All Music Guide

The experts' guide to the best recordings from thousands of artists in all types of music

THIRD EDITION

Edited by
Michael Erlewine
Vladimir Bogdanov
Chris Woodstra
Stephen Thomas Erlewine

AMG All Music Guide Series

Miller Freeman Books

San Francisco

D1010163

Published by Miller Freeman Books
600 Harrison Street, San Francisco, CA 94107
Publishers of *Guitar Player, Bass Player* and *Keyboard* magazines
Miller Freeman, Inc. is a United News and Media Company

un Miller Freeman

Distributed to the book trade in the U.S. and Canada by
Publishers Group West, P.O. Box 8843, Emeryville, CA 94662

Distributed to the music trade in the U.S. and Canada by
Hal Leonard Publishing, P.O. Box 13819, Milwaukee, WI 53213

ISBN 0-87930-423-5
Library of Congress 96-79981

Cover Design: Nita Ybarra
Cover Illustration: Paul Woods
Production: Dorothy Cox, Jan Hughes, Matt Kelsey, and Wendy Davis

Printed in the United States of America
96 97 98 99 00   5 4 3 2 1

DEDICATION & FOREWORD

I'd like to dedicate this book to . . .

> *. . . the spirit of the 60s and the music scene in*
> *Ann Arbor, Michigan, at that time.*
> *. . . my wife Margaret — I was lucky enough*
> *to find her back there and then.*
> *. . . our four children — Iotis, Anne,*
> *May, and Michael Andrew.*

Music, whatever else it may or may not be, is a great healing force. It is the best medicine for the soul that I have ever found, and it comes in all flavors. In my case, the more upset I am by life, the more music I listen to. And it takes some special music to cure those stubborn heartaches, which is how the *All Music Guide* came into being.

A simple examination of my checkbook dates makes it clear that I buy more music when my life is in turmoil than otherwise. During the period when my aging parents died, I bought and listened to a whole lot of music. If it's true that music is the best medicine for an aching heart, what I most needed at that time was some *very* good music.

But a lot had changed since the 60s, when I was a full-time musician. For one thing, almost 30 years had passed and the recordings I knew just were not around anymore. What I needed was to hear the music I most remembered and maybe try some new stuff too. I set out to find it.

By trial and error I did find some. But I made a lot of mistakes along the way, wasting my time and hard-earned money on worthless recordings, re-recordings, bad sound—you name it. I needed guidance and searched, with some success, through the many books and magazines available on music for more information. In a last-ditch effort to track down the best recordings for different artists, I called the experts themselves—music writers. This worked. They do know their stuff. I started finding some of the music that I craved.

Sharing this information with those around me, it soon became clear that I am not alone. Many people want to know where the good music is or how to venture into new music categories without fear of wasting both time and money guessing at music. This book is intended as an offering to music listeners everywhere. The driving force behind compiling the *All Music Guide* has always been my own need for the book, and I intend to be a major user.

— *Michael Erlewine*

ALL MUSIC GUIDE DATABASE

This is the third edition of the All Music Guide (AMG)—the experts' guide to the essential music from thousands of artists in all types of music. The All Music Guide is the most comprehensive database ever assembled and it is now available in many forms—books, kiosks, CD-ROMs, web sites, and commerical online services. The AMG project continues to broaden its overall coverage and, at the same time, provide increasing detail for each artist. This book contains the most significant subset of the database, the tip of the top (so to speak) of the very best music of all time. We hope you will find it useful. The All Music Guide is also available in the following formats:

Books:
All Music Guide to Jazz (Miller Freeman Books, 2nd Edition, 1996)
All Music Guide to Rock (Miller Freeman Books, 1995)
All Music Guide to the Blues (Miller Freeman Books, 1996)
All Music Guide to Country Music (Miller Freeman Books, available mid-1997)
All Music Guide to World Music (Miller Freeman Books, available late 1997)
VideoHound & All-Movie Guide Stargazer (Visible Ink, 1995)

Electronic Formats:
All Music Guide CD-ROM (Corel, release date to be announced)
All-Movie Guide CD-ROM (Corel)
MusicRoms (music and data) for Blues, Jazz, R&B, Latin, etc. (Selectware/Compton's)
All Music Guide (hard disk version) (Great Bear Technology)
World Beat CD-ROM (Medio)

In Store Kiosks:
Musicland's Soundsite
Phonolog's the Source
Sam Goody's

Internet AMG sites:
ALLMUSIC.COM
ALLMOVIE.COM
THENEWAGE.COM

Other Internet Sites:
CDNow! (CDNOW.COM)
Entertainment Connection (ECONNECTION, BBS 914-426-2285)
Music Boulevard (www.MusicBlvd.com)
CDUniverse (www.CDUNIVERSE.COM)

Other Online Sites:
Compact Disc Connection (BBS 408-730-9015)
Billboard Online
Dimple Records
Reason Ware
The Microsoft Network: New Age Forum: New Age Music

Since the All Music Guide is an ongoing project, we appreciate your feedback. Perhaps we have left out some of your favorite albums, and/or included ones that you don't consider essential. Let us know about it. We welcome criticism, suggestions, additions, and/or deletions. The All Music Guide is a work in progress. If you are knowledgeable on the recordings of a particular artist or group and would like to participate in future editions of the book and/or our larger electronic database, write or give us a call.

ALL MUSIC GUIDE
315 Marion Avenue
Big Rapids, MI 49307

616-796-3437
FAX 616-796-3060

A division of Matrix Software

CONTENTS

ABOUT THE EDITORS

Michael Erlewine

All Music Guide editor Michael Erlewine helped form the Prime Movers Blues Band in Ann Arbor, Michigan in 1965. He was the lead singer and played amplified harmonica in this pace-setting band (the first of its kind). The original band included a number of now well-known musicians including Iggy Pop (drums), "Blue" Gene Tyranny (piano; now a well-known avant-garde classical composer); Jack Dawson (bass; became bass player for Siegel-Schwall Blues Band); and Michael's brother Dan Erlewine (lead guitar; now monthly columnist for *Guitar Player* magazine). Michael has extensively interviewed blues performers, both in video and audio, and, along with his band, helped to shape the first few Ann Arbor Blues festivals. Today Michael is a systems programmer and director of Matrix Software. Aside from the company's work in music and film data, Matrix is the largest center for astrological programming and research in North America. Michael has been a practicing astrologer for more than 30 years and has an international reputation in that field.

Michael is also very active in Tibetan Buddhism and serves as the director of the Heart Center Karma Thegsum Choling, one of the main centers in North America for the translation, transcription, and publication of psychological texts and teachings of the Karma Kagyu Lineage of Tibetan Buddhism. Michael has been married for 25 years, and he and his wife Margaret live in Big Rapids, Michigan. They have four children.

Vladimir Bogdanov

Russian mathematician and programmer Vladimir Bogdanov has been involved in the design and development of *All Music Guide* databases since 1991. Having experience in many different fields such as nuclear physics, psychology, social studies and ancient chronology he now applies his knowledge to the construction of unique music reference tools utilizing the latest computer technologies. His personal interest lies in applying artificial intelligence and other mathematical methods to areas with complex semantic structures, like music, film, literature. Vladimir's ultimate goal is to provide people with the means to find what they need, even if they don't know what they are looking for.

Chris Woodstra

Chris Woodstra has had a lifelong obsession with music and is an avid record collector. He has worked many years in music retail, he was a DJ, hosting programs in every genre of music, and has been a contributing editor for several local arts and entertainment magazines. Working as an editor for the *All Music Guide* database has given him the opportunity to combine his technical skills, a B.S. in Physics and Mathematics, and his love of music for the first time in his life. Being a perfectionist by nature, Chris makes sure that that any information that goes into the database has been carefully researched and verified.

Stephen Thomas Erlewine

Stephen Thomas Erlewine studied English at the University of Michigan and was the arts editor of the school's newspaper, The Michigan Daily. In addition to editing the *All Music Guide*, Erlewine is a freelance writer and musician.

INTRODUCTION

The *All Music Guide* represents the combined efforts of over 150 experienced music writers to point out the most important artists and their best music. Most are well-known reviewers. Aside from producing scores of liner notes, they also write for magazines like *Rolling Stone, Goldmine, Detail, Pulse, Request, Billboard, Music Express, Mix, Agent/Manager, Spin, Musician, CD-Review, Rock & Roll Disc*, and many others.

Starting with extensive lists of musicians in their area of expertise, each writer picked the artists they felt should be in the book. These lists were then combined to create a master list for each genre of the most frequently selected artists. Master lists were then submitted to genre editors, further refined and commented upon, and then given to at least one other editor for still more criticism, additions, and suggestions. The final result is in your hands, the 20,000+ top albums selected from a database of over 300,000 albums.

One major difference from the previous edition is that a huge proportion of the biographies and reviews have been rewritten in much greater depth, especially in the rock, blues, jazz, and country sections. This takes more space, of course, and consequently the total number of reviews is somewhat less than in the previous edition. For some of the lower rated recordings, we have listed the title with no review, due to space restrictions—there is a definite limit to how much we can fit between two covers! We have also dropped the classical section from this edition; the scope of this book does not allow us to do justice to the subject of classical music, but we are working on plans for a separate book on this subject in the next year or so.

I would like to thank AMG editors Chris Woodstra and Stephen Thomas Erlewine for helping to make this third edition of the *All Music Guide* the best yet. These folks stayed up all hours for weeks at a time putting finishing touches on the book and coordinating all of the many contributors. My thanks also to Vladimir Bogdanov and Luda Lobenko for the required database wizardry and to all of the Matrix staff who worked to make this book possible. And last, I would like to address the readers who cared enough to call, write, fax, and e-mail us with an endless stream of suggestions, additions, and criticisms. Our thanks to you!

—Michael Erlewine, executive editor

ACKNOWLEDGMENTS

This book would not have been possible without the guidance of Andrew Gun McIver and Ven. Khenpo Karthar, Rinpoche. Special thanks to Richie Unterberger, Cub Koda, Scott Yanow, Bruce Eder, Carl Bierling, and the staff of Holland Compact Discs.

To our production staff...
Special thanks to Jonathan Ball, Sherry Batchelder, Nancy Beilfuss, Sandra Brennan, John Bush, Julie Clark, Mark Donkers, Brandy Ellison, Elizabeth Erlewine, Sarah Erlewine, Mary Anne Henry, Steve Huey, Debbie Kirby, Luda Lobenko, and Sara Sytsma.

and to all the Matrix Staff...
Kyle Alexander, Irene Baldwin, Richard Batchelder, Susan Brownlee, Stephanie Clement, Walt Crocket, Teresa Swift-Eckert, Iotis Erlewine, Margaret Erlewine, Phillip Erlewine, Stephen Erlewine, Kevin Fowler, Jeff Jawer, Rock Jensen, Mary King, Madeline Koperski, Forest Ray, and Robert Walker.

Thanks to the staffs of the following magazines, for reviews reprinted by permission: *Cadence, DOWN BEAT, Jazz Times, Coda, Jazziz, Rock & Roll Disc, Request, Pulse, Roundup Newsletter.*

All Music Guide

Editors
Michael Erlewine
Vladimir Boganov
Chris Woodstra
Stephen Thomas Erlewine

Bluegrass

Editor
David Vinopal

Contributors
Jonathan Ball
Sandra Brennan
Hank Davis
Michael Erlewine
Stephen Thomas Erlewine
Mark A. Humphrey
Linda Kohanov
Richard Lieberson
Brian Mansfield
Michael McCall
Richard Meyer
Thom Owens
Roch Parisien
Chip Renner
William Ruhlmann
Richie Unterberger
David Vinopal
Kurt Wolff
Ron Wynn

Blues

Editors
Cub Koda
Bill Dahl

Contributors
George Bedard
Myles Boisen
Sandra Brennan
Rick Clark
Bill Dahl
Hank Davis

Scott Dirks
Bruce Eder
Daniel Erlewine
Michael Erlewine
Stephen Thomas Erlewine
John Floyd
Dan Forte
Niles J. Frantz
Larry Hoffman
Steve Huey
Mark A. Humphrey
Steve James
Cub Koda
Kip Lornell
Richard Meyer
Michael G. Nastos
Jim O'Neal
Jas Obrecht
Thom Owens
Roch Parisien
Barry Lee Pearson
Bob Porter
Bruce Boyd Raeburn
William Ruhlmann
Richard Skelly
David Szatmary
Jeff Tamarkin
Richie Unterberger
Cary Wolfson
Jan Mark Wolkin
Chris Woodstra
Ron Wynn
Scott Yanow

Cajun

Editor
Jeff Hannusch

Contributors
Sandra Brennan
Bill Dahl
Hank Davis
Stephen Thomas Erlewine
Bob Gottlieb
Jeff Hannusch

Mark A. Humphrey
Leon Jackson
Cub Koda
Decibel Dennis MacDonald
Brian Mansfield
Michael G. Nastos
Liz Opoka
Thom Owens
Chip Renner
John Storm Roberts
Richie Unterberger
Ron Wynn

Celtic

Editor
Stephen Winick

Contributors
Sandra Brennan
Scott Bultman
John Bush
Danny Carnahan
Michael P. Dawson
Bruce Eder
Stephen Thomas Erlewine
Niles J. Frantz
Bob Gottlieb
Carl Hoyt
Steve Huey
Mark A. Humphrey
Leon Jackson
David Jehnzen
David L. Mayers
Richard Meyer
Michael G. Nastos
Thom Owens
Roch Parisien
Chip Renner
John Storm Roberts
William Ruhlmann
Sara Sytsma
Bob Tarte
Richie Unterberger
Stephen Winick
Ron Wynn

Country

Editors
David Vinopal
Stephen Thomas Erlewine
Chris Woodstra

Contributors
George Bedard
Myles Boisen
Sandra Brennan
John Bush
Bil Carpenter
Kenneth M. Cassidy
Rick Clark
Dan Cooper
Bill Dahl
Hank Davis
John Dougan
Bruce Eder
Michael Erlewine
Stephen Thomas Erlewine
John Floyd
Dan Heilman
Mark A. Humphrey
David Jehnzen
Cub Koda
Richard Lieberson
Brian Mansfield
Michael McCall
Richard Meyer
Thom Owens
Roch Parisien
Barry Lee Pearson
Larry Powell
Chip Renner
John Storm Roberts
Tom Roland
William Ruhlmann
Sara Sytsma
Jeff Tamarkin
Richie Unterberger
David Vinopal
Charles S. Wolfe
Kurt Wolff
Chris Woodstra
Jim Worbois
Ron Wynn

Easy Listening

Editors
Stephen Thomas Erlewine
Richie Unterberger

Contributors
Kenneth M. Cassidy
Hank Davis
Bruce Eder
Michael Erlewine
Stephen Thomas Erlewine
David Jehnzen
Cub Koda
William Ruhlmann
Sara Sytsma
David Szatmary
Richie Unterberger
Ron Wynn

Scott Yanow

Folk Contributors
Sandra Brennan
John Bush
Kenneth M. Cassidy
Rick Clark
Bill Dahl
Hank Davis
Michael P. Dawson
John Dougan
Bruce Eder
Michael Erlewine
Stephen Thomas Erlewine
Phil Fink
Mike Fleischer
John Floyd
Robert Gordon
Tom Graves
Bob Hinkle
Carl Hoyt
Steve Huey
Mark A. Humphrey
Leon Jackson
Alonso Jasso
Keith Johnson
Cub Koda
Dennis MacDonald
Brian Mansfield
Michael McCall
Bill McCaully
Richard Meyer
Michael G. Nastos
Thom Owens
Roch Parisien
Barry Lee Pearson
Chip Renner
John Storm Roberts
William Ruhlmann
Janet Schnol
Allan Shaw
Richard Skelly
Don Stevens
David Szatmary
"Blue" Gene Tyrranny
Richie Unterberger
David Vinopal
Stephen Winick
Kurt Wolff
Chris Woodstra
Jim Worbois
Ron Wynn

Folk

Editors
William Ruhlmann
Richard Meyer

Contributors
Sandra Brennan
John Bush
Rick Clark
Bill Dahl
Hank Davis
Michael P. Dawson
John Dougan
Bruce Eder

Michael Erlewine
Stephen Thomas Erlewine
Phil Fink
Mike Fleischer
John Floyd
Robert Gordon
Tom Graves
Bob Hinkle
Carl Hoyt
Steve Huey
Mark A. Humphrey
Leon Jackson
Alonso Jasso
Keith Johnson
Cub Koda
Decibel Dennis MacDonald
Brian Mansfield
Michael McCall
Bill McCaully
Richard Meyer
Michael G. Nastos
Thom Owens
Roch Parisien
Barry Lee Pearson
Chip Renner
John Storm Roberts
William Ruhlmann
Janet Schnol
Alan Shaw
Richard Skelly
Don Stevens
David Szatmary
"Blue" Gene Tyrrany
Richie Unterberger
David Vinopal
Stephen Winick
Kurt Wolff
Chris Woodstra
Jim Worbois
Ron Wynn

Gay Music

Editor
Will Grega

Contributors
Will Grega
Tom Wilson Weinberg

Gospel

Editors
Thom Granger
Ron Wynn

Contributors
Rodney Batdorf
Myles Boisen
Rob Bowman
Sandra Brennan
John Bush
Bil Carpenter
Rick Clark
Bill Dahl
Hank Davis
Michael Erlewine
Stephen Thomas Erlewine
John Floyd

Thom Granger
Carl Hoyt
Mark A. Humphrey
David Jehnzen
Cub Koda
Paul Kohler
Kip Lornell
John Lowe
Brian Mansfield
Richard Meyer
Michael G. Nastos
Opal Louis Nations
Jas Obrecht
Thom Owens
Barry Lee Pearson
John Storm Roberts
William Ruhlmann
Leo Stanley
Sara Sytsma
Richie Unterberger
Billy C. Wirtz
Charles S. Wolfe
Jim Worbois
Ron Wynn
Scott Yanow

Jazz

Editor
Scott Yanow

Contributors
Steve Aldrich
Myles Boisen
Bil Carpenter
Bill Dahl
Hank Davis
Michael P. Dawson
Bruce Eder
Michael Erlewine
Stephen Thomas Erlewine
Mark Gridley
Terri Hinte
Steve Huey
Michael Katz
Cub Koda
Paul Kohler
Stuart Kremsky
Richard Lieberson
Decibel Dennis MacDonald
Brian Mansfield
David Nelson McCarthy
Dan Morgenstern
Michael G. Nastos
Thom Owens
Roch Parisien
Bob Porter
Bruce Boyd Raeburn
John Storm Roberts
William Ruhlmann
Bob Rusch
Max Salazar
Richard Skelly
Ned Sublette
David Szatmary
"Blue" Gene Tyranny
Richie Unterberger

Ron Wynn
Scott Yanow

Sountrack/Cast

Editor
William Ruhlmann

Contributors
Jonathan Ball
Scott Bultman
Bruce Eder
Michael Erlewine
Stephen Thomas Erlewine
Tavia Hobart
Cub Koda
Linda Kohanov
Brian Mansfield
Roch Parisien
Tom Roland
Marjorie Ellen Ruhlmann
William Ruhlmann
Richie Unterberger
Ron Wynn
Scott Yanow

New Age

Editors
Linda Kohanov
Lloyd Barde

Contributors
Rodney Batdorf
Vladimir Bogdanov
Sandra Brennan
Scott Bultman
John Bush
Rick Clark
Hank Davis
Michael P. Dawson
Jim Dorsch
Bruce Eder
Michael Erlewine
Stephen Thomas Erlewine
John Floyd
Daevid Jehnzen
Linda Kohanov
Paul Kohler
Brian Mansfield
Richard Meyer
David A. Milberg
Michael G. Nastos
Thom Owens
Roch Parisien
Archie Patterson
William Ruhlmann
Janet Schnol
Sara Sytsma
David Szatmary
Bob Tarte
"Blue" Gene Tyranny
Ron Wynn
Scott Yanow

Rap

Editors
Stephen Thomas Erlewine

Ron Wynn

Contributors
Jonathan Ball
John Bush
Bil Carpenter
Sean Cooper
Stephen Thomas Erlewine
John Floyd
Dan Heilman
Steve Huey
Eddie Huffman
Ken Hunt
David Jehnzen
Cub Koda
John Storm Roberts
William Ruhlmann
Leo Stanley
Sara Sytsma
Ron Wynn

Reggae

Editors
Ron Wynn
Roger Steffans
Chris Woodstra

Contributors
Jonathan Ball
Myles Boisen
Sandra Brennan
Scott Bultman
John Bush
Rick Clark
Hank Davis
Stephen Thomas Erlewine
John Floyd
Carl Hoyt
Steve Huey
David Jehnzen
Michael G. Nastos
Thom Owens
J. Poet
John Storm Roberts
William Ruhlmann
Gene Scaramuzzo
Raissa St.Pierre
Leo Stanley
Roger Steffens
Bob Tarte
Richie Unterberger
Chris Woodstra
Ron Wynn

Rock

Editors
Stephen Thomas Erlewine
Chris Woodstra
Richie Unterberger

R&B Editor
Ron Wynn

Contributors
Steve Aldrich
Ashley S. Battel
George Bedard

Vladimir Bogdanov
Myles Boisen
John Book
Rob Bowman
Sandra Brennan
Rick A. Bueche
Scott Bultman
John Bush
Matt Carlson
Bil Carpenter
Kenneth M. Cassidy
James Chrispell
Rick Clark
Sean Cooper
Bill Dahl
Hank Davis
Michael P. Dawson
Donna DiChario
John Dougan
Bruce Eder
Iotis Erlewine
Meredith Erlewine
Michael Erlewine
Michael Anne Erlewine
Stephen Thomas Erlewine
Colin Escott
John Floyd
Dan Forte
Michael Freedberg
Robert Gordon
Bob Gottlieb
Tom Graves
Dan Heilman
Steve Huey
Eddie Huffman
Mark A. Humphrey
David Jehnzen
Julian Katz
Kit Kiefer
Cub Koda
Linda Kohanov
Paul Kohler
Larry Lapka
John Lowe
Decibel Dennis MacDonald
Brian Mansfield
Richard Meyer
Jim O'Neal
Jas Obrecht
Christine Ohlman
Thom Owens
Richard Pack
Roch Parisien
Archie Patterson
Heather Phares
Matthew Plichta
J. Poet
Bob Porter
Jim Powers
William Ruhlmann

Ali Sinclair
Leo Stanley
Sara Sytsma
David Szatmary
Jeff Tamarkin
Neal Umphred
Richie Unterberger
Stephen Winick
Kurt Wolff
Chris Woodstra
Jim Worbois
Ron Wynn
Scott Yanow

Vocal

Editors
Stephen Thomas Erlewine
Cub Koda

Contributors
Steve Aldrich
Myles Boisen
John Bush
Bil Carpenter
Kenneth M. Cassidy
Rick Clark
Bill Dahl
Hank Davis
Bruce Eder
Michael Erlewine
Stephen Thomas Erlewine
John Floyd
Dan Heilman
Mark A. Humphrey
David Jehnzen
Cub Koda
Larry Lapka
Richard Lieberson
Decibel Dennis MacDonald
Thom Owens
William Ruhlmann
David Szatmary
Jeff Tamarkin
Richie Unterberger
Charles S. Wolfe
Ron Wynn
Scott Yanow

Women's Music

Editor
Laura Post

Contributors
Sandra Brennan
John Bush
Bruce Eder
Bob Hinkle
Richard Meyer
Michael G. Nastos
Thom Owens
Roch Parisien

Laura Post
Chip Renner
William Ruhlmann
Janet Schnol
Sara Sytsma
Bob Tarte
Scott Yanow

World Music

Editor
John Storm Roberts

Contributors
Myles Boisen
Sandra Brennan
John Bush
Bil Carpenter
Hank Davis
Michael Erlewine
Stephen Thomas Erlewine
Phil Fink
John Floyd
Ted Greenwald
Don Hill
Terri Hinte
Carl Hoyt
Steve Huey
Mark A. Humphrey
Ken Hunt
Leon Jackson
Linda Kohanov
Richard Lieberson
Cliff Martin
David L. Mayers
John McCord
Terry Miller
Michael G. Nastos
J. Poet
John Storm Roberts
William Ruhlmann
David Rumpler
Max Salazar
Gene Scaramuzzo
Ned Sublette
Jeff Tamarkin
Bob Tarte
"Blue" Gene Tyrrany
Richie Unterberger
Ron Wynn
Scott Yanow

Avant-Garde

Editor
"Blue" Gene Tyranny

Contributors
"Blue" Gene Tyranny
Peter Meyer
Mary Scanlan

HOW TO USE THIS BOOK

ARTIST NAME (Alternate name in parentheses) ——— **Lonnie Johnson** (Alonzo Johnson)

VITAL STATISTICS For individual performers, date and place of birth and death, if known. —— **b.** Feb. 8, 1889, New Orleans, LA, **d.** Jun. 16, 1970 Toronto, Canada

INSTRUMENT(S) / STYLE Major instruments for each performer are listed here, followed by one or more styles of music associated with each performer or group. —— *Guitar, Vocals / Blues, Classic Jazz*

BIOGRAPHY A quick view of the artist's life and musical career. For major performers, proportionately longer biographies are provided. —— Lonnie Johnson spent most of his long career as a solo blues vocalist/guitarist, but in his early days he showed that, if he wanted to pursue it, he could have been one of the top jazz guitarists. Born in New Orleans, he played guitar and violin in Storyville. Johnson went up north by 1920, playing with Charlie Creath's band (with whom he would record in 1925) in St. Louis. In the 1920s in addition to his own solo recordings (which occasionally included some hot instrumentals), Johnson made notable appearances on records by Louis Armstrong's Hot Five and big band ("Hotter than That" finds him battling Armstrong), Duke Ellington, McKinney's Cotton Pickers, King Oliver and duets with his jazz counterpart (and only real competitor technique-wise) Eddie Lang who used the pseudonym Blind Willie Dunn. However, by the 1930s Johnson was mostly sticking to the blues, emphasizing his smooth vocals. All of his many recordings (which include a Dixieland date in 1965 with Jimmy McHarg's Metro Stompers) are of interest to jazz listeners, but his work in the 1920s in particular makes one wonder "what if?" —*Scott Yanow*

MAJOR ALBUMS These are the albums selected by our editors and contributors. An album listed here (even one without a bullet or comment) is considered an important recording. It's worth a listen. Undistinguished albums are not included here.

KEY TO SYMBOLS ● ★ ☆

☆ ESSENTIAL COLLECTIONS Albums marked with a star should be part of any good collection of the genre. Often, these are also a good first purchase (filled star). By hearing these albums, you can get a good overview of the entire genre. These are must-hear and must-have recordings. You can't go wrong with them. —— ☆ **Steppin' on the Blues** / Nov. 4, 1925–Aug. 12, 1932 / Columbia/Legacy ✦✦✦✦✦

A fine collection of nineteen blues, ragtime and pop songs from one of the best guitarists, vocalists and composers around. —*Barry Lee Pearson*

He's a Jelly Roll Baker / Nov. 2, 1939–Dec. 14, 1944 / Bluebird ✦✦✦✦✦

This 20-song collection covers 1930s and '40s material in which Johnson primarily performs blues tunes, doing salty, sassy, mournful and suggestive numbers in a distinctive, memorable fashion. His vocals on "Rambler's Blues," "In Love Again," the title cut and several others are framed by brilliant, creative playing and excellent support from such pianists as Blind John Davis, Lil Hardin Armstrong and Joshua Altheimer. This is tight, intuitive music in which Johnson set the tone and dominated the songs. If you're unaware of Lonnie Johnson's brilliant blues material, here's an excellent introduction. —*Ron Wynn*

● ★ FIRST PURCHASE Albums marked with a filled star should be your first purchase. This is where to begin to find out if you like this particular artist. These albums are representative of the best this artist has to offer. If you don't like these picks, chances are this artist is not for you. In the case of an artist (like Miles Davis) who has a number of distinct periods, you will find an essential pick marked for each period. Albums are listed chronologically when possible.

Blues By Lonnie / Mar. 8, 1960 / Original Blues Classics ✦✦✦✦

Blues & Ballads / Apr. 5, 1960 / Original Blues Classics ✦✦✦✦✦

Later Johnson, doing blues and ballads with jazz guitarist Elmer Snowden. Johnson's vocals are refined and sensitive. It is hard to hear him sing his own composition "I Found a Dream" and remain unmoved. Such a lovely album. —*Michael Erlewine*

ALBUM RATINGS: ✦ TO ✦✦✦✦✦

In addition to the stars and circles used to distinguish exceptionally noteworthy albums, as explained above, all albums are rated on a scale from one to five diamonds.

ALBUM TITLE The name of the album is listed in bold as it appears on the original when possible. Very long titles have been abbreviated, or repeated in full as part of the review, where needed. —— ● **Blues, Ballads & Jumpin' Jazz** / Apr. 5, 1960 / Original Blues Classics ✦✦✦✦✦

This is an unusual CD. In 1960 guitarists Lonnie Johnson and Elmer Snowden (along with bassist Wendell Marshall) teamed up for *Blues and Ballads*, which was primarily a showcase for Johnson's blues vocals. This previously unreleased set from the same session has six instrumentals and just four vocals with Snowden generally in the lead. The two guitarists are heard good-naturedly suggesting songs before launching into spontaneous improvisations and the results sound like an intimate concert. Highlights of this fun outing include "Lester Leaps In," "C-Jam Blues" and "Careless Love." —*Scott Yanow*

DATE The date of an album's first release, if known. For jazz albums, the date of the recording session is given whenavailable.

RECORD LABEL Record labels indicate the current (or most recent) release of this recording. Label numbers are not given because they change frequently. —— **Idle Hours** / Jul. 1961 / Original Blues Classics ✦✦✦✦

Another Night to Cry / Apr. 6, 1962 / Original Blues Classics ✦✦✦✦

REVIEWERS The name of each review's author are given at the end of the review. —— **Stompin' At The Penny** / Nov. 1965 / Columbia/Legacy ✦✦✦✦

ROCK

Rock 'n' roll, in its loosest definition, is popular music that was made after 1955. It includes rock 'n' roll, to be certain, but also R&B, soul, pop, folk-rock, heavy metal, country-rock, glam, psychedelia, pub-rock, arena rock, disco, punk, hardcore, new wave, synth-pop, jangle-pop, industrial, acid jazz, house music, alternative, lo-fi, grunge, Brit-pop, techno and any variation or fusion of any number of sub-genres. Given the vast array of styles that can be classified under "rock 'n' roll," it is nearly impossible to provide a comprehensive overview of the genre. Nevertheless, the rock section of *The All Music Guide* offers a concise and effective introduction to the music, from Little Richard and Elvis Presley to Prince and Pavement.

The rock section of *The All Music Guide* does not attempt to tell the history of rock 'n' roll—it offers a guide to the genre's essential performers and their recordings. The intent is not to draw comparisons between the artists, but to judge each artist on their own terms.

Given our space limitations, worthy artists had to be excluded, yet we included a broad range of musicians reflecting the wide range of stylistic variations rock 'n' roll has taken over the years. All of the major artists from every decade and subgenre have been included. So have cult artists of all genres and eras, just to give a suggestion of the vast variety of styles that make rock 'n' roll endlessly fascinating.

What makes rock 'n' roll so interesting is the sheer amount of variety it offers. It's been a long road from Bo Diddley and Jerry Lee Lewis to Nirvana and Oasis, and all the detours have something interesting to offer. It may be the songcraft of Neil Diamond or it could be the trance-inducing electronics of the Orb. It could be the direct rock 'n' roll of Bob Seger and John Mellencamp or the minimalist approaches of the Ramones, AC/DC and Unrest, who all take simplicity in different sonic directions. Is it all rock and roll? No, in the conventional three-chord sense it's not, but it is all popular music that owes its existence to rock 'n' roll. There's not an obvious link between Sonic Youth and Chuck Berry, yet there are links between Chuck Berry and the Velvet Underground, and the Velvet Underground and Sonic Youth.

The All Music Guide tries to explain Sonic Youth to Chuck Berry fans and, just as importantly, Chuck Berry to Sonic Youth fans. In the meantime, it explores subgenres like garage and surf rock that rarely get space in conventional rock histories. It also spotlights cult figures from the Celibate Rifles to Scott Walker that may have never gotten popular recognition, yet they had a small impact in shaping popular music—or they simply made intriguing, interesting music.

As the decades have passed, the music has changed and so have the recording formats. For the past decade, the compact disc has been the dominant medium, replacing the long-playing album. However, in the early years of rock 'n' roll, the single was the primary method of recording. Artists like Elvis Presley, Chuck Berry, Fats Domino, Buddy Holly, the Everly Brothers, and Jerry Lee Lewis

didn't think in terms of making cohesive full-length albums—they were making their next hit single. Around 1966, long-playing albums became the dominant musical format in rock 'n' roll, with British Invasion bands like the Beatles and the Kinks making records that were tied together by both lyrical and musical themes. Soon, artists were putting more thought into making cohesive albums. Initially, this meant "concept albums"—records like the Who's *Tommy*, the Kinks' *Arthur*, or the Moody Blues' *Days of Future Passed* —that told specific stories with their songs. Concept albums gave way to a wave of progressive-rock bands that wrote music that could only be told over the course of a full-length album, as well as psychedelic bands like the Grateful Dead and Jefferson Airplane, and hard rock bands like Led Zeppelin that didn't have hit singles, they had hit albums. Ever since the late '60s, bands have been concentrating their creative efforts on full-length albums, and have had long, successful careers without the benefit of hit singles. Consequently, albums were more important to the careers of '70s rockers like David Bowie and Queen than they were to Duane Eddy or the Ventures. That explains why Bowie and Queen have more albums listed than Eddy or the Ventures—it's not a critical judgment about which band is more important, it's a reflection of their particular era.

Furthermore, due to limitations in space, it was impossible to offer comprehensive discographies for each artist. Instead, selected recordings that offer a sense of the artist's history are listed. For some, that will mean just compilation, for others it means a fairly thorough listing of albums. On the other hand, musicians like James Brown and Elvis Presley have simply released too many albums for each album to be reviewed. In this case, their major records have been included, along with some interesting minor albums that help to showcase the depth of their artistry. Even when records haven't been reviewed, they have been rated, providing a guideline, if not a description.

The goal of the rock section in *The All Music Guide* is not to draw comparisons between the Carpenters and Mötley Crüe albums, or pit the Beatles against the Clash. Rather, the intent is to provide a guide a particular artist, offering a biography and description of the music, as well as to capsule reviews of their albums. Within each entry, to the right of the album's title, is a rating for the album itself, on a scale from one to five. These ratings are based on the artist, not of their overall worth (for instance, a four-star Whitney Houston album is not necessarily the same as a four-star Black Sabbath album). The only global rating in the book is a star, which signals an album that is the best of its genre—in other words, it's essential listening.

A more complete listing and exploration of rock 'n' roll is available in *The All Music Guide to Rock* but this section offers an excellent overview of the music and all of its subgenres. Hopefully, it will alert you to some terrific music you may not have heard before. —*Stephen Thomas Erlewine and Chris Woodstra*

Rock Styles

ACID HOUSE — Acid House falls somewhere between the insistent beats of House and the jazzy, free-form experimentations of Acid Jazz.

ACID JAZZ — Incorporating jazzy samples and hip-hop beats, Acid Jazz was an outgrowth of the house music scene of the late '80s. As the music progressed in the early '90s, it moved closer to its jazz roots, especially when rappers created a fusion of jazz and hip-hop and when jazz instrumentalists began performing live with a hip-hop beat. Nevertheless, acid jazz is distinguished by its thick beats, rubbery bass grooves, and its samples of bebop and soul jazz.

ACID ROCK — Acid Rock was the heaviest, loudest variation of psy-

chedelic rock. Drawing from the overblown blues improvisations of Cream and Jimi Hendrix, acid rock bands relied on distorted guitars, trippy lyrics, and long jams. Acid rock didn't last too long—it evolved and imploded within the lifespan of psychedelia—and the bands that didn't break up, became heavy metal bands.

ADULT CONTEMPORARY — Adult Contemporary is a soft-rock, easy listening genre that came into existence in the early '70s. Essentially, it is post-Beatles pop music with slight rock and soul influences. It is highly polished, without much of an edge but with a lot of melody and production. Throughout the '70s, there were string-laden easy listening bands like the Carpenters and Bread. In the '80s, synthesizers replaced strings and artists that had been relatively harder in their early career—Elton John, Billy Joel, and Sting, for instance—began to become calmer and softer. Along with pseudo-soul singers like Michael Bolton, they became the staples of adult contemporary radio in the '80s and '90s.

ALTERNATIVE COUNTRY-ROCK — Alternative country-rock keeps the sound of Gram Parsons and Neil Young alive. Though the bands are all rock 'n' roll, their dedication to replicating the sound of Parsons and Young made them more traditionalist than either the alternative rock bands of the late '80s and '90s or the country bands of the same era. Though alternative country-rock bands occasionally have louder, grungier guitars than their idols, they are traditional in their sense of songwriting and dedication to keeping the actual sound of the early '70s alive, through the use of vintage instruments. Occasionally, some alternative country-rock bands stretch the boundaries of the form, but most are simply revivalists.

ALTERNATIVE METAL — At its core, alternative metal uses the same conventions that heavy metal always has—loud guitars, bludgeoning riffs—but it subverts the genre with post-punk concepts. Instead of adhering to the traditional lightweight lyrical topics that dominate mainstream metal, alternative metal bands tackle weightier matters, much like Metallica but without the insanely fast tempos, intricate guitar solos, and hoarse, bellowed vocals. Musically, the bands tended to be more atonal than traditional metal, but that all changed after Nirvana became popular in the early '90s and grunge became the dominant form of hardrock. After Nirvana, alternative metal ranged from the grinding, dissonant Helmet to the big riffs of Stone Temple Pilots, who closely followed the formula of '70s hard-rock acts. Soon, many new metal bands were packaged as alternative acts, though there was little besides visual presentation and a trademark fuzzy distortion to distinguish them from conventional metal bands.

ALTERNATIVE POP-ROCK — Alternative pop-rock is essentially a catch-all term for post-punk bands from the mid-'80s to the mid-'90s. Though there are a variety of musical styles within alternative rock, they are all tied together because they existed outside of the mainstream. In some ways, there are two waves of alternative bands, with Nirvana's success in 1991 acting as a dividing point. In the '80s, most alternative bands were on independent labels; if they were on majors, they didn't receive as much support as most of the label's mainstream acts. During the '80s, alternative included everything from jangle-pop, post-hardcore punk, funk-metal, punk-pop, and experimental rock. After Nirvana's success in the '90s, alternative included all of these sub-genres, but many of the edges were sanded off because the music was now being marketed as part of the mainstream. Hard rock and punk-derived music were more commercially successful than the left-of-center pop that dominated late '80s alternative pop-rock, so alternative lost some of its quirkier tendencies in the '90s. Strangely, experimental bands were relegated to indie rock.

ARENA ROCK — Arena Rock developed in the mid-'70s, when hard rock and heavy metal bands began to gain popularity. The music became more commercially-oriented and radio-friendly, boasting slick productions and anthemic choruses, both on their hard rock numbers and their sweeping power ballads. Most of these bands earned their following through saturation airplay on FM radio and through constant touring. Bands like Journey, REO Speedwagon, Boston, Foreigner, and Styx became some of the most popular bands of the mid- to late '70s through this circuit.

ART-ROCK/PROGRESSIVE-ROCK — Art-rock and progressive-rock incorporates elements of European and classical music to rock 'n' roll music, resulting in long, complex instrumental passages and dramatic, grandiose flourishes. Though the movement was sparked by the Beatles' *Sgt. Pepper*, art-rock bands tend to write compositions, not songs; instrumental prowess is also emphasized. Primarily, art-rock and progressive-rock are album-oriented, not single-oriented. The album format gives the bands freedom to experiment musically and expand their ideas over the course of a side. Another tendency of art-rock bands is to tell stories—frequently, their albums are structured as rock operas. The difference between art-rock and progressive-rock is slight, but important. Art-rock bands tend to draw more heavily on classical influences and show a tendency toward medieval and mystical lyrical imagery. Progressive-rockers do have some classical elements to their music, but they also have more overt jazz and psychedelic influences, and they have a greater tendency to improvise.

BLUE-EYED SOUL — Blue-eyed soul refers to soul and R&B music performed and sung by White musicians. The term first came into play during the mid-'60s, when acts like the Righteous Brothers had hits with soulful songs like "You Lost that Loving Feeling." Throughout the late '60s, blue-eyed soul thrived, as acts like the Rascals, the Boxtops, Mitch Ryder, Tony Joe White, and Roy Head had a series of hits. During the '70s, blue-eyed soul continued to be successful as acts like Hall & Oates, Rob-

ert Palmer, Average White Band, Boz Scaggs, and David Bowie updated the blue-eyed soul formula.

BLUES-ROCK — Though much early rock 'n' roll was based in the blues, blues-rock didn't fully develop into a sub-genre until the late-'60s. Blues-rock emphasized two specific things—the traditional, three-chord blues song and instrumental improvisation. Borrowing the idea of an instrumental combo and loud amplification from rock 'n' roll, the original blues-rockers—bands like Cream, that grew out of the Alexis Korner and John Mayall tradition of British blues, as well as American bands like Paul Butterfield Blues Band and Canned Heat—also attempted to play long, involved improvisations which were commonplace on jazz records, as well as live blues shows. The hybrid became quite popular and the bands that immediately followed them were louder and more riff-oriented. Out of this approach came heavy metal and southern rock, both of which used basic blues riffs and featured extended solos. In the early '70s, the lines between blues-rock and hard rock were barely visible, as boogie-based bands like ZZ Top employed album-rock production techniques that tended to obscure their blues roots. However, blues-rock soon backed away from hard rock and there was a set number of acts that continued to play (and re-write) blues standards as well as write their own songs in the same idiom. In the '80s and '90s, blues-rock was more roots-oriented than in the '60s and '70s, even when artists like Fabulous Thunderbirds and Stevie Ray Vaughan flirted with rock stardom. By the '80s, blues-rock had become an accepted tradition, much like the blues.

BOOGIE ROCK — Boogie rock is an off-shoot of the heavy blues rock of the late '60s. Instead of emphasizing instrumental improvisation like the original blues-rock bands (Cream, Jimi Hendrix, Yardbirds, Led Zeppelin), boogie rockers concentrated on the groove, working a steady, chugling backbeat. While nearly every boogie rock band played the same 4/4 tempo, the main distinction between the groups was their instrumental attack— some groups, like Foghat, played heavier than others.

BRILL BUILDING POP — The Brill Building sound applied the concept of professional songwriters in traditional pop to rock 'n' roll. Numerous teams of professional songwriters worked at the Brill Building—a block of music publishing houses in New York City—writing songs for artists as diverse as the Coasters, the Drifters, the Shangri-las, the Ronettes, Neil Sedaka, and Connie Francis. The songs were indebted not only to rock 'n' roll and R&B, but also Tin Pan Alley pop, as the sophisticated lyrics and melodies proved. The productions on these early '60s records were also more sophisticated than most rock 'n' roll records, featuring orchestras and bands with large rhythm and guitar sections. Though it fell out of favor after the British Invasion, both British and American pop-rock demonstrated an enormous debt to the Brill Building sound for years to come.

BRIT-POP — Brit-pop evolved in the early '90s, somewhat as a response to American grunge and the anti-rock stars dominating the British-techno and indie-rock scenes. Brit-pop revived the idea of rock stars and pop songs with big, catchy melodies and hooks. Though the bands differed greatly in styles—they ranged from the massive guitar roar of Oasis and the defiantly British pop of Blur to the disco/glam-rock pastiche of Pulp—they were tied together by attitude. All of the groups were dedicated to the concept of a pop single, as well as the glamour of being a pop star. Some of the bands managed to cross over to the American market, but there had never been a generation of British rock musicians that had been less concerned with American success.

BRITISH INVASION — The British Invasion occurred in the mid-'60s, when a wave of English rock 'n' roll bands crossed over into the American market after the breakthrough success of the Beatles. Though not all of the bands sounded similar—they ranged from the hard rock of the Rolling Stones and Kinks to the sweet pop of Gerry & the Pacemakers and Herman's Hermits—each group was heavily influenced by American rock 'n' roll, blues, and R&B. British Invasion bands were either blues-based rockers or pop-rockers with ringing guitars and catchy hooks and melodies. Between 1964 and 1966, the British bands dominated the US charts, as well as the charts in the UK. In that time, there was a second wave of British Invasion bands—such as the Who and the Zombies—which were indebted to both American rock and British Invasion pop. By the late '60s, many of the bands had become rock icons but a greater number didn't survive the transition into the post-*Sgt. Pepper* era.

BRITISH METAL — British metal, in an odd way, is as much a reaction to the lumbering arena heavy-metal groups of the mid-'70s as punk rock. Taking their cue from the grimy riffs of Black Sabbath, British metal groups were faster, tougher, harder, and louder than their predecessors. Frequently dressed in leather and playing fast, pounding riffs, they stood apart from the AOR-oriented metal bands that dominated hard rock since the early-'70s. Judas Priest, Iron Maiden, and Motörhead were the leaders of the movement and they gained a dedicated following in both Europe and America, even though they didn't cross over into the mainstream. Nevertheless, they set the tone for all the metal bands that followed, from thrash to death metal.

BRITISH MUSICHALL — In terms of rock 'n' roll, British musichall derives from the music of Noel Coward and Anthony Newley, who performed pop standards and vaudevillian comedy numbers. It is characterized by kitschy dramatics, sing-along-choruses, horns, tinkling pianos, and either stomping beats or smooth crooning. During the '60s, the Beatles, the Kinks, and the Small Faces were some of the first bands to incorporate this style of British music into rock 'n' roll, followed quickly by the whimsical psychedelia of Syd Barrett-era Pink Floyd and early David Bowie. Throughout the next three decades of rock 'n' roll history, a number of British artists dabbled in this tradition, from pub rockers like Ian Dury to ska-revivalists like Madness and Brit-poppers like Blur.

BUBBLEGUM — Bubblegum is lightweight, catchy pop music that was a significant commercial force in the late '60s and early '70s. Bubblegum was targeted at a pre-teen audience whose older siblings had been raised on rock 'n' roll. It was simple, melodic, and light as feather—neither the lyrics or the music had much substance. Bubblegum was a manufactured music, created by record producers that often hired session musicians to play and sing the songs. Frequently, the session musicians were given a fake band name, to give the illusion that they were a real group. Apart from acts like the Partridge Family and Tommy Roe, most Bubblegum groups were one-hit wonders. Appropriately, the genre also had a short life span, lasting roughly five years. As the pre-teens that Bubblegum was created for grew up, they left the music behind and the following generation found other records. However, the genre had a surprisingly long legacy, as musicians that grew up with Bubblegum created songs that reflected the sunny, catchy simplicity of the music.

DANCE/CLUB-DANCE — Dance music comes in many different forms, from disco to hip-hop. Though there have been various dance crazes throughout the history of popular music, dance music became its own genre in the mid-'70s, as soul mutated into disco and whole clubs were devoted to dancing. In the late '70s, dance clubs played disco, but by the end of the decade, disco was mutating into a number of different genres. All of the genres were collected under the catch-all term "dance," though there were distinct differences between dance-pop, hip-hop, house, and techno, among other subgenres. What tied them all together was their emphasis on rhythm—in each dance subgenre, the beat remains all-important.

COUNTRY-ROCK — Essentially, country-rock is rock bands playing country music. It is country music informed by rock's counter-culture ideals, as well as its reliance on loud amplification, prominent back-beat, and pop melodies. The first country-rock bands—Flying Burrito Brothers, Gram Parsons, the Byrds, Neil Young—played straight country, as inspired by the Bakersfield sound of Merle Haggard and Buck Owens, as well as honky tonkers like Hank Williams. As the genre moved into the '70s, the rougher edges were smoothed out as the Eagles, Poco, Pure Prairie League, and Linda Ronstadt made music that was smoother and more laid-back. This became the predominant sound of country-rock in the '70s. In the late '80s, a small group of alternative rock bands began to revive the spartan sound of the original sound of Gram Parsons and Neil Young.

DANCE-POP — Dance-pop was an outgrowth of disco. Over a pounding, dance-club beat, there are simple, catchy melodies—dance-pop has more fully-formed songs than pure dance music. Dance-pop is primarily a producer's medium. The producer writes the songs and constructs the tracks, picking an appropriate vocalist to sing the song. These dance divas become stars, but frequently the artistic vision is the producer's. Naturally, there are some major exceptions—Madonna and Janet Jackson have had control over the sound and direction of their records—but dance-pop is music that is about image, not substance. It is music of the moment.

DEATH METAL — Death metal grew out of the thrash metal in the late '80s. Taking the gritty lyrics and morbid obsessions of thrash to extremes, death metal was—as its name suggests—solely about death, pain, and suffering. These relentlessly bleak lyrics were set to loud, heavy riffs that owed as much to the lumbering metal of Black Sabbath as it did to Metallica. Death metal bands also owed a debt to the complex song structures of '70s art-rockers, though most of these winding, intricate compositional methods were learned through Metallica. Death metal never attracted a wide audience, but to some diehard heavy metal fans, it was a preferable alternative to Metallica and Guns N' Roses, who were selling millions of records in the late '80s and early '90s, or the pop-metal of Poison. It kept a small, dedicated cult throughout the '90s.

DISCO — Disco marked the dawn of dance-based popular music. Growing out of the increasingly groove-oriented sound of early '70s and funk, disco emphasized the beat above anything else, even the singer and the song. Disco was named after discotheques, clubs that played nothing music for dancing. Most of the discotheques were gay clubs in New York, and the DJs in these clubs specifically picked soul and funk records that had a strong, heavy groove. After being played in the disco, the records began receiving radio play and sold well. Soon, record com-

panies and producers were cutting records created specifically for discos. Naturally, these records also had strong pop hooks, so they could have crossover success. Disco albums frequently didn't have many tracks—they had a handful of long songs that kept the beat going. Similarly, the singles were issued on 12-inch records, which allowed for extended remixes. DJs could mix these tracks together, matching the beats on each song since they were marked beats per minute. In no time, the insistent, pounding disco beat dominated the pop charts and everyone from rockers like the Rolling Stones and Rod Stewart, to pop acts like the Bee Gees and new wave artists like Blondie got in on the act. There were disco artists that became stars—Donna Summer, Chic, Village People, and KC & the Sunshine Band—but the music was primarily a producer's medium, since they created the tracks and wrote the songs. Disco lost momentum as the '70s became the '80s, but it didn't die—it mutated into a variety of different dance-based genres, ranging from dance-pop and hip-hop to acid house and techno.

DOO WOP — Doo wop was one of the most popular genres of rock 'n' roll and R&B in the late '50s. Doo wop artists were vocal groups, with each singer in the group taking a different part that interwoven with the other singers. Frequently, the backing vocalists sang nonsense words as rhythm, and the genre's name derives from this trait. Most of the doo wop groups started as a cappella bands, performing without instrumental accompaniment. The hit doo wop singles inspired countless teenagers to form their own a cappella groups, though many of them were never recorded. Despite its a cappella origins, few doo wop records were made without instrumental backing. Doo wop faded away in the early '60s, though its influence was felt throughout popular music in the following decades.

EURO-DANCE — Euro-dance is much like Euro-pop. It is lightweight, studio-constructed pop, with catchy melodies and an insistent, repetitive beat. Euro-dance draws heavily from disco, but it makes it more mechanical and synthesized.

EURO-POP — As the name suggests, Euro-pop is pop music that is made in Europe. The music is primarily lightweight pop confections, constructed in the studio by behind-the-scenes producers. ABBA defined the sound in the '70s, and hundreds of acts followed.

EXPERIMENTAL — Experimental rock owes as much to the avant garde as it does to rock 'n' roll. Like progressive-rock, experimental rock consciously pushes the boundaries by incorporating elements of classical music, avant garde, electronics, noise, etc. Not all experimental bands sound the same, but they are tied together by a willingness to be adventurous and expand the lexicon of rock 'n' roll.

FOLK-POP — Folk-pop falls into two categories. Either it is folk songs with large, sweeping pop arrangements or pop songs given intimate, acoustic-based folk arrangements. Folk-pop began to evolve in the early '60s, but it came into full force after folk-rock became a sensation in the mid-'60s. Folk-pop doesn't have ringing guitars and rougher edges of folk-rock. Instead, it is softer and gentler, and more pop-oriented.

FOLK-ROCK — Folk-rock takes the simple, direct songwriting style of folk music and melds it to a prominent rock 'n' roll backbeat. One of the most distinctive elements of folk-rock is the chiming, ringing guitar hooks, coupled with clear vocal harmonies. Folk-rock was pioneered in the mid-'60s by the Byrds, who played Bob Dylan songs as if they were from the British Invasion. The Byrds established the blueprint that many bands followed. As the '60s wound down, more folk-rock groups emphasized the acoustic origins of folk and backed away from the ringing electric arpeggios of the Byrds. In the next three decades, both the acoustic and electric folk-rock sounds were commonplace in rock 'n' roll.

FUNK — As soul began to experiment with rock textures in the late '60s, funk emerged. Funk kept the groove of soul but made it deeper. It also added a greater reliance on improvisation, much like the blues-rock and psychedelia of the era. James Brown and Sly Stone were the godfathers of funk—Brown's funk was stripped-down and spare, while Stone's was wilder and drew more from rock 'n' roll. George Clinton, the leader of Parliament and Funkadelic, was the next great funkster. Clinton expanded Stone's blueprint, adding wild conceptual fantasies derived from the psychedelia of *Sgt. Pepper* and the counterculture humor of Frank Zappa. But the main signature of Clinton's music was how he kept working one groove, how he kept jamming over a deep bass line and adding instrumental breaks. Most of the funk bands of the '70s picked up on the groove, not the concepts, though funk and hip-hop groups in the '80s and '90s would expand on both the sound and the concept.

FUNK METAL — Funk metal takes the loud guitars and riffs of heavy metal and melds them to the popping bass lines and syncopated rhythms of funk. Funk metal evolved in the mid-'80s when alternative bands like the Red Hot Chili Peppers and Fishbone began playing the hybrid with a stronger funk underpinning than metal. The bands that followed relied more on metal than funk, though they retained the wild bass lines. Like heavy metal, the genre became a way to showcase instrumental prowess.

GARAGE ROCK — Garage rock was a simple, raw form of rock 'n' roll created by a number of American bands in the mid-'60s. Inspired by British Invasion bands like the Beatles, Kinks, and Rolling Stones, these midwestern American groups played a variation on British Invasion rock. Since they were usually young and amateurish, the results were much cruder than their inspirations but that is what made the sound exciting. Most of the bands emphasized their amateurishness, playing the same three chords, bashing their guitars and growling their vocals. In many ways, the garage bands were the first wave of do-it-yourself punk rockers. Hundreds of garage bands popped up around America and a handful of them—the Shadows of Knight, the Count 5, the Seeds, the Standells—had hits, but most were destined for obscurity. In fact, nearly all of the bands were forgotten in the early '70s, but the *Nuggets* compilation brought them back to the spotlight. In the '80s, there was a garage rock revival that saw a number of bands earnestly trying to replicate the sound, style and look of the '60s garage bands.

GIRL GROUP — Falling somewhere between traditional pop and R&B, the sound of the girl groups was one of the most popular rock 'n' roll genres in the early '60s. Though there were strong elements of rock 'n' roll and R&B in the music, girl groups were decidedly more polished than earlier forms of rock 'n' roll. It was driven by producers and songwriters, who helped guide the groups and gave them material to sing. The vocalists had roots in gospel and R&B, while the songwriters and producers were schooled in traditional pop, which resulted in an exciting hybrid. The songs were innocent and yearning, with sweet, catchy melodies and driving backbeats. Though the girl groups faded away in the mid-'60s, they had a profound influence on pop-rock, particularly British Invasion acts like the Beatles.

GLAM ROCK — Glam rock combined the hard rock crunch of heavy metal with bubblegum pop melodies and a glitzy flair for theatrical dramatics. In the early '70s, it was one of the most popular styles of rock 'n' roll in Britain, as T. Rex, David Bowie, and several other similar artists dominated the charts. Though it never crossed over into the American market, it had a lasting effect on rock 'n' roll, as both heavy metal and post-punk in the late '70s and '80s demonstrated a massive debt to the riffs and look of glam rock.

GOTH-ROCK — Goth-rock grew out of the bleak post-punk rock of the Cure and Joy Division. As the name implies, goth-rock had grand, baroque arrangements performed with gloomy synthesizers and processed guitars. Lyrically, goth was equally dark, featuring a lot of cryptic, morbid poetry. Almost as remarkable as its sound was goth's image. The bands and the fans usually dressed in black and wore heavy makeup. Primarily, goth-rock was a mid-'80s British sensation—it was one of several fringe genres that occupied the space between new wave and alternative. Nevertheless, certain musical elements of goth lingered into the '90s, even if it didn't capture the imagination of alternative audiences like it did before.

GRINDCORE — Grindcore is an offspring of heavy metal and industrial music that has a fast, grinding tempo, bleak lyrics, and relentlessly loud distorted guitars.

GRUNGE — Using the sludgy, murky sound of the Stooges and Black Sabbath as a foundation, grunge was a hybrid of heavy metal and punk. Though the guitars were straight from early '70s metal, the aesthetic of grunge was far from metal. Both the lyrical approach and musical attack of grunge were adopted from punk, particularly the independent ideals of early '80s American hardcore. The first wave of grunge bands—Green River, Mudhoney, Soundgarden—were heavier than the second, which began with Nirvana. Nirvana was more melodic than their predecessors and they also had signature stop-start dynamics, which became a genre convention nearly as recognizable as fuzzy, distorted guitars. After Nirvana crossed over into the mainstream, grunge lost many of its independent and punk connections and became the most popular style of hard rock in the '90s.

HAIR METAL — Hair metal is a derisive term applied to the slick, pretty, and pop-oriented heavy-metal and hard-rock bands of the late '80s. These bands expanded the approach of the loud but safe arena rock bands, only they had a more distinctive visual image because they were living in the post-MTV era. Wearing flashy clothing, heavy makeup and large, teased hair, the bands had an appearance that was more distinctive than their music, though both their look and their sound became a curse in the early '90s. After Nirvana brought grunge and alternative music to the top of the charts in 1991, hair metal bands quickly died, losing all of their popular support. Some tried to change their sound, others struggled on with their trademark sound to no avail. Though some bands still survived in the mid-'90s, they had adopted a harder sound than they had in the '80s, but their fondness for pop hooks and melodies had not faded away.

HARD ROCK — Hard rock evolved in the late '60s, as psychedelia and blues rock began pushing the boundaries of amplification and blues-based riffs. Hard rock tends to rely less on improvisation than blues-rock and it isn't as loud as heavy metal, though it still has distorted guitars and long solos. Throughout the '70s and '80s, hard rock stayed essentially the same, though there were slight changes in production technique. At its

core, hard rock is simple, loud, anthemic and macho and it always stayed that way, no matter what decade it was.

HARDCORE PUNK — Hardcore punk was the most rigid and extreme variation of punk rock. Emerging in the early '80s, hardcore took the ideals of punk as far as it could go. The music was impossibly fast, the vocals were shouted, the riffs were simple, and the records looked (and sounded) like they were made in someone's basement. Most of the bands sounded incredibly similar to each other, but there were a handful of distinctive bands; they usually developed musically quite quickly, leaving the sound of hardcore behind, but not its ideals. Hardcore punk was primarily an American sensation, concentrated in Los Angeles and New York, but there were small, individual scenes scattered across the country. Hardcore kept going into the '90s without breaking into the mainstream, though bands influenced by the hardcore aesthetic—including Nirvana and Green Day—became major rock stars, and former hardcore punkers like Bob Mould, Henry Rollins, Mike Watt, Ian McKaye, and Dinosaur Jr.'s J Mascis became alternative icons.

HARDCORE TECHNO — Hardcore techno is distinguished by high-power, impossibly fast beats that rarely fall below 190 beats per minute. Hardcore techno is all-instrumental, performed on synthesizers and drum machines. There's not much variety within the genre, but the differences mainly lie in the arrangements of the rhythm, since there is no melody to the music.

HEAVY METAL — Heavy metal derived from the shatteringly loud blues-rock and psychedelia of the late '60s. Metal sanded away most of the blues influences and leaving the powerful, loud guitar riffs. In the early '70s, heavy metal established itself as one of the most commercially successful forms of rock 'n' roll. In the next three decades, metal adapted itself to the times and it never completely disappeared from the charts. At its core, heavy metal is an adolescent experience; teenagers —primarily white males—form the majority of its audience. Some critics dismiss metal as simplistic primal pounding. Certainly, a fair share of heavy metal is nothing but three-chord riffing, yet most metal bands place a premium on technical skill. Metal guitarists have always been innovators in technique, speed, and skill. In every subgenre of heavy metal, the guitar is the center of the music. The songs are assembled around the riff, with the guitar solo taking prominence. By and large, heavy metal is rock 'n' roll with all of the roll stripped away—the blues remains, but it doesn't swing. All the rhythms are fairly rigid, almost military in origin. Bombast is the key—from the drums to the guitars, it's about being as loud as possible.

HI-NRG — Hi-Nrg is a fast variation of disco that evolved in the '80s. Driven by a fast drum machine and synthesizers, Hi-Nrg is essentially a dance-oriented music with only slight hints of pop. There are a few hooks—generally sung by disembodied vocalists wailing in the background—but the emphasis of the music, like most dance music, is in the beat. Hi-Nrg is a predecessor to techno and house, which drew from its beats in decidedly different ways. House has a funkier, soulful rhythm while techno expanded with the mechanical beats of Hi-Nrg.

HOUSE MUSIC — House music grew out of the post-disco dance club culture of the early '80s. After disco became popular, certain urban DJs—particularly those in gay communities—altered the music to make it less pop-oriented. The beat became more mechanical and the bass grooves became deeper, while elements of electronic synth-pop, Latin soul, dub reggae, rap and jazz were grafted over the music's insistent, unvarying four-four beat. Frequently, the music was purely instrumental and when there was vocalists, they were faceless female divas that often sang wordless melodies. By the late '80s, house had broken out of underground clubs in cities like Chicago, New York, and London and had begun making inroads on the pop charts, particularly in England and Europe, but also in America under the guise of artists like M/A/R/R/S and Madonna, as well as producers like David Cole and Robert Clivilles. At the same time house was breaking into the pop charts, it fragmented into a number of subgenres, including acid house (a fusion of house and acid jazz), hip house (rap and house), and, most significantly, ambient, and techno. During the '90s, house ceased to be a cutting-edge music, yet it remained popular within clubs throughout Europe and America.

INDIE-ROCK — There have always been independent labels in the history of rock 'n' roll, but indie-rock refers to the independent rock music of the early '90s. After Nirvana inadvertently brought alternative music into the Top Ten in 1991, many alternative bands resisted the fact that their music was becoming popular, so they went further underground. They refused to sign to major labels and adhered to their independent, punk ideals. Not all of the music sounds the same, but nearly every indie-rock band is based in the post-punk guitar rock of the '80s.

INDUSTRIAL — Industrial music was a dissonant, abrasive genre that grew out of the electronic experiments of post-punk bands like Cabaret Voltaire. The music was largely electronic, with fast, pounding drum machines and samples. It was named industrial because it sounds like giant machinery, cranking away. Though industrial sometimes flirts with hard rock—Ministry and Nine Inch Nails, in particular, subvert hard rock formulas with their music—it always has experimental and dance underpinnings that keep it from falling into traditional rock 'n' roll conventions.

JANGLE-POP — Jangle-pop was an American post-punk movement of the mid-'80s which marked a return to the chiming guitars and pop melodies of the '60s. Sparked by the arrival of R.E.M., jangle-pop also had some folk-rock overtones, but it was essentially a pop-based format. But it wasn't mainstream music—the bands' lyrics were often deliberately cryptic and their sound was raw and amateurish, bearing all the signs of do-it-yourself productions. Jangle-pop was a major force between 1984 and 1987, not only were their Southern-pop bands like R.E.M. and Let's Active, there were the Paisley Underground bands on the west coast who were more psychedelic, and there were numerous bands scattered throughout the mid-west. In the late '80s, the sound fell out of favor, mainly because there were so many bands that sounded similar and were indistinguishable from each other. Though R.E.M. managed to cross over into the mainstream—in fact, become one of the most popular rock bands in the world—many of the groups (including Uncle Green and Miracle Legion) simply ran out of steam by the early '90s and disbanded.

JAZZ-ROCK — Unlike fusion, which is jazz played with rock influences, jazz-rock is essentially rock-based songs played with jazz flourishes and jazzy improvisations. When the two genres first developed in the late '60s, they were nearly identical; during the early '70s they began to branch away from each other and jazz-rock became known as a slightly more commercial version of fusion.

JUNGLE — Based almost entirely in England, jungle is a permutation of hardcore techno that emerged in the early '90s. Jungle is the most rhythmically complex of all forms of techno, relying on extremely fast polyrhythms and breakbeats. Usually, jungle is entirely instrumental—it is among the hardest of all hardcore techno, consisting of nothing but fast drum machines and deep bass. As its name implies, jungle does have more overt reggae, dub, and R&B influences than most hardcore—and that is why some critics claimed that the music was the sound of Black techno musicians and DJs reclaiming it from the White musicians and DJs who dominated the hardcore scene. Nevertheless, jungle never slows down to develop a groove—it just speeds along. Like most techno genres, jungle is primarily a singles-genre designed for a small, dedicated audience, although the crossover success of Goldie and his 1995 debut *Timeless* suggests that the music may have a broader appeal and more musical possibilities than other forms of techno.

KRAUT-ROCK — Kraut-rock refers to the legions of German bands of the early '70s that expanded the sonic possibilities of art and progressive-rock. Instead of following in the direction of their British and American counterparts, who were moving toward jazz and classical-based compositions and concept albums, the German bands became more mechanical and electronic. Working with early synthesizers and splicing together seemingly unconnected reels of tape, bands like Faust, Can, and Neu created a droning, pulsating sound that owed more to the avant garde than to rock 'n' roll. Although the bands didn't make much of an impact while they were active in the '70s, their music anticipated much of the post-punk of the early '80s, particularly industrial rock. Kraut-rock also came into vogue in the '90s, when groups like Stereolab and Tortoise began incorporating the hypnotic rhythms and electronic experiments of the German art-rock bands into their own, vaguely avant garde indie-rock.

LO-FI — During the late '80s and early '90s, lo fidelity became not only a description of the recording quality of a particular album, but it also became a genre onto itself. Throughout rock 'n' roll's history, recordings were made cheaply and quickly, often on sub-standard equipment. In that sense, the earliest rock 'n' roll records, most of the garage rock of the '60s and much of the punk rock of the late '70s, could be tagged as lo-fi. However, the term came to refer to a breed of underground indie-rockers that recorded their material at home on four-track machines. Most of this music grew out of the American underground of the '80s, including bands like R.E.M., as well as a handful of British post-punk bands and New Zealand bands like the Chills and the Clean. Often, these lo-fi bands fluctuated from simple pop and rock songs to free-form song structures to pure noise and arty experimentalism. Even when the groups kept the songs relatively straightforward, the thin quality of the recordings, the layers of tape distortion and hiss, as well as the tendency toward abstract, obtuse lyrics made the music sound different and left-of-center. Initially, lo-fi recordings were traded on homemade tapes, but several indie labels—most notably K Records, which was run by Calvin Johnson, who led the lo-fi band Beat Happening—released albums on vinyl. Several groups in the late '80s, like Pussy Galore, Beat Happening and Royal Trux, earned small cult followings within the American underground. By 1992, groups like Sebadoh and Pavement had become popular cult acts in America and Britain with their willfully noisy, chaotic recordings. A few years later, Liz Phair and Beck helped break the lo-fi aesthetic into the mainstream, albeit in a more streamlined fashion.

MOD — Technically, mod refers to a lifestyle and fashion more than music itself. During the early '60s, legions of teenagers in Great Britain began dressing in stylish, neo-Italian fashions and listening to American R&B, particularly Motown. Soon, these teens were dubbed "mods." The

original mod bands were all R&B cover bands, but soon they began writing their own material which was generally in the vein of their influences. Mod bands played R&B harder and faster than the original recordings—it was relentless, amphetamine-driven rock 'n' roll. Many of the mod bands were barely heard outside of the UK, since the lifestyle was primarily a British phenomenon. Two bands—the Small Faces and the Who—were able to crossover to the US market, but that was after both bands began developing and expanding their R&B-based sound. By the time psychedelia came around in the late '60s, Mod had died out in Britain. However, mod—both the music and the lifestyle—came back in full force in the late '70s, thanks to the Jam.

MOD-REVIVAL — In the late '70s, a group of British punk rockers inspired by the Jam brought back the mod styles and sound of mid-'60s London. The mod revivalists stuck to the R&B-informed rock 'n' roll that distinguished the original '60s mods, but the sound was harder and more frenetic, and often only implied the music's R&B roots. Since the original wave of mod bands in the '60s only included a few bands—the Small Faces, the Who, the Creation, and the Action, as well as a handful of others—there were actually more mod groups in the revival than there were in the '60s. Furthermore, since most of the original mods only performed in cover bands (with the exception of the aforementioned groups) or simply danced to Motown records, the revival was the first wave of mod bands to rely on original material. Nevertheless, the mod revival only produced a handful of popular bands. The Jam were the most popular band in Britain during the late '70s and early '80s, but groups like the Lambrettas, the Merton Parkas, Squire, and Purple Hearts managed to cultivate cult followings and occasionally have pop hits. The mod revival lasted as long as the Jam's career—after Paul Weller disbanded the trio to form the Style Council, most of the mod revivalists either split up or became new romantics, which usually resulted in a breakup as well. Despite its brief time in the spotlight, the mod revival had a lasting impact on British pop music, as many of the most popular English rock bands of the '80s and '90s—from the Smiths to Blur and Oasis—was indebted either to the Jam or to the movement in general.

MOTOWN — Motown is one of the few record labels that created a sound and style so distinct that it became known as a genre onto itself. For most R&B and pop fans, the sound of Motown instantly identifiable—strong, bouncy beat, supported with bouncy bass lines, and soulful vocals. It was R&B, but with a pop production and written with a sense of pop craftsmanship.

NEO-PSYCHEDELIA — Neo-Psychedelia represents all the legions of bands that have adapted, replicated, or interpreted the original sounds of psychedelic years after the fact. The first wave of neo-psychedelic bands arrived in the mid-'80s was largely influenced by the psychedelic sounds of the mid-'60s and generally sounded quite similar to bands like the Beatles, the Byrds, Pink Floyd, and countless garage bands. Neo-Psychedelic bands in the late '80s and '90s have tended to be more experimental and jam-oriented, much like how the first wave of psychedelia slowly evolved into the free-form jams of the late '60s.

NEW JACK R&B — New jack R&B evolved in the late '80s, when urban contemporary soul artists began incorporating hip-hop rhythms, samples, and production techniques into their sound. Some songs simply had hip-hop beats, others had rapped sections and sung choruses, but the overall result was an edgier, more street-oriented sound that seamlessly blended both the melodic qualities of soul and the funky rhythms of rap. It paved the way for the '90s soul, where the dividing line between rap and R&B was frequently indistinguishable.

NEW ROMANTIC — The new romantics were a peculiar subgenre of new wave. Wearing heavy makeup and dressed in stylish clothing, the new romantics took not only their visual cues from David Bowie and Roxy Music, but also their musical cues. Drawing from latter-day Roxy and *Station to Station*- and *Low*-era Roxy Music, new romantics created a sleek, synthesized, and danceable form of pop that was designed to be fashionable and transient. More than any other pop-rock genre, new romantics relied on style and glamour. Duran Duran was the ultimate new romantic group and they were the only one to become superstars. New romantic had died out by 1984, but it had a brief revival in the mid-'90s by the *Melody Maker*-sponsored, non-movement Romo.

NEW WAVE — During the late '70s and early '80s, "new wave" was a catch-all term for the music that directly followed punk rock; often, the term encompassed punk itself, as well. In retrospect, it's became clear that the music that followed punk could be divided, more or less, into two categories—post-punk and new wave. Where post-punk was arty, difficult and challenging, new wave was pop music, pure and simple. It retained the fresh vigor and irreverence of punk music, as well as a fascination with electronics, style, and art. Therefore, there was a lot of stylistic diversity to new wave. It meant the nervy power-pop of bands like XTC and Nick Lowe, but it also meant synth-rockers like Gary Numan, or rock revivalists like Graham Parker and Rockpile. There were edgy new wave songwriters like Elvis Costello, pop bands like Squeeze, tough rock 'n' rollers like the Pretenders, pop-reggae like the Police, mainstream rockers like the Cars, and ska revivalists like the Specials and

Madness. As important as these major artists were the countless one-hit wonders that emerged during early new wave. These one-hit groups were as diverse as the major artists, but they all shared a love of pop hooks, modernist, synthesized production, and a fascination for being slightly left of center. By the early '80s, new wave described nearly new pop-rock artist, especially those that used synthesizers like the Human League and Duran Duran. New wave received a boost in the early '80s by MTV, who broadcast endless hours of new wave videos in order to keep themselves on the air. Therefore, new wave got a second life in 1982, when it probably would have died out. Instead, 1982 and 1983 were boom years for polished, MTV-radio new wave outfits like Culture Club, Adam Ant, Spandau Ballet, Haircut 100, and A Flock of Seagulls. New wave finally died out in 1984, when established artists began to make professional videos and a new crop of guitar-oriented bands like the Smiths and R.E.M. emerged to capture the attention of college-radio and underground rock fans. Nevertheless, new wave proved more influential than many of its critics would have suspected, as the mid-'90s were dominated by bands, from Blur to Weezer, that were raised on the music.

NO WAVE — No wave was one of the first post-punk genres to emerge in the late '70s. It was an atonal, dissonant and experimental group of bands that were consciously pushing the limits of rock music; in that sense, it was more like performance art than music. Though the movement didn't exist outside of New York, it managed to worm its way into alternative music in the mid-'80s through the feedback-laden, sonic experimentations of Sonic Youth.

PAISLEY UNDERGROUND — The Paisley Underground was the most distinctive sub-genre of jangle-pop in the mid-'80s. Like jangle-pop, the bands in the Paisley Underground revived the clean, chiming textures of folk-rock, but they had a more psychedelic bent to their sound. Jangle-pop bands weren't necessarily revivalists—they updated the ringing guitars and melodies of '60s guitar-pop for the '80s—but the Paisley Underground was determined to keep the sound of the '60s alive, through their music and their appearance. The Paisley Underground gained a dedicated following in the American underground during the mid-'80s, but their audience declined in the late '80s and the scene soon disappeared.

PHILLY SOUL — Philly soul was one of the most popular forms of soul music in the early '70s. Building on the steady groove of Hi Records and Stax/Volt singles, Philly soul added sweeping strings, seductive horns, and lush arrangements to the deep rhythms. As a result, it was much smoother—even slicker—than the deep soul of the late '60s, but the vocals remained as soulful as any previous form of R&B. Philly soul was primarily a producer's medium, as Kenny Gamble & Leon Huff and Thom Bell created the instrumental textures that came to distinguish the genre. That isn't to short change the vocalists, since the Spinners, the O'Jays, Harold Melvin & the Blue Notes, and the Stylistics were among fine soul singers with distinctive voices, but the sonic elements that made Philly soul distinctive were the creation of the producers. Gamble & Huff worked with the Delfonics, Archie Bell, Harold Melvin & the Blue Notes, and the O'Jays; Bell produced the Spinners and the Stylistics, among others. The highly-produced sound of Philly paved the way for the studio constructions of disco and urban contemporary R&B.

POST-GRUNGE — Post-grunge emerged in the early '90s, after alternative music had broken into the mainstream. Where nearly all of the original grunge bands had strong ties to the indie-rock scene of the '80s, the post-grunge groups built on the angst-ridden, heavy sound of Seattle grunge. Most post-grunge was released on major labels and was consequently slicker and more polished than grunge itself—it was merely informed by the same lyrical themes, heavy instrumental attack, and visual style of grunge. Post-grunge isn't strictly grunge—it tends to draw from sources as varied as jangle-pop and AOR rock—but all of the groups are tied together by their polished, radio-ready productions, a reliance on canned distorted guitars, and self-consciously introspective lyrics.

POST-PUNK — After the punk revolution of 1977, a number of bands formed. They were all inspired by the independent spirit of punk, as well as its raw sound. Instead of replicating the sound of the Sex Pistols, many of these bands forged into more experimental territory, taking cues from Roxy Music, David Bowie, and T. Rex in addition to punk rock. The result was a group of bands tied together by their counter-culture spirit and defiance of accepted rock conventions. Many of these groups—like Joy Division or the Cure—created dark, bleak soundscapes that employed both synthesizers and guitars. Others had a lighter musical approach, but their lyrics and music were off-kilter and subverted traditional pop-rock song structures. Post-punk eventually evolved into alternative pop-rock in the '80s.

POST-ROCK/EXPERIMENTAL — Post-rock was an experimental, avant garde movement that emerged in the mid-'90s. Most post-rock was droning and hypnotic, drawing from ambient, free-form jazz, avant garde, and electronic music more than rock. The majority of post-rock groups were like Tortoise, a Chicago-based band with a rotating lineup. Tortoise viewed their music not as songs, but as ever-changing composi-

tions that they improvised nightly. Most of post-rock were defiantly anti-mainstream and anti-indie-rock in the vein of Tortoise. However, there were certain groups—like Stereolab—that essentially worked in a pop and indie-rock format, but touched on the experimental and avant garde tendencies of Tortoise.

POWER-POP — Power-pop is a cross between the crunching hard rock of the Who and the sweet melodicism of the Beatles and the Beach Boys, with the ringing guitars of the Byrds thrown in for good measure. Although several bands of the early '70s—most notably the Raspberries, Big Star, and Badfinger—established the sound of power-pop, it wasn't until the late '70s that a whole group of like-minded bands emerged. Most of these groups modeled themselves on the Raspberries (since they were the only power-pop band of their era to have hit singles), or they went directly back to the source and based their sound on stacks of British Invasion records. What tied all of these bands together was their love of the three-minute pop single. Power-pop bands happened to emerge around the same time of punk, so they were swept along with the new wave, because their brief, catchy songs fit into the post-punk aesthetic. Out of these bands, Cheap Trick, the Knack, the Romantics, and Dwight Twilley had the biggest hits, but the Shoes, the Records, the Nerves, and 20/20, among many others, became cult favorites. During the early '80s, power-pop died away as a hip movement, and nearly all of the bands broke up. However, in the late '80s, a new breed of power-pop began to form. The new bands, who were primarily influenced by Big Star, blended traditional power-pop with alternative rock sensibilities and sounds; in the process, groups like Teenage Fanclub, Material Issue, and the Posies became critical and cult favorites. While these bands gained the attention of hip circles, many of the original power-pop groups began recording new material and releasing it on independent labels. In the early '90s, the *Yellow Pills* compilation series gathered together highlights from these re-activated power-poppers, as well as new artists that worked in a traditional power-pop vein. Throughout the early and mid-'90s, this group of independent, grass roots power-pop bands gained a small, but dedicated, cult following in the US.

PROTO-PUNK — Proto-punk is a loose gathering of artists that never quite fit into the mainstream rock 'n' roll of the late '60s and early '70s. From the sonic experimentations and deceptively gentle folk-rock of the Velvet Underground to the wild, gender-bending hard rock of the New York Dolls and the song poetry of Patti Smith, proto-punk covers a diverse array of sounds and styles, but they are all tied together by an edgy, artsy attempt to subvert, ignore, and rewrite rock conventions. In the process, the spirit—if not always the music—of these artists sowed the seeds of the punk revolution of the late '70s.

PSYCHEDELIC — Psychedelic rock emerged in the mid-'60s, as British Invasion and folk-rock bands began expanding the sonic possibilities of their music. Instead of confining themselves to the brief, concise verse-chorus-verse patterns of rock 'n' roll, they moved toward more free-form, fluid song structures. Just as important—if not more so—the groups began incorporating elements of Indian and Eastern music and free-form jazz to their sound, as well as experimenting with electronically altering instruments and voices within the recording studio. Initially, around 1965 and 1966, bands like the Yardbirds and the Byrds broke down the boundaries for psychedelia, creating swirling layers of fuzz-toned guitars, sitars, and chanted vocals. Soon, numerous groups followed their pattern, including the Beatles and the Rolling Stones, who both recorded psychedelia in 1966. In no time, groups on both sides of the Atlantic embraced the possibilities of the new genre and the differences were notable. In Britain, psychedelia tended to be whimsical and surrealistic. Nevertheless, bands—most notably Pink Floyd and Traffic—played extended instrumentals that relied on improvisation as much as their American contemporaries the Grateful Dead, the Doors, Love, and Jefferson Airplane. In other corners of America, garage bands began playing psychedelic rock without abandoning their raw, amateurish foundation of three-chord rock—they just layered in layers of distortion, feedback, and effects. Eventually, psychedelic evolved into acid-rock, heavy metal, and art-rock, but there continued to be revivals of psychedelia in the decades that followed, most notably in the American underground of the mid-'80s.

PUB-ROCK — In some ways, the British phenomenon of pub-rock in the early '70s wasn't much more than roots-rock, since it basically consisted of bar bands that played back to 'n' roll, country-rock, and the blues. But there were some crucial differences, particularly in approach. If pub-rock is anything, it is loose and unpretentious—these were guys that played music for the hell of it. The members of the major pub rock bands—Brinsley Schwarz, Ducks Deluxe, Bees Make Honey, Ace, Dr. Feelgood—came from a variety of musical backgrounds, including folk-rock, blues, country-rock, and traditional rock & roll. This kind of rootsy music stood in direct contrast to the glam-rock, hard rock, and progressive-rock that dominated the British charts. Consequently, the groups had trouble finding places to play and they had to create their own circuit by playing hidden-away pubs throughout England. In no time, the unconventional venues and their defiantly good-time, back-to-basics rock 'n' roll became a rallying cry for pub-rockers. None of the pub-rock bands became stars or had hits, but their do-it-yourself attitude and stripped-down sound—as well as the creation of the pub-rock circuit itself—paved the way for punk rock. Indeed many pub-rockers—including Brinsley Schwarz's Nick Lowe, the 101ers' Joe Strummer, Flip City's Elvis Costello, Kilburn & the High Roads' Ian Dury and Graham Parker—became important figures in punk and new wave just a few years after the pub-rock scene faded away in the mid-'70s.

PUNK — Punk rock returned rock 'n' roll to the basics—three chords and a simple melody. It just did it louder and faster and more abrasively than any other rock 'n' roller in the past. Although there had been several bands to flirt with what became known as punk rock—including the garage rockers of the '60s and the Velvet Underground, the Stooges, and the New York Dolls—it wasn't until the mid-'70s that punk became its own genre. On both sides of the Atlantic, young bands began forsaking the sonic excesses that distinguished mainstream hard rock and stripping the music down to its essentials. In New York, the first punk band was the Ramones; in London, the first punk band was the Sex Pistols. Although the bands had different agendas and sounds—the Ramones were faster and indebted to bubblegum, while the Pistols played Faces riffs sloppier and louder than the Faces themselves—the direct approach of the bands revolutionized music in both the UK and the US. In America, punk remained an underground sensation, eventually spawning the hardcore and indie-rock scenes of the '80s, but in the UK, it was a full-scale phenomenon. In the UK, the Sex Pistols were thought of as a serious threat to the well-being of the government and monarchy, but more importantly, they caused countless bands to form. Some of the bands stuck close to the Pistols original blueprint, but many found their own sound, whether it was the edgy pop of the Buzzcocks, the anthemic reggae-informed rock of the Clash, or the arty experiments of Wire and Joy Division. Soon, punk splintered into post-punk (which was more experimental and artier than punk), new wave (which was more pop-oriented), and hardcore, which simply made punk harder, faster and more abrasive. Throughout the '80s, punk was identified with the hardcore scenes in both America and England. In the early '90s, a wave of punk revivalists—led by Green Day and Rancid—emerged from the American underground. The new wave of punk rockers followed the same template as the original punks, but they tended to incorporate elements of heavy metal into their sound.

PUNK REVIVAL — During the early '90s—nearly 20 years after punk happened—the US had its first punk rock hit albums and singles, as a wave of bands raised on '80s hardcore and '70s punk worked its way into the American mainstream. Essentially, these bands were all traditionalists, keeping alive the styles of groups like the Sex Pistols, the Stooges, the Jam, the Exploited, Black Flag, Dead Kennedys, the Descendants, and countless other punk and hardcore bands. Since hardcore mutated into speed-metal in the late '80s, it wasn't surprising that these punk traditionalists were heavier than their initial influences, but that is partially what made the music appealing to a mass audience in America. The first punk revivalists to break into the American mainstream were Green Day and the Offspring, and their success helped solidify cult followings for groups like Rancid, NOFX, Pennywise, and Pansy Division, as well as bring the spotlight to neglected '80s punk bands like Bad Religion and underground punk genres like the third wave of ska revival.

R&B — Evolving out of jump blues in the late '40s, R&B laid the groundwork for rock 'n' roll. R&B kept the tempo and the drive of jump blues, but its instrumentation was sparer and the emphasis was on the song, not improvisation. It was blues chord changes played with an insistent backbeat. During the '50s, R&B was dominated by vocalists like Ray Charles and Ruth Brown, as well as vocal groups like the Drifters and the Coasters. Eventually, R&B evolved into soul, which was funkier and looser than the pile-driving rhythms of R&B.

RAVE — Rave is more of an event than a genre of music. Raves were underground parties where acid house and hardcore records were played and large quantities of hallucinogens, particularly ecstasy, were consumed. Most of the music played at raves had a psychedelic quality, even before hallucinogens became a major element of the scene. DJs played at the raves, mixing stacks of house, acid jazz, and techno singles; the DJs, not the recording artists themselves, became the most recognizable names in the scene. Raves were primarily an English phenomenon during the late '80s and early '90s. They were conducted in large venues, particularly abandoned warehouses and open fields. Eventually, the British government became concerned that raves were a dangerous, anti-social phenomenon that had to be shut down, but the parties never disappeared, especially since word of the events were usually passed through word-of-mouth and handmade fliers. In the US, raves began to make some inroads in the early '90s, but they never gained a large audience, even by underground standards. Throughout the '90s, bands that were directly influenced by rave culture—particularly "baggy" bands like the Stone Roses, Happy Mondays, and Charlatans, Brit-pop acts like Pulp and Oasis, and techno artists like the Prodigy—made their way into the

mainstream, and the culture continued to capture the attention of British youth into the late '90s.

RIOT GRRRL — Riot Grrl is a subgenre of early '90s indie-rock and punk rock that is distinguished by its radical feminist lyrics and its raw, willfully amateurish musical attack. Although Riot Grrrl received a lot of press, most of it was misguided, identifying such acts as Hole and PJ Harvey as riot grrrls. All genuine Riot Grrrl bands—most notable Bikini Kill, Bratmobile, and Huggy Bear—never broke into the mainstream, mainly because their music was too abrasive for general consumption, even after alternative music broke into the mainstream.

ROCK 'N' ROLL — In its purest form, rock 'n' roll has three-chords, a strong, insistent back beat and a catchy melody. Early rock 'n' roll drew from a variety of sources, primarily blues, R&B and country, but also gospel, traditional pop, jazz, and folk. All of these influences combined in a simple, blues-based song structure that was fast, danceable, and catchy. The first wave of rock 'n' rollers—Chuck Berry, Elvis Presley, Little Richard, Jerry Lee Lewis, Buddy Holly, Bo Diddley, Bill Haley, Gene Vincent, the Everly Brothers, Carl Perkins, among many others—set the template for rock 'n' roll that was followed over the next four decades. During each decade, a number of artists replicated the sound of the first rockers, while others expanded that definition, and still others completely exploded the constrictions of the genre. From the British Invasion, folk-rock and psychedelia, through hard rock, heavy metal, glam-rock, and punk, most subgenres of rock 'n' roll initially demonstrated an allegiance to the basic structure of rock 'n' roll. Once these permutations emerged, traditional rock 'n' roll faded away from the pop charts, yet there were always artists that kept the flame alive. Some, like the Rolling Stones and the Faces, adhered to the basic rules of traditional rock 'n' roll but played the music fast and loose. Others, like proto-punk rockers the Velvet Underground, the New York Dolls, and the Stooges, kept the basic song structure, but played it with more menace. Still others, like Dave Edmunds and Graham Parker, became rock 'n' roll traditionalists, writing and recording music that never wavered from the sound of the late '50s and early '60s. Although the term "rock 'n' roll" came to refer to a number of different musics in the decades following its inception, the essential form of the music never changed.

ROCKABILLY — Rockabilly was one of the earliest forms of rock 'n' roll and it has proved to be one of the most enduring. Where rock 'n' rollers like Chuck Berry, Little Richard, Jerry Lee Lewis, and Fats Domino emphasized the blues, R&B, and pop roots of rock 'n' roll, rockabilly was backwoods hillbilly music played to boogie beat. The form emerged in the mid-'50s and it stayed the same for the next four decades, with new performers occasionally adding contemporary flairs but essentially sticking to the basic rockabilly formula.

ROOTS-ROCK — During the mid-'80s, a generation of bands reacted to the slick, pop-oriented sounds of new wave by reverting back to the traditional rock 'n' roll values of the '50s and '60s. By bringing rock back to its roots—whether that was rock 'n' roll, blues, or country—the group managed to sound like a fresh alternative, which brought them critical praise and heavy airplay from American college radio stations. Most of the leading bands of the era—such as the Beat Farmers, Del Lords, Long Ryders, and the Del Fuegos—filtered much of their traditional values through the music of Creedence Clearwater Revival, but there were an equally large number of groups that simply worked in a "rootsy" fashion, without any direct influence outside of the concept of traditional rock and blues. In the late '80s, roots-rock ceased to be a hip music in the American underground, but most of the bands continued to record and perform into the '90s. Throughout the '90s, a small number of new roots-rockers emerged, although they weren't afforded the same exposure as their predecessors.

SHOEGAZING — Shoegazing is a genre of late '80s and early '90s British indie-rock, named after the band's motionless performing style, where they stood on stage and stared at the floor while they played. But shoegazing wasn't about visuals—it was about pure sound. The sound of the music was overwhelmingly loud, with long, droning riffs, waves of distortion, and cascades of feedback. Vocals and melodies disappeared into the walls of guitars, creating a wash of sound where no instrument was distinguishable from the other. Most shoegazing groups worked off the template My Bloody Valentine established with their early EPs and their first full-length album, *Isn't Anything*, but Dinosaur Jr., the Jesus & Mary Chain, and Cocteau Twins were also major influences. Bands that followed—most notably Ride, Lush, Chapterhouse, and the Boo Radleys—added their own stylistic flourishes. Ride veered close to '60s psychedelia, while Lush alternated between straight pop and the dream-pop of the Cocteau Twins. None of the shoegazers were dynamic performers or interesting interviews, which prevented them from breaking through into the crucial US market. In 1992—after the groups had dominated the British music press and indie charts for about three years—the shoegazing groups were swept aside by the twin tides of American grunge and Suede, the band to initiate the wave of Brit-pop that ruled British music during the mid-'90s. Some shoegazers broke up within a few years (Chapterhouse, Ride), while other groups—such as the Boo Radleys and

Lush—evolved with the times and were able to sustain careers into the late '90s.

SINGER-SONGWRITER — Although many vocalists sang their own songs, including early rock 'n' rollers like Chuck Berry and Buddy Holly, the term "singer-songwriter" refers to the legions of performers that followed Bob Dylan. Most of the original singer-songwriters performed alone with an acoustic guitar or a piano. Their lyrics were personal, although they were often veiled by layers of metaphors and obscure imagery. Singer-songwriters drew primarily from folk and country, although certain writers like Randy Newman and Carole King incorporated the songcraft of Tin Pan Alley pop. The main concern for any singer-songwriter was the song itself, not necessarily the performance. However, most singer-songwriter records have a similar sound, which is usually spare, direct, and reflective, which places the emphasis on the song itself. James Taylor, Jackson Browne, and Joni Mitchell were the quintessential singer-songwriters of the '70s and most of the songwriters that followed them based themselves on their styles, or Dylan. Singer-songwriters were at the height of their popularity in the early '70s, and although they faded away from the pop chart, they never disappeared. In the late '70s, Rikki Lee Jones and Joan Armatrading crossed over into the pop charts, as did Suzanne Vega and Tracy Chapman in the late '80s. Throughout the '80s and '90s, a number of songwriters—like John Gorka and Bill Morrissey—kept the tradition alive through a series of independently-released albums.

SKA REVIVAL — Ska evolved in the early '60s, when Jamaicans tried to replicate the sound of the New Orleans R&B they heard over their radio. Instead of mimicking the sound of the R&B, the first ska artists developed a distinctive rhythmic and melodic sensibility, which eventually turned into reggae music. In the late '70s, a number of young British bands began reviving the sound of original ska, adding a nervous punk edge to the skittish rhythms. Furthermore, the ska revivalists were among the only bands of the era to feature racially integrated lineups, which was a bold political statement for the time. Indeed, ska revival was more implicitly political than any of its British punk and new wave contemporaries. The leading ska revivalist band was the Specials, who formed their own independent label, 2-Tone. Led by Jerry Dammers and fronted by Terry Hall, the Specials established the sound and approach for all of the bands that followed, and were an immediate hit in England. Through 2-Tone and a variety of tours, the Specials helped cultivate an active ska-revival scene—the group offered support for all of the major ska revivalists that followed, including Madness, the (English) Beat, and Selecter. Throughout the early '80s, ska-revival bands, particularly Madness, were very popular in the UK. The groups didn't make much headway in the US until 1982 and 1983, when MTV aired videos by all of the important (and many of the lesser) bands. By that time, most of the bands had run their peak and it was just a matter of months before the Specials, Madness, the (English) Beat, and Selecter all broke up. Although the ska-revival bands never became stars outside of the UK, they did become major cult figures in the US and inspired several generations of musicians to form similar bands. This wave of ska revivalists were equally inspired by hardcore punk and heavy metal, thereby stripping out much of the R&B groove that informed the original ska and 2-Tone artists. Nevertheless, these bands—including Rancid, Mighty Mighty Bosstones, and No Doubt—became quite popular in America during the mid-'90s. In the UK, ska revivalists influenced both Brit-pop bands like Blur and trip-hop artists like Tricky.

SKIFFLE — This refers to a mixture of jazz and country blues often played on a mixture of basically simple instruments such as the guitar, harmonica, jug, kazoo, and washtub bass. Although the term "skiffle" was originally used in the US in the '30s to describe mixtures of blues, boogie-woogie, and other popular Black music, the skiffle revival of the '50s—as typified by Lonnie Donegan's recording of "Rock Island Line"—was most pronounced the UK where it remained popular until the style was replaced by rock 'n' roll at the end of the decade. Major skiffle artists include Chris Barber and Ken Colyer.

SOFT ROCK — Soft rock emerged in the early '70s, partially as a reaction to the extreme sounds of the late '60s. Soft rock was commercial and inoffensive, taking the sound of singer-songwriter and pop-rock but smoothing out all the edges. Bands like Bread, the Carpenters, and Chicago relied on simple, melodic songs with big, lush productions. Throughout the '70s, soft rock dominated the airwaves and it eventually evolved into the synthesized sounds of adult contemporary in the '80s.

SOUL — Soul music was the result of the urbanization and commercialization of rhythm and blues in the '60s. Soul came to describe a number of R&B-based music. From the bouncy, catchy acts at Motown to the horn-driven, gritty soul of Stax/Volt, there was an immense amount of diversity within soul. During the first part of the '60s, soul music remained close to its R&B roots. However, musicians pushed the music in different directions; usually, different regions of America produced different kinds of soul. In urban centers like New York, Philadelphia, and Chicago, the music concentrated on vocal interplay and smooth productions. In Detroit, Motown concentrated on creating a pop-oriented sound

that was informed equally by gospel, R&B, and rock 'n' roll. In the south, the music became harder and tougher, relying on syncopated rhythms, raw vocals, and blaring horns. All of these styles formed soul, which ruled the Black music charts throughout the '60s and also frequently crossed over into the pop charts. At the end of the '60s, soul began to splinter apart, as artists like James Brown and Sly Stone developed funk and other artists developed slicker forms of soul. Although soul music evolved, it never went away—not only did the music inform all of the R&B of the '70s, '80s and '90s, there were always pockets of musicians around the world that kept performing traditional soul.

SOUTHERN-ROCK — Southern-rock drew from the heavy blues-rock of the late '60s, as well as honky tonk and Bakersfield country, creating a distinctive fusion of the genres. Throughout the early '70s, Southern-rock bands formed a major part of the American hard-rock band. The first Southern-rock band was the Allman Brothers, who elaborated on the improvisational tendencies and loudness of Cream and the Grateful Dead while staying closer to rock 'n' roll's blues and country roots. They were followed shortly afterward by Lynyrd Skynyrd, who played heavier and louder than the Allman Brothers; in the process, they set the template for all the Southern-rock bands that followed them. Skynyrd had three lead guitarists, so they naturally indulged themselves in long jams. They also had a sharp songwriter in Ronnie Van Zandt, who was able to fuse traditional music with contemporary rock 'n' roll and also had a gift for perceptive lyrics. The bands that followed Skynyrd often lacked a songwriter the stature of Van Zandt, but they were able to replicate the group's heavy boogie and long jams. Several bands took the music closer to its country or blues roots, while others, like the Dixie Dregs, developed skilled improvisational technique. Still, the dominant sound of Southern-rock was its loose fusion of several rootsy genres and its fondness for heavy boogie jams. The genre died out in the early '80s, after Molly Hatchet, the Marshall Tucker Band, and .38 Special experienced a string of AOR hits, but the spirit of the music lived on in '90s bands like the Black Crowes and Widespread Panic.

SPEED METAL — In the mid-'80s, speed metal became the most popular form of heavy metal in the American underground. Crossing the new wave of British heavy metal with hardcore punk, speed metal was extremely fast, abrasive, and technically demanding—the bands played fast, but their attack was precise and clean. In that sense, speed metal always remained true to its metal roots. But what it borrowed from hardcore—namely, insanely fast tempos and a defiant, do-it-yourself attitude—was equally important, since it gave the band not only a unique musical approach but also an attractive image for legions of alienated suburban youths. Led by Metallica, Megadeth, and Anthrax, this new wave of metal bands stood in direct contrast with the pop-oriented metal that dominated the charts during the '80s (Ratt, Poison, and Mötley Crüe, among countless others), but the groups managed to cultivate dedicated cult followings that would eventually allow them to go platinum with no support from mainstream media, radio, or MTV. Eventually, speed metal fractured into a number of different subgenres, most notably thrash, grindcore, and black metal.

SURF — Surf rock was one of the most popular forms of American rock 'n' roll of the early '60s. Distinguished by reverb-drenched guitar, rolling instrumentals that were designed to sound like crashing waves, and simple, three-chord songs, the music may sound similar on the surface, but it was revolutionary for its time, exploring sonic territories previously unheard in rock music. The first wave of surf rock was kicked off by Dick Dale and his single "Let's Go Trippin'." The single was a local hit in California, but it inspired countless bands to form, such as the Chantays and Surfaris, who had national hits ("Pipeline" and "Wipe Out," respectively). Nearly all of these groups were one-hit wonders that struggled to produce a second hit single. The second wave of surf rock was led by the Beach Boys, who added Four Freshmen-style pop harmonies to the basic Chuck Berry rhythms of surf rock. Groups like Jan & Dean and Ronny & the Daytonas followed, but the Beach Boys remained the ultimate surf band for many listeners, simply because they put the appeal of the beach and surfing into words instead of conveying it with impressionistic music. Nevertheless, the sounds of the instrumental surf rock echoed throughout the sonic experimentations of '60s guitarists and the genre remained popular into the '90s, thanks to the efforts of several generations of surf-rock revivalists.

SYNTH-POP — Synth-pop was one of the most distinctive subgenres of new wave. In the early '80s, a number of bands—primarily British and heavily influenced by Roxy Music and David Bowie—adapted the electronic innovations of bands like Kraftwerk for pop songs. Initially, in the hands of artists like Gary Numan, the Human League, and Depeche Mode, the sound was eerie, sterile and vaguely menacing, since the electronics droned on relentlessly without any change in inflections. However, these first stabs at synth-pop were transformed into danceable, synthesized pop by Duran Duran, who made the synthesized hooks warmer and catchier by grafting them onto a dance beat. Soon, a flood of bands followed Duran Duran's lead and although some of the groups weren't as infectious as that band, they nevertheless relied on the conventions of three-minute pop. Duran Duran became stars, while most other synth-pop groups were lucky to have more than one hit. There were some exceptions—Human League and Eurythmics had several hits, as did Howard Jones—but the field was mainly occupied by one-hit wonders like A Flock of Seagulls. By 1984, synth-pop had begun to die out, but the music had helped establish the synthesizer as a primary instrument in mainstream pop music during its time in the spotlight.

TECHNO — Techno had its roots in the electronic house music made in Detroit in the mid-'80s. Where house still had explicit connection to disco even when it was entirely mechanical, techno was strictly electronic music, designed for a small, specific audience. The first techno DJs—Kevin Suanderson, Juan Atkins, Derrick May, among others—emphasized the electronic, synthesized beats of electro-funk artists like Afrika Bambatta and synth-rock units like Kraftwerk. In the US, techno was strictly an underground phenomenon, but in the UK, it broke into the mainstream in the late '80s. In the early '90s, techno began to fragment into a number of subgenres, including hardcore, ambient, and jungle. In hardcore techno, the beats-per-minute on each record where sped up to ridiculous, undanceable levels—it was designed to alienate a broad audience. Ambient took the opposite direction, slowing the beats down and relying on watery electronic textures—it was used as come-down music, when ravers and club-goers needed a break from the acid house and hardcore techno. Jungle was nearly as aggressive as hardcore, combining driving techno beats with breakbeats and dancehall reggae—essentially. All subgenres of techno often were initially designed to be played in clubs, where they would be mixed by DJs. Consequently, most of the music was available on 12-inch singles or various artists compilations, where the songs could run for a long time, providing the DJ with a lot of material to mix into his set. In the mid-'90s, a new breed of techno artists—most notably ambient acts like the Orb and Aphex Twin, but also harder-edged artists like the Prodigy and Goldie— began constructing albums that didn't consist of raw beats intended for mixing. Not surprisingly, these artists—particularly the Prodigy— became the first recognizable stars in techno.

TEEN IDOL — It took rock 'n' roll a few years before they had a group of attractive young vocalists to claim as their own teen idols. Most of the teen idols of the late '50s and early '60s owed more to traditional pop than rock 'n' roll. They didn't have the raw sexuality of Elvis Presley, nor did they have his instinctive vocal talents. The teen idols were carefully groomed and given inoffensive, catchy material to sing. Pat Boone was the first of the teen idols of the late '50s. Boone primarily covered rock 'n' roll and R&B hits, but his clean-cut good looks and smooth vocals set the stage for singers like Paul Anka, who primarily sang ballads that were given contemporary pop-rock productions. Ricky Nelson emerged at the same time as Anka and out of all the teen idols, his music remained the closest to rock 'n' roll—Nelson performed rockabilly, R&B, and rock 'n' roll, but he played with professional studio musicians who helped give the music a cleaner attack. After Anka and Nelson, the golden age of teen idols emerged, as a number of vocalists with limited vocal skills but good looks became stars. These vocalists—like Fabian and Frankie Avalon—sang songs written by professional songwriters. Frequently, this material hearkened back to the Tin Pan Alley and traditional pop that dominated the early '50s, but the records were given rock 'n' roll productions. Teen idols continued to be popular throughout the early '60s and the genre went through a number of fads, including a string of teenage television actors who turned into singers, as well as a wave of melodramatic songs about tragic teenage deaths. Rockers like Gene Pitney, Dion, and Del Shannon were packaged as teenage idols but their music was substantial enough to essentially sustain the death of teen idols in 1963. Furthermore, there were a number of British teen idols—such as Cliff Richard and Adam Faith—who dominated the charts in the same era with similar music, but they all faded away upon the arrival of the Beatles in 1963. During the '70s, the term "teen idol" came to describe a number of AM-pop artists like the Bay City Rollers and Shaun Cassidy, who essentially updated the lightweight approach of '60s teen idols for the '70s.

TEX-MEX — Tex-Mex is a unique fusion of rock 'n' roll, blues, country, and various strains of Latin music, particularly conjunto. As far as rock 'n' roll is concerned, Tex-Mex emerged in the '60s, when garage rock bands like the Sir Douglas Quintet and vocalists like Freddy Fender began pounding out rock 'n' roll that was spiced with south-of-the-border flourishes. During the '70s, these conjunto, country, and blues roots became more pronounced and by the '80s, Tex-Mex was established as a unique genre of its own that fell between the cracks of rock, country, and Latin music.

THIRD WAVE SKA REVIVAL — The third wave of ska revival emerged in the late '80s, when certain members of the American punk underground began returning to the sounds of British ska revival and infusing it with a hardcore punk attack. During the early '80s, this third wave continued to grow—more bands continued to pop up across the country, but many of the most popular were based in California. As time wore one, the hardcore influences eventually mutated into heavy metal,

much like hardcore punk itself. Eventually, the third wave of ska revivalists broke into the American mainstream, thanks to the success of fellow Californian punk revivalists Green Day and the Offspring. The first third wave band to break big was Rancid, but they were quickly followed by groups like No Doubt, Goldfinger, Sublime, and Dancehall Crashers; the Mighty Mighty Bosstones, who were one of the leading figures of the scene in the early '90s, just missed the commercial bandwagon. Most of the bands that followed Rancid into the charts emphasized metal over ska, but some—like No Doubt—drew from new wave pop roots as well, while Rancid themselves managed to stay true to both ska revival and punk. During 1996, the third wave of ska revival became one of the most popular forms of alternative music in the US.

THRASH — Thrash is an outgrowth of hardcore punk and speed metal. Where speed metal remained true to the technical precision of heavy metal, thrash was closer to punk. By retaining the speed of hardcore but adding the relentless loudness and heaviness of metal, thrash appealed more to punks than metal fans, but it did play to the same audience of disaffected suburban adolescents. Thrash didn't evolve musically like speed metal, nor did it produce any stars—Suicidal Tendencies was the most recognizable name to emerge from the genre. During the late '80s, thrash began to die out, but certain groups kept it alive in the US underground.

TRANCE — Trance is a subgenre of techno music that emerged in the early '90s. Similar to ambient in that it emphasizes sonic textures instead of insistent beats, the difference between the two genres is that, unlike ambient, trance is still danceable. Even though it could be danced to, trance is primarily used as come down music—it is more hypnotic and soothing than the various strands of hardcore techno that usually dominate the dance floor.

TRIP-HOP — Trip-hop is a hybrid of hip-hop, soul, dub, pop, and experimental. The beats are slow and the music is atmospheric, with sampled guitars and strings. Massive Attack was the first trip-hop band, but the genre was popularized by Portishead and Tricky.

URBAN — Urban is the soul of the '80s and '90s, music that followed the smooth stylings of quiet storm. It demonstrated a debt to pop music, particularly in its polished production techniques. By the late '80s, that sheen had been dulled, thanks to the gritty sounds of hip-hop. After hip-hop, urban had a broader sonic palette, which was reflected in the music of the '90s.

URBAN FOLK — Urban folk was a movement of singer-songwriters in the '80s that grew out of punk rock. Urban folk musicians were initially inspired by punk rock but they performed solo, either with an acoustic or electric guitar. Urban folk was extremely political—the songs were ways of conveying the message, so they had basic melodies and direct, angry lyrics. Though there was only a small handful of urban folk musicians, they made a significant impact in the mid-'80s.

Artist Reviews

ABBA

Euro-Pop, Pop-Rock, Euro-Dance

During the '70s, ABBA's slick, light Euro-pop made them one of the world's most successful acts, particularly outside America. Each of the four members—Benny Andersson, Bjorn Ulvaeus, Annifrid (Frida) Lyngstad, and Agnetha Faltskog—had already enjoyed some professional success previous to the band's formation. The spirited single "Waterloo" earned ABBA much recognition when they won the 1974 Eurovision Song Contest. From there, ABBA scored a seemingly endless string of predominantly bouncy pop hits, featuring well-crafted catchy melodies (some quite good) and the band's distinctive (but occasionally shrill) multilayered female vocals. The string ran out when ABBA disbanded in 1982, with Lyngstad and Faltskog going solo and Andersson and Ulvaeus writing for the musical theater. Of the 14 American Top 40 pop hits, "Dancing Queen" was ABBA's biggest, hitting No. 1 in 1976. In Great Britain, ABBA hit the Top 40 a total of 25 times between 1974 and 1983, scoring nine No. 1 hits. ABBA's influence can be heard in such UK groups as Erasure (who recorded a tribute EP, *Abba-esque*) as well as in the Swedish groups Roxette and Ace of Base. —*Rick Clark and William Ruhlmann*

Ring Ring / 1973 / Polar ♦♦

This, the first album by the group later called ABBA (they were called Bjorn, Benny, Agnetha & Annifrid at the time), originally was released only in Sweden; England and America didn't show any interest until the group won the Eurovision Song Contest with "Waterloo" the following year, although "Ring Ring" had been a hit in several other countries. It's clear that this team has spent a lot of time listening to albums like *Abbey Road* and *Honky Chateau*, not to mention *Sweet Baby James*. But they've also been absorbing a broad range of the pop charts of the late '60s and early '70s. At the same time, they haven't put together the ABBA sound yet. For one thing, the men sing almost as much as the women, and for another, Benny Andersson and Bjorn Ulvaeus have underproduced the recordings, even as they have overarranged the music. (Eventually released in Europe, *Ring Ring* has not been released officially in the US, although import copies are readily available.) — *William Ruhlmann*

Waterloo / 1974 / Atlantic ✦✦
ABBA's second (and US-debut) album contains the title track, an American Top Ten hit and UK chart-topper, as well as "Honey, Honey," a minor US hit, and "Ring Ring," a minor British hit co-written by the ABBA team of Benny Andersson, Stig Anderson, and Bjorn Ulvaeus with Neil Sedaka and Phil Cody. It is, however, an uneven collection, ranging from reggae to near-hard rock, demonstrating that ABBA had not yet gotten its pop assembly line fully into operation. — *William Ruhlmann*

ABBA / 1975 / Atlantic ✦✦✦
ABBA appears on the cover of this album sitting in the back of a limousine and drinking champagne, which may have been intended as an ironic comment on their one-hit wonder status at the time but became an apt reflection of their status after this record's success. The lead-off track is the irresistible "Mamma Mia," their second UK chart topper and a US Top 40 hit, and also included are the equally catchy "SOS" (Top Ten in Britain, Top 40 in America) and the minor UK hit "I Do, I Do, I Do, I Do," which actually did better in the US. — *William Ruhlmann*

Arrival / Jan. 1977 / Atlantic ✦✦✦✦
ABBA's appropriately titled fourth album of new material appeared after the group had "arrived" as major stars. It featured "Dancing Queen," a tame disco number that went to No. 1 in both the US and UK, as well as "Knowing Me, Knowing You" (another UK No. 1 that hit the Top 40 in the US) and a third single, "Money, Money, Money." — *William Ruhlmann*

The Album / Feb. 1978 / Atlantic ✦✦✦✦
ABBA's fifth new studio album continued its phenomenal international success, featuring the UK No. 1 songs "The Name of the Game" and "Take a Chance on Me," and achieving ABBA's highest-ever showing in the US LP charts: it reached the Top 20 and sold a million copies in six months. It was also musically ambitious, featuring "The Girl with the Golden Hair," described as "three scenes from a mini-musical," which anticipated the theatrical ambitions Andersson and Ulvaeus would fulfill with *Chess* six years later. — *William Ruhlmann*

Voulez-Vous / Jun. 1979 / RCA ✦✦
Internationally, it was business as usual for ABBA on its sixth studio album, which included the hits "Voulez-Vous," "I Have a Dream," "Angeleyes," "Does Your Mother Know," and "Chiquitita," all of which made the UK Top Five. But America had begun to lose interest; the album stopped at gold (500,000 copies), with only "Chiquitita" getting into the Top 40. — *William Ruhlmann*

Super Trouper / Dec. 1980 / Atlantic ✦✦
Always pop-savvy, ABBA took account of the passing of disco with this release and moved back toward the pop-rock sound more typical of their early albums with this, their seventh. They were rewarded with their last big US hit, "The Winner Takes It All," plus two more American chart entries and an uptick in album sales. In the UK, they continued to roll along, with the title track becoming their final No. 1 single. — *William Ruhlmann*

The Visitors / 1981 / Atlantic ✦✦✦
ABBA's swan song was also perhaps their most musically sophisticated album. Although it was short on big hits ("The Visitors" and "When All Is Said and Done" charted in the US, "One of Us" and "Head Over Heels" in the UK, with only "One of Us" making the Top Ten), it was a consistent record imbued with a sense of the pressures that were splitting the group (the title track was subtitled "Crackin' Up"). — *William Ruhlmann*

The Singles: The First Ten Years / 1982 / Atlantic ✦✦✦✦
This 23-track double LP contains 16 of ABBA's 20 US chart entries and 22 of their 25 UK hits. Especially notable are the group's final new single, "Under Attack," and the terrific ballad "The Day Before You Came," which had previously appeared in the US only as a non-LP B-side. This collection supersedes the previous *Greatest Hits* albums, and, since ABBA was a singles band, captures their essence. — *William Ruhlmann*

ABBA Live / 1986 / Atlantic ✦✦

★ **Gold: Greatest Hits** / 1993 / Polydor ✦✦✦✦✦
A 19-track, 77-minute CD collection released in Europe in 1992 and in the US the following year to cash in on the resurgence of interest in ABBA, this is an excellent single-disc hits package, and, given that the group's catalog was sold to PolyGram in 1989, the only one that's available in the US, where the earlier *Greatest Hits; Greatest Hits, Vol. 2;* and *The Singles: The First Ten Years* (all originally released on LP by Atlantic) are out of print. — *William Ruhlmann*

More ABBA Gold / Jun. 1, 1993 / Polydor ✦✦✦✦
All of the singles and important album tracks that aren't featured on *Gold* are available on *More ABBA Gold*. — *Stephen Thomas Erlewine*

Thank You for the Music [Box] / Apr. 18, 1995 / Polydor ✦✦✦✦
Released in Europe in October 1994 and in the US six months later, *Thank You for the Music* is the ABBA box-set retrospective, tracing their ten years of record making, 1972-1982, including 52 previously released tracks on the first three discs, plus a fourth disc of rarities. Listening to all the singles, plus scattered album tracks and B-sides, provides a clear picture of the group's development. Early on, there is considerable stylistic experimentation, as these pop dabblers ape everything from Phil Spector's "Wall of Sound" rock to big-band swing. But after "Dancing Queen," they find their niche in disco, and the second disc is loaded with hit songs anchored to the familiar bass-heavy walking beat and swooping synths-meant-to-sound-like-strings that defined that most '70s of genres. On the third disc, covering their last years, ABBA returns to the more propulsive pop-rock of early classics like "SOS" and "Mamma Mia," revving up the tempo in acknowledgment of the arrival of new wave. Racked by romantic discord, they also achieve somewhat more meaningful lyrics before calling it a day. In the album's liner notes, the band members register mild protest at the inclusion of unreleased material on the fourth disc—what they finished and liked, they released, they note. Fair warning. Most prominent in a collection of alternate takes, miscellaneous B-sides, foreign-language recordings, and TV soundtracks is the 23-and-a-half-minute "ABBA Undeleted," a medley of 15 song fragments and Swedish studio chatter that suggests ABBA had a few more hits in them if they had found the time to finish them off. Nevertheless, this remains fan-only material. (This album is not to be confused with the 1983 compilation of the same title released by Epic Records in the UK.) — *William Ruhlmann*

ABC

Dance-Pop, New Wave, Pop-Rock, New Romantic
ABC was formed in 1980, when singer Martin Fry teamed up with Stephen Singleton and Mark White, who were members of the group Vice Versa. Their stylish debut, featuring Fry's cartoonishly overwrought delivery backed up by a dramatically lush dance/synth-pop sound, scored well with high-profile videos on MTV, producing the hits "The Look of Love (Part One)" and "Poison Arrow." Except for a quick sidestep into a harder rocking middle-period, Roxy Music-influenced effort with Beauty Stab, ABC has increasingly streamlined their sophisticated dance-pop. Their biggest hits have been "Be Near Me," "(How to Be A) Millionaire," and "When Smokey Sings," a tribute to Smokey Robinson. —*Rick Clark*

● **The Lexicon of Love** / 1982 / Mercury ✦✦✦✦
ABC's stylish debut successfully melded the cool detachment of Bryan Ferry and David Bowie with a more pop-oriented production than either Roxy Music or Bowie. Even if the songs tended to blend together over the course of the album, the record was successful, scoring two hits with "The Look of Love" and "Poison Arrow." — *Stephen Thomas Erlewine*

Beauty Stab / 1983 / Mercury ✦✦✦

How to Be a . . . Zillionaire! / 1985 / Mercury ✦✦✦

Alphabet City / 1987 / Mercury ✦✦✦

Up / 1989 / Mercury ✦✦

Absolutely ABC: The Best of ABC / 1990 / Mercury ✦✦✦✦
Singer-songwriter Martin Fry's Bowie/Roxy vocal affectations and sweeping productions (aided by Mark White) are showcased to great effect on this fine anthology, which contains all of this act's essential dance-pop hits. —*Rick Clark*

Paula Abdul

b. Jun. 19, 1962, Los Angeles, CA
Vocals / Dance-Pop, Urban, Adult Contemporary, Pop-Rock, Club-Dance
In the wake of Madonna's success, many dance-pop divas filled the charts, but out of them all, Paula Abdul was the only one that lasted for more than a hit or two. Abdul had two smash-hit albums not because her singing was exceptional—her voice is thin and transparent—but because she worked with savvy producers that had a knack for picking solid pop hooks; the melodies are what carried "Straight Up," "Forever Your Girl," "Cold Hearted," and "Rush Rush" to the top of the charts. Abdul's days as a cheerleader and choreographer helped her make some exciting videos, which played a major role in her rise to stardom. She has not released an album since 1991's Spellbound. — *Stephen Thomas Erlewine*

● **Forever Your Girl** / Jun. 1988 / Virgin ✦✦✦✦
Choreographer-turned-diva Abdul debuts with this upbeat collection of dance-pop that yielded a string of Top 40 hits, including four No. 1 smashes—"Straight Up," "Cold Hearted," "Opposites Attract," and "Forever Your Girl." — *Donna DiChario*

Spellbound / 1991 / Captive/Virgin ✦✦✦
This fine sophomore set includes sweet pop-soul balladry ("Rush, Rush") and the usual dance tunes ("The Promise of a New Day"). — *Bil Carpenter*

Head Over Heels / 1995 / Captive/Virgin ✦✦

AC/DC

Hard Rock, Heavy Metal
AC/DC's mammoth power-chord roar became one of the most influential hard-rock sounds of the '70s. In its own way, it was a reaction against the pompous art-rock and lumbering stadium rock of the early '70s. AC/DC's rock was minimalist—no matter how huge and bludgeoning the guitar chords were, there was a clear sense of space and restraint. Combined with Bon Scott's larynx-shredding vocals, the band spawned countless imitators over the next two decades.

AC/DC was formed in 1973 in Australia by guitarist Malcolm Young after his band, the Velvet Underground, collapsed (Young's band has no relation to the seminal American group). With his younger brother Angus as lead guitarist, the band played some gigs around Sydney. Angus was only 15 years old at the time, and his sister suggested that he should wear his school uniform on stage; the look became the band's visual trademark. While still in Sydney, the original lineup (featuring singer Dave Evans) cut a single called "Can I Sit Next to You," with ex-Easybeats Harry Vanda and George Young (Malcolm and Angus' older brother) producing.

The band moved to Melbourne the following year, where drummer Phil Rudd and bassist Mark Evans joined the band. The band's chauffeur, Bon Scott, became their lead vocalist when their singer, Dave Evans, refused to go on stage.

Previously, Scott had been a drummer for the Australian pop bands Fraternity and the Valentines. More importantly, he helped cement the group's image as brutes—he had several convictions on minor criminal offenses and *was* rejected by the Australian Army for being "socially maladjusted." And AC/DC was socially maladjusted. Throughout their career they favored crude double entendres and violent imagery, all spiked with a mischievous sense of fun.

The group released two albums—*High Voltage* and *TNT*—in Australia in 1974 and 1975. Material from the two records comprised the 1976 release *High Voltage* in the US and UK; the group also toured both countries. *Dirty Deeds Done Dirt Cheap* followed at the end of the year. Evans left the band at the beginning of 1977, with Cliff Williams taking his place. In the fall of 1977, AC/DC released *Let There Be Rock*, which became their first album to chart in the US. *Powerage*, released in spring of 1978, expanded their audience even further, thanks in no small part to their dynamic live shows (which were captured on 1978's live *If You Want Blood, You've Got It*). What really broke the doors down for the band was the following year's *Highway to Hell*, which hit No. 17 in the US and No. eight in the UK, becoming the group's first million-seller.

AC/DC's train was derailed when Bon Scott died on February 20, 1980. The coroner's report stated he had "drunk himself to death." In March, the band replaced Scott with Brian Johnson. The following month, the band recorded *Back in Black*, which would prove to be their biggest album, selling over ten million copies in the US alone. For the next few years, the band was one of the largest rock bands in the world, with *For Those About to Rock We Salute You* topping the charts in the US. In 1982, Rudd left the band; he was replaced by Simon Wright.

After 1983's *Flick of the Switch*, the band's commercial standing began to slip; they were able to reverse their slide with 1990's *The Razor's Edge*, which spawned the hit "Thunderstruck." While they haven't proved to be the commercial powerhouse they were during the late '70s and early '80s, the '90s have seen them maintain their status as a top international concert draw. In the fall of 1995, their sixteenth album, *Ballbreaker*, was released. Produced by Rick Rubin, the album received some of the most positive reviews of AC/DC's career. It entered the American charts at No. 4 and sold over a million copies in its first six months of release. — *Stephen Thomas Erlewine*

High Voltage / Oct. 1976 / Atco ✦✦✦✦
AC/DC kicked things off properly by blowing away the girders with their concussion bomb skronk. Raw, raunchy, and fun-o-plenty, its songs include "The Jack," guaranteed to offend every woman in listening radius. — *Tom Graves*

Let There Be Rock / Jun. 1977 / Atco ✦✦✦✦
A great follow-up, it proved these Aussies would be a nasty itch for a long time. There's great meltdown boogie on songs like "Let There Be Rock," "Problem Child," and "Whole Lotta Rosie." — *Tom Graves*

Powerage / May 1978 / Atco ✦✦✦
While the band still rocks with vicious authority, the quality of their songwriting on *Powerage* is slightly weaker than on its predecessor, *Let There Be Rock*. All of the musicians turn in strong performances—Angus and Malcom Young sound wild and Bon Scott is positively unhinged—but there's not enough great riffs to make *Powerage* one of the band's classics. — *Stephen Thomas Erlewine*

If You Want Blood You've Got It / Dec. 1978 / Atco ✦✦✦

☆ **Highway to Hell** / Aug. 1979 / Atco ✦✦✦✦✦
This is a classic of hard rock-heavy metal-noise-grunge-skronk-pillage-and-burn. Earlier AC/DC albums had great riffs and killer chords, but

Highway to Hell proved the boys could write too. Not a clinker on this thudfest, and songs like "Highway to Hell" and "Girls Got Rhythm" have appropriately become rock staples. — *Tom Graves*

★ **Back in Black** / Aug. 1980 / Atco ✦✦✦✦✦
Following Bon Scott's death, AC/DC came back with reinforcements and released another truly great hard-rock album. Brian Johnson ups the ante with his own tough-as-tacks vocals. Robert "Mutt" Lange's production on *Back in Black* remains one of the most powerful in all of hard rock. All in all, this is great diamond-hard, full-throttle rock 'n' roll. — *Tom Graves*

Dirty Deeds Done Dirt Cheap / Apr. 1981 / Atco ✦✦✦✦
An odds-'n'-sods collection of earlier Bon Scott-era tracks, it's worth it alone for the unforgettable title track. — *Tom Graves*

For Those About to Rock We Salute You / Nov. 1981 / Atco ✦✦✦

Flick of the Switch / Aug. 1983 / Atco ✦✦

74 Jailbreak / 1984 / Atco ✦✦✦
Actually an EP of Bon Scott-period material, it's nonetheless some of AC/DC's best and most blistering blues. In particular the title song and an incendiary "Baby, Please Don't Go" are worth the admission. — *Tom Graves*

Who Made Who / May 1986 / Atco ✦✦✦

Blow up Your Video / Feb. 1988 / Atco ✦✦✦

The Razor's Edge / 1990 / Atco ✦✦✦

AC/DC Live / 1992 / Atco ✦✦

Ballbreaker / Sep. 26, 1995 / East West ✦✦✦

Ace

Pop-Rock, Pub-Rock
Ace was a British pub-rock band formed in December 1972 by Paul Carrack (keyboards, vocals), Alan "Bam" King (guitar, vocals), Phil Harris (guitar, vocals), Terry "Tex" Comer (bass), and Steve Witherington (drums, replaced before the first album by Fran Byrne). They debuted on record with *Five-A-Side* (1974), which contained their hit "How Long," prominently featuring Carrack. They were never able to top that success, however, and split up in July 1977. Carrack has gone on to be a member of Squeeze and Mike + the Mechanics as well as maintaining a solo career. — *William Ruhlmann*

Five-A-Side / 1974 / Anchor ✦✦✦✦
Five-A-Side, Ace's debut album, is notable for introducing the world to the soulful singing talent of Paul Carrack, especially on the hit "How Long," which went to No. 1 on some charts in 1975. The band has a low-key style, frequently dominated by Carrack's piano and organ work, that is sometimes suggestive of Traffic and of the Tulsa country-rock sound of J.J. Cale, Delaney & Bonnie, and Leon Russell, although they never work up quite as much of a sweat as the last two. Already road-weary when they made this album, Ace, especially in Carrack's lyrics, comments extensively on the travails of being in a struggling rock 'n' roll band. Even "How Long," which sounds like the lament of a lover betrayed, is really about somebody quitting the group. All of which makes the irony of the song's being their sole hit all the more acute. — *William Ruhlmann*

Time for Another / Dec. 1975 / Anchor ✦✦

● **Best of Ace** / 1988 / See For Miles ✦✦✦✦

Ace of Base

Dance-Pop, Adult Contemporary, Euro-Dance, Club-Dance
Comprised of vocalists Jenny Berggren and Linn Berggren, and keyboardists Jonas "Joker" Berggren and Ulf "Buddah" Ekberg, the Swedish quartet Ace of Base became a phenomenally popular international act with their 1993 debut album, *The Sign*. Ace of Base's simple, melodic Euro-disco was equally popular on radio and in the clubs, earning the quartet three US Top Ten singles—"All That She Wants," "Don't Turn Around," and "The Sign," which spent six weeks at No. 1.

Before the group formed in 1990, sisters Jenny and Malin Berggren sang in local church choirs in Gothenburg, Sweden. Their brother, Jonas, played synthesizers and wrote songs with Ulf Ekberg. Eventually, Jonas and Ulf recruited Jenny and Linn to sing with them, and the quartet began playing dance music at local clubs in the late summer of 1990. Within a year, the group signed with Mega Records and released their debut single, "Wheel of Fortune," in 1992. By that time, the quartet had joined forces with John Ballard, who produced their recordings and wrote the majority of their songs; occasionally, Ballard co-wrote with Jonas Berggren. "Wheel of Fortune" became a hit across Scandanavia, and soon the German-based record label Metronome signed a European distribution deal with the group. "All That She Wants" was Ace of Base's first single in Europe and, thanks to heavy exposure on MTV, the song became a No. 1 hit in ten different countries. In the spring of 1993, Ace of Base released their European debut album, *Happy Nation*. "All That She Wants" was released in America in the fall of 1993 and quickly went platinum, beginning a string of platinum Top Ten singles in the US. Released in the fall of 1993, Ace of Base's American debut album *The Sign*—a reconfigured version of *Happy Nation*, featuring four new songs—quickly sold nearly two million copies in the US. Throughout 1994, Ace of Base dominated radio in America and Europe as "All That She Wants," "Don't Turn Around," and "The Sign" received heavy airplay on a number of radio formats, including Top 40, adult contemporary, urban, and, bizarrely, modern rock. By the end of the year, *The Sign* had sold over eight million copies in the US alone. Ace of Base was nominated for three Grammys that year, including Best New Artist.

Ace of Base released their second album, *The Bridge*, in the fall of 1995. Although it went platinum in its first six months of release, the record failed to duplicate the remarkable multi-platinum success of *The Sign*. —*Stephen Thomas Erlewine*

● **The Sign** / 1993 / Arista ✦✦✦✦
Ace of Base's strong point is not versatility—all of their hit singles have exactly the same beat. But that doesn't matter. On their debut album, *The Sign*, they managed to create a piece of melodic Euro-disco that was a huge hit all over the world, appealing to both dance clubs and pop radio. And with singles like "All That She Wants," "The Sign," and "Don't Turn Around," it's easy to see why they were hits—the beat is relentless and the hooks are incessantly catchy. —*Stephen Thomas Erlewine*

Bridge / Nov. 21, 1995 / Arista ✦✦✦
Ace of Base's sequel to their multi-platinum debut *The Sign* sounds like the same record on the surface. There are the same bouncy Euro-pop beats, ingratiatingly catchy melodies, and shiny production. However, underneath that gloss is an improved sense of songwriting. Ace of Base still might not be innovators, but they don't need to be. Instead, they turn out tightly constructed pop songs that are better written than they appear—songs like the hit "Beautiful Life" would sound good in different arrangements or if they were performed acoustically. And the songs on *The Bridge* are, overall, better than the ones on *The Sign*. Ace of Base might not be able to replicate the phenomenal success of their debut, but they have managed to deliver an album that is just as satisfying. —*Stephen Thomas Erlewine*

Johnny Ace (John Alexander)

b. Jun. 9, 1929, Memphis, TN, **d.** Dec. 25, 1954, Houston, TX
Piano, Vocals / R&B
The senseless death of young pianist Johnny Ace while indulging in a round of Russian roulette backstage at Houston's City Auditorium on Christmas Day of 1954 tends to overshadow his relatively brief but illustrious recording career on Duke Records. That's a pity, for Ace's gentle, plaintive vocal balladry deserves reverence on its own merit, not because of the scandalous fallout resulting from his tragic demise.

John Marshall Alexander was a member in good standing of the Beale Streeters, a loosely knit crew of Memphis youngbloods that variously included B.B. King, Bobby Bland, and Earl Forest. Signing with local DJ David Mattis' fledgling Duke logo in 1952, the rechristened Ace hit the top of the R&B charts his very first time out with the mellow ballad "My Song." From then on, Ace could do no musical wrong, racking up hit after hit for Duke in the same smooth, urbane style. "Cross My Heart," "The Clock," "Saving My Love for You," "Please Forgive Me," and "Never Let Me Go" all dented the uppermost reaches of the charts. And then, with one fatal gunshot, all that talent was lost forever (weepy tribute records quickly emerged by Frankie Ervin, Johnny Fuller, Varetta Dillard, and the Five Wings).

Ace scored his biggest hit of all posthumously. His haunting "Pledging My Love" (cut with the Johnny Otis orchestra in support) remained atop *Billboard*'s R&B lists for ten weeks in early 1955. One further hit, "Anymore," exhausted Duke's stockpile of Ace masters, so they tried to clone the late pianist's success by recruiting Johnny's younger brother (St. Clair Alexander) to record as Buddy Ace. When that didn't work out, Duke boss Don Robey took singer Jimmy Lee Land, renamed him Buddy Ace, and recorded him all the way into the late '60s. —*Bill Dahl*

● **Johnny Ace Memorial Album** / 1955 / Duke ✦✦✦✦
It's downright bizarre that Ace's catalog hasn't enjoyed a fresh reissue in 40 years. This 12-song CD is the exact same package that Don Robey rushed out following the pianist's death, with all the velvety hits ("Pledging My Love," "My Song," "The Clock," "Never Let Me Go") and a mere two blistering rockers, "How Can You Be So Mean" and "Don't You Know." A more thorough examination of Ace's discography is definitely in order! —*Bill Dahl*

Bryan Adams

b. Nov. 5, 1959, Kingston, Ontario, Canada
Guitar, Vocals / Rock 'n' Roll, Adult Contemporary, Pop-Rock
Bryan Adams was one of the most popular mainstream rock 'n' rollers to emerge in the '80s, producing a series of platinum albums and Top Ten hits. Adams wasn't an innovator on the level of Bruce Springsteen, or

even John Cougar Mellencamp. He followed in their footsteps, smoothing out their rougher edges while retaining a down-to-earth earnestness in both his straightforward rock 'n' roll and his husky voice. At the beginning of his career, he relied more on rock than pop, but as his career progressed, he became known for his ballads. But both his rockers and his slow numbers were the result of his craftsmanship, both as a writer and a performer—Adams never let anything obscure a good hook.

Born in Canada, Adams began his career as a songwriting partner of Jim Vallence, a former member of Prism. Vallence and Adams wrote songs for several Canadian rockers, including Loverboy and Bachman-Turner Overdrive, as well as Bonnie Tyler and Kiss. Adams landed a solo record contract with A&M Records in 1981, releasing an eponymous album by the end of year; it failed to make the charts. The following year, he released *You Want It, You Got It*, which managed to reach the US charts.

Bryan Adams' commercial breakthrough came in 1983 with *Cuts Like a Knife*. "Straight from the Heart," a ballad taken from the record, reached the Top Ten before the album was released. The album also made it into the Top Ten, while the title track peaked at No. 15; a third single, "This Time," reached No. 24.

Late in 1984, Adams returned with the surging, mid-tempo "Run to You," which became his second Top Ten single; it also became his first British hit, peaking at No. 11. *Reckless*, also released in late 1984, became a blockbuster success, spending two weeks at the top of the US album charts and selling over five million copies. Besides "Run to You," *Reckless* featured five other Top 15 singles, including the No. 1 "Heaven," "Summer of '69," "Somebody," "One Night Love Affair," and "It's Only Love," a duet with Tina Turner.

Released in 1987, *Into the Fire* proved to be a considerable commercial disappointment, spending 33 weeks on the charts, selling one million copies, and spawning only one Top Ten hit, "Heat of the Night." Four years later, Adams returned with "(Everything I Do) I Do It for You," the theme song for the movie *Robin Hood: Prince of Thieves*. The song became a huge hit, spending seven weeks at No. 1 in the US; in Britain, it was at the top of the charts for an astonishing 15 weeks, which was the longest stay at No. 1 since Frankie Laine's "I Believe" in 1953. The success of "(Everything I Do) I Do It for You" re-established Adams as a mainstream rock commercial powerhouse, setting the stage for the triple-platinum *Waking up the Neighbours*, released in the fall of 1991. *Waking up the Neighbours* launched the No. 2 hit "Can't Stop This Thing We Started," the minor hit "There Will Never Be Another Tonight," and two Top 15 singles, "Thought I'd Died and Gone to Heaven" and "Do I Have to Say the Words?"

The following year, Bryan Adams released a greatest hits collection, *So Far, So Good*, which featured a new track, "Please Forgive Me." The ballad became another Top Ten success, as did the similar-sounding "All for Love"—a collaboration with Rod Stewart and Sting taken from *The Three Musketeers*—which reached No. 1. In the summer of 1995, Adams had his fourth No. 1 single, "Have You Ever Really Loved a Woman?," taken from the *Don Juan DeMarco* soundtrack; the single spent five weeks at No. 1.

Bryan Adams released *18 'til I Die*, his first new studio album since 1991's *Waking Up the Neighbours*, in the summer of 1996. —*Stephen Thomas Erlewine*

You Want It You Got It / 1981 / A&M ✦✦✦

Cuts Like a Knife / Jan. 1983 / A&M ✦✦✦✦
A Top Ten breakthrough album in America for this Canadian rocker, it was carried by the strength of "Straight from the Heart." —*Donna DiChario*

Reckless / 1984 / A&M ✦✦✦✦
Radio-friendly pop-rock driven by Adams' trademark gravelly vocals that spawned three Top Ten hits, including "Heaven," "Run to You," as well as a duet with Tina Turner on "It's Only Love." —*Donna DiChario*

Into the Fire / Mar. 1987 / A&M ✦✦

Waking up the Neighbours / 1991 / A&M ✦✦✦

● **So Far So Good** / Nov. 2, 1993 / A&M ✦✦✦✦
Eliminating the filler that tends to clutter his albums, *So Far, So Good* simply gathers all of Adams' big hits (including a new one, "Please Forgive Me") in one concise package, making it the one essential Bryan Adams album and the only one that can be listened to straight through from start to finish. —*Stephen Thomas Erlewine*

Live! Live! Live! / 1995 / A&M ✦✦

18 'Til I Die / Jun. 1996 / A&M ✦✦

Aerosmith

Hard Rock, Pop-Rock, Heavy Metal
Aerosmith was one of the most popular hard-rock bands of the '70s, setting the style and sound of hard rock and heavy metal for the next two decades with their raunchy, bluesy swagger. The Boston-based quintet found the middle ground between the menace of the Rolling Stones and

the campy, sleazy flamboyance of the New York Dolls, developing a lean, dirty riff-oriented boogie that was loose and swinging and as hard as a diamond. In the meantime, they developed a prototype for power-ballads with "Dream On," a piano ballad that was orchestrated with strings and distorted guitars. Aerosmith's ability to pull off both ballads and rock 'n' roll made them extremely popular during the mid-'70s, when they had a string of gold and platinum albums. By the early '80s, the group's audience had declined as the band fell prey to drug and alcohol abuse. However, their career was far from over—in the late '80s, Aerosmith pulled off one of the most remarkable comebacks in rock history, returning to the top of the charts with a group of albums that equalled, if not surpassed, the popularity of their '70s albums.

In 1970, the first incarnation of Aerosmith formed when vocalist Steven Tyler met guitarist Joe Perry while working at a Sunapee, NH, ice cream parlor. Tyler, who originally was a drummer, and Perry decided to form a power trio with bassist Tom Hamilton. The group soon expanded to a quartet, adding a second guitarist called Ray Tabano; he was quickly replaced by Brad Whitford, a former member of Earth Inc. With the addition of drummer Joey Kramer, Tyler became the full-time lead singer by the end of year. Aerosmith relocated to Boston at the end of 1970.

After playing clubs in the Massachusetts and New York areas for two years, the group landed a record contract with Columbia Records in 1972. Aerosmith's self-titled debut album was released in the fall of 1973, climbing to No. 166. "Dream On" was released as the first single and it was a minor hit, reaching No. 59. For the next year, the band built a fan base by touring America, supporting groups as diverse as the Kinks, Mahavishnu Orchestra, Sha Na Na, and Mott the Hoople. The performance of Get Your Wings (1974), the group's second album and first produced by Jack Douglas, benefited from their constant touring, spending a total of 86 weeks on the chart.

Aerosmith's third record, 1975's Toys in the Attic, was their breakthrough album both commercially and artistically. By the time it was recorded, the band's sound had developed into a sleek, hard-driving hard rock powered by simple, almost brutal, blues-based riffs. Many critics at the time labelled the group as punk rockers, and it's easy to see why—instead of adhering to the world-music pretensions of Led Zeppelin or the prolonged gloomy mysticism of Black Sabbath, Aerosmith stripped heavy metal to its basic core, spitting out spare riffs that not only rocked, but rolled. Steven Tyler's lyrics were filled with double entendres and clever jokes and the entire band had a streetwise charisma that separated them from the heavy, lumbering arena rockers of the era. Toys in the Attic captured the essence of Aerosmith.

"Sweet Emotion," the first single from Toys in the Attic, broke into the Top 40 in the summer of 1975, with the album reaching No. 11 shortly afterward. Its success prompted the re-release of the power ballad "Dream On," which shot into the Top Ten in early 1976. Both Aerosmith and Get Your Wings climbed back up the charts in the wake of Toys in the Attic. "Walk This Way," the final single from Toys in the Attic, was released around the time of the group's new 1976 album, Rocks. Although it didn't feature a Top Ten hit like "Walk This Way," Rocks went platinum quickly, peaking at No. 3.

In early 1977, Aerosmith took a break and prepared material for their fifth album. Released late in 1977, Draw the Line was another hit, climbing to No. 11 on the US charts, but it showed signs of exhaustion. In addition to another tour in 1978, the band appeared in the movie Sgt. Pepper's Lonely Hearts Club Band, performing "Come Together," which eventually became a No. 23 hit. Live! Bootleg appeared late in 1978 and became another success, reaching No. 13. Aerosmith recorded Night in the Ruts in 1979, releasing the record at the end of the year. By the time of its release, Joe Perry had left the band to form the Joe Perry Project. Night in the Ruts performed respectably, climbing to No. 14 and going gold, yet it was the least successful Aerosmith record to date. Brad Whitford left the group in early 1980, forming the Whitsford-St. Holmes Band with former Ted Nugent guitarist Derek St. Holmes.

As Aerosmith regrouped with new guitarists Jimmy Crespo and Rick Dufay, the band released Aerosmith's Greatest Hits in late 1980; the record would eventually sell over six million copies. The new lineup of Aerosmith released Rock in a Hard Place in 1982. Peaking at No. 32, failed to match the performance of Night in the Ruts. Perry and Whitford returned to the band in 1984 and the group began a reunion tour dubbed "Back in the Saddle." Early in the tour, Tyler collapsed on stage, offering proof that the band hadn't conquered their notorious drug and alcohol addictions. The following year, Aerosmith released Done with Mirrors, the original lineup's first record since 1979 and their first for Geffen Records. Although it didn't perform as well as Rock in a Hard Place, the album showed that the band was revitalized.

After the release of Done with Mirrors, Tyler and Perry completed rehabilitation programs. In 1986, the pair appeared on Run D.M.C.'s cover of "Walk This Way," along with appearing in the video. The new "Walk This Way" became a hit, reaching No. 4 and receiving saturation airplay on MTV. "Walk This Way" set the stage for the band's full-scale comeback effort, the Bruce Fairburn-produced Permanent Vacation

(1987). Tyler and Perry collaborated with professional hard-rock songwriters like Holly Knight and Desmond Child, resulting in the hits "Dude (Looks Like a Lady)," "Rag Doll," and "Angel." Permanent Vacation peaked at No. 11 and sold over three million copies.

Pump, released in 1989, continued the band's winning streak, reaching No. 5, selling over four million copies, and spawning the Top Ten singles "Love in an Elevator," "Janie's Got a Gun," and "What It Takes." Aerosmith released Get a Grip in 1993. Like Permanent Vacation and Pump, Get a Grip was produced by Bruce Fairburn and featured significant contributions by professional songwriters. The album was as successful as the band's previous two records, featuring the hit singles "Livin' on the Edge," "Cryin'," and "Amazing." In 1994, Aerosmith released Big Ones, a compilation of hits from their Geffen years; it went double platinum shortly after its release. —Stephen Thomas Erlewine

Aerosmith / Jan. 1973 / Columbia ✦✦✦
The debut from this Boston band shows a sensitive side with their best-known ballad, "Dream On." But the focus remains on raw, aggressive garage rock style as displayed on "Mama Kin," "One Way Street," and "Make It." —Donna DiChario

Get Your Wings / Mar. 1974 / Columbia ✦✦✦✦
Aerosmith took the Yardbirds classic "Train Kept a Rollin'" and made it their own with Steven Tyler's blistering vocals and Joe Perry's ace guitar work. —Donna DiChario

☆ **Toys in the Attic** / Apr. 1975 / Columbia ✦✦✦✦✦
A solid slice of classic '70s raunch and roll, Aerosmith defined grunge rock with their best and now-classic "Sweet Emotion" and "Walk This Way." —Donna DiChario

☆ **Rocks** / May 1976 / Columbia ✦✦✦✦✦
Although the hits ("Back in the Saddle" and "Last Child") weren't as big as "Sweet Emotion" and "Walk This Way," Rocks remains Aerosmith's finest moment, full of relentlessly sleazy rock powered by some of the dirtiest guitar riffs ever committed to tape. —Stephen Thomas Erlewine

Draw the Line / Dec. 1977 / Columbia ✦✦✦

Live Bootleg / Oct. 1978 / Columbia ✦✦

Night in the Ruts / Nov. 1979 / Columbia ✦

★ **Greatest Hits** / Oct. 1980 / Columbia ✦✦✦✦✦
Although Aerosmith was an album-rock band, they only made two essential albums—Toys in the Attic and Rocks. The rest of their albums were quite uneven, even though they each had their individual stellar tracks. Greatest Hits collects all of the highlights from Aerosmith's '70s heyday, picking the best cuts from each record. Apart from a pair of relatively uninteresting obscurities—"Come Together," "Remember (Walking in the Sand)"— tacked on to the end of the album, there is no fat on Greatest Hits—the hits, from "Dream On" to "Kings and Queens," keep piling up on top of each other. This is the definitive sound of late-'70s hard rock—lean, mean grinding boogie—and it provided the blueprint for legions of bands in the late '80s. —Stephen Thomas Erlewine

Rock in a Hard Place / Aug. 1982 / Columbia ✦

Done with Mirrors / Nov. 1985 / Geffen ✦✦✦✦
Joe Perry returned to the fold in 1985, and the band turned out their finest record since Rocks. Unlike the records that preceded it, Done with Mirrors was powered by the same smart-assed lyrics and filthy guitars that formed the core of Aerosmith's best songs. It didn't receive the commercial or critical attention that Permanent Vacation did two years later, but Done with Mirrors is the better album; it marks the beginning of their remarkable comeback. —Stephen Thomas Erlewine

Classics Live / Apr. 1986 / Columbia ✦✦

Classics Live 2 / Jun. 1987 / Columbia ✦✦✦

Permanent Vacation / Aug. 1987 / Geffen ✦✦✦
Apart from the strong singles—"Dude (Looks Like a Lady)," "Angel," and "Rag Doll"—Permanent Vacation isn't as consistent or rocking a record as Done with Mirrors; too often, it relies on slick, horn-spiked production instead of genuine grit, making the moments when Joe Perry's guitar does kick into overdrive all the more splendid. —Stephen Thomas Erlewine

Gems / 1988 / Columbia ✦✦✦✦
Gems is not a greatest-hits album. Instead, it's a collection of album tracks and AOR staples ("Mama Kin," "Lord of the Thighs," "Chip Away the Stone," "Rats in the Cellar") that may not make sense as a retrospective, but rocks harder, stronger and longer than most albums they released during the 1970s. —Stephen Thomas Erlewine

Pump / Sep. 1989 / Geffen ✦✦✦✦
Where Permanent Vacation seemed a little overwhelmed by its pop concessions, Pump revels in them without ever losing sight of Aerosmith's dirty hard-rock core. Which doesn't mean the record is a sellout—"What It Takes" has more emotion and grit than any of their other power ballads; "Janie's Got a Gun" tackles more complex territory than most previous songs; and "The Other Side" and "Love in an Elevator" rock relent-

lessly, no matter how many horns and synths fight with the guitars. Such ambition and successful musical eclecticism make *Pump* rank with *Rocks* and *Toys in the Attic. — Stephen Thomas Erlewine*

Pandora's Box / 1991 / Columbia ♦♦

Get a Grip / 1993 / Geffen ♦♦♦

● **Big Ones** / 1994 / Geffen ♦♦♦♦

Big Ones serves up the hits and nothing but the hits; Aerosmith's excellent debut for Geffen, *Done with Mirrors*, is conveniently overlooked. So what's left is some of the finest mainstream hard rock of the late '80s and early '90s—the fruits of one of the most remarkable comebacks in rock 'n' roll history. Unfortunately, there's precious little of the classic Aerosmith raunch; in fact, the two new tracks are the hardest, slinkiest tracks here. Otherwise, the uptempo tracks bog down in overproduction ("Love in an Elevator"), and the frequently embarrassingly overwrought power ballads ("Angel" and "Crazy") dominate too much of the album. So what's left? The band's best stab at social commentary ("Janie's Got a Gun"), a sublime slinky throwaway ("Deuces Are Wild"), deliciously sleazy bluesrockers ("Rag Doll," "(Dude) Looks Like a Lady") and their best ballads ("What It Takes" and "Cryin' "). — *Stephen Thomas Erlewine*

Afghan Whigs

Alternative Pop-Rock
Evolving from a garage-punk band in the vein of the Replacements, Dinosaur Jr., and Mudhoney to a literate, pretentious, soul-inflected postpunk quartet, the Afghan Whigs were one of most critically acclaimed alternative bands of the early '90s. Although the band never broke into the mainstream, they developed a dedicated cult following, primarily because of lead singer-songwriter Greg Dulli's tortured, angst-ridden tales of broken relationships and self-loathing. The Afghan Whigs were one of the few alternative bands that formed in the late '90s to acknowledge R&B, attempting to create a fusion of soul and post-punk.

The Afghan Whigs were formed when the members—vocalist/rhythm guitarist Greg Dulli, bassist John Curley, lead guitarist Rick McCollum, and drummer Steve Earle—were attending the University of Cincinnati. Dulli, who was raised in Hamilton, OH, was studying film at the University of Cincinnati, where he met fellow students McCollum and Earle. Unlike the rest of the band, Curley didn't attend the university. He arrived in the city to intern as a photographer at the *Cincinnati Enquirer*, which his father—who published *USA Today*—arranged for him; for the next few years, Curley continued to shoot pictures for the paper, quitting only when the band's schedule became too busy for him to work both jobs. Dulli happened to meet Curley when visiting a friend's apartment. Soon, the two became friends and began attending concerts together. Eventually, the pair formed the Afghan Whigs in 1986 along with McCollum and Earle.

In 1988, the Afghan Whigs released their debut album, *Big Top Halloween*, on their independent record label, Ultrasuede. The album received good word-of-mouth in underground music publications and college radio. A copy of the record worked its way to the influential Seattle-based independent record label Sub Pop, and the label arranged for the Whigs to release a one-off single. The single led to a full-blown record contract with Sub Pop by 1989. For the next two years, the Afghan Whigs toured America consistently, occasionally heading over to Europe and England. In 1992, their third album, *Congregation*, was released to very positive reviews. After its release, the band was courted by a number of major labels. The band released one more record on Sub Pop, an EP of soul and R&B covers called *Uptown Avondale*, before signing to Elektra Records.

Gentlemen, the band's major label debut, was released to considerable critical acclaim in the fall of 1993. "Debonair," the first single pulled from the album, received major play from MTV and all of the reviews were positive. Nevertheless, the band wasn't able to ascend past cult status, and even all the critical praise engendered a backlash, most notably in the form of an anti-Whigs fanzine called *Fat Greg Dulli*. In the summer of 1994, the band released the *What Jail Is Like* EP to coincide with their American tour. Upon the completion of their international tour in the fall of 1994, the band took an extended break; during their time off, Curley concentrated on running Ultrasuede studios, which the Whigs founded in 1988. Since the inception of Ultrasuede, Curley had produced numerous Ohio alternative and punk bands. Steve Earle left the band in the spring of 1995; he was replaced by Paul Buchignani just before the band entered the studio to record their fifth album. *Black Love*, their second album for Elektra, was released in the spring of 1996. Again, the album received positive review but the band still failed to break out of their cult status. — *Stephen Thomas Erlewine*

Big Top Halloween / 1988 / Ultrasuede ♦♦

Up in It / 1990 / Sub Pop ♦♦♦

Congregation / Aug. 1991 / Sub Pop ♦♦♦♦

Dulli's songwriting continues to improve on their last full-length independent album, while the band itself sounds tougher and able to keep up

with the twists in the songwriting. — *Stephen Thomas Erlewine*

Uptown Avondale / 1992 / Sub Pop ♦♦♦

● **Gentlemen** / 1993 / Elektra ♦♦♦♦

With their major-label debut, *Gentlemen*, the Afghan Whigs have finally come into their own. Throughout *Gentlemen*, the Whigs act as if they were Minneapolis punks ripping through the Stax songbook as written by Paul Westerberg. It's a riveting, original album, uncompromising in its honesty and punk-soul roots—in short, with this album, the Afghan Whigs have fulfilled the promise of their earlier, independent records. — *Stephen Thomas Erlewine*

Black Love / Mar. 12, 1996 / Elektra ♦♦♦

Air Supply

Adult Contemporary, Soft Rock, Pop-Rock
With their heavily orchestrated, sweet ballads, the Australian soft-rock group Air Supply became a staple of early-'80s radio, scoring a string of seven straight Top Five singles. Air Supply, for most intents and purposes, was the duo of vocalists Russell Hitchcock and Graham Russell; other members came through the group over the years, yet they only functioned as backing musicians and added little to the group's sound. Hitchcock and Russell met while performing in a Sydney, Australia, production of *Jesus Christ Superstar* in 1976. The two singers formed a partnership and with the addition of four supporting musicians—keyboardist Frank Esler-Smith, guitarist David Moyse, bassist David Green, and drummer Ralph Cooper—Air Supply was born.

For several years, the group gained no attention outside of Australia, earning one significant hit single, "Love and Other Bruises." Their first international exposure came in the late '70s, when Rod Stewart had them as his opening act on a North American tour. Air Supply signed a record contract with Arista in 1980, releasing their first album by the end of the year. *Lost in Love*, their debut, was a major success in the US, selling over two million copies and spawning the hit singles "Lost in Love," "All Out of Love," and "Every Woman in the World." The following year they released their second album, *The One That You Love*. The title track became their only No. 1 hit and it also featured two other Top Ten hits, "Here I Am (Just When I Thought I Was Over You)" and "Sweet Dreams." With their third album, 1982's *Now and Forever*, their popularity dipped slightly—it only had one Top Ten hit, "Even the Nights Are Better," and the other two singles, "Young Love" and "Two Less Lonely People in the World," scraped the bottom of the Top 40. Air Supply released a *Greatest Hits* collection in 1983, featuring a new single, "Making Love Out of Nothing at All." The single spent two weeks at No. 2 while the album peaked at No. 7 and eventually sold over four million copies.

Two years later, they released *Air Supply*, their fourth album. It featured the No. 19 single "Just as I Am," but it was clear that their audience was shrinking—the album was their first not to go platinum. *Hearts in Motion* (1986) was even less successful, peaking at No. 84 and spending only nine weeks on the charts. After its disappointing performance, Air Supply broke up. Hitchcock and Russell reunited in 1991, releasing *Earth Is . . .*, but the album failed to make the charts as did 1993's *Vanishing Race* and 1995's *News from Nowhere*. — *Stephen Thomas Erlewine*

● **Greatest Hits** / 1988 / Arista ♦♦♦♦

This self-explanatory collection includes "Lost in Love" (No. 1), "The One That You Love" (No. 1), "Every Woman in the World" (No. 5), "All Out of Love" (No. 2), "Sweet Dreams" (No. 5), "Making Love Out of Nothing at All" (No. 2), "Even the Nights Are Better" (No. 5), and many more soft pop hits. — *Rick Clark*

The Alarm

Alternative Pop-Rock
Comparisons to U2 have dogged Welsh quartet the Alarm throughout their career, but in light of the Alarm's socially conscious lyrics, melodic rock anthems, and gravitation toward a mainstream alternative sound over their career, perhaps the comparisons are justified. Lead singer and guitarist Mike Peters was actually inspired by U2's passion and commitment to form the group in 1981 with guitarist/vocalist David Sharp, bassist Eddie MacDonald, and drummer Nigel Twist. Their early sound was energetic and largely acoustic-based, while the group's stage look encompassed skintight leather pants, gaudy belts, and spiked hair. Their first of several UK hits was "68 Guns," but didn't chart in America until 1987 with "Presence of Love," which reached No. 77 and proved to be the extent of their US singles-chart success. By that point in their career, the group had adopted a more electric guitar-based sound and had gravitated more toward the mainstream, but since U2 had hit the big time, the Alarm seemed too much like a pale imitation. The band tried something different on 1989's *Change*, which featured more traditional Celtic influences and a guest appearance from the Welsh Symphony Orchestra, but it proved to be too little too late. The Alarm broke up in the early '90s, and Mike Peters embarked on a solo career. — *Steve Huey*

● **Standards** / 1990 / IRS ✦✦✦✦
This solid anthology covers everything from early aggressive topical folk-rock anthems ("Marching On," "The Stand") to more mainstream rock hits like "Strength" and "Sold Me Down the River." —*Rick Clark*

Arthur Alexander

b. 1942, Florence, AL, **d.** Jun. 9, 1993, Nashville, TN
Vocals / Soul, R&B
Alexander was one of the first true singing/songwriting stars of country-soul, a genre that wed Southern Black R&B singers to songs written in a country format and played basically by White musicians. Alexander's "You Better Move On" (No. 24 in 1962) was the first hit to come out of Rick Hall's fledgling Muscle Shoals studio. Alexander's work is immediately appreciated by his peers in the business; those who have covered his tunes (self-penned or otherwise) read like a *Who's Who* from both sides of the Atlantic—"Anna" (Beatles); "Soldiers of Love" (Beatles and Marshall Crenshaw); "Burning Love" (Elvis Presley); "Set Me Free" (Joe Tex, Esther Phillips, Percy Sledge). The Rolling Stones' cover of "You Better Move On" led to valuable contacts for Rick Hall, and the resulting business enabled him to build the new FAME studio. It was the start of the whole Muscle Shoals sound, and Alexander's career was one of its cornerstones. He went on, after a brief retirement, to record for both Warner Bros. and Buddah.
"Anna (Go to Him)," one of Alexander's best-known tunes, epitomizes the anguished, haunting tone of his music. From the onset, the heavily echoed piano and tortured vocal set a mood that is soulful, mysterious, a little spooky, and totally mesmerizing. His work is essential to any country-soul collection. As Alexander began a comeback in 1993, he died of a heart attack. However, the album he completed before his death, *Lonely Just Like Me*, is a gentle record that is a fine way to end his career. Warner Bros. issued an Arthur Alexander retrospective anthology in 1994 featuring the early-'70s LP he recorded for them, plus some unissued tracks. —*Christine Ohlman*

Soldier of Love / 1987 / Ace ✦✦✦
Lonely Just Like Me / 1993 / Elektra/Nonesuch ✦✦✦✦
The final album from country-soul vocalist Arthur Alexander. It was like all his work—simple, unsophisticated, and sung with an earthy, direct intensity. This was part of the American Explorers series on Elektra/Nonesuch, and Alexander got some critical attention with his probing, often searing vocals. Unfortunately, he died just as this album was gaining some attention. —*Ron Wynn*

★ **The Ultimate Arthur Alexander** / 1993 / Razor & Tie ✦✦✦✦✦
Alexander's songs are better known in versions by the Beatles, Elvis Presley, and the Rolling Stones, but no one recorded better versions than Alexander himself. *The Ultimate Arthur Alexander* truly lives up to its title, gathering together the best songs (including "Anna [Go to Him]," "You Better Move On," and "Soldiers of Love") from Alexander's remarkably influential and underrated career. Absolutely essential for any R&B and soul collection. —*Stephen Thomas Erlewine*

Rainbow Road / 1994 / Warner Archives ✦✦✦✦
Songwriter and vocalist Arthur Alexander was sorely neglected during his lifetime, despite possessing a stark, compelling voice and being among pop and soul's greatest storytellers. He remained on the outside, coming close but never attaining stardom. This CD features 15 fantastic songs, most from the great 1972 Warner Bros. album recorded in Memphis that Alexander thought would finally earn him that elusive smash. There are also some singles cut in Nashville as companion records to the Memphis session. The 15 tracks range from the hypnotic title cut and "In the Middle of It All" to the uptempo burners "You Got Me Knockin'" and "Burning Love." There's also a moving gospel number, "Thank God He Came." This disc is a wonderful tribute to an unjustly ignored artist. —*Ron Wynn*

Alice in Chains

Alternative Pop-Rock, Heavy Metal, Grunge
Out of all the Seattle grunge bands of the early '90s, Alice in Chains had the strongest ties with heavy metal. Soundgarden also approximated the mammoth, heavy riffs of Black Sabbath, yet they leavened their attack with humor. On record, Alice in Chains rarely alleviates the gloom. Their music wallows in death, despair, and drugs. With guitarist Jerry Cantrell's lean, lethal riffs, drummer Sean Kinney's subtly menacing rhythms, and Layne Staley's flat, emotionless vocals, the band is relentlessly heavy. What keeps Alice in Chains from being a standard-issue metal band is Cantrell's subtly crafted songs, which rely on shifting textures and dynamics for their impact. Staley's lyrics never celebrate the darkness that he writes about; instead, they intensify the already oppressively gloomy atmosphere, making their music frighteningly claustrophobic.
Although their debut, *Facelift*, was popular in metal circles—particularly "We Die Young" and "Man in the Box"—Alice in Chains' fan base

began to build in early 1992 with their acoustic *Sap* EP. Their second full-length album, *Dirt*, expanded their audience dramatically, selling over two million copies and earning them a headlining slot on Lollapalooza 93. Before the tour began, bassist Mike Starr left the group and was replaced by Mike Inez. At the beginning of 1994, Alice in Chains released their second EP, *Jar of Flies*, which became the first EP to debut at No. 1 on the *Billboard* album charts.
Alice in Chains released their eponymous third album in the fall of 1991; it entered the charts at No. 1. In the summer of 1996, the group released an album culled from their *MTV* "Unplugged" performance; it entered the charts at No. 3. —*Stephen Thomas Erlewine*

Facelift / 1990 / Columbia ✦✦✦
Sap / Feb. 1992 / Columbia ✦✦✦✦
Before Alice in Chains delivered their second album, they released *Sap*, a five-song EP featuring acoustic-oriented material. For anyone who pigeonholed them as mere gloom-mongers after their debut, *Sap* was a shock; it showed that they were capable of playing quieter, more intricate music without losing any intensity. —*Stephen Thomas Erlewine*

● **Dirt** / Oct. 1992 / Columbia ✦✦✦✦
To say that *Dirt* is a dark album is something of an understatement. Alice in Chains convey a stark, stoic beauty to the pain of their protagonists. The violence and disturbing elements (both musical and lyrical) are offset by a mantralike feel of inner strength and acceptance. Musically, Alice In Chains' rhythm section lays down a heavy, doom-struck base over which twin guitars and double-tracked vocals slash appealingly. There are lots of interesting tempo and time-signature changes, the band veering into progressive-rock territory on occasion. —*Roch Parisien*

Jar of Flies / 1994 / Columbia ✦✦✦
Like *Sap* before it, *Jar of Flies* is a quieter, acoustic-oriented experimental EP released between full-length albums, but it also works well as a coda to the epochal *Dirt*. Although the songs are calmer, they are by no means gentle, providing harrowing examinations of loss. Thankfully, musical stretches like the instrumental "Whale & Wasp" and the swing-blues of "Swing on This" are successful, and the best material here ("I Stay Away" and "No Excuses") rivals the best tracks on *Dirt*. —*Stephen Thomas Erlewine*

Alice in Chains / Nov. 21, 1995 / Columbia ✦✦✦
Dispelling rumors of their demise due to Layne Staley's heroin addiction, *Alice in Chains* is an accomplished, detailed effort showcasing Jerry Cantrell's continually developing writing and songcrafting skills. The band relies less on metallic riffs and more on melody and complex, varying textures than their previous full-length albums, integrating some of the more delicate acoustic moods of their EPs. The lyrics deal with familiar AIC subject matter: despair, misery, loneliness, and disappointment, but in an understated fashion, making the endurance of Staley's characters more apparent than on *Dirt*. The thematic unity and consistent visceral impact *Alice in Chains* lacks in comparison to that album are more than made up for by songs like "Grind," "Brush Away," "Over Now," and the ballad "Heaven Beside You," which are easily among the band's best work. —*Steve Huey*

Unplugged / Jul. 1996 / Sony ✦✦✦

The Allman Brothers Band

Blues-Rock, Southern Rock
The Allman Brothers Band was the major instigator of the Southern rock genre of the '70s and one of the major rock acts of the first half of that decade; it continues to be popular today. In its original configuration, the group consisted of Duane Allman (b. Nov. 20, 1946, d. Oct. 29, 1971) on guitar; Gregg Allman (b. Dec. 8, 1947) on organ and vocals; Dickey Betts (b. Dec. 12, 1943) on guitar and vocals; Berry Oakley (b. Apr. 4, 1948, d. Nov. 11, 1971) on bass; and Butch Trucks and Jaimo (born John Lee Johnson, Jul. 8, 1944) on drums. This sextet was a showcase for the twin-guitar work of Duane Allman and Dickey Betts and for the bluesy singing of Gregg Allman. It cut three albums between 1969 and 1971. *Live at the Fillmore East*, the Allmans' breakthrough third album, went gold four days before bandleader Duane Allman was killed in a motorcycle accident. The group continued as a quintet, finishing its fourth album, *Eat a Peach* (1972), which was a major success. After bassist Oakley was also killed in a motorcycle accident, the group was augmented with bassist Lamar Williams (b. 1947, d. Jan. 1983) and pianist Chuck Leavell to complete its fifth album, *Brothers and Sisters*, which topped the charts and spawned the No. 2 single "Ramblin' Man." But the group split up in acrimony after the release of *Win, Lose or Draw* in 1975.
The Allmans re-formed in 1978, this time returning to the sextet format, with Allman, Betts, Trucks, and Jaimo being joined by guitarist Dan Toler and bassist David Goldflies for the gold-selling *Enlightened Rogues* (1979). Two more albums, *Reach for the Sky* and *Brothers of the Road* (for which David Toler replaced Jaimo and Mike Lawler was added on piano), were released before the band split again. Following the release of a boxed-set retrospective, *Dreams*, in 1989, the Allmans again

re-formed, with Warren Haynes on second lead guitar and Allen Woody on bass, and to date they have released four more albums and toured extensively. — *William Ruhlmann*

The Allman Brothers Band / 1969 / Polydor ✦✦✦✦
The Allmans' aggressive synthesis of blues, rock, jazz, and gospel made an impressive entrance on this 1969 debut, with soon-to-be-standards like "Whipping Post" and the dynamic, moody "Dreams." Highlights like "Don't Want You No More," "It's Not My Cross to Bear," "Black Hearted Woman," and "Trouble No More" are reasons why this was one of the greatest bands ever to emerge from the American South. — *Rick Clark*

Idlewild South / 1970 / Polydor ✦✦✦✦
The Allmans' second effort may not have been quite as strong as their powerful debut, but *Idlewild South* had more than a handful of gems with songs like the celebratory "Revival," the earthy "Midnight Rider," and the instrumental "In Memory of Elizabeth Reed," with its soaring twin-guitar counterpuntal melodies. — *Rick Clark*

☆ **Live at Fillmore East** / Mar. 1971 / Polydor ✦✦✦✦✦
The double-disc *Allman Brothers Band at Fillmore East* is one of rock's greatest live albums, featuring amazing interplay within highly dynamic arrangements. Most of the tracks exceed ten minutes, yet the Allmans never stumble. "Hot 'Lanta," "In Memory of Elizabeth Reed," and "Statesboro Blues" are highlights. Contrary to claims that these are untouched performances, *Fillmore East* actually was a skillfully edited document (courtesy of producer Tom Dowd) taken from a run of shows at Bill Graham's Fillmore. — *Rick Clark*

★ **Eat a Peach** / 1972 / Polydor ✦✦✦✦✦
Half of *Eat a Peach* consists of more fiery improvisations from the *Live at Fillmore* dates, in the form of the "Mountain Jam." Even though this was released after Duane Allman's fatal motorcycle accident, the studio sides include some tracks showcasing his soaring lead work. Creatively, the band was in peak form with great tracks like "Ain't Wastin' Time No More," "Melissa," "One Way Out," "Stand Back," "Blue Sky," and the delicate acoustic-guitar instrumental "Little Martha." — *Rick Clark*

Brothers and Sisters / 1973 / Polydor ✦✦✦✦
In spite of the inclusion of Dickey Betts' "Ramblin' Man" and "Jessica," *Brothers and Sisters* is a noticeable comedown from the previous four albums. Muddy production doesn't help matters either. — *Rick Clark*

Beginnings / 1973 / Polydor ✦✦✦✦
Beginnings is nothing more than the first two albums on a single disc. Since its release, Polygram has done a markedly improved remastering job, releasing each album separately. — *Rick Clark*

Win, Lose or Draw / 1975 / Polydor ✦✦

The Road Goes on Forever / 1975 / Polydor ✦✦

Wipe the Windows, Check the Oil, Dollar Gas / 1976 / Polydor ✦✦✦

Enlightened Rogues / 1979 / Polydor ✦✦✦

Reach for the Sky / 1980 / Arista ✦✦

Brothers of the Road / 1981 / Arista ✦✦

Dreams / 1989 / Polydor ✦✦✦✦
This is a thoughtfully compiled boxed set, containing highlights throughout the Allman Brothers' career, as well as solo projects and pre-Allman recordings. A booklet, with generous annotation and photos, is provided. The remastering is a noticeable improvement over initial CD releases of the Allman catalog. This is a worthwhile acquisition for completists and those looking for a comprehensive introduction. — *Rick Clark*

Seven Turns / Oct. 1990 / Epic ✦✦✦✦
After a nine-year absence, the Allmans return with a vengeance on *Seven Turns*, with tracks like the hard-swinging opener, "Good Clean Fun" and the powerful blues-rock workout "Gambler's Roll." The Dickey Betts-penned title track, a mystical take on life, is the album's spiritual highlight, while "True Gravity" is the musical peak, ranking with "In Memory of Elizabeth Reed" as one of the band's best instrumentals. Overall, *Seven Turns* is their strongest album since 1972's *Eat a Peach*. — *Rick Clark*

Decade of Hits 1969-1979 / 1991 / Polydor ✦✦✦
Decade of Hits 1969-1979 collects highlights from the Allman Brothers' first decade of existence and features many of their best-known songs; it provides a solid introduction to the definitive Southern rock band. — *Stephen Thomas Erlewine*

Live at Ludlow Garage: 1970 / 1991 / Polydor ✦✦✦✦
It's no *Fillmore East*, but this archival release does present the classic lineup of the Allmans at their near-peak, and fans especially will be pleased to have more Duane on disc. — *William Ruhlmann*

Shades of Two Worlds / 1991 / Epic ✦✦✦

The Fillmore Concerts / 1992 / Polydor ✦✦✦✦
Fillmore Concerts is an expanded version of the classic *Fillmore East*, featuring several songs that didn't make the original album, re-edited tracks that now run at their original length, and sterling remastered

sound; for hardcore fans, it's the ultimate version of this landmark set. — *Stephen Thomas Erlewine*

Evening with the Allman Brothers Band / Mar. 1992 / Epic ✦✦
Where It All Begins / 1994 / Epic ✦✦✦

Marc Almond

b. Jul. 9, 1959, Southport, Lancashire, England
Vocals / Dance-Pop, New Wave, New Romantic
After disbanding Soft Cell, vocalist Marc Almond pursued a solo career that followed the same vaguely sleazy, electronic dance-pop his former group had made popular. Almond's strength was never his personality—his voice tends to waver around the notes instead of hitting them—it was the atmosphere he created with the synths and drum machines. Underneath all of the electronics and disco rhythms, Almond hearkened back to the days of cabaret singers, updating that sound with his tongue-in-cheek for dance clubs of the '80s.

Before he properly started a solo career, Marc Almond formed Marc and the Mambas, a loose congregation that featured Matt Johnson of The The and Annie Hogan. *"Untitled"* (1983), the group's first album, featured covers of Lou Reed, Syd Barrett, and Jacques Brel; throughout his career, Almond would cover the songs of Brel, which he had learned from the records of Scott Walker. Like Walker, Almond used Brel's heavily orchestrated compositions and social ruminations as a starting point, both musically and lyrically—Almond added a self-conscious element of camp with his Euro-disco and occasionally sleazy lyrics. *Torment and Toreros* (1983), Marc and the Mambas' second album, explored this path in more detail than *"Untitled,"* only to an orchestral background. After its release, the group broke up.

Almond formed the backing group the Willing Sinners in 1984, releasing *Vermin in Ermine* in 1984. Almond began to hit his stride with this album, which fulfilled most of his campy cabaret fantasies. *Stories of Johnny*, released the following year, was more cohesive, spawning a British hit with the title song. Even though he maintained a cult following in England and various parts of Europe, his records were not being released in the US.

In 1987, Almond released *Mother Fist . . . and Her Five Daughters*, his first proper solo album and his bleakest work to date; a compilation, *Singles 1984-1987*, appeared the same year. *The Stars We Are*, released the following year, was a brighter, more welcoming album that revived his commercial career. In addition to a duet with Nico on "Your Kisses Burn," Almond duetted with Gene Pitney on Pitney's own "Something's Gotten Hold of My Heart," which became a No. 1 single. *Stars We Are* also became his first album released in the US since Soft Cell.

Almond followed the success of *Stars We Are* in 1990 with the pet project *Jacques*, a collection of Brel songs. That same year, he released *Enchanted*, which was more successful than *Jacques*, yet it didn't reach the heights of *Stars We Are*. In 1991, he released *The Tenement Symphony* and in 1993, a compilation entitled *Twelve Years of Tears* appeared. — *Stephen Thomas Erlewine*

● **Singles: 1984-1987** / 1987 / Some Bizarre ✦✦✦✦
This is a compilation of Almond's solo work. — *Steve Aldrich*

Stars We Are / 1988 / Capitol ✦✦✦✦
Accessible "big pop" is a fine introduction to Almond. — *Steve Aldrich*

Jacques / 1989 / Some Bizarre ✦✦✦

Memorabilia / 1991 / Mercury ✦✦✦✦
A compilation of solo material and Soft Cell sides. — *Steve Aldrich*

Tenement Symphony / Oct. 29, 1991 / Sire ✦✦

ALT

ALT is a side project (and supergroup of sorts) consisting of Andy White, Liam O'Maonlai (Hothouse Flowers), and Tim Finn (ex-Split Enz)—the name comes from the first letters of each of their first names. In 1993, the three began writing together informally in Dublin—one of the songs, "Many's the Time (in Dublin)," appeared on Finn's 1993 album, *Before & After*. In June 1994, they reconvened in Finn's Melbourne-based Periscope Studios, where they recorded their debut album, *Altitude*. *Altitude* was released by EMI-Australia in 1995 and in the US on Cooking Vinyl. — *Chris Woodstra*

● **Altitude** / 1995 / ALT ✦✦✦✦
Altitude represents the trio's drunken, post-pub jamming with the predictable result of an informal, at times sloppy, album filled with seemingly unfinished songs. While fans of any of the individual members may be put off by these qualities, there is a spirit to these sessions that not only overcomes the shortcomings in content but also gives the record a rare warmth and charm. — *Chris Woodstra*

Amazing Blondel

Art-Rock/Progressive-Rock
A progressive-rock trio who came at the music in a decidedly retrograde

manner, playing originals based on pre-19th-century musical forms (madrigals, chamber music, etc.) on authentic instruments and reproductions. The results were eloquent, stunning in their textures and timbre, but decidedly unrocklike even by the standards of the time. John David Gladwin was the trio's musical mainspring, and when he left in 1972, the duo that remained carried on with one good album before losing direction and inspiration. The group moved through a succession of labels from Bell to Island—where they did their best work—over to DJM. —Bruce Eder

Amazing Blondel / 1970 / Bell ✦✦

Evensong / 1970 / Island ✦✦✦

Fantasia Lindum / 1971 / Island ✦✦✦

England 72 / 1972 / Island ✦✦✦✦
A staggeringly beautiful collection of love songs and odes to nature. All have a distinctly pre-20th-century (indeed, pre-19th-century) feel. Exquisitely sung and played. —Bruce Eder

● **England** / 1973 / Island ✦✦✦✦
The best record ever made by the trio, a lyrical, gentle, yet ambitious expansion of their sound into a richer vein, with a wider range of instrumentation, some eerie mixes of medieval instruments and psychedelic effects, and a compelling beauty that makes this record linger long in the memory. The sound is very elegant, but this time out the group has timed and edited everything perfectly, so none of it overstays its welcome. Sort of the way the Moody Blues might've sounded circa the year 1500. —Bruce Eder

Blondel / 1973 / Island ✦✦✦

Mulgrave Street / 1974 / DJM ✦✦

Inspiration / 1975 / DJM ✦✦✦
A further effort at rocking up the folky sound, and so successful at it that one had to wonder why stick with the name or the image at all? —Bruce Eder

The Amazing Rhythm Aces

Country-Rock
One of the first and best Southern country-rock bands, the Aces were formed out of Jesse Winchester's backup band in 1974 and produced six albums bristling with rock, bluegrass, hardcore honky tonk, country, Western swing, and R&B. They scored their biggest hit with "Third Rate Romance"; supplied country singer Mel McDaniel with his hits "Big Old Brew" and "Anger and Tears"; and had minor hits with "The End Is Not in Sight (The Cowboy Song)" and "Burning the Ballroom Down." After three albums, they disbanded in 1981. Lead singer and songwriter Russell Smith pursued a solo career. —Kit Kiefer

● **Stacked Deck** / 1975 / ABC ✦✦✦✦
"Amazing" is certainly the word. In addition to "Third Rate Romance," which has been covered by artists as diverse as Earl Scruggs and Elvis Costello, this album features a collection of amazing tunes by an incredibly hot band that sound fresh 20 years after they were recorded. Look for the single of "Third Rate Romance" which features the non-LP "Mystery Train" on the flip side. —Jim Worbois

Too Stuffed to Jump / 1976 / ABC ✦✦✦
Although *Too Stuffed to Jump* isn't quite as strong a record as the debut, the album features enough good material to recommend it. Some different influences come into play on this one, like the jazzy shuffle of "Same Ole Me." And who could not hear Leon Russell in "Typical American Boy"? —Jim Worbois

Toucan Do It Too / 1977 / ABC ✦✦

Burning the Ballroom Down / 1978 / ABC ✦✦

The Amazing Rhythm Aces / 1978 / Columbia ✦✦✦

How the Hell Do You Spell Rhythum? / 1980 / Warner Bros. ✦✦

Ambrosia

Art-Rock/Progressive-Rock, Soft Rock, Pop-Rock
Los Angeles quartet Ambrosia, whose founding members included guitarist/vocalist David Pack, bassist/vocalist Joe Puerta, keyboardist Christopher North, and drummer Burleigh Drummond, fused symphonic art-rock with a slickly produced pop sound. The group was discovered in 1971 by Los Angeles Philharmonic conductor Zubin Mehta, who featured Ambrosia as part of a so-called All-American Dream Concert. However, it took them four more years to get a record contract; *Ambrosia* was released in 1975 and spawned the chart singles "Holdin' on to Yesterday" and "Nice, Nice, Very Nice." The latter was based on Kurt Vonnegut, Jr.'s *Cat's Cradle*. Ambrosia scored another hit in 1977 with a cover of the Beatles' "Magical Mystery Tour" from the film *All This and World War II*, which they also appeared in.

North left the group just before their biggest pop breakthrough in 1978, the No. 3 hit "How Much I Feel." Ambrosia followed this success in 1980 with another No. 3 hit, "Biggest Part of Me," and No. 13 follow-up

"You're the Only Woman." Their next album failed, ending their run of chart success, and the group broke up; individual members are active as session musicians and vocalists, as well as producers. —Steve Huey

● **Ambrosia** / 1975 / 20th Century ✦✦✦✦
A wonderful debut album, it was engineered by Alan Parsons. Top-notch mid-'70s art-rock, with great musicianship, it features "Holdin' on to Yesterday" and "Nice, Nice, Very Nice." —Scott Bultman

Somewhere I've Never Travelled / 1976 / Warner Bros. ✦✦✦
Their second album is more in the symphonic realm but just as good as their debut. —Scott Bultman

One Eighty / 1980 / Warner Bros. ✦✦✦
It contains their biggest pop hits, "Biggest Part of Me" and "You're the Only Woman." —Scott Bultman

America

Soft Rock, Pop-Rock
America was a light folk-rock act of the early '70s who had several Top Ten hits, including the No. 1 songs "A Horse with No Name" and "Sister Golden Hair." Vocalists/guitarists Dewey Bunnell, Dan Peak, and Gerry Beckley met while they were still in high school in the late '60s; all three were sons of US Air Force officers who were stationed in the UK. After they completed school in 1970, they formed an acoustic folk-rock quartet called Daze in London, which was soon pared down to the trio of Bunnell, Peak, and Beckley. Adopting the name America, the group landed a contract with Jeff Dexter, a promoter for the Roundhouse concert venue. Dexter had America open for several major artists and the group soon signed with Warner Bros. Records. By the fall of 1970, the group was recording their debut album in London, with producers Ian Samwell and Jeff Dexter. "A Horse with No Name," America's debut single, was released at the end of 1971. In January 1972, the song—which recalled the acoustic numbers of Neil Young—became a No. 3 hit in the UK. The group's self-titled debut album followed the same stylistic pattern and became a hit as well, peaking at No. 14. Following their British success, America returned to North America, beginning a supporting tour for the Everly Brothers. "A Horse with No Name" was released in the US that spring, where it became a No. 1 single, pushing Neil Young's "Heart of Gold" off the top of the charts; *America* followed the single to the top of the charts. "I Need You" became another Top Ten hit that summer, and the group began work on its second album with Beatles' producer George Martin. "Ventura Highway," the first single released from this collaboration, became their third-straight Top Ten hit in December 1972. In the beginning of 1973, America won the Grammy award for Best New Artist of 1972.

Homecoming was released in January 1973, becoming a Top Ten hit in the US and peaking at No. 21 in the UK. Under Martin's direction, America's essential sound didn't change, it became more polished. However, the hits stopped coming fairly soon—they had only one minor Top 40 hit in 1973. *Hat Trick*, the group's third album, was released toward the end of 1973; it failed to make it past No. 28 on the American charts. Released in the late fall of 1974, *Holiday* was the third record the group made with George Martin. It returned America to the top of the charts, peaking at No. 3 and launching the hit singles "Tin Man" and "Lonely People." "Sister Golden Hair," pulled from 1975's *Hearts*, became their second No. 1 single. That same year, the group released *History/America's Greatest Hits*, which would eventually sell over four million copies.

Although America's 1976 effort, *Hideaway*, went gold and peaked at No. 11, the group's audience was beginning to decline. At the end of 1976, Dan Peek left the group, deciding to become a Contemporary Christian recording artist. The group continued as a duo, releasing *Harbor* to a lukewarm reception. America's last Martin-produced record, *Silent Letter*, was released in 1979 to little attention. America returned to the Top Ten in 1982 with "You Can Do Magic," an adult-contemporary pop number that featured synthesizers along with their trademark harmonies. "The Border" became their last Top 40 hit in 1983, peaking at No. 33. America released their last album, *America in Concert*, in the summer of 1985, yet the group has continued to tour successfully into the '90s. —Stephen Thomas Erlewine

● **History: Greatest Hits** / 1975 / Warner Bros. ✦✦✦✦
A nice roundup of their peak years (1971-1975), it includes tracks like "A Horse with No Name," "I Need You," "Ventura Highway," "Tin Man," "Lonely People," "Sister Golden Hair," and more. —Dan Heilman

Encore: More Greatest Hits / 1991 / Rhino ✦✦✦✦
This follow-up to their *Greatest Hits* contains "The Border," "Right Before Your Eyes," "Today's the Day," and "You Can Do Magic." The rest of the tracks are album sides or previously unreleased material. —AMG

American Music Club

Alternative Pop-Rock
A traditional-sounding rock band in these postmodern times? Well, American Music Club, led by Mark Eitzel, may be an anomaly, but it's a

pretty engaging proposition on record. Eitzel's songwriting is very straightforward—good people living through hard times— and he's very much the agreeable populist. His bandmates add to this mix by playing no-nonsense, bare-bones rock 'n' roll that, if slightly derivative of blues-rock structures, is also loaded with enough panache. Smart and direct, a fine American band.

American Music Club formed in the mid-'80s when guitarist Vudi saw the Naked Skinnies, one of Eitzel's early bands perform. The Naked Skinnies had recently moved to San Francisco from Ohio, with hopes of making it big in California. Instead, the group wound up being banned from clubs. Vudi had seen one of those performances and asked Eitzel if he wanted to work together; soon the pair had formed American Music Club, adding bassist/vocalist Dan Pearson as a permanent member.

Initially, the band's music drew equally from post-punk bands like Joy Division and singer-songwriters like Nick Drake and Van Morrison, adding flourishes of experimental art-rock. The band's first album, 1986's *The Restless Stranger*, followed this pattern in particular. After its release, the group's drummer left and their record producer, Tom Mallon, played percussion and guitars on 1987's *Engine*, which featured a folk-rock influence. With their third album, 1988's *California*, the band began to build a cult following, thanks to positive reviews in underground and alternative magazines. For *California*, American Music Club was stripped down to a four-piece, with Mallon playing drums. Mallon left the band after its release; he was replaced by Mike Simms. AMC added a multi-instrumentalist, Bruce Kaphan for their next record.

American Music Club's fourth album, 1991's *Everclear*, was their breakthrough, incorporating elements of rock 'n' roll, folk, country, jazz, and schmaltzy, crooning pop into a languid, atmospheric web of sound. *Everclear* earned the band some attention, as *Rolling Stone* named it one of the best albums of the year and voted Eitzel the best songwriter. All of the attention led to a major label contract with Reprise. Before they recorded their first album for Reprise, Simms left the band and was replaced by Tim Mooney. *Mercury*, released in the spring of 1993, continued AMC's string of rave reviews and small record sales, even if it sold slightly better than their indie releases. *San Francisco*, the group's sixth album, was released in the fall of 1995. Like the band's previous albums, it was critically well-received but had little exposure on radio and MTV. —*John Dougan & Stephen Thomas Erlewine*

California / 1988 / Frontier ✦✦✦✦
Stark-sounding, highly personal songs, they cemented the reputation of bandleader Mark Eitzel. —*Steve Aldrich*

United Kingdom / 1990 / Demon ✦✦✦

Everclear / 1991 / Alias ✦✦✦✦
More expansive production and arrangements without watering down the quality of Eitzel's material, this is a brilliant album. —*Steve Aldrich*

● **Mercury** / 1993 / Reprise ✦✦✦✦
On their major-label debut, American Music Club continues to mine despair from Mark Eitzel's heart, and the results are captivating. Mitchell Froom's production polishes some of their rougher edges, but *Mercury* is by no means an easy listen. Eitzel's songs are beautifully sad, etched with grace and elegant suffering, as well as an often-overlooked self-deprecating humor. —*Stephen Thomas Erlewine*

San Francisco / 1994 / Reprise ✦✦✦

Tori Amos (Myra Ellen Amos)

b. Aug. 22, 1963, Newton, NC
Piano, Keyboards, Vocals / Singer-Songwriter, Alternative Pop-Rock
Tori Amos was one of several female singer-songwriters who combined the stark lyrical attack of alternative rock with a distinctly '70s musical approach. Her music falls between the orchestrated meditations of Kate Bush and the stripped-down poetics of Joni Mitchell. In addition to reviving the singer-songwriter traditions of the '70s, Amos revived the piano as a rock 'n' roll instrument. With her 1992 album *Little Earthquakes*, Amos built a dedicated following that continued to expand with her second album, *Under the Pink*.

Born in North Carolina but raised in Maryland, Tori Amos was the daughter of a methodist preacher. By the age of four, she was singing and playing piano in the church choir; she began writing her own songs shortly afterward. Amos won a scholarship to Baltimore's Peabody Conservatory based on her instrumental prowess. While she was studying at Peabody, she became infatuated by rock 'n' roll, particularly the music of Led Zeppelin. Amos began writing pop ballads and performing in local bars. Amos moved to Los Angeles in her late teens to become a pop singer.

Atlantic records signed her in 1987, recording an uninspired pop-metal album called *Y Kant Tori Read* the following year. The record was a complete failure, attracting no attention from radio or press and selling very few copies; nevertheless, she didn't lose her record contract. By 1990, Amos had adopted a new approach, singing sparse, haunting semi-

confessional piano ballads. Atlantic sponsored a trip to England in 1991, where she played a series of concerts in support of an EP, *Me and a Gun*.

The harrowing "Me and a Gun" was an autobiographical song, telling the tale of a rape. It gained positive reviews throughout the media, and both the EP and the concerts sold well. *Little Earthquakes*, Amos' first album as a singer-songwriter, was released in late 1991 and sold well in both the US and the UK. In 1992, she released the *Crucify* EP, which featured three covers, including Nirvana's "Smells Like Teen Spirit" and Led Zeppelin's "Thank You." Delivered in early 1994, *Under the Pink*, the full-length follow-up to *Little Earthquakes*, was a bigger hit, selling over a million copies and launching the minor hit singles "God" and "Cornflake Girl." Two years later, Amos delivered her third album, *Boys for Pele*. —*Stephen Thomas Erlewine*

● **Little Earthquakes** / 1991 / Atlantic ✦✦✦✦
The album just screams Kate Bush, from the cover shot on in. But once past that, we discover plenty of rewards. Amos engages us like few ever attempted. Her lyrical directness and the sparse production draw us almost uncomfortably close to the artist. An album as challenging as it is beautiful, *Little Earthquakes* stands as a major work. —*Steve Aldrich*

Crucify / 1992 / Atlantic ✦✦✦

Under the Pink / 1994 / Atlantic ✦✦✦✦
More difficult and ambitious than her critically acclaimed debut, the core of *Under the Pink* reveals the strong, stark presence of a compelling singer-songwriter at her piano. —*Roch Parisien*

Boys for Pele / Jan. 23, 1996 / Atlantic ✦✦✦
Highly ambitious, challenging, idiosyncratic, and confounding, *Boys for Pele* expands on the more experimental and progressive tendencies of *Under the Pink*. Amos frequently discards traditional song structures and employs wide-ranging, eclectic instrumentation in her music, while her lyrics seem to grow even more obscure, giving the album a very impressionistic feel. While there are certainly worthwhile moments, her experiments don't always work; some of the songs fail to stick, and it takes a few plays before many start to sink in. Ultimately, *Boys for Pele* is polarizing: some Amos fans will only admire her more for taking the risks she does, while others may find to their disappointment that the intimacy and personal connection that helped Amos build her fan base are too difficult to detect. —*Steve Huey*

The Angels

Girl Group
The Angels' 1963 No. 1 hit, "My Boyfriend's Back," is one of the half-dozen or so archetypal girl-group classics. Handclap beats, sassy vocals, slightly campy lyrics, and an arrangement paced by wailing horns and street-corner harmonies—it was a surefire hit and one that the group could never live up to, although they continued to record for some time.

The Angels had actually been around for a while before "My Boyfriend's Back," making the Top 20 in 1961 with the ballad "Till," and the Top 40 with a follow-up, "Cry Baby Cry." Featuring sisters Barbara and Phyllis Allibut, along with lead singer Linda Jansen, the group was at this time much more inclined toward lush doo wop, somewhat in the mold of Little Anthony & the Imperials. Jansen left near the end of 1962, to be replaced by Peggy Santiglia, who gave the trio a tougher sound. In 1963, the Angels hooked up with the songwriting/production team of Feldman-Goldstein-Gottehrer (later to oversee the McCoys and the Strangeloves), who penned and produced material more in line with the Spectorian "wall of sound" gracing the airwaves at the peak of the girl-group era.

"My Boyfriend's Back" was originally cut as a demo that music publishers hoped to shop to the Shirelles, but it turned out so well that it was released as an Angels single, after they had been freed from their prior contract to sign with Smash. Surprisingly, they would never make the Top 20 again, although they had minor hits with "Thank You and Goodnight," "I Adore Him," and "Wow Wow Wee (He's the Boy for Me)." They were decent, ebullient singers, the best of their efforts standing up well to other New York-produced groups like the Shirelles, but could never latch on to a tune like "My Boyfriend's Back" again, despite (or maybe because of) a steady supply of material from the Feldman-Goldstein-Gottehrer consortium. They worked often as session vocalists in the '60s, most notably on Lou Christie's "Lightnin' Strikes," and continued to record, unsuccessfully, throughout the '60s. —*Richie Unterberger*

● **Best of the Angels** / Jun. 18, 1996 / Polygram ✦✦✦✦
Twenty-one-song anthology of cuts from the early and mid-'60s, with all the hits, including the pre-"My Boyfriend's Back" charters "Till" and "Cry Baby Cry." Despite the spirited vocals, accomplished production, and occasional highlights like "Why Don't the Boy Leave Me Alone?," "World Without Love" (not the Lennon-McCartney song), the ska-flavored "Jamaica Joe," and the James Bond riffs of "Boy from Crosstown," nothing here lights up the room like "My Boyfriend's Back." It's certainly the best collection, though, for those who want to hear more from the group

than what's available on various-artist oldies compilations. —*Richie Unterberger*

The Animals

Rock 'n' Roll, British Invasion, Psychedelic, British Blues

One of the most important bands originating from England's R&B scene during the early '60s, the Animals were second only to the Rolling Stones in influence among R&B-based bands in the first wave of the British Invasion. The Animals had their origins in a Newcastle-based group called the Kansas City Five, whose membership included pianist Alan Price, drummer John Steel, and vocalist Eric Burdon. Price exited to join the Kontours in 1962, while Burdon went off to London. The Kontours, whose membership included Bryan "Chas" Chandler, eventually were transmuted into the Alan Price R&B Combo, with John Steel joining on drums. Burdon's return to Newcastle in early 1963 heralded his return to the lineup. The final member of the combo, guitarist Hilton Valentine, joined just in time for the recording of a self-produced E.P. under the band's new name, the Animals. That record alerted Graham Bond to the Animals; he was likely responsible for pointing impresario Giorgio Gomelsky to the group.

Gomelsky booked the band into his Crawdaddy Club in London, and they were subsequently signed by Mickie Most, an independent producer who secured a contract with EMI's Columbia imprint. A studio session in February 1964 yielded their Columbia debut single, "Baby Let Me Take You Home" (adapted from "Baby Let Me Follow You Down"), which rose to No. 21 on the British charts. For years, it has been rumored incorrectly that the Animals got their next single, "House of the Rising Sun," from Bob Dylan's first album, but more recently it has been revealed that, like "Baby Let Me Take You Home," the song came to them courtesy of Josh White. In any event, the song—given a new guitar riff by Valentine and a soulful organ accompaniment devised by Price—shot to the top of the UK and US charts early that summer. This success led to a follow-up session that summer, yielding their first long-playing record, *The Animals*. Their third single, "I'm Crying," rose to No. 8 on the British charts. The group compiled an enviable record of Top Ten successes, including "Don't Let Me Be Misunderstood" and "We've Gotta Get Out of This Place," along with a second album, *Animal Tracks*.

In May 1965, immediately after recording "We've Gotta Get Out of This Place," Alan Price left the group, citing fear of flying as the reason; subsequent biographies of the band have indicated that the reasons were less psychological. When "House of the Rising Sun" was recorded, using what was essentially a group arrangement, the management persuaded the band to put one person's name down as arranger. Price came up the lucky one, supposedly with the intention that the money from the arranger credit would be divided later on. The money was never divided, however, and as soon as it began rolling in, Price suddenly developed his fear of flying and exited the band. Others cite the increasing contentiousness between Burdon and Price over leadership of the group as the latter's reason for leaving. In any case, a replacement was recruited in the person of Dave Rowberry.

In the meantime, the group was growing increasingly unhappy with the material they were being given by manager Mickie Most. Not only were the majority of these songs much too commercial for their taste, but they represented a false image of the band, even if many were successful. "It's My Life," a No. 7 British hit and a similar smash in America, caused the Animals to terminate their association with Most and with EMI Records. They moved over to Decca/London Records and came up with a more forceful, powerful sound on their first album for the new label, *Animalisms*. The lineup shifts continued, however—Steel exited in 1966, after recording *Animalisms*, and was replaced by Barry Jenkins, formerly of The Nashville Teens. Chandler left in mid-1966 after recording "Don't Bring Me Down," and Valentine remained until the end of 1966, but essentially "Don't Bring Me Down" marked the end of the original Animals.

Burdon reformed the group under the aegis of Eric Burdon and the New Animals, with Jenkins on drums, John Weider on guitar and violin, Danny McCulloch on bass, and Vic Briggs on guitar. He remained officially a solo act for a time, releasing a collection of material called *Eric Is Here* in 1967. As soon as the contract with English Decca was up, Burdon signed with MGM directly for worldwide distribution, and the new lineup made their debut in mid-1967. Eric Burdon and the New Animals embraced psychedelia to the hilt amid the full bloom of the Summer of Love. By the end of 1968, Briggs and McCulloch were gone, to be replaced by Burdon's old friend, keyboard player/vocalist Zoot Money, and his longtime stablemate guitarist Andy Summers, while Weider switched to bass. Finally, in 1969, Burdon pulled the plug on what was left of the Animals. He hooked up with a Los Angeles-based group called War and started a subsequent solo career that continues to this day.

The original Animals reunited in 1976 for a superb album called *Before We Were So Rudely Interrupted*, which picked up right where *Animalisms* had left off a decade earlier and which was well received critically but failed to capture the public's attention. In 1983, a somewhat

longer lasting reunion came about between the original members, augmented with the presence of Zoot Money on keyboards. The resulting album, *Ark*, consisting of entirely new material, was well received by critics and charted surprisingly high, and a world tour followed. By the end of the year and the heavy touring schedule, however, it was clear that this reunion was not going to be a lasting event. The quintet split up again, having finally let the other shoe drop on their careers and history, and walked away with some financial rewards, along with memories of two generations of rock fans cheering their every note. —*Bruce Eder*

The Animals [US] / 1964 / MGM ✦✦✦

Animal Tracks [UK] / 1965 / Columbia ✦✦✦✦
The band's second British album displays far more energy and dexterity than its predecessor. Originals such as "For Miss Caulker" are paired up with excellent covers like "Bright Lights Big City," "I Ain't Got You," and "Roadrunner," along with Ray Charles' "Hallelujah I Love Her So" and "I Believe to My Soul." Note: All tracks appearing on this album are available on EMI's *Complete Animals* double CD. —*Bruce Eder*

Animalization / 1966 / PolyGram ✦✦✦✦
The best of the group's early albums, mostly sophisticated blues-based rock which, for the first time on a long-player, managed to capture the spontaneity of their live sound while also allowing them a chance to really stretch out in the studio. Around this time in the band's history, however, the albums get confusing:

Animalization, released in September 1966 by MGM in America, was simply the British *Animalisms* with three tracks missing, and four other songs ("Don't Bring Me Down," "Cheating," "Inside Looking Out," and "See See Rider") added. But MGM's *Animalism*, released two months later, consisted of tracks recorded in America during the original group's final US tour that never saw the light of day in England. —*Bruce Eder*

Animalism [US] / 1966 / MGM ✦✦✦

Animalisms / 1966 / Decca ✦✦✦✦
Very similar in lineup to the American *Animalization*, this is probably the group's best noncompilation album, with a finely developed R&B sound throughout and excellent playing, all yielding an incomparable collection of good, solid, bluesy, ballsy rock numbers, highlighted by "Gin House Blues" and "Don't Bring Me Down." —*Bruce Eder*

Winds of Change / 1967 / One Way ✦✦✦

The Best of Eric Burdon & the Animals, Vol. 2 / 1969 / MGM ✦✦✦
Actually the third Animals' hits LP to be released by MGM in the 1960s, this collection is the work of lead singer Eric Burdon with the backup group he assembled upon the breakup of the original Animals. The recordings all come from 1967 and 1968, Burdon's psychedelicized period, when he was penning praises of the Monterey Pop Festival ("Monterey," No. 15) and San Francisco ("San Franciscan Nights," No. 9). The only other Top 40 hit on the album was the antiwar epic "Sky Pilot" (No. 15), in its full seven-and-a-half-minute glory. Burdon had come a long way from his Manchester roots and his blues records, and this was the last album in his second phase; in fact, the New Animals had split by the time it was released. —*William Ruhlmann*

★ **The Best of the Animals** / 1988 / ABKCO ✦✦✦✦✦
The original Animals' American hits, including "House of the Rising Sun," "Don't Let Me Be Misunderstood," "It's My Life," and "We Gotta Get Out of This Place," in a compilation originally released in 1965. The lineup of songs is strong, but the sound is indifferent—the British *Complete Animals* covers the same territory and a lot more to much greater effect, at only twice the cost with three times the music and infinitely superior sound and notes. —*Bruce Eder*

Inside Looking Out: The 1965-1966 Sessions / 1990 / Sequel ✦✦✦✦
Together with the double-CD *The Complete Animals*, *Inside Looking Out* forms a complete retrospective of the great British Invasion band. This 22-song compilation features all of the essential recordings cut by the group in 1965 and 1966 after they broke with their original producer Mickie Most, and before Eric Burdon dissolved the core of the original lineup to pursue solo stardom with an Animals group featuring different musicians. These tracks were perhaps more soul-oriented than their previous recordings, but the group still burns on the hits "Inside Looking Out" and "Don't Bring Me Down." Despite the absence of original keyboardist Alan Price, the group continued to showcase Burdon's passionate vocals and burning, vibrant organ (by Price's replacement Dave Rowberry) on both renowned and obscure R&B tunes, with an occasional original thrown in. Besides the entirety of their final British LP *Animalisms* (from 1966) and the above-mentioned singles, the CD includes the hits "Help Me Girl" and "See See Rider" (credited to "Eric Burdon and the Animals," these were possibly Burdon solo records). The four tracks from their first release, an independently released 1963 EP featuring primitive R&B standards, are small but noteworthy bonus cuts that close this collection. —*Richie Unterberger*

★ **The Complete Animals** / Jul. 1990 / EMI ✦✦✦✦✦
This double CD includes the complete sessions that the Animals recorded with producer Mickie Most in 1964 and 1965. The 40 songs capture the band at their peak, including most of their best and biggest hits: "House of the Rising Sun," "Don't Let Me Be Misunderstood," "Bring It on Home to Me," "We Gotta Get Out of This Place," "I'm Crying," "It's My Life," and "Boom Boom." Most of the rest of the tunes don't match the excellence of these smashes, though they're solid. The great majority of them are covers of vintage R&B/rock tunes by Chuck Berry, Fats Domino, and the like, which aren't quite as durable as reinterpretations from the same era by the Stones and Yardbirds. When they hit the mark, though, the Animals produced some great album tracks that have been mostly forgotten by time, such as "I'm Mad Again" (originally by John Lee Hooker), "Worried Life Blues," and "Bury My Body." After leaving Most, the group would maintain their peak for another year or so (this period is represented on the fine import collection *Inside Looking Out*) despite the departure of one of rock's all-time finest organists, Alan Price. This compilation has everything that Price recorded with the group, including four previously unreleased cuts and the non-LP Eric Burdon original on the B-side of "It's My Life," "I'm Gonna Change the World." —*Richie Unterberger*

Paul Anka

b. Jul. 30, 1941, Ottawa, Canada
Vocals / Pop, Teen Idol, Brill Building Pop
Hugely successful vocalist from 1957 into the '80s, as well as writer of several venerable pop-music standards. The young native of Ottawa, Canada, took the US by storm in 1957 with his rock-slanted ballad "Diana," a No. 1 smash on ABC-Paramount Records. Dramatic renditions of "You Are My Destiny," "Lonely Boy," "Put Your Head on My Shoulder," and "Puppy Love" elevated the youth to teen-idol status over the next three years. Moving to RCA in 1962, the maturing Anka continued to chart regularly, although some of his most notable '60s copyrights were bequeathed to others—he wrote "My Way" for Frank Sinatra as well as the theme for TV's "The Tonight Show." Anka returned to the top pop slot in 1974 with the controversial million-seller "(You're) Having My Baby," cut in Muscle Shoals and issued on United Artists, and he enjoyed several follow-up smashes, many featuring vocalist Odia Coates. —*Bill Dahl*

● **30th Anniversary Collection** / 1989 / Rhino ✦✦✦✦
The best package of Anka's early teen-idol hits, featuring "Diana," "Puppy Love," "Put Your Head on My Shoulder," and "You Are My Destiny," as well as his '70s easy-listening hits ("My Way," "(You're) Having My Baby"). —*Cub Koda*

Adam Ant (Stuart Leslie Goddard)

b. Nov. 3, 1954
Keyboards, Vocals / New Wave, Pop-Rock, Post-Punk
One of the seminal figures of new wave, Adam Ant had several distinct phases to his career. Initially, he explored a jagged, guitar-oriented post-punk with his group Adam and the Ants before giving way to a more pop-oriented, glam-tinged direction that brought him to the top of the charts. After that had run its course, he refashioned himself as a mainstream singer, which enabled him to stretch his career out for a couple of years. Once it seemed like his musical career had evaporated, he made an unexpected comeback in the early '90s as an adult alternative artist. During all this time, he recorded several great pop singles and had a surprisingly large impact on alternative rock.

Adam Ant formed Adam and the Ants with guitarist Lester Square, bassist Andy Warren, and drummer Paul Flanagan in London in 1977. The group's approach was more theatrical than most punk groups, incorporating sadomasochistic imagery into their concerts. During this time, the group's lineup was fairly unstable, with Square being replaced by Mark Gaumont. The band released their debut, *Dirk Wears White Sox*, on the independent label Do It in 1979. *Dirk* was an ambitious and somewhat dark album, filled with jerky rhythms, angular guitar riffs, and elements of glam rock in Adam's vocals; Adam reacquired the rights to the record in 1983, reissuing it in a resequenced and remixed form.

At the time of its release, *Dirk Wears White Sox* wasn't a critical or commercial success, and the band felt the need to rework their image, so they hired Malcolm McLaren, manager of the Sex Pistols. McLaren dressed the band in pirate outfits and suggested a more accessible and pop-oriented, rhythmic variation on punk. The band followed his advice, preparing material for a new album. However, McLaren persuaded all of the Ants to leave Adam, using them as the core members of Bow Wow Wow. Adam Ant immediately formed a new version of the Ants, adding guitarist Marco Pirroni, bassist Kevin Mooney, and drummers Terry Lee Miall and Merrick (born Chris Hughes). Pirroni, in particular, became very important in the band's musical direction, co-writing the majority of the songs with Adam, thus beginning a collaboration that would continue into the '90s. Driven by a relentless beat and chanting melodies, the new band's first album, 1980's *Kings of the Wild Frontier*, became an

enormous hit in the UK, launching three Top Ten hit singles, including the No. 2 "Ant Music." The band's success was helped by a series of visually enticing videos, prominently featuring Adam Ant decked out in pirate gear. *Prince Charming*, released the following year, retained the same formula as *Kings of the Wild Frontier*, spawning two No. 1 singles, "Stand and Deliver" and "Prince Charming." Even though the album was a commercial success, the formula was beginning to wear thin.

After *Prince Charming*, Adam Ant ditched the Ants for a solo career, retaining Marco Pirroni as a songwriting collaborator and supporting musician. Adam's first solo album, *Friend or Foe*, was released in 1982 and featured the No. 1 single "Goody Two Shoes" and the Top Ten title track. Although his next album, 1983's *Strip*, had some highlights and hit singles, it marked the end of his reign as one of Britain's top pop stars.

Released in 1985, the Tony Visconti-produced *Vive le Rock* had some fun moments, but the performance was too studied and the record didn't earn any hit singles, so Adam Ant pursued a surprisingly successful career in acting. In 1990, Ant made a comeback with the catchy hit single "Room at the Top" from the *Manners & Physique* record, but the album failed to produce another hit single. For the next five years, Ant concentrated on acting.

By the time Adam Ant returned to recording in 1995, echoes of his music could be heard in the spiky singles of Elastica, the neo-goth industrial rock of Nine Inch Nails, and the pseudo-glam of Suede. Instead of capitalizing on the burgeoning new-wave revival, Adam Ant's 1995 comeback *Wonderful* had little to do with the stylish, intensely rhythmic music he made in the early '80s. Instead, the album repositioned him as a more mature pop-rocker, with crafted songs that featured acoustic guitars as prominently as electrics. The album was a moderate hit in the US and the UK, as was the single "Wonderful." —*Stephen Thomas Erlewine*

Dirk Wears White Sox / Dec. 1979 / Epic ✦✦✦✦
The debut album (originally released on Do-it Records in 1979) finds a young Adam Ant exploring the sometimes awkward fusion of punk and glam. While the somewhat pretentious lyrics and inexperienced playing are a drawback, the raw energy can stand up against later releases. A remixed version of the album was reissued in 1983. —*Chris Woodstra*

Kings of the Wild Frontier / 1980 / Epic ✦✦✦✦
Combining pounding tom-toms (from two drummers and drum kits), a guitar style adapted from Ennio Morricone movie soundtracks, and a visual motif borrowed from pirates and Native Americans, Adam and the Ants had a brief run as Britain's top band in the wake of the punk/power-pop days of the late '70s. This second album was their apex, featuring the signature tune "Ant Music." —*William Ruhlmann*

Prince Charming / 1981 / Epic ✦✦✦
The final album with the Ants is bland in comparison to the brilliant *Kings of the Wild Frontier*. While "Stand and Deliver" is one of the high points of the band's career, "Ant Rap" is certainly the low point. The essential tracks can all be found on *Antics in the Forbidden Zone*. —*Chris Woodstra*

Friend or Foe / 1982 / Epic ✦✦✦
As a solo artist, Adam Ant struck gold in the US with this album, which adopts the same musical style as that of the Ants and features the hit "Goody Two Shoes" and a version of the Doors' "Hello, I Love You." —*William Ruhlmann*

Strip / Nov. 1983 / Epic ✦✦

Vive Le Rock / 1985 / Epic ✦✦

● **Antics in the Forbidden Zone** / 1990 / Epic ✦✦✦✦
The most comprehensive overview of the band. In 22 tracks, all of the hits are represented as well as key album cuts and a rare B-side, "Beat My Guest." An essential part of any new wave collection. —*Chris Woodstra*

Manners & Physique / Feb. 1990 / MCA ✦✦

Peel Sessions / 1991 / Dutch East India ✦✦✦
A nice collection of recordings made for John Peel's radio show from 1978 to 1979. This is probably the best documentation of the early days of the band, combining tracks from *Dirk Wears White Sox*, early singles, and previously unreleased material. Essential for hardcore fans. —*Chris Woodstra*

B-side Babies! / Sep. 27, 1994 / Epic/Legacy ✦✦✦✦

Wonderful / Mar. 7, 1995 / Capitol ✦✦✦

Little Anthony & the Imperials

Vocals / R&B, Doo Wop
Featuring the high-pitched vocals of Anthony Gourdine and a brace of solid material, Little Anthony & the Imperials had a much longer chart run than the majority of doo wop groups from the '50s. When the dust finally settled, they clocked in with a total of ten entries in the Hot 100 between 1958 and 1974, including "Tears On My Pillow," "Two People in the World," "Wishful Thinking," "Oh Yeah," "So Much," "Shimmy Shimmy Ko Ko Bop" (not to be confused with the similarly titled

"Shimmy Shimmy Ko Ko Wop" by the El Capris), "When You Wish Upon a Star," "Going Out of My Head," "Better Use Your Head," and "Hurt So Bad."

Gourdine formed the group in the mid-'50s after his previous group, the Duponts, disbanded. Grabbing friends Clarence Collins, Ernest Wright, Tracy Lord, and Nat Rogers, the group was originally called the Chesters, but had their name changed to the Imperials by popular New York DJ Alan Freed. Gourdine's vocal similarities to the popular Frankie Lymon-inspired "kiddie group" sound, coupled with a tendency to chop up syllables and overstress lyrics, made theirs a style deceptively simple yet enduring. After revamping the group in 1964 down to a quartet, the sound changed from doo wop to a harder, more uptown R&B sound, best exemplified on hits like "I'm on the Outside Looking In." Still touring and from all reports, *still* knockin' em dead into their fourth decade together as a group, for many lovers of the genre, Little Anthony & the Imperials are simply New York styled doo wop at its smoothest and finest. — *Cub Koda*

Anthrax

Thrash, Heavy Metal, Speed Metal
Nearly as much as Metallica or Megadeth, Anthrax has been responsible for the emergence of speed and thrash metal. Combining the speed and fury of hardcore punk with the prominent guitars and vocals of heavy metal, Anthrax helped create a new subgenre of heavy metal on their early albums. Guitarists Scott Ian and Dan Spitz are a formidable pair, spitting out lightning-fast riffs and solos that never seem masturbatory. Unlike Metallica or Megadeth, they had the good sense to temper their often serious music with a healthy dose of humor and realism.

After their first album, *Fistful of Metal*, singer Joey Belladonna and bassist Frank Bello joined the lineup. Belladonna helped take the band further away from conventional metal clichés, and over the next five albums (with the exception of 1988's *State of Euphoria*, where the band sounded like they were in a creative straight-jacket), Anthrax arguably became the leaders of speed metal.

As the '80s became the '90s, Anthrax began to increase their experiments with hip-hop, culminating in a tour with Public Enemy in 1991 and a joint re-recording of PE's classic "Don't Believe the Hype."

After their peak period of the late '80s, Anthrax kicked Belladonna out of the band in 1992 and replaced him with ex-Armored Saint vocalist John Bush—a singer that was gruffer and deeper, fitting most metal conventions perfectly. Subsequently, their sound became less unique and their audience shrank slightly as a consequence, but it would be foolish to count Anthrax out—these guys are too clever to fade away. — *Stephen Thomas Erlewine*

Fistful of Metal / 1984 / Megaforce ◆◆◆

Armed and Dangerous / 1985 / Megaforce ◆◆◆

Spreading the Disease / 1985 / Megaforce ◆◆◆◆
An essential Anthrax album, *Spreading the Disease* demonstrates that a speed-metal band can still have the knack to create songs accessible enough for pop audiences. — *John Book*

● **Among the Living** / 1987 / Megaforce ◆◆◆◆
"The" Anthrax album to have is a high point in speed-metal history. Harsh, powerful, and strong, it's flawless from beginning to end. — *John Book*

I'm the Man / 1987 / Megaforce ◆◆◆◆
This EP consists of a few non-album tracks and some live material. The title track pokes fun at rap, the Beastie Boys, Metallica, the Mentors, and themselves. Anthrax was the first heavy-metal band to experiment with rap. — *John Book*

State of Euphoria / 1988 / Megaforce ◆◆◆

Persistence of Time / 1990 / Megaforce ◆◆◆◆
Second best to *Among the Living*, here the band makes strong political statements without sounding preachy. — *John Book*

Attack of the Killer B's / 1991 / Island ◆◆◆◆

Sound of White Noise / 1993 / Elektra ◆◆◆

Live—The Island Years / Apr. 5, 1994 / Island ◆◆◆

Stomp 442 / Oct. 24, 1995 / Elektra ◆◆

Any Trouble

Rock 'n' Roll, New Wave, Pub-Rock
Any Trouble was an underappreciated bright spot on Stiff Records, which had no shortage of talented artists. Bandleader Clive Gregson's appearance, hardened love songs, and vocal style may have led to comparisons to Elvis Costello, but they were no second-rate rip-off—each of their four albums revealed a songwriter of unique talent and a more-than-capable band to execute the songs.

Manchester-native Gregson formed the original band in 1975 while attending teaching school in Crewe, taking the group's name from a mis-

quote from the Mel Brooks film *Blazing Saddles*. After a brief moment as a folky trio, by 1976 Any Trouble had changed to a four-piece rock group, speeding up their repertoire in response to the punk movement—by this point the lineup was Gregson (vocals/guitar), Chris Parks (guitar), Phil Barnes (bass), and Mel Harley (drums). They built a strong following playing the pub circuit and released their own single, catching the attention of Radio One's John Peel, who quickly took the band and played the song on his show. This exposure started a small-scale bidding war from several labels. By 1980, the group signed with Stiff Records.

Stiff enlisted John Wood, a renowned producer to produce Any Trouble's first album. *Where Are All the Nice Girls?*, which had all the makings of a new wave classic, was met with some rave reviews but failed to rack up the big sales that were expected of it. After the record failed commercially, Stiff suggested that Gregson drop the band and redefine himself as a solo artist à la Elvis Costello—Buddy Gregson. Gregson declined, deciding instead to replace the band's weak link, drummer Harley, with the more capable Martin Hughes. They began work on the follow-up immediately.

Wheels in Motion, while certainly more accomplished, lacked the spark of the first album and the record simply didn't catch on in the UK. Any Trouble took a stab at stateside success with a small promotional tour. Halfway through the tour, the band heard by word-of-mouth that they had been dropped by Stiff and were left stranded in America. Eventually they found their way back, but the stress of the situation broke up the band temporarily—for about 18 months.

A new deal was arranged with EMI-America in 1982. Hughes left the band and was replaced by Andy Ebsworth, and Steve Gurl was added on keyboards. Chris Parks left shortly thereafter. Essentially a new band, the four-piece recorded *Any Trouble* in 1983. Again, the same story—should've been a hit, somehow overlooked. Gregson, knowing the band couldn't last much longer, talked EMI into letting them do a double album. As a parting shot, Gregson and company stretched out for *Wrong End of the Race*, a sprawling album that allowed them to show their diversity and influences over 25 tracks of new originals, remakes of earlier Any Trouble songs, and a few covers. In America, the album was distilled down to a single record. "Baby Now That I Found You" saw some airplay on MTV; the reviews were good, but the band's cult status didn't change. In December 1984, the band played their last gig and called it quits. Gregson went on to a distinguished, though still underappreciated, career both as a solo artist and as a collaborator with Christine Collister. — *Chris Woodstra*

● **Where Are All the Nice Girls?** / 1980 / Stiff ◆◆◆◆
The first album is a pure pub/pop rock delight. Leading off with the infectious "Second Choice" (one of the great "should have been hits") and ending up with the unlikely ABBA cover "Name of the Game," Gregson and company run though 12 tunes, almost all obsessed with love gone wrong. A cult favorite. — *Chris Woodstra*

Live at the Venue / 1981 / Line ◆◆◆◆
Originally released as a promo for radio, this live show from 1980 finds the band in its natural setting. Playing with higher energy than in the studio, this provides the best picture of the band at its peak. — *Chris Woodstra*

Wheels in Motion / Aug. 1981 / Stiff ◆◆◆
The playing on their sophomore effort is more sophisticated and the production is cleaner but it lacks some of the bite of the first album. Gregson's now-standard obsession makes an appearance on the album's highlight, "Trouble with Love." — *Chris Woodstra*

Any Trouble / 1983 / EMI ◆◆◆
The band's move from the Stiff label to EMI marked an attempt to crack the US market with a mainstream radio-ready album and a new lineup. Unfortunately overlooked at the time, material from this album continued to be a part of Gregson's solo sets in the '90s. — *Chris Woodstra*

Wrong End of the Race / 1984 / EMI ◆◆◆
Issued as a double LP in England and a single LP in the US, *Wrong End of the Race* compiles unnecessary re-recordings of previously released songs, some new tracks, and a few interesting covers. Their weakest set and final attempt before Gregson left to pursue a more successful solo career. — *Chris Woodstra*

Aphex Twin (Richard D. James)

Synthesizer / Ambient, Techno, Experimental, Club-Dance, Trance
Richard D. James, known as the Aphex Twin, began his musical career in rural Cornwall, making instruments with old Radio Shack gadgetry. The result of his experimentations from 1985 through 1992 is *Selected Ambient Works, Vol. 1*. Eager to cash in on the ambient-house craze, the German techno label R&S Records released *Selected Ambient Works, Vol. 1*, even though James' main work was full-throttle, nose-bleed techno. The LP caused an underground sensation, making many critics' Top Tens for 1993. James' first stateside release, under the Polygon Window moniker, was *Surfing on Sine Waves*. Amidst a great deal of hype, James released

the quadruple LP, *Selected Ambient Works, Vol. 2*, to mixed reviews in the spring of 1994. In 1995, he released *I Care Because You Do*, a schizophrenic ride of an album that unites the work on the two volumes of *Selected Ambient Works* with his distorted brand of techno. *—John Bush*

Selected Ambient Recordings 85-92 / 1993 / R&S ✦✦✦✦
A collection of electronic soundscapes by Richard James (aka Aphex Twin), arguably the leader in the ambient-techno movement, *Selected Ambient Recordings 85-92* is nothing short of stunning. Musically, much of this brings to mind Brian Eno or Kraftwerk, whom he had not heard until after he recorded this material. *—Stephen Thomas Erlewine*

Selected Ambient Works, Vol. 2 / Apr. 1994 / Sire ✦✦✦
Selected Ambient Works, Vol. 2 is a more difficult and challenging album than the Aphex Twin's previous collection. The music is all texture; there are only the faintest traces of beats and forward movement. Instead, all of these untitled tracks are long, unsettling electronic soundscapes, alternately quiet and confrontational; although most of the music is rather subdued, it is never easy listening. While some listeners may find this double-disc album dull (both discs run over 70 minutes), many listeners will be intrigued and fascinated by the intricately detailed music. *—Stephen Thomas Erlewine*

● **I Care Because You Do** / 1995 / Sire ✦✦✦✦
James' most consistent work, *I Care* fuses his earlier hardcore techno days with the smooth rhythmic and atmosphere of his ambient work, often on the same song. "Ventolin" is one of the harshest singles ever recorded; the orchestration closer "Next Heap With" is the highlight of the album. *—John Bush*

Classics / 1995 / R&S ✦✦✦

Joan Armatrading

b. Dec. 9, 1950, St. Kitts, West Indies
Guitar, Piano, Vocals / Singer-Songwriter
Born on the island of St. Kitts, British singer-songwriter Joan Armatrading was her country's first Black woman to make commercial inroads into her chosen genre— spicing her take on folk with bits of soul and reggae— and has had a remarkably long, consistent career. Emigrating to England in 1958, Armatrading met lyricist Pam Nestor in a touring production of *Hair*, and the two began collaborating on material later featured on Armatrading's 1972 debut, *Whatever's for Us*. The two ended their partnership afterward, and Armatrading resurfaced in 1975 with *Back to the Night*. Featuring former members of Fairport Convention, *Joan Armatrading* catapulted the singer into the UK Top 20 and produced her only Top Ten single, "Love and Affection." Armatrading's subsequent albums sold well in the UK to her newly established fan base, but only respectably in the US, where it took her until 1980 to have a real hit (the all-electric *Me, Myself, I*). *The Key* (1983) also did quite well, but Armatrading remained largely a cult artist with a small but devoted following in America, never quite achieving the stardom she had in Britain. She has been successful enough to record regularly up through the mid-'90s and continues to tour. *—Steve Huey*

Whatever's for Us / 1972 / A&M ✦✦

Back to the Night / 1975 / A&M ✦✦✦
Even this early on, Armatrading's basic theme—the conflict between the need for romantic attachment and the need for independence—is in place in all its paradoxical glory. She revels in the joys of love and is repelled by the threat love represents to her identity. On this release, the message overwhelms the medium, however: Armatrading hasn't yet developed the musical structures to make her lyrical concerns memorable. *—William Ruhlmann*

Joan Armatrading / Sep. 1976 / A&M ✦✦✦✦
Her third album was the one most people fell in love with, attracted by her Caribbean-flavored singing of articulate romantic lyrics and Glyn Johns's tasteful folk-rock production, especially on "Love and Affection." *—William Ruhlmann*

Show Some Emotion / Oct. 1977 / A&M ✦✦✦

To the Limit / Oct. 1978 / A&M ✦✦✦

Steppin' Out / 1979 / A&M ✦✦✦

How Cruel / Nov. 1979 / A&M ✦✦✦

Me, Myself, I / May 1980 / A&M ✦✦✦✦
On the trio of albums that made her reputation in 1976-1978, *Joan Armatrading*, *Show Some Emotion*, and *To the Limit*, Armatrading relied on the pristine production of Glyn Johns to underscore the sensitivity of her folk-based confessional songs. Here, on her first full-length album in two years, she turned to rock producer Richard Gottehrer and a session band that included Anton Fig, Chris Spedding, and members of the E Street Band, making her case for being a mainstream rocker. The songs were less serious, too, notably the title track, a UK hit. (The album's other British chart single was the ballad "All the Way from America," which was more in the style of her earlier work.) The result was the best-

selling album Armatrading has ever had in either the US or UK. *—William Ruhlmann*

Walk Under Ladders / Sep. 1981 / A&M ✦✦✦

The Key / Mar. 1983 / A&M ✦✦✦✦
The best of Armatrading's later albums, which took on a much harder rock edge. Steve Lillywhite produced, and Armatrading provided some good uptempo material, including "Drop the Pilot" and "(I Love It When You) Call Me Names." *—William Ruhlmann*

Track Record / Nov. 1983 / A&M ✦✦✦✦
A reasonable best-of that samples Armatrading's first decade of recording. *—William Ruhlmann*

Secret Secrets / Feb. 1985 / A&M ✦✦✦

Sleight of Hand / May 1986 / A&M ✦✦

The Shouting Stage / Jul. 1988 / A&M ✦✦

Hearts and Flowers / Jun. 1990 / A&M ✦✦

Square the Circle / Jun. 23, 1992 / A&M ✦✦✦

What's Inside / 1995 / RCA ✦✦

● **Greatest Hits** / Jun. 18, 1996 / A&M ✦✦✦✦
Greatest Hits features all of Joan Armatrading's biggest hits and best-known tracks, including "Love and Affection," "Show Some Emotion," and "Rosie," as well as the previously unreleased live track, "Kissin' and a Huggin." The disc is a thorough retrospective and functions as an excellent introduction to the introspective singer-songwriter. *—Thom Owens*

Army of Lovers

Euro-Dance
Army of Lovers is a European disco collective masterminded by producer Anders Wollbeck and synth programmer/vocalist Alexander Bard. On their self-titled debut album, they used a variety of lead singers and relied heavily on the work of producer/mixer Emil Hellman. With 1992's *Massive Luxury Overdose*, Bard, Jean-Pierre Barda (vocals, drums), and De La Cour (vocals, keyboards) were the featured musicians. *—Stephen Thomas Erlewine*

Army of Lovers / Aug. 13, 1991 / Giant ✦✦✦

● **Massive Luxury Overdose** / 1992 / Giant ✦✦✦✦
Superior production, with multitracked vocals and intercut rhythms, are the best things about this release. The lyrics and vocals are typical dance, exuberantly delivered, but more generic than distinctive and designed to support the beat rather than work off it. *—Ron Wynn*

The Art of Noise

New Wave, Experimental
Anne Dudley, Gary Lanagan, and J.J. Jeczalik were members of producer Trevor Horn's in-house studio band in the early '80s, before they formed Art of Noise, a techno-pop group whose music was an amalgam of studio gimmickry, tape splicing, and synthesized beats. After earning a sizable cult following in the latter half of the '80s (as well as scoring two Top 40 hits) the Art of Noise broke up in 1990. *—Stephen Thomas Erlewine*

The Art of Noise / 1983 / ✦✦✦
The Art of Noise debuted with this long (ten-track, or ten-title, anyway) EP (also called *Into Battle with the Art of Noise*), dominated by tracks like "Beat Box" (No. 1 dance-disco), a collage of steady bass drum beats and sound effects. No use looking for embedded meaning; this was surface sound all the way. If you wanted, you could dance to it, but its real function may have been as a new kind of background music. *—William Ruhlmann*

(Who's Afraid Of?) the Art of Noise! / 1984 / ZTT/Island ✦✦✦✦

● **The Best of the Art of Noise** / 1988 / China ✦✦✦✦
All of the Art of Noise's best tracks are here, including "Close (To the Edit)," "Legacy," and a cover of Prince's "Kiss" with Tom Jones on lead vocals. *—Stephen Thomas Erlewine*

Ashford & Simpson

Vocals / Soul, Disco, R&B, Urban
Nickolas Ashford (b. May 4, 1942, Fairfield, SC) and Valerie Simpson (b. Aug. 26, 1946, New York, NY) have two careers, as songwriters and as performers, with the former seemingly more important than the latter until the mid-'80s. The two met in 1964 and scored their first songwriting hit in 1966 with Ray Charles' recording of their "Let's Go Get Stoned." After a period at Scepter Records, they moved to Motown, where they wrote hits for the duo of Marvin Gaye and Tammi Terrell ("Ain't Nothing Like the Real Thing," "You're All I Need to Get By"). When Diana Ross left the Supremes for a solo career, Ashford And Simpson wrote "Reach out and Touch Somebody's Hand" for her.

Their own performing career was launched in 1973 with *Keep It Comin'* on Motown and *Gimme Something Real* on Warner Bros. Their first success came in 1977 with the gold-selling *Send It*, which contained the Top Ten R&B hit "Don't Cost You Nothing." *Is It Still Good to Ya,* a second gold album, contained the No. 2 R&B hit "It Seems to Hang On" in 1978. *Stay Free,* their third straight gold album, contained "Found a Cure," another R&B smash that also made the Top 40 on the pop chart. *A Musical Affair,* 1980, featured the hit "Love Don't Make It Right," but was not as successful as previous efforts.

Meanwhile, A&S continued to work with other artists, scoring successes with Ross, Chaka Khan ("I'm Every Woman"), and Gladys Knight. Their own career saw a resurgence in 1984 with *Solid,* which went gold and produced the R&B No. 1 "Solid" (No. 12 on the pop charts), "Outta the World," and "Babies." — *William Ruhlmann*

Is It Still Good to Ya / Aug. 1978 / Warner Bros. ♦♦♦♦
The disco arrangements are a little dated, but this is still Ashford & Simpson's best '70s album, as their two similar voices intertwine on a collection of songs about devoted love, among them the title track and "It Seems to Hang On." — *William Ruhlmann*

● **Solid** / Oct. 1984 / Warner Bros. ♦♦♦♦
Ashford & Simpson have always been the prime representatives in R&B of the joys of wedded bliss, and this extended valentine is their most consistent set as well as their biggest hit ever. — *William Ruhlmann*

● **Capitol Gold: The Best of Ashford & Simpson** / Jun. 21, 1993 / Capitol ♦♦♦♦
Ashford & Simpson scored 33 entries on the R&B singles charts between 1973 and 1990, all but one of them on Warner Bros. or Capitol. This compilation licenses the two biggest hits from the duo's tenure at Warner, "It Seems to Hang On" and "Found a Cure," both of which hit the Top Ten, and features the eight Capitol titles that made the R&B Top 40—"Street Corner," "Love It Away," "High-Rise," "Solid," "Outta the World," "Babies," "Count Your Blessings," and "I'll Be There for You." There are also six tracks culled from the five Capitol albums, bringing the disc's time to over 71 minutes. In other words, this is about as comprehensive an overview of A&S's career as could be managed by one label on one disc. There are good biographical liner notes by compiler David Nathan. — *William Ruhlmann*

Asia

Art-Rock/Progressive-Rock, Pop-Rock
When they appeared in the early '80s, Asia seemed to be a hold-over from the '70s, when supergroups and self-important progressive-rockers reigned supreme. Featuring members of such seminal art-rock bands as King Crimson (John Wetton), Emerson, Lake & Palmer (Carl Palmer), and Yes (Steve Howe), as well as Geoff Downes from the Buggles, Asia did feature stretches of indulgent instrumentals on their records. However, they also could be surprisingly poppy, and that is what brought them to the top of the charts with their debut album, *Asia,* and its hit single, "Heat of the Moment." *Alpha,* their second album, also had a couple of hits ("Don't Cry" and "The Smile Has Left Your Eyes"), but its follow-up, *Astra,* was a flop. The group disbanded in 1985, only to reunite in 1990 without John Wetton; Pat Thrall took his place. After churning out a couple of new songs for a greatest-hits collection, the band hit the road, including two sold-out dates in front of 20,000 fans in Moscow. Since then, they have toured sporadically. — *Stephen Thomas Erlewine*

Asia / 1982 / Geffen ♦♦♦♦
The debut release for this supergroup (featuring Steve Howe [Yes], John Wetton [UK], Carl Palmer [ELP], and Geoff Downes [Yes]) showcases their classy pop-rock, with several hits. — *Paul Kohler*

Alpha / 1983 / Geffen ♦♦♦

Astra / Nov. 1985 / Geffen ♦♦

● **Then & Now** / 1990 / Geffen ♦♦♦♦
This compilation includes all of their Top 40 hits—"Heat of the Moment," "Only Time Will Tell," "Don't Cry," and "The Smile Has Left Your Eyes"—as well as some unreleased tracks. — *AMG*

Aqua / 1992 / JRS ♦♦

Aria / 1994 / ♦♦

Atlantic Starr

Soul, Disco, Urban, Adult Contemporary
New York-based Atlantic Starr began in 1976. Brothers David (guitar, vocals), Jonathan (trombone), and Wayne (keyboards) Lewis started a funk-soul band, adding lead vocalist Sharon Bryant, bassist Clifford Archer, drummer Porter Carroll, saxophonist Koran Daniels, percussionist/flutist Joseph Phillips, and trumpeter William Sudderth. They signed with A&M a couple of years later, staying through 1987 and landing several hits, among them "Gimme Your Lovin'," "Circles," "When Love Calls," "Stand Up," "Silver Shadow," "One Love," and the crossover hit "Secret Lovers." Their albums *Brilliance* and *As the Band Turns* were also Top 20 pop hits, their most successful A&M LPs. They switched to Warner Bros. in 1987, and their first release, *All in the Name of Love,* included another pop smash, "Always," the group's sole No. 1 pop and

R&B hit. They enjoyed more R&B successes with Warner through the '80s. Sharon Bryant left in 1989 for Polydor; she was replaced by Barbara Weathers, who later left for a solo career as well. *Love Crazy,* in 1991, was their most recent release. — *Ron Wynn*

● **Secret Lovers: The Best of Atlantic Starr** / 1986 / A&M ♦♦♦♦
A nice anthology, although it emphasizes the ballad smashes and doesn't convey much of their earlier, harder flavor. Atlantic Starr moved to Warner Bros. in the late '80s, so their former label cranked out a greatest-hits LP to take advantage of their hit status. These songs were staples of '80s urban contemporary radio, and the ballads are still carried in the '90s on many quiet storm playlists. — *Ron Wynn*

Classics, Vol. 10 / 1987 / A&M ♦♦♦♦
This collection gathers their A&M hits, which also include "Freak-a-Ristic," "Secret Lovers" and "If Your Heart Isn't in It." But the group scored its biggest smash after moving to Warner Bros., the R&B and pop chart-topping "Always." — *Ron Wynn*

The Atlantics

Surf
One of the greatest instrumental surf groups did not even hail from America. The Atlantics, despite their name, were an Australian combo that not only emulated the sound of California surf music, but ranked among its very best practitioners. Featuring a reverb-heavy, extremely "wet" sound, the Atlantics attacked original material, standards, and movie themes with a nervy blend of precision and over-the-top intensity. As in Dick Dale's music, touches of Middle Eastern influences can be detected in the rhythms of melodies (some members of the group claimed Greek and Egyptian heritage). Their second single, "Bombora," went to the top of the Australian charts in 1963, and the follow-up "The Crusher" was also a big hit. But Beatlemania spelled commercial death for the Atlantics, as it did for US surf combos, in 1964 and 1965. After several albums and a few more equally fine instrumental singles, the Atlantics became a vocal group in the last half of the '60s, but are most renowned for their instrumental recordings. Still regarded with respect in Australia and New Zealand, they remain virtually unknown elsewhere, except to fanatical surf music specialists. — *Richie Unterberger*

The Explosive Sound of the Atlantics / 199_ / Repertoire ♦♦♦♦
This is a bit cornball compared to their best—a few of the numbers are surfizations of standards like "Secret Love," Though most of the material is original, the allusions to folk melodies sometimes make this sound like a surf band you'd find playing in a Greek restaurant. There's plenty of nifty guitar work, though, and only a couple of cuts are on *The CBS Singles Collection,* making this a fine supplement to that compilation. The original Australian LP is far harder to find than the German CD reissue, which adds some bonus cuts. — *Richie Unterberger*

● **The CBS Singles Collection 1963-1965** / Canetoad ♦♦♦♦
Both sides of their first nine singles. Includes "Bombora," "The Crusher," strong originals, and hard-boiled overhauls of "Goldfinger" and "Peter Gunn." Essential as Dick Dale but more obscure. — *Richie Unterberger*

Patti Austin

b. Aug. 10, 1948, California
Vocals / Urban
A professional since the age of five, Patti Austin was a protégé of Dinah Washington and Sammy Davis, Jr. A 1969 single for United Artists titled "Family Tree" cracked the R&B Top 50. Austin cut her debut LP, *End of a Rainbow,* for Creed Taylor's CTI label in 1976, followed by *Havana Candy* in 1977 and *Body Language* in 1980. She sang lead vocals for Japanese koto player Yutaka Yokokura on "Love Light" in 1978, did a duet with Michael Jackson on "It's the Falling in Love" on *Off the Wall,* and sang "The Closer I Get to You" on Tom Browne's album in 1979. Austin dueted with George Benson on "Moody's Mood for Love" in 1980. She sang backgrounds for sessions by Houston Person, Noel Pointer, Ralph McDonald, Angela Bofill, and Roberta Flack. Austin did vocals on Quincy Jones' *The Dude* LP in 1981, and was featured on the hit "Razzamatazz." She inked a solo deal on Jones' Qwest label, and her 1982 LP *Every Home Should Have One* included the No. 1 pop hit (No. 9 R&B) "Baby, Come to Me," which got widespread exposure via the ABC soap opera "General Hospital." The follow-up, "How Do You Keep the Music Playing," was the theme for the film *Best Friends.* Both songs paired Austin with James Ingram. She continued recording for Jones' Qwest label through the '80s, but couldn't recapture her pop or R&B success, despite working with several top producers, including Jam-Lewis in 1985. Austin switched to GRP in 1990 and recorded *Love Is Gonna Getcha,* with the singles "Through the Test of Time" and "Good in Love." She recorded *Carry On* and *Live, with Shelton Becton* in 1991 and 1992. — *Ron Wynn*

Every Home Should Have One / Sep. 1981 / Qwest ♦♦♦♦
Quincy Jones-produced pop album featuring "Baby, Come to Me," which became a belated hit when it was featured on "General Hospital," two years after the album came out. — *William Ruhlmann*

Getting Away with Murder / Oct. 1985 / Qwest ♦♦♦

● **The Real Me** / Aug. 1988 / Qwest ♦♦♦♦
And how! Austin tackles standards such as "Smoke Gets in Your Eyes" and "They Can't Take That Away from Me," and succeeds brilliantly. Her version of Comden, Green, and Bernstein's "I Can Cook, Too" is enough by itself to make this a pick. —*William Ruhlmann*

● **Best of** / 1994 / Columbia ♦♦♦♦

That Secret Place / Apr. 1994 / GRP ♦♦

Auteurs

Alternative Pop-Rock
When the Auteurs' released their debut album in 1993, the British press linked them with the massively popular Suede as part of a "glam revival." While the band can blast out guitar-drenched rockers like Suede, the Auteurs come to life when they draw from the quiet side of such distinctively English guitar-pop bands like the Kinks, the Smiths, and George Harrison. Luke Haines, the group's guitarist, vocalist, and songwriter, writes highly melodic pop songs that combine the airy melodicism of Harrison with the cutting social observations of Davies; they're sharp, intelligent songs, full of humor and gorgeous melancholy, even when they're loud rockers. With their two albums, *New Wave* and *Now I'm a Cowboy*, they've earned a devoted cult in the UK, without gathering much support in the US. By the time the group released the Steve Albini-produced *After Murder Park* in early 1996, they had even released most of their cult audience in the UK; accordingly, the album was a stiff, even on the indie charts. Before its release, Haines had dropped hints in interviews that the record may be the Auteurs' last. Six months after the release of *After Murder Park*, Haines released an album with his side project, Baddier Meinhoff. —*Stephen Thomas Erlewine*

● **New Wave** / 1993 / Plan 9/Caroline ♦♦♦♦
The debut from the Auteurs hearkens back to the golden years of British pop. The auteur of the Auteurs, Luke Haines, is as acerbic and insightful about modern British life as Ray Davies, singing about marrying showgirls and the upper classes. Songs like "Junk Shop Clothes" and "Bailed Out" have a Merseybeat quality, while "Early Years" points the way to the group's angrier sound. More than just pastiche artists, *New Wave* presents The Auteurs as a group with both wit and heart. —*Heather Phares*

Now I'm a Cowboy / 1994 / Capitol ♦♦♦♦
On the Auteurs' second album, the tunes are tighter, and the hooks and wit are sharper than "New Wave." The band rocks out (in a refined way, of course) on songs like "Lenny Valentino." Haines continues to write about the scheming rich and shabbily genteel, wrapping his words in loud guitars and sighing cellos. "New French Girlfriend" and "Chinese Bakery" are two of the gems on *Now I'm a Cowboy*, proving that the Auteurs have plenty to say and a catchy way to say it. —*Heather Phares*

After Murder Park / Feb. 1996 / Hut ♦♦♦♦

Frankie Avalon (Francis Avallone)

b. Sep. 18, 1939, Philadelphia
Vocals / Pop, Teen Idol
At the end of the '50s and beginning of the '60s, Frankie Avalon was one of the biggest teen idols around, hitting the top of the charts consistently from 1958 until the end of 1960. Avalon didn't possess a terrific voice, but he did have material that was tailor-made for a receptive teen audience. At the height of his popularity, he had five Top Ten hits in 1959, including "Dede Dinah," "Ginger Bread," "Why," and "Venus." When the '60s began in earnest, Avalon embarked on an acting career; he starred in a hugely successful series of beach movies with Annette Funicello. After he began acting, Avalon didn't return to music throughout the decade. In the '70s, he began making occasional film and TV appearances while he worked the nostalgia and club circuits; he continues to sing and act in the '90s. —*Stephen Thomas Erlewine*

● **The Best of Frankie Avalon** / 1995 / Varese Sarabande ♦♦♦♦
The definitive compilation: the original versions of 18 songs from 1958-1962, all but one of them a chart hit of some sort. Has all the Top Ten smashes and a bunch of minor post-1959 singles that found him swinging toward pop crooner material with barely any relation to rock 'n' roll whatsoever. —*Richie Unterberger*

Average White Band

Soul, Funk
The Average White Band had their name jokingly bestowed on them by Bonnie Bramlett of Delanie & Bonnie; during their prime, AWB's solid grooves and overall chemistry were anything but average. But the name did reflect their paradoxical position: they were an American-style soul band made up of native Scots. The group was formed in Glasgow, Scotland, in early 1972 by Alan Gorrie (b. Jul. 19, 1946, Perth, Scotland), bass, vocals; Michael Rosen (soon replaced by Hamish Stuart/b. Oct. 8, 1949, Glasgow, Scotland), guitar, vocals; Onnie McIntyre (b. Sep. 25, 1945, Len-

nox Town, Scotland), vocals, guitar; Robbie McIntosh (b. 1950, Scotland, d. Sep. 23, 1974, Los Angeles); Roger Ball (b. Jun. 4, 1944, Dundee, Scotland), keyboards, saxophone; and Malcolm Duncan (b. Aug. 24, 1945, Montrose, Scotland), saxophone. After their 1973 debut album, *Show Your Hand*, went unnoticed, they hooked up with producer Arif Mardin to record *Average White Band* (frequently called *AWB* because of the initials on the cover). Released in August 1974, the album topped the charts and spawned the near-instrumental dance hit "Pick Up the Pieces," which also went to No. 1. Meanwhile, tragedy struck the band, when drummer Robbie McIntosh died of a drug overdose; he was replaced by Steve Ferrone (b. Apr. 25, 1950, Brighton, England). AWB nearly replicated its success with the third album, *Cut the Cake*, and its title single, both of which reached the Top Ten. But the sameness of the group's approach and such side projects as an album with Ben E. King broke its momentum. Also, the rise of disco left its funky soul style sounding dated. AWB managed a couple more gold albums in *Person to Person* (Jan. 1977) and *Warmer Communications* (Mar. 1978), and its popularity lasted longer in the UK than in the US, but by the start of the '80s the band was permanently out of fashion. The band members have worked as session sidemen for artists ranging from Chaka Khan to Paul McCartney and Badfinger. —*Rick Clark & William Ruhlmann*

● **Pickin' up the Pieces: The Best of Average White Band (1974-1980)** / 1992 / Rhino ♦♦♦♦
All of the Average White Band's biggest hits, as well as important album tracks, are featured on this definitive 18-track collection. —*Stephen Thomas Erlewine*

Aztec Camera

Alternative Pop-Rock, New Wave, Pop-Rock
For most intents and purposes, Aztec Camera is Roddy Frame, a Scottish guitarist, vocalist, and songwriter. Several other musicians have passed through the band over the years—including founding members Campbell Owens (bass) and Dave Mulholland (drums)—but the one constant has been Frame. Throughout his career, he has created a sophisticated, lush, and nearly jazzy acoustic-oriented guitar pop, relying on gentle melodies and clever wordplay inspired by Elvis Costello. Aztec Camera released their debut album, *High Land, Hard Rain*, in 1983. Before its release, Owens and Mulholland had left the group, leaving Frame to assemble the record himself. Upon its release, the album won significant amounts of critical praise for its well-crafted, multilayered pop. After releasing a stop-gap EP, *Oblivious*, the group's second full-length record, *Knife*, appeared in 1984. Produced by Mark Knopfler, the album was more polished and immediate than the debut, featuring horn arrangements and a slight R&B influence. Three years later, Roddy Frame returned with *Love*, which featured musical support from several studio musicians. *Love* was a synthesized stab at R&B/pop, resulting in his greatest commercial success—the album launched four hit singles, including the Top Ten "Somewhere in My Heart." Two years later, Aztec Camera returned to a more guitar-oriented sound with *Stray*. It wasn't as commercially successful as *Love*, yet it was a hit with fans who missed the chiming hooks of Frame's early work. *Dreamland*, released in 1993, followed the same pattern as *Stray* and achieved about the same amount of commercial and critical success. —*Stephen Thomas Erlewine*

● **High Land, Hard Rain** / Jun. 1983 / Sire ♦♦♦♦
This intelligent and detailed, if somewhat overambitious, debut showcases vocalist/songwriter Roddy Frame's catchy and wordy acoustic-based pop songs. Imagine a folky version of Elvis Costello, with better guitar chops, and you've got the picture here. None of the Camera's other albums have come close to matching this release. —*John Floyd*

Knife / Sep. 1984 / Sire ♦♦♦

Aztec Camera / Mar. 1985 / Sire ♦♦

Love / Nov. 1987 / Sire ♦♦

Stray / Jun. 1990 / Sire ♦♦♦♦
After a lukewarm stab at soul (*Love*), Roddy Frame returns to a brilliantly textured guitar pop on *Stray*, covering rock, soul, and jazzy pop in the space of one album. It's all tied together by Frame's intelligent, sometimes precious, lyrics and melodic pop sense—it's one of Aztec Camera's finest albums. —*Stephen Thomas Erlewine*

Dreamland / May 25, 1993 / Sire ♦♦♦♦
Aztec Camera's first album since 1990's *Stray* continues singer-songwriter Roddy Frame's return to form. Highlighted by the gorgeous Motown-Byrds hybrid single "Dream Sweet Dreams" and the lush, warm ballads "Valium Summer" and "Let Your Love Decide," *Dreamland* is Aztec Camera's best effort since their debut. —*Stephen Thomas Erlewine*

Frestonia / Nov. 14, 1995 / Reprise ♦♦♦

B.T. Express

Funk, Disco
This funk-disco group was formed by Jeff Lane in Brooklyn during the

'70s. They started in 1972 as the King Davis House Rockers, and later were called the Brooklyn Trucking Express. The roster included saxophonist and vocalist Bill Risbrook, percussionist Dennis Rowe, guitarist Rick Thompson, saxophonist-flutist Carlos Ward, keyboardist Michael Jones (Kashif), lead guitarist and vocalist Wesley Hall, drummer Leslie Ming, bassist-organist-vocalist Louis Risbrook, and vocalist Barbara Joyce Lomas. Their debut LP *Do It Till You're Satisfied* had two No. 1 R&B and Top Ten pop hits in the title cut and "Express." Subsequent LPs yielded two more R&B Top Ten singles, "Give It What You Got/Peace Pipe" in 1975 and "Can't Stop Groovin' Now, Wanna Do It Some More" in 1976. After 1977's "Shout It Out," which cracked the R&B Top 20 (No. 12), the group slumped with *Shout!* They were off the charts until 1980. They made a slight comeback that year with *B.T. Express 1980*, though only the single "Give Up the Funk (Let's Dance)" made it into the Top 30 (No. 24). They later recorded for Record Shack, Earthtone, and King Davis, but couldn't duplicate their earlier success. Kashif scored hits as a producer, performer, and composer in the '80s. *—Ron Wynn*

● **Golden Classics** / Collectables ✦✦✦✦
B.T. Express exploded on the funk-disco scene in the mid-'70s with back-to-back No. 1 R&B hits, "Do It ('Til You're Satisfied)" and "Express," both of which also cracked the pop Top Ten. "Give It What You Got/Peace Pipe" was another big hit, but the group had peaked by the late '70s. This collection includes these three smashes, plus other numbers. They were never great singers, but were a good ensemble. *—Ron Wynn*

The B-52's

Alternative Pop-Rock, New Wave
Athens, GA, has been a hotbed of alternative talent for quite a while, but the town's rise to cutting-edge musical prominence was aided in no small part by the 1976 formation of the B-52's, a wildly unorthodox party band that featured a guitarist with a five-string Mosrite electric and two miniskirted, go-go-booted female singers who sported extremely bouffant hairdos. The complete original lineup was: Fred Schneider (b. Jul. 1, 1951, Newark, GA), vocals; Kate Pierson (b. Apr. 27, 1948, Weehawken, NJ), vocals, organ; Cindy Wilson (b. Feb. 28, 1957, Athens, GA), vocals; Cindy's brother Ricky Wilson (b. Mar. 19, 1953, Athens, GA, d. Oct 12, 1985), guitar; and Keith Strickland (b. Oct. 26, 1953, Athens, GA), drums. The recklessly exuberant self-titled Warner debut was a left-field success, selling tons of copies with little radio support. The follow-up, *Wild Planet*, picked up where they left off, with mixed results; nevertheless, it also enjoyed success. A dance-mix EP (*Party Mix!*), a mini-album (*Mesopotamia*), and a belated full-length third album (*Whammy!*) provided further variations on the band's sound, but the "fun" seemed increasingly forced. Ricky Wilson passed away in 1985 from AIDS before the release of the uneven *Bouncing Off the Satellites*. With Keith Strickland taking over guitar duties, the B-52's returned from an extended break and put out the hugely successful *Cosmic Thing*. Produced by Don Was and Nile Rodgers, *Cosmic Thing* successfully synthesized the band's wacky energy with just the right amount of streamlining. Its follow-up, *Good Stuff*, preceded by the departure of Cindy Wilson, was to *Cosmic Thing* what *Wild Planet* was to *The B-52's*, more of the same, but less effective and less popular. *—Rick Clark & William Ruhlmann*

★ **The B-52's** / Jul. 1979 / Warner Bros. ✦✦✦✦✦
It's all here on the debut: the "Secret Agent Man" drum/guitar tracks that compel the feet to dance, topped by shrill female vocals and the brash speak-singing of Fred Schneider giving forth with some strangest non sequiturs as though he were an overexcited carnival barker. Includes "Planet Claire" and the hit "Rock Lobster." *—William Ruhlmann*

Wild Planet / Sep. 1980 / Warner Bros. ✦✦✦
Wild Planet is more of the same, as the B-52's celebrate the joys of living in your own "Private Idaho" and the wonders of quiche lorraine. *—William Ruhlmann*

Party Mix! / Jul. 1981 / Warner Bros. ✦✦

Mesopotamia / Jan. 1982 / Warner Bros. ✦✦

Whammy! / Apr. 1983 / Warner Bros. ✦✦✦
After the still-born *Mesopotamia*, *Whammy!* is a pleasing return to the classic fun-loving wackiness of the first album, even if some of the songs sound a little forced and self-conscious. *—Stephen Thomas Erlewine*

Bouncing Off the Satellites / Sep. 1986 / Warner Bros. ✦✦

Cosmic Thing / Jun. 1989 / Reprise ✦✦✦✦
Belatedly, and despite the death of their musical leader Ricky Wilson, the B-52's found enormous commercial success with this album, which effectively recapitulates their zany virtues, especially on the two Top Ten hits "Love Shack" and "Roam." *—William Ruhlmann*

Good Stuff / Jun. 23, 1992 / Reprise ✦✦

Babyface (Kenny Edmonds)

Urban, Adult Contemporary, Club-Dance
With his friend Antonio Reid, Babyface formed a Cincinnati-based band,

---

the Deele, in the early '80s. They were introduced by members of Midnight Star to Solar Records executive Dick Griffey, who put them to work producing music for Carrie Lucas, the Whispers, and Dynasty. Since then, they've produced hits for Sheena Easton, Pebbles, Paula Abdul, and others. During the '90s, Babyface's dominance has extended beyond the production arena and into the performing circle. A series of hit releases depicting him simultaneously as a vulnerable romantic and accomplished lover turned Babyface into arguably this decade's biggest urban male vocalist. The string actually began in the mid-'80s with the underrated *Lovers*, but picked up steam with *Tender Lover* in 1989. *Tender Lover* crossed him over into pop territory and eventually sold more than two million copies, ending any doubts that Babyface would be a major solo star. The singles "Whip Appeal" and "It's No Crime" were Top Ten R&B and pop hits, and remain staples on urban radio. He followed that with *A Closer Look* in 1991, and his most recent LP, *For the Cool in You*, earned another platinum certification and ranked among 1993's biggest R&B urban albums. *—Bil Carpenter*

● **Tender Lover** / Jul. 1989 / Solar ✦✦✦✦
Babyface's second solo album yielded the first No. 1 R&B hit of the 1990s while establishing Edmonds as a major personality and performer. He wrote or co-wrote much of the material and even played several instruments. It was a combination of slick production and nicely sung sentimental tributes and heartache ballads. *—Ron Wynn*

Bachman-Turner Overdrive

Rock 'n' Roll, Pop-Rock, Arena Rock
Bachman-Turner Overdrive was formed by Randy Bachman and C.F. Turner, two expatriates of Canada's the Guess Who. They specialized in no-nonsense blue-collar rock 'n' roll; in fact, part of the band's name came from the trucking industry magazine *Overdrive*. This isn't to say that BTO was without musical sophistication, certainly evidenced in the jazzy "Lookin' Out for No. 1." The band's initial demos were rejected by over two dozen record labels before Mercury picked them up.

Several of the band's radio tracks became substantial hits, particularly "Takin' Care of Business" (No. 12 pop) and the No. 1 hit "You Ain't Seen Nothing Yet," which had a stuttering vocal hook inspired by the speech impediment of the band's first manager, Gary Bachman.

After the Top Ten success of the band's fourth album, *Four Wheel Drive* (1975), BTO's fortunes began to decline. Randy Bachman left in 1977, although the group continued without him with Jim Clench. The group officially changed its name to BTO in 1978, but by that time not many people were paying attention. After releasing *Rock N' Roll Nights* in 1979, the band called it quits.

In 1984, the group re-formed with Randy Bachman and recorded another self-titled album, which was released without much notice. Although they didn't make another album, BTO continued to tour into the '90s. *—Rick Clark*

● **The Best of B.T.O. (So Far)** / Jul. 1976 / Mercury ✦✦✦✦
Everything you need to hear, this no-frills hard-driving '70s rock showcases the band at the height of their popularity. *—Donna DiChario*

● **Greatest Hits** / 1981 / Mercury ✦✦✦✦
All the essential hits are here on this good-sounding set. The lack of liner notes keeps this from being an informative place to start, but if you are looking for just the music, the high points are here. *—Rick Clark*

The Anthology / Jul. 20, 1993 / PolyGram 3145 ✦✦✦✦
This double-disc set features fine remastering from the original masters, plus extensive liner notes. This is an ideal choice for the *true* fan who is just converting to CD and is looking for more than the basic hits package. Hit seekers will still find *BTO's Greatest Hits* more than adequate. *—Rick Clark*

Bad Brains

Alternative Pop-Rock, Hardcore Punk
Along with Black Flag and Minor Threat, the Bad Brains were the leaders of Washington, DC's hardcore punk movement in the early '80s, although they didn't sound like either band. The Bad Brains tempered their ferocious hardcore with a good dose of dub and reggae without deviating from the "hard-fast-loud" rules that were vital to the scene. Led by vocalist H.R. and the blistering guitarist Dr. Know, the Bad Brains were notorious for their exhilarating live show, which had a raw, vital energy that they rarely captured in the studio. As the years passed, the band's reggae elements became more pronounced and—like most other punk bands—their punk elements lost some of their edge, turning into an honest, brutal version of heavy metal. Throughout their career, H.R. left and rejoined the group frequently. Fifteen years after they formed, Bad Brains released their first major-label album, *Rise*, in 1993. In between those years, their eclectic, intelligent approach to punk affected a generation of rockers who enthusiastically embrace these ideas in their music. *—Stephen Thomas Erlewine*

Bad Brains / Feb. 1982 / ROIR ✦✦✦

Rock for Light / 1983 / Plan 9/Caroline ✦✦✦✦
On their Ric Ocasek-produced second album, Bad Brains were able to balance the hardcore and reggae elements more skillfully than they had on their debut, but *Rock for Light* suffers from a lack of cohesiveness. Even if it is a little inconsistent, the unique power of their vision makes the album worthwhile. — *Stephen Thomas Erlewine*

● **I Against I** / 1986 / SST ✦✦✦✦
Slick production helped the Brains make the most satisfying metal/reggae record of their career. Dr. Know's guitar is pushed way up front in the mix, and the funkier backbeat (replacing the hardcore speed blur) kicks every track into high gear. — *John Dougan*

Live / 1988 / SST ✦✦✦

Quickness / 1989 / Plan 9/Caroline ✦✦

Youth Are Getting Restless: Live in Amsterdam / 1990 / Plan 9/Caroline ✦✦✦

Rise / 1993 / Epic ✦✦

God of Love / 1995 / Maverick ✦✦

Bad Company

Hard Rock, Arena Rock
Supergroups usually don't enjoy lengthy fruitful careers, but Bad Company was a highly successful exception, producing a string of hit records from 1974 to 1982. Paul Rodgers and Simon Kirke of Free, Boz Burrell from King Crimson, and Mott the Hoople's Mick Ralphs delivered Bad Company's sparse, crunchy hard rock. Their self-titled debut, recorded in ten days, exuded an appealing unpolished sound at a time when a lot of rock seemed to be trading its visceral essence for arty pretension. After their second album (*Straight Shooter*), Bad Company began to lose some of its freshness, opting for a more processed sound.

Bad Company broke up in 1983, but by the late '80s, a new lineup with Kirke and Ralphs emerged. Brian Howe filled Rodgers' slot. Even though this lineup produced some substantial rock hits, the band's sound is disappointingly interchangeable with a load of other professional radio-rock acts. — *Rick Clark*

Bad Company / Jun. 1974 / Swan Song ✦✦✦✦
This powerhouse debut includes "Can't Get Enough," "Ready for Love," and the title track. — *Dan Heilman*

Straight Shooter / Apr. 1975 / Swan Song ✦✦✦

Run with the Pack / Jan. 1976 / Swan Song ✦✦

Burnin' Sky / Mar. 1977 / Swan Song ✦✦✦

Desolation Angels / Mar. 1979 / Swan Song ✦✦✦

● **10 from 6** / Dec. 1985 / Swan Song ✦✦✦✦
This concise collection of hits is perhaps overly brief. — *Dan Heilman*

Holy Water / Jun. 1990 / Atco ✦✦✦

Bad Religion

Punk, Alternative Pop-Rock, Hardcore Punk
Of all of the Southern Californian hardcore punk bands of the early '80s, Bad Religion has stayed around the longest. For over ten years, they have kept their underground credibility without turning out a series of records that all sound the same. It wasn't until 1993 that they released an album through a major label, and during the '90s it was much easier to sign to a major and preserve credibility. Although their major label debut, *Recipe for Hate*, didn't have the furious attack of their 1982 debut, *How Could Hell Be Any Worse?*, it didn't sell out. Between those two records, Bad Religion tightened their musical attack while adding thicker riffs and keeping lyrics righteously angry and complex. As a result, the band has leaned toward hard-rock territory on their later albums, but they remain committed to their indie-rock ethics. That dedication blazes through in their music. — *Stephen Thomas Erlewine*

How Can Hell Be Any Worse (1980-1985) / 1982 / Epitaph ✦✦✦
A tremendous collection of early Bad Religion that covers most of their hardcore and early post-hardcore period, including their debut record, *How Could Hell Be Any Worse*. Graffin's snarl is prominently displayed, and the band rages through this anthology's 28 tracks, which includes three takes of their signature theme "Bad Religion." Lots of tracks are suffused with a quasi-liberal, populist message (e.g., "Politics," "World War III," and "Oligarchy") and are more lyrically sophisticated than one might assume. An excellent introduction. — *John Dougan*

Into the Unknown / 1983 / Epitaph ✦✦✦✦
At a time when most Los Angeles bands were playing extremely fast, stripped-down rock, Bad Religion released this chunk of '70s-styled hard rock that anticipated the '70s revival by about a decade. It's a bit off-putting at first blush, mainly because the tempos are slower and more deliberate, and because of the use of swirling organs and pianos. But it's a terrific record that was perhaps more daring than anyone realized at the

time of its release. An extremely influential and interesting record, one that any fan of hard rock should own. — *John Dougan*

Back to the Known / 1984 / Epitaph ✦✦

Suffer / 1988 / Epitaph ✦✦✦✦
Featuring a reunited version of the original band, *Suffer* is a fast, stripped-down, blazing record that relentlessly tears through its songs. In terms of sheer sonic intensity, *Suffer* is their best record yet, even if it is lacking in musical diversity. — *Stephen Thomas Erlewine*

● **No Control** / 1989 / Epitaph ✦✦✦✦
No Control is even more uncompromising than *Suffer*, except that this time, Bad Religion concentrated more on songwriting and melody, making the album their most impressive straight hardcore effort. — *Stephen Thomas Erlewine*

Against the Grain / 1990 / Epitaph ✦✦✦✦
After reuniting in 1988, Bad Religion went on a recording binge that saw the release of three records in two years. All are good, with *No Control* hands-down the best of the three. What's crucial at this point in their career is that the band was concerned with simply being a good rock band and less concerned with being aging punks. As a result the music doesn't sound retrograde or tossed-off, and Graffin, Gurewitz, and Co. never come off like a pathetic bunch of middle-age punks desperately attempting to sound young. This music takes maturity head-on and deals with it in a way that gets to the roots of living in society as opposed to dying before you get old—the former being much tougher than the latter. But, even from the start Bad Religion's music was never about taking the easy way out, and these three releases are a testament to that attitude. — *John Dougan*

Generator / Mar. 13, 1992 / Epitaph ✦✦✦

Recipe for Hate / 1993 / Atlantic ✦✦✦

Stranger Than Fiction / 1994 / Atlantic ✦✦✦

Gray Race / Feb. 27, 1996 / Atlantic ✦✦

Badfinger

Power-Pop, Pop-Rock
Rarely has a recorded group had so much apparent opportunity and so much bad luck as Badfinger. Paul McCartney discovered Badfinger's demo and signed them to the Beatles' Apple label. McCartney penned their first hit, "Come and Get It," which was featured (along with a couple of their other songs) in the movie *The Magic Christian*, as well as on their debut, *Magic Christian Music*. With their follow-up, *No Dice*, Badfinger's image as a poor man's Beatles began to evaporate, due to the new sophistication found in the writing skills of all the band members. George Harrison and Todd Rundgren took turns producing their third album, *Straight Up*, which had two more international hits with "Baby Blue" and "Day After Day." Poised to take advantage of this great success, Badfinger lost momentum as Apple Records began to crumble under mismanagement and confusion.

In November 1973, Badfinger released *Ass*—a good album, but one that was a little rough around the edges. Only months later, Badfinger released their self-titled debut for Warner, who were eager to try to regain the momentum from *Straight Up*. The album was an improvement over *Ass*, but it still suffered from the hasty release. Determined to get it right, Badfinger went into the studio with Chris Thomas and produced some of their very best music in *Wish You Were Here*.

Upon discovering a questionable disappearance of monies from Badfinger's publishing escrow account, Warner pulled the record weeks after its release, in spite of glowing reviews. Undaunted but terribly upset by the situation, the band cut another album, *Head First*, which Warner also barred from release.

Depressed by personal and professional problems, Pete Ham (guitar, vocal, keys) hung himself in his garage on April 23, 1975. After a five-year break, Tom Evans (bass, vocals) and Joey Molland (guitar, vocals) regrouped and released the spotty *Airwaves* on Elektra; the subsequent *Say No More* was even weaker. In 1983, Evans, frustrated over not receiving proper royalty compensation and other endless band business problems, took his life. Molland sporadically continued with Badfinger during the rest of the '80s and '90s, hiring different sidemen for each tour, while also pursuing a solo career. — *Rick Clark*

Magic Christian Music / Feb. 16, 1970 / Capitol ✦✦✦
Magic Christian Music is Badfinger's uneven debut. The band hadn't found their sound yet. Nevertheless, tracks like "Come and Get It" and "Maybe Tomorrow" gave power-pop fans a good taste of this band's potential. — *Rick Clark*

No Dice / Nov. 9, 1970 / Capitol ✦✦✦✦
Badfinger's distinctive melodic abilities, great vocals, and solid ensemble work on *No Dice*, is a strong case that this quartet could stand on its own, apart from Apple's shadow. "I Can't Take It," "Midnight Caller," the beautifully romantic "We're for the Dark," and "No Matter What," (one of the

greatest pop singles ever), are among *No Dice*'s many highlights. —*Rick Clark*

Straight Up / Dec. 13, 1971 / Capitol ✦✦✦✦
George Harrison and Todd Rundgren took turns producing Badfinger's third album, *Straight Up,* which produced two international hits with the gorgeous "Day After Day" and the wall-of-sound pop-rock masterpiece "Baby Blue." Badfinger forges a unique sound with their sweeping, strained high harmonies, thick, edgy rhythm-guitar parts, and a drumming style that featured an exaggerated hi-hat attack on the backbeat. Check out "Take It All," "Sometimes," and the powerful "It's Over" for examples. —*Rick Clark*

Ass / Nov. 26, 1973 / Apple ✦✦✦
Badfinger / Feb. 1974 / Warner Bros. ✦✦
Wish You Were Here / Nov. 1974 / Warner Bros. ✦✦✦
Airwaves / Mar. 1979 / Elektra ✦✦
Say No More / 1981 / Radio ✦✦
The Best of Badfinger, Vol. 2 / 1989 / Rhino ✦✦✦
A decent attempt at chronicling the last half of their career, which included one of the great lost pop-rock albums of the '70s, *Wish You Were Here.* With the exception of important tracks like Joey Molland's "Love Time" and Pete Ham's "Dennis," *Wish . . .* is well represented. Key tracks from the self-titled Warner debut are included, as well as several sides from the never-released *Head First.* Also included are the only two tracks worth having from their 1979 album *Airwaves.* Until the Warner albums get released on CD stateside (which is doubtful), this is the only place you can get these fine tracks. —*Rick Clark*

● **Come and Get It: The Best of Badfinger** / 1995 / Apple ✦✦✦✦
A well-chosen 21-track best-of, wisely emphasizing their melodic, tender side rather than their oft-pedestrian hard rockers, *Come and Get It* draws from all four of their late-'60s and early-'70s Apple albums, although the absence of "We're for the Dark" from *No Dice* is a significant omission. —*Richie Unterberger*

Anita Baker

b. Dec. 20, 1957, Detroit, MI
Vocals / Soul, Urban, Adult Contemporary, Pop
Anita Baker's strong, sensual alto helped her break the doors down in the middle of the '80s. More than any other singer, she defined "quiet storm"—smooth, romantic soul for adults. Baker's music is sophisticated without being cold, romantic without being saccharine; besides soul, her singing has roots in jazz and classic pop, bringing a refined romanticism to her music. Although her 1983 debut, *The Songstress,* disappeared upon its release, her 1986 album, *Rapture,* was a modern classic that ushered in a new era of urban contemporary and modern pop singing. None of her following records were quite as good, but her singing remains impressive on each album and she was one of the most popular urban/adult contemporary singers of the '80s and '90s. —*Stephen Thomas Erlewine*

The Songstress / Jun. 1983 / Elektra ✦✦✦✦
Not too many people heard it at the time of its release, but this album contains Baker's characteristically tasteful arrangements and remarkably evocative singing. Reissued by Elektra. —*William Ruhlmann*

● **Rapture** / Mar. 1986 / Elektra ✦✦✦✦
Baker invented a new musical genre, "quiet storm," with this gorgeous album of love ballads sung in her compelling voice. Contains "Caught Up in the Rapture" and the Top Ten hit "Sweet Love." —*William Ruhlmann*

Giving You the Best That I Got / Oct. 1988 / Elektra ✦✦✦
Compositions / Jun. 1990 / Elektra ✦✦✦
Rhythm of Love / 1994 / Elektra ✦✦✦

LaVern Baker (Delores Williams)

b. Nov. 11, 1929, Chicago, IL
Vocals / R&B
LaVern Baker was one of the sexiest divas gracing the mid-'50s rock 'n' roll circuit, boasting a brashly seductive vocal delivery tailor-made for belting the catchy novelties "Tweedlee Dee," "Bop-Ting-a-Ling," and "Tra La La" for Atlantic Records during rock's first wave of prominence.

Born Delores Williams, she was singing at the Club DeLisa on Chicago's south side at age 17, decked out in raggedy attire and billed as "Little Miss Sharecropper" (the same handle that she made her recording debut under for RCA Victor with Eddie "Sugarman" Penigar's band in 1949). She changed her name briefly to Bea Baker when recording for OKeh in 1951 with Maurice King's Wolverines, then settled on the first name of LaVern when she joined Todd Rhodes' band as featured vocalist in 1952 (she fronted Rhodes' aggregation on the impassioned ballad "Trying" for Cincinnati's King Records).

LaVern signed with Atlantic as a solo in 1953, debuting with the incendiary "Soul on Fire." The coy, Latin-tempoed "Tweedlee Dee" was a

smash in 1955 on both the R&B and pop charts, although her impact on the latter was blunted when squeaky-clean Georgia Gibbs covered it for Mercury. An infuriated Baker filed suit over the whitewashing, but she lost. By that time, though, her star had ascended: Baker's "Bop-Ting-a-Ling," "Play It Fair," "Still," and the rocking "Jim Dandy" all vaulted into the R&B Top Ten over the next couple of years.

Baker's statuesque figure and charismatic persona made her a natural for TV and movies. She co-starred on the historic R&B revue segment on Ed Sullivan's TV program in November 1955 and did memorable numbers in Alan Freed's rock movies *Rock, Rock, Rock* and *Mr. Rock & Roll.* Her Atlantic records remained popular throughout the decade—she hit big in 1958 with the ballad "I Cried a Tear," adopted a pseudosanctified bellow for the rousing Leiber & Stoller-penned gospel sendup "Saved" in 1960, and cut a Bessie Smith tribute album before leaving Atlantic in 1964. A brief stop at Brunswick Records (where she did a sassy duet with Jackie Wilson, "Think Twice") preceded a late-'60s jaunt to entertain the troops in Vietnam. She became seriously ill after the trip and was hospitalized, eventually settling far out of the limelight in the Philippines. She remained there for 22 years, running an NCO club on Subic Bay for the US government.

Finally, in 1988, Baker returned to star in Atlantic's 40th anniversary bash at New York's Madison Square Garden. That led to a soundtrack appearance in the film *Dick Tracy,* a starring role in the Broadway musical *Black & Blue* (replacing her ex-Atlantic labelmate Ruth Brown), a nice comeback disc for DRG (*Woke Up This Mornin'*), and a memorable appearance at the Chicago Blues Festival. Unfortunately, illness has reportedly curtailed her musical pursuits of late. —*Bill Dahl*

Sings Bessie Smith / Jan. 27, 1958 / Atlantic ✦✦✦✦
This is an album that should not have worked. LaVern Baker, (a fine R&B singer) was joined by all-stars from mainstream jazz (including trumpeter Buck Clayton, trombonist Vic Dickenson, tenor-saxophonist Paul Quinichette and pianist Nat Pierce) for 12 songs associated with the great '20s blues singer Bessie Smith. Despite the potentially conflicting styles, this project is quite successful and often exciting. The arrangements by Phil Moore, Nat Pierce and Ernie Wilkins do not attempt to re-create the original recordings, Baker sings in her own style (rather than trying to emulate Bessie Smith), and the hot solos work well with her vocals. —*Scott Yanow*

● **Soul on Fire: The Best of LaVern Baker** / 1991 / Rhino ✦✦✦✦
The cream of this vivacious 1950s R&B belter's Atlantic catalog comprises this 20-track hits collection. Includes Baker's bouncy "Tweedlee Dee," the storming rockers "Jim Dandy" and "Bop-Ting-a-Ling," the pseudo-gospel raveup "Saved," and Baker's torchy blues ballads "Soul on Fire" and "I Cried a Tear." She imparts "See See Rider" with a lighthearted reading that contrasts starkly with Chuck Willis' Atlantic smash of a few years before. —*Bill Dahl*

Blues Side of Rock 'n' Roll / 1993 / Star Club ✦✦✦✦
This import may be of slightly dubious origins (sounds like everything was dubbed from vinyl, though the sound quality is quite acceptable), but it delves a lot deeper into LaVern Baker's Atlantic discography (26 cuts) and picks up a few essential sides ignored by Atlantic's own CD: "Tra La La," "Voodoo Voodoo," "Hey Memphis" (Baker's sequel to Elvis' "Little Sister"), and a hellacious version of "He's a Real Gone Guy" sporting a vicious King Curtis sax break. —*Bill Dahl*

Hank Ballard & the Midnighters

b. Nov. 18, 1936, Alabama
Vocals / R&B
Though born in Alabama, Ballard moved to Detroit at an early age, forming a doo wop group called the Royals by age 16. He signed to King label in early 1953. Midsize chart hits followed, and the group's name was changed to the Midnighters to avoid confusion with labelmates the Five Royales when "Work with Me Annie" became a national hit. Banned because of "explicit" lyrics, the song spawned a flurry of answer records (some by Ballard himself), most of them hitting the R&B charts as well. The hits kept coming throughout the early '60s, but the flipside of one of them became a national hit when Chubby Checker re-recorded "The Twist," spawning a national craze. Ballard's best records are informed by gospel-style harmonies and gritty guitar work, usually played by Alonzo Tucker. —*Cub Koda*

Singin' & Swingin' / Jun. 1959 / King ✦✦✦✦
Vintage red-hot R&B, shouting vocals, and frenzied instrumentals. Hank Ballard led one of the finest R&B orchestras on the '50s circuit, and his King albums are masterpieces. His singing was usually steamy, his lyrics laden with innuendo, and he kept up a furious pace throughout each album. This is one of about ten Ballard albums that have been reissued on CD and is well worth getting in any configuration. —*Ron Wynn*

★ **Sexy Ways: The Best of Hank Ballard & the Midnighters** / 1993 / Rhino ✦✦✦✦✦
Hank Ballard & the Midnighters were the 2 Live Crew of the early '50s,

burning up the airwaves and black jukeboxes with lascivious-for-the-time period tunes like "Work with Me Annie," "Annie Had a Baby," and the title track. Although Ballard would go on to write dance hits, including the original version of "The Twist," the Midnighters at their best ("Open Up the Back Door") were Black doo wop at the end of a dark alley. Forget all previous compilations on these guys, this is the one you want. — *Cub Koda*

Bananarama

Dance-Pop, New Wave, Pop-Rock
This British female dance-pop vocal trio, consisting of Sarah Dallin, Keren Woodward, and Siobhan Fahey, came on the scene just as MTV was becoming an influential force in the early '80s. Some of Bananarama's early recordings were with English artists Fun Boy Three. Their slight, airy vocals and strong grooves earned them a number of hits on both sides of the Atlantic. In the UK, their biggest singles were "He Was Really Sayin' Somethin'" (with Fun Boy Three), "Shy Boy," "Na Na Hey Hey Kiss Him Goodbye" (a remake of the hit by Steam), "Cruel Summer," "Robert De Niro's Waiting," "Venus" (a remake of the Shocking Blue hit), "Love in the First Degree," "I Want You Back," and "Help" (the Beatles hit), all Top Ten hits, while in the US they reached the Top Ten with "Cruel Summer," "Venus" (No. 1), and "I Heard a Rumour." Fahey, who married Dave Stewart of the Eurythmics in August 1987, retired from the group in December (later to form Shakespear's Sister) and was replaced by Jacqui Sullivan, who quit in mid-1991, leaving Bananarama a duo. In 1996 the band released *Ultra Violet*. — *Rick Clark*

Deep Sea Skiving / Mar. 1983 / London ✦✦✦✦
Although this was not their American breakthrough, it was their biggest UK success, hitting the Top Ten and featuring the hits "He Was Really Sayin' Somethin'," "Shy Boy," and "Na Na Hey Hey Kiss Him Goodbye." It establishes the formula for the group's success, with its untrained unison trio singing and pop exuberance. The amateurishness of the singers was what made them so appealing. — *William Ruhlmann*

Bananarama / May 1984 / London ✦✦✦

True Confessions / Jul. 1986 / Razor & Tie ✦✦✦

● **Greatest Hits Collection** / Nov. 1988 / London ✦✦✦✦
All of Bananarama's irresistible hit singles are collected on this infectious disc. — *Stephen Thomas Erlewine*

The Band

Rock 'n' Roll, Country-Rock
Composed of four Canadians and one American, the Band first came together in Toronto in the early '60s as Ronnie Hawkins' backup group. Hawkins recorded nine 45s for Roulette between 1959 and 1963. Drummer Levon Helm plays on all nine, guitarist Robbie Robertson and bass player Rick Danko can be heard on the last three, pianist Richard Manuel is on the last two, and organist Garth Hudson plays on the final outing only. Leaving Hawkins collectively in early 1964, they called themselves the Levon Helm Sextet, Levon and the Hawks, and (for a brief spell) the Canadian Squires, releasing two singles before becoming Bob Dylan's backup ensemble for his crazed electric tour of North America, Australia, and Europe in the fall of 1965 through the spring of 1966. (After a couple of gigs, Levon headed back to Arkansas.)

Playing with Dylan had a profound influence on the Band. Woodshedding for two years in Woodstock, NY, they released their debut album, *Music from Big Pink*, in the summer of 1968. Over the succeeding eight years, the Band stood completely apart from everything else happening in rock 'n' roll. There was no precedent for what they did, and there have been no antecedents. Ironically, given that they were four-fifths Canadian, their music embodied an essence of Americana that no one else in rock 'n' roll has approached. Chief writer, Torontonian Robbie Robertson, wrote about the American South, the land, rural America, tradition, and the value and richness of heritage and blood ties. The settings for his songs took place in cornfields, during the Civil War, and at carnivals at the edge of town. He was most concerned with displaced people and the passing of a way of life. Sonically, the Band was equally unique. Hudson played accordion, sax, and organ; drummer Levon Helm doubled on mandolin and guitar; pianist Manuel drummed whenever Helm was out front; bassist Rick Danko played fiddle when they needed a rural or "old-timey" feel; guitarist Robbie Robertson had a pinched, economical style that kept one teetering on the edge with tension. As a unit, they quite consciously avoided any of the current trends. They didn't want their voices to blend, because that is what everyone else was doing; they wanted their piano to sound like a funky old upright, not like a brand-spanking-new Yamaha Grand; and so on. In the process they created some of the most ethereal and evocative music imaginable. — *Rob Bowman*

☆ **Music from Big Pink** / Jul. 1, 1968 / Capitol ✦✦✦✦✦
Everything about the Band's debut album, *Music from Big Pink*, flew in the face of the current ethos of rock 'n' roll in 1968. For example, the disc opens in an unusual fashion, with a ballad, the Richard Manuel/Bob Dylan composition "Tears of Rage." There is not a guitar solo on the album, and this was a time when Jeff Beck, Eric Clapton, and Jimi Hendrix ruled the world. There was a lot of harmony singing that was deliberately ragged: together but not together, a community where the people that made up the community could be individuals. And then there were the songs, enigmatic tales such as "The Weight," "Chest Fever," and the first released version of Bob Dylan's "I Shall Be Released." An unbelievably strong debut. — *Rob Bowman*

★ **The Band** / Sep. 22, 1969 / Capitol ✦✦✦✦✦
Big Pink had been a fine, even superior debut; *The Band* was their masterpiece. Robbie Robertson's songwriting had grown by leaps and bounds. As players, all five musicians had reached a completely new level of ensemble cohesion. The sum was very much greater than the parts, and the parts were as good as any that existed. The album's single, "Up on Cripple Creek," became the Band's first and only Top 30 release. It was one of several songs on the album that had an old-timey feel. Other highlights on this masterpiece include "Rag Mama Rag," "The Night They Drove Old Dixie Down," and "King Harvest." — *Rob Bowman*

Stage Fright / Aug. 17, 1970 / Capitol ✦✦✦
Stage Fright was a reaction to a level of adulation that the Band members were unprepared for. It was conceived as a lighter, less serious, more rock 'n' roll type of album. The final product ended up somewhat darker, as the Band themselves were going through a number of changes. "The Shape I'm In" and "Stage Fright" tell the story well. Some of the original feeling manifests itself in romps such as "Strawberry Wine" and "W.S. Walcott Medicine Show." — *Rob Bowman*

Cahoots / Sep. 15, 1971 / Capitol ✦✦

Rock of Ages / Aug. 15, 1972 / Capitol ✦✦✦✦
Recorded on New Year's Eve 1971/1972, this was the Band's last gig for a year and a half. Allen Toussaint was brought in again to write horn arrangements for many of their classics. The results were inspired. Highlights are many, but of particular note are a cover of Marvin Gaye's "Baby Don't Do It" and a live recording of a track that had earlier been relegated to B-side status only, "Get Up Jake." — *Rob Bowman*

Moondog Matinee / Oct. 15, 1973 / Capitol ✦✦

Northern Lights Southern Cross / Nov. 1, 1975 / Capitol ✦✦✦✦
The first studio album of Band originals in four years, in many respects *Northern Lights Southern Cross* was viewed as a comeback. It also can be seen as a swan song. The album was the Band's finest since their self-titled sophomore effort. Totaling eight songs in all, on this album the Band explores new timbres, utilizing for the first time 24 tracks and what was (then) new synthesizer technology. "Acadian Driftwood" stands out as one of Robertson's finest compositions, the equal to anything else the Band ever recorded. — *Rob Bowman*

The Best of the Band / Jul. 15, 1976 / Capitol ✦✦✦✦
With this album, Capitol Records began the inevitable process of repackaging the music of the Band, which the company would do at increasing length without solving the fundamental problem that the Band, despite the quality of their individual songs, was not a singles act and was hard to summarize in a compilation. That said, for the real neophyte, this single-disc, 11-song album may be as good as anything. It contains the Band's two most famous songs, "The Weight" and "The Night They Drove Old Dixie Down," as well as the group's only Top 30 hit, "Up on Cripple Creek," and such songs as "Tears of Rage" and "Stage Fright" that they probably played at nearly every show they performed. It's true that if you really want to understand the Band, you have to hear all of *Music from Big Pink* and *The Band*. But if you just want a snapshot, here it is. — *William Ruhlmann*

Islands / 1977 / Capitol ✦✦

The Last Waltz / Apr. 1978 / Warner Bros. ✦✦✦✦
The Band's farewell gig was held at Winterland in San Francisco on Thanksgiving 1976. Guests from all periods of their career were invited to participate. The luminaries included Bob Dylan, Van Morrison, Neil Young, Joni Mitchell, Muddy Waters, Eric Clapton, and Paul Butterfield. The four-hour concert was one of the most spectacular in rock history. Two hours of it were released on this three-LP (now two-CD) set. Utilizing horns one more time, this was the gig of the Band's life. We are privileged that it exists in a form where we can hear it as often as we want. — *Rob Bowman*

Anthology / 1978 / Capitol ✦✦✦

● **To Kingdom Come** / 1989 / Capitol ✦✦✦✦
If (and only if) you have it in your budget for just *one* Band set, *To Kingdom Come (The Definitive Collection)* provides a good collection of their best songs, presented in remastered form. Even though the sequencing is chronological, experiencing these songs out of the context of their original albums may be disconcerting for some. In other words, the best way to *hear* this great group is to start with their first two albums, then move

on to *Rock of Ages*, and so on. Nevertheless, this is an exceptionally solid overview. —*Rick Clark*

Jericho / 1993 / Rhino ✦✦✦

Across the Great Divide / 1994 / Capitol ✦✦✦
Capitol's 1989 Band compilation *To Kingdom Come* was subtitled "The Definitive Collection," so what is this? Well, the other one was only a two-disc set, and this is a three-disc set. As the CD reissue/box set boom goes on, record companies have taken to redoing acts they've already done once, so even though the Band has one classy CD anthology (and a few tacky ones), Capitol gives us another. In this case, they've divided it into two discs' worth of the greatest hits, followed by a disc of rarities (some not so rare) and unreleased tracks that includes pre-Band recordings by the Hawks, collaborations with Bob Dylan, live tracks from the Woodstock and Watkins Glen festivals, and the like. All of which pushes its set up a price point or two from the earlier one without adding anything substantial to the story. —*William Ruhlmann*

Live at Watkins Glen / 1995 / Capitol ✦✦

High on the Hog / Feb. 27, 1996 / Rhino ✦✦

The Bangles

New Wave, Pop-Rock, Paisley Underground
The Bangles combined the chiming riffs and catchy melodies of British Invasion guitar-pop with a hint of the energy of new wave. In the process, they became one of the handful of all-female bands of the '80s to win both critical and commercial success. The critical success came first—with their self-titled debut EP and full-length album, *All Over the Place*—and popular success arrived once they polished their sound, adding some synthesizers and deviating slightly from their trademark jangling guitar hooks. Once they were selling at the platinum level, the Bangles didn't stay together long, but they left behind several pop gems.

In 1981, the original version of the group formed when guitarist/vocalist Vicki Peterson and drummer/vocalist Debbi Peterson responded to an advertisement that guitarist/vocalist Susanna Hoffs had placed in a local Los Angeles paper, *The Recycler*. Taking the name the Bangs, the trio added bassist Annette Zilinskas and released an EP, *Getting Out of Hand*, on their own independent label, Downkiddie. In early 1982, the band had to change their name to the Bangles, since there was already a New York-based group called the Bangs recording. After an appearance on a *Rodney on the ROQ* compilation and a series of local concerts, Miles Copeland signed the band to the IRS subsidiary Faulty Products and landed them an opening spot for the English Beat. That summer, the Bangles released a self-titled EP on Faulty Products.

In early 1983, the Bangles signed with CBS Records and Zilinskas left the band to join Blood on the Saddle. She was replaced by bassist/vocalist Michael Steele, a former member of the proto-punk hard-rock group the Runaways. The group released their first full-length album, *All Over the Place*, in the summer of 1984. While it didn't feature any charting singles, the record managed to climb to No. 80 on the American charts, on the strength of support from college radio and MTV, as well as strong reviews. In particular, a cover of Katrina and the Waves' "Goin' Down to Liverpool" and the original "Hero Takes a Fall" received heavy airplay on college stations.

The Bangles released their second album, *Different Light*, in the spring of 1986. It was preceded by the colorful, neopsychedelic single "Manic Monday," which was written by Prince under the pseudonym Christopher. "Manic Monday" became a No. 2 hit in both America and Britain, sending *Different Light* into the Top Five as well. A cover of Jules Shear's "If She Knew What She Wants" was a relative commercial disappointment, stalling at No. 29 on the US charts, but the third single from *Different Light*, "Walk Like an Egyptian," was a major hit, spending four weeks at No. 1 in America; it peaked at No. 3 in Britain. After the Bangles completed a summer tour, Hoffs starred in the movie *The Allnighter*, which was directed by her mother, Tamara; the film was released in the summer of 1987. "Walking Down Your Street," the final single pulled from *Different Light*, was released in early 1987 and peaked at No. 11.

Later in 1987, the Bangles recorded a hard-rocking version of Paul Simon's "Hazy Shade of Winter" for the soundtrack of *Less Than Zero;* the single peaked at No. 2 in early 1988. *Everything*, the band's third album, was released in the fall of 1988. *Everything* was a slicker affair than either of their previous albums, yet it didn't perform quite as well as *Different Light*. "In Your Room," the first single taken from the album, made it to No. 5, and the ballad "Eternal Flame" became the group's second No. 1 single in early 1989, but the record ran out of steam shortly after the release of the third single, "Be With You," which never made it past No. 30. After a brief summer tour, the group disbanded and Hoffs began a solo career. Hoffs released her debut solo album, *When You're a Boy*, in 1991; it never made it past No. 8. —*Stephen Thomas Erlewine*

Bangles / Jun. 1982 / Faulty ✦✦✦

All Over the Place / May 1984 / Columbia ✦✦✦✦
Featuring the Bangles' rich harmonies and slightly ragged folk/pop-rock ensemble work, *All Over the Place* is an absolute gem. Highlights like "Hero Takes a Fall," "Dover Beach," "Tell Me," "Live," and "Going Down to Liverpool" easily make this their best album. —*Rick Clark*

Different Light / Jan. 1986 / Columbia ✦✦✦
The Bangles' most successful album, *Different Light* presented the band with a more polished sheen, depending on a lot more outside material from professional songsmiths. Prince penned the slight (but tuneful) "Manic Monday," which became their first big hit. That was followed by the novelty-ish "Walk Like an Egyptian," their first No. 1 hit. The highlights, however, went to an inspired reading of Jules Shears' "If She Knew What She Wants" and a bouncy version of Big Star's "September Gurls." —*Rick Clark*

Everything / Oct. 1988 / Columbia ✦✦✦

● **Greatest Hits** / May 1990 / Columbia ✦✦✦✦
Greatest Hits is just that, including a great version of Simon & Garfunkel's "Hazy Shade of Winter," a hit from the *Less Than Zero* soundtrack that's not found on their other albums. Another previously unreleased track is a workmanlike reading of the Grassroots chestnut "Where Were You When I Needed You." The highlights from their weakest album, *Everything*, are provided, rendering that album inconsequential. It would've been nice if Sony had utilized the space available on CD to include more essential album tracks from their first two albums, like "September Gurls," "Live," and "James." As collections go, this is a logical place to start, but *All Over the Place* is their most appealing album. —*Rick Clark*

The Bar-Kays

Soul, Funk
Even though four group founders were killed in a 1967 plane crash along with Otis Redding, the Bar-Kays came back to reign as one of the top R&B outfits of the '70s. The original Bar-Kays were a Memphis instrumental combo that scored an R&B hit in 1967 on Volt with the rousing "Soul Finger." Guitarist Jimmy King, organist Ronnie Caldwell, drummer Carl Cunningham, and saxist Phalon Jones perished with Redding, leaving trumpeter Ben Cauley and bassist James Alexander to re-form the group. After honing their chops with session work at Stax, the new Bar-Kays kicked off a long string of R&B smashes in 1976 with "Shake Your Rump to the Funk" on Mercury. —*Bill Dahl*

Soul Finger / 1967 / Rhino ✦✦✦✦
The Bar-Kays were being trained as a second-generation Booker T and the MG's, largely by MG drummer Al Jackson. *Soul Finger* was their first album, coming off the success of their debut single, the group-written title cut. The album is in the classic Memphis-soul instrumental vein; sparse arrangements, accentuated low-end, walloping snare drum, and slightly delayed backbeat with horns taking the place of vocals. *Soul Finger* was the only album made by this particular version of the group. —*Rob Bowman*

Gotta Groove / 1969 / Stax ✦✦✦

Black Rock / Feb. 1971 / Volt ✦✦✦

● **Best of [Stax]** / 1988 / Stax ✦✦✦✦
A nice overview of this major Stax band in their second incarnation. —*Ron Wynn*

The Best of the Bar-Kays [Mercury] / May 18, 1993 / Mercury ✦✦✦✦
A solid overview of the Bar-Kays' years as a trailblazing funk outfit. —*Stephen Thomas Erlewine*

Lou Barlow

b. Jul. 17, 1966, Northhampton, MA
Bass, Guitar, Vocals / Singer-Songwriter, Alternative Pop-Rock, Lo-Fi
In many ways, Sebadoh leader Lou Barlow is the key figure of the '90s lo-fi movement. On both his band and his solo recordings, Barlow alternately turns in full-formed pop songs and sketchy sonic experiments. Sonically, there's not much difference between his Sebadoh tracks and his solo work—it's fuzzy and distorted, with chiming guitars floating through the murk every once in a while. However, Barlow's solo recordings are looser and more off-the-cuff, ranging from a cover of Bryan Adams' "Run to You" to one-joke noise rockers like "Puffin' on a Pot Pipe." Barlow's solo recordings are only for hardcore fans—he doesn't edit, apparently including everything he records on his discs—yet for his fans, everything he records is worth hearing. —*Stephen Thomas Erlewine*

Collection of Home Recordings / 1994 / Smells Like ✦✦✦✦
Lou Barlow's first *Collection of Home Recordings* is a looser affair than his albums with Sebadoh and his folkier side project, Sentridoh. Instead, it's a collection of musings that backfires as often as it connects, yet it remains intriguing and fascinating throughout its brief running time. —*Stephen Thomas Erlewine*

● **Lou Barlow and Friends: Another Collection of Home Recordings /**
1995 / Mint ◆◆◆◆
Another Collection of Home Recordings isn't all that different from Lou
Barlow's first collection—it's still him composing songs that are either
slight or significant on his portastudio, with the occasional help of some
friends and family members. However, *Another Collection* serves as a
more effective introduction to Barlow's insular world since it has more
flashes of humor than the previous record. —*Stephen Thomas Erlewine*

Lou Barlow and His Sentridoh / 1995 / City Slang ◆◆◆◆
The frontman for Sebadoh collected his previously released home
recordings on this 23-song disc. The epitome of lo-fi, most tracks are simply Barlow with a guitar or piano. The raw accompaniment complements his tender love songs perfectly, as on "Natural Nature" and "Spirit
That Kills." —*John Bush*

Syd Barrett

b. Jan. 6, 1946, Cambridge, England
Guitar, Vocals / Psychedelic
Like a supernova, Roger "Syd" Barrett burned briefly and brightly, leaving an indelible mark upon psychedelic and progressive-rock as the
founder and original singer, songwriter, and lead guitarist of Pink Floyd.
Barrett was responsible for most of their brilliant first album, 1967's *The
Piper at the Gates of Dawn*, but left and/or was fired from the band in
early 1968 after his erratic behavior had made him too difficult to deal
with (he appears on a couple tracks on their second album, *A Saucerful
of Secrets*). Such was his stature within the original lineup that few
observers thought the band could survive his departure; in fact, the original group's management decided to keep Syd on and leave the rest of
the band to their own devices. Pink Floyd never recaptured the playful
humor and mad energy of their work with Barrett.

After a period of hibernation, Barrett re-emerged in 1970 with a pair
of albums, *The Madcap Laughs* and *Barrett*, which featured considerable
support from his former bandmates (especially his replacement, David
Gilmour, who produced most of the sessions). Members of the Soft
Machine also play on these records, which have a ragged, unfinished,
and folky feel. Barrett's eccentric humor, sly wordplay, and infectious
melodies range from brilliant to chaotic on his solo work. Lacking the
taut power of his recordings with the Floyd in 1967, they nevertheless
remain fascinating and moving glimpses into a creative psyche gone
awry after (it is theorized) too much fame and too many drugs too early.
With increasing psychological problems, Barrett withdrew into near-total
reclusion after these albums. He never released any more material, and
these days rarely appears in public, let alone to play music.

Although they attracted little attention upon their release, his albums
also attracted a cult audience. Barrett's music and mystique achieved a
lasting influence that continues to grow over two decades later. Latter-
day new wave psychedelic acts like Julian Cope, the Television Personalities, and (especially) Robyn Hitchcock acknowledge Barrett's tremendous
influence on their work. The Barrett cult became large enough to warrant the release of an entire album of previously unreleased material and
outtakes, *Opel*, in the late '80s, as well as his sessions for the BBC.
—*Richie Unterberger*

● **The Madcap Laughs** / Jan. 1970 / Capitol ◆◆◆◆
While this collection bears similarities to the songs found on *The Piper at
the Gates of Dawn*, the only Pink Floyd album Barrett contributed to significantly, it nevertheless comes across more as a session of run-throughs
and demos than as a finished record. Its very roughness is its charm,
undercutting the whimsy of the songs with Barrett's ultimate strangeness. —*William Ruhlmann*

Barrett / Nov. 1970 / Capitol ◆◆◆
On his second solo album, Barrett was joined by Humble Pie drummer
Jerry Shirley and Pink Floyd members Rick Wright (organ) and Dave
Gilmour (guitar). Gilmour and Wright acted as producers as well. Instrumentally, the result is a bit fuller and smoother than the first album,
although it's since been revealed that Gilmour and Wright embellished
these songs as best they could without much involvement from Barrett,
who was often unable or unwilling to perfect his performance. The
songs, however, are just as fractured as on his debut, if not more so.
"Baby Lemonade," "Gigolo Aunt," and the nursery rhyming "Effervesc-
ing Elephant" rank among his peppiest and best-loved tunes. Elsewhere,
the tone is darker and more meandering. It was regarded as something
of a charming but unfocused throwaway at the time of its release, but
Barrett's singularly whimsical and unsettling vision holds up well.
—*Richie Unterberger*

Peel Sessions / 1987 / Dutch East India ◆◆
Opel / Apr. 1989 / Capitol ◆◆◆
For several years, the existence of "lost" material by Barrett had been
speculated on by the singer's vociferous cult, fueled by numerous patchy
bootlegs of intriguing outtakes. The release of *Opel* lived up to, and perhaps exceeded, fans' expectations. With 14 tracks spanning 1968 to 1970,

including six alternate takes and eight songs that had never been officially released in any form, it is equally as essential as his two 1970 LPs.
The tone is very much in keeping with his pair of solo albums; ragged,
predominantly acoustic, melodic, and teetering on the edge of dementia.
At the same time, it's charming and lyrically pungent, with Barrett's
inimitable sense of childlike whimsy. The production is generally more
minimal than on his other albums, even bare-bones at times, but if anything, this adds to the music's stark power. Highlights are the lengthy
brooding title track, the multi-layered swirl of "Swan Lee," the alternate
take of "Dark Globe," and the infectious "Milky Way." Meticulous liner
notes and excellent sound complete this lovingly archival package.
—*Richie Unterberger*

Octopus: The Best of Syd Barrett / May 29, 1992 / Cleopatra ◆◆◆
A well-chosen, 14-track, single-disc compilation of Barrett's solo work,
presumably discount-priced and aimed at the casual listener. But Barrett
is such a specialized taste and has such a small body of work that one
wonders why Cema Special Markets (a division of EMI) would bother.
—*William Ruhlmann*

Crazy Diamond / Apr. 19, 1994 / EMI ◆◆◆◆
A three-CD box set that enshrines Barrett's complete recorded legacy as
a solo artist. Besides including his two 1970 albums, this collection
includes the 1989 compilation of unreleased material, *Opel*. The chief
attraction of this set for Barrett fans is no less than 19 previously unreleased alternate takes from throughout his quite brief solo career. All of
those alternate takes, it's important to note, are alternate versions of
songs that appear on the three previously available albums; no entirely
unheard compositions were unearthed. Nonetheless, these alternate
takes are more interesting listening than you might expect, for a couple
of reasons. First, Barrett was so mercurial (and occasionally unfocused)
in the studio that it was difficult to get him to play a song the same way
twice. Second, the alternate takes are usually starker and more acoustic
in nature than the official versions; they're not better, but have interesting different slants. With some of the songs repeated two, three, or even
four times, this is definitely for the hardcore fan. But it's a beautifully produced document, with a meticulously detailed booklet, of a uniquely
primitive visionary and has many moments of charming and chilling
power. It includes everything salvageable that he produced, with the
exception of the *Peel Sessions*. It doesn't match his work with the original Pink Floyd, but the music continues to influence and be emulated
(most notably by Robyn Hitchcock), though never equaled. —*Richie
Unterberger*

Barry & the Remains

Rock 'n' Roll, Pop-Rock
A strong contender for the finest overlooked American band of the mid-
'60s, the Remains (led by Barry Tashian) were the most notable Boston
group of the era. But they never broke out nationally, despite signing to
Epic and copping an opening slot on the Beatles' final American tour in
1966. Sometimes described as a garage band, that designation isn't at all
accurate; the Remains shared the same British Invasion influences as
many American teen acts, but had a lot of professional finesse to their
straight-ahead attack and sharp songwriting, sometimes sounding like a
fusion of the Beatles and the Zombies with their energetic harmonies
and guitar-electric keyboard blend.

Four fine singles for Epic found little action outside of the Northeast.
Frustrated by the disparity they perceived between their studio work and
their furious live show, they cut an audition tape for Capitol, although no
offer from the label was forthcoming (the session was issued for collectors many years later). An uneven but solid debut album for Epic was
released near the end of 1966, but by that time the Remains were breaking up, dispirited by the stalemate in which their career seemed to have
been mired. Remains drummer N.D. Smart II played with Gram Parsons
and Emmylou Harris; Tashian also played with Harris and today is a
country-folk musician, often recording as a duo with his wife, Holly.
—*Richie Unterberger*

● **The Remains** / 1966 / Epic/Legacy ◆◆◆◆
A fabulous reissue that shows the group as one of the finest, and possibly
the finest, British Invasion-inspired American garage band of the mid-
'60s. The Remains had it all, except success: their first-rate original material combined tight harmonies and tuneful melodies with brash energy.
This 21-track disc repackages their entire 1966 LP and adds a wealth of
bonus cuts, including all their non-LP singles and some excellent unreleased songs. —*Richie Unterberger*

Live in Boston / 1984 / Eva ◆◆

Dave Bartholomew

b. Dec. 24, 1920, Edgard, LA
Trumpet / R&B, New Orleans R&B
A major contributor to New Orleans R&B, Bartholomew was a pivotal
figure as a writer, arranger, producer, and A&R man for Imperial. It was

Bartholomew's productions that helped make Fats Domino a major player in R&B and rock 'n' roll, and he assembled the great house band that backed Domino, Little Richard, Lloyd Price, Smiley Lewis, among others. This band included pianist Allen Toussaint, bassist Frank Fields, saxophonists Lee Allen, Alvin "Red" Tyler, and Herb Hardesty, and drummer Earl Palmer. Bartholomew recorded as a solo artist for King and others prior to taking over at Imperial, but his fame came from that stint. Bartholomew greatly reduced his activities after Domino left Imperial in the early '60s, but occasionally resurfaced to conduct his band. —*Ron Wynn*

★ **The Spirit of New Orleans: The Genius of Dave Bartholomew** / 1993 / Capitol ✦✦✦✦✦

A two-disc set featuring 50 tracks and several different artists (including Fats Domino, Smiley Lewis, T-Bone Walker, Shirley and Lee, and Earl King), *The Spirit of New Orleans* effectively conveys Bartholomew's groundbreaking achievements in R&B and rock 'n' roll. —*Stephen Thomas Erlewine*

Fontella Bass

b. Jul. 3, 1940, St. Louis, MO
Piano, Vocals / Soul, Gospel
An explosive gospel and soul singer, Fontella Bass is the daughter of the great vocalist Martha Bass and sister of David Peaston, as well as ex-wife of Art Ensemble of Chicago trumpeter Lester Bowie. But none of that family history means as much as her own skills, which include a tremendous voice, great range, and distinctive delivery. Bass, who is also a fine pianist and organist, sang in several church choirs, as her mother was a member of Clara Ward's gospel troupe. She later moved into R&B, singing in Oliver Sain's band and working with Little Milton in the early '60s. Bass teamed with Bobby McClure for two duets on Checker in 1965. "Don't Mess Up a Good Thing" reached No. 5 on the R&B charts and inched into the pop Top 30, while "You'll Miss Me When I'm Gone" got into the R&B Top 30. Bass' debut single as a solo act was her greatest; "Rescue Me" topped the R&B charts for a month, peaked at No. 4 on the pop charts, and was among the era's finest soul singles. The follow-up, "Recovery," was better than it has been credited, and reached No. 13. Bass never again attained solo stardom, but has remained busy in the ensuing years. She later sang with Bowie's group, the Art Ensemble of Chicago, and was featured on the LP *Les Stances a Sophie*. She has also been part of the gospel group From the Root to the Source and has reunited with Bowie on occasional projects. —*Ron Wynn*

● **Rescued: The Best of Fontella Bass** / 1992 / Chess ✦✦✦✦
"Rescue Me" might have been her only big hit, but Fontella Bass was a terrific gospel-influenced soul vocalist who cut several great sides for Checker/Chess Records in the mid-'60s. They might not have gotten the attention they deserved when they were released, but they have held up very well over the years. *Rescued: The Best of Fontella Bass* collects 16 of her finest tracks, including "Rescue Me," three duets with Bobby McClure and a previously unreleased song; it makes a convincing case that she should have had more hit singles than she did. —*Stephen Thomas Erlewine*

Bats

Alternative Pop-Rock
One of the shining stars of the fertile Flying Nun record label in New Zealand, the Bats were formed in 1982 in Christchurch by guitarist/vocalist Robert Scott from the Clean, bassist Paul Kean (ex-Toy Love), drummer Malcolm Grant (ex-Builders), and vocalist/multi-instrumentalist Kaye Woodward. With their fresh take on garagey folk-rock that flirts with power-pop, the band quickly became critics' favorites in the late '80s. After two generally overlooked (except by critics and specialists) albums for Communion Records, they signed to Mammoth Records in 1991, gaining only slightly more mainstream exposure. The Bats disbanded for 18 months in the mid-'90s, when Robert Scott rejoined the Clean for a reunion tour and album, but reformed in 1995, releasing their sixth album, *Couchmaster*, in the fall. —*Chris Woodstra*

Completely Bats / 1987 / Flying Nun ✦✦✦✦
Completely Bats collects the band's early output, including some non-LP rarities. —*Chris Woodstra*

● **Daddy's Highway** / 1987 / Communion ✦✦✦✦
The Bats' full-length debut immediately endears itself with the band's offbeat, at times frantic, version of jangly folk-rock with charmingly off-kilter harmonies. Robert Scott's effortless melodies and catchy hooks give an overall upbeat feeling despite a decidedly melancholy subject matter. —*Chris Woodstra*

The Law of Things / 1990 / Communion ✦✦✦
The Law of Things is essentially *Daddy's Highway, Part 2*, displaying their update on '60s pop sensibility in full force. The production is slightly slicker, but the songs continue in the same tradition that made the first album endlessly enjoyable. —*Chris Woodstra*

Fear of God / 1991 / Mammoth ✦✦✦
Silverbeet / Dec. 1992 / Mammoth ✦✦✦
Spill the Beans / 1994 / Mammoth ✦✦
Couchmaster / Oct. 24, 1995 / Matador ✦✦✦

Bauhaus

Alternative Pop-Rock, Goth-Rock, Post-Punk
Bauhaus are the founding fathers of goth-rock, creating a minimalistic, overbearingly gloomy style of post-punk rock driven by jagged guitar chords and cold, distant synthesizers. Throughout their brief career, the band explored all the variations on their bleak musical ideas, adding elements of glam rock, experimental electronic rock, funk, and heavy metal. While their following has never expanded beyond a cult, they have kept their cult alive well into the '90s, a full decade after they disbanded.

The group formed in 1978 in Northampton, England. Guitarist/vocalist Daniel Ash, bassist/vocalist David Jay (born David Jay Haskins), and drummer Kevin Haskins had played together as a trio called the Craze before forming Bauhaus with vocalist Peter Murphy. Originally, the band was called Bauhaus 1919 after the German art movement; by 1979, they had dropped the 1919 from their name.

In August 1979, the group released their debut single, "Bela Lugosi's Dead" on the independent record label Small Wonder Records. Although it did not make the pop charts, it became the de facto goth-rock anthem, staying in the UK independent charts for years. Three months later, the group signed with Beggars Banquet's subsidiary label, 4AD. The group's second single, "Dark Entries," was a remake of the B-side of "Bela Lugosi's Dead" and was released in January 1980. Following their first European tour, Bauhaus released their third single, "Terror Couple Kill Colonel," in the summer of that year, which became a hit on the indie charts. After touring America for the first time in September, the group released a version of T. Rex's "Telegram Sam." In October, they released their debut album, *In the Flat Field*, which reached No. 1 on the independent charts and No. 72 on the pop charts. The success of the album led to their first hits on the pop charts—both "Kick in the Eye" and "The Passions of Lovers" made the UK Top 60 in 1981. In October, they released their second album, *Mask*, which revealed a more ambitious musical direction; the new direction, which featured elements of metal and electronic sonic textures, made the music lighter and more accessible without abandoning its dark, foreboding core. *Mask* was a commercial success, peaking at No. 30 on the UK charts. In March 1982, Bauhaus released the EP *Searching for Satori*, which reached No. 45 on the UK charts; another successful single, "Spirit," followed in the summer. That fall, the group had a No. 15 hit with their version of David Bowie's "Ziggy Stardust." The success of the single propelled their third album, *The Sky's Gone Out*, to No. 4 on the album charts.

Peter Murphy contracted pneumonia at the beginning of 1983, which prevented him from participating in the recording sessions for Bauhaus' fourth album, *Burning from the Inside*. Consequently, the record featured substantial contributions from David Ash and David Jay, who both pursued more personal and atmospheric directions. After Murphy recovered, the band toured Japan and then returned to the UK to promote the summer release of *Burning from the Inside*. The album was another hit, peaking at No. 13. In July, Bauhaus split up.

After Bauhaus' breakup, Murphy formed Dali's Car with Japan's Mick Karn and then pursued a solo career. Ash continued with Tones on Tail, a project he began in 1981; Kevin Haskins also joined the band after Bauhaus' split. David Jay made some solo records and joined the Jazz Butcher briefly. Ash, Haskins, and Jay formed Love and Rockets in 1985 after a proposed Bauhaus reunion fell apart because Peter Murphy wasn't interested in the project. —*Stephen Thomas Erlewine*

In the Flat Field / Dec. 1980 / 4AD/Beggars Banquet ✦✦✦

Mask / Oct. 1981 / Beggars Banquet ✦✦✦
In this follow-up to *In the Flat Field*, Bauhaus matures by creating an album that stands on its own rather than a collection of scattered hits strung together with not-so-strong fillers. Feedback-driven looped guitars, fuzzy bass, and Peter Murphy's ever-haunting, commanding vocals help to create their best album. More raw than their later material, yet nicely refined next to their first, it includes "The Passion of Lovers" and "Kick in the Eye." —*Julian Katz*

The Sky's Gone Out / Oct. 1982 / A&M ✦✦✦

Burning from the Inside / Jul. 1983 / A&M ✦✦✦✦
During the recording sessions for Bauhaus' final album, *Burning from the Inside*, Peter Murphy suffered from pneumonia, leaving David Jay and Daniel Ash to complete most of the record themselves. The result is the band's most pop-oriented album; it's also their best, even if it is slightly incohesive. —*Stephen Thomas Erlewine*

● **Singles: 1979-1983** / Nov. 1985 / Beggars Banquet ✦✦✦✦
Essentially, Bauhaus was a singles band—all of their best moments were individual songs, not entire albums. And the double-disc *The Singles 1979-1983* collects them all, including some B-sides and album tracks,

making it the one essential Bauhaus purchase. — *Stephen Thomas Erlewine*

Swing the Heartache: The BBC Sessions / Jul. 1989 / Beggars Banquet ✦✦✦✦

Bay City Rollers

Power-Pop, Pop-Rock

The Bay City Rollers were a Scottish pop-rock band of the '70s with a strong following among teenage girls. The origins of the group go back to the formation of the duo the Longmuir Brothers in the late '60s, consisting of drummer Derek Longmuir (b. Mar. 3, 1952, Edinburgh) and his bass-playing brother Alan (b. Jun. 20, 1953, Edinburgh). They eventually changed their name to Saxon, adding singer Nobby Clarke and John Devine. Then they changed their name again by pointing at random to a spot on a map of the US: Bay City, MI. Their first hit was a cover of the Gentrys' "Keep on Dancing," which reached No. 9 in the UK in September 1971. In June 1972, guitarist Eric Faulkner (b. Oct. 21, 1954, Edinburgh) joined. In January 1973, singer Leslie McKeown (b. Nov. 12, 1955, Edinburgh) and guitarist Stuart Wood (b. Feb. 25, 1957, Edinburgh) replaced Clarke and Devine, stabilizing the quintet's lineup.

After flopping with three singles, they finally hit the Top Ten again in February 1974 with a cover of the Shangri-Las' "Remember (Walking in the Sand)." At this point, the Rollers became a teen sensation in Great Britain, with their good looks and tartan knickers, and they scored a series of Top Ten UK hits over the next two and a half years: "Shang-a-Lang," "Summerlove Sensation," "All of Me Loves All of You," "Bye Bye Baby" (a cover of the Four Seasons hit that went to No. 1), "Give a Little Love" (another No. 1), "Money Honey," "Love Me Like I Love You," and "I Only Wanna Be with You" (a cover of the Dusty Springfield hit). Their albums *Rollin', Once Upon a Star, Wouldn't You Like It,* and *Dedication* were also Top Ten successes, with *Rollin'* and *Once Upon a Star* getting to No. 1. They scored their first US hit with "Saturday Night," which was released in September 1975 and hit No. 1 in January 1976. It was followed by the Top Ten hits "Money Honey" and "You Made Me Believe in Magic." The Rollers also had five straight gold albums in the US: *Bay City Rollers, Rock N' Roll Love Letter, Dedication, It's a Game,* and *Greatest Hits.*

Alan Longmuir left the band in June 1976 and was replaced by Ian Mitchell (b. Aug. 22, 1958, Downpatrick, County Down, Northern Ireland) who was in turn replaced by Pat McGlynn (b. Mar. 31, 1958, Edinburgh) in June 1977. Longmuir returned in 1978, the same year that McKeown was replaced by Duncan Faure and Faulkner quit to go solo. But by then the Bay City Rollers had scored their last hits. — *William Ruhlmann*

● **Greatest Hits** / Nov. 1977 / Arista ✦✦✦✦

The Beach Boys

Rock 'n' Roll, Pop, Surf, Pop-Rock

The Beach Boys are one of the most successful American bands of the rock music era. They were formed in 1961 in Hawthorne, CA, around the three Wilson brothers: Brian (b. Jun. 20, 1942), bass, piano, vocals; Dennis (b. Dec. 4, 1944, d. Dec. 28, 1983), drums, vocals; and Carl (b. Dec. 21, 1946), guitar, vocals. Additional members were Mike Love (b. Mar 15, 1941), vocals, the Wilsons' cousin, and Al Jardine (b. Sep 3, 1942), guitar, vocals. From the start, the focus of the group's music was Brian Wilson, who combined a fascination with vocal harmony in the Four Freshmen mold with a love of Chuck Berry-derived rock 'n' roll. Added to that was the subject matter of middle-class teenage life in Southern California—surfing, cars, and girls.

The result was massive popular success for the group during the first half of the 1960s, starting with their first chart entry, "Surfin'" in 1962. "Surfin'" was released on a local record label. Subsequently, the group signed to the major label Capitol Records, where they stayed for the rest of the '60s. But their early recordings have continued to turn up on one discount label after another ever since. To date, the most complete and best-quality version of the material is to be found on the 1991 DCC album *Lost and Found! (1961-62).* The Beach Boys' first Capitol single, "Surfin' Safari," was released in June 1962 and became their first Top 40 hit. It was followed in October by a debut album of the same name. Similarly, in March 1963, Capitol released the single "Surfin' USA.," which became the group's first Top Ten hit, and the *Surfin' USA.* album, which went gold. They followed in July with "Surfer Girl," another Top Ten, and in September with a gold-selling *Surfer Girl* LP.

By this point, Brian Wilson, who was composing nearly all of the material (with lyrics by himself, Love, and others), had taken over production of the group's records as well. Given the accelerated recording schedule of the day, it was an awesome task when coupled with his onstage performing duties. This is illustrated by the release of the Beach Boys' fourth album, the million-selling *Little Deuce Coupe,* less than a

month after *Surfer Girl.* The album featured a version of their latest Top Ten hit, "Be True to Your School."

The Beach Boys dominated the pop music of 1963, but in early 1964, the Beatles arrived in the US, followed by the rest of the British Invasion, and the Beach Boys felt the competition keenly. Unlike most American recording artists, however, the group did not suffer a drop-off in popularity. In fact, 1964 was another banner year for the Beach Boys, with the Top Ten singles "Fun, Fun, Fun," "When I Grow Up (To Be a Man)," and "Dance, Dance, Dance," as well as their first No. 1 single, the gold-selling "I Get Around," and three more gold albums, *Shut Down, Vol. 2* (*Vol. 1* had been a various artists album), *All Summer Long,* and their first No. 1 LP, *Beach Boys Concert.* (There was also a Beach Boys' *Christmas Album.*)

The strain of all that work caught up with Brian Wilson, however, and at the end of 1964, he retired from onstage work with the Beach Boys, retaining his composing and producing duties. The group eventually settled on Bruce Johnston (b. Jun. 24, 1944) as his replacement.

The first product of this arrangement was the March 1965 album *The Beach Boys Today!,* which contained a version of their next No. 1 single, "Help Me, Rhonda," followed four months later by the group's eighth straight gold album, *Summer Days (And Summer Nights!!)* and its single, the Top Ten "California Girls." Such recordings gave evidence of the expansion of Brian Wilson's musical imagination, which found him taking longer to make records that were more ambitious than the group's early teen anthems.

While Wilson prepared his next opus, Capitol's release schedule was satisfied by *The Beach Boys' Party!* album, released in September, featuring a hit cover of "Barbara Ann." In March 1966, Wilson released "Caroline, No," which was billed as a solo single and made the Top 40. But he did not launch a full-fledged solo career at this time, instead completing the group's *Pet Sounds* LP (May 1966), which featured the Top Ten hits "Sloop John B" and "Wouldn't It Be Nice" and was universally hailed as one of the greatest rock albums of all time, though it did not sell as well as Beach Boys albums usually did.

Wilson trumped it with the No. 1 gold single "Good Vibrations," released in October. By this point, he was being hailed as a genius in the media, as he prepared a new album tentatively titled *Smile.* The album never appeared, however. A single, "Heroes and Villains" (Jul. 1967), offered tantalizing clues to what would become a legendary unheard, unfinished masterpiece. But Brian Wilson, whether because of the pressure to top himself and compete with the Beatles and others, internal disagreements within the group, psychological problems, or drug abuse, ceded leadership of the Beach Boys, and their next album, *Smiley Smile* (Sep. 1967), was produced by the group as a whole.

At the same time, the Beach Boys suffered a commercial decline, and though they continued to release new albums—*Wild Honey* (Dec. 1967), *Friends* (Jun. 1968), *20/20* (Feb.(Feb. 1969)—and singles through the end of the decade, they ceased to be an important force in popular music. In 1970, the group switched to the Reprise subsidiary of Warner Bros. Records for a series of albums that sometimes drew critical approval without restoring their commercial appeal—*Sunflower* (Aug. 1970), *Surf's Up* (Aug. 1971), *Carl and the Passions: So Tough* (May 1972), (initially packaged with a reissue of *Pet Sounds*), and *Holland* (Jan. 1973).

The Beach Boys returned to prominence in the mid-'70s on a wave of nostalgia and a potent concert act that focused on their early hits. Capitol Records had repackaged their catalog repeatedly, but *Endless Summer,* a June 1974 double LP compiling their early-'60s work, amazingly topped the charts, becoming their first gold album in seven years. In July 1976, the Beach Boys released *15 Big Ones,* their first new studio album in more than three years and their first album in a decade to credit Brian Wilson as producer. The album spawned a Top Ten hit in a cover of Chuck Berry's "Rock and Roll Music," but the group's commercial appeal, at least as far as new recordings, was temporary. Subsequent albums *The Beach Boys Love You* (Apr. 1977) and *M.I.U. Album* (Sep. 1978) sold less well. Brian Wilson's "comeback" also proved elusive after 1977.

The Beach Boys moved to their third major label with the release of *L.A. (Light Album)* on the Caribou subsidiary of CBS Records in March 1979. But neither that album nor its follow-up, *Keepin' the Summer Alive* (Mar. 1980), did anything to change the group's commercial status. In December 1983, Dennis Wilson drowned. In June 1985, the group returned with *The Beach Boys,* their first new album in five years, which marked the end of their Caribou contract.

The Beach Boys recorded sporadically thereafter. In 1987, they scored a surprising hit cover of "Wipeout," co-billed with rap act The Fat Boys. In 1988, minus Brian Wilson, who had finally launched a solo career, they returned to No. 1 with "Kokomo," from the hit film *Cocktail.* In 1992, they released their first new album in seven years, *Summer in Paradise.*

Especially with the dawn of the CD era, the extensive repackagings of Beach Boys material have continued apace. The year 1993 finally brought a five-CD boxed-set retrospective, *Good Vibrations: Thirty Years of the Beach Boys.* In 1995, after the resolution of various legal issues, lead singer Mike Love and Brian Wilson were working together again and there were plans for an archival release of the legendary *Smile* sessions. — *William Ruhlmann*

Surfin' Safari / Oct. 29, 1962 / Capitol ✦✦
The Beach Boys' debut album contains the Top 40 title track and the chart entries "Ten Little Indians" and "409," as well as a version of "Summertime Blues." It has a youthful exuberance but is not as accomplished as the group's albums would become shortly. — *William Ruhlmann*

Surfin' U.S.A. / Mar. 25, 1963 / Capitol ✦✦
The title track, which was really the music from Chuck Berry's "Sweet Little Sixteen" with new lyrics (he now gets the writing credit), was the Beach Boys' breakthrough hit, and the album, a gold-selling Top Ten hit, also featured the Top 40 "Shut Down" and a lovely Brian Wilson falsetto lead on "Farmer's Daughter." But the rest was filler. — *William Ruhlmann*

Surfer Girl / Sep. 23, 1963 / Capitol ✦✦
The Beach Boys' third album features the Top Ten title song, "Little Deuce Coupe"; the paean to cocooning, "In My Room"; and "Catch a Wave." It is also the first Beach Boys album to be produced by Brian Wilson. But there's still a little too much filler to merit a higher grade. — *William Ruhlmann*

Little Deuce Coupe / Oct. 21, 1963 / Capitol ✦✦

Shut Down, Vol. 2 / Mar. 23, 1964 / Capitol ✦✦
Given a confusing title and released by Capitol while the label was still trying to keep up with the Beatles' initial onslaught of popularity, this LP climbed to only No. 13, but it included the brilliant "Fun, Fun, Fun," the lovely "Don't Worry, Baby" and "The Warmth of the Sun," along with the usual filler. — *William Ruhlmann*

All Summer Long / Jul. 13, 1964 / Capitol ✦✦
The Beach Boys rebounded from the British Invasion with their first No. 1 single, "I Get Around" and this summer 1964 release, which also includes such lesser but still good tracks as "Little Honda," "Wendy," and "Don't Back Down." — *William Ruhlmann*

The Beach Boys Today! / Mar. 8, 1965 / Capitol ✦✦✦✦
The first album to be released after Brian Wilson's retirement from the stage includes a raft of hits: "When I Grow Up to Be a Man," "Dance, Dance, Dance," "Do You Wanna Dance?," "Please Let Me Wonder," and an alternate version of the Beach Boys' second No. 1, "Help Me, Rhonda." Even the filler, including "Don't Hurt My Little Sister," was improving. — *William Ruhlmann*

Summer Days (And Summer Nights!!) / Jul. 5, 1965 / Capitol ✦✦✦✦
The summer album for 1965 contains "California Girls" and the single version of "Help Me, Rhonda." Those are the only hits, but the album also contains several examples of Brian Wilson's increasing musical sophistication and eccentricity, among them "Let Him Run Wild," "You're So Good to Me," "Summer Means New Love," and the bizarre "I'm Bugged at My Old Man." — *William Ruhlmann*

The Beach Boys Party! / Nov. 8, 1965 / Capitol ✦✦✦
☆ **Pet Sounds** / May 16, 1966 / Capitol ✦✦✦✦✦
The group's most well-realized, ambitious, and well-produced album. A wistful, bittersweet, achingly beautiful foray into post-teenage angst ("God Only Knows," "Wouldn't It Be Nice," "That's Not Me") and uncertainty ("Don't Talk") augmented with one hit rock single ("Sloop John B"). The most serious record this band ever did, about teens confronting time and aging. — *Bruce Eder*

Smile / 1967 / Bootleg ✦✦✦
In 1966, Brian Wilson began work on the *Smile* LP, which was intended as the ultimate pop/progressive/psychedelic record. Many vocal and instrumental tracks were recorded, but the project was abandoned in 1967 due to accumulated pressures from Wilson's family, fellow Beach Boys, and the record company, combined with Brian's own fragile and sensitive ego. In the ensuing years, *Smile* was accorded status as the most legendary unreleased album of all time, although the record was in fact never close to being finished. Many of the tracks in progress were bootlegged in the 1980s; many, though by no means all, of these, in turn, finally surfaced on Capitol's *Good Vibrations* box set. Several bootlegs of the *Smile* sessions are still easily available, most featuring tracks that still haven't been officially released, or alternate takes and mixes of ones that did surface. A lot of these are interesting, to say the least, including the "Fire" part of the legendary "Elements" suite, the downright avant-garde "George Fell into His French Horn," and extended snippets of "Good Vibrations" and "Heroes in Villains" as works in progress. There are numerous exquisitely beautiful passages, great ensemble singing, and brilliant orchestral pop instrumentation to be found on these outtakes, but the fact is that Wilson somehow lacked the discipline needed to combine them into a pop masterpiece that was both brilliant and commercial. Search for the double-CD compilation versions of these outtakes, which, though expensive, are more thorough than the various single-disc versions available. — *Richie Unterberger*

Smiley Smile / Sep. 18, 1967 / Capitol ✦✦✦
Smiley Smile has long been underrated because of what it is not, namely Brian Wilson's unfinished masterpiece, *Smile*. What it is an exploratory album containing Wilson's two magnificent singles, "Good Vibrations" and "Heroes and Villains," plus much of the eccentric material intended for *Smile*, albeit as patched together by the other Beach Boys. It remains a curiosity, but nevertheless, some of the most imaginative music of the '60s is found here. — *William Ruhlmann*

Wild Honey / Dec. 18, 1967 / Capitol ✦✦✦
Remembered as the album on which the other Beach Boys really took over, *Wild Honey* actually features a lot of Brian Wilson, who has co-writing credits on nine of its 11 tracks, including the Top 40 title track and the Top 20 "Darlin'." Also included is the original version of "Here Comes the Night," later redone as a disco tune. — *William Ruhlmann*

Friends / Jun. 24, 1968 / Capitol ✦✦
Brian Wilson's participation is reduced here, but he still contributes the delightful curiosity "Busy Doin' Nothin'," and the album also contains the Top 50 title track and the Wilson-Jardine collaboration "Wake the World." — *William Ruhlmann*

20/20 / Feb. 3, 1969 / Capitol ✦✦
This was a contractual-obligation album, marking the end of the Beach Boys' tenure at Capitol, but it is an interesting set nevertheless, containing the singles "Do It Again," "Bluebirds Over the Mountain," and "I Can Hear Music," as well as the *Smile* outtake "Cabinessence" and Dennis Wilson's collaboration with mass murderer Charles Manson, "Never Learn Not to Love." — *William Ruhlmann*

Sunflower / Aug. 31, 1970 / Caribou ✦✦✦
The group's first new '70s album, and a highpoint for all concerned, from the transcendental doo wop music of "This Whole World" to the simple pleasantries of "Add Some Music." — *Bruce Eder*

Surf's Up [Caribou] / Aug. 30, 1971 / Caribou ✦✦✦✦
Its title notwithstanding, this album has less to do with surfing than with the band coming to terms with aging and with changing audiences—environmentalism shares space alongside the title track, a poignant, serious masterpiece of modern pop music. — *Bruce Eder*

Carl and the Passions: So Tough / May 15, 1972 / Caribou ✦✦
For reasons best known to themselves, the Beach Boys chose to package their new 1972 album as a twofer with their 1966 masterpiece *Pet Sounds*. The new album inevitably suffered in comparison, but the Brian Wilson tunes "You Need a Mess of Help to Stand Alone" and "Marcella" are standouts. — *William Ruhlmann*

Holland / Jan. 8, 1973 / Caribou ✦✦✦
The California sun mixed with mysticism and some outrageous sound experiments (all with a great beat). A failed effort to renew the group's sound with a change of venue (to Holland) that is salvaged largely by the presence of one great rock number ("Sail on Sailor") and a conceptual piece ("California Saga") that has a phenomenal middle section. — *Bruce Eder*

Endless Summer / Jun. 24, 1974 / Capitol ✦✦✦✦
A notable collection, as the record that sparked the commercial revival of the band's fortunes during the '70s, although all of the material on it has been remastered in superior form on other Capitol CDs. — *Bruce Eder*

15 Big Ones / Jul. 5, 1976 / Caribou ✦✦
A return to simplicity and the group's roots, complete with a hit Chuck Berry cover ("Rock and Roll Music") and a lot of songs about beaches, babes, and amusement parks. It was a hit too. — *Bruce Eder*

Love You / Apr. 11, 1977 / Caribou ✦✦✦
The Beach Boys had hailed the return of Brian Wilson with their 1976 album *15 Big Ones*, but it was on this follow-up, produced by Wilson, who also wrote almost all of it as well, that he was heard in all his demented glory, singing with childlike wonder about Johnny Carson, among other topics. Strange, but fascinating, especially for longtime Wilson watchers. — *William Ruhlmann*

M.I.U. Album / Sep. 25, 1978 / Caribou ✦✦✦
The group's last halfway-good album, sparked by pleasant singing, some unexpected rock cover versions, and funny wordplay by Brian Wilson. — *Bruce Eder*

L.A. (Light Album) / Mar. 16, 1979 / Caribou ✦✦
The Beach Boys went into their outtakes archive for this cobbled-together collection, which nevertheless features the lovely Brian and Carl Wilson collaboration "Good Timin'." Much of it is mediocre, however, and the nearly 11-minute disco version of "Here Comes the Night" is an embarrassment. — *William Ruhlmann*

Lost and Found! (1961-62) / 1991 / DCC ✦✦
★ **The Absolute Best, Vol. 1** / 1991 / Capitol ✦✦✦✦✦
The early hits and their best-known songs ("Surfin' USA," "Fun, Fun, Fun," etc.), and a good anthology from that standpoint—but none of all

the really interesting stuff from the albums and B-sides. It's also a little too predictable, making it okay for the unadventurous. — *Bruce Eder*

☆ **The Absolute Best, Vol. 2** / 1991 / Capitol ✦✦✦✦
The second half of this collection is much more interesting than the first, containing as it does some of their most offbeat celebrated tracks. — *Bruce Eder*

☆ **Good Vibrations: Thirty Years of the Beach Boys** / Jun. 21, 1993 / Capitol ✦✦✦✦✦
A five-CD box set— containing a whopping 142 tracks and covering the group's entire career—that manages to feel like too much and not enough at the same time. True, all of the key hits and most of their finest album tracks are here. The group's decline after 1966—and very sharp decline after 1970—is inescapable, and even though most of the material here is from the 1960s, the fourth disc especially (spanning the early 1970s to the late 1980s) is very rough sailing indeed. It's true that about 50 of these tracks are previously unreleased, but be warned that many of them are demos, backing tracks, and alternate versions of well-known songs that aren't a great deal different from the officially released versions. Also, some of the unreleased "tracks" are radio spots. That's not to say that these rare items aren't interesting for the fan; they are. It's just that it's too overwhelming a package for the non-fanatic, and a rather expensive, spotty one for the devoted fan (who will undoubtedly already have at least half the contents). By far, the most interesting unreleased tracks date from the legendary *Smile* sessions (nearly an album's worth). Never actually completed, they aren't quite the masterpiece that some have claimed, but are extremely interesting, often excursions into psychedelic production and songwriting that often resemble sound paintings more than songs. Comes with a 60-page booklet by Beach Boy historian David Leaf. — *Richie Unterberger*

20 Good Vibrations—The Greatest Hits / Apr. 4, 1995 / Capitol ✦✦✦

The Beat

New Wave, Power-Pop
A Los Angeles-based power-pop outfit formed by Paul Collins (ex-Nerves), the Beat recorded its self-titled debut LP after signing to Columbia Records in 1979. Despite good reviews and some regional success, the album failed to make much impact. A second attempt, 1982's *The Kids Are the Same* (this time credited to Paul Collins' Beat), also failed and effectively broke up the band. However, Collins returned the following year with a harder rocking lineup including Patti Smith Group drummer Jay Dee Daugherty. Their EP, *To Beat or Not to Beat*, was again ignored; it proved to be the band's last recording. While it seemed that the Beat's only claim to fame would be forcing the (English) Beat to change its name in the US, their albums are now seen as classic examples of power-pop. Paul Collins returned to a solo career in the '90s, signing to Wagon Wheel Records. — *Chris Woodstra*

● **The Beat** / 1979 / Columbia ✦✦✦✦
The Beat's great self-titled debut was produced by Bruce Botnick (the Doors), and is a must-own for lovers of melodic guitar-driven pop 'n' roll. Check out "Different Kind of Girl," "Don't Wait Up for Me" and "Walking Out on Love." Great tunes! — *Rick Clark*

The Kids Are the Same / 1982 / Columbia ✦✦✦

The Beatles

Rock 'n' Roll, British Invasion, Psychedelic, Pop-Rock
The most successful and significant rock group in history, the Beatles were formed in Liverpool, England, in the late '50s by John Lennon (b. Oct. 9, 1940—d. Dec. 8, 1980), on guitar and vocals; Paul McCartney (b. Jun. 18, 1942), on bass and vocals; and George Harrison (b. Feb. 25, 1943), on guitar and vocals. Ringo Starr (born Richard Starkey, Jul. 7, 1940), on drums and vocals, joined the group in 1962 in time for their first formal recordings.

The Beatles ingested every popular music style of their day—the raucous rock 'n' roll of Jerry Lee Lewis and Little Richard, the more sophisticated pop-rock of Buddy Holly, the soul of Motown and Phil Spector-produced girl groups, the R&B/pop of the Isley Brothers and Larry Williams, the country-rockabilly of Carl Perkins, the pop-schmaltz of Broadway show tunes—and synthesized them into a style of their own, both in their cover versions and in the original songs written by Lennon and McCartney. And that was only the beginning. By a year or so into their recording career, the Beatles had begun to throw off their influences and forge new directions in popular music, meanwhile picking up elements of classical music, Indian music, and electronic music, among other forms.

The Beatles' earliest extant recordings date from June 1961, when, while performing at a nightclub in Germany, they were hired to be the backup band for singer Tony Sheridan and cut six songs with him, plus two—"Ain't She Sweet" and an original instrumental called "Cry for a Shadow"—on their own. After they achieved fame, these recordings frequently were reissued. The best version of them is found on the Polydor

CD *The Early Tapes of the Beatles*. Another early set of recordings comes from a clandestine tape of the group's club set made on New Year's Eve 1962 and released without their authorization on various albums starting in 1977.

Prior to that, the Beatles had signed to the Parlophone subsidiary of EMI Records in the UK and released "Love Me Do" in October 1962. It was the first of 22 singles Parlophone would release through 1970, of which 21 would hit the Top Ten (all but "Love Me Do") and 17 would hit No. 1. The first of those Top Ten hits, "Please Please Me," was released in January 1963. In March came an album of the same name, the first of 11 studio LPs of new material the Beatles would release in the UK through 1970, all of which would hit No. 1.

The Beatles' success in Britain was not at first duplicated in the US, which was not surprising at the time. Until the Beatles, few British recording artists found sustained popularity in America. Capitol Records, the US subsidiary of EMI, even declined to release Beatles records in the US, and they were licensed to other small labels. For example, Vee-Jay Records released "Please Please Me" in February 1963, followed by the Beatles' third single, "From Me to You," in May and a modified version of the *Please Please Me* album, retitled *Introducing the Beatles*, in July. None of these recordings scored at the time, nor at first did the Beatles' fourth single, "She Loves You," issued by Swan Records in September. (In Britain, "She Loves You" became the best-selling single in history.)

The Beatles released their second UK album, *With the Beatles*, in November, along with their fifth single, "I Want to Hold Your Hand." These events finally convinced Capitol Records to take them on in the US, and in January 1964 the label released the single along with a modified version of *With the Beatles* retitled *Meet the Beatles!*

(A word on the "modified" versions of Beatles albums in the US In the 1960s, standard practice for album releases in the UK differed from that in the US in two important respects. First, UK albums tended to have more songs—the Beatles' early albums had up to 14 selections on them—while American policy was to have 11 or 12. Second, UK albums tended not to contain songs also released as singles, while American albums usually were built around a hit single. Since Capitol had discretion about the form in which it could release Beatles records in the US, it frequently reconfigured the UK versions, deleting tracks, adding a current single, and choosing a different title. Gathered up, the extra tracks might later turn up on an album that had no UK counterpart.)

With "I Want to Hold Your Hand" and *Meet the Beatles!*, both of which topped the charts, Beatlemania hit the US. Over the next six years, the Beatles reached the American album charts with 26 albums, 13 of which hit No. 1, 18 of which went gold, 11 of which sold at least a million copies, and nine of which sold at least two million copies. They included newly recorded studio albums, movie soundtracks, reissues of earlier recordings, and interview and documentary albums chronicling the phenomenon of their success.

On the US singles chart, the Beatles scored 64 times through 1970, including 45 Top 40 hits, 32 of which reached the Top Ten, and 20 of which hit No. 1. Twenty-one singles went gold. In addition to regular A-side releases, the chart singles included B-sides, reissues, EPs, and even a German-language version of "She Loves You." In one astonishing string, every new Beatles single released on Capitol between July 1965 and March 1970—16 records—went gold and hit the Top Ten; all but four hit No. 1.

The group's unprecedented commercial success, which redefined the record industry, was matched by their artistic accomplishments and cultural impact. Sticking to their album releases as they occurred in the UK (the format the US catalog would be brought into line with in the CD-reissue era), their third album was *A Hard Day's Night* (Jul. 1964), half of whose songs were heard in their feature film debut of the same name. Writing all 13 songs, Lennon and McCartney began to reveal an unexpected depth on such tracks as the hesitant romantic ballad "If I Fell" and the vengeful "I'll Cry Instead," alongside the automatic crowd pleasers such as the title track and "Can't Buy Me Love."

The fourth album, *Beatles for Sale* (Dec. 1964) (material from which turned up in the US on *Beatles '65* and *Beatles VI*) further demonstrated the group's evolution, notably on such tracks as "No Reply" and "I'm a Loser," although the unusually large number of cover songs—six of 14—suggested that the pace of writing new material was beginning to show. (Not that you could tell from their singles, as "I Feel Fine"/"She's a Woman," released concurrently—their sixth straight UK No. 1 and their sixth US No. 1 of 1964 alone—was as strong as any of their releases so far.)

Help! (Aug. 1965), containing many of the songs from their second movie, showed them moving more toward a country-rock style (the influence of Buddy Holly is pervasive), though it also includes "Yesterday," a ballad on which McCartney is accompanied by a string quartet that became the most popular song standard of the decade. The folkish and country influences were also heard on the Beatles' sixth album, *Rubber Soul* (Dec. 1965). The next year found the Beatles taking greater time with their recordings and stretching the releases out more. After undertaking world tours in 1964, 1965, and 1966, they retired from live performing. In the course of the year, they released only one new album, *Revolver* (Aug.) and a separate single, "Paperback Writer"/"Rain" (May). (A second single, "Yellow Submarine"/"Eleanor Rigby," was culled from the LP.) The records showed extraordinary studio experimentation and musical growth.

They were dwarfed, however, by the Beatles' next record releases, "Penny Lane"/"Strawberry Fields Forever" (Feb. 1967) and *Sgt. Pepper's Lonely Hearts Club Band* (Jun. 1967), recordings that for decades continued to top critics' polls of the greatest pop records ever made and that succeeded in bringing the public along in their inventiveness—*Sgt. Pepper* topped the charts for months and sold eight million copies in the US alone.

This may have been the Beatles' peak, though they continued to make valuable and popular music for another two years. In August 1967, their manager, Brian Epstein, died, and subsequently they suffered various reversals. Their *Magical Mystery Tour* TV film (shown in the UK in December 1967) was panned, though the accompanying music was typically successful; they launched a record company, Apple, that eventually drained their income; and there were other dubious business deals.

Meanwhile, they were working on a sprawling two-record set, *The Beatles* (Nov. 1968), immediately dubbed the "White Album" because of its blank cover, which revealed a breakdown in musical unity, with a single member dominating each track, sometimes to the point of bringing in his own sidemen in addition to the other Beatles. This was followed by an abortive film and recording project, initially called *Get Back* and abandoned after working on it in January 1969.

The Beatles reconvened for a final album project, *Abbey Road* (Sep. 1969), then broke up, with the *Get Back* project, much altered, turning up in record stores and movie theaters in May 1970 under the title *Let It Be*. All four band members launched solo careers, and all four topped the charts at one time or another, though Paul McCartney proved the most consistently popular. John Lennon was assassinated in December 1980.

Beatle music has proven perennially popular, starting with hits compilations and reissues released in the 1970s and continuing with CD reissues in the 1980s. When Capitol released a set of radio performances in December 1994, *Live at the BBC*, it sold five million copies. Meanwhile, the three surviving Beatles, having resolved various financial and personal disputes, began some recording together in connection with a video documentary project. The resulting project, entitled *Anthology*, was aired on television in the fall of 1995. The video series was accompanied by the release of a series of double-disc albums comprised entirely of outtakes and alternate takes, also entitled *Anthology*.

The first audio installment of *Anthology* was released in November 1995; the album debuted at No. 1 on the US charts, No. 2 on the UK charts. *Anthology 1* included "Free As A Bird," a John Lennon home recording from the '70s that the surviving Beatles constructed into a full-blown production. With the assistance of producer Jeff Lynne, the three remaining Beatles overdubbed instrumentation and backing vocals to Lennon's tape. The group also overdubbed another Lennon home recording, "Real Love," in the same fashion. "Real Love" appeared on *Anthology 2*, which was released in February 1996; the album debuted at No. 1 on both the US and UK charts. *Anthology 3* is scheduled for October 1996 release. A home video release of *Anthology* was scheduled for September 1996. — *William Ruhlmann*

☆ **Please Please Me** / Mar. 22, 1963 / Capitol ✦✦✦✦
Nearly 30 years after its release, the Beatles' first album still stands not only as a blueprint for what the group itself would accomplish in the next three years, but for what a large part of popular music would sound like from then on. Listening now, one revels anew in the songwriting of John Lennon and Paul McCartney (songs include "I Saw Her Standing There"), their remarkable harmonies and solo singing, and the encyclopedia of pop and rock they offer from other sources—especially light pop and hard R&B (like the show-stopping closer, Lennon's take on the Isley Brothers' "Twist and Shout"). The CD reissue is in the original mono, but Mobile Fidelity has issued the album in stereo. — *William Ruhlmann*

☆ **With the Beatles** / Nov. 22, 1963 / Capitol ✦✦✦✦✦
In only a few months, and despite a torrid schedule, the Beatles demonstrated enormous growth on their second album (growth and change would be constants throughout their remarkable career). From the forceful "It Won't Be Long" to the bouncy "All My Loving," their original songs have made a leap, especially in ensemble playing, and the covers again offer a broad range, from Broadway show music ("Till There Was You" from *The Music Man*) to two great Motown songs ("You Really Got a Hold on Me" and "Money"). The CD reissue is in mono, while Mobile Fidelity has issued it in stereo. — *William Ruhlmann*

☆ **A Hard Day's Night [UK]** / Jul. 10, 1964 / Capitol ✦✦✦✦✦
Maybe it was all the success of the previous year, but on their third (UK) album, the Beatles sound positively triumphant, roaring through exciting songs like the title tune, "Can't Buy Me Love," and "Any Time at All." On their first album to be entirely self-written, it's the material (produced

under incredible pressure) that continues to impress. "I Should Have Known Better," "If I Fell," "And I Love Her"—these are songs a generation can sing word-for-word decades later. At the same time, one can hear around the edges the beginnings of Lennon's darker side and individual voice, as more than once he refers to something he can't stand. "I'll Cry Instead" is almost bitter. *A Hard Day's Night*'s freshness has not dated an hour. — *William Ruhlmann*

☆ **Beatles for Sale** / Dec. 4, 1964 / Capitol ✦✦✦✦✦
In a sense, this fourth UK album is a step back for the Beatles, as they return to the eight-originals-with-six-covers formula of their first two albums. Fatigue is clearly setting in. But some of the originals are gems, especially Lennon's "No Reply" and "I'm a Loser," songs confirming his sense of anguish. The covers of Chuck Berry, Carl Perkins, and Little Richard are, once again, inspired recastings of formative material for the group. — *William Ruhlmann*

☆ **Help! [UK]** / Aug. 6, 1965 / Capitol ✦✦✦✦✦
The Beatles' fifth UK album contained seven songs used in their film plus seven other songs and marked a move to a softer, more reflective style. The lyrics are more prominent and thoughtful, and the sound more often features slow tempos, acoustic guitars, and other instruments. Here Lennon continued to cry for "Help!" and bitterly declared "You've Got to Hide Your Love Away" over a strummed acoustic. Here McCartney took a bluegrass-country turn in "I've Just Seen a Face" and achieved his biggest ballad with "Yesterday" (singing before a string quartet). Once again, the Beatles had exhibited remarkable growth and pointed the way for all of pop music to follow. — *William Ruhlmann*

☆ **Rubber Soul [UK]** / Dec. 3, 1965 / Capitol ✦✦✦✦
Although the Beatles' sixth (UK) album is less consistent than some of their other releases, it has its share of memorable songs, among them Lennon's "Norwegian Wood," "Nowhere Man," and "In My Life" and McCartney's "Michelle." Again, the sound is softer and more sophisticated than any of the group's 1964 material. — *William Ruhlmann*

☆ **Revolver [UK]** / Aug. 5, 1966 / Capitol ✦✦✦✦✦
The three songs that were swiped for the US album *Yesterday . . . and Today* were the least of another astonishing leap in songwriting and production that introduced "Eleanor Rigby," "Yellow Submarine," "She Said, She Said," "Good Day Sunshine," "For No One," "Got to Get You into My Life," and "Tomorrow Never Knows." If McCartney was becoming a consummate pop craftsman with a command of horns and strings, Lennon was delving into a drugged psyche while experimenting with tape loops and strange sounds. And George Harrison, whose unprecedented three songs were led by "Taxman," was finally flowering into a first-rate songwriter. — *William Ruhlmann*

☆ **Sgt. Pepper's Lonely Hearts Club Band** / Jun. 1, 1967 / Capitol ✦✦✦✦✦
The Beatles' finest album is a song cycle full of childlike whimsy and irresistibly catchy songs. Its playfulness belies an amazingly fluid arrangement of melodies, lyrics, and sounds that flow together into a whole, creating its own magical world. An open-ended embrace of light pop, hard rock, Indian music, swing, classical music, and blues, the album makes the case for musical unity-in-diversity, seemingly gathering all that came before it into surprising yet perfect combinations. The Beatles only occasionally approached this achievement in isolated moments afterward, and nobody else even came close, then or since. — *William Ruhlmann*

☆ **Magical Mystery Tour** / Nov. 27, 1967 / Capitol ✦✦✦✦✦
Six songs from the group's TV film *Magical Mystery Tour*, plus their three 1967 singles. Especially notable among them is "Penny Lane"/ "Strawberry Fields Forever," perhaps the most impressive two-sided hit ever recorded. And with songs like "All You Need Is Love," "Hello Goodbye," "The Fool on the Hill," and the title track, the rest of the album isn't too shabby, either. — *William Ruhlmann*

☆ **The Beatles [White Album]** / Nov. 22, 1968 / Capitol ✦✦✦✦
In their later recordings, the Beatles largely eschewed the elaborate arrangements and instrumentation of 1967 in favor of returning to the simpler sound of the four-piece band. They did not, however, return to the ensemble style of 1964, rather serving as backup to one of four leaders, depending on who wrote the song. On this sprawling double album, already apparent individual styles gain ascendancy; likewise, musical styles are not so much combined as separated out in pastiche form—the Beach Boys pop of "Back in the USSR," the blues of "Yer Blues," the folk of "Rocky Raccoon," the hard rock of "Birthday," the schmaltzy pop of "Good Night." The musical facility is amazing but also seems near-parodic. — *William Ruhlmann*

☆ **Yellow Submarine** / Jan. 13, 1969 / Capitol ✦✦✦
There are really only four new songs here, and even they predate the material on *The Beatles*, but this is a pleasant enough soundtrack album, dominated by the musical score written by Beatles producer George Martin. — *William Ruhlmann*

☆ **Abbey Road** / Sep. 26, 1969 / Capitol ✦✦✦✦✦
The Beatles' last unified statement finds them going out at a peak of musical achievement, from Lennon's "Come Together" to Harrison's "Something," with McCartney dominating the side two medley in which the group rocks out in fine style. *Abbey Road* is the bestselling Beatles album ever. — *William Ruhlmann*

In the Beginning: Early Tapes (Circa 1960) / May 4, 1970 / Polydor ✦✦

☆ **Let It Be** / May 8, 1970 / Capitol ✦✦✦✦✦
Flawed, botched, and overproduced by Phil Spector, the final new Beatles album to be released (most of it was recorded prior to *Abbey Road*) nevertheless included the title song, "The Long and Winding Road," an abbreviated version of "Get Back," and such lovely tunes as "Two of Us," which, for one last time, presented Paul McCartney and John Lennon and their acoustic guitars, harmonizing together. — *William Ruhlmann*

● **1962-1966** / Apr. 2, 1973 / Capitol ✦✦✦✦
A 26-track double album of the Beatles' greatest hits up through 1966. Although it is primarily devoted to singles, the collection also includes a few key album tracks. Released on CD Oct. 5, 1993. — *William Ruhlmann*

● **1967-1970** / Apr. 2, 1973 / Capitol ✦✦✦✦
Twenty-eight songs from the second half of the Beatles' career, focusing on the hits but also including key album tracks. Released on CD Oct. 5, 1993. — *William Ruhlmann*

Live at the Hollywood Bowl / May 4, 1977 / Capitol ✦✦✦

Live! at the Star-Club in Hamburg, Germany / Jun. 13, 1977 / Lingasong ✦✦

☆ **Past Masters, Vol. 1** / Mar. 7, 1988 / Capitol ✦✦✦✦✦
When EMI and Capitol released the Beatles' recordings on compact disc, it was decided to issue the albums in their original British formats in both the UK and the US. The British albums frequently did not contain singles released by the Beatles at the same time, and there were other odd tracks not included on albums. Thus two discs were necessary to gather the stray material (some of which included their biggest hits). This first volume, for example, running from 1962 to 1965, contains "She Loves You," "I Want to Hold Your Hand," and "I Feel Fine." — *William Ruhlmann*

☆ **Past Masters, Vol. 2** / Mar. 7, 1988 / Capitol ✦✦✦✦✦
Completing the CD release of the Beatles' complete EMI/Capitol catalog, this disc contains "We Can Work It Out," "Paperback Writer," "Lady Madonna," "Hey Jude," "Get Back," "Let It Be," and other later Beatles songs. — *William Ruhlmann*

Live at the BBC / 1994 / Apple/Capitol ✦✦✦✦
From 1962 to 1965, the Beatles made 52 appearances on the BBC, recording live-in-the-studio performances of both their official releases and several dozen songs that they never issued on disc. This magnificent two-disc compilation features 56 of these tracks, including 29 covers of early rock, R&B, soul, and pop tunes that never appeared on their official releases, as well as the Lennon-McCartney original "I'll Be on My Way," which they gave in 1963 to Billy J. Kramer rather than record it themselves. These performances are nothing less than electrifying, especially the previously unavailable covers, which feature quite a few versions of classics by Chuck Berry, Little Richard, Carl Perkins, and Elvis Presley. There are also off-the-beaten-path tunes by the Everly Brothers and Buddy Holly, on down to obscurities by the Jodimars, Chan Romero (a marvelous "Hippy Hippy Shake"), Eddie Fontaine, and Ann-Margret. The greatest gem is probably their fabulous version of Arthur Alexander's "Soldier of Love," which (like several of the tracks) would have easily qualified as a highlight of their early releases if they had issued it officially. Restored from existing tapes of various quality, the sound is mostly very good and never less than listenable. Unfortunately, they weren't able to include every single rarity that the Beatles recorded for the BBC; the absence of Carl Perkins' "Lend Me Your Comb," which has circulated on bootlegs in a high-fidelity version, is especially mystifying. Minor quibbles aside, these performances, available on bootlegs for years, compose the major missing chapter in the Beatles' legacy, and it's great to have them easily obtainable in a first-rate package. — *Richie Unterberger*

Anthology 1 / Nov. 21, 1995 / Apple/Capitol ✦✦✦
The first in a series of three double-CD sets of previously unreleased and rare Beatles material, released in conjunction with the mammoth *Anthology* video documentary. This covers the late '50s to the end of 1964, mixing studio outtakes, live performances, primitive recordings from the Quarrymen/Silver Beatles days, excerpts from the famous 1962 Decca audition, the most notable 1961 Tony Sheridan-era recordings, and brief spoken bits from interviews. Although this material is undeniably of vast historical importance, it can't be placed in the same company as the Beatles' proper albums, in either cohesion or quality. For that matter, for many Beatle fanatics, a good 50 percent or so of the set is no revelation, as much of this stuff has been circulating on bootleg (in somewhat

lesser audio fidelity) for quite a while. While the studio outtakes (many never even heard on bootleg) are the most enticing items, these are almost exclusively alternate versions of songs they placed on their official releases (the most notable exceptions being the 1964 R&B cover "Leave My Kitten Alone," the 1962 demo "How Do You Do It," and the unimpressive 1964 Harrison original, "You Know What to Do"). Sometimes the differences are quite interesting (a much more electric-oriented version of "And I Love Her," for example), but the alternates also illustrate how the group were virtually unerring in selecting the best arrangement and take of their songs for the final versions. The 1963-64 live material is excellent in both performance and sound quality, though offered in piecemeal extracts. The pre-1962 items are sometimes taken from private rehearsal tapes of primitive fidelity, and are really of archival value only. One could go on at great length about the many curiosities and finds unearthed by this compilation, but for most general consumers, two observations may suffice. It does not stand up to The Beatles' fully conceived albums (even *Live at the BBC*), but the Beatles' scraps and leavings are more interesting than over 95 percent of other performers' best work. By that standard, this must be judged a worthwhile collection, especially (but not solely) for dedicated Beatles fans. — *Richie Unterberger*

Anthology / Mar. 19, 1996 / Apple/Capitol ✦✦✦
As expected, the second installment of the *Anthology* series reflects the Beatles' use of the studio-as-laboratory during their "middle years." Some live material from 1965-1966 appears on the first disc, and the second "reunion" single ("Real Love") leads off the set. But the emphasis is upon alternate takes from early 1965 to early 1968, during which time the group rapidly evolved through post-Merseybeat through folk-rock to psychedelia. As with the first volume, this is nearly always interesting, but perhaps thinner on revelations that some might expect. The *Help!*-era outtakes "If You've Got Troubles" and "That Means a Lot" are on the light side but very fun, especially the latter, which Paul and the group perform much better than P.J. Proby (who covered the song shortly afterward). Some of the alternate takes are extremely different, and excellent performances on their own merits: the funkier version of "I'm Looking Through You," the less mellow arrangement of "Norwegian Wood," a wall-of-drugs reverb for "Tomorrow Never Knows," a very Byrds-like approach to "And Your Bird Can Sing" (with giggle-laden vocals), an acoustic demo of "Fool on the Hill." The earlier, much more acoustic version of "Strawberry Fields Forever" is the most notable gem. On the other hand, much of the material differs from the official cuts in fairly minute gradations and will be of greater interest to scholars than general listeners (although discoveries like a different solo on "Penny Lane" are fascinating). The seven live tracks on disc one, from the waning days of Beatlemania, are better than many would have assumed, showing the group still capable of generating heat onstage. — *Richie Unterberger*

The Beau Brummels

Country-Rock, Folk-Rock, Pop-Rock
While they only had two big hits, the Beau Brummels were one of the most important and underrated American groups of the 1960s. They were the first US unit of any sort to successfully respond to the British Invasion. They were arguably the first folk-rock group, even predating the Byrds, and also anticipated some key elements of the San Francisco psychedelic sound with their soaring harmonies and exuberant melodies. Before they finally reached the end of the string, they were also among the first bands to record country-rock in the late '60s.

The key axis of the band was formed by guitarist/songwriter Ron Elliott, who penned most of the Brummels' moody and melodious material, and singer Sal Valentino, owner of one of the finest voices in mid-'60s rock. Spotted by local DJ Tom Donahue in a club in San Mateo (just south of San Francisco), the group was signed to Donahue's small San Francisco-based label, Autumn Records, in 1964. With Sly Stewart (later Sly Stone) in the producer's chair, they made the Top 20 right off the bat with "Laugh, Laugh." The melancholy, minor-key original sounded so much like the British bands inundating the airwaves that many listeners initially mistook the Brummels for an English act. The follow-up single, "Just a Little," was another excellent, melancholy number that became their biggest hit, making the Top Ten.

The Beau Brummels made a couple of fine albums in 1965, dominated by strong original material and featuring the band's ringing guitars and multipart, mournful harmonies. The best of their early work is nearly as fine as the Byrds' first recordings, yet the band was losing ground commercially, partially because Autumn, being such a small label, lacked promotional muscle. "You Tell Me Why" was their only other Top 40 hit, though "Sad Little Girl" and the Byrds knockoff "Don't Talk to Strangers" were excellent singles. The band also shuffled personnel a few times, and Ron Elliott was unable to stay on the road because of diabetes. Autumn was sold in 1966 to Warner, who made the lunkheaded move of forcing the band to record an entire album of Top 40 covers—ignoring the fact that original material was one of the Brummels' primary fortes. Regrouping as a trio, the group recorded a critically acclaimed, more experimental album in 1967, *Triangle*. Their last Warner LP, *Bradley's Barn*, found the group branching into country-rock, a year or so before it became trendy. The Beau Brummels did reform for an unimpressive reunion album in 1975, and although Ron Elliott and Sal Valentino continued to make music and work on various low-profile projects of their own, they've never made records on par with the Brummels' vintage work. —*Richie Unterberger*

Introducing the Beau Brummels / Apr. 1965 / Sundazed ✦✦✦✦
A much stronger debut than the norm for the era. Ten of the 12 cuts are Ron Elliott originals, including the hits "Laugh Laugh," "Still in Love with You Baby," and "Just a Little." The hard-rocking numbers are the weakest, but "Stick Like Glue" and "I Would Be Happy" are fine Beatlesque numbers, and "They'll Make You Cry" is a first-rate moody folk-rocker. The CD reissue adds two bonus tracks, a demo of "Just a Little" and the single "Good Time Music." —*Richie Unterberger*

The Beau Brummels, Vol. 2 / 1965 / Sundazed ✦✦✦
No big hits on this album, but it's the best LP by the Brummels' first lineup. The 12 original songs feature several fine Ron Elliott harmony folk-rockers that stand up well to the Byrds' material from the same era, including "I Want You," "You Tell Me Why," "Sad Little Girl," and the Byrds imitation "Don't Talk to Strangers." The CD reissue adds bonus alternate versions of "Woman" and "When It Comes to Your Love." —*Richie Unterberger*

Beau Brummels '66 / Jul. 1966 / Warner Bros. ✦✦✦

Triangle / Jul. 1967 / Warner Bros. ✦✦✦✦
A beautiful venture by the surviving trio into a more authentic form of folk and country-rock, with a repertoire that recalls the more famous Everly Brothers classic, *Roots*. —*Bruce Eder*

Bradley's Barn / Oct. 1968 / Edsel ✦✦✦

From the Vaults / 1982 / Rhino ✦✦✦✦
A very solid collection of rare or previously unreleased material from the group's mid-'60s prime. Mostly Ron Elliott originals, they're easily up to the standard of the ones that made it onto their first two LPs, with "Gentle Wondering Ways," "She Loves Me," "She Sends Me," and "Love Is Just a Game" being standouts. Achingly tuneful folk-rock, it also includes an alternate, slower version of "Sad Little Girl," the silly dance-rock confection "The Jerk," and a few cuts that hint at the country-rock direction they would take in the late '60s. While over half of the cuts were finally issued on the *Autumn of Their Years* CD in 1994, a few of the better ones (notably "Gentle Wondering Ways," "Lonely Man," and the alternate "Sad Little Girl") were not. Perhaps they'll find their way onto the boxed set that Sundazed is planning, but if not, this is a worthwhile pickup, and one that is a more consistent and solid sampler of their rarities than the more extensive *Autumn of Their Years*. —*Richie Unterberger*

● **The Best of the Beau Brummels: Golden Archive Series** / 1987 / Rhino ✦✦✦✦
Probably the best (and best-sounding) anthology covering their golden years, although it lacks their brilliant, later country-based work at its best. —*Bruce Eder*

Autumn of Their Years / 1994 / Big Beat ✦✦✦

The Beautiful South

Alternative Pop-Rock, Pop-Rock
A British group formed by singer Paul Heaton (b. May 9, 1962, Birkenhead, Merseyside) after the demise of the Housemartins in 1988, characterized by melodic songs with sweet, jazz-pop arrangements that belie their witty, caustic lyrics. Other band members include Briana Corrigan (vocals), David Rotheray (guitar), Sean Welch (bass), David Hemmingway (drums/vocals), and David Stead (drums). They scored two UK Top Ten singles with "Song for Whoever" and "You Keep It All In" in 1989 and topped the charts with "A Little Time" in 1990. Their first two albums, *Welcome to the Beautiful South* (1989) and *Choke* (1990) also hit the UK Top Ten. There was a third album, *Miaow*, in 1994, and their greatest-hits album, *Carry On Up the Charts*, was the biggest UK hit of the 1994 Christmas season. —*William Ruhlmann*

Welcome to the Beautiful South / Oct. 1989 / Go! Discs ✦✦✦✦
The difference between the catchy light pop that constitutes the Beautiful South's music and the bitter, pessimistic lyrics innocently sung by Paul Heaton is so great it constitutes a kind of malevolent seduction. But that's the point. Released in the US in January 1990. —*William Ruhlmann*

Choke / Nov. 1990 / Go! Discs ✦✦✦

0898 / Apr. 1992 / Go! Discs ✦✦✦

Miaow / 1994 / Go! Discs ✦✦✦

● **Carry On Up the Charts: The Best of** / 1994 / Go! Discs ✦✦✦✦
This album was the surprise British hit of 1994, going quintuple platinum five times between its late fall release and the summer of 1995. The

success was surprising, because while the band had been modestly popular, their last few albums were sliding down the charts. However, their hits collection, *Carry On Up the Charts*, flew to No. 1 and stayed there for weeks. It's nothing more than all their singles, yet compiled together they make the most convincing case for the Beautiful South's sly, cynical sophisticated pop. *Carry on up the Charts* was finally released in the US in the fall of 1995, with fewer tracks. —*Stephen Thomas Erlewine*

Beck (Beck Hansen)

b. Jul. 8, 1970, Los Angeles, CA
Guitar, Vocals / Alternative Pop-Rock, Club-Dance, Lo-Fi, Indie Rock
With his portastudio, keyboard, drum machine, and guitar, singer-songwriter Beck created music that celebrated the junk culture of the '90s. Beck's music drew from hip-hop, folk, experimental rock, psychedelia, pop, and rock 'n' roll, recycling everything into a colorful, messy, and willfully diverse brand of post-modern rock, filled with warped, satiric imagery and clumsy poetry. With all of his rootless eclecticism, Beck is distinctly a product of the '90s; all of his influences were processed through TV and records, not real-life experiences. But that trashy, disposable quality is what makes his music unique. Beck came to national attention in early 1994, when his folky hip-hop single "Loser" began to receive airplay on alternative rock stations across America. "Loser" was released independently on a Californian label in late 1993. The single became a club hit and spread to underground and alternative radio stations. Beck became the center of a major-label bidding war; he eventually signed with DGC Records. Beck released his debut album, *Mellow Gold*, in early 1994. *Mellow Gold* received rave reviews and became a gold record as "Loser" climbed into the Top Ten. Beck's contract with DGC allows him to release records that he and the company deem as uncommercial on indie labels. Consequently, the singer-songwriter released two new records by the summer of 1994, which were both recorded roughly around the same time as *Mellow Gold*. *Stereopathic Soul Manure* was a noisy, more experimental album than his debut and was released on Flipside Records. *One Foot in the Grave* accentuated his folk roots and was released on K Records. Neither album sold on the level of *Mellow Gold*, but they sold respectably. As he prepared his second album for DGC, Beck toured with Lollapalooza Five in the summer of 1995. Beck's second major-label album, *Odelay*, finally appeared in the summer of 1996; it was released to overwhelmingly positive reviews. —*Stephen Thomas Erlewine*

Mellow Gold / 1994 / DGC ✦✦✦✦
Beck's debut album became a hit, thanks to the lazy folk/hip-hop fusion of "Loser," but the remainder of *Mellow Gold* proves he's not a one-hit wonder. From the warped TV-folk of "Pay No Mind (Snoozer)" and the pounding rhythms of "Beercan" to the trashy garage-rock of "F---in with My Head" and "Soul Suckin' Jerk," Beck turns his fascination with pop culture into exciting music that refuses to acknowledge any boundaries. —*Stephen Thomas Erlewine*

Stereopathic Soul Manure / 1994 / Flipside ✦✦

One Foot in the Grave / 1994 / K ✦✦✦

● **Odelay** / Jun. 18, 1996 / DGC ✦✦✦✦
Beck's debut, *Mellow Gold*, was a glorious sampler of different musical styles, careening from lo-fi hip-hop to folk, moving back through garage rock and arty noise. It was an impressive album, but the parts didn't necessarily stick together. The two albums that followed within months of *Mellow Gold*—*Stereopathic Soul Manure* and *One Foot in the Grave*—were specialist releases that disproved the idea that Beck was simply a one-hit wonder. But *Odelay*, the much-delayed proper follow-up to *Mellow Gold*, proves the depth and scope of his talents. *Odelay* fuses the disparate strands of Beck's music—folk, country, hip-hop, rock 'n' roll, blues, jazz, easy listening, rap, pop—into one dense sonic collage. Songs frequently morph from one genre to another, seemingly unrelated genres—bursts of noise give way to country songs with hip-hop beats, easy listening melodies transform into a weird fusion of pop, jazz, and cinematic strings; it's genre-defying music that refuses to see boundaries. All of the songs on *Odelay* are rooted in simple forms—whether it's blues ("Devil's Haircut"), country ("Lord Only Knows," "Sissyneck"), soul ("Hotwax"), folk ("Ramshackle"), or rap ("High 5," "Where It's At")—but they twist the conventions of the genre. "Where It's At" is peppered with soul, jazz, funk, and rap references, while "Novacane" slams from indie rock to funk and back to white noise. With the aid of the Dust Brothers, Beck has created a dense, endlessly intriguing album overflowing with ideas. Furthermore, it's an album that completely ignores the static, nihilistic trends of the American alternative/independent underground, creating a fluid, creative, and startlingly original work. —*Stephen Thomas Erlewine*

Jeff Beck

b. Jun. 24, 1944, Wallington, Surrey, England
Guitar / Rock 'n' Roll, Hard Rock, Fusion
Utterly distinctive and one of the most important electric lead guitarists

in rock history, Jeff Beck was the wildcard element that gave the post-Clapton Yardbirds work its futuristic quality. His pioneering experiments with feedback and various effects, particularly on the classic "Shapes of Things," influenced thousands of musicians. After leaving the Yardbirds, Beck went on to a highly successful solo career that produced an excellent debut (*Truth*), featuring Rod Stewart on vocals, Ron Wood (bass), Nicky Hopkins (keys), and Mickey Waller (drums). The next few albums contained fine moments with Stewart and replacement vocalist Bobby Tench, but during the mid-'70s Beck switched gears and released the instrumental jazz-rock fusion *Blow by Blow*, generating his greatest commercial success. Further efforts to delve into that style were less notable, but even when the material wasn't up to par, Beck's liquid, yet impulsive style has been generally amazing. *—Rick Clark*

☆ **Truth** / Aug. 1968 / Epic ✦✦✦✦✦
Along with Led Zeppelin's self-titled first album, Jeff Beck's *Truth* is considered the primo primer for what came to be known as heavy metal. Fusing the thunderous rhythm section of Ron Wood on bass and Mickey Waller on drums with his paint-blistering lead guitar and Rod Stewart's gravel-and-whiskey vocals, Beck's visionary approach to blues and rock 'n' roll influenced practically every rock band that followed on both sides of the Atlantic. Although Beck could be unpredictable and eclectic (witness his straightforward, acoustic reading of "Greensleeves"), *Truth* features the smoking "Beck's Bolero," "Rock My Plimsoul," and the wah-wah pièce de résistance, "I Ain't Superstitious." *— Tom Graves*

Beck-Ola / Jun. 1969 / Epic ✦✦✦✦
A year after Jeff Beck recorded *Truth*, he came back with the even heavier *Beck-Ola*. Although the songwriting seems diluted, and the addition of Nicky Hopkins on piano added spice in all the wrong places, *Beck-Ola* is still a gut-slamming good time. Notable tracks include "Spanish Boots" and "Plynth (Water Down the Drain)." *—Tom Graves*

Rough & Ready / Oct. 1971 / Epic ✦✦✦

Jeff Beck Group / Apr. 1972 / Epic ✦✦✦

Blow by Blow / Mar. 1975 / Epic ✦✦✦✦
When Jeff Beck announced that he was working on an all-instrumental album, few but his legion of guitar fans could have predicted the far-reaching impact of this pivotal jazz-rock fusion album. Teamed with the Beatles' ex-producer George Martin, Beck singlehandedly created a new subtext for rock 'n' roll. With his virtuosity and taste at an all-time peak, Beck let loose with such unforgettable tracks as the Roy Buchanan-inspired "Cause We've Ended as Lovers" and the percolating "Freeway Jam." This is one of rock's great instrumental works. *— Tom Graves*

Wired / May 1976 / Epic ✦✦✦✦
Nearly *Blow by Blow*'s equal, although Beck doesn't venture any further musically. Charles Mingus' "Goodbye Pork Pie Hat" is worth the price alone. (Available on Mobile Fidelity's Ultradisc.) *—Tom Graves*

Live with the Jan Hammer Group / Mar. 1977 / Epic ✦✦

There & Back / Jun. 1980 / Epic ✦✦✦

Flash / Jul. 1985 / Epic ✦✦✦

Jeff Beck's Guitar Shop / Oct. 1989 / Epic ✦✦✦✦
A guitar hero in his prime, he's full of fury and finesse, with top-notch support from Terry Bozzio and Tony Hymas. *—Jas Obrecht*

Beckology / 1991 / Epic ✦✦✦✦
Covering everything from his earliest (and terrific) tracks with the Tridents through his spot-on interpretation of Santo & Johnny's "Sleep Walk," *Beckology* features great remastering, smart packaging (resembling a vintage Fender tweed guitar case), and the essential Yardbirds and solo years material. The set (55 tracks in all) also collects the best material from weaker albums such as *Flash* and *There & Back*. A definitive overview of Beck's career would have included his work as a sideman with artists like Stevie Wonder, Rod Stewart, and Donovan; nevertheless, *Beckology* is as comprehensive a collection as one will find on this innovative guitarist. *—Tom Graves & Rick Clark*

Crazy Legs / Jun. 29, 1993 / Epic ✦✦

● **Best of Beck** / 1995 / Epic ✦✦✦✦
Basically this record exists because the record company wanted to have some product on the shelf while Beck was touring. The 14 tracks do contain some of his most often-played (by radio, at any rate) recordings, including "Shapes of Things," "Plynth," and "Beck's Bolero" from the original Jeff Beck Group days in the late '60s, and the vocoder showcase "She's a Woman" and fusion landmark "Freeway Jam" from *Blow by Blow*. It may do for casual listeners who only want one Beck CD, although more serious fans would be better off with the *Beckology* box. *—Richie Unterberger*

Best of Jeff Beck / Columbia ✦✦

The Bee Gees

Disco, Adult Contemporary, Soft Rock, Pop-Rock
One of the most successful pop groups of the 1960s and 1970s, the Bee Gees have had two careers and at present are embarked on a third. The name is an acronym for "Brothers Gibb," and the nucleus of the group has always been the brothers Barry (b. Sept. 1, 1946, Douglas, Isle of Man), Robin, and Maurice Gibb (the last two are twins, b. Dec. 22, 1949, Manchester, England), though in their first successful manifestation the group also featured guitarist Vince Melouney (b. Aug. 19, 1945, Australia) and drummer Colin Petersen (b. Mar. 24, 1946, Melbourne, Australia).

The Gibb brothers were the sons of band leader Hugh Gibb, and were performing in Manchester, England, when they were still children. The family migrated to Brisbane, Australia, in 1958, which is where the Bee Gees were organized as a pop group. After achieving some success there, they moved back to England in January 1967, where they hooked up with manager Robert Stigwood (an Australian who was an associate of Beatles manager Brian Epstein). Their first British and American single, the vibrato-laden ballad "New York Mining Disaster 1941" which appeared during the *Sgt. Pepper* Summer of Love of 1967, was in keeping with the eclectic pop scene of the time and became a Top 15 hit in both the UK and the US. It also led to charges that they were copying the Beatles. (The Bee Gees would never earn approval from rock critics.)

They enjoyed a series of hit singles and albums over the next couple of years (due to their enormous chart success, only Top Tens will be noted)—*Bee Gees' First* (US No. 7/UK No. 8, 1967); "Massachusetts" (UK No. 1, 1967); "World" (UK No. 9, 1967); "Words" (UK No. 8, 1968); "I've Gotta Get a Message to You" (UK No. 1/US No. 8, 1968); *Idea* (UK No. 4, 1968); "First of May" (UK No. 6, 1969); "I Started a Joke" (US No. 6, 1969); and their answer to *Sgt. Pepper*, the red-felt-covered double-LP *Odessa* (UK No. 10, 1969) (they also wrote the Marbles' "Only One Woman" [UK No. 5, 1968])—after which they were rent by dissension. Melouney quit in December 1968. Robin Gibb left for a solo career in the spring of 1969. He had a solo hit with "Saved by the Bell" (UK No. 2) in July, but follow-ups were less successful. Petersen was fired in August, just as the Bee Gees' "Don't Forget to Remember" (UK No. 2) was hitting the charts. In September, *Best of the Bee Gees* made UK No. 7/US No. 9. Barry and Maurice Gibb carried on as the Bee Gees, releasing *Cucumber Castle* (Apr. 1970), the soundtrack from a film in which they appeared. Each one also made a flop solo single.

The trio reformed in December 1970 and scored two reunion hits, "Lonely Days" (US No. 3, 1971) and "How Can You Mend a Broken Heart" (US No. 1, 1971). In the UK, they had "Run to Me" (No. 9, 1972). The rest of the early '70s were a rough time for them, but in April 1975 they organized a new backup group (Alan Kendall on guitar, Dennis Byron on drums, Blue Weaver on keyboards) and returned to the top of the US charts with a disco beat, falsetto vocals, and a song called "Jive Talkin'" (UK No. 5). It was followed by "Nights on Broadway" (US No. 7, 1975), "You Should Be Dancing" (US No. 1/UK No. 5, 1976), and "Love So Right" (US No. 3, 1977), while *Children of the World* (1976) and the live album *Here . . . At Last* (1977) each went to US No. 8.

In 1977, they were engaged by Stigwood to write songs for the movie *Saturday Night Fever*, and their contributions helped make the resulting double soundtrack album one of the best-selling records of all time, moving a reported 30 million copies worldwide. (As of 1993, it was certified by the Record Association of America for sales of 11 million copies in the US, making it the seventh biggest selling LP in history.) It spawned three US No. 1 Bee Gees hits, "Stayin' Alive" (UK No. 4), "Night Fever" (UK No. 1), and "How Deep Is Your Love" (UK No.3). The soundtrack also featured hits written by the Bee Gees for others: "If I Can't Have You," by Yvonne Elliman (US No. 1/UK No. 4) and Tavares' "More Than a Woman" (UK No. 7). In the late '70s, the Bee Gees wrote and produced hits for Samantha Sang ("Emotion," US No. 3, 1977), Frankie Valli ("Grease," US No. 1/UK No. 3, 1978), and Andy Gibb (the youngest Gibb brother, b. Mar. 5, 1958, Manchester, England—d. Mar. 10, 1988, Oxford, England) ("I Just Want to Be Your Everything," US No. 1, 1977; "Love Is Thicker than Water," US No. 1, 1978; "Shadow Dancing," US No. 1 1978; "An Everlasting Love," US No. 5, 1978; "[Our Love] Don't Throw It All Away," US No. 9, 1978).

At one point, five of the Top Ten singles on the *Billboard* Hot 100 had been written, produced, and/or performed by the Bee Gees. They also appeared in the film and on the soundtrack of *Sgt. Pepper's Lonely Hearts Club Band* (US No. 5, 1978), a fiasco. But *Spirits Having Flown* (1979) (UK/US No. 1) contained three more No. 1 hits in the U: "Too Much Heaven" (UK No. 3), "Tragedy" (UK No. 1), and "Love You Inside Out." They also released *Bee Gees Greatest* (US No. 1/UK No. 4, 1979).

In 1980, Barry Gibb wrote and produced Barbra Streisand's *Guilty* album (US No. 1), another multi-million-selling success that contained "Woman in Love" (US/UK No. 1) and their duets on the title track (US No. 3) and "What Kind of Fool" (US No. 10). The Bee Gees themselves, however, suffered from the backlash against disco in the '80s and sustained a second career slump, even though they reverted to their pre-disco sound with 1981's *Living Eyes*. *Staying Alive*, their soundtrack to the sequel to *Saturday Night Fever*, was a US No. 6 hit in 1983. The same year, Barry Gibb produced Kenny Rogers' *Eyes That See in the Dark* (US No. 6) and wrote Rogers's hit duet with Dolly Parton, "Islands in the

Stream" (US No. 1/UK No. 7). In 1982, Barry Gibb worked with Dionne Warwick, resulting in "Heartbreaker" (UK No. 2/US No. 10) and "All the Love in the World" (UK No. 10). In 1985, the Gibb brothers wrote and produced for Diana Ross, scoring with "Chain Reaction" (UK No. 1). (Robin and Barry Gibb also made solo records during this period.) *E.S.P.*, the Bee Gees' first new non-soundtrack studio album in six years, which reunited them with producer Arif Mardin, was released in 1987 and became a substantial hit in the UK (No. 5), along with the single "You Win Again" (No. 1), but flopped in the US. Follow-ups have seen moderate British success, while in America the single "One" (No. 7) returned them to commercial favor in 1989. Their records have sold poorly since, however. — *William Ruhlmann*

The Bee Gee's First / 1967 / PolyGram ✦✦✦
The Bee Gees' latter-day success with disco and other superficial pop pap has caused many to forget that when they first achieved international prominence, they were accomplished and serious singers and songwriters. Robin and Barry Gibb (with occasional help from Maurice) penned all of the material on the first album they recorded after moving to England (they had already previously released quite a few records in Australia). The Bee Gees were both praised and denigrated for emulating the Beatles' harmonies; in fact their songs at this point were quite brooding, even melancholy at times. The string arrangements, skirting the boundary between melodrama and mock-rococo, highlighted the pensive nature of the material and Robin's verging-on-tears vocal delivery on this strong, at times ambitious set. *First* includes the hits "To Love Somebody," "New York Mining Disaster 1941" (which evoked the most Beatle copycat cries), and "Holiday," although "In My Own Time" and "I Can't See Nobody" are overlooked highlights of similar quality. — *Richie Unterberger*

Horizontal / Jan. 1968 / Polydor ✦✦✦
This album is a little more moody than *1st* with its use of minor chords and song structure. At the same time, the Bee Gees continue to grow as songwriters and there is no shortage of good songs. The hit "Massachusetts" pretty much sets the tone for the album; if you like that one, you're sure to like the rest of the album as well. — *Jim Worbois*

Idea / Aug. 1968 / Polydor ✦✦

Odessa / Jan. 1969 / Polydor ✦✦✦✦
Odessa is the Bee Gees' finest moment of the '60s. — *AMG*

● **The Best of the Bee Gees, Vol. 1** / Jun. 1969 / Polydor ✦✦✦✦
The Best of the Bee Gees collects their greatest pop hits from the '60s. — *AMG*

Cucumber Castle / Apr. 1970 / Polydor ✦✦

Two Years On / Jan. 1971 / Polydor/Atco ✦✦✦✦
After a turbulent period in the late '60s, the Bee Gees temporarily packed it in. When they regrouped, the band consisted solely of the three brothers. What resulted was their largest commercial success to date. In addition to featuring "Lonely Days," the Bee Gees' highest-charting single to date and their first gold record, this is a fine record in its own right. It's as strong as any Bee Gees album from their early years and worth looking for. — *Jim Worbois*

Trafalgar / Sep. 1971 / Polydor ✦✦✦
Trafalgar's "How Can You Mend a Broken Heart?" was the Bee Gees' first No. 1 single. Despite this chart success, this record doesn't rate as highly as some of their other albums of this period due to somewhat lackluster material. — *Jim Worbois*

To Whom It May Concern / 1972 / Polydor ✦✦

Life in a Tin Can / Jan. 1973 / Polydor ✦✦
The Bee Gees were now recording in the US (Los Angeles, to be exact) and, if anything, that proved to be a detriment. For the most part, this is a record of "sensitive" ballads, much like everything else coming out of Southern California at the time and, for that reason, doesn't stand up against much of their earlier work. — *Jim Worbois*

The Best of the Bee Gees, Vol. 2 / Jul. 1973 / Polydor ✦✦✦✦
The Best of the Bee Gees, Vol. 2 gathers together the group's biggest and best hits from the early '70s. — *AMG*

Mr. Natural / May 1974 / Polydor ✦

Main Course / May 1975 / Polydor ✦✦✦✦
On *Main Course*, the Bee Gees began incorporating soul into their well-constructed sound, inching the group closer to their watershed disco years. Like most Bee Gees' albums, the material is fairly inconsistent, yet the strongest moments—including the hit singles "Jive Talkin'" and "Nights on Broadway"—rank with the group's best work. — *Stephen Thomas Erlewine*

Children of the World / Sep. 1976 / Polydor ✦✦

● **Bee Gees Gold, Vol. 1** / Oct. 1976 / Polydor ✦✦✦✦
Some of the best post-Beatles pop comes from the Bee Gees' first fertile era. — *Dan Heilman*

☆ **Saturday Night Fever** / Nov. 1977 / RSO ✦✦✦✦✦
One of the biggest-selling albums of all time, this double-disc soundtrack features the Bee Gees hits "Stayin' Alive," "Night Fever," and "How Deep Is Your Love"; Yvonne Elliman's "If I Can't Have You"; and a selection of popular disco hits by Tavares, K.C. & the Sunshine Band, and others. This wasn't only the soundtrack to a film, it was the soundtrack to an era. That era is over, but it's evoked by the music. — *William Ruhlmann*

1963-1966: Birth of Brilliance / 1978 / Festival ✦✦✦✦
Thirty-two-song double CD presents much of the best material from the domestic Excelsior compilations of their early years, as well as some songs that don't appear on those sets. Because of its better sound, this collection has the edge as the best compilation of their early work, though it's hard to find. — *Richie Unterberger*

Spirits Having Flown / Jan. 1979 / RSO ✦✦✦✦

● **Greatest** / Oct. 1979 / RSO ✦✦✦✦
This is the cream of their stunning string of late-'70s hits. — *Dan Heilman*

Living Eyes / 1981 / RSO ✦✦

Staying Alive / Jun. 1983 / RSO ✦✦✦

E.S.P. / Sep. 1987 / Warner Bros. ✦✦

One / Jul. 25, 1989 / Warner Bros. ✦✦✦

Tales from the Brothers Gibb / 1990 / Polydor ✦✦✦
This exhaustive four-disc boxed set contains too much for anyone but hardcore fans. — *Dan Heilman*

High Civilization / Apr. 1991 / Warner Bros. ✦✦

Size Isn't Everything / Nov. 1993 / Polydor ✦✦✦

Bel Canto

Alternative Pop-Rock
The atmospheric, melancholy, somewhat medieval soundscapes of Bel Canto (Italian for "beautiful song") mix a synth-based, chamber-rock sound with a wide range of orchestral and folk instruments and have been compared to the Cocteau Twins. The group hails from Norway and consists of ethereal vocalist Anneli Marian Drecker, plus Nils Johansen and Geir Jennsen. The group claims to draw its inspiration from powerful energy fields, including those of the female and the earth's gravitational pull; additionally, their compositions sometimes draw on world music and the ambient experiments of Brian Eno. Bel Canto released its first album, *White-Out Conditions*, in 1987. — *Steve Huey*

White-Out Conditions / 1987 / Nettwerk ✦✦✦
Bel Canto's first album is refreshing and intriguing. Although it's uneven, it is definitely more than just a search for a new style. — *Vladimir Bogdanov*

● **Birds of Passage** / 1989 / Nettwerk ✦✦✦✦
With completely professional material, it is well-composed and -performed. — *Vladimir Bogdanov*

Shimmering, Warm & Bright / 1992 / Dali ✦✦✦✦
The famous warm, "medieval electronic" sound of Bel Canto reaches the point of elaborate purity on this mature album. — *Vladimir Bogdanov*

Magic Box / Feb. 27, 1996 / Atlantic ✦✦✦

Bell Biv DeVoe

Urban, New Jack R&B
Bell Biv DeVoe was hatched in the minds of its members, New Edition's Ricky Bell, Michael Bivins, and Ronnie DeVoe, upon the departure of lead singer Bobby Brown in 1986. But it wasn't until after the group completed its supporting tour for the album *Heart Break* in 1988 that the trio gave in to the urgings of *Heart Break* producers Jimmy Jam and Terry Lewis and decided to chart its own course. Bell Biv DeVoe enlisted a variety of producers for its debut album, including Jam and Lewis and Public Enemy producers Hank and Keith Shocklee. The results were quite unlike anything in New Edition's repertoire: the beats were funkier, the lyrics and vocals were sexier, and the overall sound had a harder, hip-hop-tinged edge. The album's title track, "Poison," became a No. 3 smash, and it was followed by the equally successful "Do Me!" and the R&B hits "B.B.D. (I Thought It Was Me)," "When Will I See You Smile Again?," and "She's Dope!" The album itself went on to sell over three million copies and was followed by a remix album the next year. Meanwhile, Bivins took some time off to assemble the so-called East Coast Family, discovering and producing debut albums for Another Bad Creation and Boyz II Men. *Hootie Mack*, Bell Biv DeVoe's second proper album, was released in 1993, but didn't make as much of an impact. In 1996, all three members of Bell Biv DeVoe participated in a reunion of the New Edition. — *Steve Huey*

● **Poison** / Mar. 1990 / MCA ✦✦✦✦
BBD describe their style as "R&B on the smooth tip with a hip-hop feel," and that's just what you'll find on this hugely successful debut. Equally adept at sumptuous ballads and big-beat dance thumpers, BBD have

taken Teddy Riley's new jack innovations to both a wider audience and a new creative plateau. —*John Floyd*

Hootie Mack / 1993 / MCA ◆◆◆

Archie Bell & the Drells

b. Sep. 1, 1944, Henderson, TX
Vocals / Soul, Disco
Few groups offered good-time soul music as enjoyable, danceable, and high-spirited as Archie Bell & the Drells. The singer (from Houston, as he was eager to proclaim in the middle of some of his uptempo hits) had a left-field No. 1 smash with the limb-loosening "Tighten Up," which took off right after Bell was drafted. In 1968, Bell (who was able to fit in some recording and performing duties until his stint in the army was over) teamed with emerging Philadelphia soul mavens Kenneth Gamble and Leon Huff, who produced and wrote Bell's material over the next couple years. With sophisticated arrangements and punchy horn charts, dance hits like "I Can't Stop Dancing," "(There's Gonna Be a) Showdown," and "Do the Choo Choo" were instrumental in establishing the sound of Philadelphia as an artistic force. After a fallow period in the early '70s, Bell reunited with Gamble and Huff on the Philadelphia International for a run of successful, discofied dance soul in the mid-'70s. —*Richie Unterberger*

● **Tightening It Up: The Best of Archie Bell & the Drells** / 1994 / Rhino ◆◆◆◆
Twenty of the group's big and small hits, charting their course from Southern-fried soul through the sound of Philadelphia and disco. —*Richie Unterberger*

Chris Bell

b. Jan. 12, 1951, Memphis, TN, d. Dec. 27, 1978, Memphis, TN
Guitar, Vocals / Power-Pop
Memphis singer-songwriter Chris Bell cofounded the power-pop quartet Big Star in 1971, with Alex Chilton. Bell left the group before the release of their second album, *Radio City*, to pursue a solo career. He died in an automobile accident on December 27, 1978. It wasn't until 1992 that Bell's work was released in an album form. —*Rick Clark*

I Am the Cosmos / 1992 / Rykodisc ◆◆◆◆
A collection of the late Chris Bell's solo work, it includes mostly demos. The title track is a brilliant downer (Big Star and Badfinger at half-speed) that opens the album. "You and Your Sister" is a gorgeous heartbreaker, rendered with delicate acoustic guitars and Mellotron and guest vocalist Alex Chilton. Not everything Bell undertakes is so fragile. "I Don't Know," "Make a Scene," and "Fight at the Table" are relentless rockers. Bell's voice may be an acquired taste for some, as it occasionally gets a little whiney. When it does connect with the music, the results can be quite affecting, particularly on "You and Your Sister," "Speed of Sound," and the title track. Ryko has done a great job remastering these tapes, and the packaging is a first-rate labor of love. —*Rick Clark*

William Bell (William Yarborough)

b. Jul. 16, 1937, Memphis, TN
Piano, Vocals / Soul
William Bell was one of the first artists signed to the Stax label during its fledgling years in Memphis, and he greatly influenced the "Stax sound" as both a performer and writer. His self-penned "You Don't Miss Your Water" (1961) almost defined the genre known as country-soul, with the unmistakable gospel feel of Bell's elegant, lilting vocal over a country-church piano figure. It was this marriage of styles that became Bell's trademark at Stax and opened the door for others—most notably Otis Redding (who initially mined the same country-soul vein)—to follow. With the ascent of Redding, Bell's star began to fade somewhat. He continued to record (the beautiful, string-laden "I Forgot to Be Your Lover" in 1968) and, most importantly, to write—(his own "Tribute to a King," written after Redding's death, and Albert King's "Born Under a Bad Sign.")). After Stax's collapse in 1975, Bell moved to Mercury, where he scored his first-ever million-seller with "Tryin' to Love Two." Bell continues to live and work in Memphis. —*Christine Ohlman*

Duets / 1968 / Stax ◆◆◆
In the late '60s, Bell recorded a number of male/female duets with partners Judy Clay, Carla Thomas, and Mavis Staples; the ones with Clay were the most successful, "Private Number" and "My Baby Specializes" becoming modest R&B hits. All of his duet projects are assembled here, along with three solo sides that he cut in the 1970s. It's not among Bell's most striking work, but it's decent pop-soul, closer to Motown in feel than a lot of Stax material. I don't know what the deal is, but the version of "My Baby Specializes" here, though credited to Bell and Clay, only seems to feature Clay, unless that's Bell adding an odd backup grunt here and there. —*Richie Unterberger*

● **The Best of William Bell** / 1988 / Stax ◆◆◆◆
Southern soul singer William Bell's "I Forgot to Be Your Lover" and his cover of Booker T. Jones' "Born Under a Bad Sign" are among the 14 tracks on this collection. —*Roundup Newsletter*

A Little Something Extra / 1992 / Stax ◆◆◆

Belly

Alternative Pop-Rock
Belly's debut album, 1993's *Star*, was one of the major alternative-rock hits of the year, managing to crossover into the mainstream with the minor hit "Feed the Tree." Led by vocalist/guitarist Tanya Donelly, a former member of the Throwing Muses and the Breeders, Belly's music is more straightforward and pop-oriented than her previous bands. The group's melodies are ethereal yet catchy, supported by lush, interweaving guitar hooks. The layered, swirling guitars conceal some dark lyrical undercurrents that save the group from being too precious.

Donelly formed Belly in 1992 with former Muses bassist Fred Abong, adding brothers Tom and Chris Gorman (guitar and drums, respectively) before the group went into the studio to record their debut album. Belly released a series of British singles in 1992 that earned the band a following in both the UK and the US. Abong left the group after the recording of the album; the band recorded a handful of B-sides with various bassists before replacing him with Gail Greenwood in early 1993, after the release of their album.

Star was released in early 1993 and immediately became an alternative hit, selling more than all of the previous Muses and Breeders releases combined. "Feed the Tree," the first single from the album became a hit and the group embarked on a successful tour that ran throughout 1993. Several other alternative-radio hits followed, including "Slow Dog" and "Gepetto."

Belly returned in 1995 with *King*, their first album recorded with Greenwood. *King* failed to meet the high expectations raised by *Star*. "Now They'll Sleep" became a moderate hit on alternative radio, as did "Superconnected," but the album didn't sell in numbers comparable to *Star*, slipping out of the charts two months after its release. —*Stephen Thomas Erlewine*

● **Star** / Jan. 1993 / 4AD ◆◆◆◆
Driven by four superb singles—"Gepetto," "Feed the Tree," "Slow Dog," and "Dusted"—Belly's debut album is a terrific set of effortlessly melodic guitar-pop, alternating between bright pop songs and atmospheric ballads. Even with her sweetest melodies, lead singer/guitarist Tanya Donelly has enough realism and dark fantasies in her songs to keep *Star* from being cloying or saccharine. In fact, her songs are so good that it's a wonder she didn't start her own band sooner. —*Stephen Thomas Erlewine*

King / 1995 / Sire/Reprise ◆◆◆

Pat Benatar (Pat Andrzejewski)

b. Jan. 10, 1953, Brooklyn, NY
Vocals / Pop-Rock, Arena Rock
Benatar's polished mainstream pop-rock made her one of the more popular female vocalists of the early '80s. Although she came on like an arena rocker with her power chords, tough sexuality, and powerful vocals, her music was straight pop-rock underneath all the bluster.

Benatar began singing in New York in the late '70s; eventually she was discovered by Rick Newman at his "Catch a Rising Star" club in 1979. Under the management of Newman, Benatar signed with Chrysalis Records, releasing her debut album, *In the Heat of the Night*, that same year. The record launched her string of hit singles with the No. 23 "Heartbreaker." Featuring the Top Ten hit "Hit Me with Your Best Shot," Benatar's second album, 1980's *Crimes of Passion* was a greater success, selling over four million copies and winning the Grammy for Best Female Rock Vocal Performance. Her third album, *Precious Time* (1981), reached No. 1 on the album charts; a single from the album called "Fire and Ice" won Benatar another Grammy. She married her producer/guitarist Neil Geraldo in 1982, the same year the platinum *Get Nervous* was released. Benatar released a live album, *Live from Earth*, the following year; it contained one of her biggest hits, "Love Is a Battlefield." Although 1984's *Tropico* contained her biggest hit "We Belong" (No. 5), the album was her lowest-charting to date.

"Invincible" (1985), taken from *The Legend of Billie Jean* soundtrack, was her last Top Ten hit. Even though it included the hit single "Sex as a Weapon," Benatar's *Seven the Hard Way* (1985) became her first album not to go platinum—it didn't even go gold. She took a couple of years off before returning with *Wide Awake in Dreamland* in 1988; it didn't chart as high as *Seven the Hard Way*, yet it earned a gold record, as did *Best Shots*, a greatest-hits collection released the following year.

Benatar didn't record a new album until 1991, when she released the blues record, *True Love*. It proved a critical and commercial disaster, prompting her to return to her mainstream rock on 1993's *Gravity's*

Rainbow; nevertheless, the reversal in musical direction didn't return her to the top of the charts. —*Stephen Thomas Erlewine*

● **Best Shots** / Nov. 1989 / Chrysalis ✦✦✦✦
Multi-Grammy winner Benatar has vocal range to spare on this hits collection, including her rockers "Heartbreaker," "Fire and Ice," and "Hell Is for Children." —*Donna DiChario*

All Fired Up: The Very Best of Pat Benatar / 1994 / Chrysalis ✦✦✦✦
This double-disc collection, featuring all of her hits and popular album tracks, is the definitive collection of the popular mainstream rocker. It trims away the fat from her spotty albums, leaving the best material she recorded throughout her career. Nevertheless, it features too much material for most listeners and is only worthwhile to dedicated fans. —*Stephen Thomas Erlewine*

16 Classic Performances / 1996 / EMI ✦✦✦✦
If you're serious about your Benatar, you'll probably aim for the two-CD *All Fired Up* anthology. This 16-track single-disc compilation has many of her biggest hits (with some notable ones, like "Treat Me Right," omitted), and previously unreleased live versions of "Helter Skelter" and "Hit Me with Your Best Shot" from the early '80s. —*Richie Unterberger*

Brook Benton (Benjamin Franklin Peay)
....

b. Sep. 19, 1931, Camden, SC, **d.** Apr. 9, 1988, New York, NY
Vocals / R&B
Silky smooth: that was Brook Benton's byword from his first record to his very last, as the singer parlayed his rich baritone pipes into seven No. 1 R&B hits and eight Top Ten items. Stints on the gospel circuit preceded Benton's first secular session for Okeh in 1953, but his career didn't begin to take off until he teamed with writer/producer Clyde Otis. Benton cowrote and sang hundreds of demos for other artists before frequent collaborator Otis signed his friend to Mercury; together they pioneered a lush, violin-studded variation on the standard R&B sound, which beautifully showcased Benton's intimate vocals.

Benton crashed the top spot on the R&B charts in early 1959 with his moving "It's Just a Matter of Time," then rapidly encored with three more R&B chart-toppers—"Thank You Pretty Baby," "So Many Ways," and "Kiddio." Pairing with Mercury labelmate Dinah Washington, their delightful repartee on "Baby (You've Got What It Takes)" and "A Rockin' Good Way" paced the R&B lists in 1960.

The early '60s were a prolific period for Benton, but he left Mercury a few years later and bounced between labels before reemerging with the atmospheric Tony Joe White ballad "Rainy Night in Georgia" on Cotillion in 1970. Benton later made a halfhearted attempt to cash in on the disco craze, but his hitmaking reign was at an end long before his death in 1988. —*Bill Dahl*

● **Anthology** / 1986 / Rhino ✦✦✦✦
This is a slightly more modest version than the *40 Greatest.* —*Hank Davis*

40 Greatest Hits / 1989 / Mercury ✦✦✦✦
Everything you need to know about Benton's bluesy, sexy pop music is included here, in the duets with Dinah Washington. —*Hank Davis*

Chuck Berry (Charles Edward Anderson Berry)
....

b. Oct. 18, 1926, St. Louis, MO
Guitar, Vocals / Rock'n'Roll
Of all the early breakthrough rock'n'roll artists, none is more important to the development of the music than Chuck Berry. He is its greatest songwriter, the main shaper of its instrumental voice, one of its greatest guitarists and one of its greatest performers. Quite simply, without him, there would be no Beatles, Rolling Stones, Beach Boys, Bob Dylan nor a myriad others. There would be no standard "Chuck Berry guitar intro," the instrument's clarion call to get the joint rockin' in any setting. The clippety-clop rhythms of rockabilly would not have been mainstreamed into the now standard 4/4 rock'n'roll beat. There would be no obsessive wordplay by modern-day tunesmiths; in fact, the whole history (and artistic level) of rock'n'roll songwriting would have been much poorer without him. Like Brian Wilson said, he wrote "all of the great songs and came up with all the rock'n'roll beats." Those who do not claim him as a seminal influence or profess a liking for his music and showmanship show their ignorance of rock's development as well as his place as the music's first great creator. Elvis may have fueled rock'n'roll's imagery, but Chuck Berry was its heartbeat and original mindset.

He was born Charles Edward Anderson Berry to a large family in St. Louis. A bright pupil, Berry developed a love for poetry and hard blues early on, winning a high school talent contest with a guitar and vocal rendition of Jay McShann's big band number, "Confessin' the Blues." With some local tutelage from the neighborhood barber, Chuck progressed from a four-string tenor guitar up to an official six-string model and was soon working the local East St. Louis club scene, sitting in everywhere he could. He quickly found out that Black audiences liked a wide variety of music and set himself to the task of being able to reproduce as

much of it as possible. What he found they *really* liked—besides the blues and Nat King Cole tunes—was the sight and sound of a Black man playing White hillbilly music, and Berry's showmanlike flair, coupled with his seemingly inexhaustible supply of fresh verses to old favorites, quickly made him a name on the circuit. In 1954, he ended up taking over pianist Johnny Johnson's small combo and a residency at the Cosmopolitan Club soon made the Chuck Berry Trio the top attraction in the Black community, with Ike Turner's Kings of Rhythm their only real competition.

But Berry had bigger ideas; he yearned to make records, and a trip to Chicago netted a two-minute conversation with his idol Muddy Waters, who encouraged him to approach Chess Records. Upon listening to Berry's homemade demo tape, label president Leonard Chess professed a liking for a hillbilly tune on it named "Ida Red" and quickly scheduled a session for May 21, 1955. During the session the title was changed to "Maybellene" and rock'n'roll history was born. Although the record only made it to the mid-20s on the *Billboard* pop chart, its overall influence was massive and groundbreaking in its scope. Here was finally a Black rock'n'roll record with across-the-board appeal, embraced by White teenagers and Southern hillbilly musicians (a young Elvis Presley—still a full year from national stardom—quickly added it to his stage show), that for once couldn't be successfully covered by a pop singer like Snooky Lanson on *Your Hit Parade.* Part of the secret to its originality was Chuck's blazing 24-bar guitar solo in the middle of it, the imaginative rhyme schemes in the lyrics and the sheer thump of the record, all signaling that rock'n'roll had arrived and it was no fad. Helping to put the record over to a White teenage audience was the highly influential New York disc jockey Alan Freed, who had been given part of the writers' credit by Chess in return for his spins and plugs. But to his credit, Freed was also the first White dee jay-promoter to consistently use Berry on his rock'n'roll stage show extravaganzas at the Brooklyn Fox and Paramount theaters (playing to predominately White audiences) and when Hollywood came calling a year or so later, also made sure that Chuck appeared with him in *Rock! Rock! Rock!, Go, Johnny, Go!,* and *Mister Rock'n'Roll.* Within a year's time, Chuck had gone from a local St. Louis blues picker making $15 a night to an overnight sensation commanding over a hundred times that, arriving at the dawn of a new strain of popular music called rock'n'roll.

The hits started coming thick and fast over the next few years, every one of them about to become a classic of the genre; "Roll Over Beethoven," "Thirty Days," "Too Much Monkey Business," "Brown Eyed Handsome Man," "You Can't Catch Me," "School Day," "Carol," "Back in the USA," "Little Queenie," "Memphis, Tennessee," "Johnny B. Goode" and the tune that defined the moment perfectly, "Rock and Roll Music." Berry was not only in constant demand, touring the country on mixed package shows and appearing on television and in movies, but smart enough to know exactly what to do with the spoils of a suddenly successful show business career. He started investing heavily in St. Louis area real estate and, ever one to push the envelope, opened up a racially mixed nightspot called the Club Bandstand in 1958 to the consternation of uptight locals. These were not the plans of your average R&B singers who contented themselves with a wardrobe of flashy suits, a new Cadillac, and the nicest house in the Black section. Berry was smart with plenty of business savvy and was already making plans to open an amusement park in nearby Wentzville. When the St. Louis hierarchy found out that an underage hat-check girl Berry hired had also set up shop as a prostitute at a nearby hotel, trouble came down on Berry like a sledgehammer on a fly. Charged with transporting a minor over state lines (the Mann Act), Berry endured two trials and was sentenced to federal prison for two years as a result.

He emerged from prison a moody, embittered man. But two very important things had happened in his absence. First, British teenagers had discovered his music and were making his old songs hits all over again. Second, and perhaps most important, America had discovered the Beatles and the Rolling Stones, both of whom based their music on Berry's style, with the Stones' early albums looking like a Berry song list. Rather than being resigned to the has-been circuit, Berry found himself in the midst of a worldwide beat boom with his music as the centerpiece. He came back with a clutch of hits ("Nadine," "No Particular Place to Go," "You Never Can Tell"), toured Britain in triumph, and appeared on the big screen with his British disciples in the groundbreaking *T.A.M.I. Show* in 1964.

Berry had moved with the times and found a new audience in the bargain and when the cries of yeah-yeah-yeah were replaced with peace signs, Berry altered his live act to include a passel of slow blues and quickly became a fixture on the festival and hippie ballroom circuit. After a disastrous stint with Mercury Records, he returned to Chess in the early '70s and scored his last hit with a live version of the salacious nursery rhyme, "My Ding a Ling," yielding Berry his first "official" gold record. By decade's end, he was as in demand as ever, working every oldies revival show, TV special and festival that was thrown his way. But once again, troubles with the law reared their ugly head and 1979 saw

Berry headed back to prison , this time for income tax evasion. Upon release this time, the creative days of Chuck Berry seemed to have come to an end. He appeared as himself in the Alan Freed biopic, *American Hot Wax*, and was inducted into the Rock & Roll Hall of Fame, but stead-fastly refused to record any new material or even issue a live album. His live performances became increasingly erratic, with Berry working with terrible backup bands and turning in sloppy, out-of-tune performances that did much to tarnish his reputation with younger fans and oldtimers alike. In 1987, he published his first book, *Chuck Berry: The Autobiogra-phy* and the same year saw the film release of what will likely be his last-ing legacy, the rockumentary *Hail! Hail! Rock 'n' Roll*, which included live footage from a 60th-birthday concert with Keith Richards as musical director and the usual bevy of superstars coming out for guest turns. But for all of his offstage exploits and seemingly ongoing troubles with the law, Chuck Berry remains the epitome of rock 'n' roll, and his music will endure long after his private escapades have faded from memory. Because when it comes down to his music, perhaps John Lennon said it best, "If you were going to give rock 'n' roll another name, you might call it 'Chuck Berry.'" *—Cub Koda*

After School Session / 1958 / Chess ✦✦✦✦
While Chuck Berry's first album, *After School Session*, featured only one hit single, the Top Ten "School Day," several of the songs became rock 'n' roll standards, including "Too Much Monkey Business," "No Money Down," and "Brown Eyed Handsome Man." *After School Session* also featured a couple of stylistic variations, including the calypso-flavored "Havana Moon" and the straight blues of "Wee, Wee Hours." *—Stephen Thomas Erlewine*

One Dozen Berrys / 1958 / Chess ✦✦✦✦
The core of *One Dozen Berrys*, Chuck Berry's second album, was formed by the hit single "Sweet Little Sixteen," "Oh, Baby Doll," and "Rock and Roll Music." Besides "Reelin' and Rockin'," which failed as a single, not many of the album tracks became rock 'n' roll standards, yet the quality of the record is quite high, with "It Don't Take but a Few Minutes" and "Low Feeling" being particularly strong. *—Stephen Thomas Erlewine*

Is on Top / 1959 / Chess ✦✦✦✦
Berry's best '50s Chess album features many of his biggest hits, plus atmospheric instrumentals like "Blues for Hawaiians." *—Cub Koda*

Rockin' at the Hops / 1960 / Chess ✦✦✦

New Juke Box Hits / 1961 / Chess ✦✦✦

☆ **St. Louis to Liverpool** / 1964 / Chess ✦✦✦✦✦
Berry's first album recorded after his release from prison shows him doing more than just picking up where he left off. "No Particular Place to Go," "You Never Can Tell," "Promised Land," and "Little Marie" (his sequel to "Memphis") all charted during 1964 and present Berry doing a more mature brand of the sound he pioneered. As though aware of the British Invasion acts that were (in the cases of the Beatles and the Rolling Stones) covering his stuff extremely well, he rose to the occasion by delivering a group of more complex songs that still retain his classic sound. Those four singles and a brace of album originals make this one of Berry's most successful and enduring albums. *—Bruce Eder*

The London Sessions / 1972 / Chess ✦✦✦

★ **The Great Twenty-Eight** / 1982 / Chess ✦✦✦✦✦
A single-disc compilation of Berry's original Chess greats, every one a gem: "Maybellene," "Johnny B. Goode," "Roll Over Beethoven," "Sweet Little Sixteen," and "Little Queenie" are the music the Beatles and others cut their teeth on. Beyond essential. *—Cub Koda*

Rock 'n' Roll Rarities / 1986 / Chess ✦✦✦✦
On this follow-up to *The Great Twenty-Eight*, the songs are familiar, but the versions are not. Delving into the Chess Records archives, producer Steve Hoffman has come up with 20 tracks, many in unreleased or unusual versions. Some are demos, some are stereo recordings of songs usually heard in mono. Hoffman has remixed many of them, bringing up the '50s and '60s sound quality to near-'80s standard. Start with *The Great Twenty-Eight*, but come to this collection for interesting new ways to hear the old Berry favorites. *—William Ruhlmann*

More Rock 'n' Roll Rarities from the Golden Era of Chess Record / Aug. 1986 / Chess ✦✦✦

☆ **The Chess Box** / 1988 / Chess ✦✦✦✦✦
Over the course of three compact discs, *The Chess Box* contains all the highlights from Chuck Berry's career, including all of the hit singles. In addition to the familiar items, which are all included here, there are numerous tracks that are lesser-known but equally as good. That's partic-ularly true on the stellar first two discs, where album tracks, B-sides, and forgotten singles like "Dowbound Train," "Drifting Heart," "Havana Moon," "Betty Jean," and "The Thirteen Question Method" get equal space with "Maybellene," "Thirty Days," "No Money Down," "Roll Over Beethoven," "Too Much Monkey Business," "Brown Eyed Handsome Man," "School Day," "Rock & Roll Music," "Sweet Little Sixteen," "Johnny B. Goode," and "Carol." Toward the end of the set, the quality of the mate-

rial begins to sag a bit, but there are still forgotten gems like "Tulane" that prove that Berry's songwriting hadn't completely dried up. *The Great Twenty Eight* remains the definitive hits collection, but *The Chess Box* is an absolutely essential item for any serious fan, either of Chuck Berry or rock 'n' roll. *—Stephen Thomas Erlewine*

Missing Berries / 1990 / Chess ✦✦✦

Big Black

Alternative Pop-Rock
Proudly and self-consciously abrasive, Big Black's music is polarizing: either you think that Steve Albini's relentlessly thin, metallic, emotion-less guitar grind and distorted vocals is an uncompromising work of art or you think it's self-indulgent crap. The band's clinical noise and gro-tesque, often misogynist, lyrics easily made them the most extreme, nihilistic band in the American underground in the mid-'80s. After recording three EPs with an unstable lineup, Big Black recorded its first full album with Albini and Santiago Durango on guitar, Dave Lovering on bass and drum machine. None of their recordings show much pro-gression; instead, the band gets harder and nastier on each subsequent record. Before they recorded their final and best album, *Songs About Fucking*, Durango left the group to study law; Albini pulled the plug on the band shortly afterward.

Although Big Black's lifespan was short, Albini's influence on the American independent music scene of the late '80s and '90s has been substantial. After Big Black's breakup, he formed the equally uncompro-mising Rapeman, but Albini's real influence has been through his numerous productions. Over the years he has produced literally hun-dreds of bands; most of them are justifiably unknown, but some are quite famous—including the Pixies, the Breeders, Urge Overkill, PJ Har-vey, and Nirvana. Albini's simple production functions as a type of photo-graph, capturing the band in an aural black and white; his production shows all of the band's strengths, as well as all of their faults. He fre-quently cuts the bass levels to a minimum, leaving only a harsh guitar grind, which makes his records a bit wearing to listen to. Many young bands of the '90s have embraced his signature guitar grind, as well as his strident punk-rock ethics, as a reaction to alternative music's move into the mainstream. *—Stephen Thomas Erlewine*

Atomizer / 1986 / Homestead ✦✦✦✦

Hammer Party / 1986 / Homestead ✦✦✦

The Rich Man's 8-Track Tape / 1987 / Touch & Go ✦✦✦✦
Rich Man's 8-Track combines the *Headache* EP and *Atomizer* album on one disc. *Atomizer*, the band's first full-length album, is a self-consciously aggressive and noxious onslaught of guitars and drums, wallowing in its own depravity; for the first time, Albini and Company achieve the sound they were aiming for. *Headache* isn't as good; it's a retread of *Atomizer* without any of the surprise. *—Stephen Thomas Erlewine*

● **Songs About Fucking** / 1987 / Touch & Go ✦✦✦✦
Easily the best album Big Black ever recorded. The bleak noise of *Songs About Fucking* matches the empty nihilism of Albini's ranting lyrics; for once, the sheer force of their music actually makes the band seem threat-ening, scary, and dangerous. *—Stephen Thomas Erlewine*

Big Bopper (Jiles Perry Richardson)

b. Oct. 24, 1930, Sabine Pass, TX, **d.** Feb. 3, 1959, Clear Lake, IA
Vocals / Rock 'n' Roll
Legendary as one of the three rock greats to die in the tragic 1959 Clear Lake, IA, plane crash that also claimed the lives of Buddy Holly and Ritchie Valens, the Big Bopper (born Jiles Perry Richardson) had just established himself as a rock hitmaker with the rollicking "Chantilly Lace." Born in the heart of Texas, Richardson grew up in Beaumont and changed his first name to Jape. He broke into show biz as a DJ over KTRM radio, where he coined the nickname "The Big Bopper." He began recording for Mercury in 1957, his animated baritone scaling pop playl-ists the next year with "Chantilly Lace"—easily his top seller—and the equally raucous novelty "Big Bopper's Wedding." Richardson wrote "White Lightning," a huge country hit for George Jones, and Johnny Pre-ston's No. 1 smash "Running Bear." *—Bill Dahl*

● **Hellooo Baby!: Best of Big Bopper, 1954-59** / 1989 / Rhino ✦✦✦✦
Hellooo Baby! The Best of the Big Bopper, 1954-1959 is a single-CD compilation of The Bopper's finest, including "Chantilly Lace," "Little Red Riding Hood," and "The Big Bopper's Wedding." It's wild and fun. *—Cub Koda*

Big Brother & the Holding Company

Blues-Rock, Psychedelic
Big Brother are primarily remembered as the group that gave Janis Jop-lin her start. There's no denying that Joplin was by far the band's most striking asset, and that Big Brother would never have made a significant impression if they hadn't been fortunate enough to add her to their

lineup shortly after forming. But Big Brother also occupy a significant place in the history of San Francisco psychedelic rock, as one of the bands that best captured the era's loosest, reckless, and indulgent qualities in its high-energy mutations of blues and folk-rock.

Big Brother were formed in 1965 in the Haight-Ashbury; by the time Joplin joined in mid-1966, the lineup was Sam Andrews and James Gurley on guitar, Peter Albin on bass, and David Getz on drums. Joplin, a recent arrival from Texas, entered the band at the instigation of Chet Helms, who (other than Bill Graham) was the most important San Francisco rock promoter. Big Brother, like the Grateful Dead and Quicksilver Messenger Service, were not great songwriters or singers. They didn't entirely welcome Joplin's presence at first, and Joplin did not dominate the group right away, sharing the lead vocals with other members.

It soon became evident to both band and audience that Joplin's fiery wail—mature and emotionally wrenching, even at that early stage—had to be spotlighted to make Big Brother a contender. But Big Brother weren't superfluous to the effort, interpreting folk and blues with an inventive (if sometimes sloppy) eclecticism that often gave way to distorted guitar jamming, and matching Joplin's passion with a high-spirited, anything-goes ethos of their own.

Big Brother catapulted themselves into national attention with their performance at the Monterey Pop Festival in June 1967, particularly with Joplin's galvanizing interpretation of "Ball and Chain" (which was a highlight of the film of the event). High-powered management and record label bids rolled in immediately, but unfortunately the group had tied themselves up in a bad contract with the small Mainstream label, at a time where they were stranded on the road and needed cash. Their one Mainstream album (released in 1967) actually isn't bad at all, containing some of their stronger cuts, such as "Down on Me" and "Coo Coo." It didn't fully capture the band's strengths, and with the help of new high-powered manager Albert Grossman, they extricated themselves from the Mainstream deal and signed with Columbia. The one Big Brother album for Columbia that featured Joplin, *Cheap Thrills*, wasn't completed without problems of its own. John Simon found the band so difficult to work with that he withdrew his production credit from the final LP, which was assembled from both studio sessions and live material (recorded for an aborted concert album). *Cheap Thrills* nonetheless went to No. 1 when it was finally released, and though it, too, was an erratic affair, it contained some of the best moments of acid rock's glory days, including "Ball and Chain," "Summertime," and "Piece of My Heart."

Cheap Thrills made Big Brother superstars, a designation that was short-lived. By the end of 1968, Joplin had decided to go solo, a move from which neither she nor Big Brother ever fully recovered. That's putting matters too simply: Joplin never found a backing band as sympathetic, but did record some excellent material in the remaining two years of her life. Big Brother, on the other hand, had the wind totally knocked out of their sails. Although they did re-form for a while in the early '70s with different singers (indeed, they continue to perform in watered-down variations today), nothing would ever be the same. —*Richie Unterberger*

Big Brother & the Holding Company / 1967 / Columbia ✦✦✦
Big Brother's debut LP was a low-budget quickie, but it included a Joplin classic in the Top 50 hit "Down on Me" and was a good example of San Francisco psychedelia. —*William Ruhlmann*

★ **Cheap Thrills** / Aug. 1968 / Columbia ✦✦✦✦✦
Cheap Thrills, the major-label debut of Janis Joplin, was one of the most eagerly anticipated, and one of the most successful, albums of 1968. Joplin and Big Brother had earned extensive press notice ever since they played the Monterey Pop Festival in June 1967, but their only recorded work was a poorly produced, self-titled Mainstream album, and they spent a year getting out of their contract with Mainstream in order to sign with Columbia while demand built. When *Cheap Thrills* appeared in August 1968, it shot into the charts, reaching No. 1 and going gold within a couple of months, while "Piece of My Heart" became a Top 40 hit. Joplin, with her ear- (and vocal cord-) shredding voice, was the obvious standout. Nobody had ever heard singing as emotional, as desperate, as determined, as loud as Joplin's, and *Cheap Thrills* was her greatest moment. Big Brother's backup, typical of the guitar-dominated sound of San Francisco psychedelia, made up in enthusiasm what it lacked in precision. But everybody knew who the real star was, and Joplin played her last gig with Big Brother while the album was still on top of the charts. Neither she nor the band would ever equal it. Heard today, *Cheap Thrills* is a musical time capsule and remains a showcase for one of rock's most distinctive singers. —*William Ruhlmann*

Be a Brother / Oct. 1970 / Columbia ✦✦
Live / 1984 / Rhino ✦✦
Cheaper Thrills / 1984 / Made to Last ✦✦

Big Star

Power-Pop, Pop-Rock
Next to the Velvet Underground, Memphis's Big Star is the grandaddy of

all cult groups. The crisp, succinct pop found on their first two albums was ignored upon release in the early '70s, but by the '80s, Big Star's sound was everywhere. Everyone from the dB's, R.E.M., and the Replacements to Tommy Keene, Matthew Sweet, Teenage Fanclub, and Primal Scream has integrated Big Star's formula into their own styles, and this has turned Big Star-cofounder Alex Chilton (b. Dec. 28, 1950, Memphis, TN) into a cult icon. The group was formed by Chris Bell (b. Jan. 12, 1951, Memphis, TN, d. Dec. 27, 1978, Memphis, TN) in 1971 and, in addition to singer/guitarists Chilton and Bell, featured bassist Andy Hummell (b. Jan. 26, 1951, Memphis, TN) and drummer Jody Stephens (b. Oct. 4, 1952). Although Bell was living in the home of the blues and soul, it was the Anglo-pop stylings of the Beatles and the Kinks that rang his bell. Alex Chilton, former vocalist for the Box Tops, shared Bell's affection for Brit-pop and joined the group, rechristened Big Star after a local supermarket chain.

With producer Terry Manning, the group recorded *No.1 Record* in 1972, released on the studio's in-house Ardent label at a time when rock had become tediously pompous and self-indulgent. It was well-received in the press, and seemed like a radio natural, but poor distribution squelched whatever hit potential it had.

Chris Bell, disappointed with the poor reception of his band's debut, struck out on his own in 1972. Bell, who shared vocal and writing credits on the first album, died in a car wreck before he was able to release his solo work. His sound was equally idiosyncratic, remaining distinctly flavored by the British sound. Most of his work has since been released on a Rykodisc collection called *I Am the Cosmos*.

Chilton was left to mastermind the blistering *Radio City*. The lush charm of *No.1 Record* was replaced by Chilton's slashing, skewered guitar runs and his mangy, stray-cat vocals. The album was loaded with would-be classics ("September Gurls," "Back of a Car," "You Get What You Deserve") but again, the album was poorly distributed and fell between the cracks.

Disenchanted with the politics of the music business, and suffering from drug and alcohol abuse, Chilton hooked up with Memphis producer Jim Dickinson and vented his spleen on *Third/Sister Lovers*, recorded in 1974 but shelved until 1978. More a Chilton solo project than a group effort, the album was an erratic but sometimes brilliant emotional outcry that balanced the beautiful ("Stroke It Noel," "Blue Light") with the horrific ("Holocaust," "Kangaroo").

With the demise of Big Star, lead singer Alex Chilton pursued a renegade solo career that has taken him full circle from untamed reckless garage rock to his earthy mid-Southern musical R&B roots.

The effervescent, near-perfect guitar pop found on *No.1 Record* and *Radio City* have maintained their vitality, making them legitimate rock classics that deserve more than their cult status. It is fair to say that, in spite of almost nonexistent commercial success, Big Star has been an important influence on many of the post-punk/power-pop bands since the late '70s. —*Rick Clark*

#1 Record / 1972 / Ardent ✦✦✦✦
The problem with coming in late on an artwork lauded as "influential" is that you've probably encountered the work it influenced first, so its truly innovative qualities are lost. Thus, if you are hearing Big Star's debut album for the first time decades after its release, you may be reminded of Tom Petty and the Heartbreakers or R.E.M., who came after—that is, if you don't think of the Byrds and the Beatles, circa 1965. What was remarkable about *No.1 Record* in 1972 was that nobody except Big Star (and maybe Badfinger and the Raspberries) wanted to sound like this—simple, light pop with sweet harmonies and jangly guitars. Since then, dozens of bands have rediscovered those pleasures. But in a way, that's an advantage because, whatever freshness is lost across the years, Big Star's craft is only confirmed. These are sturdy songs, feelingly performed, and once you get beyond the style to the content, you'll still be impressed. —*William Ruhlmann*

Radio City / 1974 / Ardent ✦✦✦✦
Largely lacking co-leader Chris Bell, Big Star's second album also lacked something of the pop sweetness (especially the harmonies) of *No.1 Record*. What it possessed was Alex Chilton's urgency and sometimes desperation) on songs that made his case as a genuine rock 'n' roll eccentric. If *No.1 Record* had a certain pop perfection that brought everything together, *Radio City* was the sound of everything falling apart, which proved at least as compelling. —*William Ruhlmann*

☆ **Third/Sister Lovers** / 1978 / Rykodisc ✦✦✦✦✦
Basically an Alex Chilton solo project, it is aided by remaining bandmate Jody Stephens (drums) and a slew of Memphis players. Chilton, frustrated at the music biz and career let-downs, enlisted producer Jim Dickinson to aid in this creative tightrope-walk without a net. The result is a listening experience that's as uncompromisingly harrowing as Neil Young's *Tonight's the Night*. Not for the casual listener, it's still essential in any serious rock listener's collection. Never really finished, the album has been released several times under different titles and with different tracks since it first appeared under the name *Third* on PVC Records

(7903) in 1978. The version currently in print, Rykodisc RCD-10220, was released February 21, 1992; it resequences the material and features more of it than any earlier version, including two previously unreleased tracks. —*Rick Clark and William Ruhlmann*

★ **#1 Record/Radio City** / 1992 / Stax ✦✦✦✦✦
Their first two albums (1972, 1974) were loaded with amazing songs and performances. Mid-period Beatles, Kinks, and Byrds turned inside out and regurgitated into a unique sound. A must-own for any lover of Anglo-pop-rock. —*Rick Clark*

Big Star Live / Feb. 21, 1992 / Rykodisc ✦✦✦

Columbia: Live at Missouri University / Sep. 14, 1993 / Zoo ✦✦

Birthday Party

Post-Punk
Birthday Party was one of the darkest and most challenging post-punk groups to emerge in the early '80s, creating bleak and noisy soundscapes that provided the perfect setting for vocalist Nick Cave's difficult, disturbing stories of religion, violence, and perversity. Under the direction of Cave and guitarist Rowland S. Howard, the band tore through reams of blues and rockabilly licks, spitting out hellacious feedback and noise at an unrelenting pace. As the band's career progressed, Cave's vision got darker and their songs alternated between dirges to blistering sonic assaults.

Originally, the Australian band was called the Boys Next Door, comprising Cave, Howard, Mick Harvey (guitar, drums, organ, piano), bassist Tracy Pew, and drummer Phil Calvert. After the album *Door Door* and *Hee Haw* EP under that name, the band moved to London and switched their name to the deceptively benign Birthday Party. Once they arrived in Britain, the group's demented, knotty post-punk began to gel. They released their first international album, *Prayers on Fire*, in 1981, earning critical praise in the UK and US. While the band was preparing to record the follow-up, Pew was jailed for drunk driving; former Magazine member Barry Adamson, Harry Howard, and Chris Walsh filled in for the absent Pew on 1982's *Junkyard*.

After the release of *Junkyard*, the band fired Calvert and moved to Germany, where they began collaborating with such experimental post-punk acts as Lydia Lunch and Einsturzende Neubaten. Harvey left Birthday Party in the summer of 1983. The group briefly continued with drummer Des Heffner, but they soon disbanded after a final concert in Melbourne, Australia. Cave had the most successful solo career, recording a series of albums in the '80s and '90s that maintained his status as a popular cult figure; Harvey joined Cave's backing band, the Bad Seeds. Howard joined Crime and the City Solution, which also featured his brother Harry. —*Stephen Thomas Erlewine*

Prayers on Fire / 1981 / 4AD ✦✦✦✦
Howling, hellacious mangled art-noise. Surefire. —*John Dougan*

Drunk on the Pope's Blood / 1981 / 4AD ✦✦✦

Junkyard / 1982 / Nesak ✦✦✦

A Collection / 1985 / Missing Link ✦✦✦✦
A Collection draws from Birthday Party's *Junkyard* and *Prayers on Fire* albums, adding a few tracks from the *Hee Haw* EP and some alternate takes. The compilation has also been issued under the title *The Best and the Rarest* and provides an effective introduction to the band. —*Stephen Thomas Erlewine*

● **Hits** / 1992 / 4AD ✦✦✦✦
As an album title, *Hits* is an intentionally ironic misnomer for one of Australia's most influential rock bands of the late '70s and early '80s. Having "hits" was the furthest thing from Birthday Party's collective mind over the course of five tumultuous years that followed the group's move to England from Down Under; the members reviled anything that hinted at mainstream acceptance. Ten years on, the intensity of this music is still frightening. It's a dense, mutant hybrid that evolved from punk, progressive-rock, funk, and improvisational jazz, without directly owning up to any of these base materials. Vocalist Nick Cave (who has gone on to an equally creative solo career) didn't just sing about society's dark, depraved underbelly, he lived the experience right there on disc and on stage. —*Roch Parisien*

Björk

Keyboards, Vocals / Alternative Pop-Rock, Club-Dance
When the Sugarcubes dissolved after a string of unsuccessful albums in the early '90s, lead singer Björk Gudmundsottir rejected the band's arty guitar-rock pretensions, pursuing a dance-oriented solo career. With producer Nellee Hooper, Björk released the innovative *Debut* in 1993. Featuring the singles "Human Behaviour," "Venus as a Boy," and "Big Time Sensuality," the record became an international hit as well as establishing her as a major creative force in dance music. As she was recording the follow-up to *Debut*, Björk co-wrote the title track to Madonna's 1994 album, *Bedtime Stories*. Björk released her second album, *Post*, in the

summer of 1995; it was a hit upon its release, debuting in the American Top 40 and the British Top Ten, as well reaching the Top Ten in several European countries. —*Stephen Thomas Erlewine*

● **Debut** / Jul. 1993 / Elektra ✦✦✦✦
Björk's first album since the breakup of the Sugarcubes outshines any of her old group's albums. Covering everything from dance-pop and club music to jazzy torch songs, *Debut* reveals Björk as a fine songwriter, capable of writing wrenching ("Like Someone in Love") and intoxicating pop songs ("There's More to Life Than This"). Throughout the record, Björk's thin voice shows a surprising amount of versatility. *Debut* is one of the strongest, most musically varied and consistent dance records of the '90s. —*Stephen Thomas Erlewine*

Post / 1995 / Elektra ✦✦✦✦
Debut was a worldwide success, raising the expectations for Björk's second album, *Post*. Björk doesn't depart from the innovations of *Debut*, she refines them, pushing the jazz/dance fusions into different territories, like the big-band explosions of "It's Oh So Quiet" and the trancey "Possibly Maybe." While it's more subtle and not quite as infectious as *Debut*, the album is more accomplished and varied, switching from the menacing "Army of Me" to the graceful "Isobel" without seeming incoherent. —*Stephen Thomas Erlewine*

The Black Crowes

Rock 'n' Roll
At the time of their 1990 debut, the kind of rock 'n' roll the Black Crowes specialize in was out of style. Only Guns N' Roses came close to approximating a vintage Stones-style raunch, but they were too angry and jagged to pull it off completely. The Black Crowes replicated that Stonesy swagger and Faces boogie perfectly. Vocalist Chris Robinson appropriated the sound and style of vintage Rod Stewart while guitarist Rich Robinson fused Keith Richards' lean attack with Ron Wood's messy rhythmic sense. At their best, The Black Crowes echo classic rock without slavishly imitating their influences.

The Robinson brothers originally formed the Black Crowes in Georgia in 1984. By the time of their 1990 debut, *Shake Your Money Maker*, the group comprised Chris Robinson (vocals), Rich Robinson (guitar), Johnny Colt (bass), Jeff Cease (guitar), and Steve Gorman (drums). "Jealous Again," the first single from *Shake Your Money Maker*, was a moderate hit but it was the band's cover of Otis Redding's "Hard to Handle" that made the group a multi-platinum success. "Hard to Handle" climbed its way into the Top 40, propelling the album into the Top Ten. The acoustic ballad "She Talks to Angels" became the band's second Top 40 hit in the spring of 1991. *Shake Your Money Maker* would eventually sell over three million copies.

The Black Crowes delivered their second album, *The Southern Harmony and Musical Companion*, in the spring of 1992. It entered the charts at No. 1, but it didn't have as many hit singles as the debut; none of the singles cracked the Top 40 and only "Remedy" and "Thorn in My Pride" made the Top 100. Nevertheless, the band established themselves as a popular concert attraction that summer, selling out theaters across America. During 1992, the band added keyboardist Eddie Hersch as a permanent member. The Black Crowes' third album, *Amorica*, arrived in late 1994. *Amorica* debuted in the Top Ten, but none of the singles from the album made the charts; even though the record went gold, it slipped off the charts in early 1995.

Three Snakes & One Charm, the group's fourth album, was released in July 1996. The album entered the charts at No. 15, but it quickly slipped out of the Top 50. Nevertheless, the album received the best reviews of any Crowes album since *The Southern Harmony and Musical Companion*. —*Stephen Thomas Erlewine*

Shake Your Money Maker / 1990 / Def American ✦✦✦✦
The best ideas on the Crowes' debut are all about 20 years old, but when those ideas are replicas of vintage Stones and Faces, timeliness is not an issue. The mix of throttling rockers and acoustic ballads doesn't flow with the grace of *Beggar's Banquet*, but the best songs here—"Twice as Hard," "She Talks to Angels," "Could I've Been So Blind"—act as anchors for a strikingly confident debut. —*John Floyd*

● **The Southern Harmony and Musical Companion** / 1992 / Def American ✦✦✦✦
On *The Southern Harmony and Musical Companion*, the Crowes avoid the sophomore slump by taking the best elements of their debut and fleshing them out (and giving the rhythm section and keyboards more room to breathe). The Stones/Faces/Humble Pie comparisons are still relevant, but the band's own identity flourishes on such songs as "Remedy," "Black Moon Creeping," and "Sting Me." —*John Floyd*

Amorica / 1994 / American ✦✦✦✦
On *Amorica*, the Black Crowes finally come into their own, taking their cue from the most relaxed, groove-oriented tracks on their previous album. While the album contains no immediately obvious singles, the songs are the best band has ever written, stretching out into a hard,

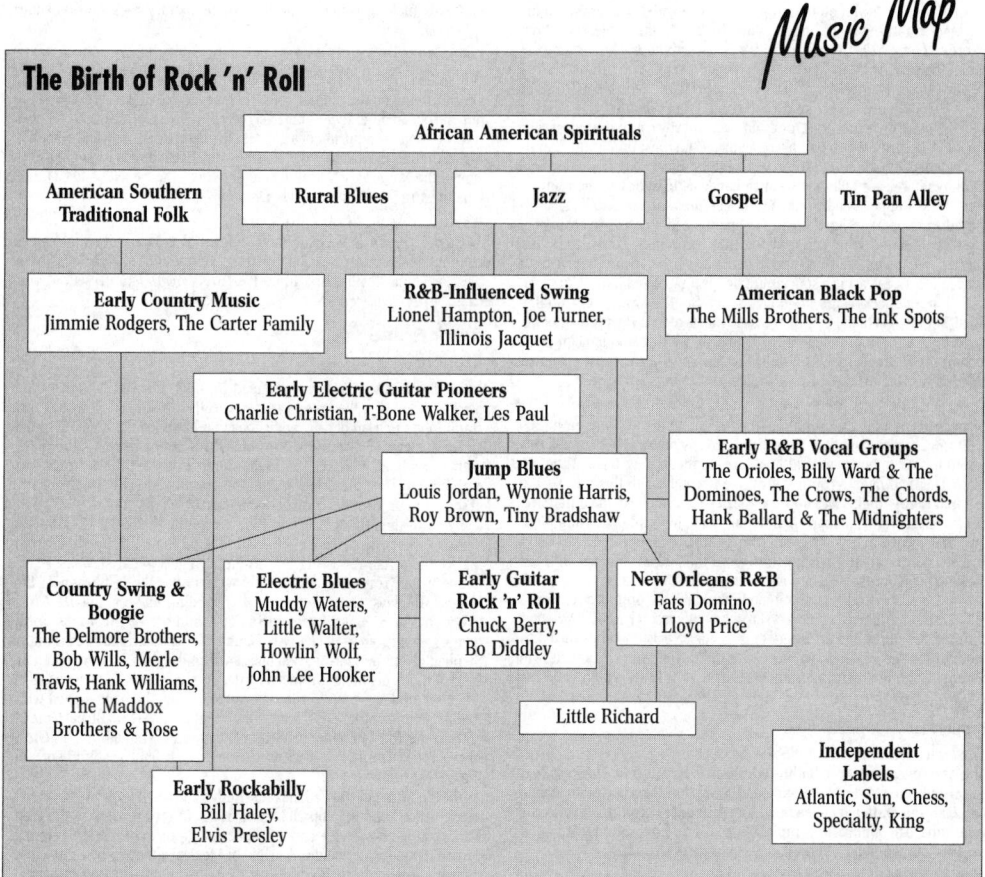

jam-oriented, funky blues-rock. The Black Crowes' influences are still discernible—no band celebrates the glory days of rock culture quite as enthusiastically—but they use the music of the Stones, the Faces, and Little Feat much the same way the Stones used the music of Chuck Berry: it's a starting point that leads the band into a new direction, incorporating different musical genres and making the music original. That sense of reinterpretation is what keeps *Amorica* fresh. —*Stephen Thomas Erlewine*

Three Snakes & One Charm / 1996 / American ♦♦♦

Black Flag

Hardcore Punk
In many ways, Black Flag were the definitive Los Angeles hardcore punk band. Although their music flirted with heavy metal and experimental noise and jazz more than that of most hardcore bands, they defined the image and the aesthetic. Through their ceaseless touring, the band cultivated the American underground punk scene—every year, Black Flag played in every area of the US, influencing countless numbers of bands. Although their recording career was hampered by a draining lawsuit early on, the band was unquestionably one of the most influential American post-punk bands. A full decade and a half before the fusion of punk and metal became popular, Black Flag created a ferocious, edgy, and ironic amalgam of underground aesthetics and gut-pounding metal. Their lyrics alluded to social criticism and a political viewpoint, but it was conveyed as seething, cynical angst. Furthermore, Black Flag demonstrated an affection for bohemia—both in musical experimentation and a fondness for poetry—that reiterated the band's underground roots and prevented it from becoming nothing but a heavy metal group. And it didn't matter who was in the band—throughout the years, the lineup changed numerous times—because the Black Flag name and three-bar logo became punk institutions.

Black Flag was formed in 1977 by guitarist Greg Ginn, a graduate of UCLA. Ginn formed the band with bassist Chuck Dukowski; the pair

soon added drummer Brian Migdol and vocalist Keith Morris. At the same time, Ginn and Dukowski formed an independent record label, SST, which released the band's first EP, *Nervous Breakdown*, in 1978. Morris and Migdol departed the following year—Morris went on to form the Circle Jerks—and they were respectively replaced with Chavo Pederast and Robo. By the release of 1980's *Jealous Again*, Black Flag had begun to tour the US relentlessly, building up a small, but dedicated, following of fans. After the release of *Jealous Again*, Black Flag went through another major lineup change. Pederast left the group and was replaced by Henry Rollins, a Washington DC fan who jumped on stage to sing with the band during a New York performance. At the same time, the band added a second guitarist, Dez Cadena, which gave the group a heavier sound.

Early in 1981, Black Flag signed a record contract with Unicorn Records, a subsidiary of MCA. The band delivered their first full-length album, *Damage*, to Unicorn and the label refused to release the record, citing that the content of the music was too dangerous and vulgar. Undaunted, Ginn released the album on SST Records. Upon its release, the album received considerable critical acclaim. Soon after the album appeared on the shelves, Unicorn sued Black Flag and SST over the release of *Damaged*. For the next two years, the band was prevented from using the name Black Flag or their logo on any records. During that time, the group continued to tour and they surreptitiously released *Everything Went Black*, a double-album retrospective that contained no mention of the band, although it listed the members on the front cover. The dispute ended in 1983, when Unicorn went bankrupt and the rights to the Black Flag name and logo reverted back to the band.

As if to make up for lost time, Black Flag became impossibly prolific when it returned to recording in 1984. A new version of the group—featuring Ginn on guitar and, under the pseudonym Dale Nixon, bass, Rollins, and drummer Bill Stevenson—recorded the albums *My War* and *Family Man*. After those two albums, the group added bassist Kira Roessler and cut *Slip It In*, its third official album of 1984. In addition to those three albums, Black Flag released the cassette-only *Live '84* and the compilation *The First Four Years* in 1984, as well as reissuing *Everything Went Black* with all the proper credits restored. The group's touring and recording pace didn't slow in 1985; they released three records—*Loose Nut, The Process of Weeding Out,* and *In My Head.* By the end of the year, Anthony Martinez replaced Stevenson on drums.

After Black Flag released the live album *Who's Got the 10 1/2?* in early 1986, Greg Ginn broke up the band. Ginn recorded two albums with the more experimental Gone, but he primarily concentrated on running SST Records, which had become one of the most important American independent labels of the era. By the time Black Flag broke up, SST had already released albums by such bands as Hüsker Dü, the Minutemen, Meat Puppets, and Sonic Youth. For most of the late '80s, Ginn retired from performing, choosing to operate SST Records instead; during this time, the label released the first recordings from bands like Soundgarden, Dinosaur Jr., and Screaming Trees. Ginn returned to music in 1993, releasing a solo album on his new record label, Cruz.

Following Black Flag's breakup, Henry Rollins formed the Rollins Band. For the rest of the '80s, he released music recorded with the Rollins Band on a variety of independent labels, as well as solo spoken-word recordings. In the early '90s, Rollins became one of the most recognizable figures of alternative music. —*Stephen Thomas Erlewine*

★ **Damaged** / 1981 / SST ✦✦✦✦✦

Perhaps the best album to emerge from the quagmire that was early-'80s California hardcore punk, the visceral, intensely physical presence of this record has yet to be equaled, although many bands have tried. Although Black Flag had been recording for three years prior to this release, the fact that Henry Rollins was now their lead singer made all the difference. His furious bellow and barely contained ferocity was the missing piece the band needed to become great. Also, guitarist/mastermind Greg Ginn wrote a slew of great songs for this record that, while suffused with the usual punk conceits (alienation, boredom, disenfranchisement), were capable of making one laugh out loud, especially the proto-slacker satire "TV Party." Extremely controversial when it was released, *Damaged* endured the slings and arrows of outrageous criticism (some reacted as though this record alone would cause the fall of America's youth) to become and remain an important document of its time. —*John Dougan*

Everything Went Black / 1983 / SST ✦✦✦

Family Man / 1984 / SST ✦✦✦

The First Four Years / 1984 / SST ✦✦✦

The best collection of pre-Rollins era Black Flag. Much of *The First Four Years* finds the band in developmental mode, but the sonic anarchy and political vituperation met head-on more than once, creating a ferociously good time. Not simply for completists, this is an important recording of the then-burgeoning L.A. hardcore scene. —*John Dougan*

Live '84 / 1984 / SST ✦✦

My War / 1984 / SST ✦✦

Slip It In / 1984 / SST ✦✦✦

In My Head / 1985 / SST ✦✦✦✦

After a rancorous three-year legal battle with their label, Unicorn, which prevented them from releasing any new material, Black Flag binged in the mid-'80s, releasing a flurry of records that had even the most devoted fans scrambling to keep up. They did, however, start this period somewhat inauspiciously with *My War,* a pretentious mess of a record with a totally worthless second side. Featuring three tracks of slower-than-Black Sabbath muck with Rollins howling like a caged animal, it was self-indulgence masquerading as inspiration and about as much fun as wading through a tar pit. Side one, however, was quite good, with the title tracks especially intimidating. *Slip It In* followed almost immediately, and while a bit better (fewer mega-volume angst drones), the band still wanders a bit, experimenting with expanding the breadth of hardcore into a newer hard rock/punk sound. This is especially true of Greg Ginn's guitar playing, which was becoming increasingly avant-garde and exciting. Rather than simply coughing up one clichéd solo after another, he wandered harmolodically up and down the fretboard as a jazz player like Blood Ulmer would, making the material more interesting than what most Black Flag-influenced bands were playing. Keeping up with this furious pace came *Live '84,* a cassette-only release of a standard (for them anyway) Black Flag gig. Opening up with an eight-and-a-half minute hardcore/punk/jazz instrumental "The Process of Weeding Out" (which came from an earlier Black Flag instrumental EP of the same title), it was abundantly clear that Black Flag was no longer just another punk band; as much as they loved to kick out the jams, they also loved destroying the audience's preconceived notions of how punk bands were supposed to behave. Running at 70 minutes, this is a terrific live recording of Black Flag at their performing peak. Hot on the heels of the live record came *Loose Nut* and *In My Head,* which showed significant improvement over *My War* and *Slip It In.* Rollins and Ginn were exploring by-now standard lyrical themes: hate, paranoia, loneliness, anomie, and violence, but framing them around music that was demanding, powerful, and exciting. *In My Head* is the slightly better of the two, primarily

because it's a little edgier and uncontrolled, but at this juncture, Black Flag was making some of the best contemporary rock music extant. —*John Dougan*

Loose Nut / 1985 / SST ✦✦✦✦

Who's Got the 10 1/2? / 1986 / SST ✦✦✦✦

Despite being on top of their game, Black Flag called it a career in 1986, but did so in fine style. The live record *Who's Got the 10 1/2?* was recorded at a barn-burner of a gig with the band (especially Ginn) sounding as though they could take on the world. Extra points for a great version of the cautionary "Drinking and Driving." The cassette and CD contain an extra 30 minutes. —*John Dougan*

Wasted . . . Again / 1987 / SST ✦✦✦✦

Wasted . . . Again is a posthumous release that is an essential career summation. For those hearing the ear-searing sounds of early-'80s SoCal hardcore punk for the first time, *Wasted . . . Again* is an essential purchase. —*John Dougan*

Black Grape

Alternative Pop-Rock, Brit-Pop

After the Happy Mondays disbanded in 1992, most observers would have guessed that the group's leader, vocalist Shaun Ryder, would succumb to the myriad of drug addictions that hastened the breakup of the group. Instead of dying, Ryder recouped his strengths and came back with a new band, Black Grape, in the summer of 1995. Black Grape was embraced by both the British public and press, making Shaun Ryder one of the more unexpected comebacks in rock 'n' roll history.

Ryder formed Black Grape in 1993, recruiting ex-Happy Monday Bez (dancing, percussion), rappers Kermit (b. Paul Leveridge) and Jed from the Ruthless Rap Assassins, and ex-Paris Angels guitarist Wags. Black Grape began recording demos only weeks after the implosion of the Happy Mondays. Over the course of recording and writing *It's Great When You're Straight,* Ryder recruited a number of musicians, most notably producer and bassist Danny Saber, keyboardist/producer Stephen Lironi, and former Bluebells and Smiths guitarist Gary Gannon. Black Grape's debut album was recorded over a period of seven weeks in late 1994 and early 1995; after it was completed, the band signed with Radioactive Records. The group's first single, "Reverend Black Grape," entered the Top Ten upon its release. The group's debut album, *It's Great When You're Straight . . . Yeah,* was released in 1995. The album entered the UK charts at No. 1.

"In the Name of the Father" and "Kelly's Heroes" followed "Reverend Black Grape" into the Top 20 later in 1995. Toward the end of the year, Kermit suffered a severe case of septicemia, a form of blood poisoning caused by bad water he drank while in Mexico; although he came close to death—bits of his heart and liver were flaking off—he had recovered by the spring of 1996. Black Grape were prepared to head to America early in 1996, when the group were denied entry into the country due to their prior drug convictions. After a couple of months, the passports were cleared and the band was admitted into the US. Due to his illness, Kermit had to miss the tour, and his spot was filled by Psycho, who became a permanent member of the band after the completion of the tour. Before Black Grape launched their US tour in spring of 1996, Bez left the band due to financial disagreements with the record company.

In May 1996, Black Grape returned with the single "Fat Neck," which entered the UK charts in the Top Ten; the song featured former Smiths member Johnny Marr on guitar. A month after the release of "Fat Neck," the group released their football anthem "England's Irie," which was recorded with Joe Strummer. Like "Fat Neck" before it, "England's Irie" became a Top Ten hit. —*Stephen Thomas Erlewine*

It's Great When You're Straight . . . Yeah / 1995 / Radioactive ✦✦✦✦

Black Sabbath

Heavy Metal

No other band has come closer to embodying heavy metal than Black Sabbath. Over the years, their lineup may have changed, but their music hasn't—it has remained the same loud, methodical guitar-based heavy rock that it was in the early '70s. Their slow, sludgy attack was part design and part accident. Because of an accident that cut the tips of his fingers, Tony Iommi tuned his guitar down a half-step because he couldn't play comfortably unless the strings were slightly slack; the lower tuning made his mammoth riffs sound heavier. Bassist Geezer Butler's lyrics reveled in black magic, fantasy, drugs, mental illness, and the occult, but never sex; Ozzy Osbourne sang them in a flat, almost tuneless, banshee wail. Butler and drummer Bill Ward never had any flair for playing around with the rhythm, preferring to let the beat plod on and on. Their songwriting never strayed from one riff, a chorus, another riff, and a guitar solo, but that is part of their appeal. Taken together, the primitive musicianship, bad poetry, obsessive fantasy world, crawling tempos, and overpowering volume represent everything good and bad about heavy metal. Critics detested them when they were at the peak of their powers in the early '70s, and they still do. But critical acclaim was never essential to the band's success. Black Sabbath was, in many ways, an underground band—parents hated them, hippies hated them, self-respecting rockers hated them. Everybody hated them except teenagers. And those were the teenagers that grew up and formed bands, from Metallica to Soundgarden to Henry Rollins. Everybody from the heaviest of metal bands to the sludgiest of grunge bands listened to Black Sabbath when they were teenagers.

Of course, after Black Sabbath hit their peak, they stuck around way too long. Some of their first six albums were great, some of them merely had good tracks, but all of them had something to recommend them. Osbourne hung around for two more records before jumping ship for good. Former Rainbow lead vocalist Ronnie James Dio replaced him in 1979; the new lineup released their first record, *Heaven and Hell*, in 1980. It was a far cry from their best, but it sounded like *Paranoid* compared to what they would later release. Throughout the '80s, the band members kept shifting, with Iommi being the only member to remain in all of the lineups. At the end of the decade, he was the only original member left in the band. Not only was Black Sabbath suffering musically, but their credibility was in question by their devoted fans as well. In 1991, Iommi persuaded Butler to rejoin and, for a brief time, Dio. Black Sabbath continues to lurch forward in the '90s, oblivious of the criticism and declining record sales, but their early records continue to inspire whole new generations of listeners. —*Stephen Thomas Erlewine*

Black Sabbath / May 1970 / Warner Bros. ✦✦✦✦
Their debut album set the tone with the title cut, "The Wizard," "Wasp," and "Warning." —*Cub Koda*

★ **Paranoid** / Jan. 1971 / Warner Bros. ✦✦✦✦✦
Paranoid, released in the UK in September 1970 and held back from US release until January 1971 to avoid cutting off sales of the still-selling debut LP, became Black Sabbath's best-selling album ever. "Paranoid" and "Iron Man" (the latter released as a single a full year after the album) became Black Sabbath's only US singles-chart entries, and the album became their only UK chart-topper. Although the album was deplored by critics at the time, the reasons for its success are easy to hear now. Subtle, it ain't (listen to the way Ozzy Osbourne sings note-for-note the same simple melodies Tony Iommi plays), but that's the point. In songs like "Paranoid" and "Iron Man," generations of teenagers heard their own insecurities writ large. —*William Ruhlmann*

☆ **Masters of Reality** / Aug. 1971 / Warner Bros. ✦✦✦✦✦
Sabbath's third album, no less potent than the first two. It includes "Into the Void," "Children of the Grave," and "Lord of This World." —*Cub Koda*

Black Sabbath, Vol. 4 / Sep. 1972 / Warner Bros. ✦✦✦✦
This is a surprisingly song-oriented set of cynical boogie. —*John Floyd*

Sabbath, Bloody Sabbath / Dec. 1973 / Warner Bros. ✦✦✦✦
Sabbath adds some synths to their sludge and comes up with a surprisingly solid album, which manages to expand on their patented slow, gloomy sound. —*Stephen Thomas Erlewine*

Sabotage / Aug. 1975 / Warner Bros. ✦✦✦✦
On *Sabotage*, the band was at their artiest, adding synths and found sounds which accentuated Iommi's tight solos and riffs. It may not be their best or most influential record, but *Sabotage* is certainly one of their most interesting. In fact, it was the last consistently impressive album they ever recorded. —*Stephen Thomas Erlewine*

We Sold Our Soul for Rock and Roll / Feb. 1976 / Warner Bros. ✦✦✦✦
Running over 70 minutes, *We Sold Our Soul for Rock and Roll* is a solid 16-track sampler from the band's first six albums, what you might call Sabbath's glory days. —*John Floyd & Cub Koda*

Never Say Die! / Oct. 1978 / Warner Bros. ✦✦
Heaven & Hell / May 1980 / Warner Bros. ✦✦✦
Black Sabbath's first album without Ozzy Osbourne curiously revitalized the band. The band's return to form had something to do with their new vocalist, Ronnie James Dio, yet it was mostly due to the fact the band had written a set of riffs that were fairly memorable. The result was their best record since *Sabotage*, and the only good record the group recorded in the '80s. —*Stephen Thomas Erlewine*

The Mob Rules / Nov. 1981 / Warner Bros. ✦✦

Frank Black (Charles Thompson)

b. 1965
Guitar, Vocals / Alternative Pop-Rock
Inverting his stage name from Black Francis to Frank Black, the former Pixies lead singer-songwriter embarked on a solo career after he broke up the band in early 1993; actually, he began recording his solo album *before* he told the band the news. Working with former Pere Ubu member Eric Drew Feldman, Black occasionally heads into the ferocious post-punk guitar territory that marked such landmark albums as *Surfer Rosa* and *Doolittle*, but more frequently he plays up his considerably underrated melodic side. His self-titled 1993 debut album was an adventurous

sketchbook of pop styles ranging from surf rock to heavy metal, from Beatlesque pop to new wave. Black's second album, 1994's *Teenager of the Year*, was a sprawling and diverse album that amplified all the best points of *Frank Black*. Although it received favorable reviews and had an alternative-radio hit with "Headache," it slipped off the charts two weeks after its release. He parted ways with Elektra and 4AD in early 1995, signing a new record contract with American. Black released his first album for American, the hard-rocking *The Cult of Ray*, in January 1996. —*Stephen Thomas Erlewine*

Frank Black / 1993 / Elektra ✦✦✦✦
On *Frank Black*, Charles Thompson (formerly Black Francis of the Pixies) brings the pop undercurrents that have always floated through his music to the forefront. The sonic onslaught of The Pixies is here in small doses (portions of "Los Angeles" and "Parry the Wind High, Low," "Czar," and the Iggy Pop tribute "Ten Percenter"), but there are more Lennon, Bowie, Brian Wilson, and surf-rock influences than Iggy; even the Ramones' tribute is a lovely pop number. "Los Angeles" encapsulates all of the album into one track; it begins with an acoustic folk section, slams into a punkish verse, and ends with a gorgeous Beatlesque coda. That Thompson can pull it off all in one song *and* make it work says volumes for his talents. —*Stephen Thomas Erlewine*

● **Teenager of the Year** / 1994 / Elektra ✦✦✦✦
Frank Black's second album is a wildly ambitious and eclectic piece of guitar-pop, ranging from the full-throttle roar of "Whatever Happened to Pong?" and "Thalassocracy" to the pure pop of "Headache" and the gorgeous, winding melodies of "Speedy Marie." It might be a little long, but *Teenager of the Year* is packed with thrilling, innovative pop. —*Stephen Thomas Erlewine*

The Cult Of Ray / Jan. 30, 1996 / Warner Bros. ✦✦

The Blasters

Roots-Rock, New Wave
Among the rock bands that emerged from the Los Angeles scene in the early '80s, the Blasters were the most-conscious, producing a sound akin to '50s rockabilly and other 25-year-old musical styles. The group was led by the Alvin brothers Phil, who sang and played rhythm guitar, and Dave, who played lead guitar and wrote songs, and included John Bazz, bass, Bill Bateman, drums, and Gene Taylor, piano.

The group issued the album *American Music* (1980) on the local Rollin' Rock label, then switched to Slash for *The Blasters* (1981), which then was included in a licensing/distribution deal with Warner Bros. Records. The Blasters drew national attention in 1982, when the album reached the Top 40. They released a live EP of rock 'n' roll covers later that year, then returned in 1983 with *Non Fiction*, which was dominated by Dave Alvin's songs. Those songs, steeped in rock, country, and blues traditions, also commented trenchantly on the current state of the American dream in much the same way Bruce Springsteen was doing at the time. They earned the Blasters greater critical respect, though sales did not expand. After *Hard Line* (1985) also proved to be a sales disappointment, Dave Alvin decamped in 1986 to join X. Phil Alvin kept the band going by hiring another guitarist, Hollywood Fats (born Michael Mann, 1954, d. Dec. 8, 1986), who died a few months later. Dave Alvin returned for a few gigs, then former X guitarist Billy Zoom took his place, but the Blasters had ceased to be a full-time entity. Both Dave and Phil Alvin have released solo albums. —*William Ruhlmann*

The Blasters / 1981 / Slash ✦✦✦✦
You might have thought the Blasters had been in suspended animation for 25 years when their major-label debut turned up in late 1981 sounding for all the world like something cut in the Sun Studios in Memphis in 1956. Dave Alvin knew all the licks and his brother Phil had the R&B/country wail down. Best of all, you couldn't tell the oldies from Dave's newly written classics. Welcome to the birth of rock 'n' roll, all over again. —*William Ruhlmann*

Over There [Live] / Oct. 1982 / Slash ✦✦✦
Non Fiction / 1983 / Slash ✦✦✦
Hard Line / 1985 / Slash ✦✦
● **The Blasters Collection** / 1991 / Slash ✦✦✦✦
One of the leading American roots bands of the '80s, this group's anthemic no-frills rock music sounds purer and more real than ever in the post-Milli Vanilli age. —*Jeff Tamarkin*

Mary J. Blige

b. 1971, Atlanta, GA
Vocals / Urban, Club-Dance
Crowned the new "Queen of Hip-Hop Soul," Mary J. Blige enjoyed a breakout year in 1992 with *What's the 411?* Such singles as "Reminisce" and "Real Love" thrust the Atlanta-born singer into the spotlight at age 21. She was raised in Yonkers and performed in local groups before

making her debut for the Uptown label. The album went platinum, and a remixed version was later issued. The single "Reminisce" had a second life when it was reworked and re-done in a rap version by the duo of Pete Rock and C.L. Smooth. —*Ron Wynn*

● **What's the 411?** / 1992 / Uptown/MCA ✦✦✦✦
Mary J. Blige's debut album, *What's the 411?*, was a revolution in disguise. Like her new jack predecessors, Blige combined R&B with hip-hop, but unlike Guy and Bobby Brown, her music was more seductive and sly. More importantly, she sounds grittier and more real than most new-jack swingers or female R&B vocalists. Blige can slip between singing and rapping with ease, which is partially the reason why *What's the 411?* is so successful. It doesn't hurt that her collaborators, from Grand Puba to Sean "Puffy" Combs, help construct backing tracks that are both melodic, relentlessly funky, and sexy. —*Stephen Thomas Erlewine*

My Life / 1994 / Suave/Relativity ✦✦✦✦

Blind Faith

Rock 'n' Roll
The calculated grafting of ex-Cream members Eric Clapton (b. Mar. 30, 1945, Ripley, Surrey, England), on guitar, vocals; and Ginger Baker (b. Aug. 19, 1939, Lewisham, England), on percussion; to ex-Traffic member Steve Winwood (b. May 12, 1948, Birmingham, England) on keyboards, guitar, and vocals; and bassist/violinist Rick Grech (b. Nov. 1, 1945, Bordeaux, France, d. Mar. 17, 1990) of the popular British group Family brought the term "supergroup" to new levels of hype. The talent involved in this amalgamation was quite impressive, but the cynical marketing minds behind this appropriately named fabrication failed to consider natural group chemistry. The volatile personalities in the lineup helped ensure that Blind Faith would be nothing more than an interesting one-off. Blind Faith debuted with a free concert before 100,000 people in London's Hyde Park on June 7, 1969. The band made an auspicious live US debut, selling out Madison Square Garden on July 12. But things soured quickly, with the members going their separate ways at the conclusion of their 20-concert, six-week US tour on August 24, and Blind Faith became yet another historical footnote in the ongoing marriage of commerce and artistic expression. In spite of unrealistic pressure to live up to fan expectations, Blind Faith delivered a single, self-titled album in July 1969 that at times almost made good on its perceived potential. It still holds up today as a listening experience, thanks to Clapton's inspiring "Presence of the Lord," Winwood's reading of Buddy Holly's "Well All Right," and his own plaintive "Can't Find My Way Home." —*Rick Clark*

● **Blind Faith** / Jul. 1969 / RSO ✦✦✦✦
More than a quarter century after the release of Blind Faith's first and last album, all the stories of hype and manipulation pall before the album's enduring appeal. Steve Winwood is especially impressive, contributing three compositions—"Had to Cry Today," "Can't Find My Way Home," and "Sea of Joy"—that continue to rank among his best, and singing with his usual soulfulness. Eric Clapton's "Presence of the Lord" is also a perennial in his repertoire, his guitar playing throughout the record is distinctive and impressive. If Ginger Baker overplays somewhat for contemporary tastes (especially on his 15-minute showcase, "Do What You Like"), late-'60s tastes were more accommodating, and Baker nevertheless demonstrates why he is among the handful of great drummers in rock. And whatever you think of the hype, the album was a notable success. —*William Ruhlmann*

Blondie

Punk, New Wave, Pop-Rock, Club-Dance
Blondie was the most commercially successful band to emerge from the much vaunted punk/new wave movement of the late '70s. The group was formed in New York City in August 1974 by singer Deborah Harry (b. Jul. 7, 1945, Miami, FL), formerly of Wind in the Willows, and guitarist Chris Stein (b. Jan. 5, 1950, Brooklyn, NY) out of the remnants of Harry's previous group, the Stilettos. The lineup fluctuated over the next year. Drummer Clement Burke (b. Nov. 24, 1955, New York) joined in May 1975. Bassist Gary Valentine joined in August. In October, keyboard player James Destri (b. Apr. 13, 1954) joined, to complete the initial permanent lineup. They released their first album, *Blondie*, on Private Stock Records in December 1976. In July 1977, Valentine was replaced by Frank Infante.

In August, Chrysalis Records bought their contract from Private Stock and in October reissued *Blondie* and released the second album, *Plastic Letters*. Blondie expanded to a sextet in November with the addition of bassist Nigel Harrison (born Princes Risborough, Buckinghamshire, England), as Infante switched to guitar. Blondie broke commercially in the UK in March 1978, when their cover of Randy And The Rainbows' 1963 hit "Denise," renamed "Denis," became a Top Ten hit, as did *Plastic Letters*, followed by a second UK Top Ten, "(I'm Always Touched by Your) Presence, Dear." Blondie turned to UK producer/songwriter Mike Chapman for their third album, *Parallel Lines*, which was released in September 1978 and eventually broke them worldwide. "Picture This" became a

UK Top 40 hit, and "Hanging on the Telephone" made the UK Top Ten, but it was the album's third single, the disco-influenced "Heart of Glass," that took Blondie to No. 1 in both the UK and the US. "Sunday Girl" hit No. 1 in the UK in May, and "One Way or Another" hit the US Top 40 in August. Blondie followed with their fourth album, *Eat to the Beat*, in October. Its first single, "Dreaming," went Top Ten in the UK, Top 40 in the US. The second UK single, "Union City Blue," went Top 40. In March 1980, the third UK single from *Eat to the Beat*, "Atomic," became the group's third British No. 1. (It later made the US Top 40.)

Meanwhile, Harry was collaborating with German disco producer Giorgio Moroder on "Call Me," the theme from the movie *American Gigolo*. It became Blondie's second transatlantic chart topper. Blondie's fifth album, *Autoamerican*, was released in November 1980, and its first single was the reggaeish tune "The Tide Is High," which went to No. 1 in the US and UK. The second single was the rap-oriented "Rapture," which topped the US pop charts and went Top Ten in the UK. But the band's eclectic style reflected a diminished participation by its members—Infante sued, charging that he wasn't being used on the records, though he settled and stayed in the lineup. But in 1981, the members of Blondie worked on individual projects, notably Harry's gold-selling solo album, *KooKoo*. *The Best of Blondie* was released in the fall of the year. *The Hunter*, Blondie's sixth and last new album, was released in July 1982, preceded by the single "Island of Lost Souls," a Top 40 hit in the US and UK. "War Child" also became a Top 40 hit in the UK, but *The Hunter* was a commercial disappointment. At the same time, Stein became seriously ill with the genetic disease pemphigus. As a result, Blondie broke up in October 1982, with Deborah Harry launching a part-time solo career while caring for Stein, who eventually recovered. —*William Ruhlmann*

Blondie / Dec. 1976 / Chrysalis ✦✦✦✦
If new wave was about reconfiguring and recontextualizing simple pop-rock forms of the '50s and '60s in new, ironic, and aggressive ways, then Blondie, which took the girl-group style of the early and mid-'60s and added a '70s archness, fit right in. True punksters may have deplored the group early on (they never had the hip cachet of Talking Heads or even the Ramones), but Blondie's secret weapon, which was deployed increasingly over their career, was a canny pop straddle—they sent the music up and celebrated it at the same time. So, for instance, songs like "X Offender" (their first single) and "In The Flesh" (their first hit, in Australia) had the tough-girl-with-a-tender-heart tone of the Shangri-Las (Brill Building songwriter Ellie Greenwich even sang backup on the latter), while going one step too far into hard-edged decadence—that is, if you chose to see that. The whole point was that you could take Blondie either way. —*William Ruhlmann*

Plastic Letters / Oct. 1977 / Chrysalis ✦✦✦✦
Blondie's second album was a less distinctive version of its first, matching the first record's bright, sharp production (courtesy of Richard Gottehrer), but marking a fall-off in songwriting. The two best tracks—both UK hits—were "Denis," a remake of an oldie, and "(I'm Always Touched By Your) Presence, Dear," written by departed bass player Gary Valentine, and that didn't bode well. Nevertheless, those songs were enough to assure the album's British success and to make some noise in the US. But Blondie would take a distinctly different approach next time out. —*William Ruhlmann*

☆ **Parallel Lines** / Sep. 1978 / Chrysalis ✦✦✦✦✦
Blondie turned to British pop producer Mike Chapman for their third album, on which they abandoned any pretensions to new wave legitimacy (just in time, given the decline of the new wave) and emerged as a pure pop band. But it wasn't just Chapman that made *Parallel Lines* Blondie's best album; it was the band's own songwriting, including Deborah Harry, Chris Stein, and James Destri's "Picture This," Harry and Stein's "Heart of Glass," and Harry and new bass player Nigel Harrison's "One Way or Another," plus two contributions from non-band-member Jack Lee, "Will Anything Happen?" and "Hanging on the Telephone." That was enough to give Blondie a No. 1 on both sides of the Atlantic with "Heart of Glass" and three more UK hits, but what impresses is the album's depth and consistency—album tracks like "Fade Away and Radiate" and "Just Go Away" are as impressive as the songs pulled for singles. The result is state-of-the-art pop-rock circa 1978, with Harry's tough-girl glamour setting the pattern that would be exploited over the next decade by a host of successors led by Madonna. —*William Ruhlmann*

Eat to the Beat / Oct. 1979 / Chrysalis ✦✦✦✦
Just as Blondie's second album, *Plastic Letters*, was a pale imitation of their debut, *Blondie*, *Eat to the Beat*, their fourth album, was a second-hand version of their breakthrough third album, *Parallel Lines*: one step forward, half a step back. There was an attempt, on such songs as "The Hardest Part" and "Atomic," to recreate the rock-disco fusion of the group's one major US hit, "Heart of Glass," without similar success, and elsewhere, the band just tried to cover too many stylistic bases. The British, who had long since been converted, made Eat to the Beat another chart-topper, but in the US, which still saw Blondie as a slightly comic

one-hit wonder, the album was greeted for what it was—slick corporate rock without the tangy flavor that had made *Parallel Lines* such ear candy. —*William Ruhlmann*

Autoamerican / Nov. 1980 / Chrysalis ✦✦✦

★ **The Best of Blondie** / 1981 / Chrysalis ✦✦✦✦✦
Although Blondie made several first-rate albums, most of their best songs were released as singles, which makes *The Best of Blondie* an essential collection. *The Best of Blondie* glosses over their punk roots—very little from the first album, apart from the vicious "Rip Her to Shreds" and the seductive "In the Flesh"—but the band's pop hits are among the finest of their era and encapsulate all of the virtues of new wave. Apart from genuine chart hits like "Heart of Glass," "One Way or Another," "Dreaming," "Call Me," "Atomic," "The Tide Is High," and "Rapture," *Best of Blondie* picks up several of the group's best album tracks, like "(I'm Always Touched By Your) Presence, Dear" and "Hanging on the Telephone." *The Best of Blondie* isn't all you need to know, but it is an excellent introduction to one of the best new wave bands. —*Stephen Thomas Erlewine*

The Hunter / Jul. 1982 / Chrysalis ✦✦

Blonde & Beyond / Nov. 16, 1993 / Chrysalis ✦✦✦
Although it is a collection of rarities, outtakes, B-sides, and forgotten singles, *Blonde & Beyond* contains enough great music to make the disc enjoyable even to casual Blondie fans. —*Stephen Thomas Erlewine*

● **Platinum Collection** / Nov. 1, 1994 / EMI ✦✦✦✦
A double-CD, 47-track collection built around Blondie's singles, including every one of their US and UK A-sides and B-sides. Not a definitive best-of, as it excludes album tracks from consideration, but pretty close. Serious fans will be most interested in five 1975 demos, recorded before the band's first LP. Bootlegged in the past, these include "Once I Had a Love," an early version of "Heart of Glass," and a cover of the Shangri-La's' "Out in the Streets." Also of interest to fanatics are the extensive liner notes, including a detailed family tree and lengthy comments from everyone in the band except Harry and Stein. —*Richie Unterberger*

Blood Sweat & Tears

Pop-Rock

For a brief period at the end of the '60s and the start of the '70s, Blood, Sweat & Tears, which fused a rock 'n' roll rhythm section to a horn section, held out the promise of a jazz-rock fusion that could storm the pop charts. The band was organized in New York in 1967 out of the remnants of the Blues Project by keyboard player/singer Al Kooper (b. Feb. 5, 1944, Brooklyn, NY) and guitarist Steve Katz (b. May 9, 1945, Brooklyn, NY) of that group and saxophonist Fred Lipsius (b. Nov. 19, 1944, New York, NY). The rhythm section consisted of bassist Jim Fielder (b. Oct. 4, 1947, Denton, TX) and drummer Bobby Colomby (b. Dec. 20, 1944, New York, NY), and the horn section was filled out by trumpeters Randy Brecker (b. Nov. 27, 1945, Philadelphia, PA) and Jerry Weiss (b. May, 1, 1946, New York) and trombonist Dick Halligan (b. Aug. 29, 1943, Troy, NY). This eight-piece band signed to Columbia Records and recorded BS&T's debut album, *Child Is Father to the Man*, which was released in February 1968. Cofounder Kooper then departed, and the group was reorganized. Singer David Clayton-Thomas (b. David Thomsett, Sept. 13, 1941, Surrey, England) was added, Halligan moved to the keyboards, and trumpeters Chuck Winfield (b. Feb. 5, 1943, Monessen, PA) and Lew Soloff (b. Feb. 20, 1944, Brooklyn, NY) replaced Brecker and Weiss, with Jerry Hyman (b. May 19, 1947, Brooklyn, NY) being added on trombone. This nine-piece unit, working with producer James William Guercio, made BS&T's self-titled second album, released in January 1969. It was a runaway hit, spawning three gold-selling Top Ten singles, "You've Made Me So Very Happy," "Spinning Wheel," and "And When I Die," selling three million copies and winning the Grammy Award for Album of the Year. It was also BS&T's highwater mark. Guercio left to work on a similar concept with Chicago Transit Authority, and BS&T increasingly became a backup group for Clayton-Thomas. Nevertheless, the third album, *Blood, Sweat & Tears 3* (1970), and the fourth, *Blood, Sweat & Tears 4* (1971), were substantial hits. Clayton-Thomas went solo in early 1972, but returned in 1974. Numerous other personnel changes took place, as the group's commercial fortunes gradually declined. BS&T left Columbia after the release of its ninth album, *More Than Ever* in 1976 and signed to ABC Records, for which it made *Brand New Day* (1977). From the late '70s on, BS&T existed largely as a group name for the concert activities of Clayton-Thomas and Colomby, who retained rights to the name. —*William Ruhlmann*

Child Is Father to the Man / Feb. 1968 / Columbia ✦✦✦✦
This is keyboard player/singer/arranger Al Kooper's finest work, an album on which he moves the folk-blues-rock amalgamation of the Blues Project into even wider pastures, taking in classical and jazz elements (including strings and horns), all without losing the pop essence that makes the hybrid work. This is one of the great albums of the eclectic post-*Sgt. Pepper* era of the late '60s, a time when you could borrow

styles from Greenwich Village contemporary folk to San Francisco acid rock and mix them into what seemed to have the potential to become a new American musical form. It's Kooper's bluesy songs, such as "I Love You More Than You'll Ever Know" and "I Can't Quit Her," and his singing, that are the primary focus, but the album is an aural delight. This is the sound of a group of virtuosos enjoying themselves in the newly open possibilities of pop music. Maybe it couldn't have lasted; anyway, it didn't. —*William Ruhlmann*

Blood, Sweat & Tears / Jan. 1969 / Columbia ✦✦✦✦
Arguably, the BS&T that made this self-titled second album, consisting of five of the eight original members and four newcomers, including singer David Clayton-Thomas, was really a different group from the one that made the debut album, *Child Is Father to the Man*, largely under the direction of singer-songwriter/keyboard player/arranger Al Kooper. BS&T Mach II had certain similarities to the original: the musical mixture of classical, jazz, and rock elements was still apparent, and the interplay between the horns and the keyboards was still occurring, even if those instruments were being played by different people. Kooper was even still present as an arranger on two tracks, notably the initial hit "You've Made Me So Very Happy." But the second BS&T, under the aegis of producer James William Guercio, was a less adventurous unit, and, as fronted by Clayton-Thomas, a far more commercial one. Not only did the album contain three songs that neared the top of the charts as singles—"Happy," "Spinning Wheel," and "And When I Die"—but the whole album, including an arrangement of "God Bless the Child" and the radical rewrite of Traffic's "Smiling Phases," was wonderfully accessible. It was a repertoire to build a career on, and BS&T did exactly that, although they never came close to equaling this album. —*William Ruhlmann*

Blood, Sweat & Tears 3 / Jun. 1970 / Columbia ✦✦✦

Blood, Sweat & Tears 4 / Jun. 1971 / Columbia ✦✦

● **Blood, Sweat and Tears' Greatest Hits** / Feb. 1972 / Columbia ✦✦✦✦
Sometimes, a greatest-hits set is timed perfectly to gather together a group's most successful and familiar performances just at the point when that group has passed the point of their maximum exposure to the public, but before the public memory has had a chance to fade. That was the case when Columbia Records assembled this compilation for release in early 1972. At that point, Blood, Sweat & Tears had released four albums and scored six Top 40 hits, each of which is heard here. But lead singer David Clayton-Thomas had just quit the group, so that the unit that recorded songs like "You've Made Me So Very Happy" was not working together anymore. And even when Clayton-Thomas returned, the band would continue to decline commercially. As such, *BS&T's Greatest Hits* captures the band's peak in 11 selections—seven singles-chart entries, plus two album tracks from the celebrated debut album when Al Kooper helmed the group, and two more from the Grammy-winning multi-platinum second album. Using the short singles edits of songs like "And When I Die" emphasizes their radio-ready punch over the more extended suitelike arrangements on the albums, but this selection gains in focus what it lacks in ambition. For the millions who learned to love BS&T in 1969 when they were all over AM radio, this is the ideal selection of their most accessible material. —*William Ruhlmann*

● **What Goes Up: Best of . . .** / Nov. 7, 1995 / Sony ✦✦✦✦
Blood, Sweat & Tears' 11-track *Greatest Hits* album, released in February 1972, contained all of the group's six Top 40 singles, plus notable tracks from its two best albums, *Child Is Father to the Man* and *Blood Sweat & Tears*. Almost 24 years later came this 32-track, 138 1/2-minute, double-CD expansion, much of it extraneous. Where *Greatest Hits* contained the single edits of songs like "You've Made Me So Very Happy" and "And When I Die," here "all titles are original album versions," as the back cover noted, which means the jazzy interludes, frequently having nothing to do with the rest of the song, remained. There were a couple of unreleased tracks, and otherwise the bloated running time was filled out by, for example, four tracks from the 1972 stiff *New Blood*, which didn't even feature singer David Clayton-Thomas. Legacy would have better served consumers by either expanding the original 41-minute *Greatest Hits* to proper CD length with a few bonus tracks or reissuing the first two albums in a double-disc set, again with a few bonus tracks to fill up the time. This compilation did not enhance the band's reputation. And the error-filled liner notes are less than worthless. —*William Ruhlmann*

Blue Nile

Pop-Rock

Glasgow's Blue Nile was formed in 1981 by vocalist/guitarist/synthesist Paul Buchanan and synthesizer manipulators Robert Bell and Joseph Moore. The independent single "I Love This Life" was picked up for distribution by the RSO label, which shortly went bankrupt. The band's demo tape wound up at Linn Products, a hi-fi company, who used it to test new equipment. The company liked what it heard and decided to venture into the recording business, signing Blue Nile and releasing its debut album, *A Walk Across the Rooftops,* in 1984. The album received high praise for its melancholy, atmospheric, haunting sound, and was eventually picked up by A&M. Blue Nile was not heard from again until 1989, when they finally released a follow-up, *Hats,* and played their first live shows ever. After a long period of inactivity, the band returned in 1996 with *Peace at Last. —Steve Huey*

A Walk Across the Rooftops / May 1984 / A&M ✦✦✦✦
This Scottish trio's 1984 debut, originally on Linn Records, is a beautifully atmospheric collection of synth-heavy songscapes. The dichotomy between the cool synthesized musical washes (with periodic percolating drum machine parts) and the yearning, passionate (yet strangely disconnected) vocals is engaging. This album could have been the soundtrack to Jonathan Pryce's lonely quenchless dreams in the Terry Gilliam movie, *Brazil.* The Linn version sounds superior to the A&M release. —*Rick Clark*

● **Hats** / Oct. 1989 / A&M ✦✦✦✦
The follow-up to *A Walk...* was five years in the making. The songs aren't as memorable, but the results are still coolly haunting. "The Downtown Lights" and "Headlights on Parade" are among the standout tracks. —*Rick Clark*

Peace at Last / 1996 / Warner Bros. ✦✦✦

Blue Öyster Cult

Hard Rock, Heavy Metal
Blue Öyster Cult was the thinking person's heavy-metal group. Put together on a college campus by a couple of rock critics, it maintained a close relationship with a series of literary figures (often in the fields of science fiction and horror), including Eric Von Lustbader, Patti Smith, Michael Moorcock, and Stephen King, while turning out some of the more listenable metal music of the early and mid '70s. The band that became Blue Öyster Cult was organized in 1967 at Stony Brook College on Long Island by students (and later rock critics) Sandy Pearlman and Richard Meltzer as Soft White Underbelly and consisted of Andy Winters (bass), Donald "Buck Dharma" Roeser (guitar), John Wiesenthal (keyboards), Allen Lanier—(keyboards), and Albert Bouchard (drums), with Pearlman managing and Pearlman and Meltzer writing songs. Initially without a lead singer, they added Les Bronstein on vocals. This quintet signed to Elektra Records and recorded an album that was never released. They then dropped Bronstein and replaced him with their road manager, Eric Bloom, as the band's name was changed to Oaxaca. A second Elektra album also went unreleased, though a single was issued under the name the Stalk-Forrest Group.

Cut loose by Elektra, they changed their name again, to Blue Öyster Cult, and signed to Columbia Records in late 1971, by which time Winters had been replaced by Albert Bouchard's brother Joe. *Blue Öyster Cult,* their debut album, was released in January 1972 and made the lower reaches of the charts. Columbia sent a promotional EP, *Live Bootleg,* to radio stations in October, and followed with BÖC's second album, *Tyranny and Mutation,* in February 1973. Their third album, *Secret Treaties,* was released in April 1974 and became their first to break into the Top 100 bestsellers. (It eventually went gold.) BÖC released a live double album, *On Your Feet or on Your Knees,* in February 1975. In May 1976 came their fourth studio album, *Agents of Fortune,* including the Top 40 (Top Ten on some charts) hit single "(Don't Fear) the Reaper" (featured in the classic John Carpenter horror film *Halloween*), which became their first gold and then platinum album. (*On Your Feet* went gold shortly after.) BÖC's sixth overall album, *Spectres,* was released in October 1977 and went gold in January 1978. In September 1978 came a second live album, *Some Enchanted Evening,* which eventually would become BÖC's second million-seller, followed by the studio album *Mirrors* in June 1979. A year later, BÖC released its ninth album, *Cultosaurus Erectus,* and the gold *Fire of Unknown Origin,* containing the Top 40 hit "Burnin' for You," following in June 1981.

In the summer of 1981, drummer Albert Bouchard was replaced by the band's tour manager and lighting designer, Rick Downey. BÖC's third live album, *Extraterrestrial Live,* was released in April 1982, followed by the studio album *The Revolution by Night* in October 1983. Downey left in 1984 and was replaced in 1985 by Jimmy Wilcox. The same year, Lanier left and was replaced by Tommy Zvonchek. BÖC released its 13th album, *Club Ninja,* in January 1986. Bassist Joe Bouchard left in 1986 and was replaced by Jon Rogers. In 1987, Lanier returned to the group, and Ron Riddle replaced Wilcox on drums. BÖC's 14th album, the concept recording *Imaginos,* became their final new album on Columbia Records in July 1988. BÖC scored the movie *Bad Channels* in 1992, by which time Chuck Burgi had replaced Ron Riddle on drums. In 1994, Blue Öyster Cult released *Cult Classic,* an album of re-recorded favorites, in connection with the use of their music in the TV miniseries of horror novelist Stephen King's, "The Stand." —*William Ruhlmann*

Blue Öyster Cult / Jan. 1972 / Columbia ✦✦✦✦
Blue Öyster Cult's debut album provided the missing link between the heavy, blues-based rock of the late '60s and the bombastic heavy metal of the '70s and beyond. You could hear major influences like Steppenwolf, with its melodic, aggressive rock, the Rolling Stones (post-1965), and even boogie bands like Canned Heat in their sound. But BÖC streamlined the approach, picked up the tempo, overlaid the guitars, brought the rhythm section up in the mix, and de-emphasized the blues, giving the music a machinelike propulsion. Manager/co-producer Sandy Pearlman (who co-wrote five songs) and lyricist Richard Meltzer (who co-wrote two) may have seen the group as a vehicle for their "clever" (in fact, pretentious) lyrics, but in fact lead vocalist Eric Bloom was the weakest element in the band, and you couldn't make out much of what he had to say over guitarist Donald "Buck Dharma" Roeser's furious power chording. What you could seemed to express some sort of mythology—or demonology; future metal bands would fill their songs with just such half-baked philosophies. *Blue Öyster Cult* was not quite full-fledged heavy metal: the production was too compressed, the playing too light and energetic. But it was the sound of something new and different in the world of hard rock. —*William Ruhlmann*

Tyranny & Mutation / Feb. 1973 / Columbia ✦✦✦✦
Co-producers Murray Krugman and Sandy Pearlman achieved a far sharper, more spacious production on Blue Öyster Cult's second album than they had in the cramped sound of its first, twinning, for instance, the high, ringing tone of Donald Roeser's lead guitar to Albert Bouchard's cymbals or Alan Lanier's keyboards and adding echo to give presence to Eric Bloom's still barely (or not quite) discernible vocals. In a sense, it's remarkable that albums like this have been categorized as heavy metal: despite the fullness of the aural attack, the fast tempos and raunchy sound give it much more the feel of old rockabilly or punk-rock-to-come. —*William Ruhlmann*

Secret Treaties / Apr. 1974 / Columbia ✦✦

On Your Feet or on Your Knees / Feb. 1975 / Columbia ✦✦

● **Agents of Fortune** / May 1976 / Columbia ✦✦✦✦
Nothing Blue Öyster Cult had produced previously prepared listeners for its infectious mid-tempo hit, "(Don't Fear) the Reaper," which propelled it into a higher commercial orbit and caused (or reflected) a change in the balance of power in the group. The song was written by guitarist Donald "Buck Dharma" Roeser and was an indication that the band was now largely doing its own songwriting; co-producer Sandy Pearlman earned only one co-writing credit on the record, while drummer Albert Bouchard had five. Poetess Patti Smith, meanwhile, not only co-wrote two tracks, but also performed on one, "The Revenge of Vera Gemini." The result was a record much more in a pop-rock vein than the vaunted metal of the first three albums and was BÖC's biggest hit ever. —*William Ruhlmann*

Spectres / Oct. 1977 / Columbia ✦✦✦
On the all-important follow-up to its commercial breakthrough with *Agents of Fortune,* Blue Öyster Cult introduced some enjoyable additions to its repertoire in "Godzilla" and "R.U. Ready 2 Rock," but did not come up with a song as memorable as "(Don't Fear) the Reaper," despite trying the same formula with "Fireworks" and "Nosferatu." Instead of consolidating its success, the group seemed to be, as one of the better songs had it, "Goin' Through the Motions," seemingly unable to follow through on the pop aspirations of the previous album and unwilling to retreat to the metal pretensions of its early records. Talk about being caught between a rock and a hard place—just when Blue Öyster Cult should have been conquering, they seemed ready to retreat. —*William Ruhlmann*

Some Enchanted Evening / Sep. 1978 / Columbia ✦✦

Mirrors / Jun. 1979 / Columbia ✦✦✦

Cultosaurus Erectus / Jun. 1980 / Columbia ✦✦✦

Fire of Unknown Origin / Jun. 1981 / Columbia ✦✦✦

Extraterrestrial Live / Apr. 1982 / Columbia ✦✦✦

The Revolution by Night / Oct. 1983 / Columbia ✦✦

Club Ninja / Jan. 1986 / Columbia ✦✦

Imaginos / Jul. 1988 / Columbia ✦✦✦

● **Workshop of the Telescopes** / Sep. 26, 1995 / Columbia/Legacy ✦✦✦✦
Blue Öyster Cult was long in need of a thorough career retrospective, and this is it. Thirty-two tracks filling up two discs with a total running time of 154:46, *Workshop of the Telescopes* traces BÖC through 14 years as the kings of lite metal, 1972-1986. Actually, as annotator Arthur Levy notes, there are at least two phases in that era. The first, running through 1974, includes the classic first two albums, *Blue Öyster Cult* and *Tyranny & Mutation,* when BÖC was one of the few acts in those pre-punk days bucking the trend toward soft rock without indulging in the more grotesque aspects of heavy metal. This material takes up disc one. Disc two leads off with "(Don't Fear) the Reaper," which launched the second phase of the band's career, when it sought to balance its hard-rocking

approach (heard especially in concert) with pop accessibility. Since this period was marked by uneven material, it is ripe for compiling, and the selection here is good. (We could have used a bit more from *Agents of Fortune*, but that's a quibble.) On the whole, *Workshop of the Telescopes* lives up to Levy's description of it as "the ultimate BÖC anthology." It's about time. —*William Ruhlmann*

Blue Rodeo

Rock 'n' Roll, Folk-Rock, Alternative Country-Rock
Blue Rodeo's style has drawn comparisons to a number of pop and rock icons, including the Beatles, Buffalo Springfield, the Band, and Bob Dylan. Formed in Toronto, the band is led by the songwriting team of vocalists/guitarists Jim Cuddy and Greg Keelor and also features bassist Bazil Donovan, drummer Glenn Milchem, and keyboardist Bob Wiseman, who also plays harmonica and accordion. Their debut album, 1987's *Outskirts*, showcased the group's harmonies and musical interplay in a classic, rootsy folk-rock style. The punchier *Diamond Mine* (1989) covered more lyrical ground, bringing a bit of social commentary into Blue Rodeo's tales of loss and heartbreak, but the recording site (an empty hall in Toronto) dulled the songs' impact somewhat. In 1990, Wiseman recorded his own solo album, *Bob Wiseman Sings Wrench Tuttle: In Her Dreams*. Producer Pete Anderson (Michelle Shocked, Dwight Yoakam) accentuated the group's vocal harmonies on the following year's *Casino*, which was well-received. Even higher praise was reserved for *Lost Together*, which synthesized the previous albums' stylistic changes into a cohesive whole. —*Steve Huey*

Outskirts / 1987 / Discoveries ✦✦✦
Outskirts is a highly likeable debut featuring mid-tempo country- rockers fleshed out by tasteful use of organ in the arrangements—a subtle touch that, along with the sheer quality of the material, distinguished Blue Rodeo from the hordes of other Gram Parsons devotees in the mid-'80s. —*Chris Woodstra*

Diamond Mine / 1989 / Discoveries ✦✦✦
Diamond Mine is a considerably more quiet affair. Beginning with the very Dylanesque "God and Country," a darker, introverted mood is set by their minimalist approach and slow tempos. —*Chris Woodstra*

● **Casino** / 1991 / Discoveries ✦✦✦✦
Casino is a more pop-oriented album. They seem to have finally established their fine blend of harmonies and laidback country-rock à la the Band and Bob Dylan. Produced by Pete Anderson (Dwight Yoakam, Michelle Shocked). —*Chris Woodstra*

Lost Together / 1992 / Discoveries ✦✦✦✦

Five Days in July / 1994 / Musicraft ✦✦✦

Nowhere to Here / Sep. 5, 1995 / Discovery ✦✦✦
Blue Rodeo continues to experiment on their latest release. Opening and closing with expansive mood pieces, it takes a bit of listening to get into this album. But sandwiched in between lies the real meat of this record. Bluesy ballads such as "Sky" and "Train" are balanced by upbeat pop tunes like "What You Want" and "Better Off as We Are." The rockin' Beatlesque "Get Through to You" shows them in top form. Every song tends to evoke th majesty of the Canadian countryside while never sounding hokey. Once you let these tunes seep into your psyche, you'll find there isn't a bum tune in the bunch. Fantastic! —*James Chrispell*

Blue Things

Folk-Rock, Pop-Rock
Along with the Remains, the Blue Things are serious contenders for the title of the Great Lost Mid-'60s American Band. The Kansas group was extremely popular in the Midwest and Texas, but remained unknown on a national level, despite a deal with RCA. Piloted by the excellent songwriting of singer/guitarist Val Stocklein, the group often sounded like a cross between the Byrds and the Beau Brummels with its melodic, energetic, guitar-oriented folk-rock and haunting harmonies. The group's sole album (*Listen & See*, 1966) and several singles chart a rapid growth from British Invasion-like material with a heavy Searchers and Buddy Holly influence to full-blown psychedelic efforts with careening guitars, organ, and backward effects. Quite innovative for the time, these 1966 psychedelic singles met with no more than regional success. The group's impetus was derailed by the departure of Stocklein at the end of 1966, although they struggled on for a bit. Stocklein went to California and recorded a disappointing MOR-folk album for Dot in the late '60s that reprised some of his Blue Things songs. —*Richie Unterberger*

Listen & See / 1966 / RCA ✦✦✦✦
One of the most underappreciated albums of the '60s. Composed of Val Stocklein originals and well-chosen covers, the group synthesized the Beatles and Dylanesque folk-rock with a skill similar to the Byrds. Ringing 12-string and acoustic guitars, melodic harmonies, passionate vocals, and strong material abound on this nearly forgotten near-classic. —*Richie Unterberger*

The Blue Things Story, Vol. 1 (1964-65) / 1987 / Cicadelic ✦✦✦
This collection of 1964 and 1965 demos, coupled with some rare early singles, shows the band at its most British Invasion-influenced. It has quite a few fine Beatlesque harmony rockers by Stocklein, along with some nifty covers. There's a marked difference between the 1964 and 1965 demos, which show the band shifting from British Invasion emulation to a more mature and far more folk-rock-influenced direction. —*Richie Unterberger*

● **The Blue Things Story, Vol. 2 (1965-66)** / 1987 / Cicadelic ✦✦✦✦
Basically a repackage of *Listen & See*, with a couple of the less impressive cover songs deleted. In their place are four fine previously unreleased demos, two of which feature the entire band, two of which are performed by Stocklein alone on acoustic guitar. The epic ballad "Desert Wind" is a special standout among the previously unreleased cuts. —*Richie Unterberger*

The Blue Things Story, Vol. 3 (1966) / 1987 / Cicadelic ✦✦✦

The Blues Brothers

Soul, R&B
During the late '70s, "Saturday Night Live" twosome Dan Aykroyd and the late John Belushi, as Elwood and Jake Blues, employed the services of Stax rhythm-section players Steve Cropped and Duck Dunn, as well as Letterman band leader Paul Shaffer, for a run-through on some soul classics. As a "Saturday Night Live" skit, this was fun. Musically, the best thing that can be said about the Blues Brothers is that they inspired a new audience to look for the real thing. —*Rick Clark*

Briefcase Full of Blues / Dec. 1978 / Atlantic ✦✦✦✦
"The Blues Brothers" began as an affectionate joke-cum-tribute to R&B music, and taken in that spirit it retained its entertainment value, even after this live album topped the charts, sold two million copies, and produced hit singles in "Rubber Biscuit" and "Soul Man." The guardians of popular music have always been entirely too reverent and humorless, however, and it wasn't long before they were leveling charges of rip-off against the Brothers and complaining that John Belushi couldn't sing as well as Otis Redding. So what? No one seems to have noticed that Belushi was as obsessive about citing his sources as Frank Sinatra is about naming his arrangers—you'd have thought those critics would have appreciated the footnotes. The beneficiaries of Belushi's encomiums didn't mind the increased exposure or the renewed royalty checks ("I suggest you buy as many blues albums as you can," Belushi told the audience), and even today, what comes across in these performances is the sincerity of feeling—that and some tasty playing from a top-notch band. —*William Ruhlmann*

The Best of the Blues Brothers / Dec. 1981 / Atlantic ✦✦✦
A solid collection, this includes the hits "Rubber Biscuit," "Soul Man," and "Gimme Some Lovin'," plus music from *The Blues Brothers* movie soundtrack. —*AMG*

● **The Definitive Collection** / 1992 / Atlantic ✦✦✦✦
The Definitive Collection is indeed the definitive Blues Brothers disc, containing all of their hits and signature songs. —*Stephen Thomas Erlewine*

The Blues Project

Group / Modern Electric Blues, Blues-Rock, Folk-Rock
One of the first album-oriented, "underground" groups in the US, the Blues Project offered an electric brew of rock, blues, folk, pop, and even some jazz, classical, and psychedelia during their brief heyday in the mid-'60s. It's not quite accurate to categorize them as a blues-rock group, although they did plenty of that kind of material; they were more like a Jewish-American equivalent to British bands like the Yardbirds, who used a blues and R&B base to explore any music that interested them. Erratic songwriting talent and a lack of a truly outstanding vocalist prevented them from rising to the front line of '60s bands, but they recorded plenty of interesting material over the course of their first three albums, before the departure of their most creative members took its toll.

The Blues Project were formed in Greenwich Village in the mid-'60s by guitarist Danny Kalb (who had played sessions for various Elektra folk and folk-rock albums), Steve Katz (a guitarist with Elektra's Even Dozen Jug Band), flutist/bassist Andy Kulberg, drummer Roy Blumenfeld, and singer Tommy Flanders. Al Kooper, in his early twenties a seasoned vet of rock sessions, joined after sitting in on the band's Columbia Records audition, although they ended up signing to Verve, an MGM subsidiary. Early member Artie Traum (guitar) dropped out during early rehearsals; Flanders would leave after their first LP, *Live at the Cafe Au-Go-Go* (1966).

The eclectic resumes of the musicians, who came from folk, jazz, blues, and rock backgrounds, was reflected in their choice of material. Blues by Muddy Waters and Chuck Berry tunes ran alongside covers of contemporary folk-rock songs by Eric Anderson and Patrick Sky, as well as the group's own originals. These were usually penned by Kooper, who had already built songwriting credentials as the co-writer of Gary Lewis' huge smash "This Diamond Ring," and established a reputation as a major folk-rock shaker with his contributions to Dylan's mid-'60s records. Kooper also provided the band's instrumental highlights with his glowing organ riffs.

The live debut sounds rather tame and derivative; the group truly hit their stride on *Projections* (late 1966), which was, disappointingly, their only full-length studio recording. While they went through straight blues numbers with respectable energy, they really shone best on the folk and jazz-influenced tracks, like "Fly Away," Katz's lilting "Steve's Song," Kooper's jazz instrumental "Flute Thing" (an underground radio standard that's probably their most famous track), and Kooper's fierce adaptation of an old Blind Willie Johnson number, "I Can't Keep from Crying." A non-LP single from this era, the pop-psychedelic "No Time Like the Right Time," was their greatest achievement and one of the best "great hit singles that never were" of the decade.

The band's very eclecticism didn't augur well for their long-term stability, and in 1967 Kooper left in a dispute over musical direction (he has recalled that Kalb opposed his wishes to add a horn section). Then Kalb mysteriously disappeared for months after a bad acid trip, which effectively finished the original incarnation of the band. A third album, *Live at Town Hall*, was a particularly half-assed project given the band's stature, pasted together from live tapes and studio outtakes, some of which were overdubbed with applause to give the impression that they had been recorded in concert.

Kooper got to fulfill his ambitions for soulful horn rock as the leader of the original Blood, Sweat & Tears, although he left that band after their first album; BS&T also included Katz (who stayed onboard for a long time). Blumenfeld and Kulberg kept the Blues Project going for a fourth album before forming Seatrain, and the group reformed in the early '70s with various lineups, Kooper rejoining for a live 1973 album, *Reunion in Central Park*. The first three albums from the Kooper days are the only ones that count, though; the best material from these is on Rhino's best-of compilation. — *Richie Unterberger*

Live at the Cafe Au-Go-Go / May 1966 / Verve/Forecast ✦✦✦

Projections / Nov. 1966 / Verve/Forecast ✦✦✦✦
Produced by Tom Wilson (Dylan, Zappa), the Blues Project's second effort was their finest hour. In less than a year the enthusiastic live band had matured into a seasoned studio ensemble. Steve Katz's dreams are lightweight folk but Al Kooper reworks two gospel themes ("Wake Me, Shake Me," "I Can't Keep from Crying") into ambitious blues-rock compositions, and Danny Kalb proves he's no mere folkie on extended versions of "Two Trains Running" and "Caress Me Baby." Bassist Andy Kulberg switches to flute and Kalb gets psychedelic on the jazzy "Flute Thing," penned by Kooper. — *Dan Forte*

Live at Town Hall / Sep. 1967 / Verve/Forecast ✦✦✦

Original Blues Project Reunion in Central Park / 1973 / MGM ✦✦✦

● **Best of the Blues Project [Forecast]** / 1989 / Verve/Forecast ✦✦✦✦
Best of the Blues Project is the best anthology of the band ever likely to be done. It encompasses their wealth of high points in better sound than ever. — *Bruce Eder*

● **The Best of the Blues Project [Rhino]** / 1989 / Rhino ✦✦✦✦
With the exception of a live version of "Flute Thing" from the Blues Project's 1973 reunion concert included only on the CD version, this compilation is culled entirely from the albums *Live at the Cafe Au-Go-Go*, *Projections*, and *The Blues Project Live At Town Hall*, all recorded and released in the period 1966-1967. Just as those individual albums do, it confirms the acclaim accorded the Blues Project at the time. The group's sophistication and ability to create a hybrid of musical styles keeps the music from sounding dated. In fact, this music not only stands as among the best of its time, but it continues to appeal where much of the music made simultaneously fails to escape its era. (Not to be confused with *Best of the Blues Project*, Verve/Forecast FTS 3077 [1969 07], which is an earlier compilation with a different selection of songs.) — *William Ruhlmann*

Blues Traveler

Rock 'n' Roll, Pop-Rock
A New York-based blues-rock quartet formed in 1988 by singer/harmonica player John Popper, guitarist Chan Kinchla, bassist Bobby Sheehan, and drummer Brendan Hill, Blues Traveler was part of a revival of the extended jamming style of '60s and '70s groups like the Grateful Dead and Led Zeppelin. Signed to A&M, they released their first album, *Blues Traveler*, in May 1990 and followed it with *Travelers & Thieves* in September 1991. Popper was in a serious car accident in 1992, leaving him unable to perform for a number of months. Fortunately, he recovered, yet he still had to perform in a wheelchair for a period of time. In April 1993, Blues Traveler released its third album, *Save His Soul*, which became its first to make the Top 100. Blues Traveler's aptly named fourth album, *Four*, released in September 1994, at first looked like a sales disappoint-

ment, but it rebounded in 1995 when "Run-Around," a single taken from it, became the group's first chart hit. — *William Ruhlmann*

● **Blues Traveler** / May 1990 / A&M ✦✦✦✦
Blues Traveler's loose jam structures on basic blues riffs mark them as a band in the tradition of such predecessors as the Grateful Dead. Unlike that communal effort, however, this group has a distinct focal point in virtuoso harmonica player and vocalist John Popper, who keeps things from meandering too much. — *William Ruhlmann*

Travelers & Thieves / Sep. 1991 / A&M ✦✦✦

Save His Soul / Apr. 1993 / A&M ✦✦✦

Four / 1994 / A&M ✦✦✦
Lacking the rootsier edge of *Save His Soul*, *Four* finds Blues Traveler retreating to their standard blues-boogie formula, with mixed results. Of course, there are some fine songs here—including their breakthrough hit single "Run-Around"— but too often the band sounds like they're coasting. *Four* is a solid record, but it shows signs that the band's formula may be wearing thin. — *Stephen Thomas Erlewine*

Live from the Fall / Jul. 1996 / A&M ✦✦✦✦

Blur

Alternative Pop-Rock, Pop-Rock, Club-Dance, Brit-Pop
Initially, Blur were one of the multitude of British bands that appeared in the wake of the Stone Roses, mining the same swirling, psuedo-psychedelic guitar-pop, only with louder guitars. Following an image makeover in the mid-'90s, the group emerged as the most popular band in the UK, establishing themselves as the heir to the Brit-pop tradition of the Kinks, the Small Faces, the Who, the Jam, Madness, and the Smiths.

Originally called Seymour, the group was formed in London in 1989 by vocalist/keyboardist Damon Albarn, guitarist Graham Coxon, and bassist Alex James, with drummer Dave Rowntree joining the lineup shortly afterward. After performing a handful of gigs and recording a demo tape, the band signed to Food Records, a subsidiary of EMI run by journalist Andy Ross and former Teardrop Explodes keyboardist Dave Balfe. Balfe and Ross suggested that the band change their name, submitting a list of alternate names for the group's approval. From that list, the group took the name Blur.

"She's So High," the group's first single, made it into the Top 50 while the follow-up "There's No Other Way" went Top Ten. Both singles were included on their 1991 Stephen Street-produced debut album, *Leisure*. Although it received favorable reviews, the album fit neatly into the dying Manchester pop scene, causing some journalists to dismiss the band as manufactured teen idols. For the next two years, Blur struggled to distance themselves from the scene associated with the sound of their first album.

Released in 1992, the snarling "Pop Scene" was Blur's first attempt at changing their musical direction. A brash, spiteful rocker driven by horns, the neo-mod single was punkier than anything the band had previously recorded, and its hooks were more immediate and catchy. Despite Blur's clear artistic growth, "Pop Scene" didn't fit into the climate of British pop and American grunge in 1992 and failed to make an impression on the UK charts. Following the single's commercial failure, the group began work on their second album, *Modern Life Is Rubbish*.

XTC's Andy Partridge was originally slated to produce *Modern Life Is Rubbish*, but the relationship between Blur and Partridge quickly soured, so Street was again brought in to produce the band. After spending nearly a year in the studio, the band delivered the album to Food. The record company rejected the album, declaring that it needed a hit single. Blur went back into the studio and recorded Albarn's "For Tomorrow," which did become a British hit. Food was ready to release the record but the group's US record company, SBK, believed there was no American hit single on the record and asked them to return to the studio. Blur complied and recorded "Chemical World," which pleased SBK for a short while. *Modern Life Is Rubbish* was set for release in the spring of 1993 when SBK asked Blur to re-record the album with producer Butch Vig (Nirvana, Sonic Youth). The band refused and the record was released in May in Britain; it appeared in the US that fall. *Modern Life Is Rubbish* received good reviews in Britain, peaking at No. 15 on the charts.

Modern Life Is Rubbish turned out to be a dry run for Blur's breakthrough album, *Parklife*. Released in April 1994, *Parklife* entered the charts at No. 1 and catapulted the band to stardom in Britain. The stylized new wave dance-pop single "Girls and Boys" entered the charts at No. 5; the single managed to spend 15 weeks in the US charts, peaking at No. 52, but the album never cracked the charts. It was a completely different story in England, as Blur had a string of hit singles including the ballad "To the End" and the mod anthem "Parklife."

With the success of *Parklife*, Blur opened the door for a flood of British indie-guitar bands that dominated British pop culture in the mid-'90s. Oasis, Elastica, Pulp, the Boo Radleys, Supergrass, Gene, Echobelly, Menswear, and numerous other bands all benefited from the band's success. By the beginning of 1995, *Parklife* had gone triple platinum and the band had become superstars. The group spent the first half of 1995 recording their fourth album and playing various one-off concerts. Blur released "Country House," the first single from their new album, in August; it became the band's first No. 1 single. *The Great Escape,* Blur's follow-up to *Parklife,* was released in September 1995, immediately entering the UK charts at No. 1. —*Stephen Thomas Erlewine*

Leisure / Sep. 1991 / Food/SBK ✦✦✦

Modern Life Is Rubbish / 1993 / SBK ✦✦✦✦
On their second album, Blur explores their influences, particularly the Kinks, David Bowie, the Smiths, and the Who. The result is an album filled with enjoyable but derivative guitar-pop singles that never manage to capture the spark of Blur's idols or create their own identity. —*Stephen Thomas Erlewine*

★ **Parklife** / Apr. 1994 / Food/SBK ✦✦✦✦✦
An audacious fusion of early-'80s new wave with the timeless guitar pop of The Kinks and the Smiths, *Parklife* is Blur's most ambitious album to date, as well as their best. For once, their songwriting has enough satisfying original hooks to make the entire record consistently enjoyable. —*Stephen Thomas Erlewine*

The Great Escape / Sep. 1995 / Food/Parlophone ✦✦✦✦
In the simplest terms, *The Great Escape* is the flipside of *Parklife.* Where Blur's breakthrough album was a celebration of the working class, drawing on British pop from the '60s and reaching through the '80s, *The Great Escape* concentrates on the suburbs, featuring a cast of characters all trying to cope with the numbing pressures of modern life. Consequently, it's darker than *Parklife,* even if the melancholia is hidden underneath the crisp production and catchy melodies. Even the bright, infectious numbers have gloomy subtexts, from the disillusioned millionaire of "Country House" and the sycophant of "Charmless Man," to the bleak loneliness of "The Globe Alone" and "Entertain Me." Naturally, the slower numbers are even more despairing, with the acoustic "Best Days," the lush, sweeping strings of "The Universal" and the stark, moving electronic ballad "Yuko and Hiro" ranking as the most affecting work Blur has ever recorded. However, none of this makes *The Great Escape* a burden or a difficult album. The music bristles with invention throughout, as Blur delves deeper into experimentation with synthesizers, horns, and strings; guitarist Graham Coxon twists out unusual chords and lead lines; and Damon Albarn spits out unexpected lyrical couplets filled with wit and venomous intelligence in each song. But Blur's most remarkable accomplishment is that it can reference the past—the Scott Walker homage of "The Universal," the Terry Hall/Fun Boy Three cop on "Top Man," the skittish, XTC-flavored pop of "It Could Be You," and Albarn's devotion to Ray Davies—while still moving forward, creating a vibrant, invigorating record. —*Stephen Thomas Erlewine*

BoDeans

Roots Rock
The BoDeans are a rock 'n' roll band formed in Waukesha, WI, by singer-songwriters/guitarists Sammy Lianas and Kurt Neumann, who had played together since junior high school, along with a rhythm section of bassist Bob Griffin and drummer Guy Hoffman. The quartet signed to Slash Records (manufactured and distributed by Warner Bros.) and released its first album, the critically well-accepted *Love & Hope & Sex & Dreams* (the title comes from a line in the Rolling Stones' song "Shattered") in 1986. *Outside Looking In* (1987), produced by Talking Head and Wisconsin native Jerry Harrison, saw the band reduced to a trio with the departure of Hoffman. It broke into the Top 100 best-sellers, as the BoDeans toured with U2, appeared on Robbie Robertson's self-titled debut solo album, and were named "Best New Band" in *Rolling Stone* magazine. By the time of the release of the third album, *Home* (1989), Michael Ramos (keyboards) and Danny Gayol (drums) had joined. This lineup stayed intact for the release of *Black and White* (1991), but the BoDeans were drummerless again as of the release of *Go Slow Down* (1993). —*William Ruhlmann*

● **Love & Hope & Sex & Dreams** / May 1986 / Slash ✦✦✦✦
When the BoDeans appeared with their first album, *Love & Hope & Sex & Dreams,* they immediately were filed under "roots rock" because of the Western twang in their guitars, their bouncy beat, and their simple, neo-rockabilly approach to songwriting, not to mention the production of T-Bone Burnett. They led off the album with "She's a Runaway," a song of spousal abuse and revenge that indicated a higher social consciousness than much of the rest of the album, which was typified by "Misery," in which the singer laments that his girlfriend sleeps around. At their best, on "She's a Runaway," "Fadeaway," and "Angels," the BoDeans came up with infectious riffs and made maximum use of the sweet-and-sour vocal interaction between the conventional voice of Kurt Neumann and Sammy Llanas' distinctive whine. Much of the album was slight, but there was enough of an individual sound to the better material to think of the BoDeans as a band of considerable promise. —*William Ruhlmann*

Outside Looking In / Sep. 1987 / Slash ✦✦

Home / Jul. 27, 1989 / Slash ✦✦✦

Black and White / Apr. 26, 1991 / Slash ✦✦✦

Go Slow Down / Oct. 12, 1993 / Slash ✦✦✦✦
The BoDeans made their best album since their debut by returning to the basic folk and rock elements that had always worked best for them. On their most acoustic outing they also rediscovered themselves as songwriters, pursuing subjects unusually close at hand, whether sex, suicide, or the frustrations of the music business. No matter what the topic, they sounded like they meant it, and for once their eclecticism worked for them, providing them with a bagful of styles to evoke without overdoing it. *Go Slow Down* may have been the statement of a band that had been through a lot and reached a point of emotional exhaustion, but the BoDeans used their experience to craft their most deeply felt and satisfying music. Two and a half years after the album's release, its lead-off track, "Closer to Free," became a hit after being made the theme song of the "Party of Five" TV series. —*William Ruhlmann*

Joe Dirt Car / Aug. 8, 1995 / Slash ✦✦

Michael Bolton (Michael Bolotin)

b. Feb. 26, 1954, New Haven, CT
Vocals / Adult Contemporary, Pop-Rock
Michael Bolton has suffered more than his fair share of criticism, no matter how much of it was deserved. After spending the '70s churning out arena-friendly hard rock with Blackjack as well as on his own, he turned to soul-inspired pop-rock in the early '80s. As long as he was a faceless hard rocker, critics and audiences paid him no mind because, frankly, he wasn't very good. He was good at pop songwriting: Laura Branigan had a hit in 1983 with his "How Am I Supposed to Live Without You," while he was struggling as an AOR singer called Michael Bolotin.

With 1987's *The Hunger,* his second album as Michael Bolton, he began charting on his own. "That's What Love Is All About" cracked the Top 20, but it was his carbon copy of Otis Redding's "(Sittin' On) The Dock of the Bay" that brought him the attention and sales that he craved, as well as the start of the blistering criticism.

To be fair, much of the criticism is unwarranted, but some of it is. When he is singing soul covers, Bolton removes any pretense of subtlety, straining any emotion from the song with his overwrought delivery. On his own material, he is drastically better. Not only does he restrain his gruff voice and sing musically, but his songs are well-constructed adult-contemporary pop songs that sound perfect on the radio.

Despite all of the criticism, Bolton continued to sell records well into the '90s, even though his writing was starting to lose some of its sharpness. It might have been a massive hit, but 1994's "Said I Loved You (But I Lied)" was his first true piece of hack work. A couple months after that single, he lost a plagiarism suit to the Isley Brothers, who claimed that he had appropriated their 1966 "Love Is a Wonderful Thing" for his 1991 hit of the same name. Bolton appealed the ruling, and the case is still in the courts. It remains to be seen whether the case will hurt his sales, but a surprising number of critics came to his defense, agreeing with him that the songs shared little more than the same title. —*Stephen Thomas Erlewine*

The Hunger / Sep. 1987 / Columbia ✦✦✦

Soul Provider / Jul. 1989 / Columbia ✦✦✦✦
Michael Bolton is no fool, and when he broke through to platinum sales with *The Hunger,* nobody had to tell him to record a follow-up devoted to more of the same. Bolton produced most of the record himself, and he teamed with the cream of the era's romantic rock ballad writers, people like Diane Warren (who gets five co-credits here) and Desmond Child, while the R&B copy this time was Ray Charles' version of "Georgia on My Mind." He also reclaimed "How Am I Supposed to Live Without You" from Laura Branigan. The result was five Top 40 hits and millions of albums sold. Maybe Bolton wasn't the king of the hockey rinks, but his voice was now stoking the romantic fires in bedrooms across America, which is nice work if you can get it. —*William Ruhlmann*

Time, Love & Tenderness / Apr. 1991 / Columbia ✦✦✦✦
Michael Bolton cloned his approach from *Soul Provider* on its follow-up, *Time Love & Tenderness,* and sold as many records for his trouble. (That's six million copies.) His key collaborator once again was Diane Warren, who applied her goldplated gift for writing contemporary love songs to six tunes, among them the hits "Time, Love and Tenderness" and "Missing You Now" (which featured saxmeister Kenny G). The obligatory R&B carbon copy was Percy Sledge's "When a Man Loves a Woman," which hit No. 1. The only unusual songs came at the beginning and the end. The album led off with "Love Is a Wonderful Thing" (a Top Ten hit), a song in standard '60s R&B mode that would be the subject of a plagiarism suit from the Isley Brothers, and it concluded with "Steel Bars," co-written by Bolton and . . . Bob Dylan? That's what it said, and if the song wasn't one of Dylan's best, it at least indicated that Bolton might have possibilities that had so far gone unnoticed. —*William Ruhlmann*

Timeless (The Classics) / Sep. 1992 / Columbia ✦✦✦

The One Thing / Nov. 1993 / Columbia ✦✦✦
● **Greatest Hits 1985-1995** / Sep. 19, 1995 / Columbia ✦✦✦✦

Bon Jovi
....
Hard Rock, Pop-Rock, Hair Metal
Bon Jovi is a hard-rock quintet from New Jersey, led by singer/guitarist Jon Bon Jovi (born John Bongiovi, Mar. 2, 1962, Perth Amboy, NJ) and featuring Richie Sambora (b. Jul. 11, 1959) on guitar, David Bryan (born David Rashbaum, Feb. 7, 1962, NJ) on keyboards, Alec John Such (b. Nov. 14, 1956) on bass, and Tico Torres (b. Oct. 7, 1953) on drums, that became one of the most popular rock acts of the late '80s and early '90s. The band was formed in Sayreville, NJ, in March 1983 and signed to Mercury Records, releasing its self-titled debut album in January 1984. The album reached the Top 100 and was followed by *7800 Degrees Fahrenheit*, which went gold. Bon Jovi achieved mass success with its third album, *Slippery When Wet* (Aug. 1986), which topped the charts and sold nine million copies. The album featured the No. 1 singles "You Give Love a Bad Name" and "Livin' on a Prayer" and the Top Ten hit "Wanted Dead or Alive." Bon Jovi's fifth album was *New Jersey* (Sep. 1988), another chart-topper that sold five million copies and spawned five Top Ten hit singles including the No. 1's "Bad Medicine" and "I'll Be There for You." The group then went on hiatus while Jon Bon Jovi and Richie Sambora made solo albums. It returned to action with *Keep the Faith* in November 1992, which hit the Top Ten, sold a million copies, and featured the Top Ten single "Bed of Roses." *Cross Road*, a greatest-hits collection, was released on October 4, 1994. It sold two million copies, reached the Top Ten, and included the Top Ten gold single "Always." —*William Ruhlmann*

Bon Jovi / Jan. 1984 / Mercury ✦✦✦

7800 Degrees Fahrenheit / Apr. 1985 / Mercury ✦✦✦

Slippery When Wet / Aug. 1986 / Mercury ✦✦✦✦
It is probably true that Bon Jovi's breakthrough success with *Slippery When Wet*, their third album, had more to do with lead singer Jon Bon Jovi's mop of curls and winning smile than with anything in the grooves of the record. Nevertheless, the album contained competent contemporary pop-rock, from its Eddie Van Halen-inspired guitar solos to the singer's enthusiastic, husky wail (which owed a lot to Bruce Springsteen). Jon Bon Jovi, guitarist Richie Sambora, and songwriter-for-hire Desmond Child had little more on their minds than girls and rock-as-mythology (even the working-class anthem "Livin' on a Prayer" featured a character who was forced to hock his "six string"), but that may only mean they had identified their audience—young white adolescent males—and were targeting it accurately. —*William Ruhlmann*

New Jersey / Sep. 1988 / Mercury ✦✦✦✦
Bon Jovi had perfected a formula for hard pop-rock by the time of this album, concentrating on sing-along choruses sung over and over again, frequently by a rough, extensively overdubbed chorus, producing an effect not unlike what these songs sounded like in the arenas and stadiums where they were most often heard. The lyrics had that typical pop twist—although they nominally expressed romantic commitment, sentiments such as "Lay Your Hands on Me" and "I'll Be There for You" worked equally well as a means for the band and its audience to reaffirm their affection for each other. The only thing that marred the perfection of this communion was Jon Bon Jovi's continuing obsession with a certain predecessor from his home state; at times, he seemed to be trying to recreate *Born to Run* using cheaper materials. —*William Ruhlmann*

Keep the Faith / Nov. 1992 / Mercury ✦✦✦
● **Cross Road** / Oct. 4, 1994 / Mercury ✦✦✦✦
While Bon Jovi always managed to stick a couple of killer album tracks on their records, their main strength has always been singles. *Cross Road* collects all of their biggest hits, adding a couple of new songs and Jon Bon Jovi's solo hit, "Blaze of Glory," for good measure. Even the band's detractors may not be able to resist the constant flow of big guitars, big hooks, and sweet melodies that pour out on *Cross Roads*. After all, this is what state-of-the-art mainstream hard rock was all about in the late '80s. —*Stephen Thomas Erlewine*

These Days / 1995 / Mercury ✦✦✦

The Graham Bond Organization (Graham John Clifton Bond)
....
b. Oct. 28, 1937, Romford, Essex, England, **d.** May 8, 1974, London, England
Organ, Saxophone / Blues-Rock, British Invasion, British Blues
An important, underappreciated figure of early British R&B, Graham Bond is known in the US for heading the group that Jack Bruce and Ginger Baker played in before they joined Cream. Originally an alto sax jazz player, he met Bruce and Baker in 1962 after joining Alexis Koerner's Blues Incorporated, the finishing school for numerous British rock and blues musicians. By the time he, Bruce, and Baker split to form their own band in 1963, Bond was mostly playing the Hammond organ, as well as

handling the lion's share of the vocals. John McLaughlin was a member of the Graham Bond Organization in the early days for a few months, and some live material that he recorded with the group was eventually issued after most of its members had achieved stardom in other contexts. Saxophonist Dick Heckstall-Smith completed Bond's most stable lineup, which cut a couple decent albums and a few singles in the mid-'60s.

In its prime, the Graham Bond Organization played R&B with a strong jazzy flavor, emphasizing Bond's demonic organ and gruff vocals. The band arguably would have been better served to feature Bruce as its lead singer—he is featured surprisingly rarely on their recordings. Nevertheless, their best records were admirably tough British R&B-rock-jazz-soul, and though Bond has sometimes been labeled as a pioneer of jazz-rock, in reality it was much closer to rock than jazz. The band performed imaginative covers and fairly strong original material, and Bond was also perhaps the very first rock musician to record with the Mellotron synthesizer. Hit singles, though, were necessary for British bands to thrive in the mid-'60s, and Bond's group began to fall apart in 1966, when Bruce and Baker joined forces with Eric Clapton to form Cream. Bond attempted to carry on with the Organization for a while with Heckstall-Smith and drummer Jon Hiseman, both of whom went on to John Mayall's Bluesbreakers and Colosseum.

Bond never recaptured the heights of his work with the Organization. In the late '60s, he moved to the US, recording albums with musicians including Harvey Brooks, Harvey Mandel, and Hal Blaine. Moving back to Britain, he worked with Ginger Baker's Airforce, the Jack Bruce Band, and Cream lyricist Pete Brown, as well as forming the band Holy Magick, who recorded a couple albums. Bond's demise was more tragic than most: he developed serious drug and alcohol problems and an obsession with the occult, and it has even been posthumously speculated (in the British Bond biography *Mighty Shadow*) that he sexually abused his stepdaughter. He committed suicide by throwing himself into the path of a London Underground train in 1974. —*Richie Unterberger*

● **The Sound of 65** / Mar. 1965 / Edsel ✦✦✦✦
Although the Organization's first album was recorded a mere year or two before Cream's debut, it bears little resemblance to Cream's pioneering hard blues-rock. Instead, it's taut British R&B with a considerable jazz influence. That influence comes not so much from the rhythm section as saxophonist Dick Heckstall-Smith and lead singer/organist Bond himself. This LP is not as exciting or rock-oriented as those of contemporaries like the Rolling Stones or John Mayall, but is respectably gritty, mostly original material, with an occasionally nasty edge. There are some obscure treasures of the British R&B explosion to be found here, including the original version of "Train Time" (later performed by Cream), the thrilling bass runs on "Baby Be Good to Me," and the group's hardboiled rearrangements of such traditional standards as "Wade in the Water" and "Early in the Morning." Even their blatant stab at commerciality (the ballad "Tammy") has its charm. —*Richie Unterberger*

There's a Bond Between Us / Nov. 1965 / Edsel ✦✦✦✦
Bond's second album stakes out similar territory as his debut in a more polished but slightly less exciting fashion. Some of the covers are a bit routine and hackneyed, and the original material isn't quite as strong (or frequent) as on the first effort. On a few tunes, the group expands from raveups to mellower, jazzier ballads that retain an R&B base. Highlights include the early Jack Bruce composition "Hear Me Calling Your Name" (to which he also contributes a fine lead vocal) and the excellent Bond tune "Walkin' in the Park," which holds up to the best early British R&B numbers. The album is also notable for being one of the very first rock LPs to feature the Mellotron, which Bond uses subtly and well. —*Richie Unterberger*

Graham Bond Organization / 1984 / Charly ✦✦

Gary "U.S." Bonds (Gary Anderson)
....
b. Jun. 6, 1939, Jacksonville, FL
Vocals / R&B, Rock 'n' Roll
After moving to the Norfolk, VA, area in the mid '50s, young Gary Anderson began plying his vocal wares, first in church, later with a local group called the Turks. When he was not yet 21, he was approached by local record producer Frank Guida to join his tiny Legrand label. Guida changed Anderson's name to US Bonds, hoping the first release would get extra airplay by disc jockeys mistaking it for a public service announcement. The result was the classic "New Orleans," combining rock-combo raunch with impassioned, scorched soul-singing that set the stage for all that would follow. Guida double- and triple-tracked Bonds's voice, and the resulting murky production gave all the hits (including "Quarter to Three," "School Is Out," and "Dear Lady Twist") a party-in-outer-space quality all their own. Though he has kept recording, making a couple of excellent solo albums in the early '80s with the help of Bruce Springsteen, Bonds is best seen today dotting the landscape of oldies shows the world over, singing the songs that made him famous. —*Cub Koda*

Dedication / Apr. 1981 / Razor & Tie ✦✦✦

On the Line / Jun. 1982 / Razor & Tie ✦✦✦

● The School of Rock 'n' Roll: Best of Gary U.S. Bonds / 1990 / Rhino ✦✦✦✦

Gary US Bonds' biggest hits—"New Orleans," "Twist, Twist Senora," and especially "Quarter to Three"—were unquestionably among the best rock 'n' roll of the early '60s. Beyond that, the going runs a bit thin. This 18-cut compilation includes all of the above hits, as well as others from his blitz of Top 40 singles in 1961 and 1962—"School Is Out," the response record "School Is In" (guess which one did worse), "Dear Lady Twist," and "Seven Day Weekend." The rest of the CD features B-sides, flop singles, and unissued material from his stay at the Legrand label in the early '60s. Most of them feature the dense production, party atmosphere, and West Indian-influenced beats that made his hits so instantly identifiable. It was nonetheless a formula, and wears thin over the course of an entire album. Two of the more interesting cuts are the original 1961 version of "Not Me," which would become a big hit for the Orlons in 1963 in a slightly sanitized version, and both parts of the 1963 single "Perdido," which works up as manic a party atmosphere as Bonds ever managed. —Richie Unterberger

Boney M

Disco, Euro-Dance

Although they never had much success in America, the Euro-disco group Boney M was a European phenomenon during the '70s. After German record producer Frank Farian (b. 1942) recorded the single "Baby Do You Wanna Bump?" (which was successful in Holland and Belgium), he created Boney M to support the song, bringing in four West Indian vocalists who had been working as session singers in Germany—Marcia Barrett (b. Oct. 14, 1948, St. Catherines, Jamaica), Liz Mitchell (b. Jul. 12, 1952, Clarendon, Jamaica), Maizie Williams (b. Mar. 25, 1951, Monserrat, West Indies), and Bobby Farrell (b. Oct. 6, 1949, Aruba, West Indies). "Daddy Cool" reached the UK Top Ten in February 1977, followed in April by a remake of Bobby Hebb's "Sunny." In July, "Ma Baker" just missed the UK No. 1 spot, and "Belfast" hit the Top Ten in December. In 1978, Boney M was at the height of its popularity with "Rivers of Babylon"/"Brown Girl in the Ring," which became the second-biggest-selling single in UK chart history. "Rivers of Babylon" also was Boney M's only US Top 40 hit. Boney M's album *Nightflight to Venus* also topped the UK charts. In October 1978, "Rasputin" became another UK Top Ten hit, followed by the seasonal chart-topper "Mary's Boy Child"/"Oh My Lord," which became the fifth-biggest selling single in UK history. In March 1979, "Painter Man" hit the UK Top Ten, followed in May by "Hooray! Hooray! It's a Holi-Holiday." In September, the album *Oceans of Fantasy* hit No. 1. The group was disbanded in 1980; their music continues to sell well in Europe, with a compilation hitting the UK Top Ten recently. Farian went on to create the late-'80s dance sensation Milli Vanilli. —Stephen Thomas Erlewine

● Magic of Boney M [20 Hits] / 1980 / Atlantic/Hansa ✦✦✦✦

Boney M's top Euro-disco creations—songs that ruled the continent for a while in the mid-'70s—are compiled on this singularly pleasing singles collection. —Stephen Thomas Erlewine

Bongos

Power-Pop, Jangle Pop

Hoboken's Bongos—founded as a trio consisting of Richard Barone (guitar, vocals), Rob Norris (bass), and Frank Giannini (drums, vocals)—made no pretense of being anything other than a pop band; fortunately, they were a good pop band, covering guitar pop from the Byrds to T. Rex, all of it pulled together by Barone's original songs. Although he was the focal point, the other members were by no means peripheral; after their first full-length album, *Drums Along the Hudson* (1982), James Mastro joined and contributed some stellar hooks. After releasing a series of singles and an EP on tiny Fetish Records in 1980 and 1981, the Bongos signed to independent PVC Records. *Drums Along the Hudson* compiled all their previously released tracks. They then moved up to major label RCA and released the five-song *Numbers with Wings EP* (1983) and the album *Beat Hotel* (1985), before leaving RCA and splitting up. (Later, *Drums Along the Hudson* and a two-fer of *Numbers with Wings* and *Beat Hotel* were reissued on CD by Razor & Tie.) At their best, the Bongos made some irresistible guitar pop. —William Ruhlmann

Drums Along the Hudson / 1982 / Razor & Tie ✦✦✦

Numbers with Wings / 1983 / RCA ✦✦✦✦

This five-song EP (now available, along with *Beat Hotel*, on a single CD) marks several upgrades in the Bongos' career. They have added second guitarist James Mastro, moved up to RCA Records, and brought in producer Richard Gottehrer. Gottehrer, who has a sharp sense of rock 'n' roll dynamics (listen to his work on the Angels' "My Boyfriend's Back"), is a felicitous choice, and the added instrumentation (and no doubt better-budgeted recording and mixing) allows the Bongos to better realize their pop sound. As a result, songs like "Numbers with Wings," with its echoed

vocals and full sound, have the kind of epic sweep Richard Barone's compositions have always suggested without achieving. Not that the band has become overblown—just fulfilled. —William Ruhlmann

Beat Hotel / 1985 / RCA ✦✦✦

● Beat Hotel/Numbers with Wings / Jul. 24, 1992 / Razor & Tie ✦✦✦✦

This is a two-fer of the Bongos' last EP and album. "Barbarella" and the title cut from the Richard Gottehrer-produced *Numbers with Wings* (1983) are the highlights on that set. *Beat Hotel* (1985) is their best-sounding effort, though the songwriting quality isn't as consistent. —Rick Clark

The Bonzo Dog Band

Psychedelic, Pop-Rock

Besides, perhaps, the Mothers of Invention (with whom they were sometimes compared), the Bonzo Dog Band was the most successful group to combine rock music and comedy. Starting off as the Bonzo Dog Dada Band, then becoming the Bonzo Dog Doo-Dah Band, and then finally just the Bonzo Dog Band, the group was started by British art college students in the mid-'60s. Initially they were inclined toward traditional jazz and vaudevillian routines, but by the time of their 1967 debut album, they were leaning further in pop and rock directions. A brief appearance in the Beatles' *Magical Mystery Tour* film bolstered their visibility, and Paul McCartney (under the pseudonym Apollo C. Vermouth) produced their single "I'm the Urban Spaceman," which reached the British Top Five in 1968. The Bonzos really hit their stride with their second and third albums, which found them adding elements of psychedelia to their already absurdist mix of pop, cabaret, and Dada. The Bonzos could be side-splitting, but their records also hold up well because they were also capable musicians and songwriters, paced by Neil Innes and Viv Stanshall (both of whom wrote the lion's share of their best material). The group attempted to move into more serious and musical realms with their 1969 LP *Keynsham*, which, not surprisingly, was acclaimed as their weakest effort. They broke up shortly afterward; Viv Stanshall made some obscure solo recordings (he was also the grandstanding narrator on Mike Oldfield's "Tubular Bells"). Neil Innes collaborated with members of Monty Python, upon whom the Bonzos were a large influence, as well as writing songs for and performing in the brilliant Beatles documentary spoof, *The Rutles.* —Richie Unterberger

Gorilla / Oct. 1967 / One Way ✦✦✦

Doughnuts in Grannys Greenhouse / Dec. 1968 / Edsel ✦✦✦✦

Taking the "Doo Dah" out of their name for this 1968 LP, the Bonzos' second album was probably their best. Although they were hardly a rock or pop group in the traditional sense, the Bonzos couldn't help absorbing some of the vibes of British psychedelia, and the heady ambience of the era is reflected in the recklessly diverse and outrageous material. Almost all of the songs were penned by the two top Dogs, Viv Stanshall and Neil Innes, who deflate British blues, psychedelia, and other pop, jazz, and music-hall styles with priceless wit. Star tracks on this saxophone-heavy album include the doo wop ode to a spacegirl ("Beautiful Zelda"), "Trouser Press" (which gave the late American underground rock magazine its name), the droll series of poker-faced spoken sketches on "Rhinocratic Oaths" (certainly an influence on Monty Python), and the boozy "My Pink Half of the Drainpipe," which ranks as one of the most ridiculous and hysterical songs released by a pop group of any era. —Richie Unterberger

Tadpoles / Aug. 1, 1969 / One Way ✦✦✦

Lets Make Up & Be Friendly / Apr. 1972 / One Way ✦✦

History of the Bonzos / May 24, 1974 / United Artists ✦✦✦✦

Necessarily, the pick among Bonzos albums is Rhino's 1990 collection *The Best of the Bonzo Dog Band,* but only because that one's in print. This compilation was released as a double-LP set in 1974 and, although out of print, is the best Bonzos compilation (and there have been quite a few). Running an hour and 42 minutes and containing 35 tracks that span the Bonzos' five albums and some of their solo work, the album effectively presents their offbeat humor and diverse musical styles, from the 1920s music-hall pop and jazz of their early period to the more rock-oriented material they made later on. The humor is absurd and whimsical rather than laugh-out-loud funny—maybe a video compilation would be the best way to appreciate them—but you can definitely hear the makings of British comedy in the Monty Python mold here. —William Ruhlmann

● The Best of the Bonzo Dog Band / 1991 / Rhino ✦✦✦✦

This is a well-chosen overview of the late-'60s British absurdists' work. Fans of Monty Python should check out this precursor. —Rick Clark

Boo Radleys

Alternative Pop-Rock, Shoegazing, Brit-Pop

Formed in Liverpool in 1988, the English guitar-pop group the Boo Radleys developed a dedicated cult following in the early '90s before crossing over into the mainstream in the middle of the decade. Originally, the group were one of the lesser lights of the loud, noisy My Bloody Valentine-inspired psychedelic trance-pop bands labelled "shoegazers" by the British weekly music press. By the mid-'90s the Boo Radleys had developed into a more straightforward pop band that didn't use noise and extended guitar workouts as a way of fleshing out their songs, instead using it as the basis of their music.

The Boo Radleys originally consisted of guitarist/songwriter Martin Carr, vocalist/guitarist Sice, bassist Timothy Brown, and drummer Steve Hewitt. The band released their first album, *Ichabod and I*, on a local independent record label in 1990; Hewitt was replaced by Rob Cieka after the release of the record. With the support of influential British DJ John Peel, the band signed with Rough Trade Records. The group released the EP *Every Heaven* in 1991; the record made it into the lower regions of the UK charts.

Rough Trade folded shortly after the release of *Every Heaven*, and the Boo Radleys moved to Creation Records, releasing *Everything's Alright Forever* in 1992. *Everything's Alright Forever* was released in the US through Creation's association with Columbia Records, but it didn't gain much attention in America. In England, it received favorable reviews and the group began to build a fan base. Topping several Best-of-the-Year lists, including *Melody Maker*'s, 1993's *Giant Steps* was a critical success in England and sold respectably. In America, the record launched the minor alternative-rock hit "Lazarus" and led to second-stage spot on Lollapalooza '94.

Released in England in the spring of 1995, the more pop-oriented *Wake Up!* was the band's commercial breakthrough, debuting at No. 1. The bright, horn-driven single "Wake Up Boo" entered in the Top Ten and stayed on the charts until the early summer, preventing the follow-up single "Find the Answer Within" from charting higher than the Top 30. *Wake Up!* was released in America in the fall of 1995. — *Stephen Thomas Erlewine*

Everything's Alright Forever / Aug. 1992 / Columbia ✦✦✦

Giant Steps / 1993 / Columbia ✦✦✦✦

Giant Steps is a pastiche of every genre of pop-rock from the British Invasion on. It's an incredibly ambitious and pretentious concept, but the Boo Radley's sense of songcraft has improved enough to make the album work. *Giant Steps* has swirling, noisy guitars, Beach Boys harmonies, the arrangements of Love and Beatlesque melodies, forming a remarkably original record, rich in detail and ultimately very rewarding. — *Stephen Thomas Erlewine*

● **Wake Up!** / 1995 / Columbia ✦✦✦✦

With their third album, the Boo Radleys abandoned the overt noise that obscured the pop sensibilities of their early work and scaled back the ambitions of *Giant Steps*. The result is *Wake Up!*, a glorious, brightly colored gem of a pop record. From the Beach Boy harmonies and trumpet fanfares of the opening "Wake Up Boo!" to the closing epic, McCartney-styled ballad "Wilder," the group winds through many styles of British pop. Much of the darkness—both musically and lyrically—of their previous music has been lifted; in its place is a sterling piece of pure pop, with all the big choruses, bright melodies, and simple hooks that word implies. *Giant Steps* had elements of this grand pop, yet it tried too hard. *Wake Up!* doesn't try for as much and in doing so, it achieves more, both musically and commercially—upon the release of the album and "Wake Up Boo!" single, the Boos became genuine Top Ten pop stars in England. The Boo Radleys were always a band with ambitions. The only difference with *Wake Up!* is that they finally fulfilled them. — *Stephen Thomas Erlewine*

Booker T. & the MG's

Soul, R&B

As the house band at Stax Records in Memphis, Booker T. & the MG's may have been the single greatest factor in the lasting value of that label's soul music—not to mention Southern soul as a whole. Their tight, impeccable grooves can be heard on classic hits by Otis Redding, Wilson Pickett, Carla Thomas, Albert King, and Sam & Dave, just to name the very most prominent examples. For that reason alone, they would deserve their spot in rock 'n' roll's hall of fame. But in addition to their formidable skills as a house band, on their own they were one of the top instrumental outfits of the rock era, cutting classics like "Green Onions," "Time Is Tight," and "Hang 'em High."

The anchors of the Booker T. sound were Steve Cropper, whose slicing, economic riffs influenced tons of other guitar players, and Booker T. Jones himself, who provided much of the groove with his floating organ lines. In 1960, Jones started working as a session man for Stax, where he met Cropper. Cropper had been in the Mar-Keys, famous for the 1961 instrumental hit "Last Night," which laid out the protoype for much of the MG's (and indeed Memphis soul's) sound with its organ-sax-guitar combo. With the addition of drummer Al Jackson and bassist Lewis Steinberg, they became Booker T. & the MG's. In a couple years or so,

Steinberg would be replaced permanently by Donald "Duck" Dunn, who, like Cropper, had also played with the Mar-Keys.

The band's first and biggest hit, "Green Onions" (No. 3, 1962), came about by accident. Jamming in the studio while fruitlessly waiting for Billy Lee Riley to show up for a session, they came up with a classic minor-key, bluesy soul instrumental, distinguished by its nervous organ bounce and ferocious bursts of guitar. For the next five years, they'd have trouble recapturing its commercial success, though the standard of their records remained fairly high, and Stax's dependence upon them as the house band ensured a decent living.

In the late '60s, the MG's really hit their stride with "Hip Hug-Her," "Groovin'," "Soul-Limbo," "Hang 'em High," and "Time Is Tight," all of which were Top 40 charters between 1967 and 1969. As a band that featured two Blacks and two Whites playing as tightly together as possible, they also set a somewhat underappreciated example of both how integrated, self-contained bands could succeed, and how both Black and White musicians could play funky soul music. As is the case with most instrumental rock bands, their singles contained their best material, and they're best appreciated via anthologies. But their albums were not inconsequential, and were occasionally ambitious (they did an entire instrumental version of the Beatles' *Abbey Road*, which they titled *McLemore Avenue* in honor of the location of Stax's studios).

Though they'd become established stars by the end of the decade, the group began finding it difficult to work together, not so much because of personnel problems, but because of logistical difficulties. Cropper was often playing sessions in Los Angeles, and Jones was often absent from Memphis while he finished his music studies at Indiana University. The band decided to break up in 1971, but were working on a reunion album in 1975 when Al Jackson was tragically shot and killed in his Memphis home by a burglar. The remaining members have been active as recording artists and session musicians since, Cropper and Dunn joining the Blues Brothers for a while in the late '70s.

The MG's got back into the spotlight in early 1992 when they were the house band for an extravagant Bob Dylan tribute at Madison Square Garden. More significantly, in 1993 they served as the backup band for a Neil Young tour, one which brought both them and Young high critical marks. The following year, they released a comeback album, arranged in much the style of their vintage '60s sides, which proved that their instrumental skills were still intact. Like most such efforts, though, it ultimately failed to recreate the spark and spontaneity it so obviously wanted to achieve. — *Richie Unterberger*

Green Onions / Oct. 1962 / Atlantic ✦✦✦✦

The title track was the signature song for Booker T. & the MG's, arguably the finest Southern soul rhythm section of all time. This early '60s album now sells in three figures for good condition copies and higher than that for sealed, mint edition. It established the immediate greatness of the organ/guitar/bass/drums lineup and demonstrated that Booker T. Jones and Steve Cropper in particular were geniuses on organ and guitar, respectively. This has been reissued on CD. — *Ron Wynn*

Soul Dressing / 1965 / Atlantic ✦✦✦

Assembled mostly from (non-hit) 1963-65 singles, this is solid stuff, but a notch below their peak collections. The best tracks ("Soul Dressing," "Tic-Tac-Toe," "Can't Be Still") are usually included on their best-of anthologies, but "Plum Nellie," featuring some ferocious, cutting-edge solos by Cropper and Jones, is an overlooked highlight. — *Richie Unterberger*

☆ **The Best of Booker T. & the MG's** / Nov. 1968 / Atlantic ✦✦✦✦✦

The Stax Records catalog ended up partially in the bands of Atlantic Records and partially with Fantasy Records, and the dividing point is 1968. That's why there are two Booker T. & the MG's hits compilations. This one, *The Best of*, presents the material owned by Atlantic. There are 12 tracks, covering the group's popular instrumental hits from "Green Onions" in the summer of 1962 to "Groovin'" in the summer of 1967. Booker T. & the MG's scored some of their biggest hits, including "Hang 'em High" and "Time Is Tight," in 1968-1969, and for those you will have to look to the Stax/Fantasy *Greatest Hits*, originally released in October 1970. Just to be confusing, in 1991 Fantasy released an album called *The Best of* that again contains only the later material. (Rhino's *The Very Best of* finally combined the two eras.) — *William Ruhlmann*

The Best of / 1986 / Fantasy ✦✦✦

Somewhat confusingly, this disc is titled identically to a CD on Atlantic that concentrates on their earlier material. This 17-cut disc draws from 1967-1971 and includes three of their four Top 20 pop hits: "Soul Limbo," "Hang 'em High," and "Time Is Tight." This perhaps lacks a bit of the edge of their mid-'60s recordings, concentrating on loping, relaxed grooves more than biting, incisive chops. The standard remains pretty high, though, with the interplay between Steve Cropper's guitar, Booker T. Jones' organ, and the rhythm section never less than telepathic. Most of the material is original, but even on the covers of period pop hits—including unlikely versions of "Something," "Eleanor Rigby," and "Mrs. Robinson"—the group is soulful and tight. This is perhaps better music for background and party listening than anything else, but within those confines it's quite good. —*Richie Unterberger*

★ **Very Best of** / 1994 / Rhino ♦♦♦♦♦
Contains 15 of Booker T. & the MG's pop-chart hits, spanning both the 1962-1967 era (now controlled by Atlantic Records) and the 1968-1971 era (now controlled by Fantasy Records). Not to be confused with the Atlantic *Best of* (81281) or the Fantasy *Best of* (60004). —*William Ruhlmann*

That's the Way It Should Be / May 24, 1994 / Sony ♦♦♦

The Boomtown Rats

New Wave, Pop-Rock
The Boomtown Rats were an Irish rock band that scored a series of British hits between 1977 and 1980 and were led by singer Bob Geldof, who organized the Ethiopian relief efforts Band Aid and Live Aid.

The Rats were formed in Dun Laoghaire, near Dublin, Ireland, in 1975 by Geldof (born Robert Frederick Zenon Geldof, Oct. 5, 1954, Dun Laoghaire, Ireland), a former journalist, Johnnie Fingers (keyboards), Gerry Cott (guitar), Garry Roberts (guitar), Pete Briquette (bass), and Simon Crowe (drums). They took their name from Woody Guthrie's novel *Bound for Glory*. The group moved to London in October 1976 and became associated with the punk-rock movement. Signing to Ensign Records, they released their debut single, "Lookin' After No. 1," in August 1977. It was the first of nine straight singles to make the UK Top 15.

Their debut album, *The Boomtown Rats*, was released in September 1977, on Ensign in the UK and on Mercury in the US. Their second album, *Tonic for the Troops* appeared in June 1978 in the UK, along with their first UK Top Ten hit, "Like Clockwork." In the fall, "Rat Trap" from the album hit No. 1. *Tonic for the Troops* was released in the US on Columbia Records in February 1979 with two tracks from *The Boomtown Rats* substituted for tracks on the UK version.

The Boomtown Rats' second straight UK No. 1 came in the summer of 1979 with "I Don't Like Mondays," a song inspired by a California teenager who had gone on a killing spree and glibly justified her action with the title line. It was contained on the Rats' third album, *The Fine Art of Surfacing*, released in October 1979, and subsequently became the band's only US singles-chart entry. The album also contained their next UK Top Ten hit, "Someone's Looking at You."

The Boomtown Rats released their final UK Top Ten hit, "Banana Republic," in November 1980, followed by their fourth album, *Mondo Bongo* in January 1981. At this point, guitarist Gerry Cott left the group, and they continued as a quintet. Their fifth album, *V Deep*, was released in the UK in February 1982. In the US, Columbia initially released only a four-song EP drawn from the album *The Boomtown Rats*, finally releasing the full LP in September, when it failed to chart. Also in 1982, Geldof starred in the movie *Pink Floyd: The Wall*.

Columbia released the six-song compilation *Ratrospective* in March 1983, but rejected the band's newly recorded sixth album, *In the Long Grass*, which was released by Ensign in England. In 1984, Geldof and Midge Ure wrote "Do They Know It's Christmas?" and organized the star-studded Band Aid group to record it for Ethiopian relief, resulting in the biggest selling single in UK history. Geldof then went on to organize the two Live Aid concerts, held on July 13, 1985, in London and Philadelphia. Geldof's increased visibility led to the belated US release of *In the Long Grass*, but when it failed to chart, the Boomtown Rats were left without a record label. The group folded in 1986, and Geldof launched a solo career. —*William Ruhlmann*

● **The Greatest Hits** / 1987 / Columbia ♦♦♦♦
Same six songs as on *Ratrospective*, plus four tracks. —*William Ruhlmann*

Pat Boone (Charles Eugene Patrick Boone)

b. Jun. 1, 1934, Jacksonville, FL
Vocals / Pop, Teen Idol
He was clean-cut, polite to his elders, and glorified the nutritional value of milk. To folks who hated everything the new music stood for, Pat Boone was the perfect '50s rock 'n' roller. But no matter how music historians judge the career of Pat Boone, nobody can dispute his enormous sales figures. The well-scrubbed crooner in the white buckskin shoes sold many millions of copies of his sanitized R&B covers during the '50s, helping to facilitate acceptance of rock 'n' roll in the pop marketplace.

Boone's family ties are impressive—he's related to frontier legend Daniel Boone through bloodlines and to country great Red Foley through marriage to his daughter. After debuting on the small Republic imprint in 1954, Boone signed with Dot and took the pop world by storm over the next couple of years with covers of R&B items by Fats Domino, Little Richard, the El Dorados, the Flamingos, Ivory Joe Hunter, and too many others to list here.

With his college-boy good looks and an affinity for smooth ballads, Boone crossed over into TV and films, scoring No. 1 hits in 1957 with

"Love Letters in the Sand," from the movie *Bernadine*, and the theme from the movie *April Love*, both of which he starred in.

"Moody River" marked Boone's last chart-topper in 1961, although he gamely tackled everything from novelty rockers ("Speedy Gonzales") to surf songs ("Beach Girl") to sustain his success. These days, you're most likely to encounter Boone and his family (which includes Debby Boone of "You Light Up My Life" fame) on the contemporary Christian circuit or doing work for charitable organizations, the white bucks and crewcut long since retired. —*Bill Dahl*

Jivin' Pat / Feb. 1986 / Bear Family ♦♦♦♦
All of Boone's rockers—cover versions of Fats Domino, Little Richard, et al.—are included with a revealing set of liner notes. You won't find these elsewhere unless you have an enormous singles collection. —*Hank Davis*

● **Greatest Hits** / 1993 / MCA ♦♦♦♦

More Greatest Hits / 1994 / Varese Sarabande ♦♦♦
Contains 17 of Pat Boone's later and lesser chart hits. —*William Ruhlmann*

Earl Bostic

b. Apr. 25, 1913, Tulsa, OK, **d.** Oct. 28, 1965, Rochester, NY
Sax (Alto) / R&B, Swing, Groove
Earl Bostic's roots and foundation were steeped in jazz and swing, but he later became one of the most prolific R&B bandleaders. His searing, sometimes bluesy, sometimes soft and moving, alto-sax style influenced many players, including John Coltrane. His many King releases, which featured limited soloing and basic melodic and rhythmic movements, might have fooled novices into thinking Bostic possessed minimal skills; but Art Blakey once said, "Nobody knew more about the saxophone than Bostic, I mean technically, and that includes Bird." Bostic worked in several Midwest bands during the early '30s, then studied at Xavier University. He left school to tour with various groups, among them a band co-led by Charlie Creath and Fate Marable. He moved to New York in the late '30s, where he was a soloist in the bands of Don Redman, Edgar Hayes, and Lionel Hampton. Bostic also led his own combos, whose members included Jimmy Cobb, Al Casey, Blue Mitchell, Stanley Turrentine, Benny Golson, and Coltrane. Bostic toured extensively through the '50s, while cutting numerous sessions for King. His recording of "Flamingo" in 1951 was a huge hit, as were the songs "Sleep," "You Go to My Head," "Cherokee," and "Temptation." Bostic recorded for Allegro, Gotham, and King from the late '40s to the mid-'60s. He made more than 400 selections for King; the label would use stereo remakes of songs with different personnel, then use the same album numbers. After a heart attack, Bostic became a part-time player. His mid-'60s albums were more soul-jazz than R&B. Several of his King LPs are available on CD. —*Ron Wynn and Michael Erlewine*

● **The Best of Earl Bostic** / 1956 / Deluxe ♦♦♦♦
A nice cross-section of this fiery alto-saxist's '50s output, it includes his hits "Sleep" and "Flamingo." —*Bill Dahl*

Boston

Hard Rock, Pop-Rock, Arena Rock
During the late '70s, Boston dominated AOR (album-oriented rock) FM with their dense, multilayered guitars and vocals. The self-titled debut effort, which was basically constructed from band leader Tom Scholz's basement demos, eventually sold over 6.5 million copies. "More Than a Feeling," their first single, is a perfect encapsulation of Boston's sound. After a two-year wait, Boston's follow-up, *Don't Look Back*, basically replicated the debut's formula. By then, Scholz was gaining a reputation as an obsessive perfectionist, further underscored by the seven-year wait for the group's third album, *Third Stage*.

During this time, Scholz applied his previous background as a senior product designer for Polaroid and started Scholz Research & Development, which marketed popular professional-musician outboard gear, like the Rockman.

After another long delay—eight years—Boston returned in 1994 with a new album, *Walk On*. —*Rick Clark*

● **Boston** / 1976 / Epic ♦♦♦♦
The album that virtually defined '70s FM rock sold over six million copies and featured the smash hits "More Than a Feeling," "Peace of Mind," and "Let Me Take You Home Tonight." —*Donna DiChario*

Don't Look Back / 1978 / Epic ♦♦♦

Third Stage / 1986 / MCA ♦♦♦

Walk On / 1994 / MCA ♦♦

Bow Wow Wow

New Wave
Bow Wow Wow was a quartet organized by UK manager Malcolm McLaren (best known as the mastermind behind the Sex Pistols) at the

start of the '80s. McLaren matched the trio of musicians who had constituted Adam Ant's Ants—Matthew Ashman (b. 1962) on guitar, Leigh
Gorman (b. 1961) on bass, and David Barbarossa (b. 1961) on
drums—with teenage singer Annabella Lwin (b. Oct. 31, 1965), retaining
the earlier group's African-derived drum sound. In 1983, Lwin quit the
group for a solo career, and the remaining three changed their name to
the Chiefs of Relief. Both Lwin and the Chiefs issued their own albums.
— William Ruhlmann

● **I Want Candy** / 1982 / RCA ++++
This album largely recompiles Bow Wow Wow's first album, plus its *Last
of the Mohicans* EP. As such, it includes the hits "Go Wild in the Country," "I Want Candy," and "Louis Quatorze" and presents the band's
urgent, rhythmic sound at its most consistent. *— William Ruhlmann*

Girl Bites Dog / 1993 / EMI ++++
A CD reissue of their first cassette-only release. Featuring a 15-year-old
Annabella Lwin singing songs with sex-obsessed themes backed by a
driving tribal beat, *Girl Bites Dog* gives a representative view of a band
with limited scope. Though it sounds a bit dated today, new wave fanatics will find this newly expanded version essential, especially for the
unreleased rarities, B-sides, and extensive discography information.
— Chris Woodstra

David Bowie (David Robert Jones)

b. Jan. 8, 1947, Brixton, England
*Guitar, Keyboards, Saxophone, Vocals / Hard Rock, Art-Rock/
Progressive-Rock, Glam Rock, Pop-Rock, Experimental,
Proto-Punk, Blue-Eyed Soul*

Although he succeeded as a singer, musician, songwriter, and film and
stage actor, David Bowie's chief artistic accomplishment may have been
his astute manipulation of his own image as a star. When he achieved
international fame in the early '70s, Bowie brought a new, highly conscious approach to stardom that involved the frequent creation of new
personae. No wonder that when he made his film acting debut in 1976,
he seemed so good at it: acting was what a large part of his career was
about. Born in Brixton, South London, as David Jones, the singer was
already playing in bands by his late teens. He changed his name to avoid
confusion with Davy Jones of the Monkees. His early-'60s work was rock
and blues oriented, then he turned to an Anthony Newley-style expressive show-music approach. But his breakthrough British hit "Space Oddity" (1969) was a folky ballad about an astronaut who doesn't come
home. By the time of *Hunky Dory* (1971), Bowie had turned again more
toward rock, using the first of many strong collaborators, guitarist Mick
Ronson.

It was Bowie's concept album *The Rise & Fall of Ziggy Stardust and
the Spiders from Mars* (1972) that made him a giant star in England,
where he adopted his fantasy rocker, with bright red hair and
futuristic stage suits. In America, "Space Oddity" became a belated
hit in 1973, the year Bowie "retired" from stage work only to return in
1974 with an even more elaborate stage show. More an established star
than a real record-seller in the US, Bowie finally hit No. 1 with "Fame"
(co-written by John Lennon and Carlos Alomar) in 1975. The late '70s
found him collaborating with electronics whiz Brian Eno. He made a
major commercial comeback in 1983 with *Let's Dance*, produced by ex-
Chic co-leader Nile Rodgers. Bowie's work in the '80s was inconsistent,
but as late as 1990 he was still able to tour the US, playing football stadiums. This was supposedly his farewell tour (again) before he turned full
attention to a group project, Tin Machine.

After releasing two unsuccessful albums with Tin Machine, Bowie
returned to his solo career in 1993, with his first solo album since 1987,
Black Tie White Noise, although it received favorable reviews, it fell off
the charts quickly. In the fall of 1995, Bowie released *Outside,* his first
collaboration with Brian Eno since *Lodger. Outside* received positive
reviews, but it became another commercial disappointment for the
singer. *— William Ruhlmann*

Space Oddity / 1969 / Rykodisc +++
Originally titled *Man of Words Man of Music,* this release was a transi-
tional effort from Bowie's earlier Anthony Newley affectations on Decca.
Tracks range from the Bob Dylan-influenced future-shock epic "Cygnet
Committee" to lightweight rockers like "Janine." This includes "Space
Oddity," Bowie's first major single and the highlight of this album.
—Rick Clark

The Man Who Sold the World / 1970 / Rykodisc ++++
After the theatrical acoustic leanings of *Space Oddity,* Bowie undertook
a dark foray into British hard rock that at times attempted Cream-style
free-for-alls, particularly "She Shook Me Cold." The strangely dense, bass-
heavy production (courtesy of Tony Visconti), coupled with Bowie's disturbing imagery, provided some powerful moments. Musically, Tin
Machine's discordant roots can be found here, on one of Bowie's better
efforts. *—Rick Clark*

☆ **Hunky Dory** / 1972 / Rykodisc +++++
This follow-up to *The Man Who Sold the World* found Bowie lightening
his sound considerably. Some of his most memorable songs are found on
this classic: the catchy pop classic "Changes" (a theme song of sorts), the
beautifully expansive "Life on Mars," the moody dynamics of "Quicksand," "The Bewlay Brothers," and "Oh, You Pretty Things." *—Rick Clark*

☆ **The Rise & Fall of Ziggy Stardust** / 1972 / Rykodisc +++++
Regarded by many to be Bowie's best album. Bowie took the melodicism
developed on *Hunky Dory* and beefed it up with a punchy, rigid, freeze-
dried "rock" setting. It's a perfect setting for Bowie's concept of a plastic
rock star, Ziggy Stardust. *The Rise & Fall of Ziggy Stardust and the Spiders from Mars,* without a doubt, was an important defining effort for the
glam-rock movement. *—Rick Clark*

Aladdin Sane / 1973 / Rykodisc ++++
It rocks harder than *Ziggy Stardust . . .* but flirts pretty closely at times
with cabaret death (courtesy of pianist Mike Garson). "Watch That Man"
is a fine rocker that manages to draw inspiration from the Stones' *Exile
on Main Street,* while not totally abandoning the tight-assed rhythmic
stiffness inherent in the glam sound. Other highlights include "Jean
Genie," "Cracked Actor," and "Panic in Detroit." *—Rick Clark*

Images 1966-1967 / 1973 / London +++

Pin-Ups / 1973 / Rykodisc +++
Bowie covers a selection of personal favorite songs from the '60s by the
Yardbirds, the Kinks, the Who, Pink Floyd, and more. It's an affectionate
tribute that makes more of a case for Bowie's excellent taste than for his
ability to transcend the original versions. It contains the hit "Sorrow."
—Rick Clark

Diamond Dogs / 1974 / Rykodisc ++
An ambitious smudge of an album, it nevertheless contains some standouts in the lean, riff-heavy hit "Rebel Rebel," the fatalistic futurism of
"1984" (an early discoish harbinger of his Thin White Duke era), and the
title track. *—Rick Clark*

Young Americans / 1975 / Rykodisc +++
Bowie affects Philly Soul and a hodgepodge of other things. Ace sidemen
can't save this spotty album, but the title track and "Fame" (co-written by
John Lennon) became worldwide hits. *—Rick Clark*

Station to Station / 1976 / Rykodisc ++++
A transitional effort, it bridges Bowie's clinical pop-disco persona to the
icy psychosis and dissonance of this next phase, working with Brian Eno.
Almost as ill-formed as *Diamond Dogs* (particularly the title track), but it
includes the Top Ten hit "Golden Years" and "TVC15." *—Rick Clark*

☆ **Low** / Jan. 1977 / Rykodisc +++++
The first of several efforts with ex-Roxy Music sound painter Brian Eno,
Low is a willful departure from Bowie's pop persona. Short songs make
their point and get out of the way on the first half, followed by four dense
synth-instrumental soundscapes. *—Rick Clark*

☆ **Heroes** / Feb. 1977 / Rykodisc +++++
With echoes of *Low's* half-sung/half-instrumental approach, this one has
longer songs (given a maniacal musical accompaniment by King Crimson's Robert Fripp) and chillingly desolate soundscapes. The brilliant
title track features one of Bowie's most passionate performances. Those
who like discordant rock should be in heaven with "Beauty and the
Beast," "Joe the Lion," and "Blackout." *—Rick Clark*

Stage / 1978 / Rykodisc +++

Lodger / 1979 / Rykodisc ++++
The third installment with Eno returns Bowie to a more conventional
(but not necessarily more commercial) song structure. Production isn't so
sharp-sounding as on *Heroes,* but it has many engaging moments, particularly the hopeful "Fantastic Voyage" and the goofy "D.J.," plus "Boys
Keep Swinging," and the hyperdrive of "Look Back in Anger." *—Rick
Clark*

Scary Monsters (and Super Creeps) / 1980 / Rykodisc ++++
One of the better post-*Low* efforts, it contains the hits "Fashion" and
"Ashes to Ashes," and the dissonant rocker "It's No Game (Part 1)." Robert
Fripp provides a wonderfully jarring racket on "It's No Game (Part 1),"
the Tom Verlaine-penned "Kingdom Come," and several others. Pete
Townshend guests on "Because You're Young." The CD includes four
bonus tracks: a nice version of Kurt Weill and Bert Brecht's "Alabama
Song," an instrumental that could've come off of *Low,* and 1979 re-
recordings of "Space Oddity" and "Panic in Detroit," of interest only to
hardcore fans *—Rick Clark*

Let's Dance / 1983 / Virgin +++
Bowie guns for big pop success and gets it on this outing, somehow
deftly sidestepping appearances of being a sellout. The title track, "China
Girl," and "Modern Love" achieved international chart success. This
album also includes a nice reworking of Metro's "Criminal World."
—Rick Clark

Love You Til Tuesday / 1984 / PolyGram ++

Tonight / 1984 / Virgin ✦✦

Never Let Me Down / 1987 / Virgin ✦✦

Sound + Vision / 1989 / Rykodisc ✦✦✦✦
An extravagantly produced three-disc-plus-CDV (video mini-disc) boxed set, it digs deeper than *Changesbowie*. This features much previously unavailable stuff but comes up short on certain primary radio tracks. It's a good complement to *Changesbowie*, in spite of a little track duplication. — *Rick Clark*

★ **Changesbowie** / 1990 / Rykodisc ✦✦✦✦✦
Except for the substitution of a "Fame '90" remix over the original No. 1 hit, this is a great sampling of big cuts from all of Bowie's many phases, from "Space Oddity" to "Ashes to Ashes." While Bowie has had some classic albums, the uninitiated should start here. — *Rick Clark*

Early On (1964-1966) / 1991 / Rhino ✦✦

Black Tie White Noise / 1993 / Virgin ✦✦

★ **Singles 1969-1993** / 1993 / Rykodisc ✦✦✦✦✦
Taking *Changesbowie* one step further, *Singles 1969-1993* collects all of David Bowie's biggest hits while picking up such overlooked gems as "Drive-In Saturday" and "Loving the Alien." The comprehensiveness and quality of the songs make *Singles* the best Bowie compilation available; fans will be pleased with the inclusion of the complete lyrics to all of the songs on this two-disc set. — *Stephen Thomas Erlewine*

Outside / Sep. 26, 1995 / RCA ✦✦✦

Buddha of Suburbia / Oct. 24, 1995 / Virgin ✦✦✦

The Box Tops

Pop-Rock, Blue-Eyed Soul
If you forget about the Rascals and the Righteous Brothers, the Memphis-based Box Tops are the finest blue-eyed soul group. Lead singer (and former Big Star honcho) Alex Chilton had a tough, swaggering voice that belied his teenage years, sounding at times as if he were in a cutting match with the young Steve Winwood. Producers Chips Moman and Dan Penn surrounded Chilton with a crack American studio band, giving the music more muscle and deep funk than you'll ever find in "Mary Mary."

Instead of knocking off lightweight teen-fodder, the Box Tops managed to add another link in the Memphis soul chain, mixing blues, Beatlesque pop, and the sound of Stax, Hi, and Goldwax. And unlike the Monkees, the Box Tops benefited from top-notch material: Dan Penn and Spooner Oldham's "Cry Like a Baby" and "I Met Her in Church"; Wayne Thompson's "The Letter" and "Soul Deep"; and the occasional Chilton-penned nugget, such as "I Must Be the Devil." The group's heyday was brief—two years, tops—but their music remains a staple on oldies stations. — *John Floyd*

● **The Ultimate Box Tops** / 1988 / Warner Bros. ✦✦✦✦
Included is everything you need by this blue-eyed soul combo, such as "The Letter," "Cry Like a Baby," and "Soul Deep." — *John Floyd*

Boyz II Men

Urban, Adult Contemporary, Club-Dance, New Jack R&B
Under the guidance of Michael Bivins of Bell Biv Devoe, the five-man vocal group Boyz II Men became a pop sensation in 1992. Although they call their music "hip-hop doo wop," there's very little traditional doo wop in it. Instead, they bring the sound of '60s and early-'70s R&B vocal groups into the '90s, adding a little new jack swing. Their 1991 debut, *Cooleyhighharmony*, featured a hit single, "Motownphilly," which exemplifies the best of their dance work. Their second single, a ballad called "It's So Hard to Say Goodbye," was an even bigger hit; its success paved the way for "The End of the Road," the group's follow-up single, which broke Elvis Presley's record for the most weeks spent at No. 1. *II* proved to be even more successful than its predecessor, selling over seven million copies by summer of 1995 and spawning the record-breaking hit "I'll Make Love to You." — *Stephen Thomas Erlewine*

Cooleyhighharmony / Nov. 2, 1993 / Motown ✦✦✦✦
Boyz II Men's retro sound dominated the 1991 pop and R&B marketplaces, with their singles "It's So Hard to Say Goodbye to Yesterday" and "Motownphilly" hitting the Top Ten on both charts. The album eventually sold over five million copies and put Boyz II Men at the forefront of a movement returning the emphasis on Black popular music to vocal harmonies and a cappella interaction. — *Ron Wynn*

● **II** / 1994 / Motown ✦✦✦✦
With their second album, Boyz II Men assured their place at the top of the charts, as well as history. "I'll Make Love to You," the album's first single, stayed on the top of the charts for over two months, only to be unseated by "On Bended Knee," the album's second single. Not surprisingly, *II* is a carefully constructed crowd pleaser, accentuating all of the finest moments from their hit debut. While there are some high-energy

dance tracks, the album's main strength is its slower numbers, where the group's vocals soar. — *Stephen Thomas Erlewine*

Billy Bragg

b. Dec. 20, 1957, Barking, Essex, England
Guitar, Vocals / Urban-Folk, Singer-Songwriter, Alternative Pop-Rock, Folk-Rock, British Folk
Finding inspiration in the righteous anger of punk rock and the socially conscious folk tradition of Woody Guthrie and Bob Dylan, Billy Bragg was the leading figure of the anti-folk movement of the '80s. For most of the decade, Bragg bashed out songs alone on his electric guitar, singing about politics and love. While his words were bitingly intelligent and clever, they were also warm and humane, filled with detail and wit. Even though his lyrics were carefully considered, Bragg never neglected to write melodies for songs that were strong and memorable. Throughout the '80s, he managed to chart consistently in Britain, yet he only gathered a cult following in America, which could be due to the fact that he sang about distinctly British subject matter, both politically and socially.

Bragg began performing in the late '70s with the punk group Riff Raff, which lasted only a matter of months. He then joined the British Army, yet he quickly bought himself out of his sojourn with 175 lbs. After leaving the Army, he began working at a record store; while he was working, he was writing songs that were firmly in the folk and punk protest tradition. Bragg began a British tour, playing whenever he had the chance to perform. Frequently he would open for bands with only a moment's notice; soon, he had built a sizable following, as evidenced by his first EP, *Life's a Riot with Spy Vs. Spy*, hitting No. 30 on the UK independent charts. *Brewing Up with Billy Bragg*, his first full-length album, climbed to No. 16 in the charts.

During 1984, Bragg became a minor celebrity in Britain, as he appeared at leftist political rallies, strikes, and benefits across the country; he also helped form the "Red Wedge," a socialist musicians collective that also featured Paul Weller. In 1985, Kirsty MacColl took one of his songs, "New England," to No. 7 on the British singles chart. Featuring some subtle instrumental additions of piano and horns, 1986's *Talking to the Taxman About Poetry* reached the UK Top Ten.

Bragg's version of the Beatles' "She's Leaving Home," taken from the *Sgt. Pepper Knew My Father* tribute album, became his only No. 1 single in 1988—as the double-A side with Wet Wet Wet's "With a Little Help from My Friends." That year, he also released the EP *Help Save the Youth of America* and the full-length *Workers Playtime*, which was produced by Joe Boyd (Fairport Convention, Nick Drake, R.E.M.). Boyd helped expand Bragg's sound, as the singer recorded with a full band for the first time. The following year, Bragg restarted the Utility record label as a way of featuring noncommercial new artists. *The Internationale*, released in 1990, was a collection of left-wing anthems, including a handful of Bragg originals. On 1991's *Don't Try This at Home*, he again worked with a full band, recording his most pop-oriented and accessible set of songs; the album featured the hit single, "Sexuality." Bragg hasn't released an album since *Don't Try This at Home*, choosing to concentrate on fatherhood, yet he remains a respected figure in British music. — *Stephen Thomas Erlewine*

Talking with the Taxman About Poetry / 1986 / Go! Discs ✦✦✦✦
Bragg's one-man approach is fleshed out on *Talking with the Taxman About Poetry*, his second long-player. "Levi Stubb's Tears" and "The Marriage" include subtle percussion and horn flourishes; "Greetings to the New Brunette" is cushioned in layers of overdubbed acoustic guitars. That makes it Bragg's most satisfying album musically, but the witty, plaintive songs listed above—in addition to "Ideology" and "The Warmest Room"—make it a stirring and evocative lyrical statement as well. — *John Floyd*

● **Back to Basics** / 1987 / Go! Discs ✦✦✦✦
This disc brings together Bragg's first three releases (*Life's a Riot with Spy vs. Spy*, *Brewing Up with Billy Bragg*, and the *Between the Wars* EP) and offers the best introduction to his confessional songwriting and uncompromising politics. Highlights include "A New England," "The Busy Girl Buys Beauty," and "A Lover Sings." — *John Floyd*

Workers Playtime / 1988 / Go! Discs ✦✦✦
Bragg's first attempt at working with a full band could be better—most of the songs are mopey and depressing, and some of his socialist manifestos are tiresome and dogmatic. Still, cuts like "She's Got a New Spell," "Must I Paint You a Picture," and "Little Time Bomb" are excellent, and "Waiting for the Great Leap Forward" is a humble and humorous explanation of Bragg's motives and intentions, both political and emotional. — *John Floyd*

Don't Try This at Home / 1991 / Go! Discs ✦✦✦✦
With full-blown production by the likes of Johnny Marr, and with musical assistance from R.E.M., this would seem like a blatant stab at the postmodern marketplace. Maybe so, but the thrust of his band turns "Accident Waiting to Happen" and "North Sea Bubble" into throttling rockers and makes "Sexuality" his best single. There are also several gorgeous

ballads, "Tank Park Salute" and "Wish You Were Here" among them. *—John Floyd*

The Peel Sessions Album / May 1992 / Dutch East India ✦✦✦

Toni Braxton

Vocals / Urban, Adult Contemporary, Club-Dance

Toni Braxton made her vocal debut with the single "Love Shoulda Brought You Home" from the *Boomerang* soundtrack. She issued her first full album in 1993, and it soared to the top of both the pop and R&B charts. Braxton eventually earned two Grammy and two Soul Train awards, saw her self-titled release go platinum, and also reaped both critical and commercial plaudits for such singles as "Love Shoulda Brought You Home" and "Just Another Sad Love Song."

In the summer of 1996, Braxton released her second album, *Secrets*, which entered the charts at No. 2 and produced the No. 1 single, "You're Makin' Me High." *—Ron Wynn*

● **Toni Braxton** / 1993 / La Face ✦✦✦✦

Toni Braxton is both an elegant and earthy songstress, nicely balancing those seemingly divergent sentiments on her self-titled debut disc. Braxton's husky, enticing voice sounds hypnotic on "Breathe Again," dismayed on "Another Sad Love Song" and disillusioned on "Love Shoulda Brought You Home." But she's never out of control, indignant, or so anguished and hurt that she fails to retain her dignity. It's a sign of how great the Babyface/L.A. Reid production team was that they didn't settle for a defining mood; they presented Braxton with enough diverse emotional settings to hold the interest of urban contemporary males and females. *—Ron Wynn*

Secrets / Jun. 18, 1996 / LaFace ✦✦✦✦

Bread

Soft Rock, Pop-Rock

Bread produced an impressive string of ultra-light pop hits from 1970 to 1976, ten of which were Top 20 pop. In spite of their rather syrupy constitution, Bread had a knack for highly crafted melodies that possessed memorable hooks. "It Don't Matter to Me," with its multiple key- and time-signature changes, is a tour de force in that genre. David Gates, the writer for all their hits, delivered the goods vocally with a silky tenor that had heart. *—Rick Clark*

● **Anthology** / 1985 / Elektra ✦✦✦✦

This album includes "Make It with You," "If," "Baby I'm-a Want You," and many other fine-tuned pop gems. *—Dan Heilman*

Retrospective / Jul. 1996 / Rhino ✦✦✦✦

This is the definitive compilation of Bread, perhaps the definitive soft-rock group of the '70s. If anything, it may be too comprehensive for most listeners. Covering the entire course of Bread's career, plus highlights from David Gates in the late '70s and early '80s, the compilation spans two very full compact discs. For those who want more than the hits but are unwilling to delve into individual albums, the collection is ideal. Listeners who want the hits might find the album tracks a little tedious. Then again, the presence of Gates' solo hits like "The Goodbye Girl" is enticing for even casual fans, since he lacks a solo compilation and there are no sets that cover both his solo career and Bread. Since *Retrospective* does cover all the Bread hits plus solid obscurities and Gates' solo highlights, it does qualify as the definitive collection. In fact, it's hard to imagine how another set could be as thorough as this. *—Stephen Thomas Erlewine*

Breeders

Alternative Pop-Rock

Initially, the Breeders were conceived as a way for Pixies' bassist Kim Deal and Throwing Muses' guitarist Tanya Donelly to let out some suppressed creative energy. Deal and Donelly both played guitar, leaving bass for Josephine Wiggs of Perfect Disaster. Taking their name from the group Deal led with her twin sister, Kelly, in their teens, the Breeders combined the spareness of Throwing Muses with the shifting dynamics and warped pop sensibilities of the Pixies. *Pod*, their critically acclaimed debut album, was released in 1990. Two years later, the group delivered *Safari*, a four-song EP that found the band getting more muscular and melodic. Soon after its recording, Donelly left the Breeders to form her own group, Belly. Kim Deal brought in her sister, Kelly, as her replacement. By this time, their permanent drummer was Jim MacPherson, who was billed as "Mike Hunt" on *Safari*.

As the Breeders were working on their new album in the beginning of 1993, the Pixies split, leaving Kim Deal able to pursue the Breeders full-time. Released late in the summer of 1993, *Last Splash* was a hazier, more disjointed continuation of the hard pop of *Safari*. With the sonic collage of "Cannonball," the Breeders had a crossover hit that catapulted the group into stardom; within a year, the album had gone platinum and

the band had a prime spot on 1994's Lollapalooza tour. *—Stephen Thomas Erlewine*

● **Pod** / 1990 / 4AD/Elektra ✦✦✦✦

At the time *Pod* was released, the Breeders were just a side project for Kim Deal and Tanya Donelly, but the album was much richer than most one-shot records. Taking a little from both the Pixies and Throwing Muses, the Breeders invent an indie-rock style of their own—a sparse, dreamy, elliptical take on guitar pop. While *Pod* may rely on the sheer uniqueness of the band's spare, raw sound, the album wouldn't be nearly as successful if it wasn't for the band's exceptional songwriting. From the wonderful, slow guitar grind of "Glorious" and "Iris" to the stripped-down pop of "Doe" and "Iris," *Pod* is full of original guitar-pop pleasures. *—Stephen Thomas Erlewine*

Safari / 1992 / 4AD/Elektra ✦✦✦

There are only four songs, but the Breeders continue to improve, growing more muscular and melodic. All of the songs here, especially "Do You Love Me Now" and a cover of the Who's "So Sad About Us," rival the best on *Pod*. *—Stephen Thomas Erlewine*

Last Splash / 1993 / Elektra ✦✦✦✦

Falling halfway between the adventurous *Pod* and the magnificent heavy guitar-pop of *Safari*, *Last Splash* is ultimately a disappointing second album from the Breeders. Nearly half of *Last Splash* is filled with song fragments and incomplete songs that sound unfinished; the songs do not sound like vital, messy garage rock from inspired amateurs—they sound lazy. However, there's no denying that when *Last Splash* is good, it's splendid. From the thrilling sonic collage of "Cannonball" to the more traditional pop melodies of "Invisible Man," "I Just Wanna Get Along," and "Drivin' on 9," the best moments on the album are truly terrific, making the underdeveloped "No Aloha," "Hag," "Mad Lucas," "Roi," and the inferior rerecording of "Do You Love Me Now?" all the more infuriating. *—Stephen Thomas Erlewine*

Brinsley Schwarz

Rock 'n' Roll, Country-Rock, Pub-Rock

Although they were one of England's best and most important bands of the early '70s, Brinsley Schwarz were forever haunted by a well-intentioned, but disastrous, publicity stunt. In order to promote their first album, the band flew nearly all of the British press, as well as many other journalists, to New York to witness their bottom-of-the-bill showcase gig at the Fillmore East. The problems began when three members of the band were denied work visas until the day of the show. On their way to New York, the reporters were grounded for four hours. Once the press got to the Fillmore, their seats had been taken; some journalists stayed, some got kicked out after they complained, some went back to the hotel. In any case, they were more than happy to pan Brinsley Schwarz in print once they got back home. Consequently, their first album was a commercial failure.

The band decided to regroup by renting a house outside of London and rehearsing for 18 months straight. It was here that they developed their Byrds-fixated sound into a distinctive, laidback country-rock that derived equally from country, R&B, and rock. Bassist/vocalist Nick Lowe became a first-rate songwriter, capable of gorgeous ballads and witty, melodic pop songs. After finding an American band playing a pub called Tally Ho in the summer of 1972, the band decided that pubs provided the perfect, relaxed atmosphere for their music. Brinsley Schwarz became regulars at Tally Ho and persuaded many other pub owners to open their doors for them.

Brinsley Schwarz soon gained a devoted following; within a year they were opening for the Wings' first UK tour. Numerous other bands, including Dr. Feelgood, began playing the same pub circuit as the Brinsleys; these were the same venues where punk rock was born several years later. Without Brinsley Schwarz, the punk movement would have been very different. At a time when rock 'n' roll was overwhelmingly pompous, the Brinsleys were modest and unpretentious; they played relaxed, rootsy music and they proved to English pub owners that it was profitable to book left-of-center acts. Without this precedent, the punks would have had nowhere to play.

After releasing six albums, Brinsley Schwarz split up in 1975. Guitarist Brinsley Schwarz and keyboardist Bob Andrews became members of Graham Parker's backing band, the Rumour; Lowe became a successful solo artist and producer in his own right. Over 20 years later, the band's music still sounds splendid and it is still underappreciated. *—Stephen Thomas Erlewine*

Brinsley Schwarz / 1970 / One Way ✦✦✦

Despite It All / 1970 / Liberty ✦✦✦

Silver Pistol / 1972 / Edsel ✦✦✦✦

Silver Pistol, the band's first consistently entertaining record, is filled with brilliant reconstructions of American country, folk, and rock 'n' roll, featuring excellent songs by both Nick Lowe and Ian Gomm, as well as

two covers of Jim Ford songs—"Niki Hoeke Speedway" and "Ju Ju Man."
—*Stephen Thomas Erlewine*

Nervous on the Road / 1972 / United Artists ✦✦✦✦
An even better collection than *Silver Pistol, Nervous on the Road* is an expertly played and superbly written set of country-rock and laidback rock 'n' roll. On the surface, it seems all pleasant and gentle, but dig a little deeper and you'll find Nick Lowe slyly subverting the conventions of the genre with his sharp sense of humor. —*Stephen Thomas Erlewine*

Please Don't Ever Change / 1973 / Edsel ✦✦✦✦
Brinsley Schwarz's fifth album is another fine set of exceptional originals and clever covers, all superbly played by the well-seasoned band. —*Stephen Thomas Erlewine*

New Favourites / 1974 / United Artists ✦✦✦✦
With their final album, Brinsley Schwarz turn in their most pop-oriented record, filled with infectious gems like "The Ugly Things," "Trying to Live My Life Without You," and "(What's So Funny 'bout) Peace, Love and Understanding." Lowe's songs were the best he had ever written and show that his ambitions were beginning to conflict with those of the rest of the band. Nevertheless, there isn't a weak song or uninspired performance on *New Favourites*, making it an excellent farewell album. —*Stephen Thomas Erlewine*

Nervous on the Road/The New Favourites of Brinsley Schwarz / 1975 / Beat Goes On ✦✦✦✦
Two of Brinsley Schwarz's finest albums, *Nervous on the Road* and *The New Favorites of Brinsley Schwarz*, have been combined on one CD. *Nervous on the Road* is the definitive pub-rock album, featuring such defining songs as "Happy Doing What We're Doing," "Play That Fast Thing One More Time," and "Home in My Hand." *The New Favorites* is a more polished, commercial collection that points toward Nick Lowe's solo career, but it also has such classic cuts as "(What's So Funny 'bout) Peace, Love and Understanding," "The Ugly Things," and "Down in the Dive." —*Stephen Thomas Erlewine*

★ **Surrender to the Rhythm** / 1991 / EMI ✦✦✦✦✦
A terrific sampler of many of Brinsley Schwarz's finest tracks, *Surrender to the Rhythm* is the perfect introduction to this highly underrated band. —*Stephen Thomas Erlewine*

Bronski Beat

New Wave
A synth-pop trio from London, everything that made Bronski Beat interesting, and at times compelling, came primarily from the larynx of Glasgow-born vocalist Jimmy Somerville. Possessing a soaring tenor voice that frequently exploded into falsetto, Somerville was a rare singer, capable of imbuing even the most rote dance songs with near-palpable heartache and layers of emotional turmoil. Openly gay, Somerville and the Bronskis, despite the rock world's implicit homophobia, became cover darlings of the British music press in 1984 after the UK success of their first two singles, "Why" and "Smalltown Boy" (the latter producing one of the best music videos of all time). From that point on, Bronski Beat seemed poised to rule the pop world (at least in England), releasing a superb cover of the Donna Summer disco hit "I Feel Love" and a remarkable debut album, 1984's *The Age of Consent*. It was only a year later that Somerville announced he was leaving Bronski Beat to form the more explicitly left-wing Communards (with pianist Richard Coles). Bronski Beat took his departure in stride, and the lead vocal slot went to a fairly anonymous singer named John Jon. There were more Bronski Beat recordings, but even fanatics would agree that the band lost everything when it lost Somerville. Ironically, the Communards got off to a fast start with a great cover of Thelma Houston's "Don't Leave Me This Way," but all in all, Somerville's work with them was far less interesting than anything he did in Bronski Beat. By 1989, Somerville was a solo act, his magnificent voice still intact and the quality of the material still in question. —*John Dougan*

● **The Age of Consent** / 1984 / London ✦✦✦✦
To say this is a great album of dance-oriented synth-pop music is to sell it extremely short; this is simply a great album, period. Somerville's soaring tenor may take some getting used to, but the songs, many of them dealing with homophobia and alienation (none more eloquently than "Smalltown Boy") are compelling vignettes about the vagaries of life as a gay man. Cynics predisposed to dismissing entire genres of music based on trendiness or a limited appeal ("dance music is for dancing, not listening") miss the point in lumping this in with more mindless forays into techno or neo-disco. As the Pet Shop Boys (the world's greatest disco band) proved a few years later, you can have substantive content and wrap it up in a compelling, visceral, dance-oriented package. Few bands understood this better, or earlier, than Bronski Beat. —*John Dougan*

The Brothers Johnson

Soul, Funk, Pop-Rock
Guitarist/vocalist George Johnson and bassist/vocalist Louis Johnson

formed the band Johnson Three Plus One with older brother Tommy and their cousin Alex Weir while attending school in Los Angeles. When they became professionals, the band backed such touring R&B acts as Bobby Womack and the Supremes. George and Louis Johnson later joined Billy Preston's band, and wrote "Music in My Life" and "The Kids and Me" for him before leaving his group in 1973.

Quincy Jones hired them to play on his LP *Mellow Madness*, and recorded four of their songs, including "Is It Love That We're Missing?" and "Just a Taste of Me." Jones took them on a Japanese tour, then produced their debut LP, *Look Out for Number 1*, after they signed with A&M, which was also his label at the time (1976). They scored a No. 1 R&B and No. 3 pop hit with "I'll Be Good to You," and enjoyed R&B chart toppers in 1977 and 1980 respectively with "Strawberry Letter 23" and "Stomp!," while sustaining a consistent hit presence via such songs as "Get the Funk Out Ma Face" and "Runnin' for Your Lovin." Jones remade "I'll Be Good to You" in 1989 with Ray Charles and Chaka Khan on his *Back on the Block* release.

The Brothers earned platinum records for *Look Out for Number 1* and *Right on Time*. Jones produced both of these, along with their third and fourth LPs, *Blam* and *Light Up the Night*. The group produced its single "The Real Thing" in 1981. It reached No. 11 on the R&B charts, and the Brothers had another hit with "Welcome to the Club" in 1982. They started doing separate ventures; Louis Johnson played bass on Michael Jackson's *Thriller* LP and recorded a gospel album, while George Johnson worked with Steve Arrington. Leon Sylvers produced their mid-'80s return LP *Out of Control;* it didn't equal their past success, but got them another R&B hit with "You Keep Coming Back" in 1984. They recorded *Kickin* in 1988, and co-wrote "Tomorrow" with Siedah Garrett for Jones' *Back on the Block* in 1989. —*Ron Wynn*

● **Greatest Hits** / Jun. 18, 1996 / A&M ✦✦✦✦
Greatest Hits contains all of the Brothers Johnson's biggest singles, including the gold singles "I'll Be Good to You" and "Strawberry Letter 23." In addition to all the familiar hits, there are some lesser-known singles that are nearly as good, making this single-disc compilation definitive retrospective. —*Stephen Thomas Erlewine*

The Crazy World of Arthur Brown

Psychedelic
One of the most electrifying one-shot artists of the '60s, British singer Brown briefly set the charts alight in 1968, as well as thrilling audiences with his theatrical performances, which saw him wearing helmets of fire and outlandish costumes. His debut album was surely one of the most left-field commercial successes of the late '60s, if not of rock history. Besides topping the British charts (and reaching No. 2 in the US) with his brilliantly demonic single "Fire," the self-proclaimed god of hellfire actually scored a Top Ten LP with his 1968 debut. Unveiling Arthur's demented, fire-obsessed lyrical visions and swooping, theatrical vocals, it showcased his band's manic, agitated psychedelic sound, which was anchored by incendiary drumming, Pete Townshend's production, and an organist who could be best described as Jimmy Smith on acid. Brown's original band broke up in early 1969; in the early '70s, he released several albums with Kingdom Come, which saw him pursuing a maddeningly obscure, and less exciting, brand of art-rock. He's recorded off and on since, but his last flash of fame was his role as a priest in the film version of *Tommy*. —*Richie Unterberger*

● **Crazy World of Arthur Brown** / 1968 / Polydor ✦✦✦✦
Though a bit over-the-top, this album was still powerful and surprisingly melodic, and managed to be quite bluesy and soulful even as the band overhauled chestnuts by James Brown and Screamin' Jay Hawkins. "Spontaneous Apple Creation" is a willfully histrionic, atonal song that gives Captain Beefheart a run for his money. Though this one-shot was not (and perhaps could not ever) be repeated, it remains an exhilaratingly reckless slice of psychedelia. The CD reissue includes both mono and stereo versions of five of the songs. Although the mono mixes lack the full-bodied power of the stereo ones, they're marked by some interesting differences, especially in the brief spoken and instrumental links between tracks. —*Richie Unterberger*

Bobby Brown

Vocals / Dance-Pop, Urban, Club-Dance, New Jack R&B
At the end of the '80s, former New Edition member Bobby Brown made the album that made new-jack swing a dominant force not only on the urban charts, but on the pop charts as well. Brown's first album, *King of the Stage*, wasn't that remarkable but 1988's *Don't Be Cruel* is the definitive new-jack album, thanks to L.A. Reid and Babyface's massive production and songs, including the hits "Don't Be Cruel," "Every Little Step," and "Roni." While recording the follow-up album, Brown married pop star Whitney Houston and they had a child; their marriage has been plagued with tabloid-fueled rumors. In 1992, Brown released *Bobby*, a follow-up record that didn't have the commercial success of *Don't Be*

Cruel, mainly because it lacked the focused songs and production that made that album such a huge success. — *Stephen Thomas Erlewine*

King of Stage / 1987 / MCA ✦✦

★ **Don't Be Cruel** / 1988 / MCA ✦✦✦✦✦
Ex-New Edition vocalist Brown released a dud debut in 1987, but his follow-up, *Don't Be Cruel,* produced by new-jack kingpin Teddy Riley, was a monster hit and a brilliant statement of Brown's creative purpose. The title cut brought a level of sensitivity into new jack, and "My Prerogative" is one of the greatest dance-groove anthems produced in the late '80s. And the man can smoke on the ballads. — *John Floyd*

Bobby / 1992 / MCA ✦✦✦
Brown's follow-up to the groundbreaking *Don't Be Cruel* isn't as innovative or consistent as his previous album, but that doesn't mean it's without any charms; the singles "Humpin' Around," "Good Enough," and "Get Away" are strong and memorable, which almost makes the abundance of filler forgivable. — *Stephen Thomas Erlewine*

James Brown

b. May 3, 1928, Macon, GA
Organ, Piano, Drums, Keyboards, Vocals / Soul, Funk, R&B
Soul Brother Number One, the Godfather of Soul, the Hardest Working Man in Show Business, Mr. Dynamite—those are mighty titles, but no one can question that James Brown has earned them more than any other performer. Other singers were more popular, others were equally skilled, but no other African-American musician has been so influential on the course of popular music in the past several decades. And no other musician, pop or otherwise, put on a more exciting, exhilarating stage show—Brown's performances were marvels of athletic stamina and split-second timing.

Through the gospel-impassioned fury of his vocals and the complex polyrhythms of his beats, Brown was a crucial midwife in not just one, but two revolutions in American Black music. He was one of the figures most responsible for turning R&B into soul; he was, most would agree, *the* figure most responsible for turning soul music into the funk of the late '60s and early '70s. Since the mid-'70s, he's done little more than tread water artistically; his financial and drug problems eventually got him a controversial prison sentence. Yet in a sense his music is now more influential than ever, as his voice and rhythms are sampled on innumerable rap and hip-hop recordings, and critics have belatedly hailed his innovations as among the most important in all of rock or soul.

Brown's rags-to-riches-to-rags story has heroic and tragic dimensions of mythic resonance. Born into poverty in the South, he ran afoul of the law by the late '40s on an armed-robbery conviction. With the help of singer Bobby Byrd's family, Brown gained parole, and started a gospel group with Byrd, changing their focus to R&B as the rock revolution gained steam. The Flames, as the Georgian group were known in the mid-'50s, were signed by Federal/King, and had a huge R&B hit right off the bat with the wrenching, churchy ballad "Please, Please, Please." By now the Flames had become James Brown and the Famous Flames, the charisma, energy, and talent of Brown making him the natural star attraction. All of Brown's singles over the next two years flopped, as he sought to establish his own style, recording material that was obviously derivative of heroes like Roy Brown, Hank Ballard, Little Richard, and Ray Charles. In retrospect, it can be seen that Brown was in the same position as dozens of other R&B one-shots—talented singers in need of better songs, or not fully on the road to a truly original sound. What made Brown succeed where hundreds of others failed was his superhuman determination, working the chitlin circuit to death, sharpening his band, and keeping an eye on new trends. He was on the verge of being dropped from King in late 1958 when his perseverance finally paid off, as "Try Me" became a No. 1 R&B (and small pop) hit, and several follow-ups established him as a regular visitor to the R&B charts.

Brown's style of R&B got harder as the '60s began, as he added more complex, Latin- and jazz-influenced rhythms on hits like "Good Good Lovin'," "I'll Go Crazy," "Think," and "Night Train," alternating these with torturous ballads that featured some of the most frayed screaming to be heard outside of the church. Black audiences already knew that Brown had the most exciting live act around, but he truly started to become a phenomenon with the release of *Live at the Apollo* in 1963. Capturing a James Brown concert in all its whirling-dervish energy and calculated spontaneity, it reached No. 2 in the album charts, an unprecedented feat for a hardcore R&B LP.

Live at the Apollo was recorded and released against the wishes of the King label. It was these kinds of artistic standoffs that led Brown to seek better opportunities elsewhere. In 1964, he ignored his King contract to record "Out of Sight" for Smash, igniting a lengthy legal battle that prevented him from issuing vocal recordings for about a year. When he finally resumed recording for King in 1965, he had a new contract that granted him far more artistic control over his releases.

Brown's new era had truly begun, however, with "Out of Sight," which topped the R&B charts and made the pop Top 30. For some time, Brown

had been moving toward more elemental lyrics which threw in as many chants and screams as words, and more intricate beats and horn charts that took some of their cues from the ensemble work of jazz outfits. "Out of Sight" wasn't called funk when it came out, but it had most of the essential ingredients. These were amplified and perfected on 1965's "Papa's Got a Brand New Bag," a monster that finally broke Brown to the White audience, reaching the Top Ten. The even more adventurous follow-up, "I Got You (I Feel Good)," did even better, making No. 3.

These hits kicked off Brown's period of greatest commercial success and public visibility. From 1965 to the end of the decade, he was rarely off the R&B charts, often on the pop listings, and all over the concert circuit and national TV, even meeting with Vice President Hubert Humphrey and other important politicians as a representative of the Black community. His music became even bolder and funkier, as melody was dispensed with almost altogether in favor of chunky rhythms and magnetic interplay between his vocals, horns, drums, and scratching electric guitar (heard to best advantage on hits like "Cold Sweat," "I Got the Feelin'," and "There Was a Time"). The lyrics were now not so much words as chanted, stream-of-consciousness slogans, often aligning themselves with Black pride as well as good old-fashioned (or new-fashioned) sex. Much of the credit for the sound he devised belonged to (and has now been belatedly attributed) his top-notch supporting musicians, such as saxophonists Maceo Parker, St. Clair Pinckney, and Pee Wee Ellis; guitarist Jimmy Nolen; backup singer and longtime loyal associate Bobby Byrd; and drummer Clyde Stubblefield.

Brown was both a brilliant bandleader and a stern taskmaster, leading his band to walk out on him in late 1969. Amazingly, he turned the crisis to his advantage by recruiting a young Cincinnati outfit called the Pacemakers, featuring guitarist Catfish Collins and bassist Bootsy Collins. Although they only stayed with him for about a year, they were crucial to Brown's evolution into even harder funk, emphasizing the rhythm and the bottom even more. The Collins brothers, for their part, put their apprenticeship to good use, helping define '70s funk as members of the Parliament/Funkadelic axis.

In the early '70s, many of the most important members of Brown's late-'60s band returned to the fold, to be billed as the J.B.'s (they also made records on their own). Brown continued to score heavily on the R&B charts throughout the first half of the 1970s, the music becoming even more and more elemental and beat-driven. At the same time, he was retreating from the White audience he had cultivated during the mid-to-late '60s; records like "Make It Funky," "Hot Pants," "Get on the Good Foot," and "The Payback" were huge soul sellers, but only modest pop ones. Critics charged, with some justification, that the Godfather was starting to repeat and recycle himself too many times. It must be remembered, though, that these songs were made for the singles-radio-jukebox market and not meant to be played one after the other on CD compilations (as they are today). By the mid-'70s, Brown was beginning to burn out artistically. He seemed shorn of new ideas, was being outgunned on the charts by disco, and was running into problems with the IRS and his financial empire. There were sporadic hits, and he could always count on enthusiastic live audiences, but by the 1980s, he didn't have a label. With the explosion of rap, however, which frequently sampled vintage JB records, Brown was now hipper than ever. He collaborated with Afrika Bambaataa on the critical smash single "Unity," and re-entered the Top Ten in 1986 with "Living in America." Rock critics, who had always ranked Brown considerably below Otis Redding and Aretha Franklin in the soul canon, began to reevaluate his output, particularly his funk years, sometimes anointing him not just as Soul Brother Number One, but as *the* most important Black musician of the rock era.

In 1988, Brown's personal life came crashing down in a well-publicized incident in which he was accused by his wife of assault and battery. After a year skirting hazy legal and personal troubles, he led the police on an interstate car chase after allegedly threatening people with a handgun. The episode ended in a six-year prison sentence that many felt excessive; he was paroled after serving two years.

It's probably safe to assume that Brown, now well into his 60s, will not make any more important recordings, although he continues to perform. Yet his music is probably more popular in the American mainstream today than it's been in over 20 years, and not just among young rappers and samplers. For a long time his cumbersome, byzantine discography was mostly out of print, with pieces available only on skimpy greatest-hits collections. A series of exceptionally well-packaged reissues on PolyGram has changed the situation; the *Star Time* box set is the best overview, with other superb compilations devoted to specific phases of his lengthy career, from '50s R&B to '70s funk. — *Richie Unterberger*

★ **Live at the Apollo** / Jan. 1963 / Polydor ✦✦✦✦✦
An astonishing record of James and the Flames tearing the roof off the sucker at the mecca of R&B theatres, New York's Apollo. When King Records owner Syd Nathan refused to fund the recording, thinking it commercial folly, Brown single-mindedly proceeded anyway, paying for it out of his own pocket. He had been out on the road night after night for a while, and he knew that the magic that was part and parcel of a James

Brown show was something no record had ever caught. Hit follows hit without a pause—"I'll Go Crazy," "Try Me," "Think," "Please Please Please," "I Don't Mind," "Night Train," and more. The affirmative screams and cries of the audience are something you've never experienced unless you've seen the Brown Revue in a Black theater. If you have, I need not say more; if you haven't, suffice to say that this should be one of the very first records you ever own. —*Rob Bowman*

Pure Dynamite! Live at the Royal / Feb. 1964 / King ✦✦✦✦
It has only eight songs, it's less than half an hour long, and two of the songs are studio tracks with overdubbed audience noise. It's not nearly as well known as his live '60s albums recorded at the Apollo, but *Pure Dynamite!*, recorded live at Baltimore's Royal Theater in 1963, is nearly as good. This is decidedly more raucous than his 1962 *Live at the Apollo*, with the balance leaning toward uptempo ravers like "Shout and Shimmy," "Signed, Sealed, and Delivered," and the set-closing "Good Good Lovin'," all of which are positively kinetic. To break up the pace, there are some R&B torch ballads, including the song without which no J.B. show was complete, "Please, Please, Please." It's also fair to say that the recording quality is primitive, even more so than on his 1962 Apollo gig; the vocals are a bit hollow, and the audience occasionally overwhelms the music with its noisy enthusiasm. Somehow, it doesn't matter much. The performances are so energetic that you can't help getting caught up in the excitement. —*Richie Unterberger*

Live at the Apollo, Vol. 2 / Aug. 1968 / Rhino ✦✦✦✦
As a whole, this double album is pretty erratic—there are a bunch of torchy R&B ballads that were somewhat anachronistic in light of the explosive funk innovations Brown was unleashing in the studio during this time, and some of those funk hits are reprised here in superbrief versions that seem to cut off before they have a chance to get started. On the other hand, some of it is as essential as anything else Brown ever recorded. In particular, the 20-minute medley of "Let Yourself Go/There Was a Time/I Feel All Right/Cold Sweat" is a magnificent, seamless ball of energy, a landmark performance in the evolution of soul and funk. Other highlights are "Bring It Up" and an 11-minute "It's a Man's, Man's, Man's World." —*Richie Unterberger*

Roots of a Revolution / 1984 / Polydor ✦✦✦✦
A double-CD retrospective of 1956-1964 recordings that charts Brown's progress from doo wop and Little Richard-influenced R&B to the verge of his groundbreaking mid-'60s funk. It doesn't include his biggest hits of the era (which are found on *Star Time*), but these are by and large equally exciting. Many fine overlooked R&B hits and B-sides like "Shout and Shimmy," "I've Got Money," the gospel-influenced "Oh Baby Don't You Weep," and "Maybe the Last Time," which inspired the Rolling Stones' "The Last Time." —*Richie Unterberger*

Messing with the Blues / 1991 / Polydor ✦✦✦
Although he is most famous for his innovations in soul and funk music, James Brown never lost sight of his blues and R&B roots. His albums often placed surprisingly rootsy covers of old chestnuts alongside his groundbreaking polyrhythmic workouts. This double CD compiles 30 of the bluesiest items from his vast recorded legacy. Cut between 1957 and 1985, most of the tracks actually date from the '60s; many of these, in turn, were laid down in the early part of the decade, when J.B. was gradually evolving from his more conventional beginnings. The artists whose songs are covered here read like a *Who's Who* of R&B pioneers: Louis Jordan, Roy Brown, Memphis Slim, Ivory Joe Hunter, Fats Domino, Chuck Willis, Little Willie John, Billy Ward, Guitar Slim, and Bobby Bland. It's quite an instructive insight into Brown's not-always-visible roots. It would be fair to say that this does not rank among his most exciting material, finding him in a smoother and more conventional style than his most innovative work. It is nonetheless always entertaining and accomplished, with Brown's love for this material shining through strongly in his committed interpretations. Especially intriguing are an 11-minute cover of Chuck Willis' "Don't Deceive Me" and a two-part, blues-based rap vamp from the early '70s, "Like It Is, Like It Was (The Blues)." The disc includes several unreleased cuts, alternate takes, and unedited versions of previously released songs. —*Richie Unterberger*

☆ **Star Time** / Jun. 1991 / Polydor ✦✦✦✦✦
One of the great box sets of all time; over four CDs, Brown's recorded legacy is traced from "Please Please Please" in 1956 through his 1984 duet with Afrika Bambaataa, "Unity Pt. 1." With 71 tracks in all, the set places the Who's Who1 R&B artist ever in his proper perspective as the prime progenitor of funk, one of the architects of soul, and the Godfather of Rap. To have done any one of these things would have been a bid for immortality; having done all three makes him a god. Four CDs at once is virtually too rich for one sitting. The well-written liner notes provide three different perspectives on Brown's career. A cornerstone of any great collection. —*Rob Bowman*

★ **20 All-Time Greatest Hits!** / Oct. 1991 / Polydor ✦✦✦✦✦
A first-rate greatest-hits package that covers the essential soul singles and some of the funk-period material as well. While the finest James

Brown package is the boxed set, if you're not going to get that, you wouldn't be far wrong getting this one instead. —*Ron Wynn*

Love Power Peace / 1992 / Polydor ✦✦✦✦
James Brown with the newly formed J.B.'s—the maestro's second great band, including Bootsy Collins, Phelps Collins, Jabo Starks, Bobby Byrd, and Fred Wesley. *Live at the Apollo* had caught James Brown, the '50s R&B/gospel singer; *Love Power Peace* captures James the funkster. In the early '70s Brown turned up the funk, recording such litanies for Black America as "Ain't It Funky Now," "Sex Machine," "Give It Up or Turn It Loose," "Super Bad," "Get Up, Get Into It, Get Involved," and "Soul Power." They're all here, along with revved-up, white-hot versions of the early- and middle-period classics. Brown had planned to release this as a triple album in 1971. When several band members left after it was recorded, Brown switched from King to Polydor Records, leading him to record a new studio album instead. In 1992, Polygram decided to make the recording available for the first time. —*Rob Bowman*

The Greatest Hits of the Fourth Decade / 1992 / Scotti Bros. ✦✦✦
Collecting Brown's 1980s hits that didn't make it onto *Star Time*, *Greatest Hits of the Fourth Decade* shows that the period was not among his most creatively fertile, even with the monster hit "Living in America." Still, the disc does pick the best tracks from a dry spell, making it a nice supplement to the box set. —*Stephen Thomas Erlewine*

Soul Pride: The Instrumentals (1960-69) / 1993 / PolyGram ✦✦✦✦
Everyone knows how hot James Brown's bands were, but not everyone's aware that he and his sidemen recorded lots of instrumental sides in the '60s. Originally scattered haphazardly over many out-of-print singles and albums, *Soul Pride* brings together the best of this work into one cohesive and chronological package. These cuts are nearly equal in power to J.B.'s vocal performances. Not only does the band cook on most of these insinuating vamps, but you can also hear the evolution of the man's sound from gritty R&B to tight-as-a-drum soul to free-form funk. Soul Brother No. 1 himself plays organ and adds unpredictable shouts and screams on most of these tracks. But the chief stars are sidemen like Maceo Parker, Fred Wesley, and Pee Wee Ellis, who broke new ground with their compulsive counterpoint riffs. This fiery two-disc, 36-track box set contains over two hours of music, as well as a few non-LP B-sides and previously unreleased tracks. —*Richie Unterberger*

Funk Power—1970: A Brand New Thang / 1996 / Polydor ✦✦✦✦
The period during which Brown was backed by the original J.B.'s (with Bootsy and Catfish Collins) lasted only a year. But it was an extremely important and influential phase of Brown's career, when he moved from soul-funk to hard funk, stretching out the grooves and putting more stress on the bottom than ever before. This 78-minute disc is the cream of his recordings from the Bootsy Collins era. The nine tracks (the tenth is a brief public-service announcement) include some of his core funk workouts—"Get Up I Feel Like Being a Sex Machine" (two versions), "Super Bad," "Give It Up or Turn It a Loose," "Talkin' Loud and Sayin' Nothing," "Get Up, Get Into It, Get Involved," and "Soul Power." It's not for those who find Brown's funk phase too monotonous, and indeed the grooves do get a bit similar when experienced all at once. But it's unquestionably the best of Brown's '70s recordings, and indeed some of the hardest funk ever waxed by anyone at any time. As a bonus, the CD has previously unreleased complete versions of "Soul Power" (12 minutes) and "Talkin' Loud and Sayin' Nothing" (14 minutes), as well as a previously unreleased version of "There Was a Time." —*Richie Unterberger*

☆ **Foundations of Funk: A Brand New Bag: 1964-1969** / Mar. 19, 1996 / Polydor ✦✦✦✦✦
There are several worthy James Brown compilations. But this is the one that presents his most fertile and innovative soul and funk material. From 1964's "Out of Sight" through 1969's "Mother Popcorn," this was Brown at the apex of his creativity, turning soul into funk in the mid-'60s, then pushing the rhythm even more to the forefront. Most of his hit singles from this five-year explosion of white heat are on this 27-track, two-CD set, including "Out of Sight," "Papa's Got a Brand New Bag," "I Got You (I Feel Good)," "Say It Loud—I'm Black and I'm Proud," and "Cold Sweat." There are some minor omissions that could be questioned (the absence of the studio version of "Bring It Up," for instance), and big James Brown fans will already have some of these tracks on the *Star Time* box and other releases. It does, however, contain minor but significant bonuses: an alternate take of "Cold Sweat," a previously unreleased live medley of "Out of Sight" and "Bring It Up," and a previously unreleased live version of "Licking Stick—Licking Stick." There are also longer versions of "I Don't Want Nobody to Give Me Nothing" (ten minutes!), "I Got the Feelin'," "The Popcorn," and "Brother Rapp" that were edited when they were prepared for official release. —*Richie Unterberger*

Maxine Brown

b. Kingstree, SC
Vocals / Soul, R&B
An underrated '60s R&B chanteuse from New York responsible for the

original "Oh No Not My Baby." With an early gospel background, Brown waxed her first secular hit, "All in My Mind," for the tiny Nomar label in 1960, and quickly encored with "Funny." Switching to Wand Records, Brown recorded some fine uptown-style R&B, including the charming and often-covered "Oh No Not My Baby" in 1964. Teamed with label-mate Chuck Jackson, Brown scored another hit the following year with a duet revival of Chris Kenner's "Something You Got." Brown later recorded for a variety of firms into the early '70s. —*Bill Dahl*

Maxine Brown's Greatest Hits / 1964 / Wand ++++
Maxine Brown had a handful of hits, most of them either laments or teary-eyed ballads, in the early '60s. They're all included on this release. Brown's timing at Scepter/Wand was unfortunate; the label was allocating most of its resources and promotional muscle to breaking Dionne Warwick in the pop market. Both she and Chuck Jackson didn't get the push they needed or deserved. —*Ron Wynn*

● **Oh No Not My Baby: The Best of Maxine Brown** / 1990 / Kent ++++
This 28-song CD is undoubtedly the best compilation of this underrated soul singer's work, featuring many of her '60s singles and several tunes from the era that were unreleased until the '80s. This disc draws from her recordings for the Wand label between 1963 and 1967, when Brown was at her artistic peak. Of course the hit title track is a highlight, but there are no clunkers in this excellent collection of overlooked '60s pop-soul, featuring the New York "uptown" production that also graced the records of fellow Wand/Scepter artists like Dionne Warwick and Chuck Jackson. Brown was one of the most versatile soul divas of the '60s, showing the influence of Brill Building pop, girl groups, Motown, and even Stax soul and supper-club ballads. As with a similar artist like Betty Everett, this versatility has worked against her in some ways. Neither full-fledged pop nor unabashedly soul, her work cannot be easily pigeonholed into a certain soul genre, and has cost her the respect that some purists reserve for "deep" soul singers. But her work holds up well. Collectors should be aware that this disc doesn't include any of the records she cut in the early '60s before joining Wand; the version of her 1961 Top 20 hit "All in My Mind" here is from a live 1964 release, not the original single. —*Richie Unterberger*

● **Greatest Hits** / 1995 / Tomato ++++
This 23-track best-of has a lot of overlap with the British import *Oh No Not My Baby;* both cover her mid-'60s period with Wand, and each has some songs not on the other. There's not a crucial difference between the pair, but the nod probably goes to the import, which has more songs and better sound. In its favor, this compilation includes five of her duets with Chuck Jackson, none of which are on the other CD (although the duets don't rank among her best material). It also has a studio version of "All in My Mind," rather than the live one on the British anthology. —*Richie Unterberger*

Something You Got / 1996 / Soul Classics/Ichiban +++
All 20 of the duet tracks that Brown and Chuck Jackson recorded for the Wand label between 1965 and 1967, comprising the entirety of their two albums for the company. It's reasonable pop-soul, but not nearly as memorable as the best male-female soul duets of the era (like the ones by Marvin Gaye and various Motown partners, or by Otis Redding and Carla Thomas). Highlights are the early compositions by the Jo Armstead-Nick Ashford-Valerie Simpson team, including a version of "Let's Go Get Stoned" that was recorded (though not released) before Ray Charles' more famous hit rendition. —*Richie Unterberger*

Ruth Brown

b. Jan. 30, 1928, Portsmouth, VA
Vocals / R&B
They called Atlantic Records "the house that Ruth built" during the 1950s, and they weren't referring to the Sultan of Swat. Ruth Brown's regal hitmaking reign from 1949 to the close of the '50s helped tremendously to establish the New York label's predominance in the R&B field. Later, the business all but forgot her—she was forced to toil as domestic help for a time—but she's back on top now, her status as a postwar R&B pioneer (and tireless advocate for the rights and royalties of her peers) recognized worldwide.

Young Ruth Weston was inspired initially by jazz chanteuses Sarah Vaughan, Billie Holiday, and Dinah Washington. She ran away from her Portsmouth home in 1945 to hit the road with trumpeter Jimmy Brown, whom she soon married. A month with bandleader Lucky Millinder's orchestra in 1947 ended abruptly in Washington, DC, when she was canned for delivering a round of drinks to members of the band. Cab Calloway's sister Blanche gave Ruth a gig at her Crystal Caverns nightclub and assumed a managerial role in the young singer's life. DJ Willis Conover dug Brown's act and recommended her to Ahmet Ertegun and Herb Abramson, bosses of a fledgling imprint named Atlantic. Unfortunately, Brown's debut session for the firm was delayed by a nine-month hospital stay caused by a serious auto accident en route to New York that badly injured her leg. When she finally made it to her first date in May of 1949, she made up for lost time by waxing the torch ballad "So Long"

(backed by guitarist Eddie Condon's band), which proved to be her first hit.

Brown's seductive vocal delivery shone incandescently on her Atlantic smashes "Teardrops in My Eyes" (an R&B chart-topper for 11 weeks in 1950), "I'll Wait for You" in 1951, 1952's "5-10-15 Hours" (another No. 1 rocker), the seminal "(Mama) He Treats Your Daughter Mean" in 1953, and a tender Chuck Willis-penned "Oh What a Dream" and the timely "Mambo Baby" the next year. Along the way, Frankie Laine tagged her "Miss Rhythm" during an engagement in Philly. Brown belted a series of her hits on the groundbreaking TV program "Showtime at the Apollo" in 1955, exhibiting delicious comic timing while trading sly one-liners with emcee Willie Bryant (ironically, ex-husband Jimmy Brown was a member of the show's house band!).

After an even two dozen R&B chart appearances for Atlantic that ended in 1960 with "Don't Deceive Me" (many of them featuring hellraising tenor sax solos by then-hubby Willis "Gator" Jackson), Brown faded from view. After raising her two sons and working a nine-to-five job, Brown began to rebuild her musical career in the mid-'70s. That comedic sense served her well during a TV-sitcom stint co-starring with McLean Stevenson in "Hello, Larry"; in a meaty role in director John Waters' 1985 sock-hop satire film *Hairspray,* and during her 1989 Broadway starring turn in *Black and Blue* (which won her a Tony Award).

There have been more records for Fantasy in recent years (notably 1991's jumping *Fine and Mellow*), and a lengthy tenure as host of National Public Radio's "Harlem Hit Parade" and "BluesStage." Brown's nine-year ordeal to recoup her share of royalties from all those Atlantic platters led to the formation of the nonprofit Rhythm & Blues Foundation, an organization dedicated to helping others in the same frustrating situation.

Factor in all those time-consuming activities, and it's a wonder Ruth Brown has time to sing anymore. But she does (quite royally, too), her pipes mellowed but not frayed by the ensuing decades that have seen her rise to stardom not once, but twice. —*Bill Dahl*

★ **Miss Rhythm (Greatest Hits and More)** / 1989 / Rhino +++++
They used to refer to Atlantic Records in its early years as "the house that Ruth built," and the 40 tracks inhabiting these two discs offer unassailable insight as to why. As one of the premier R&B divas of the early '50s, Brown's seductive, earthy style found her belting the rockers (the R&B chart-toppers "Teardrops From My Eyes," "Mama He Treats Your Daughter Mean," "5-10-15 Hours") and caressing the ballads ("So Long," "Have a Good Time," "Oh What a Dream"), backed by some of New York's finest session players (including then-hubby Willis Gator Jackson on scorching tenor sax). Covers 1949-1960 and takes Brown from the beginnings of R&B to the heyday of rock ("Wild Wild Young Men" is positively frantic, while the Bobby Darin-penned "This Little Girl's Gone Rockin'" is lightweight yet utterly charming). Essential stuff! —*Bill Dahl*

Fine and Mellow / 1991 / Fantasy +++

★ **Best of Ruth Brown** / Jun. 18, 1996 / Rhino +++++
For those who want a cheaper and more concise collection of her best Atlantic cuts than the two-CD *Miss Rhythm,* this superb 23-track CD has the cream of her '50s work, including no less than 19 Top Ten R&B singles. Charting her evolution from her jazzy debut, "So Long," through jump blues and early rock 'n' roll, it also adds a bonus of two previously unissued live cuts from 1959. —*Richie Unterberger*

Jackson Browne

b. Oct. 9, 1948, Heidelberg, Germany
Guitar, Piano, Keyboards, Vocals / Singer-Songwriter, Soft Rock, Pop-Rock
As one of the guiding lights from the sensitive '70s singer-songwriter school of pop, Jackson Browne (along with Joni Mitchell) gave the word "introspection" new meaning with his earnest musical epistles from the inside. Like Mitchell and James Taylor (somewhat), Browne provided a weighty soundtrack for scores of apprehensive '60s kids trying to come to grips with growing up and finding their place in the world.

Without a doubt, his first four albums are loaded with gems, even if his melodies tend to have a sameness. Browne has always attracted stellar sidemen for his records, many of whom can also be found on records by Linda Ronstadt and James Taylor.

During his career, Browne has proven himself to be a very capable producer for Warren Zevon and Greg Copeland.

Hardcore Browne fanatics will claim their hero ceased to perform to their expectations after his million-selling 1976 opus *The Pretender,* but his greatest commercial success took place from that album on. Granted, his highest-charting single, the lightweight "Somebody's Baby," was quite a departure from his previous work, but maybe Browne needed a breather.

In 1982 Browne's California pop-rock phase ended, and he returned with the more topical *Lawyers in Love,* which produced a hit with the title track. Subsequent albums have increasingly addressed global issues over the self-absorbed ruminations of his earlier work.

Browne returned to a more introspective style of songwriting with his 1993 album, *I'm Alive*. He followed with *Looking East* in 1996. *—Rick Clark*

☆ **Jackson Browne** / Jan. 1972 / Asylum ✦✦✦✦✦
One of the reasons that Jackson Browne's first album is among the most auspicious debuts in pop-music history is that it doesn't sound like a debut. Although only 23, Browne had kicked around the music business for several years, writing and performing as a member of the Nitty Gritty Dirt Band and as Nico's backup guitarist, among other gigs, while many artists recorded his material. So, if this doesn't sound like someone's first batch of songs, it's not. Browne had developed an unusual use of language, studiedly casual yet full of striking imagery, and a post-apocalyptic viewpoint to go with it. He sang with a calm certainty over spare, discretely placed backup—piano, acoustic guitar, bass, drums, congas, violin, harmony vocals—that highlighted the songs and always seemed about to disappear. In song after song, Browne described the world as a desert in need of moisture, and this wet/dry dichotomy carried over into much of the imagery. In "Doctor My Eyes," the album's most propulsive song and a Top Ten hit, he sang, "Doctor, my eyes/Cannot see the sky/Is this the prize/For having learned how not to cry?" If Browne's outlook was cautious, its expression was original. His conditional optimism seemed to reflect hard experience, and in the early '70s, the aftermath of the '60s, a lot of his listeners shared that perspective. Like any great artist, Browne articulated the tenor of his times. But the album has long since come to seem a timeless collection of reflective ballads touching on still-difficult subjects—suicide (explicitly), depression and drug use (probably), spiritual uncertainty and desperate hope—all in calm, reasoned tones, and all with an amazingly eloquent sense of language. *Jackson Browne*'s greater triumph is that, having perfectly expressed its times, it transcended those times as well. (The album features a cover depicting Browne's face on a water bag—an appropriate reference to its desert/water imagery—containing the words "saturate before using." Inevitably, many people began to refer to the self-titled album by that phrase, and when it was released on CD, it became official—both the disc and the spine of the jewel box read *Saturate Before Using*.) *—William Ruhlmann*

For Everyman / Oct. 1973 / Asylum ✦✦✦✦
Jackson Browne faced the nearly insurmountable task of following a masterpiece in making his second album. Having cherry-picked years of songwriting the first time around, he turned to some of his secondary older material, which was still better than most people's best and, ironically, more accessible—notably such songs as "These Days," which had been covered six times already, dating back to Nico's *Chelsea Girl* album in 1967, and "Take It Easy," a co-composition with the Eagles' Glenn Frey, which had been a Top 40 hit for the group in 1972. Browne unsuccessfully looked for another hit single with the uptempo "Red Neck Friend," reminisced about meeting his wife and starting a family in the coy "Ready or Not," and, at the end, finally came up with a new song to rank with those on the first album in the philosophical title track, which reportedly was his more positive reply to Crosby, Stills, Nash & Young's "Wooden Ships." (David Crosby sang harmony.) Musically, the album was still restrained, but not as austere as *Jackson Browne*, as the singer had hooked up with multi-instrumentalist David Lindley, who would introduce interesting textures to his music on a variety of stringed instruments for the next several years. All of which is to say that *For Everyman* was a less consistent collection than Browne's debut album. But Browne's songwriting ability remained impressive. *—William Ruhlmann*

★ **Late for the Sky** / Sep. 1974 / Asylum ✦✦✦✦✦
On his third album, Jackson Browne returned to the themes of his debut record (love, loss, identity, apocalypse), and, amazingly, delved even deeper into them. "For a Dancer," a meditation on death like the first album's "Song for Adam," is a more eloquent eulogy; "Farther On" extends the "moving on" point of "Looking Into You"; "Before the Deluge" is a glimpse beyond the apocalypse evoked on "My Opening Farewell" and the second album's "For Everyman." If Browne had seemed to question everything in his first records, here he even questioned himself. "For me some words come easy, but I know that they don't mean that much," he sang on the opening track, "Late for the Sky," and added in "Farther On," "I'm not sure what I'm trying to say." Yet his seeming uncertainty and self-doubt reflected the size and complexity of the problems he was addressing in these songs, and few had ever explored such territory, much less mapped it so well. "The Late Show," the album's thematic center, doubted but ultimately affirmed the nature of relationships, while by the end, "After the Deluge," if "only a few survived," the human race continued nonetheless. It was a lot to put into a pop music album, but Browne stretched the limits of what could be found in what he called "the beauty in songs," just as Bob Dylan had a decade before. *—William Ruhlmann*

The Pretender / Nov. 1976 / Asylum ✦✦✦
On *The Pretender*, Jackson Browne took a step back from the precipice so well defined on his first three albums, but doing so didn't seem to make him feel any better. Employing a real producer, Jon Landau (who worked with and managed Bruce Springsteen), for the first time, Browne made a record that sounded like a real contemporary-rock record for the first time—the drums boomed, the vocals had attractive, echoed presence, the songs were tightly arranged, the instrumental licks were L.A.-tasty—but this made his songs less effective. Where the uptempo drive of "Doctor My Eyes" on the first album had emphasized the disillusioned lyric tone, here the ersatz Mexican arrangement of "Linda Paloma" and the bouncy second half of "Daddy's Tune," with its horn charts and guitar solo, undercut the lyrics. But the main problem was that the man who had delved so deeply into life's abyss on his earlier albums was in search of escape this time around, whether by crying ("Here Come Those Tears Again"), sleeping ("Sleep's Dark and Silent Gate"), or making peace with estranged love ones ("The Only Child," "Daddy's Tune"). None of it worked, however, and when Browne came to the final track—traditionally the place on his albums where he summed up his current philosophical stance—he delivered "The Pretender," a cynical, sarcastic treatise on moneygrubbing and the shallow life of the suburbs. The song was primarily inner directed; the pretender was the singer, and it would be hard to find a lyric as self-hating (or as self-pitying). In a sense, the song's defeatist tone demands rejection, but it is also a quintessential statement of its time, the post-Watergate '70s. Once again, Browne had accurately described the world around him by defining his own place in it, dire as that might be, and you had to admire that kind of honesty, even as it made you wince. *— William Ruhlmann*

Running on Empty / 1977 / Asylum ✦✦✦
Having acknowledged a certain creative desperation on *The Pretender*, Jackson Browne lowered his sights (and raised his commercial appeal) considerably with *Running on Empty*, which was more a concept album about the road than an actual live album, even though its songs were sometimes recorded on stage (and sometimes on the bus or in the hotel). Although unlike most live albums, it consisted of previously unrecorded songs, Browne had less creative participation on this album than on any he ever made, solely composing only two songs, co-writing four others, and covering another four. And he had less to say—the title song and leadoff track neatly conjoined his artistic and escapist themes. Figuratively and creatively, he was out of gas, but like "the pretender," still had to make a living. The songs covered all aspects of touring, from Danny O'Keefe's "The Road," which detailed romantic encounters, and "Rosie" (co-written by Browne and his manager Donald Miller), in which a soundman pays tribute to auto-eroticism, to, well, "Cocaine," to the travails of being a roadie ("The Load-Out"). Audience noises, humorous asides, loose playing—they were all part of a rough-around-the-edges musical evocation of the rock 'n' roll touring life. It was not what fans had come to expect from Browne, of course, but the disaffected were more than outnumbered by the newly converted. (It didn't hurt that "Running on Empty" and "The Load-Out"/"Stay" both became Top 40 hits.) As a result, Jackson Browne's least ambitious, but perhaps most accessible, album ironically became his biggest seller. But it is not characteristic of his other work: for many, it will be the only Browne album they will want to own, just as others always will regard it disdainfully as *Jackson Browne Lite*. *— William Ruhlmann*

Hold Out / 1980 / Asylum ✦✦
If Jackson Browne had convincingly lowered the bar set by his first three albums on his fourth and fifth ones, his sixth, *Hold Out*, found him once again seeking some measure of satisfaction, albeit in reduced circumstances. His songs were less philosophical, but they were also more personal. In "Of Missing Persons," he once again took on a eulogy as his subject, but unlike "Song to Adam" or "For a Dancer," here the song was directed to his late friend's daughter and encouraged her recovery: it was more a song for the living than for the dead. Newly aware of the world around him ("Boulevard"), he was also newly sensitive to others, notably on the mutual dependency song "Call It a Loan." But the personal tone sometimes made him less sure-footed as a performer; "Hold On Hold Out," the traditional big, long, last song on the album, was awkwardly, not winningly intimate, just as the attention-grabbing lead-off track, "Disco Apocalypse," was merely foolish instead of whatever it may have been intended to be (satire? drama?). If Browne was still trying to write himself out of the cul-de-sac he had created for himself early on, *Hold Out* represented an earnest attempt that nevertheless fell short. *—William Ruhlmann*

Lawyers in Love / 1983 / Asylum ✦✦
Jackson Browne's messages had always seemed so important that one tended to overlook the sheer songwriting craft that went into his work, craft that was apparent, for example, on his 1982 single "Somebody's Baby," which became his biggest hit ever (and which appears on none of his albums, only being available on the soundtrack to *Fast Times at Ridgemont High*), and on songs like "Downtown," a street-life portrait on

his seventh album, *Lawyers in Love*. The craft seemed all the more important because Browne was so intent on turning his back on the conundrums that had obsessed him in the past. On "Cut It Away," he sang of his desire to remove his "desperate heart" (a phrase he had used before), to rid himself of "this crazy longing for something more/This question that I don't have the answer for." In place of such ambitions, Browne substituted the beginnings of social concern ("Say It Isn't True") and, most imaginatively, a humorous look at contemporary trash culture in the title track, one of the more exhilaratingly silly moments in Browne's generally dour catalog. But the craft, and the familiar tightness of Browne's veteran studio/live band, couldn't hide the essentially retread nature of much of this material. — *William Ruhlmann*

Lives in the Balance / 1986 / Asylum ♦♦♦
Usually among the most introspective of songwriters, Jackson Browne cast his gaze on the world outside on *Lives in the Balance* and did not like what he saw. Beginning with "For America," he lamented his previous indifference to social issues—"I went on speaking of the future/While other people fought and bled"—but immediately tried to make up for lost time. The album's context, of course, was five years of Ronald Reagan's presidency, with what the Left saw as an indifference to the plight of the poor at home and a dangerously aggressive policy against insurgent movements in the Central American countries of El Salvador and Nicaragua they feared would lead to a Vietnam-like war. Without naming those places, Browne wrote and sang passionately against poverty in the songs "Soldier of Plenty" and "Lawless Avenues" and against war in "For America," "Lives in the Balance," and "Till I Go Down." Elsewhere, his more familiar themes of romantic ("In The Shape of a Heart") and philosophical ("Black and White") disillusionment also made appearances. But, from its hard-rock sound and forceful singing to its frankly agitprop lyrics, *For America* remained primarily a political statement, and if Browne sounded more involved in his music than he had in some time, the specificity of its approach inevitably limited its appeal and its long-term significance. — *William Ruhlmann*

World in Motion / 1989 / Elektra ♦♦
I'm Alive / Oct. 1993 / Elektra ♦♦♦
Looking East / Feb. 1996 / Elektra ♦♦♦
Jackson Browne begins his most Los Angeles-oriented album standing in the Pacific Ocean "Looking East" across the country and, as usual, doing so without much approval, but with a persistent hope. After reflecting on his youth in "The Barricades of Heaven," he compares the rich and poor in "Some Bridges" and takes time out to watch a little television in "Information Wars," before considering romance in "I'm the Cat," "Culver Moon," and "Baby How Long" and childhood in "Nino." He then decides he would like to be "Alive in the World," as opposed to inside his head or "behind some wall," and declares of that world, "It Is One." Thus, we are taken on another of Jackson Browne's tours, which manages to travel to outer and inner space without leaving the county of Los Angeles. After 24 years of record-making, he remains puzzled by the same personal and philosophical issues, and he approaches them in the same way, alternately hopeful and pessimistic, but more often than not ending up determined to persevere. He now uses fewer words, such that the songs sometimes seem no more than sketches, and he continues to set them to loping rock rhythms played against slabs of ringing guitar with traces of world music. Here, he co-credits eight of the ten songs to his backup musicians, yet the haunting, long-line melodies remain familiar from his earlier work. But then, *Looking East* is a highly referential work from an artist who started where most end and has been earnestly seeking the right direction ever since. *Looking East* finds him in his own backyard, still searching. — *William Ruhlmann*

Brownsville Station

Rock 'n' Roll, Hard Rock, Boogie Rock
A Detroit-area rock 'n' roll band formed in 1969 by guitarist Cub Koda. Original members also included Mike Lutz (guitar), T.J. Cronley (drums), and Tony Driggins (bass). Initially influenced by Chuck Berry, Bo Diddley, Jerry Lee Lewis, and other '50s rockers, their early albums included inspired covers and genre-faithful originals, all presented in Marshall stack, double-bass-drum bigness. Far more effective as a live act (with Koda's onstage banter influencing everyone from J. Geils' Peter Wolf to Alice Cooper), the group finally hit paydirt in late 1973 with their No. 3 hit, the Koda-penned "Smokin' in the Boys' Room." After disbanding the group in 1979, Koda went on to a career as a solo recording artist (see separate entry) and as a journalist for several music magazines. — *Stephen Thomas Erlewine*

No B.S. / 1970 / Warner Bros. ♦♦♦♦
Their debut album, featuring pedal-to-the-metal renditions of "Road Runner," "Rumble," and "Be Bop Confidential." — *Stephen Thomas Erlewine*

Brownsville Station / 1977 / Private Stock ♦♦♦

● **Smoking in the Boys' Room: The Best of Brownsville Station** / 1993 / Rhino ♦♦♦♦
A roaring romp through The Brownsville Station's back pages compiled by Cub Koda himself, *Smokin' in the Boys' Room* makes a convincing case that these Ann Arbor, Michigan garage punks were one of the most underrated rock 'n' roll bands of the 1970s. — *Stephen Thomas Erlewine*

The Buckinghams

Pop-Rock
If everyone on the northwest side of Chicago who claims to have hung out with the Buckinghams during their heyday had faithfully bought all their releases, the rock group might have sold more records than the Beatles.

Popular attractions while still in high school, the quintet changed its name from the Pulsations to the Buckinghams to reflect the British Invasion craze and signed with Chicago's USA Records in 1966. Backing Dennis Tufano's buoyant lead vocals with prominent harmonies and punchy soul-styled brass, the group came across the wistful "Kind of a Drag," and in short order, the Buckinghams had a million-selling pop chart-topper on their hands. They quickly graduated to recording for Columbia.

As long as songwriter Jim Holvay supplied more material of the same high quality as "Kind of a Drag," the Buckinghams were sitting pretty. Holvay cowrote "Don't You Care," "Hey Baby (They're Playing Our Song)," and the pseudo-psychedelic "Susan," and they all proved to be major hits for the band. The group's R&B roots surfaced on a vocal adaptation of Cannonball Adderley's jazz standard "Mercy, Mercy, Mercy," their second-biggest hit.

But the Buckinghams' fortunes soon changed drastically—one of the top-selling rock groups of 1967, they managed only one hit after early 1968, and by 1970 the group was kaput. Two original members, guitarist Carl Giammarese and bassist Nick Fortuna, have since revived the Buckinghams for oldies tours. — *Bill Dahl*

● **Mercy Mercy Mercy (A Collection)** / 1991 / Columbia ♦♦♦♦
These mid-'60s hitmakers from Chicago hold up well with their neat blend of pop and soul. All of their hits and more can be found on this 18-song anthology. — *Jeff Tamarkin*

Tim Buckley

b. Feb. 14, 1947, Washington, DC, **d.** Jun. 29, 1975
Guitar, Vocals / Singer-Songwriter, Folk-Rock, Jazz-Rock
One of the great rock vocalists of the 1960s, Tim Buckley drew from folk, psychedelic rock, and progressive jazz to create a considerable body of adventurous work in his brief lifetime. His multi-octave range was capable of not just astonishing power, but also great emotional expressiveness, swooping from sorrowful tenderness to anguished wailing. His restless quest for new territory worked against him commercially: by the time his fans had hooked into his latest album, he was onto something else entirely, both live and in the studio. In this sense he recalled artists such as Miles Davis and David Bowie, who were so eager to look forward and change that they confused and even angered listeners who wanted more stylistic consistency. However, his eclecticism has also ensured a durable fascination with his work that has engendered a growing posthumous cult for his music, often with listeners who were too young (or not around) to appreciate it while he was active.

Buckley emerged from the same 1960s Orange County, CA, folk scene that spawned Jackson Browne and the Nitty Gritty Dirt Band. Mothers of Invention drummer Jimmy Carl Black introduced Buckley and a couple of musicians Buckley was playing with to the Mothers' manager, Herbie Cohen. Although Cohen may have first been interested in Buckley as a songwriter, he realized after hearing some demos that Buckley was also a diamond in the rough as a singer. Cohen became Buckley's manager, and helped him get a deal with Elektra.

Before Buckley had reached his 20th birthday, he'd released his debut album. The slightly fey but enormously promising effort highlighted his soaring melodies and romantic, opaque lyrics. Baroque psychedelia was the order of the day for many Elektra releases of the time, and Buckley's early folk-rock albums were embellished with important contributions from musicians Lee Underwood (guitar), Van Dyke Parks (keyboards), Jim Fielder (bass), and Jerry Yester. Larry Beckett was also an overlooked contributor to Buckley's first two albums, co-writing many of the songs.

The fragile, melancholic, orchestrated beauty of the material had an innocent quality that was dampened only slightly on the second LP, *Goodbye and Hello* (1967). Buckley's songs and arrangements became more ambitious and psychedelic, particularly on the lengthy title track. This was also his only album to reach the Top 200, where it only peaked at No. 171; Buckley was always an artist who found his primary constituency among the underground, even for his most accessible efforts. His third album, *Happy Sad*, found him going in a decidedly jazzier direction in both his vocalizing and his instrumentation, introducing congas and vibes. Though it seemed a retreat from commercial considerations at the time, *Happy Sad* actually concluded the triumvirate of recordings that are judged to be his most accessible.

The truth was, by the late '60s Buckley was hardly interested in folkrock at all. He was more intrigued by jazz; not only soothing modern jazz (as heard on the posthumous release of acoustic 1968 live material, *Dream Letter*), but also its most avant-garde strains. His songs became much more oblique in structure, and skeletal in lyrics, especially when the partnership with Larry Beckett was ruptured after the latter's induction into the army. Some of his songs abandoned lyrics almost entirely, treating his voice itself as an instrument, wordlessly contorting, screaming, and moaning, sometimes quite cacophonously. In this context, *Lorca* was viewed by most fans and critics not just as a shocking departure, but a downright bummer. No longer was Buckley a romantic, melodic poet; he was an experimental *artiste* who sometimes seemed bent on punishing both himself *and* his listeners with his wordless shrieks and jarringly dissonant music.

Almost as if to prove that he was still capable of gentle, uplifting jazzy pop-folk, Buckley issued *Blue Afternoon* around the same time. Bizarrely, *Blue Afternoon* and *Lorca* were issued almost simultaneously, on different labels. While an admirable demonstration of his versatility, it was commercial near-suicide, each album canceling the impact of the other, as well as confusing his remaining fans. Buckley found his best middle ground between accessibility and jazzy improvisation on 1970's *Starsailor*, which is probably the best showcase of his sheer vocal abilities, although many prefer the more cogent material of his earliest albums.

By this point, though, Buckley's approach was so uncommercial that it was jeopardizing his commercial survival. And not just on record; he was equally uncompromising as a live act, as the posthumously issued *Live at the Troubadour 1969* demonstrates, with its stretched-to-the-limit jams and searing improv vocals. For a time, he was said to have earned his living as a taxi driver and chauffeur; he also flirted with films for a while. When he returned to the studio, it was as a much more commercial singer-songwriter (some have suggested that various management and label pressures were behind this shift).

As much of a schism as Buckley's experimental-jazz period created among fans and critics, his final recordings have proved even more divisive, even among big Buckley fans. Some view these efforts, which mix funk, sex-driven lyrical concerns, and laidback L.A. session musicians, as proof of his mastery of the blue-eyed soul idiom. Others find them a sad waste of talent, or relics of a prodigy who was burning out rather than conquering new realms. Neophytes would be aware of the difference of critical opinion regarding this era, but on the whole his final three albums are his least impressive. Those who feel otherwise usually cite the earliest of those LPs, *Greetings from L.A.* (1972), as his best work from his final phase.

Buckley's life came to a sudden end in the middle of 1975, when he died of a heroin overdose just after completing a tour. Those close to him insist that he had been clean for some time and lament the loss of an artist who, despite some recent failures, still had much to offer. Buckley's stock began to rise among the rock underground after the Cocteau Twins covered his "Song and Siren" in the 1980s. The posthumous releases of two late-'60s live sets (*Dream Letter* and *Live at the Troubadour 1969*) in the early '90s also boosted his profile, as well as unveiling some interesting previously unreleased compositions. And Buckley's son Jeff (who had little contact with his father) is now a rising star of his own, wielding a very similar voice and very similar looks, although his material is not all that much like his father's. *—Richie Unterberger*

● **Tim Buckley** / 1966 / Asylum ✦✦✦✦
Buckley's 1966 debut was the most straightforward and folk-rock-oriented of his albums. The material has a lyrical and melodic sophistication that was astounding for a 19-year-old. The pretty, almost precious songs are complemented by appropriately baroque, psychedelic-tinged production. If there was a record that exemplified the '60s Elektra folk-rock sound, this may have been it, featuring production by Elektra owner Jac Holzman and Doors producer Paul Rothchild, Love and Doors engineer Bruce Botnick, and string arrangements by Jack Nitzsche. That's not to diminish the contributions of the band, which included his longtime lead guitarist Lee Underwood and Van Dyke Parks on keyboards. Buckley was still firmly in the singer-songwriter camp on this album, showing only brief flashes of the experimental vocal flights, angst-ridden lyrics, and soul influences that would characterize much of his later work. It's not his most adventurous outing, but it's one of his most accessible, and retains a fragile beauty. *—Richie Unterberger*

Goodbye & Hello / 1967 / Asylum ✦✦✦✦
With his second album, Buckley began exploring different sonic territory, adding exotic instruments and a distinct, winding jazz influence to his increasingly complex lyrics. *—Stephen Thomas Erlewine*

Dream Letter: Live in London / Jul. 1968 / Rhino/Bizarre ✦✦✦✦
This live double-disc set captures Buckley's jazzy folk and passionate mega-octave vocal in fine form. Lee Underwood (guitar), David Fried-

man (vibes), and Danny Thompson (bass) provide empathic support. *—Rick Clark*

Happy Sad / 1969 / Asylum ✦✦✦✦
Buckley began to turn toward softer, more introspective, and slightly jazzy tunes on his third record. This album of six lengthy compositions features some of his loveliest songs, including "Strange Feelin'," "Sing a Song for You," and the exuberant, 12-minute "Gypsy Woman." *—Richie Unterberger*

Blue Afternoon / 1969 / Rhino/Bizarre ✦✦✦✦
Buckley's atmospheric melancholy folk-jazz shines on the first four tracks, "Happy Time," "Chase the Blues Away," "I Must Have Been Blind," and "The River." Those tracks alone make this worth having. *—Rick Clark*

Lorca / 1970 / Asylum ✦✦✦
Buckley stunned and, to a rare degree, alienated fans with the dissonant, at times wearying, avant-garde exercises in vocal gymnastics that took up the entire first side of this LP. Side two was far more accessible, though Buckley's fusion of folk instrumentation with jazzy improvisation on extended compositions continued to take him further away from his folk-rock roots. *—Richie Unterberger*

Starsailor / 1970 / Rhino/Bizarre ✦✦✦✦
After his beginnings as a gentle, melodic baroque folk-rocker, Buckley gradually evolved into a downright experimental singer-songwriter who explored both jazz and avant-garde territory. *Starsailor* is the culmination of his experimentation, and alienated far more listeners than it exhilarated upon its release in 1970. Buckley had already begun to delve into jazz fusion on late-'60s records like *Happy Sad*, and explored some fairly "out" acrobatic, quasi-operatic vocals on his final Elektra LP, *Lorca*. With former Mother of Invention Bunk Gardner augmenting Buckley's group on sax and alto flute, Buckley applies vocal gymnastics to a set of material that's as avant-garde in its songwriting as its execution. At his most anguished (which is often on this album), he sounds as if his liver is being torn out—slowly. Almost as if to prove he can still deliver a mellow buzz, he throws in a couple of pleasant jazz-pop cuts, including the odd, jaunty French tune "Moulin Rouge." Surrealistic lyrics, heavy on landscape imagery like rivers, skies, suns, and jungle fires, top off a record that isn't for everybody, or even for every Buckley fan, but endures as one of the most uncompromising statements ever made by a singer-songwriter. *—Richie Unterberger*

Greetings from L.A. / 1972 / Rhino/Bizarre ✦✦✦

Sefronia / 1973 / Manifesto ✦✦

Look at the Fool / 1974 / Manifesto ✦✦

Peel Sessions / 1991 / Strange Fruit/Dutch East ✦✦

Live at the Troubadour 1969 / 1994 / Rhino/Bizarre ✦✦✦

Honeyman / Nov. 1995 / Manifesto ✦✦✦

Buffalo Springfield

Rock 'n' Roll, Country-Rock, Folk-Rock
Few American groups have produced a wealth of talent like that of Buffalo Springfield. The group's formation is the stuff of legend: driving on Sunset Boulevard in Los Angeles, Stephen Stills and Richie Furay spotted a hearse that Stills was sure belonged to Neil Young, a Canadian he had crossed paths with earlier. Indeed it was, and with the addition of fellow hearse passenger and Canadian Bruce Palmer on bass and ex-Dillard Dewey Martin on drums, the cluster of ex-folkies determined, as the Byrds had just done, to become a rock 'n' roll band.

Over a 19-month period, during 1967 and 1968, Buffalo Springfield released three impressive albums. Their debut, including their sole big hit (Stills' "For What It's Worth"), established them as the best folk-rock band in the land bar the Byrds, though the Springfield were a bit more folk and country oriented. The second, *Again*, is their masterpiece, as the group expanded their folk-rock base into tough hard rock and psychedelic orchestration. Possessing three strong songwriters with distinctly different yet complementary styles—Stills, Young, and Furay (the last of whom didn't begin writing until the second LP)—they also had strong and often conflicting egos, particularly Stills and Young. The group, which held almost infinite promise, rearranged their lineup several times, Young leaving the group for periods and Palmer fighting deportation, until disbanding in 1968. Their final album, although it contained some excellent material, clearly shows the group fragmenting into solo directions.

Even more than the Byrds, Buffalo Springfield's sound was undeniably American, drawing from rock, folk, and country. The intense clash of creative energies, however, finally caused the demise of the band in May 1968. Stephen Stills went on to Crosby, Stills & Nash. Neil Young joined that group briefly for *Deja Vu*, then went on to pursue an erratic solo career with periods of great success and brilliant music. After Springfield, Jim Messina and Richie Furay founded the country-rock group Poco. After Poco, Messina recorded a string of hits during the '70s with Kenny Loggins, as Loggins & Messina. —*Rick Clark & Richie Unterberger*

Buffalo Springfield / 1967 / Atco ✦✦✦
Their strong debut contains the Stephen Stills classic "For What It's Worth" and Neil Young's "Nowadays Clancy Can't Even Sing." "Sit Down I Think I Love You" and "Go and Say Goodbye" are also highlights. —*Rick Clark*

★ **Buffalo Springfield Again** / 1967 / Atco ✦✦✦✦✦
On what is by far their best effort, Stills, Furay, and Young each contribute some great songs: the hits "Bluebird," "Mr. Soul," and "Rock & Roll Woman," plus standouts like "A Child's Claim to Fame," "Hung Upside Down," "Broken Arrow," "Everydays," and "Expecting to Fly." Essential stuff for any good rock 'n' roll collection. —*Rick Clark*

Last Time Around / 1968 / Atco ✦✦✦
Their last album showcases a couple of gems in Furay's "Kind Woman" and Young's "On the Way Home." —*Rick Clark*

Best of Buffalo Springfield . . . Retrospective / 1969 / Atco ✦✦✦✦
This is a decent sampler for the uninitiated. It contains all their hits and some key album tracks but isn't comprehensive enough to be essential. —*Rick Clark*

● **Buffalo Springfield [Collection]** / 1973 / Atco ✦✦✦✦
Not to be confused with their self-titled debut album, this double LP, which can still be found without too much hassle, is clearly the best Springfield compilation, at least until the overdue day when a box set appears that includes everything recorded by this superb band. It does miss some good songs, especially from the first album, but zeroes in on their very best work, and includes a nine-minute version of "Bluebird" available nowhere else, as well as excellent liner notes. —*Richie Unterberger*

Buffalo Tom

Rock 'n' Roll, Alternative Pop-Rock
When they released their first album in 1989, the Boston-based trio Buffalo Tom was written off as Dinosaur Jr. junior. Admittedly, their debut was in debt to J Mascis' thundering guitar and folk-tinged songs and it didn't help that Mascis produced the record, either. Over time, Buffalo Tom stripped away their grungier influences and developed into a straightahead rock group of the early '90s, capable of throttling rockers and beautiful ballads. Comprising guitarist/vocalist Bill Janovitz, bassist/vocalist Chris Colbourn, and drummer Tom Maginnis, Buffalo Tom began to develop their own style with their second album, 1990's *Birdbrain*, which featured a noticeable improvement in songwriting. In 1992, Buffalo Tom released *Let Me Come Over,* a gritty bed of driving rock and achingly melancholy ballads; several of its tracks became alternative-radio staples, including the gorgeous ballad "Taillights Fade." Despite an increased amount of critical praise and some radio airplay, the album didn't sell. The follow-up, 1993's *Big Red Letter Day,* featured a more polished, radio-ready production, but the album received only a small push from radio and MTV. "Soda Jerk," the first single from the album, became a minor alternative-radio and MTV hit. After a year-long tour, the group returned in the summer of 1995 with *Sleepy Eyed,* a return to the more direct sound of *Let Me Come Over.* —*Stephen Thomas Erlewine*

Buffalo Tom / 1989 / SST ✦✦✦

Birdbrain / 1990 / Beggars Banquet ✦✦✦

● **Let Me Come Over** / 1992 / Beggars Banquet ✦✦✦✦
With *Let Me Come Over,* Buffalo Tom comes into its own, producing a strong album filled with exceptional songwriting. The Dinosaur Jr. comparisons are no longer accurate; now, the band sounds slightly like R.E.M. crossed with the Replacements, but that's just a starting point—it has carved out its own brand of guitar-heavy rock 'n' roll, somewhere between college-rock and traditional, classic rock. Buffalo Tom proves equally adept at pulling off the driving "Staples" and "Mountains of Your Head," the majestic folk-rock of "Mineral," and the ballads "Larry," "Frozen Lake," and the gorgeous "Taillights Fade," which is a masterpiece. *Let Me Come Over* is the breakthrough album from one of America's best rock 'n' roll bands of the 1990s. —*Stephen Thomas Erlewine*

Big Red Letter Day / 1993 / Beggars Banquet ✦✦✦✦
Following the excellent *Let Me Come Over, Big Red Letter Day* features a slightly more polished production, but it doesn't diminish the band's increasingly powerful songwriting and forceful rock 'n' roll. Buffalo Tom is America's best mainstream rock band, but is still undeservedly stuck on its fringes, as *Big Red Letter Day* proves. —*Stephen Thomas Erlewine*

Sleepy Eyed / 1995 / East West ✦✦✦

Jimmy Buffett

b. Dec. 25, 1946, Pascogoula, MS
Guitar, Vocals / Country-Rock, Singer-Songwriter, Pop-Rock
Jimmy Buffett has translated his easy-going Gulf Coast persona into more than just a successful recording career—he has expanded into

clothing, nightclubs, and literature. But the basis of the business empire that keeps him on the *Fortune* magazine list of highest-earning entertainers is his music.

Buffett moved to Nashville to try to make it in country music in the late '60s. Signed to Barnaby, he released one album, *Down to Earth* (1970), the single from which, a socially conscious song called, "The Christian?," suggested he might be more at home protesting in Greenwich Village. (Barnaby "lost" his second album, *High Cumberland Jubilee,* though they would find it and release it after he became successful.) Instead, he moved to Key West, FL, where he gradually evolved the beach bum character and tropical folk-rock style that would endear him to millions.

Signing to ABC-Dunhill Records (later absorbed by MCA), Buffett achieved notoriety but not much else with his second (released) album, *White Sport Coat & a Pink Crustacean* (1973), which featured a song called, "Why Don't We Get Drunk" (" . . . and screw?," goes the chorus). Buffett revealed a more thoughtful side on *Living & Dying in 3/4 Time* (1974), with its song of marital separation "Come Monday," his first singles-chart entry. But it took the Top Ten song "Margaritaville," and the album in which it was featured, *Changes in Latitudes, Changes in Attitudes* (1977), to capture Buffett's tropical worldview and, for a while, turn him into a pop star.

By the start of the '80s, Buffett's yearly albums had stopped going gold, and he briefly tried the country market again. But by the middle of the decade, it was his yearly summer tours that were filling his bank account, as a steadily growing core of Sun Belt fans he dubbed "Parrotheads" made his concerts into Mardi Gras-like affairs. Buffett launched his Margaritaville line of clothes and opened the first of his Margaritaville clubs in Key West. He also turned to fiction writing, landing on the book bestseller lists.

His recording career, meanwhile, languished, though a hits compilation sold millions, a 1990 live album, *Feeding Frenzy,* went gold, and a 1992 box-set retrospective, *Boats, Beaches, Bars & Ballads,* became one of the bestselling box sets ever. Buffett finally got around to making a new album in 1994, when *Fruitcakes* became one of his fastest-selling records. It was followed in 1995 by *Barometer Soup* and in 1996 by *Banana Wind.—William Ruhlmann*

Down to Earth / 1970 / Barnaby ✦✦

A White Sport Coat & a Pink Crustacean / Jun. 1973 / MCA ✦✦✦

Living & Dying in 3/4 Time / Feb. 1974 / MCA ✦✦✦

A-1-A / Dec. 1974 / MCA ✦✦✦

Rancho Deluxe / 1975 / United Artists ✦✦✦

High Cumberland Jubilee (1972) / 1976 / Barnaby ✦✦

Havana Daydreamin' / Jan. 1976 / MCA ✦✦✦✦
Buffett's best overall collection of songs yet bears the influence of Steve Goodman, who wrote "This Hotel Room" and cowrote "Woman Goin' Crazy on Caroline Street." But a personal favorite is Buffett's own "My Head Hurts, My Feet Stink, and I Don't Love Jesus." —*William Ruhlmann*

Changes in Latitudes, Changes in Attitudes / Jan. 1977 / MCA ✦✦✦✦
Buffett's biggest-selling regular release contains his biggest hit single, "Margaritaville." It's also a peak in terms of songwriting, both for the artist himself and in his covers of the work of Steve Goodman and Jesse Winchester, among others. Funny, wistful, and celebratory, the album is the definitive statement of Buffett's worldview. —*William Ruhlmann*

Son of a Son of a Sailor / Mar. 1978 / MCA ✦✦✦✦
If this album was a slight step down from its predecessor, it was almost equally successful commercially, and it contained its share of terrific material, notably the uptempo hit "Cheeseburger in Paradise" and one of Buffett's older songs, "Livingston Saturday Night." —*William Ruhlmann*

You Had to Be There / Oct. 1978 / MCA ✦✦

Volcano / Aug. 1979 / MCA ✦✦

Coconut Telegraph / Feb. 1981 / MCA ✦✦

Last Mango in Paris / Jun. 1985 / MCA ✦✦✦

● **Songs You Know by Heart** / Oct. 1985 / MCA ✦✦✦✦
If anybody ever needed a compilation, it was Jimmy Buffett, who by this time had put out 14 new studio albums in 15 years but only managed to accumulate a handful of memorable songs among them. And just about all of them are here. Unless you're a Parrothead, this will be all you'll need of Jimmy Buffett. —*William Ruhlmann*

Boats, Beaches, Bars & Ballads / May 1992 / MCA ✦✦✦✦
This four-disc, 72-track anthology is essential for Parrotheads (Buffett fans) who don't miss his concerts but aren't so hardcore that they have to own every single thing Buffett ever released. Each disc revolves around a theme (Boats, Beaches, Bars, Ballads). All of his hits and popular album tracks are here, as well as some previously unreleased material. The box includes the Parrothead Handbook, a 64-page booklet that provides a

well-assembled collection of photos, reflections from Buffett, and explanations of his songs. The sound on this set is first-rate. —*Rick Clark*

Before the Beach / May 25, 1993 / MCA ✦✦

Fruitcakes / May 24, 1994 / MCA ✦✦

Barometer Soup / 1995 / Margaritaville ✦✦

Banana Wind / Jun. 1996 / Margaritaville ✦✦✦

Sonny Burgess

b. 1931
Guitar / Rockabilly

Sonny Burgess is one of the wildest rockers to record for the legendary Sun label in Memphis. He and his band the Pacers came out of Newport, AR, with a hard-rocking style that, unlike that of most rockabillies, owed little to nothing in the way of a stylistic debt to country music. With his red-dyed hair, matching stage suit and guitar, and wild stage performances, Burgess and the Pacers made mincemeat of the competition on many of the early-'50s rock 'n' roll package tours. Though his Sun releases never brought him much in the way of commercial success, his recordings nonetheless remain landmarks of the early rockabilly style. Currently touring and recording with other Memphis alumni in the Sun Rhythm Section, the rockin' flame that is Sonny Burgess refuses to be snuffed out. —*Cub Koda*

● **We Wanna Boogie** / 1990 / Rounder ✦✦✦✦
If you want a fairly definitive compilation of the Sun material by this minor rockabilly figure, but don't want to go the whole nine yards for the expensive import double CD on Bear Family, this domestic anthology is a recommended alternative. The 13 tracks contain six sides from his '50s singles (including the most noted, "Red Headed Woman" and "My Bucket's Got a Hole in It"), and seven other cuts from the '50s that were unissued at the time. —*Richie Unterberger*

The Classic Recordings 1956-1959 / Jul. 1991 / Bear Family ✦✦✦✦
Sonny's complete output for Sun spread over two CDs. Wild and crazed, featuring Burgess's spitfire guitar and booming vocals and the relentless drive of the Pacers in support. —*Cub Koda*

Solomon Burke

b. 1936, Philadelphia, PA
Vocals / Soul

Musically and corporeally imposing, Burke was almost as important as he says he was. His account of how he invented soul music is entertaining if fanciful, but even when SB's BS count is lowered, there is no doubt he was present at the creation of '60s soul music—and at least partially responsible for it. Starting as "Solomon the Boy Wonder Preacher" in Philadelphia, he had been recording for six years when he finally broke through with "Just Out of Reach" in 1961. Burke's best recordings probably date from the early '60s, when he was working with producer Bert Berns. Songs like "Cry to Me," "I'm Hanging Up My Heart for You," "Goodbye Baby," and "The Price" collectively formed the keynote address for soul music. Some of the arrangements sound unnecessarily ornamented today, but the passion Burke brought to those recordings was that of the Boy Wonder Preacher. Live, he's still impressive, as recent recordings attest. —*Colin Escott*

Solomon Burke / 1962 / Kenwood ✦✦✦

Solomon Burke's Greatest Hits / 1962 / Atlantic ✦✦✦
Solomon Burke's booming, magnificent vocals and dramatic approach were particularly effective on a string of great early '60s tracks. The lyrics, production, and setting blended soul and country elements, and Burke was the ideal singer to convey the two genres' similarities. This includes the epic tracks "Everybody Needs Somebody to Love" and "Just Out of Reach (of My Empty Arms)." —*Ron Wynn*

You Can Run But You Can't Hide / 1987 / Mr. R&B ✦✦✦✦
You Can Run But You Can't Hide collects 20 tracks from Burke's formative years at Apollo, recorded between 1955-1959. The material tends to be more pop-oriented than his classic Atlantic sides, but his singing is nearly as impressive as it is on his hits. —*Stephen Thomas Erlewine*

● **Home in Your Heart** / 1992 / Rhino ✦✦✦✦
Home in Your Heart—The Best of Solomon Burke is a 41-track two-disc set that covers Burke's Atlantic recordings from 1961 to 1968. Seventeen of those tracks charted. All are superior examples of country-soul and gospel-soul. —*Rob Bowman*

Johnny Burnette

b. Mar. 28, 1934, Memphis, TN, **d.** Aug. 14, 1964, Clear Lake, CA
Guitar, Vocals / Rockabilly, Pop-Rock

A contemporary of Elvis Presley in the Memphis scene of the mid-'50s, Burnette played a similar brand of fiery, spare wildman rockabilly. With his brother Dorsey (on bass) and guitarist Paul Burlison forming his Rock 'n' Roll Trio, he recorded a clutch of singles for Decca in 1956 and

1957 that achieved nothing more than regional success. Featuring the groundbreaking fuzzy tone of Burlison's guitar, Johnny's energetic vocals, and Dorsey's slapping bass, these recordings—highlighted by the first rock 'n' roll version of "Train Kept a-Rollin'"—compare well to the classic Sun rockabilly of the same era. The trio disbanded in 1957, and Johnny found pop success as a teen idol in the early '60s with hits like "You're Sixteen" and "Dreamin'." Burnette died in a boating accident in 1964. His brother, Dorsey, achieved modest success as a solo act in the early '60s, and Burlison recently resurfaced as a member of the Sun Rhythm Section. —*Richie Unterberger*

● **Tear It Up** / 1978 / Solid Smoke ✦✦✦✦
Seventeen of their purest rockabilly cuts from their 1956-1957 prime. Highlights include "Train Kept a-Rollin'," "Rock Therapy," and "Honey Hush." —*Richie Unterberger*

The Best of Johnny Burnette: You're Sixteen / 1992 / Capitol ✦✦✦✦
Burnette's best pop-oriented recordings are featured on this collection, including the classic "You're Sixteen." —*Stephen Thomas Erlewine*

● **Rockabilly Boogie** / Bear Family ✦✦✦✦
All of the Johnny Burnette Trio's primal rockabilly records, including the blazing "Train Kept a-Rollin'," are collected on this single-disc compilation. The alternate takes might border on overkill, but the original takes remain powerful years after they were recorded. —*Stephen Thomas Erlewine*

Kate Bush

b. Jul. 30, 1958, Plumstead, England
Piano, Keyboards, Vocals / Art-Rock/Progressive-Rock, Pop-Rock

One of the most popular solo female acts of the past 20 years to come out of England, Kate Bush is also one of the most unusual, with her keening vocals and unusually literate and complex body of songs. As a girl, Catherine Bush amused herself playing an organ in the barn behind her parents' house. By the time she was a teenager, Bush was writing songs of her own. A family friend, Ricky Hopper, heard her music and arranged for a demo to be recorded, which brought Bush to the attention of Pink Floyd lead guitarist David Gilmour. By the time Bush was 16, she had been signed to EMI Records, though the company decidedto bring her along slowly. She studied dance, mime, and voice, and continued writing. By 1977, she was ready to enter the recording studio and begin her formal career, which she did with an original song, "Wuthering Heights," based on material from Emily Brontë's novel.

"Wuthering Heights" rose to No. 1 on the British charts. Bush became an overnight sensation at the tender age of 17 and was obligated to turn in an accompanying album in short order. This she did with *The Kick Inside*, a collection of material she had written over the previous three years; the album reached the British No. 3 position and sold over a million copies in the U K. Bush's second album, *Lionheart*, reached No. 6 but didn't achieve anything like the sales totals or critical acclaim of its predecessor. In England during the spring of 1979, Bush embarked on what proved to be the only concert tour of her career to date, playing a series of shows highlighted by 17 costume changes, lots of dancing, and complex lighting. The tour proved both exhausting and financially disastrous, and Bush has avoided any but the most limited live concert appearances since, primarily in support of certain charitable causes.

By this time, Bush was established as one of the most challenging and eccentric artists ever to have achieved success in rock music, with a range of sounds and interests that constantly challenged listeners. "Babooshka" (1980) became her first Top Five single since "Wuthering Heights," and her subsequent album *Never for Ever* entered the British charts at No. 1 in September 1980. During this period, Bush began co-producing her own work, a decisive step toward refining her sound and also establishing her independence from her record company. Although 1982's *The Dreaming* reached No. 3, the single "There Goes a Tenner" failed to reach the charts, and most observers felt that Bush had lost her audience. Bush was unfazed by the criticism, and even began taking steps to make herself more independent by establishing a home studio.

After two years' absence, Bush re-emerged in August 1985 with "Running Up That Hill," which reached No. 3 on the English charts and became her second biggest-selling single. The accompanying album, *Hounds of Love*, the first record made at her 48-track home studio, debuted on the British charts at the No. 1 position in September 1985 and remained there for a full month, and soon after "Running Up That Hill" gave Bush her long-awaited American breakthrough, reaching No. 30 on *Billboard's* charts. The changes in her sound and her development as a writer/performer were showcased in the January 1987 best-of collection *The Whole Story*. That same year, Bush won the Best British Female Artist award at the sixth annual BRIT Awards in London. In October 1989, Bush's first new album in almost four years, *The Sensual World*, reached the British No. 2 spot. Bush's next album, *The Red Shoes* (1993), debuted in the American Top 30, the first time one of her albums had ever charted that high. —*Bruce Eder*

The Kick Inside / 1978 / EMI America ✦✦✦✦
Bush's first album is her most romantic, the sound of an impressionable and highly precocious teenage singer-songwriter spreading her wings for the first time. "Wuthering Heights" was a monster hit everywhere in the world except America, and it's still an impressive debut nearly 20 years later, but Bush would do better work than this. —Bruce Eder

Lionheart / 1978 / EMI America ✦✦✦
Bush's second album was something of a disappointment, lacking the depth and certainty of direction of her debut. The title track is an enigmatic paean to her mother country, "Wow" is a strong vocal workout but somewhat on the obscure side, and the rest is enjoyable and teasing but nowhere near what Bush is capable of. —Bruce Eder

Never for Ever / 1980 / EMI America ✦✦✦
Kate Bush returned to form on her third album, which is steeped in images of violence and anger ("Babooshka," "The Wedding List") but also includes fascinating references to classical music ("Delius"). Very finely produced as well. —Bruce Eder

The Dreaming / 1982 / EMI America ✦✦

Hounds of Love / 1985 / EMI America ✦✦✦✦
Bush's strongest album to date marked her breakthrough into the American charts and yielded a set of dazzling videos. The material ranges from the sensual ("Hounds of Love," "Running Up That Hill"—the latter one of the most sensual recordings ever made) to the mystical ("Hello Earth," "The Morning Fog"). This was also the first album produced by Bush entirely at her own home studio, and the results are spellbinding, the layered instruments recalling the Beatles at the most ornate, but also displaying an exquisite timbral range, bringing out the richness of the individual instruments. Note: The British edition of this and Bush's earlier albums all have significantly better sound than their American editions and are worth finding as imports. —Bruce Eder

● **The Whole Story** / 1986 / EMI America ✦✦✦✦
Bush's first best-of is an excellent compilation/overview, encompassing all her best-known songs (including "Wuthering Heights" with an improved, re-recorded vocal track) up through the major tracks off of Hounds of Love and her follow-up single, the haunting and dramatic "Experiment IV." —Bruce Eder

The Sensual World / 1989 / Columbia ✦✦✦✦
The follow-up to Hounds of Love is almost its match, material devoted to Bush's perceptions of love and sensuality. The best track, is "This Woman's Work," from a now-forgotten feature film, a beautiful and poignant look at the female psyche at its most gentle and giving. —Bruce Eder

This Woman's Work (1978-1990) / 1990 / EMI ✦✦✦✦
Excellent box collecting all of Bush's work, including obscure B-sides, odd mixes, and other rarities in one place. The notes are skimpy, and some people who already own some of her individual CDs will be unhappy having to duplicate their purchases, but the rarities are fascinating, and because this set is from England, it uses the superior British masters on the 1978-1985 albums. (British import) —Bruce Eder

The Red Shoes / 1993 / Columbia ✦✦

Billy Butler

b. Philadelphia, PA
Guitar / Soul

The younger brother of Jerry Butler, Billy Butler wasn't as well known as his sibling, but recorded some fine Chicago soul in the 1960s. Recording for OKeh under producer Carl Davis, Butler's mid-'60s singles were quite similar to labelmates Major Lance's and (less obviously) Curtis Mayfield's as stellar examples of the finest features of the Chicago soul sound. Similar to Motown in its full, brassy production, the Chicago brand was earthier, with stronger tinges of gospel, doo wop, and Latin influences. Nor was Butler terribly similar to his brother Jerry, with a punchier, more uptempo sound. With the backing group the Enchanters, Billy recorded consistently fine singles for OKeh from 1963 to 1966, scoring R&B hits with "I Can't Work No Longer" (1965) and "Right Track" (1966). Butler left OKeh after 1966 and recorded for a variety of labels, denting the R&B charts with the singles "Get on the Chase" (1969) and "Free Yourself" (1971). A songwriter of note, he contributed material to fellow Chi-town soul greats Major Lance, Gene Chandler, and his brother Jerry. —Richie Unterberger

● **Right Track** / 1985 / Edsel ✦✦✦✦
Sixteen of the sides Butler cut for the Okeh label from 1963-1966; most of them were written by himself or Curtis Mayfield. While not quite in the same league as Mayfield, this is near-classic soul: strong material, production, and backup harmonies on this mix of uptempo numbers and ballads, paced by Butler's fluid vocals. —Richie Unterberger

Jerry Butler

b. Dec. 8, 1939, Sunflower County, MS
Vocals / Soul, R&B

It would be safer to talk about Jerry Butler's careers than about his career. Up from Mississippi, he joined Curtis Mayfield in the Impressions around 1957. They began recording the following year and broke through with For Your Precious Love, touted by some as the first soul record. Inevitably, he went solo and fell—or was pushed—into the pop mainstream. Reunited with Mayfield (the latter as a writer), Butler announced his return with He Will Break Your Heart in 1960. His subsequent recordings for Vee-Jay trod the turf where pop and R&B meet and are variable; the best are excellent.

After Vee-Jay went broke in 1966, Butler signed with Mercury and was soon placed with the team of Gamble and Huff, who produced him in Philadelphia. Jerry Butler's mellow baritone and the sweet Philly sound were a winning combination, as attested by pop and R&B hits like "Only the Strong Survive" and "Hey, Western Union Man." After the Gamble and Huff deal dissolved in 1970, Butler's career went slowly downhill. Deals with Motown and even Gamble and Huff's Philadelphia International label couldn't deliver the goods. There's something for everyone in Butler's prolificacy, but unfortunately little of it is available to sample.

Jerry Butler has made musical and political noise during the '80s and '90s. He won election to Cook County's board of supervisors in the late '80s. He also issued recordings on his own Fountain label, but they were hampered by poor distribution. He recorded Time & Faith for Urgent, a label distributed by Ichiban, in 1992. Butler has retained his soothing, dynamic sound and ability to sound simultaneously cool and soulful, even if his voice has lost some range and sheen. Mercury released Iceman: The Mercury Years Anthology in 1992, the definitive collection of his Polygram tracks, while his earlier work for Vee-Jay has also been reissued. Rhino released The Best of Jerry Butler, 1958-1969 in 1987. —Colin Escott

● **The Best of Jerry Butler [Rhino]** / 1987 / Rhino ✦✦✦✦
The primary value of this 14-song collection is that it includes material from both the VJ and Mercury eras. Butler fans are much better advised to get the compilations which cover his output for each label in much greater depth (The Ice Man for Vee-Jay, Iceman: The Mercury Years for Mercury). For the casual fan, though, it might be the best buy, as it's the only best-of spanning both labels, and includes all of his biggest hits. —Richie Unterberger

The Best of Jerry Butler [Vee-Jay] / 1987 / Vee-Jay ✦✦✦✦
Almost the same thing can be said for this one as for many other Jerry Butler hit sets, except that it's probably still available and has been issued on CD. The usual hits are here, and it's a good starting point. —Ron Wynn

★ **Iceman: The Mercury Years** / 1992 / PolyGram ✦✦✦✦✦
A glorious 44-song double-disc set, it collects Butler's best Mercury sides, with several previously unreleased songs and alternate mixes. The liner notes are crummy, though. —John Floyd

The Butthole Surfers

Alternative Pop-Rock

There was a time magazines couldn't print their name and radios couldn't say their name. Then there was a time, about ten years later, that they were in heavy rotation on MTV and starring in Nintendo commercials. Throughout it all, the Butthole Surfers haven't changed all that much; they remain the same gleefully gross noise terrorists that they were when their first record was released on Alternative Tentacles in 1983.

Although some critics may say all of their albums sound the same, the only thing that unites the Butthole Surfers' albums is their bracing vulgarity and offensiveness. Unlike many bands whose disgusting lyrics and abrasive music are calculatingly revolting, the Buttholes revel in the filth—they're not making some social commentary with their music, they simply enjoy the grotesque. Beneath all of the squalor, the Buttholes remain art-punks; their albums are never just hardcore noise, they have touches of psychedelia, country, classic rock, rockabilly, techno—anything that comes their way, really. As they get older, their songs rely more on the underpinning guitar grunge of Paul Leary, yet vocalist Gibby Haynes remains a deranged lunatic, giving the band the fuel for their gleeful nightmares. —Stephen Thomas Erlewine

Butthole Surfers / 1983 / Alternative Tentacles ✦✦✦✦
Their best album, randy and wild. Smart, stupid, and outrageous all at the same time. It may be out of print. —John Dougan

Psychic . . . Powerless . . . Another Man's Sac / 1985 / Touch & Go ✦✦✦

Rembrandt Pussyhorse / 1986 / Touch & Go ✦✦✦

● **Locust Abortion Technician** / 1987 / Touch & Go ✦✦✦✦
Good songs, real ugly execution. —John Dougan

Hairway to Steven / 1988 / Touch & Go ✦✦✦✦
Actually getting manic here! —John Dougan

Pioughd / 1991 / Capitol ✦✦

Independent Worm Saloon / 1993 / Capitol ✦✦✦

Hole Truth . . . And Nothing Butt / 1995 / Trance Syndicate ✦✦✦

Electriclarryland / 1996 / Capitol ✦✦✦

The Buzzocks

Punk

Formed in Manchester, England, in 1975, the Buzzcocks were one of the most influential bands to emerge in the initial wave of punk rock. With their crisp melodies, driving guitars, and guitarist Pete Shelley's biting lyrics, the Buzzcocks were one of the best punk bands. The Buzzcocks were inspired by the Sex Pistols' energy, yet they didn't copy the Pistols' angry political stance. Instead, they brought that intense, brilliant energy to the three-minute pop song. Shelly's alternately funny and anguished lyrics about adolescence and love were some of the best and smartest of his era; similarly, the Buzzcocks' melodies and hooks were concise and memorable. Over the years, their powerful punk-pop has proven enormously influential, with echoes of their music being apparent in everyone from Hüsker Dü to Nirvana.

Before the Buzzcocks, the teenaged Pete Shelley had played guitar in various heavy-metal bands. In 1975, he enrolled in the Bolton Institute of Technology. While he was at school, Shelley joined an electronic music society, which is where he met Howard Devoto, who had enrolled in BIT in 1972. Both Shelley and Devoto shared an affection for the Velvet Underground, while Devoto was also fascinated by the Stooges. While they were still in school, Shelley and Devoto began rehearsing with a drummer, covering everything from the Stooges to Brian Eno. The trio never performed live and soon fell apart. Shelley and Devoto remained friends and several months after their initial musical venture dissolved, the pair read the first live review of the Sex Pistols in the *NME* and decided to see the band in London. After witnessing the band twice in February 1976, they decided to form their own band, with the intent of replicating the Pistol's London impact in Manchester. Both musicians decided to change their last names—Peter McNeish became Pete Shelley and Howard Traford became Howard Devoto—and took their group's name from a review of *Rock Follies*, which ended with the quotation "get a buzz, cock." The Buzzcocks began rehearsing, picking up a local drummer and bassist Garth Smith. Shortly after their formation, Shelley and Devoto booked a local club, the Lesser Free Trade Hall, with the intent of persuading the Sex Pistols to play in Manchester. They succeeded in bringing the Pistols to Manchester, but the Buzzcocks had to pull out of their own gig when both the bassist and drummer left the group before the concert. At the Pistols show, Shelley and Devoto met Steve Diggle, who joined the Buzzcocks as their bassist, and the group found their drummer John Maher through an advertisement in the *Melody Maker.* Within a few months, the band played their first concert, opening for the second Sex Pistols show at the Lesser Free Trade Hall in July 1976. By the end of the year, the Buzzcocks had played a handful of gigs and helped establish Manchester as the second biggest punk-rock city in England, ranking just behind London.

In October of 1976, the Buzzcocks recorded their first demo tape, which remained unreleased. At the end of 1976, the group joined the Sex Pistols on their "Anarchy Tour." After thetour was completed, Shelley borrowed a couple hundred pounds from his father and the band used the money to record their debut EP, *Spiral Scratch.* The record was the first do-it-yourself, independently released record of the punk era. *Spiral Scratch* appeared on the band's New Hormones record label in January 1977; there were initially only 1,000 copies pressed. Shortly after the release of the EP, Devoto quit the group and returned to college; later in the year, he formed Magazine. Following Devoto's departure, Pete Shelley assumed the role as lead vocalist, Steve Diggle moved to guitar, and Garth Smith became the band's bassist. Two months later, the Buzzcocks played their first London gig as an opening act for the Clash. By June 1977, the Buzzcocks were attracting the attention of major record labels. By September, they had signed with United Artists Records, who gave the band complete artistic control.

The Buzzcocks certainly tested the limits of that artistic control with their debut single, "Orgasm Addict." Released in October 1977, the single didn't become a hit because its subject matter was too explicit for BBC radio, but it generated good word of mouth. Following its release, Garth Smith was kicked out of the group and was replaced by Steve Garvey. The Buzzcocks' second single, "What Do I Get?," became their first charting single, scraping the bottom of the Top 40. In March, the band released their first album, *Another Music in a Different Kitchen.* In September 1978 the Buzzcocks released their second full-length record, *Love Bites.*

The rapid pace of the band's recording and performing schedules quickly had its effects on the group. Not only were the concerts and recordings wearing the band down, the members were consuming alcohol and drugs in high numbers. Early in 1979 they recorded their third album, *A Different Kind of Tension,* which displayed some signs of wear and tear. Following the album's release in August, they embarked on their first American tour, which wasn't successful. Nevertheless, the band

was enjoying the peak of their popularity at home in Britain. Later in 1979, the singles collection, *Singles Going Steady,* was released in America.

All of the inner and outer tensions on the band culminated in 1980, when they drastically cut back their performance schedule, but they persevered with recording, cutting the EP *Parts 1-3,* which was released as three separate singles over the course of the year. During 1980, United Artists was bought out by EMI, who cut back support of the Buzzcocks. The band began working on their fourth album in early 1981, but they were prevented from recording by EMI. The label wanted to release *Singles Going Steady* in the UK before the Buzzcocks delivered their fourth album; they refused. Consequently, EMI didn't give the band an advance to cover the recording costs of the fourth album. Pete Shelley decided to break up the band instead of fight the label. The Buzzcocks broke up in 1981.

Immediately after the split, Shelley pursued a solo career that initially produced the hit single "Homosapien," but soon went dry. Steve Diggle formed Flag of Convenience with John Maher, who quit the band shortly after its formation. Steve Garvey moved to New York, where he toured with Motivation for a few years. In 1989, the group re-formed and toured the US. The following year, Maher left the band and former Smiths drummer Mike Joyce joined the band on tour. By 1990, the reunion had become permanent; after Joyce's brief tenure with the band, the final lineup of the reunited Buzzcocks featured Shelley, Diggle, bassist Tony Barber, and drummer Phil Barker. The new version of the band released their first album, *Trade Test Transmissions,* in 1993. After its release, the band toured frequently. In spring of 1996, the Buzzcocks released their fifth studio album, *All Set. —Stephen Thomas Erlewine*

Spiral Scratch / Jan. 29, 1977 / New Hormones ✦✦✦

★ **Singles Going Steady** / 1979 / IRS ✦✦✦✦✦
For those of you unwilling to jump right in and buy three CDs of Buzzcocks bliss, this single LP should convert you in a hurry—16 tracks, and not a dud among them. Everything from the hilarious sex-junkie tale "Orgasm Addict" to the frustration of "Oh Shit" and "Something's Gone Wrong Again"; this could be, track for track, one of the greatest rock albums ever made. Fast and furious, with Pete Shelley sounding wonderfully snotty, this is a piece of heaven pressed into 12 inches of vinyl. —*John Dougan*

Peel Sessions / 1988 / Dutch East India ✦✦✦

Product / 1989 / Restless ✦✦✦✦
One of the first rock 'n' roll box sets, as well as one of the finest, *Product* collects nearly every studio record the Buzzcocks ever released, with the exception of their debut EP, *Spiral Scratch. —Stephen Thomas Erlewine*

Operator's Manual: The Buzzcocks Best / 1991 / IRS ✦✦✦✦
A 25-song set, it duplicates 11 songs from the *Singles* album. It also contains the best of their three albums, only one of which was released in the US, and showcases a different side of the band. —*John Floyd*

Time's Up / 1991 / Document ✦✦✦

Entertaining Friends / 1992 / IRS ✦✦✦

A Different Kind of Tension / Buzzcocks, Pts. 1-3 / 1993 / IRS ✦✦✦✦
Even at the end of their career, the Buzzcocks were recording an amazing array of ferocious pop songs. Their last album, *A Different Kind of Tension,* featured some of Pete Shelley's best songs, including some of the most personal material he has ever written. *Parts One, Two, Three* collect the band's last three singles, which are all quite impressive. —*Stephen Thomas Erlewine*

Trade Test Transmissions / Jun. 2, 1993 / Caroline ✦✦✦

Love Bites/Another Music in a Different Kitchen / Feb. 22, 1994 / IRS ✦✦✦✦
While the Buzzcocks' singles captured the band's energetic, tightly wound pop style perfectly, the band experimented a bit more with song structures on their full-length albums. Many of the album tracks were in the vein of their classic singles, but the band also played some twisted, draining instrumental sections that were almost as impressive as their concise pop songs. Of their first two albums, the debut *Another Music in a Different Kitchen* is the stronger record, but *Love Bites* is only a shade weaker. —*Stephen Thomas Erlewine*

French / Jan. 23, 1996 / IRS ✦✦

All Set / Apr. 1996 / IRS ✦✦✦

Bobby Byrd

Organ, Piano, Vocals / Soul, Funk

As a long-running right-hand man, Bobby Byrd performed an invaluable function in the James Brown Show, warming up the crowds as a solo singer, then retreating to the sidelines as a member of the Famous Flames, Brown's backup vocal group. Indeed, without Byrd, James Brown may have never made it out of Georgia: in the early '50s, Byrd and his family sponsored Brown's parole from prison, and Byrd gave

Brown a spot in his vocal group, the Flames (which, of course, Brown eventually took over and relegated to the background). Like many of Brown's close associates and support musicians, Byrd got a chance to record his own records under Brown's direction, releasing numerous Brown-produced singles between the early '60s and early '70s. Some of these were even modest R&B hits—"We're in Love" (1965) and "I Need Help (I Can't Do It Alone)" (1970) were the biggest, making the R&B Top 20. Brown's backing musicians (and sometimes Brown himself) often figured heavily in the arrangements, and unsurprisingly the tracks often sounded like James Brown records featuring a different vocalist. The unfortunate problem was that Byrd was an average, even nondescript soul singer, sounding much more like a poor person's Sam & Dave than a facsimile of Soul Brother Number One. The records were often fine, and the early '70s hard funk singles in particular (which usually featured the J.B.'s) cook, but you can't help wondering if they might sound a lot better with B. himself on the front line. Still, fans of the James Brown groove will find a lot to like in Byrd's best recordings, in much the same way as they'll enjoy the *James Brown's Funky People* series of recordings that J.B. oversaw (but did not sing lead on). Certainly Eric B. & Rakim thought so, reworking one of Byrd's best singles (1971's "I Know You Got Soul") so faithfully that legal action ensued. After splitting from Brown in 1973, Byrd has recorded sporadically and performed often (particularly in Europe), releasing his most recent album, *On the Move*, in 1994. *—Richie Unterberger*

● **Bobby Byrd Got Soul: The Best of Bobby Byrd** / 1995 / Polydor ✦✦✦✦
As is the case with the J.B.'s and other James Brown protégés, Bobby Byrd's legacy is spread over numerous out-of-print, difficult-to-find vinyl records. So this 22-song retrospective, which gathers numerous singles and a couple of previously unreleased tracks spanning 1964 to 1973, is a welcome consolidation of his most significant work into one package. Solid stuff, covering both standard soul from the '60s and hard funk (usually featuring the J.B.'s) from the early '70s, though it sounds a lot more like a James Brown record with a different vocalist than a Bobby Byrd record that happens to benefit from James Brown's backing crew. Brown produced (and occasionally contributed to) all of the recordings here, and duets with Bobby on the 1968 single "You've Got to Change Your Mind." *—Richie Unterberger*

The Byrds

Country-Rock, Psychedelic, Folk-Rock

Although they only attained the huge success of the Beatles, Rolling Stones, and the Beach Boys for a short time in the mid-'60s, time has judged the Byrds to be nearly as influential as those groups in the long run. They were not solely responsible for devising folk-rock, but they were certainly more responsible than any other single act (Dylan included) for melding the innovations and energy of the British Invasion with the best lyrical and musical elements of contemporary folk music. The jangling, 12-string guitar sound of leader Roger McGuinn's Rickenbacker was permanently absorbed into the vocabulary of rock. They also played a vital role in pioneering psychedelic rock and country-rock, the unifying element being their angelic harmonies and restless eclecticism.

Often described in their early days as a hybrid of Dylan and the Beatles, the Byrds in turn influenced Dylan and the Beatles almost as much as Bob and the Fab Four had influenced the Byrds. The Byrds' innovations have echoed nearly as strongly through subsequent generations, in the work of Tom Petty, R.E.M., and innumerable alternative bands of the post-punk era that feature those jangling guitars and dense harmonies.

Although the Byrds had perfected their blend of folk and rock when their debut single, "Mr. Tambourine Man," topped the charts in mid-1965, it was something of a miracle that the group had managed to coalesce in the first place. Not a single member of the original quintet had extensive experience on electric instruments. Jim McGuinn (he'd change his first name to Roger a few years later), David Crosby, and Gene Clark were all young veterans of both commercial folk-pop troupes and the acoustic coffeehouse scene. They were inspired by the success of the Beatles to mix folk and rock; McGuinn had already been playing Beatles songs acoustically in Los Angeles folk clubs when Clark approached him to form an act, according to subsequent recollections, in the Peter & Gordon style. David Crosby soon joined to make them a trio, and they made a primitive demo as the Jet Set that was nonetheless bursting with promise. With the help of session musicians, they released a single on Elektra as the Beefeaters that, while a flop, showed them getting quite close to the folk-rock sound that would electrify the pop scene in a few months.

The Beefeaters, soon renamed the Byrds, were fleshed out to a quintet with the addition of drummer Michael Clarke and bluegrass mandolinist Chris Hillman, who was enlisted to play electric bass, although he had never played the instrument before. The band were so lacking in equipment in their early stages that Clarke played on cardboard boxes during their first rehearsals, but they determined to master their instruments and become a full-fledged rock band (many demos from this period would later surface for official release). They managed to procure a demo

of a new Dylan song, "Mr. Tambourine Man"; by eliminating some verses and adding instantly memorable 12-string guitar leads and Beatlesque harmonies, they came up with the first big folk-rock smash (though the Beau Brummels and others had begun exploring similar territory as well). For the "Mr. Tambourine Man" single, the band's vocals and McGuinn's inimitable Rickenbacker were backed by session musicians, although the band themselves (contrary to some widely circulated rumors) performed on their subsequent recordings.

The first long-haired American group to compete with the British Invasion bands visually as well as musically, the Byrds were soon anointed as the American counterpart to the Beatles by the press, legions of fans, and George Harrison himself. Their 1965 debut LP, *Mr. Tambourine Man*, was a fabulous album that mixed stellar interpretations of Dylan and Pete Seeger tunes with strong, more romantic and pop-based originals, usually written by Gene Clark in the band's early days. A few months later, their version of Seeger's "Turn! Turn! Turn!" became another No. 1 hit and instant classic, featuring more great chiming guitar lines and ethereal, interweaving harmonies. While their second LP (*Turn! Turn! Turn!*) wasn't as strong as their debut full-length, the band continued to move forward at a dizzying pace. In early 1966, the "Eight Miles High" single heralded the birth of psychedelia, with its druglike (intentionally or otherwise) lyrical imagery, rumbling bass line, and a frenzied McGuinn guitar solo that took its inspiration from John Coltrane and Indian music.

The Byrds suffered a major loss right after "Eight Miles High" with the departure of Gene Clark, their primary songwriter and, along with McGuinn, chief lead vocalist. The reason for his resignation, ironically, was fear of flying, although other pressures were at work as well. "Eight Miles High," amazingly, would be their last Top 20 single; many radio stations banned the record for its alleged drug references, halting its progress at No. 14. This ended the Byrds' brief period as commercial challengers to the Beatles, but they regrouped impressively in the face of the setbacks. Continuing as a quartet, McGuinn, Crosby, and Hillman would assume a much larger (actually, the entire) chunk of the songwriting responsibilities. The third album, *Fifth Dimension*, contained more groundbreaking folk-rock and psychedelia on tracks like "Fifth Dimension," "I See You," and "John Riley," although it (like several of their classic early albums) mixed sheer brilliance with tracks that were oddly half-baked or carelessly executed.

Younger Than Yesterday (1967), which included the small hits "So You Want to Be a Rock 'n' Roll Star" and "My Back Pages" (another Dylan cover), was another high point, Hillman and Crosby in particular taking their writing to a new level. In 1967, Crosby would assert a much more prominent role in the band, singing and writing some of his best material. He wasn't getting along so well with McGuinn and Hillman, though, and was jettisoned from the Byrds partway into the recording of *The Notorious Byrd Brothers*. Gene Clark, drafted into the band as a replacement, left after only a few weeks, and by the end of 1967, Michael Clarke was also gone. Remarkably, in the midst of this chaos (not to mention diminishing record sales), they continued to sound as good as ever on *Notorious*. This was another effort that mixed electronic experimentation and folk-rock mastery with aplomb, with hints of a growing interest in country music.

As McGuinn and Hillman rebuilt the group one more time in early 1968, McGuinn mused upon the exciting possibility of a double album that would play as nothing less than a history of contemporary music, evolving from traditional folk and country to jazz and electronic music. Toward this end, he hired Gram Parsons, he has since said, to play keyboards. Under Parsons' influence, however, the Byrds were soon going full blast into country music, with Parsons taking a large share of the guitar and vocal chores. In 1968, McGuinn, Hillman, Parsons, and drummer Kevin Kelly recorded *Sweetheart of the Rodeo*, which was probably the first album to be widely labeled as country-rock.

Opinions as to the merits of *Rodeo* remain sharply divided among Byrds fans. Some see it as a natural continuation of the group's innovations; other bewail the loss of the band's trademark crystalline guitar jangle, and the short-circuited potential of McGuinn's most ambitious experiments. However one feels, there's no doubt that it marked the end, or at least a drastic revamping of the "classic" Byrds sound of the 1965-68 period (bookended by the *Tambourine Man* and *Notorious* albums). Parsons, the main catalyst for the metamorphosis, left the band after about six months, partially in objection to a 1968 Byrds tour of South Africa. It couldn't have helped, though, that McGuinn replaced several of Parsons' lead vocals on *Rodeo* with his own at the last minute, ostensibly due to contractual obstacles that prevented Parsons from singing on Columbia releases. (Some tracks with Parsons' lead vocals snuck on anyway, and a few others surfaced in the 1990s on the Byrds box set).

Chris Hillman left the Byrds by the end of 1968 to form the Flying Burrito Brothers with Parsons. Although McGuinn kept the Byrds going for about another five years with other musicians (most notably former country picker Clarence White), essentially the Byrds name was a front for Roger McGuinn and backing band. Opinions, again, remain sharply divided about the merits of latter-day Byrds albums. McGuinn was (and is) such an idiosyncratic and pleasurable talent that fans and critics are inclined to give him some slack; no one else plays the 12-string as well, he's a fine arranger, and his Lennon-meets-Dylan vocals are immediately distinctive. Yet aside from some good echoes of vintage Byrds like "Chestnut Mare," "Jesus Is Just Alright," and "Drug Store Truck Drivin' Man," nothing from the post-1968 Byrds albums resonates with nearly the same effervescent quality and authority of their classic 1965-68 period. This is partly because McGuinn is an erratic (though occasionally fine) songwriter; it's also because the Byrds at their peak were very much a unit of diverse and considerable talents, not just a front for their leader's ideas.

The Byrds' diminishing importance must have stung McGuinn doubly in light of the rising profiles of several Byrds alumni as the '60s turned into the '70s. David Crosby was a superstar with Crosby, Stills, Nash & Young; Hillman, Parsons, and (for a while) Michael Clarke were taking country-rock further with the Flying Burrito Brothers; even Gene Clark, though he'd dropped out of sight commercially, was recording some respected country-rock albums on his own. The original quintet actually got back together for a one-off reunion album in 1973; though it made the Top 20, it was the first, and one of the most flagrant, examples of the futility of a great band reuniting in an attempt to recapture the lightning one last time.

The original Byrds continued to pursue solo careers and outside projects throughout the 1970s and 1980s. McGuinn, Clark, and Hillman had some success at the end of the 1970s with an adult contemporary variation on the Byrds' sound; in the 1980s, Crosby battled drug problems while Hillman enjoyed mainstream country success with the Desert Rose Band. The Byrds' legend was tarnished by squabbles over which members of the original lineup had the rights to use the Byrds name; for quite a while, drummer Michael Clarke even toured with a "Byrds" that featured no other original members. The Byrds were inducted into the Rock & Roll Hall of Fame in 1991; Gene Clark died several months later, and Michael Clarke died in 1993, permanently scotching prospects of a reunion involving the original quintet. —*Richie Unterberger*

☆ **Mr. Tambourine Man** / 1965 / Columbia ✦✦✦✦✦
One of the greatest debuts in the history of rock, *Mr. Tambourine Man* was nothing less than a significant step in the evolution of rock 'n' roll itself, demonstrating that intelligent lyrical content could be wedded to compelling electric guitar riffs and a solid backbeat. It was also the album that was most responsible for establishing folk-rock as a popular phenomenon, its most alluring traits being McGuinn's immediately distinctive 12-string Rickenbacker jangle and the band's beautiful harmonies. The material was uniformly strong, whether they were interpreting Dylan (on the title cut and three other songs, including the hit single "All I Really Want to Do"), Pete Seeger ("The Bells of Rhymney"), or Jackie De Shannon ("Don't Doubt Yourself, Babe"). The originals were lyrically less challenging, but equally powerful musically, especially Gene Clark's "I Knew I'd Want You," "I'll Feel a Whole Lot Better," and "Here Without You"; "It's No Use" showed a tougher, harder-rocking side and a guitar solo with hints of psychedelia. The CD reissue adds six less impressive (but still satisfying) bonus tracks and alternate takes from the same era. —*Richie Unterberger*

Turn! Turn! Turn! / 1966 / Columbia ✦✦✦✦
The group's second album was only a disappointment in comparison with *Mr. Tambourine Man*. They couldn't maintain such a level of consistent magnificence, and the follow-up was not quite as powerful or impressive. It was still quite good, however, particularly the ringing No. 1 title cut, a classic on par with the "Mr. Tambourine Man" single. Elsewhere they concentrated more on original material, Gene Clark in particular offering some strong compositions with "Set You Free This Time," "The World Turns All Around Her," and "If You're Gone." A couple more Dylan covers were included as well, and "Satisfied Mind" was their first foray into country-rock, a direction they would explore in much greater depth throughout the rest of the '60s. The CD adds seven decent alternate takes and bonus tracks, the most interesting being a version of Dylan's "It's All Over Now, Baby Blue," and an enigmatic Gene Clark song, "The Day Walk (Never Before)." —*Richie Unterberger*

Fifth Dimension / Feb. 1966 / Columbia ✦✦✦✦
Although *Fifth Dimension* was wildly uneven, its high points were as innovative as any rock music being recorded in 1966. Immaculate folk-rock was still present in their superb arrangements of the traditional songs "Wild Mountain Thyme" and "John Riley." For the originals, they devised some of the first and best psychedelic rock, often drawing from the influence of Indian raga in the guitar arrangements. "Eight Miles High," with its astral lyrics, pumping bass line, and fractured guitar solo, was a Top 20 hit, and one of the greatest singles of the '60s. The minor hit title track and the country-rock-tinged "Mr. Spaceman" are among their best songs; "I See You" has great 12-string psychedelic guitar solos; and "I Come and Stand at Every Door" is an unusual and moving update of a

traditional rock tune, with new lyrics pleading for peace in the nuclear age. At the same time, the R&B instrumental "Captain Soul" was a throwaway, "Hey Joe" not nearly as good as the versions by the Leaves or Jimi Hendrix, and "What's Happening?!?!" the earliest example of David Crosby's disagreeably vapid hippie ethos. These weak spots keep *Fifth Dimension* from attaining truly classic status. The CD reissue has six notable bonus tracks, including the single version of the early psychedelic cut "Why" (the B-side to "Eight Miles High"), a significantly different alternate take of "Eight Miles High," "I Know My Rider" (with some fine McGuinn 12-string workouts), and a much jazzier, faster instrumental version of "John Riley." —*Richie Unterberger*

☆ **Younger Than Yesterday** / 1967 / Columbia ✦✦✦✦✦
Younger Than Yesterday was somewhat overlooked at the time of its release during an intensely competitive era that found the Byrds on a commercial downslide. However, time has shown it to be the most durable of the Byrds' albums, with the exception of *Mr. Tambourine Man*. Crosby, McGuinn, and especially Hillman come into their own as songwriters on an eclectic but focused set blending folk-rock, psychedelia, and early country-rock. The sardonic "So You Want to Be a Rock 'n' Roll Star" was a terrific single; "My Back Pages," also a small hit, was the last of their classic Dylan covers; "Thoughts and Words," the flower-power anthem "Renaissance Fair," "Have You Seen Her Face," and the bluegrass-tinged "Time Between" are all among their best songs. The jazzy "Everybody's Been Burned" may be David Crosby's best composition, although his "Mind Gardens" is one of his most excessive. The CD reissue has six bonus tracks, including the fine Crosby-penned single "Lady Friend" and notably different alternate versions of "Mind Gardens" and "My Back Pages." —*Richie Unterberger*

★ **The Byrds' Greatest Hits** / 1967 / Columbia ✦✦✦✦✦
Even though this collection only covers the first half of their career, it contains more primo stuff than *20 Essential Tracks* on the boxed set. The mastering here isn't quite as good as that on the boxed set. —*Rick Clark*

The Notorious Byrd Brothers / Jan. 1968 / Columbia ✦✦✦✦
A classic psychedelic opus, it draws from the space-rock of *Younger*... and *Fifth*... while hinting at the country-rock to come with cuts like "Change Is Now" and "Old John Robertson." The 12-string electrics are downplayed. Production techniques like phasing, vari-speeded vocals, sound effects, and baroque string and horn arrangements play a bigger role, while the melodies and vocal execution are much spacier. Highlights include Carole King's yearning "Goin' Back," "Draft Morning," "Dolphins Smile," and "Wasn't Born to Follow" (featured in the movie *Easy Rider*). —*Rick Clark*

☆ **Sweetheart of the Rodeo** / Aug. 1968 / Columbia ✦✦✦✦✦
The Byrds made this groundbreaking country-rock classic with the songwriting aid of new member Gram Parsons. "One Hundred Years from Now" features some fine guitar and pedal-steel work from Clarence White and Lloyd Green, respectively. Versions of Dylan's "Nothing Was Delivered" and "You Ain't Going Nowhere" are pure magic, and renditions of the Louvin Brothers' "The Christian Life" and William Bell's "You Don't Miss Your Water" are standouts too. —*Rick Clark*

Preflyte / 1969 / Columbia ✦✦✦

Dr Byrd & Mr Hyde / 1969 / Columbia ✦✦
Not one of their best, this still contains two notable tracks, "This Wheel's on Fire" and "King Apathy III." There is a continued country influence, but rock still predominates. —*Rick Clark*

The Ballad of Easy Rider / Feb. 1969 / Columbia ✦✦✦✦
This is another beautiful gem with hardly a weak cut. "Gunga Din," with its delicate arpeggios, is one of the finest moments by a later incarnation of the Byrds. By this time, their characteristic 12-string sound was all but gone. —*Rick Clark*

Untitled / 1970 / Columbia ✦✦✦

In the Beginning / 1988 / Rhino ✦✦✦

Never Before / 1989 / Murray Hill ✦✦✦

☆ **The Byrds [box set]** / 1990 / Columbia ✦✦✦✦✦
With news of the original five members of the Byrds recording a new album together, speculation ran high long before this record was released. Therefore, it wasn't much of a surprise when people were disappointed at what they heard. But what no one realized was that this was a record made by *five* individuals who had once been collectively known as "The Byrds." Taken in that context, *Byrds* is a fine album indeed. Original songs as well as covers today stand up as a very strong effort, that although flawed, does not disappoint. Essential. —*James Chrispell*

20 Essential Tracks from the Boxed Set: 1965-90 / 1991 / Columbia ✦✦✦

The Cadillacs

Doo Wop
Equally adept at polished ballads or torrid rockers, the Cadillacs were

one of New York's top doo wop groups. The Harlem quintet signed with Josie in 1954 and debuted with the beautiful "Gloria," but with Earl Carroll's (b. Nov. 2, 1937) prominent energetic lead vocals, the Cadillacs became known for humorous jump material and hot choreography after "Speedoo" hit big for them in 1956. Tapping into the novelty R&B market pioneered by the Coasters, the Cadillacs cut a load of great rockers during the late '50s, such as "Peek-a-Boo" and "Please, Mr. Johnson," and performed in the quickie flick *Go, Johnny, Go!* in 1959. Carroll left to join the Coasters in 1958 but the group persevered, eventually signing with Mercury. Carroll has re-formed the Cadillacs in recent years. —*Bill Dahl*

★ **The Best of the Cadillacs** / 1990 / Rhino ✦✦✦✦✦
One of the top novelty R&B groups of the mid-'50s, these sizzling rockers also had a handful of doo wop ballads. This 18-track collects all of the group's best cuts, from "Gloria" to "Speedoo." —*Bill Dahl*

J.J. Cale (Jean Jacques Cale)

b. Dec. 5, 1938, Oklahoma City, OK
Guitar / Blues-Rock, Singer-Songwriter, Pop-Rock
Songwriter and guitarist known for his laidback style, J.J. Cale wrote several songs ("After Midnight," "Cocaine") that were recorded by Eric Clapton. —*William Ruhlmann*

Really / Dec. 1972 / Mercury ✦✦✦

Okie / May 1974 / Mercury ✦✦✦

Troubadour / Sep. 1976 / Mercury ✦✦✦✦
Producer Audie Ashworth introduced some different instruments, notably vibes and what sound like horns (although none are credited), for a slightly altered sound here. But Cale's albums are so steeped in his introspective style that they become interchangeable. If you like one of them, chances are you'll want to have them all. This one is notable for introducing "Cocaine," which Eric Clapton covered on his *Slowhand* album a year later. —*William Ruhlmann*

5 / Aug. 1979 / Mercury ✦✦

Grasshopper / Mar. 1982 / Mercury ✦✦

8 / 1983 / Mercury ✦✦

● **Special Edition** / 1984 / Mercury ✦✦✦✦
Sinuous rhythms, conversational singing, and, most of all, intricate, bluesy guitar playing characterize Cale's performances of his own songs. This compilation, covering 11 years of recording, includes the songs Eric Clapton, who borrowed heavily from Cale's style in his 1970s solo work, made famous: "After Midnight" and "Cocaine." —*William Ruhlmann*

Travel Log / Feb. 1990 / Silvertone ✦✦✦✦
Cale's first album in six years finds him taking a more aggressive stance in terms of tempos and playing, although he remains a man with a profound sense of the groove and, especially as a singer, a minimalist. But as he says, "Shuffle or die." —*William Ruhlmann*

10 / 1992 / Silvertone ✦✦✦

Guitar Man / Jun. 25, 1996 / Virgin ✦✦✦

John Cale

b. Mar. 9, 1942, Cumamman, Wales
Organ, Bass, Guitar, Piano, Harpsichord, Keyboards, Viola, Vocals / Art-Rock/Progressive-Rock, Experimental, Proto-Punk
A former member of the Velvet Underground (for whom he played viola), Cale has moved between the worlds of rock and avant-garde classical music since launching a solo career in 1969. He also worked as producer for a variety of punk and new wave artists. —*William Ruhlmann*

Vintage Violence / Mar. 25, 1970 / Columbia ✦✦✦

Church of Anthrax / Feb. 10, 1971 / Columbia ✦✦✦

The Academy in Paril / Jul. 19, 1972 / Reprise ✦✦✦

Paris 1919 / Mar. 1973 / Reprise ✦✦✦✦
John Cale's third solo album possessed a rare beauty, demonstrating that the classically trained avant-garde rock 'n' roll viola player could, when he wished, make melodic pop music with a lush elegance. (Reissued on CD in 1993.) —*William Ruhlmann*

Fear / Oct. 1, 1974 / Island ✦✦✦✦
Moving to Island Records for his fourth solo album (and third try at a pop vocal approach), Cale brought in Roxy Music guitarist Phil Manzanera and turned to a harder rocking style on the title track and "Gun." But "You Know More Than I Know" and other songs showed he retained the melodic qualities and talent for thoughtful ballads displayed on *Paris 1919*. —*William Ruhlmann*

Slow Dazzle / Mar. 25, 1975 / Island ✦✦✦

Helen of Troy / Nov. 14, 1975 / Island ✦✦✦

Sabotage/Live / Dec. 1979 / Spy ✦✦✦

Honi Soit / Mar. 10, 1981 / A&M ✦✦✦

Music for a New Society / Aug. 1982 / Island ✦✦✦✦
Cale's calmest collection of music since *Paris 1919* contains an excellent version of "Close Watch," as well as the haunting "Chinese Envoy." —*William Ruhlmann*

Caribbean Sunset / Jan. 1984 / ZE ✦✦

Comes Alive / Sep. 1984 / Mango ✦✦

Artificial Intelligence / Sep. 6, 1985 / Beggars Banquet ✦✦

Wrong Way Up / Oct. 16, 1990 / Opal ✦✦✦✦
Both Eno and John Cale have flirted with conventional pop music throughout their careers, while reserving the right to go off on less accessible experiments, which means they've held out the promise that they would make something as attractive as this collection, on which Eno comes as close to the mainstream as he has since *Another Green World* and Cale is as catchy as he's been since *Honi Soit*. The result is one of the best albums either one has ever made. —*William Ruhlmann*

Fragments of a Rainy Season / Sep. 25, 1992 / Hannibal ✦✦✦✦

● **Seducing Down the Door** / Jul. 5, 1994 / Rhino ✦✦✦✦
The range of John Cale's work can be shocking: It's hard to believe that the piano duets with minimalist composer Terry Riley on *Church of Anthrax*, the orchestral pop of *Paris 1919*, and the raucous, dissonant guitar rock of "Gun" and the rest of *Fear* are the work of the same man, much less that they were released within a four-year span. This well-chosen 38-track, 2.5-hour double-CD/cassette anthology does nothing to reconcile the musical contradictions in Cale's classical-to-punk sensibility, but it does bring coherence and consolidation to a recording career that, spread across a multitude of labels and plagued by popular indifference, has been difficult to grasp as a whole. —*William Ruhlmannn*

Island Anthology / Jul. 1996 / Polygram ✦✦✦
John Cale recorded three albums—*Fear, Slow Dazzle, Helen of Troy* (which was originally unreleased in the US)—for Island Records between 1974 and the end of 1975 and *Island Anthology* contains the complete contents of all three albums, as well as a handful of outtakes and rare B-sides over the course of two compact discs. Cale was typically eclectic during this period, playing everything from pop-rock to cutting-edge rock 'n' roll, but even so, it's not a representative collection of his entire career, just a particular part of it. The very nature of the set makes it more useful for completists, though casual fans will find isolated enthralling moments. —*Stephen Thomas Erlewine*

Camel

Art-Rock/Progressive-Rock
The British art-rock band Camel features reflective melodies within the context of extended instrumental workouts. Guitarist Andrew Latimer has been Camel's creative mainstay throughout their many incarnations, which have included keyboardists Pete Bardens and Kit Watkins. —*AMG*

Camel / 1973 / MCA ✦✦

Mirage / 1974 / Janus ✦✦

The Snow Goose / 1975 / Janus ✦✦✦

Moonmadness / 1976 / Janus ✦✦✦

Rain Dances / 1977 / Deram ✦✦✦✦
Rain Dances offers the most consistent and representative package in their saga. This is the band at its best. The addition of Caravan-cofounder Richard Sinclair proves profitable, as do a few colorist touches by Brian Eno on "Elke." Mel Collins' woodwinds are among the highlights, especially on *Tell Me* and the title track. From beginning to end, this project flows gracefully. —*Matthew Plichta*

Breathless / 1978 / Arista ✦✦✦✦
While it might not be as consistent as *Rain Dances*, *Breathless* nevertheless contains several fine tracks and remains one of their better efforts. —*Stephen Thomas Erlewine*

● **I Can See Your House from Here** / 1979 / Deram ✦✦✦✦
Although not an honest representation of the band's character, this is undoubtedly their most popular work. The one-time addition of American Kit Watkins produces some fine keyboard lead work. Rupert Hines' resourceful production and appearances by Phil Collins and Mel Collins round out this strong import release. "Survival" and "Who We Are" feature some fine orchestrations, and guitarist Latimer delivers some exceptional lead work on the album's closer, "Ice." —*Matthew Plichta*

Nude / 1981 / Decca ✦✦✦✦

The Single Factor / 1982 / Passport ✦✦

Stationary Traveller / 1984 / Decca ✦✦✦

Compact Compilation / 1986 / Rhino ✦✦✦✦
This is an excellent selection of tracks from four of Camel's best albums. —*Michael P. Dawson*

The Collection / 1986 / Castle ✦✦✦

Dust and Dreams / 1991 / Camel ✦✦✦✦
As with *Nude* and *The Snow Goose*, Camel continues refining their concept album approach, here based on Steinbeck's *The Grapes of Wrath*. Latimer maintains a symphonylike coherence throughout, with subtle character-based themes. Guest vocalist Mae McKenna has a hand in "Rose of Sharon," a gem of lyrical and musical depth. This recent album was produced and packaged by Latimer himself and may be harder to find than their others. (Available from Camel Productions, PO Box 4876, Mt. View, CA 94040.) — *Matthew Plichta*

● **Echoes: The Retrospective** / Jul. 20, 1993 / PolyGram ✦✦✦✦
There might be a song or two that die-hard fans will miss, but this double-disc set is the place to go for anyone looking for that one essential CD purchase of Camel's music. Featured are solid remastering and great liner notes and track annotation. — *Rick Clark*

Harbour of Tears / 1996 / Camel Productions ✦✦
Harbour of Tears explores the origins of Camel guitarist (and, by this time, only founding member) Andrew Latimer's family, tracing the Latimers as they emigrate from Ireland. Latimer sets the stage with a handful of descriptive, narrative songs at the beginning; by the end of the record, he's telling his story with his music. Though the album is a little rich for casual listeners, those willing to delve into Latimer's sweeping saga will find *Harbour of Tears* enthralling. — *Stephen Thomas Erlewine*

Cameo

Funk, Urban
Over the years, Cameo has reflected the numerous changes in the world of funk. When they started in 1974, they frequently toured with Parliament and Funkadelic, which is a clue to how their sound was styled. Even though they were in the hard funk vein of George Clinton's classic outfits, they were not copycats. As the '70s became the '80s, they started to play around with their sound slightly. In 1984, they found a successful style—the synth-powered title track to their album *She's Strange*. But that only hinted at what was to come. With 1986's *Word Up*, Cameo recorded a funk classic—bass-driven and synth heavy, the album was the sound of the mid-'80s. "Word Up" was also the song that broke them into the mainstream, reaching the Top Ten on the pop charts; thankfully, the album didn't have just one good song, it had a whole album's worth. Unfortunately, *Word Up* was the pinnacle of Cameo's career, with their synthesizers taking precedent over the melody and songs in their later records and the funk not being quite as strong as their earlier albums. — *Stephen Thomas Erlewine*

Word Up / 1985 / Casablanca ✦✦✦✦
Cameo's definitive album came as a surprise to those who classed them a good journeyman band. The title track became a national catch phrase in the African-American community, and "Word" remains a linguistic staple in hip-hop circles. It was also a first-rate song, with a hypnotic rhythm track and arrangement and Blackmon's best lead vocal. The follow-up singles "Candy" and "Back and Forth" were also excellent. Cameo eventually scored its only platinum album, and "Word Up" was their lone Top Ten pop hit. — *Ron Wynn*

● **The Best of Cameo** / May 18, 1993 / Casablanca ✦✦✦✦
Larry Blackmon and his Cameo mates ruled funk's domain for over a decade. Cameo evolved from its origins as a horn-based and dominated ensemble into a synthesizer-oriented group that still featured sturdy bass lines and exuberant vocals, but was in tune with urban and black America's new sensibility. These 14 selections range from the formative cuts "Rigor Mortis," "Shake Your Pants," and "It's Over" to the definitive "Word Up," "Candy," and "Back and Forth." Blackmon's alternately sneering, defiant, and aggressive vocals were the constant from Cameo's beginnings in the 1970s to their emergence as funk's reigning champions in the 1980s. — *Ron Wynn*

Best of Cameo, Vol. 2 / May 21, 1996 / Mercury ✦✦✦✦
Fifteen songs and 78 minutes for those who want a little more than what's on sale like "Freaky Dancin'," "Keep It Hot," "Be Yourself," "Insane," "We're Going out Tonight," "Feel Me," and "Alligator Woman" (the definite highlight, even if it wasn't one of their highest charters). Nona Hendryx guests on "Don't Be So Cool," and Miles Davis does the same for "In the Night." — *Richie Unterberger*

Tevin Campbell

Vocals / Urban, New Jack R&B
There's some dispute over who actually discovered Texas child sensation Tevin Campbell. Some accounts credit flutist Bobbi Humphrey, while much of the publicity material credits Quincy Jones. Campbell was in the 1988 television show *Wally & the Valentines*, and also appeared in Prince's film *Graffiti Bridge*. He made a splashy impression on Jones' *Back on the Block* LP, singing lead on "Tomorrow." He was 14 at the time. Campbell made such an impact that he earned a solo deal with Jones' Qwest label. His 1991 LP *T.E.V.I.N.* included two big R&B and pop hits, "Round and Round" and "Tell Me What You Want Me to Do." His sec-

ond release, *I'm Ready*, was issued in 1993. In June 1996 he released his third album, *Back to the World*. — *Ron Wynn*

● **T.E.V.I.N.** / Nov. 19, 1991 / Warner Bros. ✦✦✦✦
If *T.E.V.I.N.* had been recorded by an adult instead of a teenager, the album would still be impressive, but the fact that Tevin Campbell was only 14 years old when this was made makes it all the more amazing. Campbell's voice is remarkably expressive, able to handle both ballads and uptempo dance tracks without losing confidence. When he has the right material—like the hit single, Prince's "Round and Round"—the results are flawless; if the material is weak, he's merely enjoyable. — *Stephen Thomas Erlewine*

I'm Ready / 1993 / Warner Bros. ✦✦✦

Back to the World / Jun. 25, 1996 / Qwest ✦✦✦✦

Camper Van Beethoven

Vocals / Alternative Pop-Rock, Jangle-Pop
Of all of their considerable strengths, perhaps Camper Van Beethoven's strongest was the fact that, given all their ambitions and weirdness, they were never inaccessible or pretentious. It was because they never played anything as just a joke; there was always a genuine love for the music that they were playing. Whether it was country or Mideastern music, a Ringo Starr cover or a Black Flag song, Camper Van Beethoven's humor came out of a love of the music; it was not a bunch of in-jokes from a pack of hipper-than-thou, over-educated college wise-asses. For such a rough, young band, their first album, *Telephone Free Landslide Victory*, was amazingly inventive and spirited. Over the next four years, Camper Van Beethoven never lost that garagey edge to their music, no matter how arty they were (their collaborations with experimental guitarist Eugene Chadbourne) or how simple (their numerous covers, as well as originals like "Take the Skinheads Bowling" or "Eye of Fatima"). In 1990, they parted amicably, with several members making their side project, the Monks of Doom, full time; lead singer/guitarist David Lowery formed Cracker, a more straightforward band that experienced a greater commercial success in the 1990s. Camper Van Beethoven's records have not lost any charm over the years; if anything, their music sounds better a decade later than it did while they were recording. — *Stephen Thomas Erlewine*

● **Telephone Free Landslide Victory** / 1985 / IRS ✦✦✦✦
"Quirky," "eccentric," "eclectic"—all those words were used often to describe this marvelous debut by Camper Van Beethoven. The Middle East meets C&W, and skinheads go bowling. A howl. — *Jeff Tamarkin*

II & III / Jan. 1986 / IRS ✦✦✦

Camper Van Beethoven / Aug. 1986 / IRS ✦✦✦✦
Their third album is the apex of their creativity—stunning musicianship, witty lyrics, and a musical melting pot. Alternative rock at its most alternative. (The CD includes their 1987 EP *Vampire Can Mating Oven*.) — *Jeff Tamarkin*

Our Beloved Revolutionary Sweetheart / 1988 / Virgin ✦✦✦✦
Camper Van Beethoven moved to a major label and lost none of their wildly eclectic and tuneful spark. In fact, *Our Beloved Revolutionary* contains some of their finest, most accessible songs. — *Stephen Thomas Erlewine*

Key Lime Pie / 1989 / Virgin ✦✦✦

Camper Vantiquities / 1993 / IRS ✦✦✦

Canned Heat

Group / Modern Electric Blues, Blues-Rock, Alternative Pop-Rock, Boogie Rock
A hard-luck blues band of the '60s, Canned Heat was founded by blues historians and record collectors Al Wilson and Bob Hite. They seemed to be on the right track and played all the right festivals (including Monterey and Woodstock, making it very prominently into the documentaries about both) but somehow never found a lasting audience.

Certainly their hearts were in the right place. Their debut album—released shortly after their appearance at Monterey—was every bit as deep into the roots of the blues as any other combo of the time mining similar turf, with the exception of the original Paul Butterfield band. Hite was nicknamed "The Bear" and stalked the stage in the time-honored tradition of Howlin' Wolf and other large-proportioned bluesmen. Wilson was an extraordinary harmonica player, with a fat tone and great vibrato. His work on guitar, especially in open tunings (he played on Son House's rediscovery recordings of the mid-'60s, incidentally) gave the band a depth and texture that most other rhythm players could only aspire to. Henry Vestine—another dyed-in-the-wool record collector—was the West Coast's answer to Michael Bloomfield and capable of fretboard fireworks at a moment's notice. Their breakthrough moment occurred with the release of their second album, establishing them with hippie ballroom audiences as the "kings of the boogie." As a way of paying homage to the musician they got the idea from in the first place, they later collaborated on an album with John Lee Hooker that was one of the elder bluesman's most successful outings with a young White (or Black, for that matter) combo backing him up. After two big chart hits with "Goin' up the Country" and an explosive version of Wilbert Harrison's "Let's Work Together," Wilson died under mysterious (probably drug-related) circumstances in 1970, and Hite carried on with various reconstituted versions of the band until his death just before a show in 1981, from a heart seizure. —*Cub Koda & Bruce Eder*

● **The Best of Canned Heat** / 1972 / EMI America ✦✦✦✦
All of Canned Heat's best tracks and biggest hits ("Goin' up the Country," "On the Road Again") are included on this single-disc collection. —*Stephen Thomas Erlewine*

Uncanned! The Best of Canned Heat / May 17, 1994 / EMI America ✦✦✦✦
Uncanned! The Best of Canned Heat is exactly what it claims to be—the definitive portrait of the blues-soaked hippie boogie band. Spreading 41 tracks (including numerous rarities, alternate takes, and Levi commercials) over two CDs, the set is perfect for the hardcore Canned Heat collector. Casual fans might be better served by the single-disc collection, *The Best of Canned Heat.* —*Stephen Thomas Erlewine*

Freddy Cannon

b. Dec. 4, 1940, Lynn, MA
Vocals / Rock 'n' Roll
No one would claim that Freddy Cannon was one of the great early rock 'n' roll singers. His throaty rasp rated much higher for enthusiasm than impressive chops, and his 17 hit singles were often repetitious variations of his most successful tunes. Yet he did his own small part to keep the rock 'n' roll spirit burning in the late '50s and early '60s, a time at which it sometimes seemed in danger of being extinguished. He was an unabashed rock 'n' roller, for one thing, even when he was fed ancient Tin Pan Alley standards to retool for teenagers. And he was not one to let the lack of top-notch skills stand in the way of putting his heart into his vocals for all he was worth. His enthusiasm is infectious, though much of his material cannot be rescued by enthusiasm alone. Sometimes categorized as a teen idol, he was in fact too raw to fit comfortably into that mold (not to mention not quite good-looking enough). As ludicrous as it sounds, he was something of an early prototype of rock 'n' roller as Everyman, where spirit and fun counted more than conventional skill.

Cannon made his first record as part of the Spindrifts, a Boston group that went nowhere. In 1959, he hit the Top Ten with his first solo outing, "Tallahassee Lassie," a downright raw number with pounding piano, handclaps, and a raunchy guitar solo that was his best single. The Little Richard-esque shouts of "Woo" that punctuated the song would become his most familiar vocal trademark, and in fact was recycled a little too often for comfort over the next few years. "Way Down Yonder in New Orleans" (1959) made No. 3, and Cannon recorded other ancient pop tunes like "Chattanooga Shoe Shine Boy" and "Muskrat Ramble" with much more middling success—on these, he can sound something like Bobby Darin's evil doppelganger. For in-house material, he relied on Swan Records producers Bob Crewe (who would later oversee the 4 Seasons) and Frank Slay, and these were usually formulaic, if executed with spirit. His biggest hit, "Palisades Park" (which reached No. 3 in 1962), was not written by Crewe/Slay but by, of all people, future "Gong Show" host Chuck Barris.

Cannon left Swan for Warner Bros. in 1963. While the British Invasion should have spelt near-instant death, Freddy in fact managed to land a couple of his biggest hits, "Abigail Beecher" and "Action," in the mid-'60s. The latter was cut with top Los Angeles session men Hal Blaine, Leon Russell, James Burton, Glen Campbell, and David Gates—a far cry from the simpler fare of his Swan days. An artistic rebirth was not in the making, though, and Cannon never hit the charts again after "The Dedication Song" in early 1966. —*Richie Unterberger*

● **The Best of Freddy "Boom Boom" Cannon** / 1995 / Rhino ✦✦✦✦
The definitive collection. Twenty tracks, 17 of them Top 100 singles, including "Tallahassee Lassie," "Way Down Yonder in New Orleans," "Palisades Park," "Abigail Beecher," and "Action," as well as a rare 1958 single by the Spindrifts. The other selections really aren't up to the level of the best hits, despite occasional raw detours like "Buzz Buzz Buzz A-Diddle-It" and the odd novelty "If You Were a Rock and Roll Record," with the immortal line, "If you were a rock and roll record, I know they'd sell a million of you." —*Richie Unterberger*

The Capitols

Soul
The energetic Detroit-based Capitols capitalized on mid-'60s R&B dance fever with one of the most memorable entries of the genre, "Cool Jerk." Successful local producer Ollie McLaughlin signed the trio—lead singer Sam George, Donald Norman (who wrote most of the group's material under his real surname of Storball), and Richard Mitchell—to his Karen

logo, and the irresistible "Cool Jerk" made them an overnight sensation. After a couple more chart entries later that year, the trio faded quickly. George was murdered on March 17, 1982. —*Bill Dahl*

● **Golden Classics** / Collectables ✦✦✦✦
Dance-oriented mid-'60s Detroit soul, this features the notable classic "Cool Jerk." —*Bill Dahl*

The Capris

Doo Wop
The only major Capris hit, the romantic "There's a Moon Out Tonight," is a New York street-corner harmony classic. Doo wop was back in fashion by 1961, and it was no longer limited to R&B aggregations. Led by Nick Santo (born Nick Santamaria in 1941), the Capris named themselves after the Isle of Capri in Italy. The Queens, NY, natives originally cut "There's a Moon Out Tonight" for the obscure Planet imprint in 1958, but when the song was reissued on Lost Nite (and eventually on Old Town) it became a national smash its second time around in early 1961. After many moons out of the spotlight, the Capris came back triumphantly in 1981 with an album on Ambient Sound and an appearance on the PBS-TV series "Soundstage." —*Bill Dahl*

● **There's a Moon Out Tonight** / 1982 / Collectables ✦✦✦✦

There's a Moon Out Again! / 1982 / Ambient Sound ✦✦✦
Recorded in 1982, live to two-track, here's a perfect example of what a great modern-day doo wop album should be. —*Cub Koda*

Captain Beefheart

b. Jan. 15, 1941, California
Guitar, Harmonica, Keyboards, Vocals / Rock 'n' Roll, Art-Rock/Progressive-Rock, Psychedelic, Experimental, Proto-Punk
Drawing from gut-bucket Delta blues, free jazz, bare-boned rock, and the dissonance of 20th-century avant-garde chamber music, Captain Beefheart (born Don Van Vliet) and the Magic Band never sold many records, but they influenced many alternative artists, including Devo, XTC, Pere Ubu, and Sonic Youth.

Beefheart, an accomplished multi-instrumentalist, exhibited a vocal range that (some claim) spanned seven-and-a-half octaves, at times sounding like an utterly crazed incarnation of Howlin' Wolf. The first lineup of the Magic Band included Ry Cooder, and some of their first recordings on A&M were actually produced by future Bread founder David Gates.

Longtime friend and occasional musical cohort Frank Zappa signed Beefheart to his Straight label, allowing them complete artistic freedom. The result was the groundbreaking *Trout Mask Replica.*

Since then, Beefheart has put out a dozen albums, either with the Magic Band, with Zappa, or solo. Among those highlights are *Clear Spot, Bat Chain Puller, Doc at the Radar Station,* and *Ice Cream for Crow.* —*Rick Clark*

Safe as Milk / 1967 / Buddah ✦✦✦✦
Beefheart's first proper studio album is a much more accessible, pop-inflected brand of blues-rock than the efforts that followed in the late '60s—which isn't to say that it's exactly normal and straightforward. Featuring Ry Cooder on guitar, this is blues-rock gone slightly askew, with jagged, fractured rhythms, soulful, twisting vocals from Van Vliet, and more doo wop, soul, straight blues, and folk-rock influences than he would employ on his more avant-garde outings. "Zig Zag Wanderer," "Call on Me," and "Yellow Brick Road" are some of his most enduring and riff-driven songs, although there's plenty of weirdness on tracks like "Electricity" and "Abba Zaba." —*Richie Unterberger*

★ **Trout Mask Replica** / 1969 / Reprise ✦✦✦✦✦
Originally released and produced by Frank Zappa as a double album on his Bizarre/Straight label, *Trout Mask Replica* is the definitive Captain Beefheart album. To some, it is just plain weird, perhaps even anti-music. To others, it is blues with a warp or rock 'n' roll at the absolute cutting edge. Deeply rooted in blues and jazz, the Captain taught each member of the Magic Band their extremely complex individual parts over the course of a year. Playful and challenging at the same time, rhythmically kinetic, poetically beautiful, it is an absolute masterpiece. —*Rob Bowman*

Lick My Decals Off, Baby / 1970 / Bizarre/Straight ✦✦✦✦
The bookend release to *Trout Mask Replica,* this time produced by the Captain himself. Sample title "The Smithsonian Institute Blues (The Big Dig)" should give you a sense that this is not an ordinary rock 'n' roll record. Just a shade less essential than *Trout Mask Replica.* —*Rob Bowman*

Mirror Man / 1970 / One Way ✦✦✦

The Spotlight Kid / Clear Spot / 1972 / Reprise ✦✦✦✦
The Spotlight Kid (1972) and *Clear Spot* (1973) have been released on one CD. The Captain became slightly more accessible on these two early-'70s releases, accenting the rock 'n' roll ingredients. Slide guitar

abounds on some of the most asymmetrical riffs imaginable throughout *The Spotlight Kid.* The lyrics are just as playful. *Clear Spot* is the Captain at his most balanced—accessible without deserting the avant-garde. "Big-Eyed Beans from Venus" became one of his all-time classics. —*Rob Bowman*

Shiny Beast (Bat Chain Puller) / Jan. 1978 / Bizarre/Straight ✦✦✦✦
The Captain's comeback album, with the second edition of the Magic Band. As good as *Clear Spot* or *The Spotlight Kid,* with a slightly different temperament and a touch of synthesizer. —*Rob Bowman*

Doc at the Radar Station / 1980 / Blue Plate ✦✦✦✦
The masterpiece of the Captain's late-'70s/early-'80s resurrection. This time, the new Magic Band had coalesced into an ensemble of frightening power. Cross-rhythms abut each other in some of the most hyperkinetic settings imaginable. There's not a weak song or performance to be found. Buy this. —*Rob Bowman*

Ice Cream for Crow / 1982 / Blue Plate ✦✦✦✦
The Captain's last album as of this writing, with no sign that he'll ever return. A couple of changes in the Magic Band and the Captain, perhaps losing a bit of steam, make this album undistinguished. There is nothing poor here; if you are into the Captain, you will want to own this. However, everything else listed is recommended first. —*Rob Bowman*

Legendary A&M Sessions / 1984 / A&M ✦✦✦
The Best Beefheart / 1989 / Pair ✦✦✦
This is basically a combination of *Safe as Milk* and *Mirror Man* onto one CD, minus *Mirror Man's* "Tarotplane." For those who care enough about the Captain to want all or most of his material, that's a significant omission. If you're basically looking for *Safe as Milk* and not the far more avant-garde and challenging *Mirror Man,* though, this isn't a bad acquisition, maintaining the original running order of the *Safe as Milk* tracks. The *Mirror Man* songs can be viewed as bonus cuts (and, in Pair's defense, it would have been impossible to fit the lengthy "Tarotplane" onto the disc as well). —*Richie Unterberger*

Caravan

Art-Rock/Progressive-Rock
Along with the Soft Machine, Caravan was one of two eccentric, distinctively British art-rock bands to grow out of Canterbury's Wilde Flowers. Caravan itself was founded in 1968 by guitarist/vocalist Pye Hastings, keyboardist David Sinclair, bassist/vocalist Richard Sinclair, and drummer Richard Coughlan. The band immediately set itself off from the rest of the art-rock pack with its gentle melodies, complicated improvisational passages, and British folk-influenced arrangements sometimes featuring strings and woodwinds. Caravan received a fair amount of critical acclaim for its early work, particularly *In the Land of the Grey and Pink* (1971). The first of many personnel changes followed that album when David Sinclair joined Matching Mole and was replaced by former Delivery member Steve Miller for *Waterloo Lily.* Richard Sinclair left after that album and David returned for *For Girls Who Grow Plump in the Night* and *Caravan and the New Symphonia. Cunning Stunts* (1975) came out of left field to become Caravan's only charting album in the US, but critics and fans found that the group's charm had evaporated into an obsession with technical perfection. Hastings fronted the group into the '80s, and their last album, 1983's *Back to Front,* featured all the original members. The group has performed occasionally since then and played several London club dates in 1991 with several former members of Camel. —*Steve Huey*

Caravan / 1968 / Verve ✦✦
If I Could Do It All over Again I'd Do / 1970 / London ✦✦✦
In the Land of the Grey and Pink / 1971 / London ✦✦✦✦
Waterloo Lily / 1972 / London ✦✦✦
For Girls Who Grow Plump in the Night / 1973 / London ✦✦✦✦
Cunning Stunts / 1975 / BTM ✦✦✦
Blind Dog at St Dunstans / 1976 / Arista ✦✦
Best of Caravan / 1987 / London ✦✦✦
A fine single-disc collection of some of their best moments, but the double-disc *Canterbury Tales* offers a better portrait of the group. —*Stephen Thomas Erlewine*

● **Canterbury Tales: The Best of Caravan** / 1994 / Decca ✦✦✦✦
Canterbury Tales is a generous two-disc helping of this great progressive-rock band's first seven albums. The compilation draws most heavily from the albums *If I Could Do It All Over Again . . . , In the Land of the Grey and Pink, For Girls Who Grow Plump in the Night,* and *Caravan and the New Symphonia.* There are also selections from *Cunning Stunts, Waterloo Lily,* and *Caravan.* A good balance is struck between Caravan's shorter single-length pop songs and its more extended suites. The liner notes feature an informative biographical and discographical essay and lots of photographs and credits. The remastering is excellent. —*Jim Powers*

Mariah Carey

b. Mar. 22, 1970, New York, NY
Vocals / Dance-Pop, Urban, Adult Contemporary, Pop-Rock, Club-Dance
Mariah Carey has a remarkable multi-octave voice, an astonishing instrument that can reach heights only rivaled by Whitney Houston. Like Houston, Carey works the same pop-soul ballad territory, occasionally spiked by some catchy dance-oriented pop. Fortunately, Carey hasn't had a shortage of good material, either; all of her three albums feature impeccably crafted singles, designed for continuous radio play.

While she was an overnight sensation with her first single, 1990's "Vision of Love," it wasn't until 1992 that she won over many skeptical critics with her unadorned "MTV Unplugged" performance. Not that negative criticism has hurt her career any—her three albums and one EP have all sold several million copies and she has dominated the singles chart since her first album. It's a track record that very few artists can match. —*Stephen Thomas Erlewine*

Mariah Carey / 1990 / Columbia ✦✦✦
Emotions / 1991 / Columbia ✦✦✦
MTV Unplugged EP / Mar. 1992 / Columbia ✦✦✦
Music Box / 1993 / Columbia ✦✦✦✦
Mariah Carey has been stung by critical charges that she's all vocal bombast and no subtlety, soul, or shading. Her solution was to make an album in which her celebrated octave-leaping voice would be downplayed and she could demonstrate her ability to sing softly and coolly. Well, she was partly successful; she trimmed the volume on *Music Box.* Unfortunately, she also cut the energy level; Carey sounds detached on several selections. She scored a couple of huge hits, "Hero" and "Dream-lover," where she did inject some personality and intensity into the leads. Most other times, Carey blended into the background and let the tracks guide her, instead of pushing and exploding through them. It was wise for Carey to display other elements of her approach, but sometimes excessive spirit is preferable to an absence of passion. —*Ron Wynn*

● **Daydream** / Oct. 3, 1995 / Columbia ✦✦✦✦
Mariah Carey certainly knows how to construct an album. Positioning herself directly between urban R&B with tracks like "Fantasy" and adult contemporary with songs like "One Sweet Day," a duet with Boyz II Men, Carey appeals to both audiences equally because of the sheer amount of craft and hard work she puts into her albums. *Daydream* is her best record to date, featuring a consistently strong selection of songs and a remarkably impassioned performance by Carey. A few of the songs are second-rate—particularly the cover of Journey's "Open Arms"—but *Daydream* demonstrates that Carey continues to perfect her craft and that she has earned her status as an R&B/pop diva. —*Stephen Thomas Erlewine*

The Carpenters

Pop, Soft Rock, Pop-Rock
With their light, airy melodies and meticulously crafted, clean arrangements, the Carpenters stood in direct contrast with the excessive, gaudy pop-rock of the '70s, yet they became one of the most popular artists of the decade, scoring 12 Top Ten hits, including three No. 1 singles. Karen Carpenter's calm, pretty voice was the most distinctive element of their music, settling in perfectly amidst the precise, lush arrangements provided by her brother Richard. The duo's sound drew more from pre-rock pop than rock 'n' roll, but that didn't prevent the Carpenters from appealing to a variety of audiences, particularly Top 40, easy listening and adult contemporary. While their popularity declined during the latter half of the '70s, they remained one of the most distinctive and recognizable acts of the decade.

The Carpenters formed in the late '60s in Downey, CA, after their family moved from their native New Haven, CT. Richard had played piano with a cocktail jazz trio in a handful of Connecticut nightclubs and bars. Once the family had moved to California, he began to study piano while he supported Karen in a trio that featured Wes Jacobs (tuba/bass). With Jacobs and Richard forming her backup band, Karen was signed to the local Californian record label Magic Lamp, who released two unsuccessful singles by the singer. The trio won a Battle of the Bands contest at the Hollywood Bowl in 1967, which led to a record contract with RCA. Signing under the name the Richard Carpenter Trio, the group cut four songs that were never released. Jacobs left the band at the beginning of 1968.

Following Jacobs' departure, the siblings formed Spectrum with Richard's college friend John Bettis. Spectrum fell apart by the end of the year, but the Carpenters continued performing as a duo. The pair recorded some demos at the house of Los Angeles session musician Joe Osborn; the tape was directed toward Herb Alpert, the head of A&M Records, who signed the duo to his record label in early 1969.

Offering, the Carpenters' first album, was released in November 1969. Neither *Offering* or the accompanying single, a cover of the Beatles' "Ticket to Ride," made a big impression. However, the Carpenters' fortunes changed with their second single, a version of Burt Bacharach and

Hal David's "(They Long to Be) Close to You." Taken from the album *Close to You*, the single became the group's first No. 1, spending four weeks on the top of the US charts. "Close to You" became an international hit, beginning a five-year period where the duo was one of the most popular recording acts in the world. During that period the Carpenters won two Grammy Awards, including Best New Artist of 1970, and had an impressive string of Top Ten hits, including "For All We Know," "Rainy Days and Mondays," "Superstar," "Hurting Each Other," "Goodbye to Love," "Sing," "Yesterday Once More," and "Top of the World."

After 1975's No. 4 hit "Only Yesterday," the group's popularity began to decline. For the latter half of the '70s, the duo were plagued by personal problems. Richard had become addicted to prescription drugs; in 1978, he entered a recovery clinic, kicking his habit. Karen, meanwhile, became afflicted with anorexia nervosa, a disease she suffered from for the rest of her life. On top of their health problems, the group's singles had stopped reaching the Top Ten, and by 1978 they weren't even reaching the Top 40. Consequently, Karen decided to pursue a solo career, recording a solo album in 1979 with Phil Ramone; the record was never completed or released and she returned to the Carpenters later that year. The reunited duo released their last album of new material, *Made in America*, in 1981. The album marked a commercial comeback, as "Touch Me When We're Dancing" made it to No. 16 on the charts. However, Karen's health continued to decline, forcing the duo out of the spotlight. On February 4, 1983, Karen was found unconscious at her parents' home in New Haven; she died in the hospital that morning from a cardiac arrest, which was caused by her anorexia.

After Karen's death, Richard Carpenter concentrated on production work and assembling various compilations of the Carpenters' recorded work. In 1987, he released a solo album called *Time*, which featured guest appearances by Dusty Springfield and Dionne Warwick. *— Stephen Thomas Erlewine*

Close to You / Aug. 1970 / A&M ✦✦✦✦
This was the Carpenters' breakthrough album. Its title track was their first major hit, and it spawned the follow-up "We've Only Just Begun," which has been used in countless weddings since. The album also contained various pop covers of '60s hits like "Help!" and "Baby It's You," reinforcing the group's implied ties to rock while fostering the birth of a new generation of easy listening music. This album won the Carpenters a Best New Artist Grammy for 1970. *— William Ruhlmann*

● **The Singles (1969-1973)** / Nov. 1973 / A&M ✦✦✦✦
Exactly what it claims to be, this compilation contains ten of the Carpenters' 12 Top Ten hits, from "Close to You" to "Top of the World." They continued to make the charts until 1982, but the bulk of their memorable pop hits, the songs that reintroduced soft, melodic music to the masses and rolled back the rock revolution, are here. *— William Ruhlmann*

Yesterday Once More / May 1985 / A&M ✦✦✦✦
A two-CD set with 27 songs, this includes mostly their big hits, like "We've Only Just Begun" and "Mr. Postman," but there are a few sleeper cuts too. *— Bil Carpenter*

Interpretations: A 25th Anniversary Celebration / Feb. 7, 1995 / A&M ✦✦✦

James Carr

b. Jun. 13, 1942, Memphis, TN
Sax (Tenor), Vocals / Soul
Considered to be among the very greatest of "deep" Southern male soul singers, James Carr's succession of R&B hits on the Memphis Goldwax label were all gems of "country" soul, that wonderful '60s marriage of Southern Black R&B vocalists with songs written in a country format and played mostly by White musicians. Carr's dark, gospel-inflected style, marked by a subtle, rich voice that is almost frightening in its intensity and range, has been compared to that of Otis Redding and Percy Sledge; many reviewers would class him above even these formidable peers. "At the Dark End of the Street," the first songwriting collaboration between Dan Penn and Chips Moman, is Carr's undisputed masterpiece. Also recorded by Aretha Franklin, Clarence Carter, Linda Ronstadt, and Ry Cooder, it is the quintessential country-soul take on adulterous love.

Carr's career initially was short; Goldwax ceased operation in 1969, and Carr cut only one other single for Atlantic in 1971; however, he has recently emerged from retirement with a new album on Goldwax. His work stands at the apex of '60s soul—with Aretha, Otis, Percy, and Wilson—essential stuff! *— Christine Ohlman*

● **Essential James Carr** / 1995 / Razor & Tie ✦✦✦✦

Joe "King" Carrasco & the Crowns (Joseph Teutsch)

Guitar, Vocals / Tex-Mex, New Wave
Texas native Joe "King" Carrasco has devoted his career to re-creating the Tex-Mex, Farfisa organ rock 'n' roll sound of such '60s groups as the Sir Douglas Quintet and Sam the Sham and the Pharoahs. After playing in a

succession of bands around Texas in the late '60s and early '70s, Carrasco founded his band El Molino in 1976 and recorded *Tex-Mex Rock-Roll* in 1978. (The album was reissued by ROIR in 1989.) By 1979 he had formed the Crowns and was calling his music "nuevo wavo," playing especially in New York, where he appeared on stage in a cape and crown. He was signed to the UK Stiff label and Joe Boyd's Hannibal label in the US, and released *Joe "King" Carrasco and the Crowns* in 1980. By 1982 he had moved up to major label MCA for *Synapse Gap*, followed by *Party Weekend* (1983). These missed the charts, however, and although Carrasco has recorded since, turning increasingly political meanwhile, his work has been harder to find. *Bandido Rock* (1987) on Rounder was credited to Joe King Carrasco Y Las Coronas. *— William Ruhlmann*

Joe "King" Carrasco and El Molino / 1978 / Big Beat ✦✦✦
Joe "King" Carrasco and the Crowns / Nov. 1980 / Hannibal ✦✦✦
Synapse Gap / 1982 / MCA ✦✦✦✦
Joe "King" Carrasco's Crowns boasted a beefed-up sound on their major label debut, which leaned more toward guitar rock with a full rhythm section than earlier, cheesier Tex-Mex efforts. That did not constitute an improvement necessarily, though it probably was intended to broaden Carrasco's appeal. For the most part, this didn't lessen the band's effervescence, though the reggae tune was a bit trendy (it even featured harmonies by Michael Jackson!) and the overall impression was of an artist closer to the mainstream than the border. *— William Ruhlmann*

● **Anthology** / 1995 / One Way ✦✦✦✦
This is an 18-track compilation drawn from Joe "King" Carrasco's two MCA albums *Synapse Gap (Mundo Total)* (1982) and *Party Weekend* (1983). *— William Ruhlmann*

The Cars

New Wave, Pop-Rock
The Cars were one of the most popular rock bands in America between 1978 and 1985. Formed in Boston in 1976, the quintet was Rick Ocasek (guitar and vocals), Ben Orr (bass and vocals), Greg Hawkes (keyboards), Elliot Easton (guitar), and David Robinson (drums). Their 1978 debut album *The Cars*, which typified their sleek sound—new-wave energy matched to tight rhythms, disembodied vocals by Ocasek and Orr, and an affection for the sound of '60s bubblegum music—was an immediate success, spawning the singles "Just What I Needed" and "My Best Friend's Girl."

After turning out million-selling albums in 1979 (*Candy-O*), 1980 (*Panorama*), and 1981 (*Shake It Up*), the group members took a breather for solo albums before returning for their biggest album yet, *Heartbreak City* (featuring the hits "You Might Think," "Magic," and "Drive") in 1984. *Door to Door* (1987) marked a falloff in the band's popularity, and they split soon after, with Ocasek so far the most prominent solo star. *— William Ruhlmann*

The Cars / May 1978 / Elektra ✦✦✦✦
On the heels of the new wave, the Cars' debut album was a mechanized rock delight, its music spare and precise, yet undeniably catchy, with sly references to the Beatles and Tommy James and the Shondells. Vocalists Rick Ocasek and Ben Orr sounded oddly dispassionate, as if they were singing in a foreign language. But that didn't stop "Just What I Needed," "My Best Friend's Girl," and "Good Times Roll" from becoming modest hits. *— William Ruhlmann*

Candy-O / Jun. 1979 / Elektra ✦✦✦
The Cars' debut album was still charting more than a year after its release when its carbon-copy follow-up, *Candy-O*, appeared sporting a cover drawing by Vargas, noted for his *Playboy* illustrations of voluptuous women. *Candy-O* duplicated its predecessor's success, in fact outpacing the first album as the single "Let's Go" (the Cars' biggest hit so far) became one of the summer songs of the year. "It's All I Can Do" hit as well. *— William Ruhlmann*

Panorama / Aug. 1980 / Elektra ✦✦
Shake It Up / Nov. 1981 / Elektra ✦✦✦
Making extensive use of video promotion, the Cars rebounded sharply with their fourth album, whose title track was actually their first Top Ten single. The album also featured the underrated "Since You're Gone." *— William Ruhlmann*

Heartbeat City / Mar. 1984 / Elektra ✦✦✦✦
A break of three years gave the Cars plenty of time to write strong material. At the same time, Michael Jackson's *Thriller* had expanded the number of singles that could be pulled from one album, good news for the radio-friendly Cars, who scored five hits off this album, including the Top Tens "You Might Think" and "Drive." As a result, the album became the Cars' all-time best-seller. *— William Ruhlmann*

● **Greatest Hits** / Oct. 1985 / Elektra ✦✦✦✦
Ultimately, the Cars were a singles band. Here are those singles, including the biggest ones, "Drive," "Shake It Up," "You Might Think," and "Tonight She Comes." *— William Ruhlmann*

Door to Door / Aug. 1987 / Elektra ✦

Just What I Needed: The Cars Anthology / Nov. 7, 1995 / Rhino ✦✦✦✦
Over the course of two CDs and 40 tracks, *Just What I Needed: The Cars Anthology* runs through all of the Cars' greatest hits and strongest album tracks, adding exciting rarities like demos and covers of "The Little Black Egg" and "Funtime" for good measure. Even though the collection is quite comprehensive, it is never tedious, nor is it too much for the casual fan; in fact, the set works better as an album than the single-disc greatest hits collection. By including nearly all of the band's worthwhile material, *Just What I Needed* is the definitive Cars compilation. — *Stephen Thomas Erlewine*

Clarence Carter

b. Jan. 14, 1936, Montgomery, AL
Guitar, Keyboards, Vocals / Soul, R&B
A blind soul singer whose numerous hits of the late '60s and early '70s epitomized the Muscle Shoals rhythm & blues sound, Carter hit the big time with his Atlantic single "Patches" (1970) and won a lasting place in the annals of Southern soul with others like "Slip Away" and "Too Weak to Fight." In 1981 Carter broke out of a dry spell with the Venture album *Let's Burn*, featuring a track called "Workin' (On a Love Building)," which set the theme for much of what was to follow: robust, lascivious love-making boasts. More recent tracks such as his salacious reworking of Tampa Red's "Love Me with a Feeling" and the jukebox favorite "Strokin'" (too risque for some radio stations) further solidified the carnal Carter image. Still primarily a soul/R&B singer, Carter has incorporated more hard blues elements in his music recently than in the Muscle Shoals days, despite his new and unblues-minded penchant for playing and programming all the instruments on his albums. — *Jim O'Neal*

The Dr.'s Greatest Prescriptions: The Best of Clarence Carter / 198_ / Ichiban ✦✦✦✦
A selection of Carter's lascivious recent output on Ichiban Records. Classic late-'60s Muscle Shoals-soul by this deep-voiced singer, including "Slip Away" and "Patches." — *Bill Dahl*

● **Snatchin' It Back** / 1992 / Rhino ✦✦✦✦
Snatchin' It Back—The Best of Clarence Carter is a great compilation, spotlighting Carter's stellar guitar work and trademark vocals on classics like "Slip Away," "Too Weak to Fight," and "Lookin' for a Fox." His great "Tell Daddy" (covered by Etta James as "Tell Mama") is included. Dave Marsh contributes the liner notes. Soul music at its funky best, and *the* compilation to own if you're a Carter fan. — *Christine Ohlman*

Nick Cave

b. Sep. 22, 1957, Warracknabeal, Australia
Organ, Piano, Vocals / Alternative Pop-Rock, Post-Punk
After goth pioneers the Birthday Party called it quits in 1983, singer-songwriter Nick Cave assembled the Bad Seeds, a post-punk supergroup featuring former Birthday Party guitarist Mick Harvey on drums, ex-Magazine bassist Barry Adamson, and Einsturzende Neubauten guitarist Blixa Bargeld. With the Bad Seeds, Cave continued to explore his obsessions with religion, death, love, America, and violence with a bizarre, sometimes self-consciously eclectic hybrid of blues, gospel, rock, and arty post-punk, although in a more subdued fashion than his work with the Birthday Party. Cave also allowed his literary aspirations to come to the forefront; the lyrics are narrative prose, heavy on literary allusions and myth-making and taking some inspiration from Leonard Cohen. Cave's gloomy lyrics, dark musical arrangements, and deep baritone voice recall the albums of Scott Walker, who also obsessed over death and love with a frightening passion. However, Cave brings a hefty amount of post-punk experimentalism to Walker's epic dark pop.

Cave released his first album with the Bad Seeds, *From Her to Eternity*, in 1984, which contained a noteworthy cover of Elvis Presley's "In the Ghetto," foreshadowing much of Cave's style and subject matter on the follow-up *The Firstborn Is Dead*. *Kicking Against the Pricks*, an all-covers album, broke the band in England with the help of "The Singer," which hit No. 1 on the UK Independent charts. The album strengthened Cave's reputation as an original interpreter and a vocal stylist of note.

Following 1986's *Your Funeral . . . My Trial*, Cave took a two-year hiatus from recording, partially to appear in Wim Wenders' 1987 film *Wings of Desire*, and then returned with *Tender Prey*, which featured Cramps guitarist Kid Congo Powers and Cave's strongest vocal performance up to that point. Cave's productivity picked up immensely over the next two years after he kicked a heroin habit. He had two books (1988's *King Ink*, a collection of lyrics, plays, and prose, and 1989's *And the Ass Saw the Angel*, a novel) published, appeared in the 1989 Australian film *Ghosts . . . of the Civil Dead* as a prisoner, recorded a soundtrack to the film with Harvey and Bargeld, and released 1990's *The Good Son*, his most relaxed, quiet album. Cave received his due as one of the leading figures in alternative rock when he was invited to perform on the 1994 edition of the Lollapalooza tour to promote his *Let Love In* album. Early

in 1996, he released *Murder Ballads*, a collection of songs about murder. — *Stephen Thomas Erlewine & Steve Huey*

● **From Her to Eternity** / 1984 / Mute ✦✦✦✦
Desperate and ominous, this is a chilling love letter. — *John Dougan*

The Firstborn Is Dead / 1985 / Mute ✦✦✦✦
Recorded with the Bad Seeds, this album contains angst directly influenced by early American folk-blues. — *John Dougan*

Kicking Against the Pricks / 1986 / Homestead ✦✦✦✦
All covers, all unique, all recorded with the Bad Seeds. More rock from your worst nightmare. — *John Dougan*

Your Funeral . . . My Trial / 1986 / Homestead ✦✦✦

The Good Son / 1990 / Elektra ✦✦

Henry's Dream / 1992 / Mute ✦✦✦

Let Love In / 1994 / Elektra ✦✦✦

Murder Ballads / Feb. 1996 / Warner Bros. ✦✦✦

Chad & Jeremy

British Invasion, Pop-Rock
The American success of the folkish duo of Chad Stuart (b. Dec. 10, 1943, Durham, England) and Jeremy Clyde (b. Mar. 22, 1944, Buckinghamshire, England) pointed up the impact of the British Invasion led by the Beatles in February 1964. Chad & Jeremy charted only once in their native country, but their single "Yesterday's Gone," released in May 1964, was the first of 11 US chart hits they achieved through 1966. The biggest of these, and their only Top Ten, was "A Summer Song" (Jul. 1964). Adopting a lighter approach than many of their Mersey Beat contemporaries, Chad & Jeremy focused on pop revivals such as "Willow, Weep for Me" and songs from Broadway shows, such as "I Have Dreamed" from *Carousel*, both Top 40 hits for them. Having moved to Hollywood, they were frequent television guests, both on music shows such as "Hullabaloo" and series like "Batman." Their commercial progress was complicated after 1965, when they signed to Columbia Records, while Capitol Records continued to issue their earlier recordings (previously issued on the World Artists label), such that they were forced to compete with themselves. They recorded the musically ambitious *Of Cabbages and Kings* (Sep. 1967) in the wake of the Beatles' *Sgt. Pepper's Lonely Hearts Club Band*. They broke up after the commercial failure of its equally ambitious follow-up, *The Ark* (Sep. 1968). Jeremy Clyde established himself as a British stage actor. The duo reunited for a new album in 1983. — *William Ruhlmann*

Painted Dayglow Smile / Jul. 14, 1992 / Columbia/Legacy ✦✦✦✦
Chad and Jeremy signed to Columbia Records in March 1965, after spending a year on composer John Barry's Ember Records. During their three and a half years on Columbia, the duo made five albums and a couple of stray singles, as their music became increasingly ambitious and their sales declined to practically nothing. Hence, this compilation contains their last few Top 40 hits, "Before and After," "I Don't Wanna Lose You, Baby," and "Distant Shores," plus a selection of album tracks, flip singles, and rarities. The album is part of Sony's "Rock Artifacts" series, and that's a fitting subtitle. These are certainly interesting curiosities; just don't mistake this for a Chad and Jeremy greatest hits album. — *William Ruhlmann*

● **Yesterday's Gone [Greatest Hits]** / 1994 / Drive Archive ✦✦✦
This discount-priced compilation contains 14 of the 29 tracks Chad and Jeremy recorded for Ember Records (UK)/World Artists Records (US) in 1964-1965. All seven of the duo's World Artists singles are included, among them the hits "A Summer Song," "Willow, Weep for Me," "Yesterday's Gone," and "If I Loved You." An attempt to clean up the sound has been made, and there are brief, informative liner notes by Mark Humphrey. Thus, at a reduced price, this is a reasonable bare-bones presentation of Chad and Jeremy's best-known early hits. — *William Ruhlmann*

● **Best Of** / Feb. 27, 1996 / One Way ✦✦✦✦
Twenty songs from the 1964-65 World Artists era, including the hits "Yesterday's Gone," "A Summer Song," "Willow, Weep for Me," and "If I Loved You." It doesn't have any of their Columbia material, but it's the most thorough overview of their early career on CD. At its best, the folk-pop is reminiscent of a softer Peter & Gordon. However, rock-oriented listeners will find the easy listening-oriented covers, like "The Girl from Ipanema" and "September in the Rain," hard to swallow. The total absence of original dates, songwriting credits, and historical liner notes is inexcusable. — *Richie Unterberger*

Chairmen of the Board

Soul
Chairmen of the Board is one of the most dynamic acts to emerge on Holland/Dozier/Holland's Invictus label after the legendary songwriters exited Motown. Lead Norman "General" Johnson had previously fronted the Showmen, who hit in 1961 with "It Will Stand," cut in New Orleans.

Johnson's pinched, intense vocal delivery powered the pleading "Give Me Just a Little More Time," the first smash for the Chairmen in late 1969, although Danny Woods handled lead duty on the group's biggest R&B seller, "Pay to the Piper." Johnson, who wrote "Patches" for the group's first album only to see Clarence Carter score the hit, departed in 1974 to start a solo career. — *Bill Dahl*

● **Greatest Hits** / Jan. 9, 1992 / HDH ✦✦✦✦
Driving Detroit soul of the late '60s/early '70s. General Johnson's pungent lead vocals give this quartet a unique sound. Their notable hit was 1970's "Give Me Just a Little More Time." — *Bill Dahl*

Gene Chandler

b. Jul. 6, 1937, Chicago, IL
Vocals / Soul, R&B
Chandler is remembered by the rock 'n' roll audience almost solely for the classic novelty and doo wop-tinged soul ballad "Duke of Earl"; the unforgettable opening chant of the title leading the way, the song was a No. 1 hit in 1962. He's esteemed by soul fans as one of the leading exponents of the '60s Chicago soul scene, along with Curtis Mayfield and Jerry Butler. Born Eugene Dixon, he was a member of the doo wop group the Dukays, and "Duke of Earl" was actually a Dukays recording; Dixon was renamed Gene Chandler, and the single bore his credit as a solo singer. Chandler never approached the massive pop success of that chart-topper (although he occasionally entered the Top 20), but he was a big star with the R&B audience with straightforward mid-tempo and ballad soul numbers in the mid-'60s, many of which were written by Curtis Mayfield and produced by Carl Davis. Chandler's success became more fitful after Mayfield stopped penning material for him, although he enjoyed some late-'60s hits, and had a monster pop and soul smash in 1970 with "Groovy Situation." His last successes were the far less distinguished disco and dance-influenced R&B hits "Get Down" (1978) and "Does She Have a Friend?" (1980). — *Richie Unterberger*

The Duke of Earl / 1993 / Vee-Jay ✦✦✦✦
Gene Chandler exploded on the '60s soul scene with "Duke of Earl," a brilliant piece of novelty/love song material. His hit singles could be formulaic, but Chandler's expressive, haunting voice never failed to lift a trite lyric or punctuate a great one. This 23-cut set contains many songs previously available only as singles, and mixes the requisite hits with nicely done obscurities like "London Town," "Day to Day," and "Baby, That's Love." This isn't the complete Gene Chandler output, but it's certainly got most of his prime early numbers and lots of smashes. — *Ron Wynn*

● **Nothing Can Stop Me: Gene Chandler's Greatest Hits** / 1994 / Varese Sarabande ✦✦✦✦
This 20-track CD is the only collection that has all of his most popular recordings, from "Duke of Earl" through his soul hits for Constellation, Vee-Jay, Checker, Mercury, and Chi-Sound, spanning 1962 to 1980 (all but three tracks were released before 1968). Some fans might prefer *The Duke of Earl*, which focuses on his Vee-Jay years, but this has a much wider breadth, and includes "Groovy Situation." Curtis Mayfield wrote eight of the songs, although they frankly don't fully measure up to the Chicago soul he was writing for his own group, the Impressions, at the time. — *Richie Unterberger*

The Chantels

R&B, Doo Wop, Girl Group
One of the very first girl groups, the Chantels are best known for their 1957 hit "Maybe." Between 1957 and 1963, the trio racked up a number of hit singles, but none of them was ever as popular as "Maybe," which came to be regarded as one of the definitive singles of the genre.

All five members of the Chantels—Arlene Smith, Lois Harris, Sonia Goring, Jackie Landry, and Rene Minus—met as children, when they sang in the choir of Saint Anthony of Padua, a Bronx-area school. Arlene Smith was the leader of the quintet, who took their name from the name of a rival school, Saint Francis de Chantelle School. Smith wrote all of the group's early material and she was the one who convinced the other girls—whose age ranged between 14 and 17 at the time—to audition for Richard Barrett, a record producer and a member of the doo wop group the Valentines. Barrett signed the band to End Records and produced the Chantels' first single, a Smith song called "He's Gone." Released in the summer of 1957, the single scraped the charts, peaking at No. 71. However, the group's second single—another Smith composition called "Maybe"—was a smash hit, peaking at No. 2 on the R&B charts and No. 15 on the pop charts in early 1958. "Maybe" sold more copies than its chart position suggests—the single was pirated by other small record labels and none of those sales were tallied for the final chart position.

For the next year, the Chantels tried in vain to deliver a follow-up as successful as "Maybe." Two hit singles—"Every Night (I Pray)" and "I Love You So"—followed on End Records, but the label dropped them after a handful of other records failed to make an impact. Around that time,

Smith left the group to pursue a solo career (her initial solo recordings were produced by Phil Spector) and Harris had left the group. The Chantels didn't replace either singer and continued as a trio.

In the summer of 1959, the group supported Richard Barrett on his single, "Summer's Love," which peaked at No. 29 on the R&B charts. In 1961, the Chantels signed with Carlton Records, where they had two minor pop hits: "Look in My Eyes" and "Well, I Told You." Carlton dropped the group the following year and the band moved to Ludix, where they had a minor hit with "Eternally" in the spring of 1963.

The Chantels continued performing until the end of the decade; they officially disbanded in 1970. A few years later, Arlene Smith—who attended the Julliard School of Music during the '60s—re-formed the Chantels, recruiting four new members; the other original members all retired from the entertainment business. Smith continued to lead various incarnations of the Chantels into the '90s. When she wasn't touring the oldies circuit with the Chantels, Smith worked as a schoolteacher. — *Stephen Thomas Erlewine*

● **The Best of the Chantels** / 1990 / Rhino ✦✦✦✦
One of the leading girl groups of the late '50s, they were distinguished by Arlene Smith's impassioned leads. — *Bill Dahl*

Tracy Chapman

b. Mar. 20, 1964, Cleveland, OH
Guitar, Vocals / Singer-Songwriter
Tracy Chapman was the most successful folk-based performer to emerge in the '80s. Born in Cleveland, she won a scholarship to the Wooster School in Connecticut, then attended Tufts University. She began singing on street corners and in coffeehouses in the Boston area, then she signed with Elektra Records after graduating from college.

Chapman cut her debut album, prominently featuring her throaty alto and acoustic guitar, with minimal added instrumentation. Her songs were closely observed tales of lower-class life (the hit "Fast Car") and political rhetoric ("Talkin' 'bout a Revolution"), sung compellingly. Released on April 1, 1988, *Tracy Chapman* became a No. 1 international hit, selling three million copies in the US and a reported 6.5 million more overseas. Chapman toured extensively behind it, including a series of Amnesty International benefits around the world. She won three 1988 Grammy Awards, including Best New Artist. *Crossroads*, her second album, was released in 1989 and was also a million-seller. Her third album, *Matters of the Heart*, was released in 1992. — *William Ruhlmann*

★ **Tracy Chapman** / 1988 / Elektra ✦✦✦✦✦
With her choked voice and acoustic guitar, Tracy Chapman re-awakened social awareness and demonstrated the power of folk music on her debut album, singing of homelessness and desperation and "Talkin' 'bout a Revolution." Contains the Top Ten hit "Fast Car." — *William Ruhlmann*

Crossroads / 1989 / Elektra ✦✦✦
Coming after her remarkably accomplished debut, the slightly subdued follow-up *Crossroads* is a mild disappointment, but after a few plays, songs like "Bridges" and "Crossroads" reveal themselves as some of her finer work. — *Stephen Thomas Erlewine*

Matters of the Heart / 1992 / Elektra ✦✦
New Beginning / 1995 / Elektra ✦✦✦
One might assume that the difference between Tracy Chapman's third album, which spent less than three months in the charts and failed to go gold after her first two albums had sold in the millions, and her fourth, which restored her to substantial commercial success, was the album's hit single, "Give Me One Reason." In fact, after a disappointing start, *New Beginning* turned around and started selling a few months after its release and before the single took off. It went gold the week that "Give Me One Reason" hit the charts. Of course, having a hit single helps, but since "Give Me One Reason" is a nearly generic blues song that isn't particularly characteristic of Chapman or of the album, it may have brought in an audience that didn't get what it expected. Though she has added a backup band, Chapman continues to take a simple musical approach that focuses attention on her voice and to sing lyrics that alternate between intimate emotional portraits and broad political generalizations that seem more felt than deeply thought out. Three songs here, "Heaven's Here on Earth," "The Rape of the World," and the title cut, are about the state of the whole world, which is viewed in either excessively sunny or gloomy terms. As such, Chapman's relationship songs, though they too can be a little vague, register more powerfully because they are so personal. As the title suggests, Chapman is adopting a more open and hopeful posture in both her feelings and her politics on *New Beginning*, and while the surprise success of "Give Me One Reason" is heartening from a career perspective, that's the real news here. — *William Ruhlmann*

The Charlatans

Psychedelic, Folk-Rock
No relation to the British alternative rock band, the Charlatans, this San Francisco group has been widely credited as starting the Haight/Ashbury

psychedelic scene. In retrospect, their contribution was more of a social one, planting seeds of a rock counterculture with their unconventional, at times outrageous dress and attitudes. While they occasionally delved into guitar distortion and fractured, stoned songwriting, the Charlatans' music was rooted in good-time jug band blues, not psychedelic freakouts. That's not to say their records didn't have a low-key, easygoing charm, although they didn't match the innovations of the Jefferson Airplane and other peers. Cutting demos for a couple labels in 1966, most of the material they recorded at this time was unissued, and the commercial explosion of San Francisco rock passed them by. The band eventually did release a nationally distributed album in the late '60s, by which time personnel changes had diluted some of the crazy energy of the original lineup, although the LP has its engaging moments. —*Richie Unterberger*

The Charlatans / 1969 / Groucho ✦✦✦
The word is that this album failed to capture the group's essence, but it has its share of good stuff. Their good-timey sound is balanced by an engaging sincerity and folky, melodic compositions reminiscent of very early Jefferson Airplane, although there are a couple ho-hum jug band tunes. But the production and performances are too complacent and tame, lacking the spaced-out recklessness of the San Francisco scene that groups like the Airplane captured so well on record. —*Richie Unterberger*

● **Alabama Bound** / 198? / Eva ✦✦✦✦
Mid-1966 demos, recorded by Lovin' Spoonful producer Erik Jacobsen. Featuring blues, good-time music, and tentative psychedelia, it doesn't sound as crazy as one might have thought, but remains the only glimpse into the band at their most original during their early days. Also includes a live, ten-minute 1969 recording of the title track. —*Richie Unterberger*

Charlatans UK

Alternative Pop-Rock, Brit-Pop
Along with the Happy Mondays, the Charlatans (UK) were one of the two leading bands of England's Manchester bands in the late '80s and early '90s. More pop-oriented than either the Happy Mondays or the Inspiral Carpets, the Charlatans brought '60s melodies and hooks—complete with prominent Hammond organs and swirling guitar lines—together with a pulsating dance beat, creating a new psychedelia for the '90s clubgoer. Although they weren't as inventive as the Stone Roses, when the Charlatans were at the top of their form in the early, pre-grunge '90s, they made some irresistible singles that were hits in the UK. ("Then" and "The Only One I Know"); they weren't able to duplicate their success in America, where they were forced to tack "UK" to the end of their name because they shared it with a San Franciscan garage-rock band from the '60s.

As their career progressed, the Charlatans' sound became more streamlined, losing some of the neo-psychedelic club-oriented rhythm tracks that pigeonholed them as part of the Manchester scene, as the 1994 single "Can't Get out of Bed" demonstrates. All the while, they haven't lost their flair for good pop singles and each of their albums have a few gems scattered among the tracks. —*Stephen Thomas Erlewine*

● **Some Friendly** / 1990 / Beggars Banquet ✦✦✦✦
This British band combines '60s psychedelia with a '90s mentality, creating a strong retro-groove. —*Donna DiChario*

Between 10th & 11th / Apr. 14, 1992 / Beggars Banquet ✦✦✦
The Charlatans' sophomore effort is surprisingly more successful than the group's debut. While lacking the knockout punch of anything as strong as "The Only One I Know," this set steers clear of the underdeveloped material that marred much of the previous album without deviating from the basic formula. It's proof positive that the Charlatans can succeed without the hype that surrounded their arrival. —*Steve Aldrich*

Up to Our Hips / 1994 / Beggars Banquet ✦✦✦
As the Manchester craze fades further into the past, the Charlatans continue to streamline their vaguely psychedelic pop approach. On *Up to Our Hips*, the band refashions '60s British Invasion pop for the 1990s, removing most of the dance tendencies lying beneath the surface of their previous albums. As "Can't Get out of Bed" shows, their songwriting skills have continued to improve, ranking the album alongside their earlier, more popular releases. —*Stephen Thomas Erlewine*

Charlatans UK / Sep. 12, 1995 / Beggars Banquet ✦✦✦✦

Ray Charles (Ray Charles Robinson)

b. Sep. 23, 1930, Albany, GA
Piano, Vocals / Soul, R&B, Jazz Blues
Ray Charles was the musician most responsible for developing soul music. Singers like Sam Cooke and Jackie Wilson also did a great deal to pioneer the form, but Charles did even more to devise a new form of Black pop by merging '50s R&B with gospel-powered vocals, adding plenty of flavor from contemporary jazz, blues, and, (in the '60s) country. Then there is his singing—his style is among the most emotional and easily identifiable of any 20th-century performer, up there with the likes of Elvis and Billie Holiday. He's also a superb keyboard player, arranger, and bandleader. The brilliance of his 1950s and 1960s work, however, can't obscure the fact that he's made few classic tracks since the mid-'60s, though he's recorded often and tours to this day.

Blind since the age of six (from glaucoma), Charles studied composition and learned many instruments at the St. Augustine School for the Deaf and the Blind. His parents had died by his early teens, and he worked as a musician in Florida for a while before using his savings to move to Seattle in 1947. By the late '40s, he was recording in a smooth pop/R&B style derivative of Nat "King" Cole and Charles Brown. He got his first Top Ten R&B hit with "Baby Let Me Hold Your Hand" in 1951. Charles' first recordings have come in for their fair share of criticism, as they are much milder and less original than the classics that would follow, although they're actually fairly enjoyable, showing strong hints of the skills that were to flower in a few years.

In the early '50s, Charles' sound started to toughen as he toured with Lowell Fulson, went to New Orleans to work with Guitar Slim (playing piano on and arranging Slim's huge R&B hit, "The Things That I Used to Do"), and got a band together for R&B star Ruth Brown. It was at Atlantic Records that Ray truly found his voice, consolidating the gains of recent years and then some with "I Got a Woman," a No. 2 R&B hit in 1955. This is the song most frequently singled out as his pivotal performance, on which Charles first truly let go with his unmistakable gospelish moan, backed by a tight, bouncy horn-driven arrangement.

Throughout the '50s, Charles ran off a series of R&B hits that, although they weren't called "soul" at the time, did a lot to pave the way for soul by presenting a form of R&B that was sophisticated without sacrificing any emotional grit. "This Little Girl of Mine," "Drown in My Own Tears," "Hallelujah I Love Her So," "Lonely Avenue," and "The Right Time" were all big hits. But Charles didn't really capture the pop audience until "What'd I Say," which caught the fervor of the church with its pleading vocals, as well as the spirit of rock 'n' roll with its classic electric piano line. It was his first Top Ten pop hit, and one of his final Atlantic singles, as he left the label at the end of the '50s for ABC.

One of the chief attractions of the ABC deal for Charles was a much greater degree of artistic control of his recordings. He put it to good use on early-'60s hits like "Unchain My Heart" and "Hit the Road Jack," which solidified his pop stardom with only a modicum of polish attached to the R&B he had perfected at Atlantic. In 1962, he surprised the pop world by turning his attention to country & western music, topping the charts with the "I Can't Stop Loving You" single, and making a hugely popular album (in an era in which R&B/soul LPs rarely scored high on the charts) with *Modern Sounds in Country and Western Music*. Perhaps it shouldn't seem so surprising; Charles had always been eclectic, recording quite a bit of straight jazz at Atlantic, with noted jazz musicians like David "Fathead" Newman and Milt Jackson.

Charles remained extremely popular through the mid-'60s, scoring big hits like "Busted," "You Are My Sunshine," "Take These Chains from My Heart," and "Crying Time," although his momentum was slowed by a 1965 bust for heroin. This led to a year-long absence from performing, but he picked up where he left off with "Let's Go Get Stoned" in 1966. Yet by this time Charles was focusing increasingly less on rock and soul, in favor of pop tunes, often with string arrangements, that seemed aimed more at the easy-listening audience than anyone else. Charles' influence on the rock mainstream was as apparent as ever; Joe Cocker and Stevie Winwood in particular owe a great deal of their style to him, and echoes of his phrasing can be heard more subtly in the work of greats like Van Morrison.

One approaches sweeping criticism of Charles with hesitation; he's an American institution, after all, and his vocal powers have barely diminished over the years. The fact remains, though, that his work since the late '60s on record has been very disappointing. Millions of listeners yearned for a return to the all-out soul of his 1955-1965 classics, but Charles had actually never been committed to soul above all else. Like Aretha Franklin and Elvis Presley, his focus is more upon all-around pop than many realize; his love of jazz, country, and pop standards is evident, even if his more early offerings are the ones that truly broke ground and will stand the test of time. He's dented the charts (sometimes the country ones) occasionally, and can command devoted international concert audiences whenever he feels like it. For good or ill, he's ensured his imprint upon the American mass consciousness in the 1990s by singing several ads for Diet Pepsi. The CD era has seen several excellent packages that focus on various chronological/thematic phases of the legend's career. —*Richie Unterberger*

Blues & Jazz / May 26, 1950-Jun. 26, 1959 / Rhino/Atlantic ✦✦✦✦
Another easy access point for Charles' seminal Atlantic catalog. This two-disc set is evenly split between his bluesiest sides on the first disc and a selection of his greatest jazz sides on disc two (gorgeously showcasing the sax work of David "Fathead" Newman on several pieces). Charles was a masterful blues purveyor; his "I Believe to My Soul" is simultaneously invested with heartbreak and humor, while the earlier "Sinner's

Prayer," "The Sun's Gonna Shine Again," and the gospel-based "A Fool for You" emanate both hope and deep pain. —*Bill Dahl*

The Great Ray Charles / 1956 / Atlantic ✦✦✦

Ray Charles at Newport / Oct. 1958 / Atlantic ✦✦✦✦
For his appearance at the Newport Jazz Festival on July 5, 1958, Charles pulled out all the stops, performing raucous versions of "The Right Time," "I Got a Woman," and "Talkin' 'bout You." (This album was reissued in 1973 as a two-record set, packaged with *Ray Charles in Person* under the title *Ray Charles Live* [Atlantic SD 2-503].) —*William Ruhlmann*

The Genius of Ray Charles / 1959 / Atlantic ✦✦✦✦

The Genius Hits the Road / Jul. 1960 / ABC/Paramount ✦✦✦
Great blues, soul, and jazzy pop from Ray Charles, then in the midst of perhaps his most creative streak as a performer. Charles' vocals were animated, urgent, and spectacular, while the arrangements, production, material, and instrumental backing were equally splendid. —*Ron Wynn*

The Genius After Hours / 1961 / Rhino ✦✦✦✦
A great all-instrumental album, with Charles playing straight jazz, pop tunes, blues, and combinations of all those forms and more. Some equally fine solos from Fathead Newman, Hank Crawford, and Charles on keyboards and alto sax. —*Ron Wynn*

Genius + Soul = Jazz / Mar. 1961 / DCC ✦✦✦

Ray Charles & Betty Carter / Jul. 1961 / DCC ✦✦✦

☆ **Modern Sounds in Country & Western Music** / Jan. 1962 / Rhino ✦✦✦✦✦
Modern Sounds in Country & Western Music is historically important, and considered by most critics to be a classic, but some have mixed feelings about it. Charles' interpretations of songs previously recorded by Hank Williams, Eddy Arnold, Floyd Tillman, and Don Gibson are superb, but so often the arrangements by Marty Paich, Gerald Wilson, and Gil Fuller threaten to drown him in a sea of lachrymose bric-a-brac. "I Can't Stop Loving You" and "You Don't Know Me" were Top Ten pop and R&B. —*Rob Bowman*

☆ **Modern Sounds in Country & Western, Vol. 2** / Oct. 1962 / Rhino ✦✦✦✦✦
Charles' second installment of *Modern Sounds in Country and Western Music* is every bit as essential as the first, containing stellar interpretations of "Your Cheatin' Heart" and "You Are My Sunshine." —*Stephen Thomas Erlewine*

Ingredients in a Recipe for Soul / Jul. 1963 / DCC ✦✦✦✦
Ray Charles' 1963 ABC-Paramount album digitally verbatim, followed by four bonus tracks, notably the rare 1959 single "My Baby (I Love Her, Yes I Do)," an obscure Percy Mayfield goodie from 1964 ("Something's Wrong"), and Charles' 1960 version of Big Maceo's "Worried Life Blues." Charles tapped a host of disparate songwriters for this solid LP—everyone from Mel Tormé to Leroy Carr to Oscar Hammerstein—but the most memorable item is probably his irresistibly brassy remake of Harlan Howard's C&W classic "Busted." —*Bill Dahl*

Greatest Hits, Vol. 1 / 1987 / DCC ✦✦✦✦
The first of two DCC compilations to collect the best of Brother Ray's 1960s stint at ABC-Paramount Records, when he flew off in a dozen different stylistic directions. Included on this 20-track disc are Charles' immortal rendering of "Georgia on My Mind," the sinuously bluesy "Unchain My Heart," the Latin-beat instrumental "One Mint Julep," personalized remakes of the country standards "Born to Lose," "Your Cheating Heart," and "Crying Time," and his exultant rendition of the soulful "Let's Go Get Stoned." —*Bill Dahl*

Greatest Hits, Vol. 2 / 1987 / DCC ✦✦✦✦
More seminal performances from the '60s ABC catalog of the Genius (DCC split the classics evenly between the two discs, making both of them indispensable). His beloved "Hit the Road Jack" (one of several Percy Mayfield copyrights dotting Charles' repertoire), the daring country crossover "I Can't Stop Loving You," an electric-piano powered "Sticks and Stones," a wise "Them That Got," and a wonderfully mellow "At the Club" rank with the 20-song disc's standouts (though versions of the Beatles' "Yesterday" and the corny "Look What They Done to My Song, Ma" end the set on a bummer note). —*Bill Dahl*

☆ **Greatest Country Western Hits** / 1988 / DCC ✦✦✦✦✦
Collecting the highlights from Charles' two *Modern Sounds in Country and Western Music* albums, *Greatest Country Western Hits* features some of the most essential country-soul material ever recorded. —*Stephen Thomas Erlewine*

Soul Brothers/Soul Meeting / 1989 / Atlantic ✦✦✦✦
A great two-disc package that combined the pivotal Ray Charles sessions with Milt Jackson. The special release even had some bonus tracks, while the remastering and annotation were marvelous. There was no question about the quality of the tracks; Charles and Jackson were instantly compatible, with Jackson getting to display blues elements he normally sup-

pressed when playing with the Modern Jazz Quartet, and Charles getting space to present his jazz and improvising skills. —*Ron Wynn*

☆ **The Birth of Soul** / 1991 / Rhino ✦✦✦✦✦
The title isn't just hype—this absolutely essential three-disc box is where soul music first took shape and soared, courtesy of Ray Charles' church-soaked pipes and bedrock piano work. Brother Ray's formula for inventing the genre was disarmingly simple: he brought gospel intensity to the R&B world with his seminal "I Got a Woman," "Hallelujah I Love Her So," "Leave My Woman Alone," "You Be My Baby," and the primal 1959 call-and-response classic "What'd I Say." There's plenty of brilliant blues content within these 53 historic sides: Charles' mournful "Losing Hand," "Feelin' Sad," "Hard Times," and "Blackjack" ooze after-hours desperation. No blues collection should be without this boxed set, which comes with well-researched notes by Robert Palmer, a nicely illustrated accompanying booklet, and discographical info aplenty. —*Bill Dahl*

The Birth of a Legend / 1992 / Ebony ✦✦✦✦
Of all the countless compilations that have been stitched together of Ray Charles' early sides for Jack Lauderdale's Swing Time Records, this two-disc box is the only CD package that treats these enormously important works with the reverent respect that they deserve (meaning decent mono sound quality instead of murky electronic reprocessed stereo dubbed from vinyl, cogent liner notes, and full discographical annotation). This is where the Genius began, imitating Charles Brown at the very start (1949) and sounding like nobody but Brother Ray by 1952 (when he defected to Atlantic and hit the real big time). Forty-one tracks in all. —*Bill Dahl*

★ **Best of Atlantic** / 1994 / Rhino ✦✦✦✦✦
For fans who don't want to invest in the three-disc box set, this is a good single-disc collection of Charles' groundbreaking Atlantic singles. —*AMG*

The Early Years / 1994 / Tomato ✦✦✦

Genius After Hours/Great Ray / Atlantic ✦✦✦

Cheap Trick
....

Hard Rock, New Wave, Power-Pop, Pop-Rock
Combining a love for British guitar-pop songcraft with crunching power chords and a flair for the absurd, Cheap Trick provided the necessary links between '60s pop, heavy metal, and punk. Led by guitarist Rick Nielsen, the band's early albums were filled with highly melodic, well-written songs that drew equally from the crafted pop of the Beatles, the sonic assault of the Who, and the tongue-in-cheek musical eclecticism and humor of the Move. Their sound provided a blueprint for both power-pop and arena rock; it also had a surprisingly long-lived effect on both alternative and heavy metal bands of the '80s and '90s, who also relied on the combination of loud riffs and catchy melodies.

Cheap Trick's roots lie in Fuse, a late-'60s Rockford, IL, band formed by Rick Nielsen and bassist Tom Petersson, which released an unsuccessful album on Epic in 1969. After the record failed to gain any attention, the band relocated to Philadelphia and changed their name to Sick Man of Europe. The group toured Europe unsuccessfully in 1972, returning to Illinois in 1973. Upon their return to Rockford, Nielsen and Petersson changed their band's name to Cheap Trick, adding drummer Bun E. Carlos and vocalist Randy "Xeno" Hogan. Hogan was fired the following year and ex-folk singer Robin Zander joined the group.

Between 1974 and the band's first album in 1977, Cheap Trick toured constantly, playing over 200 concerts a year, including opening slots for the Kinks, Kiss, Santana, Journey, and Boston. During this time, the band built up a solid catalog of original songs that would eventually comprise their first three albums; they also perfected their kinetic live show.

Cheap Trick signed with Epic Records in 1976, releasing their debut in early 1977. The record sold well in the US, yet it failed to chart. However, the group became a massive success in Japan, going gold upon release. Later that year, the band released their second album, *In Color*, which backed away from the harder-rocking *Cheap Trick*, and featured slicker production and quieter arrangements spotlighting the band's melodic skills. Due to their constant touring, the record made it into the US charts, peaking at No. 73; in Japan it became another gold-seller.

The band realized that they were superstars in Japan when they toured the country in early 1978. Their concerts were selling out within two hours and they packed Budokan Arena. Cheap Trick's concerts at Budokan Arena were recorded for release—the record appeared after their third album, 1978's *Heaven Tonight*. *Heaven Tonight* captured both the loud energy of their debut and the hook-laden songcraft of *In Color*, leading to their first Top 100 single, "Surrender," which peaked at No. 62. However, the live performances on *At Budokan* (1979) captured the band's energetic live show, resulting in their commercial breakthrough in the US. The album stayed on the charts for over a year, peaking at No. 4 and eventually sold over three million copies; a live version of "I Want You to Want Me" pulled from the album became their first Top Ten hit. Later that year, the group released their fourth studio album, *Dream*

Police, which followed the same stylistic approach of *Heaven Tonight*. It also followed *At Budokan* into the Top Ten, selling over a million copies and launching the Top 40 hit singles "Voices" and "Dream Police." In the summer of 1980, the group released an EP of tracks recorded between 1976-79 called *Found All the Parts*.

Petersson left the group in 1980 to form a group with his wife Dagmar; he was replaced by Jon Brant. The first album recorded with Brant was the George Martin-produced *All Shook Up*, released toward the end of 1980. The album performed respectably, peaking at No. 24 and going gold, yet the single "Stop This Game" failed to crack the Top 40. Epic rejected an album the group recorded in early 1981, forcing the band back into the studio to record an entirely new record. *One on One*, the group's seventh album, appeared in 1982. Although it peaked at No. 39, the record was more successful than *All Shook Up*, eventually going platinum. Nevertheless, the group was entering a downhill commercial slide. *Next Position Please*, released in 1983, failed to launch a hit single and spent only 11 weeks on the charts. *Standing on the Edge* (1985) and *The Doctor* (1986) suffered similar fates, as the group was slowly losing its creative sparks.

Petersson rejoined the band in 1988 and the group began working on a new record with the help of several professional songwriters. The resulting record, *Lap of Luxury*, was a platinum Top 20 hit, featuring the No. 1 power ballad "The Flame" and a Top Ten version of Elvis Presley's "Don't Be Cruel." *Busted*, released in 1990, wasn't as successful as *Lap of Luxury*, peaking at No. 48 and effectively putting an end to the group's comeback. Cheap Trick signed with Warner Bros. in 1994, releasing *Wake Up with a Monster;* the record spent two weeks on the chart, peaking at 123. That same year, Epic Records released a sequel to *At Budokan, Budokan II.* Compiled from the same shows as *At Budokan*, the record provided an effective reminder of why the group was so popular in the late '70s, as well as proving that the band shaped the musical climate of the '90s, even if they were no longer selling millions of records. —*Stephen Thomas Erlewine*

Cheap Trick / 1977 / Epic ✦✦✦✦
Loaded with brain-crunching rude noises and attitude, this raucous debut plunders all the right stuff (Beatles, Who, the Move). All this supports some primo rockers like "Hot Love," "He's a Whore," "Taxman, Mr. Thief," and "Oh Candy," which ranks as one of the great lost rock singles of the '70s. Subsequent albums sound tame next to this one. Without a doubt, it's one of their best. —*Rick Clark*

In Color / 1977 / Epic ✦✦✦✦
Their second album ditches boisterous performances in favor of supertight pop-rock, with hooks galore. All the same influences are there; it's just more mannered. The lightweight "I Want You to Want Me" became their first hit. Also check out "Big Eyes," "Clock Strikes Ten," and "You're All Talk." —*Rick Clark*

☆ **Heaven Tonight** / 1978 / Epic ✦✦✦✦✦
Since Cheap Trick had dispensed with the straight medicine after an excellent debut, this third album recalibrates the band's pop smarts with an impressive handful of tunes. "Surrender," in particular, is a classic. The band wears its good taste well, with a fine cover of the Move's "California Man." —*Rick Clark*

★ **Live at Budokan** / Feb. 1979 / Epic ✦✦✦✦✦
While their records were entertaining and full of skillful pop, it wasn't until *Live at Budokan* that Cheap Trick's vision truly gelled. Many of these songs, like "I Want You to Want Me" and "Big Eyes," were pleasant in their original form, but seemed more like sketches compared to the roaring versions on this album. With their ear-shatteringly loud guitars and sweet melodies, Cheap Trick unwittingly paved the way for much of the hard rock of the next decade, as well as a surprising amount of alternative rock of the 1990s, and it was *Live at Budokan* that captured the band in all of its power. —*Stephen Thomas Erlewine*

Dream Police / Oct. 1979 / Epic ✦✦✦✦
With the big time upon them, Cheap Trick went for bigger-production sounds. Fortunately, it worked most of the time. The paranoid title cut is an effective, highly orchestrated rocker. Other notable tracks are the appealingly melodic (albeit wimpy) "Voices" and the no-frills rock of "I Know What I Want," complete with a great chorus you can shout to. In spite of its strengths, *Dream Police* marks the beginning of the band's creative decline. —*Rick Clark*

All Shook Up / 1980 / Epic ✦✦

Found All the Parts / 1980 / Epic ✦✦✦

One on One / 1982 / Epic ✦✦✦

Next Position Please / 1983 / Epic ✦✦✦

Standing on the Edge / 1985 / Epic ✦✦

The Doctor / 1986 / Epic ✦

Lap of Luxury / 1988 / Epic ✦✦✦

Busted / 1990 / Epic ✦✦

Greatest Hits / 1992 / Epic ✦✦✦✦
Hardly a passable collection, it's certainly not definitive by any standard. Nevertheless, it'll be good for those who prefer the band's more recent cookie-cutter hits, like "The Flame" and "Can't Stop Falling in Love." —*Rick Clark*

Woke up with a Monster / 1994 / Warner Bros. ✦✦✦

☆ **Budokan II** / Feb. 1994 / Epic ✦✦✦✦✦
Recorded in Japan over 1978 and 1979, this concert set amply displays everything that made Cheap Trick the great band it was—great songs set to a wall of guitars and bass, great over-the-top singing and crash and bash drumming. It's hard to pick highlights, but they absolutely make the Move's "California Man" their own. Either this album or *Live at Budokan* make a perfect introduction. —*Rick Clark*

Sex America Cheap Trick / Aug. 1996 / Sony ✦✦✦

Chubby Checker

b. Oct. 3, 1941, South Carolina
Vocals / R&B, Rock 'n' Roll
He taught America how to twist. Not just the kids, who always learned the latest steps, but everyone—from society matrons and jetsetters to the proverbial man in the street.

Rock 'n' roll was becoming complacent when Chubby Checker came along in 1960 with his note-for-note remake of Hank Ballard and the Midnighters' "The Twist" and got it moving again. The husky Philadelphia lad, known as Ernest Evans until Dick Clark's wife decided he resembled Fats Domino, had already waxed a few 45s for the local Parkway label, including a novelty called "The Class" that found him imitating Fats, Elvis, and even the Chipmunks. But it was "The Twist," a No. 1 hit not once but twice (in 1960 and 1961), that made him an international celebrity.

Checker quickly became the nation's leading dance specialist, introducing "The Hucklebuck," "The Fly," "Pony Time," and "Limbo Rock" to the gyrating masses and successfully recycling his initial routine into "Let's Twist Again" and "Slow Twistin'." While racking up monster sales figures for Parkway, Checker starred in a couple of quickie exploitation films, *Twist Around the Clock* and *Don't Knock the Twist*, later trying his hand at folk songs when the twist fad finally began to fade.

The British Invasion led to some lean years for Checker although he got a little revenge by charting with a cover of the Beatles tune "Back in the USSR." in 1969. But he continued to put on a high-energy show that inevitably led to that classic million-seller—and Chubby Checker proved every time out that he was still the king of the Twist. —*Bill Dahl*

● **Chubby Checker's Greatest Hits** / Nov. 1972 / ABKCO ✦✦✦✦
In 1972, when nostalgia for late-'50s and early-'60s rock 'n' roll was bringing Chuck Berry and others back into the charts, Allen Klein's ABKCO Records obtained the rights to reissue Chubby Checker's Cameo-Parkway singles on this 15-track hits LP. Checker actually had many more hits than just "The Twist" and "Let's Twist Again," and this LP presents both his other dance tunes—"Pony Time," "The Fly," "Limbo Rock"—and several of his later, less successful singles when he was trying to branch out into a sort of Harry Belafonte-style folk approach. But the heart of the collection is still the early-'60s dance tunes, which demonstrate that, while Checker was not a great rocker, he still, like Freddy Cannon and Gary US Bonds, was one of the people keeping the flame of rock 'n' roll flickering between the time Buddy Holly's plane went down in Iowa and the day the Beatles flew in from London. (Released on LP, this album is long out of print, and it is listed as Checker's "pick" album because, as of 1995, there is no in-print album containing his original hits.) —*William Ruhlmann*

Chemical Brothers

Acid House, Club-Dance, Trip-Hop
Manchester post-techno duo Tom Rowlands and Ed Simons, aka the Chemical Brothers, have often been described as making "techno for headbangers," referring to the somewhat lo-calorie, big-dumb-sex appeal of their music. Sample-heavy and big on dance-floor dramatics, the Brothers got their start tag-teaming the back room at London's famous Heavenly Sunday Social club after making the acquaintance of influential DJ Andrew Weatherall. The pair released a few EPs on the house-dominated Junior Boys' Own label in the early '90s under the name the Dust Brothers, and switched to their current moniker when rights were found to be owned by the US production duo of the same name (famous for their work on the Beastie Boys' *Paul's Boutique*). The Brothers found quick hype after a series of highly regarded remix projects for the Prodigy, Saint Etienne, Leftfield, Weatherall's Sabres of Paradise, and Manic Street Preachers, and released a full-length album to critical acclaim in 1995. Having toured the States a number of times with a full live act, the group also stand a good chance of breaking in the performance-centric American market. —*Sean Cooper*

● **Exit Planet Dust** / 1995 / Astralwerks ✦✦✦✦
The former Dust Brothers make oblique reference to litigation averted on their debut full-length. The Brothers' sound is big on bombast, replete with screeching guitar samples and lots of sirens and screaming divas. A breakthrough album of sorts, *Exit* was, upon its release, one of the few European post-techno albums to make any sort of headway into the stateside market. —*Sean Cooper*

The Chi-Lites

Soul
Ultra-smooth ballads were the specialty of the Chi-Lites, and they were one of the Windy City's hottest soul exports throughout most of the '70s. Changing their name from the Hi-Lites, the quartet recorded for a number of local firms before hitting in 1969 on Brunswick with "Give It Away." Lead Eugene Record's (b. Dec. 23, 1940) floating tenor caressed the R&B chart-toppers "Have You Seen Her" in 1971 and "Oh Girl" the next year, and the group scaled the soul playlists regularly through 1976, when Record went solo. Founding member Marshall Thompson keeps the group active today. —*Bill Dahl*

★ **Greatest Hits** / 1992 / Rhino ✦✦✦✦✦
All of the Chi-Lites' best songs are collected on the definitive single-disc *Greatest Hits*, making it the perfect introduction, as well as the group's most consistently enjoyable album. —*Stephen Thomas Erlewine*

Chic

Funk, Disco
Chic was the best and most influential disco band of the latter half of the '70s, earning hits with both their own records and the outside productions of co-leaders Nile Rodgers and Bernard Edwards. Beginning their career as the Big Apple Band, the group changed their name to Chic in 1977 after Walter Murphy & the Big Apple Band had a No. 1 hit with "A Fifth of Beethoven." Along with the change in name came a change in music, from fusion to disco. Edwards (bass), Rodgers (guitar), and Tony Thompson (drums) hired Norma Jean Wright and Alfa Anderson to sing, and they recorded a demo of "Dance Dance Dance." Atlantic picked it up in late 1977 after a series of rejections from other record labels; the single sold a million copies in one month, catapulting Chic into the forefront of the disco scene. After Wright left for a solo career, Luci Martin joined the band. Chic's biggest hits—"Le Freak" (No. 1), "I Want Your Love" (No. 7), and the "Good Times" (No. 1)—came in 1978-1979, and as disco started to fade, so did the group's popularity. Still, Chic's influence was apparent throughout the '80s; "Good Times" alone spawned Queen's hit "Another One Bites the Dust" (a complete rip-off), and Sugarhill Gang used the record as the foundation for "Rapper's Delight," arguably the first rap single. Nile Rodgers was one of the most successful producers of the early '80s, scoring hits with David Bowie's *Let's Dance*, Madonna's *Like a Virgin*, and Mick Jagger's solo debut, *She's the Boss*. Edwards' solo productions weren't as consistent as Rodgers', but the Power Station's album (which featured Tony Thompson on drums) was a hit. Chic re-formed in 1992, but failed to recapture the fire of its glory days. —*Stephen Thomas Erlewine*

★ **Dance Dance Dance: Best of Chic** / 1991 / Atlantic ✦✦✦✦✦
You think disco was nothing more than assembly-line funk and freeze-dried beats? Then you need to step into the crisp grooves and walloping boogie found on this stunning collection of Chic's '70s recordings. Such hits as "Good Times," "Dance Dance Dance," and "Le Freak" used the stylistic innovations of James Brown and Sly Stone as a blueprint for a new era of funk. Bernard Edwards' basslines are so provocative they seem to talk, while Nile Rodgers' skeletal guitar runs hark back to Steve Cropper's slashing style. Sure, the songs don't say much. Sure, the dance mixes collected here ramble on after about six minutes. But once you step into these grooves—grooves that influenced an entire generation of artists from David Byrne to Prince—you will realize that these were indeed good times. —*John Floyd*

The Best of Chic, Vol. 2 / 1992 / Rhino ✦✦✦✦
Filling out the gaps left by the first volume, *Best of Chic—Vol. 2* proves with its collection of album tracks and singles that Chic was not merely a great disco band, but was a great band, period. —*Stephen Thomas Erlewine*

Chicago (Chicago Transit Authority)

Adult Contemporary, Soft Rock, Pop-Rock
Chicago is second only to the Beach Boys as the most successful American rock band of all time. The group formed officially on February 15, 1967, in the city from which it eventually would take its name. The band members intended to launch a rock group with a fully integrated horn section (a novel idea at the time), so the original lineup was a sextet consisting of Walter Parazaider (b. Mar. 14, 1945) on saxophone and woodwinds, Lee Loughnane (b. Oct. 21, 1946) on trumpet, Terry Kath (b. Jan. 31, 1946, d. Jan 23, 1978) on guitar and vocals, Danny Seraphine (b. Aug.

28, 1948) on drums, James Pankow (b. Aug. 20, 1947) on trombone, and Robert Lamm (b. Oct. 13, 1944) on organ and vocals. Initially, the group did without a bass player. But in December 1967, bassist/vocalist Peter Cetera (b. Sep. 13, 1944) joined from rival band the Exceptions. Under the guidance of manager/producer James William Guercio, who initially named them Chicago Transit Authority (the name was shortened after the real C.T.A. objected), the group moved to Los Angeles and signed to Columbia Records, recording its debut album, *Chicago Transit Authority*, in January 1969. It sold over two million copies and spawned four chart singles, beginning a string of massive hits that lasted to the end of the decade, with each album cover sporting a variation on the Chicago logo and a sequential title with a roman numeral: *Chicago II, Chicago III*, etc. (Later, ordinary numbers were used.) Chicago's music was a mixture of styles, from hard rock to light pop, incorporating elements of jazz and classical, but after Cetera's "If You Leave Me Now" became a gold-selling No. 1 hit in 1976, the group became more identified with romantic ballads than anything else. Chicago went into decline after a split with Guercio in 1977 and the accidental death of Kath in 1978. But it rebounded in 1982 with "Hard to Say I'm Sorry" and the million-selling *Chicago 16*, and was able to sustain its renewed popularity despite Cetera's departure for a solo career in 1985. —*William Ruhlmann*

Chicago Transit Authority / Apr. 1969 / Chicago ✦✦✦✦
The first rock 'n' roll band to integrate a horn section into its sound successfully, Chicago Transit Authority (later Chicago), fresh from years on the Midwest bar circuit, demonstrated a wide versatility on its debut album. The band seemed capable of playing everything from lounge music to hard rock, and here it mixed ballad material with gritty funk and psychedelic guitar, often on the same song. This time capsule of the varying strands of popular music in the late '60s features the hits "Does Anybody Really Know What Time It Is?," "Beginnings," and "Questions 67 and 68." —*William Ruhlmann*

Chicago II / Jan. 1970 / Chicago ✦✦✦✦
With its second double album (now on one CD), Chicago became even more ambitious and even more successful, mounting the extended "Suite for a Girl in Buchannon," from which were excerpted the hit singles "Make Me Smile" and "Colour My World." "25 or 6 to 4" is also featured on this album. —*William Ruhlmann*

Chicago III / Jan. 1971 / Chicago ✦✦

At Carnegie Hall, Vols. 1-4 / Oct. 1971 / Chicago ✦

Chicago V / Jul. 1972 / Chicago ✦✦✦

Chicago VI / Jun. 1973 / Chicago ✦✦✦

Chicago VII / Mar. 1974 / Chicago ✦✦

Live in Japan 1972 / 1975 / Columbia ✦✦✦

Chicago VIII / Mar. 1975 / Chicago ✦✦

● **Greatest Hits** / Nov. 1975 / Chicago ✦✦✦✦
The biggest hits of Chicago's first five years of recording, including "Just You 'N' Me," "Feelin' Stronger Every Day," "Wishing You Were Here," "Call on Me," and "(I've Been) Searchin' So Long." —*William Ruhlmann*

Chicago X / Jun. 1976 / Chicago ✦✦

Chicago XI / Sep. 1977 / Chicago ✦✦

Chicago 13 / Aug. 1979 / Chicago ✦

Chicago XIV / Jul. 1980 / Chicago ✦

Chicago's Greatest Hits, Vol. 2 / 1981 / Chicago ✦✦✦
This album chronicles Chicago's gradual transformation in the second half of the '70s into a group that produced big ballads, usually sung by Peter Cetera. And here they are, starting with "If You Leave Me Now" and continuing with "Baby, What a Big Surprise" and the nostalgic "Old Days." —*William Ruhlmann*

If You Leave Me Now / 1982 / Columbia ✦✦

Chicago 16 / Jun. 1982 / Full Moon ✦✦

Chicago 17 / May 1984 / Full Moon ✦✦

Chicago 18 / Sep. 1986 / Full Moon ✦✦

Chicago 19 / Jun. 1988 / Full Moon ✦✦

● **Greatest Hits: 1982-1989** / Nov. 1989 / Full Moon ✦✦✦
Chicago returned from a career dip in 1982 with "Hard to Say I'm Sorry" and continued to hit with power ballads, among them "Hard Habit to Break" and "You're the Inspiration," all sung by Peter Cetera. But the streak continued after Cetera departed in 1985, as Jason Scheff stepped in and Chicago went on to score hits like "Will You Still Love Me?," "I Don't Wanna Live Without Your Love," and "Look Away," which are all heard here. —*William Ruhlmann*

Group Portrait / 1991 / Columbia ✦✦✦✦
If the two *Greatest Hits* collections don't look like adequate places to go, yet you want to have some Chicago in your collection, then *Group Portrait* is an extremely comprehensive boxed set that chronicles all the hits

and important album tracks. You'll probably never find a more complete history on the band than that provided in the set's booklet. —*Rick Clark*

Twenty 1 / Jan. 1991 / Full Moon ✦✦

Night & Day: Big-Band / 1995 / Giant ✦✦

The Chiffons

Girl Group, Brill Building Pop

One of the best early-'60s New York girl groups, combining sassiness and innocence on several of the style's greatest classics. The Chiffons had some singles under their belt when they reached No. 1 with "He's So Fine," whose classic "doo-lang, doo-lang" riff was appropriated by George Harrison in 1970 for his own chart-topper, "My Sweet Lord" (Harrison was subsequently ordered to pay substantial damages to the original publishers, though he always claimed the resemblance was unintentional). Their follow-up, Goffin-King's "One Fine Day," was just as good, featuring killer piano riffs from King herself. Actually cut as a Little Eva track, the Chiffons' vocal was substituted, resulting in a Top Five hit. There were a couple other memorable hits, "I Have a Boyfriend" and the Motown-influenced "Sweet Talkin' Guy," and interesting misfires like the Martha & the Vandellas-inspired "The Real Thing," as well as some singles issued under an alter ego, the Four Pennies. The group recorded quite a bit of material during the '60s, much of it derivative; the hits are their best tracks by far. —*Richie Unterberger*

● **Greatest Recordings** / 1990 / Ace ✦✦✦✦
A generous collection that not only features their greatest hits, but many forgotten songs that are surprisingly good. —*Stephen Thomas Erlewine*

● **The Best of the Chiffons** / Laurie ✦✦✦✦
Everything you need by this delicious ensemble is here, including some undeservedly obscure gems. —*John Floyd*

The Chills

Alternative Pop-Rock

The Chills were one of New Zealand's best and most popular bands of the '80s, making a small but consistent series of chiming, hook-laden guitar pop. Both the songs and the arrangements were constructed with interweaving guitar hooks and vocal harmonies, creating a pretty, almost lush, sound that never falls into cloying sentimentality. Throughout their existence, the band's personnel changed frequently—there were more than ten different lineups—with the only constant member being guitarist Martin Phillips, the band's founder.

Phillips began playing music with the New Zealand punk band the Same in 1978. Following in the footsteps of the Clean and the Enemy, the Same played mostly covers, creating a raw fusion of British Invasion and garage rock. However, the group never recorded. Phillips applied the same approach for the Chills, the band he formed in 1980 with his sister Rachel and Jane Dodd (bass) after the Same fell apart.

In 1982, the Chills signed with Flying Nun, the influential New Zealand independent record label, and released several singles that never were widely distributed in America and Europe. During this time, the group went through an enormous amount of members: future Great Unwashed member Peter Gutteridge was a member, as was the Clean's David Kilgour, keyboardist Faser Batts, bassist Terry Moore, guitarist Martin Kean, keyboardist Peter Allison, drummer Martyn Bull, and drummer Alan Haig. While these incarnations of the Chills recorded plenty of singles, they never made an album. Released on the UK record label Creation, the group's first album, *Kaleidoscope World* (1986), was a collection of their early singles; it was later released in the US on Homestead.

With the lineup of Phillips, bassist Justin Harwood, keyboardist Andrew Todd, and drummer Caroline Easther—the group's tenth lineup—the Chills recorded their first proper album, *Brave Worlds*, in 1987. Produced by Mayo Thompson, the leading figure of the cult band the Red Crayola and a former member of Pere Ubu, the band wasn't satisfied with the final result, claiming it was too loose and underproduced. The group, particularly Phillips, were more satisfied with their second full-length album, 1990's *Submarine Bells*, their first record released on an American major label. *Submarine Bells* was recorded with yet another version of the band, with Jimmy Stephenson replacing Easther, who was suffering from tinnitus. The album was well received by critics and college radio, yet it failed to break the band into the mainstream in either America or Britain. Two years later, they released *Soft Bomb*, which suffered the same fate as *Submarine Bells*. The following year, Martin Phillips broke up the Chills for the last time. —*Stephen Thomas Erlewine*

Brave Worlds / 1987 / Homestead ✦✦✦

● **Kaleidoscope World** / 1989 / Homestead ✦✦✦✦

Submarine Bells / 1990 / Slash ✦✦✦✦

Soft Bomb / 1992 / Slash ✦✦✦

Alex Chilton

b. Dec. 28, 1950, Memphis, TN

Guitar, Vocals / Rock 'n' Roll

Over the course of the last 25 years, Alex Chilton's artistic career has run the gamut from singing on classic Top Ten hit records with the Memphis, TN, group the Box Tops ("The Letter" and "Cry Like a Baby") to creating willfully chaotic solo outings with very limited commercial appeal. During the early '70s, Chilton helped form Big Star (with singer-songwriter Chris Bell). In spite of nonexistent sales, Big Star received much critical acclaim, influencing a generation of the post-punk/power-pop movement. Chilton's later solo efforts ranged from ramshackle garage rock to tight Memphis-style R&B. —*Rick Clark*

Like Flies on Sherbert / 1979 / Aura ✦

Bach's Bottom / 1981 / Razor & Tie ✦✦✦

● **19 Years: A Collection** / 1991 / Rhino ✦✦✦✦
While it draws heavily on Big Star's disturbing third album (five tracks), *19 Years* offers a surprisingly coherent and listenable overview of Chilton's wildly inconsistent solo career, collecting some of the finest songs he has written since Big Star, as well as several exuberant covers ("Can't Seem to Make You Mine," "With a Girl like You," and "Volare"). —*AMG*

Feudalist Tarts/No Sex / 1994 / Razor & Tie ✦✦✦✦
By the mid-'80s, Chilton had located to New Orleans and recorded *Feudalist Tarts*, his first album in six years. Unlike its predecessor, *Like Flies on Sherbert*, *Feudalist Tarts* marked a return to a more ordered sound that reflected Chilton's love for R&B and blues. Among the highlights are versions of Slim Harpo's "Tee Ni Nee Ni Noo," Carla Thomas' "B-A-B-Y," and his own "Lost My Job." *Feudalist Tarts* was followed by the *No Sex* EP, which is included on this disc. "Underclass" and the title track are among Chilton's finer compositions—rich in rude rootsy sounds and sarcastic deadpan humor. —*Rick Clark*

High Priest/Black List / 1994 / Razor & Tie ✦✦✦
High Priest displays a more playful Chilton with versions of Dean Martin's "Volare," Bill Black's "Raunchy," and Charlie Rich's Sun classic "Lonely Weekends." His originals "Dalai Lama" and "Thing for You" are equally fine. *Black List*, which followed *High Priest*, opens with a great send-up of the hot rod anthem "Little GTO" and Walter Lewis' bluesy "I Will Turn Your Money Green" is the high point. Chilton plays all the instruments on both of those cuts. "Magnetic Field" and "Jailbait" are solid originals. —*Rick Clark*

Cliches / 1994 / Ardent ✦✦✦

Man Called Destruction / 1995 / Ardent ✦✦

1970 / Apr. 1996 / Ardent ✦✦✦
1970 comprises the sessions that would have formed Alex Chilton's first solo album. As the title suggests, Chilton recorded these songs after he left the Box Tops but right before he joined Big Star—appropriately, the music sounds caught between the Box Tops' blue-eyed soul and Big Star's jangly power-pop. In that respect, it has more in common with his numerous solo recordings than either of his bands. And like his solo records, *1970* is wildly uneven and lacks focus. It careens between charming tributes to R&B and pop (a medley of the Archies' "Sugar, Sugar" and James Brown's "There Was a Time"), and his originals, which only hint at the heights he would reach with Big Star. If *1970* does anything, it illustrates that Chilton needs a strong collaborative force like Chris Bell to bring out the best in his music. —*Stephen Thomas Erlewine*

The Chocolate Watch Band

Psychedelic, Garage Rock

The Chocolate Watch Band never charted a record nationally. Indeed, ask most casual 1960s rock fans about them and you'll probably get little more than a blank stare. Most will probably remember their AVI Records labelmates the Standells more clearly, because they actually managed to chart a few singles. Alas, the Watch Band had the disadvantage of being a punkier band than the Standells, and also being essentially two bands as a recording unit.

The group had its start in Los Altos, CA, in 1965, where guitarist Mark Loomis joined Ned Torney (guitar) in a fledgling band that later included Danny Phay (vocals), Rich Young (bass), Jo Kemling (organ), and Gary Andrijasevich (drums). This early incarnation of the Watch Band found great, albeit short-lived popularity on the local band scene, but never recorded. Phay, Torney, and Kemling were later inducted into a rival band, the Otherside, which was formed out of a band called the Topsiders, and Young was drafted into the US Army. Loomis recruited Andrijasevich, Topsider guitarist Sean Tolby, bassist Bill Flores, and vocalist David Aguilar; this unit, also named the Chocolate Watch Band, made its debut in San Francisco and the surrounding area in the spring of 1966.

The quintet was a mod-outfitted garage punk unit par excellence, their sound founded on English-style R&B with a special fixation on the Rolling Stones at their most sneering. They eventually got a recording/management contract with Ed Cobb, a former member of the 1950s vocal ensemble the Four Preps. The group's first single was a cover of Davie Allan's "Blues Theme"; the single was a great showcase for the band, except for the fact that it was released under the alias of "The Hogs." Ironically, the band's first album, *No Way Out*, featured much tampering by the producers. By the time the record came out in June of 1967, the group had already begun breaking up. A new incarnation of the Watch Band was born in the guise of Flores and Tolby, with Tim Abbott on lead guitar, Mark Whittaker on drums, and Chris Finders on lead vocals. This lineup only lasted through the end of 1967, when Abbott and Flinders exited. Tolby moved over to lead guitar, and Aguilar returned for a few shows, but essentially the Watch Band's existence as a viable performing unit were over.

The group's producers had other ideas, however. Another album, *The Inner Mystique*, was released in February of 1968, sporting the band's name but not too much else associated with the group. Cobb would have one more go at keeping the Watch Band alive but *One Step Beyond*. By the time the record was made in the summer of 1968, all of the band had moved on to other projects, but Flores was persuaded to rejoin Tolby, Andrijasevich, Loomis (later replaced by Phil Scoma), and Phay and have one more chance in the studio.

That would probably have been the end of the group's story, but in the early 1980s, a curious thing happened—record buyers and, more particularly, young musicians in America and Europe, discovered the Watch Band. Their albums had always been collectors' items, but now the prices began escalating; a set of Australian reissues of the group's albums quickly found a market in America and Europe. More people heard the Chocolate Watch Band's music and saw their movie appearances in the 1980s than in the 1960s. Thus, it was no surprise when, in 1994, Sundazed Records reissued the complete Watch Band catalog on compact disc. *—Bruce Eder*

No Way Out / 1967 / Tower ✦✦✦
Possibly the best garage-punk album ever to make it out the door from a major label in the '60s, despite the presence of some non-Watch Band tracks. "Are You Gonna Be There (At the Love-In)" is worth the price of admission, and "Let's Talk About Girls" makes an unforgettable opening track. Reissued on Sundazed for CD, and worth owning in that form, as an original on vinyl might set you back $100 or more. *—Bruce Eder*

The Inner Mystique / 1968 / Tower ✦✦✦

One Step Beyond / 1969 / Tower ✦✦✦

● **The Best of the Chocolate Watch Band** / 1983 / Rhino ✦✦✦✦
The first CD-era collection of this hard-luck band's work was also the best compilation of the band's work, but it was a good idea done a little too early. The sound is deficient compared with Rhino's usual standard, and the notes were later outdone by Sundazed Records' reissue of the band's complete catalog. It's still a good starter, however, if one can find it. *—Bruce Eder*

The Church

Alternative Pop-Rock, Neo-Psychedelia
At their best, the Church spins out highly textured guitar psychedelia so atmospheric that the melodies work on a subconscious level or they make a guitar pop so melodic and hook-laden that it could be straight out of the Byrds and Beatles songbooks as interpreted by David Bowie. At their worst, they're ponderous and pretentious, with only their sonic textures to recommend them. Fortunately, for most of their nearly-fifteen-year career, they have been at their best, making some of the finest psychedelic-tinged guitar pop of the '80s.

Although they were always fairly popular in their native Australia, it wasn't until 1988 that they had their first (and only) hit in America, the gorgeous "Under the Milky Way." Before they had that hit single, they had recorded several albums of rougher pop and psychedelia, indebted to the Beatles and Syd Barrett. *Starfish* (1988) was their most polished record, but it also marked the culmination of the band's pop savvyness. Since that record, not only has the lineup dwindled to two members, but the music has become more concerned with texture and atmosphere, not hooks and melody. Nevertheless, they remain one of the leading guitar-driven psychedelic bands of their time. *—Stephen Thomas Erlewine*

Of Skin and Heart / 1981 / Arista ✦✦✦✦
The band's first album (now on CD with several extra tracks) is their most straightforward rock effort and one of their finest moments for this reason. "The Unguarded Moment" stands out as one of the great singles of the '80s. Issued in the US in 1982 as *The Church* with a slightly modified track listing. *—Chris Woodstra*

The Blurred Crusade / 1982 / Arista ✦✦✦
The band defined their now trademark sound on their sophomore effort. Shimmering 12-stringed guitar work from Marty Wilson-Piper more than hints at a Byrds influence. Steve Kilbey adds to the lush backdrop with his dreamy, oblique lyric delivery. *—Chris Woodstra*

Seance / 1983 / Arista ✦✦✦
While it's often seen as one of their more excessive works, this neo-psychedelic exercise is actually the culmination of the band's (especially Kilbey's) mystical obsessions. While the songs are drawn out to nearly epic length, their pop sensibility is not forgotten. *—Chris Woodstra*

Remote Luxury / 1984 / Arista ✦✦✦✦
A combination of two fine EPs, *Remote Luxury* continues to build on the sound of *Blurred Crusade*. This one takes on an even more meditative and melancholy mood. *—Chris Woodstra*

Heyday / 1986 / Arista ✦✦✦✦
The band returns to a harder, more straightahead rock album with *Heyday*. The more ambitious arrangements, adding horns for the first time, help to flesh out their now standard jangly retro-'60s sound. *—Chris Woodstra*

● **Starfish** / 1988 / Arista ✦✦✦✦
Engaging alternative rock, appealing to a wider range of listeners than their previous output. This album crystallizes the intensely atmospheric layers of bassist Steve Kilbey's lead vocals with swirling guitar work from Peter Koppes and Marty Wilson-Piper, yielding a Top 40 US hit with "Under the Milky Way." *—Donna DiChario*

Hindsight / 1988 / EMI ✦✦✦
This Australian-only double CD collects rare B-sides and EPs. Though this is obviously targeted for completists and collectors, it actually gives a good picture of the band's diversity. *—Chris Woodstra*

Gold Afternoon Fix / 1990 / Arista ✦✦✦

Priest = Aura / 1992 / Arista ✦✦

Sometime Anywhere / May 24, 1994 / Arista ✦✦✦

Eric Clapton (Eric Patrick Clapp)

b. Mar. 30, 1945, Ripley, England
Guitar, Vocals / Rock 'n' Roll, Blues-Rock, Adult Contemporary, Pop-Rock, British Blues
By the time Eric Clapton launched his solo career with the release of his self-titled debut album in August 1970, he was long established as one of the world's major rock stars due to his group affiliations—the Yardbirds, John Mayall's Bluesbreakers, Cream, and Blind Faith—affiliations that had demonstrated his claim to being the best rock guitarist of his generation. That it took Clapton so long to go out on his own, however, was evidence of a degree of reticence unusual for one of his stature. And his debut album, though it spawned the Top 40 hit "After Midnight," was typical of his self-effacing approach: It was, in effect, an album by the group he had lately been featured in, Delaney & Bonnie & Friends.

Not surprisingly, before his solo debut had even been released, Clapton had retreated from his solo stance, assembling from the D&B&F ranks the personnel for a group, Derek and the Dominos, with which he played for most of 1970. Clapton was largely inactive in 1971 and 1972, due to heroin addiction, but he performed a comeback concert at the Rainbow Theatre in London on January 13, 1973, resulting in the album *Eric Clapton's Rainbow Concert* (Sep. 1973).

But Clapton did not launch a sustained solo career until July 1974, when he released *461 Ocean Boulevard*, which topped the charts and spawned the No. 1 single "I Shot the Sheriff."

The persona Clapton established over the next decade was less that of guitar hero than arena rock star with a weakness for ballads. The follow-ups to *461 Ocean Boulevard*, *There's One in Every Crowd* (Apr. 1975), the live *E.C. Was Here* (Aug. 1975), and *No Reason to Cry* (Aug. 1976), were less successful. But *Slowhand* (Nov. 1977), which featured both the powerful "Cocaine" (written by J.J. Cale, who had also written "After Midnight") and the hit singles "Lay Down Sally" and "Wonderful Tonight," was a million-seller, and its follow-ups, *Backless* (Nov. 1978), featuring the Top Ten hit "Promises," the live *Just One Night* (May 1980), and *Another Ticket* (Apr. 1981), featuring the Top Ten hit "I Can't Stand It," were all big sellers.

Clapton's popularity waned somewhat in the first half of the '80s, as the albums *Money and Cigarettes* (Feb. 1983), *Behind the Sun* (Mar. 1985), and *August* (Nov. 1986) indicated a certain career stasis. But he was buoyed by the release of the boxed set retrospective *Crossroads* (Apr. 1988), which seemed to remind his fans of how great he was. *Journeyman* (Nov. 1989) was a return to form.

It would be his last new studio album for nearly five years, though in the interim he would suffer greatly and enjoy surprising triumph. On March 20, 1991, Clapton's four-year-old son was killed in a fall. While he mourned, he released a live album, *24 Nights* (Oct. 1991), culled from his annual concert series at the Royal Albert Hall in London, and prepared a movie soundtrack, *Rush* (Jan. 1992). The soundtrack featured a song written for his son, "Tears in Heaven," that became a massive hit single.

In March 1992, Clapton recorded a concert for *MTV Unplugged* that, when released on an album in August, became his biggest selling record ever. Two years later, Clapton returned with a blues album, *From the Cradle*. *—William Ruhlmann*

Eric Clapton / Jul. 1970 / Polydor ✦✦✦✦

Eric Clapton's eponymous solo debut was recorded after he completed a tour with Delaney & Bonnie. Clapton used the core of the duo's backing band and co-wrote the majority of the songs with Delaney Bramlett—accordingly, *Eric Clapton* sounds more laidback and straightforward than any of the guitarist's previous recordings. There are still elements of blues and rock 'n' roll, but they're hidden beneath layers of gospel, R&B, country, and pop flourishes. And the pop element of the record is the strongest of the album's many elements—"Blues Power" isn't a blues song and only "Let It Rain," the album's closer, features extended solos. Throughout the album, Clapton turns out concise solos that de-emphasize his status as guitar god, even when they display astonishing musicality and technique. That is both a good and a bad thing—it's encouraging to hear him grow and become a more fully rounded musician, but too often the album needs the spark that some long guitar solos would have given it. In short, it needs a little more of Clapton's personality. —*Stephen Thomas Erlewine*

461 Ocean Boulevard / Jul. 1974 / Polydor ✦✦✦✦

461 Ocean Boulevard is Eric Clapton's second studio solo album, arriving after his side project of Derek & the Dominos and a long struggle with heroin addiction. Although there are some new reggae influences, the album doesn't sound all that different from the rock, pop, blues, country, and R&B amalgam of *Eric Clapton*. However, *461 Ocean Boulevard* is a tighter, more focused outing that enables Clapton to stretch out instrumentally. Furthermore, the pop concessions on the album—the sleek production, the concise running times—don't detract from the rootsy origins of the material, whether it's Johnny Otis' "Willie and the Hand Jive," the traditional blues "Motherless Children," Bob Marley's "I Shot the Sheriff," or Clapton's emotional originals, "Better Make It Through Today" and "Let It Grow." With its relaxed, friendly atmosphere and strong bluesy roots, *461 Ocean Boulevard* set the template for Clapton's '70s albums. Though he tried hard to make an album exactly like it, he never quite managed to replicate its charms. —*Stephen Thomas Erlewine*

There's One in Every Crowd / Mar. 1975 / Polydor ✦✦

E.C. Was Here / Aug. 1975 / Polydor ✦✦✦

No Reason to Cry / Aug. 1976 / Polydor ✦✦✦

Slowhand / Nov. 1977 / Polydor ✦✦✦✦

After the all-star *No Reason to Cry* failed to make much of an impact commercially, Eric Clapton returned to using his own band for *Slowhand*. The difference is substantial—where *No Reason to Cry* struggled hard to find the right tone, *Slowhand* opens with the relaxed, bluesy shuffle of J.J. Cale's "Cocaine" and sustains it throughout the course of the album. Alternating between straight blues ("Mean Old Frisco"), country ("Lay Down Sally"), mainstream rock ("Cocaine," "The Core") and pop ("Wonderful Tonight"), *Slowhand* doesn't sound schizophrenic because of the band's grasp of the material. This is laidback virtuosity—although Clapton and his band are never flashy, their playing is masterful and assured. That assurance and the album's eclectic material makes *Slowhand* rank with *461 Ocean Boulevard* as Eric Clapton's best album. —*Stephen Thomas Erlewine*

Backless / Nov. 1978 / Polydor ✦✦✦

Just One Night / Apr. 1980 / Polydor ✦✦✦✦

Although Eric Clapton has released a bevy of live albums, none of them have ever quite captured the guitarist's raw energy and dazzling virtuosity. The double-live album *Just One Night* may have gotten closer to that elusive goal than most of its predecessors, but it is still lacking in many ways. The most notable difference between *Just One Night* and Clapton's other live albums is his backing band. Led by guitarist Albert Lee, the group is a collective of accomplished professionals that have managed to keep some grit in their playing. They help push Clapton along, forcing him to spit out crackling solos throughout the album. However, the performances aren't consistent on *Just One Night*—there are plenty of dynamic moments like "Double Trouble" and "Rambling on My Mind," but they are weighed down by pedestrian renditions of songs like "All Our Past Times." Nevertheless, more than any other Clapton live album, *Just One Night* suggests the guitarist's in-concert potential. It's just too bad that the recording didn't occur on a night when he did fulfill all of that potential. —*Stephen Thomas Erlewine*

Another Ticket / Feb. 1981 / Polydor ✦✦✦

Time Pieces: Best of Eric Clapton / May 1982 / Polydor ✦✦✦✦

Time Pieces is a good single-disc collection of Eric Clapton's solo hits—including "I Shot the Sheriff," "After Midnight," "Wonderful Tonight," Derek & the Domino's "Layla," and "Cocaine"—that has since been supplanted by the more thorough *The Cream of Eric Clapton*, which combines his solo work with selections of his Cream and Blind Faith work. Nevertheless, the compilation still provides a good introduction for neophyte Clapton fans, especially those that just want copies of his '70s hits. —*Stephen Thomas Erlewine*

Money and Cigarettes / Feb. 1983 / Reprise ✦✦✦✦

Recorded with some old friends—including Ry Cooder, Duck Dunn, and Albert Lee—*Money and Cigarettes* is one of Clapton's finest albums. Instead of being an empty exercise in studio professionalism, the record is an appealing, low-key effort featuring some of the smoothest blues Clapton has ever played. —*Stephen Thomas Erlewine*

Time Pieces II/Live in the '70s / 1985 / Polydor ✦✦✦

Behind the Sun / Mar. 1985 / Reprise ✦✦✦

August / Nov. 1986 / Reprise ✦✦

☆ **Crossroads** / Apr. 1988 / Polydor ✦✦✦✦✦

A four-disc box set spanning Eric Clapton's entire career—running from the Yardbirds to his '80s solo recordings—*Crossroads* not only revitalized Clapton's commercial standing, but it established the rock 'n' roll multi-disc box set retrospective as a commercially viable proposition. Bob Dylan's *Biograph* was successful two years before the release of *Crossroads*, but Clapton's set was a bona fide blockbuster. And it's easy to see why. *Crossroads* manages to sum up Clapton's career succinctly and thoroughly, touching upon all of his hits and adding a bevy of first-rate unreleased material (most notably selections from the scrapped second Derek & the Dominos album). Although not all of his greatest performances are included on the set—none of this work as a session musician or guest artist is included, for instance—every truly essential item he recorded is present on these four discs. No other Clapton album accurately explains why the guitarist was so influential, or demonstrates exactly what he accomplished. —*Stephen Thomas Erlewine*

Journeyman / Nov. 1989 / Reprise ✦✦✦✦

For most of the '80s, Eric Clapton seemed rather lost, uncertain of whether he should return to his blues roots or pander to AOR radio. By the mid-'80s, he appeared to have made the decision to revamp himself as a glossy mainstream rocker, working with synthesizers and drum machines. Instead of expanding his audience, it only reduced it. Then came the career retrospective *Crossroads*, which helped revitalize his career, not only commercially, but also creatively, as *Journeyman*—the first album he recorded after the success of *Crossroads*—proved. Although *Journeyman* still suffers from an overly slick production, Clapton sounds more convincing than he has since the early '70s. Not only is his guitar playing muscular and forceful, his singing is soulful and gritty. Furthermore, the songwriting is consistently strong, alternating between fine mainstream rock originals ("Pretending") and covers ("Before You Accuse Me," "Hound Dog"). Like any of Clapton's best albums, there is no grandstanding to be found on *Journeyman*—it's simply a laidback and thoroughly engaging display of Clapton's virtuosity. On the whole, it's the best studio album he's released since *Slowhand.* —*Stephen Thomas Erlewine*

24 Nights / Oct. 8, 1991 / Reprise ✦✦

Unplugged / Aug. 18, 1992 / Reprise ✦✦✦✦

Clapton's *Unplugged* was responsible for making acoustic-based music, and *Unplugged* albums in particular, a hot trend in the early '90s. Clapton's concert was not only one of the finest *Unplugged* episodes, but was also some of the finest music he had recorded in years. Instead of the slick productions that tainted his '80s albums, the music was straightforward and direct, alternating between his pop numbers and traditional blues songs. The result was some of the most genuine, heartfelt music the guitarist has ever committed to tape. And some of his most popular—the album sold over seven million copies in the US and won several Grammies. —*Stephen Thomas Erlewine*

From the Cradle / Sep. 13, 1994 / Reprise ✦✦✦✦

For years, fans craved an all-blues album from Clapton; he waited until 1994 to deliver *From the Cradle*. The album manages to recreate the ambience of postwar electric blues, right down to the bottomless thump of the rhythm section. If it wasn't for Clapton's labored vocals, everything would be perfect. As long as he plays his guitar, he can't fail—his solos are white-hot and evocative, original and captivating. When he sings, Clapton loses that sense of originality, choosing to mimic the vocals of the original recordings. At times, his over-emotive singing is painful; he doesn't have the strength to pull off Howlin' Wolf's growl or the confidence to replicate Muddy Waters' assured phrasing. Yet, whenever he plays, it's easier to forget his vocal shortcomings. Even with its faults, *From the Cradle* is one of Clapton's finest moments. —*Stephen Thomas Erlewine*

● **The Cream of Clapton** / Mar. 7, 1995 / Polydor ✦✦✦✦

Eric Clapton was contracted to Polydor Records from 1966 to 1981, first as a member of Cream, then Blind Faith, and later as a solo artist and as the leader of Derek and the Dominos. This 19-track, 79-minute disc surveys his career, presenting an excellent selection from the period, including the Cream hits "Sunshine of Your Love," "White Room," and "Crossroads"; "Presence of the Lord," Clapton's finest moment with Blind Faith; "Bell Bottom Blues" and "Layla" from Derek and the Dominos; and 11 songs from Clapton's solo work, among them the hits "I Shot the Sheriff," "Promises," and "I Can't Stand It." The selection is thus broader and better than that found on 1982's *Time Pieces* collection, and with excellent sound and liner notes by Clapton biographer Ray Coleman, *The Cream of Clapton* stands as the single-disc best-of to own for Clapton's greatest recordings. (Not to be confused with the popular 1987 Polydor [UK] compilation *The Cream of Eric Clapton*, which has since been retitled *The Best of Eric Clapton*.) — *William Ruhlmann*

Eric Clapton's Rainbow Concert [Expanded] / Jul. 25, 1995 / Polydor ♦♦♦

Crossroads 2: Live in the '70s / Apr. 2, 1996 / Polydor Chronicles ♦♦♦
Crossroads was a box set that appealed to both beginners and fanatics. *Crossroads 2 (Live in the Seventies)* only appeals to fanatics. Spanning four discs and consisting almost entirely of live material (there are a handful of studio outtakes), this is music that will only enthrall completists and archivists. For those listeners, there is a wealth of fascinating, compelling performances here, as well as a fair share of mediocre, uninspired tracks. The key word for the entire album is detail—it is an album for studying the intricacies of Clapton's playing and how it evolved. For example, it's easy to hear the differences and progressions between the four versions of Robert Johnson's "Rambling on My Mind." And it is Clapton that evolves, not his supporting band—although they are proficient, they are hardly exciting. However, their static, professional support provides a nice bed to chart Slowhand's growth over the course of the decade, simply because he is *always* the focal point. *Crossroads 2* may only be for a collector, but for those collectors, it is a treasure, even if some of the tracks are fool's gold. — *Stephen Thomas Erlewine*

Dave Clark Five

British Invasion
For a very brief time in 1964, it seemed that the biggest challenger to the Beatles phenomenon was the Dave Clark Five. From the Tottenham area of London, the quintet had the fortune to knock "I Want to Hold Your Hand" off the top of the British charts with "Glad All Over," and were championed (for about 15 minutes) by the British press as the Beatles' most serious threat. They were the first British Invasion band to break in a big way in the States after the Beatles, though the Rolling Stones and others quickly supplanted the DC5 as the Fab Four's most serious rivals. The Dave Clark Five reached the Top 40 seventeen times between 1964 and 1967 with memorable hits like "Glad All Over," "Bits and Pieces," "Because," and a remake of Bobby Day's "Over and Over," as well as making more appearances on the "Ed Sullivan Show" than any other English act. The DC5 were distinguished from their British contemporaries by their larger-than-life production, Clark's loud stomping drum sound, and Mike Smith's leathery vocals. Though accused by detractors of lacking finesse and hipness, they had a solid ear for melodies and harmonies, and wrote much of their early material, the best of which has endured quite well, although their albums were fairly weak. Interestingly, and unusually for that era, bandleader Dave Clark managed and produced the band himself, negotiating a much higher royalty rate than artists of that period usually received. After a couple years of superstardom, the group proved unable to either keep up with the changing times or maintain a high standard of original compositions, and called it quits in 1970. — *Rick Clark & Richie Unterberger*

● **History of the Dave Clark Five** / 1993 / Hollywood ♦♦♦♦
For many years, the Dave Clark Five were one of the few major groups of the 1960s whose work was unavailable on compact disc. This two-disc, 50-track reissue not only rectifies that situation but arguably includes more than all but devoted fans will want to hear. All of the band's mammoth mid-'60s hits —"Glad All Over," "Bits and Pieces," "Because," "Catch Us If You Can," "Any Way You Want It," and others—are included, and while they don't rival the work of British Invasion heavyweights like the Beatles, Stones, and Kinks, they still burst with exuberant melodies, harmonies, and dense production. This compilation also features worthy lesser-known hits like "Try Too Hard" and "Everybody Knows," as well as obscure but commendable beat ballads and raveups from their B-sides and albums. Nonetheless, there is a fair amount of filler, and their post-1966 work is undistinguished by either artistic growth or the hooks and heavy beat of their early material. But at their peak, the DC5 captured the *joie de vivre* of the British Invasion with a lasting power that cannot be dismissed. This reissue includes a comprehensive booklet featuring recollections from Dave Clark himself. — *Richie Unterberger*

Dave Clark Five/The Washington D.C.'s / 1993 / Repertoire ♦♦♦

Dee Clark (Delecta Clark)

b. Nov. 7, 1938, Blytheville, AR, **d.** Dec. 7, 1990
Vocals / Soul, R&B
Dee Clark was a solid R&B vocalist who had some huge hits in the late '50s and early '60s. The Arkansas-born singer moved to Chicago as a child and was in the Hambone Kids with Sammy McGrier and Ronny Strong. They recorded for Okeh in 1952; the next year Clark sang with the Goldentones (this group later became the Kool Gents), then recorded

as the Delegates for Vee-Jay in 1956. Clark went solo in 1957 and in 1958 enjoyed his first smash with "Nobody for You," an Abner release that reached No. 3 R&B and just missed the Top 20 on the pop charts. He continued a string of R&B winners with "Just Keep It Up," "Hey Little Girl," and "How About That" for Abner in 1959 and 1960. Clark teamed with guitarist Phil Upchurch to write "Raindrops" in 1961, his signature tune. The song peaked at No. 3 R&B and No. 2 pop, and was his last major hit. Clark continued performing through the '60s, '70s, and '80s, but never again was a factor, though "Raindrops" remains a staple on oldies radio. — *Ron Wynn*

● **Raindrops [Vee-Jay]** / 1994 / Vee-Jay ♦♦♦♦
Dee Clark was one of the most adaptable R&B vocalists of the '50s and early '60s, as this 25-song reissue shows. He did songs in a Little Richard mode, an Afro-Latin setting, and also performed ballads, novelty tunes ("Kangaroo Hop"), and covers ("Cupid"). Clark's gem was "Raindrops," a song with enough drama, hooks, and appeal to nearly top both the pop and R&B charts. It was his biggest hit, but not his only fine number. There are many cuts, such as "Nobody but You," "What Kind of Fool," and the newly issued "Bring Back My Heart," that equal or even top the tune that made him famous. — *Ron Wynn*

Petula Clark

b. Nov. 15, 1932, Epsom, Surrey, England
Vocals / Pop
By the time Petula Clark made her debut on American pop charts in 1964, she had already developed quite a career as an actress and singer throughout Europe, appearing in over 20 films and selling several million records. "Downtown" is the song that broke her stateside and placed her firmly in the No. 1 spot, displacing the Beatles' "I Feel Fine." Not only was she the first female artist from England to land that chart position, but her follow-up record, *I Know a Place*, went to No. 3. Only Cyndi Lauper has equaled that impressive an entry on her first two chart singles. Despite the competition, "Downtown" won the Grammy for Best Rock & Roll Recording in 1965. Over the next three years, Clark scored fifteen Top 40 pop hits.

Even though Clark's English origins helped her ride in on the first wave of the British Invasion, her music was definitely geared more towards the adult market. — *Rick Clark*

● **Greatest Hits of Petula Clark** / 1986 / GNP ♦♦♦♦
This import collection is much crisper and more vibrant-sounding than the domestic releases. All the major US hits are here, plus some British and European chart successes never heard in the US. — *Bruce Eder*

The Clash

Rock 'n' Roll, Punk
The Clash, 1976-1986, was the most accomplished band to come out of the British punk rock scene of the '70s. The group was formed by guitarist and singer Joe Strummer (b. Jan. 25, 1955), guitarist and singer Mick Jones (b. Jun. 26, 1955), bassist Paul Simonon (b. Dec. 15, 1955), and drummer Terry Chimes—replaced in 1977 by Topper Headon (b. May 30, 1955). They first gained national recognition opening for the Sex Pistols, the other major punk band. But unlike the Pistols, the Clash had a straightforward earnestness to go with their punk anger. Their music was similarly simple, loud, and abrasive.

In December 1979, the Clash released *London Calling*, a critically acclaimed double album that found them expanding their musical style from punk to a more eclectic approach. The album spawned a single in the title song, which became their biggest UK single during their existence, getting to No. 11, while the album hit No. 9 in the UK and was their first real US success at No. 27. "Train in Vain (Stand by Me)" from the album was the Clash's first US chart single, reaching No. 23.

Sandinista!, a triple-LP set released in December 1980 took the eclecticism to new lengths. The album got to a disappointing No. 19 in the UK but was a surprisingly strong No. 24 in the US. The Clash again grazed the Top 40 in the UK with the album's "The Magnificent Seven" in May 1981.

Their next, *Combat Rock* (1982), was a straightforward rock collection that was their last album with the original personnel and their most popular. It hit No. 2 in the UK and No. 7 in the US (where it sold a million copies), and its singles "Should I Stay or Should I Go?" and "Rock the Casbah" were hits on both sides of the Atlantic. Meanwhile, Headon left the band in July 1982, and Jones was fired by Strummer and Simonon in September 1983. He formed Big Audio Dynamite. Strummer and Simonon reorganized and added new members, releasing *Cut the Crap* in the fall of 1985, but by the start of 1986, the Clash was no more. — *William Ruhlmann*

☆ **The Clash** / 1977 / Epic ♦♦♦♦♦
The revised US version of the Clash's first album, containing most of the vital punk anthems of that record, plus such later tunes as "White Man in Hammersmith Palais" and "I Fought the Law." This and the sole Sex Pis-

tols album, *Never Mind the Bollocks, Here's the Sex Pistols*, tell the story of English '70s punk rock. — *William Ruhlmann*

Give 'em Enough Rope / Dec. 1978 / Epic ✦✦✦✦
In retrospect, Sandy Pearlman's production brings a welcome coherence to the Clash's sound, though they sound as aggressive as ever on such songs as "Safe European Home," "English Civil War," and "Tommy Gun." The most moving song is Mick Jones' "Stay Free," however, which may say more about the punk aesthetic than any of Joe Strummer's angry rants. — *William Ruhlmann*

★ **London Calling** / Dec. 1979 / Epic ✦✦✦✦✦
"What are we gonna do now?" asks Joe Strummer at the start of "Clamp-down," one of this album's songs. But by the time you get to that track, it's already clear that the Clash have solved that problem by taking a giant step toward making craftsmanlike rock without sacrificing the urgency that made them punk leaders. From the title track through the reggae, rock, and pop tracks that follow, this is one of the premier albums of its time. — *William Ruhlmann*

Sandinista! / Dec. 1980 / Epic ✦✦
Believe it or not, amidst this messy triple-record (two-CD) set, there are some brilliant songs—the trouble is finding them among the dub experiments, half-finished songs, and overlong jams; listening to all this filler, it's hard to believe that the Clash made a double album the year before with absolutely no weak tracks. Patient listeners will be rewarded by "The Magnificent Seven," "Charlie Don't Surf," and "Police on My Back," and a couple of other tracks that are among the band's best work; however, most will be happy to hear the highlights on Clash compilations. — *Stephen Thomas Erlewine*

Combat Rock / Jun. 1982 / Epic ✦✦✦
The Clash are still a little too individual to be as straight ahead a rock group as much of this album implies they are, but you can't fault a collection that contains the rock energy of "Should I Stay or Should I Go?" and the absurdist danceability of "Rock the Casbah." — *William Ruhlmann*

Cut the Crap / 1985 / Epic ✦✦

Story of the Clash, Vol. 1 / 1988 / Epic ✦✦✦✦
A two-disc, 28-track compilation that ranges over the Clash catalog somewhat haphazardly. Still, this is some of their essential music. — *William Ruhlmann*

Clash on Broadway / 1991 / Epic ✦✦✦✦
A three-disc, 63-track compilation that treats the catalog coherently and chronologically, with all the major songs included. It's a pricey boxed set, but if you want one album that covers the Clash's career, this is it. — *William Ruhlmann*

Super Black Market Clash / 1994 / Epic ✦✦✦✦
An expanded version of the *Black Market Clash* EP, *Super Black Market Clash* adds assorted singles and remixes to the original recording. A couple of tracks aren't that interesting, but the majority of the disc is splendid, featuring some of the band's best but unfortunately overlooked tracks, including "Armagideon Time," "The Prisoner," "Gates of the West," and "Capital Radio One." — *Stephen Thomas Erlewine*

The Clean

Alternative Pop-Rock
The Clean were one of the most influential New Zealand bands of the post-punk era. The band formed in the town of Dunedin in 1978, when Hamish Kilgour (drums) and his brother David (guitar) recruited David's school friend, guitarist Peter Gutteridge. Soon afterward, they opened for New Zealand punk rockers Enemy. The Clean were one of the first bands in the country to play original material. They carved out a distinctive, noisy but melodic sound, distinguished by David's screeching and distorted guitar. When the Kilgour brothers decided in 1979 to relocate the band to Auckland (the country's largest city), Gutteridge had already left the lineup. The Clean played with a rotating bassist before David quit the band and moved back to Dunedin. Once he was back home, he was introduced to bassist Robert Scott and the two started playing together; news of his brother's new musical relationship prompted Hamish to move back to Dunedin and begin the Clean again.

In early 1980, the group began playing around town in earnest. In early 1981, a fan named Roger Shepherd began Flying Nun Records to release a single by the Clean, "Tally Ho!" With its jagged guitar, sweet melody and persistent organ, "Tally Ho!" reached No. 19 on the charts.

As they prepared to record their first album, they discovered the small number of New Zealand engineers didn't care for the band's material. The Clean didn't fight—they backed down, deciding to record on a four-track under the guidance of Chris Knox and Doug Hood. In November, the *Boodle Boodle Boodle* EP was released; it surprised every observer by climbing to No. 4 on the New Zealand charts.

Boodle and the 1982 EP *Great Sounds Great* captured the quirky sides of the Clean's sound, since they did not have the technology to replicate the band's huge, roaring live sound. Later in 1980, the group released its loudest single yet, "Getting Older." Soon after its release,

David Kilgour exited the band, moving back to Dunedin. Robert Scott left after David's departure, forming a band of his own, the Bats. Hamish Kilgour moved to Christchurch—where Flying Nun Records was located—and bought his own four-track. After Hamish had begun writing and recording, David came up to Christchurch to help finish up the solo tracks, as well as to record some Clean songs that were never captured on tape. The resulting music, released under the name the Great Unwashed, was collected on the album *Clean out of Our Minds*. The music was a departure from the Clean's punk-injected sound; instead, it was folkier and more acoustic.

To promote the record, the Kilgours reunited with Peter Gutteridge while still using the name the Great Unwashed. On the ensuing tour, the band concentrated on Gutteridge's backlog of material; at the beginning of 1984, they recorded an EP called *Singles*. *Singles* earned quite a bit of airplay and sales, including a showing of their video on national television. Bassist Ross Humphries was added so David Kilgour and Gutteridge could both play guitar, yet the Great Unwashed wound up breaking up within a year. Hamish Kilgour formed Bailter Space with guitarist Alister Parker, Gutteridge began developing a new band called Snapper, and David stopped playing for a few years.

The Clean—the lineup featuring Robert Scott—reunited in 1988 for two concerts in London; a five-song EP culled from the shows was released a year later. The members of the band were encouraged by the results and decided to embark on a world tour. After the tour ended, the band recorded a new album, which was more straightforward and pop-oriented than their previous material. The record, *Vehicle*, was released in the spring of 1990 and the band supported its release with a world tour. After the tour's completion, the band split again. David Kilgour formed Stephen, Scott returned to the Bats, and Hamish Kilgour was inactive; the group reunited in 1994 to record a new album. — *Stephen Thomas Erlewine*

● **Compilation** / 1986 / Homestead ✦✦✦✦
This is a near-complete collection of material pre-dating the mid-'80s split. — *Steve Aldrich*

Vehicle / 1990 / Rough Trade ✦✦✦

Modern Rock / Oct. 10, 1995 / Summershine ✦✦✦

George Clinton

b. Jul. 22, 1940, Kannapolis, NC
Synthesizer, Keyboards, Vocals / Funk, Urban
George Clinton scored a few solo hits on Capitol in the early '80s, but as the president of Parliament, P. Funk, Funkadelic, and other outfits, Clinton set a new agenda for Black music during the '70s. He combined theater, sci-fi, and funk glossolalia into something that was uniquely his own. On record he loses some of his impact, but it's still the ultimate boom-box music. That Motown passed on him says much for the stripe of Clinton's music. — *Colin Escott*

● **Computer Games** / Nov. 5, 1982 / Capitol ✦✦✦✦
Former Parliament and Funkadelic leader George Clinton made a major comeback under his own name with this album, whose irresistible grooves, vocal choruses, and absurd humor were essentially identical to the music of Funkadelic's salad days. Were you wondering where that "woof-woof" cheer heard on Arsenio Hall and at Black concerts came from? Check out "Atomic Dog." — *William Ruhlmann*

You Shouldn't-Nuf Bit Fish / Dec. 1983 / Capitol ✦✦✦

Some of My Best Jokes Are Friends / Jul. 1985 / Capitol ✦✦

Best of George Clinton / 1986 / Capitol ✦✦✦
This focuses on the best early Clinton material outside of the Parliament/Funkadelic arena. Most of the tracks aren't as humorously spectacular as "Atomic Dog," but there are a couple of stone ones from other albums included besides that masterpiece, such as "Loopzilla." — *Ron Wynn*

Mothership Connection (Live from the Summit, Houston, Texas) / 1986 / Capitol ✦✦

R&B Skeletons in the Closet / Apr. 1986 / Capitol ✦✦✦

The Cinderella Theory / Aug. 1989 / Paisley Park ✦✦✦

Hey Man, Smell My Finger / Oct. 1993 / Paisley Park ✦✦✦✦
Hey Man, Smell My Finger is everything a great George Clinton album should be—conceptually disjointed, overlong, silly, sloppy, and funky as hell. Thankfully, the music here is his best since *Computer Games*, and the album proves just how responsible he is for much of the music of the 1990s, as the irresistible single "Paint the White House Black" illustrates with its numerous cameos. — *Stephen Thomas Erlewine*

Awesome Power of a Fully-Operational Mothership / Jun. 1996 / 550 Music ✦✦

The Clovers

R&B, Doo Wop
One of the earliest doo wop vocal groups, formed in the late '40s in

Washington, DC. Original members were Buddy Bailey, Matthew McQuater, Hal Lucas, Jr., and Harold Winley. Bobby Mitchell replaced Bailey by the time the group was signed to the fledgling Atlantic label in 1950. The Clovers racked up 13 Top Ten R&B hits between 1951 to 1954, all showcasing their solid harmonies and unerring rhythmic verve.

Before the early '50s, most non-gospel Black vocal groups were in the smooth pop vein of the Inkspots and Mills Brothers. Then the Clovers burst on the scene in 1951 with "Don't You Know I Love You," and things would never be the same.

Under the influence of Atlantic Records' Ahmet Ertegun (who wrote and produced most of their early songs), the Clovers combined quartet harmony, the big dance beat of the R&B jump bands, and the rawer sounds of urban blues into an exciting new blend that caught on with the young Black audience and put them consistently at the top of the R&B charts in the early '50s.

Going beyond this, just as their contemporary B.B. King was doing for blues, lead singers Buddy Bailey and later Charlie White brought a gospel influence to Ertegun's bluesy R&B songs—helping to lay the foundation for the soul music to come. — George Bedard & Cub Koda

Love Potion No. 9: The Best of the Clovers / 1991 / EMI America ◆◆◆◆
This compilation features their later sides for United Artists including the classic title track. — Cub Koda

★ **Down in the Alley: The Best of the Clovers** / 1991 / Rhino ◆◆◆◆◆
This is an excellent compilation of their best and earliest sides, including "Nip Sip," "Don't You Know I Love You," and "One Mint Julep." — Cub Koda

The Coasters

R&B, Rock 'n' Roll, Doo Wop
Possibly the most popular doo wop group of the '50s, the Coasters started on the West Coast as the Robins, scoring hits under the writing-and-production helm of Jerry Leiber and Mike Stoller. When Atlantic signed Leiber and Stoller as a production team, the group split into two factions; the core of the group became the Coasters and moved to New York to record, while the Robins continued on the West Coast to diminishing acclaim. The Coasters' hits, some of the most finely crafted, well-written, and hilarious in the genre, continued throughout the rest of the decade. Carl Gardner's sly leads and Bobby Nunn's bass singing defined their sound through numerous personnel changes. When their time on the charts came to an end a number of "Coasters" groups suddenly proliferated (much like the Drifters), many of them still dotting the landscape of a million oldies shows and still singing those classic songs. — Cub Koda

☆ **50 Coastin' Classics: Anthology** / 1992 / Rhino ◆◆◆◆◆
Although it may well be too much for the casual fan, this double CD is easily the best Coasters retrospective ever assembled. Besides featuring every one of their hits, it also contains nine strong tunes cut in the mid-'50s by the Robins, who evolved into the Coasters after some personnel changes. As for the enticing obscurities, "Three Cool Cats" and "Besame Mucho" were cut by the Beatles on unreleased recordings in the early '60s, and "Ain't That Just Like Me" would be a small hit for the Searchers. "Down in Mexico" and "Brazil" are cool R&B/Latin melodramas, and "Shoppin' for Clothes," "What About Us," and "That Is Rock & Roll" are vignettes of youthful independence that stack up against the best songs of Jerry Leiber and Mike Stoller, who wrote most of the group's material. Indeed, there's little difference in quality between the hits and the B-sides on this comp, either in the group's matchless ensemble R&B/comedy vocals or Leiber/Stoller's witty songwriting. The accompanying booklet features comments on most of the tracks by Leiber and Stoller themselves. — Richie Unterberger

★ **The Very Best of the Coasters** / 1993 / Rhino ◆◆◆◆◆
The Coasters were the 1950s' (and early rock's) dominant novelty/comic R&B ensemble, benefiting from Jerry Leiber and Mike Stoller's lyrical wit and inspired production. They weren't simply proficient clowns; the Coasters were a skilled vocal unit whose talents were utilized on slice-of-life narratives, prophetic youth manifestos, and even an occasional teen anthem, as well as the prototype humorous vehicles "Yakety Yak" and "Poison Ivy." Although Rhino has already given them the deluxe two-disc treatment, consumers who either don't want that much Coasters material or prefer only the hits are nicely served by this 18-track anthology. It contains every major release, plus valuable lesser-known selections such as "Shoppin' for Clothes" and "What About Us." — Ron Wynn

Eddie Cochran

b. Oct. 3, 1938, Oklahoma City, OK, **d.** Apr. 17, 1960, Wiltshire, England
Guitar, Vocals / Rock 'n' Roll, Rockabilly
Somehow, time has not accorded Eddie Cochran quite the same respect as other early rockabilly pioneers like Buddy Holly, or even Ricky Nelson or Gene Vincent. This is partially attributable to his very brief lifespan as a star: he only had a couple of big hits before dying in a car crash during

a British tour in 1960. He was in the same league as the best rockabilly stars, though, with a brash, fat guitar sound that helped lay the groundwork for the power chord. He was also a good songwriter and singer, celebrating the joys of teenage life—the parties, the music, the adolescent rebellion—with an economic wit that bore some similarities to Chuck Berry. Cochran was more lighthearted and less ironic than Berry, though, and if his work was less consistent and not as penetrating, it was almost always exuberant.

Cochran's mid-'50s beginnings in the record industry are a bit confusing. His family had moved to Southern California around 1950, and in 1955 he made his first recordings as half of the Cochran Brothers. Here's the confusing part: although the other half of the act was really named Hank Cochran, he was *not* Eddie's brother. (Hank Cochran would become a noted country songwriter in the 1960s.) Eddie was already an accomplished rockabilly guitarist and singer on these early sides, and he started picking up some session work as well, also finding time to make demos and write songs with Jerry Capehart, who became his manager.

Cochran's big break came about in a novel fashion. In mid-1956, while Cochran and Capehart were recording some music for low-budget films, Boris Petroff asked Eddie if he'd be interested in appearing in a movie that a friend was directing. The film was *The Girl Can't Help It*, and the song he would sing in it was "Twenty Flight Rock." This is the same song that Paul McCartney would use to impress John Lennon upon their first meeting in 1957 (Paul could not only play it, but knew all of the lyrics).

Cochran had his first Top 20 hit in early 1957, "Sittin' in the Balcony," with an echo-chambered vocal reminiscent of Elvis. That single was written by John D. Loudermilk, but Eddie would write much of his material, including his only Top Ten hit, "Summertime Blues." A definitive teenage anthem with hints of the overt protest that would seep into rock music in the 1960s, it was also a technical tour de force for the time: Cochran overdubbed himself on guitar to create an especially thick sound. One of the classic early rock singles, "Summertime Blues" was revived a decade later by proto-metal group Blue Cheer, and was a concert staple for the Who, who had a small American hit with a cover version. (Let's not mention Alan Jackson's country rendition in the 1990s.)

That, disappointingly, was the extent of Cochran's major commercial success in the US "C'mon Everybody," a chugging rocker that was almost as good as "Summertime Blues," made the Top 40 in 1959, and also gave Eddie his first British Top Tenner. As is the case with his buddy Gene Vincent, though, you can't judge his importance by mere chart statistics. Cochran was very active in the studio, and while his output wasn't nearly as consistent as Buddy Holly's (another good friend of Eddie's), he laid down a few classic or near-classic cuts that are just as worthy as his hits. "Somethin' Else," "My Way" (which the Who played in concert at the peak of psychedelia), "Weekend" (covered by the Move), and "Nervous Breakdown" are some of the best of these, and belong in the collection of every rockabilly fan. He was also (like Holly) an innovator in the studio, using overdubbing at a time when that practice was barely known on rock recordings.

Cochran is more revered today in Britain than the US, due in part to the tragic circumstances of his death. In the spring of 1960, he toured the UK with Vincent, to a wild reception, in a country that had rarely had the opportunity to see American rock 'n' roll stars in the flesh. En route to London to fly back to the States for a break, the car Cochran was riding in, with his girlfriend (and songwriter) Sharon Sheeley and Gene Vincent, had a severe accident. Vincent and Sheeley survived, but Cochran died less than a day later, at the age of 21. — Richie Unterberger

The Early Years / 1988 / Ace ◆◆◆

Box Set / 1988 / Liberty ◆◆◆
This six-LP import—which still, somehow, manages not to include every track Cochran recorded—is excessive for the non-fanatic. Nevertheless, it does include quite a few obscure, interesting pre-fame performances from the mid-'50s (some as part of the Cochran Brothers). Other bonuses include a live 1960 British TV broadcast, an album's worth of sessions and his work as a producer, and entire sides of instrumentals and stereo versions, as well as a 32-page booklet. — Richie Unterberger

★ **Legendary Masters** / 1990 / EMI America ◆◆◆◆◆
The definitive single-disc collection of Cochran's best: "Summertime Blues," "Cut Across Shorty," "Something Else," "Come on Everybody," and "Twenty Flight Rock." All the hits; all the feeling. — Cub Koda

Bruce Cockburn

b. May 27, 1945, Ottawa, Canada
Dulcimer, Guitar, Vocals / Singer-Songwriter
Immensely popular in his native Canada, Bruce Cockburn has found only cult success south of the border, in spite of a rich, varied body of work and considerable critical nods. He has won numerous Juno Awards and has kept the quality control on most of his albums at a high level. Cockburn began his musical career traveling through Europe and performing in the streets; he later enrolled at Boston's Berklee School of Music. Prior to recording his self-titled solo debut in 1970, Cockburn

played organ in a Top 40 cover band and then harmonica in a blues group. Cockburn's first decade of work (1970-1979) is largely literate, singer-songwriter folk-rock, often with a strong Christian tone and mystical, devotional lyrics. In 1979, Cockburn had his only major US single, "Wondering Where the Lions Are," which peaked at No. 21. The accompanying album, *Dancing in the Dragon's Jaw*, saw Cockburn augmenting his music with worldbeat rhythms, an approach he would continue over his next few albums. Cockburn toned down his Christian viewpoint for much of the 1980s, partially as a way of disconnecting himself from the American religious right, which he found antithetical to his own spiritual beliefs, and partially to concentrate on more humanitarian, political subject matter. Cockburn had traveled extensively across several continents, which provided him with a wide musical palette and plenty of injustice to address in his songs. In 1984, Cockburn produced an AOR hit, "If I Had a Rocket Launcher," whose accompanying video depicted conditions in war-torn Central America and gained a fair amount of MTV play. Cockburn's later 1980s work took on a more streamlined rock sound, and his political agenda was weighted towards environmental concerns, as well as oppression. In the 1990s, Cockburn has returned to a more introspective feel recalling his earlier work. He also performed at President Clinton's inaugural celebration in 1993. *—Steve Huey*

Bruce Cockburn / 1971 / Epic ♦♦

Joy Will Find a Way / 1975 / Columbia ♦♦♦

In the Falling Dark / 1976 / Columbia ♦♦♦♦
The follow-up to *Joy Will Find a Way* possesses some Cockburn standards in "Festival of Friends," the propulsive folk-jazz of "Silver Wheels," the meditative "Lord of the Starfields," and the title cut. The lyrics involve increasingly complex mystical Christian metaphors. Cockburn's exceptional guitar technique is showcased on the instrumental "Water into Wine." *—Rick Clark*

Further Adventures of Bruce Cockburn / 1978 / East Side Digital ♦♦♦

Dancing in the Dragons Jaws / 1979 / Columbia ♦♦♦♦
Cockburn's first stateside success produced a No. 21 pop hit with "Wondering Where the Lions Are," but there is much better material to be found here on one of his best albums. The lyrics tend to be spacier, and, musically, Cockburn begins to aggressively synthesize Third World rhythms with his singer-songwriter-style folk. *—Rick Clark*

Humans / Nov. 1980 / Columbia ♦♦♦♦
This follow-up isn't as accessible as *Dancing in the Dragon's Jaws*, but it's possibly Cockburn's most brilliant artistic statement, where the struggles of the general human condition and (more personally) a divorce cause this Christian mystic to dig deep and grapple with more down-to-earth issues. With some of his most powerfully poetic lyrics he maintains a fine balance between lofty intentions and grave disappointments. Musically, it is a heady dose of worldbeat folk. *—Rick Clark*

Inner City Front / 1981 / Columbia ♦♦♦

The Trouble with Normal / 1983 / Columbia ♦♦♦♦
On this, another consistently strong effort, Cockburn's brainy lyrics occasionally border on the didactic, but the imagery is usually brilliant. "Waiting for the Moon" is one of his most beautiful songs. The title cut is released in two totally different versions; the True North rendition is preferable. *—Rick Clark*

Stealing Fire / 1984 / Columbia ♦♦♦

World of Wonders / 1986 / Columbia ♦♦♦
Cockburn's noble agenda to enlighten the planet about human oppression (with numerous on-the-money observations) sometimes makes the listener feel a little bludgeoned in the process. Nevertheless, it has more than enough highlights to make this well worth seeking out, particularly "Berlin Tonight," "Call It Democracy," "Lily of the Midnight Sky," and the title cut. *—Rick Clark*

Rumours of Glory / 1986 / Plane ♦♦♦
This well-compiled 1985 anthology is heavy on Cockburn's middle period. In spite of some duplication, it's a nice complement to the *Waiting for a Miracle* double-disc. (Import) *—Rick Clark*

● **Waiting for a Miracle** / Jan. 1987 / Gold Castle ♦♦♦♦
This double-disc best-of collection is geared around Cockburn's Canadian singles—an odd approach, considering that much of his strongest material never enjoyed radio airplay. Because of that, *Waiting for a Miracle (Singles 1970-1987)* isn't definitive, but it is a very good collection (mainly because Cockburn is practically incapable of writing a bad song). Nevertheless, Cockburn has yet to receive the kind of treatment he deserves for a collection. *Waiting for a Miracle* is the best overview of Cockburn's music, by default. (Canadian Import) *—Rick Clark*

Big Circumstance / 1989 / Columbia ♦♦♦
Cockburn tries to balance the edge-rock approach of recent work with more reflective earlier sounds. He's most successful at illuminating big issues when he's focusing on his personal backyard (on "Understanding Nothing," "Don't Feel Your Touch") rather than the "Tibetan Side of

Town." Surprise element: Cockburn displays rare flashes of humor. *—Rick Clark*

Live / 1990 / Gold Castle ♦♦♦

Nothing but a Burning Light / 1991 / Columbia ♦♦♦
This T-Bone Burnett-produced effort finds Cockburn returning to the more introspective quiet spirit of his earlier work, including his most open Christian expressions in years, particularly "Cry of a Tiny Babe," a Cockburn-style Christmas story, and "Somebody Touched Me." "One of the Best Ones" is classic reflective Cockburn. Although not one of his best albums, it's a nice breather from the relentless heaviness of his last few efforts. *—Rick Clark*

Dart to the Heart / 1994 / Columbia ♦♦♦
With the exception of a few revved-up numbers (some with slide guitar and horns), this is a fairly subdued affair, featuring Cockburn's exquisite guitar work and insightful lyricism that is simultaneously grounded and mystical. It's a typically fine album for this consummate artist. *—Rick Clark*

Joe Cocker (John Robert Cocker)

b. May 20, 1944, Sheffield, England
Vocals / Adult Contemporary, Pop-Rock

After starting out as an unsuccessful pop singer (working under the name Vance Arnold), Joe Cocker found his niche singing rock and soul in the pubs of England with his superb backing group, the Grease Band. He hit No. 1 in the UK in November 1968 with his version of the Beatles' "A Little Help from My Friends." His career really took off after he sang that song at the Woodstock festival in August 1969. A second British hit came with a version of Leon Russell's "Delta Lady" in the fall of 1969 (by then, Russell was Cocker's musical director) and both of his albums, *With a Little Help from My Friends* and *Joe Cocker!*, went gold in America. In 1970, his cover of the Box Tops' hit "The Letter" became his first US Top Ten. Cocker's first peak of success came when Russell organized the "Mad Dogs & Englishmen" tour of 1970, featuring Cocker and over 40 others, and resulting in a third gold album and a concert film. Subsequent efforts were less popular, and problems with alcohol (both on stage and off) reduced Cocker's once-powerful voice to a croaking rasp. But he returned to the US Top Ten with the romantic ballad "You Are So Beautiful" in 1975 and topped the charts in a duet with Jennifer Warnes on "Up Where We Belong," the theme from the 1982 film *An Officer and a Gentleman*. He has survived, still charting into the '90s. It's unlikely we've heard the last of him, since the man still seems capable of making any song his own. *—Cub Koda & William Ruhlmann*

With a Little Help from My Friends / Apr. 1969 / A&M ♦♦♦♦
The album that foisted Joe Cocker on an unsuspecting public is full of tasteful, raucous covers, Cocker's trademark hysterical vocals, and outstanding studio backing by pros like Jimmy Page and Steve Winwood. *—Tom Graves*

Joe Cocker! / Oct. 1969 / A&M ♦♦♦♦
The rare sophomore effort that was an improvement over the first, it features great tracks (and vocals) like "Delta Lady" and "She Came in Through the Bathroom Window." Arguably, it's Cocker's most soulful album. *—Tom Graves*

Mad Dogs & Englishmen / Aug. 1970 / A&M ♦♦♦♦
A superb document of Cocker's high-energy 1970 tour, it included about a zillion musicians and hangers-on. All the goods are here, and many consider this Cocker's last great moment. *—Tom Graves*

I Can Stand a Little Rain / Aug. 1974 / A&M ♦♦♦

Jamaica Say You Will / Aug. 1975 / A&M ♦♦

Joe Cocker's Greatest Hits / Nov. 1977 / A&M ♦♦♦
Greatest Hits features most, but not all (no "She Came in Through the Bathroom Window" or "It's a Sin When You Love Somebody"), of his biggest hits from the early '70s. Nevertheless, there's plenty of fine music here, making the record a solid compilation. *—Stephen Thomas Erlewine*

● **Classics, Vol. 4** / 1987 / A&M ♦♦♦♦
A solid collection from his 1967-1976 peak, it includes "Feeling Alright," "You Are So Beautiful," and "With a Little Help from My Friends." *—Dan Heilman*

The Best of Joe Cocker / Mar. 16, 1993 / Capitol ♦♦♦♦
Although Cocker's Capitol material wasn't as consistent as his A&M work, this compilation successfully distills the highlights, including the splendid "When the Night Comes," onto a single CD. *—Stephen Thomas Erlewine*

Have a Little Faith / Sep. 8, 1994 / 550 Music/Epic ♦♦♦

Long Voyage Home / 1995 / A&M ♦♦♦♦
Long Voyage Home: The Silver Anniversary Collection is nearly the definitive Joe Cocker anthology, covering his recording career from the late '60s to the mid-'90s, featuring material from all the labels he

recorded for—A&M, Elektra, Island, and Capitol. After an early single from 1965 (a version of the Beatles' "I'll Cry Instead"), the set skips ahead to his late-'60s recordings with his Mad Dogs & Englishmen troupe. From there, the collection doesn't miss many of Cocker's greatest hits or favorite album tracks. In addition to the familiar tracks, there are a handful of unreleased cuts that are tantalizing for the collector; casual fans will find them of marginal interest. — *Stephen Thomas Erlewine*

Cocteau Twins

Alternative Pop-Rock

One of the most unique, distinctive bands of the '80s was the Cocteau Twins, an ethereal, prolific Scottish trio. Over the course of the decade, they became a major force in alternative music, although there isn't much that is forceful about their music. Instead, their music is a series of soundscapes, created with guitars, studio effects, drum machines, and Elizabeth Fraser's expansive vocals; she sings words according to their sound, not their meaning. With their atmospheric records and lush album covers, the band was the embodiment of England's arty 4AD record label during the '80s. As their career progressed, the Cocteau Twins began to harness their sound into more concrete songs, culminating in 1990's *Heaven or Las Vegas*. After one more album on 4AD, the band switched labels; with the new record company, their music started to veer slightly into new age territory, a genre that was in debt to the Cocteaus' previous records. In 1996, they released *Milk & Kisses*. — *Stephen Thomas Erlewine*

Head over Heels / 1983 / 4AD ✦✦✦✦
Where the Cocteau Twins' first album relied more on texture than songs, *Head over Heels* melds their dreamy, hazy soundscapes to actual songs. — *Stephen Thomas Erlewine*

Treasure / 1984 / 4AD ✦✦✦✦
On *Treasure*, the Cocteau Twins' rich, gauzy layers of sound are positively entrancing. It doesn't matter what Elizabeth Fraser is singing; her voice is only another element in the endless sonic textures. — *Stephen Thomas Erlewine*

Victorialand / 1986 / 4AD ✦✦✦

● **Pink Opaque** / 1986 / 4AD ✦✦✦✦
A compilation of the Cocteau Twins' first records, *Pink Opaque* offers a good introduction to their music. — *Stephen Thomas Erlewine*

● **Blue Bell Knoll** / 1988 / 4AD ✦✦✦✦
This, the first Cocteau Twins regular studio album to be released in the US, is typical of their earlier UK output: keyboards and guitars swirl together into sonic landscapes, over which (or rather, buried within which) Elizabeth Fraser sings in a high, ethereal voice reminiscent of Kate Bush and Jane Siberry, the difference being that the lyrics are utterly unintelligible. The result is classy mood music that might appeal to the new crop of Enya fans. — *William Ruhlmann*

Heaven or Las Vegas / 1990 / 4AD ✦✦✦
The song structures are more discernible, as are the lyrics, which perhaps makes this a little less mysterious than most Cocteau Twins albums, and a little more accessible, if also less characteristic. — *William Ruhlmann*

Four-Calendar Cafe / Sep. 27, 1993 / Capitol ✦✦✦

Milk & Kisses / Apr. 1996 / Capitol ✦✦✦

Leonard Cohen

b. Sep. 21, 1934, Montreal, Canada
Guitar, Vocals / Singer-Songwriter

One of the most interesting and enduring, if not the most successful singer-songwriters of the late 1960s, Leonard Cohen has retained a substantial following for more than 30 years, along with the attention of critics who long since ceased worrying about new works by most of his contemporaries.

Cohen was born nearly a decade earlier than the Beatles or the Rolling Stones, and a year before Elvis Presley, but his personal, social and intellectual background couldn't be more different than *any* rock stars of any generation, nor can he be easily compared even with any members of the generation of folk singers that came of age in the 1960's—he didn't start performing or recording until he was in his mid-30's, after he had already written several books. As an established novelist and poet, his literary accomplishments far exceed those of Bob Dylan, though as a performer, his rather monotone voice is less appealing than Dylan's singing.

Leonard Cohen was born into a middle-class Jewish family in the Montreal suburb of Westmount. His father, a clothing merchant, died when Cohen was nine years old. Cohen was raised in a progressive environment, and was encouraged to express himself at an early age. He took up the guitar at age 13, initially as a way to impress a girl, but within a year or two was singing his own songs at local cafes. He majored in English at McGill University, and despite average grades, won the McNaughton Prize in creative writing before graduating in 1955. His first book of poetry, *Let Us Compare Mythologies*, was published the following year, and became a critical success. Two more books of his poetry followed, along with an attempt to join the family business and a stint at Columbia University, but primarily Cohen wrote—his work was popular enough to pay him a modest royalty which, when coupled with government-sponsored literary grants and a family legacy, allowed him to live comfortably. He also lived a very free lifestyle, involving many women, experiments with LSD when it was still legal, and travels around the world. Cohen became almost as well known in Canada for his iconoclastic behavior as his writing, and only seemed to benefit from these extra-literary activities, in terms of recognition, especially in America.

Two novels, *The Favorite Game* (1963) and *Beautiful Losers* (1966), solidified his reputation in mid-decade. He had written songs ever since his mid-teens, and even these began attracting attention. Judy Collins, one of the top folk talents to emerge during the mid-1960's, cut a version of Cohen's "Suzanne" that proved extremely popular, garnering considerable radio airplay and becoming one of her most popular numbers, and she persuaded Cohen to join her on the folksong circuit. He made his debut during the summer of 1967 at the Newport Folk Festival, followed by a pair of sold out concerts in New York City and an appearance singing his songs and reciting his poems on the CBS network television show *Camera Three*. At around the same time, actor/singer Noel Harrison brought "Suzanne" onto the pop charts with a recording of his own.

Cohen was signed to Columbia Records, and in early 1968 his first album, *The Songs of Leonard Cohen*, was released. Despite its spare production and melancholy subject matter—or, very possibly because of it—the album was an immediate hit by the standards of the folk music world and the budding singer-songwriter community. College students by the thousands bought it—in its second year of release, the record sold over 100,000 copies. *The Songs of Leonard Cohen* was as close as Cohen ever got to mass audience success. His next album, *Songs from a Room* (1969), was characterized by a similar spirit of melancholy, but was less well received commercially and critically. The album did have a pair of tracks, "Bird On a Wire" and "The Story of Isaac," that became standards rivalling "Suzanne." Cohen's third album, *Songs of Love and Hate* (1971), showed a slackening of interest in his work, as his following retreated to well-established cult status, despite the presence of the acclaimed songs "Joan of Arc" and "Famous Blue Raincoat." *Leonard Cohen: Live Songs* was released in 1973.

Despite the critical misgivings about his vocal abilities, Cohen always had enough of a following to justify another long-player every other year or so. Meanwhile, in 1973, his music became the basis for a theatrical production called *Sisters of Mercy*, conceived by Gene Lesser and loosely based on Cohen's life, or at least a fantasy version of his life. A three-year lag ensued between *Songs of Love and Hate* and Cohen's next album, and most critics and fans just assumed he'd hit a dry spell. His 1974 release *New Skin for Old Ceremony* seemed to justify his fans' continued faith in his work. The new songs were still depressing and bleak, but also surprising in the language and their revelations. Columbia Records released *The Best of Leonard Cohen* in 1975. In 1977, Cohen reappeared with *Death of a Ladies' Man*. Cohen's most controversial album, *Death of a Ladies' Man* was produced by the reclusive and enigmatic producer Phil Spector, and suffered from the worst attributes of Cohen's and Spector's work—it was overly dense and self-consciously imposing in its sound, and it virtually bathed the listener in Cohen's depressive persona, still limited in presentation to a monotone delivery.

Cohen's next two albums, *Recent Songs* (1979) and *Various Positions* (1985, Passport Records), attracted relatively little attention despite their strong respective song lineups. *I'm Your Man* (1988, Columbia), however, benefited from the release a year earlier of Jennifer Warnes' *Famous Blue Raincoat*, a collection of Cohen's best work presented by a singer with a very attractive voice—it sold very well and served to remind the public of the worth of Cohen's music. Cohen rose to the occasion with *I'm Your Man*, introducing humor (albeit rather black humor) to his mix of pessimism and poetic conceits, with the result that the album was his best-selling record in more than a decade. Four years later, Cohen released *The Future*, an album that dwelt on the many threats facing humankind in the coming years and decades. Not the stuff of pop charts or MTV heavy rotation, it attracted Cohen's usual coterie of fans, and enough press interest as well as sufficient sales, to justify the release in 1994 of his second concert album, *Live*. — *Bruce Eder*

★ **The Songs of Leonard Cohen** / 1968 / Columbia ✦✦✦✦✦
His debut album features such standards as "Suzanne," "Sisters of Mercy," and "So Long Marianne." Many of these were featured in the 1971 Warren Beatty film, *McCabe and Mrs. Miller*. — *William Ruhlmann*

Songs from a Room / 1969 / Columbia ✦✦✦✦
Includes his versions of his classics, "Bird on a Wire" and "Story of Isaac." — *William Ruhlmann*

Songs of Love and Hate / 1971 / Columbia ✦✦✦✦
"Famous Blue Raincoat," "Joan of Arc," and more great Cohen songs. — *William Ruhlmann*

Leonard Cohen: Live Songs / 1973 / Columbia ✦✦

New Skin for Old Ceremony / 1974 / Columbia ✦✦✦

The Best of Leonard Cohen / 1975 / Columbia ✦✦✦✦
While it isn't a definitive collection, *Best of Leonard Cohen* is a fine cross-section of some of Cohen's best songs. —*Stephen Thomas Erlewine*

Death of a Ladies' Man / 1977 / Columbia ✦✦

Recent Songs / 1979 / Columbia ✦✦✦

Various Positions / 1985 / Passport ✦✦✦

I'm Your Man / 1988 / Columbia ✦✦✦✦
Pessimism, humor, and poetry add up to a profound world view in Cohen's most recent collection. —*William Ruhlmann*

The Future / Nov. 10, 1992 / Columbia ✦✦✦✦
On his latest recording, Canada's poet-musician laureate has glimpsed *The Future*, and it's not a pretty sight. Cohen's apocalyptic vision takes us through a morbid roll-call that includes torture, environmental destruction, drug abuse, abortion, sexual abuse, murder, Stalin, Charles Manson, Hiroshima, and (shudder) lousy poets. And that's just the title track. Instrumental backings focus mostly on unobtrusive textures—synths, strings, female backing vocals, and the occasional flavor of pedal steel guitar, mandolin, fiddle, and horns. —*Roch Parisien*

Live / 1994 / Columbia ✦✦

Lloyd Cole & the Commotions

Singer-Songwriter, Alternative Pop-Rock
Scottish singer-songwriter Lloyd Cole formed the Commotions, who served as his backup band, in Glasgow in 1983. The group featured guitarist Nick Clark, bassist Lawrence Donegan, keyboard player Blair Cowan, and drummer Steven Irvine. Influenced by Bob Dylan and the Band, Cole and the Commotions developed a familiar-sounding but distinctive folk-rock sound, highlighted by Cole's literate lyrics. The group signed to Polydor in 1984 and scored a series of UK hits, including "Perfect Skin." In 1989, he split the band and moved to New York, where he recorded *Lloyd Cole*, his debut solo album, with New York session players such as Voidoid and Lou Reed guitarist Robert Quine. Cole has garnered considerable critical acclaim, but so far has failed to make a commercial impact in the US. —*William Ruhlmann*

Rattlesnakes / Oct. 1984 / Capitol ✦✦✦✦
Cole's debut album reflects his Glasgow surroundings but also incorporates a Dylanish attitude toward them, with the Commotions proving to be a cohesive backup unit. Originally released in the UK by Polydor Records in 1984, *Rattlesnakes* was released in the US in 1985 by Geffen and reissued by Capitol in 1988. —*William Ruhlmann*

Easy Pieces / Nov. 1985 / Capitol ✦✦✦
Producers Clive Langer and Alan Winstanley created a shimmering pop surface for Lloyd Cole and the Commotions' second album, sweetening the tracks with string and brass counter-melodies and emphasizing the chiming highs of the guitar and keyboards for an attractive sound that echoed British bands like the Hollies and Herman's Hermits, circa 1966. It was, of course, like sugar-coating cyanide capsules, given Lloyd Cole's pleasantly sung lyrics, which detailed philosophical disillusionment, romantic discord, and attempted suicide. In the UK, *Easy Pieces* was a Top Ten hit, but no American breakthrough materialized. (*Easy Pieces* was reissued by Capitol in October 1988.) —*William Ruhlmann*

Mainstream / Sep. 1987 / Capitol ✦✦

● **1984-1989** / Jun. 1989 / Capitol ✦✦✦✦
The compilation *1984-1989* features nearly all of the best moments from Lloyd Cole and the Commotions' three albums, making it the perfect introduction to his music. —*Stephen Thomas Erlewine*

Lloyd Cole / Feb. 1990 / Capitol ✦✦✦

Don't Get Weird on Me Babe / Sep. 16, 1991 / Capitol ✦✦✦

Bad Vibes / Oct. 1993 / Rykodisc ✦✦✦

Love Story / Oct. 3, 1995 / Rykodisc ✦✦✦

Natalie Cole

b. Feb. 6, 1950, Los Angeles, CA
Piano, Vocals / Soul, Urban, Adult Contemporary
The daughter of jazz and pop legend Nat "King" Cole, Natalie Cole has forged a successful career in two phases, doing R&B/Urban Contemporary and then jazz-based pop. She made her stage debut at age 11 and sang in college. Cole met the writing and producing team of Chuck Jackson and Marvin Yancey in 1973. The next year they collaborated on some sessions that were recorded at Curtis Mayfield's Curtom studios in Chicago. These helped her land a deal with Capitol, and she teamed with Jackson/Yancey for a string of hit albums and singles from 1975 until 1983. Such LPs as *Inseparable, Natalie, Thankful, Unpredictable*, and *I Love You So* yielded five No. 1 R&B hits between 1975 and 1977. These included "This Will Be," "Inseparable," "Our Love," and "I've Got Love on My Mind." She stayed with Capitol until 1983, then switched to Epic for

her final album with the Jackson/Yancey tandem. Cole made duets with Peabo Bryson in 1979 and 1980 and Ray Parker, Jr., in 1987. She scored more hits with "Jump Start," "I Live for Your Love," and "Over You" in 1987, and "Pink Cadillac," a cover of a Bruce Springsteen tune, in 1988, and then made her stylistic shift. Cole eased into the transition with "When I Fall in Love," a number her father recorded in 1957. It was included on her 1987 LP, *Everlasting*. She fully embraced the move with the 1991 LP *Unforgettable with Love*, earning Grammy awards and landing a No. 1 pop album that eventually sold over five million copies. The title track featured her doing a duet with her father via electronic elaboration. She continued the jazzy trend with *Take a Look* in 1993, and has toured and done television specials working with a large orchestra conducted by Nelson Riddle. Cole was among several African-American artists who teamed with country stars on the 1994 LP *Rhythm, Country and Blues*. It proved a smash on the R&B, country, and pop charts. —*Ron Wynn*

The Collection / 1988 / Capitol ✦✦✦✦
This contains the finest soul and sophisticated pre-rock pop tracks from Cole's days at Capitol (1975-1981). Cole made some superb singles in her early days, especially "This Will Be" and "Inseparable." At the same time, she laid the foundation for the early-'90s change that would surprise those who slept on "Mr. Melody" or "I've Got Love on My Mind." Her voice was actually more suited for these songs than the soul numbers, which were as much production and arranging triumphs as vocal victories. —*Ron Wynn*

● **Unforgettable** / 1991 / Elektra ✦✦✦✦
Natalie Cole found new glory with pre-rock pop in 1991. She earned commercial and critical success with an electronically manipulated duet with her father Nat on "Unforgettable." The subsequent album also contained some fine vocals by Natalie, doing decent renditions of such songs as "Avalon" and "Lush Life," but it was the title cut that recreated her as a diva in the Anita Baker mode. The album sold over five million copies. —*Ron Wynn*

Take a Look / 1993 / Elektra ✦✦✦✦
Those who questioned whether Natalie Cole had either the will or skill to succeed with another session of pre-rock popular music need wonder no more. There are another 18 jazz-tinged and early pop numbers, with some unexpected pleasures ("Calypso Blues," "It's Sand Man") and spectacular triumphs ("Cry Me a River," "Fiesta in Blue," "I'm Beginning to See the Light"). Cole is now completely comfortable with the pacing, flow, and sensibility of pre-rock material; she has no problems with articulation or delivery, either. —*Ron Wynn*

Collins Kids

Rockabilly
By the time Lawrence (b. 1944) and Lawrencine (b. 1942) Collins were 11 and 13, respectively, they were already tearing it up on country package shows, recording for Columbia Records, and performing on national TV almost weekly. Older sister Lorrie held up the cowgirl fringe-rustling-against-nylons teenage-sensuality department; kid brother Larry was a bundle of hyperkinetic energy, bopping all over the place while laying down exciting, twangy guitar breaks learned firsthand from the "King of Doublenecked Mosrite," Joe Maphis. The Collins' recordings as time went on veered from mawkish brother/sister country-style duets to white-hot rockabilly, and they were just reaching their peak when Lorrie eloped, effectively breaking up the act. Revered by rockabilly collectors the world over, their filmed television appearances and recordings are testimony to the fact that the Collins Kids weren't just "good for their age," they were just plain good, period. —*Cub Koda*

Introducing Larry and Lorrie / 1958 / Columbia Special Products ✦✦✦
For those who don't want to spring for the lengthy and expensive Bear Family box, this is an excellent distillation of 12 of their best late-'50s rockabilly sides. "Hoy Hoy," "Whistle Bait," "Mercy," "Just Because," and "Party" rank among the most smokin' rockabilly sides ever waxed. —*Richie Unterberger*

● **Hop Skip & Jump** / Aug. 1991 / Bear Family ✦✦✦✦
A two-CD boxed set covering the Kids' entire career. —*Cub Koda*

Rockin' on T.V. / 1993 / Krazy Kat ✦✦✦✦
Thirty-one performances taken from various *Town Hall Party* television performances from 1957 to 1961. Sound is suspect in spots, naturally, but the energy level makes such arguments superfluous. Highlights include "Kokomo," "Chantilly Lace," "Lonesome Road," "Way down Yonder in New Orleans," and decidedly left-field takes on three Buddy Holly songs. Highly recommended. —*Cub Koda*

Phil Collins

b. Jan. 31, 1951, London, England
Drums, Vocals / Adult Contemporary, Pop-Rock
Phil Collins' ascent to the status of one of the most successful pop and adult-contemporary singers of the '80s and beyond was probably as

much of a surprise to him as it was to many others. Balding and diminutive, Collins was almost 30 years old when his first solo single, "In the Air Tonight," became a No. 2 hit in his native UK (the song was a Top 20 hit in the US). Between 1984 and 1990, Collins had a string of 13 straight US Top Ten hits. Long before any of that happened, however, Collins was a child actor/singer who appeared as the Artful Dodger in the London production of *Oliver!* in 1964. (He also has a cameo in *A Hard Day's Night*, among other films.) He got his first break in music at the end of his teens, when he was chosen to be a replacement drummer in the British art-rock band Genesis in 1970. (Collins maintained a separate jazz career with the band Brand X, as well.) Genesis was fronted by singer Peter Gabriel. They had achieved a moderate level of success in the UK and the US, with elaborate concept albums, before Gabriel abruptly left in 1974. Genesis auditioned 400 singers without success, then decided to let Collins have a go.

The result was a gradual simplifying of Genesis' sound and an increasing focus on Collins' expressive, throaty voice. *And Then There Were Three...* went gold in 1978, and *Duke* was even more successful. Collins made his debut solo album *Face Value* in 1981, which turned out to be a bigger hit than any Genesis album. It concentrated on Collins' voice, often in stark, haunting contexts such as the piano-and-drum dirge "In the Air Tonight," which sounded like something from John Lennon's debut solo album, *John Lennon/Plastic Ono Band*. Collins' continuing solo work has not meant the end of Genesis. In fact, he balances group and solo careers with enormous success. In 1992, Genesis released *We Can't Dance* and began an extensive tour, and it seems likely that Collins' double success will continue. — *William Ruhlmann*

Face Value / 1981 / Atlantic ♦♦♦♦
Collins proves himself a passionate singer (and distinctive drummer) with a gift for both deeply felt ballads and snarling rockers. His debut album transformed him from the frontman of Genesis to a solo star who happened to be in Genesis, too. Contains "In the Air Tonight" and "I Missed Again." — *William Ruhlmann*

Hello, I Must Be Going / 1982 / Atlantic ♦♦♦
As his hit cover of "You Can't Hurry Love" demonstrates, Collins began to inject his highly melodic pop songwriting with more soul and R&B influences on his second solo album. While some of the material was successful, much of it showed that he was still coming to grips with how to incorporate R&B techniques into his style; in retrospect, *Hello, I Must Be Going* laid the groundwork for his breakthrough album, *No Jacket Required*. — *Stephen Thomas Erlewine*

● **No Jacket Required** / 1985 / Atlantic ♦♦♦♦
From ballads like the No. 1 "One More Night" to uptempo funk like the No. 1 "Sussudio," another tour de force in what was by now one of the most identifiable styles in pop music. The 1985 Grammy winner for Album of the Year. — *William Ruhlmann*

But Seriously / 1989 / Atlantic ♦♦♦

Serious Hits...Live! / 1990 / Atlantic ♦♦

Both Sides / 1993 / Atlantic ♦♦♦

Colourfield
New Wave
By the summer of 1983, the Fun Boy Three were peaking in popularity and Hall disbanded the group. Hooking up with ex-Swinging Cats members Toby Lyons and Karl Shale, Terry Hall moved to Manchester and formed the Colourfield, a more lush and melodic outfit than the Fun Boy Three. In January of 1984, the band released their first single, "The Colourfield," which just missed the Top 40. It was followed later that summer with "Take," which didn't come close to the Top 40. The Colourfield had its first hit in January of 1985, when "Thinking of You" reached No. 12. It was followed by "Castles in the Air," another failed single that preceded the release of their debut album, *Virgins and Philistines*, by just a few weeks. Like the band's singles, *Virgins and Philistines* failed to gain a large audience for the Colourfield. The band released a second album, *Deception*, in the spring of 1987. During the sessions, Lyons left the band, leaving Hall to finish the album by himself; to complete the album, Hall hired Raquel Welch's band. — *Stephen Thomas Erlewine*

● **Virgins & Philistines** / Jan. 1985 / Chrysalis ♦♦♦♦
A good mix of folk and rock comes from this band led by Terry Hall (ex-Specials, Fun Boy Three). Hall is an interesting if somewhat gloomy writer. — *Kenneth M. Cassidy*

The Colourfield / 1986 / Chrysalis ♦♦♦

Deception / Apr. 1987 / Chrysalis ♦♦

Shawn Colvin
b. Jan. 10, 1958, Vermillion, SD
Guitar, Vocals / Singer-Songwriter
Singer and songwriter Shawn Colvin was born in South Dakota and has lived in London (Ontario) and in Carbondale, IL, where she graduated

from high school. She dropped out of Southern Illinois University to join a hard-rock group, later playing with the Dixie Diesels, a Western swing band in Austin. After a sojourn in San Francisco, she moved to New York City in 1980 and gradually worked her way up the folk circuit, also appearing in such off-Broadway shows as *Pump Boys and Dinettes*, *Diamond Studs*, and *Lie of the Mind*. Her work appeared in *The Fast Folk Musical Magazine*, and she got her first real break in 1987, singing backup on a Suzanne Vega tour. Recruited by Vega's management, she signed to Columbia Records in 1988 and released her debut album, *Steady On*, in 1989. — *William Ruhlmann*

● **Steady On** / Oct. 1989 / Columbia ♦♦♦♦
Sharp production, surprising arrangements, and Shawn Colvin's alternately breathy and ringing vocals give the best possible forum to her astute reflections on life and love. The album's roots go into rock and country as well as folk. — *William Ruhlmann*

Fat City / Oct. 1992 / Columbia ♦♦♦♦
Produced by bassist Larry Klein, Colvin's second album is looser than the first with a great cover of Warren Zevon's "Tenderness on the Block," and her own "Another Round of Blues." Various singles have been issued with non-CD tracks. — *Richard Meyer*

Cover Girl / Aug. 23, 1994 / Columbia ♦♦

Live '88 / Oct. 1995 / Plump ♦♦♦

Combustible Edison
Alternative Pop-Rock
What to do if you've been slogging away in the rock underground for a decade to slight critical acclaim without making any appreciable artistic or commercial headway? In the mold of David Johansen/Buster Poindexter, the band Christmas decided to retool themselves as lounge lizards. On their debut album, the Providence, RI, group plays cocktail jazz, exotica, torch ballads, and B-movie spy/guitar themes. To complete their transformation, the band has adopted ice cream-colored tuxedoes in their live performances; one member of the group has adopted the pseudonym "The Millionaire," and former Christmas singer Liz Cox calls herself "Miss Lily Banquette" as she croons languid jazz-pop tunes. — *Richie Unterberger*

● **I, Swinger** / Mar. 1994 / Sub Pop ♦♦♦♦
Combustible Edison's goofy and irreverent mix owes a lot more to the music of the 1950s and early '60s than to new wave; they sound as if they've stumbled on a treasure trove of dime-store albums in their aunt's attic and can't quite get over the experience. Their immaculate recreation of late-'50s/early-'60s cheese is fun...to a point. Treading the line between self-conscious irony and the ridiculous, it probably won't prove to be more durable than those old Christmas (the band, not the season) albums. But then, nobody could have predicted the Martin Denny revival, either. — *Richie Unterberger*

Schizophonic / Feb. 27, 1996 / Sub Pop ♦♦♦

Commander Cody
Country-Rock
Commander Cody and the Lost Planet Airmen were equally adept at stripped-down basic rock 'n' roll, R&B, and gritty country-rock. Commander Cody's country-rock rocked harder than the Eagles or Poco—essentially, the group was a bar band. Much like English pub-rock bands like Brinsley Schwarz and Ducks Deluxe, Commander Cody resisted the overblown and bombastic trends of early-'70s rock, preferring a basic, no-frills approach. Commander Cody and the Lost Planet Airmen never had the impact of the British pub-rockers, yet their straightforward energy gave their records a distinguishing drive; they could play country, western swing, rockabilly, and R&B, and it all sounded convincing.

The group originally formed in 1967 in Ann Arbor, MI; Commander Cody (born George Frayne, IV; piano), John Tichy (lead guitar), Steve Schwartz (guitar), Don Davis (bass), Don Bolton (aka the West Virginia Creeper; pedal steel guitar), and Ralph Mallory (drums) formed the original lineup. When the group relocated to San Francisco the following year, only Frayne, Bolton, and Tichy made the move; the group's membership included Billy C. Farlowe (vocals, harp), Andy Stein (fiddle, saxophone), guitarist Billy Kirchen, bassist "Buffalo" Bruce Barlow, and drummer Lance Dickerson at the time of their 1971 debut album, *Lost in the Ozone*. The following year the group scored a fluke Top Ten hit with "Hot Rod Lincoln," taken from their second album, *Hot Licks, Cold Steel and Trucker's Favourites*. Commander Cody was never able to capitalize on the single's success, partially because their albums never completely captured their live energy. They continued to release albums until Tichy left the band in 1976. Commander Cody released his first solo album, *Midnight Man*, in 1977, then he re-formed the group as the Commander Cody Band. The group recorded three albums between 1977 and 1980. — *Stephen Thomas Erlewine*

Lost in the Ozone / 1971 / MCA ✦✦✦

Country Casanova / 1973 / MCA ✦✦✦

Very Best of . . . Plus / 1986 / See For Miles ✦✦✦✦
With more tracks than their US best-of and costlier, this collection provides a grand overview of one of the saving graces of '70s rock. —*Jeff Tamarkin*

Sleazy Roadside Stories / 1988 / Relix ✦✦✦

Aces High / 1990 / Relix ✦✦✦

● **Too Much Fun: Best of Commander Cody** / 1990 / MCA ✦✦✦✦
Not only could they play the hell out of their instruments, but C.C. and his Lost Planet Airmen were a virtual melting pot of American music—country, R&B, rockabilly, Western swing. And always too much fun. —*Jeff Tamarkin*

Deep in the Heart of Texas / 1991 / MCA ✦✦✦

The Commodores

Soul, Funk, Urban, Pop-Rock
The Commodores got their start by being the opening act for the Jackson 5. Largely through the prolific lyrics of Lionel Richie, the band broke out nationally in the mid-'70s. Their initial success was mainly with dance tunes, but in the late '70s Richie began turning out love ballads such as "Easy," "Still," and "Three Times a Lady." His departure for solo stardom crippled the band, but not before they had one more huge success with "Nightshift" in 1985. Today the group plays state fairs and oldies venues. Members included Lionel Richie (replaced in 1984 by J.D. Nicholas), Thomas McClary (who left in 1984), Ronald LaPread, William King, Walter Orange, and Milan Williams. —*Rick A. Bueche*

● **All the Greatest Hits** / Nov. 1982 / Motown ✦✦✦✦
While there are many Commodores greatest hits packages available, *All the Great Hits* offers most of their biggest hits, making it ideal for the casual fan. —*Stephen Thomas Erlewine*

Commodores Anthology / Apr. 1983 / Motown ✦✦✦✦
The anthology series was Motown's best greatest hits line until they issued the two boxed-set *Hitsville* packages in '93. They compiled not just the hits but the important singles onto the Commodores anthology, and the sound quality was better than on either *Command Performances* or the two-in-one line. —*Ron Wynn*

Anthology: The Best of the Commodores / 1995 / Motown ✦✦✦✦
The revamped 1995 edition of *Anthology* includes all of the group's hit singles, as well as significant album tracks and singles that didn't chart, making it the definitive portrait of the popular, groundbreaking urban contemporary group. —*Sara Sytsma*

● **Very Best Of** / 1995 / Motown ✦✦✦✦

Con Funk Shun

Funk
This Memphis-based group was among the premier funk and soul ensembles of the '70s and '80s. Lead vocalist and guitarist Michael Cooper and drummer Louis McCall formed Project Soul as California high school students. They became Con Funk Shun in 1972, when Cooper and McCall moved to Memphis. They added bassist/keyboardist Cedric Martin, keyboardist Danny Thomas, saxophonist Karl Fuller, keyboardist/vocalist Melvin Carter, and saxophonist/percussionist Zebulon Paulle Harrel. Con Funk Shun began as an in-house band at Stax, backing various acts, while recording their own material. Some of this was later issued on Fretone, a Memphis label. They signed with Mercury in 1976, and had a long run with them until the mid-'80s. "Ffun" topped the R&B charts in 1977, and through 1986, Con Funk Shun had eight Top Ten R&B hits overall on Mercury, although they never scored a single Top Ten or Top 20 pop hit. Their sound and appeal was completely tailored to funk, soul, and later urban contemporary audiences. They did danceable ditties, comic pieces, and competent love songs and ballads, especially "Baby, I'm Hooked (Right into Your Love)." Deodato and Leon Ware were two of their producers at various times. Cooper became a star in his own right after Con Funk Shun disbanded in the late '80s. —*Ron Wynn*

● **The Best of Con Funk Shun** / 1992 / PolyGram ✦✦✦✦
This is a solid compilation of Con Funk Shun's influential late '70s and early '80s funk. —*AMG*

Best of Con Funk Shun, Vol. 2 / May 21, 1996 / Mercury ✦✦✦
A mix of LP cuts and moderate-to-big R&B hits, the most famous of those being the novelty "Electric Lady," and "Too Tight" (presented here in an extended version). —*Richie Unterberger*

The Contours

Soul, R&B, Motown
One of Berry Gordy's earliest discoveries at Motown, the hard-rocking Contours cultivated a new generation of fans when their "Do You Love

Me" was featured in the 1987 hit movie *Dirty Dancing.* Led by gravelly-voiced Billy Gordon, the quintet scored an R&B chart-topper in 1962 with the rollicking "Do You Love Me" on Gordy's label, then smoothed out their sound just a bit for the mid-'60s soul classics "First I Look at the Purse" and "Just a Little Misunderstanding." Dennis Edwards, who joined the group well after "Do You Love Me," was recruited to replace David Ruffin as lead of the Temptations in 1968. —*Bill Dahl*

● **Do You Love Me** / 1962 / Motown ✦✦✦✦
This rough-edged, early-'60s Motown group deserves more than its enduring one-hit status for "Do You Love Me?" —*Bill Dahl*

Ry Cooder

b. Mar. 15, 1947, Los Angeles, CA
Guitar, Vocals / Modern Electric Blues, Modern Acoustic Blues, Blues-Rock, Country-Rock, Ethnic Fusion, Roots-Rock
Whether serving as a session musician, solo artist, or soundtrack composer, Ry Cooder's chameleon-like fretted instrument virtuosity, songwriting, and choices of material encompasses an incredibly eclectic range of North American musical styles, including rock 'n' roll, blues, reggae, Tex-Mex, Hawaiian, Dixieland jazz, country, folk, R&B, gospel, and vaudeville. The 17-year-old Cooder began his career in 1963 in a blues band with Jackie DeShannon and then formed the short-lived Rising Sons in 1965 with Taj Mahal and Spirit drummer Ed Cassidy. Cooder met producer Terry Melcher through the Rising Sons and was invited to perform at sessions with Paul Revere and the Raiders. During his subsequent career as a session musician, Cooder's trademark slide guitar work graced the recordings of such artists as Captain Beefheart (*Safe as Milk*), Randy Newman, Little Feat, Van Dyke Parks, the Rolling Stones (*Let It Bleed, Sticky Fingers*), Taj Mahal, and Gordon Lightfoot. He also appeared on the soundtracks of *Candy* and *Performance.*

Cooder made his debut as a solo artist in 1970 with a self-titled album featuring songs by Leadbelly, Blind Willie Johnson, Sleepy John Estes, and Woody Guthrie. The follow-up, *Into the Purple Valley,* introduced longtime cohorts Jim Keltner on drums and Jim Dickinson on bass, and it and *Boomer's Story* largely repeated and refined the syncopated style and mood of the first. In 1974, Cooder produced what is generally regarded as his best album, *Paradise and Lunch,* and its follow-up, *Chicken Skin Music,* showcased a potent blend of Tex-Mex, Hawaiian, gospel, and soul music and featured contributions from Flaco Jimenez and Gabby Pahuini. In 1979, *Bop till You Drop* was the first major-label album to be recorded digitally. In the early '80s, Cooder began to augment his solo output with soundtrack work on such films as *Blue Collar, The Long Riders,* and *The Border;* he has gone on to compose music for *Southern Comfort, Goin' South, Paris Texas, Streets of Fire, Bay, Blue City, Crossroads, Cocktail, Johnny Handsome, Steel Magnolias,* and *Geronimo. Music by Ry Cooder* (1995) compiled two discs' worth of highlights from Cooder's film work. In 1992, Cooder joined Keltner, John Hiatt, and renowned British tunesmith Nick Lowe, all of whom had played on Hiatt's *Bring the Family,* to form Little Village, which toured and recorded one album. Cooder next turned his attention to world music, recording the album *A Meeting by the River* with Indian musician V.M. Bhatt. Cooder's next project, a duet album with renowned African guitarist Ali Farka Toure titled *Talking Timbuktu,* won the 1994 Grammy for Best World Music Recording. —*Steve Huey*

Ry Cooder / 1970 / Reprise ✦✦✦
His debut serves as a neat prototype, with its Sleepy John Estes and Woody Guthrie covers. It also introduces a most talented musician in its leader. But it's still a prototype; the best was yet to come. —*Jeff Tamarkin*

Into the Purple Valley / Jan. 1971 / Reprise ✦✦✦✦
First, there are no other credits for musicians, but because of his reputation for honesty in music, I will assume that he plays all the instruments including the ones with no strings. He is known as a virtuoso on almost every stringed instrument, and on this CD he demonstrates this ability on a wide variety of instruments. The main focus of the music here is on the era of the Dust Bowl, and what was happening in America at the time, socially and musically. There is one song by Woody Guthrie, and one by Leadbelly and a variety of other people all showing Ry's encyclopedic knowledge of the music of this time combined with an instinctive feel for the songs. Phenomenal is the descriptive word to describe his playing, whether it is on guitar, Hawaiian "slack key" guitar, mandolin, or some more arcane instrument he has found. This is a must for those who love instrumental virtuosity, authentic reworkings of an era, or just plain good music. —*Bob Gottlieb*

Boomer's Story / Feb. 1972 / Reprise ✦✦✦✦
Largely laidback and bluesy, this album features a number of paeans to an America long lost. —*Jeff Tamarkin*

● **Paradise & Lunch** / 1974 / Reprise ✦✦✦✦
Working with an intriguing collection of veteran musicians, the master musician and archivist turns in a stunning set of timeless remakes and new compositions. —*Jeff Tamarkin*

Chicken Skin Music / 1976 / Reprise ++++
Hawaiian traditional music meets Leadbelly and Ben E. King on
Cooder's gospelization of rock and soul. —*Jeff Tamarkin*

Show Time / 1976 / Reprise +++

Jazz / 1978 / Reprise +++

Bop till You Drop / 1979 / Reprise ++

The Slide Area / 1982 / Reprise ++

Get Rhythm / 1987 / Reprise +++

Music By Ry Cooder / 1995 / Reprise ++++
Since he's a limited vocalist with erratic songwriting skills, one could
argue that the soundtrack medium is the best vehicle for Cooder's talents, allowing him to construct eclectic, chiefly instrumental pieces drawing upon roots music and ethnic flavors (often employing his excellent
blues and slide guitar). This two-CD, 34-song compilation gathers
excerpts from 11 of the soundtracks he worked on between 1980 and
1993 (three of the cuts, from the 1981 film *Southern Comfort*, are previously unreleased). As few listeners (even Cooder fans) are dedicated
enough to go to the trouble of finding all of his individual soundtracks,
this is a good distillation of many of his more notable contributions in
this idiom, although it inevitably leaves out some fine moments. Still, it's
well programmed and evocative, often conjuring visions of ghostly landscapes and funky border towns. —*Richie Unterberger*

Sam Cooke (Sam Cook)

b. Jan. 22, 1931, Chicago, IL, **d.** Dec. 11, 1964, Los Angeles, CA
Vocals / Soul, R&B, Pop-Rock

Gospel, R&B, and pop singer-songwriter Sam Cooke enjoyed two careers
of nearly equal duration and success, first in the religious, and later in the
secular music fields. The son of a minister, Cooke began singing in gospel groups at an early age, and from 1950, when he was only 20, was the
lead singer of the Soul Stirrers. His flexible tenor made him a standout
star in gospel and an obvious candidate for secular stardom. He moved
to performing nonreligious material in 1956, which caused a split from
the group and its record label, Specialty, as well as an ongoing controversy among music fans, just as his concentration on pop-oriented material over grittier R&B led some to question his intentions. Nevertheless,
his pop successes were overwhelming. Keen Records released "You Send
Me" (Oct. 1957), Cooke's recording of a song written by his brother, and
saw it top the charts. "I'll Come Running Back to You" (Dec. 1957),
released by Specialty in the wake of Cooke's success, topped the R&B
charts. Cooke's hits of 1959 included "Everybody Likes to Cha Cha Cha"
and "Only Sixteen," the former with a songwriting credit to "Barbara
Campbell" (actually Cooke, Herb Alpert, and Lou Adler), the latter written by Cooke.

Cooke signed to RCA Victor Records in January 1960, though Keen
scored one more hit with a "Wonderful World" (another "Barbara
Campbell" composition). He then had his biggest hit since "You Send
Me" with his own "Chain Gang" (Jul. 1960). In 1962 and 1963, he
released nine consecutive R&B Top Ten hits, including the chart-topping
"Twistin' the Night Away" (Jan. 1962) and "Another Saturday Night" (Apr.
1963); both also made the pop Top Ten, and were his compositions. (The
notion that Cooke was some sort of puppet of White pop entrepreneurs
was always belied by his songwriting as well as his acute business acumen, including the founding of his own record label, Sar.) Cooke's last
giant single was the two-sided "Shake"/"A Change Is Gonna Come" (Dec.
1964), released the same month as his untimely death.

Cooke proved a major influence on R&B singers like Otis Redding,
rock singers like Rod Stewart, and pop singers like Art Garfunkel, all of
whom covered his songs. His work has remained popular, and in 1985 the
release of the album *Sam Cooke Live at the Harlem Square Club, 1963*,
which showed him performing an uninhibited, soulful set before an African-American audience, further fueled the debate about him as a crossover artist. However that debate is resolved (if it ever is), Cooke's influence
on popular music will remain profound, as many of his songs have long
since become standards. —*William Ruhlmann*

Night Beat / Aug. 1963 / ABKCO ++++
Intense, spiraling uptempo numbers, gripping ballads, and simply marvelous performances by a legend who sadly wouldn't be around much
longer. Originally released in August 1963, *Night Beat* [RCA 2709] was
reissued on CD on June 6, 1995 [ABKCO 1124]. —*Ron Wynn*

Sam Cooke at the Copa / Oct. 1964 / ABKCO +++
Cooke's classic live album is a mixed bag—he was playing to a White
supper-club audience and altered his sound accordingly, favoring ballads
and folk songs over most of his celebrated classic soul numbers. The
voice is there, and the style, but he never does cut loose completely, and
the backing band is too clean. —*Bruce Eder*

The Legendary Sam Cooke / 1974 / Candlelite Music/RCA Special
    Products ++++
Usually it's best to steer way clear of these sort of budget packages, but

this is an exception, primarily because Cooke's catalog has been handled
so poorly. This triple album has 30 songs from Cooke's RCA peak, including all the big smashes, and quite a few big and small hits ("Little Red
Rooster," "Good News," "Sugar Dumplin'," "Sad Mood," "That's It, I Quit,
I'm Movin' On") that don't appear on the only decent Cooke anthology
currently in print (*The Man and His Music*). That makes it a decent
pickup if you find a cheap used copy, but the real solution would be to
have RCA finally get its act together and give the man the multi-disc retrospective he deserves. —*Richie Unterberger*

☆ **Live at the Harlem Square Club** / Jun. 1985 / RCA +++++
Long believed lost, this live album—rejected for release in 1963 by
Cooke's managers, who wanted to broaden his appeal to White listeners—captures Cooke playing to a largely Black crowd, and it couldn't be
more different from his *At the Copa* live album. A hot, sweaty performance, with Cooke and a proper band luxuriating in his most soulful
material in its most wrenching and impassioned form. —*Bruce Eder*

★ **The Man & His Music** / Feb. 1986 / RCA +++++
The ultimate Sam Cooke collection, and the only one worth owning, covering his post-1957 career from his pop music breakthrough ("You Send
Me") to his final impassioned soul statement, "A Change Is Gonna Come"
(which is included in its seldom-heard uncut version). Few stones are left
unturned, the sound is clean and sharp, and the tragedy of Cooke's death
is recalled with each play. —*Bruce Eder*

His Earliest Recordings / 1991 / Specialty ++++
A superb collection of 25 recordings made by Sam Cooke, including
"Touch the Hem of His Garment." —*Stephen Thomas Erlewine*

Rhythm and the Blues / Oct. 24, 1995 / RCA ++++
From the title, you might infer that this 20-track compilation—taken
from early-'60s sessions, and principally composed of LP-only
cuts—aims to showcase Cooke's most soulful side. That's true to some
degree, but this isn't his funkiest stuff; for that, look to *Live at the Harlem
Square Club 1963*, or even his most uptempo singles. Most of this is in
fact suave pop/R&B, the emphasis sometimes falling on the pop, with
lightly swinging, jazzy arrangements and some orchestration. Cooke
didn't write most of the material here, and while "Little Red Rooster" (a
hit single) represents the earthiest extreme that the CD touches upon,
there are also quite a few songs that were originally performed by jazz/
popsters from the '20s, '30s, and '40s. Certainly these are decent offerings; Cooke's a great singer and interpreter, and the arrangements are
smooth without being overdone. But it's neither Cooke at his very best
(the hits compilation *Man and His Music* is much better) or his grittiest
(that honor belongs to *Harlem Square*). It does restore much of his better
obscure material to wide availability and is recommended to those who
have the above-mentioned albums and want more Cooke, although the
1963 LP *Night Beat* (reissued on CD in 1995) is a bluesier and better one
to check out first. —*Richie Unterberger*

Alice Cooper (Vincent Damon Furnier)

b. Feb. 4, 1948, Detroit, MI
Vocals / Hard Rock, Heavy Metal

During the first half of the '70s, Alice Cooper (born Vincent Furnier, son
of a preacher), made a name for himself as the king of gross-out, horror
hard-rock, touring with guillotines, boa constrictors, and mutilated baby
dolls, among other shock props. Fortunately, Cooper's theatrical hard-
rock anthems generally weren't upstaged by his performance antics,
thanks to smart choices of song covers and crafty plunderings of show-
tune melodies. Songs like "I'm Eighteen" and "School's Out" are among
some of rock's finest expressions of teen discontent. Cooper fired his original classic lineup in 1974 to pursue a solo career that, while giving him
his biggest chart hits, reduced him to an odd middle-of-the-road balladeer. He returned to his old schtick with blood and guts in the late '80s,
enjoying something of a comeback. —*Rick Clark*

Pretties for You / 1969 / Bizarre/Straight +++
Alice Cooper's debut album had none of his legendary grotesque hard
rock; instead, *Pretties for You* was an earnest, but flawed, stab at psychedelia that occasionally catches fire. —*Stephen Thomas Erlewine*

Love It to Death / Jan. 1971 / Warner Bros. ++++
The best studio album by Cooper features the classic "Eighteen." Other
standouts: "Caught in a Dream," "Long Way to Go," and "Black Juju."
—*Rick Clark*

Killer / Feb. 1971 / Warner Bros. ++++
Some of the more theatrical pieces undermine the album's strengths. It
contains the hits "Under My Wheels" and "Be My Lover." —*Rick Clark*

School's Out / 1972 / Warner Bros. ++++
The title cut of one of Cooper's best albums was a Top Ten hit. —*Rick
Clark*

Billion Dollar Babies / 1973 / Warner Bros. ++++
It's not as mindbendingly outrageous or hard-rocking as *School's Out*,
Killer, or *Love It to Death*, but with its conscious attempt at pop cross-

over ("No More Mr. Nice Guy" and "Elected"), *Billion Dollar Babies* is just as perverse as the earlier records, as well as being more consistent than any of his other proper albums. Sometimes selling out just a little bit might not be such a bad thing. —*Stephen Thomas Erlewine*

★ **Greatest Hits** / 1974 / Warner Bros. ✦✦✦✦✦
While he made many classic hard-rock singles, Alice Cooper never made a consistently enjoyable album, making *Greatest Hits* a necessity. It might not cover *all* of his best tracks, but everything you need to know is here. —*Stephen Thomas Erlewine*

Welcome to My Nightmare / 1975 / Atlantic ✦✦✦✦
Cooper's solo-artist debut contains "Only Women Bleed." It's the best of his solo efforts. —*Rick Clark*

Julian Cope

b. Oct. 21, 1957, Deri, Mid Glamorgan, Wales
Organ, Guitar, Vocals / Alternative Pop-Rock, Post-Punk
Midway through the recording of the Teardrop Explodes' third album, leader Julian Cope decided to go solo and dissolved the band. Cope's reputation as a rock eccentric was already well established, and following his solo debut, *World Shut Your Mouth*, many believed he was downright deranged. The music strongly echoed the garage rock of Roky Erickson and the psychedelia of Syd Barrett, two of rock's most notorious LSD addicts, while Cope himself intentionally slashed his stomach with a broken microphone and gave interviews advocating the use of hallucinogens during his supporting tour. Cope strengthened his image of mental imbalance on the cover of his second album, *Fried*, by picturing himself cowering naked under a giant tortoise shell.

In 1986, Cope scored a surprise UK Top 20 hit with a re-recorded version of "World Shut Your Mouth," and Island attempted to introduce the singer to US audiences with the *Julian Cope* EP. Cope followed his success with *Saint Julian* in 1987, his first album since recovering from his earlier mental difficulties. However, he was forced to cancel a supporting tour for the follow-up LP *My Nation Underground* due to illness. While Cope took a break from the public eye, he released *Skellington*, a follow-up to *Fried* rejected by Mercury, and *Droolian*, a series of demos and experiments, in 1989 and 1990, respectively, through his fan club. He served notice of his return in 1990 by showing up at an anti-poll tax demonstration in London dressed as an alien named Mr. Sqwubbsy, and the following year, he scored a UK hit with "Beautiful Love" and released the critically acclaimed double album *Peggy Suicide*. *Peggy Suicide* set a tone for much of Cope's subsequent work; it was an ambitious concept album addressing political, environmental, and spiritual issues in Cope's own idiosyncratic, sometimes confusing way. *Jehovahkill* and *Autogeddon*, the latter of which examined social evils through the metaphor of an automobile, followed but were less successful artistically and attracted less critical attention. —*Steve Huey*

Julian Cope / 1986 / Island ✦✦✦

Saint Julian / Mar. 1987 / Island ✦✦✦

My Nation Underground / Oct. 1988 / Island ✦✦✦✦
Julian Cope's follow-up to *Saint Julian* is another hard-edged pop-rock collection, paced by its leadoff track, a medley of two 1965 hits, the Vogues' "Five O'Clock World" and Petula Clark's "I Know a Place," with Cope's apocalyptically altered lyrics—in his version, it's the missiles that blow, not the whistle. Cope follows this pessimistic vision throughout the album, but that doesn't keep him from making accessible music that drives home his message. —*William Ruhlmann*

Peggy Suicide / Mar. 1991 / Island ✦✦✦✦
Peggy Suicide is Cope's idiosyncratic and complexly layered treatise on the state of the earth. Initially inspired by a vision that involved his own self-created mythological characters (Peggy Suicide as Mother Earth, Pollutio as destructive siren), Cope expands his cosmic tragedy beyond the larger political, social, and ecological issues with a healthy dose of mesmerizing psychedelic state-of-the-mind profiles. The unpolished production quality gives *Peggy Suicide* a more immediately believable delivery. Cope juxtaposes pure garage rock next to marimbas, loopy keyboard sounds, and loose-limbed percussion into a spellbinding tapestry. Among the many highlights are the ominous AIDS/death epic "Safesurfer" and "Drive, She Said," which is a trashy synthesis of Bowie's Velvet Underground send-ups. —*Rick Clark*

● **Floored Genius: The Best of Julian Cope & the Teardrop Explodes 1979-1991** / Oct. 20, 1992 / Island ✦✦✦✦
A sprawling compilation that gives a good sense of the variety of Cope's career, even if it's a bit too scattered to be thoroughly listenable. —*Stephen Thomas Erlewine*

Jehovahkill / Dec. 8, 1992 / Island ✦✦

Autogeddon / 1994 / American ✦✦

20 Mothers / 1995 / Echo ✦✦✦✦
Another lengthy grab-bag of contrasting musical styles and left-wing world politics mixed with eccentric personal concerns, *20 Mothers* is a

---

Music Map

Doo Wop

Gospel	Early Black Pop Vocal Groups The Mills Brothers, The Ink Spots

Early R&B Vocal Groups
The Orioles, The Ravens, The Clovers

Early Doo Wop Groups
The Crows, The Penguins, The El Dorados, The Turbans

Doo Wop Stars
The Platters, The Coasters, The Moonglows, Frankie Lymon & The Teenagers, The Flamingos

Italian-American Doo Wop Dion & The Belmonts, The Mystics	Early '60s Doo Wop The Marcels, Shep & The Limelites	Early Soul and Girl Groups The Miracles, The Impressions, The Shirelles

'60s Doo Wop-Influenced Acts
Dion, The 4 Seasons, The Beach Boys, Jan & Dean

---

more produced effort than its ramshackle predecessor, *Autogeddon*, though at times it descends to the near-demo offhandedness characteristic of that effort. Just as often, however, Cope turns out blistering rock (the ironically titled "By the Light of the Silvery Moon") or Depeche Mode/Erasure-style synth-dance pop ("Just like Pooh Bear"). Generally speaking, as one song ends, it's anybody's guess what may come next. But whether playing acoustic folk or psychedelic rock, whether commenting on crop circles or Kurt Cobain, Julian Cope retains a nervy confidence. He may be a gadfly with a thousand offbeat opinions, but he isn't tentative about them. Still, the tone combined with the viewpoint tends to mean he is more likely to amuse you than to involve you: The downside of being a gadfly is that you can be easily dismissed as a harmless nut. —*William Ruhlmann*

Elvis Costello

b. Aug. 25, 1955, Liverpool, England
Guitar, Keyboards, Vocals / Rock 'n' Roll, Singer-Songwriter, New Wave, Pop-Rock
When Elvis Costello's first record was released in 1977, his bristling cynicism and anger linked him with the punk and new wave explosion. A cursory listen to *My Aim Is True* proves that the main connection that Costello had with the punks was his unbridled passion. He tore through rock's back pages taking whatever he wanted, as well borrowing from country, Tin Pan Alley pop, reggae, and many other musical genres. Over his career, that musical eclecticism has distinguished Costello's records as much as his fiercely literate lyrics. Because he supports his lyrics with his richly diverse music, Costello is one of the most innovative, influential, and best songwriters since the Bob Dylan.

The son of British bandleader Ross MacManus, Costello (born Declan McManus) worked as a computer programmer during the early '70s, performing under the name D.P. Costello in various folk clubs. In 1976, he became the leader of country-rock group Flip City. During this time, he recorded several demo tapes of his original material with the intention of landing a record contract. A copy of these tapes made its way to Jake Riviera, one of the heads of the fledgling independent record label Stiff. Riviera signed Costello to Stiff as a solo artist in 1977; the singer-songwriter adopted the name Elvis Costello at this time, taking his first name from Elvis Presley and his last name from his mother's maiden name.

With former Brinsley Schwarz bassist Nick Lowe producing, Costello began recording his debut album with the American band Clover providing support. "Less than Zero," the first single released from these sessions, appeared in April of 1977. The single failed to chart, as did its follow-up, "Alison," which was released the following month. By the summer of 1977, Costello's permanent backing band had been assembled. Featuring bassist Bruce Thomas, keyboardist Steve Nieve, and drummer Pete Thomas (no relation to Bruce), the group was named the Attractions; they made their live debut in July of 1977.

My Aim Is True, his debut album, was released in the summer of 1977 to positive reviews; the album climbed to No. 14 on the British charts but it wasn't released on his American label, Columbia Records, until later in the year. Along with Nick Lowe, Ian Dury, and Wreckless Eric, Costello participated in the *Stiffs Live* package tour in the fall. At the end of the year, Jake Riviera split from Stiff Records to form Radar Records, taking Costello and Lowe with him. Costello's last single for Stiff, the reggae-inflected "Watching the Detectives," became his first hit, climbing to No. 15 at the end of the year.

This Year's Model, Costello's first album recorded with the Attractions, was released in the spring of 1978. A rawer, harder-rocking record than *My Aim Is True*, *This Year's Model* was also a bigger hit, reaching No. 4 in Britain and No. 30 In America. Released the following year, *Armed Forces* was a more ambitious and musically diverse album than either of his previous records. It was another hit, reaching No. 2 in the UK and cracking the Top Ten in the US. "Oliver's Army," the first single from the album, also peaked at No. 2 in Britain; none of the singles from *Armed Forces* charted in America. In the summer of 1979, he produced the self-titled debut album by the Specials, the leaders of the ska-revival movement.

In February of 1980, the soul-influenced *Get Happy!!* was released; it was the first record on Riviera's new record label, F-Beat. *Get Happy!!* was another hit, peaking at No. 2 in Britain and No. 11 in America. Later that year, two collections of B-sides, singles, and outtakes called *Taking Liberties* was released in America; in Britain, a similar album called *Ten Bloody Marys and Ten How's Your Fathers* appeared as a cassette-only release, complete with different tracks than the American version.

Costello and the Attractions released *Trust* in early 1981; it was his fifth album in a row produced by Nick Lowe. *Trust* debuted at No. 9 in the British charts and worked its way into the Top 30 in the US. During the spring of 1981, Costello and the Attractions began recording an album of country covers with famed Nashville producer Billy Sherrill, who recorded hit records for George Jones and Charlie Rich, among others. The resulting album, *Almost Blue*, was released at the end of the year to mixed reviews, although the single "A Good Year for the Roses" was a British Top Ten hit.

Costello's next album, *Imperial Bedroom* (1982), was an ambitious set of lushly arranged pop produced by Geoff Emerick, who engineered several of the Beatles' most acclaimed albums. *Imperial Bedroom* received some of his best reviews, yet it failed to yield a Top 40 hit in either England or America; the album did debut at No. 6 in the UK. For 1983's *Punch the Clock*, Costello worked with Clive Langer and Alan Winstanley, who were responsible for several of the biggest British hits in the early '80s. The collaboration proved commercially successful, as the album peaked at No. 3 in the UK (No. 24 in the US) and the single "Everyday I Write the Book" cracked the Top 40 in both Britain and America. Costello tried to replicate the success of *Punch the Clock* with his next record, 1984's *Goodbye Cruel World*, but the album was a commercial and critical failure.

After the release of *Goodbye Cruel World*, Costello embarked on his first solo tour in the summer of 1984. Costello was relatively inactive during 1985, releasing only one new single ("The People's Limousine," a collaboration with singer-songwriter T-Bone Burnett released under the name the Coward Brothers) and producing *Rum, Sodomy and the Lash*, the second album by the punk-folk band the Pogues. Both projects were indications that he was moving toward a stripped-down, folky approach and 1986's *King of America* confirmed that suspicion. Recorded without the Attractions and released under the name the Costello Show, *King of America* was essentially a country/folk album and it received the best reviews of any album he had recorded since *Imperial Bedroom*. It was followed at the end of the year by the edgy *Blood and Chocolate*, a reunion with the Attractions and producer Nick Lowe. Costello would not record another album with the Attractions until 1994.

During 1987, Costello negotiated a new worldwide record contract with Warner Bros. Records and began a songwriting collaboration with Paul McCartney. Two years later, he released *Spike*, the most musically diverse collection he had ever recorded. *Spike* featured the first appearance of songs written by Costello and McCartney, including the single "Veronica." "Veronica" became his biggest American hit, peaking at No. 19. Two years later, he released *Mighty like a Rose*, which echoed *Spike* in its diversity, yet it was a darker, more challenging record. In 1993, Costello collaborated with the Brodsky Quartet on *The Juliet Letters*, a song cycle that was the songwriter's first attempt at classical music; he also wrote an entire album for former Transvision Vamp singer Wendy James called *Now Ain't the Time for Your Tears*. That same year, Costello

licensed the rights to his pre-1987 catalog (*My Aim Is True* to *Blood and Chocolate*) to Rykodisc in America.

Costello re-united with the Attractions to record the majority of 1994's *Brutal Youth*, the most straightforward and pop-oriented album he had recorded since *Goodbye Cruel World*. The Attractions backed Costello on a worldwide tour in 1994 and played concerts with him throughout 1995. In 1995, he released his long-shelved collection of covers, *Kojak Variety*. In the spring of 1996, Costello released *All This Useless Beauty*, which featured a number of original songs he had given to other artists, but never recorded himself. — *Stephen Thomas Erlewine*

☆ **My Aim Is True** / Aug. 1977 / Rykodisc ✦✦✦✦✦
Elvis Costello's debut album is a pop landmark that indicates the future that may exist for the spirit of punk in the wider genre of rock music. Backed by the American group Clover (featuring then-future Doobie Brother John McFee but not harmonica player Huey Lewis), Costello displays all the characteristics that would serve him throughout his career: a caustic wit he uses to savage himself and others, a broad imagination—"(The Angels Wanna Wear My) Red Shoes" is one of the best pieces of rock whimsy ever written—an unsentimental but compelling sense of romance ("Alison"), and an astonishing verbal facility, all enmeshed with a pop encyclopedist's musical knowledge. One of the greatest first albums in pop history. — *William Ruhlmann*

☆ **This Year's Model** / Jul. 1978 / Rykodisc ✦✦✦✦✦
Where *My Aim Is True* implied punk rock with its lyrics and stripped-down production, *This Year's Model* sounds like punk. Not that Costello's songwriting has changed—*This Year's Model* is comprised largely of left-overs from *My Aim Is True* and songs written on the road. It's the music that changed. After releasing *My Aim Is True*, Costello assembled a backing band called the Attractions, which were considerably tougher and wilder than Clover, who played on his debut. The Attractions were a rock 'n' roll band, which gives *This Year's Model* a reckless, careening feel. It's nervous, amphetamine-fueled, nearly paranoid music—the group sounds like they're spinning out of control as soon as they crash in on the brief opener, "No Action," and they never get completely back on track, even on the slower numbers. Costello and the Attractions speed through *This Year's Model* at a blinding pace, which gives his songs—which were already meaner than the set on *My Aim Is True*—a nastier edge. "Lipstick Vogue," "Pump It Up," and "(I Don't Want to Go to) Chelsea" are all underscored with sexual menace, while "Night Rally" touches on a bizarre fascination with fascism that would blossom on his next album, *Armed Forces*. Even the songs that sound relatively lighthearted—"Hand in Hand," "Little Triggers," "Lip Service," "Living in Paradise"—are all edgy, thanks to Costello's breathless vocals, Steve Nieve's carnivalesque organ riffs, and Nick Lowe's bare-bones production. Of course, the songs on *This Year's Model* are typically catchy and help the vicious sentiments sink into your skin, but the most remarkable thing about the album is the sound—Costello and the Attractions never rocked this hard, or this vengefully, ever again. (The 1993 compact disc reissue standardized the sequencing of *This Year's Model* on both sides of the Atlantic, restoring the album to its original British running order and adding six bonus tracks. The first three tracks are singles and B-sides, including the classic rant "Radio, Radio," the organ-driven '60s pop of "Big Tears," and the frenetic "Crawling to the USA." The remaining three tracks—"Running Out of Angels," "Greenshirt," and "Big Boys"—are all demos.) — *Stephen Thomas Erlewine*

☆ **Armed Forces** / 1979 / Rykodisc ✦✦✦✦✦
Lavishly produced by Nick Lowe, and masterfully programmed, this is Costello's most political album and his most melodic. His bitterness is somewhat subdued, but his passion informs every song. — *John Floyd*

☆ **Get Happy!!** / 1980 / Rykodisc ✦✦✦✦✦
Featuring 20 tracks of energetic, amphetamine-driven soul, *Get Happy!!* captures Costello at his most vicious and clever. While his words and puns are pithy, it's the constant barrage of songs that make the album work. Not all of the songs are first-rate, but the great majority are. — *Stephen Thomas Erlewine*

☆ **Trust** / Feb. 1981 / Rykodisc ✦✦✦✦✦
Some of the songs are too obtuse to really stick, but the Attractions turn the best of them into edgy and brittle mini-masterpieces. — *John Floyd*

Almost Blue / Nov. 1981 / Rykodisc ✦✦✦
Costello's "country record" is usually written off as a vanity project, but *Almost Blue* is quite a bit more than that. It's one of the most entertaining cover records in rock 'n' roll, simply because of its enthusiasm. The album begins with a roaring version of Hank Williams' "Why Don't You Love Me" and doesn't stop. Costello sings with conviction on the tear-jerking ballads, as well as barn burners like "Tonight the Bottle Let Me Down." It's clear that Costello knows this music, and it's also clear who he learned it from—Gram Parsons. Costello covers Parsons' "Hot Burrito No. 1" and "How Much I Lied," and all of the music on *Almost Blue* recalls Parsons' taste for hardcore honky-tonk and weepy ballads. It's to Costello's credit that he made a record relying on emotion to pay tribute. — *Stephen Thomas Erlewine*

☆ **Imperial Bedroom** / Jul. 1982 / Rykodisc ✦✦✦✦✦
This ornately orchestrated and lush set is Costello's version of *Blood on the Tracks*. It's a musically sophisticated and emotionally devastating tour through the crumbling heart of an incurable romantic. —*John Floyd*

Punch the Clock / 1983 / Rykodisc ✦✦✦
An upbeat set of fairly clear and concise pop songs, it is supplemented by some punchy horn charts. —*John Floyd*

Goodbye Cruel World / 1984 / Rykodisc ✦✦
King of America / Jan. 1986 / Rykodisc ✦✦✦✦
Although this is linked thematically to *Imperial Bedroom*, Costello's newfound clarity and the mostly acoustic accompaniment distinguish it from anything in his canon. Remarkable. —*John Floyd*

Blood & Chocolate / Feb. 1986 / Rykodisc ✦✦✦✦
A hard-rocking but inconsistent set is made worthwhile by "I Want You," "I Hope You're Happy Now," and "Next Time Round," all emotional stunners. —*John Floyd*

Out of Our Idiot / 1987 / Demon ✦✦✦
Spike / 1989 / Warner Bros. ✦✦
Throughout his career Elvis Costello has always been prolific; thus it was surprising, even given the change in record labels for the US, when he took a whole 20 months between *Blood & Chocolate* and this follow-up. But the musical growth he exhibits makes the wait worthwhile. The musical settings range from the stark folk of "Tramp the Dirt Down" to the pop sprightliness of "Veronica" (a collaboration with Paul McCartney that became Costello's first American Top 20 hit) and the New Orleans jazz sound of "Deep Dark Truthful Mirror," featuring the Dirty Dozen Brass Band. The lyrics are among his best. —*William Ruhlmann*

Mighty like a Rose / 1991 / Warner Bros. ✦✦
The lyrical concerns here are cumbersome and pretentious, and the music is ponderous and indulgent. But a few decent songs—especially "The Other Side of Summer"—make this 1991 set worthwhile. —*John Floyd*

The Juliet Letters / 1993 / Warner Bros. ✦✦✦
Costello's collaboration with the Brodsky Quartet is an intriguing, if flawed, attempt at crossing pop with chamber music. Some songs rely too much on clever arrangements, but most of the tracks are surprisingly successful. —*Stephen Thomas Erlewine*

2 1/2 Years / Oct. 12, 1993 / Rykodisc ✦✦✦✦
Rykodisc launched its Elvis Costello reissue series with this box set featuring his first three albums together with the previously promotional-only *Live at the El Mocambo* (available only in the box). Costello fans know the studio albums by heart and will be pleased by the remastering and bonus tracks, while the highly sought-after *Live at the El Mocambo* proves that in addition to being an extremely talented songwriter, Costello was a hell of a rocker. —*Stephen Thomas Erlewine*

Brutal Youth / 1994 / Warner Bros. ✦✦✦
Costello's first album with the Attractions since *Blood and Chocolate*, *Brutal Youth* suffers from soft production and the inclusion of too many songs. Apart from these two flaws, the record is enjoyable, recalling the eclecticism of *Trust* and the force of *This Year's Model*. Costello's songs are strong; it's his least affected and pretentious writing since *Blood and Chocolate*. —*Stephen Thomas Erlewine*

● **The Very Best of Elvis Costello and the Attractions** / 1994 / Rykodisc ✦✦✦✦
A solid complement to Ryko's Costello reissue series if you don't want to pick up each individual album. Of course, the 22 tracks (drawn from his first 11 albums and, according to the liner notes, "hand-picked by Elvis himself") also sport the crisply remastered sound featured on the rest of the series. "The Very Best Of" halts abruptly at 1986's *Blood and Chocolate*, his last release for Columbia. —*Roch Parisien*

Kojak Variety / 1995 / Warner Bros. ✦✦
Deep Dead Blue, Live at Meltdown / Nov. 1995 / Nonesuch ✦✦
All This Useless Beauty / May 14, 1996 / Warner Bros. ✦✦✦
Following his second covers album, *Kojak Variety*, Elvis Costello set out to assemble a collection of songs he had written for other artists, but he never recorded himself—sort of a reverse covers album. As it turned out, that idea was only used as a launching pad—the resulting album, *All This Useless Beauty*, is a mixture of nine old and three new songs. Given its origins, it's surprising that the record holds together as well as it does. The main strength of *All This Useless Beauty* is the quality of the individual songs—each song can stand on its own as an individual entity, as the music is as sharp as the lyrics. Although the music is certainly eclectic, it's accessible, which wasn't the case with *Mighty like a Rose*. Furthermore, the production is much more textured and punchier than Mitchell Froom's botched job on *Brutal Youth*. *All This Useless Beauty* doesn't quite add up to a major statement, but the simple pleasures it offers makes it one of the more rewarding records of the latter part of Costello's career. —*Stephen Thomas Erlewine*

Count Five

Psychedelic, Garage Rock
This San Jose quintet scored one of the biggest garage-psychedelic hits of the '60s with "Psychotic Reaction," a derivative but riveting American adaptation of the Yardbirds' guitar rave-ups. The single reached No. 5 in late 1966, but the group was unable to come anywhere close to duplicating its success. Their sole album and collectible follow-up flop singles, like "Psychotic Reaction," emulate the Yardbirds, Rolling Stones, and Who with less memorable results, although they have their moments. —*Richie Unterberger*

● **Psychotic Reaction: The Complete Psychotic Reaction** / 1994 / Performance ✦✦✦✦
Replaces previous Count Five collections as the most thorough retrospective of the group, with 18 of their tracks from the 1960s. —*Richie Unterberger*

Counting Crows

Alternative Pop-Rock
With their angst-filled hybrid of Van Morrison, the Band, and R.E.M., Counting Crows became an overnight sensation in 1994. Only a year earlier, the band was a group of unknown musicians, filling in for the absent Van Morrison at the Rock & Roll Hall of Fame ceremony; they were introduced by an enthusiastic Robbie Robertson. Early in 1993, the band recorded their debut album, *August & Everything After*, with T-Bone Burnett. It was a dark, somber record, driven by the morose lyrics and expressive vocals of Adam Duritz; the only uptempo song, "Mr. Jones," became their ticket to stardom. What made Counting Crows was how they were able to balance Duritz's tortured lyrics with the sound of the late '60s and early '70s; it made them one of the few alternative bands to appeal to listeners who thought that rock 'n' roll died in 1972. —*Stephen Thomas Erlewine*

August & Everything After / 1993 / DGC ✦✦✦✦
Counting Crows became the surprise success story of 1994 with *August & Everything After*, which skillfully filters the classic rock of Van Morrison and the Band through the post-punk sensibilities of R.E.M. and the Cure. With his verbose lyrics and twisting melodies, lead singer and songwriter Adam Duritz resembles a cross between Morrison and Rick Danko, and his songs are more weathered than one might expect on a debut. Apart from the single "Mr. Jones," the album is rather gloomy, with melancholy, jangling guitars and a somber, solemn mood. Counting Crows crossed over because they were able to keep that gloom from resembling Joy Division or the Cure (or even *Automatic for the People*), instead sounding like something straight out of the classic years of 1968 to 1972. It's modern music for people who don't like modern music. —*Stephen Thomas Erlewine*

Country Joe & the Fish

Psychedelic
One of the original and most popular San Francisco Bay Area psychedelic bands, Country Joe & the Fish, was formed by lead singer Country Joe McDonald (b. Jan. 1, 1942). The Berkeley group still had one foot in the jug band sound on their first EP, released in 1965 (featuring a folk version of their anthem "I Feel like I'm Fixin' to Die Rag"). By the time of their second EP in 1966, though, they had plunged full-tilt into the burgeoning psychedelic sound, with raga-ish, heavily distorted guitars and farfisa organ, displayed to its full glory on the instrumental "Section 43." Versions of songs from those limited edition EPs were combined with other material for their first and best album, *Electric Music for the Mind and Body*. McDonald and his group combined protest politics, free love, and psychedelic drugs with a good-time humor on this 1967 release. After a similar, less impressive follow-up, the band began to disintegrate, and never recaptured the highs of their early days. McDonald went on to an intermittently successful, more folk-rock-oriented solo career, achieving his greatest moment of notoriety with his version of "Fixin' to Die" (complete with the obscene "Fish Cheer") at the Woodstock festival. —*Richie Unterberger*

Live at the Fillmore West / Mar. 12, 1996 / Vanguard ✦✦

Don Covay

b. Mar. 1938, Orangeburg, SC
Vocals / Soul
An R&B and soul songwriting great, Don Covay compositions have been recorded by everyone from the Rolling Stones to Jimi Hendrix, Gladys Knight to Wilson Pickett, and many others. Covay was the son of a Baptist preacher. He sang in his family's gospel group, the Cherry-Keys, as a youngster. Covay was born in Orangeburg, SC, but grew up in Washington, D.C., and joined The Rainbows alongside Marvin Gaye, John Berry, and Billy Stewart in the '50s. Covay also performed as a solo singer with Little Richard, who recorded Covay as "Pretty Boy" on the Atlantic

release "Bip Bop Bip." Covay had moderate success with the single "Pony Time," which he co-wrote with Berry, for the Arnold label in 1960. He began to hit his stride in 1964. Besides fronting Don Covay and the Goodtimers, he wrote "Mercy Mercy," "Sookie Sookie," and "See Saw," and had tunes recorded by Gene Chandler and Aretha Franklin. Covay did both blues and soul numbers for Janus and Mercury labels in the '70s. His biggest hit as a performer was "See Saw," which made it to No. 5 on the R&B charts in 1965. But his most electrifying number was 1973's "I Was Checkin' out While She Was Checkin' In," which made it to No. 6. Covay was also part of the short-lived Soul Clan, with Solomon Burke, Arthur Conley, Ben E. King, and Joe Tex in 1968. Their collaboration "Soul Meeting" made it to No. 34, but wasn't quite the elaborate or explosive number everyone had envisioned. Covay made one LP for Gamble and Huff's Philadelphia International label in 1976, but *Travelin' in Heavy Traffic* proved a disappointment. Covay recorded for Newman in 1980, and got his last chart single with "Badd Boy." Some of his singles were reissued on a 1992 Mercury release, *Checkin' in with Don Covay.* An all-star gathering that included Ron Wood, Robert Cray, Bobby Womack, Iggy Pop, Peter Wolf, King, Todd Rundgren, Billy Squier, and Jimmy Witherspoon recorded a tribute album to Covay in 1993. —*Ron Wynn*

● **Mercy Mercy: The Definitive Don Covay** / 1995 / Razor & Tie ◆◆◆◆
Mercy Mercy: The Definitive Don Covay compiles 23 tracks from throughout the soul singer's career. Encompassing everything from the R&B stomp of "Bip Bop Bip" and "Pony Time" to the seductive soul of "I Was Checkin' out While She Was Checkin' In" and "No Tell Motel," the disc makes a convincing argument that Covay was one of the great overlooked R&B/soul artists of the '60s. —*Stephen Thomas Erlewine*

Cowboy Junkies

Alternative Pop-Rock
Although it was solely a way to gain attention, the Cowboy Junkies' name goes a long way in describing the Canadian band's sound. At its core, the group's music is based in country and folk traditions, except their tempos are slow and lethargic, their guitars are languid, and Margo Timmins' vocals are lovely, yet hauntingly detached.

The Cowboy Junkies have their roots in the Hunger Project, an unsuccessful Toronto-based group formed by guitarist/songwriter Michael Timmins and bassist Alan Anton in 1979. After the band failed, the duo moved to the United Kingdom and formed an experimental instrumental group called Germinal. It was also unsuccessful, so the two musicians moved back to Toronto, where they began playing with Timmins' sister Margo and his drummer brother, Peter. Under the name Cowboy Junkies, the group recorded their first album, *Whites off Earth Now!!,* in 1986, releasing it on a Canadian independent label. Two years later, they recorded *The Trinity Sessions* in an abandoned church, using only one microphone. The album may have only cost $250 to record, but it sparked a small sensation, with the band's reworkings of "Blue Moon," "I'm So Lonesome I Could Cry," "Walking After Midnight," and "Sweet Jane" earning them a diverse and dedicated cult following.

The success of *The Trinity Sessions* allowed the band to record on a bigger budget. The result was 1990's *The Caution Horses,* which featured more of Michael Timmins' original songs. *The Caution Horses* didn't earn as much press as their previous album, yet they maintained a sizable cult, which stuck by the band through their next two records, *Black-Eyed Man* (1992) and *Pale Sun, Crescent Moon* (1993). After the stop-gap live album in late 1995, *200 More Miles, Live Performances 1985-1994,* the Cowboy Junkies returned with *Lay It Down* in 1996. —*Stephen Thomas Erlewine*

Whites off Earth Now!! / 1986 / RCA ◆◆◆

● **The Trinity Sessions** / 1988 / RCA ◆◆◆◆
Recorded with one microphone in an abandoned church, their second album achieves a haunting ambience. —*John Floyd*

The Caution Horses / 1990 / RCA ◆◆

Black-Eyed Man / 1992 / RCA ◆◆◆
The Cowboy Junkies stick with their style of low-key songs steeped in country blues. Songwriter and guitarist Michael Timmins writes story-songs full of rain and street life and regret, and they are movingly sung by Margo Timmins. Two Townes Van Zandt songs, including his classic "To Live Is to Fly," fit right in. —*William Ruhlmann*

Pale Sun, Crescent Moon / 1993 / RCA ◆◆◆◆
A refreshed, revitalized sound that doesn't sacrifice the delicate touches that first made them unique; rugged, but still pristine. Much of the new spark emanates from the strings of honorary Junkie Ken Myhr, who peals out intense, biting lead guitar throughout. Especially prominent is his incendiary slide work on "Seven Years" and a spectacular cover of Dinosaur Jr.'s "The Post." Still, it's hard to imagine a ballad instrument more haunting and ethereal than Margo Timmins' voice. —*Roch Parisien*

200 More Miles, Live Performances 1985-1994 / Oct. 10, 1995 / RCA ◆◆◆

Lay It Down / Feb. 27, 1996 / Geffen ◆◆◆

Cracker

Alternative Pop-Rock
While he was the front man for Camper Van Beethoven, it seemed that it would take nothing short of a miracle to make guitarist/singer David Lowery a favorite of mainstream rockers, but that's what he and his second band, Cracker, have become. Led by Lowery and guitarist Johnny Hickman, Cracker is much more straightforward than Camper; Cracker concentrates on rock and country, creating a twisted, rootsy rock 'n' roll that sounds like a post-punk Rolling Stones or Little Feat. While their self-titled 1992 debut had moments of raw brilliance, Cracker's second album, 1993's *Kerosene Hat,* fulfilled their promise. Powered by the hit single "Low," the album was a hard-rocking meeting of traditional rock and post-punk sensibilities. Like Camper Van Beethoven's albums, it deserved to be heard by a wide audience; this time Lowery found a larger audience—*Kerosene Hat* eventually went gold.

Cracker released their third album, *The Golden Age,* in the spring of 1996. The album didn't repeat the success of its predecessor, falling off the charts within three months of its release.—*Stephen Thomas Erlewine*

Cracker / 1992 / Virgin ◆◆◆◆
Apart from David Lowery's tendency to slip in some smug, self-serving lyrics, Cracker's debut is a terrific rock 'n' roll record, full of energetic three-chord bashers and surprisingly moving ballads. —*Stephen Thomas Erlewine*

● **Kerosene Hat** / 1993 / Virgin ◆◆◆◆
With their second album, Cracker has lost the smarmy self-righteousness that plagued their otherwise fine debut, replacing it with a surprisingly solid, rocking core. *Kerosene Hat* is David Lowery's least affected album yet—its humor is no stranger than the Stones' "Dead Flowers" or Little Feat's "Fat Man in a Bathtub," two groups that Cracker strongly recall throughout the album. *Kerosene Hat* is more blues- and country-based than their debut, but it sounds natural, since their songwriting has improved and the band has grown tighter. —*Stephen Thomas Erlewine*

The Golden Age / Apr. 2, 1996 / Virgin ◆◆◆

The Cramps

Rockabilly, Alternative Pop-Rock, Post-Punk
The Cramps' unique sound synthesizes classic rockabilly, touches of psychedelia, and lyrical fare devoted mostly to monster movies and sleazy sex into an infectious, gloriously tasteless conglomeration of American trash culture. While their subject matter may verge on offensive to some, their obvious sense of humor and the fun, disposable feel of their best work prevent the listener from ever taking things more seriously than they should. The group was formed by vocalist Erick "Lux Interior" Purkhiser and guitarist Kirsty "Poison Ivy Rorschach" Wallace, who met in Sacramento and found they shared an affinity for obscure '50s rockabilly and surf records and junk culture. The two moved back to Interior's native Ohio and then to New York in 1975, where they formed the Cramps as a vehicle for indulging their obsessions with guitarist Bryan Gregory and his sister Pam "Balam" Gregory on drums. Miriam Linna replaced Pam Balam after a few months, and the Cramps became favorites at the renowned punk club CBGB's. Linna left in 1977 to join Nervus Rex; she later cofounded *Kicks* magazine and the '50s rock 'n' roll-oriented Norton Records label.

After drummer Nick Knox joined the fold, the Cramps went to the legendary Sun studio with cult icon Alex Chilton producing to record several singles, later released on the *Gravest Hits* EP. Chilton also produced their minimalistic 1980 debut album, *Songs the Lord Taught Us.* Gregory left the band very suddenly afterwards without explanation; he reportedly tried his hand at being a warlock, sex-shop owner, and tattoo artist afterwards. He was replaced by ex-Gun Club guitarist "Kid Congo" Powers for *Psychedelic Jungle.* Following the 1983 live EP *Smell of Female,* the Cramps sued I.R.S. for lack of support; the case was settled out of court and resulted in the Cramps being released from the label. Nothing more was heard from the band in the way of new material for years; their only new album prior to 1990, 1986's *A Date with Elvis,* was not released in the US until four years later. In the meantime, they toured extensively with a succession of female guitarists and new bassist Candy Del Mar, who was on board for their 1990 Poison Ivy-produced album *Stay Sick!* Lux Interior and Poison Ivy continue to tour with a Cramps lineup featuring bassist Slim Chance and drummer Jim Sclavunos. —*Steve Huey*

Songs the Lord Taught Us / May 1980 / IRS ◆◆◆◆
. . . a virtual textbook of obscure '50s and '60s rock 'n' roll. Sixties and '70s punk, surf instrumental dementia, and rockabilly are all brought to a boil in a stew that is anything but a stuffy history lesson. —*John Floyd, Rock & Roll Disc.*

Psychedelic Jungle / May 1981 / A&M ✦✦✦✦
Contained is their second album (not as wild as the first but still a ton of fun) and their debut EP material, featuring the epochal "Human Fly" and a pulverizing cover of Roy Orbison's "Domino." —*John Floyd*

The Smell of Female / 1983 / Enigma ✦✦✦

● **Bad Music for Bad People** / 1984 / IRS ✦✦✦✦
A solid collection of singles, B-sides, and album cuts, this decent introduction is made great by "Drug Train" and "New Kind of Kick." —*John Floyd*

Cream

Blues-Rock, Hard Rock, Psychedelic
Although Cream were only together for a little more than two years, their influence was immense, both during their late-'60s peak and in the years following their breakup. Cream were the first top group to truly exploit the power-trio format, in the process laying the foundation for much blues-rock and hard rock of the 1960s and 1970s. It was with Cream, too, that guitarist Eric Clapton truly became an international superstar. Critical revisionists have tagged the band as overrated, citing the musicians' emphasis upon flash, virtuosity, and showmanship at the expense of taste and focus. This was sometimes true of their live shows in particular, but in reality the best of their studio recordings were excellent fusions of blues, pop, and psychedelia, with concise original material outnumbering the bloated blues jams and overlong solos.

Cream could be viewed as the first rock supergroup to become superstars, although none of the three members were that well known when the band formed in mid-1966. Eric Clapton had the biggest reputation, having established himself as a guitar hero first with the Yardbirds, and then in a more blues-intensive environment with John Mayall's Bluesbreakers. (In the States, however, he was all but unknown, having left the Yardbirds before "For Your Love" made the American Top Ten.) Bassist/singer Jack Bruce and drummer Ginger Baker had both been in the Graham Bond Organization, an underrated British R&B combo that drew extensively upon the jazz backgrounds of the musicians. Bruce had also been, very briefly, a member of the Bluesbreakers along Clapton, and also briefly a member of Manfred Mann when he became especially eager to pay the rent.

All three of the musicians yearned to break free of the confines of the standard rock/R&B/blues group, to form a unit that would allow them greater instrumental and improvisational freedom, somewhat in the mold of a jazz outfit. Eric Clapton's stunning guitar solos would get much of the adulation, yet Bruce was at least as responsible for shaping the group's sound, singing most of the material in his rich voice. He also wrote their best original compositions, sometimes in collaboration with outside lyricist Pete Brown.

At first Cream's focus was electrified and amped-up traditional blues, which dominated their first album, *Fresh Cream*, which made the British Top Ten in early 1967. Originals like "N.S.U." and "I Feel Free" gave notice that the band were capable of moving beyond the blues, and they truly found their voice on *Disraeli Gears* in late 1967, which consisted mostly of group-penned songs. These they fashioned invigorating, sometimes beguiling hard-driving psychedelic pop, which included plenty of memorable melodies and effective harmonies along with the expected crunching riffs. "Strange Brew," "Dance the Night Away," "Tales of Brave Ulysses," and "S.W.L.A.B.R." are all among their best tracks, and the album broke the band bigtime in the States, reaching the Top Five. It also generated their first big US hit single, "Sunshine of Your Love," which was based around one of the most popular hard-rock riffs of the '60s.

With the double album *Wheels of Fire*, Cream topped the American charts in 1968, establishing themselves alongside the Beatles and Hendrix as one of the biggest rock acts in the world. The record itself was a more erratic affair than *Disraeli Gears*, perhaps dogged by the decision to present separate discs of studio and live material; the concert tracks in particular did much to establish their reputation, for good or ill, for stretching songs way past the ten-minute mark on stage. The majestically doomy "White Room" gave Cream another huge American single, and the group were firmly established as one of the biggest live draws of any kind. Their decision to disband in late 1968—at a time when they were seemingly on top of the world—came as a shock to most of the rock audience.

Cream's short lifespan, however, was in hindsight unsurprising given the considerable talents, ambitions, and egos of each of its members. Clapton in particular was tired of blowing away listeners with sheer power, and wanted to explore more subtle directions. After a farewell tour of the States, the band broke up in November 1968. In 1969, however, they were in a sense bigger than ever—a posthumous album featuring both studio and live material, *Goodbye*, made No. 2, highlighted by the haunting Eric Clapton-George Harrison composition "Badge," which remains one of Cream's most beloved tracks.

Clapton and Baker would quickly resurface in 1969 as half of another short-lived supergroup, Blind Faith, and Clapton of course went on to

one of the longest and most successful careers of anyone in the rock business. Bruce and Baker never attained nearly as high a profile after leaving Cream, but both have kept busy in the ensuing decades with various interesting projects in the fields of rock, jazz, and experimental music. —*Richie Unterberger*

Fresh Cream / Dec. 1966 / Polydor ✦✦✦
Cream's debut album was largely rooted in the blues, and included here highly charged versions of such standards as Willie Dixon's "Spoonful," Muddy Waters' "Rollin' and Tumblin'," and bassist Jack Bruce's "N.S.U."—which took on a whole new life on stage. On this record they sound somewhat flat and uninspired. —*Rob Bowman*

Disraeli Gears / Nov. 1967 / Polydor ✦✦✦✦
Cream's sophomore effort was a substantial step forward. Interestingly, part of the reason seems to be that they stopped covering American blues musicians and started writing their own psychedelic blues-based hybrids. "Sunshine of Your Love" was the big AM radio hit and "Tales of Brave Ulysses," "Strange Brew," and "S.W.L.A.B.R." received substantial FM play. —*Rob Bowman*

Wheels of Fire / Jun. 1968 / Polydor ✦✦✦✦
Wheels of Fire is a two-album set, one disc recorded in the studio, the second disc recorded on stage in San Francisco. Side Three contains the definitive live version of what became Clapton's signature piece, Robert Johnson's "Crossroads," plus a version of "Spoonful." On such pieces, Cream approached blues-based rock with a jazz aesthetic, using the song as a framework to begin and end a performance. The strength of the performance is in the improvisation. When it worked, as it does on "Spoonful," it was brilliant. When it didn't, as on "Traintime" and "Toad," they became excess incarnate. The studio disc contained their second Top Ten single, Jack Bruce's "White Room," as well as a stunning cover of Albert King's "Born Under a Bad Sign." Other tracks, particularly those written by Ginger Baker, do not hold up. —*Rob Bowman*

Goodbye / Jan. 1969 / Polydor ✦✦✦
As the title implies, this is Cream's farewell. By the time it was issued, the band had broken up. Three studio recordings that were left were coupled with extended live versions of "I'm So Glad," "Politician," and "I'm Sitting on Top of the World." The live tracks burn. Clapton, Bruce, and Baker each take credit for one of the studio tracks. Clapton's cut, "Badge," was co-written by George Harrison and remains what was surely the prettiest melody to ever grace a Cream recording. —*Rob Bowman*

Live Cream, Vol. 1 / Apr. 1970 / Polydor ✦✦✦

Live Cream, Vol. 2 / Mar. 1972 / Polydor ✦✦✦

Strange Brew: The Very Best of Cream / 1983 / Polydor ✦✦✦
What the title implies, all the finest tracks from the band's four studio albums. The best was brilliant. —*Rob Bowman*

★ **The Very Best of Cream** / 1995 / Chronicles ✦✦✦✦✦
There have been many compilations drawn from the four albums Cream originally released between 1966 and 1969. But the one most commonly available since the early 1980s was the ten *Strange Brew: The Very Best of Cream* (1983), a bare-bones collection focusing on the group's hit singles. Note that this album, despite the similar title, is a newly compiled 1995 CD/cassette containing all of the recordings on *Strange Brew*, plus ten more. It is the most comprehensive Cream anthology on the market, including all the group's essential tracks on a single disc with superior sound. —*William Ruhlmann*

Creation

Rock 'n' Roll, British Invasion, Psychedelic
No other band came closer to emulating the feedback-ridden autodestruction of the early Who than the Creation, who had a couple minor UK hit singles in 1966 with "Making Time" and "Painter Man." The sonic resemblance is hardly surprising; the Creation were produced by Shel Talmy, who also produced the Who's earliest records, and lead guitarist Eddie Phillips was even asked by Pete Townshend to join the Who as second guitarist. Phillips' feedback freakouts were grounded by solid mod power chords and British Invasion harmonies. The Creation produced several interesting singles between 1966 and 1968, and although they achieved brief stardom in Germany, they never made it big in the UK Ronnie Wood was briefly a member before the group disbanded in 1968. —*Richie Unterberger*

● **How Does It Feel to Feel** / 1982 / Edsel ✦✦✦✦
Unquestionably the best of the several Creation repackages floating around. Includes virtually all of their 1966-68 singles and a few other stray tracks of interest from the same period. —*Richie Unterberger*

Creedence Clearwater Revival

Rock 'n' Roll
At a time when rock was evolving further and further away from the forces that had made the music possible in the first place, Creedence Clearwater Revival brought things back to their roots with their concise

synthesis of rockabilly, swamp pop, R&B, and country. Though CCR were very a much a group in their tight, punchy arrangements, their vision was very much singer, songwriter, guitarist, and leader John Fogerty's. Fogerty's classic compositions for Creedence both evoked enduring images of Americana and reflected burning social issues of the day. The band's genius was their ability to accomplish this with the economic, primal power of a classic rockabilly ensemble.

The key elements of Creedence had been woodshedding in bar bands for about a decade before their breakthrough to national success in the late '60s. John's older brother Tom formed the Blue Velvets in the late '50s in El Cerrito, CA, a tiny suburb across the bay from San Francisco. By the mid-'60s, with a few hopelessly obscure recordings under their belt, they'd signed to Fantasy, releasing several singles as the Golliwogs that went nowhere. In fact, there's little promise to be found on those early efforts, primarily because Tom, not John, was doing most of the singing. The group only found themselves when John took firm reigns over the band's direction, singing and writing virtually all of their material.

On their first album as Creedence Clearwater Revival in 1968, the group played it both ways, offering extended, quasi-psychedelic workouts of the '50s classics "I Put a Spell on You" and "Suzy Q." The latter song became their first big hit, but the band didn't really bloom until "Proud Mary," a No. 2 single in early 1969 that demonstrated John's talent at tapping into Southern roots music and imagery with a natural ease. It was the start of a torrent of classic hits from the gritty, Little Richard-inspired singer over the next two years, including "Bad Moon Rising," "Green River," "Down on the Corner," "Travelin' Band," "Who'll Stop the Rain," "Up Around the Bend," and "Lookin' out My Back Door."

Creedence also made good albums, but their true forte was as a singles band—their LPs contained some filler, both in the forms of average original material and straightforward covers of rock 'n' roll chestnuts. When the Beatles broke up in early 1970, CCR were the only other act that provided any competition in the fine art of crafting bold, super-catchy artistic statements that soared to the upper reaches of the charts every three or four months. Although they hailed from the San Francisco area, they rarely succumbed to the psychedelic indulgences of the era. John Fogerty also proved adept at voicing the concerns of the working class in songs like "Fortunate Son," as well as partying with as much funk as any White rock band would muster on "Travelin' Band" and "Down on the Corner."

With John Fogerty holding such a strong upper hand, Creedence couldn't be said to have been a democratic unit, and Fogerty's dominance was to sow the seeds of the group's quick dissolution. Tom Fogerty left in 1971 (recording a few unremarkable solo albums of his own), reducing the band to a trio. John allowed drummer Doug Clifford and bassist Stu Cook equal shares of songwriting and vocal time on the group's final album, *Mardi Gras* (1972), which proved conclusively that Fogerty's songs and singing were necessary to raise CCR above journeyman status.

It was John Fogerty, of course, who produced the only notable work after the quartet broke up. Even his solo outings, though, were erratic and, for nearly ten years, nonexistent as he became embroiled in a web of business disputes with Fantasy Records. His 1984 album *Centerfield* proved he could still rock in the vintage Creedence mode when the spirit moved him, but Tom Fogerty's death in 1990 ended any hopes of a CCR reunion with the original members intact. *—Richie Unterberger*

Creedence Clearwater Revival / 1968 / Fantasy ✦✦✦
The band's unique swampy crunch was already well-developed on this fine debut. It opens with a riveting version of Screamin' Jay Hawkins' hit "I Put a Spell on You." A gritty psychedelic version of Dale Hawkins's creation "Suzy Q" was Creedence's first hit. *—Rick Clark*

Bayou Country / 1969 / Fantasy ✦✦✦
John Fogerty's songwriting voice gains new focus, particularly in "Proud Mary," the band's most popular song, and "Penthouse Pauper." "Bootleg" features a powerfully spare groove, and "Born on the Bayou," with its rock-solid pulse and economical lead-guitar work, is one of the band's better attempts at stretching out. Nevertheless, the long jams found here cause the album to lose some steam. *—Rick Clark*

☆ **Green River** / 1969 / Fantasy ✦✦✦✦✦
Fogerty tightens things up with this great collection of songs. It contains the truly great hits "Green River," "Lodi," and "Bad Moon Rising." "Wrote a Song for Everyone," "Cross-tie Walker," and "Tombstone Shadow" are classic Fogerty. There's a super version of "The Night Time Is the Right Time." *—Rick Clark*

☆ **Willy & the Poor Boys** / 1969 / Fantasy ✦✦✦✦✦
There's not a weak cut here, just more hits like "Down on the Corner" and the relentless wrong-side-of-the-tracks railing of "Fortunate Son." By the time of *Willy*, this California band had captured the spirit of the South more believably than most bands from that region. Versions of "The Midnight Special," "Cotton Fields," and instrumentals like the

down-home "Poorboy Shuffle" and "Side O' the Road," with its Booker T. groove, helped underscore that perception. *—Rick Clark*

Cosmo's Factory / 1970 / Fantasy ✦✦✦✦
"Ramble Tamble" and a masterful version of "I Heard It Through the Grapevine" may run a little too long, but the remainder of the album is letter-perfect. Pointing out highlights here is useless. Most of these tracks were hits as well. *—Rick Clark*

Pendulum / 1970 / Fantasy ✦✦✦

Creedence Gold / 1972 / Fantasy ✦✦✦✦
Creedence Gold is a good collection of Creedence Clearwater Revival's hit singles that was supplanted by the thorough *Chronicle*. *—Stephen Thomas Erlewine*

Mardi Gras / 1972 / Fantasy ✦✦✦

★ **Chronicle, Vol. 1** / 1976 / Fantasy ✦✦✦✦✦
An essential disc for any serious lover of rock 'n' roll, it contains almost all of the Creedence hits, plus a generous helping of key album tracks. *—Rick Clark*

The Royal Albert Hall Concert / 1980 / Fantasy ✦✦✦

☆ **Chronicle, Vol. 2** / 1986 / Fantasy ✦✦✦✦✦
Chronicle, Vol. 2 effectively compiles all of the highlights from Creedence Clearwater Revival's career that weren't on the first volume. All of the singles were included on *Chronicle*, so *Chronicle, Vol. 2* is comprised solely of album tracks. That doesn't mean these are lesser items. On the contrary, the majority of these songs—"Born on the Bayou," "Tombstone Shadow," "Wrote a Song for Everyone," "It Came out of the Sky," "Midnight Special"—rank among their best performances. Of course, a couple of great tracks remain on CCR's individual albums, notably "Bootleg," but *Chronicle, Vol. 2* is an ideal choice for listeners that want a little more than the hits but are unwilling to delve into the proper albums. *—Stephen Thomas Erlewine*

Marshall Crenshaw

b. 1954, Detroit, MI
Guitar, Vocals / Rock 'n' Roll, New Wave, Pop-Rock
When Marshall Crenshaw burst onto the 1982 music scene, his tight well-crafted songs (part Buddy Holly, part Beatles) and exuberant performances were a fresh breeze at a time when robotic pop by Human League and Tony Basil, as well as soul-numbing ballads like Lionel Richie's "Truly," reigned on the airwaves. He even managed a Top 40 hit with the timeless-sounding "Someday, Someway." Crenshaw's albums have been mostly enjoyable. Only on 1989's *Good Evening* does Crenshaw seem creatively adrift. *—Rick Clark*

● **Marshall Crenshaw** / 1982 / Warner Bros. ✦✦✦✦
His incredible debut revealed Crenshaw to be a fully formed songwriter in the Beatles and Buddy Holly super-melodic pop tradition. Like the work of those influences, the best material here seems timeless. "Someday, Someway" (No. 36) was a moderate hit, even though it (and others like "Cynical Girl," "Girls," "The Usual Thing," and "Mary Anne") seemed written in stone. Crenshaw does include one fine cover of "Soldier of Love," recorded originally by Arthur Alexander and later by the Beatles. Criticism: Why has Warner chosen not to include Crenshaw's fine B-sides as bonus tracks from this period on this or his other CDs? *—Rick Clark*

Field Day / 1983 / Warner Bros. ✦✦✦✦
For those expecting a repeat of his fine debut effort, Crenshaw made an unexpected left turn and sought out in-demand producer Steve Lillywhite, whose credits (Psychedelic Furs, XTC, U2, Ultravox) read like an alternative rock Who's Who. The heavily treated drum sounds and walls of guitar may have initially put off some fans, but *Field Day* demonstrated that Crenshaw was making impressive strides as a songwriter and musician. "Whenever You're on My Mind" (a great single that should've been a hit), "Our Town," "All I Know Right Now," and "Monday Morning Rock" are highlights. *—Rick Clark*

Downtown / 1985 / Warner Bros. ✦✦✦✦
With the help of producer T-Bone Burnett and a handful of session sidemen, Crenshaw delivered a strong collection of originals and covers. Highlights include a version of Ben Vaughn's "I'm Sorry (But So Is Brenda Lee)" and Crenshaw's own "The Distance Between." This is one of Crenshaw's best efforts. *—Rick Clark*

Mary Jean & 9 Others / 1987 / Warner Bros. ✦✦✦✦
Not quite as strong as his first three full-length albums, *Mary Jean* does possess some standout tracks in "Calling our for Love (at Crying Time)," a version of Peter Case's "Steel Strings," and the title cut. It was produced by Don Dixon, whose credits include the Smithereens. *—Rick Clark*

Good Evening / 1989 / Warner Bros. ✦✦
This effort drew heavily on outside material, with songs by Richard Thompson, Dianne Warren, John Hiatt, the Isley Brothers, and Bobby Fuller. David Kershenbaum's production is typically classy, but is unable to keep this from being Crenshaw's weakest release. *—Rick Clark*

Life's Too Short / 1991 / MCA ✦✦✦
Live: My Truck Is My Home / 1994 / Razor & Tie ✦✦✦

The Crests

Doo Wop
One of the most successful integrated doo wop groups, the Crests waxed the classic ballad "16 Candles" in 1959. Formed in 1956, they began recording the next year for Joyce, where they inched onto the pop lists with "Sweetest One." Moving to the brand-new Coed logo, Johnny Maestro's (b. May 7, 1930) warm tenor made "16 Candles" a national smash, and pop/R&B hybrids like "The Angels Listened In" and "Step by Step" also did well. Maestro went solo in 1960, scoring the next year with "Model Girl" on Coed, while the Crests attempted to survive on their own. Maestro eventually reclaimed stardom as leader of Brooklyn Bridge, an 11-piece aggregation that hit with "Worst That Could Happen" in 1968. *—Bill Dahl*

● **The Best of the Crests** / 1990 / Rhino ✦✦✦✦
All of the Crests' hits, including the classic "16 Candles" and "Trouble in Paradise," are collected on this splendid 18-track disc. *—Stephen Thomas Erlewine*

Jim Croce

b. Jan. 10, 1943, Philadelphia, PA, d. Sep. 20, 1973, Natchitaches, LA
Guitar, Vocals / Singer-Songwriter
A singer-songwriter whose enormous pop success of the early '70s was cut short by his death in a plane crash. A Philadelphia native who had worked the coffeehouse circuit for almost ten years when he was signed to ABC Records in 1971, Croce had a warm singing voice that served him well on his comic uptempo hits ("You Don't Mess Around with Jim," "Bad, Bad Leroy Brown") as well as his sincere ballads ("Operator"). The latter became predominant after his death, with "I Got a Name," "Time in a Bottle," and "I'll Have to Say I Love You in a Song," all of which were posthumous Top Ten hits. *—William Ruhlmann*

You Don't Mess Around with Jim / 1972 / ABC ✦✦✦

● **Photographs & Memories: His Greatest Hits** / 1974 / Atlantic ✦✦✦✦
Photographs & Memories: His Greatest Hits is a compilation containing Croce's best songs and biggest hits, including the No. 1 hits "Bad, Bad Leroy Brown" and "Time in a Bottle." *—William Ruhlmann*

Time in a Bottle/Greatest Love Songs / 1977 / Atlantic ✦✦✦✦
Since it contains only his love ballads, fans who prefer his sweetly sentimental songs like "Operator" and "Time in a Bottle" to story-songs like "Bad, Bad Leroy Brown" and "You Don't Mess Around with Jim" will find *Time in a Bottle* the essential compilation; despite the amount of good material here, *Photographs and Memories* remains a better collection, because it presents both sides of the popular singer-songwriter. *—Stephen Thomas Erlewine*

The 50th Anniversary Collection / 1992 / Saja ✦✦✦✦
While it has too much material for the casual listener, the two-disc *50th Anniversary Collection* is the definitive package for the hardcore Jim Croce fan, covering all of his hits, as well as many forgotten album tracks. *—Stephen Thomas Erlewine*

Crosby Stills & Nash (and Young)

Singer-Songwriter, Folk-Rock, Pop-Rock
The musical partnership of David Crosby (b. Aug. 14, 1941), Stephen Stills (b. Jan. 3, 1945), and Graham Nash (b. Feb. 2, 1942), with and without Neil Young (b. Nov. 12, 1945), not only was one of the most successful touring and recording acts of the late '60s, '70s, and early '80s—with the colorful, contrasting nature of the members' characters and their connection to the political and cultural upheavals of the time—it was the only American-based band to approach the overall societal impact of the Beatles. The group was a second marriage for all the participants when it came together in 1968: Crosby had been a member of the Byrds, Nash was in the Hollies, and Stills had been part of Buffalo Springfield. The resulting trio, however, sounded like none of its predecessors and was characterized by a unique vocal blend and a musical approach that ranged from acoustic folk to melodic pop to hard rock. CSN's debut album, released in 1969, was perfectly in tune with the times, and the group was an instant hit. By the time of their first tour (which included the Woodstock festival), they had added Young, also a veteran of Buffalo Springfield, who maintained a solo career. The first CSN&Y album, *Deja-vu*, was a chart-topping hit in 1970, but the group split acrimoniously after a summer tour. *Four Way Street*, a live double album issued after the breakup, was another No. 1 hit. (When it finally was released on CD in 1992, it was lengthened with more live material.) In 1974, CSN&Y reformed for a summer stadium tour without releasing a new record. Nevertheless, the compilation *So Far* became their third straight No. 1. Crosby, Stills and Nash reformed without Young in 1977 for the album *CSN*, another giant hit. They followed with *Daylight Again* in 1982, but

by then Crosby was in the throes of drug addiction and increasing legal problems. He was in jail in 1985-1986, but cleaned up and returned to action, with the result that CSN&Y reunited for only their second studio album, *American Dream*, in 1988. CSN followed with *Live It Up* in 1990, and though that album was a commercial disappointment, the trio remains a popular live act; it embarked on a 25th anniversary tour in the summer of 1994 and released a new album, *After the Storm.* *—William Ruhlmann*

Crosby, Stills & Nash / May 29, 1969 / Atlantic ✦✦✦✦
The group's debut album is a scintillating blend of personal poetry, topical politics, and splendid, spare production. "Suite: Judy Blue Eyes" caught everybody's ear, but every track here is worthwhile, and the success of the album can be measured by the fact that every song here could have been a single or a B-side. "Marrakesh Express," "Pre-Road Downs," and "Lady of the Island" stand out. *—Bruce Eder*

☆ **Deja-vu** / Mar. 11, 1970 / Atlantic ✦✦✦✦✦
This was the group's triumph, displaying a broader musical scope than that found on the CSN debut record. Each of the four members contributed high-quality material, with Stills turning in the leadoff track, "Carry On," Nash contributing such standards as "Teach Your Children" and "Our House," Crosby presenting the title track, and Young adding the characteristic "Helpless." There was also the hit version of Joni Mitchell's "Woodstock." Flawless harmonies, thoughtful lyrics, accomplished playing: this is state-of-the-art '70s rock music and continues to be the best explanation of CSN&Y's enormous stature and enduring legacy. *—William Ruhlmann*

Four Way Street / Apr. 7, 1971 / Atlantic ✦✦✦✦
This 1992 expanded version of the original double live album (originally released on April 7, 1971) by CSN&Y is now an indispensable part of any collection, with additional Neil Young and Graham Nash material (and even a version of "King Midas in Reverse," the old Hollies tune) that any serious listener will want. Some of the extended guitar jams between Stills and Young ("Southern Man") go on longer than strict musical sense would dictate, but it seemed right at the time, and they capture a form that was far more abused in other hands after this group broke up. *—Bruce Eder*

● **So Far** / Aug. 1974 / Atlantic ✦✦✦✦
Released to coincide with CSN&Y's 1974 reunion tour, this compilation remains the best representation of the group's early work, featuring such hits as "Teach Your Children" and "Suite: Judy Blue Eyes." It also put the one-off single "Ohio/Find the Cost of Freedom" (CSN&Y's response to the shooting of four anti-war student protestors at Kent State University) on an album for the first time. *—William Ruhlmann*

CSN / Jun. 17, 1977 / Atlantic ✦✦✦
A fair and somewhat slick reprise, highlighted by "Dark Star." A valiant attempt to re-create the good spirits of the first album amid the malaise of the '70s. *—Bruce Eder*

Daylight Again / Jun. 21, 1982 / Atlantic ✦✦✦
American Dream / Nov. 3, 1988 / Atlantic ✦✦
Live It Up / Jun. 11, 1990 / Atlantic ✦✦
Crosby, Stills & Nash Box Set / Oct. 1991 / Atlantic ✦✦✦✦
Seventy-seven tracks make up this four-CD boxed set retrospective of the various permutations of Crosby, Stills and Nash (and Young) from 1968 to 1990. The set is dotted with unreleased tracks from abortive album sessions (CSN&Y may have recorded only two studio albums, but they sure tried a lot of other times), and there are also good choices from both solo work and the well-known material. For a neophyte, it may be on the long side, but seasoned fans can welcome this lavish tribute. *—William Ruhlmann*

Sheryl Crow

b. Feb. 11, 1963, Kernett, MO
Vocals / Singer-Songwriter, Pop-Rock
After many years of paying her dues as a backup singer for Don Henley, Eric Clapton, Rod Stewart, and Michael Jackson, Sheryl Crow finally got a chance to make her own album in 1993. Growing out of a series of informal jam sessions with Los Angeles studio veterans, the relaxed yet gritty blues-rock of *Tuesday Night Music Club* became a hit in the Spring of 1994, thanks to the single "Leaving Las Vegas," a slightly surreal travelogue which only shows the beginning of her talent. Later that summer, the laidback "All I Want to Do" was released and it became an across-the-boards success, pushing *Tuesday Night Music Club* into the Top Ten and into multi-platinum status. *—Stephen Thomas Erlewine*

Tuesday Night Music Club / Aug. 3, 1993 / A&M ✦✦✦✦
Sheryl Crow's debut album *Tuesday Night Music Club* is a loose, melodic, gritty record with subtle country underpinnings. Throughout the album, she shows that not only does she have an impressive, bluesy voice, but is also a considerably talented songwriter, as "Leaving Las Vegas" and "Run Baby Run" prove. *—Stephen Thomas Erlewine*

Crowded House

Pop-Rock

An institution in their homeland, a two-hit wonder in the US and, during the last half of their ten-year career, bona fide stars in the UK and most of Europe, Crowded House recorded some of the best pop music of the late '80s and early '90s. Leader Neil Finn's carefully crafted songs, meticulous eye for lyrical detail, and gift for melody are matched by few other songwriters.

Crowded House formed in 1985 when Neil Finn dissolved Split Enz rather than carry on after his brother Tim, the group's founding member, left to pursue a solo career. Instead of carrying through with the new wave direction of latter-day Split Enz, Neil moved in favor of a stripped down, back-to-basics combo featuring ex-Enz drummer Paul Hester, bassist Nick Seymour, and guitarist Craig Hooper. Initially, the group named themselves after Finn's middle name, touring Australia and recording demos under the name the Mullanes; Hooper was dropped shortly after this formative period. In June of 1985, the group headed to Los Angeles to shop for a record label, eventually signing with Capitol Records. Capitol requested that the band change their name and the group settled on Crowded House, a reflection of their living conditions in Los Angeles. They began work on their debut, enlisting the help of then-unknown producer, Mitchell Froom. A partnership between the band and the producer formed, making Froom nearly a fourth member. The partnership benefited both the band and the producer—the band was helped by Froom's direct, simple approach and more "American" sound as well as his input as a musician, and Froom was able to build a career as a high-profile producer.

Crowded House's self-titled debut didn't gain much attention upon its release in the summer of 1986, due to insufficient promotion from Capitol Records. In wake of the weak support from Capitol, the band took matters into their own hands. Rather than setting out on an expensive large-scale tour, the band took a more low-profile route, playing acoustic sets for industry insiders and for small crowds at ethnic restaurants and in record stores. This unorthodox approach began a buzz within the industry. On the talk show circuit, they won over American and Canadian audiences with their charm and wit as well as their wacky antics. By February of 1987, the album broke into the American Top 40, eventually peaking at No. 12. The album spawned the No. 2 hit single "Don't Dream It's Over" and "Something So Strong," which reached No. 7. In Australia and New Zealand, multi-platinum success followed.

Released in 1988, *Temple of Low Men*, was anything but a sophomore slump—Neil Finn's new songs were among his finest, showcasing a notable progression in his songcraft. The album's slightly darker material, however, made for a more difficult listen and, although the material was stronger, the record lacked the immediate appeal of the debut. This, coupled with Capitol's lack of promotional support, led to disappointing sales—the album barely broke the US Top 40 and the single, "Better Be Home Soon," stalled at No. 42. Since hope had basically run out for the album, they abandoned plans for a major US tour. A three-month break in touring revitalized the band for an well-received Australian and Canadian tour, but by mid-1989 the band had effectively broken up.

Late in 1989, Neil reunited with his brother Tim and the duo began writing songs together for the first time, with the intention of releasing the material on a proposed Finn Brothers album. The collaboration was successful and the duo was prolific, writing 14 songs in a very short time; these songs were among the finest either had ever written. After the initial sessions with Tim, Neil began working on a new set of songs, designed for the next Crowded House album, but he soon found the new material unsatisfactory. Neil decided to combine the better moments of the Finn Brothers project and the scrapped third album, adding his brother as a fourth member of Crowded House.

Crowded House's third album, *Woodface,* released in 1991, proved the decision to combine the material from the two scrapped records was sound. Although the choice of "Chocolate Cake" as a leadoff single was both misleading and off-putting to American audiences, effectively sinking the album's chances of success in the US, England and Europe embraced the band for the first time. After about six months of dormancy, they began charting in the UK and Europe with several singles including the smash "Weather with You." The British success of "Weather with You" helped *Woodface* achieve platinum status in the UK, and led the group to several headlining concerts at Wembley Arena. Tim, for all of his invaluable contributions in the writing and recording of *Woodface*, proved extraneous to the band's live show. He left the band in November 1991, as the band was in the middle of their tour and just prior to their breakthrough success in England. Following the success of *Woodface*, both Neil and Tim Finn were awarded OBEs from the Queen of England in 1993; the honor was bestowed for their contribution to the arts.

In early 1993, Crowded House regrouped to record their fourth album, adding American guitarist Mark Hart (who had briefly toured with the band around the time of *Temple of Low Men*) to the band and dropping Mitchell Froom as their producer, opting instead for ex-Killing Joke

member Youth, who developed a reputation as a hip producer in the early '90s. *Together Alone* was released in October 1993 (Jan. 1994 in North America) to unanimously positive reviews and solid sales in every country except the US. Upon its release, *Together Alone* entered the English charts at No. 4; at the time, *Woodface* was still in the UK charts. After the album was released, Crowded House embarked on a successful European tour. They were beginning an American tour when Paul Hester decided to leave the band to spend more time with his new family. Hiring a session drummer, the band rounded out the tour, eventually returning to Australia.

By the end of 1994, Neil Finn decided to cut back on the touring to work on side projects which included some production work for Dave Dobbyn and a second try at a Finn Brothers album with Tim. The Finn Brothers finally released their long-awaited duet album in the fall of 1995. In June of 1996, Neil officially broke up Crowded House. That same month, *Recurring Dream: The Very Best of Crowded House* was released, entering the UK and Australian charts at No. 1. —*Chris Woodstra*

Crowded House / 1986 / Capitol ✦✦✦

Their Top 40 debut is loaded with highly melodic, pop gems. Strong, upbeat songwriting and vocal harmonies from this talented trio, featuring the hits "Don't Dream It's Over" and "Something So Strong." —*Scott Bultman*

Temple of Low Men / 1988 / Capitol ✦✦✦✦

Following the success of Crowded House's debut and the band's gruelling promotion schedule, Neil Finn was clearly showing signs that he was no longer happy being New Zealand's zany ambassador to the US. While the material on *Temple of Low Men* demonstrates great leaps in quality over its predecessor, it is a darkly difficult album, especially for those expecting *Crowded House, Pt. 2*—in short, there are no immediately accessible singles. Instead, Finn digs into the depths of his emotional psyche with obsessive detail, crafting a set of intense, personal songs that range from the all-too-intimate look at infidelity of "Into Temptation" to the raucous exorcism of "Kill Eye." Through all of this introspective soul searching, Finn reveals most of all his true mastery of melody. —*Chris Woodstra*

Woodface / 1991 / Capitol ✦✦✦✦

Where Crowded House's previous album, *Temple of Low Men*, showcased the often dark side of a man alone with his thoughts, *Woodface* represents the joy of reunion and the freedom of a collaborative effort—more than half of the album was originally conceived as a Finn Brothers project, which was Tim and Neil's first crack at writing together. The songs are easily their finest to date, combining flawless melodies and the outstanding harmonies of the brothers' perfectly matched voices. —*Chris Woodstra*

Together Alone / 1993 / Capitol ✦✦✦

More experimental and musically varied than any of their previous releases, *Together Alone* finds Crowded House branching out into traditional Maori music and heavy guitars, as well as the shining pop songcraft that is Neil Finn's trademark. Picking up a new guitarist and adding the production skills of ex-Killing Joke member Youth, Crowded House energizes their sound without losing sight of Neil Finn's classic pop songwriting, as "Locked Out" and "Distant Sun" prove. —*Stephen Thomas Erlewine*

● **Recurring Dream: The Very Best of Crowded House** / Jun. 1996 / EMI ✦✦✦✦

Recurring Dream is a 19-track collection which assembles most of the band's singles and adds three new studio tracks to entice fans—"Not the Girl You Think You Are," "Instinct," and "Everything Is Good for You." As a career summary, the collection works fairly well, though the nonchronological sequencing makes for a slightly confusing listen. Nevertheless, for a band with no shortage of great material (there's not a bad album in the bunch), *Recurring Dream* is a good place to get acquainted with them. Initial pressings also came with a second disc which compiles highlights from the band's always entertaining live shows. Maybe a disc of non-album rarities and B-sides would have been a better choice, but for fans this is an essential addition. —*Chris Woodstra*

The Cryan' Shames

Pop-Rock

The Cryan' Shames were a big deal in Chicago in the mid- and late '60s, when a bunch of their singles hit the local Top Ten; some of them were small national hits as well. The biggest of these was "Sugar and Spice," a cover of a Searchers' song (itself a cover of a Drifters' hit) that made the Top 50 in 1966, and was later featured in the *Nuggets* anthology of '60s garage bands. In their original incarnation, the Shames leaned toward the pop end of the garage, but did quite a good job. Borrowing heavily from the Beatles, Byrds, and Yardbirds, guitarist Jim Fair wrote a clutch of energetic guitar pop-rockers with sparkling harmonies. After 1966, unfortunately, the group pursued an increasingly mainstream pop direction featuring saccharine arrangements and material. In this respect they uncannily mirrored the devolution of local rivals the New Colony Six, who also shifted from tough pop-rock to MOR in their bid for national success. — *Richie Unterberger*

● **Sugar & Spice (A Collection)** / 1992 / Columbia ✦✦✦✦
This 18-song compilation spans 1966 to 1969 and features their singles and key album cuts. Despite its good intentions, this well-packaged retrospective runs out of octane after the first half dozen songs. — *Richie Unterberger*

The Crystals

Girl Group
This Brooklyn female vocal group had R&B roots, but the Crystals were really a pop ensemble whose best songs perfectly expressed the romantic innocence of the early '60s. Barbara Alston, Lala Brooks, Dee Dee Kennibrew, Mary Thomas, and Patricia Wright were the original lineup formed by Benny Wells while still in high school. Wells served as their first manager. The remarkable producer Phil Spector heard them rehearsing and eventually signed them to his Philles label, where they had several classic songs. "There's No Other like My Baby" got things started in 1961, making it to No. 5 on the R&B charts and to No. 20 on the pop charts. "Uptown" cracked the R&B and pop Top 20, then came "He's a Rebel," arguably their finest song and one of the era's landmarks. Darlene Love was lead vocalist, and both it and the successful follow-up "He's Sure the Boy I Love" featured Love and the Blossoms but were credited to the Crystals. The actual Crystals returned in 1963 minus Mary Thomas, who left to get married. They had two more huge hits, "Da Doo Ron Ron (When He Walked Me Home)" and "Then He Kissed Me" in 1963, each one making the Top Ten on both the R&B and pop lists. But the party ended in 1964, as their final two singles for Philles both flopped and relations between them and Spector degenerated. Wright left and was replaced by Frances Collins. They bought themselves out of their Philles contract in 1965 and signed with United Artists, only to get dropped a year later. They disbanded, then re-formed in 1971. Since then, various editions of the Crystals have been plentiful on the oldies circuit, but at last account, only Kennibrew was still involved out of the originals. — *Ron Wynn*

● **The Best of the Crystals** / 1992 / ABKCO ✦✦✦✦
All of the Crystals' biggest hits are included on this comprehensive collection, which also features many forgotten singles and album tracks; while some of the lesser-known material might not match the standards of the classic singles, many songs do come close. — *Stephen Thomas Erlewine*

The Cult

Hard Rock
Singer Ian Astbury formed the Southern Death Cult in England in 1982 as a doom-rock band. Reorganized in 1983 as Death Cult with guitarist Billy Duffy, by 1984 the rock quartet, quickly moving toward heavy metal, had become simply the Cult. Their hard-rock set *Electric* (1987) was a commercial breakthrough. *Sonic Temple* (1989) was an even bigger success, hitting the Top Ten (No. 3 in the UK) and selling over a million copies. However, that proved to be the band's commercial peak, as subsequent records failed to chart as highly. After 1994's self-titled album failed to make an impression in either the US or the UK, the Cult disbanded in early 1995. — *William Ruhlmann*

Love / 1985 / Sire ✦✦✦
Apart from the monolithic rock 'n' roll masterpiece "She Sells Sanctuary," *Love* is devoid of memorable riffs and melodies. — *Stephen Thomas Erlewine*

● **Electric** / 1987 / Sire ✦✦✦✦
After four years of evolving from a goth-rock band with two longer names (Southern Death Cult, Death Cult), the Cult emerged on this Rick Rubin production as a full-fledged heavy metal band. Billy Duffy pulls out monstrous guitar riffs and lead singer Ian Astbury declaims like a latter-day Jim Morrison. It also contains "Love Removal Machine." — *William Ruhlmann*

Sonic Temple / 1989 / Sire ✦✦✦
A change of producer and drummers has no discernible impact on the Cult's driving metal assault. — *William Ruhlmann*

Ceremony / 1991 / Sire ✦✦✦
Ceremony continued the straightforward attack of *Sonic Temple*, and while the songs weren't quite as strong as those on the previous record, it delivered a bracing heavy-metal roar. — *David Jehnzen*

The Cult / 1994 / Sire ✦✦

Culture Club

New Wave, Pop-Rock
Culture Club was a successful pop-rock group of the early '80s, led by

singer Boy George O'Dowd (b. Jun. 14, 1961). It was as well known for O'Dowd's flamboyant fashion sense as it was for its music, but when it was hot, it was hot: Culture Club racked up six straight Top Ten hits in 1983-1984. The group was formed in London in 1981. In addition to O'Dowd, it consisted of bassist Mikey Craig (b. Feb. 15, 1960), guitarist Roy Hay (b. Aug. 12, 1961), and drummer Jon Moss (b. Sep. 11, 1957). They topped the charts with their debut single, "Do You Really Want to Hurt Me." The band's visual flair helped them in the US, where music video had recently become an important promotional tool, and the single hit Stateside by early 1983.

Culture Club's music was light, bouncy pop, topped by O'Dowd's appealing tenor. It was anything but outrageous, although O'Dowd's elaborate costumes made the group seem more daring than it was. *Kissing to Be Clever,* their debut album, was a million-seller and included "I'll Tumble 4 Ya," another Top Ten hit. The fall of 1983 brought a second album, *Colour by Numbers,* and more hits: "Church of the Poison Mind," "Karma Chameleon" (a No. 1), and "Miss Me Blind."

Unfortunately, the group's very novelty was its undoing. The third album, *Waking up with the House on Fire* (1984), went platinum by momentum but its singles were not big hits, and the fourth album, *From Luxury to Heartache,* was a relative flop in 1986, the same year O'Dowd's heroin addiction became a matter of public knowledge. In 1987 O'Dowd cleaned up, split up Culture Club, and embarked on a solo career. — *William Ruhlmann*

Kissing to Be Clever / 1982 / Virgin ✦✦✦✦
Appealing lightly synthesized '80s pop music, featuring the infectious ballad hit "Do You Really Want to Hurt Me." — *William Ruhlmann*

Colour by Numbers / 1983 / Virgin ✦✦✦✦
More melodic bouncy pop led by Boy George's engaging singing on "Karma Chameleon" and other songs. — *William Ruhlmann*

Waking up with the House on Fire / 1984 / Virgin ✦✦

From Luxury to Heartache / 1986 / Virgin ✦✦

● **At Worst . . . The Best of Boy George and Culture Club** / 1993 / Virgin ✦✦✦✦
The success of "The Crying Game" marked a comeback for Boy George, especially in the US, where his solo career had never taken hold beyond the dance clubs, and SBK (distributor of his label, Virgin) took advantage of his resurgence by compiling this 75-minute, 19-track album, which combines his former group Culture Club's biggest hits with selections from his solo work. The ten Culture Club tracks are of a piece, from 1982's "Do You Really Want to Hurt Me" (which here leads off with an ominous voice intoning, "Popularity breeds contempt") to "Love Is Love," which wasn't a hit, but is a better choice than the missing "The War Song," which was. The solo tracks are a more mixed batch, and not only because Top 40 UK hits like "Keep Me in Mind," "Sold," and "To Be Reborn" are missing. They often rely on loud percussion tracks that strand Boy George's tender tenor somewhere in the distance. He remains most effective on rhythmic ballads, whether "Do You Really Want to Hurt Me," "Everything I Own" (his chart-topping first UK solo hit), or "The Crying Game." — *William Ruhlmann*

The Cure

Alternative Pop-Rock, Post-Punk
Out of all the bands that emerged in the immediate aftermath of punk rock in the late '70s, the Cure was one of the most enduring and popular. Led through numerous incarnations by guitarist/vocalist Robert Smith (b. Apr. 21, 1959), the band became notorious for their slow, gloomy dirges and Smith's ghoulish appearance. But the public image often hid the diversity of the Cure's music. At the outset, they played jagged, edgy pop songs and they slowly evolved into a more textured outfit. As one of the bands that laid the seeds for goth-rock, the group created towering layers of guitars and synthesizers, but by the time goth caught on in the mid-'80s, the Cure had moved away from the genre. By the end of the '80s, the Cure had crossed over into the mainstream not only in their native England, but also in the US and in various parts of Europe.

Originally called the Easy Cure, the band was formed in 1976 by schoolmates Robert Smith (vocals, guitar), Michael Dempsey (bass), and Laurence "Lol" Tolhurst (drums). Initially, the band was playing dark, nervy guitar pop with pseudo-literary lyrics, as evidenced by the Albert Camus-inspired "Killing an Arab." A demo tape, featuring "Killing an Arab," arrived in the hands of Chris Parry, an A&R representative at Polydor Records; by the time he received the tape, the band's name had been truncated to the Cure. Parry was impressed with the song and arranged for its release on the independent label Small Wonder in December 1978. Early in 1979, Parry left Polydor to form his own record label, Fiction, and the Cure was one of the first bands he signed to the label. "Killing an Arab" was re-released in February of 1979, and the Cure set out on their first tour of England. The Cure's debut album, *Three Imaginary Boys,* was released in May 1979 to good reviews in the British music press. Later that year, the group released the non-LP singles "Boys

Don't Cry" and "Jumping Someone Else's Train." That same year, the Cure embarked on a major tour with Siouxsie and the Banshees. During the tour, the Banshees' guitarist John McKay left the group and Robert Smith stepped in for the missing musician; for the next decade or so, Smith would frequently collaborate with members of the Banshees.

At the end of 1979, Dempsey was replaced by Simon Gallup at the beginning of 1980. At the same time, the Cure added a keyboardist, Matthieu Hartley, to their lineup. The band's second album, *17 Seconds*, was released in the spring of 1980. The addition of a keyboardist expanded the group's sound—it was now more experimental, and frequently they would immerse themselves in slow, gloomy dirges. Nevertheless, the band still wrote pop hooks, as demonstrated by the group's first UK hit single, "A Forest," which peaked at No. 31. After the release of *17 Seconds*, the Cure began their first world tour. Following the Australian leg of the tour, Matthieu Hartley left the band and the group chose to continue without him. In 1981, they released their third album, *Faith*, which peaked at No. 14 in the charts and spawned the minor hit single "Primary." The Cure's fourth album, the doom-laden, *Pornography*, was released in 1982. *Pornography* expanded their cult audience even further and it cracked the UK Top Ten. After the *Pornography* tour was completed, Simon Gallup quit the band and Lol Tolhurst moved from drums to keyboards. At the end of 1982, the Cure released a new single, the dance-tinged "Let's Go to Bed."

Robert Smith devoted most of the beginning of 1983 to Siouxsie and the Banshees, recording the *Hyaena* album with the group and appearing as the band's guitarist on the album's accompanying tour. Smith also formed a band with Banshees bassist Steve Severin called the Glove that same year. The Glove released their only album, *Blue Sunshine*, later in 1983. By the late summer of 1983, a new version of the Cure—featuring Smith, Tolhurst, drummer Andy Anderson, and bassist Phil Thornalley—was assembled and they recorded a new single, the jaunty "The Lovecats." The song was released in the fall of 1983 and became the group's biggest hit to date, peaking at No. 7 on the UK charts. The new lineup of the Cure released *The Top*, in 1984. Despite the pop leanings of the No. 14 hit "The Caterpillar," *The Top* was a return to the bleak soundscapes of *Pornography*. During the world tour supporting *The Top*, Anderson was fired from the band. In early 1985, following the completion of the tour, Thornalley left the band. The Cure revamped its lineup after his departure, adding drummer Boris Williams, guitarist Porl Thompson, and bassist Simon Gallup. Later in 1985, the Cure released their sixth album, *The Head on the Door*. The album was the most concise and pop-oriented record the group had ever released, which helped send it into the UK Top Ten and to No. 59 in the US—the first time the band had broken the American Hot 100. "In Between Days" and "Close to Me"—both pulled from *The Head on the Door*—became sizable UK hits, as well as popular underground and college-radio hits in the US.

The Cure followed the breakthrough success of *The Head on the Door* in 1986 with the compilation *Standing on a Beach: The Singles*. *Standing on a Beach* reached No. 4 in the UK but more importantly, it established the band as a major cult act in the US—the album peaked at No. 48 and went gold within a year. In short, *Standing on a Beach* set the stage for 1987's double album *Kiss Me, Kiss Me, Kiss Me*. The album was eclectic but it was a hit, spawning four hit singles in the UK and the group's first American Top 40 hit. Following the supporting tour for *Kiss Me, Kiss Me, Kiss Me*, the Cure's activity slowed to a halt. Before the Cure began working on their new album in early 1988, the band fired Lol Tolhurst, claiming that relations between him and the rest of the band had been irrevocably damaged. Tolhurst would soon file a lawsuit, claiming that his role in the band was greater than stated in his contract and, consequently, he deserved more money.

In the meantime, the Cure replaced Tolhurst with former Psychedelic Furs keyboardist Roger O'Donnell and recorded their eighth album, *Disintegration*. Released in the spring of 1989, the album was more melancholy than its predecessor but it was an immediate hit, reaching No. 3 in the UK and No. 14 in the US, and spawning a series of hit singles. "Lullaby" became the group's biggest British hit in the spring of 1989, peaking at No. 5. In the late summer, the band had their biggest American hit with "Lovesong," which climbed to No. 2. On the *Disintegration* tour, the Cure began playing stadiums across the US and the UK. In 1990, the Cure released *Mixed Up*, a collection of remixes featuring a new single, "Never Enough."

Following the *Disintegration* tour, Roger O'Donnell left the band and the Cure replaced him with their roadie, Perry Bamonte. In the spring of 1992, the band released *Wish*. Like *Disintegration*, *Wish* was an immediate hit, entering the British charts at No. 1 and the American charts at No. 2, as well as launching the hit singles "High" and "Friday I'm in Love." The Cure embarked on another international tour after the release of *Wish*. One concert, performed in Detroit, was documented on a film called *Show* and on two albums, *Show* and *Paris*. The movie and the albums were released in 1993.

Porl Thompson left the band in 1993 to join Jimmy Page and Robert Plant's band. After his departure, Roger O'Donnell re-joined the band as

a keyboardist and Perry Bamonte switched from synthesizers to guitars. During most of 1993 and early 1994, the Cure were sidelined by the then-ongoing lawsuit from Lol Tolhurst. Following the settlement in the band's favor in the fall of 1994, the group were set to record a follow-up album to *Wish*, but drummer Boris Williams quit just as they were about to begin the record. The Cure recruited a new drummer through advertisements in the British music papers—by the spring of 1995, Jason Cooper had replaced Williams. Throughout 1995, the Cure recorded their tenth proper studio album, pausing to perform a handful of European musical festivals in the summer. The album, titled *Wild Mood Swings*, was finally released in the spring of 1996. —*Stephen Thomas Erlewine*

Three Imaginary Boys / Jun. 1979 / Fiction ✦✦✦✦
Bursting with high-energy playing and bare-bones production, the band's first album showcases Robert Smith's most concise songwriting. The now common themes of isolation and despair are present, this time presented in perfect three-minute form. *Three Imaginary Boys* ends up sounding like a more tuneful version of Wire's *Pink Flag*. —*Chris Woodstra*

Boys Don't Cry / Jan. 1980 / Elektra ✦✦✦✦
Combining the finer moments from *Three Imaginary Boys* with early singles, this is the best representation of the band's early pop-oriented days. A post-punk masterpiece. —*Chris Woodstra*

Seventeen Seconds / May 1980 / Elektra ✦✦✦
Still a pop album in many ways, the second proper album marks a move toward despair, depression, and epic songwriting. The playing is slowed considerably with synthesizers barely rising above the minimalist arrangements. The hooks are present but in smaller numbers. —*Chris Woodstra*

. . . Happily Ever After / 1981 / A&M ✦✦✦
A double album combination of *Seventeen Seconds* and *Faith*. An ideal package for two albums that flow together perfectly. —*Chris Woodstra*

Faith / Sep. 1981 / Elektra ✦✦✦
Continuing the trend of the previous album, *Faith* is an even darker affair. Smith sings with suicidal resignation through eight somber epics, raising the tempo only for the single, "Primary." Typified by the title track and "Funeral Party," the album is chilling even though not particularly memorable. —*Chris Woodstra*

Pornography / 1982 / Elektra ✦✦✦

Japanese Whispers / 1984 / Sire ✦✦✦
This collection of the band's mid-'80s lightweight pop singles is a refreshing contrast to the somber albums that preceded it. —*Chris Woodstra*

The Top / 1984 / Sire ✦✦

Concert: Live / 1984 / Fiction ✦✦

The Head on the Door / 1985 / Elektra ✦✦✦✦
Head on the Door represents the band's creative high point and most accessible moment. The songs successfully walk a fine line between gloom and pop, including the danceable hits "In Between Days" and "Close to Me." This move toward the mainstream made them stars in the UK and helped them make some inroads into the US market. —*Chris Woodstra*

★ Standing on a Beach: The Singles / 1986 / Elektra ✦✦✦✦✦
The Cure's gloom-and-doom (but danceable) greatest hits, 1979-1985. Though not hits in the US, these helped set the stage for the group's later Stateside success. —*William Ruhlmann*

Kiss Me, Kiss Me, Kiss Me / 1987 / Elektra ✦✦✦
The Cure's breakthrough US success, a double album containing "Why Can't I Be You?," "Just like Heaven," and "Hot Hot Hot!!!" —*William Ruhlmann*

Disintegration / 1989 / Elektra ✦✦✦✦
The Cure became a top-selling group in the US with this album, which sold a million copies and contains their No. 2 hit, "Love Song." —*William Ruhlmann*

Mixed Up / 1990 / Elektra ✦✦

Wish / 1992 / Elektra ✦✦✦
Early notices for this album suggested that Robert Smith and company were getting more optimistic. To be sure, "Doing the Unstuck" contains the lyric "Kick out the gloom," but the chorus to that song is more ambiguous: "It's a perfect day to throw back your head and kiss it all goodbye." In fact, much of this album, from its dirge-like tempos to Smith's just-off-key vocals, bespeaks the depressed state typical of the Cure. There are oddly bouncy pop songs here and there, too ("Friday I'm in Love") but the Cure remains the band its fans love to mope to. —*William Ruhlmann*

Show / 1993 / Elektra ✦✦

Paris / 1993 / Elektra ✦✦

Wild Mood Swings / 1996 / Fiction/Elektra ✦✦✦
After the relatively straightforward pop of *Wish*, the Cure moved back toward stranger, edgier territory with *Wild Mood Swings*. Actually, that's

only part of the truth. As the title suggests, there's a vast array of textures and emotions on *Wild Mood Swings*, from the woozy mariachi lounge horns of "The 13th" to the perfect pop of "Mint Car" and the monolithic dirge of "Want." In between the extremes, Robert Smith and the Cure—which now features a radically reworked lineup, with several key players from *Wish* now missing—explore some simpler territory, from contemplative acoustic numbers tinged with strings to swooning neo-psychedelia. But what ties it all together is conviction—Smith sounds more content than he ever has, but he sings with more passion than he has for a number of years. Of course, the Cure haven't significantly changed their sound—tinny synthesizers and guitar effects that haven't appeared on an album since 1988 are in abundance throughout the record—but the variety of sounds and strength of performance offers enough surprises to make *Wild Mood Swings* more than just another Cure record. —*Stephen Thomas Erlewine*

King Curtis (Curtis Ousley)

b. Feb. 7, 1934, Fort Worth, TX, **d.** Aug. 14, 1971, New York, NY
Sax (Tenor) / R&B, Groove
King Curtis was the last of the great R&B tenor sax giants. He came to prominence in the mid-'50s as a session musician in New York, recording, at one time or another, for most East Coast R&B labels. A long association with Atlantic/Atco began in 1958, especially on recordings by the Coasters. He recorded singles for many small labels in the '50s—his own Atco sessions (1958-1959), then Prestige/New Jazz and Prestige/TruSound for jazz and R&B albums (1960-1961). Curtis also had a No. 1 R&B single with "Soul Twist" on Enjoy Records (1962). He was signed by Capitol (1963-1964), where he cut mostly singles, including "Soul Serenade." Returning to Atlantic in 1965, he remained there for the rest of his life. He had solid R&B single success with "Memphis Soul Stew" and "Ode to Billie Joe" (1967). Beginning in 1967, Curtis started to take a more active studio role at Atlantic—leading and contracting sessions for other artists, producing with Jerry Wexler and later on his own. He also became the leader of Aretha Franklin's backing unit, the Kingpins. He compiled several albums of singles during this period. All aspects of his career were in full swing at the time he was murdered in 1971. —*Bob Porter*

The Cyrkle

Pop-Rock
Cyrkle's biggest hit in 1966, "Red Rubber Ball," was co-written by Bruce Woodley, a member of the Seekers, and Paul Simon. With Tom Dawes and Don Dannemann as lead vocalists, the folk-tinged group managed by Beatles manager Brian Epstein came together at a Pennsylvania college and signed with Columbia. After "Red Rubber Ball" bounced up the charts, the group scored with another major seller, "Turn-Down Day." They made their last pop-chart appearance in late 1967. —*Bill Dahl*

● **Red Rubber Ball (A Collection)** / 1966 / Columbia ✦✦✦✦
Basically a two-hit wonder of the mid-'60s ("Red Rubber Ball," "Turn-Down Day"), the Cyrkle had Beatles and Paul Simon connections and were themselves fine examples of lightweight folkie pop. Everything of note they ever did is on this album. —*Jeff Tamarkin*

Dick Dale & Del-Tones

Surf
The father of surf music, guitarist Dick Dale to a large degree invented and defined the form in the early '60s with his pioneering use of Fender reverb, dazzling staccato playing, and thundering instrumentals that incorporated Middle Eastern and Latin melodic influences. Playing guitars strung for right-handers with his left hand (as Hendrix would years later), he had an agreement with Fender instruments to "road test" new amplification equipment before it was manufactured for the general public, and found that its hollow, sustained tones evoked the mood of surfing, then catching on in a big way in his Southern California stomping grounds. Dale's impact was largely limited to Southern California, but his influence was vast, helping ignite surf music and contributing several of the genre's most enduring classics, especially "Let's Go Trippin'" and "Miserlou" (both of which were covered by the Beach Boys on their early albums). In the 1990s, Dale made an unexpectedly successful comeback with newly recorded material that closely echoed his vintage sides. —*Richie Unterberger*

★ **King of the Surf Guitar: Best of Dick Dale** / 1989 / Rhino ✦✦✦✦✦
King of the Surf Guitar: Best of Dick Dale is the definitive compilation of the father of surf rock, containing 18 of his best-known songs, including all of his biggest hits ("Miserlou," "Let's Go Trippin'," "The Scavenger"), all presented in their original versions and in excellent audio. In addition to showcasing the roots of surf, *King of the Surf Guitar* demonstrates what a skilled and eclectic guitarist Dale was. Dale was one of the first guitarists in rock 'n' roll to rely on studio and guitar effects and fuse elements of world musics to his sound, and every one of his experiments is captured on this disc. It's a definitive retrospective. —*Stephen Thomas Erlewine*

The Damned

Punk
While the Sex Pistols are often considered to be the first English punk band, a motley group of louts called the Damned managed to steal some of their thunder. Not only were the Damned the first punk band to release a proper album (1977's *Damned Damned Damned*), they released the first punk single in the UK ("New Rose"), and they were also the first to tour the US. Not only are the Damned historically important, but much of their music retained its power over the years; "New Rose" is a classic, breathless rocker and the album, produced by Nick Lowe and released on Stiff Records, followed through on its promise. However, they quickly fell out of favor with their second album, *Music for Pleasure*, which was produced by Nick Mason of Pink Floyd. With their credibility under attack from fans and the press, the band was dropped from Stiff; they briefly parted ways in 1978, with original members bassist Captain Sensible, drummer Rat Scabies, and singer Dave Vanian assembling a new version of the band at the end of the year. The new lineup's *Machine Gun Etiquette* was surprisingly good, yet it was the last good record the band ever released. During the '80s, the band's lineup changed several times with Vanian and Scabies remaining as the only original members; their '80s records are, not surprisingly, directionless, ranging from near power-pop to goth-rock and hard rock back to psychedelia. In 1989, the original Damned reunited for a successful US tour; after the tour, the band called it quits for the last time. —*Stephen Thomas Erlewine*

★ **Damned Damned Damned** / Apr. 16, 1977 / Frontier ✦✦✦✦✦
With its raw, stripped-down production and primal three-chord bashing, the Damned's debut was a landmark punk album. It never deviated from the sound of "New Rose," but that didn't matter—with its simplistic approach and relentless energy, *Damned Damned Damned* defined an era. —*Stephen Thomas Erlewine*

Music for Pleasure / Nov. 1977 / Demon ✦✦
Quickly dismissed by critics at the time as a shocking misstep, *Music for Pleasure* is not quite as bad as the Nick Mason (Pink Floyd) production would lead you to believe—though close. Its failure led to Stiff Records dropping them and the first of many temporary breakups. —*Chris Woodstra*

Machine Gun Etiquette / Dec. 1979 / Roadrunner ✦✦✦✦
A newly reformed version of the Damned (with a new lineup) makes a surprising return to form with 1979's *Machine Gun Etiquette*, a psychedelic-tinged punk masterpiece. With the punk anthem "Smash It Up" and the UK hits "Love Song" and "I Just Can't Be Happy Today," the band proves that it hasn't given up the fight yet. —*Chris Woodstra*

Black Album / Dec. 1980 / Chiswick ✦✦✦
The band's most accomplished and mainstream effort (at least attempt) to date, this sprawling double album obviously takes its inspiration from the Beatles' *White Album* for its title and attempts at stylistic diversity—ranging from power-pop to a bloated quasi-concept side to raw rock 'n' roll. Unfortunately, despite several gems, the end result is a fairly inaccessible album. It was released as an edited single LP in America but was virtually overlooked. —*Chris Woodstra*

Live at Shepperton / 1982 / Ace ✦✦

Strawberries / 1982 / Bronze ✦✦✦
A more cohesive album, *Strawberries* finally achieves the pop sound and diversity they were looking for on *Black Album*. Easily their finest moment since leaving punk behind, the band seems comfortable (and unexpectedly competent) stretching out with strings and horns embellishing the arrangements. —*Chris Woodstra*

Phantasmagoria / 1985 / Off Beat ✦✦✦
Now essentially Dave Vanian's vehicle, the Damned make an attempt to jump on the goth-rock bandwagon. Unfortunately for the band, they end up sounding more like a parody of the genre than anything else. Only on "Grimly Fiendish," which is pleasantly reminiscent of Madness, and "Is It a Dream" does the band make a lasting impression with better-than-average Brit-pop. —*Chris Woodstra*

Anything / 1986 / MCA ✦

The Light at the End of the Tunnel / 1987 / MCA ✦✦✦✦
While it would have been much more effective if it was sequenced chronologically, *The Light at the End of the Tunnel* is a fine compilation of the Damned's long and surprisingly varied career. —*Stephen Thomas Erlewine*

Danzig

Hard Rock, Heavy Metal
Most heavy-metal bands that sing about Satan aren't threatening because their lyrics and music are never as menacing as their album covers. Danzig is the exception that proves the rule. Led by singer-songwriter Glenn Danzig, the band has created a dark, bluesy metal that walks the line between being horrifying and being a parody. As the band

churns out a bluesy Sabbath/Zeppelin/AC/DC hybrid, he sings about death and evil, but with a knowing wink. All of the satanism is too exaggerated to be taken seriously, but beneath the cartoonish bluster there are some genuinely disturbing imagery and music. This duality, along with some undeniably powerful riffs, have made Danzig one of the best heavy-metal bands since Metallica. Before forming Danzig in the mid-'80s, Glenn Danzig performed with the seminal hardcore punk band the Misfits and a transitional metal-punk group, Samhain. With Danzig, his morbid visions flowered. Throughout the late '80s and early '90s, the band's cult grew steadily without the benefit of a hit. In 1994, a live version of the first album's "Mother" became a hit single, thanks to MTV's incessant airing of the video. *Danzig 4*, released in the fall of 1994, failed to capitalize on the success of "Mother," making it the band's first album not to significantly expand its audience. —*Stephen Thomas Erlewine*

● **Danzig** / 1988 / Def American ✦✦✦✦
Danzig's debut album has some incredibly dark and morbid lyrics, including such songs as "Twist of Cain" and "Mother." —*John Book*

Danzig II: Lucifuge / 1990 / Def American ✦✦✦
Danzig's second release is also their most diversified. They explore their blues roots here with a couple of boogies, a slow shuffle, and a slide number, throwing in a '60s-reminiscent ballad in waltz time for good measure. Glenn Danzig's theatrical vocals don't prevent these numbers from working surprisingly well, except when he attempts a Mississippi Delta accent on "Killer Wolf." The simple, somewhat standard blues-metal riffs of their debut are here, but not as plentiful, and the songs done in that style are generally more interesting. —*Steve Huey*

Danzig III: How the Gods Kill / 1992 / Def American ✦✦✦
Danzig's most accessible album to date has songs that could even cross over into mainstream audiences. Glenn Danzig's vocals aren't as raw as they used to be; they're rather more defined and toned down like a real heavy-metal vocalist. John Christ's guitar playing is great throughout, and it shows his progression from the band's debut. The cover artwork is by H.R. Giger. —*John Book*

Black Aria / 1993 / Plan 9/Caroline ✦✦
Thrall: Demonsweatlive / May 25, 1993 / Def American ✦✦✦
Danzig 4 / 1994 / American ✦✦✦

Bobby Darin

b. May 14, 1936, Bronx, NY, **d.** Dec. 20, 1973, Los Angeles, CA
Vocals / Pop, Pop-Rock, Brill Building pop
Who was the real Bobby Darin? Was it the finger-poppin' crooner, the slick '50s rocker, or the introspective folkie of the late '60s? In the end, it really doesn't matter, for Bobby Darin was all of these things and played each of these roles exceedingly well. The show-biz legend suffered from a number of hardships, health problems in particular, that in the end make his achievements even more impressive. He was one of the first of that breed of whitebread late-'50s pop singers, but Darin did indeed rock. Best known for his ring-a-ding-ding style, Darin came across at the outset as a punk Sinatra; he was damn good, and he wasn't about to let you forget it. There was still the much underrated side of Darin that first turned to the music of Tim Hardin and then started his own record label to record the kind of music he felt deeply about, often as the revision of show-biz buddies who were confused by his moves. Over the years, Bobby Darin has been bagged as kind of a jive, glossy cat and something of an also-ran. But in the end, quite the opposite was true; he gave everything to all his phases and acted honestly on his instincts and accomplished what most others would have never attempted. —*Steve Aldrich*

● **The Ultimate Bobby Darin** / Jun. 1988 / Warner Bros. ✦✦✦✦
It offers a thorough look at Darin's rock and pop hits, including "Mack the Knife," "Dream Lover," "Splish Splash," and the breathtaking "Beyond the Sea." —*John Floyd*

Capitol Collectors Series / 1989 / Capitol ✦✦✦✦
A compilation of Darin's mid-'60s singles, which showcase Darin's diversity even if the majority of the set leans heavily on his pop material. Comprehensive liner notes, intelligent track selection, and great fidelity make this worth picking up. —*Stephen Thomas Erlewine*

Splish Splash / 1991 / Atco ✦✦✦✦
The first installment of a definitive two-volume Bobby Darin retrospective, *Splish Splash* concentrates on his earlier hits, including "Dream Lover," "Baby Face," "You Must Have Been a Beautiful Baby," "Multiplication," and the title track. —*Stephen Thomas Erlewine*

Mack the Knife / 1991 / Atco ✦✦✦✦
Darin's later hits, including "Mack the Knife," "Beyond the Sea," "Guys and Dolls," "Black Coffee," and "Artificial Flowers," are collected on this second volume of Atco's fine retrospective. —*Stephen Thomas Erlewine*

As Long as I'm Singing: The Bobby Darin Collection / 1995 / Rhino ✦✦✦✦
A four-CD box set spanning several styles, labels, and eras, this will stand as the most thorough retrospective of Darin's eclectic career. Thorough,

however, doesn't necessarily mean the best. There's a lot of material here—96 songs, including not only the hits but obscure flops, B-sides, album cuts, and 11 previously unreleased tracks. Too much material, really, if you're not a committed fan. Because Darin covered a lot of different genres, it's not programmed chronologically, but by style—one disc for "The Rock 'n' Roll Years" (which, truth be told, were often closer to pop than rock), two to his pop sides, and one to his folk and country outings. In hindsight (and in the enclosed 64-page book), much has been made of Darin's versatility. But while it's true he could handle a range of genres competently, versatility does not automatically equate with quality. Just as a baseball player who can play all the positions is not necessarily a great player, Darin's unusual eclecticism did not mean that he was as great a singer as some legends who concentrated only on rock, or only on pop, or only on folk. There are some neat surprises here—the mid-'60s protest folk-rock of "We Didn't Ask to Be Brought Here," the full-bodied pop of "When I Get Home" (covered by the Searchers for a British hit), the fine rendition of "Nature Boy," and the reasonably cogent and sincere late-'60s folk-rock (when he briefly billed himself as "Bob" Darin). But a lot of it is not more than competent, and some of it (especially the slighter rock efforts) are less than that. And the almost diametrically opposed range of sounds (it's a long way from "Splish Splash" to "Mame" and "If I Were a Carpenter," after all) means that not many listeners except Darin fanatics will be able to get through the whole set without skipping over a lot of the tracks—the pop sides may hold little appeal for the rock-folk fans, and vice versa. —*Richie Unterberger*

Spotlight on . . . Bobby Darin / 1995 / Capitol ✦✦✦

Spencer Davis Group

Guitar / British Invasion
His ferocious soul-drenched vocals belying his tender teenage years, Stevie Winwood powered the Spencer Davis Group's three biggest US hits during their brief life span as one of the British Invasion's most convincing R&B-based combos. Guitarist Davis formed the band with Winwood on organ, his brother Muff Winwood on bass, and drummer Peter York. Signing on with producer Chris Blackwell, the quartet got their first hit (the blistering "Keep on Running") from another of Blackwell's acts, West Indian performer Jackie Edwards. After topping the British charts in 1965, the song struggled on the lower reaches of the US Hot 100. The group's two hottest sellers were self-penned projects. "Gimme Some Lovin'" and "I'm a Man" were searing showcases for the adolescent Winwood's gritty vocals and blazing keyboards and the band's pounding rhythms. Although they burned up the charts even on this side of the ocean in 1967, the quartet never capitalized on their fame with an American tour. At the height of their power, Winwood left to form Traffic, leaving Davis without his dynamic front man. The bandleader focused on producing other acts, including a Canadian ensemble called the Downchild Blues Band during the early '80s. —*Bill Dahl*

● **Golden Archive Series** / 1984 / Rhino ✦✦✦✦
The best compilation of their best moments—14 songs, including both of their US hits, "I'm a Man" and "Gimme Some Lovin'"; the UK chart-toppers "Keep on Running" and "Somebody Help Me," the smaller UK hit "When I Come Home," and several fine R&B covers, all from 1964 to 1966. —*Richie Unterberger*

● **Best of the Spencer Davis Group** / 1985 / EMI America ✦✦✦✦
This contains "Gimme Some Lovin'" and many good lesser-known songs. —*Dan Heilman*

Eight Gigs a Week: The Steve Winwood Years / 1996 / Island/Chronicles ✦✦✦✦
Unfortunately, this two-CD, 51-song set—which covers virtually everything the group recorded with Steve Winwood in the lineup from 1964-1967—was only available as a British import as of mid-1996. The gap between the band's best and worst material was considerable; quite a few of their R&B covers are surprisingly routine, and the occasional cuts that don't have Winwood on lead vocals are downright pedestrian. Because of this inconsistency, the general fan's better off with the Rhino best-of, if it can be found. If you want to get more, though, this is the first and last place to go, with all the hit singles, everything from their three albums, and some E.P., some B-sides, and a couple of previously unissued tracks. And some of the obscure material is really good, whether in a straight R&B-blues or more soulful vein. Be aware that the version of "Gimme Some Lovin'" here is the less dynamic, original British mix, minus some backup vocals and percussion. —*Richie Unterberger*

Tyrone Davis

b. May 4, 1938, Greenville, MS
Vocals / Soul
Perennially a ladies' choice, Tyrone Davis just seems to naturally appeal to women. That's not to say that gents haven't bought his churning Chicago soul records too—his impressive hit-making career harks back to 1968, and there's no end in sight. His mentor, noted singer Harold Bur-

rage, coached his charge well, and Davis debuted on wax in 1965 as "Tyrone the Wonder Boy" on the local Four Brothers logo. Far more wondrous were Davis's classy efforts for Chicago's Dakar label, commencing with the remorseful R&B chart-topper "Can I Change My Mind" in 1968, continuing with "Is It Something You've Got" in 1969, and the million-selling classic "Turn Back the Hands of Time" in 1970. With Willie Henderson producing, the cats at Dakar were forging a fresh, vital new Chicago soul sound, and Tyrone Davis was right there at its forefront.

Davis remained with Dakar into 1976, his warm, assured vocals powering the likes of "I Had It All the Time" and "Turning Point," before moving over to Columbia without missing a beat. These days, Tyrone hops from one label to the next, seemingly with each new release—but he's still no stranger to the urban contemporary charts, and the women still love him. What more could he possibly ask for? —Bill Dahl

● **Greatest Hits [Rhino]** / 1992 / Rhino ✦✦✦✦
Tyrone Davis combined influences from hard-edged, country-tinged urban blues and more tightly arranged, horn-dominated soul. He sang surging uptempo tunes, churning ballads, heartache songs and tribute numbers, and moved from material dominated by brassy arrangements to numbers reliant on his narratives and persona. This 17-track CD begins with his earliest hits, such as "Can I Change My Mind" and "Is It Something You've Got," and continues into smoother but no less urgent tunes such as "Turning Point," "There Is Is," and "One Way Ticket." Because this collection only covers his Dakar material, things end at 1976, after which he left for Columbia. But for soul fans, Tyrone Davis' greatest music came on Dakar. —Ron Wynn

Bobby Day

b. Jul. 1, 1932, Fort Worth, TX, **d.** Jul. 15, 1990
Vocals / Rock 'n' Roll, Doo Wop
An important cog in Los Angeles's doo-wop community during the '50s, Day wrote three often-covered early rock classics in 1957-1958. Day was part of the Hollywood Flames, one of the area's top R&B vocal groups, and briefly part of Bob and Earl, later to hit without Day on "Harlem Shuffle." Day formed his own group, the Satellites, in 1957, cutting the original "Little Bitty Pretty One" for Class Records. A nearly identical cover by Thurston Harris beat the original out, so Day countered with the driving "Rockin' Robin" in 1958, an R&B chart-topper. Its flip, "Over and Over," was a hit in its own right, although The Dave Clark Five's 1965 revival is better remembered today. Day waxed a few more hits for Class in 1959, including "That's All I Want" and a derivative "The Bluebird, the Buzzard & the Oriole," flitting from label to label during the '60s. —Bill Dahl

● **The Original Rockin' Robin** / 1991 / Ace ✦✦✦✦
Bobby Day's "Rockin' Robin" remains a classic. That and 25 other original recordings show up on this solid British import. —Jeff Tamarkin

The dB's

Alternative Pop-Rock, Power-Pop, Jangle-pop
Along with Let's Active, the dB's defined the Southern power-pop/jangle-pop movement of the early-to-mid-'80s. The band's music was a quirky blend of smart pop and psychedelia crossed with the more experimental side of new wave. Though they never received widespread recognition outside of critical acclaim, they provided a key link between Big Star and '80s alternative guitar acts such as R.E.M.

Formed in 1978 in Winston-Salem, NC, the original lineup of the band featured Chris Stamey (guitar, vocals, keyboards), Gene Holder (bass), and Will Rigby (drums). All three members had spent time in Stamey's legendary group, the Sneakers, a group he co-founded with Mitch Easter. After relocating to New York, the dBs released their debut single, "(I Thought) You Wanted to Know" for Stamey's Car label. Guitarist/vocalist/keyboardist Peter Holsapple, who had worked with Stamey in the band Rittenhouse Square in the early-'70s, joined the band by the end of 1978. Holsapple and Stamey shared the songwriting chores during the band's early years.

The dB's were unable to secure a US recording contract, so they signed to the British Albion label. They released two albums on Albion: *Stands for Decibels* (1981) and *Repercussions* (1982). Both records received rave reviews but little sales. Stamey left in 1983 to resume a solo career. Rick Wagner was added on bass but was replaced shortly by Jeff Beninato. With Holsapple fronting the group, they signed to Bearsville in 1984 and released *Like This*, a more conventional jangle-pop album with strong country leanings. Bearsville's internal problems doomed the album despite its obvious hit potential. They eventually left to sign with I.R.S. Records in 1987 where they released *The Sound of Music*. The album managed to break the Top 200 and college radio support was strong. The dB's received some crucial exposure when they opened for R.E.M. on their *Document* tour in the end of 1987, but by the end of 1988, the band decided break up.

Holsapple and Stamey reunited in 1991 for a duo project, releasing *Mavericks* later that year. *Mavericks* was the only album the duo ever

released. Following its release, Stamey continued with solo projects; he also continued to contribute to the Golden Palominos. Holder went on to join the Wygals and more recently has worked a producer and guest musician for other artists. Will Rigby released one solo album, *Sick Phenomenon* in 1985. Holsapple joined R.E.M. as an occasional touring member in 1991 and formed his own band, the Continental Drifters with wife Susan Cowsill. In 1994, Holsapple, Rigby, Beninato plus new member Eric Peterson (guitar) re-formed the dBs and recorded *Paris Avenue*, which was released on the Monkey Hill label. —Chris Woodstra

Dead Can Dance

Alternative Pop-Rock
Dead Can Dance combines elements of European folk music—particularly music from the Middle Ages and the Renaissance—with ambient pop and worldbeat flourishes. Their songs are of lost beauty, regret and sorrow, inspiration and nobility, and of the everlasting human goal of attaining a meaningful existence.

Over the course of their career, Dead Can Dance has featured a multitude of members, but two musicians have remained at the core of the band—guitarist Brendan Perry and vocalist Lisa Gerrard. Perry had previously been the lead vocalist and bassist for the Australian-based punk band the Scavengers, a group who were never able to land a recording contract. In 1979, the band changed their name to the Marching Girls, but they still weren't able to sign a contract. The following year, Perry left the group and began experimenting with electronic music, particularly tape loops and rhythms. In 1981, Perry formed Dead Can Dance with Lisa Gerrard, Paul Erikson, and Simon Monroe. By 1982, Perry and Gerrard decided to relocate to London; Erikson and Monroe decided to stay in Australia.

Within a year, Dead Can Dance had signed a record deal with 4AD. In the spring of 1984, they released their eponymous debut album, comprised of songs the pair had written in the previous four years. By the end of the year, the group had contributed two tracks to *It'll End in Tears*, the first album by This Mortal Coil, and had released an EP called *Garden of the Arcane Delights*. In 1985, Dead Can Dance released their second album, *Spleen and Ideal*. The album helped build their European cult following, peaking at No. 2 on the UK indie charts.

For the next two years, Dead Can Dance were relatively quiet, releasing only two new songs in 1986, both which appeared on the 4AD compilation *Lonely Is an Eyesore*. *Within the Realm of a Dying Sun*, the group's third album, appeared in 1986. In 1988, the band released their fourth album, *The Serpent's Egg*, and wrote the score for the Agustin Villarongas film, *El Nino de la Luna*, which also featured Lisa Gerrard in her acting debut.

Aion, Dead Can Dance's fifth album, was released in 1990. Also in 1990, the group toured America for the first time, earning rave reviews. The following year, the group was involved in various festivals and theatrical productions. In 1992, the compilation *A Passage in Time* was released on Rykodisc, making it the first American release of Dead Can Dance music. Early in 1993, the group provided the score to *Baraka* and contributed songs to *Sahara Blue*. In the fall of 1993, the group released *Into the Labyrinth*, which became their first proper studio album to receive an American release. *Into the Labyrinth* was a cult success throughout the US and Europe. It was followed by another American and European tour, which was documented on the 1994 album and film, *Toward the Within*. In 1995, Lisa Gerrard released her debut solo album, *The Mirror Pool*. In the summer of 1996, Dead Can Dance released *Spiritchaser* and embarked on an international tour. —Stephen Thomas Erlewine & Vladimir Bogdanov

Dead Can Dance / 1984 / Warner Bros. ✦✦✦
These are just experiments, without any definite style or direction. It's interesting only as a history of the group. —Vladimir Bogdanov

Spleen & Ideal / 1985 / Warner Bros. ✦✦✦
Well balanced in terms of both mood and style, this album brings the whole new world of hopeless hope and aimless urge and search. —Vladimir Bogdanov

Within the Realm of a Dying Sun / 1987 / Warner Bros. ✦✦✦✦
Probably their most subtle and intelligent album, it touches the deepest levels of our identity. —Vladimir Bogdanov

The Serpent's Egg / 1988 / Warner Bros. ✦✦✦
This is an interesting combination of Slavonic and European medieval music. —Vladimir Bogdanov

Aion / 1990 / Warner Bros. ✦✦✦✦
True medieval sound is combined with all the variety of modern studio techniques, no imitation at all, it's just enriched with an old musical tradition. —Vladimir Bogdanov

● **A Passage in Time** / Oct. 1991 / Rykodisc ✦✦✦✦
Dead Can Dance has long been known for their hauntingly beautiful weaving of traditional and modern music, stunningly presented on their compilation *A Passage in Time*. The tracks represent a healthy serving

from their previous albums and include two new pieces unavailable elsewhere. Using an eclectic mixture of gothic, descant, Middle Eastern, medieval and early Renaissance music, as well as sacred music of the 18th and 19th centuries, Dead Can Dance is truly unique. Vocals by Brendan Perry and Lisa Gerrard are featured, less than half of which are sung in English; Gerrard's gorgeously chilling vocals are consistent high points. Instruments like the Turkish saz, Chinese yang ch'in and the hurdy-gurdy blend with synth and strings. For their many fans, *A Passage in Time* is a valued addition; for those new to the territory, this release will leave no doubt as to why people rave about this group. —*Backroads Music/Heartbeats*

Into the Labyrinth / 1993 / Warner Bros. ✦✦✦
Into the Labyrinth explores worldbeat territory more heavily than Dead Can Dance's previous releases and the results are impressive, if not altogether perfect. *Into the Labyrinth* also marks the inclusion of more vocal tracks, some of which could even be labeled pop songs, and not bad ones at that. —*AMG*

Toward the Within / 1994 / Warner Bros. ✦✦✦
Dead Can Dance's albums are so meticulously constructed that the mere thought of a live album seems ridiculous. However, Dead Can Dance are more clever than the average band. When it came time for them to record a live album, they came upon an ingenious solution: instead of capturing their classics live, they decided to record an album of all-new material. Naturally, the result still appeals to the hardcore fan as much as the standard live formula, yet *Toward the Within* shows that Dead Can Dance's mesmerizing music continues to evolve, incorporating different strands of world music all the while. —*Stephen Thomas Erlewine*

Spiritchaser / Jun. 25, 1996 / 4AD ✦✦✦

Dead Kennedys

Hardcore Punk
The Dead Kennedys merged revolutionary politics with hardcore punk music and, in the process, became one of the defining hardcore bands. Often, they were more notable for their politics than their music, but that was part of their impact. The Kennedys were more inspired by British punk and the fiery, revolutionary-implied politics of the Sex Pistols than the artier tendencies of New York punk rockers. Under the direction of lead vocalist Jello Biafra, the Dead Kennedys became the most political and—to the eyes of many observers, including Christians and right-wing politicians—the most dangerous band in hardcore. By the mid-'80s, the band had become notorious enough to open themselves up to a prosecution for obscenity (concerning a poster inserted into their 1985 *Frankenchrist* album), and the ensuing court battle sped the band toward a breakup, but they left behind a legacy that influenced countless punk bands that followed.

Biafra (vocals; born Eric Boucher) formed the Dead Kennedys in 1978 in San Francisco; the other members included guitarist East Bay Ray, bassist Klaus Flouride, and drummer Ted (born Bruce Slesinger). The band played locally for the first two years of their career, occasionally venturing outside the Bay Area. Within a year, the band released their first independent single, "California Uber Alles," an attack on the then-current governor, Jerry Brown. It was followed shortly afterward by their second single, "Holiday in Cambodia." In 1979, Biafra ran for mayor of San Francisco; he finished fourth. By this time, the band had become quite popular in both the American and British underground. Finally, in 1980, the band released their debut album, *Fresh Fruit for Rotting Vegetables*, on IRS Records. After its release, Ted left the band; he was replaced by drummer Darren H. Peligro.

Following the release of *Fresh Fruit for Rotting Vegetables*, the Dead Kennedys formed their own independent record label, Alternative Tentacles, in 1981. The first release on the label was the Kennedys' EP, *In God We Trust*. That same year, the single "Too Drunk to Fuck" scraped the bottom of Britain's pop Top 40, despite being banned from airplay. In 1982, the Kennedys released their second full-length album, *Plastic Surgery Disasters*. After its release, the band took a hiatus, during which band members—most notably Klaus Flouride—performed with various side projects. During that time, Alternative Tentacles began to establish itself as a major force in the American underground.

The Dead Kennedys returned in 1985 with *Frankenchrist*, which was the record that earned the band its greatest notoriety. Included with the album was a poster of the Swiss artist H.R. Giger's *Landscape No.XX*, a garish illustration of penises and anuses. A year after the release of the album, the Kennedys and Alternative Tentacles were prosecuted under revised Californian anti-obscenity laws for distributing pornography to minors because of the poster. For the next two years, the band was embroiled in a bitter legal battle, during which Biafra emerged as one of the most articulate advocates for free speech and vocal opponents of the PMRC. In the summer of 1987, the case ended with a hung jury and was dismissed.

Although the Dead Kennedys emerged victorious from the court battle, they didn't remain a band for much longer. Just before the prosecu-

tion began in 1986, the band released *Bedtime for Democracy*, which turned out to be their last official album. After the case was settled, the Kennedys split, releasing the posthumous compilation *Give Me Convenience or Give Me Death* in 1987. Biafra embarked on a solo career, releasing musical and spoken word recordings sporadically over the next decade and a half. Flouride returned to his fledgling solo career, releasing two albums in the late '80s and early '90s. —*Stephen Thomas Erlewine*

★ **Fresh Fruit for Rotting Vegetables** / 1980 / Alternative Tentacles ✦✦✦✦✦
The DK's 1980 debut was as important to the West Coast hardcore scene as the Sex Pistols' *Bollocks* was to disenfranchised British punks. Despite a few clunkers, *Fresh Fruit* is an explosive and scalding blast of political and social fury, underpinned by Jello Biafra's wise-ass vocals and Klaus Flouride's pseudo-surf guitar wailing. Most of the band's best songs are here. —*John Floyd*

In God We Trust, Inc. / Feb. 1981 / Alternative Tentacles ✦✦✦

Plastic Surgery Disasters/In God We Trust, Inc. / 1982 / Alternative Tentacles ✦✦✦✦
Their second effort captures their frenetic live set, full of mayhem and confusion, but with an underlying feeling of greatness. Nonconformist, anti-establishment sentiment is eloquently made sensible by talented frontman Jello Biafra. Punk at its best, musically and lyrically, it includes "Terminal Preppie," "Government Flu," and "Winnebago Warrior." —*Julian Katz*

Frankenchrist / 1985 / Alternative Tentacles ✦✦✦

Bedtime for Democracy / 1986 / Alternative Tentacles ✦✦

Give Me Convenience or Give Me Death / 1987 / Alternative Tentacles ✦✦✦
A useful compilation, it not only collects many essential nonalbum cuts but rounds up the best material from the otherwise desultory follow-ups to *Fresh Fruit*. —*John Floyd*

Chris Deburgh

b. Oct. 15, 1948, Argentina
Guitar, Vocals / Adult Contemporary, Soft Rock, Pop-Rock
An art-rocker that occasionally writes pop-oriented material, Chris Deburgh has never been as popular in his native Britain or the US as he was in other areas of the world. In America, he's only managed two Top 40 hits—1983's "Don't Pay the Ferryman" (No. 34) and the No. 3 ballad "The Lady in Red" (1987). In Britain, he's had the same number of Top 40 singles—"The Lady in Red" was a No. 1 hit and "Missing You" peaked at No. 3—yet he's had a number of minor hits. Nevertheless, he has gained an astounding popularity in other countries, particularly Norway and Brazil.

Deburgh signed with A&M Records in 1974, releasing his debut album the following year. Before its release, he supported Supertramp on their *Crime of the Century* tour, building himself a small fan base. His debut, *Far Beyond These Castle Walls*, was a folk-tinged stab at fantasy in the tradition of the Moody Blues that failed to chart upon its release in February of 1975. That July, he released a single from the album called "Flying." It didn't make an impression in the UK, but it stayed on top of the Brazilian charts for 17 weeks. This became a familiar pattern for the singer-songwriter, as every one of his '70s albums failed to chart in the UK or US while they racked up big sales in European and South American countries. In 1981, he had his first UK chart entry with *Best Moves*, a collection culled from his early albums. It set the stage for 1982's Rupert Hine-produced *The Getaway*, which reached No. 30 on the UK charts and No. 43 in the US, thanks to the eerie single "Don't Pay the Ferryman." Deburgh's follow-up album, *Man on the Line*, also performed well, charting at 69 in the UK and 11 in the US.

Deburgh had an across-the-board success with the languid ballad "The Lady in Red" in late 1986; the single became a No. 1 hit in England (No. 3 in America) and its accompanying album, *Into the Light*, reached No. 2 in the UK (No. 25 in the US). That Christmas season, a re-release of Deburgh's 1976 holiday song "A Spaceman Came Travelling" became a Top 40 hit in the UK. *Flying Colours*, his follow-up to *Into the Light*, entered the British charts at No. 1 upon its 1988 release, yet it failed to make the American charts. Deburgh never hit the US charts again and his commercial fortunes began to slide slightly in Britain in the early '90s, yet he retained a devoted following around the world. —*Stephen Thomas Erlewine*

Far Beyond These Castle Walls / 1975 / A&M ✦✦
Chris Deburgh's debut album clearly stated his musical roots in classic melodic rock and folk ballads; sometimes his songwriting developed into complete fantasy tales. —*Vladimir Bogdanov*

Spanish Train & Other Stories / 1976 / A&M ✦✦

At the End of a Perfect Day / 1977 / A&M ✦✦

Crusader / 1979 / A&M ✦✦✦
Although it features ambitious and sometimes overweighted compositions, *Crusader* still has Deburgh's usual melodic beauty and straightforward rhythmic arrangements. —*Vladimir Bogdanov*

Eastern Wind / 1980 / A&M ✦✦
This transitional album was no doubt a step forward from *Spanish Train . . .*, but it never was a major success, except in Scandinavia, where it outsold the Beatles' *Let It Be.* —*Vladimir Bogdanov*

The Getaway / 1982 / A&M ✦✦✦
A powerful, strong collection of well-produced, well-balanced songs that show his vocal and writing skills at their best. "Don't Pay the Ferryman" is one of the best known of all of his recordings, but there is something on *The Getaway* for every mood and temperament: "Borderline," a wartorn ballad, soars with pain and hope from its quiet piano backing with just-the-right touch of plaintive lead guitar; "I'm Counting on You" portrays a father's hopes and doubts; and "The Getaway" is fun, cheerful, and strong. A good album and one of Deburgh's best. —*Ali Sinclair*

Man on the Line / May 1984 / A&M ✦✦✦

Into the Light / 1986 / A&M ✦✦✦✦
Chris Deburgh's eighth album, *Into the Light*, released in his 11th year as a recording artist, finally broke him through to the two major record markets he had not conquered previously, the UK and the US. The reason was simple: The album contained a romantic ballad hit, "The Lady in Red," which topped the British charts and came close to doing the same thing in America. Heard within the context of *Into the Light*, however, Deburgh's big Anglo-American hit sounds like a slight tune, buried as the fourth track on the first side. On the rest of the album, it's easy to hear why Deburgh was such a success in South America and Europe before his breakthrough. *Into the Light* is an album full of simple melodic songs set to two kinds of Eurodisco beats—medium tempo and slow tempo. Deburgh delivers hooks as reliably as any pop performer; if a phrase, usually the song title, is worth singing once, it's worth singing 15 or 20 times more. In fact, these are songs for people for whom English is a second language. The imagery is all primary—sun, moon, fire, water—and the statements are all easily translatable into any European language (though they'd sound more complicated in German, of course). And the sentiments have a European tinge. In addition to the idealized love songs (including "The Lady in Red," which is part of that limited genre, of "Gee, honey, you really dolled yourself up" songs, along with Eric Clapton's "Wonderful Tonight"), DeBurgh has politics on his mind, though he expresses it in terms just as simple as those in the love songs. "Last Night" tells us war is bad, "Say Goodbye to It All" tells us war is bad, "The Spirit of Man" tells us to hang on anyway, and the album-closing trilogy, "The Leader/The Vision/What About Me?," introduces that perennial European favorite, fascist dictatorship. Which is bad, too, though Deburgh gets close to the end before he gets around to saying so. —*William Ruhlmann*

Flying Colours / 1988 / A&M ✦✦✦✦
A No. 1 album in Great Britain, *Flying Colours* is by far Deburgh's most pop-oriented album. Crisp and clear arrangements, catchy melodies and simple lyrics make it a favorite of fans. —*Vladimir Bogdanov*

● **Lady in Red: Very Best of Chris Deburgh** / 1991 / A&M ✦✦✦✦

Joey Dee & Starliters
....
Rock 'n' Roll
Joey Dee led the house band at New York's Peppermint Lounge, immortalizing the joint in his 1961 chart-topper "Peppermint Twist." Born Joseph DiNicola in Passaic, NJ, Dee teamed with veteran producer Henry Glover to cut "Peppermint Twist" for Roulette, and the huge hit led to a starring role in the film *Hey, Let's Twist.* Most of Dee's hits, including a supercharged revival of the Isley Brothers hit "Shout" in 1962, were firmly in the Twist mode, although he took a successful stab at a softer sound that year with a Johnny Nash tune, "What Kind of Love Is This." Dee gave several future stars early breaks with the Starliters, notably the Ronettes, three-quarters of the Young Rascals, and Jimi Hendrix. Dee is still active on the oldies circuit. —*Bill Dahl*

● **Best of Joey Dee & Starliters: Hey Let's Twist** / 1990 / Rhino ✦✦✦✦
Best of Joey Dee & Starliters: Hey Let's Twist is a representative early-'60s compilation by the man who made the "Peppermint Twist" a national craze. —*Bill Dahl*

Deee-Lite
....
Dance-Pop, House Music, Club-Dance
Most dance bands based in the house movement of the early '90s concentrated more on the groove than the song; Deee-Lite did not. While they had a strong groove, they also had a strong sense of melody and song structure, as well as a campy, stylish retro-'70s look and a social conscience. Their music is a heady rush of beats, samples, and hooks, with

pop songs—like the hit "Groove Is in the Heart"—that distinguish them from other dance combos. —*Stephen Thomas Erlewine*

● **World Clique** / 1990 / Elektra ✦✦✦✦
Deee-Lite's first and most consistent album, *World Clique* blends DJ Dmitry's and DJ Towa Tei's groovy, neo-retro house beats with Lady Miss Kier's sultry voice. The result is a nonstop dance album with as much artistic integrity as booty-shakin' power. Even though "Groove Is in the Heart" was the breakout hit from this album, tracks like "Smile On," "What Is Love?," and "World Clique" make this one of the best dance albums of the '90s. —*Heather Phares*

Infinity Within / 1992 / Elektra ✦✦✦

Dewdrops in the Garden / 1994 / Elektra ✦✦✦✦
Dewdrops in the Garden sees DJ Towa Tei take a vacation from the band, replaced with DJ On-E—just one of the album's not-so-subtle rave references. The tracks on *Dewdrops in the Garden* are either pseudo-rave instrumentals or witty, funky showcases for Lady Kier's rich vocals. While it's somewhat inconsistent, songs like "Apple Juice Kissin'," "Picnic in the Summertime," and "Call Me "radiate with the group's innate charisma. —*Heather Phares*

Deep Purple
....
Hard Rock, Heavy Metal, Arena Rock
Formed in 1968, Deep Purple's initial success was on Bill Cosby's Tetragrammaton label with remakes of Joe South's "Hush" (No. 4) and Neil Diamond's "Kentucky Woman" (No. 38). When Tetragrammaton went under shortly afterward, Deep Purple switched to Warner, with a change in lineup, including the addition of dramatic lead singer Ian Gillan.

Their first effort on Warner, Jon Lord's *Concerto for Group and Orchestra*, was a ponderously overblown affair that died a quick death in the marketplace. From there on out, the band pursued a hard-rock direction, generating their greatest successes on *Machine Head*, *Burn*, and the live double record set *Made in Japan.* In 1975 Deep Purple earned the dubious distinction of being named the "world's loudest band" in the *Guinness Book of World Records.*

Much of Deep Purple's appeal during their heyday (from 1970's *In Rock* to 1973's *Made in Japan*) came from the lightning-fast duels between keyboardist Jon Lord and lead guitarist Ritchie Blackmore.

Deep Purple successfully carried on after Blackmore, Gillan, and bassist Roger Glover departed (at different times), with a lineup featuring ex-Trapeze member Glen Hughes (bass, vocals), Tommy Bolin (lead guitar, vocals), and David Coverdale (lead vocals). Coverdale would later front the popular MTV/AOR band Whitesnake. —*Rick Clark*

Shades of Deep Purple / 1968 / Tetragrammaton ✦✦✦✦
This is worthwhile mainly for their psychedelic cover of Joe South's "Hush," which pits Ritchie Blackmore's flame-throwing guitar bursts against Jon Lord's chugging organ. —*Tom Graves*

Deep Purple in Rock / 1970 / Warner Bros. ✦✦✦✦
The album on which Deep Purple decided they were rockers after all—they turned up the amps to prove it. Ian Gillan on vocals (added at this time) became the archetype for heavy metal screamers thereafter. Check out "Speed King," "Bloodsucker," and "Flight of the Rat" for your daily dose of high voltage. —*Tom Graves*

Fireball / 1971 / Warner Bros. ✦✦✦✦
Fireball solidified the band's reputation as purveyors of maximum-dosage heavy metal. Ritchie Blackmore steals the show with a wall of grinding chords and greased-lightning lead flourishes. At this juncture the band began to challenge Led Zeppelin's position as hard rock's most successful act. —*Tom Graves*

★ **Machine Head** / 1972 / Warner Bros. ✦✦✦✦✦
The definitive '70s heavy-metal album, each locomotive song ("Highway Star," "Space Truckin'") blasts off like World War III. The highlight is the AOR staple "Smoke on the Water," which has a mandatory riff for anyone owning a guitar. It still fries ears 20 years after the fact. —*Tom Graves*

Purple Passages / 1972 / Warner Bros. ✦✦

Who Do We Think We Are / Jan. 1973 / Warner Bros. ✦✦✦
The last gasp for the classic Deep Purple lineup, *Who Do We Think We Are* isn't as rock-solid as their previous records, but its best moments, including the deliriously stupid "Woman from Tokyo," are bludgeoning hard rock of the highest order. —*Stephen Thomas Erlewine*

Made in Japan / Apr. 1973 / Warner Bros. ✦✦✦✦
Not only could they kick ass in the studio, they could stir up a hornet's nest on stage, too. This double-album (one CD) set recorded in Japan includes most of their best material ("Highway Star," "Smoke on the Water") and pushes the metal envelope even further. Ritchie Blackmore is in peak form throughout. —*Tom Graves*

Burn / 1974 / Warner Bros. ✦✦✦
Burn is Deep Purple's first album with lead singer David Coverdale. While it's not quite up to the standards of *Machine Head* and *Made in*

Japan, it featured enough hot riffs and well-constructed heavy rockers to make it a Top Ten success and an album rock favorite. *—Stephen Thomas Erlewine*

Come Taste the Band / 1975 / Metal Blade ♦♦♦
The addition of guitarist Tommy Bolin adds some fire to the performances on *Come Taste the Band,* yet the group didn't come up with enough good songs to make the record memorable for anything besides Bolin's exceptional playing. *—Stephen Thomas Erlewine*

When We Rock, We Rock & When We Roll, We Roll / 1978 / Warner Bros. ♦♦♦♦
When We Rock, We Rock & When We Roll, We Roll is a solid, if incomplete collection from their 1968-1974 peak years. *—Dan Heilman*

Best of Deep Purple in the 80's / 1994 / Mercury ♦♦♦
This compilation may be inconsistent and unsatisfying, but that's an accurate reflection of the group's career during the decade. Even though it's fitfully entertaining, *Best Of* features all of the highlights the group recorded during the '80s and its preferable to the albums they released during the era. *—Stephen Thomas Erlewine*

Def Leppard

Hard Rock, Pop-Rock, Heavy Metal
Def Leppard's catchy, guitar-driven, power pop-rock was one of the most imitated styles of the '80s. Leppard's hit albums are polished syntheses of heavy, hummable guitar riffs, memorable pop melodies, and simple teen-oriented lyrics. Originally the band (Joe Elliot, vocals; Pete Willis, guitar; Steve Clark, guitar; Rick Savage, drums; Rick Allen, drums) was associated with the new wave of British heavy-metal bands, releasing two albums (*On Through the Night* and *High 'n' Dry*) that made a small impact in the US. Robert "Mutt" Lange produced *High 'n' Dry,* which contained the seeds of the signature Leppard sound. Before the recording of their next album, Pete Willis left and was replaced by Phil Collen, who used to play in the glam-rock band Girl. *Pyromania,* released in 1983, was a monster success selling over 6.5 million copies in the US and featuring three Top 40 hits ("Photograph," "Rock of Ages," and "Foolin'"). The album showcased the refinement of Def Leppard's twin-guitar attack, where both parts worked together to create a huge sound instead of merely repeating the riff. In 1984, the group made two attempts to record a follow-up, one with the exhausted Lange and another with Jim Steinman, both ending with the dismissal of the producer. On New Year's Eve, Allen lost his left arm in an auto accident. Despite this, the band wanted Allen in the group; he was equipped with a customized electronic drum kit to ease his playing. In 1987, the long-awaited *Hysteria* (also produced by Lange) was released. Although *Hysteria* was a bigger success than *Pyromania,* it took considerable time for it to gain its sales—after 49 weeks, the album reached No. 1. Recording for the follow-up to *Hysteria* was under way when Clark was found dead in his apartment after a drinking binge in January 1991. Def Leppard continued the album, with Collen playing all the guitars. *Adrenalize* shot to the top of the charts upon its release in April 1992. Vivian Campbell, former guitarist for Whitesnake, was announced as Clark's replacement in spring of 1992. Def Leppard released a greatest hits collection, *Vault,* in 1995. The following year, the group released the follow-up to *Adrenalize, Slang.* *—Stephen Thomas Erlewine*

☆ **Pyromania** / 1983 / Mercury ♦♦♦♦♦
Although Def Leppard's first two workmanlike metal albums, *On Through the Night* and *High 'n' Dry,* had already established the band in both England and the US, it was *Pyromania* that broke the sound (and sales) barrier for them. *Pyromania*'s acute emphasis on pop sensibilities in songs like "Photograph" and "Rock Rock ('til You Drop)" over numbing thonk made the album a huge crossover success with the more conservative AOR market. MTV video saturation with key *Pyromania* songs didn't hurt either. *—Tom Graves*

☆ **Hysteria** / 1987 / Mercury ♦♦♦♦♦
If *Pyromania* was great pop-metal, *Hysteria* upped the ante a few more notches. With dense, elaborate instrumental layering and meticulous engineering, the album became known almost as much for its production values as for its terrific music. Drummer Rick Allen, who lost an arm in an automobile accident, adds an even harder core of bottom end with his specially rigged drum kit. As hardhitting as it is slick-sounding, *Hysteria* became the standard-bearer for pop metal with anthemic tracks like "Rocket" and "Pour Some Sugar on Me." This is one of the masterpieces of the '80s that renewed the faith, for many, in sensible hard rock. *—Tom Graves*

Adrenalize / 1992 / Mercury ♦♦♦

Retro Active / Oct. 5, 1993 / Mercury ♦♦♦

● **Vault: Def Leppard's Greatest Hits** / Oct. 31, 1995 / Mercury ♦♦♦♦
Def Leppard was untouchable in the '80s. Over the course of four albums, the band established themselves as one of the best and most popular hard-rock/heavy-metal groups of the decade, scoring a long list of hit singles. *Vault: Def Leppard's Greatest Hits—1980-1995* compiles

the biggest of those hits, as well as selections from their first album of the '90s, *Adrenalize,* and the outtakes collection *Retro Active.* Essentially, Def Leppard's legacy rests on two albums, 1983's *Pyromania* and 1987's *Hysteria.* On both records, the group created a sleek, shiny brand of hard rock powered by huge, catchy melodies and guitar hooks that owed more to Mott the Hoople and T. Rex than Deep Purple and Black Sabbath. It was a polished but potent sound, whether the band turned out rockers ("Photograph," "Rocket") or ballads ("Bringin' on the Heartbreak," "Love Bites"). *Vault* has all of the necessary items, from "Pour Some Sugar on Me" to "Rock of Ages." It's not a perfect collection—it's not sequenced chronologically, it includes too much material from *Adrenalize,* and the new "When Love & Hate Collide" is simply average—but that doesn't stop *Vault* from being a great greatest hits collection. *—Stephen Thomas Erlewine*

Slang / May 14, 1996 / Mercury ♦♦♦

Del Amitri

Folk-Rock, Pop-Rock
Glasgow's Del Amitri has gained a strong cult following for their country- and folk-inflected rock 'n' roll and the quality songwriting of bassist/vocalist Justin Currie and guitarist Iain Harvie, plus the frequently ironic lyrics of the former. Currie and Harvie formed the band in 1982, releasing the independent single "Sense Sickness" in 1983 with guitarist Bryan Tolland and drummer Paul Tyagi. In 1984, the band was invited to record for BBC DJ John Peel, and tours with acts like the Fall and the Smiths helped the group build a fan base and get a deal with Chrysalis. Del Amitri's self-titled debut album was released in 1985 and featured a country-, and new wave-influenced brand of pop-rock, but unfortunately, the group had appeared on the cover of *Melody Maker* two months before its release; critics slammed the album in the wake of excessive hype, while potential fans perceived the lack of product in record stores as a sign of the album's quality. However, a network of fans helped organize a low-budget Del Amitri tour of the US. Encouraged, the band returned to England and hammered out new material, which helped get them signed to A&M in 1987. Tolland was replaced by guitarist David Cummings, and Tyagi by drummer David Cummings; the group also added keyboardist Andy Alston. 1990's *Waking Hours* accentuated Del Amitri's roots-rock feel and produced the British singles "Kiss This Thing Goodbye," "Nothing Ever Happens," and "Spit in the Rain"; the former scraped the lower reaches of the US Top 40. The 1992 follow-up, *Change Everything,* solidified their popularity in the UK and produced another minor American chart single, "Always the Last to Know." McDermott left the band in 1994 and was replaced by Ashley Soan. *Twisted* was released early in 1996. *—Steve Huey*

Del Amitri / 1985 / Chrysalis ♦♦♦

● **Waking Hours** / 1989 / A&M ♦♦♦♦
The sound on this effort has more of a mainstream rock sheen to the production than the debut. *—David Szatmary*

Change Everything / Jun. 9, 1992 / A&M ♦♦♦♦
Del Amitri serves up a slice of Scottish folk-rock on 1992's *Change Everything.* Gritty vocals often hinting at sadness drape themselves over chiming guitars and tasty harmonies; vague memories of Van Morrison in his rockier days. *—Roch Parisien*

Twisted / 1995 / A&M ♦♦♦♦
Del Amitri hasn't changed their style for *Twisted*—they're still a bright, catchy folk-rock combo. However, the songs and performances don't match those on *Change Everything.* The songs don't have the same quality hooks, nor do the performances match anything on *Change Everything,* yet for fans of their sound, it's a fine effort. *—Sara Sytsma*

Del Fuegos

Roots-Rock
Originally including Dan and Warren Zanes (who have the vocalist and guitarist duties, respectively), bassist Tom Lloyd, and drummer B. Woody Giessmann, this Boston-based band pounds out Rolling Stones-style rock. After critics panned *Stand Up,* Giessmann left the group. The band added horns for a more Stax-oriented sound on *Smoking in the Fields.* Guest appearances on their albums include James Burton and Tom Petty (*Stand Up*) and Rick Danko (*Smoking*). *—David Szatmary*

The Longest Day / 1984 / Slash ♦♦♦♦
An explosive garage-meets-roots-rock debut from the Boston rockers. *—David Szatmary*

● **Boston, Mass.** / 1985 / Slash ♦♦♦♦
It features more guitar-driven crunch. *—David Szatmary*

Stand Up / 1987 / Slash ♦♦♦

Dell-Vikings

R&B, Doo Wop
One of the first integrated acts during rock 'n' roll's infancy, the Dell-

Vikings recorded a beloved classic in 1956, "Come Go with Me." The quintet was formed at Pittsburgh's Air Force Serviceman's Club in 1955 while the members were stationed there. They recorded their immortal "Come Go with Me," written by bass singer Clarence Quick, in the basement of a local DJ and sold the master to tiny FeeBee Records. When given national distribution on Dot, the upbeat tune proved a monster hit. Upon their discharge, four members split to form a new "Del Vikings" on Mercury, hitting in 1957 with "Cool Shake." Kripp Johnson, meanwhile, stayed with Dot, assembling a new lineup of "Dell-Vikings" that included a young Chuck Jackson, and hitting at precisely the same time with "Whispering Bells." All the confusion about the two groups may have ultimately sunk both, since those were the last hits for either lineup. —*Bill Dahl*

● **Dell-Vikings** / 1988 / Collectables ◆◆◆◆
Solid hits by one of doo wop's first integrated groups. —*Bill Dahl*

The Best of the Dell- Vikings: The Mercury Years / 1996 / Mercury ◆◆◆
Read the title carefully, because the Dell-Vikings' two great doo wop hits—"Come Go with Me" and "Whispering Bells"—were not recorded for Mercury, and so are not contained on this compilation. This disc has 22 sides they recorded for Mercury in 1957-1958, with a lineup that had some but not all of the members that recorded "Come Go with Me" and "Whispering Bells." (To make matters more confusing, a different Dell-Vikings, led by Kripp Johnson, who had sung lead on "Whispering Bells," kept recording for a different label.) The Mercury Dell-Vikings did have a Top 20 hit right out of the box, "Cool Shake" (included here), but never had a big single again. Most of this is routine doo wop that's below the standards of their Dot sides, sometimes clouded by inadvisable attempts at pop-oriented material and production. It's only of value to hard-core doo wop bugs, who will appreciate the inclusion of many tracks only available on rare EPs, singles, and compilations, as well as one previously unissued in the US. The intro to "The Bells," by the way, bears a close similarity to the famous wordless scats that kicked off the Marcels' classic "Blue Moon" several years later. —*Richie Unterberger*

The Delfonics
Soul
A sweet ballad-oriented Philadelphia vocal trio, the Delfonics proved highly popular in the late '60s and early '70s. Lead singer William Hart's high-pitched tenor effortlessly sailed into falsetto range on their first hit in 1968, "La-La—Means I Love You," a typically smooth ballad filled with swirling strings. Hart and co-producer Thom Bell wrote most of the group's early smashes, including "Didn't I (Blow Your Mind This Time)" in 1970. The group's hit-making reign ended in 1974. —*Bill Dahl*

● **The Best of the Delfonics** / 1990 / Arista ◆◆◆◆
The Delfonics were arguably the premier sweet soul band of the late '60s and early '70s; their shimmering harmonies and William Hart's agonizing falsetto, coupled with Stan Watson's production and Thom Bell's arranging and writing touches, created many unforgettable love songs. While their hits have been frequently collected and reissued, this short CD set (37 minutes) includes among its 12 tracks every major hit except "Over and Over." Engineering guru Bill Inglot used original masters, fully capturing the trio's marvelous interaction, the songs' sweeping arrangements, and the great mix of vulnerability, hurt, and poignance that characterized their finest hits. —*Ron Wynn*

Golden Classics / Collectables ◆◆◆◆
The Delfonics were arguably the greatest "sweet" soul trio of all time and certainly among the top two or three. Unfortunately, there are almost as many Delfonics anthologies as Sam Cooke collections, and most are just as bogus. This is actually a good one, and Collectables, a label notorious for poor quality, badly transferred CDs, have done pretty well with their soul releases. —*Ron Wynn*

The Dells
Soul, Doo Wop
After nearly four decades of recording an incredible legacy of hits, the Dells have made only one personnel change in their entire professional career. Perhaps that's why the venerable R&B vocal group can boast such a remarkably consistent track record.

The quintet from Chicago's south suburbs has weathered stylistic shifts from doo wop and soul to disco and urban contemporary, and every permutation in between. Their harmony remains as striking as ever, with Marvin Junior's earthshaking lead enduring as the group's focal point.

Signing with Vee-Jay in 1955, their creamy vocal blend on "Oh, What a Night" gave the Dells their first major R&B hit the next year, but it would be nearly a decade before they returned to the winner's circle with another dreamy classic, "Stay in My Corner." By then Chicago's R&B sound had changed drastically—doo wop was dead and soul was king—but the Dells adapted effortlessly, regularly scaling the charts for

the Chess subsidiary Cadet with "There Is," "Always Together," "Give Your Baby a Standing Ovation," and a marathon remake of "Stay in My Corner" that afforded Junior's booming baritone room to roam.

Seemingly an indestructible force (turning up on the R&B charts as recently as 1984), the succinct harmonies of the Dells span entire generations of R&B history. —*Bill Dahl*

★ **On Their Corner** / 1992 / Chess ◆◆◆◆◆
Excellent compilation of their late-'60s sides, like "Oh What a Night," "Stay in My Corner," "The Love We Had Stays on My Mind," and "Give Your Baby a Standing Ovation." —*Stephen Thomas Erlewine*

Dreams of Contentment / 1993 / Vee-Jay ◆◆◆◆
The Dells never made it over the hump while at Vee-Jay, despite making impressive singles. They were a top-flight doo wop group, but they couldn't find a way to advance beyond the R&B margins. Only when they moved to Chess, changed their style, and made Marvin Junior the lead singer did they enjoy the success they deserved. As this 24-track reissue shows, there wasn't anything wrong with the Vee-Jay output. They experimented on such numbers as "Lil Darlin'," "It's Not for Me to Say," and "It's Not Unusual" with jazz-pop harmonies and covers. In addition, songs like "Now I Pray" and "Pain in My Heart" are wonderfully sung and harmonized, even if they weren't huge sellers. —*Ron Wynn*

Passionate Breezes: Best of 1975-1991 / Oct. 1995 / Mercury ◆◆◆
By the last half of the '70s, the Dells had already gone through two phases in their career, transforming themselves from an R&B vocal group into a smooth soul outfit and scoring hits in both incarnations. During the late '70s and '80s, the group continued to perform, usually in the same vein as their early-'70s hits. Even if the strength of their voices hadn't diminished, their audience had. Nevertheless, much of the material they recorded during this era was fine, as *Passionate Breezes: Best of 1975-1991* proves. It's not as compulsively listenable as the group's doo wop hits or their early-'70s material, but there is still enough first-rate music here to satisfy fans. —*Stephen Thomas Erlewine*

John Denver (John Henry Deutchendorf)
b. Dec. 31, 1943, Roswell, NM
Guitar, Vocals / Singer-Songwriter, Soft Rock, Folk-Rock
In the '70s, John Denver's simple, melodic, light folk-pop made him one of the decade's biggest stars. In the '60s, he played with his idols the Chad Mitchell Trio, turning into a talented songwriter while he was with the group. Denver left for a solo career in 1969; later in the year, his "Leaving on a Jet Plane" became a big hit for Peter, Paul and Mary. In no time, Denver established himself as a star in his own right, with songs like "Take Me Home, Country Roads," "Rocky Mountain High," "Sunshine on My Shoulders," "Annie's Song," and "Thank God I'm a Country Boy" becoming pop standards of the decade. After the '70s were over, Denver's career began to lose its commercial momentum and he turned to social work, while recording the occasional album. Denver continues to record and perform in the '90s, consistently pleasing his fans. —*Stephen Thomas Erlewine*

● **Greatest Hits** / 1973 / RCA ◆◆◆◆
A good collection of his early (and best) era, 1969-1973. Note that John Denver re-recorded some of his hits for this collection. —*Dan Heilman*

Greatest Hits, Vol. 2 / 1977 / RCA ◆◆◆◆
More pop, less folk, and more hits. —*Dan Heilman*

Greatest Hits, Vol. 3 / 1985 / RCA ◆◆◆◆
Not many hits, but it still features notable '80s tracks. —*Dan Heilman*

Depeche Mode
Alternative Pop-Rock, Post-Punk
In 1980, Depeche Mode (the name means "fast fashion") was formed in Basildon, Essex, England, by Andy Fletcher (b. Jul. 8, 1961), Martin Gore (b. Jul.23, 1961), Vince Clarke, and Dave Gahan. All four played synthesizers, and Gahan sang. They were signed to tiny Mute Records in England in 1982 (distributed by Sire/Warner Bros. in the US) and scored two Top 20 hits, "New Life" and "Just Can't Get Enough," and a Top Ten album, *Speak and Spell*, by the end of the year. At that point, Clarke quit and was replaced by Alan Wilder. The band's style—pop songs with ominous lyrics sung in Gahan's distinct baritone and backed by intricate synthesized dance music—did not change, and its commercial success continued as well. The group only gradually built a following in the US, finally breaking the Hot 100 with "People Are People," which reached No. 13 in 1985. The first album to reach the American Top 100 was *Black Celebration* in 1986; then *Music for the Masses* went gold in 1987. By 1989, Depeche Mode was big enough in the US to play a concert at the Rose Bowl in California, and that show was recorded for the live album *101*. But it wasn't until the 1990 album *Violator* and the single "Enjoy the Silence" that Depeche Mode made the Top Ten in the US. By then, they'd also conquered the rest of the world and become one of the most popular "modern" or "alternative" rock groups of the '80s and early '90s. —*William Ruhlmann*

Speak & Spell / 1981 / Sire ✦✦✦
Vince Clarke's only album with Depeche Mode is dominated by him (he wrote nine of 11 tracks), and the band was never this imaginative or infectious again. Especially notable is the UK Top Ten hit, "Just Can't Get Enough," which remains the best single track they ever recorded. — *William Ruhlmann*

A Broken Frame / 1982 / Sire ✦✦✦

Construction Time Again / 1983 / Sire ✦✦✦

People Are People / 1984 / Sire ✦✦✦✦

Some Great Reward / 1984 / Sire ✦✦✦✦
Depeche Mode's most consistent post-Clarke album contains some of its most provocative material, notably "Blasphemous Rumours" and "Master and Servant," which concern, respectively, religion and sexual domination. — *William Ruhlmann*

● **Catching up with Depeche Mode** / 1985 / Sire ✦✦✦✦
A US-only compilation that's a well-put-together best-of, from the band's early singles to its current state. If you want to know what Depeche Mode is about, this is the record that will tell you. — *William Ruhlmann*

Black Celebration / 1986 / Sire ✦✦✦✦
Depeche Mode are frequently called gloom-mongers, and much of that criticism stems from this relentlessly bleak album, which is undoubtedly the most desolate record they have ever made. — *Stephen Thomas Erlewine*

Music for the Masses / 1987 / Sire ✦✦✦✦
Music for the Masses backs away from the dark brooding *Black Celebration*, but only slightly. Though the sound of *Music for the Masses* is slightly brighter, Depeche Mode's synths still create a gloomy, atmospheric mood. The real step forward on the record is in terms of pop sensibility—Martin Gore is beginning to show a melodic flair that the band has largely lacked since Vince Clarke's departure, as "Never Let Me Down Again" proves. — *Stephen Thomas Erlewine*

101 / 1989 / Sire ✦✦✦

Violator / 1990 / Sire ✦✦✦
Depeche Mode's commercial breakthrough album is a mixed bag. Unlike their previous album, *Violator* truly is music for the masses. Throughout the album, occasional spells of catchy hooks emerge from beneath the thudding machines (most notably on the excellent "Personal Jesus" and the hit single "Enjoy the Silence). On the strength of these flashes of melody, the album crossed over into the mainstream, but for the most part *Violator* is a dull, tedious drag. — *Stephen Thomas Erlewine*

Songs of Faith & Devotion Live / May 1993 / Sire ✦

Derek & the Dominos

Group / Rock 'n' Roll, Blues-Rock
Derek & The Dominos was a group formed by guitarist/singer Eric Clapton (born Eric Patrick Clapp, Mar. 30, 1945, Ripley, Surrey, England) with other former members of Delaney & Bonnie & Friends, in the spring of 1970. The rest of the lineup was Bobby Whitlock (b. 1948, Memphis, TN) on keyboards, vocals; Carl Radle (b. 1942, Oklahoma City, OK, d. May 30, 1980) on bass; and Jim Gordon (b. 1945, Los Angeles) on drums. The group debuted at the Lyceum Ballroom in London and undertook a summer tour of England. From late August to early October, they recorded the celebrated double album *Layla and Other Assorted Love Songs* (Nov. 1970) with guitarist Duane Allman sitting in. They then returned to touring in England and the US, playing their final date on December 6.

The *Layla* album was successful in the US, where "Bell Bottom Blues" and the title song charted as singles in abbreviated versions, but it did not chart in the UK. The Dominos reconvened to record a second album in May 1971, but split up without completing it. Clapton then retired from the music business, nursing a heroin addiction.

In his absence, and in the wake of Allman's death in a motorcycle accident on October 29, 1971, the Dominos and *Layla* gained in stature. Re-released as a single at its full, seven-minute length in connection with the compilation album *History of Eric Clapton* (Mar. 1972), "Layla" hit the Top Ten in the US and the UK in the summer of 1972. (It would return to the UK Top Ten in 1982.) A live album, *Derek and the Dominos in Concert* (Jan. 1973), taken from the 1970 US tour, was also a strong seller.

Time has only added to the renown for the group, which is now rated among Eric Clapton's most outstanding achievements. The 1988 Eric Clapton boxed set retrospective *Crossroads* featured material from the abortive second album sessions. *The Layla Sessions* was a 1991 boxed set expanding that album across three CDs/cassettes. And *Live at the Fillmore* (1994) offered an expanded version of the *In Concert* album. — *William Ruhlmann*

★ **Layla & Other Assorted Love Songs** / Nov. 1970 / Polydor ✦✦✦✦✦
Quite simply, this is Eric Clapton's finest moment, full of gutsy, impassioned playing and tortured vocals. None of the love songs are simple,

and the band rocks away their blues in a series of long jams that are never boring. — *Stephen Thomas Erlewine*

The Layla Sessions / Sep. 1990 / Polydor ✦✦✦

Live at the Fillmore / Feb. 22, 1994 / Polydor ✦✦✦

Jackie DeShannon

b. Aug. 21, 1944, Hazel, KY
Guitar, Vocals / Singer-Songwriter, Folk-Rock, Pop-Rock, Brill Building Pop
Few performers have enjoyed as versatile a career as Jackie DeShannon, and although she made a couple of well-remembered Top Ten pop hits in the '60s, she's never achieved the level of success or artistic recognition she deserves. Starting as a pop-rockabilly singer as a teenager in the late '50s, she quickly developed into one of the L.A. pop scene's hottest songwriters, penning hits for Brenda Lee, the Fleetwoods, and Irma Thomas, and often collaborating with fellow noted songwriter Shari Sheeley. One of the first established rock figures to see the potential for crossbreeding rock and folk, she was a crucial midwife to the birth of folk-rock, with the wonderful singles "Needles and Pins" and "When You Walk in the Room." Using the circular, jangling guitar lines that would become a prime feature of early folk-rock, both of those songs were covered by the Searchers for much bigger hits; she also wrote "Don't Doubt Yourself Babe," covered by the Byrds on their first album, and penned a couple of Marianne Faithfull's early hits. In the mid-'60s, she also found time to write some songs with then-sessionman Jimmy Page, and perform as an opening act for the Beatles on the group's first big American tour.

DeShannon's famous affiliations and success as a songwriter have sometimes obscured her own enormous talents. She's a superb singer, capable of both sweet ballads and (more satisfyingly) a gutsy, soulfully husky delivery. She performed her own material with an honest, vulnerable, intelligent intensity that pre-figured the singer-songwriter movement by several years, and demonstrated command of pop, soul, hard rock, girl group, and country styles. Her greatest success, however, came not with her own material, but with Bacharach-David's "What the World Needs Now Is Love," which made the Top Ten in 1965. Perhaps as a result, she gravitated toward more middle-of-the-road pop sounds in the last half of the '60s, though she cut a good deal of strong material, by both herself and emerging writers like Randy Newman, Tim Hardin, and Warren Zevon. The soft-rock "Put a Little Love in Your Heart" gave her another Top Ten hit in 1969, and she made some well-received singer-songwriter albums in the 1970s. One of the songs from her '70s LPs, "Bette Davis Eyes," became a No. 1 hit for Kim Carnes in 1981. — *Richie Unterberger*

This Is Jackie DeShannon / 1965 / Imperial ✦✦✦

You Won't Forget Me / 1965 / Imperial ✦✦✦

Put a Little Love in Your Heart / 1969 / Imperial ✦✦✦

New Arrangement / 1975 / Columbia ✦✦✦

● **Pop Princess** / 1981 / EMI Australia ✦✦✦✦
Rhino and EMI have come out with fairly extensive CD compilations of DeShannon's work, but this 23-song Australian album—if it can be found—is probably the best. It concentrates almost solely on her '60s recordings (one 1959 track is included), which remains her most fertile era. It also has a few excellent singles that didn't make it onto either compilation. These include the early-'60s girl group-type efforts "It's Love Baby," "Baby (When Ya Kiss Me)," "I Won't Turn You Down," and "Should I Cry?"— most written by DeShannon, all flops, and all worth hearing. Later, more mainstream efforts like "A Proper Girl" and Jim Webb's "The Girls' Song" are also not included on other reissues, and also worth a listen. The gatefold package contains informative liner notes, photos, and an exhaustive discography which also lists dozens of songs she wrote for other performers. — *Richie Unterberger*

The Best of Jackie Deshannon / 1991 / Rhino ✦✦✦✦
This set contains all of DeShannon's best-known singles, as well as other notable original songs like "Bette Davis Eyes." — *Rick Clark*

Trouble with Jackie Dee / 1991 / Teenager ✦✦

● **What the World Needs Now . . . : The Definitive Collection** / 1994 / EMI ✦✦✦✦
DeShannon's work is actually too diverse to be satisfactorily captured on an anthology, even one that includes 28 tracks, as this one does. Still, considering how hard the one DeShannon anthology that might be better than this one is to find (the Australian import *Pop Princess*), this has to be cited as the recommended first purchase. Focusing on her output for Liberty between 1959 and 1970, it has all the essentials: her two Top Ten hits, the minor hits like "A Lifetime of Loneliness," the original versions of "Needles and Pins" and "When You Walk in the Room," and a host of fine girl group, ballad, folk-rock, and singer-songwriter flop singles. From the collector's viewpoint, the most interesting songs are the rarities. The six previously unreleased tracks include the exuberant "Breakaway," a hit for Irma Thomas; the rocker "Dream Boy," cut in 1964 in

Britain with Jimmy Page on guitar; and a cover of Tim Hardin's "Reason to Believe." A couple of interesting rarities are "For Granted" (from the little-seen movie *C'mon, Let's Live a Little*) and the 45 version of "Splendor in the Grass," a somewhat sloppy folk-rock performance on which Jackie was backed by the Byrds. —*Richie Unterberger*

Devo

New Wave
Made up of two sets of brothers (Mark and Bob Mothersbaugh and Jerry and Bob Casale), Devo was one of the first new-wave groups to get mass-market attention. An Akron, OH, band, they had their own philosophy, "de-evolution"—a sci-fi/satirical view of post-modern cultural values complete with strange costumes and behavior. Their sound was appropriately nervous and jerky, with a heavy emphasis on synthesizers. Their debut album, *Q: Are We Not Men? A: We Are Devo!*, was produced by Brian Eno and featured a great cover of the Rolling Stones' "Satisfaction." After a less interesting second album, they rebounded with the self-produced album *Freedom of Choice*, containing the hit "Whip It." As one of new wave's most cartoonish and successful bands, they helped define the genre with a minimalistic synth sound and a nihilistic attitude. Although each successive album provided a new look and theme, their sound became more glossy and less challenging, heading toward straight synth/dance-pop grooves. While both sets of brothers remain musically active on soundtrack work like *Pee Wee's Playhouse* and the theme for *Davis Rules*, most Devo discs of late have been repackage/remix efforts, live recordings, or instrumental works. —*Scott Bultman*

Q: Are We Not Men? A: We Are Devo! / Jul. 1978 / Warner Bros. ✦✦✦✦
Devo's debut shows why the band still has a small but rabidly dedicated following well after their artistic peak. Their sound here is mostly guitar-based, with odd melodies and crazily jerky rhythms. With songs about masturbation ("Uncontrollable Urge"), freaks ("Mongoloid"), and technology ("Space Junk"), plus their patented de-evolution philosophy (the anthem "Jocko Homo," about the regression of mankind) and a wickedly deranged deconstruction of "(I Can't Get No) Satisfaction," Devo took punk's anti-mainstream, D.I.Y. spirit and filtered it through the sensibilities of weirdos, nerds, and outcasts, relentlessly (and bizarrely) satirizing American culture and briefly picking up, attitude-wise, where the Mothers of Invention left off. —*Steve Huey*

Duty Now for the Future / Jul. 1979 / Warner Bros. ✦✦✦✦
Most of the aural weirdness on Devo's second album comes from the band's experiments with homemade synthesizer technology. As a result, both the guitars and jerky rhythms play a lesser role in their sound. Although it isn't quite as interesting, it's still appropriately strange, and Devo still doesn't sound quite like anyone else. *Duty* is loosely structured around the theme of everyday corporate drudgery and its effects on individuals. —*Steve Huey*

Freedom of Choice / Jul. 1980 / Warner Bros. ✦✦✦

New Traditionalists / 1981 / Warner Bros. ✦✦✦

Oh, No! It's Devo / 1982 / Warner Bros. ✦✦✦

● **The Greatest Hits** / 1990 / Warner Bros. ✦✦✦✦
This isn't the best Devo collection around; there's an import with better selections, but few distributors carry it and it's difficult to find. Devo's present-day cult is quite intense; if they sound like your thing, chances are that you'll want as much as you can get, so start with *Q: Are We Not Men?* and buy the albums. If Devo simply sounds like an interesting novelty to you, or if you don't enjoy them enough to listen to their more uneven albums, this will suffice if you can't find the import. —*Steve Huey*

Dexy's Midnight Runners

Rock'n'Roll, New Wave, Pop-Rock
When Dexy's Midnight Runners were at their peak in the early '80s, UK critics hailed their lead singer-songwriter Kevin Rowland as a genius, capable of fusing soul, pop, Irish folk, new wave, and rock into one seamless, unique mix. Although the band wasn't able to fulfill their promise, the best of their music was remarkable. On their first album, *Searching for the Young Soul Rebels*, the group featured scores of horns along with accomplished songwriting from Rowland. It became a sensation in England, although it didn't dent the charts in America. After the album's release, three members of the band split and formed the Bureau, leaving Rowland to refashion Dexy's Midnight Runners. What he came up with was a departure from the debut, although it shared the same spirit. Instead of soul, the band was rooted in folk and celtic music on their second album, *Too-Rye-Ay*, which produced the enormous international hit, "Come on Eileen." Rowland seemed lost in the wake of his success, lacking a new idea for his music; the last Dexy's album was bland and directionless, as was his solo album, 1988's *The Wanderer*. Rowland hasn't been making music since the late '80s but his band's first records remain searing displays of passion and musical inventiveness. —*Stephen Thomas Erlewine*

Searching for the Young Soul Rebels / Jul. 1980 / EMI America ✦✦✦✦
While it's a fascinating fusion of punk and soul, Dexy's Midnight Runners' debut album isn't quite as wonderful as the band's cult claims it is, but it does offer a number of genuinely impressive and impassioned songs. —*Stephen Thomas Erlewine*

● **Too-Rye-Ay** / Aug. 1982 / Mercury ✦✦✦✦
For the second Dexy's Midnight Runners album, Kevin Rowland refashioned the band as country/folk/punk rockers. Much like *Searching for the Young Soul Rebels*, *Too-Rye-Ay* is more interesting in theory than in practice, but it's the strongest of the two records, thanks to the irresistible hit single "Come on Eileen." —*Stephen Thomas Erlewine*

Don't Stand Me Down / Sep. 1985 / Mercury ✦✦

It Was Like This / 1996 / EMI Premier ✦✦✦✦
It Was Like This collects the entirety of *Searching for the Young Soul Rebels* and adds all the B-sides from the album, plus alternate mixes of "Geno" and "Dance Stance," plus a version of "Respect" recorded for the BBC. The reissue is packaged with care and attention to detail, highlighted by Kevin Rowland's liner notes, making the compact disc the definitive version of Dexy's debut album. —*Stephen Thomas Erlewine*

Very Best of Dexy's Midnight Runners / Mercury ✦✦✦✦
Very Best of Dexy's Midnight Runners, a 19-track collection, gives a comprehensive look at the band. Though the import price tag may be prohibitive, it is notable for the inclusion of the rare "Because of You"—the charming theme to the British television show "Brush Strokes"—unavailable elsewhere. —*Chris Woodstra*

Neil Diamond

b., Jan. 24, 1941, Brooklyn, NY
Guitar, Vocals / Adult Contemporary, Pop, Soft Rock, Pop-Rock
Neil Diamond built a career, first as a pop songwriter, and then as a pop singer, that has withstood the changing fashions of music, especially rock, over more than 25 years. Born in Brooklyn, Diamond was writing and recording in New York in his teens, though he graduated from Erasmus High School and attended New York University for a time. In 1965, he signed to Bang Records as an artist while also working as a songwriter. In 1966, he reached the Top Ten with his "Cherry, Cherry," while The Monkees took his "I'm a Believer" to No. 1. "Cherry, Cherry" was the first of five straight Top 20 hits, among them "Girl, You'll Be a Woman Soon."

Diamond began to develop into more of an individual writer in the mold of Bob Dylan and Paul Simon in the late '60s, and this led to his move to Uni Records in 1968, where he continued to score hits like "Sweet Caroline," "Holly Holy," and "Cracklin' Rosie," in a pop-rock style laced with gospel and country influences. His albums also began to go gold consistently beginning with 1969's *Touching You, Touching Me*.

Diamond signed a lucrative contract with Columbia Records in 1973 that began with his soundtrack to the film *Jonathan Livingston Seagull*. His 1976 album, *Beautiful Noise*, was produced by Robbie Robertson of the Band; it was his first album to go platinum. In 1980, Diamond starred in a remake of the film *The Jazz Singer*. Its soundtrack was another million-seller for him.

Diamond had developed into a dynamic live performer over the years, and his concert recordings were among his most successful. In the late '80s and early '90s, while updating his sound, he faded from the singles charts though his albums continued to sell consistently. And his shows continued to sell out: According to *Amusement Business*, he was the top concert draw in the US for the first six months of 1992.

In early 1996, Diamond released *Tennessee Moon*, a country music album that was his first set of newly recorded material in five years. *Tennessee Moon* became a hit on the country charts, peaking at No. 3 and going gold within six months of its release. —*William Ruhlmann*

Hot August Night / 1972 / MCA ✦✦✦✦
This double-record set is the album that established Diamond's reputation as a live performer. Containing passionately performed versions of his biggest hits up to this time, it sold the best of any album he'd had so far, going gold the month of its release. —*William Ruhlmann*

★ **His Twelve Greatest Hits** / 1974 / MCA ✦✦✦✦✦
Actually, this is 12 songs that were hits for Diamond on Uni between 1969 and 1972. "Cracklin' Rosie" is here, along with Diamond's other chart-topper of the period, "Song Sung Blue," and the Top Ten hits "Sweet Caroline" and "Holly Holy." —*William Ruhlmann*

The Jazz Singer / 1980 / Capitol ✦✦✦✦
Diamond's only notable screen appearance was his starring role in this remake of the 1927 movie that was Hollywood's first real talkie and originally featured Al Jolson. Diamond wrote a new score, featuring his biggest latter-day hits, "Love on the Rocks," "Hello Again," and "America," and as a result this soundtrack album became his biggest seller ever—five million copies and counting. —*William Ruhlmann*

12 Greatest Hits, Vol. 2 / May 1982 / Columbia ✦✦✦✦

Keying off the title of an earlier hits collection on another label, Columbia's *12 Greatest Hits Volume 2* summed up Neil Diamond's first eight years with the label, 1973-1981, as well as his successful 1980 soundtrack for *The Jazz Singer* on Capitol Records. Five of the 12, "Longfellow Serenade," "You Don't Bring Me Flowers" (with Barbra Streisand), "Love on the Rocks," "Hello Again," and "America," were Top Ten hits. Another six, "Be," "If You Know What I Mean," "Desiree," "Forever in Blue Jeans," "September Morn," and "Yesterday's Songs," made the Top 40, and the last, "Beautiful Noise," was the title track of Diamond's best album of the period. The songs shared a catchiness that belied Diamond's shallow philosophizing and thinly veiled lust, and they made for a consistent collection out of what had been a series of uneven albums. And, since Diamond only made the Top Ten one more time, the album capped his hit-making days. This is the record to buy instead of investing in the Columbia catalog. — *William Ruhlmann*

★ **Classics: The Early Years** / 1983 / Columbia ✦✦✦✦✦

A terrific collection featuring his earliest and best songs, like "Kentucky Woman," "Girl, You'll Be a Woman Soon," "Cherry, Cherry," "Thank the Lord for the Night Time," "Solitary Man," "I'm a Believer," and "Red Red Wine." — *Stephen Thomas Erlewine*

The Greatest Hits (1966-1992) / 1992 / Columbia ✦✦✦✦

Columbia has been Diamond's label since 1973, and it acquired the rights to his Bang material of 1966-1968. But MCA still controls the recordings from 1968-1973. That's why (although you won't find out by reading the album cover) this two-disc, 37-track retrospective consists of the original versions of such hits as "Cherry, Cherry" (1966) and "You Don't Bring Me Flowers" (1978) but covers the middle period with re-recordings and live renditions of 13 of Diamond's biggest hits. As such, this collection gets only a qualified recommendation. — *William Ruhlmann*

Glory Road: 1968 to 1972 / 1992 / MCA ✦✦✦✦

A fine two-disc retrospective of Diamond's late-'60s and early-'70s tracks, it includes some of his biggest hits—"Cracklin' Rosie," "Sweet Caroline," and "Song Sung Blue," among others. If his *12 Greatest Hits* doesn't offer enough material, *Glory Road* is the definitive retrospective of his years with Uni/MCA. — *AMG*

The Dictators

Hard Rock, Proto-Punk

Formed in 1974, NYC's Dictators were one of the finest and most influential proto-punk bands to walk the earth. Alternately reveling in and satirizing the wanton excesses of a rock 'n' roll lifestyle and lowbrow culture (e.g., wrestling, TV, fast food), the Dictators, whose worldview was defined by bassist/keyboardist and former fanzine publisher (*Teenage Wasteland Gazette*) Andy (occasionally Adny) Shernoff and renegade rock critic/theorist Richard Meltzer, played loud, fast rock 'n' roll fueled by a love of '60s American garage rock, British Invasion pop and the sonic onslaught of the Who. Driven by the guitar barrage of Scott "Top Ten" Kempner and Ross "The Boss" Funichello, and fronted by indefatigable ex-roadie and wrestler Handsome Dick Manitoba (aka Richard Blum), it seemed that nothing stood in the way of the Dictators and mega-popularity. But that's not what happened. There were complications with record companies, personnel changes (one-time bassist Mark Mendoza left for Twisted Sister; original drummer Stu Boy King was replaced by Richie Teeter), radio hated them, critical response was lukewarm, and lots of audiences didn't get the jokes; supporters remained loyal and vociferous (especially Meltzer), but it didn't turn into anything tangible. Ironically, what didn't help at all was the rise of the New York punk scene, which only diverted attention away from them and onto bands they influenced (e.g., the Ramones). They did manage to release three fine albums, but by 1978, it was over, and the Dictators broke up in the face of the public apathy and overstated accusations of sellout that greeted what was to be their final album, *Bloodbrothers*. Since then, individual members have kept busy: Kempner put together the Del-Lords and now records as a solo act; Ross the Boss spent a few years in the goofy, macho heavy-metal band Manowar and later joined Shernoff and Manitoba in the punk/metal combo Manitoba's Wild Kingdom; Shernoff also works as a producer. In 1991, there was a brief reunion tour (with Top Ten) that proved they hadn't lost a step after all these years. — *John Dougan*

● **Go Girl Crazy** / 1975 / Epic ✦✦✦✦

A great debut release that went almost totally ignored in its day. Although Manitoba appears on the LP cover, it's Shernoff who does the bulk of the lead singing. Many of the songs—"The Next Big Thing," "Master Race Rock," "Teengenerate," and "(I Live For) Cars and Girls"—became live staples and are accurate example of the Dictators' style and abundant sense of humor. — *John Dougan*

Manifest Destiny / 1977 / Asylum ✦✦✦

Bloodbrothers / 1978 / Asylum ✦✦✦

Live, Fuck 'em If They Can't Take a Joke / 1981 / ROIR ✦✦✦

Bo Diddley (Ellas Otha Bates McDaniels)

b. Dec. 30, 1928, McComb, MS

Guitar, Violin, Vocals / R&B, Rock 'n' Roll

He only had a few hits in the 1950s and early '60s, but as Bo Diddley sang, "You Can't Judge a Book by Its Cover." You can't judge an artist by his chart success, either, and Diddley produced greater and more influential music than all but a handful of the best early rockers. The Bo Diddley beat—bomp, ba-bomp-bomp, bomp-bomp—is one of rock 'n' roll's best-rock rhythms, showing up in the work of Buddy Holly, the Rolling Stones, and even pop-garage knockoffs like the Strangeloves' 1965 hit "I Want Candy." Diddley's hypnotic rhythmic attack and declamatory, boasting vocals stretched back as far as Africa for their roots, and looked as far into the future as rap. His trademark otherwordly vibrating, fuzzy guitar style did much to expand the instrument's power and range. But even more important, Bo's bounce was fun and irresistibly rocking, with a wisecracking, jiving tone that epitomized rock 'n' roll at its most humorously outlandish and freewheeling.

Before taking up blues and R&B, Diddley had actually studied classical violin, but shifted gears after hearing John Lee Hooker. In the early '50s, he began playing with his longtime partner, maraca player Jerome Green, to get what Bo's called "that freight train sound." Billy Boy Arnold, a fine blues harmonica player and singer in his own right, was also playing with Diddley when the guitarist got a deal with Chess in the mid-1950s (after being turned down by rival Chicago label Vee-Jay).

His very first single, "Bo Diddley"/"I'm a Man" (1955), was a double-sided monster. The A-side was soaked with futuristic waves of tremolo guitar, set to an ageless nursery rhyme; the flip was a bump-and-grind, harmonica-driven shuffle, based around a devastating blues riff. But the result was not exactly blues, or even straight R&B, but a new kind of guitar-based rock 'n' roll, soaked in the blues and R&B, but owing allegiance to neither. Diddley was never a top seller on the order of his Chess rival Chuck Berry, but over the next half-dozen or so years, he'd produce a catalog of classics that rival Berry's in quality. "You Don't Love Me," "Diddley Daddy," "Pretty Thing," "Diddy Wah Diddy," "Who Do You Love?," "Mona," "Road Runner," "You Can't Judge a Book by Its Cover"—all are stone-cold standards of early, riff-driven rock 'n' roll at its funkiest. Oddly enough, his only Top 20 pop hit was an atypical, absurd back-and-forth rap between him and Jerome, "Say Man," that came about almost by accident as the pair were fooling around in the studio.

As a live performer, Diddley was galvanizing, using his trademark square guitars and distorted amplification to produce new sounds that anticipated the innovations of '60s guitarists like Jimi Hendrix. He'd record with ongoing and declining frequency, but after 1963, he'd never write or record any original material on par with his early classics. Whether he'd spent his muse, or just felt he could coast on his laurels, is hard to say. But he remains a vital part of the collective rock 'n' roll consciousness, occasionally reaching wider visibility via a 1979 tour with the Clash, a cameo role in the film *Trading Places*, a late-'80s tour with Ronnie Wood, and a 1989 television commercial for sports shoes with star athlete Bo Jackson. — *Richie Unterberger*

Bo Diddley in the Spotlight / 1960 / Chess ✦✦✦✦

Another excellent original Checker album from 1960 that features some of Bo Diddley's better work (including the soaring smash "Road Runner"), transferred verbatim to CD (no bonus items this time). He was in an amazingly prolific groove during this time frame, churning out album after album, and they're all worth collecting. — *Bill Dahl*

Bo Diddley Is a Gunslinger / 1963 / Chess ✦✦✦✦

Not only does it sport one of the most striking album covers of its era (Diddley decked out in cowboy finery, about to get the drop on some unfortunate varmint with one of his fieriest guitars lying at his feet), this 1963 album contains some fine music. The title track continues the legend of you-know-who, while "Ride on Josephine" and "Cadillac" rock like hell (and Ed Sullivan must have been glad to see that Diddley finally learned "Sixteen Tons"). Two bonus cuts, "Working Man" and "Do What I Say," make this one a must. — *Bill Dahl*

Bo Diddley's Beach Party / 1963 / Checker ✦✦✦✦
A blistering live album. Currently out of print but well worth any search. —*Cub Koda*

Two Great Guitars / 1964 / Chess ✦✦

☆ **Bo Diddley/Go Bo Diddley** / 1986 / Chess ✦✦✦✦✦
There are precious few weak tracks on this combination of Bo Diddley's first two late-'50s albums for Chess/Checker, which boasts a plethora of classics ("Bo Diddley," "I'm a Man," "Before You Accuse Me," "Crackin' Up," "Little Girl," even his electric violin workout "The Clock Struck Twelve"). The only drawback: someone failed to notice that "Dearest Darling" was on both LPs, so . . . it's on here twice! —*Bill Dahl*

★ **The Chess Box** / 1990 / MCA ✦✦✦✦✦
Not every single track you'll ever want or need by the legendary shave-and-a-haircut R&B/rock pioneer, but a great place to begin. Two discs (45 songs) in a great big box with a nice accompanying booklet contain the groundbreaking introduction "Bo Diddley" (never again would he be referred to as Ellas McDaniel), its swaggering flipside "I'm a Man," the killer follow-ups "Diddley Daddy," "I'm Looking for a Woman," "Who Do You Love?," and "Hey Bo Diddley," signifying street-corner humor ("Say Man"), pile-driving rockers ("Road Runner," "She's Alright," "You Can't Judge a Book by Its Cover"), and numerous stunning examples of his daringly innovative guitar style. —*Bill Dahl*

Rare & Well Done / Sep. 10, 1991 / Chess ✦✦✦✦
Sixteen extreme rarities from the deepest recesses of the Chess vaults that date from 1955-1968. The grinding "She's Fine, She's Mine" and snarling "I'm Bad" are comparatively well known, at least to collectors; far more obscure are the previously unissued "Heart-O-Matic Love," "Cookie-Headed Diddley," and "Moon Baby." —*Bill Dahl*

Bo's Blues / 1993 / Ace ✦✦✦✦
Twenty-two of Bo Diddley's best blues-oriented sides from the Chess catalog, including some rare stuff—the rip-roaring 1959 outing "Run Diddley Daddy," a jive-loaded "Cops and Robbers" from 1956 that features maraca shaker Jerome Green more than Diddley, and a surging "Down Home Special." If you think that everything Bo Diddley ever made has that same shave-and-a-haircut beat, this collection will set you straight! —*Bill Dahl*

Bo Diddley Is a Lover . . . Plus / 1994 / See For Miles ✦✦✦✦
Very welcome digital British import reissue of Bo's 1961 Checker album, bolstered by a handful of bonus tracks (including his rendering of Willie Dixon's "My Babe"). On second guitar for many of these sides is Peggy Jones, one of Diddley's prize pupils. Some of the better-known sides include "Not Guilty," "Hong Kong, Mississippi," and the bragadocious title cut. —*Bill Dahl*

Let Me Pass Plus / 1994 / See For Miles ✦✦✦

Dinosaur Jr.

Alternative Pop-Rock
Led by J. Mascis' massive guitar roar and drawling vocals, Dinosaur Jr. were one of the most distinctive and influential alternative bands of the late '80s. Taking hardcore punk and Neil Young's splattered electric folk as their starting points, Dinosaur Jr. created a loud, sprawling rock 'n' roll that frequently spun off into the white noise territory of Sonic Youth but just as frequently stayed in Mascis' lazily melodic, folk-based songs.

Initially, Dinosaur Jr. was a trio called Dinosaur. Mascis and bassist Lou Barlow played in a Massachusetts-area hardcore combo called Deep Wound, with Mascis on drums. After Deep Wound had run its course, former All White Jury drummer Murph was brought into the lineup and Mascis switched to guitar. The group released its self-titled debut for Homestead Records in 1985. Around the time of their second album, 1987's *You're Living All over Me*, a '60s rock group called the Dinosaurs forced the band to change their name; at Mascis' suggestion, the band added "Jr."

The following year Lou Barlow recorded his last album with the band, *Bug;* he formed Sebadoh in the same year. Barlow wasn't immediately replaced. Instead, J. Mascis recorded the next album, *Green Mind,* almost entirely by himself, which began a practice that Dinosaur Jr. would follow throughout their career. Frequently, Mascis recorded the majority of the album, with various musicians filling out the parts. Bassist Mike Johnston joined with 1993's *Where You Been* and Murph was kicked out before the sessions for 1994's *Without a Sound.*

Without Barlow, the band became more direct and accessible, although Mascis' guitar would still frequently veer into wrenching noise. One of the few traditional lead guitarists in alternative rock, Mascis' fluid, feedback-drenched guitar expressed all of the emotions that his lyrics alluded to. Mascis also is one of the most respected songwriters in alternative rock; his songs have been covered by several artists, including the Cowboy Junkies. Since their first release in 1985, Dinosaur Jr. have influenced a generation of young guitar bands; along with the Pixies and Sonic Youth, they provide the link between the post-punk rock of

Hüsker Dü and Replacements and the grunge rock of the '90s. —*Stephen Thomas Erlewine*

Dinosaur / 1985 / Positive ✦✦✦

★ **You're Living All over Me** / 1987 / SST ✦✦✦✦✦
A colossal slab of snarling indie-rock guitar noise, Dinosaur Jr's second album was one of the landmark underground rock records of the late '80s; with its huge sheets of white noise and sighing melodies, it paved the way for the grunge movement of the early '90s. —*Stephen Thomas Erlewine*

Bug / 1988 / SST ✦✦✦✦
Bug is as noisy as *You're Living All over Me,* but this time out, Mascis' songwriting has sharpened a bit, as evidenced by the brilliant single "Freak Scene." —*Stephen Thomas Erlewine*

Fossils / 1991 / SST ✦✦✦
A good collection of non-LP singles and rarities, *Fossils'* high points include strangely appropriate covers of Peter Frampton's "Show Me the Way" and the Cure's "Just like Heaven." —*Stephen Thomas Erlewine*

Green Mind / 1991 / Sire ✦✦✦✦
Many consider *Green Mind* to be a weak, uninspired effort, but Dinosaur Jr's major-label debut is a strong, varied album, featuring some of J. Mascis' best songwriting, as well as some of his best, most fluid guitar work. Essentially a solo effort by Mascis (Murph only appears on three tracks), *Green Mind* finds him stretching and expanding his traditional sonic assault with more acoustic guitars and tighter melodies. With its gentle Mellotron and lovely, sighing melody, "Thumb" stands as one of Mascis' finest songs; "Muck" is a surprisingly enjoyable stab at funk, "How'd You Pin That One on Me" is a great guitar workout, "Puke & Cry" and "I Live for That Look" are impressive folk-punk, and "The Wagon" rivals "Freak Scene" in its depiction of the underground scene. —*Stephen Thomas Erlewine*

Whatever's Cool with Me / Oct. 22, 1991 / Sire ✦✦✦
"Whatever's Cool with Me" is definitive Dinosaur Jr.—roaring rhythm guitars, legato solos, weary lyrics and a winding, penetrating melody. The other five B-sides on the EP are solid, but unremarkable, highlighted by a tongue-in-cheek rewrite of David Bowie's "Quicksand." —*Stephen Thomas Erlewine*

Where You Been / 1993 / Warner Bros. ✦✦✦✦
Dinosaur Jr's full-throttle punk roar keeps diminishing as time goes by, but that doesn't mean the music is any less powerful; if anything, it's getting stronger. *Where You Been* sounds similar to most other Dinosaur Jr. albums—there's no mistaking J Mascis' trademark wrenching guitar and vocals—but the album is filled with terrific songs like "Get Me" and "Start Choppin'," even if the guitar meanders a bit too much. —*Stephen Thomas Erlewine*

Without a Sound / 1994 / Warner Bros. ✦✦

Dion & the Belmonts

Rock 'n' Roll, Doo Wop, Teen Idol
Bridging the era between late-'50s rock and the British Invasion, Dion DiMucci (b. Jul. 18, 1939) was one of the top White rock singers of his time, blending the best elements of doo wop, teen idol, and R&B styles. Some revisionists have tried to cast him as a sort of early blue-eyed soul figure, although he was probably more aligned with pop-rock, at first as the lead singer of the Belmonts, and then as a solo star. Drug problems slowed him down in the mid-'60s, yet he made some surprisingly interesting progressions into blues-rock and folk-rock as the decade wore on, culminating in a successful comeback in the late 1960s, although he was unable to sustain its commercial and artistic momentum for long.

When Dion began recording in the late 1950s, it was as the lead singer of a group of friends that sang on Bronx street corners. Billing themselves as Dion and the Belmonts (Dion had released a previous single with the Timberlanes), their first few records were prime Italian-American doo wop; "I Wonder Why" was their biggest hit in this style. His biggest single with the Belmonts was "A Teenager in Love," which pointed the way for the slightly self-pitying, pained odes to adolescence and early adulthood that would characterize much of his solo career.

Dion went solo in 1960 (the Belmonts did some more doo wop recordings on their own), moving from doo wop to more R&B/pop-oriented tunes with great success. He handled himself with a suave, cocky ease on hits like "The Wanderer," "Runaround Sue," "Lovers Who Wander," "Ruby Baby," and "Donna the Prima Donna" cast him as either the jilted, misunderstood youngster or the macho lover, capable of handling anything that came his way (on "The Wanderer" especially).

In 1963, Dion moved from Laurie to the larger Columbia label, an association that started promisingly with a couple of big hits right off the bat, "Ruby Baby" and "Donna the Prima Donna." By the mid-'60s, his heroin habit (which he'd developed as a teenager) was getting the best of him, and he did little recording and performing for about five years. When he did make it into the studio, he was moving in some surprisingly bluesy directions; although much of it was overlooked or unissued at the time, it can be heard on the *Bronx Blues* reissue CD.

In 1968 he kicked heroin and re-emerged as a gentle folk-rocker with a No. 4 hit single, "Abraham, Martin and John." Dion would focus upon mature, contemporary material on his late-'60s and early-'70s albums, which were released to positive critical feedback, if only moderate sales. The folk phase didn't last long; in 1972 he reunited with the Belmonts, and in the mid-'70s cut a disappointing record with Phil Spector as producer. He's been recording and performing fairly often over the last two decades (sometimes singing Christian music) to indifferent commercial results. But his critical rep has risen steadily since the early '60s, with many noted contemporary musicians showering him with praise and citing his influence, such as Dave Edmunds (who produced one of his periodic comeback albums) and Lou Reed (who guested on that record). *—Richie Unterberger*

Runaround Sue / 1961 / The Right Stuff ◆◆◆

Lovers Who Wander / 1962 / The Right Stuff ◆◆◆

Dion / 1968 / The Right Stuff ◆◆◆◆
Featuring his Top Five comeback single "Abraham, Martin and John," this folk-rock and blues-flavored effort remains his most fully realized album. In addition to the impressive anti-war original "He Looks a Lot like Me," it contains mature interpretations, arranged both acoustically and with strings, of songs by Fred Neil, Joni Mitchell, Leonard Cohen, Bob Dylan, and Lightnin' Hopkins (though the florid version of Jimi Hendrix's "Purple Haze" is embarrassing). The CD reissue adds the highly sought-after non-LP B-side "Daddy Rollin'," a Dion original that ranks as his most country-blues-influenced performance. *—Richie Unterberger*

☆ **Everything You Always Wanted to Hear by Dion** / 1976 / Laurie ◆◆◆◆◆
The best overall collection of their classic sides. Includes "Teenager in Love," "Where or When," and "I Wonder Why." White New York doo wop at its best. *—Cub Koda*

★ **24 Golden Greats** / 1983 / Arista ◆◆◆◆◆
24 Golden Greats contains all of Dion & the Belmonts' biggest hits, plus all of Dion's solo hits from the late '60s and early '70s, making it the definitive compilation of the vocalist's long, successful career. *—Stephen Thomas Erlewine*

Greatest Hits / 1987 / Columbia ◆◆◆◆
A solid compilation of Dion's solo sides, including "Donna the Prima Donna," "Ruby Baby," and others. *—Cub Koda*

Bronx Blues: The Columbia Recordings / 1991 / Columbia ◆◆◆◆
In the mid-'60s, Dion turned away from teen-idol doo wop material and cut several sides in a solid R&B/blues/folk vein. The best of those sides are collected here. *—Cub Koda*

Celine Dion

Vocals / Adult Contemporary, Pop-Rock, Club-Dance
In her native Canada as well as France, Celine Dion was a popular singer since she was a teenager. Dion's polished yet soulful adult contemporary pop didn't break in the US until 1991 (when she released a record recorded in English), but when it did there was no stopping the hits; from "Where Does My Heart Beat Now" to the theme to *Beauty and the Beast*, Dion has been a fixture on the American pop charts since 1992.

In 1996, Celine Dion enjoyed her biggest hit to date with "Because You Loved Me," the theme from the film *Up Close & Personal*. The song became the biggest adult contemporary hit of all time and propelled her own album, *Falling into You*, into the pop Top Ten and multi-platinum status. *—Stephen Thomas Erlewine*

Unison / 1990 / Epic ◆◆◆

● **Celine Dion** / Mar. 31, 1992 / Epic ◆◆◆◆
Featuring the hit singles "Beauty and the Beast," "Love Can Move Mountains," and "If You Asked Me To," Celine Dion's follow-up to her successful American debut is an even stronger and more accomplished record than her previous album. *—Stephen Thomas Erlewine*

The Colour of My Love / Nov. 9, 1993 / 550 Music/Epic ◆◆◆

Falling into You / Mar. 12, 1996 / 550 Music/Epic ◆◆◆◆

Dire Straits

Rock 'n' Roll, Pop-Rock
In 1977 disco reigned and the new wave/punk movements were heralding the death of tired FM rock. It was then that Dire Straits came along with a unique blend of atmospheric blues-flavored rock and literate Dylanesque story-type lyrics. Singer, songwriter, and lead guitarist Mark Knopfler's dry, low-key vocal delivery and economical, clean guitar playing immediately hit a nerve with the public.

Aside from *Communique*, the band's sophomore effort, Dire Straits increasingly developed a cinematic approach to songwriting and production. *Love over Gold* is a particular highlight. It was only a natural side-

step for Knopfler to score the highly acclaimed soundtracks for *Local Hero* (1983) and *The Princess Bride* (1987). *Alchemy,* a double-record live set, was released in 1984.

In 1985 *Brothers in Arms* was released, becoming one of the biggest internationally selling albums of the '80s. The song "Money for Nothing" became free advertising for MTV, with the hook "I want my MTV."

Knopfler undertook various side projects, including the Notting Hill-billies and a fine duet album with Chet Atkins (*Neck and Neck*). Six years after the release of *Brothers in Arms, On Every Street* was released. *—Rick Clark*

☆ **Dire Straits** / Oct. 1978 / Warner Bros. ◆◆◆◆◆
Even after all the success, the debut is the best example of the intricate style of Dire Straits, dominated by the electric finger-picking of guitarist Mark Knopfler, his smoky voice and poetic lyrics. Features their first hit, "Sultans of Swing." *—William Ruhlmann*

Communiqué / Jun. 1979 / Warner Bros. ◆◆

Making Movies / Oct. 17, 1980 / Warner Bros. ◆◆◆◆
The third album displays Knopfler's expanding ambitions as a songwriter with, as the title suggests, a cinematic sweep on such songs as "Tunnel of Love" and "Romeo and Juliet." *—William Ruhlmann*

Love over Gold / Sep. 1982 / Warner Bros. ◆◆◆◆
The fourth Dire Straits album is their most atmospheric effort, featuring the spacious title track as well as the epic "Telegraph Road," with the extended guitar workout at its conclusion. *—Rick Clark*

Twisting by the Pool [EP] / Feb. 1983 / Warner Bros. ◆◆◆

Alchemy: Dire Straits Live / Mar. 1984 / Warner Bros. ◆◆◆

Brothers in Arms / May 1985 / Warner Bros. ◆◆◆◆
Their biggest-selling album, containing the mega-hit "Money for Nothing" as well as "Walk of Life" and "So Far Away." *—William Ruhlmann*

● **Money for Nothing** / Oct. 1988 / Warner Bros. ◆◆◆◆
This best-of collection contains Dire Straits' biggest hits as well as some key album tracks. "Sultans of Swing," "Walk of Life," "Money for Nothing," plus a live version of "Telegraph Road" from *Love over Gold*, are among the highlights. Even though this may be a fairly representative sampler, listening to the better albums in their entirety is the best way to hear this band. *—Rick Clark*

On Every Street / Sep. 1991 / Warner Bros. ◆◆

On the Night / May 11, 1993 / Warner Bros. ◆◆

Live at the BBC / 1995 / Winsong ◆◆◆

Don Dixon

Bass, Guitar, Keyboards, Vocals / Singer-Songwriter, Pop-Rock, Jangle-Pop
While his own records never reached a mass audience, Don Dixon was one of the major figures in the post-punk Southern guitar pop of the '80s. Dixon produced R.E.M., Let's Active, the Smithereens, and Marti Jones during the decade, bringing his sharp pop sensibilities to their already highly melodic songs. But his true talents shine in his solo albums. Dixon is successfully able to recall everything from Beatlesque pop and Southern soul to gritty country and R&B with his lean, muscular pop; he adds an engagingly twisted lyrical view to his effortlessly eclectic music, making him one of the best subversive pop singer-songwriters since Nick Lowe. *—Stephen Thomas Erlewine*

Most of the Girls Like to Dance but Only Some of the Boys Do / 1985 / Enigma ◆◆◆◆
Dixon put together this album out of demos cut from 1981-1984. It's a kind of best-of from a man with a pure pop sensibility and a wicked sense of humor when it comes to matters romantic. (The 1986 CD version adds two songs to make a total of 16.) *—William Ruhlmann*

Romeo at Juilliard / Sep. 1987 / Enigma ◆◆◆◆
Dixon's domestic debut featured more of his skewed songs, and here he was aided and abetted by such compatriots as Mitch Easter and Marti Jones (who is his wife). *—William Ruhlmann*

Chi-Town Budget Show / 1988 / Enigma ◆◆◆

Eee / Sep. 20, 1989 / Enigma ◆◆◆

● **If I'm a Ham, Well You're a Sausage** / Mar. 3, 1992 / Restless ◆◆◆◆
While he is known mainly through his production work, this extensive best-of collection shows Dixon to be an equally sharp songwriter and performer. *—Chris Woodstra*

Romantic Depressive / Mar. 28, 1995 / Sugar Hill ◆◆◆
Don Dixon produces another set of well-crafted mid-'60s-style pop-rock songs on his Sugar Hill Records debut, playing most of the instruments and singing in his husky voice. The album title catches the tone of many of the lyrics, which turn on romantic reversals. Though Dixon continues to sound like a man who never got over the British Invasion of 1964, he does locate one song several years later, reminiscing in "Lottery of Lives"

about a point in the Vietnam Era when his student deferment was in doubt. —*William Ruhlmann*

Dr. Feelgood

Rock 'n' Roll, Pub-Rock
Although they never strayed from their gritty R&B-based sound, Dr. Feelgood was a fixture of England's rock 'n' roll scene since the early '70s. While their music wasn't particularly influential, their method of playing was. Dr. Feelgood constantly traveled England, playing to sold-out clubs across the country; with their devoted following, they helped create the pub-rock scene in the UK—venues where rough rock 'n' roll bands could pound out anything from R&B to pop to simple, three-chord rock. By proving these clubs were profitable, the band helped pave the way for the success of punk rock in England; punk bands played the same bars and clubs that Dr. Feelgood, Brinsley Schwarz, and other pub-rockers played in the early '70s. Over the years, the band's lineup changed frequently with vocalist/harmonica player Lee Brilleaux being the only constant member. Brilleaux's energy never diminished as he got older; his consistently vibrant live performances were the reasons why Dr. Feelgood was such a concert draw.

Even though he had been performing for over twenty years, Brilleaux remained a force to be reckoned with when he was on stage, right until his untimely death in April of 1994. —*Stephen Thomas Erlewine*

Down by the Jetty / Jan. 1975 / United Artists ✦✦✦
Dr. Feelgood's debut album is on a par with the early Rolling Stones albums as a demonstration of R&B fervor. Every track burns. —*Bruce Eder*

● **Malpractice** / Feb. 1975 / Columbia ✦✦✦✦
Guitarist Wilko Johnson's songs shine against such inspired covers as "Riot in Cell Block No.9." And his Stonesy playing takes no prisoners. —*Bruce Eder*

Sneakin' Suspicion / 1977 / Columbia ✦✦✦✦
Wilko Johnson's last album with Dr. Feelgood continues to be dominated by his tough guitar playing, although fewer of his songs are heard. —*Bruce Eder*

Be Seeing You / 1977 / United Artists ✦✦✦✦
The Nick Lowe-produced *Be Seeing You*, Dr. Feelgood's first album with guitarist John Mayo, was only slightly weaker than the group's previous records. Although Mayo was still working his way into the band's sound, Dr. Feelgood retained their tough, hard-rocking appeal. —*Stephen Thomas Erlewine*

Singles (The UA Years) / 1989 / Liberty ✦✦✦✦

Looking Back / Nov. 1995 / EMI ✦✦✦

Dr. John

Piano, Vocals / R&B, Rock 'n' Roll, New Orleans R&B
Although he didn't become widely known until the '70s, Dr. John had been active in the music industry since the late '50s, when the teenager was still known as Mac Rebennack. A formidable boogie and blues pianist with a lovable growl of a voice, his most enduring achievements have fused New Orleans R&B, rock, and Mardi Gras craziness to come up with his own brand of "voodoo" music. He's also quite accomplished and enjoyable when sticking to purely traditional forms of blues and R&B. On record, he veers between the two approaches, making for an inconsistent and frequently frustrating legacy that often makes the listener feel as if the Night Tripper (as he's nicknamed himself) has been underachieving.

In the late '50s, Rebennack gained prominence in the New Orleans R&B scene as a session keyboardist and guitarist, contributing to records by Professor Longhair, Frankie Ford, and Joe Tex. He also did some overlooked singles of his own, and by the 1960s had expanded into production and arranging. After a gun accident damaged his hand in the early '60s, he gave up the guitar to concentrate on keyboards exclusively. Skirting trouble with the law and drugs, he left the increasingly unwelcome environs of New Orleans in the mid-'60s for Los Angeles, where he found session work with the help of fellow New Orleans expatriate Harold Battiste.

Rebennack renamed himself Dr. John the Night Tripper when he recorded his first album, *Gris Gris*. According to legend, this was hurriedly cut with leftover studio time from a Sonny & Cher session, but it never sounded hastily conceived. In fact, its mix of New Orleans R&B with voodoo sounds and a tinge of psychedelia was downright enthralling, and may have resulted in his greatest album. He began building an underground following with both his music and his eccentric stage presence, which found him conducting ceremonial-type events in full Mardi Gras costume.

Dr. John was nothing if not eclectic, and his next few albums were granted mixed critical receptions because of their unevenness and occasional excess. They certainly had their share of admirable moments, though, and Eric Clapton and Mick Jagger helped out on *The Sun Moon*

and Herbs in 1971. The following year's *Gumbo*, produced by Jerry Wexler, proved Dr. John was a master of traditional New Orleans R&B styles, in the mold of one of his heroes, Professor Longhair. In 1973, he got his sole big hit, "In the Right Place," which was produced by Allen Toussaint, with backing by the Meters. In the same year, he also recorded with Mike Bloomfield and John Hammond, Jr. for the *Triumvirate* album.

The rest of the decade, unfortunately, was pretty much a waste musically. Dr. John could always count on returning to traditional styles for a good critical reception, and he did so constantly in the 1980s. There were solo piano albums, sessions with Chris Barber and Jimmy Witherspoon, and *In a Sentimental Mood* (1989), a record of pop standards. These didn't sell all that well, though. A more important problem was that he's capable of much more than recastings of old styles and material. In fact, by this time he was usually bringing in the bacon not through his own music, but via vocals for numerous commercial jingles.

It's continued pretty much in the same vein throughout the 1990s: New Orleans supersessions for the *Bluesiana* albums, another outing with Chris Barber, an album of New Orleans standards, and *another* album of pop standards. In 1994, *Television* did at least offer some original material. However, at this point it seems like he will usually rely upon cover versions for the bulk of his recorded work, though his interpretive skills will always ensure that these are more interesting than most such efforts. His autobiography, *Under a Hoodoo Moon*, was published by St. Martin's Press in 1994. —*Richie Unterberger*

Gris Gris / 1968 / Repertoire ✦✦✦✦
The most exploratory and psychedelic outing of Dr. John's career, a one-of-a-kind fusion of New Orleans Mardi Gras R&B and voodoo mysticism. Great rasping, bluesy vocals, soulful backup singers, and eerie melodies on flute, sax, and clarinet, as well as odd Middle Eastern-like chanting and mandolin runs. It's got the setting of a strange religious ritual, but the mood is far more joyous than solemn. —*Richie Unterberger*

Babylon / 1969 / Atco ✦✦✦

Dr. John's Gumbo / Apr. 1972 / Atco ✦✦✦✦
Gumbo bridged the gap between post-hippie rock and early rock 'n' roll, blues and R&B, offering a selection of classic New Orleans R&B, including "Tipitina" and "Junko Partner," updated with a gritty, funky beat. There are not as many psychedelic flourishes as there were on his first two albums, but the ones that are present enhance his sweeping vision of American roots music. And that sly fusion of styles makes *Gumbo* one of Dr. John's finest albums. —*Stephen Thomas Erlewine*

In a Sentimental Mood / Apr. 1989 / Warner Bros. ✦✦✦

Goin' Back to New Orleans / Jun. 23, 1992 / Warner Bros. ✦✦✦

Anthology / 1993 / Rhino ✦✦✦✦
Over his 35 years of recording, Mac "Dr. John" Rebennack has worn many hats, from '50s greasy rock 'n' roller to psychedelic '70s weirdo to keeper of the New Orleans music flame. All of these modes, plus more, are excellently served up on this two-disc anthology. From the early New Orleans sides featuring Rebennack's blistering guitar work ("Storm Warning" and "Morgus the Magnificent") to the fabled '70s sides as the Night Tripper to his present day status as repository of the Crescent City's noble musical tradition, this is the one you want to have for the collection. —*Cub Koda*

● **The Very Best of Dr. John** / 1995 / Rhino ✦✦✦✦
The Very Best of Dr. John compiles the best moments from the comprehensive double-disc *Anthology*, making it a more effective, and cheaper, introduction for casual fans. —*Stephen Thomas Erlewine*

Thomas Dolby

b. Oct. 14, 1958, Cairo, Egypt
Guitar, Keyboards / Synth-Pop, New Wave
This British musician and producer was one of the first artists to explore the possibilities of synthesizers and digital samplers in a straight pop music context. Besides his dance hits "She Blinded Me with Science" and "Hyperactive!," Dolby has played on Foreigner's *4* album, produced albums for Joni Mitchell and Prefab Sprout, collaborated with George Clinton (on their respective solo albums and the Dolby's Cube project), and written music for the films *Howard the Duck* and *Gothic.*

He began his career working with Lene Lovich (he wrote "New Toy" for her) and with Bruce Wooley & The Camera Club, a group that also featured Trevor Horn (Yes, Buggles), Geoff Downes (Yes, Asia), and Matthew Seligman (Soft Boys). —*Scott Bultman*

The Golden Age of Wireless / Mar. 1983 / Capitol ✦✦✦✦
This contains Dolby's biggest hit, the humorously quirky "She Blinded Me with Science." Highlights include "Radio Silence," "Europa and the Pirate Twins," "Windpower," "One of Our Submarines," and "Airwaves"—a track that should've been a single. All in all, this is a very solid collection of early-'80s synth-pop. (*The Golden Age of Wireless* originally was released in May 1982 as Harvest/Capitol 12203. In the wake of the success of "She Blinded Me with Science," it was reissued in March 1983

with that track and another added (and two others dropped) as Harvest/ Capitol 12271, later reissued on CD as Capitol 46009.) —*Rick Clark*

The Flat Earth / Feb. 1984 / Capitol ✦✦✦
A departure from the style of his debut, this moody and atmospheric album adds jazz and Joni Mitchell-esque elements to warm his synth textures. Only "White City" and the single, "Hyperactive!," feature the hard dance beats of his early hits. —*Scott Bultman*

Aliens Ate My Buick / Apr. 1988 / EMI-Manhattan ✦✦

Gate to the Mind's Eye / Oct. 18, 1994 / Giant ✦✦✦

● **Best of Thomas Dolby: Retrospectacle** / Apr. 4, 1995 / Capitol ✦✦✦✦
After what had seemed like a promising start with "She Blinded Me with Science" in 1983, Thomas Dolby only charted with two other singles in the US (though he had nine chart singles in his native UK, 1981-1992). This 16-track compilation, embracing both his Capitol/EMI and Warner Bros. recordings, demonstrates that Dolby deserved better. His synthesizer-based songs are consistently catchy and clever, and especially notable are early songs like "Urges" and "Leipzig" that have not previously appeared on a US album. "One of Our Submarines," Dolby's cover of Dan Hicks's "I Scare Myself," and "Hyperactive!" all hold up well. Some of the later (non-hit) material from the albums *Aliens Ate My Buick* and *Astronauts & Heretics* is less impressive; a better choice could have been made from those records. But for the most part, this is an efficient collection that justifies its name. —*William Ruhlmann*

Fats Domino

b. Feb. 28, 1928, New Orleans, LA
Piano, Vocals / R&B, Rock 'n' Roll, New Orleans R&B
The most popular exponent of the classic New Orleans R&B sound, Fats Domino sold more records than any other Black rock 'n' roll star of the 1950s. His relaxed, lolling boogie-woogie piano style and easygoing, warm vocals anchored a long series of national hits from the mid-'50s to the early '60s. Through it all, his basic approach rarely changed. He may not have been one of early rock's most charismatic, innovative, or threatening figures, but he was certainly one of its most consistent.

Domino's first single, "The Fat Man" (1950), is one of the dozens of tracks that have been consistently singled out as a candidate for the first rock 'n' roll record. As far as Fats was concerned, he was just playing what he'd already been doing in New Orleans for years, and would continue to play and sing in pretty much the same fashion even after his music was dubbed "rock 'n' roll."

The record made No. 2 on the R&B charts, and sold a million copies. Just as important, it established a vital partnership between Fats and Imperial A&R man Dave Bartholomew. Bartholomew, himself a trumpeter, would produce Domino's big hits, co-writing many of them with Fats. He would also usually employ New Orleans session greats like Alvin Tyler on sax and Earl Palmer on drums—musicians who were vital in establishing New Orleans R&B as a distinct entity, playing on many other local recordings as well (including hits made in New Orleans by Georgia native Little Richard).

Domino didn't cross over into the pop charts in a big way until 1955, when "Ain't That a Shame" made the Top Ten. Pat Boone's cover of the song stole some of Fats' thunder, going all the way to No. 1 (Boone was also bowdlerizing Little Richard's early singles for pop hits during this time). Domino's long-range prospects weren't damaged, however; between 1955 and 1963, he racked up an astonishing 35 Top 40 singles. "Blueberry Hill" (1956) was probably his best (and best-remembered) single; "Walking to New Orleans," "Whole Lotta Loving," "I'm Walking," "Blue Monday," and "I'm in Love Again" were also huge successes.

After Fats left Imperial for ABC-Paramount in 1963, he would only enter the Top 40 one more time. The surprise was not that Fats fell out of fashion, but that he'd maintained his popularity so long while the essentials of his style remained unchanged. This was during an era, remember, when most of rock's biggest stars had their careers derailed by death or scandal, or were made to soften up their sound for mainstream consumption. Although an active performer in the ensuing decades, his career as an important artist was essentially over in the mid-'60s. He did stir up a bit of attention in 1968 when he covered the Beatles' "Lady Madonna" single, which had been an obvious homage to Fats' style. —*Richie Unterberger*

★ **My Blue Heaven: Best of Fats Domino** / Jul. 30, 1990 / EMI America ✦✦✦✦✦
For the budget-minded fan, this 20-track single disc compilation of Fats Domino's Imperial smashes will serve nicely. Not much of his early pre-rock stuff—"The Fat Man" and "Please Don't Leave Me" are all that's here—but there's plenty of his hit-laden output from 1955 on—"Ain't It a Shame," "Blue Monday," "I'm in Love Again," "Blueberry Hill," "I'm Ready," etc. One small but substantial difference between this set and the larger packages: it uses non-sped-up masters of his mid-'50s material (some of his hits from this era were mastered slightly faster than true

pitch). Even if they're not historically correct, these versions actually sound better! —*Bill Dahl*

☆ **They Call Me the Fat Man . . . : The Legendary Imperial Recordings** / 1991 / EMI America ✦✦✦✦✦
If you can't quite finance the Bear Family box, this four-disc compilation is the next best thing—an even 100 of the best Imperial sides, including a great many from 1958 on that turn up in crystal-clear stereo (as they also do on the Bear Family package). All the hits are aboard, along with a nice cross-section of the important non-hits. The saxes (usually including Herb Hardesty and sometimes Lee Allen) roar with typical Crescent City power, Fats rolls the ivories, and magic happens—over and over again! Another nice booklet with plenty of photos (but a less detailed discography without sideman credits). —*Bill Dahl*

☆ **Out of New Orleans** / 1993 / Bear Family ✦✦✦✦✦
An amazing piece of work—a massive eight-disc boxed set that contains every one of Fats Domino's 1949-1962 Imperial waxings. That's a tremendous load of one artist, but the legacy of Domino and his partner Dave Bartholomew was so consistently innovative and infectious that it never grows tiresome for a second. From the clarion call of "The Fat Man," Domino's 1949 debut, to the storming "Dance with Mr. Domino" in 1962, he typified everything charming about Crescent City R&B, his Creole patois and boogie-based piano a non-threatening vehicle for the rise of rock 'n' roll. A thick, photo-filled book accompanies the disc, and there's an exhaustive discography that makes sense of Fats Domino's many visits to Cosimo Matassa's studios. If you care about Fats Domino, this is the package to purchase! —*Bill Dahl*

Fat Man: 25 Classic Performances / Aug. 20, 1996 / Capitol ✦✦✦✦
Ostensibly replacing the compact disc *My Blue Heaven* as the definitive single-disc collection of Fats Domino's biggest hits singles, *Fat Man: 25 Classic Performances* features most of Fats Domino's biggest hits, but it inexplicably neglects such hits as "Walking to New Orleans," "Be My Guest" and "I'm Gonna Be a Wheel Someday." The only justification for the omission of so many hits is that the intent of the collection is to portray Fats Domino as the R&B heavyweight that he undoubtedly is, but seldom receives credit for being. Nevertheless, *Fat Man* masquerades as a greatest hits collection, billing itself as "25 Classic Performances," which leads you to believe that it is simply another hits collection. As an R&B compilation, *Fat Man* is strong—and, like any proper R&B collection, it presents the singles at the speed they were recorded at, not the sped-up versions that became hits—but because it lacks these hits, *My Blue Heaven* remains a preferable collection and introduction to Fats. —*Stephen Thomas Erlewine*

Don & Dewey

R&B
Wailing in tandem like twin Little Richards, Don & Dewey cut numerous blistering rockers for Specialty from 1957 to 1959 without registering a single hit, only to see other acts revive their songs to much greater acclaim. Don Harris (b. 1938) and Dewey Terry (b. 1938) were born and raised in Pasadena, CA, joining a group called the Squires and recording for Vita before branching off on their own. Their Specialty output included the savage rockers "Jungle Hop," "Koko Joe" (written by Sonny Bono), and "Justine," the latter pair later covered by the Righteous Brothers. Don & Dewey's Specialty discography also includes the original "I'm Leavin' It up to You," a hit for Dale & Grace; "Big Boy Pete," ditto for the Olympics; and "Farmer John," the Premiers' only smash. Don laid down his guitar for a violin during the '60s and, billed as "Sugarcane" Harris, sawed his rocked-out fiddle beside John Mayall and Frank Zappa. —*Bill Dahl*

● **Jungle Hop** / 1991 / Specialty ✦✦✦✦
Wild '50s rock 'n' roll duets from Don "Sugarcane" Harris and Dewey Terry, backed by the same Specialty house band that recorded with Little Richard and others. A lot of these songs were covered by other people, but *nobody* cut these guy's versions. —*George Bedard*

Lonnie Donegan (Anthony James Donegan)

b. Apr. 29, 1931, Glasgow, Scotland
Banjo, Guitar, Vocals / Skiffle, Pop-Rock
In Britain, Lonnie Donegan was the king of skiffle, a joyously amateurish interpretation of American folk, blues, and country songs that pre-dated rock 'n' roll. In 1954, Donegan's version of Leadbelly's "Rock Island Line" was an enormous hit in the UK (it also was successful in the US) and set off a skiffle craze—thousands of teenagers formed their own skiffle combos and tried to emulate his spare sound with washboards, broomsticks, and other household items.

Donegan remained a star until Britain raised its own rock superstars with the Beatles in 1962. Although he stopped having hits, he never stopped performing, and he continued to explore different traditional music, from Cajun and Appalachian styles to old time, vaudeville-style pub favorites right through the '80s. In the '90s, Donegan is not in perfect health, yet he continues to perform occasionally. —*Stephen Thomas Erlewine*

● **The EP Collection** / 1992 / See For Miles ✦✦✦✦
The EP Collection, Vol. 2 / 1994 / See For Miles ✦✦✦
Surprisingly strong (and nearly as important as Volume One) collection of the rest of Donegan's classic skiffle material, including the complete contents of his live EP *Donegan on Stage*. The novelty tunes share space with some surprisingly solid early rock 'n' roll, and all of it is fast-paced and entertaining. —*Bruce Eder*

Donovan (Donovan Leitch)

b. Feb. 10, 1946, Glasgow, Scotland
Guitar, Harmonica, Vocals / Singer-Songwriter, British Invasion, Psychedelic, Folk-Rock, British Folk
When Donovan first appeared on the British pop scene in the mid-'60s, he was touted as the British Invasion's answer to Bob Dylan. The unfortunate comparison led to a battle of the bands of sorts, immortalized in the Dylan documentary *Don't Look Back*, where Dylan shot down one of Donovan's pretty acoustic ditties with "It's All over Now, Baby Blue." All of which has cast a harsher light on Donovan's early work than it merits. Certainly he wasn't as deep as Dylan, but the acoustic tracks he recorded in the mid-'60s, including the British hits "Catch the Wind" and "Colours," were affecting, thoughtful, and tuneful, especially considering he was still in his teens at the time.

In late 1965, Donovan hooked up with manager Allen Klein and a new producer, Mickie Most (who also worked with the Animals, Herman's Hermits, and Lulu), who steered the young singer away from acoustic folk and into psychedelic pop. His more excessively cosmic lyrics haven't worn well, but in general the combination was quite successful, with seductive and ornate arrangements backing Donovan's gentle musings, which could be more humorous and biting than he's been given credit for. Between 1965 and 1969, he scored a series of memorable hits, including "Sunshine Superman," "Mellow Yellow" (containing a Paul McCartney cameo), "Hurdy Gurdy Man" (with Jeff Beck), and "Atlantis." His initial pair of psychedelic albums, *Sunshine Superman* and *Mellow Yellow*, were quite strong, but after a while his full-length efforts began to sound unduly repetitive and overly florid. By the early '70s, Donovan had begun to fade and struggle for relevancy, although he's been an active performer since, and has periodically mounted comebacks. —*Rick Clark & Richie Unterberger*

Catch the Wind / Jun. 1965 / Hickory ✦✦
Fairytale / Nov. 1965 / Hickory ✦✦
Sunshine Superman / Sep. 1966 / Epic ✦✦✦✦
Probably the singer-songwriter's best album, embracing folk, blues, and a druggy psychedelia, and driven by crisp rhythm guitars (especially on the title track). It starts to sound the same after a bit, but at its release, even this was a point of recommendation—it set a hazy, drugged-out mood. The use of the mono master helps, because it's punchier. —*Bruce Eder*
Mellow Yellow / Jan. 1967 / Epic ✦✦✦
Wear Your Love like Heaven / Dec. 1967 / Epic ✦✦✦
A Gift from a Flower to a Garden / Dec. 1967 / Epic ✦✦✦
A blast from hippie past—a flower-decorated double album made up of precious trippy music spiced with a haunting melody or two ("Wear Your Love like Heaven"). —*Bruce Eder*
Hurdy Gurdy Man / Oct. 1968 / Epic ✦✦✦
For this performer, this is a hard-rocking album, driven by some loud electric guitar subbing for sitar, which dresses up the plainer folk melodies and turns the title tune into a near-classic. —*Bruce Eder*
● **Donovan's Greatest Hits** / Jan. 1969 / Epic ✦✦✦✦
Entertaining but flawed collection of Donovan's psychedelic-era hits, fleshed out with too-languid re-recordings of his pre-CBS folk successes, including "Colours." It's unfortunate that the producers used the stereo versions, which don't sound nearly as good as the mono. —*Bruce Eder*
Barabajagal / Aug. 11, 1969 / Epic ✦✦✦✦
Donovan was moving beyond his hippie-dippie phase by this point, collaborating with the Jeff Beck Group on the title track, protesting the Vietnam War with "Susan on the West Coast Waiting," adapting the epic style of Beatles songs like "Hey Jude" on the hit "Atlantis" (which features Paul McCartney) and turning in two of his most charming, childlike songs in "Happiness Runs" and "I Love My Shirt." Overall, this may be Donovan's strongest collection of original songs, other than his compilations. —*William Ruhlmann*
Open Road / 1970 / Epic ✦✦✦
Spotlight / 1981 / PRT ✦✦✦✦
Donovan's acoustic, pre-psychedelic work was shoddily packaged in the US, spread out over several albums in a haphazard fashion. This 24-track double LP reissue covers most of his work from this period (basically,

1965), including the hits "Catch the Wind" and "Colours," as well his cover of Buffy St. Marie's "Universal Soldier" and the memorable originals "Josie" and "Hey Gyp." This early phase is often unfairly dismissed as sub-Dylan musings by critics; Donovan was indeed the closest counterpart to Bob in the mid-'60s, but was distinctly more pop-oriented, and had a gentle, wistful songwriting voice all his own, even if it wasn't as complex as Dylan's. While this material lacks the punch of his best psychedelic work, it is of a consistently high standard, and lacks the occasional overly cosmic vision that has dated some of his later '60s recordings. While this reissue captures all the essential highlights of Donovan's pre-electric career, it's missing a few cuts and is packaged rather tackily; a comprehensive double CD compilation of the 30 or so tracks he recorded for the British Pye label during this time would be welcome. —*Richie Unterberger*
● **Troubadour: The Definitive Collection 1964-1976** / Aug. 4, 1992 / Epic ✦✦✦✦
This two-disc, 44-track retrospective album (initially released as a boxed set) chronicles Donovan's decade-long career at Epic Records, with the few folk hits he recorded before joining the label and a couple of early demos added. All the hippie hits of the '60s are included, plus a judicious selection of the less successful '70s recordings. Good liner notes by Brian Hogg and Derek Taylor. —*William Ruhlmann*

The Doobie Brothers

Pop-Rock
The Doobie Brothers ("doobie" being slang for a marijuana joint) straddled FM rock and Top 40 pop better than most bands of the '70s, with their good-time grooves and melodies and solid musicianship. During the first part of their career (1970 to 1975), the Doobie Brothers scored with a batch of radio classics: "Listen to the Music" (No. 11), "Long Train Running" (No. 8), "China Grove" (No. 15), and the No. 1 hit "Black Water." With the arrival of soulful Steely Dan singer and keyboardist Michael McDonald, the Doobie Brothers took on a mellower, more sophisticated musical direction, giving passing nods to jazz and light funk along the way. "Takin' It to the Streets" (No. 13) showcased McDonald's contribution to fine effect. The 1977 album *Living on the Fault Line* is an artistic pinnacle of the band's new direction, but the No. 1 follow-up, *Minute by Minute*, was a much bigger success, containing the hits "What a Fool Believes" and the title cut.

By the time *One Step Closer* was released in 1980, the Doobies' brand of slick California pop reached the saturation point in fern bars across the land. The fact that Michael McDonald's aching vocals seemed to appear on every record from the West Coast ensured overkill. The band called it quits in 1981. The pre-McDonald lineup re-formed in 1987 and enjoyed a successful comeback. —*Rick Clark*

● **Best of the Doobies** / 1976 / Warner Bros. ✦✦✦✦
This formidable bunch of hard-rock hits appeared from 1972-1976. —*Dan Heilman*
The Best of the Doobies, Vol. 2 / 1981 / Warner Bros. ✦✦✦✦
This is the best of the Michael McDonald era. —*Dan Heilman*
Cycles / 1989 / Capitol ✦

The Doors

Rock 'n' Roll, Psychedelic
The Doors, one of the most influential and controversial rock bands of the 1960s, were formed in Los Angeles in 1965 by UCLA film students Ray Manzarek, keyboards, and Jim Morrison, vocals, with drummer John Densmore, and guitarist Robby Krieger. The group never added a bass player, and their sound was dominated by Manzarek's electric organ work and Morrison's deep, sonorous voice, with which he sang and intoned his highly poetic lyrics. The group signed to Elektra Records in 1966 and released its first album, *The Doors*, featuring the hit "Light My Fire," in 1967.

Like "Light My Fire," the debut album was a massive hit, and endures as one of the most exciting, groundbreaking recordings of the psychedelic era. Blending blues, classical, Eastern music, and pop into sinister but beguiling melodies, the band sounded like no other. With his rich, chilling vocals and somber poetic visions, Morrison explored the depths of the darkest and most thrilling aspects of the psychedelic experience. Their first effort was so stellar, in fact, that the Doors were hard-pressed to match it, and although their next few albums contained a wealth of first-rate material, the group also began running up against the limitations of their recklessly disturbing visions. By their third album, they had exhausted their initial reservoir of compositions, and some of the tracks they hurriedly devised to meet public demand were clearly inferior to, and imitative of, their best early work.

On *The Soft Parade*, the group experimented with brass sections, with mixed results. Accused (without much merit) by much of the rock underground as pop sellouts, the group charged back hard with the final two albums they recorded with Morrison, on which they drew upon stone-cold blues for much of their inspiration, especially on 1971's *L.A. Woman.*

From the start, the Doors' focus was the charismatic Morrison, who proved increasingly unstable over the group's brief career. In 1969, Morrison was arrested for indecent exposure during a concert in Miami, an incident that nearly derailed the band. Nevertheless, the Doors managed to turn out a series of successful albums and singles through 1971, when, upon the completion of *L.A. Woman,* Morrison decamped for Paris. He died there, apparently of a drug overdose. The three surviving Doors tried to carry on without him, but ultimately disbanded. Yet the Doors' music and Morrison's legend continued to fascinate succeeding generations of rock fans: In the mid-'80s, Morrison was as big a star as he'd been in the mid-'60s, and Elektra has sold numerous quantities of the Doors' original albums plus reissues and releases of live material over the years, while publishers have flooded bookstores with Doors and Morrison biographies. In 1991, director Oliver Stone made *The Doors,* a feature film about the group starring Val Kilmer as Morrison. —*William Ruhlmann & Richie Unterberger*

☆ **The Doors** / Jan. 1967 / Elektra ✦✦✦✦✦
One of the most remarkable debut albums in rock history introduced the powerful singing of Jim Morrison, his provocative lyrics, and the group's spare, direct guitar/organ sound. "Light My Fire" became an instant standard but the album also contained such Doors classics as "Break on Through (to the Other Side)," "Twentieth Century Fox," and, of course, that Oedipal odyssey "The End." —*William Ruhlmann*

Strange Days / Oct. 1967 / Elektra ✦✦✦
The band's second effort isn't as consistently stunning as their debut, but is overall a very successful continuation of the themes of their classic first album. Besides the hit "People Are Strange," it includes "You're Lost Little Girl," "Love Me Two Times," and "Moonlight Drive," which remain among the group's finest songs. —*Richie Unterberger*

Waiting for the Sun / Jul. 1968 / Elektra ✦✦✦
Singles like "Hello, I Love You" and "The Unknown Soldier" are on *The Best of the Doors,* but many of the standouts on this album are gentle songs like "Summer's Almost Gone," "Yes, the River Knows," and "Wintertime Love," which demonstrate that Morrison & Co. can be lyrical without losing their power. —*William Ruhlmann*

The Soft Parade / Jul. 1969 / Elektra ✦✦✦
Probably the most underrated Doors collection because the addition of horns and strings ("Wishful Sinful") turns it into a more exploratory album than their more basic music usually attempted. But "Tell All the People" is the group at its most revolutionary, and the long title track is among its most ambitious. This included the hit "Touch Me" as well as "Wild Child," one of their best rockers. —*William Ruhlmann*

Morrison Hotel/Hard Rock Cafe / 1970 / Elektra ✦✦✦✦
A bluesy, hard-rock album that nevertheless contains some of Morrison's most visionary poetry. —*William Ruhlmann*

13 / Feb. 1970 / Elektra ✦✦✦✦
A one-disc hits compilation issued before the Doors' final album and thus lacking "Riders on the Storm," but nevertheless a good sampler of the singles that maintained the Doors' enormous popularity in the late '60s and remain rock standards today. —*William Ruhlmann*

Absolutely Live / Sep. 1970 / Elektra ✦✦
L.A. Woman / Apr. 1971 / Elektra ✦✦✦✦
Morrison's final testament shows him at the height of his ability to bring striking images to the lyrics of rock music, and the group produces some of its most trancelike music. —*William Ruhlmann*

Alive, She Cried / Oct. 1983 / Elektra ✦✦
★ **The Best of the Doors** / 1985 / Elektra ✦✦✦✦✦
A well-chosen, 18-track compilation balancing the radio hits with the longer, more complex song poems. It's a good sampler, but this is one group for whom you need to hear the whole story. Reissued on CD in 1991 with one bonus track. —*William Ruhlmann*

Lee Dorsey

b. Dec. 24, 1924, New Orleans, LA, d. Dec. 1, 1986, New Orleans, LA
Vocals / Soul, R&B, New Orleans R&B
The effervescent approach of Lee Dorsey perfectly summarizes the infectious charm of early-'60s New Orleans R&B. Dorsey specialized in good-humored music with a touch of second-line funk thrown in to make it all the more irresistible. Although he had already waxed a couple of singles, Dorsey caught the country by total surprise in 1961 with his deceptively simple nursery-rhyme-style "Ya Ya" on Bobby Robinson's Fury label. Arranged by prolific New Orleans pianist Allen Toussaint, the track proved an R&B chart-topper and a major pop hit to boot.

Dorsey's laconic vocal charms served him well on "Ya Ya" and the Earl King-penned follow-up "Do Re Mi," and the mid-'60s found him working with Toussaint on the funky smashes "Ride Your Pony" and "Working in the Coal Mine," this time for Amy Records. It's little remembered that

Dorsey was responsible for the original 1970 version of Toussaint's "Yes We Can," revived to much greater acclaim by the Pointer Sisters (who tacked on an extra "Can"). From all accounts, Dorsey remained an exceedingly humble R&B star who preferred tinkering with cars to extensively touring the country. He died of emphysema in 1986. —*Bill Dahl*

Ya Ya / 1962 / Relic ✦✦✦✦
This terrific overview of the good-humored New Orleans singer's early-'60s classics (for Bobby Robinson's Fury label) features direct-from-masters sound quality. —*Bill Dahl*

● **Holy Cow!: Best of Lee Dorsey** / 1985 / Arista ✦✦✦✦
A nice single-disc anthology featuring the best-known cuts and biggest pop hits of New Orleans R&B and soul singer Lee Dorsey, one of the Crescent City's best comic/novelty artists and a fine traditional R&B vocalist as well. The title track, "Working in a Coal Mine," and "Ride Your Pony" are superb songs that use the second line rhythm and boast outstanding arrangements, clever lyrics, and great vocals. —*Ron Wynn*

Downliners Sect

British Invasion
Of all the British R&B bands to follow the Rolling Stones' footsteps, the Downliners Sect were arguably the rawest. The Sect didn't as much interpret the sound of Chess Records as attack it, with a finesse that made the Pretty Things seem positively suave in comparison. Long on crude energy and hoarse vocals, but short on originality and songwriting talent, the band never had a British hit, although they had some sizable singles in other European countries. Despite their lack of commercial success or appeal, the band managed to record three albums and various EPs and singles between 1963 and 1966, with detours into country-rock and an EP of death-rock tunes. Although they recorded afterwards, it is the Sect's early work that continues to attract connoisseurs of '60s garage and punk. —*Richie Unterberger*

● **The Sect** / 1964 / Columbia ✦✦✦✦
Their rawest and most R&B-oriented, firmly rooted in the same influences as the Stones and Pretty Things. Includes punk covers of Chuck Berry, Bo Diddley, Muddy Waters, Jimmy Reed, et al., and a few originals in the same vein. —*Richie Unterberger*

Nite at Gt. Newport Street / 1964 / RBC ✦✦
The Country Sect / 1965 / Columbia ✦✦
Sect Sing Sick Songs / 1965 / Columbia ✦✦
The Rock Sects In / 1966 / Columbia ✦✦✦
I Want My Baby Back / 1978 / Charly ✦✦✦
Definitive Downliners Sect: Singles A's & B's / 1994 / See For Miles ✦✦

Dramatics

Soul
Popular Detroit R&B vocal aggregation that scored numerous hits for Volt and maintained their momentum through the disco era. The early Dramatics hits for Volt lived up to their billing with the emphatic vocals of Ron Banks (b. May 10, 1951) powering the funky "Whatcha See Is Whatcha Get," their first big-seller in 1971, and the R&B chart-topping ballad "In the Rain" the next year. The quintet was just as successful later in the decade, signing with ABC in 1975 and scoring repeatedly throughout disco-fever days. —*Bill Dahl*

● **The Best of the Dramatics** / 1976 / Stax ✦✦✦✦
A solid compilation, it includes the hits "Whatcha See Is Whatcha Get" (No. 9), "In the Rain" (No. 5), "Fell for You" (No. 45), and other equally good but lesser-known tracks. —*AMG*

ABC Years 1974-1980 / Nov. 21, 1995 / Soul Classics ✦✦✦
The Dramatics were one of the best soul groups of the early '70s, scoring a series of hits for Volt Records. After leaving Volt, they went to ABC Records in 1974 and stayed there until the end of the decade. The hits began to become a little bit smaller, and that's partially because they were either covering other people's hits ("Me and Mrs. Jones") or lacked solid material. *ABC Years 1974-1980* collects their biggest hits from this period. While the music on the collection isn't as consistently thrilling as their early-'70s hits, there are a couple of gems buried in these 11 tracks that makes the album worthwhile for dedicated fans. —*Stephen Thomas Erlewine*

Best of Volt / Stax ✦✦✦✦
The Dramatics were one of Stax's finest soul vocal groups, using Ron Banks' rising soprano, L.J. Reynolds' booming baritone, and Willie Ford's emphatic bass to create enticing love songs with excellent harmonizing at the top, in the middle, and at the bottom of the scale. Their albums tended to be erratic affairs, with outstanding love songs and sometimes dismal, formulaic dance tunes. This is one of many collections that spotlight their hits on the Stax/Volt label. —*Ron Wynn*

Dream Syndicate

Alternative Pop-Rock, Paisley Underground, Jangle-Pop
Of all of the so-called "paisley underground" Los Angeles bands of the '80s, the Steve Wynn-led Dream Syndicate was the one that gained the largest audience and was arguably the best of the lot. Instead of lifting their riffs from old Pink Floyd, Jefferson Airplane, or Byrds albums, Wynn relied on the darker sounds of the Velvet Underground and Neil Young, creating a dense, guitar-based pseudo-psychedelia that either soared on ballads or drilled on mid-tempo rockers; it was tailor-made for college radio success, where they received a fair amount of airplay. Dream Syndicate recorded several impressive records over their career, yet they never became big rock stars; the band called it quits in 1989, with Wynn pursuing a solo career. —*Stephen Thomas Erlewine*

The Days of Wine & Roses / 1982 / Slash ✦✦✦
Karl Precoda plays the kind of noisy guitar associated with the Velvet Underground, while lead singer Steve Wynn pursues his private demons on this perfectly realized low-budget '80s rock record. —*William Ruhlmann*

Ghost Stories / 1988 / Restless ✦✦✦
Paul B. Cutler plays the kind of noisy guitar associated with Neil Young and Crazy Horse, while lead singer Steve Wynn continues to pursue his private demons on what is nevertheless more of a mainstream rock record, maybe courtesy of Young's producer, Elliot Mazer. —*William Ruhlmann*

● **Tell Me When It's Over: The Best of Dream Syndicate** / 1992 / Rhino ✦✦✦✦
These 15 tracks contain the cream of the crop of this Los Angeles band's independent and major label work. Among the highlights are "When You Smile," "Tell Me When It's Over," and "Halloween" from their 1982 Ruby/Slash EP *Days of Wine and Roses*. The collection captures their dense Velvet Underground-style rock in all its trashy glory. The booklet is loaded with a detailed history, many photos, lyrics, and track and personnel listings. —*Rick Clark*

The Drifters

R&B, Doo Wop
Originally a backup group formed around the soaring vocal talents of Clyde McPhatter, the Drifters—like their '50s counterparts, the Platters and the Coasters—have turned out to be one of the most enduring "franchises" in rock 'n' roll. Though it's been years since any of the original members have been involved (almost all of them being long deceased), chances are if there's an oldies but goodies stage show happening somewhere tonight, there's a 50-50 shot that some form of the Drifters will be up on that stage, singing the hits that made the original group a legend. Unlike other groups who lost key members along the way and never regained their artistic or commercial footing, the various incarnations of the Drifters produced distinctly memorable material every step of the way. Depending on what time frame you come in on during their 40-plus years as a group, you'll discover that they turned from a hard rhythm and gospel doo wop aggregation to one of the smoothest and most romantic ever to grace an AM radio. One of the first Black R&B groups to utilize a string section on their records ("There Goes My Baby," 1959), their middle period sound defined universal love and the good life as seen through the eyes of the ghetto, an arresting combination that won them crossover appeal. That they not only moved, but prospered, with the times is testimony enough to their rightly deserved longevity.

In 1953, Clyde McPhatter already held a reputation in the R&B community as one of its finest tenor lead voices. He had been plucked from a gospel group to become a member of Billy Ward and the Dominoes, a doo wop aggregation that combined classic "blow harmony" sounds with Clyde's agonized, fervent vocals. Originally McPhatter was so concerned about the backlash from the gospel community over the way he sang secular material that he claimed to be related to the group's leader, appearing in magazine articles and such as "Clyde Ward." But with the back to back success of "Have Mercy Baby," "The Bells," and others, McPhatter soon grew restless to be out on his own. The promise of an Atlantic recording contract prompted him to leave the group and come to New York to form the original version of the Drifters with Bill Pinkey (aka Pinkney) and Andrew and Gerhard Thrasher from the gospel quartet the Wonderland Thrashers.

The sound of the new group combined with Atlantic's production expertise was an ideal marriage, both aesthetically and commercially, and almost immediately the hits started coming, one after another; "Money Honey," "Let the Boogie Woogie Roll," "Such a Night," "Honey Love," and a bizarre arrangement of Irving Berlin's "White Christmas" all made the Top Ten on the R&B charts. But this run would soon be interrupted as Clyde was drafted into military service, a move that had far-reaching effects on the rest of his career.

They quickly regrouped with Johnny Moore replacing McPhatter and scored three more hits, "Ruby Baby," "Adorable," and "Your Promise to Be Mine." In 1958, manager George Treadwell disbanded the group but, realizing that they still had a few years to go on their Atlantic contract and a yearly commitment to perform at the Apollo Theater, tapped an unknown group called the Five Crowns—with lead singer Ben E. King—to become the new Drifters. This incarnation of the group is the one most fans readily remember as King's lead vocals, combined with Lieber and Stoller's excellent songwriting, produced groundbreaking hits such as "Save the Last Dance for Me," "There Goes My Baby," "Dance with Me," "Lonely Winds," and "This Magic Moment." King went solo in 1960 and Rudy Lewis stepped in as the new lead singer, producing seven Top 40 hits including the classics "On Broadway" (featuring a young Phil Spector on lead guitar) and "Up on the Roof." After Lewis' drug-related death in 1964, Johnny Moore once again stepped in as lead singer, producing their final hits, "Under the Boardwalk" and "Saturday Night at the Movies." When the group's Atlantic contract finally ran out in 1972 (!), Moore took the group to England and signed with Bell Records, producing three more UK Top Ten hits before leaving the group in 1980. Since that time, various versions of the group—some legal, most not—have dotted the landscape of the oldies circuit and any lineup could feature any combination of the 50-odd members who passed through their ranks over the years. —*Cub Koda*

☆ **Let the Boogie Woogie Roll: Greatest Hits** / 1988 / Rhino ✦✦✦✦✦
Let the Boogie Woogie Roll: Greatest Hits is the definitive account of the early group (1953-1958) and Clyde McPhatter's greatest sides. —*Bruce Eder*

☆ **All-Time Greatest Hits & More: 1959-1965** / 1988 / Rhino ✦✦✦✦✦
This is a towering and magnificent collection of some of the best popular R&B ever done this side of Sam Cooke. —*Bruce Eder*

★ **The Very Best of the Drifters** / 1993 / Rhino ✦✦✦✦✦
Combining all the greatest hits from both the Clyde McPhatter and Ben E. King eras, the single-disc *The Very Best of the Drifters* serves as the perfect introduction to the seminal R&B vocal group. —*Stephen Thomas Erlewine*

☆ **Rockin' & Driftin': The Drifters Box** / 1996 / Rhino ✦✦✦✦✦
A three-CD, 79-song box spanning all incarnations of the group, from 1953 to 1976 (although only six of the tracks date from after 1966). Sure, there's a lot of classic music here: All of the big hits, and many interesting flops and B-sides. Assuming, however, that the audience for this set is mostly limited to serious Drifters fans, it's likely that many or most of the listeners falling into that category already have the *Let the Boogie Woogie Roll* and *All-Time Greatest Hits & More* compilations, which covers just about all of the essential cuts from the box. If you already own those CDs, you may well want to pass this up, but if you have yet to build a serious Drifters collection, this will supply virtually everything you need. And, frankly, then some; some of this is pretty extraneous, particularly the '70s cuts. A bonus is their previously unreleased 1963 version of "Only in America," a song which was ultimately given to Jay & the Americans (who had a hit with it) because it was deemed too controversial for a Black group to release. —*Richie Unterberger*

Ducks Deluxe

Rock 'n' Roll, Pub-Rock
If the old scientific adage is true—that for every action there is an equal and opposite reaction—than British pub-rockers Ducks Deluxe were purely and simply a reaction. With the mid-'70s English pop scene dominated by glitter glam rockers like Gary Glitter, the Sweet, or blustery, chops-heavy art-rockers like Yes, Tull, Genesis, etc., then Ducks Deluxe represented none of the above. One of the first pub-rock bands, the Ducks played basic American-style blues and boogie with remarkable panache and thorough disregard for the whims of the zeitgeist. They never were hugely popular, but the unpretentious, do-it-yourself, working-class attitude they and their contemporaries (most notably seminal pub-rockers Dr. Feelgood) exuded influenced the English punk scene that was right around the corner. With friends like Dave Edmunds producing their records, the Ducks (guitarist/vocalist Sean Tyla, guitarist Martin Belmont, bassist Nick Garvey, and keyboardist Andy McMasters) came up with engaging, though not life-changing, records that celebrated the simple joys of rock 'n' roll. Sure, much of it sounds like recycled Chuck Berry, but there's an infectious enthusiasm that the fan in you, who simply wants to hoist a pint of lager and hear some Little Richard, will love. Ironically, to get the biggest promotional boost in America, the Ducks Deluxe LP was released three years after they'd split up. This little bit of shift marketing came as a result of ex-Ducks going on to more prominent bands like the Motors, the Rumour and the Tyla Gang. —*John Dougan*

● **Ducks Deluxe/Taxi to the Terminal Zone** / 1974 / Edsel ✦✦✦✦
Both of the group's albums, *Ducks Deluxe* and *Taxi to the Terminal Zone*, compiled on one CD with one song from each removed to fit the format's time restriction—really a best-of, and worth any three Led Zeppelin albums. —*Bruce Eder*

Don't Mind Rockin' Tonite / 1978 / RCA ✦✦✦

The Dukes of Stratosphear

Alternative Pop-Rock, Psychedelic
In 1985, the British pop band XTC recorded an EP of affectionate parodies of '60s psychedelia and guitar pop called *25 O'Clock*. Instead of
releasing the EP under their own name, they released the record under
the name the Dukes of Stratosphear and claimed that they had nothing
to do with the project. Two years after the appearance of *25 O'Clock*, the
Dukes of Stratosphear released a full album, *Psonic Psunspot*. By the
time *Psonic Psunspot* appeared in 1987, XTC were beginning to admit in
interviews that they were indeed the Dukes of Stratosphear. Later in
1987, both the EP and album were released on a single compact disc,
Chips from the Chocolate Fireball. —*Stephen Thomas Erlewine*

● **Chips from the Chocolate Fireball** / 1987 / Geffen ✦✦✦✦
Fans of late-'60s psychedelia will love this affectionate Rutles-esque col-
laboration between XTC (posing as the Dukes) and producer John Leckie
(Posies, Let's Active, House of Freaks). *Chips from the Chocolate Fireball*
is loaded with playful tips of the hat to artists like The Move, the Electric
Prunes, early Pink Floyd, the Yardbirds, Spirit, the Zombies, the Beach
Boys, and (of course) the Beatles. By the way, this is a compilation of the
Dukes' *25 O'Clock* EP and the full-length album *Psonic Psunspot*. —*Rick
Clark*

Duran Duran

Dance-Pop, New Wave, Pop-Rock, Club-Dance, New Romantic
The major teen-pop band of the '80s (Nick Rhodes, keyboards; John Taylor, bass; Simon Le Bon, vocals; Andy Taylor, guitar; Roger Taylor, drums)
formed in 1978 in Birmingham, England, although the final lineup was
not set until the addition of Simon Le Bon in 1980. Taking their name
from a character in the Jane Fonda film *Barbarella*, their style of dance
music was quickly drawn into the new romantic movement of the British punk/new wave scene. These so-called haircut bands were inspired to
their fashion-centered look and hip synthesizer, neo-disco style by bands
like Roxy Music. Duran Duran's lush arrangements and distinct vocal
sound, combined with an aggressive new wave, funk-rhythm section,
caught the attention of the mass market. But it was their visual appeal
and exotic/erotic videos for "Girls on Film," "Hungry like the Wolf," and
"Rio" on the newborn MTV that catapulted them into concert arenas and
multi-platinum stardom. Although unabashed teen idols, the members
tried to gain more critical respect with sideline efforts like Power Station
(for John & Andy Taylor) and Arcadia (for Le Bon, Roger Taylor, and
Rhodes). After these experiments, the band went through a series of
lineup changes and artistic wanderings as their teenage fans began to
outgrow them. But none of their later works were as successful as *Rio* or
Seven and the Ragged Tiger. With the end virtually in sight, Duran
Duran released the hits/retrospective package *Decade* and one final studio album before the band temporarily disbanded.
   In 1993, the band returned with a self-titled album that became a sur-
prise success, thanks to two hit singles—"Ordinary World" and "Come
Undone." Two years later, the band received some of the harshest reviews
of their career for their covers album, *Thank You*. Even with the bad
press, Duran Duran's version of Grand Masterflash's "White Lines (Don't
Don't Do It)" received a significant amount of play in dance clubs.
—*Scott Bultman*

Duran Duran [First] / 1981 / Capitol ✦✦✦✦
Duran Duran's self-titled debut effectively established their slick, catchy
synth-pop sound. Featuring the decadent "Girls on Film" and "Planet
Earth," the album set the pace for scores of new wave bands in the early
'80s, which were subsequently dubbed the new romantics. —*Stephen
Thomas Erlewine*

Rio / 1982 / Capitol ✦✦✦✦
Rio was Duran Duran's breakthrough album, selling over two million
copies in the US. The album's success was helped immeasurably by slick,
big-budget videos that featured the band cavorting in various exotic
locations. However, the music on the album was as noteworthy as the
accompanying videos. *Rio* featured more ambitious arrangements, with
the group pursuing a more dance-oriented direction without losing its
sense of pop songcraft. With the hit singles "Hungry like the Wolf," "Rio"
and "Save a Prayer" forming the core of the record, *Rio* stands as their
best, most accomplished record. —*Stephen Thomas Erlewine*

Seven and the Ragged Tiger / 1983 / Capitol ✦✦✦
Seven and the Ragged Tiger was released at the height of Duran Duran-
mania and it shows. Throughout the album, the group replicates the
sound of *Rio*, yet they have failed to write strong material. Although they
are catchy, the singles "Union of the Snake" and "The Reflex" aren't on
par with "Hungry like the Wolf" and "Rio." Only the brooding "New
Moon on Monday" matches the inspired pop-craft of *Rio*. —*Stephen Thomas Erlewine*

Arena / 1984 / Capitol ✦✦

Notorious / 1986 / Capitol ✦✦✦
Big Thing / 1988 / Capitol ✦✦
● **Decade: Greatest Hits** / Nov. 15, 1989 / Capitol ✦✦✦✦
All their hits—"Hungry like the Wolf," "Rio," "Is There Something I
Should Know?," "Union of the Snake," "The Wild Boys," "Notorious," "I
Don't Want Your Love," and the No. 1 hits "The Reflex" and "A View to a
Kill"—are included in a well-selected package. —*Dan Heilman*

Liberty / Aug. 13, 1990 / Capitol ✦
Duran Duran [1993] / 1993 / Capitol ✦✦✦✦
Duran Duran came back out of nowhere in early 1993 with a new album
and a huge hit, "Ordinary World." The group sounds more relaxed and
mature than it did during their glory days, but not much has changed;
instead of personifying the days of early-'80s synthesized dance-pop, the
music is smooth dance-pop for the '90s. Taken on its own terms, *Duran
Duran* works every bit as well as *Duran Duran, Rio*, or *Seven and the
Ragged Tiger*. "Ordinary World" and "Come Undone" are wonderful pop
singles that sit between some passable album tracks and the occasional
embarrassment, namely the wretched cover of the Velvet Underground's
"Femme Fatale." In other words, Duran Duran are back and as good as
they ever were. —*Stephen Thomas Erlewine*

Thank You / Apr. 1995 / Palophone/EMI ✦

Ian Dury

b. May 12, 1942, Upminster, Essex, England
Vocals / Disco, Rock 'n' Roll, New Wave, Pub-Rock
When Ian Dury released his first record in 1977, he was 35 years old, yet
he fit in perfectly with the UK punk scene. Dury had energy to spare with
his raucous rock 'n' roll and surprisingly incisive lyrics, possibly fueled
by anger over the lasting effects of childhood polio. Yet Dury's music
wasn't full of bile—it was joyful noise-making. Dury never became a star
in the US—perhaps his thick Cockney accent was impenetrable—yet he
became a beloved figure in the UK, releasing records until 1984 and performing throughout the '80s and '90s. —*Stephen Thomas Erlewine*

New Boots & Panties!! / 1977 / Edsel ✦✦✦✦
Ian Dury's debut album positively seethes with energy, as he tears
through a set of raw and funny punk rockers like the frenetic "Blockheads." However, the emotional core of the record lies in the slightly
slower, but no less inspired, number like "Sweet Gene Vincent," "My Old
Man," and "Wake up and Make Love with Me," which provide the context
for his raging anthems. —*Stephen Thomas Erlewine*

Do It Yourself / 1979 / Edsel ✦✦✦
Laughter / 1980 / Stiff ✦✦✦
Lord Upminster / Nov. 1981 / Polydor ✦✦
● **Sex & Drugs & Rock 'n' Roll: Best of Ian Dury and the Blockheads** /
1992 / Rhino ✦✦✦✦
Everything you'd ever want in one package. This does an excellent job of
combining Dury's rock with his slippery funk/disco and does so in such a
way that it sounds perfectly natural. Every home should have a copy of
the song "Sex & Drugs & Rock & Roll," but a big plus is having the salacious and horny "Wake Up and Make Love with Me." Durable, funny, and
energetic to the core, this is indispensable. —*John Dougan*

Bob Dylan

b. May 24, 1941, Duluth, MN
*Guitar, Harmonica, Piano, Keyboards, Vocals / Rock 'n' Roll, Country-
RockCountry-Rock, Singer-Songwriter, Folk-Rock*
The greatest songwriter of his generation and a figure of incalculable
influence on popular music from the '60s on, Bob Dylan is also, with the
possible exception of Elvis Presley, the most important individual in rock
music ever.
   Dylan came from Minnesota to New York City in 1961, at the age of
19, as an acolyte of folksinger Woody Guthrie, although he had played
rock music in the late '50s. He met Guthrie (who was slowly dying in a
hospital) and was quickly taken up by the New York folk community. He
signed to Columbia Records and, in March 1962, released his first album,
Bob Dylan, consisting largely of folk-blues covers. By this time, however,
he had begun to write original songs, many in the philosophical/political
style of his Greenwich Village compatriots (though far superior in quality), the best early example being "Blowin' in the Wind." Many of these
songs were on Dylan's second album, *The Freewheelin' Bob Dylan*,
released in May 1963. That summer, the popular folk group Peter, Paul &
Mary took "Blowin' in the Wind" to the Top Ten in the national charts.
Thereafter, Bob Dylan songs became favorites among many pop and
folk performers. As the result of such exposure, *Freewheelin'* became a
chart hit in September 1963.
   Dylan followed with two albums in 1964, the heavily protest-oriented
The Times They Are a-Changin' and the more introspective *Another Side
of Bob Dylan*. In 1965, he began recording and playing concerts with
rock musicians, which vastly increased his following but also led to con-

troversy within the folk community. His singles "Like a Rolling Stone" and "Positively 4th Street" were Top Ten hits, as were the albums *Bringing It All Back Home* and *Highway 61 Revisited*, and the "folk-rock" sound of his music could be heard on any number of other artists' records, many of them written by Dylan himself. Dylan undertook a world tour in 1966 to promote the double album *Blonde on Blonde*, which featured the Top Ten single "Rainy Day Women No.12 & 35." That summer he was in a motorcycle accident and withdrew from public view for a year and a half, meanwhile recording the informal material later released as *The Basement Tapes*.

When Dylan returned to action in late 1967, it was with the quieter *John Wesley Harding* album, followed in 1969 by the country-flavored *Nashville Skyline* and its Top Ten single "Lay Lady Lay." Critics expecting Dylan's more complex work were disappointed and they savaged his two-disc *Self-Portrait* in 1970, though most saw *New Morning*, released only a few months later, as a return to form.

Dylan was not much heard from in the early '70s (he played at George Harrison's Bangladesh benefit concert in 1971, and in 1973 he appeared in the film *Pat Garrett and Billy the Kid* and wrote its score), but he returned in 1974 with a national concert tour and the No. 1 album *Planet Waves*. This was followed in 1975 by *Blood on the Tracks*, regarded by many as his best collection of the decade. The same year, Dylan organized a roving band of musicians as the Rolling Thunder Revue and toured the Northeast, later appearing in other parts of the country in 1976.

A film crew was part of the entourage, and Dylan put together a sprawling film, *Renaldo & Clara*, released in 1978. With that done, he went on an international tour and released a new album, *Street Legal*. In 1979, Dylan converted to Christianity and released the first of three overtly religious albums, *Slow Train Coming*.

The religious fervor became less apparent by the time of *Infidels* in 1983, and Dylan has released several excellent albums since, while touring more or less continually. The '80s and early '90s have also seen the welcome legitimate release of much previously unissued vintage Dylan material (some of it widely available on bootlegs). — *William Ruhlmann*

Bob Dylan / Mar. 19, 1962 / Columbia ♦♦♦
For the most part, Bob Dylan's debut album positions him as an interpretive singer of rural folk songs, and already influential at that. The Animals found "House of the Rising Sun" on this album, while Led Zeppelin borrowed "In My Time of Dyin'." But the most striking track is the Dylan original "Song to Woody," his tribute to Woody Guthrie, which leaves no doubt he intends to carry on in his mentor's footsteps. — *William Ruhlmann*

☆ **The Freewheelin' Bob Dylan** / May 27, 1963 / Columbia ♦♦♦♦♦
The most important collection of original songs issued in the '60s. "Don't Think Twice, It's All Right," "Girl from the North Country," "A Hard Rain's a-Gonna Fall," "Masters of War," and, especially, "Blowin' in the Wind" have long since become standards, and their sheer range, from bitter protest to wry romantic regret, is astonishing, not to mention the absurd apocalyptic humor of some of the album's other tracks. The songs were so strong that they put across Dylan's limited, rough vocal style at a time when such a voice normally would have seemed completely unacceptable in a professional singer. This album transformed the notion of what "good" singing was. — *William Ruhlmann*

The Times They Are a-Changin' / Jan. 13, 1964 / Columbia ♦♦♦♦
Dylan devoted most of his third album to hard, uncompromising topical or "protest" songs, starting with the anthemic title track and continuing through "The Lonesome Death of Hattie Carroll," "Ballad of Hollis Brown," "Only a Pawn in Their Game," and "With God on Our Side." — *William Ruhlmann*

☆ **Another Side of Bob Dylan** / Aug. 8, 1964 / Columbia ♦♦♦♦♦
The first of two transitional albums in which Dylan moved beyond protest, and then beyond folk music. Here, in songs like "Chimes of Freedom" and "My Back Pages," he suggested that social issues were much more complicated than the increasingly polarized times made them seem. His lyrics, meanwhile, also became more complicated and poetic. Other singers would mine this album for hits with "All I Really Want to Do" and "It Ain't Me, Babe." — *William Ruhlmann*

☆ **Bringing It All Back Home** / Mar. 22, 1965 / Columbia ♦♦♦♦♦
Dylan added a bluesy rock-band backing for the first half of this album, and the lyrics of the new songs are compendiums of allusions and witticisms—"Subterranean Homesick Blues," "Maggie's Farm," "Mr. Tambourine Man," "It's All Right, Ma (I'm Only Bleeding)." Even the love songs achieve a new poetic height—"She Belongs to Me," "Love Minus Zero/No Limit," "It's All Over Now, Baby Blue." — *William Ruhlmann*

☆ **Highway 61 Revisited** / Aug. 30, 1965 / Columbia ♦♦♦♦♦
Dylan only upped the ante, making more extensive use of a crack backup band including Al Kooper and Michael Bloomfield to play his signature song, "Like a Rolling Stone," and other articulate, poetic, and incredibly bitter songs, notably "Ballad of a Thin Man" and "Desolation Row." — *William Ruhlmann*

☆ **Blonde on Blonde** / May 16, 1966 / Columbia ♦♦♦♦♦
The bitterness was transmuted into humor and absurdity on this remarkable album, in which Dylan's gush of wordplay seems endlessly inventive, his wit razor sharp, and his world-weariness overwhelming. The music, meanwhile, has coalesced into a rock backing that influences every musician who hears it. — *William Ruhlmann*

★ **Bob Dylan's Greatest Hits** / Mar. 27, 1967 / Columbia ♦♦♦♦♦
A ten-song retrospective of the work of the most impressive—and most protean—singer-songwriter of the period 1963 to 1966. Please note that, while this album is listed as the "pick" of this period of Dylan's career due to its general accessibility, a full understanding of the popular music of the '60s is impossible unless the listener is familiar with its three predecessors. *Greatest Hits* combines folk-protest standards like "Blowin' in the Wind" and "The Times They Are a-Changin'" with his folk-rock hits "Like a Rolling Stone" and "Rainy Day Women No.12 & 35." — *William Ruhlmann*

☆ **John Wesley Harding** / Dec. 27, 1967 / Columbia ♦♦♦♦♦
A quieter, simpler album than those Dylan had made in the mid-'60s, this "comeback" record nevertheless contained open-ended, parable-like songs, the most memorable of which has turned out to be "All Along the Watchtower." — *William Ruhlmann*

☆ **Nashville Skyline** / Apr. 9, 1969 / Columbia ♦♦♦♦♦
Dylan reached a sales peak with this album of simple, country-inflected songs (including "Lay Lady Lay"). — *William Ruhlmann*

Self-Portrait / Jun. 8, 1970 / Columbia ♦♦
That Dylan was suffering writer's block should have been apparent from the skimpy *Nashville Skyline*, but he shocked his following by turning out this two-record set mostly devoted to covers of songs by the Everly Brothers and Simon and Garfunkel. A few tracks were drawn from Dylan's concert performance at the Isle of Wight on Aug. 31, 1969, and they proved ragged. For an audience accustomed to Dylan's classic '60s albums, this first album of the '70s was a crushing disappointment. — *William Ruhlmann*

New Morning / Oct. 21, 1970 / Columbia ♦♦♦♦
While retaining some of the bucolic, sunny outlook of his recent work, Dylan partially turned back to a grittier rock sound (Al Kooper again in the mix) and to the more ironic, poetic lyrics of his mid-'60s songs. — *William Ruhlmann*

★ **Bob Dylan's Greatest Hits, Vol. 2** / Nov. 17, 1971 / Columbia ♦♦♦♦♦
A grab bag of material dating back to 1963, this sprawling two-disc set is notable for its rarities, especially the 1971 single "Watching the River Flow" and the 1963 live performance of "Tomorrow Is a Long Time." — *William Ruhlmann*

Pat Garrett & Billy the Kid [soundtrack] / Jul. 13, 1973 / Columbia ♦♦
Dylan's soundtrack for this Sam Peckinpah-directed Western in which he co-starred consists of some folkish instrumentals, several takes of a ballad called "Billy," and "Knockin' on Heaven's Door," a simple song that has become one of his best-remembered compositions. — *William Ruhlmann*

Dylan / Nov. 16, 1973 / Columbia ♦
When Dylan signed to Geffen Records, Columbia Records retaliated by releasing this, which consists of outtakes from the sessions that produced his worst album, *Self-Portrait*. There oughta be a law. — *William Ruhlmann*

Planet Waves / Jan. 17, 1974 / Columbia ♦♦♦
A companion work to its predecessor, *New Morning*, this first album to be recorded with Dylan's backup group, the Band, mixes pronouncements of marital and familial contentment with severe criticisms of the singer himself and others. Contains "Forever Young." — *William Ruhlmann*

Before the Flood / Jun. 20, 1974 / Columbia ♦♦♦
This double album chronicles Bob Dylan and the Band's US tour of January and February 1974. It features souped-up performances of many of Dylan's hits and best songs as well as a good selection of work by the Band. — *William Ruhlmann*

★ **Blood on the Tracks** / Jan. 17, 1975 / Columbia ♦♦♦♦♦
A stunning, mature statement in which the songwriter faced the conflicting elements of his life, the uncertainties of life in general, and the virtues of kindness and generosity. Incidentally, he also invented new songwriting structures and composed some of the most appealing music of his career. Perhaps Dylan's most listenable and compelling album, this best represents his post-'60s work. — *William Ruhlmann*

☆ **The Basement Tapes** / Jun. 26, 1975 / Columbia ♦♦♦♦♦
A two-disc set of ad hoc performances from 1967, albeit refurbished slightly for this release, *The Basement Tapes* provides the missing link between Dylan's long, poetic songs of the mid-'60s and the shorter, more direct songs of the late '60s. Some of the songs had already become well known: "Too Much of Nothing," "Tears of Rage," "This Wheel's on Fire," and "You Ain't Goin' Nowhere." — *William Ruhlmann*

Desire / Jan. 16, 1976 / Columbia ✦✦✦✦
A rough-and-tumble collection cut with a band Dylan was assembling for the *Rolling Thunder* tour. "Hurricane" recounts the tale of an unjustly imprisoned boxer, "Romance in Durango" and "Black Diamond Bay" are short stories in song, and "Sara" is a last plaintive plea from the singer to his wife. — *William Ruhlmann*

Hard Rain / Sep. 10, 1976 / Columbia ✦✦

Street Legal / Jun. 15, 1978 / Columbia ✦✦✦
Using a big band assembled for a world tour, Dylan presents a group of songs, some of which are as imagistic—and as bitter—as his mid-'60s material. Particularly notable are the tone poem "Changing of the Guards" and the desperate but moving "Senor." — *William Ruhlmann*

At Budokan / 1979 / Columbia ✦✦

Slow Train Coming / Aug. 18, 1979 / Columbia ✦✦✦
Among Dylan's best-played (members of Dire Straits participate) and best-produced recordings, this album reflects Dylan's religious conversion. At its best, on "Gotta Serve Somebody" and "When You Gonna Wake Up," the album presents cautionary messages similar to those Dylan had served up throughout his career. — *William Ruhlmann*

Saved / Jun. 20, 1980 / Columbia ✦✦
Just as fervent as he was on *Slow Train Coming*, Dylan is less inspired (sorry) as a songwriter here, and his preachiness is likely to be a bit much even for believers. — *William Ruhlmann*

Shot of Love / Aug. 12, 1981 / Columbia ✦✦
Dylan's need to sing only about his faith recedes, and his muse returns, notably on "Every Grain of Sand," one of his finest '80s songs. In 1985, this album was re-released with the non-LP B-side "The Groom's Still Waiting at the Altar," another of Dylan's better later songs, added. — *William Ruhlmann*

Infidels / Nov. 1, 1983 / Columbia ✦✦✦
Dylan emerged from his overt references to Christianity with his sense of moral outrage reawakened. He expressed it in songs defending Israel and attacking unions on this impassioned collection, which also includes "Jokerman," as impressive a piece of socially conscious poetry as he'd ever produced, and the love songs "Sweetheart like You" and "Don't Fall Apart on Me Tonight." — *William Ruhlmann*

Real Live / Dec. 3, 1984 / Columbia ✦✦✦

Empire Burlesque / Jun. 8, 1985 / Columbia ✦✦✦✦
Dylan's strongest song collection since *Blood on the Tracks*, this album also benefits from excellent backup work by members of Tom Petty's Heartbreakers, among others, and a remix by dance expert Arthur Baker. Dylan himself sounds unusually engaged as well, especially on such songs as "Emotionally Yours" (later an R&B hit for the O'Jays) and the moving autobiographical folk ballad "Dark Eyes." — *William Ruhlmann*

☆ **Biograph** / Oct. 28, 1985 / Columbia ✦✦✦✦✦
A five-LP, three-CD retrospective of Dylan's first 20 years of recording, with an emphasis on presenting some of the mountain of unreleased songs that began leaking out unofficially in the late '60s. The only reason this massive, brilliantly executed album is not listed as an essential pick is its expense—in fact, it's not a bad place to start in trying to appreciate the whole of Dylan's achievement. — *William Ruhlmann*

Knocked out Loaded / Aug. 8, 1986 / Columbia ✦✦
A hodgepodge of tracks recorded between 1984 and 1986, some written by others, some in collaboration. Mostly dispensable, it is saved from a "Poor" rating by the rambling "Brownsville Girl," co-written with playwright Sam Shepard. — *William Ruhlmann*

Royal Albert Hall / 1989 / Bootleg ✦✦✦✦
Recorded in May 1966 during Dylan's British tour with the Hawks (soon to become the Band), this documents a landmark in the history of Dylan, folk-rock, and rock itself. Although Dylan had been recording electric rock 'n' roll for a year at this point, his appearances with a full band continued to arouse tremendous controversy and even hostility, as much of the folk audience that formed his original constituency viewed him as a sellout. He divided his sets between acoustic and rock formats; this bootleg comes from the electric half, in which he performed eight of his mid-'60s tunes, including "Like a Rolling Stone," "Just like Tom Thumb's Blues," "Ballad of a Thin Man," the unreleased "Tell Me Mama," and radically reworked arrangements of "I Don't Believe You" and "One Too Many Mornings," which had appeared in plaintive acoustic versions on his albums. The songs are delivered with a fierceness and tight ensemble backing that exceeds the energy of his mid-'60s albums, and must have been quite a revelation for the more open-minded members of the audience. Some of the less open-minded customers are heard heckling Dylan on this recording, to which he responds by heckling right back and charging into a stormy version of "Like a Rolling Stone" that holds nothing in reserve. It's been said that this isn't actually from Albert Hall, but wherever the tape dates from (it is certainly from the 1966 British tour), it's way, way overdue for official release, though most Dylan fans and many serious rock scholars have a copy already. — *Richie Unterberger*

Dylan & the Dead / Feb. 6, 1989 / Columbia ✦
Quite possibly the worst album by either Bob Dylan or the Grateful Dead, the live *Dylan and the Dead* completely squanders its promise. Working from an intriguing selection of songs—it includes staples like "Knockin' on Heaven's Door" and more obscure gems like "Joey"—the Dead and Dylan contribute listless, meandering versions that are simply boring. Both artists have done much better—reportedly they have done better together, according to various bootleg fans—but *Dylan and the Dead* is a sad, disheartening document. — *Stephen Thomas Erlewine*

Oh Mercy / Sep. 22, 1989 / Columbia ✦✦✦
This stunning album demonstrated that, after more than 25 years, Dylan was perfectly capable of writing songs of topical concern, high poetry, and unflinching self-examination to match any of his best work of the '60s and '70s. — *William Ruhlmann*

Under the Red Sky / Sep. 11, 1990 / Columbia ✦✦

Bootleg Series / Mar. 26, 1991 / Columbia ✦✦✦✦
The floodgates opened with the release of this 58-song collection of outtakes and unreleased songs from throughout Dylan's career, an outpouring that demonstrated what all the bootleggers and their customers had known all along: that Dylan's throwaways were better than everyone else's keepers. It's amazing to think that, while turning out some of the most impressive albums of his time, Dylan was holding back material often equally good. — *William Ruhlmann*

Good as I Been to You / Oct. 27, 1992 / Columbia ✦✦✦

World Gone Wrong / Oct. 28, 1993 / Columbia ✦✦✦

Greatest Hits, Vol. 3 / Nov. 15, 1994 / Columbia ✦✦✦
Dylan's first greatest hits album was released in 1967, and his second in 1971. Twenty-three years later comes his third, and it's a reasonable compilation of the better-known songs he has produced over the period, notably standards like "Knockin' on Heaven's Door" and "Forever Young," Dylan chart hits like "Tangled up in Blue" and "Hurricane," songs that have been covered extensively by other singers, such as "Ring Them Bells," and some of the better album tracks, such as "Changing of the Guard" and "Brownsville Girl." In an effort to span the period, a few lesser, later songs, such as "Silvio" and "Under the Red Sky" are included, while some stronger, earlier songs are not ("Simple Twist of Fate," "Senor," "Emotionally Yours," and "Everything Is Broken"). But on the whole, the selection is excellent, and this is the album to get for that Dylan fan who stopped listening to him at the end of the '60s. (Includes the previously unreleased 1989 track "Dignity.") — *William Ruhlmann*

MTV Unplugged / Apr. 25, 1995 / Columbia ✦✦

The Eagles
....

Country-Rock, Soft Rock, Pop-Rock
The Eagles were among the most successful rock groups of the '70s, and their blend of country, folk, and rock continues to sell well in catalog. The group's four original members were Los Angeles session and group veterans assembled by producer John Boylan in 1970 as backup musicians for Linda Ronstadt on her *Silk Purse* album. They then served as her backup band for two years. The four were Glenn Frey (b. Nov. 6, 1948), guitarist; Bernie Leadon (b. Jul. 19, 1947), who played banjo and mandolin; Randy Meisner (b. Mar. 8, 1948) on bass; and Don Henley (b. Jul. 22, 1947) on drums. All four sang, though Henley and Frey took most leads. Signed to Ronstadt's label, Asylum, they issued their first album, *The Eagles*, in June 1972. It was a moderate hit (going gold a year and a half later) and produced the Top 40 hits "Take It Easy" (written by Frey and Jackson Browne), "Witchy Woman," and "Peaceful Easy Feeling."

The second Eagles LP, a semi-concept album called *Desperado* (1973) that emphasized an "outlaw" image, was somewhat less successful. For their third album, *On the Border* (1974), the group added guitarist Don Felder. This was a breakthrough record, going gold in three months and producing the No. 1 hit "Best of My Love," which didn't top the charts until almost a year after the album's release, just in time to set up their fourth album. *One of These Nights* (1975), the first of four straight albums to top the charts, featured the title track, "Lyin' Eyes," and "Take It to the Limit," both Top Ten hits.

The Eagles released a greatest-hits album in 1976 (it now stands at 14 million sales, the best-selling hits record of all time) and suffered the loss of Leadon, who was replaced by former James Gang leader Joe Walsh (b. Nov. 20, 1947). At the end of the year, they released *Hotel California*, which has now sold nine million copies. Its hits included the ominous title track, "New Kid in Town," and "Life in the Fast Lane."

In 1977, Meisner left the band and was replaced by former Poco member Timothy B. Schmit (b. Oct. 30, 1947). It took the Eagles until the fall of 1979 to complete *The Long Run*, another million-seller, featuring the chart-topper "Heartache Tonight" and Top Ten successes in the title track and "I Can't Tell You Why." The next year saw the release of a live album, but by 1981 the Eagles had split up. All five members have since released solo albums, the most successful of which have been by Henley and Frey.

In 1994, the Eagles reunited for a summer stadium tour and recorded an album as part of an appearance on the TV show *MTV Unplugged* that featured several new songs. The resulting album, *Hell Freezes Over*, was released in November of 1994; it debuted at No. 1 and sold over five million copies by June of 1995. — *William Ruhlmann*

The Eagles / Jun. 1972 / Asylum ✦✦✦
The Eagles' tentative debut album is notable for its single hits, "Take It Easy," "Witchy Woman," and "Peaceful Easy Feeling." (It also contains a rare Jackson Browne composition, "Nightingale.") The album has more of a bluegrass tone (courtesy of Bernie Leadon) than the band would later pursue. — *William Ruhlmann*

Desperado / Apr. 1973 / Asylum ✦✦✦
A concept album equating rock 'n' roll musicians with Old West outlaws, the Eagles' second album contains the hit "Tequila Sunrise," the song "Desperado," which has become a standard, and the recurring "Doolin-Dalton," cowritten with J.D. Souther and Jackson Browne. — *William Ruhlmann*

On the Border / Mar. 1974 / Asylum ✦✦✦
A transitional Eagles album (and their commercial breakthrough), this contained songs like "Already Gone" and "James Dean" (cowritten by Jackson Browne) that hark back to their earlier uptempo rock style, but also "Best of My Love" and Tom Waits' "Ol' 55," ballads that showed off their harmonies and won them a whole new audience. — *William Ruhlmann*

One of These Nights / Jun. 1975 / Asylum ✦✦✦
The Eagles' breakthrough album, a convincing mix of heady rockers and lush ballads, featuring the Top Ten hits "One Of These Nights," "Lyin' Eyes," and "Take It to the Limit." — *William Ruhlmann*

★ **Their Greatest Hits (1971-1975)** / Feb. 1976 / Asylum ✦✦✦✦✦
The reason this is such a great greatest-hits album is that it includes almost all the best tracks from the Eagles' first four albums, eight Top 40 hits including the No. 1 hits "Best of My Love" and "One of These Nights," plus the favorites "Tequila Sunrise" and "Desperado." This is the essential Eagles for the period. (As of mid-1995, *Their Greatest Hits (1971-1975)* was the second-best-selling album of all time in the US, with certified sales of 22 million copies.) — *William Ruhlmann*

☆ **Hotel California** / Dec. 1976 / Asylum ✦✦✦✦✦
A concept album about the dissipated life of Southern California rock stars, from being the "New Kid in Town" to living "Life in the Fast Lane" to holing up in the "Hotel California" fearing it's all been "Wasted Time" and turning to "The Last Resort." This album and Pink Floyd's *The Wall* are aural versions of *A Star is Born* for the rock generation. — *William Ruhlmann*

The Long Run / Sep. 1979 / Asylum ✦✦✦
The long-awaited follow-up to *Hotel California* and the Eagles' last studio album proved a considerable disappointment, although it sold in the expected multimillions and included the hits "Heartache Tonight," "The Long Run," and "I Can't Tell You Why." — *William Ruhlmann*

Eagles Live / Nov. 1980 / Asylum ✦✦

Eagles Greatest Hits, Vol. 2 / Oct. 1982 / Asylum ✦✦✦
This will save you from having to buy *The Long Run*, an inconsistent album best remembered for its hit songs, all of which are here, along with the ones from *Hotel California*. — *William Ruhlmann*

Hell Freezes Over / Nov. 8, 1994 / Geffen ✦✦

Earth, Wind & Fire

Soul, Funk, Disco, Urban
Earth, Wind & Fire was the most successful R&B group of the second half of the '70s. EW&F was founded by Maurice White (b.Dec 19, 1942) and his brother Verdine (b.Jul 25, 1951) in Chicago in 1969, and they released their self-titled debut album on Warner Bros. in 1970. After the 1971 release of the second album, *The Need of Love*, White reorganized the group, bringing in Philip Bailey (b.May 8, 1951) as co-lead singer for the recording of the third album, *Last Days and Time* on Columbia.

EW&F encapsulated many strains of Black pop from before their time. Their high-pitched harmony vocals called to mind groups such as the Temptations, while their funkiness was reminiscent of Sly and the Family Stone, and their horn section sometimes evoked the work of James Brown and others. Over this, Maurice White laid his own brand of African-inspired kalimba music for a thorough synthesis that nonetheless bore a particular musical stamp unique to Earth, Wind and Fire.

The band began to break through with its fourth album, *Head to the Sky*, in 1973. EW&F's first R&B Top Ten hit was "Mighty Mighty," from their first gold album, *Open Our Eyes*, which went to No. 15 in the pop charts and also contained the R&B hit "Kalimba Story." EW&F's breakthrough to a mass audience, however, came in 1975 with the release of *That's the Way of the World*, the soundtrack to a film in which the group

appeared. Led by its gold-selling No. 1 single, "Shining Star," the album topped the pop charts.

Equally successful were the partially live *Gratitude* (1975), *Spirit* (1976), *All 'n All* (1977), *The Best of Earth, Wind & Fire, Vol. 1* (1978), and *I Am* (1979). Several albums in the early '80s did almost as well, but after the relative failure of *Electric Universe* in 1983, EW&F disbanded. It reformed for the 1987 release *Touch the World*.

Earth, Wind & Fire returned to the R&B/urban universe in 1990 with the LP *Heritage*, an attempt to update their sound with hip-hop and new jack ingredients. Hammer and the Boys, as well as old school veteran Sly Stone, made guest appearances, but couldn't rekindle the old magic. They tried again in '93 with *Millennium*, switching labels to Reprise and ending a relationship with Columbia dating back to 1972. Columbia issued a deluxe boxed set of their greatest hits in 1992, *The Eternal Dance*. — *William Ruhlmann and Ron Wynn*

★ **The Best of Earth, Wind & Fire, Vol. 1** / Nov. 1978 / Columbia ✦✦✦✦✦
Best of Earth, Wind & Fire, Vol. 1, contains the bulk of their hits from the mid-'70s, including "Shining Star," "September," "Got to Get You into My Life," "Sing a Song," "Getaway," and several other hits. — *Stephen Thomas Erlewine*

The Best of Earth, Wind & Fire, Vol. 2 / 1988 / Columbia ✦✦✦✦
The second collection covering hit singles from the '70s top funk and soul band, Earth, Wind & Fire. This anthology has recently been supplanted by a boxed set covering virtually all of their big Columbia singles and some early Warners material. If you enjoyed their disco and late '70s cuts more than the early tracks, this anthology is worth getting. — *Ron Wynn*

The Eternal Dance / Sep. 8, 1992 / Columbia ✦✦✦✦
Covering three discs and including all the hits, as well as a healthy selection of rarities, *The Eternal Dance* is not designed for the casual listener; only hardcore fans will remain enthralled through the numerous rarities. Most listeners will be content with the two greatest hits collections, but this comprehensive box set remains essential for hardcore Earth, Wind & Fire fans. — *Stephen Thomas Erlewine*

The Easybeats

Pop-Rock
The most successful Australian rock group of the 1960s, the Easybeats were nearly as popular as the Beatles in their homeland in the mid-'60s. In 1965 and 1966, they ran off a rapid string of seven Top Ten singles in Australia with peppy variations on the early Beatle and Merseybeat sound. With a nervous energy that featured staccato guitar lines, unexpected tempo changes, and strong original material, they also betrayed strong debts to the Kinks, the Who, and the Small Faces, although their songs were generally cheerier and more lightweight. Like all of the aforementioned bands, the Easybeats stand as one of the earliest and foremost exponents of pure power-pop. In late 1966, The Easybeats moved to London and hooked up with legendary producer Shel Talmy (Who, Kinks) in an attempt to crack the international pop market. Against all the odds, they did so the first time out with the classic "Friday on My Mind," which hit the British Top Ten and the American Top 20. Some ill-chosen follow-ups, however, deflated their momentum, although the group—led by the increasingly adventurous combination songwriting/production team of guitarists George Young and Harry Vanda—were keeping up with the tenor of their times by expanding the scope of their lyrics and arrangements. Cuts like "Falling off the Edge of the World," "Come in You'll Get Pneumonia," and "Good Times" drew raves from peers like Lou Reed and Paul McCartney, although few listeners actually heard them at the time. After a few generally dispiriting years in London (during which they were nonetheless quite active in the studio), the group disbanded in late 1969 after a homecoming tour of Australia, where they had been superstars throughout the decade. Vanda and Young remained international cult figures with their extensive production work, and recaptured pop success for a time as masterminds of Flash & the Pan. — *Richie Unterberger*

Easy / 1965 / Repertoire ✦✦✦

It's 2 Easy / 1966 / Repertoire ✦✦✦

Volume 3 / 1966 / Albert ✦✦✦

Friends / 1969 / Repertoire ✦✦

The Shame Just Drained / 1977 / Albert ✦✦✦

Absolute Anthology / 1980 / EMI ✦✦✦✦
A two-CD package from Australia, with ear-stunning sound and two hours of golden classics. The collection of choice. — *Bruce Eder*

Raven EP LP, Vol. 2 / 1982 / Raven ✦✦✦

● **The Best of the Easybeats** / 1985 / Rhino ✦✦✦✦
A well-devised collection that pales in sound and content next to its Australian competitor. — *Bruce Eder*

Echo & the Bunnymen

Alternative Pop-Rock, Post-Punk

Echo & the Bunnymen's dark, swirling fusion of gloomy post-punk and Doors-inspired psychedelia brought the group a handful of British hits in the early '80s, while attracting a cult following in the US. The Bunnymen grew out of the Crucial Three, a late '70s trio featuring vocalist Ian McCulloch, Pete Wylie, and Julian Cope. Cope and Wylie left the group by the end of 1977, forming Teardrop Explodes and Wah!, respectively. McCulloch met guitarist Will Sargeant in the summer of 1978, and the pair began recording demos with a drum machine, which the duo called "Echo." Adding bassist Les Pattinson, the band made its live debut at the Liverpool club Eric's at the end of 1978, calling themselves Echo & the Bunnymen.

In March of 1979, the group released their first single, "Pictures on My Wall"/"Read It in Books," on the local Zoo record label. The single and their popular live performances led to a contract with Korova. After signing the contract, the group discarded the drum machine, adding drummer Pete de Freitas.

Released in the summer of 1980, their debut album *Crocodiles* reached No. 17 on the UK charts. *Shine so Hard*, an EP released in the fall, became their first record to crack the UK Top 40. With the more ambitious and atmospheric *Heaven up Here* (1981), the group began to gain momentum, thanks to positive reviews and increased sales; it became their first UK Top Ten album. Two years later, *Porcupine* appeared, becoming the band's biggest hit (peaking at No. 2 on the UK charts) and launching the Top Ten single, "The Cutter."

"The Killing Moon" became the group's second Top Ten hit at the beginning of 1984, yet its follow-up, "Silver," didn't make it past 30 when it was released in May. *Ocean Rain* was released that same month to great critical acclaim; peaking at No. 4 in Britain, the record became the Bunnymen's first album to chart in the US Top 100. The following year was a quiet one for the band, as they released only one new song, "Bring on the Dancing Horses," which was included on the compilation, *Songs to Learn and Sing*. De Freitas left the band at the start of 1986 and was replaced by former Haircut 100 drummer Mark Fox; by September, de Freitas rejoined the group.

Echo & the Bunnymen returned with new material in the summer of 1987, releasing the single "The Game" and a self-titled album. *Echo & the Bunnymen* became their biggest American hit, peaking at No. 51; it was a success in England as well, reaching No. 4. However, the album indicated that the group was in a musical holding pattern. At the end of 1988, McCulloch left the band to pursue a solo career; the rest of the band decided to continue without the singer. Tragedy hit the band in the summer of 1989, when de Freitas was killed in an auto accident. McCulloch released his first solo album, *Candleland*, in the fall of 1989; it proved a respectable commercial success, peaking a No. 18 in the UK and No. 159 in the US. Echo & The Bunnymen released *Reverberation*, their first album recorded without McCulloch, in 1990; it failed to make the charts. McCulloch released his second solo album, *Mysterio*, in 1992. Two years later, Ian McCulloch and Will Sergeant formed Electrafixion, releasing their first album in 1995. —*Stephen Thomas Erlewine*

Crocodiles / 1980 / Sire ✦✦✦✦
Arguments rage about these guys, but I prefer this—their debut—when their pop was spacier, moodier, and less coherent; in other words, before they started reading their press clippings. —*John Dougan*

Ocean Rain / 1984 / Sire ✦✦✦✦
Lots of strings on this one, but the pop is still delivered with flair. Lacks direction, though. —*John Dougan*

● **Songs to Learn and Sing** / 1985 / Sire ✦✦✦✦
A fine anthology collecting all of the singles from their golden period of 1980 to 1985. In the end, Echo & the Bunnymen were a great singles band, so this is the ideal way to either get acquainted with the group or revisit them. —*Chris Woodstra*

Echo & the Bunnymen / 1987 / Sire ✦✦✦
Their "mature" record. Actually, the sound hadn't varied all that much since the early '80s; it just lost a little wallop. —*John Dougan*

Eddie & the Hot Rods

Rock 'n' Roll, New Wave, Pub-Rock

Although their music might sound like conventional rock 'n' roll today, Eddie & The Hot Rods played an important role in the birth of UK punk rock. The Hot Rods are the bridge between the pub-rock of Dr. Feelgood and the punk rock of the Sex Pistols; tougher, louder, and wilder than Dr. Feelgood, the band gathered a large following in England's clubs, culminating with the release of their 1976 album *Teenage Depression*. At a time when pompous hard rock was dominating rock 'n' roll, the simple pleasures of the joyous, R&B rockers on the album were a refreshing—and important—change of pace. Released during the beginning of England's punk revolution, 1977's *Life on the Line* featured an equally inspired set of songs that were more pop-oriented than their predeces-

sors. However, it was the last time Eddie & the Hot Rods had any impact in Britain. When *Thriller* was released in 1979, the band no longer was on the cutting edge; they couldn't compete with the bands they inspired. After one more lackluster album, the group called it quits; they reunited briefly in 1985. —*Stephen Thomas Erlewine*

Live at the Marquee / Aug. 1976 / Island ✦✦✦✦
Eddie & the Hot Rods were first and foremost a great live band, so it makes perfect sense for their debut EP to show the band in their natural setting. *Live at the Marquee*, though only four songs (all covers), clearly shows how the band's wild and raw energy helped to inspire the punk explosion. —*Chris Woodstra*

Teenage Depression / Dec. 1976 / Island ✦✦✦
The band's first studio album is a fine effort in the spirit of Dr. Feelgood, bridging the gap between pub-rock and punk rock. Wild, raw, and rebellious—everything a rock 'n' roll album should be. —*Chris Woodstra*

Life on the Line / 1977 / Island ✦✦✦✦
Life on the Line adds guitarist Graeme Douglas (ex-Kursaal Flyers), helping to bring out the band's pure pop sensibility. This is their finest moment and also their last really great album. Includes the brilliant "Do Anything You Want to Do," a British hit. —*Chris Woodstra*

Thriller / 1977 / Island ✦✦

● **End of the Beginning: Best Of** / 1994 / Island ✦✦✦✦
A nearly flawless collection, *End of the Beginning* documents the band's golden period of 1976-1979 with the infectious singles, inspired live workouts, album tracks, and a rarity or two for the collectors. An important part of punk rock's roots that shouldn't be missed. —*Chris Woodstra*

Duane Eddy

b. Apr. 26, 1938, Corning, NY
Guitar / Rock 'n' Roll, Instrumental Rock

If Duane Eddy's instrumental hits from the late '50s can sound unduly basic and repetitive (especially when taken all at once), he was vastly influential. Perhaps the most successful instrumental rocker of his time, he may have also been the man most responsible (along with Chuck Berry) for popularizing the electric rock guitar. His distinctively low, twangy riffs could be heard on no less than 15 Top 40 hits between 1958 and 1963. He was also one of the first rock stars to successfully crack the LP market.

That low, twangy sound was devised in collaboration with producer Lee Hazlewood, an Arizona disc jockey whom Eddy had met while hanging out at a radio station as a teenager. By the late '50s, Hazlewood had branched out into production. Before Duane began recording, his principal influence had been Chet Atkins, but at Hazlewood's suggestion, he started concentrating on guitar lines at the lower end of the strings. His opening riff of his debut single, "Movin' and Groovin'," would be lifted for the Beach Boys five years later to open "Surfin' USA." It was the next 45, "Rebel Rouser," that would really make him a national star, reaching the Top Ten in 1958. Opening with a down-and-dirty, heavily echoed guitar riff, it remains the tune with which he's most often identified.

Eddy's phenomenally successful run of hits over the next few years was to some extent a variation on the "Rebel Rouser" theme. With cowboy whoops from the backup band helping to drive things along, they weren't nearly as innovative as the work of Link Wray during the same era, but they were much more popular. The singles—"Peter Gunn," "Cannonball," "Shazam," and "Forty Miles of Bad Road"—were probably the best—also did their part to help keep the raunchy spirit of rock 'n' roll alive, during a time in which it was in danger of being watered down. Much of that raunch was not solely due to Eddy himself, but to the honking sax solos of Steve Douglas, who would go on to become one of the top session players in the industry. Duane would have his biggest hit, however, in 1960, when he sweetened the twang with strings for the movie theme "Because They're Young."

Eddy's records were also huge influences on legions of budding guitar players. In England, the Shadows no doubt took Eddy as one of their chief inspirations for their spare, moody sound, as one listen to their most famous hit, "Apache," makes obvious. More subtly, his influence can also be heard in the work of George Harrison. For evidence, listen to the growling riffs that decorate the verse of "I Want to Hold Your Hand."

Eddy started to lose momentum in the early '60s, and left the Jamie label in 1962 for the much bigger RCA. "(Dance with the) Guitar Man," which featured an atypical chorus of female vocals, would be his last Top 20 hit that same year. His albums—often based on loose themes, like *A Million Dollars Worth of Twang*, *Twisting with Duane Eddy*, and *Surfing with Duane Eddy*—kept him afloat to some degree. But his style doggedly refused evolution, although scattered cuts indicate he was capable of abandoning the twang for more bluesy or straight-out rock sounds. The British Invasion wiped Duane out commercially, although he recorded intermittently over the next couple of decades. In 1986, he enjoyed a brief comeback when the Art of Noise built their "Peter Gunn" hit around his guest contributions; Paul McCartney, George Harrison, Ry

Cooder, and Jeff Lynne all helped produce a 1987 album. It's that run of late-'50s and early-'60s hits, though, for which he'll principally be remembered. —*Richie Unterberger*

★ **Twang Thang: Anthology** / May 18, 1993 / Rhino ✦✦✦✦✦

Duane Eddy was America's first bona fide rock 'n' roll guitar hero, playing minimalistic riffs that any kid with a pawnshop guitar could aspire to with a little determination and elbow grease. This two-CD anthology offers the finest retrospective of his career available, with all facets of his career being well documented, from the early hits to later collaborations with the famous rockers he initially inspired. Featuring just enough rarities to keep it from being merely a greatest-hits package, this truly showcases Duane at his best. —*Cub Koda*

Twangin' from Phoenix to L.A. / 1994 / Bear Family ✦✦✦✦

Dave Edmunds

b. Apr. 15, 1944, Cardiff, Wales
Bass, Guitar, Keyboards, Vocals / Rock 'n' Roll, Roots-Rock, New Wave, Pub-Rock

Dave Edmunds may not be a musical innovator, but that doesn't mean he's not an original. Where other roots-rockers sound stiff and respectable, Edmunds sounds alive and passionate even on the tracks he recorded completely by himself. He's not much of a songwriter—all of his best compositions were co-written with Nick Lowe—but he has a great ear for material; he's able to not only pick the overlooked oldies, but new material that sounds like classic rock 'n' roll (Elvis Costello's "Girls Talk," Graham Parker's "Back to Schooldays"). Edmunds' skills as a producer are formidable; he can replicate and update everything from the sound of Sun Studios and Phil Spector's wall of sound to the crisp guitars of the Everly Brothers and the driving rhythms of Chuck Berry. Although his records after 1982's *D.E. 7th* suffer from lackluster material and sound like he's trying to keep up with trends, all of the albums he recorded in the previous decade are brilliant re-creations of the best of '50s and '60s rock 'n' roll, played with energy and flair.

After spending some time as the lead guitarist of Love Sculpture, Edmunds built his own recording studio in the late '60s. In 1971, he had his only big hit single with a revamped version of Smiley Lewis' "I Hear You Knocking." As he recorded his own albums, he produced several other artists, including Brinsley Schwarz and the Flamin' Groovies. *Get It* featured former Brinsley bassist Nick Lowe, who also contributed several songs, including the single "I Knew the Bride." Lowe and Edmunds formed Rockpile with guitarist Billy Bremner and drummer Terry Williams. Rockpile backed both Edmunds and Lowe on their solo records; during concerts everyone traded songs. With their support, Edmunds' solo records became tougher and looser; the two albums he recorded entirely with the group—*Tracks on Wax 4* and *Repeat When Necessary*—are his finest.

Rockpile recorded one album as a group before they split in 1980. During the '80s, Edmunds produced several artists, including the Fabulous Thunderbirds, a Carl Perkins television special, and the Everly Brothers. After releasing a couple of albums that lacked hit singles, he turned to Jeff Lynne for production help in 1983; the teaming resulted in two stiff, synth-dominated records. By 1990's *Closer to the Flame*, Edmunds had shed Lynne and returned to the straightforward rock 'n' roll of his earlier records. 1994's *Plugged In* found Edmunds making a one-man band record again, for the first time since *Subtle as a Flying Mallet*. —*Stephen Thomas Erlewine*

Subtle as a Flying Mallet / 1975 / RCA ✦✦✦

Get It / 1977 / Swan Song ✦✦✦✦

Driven by the raucous rockers "Get out of Denver," "I Knew the Bride," and "JuJu Man," *Get It* is one of Dave Edmunds' strongest albums. —*Stephen Thomas Erlewine*

Tracks on Wax 4 / 1978 / Swan Song ✦✦✦✦

A pile-driving set of new written-to-orders and covers is powered by Edmunds' dexterous vocals and the bar-band boogie of Rockpile. —*John Floyd*

Repeat When Necessary / 1979 / Swan Song ✦✦✦✦

His creative breakthrough mines the usual retro-terrain, only the nuevo-oldies are the best he's ever had. Both Edmunds' and Rockpile's finest moment. —*John Floyd*

Single's A's & B's / 1980 / Harvest ✦✦✦

With 20 tracks Edmunds issued with Love Sculpture and Rockpile in the late '60s and early '70s, this import collection is certainly the best retrospective of his early years, if you can find it. Edmunds' image is that of a roots-rocker, and you'll find a lot of that here, ranging from the huge 1970 hit "I Hear You Knocking" to pedestrian oldies covers. Actually, though, he wasn't at all settled on this identity at the time, also cutting some psychedelia, folk-rock, and primitive art-rock. The magnificent Love Sculpture version of Khachaturian's "Sabre Dance," featuring faster-than-light riffs by Edmunds, was a British Top Ten hit; "Farandole" was an unsuccessful attempt to do the same for Bizet. Cuts like "Seagull," Tim Rose's

oft-covered "Morning Dew," "In the Land of the Few," and the Moody Blues-like "River to Another Day" are uncharacteristically wistful reflections of late-'60s hippie rock. The album also includes the rare 1967 single by Edmunds' pre-Love Sculpture band, the Human Beans. —*Richie Unterberger*

Twangin' / 1981 / Swan Song ✦✦✦

Twangin' . . . , Edmunds' first post-Rockpile album, is an inconsistent but enjoyable record, highlighted by the pseudo-new wave of John Hiatt's "Something Happens," the insistent groove of "You'll Never Get Me Up (In One of Those)," and the gorgeous Everly Brothers-style ballad "(I'm Gonna Start) Living Again if It Kills Me." —*Stephen Thomas Erlewine*

The Best of Dave Edmunds / 1981 / Swan Song ✦✦✦✦

D.E. 7th / 1982 / Columbia ✦✦✦

● **The Dave Edmunds Anthology (1968-1990)** / 1993 / Rhino ✦✦✦✦

By trying to represent all aspects of his career accurately, this double-disc set overlooks a lot of Edmunds' finest material, but the 41 songs on *The Dave Edmunds Anthology (1968-1990)* do offer a good portrait of his career, from his beginnings with Love Sculpture, through Rockpile, and his solo hits. —*AMG*

Plugged In / 1994 / Forward ✦✦

The Edsels

Doo Wop

A brief encounter with fame came for the Edsels when they recorded the doo wop masterpiece "Rama Lama Ding Dong." Originally released in 1959, the single became a hit some three years after its intial release, thanks to the efforts of diligent record collectors and disc jockeys.

Taking their name from Ford's legendary failed automobile, the Edsels formed in the tiny mill town of Campbell, OH, in the late '50s. The group consisted of lead vocalist George Jones Jr., James Reynolds, Marshall Sewell, Harry Greene, and Larry Greene. The group audtioned for a local Ohio music publisher in 1958. Through the publisher, the group landed a record deal with the small Dub Records. The Edsels' first single was a song Jones had written, "Rama Lama Ding Dong." The first pressings on Dub Records were mislabeled "Lama Lama Ding Dong."

"Rama Lama Ding Dong" became a local hit, but made no impact nationally. In 1961, disc jockeys began playing the song again because it sounded similar to the Marcels' current hit, "Blue Moon." Within a few months, the single was re-released on Twin Records—this time with the correct song title—and it quickly scaled the pop charts, peaking at No. 21. Ironically, the group had broken up by the time "Rama Lama Ding" became a hit in 1961. —*Stephen Thomas Erlewine & Cub Koda*

● **Rama Lama Ding Dong** / 1992 / Relic ✦✦✦✦

A complete collection of the group's best sides; one of the great nonsense doo-wop sides of all time. —*Cub Koda*

Elastica

Alternative Pop-Rock, Brit-Pop

Elastica's brief, angular, and catchy punk rock became a hit on both sides of the Atlantic in 1995. While the group reworks both the sound and the image of new wave and punk rockers like Adam & the Ants, Wire, the Buzzcocks, and Blondie, the band's songs are more pop-oriented and hook-driven than most of their influences, and Justine Frischmann's cool sexuality is earthier, yet more detached, than Debbie Harry's.

Guitarist/vocalist Justine Frischmann began performing professionally in the early '90s, forming Suede with her boyfriend Brett Anderson. In addition to naming the band, Frischmann was the group's original guitarist and continued to perform with them once lead guitarist Bernard Butler joined. However, she left the group soon after her relationship with Anderson ended. Frischmann formed Elastica after leaving Suede in 1991. Recruiting guitarist Donna Matthews, drummer Justin, and bassist Annie Holland through advertisements, the final lineup of the band was set in 1993. Elastica released their first single, the roaring three-chord, two-minute punk rocker "Stutter," at the end of 1993. The single was a limited-edition run and it quickly sold out, thanks to radio airplay and rave reviews. "Line Up" followed a few months later. It also sold very well, yet some critics claimed the band appropriated the melody from Wire's "I Am the Fly" for the song. For most of 1994, the group was relatively quiet, playing the occasional concert and recording; nevertheless, the band's name stayed in the British press, largely due to Frischmann's romance with Damon Albarn, the lead singer for Blur, England's most popular band of 1994. Released in the fall of that year, "Connection," their biggest hit yet, suffered the same criticism, this time for taking the keyboard riff from Wire's "Three Girl Rhumba." On the eve of the March 1995 release of their debut album, the group was taken to court by Wire's publishers, as well as the publishers of the Stranglers (who claimed Elastica's new single, "Waking Up," took the riff from the punk band's "No More Heroes"); both cases were settled out of court before the album was released. Entering the charts at No. 1, Elastica's self-titled first album became the fastest-selling debut in the UK, beating the record Oasis' *Definitely Maybe* set only seven months earlier. As well as being a popular success, the record received overwhelmingly positive reviews. Like Oasis, Elastica managed to have a hit single in America with "Connection"; the single was a major modern rock radio hit, as well as reaching the Top 60 on the singles chart. Elastica continued to make headway in America by replacing Sinead O'Connor on the 1995 Lollapalooza tour. —*Stephen Thomas Erlewine*

● **Elastica** / 1995 / DGC ✦✦✦✦
Elastica's debut album may cop a riff here and there from Wire or the Stranglers, yet no more than Led Zeppelin did with Willie Dixon, or the Beach Boys with Chuck Berry. The key is context. Elastica can make the rigid artiness of Wire into a rocking, sexy single with more hooks than anything on *Pink Flag* ("Connection") or rework the Stranglers' "No More Heroes" into a more universal anthem that loses none of its punkiness ("Waking Up"). But what makes *Elastica* such an intoxicating record is not only how the 16 songs speed by in 40 minutes, but that the songs are nearly all classics. The riffs are angular like early Adam & the Ants, the melodies tease like Blondie, and the entire band is as tough as the Clash, yet they never seem anything less than contemporary. Justine Frischmann's detached sexuality adds an extra edge to her brief, spiky songs—"Stutter" roars about a boyfriend's impotence, "Car Song" makes sex in a car actually sound sexy, "Line Up" slags off groupies, and "Vaseline" speaks for itself. Even if the occasional riff sounds like an old wave group, the simple fact is that hardly any new wave band made records this consistently rocking and melodic. —*Stephen Thomas Erlewine*

Electric Flag

Blues-Rock
The Electric Flag were a horn-dominated rock band led by guitarist Michael Bloomfield (1944-1981) and featuring drummer and vocalist Buddy Miles, bassist Harvey Brooks (born Goldstein), and vocalist Nick Gravenites. Whereas later, more successful horn-based groups like Chicago and Blood, Sweat & Tears worked from jazz and pop influences, the Electric Flag used the Stax/Volt sound, James Brown, and B.B. King's large groups as role models. Bloomfield left after their first album, with Miles taking over the leadership role for the second album. They reformed with Bloomfield in 1974 for one quick album released to scant acclaim, but its influence as a trendsetter far exceeds its record sales. —*Cub Koda*

Trip [O.S.T.] / 1967 / Edsel ✦✦✦

A Long Time Comin' / 1968 / Columbia ✦✦✦✦
Ex-Butterfield Band guitarist/drummer Miles and others put this soulrock band together in 1967. This debut is a testament to their ability to catch fire and keep on burnin'. —*Jeff Tamarkin*

● **Old Glory: The Best of Electric Flag** / Oct. 1995 / Columbia/Legacy ✦✦✦✦
A near-definitive anthology, including almost all of the debut LP (but not every last item), key songs from the second album, and some previously unissued demos, alternate takes, and performances from the 1967 Monterey Pop Festival. —*Richie Unterberger*

Electric Light Orchestra

Art-Rock/Progressive-Rock, Pop-Rock
Formed in 1971 from the ashes of one of Britain's greatest eccentric rock bands, the Move, the Electric Light Orchestra drew heavily from the ornately lumbering "I Am the Walrus"-period Beatles. This is shown to extreme effect on their oddly engaging debut, *No Answer*. Of particular note is the track "10538 Overture."

Move expatriates Roy Wood, Jeff Lynne, and Bev Bevan formed the initial nucleus of ELO, but multi-instrumentalist Wood split after *No Answer* to form the bizarrely '50s-influenced Wizzard. Their sophomore release, *ELO II*, retained some of the off-key crunch of the debut, but it is clearly a transition to what became a very slick, highly orchestrated pop-hit factory. Between 1975 and 1981, ELO managed 17 Top 40 hits, among which were "Evil Woman" (No. 10), "Telephone Line" (No. 7), "Don't Bring Me Down" (No. 4), "Hold on Tight" (No. 10), "Shine a Little Love" (No. 8), and the wonderful "Can't Get It out of My Head" (No. 9). ELO also scored a No. 24 hit with "Do Ya," which was the Move's only stateside chart hit. ELO increasingly became a side project to leader Jeff Lynne's successful outside artist productions, which included Brian Wilson, Dave Edmunds, Tom Petty, the Traveling Wilburys, Randy Newman, and George Harrison. —*Rick Clark*

No Answer / 1972 / Jet ✦✦✦✦
Their most lively album, this debut is driven by Roy Wood's manic musical sensibilities. An energetic offshoot of the Move's final album. —*Bruce Eder*

On the Third Day / 1973 / Jet ✦✦✦✦
ELO's sound came togther here, hooked around rocked-up classics and Jeff Lynne's guitar. —*Bruce Eder*

Electric Light Orchestra 2 / 1973 / Jet ✦✦

Eldorado / 1975 / Jet ✦✦✦✦
Pretentious pseudo-concept rock with some hot old-style rock 'n' roll grace notes. —*Bruce Eder*

Face the Music / 1975 / Jet ✦✦✦✦
Superb production and a good song lineup featuring "Evil Woman" and "Strange Magic." —*Bruce Eder*

Ole' Elo / 1976 / Jet ✦✦✦✦
The early hits, marred only by the unnecessary cutting of "Roll over Beethoven." —*Bruce Eder*

A New World Record / 1976 / Jet ✦✦✦

Out of the Blue / 1977 / Jet ✦✦✦

● **Elo's Greatest Hits** / 1979 / Jet ✦✦✦✦
Most of ELO's biggest and best hits—"Evil Woman," "Rockaria," "Telephone Line"—are included on this solid but slightly skimpy collection. —*Stephen Thomas Erlewine*

Afterglow / 1990 / Epic ✦✦✦✦
Although it contains all the hits and the remastering sounds superb, the three-disc box set *Afterglow* is likely to be more ELO than anyone but the most devoted fans would want from an anthology. —*Stephen Thomas Erlewine*

Strange Music: The Best of Electric Light Orchestra / Apr. 11, 1995 / Epic/Legacy ✦✦✦✦
Strange Music concentrates more on ELO's pop hits than *Afterglow*, which makes for a better, more listenable collection. All of the hits are accounted for, along with the group's '70s AOR staples, making it the one definitive collection. ELO may have been an album rock band, but their best moments were individual songs; consequently, *Strange Music* doesn't ignore their best attributes, it accentuates them. —*Stephen Thomas Erlewine*

The Electric Prunes

Psychedelic
The Electric Prunes were not so much a self-contained group as a front for some talented Los Angeles songwriters and producers; they by and large played the music on their records, but the vision and inspiration came from elsewhere. Nonetheless, they produced a few great psychedelic garage songs, especially the scintillating "I Had Too Much to Dream Last Night," which mixed distorted guitars and pop hooks with inventive oscillating reverb. Songwriters Annette Tucker and Nancie Mantz wrote much of the Prunes' material, much of which in turn was crafted in the studio by Dave Hassinger, who had engineered some classic Rolling Stones sessions in the mid-'60s. "Too Much to Dream" was a big hit in 1967, and the psychedelized Bo Diddley follow-up "Get Me to the World on Time" was just as good, and also a hit. Nothing else by the group made it big, and their initial pair of albums were quite erratic, although a few scattered tracks were nearly as good as those singles. Although they began to write more of their own material on their second album, their subsequent releases were apparently the products of personnel that had little to do with the original lineup. Their third LP, *Mass in F Minor*, was a quasi-religious concept album of psychedelic versions of prayers; a definitively excessive period piece, its best song ("Kyrie Eleison") was lifted for the *Easy Rider* soundtrack. None of the original Prunes were still in the lineup when the band dissolved, unnoticed, at the end of the '60s. —*Richie Unterberger*

● **Long Day's Flight** / 1986 / Edsel ✦✦✦✦
This 18-track compilation includes the best cuts from their first two albums, as well as a couple of non-LP singles. Pruned down to the best six or seven cuts, it would have made a ferocious EP; some of the material is simply unmemorable, as the band pounds away in a sub-Stones bluesy fuzz style in the mode of the Standells or Chocolate Watch Band. Besides the two hits, there are a few first-rate cuts that meld garage pop to inspired psychedelic production, like "Train for Tomorrow," "Hideaway," "Long Day's Flight," "You Never Had It Better," "Sold to the Highest Bidder" (featuring an organ made to sound like a balalaika), and their cover of Goffin/King's "I Happen go Love You." —*Richie Unterberger*

Eleventh Dream Day

Alternative Pop-Rock
One of the more underrated American bands currently occupying the ever-changing "alternative rock" scene, Chicago-based Eleventh Dream Day has managed to record three remarkable albums of driving rock 'n' roll propelled by a swirling, intoxicating din of country-tinged, feedback-drenched guitars. As did the Los Angeles band X nearly a decade earlier, EDD deals intelligently with complex human and social relationships, the narratives spilling forth from the pens of Rick Rizzo and Janet Beveridge Bean. Unlike a number of alternative-rock bands who simply cannot write songs, EDD eschews a marketable pose and lets the music do

the talking. Having been bounced from a major label to an indie, here's hoping the future is kind to them. — *John Dougan*

Beet / 1989 / Atlantic ✦✦✦

● **Lived to Tell** / 1991 / Atlantic ✦✦✦✦
The underrated album of 1991. *Lived to Tell* is a resounding triumph exhibiting all of Eleventh Dream Day's strengths without ever sounding like generic alternative rock. Sad, combative, and raging, this is a record that reveals more with each play. — *John Dougan*

El Moodio / 1993 / Atlantic ✦✦✦✦
EDD got the big heave-ho from Atlantic when *El Moodio* stiffed. But I can't come up with a single reason as to why this album didn't make them the toast of MTV's Buzz Bin. Perhaps not as galvanizing as *Lived to Tell*, but there's no dross here, just lots and lots of guitars, passion, and energy. — *John Dougan*

Ursa Major / 1994 / Atavistic ✦✦✦

Emerson, Lake & Palmer

Art-Rock/Progressive-Rock
By the end of the '60s, many artists became swept up in the wake of the Beatles and their aggressive exploration of the possibilities of pop and rock. In the minds of many young, schooled musicians who found release in rock's energy, expanding the form by incorporating motifs and highly arranged extended compositions seemed an appealing notion. The results of this concept became known as art-rock.

Depending on your point of view, Emerson, Lake & Palmer was guilty of encouraging such tonal indulgence, or they delivered some of the genre's better moments. Pianist Keith Emerson had already met much success in Britain with his theatrical pyrotechnics in the Nice. Greg Lake was the vocalist/bassist for the explosively dark King Crimson, and percussionist Carl Palmer backed up the heavy blues-based Atomic Rooster, a band that also contained eventual Fleetwood Mac member Christine McVie.

Months before the arrival of Emerson, Lake & Palmer's self-titled debut, expectations began running high about what the band would contribute to the expansion of rock. The debut was impressive, ranging from delicate acoustic piano and guitar interplay to explosive free-for-alls, but with the second album (*Tarkus*) it became obvious that the band often placed an enormous amount of finesse on playing to the back of the bleachers, rather than focusing that energy into a consistently satisfying musicality.

Nevertheless, Emerson, Lake & Palmer became a staple of FM rock radio during the '70s, even scoring a couple of hits with "Lucky Man" (No. 48) and "In the Beginning" (No. 39). — *Rick Clark*

Emerson, Lake & Palmer / 1970 / Atlantic ✦✦✦✦
Lively, ambitious, largely successful debut album, made up of daring instrumentals ("Three Fates," "The Barbarian") and romantic ballads ("Lucky Man"), showcasing three very daunting talents. "Take a Pebble" is rewarding and pretentious enough to have been a Moody Blues track, except that the Moodies could never solo like Keith Emerson. The trio would never be as concise or precise in their work again. — *Bruce Eder*

Tarkus / 1971 / Atlantic ✦✦✦

Pictures at an Exhibition / 1971 / Atlantic ✦✦✦
A live recording of the Mussorgsky piece which, despite its wildness, holds up well as a psychedelic art-rock showcase. — *Bruce Eder*

Trilogy / 1972 / Atlantic ✦✦✦

Brain Salad Surgery / 1973 / Atlantic ✦✦✦✦
Science-fiction rock, virtually a soundtrack to a nonexistent film. Well-produced and overpowering, but fully rewarding only on the tracks that fall outside the concept. — *Bruce Eder*

Ladies & Gentlemen (Welcome Back My Friends to the Show That Never Ends) / 1974 / Manticore ✦✦

Works, Vol. 1 / Oct. 1977 / Atlantic ✦✦✦
The trio's last great album, a double-disc set that essentially allowed each of the members a side of his own to produce and a fourth side on which they worked as a team. Emerson's Piano Concerto is over-extended but probably the best work of its kind (and there are quite a few from this period) by a rock figure. Lake's solo material is a little too soft and romantic, while Palmer comes off best, with a percussion/production tour de force. The group material (including "Fanfare for the Common Man") isn't a major advance (except in dimension) from the preceding record. — *Bruce Eder*

● **The Atlantic Years** / 1992 / Atlantic ✦✦✦✦
This double-disc set is a solid two-and-a-half hours' overview of ELP's career highlights, including "The Endless Enigma (Parts 1 & 2)," "Fugue," "Knife-Edge," "Take a Pebble," "Lucky Man," "From the Beginning," "Fanfare for the Common Man," "Still... You Turn Me On," Greg Lake's "Father Christmas," and excerpts from *Pictures at an Exhibition*. — *AMG*

The Return of the Manticore / Nov. 16, 1993 / Victory ✦✦

The Emotions

Soul
A trio of sisters with a strong gospel base, the Emotions (based in Chicago) were one of the leading female R&B acts of the '70s. Lead singer Sheila Hutchinson and her sisters Wanda and Jeanette were only teenagers when they crashed the soul charts in 1969 with the engaging "So I Can Love You," but they sang gospel as children and enjoyed secular fame locally before signing with Memphis-based Volt and working with producers Isaac Hayes and David Porter. When Stax folded in 1975, the group hooked up with Maurice White of Earth, Wind & Fire, an association that led to the No. 1 pop/R&B hit "Best of My Love" in 1977.

Two years after *Best of My Love*, Maurice White and the Emotions collaborated on "Boogie Wonderland," which was both a No. 2 R&B and No. 6 pop hit. They issued three more albums on White's ARC label from 1979 to 1981, but were unable to duplicate their earlier success. They moved to the Red label for the 1984 LP *Sincerely*, which included the single "All Things Come in Time." They issued three other singles from the album, but none made much impact, though each one charted. They then signed with Motown, but issued only one album, *If I Only Knew*. Sheila Hutchinson was a featured vocalist on Garry Glenn's "Feels Good to Feel Good" in 1987. Pam and Jeanette Hutchinson did background vocals on Helen Baylor's gospel song "There's No Greater Love" in 1990. Wanda Hutchinson and Jeanette sang on Earth, Wind & Fire's *Heritage* in 1990. — *Bill Dahl and Ron Wynn*

● **Best of My Love: The Best Of** / Mar. 12, 1996 / Columbia/Legacy ✦✦✦✦
This 16-track, 69-minute disc surveys the Emotions' five-year, five-album stay on Columbia Records (and the custom label ARC), which was the group's most successful period, featuring the gold No. 1 hit "Best of My Love" and the gold Top Ten hit "Boogie Wonderland" (on which the Emotions backed their mentors, Earth, Wind & Fire), both of which are heard here, along with four other songs that saw action on the pop charts. Surprisingly, the Emotions' five singles that only made the R&B charts are excluded in favor of album tracks. Unlike their earlier period at Stax, at Columbia the Emotions essentially were an adjunct to EW&F and its leader, Maurice White, and since EW&F featured tenor and falsetto vocals, the similarity was often heightened, especially on "Boogie Wonderland." Nevertheless, the sisters sang well over the horns and disco rhythms that characterized the pop/R&B music of the period. — *William Ruhlmann*

En Vogue

Urban, Club-Dance, New Jack R&B
The female vocal quartet En Vogue was conceived and put together by the production team of Denzil Foster and Thomas McElroy, both former members of Club Nouveau. Foster and McElroy wanted a vocal group who could exude sultriness and intelligence in addition to vocal proficiency, and as producers, they wanted material that would fuse R&B and girl-group traditions with hip-hop and new jack swing rhythms. The two held auditions and settled on a membership of former Miss Black California Cindy Herron, Maxine Jones, Dawn Robinson, and Terry Ellis. The new group performed two songs on Foster and McElroy's *FM2* album, and the producers crafted an image of them as stylish, sophisticated, and sexy. Originally called For You, the women switched to the more elegant Vogue, and then En Vogue after learning of another group with a very similar name.

En Vogue's debut album, *Born to Sing*, appeared in 1990 and launched the pop crossover smash "Hold On," which peaked at No. 2 and helped the album go platinum. The group attracted comparisons to the Supremes, even though group members shared lead vocals and intentionally designated no particular singer the "star." In between albums, Herron appeared in the film *Juice*. When En Vogue returned in 1992 with *Funky Divas*, critical and commercial response was overwhelming. The album's wide array of styles, from pop, rock, and R&B to rap, rock, and reggae, were lauded in print; the first three singles—"My Lovin' (You're Never Gonna Get It)," "Giving Him Something He Can Feel" (both covers of songs written by Curtis Mayfield), and "Free Your Mind" (which borrowed a chorus line from George Clinton)—reached the Top Ten, and the album went multiplatinum. En Vogue were in the Top Ten again in 1993, backing Salt-N-Pepa on their hit "Whatta Man." — *Steve Huey*

Born to Sing / 1991 / Atlantic ✦✦✦

● **Funky Divas** / 1992 / East West ✦✦✦✦
En Vogue are incredible singers, which is what makes *Funky Divas* a delight. Naturally, the singles are the high points on the album, but the rest of the disc is hardly filler—it proves that En Vogue possess great talent. — *Stephen Thomas Erlewine*

The English Beat

New Wave, Ska-Revival
One of the earliest and most important ska-revivalist groups, Birming-

ham's the Beat formed in 1978 (the band had to change their name to the English Beat in the US to avoid confusion with Paul Collins' band of the same name). The multiracial band carved a distinct sound through the use of alternating lead vocals by guitarist Dave Wakeling and punk-toaster/rapper Ranking Roger, supported by a tight band consisting of Andy Cox (guitar), Dave Steel (bass), and Everett Moreton (drums). The addition of 50-year-old saxophonist Saxa, who originally played with Prince Buster and Desmond Dekker, gave the band credibility and fleshed out its sound. An opening spot for the Selecter led to the band's signing to 2-Tone, where they released the hit single "Tears of a Clown," a wonderful version of the Smokey Robinson classic. In 1980, the band decided to form their own 2-Tone inspired label, Go-Feet (distributed by Arista). A string of hit singles followed in the UK, including "Mirror in the Bathroom." Their debut LP, *I Just Can't Stop It*, combined the early hits with other pop/ska-oriented material. "Stand Down Margaret," with its anti-Thatcher stance, found the band moving in a more political direction, leading to several benefit gigs for "radical" causes. Musically, the Beat slowed down the tempo for a more traditional reggae sound showcased on 1981's *Wha'ppen?*. This direction failed to bring the chart success of its predecessor. Featuring a more pop-oriented approach, 1982's *Special Beat Service* helped the band increase its US fan base through MTV exposure of "Save it for Later" and "I Confess," but the band members decided to call it quits later that same year. Wakeling and Ranking Roger went on to form General Public, and Cox and Steel formed Fine Young Cannibals. — *Chris Woodstra*

☆ **I Just Can't Stop It** / Oct. 1980 / IRS ✦✦✦✦✦
The Beat's debut is a true landmark of the period, perfectly blending intense politics with a playful, yet driving dance beat. While the sound could be mimicked by other revivalists, the top-notch songwriting represented on this album is what set them apart. *I Just Can't Stop It* plays like a *Greatest Hits* album (most of their hits are found here) and still holds up today. — *Chris Woodstra*

Wha'ppen? / Jun. 1981 / IRS ✦✦✦
After the nearly perfect debut, the Beat seem somewhat directionless on *Wha'ppen?*. No longer instantly danceable, the tunes have slowed to sub-reggae tempo with more political content (though less focused this time around). The two unmemorable singles, "Drowning" and "Doors of Your Heart," failed to make an impact in the charts and only "Dreamhome in N.Z." leaves a lasting impression. — *Chris Woodstra*

Special Beat Service / 1982 / IRS ✦✦✦✦
The final Beat album focuses less on politics and more on the subject of personal relationships. Their most polished effort, the band leaves behind their early ska influences in favor of jangly pop that, at times, delves into African and Latin rhythms. Includes the flawless singles "Save It for Later" and "I Confess." — *Chris Woodstra*

● **What Is Beat?** / 1983 / IRS ✦✦✦✦
While the best introduction to Beat is still the first album, *What Is Beat* does a good job of collecting the hits from each of the three albums. The live tracks and remixes are a nice addition for completists but are generally unnecessary for anyone else. — *Chris Woodstra*

The Beat Goes On / 1991 / IRS ✦✦✦

Enigma

Club-Dance
With their 1991 hit, "Sadeness," Enigma brought the new age fascination with Gregorian chants and old-world culture to the clubs; the resulting single was both unique and irresistible. The rest of the album followed that pattern successfully, although without quite matching the stunning success of the hit single. On their second album, 1994's *Cross of Changes*, some of the old-world elements remained, but the new age angle came to the forefront in a set of slick, radio-friendly dance-pop tunes. — *Stephen Thomas Erlewine*

● **MCMXC A.D.** / 1990 / Charisma ✦✦✦✦
Driven by the Gregorian chants of the hit single "Sadeness Part I," Enigma's debut album is an interesting fusion of new age sensibilities and dance-floor rhythms. — *Stephen Thomas Erlewine*

The Cross of Changes / Feb. 8, 1994 / Charisma ✦✦✦
On Enigma's second album, their latent new age tendencies come to the forefront and occasionally obscure their usually captivating dance tracks. — *Stephen Thomas Erlewine*

Brian Eno

b. May 15, 1948, Woodbridge, England
Synthesizer / Electronic, Ambient, Art-Rock/Progressive-Rock, Experimental
Brian Eno may not be a household name, but his influence has been felt on a number of rock's most unique records. Eno first made his appearance as a founding member of British art-pop rockers Roxy Music in 1971. Eno, who fancied himself a manipulator of "treated" sound rather

than a formally titled musician, provided Roxy with sweeping tonal washes, peculiar noises, and bleeps and blips on electronic keyboards and tapes. After leaving Roxy Music, Eno pursued a fascinating career as a solo artist and producer.

Eno's solo career perhaps has been the most rewarding in the pantheon of art-rock. His ground-breaking early work influences a slew of budding art-punk rockers, his experiments with synthesized atmospheria serve as intriguing Muzak for rock fans, and his innovative production skills have been enlisted by rockers as varied as David Bowie, U2, Ultravox, Devo, and Talking Heads. He's also collaborated with John Cale, Robert Fripp, Daniel Lanois, David Byrne, and his brother, Roger Eno. Eno's interest in creating "sound landscapes" with sophisticated manipulations of echo and timbre led to the establishment of his "ambient music" ideal in the late '70s, through a series of influential solo albums and ethereal collaborations with Laraaji, Jon Hassell, and Harold Budd. By creating this new subgenre, he unwittingly became one of the fathers of new age music, a genre he was quick to criticize for not encompassing enough "evil and doubt." The intention and effect of Eno's style, however, is markedly different from the soothing sound baths associated with many new age and contemporary electronic recordings, notoriously one-dimensional in their approach to sound construction. Eno makes soundscapes that challenge the listener.

In recent years, Eno has created increasingly sophisticated ambient soundtracks for his own multimedia installations, which have graced galleries in Venice, Milan, and Tokyo. Eno continues to release albums in both pop and contemporary instrumental genres. — *Rick Clark, John Floyd, and Linda Kohanov*

No Pussyfooting / Nov. 1973 / EG ✦✦✦✦
Robert Fripp's collaboration with Brian Eno. A musical landscape made up of sedate guitar feedback echoed, repeated, and otherwise treated by tape recorder. Today this would be classified under "new age." The follow-up, *Evening Star*, is similar. — *William Ruhlmann*

Here Come the Warm Jets / Jan. 1974 / EG ✦✦✦✦
Eno's solo debut features complex but tight pop songs with bizarre and often hilarious lyrics, which puncture the treated guitar and keyboard textures. — *John Floyd*

Taking Tiger Mountain (by Strategy) / Nov. 1974 / EG ✦✦✦✦
They lack the vibrant and energetic rock-laced enthusiasm of *Here Come the Warm Jets*, but these experimentations within the pop format give art-rock a good name. — *John Floyd*

Evening Star / 1975 / Antilles ✦✦✦

★ **Another Green World** / Nov. 1975 / EG ✦✦✦✦✦
Eno's masterpiece contains a sumptuous aural mélange of dense ambient instrumental snippets and rich, often beautiful pop melodies. This is one of those albums that should be enjoyed in one concentrated sitting. — *John Floyd*

After the Heat / 1978 / Sky ✦✦✦

☆ **Before & After Science** / May 1978 / EG ✦✦✦✦✦
This thrashing partial return to more basic song structures is punctuated by the exhilarating "King's Lead Hat." — *John Floyd*

Ambient 1: Music for Airports / Mar. 1979 / EG ✦✦✦✦
Four subtle, slowly evolving pieces grace Eno's first conscious effort at creating ambient music. The composer was in part striving to create music that approximated the effect of visual art. Like a fine painting, these evolving soundscapes don't require constant involvement on the part of the listener. They can hang in the background and add to the atmosphere of the room, yet the music also rewards close attention with a sonic richness absent in standard types of background or easy-listening music. — *Linda Kohanov*

Ambient 4: On Land / Apr. 1982 / EG ✦✦✦✦
Eno's most masterful ambient effort to date was created as a musical antidote to the confusion of life in New York City. An earthy sense of repose underlies intricate sonic essays. — *Linda Kohanov*

Nerve Net / Sep. 1992 / Opal ✦✦

The Shutov Assembly / Oct. 1992 / Opal ✦✦✦

Eno Box II / 1993 / Virgin ✦✦✦✦
The first of two retrospective box sets devoted to the groundbreaking work of Brian Eno, *II* concentrates on his pop and vocal material, including some selections from the unreleased *My Squelchy Life*. Although his music still makes the most sense in the context of his albums, *II* is a solid crash-course introduction to his work, which remains as revolutionary today as it was when it was released. — *Stephen Thomas Erlewine*

Eno Box I / Mar. 22, 1994 / Virgin ✦✦✦✦
Box I features a cross-section of Eno's influential ambient music; while this music often works better in its original context, the box offers a good introduction to Eno's innovative instrumental work. — *Stephen Thomas Erlewine*

Erasure

Dance-Pop, Alternative Pop-Rock, Club-Dance

After Vince Clarke left Depeche Mode in the early '80s, he formed the synth-based dance-pop band Yaz before forming Erasure in 1985 with singer Andy Bell. Clarke wrote and played the majority of the material; the extravagant Bell provided the duo with a voice and image. Like Depeche Mode or the Pet Shop Boys, Erasure sounds cold and detached while singing about love and alienation, yet they still have a knack for crafting successful pop singles like "Chains of Love." Over the years, the duo's following has expanded with each release and they have edged their way into the pop mainstream. —*Stephen Thomas Erlewine*

Wonderland / May 1986 / Sire ✦✦✦✦
Vince Clarke's inventive synthesizer music is immediately identifiable no matter who the singer is. Here the former Depeche Mode/Yaz leader does his electronic wonders behind emotive singer Andy Bell (who bears a certain vocal resemblance to Yaz's Alison Moyet). Clarke's irresistible music is the best argument there is for synthesizers, and Bell is an appealing front man. —*William Ruhlmann*

The Circus / Mar. 1987 / Sire ✦✦✦
Erasure broke through to mass acceptance in their native UK with their second album, *The Circus*, which contained four chart singles, three of which made the Top Ten. The album stayed in the charts more than two years. In America, the group's relentless synthesizer-based music, heavy beat, and emotive, romantically tinged vocals marked them as a dance music phenomenon. "Victim of Love" became a major club hit, and *The Circus* was Erasure's first album to reach the charts, however briefly. Vince Clarke and Andy Bell were simply continuing to turn out inventive pop tracks, the best (which is to say, the catchiest) being "Sometimes" and "Victim of Love." —*William Ruhlmann*

Two Ring Circus / Dec. 1987 / Sire ✦✦

The Innocents / Apr. 1988 / Sire ✦✦✦✦
Erasure emerged from the dance clubs with this million-selling US breakthrough album, which contains the Top 15 hits "A Little Respect" and "Chains of Love." —*William Ruhlmann*

Crackers International / Apr. 1989 / Sire ✦✦✦

Wild! / Oct. 1989 / Sire ✦✦

Chorus / Oct. 1991 / Sire ✦✦

● **Erasure Pop! The First 20 Hits** / Nov. 24, 1992 / Sire ✦✦✦✦
This album is exactly what it claims to be—a collection of Erasure's biggest singles, which makes it the best place to get acquainted with this synth-pop band. —*Stephen Thomas Erlewine*

I Say I Say I Say / May 17, 1994 / Mute/Elektra ✦✦✦
I Say I Say I Say, Erasure's sixth full-length album, was something of a new start for the group following its successful EP of Abba covers and greatest hits compilation. And it earned them their long-awaited third US Top 40 hit with "Always." But while the group maintained a mass following in Britain and a dance following in America, Erasure still seemed like proponents of a style that had long since peaked and passed into decline, which may have accounted for the wistful, vaguely spiritual tone of Andy Bell's lyrics. Early on, Erasure had seemed to represent a radical change in the sound of pop music, but nine years, six albums, and several EPs later, they just seemed like another weightless British pop band who happened to use synthesizers a lot. —*William Ruhlmann*

Erasure / Oct. 24, 1995 / Elektra ✦✦✦
It's been a long way from the bouncy dance hits of Erasure's early days to this thoughtful, expansive collection whose eponymous title suggests a new beginning. The 11 tracks run 71 1/2 minutes, leaving room for extended instrumental passages. (The lack of breaks between the songs contributes to the sense of a single long musical piece.) But it isn't so much the length as the slower tempos and reflective lyrics, which often conflate romance with religion, that make *Erasure* the group's most ponderous album. "Fingers & Thumbs (Cold Summer's Day)" is the obvious uptempo dance-floor hit, but that's an atypical track on an album that finds Andy Bell singing about fear and grace and sanctuary. Maybe AIDS is the subtextual subject in all this, or maybe Bell and Clarke are just getting philosophical after seven albums. Whatever the reasons, they are becoming the Pink Floyd of the synth-pop set. —*William Ruhlmann*

Roky Erickson

b. Jul. 15, 1957, Dallas, TX
Guitar, Vocals / Rock 'n' Roll, Psychedelic

Aside from Syd Barrett, Erickson is rock's most notorious looney-toon. After forming the 13th Floor Elevators, the quintessential acid-rattled '60s punk band, Erickson embarked on a solo career that has explored his emotional crumbling (due mostly to his nasty penchant for LSD). He's spent several years in institutions, and his voluminous and scattered solo catalog reflects the peculiarities of his vision. At its best, Erickson's music is truly scarifying. —*John Floyd*

Holiday Inn Tapes / 1987 / Fan Club ✦✦✦

● **You're Gonna Miss Me**—The Best of Roky Erickson / Sep. 27, 1991 / Restless ✦✦✦✦
Erickson's peculiar rock vision has been too schizophrenic to produce one essential album. *You're Gonna Miss Me* rounds up the finest cuts from Erickson's solo career, from a remake of "Bermuda" up to the slashing "Don't Slander Me" and "Don't Shake Me Lucifer." An alternately rocking and frightening compilation, it has fine liner notes by John Morthland. —*John Floyd*

Gloria Estefan & Miami Sound Machine

Dance-Pop, Latin Pop, Adult Contemporary, Pop-Rock, Club-Dance

More than any other pop group, Miami Sound Machine and lead singer Gloria Estefan (b. Jan. 9, 1957) have brought Latin-American (particularly Cuban) music into the mainstream. They originated out of the Miami Cuban community, and many of their early recordings were sung in Spanish. Their hits have included "Conga" (No. 10), "Bad Boy" (No. 8), "Words Get in the Way" (No. 5), "Anything for You" (No. 1), "1-2-3" (No. 9), and "Rhythm Is Gonna Get You" (No. 5).

In 1987, the group officially changed their name to Gloria Estefan & Miami Sound Machine. Not surprisingly, the following two years saw the direction of the group's music shift towards her vocals. In 1989, Estefan released her first solo album, *Cuts Both Ways*, which spawned the No. 1 hit "Don't Wanna Lose You."

The following year the group's tour bus was in a serious accident when traveling in New York. Estefan's vertebra was broken, and she underwent a successful surgery. Estefan's and the group's career was postponed for nearly a year due to the accident. She released *Into the Light* in 1991, which showed her inching toward adult-contemporary territory. She followed *Into the Light* with a Latin album, *Mi Tierra*, in 1993. The following year, she released a collection of covers called *Hold Me Thrill Me Kiss Me*. In 1995, Estefan released her second Latin album, *Abriendo Puertas*. The next year, she released *Destiny*. —*Rick Clark*

Eyes of Innocence / 1984 / Epic ✦✦

Primitive Love / 1986 / Epic ✦✦✦

Let It Loose / 1988 / Epic ✦✦✦✦
The group was still billed as "Gloria Estefan & Miami Sound Machine" on this album, which showed the singer and her bandleader husband, Emilio, retaining the jazzy, Latino flavor of their earlier music while moving determinedly into the pop mainstream and incidentally positioning Gloria as a superstar. Such goals were reached by a record that sold two million copies, went Top Ten, and produced the hits "Rhythm Is Gonna Get You," "Betcha Say That," "Can't Stay Away from You," "Anything for You," and "1-2-3." —*William Ruhlmann*

Cuts Both Ways / 1989 / Epic ✦✦✦
Dispensing with the "Miami Sound Machine" name, Estefan continued to successfully mix Latin-tinged dance numbers with strong ballads on this million-selling Top Ten solo album, which included "Don't Wanna Lose You," "Get on Your Feet," and "Here We Are." —*William Ruhlmann*

Into the Light / 1991 / Epic ✦✦✦
With this successful album, Estefan demonstrated that she had recovered from her serious accident of 1990. The album contains the telling hit "Coming out of the Dark" but showed her moving even farther toward the middle of the road and sacrificing her younger fans in the process—most of the singles from this album performed better on the adult-contemporary charts than on the Hot 100. —*William Ruhlmann*

● **Greatest Hits** / Oct. 6, 1992 / Epic ✦✦✦✦
All of Gloria Estefan's hits, with and without the Miami Sound Machine, are here, making *Greatest Hits* the best Estefan CD available. —*AMG*

Mi Tierra / Jun. 22, 1993 / Sony ✦✦✦✦

Hold Me Thrill Me Kiss Me / 1994 / Epic ✦✦✦

Abriendo Puertas / Sep. 26, 1995 / Epic ✦✦✦

Destiny / Jun. 1996 / Epic ✦✦✦

Melissa Etheridge

Guitar, Vocals / Rock 'n' Roll, Blues-Rock, Singer-Songwriter

Melissa Etheridge's gutsy electric blues-rock has earned her favorable comparisons to Rod Stewart and Janis Joplin, as well as a considerable fan base across America. Not only is she a solid live performer, but she has written several songs that have become AOR favorites since the late '80s, including "Bring Me Some Water" and "Similar Features." Although she earned some fans with her debut in 1988, her audience has increased with each new album. When she revealed that she is a lesbian in 1992, her commercial fortunes were not hurt at all; in fact, her audience continued to grow. Because it is rooted in the heart-break and turmoils of everyday life, Etheridge's music has a widespread appeal that makes her one of the top concert draws and AOR acts of the '90s. —*Stephen Thomas Erlewine*

● **Melissa Etheridge** / 1988 / Island ✦✦✦✦
A powerful debut with occasionally strident performances, it includes "Bring Me Some Water," a fine acoustic rocker. "Similar Features," a scathing indictment of a former lover, is a standout. *—Rick Clark*

Brave & Crazy / 1989 / Island ✦✦✦
A little more laidback offering than her self-titled debut, it includes reflective numbers like "Testify" and "You Used to Love to Dance." There are a few acoustic rockers like "My Back Door," "Skin Deep," and "Let Me Go." *—Rick Clark*

Never Enough / 1992 / Island ✦✦✦
Nothing here matches the raw power of "Bring Me Some Water," but this outing blends the thoughtful virtues of *Brave & Crazy* with the more rocking elements of her debut. Etheridge also synthesizes urban-dub rhythms and rap on tracks like "2001" (a single) and "Must Be Crazy for Me." It also includes the single "Ain't It Heavy." *—Rick Clark*

Yes I Am / 1993 / Island ✦✦✦✦
Etheridge's gutsy acoustic guitar-based rock is given a slightly more atmospheric treatment on this outing. Her voice is front and center in the mix and the instrumentation conveys power, but there is an evenness to the dynamics here that keep her natural theatrical delivery from totally getting across. Nevertheless, "All American Girl" is a highlight, as is "I'm the Only One." A good album, it's not her best. *—Rick Clark*

Your Little Secret / Nov. 14, 1995 / Island ✦✦

Eurythmics

Synth-pop, New Wave, Pop-Rock
Formed in December 1980 out of the ashes of the British band the Tourists, Eurythmics (comprising Dave Stewart and Annie Lennox) initially embraced the cool, clinical, synth-heavy sound of German ensembles like Kraftwerk or Can.

The musical element that immediately set Eurythmics apart from other techno artists was Lennox's powerful yet subtle voice, which could be extremely icy or soulful, depending on the requirements of the material. Stewart's production skills and multi-instrumental strengths usually provided all the right support.

Visually, Lennox toyed with androgyny as aggressively as David Bowie. As the '80s wore on, Eurythmics progressively infused soul and garage rock into their sound, producing an impressive string of hits. *—Rick Clark*

In the Garden / 1981 / RCA ✦✦

Sweet Dreams (Are Made of This) / Jan. 1983 / RCA ✦✦✦✦
Much commotion was caused by the MTV video clip for the hit title track from their breakthrough second album, which played up vocalist Annie Lennox's androgynous image. *—Donna DiChario*

Touch / Nov. 1983 / RCA ✦✦✦✦
The follow-up to the success of *Sweet Dreams* showed a more confident Lennox and Stewart, ready to expand their stylistic range. It contains the Top 40 hits "Here Comes the Rain Again," "Who's That Girl," and "Right by Your Side." *—Scott Bultman*

1984 (For the Love of Big Brother) / Nov. 1984 / RCA ✦✦

Be Yourself Tonight / May 1985 / RCA ✦✦✦✦
Showing sparks of Motown influence with the hit "Would I Lie to You?" and others, Stevie Wonder adds a harmonica solo to "There Must Be an Angel." *—Donna DiChario*

Revenge / Jul. 1986 / RCA ✦✦✦

Savage / Nov. 1987 / RCA ✦✦

We Too Are One / Sep. 1989 / Arista ✦✦✦

● **Greatest Hits** / 1991 / Arista ✦✦✦✦
Whether cool and sophisticated or impassioned and soulful, this duo of singer Annie Lennox and guitarist Dave Stewart creates stylish and compelling rock. *—Donna DiChario*

Live 1983-1989 / 1993 / Arista ✦✦

Betty Everett

Piano, Vocals / Soul
Betty Everett sang gospel growing up in Greenwood, MS, before relocating to Chicago and moving into secular music. She began recording for Cobra in 1958, then joined Vee-Jay in the early '60s and started to land hit records. Her original version of "You're No Good," though sung with fire and verve, didn't make much impact until it was turned into a No. 1 pop hit by Linda Ronstadt in 1975. Her next single, "The Shoop Shoop Song (It's in His Kiss)" was her first major release, peaking at No. 6 pop in 1964. Her next success was the duet "Let It Be Me" with Jerry Butler, a soul version of the Everly Brothers tune that reached No. 5 R&B that same year. Everett's finest song as a solo act was 1969's "There Comes a Time," which reached No. 2 on the R&B charts and also cracked the pop Top 30 at No. 26. Everett was now on Uni, where she remained until

1970. She continued recording for Fantasy until 1974 and made one other record for United Artists in 1978. *—Ron Wynn*

There'll Come a Time / 1969 / Varese Sarabande ✦✦✦✦
Everett made her best records for Vee-Jay in the mid-'60s, but this album, originally released on Uni in 1969, isn't far behind in merit. Featuring her No. 2 R&B single (and Top 40 pop hit) "There'll Come a Time," this has much more of a sweet soul flavor than her Vee-Jay sides, at times blending the trademarks of her brassy native Chicago scene with a Philadelphia influence. It's far from *too* sweet, though, with strong material, punchy arrangements, and Everett's always dependably energetic and warm vocals. Also contains the R&B hit "I Can't Say No to You"; the CD reissue adds three valuable 1969-70 singles that were previously unavailable on album, including the Top 20 R&B hit "It's Been a Long Time," arranged by Donny Hathaway and written by Kenny Gamble, Leon Huff, and Jerry Butler. *—Richie Unterberger*

● **The Shoop Shoop Song** / 1993 / Vee-Jay ✦✦✦✦
Though sometimes classified as a "girl group" singer because of the Top Ten success of "The Shoop Shoop Song," Betty Everett's main thrust was much more in the R&B/soul vein. This excellent 25-track anthology of her 1963-65 material shows her facility with various soul, R&B, and pop styles. She had three other minor hits—the original hit version of "You're No Good," the energetic Goffin/King pop-rocker "I Can't Hear You," and Van McCoy's soulful "Gettin' Mighty Crowded"—all of which are featured here. But most of the other material is equally enjoyable, including other early efforts by McCoy, Valerie Simpson, Nick Ashford, and even P.F. Sloan (whose "Can I Get to Know You" is presented in a much earlier, slower version here than the Turtles' rendition several years later). This CD doesn't include her hit duets with fellow Chicago soulster Jerry Butler, but is a consistently enjoyable retrospective of an underrated singer who straddled the soul and pop worlds. *—Richie Unterberger*

The Fantasy Years / 1995 / Fantasy ✦✦✦

The Everly Brothers

Rock 'n' Roll, Country-Rock, Pop-Rock
The Everly Brothers were not only among the most important and best early rock 'n' roll stars, but also among the most influential rockers of any era. They set unmatched standards for close, two-part harmonies, and infused early rock 'n' roll with some of the best elements of country and pop music. Their legacy was and is felt enormously in all rock acts that employ harmonies as prime features, from the Beatles, Simon & Garfunkel, and legions of country-rockers to modern-day roots rockers like Dave Edmunds and Nick Lowe (who once recorded an EP of Everlys songs together).

Don (b. Feb. 1, 1937) and Phil (b. Jan. 19, 1939) were professionals way before their teens, schooled by their accomplished guitarist father Ike, and singing with their family on radio broadcasts in Iowa. In the mid-'50s, they made a brief stab at conventional Nashville country with Columbia. When their single flopped, they were cast adrift for quite a while until they latched onto Cadence. Don invested their first single for the label, "Bye Bye Love," with a Bo Diddley beat that helped lift the song to No. 2 in 1957.

"Bye Bye Love" began a phenomenal three-year string of classic hit singles for Cadence, including "Wake Up Little Susie," "All I Have to Do Is Dream," "Bird Dog," "'Til I Kissed You," and "When Will I Be Loved." The Everlys sang of young love with a heart-rending yearning and compelling melodies. The harmonies owed audible debts to Appalachian country music, but were imbued with a keen modern pop sensibility that made them more accessible without sacrificing any power or beauty. They were not as raw as the wild rockabilly men from Sun Records, but they could rock hard when they wanted. Even their mid-tempo numbers and ballads were executed with a force missing in the straight country and pop tunes of the era. The duo enjoyed a top-notch support team of producer Archie Bleyer, great Nashville session players like Chet Atkins, and the brilliant songwriting team of Boudleaux and Felice Bryant. Don, and occasionally Phil, wrote excellent songs of their own as well.

In 1960, the Everlys left Cadence for a lucrative contract with the then-young Warner Bros. label (though it's not often noted, the Everlys would do a lot to establish Warners as a major force in the record business). It's sometimes been written that the duo never recaptured the magic of their Cadence recordings, but actually Phil and Don peaked both commercially and artistically with their first Warners releases. "Cathy's Clown," their first Warners single, was one of their greatest songs and a No. 1 hit. Their first two Warners LPs, employing a fuller and brasher production than their Cadence work, were not just among their best work, but two of the best rock albums of the early '60s. The hits kept coming for a couple of years, some great ("Walk Right Back," "Temptation"), some displaying a distressing, increasing tendency toward soft pop and maudlin sentiments ("Ebony Eyes," "That's Old Fashioned").

Don and Phil's personal lives came under a lot of stress in the early '60s: They were drafted into the Army (together), and studied acting for six months, but never made a motion picture. More seriously, Don developed an addiction to speed and almost died of an overdose in late 1962. By that time, their career as chart titans in the US had ended; "That's Old Fashioned" (1962) was their last Top Ten hit. Their albums became careless, erratic affairs, which was all the more frustrating because many of their flop singles of the time were fine, even near-classic efforts that demonstrated they could still deliver the goods. Virtually alone among first-generation rock 'n' roll superstars, the Everlys stuck with no-nonsense rock 'n' roll and remained determined to keep their sound contemporary, rather than drifting toward soft pop or country like so many others. Although their mid-'60s recordings were largely ignored in America, they contained some of their finest work, including a ferocious Top 40 single in 1964 ("Gone, Gone, Gone"). They remained big stars overseas—in 1965, "Price of Love" went to No. 2 in the UK at the height of the British Invasion. They incorporated jangling (Beatle-Byrdesque) guitars into some of their songs, and recorded a fine album with the Hollies (who were probably more blatantly influenced by the Everlys than any other British band of the time). In the late '60s, they helped pioneer country-rock with the 1968 album *Roots*, their most sophisticated and unified full-length statement. None of this revived their career as hit-makers, though they could always command huge audiences on international tours, and hosted a network TV variety show in 1970.

The decades of enforced professional togetherness finally took their toll on the pair in the early '70s, which saw a few dispirited albums and, finally, an acriminious breakup in 1973. They spent the next decade performing solo, which only proved—as is so often the case in close-knit artistic partnerships—how much each brother needed the other to sound his best. In 1983, enough water had flowed under the bridge for the two to resume performing and recording together. The tours, with a backup band led by guitarist Albert Lee, proved they could still sing well. The records (both live and studio) were fair efforts that, in the final estimation, were not in nearly the same league as their '50s and '60s classics, although Paul McCartney penned a small hit single for them ("On the Wings of a Nightingale"). Although it was one of the most successful and dignified reunions in rock annals, this, too, could not last; as of this writing, the Everlys have not performed or recorded together since the early '90s. —*Richie Unterberger*

The Everly Brothers [Cadence] / 1958 / Cadence ♦♦♦♦
Although the Everlys hadn't quite fully matured as artists, their debut is a fine, consistent effort divided between original material and respectably energetic covers of early rockers by Little Richard, Gene Vincent, and Ray Charles. Besides their first few hits, it includes some superb, underappreciated tracks that are nearly as good, like "Should We Tell Him" and "I Wonder If I Care as Much." —*Richie Unterberger*

Songs Our Daddy Taught Us / 1958 / Rhino ♦♦♦
The Everlys had reached their commercial peak when they made this album of sparsely arranged traditional songs, a concept that was quite a surprise from a top rock 'n' roll act, and considerably ahead of its time. It's actually not as enduring as their early rockers and pop ballads, but the singing is superb in their interpretations of standards like "Barbara Allen" and "Kentucky." —*Richie Unterberger*

The Fabulous Style of the Everly Brothers / 1960 / Rhino ♦♦♦♦
The best of their original Cadence albums, packed with hits ("Bird Dog," "All I Have to Do Is Dream," "When Will I Be Loved," "'Til I Kissed You"), and other classic tracks ("Devoted to You," "Let It Be Me," "Since You Broke My Heart," "Like Strangers"). Almost all of the songs show up on their greatest hits collections, so it might be a superfluous purchase for all but serious fans, despite its top-drawer quality. —*Richie Unterberger*

It's Everly Time / 1960 / Warner Bros. ♦♦♦♦
While the Everlys' sound was diluted by more elaborate production in the '60s, that's not at all true on this LP, which is one of their very best. Not a stiff among the 12 tracks, most of which are barely known outside of serious Everly fans. Includes six stellar contributions by Boudleaux and Felice Bryant, one of Don Everly's best compositions ("So Sad"), and incredible harmony singing throughout. —*Richie Unterberger*

A Date with the Everly Brothers / 1961 / Warner Bros. ♦♦♦♦
Although the material is not on the killer level of *Everly Time*, there are some very fine songs on their second Warner LP. Includes "Cathy's Clown," their raucous cover of Little Richard's "Lucille," "Love Hurts" (which preceded Roy Orbison's hit version), and "So How Come" (covered by the Beatles in 1963 on the BBC). —*Richie Unterberger*

The Very Best of the Everly Brothers [Warner Bros.] / Aug. 1964 / Warner Bros. ♦
The operative word here is: Beware. This does indeed have 12 of their biggest hits, but half of them are re-recorded versions of Cadence-era material. It's not that they're bad or radically different (after all, they were recorded only a few years later). But why settle for these when only the originals will do? —*Richie Unterberger*

Two Yanks in England / 1966 / Demon ♦♦♦

Roots / 1968 / Warner Bros. ♦♦♦♦
Considered one of the finest early country-rock albums, this showed the

Everlys, unlike virtually every other top rock 'n' roll act of the '50s, keeping abreast of contemporary rock and pop trends. In the manner of their 1958 LP *Songs Our Daddy Taught Us*, the concept was to cover songs by performers and composers that had been influential on the duo, including Jimmie Rodgers, Merle Haggard, traditional standards, and a couple of numbers by Ron Elliott of the Beau Brummels. Although this laid-back, tasteful, acoustic-oriented recording isn't as outstanding as their classic early hits, the vocals are superb, conveying qualities of innocence tempered by experience. —*Richie Unterberger*

All They Had to Do Was Dream / 1985 / Rhino ♦♦♦
Alternate takes of much of their strongest material from the Cadence era, cut between 1957 and 1960. A bit more tentative than the familiar renditions, these aren't as good as the versions that ended up on official releases, but are enjoyable and fascinating glimpses of works in progress, and the singing is excellent throughout. Includes different versions of hits like "Wake Up, Little Susie," "All I Have to Do is Dream," "'Til I Kissed You," and "When Will I Be Loved." —*Richie Unterberger*

★ **Cadence Classics: Their 20 Greatest Hits** / 1986 / Rhino ♦♦♦♦♦
The single-disc collection *Cadence Classics: Their 20 Greatest Hits* compiles all of the Everly Brothers' hits, plus many terrific album tracks, from the duo's recordings for Cadence Records in the late '50s. Every one of the Everlys' biggest hits, including "Bye Bye Love," "I Wonder If I Care as Much," "Wake Up, Little Susie," "This Little Girl of Mine," "All I Have to Do Is Dream," "Claudette," "Bird Dog," "Devoted to You," "Problems," "Message to Mary," "('Til) I Kissed You," "Let It Be Me," and "When Will I Be Loved." *Cadence Classics* misses no essential track, making it a definitive collection and the perfect introduction to the duo's sound. —*Stephen Thomas Erlewine*

Hidden Gems from the Warner Years / 1989 / Ace ♦♦♦♦
This collects 14 songs that originally appeared on nonhit singles between 1962 and 1965; many of them had never been on LP. This material strongly counters the view that the Everlys faded artistically after "Cathy's Clown." The writing credits for these strong compositions read a bit like a who's who of early-'60s pop-rock, with contributions from Gerry Goffin, Mann/Weill, Doc Pomus & Mort Shuman, Sonny Curtis, Boudleaux and Felice Bryant, and the Everlys themselves. The singing is fabulous, and the arrangements still strong, rock-oriented, and tastefully produced. Tracks like "Nancy's Minuet" (1963), a great Don Everly original and one of their best paeans to lovelorn melancholia, and "You're the One I Love" (1964), a fine, brooding midtempo rocker, stand with their very best work. Only three of these appear on the '60s Everlys anthology *Walk Right Back*, making this a necessary purchase for Everlys fans. —*Richie Unterberger*

☆ **Walk Right Back: The Everly Brothers on Warner Bros.** / 1993 / Warner Archives ♦♦♦♦♦
This two-CD, 50-track compilation assembles the Everly Brothers' most memorable recordings of the 1960s. Although their work from this period has sometimes been criticized as inferior to their classic '50s recordings for Cadence, the best of these songs are a match for anything the duo recorded. As it happens, the strongest of these tunes are drawn from their first two albums for Warners in the 1960s, including the hits "Cathy's Clown" and "So Sad." In the following years, their material suffered from increasing inconsistency and ill-suited production. Yet the Brothers continued to intermittently hit the mark squarely—not only with early-'60s hits like "Crying in the Rain" and "Temptation," but neglected flop singles like "Nancy's Minuet" and "You're the One I Love," as well as the hard-rocking minor 1964 hit "Gone Gone Gone" (their last Top 40 single). They also showed a willingness to incorporate the hard-rocking beat of the British Invasion into their work that was not shared by any of the other major stars of the '50s. This compilation misses a number of fine B-sides and nonhit singles from the early and mid-'60s (check the Ace import collection *Hidden Gems* for those), and perhaps leans too heavily on their tepid late-'60s country-rock. But it's a good overview of a body of work that is often unfairly overlooked. —*Richie Unterberger*

The Mercury Years / Jul. 20, 1993 / Mercury ♦♦♦♦

☆ **Heartaches & Harmonies [Box Set]** / 1994 / Rhino ♦♦♦♦♦
This four-CD, 102-song set includes all of their key performances, as well as many overlooked ones, dating from a previously unreleased 1951 radio performance of "Don't Let Our Love Die" to a 1990 live rendition of the very same tune. Opening with a disc's worth of classic Cadence performances, most of the next five CDs are given over to their largely overlooked Warner Bros. '60s output, including many interesting flop singles and album tracks, as well as top-notch rarities like an alternate version of the supremely moody "Nancy's Minuet" and the mid-'60s outtake "And I'll Go." Fine liner notes with detailed comments from the Everlys themselves, but it still manages to miss some great tunes (like the 1964 single "You're the One I Love" and various tracks from their late-'50s and early-'60s LPs), and shouldn't be considered a definitive collection of all their great performances. And the hard fact is, a lot of their

post-1966 material (which comprises some of disc three and all of disc four) is kind of boring. —*Richie Unterberger*

Everything but the Girl

Alternative Pop-Rock, Pop-Rock, Club-Dance
As Everything but the Girl, the duo of Ben Watt (guitars, keyboards, vocals) and Tracey Thorn (guitar, vocals) first found success at the forefront of the British neo-jazz-pop movement of the mid-'80s, typified by other artists such as Sade and Swing out Sister. The two met while students at Hull University and took their name from a local furniture shop slogan; both had recorded solo, Watt had worked with Robert Wyatt, and Thorn had been a member of the Marine Girls. Their 1984 debut *Eden* was also one of their best, effectively showcasing the group's unique, sophisticated sound and Thorn's vocal talent. Everything but the Girl scored a No. 3 UK hit in 1988 with a cover of Danny Whitten's "I Don't Want to Talk About It." Subsequent releases found the duo moving towards mature, adult love songs, but American audiences largely missed out; Everything but the Girl was too light for rock radio and too distinctive for light-rock airplay. However, that all changed in 1995, when the track "Missing," from the previous year's *Amplified Heart*, was remixed and became a US pop smash, peaking at No. 2 in *Billboard*. The exposure helped their next album, *Walking Wounded*, reach their highest chart position to date in America. —*Steve Huey*

Everything but the Girl / 1984 / Sire ✦✦✦

Love Not Money / Apr. 1985 / Sire ✦✦✦

Baby, the Stars Shine Bright / Aug. 1986 / Sire ✦✦✦

● **Idlewild** / Feb. 1988 / Sire ✦✦✦✦
Thorn and Watt made a couple of albums with a cocktail-jazz backup and one with strings before trying a small unit for the intimate songs of their most accessible recording. The setting is perfect for such moving compositions as "Love Is Here Where I Live" and "Apron Strings." Start here, then go on to the rest of this remarkable group's catalog. —*William Ruhlmann*

The Language of Life / Jan. 1990 / Atlantic ✦✦

Worldwide / Sep. 1991 / Atlantic ✦✦✦

Acoustic / Jun. 1992 / Atlantic ✦✦

Amplified Heart / Jul. 19, 1994 / Atlantic ✦✦✦
Despite its title, *Amplified Heart* is one of Everything but the Girl's more acoustic works. A simple instrumentation of guitars and keyboards, augmented here and there by British folk-rock veterans like Richard Thompson, Danny Thompson, and Dave Mattacks, serves to set up a series of songs of romantic disillusionment. Declaring "My life is just an image of a roller coaster, anyway" and "I don't understand anything," among other things, over and over the songs speak of confusion and disappointment deriving from failed love affairs. The approach is much more introspective than that taken on the group's last new original album, *Worldwide*, but Tracey Thorn and Ben Watt's musical restraint supports it well. This is an album to listen to when you've just broken up with your lover, or even when you're just in the mood to think about lost lovers from long ago—self-pity set to music. —*William Ruhlmann*

Walking Wounded / May 21, 1996 / Atlantic ✦✦✦✦
With *Walking Wounded*, Everything but the Girl put an acceptable face on trip-hop, jungle, and techno, opening up the world of experimental dance music to a new audience. At its core, Everything but the Girl is a pop group, which means they automatically abandon the free-form song structures that characterize most of trip-hop and techno. In a sense, that dilutes the impact of the music, but the duo has found a way around that by seamlessly incorporating the rhythms into carefully crafted songs. They work the same ground as Massive Attack, but their songwriting is more accessible and less adventerous than the ground-breaking Bristol group. Furthermore, Everything but the Girl never approach the tarnished glamour of Portishead, the kineticism of Björk, or the brilliantly evocative soundscapes of Tricky. Essentially, the beats are used as window dressing—the group's music hasn't changed that much. And while the change of pace is refreshing, it only adds a slight new dimension to the duo's sound and that is at the expense of the music they are trying to incorporate into their own style. —*Stephen Thomas Erlewine*

The Exciters

Girl Group
Despite the presence of lone male Herb Rooney, the Exciters made some of the best girl-group records of the early '60s. Led by vibrant-voiced Brenda Reid, the originally all-female quartet came from Jamaica, NY, as the Masterettes. After signing on with saxist Al Sears as their manager, they switched their name to the Exciters and cut "Tell Him" in 1962 for United Artists. Produced by Jerry Leiber and Mike Stoller, the brilliant uptown soul effort proved a major smash. Reid's roaring pipes were expertly spotlighted on the follow-ups "He's Got the Power," "Get Him," and their original reading of "Do-Wah-Diddy," immortalized later that

year by Manfred Mann. The group later appeared on Roulette, Band, Shout, and RCA. Reid and Rooney were married for a time, and Reid now performs with her children backing her. —*Bill Dahl*

● **Tell Him /EMI Legends of Rock 'n' Roll Series** / 1991 / EMI America ✦✦✦✦
This girl-group R&B have full-fledged, violin-laden productions backing Brenda Reid's soul-drenched lead vocals. —*Bill Dahl*

Fabian

Vocals / Pop, Teen Idol, Brill Building Pop
Thanks to a series of performances on Dick Clark's "American Bandstand," Fabian rocketed to stardom in the late '60s. With his stylish good looks and mild rock 'n' roll, he became one of the top teen idols of the era; luckily, he had the support of the legendary songwriting team of Doc Pomus and Mort Shuman, who provided him with "Turn Me Loose," "Hound Dog Man," and "I'm a Man," among other songs. Fabian's fame peaked in 1959 with the million-selling "Tiger" single; after that, he valiantly tried to become a movie star. When Congress fingered him as one of the performers who benefited from payola, his already ailing career was given a nearly fatal blow; under questioning, Fabian explained that his records featured a substantial amount of electronic doctoring in order to improve his voice. After the hearings, he starred in some more movies in the '60s, without regaining the audience of his peak years. —*Stephen Thomas Erlewine*

● **The Best of Fabian** / 1995 / Varese Vintage ✦✦✦✦
Compared to some import collections that are available, this ten-song CD is on the skimpy side. But it does include all of his late-'50s and early-'60s chart hits, which should satisfy all but obsessively rabid collectors, and as a domestic release, it's considerably cheaper and more readily available than the other comps. —*Richie Unterberger*

The Fabulous Thunderbirds

Group / Rock 'n' Roll, Blues-Rock, Electric Texas Blues
The Fabulous Thunderbirds are one of the finest examples of Texas roadhouse R&B-electric blues. The original lineup featured the taut lead-guitar work of Jimmie Vaughan (Stevie Ray's brother). Kim Wilson, the band's frontman, is a master of rude harmonica playing. After years of fine album releases and endless gigging, this journeyman Austin band hit it big in 1986 with the No. 10 title cut off the Dave Edmunds-produced *Tuff Enuff*. Since then they've continued to enjoy a string of hits, including a remake of Sam & Dave's "Wrap It Up," "Stand Back," and "Powerful Stuff," featured in the Tom Cruise film *Cocktail*. In 1990 Vaughan left the group and was replaced by Kid Bangham and Duke Robillard. After one more album, the group called it quits, with Wilson pursuing a solo career. —*Rick Clark*

Fabulous Thunderbirds / 1979 / Chrysalis ✦✦✦✦
Their debut album, with the original lineup of Wilson, Vaughn, Buck, and Ferguson stompin' through a roadhouse set of covers and originals. One of the few White blues albums that works. —*Cub Koda*

What's the Word / 1980 / Chrysalis ✦✦✦✦
Second album, equally powerful. Some of their best, including the off-kilter "Los Fabulosos Thunderbirds" and "Running Shoes." —*Cub Koda*

Tuff Enuff / 1986 / Epic ✦✦✦

Hot Number / 1987 / Epic ✦✦

Powerful Stuff / 1989 / Epic ✦✦

The Essential / 1991 / Chrysalis ✦✦✦✦
Nice compilation of the early Chrysalis albums. —*Cub Koda*

Walk That Walk, Talk That Talk / Dec. 1991 / Epic ✦✦✦

● **Hot Stuff: The Greatest Hits** / 1992 / Epic ✦✦✦✦
The best tracks from the Fabulous Thunderbirds' more rock-oriented years at CBS Associated Records are collected on this single-disc compilation. —*Stephen Thomas Erlewine*

Roll of the Dice / 1995 / Private Music ✦✦✦
The Fabulous T-Birds' second album without Jimmie Vaughan is an improvement over *Walk That Walk, Talk That Talk*, featuring a tighter, more focused band and hotter playing. Nevertheless, the band takes a couple of missteps, particularly with a limp version of "Zip-a-Dee-Doo-Dah." —*Stephen Thomas Erlewine*

Faces

Rock 'n' Roll
When Steve Marriott left the Small Faces in 1969, the three remaining members brought in guitarist Ron Wood and lead singer Rod Stewart to complete the lineup and changed their name to the Faces, which was only appropriate since the group now only slightly resembled the mod-pop group of the past. Instead, the Faces were a rough, sloppy rock 'n' roll band, able to pound out a rocker like "Had Me a Real Good Time," a blues ballad like "Tell Everyone," or a folk number like "Richmond" all in

one album. Stewart, already becoming a star in his own right, let himself go wild with the Faces, tearing through covers and originals with abandon. While his voice didn't have the power of Stewart, bassist Ronnie Lane's songs were equally as impressive and eclectic. Wood's rhythm guitar had a warm, fat tone that was as influential and driving as Keith Richards' style.

Notorious for their hard-partying and ragged concerts, the Faces lived the rock 'n' roll life-style to the extreme. When Stewart's solo career became more successful than the Faces', the band slowly became subservient to his personality; after their final studio album, *Ooh La La*, in 1973, Lane left the band. After a tour in 1974, they called it quits. Wood joined the Rolling Stones, drummer Kenny Jones eventually became part of the Who, and keyboardist Ian McLagan came to become a sought-after supporting musician; Stewart became a superstar, although he never matched the simple charms of the Faces.

While they were together, the Faces never sold that many records and were never considered as important as the Stones, yet their music has proven vastly influential over the years. Many punk rockers in the late '70s learned how to play their instruments by listening to Faces records; in the '80s and '90s, guitar-rock bands from the Replacements to the Black Crowes took their cue from the Faces as much as the Stones. Their reckless, loose, and joyous spirit has stayed alive in much of the best rock 'n' roll of the past two decades. *—Stephen Thomas Erlewine*

First Step / 1970 / Warner Bros. ♦♦♦♦
On their first album, the Faces established the pattern they would follow throughout their four albums—a ragged mix of breakneck rockers ("Shake, Shudder"), sensitive yet gritty ballads ("Devotion"), folk songs ("Stone"), revelatory covers (Bob Dylan's "Wicked Messenger"), and relaxed, friendly rockers ("Three Button Hand Me Down"). Although two instrumentals on the second side is one too many (Ron Wood's "Pineapple and the Monkey" is pretty great), the Faces seldom got better than the first half of *First Step*. *—Stephen Thomas Erlewine*

☆ **Long Player** / 1971 / Warner Bros. ♦♦♦♦♦
With their second effort, the Faces grew more muscular and loose, rocking with loose abandon on "Bad N' Ruin" and "Had Me a Real Good Time," two of their best songs. At the same time, their ballads also improved, with Stewart's "Tell Everyone" and Lane's "Richmond" rivaling each other for the most touching number on the album. Out of the two live tracks, "Balling the Jack" goes on a little too long, but "Maybe I'm Amazed" is tremendous—the Faces tear into the song, transforming it from a McCartney ballad to a heartfelt cry of devotion. *Long Player* is a sloppy, terrific record; although it may have a couple of weak moments, it has the heart and soul of the band. *—Stephen Thomas Erlewine*

★ **A Nod Is as Good as a Wink . . . to a Blind Horse** / 1971 / Warner Bros. ♦♦♦♦♦
Boasting "Stay with Me," the only hit the Faces ever had, *A Nod is as Good as a Wink* is their most consistent record, and arguably their best. "Stay with Me" and "Miss Judy's Farm" showcase the band at their best—they're all over the place, threatening to fall apart altogether before they snap it all back into place. Nobody rocked better than this, and the album is full of such terrific moments, including a rollicking cover of Chuck Berry's "Memphis." As with all of the Faces' albums, it's a little messy, but it is a classic rock 'n' roll band at the top of their form. *—Stephen Thomas Erlewine*

Ooh La La / 1973 / Warner Bros. ♦♦♦

Snakes & Ladders / 1976 / Warner Bros. ♦♦♦

Donald Fagen

b. Jan. 10, 1948, Passaic, NJ
Keyboards / Soft Rock, Pop-Rock
Donald Fagen was one of the two masterminds behind Steely Dan, the seminal jazz-pop band of the '70s. Fagen's solo work has been a continuation of the band's work of the early '80s—carefully constructed and arranged, intricately detailed pop songs that are more substantial than their stylish surface may indicate. His 1982 solo debut, *The Nightfly*, was the best album he had made in years; it covered the same ground as the last two Steely Dan albums, yet surpassed it in terms of ambition and achievement.

After the success of *The Nightfly*, Fagen suffered a case of writer's block; for the rest of the decade he contributed music to the occasional film and briefly wrote a column for *Premiere* magazine in the mid-'80s. In the early '90s, he toured with the New York Rock & Soul Revue as he finished the material for his second album. With his former Steely Dan partner Walter Becker producing, 1993's *Kamakiriad* sounded like *Aja* recorded with '90s technology. It had some success on the adult-contemporary charts, but it was overshadowed by the duo's decision to re-form Steely Dan and tour for the first time in nearly 20 years; the tour was a massive success. *—Stephen Thomas Erlewine*

★ **The Nightfly** / Oct. 1982 / Warner Bros. ♦♦♦♦♦
For his debut solo album after leaving Steely Dan, Fagen turned in a typ-

ically sophisticated jazz-pop collection tied to a lyrical theme concerning the late '50s and early '60s. One song takes the Kennedy administration's slogan, "The New Frontier," as a title, while another, "The Goodbye Look," is set in Cuba around the time of Castro's takeover. Steely Dan lovers will feel right at home. *—William Ruhlmann*

Kamakiriad / May 25, 1993 / Reprise ♦♦♦♦
After 11 years, Donald Fagen delivered his second album, *Kamakiriad*, in the summer of 1993. Where the sophisticated eclecticism of *The Nightfly* was warm and welcoming, *Kamakiriad* is insular; it takes several listens before all of the pieces fall into place. While all of the album *sounds* terrific, the melodies are subtler and tend to get buried under the meticulous arrangements. However, the hooks and melodies emerge after a couple of plays, as do Fagen's wry, witty lyrics. *—Stephen Thomas Erlewine*

Fairport Convention

Folk-Rock, British Folk
The best British folk-rock band of the late '60s, Fairport Convention did more than any other act to develop a truly British variation on the folk-rock prototype by drawing upon traditional material and styles indigenous to the British Isles. While the revved-up renditions of traditional British folk tunes drew the most critical attention, the group were also (at least at the outset) talented songwriters as well as interpreters. They were comfortable with conventional harmony-based folk-rock as well as tunes that drew upon more explicitly traditional sources, and boasted some of the best singers and instrumentalists of the day. A revolving door of personnel changes, however, saw the exit of their most distinguished talents, and basically changed the band into a living museum piece after the early '70s, albeit an enjoyable one with integrity.

When Fairport formed around 1967, their goal was not to revive British folk numbers, but to play harmony- and guitar-based folk-rock in a style influenced by Californian groups of the day (especially the Byrds). The lineup that recorded their self-titled debut album in 1968 featured Richard Thompson, Ian Matthews, and Simon Nicol on guitars; Ashley Hutchings on bass; Judy Dyble on vocals; and Martin Lamble on drums. Most of the members sang, though Matthews and Dyble were the strongest vocalists in this early incarnation; all of their early work, in fact, was characterized by blends of male and female vocals, influenced by such American acts as the Mamas and the Papas and Ian & Sylvia. While their first album was derivative, it had some fine material, and the band was already showing a knack for eclecticism, excavating overlooked songs by Joni Mitchell (then virtually unknown) and Emitt Rhodes.

Fairport didn't reach their peak until Dyble was replaced after the first album in 1968 by Sandy Denny, who had previously recorded both as a solo act and with the Strawbs. Denny's penetrating, resonant style qualified her as the best British folk-rock singer of all time, and provided the band with the best vocalist they would ever have. *What We Did on Our Holidays* (1968) and *Unhalfbricking* (1969) are their best albums, mixing strong originals, excellent covers of contemporary folk-rock songs by the likes of Mitchell and Dylan, and imaginative revivals of traditional folk songs that mixed electric and acoustic instruments with a beguiling ease.

Matthews had left the band in early 1969, and Lamble (still in his teens) died in an accident involving the group's equipment van in mid-1969. That forced Fairport to regroup, replacing Lamble with Dave Mattacks, and adding Dave Swarbrick on fiddle. Their repertoire, too, became much more traditional in focus, and electrified traditional folk numbers would dominate their next album, *Liege and Lief* (1969). Here critical thought diverges; some insist that this is unequivocally their peak, marking a final escape from their '60s folk-rock influences into a much more original style. This school of thought severely underestimates their songwriting talents, and others feel that they were at their best when mixing original and outside material, and contemporary and traditional styles, in fact becoming more predictable and derivative when they opted to concentrate on British folk chestnuts.

The *Liege and Lief* lineup didn't last long; by the end of the '60s, Ashley Hutchings had left to join Steeleye Span, replaced by Dave Pegg. More crucially, Denny was also gone, helping to form Fotheringay. Thompson was still on board for *Full House* (1970), but by the beginning of 1971 he too, had departed, leaving Nicol as the only original member.

Fairport have kept going, on and off (mostly on), for the last 25 years, touring and performing frequently. It may be too harsh to dismiss all of their post-Thompson records out of hand; *Angel Delight* (1971), the first recorded without the guitarist on board, was actually their highest-charting LP in the UK, reaching the Top Ten. Nicol's exit in late 1971 erased all vestiges of connections to their salad days. Fairport was now not so much a continuous entity as a concept, carried on by musicians dedicated to the electrified British folk style that had been mapped out on *Liege and Lief*.

So it continues to this day, supported by a devoted fan base (*Dirty Linen*, the top American roots music magazine, originally began as a

Fairport Convention fanzine). Denny would actually return to the group for about a year and a half in the 1970s, prior to her death in 1978; Nicol rejoined in 1976. Keeping track of Fairport's multitudinous lineup changes is a daunting task, and the group has coexisted on an erratic basis with the various other projects of the most frequent members (Nicol, Mattacks, and Pegg, the last of whom has played with Jethro Tull since the late '70s). They have played annual reunion concerts during the '80s and '90s (sometimes joined onstage by Fairport alumni like Thompson), events that have turned into one of the most popular folk festivals in Europe. They've also released some albums of new material intermittently throughout the last couple of decades, mostly pleasant, unexceptional traditional-oriented outings that appeal mainly to diehards.

The most distinguished graduates of Fairport, however, have continued to shape the British folk and folk-rock scene with notable solo and group projects. Richard Thompson is one of the most critically acclaimed singer-songwriters in the world; Ian Matthews made some interesting recordings as a solo act, and with Plainsong and Matthews Southern Comfort; Denny sang with Fotheringay, and released several solo albums, before her death; and Hutchings carried on the most traditional face of British folk-rock with Steeleye Span, the Albion Band, and the Etchingham Steam Band. — *Richie Unterberger*

Fairport Convention [1st] / Jun. 1968 / Polydor ✦✦✦✦
By far the most rock-oriented of Fairport's early albums, this was recorded before Denny joined the band (Judy Dyble handles the female vocals). Unjustly overlooked by listeners who consider the band's pre-Denny output insignificant, this is a fine folk-rock effort that takes far more inspiration from West Coast '60s sounds than traditional British folk. Good originals and excellent covers of a variety of obscure tunes by Joni Mitchell, Dylan, Emmitt Rhodes, and Jim & Jean. — *Richie Unterberger*

What We Did on Our Holidays / Jan. 1969 / Hannibal ✦✦✦✦
Sandy Denny's haunting, ethereal vocals give Fairport a big boost on her debut with the group. A more folk-based album than their initial effort, divided between original material and a few well-chosen covers. This contains several of their greatest moments: Sandy Denny's "Fotheringay," Richard Thompson's "Meet on the Ledge," the obscure Joni Mitchell composition "Eastern Rain," the traditional "She Moves Through the Fair," and their version of Dylan's "I'll Keep It with Mine." — *Richie Unterberger*

★ **Unhalfbricking** / Jul. 1969 / Hannibal ✦✦✦✦✦
Richard Thompson and Sandy Denny at their Fairport peak; three Dylan tunes, including the hit "Si Tu Dois Partir," and Denny's "Who Knows Where the Time Goes." This is worth owning just for the apocalyptic "A Sailor's Life." — *William Ruhlmann & Bruce Eder*

☆ **Liege and Lief** / Dec. 1969 / A&M ✦✦✦✦✦
This was Sandy Denny's exit album, highlighted by the scintillating "Tam Lin" and "Matty Groves." Voted the Best Folk Album of All Time by the readers of Britain's *Folk Roots* magazine, it features Thompson and Denny along with fiddler Dave Swarbrick. — *Steve Winick & Bruce Eder & William Ruhlmann*

Full House / Jul. 1970 / Hannibal ✦✦✦
Denny and bass player Ashley Hutchings are gone. Thompson and Swarbrick take over as singers, while Dave Pegg (now also of Jethro Tull) plays bass. — *Steve Winick*

Angel Delight / Jun. 1971 / A&M ✦✦✦
After Richard Thompson's departure, Fairport continued as a guitar-fiddle-bass-drums quartet, its dominant presence being violinist/singer Dave Swarbrick, who led the group in even more of a traditional British folk vein. But the loss of Fairport's big guns, Sandy Denny and Thompson, was felt, and this was a minor, if pleasant, effort. — *William Ruhlmann*

Babbacombe Lee / Nov. 1971 / A&M ✦✦✦
This concept album relates the story of John "Babbacombe" Lee, the man they could not hang. — *Steve Winick*

Rosie / Mar. 1973 / A&M ✦✦✦
Simon Nicol, the last original member of Fairport, had departed by the time of this, the group's eighth album, and was replaced by two guitarists, Jerry Donahue and Trevor Lucas. The reconstituted band made a renewed effort at writing new material, the best of which was Dave Swarbrick's title tune (which featured ex-Fairporters Sandy Denny and Richard Thompson, and Thompson's future wife, Linda Peters, as guests). — *William Ruhlmann*

Nine / Oct. 1973 / A&M ✦✦
The second album by the Mattacks/Pegg/Swarbrick/Donahue/Lucas lineup finds the last two asserting themselves more and moving Fairport Convention toward more of a conventional pop sound. But nothing here is particularly memorable. — *William Ruhlmann*

A Fairport Live Convention / Jul. 1974 / Island ✦✦✦

Rising for the Moon / Jun. 1975 / Island ✦✦✦
Fairport turned to rock producer Glyn Johns for a more contemporary sound on its tenth studio album. The band continued to suffer personnel changes, with Dave Mattacks leaving before the album was complete and being replaced by Bruce Rowland. On her first studio album with Fairport since *Liege and Lief* six years before, Sandy Denny dominates the proceedings, writing or co-writing six of the 11 tracks, including the title track and the haunting "What Is True." With typical Fairport luck, however, this was Denny's last album with the group. — *William Ruhlmann*

● **Fairport Chronicles** / 1976 / A&M ✦✦✦✦
A well-chosen early best-of collection. — *William Ruhlmann*

Gottle O'Geer / May 1976 / Island ✦✦

Bonny Bunch of Roses / Feb. 1977 / Vertigo ✦✦

Tipplers Tales / May 1978 / Vertigo ✦✦✦
Some of Fairport's finest traditional song performances are here, from yet another lineup. Singer/guitarist Simon Nicol, the only original Fairporter left, begins to take a more active role. — *Steve Winick*

Farewell, Farewell / 1979 / Simon's ✦✦✦

Moat on the Ledge / 1982 / Stony Plain ✦✦✦

Glady's Leap / 1985 / Varrick ✦✦✦

Expletive Delighted! / 1986 / Varrick ✦✦✦

House Full / 1986 / Hannibal ✦✦✦
A revised version of the 1977 album *Live at the L.A. Troubadour*, which, in turn, is taken from a concert performance by the Richard Thompson-led 1970 lineup of Fairport, one of its strongest units. Long versions of "Sloth" and "Matty Groves" dominate. — *William Ruhlmann*

Heyday / 1987 / Hannibal ✦✦✦✦
This collection of 14 BBC performances from 1968 and 1969 is just as outstanding as their late-'60s studio albums, and shows their mastery of an astonishing range of material. Most of these songs were not recorded on the group's official releases, and include covers of gems by Joni Mitchell, Eric Anderson, Johnny Cash, Leonard Cohen, Gene Clark, Richard Farina, the Everlys, and Bob Dylan. — *Richie Unterberger*

In Real Time: Live '87 / 1987 / Island ✦✦

Red & Gold / 1989 / Rough Trade ✦✦✦

Five Seasons / Dec. 1990 / Rough Trade ✦✦✦

Jewel in the Crown / 1995 / Green Linnet ✦✦✦

Faith No More

Alternative Pop-Rock, Heavy Metal, Funk Metal
With their fusion of heavy metal, funk, hip-hop, and progressive-rock, Faith No More has earned a substantial cult following. By the time they recorded their first album in 1985, the band had already had a string of lead vocalists, including Courtney Love; their debut, *We Care a Lot*, featured Chuck Mosley's abrasive vocals but it was driven by Jim Martin's metallic guitar. Faith No More's next album, 1987's *Introduce Yourself*, was a more cohesive and impressive effort; for the first time, the rap and metal elements didn't sound like they were fighting each other.

In 1988, the rest of the band fired Mosley; he was replaced by Bay Area vocalist Mike Patton during the recording of their next album, *The Real Thing*. Patton was a more accomplished vocalist, able to change effortlessly between rapping and singing, as well as adding a considerably more bizarre slant to the lyrics. Besides adding a new vocalist, the band had tightened their attack and the result was the genre-bending hit single, "Epic," which established them as a major hard-rock act.

Following up the hit wasn't as easy, however. Faith No More followed their breakthrough success with 1992's *Angel Dust*, one of the more complex and simply confounding records ever released by a major label. Although it sold respectably, it didn't have the crossover potential of the first album. When the band toured in support of the album, tensions between the band and Martin began to escalate; rumors that his guitar was stripped from some of the final mixes of *Angel Dust* began to circulate. As the band was recording its fifth album in early 1994, it was confirmed that Martin had been fired from the band.

Faith No More recorded *King for a Day, Fool for a Lifetime* with Mr. Bungle guitarist Trey Spruance. During tour preparations he was replaced by Dean Mentia. — *Stephen Thomas Erlewine*

Introduce Yourself / 1987 / Slash ✦✦✦

● **The Real Thing** / 1989 / Slash ✦✦✦✦
An unusual combination of heavy metal, rap, and hard rock, appealing to head bangers and popsters alike. — *Donna DiChario*

Angel Dust / 1992 / Slash ✦✦✦✦
It's quite diverse and eclectic, with its range of styles going from lounge jazz to power-pop and all-out industrial grindcore. The songwriting shows a lot of talent, especially from Mike Patton, whose vocal range is used to its full potential on this album, the band's fourth. — *John Book*

King for a Day/Fool for a Lifetime / Mar. 28, 1995 / Slash ◆◆

Marianne Faithfull

b. Dec. 29, 1946, London, England
Vocals / Pop-Rock, Girl Group

Few stars of the 1960s have reinvented themselves as successfully as Marianne Faithfull. Coaxed into a singing career by Rolling Stones manager Andrew Loog Oldham in 1964, she had a big hit in both Britain and the US with her debut single, the Jagger/Richards composition "As Tears Go By" (which prefaced the Stones' own version by a full year). Considerably more successful in her native land than the states, she had a series of hits in the mid-'60s that set her high, fragile voice against delicate orchestral pop arrangements—"Summer Night," "This Little Bird," Jackie De Shannon's "Come and Stay with Me." Not a songwriter at the outset of her career, she owes more of her fame as a '60s icon to her extraordinary beauty and her long-running romance with Mick Jagger, although she offered a taste of things to come with her compelling 1969 single "Sister Morphine," which she co-wrote (and which the Stones released themselves on *Sticky Fingers* later).

In the 1970s, Faithfull split up with Jagger, developed a serious drug habit, and recorded rarely, with generally dismal results. Until late 1979, when she pulled off an astonishing comeback with *Broken English*. Displaying a croaking, cutting voice that had lowered a good octave since the mid-'60s, Faithfull had also begun to write much of her own material, and addressed sex and despair with wrenching realism. After allowing herself to be framed as a demure chanteuse by songwriters and arrangers throughout most of her career, Marianne had found her own voice, and suddenly sounded more relevant and contemporary than most of the stars she had rubbed shoulders with in the '60s. Faithfull's recordings in the 1980s and 1990s have been sporadic and erratic, but generally quite interesting; *Strange Weather*, a Hal Willner-produced 1987 collection of standards and contemporary compositions that spanned several decades for its sources, was her greatest triumph of the decade. In 1994, she published her self-titled autobiography; the recent biography *As Tears Go By*, by Mark Hodkinson, is a more objective and thorough account of her life and times. One continues to look forward to unexpected twists on forthcoming recordings—a statement one can apply to few other performers who emerged during the 1960s. *—Richie Unterberger*

Marianne Faithfull / May 1965 / London ◆◆◆
Her erratic, self-titled debut features lovely baroque arrangements by Mike Leander and decent tunes like "As Tears Go By," Jackie DeShannon's "Come and Stay with Me" and "In My Time Of Sorrow," and Bacharach-David's "If I Never Get to Love You," as well as fairly crummy covers of hits by the Beatles, Herman's Hermits, and Petula Clark. Look for the Japanese CD reissue: It adds six non-LP bonus tracks from mid-'60s singles, including a couple (the girl-groupish "The Sha La La Song," the melancholy "The Morning Sun") that rank among her best '60s recordings. *—Richie Unterberger*

Faithless / Mar. 1978 / Sony ◆◆◆

● **Broken English** / Nov. 1979 / Island ◆◆◆◆
After a lengthy absence, Faithfull resurfaced on this 1979 album, which took the edgy and brittle sound of punk rock and gave it a shot of studio-smooth dance rock. Faithfull's whiskey-worn vocals perfectly match the bitter and biting "Why'd Ya Do It" and revitalize John Lennon's "Working Class Hero." *—John Floyd*

A Child's Adventure / Mar. 1983 / Island ◆◆

Marianne Faithfull's Greatest Hits / 1987 / ABKCO ◆◆◆◆
While missing a few fine album tracks, this is an excellent 16-song distillation of her '60s recordings. Includes all of her British and American hits—"As Tears Go By," "This Little Bird," "Summer Nights," and "Come and Stay with Me." Bonuses include "In My Time of Sorrow," an obscure mid-'60s folk-rocker co-written by Jackie DeShannon and Jimmy Page, and her 1969 single "Sister Morphine" (co-written with the Rolling Stones), predating the *Sticky Fingers* version; it's easily her most powerful performance of the decade. *—Richie Unterberger*

Strange Weather / Jul. 1987 / Island ◆◆◆◆
Faithfull's 1987 release recast her as a nicotine-stained chanteuse, approaching such standards as "Boulevard of Broken Dreams" and "Penthouse Serenade" with a ravaged, world-weary demeanor that recalls the latter-day recordings of Billie Holiday. She also tackles some blues and jazz material and turns "As Tears Go By" into the gut-wrenching torch ballad neither the Stones nor Faithfull could ever have done in the '60s. A dark, challenging masterpiece. *—John Floyd*

Blazing Away / Mar. 1990 / Island ◆◆◆

Faithfull: A Collection of Her Best Recordings / Aug. 23, 1994 / Island ◆◆◆
This best-of basically covers the years 1979 to 1994, though it reaches back to 1964 for Marianne Faithfull's first recording and first hit, "As Tears Go By," and includes "She," slated for the upcoming 1995 album *A*

Secret Life. Five of the 11 songs are drawn from Faithfull's strongest album, 1979's *Broken English*, including the bitter title track and "Why'd Ya Do It." Otherwise, compiler Chris Blackwell makes little attempt to present a balance among Faithfull's recordings—there is nothing at all from *Dangerous Acquaintances* or *A Child's Adventure*, and only one track each from *Strange Weather* and *Blazing Away*. But there is a good newly recorded cover of Patti Smith's "Ghost Dance" co-produced by Keith Richards and featuring other members of the Rolling Stones, and Blackwell rescues Faithfull's rendition of the title theme for the movie *Trouble in Mind* from the soundtrack album. It adds up to an excellent compilation that highlights Faithfull's strengths as a singer. *—William Ruhlmann*

The Falcons

Soul

Often credited as having cut the first true soul record in 1959 with "You're So Fine," a host of '60s soul stars called themselves Falcons at one time or another, including founder Eddie Floyd, Wilson Pickett, Sir Mack Rice, and 100 Proof Aged in Soul's Joe Stubbs. Originally an integrated R&B group headed by Floyd, the Falcons debuted on Mercury in 1955. Under the production aegis of Robert West, the Falcons' sound became more gospel-based as time passed, and with Stubbs as lead, the seminal "You're So Fine" was a major hit in 1959. Pickett screamed the gospel-fired ballad "I Found a Love" to national prominence on West's LuPine label in 1962, backed by guitarist Robert Ward's Ohio Untouchables. When Pickett went solo shortly thereafter, the members went their separate ways. West recruited another group, the Fabulous Playboys, who took over the Falcons name, but with little success. *—Bill Dahl*

● **I Found a Love** / 1986 / Relic ◆◆◆◆
A more incendiary collection, thanks to the addition of Wilson Pickett as the Falcons' front man. *—Bill Dahl*

You're So Fine / 1986 / Relic ◆◆◆◆
Prototypical early Detroit soul from this rough-edged vocal group that featured Eddie Floyd and Joe Stubbs. *—Bill Dahl*

The Fall

Post-Punk

While the band's audience has never been expanded beyond a rabidly devoted cult following across the world, the Fall has had a significant impact on the post-punk music of the '70s, '80s, and '90s. Many fans of the group have gone on to form their own band, leaving the rock underground with a wealth of bands replicating and expanding the Fall's harsh, jagged guitar experimentalism.

Under the leadership of guitarist/vocalist Mark E. Smith, the band has released an enormous amount of albums since their debut in 1977. Every album is a complex, challenging piece of rock 'n' roll yet none of them sounds the same; with each album, the Fall explores new territory, from guitar noise to club music. Through every incarnation, Smith has retained his reputation as one of rock's foremost experimental artists. *—Stephen Thomas Erlewine*

Live at the Witch Trials / 1979 / A&M ◆◆◆◆

Grotesque / 1980 / Rough Trade ◆◆◆

Early Years 77-79 / 1981 / Step Forward ◆◆◆

Perverted by Language / 1983 / Rough Trade ◆◆◆◆
With the most prodigious catalog of all the late-'70s punk rock bands, the Fall's recorded output can be, for sanity's sake, broken down into three periods covering roughly 20 years. Early Fall (1977-1983) contains their harshest and most extreme music. Truthfully, only hardcore Fall fans will detect the differences among albums of any period, but with a catalog this large, collecting significant recordings of each era will help (and hopefully encourage) adventuresome neophytes to plunge headfirst into the dazzling, unpredictable world of the Fall. This is, to be sure, not every Fall album available; it is rather a subjective sampling. Perhaps of the early material, the best place to start is *Live at the Witch Trials*. Under the guidance of producer Bob Sargeant, this harnesses the essence of the Fall's early sound: jagged, colliding guitars; stiff, repetitive percussion; and Mark E. Smith's nasal, singsong ranting. It's dissonant, but not so harsh as to be totally unapproachable. In fact, Sargeant (who later went on to produce records by far poppier bands like the English Beat) accents the rhythmic bottom, so that even when the music lurches like a drunken Frankenstein's monster, it does swing enough to be captivating. Of course, this is assuming that Smith's vocals haven't prevented you from enjoying this (and really, they shouldn't). Tunes like "Rebellious Jukebox" and "Music Scene" will win you over with their caustic appeal. Both *Grotesque* and *Early Years 77-79* are more extreme. Extreme in the sense that traditional song form is almost totally dispensed with for a din of cacophony built around thuddingly simple guitar riffs. It's not totally alienating, but it's not where potential Fall fans (unless you have a jones for barely structured rock noise) should start. Oddly, despite both records being anti-rock to the point of almost being anti-music, there are some

great songs that emerge through the trebly crashing and bashing ("Rowche Rumble," "Pay Your Rates," "Bingo Masters Breakout," and "New Face on Hell"). Closing the early Fall period is *Perverted by Language*, which also starts the (what I call) "Brix Period." It was during this time that Smith married American guitarist Brix (birth surname unknown to this writer), who brought a stronger pop sense to the band. Suddenly, Fall albums, although still essentially abrasive, were more tuneful, and loaded with fuzztone garage-raunch guitar playing. Brix's first effort as a full-time Fall member is a winner, with tracks like "I Feel Voxish" and the parody of the excessively health-conscious "Eat Y'self Fitter," pushing the Fall into a new terrain that would bring them (surprise!) chart success in England. —*John Dougan*

The Wonderful and Frightening World Of / 1984 / Beggars Banquet ✦✦✦✦

This Nation's Saving Grace / 1985 / Beggars Banquet ✦✦✦✦
Driven by an unrelenting, tense performance by the band and filled with fractured melodies and elliptical guitar hooks, *This Nation's Saving Grace* is the Fall's masterpiece. —*Stephen Thomas Erlewine*

The Frenz Experiment / 1988 / Beggars Banquet ✦✦

I Am Curious Oranj / 1988 / Beggars Banquet ✦✦✦
The high point of the "Brix Period" may well have been the release of the *Wonderful and Frightening World of the Fall*. Where before the music was tense, jumpy, and anarchic, here it was focused, harder-hitting, and rocked more. To some, it signaled the end of the Fall, but that was an unfair assessment. Granted, the music changed slightly, but it didn't diminish the band's potency. And, for all the time that Mark Smith had dominated the band, it was becoming clear that Brix's talents as a writer and musician were formidable, and she deserved to take some of the spotlight. The records from *Wonderful* to roughly the end of the decade are solid, at times excellent forays into increasingly commercial rock. *This Nation's Saving Grace* could almost qualify as a dance record if it were a little smoother, but the songs are catchy, and for the Fall, almost upbeat. As far as solid groove goes, this is their toughest, funkiest record. Both *The Frenz Experiment* and *I Am Curious Oranj* sound as if they were recorded on the same day, although the latter was a score commissioned for an experimental ballet. *Frenz* has a great cover of the Kinks' "Victoria," as well as production values never before heard on Fall records (high quality). *Oranj* isn't as completely satisfying, but was (so I am told) much better than the ballet. The anomalous release during this period was *A Palace of Swords Reversed*, which is a collection of non-LP tracks and assorted odds and sods from 1980-83. Despite its patchwork arrangement, it's a remarkably cohesive document and one of the Fall's best efforts. There was also a live recording made during this period (*Seminal Live*), but it's thoroughly mediocre and not worth the bother. —*John Dougan*

458489 B-Sides / 1990 / Beggars Banquet ✦✦✦✦

★ **458489 A-Sides** / 1990 / Beggars Banquet ✦✦✦✦✦
Bypassing their edgy, early singles and concentrating on their artier, more eclectic work of the mid- and late '80s, *458489 A Sides* encapsulates nearly all of the Fall's many attributes. All of the singles on *A Sides* are culled from the era when Brix Smith was in the band, arguably the band's most cohesive and rewarding years. Drawing from their strongest albums—*The Wonderful and Frightening World of the Fall, This Nation's Saving Grace, Bend Sinister, The Frenz Experiment*—*A-Sides* offers an excellent introduction to the Fall. It is both a useful retrospective and a kind of road map, pointing out the differences between albums. For neophytes and the uninitiated, there is no better sampler, and for longtime fans, the collection reiterates what a fine singles band the Fall were in their heyday. —*Stephen Thomas Erlewine*

Extricate / 1990 / Fontana ✦✦✦✦

Code: Selfish / 1991 / Fontana ✦✦✦

Middle Class Revolt / 1994 / Matador ✦✦✦
This is the late Fall period also known (by me, anyway) as the "post-Brix" years. The Smiths had divorced around the time of *Extricate*, but Brix's presence could still be felt on Fall records. Some thought the mid-'80s signaled an end to the ragged, jagged Fall of old; the '90s must have made them apoplectic. Working with producers Rex Sergeant, Craig Leon, and Adrian Sherwood, the post-apocalyptic sound of the '70s had been smoothed to a sheen. There were still moments of anarchy and dissonance, but generally they were swaddled in synth-driven beats and high-tech production that smoothed out any remaining rough edges. Again, this was not a bad thing; after all, Mark Smith was still up front and still ranting, but he was singing even more, and shocking as that was, it made for even better music. Although *Shiftwork* and *Code: Selfish* are very good, they are almost indistinguishable from one another and the sameness works against them. That being said, let me contradict myself and suggest you buy *Code: Selfish*, which is notable for "Birmingham School of Business School" and a cover of Hank Williams' "Just Waiting." For this period, the place to start is *Extricate*, which proved beyond a doubt that the Fall were not too old to still be a part of this

punk rock thang. Since this record follows on the heels of the Smiths' divorce, it's tempting to assume that Mark Smith's ranting has a more conspicuous target, but enigmatic as he tends to be, this is mere speculation. Still, "Sing! Harpy" and the title track will give you pause as to the source of Smith's considerable consternation. The band sounds great, especially longtime members Stephen Hanley and Craig Scanlon. Extra kudos to the solid backbeat provided by Simon Wolstencroft. During this time, Fall recordings were less likely to automatically be released in America. Still, hip American indie label Matador decided that these seminal punksters deserved better, and their last two records were made available in America (on vinyl no less!). *Infotainment Scam* is the better of the two, if only because *Middle Class Revolt* sounds carelessly conceived, but the sound that has defined the Fall in the '90s remains intact. In fact, *Infotainment Scam* was followed by the Fall's biggest American tour in some time, but it did little to stimulate interest and sales. A great collection of singles was also released during this time; *458489 A-Sides* is essential Fall—lean, mean, and nasty. —*John Dougan*

Merrell Fankhauser

Singer-Songwriter, Art-Rock/Progressive-Rock, Psychedelic
One of the most interesting cult figures in rock history, Fankhauser's best work came as the leader of several interesting groups during the '60s and early '70s: the Impacts (instrumental surf), Merrell & the Exiles (solid British Invasion-style rock), Fapardokly (great Byrdsish folk-rock), the H.M.S. Bounty (fine late '60s folk-rock), and Mu (spaced-out progressive blues/psychedelia).

When Mu broke up in the mid-'70s, Fankhauser began working as a solo artist, issuing a series of independent albums that continue to this day. These usually show him in a considerably mellower and more mainstream folk-rock mood than his best, earlier work, sometimes recalling Crosby, Stills & Nash, and often featuring violinist Mary Lee. —*Richie Unterberger*

● **The Maui Album** / 1988 / Reckless ✦✦✦✦
Fankhauser's first solo outing, originally titled *Merrell Fankhauser* and released in 1976, remains his best post-Mu work. Very light and serene folk-rock that owes little to trends of its era, predominantly acoustic in feel, often featuring Mary Lee on violin and harmony vocals. The 1988 reissue is enhanced by four previously unreleased Mu tracks, dating from 1974. —*Richie Unterberger*

Early Years 1964-1967 / 1994 / Legend Music ✦✦

Merrell Fankhauser & H.M.S. Bounty

Singer-Songwriter, Art-Rock/Progressive-Rock, Psychedelic
After cutting some fine folk-rock and psychedelia on ultra-rare records with his group the Exiles, guitarist, singer, and songwriter Merrell Fankhauser moved to Los Angeles, retitled his backing group H.M.S. Bounty, and recorded a fine, if obscure, slice of pop-psychedelia in 1968, *Things*. The diverse offerings on the group's sole LP recalled such fellow Californian heavyweights as the Byrds, Buffalo Springfield, Moby Grape, and even Captain Beefheart. They weren't quite in the same league as those legends, but the album has a light and enigmatic air all its own, and is well worth investigation by fans of late-'60s West Coast psychedelia. The group evolved into the interesting mystical avant garde-blues-progressive-rock group Mu in the early '70s. —*Richie Unterberger*

● **Things** / 1968 / Shamley ✦✦✦✦
Fine, tuneful '60s psychedelia with a pop edge, featuring Fankhauser's first-rate songwriting and warm vocals. About half of the tunes are excellent, especially the country-rocker "Your Painted Lives," the folk-rock ballad "Ice Cube Island," and "A Visit with Ashiya," one of the best raga-rock songs ever cut. The reissue adds a bluesy non-LP B-side, "Flying Home," that looks forward to the innovations of Mu; it also includes fine, lengthy liner notes detailing Fankhauser's fascinating and winding career. —*Richie Unterberger*

Fapardokly

Psychedelic, Folk-Rock
An enigma in the world of '60s rock collectibles that would be barely worth explaining if the music wasn't so fine. There was never a group called Fapardokly; the 12 songs on their self-titled album were recorded by Merrell & the Exiles, a Southern California group headed by legendary cult folk-rocker Merrell Fankhauser. That group cut several singles for the tiny Glenn label, some of which are collected here, before heading off in a psychedelic direction and mutating into H.M.S. Bounty. The equally tiny UIP label decided to gather a few of the Glenn singles, add a few more psychedelically oriented tracks that Merrill and his group had recorded, and release the package as the work of a group called Fapardokly. Although it was not recorded or intended as a unified work, it stands as one of the great lost folk-rock classics of the 1960s. Fankhauser went on to make more excellent obscure recordings with H.M.S. Bounty in the late '60s and Mu in the early '70s. —*Richie Unterberger*

● **Fapardokly** / 1967 / Sundazed ✦✦✦✦
One of the most sought-after rock rarities of the '60s, this album was sty-listically uneven, as can be expected from an LP cobbled together from recordings spanning a few years. About half, however, is sparkling psy-chedelic folk-rock, recalling *Fifth Dimension* Byrds with its shimmering 12-string guitars, multipart harmonies, and occasional trippy lyrics. Although the early material is more pop-oriented and doesn't fit in as well, it's pretty solid, recalling the Zombies and (in the very earliest tracks) Ricky Nelson. "Lila," "Tomorrow's Girl," and "Super Market" are genuine lost '60s treasures, and much of the rest of the album isn't far behind. After a couple of European LP reissues, it was finally reissued on CD, with three bonus tracks, in 1995. —*Richie Unterberger*

Mylene Farmer

Vocals / Art-Rock/Progressive-Rock, Euro-Pop, Club-Dance
Since 1985, Mylene Farmer (born in Quebec, but raised in France) and her musical collaborator, Laurent Boutonnat, have expanded the Birkin-Gainsbourg bedroom fantasy song into an entire cosmology of sighing songs, pensive and melancholy and fitfully melodic dances in which *fin de siecle libertinism* is the motive principle and intoxicated hallucina-tion the saving grace. It's popular throughout Euro-land and not unknown even in the US. —*Michael Freedberg*

Ainsi Soit Je . . . / 1988 / ✦✦✦✦
Ambitiously stylish, this thick mix of powerful dance rhythms and sen-sual melodies is both accessible and subtle. Sometimes uneven in its overall composition, it offers superb sound quality of the mature artist. —*Vladimir Bogdanov*

En Consert / 1989 / Polydor ✦✦✦
● **L'Antre . . .** / 1991 / ✦✦✦✦
Marked with the same stylistic integrity as her previous albums, this is without a doubt Mylene Farmer's masterpiece. Compositions are still elaborate and carefully designed but have now more refined transparent feel. Deep, dark reflection of life, so typical for the artist, is enriched by the sparkling energy of her powerful, sometimes hysterical irony and calm confidence of her velvet-soft voice. —*Vladimir Bogdanov*

Cendres De Lune / Polydor ✦✦

The Feelies

Alternative Pop-Rock, Jangle-pop
The Feelies, consisting of Glenn Mercer (guitar/vocals), Bill Million (gui-tar/vocals), Keith DeNunzio (bass), Vinny DeNunzio (drums), and part-time member Anton Fier (drums), formed in New Jersey in 1977. In 1980, they released their debut avant-pop masterpiece, *Crazy Rhythms*, to criti-cal acclaim but to no commercial response. Mercer and Million left the band dormant while working on outside projects such as the Trypes, Wil-lies and Yung Wu; Fier left to work on his own Golden Palominos projects. Revived interest in the band, thanks in part to R.E.M.'s Peter Buck citing the band as an influence, led to a reactivated version of the Feelies in 1986, featuring Brenda Sauter on bass and Dave Weckerman on percussion. Produced by Peter Buck, *The Good Earth* was released in 1986 by Coyote to an enthusiastic college radio audience. They contin-ued to be college radio mainstays for the rest of the decade, though mainstream success has eluded them. —*Chris Woodstra*

● **Crazy Rhythms** / Apr. 1980 / A&M ✦✦✦✦
The Feelies' debut picks up where the Velvet Underground and Televi-sion left off, using unconventional structures to create an album that is stark, nervous, and detached. While it was virtually ignored at the time, *Crazy Rhythms* would prove to be a blueprint for much of the mid-'80s' guitar-based alternative rock. —*Chris Woodstra*

The Good Earth / 1986 / Coyote ✦✦✦
After a six-year break, the Feelies return with R.E.M.'s Peter Buck produc-ing. The result, not so surprisingly, is a fine alternative folk-pop album in the spirit of early R.E.M. Though not matching the debut's brilliance, *The Good Earth* creates a pleasant enough atmosphere and is a welcome return. —*Chris Woodstra*

Only Life / 1988 / A&M ✦✦✦✦
Only Life moves from the light acoustic strumming of 1986's *The Good Earth* into a slightly harder acoustic sound while still retaining much of the textured and atmospheric qualities that made its predecessor so charming. There is more of a return to the driving rhythms of the first album, and the entire album has a feeling of the Velvet Underground revisited. —*Chris Woodstra*

Time for a Witness / 1991 / A&M ✦✦

Bryan Ferry

b. Sep. 26, 1945, Washington, Durham, UK
Harmonica, Piano, Keyboards, Vocals / Pop-Rock
Bryan Ferry has been recording solo albums since Roxy Music's early- to mid-'70s heyday, in a bizarre and confounding hodgepodge of styles. His first few solos incorporated mostly eclectic covers that wander every-where from early rock and soul hits up to Dylan and Beatles tunes; musi-cally, they share a lot of common ground with his full-time group. —*John Floyd*

These Foolish Things / Oct. 1973 / Reprise ✦✦✦✦
As a side project during his Roxy Music tenure, Ferry recorded this album of drastic rearrangements of a variety of standards, most of them from the '60s. The Beatles, the Rolling Stones, and especially Bob Dylan never sounded like this before. —*William Ruhlmann*

Another Time, Another Place / Jul. 1974 / Reprise ✦✦✦
Same concept, different songs, as the suave Ferry recasts "Smoke Gets in Your Eyes," Sam Cooke, and several country standards. —*William Ruhl-mann*

Let's Stick Together / Sep. 1976 / Reprise ✦✦✦
In Your Mind / Feb. 1977 / Reprise ✦✦
The Bride Stripped Bare / Sep. 1978 / Reprise ✦✦
Boys and Girls / May 1985 / Reprise ✦✦✦✦
With the second (and presumably final) disbanding of Roxy Music, Ferry turned full time to his solo career, so this album is more of a follow-up to 1982's *Avalon*, the last Roxy album, than to 1978's *The Bride Stripped Bare*, the previous Ferry solo release. It brilliantly continues the ethereal dance-floor charm of *Avalon*. —*William Ruhlmann*

● **Street Life: 20 Greatest Hits** / Apr. 1986 / EG ✦✦✦✦
Covering both Ferry and Roxy Music's best-known songs, *Street Life* is the best introduction to the stylish art-rocker's career. —*Stephen Thomas Erlewine*

Bête Noire / Oct. 1987 / Reprise ✦✦✦✦
Enlisting Madonna producer Patrick Leonard to assist, Ferry matches his studiedly languorous vocals to densely percussive dance tracks. —*Will-iam Ruhlmann*

Taxi / Mar. 1993 / Reprise ✦✦
Mamouna / Sep. 20, 1994 / Capitol ✦✦✦✦
Ferry's first album of original material since *Bête Noire* finds the ex-Roxy Music singer in a familiar seductive mood. While working within his standard dance-oriented darkness, Ferry incorporates several new touches—namely, several pseudo-world music touches. None of it would have worked if Ferry hadn't blended them in so seamlessly with his styl-ish pop, which hasn't dated in the seven years that he's been away. —*Stephen Thomas Erlewine*

5th Dimension

Pop-Rock
They didn't sound anything like an R&B group, and their soaring, lighter-than-air harmonic blend frequently proved more palatable to pop audiences than to Black record buyers. But do not suggest, even for a sec-ond, that the 5th Dimension was in any way lacking in soul.
    Formed as the Versatiles in 1965, the slick quintet changed its name at the request of Johnny Rivers, who had just signed them to his brand-new label, Soul City. Up-and-coming songwriter Jimmy Webb supplied the group with their first pop smash "Up, Up and Away," in 1967, and the group's monumental rise mirrored the song's high-flying imagery. Another prolific composer, Laura Nyro, handed the 5th Dimension sev-eral megahits, notably "Stoned Soul Picnic" and "Wedding Bell Blues," but their biggest seller hailed from the ground-breaking musical *Hair*. The Grammy-winning "Aquarius/Let the Sunshine In" held down the No. 1 slot on the pop lists for six weeks in 1969.
    After several more hits, Marilyn McCoo and Billy Davis, Jr., who had married while part of the group, successfully branched off as a duo, while Lamonte McLemore, Ron Townson, and Florence LaRue kept the 5th Dimension on the soul charts, losing a head-to-head battle with Diana Ross for hit status on "Love Hangover" in 1976. —*Bill Dahl*

● **Greatest Hits on Earth** / Sep. 1972 / Arista ✦✦✦✦
Until Rhino issued its anthology, this was the best-hits package for the 5th Dimension, a group that in its peak was among the best at doing lighthearted pop with a soulful foundation. Certainly, they weren't a hardcore R&B or earthy singing group, but they did put some punch into songs that were really kind of silly otherwise, like "Wedding Bell Blues." —*Ron Wynn*

Anthology 1967-1973 / 1986 / Rhino ✦✦✦✦
This complete compilation represents the best of this California soul quintet. —*Rick A. Bueche*

Fine Young Cannibals

Pop-Rock
When the English Beat splintered in two, bassist David Steele and guitar-ist Andy Cox formed the Fine Young Cannibals with Roland Gift. Although the band's fusion of rock, Motown-style R&B, pop, and modern dance is tight and loaded with hooks, the real attraction is Gift's soaring

falsetto—he sounds like a classic soul singer. Their 1985 debut album was critically acclaimed, but it was the 1989 follow-up, *The Raw & the Cooked*—with the No. 1 singles "She Drives Me Crazy" and "Good Thing"—that made the band major hit makers. Apart from a remix album in 1990 and Gift's occasional film role, the group has been quiet since their breakthrough success. *—Stephen Thomas Erlewine*

Fine Young Cannibals / Dec. 1985 / IRS ✦✦✦

● **The Raw & the Cooked** / Feb. 20, 1989 / IRS ✦✦✦✦
FYC rode to massive success on the tender-and-terrified singing of Roland Gift and the neo-Motown sheen of the No. 1 hits "She Drives Me Crazy" and "Good Thing." *—William Ruhlmann*

Finn Brothers

Pop-Rock
Brothers Tim and Neil Finn have been making music together since their childhood in Te Awamutu, New Zealand, continuing through to international success in Split Enz and Crowded House. However it wasn't until late 1989 that they actually started writing together—a reunion that yielded more than a dozen songs for a proposed Finn Brothers side project. That album was scrapped and most of the material was absorbed by Crowded House's *Woodface* (1991) and *Together Alone* (1993), as well as Tim's 1993 solo album, *Before & After*. The brothers' project resumed in late 1994, and in four weeks, they completed an album called simply *Finn*. The album, released in the fall of 1995 (the summer of 1996 in the US), showed a much more casual side of the Finns and was less pop-oriented than their previous musical collaborations—the brothers play nearly all of the instruments themselves, ranging from the primitive to the exotic. After initial pressings of *Finn*, the duo changed their name to the Finn Brothers to avoid confusion with a band going under a similar name. *—Chris Woodstra*

● **Finn** / Oct. 1995 / Parlophone ✦✦✦✦
Finn is the long rumored and awaited collaboration between brothers Tim and Neil Finn. The first reports of the project in 1990 promised an album of "just acoustic guitars and lots of harmonies," and when that material was absorbed by Crowded House for *Woodface*, it was proven that the team was capable of making near-perfect pop. Those expecting *Woodface Part 2*, however, are in for a surprise—*Finn* is a moody, atmospheric album that shows a more spontaneous and experimental side with the brothers playing all of the instruments, including ukuleles, Chamberlain keyboards, Mellotron, and tea chest bass. Though most projects of this nature get hung up on the "concept," this one succeeds because the Finns' pop songwriting sense allows the songs to come first. Despite the lack of polish and the odd setting, the material on this album is among the pair's finest, together or apart. *—Chris Woodstra*

Tim Finn

b. Jun. 25, 1952, Te Awamutu, New Zealand
Keyboards, Vocals / Pop-Rock
Singer-songwriter keyboardist/guitarist Tim Finn was born in Te Awamutu, New Zealand. Influenced by not only British Invasion acts like the Beatles, the Move, and the Kinks, but also his Catholic upbringing and the communal sing-alongs of the native Maori people, Finn founded the '70s art-rock-turned-new-wave band Split Enz, leading the band through several albums to moderate international success. The success of the between-albums solo project, *Escapade*, led to his leaving the band in 1983. He followed with the more ambitious second album, *Big Canoe* (1985), which went virtually ignored (it was unreleased in the US until the success of his brother's band, Crowded House, stirred up enough interest by 1988). Finn returned in 1989 with a self-titled album for Capitol Records. Despite good reviews, this, too, failed to make much impact. He joined his brother Neil's band, Crowded House, for their *Woodface* album but left mid-tour and released his fourth solo album, *Before and After* in 1993. In 1995, he joined with Hothouse Flowers' Liam O Maonlai and Andy White, releasing an album under the group name ALT. A long-rumored collaboration between the Finn brothers was finally released in late 1995 under the name Finn Brothers (it was released in the spring of 1996 in the US). Finn returned to his solo career by the fall of 1996. *—Scott Bultman and Chris Woodstra*

Escapade / 1983 / A&M ✦✦✦
On his solo debut, Finn broke from Split Enz to exorcise these charming, light, melodic pop songs that didn't quite fit the band's style. Sweet and sappy, his soaring vocal style and introspective lyrics make this worthwhile. *—Scott Bultman*

Big Canoe / 1985 / Virgin ✦✦✦✦
Much production glitz here from producer Nick Launay, competing for attention with Finn's voice and songs. A very melodic and musical second solo effort, the highlights include "Don't Bury My Heart" and "Hyacinth." *—Scott Bultman*

● **Tim Finn** / 1989 / Capitol ✦✦✦✦
His third album is his most sparsely produced effort. Supported by Los Angeles session musicians and producer Mitchell Froom (Crowded House), Finn is as accessible here as he's ever been. Great melodies, well-turned phrases, and seamless backing vocals from brother Neil Finn of Crowded House make this one his best. *—Scott Bultman*

Before & After / 1993 / Capitol ✦✦✦✦
On his fourth solo album, Finn dabbles in dance-pop, pseudo-reggae, and folky ballads, with a different set of producers on nearly every track. While this leads to a certain lack of consistency, Finn's songwriting has never been stronger. He has the most success on the self-produced, stripped-down tracks where his strong sense of melody and knack for catchy pop hooks are allowed to be in the forefront. "Persuasion," co-written by Richard Thompson, and "In Love with It All," written with his brother Neil Finn (Crowded House), are highlights. *—Chris Woodstra*

fIREHOSE

Alternative Pop-Rock
In 1985, after D. Boon's tragic death at age 28 signaled the end of the Minutemen, bassist Mike Watt and drummer George Hurley threw in their lot with then-22-year-old former Ohio State University student, guitar player and Minuteman fanatic Ed Crawford to form Firehose. Taking their group name from a line in Bob Dylan's "Subterranean Homesick Blues," Firehose continued in the Minuteman tradition of breathtaking musicianship combined with caustic lyrical fusillades inspired by the writing of the Beat Generation and the erect-middle-finger indignation of the Blank Generation. However, with Crawford's decidedly folkie bent insinuating itself into the mix, fIREHOSE songs began to expand into more traditional verse-chorus-verse songwriting symmetry. And although fIREHOSE never equaled the Minutemen's output in terms of sheer audacity and emotional depth, Crawford, Watt, and Hurley recorded rock that was muscular, dense, and daring, along with being tremendously heartfelt. They never patronized audiences or comported themselves as "rock stars"; they were instead the quintessential post-punk "people's band." Although they achieved wider notoriety than did the Minutemen (eventually recording for a major label), fIREHOSE called it quits in early 1994 after a desultory, dispirited final LP (*Mr. Machinery Operator*). Still, nearly all of their recorded work stands as some of the best late-'80s/early-'90s indie rock. *—John Dougan*

Ragin', Full-On / 1986 / SST ✦✦✦
The title is a bit of a misnomer, since this record seethes more than it rages, but all and all, it was a fine debut. Crawford's (here he was referred to as Ed Fromohio) singing is tentative and a bit wan, but the songs are strong, and Watt and Hurley are one of rock's great rhythm sections. *—John Dougan*

● **If'n** / 1987 / SST ✦✦✦✦
On release number two, Crawford's guitar is assertive and drives the band more. Just as important, however, is that the songwriting has grown sharper and more compelling (especially on the romping "Sometimes"), and Crawford sings with more reckless abandon here. No sophomore slump, not by a long shot. *—John Dougan*

Sometimes / 1988 / SST ✦✦

Fromohio / 1989 / SST ✦✦✦✦
A bit of a retrenchment and perhaps not a wholly successful record. Here, fIREHOSE sounds like a band reevaluating its place in the world and only occasionally coming up with compelling answers. An easy record to slough off as more of the same. But while it may not be an essential record, it isn't bad either. *—John Dougan*

Flyin' the Flannel / 1991 / Columbia ✦✦✦

Live Totem Pole / 1992 / Columbia ✦✦✦

Mr. Machinery Operator / Feb. 16, 1993 / Columbia ✦✦

The "5" Royales

R&B
The "5" Royales were a relatively unheralded, but significant, link between early R&B and early soul in their combination of doo wop, jump blues, and gospel styles. Their commercial success was relatively modest—they had seven Top Ten R&B hits in the 1950s, most recorded in the span of little over a year between late 1952 and late 1953. A few of their singles would prove extremely popular in cover versions by other artists, though—James Brown and Aretha Franklin tore it up with "Think," Ray Charles covered "Tell the Truth," and the Shirelles (and later the Mamas and the Papas) had pop success with "Dedicated to the One I Love." Almost all of their material was written by guitarist Lowman Pauling, who influenced Steve Cropper with his biting and bluesy guitar lines, which at their most ferocious almost sound like a precursor to blues-rock.

Pauling's guitar is pretty muted on their early sides, though, which sometimes walk the line between gospel and R&B. The gospel elements aren't surprising, given that the Royales were originally known as the Royal Sons Quintet when they formed in Winston-Salem, NC. In fact, they were still known as the Royal Sons Quintet when they began recording for Apollo in the early '50s, although they had six members. They would change their name to the "5" Royales in 1952, although they would, confusingly, remain a six-man outfit for a while; the quotes around the 5 in their billing were designed to alleviate some of the confusion. The Apollo singles "Baby Don't Do It" and "Help Me Somebody" made No. 1 on the R&B charts in 1953, and they had a few other hits for Apollo before being lured away to King Records in 1954.

Although the group would remain on King for the rest of the 1950s, they would only enter the R&B Top Ten two more times, with "Think" and "Tears of Joy" (both in 1957). Their later sides, however, are their best, as Pauling became much more assertive on the guitar, dashing off some piercing and fluid solos. Some of these solos are among the heaviest and wildest in '50s rock, on both relatively well-known cuts like "Think," and virtually unknown numbers like "The Slummer the Slum." Greil Marcus once wrote something to the effect that a young Eric Clapton would have once paid to hold Pauling's coat. They remained primarily a harmony vocal group, though, and if their late-'50s sides are considerably more modernized than their early Apollo hits, they're still a lot closer to doo wop than soul.

Even when their records weren't selling, the "5" Royales were a popular touring band. Their constant activity at King Records, in all likelihood, had some influence on the young James Brown, then starting his career on the same label; one of Brown's first big R&B hits was a frenetic cover of "Think." They couldn't sustain themselves without more hits, though. After leaving King and recording some more sides in the early '60s, they finally broke up by 1965. —*Richie Unterberger*

★ **Monkey Hips and Rice: The "5" Royales Anthology** / 1994 / Rhino ✦✦✦✦✦

The "5" Royales certainly did their share of forgettable period-piece tunes, but they also had transcendent songs like "Think," "Just as I Am," and "Dedicated to the One I Love." They enjoyed a lengthy run, creating many hits plus a few gems, which are all available on this sparkling two-disc set. The opening disc sets the stage, showing their gospel origins and also the rather routine cuts the band did in its formative period. They began to evolve into a more substantial unit in the mid-'50s, and by the late '50s were a sterling unit cutting emphatic, appealing numbers. Most of these appear on the second disc. By the early '60s, they had run their course, but their legacy and impact was secure. This offers the most complete picture of the "5" Royales and their superb music. —*Ron Wynn*

The Five Satins

Doo Wop

The Five Satins are best-known for the doo wop classic "In the Still of the Night," a song that was popular enough to make the group one of the most famous doo wop outfits, although they never had another hit of the same magnitude. The origins of the Five Satins lie in the Scarlets, a New Haven, CT, doo wop group led by Fred Parris. The Scarlets formed in 1953, while Parris was still in high school. The group had a local hit with "Dear One" the following year. In 1954, Parris formed the Five Satins with vocalists Al Denby, Ed Martin, and Jim Freeman. Within the next year, Parris had the group record "In the Still of the Night," a song he had recently written, in the basement of a local church. The first single the group released was "In the Still of the Night." The single was released on Standard Records in the spring of 1956. By the end of the year, it had been leased to Ember and became a huge hit, peaking at No. 3 on the R&B charts and No. 25 on the pop charts.

By the time "In the Still of the Night" scaled the charts, Parris had been drafted into the army. He was stationed in Japan when the song became a hit, and he was still stationed in Japan when the group recorded the follow-up single, "To the Aisle." For that single, Bill Baker handled the lead vocals. "To the Aisle" became a Top Ten R&B hit in the summer of 1957. Parris returned from the army in 1958. Upon his return, he re-organized the group, adding Richie Freeman, Sylvester Hopkins, West Forbes, and Lou Peeples. This incarnation of the group had a minor hit in the fall of 1959 with "Shadows." In 1960, "In Still of the Night" re-entered the pop charts thanks to its exposure on Art Laboe's first *Oldies but Goodies* compilation. The repeated success of the single sparked a another minor hit for the band in 1960, a cover of the standard "I'll Be Seeing You." During the remainder of the '60s, Parris led various incarnations of the Five Satins through oldies revues in America and Europe; they also recorded occasionally during this time.

In 1974, the group signed a contract with Kirsner Records and released a single, "Two Different Worlds." Two years later, they briefly changed their name to Black Satin and released a single called "Everybody Stand Up and Clap Your Hands (For the Entertainer)," which became a Top 50 R&B hit. Shortly afterward, the group reverted to the Five Satins name.

In 1982, the Five Satins had their last hit with a doo wop medley entitled "Memories of Days Gone By." The single, which was released on Ele-

ktra Records, peaked at No. 71 on the pop charts. For the remainder of the '80s and the '90s, Fred Parris led various lineups of the Five Satins and the group performed regularly at oldies shows in America and Europe. —*Stephen Thomas Erlewine*

● **In the Still of the Night** / 1990 / Relic ✦✦✦✦

Everything you need from this sumptuous and smoochy late-night doo wop quintet is here. The title cut is a work of art worth listening to over and over. —*John Floyd*

The Five Stairsteps

Soul

The Five Stairsteps were a Windy City family affair initially consisting of four brothers and a sister; later on, five-year-old Cubie Burke toddled aboard, and even mom and pop got into the act. Curtis Mayfield discovered the group at a talent contest, and they debuted in 1966 on his Windy C logo with the tender "You Waited Too Long," their first hit. Lead singer Clarence Burke, Jr., was only 15 years old in 1966, yet his attractive leads on "World of Fantasy" and "Come Back" displayed a wealth of emotion. The group enjoyed its biggest pop hit in 1970 with the classic "O-o-h Child" for Buddah. After a few years apart, the group re-formed and notched a final hit, "From Us to You," on George Harrison's Dark Horse label in 1976. Four of the Burkes recorded as the Invisible Man's Band, scoring a sizable seller in 1980 with "All Night Thing," and bassist Keni Burke has recorded as a solo artist. —*Bill Dahl*

● **Greatest Hits** / Collectables ✦✦✦✦

This hits package examines the adolescent Chicago soul group from their mid-'60s beginning with their 1970 bubblegum soul hit "O-o-h Child." —*Bill Dahl*

The Fixx

New Wave, Pop-Rock

A London-based new wave group that managed to sustain a successful career in America for several years in the mid-'80s, the Fixx always flirted with mainstream pop with their catchy, keyboard-driven pop. Formed by college friends vocalist/keyboardist Cy Curnin and drummer Adam Woods in the early '80s, the pair advertised in the music press for additional members; the remaining members of the group—guitarist Jamie West-Oram, keyboardist Rupert Greenall, and bassist Charlie Barret—all responded to the ad. Taking the name the Portraits, the band recorded a single for Ariola Records, "Hazards in the Home," which failed to gather much attention. Within a year, the band had changed their name to the Fixx and recorded "Lost Planes," the single that led to a record contract with MCA.

The Fixx released their debut album, the Rupert Hine-produced *Shuttered Room*, in 1982. The record spawned to minor UK hits, "Stand or Fall" and "Red Skies," and spent a short time in the charts. In America, none of the singles were hits, yet the album stayed on the charts for nearly a year. After *Shuttered Room*, Barret left the group and was replaced by Dan K. Brown. *Reach the Beach*, released in 1983, established them as a hit-making force in the US. The terse, pulsating "One Thing Leads to Another" became a No. 4 hit, sending the album into the Top Ten. *Reach the Beach* would go platinum by the end of the year, launching two more Top 40 singles—"Saved by Zero" and "Sign of Fire." Despite all of their American success, the Fixx failed to break back into the British charts with *Reach the Beach*; in fact, they never had another British hit in their career.

The Fixx returned in 1984 with *Phantoms*. While it performed well—it peaked at No. 19 and went gold—it didn't match the success of *Reach the Beach*; after it launched the No. 15 single "Are We Ourselves," the record fell off the charts. Although their audience was shrinking, the band kept their basic, synth-driven sound intact for 1986's *Walkabout*, which featured the hit "Secret Separation." After *Walkabout*, the Fixx stopped working with producer Rupert Hine, which resulted in a harder, more guitar-oriented sound for 1988's *Calm Animals*. The album charted at No. 72, but it spawned no hit singles. *Ink* (1991), the group's last album, didn't reverse their declining fortunes, even though they tried to update their sound with an emphasis on guitars and slick, dance-ready beats. After the record failed to recapture their mainstream audience, the Fixx quietly faded away. —*Stephen Thomas Erlewine*

● **One Thing Leads to Another: Greatest Hits** / 1989 / MCA ✦✦✦✦

All their hits are here, including "One Thing Leads to Another," "Are We Ourselves," "The Sign of Fire," "Secret Separation," "Stand or Fall," and "Saved by Zero." —*Larry Lapka*

Roberta Flack

b. Feb. 10, 1939, Ashville, NC

Piano, Vocals / Soul, Urban, Pop-Rock

Classy, urbane, reserved, smooth, and sophisticated—all of these terms have been used to describe the music of Roberta Flack, particularly her string of romantic, light-jazz ballad hits in the '70s, which continue to enjoy popularity on MOR-oriented adult contemporary stations. Flack was the daughter of a church organist and started playing piano early enough to get a music scholarship and eventual degree from Howard University. After a period of student teaching, Flack was discovered singing at a club by jazz musician Les McCann and signed to Atlantic. Her first two albums were well-received but produced no hit singles; however, that all changed when a version of Ewan MacColl's "The First Time Ever I Saw Your Face," from her first LP, was included in the soundtrack of *Play Misty for Me*. The single zoomed to No. 1 in 1972 and remained there for six weeks, becoming that year's biggest hit. Flack followed it with the first of several duets with Howard classmate Donny Hathaway, "Where Is the Love." "Killing Me Softly with His Song" became Flack's second No. 1 hit (five weeks) in 1973, and after topping the charts again in 1974 with "Feel Like Makin' Love," Flack took a break from performing to concentrate on recording and charitable causes. She charted several more times over the next few years, but a major blow struck in 1979 when Hathaway committed suicide. Devastated, Flack was forced to find another partner and eventually did in Peabo Bryson, with whom she toured in 1980. The two recorded together in 1983, scoring a hit duet with "Tonight, I Celebrate My Love." Flack spent the remainder of the '80s touring and performing, often with orchestras, and also several times with Miles Davis. She returned to the Top Ten once more in 1991 with "Set the Night to Music," a duet with Maxi Priest. —*Steve Huey*

The Best of Roberta Flack / 1980 / Atlantic ✦✦✦✦
Showcases her biggest ballads, including "First Time Ever I Saw Your Face," "Feel Like Making Love," and "Killing Me Softly with His Song," as well as her duets with Donny Hathaway, "Where Is the Love" and "The Closer I Get to You." —*Bil Carpenter*

● **Softly with These Songs: The Best of Roberta Flack** / Jun. 22, 1993 / Atlantic ✦✦✦✦
While it includes almost everything on *Best of Roberta Flack*, *Softly with These Songs* covers material after 1980, including the hits "Tonight, I Celebrate My Love" and "Making Love," which makes it the preferable compilation. —*Stephen Thomas Erlewine*

The Flamin' Groovies

Rock 'n' Roll, Power-Pop
One of America's greatest, most influential, and legendary cult bands, the Flamin' Groovies came out of the San Francisco area in 1965 playing greasy, bluesy, rock 'n' roll dashed with a liberal sprinkling of British Invasion panache in an era soon to be dominated by hippie culture and hyperextended raga-rock freakouts. Caught in a double bind of playing the wrong kind of music at the wrong time (as well as not looking the part), the Groovies were almost completely forgotten as the Fillmore/ Avalon Ballroom scenes, dominated by the Dead, the Jefferson Airplane, et al., rendered them anachronistic. The plain truth, however, was that despite not being in tune with the zeitgeist, the Groovies made great music, and managed to sustain a career that lasted for over two decades.

What made the Groovies such a formidable band was the double dynamite supplied by guitarist Cyril Jordan and singer/wildman Roy A. Loney. Together they formed an uneasy partnership that guided the band through its most fertile period, from 1968 to 1971. In 1968, for next to nothing, the band recorded a seven-song EP entitled *Sneakers*. This little bit of DIY ingenuity resulted in a contract with Epic and the huge sum of $80,000 (1968 dollars, mind you) to be spent on their debut recording, *Supersnazz*. It was a great album that didn't sell but did get them dropped from Epic. Quickly singing with Kama Sutra, the Groovies closed the '60s and started the '70s with two terrific records (*Flamingo* and *Teenage Head*), but public apathy and the increasingly tempestuous relationship between Jordan and Loney led to the latter's departure for a solo career in 1971. Jordan, now free to run the band as a "benevolent" dictator and indulge his passion for a more folk-rock (read: Byrds) focus, hired guitarist/vocalist Chris Wilson, curiously added the apostrophe to their first name, and in 1972 moved the band to England.

Oddly enough, the Groovies had a larger, more enthusiastic following in Europe (especially in England and Germany) than they did in the states, and it seemed perfectly reasonable to assume that if great rewards were to be reaped, it would happen in Europe first. Hooking up with Dave Edmunds, who was keen to produce them, Jordan and company recorded a handful of songs as early as 1972. However, this seemingly natural collaboration yielded little until 1976, when the Groovies released their finest post-Loney effort, *Shake Some Action*. Loaded with ringing guitars, great covers, and Edmunds' spongy, bass-heavy production, *Shake Some Action* became a well-received album in punk-era Britain, as was the fine follow-up, *Flamin' Groovies Now*. This new notoriety brought renewed interest in the Groovies in America, but the string of good albums ended abruptly with the mostly covers and mostly forgettable *Jumpin' in the Night* in 1979. Clearly, the band had run out of gas. That fact, however, did little to convince Cyril Jordan that the Flamin' Groovies in any form were no longer viable. So, after five or six years of no new music—there were instead countless repackagings, anthologies,

and lousy bootlegs—the band ended up in Australia, now reduced to Jordan and a bunch of unknowns (with the exception of longtime bassist George Alexander), shamelessly covering '60s material and living off the band's legend. Apparently Jordan, 20-plus years since the Groovies' first record, still flogs a version of the band to anyone willing to listen. Expectations for quality new music by the Groovies are at an all-time low. It should be noted that after his departure in 1971, Roy Loney, after a couple of music industry jobs, made (and still makes) some wonderful records with his band the Phantom Movers (with ex-Groovies drummer Danny Mihm). Loney still occasionally works behind the counter at Jack's Record Cellar in San Francisco (stop in and say hello), and has most recently been recording with the Young Fresh Fellows. —*John Dougan*

Supersnazz / 1968 / Epic ✦✦✦
For an unknown band, Epic sank a lot of money into this record, and wasn't happy when it didn't sell. But that's hardly the fault of the band, who sound great despite the intrusive overproduction of novice knob-twiddler Steve Goldman. Loney's yelping lead vocals are in fine form, and the rest of the band rocks with a reckless abandon and stunning succinctness that was totally out-of-step with the times. —*John Dougan*

Flamingo / 1970 / Kama Sutra ✦✦✦✦
Licking their wounds after the Epic fiasco, the Groovies resurfaced on the much smaller Kama Sutra label and tore off this chunk of delirium that marked their best early-'70s work. Jordan and second guitarist Tim Lynch fire off salvo after salvo of James Burton-tinged riffing, while Loney is, well, himself; his twitchy, rockabilly-styled vocalizing never wears thin. There's a great cover of Little Richard's "Keep a-Knockin'," and even better is Loney's hip and hilarious "Second Cousin." —*John Dougan*

Teenage Head / 1971 / Big Beat ✦✦✦✦
The last and best Flamin' Groovies record made with Roy Loney, *Teenage Head* is probably the most influential record they ever made. A favorite of the hip New York rock crowd (many of whom are thanked on the album jacket), this is a rip-snorter from the Loney/Jordan-penned "High Flyin' Baby" to the cover of Randy Newman's "Have You Seen My Baby?" —*John Dougan*

☆ **Shake Some Action** / 1976 / Sire ✦✦✦✦✦
The Groovies disappeared into the wilds of Europe after *Teenage Head*, which barely earned them a cult following over here. Then came *Shake Some Action*, the debut of the Flamin' Groovies' Mark II, where they rocked out British-style for most of it (while still acknowledging their American roots), only louder and more passionately than any British Invasion band had played since 1964. The sound was a complete anachronism in the mid-'70s, but it got them noticed and earned them a cult following. The guitar sound is straight 1964 Beatles alternating with Kinks material of the same era, the vocals are the plaintive wailing of lovesick young rock gods, and the effect is stunning even 20 years on. Reissued by Australia's AIM Records on CD, and well worth tracking down as an import. —*Bruce Eder*

Still Shakin' / 1976 / Buddah ✦✦✦✦
Buddah Records, the successor to Kama Sutra, seeing that the boys were finally getting their due in the rock press, put together this cool little cash-in effort, which combined the best tracks from *Flamingo* and *Teenage Head* with a bunch of outtakes into a sort of "best-of" the Mark I Groovies. The leftover tracks are even rawer and better than the released material, and this record only added to the passion that fans old and new felt for the band. —*Bruce Eder*

The Flamin' Groovies Now! / 1978 / Sire ✦✦✦✦
So the group is getting all kinds of great press, and even some radio play from their comeback album on Sire, and embark on a national tour, playing clubs like the Bottom Line in New York before every rock V.I.P. who could write a ticket. And to accompany the tour, they put out an album of yet more British Invasion-style tracks. The sound on this record was a notable improvement over *Shake Some Action*, and the group had lost none of its flair for the period or the style, but there was also precious little new ground covered. And their cover of the Gene Clark/Byrds classic rocker "Feel a Whole Lot Better" was one of the best remakes of a '60s classic ever recorded, outdoing the original at every turn. —*Bruce Eder*

Jumpin' in the Night / 1979 / Sire ✦✦✦
The Groovies' third British Invasion-revival style album was actually even better than the second, but Sire by this time was hedging its bets, replacing a cover of the Rolling Stones' "19th Nervous Breakdown" with Warren Zevon's "Werewolves of London" on the US version. By this time, the record company was losing interest and the band was going through major personnel changes as well, and it would be a while before the Groovies turned up on another full-length album again. —*Bruce Eder*

Flamin' Groovies Studio '68 / 1984 / Eva ✦✦✦

● **Groovies' Greatest Grooves** / 1989 / Sire ✦✦✦✦
More or less what it says, a 24-song best-of including much of their finest Sire Records material, including a few rarities and outtakes, rounded out with a few of the better tracks from the pre-Sire Kama Sutra period. The

notes are voluminous and enjoyable, and the music holds up even two decades later. An essential part of any serious rock record collection. —*Bruce Eder*

The Flamingos

Doo Wop
The Flamingos may have been the greatest harmonizing vocal ensemble ever, and were certainly among the premier units of the doo wop/R&B era. Cousins Jake and Zeke Carey moved to Chicago from Baltimore in 1950. They met Paul Wilson and Johnny Carter at the Church of God and Saints of Christ Congregation, a black Jewish church. They began singing in the choir, and the foursome met Earl Lewis (not the Channels' lead vocalist) through one of the members' sisters, who was his girlfriend at the time. They originally called themselves the Swallows, but had to change names when they found out that a Baltimore group already had the name. Carter suggested El Flamingos, which was changed to the Five Flamingos, and later the Flamingos. Ralph Leon of the King Booking Agency eventually became their manager. Sollie McElroy replaced Lewis as their lead singer in the early '50s, with Lewis joining the Five Echoes. They recorded with Chance in 1953, and "If I Can't Have You" attracted some attention and did well in the Midwest and on the East Coast. "That's My Desire" and "Golden Teardrops" were marvelously sung numbers, particularly "Golden Teardrops," with its sweeping harmonies on top and bottom framing McElroy's wondrous lead. But none of their great Chance recordings generated enough national attention to make the R&B charts, nor did the three numbers they recorded for Parrot. McElroy departed and was replaced by Nate Nelson. They enjoyed their first chart success with Checker in the late '50s, scoring a Top Ten R&B hit with "I'll Be Home" in 1956. They temporarily disbanded in 1956 and regrouped in 1957 with Nelson, Jake Carey, Paul Wilson, and Tommy Hunt as the lineup, and the group now a quartet. Zeke Carey returned in 1958, and they signed with End late that year. "I Only Have Eyes for You" in 1959 was their biggest hit, peaking at No. 3 R&B and No. 11 pop. It was a cover of a song that had been a huge hit for Eddy Duchin in 1934, and was the start of a productive period that saw the Flamingos issue four albums for End and get two more R&B Top 30 singles, one the Sam Cooke composition "Nobody Loves Me Like You" in 1960. Hunt left in 1961, and the group returned briefly to Checker in 1964. They later recorded for Phillips, Julman, and Polydor, but couldn't regain their former standing. They remained among the genre's most beloved groups, and anthologies of their material on Chance and Checker have been reissued. In 1993, *The Flamingos Meet the Moonglows* was reissued by Vee-Jay. —*Ron Wynn*

★ **The Doo Bop She Bop: Best of the Flamingos** / 1990 / Rhino ✦✦✦✦✦
This 18-track collection that compiles all of the Flamingos' biggest hits and best songs. *The Doo Bop She Bop* ignores the group's latter-day soul hits and concentrates solely on their doo-wop material, which makes for a stronger, more cohesive collection. "I Only Have Eyes for You" is the acknowledged classic, while "I'll Be Home" and "A Kiss from Your Lips" were hits in their own right, but the compilation proves that the Flamingos were one of the greatest doo wop groups with its lesser-known numbers like "The Vow" and "The Ladder of Love." —*Stephen Thomas Erlewine*

Fleetwood Mac

Group / Blues-Rock, Pop-Rock, British Blues
Fleetwood Mac, formed in 1967, initially began as one of Britain's great blues-influenced rock ensembles. Over the course of many lineup changes and a relocation to Los Angeles in 1974, "Big Mac" evolved into one of the most successful pop-rock units in commercial music history.

During the early years, Fleetwood Mac endured a succession of unstable (but brilliant) lead-guitarist/singer-songwriters in Peter Green, Danny Kirwan, and Jeremy Spencer. Green and Spencer eventually jumped ship for cultish religious pursuits, and Kirwan (who ended up in a psychiatric hospital) was fired in 1972 for refusing to go on stage at a Munich gig. Green, in particular, wrote some classics in "Oh Well," "Black Magic Woman" (later a hit for Santana), and "The Green Manalishi (With the Two-Pronged Crown)." Danny Kirwan contributed many of the standout tracks on albums like *Bare Trees*, including the haunting "Dust," the ethereal "Sunny Side of Heaven," and the propulsive title track.

Bob Welch, a Los Angeles resident, was brought on board in 1971. During his time with Fleetwood Mac, Welch penned some standouts as well, like "Hypnotized" and "Sentimental Lady." During all these changes, drummer Mick Fleetwood, bassist John McVie, and vocalist and keyboardist Christine McVie (also a fine songwriter) provided the glue for the proceedings.

In January of 1975 Welch left, and engineer and producer Keith Olsen turned the band on to a tape of Lindsey Buckingham and Stevie Nicks (who had previously released a much-sought-after debut on Polydor called *Buckingham Nicks*). They were hired onto Fleetwood Mac, and the rest is history. *Fleetwood Mac*, the first album featuring the new lineup, became a gold mine, eventually hitting No. 1 in September 1976, fourteen

months after its release. After much inner turmoil, Fleetwood Mac put out *Rumours*, which topped charts around the world and became one of the biggest albums in history. Mac never duplicated the impact of *Rumours*, but subsequent albums (*Tusk, Fleetwood Mac Live, Mirage, Tango in the Night*) have been substantial successes.

Buckingham (who left in 1987) and Nicks have enjoyed solid solo careers, and Christine McVie had a No. 10 hit in 1984 with "Got a Hold on Me" from her self-titled solo album.

Fleetwood Mac reunited with two new guitarists in 1989, releasing the lackluster *Behind the Mask*.

In November 1993, confirming the departure of Stevie Nicks and guitarist Billy Burnette, Fleetwood Mac announced the addition of vocalist Bekka Bramlett and veteran singer, songwriter, and guitarist Dave Mason to the band's lineup, joining Fleetwood and the McVies. This lineup released *Time* (Oct. 1995), which was a commercial disappointment. —*Rick Clark and William Ruhlmann*

Peter Green's Fleetwood Mac / Feb. 1968 / Blue Horizon ✦✦✦✦
Fleetwood Mac's debut LP was a highlight of the late '60s British blues boom. Green's always inspired playing, the capable (if erratic) songwriting, and the general panache of the band as a whole placed them leagues above the overcrowded field. Elmore James is a big influence on this set, particularly on the tunes fronted by Jeremy Spencer ("Shake Your Moneymaker," "Got to Move"). Spencer's bluster, however, was outshone by the budding singing and songwriting skills of Green. The guitarist balanced humor and vulnerability on cuts like "Looking for Somebody" and "Long Grey Mare," and with "If I Loved Another Woman," he offered a glimpse of the Latin-blues fusion that he would perfect with "Black Magic Woman." The album was an unexpected smash in the UK, reaching No. 4 on the British charts. —*Richie Unterberger*

English Rose / Jan. 1969 / Epic ✦✦✦✦
Under the direction of Peter Green, Fleetwood Mac is heard as a British blues group, although its most notable performances are on Green's original tunes "Black Magic Woman" and "Albatross," both British hits. —*William Ruhlmann*

Then Play On / Oct. 1969 / Reprise ✦✦✦
The most diverse and accomplished album by the Peter Green-led lineup. Features some wrenching, introspective originals that draw from both blues and progressive-rock, highlighted by the doomy British hit single "Oh Well." —*Richie Unterberger*

Kiln House / Sep. 1970 / Reprise ✦✦✦
Fleetwood Mac's first album after the departure of their nominal leader, Peter Green, finds the remaining members, Mick Fleetwood, John McVie, Jeremy Spencer, and Danny Kirwan (plus McVie's wife, Christine) trying to maintain the band's guitar-heavy, blues-rock approach, with the burden falling on Spencer and Kirwan. They don't embarrass themselves, but none of this is of the caliber of Green's work. —*William Ruhlmann*

Future Games / Nov. 1971 / Reprise ✦✦✦
By the time of this album's release, Jeremy Spencer had been replaced by Bob Welch and Christine McVie had begun to assert herself more as a singer and songwriter. The result is a distinct move toward folk-rock and pop; this album sounds almost nothing like Peter Green's Fleetwood Mac. Welch's eight-minute title track has one of his characteristic haunting melodies, and with pruning and better editing could have been a hit. Christine McVie's "Show Me a Smile" is one of her loveliest ballads. Initial popular reaction was mixed: the album didn't sell as well as *Kiln House*, but it sold better than any of the band's first three albums in the US. In the UK, *Future Games* didn't chart at all, the same fate that would befall the rest of its albums until the Lindsey Buckingham-Stevie Nicks era. —*William Ruhlmann*

Bare Trees / Mar. 1972 / Reprise ✦✦✦✦
On *Bare Trees*, Fleetwood Mac married the gritty electric blues-rock of their earlier incarnations to the classic pop sensibilities that would later become fully realized in 1975's *Fleetwood Mac*. Bob Welch's "Sentimental Lady" and Christine McVie's soulful "Spare Me a Little of Your Love" are highlights. Danny Kirwin revealed an ability to compose highly melodic material that didn't constrain the band's legendary musical chemistry. —*Rick Clark*

Penguin / Mar. 1973 / Reprise ✦✦

Mystery to Me / Oct. 1973 / Reprise ✦✦✦
At this point, Fleetwood Mac is a mainstream rock band whose songs alternate between guitarist/singer Robert Welch and keyboard player/singer Christine McVie. —*William Ruhlmann*

Heroes Are Hard to Find / Sep. 1974 / Reprise ✦✦✦
Welch's peak as a songwriter (with new highs by Christine McVie) is also his swan song with the group. —*William Ruhlmann*

Fleetwood Mac in Chicago / 1975 / Sire ✦✦

☆ **Fleetwood Mac** / Jul. 1975 / Reprise ✦✦✦✦✦
The addition of Lindsey Buckingham and Stevie Nicks, plus the increasing quality of Christine McVie's songs, results in massive success. This

No. 1 album, one of the finest collections of pop-rock in the decade, contains the hits "Rhiannon," "Over My Head," and "Say You Love Me." —*William Ruhlmann*

Original Fleetwood Mac / 1977 / Sire ✦✦

T★**Rumours** / Feb. 4, 1977 / Reprise ✦✦✦✦✦
Among the best-selling albums of all time, this brilliant song cycle about the travails of love features "Dreams," "Don't Stop," "Go Your Own Way," and "You Make Loving Fun." —*William Ruhlmann*

Tusk / Oct. 1979 / Reprise ✦✦✦✦
In some ways even more impressive than *Rumours*, this two-record set is an ambitious effort full of unusual arrangements and striking instrumental passages, plus a wealth of topflight songwriting. —*William Ruhlmann*

Fleetwood Mac Live / Dec. 1980 / Reprise ✦✦✦

Mirage / Jun. 1982 / Reprise ✦✦✦
A tuneful, tastefully produced album that makes up in songcraft ("Hold Me," "Gypsy") what it lacks in the anguished passion that was once Fleetwood Mac's stock in trade. —*William Ruhlmann*

Tango in the Night / 1987 / Reprise ✦✦✦

● **Greatest Hits [Reprise]** / Nov. 1988 / Reprise ✦✦✦✦
A well-chosen best-of. The cassette version has three more tracks than the LP. —*William Ruhlmann*

Behind the Mask / Apr. 10, 1990 / Reprise ✦✦✦

25 Years: The Chain / Nov. 24, 1992 / Reprise ✦✦✦

Peter Green's Fleetwood Mac Live at the BBC / Oct. 1995 / Raw Power ✦✦

Time / Oct. 10, 1995 / Warner Bros. ✦✦

The Fleetwoods

Pop, Doo Wop, Pop-Rock
Although the Fleetwoods' sound was smooth, without many of the rougher edges of doo wop groups, they were one of the few White vocal groups of the late '50s and early '60s to enjoy success not only on the pop charts, but also the R&B charts. The Fleetwoods' forte was ballads—beginning with their 1959 debut single, "Come Softly to Me," the group racked up a number of hits over the next three years, and nearly all of them were ballads. The group broke up in 1963, but their songs—particularly "Come Softly to Me"—became pop-rock classics of the pre-British Invasion era.

Gretchen Christopher, Barbara Ellis, and Gary Troxell formed the Fleetwoods while attending high school in Olympia, WA. Originally, the group consisted only of Christopher and Ellis, but the duo soon asked Troxell to accompany them on trumpet. Shortly after his arrival in the group, Troxell abandoned the trumpet and concentrated on singing once the other two members heard a portion of a song he had written. Following some contributions from Christopher and Ellis, the group had written "Come Softly to Me." They began performing the song at various events around Olympia, eventually gaining the attention of Bob Reisdorff, who ran the Seattle-based label, Dolphin Records.

Dolphin released "Come Softly to Me" early in 1959 and the song became an instant hit, climbing to No. 1 on the pop charts and No. 5 on the R&B charts; it also reached the Top Ten in UK. The Fleetwoods weren't able to immediately produce a follow-up single as successful as their debut, but their third single, "Mr. Blue," was a No. 1 pop and Top Five R&B hit in the US in late 1959. By the time of its release, Dolphin had changed its name to Dolton. For the next three years, the Fleetwoods had a string of minor pop hits. The group wasn't able to consistently place singles in the upper regions of the charts partially because Troxell was drafted into the navy at the height of the group's popularity at the end of 1959. Troxell was replaced by Vic Dana, who would later have a string of his own hit singles in the early '60s.

The Fleetwoods last Top Ten single arrived in the spring of 1961, when "Tragedy" climbed the US charts. The group disbanded two years later, after releasing their final single, a cover of Jesse Belvin's "Goodnight My Love." Over the next three decades, the Fleetwoods reunited occasionally to perform concerts and oldies revues. In 1973, the group recorded an album with producer Jerry Dennon, but the resulting recordings were unsuccessful. In 1990, the Fleetwoods—featuring Christopher, Troxel, and instead of Ellis a singer called Cheryl Huggins—played a tour on the American oldies circuit after Rhino released the compact disc collection, *Best of the Fleetwoods*. —*Stephen Thomas Erlewine*

● **The Best of the Fleetwoods** / 1990 / Rhino ✦✦✦✦
Rhino's *Best of the Fleetwoods* contains all of their hits ("Come Softly to Me," "Mr. Blue," and 16 other songs) on a smartly assembled collection. —*Stephen Thomas Erlewine*

Come Softly to Me: The Very Best of the Fleetwoods / Aug. 10, 1993 / EMI ✦✦✦✦
This single-disc collection is a treasure for devoted fans, featuring alter-

nate takes, radio commercials, a comprehensive discography, fine liner notes, and unreleased tracks. Casual listeners may find all of this material extraneous; they will find everything they need on Rhino's collection. —*Stephen Thomas Erlewine*

A Flock of Seagulls

New Wave, New Romantic
A Liverpool new wave group with a name derived from the novel *Jonathan Livingston Seagull*, featuring lead singer/keyboard player Mike Score (b. Nov. 5, 1957), his brother Ali (drums), Paul Reynolds (guitar), and Frank Maudsley (drums). They formed in 1979, hit with "I Ran (So Far Away)" in 1982, split up in 1986, and have since re-formed. —*William Ruhlmann*

A Flock of Seagulls / 1982 / Jive ✦✦✦✦
A Flock of Seagulls scored one big hit, "I Ran," in the driving, quick-tempo dance style that characterized most of their work. It's here, along with several similar tracks. —*William Ruhlmann*

The Story of a Young Heart / Aug. 1984 / Jive/Arista ✦✦

● **The Best of A Flock of Seagulls** / 1987 / Jive ✦✦✦✦
Every good song A Flock of Seagulls ever recorded is available on this fine collection, including the new wave classic "I Ran (So Far Away)." —*Stephen Thomas Erlewine*

Eddie Floyd

b. Jun. 25, 1935, Montgomery, AL
Vocals / Soul
Floyd came aboard the good ship Stax at the behest of his friend Al Bell and immediately made himself useful as a composer for labelmates Carla Thomas, William Bell, Otis Redding (originally intended to be the recipient of "Knock on Wood"), and Atlantic's Wilson Pickett.

Floyd's own mid-'60s output included "Raise Your Hand," which utilized the same Booker T. & the MGs-powered thrust as "Knock on Wood," and "Big Bird," written partially in shocked response to the tragic death of Redding. Floyd remained loyal to Stax right up to its bitter demise, his engaging vocals resulting in major hits with the gentle "I've Never Found a Girl" and a lively remake of Sam Cooke's "Bring It on Home to Me."

Whenever Floyd re-teams with his old Stax pals—guitarist Steve Cropper, bassist Duck Dunn, and sometimes Booker T. Jones on organ—the long-ago Memphis magic instantly returns. With Floyd happily leading the throngs through "Raise Your Hand" and "Knock on Wood," it's 1966 all over again. —*Bill Dahl*

● **Chronicle** / 1979 / Stax ✦✦✦✦
Singer-songwriter/producer Eddie Floyd, a former member of the Falcons, shines on originals such as "Soul Street" and "I've Got to Have Your Love" as well as covers such as Sam Cooke's "Bring It on Home to Me" and Smokey Robinson's "My Girl." This 1979 collection includes all of Floyd's singles between 1968 and 1974.

Rare Stamps / 1993 / Stax ✦✦✦✦
A pair of remarkable soul hits, "Knock on Wood" and "I've Never Found a Girl," enabled Eddie Floyd to attain national success in 1968. But the longtime singer and composer, whose roots dated back to the Detroit group the Falcons in the late '50s, was a steady, if not spectacular, performer for many years before and after those two songs. Several of Floyd's finest pieces are compiled on the 25-track CD *Rare Stamps*, including a wonderful testimonial to Otis Redding, "Big Bird." There are also two super duets with Mavis Staples, "Never Let You Go" and "Ain't That Good," which rank with anything that the label issued. —*Ron Wynn*

The Flying Burrito Brothers

Country-Rock
The Flying Burrito Brothers helped forge the connection between rock and country, and with their 1969 debut album, *The Gilded Palace of Sin*, they virtually invented the blueprint for country-rock.

Originally, the Flying Burrito Brothers were a group of Los Angeles musicians who gathered together to jam. Gram Parsons and Chris Hillman took the band's name when they were forming their own band after leaving the Byrds. Parsons helped steer the Byrds toward a country direction during his brief stint with the band, as captured on the 1968 album *Sweetheart of the Rodeo*. He left the Byrds, followed shortly afterward by Hillman. The duo added pedal steel guitarist "Sneaky" Pete Kleinow and bassist Chris Ethridge to the band and set about recording their debut album with a variety of session drummers.

The Gilded Palace of Sin, the Flying Burrito Brothers' debut album, was released in the spring of 1969. Although the album only sold 40,000 copies, the band developed a devoted following, which happened to include many prominent musicians in Los Angeles, Bob Dylan, and the Rolling Stones. The Stones were so impressed with the album that they hired the Burrito Brothers to play their Altamont festival. Around this time, Parsons and Stones guitarist Keith Richards became good friends, which led to Parsons losing interest in the Burritos. Before the band recorded their second album, Ethridge left the band and was replaced by Bernie Leadon, and the group hired ex-Byrd Michael Clarke as their permanent drummer.

Burrito Deluxe, the group's second album, was released in the spring of 1970. After its release, Gram Parsons left the group and was replaced by Rick Roberts, a local Californian songwriter. Roberts' first album with the band, *The Flying Burrito Brothers*, was released in 1971. After its release, Kleinow left the band to become a session musician and Leadon departed to join the Eagles. The Burritos hired pedal steel guitarist Al Perkins and bassist Roger Bush to replace them, as well as adding guitarist Kenny Wertz and fiddler Byron Berline to the lineup. This new version of the group recorded the live album *The Last of the Red Hot Burritos*, which was released in 1972. Before its release, the band splintered apart. Berline, Bush, and Wertz all left to form the bluegrass group Country Gazette, while Hillman and Perkins joined Manassas. Roberts assembled a new band to tour Europe in 1973 and then dissolved the group, choosing to pursue a solo career. Roberts would later form Firefall with Michael Clarke.

Close up the Honky Tonks, a double-album Flying Burrito Brothers compilation, was released in 1974 because of the burgeoning interest in Gram Parsons. Capitalizing on the collection and the cult forming around Parsons, Sneaky Pete Kleinow and Chris Ethridge formed a new version of the Flying Burrito Brothers in 1975. The duo recruited Floyd "Gib" Gilbeau (vocals, guitar, fiddle), bassist Joel Scott Hill, and drummer Gene Parsons and recorded *Flying Again*, which was released on Columbia Records in 1975. Ethridge left the band after the release of *Flying Again;* he was replaced by Skip Battin, who appeared on the 1976 album *Airborne*. Following its release, Gene Parsons left the group. Also in 1976, a collection of Gram Parsons-era outtakes entitled *Sleepless Nights* was released on A&M Records.

For the two decades following their 1975 reunion, the Flying Burrito Brothers performed and recorded sporadically. In 1979, the group released *Live from Tokyo* on Regency Records; the album spawned their first country hit, a cover of Merle Haggard's "White Line Fever," which hit the charts in 1980. Also in 1980, the group abbreviated its name to the Burrito Brothers when they signed a contract with Curb Records. The band's first release under the name the Burrito Brothers was 1981's *Hearts on the Line*, a record that spawned three minor country chart hits. *Sunset Sundown*, the Brothers second Curb album, appeared in 1982 and like its predecessor produced three minor hits. Following the release of *Sunset Sundown*, Sneaky Pete Kleinow left the band to become an animator and special effects creator in Hollywood. The group carried on without him, led by Gib Gilbeau and John Beland. That incarnation of the band fell apart in 1985, the same year that Kleinow assembled yet another version of the band, and for the next three years, this incarnation of the Flying Burrito Brothers toured America and Europe. In 1988, the group split apart again, although it did occasionally reunite for further tours and recordings in the '90s. —*Stephen Thomas Erlewine*

☆ **The Gilded Palace of Sin** / Feb. 1969 / A&M ✦✦✦✦✦
The birth of country-rock. Gram Parsons and Chris Hillman, aided by Sneaky Pete Kleinow and Chris Ethridge, create a hybrid by combining rock attitude with country sentiments and change the course of popular music. Really. —*William Ruhlmann*

Burrito Deluxe / Apr. 1970 / A&M ✦✦✦✦
The follow-up to the brilliant *Guilded Palace of Sin* finds the band somewhat directionless with Gram Parsons losing interest and playing a less active role. While the Parsons/Hillman-penned "Cody Cody" and a touching rendition of the Rolling Stones' "Wild Horses" capture some of the previous album's magic, *Burrito Deluxe* is somewhat a letdown. Parsons left for a solo career shortly after. —*Chris Woodstra*

The Flying Burrito Brothers / May 1971 / A&M ✦✦✦
On their first post-Parsons album, the Burritos (now led by Hillman and Rick Roberts, and with future Eagle Bernie Leadon replacing Ethridge) make an honest step forward in country-rock. Includes the Roberts song "Colorado." —*William Ruhlmann*

The Last of the Red Hot Burritos / Apr. 1972 / A&M ✦✦
Close up the Honky Tonks / Jun. 1974 / A&M ✦✦✦✦
A&M Records seemed to close the book on The Flying Burrito Brothers with *Close up the Honky Tonks*, a 23-track, double-LP compilation. A combination best-of and odds-and-sods career wrap-up, the album contained one LP given over to tracks from The Burritos' first two records, *The Gilded Palace of Sin* and *Burrito Deluxe*, plus the non-LP single "The Train Song." The second disc presented 11 previously unreleased tracks, most of them cover songs, ranging from the Bee Gees' "To Love Somebody" to the Everly Brothers' "Wake Up, Little Susie." Co-founder Gram Parsons was featured on the five songs on Side Three, while Side Four came from the Rick Roberts era of the band. The Burritos would lack a one-disc best-of until A&M came up with the CD/cassette release *Farther Along* in 1988. So, for more than a decade, *Close up the Honky*

Tonks was the definitive Burritos compilation, and even now, when it is out of print, it contains some excellent performances available nowhere else. —*William Ruhlmann*

Flying Again / Sep. 1975 / Columbia ✦✦
Sleepless Nights / Apr. 1976 / A&M ✦✦✦
Dim Lights, Thick Smoke and Loud, Loud Music / Mar. 1987 / Edsel ✦✦✦

★ **Farther Along: Best Of** / 1988 / A&M ✦✦✦✦✦
Farther Along: The Best of the Flying Burrito Brothers is a nearly flawless compilation, containing a full 21 tracks of the pioneering group's best material. All but two of the songs from *The Gilded Palace of Sin* are included on the collection, as are all of the highlights from *Burrito Deluxe* and a handful of rarities and outtakes. In short, it's a definitive collection containing all of the Burrito Brothers' finest moments. It's indespensible to any rock or country collection. —*Stephen Thomas Erlewine*

Close Encounters to the West Coast / 1991 / Relix ✦✦

John Fogerty

b. May 28, 1945, Berkeley, CA
Guitar, Vocals / Rock 'n' Roll
John Cameron Fogerty achieved fame as the lead singer-songwriter and guitarist in Creedence Clearwater Revival and has since gone on to a chart-topping solo career. Born in Berkeley, CA, Fogerty and his brother Tom organized the group that would become Creedence and the Golliwogs in the late '50s. As Creedence, they released nine Top Ten singles, all written by Fogerty, between 1969 and 1971, starting with the standard "Proud Mary." They also scored eight gold albums between 1968 and 1972, all fueled by Fogerty's simple, driving rock songs and his burly baritone, intoning deceptively poetic ("Bad Moon Rising") and even political ("Fortunate Son") lyrics.

Creedence split up in 1972. Fogerty at first confused his considerable following by releasing an album of covers, on which he played all the instruments, under the name the Blue Ridge Rangers in 1973. This was followed by a formal solo album, *John Fogerty*, in 1975, and then silence for more than nine years while the artist worked out business problems with Creedence's old label. But Fogerty returned at the end of 1984 with a Top Ten single, "The Old Man Down the Road," and a No. 1 album, *Centerfield. Eye of the Zombie* was a less successful follow-up in 1986. —*William Ruhlmann*

Blue Ridge Rangers / 1973 / Fantasy ✦✦✦
John Fogerty / 1975 / Asylum ✦✦
● **Centerfield** / Apr. 1985 / Warner Bros. ✦✦✦✦
The comeback album that proved the ex-Creedence firebrand still knew how to rock and make it count. Includes "The Old Man Down the Road," "Rock and Roll Girls," and "Centerfield." —*Jeff Tamarkin*

Eye of the Zombie / 1986 / Warner Bros. ✦✦

Foo Fighters

Alternative Pop-Rock, Grunge
While he was drumming with Nirvana, Dave Grohl was recording original songs at home that never received public release. Those tapes would become the foundation of the Foo Fighters, the band he formed in 1995, after the death of Kurt Cobain. Like Nirvana, the Foo Fighters melded loud, heavy guitars with pretty melodies and mixed punk sensibilities with a sharp sense of pop songwriting. They might not have had the revolutionary spark of Nirvana, but they satisfied the immediate desires of many Nirvana fans, as their platinum success proved.

Dave Grohl began playing guitar and writing songs in his early teens, as well as performing with a variety of obscure hardcore punk bands. In the late '80s, when he was still in his teens, he joined the Washington, DC-area hardcore band Scream as their drummer. During the final days of Scream, Grohl began writing and recording his own material in the basement studio of his friend, Barrett Jones. Some of Grohl's songs appeared on Scream's final album, *Fumble*. After Scream's 1990 summer tour, Grohl joined Nirvana and moved to Seattle.

After Nirvana recorded *Nevermind*, Grohl went back to the DC-area and recorded a handful of tracks that would appear on *Pocketwatch*, a cassette released by Simple Machines. For most of 1992, he was busy with Nirvana, but when the band stayed off of the road, he recorded solo material with Jones, who had moved to Seattle. The pair kept recording throughout early 1993, when Grohl returned to Nirvana to record *In Utero*. Grohl had toyed with the idea of releasing another independent cassette in the summer of 1993, but the plans never reached fruition. Following Kurt Cobain's suicide in 1994, the drummer kept quiet for several months. In the fall of 1994, booking time in a professional studio, Grohl and Jones recorded the album that became the Foo Fighters' debut album in a week. Boiling down his backlog of songs to about 15 tracks, Grohl played all of the instruments on the album. He made 100 copies of the tape, passing it out to friends and associates. In no time, Dave Grohl's solo project became the object of a fierce record company bidding war.

Instead of embarking on a full-fledged solo career, Grohl decided to form a band. Through his wife he met Nate Mendel, the bassist for Sunny Day Real Estate. Shortly before the pair met, Jeremy Enigk, the leader of Sunny Day Real Estate, had converted to Christianity and quit the band, effectively ending the group's career. Not only did Mendel join Grohl's band, but so did Sunny Day's drummer, William Goldsmith; former Germs and Nirvana guitarist Pat Smear rounded out the lineup. The band, named the Foo Fighters after a World War II secret force that allegedly researched UFOs, and signed a contract with Capitol Records. The band's self-titled debut, consisting solely of Dave Grohl's recordings, was released on July 4, 1995. It was an instant success in America, as "This Is a Call" garnered heavy alternative and album rock airplay. By early 1995, the album was certified platinum in the US. — *Stephen Thomas Erlewine*

Foo Fighters / 1995 / Roswell/Capitol ✦✦✦✦
Essentially a collection of solo home recordings by Dave Grohl, the Foo Fighters' eponymous debut is a modest triumph. Driven by big pop melodies and distorted guitars, Foo Fighters does strongly recall Nirvana, only with a decidedly lighter approach. If Kurt Cobain's writing occasionally recalled John Lennon, Dave Grohl's songs are reminiscent of Paul McCartney—they're driven by large, instantly memorable melodies, whether it's the joyous outburst of "This Is a Call" or the gentle pop of "Big Me." That doesn't mean Grohl shys away from noise; toward the end of the record, he piles on several thrashers that make more sense as pure aggressive sound than songs. Since he recorded the album by himself, they aren't as powerful as most band's primal sonic workouts, but the results are impressive for a solo musician. Nevertheless, they aren't as strong as his fully formed pop songs, and that's where the heart of the album lies. *Foo Fighters* has a handful of punk-pop gems that show, given the right musicians and songwriters, the genre had not entirely become a cliché by the middle of the '90s. — *Stephen Thomas Erlewine*

Steve Forbert

b. 1955, Meridian, MS
Guitar, Harmonica, Vocals / Singer-Songwriter, Pop-Rock
Mississippi-born Forbert was one of the better received folk-based singer-songwriters of the late '70s. In recent years, he has written hits for country artists as well as continuing to record albums himself. — *William Ruhlmann*

Alive on Arrival / 1978 / Nemperor ✦✦✦✦
Forbert takes the folk-rock singer-songwriter format, already 13 years old at this point, and gives it a fresh, exuberant, almost punkish appeal. — *William Ruhlmann*

Jackrabbit Slim / Oct. 1979 / Nemperor ✦✦✦✦
Forbert's more elaborately produced second album continues the songwriting quality of his first and includes his No. 11 hit single "Romeo's Tune." — *William Ruhlmann*

Little Stevie Orbit / Sep. 1980 / Nemperor ✦✦✦
Little Stevie Orbit was seen as a disappointment at the time of its release because it did not generate a hit single on the order of "Romeo's Tune," and thus failed to consolidate the commercial success Steve Forbert had achieved with his second album, *Jackrabbit Slim*. In retrospect, however, it is a spirited, rollicking collection on which Forbert sounds increasingly comfortable fronting a rock band on a series of lighthearted songs such as "I'm an Automobile" and "If You've Gotta Ask You'll Never Know." It may not have made him a superstar, but *Little Stevie Orbit* provided some strong additions to Steve Forbert's concert repertoire for years to come. — *William Ruhlmann*

Steve Forbert / Jul. 1982 / Nemperor ✦✦
Streets of This Town / Apr. 1988 / Geffen ✦✦✦
Coming back after a six-year layoff, Forbert displays a previously unheard edge of bitterness that only deepens his thoughtful lyrics. And he rocks harder than ever. — *William Ruhlmann*

The American in Me / Jan. 1992 / Geffen ✦✦✦
● **Best of: What Kinda Guy?** / 1993 / Columbia/Legacy ✦✦✦✦
Excellent compilation featuring a generous 19 tracks, including his hit "Romeo's Tune." A great place to get acquainted with this underrated singer-songwriter. — *Stephen Thomas Erlewine*

Mission of the Crossroad Palms / 1995 / Giant ✦✦✦

Foreigner

Hard Rock, Pop-Rock, Arena Rock
Foreigner was formed in 1976 by Mick Jones (ex-Spooky Tooth) and Ian McDonald (ex-King Crimson). The band was an instant success with the release of their debut album in 1977, which showcased the talents of guitarist Jones and lead singer Lou Gramm. Jones and Gramm also wrote most of the band's material. The songs, mainly hard rock, boasted strong

melodies and memorable guitar riffs. The band never strayed far from this formula but, to keep things fresh, added some interesting touches. For example, Junior Walker's sax on "Urgent" and the gospel vocals of Jennifer Holliday and the New Jersey Mass Choir on "I Want to Know What Love Is" helped elevate these songs above the ordinary. Gramm left the band in the late '80s for a solo career. Foreigner recruited a new lead singer but Gramm's writing and distinctive vocals are sorely missed. —*Kenneth M. Cassidy*

Foreigner / 1977 / Atlantic ✦✦✦
Double Vision / 1978 / Atlantic ✦✦✦
4 / 1981 / Atlantic ✦✦✦✦
The strength of Lou Gramm's powerhouse vocals and the band's synth-pop texturing carried this album to No. 1. It produced several major hits, including "Urgent," which featured a sax solo by Junior Walker, and "Waiting for a Girl like You." —*Donna DiChario*

Records / 1982 / Atlantic ✦✦✦✦
All the band's early (including those from *4*) radio-friendly hits are here in this collection of straightahead rock 'n' rollers. It includes "Waiting for a Girl like You," "Hot Blooded," and more. —*Donna DiChario*

● **The Very Best . . . and Beyond** / 1992 / Atlantic ✦✦✦✦
Very Best . . . and Beyond not only collects all the major hits from Foreigner's early years ("Feels Like the First Time," "Head Games," "Hot Blooded"), but also features their hits from the late '80s ("I Want to Know What Love Is," "Say You Will"), making the set preferable to *Records*. —*Stephen Thomas Erlewine*

Four Seasons

Pop-Rock
Although they were one of the very biggest rock 'n' roll groups of the 1960s, the Four Seasons—unlike, say, the Beatles, Rolling Stones, or the Byrds—don't excite virtually automatic respect from listeners and critics. A big factor is their most distinguishing trademark, the shrill falsetto vocals of their lead singer, Frankie Valli. Many also find their material—gently moralistic, romantic tunes with tightly arranged group harmonies that updated doo wop ethos into the 1960s—too cornball and clean-cut.

Whatever your feelings about the group, though, there's no denying their considerable importance. No other White American group of the time save the Beach Boys boasted such intricate harmonies, though the Four Seasons were much more firmly in the Italian-American doo wop tradition. Their uptown production values were contemporary and, in certain respects, innovative. The R&B influence in their music was large, and some of their early singles enjoyed success with the R&B audience; in fact, some listeners thought that the Four Seasons were Black when the group landed their first hits. And they were immensely successful, making the Top Ten thirteen times between 1962 and 1967 with hits like "Sherry," "Big Girls Don't Cry," "Dawn," "Rag Doll," and "Let's Hang On."

The Four Seasons had been around for a long time before they got their first hit in 1962. Frankie Valli had made his first record way back in 1953, and in 1956 made a little noise with the Four Lovers' "Apple of My Eye." The Newark, NJ group also included future Four Season Tommy DeVito on guitar, and in subsequent years Valli would record flops for RCA, Decca, Cindy, and Gone, sometimes as a soloist, sometimes with groups. In the early '60s, the group, now known as the Four Seasons, were doing backup vocals for other artists.

Philadelphia producer Bob Crewe started working with the Seasons in 1962, and his contributions would be inestimable in the following years. Not only did he produce all of their big '60s hits, but he would write much of their material in collaboration with group member Bob Gaudio. It was Valli's near-soprano, though, that dominated their No. 1 hit "Sherry," as it would on the rest of their hits. "Big Girls Don't Cry," "Walk like a Man," and "Candy Girl" all followed within the next year—big smashes all, the first two (like "Sherry") featuring stomping, almost martial hand claps. "Candy Girl" offered evidence of versatility, with its samba-like rhythms and glissando flourishes.

The British Invasion did little to diminish the Seasons' fortunes, at least initially. In 1964, they moved from Vee-Jay (which also, for a brief time, had rights to the Beatles) to Philips. Their production became more sophisticated and dramatic while remaining unabashedly pop, and in 1964 they had several of their biggest hits: "Dawn," "Ronnie," "Rag Doll," "Save It for Me," and "Big Man in Town" (as well as a gem-like B-side, "Silence Is Golden," which would be a hit in 1967 for the Tremeloes). The Four Seasons' influence, oddly, was also felt on a couple of tracks by the biggest British Invasion bands: the Beatles' "Tell Me Why" and the Rolling Stones' "The Singer Not the Song" both launched into ear-straining falsettos at points, whether as a satire, tribute, or both.

The winning streak basically continued through 1967, although they would never again be as huge. "Let's Hang On," "Working My Way Back to You," "Opus 17," "I've Got You Under My Skin," "Beggin'," and "Marianne" were all big hits from the time, though, working in some mild soul influences. They also, just for kicks, released a couple of silly singles under a pseudonym, the Wonder Who?, that even pre-teens quickly identified as the Seasons under disguise. The Wonder Who?'s 1965 Top 20 hit, "Don't Think Twice," easily qualifies as the most ridiculous Dylan cover ever to hit the Top 40.

Guitar-oriented, more socially conscious rock and soul had been making inroads into the Four Seasons' audience for a while, but the times really caught up with them by the end of 1967. The group would only make the Top 40 one more time before their mid-'70s reunion. In the late '60s Valli, while maintaining his position in the Seasons, had kicked off a solo career that went straight for the heart of show-bizzy pop on his biggest single, the No. 2 hit "Can't Take My Eyes off You." The Four Seasons did attempt to address social concerns of the day on the late-'60s album *Genuine Imitation Life Gazette*, which usually met with derisive snickers from the few that heard it.

The Four Seasons struggled on into the 1970s; by the time they signed with a Motown subsidiary in 1971, Valli and Gaudio were the only original members left. They briefly returned to the top of the charts in the mid-'70s with "Who Loves You" and the nostalgic "December, 1963 (Oh, What A Night)"; at the same time, Valli had a resurgence as a soloist, reaching No. 1 with "My Eyes Adored You" and making the Top Ten with "Swearin' to God." It couldn't last, any more than the group could turn back the clock to December 1963, that last moment when they reigned as the most successful White rock group in the world, unaware of the oncoming invasion by the Beatles. They've remained active off and on during the last two decades on the nostalgia circuit, without gaining any notable successes on record. *—Richie Unterberger*

25th Anniversary Collection / 1987 / Rhino ♦♦♦♦
Frankie Valli and the Four Seasons scored hits from 1962 to 1978 under a variety of guises. Lead singer Valli started making solo records in 1965, and he had his own hits. They are all included in this long-overdue four-disc set, which runs from the Seasons' "Sherry" to Valli's "Grease." *—William Ruhlmann*

★ **Anthology** / 1988 / Rhino ♦♦♦♦♦
Over the course of 20 tracks, *Anthology* covers all of the Four Seasons' essential hits, as well as Valli's solo "Can't Take My Eyes off You"; it's the definitive collection. *—Stephen Thomas Erlewine*

Four Tops

Soul, R&B, Motown
The Four Tops are the most stable, consistent, and dependable of the successful R&B/pop vocal acts to emerge from Motown Records in the 1960s. Unlike the Temptations, they have had no personnel changes; unlike the Supremes and the Miracles, their lead singer never felt the need to step out on his own. At the same time, the Four Tops personified the musical hybrid Motown sought—they had the grittiness of gospel and R&B, but they were smooth enough to appeal to pop audiences.

The group was formed in Detroit in 1953 by lead singer Levi Stubbs, Jr., Renaldo "Obie" Benson, Lawrence Payton, and Abdul "Duke" Fakir when they were still in high school. They recorded for several labels before signing to Motown in 1963. "Baby, I Need Your Loving" (Jul. 1964), written and produced by the team of Brian Holland, Lamont Dozier, and Eddie Holland, was their first substantial hit, setting the pattern for a series of songs showcasing Stubbs's emotive wail set against the Benson-Payton-Fakir harmony line. Need and longing would be the hallmarks of Stubbs' singing on such songs as "Ask the Lonely" (Jan. 1965), which launched a string of Pop Top Ten/pop Top 40 hits over the next two years. Its follow-up, "I Can't Help Myself" (Apr. 1965), hit No. 1 and was itself followed by "It's the Same Old Song" (Jul. 1965), "Something About You" (Oct. 1965), "Shake Me, Wake Me (When It's Over)" (Feb. 1966), "Loving You Is Sweeter than Ever" (May 1966), a second No. 1, "Reach Out, I'll Be There" (Aug. 1966), "Standing in the Shadows of Love" (Nov. 1966), "Bernadette" (Feb. 1967), "7 Rooms of Gloom" (May 1967), and "You Keep Running Away" (Aug. 1967).

At that point, the Holland-Dozier-Holland team left Motown, depriving the Four Tops of their writing and producing talent. The label at first had some trouble finding material for them, having them cover songs like "Walk Away Renee" and "If I Were a Carpenter." In 1970, however, they rebounded with "It's All in the Game," "Still Water (Love)," a duet with the Supremes on "River Deep—Mountain High," and "Just Seven Numbers (Can Straighten out My Life)," all of which made the R&B Top Ten and the pop Top 40. They scored one more R&B Top Ten on Motown with "(It's the Way) Nature Planned It" before moving to Dunhill (later acquired by ABC, then by MCA) Records, where they enjoyed another string of hits, including "Keeper of the Castle" (Oct. 1972), the gold-selling "Ain't No Woman (Like the One I Got)" (Jan. 1973), "Are You Man Enough" (Jun. 1973), "Sweet Understanding Love" (Sep. 1973), "One Chain Don't Make No Prison" (Apr. 1974), and "Midnight Flower" (Jul. 1974). They returned to the R&B Top Ten with "Catfish" (Aug. 1976), and moved to Casablanca (since acquired by PolyGram) for the R&B No. 1 "When She Was My Girl" (Sep. 1981). The Four Tops returned to Motown

in 1983, and by 1988 were signed to Arista. Their hit-making days presumably behind them, they remain a solid concert act with a repertoire of favorites and a catalog that continues to be repackaged successfully. *—William Ruhlmann*

● **The Greatest Hits** / Aug. 1967 / Motown ♦♦♦♦
The first of what would be many greatest hits and anthology packages featuring the Four Tops. At this point, they had had enough chart hits for a good single album set, which is what this is. It has long since lost its value with the release of numerous superior packages. *—Ron Wynn*

Keeper of the Castle / 1972 / Motown ♦♦♦

★ **Anthology** / Jul. 1974 / Motown ♦♦♦♦♦
Until they get the deluxe box set CD treatment, this three-record/two-CD set qualifies as the ultimate Four Tops Motown statement. It includes all the landmark hits, plus good numbers from their final days at Motown in the 1970s (they did return in the mid-'80s), such as "Still Water" and "Just Seven Numbers." *—Ron Wynn*

Until You Love Someone: More of the Best (1965-1970) / 1993 / Rhino ♦♦♦
This compilation gathers 18 nonhit album tracks from eight LPs that the Four Tops cut for Motown between 1965 and 1970 (some of which appeared on B-sides). A major soul group they might have been, but the Tops' pinnacle was actually quite brief, and that's reflected in this collection. No less than two-thirds of the songs date from 1965 and 1966, six from 1965's *Second Album* alone. Not so coincidentally, all but one of those cuts were written by the legendary Holland/Dozier/Holland songwriting team. The production is faultless, the songs very characteristically HDH, and Levi Stubbs' lead vocals are unfailingly gritty and pleasurable. Yet none of these have the unforgettable hooks of their hit singles of the period like "Reach Out, I'll Be There" and "I Can't Help Myself." As enjoyable as the formula is, the uniformity of the sound limits this disc's appeal to serious Motown and soul collectors. Curiosities among the non-HDH cuts include little-known tunes by Smokey Robinson and Stevie Wonder, and a nonhit single from 1969, "What Is a Man." *—Richie Unterberger*

The Best of the Four Tops (1972-1976) / MCA ♦♦♦♦
This collection covers their best Dunhill tracks from the 1970s, which did include two big hits in "Ain't No Woman (Like the One I Got)" and "Are You Man Enough." "Keeper of the Castle" was also a Top Ten R&B single, and it seemed as if the Four Tops were in stride again. The Dunhill period yielded two more Top Ten R&B smashes with "One Chain Don't Make No Prison" and "Midnight Flower," and is a much better period than some fans consider. *—Ron Wynn*

Peter Frampton

b. Apr. 22, 1950, Beckenham, England
Guitar, Vocals / Pop-Rock, Arena Rock
Before he shot to solo superstardom in the mid-'70s, guitarist Peter Frampton was a British teen idol in the late '60s thanks to his work with the Herd and looks worthy of being named "Face of 1968" in several British magazines. The following year, Frampton joined ex-Small Faces front man Steve Marriott in Humble Pie, remaining for two years before departing for a solo career. After performing on George Harrison's *All Things Must Pass* and Nilsson's *Son of Schmilsson*, Frampton recorded his solo debut *Wind of Change* in 1972 and formed a backing band, Frampton's Camel, to support him on tour. Members included ex-Spooky Tooth drummer Mick Kellie, ex-Cochise keyboardist Mickey Gallagher, and former Bell and Arc bassist Rick Wills. Frampton toured extensively for the next few years but broke up Frampton's Camel in 1974, a year before his *Frampton* LP went gold. Recorded at San Francisco's Winterland, 1976's double album *Frampton Comes Alive* was a staggering success, selling over six million copies and becoming the biggest-selling live rock album ever at that time. It showcased Frampton's mastery of the talk-box guitar effect and his penchant for in-concert theatrics, and produced three hit singles ("Show Me the Way," "Baby, I Love Your Way," and "Do You Feel Like We Do"). The follow-up LP, *I'm in You*, produced Frampton's biggest hit in the title track, but his career was temporarily put on hold by a near-fatal car crash in the Bahamas in 1978. Frampton had made his acting debut as Billy Shears in that year's ill-received film version of *Sgt. Pepper's Lonely Hearts Club Band*, directed by Robert Stigwood. Personal problems halted a full-scale comeback following Frampton's recovery; he recorded sporadically throughout the '80s, but none of these efforts caught fire with the public. He had been planning a Humble Pie reunion with Steve Marriott in 1991 when Marriott's home burned down, killing him. Nevertheless, Frampton released a self-titled album for Relativity in 1994. *—Steve Huey*

Frampton Comes Alive / 1976 / A&M ♦♦♦♦
Fueled by Frampton's voice-box guitar technique and accessible radio-friendly pop-rock songs like "Show Me the Way" and "Baby, I Love Your Way," the double album *Frampton Comes Alive* became the biggest-selling live album in rock history, topping the ten million mark. It's a sensi-

ble place to start, since Frampton seems to be in his element here, and the song selection includes the cream of his first four albums. —*Donna DiChario*

Shine on: A Collection / Oct. 20, 1992 / A&M ✦✦✦✦
This two-disc set—featuring all the hits, stellar sound, and insightful liner notes—is the essential collection for anyone looking for a great overview of Frampton. —*Rick Clark*

● **Greatest Hits** / Jun. 18, 1996 / A&M ✦✦✦✦
By compiling all of Peter Frampton's biggest hits—in their hit versions, so "Show Me the Way" and "Baby, I Love Your Way" are from *Frampton Comes Alive*, not the studio albums—onto one disc, *Greatest Hits* functions as the definitive retrospective on the guitarist. It has a better selection than the single disc *Classics, Vol. 12*, and it is more concise and listenable than the double-disc box *Shine On: A Collection*, which means it's the only collection that provides an effective, manageable overview of Frampton. —*Stephen Thomas Erlewine*

Connie Francis

b. Dec. 12, 1938, Newark, NJ
Vocals / Pop, Brill Building Pop
Considered the leading pop female singer of her era, Connie Francis usually sang of her latest broken heart with a teardrop in her voice. The Newark, NJ, native started performing as a child, signing with MGM Records in 1955, but she suffered two years of bombs before the torch ballad "Who's Sorry Now" shot up the charts in 1958. Although she specialized in sobbing tales of woe, Francis proved she could rock with Neil Sedaka's "Stupid Cupid" in 1958 and "Lipstick on Your Collar" the next year. Francis scored two No. 1 hits in 1960—the twangy "Everybody's Somebody's Fool" and "My Heart Has a Mind of Its Own," and she branched into acting with a starring role in *Where the Boys Are*, the archetypal spring-break movie. "Don't Break the Heart That Loves You" was Francis' last pop chart-topper in 1962, but she continued to rank high in the pop pantheon throughout the decade, with forays into ethnic and country idioms. —*Bill Dahl*

● **The Very Best of Connie Francis** / Oct. 1963 / Polydor ✦✦✦✦
Though many best-of's exist on the market, this one leans more heavily toward her earlier rock 'n' roll hits. (Originally released in October 1963 as a 15-track LP by MGM Records, *The Very Best of Connie Francis* was reissued in 1986 on CD with six bonus tracks by Polydor Records.) —*Cub Koda*

White Sox, Pink Lipstick . . . & Stupid Cupid / Jul. 1993 / Bear Family ✦✦✦✦

Frankie Goes to Hollywood

Dance-Pop, New Wave
Under the production hand of Trevor Horn, this Liverpool group took the "hi-NRG" dance sound into British and American charts in 1984 with the homoerotic "Relax" and the politically trenchant "Two Tribes." The group, however, was a victim of overhype, and by the time their debut album was released, Frankie's fad had worn thin. —*John Floyd*

Welcome to the Pleasuredome / 1984 / ZTT/Island ✦✦✦✦
Upbeat British dance music with melodramatic vocals and lyrics that are sexually and politically provocative. The sound of Frankie Goes to Hollywood swept Britain in the years 1983-1985. Here is the wide-screen debut double album, containing the hits "Relax," "Two Tribes," "The Power of Love," and the title track. —*William Ruhlmann*

● **Bang! Greatest Hits** / 1994 / ZTT/Island ✦✦✦✦
This good collection includes all the worthwhile songs Frankie Goes to Hollywood ever recorded. —*AMG*

Aretha Franklin

b. Mar. 25, 1942, Memphis, TN
Piano, Vocals / Soul, R&B, Gospel, Urban, Club-Dance
Appropriately dubbed "Lady Soul," Aretha Franklin made several false starts before finding consistent artistic direction. It was only when she began integrating her gospel phrasing and passion (heard in its embryonic form on the Chess album) into secular material that she, like Ray Charles before her, elevated herself from the ranks of the also-rans. There were hints of what was to come in her Columbia recordings, but the flowering of Aretha Franklin coincided with her arrival at Atlantic. From the moment "I Never Loved a Man" broke through in early 1967, Aretha rarely put a wrong foot forward for five or six glorious years. When she went wrong, it was usually because of her poor choice of other people's songs to record, but even then, Aretha could sometimes turn dross into gold. By the late '70s, though, the partnership with Atlantic had become stale, and it took a deal with Arista to recharge her chart career. She still has the vocal chops, but many consider that market considerations alone will ensure she will never surpass the artistic high-water mark of her early Atlantic recordings. —*Colin Escott*

☆ **I Never Loved a Man (The Way I Love You)** / 1967 / Atlantic ✦✦✦✦✦
This is Franklin's first Atlantic album—an electrifying breakthrough in her somewhat stymied (Columbia) career. The Muscle Shoals sound featured here became legendary. —*George Bedard*

Aretha Arrives / 1967 / Atlantic ✦✦✦

☆ **Lady Soul** / 1968 / Atlantic ✦✦✦✦✦
Great personnel again—King Curtis, Bobby Womack, Frank Wess, and others, including a guest spot by Eric Clapton—and several classic songs. —*George Bedard*

Aretha Now / 1968 / Atlantic ✦✦✦✦
Though short on running time, this still caught Franklin at the peak of her early form. "Think," "I Say a Little Prayer," "See Saw," and "I Can't See Myself Leaving You" were all big hits. Her choice of cover material included some of her most R&B-drenched early Atlantic cuts, like "Night Time Is the Right Time," "You Send Me," and "I Take What I Want." —*Richie Unterberger*

Aretha in Paris / 1968 / Atlantic ✦✦✦

Soul '69 / 1969 / Atlantic ✦✦✦✦
One of her most overlooked '60s albums, on which she presented some of her jazziest material, despite the title. None of these cuts were significant hits, and none were Aretha originals; she displayed her characteristically eclectic taste in the choice of cover material, handling compositions by Percy Mayfield, Sam Cooke, Smokey Robinson, and, at the most pop-oriented end of her spectrum, John Hartford's "Gentle on My Mind" and Bob Lind's "Elusive Butterfly." Her vocals are consistently passionate and first-rate, though, as is the musicianship; besides contributions from the Muscle Shoals rhythm section, session players include respected jazzmen Kenny Burrell, Ron Carter, Grady Tate, David Newman, and Joe Zawinul. —*Richie Unterberger*

This Girl's in Love with You / 1970 / Atlantic ✦✦✦
The title song (a cover of Herb Alpert's "This Guy's in Love with You") might lead you to believe this is one of Aretha's more pop-oriented albums, but in fact, this is the only song of the sort on this solid and fairly earthy effort. Besides the hit singles "Call Me" and "Share Your Love With Me," it also includes her most well-known Beatle covers ("Eleanor Rigby" and "Let It Be"), and her interesting version of "The Weight," a Top 20 single featuring slide guitar by Duane Allman. —*Richie Unterberger*

Spirit in the Dark / 1970 / Atlantic ✦✦✦✦
Spirit in the Dark was one of Aretha Franklin's more overlooked albums from her Atlantic prime, despite the inclusion of a couple hit singles (the title track and "Don't Play That Song"). The disc includes five of her own compositions (the most she ever recorded for a single album) and her usual eclectic choice of cover material. On this record, the covers ranged from B.B. King and Dr. John to Jimmy Reed and Goffin/King's "Oh Not My Baby." The album also benefits from great backup players: Both the Muscle Shoals rhythm section and the Dixie Flyers contributed to the sessions, and Duane Allman lends his guitar to a couple of tracks. Though it doesn't rank with her very best Atlantic LPs, it's an exuberant and remarkably consistent effort. The 1993 CD reissue has detailed liner notes on the songs and sessions by David Nathan. —*Richie Unterberger*

Live at Fillmore West / 1971 / Atlantic ✦✦✦

☆ **Amazing Grace** / 1972 / Atlantic ✦✦✦✦✦
Aretha Franklin disproved the notion that once you leave the church, you can't go back. She returned in triumph on this 1972 double album, making what might be her greatest release ever in any style. Her voice was chilling, making it seem as if God and the angels were conducting a service alongside Franklin, Rev. James Cleveland, the Southern California Community Choir, and everyone else in attendance. Her versions of "How I Got Over" and "You've Got a Friend" are legendary. —*Ron Wynn*

Hey Now Hey / 1973 / Atlantic ✦✦✦

With Everything I Feel in Me / 1974 / Atlantic ✦✦✦

Let Me in Your Life / 1974 / Atlantic ✦✦✦

You / 1975 / Atlantic ✦✦

Sparkle / 1976 / Rhino ✦✦✦✦

Jump to It / 1982 / Arista ✦✦✦
Aretha Franklin scored some hits with this early '80s album and managed to make concessions to urban contemporary tastes without totally distorting her classic soul sound. While it's certainly not in the class of past recordings, the title cut gave Franklin her first No. 1 hit of the '80s, and "Love Me Right" was a decent follow-up. —*Ron Wynn*

Get It Right / 1983 / Arista ✦✦✦

Who's Zoomin' Who? / 1985 / Arista ✦✦✦
Franklin continued finding ways to accommodate the urban contemporary production style and retain her soulfulness. The single "Freeway of Love" was a monster hit in both clubs and on radio, while the title track and "Another Night" also did well across the board. The cut with the Eurythmics even got a little attention at rock stations. —*Ron Wynn*

★ **30 Greatest Hits** / 1986 / Atlantic ◆◆◆◆◆
The double-disc set *30 Greatest Hits* contains all of Aretha Franklin's greatest hits from the '60s and early '70s, from 1967's "I Never Loved a Man (The Way I Love You)" and "Respect" to 1973's "Until You Come Back to Me (That's What I'm Gonna Do)." It's an essential, comprehensive collection—the ideal purchase for fans that want more than just the biggest hits, but don't want to invest in the box set. —*Stephen Thomas Erlewine*

One Lord, One Faith, One Baptism / 1987 / Arista ◆◆◆

Jazz to Soul / 1992 / Columbia ◆◆◆

☆ **Queen of Soul: The Atlantic Recordings** / 1993 / Rhino ◆◆◆◆◆
This four-disc, 86-track collection is a comprehensive look at Franklin's soul genius. All of her great Atlantic hits are here, as well as many key performances. —*AMG*

Greatest Hits (1980-1994) / 1994 / Arista ◆◆◆
This album rounds up the biggest hits from the latter part of Aretha Franklin's career, including "Jump to It," "Freeway of Love," and "Who's Zoomin' Who." The album does a good job of selecting the highlights from a slightly uneven era. —*Stephen Thomas Erlewine*

Very Best Of, Vol. 1 / 1994 / Rhino ◆◆◆◆

Very Best Of, Vol. 2 / 1994 / Rhino ◆◆◆◆

Freakwater

Alternative Country-Rock
An acoustic side project of the Eleventh Dream Day family tree, featuring Dream Day drummer/singer Janet Bean (who plays guitar in Freakwater) and her friend Catherine Ann Irwin, with contributions from various other musicians. This is only "alternative rock" in the marketing sense; the Kentucky-bred singers largely stick to acoustic folk/country with close harmonies and strong Appalachian overtones, sometimes employing fiddle, pedal steel, mandolin, and dobro. Mixing strong original material (mostly written by Irwin) with traditional numbers and songs by the likes of Bill Monroe, Freakwater's albums stand as some of the finest maverick, progressive acoustic records of recent years. —*Richie Unterberger*

Freakwater / 1989 / Amoeba ◆◆◆
Their debut, a short LP, or a long EP, depending on how you look at it, presents plaintive, raw country-folk in a modern context without sounding forced. —*Richie Unterberger*

● **Dancing Under Water** / 1991 / Amoeba ◆◆◆◆
A bit more polished than their debut, but hardly slick, with harmonies and the sobbing lead vocals of Irwin at the fore. This is recommended above the debut for a simple reason: The CD includes all of the songs from *Freakwater* as bonus tracks, eliminating the need to look for the first album. —*Richie Unterberger*

Old Paint / Oct. 10, 1995 / Thrill Jockey ◆◆◆◆
After a four-year gap since their second album, Freakwater returned with another solid effort that's not as bare-bones as their debut, but a little earthier than *Dancing Under Water*. Not a lot of new ground is broken, yet it somehow doesn't sound at all tiresome. All of their strengths remain in place: fine, mournful harmonies, good original songs, some well-chosen covers (Loudon Wainwright's "Out of This World" is a particular highlight), and nice unobtrusive touches of pedal steel and fiddle embellishing the acoustic guitars. This is modern country-folk at its best, and in fact would really be more suitable for the roots-country audience, except that the execution is too direct, the production too basic, and the songwriting too heartfelt for the contemporary country marketplace. Thus it is that the group's primary listenership is the alternative rock community, which is country's loss: Few performers today are performing roots music so convincingly, without sounding forced or dated. —*Richie Unterberger*

John Fred & The Playboys

Vocals / Rock 'n' Roll, Pop-Rock
Remembered only for his fluke 1968 No. 1 hit "Judy in Disguise," John Fred actually made quite a few records in the '60s. Though he was from Louisiana, Fred's vocals strongly recall Eric Burdon at times, and Georgie Fame's at others. A capable songwriter ("Judy in Disguise" was an original), he also cut several fine, deep Southern soul ballads that distinguish him as one of the best American White R&B singers. —*Richie Unterberger*

● **History of John Fred & the Playboys** / 1991 / Paula ◆◆◆◆
Eclectic 26-song assortment of pop-rock-soul-R&B. Highlights are his 1964 cover of John Lee Hooker's "Boogie Chillen," which stands up to the best early British R&B; the odd, moody "Agnes English" and "Sun City," which shows a strong Animals influence, and of course "Judy In Disguise." A 1958 track that he cut as a teenager recalls a frat-rock Frankie Ford with its low-wattage emulation of the New Orleans sound. Unfortunately there are little in the way of liner notes here, but the grooves prove

Fred to be a versatile stylist with much greater depth than the usual one-shot. —*Richie Unterberger*

Free

Blues-Rock, Hard Rock
Free, an English quartet formed in 1968 with Paul Rodgers, Andy Fraser, Paul Kossoff, and Simon Kirke, took the then-popular heavy British blues-rock sound and stripped it down to a hard yet open minimalistic sound.

Rodgers quickly earned a reputation as one of the greatest singers of the genre, able to deliver lyrics with gritty dark sensuality as well as playful toss-offs. Drummer Simon Kirke was the hard-rock equivalent to soul music's Al Jackson, speaking volumes with a no-nonsense groove. Paul Kossoff's wide sustain leads and rhythm work filled in the band's sounds, allowing Andy Fraser great freedom to pursue his inventive style of very spare, open but melodic, bass playing.

The band's sound coalesced into some great moments, particularly the No. 4 hit "All Right Now," "Fire and Water," and "The Stealer." After some lineup changes and an uneven album (*Heartbreaker*) in 1973, Free disbanded. Rodgers and Kirke went on to form Bad Company. Fraser and Kossoff released spotty solo efforts, and Kossoff died of heart failure on March 19, 1976. —*Rick Clark*

Tons of Sobs / 1968 / A&M ◆◆

Free / 1969 / A&M ◆◆◆

Fire & Water / 1970 / A&M ◆◆◆◆
This classic Free album features their biggest hit, "All Right Now," as well as key Free tracks, "Heavy Load," "Mr. Big," and the title track. —*Rick Clark*

Highway / Feb. 1971 / A&M ◆◆◆

Free Live / Sep. 1971 / A&M ◆◆

Free at Last / 1972 / A&M ◆◆◆

● **The Best of Free** / 1973 / A&M ◆◆◆◆
A solid compilation showcasing "All Right Now" and other semi-hits, this is a worthwhile sampler for the uninitiated. —*Dan Heilman*

Heartbreaker / 1973 / PolyGram ◆◆

● **Molten Gold: The Anthology** / Oct. 5, 1993 / A&M ◆◆◆◆
With their big riffs and bluesy melodies, Free virtually defined hard rock in the early '70s, and *Molten Gold: The Anthology* shows that this wasn't such a meager achievement. Throughout the two discs, it becomes clear that the key to Free's rock 'n' roll was their rhythm section, which powered their riffs to perfection. This is the definitive Free, two discs of pure hard rock. —*Stephen Thomas Erlewine*

Friends of Dean Martinez

Alternative Pop-Rock
A Southwestern alternative rock supergroup of sorts, Arizona's Friends of Dean Martinez features past and present members of Giant Sand and Naked Prey. Giant Sand leader Howe Gelb, though not a member of the group, plays guest keyboards on their debut album, *The Shadow of Your Smile*, a surprisingly retro set of guitar-based instrumentals inspired by instrumental and surf music of the late '50s and early '60s. With plenty of lounge music and desert country guitar twang thrown in, it's certainly retro in feel, but not revivalist; with Bill Elm's keening steel guitar at the forefront and occasional insertions of found sound and experimental bits, they evoke open dusty landscapes with wit and, one suspects, a bit of tongue-in-cheek irony. At any rate, it's a refreshing change from the often too-serious alternative rock paths that the musicians pursue in their full-time bands. —*Richie Unterberger*

The Shadow of Your Smile / 1995 / Sub Pop ◆◆◆
A post-modern fusion of Santo & Johnny, Dick Dale, and the Ventures, with a heaping side order of Tex-Mex border music. Whether or not the musicians are playing this straight or not, they're playing it very well, and the result is good fun, even if it's totally uncharacteristic of the material offered by the Giant Sand/Naked Prey axis in the past. —*Richie Unterberger*

Front 242

Industrial, Alternative Pop-Rock, Techno
When the Belgian synth-dance group began recording in 1982, their style followed the cold, clinical work of Kraftwerk and Cabaret Voltaire yet their music had none of the mystery or threat of those early electronic bands. As the decade progressed, they captured that mystery; by the end of the decade, Front 242 were on the cutting edge of the experimental industrial dance groups, combining political sound bites with their dance samples and beats. Their 1988 club hit, "Headhunter," cemented their reputation and provided an example of their aggressive style. After their 1988 album, *Front by Front*, the group left the seminal industrial record label Wax Trax for a major label, Epic. Front 242's first major label

release, 1991's *Tyranny for You,* showed no concessions and was another strong statement. However, their subsequent albums in the '90s showed that the group was beginning to slip from the cutting edge, although each album had some highlights. — *Stephen Thomas Erlewine*

Official Version (1986-1987) / 1987 / Epic ✦✦✦✦
With its dense, claustrophobic mix of samples and relentless, hard beats, *Official Version* was the first consistently impressive Front 242 record. — *Stephen Thomas Erlewine*

Back Catalogue / 1987 / Wax Trax! ✦✦✦
A collection of early 12-inch singles, *Back Catalogue* is the best way to get acquainted with Front 242's early days. — *Stephen Thomas Erlewine*

● **Front by Front** / 1988 / Epic ✦✦✦✦
While it reiterates the music of *Official Version, Front by Front* features a stronger political message, as well as their signature single, "Headhunter." — *Stephen Thomas Erlewine*

Tyranny (for You) / 1991 / Epic ✦✦✦✦
More aggressive and militant than its predecessors, *Tyranny (for You)* is an impressionistic, angry album that captured the underlying chaos of the early '90s with its dark, brutal rhythm tracks alone. — *Stephen Thomas Erlewine*

06:21:03:11 up Evil / May 25, 1993 / Epic ✦✦✦

Fugazi

Alternative Pop-Rock, Hardcore Punk
Fugazi is as famous for its strident anti-corporate stance as they are for their music. Fugazi's leader, singer/guitarist Ian MacKaye, refuses to charge over five dollars for a concert and keeps the prices of their recordings low by releasing the band's recordings through his own record label, Dischord. As such, their vehement political stance can overshadow their musical accomplishments; they are one of the few bands that prove it's possible for hardcore punk to expand beyond its rigid structures. With the seminal D.C. hardcore band Minor Threat, MacKaye defined straight-edge hardcore; with Fugazi, he breaks and rewrites the very rules he established.

Since their 1988 debut EP, Fugazi has gained a substantial fan base without the help of mainstream press and MTV airplay; the band would rather talk to fanzines than to the mainstream press, so they never talk to *Rolling Stone.* By the time of their 1993 album, they charted on *Billboard's* Top 200 without any commercial push. Through their anti-rock star stance, Fugazi have become rock stars. — *Stephen Thomas Erlewine*

● **13 Songs** / 1990 / Dischord ✦✦✦✦
A CD combination of their first two EPs, *Fugazi* and *Margin Walker.* — *Meredith Erlewine*

Repeater + 3 Songs / 1990 / Dischord ✦✦✦✦
Not quite as polished as *13 Songs,* but a great album. — *Meredith Erlewine*

Steady Diet of Nothing / 1991 / Dischord ✦✦✦

In on the Kill Taker / 1993 / Dischord ✦✦✦✦

Red Medicine / Jun. 1995 / Dischord ✦✦✦

The Fugs

Rock'n'Roll, Folk-Rock
Arguably the first "underground" rock group of all time, the Fugs formed at the Peace Eye bookstore in New York's East Village in late 1964. The nucleus of the band throughout its many personnel changes was Peace Eye owner Ed Sanders, and fellow poet Tuli Kupferberg. Sanders and Kupferberg had strong ties to the beat literary scene, but charged, in the manner of their friend Allen Ginsberg, full steam ahead into the maelstrom of '60s political involvement and psychedelia. Surrounded by an assortment of motley refugees from the New York folk and jugband scene (including Steve Weber and Peter Stampfel of the Holy Modal Rounders), some of whom could barely play their instruments, the group nonetheless was determined to play rock'n'roll their way—which meant rife with political and social satire, as well as explicit profanity and sexual references, all downright unheard of in 1965. Starting on the legendary avant garde ESP label, the Fugs' debut was full of equal amounts of chaos and charm, but their songwriting and instrumental chops improved surprisingly quickly, resulting in a great second album that was undoubtedly the most shocking and satirical recording ever to grace the Top 100 when it was released. After cutting an unreleased album for Atlantic, they moved on to Frank Sinatra's Reprise label, unleashing a few more albums of equally satirical material that were more instrumentally polished, but equally scathing lyrically. Breaking up around 1970, Sanders and Kupferberg have continued to write prose and poetry, and sometimes write and perform music, both on their own and as part of Fugs reunions. By breaking lyrical taboos of popular music, they helped pave the way for the even more innovative outrage of the Mothers of Invention, the Velvet Underground, and others. — *Richie Unterberger*

The Fugs First Album / 1965 / Fantasy ✦✦✦
Engagingly sloppy, even raw performances on their debut, which draws on leftist politics, the poetry of William Blake, and the joys of sex. Some of this is wearily cacophonous, but "Slum Goddess," "Supergirl," "I Couldn't Get High," and "Nothing" are among their funniest songs. The CD reissue adds 11 bonus tracks: seven studio cuts from the same era (the sarcastic "CIA Man" is a highlight), three live songs from 1965, and an eight-minute spoken word piece. — *Richie Unterberger*

● **The Fugs** / 1966 / Fantasy ✦✦✦✦
At the time of its release, the Fugs' second (self-titled) album contained the most outrageous lyrics ever heard on a Top 100 rock'n'roll LP. The group, with roots in New York's underground folk and poetry scenes, flung themselves wholeheartedly into all-out rock'n'roll on this 1966 record, which addresses concerns like free love, the madness of war, and government repression. The CD reissue of this classic includes two previously unreleased live performances and three tracks from the unreleased album they recorded for Atlantic in 1967. — *Richie Unterberger*

Tenderness Junction / 1967 / Reprise ✦✦✦
The band opted for a considerably more conventional rock sound more in keeping with the era's psychedelic tenor on their first major-label release. The material isn't as strong and the satirical humor not as biting as their earlier efforts, though it's characteristically witty stuff. Highlights include "Turn On/Tune In/Drop Out" and "War Song"; "Aphrodite Mass" is an ambitious if not terribly memorable five-part suite. — *Richie Unterberger*

Bobby Fuller Four

Vocals / Rock'n'Roll
With his blatant reverence for Buddy Holly, fellow Texan Bobby Fuller was a bit of an anomaly in the mid-'60s. With his Stratocaster guitar and brash, full sound, at his best Fuller sounded like Holly might have had he survived into the '60s. Cracking the Top 30 in 1966 with a cover of Holly's "Love's Made a Fool of You," and then the Top Ten with "I Fought the Law" (written by one-time Cricket Sonny Curtis), Fuller had just become a star when he died in mysterious circumstances in a parked car in Hollywood (the police thought it was a suicide, but just about everyone who knew him disagreed). Fuller's relatively short period of national stardom actually crowned a good half-dozen years of recording, during which he released many outstanding tracks. After a few local singles in his hometown of El Paso in the early '60s, he moved to California with his combo in 1964, and briefly had aspirations of playing surf music before hooking up with producer Bob Keene. In the short time he recorded for Mustang in 1965 and 1966, he waxed quite a few fine tracks (most self-penned) besides his hits, including "Let Her Dance," "Another Sad and Lonely Night," "My True Love," "Never to Be Forgotten," "Fool of Love," and "The Magic Touch." Rocking, tuneful, and infectiously joyous, they showed Fuller to be a worthy inheritor of early rock'n'roll and rockabilly traditions without sounding self-consciously revivalist. While it's hard to imagine Fuller maintaining his success in the era of psychedelia, he no doubt would have gone on to produce interesting work. A talented and prolific songwriter and a studio wiz who drew from Eddie Cochran and (though only slightly) the full guitar sound of the British Invasion as well as Buddy Holly, he recorded a great deal of unreleased studio and live material that was issued in the 1980s, when the depth of his loss began to be appreciated. — *Richie Unterberger*

● **The Best of Bobby Fuller Four** / 1981 / Rhino ✦✦✦✦
A great 18-track compilation of his best work that is truly all killer, no filler. While there's some other good Fuller to be found, this is definitely the prime stuff from his mid-'60s recordings for Mustang: "I Fought the Law," "Let Her Dance," "The Magic Touch," "Love's Made a Fool of You," "Fool of Love," "My True Love," and other equally fine if lesser-known sides. — *Richie Unterberger*

Bobby Fuller Tapes, Vol. 1 / 1983 / Rhino ✦✦✦

Live Again / 1984 / Eva ✦✦✦

Bobby Fuller Tapes, Vol. 2 / 1984 / Voxx ✦✦✦

Bobby Fuller Instrumental Album / 1985 / Rockhouse ✦✦✦

Fun Boy Three

New Wave
The Specials were one of the most popular and influential bands in the UK, scoring a streak of seven straight Top Ten singles. Their popularity culminated with the prophetic "Ghost Town," which spent three weeks at No. 1 in the summer of 1981. The "Ghost Town" single was the last to feature Terry Hall and the original lineup—after its release Hall split with the group's other two vocalists, Lynval Golding and Neville Staples, to form the Fun Boy Three.

Where the Specials were a ska-revival band, the Fun Boy Three was a new wave pop group with distinctly weird, skeletal, and experimental overtones. The band released their first single, "The Lunatics (Have

Taken over the Asylum)," shortly after they departed from the Specials. The single peaked at No. 20 late in 1981. Early in 1982, the group charted again with "It Ain't What You Do (It's the Way That You Do It)," a duet with Bananarama on an old Jimmie Lunceford song. The Fun Boy Three finally released their eponymous debut in the spring of 1982. That summer, they had a hit with a cover of George Gershwin's "Summertime." The group recorded a second album with Talking Heads leader David Byrne late in 1982. The resulting album, *Waiting*, appeared in the spring of 1983, concurrently with the Top Ten singles "The Tunnel of Love" and "Our Lips Are Sealed," a song Hall wrote with Jane Wiedlin, who already made it into a hit the previous year with her group, the Go-Go's.

By the summer of 1983, the Fun Boy Three were peaking in popularity and Hall disbanded the group. —*Stephen Thomas Erlewine*

The Fun Boy Three / Mar. 1982 / Chrysalis ✦✦✦
Hall sings lead and Staples and Golding chant behind him on the group's beat-heavy ballads on such hits as "It Ain't What You Do . . . ," on which they are joined by Bananarama. —*William Ruhlmann*

Waiting / Feb. 1983 / Chrysalis ✦✦
● **The Best of the Fun Boy Three** / 1984 / Chrysalis ✦✦✦✦
This collects all of the essential moments of the short-lived band. Two non-LP tracks are an added bonus: a cover of Gershwin's "Summertime" and their collaboration with Bananarama, "Really Saying Something." —*Chris Woodstra*

Funkadelic

Soul, Funk, Rock 'n' Roll, Psychedelic
Funkadelic was the more politicized of George Clinton's psycho-funk spinoffs. Where Parliament offered the butt-tugging ecstasy of "Tear the Roof off the Sucker" and "Flashlight," Funkadelic tackled racial conflict ("You and Your Folks, Me and My Folks"), government corruption ("America Eats Its Young"), and the power of the boogie ("One Nation Under a Groove"). They were never the singles act Parliament turned out to be, but Funkadelic tackled tougher issues and made them wiggle and wobble as surely as anything that ever bore Clinton's stamp. —*John Floyd*

Funkadelic / 1970 / Westbound ✦✦✦
The music is serious but George Clinton is as tongue-in-cheek as ever. The album opens up with his voice, proposing "If you will suck my soul, I will lick your funky emotions," and proceeds in and out of that vein for 40 minutes. This album is raw and pure funk, with often twangy guitars and deep, low, yet prominent bass lines. It takes the quirky, basic groove of The Meters and renders it heavy and grungy, while maintaining the straight-faced humor that Clinton has made famous. —*Julian Katz*

Free Your Mind and Your Ass Will Follow / 1970 / Westbound ✦✦✦
Not quite as promising as its title would indicate, *Free Your Mind and Your Ass Will Follow* is full of faux religious rambling and spacey studio overdubs and effects, yet still manages to pull it off in the endearing Clinton style of blending soul, heavy metal, gospel, and bad sci-fi movies, coming up with gems such as "Friday Night, August the Fourteenth," and "Funky Dollar Bill." —*Julian Katz*

☆ **Maggot Brain** / 1971 / Westbound ✦✦✦✦✦
The best early Funkadelic record. There's some indulgent stuff here that may conjure some art-rock nightmares, but at its best—"You and Your Folks, Me and My Folks"—this is a brave and pioneering recording. —*John Floyd*

America Eats Its Young / 1972 / Westbound ✦✦✦
Some fantastic extended guitar jams and bitter, prophetic lyrics made this one of Funkadelic's most ambitious and remarkable albums. Few were ready in the early '70s for a Black band that blended acid rock riffs and angry rhetoric. It wasn't all political, however; there were also some silly, joyous tunes and the band's trademark biting satires on their rivals. —*Ron Wynn*

Cosmic Slop / 1973 / Westbound ✦✦✦✦
Another classic, with furious guitar riffs, inspired, bizarre lyrics, marvelous production, and loose, chaotic, brilliant arrangements. Funkadelic was the most musically ambitious, energized band in the Clinton empire, and every one of their Westbound albums was a triumph. —*Ron Wynn*

Standing on the Verge of Getting It On / 1974 / Westbound ✦✦✦
Let's Take It to the Stage / 1975 / Westbound ✦✦✦✦
The title track was one of their funniest funk jams, while the other songs run the gamut from blistering rock to zany R&B. George Clinton was in the midst of his greatest commercial/creative run, and this one ranks right alongside the other magical Funkadelic releases of the '70s. —*Ron Wynn*

Hardcore Jollies / 1976 / Warner Bros. ✦✦✦✦
Their major-label debut from 1976 lacks the manic drive of the early stuff, but tightens the grooves and adds some sharp melodies. —*John Floyd*

Tales of Kidd Funkadelic / 1976 / Westbound ✦✦✦
★ **One Nation Under a Groove** / 1978 / Warner Bros. ✦✦✦✦✦
Early on *One Nation Under a Groove* George Clinton asks the rhetorical question "Who Says a Funk Band Can't Play Rock?" Only a fool needs to ask for the answer, since the answer is the album itself. *One Nation Under a Groove* is the most fully-realized slice of P-Funk. Parliament put out albums as funky as this, but they got bogged down in their concepts, while Funkadelic always traded too heavily in psychedelic clichés and art-rock trappings to really let loose. But that's not the case with *One Nation*. On this record, the concept is underplayed, letting the funk come to the forefront. Some died-in-the-wool Funkadelic fans might lament the lack of electric guitar freak-outs, but no matter—this is music of a supreme vision. Besides, the guitars are there, pushing along the funk in an effortless fashion, which helps draw attention to the vocals, which are alternately sexy and downright hilarious. Don't think of *One Nation Under a Groove* as a collection of songs. Think of it as one sustained funk symphony, and you'll be on the right track. Clinton never got this consistently funky again. —*Leo Stanley*

Uncle Jam Wants You / 1979 / Warner Bros. ✦✦✦✦
It doesn't keep moving like its immediate predecessor, but this is where you'll find "Not Just Knee Deep," a wonderful piece of erotic esoterica. —*John Floyd*

The Electric Spanking of War Babies / 1981 / Warner Bros. ✦✦✦✦
★ **Music for Your Mother** / 1993 / Westbound ✦✦✦✦✦
This two-disc set collects all the great Funkadelic singles and B-sides and presents them in remastered glory. The list includes such gems as "Funky Dollar Bill," "Cosmic Slop," "Let's Take It to the Stage," and "I'll Bet You." Unfortunately, some of Funkadelic's finest efforts were album-length and/or suite pieces, so some brilliant material not issued on singles was omitted. But it's as comprehensive a collection as possible under the circumstances, and Rob Bowman's notes are extensive and nicely done. —*Ron Wynn*

Live: Meadowbrook, Rochester, Michigan 12th September 1971 / 1996 / Westbound ✦✦✦

Billy Fury

b. Apr. 17, 1941, Liverpool, England, **d.** Jan. 28, 1983
Vocals / Rock 'n' Roll, British Invasion
England's best rock singer of the pre-Beatles era, Fury, born in Liverpool, was the most talented of England's Elvis clones and near-clones of the very early '60s; he also wrote some of his own songs. A strong singer with a very suggestive stage presence, Fury also had the benefit of a fine backing band, including rockabilly guitarist Joe Brown. His recordings from 1963 onward, backed by the Tornados (of "Telstar" fame), lack this power, but Fury still made the charts through the mid-'60s, and, prior to his death in the mid-'80s, retained the respect and admiration of the British rock establishment he helped to form. —*Bruce Eder*

Billy Fury / 1963 / Beat Goes On ✦✦
We Want Billy / 1963 / Beat Goes On ✦✦
The Billy Fury Story / 1977 / Decca ✦✦✦
● **Sound of Fury Plus 10** / 1988 / PolyGram ✦✦✦✦
The best rock album recorded in England before the rise of the Beatles (Andy White, the guest drummer on "Love Me Do," plays the skins on this, too). A hard-rocking gem driven by Fury's powerful voice and Joe Brown's superb guitar. This reissue has ten bonus tracks. —*Bruce Eder*

Peter Gabriel

b. May 13, 1950, England
Synthesizer, Percussion, Keyboards, Vocals / Art-Rock/, Progressive-Rock, Pop-Rock
Peter Gabriel was one of the founding members of Genesis when it was formed in 1965. Gabriel left Genesis in 1975 to pursue an idiosyncratic but highly successful solo career. He initially drew from the art-rock sounds of his time with Genesis but increasingly infused worldbeat and extremely dissonant rock, and eventually some R&B, into his sound.

Gabriel has always surrounded himself with first-class producers (Bob Ezrin, Robert Fripp, Daniel Lanois, Steve Lillywhite) who could sonically push the envelope into new frontiers. Thematically Gabriel's lyrics progressively abandoned the journey through the dark side of the psyche in favor of reaching out with awareness-elevating sentiment. That transition helped expand Gabriel's audience significantly in 1986 with the multi-platinum hit album *So*, which peaked at No. 2.

Gabriel followed *So* three years later with *Passion*, a collection of music used in the film *The Last Temptation of Christ*. It wasn't until 1992 that he delivered *Us*, the proper follow-up to *So*. Although it sold respectably and had a Top 40 hit, the "Sledgehammer" knock-off "Steam," it proved a relative commercial disappointment. —*Rick Clark*

Peter Gabriel [1] / 1977 / Atco ✦✦✦✦
His strong debut, produced by Bob Ezrin (Pink Floyd, Alice Cooper), features the hit "Solsbury Hill," which addressed Gabriel's breakup with Genesis. The sound reflects some of Genesis's art-rock sensibilities ("Moribund the Burgermeister"), while charting some more accessible styles (in Gabriel's eccentric fashion) like the fairly straightahead rock of "Modern Love." Other highlights include the portentous "Here Comes the Flood" and "Humdrum." —*Rick Clark*

Peter Gabriel [2] / 1978 / Atco ✦✦✦
King Crimson's Robert Fripp produced this follow-up. Overall, this effort is more uneven, but there are some real highlights in the form of "D.I.Y." and the dissonant rocker "On the Air." —*Rick Clark*

★ **Peter Gabriel [3]** / 1980 / Geffen ✦✦✦✦✦
On this, the third of three self-titled efforts, Gabriel teams up with producer Steve Lillywhite (XTC, Psychedelic Furs, U2) and produces a masterpiece. From the chilling opener, "Intruder," to "Biko," an impassioned tribute to murdered South African poet and activist Steven Biko, Lillywhite's experimental (and very left-of-center) approach to sound is a perfect match for Gabriel's convoluted tales from the dark side of human nature. Arguably, it is Gabriel's best work thus far. —*Rick Clark*

Security / 1982 / Geffen ✦✦✦
Produced by David Lord and Gabriel, this is really a transitional album, borrowing from the heavily treated approach to sound found on the Lillywhite work while embracing more worldbeat rhythms. The music is less dissonant. Thematically, Gabriel picks up the human-rights thread he started with "Biko" on "Wallflower." "Kiss of Life" suggests a hopefulness emerging in his work. It includes the hit "Shock the Monkey." —*Rick Clark*

Plays Live / 1983 / Geffen ✦✦✦

Music from the Film "Birdy" / 1985 / Geffen ✦✦✦

So / 1986 / Geffen ✦✦✦✦
After a four-year layoff from his last studio album *(Security)*, Gabriel returned with his most upbeat record, infusing funk, worldbeat, and gospel. The more accessible production, by Daniel Lanois (U2) and Gabriel, helped make this album a worldwide commercial success. It includes the hits "In Your Eyes," "Sledgehammer," "Big Time." —*Rick Clark*

Passion / 1989 / Geffen ✦✦✦

Shaking the Tree: Sixteen Golden Greats / 1990 / Geffen ✦✦✦✦
This is an odd best-of collection. True, it includes his hits, but Gabriel isn't merely a singles artist. As a result, there are many important album tracks that are glaring omissions from a more well-rounded picture of Gabriel's artistry. The title, no doubt, is an indicator of the tossed-off nature of this set. —*Rick Clark*

Us / 1992 / Geffen ✦✦✦
Us marks Peter Gabriel's first (nonsoundtrack) studio effort since 1986's *So* and, more importantly, his most introspective and self-analytical work since leaving Genesis in 1975. Gabriel has done much to promote international music in recent years through his Real World record label, and he calls in a fistful of IOU's for *Us*. The most distinctive imports are exotic percussion sounds which percolate subtly throughout the recording. Intensely personal portrayals of love, longing, loss, and the dark emotions they can generate permeate atmospheric pieces such as "Blood of Eden," "Only Us," "Washing in the Water," and "Secret World." Gabriel makes group therapy a fascinating place to spend an hour and, thankfully, never loses sight of those rays of hope that pierce through from the other side. —*Roch Parisien*

Revisited / 1992 / Atlantic ✦✦✦

Secret World Live / 1994 / Geffen ✦✦

Galaxie 500

Alternative Pop-Rock
While many bands picked up on the Velvet Underground's more rocking traits, this Boston-based trio reveled in their slower doings. Sparse and not upbeat, they are not dour either. Galaxie 500 released three albums between 1987 and 1990 before lead singer/guitarist Dean Wareham left the band, effectively causing their breakup; Wareham formed Luna soon afterward. Bassist Naomi Yang and drummer Damon Krukowski have worked as Pierre Etoile and Damon & Naomi, and are currently in Magic Hour. —*Bruce Eder*

● **Today** / 1987 / Rough Trade ✦✦✦✦
Working the slow side of the Velvet Underground, it's melodic and intense. —*Robert Gordon*

On Fire / 1989 / Rough Trade ✦✦✦

This Is Our Music / 1990 / Rough Trade ✦✦✦✦
With more of the same as on *Today*, they knew their trick and stuck to it. —*Robert Gordon*

Game Theory

Alternative Pop-Rock, Power-Pop, Jangle-Pop
One of the most visible and longest-lived bands of California's Paisley Underground movement of the early '80s, Game Theory was also one of the only bands able to transcend that somewhat limited and highly derivative genre. Leader Scott Miller's song craft, distinctive voice (self-described as a "miserable whine") and intelligent lyrics (often obscure but rarely pretentious) carved a sound that, while firmly rooted in traditional pop, was truly original and defined an era of college rock.

Formed in Sacramento in 1982, the first incarnation included ex-Alternative Learning member Scott Miller (singer-songwriter, guitarist), Fred Juhos (bass), Nancy Becker (keyboards), and Michael Erwin (drums). Within four months of forming and before ever playing a live gig, the band recorded their first album, *Blaze of Glory*, in Miller's bedroom. Only 500 copies were pressed and sent out to college radio (according to the legend, wrapped in trash bags). The album, while a pleasant amalgam of '60s pure pop and the quirkier elements of new wave, only hinted at the band's potential. They began playing live in the same circles with Dream Syndicate and Thin White Rope—rumblings of the Paisley Underground scene were just beginning. The *Pointed Accounts of People You Know* EP in 1983 and the *Distortion* EP (produced by Michael Quercio of paisley-peers the Three O'Clock) the following year quickly earned the band a following and drew favorable comparisons to Big Star.

In 1985, with the help of producer Mitch Easter, they recorded their first proper album—*Real Nighttime*—for Enigma Records. Internal tensions broke the band up before its release, leaving Miller to carry on with a new lineup consisting of Shelley LaFrenier (keyboard), Gil Ray (drums), and Suzie Ziegler (bass)—Easter would continue as the band's producer and essentially a fifth member in the studio throughout the rest of their career. The new group immediately began recording *Big Shot Chronicles* by late 1985—the album once again showing great leaps in quality. By this time, they had become staples of college radio, though mainstream recognition eluded them. Miller seemed to accept the destiny of the band (obscurity) when he created his most excessive, and ultimately most enjoyable, album—1987's *Lolita Nation*—a sprawling double album packed with obscure pop-culture references, and riddled with experimental sounds and song fragments. *Lolita Nation* also marked the addition of guitarist/vocalist Donnete Thayer.

They took one more stab at the mainstream with the more accessible *Two Steps from the Middle Ages* in 1988, but its commercial failure took its toll on the band, leading to several more personnel changes—which included the temporary exit of Miller himself. Miller finally dissolved the band in 1990 to form the similar-sounding, though more eclectic, Loud Family. —*Chris Woodstra*

Blaze of Glory / 1982 / Rational ✦✦

Real Nighttime / 1985 / Alias ✦✦✦
This is the band's first effort with Mitch Easter (R.E.M., Let's Active) producing. Miller's Alex Chilton fixation comes to the fore here, and it generally works nicely. "24" was a breezy alternative college hit. Other highlights include "Curse of the Frontierland," with its Big Star-influenced guitar figure, and the delicately reflective "If and When It All Falls Apart." —*Rick Clark*

Big Shot Chronicles / 1986 / Alias ✦✦✦✦
The band's sound and Miller's songwriting are more aggressive here, delivering an appealingly punchy power-pop sound. It's a fine album with many tracks to recommend; "I've Tried Subtlety" is a strong, overamped T-Rex number, while "Like a Girl Jesus" shines with Easter's mildly psychedelic production touches. "Erica's World" is a wonderfully quirky rocker, and "Regenisraen" showcases the band's harmonic capabilities. —*Rick Clark*

Lolita Nation / 1987 / Enigma ✦✦✦✦
Many fans of the band claim that this is a creative peak for Game Theory. *Lolita Nation* is loaded with odd juxtapositions of experimental sounds and spoken passages. The material, while dazzling in places, is rather inconsistent. "The Real Sheila" and "We Love You, Carol and Alison" are highlights, and both of them are found on *Tinker*. —*Rick Clark*

Two Steps from the Middle Ages / 1988 / Enigma ✦✦
With *Two Steps from the Middle Ages*, it seems Scott Miller was having second thoughts about the band's direction. Where *Lolita Nation* jumped wildly through experimental territory, this time out, they opted for a more radio-ready approach—unfortunately though, not college radio where their real support was. And while there is no shortage of good pop music here, overall the results are somewhat bland compared to previous efforts. —*Chris Woodstra*

● **Tinker to Evers to Chance (Selected Highlights 1982-1989)** / 1990 / Enigma ✦✦✦✦
For the uninitiated, this collection of highlights from 1982 to 1989 is the best place to start, containing a healthy selection from their later Mitch Easter-produced albums. —*Rick Clark*

Distortion of Glory / 1994 / Alias ✦✦

Distortion of Glory collects the band's early (and long out-of-print) EPs. An interesting look at their formative years but only fans need to bother. *—Chris Woodstra*

Gang of Four

Alternative Pop-Rock, New Wave, Post-Punk

Formed in 1977 by Leeds University students Jon King (vocals), Andy Gill (guitar), Dave Allen (bass), and Hugo Burnham (drums), Gang of Four (along with the Fall, Mekons, and Liliput) produced some of the most exhilarating and lasting music of the early English post-punk era of 1978-1983. Fueled by the fury of punk rock and radical political theory, Gang of Four successfully welded the two in an inspired display of polemics and music that addressed the vagaries of life in the modern world (including love and romance) as matters of political inquiry. Despite the fact that this sounds rife with the potential for being long on rhetoric and short on groove, such was not the case. What made Gang of Four's polemical clang 'n' roll so compelling was that it worked as harsh, bracing, and ultimately liberating rock 'n' roll. With Allen and Burnham combining as a formidable and frequently very funky rhythm section, Gill didn't play guitar as much as emit thick wads of semituneful distortion, while King "sang" in a dry, declamatory fashion similar to that of the Fall's Mark E. Smith. The rhythms were stripped down and jagged; at times Gill would dispense with guitar solos entirely and "play" nonsolos, which were (surprise!) silence. Song titles sounded like the titles of radical political essays: "At Home He's a Tourist," "Damaged Goods," "It's Her Factory," "Love like Anthrax," "To Hell with Poverty," all of it openly challenging the audience's preconceived notions about rock music, performance, the cult of celebrity, and the nature of politics. And in doing so, GOF conveyed rage, confusion, and loss of identity as well as any band of its time.

After three consecutive sensational albums, as well as a handful of EPs and singles, Allen left in 1982 to form the more danceable and less overtly political Shriekback, while Gill, King, and Burnham recorded the misguided "radical soul/R&B" record *Hard* with veteran American producers Ron and Howard Albert (who'd previously worked with Stephen Stills' Manassas and Firefall). A near total disaster, *Hard* signalled that the end was nigh. Gill and King, who by this point had final say-so on the band's musical and political direction, sacked Burnham, and the now Gang of Two released a so-so live album *(At the Palace)* and called it quits in 1984. But legends die hard, and Gang of Four experienced a mini-renaissance in the early '90s with the release of two excellent collections *(A Brief History of the Twentieth Century* and *The Peel Sessions Album)*. King and Gill put together a new Gang of Four and released the tepid but not disgraceful *Mall* in 1991. Despite the clumsy and haphazard finish, Gang of Four remains, to the ears of those opened wide by punk rock, an extremely important band. *—John Dougan*

★ **Entertainment!** / 1979 / Infinite Zero ✦✦✦✦✦

With songs like "Love like Anthrax" and "Damaged Goods," you soon realize that the title of this release is heavy on sarcasm. Still, a decade and a half after its debut, *Entertainment!* still sounds direct, exciting, and uncompromising. And, in spite of GOF's anti-pop tendencies, songs like "I Found That Essence Rare" explode into a sing-along chorus that is delightfully shocking. True to their collectivist spirit, Gill, King, Burnham, and Allen are a forceful musical unit, and the strength in this unity makes for a great fusion of punk, pop, and politics. Easily one of the best records of the post-punk era. Issued on CD by Infinite Zero in 1995. *—John Dougan*

Solid Gold / May 1981 / Warner Bros. ✦✦✦✦

Another tongue-in-cheek title, another great record. A little more abstract and anti-pop than *Entertainment!, Solid Gold* is, arguably, the most abrasive record GOF ever made. Burnham and Allen play dance-defiant, choppy grooves, while King and Gill explore more contentious political terrain. Some of *Solid Gold*'s best songs are the most challenging and confrontational ("Why Theory?" and "Paralysed"). Clearly hitting its stride as a band, by this time GOF was a force to be reckoned with, and without a doubt post-punk's best band. *—John Dougan*

Songs of the Free / 1982 / Warner Bros. ✦✦✦✦

Recorded under the influence of Chic records and a burgeoning post-punk dance culture, *Songs of the Free* is the most accessible of GOF's first three records, but in no way indicates a compromise of principles or an egregious attempt to sell out. The more polished arrangements, backup vocalists, and slight studio sweetening does little to mask the sarcasm and ironic intent of songs like "I Love a Man in a Uniform" (a dance club "hit" in the early '80s) or the bitter "We Live As We Dream, Alone." A record that appeals to the aficionado as well as the benighted, *Songs of the Free* indicated that the GOF could simultaneously embrace and attack pop music without sounding disingenuous. Music for the mind and body. *—John Dougan*

Peel Sessions / 1990 / Strange Fruit/Dutch East ✦✦✦

● **Brief History of the Twentieth Century** / 1990 / Warner Bros. ✦✦✦✦

A great starting point. This 20-track anthology covers all of GOF's best album material (even the one good song from the execrable *Hard*) and includes a wonderful liner essay by longtime GOF fan and fellow theorist Greil Marcus. Although *Entertainment!* is perhaps the most striking Gang release available, this compilation, due to its length, breadth, and quality, is the best place to become acquainted with this formidable band. *—John Dougan*

Gap Band

Soul, Funk, Club-Dance

A funk septet led by brothers Ronnie (vocals, trumpet, keyboards), Charles (lead vocals, keyboards), and Robert Wilson (vocals, bass), all cousins of Bootsy Collins, the Gap Band enjoyed a successful run on the R&B charts during the '80s with its Sly Stone-influenced boogie. The group took their name from the initials of three streets—Greenwood, Archer, and Pine—in their Tulsa, OK, neighborhood.

The brothers met Leon Russell in 1974, who signed them to his Shelter label; this led to a recording session with A&M, a self-titled debut on Tattoo/RCA, and a deal with Mercury. A string of R&B Top Ten hits followed, including "I Don't Believe You Want to Get Up and Dance (Oops, Up Side Your Head)"; by the time of *Gap Band III*, the group was established as hitmakers, and the album and its follow-up went platinum on the strength of hits like "Burn Rubber (Why You Wanna Hurt Me)," "Early in the Morning," and "Outstanding." The group recorded the title song to Keenen Ivory Wayans' blaxploitation parody *I'm Gonna Git You Sucka* in 1988 as their chart success continued. Charles Wilson and Eurythmic Dave Stewart co-wrote the soundtrack to the 1990 film *Rooftops;* Wilson then joined the Eurythmics' backing band in 1990 and guested on their *We Too Are One.* He remained with the Gap Band, though, which continued to tour and resumed recording after a six-year hiatus in 1995 with *Ain't Nothin' But a Party. —Steve Huey*

● **Best Of** / 1995 / Mercury ✦✦✦✦

The Best of the Gap Band collects nearly every hit and key album track by the seminal funk group, making it the perfect introduction and arguably their only essential record. *—David Jehnzen*

Garbage

Alternative Pop-Rock

Garbage built on the sonic landscapes of My Bloody Valentine, Curve, and Sonic Youth, adding a distinct sense of accessible pop songcraft.

Garbage was the brainchild of producers Butch Vig, Duke Erikson, and Steve Marker. Initially, Garbage was an informal jam session between the three producers held in Marker's basement, but they eventually recruited vocalist Shirley Manson, who had previously sang with Angelfish and Goodbye Mr. MacKenzie.

Vig is a native of Viroqua, WI, who learned to play piano as a child and drums as a teenager. He attended the University of Wisconsin with plans of becoming a doctor, but he dropped out and pursued a career in music instead. The first band he joined after leaving college was Spooner, whom he played drums with. Also in Spooner was Erikson, a native Nebraskan who sang and played guitar with the band. Marker was a native of New York who moved to Wisconsin to study film. He became a fan of Spooner and began recording their songs. Vig left Spooner shortly after Marker began recording their songs, but he kept in touch with the band. After a few years, Spooner became Firetown and Vig played drums for the new outfit. Firetown broke up in the late '80s, without achieving much success. Prior to the formation of Firetown, Vig and Marker bought an eight-track cassette recorder together and set up a makeshift studio in a local warehouse. This studio was dubbed Smart Studios and Vig recorded numerous local punk and alternative bands at the warehouse. By the late 80's, Smart had become one of the hippest recording studios in America. Many records released on Touch & Go, Sub Pop, and Twin/Tone, among other indie labels, were made at Smart. Vig and Smart broke into the big-time in 1991, after he produced Nirvana's *Nevermind. Nevermind* elevated Butch Vig to the status of a superstar producer and for the next two years, he produced numerous American alternative superstars, including Sonic Youth, Smashing Pumpkins, and L7.

Shortly after Vig became a star, he and Marker began playing together, eventually asking Erikson to join them. Hence, Garbage was officially formed in 1993, after Erikson joined the duo. After a year of playing, they hired Shirley Manson after seeing Angelfish's "Suffocate Me" video on MTV. Manson began her musical career at an early age, joining Goodbye Mr. MacKenzie as a teenager; she played keyboards and sang backing vocals in the band. For the next few years, she toured with the band before leaving to form Angelfish, whom she led through an eponymous 1994 album.

Garbage recorded their debut album in late 1994 and early 1995. Their eponymous first album appeared in the fall of 1995 on Almo Sounds. After receiving support from radio and MTV, the album began to climb the charts toward the end of 1995, when the second single,

"Queer," received heavy airplay. By the summer of 1996, *Garbage* had gone gold in the US. — *Stephen Thomas Erlewine*

Garbage / 1995 / Almo Sounds ✦✦✦✦
Garbage's self-titled debut has all the trappings of alternative rock, but it comes off as pop, thanks to the glossy production courtesy of bassist Butch Vig. Not only is the sound of the record slick and professional, but all the songs are well-crafted pop songs. Unfortunately, only a handful of the songs are memorable, but those that are—"Vow" and "Queer," in particular—are small, trashy alternative pop gems. — *Stephen Thomas Erlewine*

Jerry Garcia

b. Aug. 1, 1942, San Francisco, CA, **d.** Aug. 9, 1995
Guitar, Vocals / Rock 'n' Roll, Country-Rock, Folk-Rock
Jerry Garcia was the lead guitarist, vocalist, and spokesman for the seminal '60s rock 'n' roll band the Grateful Dead. Throughout his career, he led the Dead through numerous changes, becoming one of the most famous figures in the history of rock 'n' roll. Simultaneously, Garcia pursued an eclectic array of side projects, ranging from the bluegrass group Old & In the Way to his folky solo recordings. Garcia stayed active as a member of the Grateful Dead and as a solo performer until his death in 1995.

Garcia learned to play guitar when he was 15 years old, originally playing folk and rock 'n' roll. In 1959, when he was 17 years old, he spent a brief time in the army. When he left the military after a matter of months, he moved to Palo Alto, CA, where he met and became friends with Robert Hunter, who would later become his lyricist. Garcia bought a banjo in 1962 and began playing in local bluegrass bands. Within a few years, he was a member of Mother McCree's Uptown Jug Champions, a popular local bluegrass and folk band whose membership also included Bob Weir and Pigpen. In 1965, this group evolved into the Warlocks, which would in turn become the Grateful Dead in 1966.

Over the course of the next five years, the Grateful Dead began building a reputation as a mesmerizing live act. During this time, Garcia guested with a number of bands, both in concert and in the studio; among the artists he appeared with are the New Riders of the Purple Sage (a band which he helped form), Jefferson Starship, and Crosby, Stills, Nash, and Young. In 1970, they began to shift their music back toward their folk, country, and bluegrass roots with the albums *Workingman's Dead* and *American Beauty*. The following year, Garcia began a solo career with *Hooteroll?*, which was released on Douglas Records. For the next few years, Garcia recorded solo albums frequently, often with keyboardist Merl Saunders. In 1973, he was one of the founding members of the bluegrass supergroup Old & In the Way, which also featured David Grisman, Vassar Clements, and John Kahn.

Garcia's solo efforts slowed in the early '80s, as he battled heroin addiction and diabetes. After the Grateful Dead scored their first hit album in 1987 with *In the Dark*, Garcia pursued a number of solo projects, including several acoustic duet records with David Grisman and a handful of live tours and albums with the Jerry Garcia Acoustic Band. For the first half of the '90s, Garcia concentrated on Grateful Dead tours and albums, as the band confirmed their status as one of the most popular concert acts in America. However, the guitarist slowly sank back into heroin addiction. Late in the summer of 1995, he entered Serenity Knolls, a drug rehabilitation facility in Forest Knolls, CA. While he was attempting to recover, Garcia died in his sleep of a heart attack on August 9, 1995. Several months after his death, the Grateful Dead announced their disbandment. — *Stephen Thomas Erlewine*

Hooteroll? / 1971 / Grateful Dead ✦✦✦
Howard Wales, who is co-credited on this album, is a keyboard player, and Jerry Garcia's first non-Grateful Dead album release finds the two, along with such Garcia band stalwarts as drummer Bill Vitt and bassist John Kahn, playing exploratory instrumental music that touches on jazz and rock. Originally released in 1971 on Douglas Records, the album was reissued on CD on Grateful Dead Records in 1987 with two added tracks. — *William Ruhlmann*

● **Garcia** / Jan. 1972 / Grateful Dead ✦✦✦✦
In essence, this is a Grateful Dead record, featuring as it does the band's leader/singer/guitarist, its drummer, and its lyricist. Except for the few instrumental/experimental cuts, the material has been incorporated into the Dead's concert repertoire. In fact, this is a perfect follow-up to the folk-rock song albums the Dead produced in 1970, *Workingman's Dead* and *American Beauty*—albums the band itself has never really followed up. — *William Ruhlmann*

Live at the Keystone / 1973 / Fantasy ✦✦
Reflections / Jan. 1976 / Grateful Dead ✦✦✦
Again, a Dead album in everything but name, with several tracks featuring the entire band, perhaps most memorably on "It Must Have Been the Roses." — *William Ruhlmann*

Cats Under the Stars / 1978 / Arista ✦✦✦

Run for the Roses / 1982 / Arista ✦✦✦
Almost Acoustic / Dec. 1988 / Grateful Dead ✦✦✦
Compliments of Garcia / 1989 / Grateful Dead ✦✦
Jerry Garcia Band / 1991 / Arista ✦✦✦
Jerry Garcia & David Grisman / 1991 / Acoustic Disc ✦✦✦✦
A guitar-and-mandolin duet album, exquisitely produced, with this pair trying a variety of styles from Garcia's "Friend of the Devil" to the ambitious instrumental "Arabia." — *William Ruhlmann*

Marvin Gaye (Marvin Pentz Gay, Jr.)

b. Apr. 2, 1939, Washington, DC, **d.** Apr. 1, 1984, Los Angeles, CA
Keyboards, Vocals / Soul, R&B, Urban, Motown
Of the important R&B-pop artists to emerge on Motown Records in the 1960s, Marvin Gaye was one of two (the other being Stevie Wonder) to adapt effectively to the musical changes of the '70s. A singer of dance hits and light romantic ballads early on, he turned to album-length treatments of social concerns and erotic pleasures, with complex music that took on elements of rock and funk.

The son of a minister, Gaye got his start singing in church and in the '50s was a member of the vocal group the Moonglows. He was an early recruit to Motown, for which he began recording on its Tamla label in 1961, the same year he married Anna Gordy, sister of Motown chief Berry Gordy, Jr. His first recording success came with "Stubborn Kind of Fellow" (Sep. 1962), which reached the R&B Top Ten and entered the pop charts. "Hitch Hike" (Dec. 1962) brought him into the pop Top 40 and "Pride and Joy" (May 1963) into the pop Top Ten.

Gaye continued to chart in 1964, sometimes in duets with Mary Wells and with Kim Weston, and his next major success came with "How Sweet It Is (To Be Loved by You)" (Nov. 1964). Its follow-up, "I'll Be Doggone" (Mar. 1965) topped the R&B chart, where nearly all of his singles would reach the Top Ten for the next eight years. His next major pop success was "Ain't That Peculiar" (Sep. 1965), which also went to No. 1 R&B. Gaye enjoyed the biggest hit of his career with his sultry treatment of "I Heard It Through the Grapevine" (Nov. 1968), which had been a No. 1 hit for Gladys Knight and the Pips only a year before. His next two singles, "Too Busy Thinking About My Baby" (Apr. 1969) and "That's the Way Love Is" (Aug. 1969), also hit the pop Top Ten.

Gaye was profoundly affected by the death of his singing partner Tammi Terrell of a brain tumor on March 16, 1970. (Their hits together had included "Your Precious Love" [August 1967], "If I Could Build My Whole World Around You" [November 1967], "Ain't Nothing like the Real Thing" [March 1968], and "You're All I Need to Get By" [July 1968]). He went into seclusion. At the same time, he was attempting to wrest greater creative control over his music from Motown. He re-emerged with a masterwork, "What's Going On" (Feb. 1971), the centerpiece of his first pop Top Ten album *What's Going On* (May 1971), which also featured the hits "Mercy Mercy Me (The Ecology)" and "Inner City Blues (Make Me Wanna Holler)," songs that were a far cry from Gaye's '60s love songs.

Gaye next turned to movie scoring, producing the soundtrack to *Trouble Man* (Dec. 1972), before topping the commercial success of *What's Going On* with the lusty *Let's Get It On* (Aug. 1973). *Marvin Gaye Live!* (Jun. 1974) and *I Want You* (Mar. 1976) were also Top Ten hits, and *Marvin Gaye Live at the Palladium* (Mar. 1977) returned him to the top of the pop charts with the irresistible funk song "Got to Give It Up."

Gaye suffered personal and business problems thereafter, however, divorcing Anna Gordy in an extraordinary settlement that awarded her the proceeds from his next album (he dubbed it *Here, My Dear* [December 1978]) and getting into a dispute over back taxes with the IRS. Gaye left Motown and the US, living in Europe for several years, then returned with the comeback album *Midnight Love* (Nov. 1982) and its single "Sexual Healing." In 1984, Gaye was shot to death by his father during an argument. — *William Ruhlmann*

☆ **Marvin Gaye's Greatest Hits, Vol. 2** / 1967 / Motown ✦✦✦✦✦
Other than the *Anthology* line, this was for quite a while the best single album set featuring Gaye's early and mid-'60s hits. There isn't a dud in the bunch, but both the *Super Hits* and Anthology line give you more cuts, while the boxed set has more variety. But this isn't by any stretch a bad release. — *Ron Wynn*

Super Hits / 1970 / Motown ✦✦✦✦
A fabulous anthology, one of the best ones Motown ever released. Both *Super Hits* packages were crammed full for albums of the era, and the sound and selections were first rate. Motown has issued the first volume on CD, but thus far not the second—a major mistake. — *Ron Wynn*

☆ **What's Going On** / May 20, 1971 / Motown ✦✦✦✦✦
Shortly after Marvin Gaye turned 30, he became the first Motown artist with a measure of creative control. *What's Going On* was the result, surely Marvin's finest moment and, along with a number of Stevie Wonder's early-'70s releases, one of a handful of *great* Motown albums. A concept album, *What's Going On* chronicled a multitude of societal ills. Ironically, Motown owner Berry Gordy did not want to release it. He was

convinced it held no commercial potential. Gordy couldn't have been more wrong: *What's Going On* catapulted Marvin Gaye into superstardom. Three No. 1 singles were pulled from the album: the title song, "Mercy Mercy Me (The Ecology)," and "Inner City Blues (Make Me Wanna Holler)." This was the first album where Marvin overdubbed his voice multiple times, creating a one-man vocal group. The result was a level of timbral integration in the harmonies that became a Gaye trademark. — *Rob Bowman*

Trouble Man / Dec. 8, 1972 / Motown ◆◆◆
Marvin Gaye turned to soundtracks in the early '70s, and came out with one that ranked right alongside the epic scores done by Curtis Mayfield and Isaac Hayes. The film itself was a typical '70s "blaxploitation" effort, but Gaye's vocals, seamless production, and a nice mix of uptempo funk, light ballads, and pseudo-macho camp were brilliant. — *Ron Wynn*

☆ **Let's Get It On** / Aug. 28, 1973 / Motown ◆◆◆◆◆
Let's Get It On is one of the most erotic recordings known to mankind. Inspired by Gaye's obsession with a teenage girl, Janis Hunter, who would later become his second wife, side one is a self-contained suite. Side two, including "You Sure Love to Ball," is nearly pornographic. Over time, five songs would chart from the album, including one of his concert standards, "Distant Lover." — *Rob Bowman*

★ **Anthology** / 1974 / Motown ◆◆◆◆◆
With *Anthology* you can get an overview of Gaye's Motown work without having to plunk the money down for *The Marvin Gaye Collection* boxed set. The two-disc set contains most of his major hits (although not his No. 1 hit "Let's Get It On"), including "Inner City Blues (Make Me Wanna Holler)," "Mercy Mercy Me (The Ecology)," "I Heard It Through the Grapevine," "Trouble Man," "I'll Be Doggone," "What's Going On," "Hitch Hike," "Can I Get a Witness," and "Pride and Joy," as well as his numerous duets with Kim Weston and Tammi Terrell, like "Ain't No Mountain High Enough," "Ain't Nothing like the Real Thing," "It Takes Two," and "Your Precious Love." — *AMG*

I Want You / Mar. 16, 1976 / Motown ◆◆◆

Here My Dear / Dec. 15, 1978 / Motown ◆◆◆◆
On one of the stranger releases in popular music, *Here, My Dear*, Gaye stands emotionally naked. Over the course of this two-album set, Marvin chronicles the dissolution of his marriage (to company president Berry Gordy's sister Anna). The level of detail is nearly painful as Marvin accuses Anna of keeping him from seeing his son, having a restraining order issued against him, and holding their separation up for ransom. Marvin also tells us of his cocaine habit and his obsession with prostitutes. In a trace of irony not lost on the singer, Anna received all royalties from the album as per their divorce agreement. Upon hearing it, she reportedly contemplated suing for invasion of privacy. — *Rob Bowman*

In Our Lifetime / Jan. 15, 1981 / Motown ◆◆◆

Midnight Love / Oct. 1982 / Columbia ◆◆◆◆
Gaye's comeback album contains its share of fluff but "Sexual Healing" is one of the greatest R&B singles of all time. Black radio felt that way as well; the song stayed No. 1 for ten weeks, remaining on the charts for a total of 27 weeks. — *Rob Bowman*

The Marvin Gaye Collection / 1990 / Motown ◆◆◆
Marvin Gaye has more than enough great music to make a superb box set, but the haphazard *Marvin Gaye Collection* isn't it. The four discs within the set are arranged thematically—one terrific disc of hits, one good disc of duets, one largely uninteresting disc of rarities, and one wildly uneven disc of ballads. By spreading out the material this way, Motown shortchanges Gaye's musical accomplishments; there is no sense of growth or innovation. Although many of the songs are wonderful, some of the selections are puzzling—they seem to be chosen because they're arcane, not because they're significant. This very quality makes *The Marvin Gaye Collection* essential for his most devoted fans; however, most fans will find this box set disappointing. — *Stephen Thomas Erlewine*

Norman Whitfield Sessions / 1994 / Motown ◆◆◆

The Master 1961-1984 / Apr. 25, 1995 / Motown ◆◆◆◆
The average fan is better off with *Anthology*, which covers almost all of Gaye's true classics. But for those who want the hits and then some, and have the budget and interest to go further, this four-CD box set is an excellent retrospective of his career. The 89 tracks include all the chart hits (both on his own and with Mary Wells, Kim Weston, Tammi Terrell, and Diana Ross) and many interesting B-sides, album tracks, and misses. There are also over a dozen previously unreleased cuts, most dating from the early part of his career; they don't rank among his best work, but they're almost all good and interesting. With a long essay by his biographer, David Ritz, this is the best overview of Gaye's evolution and versatility, and a much-recommended alternative to the previous Gaye box, *The Marvin Gaye Collection*. — *Richie Unterberger*

★ **Anthology [1995]** / Aug. 22, 1995 / Motown ◆◆◆◆◆
The Marvin Gaye Anthology released in August 1995 is an entirely dif-

ferent compilation from the three-LP *Anthology* originally released in April 1974 and reissued as a double-CD in August 1986. The earlier version contained 40 tracks, starting with "Stubborn Kind of Fellow" and running through "Trouble Man." The new one, on two CDs or cassettes, contains 47 tracks, also starting with "Stubborn Kind Of Fellow," but running through "Heavy Love Affair". As such, it is more comprehensive, containing such later hits as "Let's Get It On," "I Want You," and "Got To Give It Up—Pt. 1" that were not featured on the earlier edition (but not "Sexual Healing," which Gaye recorded after leaving Motown). Only a couple of Gaye's Top Ten R&B/Top 40 pop hits are missing, and there is a smattering of rarities. The 1995 *Anthology* falls neatly between the single-disc *Every Great Motown Hit* and the four-disc boxed set *The Master 1961-1984* as a thorough hits collection at a reasonable price. — *William Ruhlmann*

Gloria Gaynor

b. Sep. 7, 1949, Newark, NJ
Vocals / Disco
Gaynor sang with the Soul Satisfiers band before being discovered at the Wagon Wheel in New York in the early '70s. Probably the first "disco queen," Gaynor helped popularize, through her music, the "segue" or "extended mix" that came to represent disco music. Her 1979 cut, "I Will Survive," became a woman's anthem in the vein of Helen Reddy's "I Am Woman." She continued to thrive in Europe during the '80s. — *Bil Carpenter*

● **Greatest Hits** / 1982 / Polydor ◆◆◆◆
Includes "Never Can Say Goodbye" and other disco hits. — *Bil Carpenter*

J. Geils Band

Rock 'n' Roll, Blues-Rock, Pop-Rock
The J. Geils Band from Boston (formed 1967) embraced the idioms of doo wop, blues, and R&B at a time when many of their peers were diving headfirst into psychedelia. While everyone else grew their hair out, many of the Geils Band slicked their hair back like greasers. Jerome Geils was the band's lead guitarist, but it was Peter Wolf (Blankfield), a former WBCN-FM Boston DJ, who was the group's captivating frontman.

During the '70s, the J. Geils Band toured incessantly and enjoyed the occasional near-hit album or single, but the band struck multi-platinum with *Freeze Frame* (No. 1) in 1982, one of the biggest albums of that year. Excellent video exposure on the fledgling MTV helped considerably. With success came numerous problems, including substance abuse. A live album, *Showtime*, (No. 23), followed before Wolf jumped ship for a solo career. The group's first post-Wolf studio effort *(You're Getting Even While I'm Getting Odd)* was a major stumble chartwise (No. 80), and the group disbanded shortly afterwards. — *Rick Clark*

The J. Geils Band / 1970 / Atlantic ◆◆◆◆
Their debut paid homage to the likes of Otis Rush, John Lee Hooker, and Motown through blistering covers, but originals such as "Wait" and "What's Your Hurry" more than hold their own. Magic Dick steals the show on this one. — *John Floyd*

Monkey Island / 1977 / Atlantic ◆◆◆◆
One of the great lost albums, *Monkey Island* is where the Geils Band make the blues their own. It's an elaborately produced, adventurous set that analyzes their commerical failure and looks for answers to hard-to-ask questions. Unlike their 1972 album *Full House*, *Monkey Island* refuses to pander to blues conservatists or boogie-rock hammerheads; the album is steeped in the kind of pathos and bitterness that infuse the Stones' *Sticky Fingers*. The album flopped, but it remains the group's most personal statement. — *John Floyd*

Sanctuary / 1978 / EMI America ◆◆◆

The Best of the J. Geils Band / 1979 / Atlantic ◆◆◆◆
Pulling the decent material from these otherwise unspectacular mid-'70s albums makes this an adequate overview of the band's achievements. It's the best place to sample such minor hits as "Must of Got Lost" and "Give It to Me." — *John Floyd*

Love Stinks / 1980 / EMI America ◆◆◆
The title cut brought the band an across-the-board hit, and the near new wave production touches don't get in the way of the crack rhythm section or Geils' tasty leads. A new sound for a new decade. — *John Floyd*

Freeze Frame / 1981 / EMI America ◆◆◆◆
A stylistic retread, it nonetheless cemented the band's newfound popularity, thanks to the naggingly catchy "Centerfold" and the nuevo-funky "Flamethrower." "Piss on the Wall" and "Rage in the Cage" are blistering rockers. — *John Floyd*

Flashback / 1988 / EMI America ◆◆◆

● **Houseparty: Anthology** / 1992 / Rhino ◆◆◆◆
The superb two-disc anthology *Houseparty* concentrates on the rousing, full-throttle blues-boogie of their heyday, including a full album's worth of live material (ten songs from their three live albums). The pop success

of *Love Stinks* and *Freeze Frame* makes sense in the context of the set, but the songs that cut the deepest are the blues-rock numbers on the first disc and the live songs. Thankfully, the compilers (*Trouser Press* editor Ira Robbins and band members Peter Wolf and Seth Justman) end *Houseparty* with three songs from *Sanctuary*, helping secure the image of the J. Geils Band as one of America's top rock 'n' roll groups. —*Stephen Thomas Erlewine*

Gene

Alternative Pop-Rock, Brit Pop

To say that Gene sound like the Smiths is a bit like saying the Rolling Stones sound like Chuck Berry—although there are clear traces of their primary influence, the band has incorporated them into a familiar but re-energized sound. Gene don't treat the Smiths' catalog as sacred texts; the music serves as a launching point for tales of debauchery and loneliness that Morrissey would never bother to chronicle. Gene's attack is more muscular and straightforward as well, relying less on layers of guitars than a simple intertwining of two guitar parts. Before the release of their 1995 debut, the band had developed a dedicated following based on the strength of their singles "Be My Light, Be My Guide" and "Sleep Well Tonight" and extensive coverage in the British music weeklies. Upon its release, *Olympian* received mixed reviews, yet it sold well in the UK; however, the band failed to break big in the US. —*Stephen Thomas Erlewine*

● **Olympian** / 1995 / Polydor ✦✦✦✦

Kicking off with the sprightly "Haunted by You," *Olympian* immediately conjures images of the Smiths, particularly "This Charming Man." Martin Rossiter's voice also sways like Morrissey, yet his band plays their songs as if they were hard rockers, bringing a desperate edge to their best material. Most of *Olympian*'s finest moments were singles—aside from "Haunted by You," the epic sweep of "Sleep Well Tonight" and the gentle urgency of the title track form the heart of the album; two other singles were added to the American version, including the stellar "Be My Light, Be My Guide." While Gene manages to carve out an identity indebted to the Smiths but not dominated by them, they also fail to produce an album of consistently compelling material—considering that it's a debut album, that's not a fatal flaw. And Gene's best material shows they are capable of transcending their influences. —*Stephen Thomas Erlewine*

To See the Lights / Jan. 1996 / Costermager ✦✦✦✦

The easy joke is, *To See the Lights* is Gene's *Hatful of Hollow*. True, the album is a collection of B-sides, nonalbum singles, radio sessions, and live tracks but, like the Smiths' *Hatful of Hollow* before it, the album illustrates the band's strengths more effectively than their debut album, *Olympian*. Several of Gene's greatest songs, including the roaring title track, the anthemic "Be My Light, Be My Guide," and the gorgeous "I Can't Decide If She Really Loves Me," are rounded up on the album and they are stronger than some of the material that appeared on the debut. Also, the live versions of the *Olympian* singles are better, illustrating that the band can rock with a vengeance. It might appear to be an album designed solely for fans, but *To See the Lights* is a better, more compulsively listenable album than *Olympian*. —*Stephen Thomas Erlewine*

Generation X

Punk

An early London punk band (1978-1981), Generation X featured Billy Idol and Tony James (later to form Sigue Sigue Sputnik). Often criticized as being too commercially minded, Gen X was definitely the smoothest and most pop-oriented of their rebellious crowd. Their first album is considered the best, with the US version offering a slightly improved song set. Their third and last, *Kiss Me Deadly*, was more an Idol/James project than a band effort and was produced by Keith Forsey, who shaped Idol's solo sound. This album contained an early version of "Dancing with Myself," which was eventually Idol's first big solo pop success. As to whether they were a band of crass opportunists or true champions of the punk spirit, Billy Idol's career and Sigue Sigue Sputnik's dubious distinction of having the first advertisement on a pop record speak volumes. —*Scott Bultman*

Generation X / 1979 / Chrysalis ✦✦✦✦

Generation X had punk attitude and subject matter on their debut album, which includes their answer song to the Who, "Your Generation," and the generic "One Hundred Punks." But the group's music already had more of a melodic mainstream rock sound than punk's raw assault, and frontman Billy Idol's snarl was straight out of Elvis Presley. —*William Ruhlmann*

Kiss Me Deadly / 1981 / Chrysalis ✦✦✦

● **Best of Generation X** / 1985 / Chrysalis ✦✦✦✦

Collecting the highlights from their three uneven albums as well as their EP, *Best of Generation X* features nearly everything of value the band recorded. —*Stephen Thomas Erlewine*

Genesis

Art-Rock/Progressive-Rock, Pop-Rock

Genesis has been both a successful progressive art-rock band of the 1970s and a successful pop-rock band of the 1980s and '90s, though fans of their earlier work and of their later work might not share the same taste in music. The group's evolution began at the elite British prep school Charterhouse, attended by all of its original members—Tony Banks (b. Mar. 27, 1951, East Heatbly, Sussex, England) (keyboards), Peter Gabriel (b. May 13, 1950, London, England) (vocals), Anthony Phillips (guitar), Mike Rutherford (b. Oct. 2, 1950) (guitar), and Chris Stewart (replaced by John Silver) (drums). This lineup signed to Decca Records in the UK and released *From Genesis to Revelation* (Mar. 1969). Leaving school and turning professional, the group replaced Silver with John Mayhew, signed to Charisma Records, and released *Trespass* (Oct. 1970). But by the time it appeared, Phillips and Silver had dropped out and been replaced by Steve Hackett (b. Feb. 12, 1950, London, England) (guitar) and Phil Collins (b. Jan. 31, 1951, London, England) (drums), and this unit made the third album, *Nursery Cryme* (Nov. 1972).

Up to this point, Genesis hadn't sold enough records to make the charts, but they developed a highly visual stage show centered on Gabriel and toured extensively. Their fourth album, *Foxtrot* (Oct. 1972), finally broke into the UK charts, and from then on they were a big success in their native country. Their live show was documented on *Genesis: Live* (Jun. 1973), which soared into the UK Top Ten. (From here on, every new Genesis album would reach the Top Ten in Britain.)

Selling England by the Pound (Nov. 1973) spawned Genesis's first UK single hit, "I Know What I Like (In Your Wardrobe)," and were their first album to chart in the US, where it eventually went gold. An even greater success was the two-LP concept album *The Lamb Lies Down on Broadway* (Nov. 1974). Then, just as Genesis seemed to be entering the top ranks of '70s rock groups, Peter Gabriel quit to start a solo career.

The remaining quartet auditioned singers but finally settled on drummer Phil Collins, whose voice bore some similarity to Gabriel's. They returned to action with *A Trick of the Tail* (Mar. 1976), which turned out to be their most successful album yet. After *Wind and Wuthering* (Jan. 1977) and a second live set, *Seconds Out* (Nov. 1977), Hackett also decamped, and the remaining trio of Banks, Rutherford, and Collins continued on as Genesis, augmenting themselves with hired musicians on stage.

As their next album, *And Then There Were Three* (Mar. 1978), demonstrated, fans liked Genesis even better as a trio than they had as a quartet or quintet. The album went platinum and produced Genesis's first US Top 40 hit, "Follow You, Follow Me"; in the UK, it was their first Top Ten hit. By the time of *Duke* (Apr. 1980), any resemblance to the art-rock style of the early Genesis was gone, and the result was another million-seller in the US In the UK, *Duke* was the first Genesis album to go to No. 1, and each of the band's next four studio albums would do the same.

Genesis's status was only enhanced by *Face Value* (Feb. 1981), Collins' debut solo album, which was a far bigger hit than any Genesis album so far. Nevertheless, he stayed with the group, which now began to alternate periods of solo and band work. (Mike Rutherford achieved separate success as of the release of the self-titled debut album by his spin-off group, Mike & the Mechanics, in Nov. 1985.)

Not surprisingly, *Abacab* (Nov. 1981), the next Genesis album, was the group's biggest hit yet, soaring into the US Top Ten. *Three Sides Live* (Jun. 1982) was another concert collection, followed by *Genesis* (Oct. 1983), which featured the group's first US Top Ten hit, "That's All!"

Three years passed before the release of *Invisible Touch* (Jun. 1986), long enough to build up tremendous demand among fans, who bought five million copies of it in the US alone and put five of its songs into the Top Ten, including the No. 1 title song, "Throwing It All Away," "Land of Confusion," "Tonight, Tonight, Tonight," and "In Too Deep."

Genesis waited five years before releasing its next album, *We Can't Dance* (Oct. 1991), which did not match the success of its predecessor, though with three million in US sales and another five chart singles, including the Top Ten hit "I Can't Dance," it didn't do too badly. Following a world tour, Genesis released a two-part concert album under the title *Live/The Way We Walk, Vol. One: The Shorts* (Nov. 1992), which contained more concise pop songs, while *Vol. Two: The Longs* (Feb. 1993) contained more extended performances.

Genesis's popular momentum seemed to be slowing in the mid-'90s, as group albums and spin-off records ceased to trace new sales peaks with each release. In March 1996, Phil Collins quit the group, leaving the remaining duo of Mike Rutherford and Tony Banks to audition new singers and hope Genesis could begin yet another chapter in its career. But both its more challenging early work and its more radio-friendly later work had a major impact on the music of the '70s and '80s. —*William Ruhlmann*

From Genesis to Revelation / Mar. 1969 / DCC ✦✦

Trespass / Oct. 1970 / MCA ♦♦
Genesis had changed considerably by the release of their second album (which was their first to be issued in the US, by the Impulse! division of ABC-Dunhill Records, now part of MCA). For one thing, they'd finished school, turned professional and started playing out. For another, drummer John Silver had left and been replaced for the album by John Mayhew. (Before the release of *Trespass*, both Mayhew and Anthony Phillips left. The group then recruited guitarist Steve Hackett and former child actor Phil Collins as new drummers.) Genesis's individual sound began to appear on *Trespass*, with its complex structures and long songs. The driving rocker "Knife," at nine minutes the longest track, remains the highlight. — *William Ruhlmann*

Nursery Cryme / Nov. 1971 / Atlantic ♦♦♦
On their third album, released in the UK in November 1971 and in the US in 1972, Genesis is beginning to find a place in the British art-rock movement of the early '70s, as Peter Gabriel constructs elaborate musical set pieces, the most impressive of which is the 10.5-minute leadoff track, "The Musical Box." The dense structures, tempo changes, organ/guitar interplay, and fanciful lyrics are not unlike what Yes was doing at the same time, and fans of that band will find music to their liking here. — *William Ruhlmann*

Foxtrot / Oct. 1972 / Atlantic ♦♦♦
On its fourth album, Genesis's ambitious music finally starts to show individual identity and accomplishment, mixing elaborate arrangements with stirring rhythms and highly poetic lyrics. Contains "Watcher of the Skies" and the 22-minute "Supper's Ready." — *William Ruhlmann*

☆ **Selling England by the Pound** / Jan. 1973 / Atlantic ♦♦♦♦♦
One of the best examples of '70s British art-rock, this album incorporates a variety of styles, showcasing the musical dexterity of the players as well as the lyrics to story-songs like "I Know What I Like (In Your Wardrobe)," the first Genesis British hit. — *William Ruhlmann*

Genesis: Live / Jun. 1973 / Atlantic ♦♦♦

★ **The Lamb Lies Down on Broadway** / Nov. 1974 / Atlantic ♦♦♦♦♦
This, the last Genesis album with Peter Gabriel, is a sprawling two-disc thematic album concerning a character named Rael. Keeping with that theme, it includes pastiches of Broadway show music, plus the group's typical mixture of folk, rock, and classical influences. If this is not the first Gabriel Genesis album to buy, it ultimately may prove the most satisfying. — *William Ruhlmann*

Trick of the Tail / Mar. 1976 / Atlantic ♦♦♦
At the time of its release in March 1976, Genesis's seventh studio album was a remarkable document if only because the group had managed to survive the departure of its frontman, Peter Gabriel, not only by locating a worthy (and similar-sounding) vocalist in drummer Phil Collins, but also by writing material that was respectable, even if it lacked Gabriel's vision and imagination. As a result, the album hit No. 3 in the UK and maintained the band's following in the US, assuring them a future. In retrospect, it isn't a very impressive effort (with the exception of "Robbery, Assault and Battery," which has some of the old spirit), although it gives hints of the pop assembly line Genesis would develop in the coming years. — *William Ruhlmann*

Wind and Wuthering / Jan. 1977 / Atlantic ♦♦
Less impressive than the first Genesis quartet album, *A Trick of the Tail*, *Wind and Wuthering* nevertheless marked another step in the band's gradual transformation into more of a pop act, containing its first US (and only its second UK) chart single, "Your Own Special Way." — *William Ruhlmann*

Seconds Out / Nov. 1977 / Atlantic ♦♦

And Then There Were Three / Mar. 1978 / Atlantic ♦♦♦
The birth of the modern Genesis, a pop-rock trio led by singer/drummer Phil Collins, playing tightly constructed, short, catchy songs. The best of the bunch here is "Follow You, Follow Me," a hit on both sides of the Atlantic. (The first Genesis gold album in the US) — *William Ruhlmann*

Duke / Apr. 1980 / Atlantic ♦♦♦
Released in April 1980, *Duke* found Genesis geared up as a maker of concise, appealing pop singles, and it was an immediate, across-the-board hit, topping the UK chart and almost making the US Top Ten, while the singles "Misunderstanding" and "Turn It On Again" became radio favorites on both sides of the Atlantic. — *William Ruhlmann*

● **Abacab** / Sep. 1981 / Atlantic ♦♦♦♦
Genesis had perfected its rhythmic, densely chorded, passionate trio music with this, their first US million-seller and Top Ten hit, which includes the Top 40 singles "Abacab," "No Reply at All," and "Man on the Corner." — *William Ruhlmann*

Three Sides Live / Jun. 1982 / Atlantic ♦♦♦

Genesis / Oct. 1983 / Atlantic ♦♦♦♦
Genesis' third straight No. 1 studio album in the UK was also its biggest seller yet in the US, making the Top Ten and selling three million copies.

Its big US hit was "That's All," while Britain preferred "Mama." "Illegal Alien" and "Taking It All Too Hard" also charted. — *William Ruhlmann*

Invisible Touch / Jun. 1986 / Virgin ♦♦♦
The biggest Genesis hit to date, this multi-million-selling release features five Top Five hits, including the No. 1 title track, "Throwing It All Away," "Land of Confusion," "Tonight, Tonight, Tonight," and "In Too Deep." — *William Ruhlmann*

We Can't Dance / Oct. 28, 1991 / Atlantic ♦♦♦

Genesis Live: The Way We Walk, Vol. 1 (The Shorts) / Nov. 17, 1992 / Atlantic ♦♦

Genesis Live: The Way We Walk, Vol. 2 (The Longs) / Feb. 9, 1993 / Atlantic ♦♦

Barbara George

b. Aug. 16, 1942, New Orleans, LA
Vocals / Soul, New Orleans R&B
George's "I Know (You Don't Love Me No More)" topped the R&B charts in 1961 and has proven a popular cover item ever since. The New Orleans native had never been in the studio before she brought her extremely catchy melody to Harold Battiste's fledgling A.F.O. label. Benefiting from her pleasing, unpolished vocal and a melodic cornet solo by Melvin Lastie, the tune caught fire, vaulting high on pop playlists. Amazingly, nothing else George did ever dented the charts, although she waxed some listenable follow-ups for A.F.O. and Sue. — *Bill Dahl*

● **I Know (You Don't Love Me Anymore)** / 1962 / Collectables ♦♦♦♦
This catchy New Orleans R&B from the early '60s features coy and charming vocals by George. — *Bill Dahl*

Lowell George

b. 1945, d. Jun. 29, 1979, Arlington, VA
Guitar, Vocals / Rock 'n' Roll
As Little Feat was disbanding in late 1978, their lead guitarist/songwriter Lowell George recorded a solo album, *Thanks I'll Eat It Here*, that sounded as loose and funky as the band in their prime. After its release the following year, he set out on tour to support the album. Sadly, George died of a heart attack while on the road; he left behind a body of gritty, eclectic, and funky rock 'n' roll. On the first five Little Feat albums, his songwriting and instrumental talents are more apparent than on his solo effort, yet that doesn't detract from the record's pleasures. — *Stephen Thomas Erlewine*

● **Thanks I'll Eat It Here** / 1979 / Warner Bros. ♦♦♦♦
While it's surprisingly short on original songs, Lowell George's solo album *Thanks I'll Eat It Here* is as relaxed and funky as any Little Feat album from the last half of the 1970s. — *Stephen Thomas Erlewine*

Lightning-Rod Man / 1993 / Bizarre/Straight ♦♦♦

Georgia Satellites

Rock 'n' Roll
At a time when rock 'n' roll didn't care about its roots, the Georgia Satellites came crashing into the charts with a surprise hit single to remind everybody where the music had come from. The hit single, 1986's "Keep Your Hands to Yourself," rocked as hard as an old Chuck Berry song, as well as being almost as clever. The Satellites weren't a back-to-basic roots band, either—their straightforward sound borrowed equally from Berry, the Rolling Stones, the Faces, Little Feat, and AC/DC, with a Southern backwoods bent. At their best, the Satellites were just a damn good rock 'n' roll band, driven by the classic, yet fresh, songwriting of lead singer/guitarist Dan Baird. On the strength of "Keep Your Hands to Yourself," their first major-label album sold well, but the follow-up, *Open All Night*, did not; radio and MTV had treated the band as a kind of novelty—a bunch of hicks kicking out rock 'n' roll offered a break between the slick pop-metal of Bon Jovi and Peter Gabriel's introspective pop. By the time they released *Open All Night* in 1988, no one was interested, even if the album was only slightly weaker than the debut. After one more album, 1989's *In the Land of Salvation and Sin*, the band called it quits. Guitarist Rick Richards joining Izzy Stradlin's Ju Ju Hounds three years later; Baird pursued a solo career and had a small hit in late 1992 with "I Love You Period." — *Stephen Thomas Erlewine*

Georgia Satellites / 1986 / Elektra ♦♦♦♦
Dirty Rolling Stones-like guitar grunge played by Rick Richards and topped by the adenoidal singing of Dan Baird. Especially enjoyable on the hits "Keep Your Hands to Yourself" and "Battleship Chains." — *William Ruhlmann*

Open All Night / 1988 / Elektra ♦♦♦

In the Land of Salvation and Sin / 1989 / Elektra ♦♦♦

● **Let It Rock: The Best of the Georgia Satellites** / 1993 / Elektra ♦♦♦♦
Most of the band's best tracks are on this generous compilation, which not only features their hits ("Keep Your Hands to Yourself" and "Battle-

ship Chains"), but also includes rarities like their sublime John Fogerty medley "Almost Saturday Night/Rockin' All Over the World" from the out-of-print *Rubaiyat* collection. —*Stephen Thomas Erlewine*

Lisa Germano

Fiddle, Violin, Vocals / Alternative Pop-Rock
Violinist Lisa Germano became known for her fluid, gutsy style through her work with John Mellencamp, which is captured on the *Big Daddy* and *Lonesome Jubilee* albums. Germano's solo work is much darker and atmospheric than Mellencamp's albums; her 1991 solo debut, *On the Way Down from Moon Palace*, displayed some promising songwriting along with her acclaimed instrumental prowess. Germano's second album, 1993's *Happiness*, was even better, but the record didn't sell very well when it was first released on Capitol, prompting her to change record labels in 1994. She signed with 4AD, who released a resequenced and remixed *Happiness* in the spring of 1994; the new version of the album emphasized her music's underlying dark melancholy, which the original version only hinted at. —*Stephen Thomas Erlewine*

On the Way Down from Moon Palace / 1991 / Major Bill ✦✦✦

● **Happiness** / 1993 / Capitol/EMI ✦✦✦✦
Germano's sophomore effort is a harrowing descent into black humor, anger, and general miserableness. With her deadpan little girl voice, Germano makes "You Make Me Want to Wear Dresses" sound like that is the last thing she wants to do, while she drives the point home on the transcendent dissonance of "Puppet." —*Rick Clark*

Geek the Girl / 1994 / 4AD ✦✦✦✦
Geek the Girl manages to eclipse both of Germano's previous albums by accentuating both the folkiness in her music and its awkward, dreamy qualities. The album is a song cycle about a young girl trying to come of age, both emotionally and sexually, but the story never overwhelms the tensely charming songs. It's musically richer than the average alternative angst-fest, incorporating traditional Italian melodies into Germano's folky songwriting, which touches on everything from unstructured stream-of-consciousness melodies to tight pop songs. But what makes *Geek the Girl* even more satisfying is that Germano doesn't take the easy way out and wallow in self-pity. Instead, she offers a glimmer of hope with the last two songs, making *Geek the Girl* a richly rewarding and moving record. —*Stephen Thomas Erlewine*

The Germs

Punk
One of the first (but certainly not the best) Los Angeles punk groups. Lead singer Darby Crash was a live-fast/die-young nihilist who bemoaned the stodginess of his sunny suburban surroundings. The group recorded from 1977 until 1979, when Crash died of a heroin overdose, like his idol Sid Vicious. —*John Floyd*

GI / 1979 / Slash ✦✦✦✦
It captures the black, foreboding explosiveness of West Coast punk during the late '70s and highlights the sandpaper cries of Darby Crash (who died of a self-induced drug overdose shortly after the album was recorded). —*David Szatmary*

● **M.I.A.** / Aug. 3, 1993 / Slash ✦✦✦✦
The essential Germs anthology contains all of *(GI)* as well as some of the best tracks from *What We Do Is Secret*, and a handful of recordings made for the William Friedkin film, *Cruising*. (the filmmaker best known for *The Exorcist* reportedly saw the Germs live and was knocked out by their extreme performance.) Some of the early stuff, especially "Forming" and the live "Sex Boy," wander into avant-garde noise rock; all meandering atonality and screeching hysteria, still it's pretty good. But the material from *(GI)* still sounds great and proves conclusively that the Germs had, in spite of themselves, turned into a tight, explosive rock band. Generous at 30 tracks, this is seminal late-'70s Los Angeles punk that set the stage for a generation of hardcore bands to follow. —*John Dougan*

Lisa Gerrard

Vocals / Alternative Pop-Rock
In collaboration with Brendan Perry, Lisa Gerrard is half of the duo Dead Can Dance, which has been releasing arty goth-rock on the 4AD label since the mid-'80s. Gerrard began her solo career with the 1995 release *The Mirror Pool*, which contained a lot of work that wouldn't fit comfortably into the DCD oeuvre. Combining these fragments with music that she composed and arranged digitally before reconfiguring them into scores that could be performed, it also draws on a composition by Handel and traditional Iranian music. Recorded and produced largely at her home in rural Australia, it extends the world music inclinations of recent Dead Can Dance albums by featuring bouzouki, tablas, and camel drums, though the somber, orchestrated pomp of Dead Can Dance is also present in her operatic, often wordless vocals, and string/woodwind pas-

sages (some of which were performed by Australia's Victorian Philharmonic Orchestra). —*Richie Unterberger*

The Mirror Pool / 1995 / 4AD/Warner Bros. ✦✦✦
If this is rock, it's rock of the artiest and most ambitious sort, focusing on both the gloomy orchestration that has graced much of Dead Can Dance's output, and melismatic vocal workouts that owe much to Indian and Middle Eastern music. It's sometimes a wearyingly downbeat affair, the most orchestrated sections sounding much like highly accomplished soundtrack music for very serious art house films. But these are outweighed by lengthy movements of dignified beauty, most often when Gerrard sings in her Persian cantorial style (although the purely instrumental pieces have their highlights as well). It's a challenging work, but like Dead Can Dance's most recent albums, it may actually find a wider audience than the goth-rock with which Gerrard first made her mark, due both to its wider palette of sounds and its greater emotional range. —*Richie Unterberger*

Gerry & the Pacemakers

British Invasion
The second group out of the Liverpool starting gate in the early '60s, Gerry and the Pacemakers shared manager Brian Epstein and producer George Martin with the Beatles—and even got the Beatles' hand-me-down material. Their first (UK) hit was "How Do You Do It," a song the Fab Four had declined to release. It was a No. 1 for Gerry.
The group was formed in 1959 by singer and guitarist Gerry Marsden, with his brother Freddie on drums, and Les Chadwick on bass. Pianist Les Maguire completed the lineup in 1961. They followed the same path to success as the Beatles, including making trips to Hamburg and hooking up with Epstein and Martin. And shortly after the Beatles topped the charts with "Please Please Me," Gerry and the Pacemakers did so with "How Do You Do It."
Like the Beatles, the group went over to America in 1964 and debuted on the "Ed Sullivan Show," resulting in a hit with their ballad "Don't Let the Sun Catch You Crying." Like the Beatles, they then made a movie (theirs was called *Ferry Cross the Mersey*). But unlike the Beatles, Gerry and the Pacemakers faltered commercially after 1964 and failed to develop musically. As a result, they split up in 1966, with Gerry going solo. By 1975, he had put together a new Pacemakers group and toured on the oldies circuit, his voice still appealing and the Mersey Beat still bouncing. —*William Ruhlmann*

The EP Collection / 1987 / See for Miles ✦✦✦✦
A truly definitive collection, with all the hits and the most interesting nonhits. Includes the ultra-rare live *Gerry in California* concert recording from 1966. —*Bruce Eder*

● **Best of Gerry & the Pacemakers: The Definitive Collection** / 1991 / EMI America ✦✦✦✦
The title promises more than it really delivers in content, if not sound. It'll do for the casual listener. —*Bruce Eder*

The Gerry Cross the Mersey: All the Hits of Gerry and the Pacemakers / Oct. 1995 / Razor & Tie ✦✦✦✦
Sixteen-track best-of includes all of their British and American hits, as well as some of their best B-sides. The more extensive EMI America best-of has all of these songs and more, and so is still recommended as the first purchase. But for just about everybody, this has all the Gerry you need, and all but two of the songs are in stereo, if that's an important consideration. —*Richie Unterberger*

Gin Blossoms

Pop-Rock
After an impressive debut EP, the Gin Blossoms rocketed out of the college pop charts and into the mainstream with their 1993 hit single, "Hey Jealousy." Combining the ringing guitar hooks of the Byrds and R.E.M. with a solid, rootsy drive, the band's breakthrough full-length album, *New Miserable Experience*, was filled with songs equally as strong as "Hey Jealousy," including the second hit single, "Found Out About You." *New Miserable Experience* and its singles dominated radio and MTV for the following year—both "Hey Jealousy" and "Found Out About You" were in heavy radio rotation nearly a year after their initial release—pushing the sales of their debut album over a million copies.
During 1995, the Gin Blossoms recorded their second album. In the summer of that year, the group contributed "Till I Hear It from You," a song they co-wrote with Marshall Crenshaw, to the soundtrack of *Empire Records.* "Till I Hear It from You" became a major radio hit, but it was never released as an official single until it was the B-side of "Follow You Down," the first single from the group's second album, *Congratulations... I'm Sorry.* Upon its release in February of 1996, *Congratulations... I'm Sorry* charted well, but within six months of its release, it had disappeared from the charts. —*Stephen Thomas Erlewine*

Up & Crumbling / 1992 / A&M ✦✦✦

● **New Miserable Experience** / 1992 / A&M ◆◆◆◆
With their rootsy, melodic fusion of R.E.M. and The Byrds, the Gin Blossoms carry jangle into the '90s with their breakthrough album. Powered by the hit singles "Hey Jealousy" and "I Found Out About You," *New Miserable Experience* is a solid, consistent album that offers an exciting vision of contemporary heartland rock. —*AMG*

Congratulations . . . I'm Sorry / Feb. 13, 1996 / A&M ◆◆◆

Ginger

Pop-Rock
When vocalist/guitarist and founding member Kevin Kane left Canada's acclaimed Grapes of Wrath due to the cliched musical and personal differences, the remaining members—Chris Hooper (drums), Tom Hooper (vocals, bass, guitars), and Vincent Jones (keyboards)—carried on with the like-sounding and equally enjoyable Ginger. The band returned to Nettwerk Records, releasing a self-titled, Canadian-only EP in 1993 and the full-length *Far Out* in 1994. *Far Out* was eventually released in the US in 1995. —*Chris Woodstra*

Ginger / 1993 / Nettwerk ◆◆◆
The combo's first release picks up effectively where Grapes of Wrath left off with five songs of pleasantly jangly folk-pop that occasionally flirt with pseudo-psychedelia. Only "The Earth Revolves Around You" appears on *Far Out*, so fans are advised to seek this out. —*Chris Woodstra*

● **Far Out** / Nettwerk ◆◆◆◆
Far Out is a well-paced album that clearly stands alongside the finer moments of Grapes of Wrath, alternating quieter, introspective moments with upbeat rockers and pure Beatle-esque pop. —*Chris Woodstra*

Gary Glitter (Paul Gadd)

b. May 8, 1940, Banbury, Oxfordshire, England
Vocals / Rock 'n' Roll, Glam Rock
After many years of trying to become a star, Paul Gadd finally hit the winning formula in 1972—the glam-rock king, Gary Glitter. Complete with extravagant makeup, silver outfits, and high boots, Glitter looked as trashy as his music sounded. Glitter and producer Michael Leander created pop records that weren't intended to be serious music—infectious singles that sounded perfect for the three minutes that they were playing; after they were finished, they seemed slightly embarrassing. With its mammoth drum beat, growling guitar, dumb instrumental hook, and incessant chorus of "hey!," his debut single, "Rock and Roll, Part Two," was a huge hit in both the UK and the US. Although he never had another hit in America, Glitter was a superstar in Britain throughout the mid-'70s, scoring three No. 1 singles. Surprisingly, Glitter's cheerfully idiotic, catchy glam rock became somewhat influential over the next decade; Joan Jett covered several of his songs, as did the Human League, Generation X, Planet Control, and the Brownsville Station. —*Stephen Thomas Erlewine*

● **Rock 'n' Roll: The Best of Gary Glitter** / 1990 / Rhino ◆◆◆◆
Although he's best known for the knuckle-headed sports anthem "Rock & Roll Part Two," Glitter had plenty of other glam-rock delights that were equally as good, if not better. *Rock 'n' Roll—The Best of Gary Glitter* lovingly collects his best singles, from "Rock & Roll Part Two" to such unsung riff-rockers as "Do You Wanna Touch Me (Oh Yeah!)" and "I'm the Leader of the Gang (I Am!)." It's dumb, it's catchy, it's loud—everything good rock 'n' roll should be. A nice guilty pleasure. —*Stephen Thomas Erlewine*

The Go-Go's

New Wave, Pop-Rock
The Go-Go's were the most popular all-female band to emerge from the punk/new wave explosion of the late '70s and early '80s, becoming one of the first commercially successful female groups that wasn't controlled by male producers or managers. While their hit singles—"We Got the Beat," "Our Lips Are Sealed," "Vacation," "Head over Heels"—were bright, energetic new wave pop, the group was an integral part of the Californian punk scene. And they did play punk rock, even if many of their rougher edges were ironed out by the time they recorded their first album, 1981's *Beauty and the Beat*. Even as they became America's darlings, the Go-Go's lived the wild life of rockers, swallowing as many pills and taking as much cocaine as possible, trashing hotel rooms and just generally being bad. More importantly, their earliest music—now collected on *Return to the Valley of the Go-Go's*—was raw and rocking; it may not have directly inspired the female alternative rockers and riot grrrls of the '90s, but it certainly foreshadowed it.

Originally formed in 1978 as the Misfits, the group featured Belinda Carlisle (vocals), Jane Wiedlin (guitar, vocals), Charlotte Caffey (lead guitar, keyboards), Margot Olaverra (bass), and Elissa Bello (drums); the group soon changed their name to The Go-Go's and began playing local parties and small clubs in California. In 1979, Gina Schock became the

group's drummer. During that year, the band recorded a demo and supported the British ska revival group Madness in both Los Angeles and England. The Go-Go's spent half of 1980 touring England, earning a sizable following and releasing "We Got the Beat" on Stiff Records. An import copy of "We Got the Beat" became an underground club hit in the US, which meant the band was popular enough to sell out concerts yet they had a difficult time landing a record contract.

At the end of 1980, bassist Olaverra became ill and had to stop performing; she was replaced by Kathy Valentine, a guitarist who had never played bass before. Early in 1981, the Go-Go's signed with IRS Records. Released in the summer of 1981, their debut album, *Beauty and the Beat*, became one of the surprise hits of the year, staying at No. 1 for six weeks and selling over two million copies; "Our Lips Are Sealed" hit No. 20 and a re-recorded version of "We Got the Beat" spent three weeks at No. two. The following year, the group released *Vacation*. Although it sold well—the album made the Top Ten and it went gold, spawning the Top Ten hit single "Vacation"—it failed to keep the momentum of the first record. During the next year the band was unable to perform as Caffey recovered from a broken wrist. In 1984, the Go-Go's returned with *Talk Show*, their most musically ambitious album. While it had two Top 40 hits—the No. 11 "Head over Heels" and "Turn to You"—it failed to even go gold. By the end of the year, Wiedlin had left the band; the Go-Go's broke up in May of 1985. Belinda Carlisle became the most successful solo artist, scoring a string of mainstream pop singles in the late '80s, including the No. 1 single "Heaven Is a Place on Earth." For a while, Charlotte Caffey was in Carlisle's backing group; she eventually formed the Graces, who released *Perfect View* in 1990. Jane Wiedlin recorded two solo albums and acted in a few films. Wiedlin also organized the group's brief 1990 reunion, where they performed at a benefit for People for the Ethical Treatment of Animals; they also recorded a version of "Cool Jerk" for their 1990 *Greatest Hits* album. The Go-Go's reunited once more in 1994, recording three new songs for the double-disc compilation *Return of the Valley of the Go-Go's*; after recording the songs, the group decided to continue as a full-time unit. —*Stephen Thomas Erlewine*

Beauty & the Beat / Jul. 1981 / IRS ◆◆◆◆

Vacation / Aug. 1982 / IRS ◆◆◆

Talk Show / 1984 / IRS ◆◆◆

● **Greatest** / 1990 / IRS ◆◆◆◆
An adequate collection of hits, it includes "Our Lips Are Sealed," "We Got the Beat," "Vacation," and "Head over Heels." —*Dan Heilman*

● **Return to the Valley of the Go-Go's** / 1994 / IRS ◆◆◆◆
Because it doesn't ignore the group's punk and new wave roots, the double-disc set *Return to the Valley of the Go-Go's* is far more entertaining than the single-disc collection *Greatest Hits*. All of the hits are included, as well as many rarities as good as anything they officially released. Not only is the music intoxicating, but the liner notes are filled with priceless photos and memorabilia, which makes the set the one definitive Go-Go's album. —*Stephen Thomas Erlewine*

The Golden Palominos

Alternative Pop-Rock
Led by drummer Anton Fier, this progressive project band from New York features an ever-changing lineup of current alternative players. At various times, the Golden Palominos have included Michael Stipe of R.E.M., John Lydon, Richard Thompson, Chris Stamey, Jack Bruce, Arto Lindsay, Carla Bley, Bob Mould, and others. —*Iotis Erlewine*

The Golden Palominos / 1983 / Celluloid ◆◆◆

Visions of Excess / 1985 / Celluloid ◆◆◆◆
There's a great eclectic mix of alternative-rock songcraft and great musicianship from Jack Bruce, Richard Thompson, and others. Syd Straw shines on "(Kind Of) True" as does Michael Stipe on "Omaha." —*Scott Bultman*

Blast of Silence / 1986 / Celluloid ◆◆◆

Drunk with Passion / 1991 / Charisma ◆◆◆◆
Fier and Bill Laswell are joined by Stipe, Thompson, Carla Bley, and former Hüsker Dü singer-songwriter and guitarist Bob Mould on this album. —*William Ruhlmann*

● **A History (1982-1985)** / 1992 / Metrotone ◆◆◆◆
This is a fine sampler of the Golden Palominos' first two records. —*AMG*

● **A History (1986-1989)** / 1992 / Metrotone ◆◆◆◆
This is a fine sampler of the Golden Palominos' third and fourth records. —*AMG*

This Is How It Feels / 1993 / Restless ◆◆◆◆
Anton Fier and Bill Laswell use Lori Carson as their regular vocalist here, with three songs sung by Lydia Kavanaugh. Guest musicians include Bootsy Collins, Nicky Skopelitis, and Bernie Worrell. The key figure, however, is Carson, who co-wrote all the songs on which she sings, making this, in effect, a Lori Carson solo album. Carson explores the

argumentative, often brutal aspects of romance in songs that have a dreamy effect despite the involved rhythm tracks. Her double-tracked, interweaving vocals, with their repeated phrases and blunt sentiments, have a disorienting, yet compelling force. — *William Ruhlmann*

Pure / 1994 / Restless ✦✦✦✦
The Golden Palominos manage to convey much of the same darkly seductive atmosphere as their other shimmering experimental pop records. — *Stephen Thomas Erlewine*

No Thought, No Breath, No Eyes, No Heart / 1995 / Restless ✦✦✦

Lesley Gore

b. May 2, 1946, New York, NY
Vocals / Girl Group, Brill Building Pop
The most commercially successful solo singer to be identified with the girl group sound, Lesley Gore hit the No. 1 spot with her very first release, "It's My Party," in 1963. Produced by Quincy Jones, who fattened the teenager's sound with double-tracked vocals and intricate backup vocals and horns, she reeled off a few more big hits in 1963 and 1964, including "Judy's Turn to Cry," "She's a Fool," "You Don't Own Me," "That's the Way Boys Are," and "Maybe I Know." She wasn't the most soulful girl group singer by a long shot, but she projected an archetype of female adolescent yearning. Her best songs survive as classics, particularly the irresistibly melodic "Maybe I Know" and "Look of Love" (both written by Ellie Greenwich and Jeff Barry) and "You Don't Own Me," an anthem of independence with a feminist theme that was considerably advanced for early 1964.

So what was Quincy Jones doing producing a White suburban teenager who had never recorded before? A couple of demos she recorded with her vocal coach made their way to Mercury's president, who recommended her to Jones, the label's A&R head. For their first session, Gore and Jones picked "It's My Party" out of a pile of about 200 demos. The "It's My Party" single was rush-released when Jones found out that Phil Spector had plans to record the same song with the Crystals.

"It's My Party" and the weaker sequel, "Judy's Turn to Cry," have given Gore a somewhat unfair bratty image. Those are the hits that are remembered the most, but much of her subsequent material was both more mature (or, perhaps more accurately, less immature) and stronger. The singles were also very well produced, with orchestral arrangements (by Claus Ogermann) that hewed closer to mainstream pop than Phil Spector's Wall of Sound. Retrospectives of Quincy Jones' career usually downplay or omit his work with Gore, although it was among his most commecially successful; he's known now for recordings that are, well, funkier. But his success with Gore did a lot to build his already impressive résumé within the industry. Gore appeared on the legendary *T.A.M.I. Show* alongside such heavyweights as the Rolling Stones, James Brown, and Smokey Robinson, but after 1964 her star plummeted rapidly. Mercury was still investing a lot of care in her sessions throughout the rest of the '60s, and her material and arrangements showed her capable of greater stylistic range than many acknowledged. But after the mid-'60s, Jones no longer worked with the singer on a regular basis. "Sunshine, Lollipops and Rainbows" (1965) and "California Nights" (1967), both of which were co-written by Marvin Hamlisch, would be her only Top 20 entries after 1964. She played the cabarets after her days as an active recording artist, and eventually had some success as a songwriter for other performers. — *Richie Unterberger*

● **Anthology** / 1986 / Rhino ✦✦✦✦
Superlative compilation of Leslie's best sides, including "It's My Party," "Judy's Turn to Cry," and "You Don't Own Me." — *Cub Koda*

● **It's My Party: Mercury Anthology** / Jun. 18, 1996 / Mercury ✦✦✦✦
Fifty-two-track double CD has all the hits and then some. It may seem excessive for those who *only* want the hits, and some of the selections (particularly from the late '60s) are weak. But Gore had more worthy B-sides, album cuts, and low-charting singles than most people assume, and there are a good number of those on this collection: "Wonder Boy" (a White Martha & the Vandellas cop), "Off and Running" (covered by the Mindbenders in the *To Sir with Love* film), "Look of Love" (one of Greenwich-Barry's greatest girl group-style songs), a cover of Laura Nyro's "Wedding Bell Blues" (which lost out on the charts to the Fifth Dimension's version), and interesting little-known compositions by Goffin-King, Paul Anka, Van McCoy, Marvin Hamlisch, and Lesley herself. Gore covered more territory than the teen self-pity anthems for which she's most remembered, and this anthology, while not enough to make you demand her election to the Rock and Roll Hall of Fame, is not nearly as relentlessly lightweight as her detractors would have you imagine. Includes some tracks that were previously unavailable on album, or previously unreleased in the US. — *Richie Unterberger*

Grand Funk Railroad

Hard Rock, Arena Rock
In spite of the fact that Grand Funk Railroad was almost universally

reviled by the critical community, FM rock radio and millions of hard rock fans couldn't get enough. Conceived as a trio in 1968, Grand Funk was signed by Capitol after the label caught them live at the 1969 Atlanta Pop Festival. Unlike Cream or the Jimi Hendrix Experience, Grand Funk dispensed with wild interplay and focused on good-time boogie grooves and no-nonsense workmanlike arrangements. Their first album, *On Time*, featuring Mark Farner's earnestly untrained tenor and buzz-saw guitar, Mel Schacher's buffalo-fart bass, and Don Brewer's bashola drumming, was an immediate hit.

The self-titled follow-up stripped down the band's sound to utter basics, but the third effort, *Closer to Home*, showed the band utilizing strings and sound effects to widen their sound. By 1970 the band had sold more albums than any other American band. They broke the Beatles' record at Shea Stadium in 1971.

The band became a four-piece in 1973, and Todd Rundgren produced the hit albums *We're an American Band* and *Shinin' On*. The Jimmy Jenner-produced *All the Girls in the World Beware!!!* continued their winning streak. Subsequent releases did progressively worse, and the band formally disbanded in 1983. — *Rick Clark*

More of the Best / 1991 / Rhino ✦✦✦✦
This set does a decent job of picking key tracks not found on the *Capitol Collectors Series* album. Included is the fuzz-bass-heavy "Paranoid" and boogie numbers like "Are You Ready?" and "Got This Thing on the Move." Fans may wish for a more incisive selection from their first three albums. — *Rick Clark*

● **Capitol Collectors Series** / 1991 / Capitol ✦✦✦✦
This is the place to start. All of Grand Funk's hits are here: the classic "We're an American Band," Todd Rundgren's perverse production of "Loco-Motion," their thudding remake of yhe Animals' "Inside Looking Out," the epic "Closer to Home/I'm Your Captain," "Heartbreaker," and other big favorites. — *Rick Clark*

Grant Lee Buffalo

Alternative Pop-Rock
Under the leadership of guitarist/songwriter Grant Lee Phillips, Grant Lee Buffalo became a major buzz band in 1993 with their debut album, *Fuzzy*. The band's searching, often political, folk-rock has shades of everyone from David Bowie and John Lennon to R.E.M. and Bob Mould. Phillips' songwriting received a large amount of critical praise, as did their electrifying live performances. The band captured a larger following in Europe than their native America, earning near-universal critical praise upon the release of *Fuzzy*. During 1993, the band toured constantly, building a solid cult following all over the world. The following year they delivered their second record, *Mighty Joe Moon*. In 1996, they released *Copperopolis*. — *Stephen Thomas Erlewine*

● **Fuzzy** / 1993 / Warner Bros. ✦✦✦✦
While Grant Lee Phillips' songwriting is quite impressive, what makes Grant Lee Buffalo's debut album, *Fuzzy*, memorable is the band's muscular folk-rock. Equally adept at propulsive rock 'n' roll and haunting ballads, the band turns Phillips' best songs into rough gems, as "Jupiter and Teardrop" and "Fuzzy" prove. — *Stephen Thomas Erlewine*

Mighty Joe Moon / 1994 / Warner Bros. ✦✦✦✦
With their second album, Grant Lee Buffalo strips back their sound to its bare essentials, which accentuates Grant Lee Phillips' rural myths. Not only does the approach make songs like "Lone Star Song" rock viciously, but it also makes the bittersweet beauty of ballads like the gorgeous "Mockingbirds" all the more poignant. — *Stephen Thomas Erlewine*

Copperopolis / Jun. 1996 / Slash/Reprise ✦✦✦

Grapes of Wrath

Alternative Pop-Rock, Jangle-Pop
Grapes of Wrath was a jangly alternative folk-pop quartet formed in Kelowna, British Columbia, in 1983 by brothers Chris Hooper (drums) and Tom Hooper (bass) along with vocalist/guitarist Kevin Kane and keyboardist Vincent Jones. In 1984, they signed to Nettwerk Records and relocated to Vancouver where they recorded a four-song self-titled EP that earned the band some initial local exposure. 1985's full-length *September Bowl of Green*, however, gave them national recognition and critical acclaim. Ready to make a stab at the US, they enlisted the help of Tom Cochrane (ex-Red Rider) for production of the follow-up *Tree House*. Though it failed to break big, it did yield a hit single in Canada with "Peace of Mind." Subsequent singles and two more albums, *Now and Again* (1989) and *These Days* (1991), did well in their homeland but earned little sales elsewhere. In 1992, Kane left the band and the remaining members went on to become Ginger. — *Chris Woodstra*

September Bowl of Green / 1986 / Capitol ✦✦✦
Their first LP shows a band unsure whether to follow R.E.M.'s folky lead or post-punk's dreamy abstraction. Fortunately, the jangly guitars and harmonies win out for a pleasing, though unspectacular, debut. Highlights include the single "Misunderstanding," as well as "Love Comes

Music Map

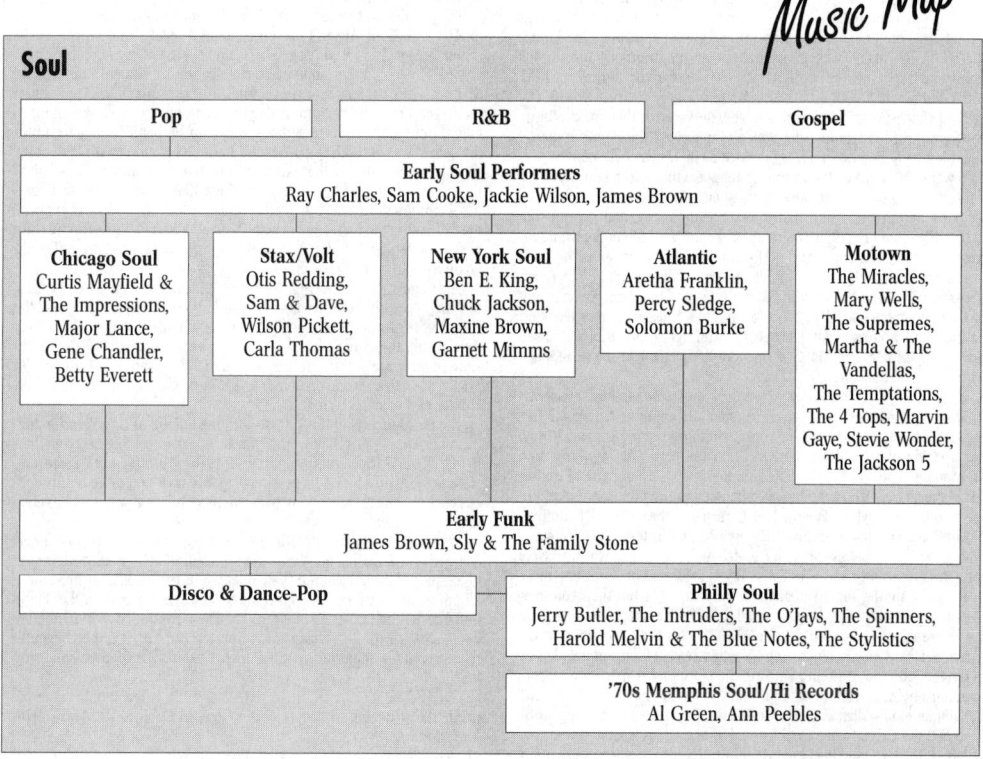

Soul

Pop	R&B	Gospel

Early Soul Performers
Ray Charles, Sam Cooke, Jackie Wilson, James Brown

Chicago Soul	Stax/Volt	New York Soul	Atlantic	Motown
Curtis Mayfield & The Impressions, Major Lance, Gene Chandler, Betty Everett	Otis Redding, Sam & Dave, Wilson Pickett, Carla Thomas	Ben E. King, Chuck Jackson, Maxine Brown, Garnett Mimms	Aretha Franklin, Percy Sledge, Solomon Burke	The Miracles, Mary Wells, The Supremes, Martha & The Vandellas, The Temptations, The 4 Tops, Marvin Gaye, Stevie Wonder, The Jackson 5

Early Funk
James Brown, Sly & The Family Stone

Disco & Dance-Pop	Philly Soul
	Jerry Butler, The Intruders, The O'Jays, The Spinners, Harold Melvin & The Blue Notes, The Stylistics

'70s Memphis Soul/Hi Records
Al Green, Ann Peebles

Around" and "A Dream (About You)." The CD version adds two previously unreleased tracks. —*Chris Woodstra*

Treehouse / 1987 / Capitol ✦✦✦✦
Early comparisons to R.E.M. are clearly justified on *Treehouse*, a jangly folk-pop masterpiece. On this, their second album, the band seem considerably more confident and focused. Crisp and bright production, courtesy of Tom Cochrane (ex-Red Rider), compliment the glorious harmonies and melancholy songs perfectly. A sadly overlooked classic of '80s guitar rock. —*Chris Woodstra*

● **Now & Again** / 1989 / Capitol ✦✦✦✦
Producer Anton Fier, leader/drummer of the Golden Palominos, imbues this Vancouver quartet's third full-length album with a lush early-'70s sound, at times approaching an Elton John/*Tumbleweed Connection*-style blend of orchestration and occasional pedal-steel augmentation (by Sneaky Pete Kleinow). Chuck Leavell plays keys on this outing as well. Melodically, the band tends to sound the same throughout, partly attributable to the band's rather light singing tonalities. Highlights include the reflective "All the Things I Wasn't." —*Rick Clark*

These Days / 1991 / Capitol ✦✦✦
John Leckie (the Posies, Let's Active) produces this follow-up to *Now & Again*, by giving the band a slightly heavier, more organic bandlike sound. In spite of an improved performance edginess, the band still lacks the proper dynamics for their melodies to stand out in relief memorably. Leckie's production, while loaded with nice touches, fails to help the band in overcoming their limitations. —*Rick Clark*

Seems like Fate 1984-1992 / 1994 / Nettwerk/EMI ✦✦✦
Seems like Fate is a 20-track collection which attempts to chronicle the band's career. Unfortunately the disc's emphasis on non-LP material, unnecessary remixes over the original single versions, and nonchronological sequencing creates confusion, ultimately doing a disservice to one of Canada's best bands of the late '80s. As an introduction, it fails miserably, though as a rarities compilation, fans will probably find it an essential addition to their collection. —*Chris Woodstra*

Grass Roots

Pop-Rock
The Grass Roots had a series of major hits—most notably "Let's Live for Today," "Midnight Confessions," "Temptation Eyes" and "Two Divided by

Love"—that help define the essence of the era's best AM radio. Although the group's members weren't even close to being recognizable, and their in-house songwriting was next to irrelevant, the Grass Roots managed to chart 14 Top 40 hits, including seven gold singles and one platinum single, and two hits collections that effortlessly went gold. The group's history is also fairly complicated, because there were at least three different groups involved in the making of the songs identified as being by "the Grass Roots."

The Grass Roots was originated by the writer/producer team of P.F. Sloan and Steve Barri as a pseudonym under which they would release a body of Byrds/Beau Brummels-style folk-rock. Sloan and Barri were contracted songwriters for Trousdale Music, the publishing arm of Dunhill Records, which wanted to cash in on the folk-rock boom of 1965. Dunhill asked Sloan and Barri to come up with this material, and a group alias under which they would release it. The resulting "Grass Roots" debut song, "Where Were You When I Needed You," sung by Sloan, was sent to a Los Angeles radio station, which began playing it. The problem was, there was no "Grass Roots." The next step was to recruit a band that could become the Grass Roots. Sloan found a San Francisco group called the Bedouins that seemed promising on the basis of their lead singer, Bill Fulton. Fulton recorded a new vocal over the backing tracks laid down for the P.F. Sloan version of the song. The Bedouins were, at first, content to put their future in the hands of Sloan and Barri as producers, despite the fact that the group was more blues-oriented than folk-rock. However, the rest of the group was offended when Fulton was told to record their debut single, a cover of Bob Dylan's "The Ballad of a Thin Man," backed by studio musicians. When that single, released in October of 1965, became only a modest hit, the Bedouins—except for their drummer, Joel Larson—departed for San Francisco, to re-form as the Unquenchable Thirst. Sloan and Barri continued to record; "Where Were You When I Needed You" was released in mid-1966 and peaked at No. 28, but the album of the same name never charted.

Amid the machinations behind *Where Were You When I Needed You*, no "real" Grass Roots band existed in 1966. A possible solution came along when a Los Angeles band called the 13th Floor submitted a demo tape to Dunhill. This group, consisting of Warren Entner (vocals, guitar, keyboards), Creed Bratton (lead guitar), Rob Grill (vocals, bass), and Rick Coonce (drums), was recruited and offered the choice of recording under their own name, or to take over the name the Grass Roots, put themselves in the hands of Sloan and Barri, and take advantage of the Grass

Roots' track record. They chose the latter, with Rob Grill as primary lead vocalist. The first track cut by the new Grass Roots in the spring of 1967 was "Let's Live for Today," a new version of a song that had been an Italian hit, in a lighter, more uptempo version, for a band called the Rokes. "Let's Live for Today" was an achingly beautiful, dramatic, and serious single and it shot into the Top Ten upon its release in the summer of 1967. An accompanying album, *Let's Live for Today*, only reached No. 75. The group began spreading its wings in the studio with their next album, *Feelings*, recorded late in 1967, which emphasized the band's material over Sloan and Barri's. This was intended as their own statement of who they were, but it lacked the commercial appeal of anything on *Let's Live for Today*, sold poorly, and never yielded any hit singles. Eleven months went by before the group had another chart entry, and during that period, Sloan and Barri's partnership broke up, with Sloan departing for New York and an attempt at a performing career of his own. The band even considered splitting up as all of this was happening. The Grass Roots' return to the charts (with Barri producing), however, was a triumphant one—in the late fall of 1968, "Midnight Confessions" reached No. 5 on the charts and earned a gold record. "Midnight Confessions" showed the strong influence of Motown, and the R&B flavor of the song stuck with Barri and the band.

In April of 1969, Creed Bratton left the band, to be replaced by Denny Provisor on keyboards and Terry Furlong on lead guitar. Now a quintet, the Grass Roots went on cutting records without breaking stride, enjoying a string of Top 40 hits that ran into the early '70s, peaking with "Temptation Eyes" at No. 15 in the summer of 1971. Coonce and Provisor left at the end of 1971, to be replaced by Reed Kailing on lead guitar, Virgil Webber on keyboards, and Joel Larson—of the original Bedouins/ Grass Roots outfit—on drums. They arrived just in time to take advantage of the No. 16 success of "Two Divided by Love," which was the last of the Grass Roots' big hits. The Grass Roots soldiered on for a few more years, reaching the Top 40 a couple of times in 1972, but their commercial success slowly slipped away during 1973. They kept working for a few more years, but called it quits in 1975. Rob Grill remained in the music business on the organizing side, and by 1980 was persuaded by his friend John McVie to cut a solo album, *Uprooted*, which featured contributions by Mick Fleetwood and Lindsay Buckingham. By 1982, amid the burgeoning oldies concert circuit and the respect beginning to be accorded the Grass Roots, Grill formed a new Grass Roots—sometimes billed as Rob Grill and the Grass Roots—and began performing as many as 100 shows a year. Their presence on various oldies package tours have seen to it that the Grass Roots name remains visible in the '90s. —*Bruce Eder*

Where Were You When I Needed You? / 1966 / Varese Sarabande ✦✦✦✦

Before the Grass Roots reached the peak of their pop-rock popularity, they were a much more folk-rock-oriented outfit. Indeed, this debut album is a matter of much confusion; apparently the original Grass Roots are pretty much a front for the songwriting team of P.F. Sloan and Steve Barri, who ended up performing on much of the album themselves. In any case, this is decent, though not top-of-the-line, early folk-rock, falling about halfway between the Byrds and more pop-oriented peers like the Turtles and the Mamas and the Papas. Highlights include the hit title track and other Sloan-Barri originals like "Lollipop Train," "Look Out Girl," "This Is What I Was Made For," and "You Baby," which was a hit for the Turtles. The CD reissue adds six bonus tracks from rare singles, the best of which is the uncharacteristically tough "Tip of My Tongue" (not the obscure Lennon-McCartney composition). —*Richie Unterberger*

● **Anthology: 1965-1975** / 1991 / Rhino ✦✦✦✦

It may be expensive, and two CDs of their work may seem like overkill, but this double-disc set is the one to get. Not only does it contain every hit and each single, and every B-side, from 1965's "Where Were You When I Needed You" through 1975's glorious "Mamacita," but the sound is extraordinary, far better than on any of the other hits compilations, and provides several revelations about the quality of their work. Highlights, in addition to the expected hits "Let's Live for Today," "Midnight Confessions," "Two Divided by Love" etc., include tracks like "Is It Any Wonder," with a chorus as radiant as anything the Mamas and the Papas ever recorded, and the seldom heard, vibrant "Mamacita." If you could never imagine listening to 120 minutes of Grass Roots material (this reviewer couldn't, either), this set will make you feel differently. —*Bruce Eder*

All Time Greatest Hits / Jul. 1996 / MCA ✦✦✦✦

The Grateful Dead

Rock 'n' Roll, Country-Rock, Psychedelic, Folk-Rock
The Grateful Dead are the longest lived of the San Francisco "acid rock" groups of the '60s. In the '90s, after more than 25 years in action, the Dead were still playing to enough satisfied customers on the road (most

of them "Deadheads") to make them one of the top-grossing concert acts in the music business.

The group was formed in 1965 by bluegrass enthusiast Jerry Garcia (b. Aug 1, 1942—d. Aug 9, 1995) on guitar and vocals, Ron "Pigpen" McKernan (b. Sep 8, 1945—d. Mar 8, 1973) on vocals and organ, Bob Weir (b. Oct 16, 1947) on guitar and vocals, classical music student Phil Lesh (b. Mar, 15, 1945) on bass and vocals, and Bill Kreutzmann (b. Apr 7, 1946) on drums. From the beginning, they brought together a variety of influences, from Garcia's country background to Pigpen's feeling for blues (his father was an R&B radio DJ) and Lesh's education in contemporary "serious" music. Add to that the experimentation encouraged at some of the group's first performances at novelist Ken Kesey's "acid test" parties—multimedia events intended to replicate (or accompany) the experience of taking the then-legal drug LSD—and you had a musical mixture of styles often played with extended improvisational sections that could go off in nearly any direction.

The band signed to Warner Bros. in 1967, experiencing some difficulties early on with the restrictions of standard recording practices and the company's interest in producing a conventionally commercial product. As a result, the group's first few albums were somewhat tentative but showed promise for the future, especially with the key additions of Mickey Hart as a second drummer in 1967 and Garcia's old friend Robert Hunter as the band's lyricist.

The Dead finally hit their stride with the release of *Live/Dead*, a double album, in 1969. (They were always more comfortable on stage than in the studio.) Two studio albums in 1970, *Workingman's Dead* and *American Beauty*, found them exploring folk-rock and more tightly constructed song forms and, along with extensive touring, won them a much larger audience.

In the second half of the '70s, the Dead recorded a series of commercially oriented albums for Arista, then concentrated on road work for the better part of the '80s. *In the Dark*, released in 1987, was their first studio album in seven years. It sold a million copies and produced the band's first Top Ten hit in "Touch of Grey." The Dead continued to tour, notably doing shows with Bob Dylan, and at the start of the '90s, they began to release vintage material on their own Grateful Dead merchandising label.

Garcia died of heart failure on August 9, 1995. A few months after his death, the surviving members of the Grateful Dead disbanded. —*William Ruhlmann*

The Grateful Dead / Mar. 17, 1967 / Warner Bros. ✦✦

Anthem of the Sun / Jul. 18, 1968 / Warner Bros. ✦✦✦
The Grateful Dead spent six months recording their second album in studios and at concerts. The result came closer to an accurate portrait of them, highlighted by the four-part, 12-minute "That's It for the Other One." Still, the extensive mixing and editing made the sound dense and uninviting, especially to those not yet converted to the group's approach. —*William Ruhlmann*

Aoxomoxoa / Jun. 20, 1969 / Warner Bros. ✦✦✦
The addition of poet Robert Hunter as lyricist marked the beginning of a consistent set of imagery in the Dead's words to match their musical interplay, especially on songs like "St. Stephen" and "China Cat Sunflower." But the aural experiments were still making for trying listening as the Dead continued to search for a way to capture their concert feel on disc. —*William Ruhlmann*

Live/Dead / Nov. 10, 1969 / Warner Bros. ✦✦✦✦
Long, trancelike songs with allusive lyrics (such as the classic "Dark Star") and R&B workouts featuring Pigpen's bluesy voice characterize this album, which is the basic document in the early Dead catalog—it's what most fans would like them to sound like every night. —*William Ruhlmann*

☆ **Workingman's Dead** / May 1970 / Warner Bros. ✦✦✦✦✦
A folk-rock, tightly arranged Dead, singing (in harmony!) some of their best songs, from "Uncle John's Band" to "Casey Jones." —*William Ruhlmann*

★ **American Beauty** / Nov. 1970 / Warner Bros. ✦✦✦✦✦
Workingman's Dead, part two—more of the songs that have served as the band's basic repertoire ever since these albums were released. Includes "Box of Rain," "Friend of the Devil," "Sugar Magnolia," "Ripple," and, of course, "Truckin'." —*William Ruhlmann*

Grateful Dead / Oct. 1971 / Warner Bros. ✦✦✦
The Dead's second double live album (now on a single CD) introduces a couple of excellent Garcia-Hunter compositions, "Bertha" and "Wharf Rat," and allows Bob Weir to indulge his taste for what Deadheads would come to call "cowboy songs": Merle Haggard's "Mama Tried" and Kris Kristofferson's "Me & Bobby McGee." The album became the Dead's first gold record, probably on the momentum of *Workingman's Dead* and *American Beauty*. It also failed to match *Live/Dead* as a concert album, so that, coming off the band's recent peaks, it seemed less effective than it was. Now, it seems like one of the Dead's better, more coherent records.

(Not to be confused with *The Grateful Dead*, the band's debut album. They resorted to *Grateful Dead* as a title when Warner wouldn't let them call the album *Skull Fuck*.) — *William Ruhlmann*

Europe '72 / Nov. 1972 / Warner Bros. ♦♦♦♦
Released as a three-record set, *Europe '72* is now a double CD. But it's still a long album, notable for introducing more Garcia-Hunter songs, especially "Brown-Eyed Woman," and for incorporating onto one album the variety of musical styles to be heard at a Dead concert, as well as the sheer duration necessary to appreciate the experience. Which means that, while this may not be the place a new fan wants to start, it's a Deadhead favorite. — *William Ruhlmann*

History of the Grateful Dead, Vol. 1 (Bear's Choice) / Jul. 13, 1973 / Warner Bros. ♦♦♦
This is a contractual obligation album, a record given to Warner Bros. Records to complete the Dead's commitment to the label. It was recorded in February 1970 and is something of a tribute to the late keyboardist/vocalist Ron "Pigpen" McKernan, who is heard frequently. Pigpen highlights an 18-minute version of Howlin' Wolf's "Smokestack Lightnin'," But this is a nonessential Dead album. "Bear" is the band's friend/soundman/drug manufacturer Owsley Stanley. The album is misnamed: it does not provide a "history" and there was never any Vol. 2. — *William Ruhlmann*

Wake of the Flood / Nov. 15, 1973 / Grateful Dead ♦♦♦♦
The Grateful Dead's first studio album in three years was also their first for their own record label. It's a strong collection, featuring such Garcia-Hunter songs as "Mississippi Half-Step Uptown Toodleoo," "Row Jimmy," and "Stella Blue," songs that would become concert staples, as well as Bob Weir's "Weather Report Suite." — *William Ruhlmann*

Skeletons from the Closet: The Best of The Grateful Dead / 1974 / Warner Bros. ♦♦♦
This is an 11-song compilation, five of whose songs come from *Workingman's Dead* or *American Beauty*. It presents a sampling of the Dead's 1967-1972 period, focusing on their more accessible material. In that sense, it is recommended to the uninitiated who want to get a feel for the group; not surprisingly, it is a perennial seller, turning up week after week on *Billboard* magazine's Top Pop Catalog chart. The initiated, however, despise it: In a survey of Deadheads conducted by *DeadBase*, it was rated above only *Dylan & the Dead* as the worst Grateful Dead album. — *William Ruhlmann*

Grateful Dead from the Mars Hotel / Jun. 27, 1974 / Grateful Dead ♦♦♦
The Grateful Dead's second independent album was an uneven one, containing favorites like "Scarlet Begonias," "US Blues," and "China Doll," but also a fair amount of filler. — *William Ruhlmann*

Blues for Allah / Sep. 1, 1975 / Grateful Dead ♦♦♦♦
Opening with the suite that has become a concert favorite, "Help on the Way"/"Slip Knot!"/"Franklin's Tower," and also containing the anthemic "The Music Never Stopped," *Blues for Allah* is another Grateful Dead album containing a few band classics and a lot of filler. Note, however, that some fans seem to like the filler. In its survey of Deadheads, *DeadBase* found *Blues for Allah* to be the band's most popular studio album after *Workingman's Dead* and *American Beauty*. — *William Ruhlmann*

Steal Your Face / Jun. 26, 1976 / Grateful Dead ♦♦
● **What a Long Strange Trip It's Been** / 1977 / Warner Bros. ♦♦♦♦
This is a two-disc compilation of The Grateful Dead covering its tenure at Warner Bros. Records, 1967-1972, and as such the most extensive sampler of their work in existence. Well-chosen, it contains many of their best songs from the period and is notable for giving album release to the studio-recorded single version of "Dark Star," the Dead's most requested song. Relative newcomers to the band (those who bought *Skeletons from the Closet* and liked it) can get a stronger dose here, and then perhaps go on to the individual albums. Of course, Deadheads hate this record. — *William Ruhlmann*

Terrapin Station / Jul. 27, 1977 / Arista ♦♦♦
Shakedown Street / Nov. 15, 1978 / Arista ♦♦
Using Little Feat leader Lowell George as producer should have been a great idea, but somehow it didn't work out. The Dead have salvaged "Fire on the Mountain" and "I Need a Miracle" for live work from this collection, but it's one of their least satisfactory studio ventures. — *William Ruhlmann*

Go to Heaven / Apr. 28, 1980 / Arista ♦♦
Reckoning / Apr. 1, 1981 / Arista ♦♦♦
Having given up on studio work after the disaster of *Go to Heaven*, the Dead recorded a series of concerts in New York and San Francisco in October 1980 for two live albums. This is the first, a set of acoustic material that will remind many listeners of the rustic feel of the classic *Workingman's Dead* and *American Beauty* albums, although much of it consists of traditional and bluegrass material favored by Jerry Garcia. (The original two-LP set was fit onto one CD in 1987 by eliminating The

Dead's cover of Elizabeth Cotten's "Oh Babe It Ain't No Lie.") — *William Ruhlmann*

Dead Set / Aug. 1981 / Arista ♦♦♦
In the Dark / Jul. 6, 1987 / Arista ♦♦♦♦
The comeback, with "Touch of Grey," "West L.A. Fadeaway," and "Black Muddy River." For anyone who wondered how these old hippies could have such a following 20 years after the hippies disappeared, here's the answer. — *William Ruhlmann*

Built to Last / Oct. 31, 1989 / Arista ♦♦
Without a Net / Sep. 1990 / Arista ♦♦♦
One from the Vault / Apr. 15, 1991 / Grateful Dead ♦♦♦
Infrared Roses / Nov. 1, 1991 / Grateful Dead ♦♦
Two from the Vault / 1992 / Grateful Dead ♦♦♦
Dick's Picks, Vol. 1 / Dec. 1993 / Grateful Dead ♦♦♦
This recording of a Grateful Dead concert performed in Tampa, FL, on December 19, 1973, inaugurates a new series of archival releases that differs from the band's already established *From the Vaults* series in that it is to feature somewhat lower fidelity, "what you hear is what you get" tapes as the liner notes put it, subject to editing problems, incompleteness, etc. Perhaps to make up for that, this double-CD album was not offered to retail, but distributed only through mail order, and it was sold at a discount price. For all that, this is a good, if laidback, Dead set, led off by a 14-minute version of "Here Comes Sunshine." That song comes from *Wake of the Flood*, which was the band's current album release at the time, and much of that LP's other material turns up, notably a complete, 16-minute "Weather Report Suite," along with favorites like "Truckin'" and "Playing in the Band," the latter at a running time of 21 minutes. As promised, the recording quality is noticeably unenhanced, but Deadheads won't mind, and casual fans won't bother. — *William Ruhlmann*

Dick's Picks, Vol. 2 / 1995 / Grateful Dead ♦♦♦
Hundred Year Hall / Sep. 26, 1995 / Grateful Dead ♦♦♦
Dick's Picks, Vol. 3 / Nov. 7, 1995 / Grateful Dead ♦♦♦
☆ **Dick's Picks, Vol. 4** / Mar. 1, 1996 / Grateful Dead ♦♦♦♦♦
Though this is the third Grateful Dead album to be released since the death of bandleader Jerry Garcia and the group's subsequent decision to disband, it is the first one that wasn't in the pipeline already. Its release offers evidence that the Dead organization, which had begun releasing selected recordings of live shows as a courtesy to fans while raking in most of its revenues through roadwork, has changed its priorities. *Dick's Picks, Vol. 4* isn't just another Grateful Dead concert recording, it's *the* recording: February 13-14, 1970, the Dead's debut at the Fillmore East, and a show consistently ranked by Deadheads as among the five best live tapes ever. This stand, some of which was released in 1973 on the *History of the Grateful Dead, Vol. 1 (Bear's Choice)* (there is no overlap with this album) finds the Dead gearing up to record *Workingman's Dead*, and already songs like "Casey Jones" and "Dire Wolf" have crept into the set. But there is so much more: half-hour versions of "That's It for the Other One," "Turn on Your Lovelight" (a showcase for Pigpen), and, in a near-definitive performance, the Dead's signature song, "Dark Star." Much of the then recently released *Live/Dead* material is heard, not to mention a rare performance of "Haven's Children." But it isn't just the set list that makes this a legendary show, it's the playing, amazing interaction among the players on every song, with Garcia noodling his way to nirvana. While it would be an exaggeration to say that if you own this three-CD, three-hour-and-ten-minute album you have all you need of the Grateful Dead on disc, the overstatement is only slight. As Bob Weir says at the outset, "This ain't a show, it's a party." — *William Ruhlmann*

The Great Society

Psychedelic
Before joining the Jefferson Airplane, Grace Slick sang lead and played various instruments for the Great Society, who were nearly as popular as the Airplane in the early days of the San Francisco psychedelic scene. Instrumentally, the Great Society were not as disciplined as the Airplane. But they were at least their equals in imagination, infusing their probing songwriting with Indian influences, nifty minor key melodic shifts, and groundbreaking, reverb-soaked psychedelic guitar by Grace's brother-in-law, Darby Slick. Darby was also responsible for penning "Somebody to Love," which Grace brought with her to the Airplane, who took it into the Top Five in 1967. The Great Society broke up in late 1966 after recording only one locally released single; after the Airplane became stars, Columbia issued a couple of live albums of the Great Society performing at San Francisco's Matrix Club in 1966. — *Richie Unterberger*

● **Collector's Item** / 1966 / Columbia ♦♦♦♦
This CD reissue combines both of the Great Society's live albums onto one disc, and features "Somebody to Love" in its original slower, more menacing version. It also includes the Society's extended version of

Grace Slick's "White Rabbit," along with several other haunting originals which strike an exhilarating balance between tight songwriting and psychedelic jamming. This is far more than a "Collector's Item"; it's a genuinely exciting glimpse into the birth of psychedelic music. *—Richie Unterberger*

Born to Be Burned / 1995 / Sundazed ✦✦✦

Green Day

Alternative Pop-Rock, Punk Revival
Although these brash, third-generation California punks had made a name for themselves in the independent scene in the early '90s, it wasn't until they signed to a major label that they became alternative stars. And when their major-label debut, 1994's *Dookie*, was released, the infectious punk-pop of "Longview" became more than an alternative hit—it quickly crossed over into the mainstream. Green Day come off as bratty punks, not threatening revolutionaries, but it's actually for the music's benefit; without their healthy, snotty attitude, their speedy, loud guitars and highly melodic hooks wouldn't be nearly as appealing as they are. *—Stephen Thomas Erlewine*

1039/Smoothed Out Slappy Hour / 1991 / Lookout ✦✦

Kerplunk / 1992 / Lookout ✦✦✦

● **Dookie** / 1994 / Reprise ✦✦✦✦
After two albums of indie guitar punk, Green Day made the jump to the majors with *Dookie*. Based on MTV's constant playing of "Longview," the band became a major crossover success; *Time* even hailed the album as the best rock 'n' roll record of 1994. While *Dookie* isn't that good, it is quite good. For once, Green Day has genuine songs and hooks to go along with their muscular, roaring guitars, making *Dookie* not only their most accessible album, but also their best. *—Stephen Thomas Erlewine*

Insomniac / Oct. 10, 1995 / Reprise ✦✦✦

Green River

Alternative Pop-Rock, Grunge
In the mid-'80s, Before the word "grunge" became a specific musical style, before Sub Pop was considered as a training league for major labels, many post-punk rock fans didn't believe Seattle had a worthwhile musical scene. Green River helped change that. With its ugly, loud, sub-Stooges guitar grind, Green River was the first band to make Sub Pop a hip underground label. At their best, the band made a powerful, brutal guitar rock that merged '70s heavy metal and '60s garage punk with '80s post-punk; at their worst, they were a sludgy, depressing mess.

Green River were together for three years before the band splintered apart. Singer Mark Arm and occasional guitarist Steve Turner formed Mudhoney. Guitarist Stone Gossard and bassist Jeff Ament formed Mother Love Bone after the band's demise, which would eventually turn into Pearl Jam. The roots of Mudhoney's garage grunge and Pearl Jam's revisionist '70s hard rock can be heard on Green River's two EPs and their one album. *—Stephen Thomas Erlewine*

● **Rehab Doll** / 1988 / Sub Pop ✦✦✦✦
Green River's only album is a brutal collection of primal Stooges-style guitar grind and punked-up metal riffing. The CD includes the equally powerful *Dry as a Bone* EP. *—Stephen Thomas Erlewine*

Al Green

b. Apr. 13, 1946, Forest City, AR
Vocals / Soul, R&B, Gospel
Born in 1946 in Forest City, AR, and raised in Grand Rapids, MI, Al Green became the premier soul singer in the '70s, in the process being the last great purveyor of a music whose time had come and gone. When he was thirteen, Green started singing with a family gospel group, the Greene Brothers. By 1967, he was singing secular and solo, scoring a hit with "Back Up Train" on the Hot Line Music Journal label. Touring the chitlin circuit on the strength of the record, Green found himself playing the same bill in Midland, TX, as Memphis trumpeter and producer Willie Mitchell. Mitchell signed Green to Memphis's Hi Records, and, as they say, the rest is history.

Between 1970 and 1977, Green placed 23 records on the R&B charts and 18 on the pop charts, including seven Top Tens. The Green/Mitchell/Hi rhythm section sound was incredibly consistent, making most of the albums listed below somewhat interchangeable. The records are ultra cool; there is little overt sweat. Green's phrases are disjointed, generally behind the beat, always surprising. At regular intervals he dips into his unreal falsetto. Soft girl backup singing is employed, as is a string orchestra. Drummers Al Jackson and Howard Grimes eschew the cymbals, replacing them with a ride pattern on the tom-toms. All of this is executed in the context of compositions by Mitchell, Green, Jackson, and guitarist Teenie Hodges such as "Love and Happiness," "Take Me to the River," "Let's Stay Together," and "Tired of Being Alone." Green became "born again" in 1976, splitting from Mitchell a year later and electing to

record gospel music only for most of the next decade and a half. In 1985, he reunited with Mitchell for the album *He Is the Light*. *—Rob Bowman*

Green Is Blues / 1970 / The Right Stuff ✦✦✦

Let's Stay Together / Feb. 1972 / The Right Stuff ✦✦✦✦
Green's third album for Hi and the first of a string of brilliant releases. The title song was the big hit but an extended version of the Bee Gees' "How Can You Mend a Broken Heart?" remained a staple for years. *—Rob Bowman*

☆ **I'm Still in Love with You** / Dec. 1972 / The Right Stuff ✦✦✦✦✦
Green's fourth album for Hi finds him exploring country-soul with an achingly beautiful take on Kris Kristofferson's "For the Good Times." The hits were the title song and "Look What You Done for Me." *—Rob Bowman*

☆ **Call Me** / Jul. 1973 / The Right Stuff ✦✦✦✦✦
Three R&B Top Ten hits, the title song, "Here I Am (Come and Take Me)," and "You Ought to Be with Me," dominate what is probably his finest album. Once again he tackles some country-soul, turning in moving versions of Hank Williams' "I'm So Lonesome I Could Cry" and Willie Nelson's "Funny How Time Slips Away." Green also returns to the gospel vein on "Jesus Is Waiting." *—Rob Bowman*

Livin' for You / Dec. 1973 / The Right Stuff ✦✦✦
A cut below the albums listed above, *Livin' for You* is still mighty fine. The title cut and "Let's Get Married" were both Top Ten R&B hits. *—Rob Bowman*

Al Green Explores Your Mind / 1974 / The Right Stuff ✦✦✦
Only one Hi single this time out with "Sha-La-La (Make Me Happy)." *Explores Your Mind* also contains what may have become Green's best-known song, "Take Me to the River." *—Rob Bowman*

★ **Al Green's Greatest Hits** / Apr. 1975 / The Right Stuff ✦✦✦✦✦
Upon its original release in 1975, *Al Green's Greatest Hits* pretty much summed up everything about Green, containing his ten biggest hits up to that point. A few years later, it was followed by a second volume, which contained hit singles that charted since the release of the first collection. In 1995, the Right Stuff reissued *Al Green's Greatest Hits*, adding six of the highlights from the second volume of greatest hits as bonus tracks. The result was a definitive single-disc compilation, featuring 16 of Green's absolute best songs, including "Tired of Being Alone," "Let's Stay Together," "I'm Still in Love with You," "Call Me," "Here I Am," "Sha-La-La (Make Me Happy)," "L-O-V-E (Love)." The original version of *Greatest Hits* was great, but the revision made it nearly perfect. *—Stephen Thomas Erlewine*

Al Green Is Love / Oct. 1975 / The Right Stuff ✦✦✦
Two more Top Ten hits with "L-O-V-E (Love)" and "Oh Me, Oh My (Dream's in My Arms)." *—Rob Bowman*

Full of Fire / Apr. 1976 / Hi ✦✦✦

Have a Good Time / Dec. 1976 / Hi ✦✦✦

☆ **Al Green's Greatest Hits, Vol. II** / Jul. 1977 / The Right Stuff ✦✦✦✦✦
As good as *Vol. 1*, augmented by nonchart items that might have been hits anyway, like "Love and Happiness," "Take Me to the River," and "For the Good Times." *—Rob Bowman*

The Belle Album / Dec. 1977 / The Right Stuff ✦✦✦✦
Al Green severed his ties with longtime producer Willie Mitchell in 1977, establishing his own backup band and seizing the production reins. But he hadn't yet made the final break with soul; this was the last secular work he would make for many years, and it was brilliant, even though it didn't come close to equaling his previous commercial heights. In retrospect, many just didn't understand where he was going, while others were turned off by the blurred lyrical focus of songs like "Belle." But "I Feel Good" had as much danceable energy and soulful fire as any Green uptempo tune, and "Lovin' You" and "Dream" were sorely underrated compositions. *—Ron Wynn*

The Lord Will Make a Way / 1980 / Myrrh ✦✦✦✦
One of the best gospel albums by Rev. Green. The R&B and pop hits had stopped coming but the sacred peaks were the equal of any of his secular material. In 1992 Green was still performing the title song and "In the Holy Name of Jesus." *—Rob Bowman*

Tokyo Live / 1981 / The Right Stuff ✦✦✦✦
A wonderful live set that serves as both a retrospective and a defining release showing that Green sang the same way regardless of musical and lyrical content. He did many of his greatest soul hits, performing them with the relaxed, powerful grace that made him the '70s' finest soul vocalist and the '80s' best male gospel artist. *—Ron Wynn*

Higher Plane / Feb. 1981 / Hi ✦✦✦✦
Another superior sacred recording, most notable for a stellar version of the Impressions' "People Get Ready." *—Rob Bowman*

He Is the Light / 1985 / A&M ✦✦✦✦
At the time of writing, this was Green's last truly great recording. Back with Willie Mitchell, the Hi rhythm section, and the Memphis Horns,

Green has great material and delivers the goods. —*Rob Bowman*

I Get Joy / 1989 / A&M ✦✦✦✦
Some exuberant, rocking gospel and slower, less energetic, but equally reverent material from Rev. Al Green. Although he's not doing soul, Green still slips in some of the vocal maneuvers, sliding falsetto effects, and mannerisms that made his secular material electrifying. His '80s gospel albums were no less moving. —*Ron Wynn*

Love Ritual / 1989 / MCA ✦✦✦✦
Don't let the title lead you into thinking that these are second-rate left-overs, because this album (originally compiled for the British Demon label) is loaded with gems. Highlights are hard to pin down, but one surprise is a spirited version of The Beatles' "I Want to Hold Your Hand"; it should've been a single. Every track except "Ride Sally Ride" has been digitally remixed from the original multi-tracks. The sound is great, being faithful to the spirit of Willie Mitchell's production and mixing style, and the disc includes detailed liner notes. All in all, Green fans should pick this up. —*Rick Clark*

One in a Million / 1990 / Word ✦✦✦✦
A compilation from Green's gospel recordings, it reveals the emotional depth of his religious work. —*Brian Mansfield*

Love Is Reality / 1992 / Word ✦✦✦
Your Heart's In Good Hands / Nov. 7, 1995 / MCA ✦✦✦

The Guess Who

Pop-Rock
While the Guess Who did have several hits in the US, they were super-stars in their home country of Canada during the '60s and early '70s. The band grew out of vocalist/guitarist Chad Allan (born Allan Kobel) and guitarist Randy Bachman's Winnipeg-based group Chad Allan and the Expressions (originally known as first the Silvertones and then the Reflections). The remainder of the lineup featured bassist Jim Kale, pianist Bob Ashley, and drummer Garry Peterson. The Expressions recorded a cover of Johnny Kidd and the Pirates' "Shakin' All Over" in 1965, which became a surprise hit in Canada and reached the US Top 40. When the Expressions recorded an entire album of the same name, its record company, Quality, listed their name as "Guess Who?" on the jacket, hoping to fool record buyers into thinking that the British Invasion-influenced music was actually by a more famous group in disguise. Ashley had been replaced by keyboardist/vocalist Burton Cummings, who became lead vocalist when Allan departed in 1966. The Guess Who embarked on an unsuccessful tour of England and returned home to record commercials and appear on the television program *Let's Go*, hosted by Chad Allan. However, further US success eluded the Guess Who until the 1969 Top Ten hit "These Eyes," the recording session for the accompanying album, *Wheatfield Soul*, was paid for by producer Jack Richardson, who mortgaged his house to do so. *Canned Wheat Packed by the Guess Who* produced three Top 40 singles later that year. In 1970, the Guess Who released the cuttingly sarcastic riff-rocker "American Woman," which, given its anti-American putdowns, ironically became their only US chart-topper. The album of the same name became their first US Top Ten and first gold album.

Trouble was brewing on the horizon, though. Guitarist Bachman, having recently converted to Mormonism, took issue with the band's typical rock 'n' roll lifestyle, leading to clashes with Cummings. Finding the atmosphere unbearable, Bachman left the group in July 1970 and formed Brave Belt with Chad Allan, which later evolved into Bachman-Turner Overdrive. His place in the Guess Who was taken by Kurt Winter and Greg Leskiw, and the title track from their next album, "Share the Land," climbed into the Top Ten later that year, and several more singles charted afterwards. The group returned to the Top Ten one last time in 1974 with the novelty single "Clap For the Wolfman," featuring dialogue by deejay Wolfman Jack. Burdened by shifting personnel and loss of direction, Cummings broke up the band in 1975 and tried a solo career. The lineup from the Guess Who's glory years reunited in 1983, and a version of the group with constantly shifting musicians continues to tour. —*Steve Huey*

● **The Best of Guess Who** / 1971 / RCA ✦✦✦✦
A fine single-disc collection of most of the band's greatest hits, it's perfect for listeners who don't want to invest in the double-disc *Track Record*. —*AMG*

Track Record: The Guess Who Collection / 1988 / RCA ✦✦✦✦
A perfect collection, covering the band's whole history on two CDs. Includes the hits "These Eyes," "Laughing," "Undun," "No Time," "American Woman/No Sugar Tonight," "Share the Land," and the noveltyish "Clap for the Wolfman." —*Bruce Eder*

Guided by Voices

Alternative Pop-Rock, Lo-Fi, Indie Rock
Throughout the '80s, the Dayton, OH, guitar-pop group Guided by Voices released a series of independent albums; most of them never made it out of their own hometown. Led by vocalist Robert Pollard, the group featured a fluctuating lineup that recorded their albums in their spare time and rarely performed live. While their records are frequently muddy, full of tape hiss, and always lacking in clarity, their hooks are simple and catchy, and their songs are quite brief; their sound evokes Wire and mid-'60s British pop.

Guided By Voices became a hip name to drop in 1994, thanks to numerous accolades from Kim Deal, the leader of the Breeders. The group landed a slot on Lollapalooza's second stage and their album *Bee Thousand* received rave reviews. All the attention led to the reissue of all of their albums, as well as a record contract with the influential independent record label Matador. *Alien Lanes*, the group's first release for Matador Records, appeared in March of 1995. Exactly a year later, Guided By Voices released their second Matador record, *Under the Bushes, Under the Stars*. —*Stephen Thomas Erlewine*

Vampire on Titus / 1993 / Scat ✦✦✦
After years of impressive but flawed records, *Vampire on Titus* was Guided By Voices' first consistent record, with more than half of the 18 songs being blessed with memorable melodies or hooks. The CD version includes *Propeller*, which showed Robert Pollard's songwriting beginning to become more refined and accessible. —*Stephen Thomas Erlewine*

● **Bee Thousand** / 1994 / Scat ✦✦✦✦
Sonically, *Bee Thousand* isn't that different from Guided By Voices' previous albums. The band still is creating brief, minimalistic homages to British Invasion pop and art-rock, except the songs are better constructed, with hooks that are immediately memorable. —*Stephen Thomas Erlewine*

Box / 1995 / Scat ✦✦✦
Compiling all of Guided By Voices' '80s albums—*Devil Between My Toes*, *Sandbox*, *Self-Inflicted Aerial Nostalgia*, and *Same Place the Fly Got Smashed* (the vinyl version includes *Propeller*, which was on the *Vampire on Titus* CD)—and adding a collection of rarities called *King Shit and the Golden Boys*, *Box* is a bit of an intimidating listen for some devoted fans, let alone beginners. On each of their albums, Guided By Voices packs their records full of brief songs—if they reach the three-minute mark, it's an epic for the band. That can make such a massive collection of music rather daunting; it all seems to speed by without much distinction, if you're listening casually, but on closer inspection, it withstands repeated listens. The first records, *Devils* and *Sandbox*, are unpolished versions of R.E.M.'s *Murmur*. On the next two albums, the group's distinctive, British Invasion-inspired abbreviated pop begins to coalesce; their music sounds more like messages than songs, albeit messages that are driven by undeniable hooks. Retailing for under $50, *Box* is a worthwhile investment for dedicated fans. —*Stephen Thomas Erlewine*

Alien Lanes / Mar. 28, 1995 / Matador ✦✦✦
Featuring a slightly cleaner production and more straightforward melodies, *Alien Lanes*, the first record Guided By Voices released since their breakthrough *Bee Thousand*, is only slightly less impressive than their previous record. —*Stephen Thomas Erlewine*

Under the Bushes, Under the Stars / Mar. 26, 1996 / Matador ✦✦✦✦
Only Guided By Voices devotees can distinguish between their albums, but that doesn't make them any less enjoyable. *Under the Bushes, Under the Stars* delivers all of the standard GBV trademarks—the sharp, catchy melodies and hooks, the brief songs, the defiant lo-fi sound—without improving on the formula. Nevertheless, the album isn't any weaker than the previous *Alien Lanes;* in fact, it might even be a bit more consistent, with a stronger batch of songs. *Under the Bushes, Under the Stars* isn't the kind of album that will win the band new fans, but it will certainly fulfill the wishes of their legions of fans. —*Stephen Thomas Erlewine*

Guns N' Roses

Hard Rock, Heavy Metal
At a time when pop was dominated by dance music and pop metal, Guns N' Roses brought raw, ugly rock 'n' roll crashing back into the charts. They were not nice boys; nice boys don't play rock 'n' roll. They were ugly, misogynist, violent; they were also funny, vulnerable, and occasionally sensitive, as their breakthrough hit "Sweet Child o' Mine" showed. While Slash and Izzy Stradlin ferociously spit out dueling guitar riffs worthy of Aerosmith or the Stones, Axl Rose screeched out his tales of sex, drugs, and apathy in the big city; bassist Duff McKagan and drummer Steven Adler were a limber rhythm section that kept the music loose and powerful. Guns N' Roses' music was basic and gritty, with a solid hard, bluesy base; they were dark, sleazy, dirty, and honest—everything that good hard rock and heavy metal should be.

Guns N' Roses released their first EP in in 1986, which led to a contract with Geffen; the following year, the band released their debut album, *Appetite for Destruction*. They started to build a following with their numerous live shows, but the album didn't start selling until almost a year later, when MTV started playing "Sweet Child o' Mine." Soon, the album shot to No. 1 and Guns N' Roses became one of the biggest bands in the world. By the end of 1988, they released *G N' R Lies*, which paired four new, acoustic-based songs with their first EP.

Guns N' Roses began to work on the follow-up to *Appetite* at the end of 1990. In October of that year, the band fired Adler, claiming that his drug dependency caused him to play poorly; he was replaced by Matt Sorum from the Cult. During recording, the band added Dizzy Reed on keyboards. By the time the sessions were finished, the new album had become two new albums. After being delayed for nearly a year, the albums, *Use Your Illusion I* and *II*, were released in the fall of 1991. The *Illusions* showcased a more ambitious band; while there were still a fair number of full-throttle guitar rockers, there were stabs at Elton John-style balladry, acoustic blues, horn sections, female backup singers, ten-minute songs with several different sections, and a good number of introspective, soul-searching lyrics. In short, they were now making art; amazingly, they were successful at it.

While the albums sold very well initially, the band soon fell out of favor. Stradlin left the band by the end of 1991 and with his departure the band lost their best songwriter. Once Nirvana's *Nevermind* hit the top of the charts in early 1992, there was a distinct division between what was cool in hard rock and what wasn't; Guns N' Roses—with all of their pretensions, impressionistic videos, models, and rock star excesses—were very uncool. The band didn't fully grasp the change until 1993, when they released their album of punk songs, *The Spaghetti Incident?*; it received some good reviews, but the band failed to capture the reckless spirit of not only the original versions, but their own *Appetite for Destruction*. By the middle of 1994, there were rumors flying that the band was about to break up, since Rose wanted to pursue a new, more industrial direction and Slash wanted to stick with their blues-inflected hard rock. *—Stephen Thomas Erlewine*

★ **Appetite for Destruction** / 1987 / Geffen ✦✦✦✦✦
Aggressive, brash, and well-executed hard rockers and ballads, they never stray from their chosen target. This major-label debut is one of the finest examples of late-'80s hard rock. "Welcome to the Jungle," "Sweet Child o' Mine," and "Paradise City" were key tracks from this classic. *—Donna DiChario & Rick Clark*

G N' R Lies / 1989 / Geffen ✦✦✦
The first side of *Lies* features their primitive independent debut EP, full of raw, vital rock 'n' roll. Despite its disturbing lyrics, the second side is even more impressive musically, containing everything from the stark acoustic balladry of "Patience" to the country-rock boogie of "Used to Love Her." *—Stephen Thomas Erlewine*

Use Your Illusion I / Jan. 1991 / Geffen ✦✦✦✦

Use Your Illusion II / Feb. 1991 / Geffen ✦✦✦✦
Both CDs are full of what made classic rock classic, namely forceful band chemistry and an uncompromising spirit that approach staples like the Stones' *Exile on Main Street, Led Zeppelin IV,* or Aerosmith's *Rocks*. These two separately (but simultaneously) released volumes were a neat sidestep from the indulgent double-album concept. Musically, the band has never sounded better—or rawer. Lyrically, W. Axl Rose still spews out enough venom to offend half the planet, but you'd have to listen hard to catch it through the band-heavy sound mix. Nevertheless, Rose has seasoned his railings with some insights that the world around him isn't hopeless. In spite of his sloppy target shooting, his raw sentiments and delivery are bracing compared to the bulk of rock bands pounding the circuits. Highlights on Vol. 1 are "Right Next Door to Hell," "November Rain," "Perfect Crime," "You Ain't the First," and "Don't Cry." Vol. 2's standout tracks are "Civil War," "You Could Be Mine," "Locomotive," "Breakdown," and "Pretty Tied Up." Of the two albums, the first one is the better choice, but fans of hard rock should get both. *—Rick Clark*

Spaghetti Incident? / 1993 / Geffen ✦✦✦

Guy

Vocals / Urban, Club-Dance, New Jack R&B
This seminal R&B trio was the first group to sport the new jack swing sound, essentially traditional soul vocals melded to hip-hop beats, with credit for the genre's invention going to founder, multi-instrumentalist, and superproducer Teddy Riley. Riley formed his first band, Wreckx-N-Effect, while still a teenager, with brothers Markell Riley and Brandon Mitchell; Guy followed a few years later in 1987. Its first incarnation featured vocalists Aaron Hall and Timmy Gatling. Their self-titled debut album was an instant smash, producing the R&B hits "I Like," "Groove Me," "Spend the Night," and "Teddy's Jam." Meanwhile, Riley found himself in strong demand as a songwriter and producer; in 1988, Riley produced Bobby Brown's *Don't Be Cruel*, the album that helped new jack swing cross over into the pop mainstream. Riley has also worked with Kool Moe Dee, Michael Jackson (*Dangerous*), Stevie Wonder, Keith Sweat, Jane Child, and SWV, among others. In between albums, Guy con-

tributed songs to the soundtracks of *Do the Right Thing* and *New Jack City*.

By 1989, Guy was in turmoil; Riley's brother Brandon Mitchell was killed in a shooting, and Guy became involved in an acrimonious split with manager Gene Griffin over money. 1990's *The Future* featured Hall's brother Albert Damion Hall in place of Gatling and spawned R&B hits in "Let's Chill," "Do Me Right," "D-O-G Me Out," and "Long Gone." However, by the time Riley and Guy finally started to attract media attention for their innovative and influential work, the trio had broken up. Riley concentrated on his production and songwriting career for several years before forming the band Blackstreet with vocalists Chauncey "Black" Hannibal, Dave Hollister, and Levi Little. The quartet released a self-titled debut in 1994. Aaron Hall released his solo debut, *The Truth*, in 1993; brother Damion followed in 1994 with *Straight to the Point*. *—Steve Huey*

★ **Guy** / 1988 / MCA ✦✦✦✦✦
The hottest trend of the late '80s was new jack swing, in which hip-hop production met vintage R&B/soul singing. The man credited with perfecting this style, of course, was Guy's Teddy Riley. The New York City threesome roared out of the chute with this album, which eventually became a platinum success, and the hit "I Like" was extremely influential. "Spend the Night" and "Teddy's Jam" were other strong singles, but the key hit was "Groove Me," one of the year's hottest records and Guy's finest single. It had hypnotic beats, was superbly produced, and featured riveting vocals. *—Ron Wynn*

The Future / 1990 / Uptown/MCA ✦✦✦✦
The second and final album from new jack trio Guy matched the platinum credentials of its predecessor, but didn't have the same dynamic grooves or inspired mix of soulful harmonies and futuristic beats. Once more, brothers Aaron and Damion Hall teamed with singer and producer Teddy Riley, but only the singles "I Wannna Get with U" and "Let's Chill" came close to generating the buzz and the heat of earlier hits. *—Ron Wynn*

Sammy Hagar

b. Oct. 13, 1947, Monterey, CA
Guitar, Vocals / Hard Rock, Heavy Metal, Arena Rock
After spending several years as the lead vocalist and rhythm guitarist for the mid-'70s hard-rock band Montrose, Sammy Hagar began a solo career that produced several hits and made him an album rock favorite. Hagar became a true star once he joined Van Halen in 1985, but he was a popular hard rocker ever since his first album with Montrose.

After giving up a boxing career, Hagar began singing in the late '60s, performing with various California bands including Skinny, the Fabulous Catillas, Justice Brothers, and Dust Cloud. During this time, he built up a solid reputation in the Californian hard-rock scene. Former Edgar Winter guitarist Ronnie Montrose asked Hagar to join his band, Montrose, in 1973. Hagar recorded two albums with Montrose before going solo in 1976, taking the group's bassist Bill Church. Montrose's drummer Denny Carmassi later joined Hagar's band, along with keyboardist Geoff Workman. Hagar's self-titled *Sammy Hagar* was his first chart entry; it eventually went gold. In 1979, he created a new supporting band featuring Workman, Church, guitarist Gary Pihl, and drummer Chuck Ruff. This lineup played on Hagar's most popular solo albums, including 1981's platinum *Standing Hampton* and 1982's gold *Three Lock Box*. After *Three Lock Box* and its No. 13 hit single "Your Love Is Driving Me Crazy," Hagar toured with guitarist Neal Schon, bassist Kenny Aaronson, and drummer Mike Shrieve; the group recorded a live album under the name HGAS, as well as a studio version of Procol Harum's "A Whiter Shade of Pale." His 1984 album *VOA* contained the hit single "I Can't Drive 55," which peaked at No. 26.

In 1985, Hagar replaced David Lee Roth in Van Halen; his first album with the group was 1986's *5150*. Hagar released his last solo album, *Sammy Hagar*, in 1987; the title of the record was changed to *I Never Said Goodbye* in a MTV contest, but no copies of the record were issued with that name. *—Stephen Thomas Erlewine*

Standing Hampton / 1982 / Geffen ✦✦✦✦
After releasing several competent but more or less undistinguished albums on Capitol, Sammy Hagar switched to Geffen in 1981 and released *Standing Hampton*, a polished but tough record that showed a surprising amount of pop songcraft. The added production gloss and improved melodic sense proved commercially successful—the album was his first million-seller and it cracked the Top 30—and artistically successful as well; the record was the most consistent and memorable album he recorded to date, featuring the singles "I'll Fall in Love Again," "Baby's on Fire," and "There's Only One Way to Rock." *—Stephen Thomas Erlewine*

Rematch / 1982 / Capitol ✦✦✦✦
As Sammy Hagar's career was at its height in the early '80s, Capitol, his '70s record label, released *Rematch*, a compilation of highlights from his six albums with the label. Like *All Night Long* before it, *Rematch* cuts

away all the fat from Hagar's '70s catalog, leaving only his best rockers, including the scorching "I've Done Everything for You," "Plain Jane," "Turn Up the Music," and "Trans Am (Highway Wonderland)." Even though the track listing is well chosen, his Capitol records weren't as impressive as his albums for Geffen, meaning *Rematch* is only the best of a specific era of Hagar's career, not his entire career. *—Stephen Thomas Erlewine*

Three Lock Box / 1983 / Geffen ✦✦✦✦
Continuing the sleek, driving pop-oriented sound of Hagar's breakthrough *Standing Hampton, Three Lock Box* equals its predecessor, featuring such highlights as the double entendres of the title track and the hit single "Your Love Is Driving Me Crazy." *—Stephen Thomas Erlewine*

VOA / 1983 / Geffen ✦✦✦✦
VOA was the last album Hagar recorded before he became the lead singer of Van Halen and the record shows why he was invited to join the band. With songs like "I Can't Drive 55" he adds a simple melody to the song which never distracts from the all-important hard-driving riff. On "Two Sides of Love," he shows that he has the ability to pull off a power ballad, wrenching every bit of feeling out of the song. Like Hagar himself, *VOA* is never subtle, but in hard rock, that's a positive attribute. *—Stephen Thomas Erlewine*

Sammy Hagar / 1987 / Geffen ✦✦✦
The Best of Sammy Hagar / Nov. 16, 1992 / Capitol ✦✦✦✦
A CD-era collection of Hagar's Capitol work that supplants *Rematch, The Best of Sammy Hagar* has a nearly identical track listing as the previous collection and suffers from the same flaws. *—Stephen Thomas Erlewine*

● **Unboxed** / 1994 / Geffen ✦✦✦✦
Collecting the best of Hagar's prime years at Geffen, *Unboxed* has most of his hits from the early '80s—including "I Can't Drive 55," "There's Only One Way to Rock," "Three Lock Box," and "Give to Live"—but there's a noticeable absence of "Your Love Is Driving Me Crazy," which was his biggest hit. Nevertheless, *Unboxed* is a good introduction to his best years. *—Stephen Thomas Erlewine*

Bill Haley (William John Clifton Haley)

b. Jul. 6, 1925, Highland Park, MI, d. Feb. 9, 1981, Harlingen, TX
Guitar, Vocals / Rock'n'Roll, Rockabilly
The Bill Haley and the Comets recording of "Rock Around the Clock," which topped the charts for eight weeks in 1955, is remembered as the beginning of the rock era. Though it also represented Haley's peak as a performer, his career had begun some time before and would continue for a long time after. Born in Michigan, Haley began leading Western swing bands under various names in the late '40s, slowly starting to incorporate elements of R&B. Soon after he began recording for Essex in the early '50s, his backup band was named the Comets.

Because of his somewhat square image and his undeniably white sound, Haley, it could be argued, has been short-changed by latter-day rock historians. He was among the first performers—perhaps he was even the very first—of any color to combine R&B and C&W in a way that can readily be identified by listeners of any era as bonafide rock 'n' roll. Although their initial impact was regional, his early '50s sides rank among his most exciting, steering country and Western and big band forms into uncharted regions that were more frenetic and reckless. Haley also wrote much of his own material, and one of his compositions, "Crazy, Man, Crazy," became one of the first Top 20 rock 'n' roll hits in 1953. In 1954, he moved to the major Decca label, where his sides became increasingly formulaic, though for a time very successful, after "Rock Around the Clock."

It is his Decca sides, however, that are his most famous. In 1954, he went to No. 12 with "Shake, Rattle and Roll," and in 1955 he hit with "Dim, Dim the Lights," "Mambo Rock," and "Birth of the Boogie." But it was "Rock Around the Clock," previously recorded and released as a B-side in 1954 and reissued as the theme song for the movie *Blackboard Jungle*, that became his biggest hit. At that time the band consisted of Haley on guitar and vocals, Danny Cedrone on lead guitar, Joey D'Ambrose on sax, Billy Williamson on steel guitar, Johnny Grande on piano, Marshall Lytle on bass, and Dick Richards on drums.

Following the success of "Rock Around the Clock," Haley And The Comets placed nine more records in the Top 40 over the next three years, among them the Top Tens "Burn That Candle" and "See You Later, Alligator." Haley was largely eclipsed as the king of rock 'n' roll by Elvis Presley and other more flamboyant performers who followed him from 1956 on. Nevertheless, he continued to perform overseas and in oldies shows in the US, and "Rock Around the Clock" even got back into the Top 40 in 1974. *—William Ruhlmann & Richie Unterberger*

Greatest Hits / 1985 / MCA ✦✦✦
● **From the Original Master Tapes** / 1985 / MCA ✦✦✦✦
The best-sounding Haley collection, but its 20 songs are probably ten more than anyone but the most hardcore fan needs. *—Bruce Eder*

Rock the Joint! / 1995 / Schoolkids ✦✦✦✦
A 22-track collection which collects sides from 1951-53. Those who haven't heard this material before will be astonished to discover bonafide rock 'n' roll dating from three to four years earlier than the era ('54-55) more commonly associated with the music's birth. Haley's sound is similar to the country-boogie of the late '40s, retaining the steel guitar prominent in much of the era's country music, but it's clearly more driving and forward-looking. The songs owe a lot to jump R&B, but are transformed into the basic model of rock 'n' roll with slapping bass, ricky-tick drums, and extended electric guitar riffing. Listen to his version of Jackie Brenston's "Rocket 88" (which has itself been pegged as one of the first rock 'n' roll records) and you'll be astounded to note the basics of rockabilly already in place—in 1951. The low buzzing, distorted guitar on "Green Tree Boogie" (also from 1951) is also a revelation, as is the guitar solo on 1952's "Rock the Joint," which is almost identical to the much more famous one on "Rock Around the Clock" a couple of years later. The later sides introduce a honking sax, which would become such a prominent feature in '50s rock »n» roll. Includes "Crazy Man Crazy," the first rock 'n' roll song to make the Top 20. *—Richie Unterberger*

Half Japanese

Alternative Pop-Rock, Soft Rock, Experimental, Post-Punk, Indie Rock
Depending on your point of view, Half Japanese is either a celebration of the pure, amateurish do-it-yourself rock 'n' roll spirit or a pretentious, highly irritating example of noisy, self-conscious experimental rock at its most extreme. Formed by Jad and David Fair in 1977, the group started bashing out music in their parents' basement in Maryland, recording their debut EP by themselves. By the time the Fairs recorded their debut album, the three-record box set *1/2 Gentlemen/Not Beasts*, they had acquired a full-time drummer plus a saxophonist, yet their music was no less noisy and primitive; if anything, it was more atonal and difficult than before.

For the rest of their career, the band has proudly displayed nothing approaching instrumental virtuosity. David Fair left the band after their third record, rejoining briefly for 1988's *Charmed Life*. Throughout the years, the lineup has changed frequently—at times it has included Velvet Underground drummer Maureen Tucker and guitarist Don Fleming, as well as occasional contributions from Fred Frith and John Zorn—but Jad Fair has remained. That doesn't necessarily mean the music hasn't changed; their later records are slightly more musically varied and accessible, yet no less challenging. Fair has released a few solo albums that are stranger (believe it or not) than the typical Half Japanese release. *—Stephen Thomas Erlewine*

1/2 Gentlemen/Not Beasts / 1980 / Armageddon ✦✦✦✦
As with any album that is three records long, *1/2 Gentlemen/Not Beasts* unwittingly shows Half Japanese's true roots. Over the three records, the band "covers" such minimalists as the Velvet Underground, the Stooges, and Jonathan Richman, as well as deconstructing such wordsmiths as Bruce Springsteen and Bob Dylan. Although they would have you believe that their untuned, almost unlistenable, instrumental clatter is the result of being so enthusiastic that they didn't bother to learn how to play their instruments, it's just the logical, inevitable intellectual extension of Richman's naivete and the Velvet Underground's stripped-down guitar. Half Japanese is consciously primitive and amateurish. *—Stephen Thomas Erlewine*

● **Charmed Life** / 1988 / 50 Skidillion Watts ✦✦✦✦
While *Charmed Life* is the band's most accessible record, it doesn't even come close to the mainstream's concept of what constitutes pop music. Yet when Jad Fair sings about love and joy on *Charmed Life*, he is as straightforward and direct as he ever gets. *—Stephen Thomas Erlewine*

The Band That Would Be King / 1989 / 50 Skidillion Watts ✦✦✦✦
Featuring contributions from John Zorn and Fred Frith, *The Band That Would Be King* is one of the most diverse and challenging records Half Japanese has recorded. It's also one of their most rewarding. *—Stephen Thomas Erlewine*

● **Greatest Hits** / 1995 / Safe House ✦✦✦✦
Half Japanese began their career with a three-LP box set, so it's little wonder that their *Greatest Hits* encompasses two CDs. Under the guidance of Jad Fair, the group has become more accessible over the years, but that's only a relative term. Fair has remained doggedly amateurish and noisy, letting the twisted pop structures peak out only once in awhile. There's a lot of subtle differences between albums which only fans can tell, so *Greatest Hits* serves as a good introduction to Half Japanese as well as a kind of roadmap of their career. *—Stephen Thomas Erlewine*

Hall & Oates

Soft Rock, Folk-Rock, Pop-Rock, Blue-Eyed Soul
From their first hit in 1974 through their heyday in the '80s, Daryl Hall and John Oates' smooth, catchy take on Philly soul brought them enor-

mous commercial success—including six No. 1 singles and six platinum albums—yet little critical success. Hall & Oates' music was remarkably well-constructed and produced; at their best, their songs were filled with strong hooks and melodies that adhered to soul traditions without being a slave to them by incorporating elements of new wave and hard rock.

Daryl Hall began performing professionally while he was a student at Temple University. In 1966, he recorded a single with Kenny Gamble and the Romeos; the group featured Gamble, Leon Huff and Thom Bell, who would all become the architects of Philly soul. During this time, Hall frequently appeared on sessions for Gamble and Huff. In 1967, Hall met John Oates, a fellow Temple University student. Oates was leading his own soul band at the time. The two students realized they had similar tastes and began performing together in an array of R&B and doo wop groups. By 1968, the duo had parted ways, as Oates transferred schools and Hall formed the soft-rock band Gulliver with singer-songwriter Tim Moore and producer Tom Sellers; the group released one album on Elektra in the late '60s before disbanding.

After Gulliver's breakup, Hall concentrated on session work again, appearing as a backup vocalist for the Stylistics, the Delfonics, and the Intruders, among others. Oates returned to Philadelphia in 1969, and he and Hall began writing folk-oriented songs and performing together. Eventually they came to the attention of Chappell Music representative Tommy Mottola, who quickly became their manager, securing the duo a contract with Atlantic Records. On their first records—*Whole Oates* (1972), *Abandoned Luncheonette* (1973), *War Babies* (1974)—the duo were establishing their sound, working with producers like Arif Mardin and Todd Rundgren and removing much of their folk influences. At the beginning of 1974, the duo relocated from Philadelphia to New York. During this period, they only managed one hit—the No. 60 "She's Gone" in the spring of 1974.

After they moved to RCA in 1975, the duo landed on its successful mixture of soul, pop, and rock, scoring a Top Ten single with "Sara Smile." The success of "Sara Smile" prompted the re-release of "She's Gone," which rocketed into the Top Ten as well. Released in the summer of 1976, *Bigger than the Both of Us* was only moderately successful upon its release. The record took off in early 1977, when "Rich Girl" became the duo's first No. 1 single.

Although they had several minor hits between 1977 and 1980, the albums Hall & Oates released at the end of the decade were not as successful as their mid-'70s records. Nevertheless, they were more adventurous, incorporating more rock elements into their blue-eyed soul. The combination would finally pay off in late 1980, when the duo released self-produced *Voices*, the album that marked the beginning of Hall & Oates' greatest commercial and artistic success. The first single from *Voices*, a cover of the Righteous Brothers' "You've Lost That Lovin' Feeling," reached No. 12, yet it was the second single, "Kiss on My List," that confirmed their commercial potential by becoming the duo's second No. 1 single; its follow-up, "You Make My Dreams" hit No. 5. They quickly released *Private Eyes* in the summer of 1981; the record featured two No. 1 hits, "Private Eyes" and "I Can't Go for That (No Can Do)," as well as the Top Ten hit "Did It in a Minute." "I Can't Go for That (No Can Do)" also spent a week at the top of the R&B charts—a rare accomplishment for a White act. *H2O* followed in 1982 and it proved more successful than their two previous albums, selling over two million copies and launching their biggest hit single, "Maneater," as well as the Top Ten hits "One on One" and "Family Man." The following year, the duo released a greatest hits compilation, *Rock 'n' Soul, Part 1*, that featured two new Top Ten hits—the No. 2 "Say It Isn't So" and "Adult Education."

In April of 1984, the Recording Industry Association of America announced that Hall & Oates had surpassed the Everly Brothers as the most successful duo in rock history, earning a total of 19 gold and platinum awards. Released in October of 1984, *Big Bam Boom* expanded their number of gold and platinum awards, selling over two million copies and launching four Top 40 singles, including the No. 1 "Out of Touch." Following their contract-fulfilling gold album *Live at the Apollo with David Ruffin & Eddie Kendrick*, Hall & Oates went on hiatus. After the lukewarm reception for Daryl Hall's 1986 solo album, *Three Hearts in the Happy Ending Machine*, the duo regrouped to release 1988's *Ooh Yeah!,* their first record for Arista. The first single, "Everything Your Heart Desires," went to No. 3 and helped propel the album to platinum status. However, none of the album's other singles broke the Top 20, indicating that the era of chart dominance had ended. *Change of Season*, released in 1990, confirmed that fact. Although the record went gold, it only featured one Top 40 hit—the No. 11 single, "So Close." The duo hasn't released an album since 1990. —*Stephen Thomas Erlewine*

Daryl Hall & John Oates / 1976 / RCA ✦✦✦✦
Switching to RCA, Daryl Hall & John Oates recorded a self-titled album that fulfilled their early promise as pop-savvy blue-eyed soul craftsmen. A few of the tracks fall flat—including the reggae-tinged "Soldering" and the pompous "Ennui on the Mountain"—but much of the album is lush and catchy, featuring ballads and mid-tempo numbers that are nearly as

engaging as their breakthrough single "Sara Smile." —*Stephen Thomas Erlewine*

Voices / 1980 / RCA ✦✦✦✦
This is the album that took Hall & Oates from being a successful '70s pop duo to being one of the four biggest singles acts of the '80s (the others: Michael Jackson, Prince, and Madonna). The sound is a wonderful pop pastiche, from the Beatlesque "How Does It Feel to Be Back" to the neo-Philadelphia soul of the hits "Kiss on My List" and "You Make My Dreams." —*William Ruhlmann*

Private Eyes / 1981 / RCA ✦✦✦✦
More bouncy, soulful rock 'n' roll, led by the No. 1 hits "Private Eyes" and "I Can't Go for That (No Can Do)." —*William Ruhlmann*

H2O / 1982 / RCA ✦✦✦✦
From the Motown beat of "Maneater" to the lush ballad "One on One," Hall & Oates continue to make the top pop of the early '80s. Also contains "Family Man." —*William Ruhlmann*

★ **Rock 'n' Soul Pt. 1: Greatest Hits** / 1983 / RCA ✦✦✦✦✦
The best of Hall & Oates, 1974 to 1983, including their biggest '70s hits, "She's Gone," "Sara Smile," and "Rich Girl," plus the '80s chart-toppers and two new hits: "Say It Isn't So" and "Adult Education." —*William Ruhlmann*

Big Bam Boom / 1984 / RCA ✦✦✦
Atlantic Collection / Jan. 23, 1996 / Rhino ✦✦✦✦
Drawing from Hall & Oates' four Atlantic albums and adding one previously unreleased song, *Atlantic Collection* is a definitive overview of the duo's early years. Although they only had one hit during this period—"She's Gone," which is included here in its full-length album version—their early recordings contained some of their richest, most diverse music. Much of the material is based in soul, particularly the smooth Phillie soul of the early '70s, yet it also has strong folk overtones, as well as distinct pop-rock leanings. Within these 21 tracks, it is possible to hear the roots of their later hits, as well as directions they never wound up pursuing. For serious Hall & Oates fans, *The Atlantic Collection* can be a revelatory listen. —*Stephen Thomas Erlewine*

Happy Mondays

House Music, Alternative Pop-Rock
Along with the Stone Roses, the Happy Mondays were the leaders of the late '80s/early '90s dance club-influenced Manchester scene, experiencing a brief moment in the spotlight before collapsing in 1992. While the Stone Roses were based in '60s pop, adding only a slight hint of dance music, the Happy Mondays immersed themselves in the club and rave culture, eventually becoming the most recognizable band of that drug-fueled scene. The Mondays' music relied heavily on the sound and rhythm of house music, spiked with '70s soul licks, and swirling '60s psychedelia. It was bright, colorful music that had fractured melodies that never quite gelled into cohesive songs.

Unwittingly or not, the Happy Mondays personified the ugly side of rave culture. They were thugs, pure and simply—they brought out the latent violence that lay beneath the surface of any drug culture, even one as seemingly beatific as England's late '80s/early '90s rave scene. Under the leadership of vocalist Shaun Ryder, the group sounded and acted like thugs, especially in comparison with their peace-loving peers, the Stone Roses. Ryder's lyrics were twisted and surrealistic, loaded with bizarre pop culture references, drug slang, and menacing sexuality. Appropriately, their music was as convoluted. The Happy Mondays were one of the first rock bands to integrate hip-hop techniques into their music. They didn't sample, but they borrowed melodies and lyrics and, in the process, committed rock blasphemy. For a band that celebrated their vulgarity and excessiveness, the Happy Mondays appropriately came undone by their addictions, but they left behind a surprisingly influential legacy, apparent in everyone from dance bands like the Chemical Brothers to rock 'n' rollers like Oasis.

With their second album, 1988's *Bummed*, the Happy Mondays became British superstars, particularly lead singer Shaun Ryder. *Pills 'n' Thrills and Bellyaches*, released in 1990, marked the height of the band's popularity, creativity, and influence; although the record made the Top 100 albums chart in America, it didn't establish them as stars in the US.

After that, the fall was quick. By the time they released their last studio album, *Yes, Please*, Manchester had disappeared from public consciousness; it sold respectably, but the group didn't have the commercial impact that they had just two years before. Besides the lack of public interest, Shaun Ryder had become addicted to heroin, tearing the band apart in the process. At a high-level record contract meeting, Ryder walked out for some "Kentucky Fried Chicken," which was the band's slang for heroin. Ryder never returned and the group quickly fell apart.

Shaun Ryder and the Mondays' full-time dancer Bez re-emerged in the mid-'90s with Black Grape. The band released their critically acclaimed debut, *It's Great When You're Straight... Yeah!,* late in the summer of 1995. Black Grape's sound pursued the same direction as the

Mondays, only with a harder, grittier edge to their sound and lyrics. —*Stephen Thomas Erlewine*

Squirrell & G Man Twenty Four Hour Part People Plastic Face Carnt Smile / 1987 / Factory ✦✦

Bummed / 1988 / Elektra ✦✦✦✦
The second album by the band, *Bummed*, established them as premier dance rockers and helped publicize the Manchester scene internationally. —*David Szatmary*

● **Pills 'n' Thrills & Bellyaches** / 1990 / Elektra ✦✦✦✦
The Mondays sound more kaleidoscopic and more soulful than ever, with '70s soul emerging as the primary stepping-off point. "Kinky Afro" lifts the groove from LaBelle's "Lady Marmalade" for a chilling effect. The group also covers John Kongos' "Step On." More varied and better produced than their previous efforts—the Manchester scene is likely to run out of ideas before the Mondays do. —*Brian Mansfield*

Live / 1991 / Elektra ✦✦

Yes, Please / 1992 / Elektra ✦

Double Easy: The US Singles / 1993 / Elektra ✦✦✦
The Happy Mondays' drug-soaked vision worked best on individual songs, so the concept of a singles collection seems ideal. However, the band's two groundbreaking and popular albums—*Bummed* and *Pills 'n' Thrills and Bellyaches*—have distinct musical visions, and work better as records than *Double Easy*, which fails to be a captivating listen, even though it includes nearly every one of their finest songs. —*Stephen Thomas Erlewine*

Loads (& Loads More) / Jan. 1996 / London ✦✦✦✦

John Wesley Harding

Guitar / Urban-Folk, Singer-Songwriter, Alternative Pop-Rock
John Wesley Harding takes his name from a Bob Dylan song and he's a modern-day folk singer, but with his biting, cynical, clever songwriting, his true forefather is Elvis Costello. On occasion, he also dips into the political commentary of Billy Bragg. Harding's records never slip into self-absorbed, singer-songwriter mush, thanks to his sharp melodies. At times, his approach is a little too much like Costello's for comfort, yet his lyrical and musical style is distinctly his own. —*Stephen Thomas Erlewine*

It Happened One Night / 1988 / Rhino ✦✦✦✦
This solo acoustic outing, recorded live in England in 1988, seems like an odd choice for a debut, but it comes off very well. Capturing both John Wesley Harding's folk roots and a wonderful sense of humor, *It Happened One Night* gives a very representative picture of the singer-songwriter. Included are early versions of songs appearing on the following two albums as well as unreleased gems such as his fun account of Live Aid ("July 13th 1985") and a cover of Prince's "Kiss." —*Chris Woodstra*

● **Here Comes the Groom** / 1989 / Sire ✦✦✦✦
His second album has him working in the studio with a band called the Good Liars, including Pete Thomas, and Bruce Thomas of the Attractions. Not surprisingly, *Here Comes the Groom* has a feel similar to classic Elvis Costello. Harding's articulate and biting vocal delivery, also reminiscent of Costello, retains a good dark sense of humor. —*Chris Woodstra*

The Name Above the Title / 1991 / Sire ✦✦✦
The follow-up to *Here Comes the Groom* continues in the same direction. This time the arrangements are filled out with horn sections and strings, but the overall folky feel remains. —*Chris Woodstra*

Why We Fight / Mar. 1992 / Sire ✦✦✦
This 1992 release is more low-key and moody than any of his previous work. The subject matter is darker, though the melodies are still catchy and instantly memorable as always, this time with smoother production. Even a discussion about Hitler ("Hitler's Tears") is musically irresistible, placing him in the ranks of Nick Lowe and Elvis Costello. —*Chris Woodstra*

New Deal / Feb. 13, 1996 / Rhino ✦✦✦
Four years have passed since John Wesley Harding's last full-length album and it seems he spent the time "growing up" a bit, shaking once-and-for-all the image of Elvis Costello's smart-ass kid brother. *New Deal* (the title presumably referring to his parting of ways with Sire and his new signing to Forward Records) finds a gentler Harding doing some soul searching on his most introspective outing to date. Continuing in the trend set by 1992's *Why We Fight*, the album's warmer production—bare-boned arrangements consisting mainly of acoustic guitar with subtle use of violin, cello, hammond organ, and pedal steel—create the appropriate intimate setting for the subject matter. Thankfully the new John Wesley Harding's songs are still as clever as ever and, in a different way, just as catchy and memorable. —*Chris Woodstra*

Dynablob / Jun. 1996 / Mod Lang ✦✦✦
Dynablob is a collection of previously unreleased studio recordings from

John Wesley Harding's first recording session in 1986 to 1994 with track-by-track commentary by Wes himself. This is obviously an essential purchase for fans, but it is also surprisingly consistent enough to offer a good listen and a good look at the artist in a more traditional singer-songwriter setting. Points should also be given for the detail of the Dylan-esque cover design. —*Chris Woodstra*

Francoise Hardy

b. Jan. 17, 1944, Paris, France
Guitar, Vocals / Pop, Girl Group
Usually thought of as a middle-of-the-road popular singer, Francoise Hardy—at the beginning of her career, at least—covered more stylistic ground and owed more debts to pop-rock than she's given credit for. Immensely popular in her native France, the chanteuse first displayed her breathy, measured vocals in the early and mid-'60s. Her (mostly self-penned) recordings from that era draw from French pop traditions, lightweight '50s teen-idol rock, girl groups, and sultry jazz and blues—sometimes in the same song. The material is perhaps too unreservedly sentimental for some (in the French tradition), but the songs are invariably catchy and the production, arrangements, and near-operatic backup harmonies excellent, at times almost Spector-esque. Fans of Mariane Faithfull's mid-'60s work can find something of a French equivalent here, though Hardy's material was stronger and her delivery more confident.

In the 1950s, Hardy was inspired by early rock recordings to pick up guitar, and was already writing her own songs by the time she was a teenager. By the age of 17, she was already singing her own compositions in French clubs, and successfully auditioned for Vogue Records in France in late 1961. Her debut EP appeared the following year, inaugurating successful EPs and albums that would last through the '60s.

Hardy sang of young love with both fetching moodiness and unrestrained ebullience; although she often wrote both her music and lyrics, she often co-wrote tunes with others as well. She was greatly aided by a number of talented arrangers who seemed to be attempting (usually successfully) to blend American and British production sophistication with a Continental European sensibility. Charles Blackwell was the most notable and effective of these figures; in 1964, interestingly, she recorded some tracks under the direction of the great American R&B guitarist Mickey Baker, who was then based in France.

Starting in 1964, Hardy made periodic attempts to capture the international market with English recordings. Although these weren't entirely unsuccessful, by the late '60s she was concentrating on more mainstream, middle-of-the-road material and arrangements on both her French and English sessions. She has remained popular in France until the present. —*Richie Unterberger*

All over the World / 1988 / Vogue ✦✦

Story 1962-64 / 1989 / Vogue ✦✦✦
The *Story* series, with three separate volumes covering the period from 1962-1967, presents this immensely popular French chanteuse at her best. This first volume, which features 20 songs, is perhaps the most innocuous of the lot, which isn't to say it isn't good. Her 1962 single "Le Temps De L'Amour" is perhaps her best recording, featuring snaky spy guitars and a minor-key melody in an unlikely but wonderful marriage of early-'60s rock and a film-noirish atmosphere. —*Richie Unterberger*

● **Story 1964-65** / 1989 / Vogue ✦✦✦✦
Perhaps Hardy's finest compilation, although *Story 1962-64* is almost as good. This 20-song CD finds her at her most girl group-influenced; you don't need to understand French to catch the infectious melodies and sultry, almost hushed vocals. Highlights include the magnificently moody ballad "Tu Peux Bien"; "Non Ce N'est Pas Un Reve," with melodramatic Spectorish production that recalls the Righteous Brothers at their peak; and the tense, romantic yearning of "Il Se Fait Tard." All of these *Story* discs have apparently been remixed for CD release, although the differences are slight, giving more prominence to the percussion and Hardy's vocals. —*Richie Unterberger*

Story 1965-67 / 1989 / Vogue ✦✦✦
The third 20-song anthology of work from Hardy's early (and best) years is perhaps the least essential of the trio. Several of the ballads and acoustic numbers are unmemorable, suffering from weak material and/or soppy, orchestrated arrangements. These sometimes recall a modified Petula Clark, which can be good or (more often) bad. But the best cuts here stand up to her best material from the decade. "Surtout Ne Vous Retournez Pas" and "Qu'ils Sont Hereux" are among her best ballads, "Je Ne Suis La Pour Personne" is a snappy folk-rocker, and "Voila" is her best grandiose, heart-on-the-sleeve orchestral production. All of the aforementioned highlights were Hardy originals. In the late '60s, Hardy moved towards more middle-of-the-road material (often sung in English), perhaps in an attempt to crack the international market; the three volumes of *Story* remain her most impressive work. —*Richie Unterberger*

L'Integrale Disques Vogue 1962/1967 (The Complete Vogue Recordings) / 1995 / Vogue ✦✦✦✦
Four-CD, 83-track box retrospective of her first five (and best) years on record, including everything except the English-language versions she recorded for foreign markets. It's expensive, and hard to find in the US. But it's worth the investment for Hardy fans, as her early material was very consistent, and has usually been reissued in piecemeal fashion; this puts it all in one place, chronologically sequenced. —*Richie Unterberger*

George Harrison

b. Feb. 25, 1943, Liverpool, England
Guitar / Singer-Songwriter, Pop-Rock
As lead guitarist for the Beatles, George Harrison provided the band with a lyrical style of playing in which every note mattered. Harrison was one of millions of young Britons inspired to take up the guitar by British skiffle king Lonnie Donegan's recording of "Rock Island Line." But he had more dedication than most, and with the encouragement of a slightly older school friend—Paul McCartney—he advanced quickly in his technique and command of the instrument. Harrison developed his style and technique slowly and painstakingly over the several years, learning everything he could from the records of Carl Perkins, Duane Eddy, Chet Atkins, Buddy Holly, and Eddie Cochran. By age 15, he was allowed to sit in with the Quarry Men, the Liverpool group founded by John Lennon, of which McCartney was a member; by 16 he was a full-fledged member of the group.
The Beatles finally coalesced around Lennon, McCartney, Harrison, and drummer Ringo Starr in 1962, with Harrison established on lead guitar. The Beatlemania years, from 1963 through 1966, were a mixed blessing for Harrison. The Beatles' studio sound was generally characterized by very prominent rhythm guitar parts, and on many of the Beatles' early songs, Harrison's lead guitar was buried beneath the chiming chords of Lennon's instrument. Additionally, he was thwarted as a songwriter by the presence of Lennon and McCartney—the quality and prolificacy of their output left very little room on the group's albums for songs by anyone else. Despite these problems, Harrison grew markedly as a musician between 1963 and 1966, writing a handful of good songs and one classic ("If I Needed Someone"), and also making his first acquaintance of the sitar, an Indian instrument whose sound fascinated him.
In 1966, Harrison finally seemed to find his voice, with two of his songs on the *Revolver* album, "Taxman" and "Love You Too." In the wake of the group's decision to stop touring, Harrison's playing and songwriting grew exponentially. The period from 1968 onward was Harrison's richest with the Beatles. He displayed a smooth, elegant slide guitar technique that showed up on their last three albums, and contributed two classic songs, "While My Guitar Gently Weeps" and "Here Comes the Sun," along with "Something," which became the first Harrison song on the A-side of a Beatles single.
Although never known as a strong singer, Harrison's vocals were always distinctive, especially when placed in the right setting—for his first solo record following the group's 1970 break-up, *All Things Must Pass*, Harrison collaborated with producer Phil Spector, whose so-called "wall of sound" technique adapted well to Harrison's voice. *All Things Must Pass* and the accompanying single "My Sweet Lord" had the distinction of being the first solo recordings by any of the Beatles to top the charts following their breakup. Unfortunately, Harrison was later successfully sued by the publisher of the 1962 Chiffons hit "He's So Fine," which bore a striking resemblance to "My Sweet Lord."
Harrison followed *All Things Must Pass* with rock's first major charity event, *The Concert for Bangladesh*, which was staged as two shows at New York's Madison Square Garden in 1971 to help raise money for aid to that famine-ravaged nation. The second of the two all-star shows was released as a movie and a live triple album. Harrison's next studio album, *Living in the Material World*, initially sold well, but its leaner, less opulent production lacked the majestic force of *All Things Must Pass*, and it lacked the earlier album's mass appeal. Subsequent Harrison albums from the 1970s into the 1980s always had an audience, but except for *Somewhere in England* (1981), released in the wake of the murder of John Lennon with the memorial song "All Those Years Ago," none seemed terribly well-crafted or executed. During this same period, Harrison embarked on a successful career as a movie producer with the founding of Handmade Films.
In 1987, Harrison made a return to the top of the charts with his album *Cloud Nine*, which featured his most inspired work in years, most notably a cover of an old Rudy Clark gospel number called "Got My Mind Set on You," which reached No. 1 on the charts. In 1988, Harrison, Bob Dylan, Tom Petty, Jeff Lynne, and Roy Orbison formed The Traveling Wilburys, who have since released two very successful albums. —*Bruce Eder*

Wonderwall Music / Dec. 2, 1968 / Capitol ✦✦
★ **All Things Must Pass** / Nov. 27, 1970 / Capitol ✦✦✦✦✦
Without a doubt, Harrison's first solo recording, originally issued as a tri-

ple album, is his best. Drawing on his backlog of unused compositions from the late Beatle era, George crafted material that managed the rare feat of conveying spiritual mysticism without sacrificing his gifts for melody and grand, sweeping arrangements. Enhanced by Phil Spector's lush orchestral production and Harrison's own superb slide guitar, nearly every song is excellent: "Awaiting on You All," "Beware of Darkness," the Dylan collaboration "I'd Have You Anytime," "Isn't It a Pity," and the hit singles "My Sweet Lord" and "What Is Life" are just a few of the highlights. A very moving work, with a very significant flaw: the jams that comprise the final third of the album are entirely dispensable, and have probably only been played once or twice by most of the listeners that own this record. —*Richie Unterberger*

The Concert for Bangladesh / Dec. 20, 1971 / Capitol ✦✦✦
Living in the Material World / May 30, 1973 / Capitol ✦✦✦
Harrison had a lot of songs stored up for his first major solo work, *All Things Must Pass*, and it launched his post-Beatles career with a bang. Two and a half years later, he released its follow-up, which, although it contained some good playing by his band of superstar friends and some good tunes, notably the No. 1 hit "Give Me Love (Give Me Peace on Earth)," indicated that the first album had contained his best effort and the most he'd be able to do in the future would be to repeat it. —*William Ruhlmann*

Dark Horse / Dec. 9, 1974 / Capitol ✦✦
Rushed through in the preparations for Harrison's first (and last) North American tour, his third solo album found him with a strained throat and not enough first-rate material. Most embarrassing was a rewrite of "Bye Bye Love" in which he commented on the romantic triangle between himself, his wife, and his best friend, Eric Clapton (who later married her). The title track and "Ding Dong, Ding Dong" were Top 40 hits. —*William Ruhlmann*

Extra Texture / Sep. 22, 1975 / Capitol ✦✦
"You," a Top 20 hit, was a terrific pop song, but much of this album is expendable, including an update of the old Beatles song "While My Guitar Gently Weeps" called "This Guitar (Can't Keep from Crying)." From the superstar status of *All Things Must Pass*, Harrison had declined rapidly. —*William Ruhlmann*

The Best of George Harrison / Nov. 8, 1976 / Capitol ✦✦✦
The Harrison material is matched with some Beatles numbers in a good but routine collection. —*Bruce Eder*

33 & 1/3 / Nov. 24, 1976 / Dark Horse ✦✦✦✦
Having suffered the humiliation of being sued successfully over "My Sweet Lord," Harrison turned the ordeal into music, writing "This Song," a Top 25 hit. Even better was "Crackerbox Palace," which would have fit in nicely on any Beatles album. The rest was slight, although Harrison covering Cole Porter's "True Love" is an interesting idea. This was Harrison's first album on his Dark Horse custom label, formed after the completion of his contract with EMI/Capitol in June 1976 and initially distributed by A&M. —*William Ruhlmann*

George Harrison / Feb. 14, 1979 / Dark Horse ✦✦
Harrison's sixth solo studio album (released after a two-year hiatus) was another slight affair, boasting the Top 20 single "Blow Away," but otherwise unremarkable. "Not Guilty" was a Beatles-era song once short-listed for their *White Album*. "Here Comes the Moon" was a tepid sequel to "Here Comes the Sun." —*William Ruhlmann*

Somewhere in England / Jun. 1, 1981 / Dark Horse ✦✦
Harrison had trouble getting Warner Bros. Records, which now distributed his Dark Horse label, to accept this album (an early, rejected version even turned up in collecting circles). It finally appeared, heavily revised, featuring a song originally intended for Ringo Starr and with different lyrics, "All Those Years Ago." Now pitched as a tribute to the late John Lennon, the song (featuring Starr and Paul McCartney) became a substantial hit and carried the mediocre album, which also features two Hoagy Carmichael songs. —*William Ruhlmann*

Gone Troppo / Oct. 27, 1982 / Dark Horse ✦✦
Cloud Nine / Nov. 2, 1987 / Dark Horse ✦✦✦✦
A great collection of bright, hard-rocking numbers, even embracing gospel. —*Bruce Eder*

The Best of Dark Horse (1976-1989) / 1989 / Dark Horse ✦✦✦✦
The best of a less-than-satisfying era. The only way to take it in. —*Bruce Eder*

Live in Japan / Jul. 1992 / Dark Horse ✦✦

P.J. Harvey

Alternative Pop-Rock
In terms of sound as well as subject, Polly Jean Harvey is the most challenging female singer-songwriter to emerge in the early '90s. With her band, PJ Harvey, she staked out a distinctly personal territory with her brutally honest, darkly humorous songs about sex, love, and hate. At

their core, her songs are structured like the blues, but played with the raw aggression of punk. Harvey's voice is equally uncompromising, squeezing all of the emotion out of a song. The sheer overpowering sonic rush of her music can overshadow the fact that her songs are not bitterly angry and violent—they only sound that way; her music has a very human core.

Harvey became an indie rock sensation, especially in her native Britain, with the 1992 release of their debut, *Dry*. All of the subsequent media attention helped her build a substantial cult following. Instead of expanding her cult, Harvey's uncompromising second album, 1993's *Rid of Me*, only made her fans more devoted; in the fall of 1993, it was followed by *4-Track Demos*, a collection of Harvey's original recordings for the album, plus several unreleased songs.

During the *Rid of Me* tour, Harvey's drummer and backing vocalist Rob Ellis left the band; for a short time, bassist Steven Vaughan also left, only to return by the end of the year. During 1994, Harvey broke up the original trio, recording her new album with a group of studio musicians, including Joe Gore, who played on Tom Waits' *Bone Machine*. Released in early 1995, the resulting *To Bring You My Love* was Harvey's most ambitious and accessible album to date. The album debuted in the American Top 40 and featured the alternative hit "Down by the Water." *—Stephen Thomas Erlewine*

Dry / 1992 / Indigo/Too Pure/Island ✦✦✦✦
Dry is the stunning debut album from singer-songwriter Polly Jean Harvey's trio PJ Harvey. Although Harvey has her share of post-feminist anger, the album doesn't lack humor ("Dress" and "Sheela-Na-Gig"). However, Harvey really makes her mark through her music, a fierce combination of punk rage, sharp songwriting, and surprisingly melodic hooks. *Dry* is one of the most distinctive debut albums ever recorded. *—Stephen Thomas Erlewine*

Rid of Me / May 4, 1993 / Indigo/Island ✦✦✦✦
Thanks to Steve Albini's production, PJ Harvey's second album is a harsher, more abrasive affair. Albini has taken the dynamics of Polly Harvey's songwriting to extremes; sometimes it's nearly impossible to hear the beginning of a song until an explosive rush of guitars obliterates the silence a minute later. Still, most of the uneasiness of *Rid of Me* can be mainly attributed to Harvey herself. Although the best songs here ("Rid of Me," "50 Ft. Queenie," "Yuri G," "Man-Sized") are better than the best on *Dry*, they're more difficult to listen to. Harvey's songs have become harder and angrier, but she hasn't completely stripped away the humor that enlivened *Dry*. *Rid of Me* is an impressive artistic achievement, but is difficult listening precisely because of its accomplishment. *—Stephen Thomas Erlewine*

4-Track Demos / Nov. 1993 / Indigo/Island ✦✦✦

● **To Bring You My Love** / Feb. 28, 1995 / Island ✦✦✦✦
Harvey's third proper album is her first true solo album, recorded without the rhythm section that gave *Dry* and *Rid of Me* their savage roar. Instead, she has headed into the studio with Flood (U2/Depeche Mode/Nine Inch Nails), creating an album that is easily as dark as the blackest moments of *Rid of Me*, only with more sonic textures and colors, including the menacing rhythms of "Down by the Water," the bluesy stomp of "Meet Ze Monsta," and the layered guitars of "C'Mon Billy." Instead of diluting the impact of Harvey's music, the expanded palette results in a more satisfying and uncompromising album that becomes more rewarding with each listen. *—Stephen Thomas Erlewine*

Juliana Hatfield

Bass, Guitar, Vocals / Alternative Pop-Rock
After leaving the Blake Babies, singer/guitarist Juliana Hatfield pursued a solo career that easily eclipsed her former band, both in commercial and artistic terms. Hatfield's thin, girlish voice accentuates her unassuming, catchy pop songs that can either be sweet and happy ("Spin the Bottle") or surprisingly honest and moving ("Ugly"). Her first solo album, 1992's *Hey Babe*, was a small gem, full of well-constructed songs that effortlessly evoked the pain and charm of adolescence; rarely had anyone captured teenagers from a female perspective so accurately. It was a college-radio hit that made a small dent in the mainstream, particularly with teenage girls. Afraid that she wasn't being taken seriously as an artist, Hatfield hooked up with a grungy male rhythm section for her next album, 1993's *Become What You Are.* She kept the effortless melody of her first album, while turning up the volume on the amplifiers, resulting in a more commercially successful album. After assembling a new band in late 1994, Hatfield returned in the spring of 1995 with *Only Everything*, which featured the minor hit single "Universal Heartbeat." *—Stephen Thomas Erlewine*

● **Hey Babe** / 1992 / Mammoth ✦✦✦✦
Hey Babe is Juliana Hatfield's terrific solo debut, filled with effortless melodies and catchy guitar riffs. Hatfield's thin, girlish voice can be slightly wearing over the course of an entire album, but her intelligent,

hook-laden songs make up for that minor flaw. *—Stephen Thomas Erlewine*

Become What You Are / 1993 / Mammoth/Atlantic ✦✦✦

Only Everything / 1995 / Mammoth/Atlantic ✦✦✦

Donny Hathaway

b. Oct. 1, 1945, Chicago, IL, **d.** Jan. 13, 1979, New York, NY
Piano, Keyboards, Vocals / Soul
Donny Hathaway was a marvelous composer and vocalist. His sound, delivery, and timbre have influenced singers from Stevie Wonder to George Benson, while his compositions have been recorded by an array of artists from Cold Blood to Jerry Butler, the Staple Singers, Carla Thomas, and Aretha Franklin. Hathaway was born in Chicago, but grew up in St. Louis and began singing gospel at age three. He attended Howard University on a fine arts scholarship and was a classmate of Roberta Flack. He began recording for Curtis Mayfield's Curtom label in 1969, then signed with Atco. His single "The Ghetto" was a mild hit, but the duet "You've Got a Friend" with Flack was his first Top Ten R&B hit. The duo would later score two No. 1 hit duets, "Where Is the Love" and "The Closer I Get to You," each of which was also a Top Ten pop hit. The duo had two final hits, "You Are My Heaven" and "Back Together Again," in 1980, after Hathaway stunned everyone by committing suicide in 1979 at age 33. *—Ron Wynn*

Extension of a Man / 1973 / Atlantic ✦✦✦✦
This 1973 album (reissued on CD in 1993) was among Hathaway's most ambitious. It included a stunning two-part gospel tune, "I Love the Lord," a revamped version of "Valdez in the Country," a magnificent "We'll All Be Free" and a soulful remake of Blood, Sweat & Tears' "I Love You More Than You'll Ever Know." Hathaway's gorgeous voice and superb delivery, timing, pacing, and style made him unsurpassed among soul artists of his generation, and his arranging skills were equally brilliant. This album ranks as a masterpiece, along with his self-titled debut. *—Ron Wynn*

● **Collection** / 1990 / Atlantic ✦✦✦✦
A hits compilation including "The Ghetto" and "Givin' Up Your Love Is Like (Givin' Up the World)," as well as the hit duets with Roberta Flack "Where Is the Love" and "You've Got a Friend." *—Bil Carpenter*

Dale Hawkins

Guitar, Vocals / Rockabilly
This Louisiana guitarist's 1957 hit "Suzy Q," with its crackling bluesy guitar and insistent cowbell, was one of the most exciting early rockabilly singles. Recording for Chess (as one of its few White artists) between 1956 and 1961, Hawkins never quite duplicated its success, either commercially or artistically, but came close enough on a number of occasions to warrant respect as one of the better rockabilly singers. His drawling delivery, sense of humor, affinity for blues, and sharp guitar work (which was actually provided by such ace players as Roy Buchanan, Scotty Moore, and James Burton) are heard to good effect on his 1958 album and a number of nonhit singles. Hawkins went on to become a producer of some note in the 1960s, working with the Five Americans and Bruce Channel. *—Richie Unterberger*

Susie Q / 1958 / Chess ✦✦✦✦
A way-above-average '50s rock 'n' roll album, including both sides of Dale's first four singles. Highlights are "Suzie Q," its killer B-side ("Don't Treat Me This Way"), and the goofy "See You Soon Baboon" and "Mrs. Mergitory's Daughter." *—Richie Unterberger*

My Babe / 1987 / Argo ✦✦✦

● **Oh Suzy Q** / Oct. 24, 1995 / Chess ✦✦✦✦
Eighteen tracks from Hawkins' Chess prime, all but one from the late '50s. Includes "Susie Q" and some obscure rockabilly cuts that are nearly as good, such as "Don't Treat Me This Way," "Liza Jane," and "Ain't That Lovin' You Babe." James Burton, Roy Buchanan, and Scotty Moore are the most prominent of the excellent guitarists to be heard on these sides. One could quibble over the absence of "Mrs. Mergitory's Daughter," "Yea Yea (Class Cutter)," and the post-Chess single "Stay at Home Lulu," but this is definitely the best Hawkins compilation ever assembled. *—Richie Unterberger*

Ronnie Hawkins

Guitar, Vocals / Rockabilly
Hawkins is a rockabilly singer who formed his original backing band, the Hawks, while attending the University of Arkansas. After auditioning unsuccessfully for Sun in 1957, he started working regularly in Canada the following year, eventually taking up permanent residence there. After one release on the Canadian Quality label, he signed with Roulette in New York in 1959, having hits with "Forty Days" and "Mary Lou." The live fervor of Hawkins (known as Mr. Dynamo) & the Hawks' show continued in Canada after all the original members except Levon Helm

headed back to the US. Hawkins quickly hired Canadian players Robbie Robertson, Garth Hudson, Rick Danko, and Richard Manuel as the new Hawks. They stayed with him until 1963, but later became Bob Dylan's backing group and went on to a career of their own as the Band. Hawkins has remained a legend in Canada, recording unrepentant rockabilly sides and gigging constantly. He's still the original Mr. Dynamo, capable of shaking the walls down any old time he feels like it. —*Cub Koda*

● **The Best of Ronnie Hawkins & His Band** / 1990 / Rhino ✦✦✦✦
In the late 1950s and early 1960s, Ronnie Hawkins was one of the few rock 'n' rollers committed to performing and recording unapologetic rockabilly while others were returning to their country roots or going the teen-idol route. This 18-song compilation focuses mostly on his initial burst of activity for Roulette in 1959 and 1960, with a few later odds and ends thrown in. While he deserves respect for keeping the torch of rock 'n' roll's roots burning during some of its leaner years, he didn't match the greatness of rockabilly's kingpins. His voice and performance was energetic but not brilliant; his material was a bit pedestrian. The best of these tunes are "Mary Lou" (his sole Top 30 hit), "Forty Days" (an update of Chuck Berry's "Thirty Days"), and "One of These Days" (later covered by the Searchers). What he's really known for, of course, is giving a bunch of mostly Canadian kids their start as his backing band, the Hawks. A later edition of the Hawks eventually toured with Bob Dylan and evolved into the Band. Only two of these songs, though, feature that lineup (the 1963 single "Bo Diddley"/"Who Do You Love"). On "Who Do You Love" especially, Robbie Robertson lets rip with a roaring solo that's a good few years ahead of its time in its manic distorted intensity. It's by far the most exciting track on this compilation of a respectable but minor performer from rock's early days. —*Richie Unterberger*

Screamin' Jay Hawkins

b. Jul. 18, 1929, Cleveland, OH
Vocals / R&B, Rock 'n' Roll
Screamin' Jay Hawkins was the most outrageous performer extant during rock's dawn. Prone to emerging out of coffins onstage, a flaming skull named Henry his constant companion, Screamin' Jay was an insanely theatrical figure long before it was even remotely acceptable.

Hawkins' life story is almost as bizarre as his onstage shtick. Originally inspired by the booming baritone of Paul Robeson, Hawkins was unable to break through as an opera singer. His boxing prowess was every bit as lethal as his vocal cords; many of his most hilarious tales revolve around Jay beating the hell out of a musical rival!

Hawkins caught his first musical break in 1951 as pianist/valet to veteran jazz guitarist Tiny Grimes. He debuted on wax for Gotham the following year with "Why Did You Waste My Time," backed by Grimes and his Rockin' Highlanders (they donned kilts and tam-o'-shanters on stage). Singles for Timely ("Baptize Me in Wine") and Mercury's Wing subsidiary (1955's otherworldly "[She Put The] Wamee [On Me]," a harbinger of things to come) preceded Hawkins' immortal 1956 rendering of "I Put a Spell on You" for Columbia's Okeh imprint.

Hawkins originally envisioned the tune as a refined ballad. After he and his New York session aces (notably guitarist Mickey Baker and saxist Sam "The Man" Taylor) had imbibed to the point of no return, Hawkins screamed, grunted, and gurgled his way through the tune with utter drunken abandon. A resultant success despite the protests of uptight suits-in-power, "Spell" became Screamin' Jay's biggest seller ("Little Demon," its rocking flip, is a minor classic itself).

Hawkins cut several amazing 1957-58 follow-ups in the same crazed vein—"Hong Kong," a surreal "Yellow Coat," the Jerry Leiber/Mike Stoller-penned "Alligator Wine"—but none of them clicked the way "Spell" had. Deejay Alan Freed convinced Screamin' Jay that popping out of a coffin might be a show-stopping gimmick by handing him a $300 bonus (long after Freed's demise, Screamin' Jay Hawkins is still benefiting from his crass brainstorm). Hawkins' next truly inspired waxing came in 1969 when he was contracted to Philips Records (where he made two albums). His gross "Constipation Blues" wouldn't garner much airplay, but remains an integral part of his legacy to this day.

The cinema has been a beneficiary of Screamin' Jay's larger-than-life persona in recent years. His featured roles in *Mystery Train* and *A Rage in Harlem* have made Hawkins a familiar visage to youngsters who've never even heard "I Put a Spell on You." Hawkins remains musically active, though his act doesn't seem all that bizarre anymore. —*Bill Dahl*

● **Voodoo Jive: Best of Screamin' Jay Hawkins** / 1990 / Rhino ✦✦✦✦
Some maintain that Hawkins was a one-hit fluke and a one-dimensional performer with a limited singing voice and no other discernible skills. Others insist that Hawkins was a decent R&B and blues singer and an excellent entertainer and personality whose talents were overshadowed by the success of "I Put a Spell on You." This anthology doesn't answer the argument, but it does collect 17 Hawkins singles from Okeh, Enrica, and Phillips, including all of his major hits. The high (or low) point is perhaps 1969's "Constipation Blues." —*Ron Wynn*

Hayden

Vocals / Alternative Pop-Rock
Hayden's *Everything I Long For* is bound to draw comparisons with alternative faves like Beck, J Mascis, and Palace; the low, prematurely wizened vocals, the plain acoustic (though not quite lo-fi) arrangements, the downbeat whimsy. The post-punk gloom is leavened by the sweetly melancholic guitars (something like Neil Young's *Four Way Street* version of "Cowgirl in the Sand") and heartfelt, sometimes heartrending throaty vocals with shades of Tom Waits and Captain Beefheart. Despite the abundant reference points, it's an original sound, and one whose left-field charm is likely to cause a warranted stir in the alternative audience. —*Richie Unterberger*

Everything I Long For / May 21, 1996 / Outpost ✦✦✦✦
Solitary, rootsy post-punk of the best kind, delving into somewhat dark and twisted terrrain, but invested with a lot of passion and unflinching grit. The sparse and haunting arrangements put acoustic guitars at the forefront, but vary the pace with occasional searing licks, eerie solo piano, and harmony vocals. It's one of the relatively few releases of this type that will find a comfortable home in the collections of those with an ear for either stark folk-rock or grunge. —*Richie Unterberger*

Isaac Hayes

b. Aug. 29, 1942, Covington, TN
Piano, Saxophone, Vocals / Soul, Funk, Disco, R&B
From the tough urgency of the Stax studio (for whom he was a prolific writer and arranger), Isaac Hayes went on to develop an overwrought style that utilized the potential of the album. To that point, most R&B and soul albums had been a mixture of two-and-a-half minute singles and filler. Hayes concocted mini-symphonies of extraordinary length, which, allied with his visual presence (shaved head, designer African clothes, shades, and bizarre jewelry), made him more than a musician: he became an instantly recognizable cultural icon in early-'70s Black music. One album title, *Black Moses*, was probably Hayes' own succinct self-appraisal. Some might argue that his legacy is better represented by his workaday compositions and his arrangements, which include Sam & Dave's immortal "Soul Man" and "Hold On, I'm Comin." —*Colin Escott*

☆ **Hot Buttered Soul** / 1969 / Stax ✦✦✦✦✦
Isaac Hayes had already co-written many immortal soul singles in the late '60s when he began forging a solo career. Hayes helped focus attention on the album as a creative source in soul and R&B. This seminal album went against the grain in several ways. There were only four cuts, three of them at least nine minutes. There were two with extensive monologues, and he used symphonic backing and elaborate production. The album went gold, cracked the Top 100 and helped usher soul and R&B into the concept album era. It also featured some superb vocals and fine keyboard work by Hayes. —*Ron Wynn*

Isaac Hayes Movement / 1970 / Stax ✦✦✦✦
His second huge hit album and a great follow-up to the superb *Hot Buttered Soul*. Those critics who thought there was no way Hayes could repeat that triumph got fooled. He included a brilliant remake of Jerry Butler's "I Stand Accused" and also did a 12-minute version of the Beatles' "Something," complete with a wailing violin solo from jazz-rocker John Blair. This album showed that Hayes was going to be around for a long time and perform just as consistently on his own as he did teaming with Porter. —*Ron Wynn*

To Be Continued / 1970 / Stax ✦✦✦
Black Moses / 1971 / Stax ✦✦✦
Isaac Hayes followed his Oscar-winning soundtrack LP *Shaft* with another two-record set blending remakes of soul and pop hits, extended monologues, symphonic orchestrations and backing, and other production devices that made him one of the 1970s' most successful producers and performers. Although *Black Moses* wasn't nearly as commercially dominant as earlier albums, it did make the Top Ten briefly and was on the charts for over 30 weeks. But it was also an indication that he was beginning to run a bit dry in the material department. —*Ron Wynn*

Shaft / 1971 / Stax ✦✦✦✦
Isaac Hayes surprised many in the film and R&B/soul world when he produced, arranged, and composed the music for *Shaft*. Only three of the 15 tracks featured vocals, and Hayes displayed a finesse and capability with strings and mood pieces that his fans already knew he possessed from earlier albums, but which the general audience might have missed. This was a No. 1 pop LP and eventually earned Hayes an Oscar. It's also held up much better than the film. —*Ron Wynn*

Double Dynamite / 1974 / Stax ✦✦✦
Isaac Hayes not only was an innovative composer, songwriter, producer, and performer in his '60s and '70s, he was also an actor and appeared in several "blaxploitation" films during the early '70s. Hayes did double duty on these projects, writing and conducting the soundtracks for several, including the two featured on this twin-CD reissue. Neither *Truck*

Turner nor *Tough Guys* was a particularly memorable film, but Hayes' effective use of symphony orchestras and strings against a vocal backdrop often made the music the best part of the movie. —*Ron Wynn*

Chocolate Chip / 1975 / ABC ✦✦✦

● **Best of Isaac Hayes, Vol. 1** / 1986 / Stax ✦✦✦✦
A decent attempt to present some of Isaac Hayes' past hits on an anthology. But as one of R&B and soul's first concept and album artists, it's impossible to appreciate his contributions out of sequence. His early and mid-'70s albums helped change the course of contemporary African-American music production approaches, and that can't be understood by listening to condensed versions of hit singles, or even just by hearing the singles themselves removed from the album context. —*Ron Wynn*

● **Best of Isaac Hayes, Vol. 2** / 1986 / Stax ✦✦✦✦
These two compilations dutifully boil down Isaac Hayes' sometimes long-winded albums to their essential parts—in other words, they're both singles collections, highlighted by '70s landmarks such as "Theme from *Shaft*" and "By the Time I Get to Phoenix." Fanatics may want to investigate Hot Buttered Soul and Black Moses. —*John Floyd*

● **Greatest Hit Singles** / 1991 / Stax ✦✦✦✦
The place to start (and probably the place to end), with nearly an hour of music and 12 of his best-known singles, including "Shaft," "By the Time I Get to Phoenix," "Walk on By," "Never Can Say Goodbye," "Do Your Thing," and "Joy (Part 1)." There's a separate two-volume series of Stax Hayes hits for those who want a little more, but this is the essential dose. —*Richie Unterberger*

Roy Head

b. Jan. 9, 1943, Three Rivers, TX
Vocals / R&B, Rock 'n' Roll
Actually a country and rock vocalist rather than an R&B star, Roy Head nevertheless cut one of the great pieces of uptempo soul in the mid-'60s. "Treat Her Right" on Back Beat made it to No. 2 on the R&B charts and No. 2 pop, and the fact that Head was White was soft-pedaled in R&B circles while the song made its way up the charts. That performance alone was enough to qualify Head as one of the finest blue-eyed soul singers of the 1960s. But in fact, Roy was one of the most versatile stylists of the era, capable of hard R&B/rock tunes (even cutting material with a pre-fame Johnny Winter on backup guitar), mournful, soul-tinged country, and straight R&B and blues covers. Head was also an excellent entertainer, and his live shows of the period even included some fancy footwork clearly under the influence of James Brown. The Texan singer is remembered as a one-shot artist, but he actually cut many records (some under the auspices of noted producer Huey Meaux) throughout the 1960s on a confusing variety of labels. A few of these were tiny hits in the wake of "Treat Her Right," only a couple ("Just a Little Bit" and "Apple of My Eye") sneaking into the Top 40. Quite a few of his records were dynamic, sleek hybrids (in varying degrees) of soul, rock, and country, all featuring Head's cocky, confident vocals. In a sense, though, he was damned by his versatility, not fitting comfortably into any niche or marketing plan; the tiny labels he recorded for lacked national promotional muscle in any case. In the 1970s, after several years without success in the rock or R&B fields, Head returned to country, and landed quite a few chart hits in the arena between 1974 and 1985. —*Ron Wynn & Richie Unterberger*

Slip Away: His Best Recordings / 1993 / Collectables ✦✦✦
Not only are these not a few very good cuts here that aren't on The Best of Roy Head, such as the talking soul rap "Slip Away," the deep soul ballad "The Feeling Is Gone," and the zany psychedelic/jazz-flavored "Easy Loving Girl" (written by Johnny Winter, who plays fuzz guitar on the song). Just be warned that this is a carelessly assembled package, much inferior to the Varese Sarabande compilation, if you only want one disc. —*Richie Unterberger*

● **Treat Her Right: Best of Roy Head** / 1995 / Varese Vintage ✦✦✦✦
A long overdue anthology of Head's best sides, mostly recorded for the Back Beat label in the mid-'60s. Besides "Treat Her Right," it has all five of his other singles that dented the charts at the time. These aren't necessarily the highlights of these 18 tracks; "Pain" is country-soul moan at its best (although it's a thinly veiled rewrite of Lonnie Mack's "Why"), "To Make a Big Man Cry" is his best foray into country-pop from the period, and "You're (Almost) Tuff" is one of his toughest rockers, with a sound that almost verges on Texas garage. This collection is the most solid evidence of Head's superb talents, which were never rewarded with the consistent material or national recognition he deserved. —*Richie Unterberger*

Heart

Hard Rock, Pop-Rock
This Seattle band, led by sisters Ann and Nancy Wilson, has been a staple on FM-rock radio ever since their first hit in 1976, "Crazy on You." It was lead singer Ann Wilson's powerful voice that gave the band an immediate appeal. Heart synthesized Led Zeppelin-style riff-heavy rock and

shades of folk. Over the years, the band has continued to churn out hit after hit. In spite of a recent resurgence in the band's popularity, their hits are sounding increasingly formulaic. —*Rick Clark*

Dreamboat Annie / Mar. 1976 / Capitol ✦✦✦✦
Their striking first album was one of the top-selling debuts ever. —*Dan Heilman*

Little Queen / May 1977 / Portrait ✦✦✦✦
Little Queen continued the arena-rock formula of Heart's debut album, streamlining the bombast of Led Zeppelin into a glossy, pop-friendly but tough variation of hard rock. And with material as catchy as "Barracuda" and "Little Queen," it didn't seem like the band was treading water—it seemed like they were using their strength to the best of their abilities. —*Stephen Thomas Erlewine*

Magazine / Apr. 1978 / Capitol ✦✦

● **Heart Greatest Hits/Live** / Nov. 1980 / Epic ✦✦✦✦
This set includes all of the significant rock radio hits that made Heart such a staple during the '70s and early '80s, such as "Crazy on You," "Straight On," "Dreamboat Annie," "Even It Up," "Magic Man," "Heartless," and "Dog & Butterfly." Filling out the disc are six live tracks, including versions of Led Zeppelin's "Rock and Roll" and the Beatles' rave-up "I'm Down." —*Rick Clark*

Heart / Jun. 1985 / Capitol ✦✦✦✦
Just when it seemed that Heart was yesterday's news on the radio, they changed labels and experienced a resurgence of huge success with this, their self-titled Capitol debut. Includes the hits "If Looks Could Kill," "What About Love?," "Never," "Nothin' at All," and "These Dreams." —*Rick Clark*

Bad Animals / May 1987 / Capitol ✦✦✦

The Heartbeats

Doo Wop
Lead singer James "Shep" Sheppard cowrote a series of velvety doo wop ballads for the Heartbeats during the mid-'50s; one entry, "A Thousand Miles Away," was a huge R&B seller in 1956. The Queens, NY, quintet began their string of street-corner classics with "Crazy for You" and "Darling How Long," culminating with "A Thousand Miles Away." The Heartbeats recorded for Hull, Rama, Roulette, Gee, and Guyden before packing it in. In 1961 the lead singer formed a new trio, Shep & the Limelites, and scored on the charts with a heartwarming sequel to his first hit, "Daddy's Home," for Hull. "Our Anniversary" also sold well for the trio the next year, but they broke up soon thereafter. Sheppard was found dead in his auto on the Long Island Expressway in 1970. —*Bill Dahl*

● **The Best of the Heartbeats** / 1990 / Rhino ✦✦✦✦
This silky smooth New York quintet appeared from the mid-'50s. The album includes five tracks by lead James Sheppard's early-'60s vocal trio, Shep & The Limelites. —*Bill Dahl*

Hearts & Flowers

Country-Rock, Folk-Rock
Of the many folk-rock groups in southern California in the 1960s, Hearts & Flowers was one of the relatively few that were closer to "folk" than "rock." Founding guitarist Larry Murray was a member of the Scottsville Squirrel Barkers bluegrass group in the late '50s and early '60s; Chris Hillman and Bernie Leadon were also members of that group for a time. Murray teamed up with David Dawson and Rick Cunha to form Hearts & Flowers, a self-described "Georgia country-folk meets Hawaiian ukelele folk-rock" group, in the mid-'60s. They released a couple albums of pleasant but inessential country-folk-rock in the late '60s. —*Richie Unterberger*

Now Is the Time for Hearts and Flowers / 1967 / Capitol ✦✦✦✦
This debut album is an overlooked precursor to country-rock, echoing the late-'60s Byrds, Stone Poneys, Gene Clark, and most especially, as Brian Hogg points out in his lengthy liner notes, The Dillards. Earnest vocals and conscientious harmonies on this subdued, acoustic, and countrified take on folk-rock, with mild Eastern/psychedelic dabs of autoharp. The songs mix original tunes with covers of Donovan, Tim Hardin, Hoyt Axton, Kaleidoscope, and Carole King. There's little to criticize, but it lacks the innovative spark that characterizes the best of folk-rock of the time. —*Richie Unterberger*

Of Horses, Kids and Forgotten Women / 1968 / Capitol ✦✦✦✦
Future Flying Burrito Brother/Eagle Bernie Leadon replaced Rick Cunha for the group's second and final album, which is actually a considerably more L.A. pop-flavored production than their debut. Country-seasoned folk-rock remains at the core of the group's sound, but producer Nik Venet provides occasional tasteful, psychedelic-tinged orchestral arrangements. The material—about half original—is fairly strong, especially their covers of Arlo Guthrie's "Highway in the Wind" and Jesse Lee Kincaid's "She Sang Hymns Out of Tune" (also covered by Harry Nilsson on his first album). The unquestioned highlight is Larry Murray's "Ode to

a Tin Angel"; by far the group's most psychedelic slice of folk-rock, with its swimming strings, tripped-out lyrics, and sweet harmonies, it's also their most atypical track. A slicker, but better, album than their first effort. —*Richie Unterberger*

● **Now Is the Time for Hearts and Flowers/Of Horses, Kids and Forgotten Women** / 1995 / Edsel ♦♦♦♦
Edsel does '60s collectors a favor by combining both of Hearts & Flowers' hard-to-find LPs onto one compact disc, which puts the group's entire repertoire in one place. —*Richie Unterberger*

Helium

Alternative Pop-Rock, Indie Rock
Helium is essentially the project of Mary Timony, formerly of the girl-punk band Autoclave. Helium formed with Brian Dunton on bass and Shawn King Devlin in 1992, and started releasing seven-inches like "The American Jean" in 1993. 1994 saw the band release the *Pirate Prude* EP, an interesting but somewhat inaccessible exercise in mixing radical feminism with punk rock. *The Dirt of Luck*, released in 1995, was an improvement and embellishment of the sound laid forth in *Pirate Prude:* heavy, sluggish guitars, spooky keyboards, and Timony's breathy alto laid over an understated rhythm section. That year, Polvo's Ash Bowie also joined the lineup, replacing Dunton on bass. Helium are a challenging listen, but also a rewarding one. —*Heather Phares*

Pirate Prude / 1994 / Matador ♦♦♦

● **The Dirt of Luck** / Apr. 1995 / Matador ♦♦♦♦
Helium's first full-length album expands on Timony's feminist lyrical bent and adds more colors to the band's musical palette. Full of what Timony calls "cartoon and monster movie music" *The Dirt of Luck* is a tight, focused album that is also diverse. The sludgy "Pat's Trick" mingles with the sweet-sounding and sweetly named "Honeycomb," which shares space with the nasty-sultry sounds of "Medusa" and the shimmery drone-pop of "Baby's Going Underground." It's tied together by the album's spacious sound and Timony's singing, which is fuller and richer than on the group's debut. —*Heather Phares*

Richard Hell & the Voidoids

Punk, Proto-Punk
Some people will tell you Richard Hell was the main catalyst behind the birth of New York punk and its sensibilities. That's hardly true, but he's been around forever and did influence a number of budding punks (the Sex Pistols among them). In 1971 Hell and former high school buddy Tom Verlaine formed a group called the Neon Boys, who later became Television; he also cofounded the Heartbreakers with ex-New York Doll Johnny Thunders. In 1976 Hell formed the Voidoids, a caustic congregation that included guitarists Ivan Julian and Robert Quine and soon-to-be Ramones drummer Marc Bell. Hell's apocalyptic lyrics were steeped in alienated poetry, and his anguished howl of a voice set the pattern for scores of Bowery rockers. —*John Floyd*

● **Blank Generation** / 1977 / Sire ♦♦♦♦
Hell's debut isn't a masterpiece but it manages to re-create the intensity and exhilaration of the burgeoning days of American punk. "Love Comes in Spurts" defines Hell's romantic outlook, and the title cut is a classic piece of angst rock. —*John Floyd*

Destiny Street / 1982 / Combat ♦♦♦

R.I.P. / 1984 / Combat ♦♦♦

Helmet

Alternative Pop-Rock, Heavy Metal, Alternative Metal
Led by ex-Band of Susans guitar monster and university-trained musician Page Hamilton, Helmet boils away the excess of hard rock and heavy metal and serves up a wad of aural assault that values power, volume, and simplicity. Hamilton does a great job of creating songs that emphasize lacerating riffs, hypnotically repetitive distortion, and, at times, slower-than-a-lingering-death tempos. When the gears mesh on this monstrous machine, Helmet is one intimidating proposition. But by distilling hard rock to its feral core without the wit and panache that mark the careers of other, better, like-minded bands (e.g., Motörhead, the Melvins), one may not need a lot of Helmet to live a long and happy life. Hamilton does deserve credit for coming up with one killer record and scoring a sizable contract with a major label after the buzz surrounding their 1990 indie-label debut, *Strap It On*. —*John Dougan*

Strap It On / 1990 / Interscope ♦♦♦

● **Meantime** / 1992 / Interscope ♦♦♦♦
This is all the Helmet you will ever need. *Meantime* is a ferocious, sonic onslaught akin to hearing multiple explosions or living through a series of train accidents. Intense beyond description, *Meantime* will, with few exceptions, destroy nearly everything in its path, including Helmet's two other records. —*John Dougan*

Betty / 1994 / Interscope ♦♦♦♦
Although I cannot imagine wanting more Helmet than *Meantime*, if you've become a volume junkie and want a new fix, *Betty* might do the trick. Not as brutal or overpowering as *Meantime*, it has its moments, but indicates that Helmet's rage and fury may be changing into something slightly less aggressive. —*John Dougan*

Jimi Hendrix

b. Nov. 27, 1942, Seattle, WA, **d.** Sep. 18, 1970, London, England
Guitar / Rock 'n' Roll, Blues-Rock, Hard Rock, Psychedelic
In his brief four-year reign as a superstar, Jimi Hendrix expanded the vocabulary of the electric rock guitar more than anyone before or since. Hendrix was a master at coaxing all manner of unforeseen sonics from his instrument, often with innovative amplification experiments that produced astral-quality feedback and roaring distortion. His frequent hurricane blasts of noise, and dazzling showmanship—he could and would play behind his back and with his teeth, and set his guitar on fire—has sometimes obscured his considerable gifts as a songwriter and singer, and master of a gamut of blues, R&B, and rock styles.

When Hendrix became an international superstar in 1967, it seemed as if he'd dropped out of a Martian spaceship, but in fact he'd served his apprenticeship the long, mundane way in numerous R&B acts on the chitlin circuit. During the early and mid-'60s, he worked with such R&B/ soul greats as Little Richard, the Isley Brothers, and King Curtis as a backup guitarist. Occasionally he recorded as a session man (the Isley Brothers' '64 single "Testify" is the only one of these early tracks that offers even a glimpse of his future genius). But the stars didn't appreciate his show-stealing showmanship, and Hendrix was straightjacketed by sideman roles that didn't allow him to develop as a soloist. The logical step was for Hendrix to go out on his own, which he did in New York in the mid-'60s, playing with various musicians in local clubs, and joining White blues-rock singer John Hammond, Jr.'s band for a while.

It was in a New York club that Hendrix was spotted by Animals bassist Chas Chandler. The first lineup of the Animals was about to split, and Chandler, looking to move into management, convinced Hendrix to move to London and record as a solo act in England. There a group was built around Jimi, also featuring Mitch Mitchell on drums and Noel Redding on bass, that was dubbed the Jimi Hendrix Experience. The trio became stars with astonishing speed in the UK, where "Hey Joe," "Purple Haze," and "And the Wind Cries Mary" all made the Top Ten in the first half of 1967. These tracks were also featured on their debut album, *Are You Experienced?*, a psychedelic meisterwerk that became a huge hit in the US after Hendrix created a sensation at the Monterey Pop Festival in June of 1967.

Are You Experienced? was an astonishing debut, particularly from a young R&B veteran who had rarely sung, and apparently never written his own material, before the Experience formed. What caught most people's attention at first was his virtuosic guitar playing, which employed an arsenal of devices, including wah-wah pedals, buzzing feedback solos, crunching distorted riffs, and lightning, liquid runs up and down the scales. But Hendrix was also a first-rate songwriter, melding cosmic imagery with some surprisingly pop-savvy hooks and tender sentiments. He was also an excellent blues interpreter and passionate, engaging singer (although his gruff, throaty vocal pipes were not nearly as great assets as his instrumental skills). *Are You Experienced?* was psychedelia at its most eclectic, synthesizing mod pop, soul, R&B, Dylan, and the electric guitar innovations of British pioneers like Jeff Beck, Pete Townshend, and Eric Clapton.

Amazingly, Hendrix would only record three fully conceived studio albums in his lifetime. *Axis: Bold as Love* and the double-LP *Electric Ladyland* were more diffuse and experimental than *Are You Experienced?* On *Electric Ladyland* in particular, Hendrix pioneered the use of the studio itself as a recording instrument, manipulating electronics and devising overdub techniques (with the help of engineer Eddie Kramer in particular) to plot uncharted sonic territory. Not that these albums were perfect, as impressive as they were; the instrumental breaks could meander, and Hendrix's songwriting was occasionally half-baked, never matching the consistency of *Are You Experienced?* (although he exercised greater creative control over the later albums).

The final two years of Hendrix's life were turbulent ones musically, financially, and personally. He was embroiled in enough complicated management and record company disputes (some dating from ill-advised contracts he'd signed before the Experience formed) to keep the lawyers busy for years. He disbanded the Experience in 1969, forming the Band of Gypsies with drummer Buddy Miles and bassist Billy Cox to pursue funkier directions. He closed Woodstock with a sprawling, shaky set, redeemed by his famous machine-gun interpretation of "The Star-Spangled Banner." The rhythm section of Mitchell and Redding were underrated keys to Jimi's best work, and the Band of Gypsies ultimately couldn't measure up to the same standard, although Hendrix did record an erratic live album with them. In early 1970, the Experience re-formed again—and disbanded again shortly afterwards. At the same time, Hendrix felt torn in many directions by various fellow musicians, record-company expectations, and management pressures, all of whom had their own ideas of what Hendrix should be doing. Coming up on two years after *Electric Ladyland*, a new studio album had yet to appear, although Hendrix was recording constantly during the period.

While outside parties did contribute to bogging down Hendrix's studio work, it also seems likely that Jimi himself was partly responsible for the stalemate, unable to form a permanent lineup of musicians, unable to decide what musical direction to pursue, unable to bring himself to complete another album despite jamming endlessly. A few months into 1970, Mitchell—Hendrix's most valuable musical collaborator—came back into the fold, replacing Miles in the drum chair, although Cox stayed in place. It was this trio that toured the world during Hendrix's final months.

It's extremely difficult to separate the facts of Hendrix's life from rumors and speculation. Everyone who knew him well, or claimed to know him well, has different versions of his state of mind in 1970. Critics have variously mused that he was going to go into jazz, that he was going to get deeper into the blues, that he was going to continue doing what he was doing, or that he was too confused to know what he was doing at all. The same confusion holds true for his death: contradictory versions of his final days have been given by his closest acquaintances at the time. He'd been working intermittently on a new album, tentatively titled *First Ray of the New Rising Sun*, when he died in London on September 18, 1970, from drug-related complications.

Hendrix recorded a massive amount of unreleased studio material during his lifetime. Many of these (as well as entire live concerts) were issued posthumously; several of the live concerts were excellent, but the studio tapes have been the focus of enormous controversy for over 20 years. These initially came out in haphazard drabs and drubs (the first, *The Cry of Love*, was easily the most outstanding of the lot). In the mid-'70s, producer Alan Douglas took control of these projects, posthumously overdubbing many of Hendrix's tapes with additional parts by studio musicians. In the eyes of many Hendrix fans, this was sacrilege, destroying the integrity of the work of a musician known to exercise meticulous care over the final production of his studio recordings. Even as late as 1995, Douglas was having ex-Knack drummer Bruce Gary record new parts for the typically misbegotten compilation *Voodoo Soup*. After a lengthy legal dispute, the rights to Hendrix's estate, including all of his recordings, returned to Al Hendrix, the guitarist's father, in July of 1995. This may or may not mean that greater care will be exercised in packaging Jimi's legacy in the future. —*Richie Unterberger*

☆ **Are You Experienced?** / 1967 / Reprise ✦✦✦✦
One of the most stunning debuts in rock history, and one of the definitive albums of the psychedelic era. On *Are You Experienced?*, Hendrix synthesized various elements of the cutting edge of 1967 rock into music that sounded both futuristic and rooted in the best traditions of rock, blues, pop, and soul. It was his mind-boggling guitar work, of course, that got most of the ink, building upon the experiments of British innovators like Jeff Beck and Pete Townshend to chart new sonic territories in feedback, distortion, and sheer volume. It wouldn't have meant much, however, without his excellent material, whether psychedelic frenzy ("Foxy Lady," "Manic Depression," "Purple Haze"), instrumental freakout jams ("Third Stone from the Sun"), blues ("Red House," "Hey Joe"), or tender, poetic compositions ("The Wind Cries Mary") that demonstrated the breadth of his songwriting talents. Not to be underestimated were the contributions of drummer Mitch Mitchell and bassist Noel Redding, who gave the music a rhythmic pulse that fused parts of rock and improvised jazz. Many of these songs are among Hendrix's very finest; it may be true that he would continue to develop at a rapid pace throughout the rest of his brief career, but he would never surpass his first LP in terms of consistently high quality. The British and American versions of the album differed substantially when they were initially released in 1967; MCA's 17-song 1993 reissue does everyone a favor by gathering all of the material from the two records in one place, adding a few B-sides from early singles as well. —*Richie Unterberger*

☆ **Axis: Bold as Love** / 1967 / Reprise ✦✦✦✦✦
When the Experience recorded their second album, they were solidifying their international stardom. That meant access to more studio time and more sophisticated technology, but not, alas, a great deal of time to write the material. That may be why *Axis* isn't quite as much of a tour de force as *Are You Exerienced?*, but it's nevertheless another major effort, showing Hendrix continue to grow, particularly in his increasing mastery of the studio and more sophisticated lyrics. Soul and R&B influences are more prominent here than on his debut, though psychedelic experimentalism ran rampant (to great effect) on "If 6 Was 9," "Spanish Castle Magic," "Up from the Skies," "You Got Me Floatin'," and "Castles Made of Sand" all had funky grooves that gave the spiraling guitars and crunchy rhythm section a much-needed buoyancy. The best song, though, might have been the mellowest: "Little Wing" was Hendrix at his most delicate, and perhaps his most personal. —*Richie Unterberger*

Smash Hits / Jan. 1968 / Reprise ✦✦✦✦
Smash Hits is a solid collection of his most popular radio tracks, as well as featuring the bluesy "Red House" and "Stone Free," which were not found on previous albums. —*Rick Clark*

☆ **Electric Ladyland** / Feb. 1968 / Reprise ✦✦✦✦✦
With *Electric Ladyland*, Hendrix took psychedelic experimentation as far as he could within the original Experience trio format. That meant pushing the barriers of late '60s studio technology as far as they could bend, particularly with regard to multitracking and effects that could only be achieved through certain treatments and manipulation of the tape itself. It also meant greater freedom and looseness in the playing and the songwriting, which could be both a plus and a drawback, as the compositions became both less constricted and less concise. Not all of the material here is top-of-the-line, but certainly much of this is Hendrix at his best: the dreamy wah-wah guitars of "Rainy Day, Dream Away" were only matched by the dreaminess of the lyrics, and "Have You Ever Been (To Electric Ladyland)" and "Gypsy Eyes" were also standouts. "1983 . . . (A Merman I Should Turn to Be)" and "Voodoo Chile" were lengthy cuts dominated by jam-like instrumental passages; "Crosstown Traffic" and a cover of Dylan's "All Along the Watchtower," by contrast, were two of his catchiest and most pop-friendly tunes. "Voodoo Chile," "Voodoo Child (Slight Return)," and a cover of Earl King's "Come On" are three of his most determined forays into the blues, albeit the blues as fed through a nearly avant-garde filter. Originally released as a double album, the CD reissue fits the entire recording onto one 75-minute disc. —*Richie Unterberger*

Band of Gypsys / 1970 / Capitol ✦✦✦✦
Hendrix, sans the Experience, hooked up with bassist Billy Cox and drummer Buddy Miles to record this hard electric funk outing live at the Fillmore East in New York on December 31, 1969. While the rhythm section may have lacked the chops for wild free-form excursions, they provided Hendrix with a no-nonsense groove for his funkier R&B experiments. "Machine Gun," the album's highlight, features some of Hendrix's greatest playing. His dramatically violent soundscapes convey the horror of the war experience, with brilliantly controlled use of feedback and rapid-fire bursts of notes. —*Rick Clark*

The Cry of Love / 1971 / Reprise ✦✦✦✦
The posthumously released *The Cry of Love* revealed Hendrix turning toward a more subdued, less psychedelic style, with songs like "Night Bird Flying" and "Angel." Hendrix does deliver a few strong rockers with "Freedom," "Ezy Ryder," and "Astro Man." —*Rick Clark*

Plays Monterey / 1986 / Reprise ✦✦✦✦
Hendrix's show at the 1967 Monterey Pop Festival was the performance that broke him in the US. While half of this was previously available as one side of an LP that also featured a side of live Otis Redding from the same event, this has his whole performances. Jimi and the Experience were in fine, lean, fiery form on this nine-song set, which showcased the most well-known tunes from the *Are You Experienced?* album and covers of "Killing Floor," "Like a Rolling Stone," "Rock Me Baby," and "Wild Thing." —*Richie Unterberger*

Live at Winterland / 1987 / Rykodisc ✦✦✦✦
Jimi Hendrix's sonic assaults and attacks hypnotized, frightened, and amazed audiences in the late '60s. His studio recordings helped him attain his reputation, but his live works validated it. That's the case on the 13 songs from a 1968 Winterland concert that made their way onto CD in 1987. Whether he was doing short, biting songs like "Fire" or stretching out for blues statements like "Red House" and "Killing Floor," Jimi Hendrix turned the guitar into a battering ram, forcing everyone to notice and making every solo and note a memorable one. —*Ron Wynn*

Radio One / 1989 / Rykodisc ✦✦✦✦
Seventeen songs from 1967 BBC broadcasts, when the Experience had yet to burn out from the wheel of constant touring, management hassles, and internal strife. They're in good, enthusiastic form as they run through early gems like "Hey Joe," "Foxy Lady," "Fire," and "Stone Free," the lack of studio polish giving these versions a loose feel. The Experience studio albums are still considerably superior to this set, but it's certainly worth acquiring by any serious Hendrix fan, not least because it has several covers that didn't make it onto the three proper Experience LPs. Several of these ("Hoochie Koochie Man," "Killing Floor," "Catfish Blues") reveal his sometimes overlooked affinity for Chicago-style electric blues; there are also a couple of surprises ("Hound Dog" and "Day Tripper"). With good sound, it's a solid addition to the Hendrix library, demonsrating his versatility in various rock, soul, and blues styles. —*Richie Unterberger*

● **The Ultimate Experience** / Apr. 27, 1993 / MCA ✦✦✦✦
As a single-disc compilation, *The Ultimate Experience* is hard to beat. Drawing from the original Jimi Hendrix Experience albums, the 20-track collection hits all of the highpoints—"Purple Haze," "All Along the Watchtower," "Little Wing," "Red House," "The Wind Cries Mary," "Highway Chile," "Angel"—and gives an accurate impression of why Hendrix was

so revolutionary and influential. All three of Hendrix's completed studio albums are mandatory listening, but *The Ultimate Experience* is a terrific introduction to the guitarist. — *Thom Owens*

☆ **Jimi Hendrix: Blues** / 1994 / MCA ✦✦✦✦✦
While Hendrix remains most famous for his hard rock and psychedelic innovations, more than a third of his recordings were blues-oriented. This CD contains eleven blues originals and covers, eight of which were previously unreleased. Recorded between 1966 and 1970, they feature the master guitarist stretching the boundaries of electric blues in both live and studio settings. Besides several Hendrix blues-based originals, it includes covers of Albert King and Muddy Waters classics, as well as a 1967 acoustic version of his composition "Hear My Train A-Comin'." — *Richie Unterberger*

Jimi Hendrix: Woodstock / 1994 / MCA ✦✦✦

Voodoo Soup / Apr. 1995 / MCA ✦✦✦

Don Henley

b. Jul. 22, 1947, Gilmer, TX
Drums, Keyboards, Vocals / Singer-Songwriter, Pop-Rock
Out of all of the Eagles, Don Henley had the most successful solo career. After the group broke up in 1982, Henley released his first solo album, *I Can't Stand Still*. Although it wasn't as successful as an Eagles record, the album peformed respectably, launching the No. 3 single "Dirty Laundry" and going gold. *Building the Perfect Beast* followed two years later and established Henley as a solo star in his own right. Featuring the Top Ten hits "Boys of Summer" and "All She Wants to Do Is Dance," as well as the Top 40 singles "Not Enough Love in the World" and "Sunset Grill," the album sold over two million copies and stayed on the charts for over a year. Henley's third album, 1989's *The End of the Innocence*, was his most ambitious record yet, as well as his most commercially successful. The album sold over three million copies and stayed on the charts for nearly three years, launching the hit singles "The End of the Innocence," "Heart of the Matter," "New York Minute," "How Bad Do You Want It?," and "The Last Worthless Evening." Henley reunited with the Eagles in 1994, embarking on a worldwide tour. The group released a live album culled from an appearance on *MTV Unplugged* called *Hell Freezes Over*; the record also featured a handful of new studio tracks. *Hell Freezes Over* was a major success, selling over five million copies by the summer of 1995. However, the group decided not to pursue any more projects together and Henley continued working on his fourth solo album in 1995. — *Stephen Thomas Erlewine*

I Can't Stand Still / 1982 / Asylum ✦✦✦

Building the Perfect Beast / 1984 / Geffen ✦✦✦✦
His commercial breakthrough defined his solo formula with songs like "The Boys of Summer" and "All She Wants to Do Is Dance," which responded to political and romantic breakdowns. — *John Floyd*

The End of the Innocence / 1989 / Geffen ✦✦✦
A conceptual elaboration on his *Beast* album, this frames some wonderfully sarcastic rockers around "The Heart of the Matter," one of the finest ballads of the '80s. — *John Floyd*

● **Actual Miles: Henley's Greatest Hits** / Nov. 21, 1995 / Geffen ✦✦✦✦
Although it is drawn from only three albums (with only one track, "Dirty Laundry," from *I Can't Stand Still*), *Actual Miles* was a well-chosen best-of from an artist who had had just enough hits to justify one. Five tracks each came from *Building the Perfect Beast* and *The End of the Innocence*, and they included all of Don Henley's Top 40 hits. The album was filled out with a cover of Leonard Cohen's "Everybody Knows" and two new tracks, among them the ambitious "The Garden of Allah," which seemed to be an attempt to create a new allegorical masterpiece along the lines of "Hotel California," but managed to be only pretentious. Still, the bulk of this album was the sound of AOR radio in the mid-1980s. That, of course, was the catch—this album should have come out about four years before it did, and probably would have if Henley hadn't been suing Geffen Records. Though destined to be a successful catalog item, in 1995 it was more a historical artifact than a major release. — *William Ruhlmann*

Clarence Henry

b. Mar. 19, 1937, Algiers, LA
Piano, Trombone, Vocals / R&B, New Orleans R&B
A bit more eccentric and unpredictable than Fats Domino, as contemporary or inventive as, say, Lee Dorsey, New Orleans pianist Clarence "Frogman" Henry's vocals were consistently warm and humorous, his recordings always polished. Scoring an unexpected novelty hit with "Ain't Got No Home" in 1956, Henry disappeared from the charts for four years before roaring back with two smashes in the early '60s: "(I Don't Know Why) But I Do" and "You Always Hurt the One You Love."
On his early-'60s singles, Clarence added beefier horn sections that occasionally reached back to the spirit of Dixieland. Crescent City leg-

ends like saxophonist Lee Allen and pianists Allen Toussaint and Paul Gayten cropped up on his sessions. When Henry traveled to Memphis to record, he was backed by the all-star band of Bill Justis (guitar), Boots Randolph (sax), and Floyd Cramer (piano). He went on to record a fair number of singles for Chess's Argo subsidiary in the relaxed New Orleans R&B style of his big hits. — *Richie Unterberger*

But I Do / 1994 / Charly ✦✦✦✦
Twenty Argo waxings by the roly-poly pianist—much duplication with the easier-to-locate MCA disc as far as the hits go, though the inclusion of the sequel "I Found a Home" and the lesser-known rockers "Steady Date," "Oh Why," and "Live It Right" certainly make this one worth looking for. — *Bill Dahl*

● **Ain't Got No Home: Best of Clarence "Frogman" Henry** / 1994 / MCA ✦✦✦✦
The New Orleans R&B singer with the joyous frog's croak in his voice is served well by this 18-song collection of his 1956-1964 output for the Chess subsidiary Argo Records. Begins with his definitive "Ain't Got No Home," follows with his vicious Crescent City rockers "Troubles, Troubles," "It Won't Be Long," and "I'm in Love," and visits his comeback hits "But I Do" and "You Always Hurt the One You Love." — *Bill Dahl*

Joe Henry

Guitar, Vocals / Singer-Songwriter
Joe Henry is best known for his two country-influenced albums, 1992's *Short Man's Room* and 1993's *Kindness of the World*, both of which feature members of the country-rock band the Jayhawks, but his musical direction has actually changed several times over the course of his recording career, reflecting his restless, adventurous spirit.
Henry was born in North Carolina, grew up in Michigan, spent the early part of his music career in New York City, and finally settled in Los Angeles in 1990 with his wife and son. After his little-heard 1986 debut, "Talk of Heaven," Henry debuted on A&M in 1989 with the rock 'n' roll album *Murder of Crows*, which was produced by Anton Fier and featured Mick Taylor on guitar.
From there he pared down to the quiet, entirely acoustic moods of *Shuffletown* (1990) before shifting into the country- and folk-influenced territory of "Short Man's Room" and "Kindness of the World." The latter two albums earned him an excellent reputation among fans of alternative rock and country as a superb singer and songwriter. He followed *Kindness* with the five-song EP *Fireman's Wedding* a year later.
Henry's lyrics are a central focus of his songwriting, but even though he often writes in the first person, his songs are not "personal" in the manner of musicians who are often called singer-songwriters (a genre he doesn't like to be associated with). He's recorded some excellent country covers, but he's equally interested in soul, funk, and rock 'n' roll.
On *Trampoline*, released in 1996, Henry veered his music in an edgier, more rhythm-oriented direction. While he still employs acoustic instruments and even a pedal-steel guitar on several songs, "Trampoline" (much of which Henry recorded at a studio he set up in his garage) is more clearly defined by its drum loops, loud electric guitars, mysterious voices, and curious sonic textures. For this album Henry recruited guitarist Page Hamilton from the band Helmet and drummer Carla Azar from the band Edna Swap. — *Kurt Wolff*

Shuffletown / 1990 / A&M ✦✦✦

● **Short Man's Room** / Jun. 16, 1992 / Mammoth ✦✦✦✦
Working with country-rockers the Jayhawks, singer-songwriter Joe Henry turned in one of his strongest records with *Short Man's Room*. The Jayhawks help bring out the country leanings in Henry's songs and the results are quite impressive. As always, the songwriter's eye for detail is sharp, bringing his characters to vivid life. The gritty, rootsy music increases the impact of the writing, making *Short Man's Room* an emotional, affecting record. — *Stephen Thomas Erlewine*

Kindness of the World / 1993 / Mammoth ✦✦✦✦
On this album of more strong songs, some have definite country leanings. Henry covers Tom T. Hall's "I Flew over Our House Last Night," and he wrote "She Always Goes" with George Strait in mind. — *Brian Mansfield*

Fireman's Wedding / 1994 / Mammoth ✦✦

Trampoline / Mar. 26, 1996 / Mammoth/Atlantic ✦✦✦
On *Trampoline*, Joe Henry moves away from the country-rock that earned his reputation in the early '90s. Though there are still some remnants of his Gram Parsons and Neil Young influences, Henry attempts a more atmospheric, rock-based sound on *Trampoline*, which explains his choice of Helmet guitarist Page Hamilton as musical collaborator. The shift in sound is effective, but it does sound as if the singer-songwriter is still trying to become comfortable with his new direction. It doesn't help that the album is slightly uneven, as Henry tries to write more literate lyrics, making his songs almost into short stories. When his ambitions do work, *Trampoline* is a stark, affecting listen, and even when they don't, the album is admirable. — *Stephen Thomas Erlewine*

Herman's Hermits

British Invasion, Pop-Rock

Herman's Hermits began life in 1963 in Manchester, England, as the Heartbeats, the group consisting of Keith Hopwood (b. Oct. 26, 1946, Manchester, England), guitar; Karl Green (b. Jul. 31, 1947, Salford, England), guitar, harmonica; Derek Leckenby (b. May 14, 1945, Leeds, England), guitar; and Barry Whitwam (b. Jul. 21, 1946, Manchester, England), drums. They got the name Herman's Hermits when they were joined by 16-year-old TV actor Peter Noone (b. Nov. 5, 1947, Manchester), vocals, piano, and guitar. Pop producer Mickie Most, induced to see the group by their managers, thought Noone looked like a young John Kennedy and agreed to sign them. Most chose the group's material, from revamped oldies and pub songs to tunes submitted by professional songwriters like Gerry Goffin and Carole King, and produced the recordings, generally using Noone as singer and a group of studio musicians.

The result was two years of solid hits, starting with "I'm into Something Good," which topped the UK charts and broke the group in America. There were 11 Top Ten hits in the US through 1967, among them the No. 1 gold singles "Mrs. Brown You've Got a Lovely Daughter" and "I'm Henry VIII, I Am." Herman's Hermits had ten Top Ten hits in Britain through 1970. Inevitably, the group's teenage heartthrob appeal waned, and they never became the kind of self-sustaining musical unit that could outlive that initial infatuation. The group split in 1971, though it has re-formed, with and without Noone, for oldies performances. — *William Ruhlmann*

● **Their Greatest Hits** / 1973 / ABKCO ✦✦✦
Basic hits package, but too brief and under par sound-wise. (Originally released as a 15-track LP in 1973, *Their Greatest Hits* was reissued as a 16-track CD in 1987.) — *Jeff Tamarkin*

The EP Collection / Jan. 1990 / See For Miles ✦✦✦✦
This 22-track CD also features most of the major Herman hits, with a handful of obscurities thrown in. — *Jeff Tamarkin*

The Collection / Jun. 1990 / Castle ✦✦✦✦
All of the hits by Peter Noone and company, with room to spare for some nice surprises. — *Jeff Tamarkin*

Kristin Hersh

b. Aug. 7, 1966, Atlanta, GA

Guitar, Vocals / Singer-Songwriter, Alternative Pop-Rock

Kristin Hersh, the lead singer-songwriter of Throwing Muses, released her first solo album, the acoustic *Hips and Makers*, in early 1994; she followed it a couple of months later with the *Strings* EP, which featured versions of selected songs from the album recorded with a string quartet. After releasing the record, Hersh did a solo tour and finished the next Throwing Muses record, *University*, which was released in February 1995. — *Stephen Thomas Erlewine*

● **Hips and Makers** / 1994 / Sire/Reprise ✦✦✦✦
Hersh dug into her backlog of compositions for material of an intensely personal nature that she felt wouldn't be suitable for her band on her solo debut, *Hips and Makers*. In stark contrast to her work with Throwing Muses, *Hips and Makers* is almost entirely acoustic. Hersh embellishes her waifish voice and acoustic guitar with touches of cello and piano on this album, which offers a despairing and introspective tone that fails to submerge her considerable inner strength and fortitude. Recorded in a mere two weeks, this collection of haunting and confessional songs was produced by ex-Patti Smith Group guitarist Lenny Kaye, who has also produced Suzanne Vega. Hersh's voice and lyrical tone, however, are considerably brittler and coarser than Vega's. The opening track, "Your Ghost," features a duet with R.E.M. singer Michael Stipe. — *Richie Unterberger*

Strings / 1994 / Sire ✦✦✦✦
A beautiful EP featuring several tracks that didn't make *Hips and Makers*, as well as excellent re-recorded versions of several of the tracks that did. — *Stephen Thomas Erlewine*

John Hiatt

b. 1952, Indianapolis, IN

Guitar, Piano, Vocals / Rock 'n' Roll, Country-Rock, Singer-Songwriter

One of the longest-gestating singer-songwriters of the last quarter-century, and one of the best, John Hiatt left his native Indianapolis in 1970 (after high school) to go to Nashville and write songs. He signed up with Epic Records and made two albums, *Hangin' Around the Observatory* (1974) and *Overcoats* (1975), which demonstrated his powerful songwriting ability but didn't draw customers. He signed to MCA in Los Angeles in the late '70s and released *Slug Line* (1979) and *Two Bit Monsters* (1980), still without gaining a commercial following. Then came a stint on Geffen that produced *All of a Sudden* (1982), *Riding with the King*

(1983), and *Warming Up to the Ice Age* (1985). All increased his visibility without really breaking through.

But in 1987, Hiatt went into the studio with old friends Ry Cooder and Nick Lowe, plus drummer Jim Keltner, and came out with his first chart album, *Bring the Family*. That album's follow-ups, *Slow Turning* (1988), *Stolen Moments* (1990), and *Perfectly Good Guitar* (1993), have demonstrated Hiatt's maturity as a writer and his flowering as a performer, resulting in some of the best singer-songwriter rock of the era. In 1992, Hiatt again teamed with Cooder, Lowe, and Keltner, this time in a group called Little Village that released a well-received debut album. — *William Ruhlmann*

Hangin' Around the Observatory / 1974 / Epic ✦✦✦

Overcoats / 1975 / Epic ✦✦

Slug Line / 1979 / MCA ✦✦✦

Two Bit Monsters / 1980 / MCA ✦✦✦

All of a Sudden / 1982 / Geffen ✦✦✦

Riding with the King / 1983 / Geffen ✦✦✦✦
One half of Hiatt's best Geffen album is played by him and Scott Matthews, while the other half features a band including Paul Carrack and Nick Lowe. But what matters is the songs: Hiatt's trenchant observations on life and love, especially the perceptive and painfully funny "She Loves the Jerk." — *William Ruhlmann*

Warming Up to the Ice Age / Jan. 1985 / Geffen ✦✦✦

★ **Bring the Family** / May 1987 / A&M ✦✦✦✦✦
Not only is the small-band playing impeccable, but this is Hiatt's best collection of songs, which is saying a lot for so talented a writer. "Memphis in the Meantime" is a knowledgeable look at the fame game, "Your Dad Did" perfectly skewers domestic life, and "Have a Little Faith in Me" is a touching evocation of persistent love. And that's just three of them. — *William Ruhlmann*

Slow Turning / 1988 / A&M ✦✦✦✦
Only a notch below *Bring the Family*, with such strong songs as "Drive South" and the wild criminals-on-the-loose song "Tennessee Plates." — *William Ruhlmann*

Y'all Caught? The Ones That Got Away 1979-1985 / 1989 / Geffen ✦✦✦✦

Stolen Moments / Jun. 1990 / A&M ✦✦✦
John Hiatt's highest charting album yet is a step down from the dizzy heights of *Bring the Family* and *Slow Turning*, as he abandons his more acid commentaries and turns in a self-deprecating set full of promises of reformation and celebrations of marriage and family life. But the observations remain acute, and Hiatt's singing (so much camouflaged in his early days) is becoming his secret weapon. — *William Ruhlmann*

Perfectly Good Guitar / 1993 / A&M ✦✦

Hiatt Comes Alive at Budokan? / Nov. 22, 1994 / A&M ✦✦✦

Walk On / Oct. 24, 1995 / Capitol ✦✦✦

Living a Little, Laughing a Little / Raven ✦✦✦✦
Living a Little, Laughing a Little does a good job as an early-career summary, drawing material from his albums released from 1974 to 1985—*Hangin' Around the Observatory, Overcoats, Slug Line, Two Bit Monster, All of a Sudden, Riding With the King*, and *Warming Up to the Ice Ages*. For those who are only familiar with his critically acclaimed work from the late-'80s on, this provides a introduction to the formative years and a facinating look at a man finding his voice—from an average '70s-style singer-songwriter to a rocker à la Elvis Costello to the first hints of his better known, later rootsy incarnation. A 1985 interview and a track Hiatt contribute to the *Cruisin'* soundtrack have been added as a bonus to those who already have the albums. — *Chris Woodstra*

High Llamas

Alternative Pop-Rock, Post-Rock/Experimental

Although the High Llamas are nominally a group, they're pretty much the brainchild of singer and guitarist Sean Hogan. Hogan did some time in the London-by-way-of-Dublin band Microdisney, in which he was the songwriting partner of Cathal Coughlan. After Microdisney split in 1988 (Coughlan forming Fatima Mansions), Hogan released a couple of import-only solo albums before forming the High Llamas. The Llamas issued their debut, *Gideon Gaye*, in 1994 to high praise in the British press; it was released in the States a year later almost as an afterthought, with virtually no fanfare. Comparisons of the High Llamas/Hogan to Brian Wilson/the Beach Boys are unavoidable, and not just from arcane critics. Anyone with a large Beach Boys collection will detect the uncanny resemblance to 1966-70 Beach Boys, with the sophisticated melodies, the beautiful harmonies, and the elaborate production, with the emphasis on layered keyboards and orchestration. Echoes of *Pet Sounds, Smile, Wild Honey*, and *Surf's Up* predominate, though Hogan also claims Burt Bacharach as a major inspiration. At this point, however, the strong resemblance to Wilson's meisterwerks place Hogan closer to imitation than originality. Considering that he's been making records for about a decade, he might want to start aiming his sights higher. — *Richie Unterberger*

Gideon Gaye / 1994 / Sony ✦✦✦

Despite what Don Was, Van Dyke Parks, and others might be claiming, Brian Wilson is *not* going to return to the peak of his powers. In his absence, Sean Hogan might be the best available substitute. He's obviously done his homework, listening not only to all the albums between *Pet Sounds* and *Surf's Up*, but the widely circulated *Smile* bootlegs as well. Cheeky references to cuts like "Let's Get Away for a While" and "Surf's Up" pop up from time to time on this lush set, which takes its cues from both Wilson's most melodic and most eccentric qualities (though the ten-minute flute solo on "Track Goes By" does this to excess). It's an impressive outing that sounds like little else in the alternative rock world of the mid-'90s. But it only establishes Hogan and his various pals as charming emulators, rather than true innovators. — *Richie Unterberger*

His Name Is Alive

Alternative Pop-Rock, Experimental

His Name Is Alive create some of the most beautiful and complex independently released music in recent memory, ranging from simple, folky ballads to electrifying guitar maelstroms. The brainchild of guitarist Warren Defever (also of shockabilly group Elvis Hitler), His Name Is Alive features the voices of Karin Oliver, Melissa Elliott, Denise James, and Karen Neal, and the drumming of Damian Lang and Trey Many (also of Licorice). The band's sound is as ever-changing as its lineup; each of the group's releases, from the haunting, near-gothic *Livonia* (named after the group's Michigan hometown) to the sunny-sounding *Mouth by Mouth*, shows innovation and continual change. — *Heather Phares*

Livonia / 1990 / Rykodisc ✦✦✦

The group's artiest release, *Livonia*, was recorded when Defever was a mere 19 years old. Karin Oliver's wide vocal range and elegant harmonies mix with Defever's guitar maelstroms and tape loops in a unique and usually successful way. "E-Nicolle," "How Ghosts Affect Relationships" and "Caroline's Supposed Demon" are good examples of *Livonia's* mix of sonic beauty and experimentalism. — *Heather Phares*

Home Is in Your Head / 1992 / Rykodisc ✦✦✦✦

Home Is in Your Head completes His Name Is Alive's moody, neo-gothic period. A dark and disturbing, but also very beautiful record, *Home Is in Your Head* features song titles like "Put Your Finger in Your Eye," "Why People Disappear," "Chances Are We Are Mad" and "Are We Still Married?" The album is musically diverse, ranging from gentle folk ballads to ethereal instrumentals to harsh guitar blasts. The Rykodisc re-release also includes the group's *The Dirt Eaters* EP, which contains a creepy remix of "Are We Still Married?" as well as one of His Name Is Alive's best songs, "We Hold the Land in Great Esteem." — *Heather Phares*

● **Mouth by Mouth** / 1993 / 4AD ✦✦✦✦

His Name Is Alive's third release is actually half HNIA songs and half Dirt Eaters (HNIA's sister band) songs. The two groups' songs work together brilliantly, creating one of the best and most varied albums in alternative music. The Dirt Eaters' songs, like "Baby Fish Mouth," "In Every Ford," and "Sick" are loud, catchy art-pop songs with lots of distorted guitars. His Name Is Alive's tunes, in contrast, feature the pristine harmonies and crisp cellos of "Cornfield," the pseudo-gamelan on "Sort Of," and the disturbing dead calm of "Can't Go Wrong Without You" and "Ear." The light and shadow that the bands create with their harmonious yet distinct styles make *Mouth by Mouth* fascinating and rewarding on each listen. — *Heather Phares*

Stars on ESP / Jul. 1996 / 4AD ✦✦✦✦

As usual, Michigan-based sonic envelope-pushers His Name Is Alive continue to boggle expectations with their beautiful, exciting music. On their fourth album for 4AD, *Stars on ESP*, the group mixes dub, dreampop, surf, country and *Pet Sounds*-era Beach Boys into something altogether unique. The songs range from the deceptively simple, folky "Answer to Rainbow at Midnight" and "Famous Goodbye King" to bouncy pop like "Bad Luck Girl," "The Bees" and "Across the Street." Then there's songs that defy easy description, like the beautiful, lilting "Dub Love Letter," and the "Good Vibrations" pastiche "Universal Frequencies." On the whole, *Stars on ESP* is their most acoustic since 1992's *Home Is in Your Head* and their brightest sounding since *Mouth by Mouth*. However, the trademark strange, spacy noises that peppered the band's other releases can still be found on this album, particularly on "What Else Is New List" and "Wall of Speed." An eclectic, unique album—it even includes a gospel song—from an eclectic, unique band, *Stars on ESP* features His Name Is Alive at their most accessible and exciting. — *Heather Phares*

Robyn Hitchcock

b. 1952

Guitar, Vocals / Alternative Pop-Rock, Neo-Psychedelia

British alternative singer-songwriter Robyn Hitchcock built up a large

cult following and critical acclaim for his highly poetic, if somewhat obscure, songs, especially after his work began to be more generally available in the US after 1985. Born in London, Hitchcock formed the Soft Boys with Andy Metcalfe and Morris Windsor in 1976; the band continued until 1981, when Hitchcock released his first solo album, *Black Snake Diamond Role*. This was followed by *Groovy Decay* (1982) and *I Often Dream of Trains* (1984). In 1984, Hitchcock formed a backing band called the Egyptians, consisting of Metcalfe, Windsor, Otis Horns Fletcher, and Roger Jackson, and began playing concerts for the first time in two and a half years. The first recorded output of this band, and the first US Hitchcock album, was *Fegmania!* (1985). It was followed by the live album *Gotta Let This Hen Out!* (1985), *Element of Light* (1986), and a compilation called *Invisible Hitchcock* (1986), all of which built up Hitchcock's following to the point that he was signed by A&M Records, resulting in his major-label debut *Globe of Frogs* (1988), which reached No. 111. *Queen Elvis*, Hitchcock's second A&M album, reached No. 139 in 1989. He then made *Eye* (1990), an acoustic solo album released on Twin/Tone Records. Two other albums for A&M—1991's *Perspex Island* and 1993's *Respect*—followed before his contract with the label ended. In 1995, his pre-A&M catalog was reissued by Rhino Records. In 1996, he signed with Warner Bros. Records and released *Moss Elixir* in the summer of that year. — *William Ruhlmann*

Black Snake Diamond Role / 1981 / Rhino ✦✦✦

I Often Dream of Trains / 1984 / Rhino ✦✦✦✦

Hitchcock was so shaken by the entire *Groovy Decay* disaster that he retired from recording for two years. When he returned in 1984 with *I Often Dream of Trains*, it was clear that the time off had affected his music. A collection of spare, acoustic-based pop-folk songs, *I Often Dream of Trains* is one of Hitchcock's most introspective and charming records. Instead of creating an impenetrably personal album, the stripped-down instrumentation actually opens up the songwriter's world, allowing the ballads ("Trams of Old London," "Cathedral," "Flavour of Night") to sit comfortably next to the jokes ("Uncorrected Personality Traits"). Alternating between acoustic guitars and solo piano, the music is never fragile, adding a strong support to Hitchcock's eccentric lyrics. — *Stephen Thomas Erlewine*

Fegmania! / Mar. 1985 / Rhino ✦✦✦✦

After the stripped-back collection *I Often Dream of Trains*, Hitchcock slowly formed a backing band called the Egyptians with ex-Soft Boys Andy Metcalfe and Morris Windsor and keyboardist Roger Jackson over the course of the next year. *Fegmania!*, the Egyptians' first album, was a distinct departure from both the Soft Boys and Hitchcock's previous solo work, featuring layered, intertwining guitars and keyboards that created lush and thick sonic textures. Even with the more detailed arrangements, the songs remained twitchy and off-kilter, with melodies that usually went in willfully unpredictable directions, yet remained catchy all the while. *Fegmania!* was Hitchcock's most consistent work to date, featuring such highlights as the Eastern-tinged "Egyptian Cream," the creepy "My Wife & My Dead Wife," and the relatively straightforward "The Man with the Lightbulb Head." — *Stephen Thomas Erlewine*

● **Gotta Let This Hen Out** / Oct. 1985 / Rhino ✦✦✦✦

Recorded at the Marquee in London shortly after the release of *Fegmania!*, the live *Gotta Let This Hen Out!* is a tense and exciting record, finding the raw energy that usually goes untapped in Hitchcock's music. Although the album makes The Egyptians sound more like a rock 'n' roll band than they actually were—they never played with such wreckless abandon before or since—the driving performances don't wreck the melodic and lyrical eccentricities of the songs; instead, the increased vigor gives the music a searing power, obliterating the notion that his songs are delicate and precious. The set list also accentuates Hitchcock's strengths, relying on his most accessible and melodic material, whether it's recent material like "Egyptian Cream," "Sometimes I Wish I Was a Pretty Girl," and "Acid Bird" or Soft Boys' tracks like "Kingdom of Love," "Only the Stones Remain," "The Face of Death," and "Leppo and the Jooves." — *Stephen Thomas Erlewine*

Element of Light / 1986 / Rhino ✦✦✦✦

Element of Light, Hitchcock's second studio album with the Egyptians, remains one of his finest moments and offers a convincing argument for his talents as a pop craftsman. Using John Lennon's work for *Revolver* and *The Beatles* as a template, Hitchcock wrote an elegant set of songs for *Element of Light*, songs that contained all of his cryptic lyrical sensibilities, yet featured more refined melodies and song structures. The Egyptians play with a subtle grace, moving between the stately "Winchester" and light psychedelia of "If You Were a Priest" to the bracing attack of "Tell Me About Your Drugs" with ease. While it sacrifices some of the edgy tension of Hitchcock's earlier work, *Element of Light* is his most melodic and eerily beautiful record. — *Stephen Thomas Erlewine*

Invisible Hitchcock / 1986 / Rhino ✦✦✦

● **Globe of Frogs** / 1988 / A&M ✦✦✦✦

Hitchcock has a considerable catalog, but neophytes might wish to begin with this relatively recent collection, which finds him playing in a folk-rock style while singing highly imagistic lyrics, the tone of which can be suggested by noting some of the titles: "Balloon Man," "Tropical Fish Mandala," "Sleeping with Your Devil Mask," and "The Shapes Between Us Turn into Animals." Hitchcock is an original eclectic, well worth hearing, if not an acquired taste. *— William Ruhlmann*

Queen Elvis / 1989 / A&M ✦✦
Hitchcock earned some radio play for this album's leadoff track, "Madonna of the Wasps," which, like several tracks here, features the distinctive guitar of R.E.M.'s Peter Buck. *— William Ruhlmann*

Eye / 1990 / Rhino ✦✦✦✦
Robyn Hitchcock recorded *Eye*, his fourth proper solo album, after the disappointing *Queen Elvis*. *Eye* marked a return to the acoustic-oriented folk-pop of *I Often Dream of Trains*, featuring a collection of his most personal songs. Where *I Often Dream of Trains* was a kaleidoscopic journey through a colorfully twisted world, *Eye* sounds more confessional, although Hitchcock's exact lyrical sentiments can be difficult to sort out through his dense and willfully obscure imagery. Nevertheless, the immediacy of the music—which is delivered on acoustic guitars and piano—and the simple, delicate grace of Hitchcock's melodies make even the most cryptic lines sound direct and straightforward. *— Stephen Thomas Erlewine*

Perspex Island / 1991 / A&M ✦✦✦
Respect / Feb. 23, 1993 / A&M ✦✦
Gravy Deco / Jan. 1995 / Rhino ✦✦
You & Oblivion / Mar. 1995 / Rhino ✦✦
Moss Elixir / Aug. 1996 / Warner Bros. ✦✦✦

Hole

Alternative Pop-Rock, Grunge
Throughout Hole's career, vocalist/guitarist Courtney Love's notorious public image has overshadowed her band's music. In its original incarnation, Hole was one of the noisiest, most abrasive alternative bands performing in the early '90s. By the time of their second album, 1994's *Live Through This*, the band had smoothed out many of their rougher edges, as well as adding more melody and hooks to their songwriting. Through both versions of Hole, Love's combative, assaultive persona permeated both the group's music and lyrics, giving the band a tense, unpredictable edge even at their quietest moments.

Love formed Hole in Los Angeles in 1989, recruiting guitarist Eric Erlandson through a newspaper ad. Love had played in numerous bands before Hole, including an early version of Babes In Toyland and Faith No More. Erlandson and Love eventually drafted bassist Jill Emery and drummer Caroline Rue into the band, recording their first album with producer Kim Gordon, the bassist of Sonic Youth. The violent and uncompromising *Pretty on the Inside*, Hole's debut record, was released on Caroline Records in 1991, to numerous positive reviews, especially in the British weekly music press.

In early 1992, Courtney Love married Kurt Cobain, the lead singer-songwriter of Nirvana. For a couple of months, the couple were the king and queen of the new rock world; soon, that world came crashing in. Cobain became addicted to heroin and the couple fought to keep custody of their baby after a piece in *Vanity Fair* accused Love of shooting heroin while pregnant, charges which she vehemently denied at the time; she would later admit that she had taken small quanities of the drug. By 1993, their private world had settled down somewhat, with Cobain and Love recording new albums with their respective bands.

Halfway through 1993, Love reassembled Hole with Erlandson, adding bassist Kristen M. Pfaff and drummer Patty Schemel. Hole was set to release their first major-label album, the more pop-oriented *Live Through This*, on DGC Records in April of 1994. Advance word on the album was overwhelmingly positive, with many critics calling it one of the best records of the year. Four days before the album was released, Kurt Cobain's body was discovered in the couple's Seattle home; he had died of a self-inflicted shotgun wound three days before.

Two months after Cobain's death, Kristen M. Pfaff was found dead of a heroin overdose in a Seattle apartment. Two months later, Hole began touring again, with bassist Melissa Auf Der Maur taking Pfaff's place. "Doll Parts" was released as a single late in 1994, climbing into the Top 60 by the beginning of 1995. *Live Through This* topped many critics' polls at the end of the year, including *Rolling Stone* and the *Village Voice*. After *Live Through This* went gold in the summer of 1995, Hole toured with the fifth Lollapalooza tour. *— Stephen Thomas Erlewine*

Pretty on the Inside / 1991 / Caroline ✦✦✦
● **Live Through This** / 1994 / DGC ✦✦✦✦
On their second album, Hole's sound matures without losing its vital edge. Love's songwriting is more melodic and succinct, which makes the band's raging guitars and naked honesty all the more effective. *— Stephen Thomas Erlewine*

Hollies

British Invasion, Pop-Rock
One of the best and most commercially successful pop-rock acts of the British Invasion, when the Hollies began recording in 1963, they relied heavily upon the R&B/early rock 'n' roll covers that provided the staple diet for countless British bands of the time. They quickly developed a more distinctive style of three-part harmonies (heavily influenced by the Everly Brothers), ringing guitars, and hook-happy material, penned by both outside writers (especially Graham Gouldman) and themselves, eventually composing most of their repertoire on their own. The best early Hollies records evoke an infectious, melodic cheer similar to that of the early Beatles, although the Hollies were neither in their class (not an insult: nobody else was) nor demonstrated a similar capacity for artistic growth. They tried, though, easing into somewhat more sophisticated folk-rock and mildly psychedelic sounds as the decade wore on, especially on their albums (which contain quite a few overlooked highlights).

Allan Clarke (lead singer) and Graham Nash (vocals, guitar) had been friends since childhood in Manchester, and formed the nucleus of the Hollies in the early '60s with bassist Eric Haydock. In early 1963, EMI producer Ron Richards signed the group after seeing them at the famous Cavern Club in Liverpool. Guitarist Vic Steele left before the first session, to be replaced by 17-year-old Tony Hicks. Drummer Don Rathbone only lasted for a couple of singles before being replaced by Bobby Elliott, who had played with Hicks in his pre-Hollies group, the Dolphins. The lineup changes were most fortuitous: Hicks contributed a lot to the group with his ringing guitar work and songwriting, and Elliott was one of the very finest drummers in all of pop-rock.

Although their first singles were R&B covers, the Hollies were no match for the Rolling Stones (or for that matter the Beatles) in this department, and were much more at home with pop-rock material that provided a sympathetic complement to their glittering harmonies. They ran off an awesome series of hits in the UK in the '60s, making the Top 20 almost 20 times. Some of their best mid-'60s singles, like "Here I Go Again," "We're Through," and the British No. 1 "I'm Alive," passed virtually unnoticed in the US, where they couldn't make the Top 40 until early 1966, when Graham Gouldman's "Look Through Any Window" did the trick. In 1966, Eric Haydock left the group under cloudy circumstances, replaced by Bernie Calvert.

The Hollies really didn't break in America in a big way until "Bus Stop" (1966), their first stateside Top Tenner; "On a Carousel," "Carrie Ann," and "Stop Stop Stop" were also big hits. Here the Hollies were providing something of a satisfying option for pop-oriented listeners who found the increasingly experimental outings of groups like the Beatles and Kinks too difficult to follow. At the same time, the production and harmonies were sophisticated enough to maintain a broader audience than more teen- and bubblegum-oriented British Invasion acts like Herman's Hermits. Their albums showed a more serious and ambitious side, particularly on the part of Graham Nash, without ever escaping the truth that their forte was well-executed pop-rock, not serious statements.

Nash, however, itched to make an impression as a more serious artist, particularly on the "King Midas in Reverse" single (1967). Its relatively modest commecial success didn't augur well for his influence over the band's direction, and their next 45s were solidly in the more tried-and-true romantic tradition. By 1968, though, Nash really felt constrained by the band's commercial orientation, and by the end of the year he was gone, leaving for the States to help found Crosby, Stills, & Nash. His departure really marked the end of the group's peak era.

In 1969, the band tried to have their cake and eat it too by doing a whole album of Hollie-ized Dylan songs, which was received poorly by some critics, although it was a decent seller in Britain. Nash was replaced by Terry Sylvester (formerly of Liverpool bands the Escorts and Swinging Blue Jeans), and the hit streak continued for a while. "He Ain't Heavy, He's My Brother," in fact, was one of their biggest international singles. But the group was really reaching a cul de sac; they'd managed a remarkably long run at the top considering that they hadn't changed their formula much since the mid-'60s, adding enough sophistication to the lyrics and arrangements to avoid sounding markedly dated. It was apparent they really weren't capable of producing long-playing works striking enough to appeal to the album audience, though, and their singles, though still hits on occasion, weren't as memorable as their best '60s work.

A modest slide in the early '70s was arrested by "Long Cool Woman in a Black Dress," a Creedence Clearwater Revival-type rocker that made No. 2 in the States in 1972. The timing wasn't ideal; by the time it became a smash, Clarke, who had sung lead on the single, had left to go solo, to be replaced by Swedish vocalist Mikael Rikfors. Clarke rejoined in mid-1973, and the group had one last international monster, "The Air That I Breathe," which made No. 6 in the US in 1974. The Hollies recorded several other albums in the 1970s and 1980s, and toured often; Graham Nash even rejoined them for a 1983 album. Their post-mid-'70s output, however, is only for fanatics; it's the '60s classics that continue to hold enduring appeal. —*Richie Unterberger*

Evolution / 1967 / Epic ✦✦

The EP Collection / Apr. 1987 / See For Miles ✦✦✦

● **All Time Greatest Hits** / 1990 / Curb ✦✦✦✦
A 12-track all-singles compilation that includes the Hollies' biggest US hits on both Imperial ("Bus Stop," "Stop, Stop, Stop") and Epic Records from 1964 to 1975. —*William Ruhlmann*

● **Epic Anthology** / 1990 / Epic ✦✦✦✦
A 20-track compilation that picks up when The Hollies signed with Epic in 1967 and presents their biggest hits plus select album tracks and rarities through 1975. Includes "Carrie-Anne," "He Ain't Heavy, He's My Brother," "Long Cool Woman (In a Black Dress)," and "The Air That I Breathe." —*William Ruhlmann*

Thirtieth Anniversary Collection 1963-1993 / 1993 / EMI America ✦✦✦✦
This three-CD, 57-track box set does a good if imperfect job of encapsulating the legacy of one of the British Invasion's better bands. This includes all of the Hollies' singles, A- and B-sides, from the '60s, as well as five previously unreleased tunes. The hits—"I'm Alive," "Bus Stop," "On a Carousel," and others—contain some of the finest beat harmonizing not done by the Beatles. The B-sides—many of them originals, some of them never before available in the US—are often nearly equal in quality to the classic material. The compilation wisely touches upon only the essentials of their post-1970 singles ("Long Cool Woman" and "The Air That I Breathe"), and unwisely closes with three forgettable tracks from the early '90s. Don't be misled, however, that this box contains all of their best material—their early albums, though inconsistent, featured a fair number of strong original tunes which remain little known beyond collector circles. It's a good set, with an excellent booklet and thoroughly annotated discography, but not definitive. —*Richie Unterberger*

Brenda Holloway

b. Jun. 21, 1946, Atascadero, CA
Violin, Vocals / Soul, Motown
This sultry '60s addition to the Motown roster waxed several memorable ballads for the firm. One of Motown's first Los Angeles signings, Holloway's Tamla debut, "Every Little Bit Hurts," was a soaring ballad that sailed up the pop charts in 1964, which the Smokey Robinson wrote and produced Holloway's 1965 smash "When I'm Gone." The voluptuous vocalist opened several concerts for the Beatles on their 1965 US tour, including their Shea Stadium show. In 1967 Holloway co-wrote and recorded the original version of "You've Made Me So Very Happy," later a gigantic hit for Blood, Sweat & Tears. —*Bill Dahl*

Every Little Bit Hurts / 1964 / Motown ✦✦✦

● **Greatest Hits & Rare Classics** / 1991 / Motown ✦✦✦✦
Brenda Holloway was Motown's second big solo female star, but she spent even less time at the label than Mary Wells. A hard-edged, gospel-tinged belter, Holloway scored two Top 20 hits in the mid-'60s with "Every Little Bit Hurts" and "When I'm Gone," and her single "You've Made Me So Very Happy" was later a huge smash for Blood, Sweat & Tears. Holloway lasted on Motown until 1967, then departed after becoming a born-again Christian. This album includes her biggest singles for Tamla, plus some other good, though not necessarily classic, 1960s soul numbers. —*Ron Wynn*

Buddy Holly (Charles Hardin Holley)

b. Sep. 7, 1936, Lubbock, TX, d. Feb. 3, 1959, Mason City, IA
Guitar, Vocals / Rock 'n' Roll, Rockabilly
An enormously important and influential performer, Buddy Holly started in his native Texas doing country music with boyhood friend Bob Montgomery, eventually adding R&B numbers to the set list after meeting Elvis Presley. He recorded early rockabilly sides in Nashville, resulting in the Decca singles "Blue Days, Black Nights" (Apr. 1956) and "Modern Don Juan" (Dec. 1956). But success didn't come until he formed the Crickets and recorded in Norman Petty's New Mexico studio, producing the No. 1 hit "That'll Be the Day" (May 1957). Holly and Petty experimented in the studio, utilizing double-tracking ("Words of Love" [June 1957]), different forms of echo ("Peggy Sue" [September 1957], a second gold-selling Top Ten hit), and close-miking techniques, now commonplace in the industry. Holly recorded under his own name and the name of the Crickets interchangeably ("That'll Be the Day" was credited to the group, "Peggy Sue" to him alone). With the Crickets, he had the further chart hits "Oh, Boy!" (Oct. 1957) (another Top Ten), "Maybe Baby" (Feb. 1958), and "Think It Over"/"Fool's Paradise" (May 1958), while "Rave On" (Apr. 1958) was a Holly "solo" hit. Holly went solo for real during 1958, however, marrying and relocating to New York. He charted with "Early in the Morning" (Jul. 1958) and "Heartbeat" (Nov. 1958), and released "It Doesn't Matter Anymore"/"Raining in My Heart" (Jan. 1959) before

embarking on the Winter Dance Party package tour, during which he, the Big Bopper, and Ritchie Valens were killed in an airplane crash.

After Holly's death, much of his earlier pre-Crickets music was overdubbed by Petty, using the Fireballs, to keep up with fan demand for more product. In England, where "It Doesn't Matter Anymore" went to No. 1 in the wake of his death, Holly continued to score hits through the mid-'60s, and he exerted tremendous influence on the developing beat groups both for his music and for his self-contained approach to his work—writing his own songs, playing them with his own group. As late as 1978, Holly could still top the UK charts with a hits collection, *20 Golden Greats*.

Buddy Holly's moment in the spotlight lasted barely 18 months, and the movie version of his life story only got it about half right, but his music still sounds fresh and continues to influence musicians to this day. —*Cub Koda & William Ruhlmann*

The Chirping Crickets / 1957 / MCA ✦✦✦✦
The debut album by the Crickets and the only one featuring Buddy Holly released during his lifetime, *The Chirping Crickets* contains the group's No. 1 single "That'll Be The Day" and its Top ten hit "Oh, Boy!" Other Crickets classics include "Not Fade Away," "Maybe Baby," and "I'm Looking for Someone to Love." The rest of the 12 tracks are not up to the standard set by those five, but those five are among the best rock 'n' roll songs of the 1950s or ever, making this one of the most significant album debuts in rock 'n' roll history, ranking with *Elvis Presley* and *Meet the Beatles*. —*William Ruhlmann*

☆ **The Complete Buddy Holly** / 1979 / MCA ✦✦✦✦✦
In the wake of the No. 1 British ranking for *20 Golden Greats* in 1978 and the release of the feature film *The Buddy Holly Story*, MCA UK assembled this six-LP box set (which finally was released in the US in February 1981). It traces Buddy Holly's career from his country & western duo with Bob Montgomery in 1954/1955 to his 1956 Nashville sessions for Decca Records, the Clovis, NM, recordings with the Crickets and producer Norman Petty that launched his career in 1957, the New York sessions of 1958, the final 1958 demo recordings, the various posthumously overdubbed versions of the demos, and other assorted rarities. In other words, all the material that Decca/MCA previously had spread across seven LPs—*The "Chirping" Crickets, Buddy Holly, That'll Be the Day, Reminiscing, Showcase, Holly in the Hills,* and *Giant*—between 1957 and 1969 (not counting the many compilations) was here, plus more. The box also contained an extensive scrapbook, lots of liner notes, and a detailed discography. It was, thus, the state of the art in box sets just prior to the CD era, and given Holly's importance in the history of rock 'n' roll, an essential album for any serious collector. With the passing of the LP era, it is out of print, and MCA claims to be gathering more unreleased material for some comparable box set, though years go by without its appearing. Meanwhile, if you needed one record album to demonstrate what the most popular music of the second half of the 20th century sounded like, this would be it. —*William Ruhlmann*

★ **From the Original Master Tapes** / 1985 / MCA ✦✦✦✦✦
From the Original Master Tapes is the best single-disc collection of Buddy Holly, featuring 20 of his biggest hits. Although the songs aren't presented in chronological order, the disc flows well, running through every one of his hits and all of his best-known songs—"That'll Be the Day," "Peggy Sue," "Oh, Boy!," "Maybe Baby," "Rave On," "Think It Over," "Heartbeat," "It Doesn't Matter Anymore," "Raining in My Heart," "Everyday," "Not Fade Away," "Well . . . All Right," and many others. A few terrific songs are missing, but *From the Original Master Tapes* remains a first-rate introduction and a nearly definitive retrospective of Holly's brief career. —*Stephen Thomas Erlewine*

☆ **The Buddy Holly Collection** / 1993 / MCA ✦✦✦✦✦
The first comprehensive, remastered CD retrospective of Holly's work, including early tracks recorded in the Holly family garage, the Owen Bradley-produced singles, all the rockin' hits, orchestrated ballads, and tracks overdubbed with instrumentation after Holly's tragic death. Two discs, solid liner notes. —*Roch Parisien*

Hollywood Flames

Doo Wop
Long-lasting Los Angeles doo wop aggregation with a very fluid personnel roster. Bobby Day was one of the group's founders in 1950, and they recorded prolifically for Hollywood, Specialty, Lucky, Swingtime, Money, and other firms before cutting their one major hit, the rocking "Buzz Buzz Buzz," in 1957 for Ebb Records. Earl Nelson, who was later half of Bob and Earl, sang lead on the tune, and some of their subsequent Ebb 45s were rocking novelties. Day went on to solo success with "Rockin' Robin," and the group managed one more chart item, "Gee," for Chess in 1961 with Donald Height as lead. —*Bill Dahl*

● **The Hollywood Flames** / 1992 / Specialty ✦✦✦✦
Rockers and doo wop are included from this respected West Coast '50s R&B vocal group, including the Top Ten "Buzz Buzz Buzz." —*Bill Dahl*

Holsapple-Stamey

Power-Pop

During the early '80s, guitarist/vocalist Chris Stamey and keyboardist/guitarist/vocalist Peter Holsapple led the dB's, one of the premier jangle-pop bands of the American pop underground. Stamey left the group in 1983, but Holsapple led the band until its final album, 1987's *The Sound of Music.* Four years after the dB's broke up, Holsapple and Stamey reunited to record an album that was in the vein of their previous collaborations. Released in 1991, *Mavericks*—the only album they ever released as a duo—received good reviews but didn't sell well. After the release of *Mavericks,* Stamey returned to his solo career and Holsapple formed the Continental Drifters with his wife Susan Cowsill. In 1994, Holsapple re-formed the dB's and the group released *Paris Avenue* later in the year. —*Stephen Thomas Erlewine*

Mavericks / 1991 / Rhino ✦✦✦✦
A charming low-key power-pop effort, "Geometry" is a perfect Gary Lewis & the Playboys-style sendup. "Angels" is pure power-pop magic. The softer acoustic numbers, "Close Your Eyes" and "Anymore," recall the duo's work on *Repercussions.* —*Rick Clark*

The Honeycombs

British Invasion

Mostly renowned for their 1964 Top Five hit "Have I the Right," the Honeycombs were pretty much a front for producer Joe Meek and their songwriting-management team of Ken Howard and Alan Blaikley. With bee-sting guitar leads and lead singer Dennis O'Dell's wobbling vocals, which sounded like a Gene Pitney unable to hold notes, "Have I the Right" was a single that you either loved or hated, but couldn't forget. The relatively faceless group afforded Meek perhaps his fullest artistic expression in the studio; all the Honeycombs' singles and albums feature vari-speed vocals, ghostly organ, unpredictable clavoline runs, majestically thudding drums, and super-compressed sonics. The group managed a couple more minor American hits, "Is It Because" and the thrilling "I Can't Stop," as well as another British Top 20 hit, "That's the Way," and cut quite a few singles and two albums before Meek's death in early 1967 effectively finished the group as well. The Honeycombs' material can be annoyingly cloying and lightweight, but the eerie melodies and production continue to fascinate. —*Richie Unterberger*

● **The Honeycombs** / 1964 / Repertoire ✦✦✦✦
Most famed for their 1964 one-shot British Invasion hit "Have I the Right" and for being the first rock band of any renown to feature a female drummer, the Honeycombs recorded a surprising amount of material in the mid-'60s. Even for collectors, this definitely falls into the "guilty pleasure" category. Lead singer Dennis O'Dell's wobbly voice sounds like a speeded-up Gene Pitney, and the material, though peppy and catchy, is exceedingly trite and innocuous. The group's chief asset, actually, was producer Joe Meek, who found the band to be a perfect vehicle for his eccentric production techniques. Meek used compression to the point of squashing, and used all manners of odd vari-speed vocals, bee-stinging guitars, tinny keyboards, and echo to achieve a sound that was quite otherwordly by 1964 standards. Besides "Have I the Right," this 1964 debut LP includes the British Top 20 hit "That's the Way" (featuring drummer Honey Lantree on vocals) and the ghostly ballads "Without You It Is Night" and "This Too Shall Pass Away," though most of the rest of the material is slight. This 1990 reissue adds seven bonus tracks from non-LP singles, including a German recording of "Have I the Right" and the manic, irresistible "I Can't Stop," which was a minor hit for the band in the US. —*Richie Unterberger*

All Systems Go / 1965 / Repertoire ✦✦✦

Best of the Honeycombs / 1988 / PRT ✦✦✦
The German Repertoire label has reissued both of the Honeycombs' studio LPs with bonus tracks; oddly, they don't include quite a few of the group's A-sides. All six of those missing singles can be found on this reissue, along with most of their other best-known songs. Two of these A-sides are standouts: "Is It Because," a small hit in the UK, is a driving number, and "Eyes" one of the spookiest productions from a man (Joe Meek) who specialized in them. If you pick this up thinking you'll forego the fanatically repackaged CDs for a 14-song greatest hits collection of this interesting but minor British Invasion band, be warned: the version of "I Can't Stop," the minor US hit that was their best song, included here is not the original, but an inferior remake from their second album. —*Richie Unterberger*

Hootie & The Blowfish

Pop-Rock

Hootie & the Blowfish's mainstream pop variation of blues-rock brought the band to the top of the charts in 1995. Formed at the University of South Carolina, the group features lead vocalist/guitarist Darius Rucker, Mark Bryan, Dean Felber, and Jim "Soni" Sonefeld; the name refers to

two friends of the band, not Rucker and the group itself. *Cracked Rear View,* the group's first album, was released in the fall of 1994 and a single, "Hold My Hand," worked its way into the Top Ten by the beginning of 1995. Its success propelled the album to No. 1, as well as launching a second hit, "Let Her Cry," which was quickly followed by "Only Wanna Be with You."

Cracked Rear View had become a massive success by the fall of 1995, going platinum several times over. By the time the group released their second album, *Fairweather Johnson,* in the spring of 1996, the debut had sold 13 million copies in the US alone. *Fairweather Johnson* initially didn't replicate that success. It entered the charts at No. 1 and sold two million copies within its first four months of release, but it didn't produce any hit singles on the level of the debut's "Hold My Hand" or "Let Her Cry." —*Stephen Thomas Erlewine*

● **Cracked Rear View** / 1994 / Atlantic ✦✦✦✦
Hootie and the Blowfish's debut album *Cracked Rear View* was the success story of 1994/1995, selling over 12 million copies. It's a startling large number, especially for a new band, but in some ways, the success of the record isn't that surprising. Although Hootie and the Blowfish aren't innovative, they deliver the goods, turning out an album of solid, rootsy folk-rock that have simple, powerful hooks. "Hold My Hand" has a sing-along chorus that epitomizes the band's good-times vibes. None of the tracks transcend their generic status, but they are strong songs for their genre, with crisp chords and bright melodies. Still, the songs wouldn't be convincing without the emotive vocals of Darius Rucker, whose gruff baritone has more grit than the actual songs. At their core, Hootie and the Blowfish is a bar band, but they managed to convince millions of listeners that they were the local bar band, and that's why *Cracked Rear View* was a major success. —*Stephen Thomas Erlewine*

Fairweather Johnson / Apr. 1996 / Atlantic ✦✦✦

Bruce Hornsby & the Range

b. Nov. 23, 1954, Williamsburg, VA

Adult Contemporary, Pop-Rock

Hornsby was born in Williamsburg, VA, and grew up in that combination college town and tourist center, later attending the University of Miami and the Berklee School of Music. He then spent years playing in bars and sending demo tapes to record companies. In 1980, he and his brother (and songwriting partner) John Hornsby moved to Los Angeles, where they spent three years writing for 20th Century Fox. There Bruce Hornsby met Huey Lewis, who would eventually produce him and record his material. Hornsby finally signed his band, the Range, to RCA in 1985.

Their debut album, *The Way It Is,* was released in August 1986. It eventually produced three Top 20 hits, the biggest of which was the socially conscious "The Way It Is," which featured Hornsby's characteristically melodic right-hand piano runs. The album stayed in the charts almost a year and a half, and sold two million copies. Hornsby and the Range won the Best New Artist Grammy Award for 1986.

Hornsby's second album, *Scenes from the Southside,* was not as successful as his debut, though it sold a million copies, and produced the Top Ten single "The Valley Road." Hornsby also began to make his mark as a songwriter for others: Huey Lewis had a hit with his "Jacob's Ladder," as did Don Henley with "The End of the Innocence."

Hornsby worked extensively as a producer and sideman in the early '90s, notably doing temporary duty in the Grateful Dead after their keyboardist, Brent Mydland, died in July 1990, and producing a comeback album for Leon Russell, an idol of Hornsby's. He also became the father of twin sons. He finally turned in his fourth album, *Harbor Lights,* for release in 1993. This solo album, which did not feature his backup band, the Range, went gold, and Hornsby toured the US and Canada through the end of the year. He followed it with a similar effort, *Hot House,* in July 1995. —*William Ruhlmann*

● **The Way It Is** / Aug. 1986 / RCA ✦✦✦✦
One of the best collections of new songs released in the 1980s, performed to perfection by a versatile band led by a seasoned (if new to the listener) artist. The songs provide an American panorama, in terms both of landscape and social mores. This is smart, compassionate music for thinking adults . . . and you can dance to it, too. Includes "The Way It Is" and "Mandolin Rain." —*William Ruhlmann*

Scenes from the Southside / 1988 / RCA ✦✦✦✦
The Way It Is, part two, featuring some wonderful story songs, not only on the hits "Jacob's Ladder" and "The Valley Road" but also "Defenders of the Flag" and "The Road Not Taken." Hornsby continues to mine a rich American vein on this album. —*William Ruhlmann*

A Night on the Town / Jun. 1990 / RCA ✦✦✦

Harbor Lights / 1993 / RCA ✦✦✦

Hot House / 1995 / RCA ✦✦✦

House of Love

Alternative Pop-Rock

The post-Smiths guitar pop of the House of Love was popular for a short time in the late '80s, as many college and alternative-rock fans became converts to their mixture of shiny ringing guitars, pseudo-psychedelic melodies and bursts of noise. The British group formed in 1986; it featured Guy Chadwick (vocals, guitar), Terry Bickers (guitar), Andrea Heukamp (vocals, guitar), Pete Evans (drums), and Chris Groothuizen (bass). Their demo tape attracted the attention of Alan McGee, the head of Creation Records. McGee signed the band for a single, "Shine On," which was released in May of 1987 to some critical acclaim; it and its follow-up, "Real Animal," both sold poorly. Following a tour supporting the singles, Heukamp left the group. Instead of replacing her, the House of Love continued as a quartet, releasing their untitled debut album in the spring of 1988. Many UK critics called it one of the finest records of the year, and the band built up a cult audience.

The following year the band moved over to PhonoGram Records (PolyGram in the US) and released two singles, "Never" and "I Don't Know Why I Love You," that failed to crack the British Top 40. By the end of 1989, Bickers left the group; he was replaced by Simon Walker. The House of Love's second untitled album (commonly called *Fontana*) was released in early 1990 to lukewarm sales and reviews; the band's revivalist guitar pop didn't fit in with England's club-conscious pop scene, spearheaded by the Stone Roses and Happy Mondays. After the group's 1990 tour, Walker left the group and was replaced by Andrea Heukamp. The House of Love returned in early 1992 with *Babe Rainbow*, which received favorable reviews yet weak sales. The continuing lack of commercial success began to wear on the band, leading to their disbandment in 1994. — *Stephen Thomas Erlewine*

● **House of Love ['88]** / 1988 / Combat ✦✦✦✦
This brilliant debut established a pattern oft-imitated: a layered, swirling guitar sound and outstanding songs as well. — *Steve Aldrich*

House of Love ['90] / 1990 / Fontana ✦✦✦
A strong second album, it never quite reaches the highs of their debut. — *Steve Aldrich*

Spy in the House of Love / 1990 / Fontana ✦✦✦

Babe Rainbow / 1992 / Fontana ✦✦✦

Audience with the Mind / 1994 / PolyGram ✦✦

Housemartins

Alternative Pop-Rock, Pop-Rock

The Housemartins were formed in Hull, England, in 1984 and included singer/guitarist Paul Heaton, bassist Stan Cullimore, drummer Hugh Witaker, and Ted Key. They signed to the independent Go! Discs label in October 1985. Shortly after, vocalist Norman Cook (b. Jul 31, 1963) replaced Key. The group's first substantial success came with its third single, "Happy Hour," which reached No. 3 in the UK in June 1986. The Housemartins' debut album, *London 0 Hull 4*, reached the same position in the album chart. More success followed with the singles "Think for a Minute" and the chart-topping cover of Isley-Jasper-Isley's "Caravan of Love." In 1987, the Housemartins continued to hit in the UK, while suffering adverse press and personnel conflicts that eventually convinced them to split in 1988. They released two more albums, *The People Who Grinned Themselves to Death* (1987) and *Now That's What I Call Quite Good* (1988), the latter a double-disc compilation that has not been released in the US. Heaton went on to form the Beautiful South. — *William Ruhlmann*

● **London 0 Hull 4** / 1986 / Go! Discs ✦✦✦✦
The Housemartins had a bouncy pop-rock sound that was reminiscent of the British beat groups of the mid-'60s. This album is full of catchy tunes, although the lyrics are sometimes more serious than the music might suggest. — *William Ruhlmann*

The People Who Grinned Themselves to Death / 1987 / Go! Discs ✦✦✦✦
Not quite on par with their debut, their second album nevertheless contains some bright moments of bouncy Brit pop. The band takes a more abstract lyrical approach but the song craftsmanship can't be denied. The band broke up shortly after its completion. — *Chris Woodstra*

Now That's What I Call Quite Good / 1988 / Go! Discs ✦✦✦✦
A solid collection of singles, B-sides and rarities released in the UK. This, combined with the two albums, represents most of the band's recorded output. Clocking in at over 70 minutes, this is not a bad place to start, though the actual albums should be heard as well. — *Chris Woodstra*

Cissy Houston

Soul

A terrific soul singer who is known primarily as Whitney Houston's mother rather than for her own considerable talents, Houston was born

Emily Drinkard, and began her career as a member of her family's gospel group, the Drinkards. In the early '60s, she joined forces with a floating group of singers, known simply as "the Group" (including at various points Doris Troy and Dee Dee Warwick), to provide backup vocals on numerous soul, pop, and rock sessions. They contributed to many Atlantic sessions in particular, and Atlantic executive Jerry Wexler signed the act to the label in 1967. Named the Sweet Inspirations, they recorded some excellent gospel-flavored soul in the late '60s, managing a few hits (as well as continuing to back up other artists, most notably Aretha Franklin) before Cissy left to go solo at the end of 1969. Houston recorded an impressive album for Commonwealth United in 1970, *Presenting Cissy Houston*, which yielded a couple small R&B/pop hits, "I'll Be There" and "Be My Baby." Much in the manner of the Sweet Inspirations, although the material consisted of fairly well-worn soul, rock, and pop tunes, the state-of-the-art arrangements and gospelish vocals made them sound fresh. Her contract was sold to Janus Records later in the year, and while she issued a few fine singles there until the middle of the 1970s, she never received the support and promotion she deserved. A case in point was her little-known original version of "Midnight Train to Georgia," taken to the top of the charts about a year later by Gladys Knight & the Pips. Houston recorded several albums for Private Stock beginning in the late '70s, as well as continuing her regular work on sessions and commercial jingles. She recorded a duet with daughter Whitney ("I Know Him So Well") in 1987, and cut a duet album with veteran soul singer Chuck Jackson in 1992. — *Richie Unterberger*

● **Midnight Train to Georgia: The Janus Years** / 1995 / Ichiban Soul Classics ✦✦✦✦
Fine 21-track compilation of almost everything she recorded between 1970 and 1975, including most of her 1970 album *Presenting Cissy Houston*, ten songs that were previously available only on singles, and a couple that were previously unreleased in the US. Highlights include excellent interpretations of two Bacharach-David classics ("I Just Don't Know What to Do with Myself," "This Empty Place") and Tim Hardin's "Hang On to a Dream," as well as the original version of "Midnight Train to Georgia." — *Richie Unterberger*

Penelope Houston

Autoharp, Vocals, Melodica / Singer-Songwriter, Alternative Pop-Rock

Houston is one of the most shocking reincarnations from the original punk era. She was the lead singer of the San Francisco band the Avengers, one of the very first full-out American punk acts, opening for the Sex Pistols on the last show of their legendary US tour. After the group broke up in 1979, Houston worked for a time with Howard Devoto, and released a 1986 single fronting the short-lived -30-, finally releasing her debut album in 1988. To the shock of those who remembered her work with the Avengers, Houston had transformed into a folk-rock singer-songwriter with alternative rock sensibilities. As a solo act, her material emphasizes acoustic textures, haunting melodies, and her gentle soprano voice. Popular as a performing act in San Francisco, she has had trouble finding recording deals. Her similar, somewhat more fully produced second album did not appear until 1993 (a couple cassette-only releases mixing live and studio material appeared in the interim). Fans of singer-songwriters like Suzanne Vega, Shawn Colvin, and Christine Lavin looking for something similar but darker would do well to check Houston out. — *Richie Unterberger*

● **Birdboys** / 1988 / Subterranean ✦✦✦✦
A moody, melodic debut that evokes the spirit of Nick Drake and Sandy Denny with its brooding images of loss. Mandolins, accordion, acoustic bass, and sparse percussion (usually tambourines and bells) almost qualify this as a contemporary folk album, but Houston's biting and somber approach draws from her punk and alternative-rock roots. The writing is inconsistent, and Houston's fragile voice is sometimes not as forceful as the material seems to demand, but overall this is one of the more underrated alternative music statements of the late 1980s. — *Richie Unterberger*

The Whole World / 1993 / Heyday ✦✦✦
Similar in tone to her debut, but bouncier and more engaging, prominently featuring her husband Mel Pappas on mandolin. Mature and introspective works that do their best to examine romance, innocence, aging, and compassion without sounding hackneyed, but it doesn't quite match the haunting power of her first album. — *Richie Unterberger*

Cut You / Mar. 5, 1996 / Reprise ✦✦✦
A curious disc in that it's more of a career survey than a collection of newly minted material, although all of these tracks were recorded shortly before the album was issued, as is the standard for new releases. Many of the songs were released in different versions on previous albums, some as long ago as 1988. This could be because it's Houston's first effort to benefit from major-label distribution, meaning that it will mark the first time that many listeners outside of the San Francisco Bay Area will be exposed to her material. That may make it a disappointment for those who've followed her career and have the original ver-

sions. But it's a solid set of melodic and inventively arranged folk-rock, with arrangements that differ from the originals in interesting ways that avoid redundancy. It also offers proof that Houston helped pioneer the melodic-yet-hard-hitting alternative rock currently mined by such performers as Liz Phair and Aimee Mann. Ironically, because of the timing of the release, it may be perceived as being just the opposite. —*Richie Unterberger*

Whitney Houston

b. Aug. 9, 1963, Newark, NJ
Vocals / Dance-Pop, Urban, Adult Contemporary, Pop-Rock, Club-Dance
Coming from a solid musical background, this daughter of soul singer Cissy Houston and cousin of Dionne Warwick debuted in 1985. Her first album, *Whitney Houston*, was the first in *Billboard* chart history by a woman to enter at No. 1; it sold 14 million copies. She scored heavily on MTV with classy videos, helping to break the "color barrier" originally knocked down by Michael Jackson. Her second album, *Whitney*, was just as popular, scoring seven consecutive No. 1s in the US, shattering the previous record held by the Beatles.

After the disappointing performance of her third album, *I'll Be Your Baby Tonight*, Houston rocketed back to the top of the charts in late 1992 with the soundtrack from her first movie, *The Bodyguard*. The love theme from the movie, a version of Dolly Parton's "I Will Always Love You," broke all previous sales and airplay records, becoming the biggest single in pop music history; it also won her an almost innumerable amount of awards, including several Grammies.

With pure pop music melded to stunning beauty, Houston's star shines bright whether she is singing ballads, uptempo dance material, the national anthem, or cola commercials. Almost ten years after her first album, she is one of the biggest stars in pop music. —*Cub Koda & Stephen Thomas Erlewine*

● **Whitney Houston** / 1985 / Arista ◆◆◆◆
The legend of Whitney Houston began with this self-titled album. It marked her shift away from the experimental songs she did with the group Material and a move into heavily produced, very slick urban contemporary and adult pop. Although Houston had learned her craft working in New York nightclubs and singing in a Baptist church in Newark, she was steered into radio-friendly ballads that emphasized style over substance. The album did yield an unprecedented string of No. 1 hits, but "Saving All My Love for You" and "How Will I Know" created an impression of an incredibly talented vocalist using only a minimum of her skills. It also contained one of her few legitimate soul workouts in "The Greatest Love of All." —*Ron Wynn*

Whitney / 1987 / Arista ◆◆◆◆
Whitney Houston became an international star with this album. It sold more than 13 million copies around the world, yielded a string of hit singles across the board like "How Will I Know," "Saving All My Love for You," and "You Give Good Love," and established Houston as the era's top female star. She has since gone to more than solidify that status, with other hit albums and now a budding film career. While this is a far cry from soul, it's the ultimate in polished, super-produced urban contemporary material. —*Ron Wynn*

I'm Your Baby Tonight / 1990 / Arista ◆◆

H.P. Lovecraft

Psychedelic
Featuring two strong singers (who often sang dual leads), hauntingly hazy arrangements, and imaginative songwriting that drew from pop and folk influences, H.P. Lovecraft were one of the better psychedelic groups of the late '60s. The band was formed by ex-folkie George Edwards in Chicago in 1967. Edwards and keyboardist Dave Michaels, a classically trained singer with a four-octave range, handled the vocals, which echoed The Jefferson Airplane's in their depth and blend of high and low parts. Their self-titled 1967 LP was an impressive debut, featuring strong originals and covers of early compositions by Randy Newman and Fred Neil, as well as one of the first underground FM radio favorites, "White Ship." The band moved to California the following year; their second and last album, *H.P. Lovecraft II*, was a much more sprawling and unfocused work, despite some strong moments. A spin-off group, Lovecraft, released a couple LPs in the '70s that bore little relation to the first incarnation of the band. —*Richie Unterberger*

H.P. Lovecraft / 1967 / Philips ◆◆◆◆
With the exception of a couple of badly dated tracks, this is one of the best second-division psychedelic albums, with strong material that shows the immediately identifiable Edwards-Michaels vocal tandem at its best. According to the LP notes, the songs were largely inspired by novelist H.P. Lovecraft's "macabre tales and poems of Earth populated by another race." It's more haunting than gloomy, though, with deft touches of folk, jazz, and horns. —*Richie Unterberger*

H.P. Lovecraft II / 1968 / Philips ◆◆◆
Much more progressive than their first effort, the album also showed the band losing touch with some of their most obvious strengths, most notably their disciplined arrangements and incisive songwriting. The arrangements are more swirling and far denser on this follow-up. Unsurprisingly, the more concise, dual harmony numbers that bear the closest resemblance to the first album work best, especially "At the Mountains of Madness." —*Richie Unterberger*

● **At the Mountains of Madness** / 1988 / Edsel ◆◆◆◆
A superb double-album package of all of their studio material. Includes both LPs, historical liner notes, and a 1967 non-LP single (released prior to their debut) that is much poppier than their albums. —*Richie Unterberger*

Live May 11, 1968 / 1991 / Sundazed ◆◆◆

Human League

Dance-Pop, New Wave, Club-Dance, New Romantic
The Human League scored a number of hits in the '80s that crossed the line between post-new wave rock and dance-pop, though that was a very different style from the music the group played at first. The Human League was formed in Sheffield, England, in 1977 by synthesizer players Martin Ware (b. May 19, 1956) and Ian Marsh (b. Nov 11, 1956), along with Addy Newton and singer Philip Oakey (b. Oct 2, 1955). Newton was soon replaced by Adrian Wright and the lineup held for the first two Human League albums, *Reproduction* (1979) and *Travelogue* (1980).

Ware and Marsh left The Human League in October 1980 (they subsequently formed Heaven 17). Oakey and Wright recruited bassist Ian Burden (b. Dec 24, 1957) and backup singers Joanne Catherall (b. Sep 18, 1962) and Susanne Sulley (b. Mar 22, 1963), resulting in a much more pop-sounding version of the band. Synth player Jo Callis (b. May 2, 1955) was added to the group.

The Human League's third album, *Dare*, was its commercial and international breakthrough. Released in October 1981 in the UK and in February 1982 in the US, it went to No. 1 in England and No. 3 in the US, largely on the strength of the single "Don't You Want Me," which topped the charts in both countries. Subsequent hits in 1982 and 1983 included "(Keep Feeling) Fascination" and "Mirror Man."

Hysteria (1984) was far less successful, and the group agonized over a follow-up. *Crash* appeared in 1986, produced by Jimmy Jam and Terry Lewis (responsible for Janet Jackson's *Control*, among other hits). Largely a studio creation, it was nevertheless successful, producing the No. 1 hit "Human." The Human League's sixth album, *Romantic?*, was released in 1990. —*William Ruhlmann*

Dare / 1981 / A&M ◆◆◆◆
Martin Rushent's fresh, clean production keeps the synthesized music from being too cluttered, while Philip Oakey's voice is used for its self-consciously melodramatic effect and contrasted with the untrained singing of Joanne Catherall and Susanne Sulley. The hits are "Don't You Want Me" and (in England) "The Sound of the Crowd," "Love Action (I Believe in Love)," and "Open Your Heart," but the album also works as a consistent piece. —*William Ruhlmann*

Fascination! / 1983 / A&M ◆◆◆

● **Greatest Hits** / 1988 / A&M ◆◆◆◆
Greatest Hits reminds that popular tracks like "Don't You Want Me" successfully bridged the gap between dance, pop, and rock audiences. With "Being Boiled," the 16-strong collection even offers a token sample of the League's earliest, more experimental machine music approach—although their atmospherically funereal cover of the Righteous Brothers' "You've Lost That Loving Feeling" should also have made the cut. Includes the rather engaging new recording "Stay with Me Tonight" from the currently active version of Phil Oakey and friends. —*Roch Parisien*

Humble Pie

Blues-Rock, Hard Rock
When Humble Pie was formed in 1969, there was much excitement about the possibilities. After all, its founding members came from very popular English bands. Humble Pie comprised vocalist and guitarist Steve Marriott, previously with the Small Faces; Greg Ridley, former bassist for Spooky Tooth; Peter Frampton, the Herd's frontman and guitarist; and drummer Jerry Shirley of Little Women.

The band's initial albums (on Andrew Oldham's Immediate Records) were surprisingly laidback and melodic. 1971 turned out to be the band's breakthrough to major success, due to a hard and loud double live album, *Performance—Live at the Fillmore*, which went to No. 21. Frampton left shortly thereafter to pursue a successful solo career, and Humble Pie progressively turned toward an over-amped boogie style of rock. During the next two years, Humble Pie made three more forays onto the album charts with *Smoking* (No. 6), *Eat It* (No. 13), and *Lost and Found* (No. 37), an anthology of their earlier Immediate label work.

In spite of substantial album popularity, Humble Pie never had a major single, with their only chart titles being "I Don't Need No Doctor" (No. 73) and "Hot 'N' Nasty" (No. 52). The group disbanded in 1981 and Steve Marriott later passed away. —*Rick Clark*

The Best of Humble Pie / 1982 / A&M ✦✦✦✦
A brief but entertaining collection of Humble Pie's finest moments, *The Best of Humble Pie* is an effective introduction to the group's loud boogie. —*Stephen Thomas Erlewine*

● **Classics, Vol. 14** / 1987 / A&M ✦✦✦✦
If you are looking for the one place to go for Humble Pie, this best-of collection covers the essentials, such as "I Don't Need No Doctor," "Stone Cold Fever," "30 Days in the Hole," "Hot N' Nasty," "C'Mon Everybody," and "Take Me Back." —*Rick Clark*

Hot N' Nasty—The Anthology / 1994 / A&M ✦✦✦✦
Album rock artists that never made great albums, Humble Pie are well served by *Hot N' Nasty*, a double-disc set that collects the hits and highlights from throughout their career. —*Stephen Thomas Erlewine*

Ian Hunter

b. Jun. 3, 1946, Shrewsbury, England
Guitar, Vocals / Rock 'n' Roll, Hard Rock
With Mott the Hoople, guitarist/vocalist Ian Hunter established himself as one of the toughest and most inventive hard-rock songwriters of the early '70s, setting the stage for punk rock with his edgy, intelligent songs. As a solo artist, Hunter never attained the commercial heights of Mott the Hoople but he cultivated a dedicated cult following.

Hunter was born in Shrewsbury but raised in cities throughout England, since his father worked in the British Intelligence agency called MI5 and had to move frequently. Eventually, the family returned to Shrewsbury, where the teenaged Hunter joined a band called Silence in the early '60s. Silence released an album, but it received no attention. In the years following Silence, Hunter played in a handful of local bands and worked a variety of jobs.

In 1968, Hunter began playing bass with Freddie "Fingers" Lee and the duo played around Germany. Shortly afterward, Hunter became the vocalist for Mott the Hoople. During the next six years, Hunter sang and played piano and guitar with the band, becoming its lead songwriter within a few albums. Although few of their records sold, Mott the Hoople was one of the most popular live bands in England, drawing large, fanatical crowds. In 1972, David Bowie produced their breakthrough album, *All the Young Dudes*, which brought the band into the British Top Ten and the American Top 40. For the next two years, the group had a consistent stream of hits in both the UK and the US. Toward the end of 1973, the band began to fall apart, as founding member and lead guitarist Mick Ralphs left the band. Ian Hunter carried through another album but he left the group in late 1974, taking along former Bowie guitarist Mick Ronson who had just joined Mott the Hoople. Just prior to leaving the group, Hunter published *Diary of a Rock Star*, an account of his years leading Mott the Hoople, in June of 1974.

Hunter moved to New York, where he and Ronson began working on his solo debut. Released in 1975, *Ian Hunter* spawned "Once Bitten, Twice Shy," a Top 20 UK hit. Following its release, Hunter and Ronson embarked on a tour. After its completion, the pair parted ways, although they would reunite later in the '80s. *All-American Alien Boy*, Hunter's second solo album, was recorded with a variety of all-star and session musicians, including members of Queen. Released in the summer of 1976, *All-American Alien Boy* was a commercial failure. It was followed in 1977 by *Overnight Angels*, an album that saw Hunter moving closer to straightforward rock 'n' roll; disappointed with the completed album, Hunter decided to leave the album unreleased in America.

Following the mainstream approach of *Overnight Angels*, Hunter became involved with England's burgeoning punk rock movement, producing Generation X's second album, 1979's *Beyond the Valley of the Dolls*. For Hunter's next solo album, he reunited with Mick Ronson, who produced and arranged 1979's *You're Never Alone with a Schizophrenic*. The album was a hit, especially in America where it peaked at No. 35. Hunter and Ronson set out on another tour, which resulted in the 1980 double live album, *Ian Hunter Live / Welcome to the Club*. In 1981, Ian Hunter released *Short Back and Sides*, which was produced by the Clash's Mick Jones. Two years later, he released *All of the Good Ones Are Taken*.

After *All of the Good Ones Are Taken*, Ian Hunter became a recluse, spending the next six years in silence; occasionally, he contributed a song to a movie soundtrack. In 1989, Hunter resumed recording, releasing *Yui Orta* with Mick Ronson. After its release, Hunter remained quiet during the '90s, appearing only on Ronson's posthumous 1994 album *Heaven and Hull* and at tribute concerts for Ronson in 1994 and Freddie Mercury in 1992. —*Stephen Thomas Erlewine*

Ian Hunter / 1975 / Columbia ✦✦✦✦
A spotty debut, but "Once Bitten Twice Shy," "Who Do You Love," and "I Get So Excited" rank with the best Mott the Hoople material. —*John Floyd*

All American Alien Boy / 1976 / Columbia ✦✦✦

Overnight Angels / 1977 / Columbia ✦✦

Shades of Ian Hunter / 1979 / Chrysalis ✦✦✦✦
A fine, if somewhat inconsistent, collection that features highlights from the early part of Ian Hunter's solo career as well as selections from Mott the Hoople's catalog, *Shades of Ian Hunter* is a good introduction to his work, even if it doesn't feature many of his best songs. —*Stephen Thomas Erlewine*

● **You're Never Alone with a Schizophrenic** / 1979 / Razor & Tie ✦✦✦✦
Hunter's post-punk return salutes the genre he helped spawn and brings that old Mott crunch to a fine set of energetic, if somewhat dated, rock 'n' roll. —*John Floyd*

Ian Hunter Live / Welcome to the Club / 1980 / Chrysalis ✦✦✦

Short Back and Sides / 1981 / Chrysalis ✦✦✦✦
Ian Hunter had been revitalized by punk rock, as *Short Back and Sides* shows. Featuring the Clash's Mick Jones on guitar, the music is a tougher and spikier take on Hunter's rock 'n' roll, and his songwriting is at a near-peak. —*Stephen Thomas Erlewine*

All of the Good Ones Are Taken / 1983 / Columbia ✦✦✦

Yui Orta / 1990 / Mercury ✦✦✦✦
Overlooked upon its release, this is Hunter's most lyrically ambitious and mature disc, with tight rockers and melancholy ballads working gloriously off one another. —*John Floyd*

Hüsker Dü

Alternative Pop-Rock, Hardcore Punk
Hüsker Dü and R.E.M. were the two American post-punk bands of the '80s that changed the direction of rock 'n' roll. R.E.M. became superstars; Hüsker Dü never was more than a cult favorite. Nevertheless, their albums between 1981 and 1987 have proven remarkably influential; they provided the sonic blueprint for the roaring punk-pop hybrid that crossed over into the mainstream in the early '90s. Not only did they shape the sound of the music, they shaped the way independent bands made the transition to the major labels; they showed other bands that it was possible to record uncompromising music on a major label without losing any integrity or creative control. From the Replacements to Nirvana, the Pixies to Superchunk, nearly every major and minor band that appeared in the alternative underground in the late '80s and '90s owed a major debt to Hüsker Dü, whether they were aware of it or not.

The band's two songwriters, guitarist Bob Mould and drummer Grant Hart, both had a knack for writing songs that essentially followed conventional pop structures, complete with memorable melodies, but were still punk songs. Hüsker Dü took the Buzzcocks' pioneering punk pop and made it harder, both musically and lyrically. Throughout their career, Hüsker Dü never lost their edge, never turned down their amplifiers, never compromised their music. While Hart and bassist Greg Norton were an unflailingly strong rhythm section, Mould would prove to be one of the most influential guitarists of the decade. With his slashing rhythms, distorted strumming, and blazing leads, he set the stage for the alternative guitar heroes of the late '80s and the '90s.

Hüsker Dü formed in Minneapolis, MN, in 1979. Guitarist/vocalist Bob Mould was studying at Macalester College in St. Paul, MN, and working at a record store, which is where he met drummer/vocalist Grant Hart and bassist Greg Norton. The three musicians had diverse tastes, but all shared a love for hardcore punk music. Naming themselves Hüsker Dü after a '50s Swedish boardgame (the name means "do you remember?"), the trio began rehearsing in Norton's basement.

In the early '80s, Hüsker Dü developed a strong local following—nearly every local band, from the Replacements to Soul Asylum, sounded like the Hüskers. Both Mould and Hart wrote songs and sang lead. In 1981, they released their first single, "Statues," on the local label Reflex, which was quickly followed by their debut album, *Land Speed Record*, which was released on New Alliance Records. Recorded live, *Land Speed Record* boasted 17 songs that lasted a full 26 minutes. Later that year, they released an equally fast and hard EP, *In a Free Land*.

In 1982, they moved backed to Reflex, where they released *Everything Falls Apart*, their first album recorded in a studio. By this time, Hüsker Dü had begun touring the US relentlessly, travelling across the country in a van and playing small clubs throughout the country. Along with the Minutemen, R.E.M., Black Flag, the Meat Puppets, and the Replacements, Hüsker Dü formed the core of a group of independent rock 'n' roll bands that carved out a reputation by touring ceaselessly and getting their records played through college radio stations. Hüsker Dü concerts were a nonstop barrage: The band rarely spoke to the audience and each song segued directly into the next, without interruption. In addition to touring constantly, Hüsker Dü was recording quickly, turning out the *Metal Circus* EP in 1983.

After *Metal Circus*, Hüsker Dü developed musically at a rapid pace, with Mould and Hart coming into their own as songwriters on 1984's *Zen Arcade*, their first album for SST Records and their critical breakthrough. *Zen Arcade* was a double album—something that was completely unheard of in the underground—that showed the band stretching out musically, writing sharper pop songs, as well as lengthy abrasive instrumentals. Critics embraced the record, as did independent rock fans. At the end of 1984, they released "Eight Miles High," a cover of the Byrds' song that was only available as a single.

Hüsker Dü continued to record at tour at a blindingly fast speed throughout 1984 and 1985. Mould and Hart were beginning to develop an unspoken rivalry, as well as a dependency on alcohol and speed. Nevertheless, the group was at their peak in 1985, turning out two albums. The first, *New Day Rising*, was released in the spring and showed the band moving closer to concise pop songwriting while accentuating their fierce sonic barrage. *Flip Your Wig* (1985) featured their cleanest, most accessible production, without making any concessions to mainstream rock. Both albums received excellent reviews, both in fanzines and some mainstream rock publications.

Following the release of *Flip Your Wig*, Hüsker Dü became the first of the mid-'80s independent post-punk bands to sign a contract with a major label, as they closed a deal with Warner Bros. *Candy Apple Grey*, the band's first major-label album, appeared in 1986. During that year, tensions between Bob Mould and Grant Hart escalated. Mould began to clean up and Hart continued to sink further into drug and alcohol addiction. Nevertheless, they managed to write and record another double album, *Warehouse: Songs and Stories*. Although Warner didn't want the band to release another double record, *Warehouse* was released in the spring of 1987, to uniformly positive reviews.

Hüsker Dü was preparing to launch a series of concerts to support *Warehouse* when their manager, David Savoy, committed suicide the night before the start of the tour. Hüsker played the tour anyway—they ran through the new album in order every night, without interruption—but Savoy's suicide helped the interband turmoil reach a peak. Hart showed no signs of sobering—he was developing a heroin addiction—while Mould was clean. Following the *Warehouse* tour, the band played no more concerts for the rest of the year, which caused speculation that the group was breaking up. Those rumors were confirmed in January of 1988, when Hart was fired and the band broke up.

Hart would released a solo EP, *2541*, on SST later that year, followed by a full-length album called *Intolerance* a year later. After its release, Hart shook loose his addictions and formed a new band, Nova Mob. Nova Mob released their debut album, *The Last Days of Pompeii*, in 1991; a self-titled second album appeared in 1994. Greg Norton became a chef in Minneapolis.

Immediately after the breakup of Hüsker Dü, Bob Mould embarked on a solo career. After releasing two solo albums—*Workbook* (1989) and *Black Sheets of Rain* (1990)—he formed a trio called Sugar in 1992. Between 1992 and 1994, Sugar released two albums—*Copper Blue* (1992) and *File Under: Easy Listening* (1994). Mould broke up the band in 1995 and returned to a solo career the following year. —*Stephen Thomas Erlewine*

Land Speed Record / 1981 / SST ♦♦

Everything Falls Apart / 1982 / Reflex ♦♦♦

Metal Circus / 1983 / SST ♦♦♦
This five-songer, which followed a furiously paced debut, hinted that the confines of hardcore punk couldn't contain the group's collective vision. —*John Floyd*

☆ **Zen Arcade** / 1984 / SST ♦♦♦♦♦
In many ways, it's impossible to overestimate the impact of Hüsker Dü's *Zen Arcade* on the American rock underground in the '80s. It's the record that exploded the limits of hardcore and what it could achieve. Hüsker Dü broke all of the rules with *Zen Arcade*. First and foremost, it's a sprawling concept album, even if the concept isn't immediately clear or comprehensible. More important are the individual songs. Both Bob Mould and Grant Hart abandoned the strict "fast, hard, loud" rules of hardcore punk with their songs for *Zen Arcade*. Without turning down the volume, Hüsker Dü tries everything—pop songs, tape experiments, acoustic songs, pianos, noisy psychedelia. Hüsker Dü willed themselves to make such a sprawling record—as the liner notes state, the album was recorded and mixed within 85 hours and consists almost entirely of first takes. That reckless, ridiculously single-minded approach does result in some weak moments—the sound is thin and the instrumentals drag on a bit too long—but it's also the key to the success of *Zen Arcade*. Hüsker Dü sounds phenomenally strong and possessed, as if they could do anything. The sonic experimentation is bolstered by Mould and Hart's increased sense of songcraft. Neither writer is afraid to let their pop influences show on *Zen Arcade*, which gives the songs—from the unrestrained rage of "Something I Learned Today" and the bitter, acoustic "Never Talking

to You Again" to the eerie "Pink Turns to Blue" and anthemic "Turn On the News"—their weight. It's music that is informed by hardcore punk and indie-rock ideals without being limited by it. —*Stephen Thomas Erlewine*

★ **New Day Rising** / Jan. 1985 / SST ♦♦♦♦♦
For *New Day Rising*, the follow-up to their breakthrough double-album *Zen Arcade*, Hüsker Dü replaced concept with conciseness, concentrating on individual songs delivered as scalding post-hardcore pop. *New Day Rising* is not only a more vicious and relentless record than *Zen Arcade*, it's more melodic. Bob Mould and Grant Hart have written tightly crafted, melodic pop songs that don't compromise Hüsker's volcanic, unchecked power. Mould and Hart's songs owe a great deal to '60s pop, as the verses and choruses ebb and flow with immediately catchy hooks. Occasionally, the razor-thin production and waves of noise mean that it takes a little bit of effort to pick out the melodies, but more often the furious noise and melodies fuse together to create an overwhelming sonic force. It's possible to hear the rivalry between Mould and Hart on the album itself—each song is like a game of oneupmanship, as Mould responds to "The Girl Who Lives on Heaven Hill" with "Celebrated Summer." Neither songwriter slips—both turn in songs that are catchy, clever, and alternately wracked with pain or teeming with humor. *New Day Rising* is a positively cathartic record and ranks as Hüsker Dü's most sustained moment of pure power. —*Stephen Thomas Erlewine*

☆ **Flip Your Wig** / Feb. 1985 / SST ♦♦♦♦♦
Spot—SST's house producer who manned the boards for *Zen Arcade* and *New Day Rising*—didn't produce *Flip Your Wig*, Hüsker Dü's second album of 1985, and the difference is immediately noticeable. Everything on *Flip Your Wig* is cleaner and brighter than on its two immediate predecessors, which is appropriate, considering that Bob Mould and Grant Hart have only increased their debt to '60s pop. The hooks and melodies are on the surface, right from the kick-start call-and-response of the title track. On paper, it might sound as if Hüsker Dü have watered down their hardcore ideals, but it doesn't play that way. *Flip Your Wig* is pop played as punk, as if this is the only time these songs could ever be heard. Which means Hart's love song "Green Eyes" and Mould's pure pop single "Makes No Sense at All" are delivered with the same rage and passion as Mould's blistering "Divide and Conquer" and Hart's "Keep Hanging On," or the pair of surging, neo-psychedelic and noise-wracked instrumentals that close the album. *Flip Your Wig* would be a remarkable record on its own terms, but the fact that it followed *New Day Rising* by a matter of months and *Zen Arcade* by just over a year is simply astonishing. —*Stephen Thomas Erlewine*

Candy Apple Grey / 1986 / Warner Bros. ♦♦♦
The band's major-label debut coincidentally happens to be their most lyrically optimistic. Musically, it reiterates *Flip Your Wig*. —*John Floyd*

☆ **Warehouse: Songs & Stories** / 1987 / Warner Bros. ♦♦♦♦♦
It's cleaner and more produced than any of their records, which is one reason why many Hüsker Dü fans have never fully embraced their second double-album, *Warehouse: Songs and Stories*. Granted, *Warehouse* boasts a fuller production—complete with multitracked guitars and vocal, various percussion techniques and endless studio effects—that would have seemed out of place a mere two years before its release. However, *Flip Your Wig* and *Candy Apple Grey* both suggested

Everything Falls Apart and More / 1993 / Rhino ♦♦♦
Rhino's reissue of Hüsker Dü's shattering first studio album includes a couple of rare singles, making it a must-have for the band's fans, as well as anyone interested in hardcore punk rock. Anyone unfamiliar with Hüsker Dü's early work should brace themselves for a breakneck force like no other. Not for the faint of heart. —*Stephen Thomas Erlewine*

The Living End / Oct. 1994 / Warner Bros. ♦♦♦
Recorded on their final tour, *The Living End* is an invigorating document of Hüsker Dü's blistering live power, highlighted by a couple unreleased songs and a manic cover of "Sheena Is a Punk Rocker." —*Stephen Thomas Erlewine*

Janis Ian (Janis Eddy Fink)

b. Apr. 7, 1951, New York, NY
Guitar, Vocals / Singer-Songwriter, Folk-Rock
A folk-pop singer-songwriter who gained fame at age 16 for her socially conscious ballad "Society's Child" and scored all over again at age 24 with "At Seventeen." Lately she is living and writing songs in Nashville. —*William Ruhlmann*

Janis Ian / Jan. 1967 / Verve ♦♦♦♦
An amazingly precocious set of songs, including the civil rights anthem "Society's Child" and songs touching on religion, prostitution, politics, and other urban concerns, all from the viewpoint of an intelligent teenager. —*William Ruhlmann*

Aftertones / 1975 / Columbia ♦♦♦
Following only nine months after Ian's masterpiece, *Between the Lines*, *Aftertones* was something of a coda to that album, again tastefully pro-

duced by Brooks Arthur and featuring songs in the same mood. Although none came up to the standard of "At Seventeen," "I Would Like to Dance" presents much the same delicacy of expression. — *William Ruhlmann*

Breaking Silence / Jun. 8, 1993 / Morgan Creek ✦✦✦✦
Breaking Silence finds Ian ditching her past waifishness for a confident, mature, contemporary acoustic approach relying mostly on spare guitar and piano textures. Opening with "All Roads to the River" (also recorded by John Mellencamp), *Breaking Silence* includes among its highlights the Holocaust-survivor tale "Tattoo" and the dramatic half-a cappella, half-syncopated-rocker title track. — *Roch Parisien*

Society's Child: The Verve Recordings / Aug. 22, 1995 / Polydor ✦✦✦✦
The 41 songs on this double CD contain almost everything from the four albums that the singer-songwriter recorded for Verve in the late '60s. While it is true that Ian's early work may have been unduly savaged by unsympathetic rock critics, it's also true that the magnitude of her talent isn't large enough to merit a box set. As others have pointed out over the years, these compositions are often overly wordy, didactic, and self-absorbed, though these flaws are understandable (to a degree) given that Ian was in her mid- and late teens when they were recorded. At the same time, the grooves make a fairly strong case that Ian is underrated, if hardly a major figure; some of the songs are affecting, the arrangements (especially the early ones by Shangri-Las producer Shadow Morton) have a '60s-period charm, and she's a pretty strong singer. Although some Laura Nyro fans might find the comparison insulting, there's a similarity to be found in Ian's bluesier and more soulful vocals, especially on her later Verve records. So while this couldn't be classified as a milestone of the early singer-songwriter era, it's more enjoyable and impressive than a lot of listeners would expect, although two-and-a-half hours is too much to take at once. — *Richie Unterberger*

Billy Idol (William Broad)

b. Nov. 30, 1955, Middlesex, England
Vocals / Hard Rock, Pop-Rock
Billy Idol represents the bridge between punk rock and hard rock/metal, a logical enough connection that somehow seemed unlikely until he made the transition. Idol left Sussex University in 1976 to join the punk movement, specifically the group of rabid Sex Pistols fans called the Bromley Contingent. Many of the members formed their own bands, and Idol began Generation X with Tony James. Generation X became a moderate success during the punk heyday of the late '70s, especially in England, with Idol on snarling lead vocals.

When the band split in 1981, Idol went to New York and hooked up with manager Bill Aucoin (who had handled Kiss, among others). This resulted in Idol's grooming as more of a mainstream rock figure. His debut album, *Billy Idol*, came out in 1982 and spent two years on the charts as the result of such video hits as "White Wedding" and "Hot in the City." But it was Idol's second album, *Rebel Yell*, that was his big breakthrough, selling two million copies and spawning hits in the raucous title track and the ballad "Eyes without a Face." Idol followed it up with *Whiplash Smile* in 1986 and *Charmed Life* in 1990.

Idol's first commercial failure came in 1993, with *Cyberpunk*, his stab at techno-influenced rock. — *William Ruhlmann*

Billy Idol / Jul. 1982 / Chrysalis ✦✦✦✦
Billy Idol's self-titled debut album was a snarling take on hard rock, injected with the spite and attitude of punk and new wave. While the record is spotty, Idol pulls it all together on the classic single "White Wedding." — *Stephen Thomas Erlewine*

● **Rebel Yell** / 1983 / Chrysalis ✦✦✦✦
Tight rock arrangements featuring Steve Stevens' slashing guitar playing and Idol's vocal sneer. The dance-rock of "Rebel Yell" is alternated with power-ballads like "Eyes without a Face" for a well-rounded pop package. — *William Ruhlmann*

Whiplash Smile / 1986 / Chrysalis ✦✦✦
Charmed Life / 1990 / Chrysalis ✦✦✦✦
Like any Billy Idol album, *Charmed Life* is wildly inconsistent, but it has enough strong songs—like the gloriously tongue-in-cheek hard rock of "Cradle of Love"—to make most of the filler on the record forgivable. — *Stephen Thomas Erlewine*

Cyberpunk / Jun. 29, 1993 / Chrysalis ✦✦✦✦

The Impressions

Soul, R&B
The first Impressions hit, "For Your Precious Love," was an anachronism when released in 1958. Jerry Butler's robust, yearning vocal was a throwback to deep-South gospel, and Curtis Mayfield's arrangement was decidedly barebones. But this song also precipitated the changes coming in R&B; you can hear the groundwork for soul music being laid, from the

melisma of Butler's phrasing to Mayfield's skeletal guitar. The song literally flew in the face of then-popular doo wop formulas.

Butler left the group in 1960, but the pared-down trio, led by Mayfield, cut a path that altered the R&B map. Mayfield's high falsetto and the trade-off vocals of Fred Cash and Sam Gooden framed a new kind of R&B: smooth and graceful, at times lilting, soaked in the history of gospel, and, thanks to Mayfield's lyrical examinations of racism and urban decay, the catalyst for the wave of socially aware Black hits recorded in the '70s.

The group's hits varied from supple statements of affirmation ("It's All Right," "People Get Ready") and romantic declarations ("Talking About My Baby," "I'm So Proud") to songs that were sociopolitical ("Choice of Colors," "This Is My Country") or mystical ("Gypsy Woman"). Mayfield's outside production work yielded similar-sounding hits for the likes of Major Lance, Walter Jackson, and Billy Butler (and the sound of the Impressions was imitated by the likes of the Viscounts and the Knight Brothers). Their chart run ended by the late '60s, as did Mayfield's Midas touch; after recording the brilliant *Superfly* in 1972, his talents ran dry. Nonetheless, Mayfield's reputation as one of soul's supreme innovators cannot be exaggerated. — *John Floyd*

● **Greatest Hits** / 1965 / MCA ✦✦✦✦
This skimpy but solid collection of Curtis Mayfield's early-'60s soul landmarks includes "It's All Right" and "Gypsy Woman," defining the formula of early-'60s soul. — *John Floyd*

The Complete Vee-Jay Recordings / 1993 / Vee-Jay ✦✦✦✦
The Impressions' early music has taken a back seat to what they did after Jerry Butler departed and Mayfield began doing the lead vocals, writing, producing, and arranging. This excellent 18-track disc helps put the early years into focus, with Butler showcased on seven cuts and Mayfield on eight. The Impressions weren't a bad five-member harmony unit; they just were not a great one in an era when you had to be fantastic simply to break out of the pack. These are mostly nice love songs, and they aren't lyrically different from thousands of similar tracks, but they did deserve a better fate than to be dropped from the Vee-Jay label in 1959. — *Ron Wynn*

This Is My Country/The Young Mods' Forgotten Story / 1996 / Sequel ✦✦✦✦
Two fine late-'60s albums, combined onto one CD, including some hits and a wealth of good overlooked Mayfield compositions that touched on sensitive racial issues as well as romance. Offering excellent value, the CD is a recommended alternative to tracking down the hard-to-find original vinyl editions. — *Richie Unterberger*

Keep on Pushing/People Get Ready / 1996 / Kent ✦✦✦✦
Two good Impressions albums from the mid-'60s, combined onto one CD, making them handier to collect in this fashion than hunting down good-quality copies of the rare original vinyl editions. As usual, the singles ("Keep On Pushing," "People Get Ready," "Amen," "I've Been Trying," "Woman's Got Soul," "You Must Believe Me") overshadow the LP-only cuts. But the Impressions made a higher standard of albums than most '60s soul groups, investing a lot of care in the songwriting and production, making this a decent pickup for those who want to go beyond the greatest-hits anthologies. — *Richie Unterberger*

Further Impressions: More Soulful Classics / Jul. 1996 / HIPP ✦✦✦✦
Featuring a selection of 14 songs making their compact disc debut, *Further Impressions: More Soulful Classics* fills in the gaps left by the single-disc MCA *Greatest Hits* collection and the more comprehensive double-disc anthology. Only four R&B hits are present, but the remaining ten songs are all first-rate album tracks that are nearly equal in quality. *Further Impressions* doesn't overlap at all with MCA's two previous Impressions sets, so it is a necessary addition to any fan's CD library. — *Stephen Thomas Erlewine*

Indigo Girls

Singer-Songwriter, Folk-Rock
While they came into prominence as part of the late-'80s folky-singer-songwriter revival, the Indigo Girls have had staying power where other artists from the same era quickly faded. Their two-women-with-guitars formula may not seem very revolutionary on paper, but the combination of two distinct personalities and songwriting styles provides a tension and an interesting balance—Emily Saliers, hailing from the more traditional Joni Mitchell school, has the gentler sound, is more complex musically, and often leans toward the abstract and spiritual while Amy Ray draws heavily from the singer-songwriter aspects of punk rock, citing influences such as the Jam, the Pretenders, and Hüsker Dü for her more abrasive and direct approach. In more than a decade of recording, they have managed respectable mainstream success as well as keeping their rabid core following.

Amy Ray and Emily Saliers first took the name Indigo Girls while living in Atlanta in 1985, although they had been performing together since the early '80s, at times under the name the B-Band. In 1986, they recorded an independent self-titled EP and followed in 1987 with the full-length *Strange Fire*—only 7,000 copies were pressed and very little interest was generated. Things changed quickly in 1988 when, in the wake of the success of Suzanne Vega, Tracy Chapman, and 10,000 Maniacs, they seemed to fit nicely into "the next big thing." Epic Records was quick to sign them.

Indigo Girls, released in 1989, was an excellent national debut. Featuring a guest vocal by R.E.M.'s Michael Stipe ("Kid Fears") gave them initial college radio credibility and the single "Closer to Fine" was a hit—the album eventually broke the Top 30 and earned a Grammy for Best Folk Recording that year. By the end of 1991, it achieved platinum sales. *Strange Fire* was reissued in the fall with a cover of "Get Together," replacing one of the original tracks.

The follow-up, 1990's *Nomads Indians Saints*, didn't fare quite as well. It was nominated for a Grammy and eventually reached gold status but the material wasn't nearly as strong. A live EP, *Back on the Bus, Y'All*, was released in 1991 while they regrouped. It was also certified gold and was nominated for a Grammy.

In spring of 1992, they made a comeback with *Rites of Passage*, which debuted at No. 22 and went platinum by year's end. The album showed an increasing diversity and some of their strongest songs to date. Almost exactly two years later, *Swamp Ophelia* was released and entered the charts at No. 9; it went gold by the end of the year. A double-live album, *1200 Curfews*, was released in 1995.

In addition to her work as part of the Indigo Girls, Amy Ray also set up and presides over Daemon Records, a nonprofit label to nurture new talent with an emphasis on like-minded singer-songwriters. The label's releases include albums by Kristen Hall, Ellen James Society, James Hall, a remake of *Jesus Christ Superstar* (which includes performances by both Ray and Sailers), and a gun control benefit. —*Chris Woodstra*

Strange Fire / 1987 / Epic ✦✦

● **Indigo Girls** / 1989 / Epic ✦✦✦✦
This major-label debut is a strong showcase for this duo's harmonic skills and songwriting virtues. "Closer to Fine" (No. 52) was a moderate hit. Emily Saliers's "History of Us" is particularly affecting. Other highlights include "Secure Yourself," "Tried to Be True," and "Kid Fears," which featured R.E.M. vocalist Michael Stipe on backups. Hothouse Flowers also provides support. —*Rick Clark*

Nomad Indians Saints / 1990 / Epic ✦✦✦
Not as dynamic as *Indigo Girls*, this effort includes a few nice songs with "Welcome Me," "Watershed," and "Southland in the Springtime." The dichotomy between Ray's occasionally abrasive vocal strain and Saliers's delicately earthy alto are more apparent, making their delivery feel less focused. Their overreaching lyrics also undermined the success of this outing. —*Rick Clark*

Live: Back on the Bus Y'all / 1991 / Epic ✦✦

Rites of Passage / Feb. 1992 / Epic ✦✦✦
Not straying too far from their nearly formulaic sound, *Rites of Passage* shows great strides in songwriting maturity. The tension between Amy Ray's harsher rock style and Emily Salier's sweeter melodic sense makes for a beautiful combination. Only a ridiculous cover of Dire Straits' "Romeo and Juliet" misses the mark. —*Chris Woodstra*

Swamp Ophelia / 1994 / Epic ✦✦✦
The most sophisticated sounding Indigo Girls production to date, *Swamp Ophelia* features some fine material, like "Touch Me Fall," "Mystery," "Language or the Kiss," "Power of Two," and "Least Complicated." For the most part, Amy Ray's occasional over-the-top stridency is fortunately restrained, while Emily Saliers' warm, earthy voice continues to pull the listener into considering her lyrical sentiments. As usual, when the two sing together, it's a wonderful sound. —*Rick Clark*

4.5 The Best Of / 1995 / Epic ✦✦✦
4.5 is a 15-track import collection covering the Indigo Girls' career from their self-titled Epic Records debut to *Swamp Ophelia*. While it certainly does the job of introducing the band to the foriegn market, its lack of rarities and prohibitive import price, make it unnecessary for the US.—the self-titled album is still the best place to start. —*Chris Woodstra*

1200 Curfews / Oct. 24, 1995 / Epic ✦✦✦✦

James Ingram

b. Feb. 16, 1956, Akron, OH
Keyboards, Vocals / Soul, Urban, Adult Contemporary
Ingram began performing with the band Revelation Funk in the early '70s, moving from Akron, OH, to Los Angeles in 1973. During the '70s, Ingram supported Ray Charles on the road with backup vocals and piano, played keyboards behind the Coasters on Dick Clark's oldies revues, and was Leon Haywood's musical director. After hearing a demo of him singing "Just Once," Quincy Jones asked Ingram to perform on his new album. Released in 1980 on *The Dude*, the No. 17 "Just Once" was Ingram's first success, resulting in three Grammy nominations—Best New Artist, Best Pop Male Vocal, and Best R&B Vocal—winning in the

two latter categories. Throughout the '80s, Ingram had steady popular success singing duets, but all of his solo albums failed to make a dent in the charts; in 1990 he scored his first solo hit, "I Don't Have the Heart." —*Stephen Thomas Erlewine*

Never Felt So Good / 1988 / Qwest ✦✦✦

● **The Power of Great Music: Best of James Ingram** / 1991 / Qwest ✦✦✦✦
Includes his Top 40 duets—"Yah Mo B There" (recorded with Michael McDonald), "Somewhere Out There" (recorded with Linda Ronstadt), "Baby, Come to Me" (recorded with Patti Austin), and his first solo hit, "I Don't Have the Heart"—as well as songs that have scored the urban charts. —*Ron Wynn*

Luther Ingram

b. Nov. 30, 1944, Jackson, TN
Vocals / Soul
This Jackson, TN, Southern-soul singer was one of the top artists at Stax during the early '70s. Hooking up with producer Johnny Baylor's tiny KoKo label, Ingram appeared regularly on the R&B charts after Baylor brought his firm into the Stax fold in 1969. Ingram's intimate vocal approach was well suited to ballads, and his 1970 hit revival of "Ain't That Loving You (For More Reasons than One)" set the stage for his R&B chart-topping classic "(If Loving You Is Wrong) I Don't Want to Be Right" two years later. Long after Stax had folded, Ingram was still releasing hit singles—clear into 1987. —*Bill Dahl*

I've Been Here All the Time / 1972 / KoKo ✦✦✦

If Loving You Is Wrong (I Don't Want to Be Right) / 1972 / KoKo ✦✦✦✦
Luther Ingram earned his biggest R&B and pop hit with the title track, one of the last hurrahs for gospel-tinged and country-flavored confessional soul. The song would later become a country hit for Barbara Mandrell. Ingram landed one other Top Ten R&B single with "I'll Be Your Shelter (In Time of Storm)," and the album contained some other earnest soul ballads that weren't hits in "I Can't Stop" and "Help Me Love." Ingram never again enjoyed similar crossover heights, and the tide was turning against deep soul in both pop and R&B camps. —*Ron Wynn*

Luther Ingram / 1986 / Profile ✦✦✦✦
Luther Ingram made a brief return to the R&B charts with this 1986 LP issued on a predominantly dance-oriented label, which mixed his classic soul voice with urban contemporary production. It wasn't an early new jack swing number, as there were no hip-hop or rap elements, but it did contain drum machine tracks and synthesizer-dominated arrangements. Otherwise, Ingram was still singing heartache ballads, doing confessional country-soul and sounding raw and urgent on "Baby Don't Go Too Far" and "Don't Turn Around." The album also contained an interesting, although flawed, remake of Bob Dylan's "Gotta Serve Somebody." —*Ron Wynn*

● **Greatest Hits** / Apr. 1996 / The Right Stuff ✦✦✦✦

INXS

Rock 'n' Roll, New Wave, Pop-Rock, Club-Dance
After several years as a moderately successful dance-oriented new wave band, INXS began to accentuate the underlying dance and funk elements of their music, as well as vocalist Michael Hutchence's Jaggeresque sexuality. With the strong, funky single "The Original Sin," 1984's *The Swing* was the first album that featured their change in direction; for the first time, INXS had a hit outside of their native Australia. 1985's *Listen like Thieves* was even more successful, both commercially and artistically; its title track was a hit on the charts and on MTV, but it was "What You Need" and its stylish, funky rock 'n' roll that gave them their first Top Ten hit outside of Australia. But that was nothing compared to the worldwide success of 1987's *Kick*, which sold over four million copies in the US alone. From the slow, simmering sexuality of "Need You Tonight" to the lovely ballad "Never Tear Us Apart," the album had no less than four huge hit singles.

Although its 1990 follow-up, *X*, sold well, the record was a carbon copy of *Kick*, signalling the beginning of INXS's commercial decline. The band released their most consistent and musically adventurous album, *Welcome to Wherever You Are*, in 1992 but it almost had no impact on the chart; 1993's *Full Moon, Dirty Hearts* was even more disappointing, falling off the charts only a few weeks after its release. —*Stephen Thomas Erlewine*

Inxs / 1980 / Atlantic ✦✦

Underneath the Colours / 1981 / Atlantic ✦✦

Shabooh Shoobah / 1982 / Atlantic ✦✦✦

Dekadance / 1983 / Atlantic ✦✦

The Swing / 1984 / Atco ✦✦✦

Listen Like Thieves / 1985 / Atlantic ✦✦✦✦
INXS completes its transition into an excellent rock 'n' roll singles band with this album. Unfortunately, the new configuration only works for three songs: "What You Need," "Listen like Thieves," and "Kiss the Dirt (Falling Down the Mountain)." But these three songs are so strong that the album cannot be dismissed completely. The album is worth its price just for "What You Need," a strong Stonesy groove with Michael Hutchence singing more warmly than he ever has. —*Stephen Thomas Erlewine*

Kick / 1987 / Atlantic ✦✦✦✦
Kick, INXS's commercial and artistic breakthrough, overflows with hit singles, including "Need You Tonight," "Devil Inside," "New Sensation," and "Never Tear Us Apart." The band's mix of Stonesy rock 'n' roll, melodic pop, and dance-oriented beats has never sounded fresher—even the album tracks are fully developed songs that never seem like filler. It's easily their best album. —*Stephen Thomas Erlewine*

X / 1990 / Atlantic ✦✦✦
The follow-up to the smash *Kick* isn't quite as successful as its predecessor, but it packs quite a punch. Although "Suicide Blonde," "The Stairs," "Bitter Tears" and "Disappear" are as good as anything on *Kick*, the album suffers from songs that sound too similar. —*Stephen Thomas Erlewine*

Live Baby Live / 1991 / Atlantic ✦

Welcome to Wherever You Are / Aug. 4, 1992 / Atlantic ✦✦✦✦

Full Moon, Dirty Hearts / 1993 / Atlantic ✦✦

● **The Greatest Hits** / 1994 / Atlantic ✦✦✦✦
While INXS have made a few consistent albums, singles are the best format for the group's stylish dance-rock. Throughout the '80s and early '90s, the group racked up nine Top 40 hits and seven of those singles hit the Top Ten. *Greatest Hits* collects all of those hits—including "Need You Tonight," "What You Need," "Devil Inside," "New Sensation," "Disappear," "Suicide Blonde," and "Never Tear Us Apart"—adding minor hits like "Original Sin" and "Listen like Thieves," but curiously bypassing the pivotal "Don't Change" and excellent "Bitter Tears," which was a bigger hit than several songs on the record. Nevertheless, *Greatest Hits* lives up to its title and provides a fine introduction to the band. —*Stephen Thomas Erlewine*

Iron Butterfly

Hard Rock, Psychedelic, Heavy Metal, Acid Rock
Formed in 1966, Iron Butterfly performed a heavy, minor-key style of psychedelic rock-pop. Their debut album *Heavy* was a promising start, but the follow-up effort, *In a Gadda Da Vida* (No. 4) became the biggest-selling album in Atlantic Records history until the advent of Led Zeppelin. This was primarily due to the 17-minute title track, which became a staple on the emerging progressive-FM rock format. An edited version became a No. 30 hit. The follow-up album, *Ball*, did one better at No. 3.

Besides "In-a-Gadda-Da-Vida," Iron Butterfly charted with "Soul Experience," "In the Time of Our Lives," and "Easy Rider (Let the Wind Pay the Way)," from the movie *Easy Rider*. The band attempted a reunion in 1975 with two albums, *Scorching Beauty* and *Sun and Steel*, before breaking up again. —*Rick Clark*

In a Gadda Da Vida / 1968 / Atco ✦✦✦✦

● **Light and Heavy: The Best of Iron Butterfly** / 1993 / Rhino ✦✦✦✦
Although the compilation is quite generous, featuring 21 tracks on CD, *Light and Heavy: The Best of Iron Butterfly* isn't all that entertaining, due to Iron Butterfly's difficulties with producing compelling material. All of the group's highlights from 1968-1970 are included, although the career-making, 17-minute "In A Gadda Da Vida" is presented in its three-minute single edit. Since that is the only Iron Butterfly song most listeners know, the lack of the full-length version could potentially sink the album, but the fact of the matter is, "In A Gadda Da Vida" gets quite repetitive over the course of nearly 20 minutes. While the quality of the rest of *Light and Heavy* is spotty—ranging from heavy psychedelic rock to light psychedelic pop—it is a more intriguing listen than *In-A-Gadda-Da-Vida*, even if it doesn't have the period-piece charm of the original hit record. —*Stephen Thomas Erlewine*

Iron Maiden

Heavy Metal, British Metal
From their origins as a bar band in the mid-'70s to the present, England's Iron Maiden has become one of the most imitated bands in heavy metal. The man who has held the group together through the rough times is bassist Steve Harris. Some of their theatrics were somewhat tacky in the early days, but by the late '70s they were already gaining a respectable following. EMI released their self-titled debut album in 1980, featuring Paul Di'Anno on vocals and Dave Murray on guitar. In the US, the album was released on Harvest. The band's second album helped them gain a huge following all over Europe and America, but within the band there

were problems. Out went Di'Anno and in came Bruce Dickenson, former vocalist for the band Samson. Another change was the addition of guitarist Adrian Smith (who joined just before the *Killers* album, replacing Dennis Stratton), and it was this lineup (along with drummer Clive Burr) that took them over the top. The band's impact has been immense, selling millions, and their sound has easily distinguished them from other bands. —*John Book*

Iron Maiden / 1980 / Capitol ✦✦✦✦
This is the debut album that started it all for this band; many of the songs remain all-time metal classics, including "Sanctuary" and "Running Free." —*John Book*

Killers / 1981 / Capitol ✦✦✦✦
Album No. 2 by Iron Maiden is not as aggressive or as addicting as their self-titled debut but still an essential part of their career. This was the last studio album to feature vocalist Di'Anno; he later formed Paul Di'Anno's Battlezone. —*John Book*

Maiden Japan / 1981 / Capitol ✦✦

● **The Number of the Beast** / 1982 / Capitol ✦✦✦✦
The first Maiden album to feature ex-Samson vocalist Bruce Dickenson, this is powerful with some great guitar work from Dave Murray and Adrian Smith and fantastic bass playing from Steve Harris. This is the album that brought the band success in the US, and it features the classics "Run to the Hills" and the title track. —*John Book*

Piece of Mind / 1983 / Capitol ✦✦✦✦
The first Maiden album to feature drummer Nicko McBrain, *Peace of Mind* is easily one of their best efforts. Lead guitarists Adrian Smith and Dave Murray play their most creative work here, and the whole band is in top form. —*John Book*

Powerslave / 1984 / Capitol ✦✦✦

Live After Death (The World Slavery Tour) / 1985 / Capitol ✦✦✦✦
Documenting the band at their peak, this is a great live double album with a wide range of songs, going as far back as their first album. It's also available as a home video. —*John Book*

Somewhere in Time / 1986 / Capitol ✦✦

Seventh Son of a Seventh Son / 1988 / Capitol ✦✦✦✦
The band's first attempt at a concept album includes keyboardist/synthesizer sounds, but is not as annoying as the *Somewhere in Time* album. A good set of songs includes "Can I Play with Madness?," "The Clairvoyant," and the haunting title track. —*John Book*

No Prayer for the Dying / 1990 / Epic ✦✦

Fear of the Dark / May 12, 1992 / Epic ✦✦

X Factor / Oct. 10, 1995 / CMC International ✦✦

Chris Isaak

b. Jun. 26, 1956, Stockton, CA
Guitar, Vocals / Roots-Rock, Pop-Rock
Chris Isaak clearly loves the reverb-laden rockabilly and country of Sun Studios. In particular, he transfers the sweeping melancholy of Roy Orbison's sweeping, classic melancholy Monument singles ("Crying," "Oh, Pretty Woman," "In Dreams") to the more stripped-down, rootsy sound of Sun. His stylized take on '50s and '60s rock 'n' roll eventually made him into a star in the early '90s, thanks to the hit single "Wicked Game."

Isaak began performing after he graduated from college, forming the rockabilly band Silvertone. The group, which featured guitarist James Calvin Wilsey, bassist Rowland Salley, and drummer Kenney Dale Johnson, would become the singer/guitarist's permanent supporting band. Isaak released his first album, *Silvertone*, on Warner Bros. Records in 1985. It was crtically well-received, yet it didn't sell. Two years later, he released *Chris Isaak* which managed to scrape into the Top 200 album charts. After its release, the singer began an acting career with a bit part in Jonathan Demme's 1988 film, *Married to the Mob*; he would later have parts in *Wild at Heart* and *The Silence of the Lambs*.

Released in 1989, *Heart Shaped World* initially sold more than *Chris Isaak*, yet it didn't manage to break big until late 1990, when the single "Wicked Game" was featured in David Lynch's *Wild at Heart*. Soon, the single became a Top Ten hit; the album also made it into the Top Ten and sold over a million copies. Both 1993's *San Francisco Days* and 1995's *Forever Blue* mine essentially the same vein as *Heart Shaped World*, yet he has managed to keep the formula from growing stale; in the meantime, he has been able to score a handful of hits in both the pop and adult contemporary charts. —*Stephen Thomas Erlewine*

Silvertone / 1985 / Warner Bros. ✦✦✦✦
Chris Isaak's debut album, *Silvertone*, named after his three-piece backup group, sets the pattern for his subsequent albums in its meticulously constructed retro sound. Isaak enters a time machine and emerges around 1960, when Roy Orbison is ruling the charts with his melodramatic ballads and Elvis Presley has just returned from the Army. Of course, what passed for a style 25 years before is in Isaak's hands styliza-

tion, and when he wails in an Orbison falsetto of romantic desperation, then does a flat, Presley-like recitation in the album-closing "Western Skies," it all seems over the top. But he is just about sincere enough to pull it off, and James Calvin Wilsey is a strong enough guitarist to keep the arrangements on track. So, to the extent that you can resist the "Is this guy kidding?" impression, the music is appealing. — *William Ruhlmann*

Chris Isaak / Dec. 1986 / Warner Bros. ✦✦✦

● **Heart Shaped World** / 1989 / Warner Bros. ✦✦✦✦
The album that really broke Isaak through to a mainstream audience, this features the title cut, "I'm Not Waiting," "Wrong to Love You," a driving rendition of "Diddley Daddy," and the surprise No. 6 hit "Wicked Game." Brooding and intense. — *Cub Koda*

San Francisco Days / 1993 / Reprise ✦✦✦✦
Chris Isaak's records are eerily out of time; the production is too clean and sterile to sound as if it was recorded at Sun Studios (a sound he clearly admires), but his music doesn't fit neatly into the sounds of contemporary radio. Accordingly, his sound is original yet familiar, appealing both to fans of early-'60s rock 'n' roll and a modern audience. At times, Isaak tries too hard to emulate his idols—for instance, his strained Orbison-esque falsetto on "Two Hearts"—but when he doesn't try too hard, the results are often startling. *San Francisco Days* is Isaak's most musically diverse album yet. — *Stephen Thomas Erlewine*

Forever Blue / 1995 / Warner Bros. ✦✦✦

The Isley Brothers

Soul, Funk, R&B, Urban
They're still at it: recording artists since 1957, and hitmakers for almost as long. Inevitably, their music has changed, but this group's chief claim to fame remains their secularization of gospel call-and-response. They found that particular groove on "Shout" (cut for RCA in 1959), later followed by "Twist and Shout" on Wand in 1962—definitely one of the ballsier twist records. Four years in the commercial wilderness followed before they signed with Tamla and came up with "This Old Heart of Mine."

They didn't work long on the Motown assembly line, though, and in 1969 revived their own T-Neck Records. Twenty years later they were still grinding out hits on the label, although their first T-Neck smash, "It's Your Thing," remains their biggest. Brothers have come and gone, as have sidemen—including Jimi Hendrix at one point. Still, the family that plays together stays together, although the group trading as the Isley Brothers today includes elements of Isley-Jasper-Isley (two younger brothers and a cousin), who had a hit with "Caravan of Love" in 1985.

The great second-generation family unit 3 + 3 finally disbanded in 1984. At that time the original trio continued recording for Warner Bros., while the younger threesome worked as Isley-Jasper-Isley. When O'Kelly suffered a heart attack in 1986, Ronald and Rudolph continued without him. Ronald Isley's wife, Angela Winbush, contributed production and compositions, as well as sang backgrounds for the 1987 *Smooth Sailing* LP. Their most recent release was *Tracks of Life* in 1992. Ronald Isley became her manager and collaborator on her projects. After working together until 1990, Isley-Jasper-Isley split into various groups as well. Ernie Isley and Chris Jasper became solo artists. — *Colin Escott and Ron Wynn*

Twist & Shout! / 1962 / Sundazed ✦✦✦

3 Plus 3 / 1973 / T Neck ✦✦✦✦
A masterpiece, one of the defining albums for '70s Black music. The original Isley frontline of Ronald, Rudolph, and O'Kelly merged with the next generation featuring younger brothers Marvin and Ernie, plus cousin Chris Jasper. The lead single "That Lady" established their new sound and identity on Epic, and was just one of four monster songs that came from the album. — *Ron Wynn*

The Isley Brothers Live It Up / 1974 / T Neck ✦✦✦✦
The album that cemented the revolution begun by the 3 + 3 LP. The title song was a blazing triumph, landing them on *Soul Train* and getting widespread pop and club attention, although it didn't prove to be their biggest hit in those areas. Ernie Isley made his first significant impact as a guitar soloist, and the group also began attracting fans who hadn't heard their earlier cuts, while alerting the faithful they were really back on the scene. — *Ron Wynn*

Greatest Hits & Rare Classics / 1991 / Motown ✦✦✦✦
Although the Isleys recorded some good stuff for Motown in the late '60s, it's generally true that the label's attempts to fit them into the standard Motown production line inhibited their creativity and individuality. This 22-track retrospective of their Motown days is dominated by material from in-house songwriters such as Eddie Holland, Smokey Robinson, and Ivory Joe Hunter, and doesn't rank among the Isleys' best work, though it's respectable enough. The best tracks—the Top Ten hit "This Old Heart of Mine," "Behind a Painted Smile," and "Take Some Time Out for Love"—are available on the Rhino best-of, but Isleys fans will find this a

worthwhile summary of their brief Motown stay. Includes the original versions of two of their biggest hits cut for other labels, "Twist & Shout" and "It's Your Thing." — *Richie Unterberger*

★ **The Isley Brothers Story, Vol. 1** / 1991 / Rhino ✦✦✦✦✦
Rhino's two Isley Brothers compilations provide the definitive portrait of the group. *Vol. 1: Rockin' Soul (1959-1968)* focuses on the Isleys' R&B beginnings, including both parts of "Shout," "This Old Heart of Mine (Is Weak for You)," and "Twist and Shout." — *Stephen Thomas Erlewine*

★ **The Isley Brothers Story, Vol. 2** / 1991 / Rhino ✦✦✦✦✦
The Isley Brothers founded their own record label, T-Neck, in 1969, and along with the new label came a new direction and sound for the group. Funkier and harder, the Isleys charted more frequently than ever before in their career with such singles as "That Lady" (No. 6), "Fight the Power" (No. 4), and the No. 2 hit "It's Your Thing." This completes the picture that *Vol. 1* began and is essential for any collection of early-'70s soul. — *Stephen Thomas Erlewine*

Mission to Please / 1996 / T-Neck/Island ✦✦✦✦

Shout: RCA Sessions / Jul. 1996 / RCA ✦✦✦✦
The Isley Brothers spent a year at RCA Records, during which time they only had one hit—"Shout"—which barely scraped the charts. Of course, Joey Dee & the Starliters would later take the song into the Top Ten, but at the time it was an inauspicious beginning to a long, illustrious career. "Shout" and the rest of the recordings the Isleys made for RCA Records are collected on *Shout: RCA Sessions*. Although it's only a single-disc collection, the material is too uneven to be a thoroughly compelling listen, although it is certainly valuable as a historical compilation. — *Stephen Thomas Erlewine*

The Jackson 5

Soul, Motown, Philly Soul
The Jackson 5 was Motown's last great pop group and among the most successful singles acts of the '70s. The group consisted of five brothers—Jackie (b. May 4, 1951), Tito (b. Oct 15, 1953), Jermaine (b. Dec 11, 1954), Marlon (b. Mar 12, 1957), and Michael Jackson (b. Aug 29, 1958). They grew up in Gary, IN, and were first organized as a group by their father, Joe Jackson, in 1966. In essence, the group was a vocal ensemble centered on Michael, who, though the youngest, was clearly the most talented. The group came to the attention of Motown and was signed in 1969. Their first four singles, "I Want You Back," "ABC," "The Love You Save," and "I'll Be There," all hit No. 1 in 1970; "Mama's Pearl" and "Never Can Say Goodbye" did almost as well in 1971.

In 1972, Motown launched both Michael Jackson and Jermaine Jackson as solo acts, and the group's efforts were gradually less successful in the following years, though "Dance Machine" was a big hit in 1974. In 1975, Jackie, Tito, Marlon, and Michael signed to Epic Records, adding brother Randy (b. Oct 29, 1961), and became the Jacksons (the name the Jackson 5 was owned by Motown). (Although Jermaine stayed at Motown, he rejoined the group in 1984.) — *William Ruhlmann*

The Jacksons / 1976 / Epic ✦✦✦

☆ **Anthology** / 1976 / Motown ✦✦✦✦✦
This three-LP set contains all 18 of the Jackson 5's pop-chart hits, plus solo hits by Jermaine and Michael Jackson, among its 33 cuts. It's the definitive collection and a good sampler of the sound of pop/R&B, circa 1969-1975. (Originally released as a 33-track, three-LP set by Motown on June 15, 1976, as Motown 868, *Anthology* was reissued as a 40-track, two-CD set in August 1986 as Motown 6194.) — *William Ruhlmann*

Goin' Places / 1977 / Epic ✦✦✦

Destiny / 1978 / Epic ✦✦✦✦
The Jacksons are finally turned loose to write and produce themselves, and the result is their best (non-hits collection) ever. The dance tracks still sound fresh—"Blame It on the Boogie," "Shake Your Body (Down to the Ground)"—and the ballads are heartfelt and smooth. This album is a dry run for Michael Jackson's adult solo career. — *William Ruhlmann*

Triumph / 1980 / Epic ✦✦✦✦
An excellent follow-up, featuring the hits "Can You Feel It" and "Heartbreak Hotel." — *William Ruhlmann*

Victory / 1984 / Epic ✦✦✦

2300 Jackson Street / 1989 / Epic ✦✦✦

Soulsation! / 1995 / Motown ✦✦✦✦
Nineteen years after the release of *Anthology*, Motown finally tops that 33-track, three-LP compilation with this 82-track, four-and-a-half-hour, four-CD/cassette box set. The Jackson 5 were long overdue for box set treatment, and this one is well done. All the hits by the group as well as those by Michael and Jermaine Jackson are here (that is, from 1969-1975, the J5's tenure at Motown), along with a representative sampling of album cuts. The J5's albums were afterthoughts to their singles, but some of these songs are nevertheless interesting, whether the group is covering Sly and the Family Stone or Jackson Browne (!). An entire disc is

given over to previously unreleased or rare tracks from the Motown vaults. Taken together, it may be more than all but the most diehard fan wants to hear, which may be why Motown rushed out yet another single-disc hits collection, *The Ultimate Collection*, a couple of months later. But if you want the Jackson 5 on Motown, a big chunk of it is here. —*William Ruhlmann*

Greatest Hits / 1995 / Epic ✦✦✦

While they were with Epic, the Jacksons mainly recorded disco and dance-pop, with a few romantic ballads thrown in. *Greatest Hits* collects the majority of their hit singles from the late '70s and early '80s, although *Destiny* and *Triumph* remain more consistent and enjoyable albums than this compilation. —*Stephen Thomas Erlewine*

★ **The Ultimate Collection** / Aug. 15, 1995 / Motown ✦✦✦✦✦

Not quite as extensive as the 33-song *Anthology*, this 21-song single disc does include the group's biggest Motown hits, as well as early solo hits by Michael Jackson and Jermaine Jackson. *Anthology* is still the best way to go for those whose interest isn't deep enough to spring for the *Soulsation!* box. However, if you're on a budget, this does nail down most or all of the key cuts that most listeners want or need. —*Richie Unterberger*

Chuck Jackson

b. Jun. 22, 1937, Latta, SC
Vocals / Soul, R&B

He's relatively forgotten today, and his brand of "uptown" soul is dismissed by the relatively vocal clique of critics who prefer their soul deep and down-home. But Chuck Jackson was a regular visitor to the R&B charts (and an occasional one to the pop listings) in the early '60s with such early pop-soul concoctions as "I Don't Want to Cry," "Any Day Now," and "Tell Him I'm Not Home." His records were very much of a piece with New York pop-rock-soul production, with cheeky brass, sweeping strings, and female backup vocalists. Those production trills make his work sound dated to some listeners, and his hoarse, emotional vocals weren't as subtle or commanding as peers like Ben E. King or Wilson Pickett. On its own terms, though, his best work is quite good, whether you prefer pop to soul or vice versa.

Jackson sang with one of the best doo wop groups, the Dell-Vikings, for a while in the late '50s (although he doesn't appear on their hit singles). Spotted by Scepter Records while performing with Jackie Wilson's Revue, he started recording for the label in 1961. As was the case with labelmates Dionne Warwick and the Shirelles, Jackson's early-'60s arrangements blended pop, R&B, and New York session professionalism. Like Warwick, Jackson was one of the first singers to successfully record Bacharach-David material; one of his best singles, "I Keep Forgettin'" (1962), was written and produced by Leiber-Stoller. Chuck had some success with some duets with Maxine Brown in the mid-'60s, but he left Wand in 1967 for Motown, at the urging of Smokey Robinson. Jackson was (perhaps understandably) lost in the shuffle during his four years at Motown, and he's barely been heard from since, although he remains a favorite on England's "Northern soul" scene. —*Richie Unterberger*

Mr. Emotion / 1984 / Kent ✦✦✦

● **The Great Recordings** / 1995 / Tomato ✦✦✦✦

This 46-song, double-CD compilation of Wand-era recordings is the most extensive Jackson retrospective, though it doesn't include every last worthwhile track. It does contain his most important songs, as well as a few of his duets with Maxine Brown, but the programming leaves something to be desired, inserting some half-baked instrumentals, live cuts, and Elvis Presley covers among the prime stuff. —*Richie Unterberger*

Janet Jackson

b. May 16, 1966, Gary, IN
Vocals / Dance-Pop, Urban, Adult Contemporary, Pop-Rock, Club-Dance

Janet Jackson is the ninth and last child in the musically talented Jackson family that includes the Jackson 5, Michael Jackson, and Jermaine Jackson. Janet Jackson performed on stage with her brothers at the age of seven. At ten, she acted in the TV series *Good Times* and was later seen in *Diff'rent Strokes* and *Fame*. She released her first album, *Janet Jackson*, in 1982 and her second, *Dream Street*, in 1984, but neither of these records was notably successful. Then, in 1985, Jackson turned to the production team of Jimmy Jam and Terry Lewis (formerly of the Time) for the album *Control*, which, ironically, emphasized the artist's new maturity and independence, even though most of the songs were co-compositions of the three. *Control* was a massive hit: it topped the charts, selling more than four million copies, and spawned five Top Ten hits, including the No. 1 "When I Think of You." The follow-up, *Rhythm Nation 1814*, did even better, spawning seven Top Ten hits, among them the No. 1s "Miss You Much," "Escapade," and "Black Cat." In 1991, Jackson signed a new recording contract with Virgin Records for a reported $32 million.

1993's *janet*. proved to be as successful as her previous two releases, featuring a series of Top Ten singles including "If" and "That's the Way Love Goes." —*William Ruhlmann*

Janet Jackson / 1982 / A&M ✦✦

Dream Street / 1984 / A&M ✦✦

☆ **Control** / 1986 / A&M ✦✦✦✦✦

Jam and Lewis tailor their contemporary dance-pop to the emerging personality of Jackson, who is attempting to take "Control" of her life on this record. In the course of that attempt, she comes across as an aggressive, independent woman, notably on "What Have You Done for Me Lately." But the album is primarily a production showcase; it may be tailored to Jackson's persona, but the real artists are Jam and Lewis. —*William Ruhlmann*

Rhythm Nation 1814 / 1989 / A&M ✦✦✦✦

Jam and Lewis have more beats up their sleeves, and the singer's own personality is even more submerged than it was on *Control*, but this is the height of '80s dance-pop. —*William Ruhlmann*

janet. / May 18, 1993 / Virgin ✦✦✦

Janet Jackson returns with *janet.*, a long (75 minutes), ambitious album declaring her sexual maturity. There are good moments here, but it's marred by the torturously long running time and the intros cluttering the entire album. With a CD player, it's possible to program these excesses out and enjoy *janet.* as a solid successor to *Control* and *Rhythm Nation 1814*. —*Stephen Thomas Erlewine*

★ **Design of a Decade 1986-1996** / Oct. 10, 1995 / A&M ✦✦✦✦

Design of a Decade: 1986-1996 is a misleading title. The bulk of Janet Jackson's greatest hits collection concentrates on *Control* and *Rhythm Nation 1814*, simply by contractual necessity. That is far from a fatal flaw. The hits from those two albums were state-of-the-art dance-pop productions at the time of their release, filled with bottomless beats and memorable, catchy hooks. None of the songs have lost any of their impact, from the funk of "Miss You Much" and "What Have You Done for Me Lately" to the ballads "Let's Wait Awhile" and "Come Back to Me." In addition to all 13 Top 40 hits from *Control* and *Rhythm Nation*—all but one went into the Top Five—*Design of a Decade* includes the biggest and best hit from *janet.*, the sultry "That's the Way Love Goes," and two new songs, "Runaway" and "Twenty Foreplay." It's a credit to Janet Jackson that the two new numbers feel like genuine hits, not tacked-on filler, and help make the album a compulsively listenable greatest hits collection. —*Stephen Thomas Erlewine*

Joe Jackson

b. Aug. 11, 1955, Burton-on-Trent, England
Piano, Vocals / Singer-Songwriter, New Wave, Pop-Rock

Although Joe Jackson initially appeared to fit in neatly with such new wave singer-songwriters as Elvis Costello and Graham Parker when he appeared in the late '70s, he has displayed a much broader range on his numerous record releases since. Born in Burton-on-Trent, England, Jackson studied piano as a youth and earned a piano scholarship to the Royal College of Music, which he attended from 1971 to 1974. *Look Sharp!*, his debut album released in 1979, featured a fast-paced, guitar-driven rock style, with Jackson spitting out sometimes bitter, sometimes vulnerable lyrics, notably on the single "Is She Really Going Out with Him?," which hit No. 21 in the US. The album got to No. 20 and went gold. *I'm the Man*, an album in the same style released in October, got to No. 22.

Jackson then began the first of his many changes of style. *Beat Crazy*, released in the fall of 1980, marked a sharp turn toward reggae and a drop in Jackson's commercial fortunes. *Joe Jackson's Jumpin' Jive* (1981) contained big-band and jump-blues standards from the '40s. In 1982, Jackson moved to New York City, adopting some of the sophisticated style of Cole Porter and some of the small-band jazz music found in the city's clubs for *Night and Day*, released in June. The album was Jackson's biggest hit, going to No. 4 and producing the hit singles "Steppin' Out" and "Breaking Us in Two."

Jackson composed a film soundtrack, *Mike's Murder*, in 1983, then made *Body and Soul* in a style similar to *Night and Day*. It hit No. 20 and included the Top 15 hit "You Can't Get What You Want (Till You Know What You Want)." In 1985 Jackson composed music for the Japanese film *House of the Poet*. Some of the music was later released on his album *Will Power*. Jackson's 1986 album was the three-sided *Big World*, which reached No. 34. *Will Power*, issued in 1987, was an instrumental album combining classical and jazz styles. It was followed in 1988 by the double *Live 1980–1986* and the soundtrack to the film *Tucker*. After his next pop album, *Blaze of Glory* (1989), did not succeed commercially, Jackson jumped to Virgin Records, which issued *Laughter and Lust* (1991). —*William Ruhlmann*

★ **Look Sharp!** / Apr. 1979 / A&M ✦✦✦✦✦

Hyperactive new wave rock overlaid with the intelligent, caustic worldview of a man as angry as any punk, but far more perceptive. Includes the hit "Is She Really Going Out with Him?" —*William Ruhlmann*

I'm the Man / Oct. 1979 / A&M ✦✦✦✦

Nearly a rewrite of *Look Sharp!* and capturing all of its brilliance, *I'm the Man* is pure power-pop—hook filled, concise, and fun. Includes the won-

derful "It's Different for Girls," a marginal hit in both the US and UK.
—Chris Woodstra

Beat Crazy / 1980 / A&M ✦✦✦✦
Credited to the Joe Jackson Band, *Beat Crazy* completes Jackson's power-pop period. Jackson begins to stretch a bit stylistically, flirting with reggae and more experimental styles while in the confines of the three-minute form he would later dismiss. Every bit as charming as the first two. *—Chris Woodstra*

Jumpin' Jive / 1981 / A&M ✦✦✦✦
A delightful trip back to '40s and '50s jump blues and big-band swing. With faithful covers of Louis Jordan and Cab Calloway, Jackson appears to be having fun, while helping a new generation discover these classics. *—Chris Woodstra*

Night & Day / 1982 / A&M ✦✦✦✦
Since Jackson has already demonstrated his broad musical tastes by turning from rock to "jumpin' jive" on his last album, that he was able to incorporate Latin, dance, and sophisticated ballad styles into his music wasn't so surprising. But that he could do it all so well was delightful. Includes "Steppin' Out" and "Breaking Us in Two." *—William Ruhlmann*

Body & Soul / 1984 / A&M ✦✦✦
Continuing in his move away from pop music that began with *Night and Day*, Jackson shows his love of '50s jazz with detail best represented by the cover photo (nearly identical to the Sonny Rollins album of the same name). Features his last US hit, "You Can't Get What You Want" and the beautiful "Be My Number Two." *—Chris Woodstra*

Big World / 1986 / A&M ✦✦✦
A brilliant collection of songs, running over an hour, finds Jackson as biting as ever as he surveys the world, but also tenderly reflective on "Home Town." *—William Ruhlmann*

Will Power / 1987 / A&M ✦✦

Live . . . 1980-1986 / 1988 / A&M ✦✦✦

Blaze of Glory / 1989 / A&M ✦✦✦

Laughter & Lust / 1991 / Virgin ✦✦✦

Night Music / 1994 / Virgin ✦

Michael Jackson
....
b. Aug. 29, 1958, Gary, IN
Vocals / Soul, Dance-Pop, Funk, Urban, Motown, Pop-Rock, Club-Dance, New Jack R&B
As part of the Jackson 5, a group made up of his brothers, Michael Jackson was among the most popular singing stars of the '70s. On his own, he was the biggest pop star of the '80s. Jackson was always the visual and vocal focus of the Jackson 5, who broke through to national success on the Motown label in 1970, when he was 11, with the first of four straight No. 1 hits, "I Want You Back." Jackson was also promoted as a solo artist, and he scored his first hit, "Got to Be There," in 1971. Subsequent hits included his remake of "Rockin' Robin" and "Ben" in 1972.

Jackson's and the Jackson 5's fortunes declined somewhat after the early '70s, and the group moved to Epic at mid-decade, with Michael temporarily abandoning his solo career and subsuming his group leadership to other members of what was now called the Jacksons. The group gradually built back its popularity by writing its own material. Jackson returned to solo work in 1979 with *Off the Wall*, a mature combination of driving dance songs ("Don't Stop Til You Get Enough") and feelingly sung ballads ("She's Out of My Life") that outsold any previous group or solo effort, and spawned four Top Ten hits.

Jackson again recorded and toured with the Jacksons, but his next album, *Thriller* (1982), became a musical phenomenon. It was the biggest-selling album of all time, moving 20 million copies in the US alone and including seven Top Ten hits. Clearly Jackson had grown beyond his brothers, but he stayed with them for one more album and tour in 1984.

His follow-up album, *Bad* (1987), accompanied by a solo world tour, sold six million copies domestically. Only six of its seven singles hit the Top Ten, but five in a row hit No. 1.

In late 1991, Jackson returned with *Dangerous*, which, by mid-1992, had sold four million copies and spawned the hits "Black and White," "Remember the Time," "In the Closet," and "Jam." Jackson's second world tour, launched in Europe in June 1992, continued into 1993.

Although numerous rumors had circled around Jackson throughout his career, his reputation remained clean. It wasn't until 1993 that he suffered serious damage to his image. Jackson was accused of child abuse by a teenage friend, sparking a major media frenzy. Through it all, Jackson vehemently denied the accusations. The civil case was settled out of court in early 1994. Jackson began working on *HIStory* soon after the settlement. *HIStory* contained one disc of Jackson's greatest hits and one disc of new material. It was released on June 20, 1995. *—William Ruhlmann*

☆ **Off the Wall** / 1979 / Epic ✦✦✦✦✦
If you were listening to the Jacksons's *Destiny* from the previous year, maybe you were less surprised than many that Michael Jackson was capable of making an album this accomplished and assured. From the first moments, he seems bursting with the wide range of music included, from the first side's clutch of irresistible dance tracks ("Don't Stop 'Til You Get Enough," "Rock with You," "Working Day and Night") to the light pop and ballads ("She's Out of My Life," "Off the Wall") of side twp. Throughout, Jackson's flexible tenor coos and growls by turns, always goosing the songs along. Deservedly a massive hit, this is less dated today than much of the dance music of that era. *—William Ruhlmann*

The Best of Michael Jackson / 1981 / Motown ✦✦✦

★ **Thriller** / 1982 / Epic ✦✦✦✦✦
What impresses after a decade is Jackson's range of musical expression, one that touches the schmaltzy pop of Paul McCartney (his duet partner on "The Girl Is Mine") on one side and the hard rock of Van Halen (whose lead guitarist, Eddie Van Halen, is heard on "Beat It") on the other, with plenty of mainstream rock-pop and dance music in between. It's no accident that the record found a home in so many record collections—there's good music here for everyone. And of course, by summing up the state of pop music, Jackson also redefined it—this was a high-water mark for pop music never equaled since, even in his subsequent music. *—William Ruhlmann*

Anthology / 1986 / Motown ✦✦✦✦
Michael Jackson's greatest hits (1971-1975) emphasize his waiflike charm and youth (he was 13 years old when the first of these songs appeared) in ballads such as "Got to Be There," "Ben" (even if it is a love song to a rat), and "I Wanna Be Where You Are." The upbeat cover of "Rockin' Robin" is equally appealing. The digitally remastered, double-CD version includes a few additional tracks. *—William Ruhlmann*

Bad / 1987 / Epic ✦✦✦✦
A partially successful attempt to remake *Thriller*. Interestingly, Jackson did not turn to a softer, more broadly commercial approach but instead upped the dance-rock ante. Songs such as "Dirty Diana" and "Smooth Criminal" found him striding forward in terms of rhythm and beat. And with seven hit singles out of ten tracks (five at No. 1), this, like *Thriller*, is in effect a Michael Jackson greatest-hits record, covering 1987-1989. *—William Ruhlmann*

Dangerous / 1992 / Epic ✦✦✦
Wisely, Jackson altered his creative process here, jettisoning producer Quincy Jones in favor of Teddy Riley and bringing in several songwriting collaborators. The result is an updated dance-floor success (the drums are way up in the mix), though the songwriting sometimes seem schematic. When Jackson is left more or less to himself, he is less R&B-oriented, notably on the pop ballad "Heal the World" and the guitar-driven pop-rock song "Black or White" (a Stones riff, though taken at a tempo the Stones never attempted). Rather than resting on his laurels, Jackson continues to work hard to maintain and further the quality of his work. *—William Ruhlmann*

HIStory: Past, Present And Future Book 1 / 1995 / Epic ✦✦✦
However, *HIStory Continues* reiterates musical ideas Jackson has been exploring since *Bad*. Jackson certainly tries to stay contemporary, yet he has a tendency to smooth out all of his rougher musical edges with show-biz schmaltz. Occasionally, Jackson produces some well-crafted pop that ranks with his best material: R. Kelly's "You Are Not Alone" is seductive, "Scream" improves on the slamming beats of his earlier single "Jam," and "Stranger in Moscow" is one of his most haunting ballads. Nevertheless, *HIStory Continues* stands as his weakest album since themid-'70s. *—Stephen Thomas Erlewine*

The Jam
....
Rock'n'Roll, Punk, Pop-Rock, Mod-Revival
The Jam were the most popular band to emerge from the initial wave of British punk rock in 1977; along with the Sex Pistols, the Clash, and the Buzzcocks, the Jam had the most impact on pop music. While they could barely get noticed in America, the trio became genuine superstars in Britain, with an impressive string of Top Ten singles in the late '70s and early '80s. The Jam could never have a hit in America because they were thoroughly and defiantly British. Under the direction of guitarist/vocalist/songwriter Paul Weller, the trio spearheaded a revival of mid-'60s mod groups, in the style of the Who and the Small Faces. Like the mod bands, the group dressed stylishly, worshipped American R&B, and played it loud and rough. By the time of the group's third album, Weller's songwriting had grown substantially, as he was beginning to write social commentaries and pop songs in the vein of the Kinks. Both his political songs and his romantic songs were steeped in British culture, filled with references and slang in the lyrics, as well as musical allusions. Furthermore, as the Jam grew more popular and musically accessible, Weller became more insistent and stubborn about his beliefs, supporting leftist causes and adhering to the pop aesthetics of '60s British rock without

ever succumbing to hippie values. Paradoxically, that meant even when their music became more pop than punk, they never abandoned the punk values—if anything, Weller stuck to the strident independent ethics of 1977 more than any other punk band just by refusing to change.

Weller formed the Jam with drummer Rick Buckler, bassist Bruce Foxton, and guitarist Steve Brookes while they were still in school in 1975; Brookes quickly left the band and they remained a trio for the rest of their career. For the next year, the band played gigs around London, building a local following. In February 1977, the group signed a record contract with Polydor records; two months later, they released their debut single, "In the City," which reached the UK Top 40. The following month, the group released their debut album, also called *In the City*. Recorded in just 11 days, the album featured a combination of R&B covers and Weller originals, all of which sounded a bit like faster, more ragged versions of the Who's early records. Their second single, "All Around the World," nearly broke into the British Top Ten and the group embarked on a successful British tour. During the summer of 1977, they recorded their second album, *This Is the Modern World*, which was released toward the end of the year. "The Modern World" made it into the Top 40 in November, just as the Jam were beginning their first American tour. Although it was brief, the tour was not successful, leaving bitter memories of the US in the minds of the band.

This Is the Modern World peaked in the British charts at No. 22, yet it received criticism for repeating the sound of the debut. The band began a headlining tour of the UK, but was derailed shortly after it started when the group got into a nasty fight with a bunch of rugby players in a Leeds hotel. Weller broke several bones and was charged with assault, although the Leeds Crown Court would eventually acquit him. The Jam departed for another American tour in March of 1978 and it was yet another unsuccessful tour, as they opened for Blue Öyster Cult. It did nothing to win new American fans, yet their star continued to rise in Britain. Bands copying the group's mod look and sound popped up across Britain and the Jam itself performed at the Reading Festival in August. *All Mod Cons*, released late in 1979, marked a turning point in the Jam's career, illustrating that Weller's songwriting was becoming more melodic, complex, and lyrically incisive, resembling Ray Davies more than Pete Townshend. Even as their sound became more pop-oriented, the group lost none of their tightly controlled energy. *All Mod Cons* was a major success, peaking at No. 6 on the UK charts, even if it didn't make it into the US. Every one of the band's singles were now charting in the Top 20, with the driving "Eton Rifles" becoming their first Top Ten in November 1979, charting at No. 3.

Setting Sons, released at the end of 1979, climbed to No. 4 in the UK and marked their first charting album in the US, hitting No. 137 in spring of 1980. At that time, the Jam had become full-fledged rock stars in Britain, with their new "Going Underground" single entering the charts at No. 1. During the summer, the band recorded their fifth album, with the "Taxman"-inspired "Start" released as a teaser single in August; "Start" became their second straight No. 1. Its accompanying album, the ambitious *Sound Affects*, hit No. 2 in the UK at the end of the year; it was also the band's high-water mark in the US, peaking at No. 72. "That's Entertainment," one of the standout tracks from *Sound Affects*, charted at No. 21 in the UK charts as an import single, confirming the band's enormous popularity.

"Funeral Pyre," the band's summer 1981 single, showed signs that Weller was becoming fascinated with American soul and R&B, as did the punchy, horn-driven "Absolute Beginners," which hit No. 4 in the fall of the year. As the Jam were recording their sixth album, Weller suffered a nervous breakdown, which prompted him to stop drinking. In February 1982, the first single from the new sessions—the double-A-sided "Town Called Malice"/"Precious"—became their third No. 1 single and the band became the first group since the Beatles to play two songs on BBC's *Top of the Pops*. The Gift, released in 1982, showcased the band's soul infatuation and became the group's first No. 1 album in the UK. "Just Who Is the 5 O'Clock Hero" hit No. 8 in July, becoming the group's second import single to make the UK charts.

Although the Jam was at the height of its popularity, Paul Weller was becoming frustrated with the trio's sound and made the decision to disband the group. On the heels of the No. 2 hit "The Bitterest Pill," the Jam announced their breakup in October of 1982. The band played a farewell tour in the fall and their final single, "Beat Surrender," entered the charts at No. 1. *Dig the New Breed*, a compilation of live tracks, charted at No. 2 in December of 1982. All 16 of the group's singles were re-released by Polydor in the UK at the beginning of 1983; all of them recharted simultaneously. Bruce Foxton released a solo album, *Touch Sensitive*, and Rick Buckler played with the Time UK; neither of the efforts were noteworthy as the Jam biography the two wrote in the early '90s, which contained many vicious attacks on Paul Weller.

Immediately after the breakup of the Jam, Weller formed the Style Council with Mick Talbot, a member of the Jam-inspired mod-revival band the Merton Parkas. After a handful of initial hits, the Style Council proved to be a disappointment and Weller fell out of favor, both critically

and commercially. At the end of the decade he disbanded the group and went solo in the early '90s; his solo albums have been both artistic and popular successes, returning him to the spotlight in the UK. The legacy of the Jam is apparent in nearly every British guitar pop band of the '80s and '90s, from the Smiths to Blur and Oasis. More than any other group, the Jam kept the tradition of three-minute, hook-driven British guitar pop alive through the '70s and '80s, providing a blueprint for generations of bands to come. —*Stephen Thomas Erlewine*

In the City / May 1977 / Polydor ✦✦✦
A spunky and abrasive debut, it mixes a mod's penchant for soul grooves with some fine piss-and-vinegar originals. —*John Floyd*

This Is the Modern World / Nov. 1977 / Polydor ✦✦✦
While it essentially repeats the formula of their debut, *This Is the Modern World* is an exciting, energetic record. —*Stephen Thomas Erlewine*

☆ **All Mod Cons** / 1978 / Polydor ✦✦✦✦✦
All Mod Cons marks a great leap for the band in songwriting maturity and sense of purpose. For the first time, they are able to build on rather than fall back on their influences, creating a sound all their own. Weller's story-song style, using invented characters, vivid British imagery, a youthful perspective, and an impassioned delivery begs for the "voice of a generation" tag and clearly places him in the ranks of Ray Davies. Nothing short of a masterpiece. —*Chris Woodstra*

☆ **Setting Sons** / 1979 / Polydor ✦✦✦✦
Setting Sons was originally planned as a concept album about three childhood friends who, upon meeting up after some time apart, discover that they've grown apart. Though only about half of the songs follow the concept, Weller successfully depicts British life, male relationships, and coming to terms with entry into adulthood. Oddly enough, while the lyrics are among Weller's darkest and most cynical, the production is their smoothest and the music is their most melodic to date. —*Chris Woodstra*

☆ **Sound Affects** / 1980 / Polydor ✦✦✦✦✦
A return to the expansive sound and love-and-politics of *All Mod Cons*, it's highlighted by the snarling "Pretty Green," "Set the House Ablaze," and "Start!," a fiery rewrite of the Beatles hit "Taxman." —*John Floyd*

The Gift / Jan. 1982 / Polydor ✦✦
A blatant stab at expanding their soul roots, it's pretty spotty, really, but "Town Called Malice," "Ghosts," and "Just Who Is the 5 O'Clock Hero?" are among the band's best work. —*John Floyd*

Dig the New Breed / Feb. 1982 / Polydor ✦✦✦

★ **Snap!** / 1983 / Polydor ✦✦✦✦✦
Snap! collects all of the Jam's singles, from "In the City" to "Beat Surrender," including several B-sides ("A' Bomb in Wardour Street," "Dreams of Children") and a handful of rarities, like a demo of "That's Entertainment" and the rock version of "Smithers-Jones." For its compact disc release, several songs were trimmed, but *Snap!* remains a brilliant summation of why the Jam were one of the most important and beloved British bands of their era. The latter-day collection *Greatest Hits* covers much the same ground as *Snap!*, but the earlier compilation remains preferable because of sequencing and its inclusion of essential items like "A' Bomb in Wardour Street" and "Dreams of Children." —*Stephen Thomas Erlewine*

Extras: A Collection of Rarities / 1992 / Polydor ✦✦✦✦
Paul Weller has yet to receive his due in North America as one of Britain's major rock writers. His group the Jam began in the late '70s as a mod-revival combo influenced by the Who and the Small Faces. By 1982, backed by a fusion of pop, soul, R&B, and rock, Weller's lyrical insights into his country's psyche had positioned him as the Ray Davies of his generation. The exhaustive 26 tracks on *Extras* may not be the ideal introduction to newcomers but make up an essential item for fans. As the title suggests, the disc collects single B-sides, demos of well-known songs, cover versions, and overlooked album tracks. Of interest are two never-before-released numbers, a 1980 demo called "No One in the World," and "Hey Mister," recorded in 1979. UK music journalist Paolo Hewitt's seven-page essay is insightful, if a bit gushy. —*Roch Parisien*

Greatest Hits / 1992 / Polydor ✦✦✦✦
Greatest Hits covers nearly the same ground as *Snap!*, with all the tracks but "Just Who Is the Five O'Clock Hero" included on the previous compilation. Granted, "That's Entertainment" is presented in the album version and "Funeral Pyre" in its original mix, but the album isn't quite as strong as *Snap*. Nevertheless, it has all of their hit singles, making it a thoroughly entertaining record, as well as an effective introduction to the group. —*Stephen Thomas Erlewine*

Live Jam / 1993 / Polydor ✦✦

The Jam Collection / 1996 / Polydor ✦✦✦

James Gang

Rock 'n' Roll, Hard Rock
For a brief period in the early '70s, the James Gang was one of the top

hard-rock acts in America, thanks to the songwriting and inventive instrumental work of singer/guitarist Joe Walsh. The band was founded in Cleveland by drummer Jim Fox; its first lineup was fleshed out by bassist Tom Kriss and guitarist Glen Schwartz. The group toured the Midwest and built a name for itself, but Schwartz left the band in 1969. Walsh stepped in admirably, and word of the new guitar phenom spread quickly; the James Gang recorded its debut, *Yer Album*, later that year. The follow-up, *The James Gang Rides Again*, proved to be arguably the group's strongest and contained their best-known song, "Funk No.49" (they never had a hit single). The album went gold, as did their next two, and hit the Top 20. James Gang fan Pete Townshend invited the group to open for the Who on a European tour in 1971; shortly thereafter, Walsh left the group, feeling constrained by the power-trio formula. He first formed Barnstorm; later, he recorded several solo albums and joined the Eagles for *Hotel California* and *The Long Run*. Dominic Troiano served as guitarist until 1973, when he joined the Guess Who; Tommy Bolin played on the *Bang* and *Miami* albums, but when he left to join Deep Purple, it essentially spelled the end of the James Gang, whose sales declined steadily following. The James Gang finally broke up for good in 1976. —*Steve Huey*

Yer' Album / 1969 / One Way ✦✦✦

● **Rides Again** / 1970 / MCA ✦✦✦✦
With their second album *The James Gang Rides Again*, the James Gang came into their own. Under the direction of guitarist Joe Walsh, the group—now featuring bassist Dale Peters—began incorporating keyboards into their hard rock, which helped open up their musical horizons. For much of the first side of *Rides Again*, the group tears through a bunch of boogie numbers, most notably the heavy groove of "Funk No.49." On the second side, the James Gang departs from their trademark sound, adding keyboard flourishes and elements of country-rock to their hard rock. Walsh's songwriting had improved, giving the band solid support for their stylistic experiments. What ties the two sides of the record together is the strength of the band's musicianship, which burns brightly and powerfully on the hardest rockers, as well as on the sensitive ballads. —*Stephen Thomas Erlewine*

Thirds / 1971 / One Way ✦✦✦✦
Thirds wasn't quite as satisfying as *The James Gang Rides Again*, lacking the consistently strong songwriting of the previous album. Nevertheless, the interplay between the musicians is impressive throughout the record and whenever Walsh turns in a killer song, like "Walk Away" or "Midnight Man," the band drives it home for all it's worth. —*Stephen Thomas Erlewine*

Bang / 1973 / Atco ✦✦✦

The Best of the James Gang / 1973 / ABC ✦✦✦✦
A good collection of their innovative hard rock features "Walk Away" and "Funk 49." —*Dan Heilman*

Rick James (James Johnson)

b. Feb. 1, 1952, Buffalo, NY
Bass, Guitar, Vocals / Funk, Urban
Never quite as musically exciting as his cheerfully sleazy image suggests, Rick James was a major funk figure for a short time in the late '70s and early '80s. He called his music "punk funk," which is a reasonable description of his style. James took the basic sound of George Clinton's P-Funk, sang it like was rock, and added cloying drug and sex references. Too often, his music sounded like a string of hooks without any song, but when the hooks worked, as on "Super Freak," the results were undeniably funky and frequently brought him to the top of the R&B and pop charts.

In the early '80s, he brought a number of groups to Motown, most prominently the Mary Jane Girls. Not only did he produce their records, he controlled the direction of their career. However, there was only so far his music could take these artists, not to mention himself, and by 1983 his career had started to slip. By the end of the decade, his music wasn't funk, it was slick urban contemporary R&B; even a change in style couldn't send James back to the top of the charts. Throughout the '90s, his comeback attempts have been plagued by persistent drug and legal problems. The last time he hit the charts was not even as a solo artist, it was as a featured sample in MC Hammer's smash hit, "U Can't Touch This." —*Stephen Thomas Erlewine*

Bustin' Out of L Seven / 1979 / Gordy ✦✦✦

Street Songs / 1981 / Motown ✦✦✦✦
Rick James peaked on this album. His vocals were never more aggressive or better produced than on the singles "Super Freak" and "Give It to Me Baby." James became a crossover sensation, as the LP peaked at No. 3 on the pop album chart and eventually went platinum. "Give It to Me Baby" topped the R&B charts for five weeks, while "Super Freak" was also a Top Ten single. —*Ron Wynn*

● **Reflections: Greatest Hits** / 1984 / Motown ✦✦✦✦
A nice collection featuring the best uptempo and left-field ballad hits by Rick James. The anthology shows that James functioned best when riding the rhythm; he was a moderately talented (at best) vocalist, better at yelling and exhorting than trying to interpret lyrics, pace a slow song, or vary a mood. The only significant ballad hit he had was a duet where the contrast between his voice and Smokey Robinson's generated enough response to sell the song. —*Ron Wynn*

● **Greatest Hits** / 1986 / Motown ✦✦✦✦
The best of his "punk-funk" includes "Super Freak," "Give It to Me Baby," and "You & I." —*Rick A. Bueche*

Bustin' Out: The Very Best Of / 1994 / Motown ✦✦✦✦
A definitive double-disc anthology, it's essential for devoted fans. —*AMG*

Tommy James & the Shondells

Pop-Rock, Bubblegum, Brill Building Pop
During the last half of the '60s, Tommy James & the Shondells were one of America's most successful pop acts, generating 14 Top 40 hits between 1966 and 1969. James formed the original Shondells at the age of 12, in 1960. In 1963, they recorded a Jeff Barry-Ellie Greenwich song called "Hanky Panky" for the Snap label. Two years later, a Pittsburgh DJ picked up on the song and made it into a regional hit. James and the original Shondells parted ways because the band members didn't want to relocate from Indiana, and James formed a new Shondells by taking on a group called the Raconteurs. In 1966 they signed to Morris Levy's Roulette, which reissued "Hanky Panky" (it became a No. 1 million-seller).

For the next two years, they embodied lightweight chewy pop with hits like "I Think We're Alone Now" and "Mirage." The group developed a heavier sound with the percussive 1968 hit "Mony Mony." In keeping with the times, they became more psychedelic, best captured in their No. 1 "Crimson and Clover." The Shondells continued to chart until James left for a moderately successful solo career in 1970. James' biggest hit was "Draggin' the Line." The Shondells changed their name to Hog Heaven to no appreciable success. During the '80s, the Shondells' material enjoyed a resurgence of popularity among various pop and rock artists. Joan Jett scored with "Crimson and Clover," while Billy Idol's version of "Mony Mony" and Tiffany's "I Think We're Alone Now" took turns at the No. 1 position in November of 1987. —*Rick Clark*

● **Anthology** / 1990 / Rhino ✦✦✦✦
James and his band had a remarkable string of hits from the mid-'60s to the early '70s, largely because of an uncanny ability to keep current with fast-changing pop trends, from their first garage-band hit, "Hanky Panky," to their psychedelicized songs like "Crimson and Clover." Even more remarkable, the music holds up entertainingly today, and this well-annotated, 27-track compilation contains all the hits and more. —*William Ruhlmann*

Solo Years (1970-81) / 1991 / Rhino ✦✦✦✦

Jan & Dean

Surf, Pop-Rock
Besides the Beach Boys, no other vocal group captured the sound of California surf music with as much success—both commercial and artistic—as Jan & Dean. The duo actually began as a doo wop-soaked harmony act in the late '50s, reaching the Top Ten with the goofy "Baby Talk" and scoring minor hits with doo wop updates of standards like "A Sunday Kind of Love" and "Heart and Soul." When the Beach Boys began their climb to superstardom, Jan & Dean changed gears and followed suit with a series of surf and hot rod hits that featured falsetto harmonies, chugging guitars, and Jan Berry's clean production. Brian Wilson himself sang backup vocals on their biggest hit (which he co-wrote with Jan), "Surf City," in 1963.

While they lacked the Beach Boys' depth and capacity for artistic growth, Jan & Dean's hits from 1963 and 1964—which also included "The Little Old Lady (From Pasadena)," "Drag City," "Honolulu Lulu," and the mini-soap opera "Dead Man's Curve"—are in the same class as the Beach Boys' early work in their infectious, energetic invocation of good times and California sunshine. They added an irresistibly reckless humor to the genre, and were well cast as the fun-loving hosts of the classic 1964 rock 'n' roll hootenanny film *The T.A.M.I. Show* (for which they performed the rip-roaring theme, "(Here They Come) From All over the World"). The duo's success, already on the wane a bit, was tragically cut short by Jan Berry's near-fatal auto accident in April 1966, which had been eerily foreshadowed by the lyrics of "Dead Man's Curve." —*Richie Unterberger*

● **Surf City: The Best of Jan & Dean** / 1990 / EMI America ✦✦✦✦
Remembered mostly for their surfing hits, Jan & Dean had a bit more range than they're generally given credit for. Their roots were in doo wop, and after scoring surf and hot rod hits, they also cut some decent straight pop-rock songs and zany singles that verged on pop satire. *Surf City*

includes just about all the material you'd want from the duo. The 22 songs include the big hits "Surf City," "Dead Man's Curve," and "The Little Old Lady (From Pasadena)," of course, but also feature nifty smaller successes like "Honolulu Lulu," "The New Girl in School," and "Ride ihe Wild Surf." The pair was second only to ihe Beach Boys in blending high, soaring harmonies with driving vocal surf 'n' hot rod sounds. Of course, they weren't nearly as talented as Brian Wilson's group, but even their minor material has an irrepressible sense of fun and sparking L.A. pop-rock production and melodies. Other highlights include their rearrangement of the old standard "Linda" and the 1965 Top 40 hit "I Found a Girl," written by P.F. Sloan and Steve Barri. Sloan-Barri also penned their infectious theme for the classic rock film *The T.A.M.I. Show,* "(Here They Come) From All over the World," which deserved to be a bigger hit than it was. The only major omissions of this well-packaged set are their early, heavily doo wop-influenced hits "Jennie Lee," "Baby Talk," and "Heart and Soul," which weren't recorded for EMI. — *Richie Unterberger*

Teen Suite 1958-1962 / Jul. 4, 1995 / Varese Sarabande ◆◆◆

Golden Hits, Vols. 1-3 / 1996 / One Way ◆◆◆

Jan & Dean [K-Tel] / Jun. 1996 / K-Tel ◆◆◆◆

Jane's Addiction

Hard Rock, Alternative Pop-Rock, Heavy Metal
Jane's Addiction were one of the most hotly pursued rock bands when they gained notice in Los Angeles in the mid-'80s, with record companies at their feet. Flamboyant frontman Perry Farrell, formerly of the band Psi Com, has an undeniable charisma and an interest in provocative art (he designed the band's album covers) and Jane's Addiction plays a hybrid of rock music—metal with strains of punk, folk, jazz, or you-name-it.

The quartet comprising Farrell, bassist Eric Avery, drummer Stephen Perkins, and guitarist Dave Navarro had already released their debut album as well, in the form of a live recording from the Roxy in Hollywood. Finally, Warner Bros. won the bidding war and released *Nothing Shocking* in 1988. The band's abrasive sound and aggressive atttitude (typified by the nude sculpture on the cover) led to some resistance, but Jane's Addiction began to break through to an audience: the album spent 35 weeks in the charts.

Ritual de lo Habitual followed in 1990 and was the band's commercial breakthrough, reaching the Top 20 and going gold. Farrell designed the travelling rock festival Lollapalooza as a farewell tour for Jane's Addiction. After the tour was completed at the end of the summer of 1991, the group split. Farrell would continue to be involved with the organization of the annual Lollapalooza festival for the next several years; he also formed Porno for Pyros with Perkins in 1992, releasing their debut record the following year. After a couple of quiet years—which included forming Deconstruction, a band that didn't release any records until 1994, with Avery—Navarro joined The Red Hot Chili Peppers at the end of 1993. — *William Ruhlmann*

Jane's Addiction / 1987 / Triple X ◆◆◆

Nothing's Shocking / 1988 / Warner Bros. ◆◆◆◆
The cover (a sculpture of two naked females joined at the hips with their hair ablaze) screams that this is an artsy album, and it is. Jane's Addiction, under the direction of lead vocalist Perry Farrell, brings the aesthetics of performance art to heavy metal. Some of the results are provoking, but the group's ambitions are usually irritating. Farrell's voice wears thin after a few songs, and it's not helped much by the post-Zeppelin stumble of the band—Dave Navarro may be a fluid guitarist, but he can't write riffs as powerful and catchy as Jimmy Page. Nevertheless, *Nothing's Shocking* works on occasion, particularly "Summertime Rolls" and the re-recorded version of "Jane Says." — *Stephen Thomas Erlewine*

● **Ritual de lo Habitual** / 1989 / Warner Bros. ◆◆◆◆
Throughout the first half of *Ritual,* Jane's Addiction manages to groove, creating the best rock 'n' roll of their short career. The two Bo Diddley knock-offs, "Stop!" and "Been Caught Stealing," in particular, sound tight and exciting, but on the second half, the indulgent ten-minute songs are hauled out, beginning with the insufferable *menage à trois* magnum opus "Three Days." Still, the band manages to salvage the album with the majestic "Classic Girl," one of their best songs. — *Stephen Thomas Erlewine*

Jason & the Scorchers

Rock 'n' Roll, Country-Rock, Roots-Rock
A country/hard-rock band formed by Illinois native Jason Ringenberg in 1981, Jason and the Scorchers came careening onto the indie-rock scene seemingly out of nowhere (truth was, it was Nashville) with a debut EP whose most killer track (among a slew of killer tracks) was a fire-breathing cover of Bob Dylan's "Absolutely Sweet Marie." This amalgam of speedy hard rock fused with Ringenberg's decidedly country twang, along with the band's ability to deftly negotiate between Rolling Stones-style stomps and quieter, more melodic acoustic country music, led to Jason and the Scorchers becoming a critically lauded and fairly popular

'80s band. Capitalizing quickly on the notoriety brought by their debut EP, the Scorchers kicked out two fine LPs (*Lost & Found* and *Still Standing*) that sounded perfect for radio, but not so slick as to sound manufactured. With Ringenberg's yowling voice pushed way up front, the band's sonic power came from the synchronous playing of Nashville rock veterans Warner Hodges (guitar), Jeff Johnson (bass), and Perry Baggs (drums). Sharing similar musical backgrounds that valued the music of Hank Williams and Johnny Cash as much as the Stones or Beatles, these guys could crank out mega-amped hard rock one minute and sound like the Flying Burrito Brothers the next, all of it done with great skill and excitement. Despite their obvious talent, by the release of 1986's *Still Standing,* it seemed as though the band wasn't going anywhere. They had achieved a modicum of success, but weren't able to break through to mass acclaim, partly because they came along just before the explosion of country radio in the late '80s/early '90s. Hence, rock radio was reluctant to play them because they sounded too country, and country radio thought they were too rock; it's an old story that usually spells doom for the band in question. After a three-year break that saw Johnson's departure, the Scorchers released a desultory third album (*Thunder and Fire*) that sounded like a desperate attempt at hard-rock credibility. They broke up soon after. Ringenberg went on to record country-oriented solo work, re-formed the original Scorchers in 1994, and released a modest reunion record (*A Blazing Grace*) that sounded like the Scorchers of old. —*John Dougan*

Fervor / 1983 / EMI America ◆◆◆◆
Their debut EP has "Absolutely Sweet Marie" (which you'll play over and over and over), as well as some wonderful country-rock like "Hot Nights in Georgia." Ringenberg's twangy voice is a hoot to listen to, and Warner Hodges plays some great guitar. A wonderful, if too brief, record and a harbinger of some great rock 'n' roll to come. R.E.M.'s Michael Stipe contributes a song ("Both Sides of the Line") and some backup vocals. —*John Dougan*

Lost & Found / 1985 / EMI America ◆◆◆◆
Of the Scorchers' three full-length LPs, this is by far the best. There is so much pent-up energy and excitement on this record, it sounds as if it will fly off your turntable at any moment. With Hodges (as usual) driving this machine, Ringenberg's wild-eyed country-punk persona is here in full fury, and the good times never let up. This should have been the album that made them stars, but it did solidify their audience and place them in larger concert venues, where they tore it up. —*John Dougan*

Still Standing / 1986 / EMI Australia ◆◆◆

● **Essential, Vol. 1 (Are You Ready for the Country)** / 1992 / Capitol ◆◆◆◆

Jayhawks

Alternative Country-Rock
On a series of independent albums in the late '80s, the Jayhawks staked out the same territory as Gram Parsons and Neil Young, recording some of the best, grittiest country-rock of the decade. When the band signed to American Records in the early '90s, they started getting a substantial amount of press; many critics called their 1992 album, *Hollywood Town Hall,* one of the best of the year. While the Jayhawks do nothing particularly new, they do it well; not only do they sound like the classic country-rock of the '70s, they have the songs to support their sound, which keeps them from being an empty exercise in nostalgia. —*Stephen Thomas Erlewine*

Blue Earth / 1989 / Twin/Tone ◆◆◆

● **Hollywood Town Hall** / 1992 / Def American ◆◆◆◆
Darn if that old Neil Young influence hasn't spun off another winner. Right from the distorted, rootsy, opening chords of lead track "Waiting for the Sun," you can tell that Minneapolis combo the Jayhawks is well versed in early Crazy Horse. Gary Louris' electric chording is offset by Mark Olson's full-bodied acoustic guitar and harmonica textures. The disc was recorded partly in a home state, backwoods studio and partly in posher L.A. facilities. This contrast highlights the blend of—and tension between—rural and urban elements that give *Hollywood Town Hall* its edge. —*Roch Parisien*

Tomorrow the Green Grass / 1995 / American ◆◆◆◆
Even the title of the Jayhawks' follow-up, *Tomorrow the Green Grass,* shows that the band is headed for lusher pastures. The addition of a full-time keyboardist opens up their sound, as does the subtle string arrangements. The result is an album that is steeped in the early '70s, yet not in the dusty Gram Parsons tribute of *Hollywood Town Hall.* Instead, it sounds like what Parsons or Neil Young would have sounded like if they were produced in Nashville. —*Stephen Thomas Erlewine*

The JB's

Soul, R&B, Soul Jazz
Maceo Parker joined James Brown's fabled band in 1964, Alfred "Pee

Wee" Ellis joined the fold two years later, and Fred Wesley came on board in 1968. Ellis co-wrote such classics as "Cold Sweat" and "Say It Loud—I'm Black and I'm Proud," and both he and Wesley at various points were musical director of The JB's. Parker was immortalized in Brown's famous incantation "Maceo, come blow your horn." Ellis also served as musical director for Van Morrison, while Wesley and Parker were part of the Parliament/Funkadelic gang at their peak in the mid and late '70s. The three of them have recorded in various permutations as Maceo and All the King's Men, Maceo and the Macks, the JB's, Fred Wesley and the New JB's, Fred Wesley and the Horny Horns, the John Book Horns and simply under any one of their individual names. In the '80s and early '90s, with the resurgence of interest in James Brown and Parliament/Funkadelic, the three horn men have been involved in a plethora of recordings. (Note: All of the albums made by Parker, Ellis, and Wesley in their various permutations have been included here; the artist credited with the album appears at the end of the review.) —*Rob Bowman*

Doing Their Own Thing / 1970 / House of the Fox ✦✦✦

Doing It to Death / 1973 / People ✦✦✦✦
Extended live "funkafizing" including a ten-minute version of the No. 1 R&B hit "Doing It to Death." Written, produced, and arranged by James Brown. —*Rob Bowman*

Breakin' Bread / 1974 / People ✦✦✦

A Blow for Me: A Toot for You / 1977 / Atlantic ✦✦✦✦
Produced by George Clinton and Bootsy Collins and recorded with the company of much of the P-Funk Mob, *A Blow for Me, A Toot for You* showcases a new, slinkier, more produced and less hard-edged edition of the JB Horns. The lead cut, a remake of Parliament's "Up for the Down Stroke," received a little R&B airplay. —*Rob Bowman*

New Friends / 1990 / Antilles ✦✦✦

Roots Revisited / 1990 / Verve ✦✦✦

Mo' Roots / 1991 / Verve ✦✦✦

● **Funky Good Time: The Anthology** / 1995 / Polydor Chronicles ✦✦✦✦
The JB's recorded under various billings in the early '70s, including the JB's, Fred Wesley & the JB's, Maceo & the Macks, the First Family, the Last Word, and others. This double CD gathers 30 of the prime tracks by all of the above configurations from the first half of the '70s, including all nine of their chart hits and quite a few rare singles and long versions. Often, James Brown himself chirps in with incidental vocals (though this is mostly instrumental) and keyboards. The two-and-a-half-hour program can start to sound monotonous if taken all at once, but it's prime, often riveting funk, jammed with lockstep grooves that vary between basic R&B vamps and imaginative, almost jazzy improvisation. —*Richie Unterberger*

Jefferson Airplane / Starship

Rock 'n' Roll, Hard Rock, Psychedelic, Folk-Rock, Arena Rock
Jefferson Airplane was the first of the San Francisco psychedelic rock groups of the 1960s to achieve national recognition, and in its later configurations, billed as Jefferson Starship or simply Starship, it remained a significant popular recording act well into the 1980s. The band was organized in the summer of 1965 by singer-songwriter Marty Balin (b. Jan. 30, 1943, Cincinnati), who recruited a band to play at the Matrix, a club he was planning to launch in San Francisco. Balin brought in guitarist/singer Paul Kantner (b. Mar. 12, 1941, San Francisco), guitarist/singer Jorma Kaukonen (b. Dec. 23, 1940, Washington, DC), and singer Signe Anderson (b. Sept. 15, 1941, Seattle). After the original rhythm section didn't work out, Balin persuaded guitarist Skip Spence (b. Apr. 18, 1946, Ontario, Canada) to switch to drums, and Kaukonen invited his friend Jack Casady (b. Apr. 13, 1944, Washington, DC) to join on bass. RCA signed the Airplane and released their debut album, *Jefferson Airplane Takes Off* (Sep. 1966) to little commercial response. Anderson and Spence then left the group. Spence (who went on to form Moby Grape) was replaced by Spencer Dryden (b. Apr. 7, 1943). In Anderson's place, the group invited in the lead singer of a rival group, Grace Slick (b. Oct. 30, 1939, Chicago) of the Great Society. The new lineup released *Surrealistic Pillow* (Feb. 1967), a gold-selling Top Ten hit that spawned the Top Ten singles "Somebody to Love" (which Slick brought with her from the Great Society) and "White Rabbit" (which Slick wrote). This success made Jefferson Airplane the top San Francisco group during the 1967 Summer of Love and helped touch off the national craze for psychedelic music, the hippie lifestyle, and youthful drug-taking.

After Bathing at Baxter's (Nov. 1967) was a more experimental effort that was less successful. But *Crown of Creation* (Sep. 1968) was another gold-selling Top Ten hit, despite the lack of a successful single. *Bless Its Pointed Little Head* (Feb. 1969) was a live album, followed by *Volunteers* (Nov. 1969), another gold studio album. At this point, Dryden left and was replaced by Joey Covington. Violinist Papa John Creach (b. May 28, 1917, Beaver Falls, PA, d. Feb. 22, 1994) joined in 1970, and Balin quit in early 1971. The group began to release solo and offshoot albums includ-

ing Kantner's *Blows Against the Empire* (Dec. 1970) and recordings by Kaukonen and Casady's Hot Tuna.

The next Airplane album was *Bark* (Aug. 1971), which went gold, as did its follow-up, *Long John Silver* (Jul. 1972) (by which time Covington had been replaced by John Barbata). Ex-Quicksilver Messengers member David Freiberg was brought in to belatedly replace Balin as male lead singer, and the group made a second live album, *Thirty Seconds over Winterland* (Apr. 1973).

Kaukonen and Casady then left, and were replaced by guitarist Craig Chaquico (b. Sep. 26, 1954, Sacramento) and (after a brief stint by Kaukonen's brother Peter) bassist Pete Sears (b. England), as the group name was changed to Jefferson Starship. This new aggregation made *Dragon Fly* (Oct. 1974), a gold-selling hit that also featured one song sung by Marty Balin. Balin joined Jefferson Starship full-time for *Red Octopus* (Jul. 1975), contributing "Miracles," which hit the Top Ten as the album topped the charts. The next two albums, *Spitfire* (Jun. 1976) and *Earth* (Feb. 1978) were Top Ten million-sellers.

Then Slick, Balin, and Barbata left the group. Veteran drummer Aynsley Dunbar (b. Jan. 10, 1946, Liverpool) and ex-Elvin Bishop Group singer Hickey Thomas (b. Cairo, GA) joined, and the next album, *Freedom at Point Zero* (Nov. 1979) went gold and reached the Top Ten. Slick rejoined for *Modern Times* (Mar. 1981), which was followed by *Winds of Change* (Oct. 1982), after which Don Baldwin replaced Dunbar. *Nuclear Furniture* (May 1984) was the group's final album, after which Kantner (the last original Airplane member) and Freiberg left and the remaining lineup of Slick, Thomas, Chaquico, Sears, and Baldwin carried on as Starship. (See Starship.)

In 1989, Jefferson Airplane reunited with original members Balin, Kantner, Kaukonen, Casady, and Slick for a tour and an album, *Jefferson Airplane* (Sep. 1989). In 1995, a new edition of Jefferson Starship featuring Kantner, Balin, and Casady, released *Deep Space/Virgin Sky*. —*William Ruhlmann*

Takes Off / Sep. 1966 / RCA ✦✦✦
The original group's pre-Grace Slick debut album, really closer in spirit to the Mamas & Papas in some respects, as a kind of folk-pop album. Signe Anderson and Marty Balin handle most of the vocals, and the instrumental textures are largely acoustic (Jorma Kaukonen contributes some excellent playing, however) and the political sensibilities are almost nonexistent. —*Bruce Eder*

★ **Surrealistic Pillow** / Feb. 1967 / RCA ✦✦✦✦✦
Their groundbreaking folk-based psychedelic album hit like a shot heard round the world. From "White Rabbit" and "Somebody to Love" to the sublime "3/5 of a Mile in 10 Seconds," the sensibilities are fierce, and the material is melodic, and the performances, sparked by new member Grace Slick on most of the lead vocals, are magnificent and inspired. —*Bruce Eder*

After Bathing at Baxter's / Dec. 1967 / RCA ✦✦✦

Crown of Creation / Sep. 1968 / RCA ✦✦✦
An impressive but meandering journey through the drugged-out sensibilities of 1967. The science-fiction content gives it some cohesiveness, but not enough. —*Bruce Eder*

Bless Its Pointed Little Head / Feb. 1969 / RCA ✦✦✦

Volunteers / Nov. 1969 / RCA ✦✦✦
The band's most political album is a somewhat dated statement but also a very joyous and rewarding one. "We Can Be Together" is still a compelling anthem. —*Bruce Eder*

Bark / Sep. 1971 / RCA ✦✦✦

Long John Silver / Jul. 1972 / RCA ✦✦

Thirty Seconds over Winterland / Apr. 1973 / RCA ✦✦

● **Red Octopus** / 1975 / RCA ✦✦✦✦
The masterpiece, and a massive seller, too. Grace Slick sings expressively, especially on "Fast Buck Freddie" and "Play on Love," but the real story is the integration of Marty Balin fully into the band, and again he brings a timeless ballad along in the hit "Miracles." —*William Ruhlmann*

Earth / 1978 / Grunt ✦✦

Freedom at Point Zero / 1979 / Grunt ✦✦✦

Gold / 1979 / RCA ✦✦✦✦
Well-chosen best-of covering the years 1974-1979, after which the band personnel changed significantly. —*William Ruhlmann*

Modern Times / 1981 / RCA ✦✦✦

● **2400 Fulton Street: An Anthology** / Mar. 1987 / RCA ✦✦✦✦
A more-than-adequate retrospective on the group (at least until the boxed set anticipated for late 1992 arrives), with every major song and a lot of oddball favorites as well, all remastered from sources far superior to those used on the original albums. Some of it will be redundant (virtually the whole *Surrealistic Pillow* album is here) but the quality and the order of the programming is rewarding. —*Bruce Eder*

Jefferson Airplane Loves You / Oct. 1992 / RCA ✦✦✦
A three-disc box set loaded with rarities, *Jefferson Airplane Loves You* is necessary for hardcore fans, but the double-disc *2400 Fulton Street* offers a better portrait of the band and is the essential purchase for casual fans. —*Stephen Thomas Erlewine*

Jesus & Mary Chain

Alternative Pop-Rock, Post-Punk
This Scottish combo burst out of East Kilbraid in 1984 with a style that piled thick gobs of squalling guitars over tugging Beach Boy harmonies and the lyrical cynicism of Velvets-era Lou Reed. Brothers Jim and William Reid eventually toned down the feedback just a tad—replacing their rhythm section with a drum machine—and have managed to keep their sound fresh, primarily through clever melodies and the occasional inspired lyric hook. —*John Floyd*

● **Psychocandy** / 1985 / Def American ✦✦✦✦
This fuzzy, super-loud release introduced JMC to American audiences. —*John Floyd*

Darklands / 1987 / Warner Bros. ✦✦✦✦
This was the subdued, depressing followup to *Psychocandy*. —*John Floyd*

Barbed Wire Kisses / 1988 / Def American ✦✦
Automatic / 1989 / Warner Bros. ✦✦✦
The drum-machine beats are too stiff, but this set contains their best songs, including the sorta-hit "Head On." —*John Floyd*

Honey's Dead / May 1992 / Def American ✦✦✦✦
If Mary Chain albums share that common thread with, say, The Ramones or Motörhead—in that as good as they are they're all pretty much interchangeable—then know that *Honey's Dead* still stands out. The Reid brothers deliver their concoction of melodic noise with craftsmen-like ability, and this latest collection stands above much of their previous output. —*Steve Aldrich*

Stoned & Dethroned / 1994 / Warner Bros. ✦✦✦
More subdued than any of their previous records, The Jesus & Mary Chain explore a calmer, almost acoustic-oriented direction for part of *Stoned & Dethroned*. Apart from the hit duet with Mazzy Star's Hope Sandoval, "Sometimes Always," the fuzz-drenched pseudo-psychedelic pop that has become the group's trademark is more effective than any of the band's musical experiments. —*Stephen Thomas Erlewine*

Jesus & Mary Chain Hate Rock N' Roll / Sep. 26, 1995 / American ✦✦

Jethro Tull

Hard Rock, Art-Rock/Progressive-Rock
Centered around wildman flutist, singer, and songwriter Ian Anderson, Jethro Tull has been churning out an oddball synthesis of British Isles folk and progressive hard rock since the late '60s. During their heyday (the '70s), Tull became one of the biggest concert draws, due to Anderson and the band's clownish stage antics and their amazingly complex interplay.

Their earlier albums, *This Was* (No. 62), *Stand Up* (No. 20), and *Benefit* (No. 11), laid the groundwork for Tull's success, but it was 1971's *Aqualung* (No. 7) that put them over the top.

Not unlike many bands attempting to take rock to new levels through extended pieces, Tull released two back-to-back albums (*Thick as a Brick*, *Passion Play*) containing one musical piece on each. Unlike many of those bands, both of these albums went to No. 1.

Jethro Tull also managed a couple of hits with "Living in the Past" (No.11) and "Bungle in the Jungle" (No. 12). The band continues to release albums and tour. —*Rick Clark*

This Was / 1968 / Chrysalis ✦✦✦
Stand Up / 1969 / Chrysalis ✦✦✦✦
Tull's second album was as impressive as *This Was*. Anderson's flute dominates this outing. The instrumental "Bouree" became a signature song for the band's early sound. Other highlights included "A New Day Yesterday," "Fat Man," and "Nothing Is Easy." —*Rick Clark*

Benefit / 1970 / Chrysalis ✦✦✦
★ **Aqualung** / 1971 / Chrysalis ✦✦✦✦✦
It was with *Aqualung* that Tull became a staple on FM rock radio, thanks to dynamic riff-heavy tracks like "My God," "Hymn 43," "Locomotive Breath," "Cross-eyed Mary," "Wind-Up," and the title track. Thematically, many of these songs were vehicles for Anderson's railings about how organized religion had restricted man's relationship with God. —*Rick Clark*

Thick as a Brick / 1972 / Chrysalis ✦✦
Living in the Past / 1972 / Chrysalis ✦✦✦✦
Living in the Past was essentially an anthology of key tracks from Tull's first five albums. Included are extended live tracks as well as popular numbers like "Christmas Song," "Song for Jeffery," "Hymn 43," and their

biggest hit, "Living in the Past." The CD version has curiously omitted two of Tull's better early tracks—"Teacher" and "Bouree." Besides "Hymn 43," *Living in the Past* doesn't include any key tracks from *Aqualung*. —*Rick Clark*

Minstrel in the Gallery / 1975 / Chrysalis ✦✦✦
M.U.: The Best of Jethro Tull / 1976 / Chrysalis ✦✦✦
Songs from the Wood / 1977 / Chrysalis ✦✦✦✦
On *Songs from the Wood*, Tull's aggressive rock interplay and Ian Anderson's fascination with early folk melodies from the British Isles produced a particularly appealing collection of songs. "Cup of Wonder" and "The Whistler" are particularly successful. —*Rick Clark*

A / 1980 / Chrysalis ✦✦✦✦
With the addition of ex-Roxy Music violinist and keyboardist Eddie Jobson and ex-Fairport Convention bassist Dave Pegg, Tull produced their most overt (and fully realized) folk-rock album. "Batteries Not Included," "Black Sunday," and "Crossfire" are highlights. —*Rick Clark*

20 Years of Jethro Tull: Highlights / 1988 / Chrysalis ✦✦✦✦
20 Years of Jethro Tull / 1988 / Chrysalis ✦✦✦
Fans of Tull should enjoy this collection that amply documents the band's entire career. There are loads of live performances, TV appearances, and good interviews. The sound quality is quite good. —*Rick Clark*

25th Anniversary / Apr. 20, 1993 / Capitol ✦✦

Joan Jett

b. Sep. 22, 1960, Philadelphia, PA
Guitar, Vocals / Rock 'n' Roll, Hard Rock
By playing pure and simple rock 'n' roll without making an explicit issue of her gender, Joan Jett became a figurehead for several generations of female rockers. Jett's brand of rock 'n' roll is loud and stripped-down, yet with overpowering hooks—a combination of The Stones tough, sinewy image and beat, AC/DC chords, and glam-rock hooks. As the numerous covers she has recorded show, she adheres both to rock tradition and breaks with it—she plays classic three-chord rock 'n' roll, yet she also loves the trashy elements (in particular, Gary Glitter) of it as well, and she plays with a defiant sneer. From her first band, The Runaways, through her hit-making days in the '80s with the Blackhearts right until her unexpected revival in the '90s, she hasn't changed her music, yet she's kept her quality control high, making one classic single ("I Love Rock-n-Roll") along the way.

Jett was born in Philadelphia, PA; her family moved to Los Angeles when she was 12 years old. By the time she was 15, she had formed her first band and was performing around town. Kim Fowley, a Los Angeles record producer, discovered the band at one of their gigs and became their manager; soon, he renamed the all-female group the Runaways and secured them a contract with Mercury Records. The band released three albums that never had much commercial success in America, yet were very popular in Japan; the group were popular in both the Los Angeles hard-rock and punk scenes, which led to Jett's production of the Germs' first record, *G.I.* The Runaways group broke up in 1980 and Jett moved to New York to begin a solo career.

Teaming up with producer/manager Kenny Laguna, Jett independently released her self-titled debut album in 1980 in America, since no labels were interested in signing her. The record was a more traditional rock 'n' roll record than the punky Runaways, yet it retained her previous band's defiant attitude. The record sold very well for an independent release, leading to a contract with Boardwalk Records, who reissued the album under the title *Bad Reputation;* it soon climbed to No. 51 on the American charts.

Jett formed The Blackhearts between *Bad Reputation* and her second album, 1981's *I Love Rock-n-Roll;* the group included guitarist Ricky Byrd, bassist Gary Ryan, and drummer Lee Crystal. Released at the end of 1981, *I Love Rock-n-Roll* became her greatest success, sending her into the Top Ten. Originally the B-side of an Arrows single, the title track was an enormous success, spending seven weeks at No. 1 in the spring of 1982. The follow-up single, a version of Tommy James And The Shondells' "Crimson and Clover," went Top Ten as well; a single of Gary Glitter's "Do You Wanna Touch Me (Oh Yeah)," taken from the *Bad Reputation* album reached No. 20 in the summer of 1982. *Album*, released in 1983, went gold yet it had no hits that compared with either "I Love Rock-n-Roll" or "Crimson and Clover."

Jett starred in Paul Schrader's 1987 film *Light of Day*, which featured the Top 40 title song, yet she didn't have another Top Ten hit until 1988, when "I Hate Myself for Loving You," taken from the *Up Your Alley* album, hit No. 8; the album became her second platinum record. After the album's success, her career had another slow period, with 1990's all-covers album *The Hit List* making it to No. 36 and 1991's *Notorious* failing to chart. Between *Notorious* and 1994's *Pure and Simple*, a new generation of female rockers came of age and everyone from hard alternative rockers like L7 to the minimalist, riot grrrl punk rockers like Bikini Kill claimed Jett and the Runaways as an influence. Consequently, *Pure and Simple* featured contributions from L7, Bikini Kill, Babes in Toyland's Kat Bjelland, received more press and positive reviews than any of her albums since the mid-'80s. In 1995, Jett recorded the live album *Evilstig* with the remaining members of the Gits, a Seattle punk rock band whose lead singer, Mia Zapata, was raped and murdered in 1993. — *Stephen Thomas Erlewine*

Bad Reputation / 1981 / Blackheart ✦✦✦
Her debut suffers from a lack of one coherent sound, but it's an impassioned homage to her glitter-and-punk roots. — *John Floyd*

I Love Rock 'n' Roll / 1981 / Blackheart ✦✦✦✦
The title track was an inescapable hit in 1981, and Jett's new band, the Blackhearts, gave her a big crunching hard-rock sound. She could've used some better songs though. — *John Floyd*

Album / 1983 / Blackheart ✦✦✦✦
With her best set of songs and big-time production, this is an astonishing statement of purpose, full of gritty Rolling Stones-like boogie and a cover of Sly Stone's "Everyday People" that works better than you'd think. But it's all spectacular. — *John Floyd*

Glorious Results of a Misspent Youth / 1984 / Blackheart ✦✦✦✦
Another masterful blast of fury and celebration, it shifts from a blazing cover of the Runaway's "Cherry Bomb" to her best song, "I Got No Answers." Besides the Pretenders' early work, *Glorious Results...* ranks with the best rock of the '80s, focused through a female point of view. — *John Floyd*

Good Music / 1986 / Epic ✦✦✦

Up Your Alley / 1988 / Epic ✦✦

The Hit List / 1990 / Epic ✦✦

Notorious / 1991 / Epic ✦✦✦

● Flashback / 1994 / Blackheart ✦✦✦✦
While it includes a healthy share of rarities, nothing on Joan Jett's career overview, *Flashback*, is second rate. Even though she vascillated between punky hard rock and smoothed-out arena-rock for much of the '80s, the disc accentuates her rebellious nature, making *Flashback* an effective introduction to her career. Besides, it rocks like hell. — *Stephen Thomas Erlewine*

Pure and Simple / 1994 / Warner Bros. ✦✦✦

Jive Five

Soul, R&B, Doo Wop
Best known for the No. 1 R&B hit "My True Story," the Jive Five were one of the few vocal groups to survive the transistion from the '50s to the '60s. In the process, they helped move the music itself forward, providing a key link between doo wop and '60s soul. Formed in Brooklyn, NY, the group originally consisted of Eugene Pitt (lead), Jerome Hanna (tenor), Richard Harris (tenor), Billy Prophet (baritone), and Norman Johnson (bass). The group's first hit, "My True Story," was their biggest, peaking at No. 1 on the R&B charts and No. 3 on the pop charts in the summer of 1961. None of the band's subsequent singles—including the minor R&B hit, 1962's "These Golden Rings"—were as popular, but the group managed to keep performing and recording. Under the direction of Eugene Pitt and Norman Johnson, the Jive Five refashioned themselves as a soul band in 1964, forming a new lineup with Casey Spencer (tenor), Webster Harris (tenor), and Beatrice Best (baritone). This new incarnation of the band signed to United Artists Records. The group only had one hit on UA, 1965's "I'm a Happy Man."

In 1966, the Jive Five left United Artists and signed with Musicor, where they had the 1968 R&B hit "Sugar (Don't Take Away My Candy)." They changed labels again in 1970, signing with Decca. That same year, they changed their name to the Jyve Fyve, in order to appear more contemporary. The Jyve Fyve had only one minor R&B hit, 1970's "I Want You to Be My Baby."

The group continued to perform and record for a variety of small labels during the '70s, but they never had another hit. Throughout the '70s and '80s, the only constant member was Eugene Pitt. In 1975, Pitt changed the name of the group to Ebony, Ivory, and the Jades, but this new incarnation failed to gain much attention. In 1982, Pitt changed the name of the group back to the Jive Five and the band recorded two albums for the indie label, Ambient Sound. For the rest of the '80s and the '90s, the Jive Five were regulars on the oldies circuit. — *Stephen Thomas Erlewine*

● The Jive Five / 1989 / United Artists ✦✦✦✦
A superb 25-track collection, it features The Jive Five's finest material, recorded in the early '60s for Lescay/Belton; songs include "Rain," "My True Story," "No Not Again," "What Time Is It?," and "Hurry Back." — *AMG*

The Complete United Artists Recordings... / 1992 / Capitol ✦✦✦✦
A superior 21-track collection, it highlights the Jive Five's material for United Artists, recorded in the mid-'60s. — *AMG*

My True Story / Relic ✦✦✦
These hard-hitting doo woppers testify on the title cut, "What Time Is It?," and on "Hully Gully Callin' Time." Eugene Pitts is one of the era's most evocative singers. — *John Floyd*

Jodeci

Urban, Club-Dance
A new jack swing ensemble whose debut album was a huge hit, Jodeci pairs North Carolina brothers Joel and Cedric Halley (also called Jo-Jo and K-Ci) and Dalvin and Donald Degrate Jr. (the latter better known as Devante Swing). *Forever My Lady* made them huge stars in 1991, selling over two million copies and securing a Top 20 pop hit with "Come and Talk to Me." "Forever My Lady" and "Stay" were also major R&B successes, as was their cover of Stevie Wonder's "Lately," which was featured on the Uptown Unplugged release. Jodeci followed that in 1994 with *Diary of a Mad Band*, which debuted at the top of the R&B charts. — *Ron Wynn*

Forever My Lady / 1991 / Uptown/MCA ✦✦✦

● Diary of a Mad Band / 1993 / Uptown/MCA ✦✦✦✦
Jodeci juggles new jack swing and vintage soul on their second album, and wind up with a jarring, mismatched release. The disc's love songs, particularly "Cry for You," "What About Us," and "My Heart Belongs to You," are tender, passionately sung, sincere expressions of romance and love. But they diminish these with a string of innuendo-laden come-on numbers, complete with explicit language, tired raps and samples, and the kind of sentiments and appeals better suited to a *Penthouse Forum* entry than an album. — *Ron Wynn*

The Show, the After Party, the Hotel / 1995 / Uptown ✦✦✦

Billy Joel

b. May 9, 1949, Long Island, NY
Organ, Synthesizer, Harmonica, Piano, Keyboards, Vocals / Singer-Songwriter, Pop-Rock
Although Billy Joel never was a critic's favorite, the pianist emerged as one of the most popular singer-songwriters of the latter half of the mid-'70s. Joel's music consistently demonstrates an affection for Beatlesque hooks and a flair for Tin Pan Alley and Broadway melodies. His fusion of two distinct eras made him a superstar in the late '70s and '80s, as he racked an impressive string of multi-platinum albums and hit singles.

Joel was raised in the Bronx suburb Levittown, where he learned to play piano as a child. Upon seeing the Beatles on the *Ed Sullivan Show* in 1964, Joel decided to pursue a musical career and set about finding a local band to join. Eventually, he found the Echoes, a group that specialized in British Invasion covers. Shortly after he joined the group, the Echoes became a popular New York attraction. While he was still a member of the group, Joel began playing recording sessions in 1965, playing piano on recordings George "Shadow" Morton produced as well as several records released through Kama Sutra Productions. Soon, his musical commitments occupied all of his time and Joel dropped out of high school, just a few months shy of his graduation. In 1967, he joined the Hassles, a Long Island rock 'n' roll band that had a recording contract with United Artists. Over the next year and a half, the Hassles released two albums and four singles, all of which failed commercially. In 1969, the Hassles broke up. Joel and the band's drummer, Jon Small, formed an organ and drums duo called Attila. In Attila, Joel played his organ through a variety of effects pedals, creating a heavy psychedelic hard-rock album completely without guitars. Epic released *Attila* early in 1970; sporting a cover featuring the duo dressed as barbarians, the album was a bomb and the band broke up. While the group was still together, Joel began a romance with Small's wife, Elizabeth; she would eventually leave the drummer and marry the pianist in 1973. After Attila's embarrassing failure, Joel wrote rock criticism and played on commercial jingles.

Billy Joel signed a deal with Family Productions in 1971. Under the terms of the contract, Joel signed to the label's parent company, Ripp, for life; the pianist was unaware of the clause at the time. Joel refashioned himself as a sensitive singer-songwriter for his debut album, *Cold Spring Harbor*, which was released in November of 1971. Upon Joel's completion of a small US tour, Family Productions were experiencing legal and financial difficulties, which prevented Joel from recording an immediate follow-up. Early in 1972, he moved out to Los Angeles with Elizabeth. Joel adopted the name Bill Martin and spent half a year playing lounge piano at the Executive Room. Toward the end of the year, he began touring, playing various nightclubs across the country. Around the beginning of 1973, a Philadelphia radio station began playing a live version of "Captain Jack." Soon, record companies were eager to sign the pianist, and he eventually signed with Columbia Records. In order for Joel to sign with Columbia, the major label had to agree to pay Ripp Productions 25 cents for each album sold, plus display the Family and Remus logos on each record Joel released. By the end of 1973, Billy Joel's first album for

Columbia Records, *Piano Man,* had been released. The record slowly worked its way up the charts, peaking at No. 27 in the spring of 1974. The title track—culled from experiences he had while singing at the Executive Room—became a Top 40 hit single. At the end of the summer, Joel assembled a touring band and undertook a national tour. By the end of 1974, he had released his album, *Streetlife Serenade,* which reached No. 35 early in 1975. After its success, Joel signed a contract with James William Guercio and Larry Fitzgerald's management company, Caribou, and moved from California to New York, where he recorded his 1976 album *Turnstiles.* The sessions for *Turnstiles* were long and filled with tension, culminating with Joel firing the album's original producer, Guercio, and producing the album himself. Once he fired Guercio, Joel also left Caribou, hired his wife as his new manager and recorded his new album with his touring band.

Turnstiles stalled on the charts, only reaching No. 122. Billy Joel was at the make-or-break point for his career and the resulting album, *The Stranger,* catapulted him into superstardom. Produced by Phil Ramone, *The Stranger* was released in the fall of 1977—by the end of the year, it peaked at No. 2 and had gone platinum and, within the course of a year, it spawned the Top 40 singles "Just the Way You Are," "Movin' Out (Anthony's Song)," "She's Always a Woman," and "Only the Good Die Young." Joel followed *The Stranger* with *52nd Street,* which was released in the fall of 1978. *52nd Street* spent eight weeks at No. 1 in the US, selling over two millions copies within the first month of its release. The album spawned the hit singles "My Life," "Big Shot," and "Honesty," and won the Grammy award for Album of the Year in 1980. In the spring of 1980, Joel released *Glass Houses,* theoretically a harder-edged album that was a response to the punk and new wave movement. By the summer of 1980, *Glass Houses* had reached No. 1 in America, where it stayed for six weeks; the album spawned the Top 40 singles "You May Be Right," "It's Still Rock'N'Roll to Me," "Don't Ask Me Why," and "Sometimes a Fantasy" and won the Grammy for Best Rock Vocal Performance, Male in 1981. In the fall of 1981, Joel released *Songs in the Attic,* a live album that concentrated on material written and recorded before he became a star in 1977.

Songs in the Attic bought Joel some time as he was completing an album he had designed as his bid to be taken seriously as a composer. The recording was long and plagued with problems, most notably Joel's divorce. The record, called *The Nylon Curtain,* was finally released in the fall. The album was a commercial disappointment, only selling a million copies, but it did earn him some of his better reviews, as well as spawning the Top 20 hits "Pressure" and "Allentown." Joel quickly followed the album in 1983 with the oldies pastiche *An Innocent Man,* which restored Joel to his multi-platinum status. The album also launched the hit singles "Uptown Girl," "Tell Her About It," "An Innocent Man," and "Keeping the Faith." During 1983 and 1984, Joel became one of the first '70s stars to embrace MTV and music videos, shooting a number of clips for the album which were aired frequently on the network.

Billy Joel released a double-album compilation, *Greatest Hits, Vols. 1 & 2* in the summer of 1985. Two new songs—including the Top Ten "You're Only Human (Second Wind)"—were added to the hits collection; the album itself peaked at No. 6. In the summer of 1986, Joel returned with the Top Ten single "Modern Woman," which was a teaser for his new album, *The Bridge,* which was released in August. *The Bridge* peaked, sold over two million copies, and launched the Top 40 hits "A Matter of Trust" and "This Is the Time." In the spring of 1987, Billy Joel embarked on a major tour of the USSR. His Leningrad concert was recorded and released in the fall of 1987 as the double-live album *Kohuept.*

Billy Joel fired his long-time manager and former brother-in-law Frank Weber in August of 1989, after an audit revealed that there were major discrepancies in Weber's accounting. Following Weber's dismissal, Joel sued Weber for $90 million claiming fraud. Immediately after filing suit, Joel was hospitalized with kidney stones. All of this turmoil didn't prevent the release of his twelfth studio album, *Storm Front,* in the fall of 1989. It was preceded by the single "We Didn't Start the Fire," which became a No. 1 hit. *Storm Front* marked a significant change for Billy Joel—he fired his band, keeping only Liberty DeVito, and ceased his relationship with producer Phil Ramone, hiring Mick Jones of Foreigner to produce the album. *Storm Front* was another hit for Joel, reaching No. 1 in the US and selling over three million albums. During 1990, Joel embarked on a major US tour that ran well into 1991. In January, the court awarded Joel two million dollars in a partial judgement against Frank Weber. At the end of the year, the National Academy of Recording Arts and Sciences honored Billy Joel with a Grammy Living Legend award. Following the *Storm Front* world tour, Billy Joel spent the next few years quietly. Joel returned in the summer of 1993 with *River of Dreams,* which entered the charts at No. 1 and spawned the Top Ten title track. —*Stephen Thomas Erlewine*

Cold Spring Harbor / 1971 / Columbia ✦✦✦
Joel's debut solo album finds him sounding like a romantic singer-songwriter with a strong sense of melody. The album's single, "She's Got a

Way," later turned up in his concerts. The original 1971 album released by Family Productions was mastered wrong and speeds up the tape; in 1984, Columbia Records released a corrected version. —*William Ruhlmann*

Piano Man / Nov. 1973 / Columbia ✦✦✦
Joel presents a personal perspective of middle-class teen life in the suburbs ("Captain Jack," "The Ballad of Billy the Kid") followed by life in a cocktail lounge ("Piano Man"), and concludes, "Worse comes to worst, I'll get along." But his already apparent sense of melody and supple singing voice indicate much more promise than that. —*William Ruhlmann*

Streetlife Serenade / Oct. 1974 / Columbia ✦✦✦
Extending a mean streak he'd already revealed more than once, Joel looks upon the star-making machinery that broke him the year before and scorns it. But he has such a gift for the putdown, notably in "Los Angelenos" and "The Entertainer," and the melodies are so good that you can't help singing along and agreeing with him. If you didn't already, that is. —*William Ruhlmann*

Turnstiles / May 1976 / Columbia ✦✦✦✦
Billy Joel's best, most consistent, most accessible record, even if not his best seller. From "Say Goodbye to Hollywood," which signals his return to the Big Apple with a drumbeat borrowed from the Ronettes, through the Sinatra ballad "New York State of Mind," the reflective "Summer, Highland Falls," and the hilarious "Miami 2017," Joel has never been more imaginative or more tuneful. Of course, "Angry Young Man" shows him to be as mean-spirited as ever, but the music carries even that one home. This record was the prototype to a virtual hit assembly line. —*William Ruhlmann*

The Stranger / Sep. 1977 / Columbia ✦✦✦✦
The breakthrough to superstardom, containing the hits "Just the Way You Are," "Movin' Out (Anthony's Song)," "Only the Good Die Young," and "She's Always a Woman." All those are on *Greatest Hits*—Vols. I & II, but "Scenes from an Italian Restaurant," one of Joel's most compelling storysongs, is not. —*William Ruhlmann*

52nd Street / Oct. 1978 / Columbia ✦✦✦✦
Joel consolidated his position with this somewhat harder rocking followup to *The Stranger,* which contained the hits "My Life," "Big Shot," and "Honesty." —*William Ruhlmann*

Glass Houses / Mar. 1980 / Columbia ✦✦✦
Billy Joel's response to punk, which, being a snotty kid himself, he felt a certain affinity with, and which allowed his usual belligerence unusually free rein (an aspect of his work that can be tolerated only because it is unflinchingly honest and as often directed at himself as at others). Again, most of the best songs are on the *Greatest Hits,* but this is the only place you can get "Sometimes a Fantasy." —*William Ruhlmann*

Songs in the Attic / Sep. 1981 / Columbia ✦✦✦
Joel used his first live album to refocus attention on his pre-*Stranger* catalog, turning in new versions of worthy songs like "She's Got a Way" and "Say Goodbye to Hollywood," both of which now became Top 25 hits. —*William Ruhlmann*

The Nylon Curtain / Sep. 1982 / Columbia ✦✦✦✦
Upon release, Joel's eighth studio album was hailed by critics who had previously scorned him because he had decided to take on social concerns—the stress of modern life in "Pressure," unemployment in "Allentown," and the Vietnam War in "Goodnight Saigon." In retrospect, those songs were the best of an uneven collection. —*William Ruhlmann*

An Innocent Man / Aug. 1983 / Columbia ✦✦✦
A brilliant evocation of popular styles of the early '60s, from doo wop to R&B, that is much more than a period exercise because it obviously is so deeply felt and because it is so well executed. And no one has sounded quite so guilty as the singer of the title track, whether he realized it or not. —*William Ruhlmann*

● **Greatest Hits, Vols. 1 & 2 (1973-1985)** / 1985 / Columbia ✦✦✦✦
Although it's missing a few important (not to mention big) hits, *Greatest Hits, Vols. 1 & 2* is an excellent retrospective of the first half of Billy Joel's career. Beginning with "Piano Man," the first disc runs through a number of early songs before arriving at the hit-making days of the late '70s; some of these songs, including "Captain Jack" and "New York State of Mind," weren't strictly hits, but were popular numbers within his stage show and became radio hits. Once the songs from *The Stranger* arrive halfway through the first disc, there's no stopping the hits (although "Scenes from an Italian Restaurant," an album track from *The Stranger,* manages its way onto the collection). In fact, over the next disc and a half, there are so many hits, it's inevitable that some are left off—to be specific, "Honesty," "Sometimes a Fantasy," "An Innocent Man," "Leave a Tender Moment," and "Keeping the Faith" aren't included. But all the other hits—including "Just the Way You Are," "Only the Good Die Young," "My Life," "You May Be Right," "It's Still Rock and Roll to Me," "Don't Ask Me Why," "Allentown," "Tell Her About It" and "Uptown Girl," among many others—are

The Bridge / Jul. 1986 / Columbia ✦✦

The hits are "Modern Woman," "A Matter of Trust," and "This Is the Time," all melodic rockers in Joel's patented style. There is also "Baby Grand," a duet with Ray Charles. But, three years on, this wasn't a patch on *An Innocent Man* and suggested Joel's best work might be behind him. —*William Ruhlmann*

Kohuept (Live in Leningrad) / Oct. 1987 / Columbia ✦✦

Storm Front / 1989 / Columbia ✦✦

Joel caused a stampede for high school social science classes with the patter song "We Didn't Start the Fire," a cross between Gilbert and Sullivan and rock 'n' roll that listed events in the news over the last 40 years, broken up by chants of the title. "I Go to Extremes" was a confession of emotional instability set to a strong melody and a rocking beat. There were also minor entries, such as "The Downeaster 'Alexa,'" which was about Long Island fishermen, and "Shameless," which Garth Brooks turned into a country smash. And, as usual, there was about a side's worth of worthless filler. —*William Ruhlmann*

River of Dreams / Aug. 10, 1993 / Columbia ✦✦

Joel has reached middle age and he is still restless and angry. Fortunately, this results in some fine, adventurous music, making *River of Dreams* his strongest effort since *The Nylon Curtain.* Joel explores all of his favorite musical territory on this album, reaching back to doo wop, moving through Beatlesque pop, towards his trademark balladry. —*Stephen Thomas Erlewine*

Elton John (Reginald Dwight)

b. Mar. 25, 1947, Pinner, England
Piano, Vocals / Rock 'n' Roll, Singer-Songwriter, Adult Contemporary, Soft Rock, Pop-Rock, Club-Dance

Elton John was the single most successful pop artist of the '70s, and he continued to score hits for decades after his initial reign of popularity. Born Reginald Dwight in Pinner, England, he showed an early aptitude for the piano and received classical training, winning a scholarship to the Royal Academy of Music at the age of 11. But after six years he turned to pop music, and struggled as a songwriter, sideman, and member of unsuccessful groups for the rest of the '60s.

During this period, he hooked up with lyricist Bernie Taupin through a newspaper advertisement, and the two were signed as songwriters to publisher Dick James, who was to have a tremendous impact on John's early career.

A debut album sponsored by James, *Empty Sky,* flopped in 1969, but in 1970, with the album *Elton John* and the single "Your Song," Elton John took off, scoring especially well in America. For the next five years, his output—and the sales that material racked up—was enormous. John always had an ability to hit with ballads like the wistful "Daniel," then turn around and rock as hard as the Rolling Stones on a song like "Saturday Night's Alright for Fighting." There hardly seemed a day from 1972, when "Rocket Man" began a streak of 16 straight Top 20 hits (15 of which went Top Ten), to 1976, when John took a breather, that his songs were not dominating the airwaves and the record charts.

The late '70s seem to have been a period of recovery and indecision for the singer, but by 1980 he had settled into making one well-crafted album a year, and many of them tossed off hits, if not with such consistency as before. "Little Jeannie" (1980), "I Guess That's Why They Call It the Blues" and "Sad Songs (Say So Much)" (both 1984), and "Nikita" (1986) all showed John could still hit the upper reaches of the charts, especially with his trademark ballads. The late '80s again saw a slowing in John's record success, but by the start of the '90s he had gone public about drug and alcohol problems he said were behind him, and he looked poised for a new start.

After several more years of adult contemporary hits in the early '90s, John moved into film, writing the music for Walt Disney's 1994 film *The Lion King.* The soundtrack was an enormous success and John's version of "Can You Feel the Love Tonight" was his biggest hit in years. —*William Ruhlmann*

Empty Sky / 1969 / MCA ✦✦

Elton John / Aug. 1970 / MCA ✦✦✦

Ironically, Elton John's breakthrough album (and US debut) is uncharacteristic of his other work, heavily featuring Paul Buckmaster's dramatic string arrangements. John is never overwhelmed by strings or choirs and turns in some powerful performances. Contains "Your Song." —*William Ruhlmann*

☆ **Tumbleweed Connection** / Jan. 1971 / MCA ✦✦✦✦✦

Elton John's followup was a thematic album about the American Old West (a Taupin fascination) that allowed John to rock out on several numbers. There are no hits here, but the album stands up well two decades later on. —*William Ruhlmann*

11-17-70 / Mar. 1971 / MCA ✦✦✦

Madman Across the Water / Nov. 1971 / MCA ✦✦✦✦

One of John's best-ever collections of songs, containing "Levon," "Tiny Dancer," and the title track, all of which survive in the memory better than they did in the charts. —*William Ruhlmann*

Honky Chateau / May 1972 / MCA ✦✦✦✦

Notable not only for the hits "Honky Cat" and "Rocket Man" but also for "I Think I'm Gonna Kill Myself" and "Mona Lisas and Mad Hatters." The first of John's seven US No. 1 albums. —*William Ruhlmann*

Don't Shoot Me I'm Only the Piano Player / Jan. 1973 / MCA ✦✦✦

The hits were the ballad "Daniel" and the nuevo-retro rocker "Crocodile Rock," but there were also such excellent album tracks as "Elderberry Wine" and "I'm Going to Be a Teenage Idol" to keep things moving. —*William Ruhlmann*

Goodbye Yellow Brick Road / Oct. 1973 / MCA ✦✦✦✦

Almost certainly Elton John's biggest seller, save his first greatest hits collection. The hits on this sprawling double-disc set include "Saturday Night's Alright for Fighting," the title track, and "Bennie and the Jets," and the album tracks include "Love Lies Bleeding" and "Candle in the Wind" (which became a hit 15 years later in a live version). —*William Ruhlmann*

Caribou / Jun. 1974 / MCA ✦✦

Enjoying the hottest career in the music business at this point, Elton John was also amazingly prolific: *Caribou* was his eighth LP of new, original songs to be released within four years. Finally, the pace was beginning to tell. There were the expected hits in "The Bitch Is Back" and "Don't Let the Sun Go Down on Me," but the rest of this album was filler, with the nonsense song "Solar Prestige a Gammon" giving testimony to the facile and vapid approach to writing John and Taupin could take in their haste. —*William Ruhlmann*

★ **Greatest Hits** / Nov. 1974 / MCA ✦✦✦✦✦

Rarely has a greatest hits collection been as effective as Elton John's first compilation of *Greatest Hits.* Released at the end of 1974, after *Goodbye Yellow Brick Road* and *Caribou* had effectively established him as a superstar, *Greatest Hits* is exactly what it says it is—it features every one of his Top Ten singles ("Your Song," "Rocket Man," "Honky Cat," "Crocodile Rock," "Daniel," "Goodbye Yellow Brick Road," "Bennie and the Jets," "Don't Let the Sun Go Down on Me"), plus the No. 12 "Saturday Night's Alright for Fighting" and radio and concert favorites "Border Song" and "Candle in the Wind." Despite the exclusion of a couple of lesser hits from this era, most notably "Levon" and "Tiny Dancer," *Greatest Hits* is a nearly flawless collection, offering a perfect introduction to Elton John and providing casual fans with almost all the hits they need. —*Stephen Thomas Erlewine*

Captain Fantastic & The Brown Dirt Cowboy / May 1975 / MCA ✦✦✦✦

Bernie Taupin's most ambitious lyrical effort, *Captain Fantastic & the Brown Dirt Cowboy* is an autobiographical song cycle that also drew an unusually strong musical effort from John, resulting in perhaps his strongest overall record since *Tumbleweed Connection.* —*William Ruhlmann*

Rock of the Westies / Oct. 1975 / MCA ✦✦

The title signals that this album is short on ballads and long on bouncers; the hit was "Island Girl," but the real key to this album's thinness is that it came a mere five months after its ambitious predecessor, and even for Elton and Bernie, that's a bit too soon to expect much quality. —*William Ruhlmann*

Here & There / May 1976 / MCA ✦✦

Blue Moves / Oct. 1976 / MCA ✦✦

An unprecedented year in the making, the two-record *Blue Moves* was Elton John's opening farewell, a dreary song cycle full of self-pity and recycled melodies by an artist who had finally run out of gas. The inevitable hit was "Sorry Seems to Be the Hardest Word," although "Tonight," the album's other memorable song, was just as indicative of the low emotional ebb of the John-Taupin team. As the Mamas and the Papas once said in an LP title, "Farewell to the first golden era." —*William Ruhlmann*

☆ **Greatest Hits, Vol. 2** / Sep. 1977 / MCA ✦✦✦✦✦

More of the hottest hit streak of the decade, including such otherwise nonalbum singles as "Lucy in the Sky with Diamonds" and "Philadelphia Freedom." —*William Ruhlmann*

A Single Man / Oct. 1978 / MCA ✦✦✦

Victim of Love / 1979 / MCA ✦

21 at 33 / May 1980 / MCA ✦✦✦

The Fox / 1981 / MCA ✦✦

Jump Up! / Apr. 1982 / MCA ✦✦✦

John began finding his greatest successes with ballads in the 1980s, and this album still finds him mixing collaborators, including Tim Rice (with whom he would write the 1994 soundtrack to *The Lion King*), this time to good effect: Gary Osborne contributes "Blue Eyes," while Bernie Taupin effectively eulogizes John Lennon in "Empty Garden." Originally on Geffen, this album has since been acquired by MCA. — *William Ruhlmann*

Too Low for Zero / May 1983 / Geffen ✦✦✦✦
With Taupin (and his old band) on board full-time, John turned out one of his best '80s albums—one full of remorse ("Cold as Christmas") and fierce reaffirmation ("I'm Still Standing"), not to mention such irresistible tunes as "Kiss the Bride" and "I Guess That's Why They Call It the Blues." — *William Ruhlmann*

Breaking Hearts / Jul. 1984 / Geffen ✦✦✦

Ice on Fire / Nov. 1985 / Geffen ✦✦

Leather Jackets / 1986 / Geffen ✦✦

Elton John Live in Australia (With the Melbourne Symphony Orchestra / Jun. 1987 / MCA ✦✦

Greatest Hits, Vol. 3 (1979-1987) / Sep. 1987 / Geffen ✦✦✦✦
The best of the Geffen years is very good indeed. — *William Ruhlmann*

The Complete Thom Bell Sessions / 1989 / MCA ✦✦✦

Sleeping with the Past / 1989 / MCA ✦✦

To Be Continued . . . / 1990 / MCA ✦✦✦✦
The inevitable Elton John box set is a four-disc, 68-track affair covering 25 years of the biggest pop star since the Beatles. Hit after hit is heard, plus good album tracks and rarities. There's a big booklet with commentary by John and his lyricist, Bernie Taupin. In a pinch, you can get by with the two MCA and one Geffen greatest hits collections, but for a complete overview of Elton John's career, this is the place to come. — *William Ruhlmann*

Greatest Hits, 1976-1986 / 1992 / MCA ✦✦✦
It covers much of the same ground as Geffen's *Greatest Hits—Vol. 3* but there's no denying that the hits on *Greatest Hits 1976-1986* are worth owning in any format by any Elton John fan. —*AMG*

The One / 1992 / MCA ✦✦

Rare Masters / 1992 / PolyGram ✦✦✦✦
A two-disc collection of rarities from the early '70s, it includes B-sides and the entire *Friends* soundtrack, which has previously been unavailable on CD. *Rare Masters* is essential for any hardcore Elton John fan. —*AMG*

Duets / Nov. 23, 1993 / MCA ✦✦

Made in England / 1995 / Rocket ✦✦✦

Freedy Johnston

Guitar, Vocals / Singer-Songwriter, Folk-Rock
A fine lyricist from Kansas who resettled in Hoboken, Johnston brought his heartland rock to the more brash Northeast, and after a shaky start has become a very exciting artist.
   Johnston's 1992 album *Can You Fly* received a generous amount of critical praise; his direct, Midwestern viewpoint graced some of the finest folk-rock of the decade. Two years later, the singer-songwriter had become a hot property and he followed through on his promise with the Butch Vig-produced *This Perfect World*, which easily matched *Can You Fly?* with its spare beauty. —*Bruce Eder*

Trouble Tree / 1990 / Bar/None ✦✦✦✦
Featured are provocative lyrics, with a Neil Young-ish voice. —*Robert Gordon*

● **Can You Fly** / Apr. 14, 1992 / Bar/None ✦✦✦✦
Freedy Johnston's second album is a supremely engaging set of folk-rock that showcases Johnston's considerable talent for writing melodic, literate songs. —*AMG*

Unlucky / 1993 / Restless ✦✦✦

This Perfect World / 1994 / Elektra ✦✦✦✦
The follow-up to the critically acclaimed *Can You Fly* is a collection of catchy, intelligent folk-rock that confirms Johnston's status as one of the 1990s' finest singer-songwriters. —*Stephen Thomas Erlewine*

Howard Jones (John Howard Jones)

b. Feb. 23, 1955, Southampton, Hampshire, England
Keyboards, Vocals / Synth-Pop, New Wave, Pop-Rock
Howard Jones was one of the defining figures of mid-'80s synth-pop. Jones' music merged the technology-intensive sound of new wave with the cheery optimism of hippies and late '60s pop. Jones racked up a string of hits in the mid- and late '80s before he retreated into being a cult figure in the '90s.
   A native of Southampton, England, Jones learned how to play piano at the age of seven. By the time he was a teenager, his family had relocated to Canada, which is where he joined his first band, a progressive-rock group called Warrior. Eventually, Jones moved back to England, where

he played in a number of different groups. In the mid-'70s, he enrolled in the Royal Northern College of Music in Manchester. After he dropped out of college, he played with a variety of local Southampton jazz and funk bands. Eventually, Jones began performing as a solo artist. At these solo shows, Jones performed only with synthesizers, drum machines. For these one-man concerts, Jones had a mime called Jed Hoile perform and act out his interpretations of Jones' music. After a few years of solo performing, Jones attracted the attention of John Peel, who offered the keyboardist a BBC session. Soon, Jones was opening for new wave synth-pop acts across England. By 1983, he had signed with WEA in England and Europe; in America, he signed to Elektra.
   Howard Jones released his first single, "New Song," in England in the fall of 1983 and it became a big hit, peaking at No. 3. His second single, "What Is Love," was released a few months later and it reached No. 2. *Humans Lib*, Jones' debut album, was released in the spring of 1984 and quickly rose to No. 1 in England. Thanks to repeated exposure on MTV, the album became a moderate hit in the US. Later in 1984, "New Song" and "What Is Love" became American Top 40 hits, while "Pearl in the Shell" became his third British Top Ten single.
   In 1985, Jones phased Hoile out of his live show, formed a touring band and released his second album, *Dream into Action*. The record became his most successful album, reaching No. 10 and going platinum in the US and spawning the hit singles "Things Can Only Get Better," "Like to Get to Know You Well," "Life in One Day," and "Look Mama." In the spring of 1986, he released *Action Replay*, an EP of remixes that featured a new version of "No One Is to Blame" from *Dream into Action*. "No One is to Blame" became Jones' biggest US hit, peaking at No. 4; in the UK, the single reached No. 16. The relatively weaker chart placement in the UK was indicative of his future in England—his next single, "You Know I Love You . . . Don't You?," taken from his third album *One to One*, became his last UK Top 40 hit.
   Jones released his fourth album, *Cross That Line*, in the spring of 1989. The first single from the album, "Everlasting Love," became a No. 1 adult-contemporary hit in America, reaching No. 13 on the pop charts. However, the album stalled at No. 65. Jones returned three years later with *In the Running*, a set that saw him abandoning synthesizers for piano. Predictably, it didn't make the charts. Following the release of *The Best of Howard Jones* in 1993, Elektra dropped him. Instead of seeking a new record contract with another major label, Jones hit the road in 1994, performing acoustic shows. At the 1994 shows, he sold *Working in the Backroom*—an album he recorded at his home studio and released on his own label, Dtox Records—at his concerts. For the next two years, Jones continually toured America and Europe. In 1996, he released *Live Acoustic America* on PLM Records. —*Stephen Thomas Erlewine*

Human's Lib / 1984 / Elektra ✦✦✦✦
His debut album is almost entirely performed on synthesizers. The material on *Human's Lib*, like all of the following albums, is very inconsistent; Jones either writes hits or flops, with very little in between. Contains two of Jones' best songs, "New Song" and "What Is Love?" —*Iotis Erlewine*

Dream into Action / 1985 / Elektra ✦✦✦✦
This album shows the synthesizer pop idol at the height of his creativity—*Dream into Action* is definitely the most interesting of Jones' albums. It contains some of his best songs—"Things Can Only Get Better," "Life in One Day," and "No One Is to Blame." The CD includes two bonus tracks, "Bounce Right Back" and "Like to Get to Know You Well," both of which are worthwhile additions. —*Iotis Erlewine*

Action Replay / 1986 / Elektra ✦✦

One to One / 1986 / Elektra ✦✦

Cross That Line / 1989 / Elektra ✦✦✦

In the Running / 1992 / Elektra ✦✦

● **The Best of Howard Jones** / Jun. 29, 1993 / Elektra ✦✦✦✦
The Best of Howard Jones successfully distills all the hits and highlights from his albums onto one disc. It could be all the Howard Jones you'll ever need. —*AMG*

Live Acoustic America / Feb. 13, 1996 / Plump ✦✦✦

Rickie Lee Jones

b. Nov. 8, 1954, Chicago, IL
Guitar, Keyboards, Vocals / Singer-Songwriter
A singer-songwriter who emerged in 1979 with a million-selling album and the Top Ten hit "Chuck E's in Love." Born in Chicago, Jones grew up in Arizona and Washington State and was taught music by her father. Moving to Los Angeles in 1973, she started as a performer by doing rhythmic "beat" monologs. She began to gain notice after hooking up with singer-songwriter Tom Waits in 1977, and in 1979 Little Feat leader Lowell George recorded her "Easy Money" on his debut solo album. Signed to Warner Bros., Jones recorded her own debut, *Rickie Lee Jones* (a combination of folk, jazz, and rock styles), its lyrical songs populated

by bohemian characters and sung in Jones' slightly slurred voice. It hit, and Jones won the Best New Artist Grammy for 1979.

She returned in 1981 with the even more ambitious *Pirates*, which hit and went gold. *Girl at Her Volcano* was a 1983 EP made up mostly of cover songs. Jones' next full-length album was *The Magazine*, which hit the Top 50 in 1984. In the second half of the '80s, Jones married and gave birth to a daughter. She returned to recording with the Top 40 *Flying Cowboys* in 1989, and in 1991 she released another record of covers, *Pop Pop*. Her fifth album of original songs, *Traffic from Paradise*, arrived in 1993, followed by an "unplugged"-style live album, *Naked Songs*, in 1995. — *William Ruhlmann*

★ **Rickie Lee Jones** / Mar. 1979 / Warner Bros. ✦✦✦✦✦
One of the most impressive debuts for a singer-songwriter ever, this infectious mixture of styles not only features a strong collection of original songs (the hits are "Chuck E's in Love" and "Young Blood," but "Danny's All-Star Joint" and "Coolsville" are just as good) but also a singer with a savvy, distinctive voice that can be streetwise, childlike, and sophisticated, sometimes all in the same song. — *William Ruhlmann*

Pirates / Jul. 1981 / Warner Bros. ✦✦✦✦
If the songs are less immediately accessible than on Jones' first album, repeated listenings are likely to lead to even greater rewards. Open-ended song structures allow Jones to explore more fully her closely observed portraits of lowlife characters, and her singing remains entrancing. — *William Ruhlmann*

The Magazine / Sep. 1984 / Warner Bros. ✦✦✦

Flying Cowboys / Sep. 1989 / Geffen ✦✦✦✦

Traffic from Paradise / Sep. 14, 1993 / Geffen ✦✦✦✦
"Just give me many chances . . . time to learn to crawl," sings Rickie Lee Jones on this, her fifth album of new material in 14 years. Clearly, she's had a lot of chances already, and some have paid off big. Here, however, Jones has made a record of what sound like rough performances of musical ideas that might at some point become songs and then, with some work, acceptable recordings. As it is, the record is vague and unfocused, only aspiring to coherence when someone other than Jones is heard from, such as the two songs co-written by Leo Kottke. Too much of the time, Jones sounds like she's singing half-forgotten songs, and the result is wispy and fragmentary. — *William Ruhlmann*

Naked Songs / Sep. 19, 1995 / Reprise ✦✦✦✦
Rickie Lee Jones "unplugged"—in fact, solo with an acoustic guitar or piano on all but a couple of tunes—*Naked Songs* is otherwise a retrospective concert album on which Jones cherrypicks songs from her five studio albums, including the hits "Chuck E's in Love" and "Young Blood," and others from her breakthrough debut record. The studio album arrangements always tried to support and augment Jones' idiosyncratic writing and playing style, which sounds less unusual when she is simply accompanying herself, and in many ways more effective. "Altar Boy," a previously unreleased song, strays into Leonard Cohen territory, mixing religion with eroticism. — *William Ruhlmann*

Tom Jones (Thomas Jones Woodward)

b. Jun. 7, 1940, Pontypridd, Mid-Glamorgan
Vocals / Pop, Pop-Rock, Club-Dance
Tom Jones became one of the most popular vocalists to emerge from the British Invasion. Since the mid-'60s, Jones has sang nearly every form of popular music—pop, rock, show tunes, country, dance, and techno. His actual style—a full-throated, robust baritone that had little regard for nuance and subtlety—never changed, he just sang over different backing tracks. On stage, Jones played up his sexual appeal; it didn't matter whether he was in an unbuttoned shirt or a tuxedo, he was always radiated a raw sexuality, which earned him a large following of devoted female fans who frequently threw underwear on stage. Jones' following never diminished over the decades; he was able to exploit trends, earning new fans while retaining his core following.

Born Thomas Jones Woodward, Tom Jones began singing professionally in 1963, performing as Tommy Scott with the Senators, a Welsh beat group. In 1964 he recorded a handful of solo tracks with record producer Joe Meek and shopped them to various record companies to little success. Later in the year, Decca producer Peter Sullivan discovered Tommy Scott performing in a club and directed him to manager Phil Solomon. It was a short-lived partnership and the singer soon moved back to Wales, where he continued to sing in local clubs. At one of the shows, he gained the attention of former Viscounts singer Gordon Mills, who had become an artist manager. Mills signed Scott, renamed him Tom Jones and helped him record his first single for Decca, "Chills and Fever," which was released in late 1964. "Chills and Fever" didn't chart but "It's Not Unusual," released in early 1965, became a No. 1 hit in the UK and a Top Ten hit in the US. The heavily orchestrated, over-the-top pop arrangements perfectly meshed with Jones' swinging, sexy image, guaranteeing him press coverage, which translated into a series of hits, including "Once upon a Time," "Little Lonely One," and "With These Hands." During 1965, Mills also secured a number of film themes for Jones to record, including the Top Ten hit "What's New Pussycat?" (Jun. 1965) and "Thunderball" (Dec. 1965).

Jones' popularity began to slip somewhat by the middle of 1966, causing Mills to redesign the singer's image into a more respectable, mature tuxedoed crooner. Jones also began to sing material that appealed to a broad audience, like the country songs "Green, Green Grass of Home" and "Detroit City." The strategy worked, as he returned to the top of the charts in the UK and began hitting the Top 40 again in the US. For the remainder of the '60s, he scored a consistent string of hits in both Britain and America. At the end of the decade, Jones relocated to America, where he hosted the television variety program, "This Is Tom Jones." Running between 1969 and 1971, the show was a success and laid the groundwork for the singer's move to Las Vegas in the early '70s. Once he moved to Vegas, Jones began recording less, choosing to concentrate on his lucrative club performances. After Gordon Mills died in the late '70s, Jones' son, Mark Woodward, became the singer's manager. The change in management prompted Jones to begin recording again. This time, he concentrated on the country market, releasing a series of slick Nashville-styled country-pop albums in the early '80s that earned him a handful of hits.

Jones' next image makeover came in 1988, when he sang Prince's "Kiss" with the electronic dance outfit, the Art of Noise. The single became a Top Ten hit in the UK and reached the American Top 40, which led to a successful concert tour and a part in a recording of Dylan Thomas' voice play, *Under the Milk Wood*. The singer then returned to the club circuit, where he stayed for several years. In 1993, Jones performed at the Glastonbury festival in England, where he won an enthusiastic response from the young crowd. Soon, he was on the comeback trail again, releasing the alternative-dance-pop album *The Lead and How to Swing It* in the fall of 1994; the record was a moderate hit, gaining some play in dance clubs. — *Stephen Thomas Erlewine*

Things That Matter Most to Me / 1987 / Mercury ✦✦✦✦
Things That Matter Most to Me compiles Jones' greatest country-pop hits. Taken in one sitting, the singles sound stronger than they do on the albums, and show that Jones can deliver country-flavored material convincingly. — *Stephen Thomas Erlewine*

● **The Complete Tom Jones** / Aug. 17, 1993 / PolyGram ✦✦✦✦
Collecting almost all of his hit singles on one album, *Complete Tom Jones* is the singer's most entertaining album, devoid of the filler that clutters all of his studio records. — *Stephen Thomas Erlewine*

Janis Joplin

b. Jan. 19, 1943, Port Arthur, TX, **d.** Oct. 4, 1970, Los Angeles, CA
Vocals / Rock 'n' Roll, Blues-Rock
The greatest White rock singer of the 1960s, Janis Joplin was also a great blues singer, making her material her own with her wailing, raspy, supercharged emotional delivery. First rising to stardom as the frontwoman for San Francisco psychedelic band Big Brother & the Holding Company, she left the group in the late '60s for a brief and uneven (though commercially successful) career as a solo artist. Although she wasn't always supplied with the best material or most sympathetic musicians, her best recordings, with both Big Brother and on her own, are some of the most exciting performances of her era. She also did much to redefine the role of women in rock with her assertive, sexually forthright persona and raunchy, electrifying onstage presence.

Joplin was raised in the small town of Port Arthur, TX, and much of her subsequent personal difficulties and unhappiness has been attributed to her inability to fit in with the expectations of the conservative community. She'd been singing blues and folk music since her teens, playing on occasion in the mid-'60s with future Jefferson Airplane guitarist Jorma Kaukonen. There are a few live pre-Big Brother recordings (not issued until after her death), reflecting the inspiration of early blues singers like Bessie Smith, that demonstrate she was well on her way to developing a personal style before hooking up with the band. She had already been to California before moving there permanently in 1966, when she joined a struggling early San Francisco psychedelic group, Big Brother & the Holding Company.

Big Brother's story is told in more detail in their own entry. Although their loose, occasionally sloppy brand of bluesy psychedelia had some charm, there can be no doubt that Joplin—who initially didn't even sing lead on all of the material—was primarily responsible for lifting them out of the ranks of the ordinary. She made them a hit at the 1967 Monterey Pop Festival, where her stunning version of "Ball and Chain" (perhaps her very best performance) was captured on film. After a debut on the Mainstream label, Big Brother signed a management deal with Albert Grossman, and moved on to Columbia. Their second album, *Cheap Thrills*, topped the charts in 1968, but Joplin left the band shortly afterwards, enticed by the prospects of stardom as a solo act.

Joplin's first album, *I Got Dem Ol' Kozmic Blues Again Mama!*, was recorded with the Kozmic Blues Band, a unit that included horns, and retained just one of the musicians that had played with her in Big Brother (guitarist Sam Andrew). Although it was a hit, it wasn't her best work; the new band, though more polished musically, were not nearly as sympathetic accompanists as Big Brother, purveying a soul-rock groove that could sound forced. That's not to say it was totally unsuccessful, boasting one of her signature tunes in "Try (Just a Little Bit Harder)."

For years, Joplin's life had been a roller coaster of drug addiction, alcoholism, and volatile personal relationships, documented in several biographies. Musically, however, things were on the upswing shortly before her death, as she assembled a better, more versatile backing outfit, the Full Tilt Boogie Band, for her final album, *Pearl* (ably produced by Paul Rothschild). Joplin was sometimes criticized for screeching at the expense of subtlety, but *Pearl* was solid evidence of her growth as a mature, diverse stylist who could handle blues, soul, and folk-rock. "Mercedes Benz," "Get It While You Can," and Kris Kristofferson's "Me and Bobby McGee" are some of her very best tracks. Tragically, she died before the album's release, overdosing on heroin in a Hollywood hotel in October 1970. "Me and Bobby McGee" became a posthumous No. 1 single in 1971, and thus the song with which she is most frequently identified. —*Richie Unterberger*

I Got Dem Ol' Kozmic Blues Again Mama / 1969 / Columbia ✦✦✦
Joplin's only solo album to be released during her lifetime heavily employs horns and an R&B band feel, but the dominant sound remains Joplin's impassioned singing on such songs as "Try." —*William Ruhlmann*

☆ **Pearl** / Feb. 1971 / Columbia ✦✦✦✦✦
Backed by a tight rock band, Full Tilt Boogie, Joplin puts her mark on everything from the bluesy "Cry Baby" to her hit version of Kris Kristofferson's "Me & Bobby McGee." —*William Ruhlmann*

In Concert / May 1972 / Columbia ✦✦✦

● **Janis Joplin's Greatest Hits** / Jul. 1973 / Columbia ✦✦✦✦
Well-chosen best-of gathers together tracks from Big Brother and the Holding Company and solo material. —*William Ruhlmann*

Farewell Song / 1982 / Columbia ✦✦✦

Janis / Nov. 23, 1993 / Columbia/Legacy ✦✦✦✦
This 3-CD box set is the most thorough and valuable retrospective of Janis Joplin's career. Besides including all of her most essential recordings with and without Big Brother and the Holding Company, this 49-song package features quite a few enticing rarities; 18 of the tracks were previously unissued. These include a 1962 home recording of the Joplin original "What Good Can Drinkin' Do," which marked the first time her singing was captured on tape, a pair of acoustic blues tunes from 1965 with backup guitar by future Jefferson Airplane star Jorma Kaukonen, an acoustic demo of "Me and Bobby McGee," a 1970 birthday song for John Lennon, and live performances from her appearance on "The Ed Sullivan Show" in 1969. The real showstopper is the previously unissued, eight-minute version of "Ball and Chain" from Big Brother's first set at the 1967 Monterey Pop Festival (the cut on the *Monterey Pop* box set is from their second set). The more forgettable tracks from her solo albums are wisely excised, as are the Big Brother songs which did not feature her vocals. This is the rare multidisc set of a major artist which manages to cover all the official milestones and present a bounty of worthwhile rarities at the same time. —*Richie Unterberger*

18 Essential Songs / 1995 / Columbia/Legacy ✦✦✦✦
18 Essential Songs is a one-disc distillation of the triple-disc *Janis* box set. Running 70 minutes, it is a more extensive best-of than the ten-track 1973 *Janis Joplin's Greatest Hits* album. But it is denied "first pick" status because, unlike that album, it does not contain the hit version of Joplin's only No. 1 single, "Me and Bobby McGee." (It does, however, contain an alternate demo version of that song.) —*William Ruhlmann*

Journey

Pop-Rock, Arena Rock
During its 14-year existence (1973-1987), Journey altered its musical approach and its personnel extensively while becoming a top touring and recording band. The only constant factor was guitarist Neal Schon (b. Feb 27, 1954), a music prodigy who had been a member of Santana in 1971-1972. The original unit, which was named in a contest on KSAN-FM in San Francisco, featured Schon, bassist Ross Valory, drummer Prairie Prince (replaced by Aynsley Dunbar), and guitarist George Tickner (who left after the first album). Another former Santana member, keyboard player and singer Gregg Rolie, joined shortly afterwards. This lineup recorded *Journey* (1974), the first of three moderate-selling jazz-rock albums given over largely to instrumentals.

By 1977, however, the group decided it needed a strong vocalist/frontman and hired Steve Perry (b. Jan 22, 1953). The results were immediately felt on the fourth album, *Infinity* (1978), which had sold a million copies by the end of the year. (By this time, Dunbar had been replaced by Steve Smith.) *Evolution* (1979) was similarly successful, as was *Departure* (after which Rolie was replaced by Jonathan Cain). After a live

album, *Captured* (1981), Journey released *Escape*, which broke them through to the top ranks of pop groups by scoring three Top Ten hit singles, all ballads featuring Perry's smooth tenor: "Who's Crying Now," "Don't Stop Believin'," and "Open Arms." The album topped the charts and had sold seven million copies by 1989.

Frontiers (1983), featuring the hit "Separate Ways," was another big success, after which Perry released a successful solo album, *Street Talk* (1984). When the group got back together to make a new album, Valory and Smith were no longer in the lineup, and *Raised on Radio* (1986) was made by Schon, Perry, and Cain, who added other musicians for a tour. This, however, was the end of Journey, as Perry and Cain went off to form Bad English. —*William Ruhlmann*

Evolution / 1979 / Columbia ✦✦✦✦
Journey got major US radio airplay with "Just the Same Way," "Lovin', Touchin', Squeezin'," and "City of Angels." —*Donna DiChario*

Escape / 1981 / Columbia ✦✦✦✦
Jonathan Cain (ex-Babys keyboardist) replaced Gregg Rolie on the band's most popular album to date. On the strength of the hits "Who's Crying Now" and "Don't Stop Believin'," this album spent more than a year in the Top 20. —*Donna DiChario*

Frontiers / 1983 / Columbia ✦✦✦✦
The ballads "Faithfully" and "Send Her My Love" reap the benefits of Steve Perry's crystal-clear vocals. —*Donna DiChario*

Raised on Radio / 1986 / Columbia ✦✦✦

● **Greatest Hits** / 1988 / Columbia ✦✦✦✦
A collection of Journey's '70s and '80s radio staples, the band's best-known rockers and ballads are here, including "Open Arms," "Who's Crying Now," "Any Way You Want It," and "Separate Ways (Worlds Apart)." —*Donna DiChario*

Time 3 / Dec. 1, 1992 / Columbia ✦✦✦

Joy Division

Post-Punk
The unchallenged Kings of Angst, Joy Division would ultimately be recognized as England's most important band of the immediate post-punk era. Starting out as Warsaw, the band failed to distinguish itself beyond the psychotic-looking onstage behavior of singer Ian Curtis and the handful of sides the band issued were largely ignored. All of that changed with the release of Joy Division's debut album, *Unknown Pleasures*. The music was built around Peter Hook's dominant bass lines, winding their way around brooding minor-key melodies, while Curtis established himself as a Jim Morrison-like presence, with his rigid delivery and often disturbing lyrics. The album was hailed as an immediate classic.

As difficult and gloomy as Joy Division's music appeared to be, there was also an oddly warmer and sometimes beautiful side to this group, as evidenced by the non-LP single "Atmospheres." Their upcoming recorded work was highly anticipated, but just prior to its release came the shocking news that Curtis had taken his own life. The ensuing single, "Love Will Tear Us Apart," came packaged in tombstone-style graphics, and housed Joy Division's masterpiece. The group continued as New Order; only their earliest work was directly connected with Joy Division's music, before finding a voice of their own, away from the spectre of Curtis. Despite the near-hysteria after Curtis' death and the numerous tortured souls who attempted to ape the formula, Joy Division's music stands as an impressive and still-riveting achievement. —*Steve Aldrich*

☆ **Unknown Pleasures** / 1979 / Qwest ✦✦✦✦✦
Their debut is a stark, almost gothic, masterpiece of emotional destruction and inner pain, expressed both lyrically and musically. —*John Floyd*

☆ **Closer** / 1980 / Qwest ✦✦✦✦✦
An even gloomier set, their second album was released just after Curtis' death. Guitars take a backseat to swirling layers of synthesizer, while Curtis' lyrics expand to examine the decay of not only the heart but society. —*John Floyd*

Still / 1981 / Qwest ✦✦✦
A double album, it contains nine worthwhile studio outtakes, a live version of the Velvet Underground's "Sister Ray," and ten cuts from a 1980 gig. Of interest only to hardcore fans. —*John Floyd*

★ **Substance** / 1988 / Qwest ✦✦✦✦✦
Collecting some riveting and rare material previously available only on singles and compilations, this offers a more diverse portrait of the band and works as both an introduction and a supplement to the original release. —*John Floyd*

Permanent / 1995 / Warner Bros. ✦✦✦
Featuring selected highlights from *Unknown Pleasures* and *Closer, Permanent* contains some of Joy Division's best songs, but the compilation isn't as useful as *Substance*, which featured early demos and B-sides, nor is it as mesmerizing as the band's two original studio albums. Consequently, *Permanent* is not only useless for dedicated fans, it's an incom-

plete and misleading introduction for casual fans, even though it contains a wealth of brilliant music. — *Stephen Thomas Erlewine*

Judas Priest

Hard Rock, Heavy Metal, British Metal

Judas Priest was one of the most influential heavy-metal bands of the '70s, spearheading the "new wave of British heavy metal" late in the decade. Decked out in leather and chains, the band fused the gothic doom of Black Sabbath with the riffs and speed of Led Zeppelin, as well as adding a vicious two-lead guitar attack; in doing so, they set the pace for much popular heavy metal from 1975 until 1985, as well as laying the groundwork for the speed- and death-metal of the '80s.

Formed in Birmingham, England, in 1970, the group's core members were guitarist K.K. Downing and bassist Ian Hill. Joined by Alan Atkins and drummer John Ellis, the band played their first concert in 1971. Atkins' previous band was called Judas Priest, yet the members decided it was the best name for the new group. The band played numerous shows throughout 1971; during the year, Ellis was replaced by Alan Moore; by the end of the year, Chris Campbell replaced Moore. After a solid year of touring the UK, Atkins and Campbell left the band in 1973 and were replaced by vocalist Rob Halford and drummer John Hinch. They continued touring, including a visit to Germany and the Netherlands in 1974; by the time the tour was completed, they had secured a record contract with Gull, an independent UK label.

Before recording their debut album, *Rocka Rolla,* Judas Priest added guitarist Glenn Tipton. They released the record in September of 1974 to almost no attention. The following year they gave a well-received performance at the Reading Festival and Hinch departed the band; he was replaced by Alan Moore. Later that year, the group released *Sad Wings of Destiny,* which earned some positive reviews. However, the lack of sales were putting the band in a dire financial situation, which was remedied by an international contract with CBS Records.

Sin After Sin (1977) was the first album released under that contract; it was recorded with Simon Phillips, who replaced Moore. The record received positive reviews and the band departed for their first American tour, with Les Binks on drums. When they returned to England, Judas Priest recorded 1978's *Stained Class,* the record that established them as an international force in metal. Along with 1979's *Hell Bent for Leather* (*Killing Machine* in the UK), *Stained Class* began the "new wave of British heavy metal" movement. A significant number of bands adapted Priest's leather-clad image and hard, driving sound, making their music harder, faster, and louder.

After releasing *Hell Bent for Leather,* the band recorded the live album *Unleashed in the East* (1979) in Japan; it became their first platinum album in America. Les Binks left the band in 1979; he was replaced by former Trapeze drummer Dave Holland. Their next album, 1980's *British Steel,* entered the British charts at No. 3, launched the hit singles "Breaking the Law" and "Living After Midnight," and was their second American platinum record; *Point of Entry,* released the following year, was nearly as successful.

At the beginning of the '80s, Judas Priest was a top concert attraction around the world, in addition to being a best-selling recording artist. Featuring the hit single "You've Got Another Thing Comin'," *Screaming for Vengeance* (1982) marked the height of their popularity, peaking at No. 17 in America and selling over a million copies. Two years later, *Defenders of the Faith* nearly matched its predecessor's performance, yet metal tastes were beginning to change, as Metallica and other speed/thrash-metal groups started to grow in popularity. That shift was evident on 1986's *Turbo,* where Judas Priest seemed out of touch with current trends; nevertheless, the record sold over a million copies in America on the basis of name recognition alone. However, 1987's *Priest . . . Live!* was their first album since *Stained Class* not to go gold. *Ram It Down* (1988) was a return to raw metal and returned the group to gold. Dave Holland left after this record and was replaced by Scott Travis for 1990's *Painkiller.* Like *Ram It Down, Painkiller* didn't make an impact outside the band's diehard fans, yet the group was still a popular concert act. In the late '80s Rob Halford began his own thrash band, Fight, and soon left Judas Priest. The rest of the band quietly faded away. — *Stephen Thomas Erlewine*

Rocka Rolla / 1974 / RCA ✦✦✦

Sad Wings of Destiny / 1976 / RCA ✦✦✦

Sin After Sin / 1977 / Columbia ✦✦✦

Stained Class / Apr. 1978 / Columbia ✦✦✦✦
Judas Priest came into its own on *Stained Class,* a lean and lethal collection of brutal riffs. Halford's lyrics were deliberately morbid—"Beyond the Realms of Death" and "Saints in Hell" are about as bleak as heavy metal gets—but he sang them with a salacious glee, as the band hammered out a series of relentless power chords. *Stained Class* sounded like nothing else in heavy metal at the time and it sowed the seeds of the death-metal movement of the '80s. — *Stephen Thomas Erlewine*

Hell Bent for Leather / Mar. 1979 / Columbia ✦✦✦✦
Hell Bent for Leather (titled *Killing Machine* in the UK) continued the style and sound of Judas Priest's breakthrough, *Stained Class,* yet its overall tone was lighter, as anthems like "Rock Forever" and the title track vied for space with "Evil Fantasies." While the lyrics weren't quite as dark as its predecessor's, the musical attack was just as heavy and the band's songwriting hadn't slipped at all. — *Stephen Thomas Erlewine*

Unleashed in the East (Live in Japan) / Oct. 1979 / Columbia ✦✦✦✦
Recorded live in Japan, this was the album that helped Judas Priest finally break through in America with support from critics and radio airplay. The album is an exceptional live performance. The songs chosen are a good example of their material from the '70s. — *John Book*

● **British Steel** / 1980 / Columbia ✦✦✦✦
British Steel added something that *Stained Class* and *Hell Bent for Leather* were missing—melody. Halford had managed to write some strong pop hooks for the album, particularly on the driving "Breaking the Law" and "Living After Midnight." Instead of diluting the group's power, the melodic hooks made them more forceful, arguably making *British Steel* their finest moment. — *Stephen Thomas Erlewine*

Point of Entry / 1981 / Columbia ✦✦✦

Screaming for Vengeance / 1982 / Columbia ✦✦✦✦
Screaming for Vengeance was Judas Priest's most successful album, featuring the hit single "You've Got Another Thing Comin'." While the group had backed away from the blitzkrieg attack of their late-'70s albums, they had increased the volume, turning in a set of thundering, heavy riffs that managed to stay melodic and catchy. The result was one of the band's finest albums; along with *British Steel,* it is their most accessible and memorable work. — *Stephen Thomas Erlewine*

Defenders of the Faith / 1984 / Columbia ✦✦✦

Turbo / 1986 / Columbia ✦✦✦

● **Metal Works '73-'93** / 1993 / Columbia ✦✦✦✦
Over two discs, *Metal Works '73-'93* winds its way through Judas Priest's 20-year career, hitting most of the high points as well as the low points and somehow managing to overlook seven of their eleven UK hits. Still, there isn't a better place to get acquainted with the band, which really was one of the most important metal acts of the late '70s and early '80s. — *AMG*

Jules & the Polar Bears

Rock 'n' Roll

After the demise of The Funky Kings, singer-songwriter Jules Shear formed his own band consisting of Stephen Hague (keyboards and, later, a noted producer), Richard Bredice (guitar), David White (bass), and David Beebe (drums). They were signed to Columbia Records in 1978 solely on the basis of Shear's demos—at the time, the band had never played live together. They recorded their first LP, *Got No Breeding,* in 1978, which quickly found critical acclaim, drawing favorable comparisons to Jackson Browne, the Kinks, Bob Dylan, and Bruce Springsteen. Unfortunately, it failed to sell when Columbia tried to lump the band in with its new wave promotion. 1979's *Fenetiks,* another fine effort, went virtually unnoticed as well. A third LP, *Bad for Business,* was recorded, but Columbia decided to pass on it and the band folded. Shear moved on to a distinguished, though commercially unsuccessful, solo career, and Hague focused on production. The albums, especially *Got No Breeding,* remain cult favorites. *Bad for Business* was finally released in late '96 by Columbia/Legacy. — *Chris Woodstra*

Got No Breeding / 1978 / Columbia ✦✦✦✦
Though it is packed with memorable hooks and Jules Shear's subtle twist-of-phrase, *Got No Breeding* was virtually ignored upon release, due in part to Columbia Records mis-marketing the band as part of the new wave. The Polar Bears were, in reality, just a good, hard-working rock band jamming with a sometimes over-enthusiastic Shear. The songs are among Shear's finest and the album is one of his most consistently enjoyable. — *Chris Woodstra*

Phonetics/Fenetiks / 1979 / Columbia ✦✦✦
The second Polar Bears album follows much of the same formula as *Got No Breeding,* with less memorable results. The band still rocks in places but the overall production is slicker and a little more synthesizer heavy. Shear's songwriting is top-notch ranging from pure pop, "Good Reason," to beautiful ballads, "Real Enough to Love." His delivery seems more restrained this time around. — *Chris Woodstra*

Kaleidoscope

Psychedelic, Folk-Rock

Kaleidoscope were arguably the most eclectic band of the psychedelic era, weaving together folk, blues, Middle Eastern, and acid more often and seamlessly than any other musicians. The California group was formed around the nucleus of multi-instrumentalists David Lindley and Chris Darrow in the mid-'60s. Adding fiddle, banjo, and various exotic string instruments to the traditional rock lineup, Kaleidoscope complemented their experimental sounds with taut and witty (if lyrically eccentric) songwriting. With the exception of their mawkish forays into old-timey music, their work holds up well. Their first three albums were their best, highlighted by the lengthy tracks "Taxim" and "Seven-Ate Sweet," which are groundbreaking fusions of Middle Eastern music and rock. —*Richie Unterberger*

Side Trips / 1967 / Epic ✦✦✦✦

Rampe Rampe / 1984 / Edsel ✦✦✦

Bacon from Mars / 1986 / Edsel ✦✦✦
The most intelligent compilation of their more accessible songs. Includes highlights of their first three albums, three tracks from non-LP singles, and a lengthy history of the band. —*Richie Unterberger*

● **Egyptian Candy (A Collection)** / 1991 / Epic ✦✦✦✦

Kansas

Art-Rock/Progressive-Rock, Pop-Rock, Arena Rock
Popular prog-rock group from Topeka, whose ranks included Steve Walsh (vocals, keyboards), Kerry Livgren (guitar, keyboards), Rich Williams (guitar), Robby Steinhardt (violin), Dave Hope (bass), and Phil Ehart on percussion. Kansas' music leaned more towards progressive arena rock than the artsier, more symphonic music of other groups like Yes and King Crimson. Hits like "Carry On Wayward Son" and "Point of Know Return" cemented that reputation and resulted in multi-platinum success in the late '70s. Walsh, unhappy with the commercial direction the band had taken, left the group in the early '80s and recorded a solo album. He was replaced by John Elefante. Without Walsh, their primary songwriter, the band lost direction and broke up in 1983. Livgren subsequently became a contemporary Christian artist. Walsh, Williams, and Ehart re-formed in 1986 with ex-Dixie Dregs guitarist Steve Morse and bassist Billy Greer joining the band. —*Steve Huey*

● **The Best of Kansas** / 1984 / Epic ✦✦✦✦
It contains the essential rock radio hits "Dust in the Wind," "Carry On Wayward Son," and "Point of Know Return," as well as improved remastering from the original tapes. —*Rick Clark*

Box Set / 1994 / Epic ✦✦✦✦

KC & the Sunshine Band

Disco
In the early '70s, two White men, Harry "KC" Casey (b. Jan 31, 1951) and Richard Finch (b. Jan 25, 1954), created a racially integrated disco band that based its music on various soul styles. They became one of the most commercially successful groups of the early disco era. KC & the Sunshine Band's disco was funky enough to be a staple in the clubs, while remaining melodic and sweet enough to be huge pop hits. The group continued to have hits until the early '80s; their last hit single, "Give It Up," was credited to KC in the US. —*Bil Carpenter*

● **The Best of KC & The Sunshine Band** / 1990 / Rhino ✦✦✦✦
A percussive mix of steel drums, whistle flutes, and funky group harmonies, this most soulful disco set includes all of their hits—"Get Down Tonight," "Please Don't Go," "That's the Way (I Like It)," "I'm Your Boogie Man," "(Shake, Shake, Shake) Shake Your Booty," and KC's solo hit, "Give It Up." —*Bil Carpenter*

R. Kelly

Urban, Club-Dance
Urban R&B producer/vocalist/multi-instrumentalist/songwriter R. Kelly and his supporting band Public Announcement began recording in 1992 at the tail end of the new jack swing era, yet he was able to keep much of its sound alive while remaining commercially successful. While he's created a smooth, professional mixture of hip-hop beats, soul-man crooning, and funk, the most distinctive element of Kelly's music is its explicit carnality. Over the course of two albums, the singer has been able to make songs like "Sex Me," "Bump N' Grind," and "Your Body's Callin'" into hits because his production has been seductive enough to sell such blatant come-ons. Kelly and Public Announcement released their debut album, *Born into the '90's*, at the beginning of 1992. It was an instant R&B smash, while earning a fair amount of pop airplay; "Honey Love" and "Slow Dance (Hey Mr. DJ)" were No. 1 R&B hits, while "Dedicated" was his biggest pop hit at No. 31. *12 Play*, released in the fall of 1993, established R. Kelly as an R&B superstar. The first single pulled from the album, "Sex Me (Parts I & II)," became a gold single and the second, "Bump n' Grind" hit No. 1 on both the pop and R&B charts in 1994; "Bump N' Grind" stayed on the top of the R&B charts for an astonishing 12 weeks, while it logged four weeks at the top of the pop charts. "Your Body's Callin'" was another gold single for Kelly, peaking at No. 13 on the pop charts. In 1994, he also produced *Age Ain't Nothin' But a Number*, the debut album for Aaliyah, a 15-year-old R&B singer from Detroit; it featured two Top Ten pop singles, "Back & Forth" and "At Your Best

(You Are Love)." Late in 1994, it was revealed that Kelly and Aaliyah had wed in August. The news sparked a small storm of controversy in the media, yet it didn't appear to hurt the careers of either singer. Kelly wrote and co-produced "You Are Not Alone," the second single from Michael Jackson's *HIStory* album, which was released in the summer of 1995. —*Stephen Thomas Erlewine*

Born into the 1990's / Jan. 14, 1992 / Jive ✦✦✦
One of the last popular new jack groups, this East Coast unit had some smash singles in '92 doing both conventional R&B/soul and hip-hop/new jack tracks. They did both originals and covers, had an enthusiastic attitude, were well produced, and stayed on the urban contemporary outlets throughout the year. —*Ron Wynn*

● **12 Play** / Nov. 9, 1993 / Jive ✦✦✦✦
new jack swing may be on its way out as a primary R&B sound, but R. Kelly hasn't lost any points by employing it here. Kelly skillfully mixes '70s-style funk beats, '90s hip-hop production and his own raps, as well as those of Deandre Boykins and Carey Kelly. Sometimes things come perilously close to sounding corny, but he manages to bring things off successfully. Kelly is a competent vocalist, but a master at striking a heated mood, keeping a light touch no matter how explicit the language gets and giving this album distinction even as it mines territory that's essentially played out. —*Ron Wynn*

R. Kelly / Nov. 14, 1995 / Jive ✦✦✦✦
With the salacious *12 Play*, R. Kelly established himself as one of the top R&B hitmakers of the mid-'90s, rivalled only by Babyface and Dr. Dre for overall consistency. *12 Play* was marred by occasionally slight tunes which were obscured by the explicit sexuality of the lyrics. *R. Kelly* isn't hampered by those flaws, although it isn't a perfect record by any means. Throughout the album, Kelly relies on melody and grooves instead of overtly carnal imagery. But that doesn't mean he has cleaned up—Kelly remains a sly, seductive crooner, and his sexiness is more effective when it is suggestive. Nevertheless, his lyrics and music are never subtle, which can make *R. Kelly* tiresome if taken as a whole. Taken as individual songs, the album works better than anything he has recorded to date. —*Stephen Thomas Erlewine*

Chris Kenner

b. Dec. 25, 1929, d. Jan. 25, 1976
Vocals / New Orleans R&B
Kenner wrote a number of enduring New Orleans R&B classics, although subsequent cover versions eclipsed all but "I Like It like That," his Grammy-nominated greatest hit in 1961. Kenner co-wrote "Sick and Tired" with Fats Domino and charted with it in 1957 on Imperial, but Domino's version blew it out of the water. Signing with Joe Babashak's Instant label, Kenner's "I Like It like That," "Land of 1000 Dances," and "Something You Got" sported Allen Toussaint's rolling piano behind Kenner's raw vocals. —*Bill Dahl*

Land of a Thousand Dances / 1966 / Atlantic ✦✦✦✦
Slashing soul by the writer of the title cut, this is one of the great forgotten albums. —*David Szatmary*

● **I Like It like That: Golden Classics** / 1987 / Collectables ✦✦✦✦
Vocalist Kenner's early-'60s sides for Instant, with Allen Toussaint laying down rolling piano behind him, represent New Orleans R&B at its most infectious. —*Bill Dahl*

Chaka Khan

b. Mar. 23, 1953, Great Lakes, IL
Vocals / Soul, Funk, Urban, Club-Dance
The lead singer of the R&B band Rufus from 1972 to 1978, Khan went solo with *Chaka* and the single "I'm Every Woman." Since 1978 she has released several solo albums. The Grammy-winning Khan has also done vocal work for Prince, Steve Winwood, David Bowie, and Quincy Jones. —*William Ruhlmann*

Chaka Khan / 1982 / Warner Bros. ✦✦✦✦
An excellent album from Chaka Khan, mixing tingling uptempo tunes with her characteristic soaring, glorious vocals. "Got to Be There" reached No. 5 on the R&B charts, but it actually wasn't the album's high point. That was the marvelous "Be Bop Medley," which later led hardcore jazz purist Betty Carter to proclaim Khan the one female singer working outside the jazz arena with legitimate improvising credentials. —*Ron Wynn*

● **I Feel for You** / 1984 / Warner Bros. ✦✦✦✦
Smoothly produced funk outing features the Prince-composed title track, an R&B No. 1, and two more R&B Top 20 hits, "This Is My Night" and "Through the Fire." —*William Ruhlmann*

Destiny / 1986 / Warner Bros. ✦✦✦

Life Is a Dance (The Remix Project) / 1989 / Warner Bros. ✦✦

Johnny Kidd & the Pirates

Rock 'n' Roll
Pioneering British hard-rock act in the pre-Beatles era, Kidd (born Fred Heath) and his backing trio the Pirates had a lean, loud, muscular approach to R&B that strongly influenced the Who and the Small Faces, among other bands. When they weren't recording dross like "The Birds and the Bees" at EMI's behest, they were making history with original numbers like "Shakin' All Over" (written by Heath) and a brilliant set of (mostly unreleased at the time) R&B covers. Pirates guitarist Mick Green later became well known in his own right. Kidd was in the process of reviving the group in the mid '60s when his life was ended in a car crash. —*Bruce Eder*

● **Hits & Rarities** / 1983 / See For Miles ✦✦✦✦
This collection is the best of three now available. It contains the strongest of Kidd's singles plus superb vault finds. Considered too rough for release in the '60s, they hold up splendidly. —*Bruce Eder*

Complete Johnny Kidd / 1994 / EMI ✦✦✦✦
A double CD of everything this underrated band ever recorded, assembled chronologically and beautifully remastered and annotated. This is the collection to own, especially since it has been issued at mid-price. And fans of the Who or the Small Faces can double the priority of owning this collection. —*Bruce Eder*

Greg Kihn

b. 1952, Baltimore, MD
Guitar, Vocals / Rock 'n' Roll, New Wave, Pop-Rock
Greg Kihn began his career in his hometown of Baltimore, MD, working in the singer-songwriter mold, but switched to straightforward rock 'n' roll when he moved to San Francisco in 1974. The following year, he became one of the first artists signed to Matthew Kaufman's now legendary Beserkley Records. Along with Jonathan Richman, Earthquake, and the Rubinoos, Kihn helped to carve the label's sound—melodic pop with a strong '60s-pop sensibility—a refreshing alternative to the bloated prog-rock of the time. In 1976, after his debut on the compilation *Beserkley Chartbusters*, he recorded his first album with his own band consisting of Ronnie Dunbar (guitar), Steve Wright (bass), and Larry Lynch (drums). Through the '70s, he released an album each year and built a strong cult following through constant touring, becoming Beserkley's biggest seller. In 1981, he earned his first bonafide hit with the Top 20 single, "The Breakup Song (They Don't Write 'Em)," from the *Rockihnroll* album. He continued in a more commercial vein through the '80s with a series of pun-titled albums; *Kihntinued* (1982), *Kihnspiracy* (1983), *Kihntageous* (1984), and *Citizen Kihn* (1985). He scored his biggest hit with 1983's "Jeopardy" (No. 2) from the *Kihnspiracy* album. One more single broke the Top 40, 1985's "Lucky," but by the time *Love and Rock and Roll* was released in 1986, the puns had run out and so had the hits. Kihn has kept a relatively low profile throughout the '90s, releasing only one album, 1994's *Mutiny*. —*Sara Sytsma*

Greg Kihn / 1976 / Beserkley ✦✦✦

Greg Kihn Again / 1977 / Beserkley ✦✦✦✦
A fine follow-up to *Greg Kihn* as Kihn continues to grow as an artist and songwriter. His version of "For You" received some favorable comments from Springsteen as well as first dibs on an original Springsteen tune for a later album. —*Jim Worbois*

Next of Kihn / 1978 / Beserkley ✦✦✦

With the Naked Eye / 1979 / Beserkley ✦✦✦

Rockihnroll / 1981 / Beserkley ✦✦✦✦
With this album Kihn finally has the hit he long ago deserved ("Breakup Song"). He also manages to recapture some of what made the early records so enjoyable. Once again, with both the material and the performance, Kihn sounds as if he is enjoying himself. —*Jim Worbois*

Kihntinued / 1982 / Beserkley ✦✦✦✦
A couple of the tracks, like "Everyday/Saturday" and "Testify," are more memorable than nearly anything on the previous record, but still not up to the potential Kihn hinted at on his first couple albums. —*Jim Worbois*

Kihnspiracy / 1983 / Beserkley ✦✦

Citizen Kihn / 1985 / EMI ✦✦

Love & Rock & Roll / 1986 / Beserkley ✦✦

● **Kihnsolidation: The Best of Greg Kihn** / 1989 / Rhino ✦✦✦✦
A fine sampling of Kihn's pop sensibility. Drawing from each of his albums, it includes the hits "The Breakup Song" and "Jeopardy" as well as his better album cuts. —*Chris Woodstra*

Killing Joke

Alternative Pop-Rock, New Wave, Post-Punk
Heavy and slow, Killing Joke (at least early in their career) was a quasi-metal band dancing to a tune of doom and gloom. They eventually became less heavy and more arty (the latter seems almost impossible), more danceable even, but early on they made some urgent slabs of molten dynamite that oozed with the power of thick guitars, thudding drums, and over-the-top singing. —*John Dougan*

Killing Joke / May 1981 / EG ✦✦✦✦
Killing Joke's self-titled debut album is a throttling merger of heavy metal, new wave, and noise. It's a dense, claustrophobic record that basically sketched out the path the band would follow over the next decade. —*Stephen Thomas Erlewine*

● **Incomplete Collection 1980-85** / 1990 / EG ✦✦✦✦

Democracy / Apr. 1996 / Zoo ✦✦

King Crimson

Art-Rock, Progressive-Rock
If the Moody Blues provided a heavenly Mellotron-soaked soundtrack for millions of late-'60s cosmic rockers, King Crimson (formed in 1969) balanced the scales with disturbingly dense and explosive sonic trips into the dark side. Even when the band was playing something relatively peaceful, there was a sense that something wasn't quite settled. Founded by guitarist Robert Fripp and saxophonist Ian McDonald, the group burst forth with an ornate, majestic, savage sound and an approach that owed a great deal to modern jazz. McDonald left after the first tour, followed by the rest of the band, except for Fripp, who re-formed the band in ever-changing configurations up through 1974, when the final breakup came. The latter-day King Crimson (with Adrian Belew on guitar with Fripp) is the most daring version, but has virtually no connection with the original except its name. —*Bruce Eder & Rick Clark*

★ **In the Court of the Crimson King** / 1969 / EG ✦✦✦✦✦
Definitive debut album, which was almost too good (it took years for them to come up with a record as concise and distinctive); an orchestrated vision of apocalyptic doom dominated by Ian McDonald's Mellotron, Greg Lake's dignified voice, and the ferocious guitar playing of Robert Fripp. The latter would be the only survivor onto subsequent albums. —*Bruce Eder*

In the Wake of Poseidon / 1970 / EG ✦✦✦✦
A more carefully produced and better-crafted but more diffuse second album. Fripp took over the keyboards as well as all the compositional chores, with help from Gustav Holst (*The Planets*). —*Bruce Eder*

Lizard / 1970 / EG ✦✦✦

Islands / 1971 / EG ✦✦✦
A flawed album by what looked like the most stable Crimson lineup in some time (this band actually got to tour), with too much weak material expanded to mammoth proportions. The one compensation is the return of the sense of humor missing since the first two albums. —*Bruce Eder*

Larks' Tongues in Aspic / 1973 / EG ✦✦✦✦
The new King Crimson makes their debut with a violin (courtesy of David Cross) now sharing center stage with Fripp's guitar, and the Mellotron pushed somewhat into the background. The material itself is the most experimental that Fripp has come up with up to this time, and John Wetton's vocals are the strongest since the departure of Greg Lake in 1970. —*Bruce Eder*

Red / 1974 / EG ✦✦✦
Some final thoughts before Fripp pulled the plug on Crimson—the material is longer, the playing more ferocious, and the whole album seems rushed toward the breaking point of dissolution for the band. The culmination of five years of doom-rock. —*Bruce Eder*

Starless & Bible Black / 1974 / EG ✦✦✦✦
An intriguing follow-up, and overall the band's most satisfying album. —*Bruce Eder*

Discipline / 1981 / EG ✦✦✦✦
The new King Crimson, harder and heavier. —*Bruce Eder*

Beat / 1982 / EG ✦✦✦✦
A superior mid-'80s follow-up with better material. —*Bruce Eder*

Frame by Frame / 1991 / Caroline ✦✦✦✦
Frame by Frame is a four-disc box set, compiled by bandleader Robert Fripp, that does a good job providing primo samples of each of Crimson's musical periods. Sonically, the excellent remastering makes this the best this band has ever sounded on disc. Three of the discs cover their studio work, while the fourth is a collection of live work, spanning the band's entire career. Enclosed is a richly detailed diary (written by Fripp) of Crimson's entire history, plus interviews with band members, and glowing and hateful reviews from critics. Typical of Crimson, precious little of the music on this set would qualify for casual listening. However, those whose taste run toward the dark side of prog-rock will find this set rewarding. —*Rick Clark*

The Great Deceiver (Live 1973-1974) / 1992 / Caroline ✦✦✦✦
Four CDs full of live King Crimson from 1973 and 1974, an era that many consider their best. Although some songs are repeated, they're never

played the same way twice. If you're a King Crimson fan, that's enough of an incentive for purchase; if you're not, the musical expertise of the band might convert you, providing you have the money for a box set. —*Stephen Thomas Erlewine*

Thrak / Apr. 1995 / Virgin ✦✦✦

Thrakattak / 1996 / DPL ✦✦✦

Ben E. King

b. Sep. 23, 1938, Henderson, NC
Vocals / Soul, R&B, Brill Building pop
Swirling strings, subtly shaded orchestrations, and Ben E. King's assured baritone were a blueprint for uptown soul success during the early '60s. King and his vocal group, the Five Crowns, were in the right place at the right time when, in 1959, the manager of the Drifters decided to sack his entire group and solicit replacements. As new lead singer for the Drifters, King crooned the soulful smashes "There Goes My Baby," "Save the Last Dance for Me," and "I Count the Tears" before heading out on his own in 1960. The vocalist's own Atco singles mirrored the sumptuous production of his Drifter sides, and "Spanish Harlem," "Don't Play That Song (You Lied)," and the R&B chart-topping "Stand by Me" were all huge successes. King remained with Atco through 1969, then triumphantly returned to Atlantic in 1975 with another No. 1 soul hit, "Supernatural Thing (Part 1)." With the re-release of *Stand by Me* as the theme to the 1986 film of the same title, King was in demand all over again, the stirring song improbably scaling the charts for a second time, despite being a quarter-century old. —*Bill Dahl*

The Ultimate Collection / 1987 / Atlantic ✦✦✦✦
The rich baritone of this ex-Drifter lead is matched by the majestic, violin-drenched, uptown soul arrangements on these early-'60s classics. —*Bill Dahl*

● **Anthology** / 1993 / Rhino ✦✦✦✦
This two-disc, 50-song box set thoroughly documents the recordings that Ben E. King cut for Atlantic. Starting as the lead voice of the Drifters on such hits as "There Goes My Baby" and "Save The Last Dance for Me," King went on to a successful solo career with a string of singles that matched his smooth, sexy baritone with tastefully arranged string sections and Latin rhythms. All of those early hits—"Stand by Me" and "Spanish Harlem" were the biggest—are included here, along with non-hit 45s by the likes of Leiber/Stoller, Doc Pomus, Mort Shuman, Phil Spector, and Goffin/King that were nearly equal in worth. As the '60s progressed, King moved toward a more mainstream, heavier soul sound and less distinctive material, culminating in his parting from Atlantic in 1969. He returned to the label in the mid-'70s for a string of mainstream R&B successes. This compilation includes 16 non-LP singles from the '60s, which together with the hits constitute the definitive overview of this influential soul singer's work. —*Richie Unterberger*

Carole King

b. Feb. 9, 1942, Brooklyn, NY
Synthesizer, Guitar, Piano, Keyboards, Vocals / Singer-Songwriter, Adult Contemporary, Soft Rock, Pop-Rock, Brill Building Pop
During the early '70s, the singer-songwriter movement emerged as a reflective, folky alternative to rock and pop. Among the genre's more notable avatars were James Taylor, Joni Mitchell, Cat Stevens, and Carole King. Unlike many of the other artists, King was well-grounded in the pop songcrafting tradition, primarily from her tenure as a writer during the glory days at the Brill Building in New York. It was while she was at the Brill Building, beginning in 1958, that King met Neil Diamond and Paul Simon and began a very successful string of collaborations with Gerry Goffin, whom she would later marry. To list all of those hits would fill a page, but classics like "Up on the Roof," "(You Make Me Feel Like) A Natural Woman," "Will You Still Love Me Tomorrow," "The Locomotion," "Don't Bring Me Down," "Hey Girl," "One Fine Day," "Pleasant Valley Sunday," "Some Kind of Wonderful," and "You've Got a Friend" are a few.

In 1962, King scored a No. 22 hit as a solo artist with "It Might as Well Rain until September." With guitarist Danny Kortchmar and her second husband, bassist Charles Larkey, King formed The City, releasing an album titled *Now That Everything's Been Said* on Lou Adler's Ode label. The project fell apart and King focused on her solo career in 1970 with *Writer: Carole King*. That album went nowhere, but its follow-up, *Tapestry*, became one of the biggest-selling albums of the '70s, holding the No. 1 position for 15 weeks and remaining on the charts for 302 consecutive weeks. *Tapestry*, which featured a blend of old King standards and new compositions, fused the introspection of the singer-songwriter genre with a warm, homey soulfulness and believable passionate delivery. Since then, King's intimate delivery and quality work have given her a long, rewarding career. In 1987, King was inducted into the Songwriters Hall of Fame. A few of her many hits include "It's Too Late"/"I Feel the Earth Move" (No. 1), "So Far Away" (No. 14), "Sweet Seasons" (No. 9), "Jazzman" (No. 2), and "Nightingale" (No. 9). —*Rick Clark*

★ **Tapestry** / Mar. 1971 / Epic ✦✦✦✦✦
In the world of popular music, the word "classic" gets bandied about like the word "improved" on ad campaigns, ceasing to mean anything after a while. *Tapestry*, however, is a *classic*, no two ways about it. King (already a very successful songwriter) assembled a collection of her best-known songs, plus some new ones, and gave them intimate heartfelt readings. King's voice had a warm earthy quality, with just the right amount of urgency. Listing highlights is fairly pointless, as the whole album is stunning. —*Rick Clark*

Music / Dec. 1971 / Epic ✦✦✦✦
Without the reserve of self-penned standards to draw upon, *Music* lacked the powerful resonance of its predecessor, *Tapestry*. Nevertheless, songs like "Sweet Seasons," "Brother Brother," "Some Kind of Wonderful," and "Song of Long Ago" make this one of her better efforts. —*Rick Clark*

Rhymes & Reasons / Nov. 1972 / Epic ✦✦✦
On her second follow-up to *Tapestry* and third new album in less than two years, King turned entirely to new compositions—most of them co-written with Toni Stern—rather than relying partly on songs from her back catalog. The result was a thinner collection than *Tapestry* or *Music*, although the album still went to No. 2 and featured the Top 25 hit "Been to Canaan," as well as the warm love song "The First Day in August." —*William Ruhlmann*

Fantasy / Jun. 1973 / Epic ✦✦✦

Really Rosie / 1975 / Caedmon ✦✦✦✦
This winning soundtrack collaboration for a children's TV special (with children's author Maurice Sendak) was a return to form for King. *Really Rosie* contains some of King's best solo material. This is an enjoyable listening experience for children and adults alike. —*Rick Clark*

Thoroughbred / Jan. 1976 / Epic ✦✦✦

Simple Things / Jul. 1977 / Capitol ✦✦

Welcome Home / 1978 / Capitol ✦✦

Her Greatest Hits / Mar. 1978 / Epic ✦✦✦✦
All of King's major hits are here, plus a few key album tracks. It's a decent starting place for the uninitiated, but *Tapestry* is a richer listening experience. —*Rick Clark*

City Streets / Apr. 1989 / Capitol ✦✦

Colour of Your Dreams / 1993 / Rhythm Safari ✦✦

● **A Natural Woman: The Ode Collection (1968-1976)** / 1994 / Ode ✦✦✦✦
Carole King had already written an enormous amount of pop classics by the time she began her solo career in earnest in the late '60s. With her second album, *Tapestry*, King became one of the most popular and artistically successful singer-songwriters of the early '70s. King never matched the consistent brilliance of *Tapestry*, yet managed to record many fine songs during the rest of the decade. *A Natural Woman* collects all of her finest moments over the course of two discs. *Tapestry* is included in its entirety, along with the highlights from her other albums, making *A Natural Woman* the one essential King album—apart from *Tapestry* itself, of course. —*Stephen Thomas Erlewine*

The Kingsmen

Rock 'n' Roll
A rock 'n' roll band from Portland, OR, the Kingsmen's one big hit "Louie, Louie" defined the garage-band style and became one of the all-time classics. The original lineup included Jack Ely (lead singer and guitar), Lynn Easton (drums), Mike Mitchell (lead guitar), Bob Nordby (bass), and Don Galucci (piano). After Ely had "incorrectly" taught the rest of the band The Wailers version of Richard Berry's "Louie Louie," they recorded it for 50 dollars at a primitive local recording studio with only three mikes, Ely hollering the lyrics into an overhead boom mike suspended ten feet in the air. Released on a local label, the record went nowhere after Paul Revere & The Raiders quickly covered it in the Northwest market, although it had quickly become a standard for all teen bands in that area. In 1964, the record started to break nationally, causing the breakup of the original lineup when Easton copyrighted the group's name, informing the other members that he was now sole owner of The Kingsmen and its new lead singer. Ely formed his own Kingsmen, touring at the same time as Easton, who was lip-synching the record whenever possible. Only Easton and Mitchell were left from the original lineup, but they kept scoring big with frat-band versions of "Money" and "Little Latin Lupe Lu," reaching their peak with "The Jolly Green Giant," while Ely languished in relative obscurity and Gallucci formed Don & The Goodtimes. By the early '90s, history had redressed itself somewhat. When replacement members from the Easton version of the band toured as the "original" Kingsmen, Jack Ely finally received some of his due, headlining the 30th Anniversary Louie Louie tour. Though the song itself has been covered repeatedly, the version by Ely and the original lineup remains definitive. —*Cub Koda*

The Kingsmen in Person / 1963 / Sundazed ✦✦✦
CD reissue of the group's first album, including the rock anthem "Louie Louie," issued here for the first time minus the annoying overdubbed crowd noises. Also nice is the inclusion of three bonus tracks. —*Cub Koda*

The Kingsmen, Vol. 2 / 1964 / Sundazed ✦✦✦
Supposedly another "live" album, finally issued here without the audience overdubs. Highlights include "Little Latin Lupe Lu," "Long Green," and "David's Mood," plus two CD bonus tracks. —*Cub Koda*

The Kingsmen, Vol. 3 / 1965 / Sundazed ✦✦✦
The group's third album, again issued here without the overdubbed crowd noises. This features their hit "Jolly Green Giant" plus three CD bonus tracks. —*Cub Koda*

● **The Best of the Kingsmen** / 1989 / Rhino ✦✦✦✦
All the hits; great sound. —*Cub Koda*

The Kinks

Rock 'n' Roll, Hard Rock, British Invasion, Pop-Rock
Although they weren't as boldly innovative as the Beatles or as popular as the Rolling Stones or the Who, the Kinks were one of the most influential bands of the British Invasion. Like most bands of their era, the Kinks began as an R&B/blues outfit. Within four years, the band had become the most staunchly English of all their contemporaries, drawing heavily from British music hall and traditional pop, as well as incorporating elements of country, folk, and blues.

Throughout their long, varied career, the core of the Kinks remained Ray (b. June 21, 1944) and Dave Davies (b. February 3, 1947), who were born and raised in Muswell Hill, London. In their teens, the brothers began playing skiffle and rock 'n' roll. Soon, the brothers recruited a schoolmate of Ray's, Peter Quaife, to play with them; like the Davies brothers, Quaife played guitar, but he switched to bass. By the summer of 1963, the group had decided to call itself the Ravens and had recruited a new drummer, Mickey Willet. Eventually, their demo tape reached Shel Talmy, an American record producer who was under contract to Pye Records. Talmy helped the band land a contract with Pye in 1964. Before signing to the label, the Ravens replaced drummer Willet with Mick Avory.

The Ravens recorded their debut single, a cover of Little Richard's "Long Tall Sally," in January 1964. Before the single was released, the group changed their name to the Kinks. "Long Tall Sally" was released in February of 1964 and it failed to chart, as did their second single, "You Still Want Me." The band's third single, "You Really Got Me," was much noisier and dynamic, featuring a savage, fuzz-toned two-chord riff and a frenzied solo from Dave Davies. Not only was the final version the blueprint for the Kinks' early sound, but scores of groups used the heavy power chords as a foundation. "You Really Got Me" reached No. 1 within a month of its release; released on Reprise in the US, the single climbed into the Top Ten. "All Day and All of the Night," the group's fourth single, was released late in 1964 and it rose all the way to No. 2; in America, it hit No. 7. During this time, the band also produced two full-length albums and several EPs.

Not only was the group recording at a breakneck pace, they were touring relentlessly, as well, which caused much tension within the band. At the conclusion of their summer 1965 American tour, the Kinks were banned from re-entering the US by the American government for unspecified reasons. For four years, the Kinks were prohibited from returning to the US, which not only meant that the group was deprived of the world's largest music market, but that they were effectively cut off from the musical and social upheavals of the late '60s. Consequently, Ray Davies' songwriting grew more introspective and nostalgic, relying more on overtly English musical influences, such as music hall, country and English folk, than the rest of his British contemporaries. The Kinks' next album, *The Kinks Kontroversy*, demonstrated the progression in Davies' songwriting. "Sunny Afternoon" was one of Davies' wry social satires, and the song was the biggest hit of the summer of 1966 in the UK, reaching No. 1. "Sunny Afternoon" was a teaser for the band's great leap forward, *Face to Face*, a record that featured a vast array of musical styles. In May of 1967, they returned with "Waterloo Sunset," a ballad that reached No. 2 in the UK in the spring of 1967. Released in the fall of 1967, *Something Else* continued the progressions of *Face to Face*. Despite the Kinks' musical growth, their chart performance was beginning to stagnate. Following the lackluster performance of *Something Else*, the Kinks rushed out a new single, "Autumn Almanac," which became another big UK hit for the band. Released in the spring of 1968, the Kinks' "Wonderboy" was the band's first single not to crack the Top Ten since "You Really Got Me." They recovered somewhat with "Days," but the band's commercial decline was evident by the lack of success of *The Village Green Preservation Society*.

Released in the fall of 1968, *Village Green Preservation Society* was the culmination of Ray Davies' increasingly nostalgic tendencies. While the album was unsuccessful, it was well-received by critics, particularly in the US.

Peter Quaife soon grew tired of the band's lack of success, and he left the band by the end of the year, being replaced by John Dalton. In early 1969, the American ban upon the Kinks was lifted, leaving the band free to tour the US for the first time in four years. Before they began the tour, the Kinks released *Arthur (or the Decline and Fall of the British Empire)*. Like its two predecessors, *Arthur* contained distinctly British lyrical and musical themes, but it was a modest success. As they were recording the follow-up to *Arthur*, the Kinks expanded their lineup to include keyboardist John Gosling. The first appearance of Gosling on a Kinks record was "Lola." Featuring a harder rock foundation than their last few singles, "Lola" was a Top Ten hit in both the UK and the US. Released in the fall of 1970, *Lola Vs. the Powerman and the Money-go-round, Part One* was their most successful record since the mid-'60s in both the US and UK, helping the band become concert favorites in the US.

The band's contract with Pye/Reprise expired in early 1971, leaving the Kinks free to pursue a new record contract. By the end of 1971, the Kinks had secured a five-album deal with RCA Records, which brought them a million dollar advance. Released in late 1971, *Muswell Hillbillies*, the group's first album for RCA, marked a return to the nostalgia of the Kinks' late-'60s albums, only with more pronounced country and music hall influences. The album failed to be the commercial blockbuster RCA had hoped for. A few months after the release of *Muswell Hillbillies*, Reprise released a double-album compilation callled *The Kink Kronikles*, which outsold their RCA debut. *Everybody's in Showbiz* (1973), a double record set consisting of one album of studio tracks and another of live material, was a disappointment in the UK, although the album was more successful in the US.

In 1973, Ray Davies composed a full-blown rock opera called *Preservation*. When the first installment of the opera finally appeared in late 1973, it was harshly criticized and given a cold reception from the public. *Act 2* appeared in the summer of 1974; the sequel received worse treatment than its predecessor. Davies began another musical, *Starmaker*, for the BBC; the project eventually metamorphosed into *Soap Opera*, which was released in the spring of 1975. Despite poor reviews, *Soap Opera* was a more commercially successful record than its predecessor. In 1976, the Kinks recorded Davies' third straight rock opera, *Schoolboys in Disgrace*, which rocked harder than any album they released on RCA.

During 1976, the Kinks left RCA and signed with Arista Records. On Arista, the band refashioned themselves as a hard rock band. Bassist John Dalton left the group near the completion of their debut Arista album; he was replaced by Andy Pyle. *Sleepwalker*, the Kinks' first album for Arista, became a major hit in the US. As the band was completing the follow-up to *Sleepwalker*, Pyle left the group and was replaced by the returning Dalton. *Misfits*, the band's second Arista album, was also a US success. After a British tour, Dalton left the band again, along with keyboardist John Gosling; bassist Jim Rodford and keyboardist Gordon Edwards filled the vacancies. Soon, the band was playing arenas in the USUS. Even though punk rockers like the Jam and the Pretenders were covering Kinks songs in the late '70s, the group was becoming more blatantly commercial with each release, culminating in the heavy rock of *Low Budget* (1979), which became the group's biggest American success, peaking at No. 11. The Kinks' next album, *Give the People What They Want*, appeared in late 1981; the record peaked at No. 15 and went gold. For most of 1982, the band was on tour. In the spring of 1983, "Come Dancing" became the group's biggest American hit since "Tired of Waiting for You," thanks to the video's repeated exposure on MTV; in the US, the song peaked at No. 6, in the UK it climbed to No. 12. *State of Confusion* followed the release of "Come Dancing," and it was another success, peaking at No. 12 in the US. For the remainder of 1983, Ray Davies worked on a film project, *Return to Waterloo*, which caused considerable tension between himself and his brother. Instead of breaking up, the Kinks merely reshuffled their lineup, but there was a major casualty—Mick Avory, the band's drummer for 20 years, was fired and replaced by Bob Henrit. As Ray finished post-production duties on *Return to Waterloo*, he wrote the next Kinks album, *Word of Mouth*. Released in late 1984, the album was similar in tone to the last few Kinks records, but it was a commercial disappointment and began a period of decline for the band—they never released another record that cracked the Top 40.

Word of Mouth was the last album they would record for Arista Records. In early 1986, the band signed with MCA Records in the US, London in the UK. *Think Visual*, their first album for their new label, was released in late 1986. It was a mild success but there were no hit singles from the record. The following year, the Kinks released another live album, appropriately titled *The Road*, which spent a brief time on the charts. Two years later, the Kinks released their last studio record for MCA, *UK Jive*. During 1989, keyboardist Ian Gibbons left the band. The Kinks were inducted into the Rock & Roll Hall of Fame in 1990, but the induction did not help revive their career. In 1991, a compilation of their MCA records, *Lost & Found (1986-1989)*, appeared, signalling that their contract with the label had expired. Later in the year, the band signed with Columbia Records and released an EP called *Did Ya*, which didn't chart. The Kinks' first album for Columbia, *Phobia*, arrived in 1993 to fair reviews but poor sales. By this time, only Ray and Dave Davies remained from the original lineup. In 1994, the band was dropped from Columbia Records, leaving the group to release the live *To to the Bone* on an independent label in the UK; the band was left without a record label in the US.

Despite a lack of commercial success, the band's public profile began to rise in 1995, as the group was hailed as an influence on several of the most popular British bands of the decade, including Blur and Oasis. Ray Davies was soon on popular television shows again, acting the godfather to the bands and promoting his autobiography, *X-Ray*, which was published in early 1995 in the UK Dave Davies' autobiography, *Kink*, was published in the spring of 1996. — *Stephen Thomas Erlewine*

You Really Got Me / 1964 / Rhino ♦♦
The highlight of this rather spotty debut (consisting of a sampling of originals and covers the Kinks churned out at gigs) was, without a doubt, the title track, which single-handedly pioneered riff-oriented hard rock. "Stop Your Sobbing," a song later recorded by thePretenders, was also a standout track, but producer Shel Talmy's "Bald Headed Woman" was an absolute low point. — *Rick Clark*

Kinda Kinks / 1965 / Rhino ♦♦♦
Album number two featured a rewrite of "You Really Got Me," with the equally fine "All Day and All of the Night." Ray Davies, however, delivered a strong set of tunes that went beyond riff-rockers with the exuberant "Come on Now" and "You Shouldn't Be Sad." His penchant for memorable melodies emerged with tracks like "Something Better Beginning" and "Tired of Waiting for You." — *Rick Clark*

Kink-Size/Kinkdom / 1965 / Rhino ♦♦♦♦
This Rhino reissue contains theKinks' third and fourth albums, *Kink-Size* and *Kinkdom*, respectively, plus some non-album sides from the same period. *Kink-Size* featured the hit "Set Me Free," another Kinks classic, as well as "Everybody's Gonna Be Happy." By the release of *Kinkdom*, the Kinks had developed an instantly identifiable sound, built around Davies' wavering lower tenor and the group's airy falsetto background vocals and ragged garage rock-like ensemble work. "Dedicated Follower of Fashion," a noisy dance-hall rocker, was a wonderful poke at a Carnaby Street fop in his "frilly nylon panties." Other hits included "Who'll Be the Next in Line?" and "A Well Respected Man." This disc also includes the assertive "I'm Not Like Everybody Else" (originally written as a pitch for the Animals, and the B-side to "Sunny Afternoon"). — *Rick Clark*

Kink Kontroversy / 1965 / PRT ♦♦♦
This great album is still only available as a British import. The Kinks sludge out some fine trashy rockers with "Where Have All the Good Times Gone?" (later re-recorded by Van Halen) and "Till the End of the Day" (No. 50), a moderate hit. Other highlights included "It's Too Late," "You Can't Win," and "I'm on an Island." — *Rick Clark*

☆ **Face to Face** / 1966 / Reprise ♦♦♦♦♦
Face to Face was another extraordinary Kinks album, this time featuring the hit "Sunny Afternoon" and other gems like "Holiday in Waikiki," "Fancy," "Too Much on My Mind," and "Rainy Day in June." — *Rick Clark*

Live at Kelvin Hall / 1967 / Reprise ♦♦♦

☆ **Something Else by the Kinks** / 1967 / Reprise ♦♦♦♦♦
The follow-up to *Face to Face* was equally impressive, featuring the wistful "Waterloo Sunset," one of Davies' finest compositions. Other highlights included "Situation Vacant," "David Watts," "Love Me Till the Sun Shines," and Dave Davies' "Death of a Clown." Highly recommended! — *Rick Clark*

☆ **The Village Green Preservation Society** / 1968 / Reprise ♦♦♦♦♦
On *The Kinks Are the Village Green Preservation Society*, Ray Davies' eye for the little lyrical details that speak volumes about everyday people hit a zenith. Initially inspired by Dylan Thomas' portrayal of an indolent Welsh village (*Under the Milkwood*), this was the Kinks' finest conceptual album. Their first album produced without Shel Talmy, it projected an unassuming, low-key quality. It is amazing that this album failed to dent the charts. Fortunately, Warner has released it on CD. Highlights include "Picture Book," "Animal Farm," "Big Sky," "Johnny Thunder," "Wicked Annabella," and the title track. — *Rick Clark*

☆ **Arthur (or the Decline and Fall of the British Empire)** / 1969 / Reprise ♦♦♦♦♦
After the commercial disaster of *Village Green Preservation Society*, Ray Davies turned his attentions to collaborating on a TV musical titled *Arthur (Or the Decline and Fall of the British Empire)* with writer Julian Mitchell. Even though the show got canned, the album received much acclaim, placing the Kinks back on the charts. "Victoria" (No. 62) became a moderate hit. Other highlights included "Brainwashed," "Australia," "Shangri-la," and the title cut. — *Rick Clark*

Lola vs. the Powerman & the Money-Go-Round, Part One / 1970 / Reprise ♦♦♦♦
Thanks to the No. 9 hit single "Lola," this album became a comeback of sorts for the Kinks. Overall, this album is a Davies-eye view of life as an artist coping with the road ("This Time Tomorrow") and the music industry, which includes blackly humorous portrayals of the musician's union ("Get Back in Line"), music publishers ("Denmark Street"), making it big ("Top of the Pops"), and greed ("Money-go-round"). This might be a whinefest from a successful pop artist, but his observations aren't that far off base. Musically, the Kinks still had their ragged delivery, but they increasingly employed more acoustic instrumentation, giving the arrangements a slightly folky quality at times. — *Rick Clark*

Percy [O.S.T.] / 1971 / Pye ♦♦

Muswell Hillbillies / 1971 / Rhino ♦♦♦♦
For their first outing on the RCA label, the Kinks adopted a more laid-back rootsy sound that even sported traces of country ("Holloway Jail") and dancehall/cabaret theater styles ("Skin and Bones," "Holiday," "Alcohol"). "Twentieth Century Man" is a nice medium-tempo rocker but lacks the reckless fire of their earlier efforts. — *Rick Clark*

Everybody's in Show-Biz / 1972 / Rhino ♦♦♦
One half of this release is a document of the Kinks' spirited live slopfest, including versions of "Top of the Pops," "Holiday," and the "Banana Boat Song." The other half contains a couple of gems like "Celluloid Heroes" and "Sitting in My Hotel," as well as "Motorway," and "Maximum Consumption." — *Rick Clark*

★ **The Kink Kronikles** / 1972 / Reprise ♦♦♦♦♦
Anyone wanting a well-chosen sampler of the best Kinks work, from half of their stay at Reprise, should start here. Many of the essential tracks are here. — *Rick Clark*

Great Lost Kinks Album / 1973 / Reprise ♦♦♦♦
An aptly titled collection; out of print for many years, there are even some Kinks cultists who have never been able to hear this ragtag but worthy collection of late-'60s and early-'70s outtakes and rarities. Most of these were recorded around the same time as the 1968 LP *Village Green Preservation Society;* these low-key, wry, bouncy tunes would have fit in well with that record. Lyrically, they're on the whole slighter than much of their late-'60s work, perhaps accounting for why the group did not deign to release them at the time. Still, songs like "Rosemary Rose," "Misty Water," and "Mr. Songbird" would have hardly embarrassed the group, and rank as the highlights of this anthology. Besides 1969-era outtakes, it includes the single "Plastic Man," a couple of okay wax-obscure B-sides featuring Dave Davies, and some songs penned for long-forgotten film and television productions. It also has the dynamite 1966 B-side "I'm Not Like Everybody Else," though that's available on reissue these days. That's not the case for most of the rest of this album; Kinks fans will find it quite worthwhile, and should be on the lookout for it in the used bins. — *Richie Unterberger*

Preservation: Acts 1 & 2 / 1973 / Rhino ♦♦♦
Initially intended as an extension of *The Village Green Preservation Society*, *Preservation* offered relatively little in the way of great songwriting or spirited performances, something *Village Green* had in spades. "Money Talks" is a nice mid-tempo rocker. The Rhino CD includes the single, "Preservation." — *Rick Clark*

The Kinks Present Schoolboys in Disgrace / 1975 / Rhino ♦♦
As the last of the Kinks' overt conceptual exercises, *Schoolboys* was further proof that Ray Davies' best "plays" happened when he focused his observational skills into singular songs, rather than fleshing out an idea over the course of a whole album. Like *Soap Opera*, this is only recommended for hardcore completists. — *Rick Clark*

The Kinks Present a Soap Opera / 1975 / Rhino ♦♦
Davies' obsession with concept albums reached a nadir with *Soap Opera*. At this point, Davies and company were so busy pandering to their live audiences, they seemed to forget how to make truly memorable music. The lifeless production, indicative of this era of their music, didn't help matters either. Nevertheless, "You Make It All Worthwhile," "Face in the Crowd," and "Everybody's a Star" were highlights from this spotty set. — *Rick Clark*

The Kinks' Greatest: Celluloid Heroes / 1976 / RCA ♦♦♦
This is a good collection comprising the cream of The Kinks' RCA years. It includes "Sitting in My Hotel," "Twentieth Century Man," "Alcohol," and "Everybody's a Star." — *Rick Clark*

Sleepwalker / 1977 / Arista ♦♦♦
For their first release on Clive Davis' Arista label, The Kinks ditched the concept albums, and knuckled down to a workmanlike, but unexceptional batch of songs. "Full Moon" and "Juke Box Music" are among the stronger tracks. — *Rick Clark*

Misfits / 1978 / Arista ♦♦♦♦
A slight improvement over *Sleepwalker*, *Misfits* boasted their first Top 40 hit in eight years, "A Rock 'n' Roll Fantasy." — *Rick Clark*

Low Budget / 1979 / Arista ✦✦✦

One for the Road / 1980 / Arista ✦✦

Give the People What They Want / 1981 / Arista ✦✦✦
The Kinks delivered their interpretation of the mainstream FM rock sound on this effort, producing three moderate radio hits with "Destroyer," "Better Things" and the title cut. —*Rick Clark*

State of Confusion / 1983 / Arista ✦✦✦
State of Confusion had its share of glossy hard rock in the vein of "Low Budget" and "Destroyer," but the record came to life on the quieter numbers, whether it's the elegiac "Don't Forget to Dance," the wistful pop of "Long Distance," or the buoyant nostalgia of "Come Dancing," which became the group's biggest hit since "Tired of Waiting for You." —*Stephen Thomas Erlewine*

Word of Mouth / 1984 / Arista ✦✦

Come Dancing with the Kinks: The Best of the Kinks 1977-1986 / Jul. 1986 / Arista ✦✦✦✦
A sampling of the their Arista years (1977-1986), most of the essential tracks are here, including all of their hits from that period. "Come Dancing," "A Rock 'n' Roll Fantasy," "Juke Box Music," "Destroyer," and "(Wish I Could Fly Like) Superman" are among the titles found here. —*Rick Clark*

Think Visual / Dec. 1986 / MCA ✦✦

The Kinks Live: The Road / 1988 / MCA ✦✦

UK Jive / 1989 / MCA ✦✦

★ **Greatest Hits, Vol. 1** / 1989 / Rhino ✦✦✦✦✦
If you are going to budget for only one Kinks disc, this is the one to get. It features all of their biggest '60s chart hits, plus some key B-sides. Nevertheless, their albums from this period feature many fine album cuts worth having, so consider this an excellent primer but not a definitive package. —*Rick Clark*

Lost & Found (1986-89) / 1991 / MCA ✦✦

Phobia / 1993 / Columbia ✦✦

To the Bone / 1994 / Grapevine ✦✦✦

Kiss

Hard Rock, Heavy Metal, Hair Metal, Arena Rock
Rooted in the campy theatrics of Alice Cooper and the sleazy hard rock of glam rockers the New York Dolls, Kiss became an favorite for American teenagers in the '70s. Most kids were infatuated with the look of Kiss, not their music. Decked out in outrageously flamboyant costumes and makeup, the band fashioned a captivating stage show featuring dry ice, smoke bombs, elaborate lighting, blood spitting, and fire breathing that captured the imaginations of thousands of kids. But Kiss' music shouldn't be dismissed out of hand—it was a commercially potent mix of anthemic, fist-pounding hard rock driven by sleek hooks and ballads powered by loud guitars, cloying melodies and sweeping strings. It was a sound that laid the groundwork for both arena rock and the pop-metal that dominated rock in the late '80s.

Kiss was the brainchild of Gene Simmons (bass, vocals) and Paul Stanley (rhythm guitar, vocals), former members of the New York-based hard rock band Wicked Lester; the duo brought in drummer Peter Criss through his ad in *Rolling Stone* and guitarist Ace Frehley responded to an advertisement in *The Village Voice*. Even at their first Manhattan concert in 1973, the group's approach was quite theatrical; Flipside producer Bill Aucoin offered the band a management deal after the show. Two weeks later, the band was signed to Neil Bogart's fledgling record label Casablanca. Kiss released their self-titled debut in February of 1974; it peaked at No. 87 on the US charts. By April of 1975, the group had released three albums and had toured America constantly, building up a sizable fan base. Culled from those numerous concerts, *Alive!* (released in the fall of 1975) made the band rock 'n' roll superstars; it climbed into the Top Ten and its accompanying single, "Rock'N'Roll All Nite" made it to No. 12. Their follow-up, *Destroyer*, was released in March of 1976 and became the group's first platinum album; it also featured their first Top Ten single, Peter Criss' power ballad "Beth."

A 1977 Gallup poll named Kiss the most popular band in America. Kiss mania was in full swing and thousands of pieces of merchandise hit the marketplace. The group had two comic books released by Marvel, they had pinball machines, makeup and masks, board games, and an animated television special, *Kiss Meet the Phantom of the Park*. The group was never seen in public without wearing their makeup and their popularity was growing by leaps and bounds; the membership of the Kiss Army, the band's fan club, was now in the six figures. Even such enormous popularity had its limits and the band reached them in 1978, when all four members released solo albums on the same day in October. Simmons' record was the most successful, reaching No. 22 on the charts, yet all of them made it into the Top 50. *Dynasty*, released in 1979,

continued their streak of platinum albums, yet it was their last recorded with the original lineup—Criss left in 1980.

Kiss Unmasked, released in the summer of 1980, was recorded with session drummer Anton Fig; Criss' permanent replacement, Eric Carr, joined the band in time for their 1980 world tour. *Kiss Unmasked* was their first record since *Destroyer* to fail to go platinum and 1981's *Music from the Elder*, the first album recorded with Carr, didn't even go gold—it couldn't even climb past No. 75 on the charts. Ace Frehley left the band after its release; he was replaced by Vinnie Vincent in 1982. Vincent's first album with the group, 1982's *Creatures of the Night*, fared better than *Music from the Elder*, yet it couldn't make it past No. 45 on the charts.

Sensing it was time for a change, Kiss dispensed with their makeup for 1983's *Lick It Up*. The publicity worked, as the album became their first platinum record in four years. *Animalize*, released the following year, was just as successful and the group had recaptured its niche. Vincent left after *Animalize* and was replaced by Mark St. John; St. John soon taken ill with Reiter's Syndrome and left the band. Bruce Kulick became Kiss' new lead guitarist in 1984. For the rest of the decade, Kiss turned out a series of best-selling albums, culminating in the early 1990 hit ballad "Forever," which was their biggest single since "Beth."

Kiss were scheduled to record a new album with their old producer Bob Ezrin in 1990 when Eric Carr became severely ill with cancer; he died in November of 1991 at the age of 41. Kiss replaced him with Eric Singer and recorded *Revenge* (1992), their first album since 1989; it was a Top Ten hit and went gold. Kiss followed it with the release of *Alive III* the following year; it performed respectably, but not up to the standards of their two previous live records. IIn 1996, the original lineup of Kiss—featuring Simmons, Stanley, Frehley, and Criss—reunited to perform an American tour, complete with their notorious makeup and special effects. —*Stephen Thomas Erlewine*

Kiss / Apr. 1974 / Casablanca ✦✦✦✦
Compared to their later albums, Kiss' self-titled debut is a raw, riveting dose of heavy metal. At the time of its recording, the group was still working out their sound, trying to develop their loud, lumbering guitar riffs into sleek, melodic heavy hooks. Kiss only succeeds in streamlining their bombast on a couple of tracks—"Deuce," "Black Diamond," "Firehouse," "Strutter"—but the rest of the record sounds vigorous and forceful, making up for the lapses in songwriting quality. —*Stephen Thomas Erlewine*

Hotter Than Hell / Nov. 1974 / Casablanca ✦✦✦

Dressed to Kill / Apr. 1975 / Casablanca ✦✦✦✦
With *Dressed to Kill*, Kiss began to write songs that delivered on the promise of their live shows. Driven by the pounding, but catchy, hooks of "Rock 'n' Roll All Nite" and "She," the album increases the amount of melody Kiss works into their songs. Kiss also increases their sleaze content, delivering leering double entendres like "Room Service," "Love Her All I Can," and "Ladies in Waiting" throughout. But the hooks make the sleaze appealing, and when they can't come up with convincing melodies, the group has polished their sound enough to make the filler enjoyable. —*Stephen Thomas Erlewine*

★ **Alive!** / Oct. 1975 / Casablanca ✦✦✦✦✦
Given the wildly inconsistent quality of Kiss' first three albums, the high quality of *Alive!* comes as somewhat of a surprise. Then again, Kiss were showmen, not songwriters, which means they were always at their best when they were on stage. Part of that show—the makeup, the explosions, the lights, the dry ice—could not be replicated on record, but the group was invigorated by the live setting, adding passion and conviction to their thunderously loud riffs. Of course, some of the material still falls flat, but most of *Alive!* seethes with energy, making their finest moments—"Rock'N' Roll All Nite," "Deuce," "Strutter," "Black Diamond," "She," "Hotter than Hell"—seem like hard rock classics. —*Stephen Thomas Erlewine*

Destroyer / 1976 / Casablanca ✦✦✦✦
Kiss followed the breakthrough Top Ten success of *Alive!* with *Destroyer*, the most pop-oriented record they had ever recorded. Under the direction of producer Bob Ezrin (Alice Cooper), the group's recorded sound became as theatrical as their live shows, featuring strings, sound effects, multi-layered guitars and vocals. That doesn't necessarily mean *Destroyer* is a better record than *Dressed to Kill*—it means the album is a set of slick pop-rock that hides its lack of improved songwriting with stylish production flourishes. Despite the presence of the throttling "Shout It Out Loud" and "Detroit Rock City," none of the rockers are quite as direct and memorable as "Rock 'N' Roll All Night," but that's remedied by the heavily orchestrated proto-power-ballad "Beth." —*Stephen Thomas Erlewine*

Rock and Roll Over / 1976 / Casablanca ✦✦✦✦
Rock and Roll Over was Kiss' second straight No. 11 album, and it was a marginally better album than the previous *Destroyer*, featuring a harder, more direct production and improved songwriting, as illustrated by the hit singles "Calling Dr. Love" and "Hard Luck Woman." —*Stephen Thomas Erlewine*

Love Gun / Jul. 1977 / Casablanca ✦✦✦✦
By the time of *Love Gun*, Kiss had perfected their gimmick, turning in a set of sleek, slick hard rock that celebrated its silly, tongue-in-cheek jokes and grotesque imagery. The group had polished all of the rough edges out of their sound, leaving a collection of hard-driving riffs that were more catchy than heavy. Songwriting was still a problem for the band, but *Love Gun* was one of their most consistent albums, featuring the concert staples "Christine Sixteen," "Plaster Caster," and "Love Gun." —*Stephen Thomas Erlewine*

Alive II / Nov. 1977 / Casablanca ✦✦✦

Double Platinum (Greatest Hits) / 1978 / Casablanca ✦✦✦✦
An imperfect collection, it still represents the best of their early peak years. —*Dan Heilman*

Dynasty / 1979 / Casablanca ✦✦✦

Kiss Unmasked / 1980 / Casablanca ✦✦

Music from the Elder / 1981 / Casablanca ✦✦

Lick It Up / 1983 / Mercury ✦✦✦

Animalize / 1984 / Mercury ✦✦

Crazy Nights / 1987 / Mercury ✦✦✦

Smashes, Thrashes & Hits / 1988 / Casablanca ✦✦✦✦
The companion volume to the above, from their later makeup-less period, including "Lick It Up," "Let's Put the X in Sex," and "Love Gun." —*Dan Heilman*

Revenge / 1992 / Mercury ✦✦✦

Alive III / May 18, 1993 / PolyGram ✦✦

Unplugged / Mar. 12, 1996 / Mercury ✦✦✦

The Knack

New Wave, Power-Pop
The Knack made a nod to the '60s power-pop sound, pushing the image of themselves as the American Beatles on their 1979 debut album cover. All of the members were experienced musicians and they didn't try to hide their attempt to market their way to the top. Cleverly crafted pop songs like their smash hit "My Sharona," which sold over five million copies, were aimed straight at the teen-pop market. "Good Girls Don't," the follow-up single to "My Sharona," was another strong hit. Their subsequent albums tried to repeat this initial success, even using blatant copies of previous songs, but failed. After the third album, The Knack folded; some members stayed together as The Game, while vocalist Doug Fieger started the band Taking Chances. In the '90s, the band reformed with a new drummer, Billy Ward, but didn't make much of a splash. —*Scott Bultman*

● **Get the Knack** / 1979 / Capitol ✦✦✦✦
The band attempted to update the Beatles sound for the new wave era on their debut. A good idea that was well executed, but critics cried "foul" when millions sold after Capitol's pre-release hype (it went gold in 13 days and eventually sold five million copies, making it one of the most successful debuts in history). *Get the Knack* is at once sleazy, sexist, hook-filled and endlessly catchy—above all, it's a guilty pleasure and an exercise in simple fun. When is power-pop *legitimate* anyway? Includes the unforgettable hits "My Sharona" and "Good Girls Don't." —*Chris Woodstra*

... but the Little Girls Understand / Dec. 1979 / Capitol ✦✦✦
Mike Chapman summed it up best in the liner notes—"The songs are an assortment of feelings and emotions expressed redundantly as only the Knack can . . . This record is very dear to me and my bank manager." The self-deprecating title (which quotes Willie Dixon's "Back Door Man") isn't really an attempt to apologize but rather to let everyone know that they were in on the joke all along—and they're laughing all the way to the bank. This is essentially a rewrite of the debut, especially evident on the lead-off single "Baby Talks Dirty." It's not as good as *Get the Knack* and didn't sell nearly as well, but it *is* a good time for those who don't take rock 'n' roll too seriously. —*Chris Woodstra*

Round Trip / 1981 / Capitol ✦✦

Serious Fun / 1991 / Charisma ✦✦

Retrospective: The Best of the Knack / Nov. 16, 1992 / Capitol ✦✦✦✦
A fine greatest hits set that collects the best from their debut and their two weaker follow-ups. —*Stephen Thomas Erlewine*

Knickerbockers

Pop-Rock
In early 1966, the Knickerbockers hit the Top 20 with "Lies," the best and most accurate early Beatle imitation ever recorded; the lead vocals were a dead ringer for John Lennon, and the whole production could have fit in snugly on the second side of *A Hard Day's Night*. Actually a frat-rock band from New Jersey who didn't write much of their own material, they never made anything else as successful or good. A couple decent follow-

ups, "One Track Mind" and the similarly mock British Invasion "High on Love," were small hits, but their albums were even blander than many of the era's other one-shot artists. Their three noteworthy singles were all featured in Rhino's *Nuggets* series, and everyone but '60s completists would be advised to stick with those tracks. Drummer and singer Jimmy Walker briefly replaced Bill Medley in the Righteous Brothers. —*Richie Unterberger*

Lies / 1965 / Challenge ✦✦

● **The Fabulous Knickerbockers** / 1988 / Sundazed ✦✦✦✦
This "best-of" collection includes the hits "Lies" (one of the greatest mid-'60s singles) and "One Track Mind." Tracks like "I Can Do It Better," "Rumors, Gossip, Words Untrue" and "High on Love" are more period highlights. This set contains ample annotation and great sound. —*Rick Clark*

Great Lost Album / Sundazed ✦✦✦

Gladys Knight & The Pips

Soul, R&B, Motown, Club-Dance
One of the great soul singers, Gladys Knight was a performer from her childhood years, forming the Pips with her brother Merald and a couple cousins. They made the Top Ten in 1961 with the heavily doo wop-influenced "Every Beat of My Heart," and recorded some fine, nowadays overlooked, pop-soul sides for the Fury and Maxx labels in the early and mid-'60s, sometimes under the direction of songwriter Van McCoy. A couple singles from this period, "Letter Full of Tears" and "Giving Up," made the Top 40, but Knight didn't hit her commercial stride until she moved to Motown in 1966. Steeped in the gospel tradition, like so many soul singers, Knight & the Pips developed into one of Motown's most dependable acts, although they never quite scaled the commercial or artistic heights of fellow stars on the label like the Supremes, Marvin Gaye, and the Temptations. With Norman Whitfield providing the production and much of the songwriting, the Pips fit into the mainstream of Motown's machine well, scoring big hits with some rabble-rousers (like "Friendship Train" and the original version of "I Heard It Through the Grapevine"), mainstream mid-tempo soul ("It Should Have Been Me" and "The End of Our Road"), and smooth ballads like "If I Were Your Woman."

In 1973, Knight had her biggest Motown hit with "Neither One of Us," which made No. 2; shortly afterwards, she and the Pips left Motown for Buddah. The group were briefly superstars in 1973-74, reeling off the smashes "Midnight Train to Georgia" (their only No. 1), "I've Got to Use My Imagination," and "Best Thing That Ever Happened to Me." This ranked as some of their best material, but Knight soon moved toward an easy listening, adult contemporary direction, one that she's maintained to this day. Now performing separately from The Pips (who have retired), her days as a high-charting star ended after the mid-'70s, although she remains fairly popular. —*Richie Unterberger*

Letter Full of Tears / 1961 / Collectables ✦✦✦

● **Anthology** / 1974 / Motown ✦✦✦✦
Atlanta family-group Gladys Knight & The Pips had performed together for 14 years before signing with Motown in 1966. Earlier recordings for Huntom (the master recordings were later sold to Vee-Jay), Fury, and Maxx had generated five chart hits, including the Top Ten R&B smashes "Every Beat of My Heart" and "Letter Full of Tears," but it was on the Motown subsidiary Soul that Gladys Knight and company hit their stride. This compilation more than adequately covers this period of the Pips' career. Working primarily with producer Norman Whitfield from 1967 through 1969, the group created such Motor City classics as "Everybody Needs Love," "I Heard It Through the Grapevine," "The End of Our Road," and "Friendship Train." From 1970 through 1973 the Pips worked with a variety of Motown producers, concentrating on ballads. Although they were perhaps a little less consistent, there was no shortage of hits, the most notable being 1970's "If I Were Your Woman" and 1973's "Neither One of Us (Wants to Bob Be the First to Say Goodbye)." The updated double-CD version of *Anthology*, featuring digitally remastered sound, replaces about a dozen songs with different ones, though this 40-track collection still contains all of the essential hits and adds lengthy liner notes. Be aware that the three early-'60s hits that lead off the volume (on both versions of *Anthology*) are Motown re-recordings, not the originals. —*Rob Bowman*

Every Beat of My Heart / 1989 / Chameleon ✦✦✦
The best collection of Knight's pre-Motown sides, including both of their big early-'60s hits (the title track and "Letter Full of Tears"), but concentrating more heavily on their mid-'60s sessions. These were overseen by Van McCoy, who supplied the group with several of his own compositions as well. McCoy was one of the most melodically ambitious pop/soul composers of the era, and his songs on this compilation—"Either Way I Lose," "Why Don't You Love Me," "Lovers Always Forgive"—are achingly beautiful and rife with unexpected key changes. His "Stop and Get a Hold of Myself," on the other hand, is a more conventional (but equally first-rate) uptempo soul stomper. If there's any criticism of these

sides, it's that Knight and the group don't establish a strong identity, handling doo wop-like ballads, girl-group-tinged pop, McCoy's idiosyncratic songs, and more modern pop-soul with chameleon-like skill. In the end, that doesn't detract from the strength of this CD, which is a collection of fine early to mid-'60s pop/soul. The major flaw is the inexplicable omission of the McCoy composition "Giving Up," a Top 40 hit for the group in 1964. *—Richie Unterberger*

● **Soul Survivors: The Best of Gladys Knight & the Pips** / 1990 / Rhino ✦✦✦✦
Soul Survivors picks up where the Motown anthology left off, containing the most important singles that Gladys Knight And The Pips recorded for Buddah, Columbia, and MCA from the early '70s until the late '80s. The Buddah tracks, highlighted by the Jim Weatherly-written "Midnight Train in Georgia" and "Best Thing That Ever Happened to Me," contain some of Knight's most impassioned vocal performances. *—Rob Bowman*

Every Beat of My Heart [U.K. reissue compilation] / 1992 / Charly ✦✦✦✦
Twenty-track compilation of Knight's pre-Motown material, including most of the songs from the US anthology of the same name (on Chameleon). This has the slight edge, mostly due to the inclusion of the Top 40 single "Giving Up," and an odd version of Holland-Dozier-Holland's "Come See About Me" that is very different than the hit rendition by the Supremes. Unfortunately, the packaging is ugly, and the liner notes nonexistent. *—Richie Unterberger*

Blue Lights in the Basement / Apr. 1996 / RCA ✦✦✦
Knight's stint for the Buddah label in the mid-'70s found her commercial success at its peak, landing hits like "Midnight Train to Georgia," "Best Thing That Ever Happened to Me," "Part Time Love," and "The Way We Were" (all included here). But this 17-track survey of 1973-78 material is not nearly as artistically satisfying as her Motown and Vee-Jay recordings, finding her and the Pips easing into a middle-of-the-road sound that helped pave the way for mellow urban contemporary music. What's more, this compilation is not truly representative of the era, omitting the huge hit "I've Got to Use My Imagination," presumably because it's too uptempo to find a place on an anthology geared toward the "quiet storm" audience. *—Richie Unterberger*

Buddy Knox (Wayne Knox)

b. Jul. 20, 1933, Happy, TX
Guitar, Vocals / Rockabilly
The brand of Texas rockabilly that Buddy Knox cooked up around 1957 wasn't quite as raw as that of his Memphis cohorts at Sun, but it was just as commercially potent. Knox sported a light, almost gentle vocal style, and his band, the Rhythm Orchids, obliged with upbeat backing that suited him well. Formed at West Texas State University, the Rhythm Orchids also included Jimmy Bowen on upright bass, and it was Bowen's equally lighthearted vocal on "I'm Stickin' with You" that originally graced the flip side of Knox's first smash, "Party Doll." Roulette Records astutely picked up the master from the tiny Triple-D logo, separated the sides, and the fledgling label enjoyed two giant hits for the price of one.
"Party Doll" soared to the very top of the pops, and Knox encored with the equally tuneful "Rock Your Little Baby to Sleep" and "Hula Love," which he performed in the 1957 rock flick *Jamboree*. Knox waxed the fine rockabilly-based "Swingin' Daddy," "Devil Woman," and a cover of Ruth Brown's "Somebody Touched Me" for Roulette before moving to Liberty and hitting with a pop-flavored rendition of The Clovers' song "Lovey Dovey" in 1960. Over three decades later, the Texas rocker remains a popular act on the oldies front. *—Bill Dahl*

● **The Best of Buddy Knox** / 1990 / Rhino ✦✦✦✦
This gentle, catchy Texas rockabilly has a pop slant. *—Bill Dahl*

The Complete Roulette Recordings / 1996 / Sequel ✦✦✦
Knox only issued one-half of this double CD; the second disc is devoted to tracks by his friend and contemporary, Jimmy Bowen. The approach isn't as odd as it seems: When Knox and Bowen began their recording careers, they were both part of the Rhythm Orchids, and a similar lineup of Orchids backs each solo singer on their respective recordings. Most listeners will be much better off with Rhino's briefer, more selective Knox best-of. Completists, however, will find all 30 of Knox's 1956-60 Roulette tracks on disc one of this two-pack. Including five previously unreleased songs, it's pleasant Tex-Mex rockabilly, tamer than Buddy Holly, but far gutsier than the Jimmy Bowen solo cuts that take up all of disc two. *—Richie Unterberger*

Cub Koda

b. Oct. 1, 1948, Detroit, MI
Guitar, Vocals / Rock 'n' Roll, Electric Chicago Blues, Blues-Rock, Rockabilly
Founder and leader of the rowdy '70s rock group Brownsville Station ("Smokin' in the Boy's Room," "The Martian Boogie"), Koda has gone on to a solo career as a high-spirited archivist of obscure rock, blues, coun-

try, and R&B songs and artists. As a producer, Koda unearthed the "world's worst bar band," King Uszniewicz & the Uszniewicztones. As the frontman for Hound Dog Taylor's resurrected Houserockers, he recorded two raucous albums that are encyclopedic in their array of blues songs and styles. But perhaps Koda's most lasting contribution to music is as a writer of liner notes and the long-running "Vinyl Junkie" column for the record-collecting magazine Goldmine. *—Kit Kiefer*

Cub Koda & the Points / 1980 / Fan Club ✦✦✦✦
Koda's first solo album after Brownsville Station. Highlights include "Jail Bait" and "Welcome to My Job." *—Stephen Thomas Erlewine*

It's the Blues / 1981 / Fan Club ✦✦✦

Cub Digs Chuck / 1989 / Garageland ✦✦✦
Koda's tribute album to Chuck Berry, featuring blistering versions of "Johnny B. Goode," "Maybellene," and others. *—Stephen Thomas Erlewine*

● **Live at B.L.U.E.S. 1982** / 1991 / Wolf ✦✦✦✦
What's wrong with this picture? The sawed-off bespectacled singer/guitarist from Brownville Station fronting the late Hound Dog Taylor's ex-rhythm section, the Houserockers—blasphemy, you say? Get a life. Koda smokes like he's: 1) out to dispel any doubts about his legitimacy, and 2) having the time of his life. Opening with Howlin' Wolf's "Highway 49" (a rather tall order), the Cubmaster grabs the Chicago crowd by its collective neck and shakes it into submission. His guitar trade-offs with Brewer Phillips (no bass in this band) are a delight, and by "You Can't Sit Down" drummer Ted Harvey is blowing his police whistle—signalling that things be rockin'! Eddie Clearwater sits in on one tune, and Koda tips his hat to the guitarist with a stellar rendition of Eddie's "Hillbilly Blues." This is worthy of wider release, not to mention an encore. *—Dan Forte*

Cub Digs Bo / 1991 / Garageland ✦✦✦✦
Koda's tribute album to Bo Diddley, including powerhouse renditions of "Mumblin' Guitar," "Roadrunner," and "Background to a Music." *—Stephen Thomas Erlewine*

● **Welcome to My Job: the Cub Koda Collection 1963-93** / 1993 / Blue Wave ✦✦✦✦
Covering everything from his pre-Brownsville Station days to two brand-new songs, *Welcome to My Job* is the definitive collection of Cub Koda's versatile solo career. *—Stephen Thomas Erlewine*

Abba Dabba Dabba: A Bananza of Hits / 1994 / Schoolkids' ✦✦✦✦
Cub Koda's first album for Schoolkids' Records is his wildest, funniest, and simply best album in years. *—Stephen Thomas Erlewine*

● **The Joint Was Rockin'** / 1996 / Deluxe ✦✦✦✦

Kool & the Gang

Soul, Funk, Urban, Pop-Rock
One of the leading funk outfits of the '70s and '80s, with gold and platinum platters galore. Formed by bassist Robert "Kool" Bell (b. 1950) as the Jazziacs in Jersey City, The Gang also featured his brothers Robert and Ronald Bell. The crew signed with De-Lite Records in 1969 and began churning out massively funky grooves, hitting full stride in 1973-1974 with "Jungle Boogie," "Hollywood Swinging," and "Higher Plane." The Gang topped the soul charts in 1979 with the high-stepping disco favorite "Ladies Night"—the same year they hired J.T. Taylor as their new lead singer. "Celebrate!," a staple of every respectable wedding reception of the last dozen years, went platinum for the group in 1980, and their nonstop string of incendiary successes stretched into the mid-'80s with "Fresh" and "Cherish." Taylor went solo in 1988. *—Bill Dahl*

● **Greatest Hits & More** / 1988 / Polydor ✦✦✦✦
The best of their later-era hits, featuring "Cherish" and the anthemic "Celebrate!" *—Cub Koda*

● **The Best of Kool & The Gang** / May 18, 1993 / Mercury ✦✦✦✦
Although Kool & the Gang became pop superstars in the 1980s on the strength of J.T. Taylor's silky voice and several catchy arrangements, R&B fans regard their true glory days as the 1970s. The New Jersey-based ensemble patented a jazz-tinged funk approach keyed by Robert "Kool" Bell's bass lines, red-hot horn lines, chunky keyboards and guitar riffs, and functional vocals. Although they seldom ventured beyond the R&B charts during this era, their music had far more bite than their later pop hits. These 16 cuts pay homage to Kool and the Gang's funk roots, and should be a revelation to those who only know them as the light ensemble behind J.T. Taylor. *—Ron Wynn*

● **Funk Essentials Series: Celebration Best Of (1979-87)** / 1994 / Mercury ✦✦✦✦

Kraftwerk

Electronic
In the mid-'70s, the German quartet Kraftwerk laid the groundwork for most of the electronic and synth-rock bands that followed them in the

next two decades. Each of the members played synthesizers, creating a cold, precise, almost mechanical music that was hypnotic in its repetitiveness. For the rest of the '70s, the band was on the cutting edge of rock and dance music, influencing numerous musicians in the process. As the '80s progressed, the group's records became less and less innovative, but they still made a number of albums that were very impressive; the band continues to record in the '90s.

Echoes of Kraftwerk's music can be heard in everyone from David Bowie and Tangerine Dream to Depeche Mode and the Human League. Hip-hop is also unwittingly in debt to the band's innovative use of electronics. But the underground techno scene of the '80s and '90s owes a great debt to Kraftwerk, as artists like Aphex Twin, Orbital, Vapourspace, and the Orb bring the band's trance-like electronics to new heights, adding a warm, human dimension that Kraftwerk never had when they recorded *Autobahn* in 1974. —*Stephen Thomas Erlewine*

Kraftwerk 2 / 1972 / Philips ✦✦✦

★ **Autobahn** / 1974 / Warner Bros. ✦✦✦✦✦
Although Kraftwerk's first three albums were groundbreaking in their own right, *Autobahn* is where the group's hypnotic electro-pulse genuinely came into its own. The main difference between *Autobahn* and its predecessors is how it develops an insistent, propulsive pulse which makes the repeated rhythms and riffs of the shimmering electronic keyboards and trance-like guitars all the more hypnotizing. The 22-minute title track, in a severely edited form, became an international hit single and remains the peak of the band's achievements—it encapsulates the band and why they are important within one track—but the rest of the album provides soundscapes equally as intriguing. Within *Autobahn*, the roots of electro-funk, ambient, and synth-pop are all evident—it's a pioneering album, even if its electronic trances might not capture the attention of all listeners. —*Stephen Thomas Erlewine*

Billy J. Kramer & The Dakotas

British Invasion
At the outset of the British Invasion in 1964, Billy J. Kramer & the Dakotas was one of the hottest bands of the movement's initial wave. Beatles manager Brian Epstein paired young Liverpool vocalist Kramer with the Dakotas and gave them a surefire hit—the Lennon/McCartney composition "Do You Want to Know a Secret?," which established the group in England. The group broke in America with the two-sided smash "Little Children"/"Bad to Me" in 1964 on Imperial, the latter another Lennon/McCartney effort. Their next two smashes, "I'll Keep You Satisfied" and "From a Window," were also penned by the prolific duo, although Kramer's last US hit, "Trains and Boats and Planes," was written by Burt Bacharach and Hal David. The group appeared in the popular 1964 movie *The T.A.M.I. Show*, but by 1967 the musicians and Kramer had gone their separate ways, the vocalist recording as a solo in Britain. —*Bill Dahl*

● **Best of Billy J. Kramer** / 1991 / EMI America ✦✦✦✦
A strong collection that presents all of his best—including a number of songs written by John Lennon and Paul McCartney—in excellent sound. —*Bruce Eder & Jeff Tamarkin*

Lenny Kravitz

b. May 6, 1964 , New York, NY
Bass, Guitar, Drums, Vocals / Rock 'n' Roll, Pop-Rock
As a musician and a producer, Lenny Kravitz is unquestionably gifted. He can successfully recreate the sound and feeling of countless groups from the past; his music recalls everyone from Lennon, Hendrix, and Bowie to the Velvet Underground, Curtis Mayfield and Prince. What Kravitz can't do is synthesize these influences into a distinctive style—every song on each of his albums sounds like it was recorded by a different artist. However, that's not entirely a bad thing, because Kravitz *can* reproduce the sound of his favorite artists exactly; "It Ain't Over 'Til It's Over" sounds like it was recorded in 1972, "Are You Gonna Go My Way" sounds like a forgotten track from 1968. His music might not be original, but it is quite enjoyable. Since his 1989 debut, *Let Love Rule*, Kravitz's songwriting and production skills have been consistently improving. His second album, *Mama Said*, gave him a No. 2 hit with "It Ain't Over 'Til It's Over." *Are You Gonna Go My Way*, Kravitz's third album, was released in 1993; it was a stronger album than anything he had released in the past and it is his most commercially successful record yet. —*Stephen Thomas Erlewine*

Let Love Rule / 1989 / Virgin ✦✦✦✦
Kravitz plays the majority of the instruments on this self-produced debut of catchy retro-pop. Most of the songs are exceptionally well-crafted, evoking everyone from the Velvet Underground and John Lennon to Prince and Sly Stone. Musically, *Let Love Rule* is an impressive debut, but lyrically Kravitz tends to rely on clichés and simple rhymes, including some embarrassingly sophomoric lyrics from his current wife Lisa

Bonet. Nevertheless, his musical talent obscures most of the lyrical shortcomings. —*Stephen Thomas Erlewine*

Mama Said / 1991 / Virgin ✦✦✦
Like his debut, Kravitz's second album, *Mama Said*, works best on the surface. *Mama Said* abandons the hippie folk leanings of *Let Love Rule* for a sleek update of Philly soul, acid rock, psychedelia, hard rock, and '60s pop. It's a more polished and musically accomplished record than his debut, resulting in the breakthrough No. 2 hit single "It Ain't Over 'Til It's Over." Again, Kravitz plays the majority of the instruments, with Slash contributing some fine guitar to "Always on the Run" and "Fields of Joy." While the music never sounds insular and self-involved, since Kravitz works in familiar pop idioms and has a knack for warm, organic production. the lyrics—which mainly concentrate on the breakup of his marriage to actress Lisa Bonet—*are* insular and self-involved; however the music makes it easy to ignore what he's saying. —*Stephen Thomas Erlewine*

● **Are You Gonna Go My Way?** / 1993 / Virgin ✦✦✦✦
Opening with the pounding Hendrix-styled title track, Lenny Kravitz continues his rampage through the back pages of pop music history. On *Are You Gonna Go My Way*, Kravitz follows the same basic formula as *Mama Said*, concentrating on early-'70s soul and psychedelic hard rock, but his songwriting has improved, making the record his most consistent and coherent album. —*Stephen Thomas Erlewine*

Circus / Sep. 12, 1995 / Virgin ✦✦

Kursaal Flyers

Rock 'n' Roll, New Wave, Power-Pop, Pub-Rock
The Kursaal Flyers bridged the gap between pub-rock and power-pop, turning out a handful of fine albums and great singles in their brief two-year career. Comprised of Paul Shuttleworth (vocals), Graeme Douglas (guitar), Vic Collins (guitar, steel guitar, vocals), Riche Bull (bass, vocals), and Will Birch (drums), the band released their first album *Chocs Away* in 1975; it was followed soon afterward by *The Great Artiste*. Both records showed a grasp of country and roots-rock, as well as pure pop. They would begin to emphasize their pop elements with 1976's *Golden Mile*, released by CBS Records. The union with the major label helped the single "Little Does She Know" reach the British Top 20. Douglas left to join Eddie and the Hot Rods before the recording of their final album, *Five Live Kursaals* (1977); he was replaced by Barry Martin. The band broke up after the release of punk and power-pop injected *Five Live Kursaals*. Out of the members, only Will Birch and John Wicks stayed active—they formed the Records immediately after the Kursaal Flyers' disbandment. The Kursaal Flyers reunited in 1988, recording *A Former Tour de Force Is Forced to Tour*, which picks up right where they left off in 1977. —*Stephen Thomas Erlewine*

● **In for a Spin: The Best of the Kursaal Flyers** / 1985 / Edsel ✦✦✦✦

L7

Hard Rock, Alternative Pop-Rock, Heavy Metal, Grunge
L7's heavy, punk-inflected, riff-oriented guitar grind—a mix of the Ramones, Motörhead, and Joan Jett—was what earned them a dedicated following of fans in the early '90s, not the fact that they were female. While the band is strongly feminist, they never let their rhetoric stand in the way of their roaring guitars. L7 always relies on the sheer sonic aggression of rock, not its lyrical power.

When the group was on Sub Pop early in the '90s, the band sounded punkier and more abrasive; signing to a major label didn't cause them to lose that aggression—they just had a better production, courtesy of Butch Vig (Nirvana, Smashing Pumpkins, Sonic Youth). Featuring "Pretend We're Dead," 1992's *Bricks Are Heavy* was a major alternative hit; their second major-label album, the coarse *Hungry for Stink*, was released right before L7 toured with 1994's Lollapalooza. —*Stephen Thomas Erlewine*

L7 / 1990 / Epitaph ✦✦✦

Smell the Magic / Jul. 12, 1991 / Sub Pop ✦✦✦✦
A wonderfully abrasive set of thrashing guitars and growling vocals. —*Stephen Thomas Erlewine*

● **Bricks Are Heavy** / 1992 / Slash ✦✦✦✦
While their major-label debut is hampered by Butch Vig's rather tame production, it does show that L7 has some strong pop sensibilities underneath their burning guitars, as "Pretend We're Dead" and "Everglade" prove. —*Stephen Thomas Erlewine*

Hungry for Stink / 1994 / Slash/Reprise ✦✦✦

The La's

Alternative Pop-Rock
When the La's released their debut album in 1990, it made immediate waves in the British pop scene, as well as American college radio. Drawing from the hook-laden, ringing guitars of mid-'60s British pop as well

as the post-punk pop of the Smiths, the La's self-titled first album had a timeless, classic feel. It seemed like effortless music, yet that was not the case. From their inception in 1986 to the present day, lead singer/guitarist/songwriter Lee Myers has been a perfectionist with a nearly obsessive eye for detail. Consequently, the La's have never been able to totally fulfill their promise.

Myers formed the group in Liverpool with bassist John Power, guitarist Paul Hemmings, and drummer John Timson. On the strength of their demo tapes, Go! Discs signed the band in 1987, releasing the single "Way Out"; it received good reviews, yet it wasn't a chart success. Similarly, the following year's "There She Goes" received good press yet stalled on the charts. With a new lineup featuring bassist James Joyce, guitarist Cammy (born Peter James Camell), and Lee's brother Neil on drums, the La's began recording their debut album that same year. The record didn't appear until 1990. Even though Myers claimed it was rush-released, the Steve Lillywhite-produced The La's received glowing reviews and strong sales; a re-released "There She Goes" entered the UK Top 20 and hit No. 49 in America. For most of 1991, the band was on tour. At the end of the year, they went back to the studio to record their follow-up. This time, Lee Myers was in complete control and he took his time to perfect the album, re-recording tracks and rewriting songs. The La's disappeared without a trace from the pop music scene. Myers and a reconstituted band resurfaced in the spring of 1995, playing a handful of supporting concerts that featured a couple of new songs; the band began recording their second album the following summer. —*Stephen Thomas Erlewine*

The La's / 1990 / London ✦✦✦✦
This was one of the strongest debuts on the 1991 alternative music scene. "There She Goes" was a hit single with its mid-'60s-influenced Brit Invasion sound and interweaving hooks. Most of the album should be a joy to hear for fans of alternative pop. Highlights include "Son of a Gun," "Way Out," "Freedom Song," and "I.O.U." —*Rick Clark*

Labelle

Soul, Funk, Disco, R&B
A girl-group from Philadelphia, they formed in 1962. Initially known as The Blue Belles, and then Patti LaBelle and the Blue Belles, the group's personnel consisted of Patti LaBelle, Cindy Birdsong, Sarah Dash, and Nona Hendryx. The quartet scored six R&B hits from 1962 through 1967 before Birdsong departed to join Diana Ross and The Supremes. Continuing as a trio, for the next seven years the group languished in obscurity. British manager Vicki Wickham remade their image in the early '70s and shortened the name to Labelle. Decked out in ersatz futuristic garb, the threesome appeared as whirling dervishes delivering an explosive gospel/funk hybrid. Between late 1974 and late 1976, Labelle enjoyed five R&B hits, the first, "Lady Marmalade," reaching the No. 1 spot on the R&B and pop charts. Labelle split up in early 1977. —*Rob Bowman*

Nightbirds / 1974 / Epic ✦✦✦✦
The finest of the three Labelle albums, *Nightbirds* was recorded in New Orleans with funkmeister Allen Toussaint handling the production and, one assumes, members of the Meters taking care of the session work. Worth the price of admission for the Bob Crewe-written "Lady Marmalade" alone, the album veers between the strutting New Orleans, horn-laden singles and more mainstream pop material. —*Rob Bowman*

● **Lady Marmalade: The Best of Patti and Labelle** / 1995 / Epic/Legacy ✦✦✦✦
Lady Marmalade: The Best of Labelle features eight of the group's best tracks—including their two hits, "Lady Marmalade" and "What Can I Do for You?"—as well as eight of Patti LaBelle's R&B hits from the late '70s, which were among the funkiest tracks she ever recorded. —*Stephen Thomas Erlewine*

Patti LaBelle (Patricia Holt)

b. May 24, 1944, Philadelphia, PA
Vocals / Soul, Urban, Club-Dance
Born Patricia Holt in Philadelphia, Patti LaBelle has enjoyed a 30-year-plus career, having sung early-'60s girl-group material, soul, funk, and '80s ballad and dance music. From 1962-1976 she was a founding member of both Patti LaBelle & the Blue Belles and Labelle. She began her solo career in 1977. Over the ensuing six years, she scored a number of lower-rung R&B hits with Epic, coming into her own on Gamble and Huff's Philadelphia International label in 1984 with the No. 1 R&B hit, "If Only You Knew." She has been a consistent chartmaker ever since, renowned for a gospel-trained voice with stunning power and range, capable of exhilarating aural gymnastics. One of the most gifted, idiosyncratic voices in R&B. —*Rob Bowman*

Patti LaBelle / 1977 / Epic ✦✦✦
● **The Best of Patti LaBelle** / 1986 / Epic ✦✦✦✦
This anthology includes the biggest pop hit that the trio Labelle scored, the classic "Lady Marmalade," plus other staples from Patti LaBelle's solo phase, including "You Are My Friend," "Joy to Have Your Love" and "I

Don't Go Shopping." LaBelle didn't make her best or most successful records while on Epic, so these aren't the tunes currently associated with her. They were decently produced and often well performed, but lack the depth of her best MCA cuts. —*Ron Wynn*

Winner in You / 1986 / MCA ✦✦✦
Be Yourself / 1989 / MCA ✦✦✦
Burnin' / 1991 / MCA ✦✦✦
● **Over the Rainbow: The Atlantic Years** / 1994 / Ichiban ✦✦✦✦
The Bluebelles' stint with Atlantic in the '60s was not a great commercial success, yielding only a couple minor R&B hits ("I'm Still Waiting" and "Take Me for a Little While," both included here), but that wasn't due to any shortcomings on the records themselves, either in performance or material. Patti and the group recorded fine sides in pop-soul, Motown, Aretha Franklin, and early Philly soul styles, making full use of their powerful gospel-derived lead vocals and harmonies. This 22-track anthology features most of the singles (many previously non-LP) and some key album tracks that they recorded for Atlantic between 1965 and 1969, using top-notch writers like Carole Bayer, Pam Sawyer, Lori Burton, Bert Berns, Jeff Barry, Bacharach-David, Lorraine Ellison, Spooner Oldham, Dan Penn, and Curtis Mayfield (who produced some of the later sides), as well as The Bluebelles' own Nona Hendryx and Sarah Dash. Highlights include the original version of "Groovy Kind of Love" (a big hit for The Mindbenders), The Supremes-like "Tender Words," the dramatic "All or Nothing," and the moody Oldham-Penn ballad "Dreamer." —*Richie Unterberger*

● **The Best of the Bluebelles** / Relic ✦✦✦✦
This anthology collects the early, often charming and sometimes overly cute singles from Patti LaBelle and the Bluebelles. Besides the classic "I Sold My Heart to the Junkman" (which was really LaBelle backed by the Starlets), there are lesser-known numbers like "Down the Aisle (The Wedding Song)" and "I'm Still Waiting." Overall, this is competent period-piece material, but it's clear that LaBelle and company preferred more aggressive and assertive material and were never quite comfortable with most of these songs. —*Ron Wynn*

Lambchop

Indie Rock, Alternative Country-Rock
One of the hands-down weirdest groups to appear on the alternative scene in the mid-'90s (although they had been active for some years before that), it's hard to tell whether Lambchop play alternative rock with a heavy Nashville country influence, straight country music with a heavy alternative rock influence, or whether the whole thing is just an ironic joke. The group are actually from Nashville, and number about ten members (although the lineup fluctuates). The chief of this zany crew, however, is singer-songwriter/guitarist Kurt Wagner, whose stream-of-consciousness laments are distinctly at odds with the (usually) comfortably normal-sounding country-pop arrangements.

Musically, Lambchop can (and often does) offer a reasonable facsimile of the MOR Nashville country devised by producers such as Billy Sherill (who handled Charlie Rich's most popular work, and worked with Tammy Wynette and Tanya Tucker in the '70s). It is doubtful, however, that any release on the Merge label (also home to acts like Magnetic Fields and Superchunk) is aimed at the mainstream country music audience. Lambchop subverts the clichés of Nashville country with lyrics about suicide, bowling, and Theodore Dreiser-ish narratives about mundane everyday activities. There are also occasional interjections of post-punk guitar, thrash, clarinets, organ, and recorders that will not find a home in many trailer parks. Nor will Wagner's uneasy mumbling vocal style, which has more in common with Morrissey than Garth Brooks.

This is not the solace that most listeners turn to country-pop for as a respite from their day-to-day activities; it *is* their day-to-day activities, rendered too unflinchingly for comfort. Nor is it, despite considerable critical acclaim, the art statement some make it out to be, with plenty of what's-the-point lyrics and a nagging suspicion that the whole thing is a tongue-in-cheek art-school project that's gotten out of hand. Of their two albums, the debut is by far the more rock-influenced; 1995's *How I Quit Smoking* embraces mushy country production values much more wholeheartedly, without much alteration to the off-kilter, unsettling (and occasionally profane) tone of the lyrics. —*Richie Unterberger*

I Hope You're Sitting Down [aka Jack's Tulips] / 1994 / Merge ✦✦✦
A mix of post-modernism and straight (not roots) country music. The spooky organ fills, saxes, clarinets, and cello make this sound at times like the Art Ensemble of Chicago-as-country-band. Kurt Wagner's morose, resigned lyrics and dry, almost spoken delivery can get hard to take over the course of the hour-plus disc. "Soaker in the Pooper," a song about suicide in the bathroom, gave Wagner almost instant notoriety, and many of the other songs deal with similarly downbeat matters, although usually not as directly. —*Richie Unterberger*

● **How I Quit Smoking** / Jan. 30, 1996 / Merge ✦✦✦✦
Bona fide string arrangements give Lambchop's second album a much more "authentic" Nashville country feel than the first—meaning, ironically, that it sometimes sounds as gloppy, sentimental, and superficial as "real" Nashville country records. The arrangements are more inventive as well, mixing conventional country instruments like steel and acoustic guitars with saxes, clarinet, cornet, banjo, tin whistle, and more, along with the same kind of off-center organ featured on the first album. Wagner continues to mine the same offbeat lyrical territory, though unlike other audio verité talents like (say) Lou Reed, he doesn't bring much passion to his inner monologues. —*Richie Unterberger*

The Lambrettas

Power-Pop, Pop-Rock, Mod-revival
This Brighton-based band featuring Jez Bird (guitar/vocals), Doug Saunders (guitar), Mark Ellis (bass) and Paul Wincer (drums), jumped on the mod-revival bandwagon of the late '70s, dressing in matching mohair suits and naming themselves after one of the mod-favored motor scooters. Led by Bird's catchy songwriting, the Lambrettas proved to be more (if only slightly more) than just Jam-soundalikes, leaving behind mod-life arrogance/elitism in favor of a pure pop sensibility. The band signed to Elton John's Rocket Records in 1979 and after one failed single, "Go Steady," had a UK hit with their cover of Leiber and Stoller's "Poison Ivy." The follow-up singles "D-a-a-ance" and "Another Day (Another Girl)" also charted in the UK. The latter (originally titled "Page Three"), with its not-so-thinly veiled jabs at *The Sun* newspaper's practice of placing photos of topless women on page three, earned them some notoriety when the newspaper threatened legal action. *Beat Boys in the Jet Age*, their debut LP, released in 1979, collected the early singles and other similar-sounding originals. Though it did make it into the British charts, the mod-revival was fading fast. Subsequent singles and a second album, 1981's *Ambience*, were commercial flops despite efforts to break from the mod mold. The band called it quits in 1981 and faded quickly into obscurity. Bird regrouped the band in the '90s, playing small venues in England and recorded several demos for a new album yet to be released. —*Chris Woodstra*

Beat Boys in the Jet Age / 1980 / Rocket ✦✦✦✦
The band's debut picks up on all of the elements that made the early Jam albums brilliant—a certain reverence for '60s pop with a youthful, forward-looking attitude, punk's high-charged energy and strong songwriting. This sadly overlooked album features some of the era's best teen anthems. The CD version adds three bonus tracks. —*Chris Woodstra*

Ambience / 1981 / Rocket ✦✦✦
As the mod-revival was running out of steam, the band took a step away from the sound for a more mature and varied album. No longer is their main concern motor scooters, girls, and living for today as evident in the haunting "Good Times" and "Decent Town." Though it failed commercially, *Ambience* is a fine collection of Brit-pop worth seeking out. —*Chris Woodstra*

● **Best of the Lambrettas: The Singles Collection** / 1995 / ✦✦✦✦
Like so many bands of the era, the Lambrettas are best represented by their singles; *Best of the Lambrettas* collects all of the A and B-sides (as well as a newly recorded demo) in one place for the first time, providing the best introduction to the band. The songs are certainly of the time, but they've aged well, sounding as fresh as they did originally. —*Chris Woodstra*

Major Lance

b. Apr. 4, 1941, Chicago, IL, d. Sep. 3, 1994
Vocals / Soul
Few vocalists better epitomize the breezy danceability of '60s Chicago soul than whippet-thin Major Lance. Local deejay Jim Lounsbury discovered the loose-limbed singer and arranged his first contract with Mercury in 1959, but Lance needed expert guidance—and he received plenty from innovative producer Carl Davis after joining the OKeh label in 1962. Armed with exceptional dance material by Curtis Mayfield and the brass-heavy, often Latin-tinged charts of Johnny Pate, Lance blasted off with "The Monkey Time" and "Hey Little Girl" in 1963 and followed with the mysterious "Um Um Um Um Um Um" and "The Matador" the next year. When the influence of Mayfield and Davis dimmed, the hits became lesser in magnitude, and Lance left OKeh in 1968, bouncing from Dakar to Curtom to Volt with moderate success. Lance did a three-year prison stretch from 1978 to 1981 for drug dealing, but had returned to the stage shortly before his death. —*Bill Dahl*

● **Best of Major Lance: Everybody Loves a Good Time!** / 1995 / Epic/ Legacy ✦✦✦✦
Delightful 40-song, double-CD compilation of Lance's best work for Okeh between 1962 and 1967, including all of the chart singles, quite a few misses and B-sides, five previously unreleased cuts, and some Curtis Mayfield songs from his debut LP. The later tracks, recorded after producer Carl Davis and songwriter Mayfield had moved on to other projects, suffer in comparison with Lance's 1963-65 output, as he tried to keep abreast of contemporary soul trends, especially Motown. For many listeners, a briefer best-of Lance compilation will suffice. But for soul fans, this is prime stuff, dominated by the classic Latin-influenced Chicago soul sound of the Davis-produced tracks. —*Richie Unterberger*

Mark Lanegan

Guitar, Vocals / Alternative Pop-Rock
Mark Lanegan's solo albums are sufficiently dissimilar in tone from those of the group he usually fronts, Screaming Trees, to make listeners wonder where his true interests lie. His two records to date employ a much more acoustic tone, and address much more serious, personal concerns. Quite a few critics and listeners find them more impressive than the Screaming Trees' efforts, although he apparently has no plans to quit the band for a solo career. When Lanegan was planning his first solo recording, the original plan was to do an EP of blues songs with Nirvana's Kurt Cobain and Chris Novoselic, as well as Screaming Trees drummer Mark Pickerel. That didn't work out, and the first album ended up being recorded with Pickerel, guitarist Mike Johnson (later bassist in Dinosaur Jr.), and noted producer Jack Endino on bass. Despite a good reception from the underground, it took over three years for the follow-up, *The Winding Sheet*, to surface, again featuring Johnson in a prominent role. —*Richie Unterberger*

The Winding Sheet / 1990 / Sub Pop ✦✦✦✦
A dark side of this Screaming Trees vocalist. —*Robert Gordon*

● **Whiskey for the Holy Ghost** / 1994 / Sub Pop ✦✦✦✦
As a member of the Washington state alternative rock group Screaming Trees, Lanegan sings a somewhat lightweight and goofy blend of punk, hard rock, and psychedelia. On his own, he pursues an altogether more somber, acoustic, and bluesier vision. Like his debut release *The Winding Sheet*, Lanegan's second effort features his deep, husky-voiced musings, evocative mystic imagery, and brooding meditations on mortality. His dark but passionate vision is underscored by forceful acoustic guitars, harmonica, and occasional female backup harmonies. Sonically, Lanegan strongly resembles post-punk god Nick Cave, but his vision is ultimately more optimistic and accessible. —*Richie Unterberger*

Latimore

Keyboards, Vocals / Soul, Funk, Disco, Urban
Deep-voiced Latimore's sultry mid-'70s output for Miami's Glades label was a steamy marriage of soul and blues. Initially billed as Benny Latimore, the Tennessean began recording for Miami mogul Henry Stone in 1965, and his late-'60s Dade singles are solid deep-soul. Dropping his first name on Glades, Latimore finally found stardom in 1973 with a jazzy reading of T-Bone Walker's "Stormy Monday." He topped the soul lists in 1974 with the anguished "Let's Straighten It Out," a simmering soul/blues hybrid, and encored with the incendiary "Keep the Home Fires Burnin'" the next year. Most of Latimore's Glades sides were produced in Miami by Steve "Everyday I Have to Cry" Alaimo, and when he wasn't cutting his own hits, Latimore acted as a house pianist for parent TK Records. Latimore moved to Malaco during the '80s, his appeal undiminished. —*Bill Dahl*

● **Straighten It Out: The Best of Latimore** / 1995 / Rhino ✦✦✦✦
All of Latimore's greatest hits are included on this 17-track collection *Straighten It Out: The Best of Latimore*, making the album the best overview of the seductive '70s soul balladeer's career. —*Stephen Thomas Erlewine*

Cyndi Lauper

b. Jun. 20, 1953, Queens, NY
Guitar, Vocals / New Wave, Pop-Rock
As a guitarist, Lauper gigged with several bands in the '70s before co-founding Blue Angel in 1977, which released a highly acclaimed rock 'n' roll album on Polydor three years later. She went solo in 1983 and became a musical and MTV sensation with her pop-feminist song "Girls Just Want to Have Fun" and her tender ballad "Time after Time." She won the 1984 Grammy for Best New Artist.
Although she has had several hits since her debut, most notably the hit ballad "True Colors," Lauper was never able to recapture the excitement that surrounded her debut, *She's So Unusual*. She was still recording in the '90s, scoring a hit every now and then. —*Bil Carpenter & Donna DiChario*

● **She's So Unusual** / 1984 / Portrait ✦✦✦✦
This quirky diva created a musical and MTV sensation with her pop-feminist "Girls Just Want to Have Fun" and her tender ballad "Time After Time." She won the 1984 Grammy for Best New Artist. —*Donna DiChario*

True Colors / 1986 / Portrait ✦✦✦
Included is the Top Five title track ballad and her Top 20 faithfully
remade cover of Marvin Gaye's "What's Going On." Also included is the
harder-edged "Change of Heart." —*Donna DiChario*

A Night to Remember / 1989 / Epic ✦✦

A Hat Full of Stars / 1992 / Epic ✦✦

12 Deadly Cyns / Jul. 18, 1995 / Epic ✦✦✦✦
Thankfully bypassing the Top Ten hit "The Goonies 'R' Good Enough,"
12 Deadly Cyns features almost all of Cyndi Lauper's Top 40 hits, tacking
on a handful of new tracks at the end, including "Hey Now (Girls Still
Wanna Have Fun)," an updated version of her breakthrough hit single,
"Girls Just Wanna Have Fun." As hits collections go, the album is fine, but
with the exception of the ballad "True Colors" and the pop confection
"Change of Heart," all of her finest songs and biggest hits were on *She's
So Unusual*, which is a more consistent and entertaining album.
—*Stephen Thomas Erlewine*

Amanda Lear

Vocals / Disco, Euro-Dance
Amanda Lear first surfaced in the early '70s as a fetishistically-clothed
album-cover model for Roxy Music. She was said to be a transsexual but,
as she told *Interview* magazine, that was just a ruse dreamed up by her
sponsor, David Bowie, to draw attention. Her importance to disco fans,
however, began in 1977, when, in Germany with production help from
Tony Monn, she recorded *I Am a Photograph*, the first of six sleazy, hard-
to-find albums in which she flaunts a voice so heavy with low notes you
wonder if she really isn't a man after all. But no, Lear's slow notes are
simply an exaggeration of the whisky-voiced sultryness created by Marlene Dietrich. Which isn't to say that Lear's lyrics—or the music's inverted
proportions—don't exploit her mythology as a kinky concoction to the
bursting point. —*Michael Freedberg*

I Am a Photograph / 1977 / Chrysalis ✦✦✦✦
Lear, previously known as a Roxy Music album cover model and a protégé of Salvador Dali, appears here as a cabaret countess. She enunciates
sexually naughty suggestions in a smoke-and-velvet rasp. Her best sub-
versions hit a dancer's most salacious fantasies dead on. Most of these
songs support their studied lewdness with absurdly different music, creating tangible friction (i.e. "Alligator"—funk bottom, frothy violins on top)
that makes Lear's tape-loop voice feel even naughtier. All of Lear's tempos assault disco norms, either as sleaze or ultra-fast high-energy. An
album not to be missed. —*Michael Freedberg*

Sweet Revenge / 1978 / Chrysalis ✦✦✦✦
Producer Anthony Monn parades every effect known to Euro-dream
imagery in support of Lear as disco vamp: whispers from inside a tunnel,
rhythms that filter in subliminally, themes that scale up to soprano
range, choirs of angels singing, guitar rhythm rock-ons, and, of course,
Lear's voice. Lear's singing is perhaps Monn's greatest effect: androgynous, sultry, out of reach and horny at the same time, Lear works hard to
pretend at playing the merciless siren. She can't properly sing even one
note, but what's that got to do with anything? —*Michael Freedberg*

● **Super 20** / Ariola ✦✦✦✦

The Leaves

Folk-Rock
One of the first Los Angeles folk-rock groups to spring up in the wake of
the Byrds in the mid-'60s, The Leaves are most remembered for recording the first—and one of the most successful—rock versions of "Hey Joe,"
which reached the Top 40 (and was a huge Californian hit) in 1966. None
of their other releases approached this success (although "Too Many People" was a local hit), but the group recorded a fair number of strong covers and original songs during their brief existence. More explicitly
Stones and Beatles-influenced than the Byrds, they didn't project as
strong an identity as competitors like the Byrds or Love, despite displaying considerable talent for harmony rockers in both the folk-rock and
British Invasion styles. After cutting some singles and a decent album for
the tiny Mira label, they moved to Capitol, and disbanded after a disappointing follow-up (*All the Good That's Happening*, 1967) that offered
less distinguished material and a more diluted sound. Leaves bassist Jim
Pons went on to join the Turtles for a while in the late '60s. —*Richie
Unterberger*

Hey Joe / 1966 / One Way ✦✦✦
Their spotty first album includes the hit title track, the strong beat ballad
"Just a Memory," the Bo Diddley-esque folk-rocker "Dr. Stone," "Back on
the Avenue" (a ripoff of the Stones' "2120 South Michigan Avenue"), and
a pre-Monkees version of "Words." The CD reissue on One Way adds five
bonus tracks. —*Richie Unterberger*

● **1966** / 1982 / Fan Club ✦✦✦✦
Somewhat hard to find these days, this well-chosen best-of compilation
includes the best cuts from the *Hey Joe* album and a clutch of fine rare

and unreleased tracks. Highlights among these are the raw, original 45
version of "Too Many People," the Beatlesque B-side "Funny Little
World," a Byrds-like folk-rock cover of Dylan's "Love Minus Zero," and
"Be with You," a superb ripoff of the Byrds' "All I Really Want to Do."
Liner notes by Leaves member Jim Pons top off a fine package. —*Richie
Unterberger*

Led Zeppelin

Blues-Rock, Hard Rock, Heavy Metal
Led Zeppelin was the definitive heavy metal band. It wasn't just their
crushingly loud interpretation of the blues—it was how they incorporated mythology, mysticism, and a variety of other genres (most notably
world music and British folk) into their sound. Led Zeppelin had mystique. They rarely gave interviews, since the music press detested the
band. Consequently, the only connection the audience had with the band
was through the records and the concerts. More than any other band, Led
Zeppelin established the concept of album-oriented rock, refusing to
release popular songs from their albums as singles. In doing so, they
established the dominant format for heavy metal, as well as the genre's
actual sound.
    Led Zeppelin formed out of the ashes of the Yardbirds. Jimmy Page
had joined the band in its final days, playing a pivotal role on their final
album, 1967's *Little Games*, which also featured string arrangements
from John Paul Jones. During 1967, the Yardbirds were fairly inactive.
While the Yardbirds decided their future, Page returned to session work
in 1967. In the spring of 1968, he played on Jones' arrangement of Donovan's "Hurdy Gurdy Man." During the sessions, Jones requested to be
part of any future project Page would develop. Page would have to
assemble a band sooner than he had planned. In the summer of 1968,
the Yardbirds' Keith Relf and James McCarty left the band, leaving Page
and bassist Chris Dreja with the rights to the name, as well as the obligation of fulfilling an upcoming fall tour. Page set out to find a replacement
vocalist and drummer. Initially, he wanted to enlist Procol Harum's
singer Terry Reid and the band's drummer B.J. Wilson, but neither musician was able to join the group. Reid suggested that Page contact Robert
Plant, who was singing with a band called Hobbstweedle. After hearing
him sing, Page asked Plant to join the band in 1968, the same month the
Yardbirds' bassist Chris Dreja dropped out of the new project. Following
Dreja's departure, John Paul Jones joined the group as its bassist. Plant
recommended that Page hire John Bonham, the drummer for Plant's old
band, the Band of Joy. Bonham had to be persuaded to join the group, as
he was being courted by other artists who offered the drummer considerably more money. By September, Bonham agreed to join the band.
    Performing under the name the New Yardbirds, the band fulfilled the
Yardbirds' previously booked engagements in late September 1968. The
following month, they recorded their debut album in just under 30
hours. Also in October, the group switched their name to Led Zeppelin.
The band secured a contract with Atlantic Records in the US before the
end of the year. Early in 1969, Led Zeppelin set out on their first American tour, which helped set the stage for the January release of their eponymous debut album. Two months after its release, *Led Zeppelin* had
climbed into the US Top Ten. Throughout 1969, the band toured relentlessly, playing dates in America and England. While they were on the
road, they recorded their second album, *Led Zeppelin II*, which was
released in October of 1969. Like its predecessor, *Led Zeppelin II* was an
immediate hit, topping the American charts two months after its release
and spending seven weeks at No. 1. The album helped establish Led Zeppelin as an international concert attraction, and for the next year, the
group continued to tour relentlessly.
    Led Zeppelin's sound began to deepen with *Led Zeppelin III*. Released
in October of 1970, the album featured an overt British folk influence.
The group's infatuation with folk and mythology would reach a fruition
on the group's untitled fourth album, which was released in November of
1971. *Led Zeppelin IV* was the band's most musically diverse effort to
date, featuring everything from the crunching rock of "Black Dog" to the
folk of "The Battle of Evermore," as well as "Stairway to Heaven," which
found the bridge between the two genres. "Stairway to Heaven" was an
immediate radio hit, becoming the most played song in the history of
album-oriented radio; the song was never released as a single. Despite
the fact that the album never reached No. 1 in America, *Led Zeppelin IV*
was their biggest album ever, selling well over 16 million copies over the
next two and a half decades.
    Led Zeppelin did tour to support both *Led Zeppelin III* and *Led Zeppe-
lin IV*, but they played fewer shows than they did on their previous tours.
Instead, they concentrated on only playing larger venues. After completing their 1972 tour, the band retreated from the spotlight and recorded
their fifth album. Released in the spring of 1973, *Houses of the Holy* continued the band's musical experimentation, featuring touches of funk
and reggae among their trademark rock and folk. *Houses of the Holy*
debuted at No. 1 in both America and Britain, setting the stage for a
record-breaking American tour. Throughout their 1973 tour, Led Zeppelin broke box office records—most of which were previously held by the

Beatles—across America. The group's concert at Madison Square Garden in July was filmed for use in the feature film *The Song Remains the Same*, which was released three years later. After their 1973 tour, Led Zeppelin spent a quiet year during 1974, releasing no new material and performing no concerts. They did, however, establish their own record label, Swan Song, which released all of Led Zeppelin's subsequent albums, as well as records by Dave Edmunds, Bad Company, the Pretty Things, and several others. *Physical Graffiti*, a double album released in the spring of 1975, was the band's first release on Swan Song. The album was an immediate success, topping the charts in both America and England. Led Zeppelin planned to launch a large American tour in the late summer of 1975 when Robert Plant and his wife suffered a serious car crash while vacationing in Greece. Plans for the tour were cancelled and Plant spent the rest of the year recuperating from the accident.

Led Zeppelin returned to action in the spring of 1976 with *Presence*. Although the album debuted at No. 1 in both America and England, the reviews for the album were lukewarm, as was the reception to the live concert film *The Song Remains the Same*, which appeared in the fall of 1976. The band finally returned to tour America in the spring of 1977. A couple of months into the tour, Plant's six-year-old son Karac died of a stomach infection. Led Zeppelin immediately cancelled the tour and offered no word whether or not it would be rescheduled, causing widespread speculation about the band's future. For a while, it did appear that Led Zeppelin was finished. Robert Plant spent the latter half of 1977 and the better part of 1978 in seclusion. The group didn't begin work on a new album until late in the summer of 1978, when they began recording at ABBA's Polar studios in Sweden. A year later, the band played a short European tour, performing in Switzerland, Germany, Holland, Belgium, and Austria. In August of 1979, Led Zeppelin played two large concerts at Knebworth; the shows would be their last English performances.

In Through the Out Door, the band's much-delayed eighth studio album, was finally released in September of 1979. The album entered the charts at No. 1 in both America and England. In May of 1980, Led Zeppelin embarked on their final European tour. In September, Led Zeppelin began rehearsing at Jimmy Page's house in preparation for an American tour. On September 25, John Bonham was found dead in his bed—following an all-day drinking binge, he had passed out and choked on his own vomit. In December of 1980, Led Zeppelin announced they were disbanding, since they could not continue without Bonham.

Following the breakup, the remaining members all began solo careers. John Paul Jones never released a solo album. Instead, he returned to producing and arranging. After recording the soundtrack for *Death Wish II*, Jimmy Page compiled the Zeppelin outtakes collection, *Coda*, which was released at the end of 1982. That same year, Robert Plant began a solo career with the *Pictures at Eleven* album. In 1984, Plant and Page briefly reunited in the all-star oldies band the Honeydrippers. After recording one EP with the Honeydrippers, Plant returned to his solo career and Page formed the Firm with former Bad Company singer Paul Rogers. In 1985, Led Zeppelin reunited to play Live Aid, sparking off a flurry of reunion rumors; the reunion never materialized. In 1988, the band re-formed to play Atlantic's 25th Anniversary Concert. During 1989, Page remastered the band's catalog for release on the 1990 box set, *Led Zeppelin*. The four-disc set became the biggest selling multidisc box set of all time. In 1994, Jimmy Page and Robert Plant reunited to record a segment for *MTV Unplugged*, which was released as *Unledded* in the fall of 1994. Although the album went platinum, the sales were disappointing considering the anticipation of a Zeppelin reunion. The following year, Page and Plant embarked on a successful international tour. —*Stephen Thomas Erlewine*

☆ **Led Zeppelin** / Jan. 12, 1969 / Swan Song ✦✦✦✦✦
Led Zeppelin's debut album provided a blueprint for its overall approach—hard rock with ornate guitar textures and powerful riffs, topped by singer Robert Plant's high-pitched singing on roaring rockers like "Good Times Bad Times" and "Communication Breakdown," plus drawn-out blues performances like "Dazed and Confused." —*William Ruhlmann*

☆ **Led Zeppelin II** / Oct. 22, 1969 / Swan Song ✦✦✦✦✦
Recorded quickly during Led Zeppelin's first American tours, *Led Zeppelin II* provided the blueprint for all the heavy metal bands that followed it. Since the group could only enter the studio for brief amounts of time, the material that comprises *II* is almost entirely re-worked blues and rock 'n' roll standards that the band were performing onstage at the time. Not only did the short amount of time result in a lack of original material, it made the sound more direct. Jimmy Page still provided layers of guitar overdubs, but the overall sound of the album is heavy and hard, brutal and direct. "Whole Lotta Love," "The Lemon Song," and "Bring It on Home" are all based on classic blues songs, only the riffs are simpler and louder, and each song has an extended section for instrumental songs. Out of the remaining six songs, two sport light acoustic touches ("Thank You," "Ramble On"), but the other four are straightahead heavy rock, that follow the formula of the revamped blues songs. While *Led Zeppelin II* doesn't have the eclecticism of their debut, it was arguably

more influential. After all, nearly every one of the hundreds of Zeppelin imitators used this record, with its lack of dynamics and its pummeling riffs, as a blueprint. —*Stephen Thomas Erlewine*

☆ **Led Zeppelin III** / Oct. 5, 1970 / Swan Song ✦✦✦✦✦
After the bone-crunching hard rock of *Led Zeppelin II*, Page, Plant, Bonham, and Jones tracked a collection of more acoustic-flavored numbers. Songs like "Gallows Pole" and "Bron-Y-Aur Stomp" were essentially their trademark rockers played on folk instruments, but the reflective "That's the Way" and "Tangerine" indicated a new maturity. A handful of heavy riff-rockers like "Immigrant Song," "Out on the Tiles," "Celebration Day," and the hard blues raveup "Since I've Been Loving You" more than rounded out this solid (but transitional) effort. —*Rick Clark*

★ **Led Zeppelin IV** / Nov. 8, 1971 / Swan Song ✦✦✦✦✦
The perfect mixture of Zeppelin's trademark heavy rock, plus some old-time rock 'n' roll and the band's folkie influences, all of which culminated in its greatest song, "Stairway to Heaven." —*William Ruhlmann*

☆ **Houses of the Holy** / Mar. 28, 1973 / Swan Song ✦✦✦✦✦
Houses of the Holy follows the same basic pattern as *Led Zeppelin IV*, but the approach is looser and more relaxed. Jimmy Page's riffs rely on ringing, folky hooks as much as thundering blues-rock, giving the album a lighter, more open atmosphere. While the pseudo-reggae of "D'Yer Mak'er" and the affectionate James Brown send-up "The Crunge" suggest that the band was searching for material, they actually contribute to the musical diversity of the album. "The Rain Song" is one of their finest moments, featuring a soaring string arrangement and a gentle, aching melody. "The Ocean" is just as good, starting with a typically heavy, but funky, guitar groove before slamming into an a cappella section and ending with a swinging, doo wop-flavored raveup. With the exception of the rampaging opening number "The Song Remains the Same," the rest of *Houses of the Holy* is fairly straightforward, ranging from the foreboding "No Quarter" and the strutting hard rock of "Dancing Days" to the epic folk/metal fusion "Over the Hills and Far Away." Throughout the record, the band's playing is excellent, making the eclecticism of Page and Plant's songwriting sound coherent and natural. —*Stephen Thomas Erlewine*

☆ **Physical Graffiti** / Feb. 24, 1975 / Swan Song ✦✦✦✦✦
A lengthy two-disc set whose bluesy workouts (plus such new explorations as the Middle Eastern "Kashmir") mark it as the most "Zeppelinish" of Led Zeppelin albums. —*William Ruhlmann*

The Song Remains the Same / 1976 / Swan Song ✦✦

Presence / 1976 / Swan Song ✦✦✦
Presence scales back the size of *Physical Graffiti* to a single album, but it retains the grandiose scope of the double album. If anything, *Presence* has more majestic epics than its predecessor, opening with the surging ten-minute "Achilles Last Stand" and closing with the meandering, nearly ten-minute "Tea for One." In between, Zeppelin adds the lumbering blues workout "Nobody's Fault but Mine" and the terse, menacing "For Your Life," which is the best song on the album. These four tracks take up the bulk of the album, leaving three lighthearted throwaways to alleviate the foreboding atmosphere of the epics, as well as their pretensions. If all of the throwaways were as focused and funny as those on *Physical Graffiti* or *Houses of the Holy*, Zeppelin would have had another classic in their hands. However, the Crescent City love letter of "Royal Orleans" sags in the middle and the ersatz rockabilly of "Candy Store Rock" doesn't muster up the loose, funky swagger of "Hots on for Nowhere," which it *should* in order to work. The three throwaways are also scattered haphazardly throughout the album, making it seem more ponderous than it actually is, and the result is the weakest album they had yet recorded. —*Stephen Thomas Erlewine*

In Through the Out Door / 1979 / Swan Song ✦✦✦
Between *Presence* and *In Through the Out Door*, disco, punk, and new wave had overtaken rock 'n' roll, and Led Zeppelin chose to tentatively embrace the pop revolutions, adding synthesizers to the mix and emphasizing Bonham's inherent way with a groove. The album's opening number "In the Evening," with its stomping rhythms and heavy, staggered riffs, suggests that the band hasn't strayed from their course, but by the time the rolling shuffle of "South Bound Suarez" kicks into gear, it's apparent that the group have regained their sense of humor. After "South Bound Suarez," the group try a variety of styles, whether it's an over-driven homage to Bakersfield country called "Hot Dog," the layered, Latin-tinged percussion and pianos of "Fool in the Rain," or the slickly seductive ballad "All My Love." "Carouselambra," a lurching, self-consciously ambitious synth-driven number, and the slow blues "I'm Gonna Crawl" aren't quite as impressive as the rest of the album, but the record is a graceful way to close their career, even if it wasn't intended as the final chapter. —*Stephen Thomas Erlewine*

Coda / 1982 / Swan Song ✦✦✦
An odds-n-sods collection assembled after Bonham's death, *Coda* is predictably a hit-or-miss affair. The best material comes from later in their career, including the ringing folk stomp of "Poor Tom," the jacked-up

'50s rock 'n' roll of "Ozone Baby," and their response to punk rock, the savage "Wearing and Tearing." The rest of the album, sadly including the Bonham showcase "Bonzo's Montreux," is average, despite the presence of some stellar playing, especially on the early blues-rock blitzkrieg "I Can't Quit You Baby" and "We're Gonna Groove." —*Stephen Thomas Erlewine*

Led Zeppelin [Box Set] / 1990 / Swan Song ✦✦✦
Led Zeppelin Remasters / 1992 / Swan Song ✦✦✦
Boxed Set 2 / 1993 / Atlantic ✦✦✦
Complete Studio Recordings / 1993 / Atlantic ✦✦✦

The Left Banke

Pop-Rock
This New York group pioneered "Baroque'n'Roll" in the '60s with their mix of pop-rock and grand, quasi-classical arrangements and melodies. Featuring teenage prodigy Michael Brown as keyboardist and chief songwriter, the group scored two quick hits with "Walk Away Renee" (No. 5) and "Pretty Ballerina" (No. 15). Chamber-like string arrangements, Steve Martin's soaring, near-falsetto lead vocals, and tight harmonies that borrowed from British Invasion bands like the Beatles and the Zombies were also key elements of the Left Banke sound. Though their two hits are their only well-remembered efforts, their debut album (*Walk Away Renee/Pretty Ballerina*) was a strong, near-classic work that matched the quality of their hit singles in songwriting and production.

Unfortunately the group, which showed such tremendous promise, was quickly torn asunder by dissension. Brown left in 1967, and most of the group's second and final album, *The Left Banke Too*, was recorded without him. While it still sported baroque arrangements and contained some fine moments, Brown's presence was sorely missed, and the record pales in comparison to their debut. Brown went on to form a Left Banke-styled group, Montage, which released a fine and underappreciated album in the late '60s. He later teamed up to form Stories with vocalist Ian Lloyd. —*Richie Unterberger*

● **There's Gonna Be a Storm: Complete Recordings 1966-69** / 1992 / Mercury ✦✦✦✦
Though it's missing a few rarities—namely the Steve Martin single for Buddha that reunited him with Michael Brown—this is the most definitive Left Banke compilation. It features the entirety of their two late-'60s albums, as well as a couple of singles that didn't make it onto LPs at the time (though they later appeared on Rhino's *History*) and a previously unissued cut, "Men Are Building Sand." Their debut 1967 LP, *Walk Away Renee/Pretty Ballerina*, is an underrated classic of the time, matching smart harmonies and pop hooks to baroque orchestration. Its brilliance casts a bit of a shadow over the rest of this collection. The group's 1968 album *Too* suffered from bloated production and, more importantly, the absence of chief songwriter/arranger Michael Brown. In turn, the 1967 single Brown cut under the Left Banke moniker with singer Bert Sommer suffers from the absence of lead vocalist Steve Martin. By the time Brown and Martin tenuously reunited for a late-1969 single, some of the spark had gone. All of the aforementioned highs and lows of this prodigiously talented but strife-ridden group are on this disc. —*Richie Unterberger*

Lemonheads

Alternative Pop-Rock, Hardcore Punk, Pop-Rock
Evan Dando was a hardcore punk when the Lemonheads released their first album, *Hate Your Friends*, in 1987; five years later, he was a teenage heart-throb, thanks to the memorable, punky power-pop of *It's a Shame About Ray*. Between those two albums, the rest of the band quit, leaving guitarist/vocalist Dando as the only Lemonhead. The membership wasn't the only thing that changed. Over the years, Dando began to accentuate his fondness for pure pop, which was apparent even on the band's harder earlier records. The Lemonheads moved to a major label in 1990 and released *Lovey*. Dando recorded most of the album by himself, which makes its mix of loud guitars, bright melodies, and charming, simple lyrics all the more impressive; this was the path he would follow to stardom. On the band's next album—1992's *It's a Shame About Ray*, which was recorded with a full band—Dando's songwriting blossomed. Not only could he write catchy, brash power-pop, he was able to seamlessly incorporate touches of folk and country-rock. Thanks to a loud, irreverent cover of Simon & Garfunkel's "Mrs. Robinson," the Lemonheads began getting mainstream attention; with their next album, 1993's *Come on Feel the Lemonheads*, the band gained an even bigger audience, even if the album was more inconsistent. Even with its dull spots, the album showed that Dando continued to grow as a songwriter, as his country influences became more pronounced and genuine. —*Stephen Thomas Erlewine*

Lick / 1989 / Taang! ✦✦✦✦
On their last independent release, the Lemonheads turn in an engaging but incoherent album that bounces back and forth between inspired

melodic punk-pop, hardcore, and the occasional ballad; the whole charming mess is highlighted by a muscular cover of Suzanne Vega's "Luka." —*Stephen Thomas Erlewine*

Create Your Friends / 1989 / Taang! ✦✦
The Lemonheads' first two albums show that beneath the band's relentless hardcore guitar grind, Evan Dando had written some very good songs with strong melodies. It just takes some effort to *hear* the melodies. —*Stephen Thomas Erlewine*

Lovey / 1990 / Atlantic ✦✦✦
Alternating between melodic hard rock and gentle country and folk-rock, *Lovey* was the band's most refined album to date, but only half the songs (including "Stove," "Half the Time," "(The) Door," and Gram Parsons' "Brass Buttons") make a lasting impression. —*Stephen Thomas Erlewine*

● **It's a Shame About Ray** / 1992 / Atlantic ✦✦✦✦
It's a Shame About Ray is a nearly perfect pop album—short, concise, and overflowing with memorable melodies. Although Evan Dando keeps every song between two and three minutes, he isn't cheating the audience by any measure; the 12-song, under-30-minute blitz of *It's a Shame About Ray* provides more quality music than most of today's bloated, 70-minute epics. Dando's songs prove that his true talents as a pop songwriter are just beginning to emerge. (Note: After the fall of 1992, the album was issued with the band's raucous power-pop take on Simon & Garfunkel's "Mrs. Robinson.") —*Stephen Thomas Erlewine*

Come on Feel the Lemonheads / 1993 / Atlantic ✦✦✦
More confused and muddled than *It's A Shame About Ray*, *Come on Feel the Lemonheads* has a number of power-pop pleasures, but they're buried among several lazy, half-hearted numbers and a ridiculous solo piano piece. When Evan Dando does hit home—as on "The Great Big No," "Down About It," and the cover, "Into Your Arms"—the results are irresistible; the moving, introspective "Favorite T" and the country-rock of "Being Around" and "Big Gay Heart" are also strong. Unfortunately, these songs are hard to find amidst the bloated directionlessness of the rest of the album. —*Stephen Thomas Erlewine*

John Lennon

b. Oct. 9, 1940, Liverpool, England, **d.** Dec. 8, 1980, New York, NY
Guitar, Vocals / Rock 'n' Roll, Singer-Songwriter, Pop-Rock
John Lennon was a singer, songwriter, guitarist, record producer, author, actor, filmmaker, artist, and political spokesman, and one of the greatest figures in postwar popular music. Lennon was born in Liverpool, England, and became involved in music in the '50s. The group he founded as the Quarrymen eventually evolved into the Beatles, and from 1963 to 1970 they were the most successful rock group in history. Lennon, the group's leader, played an important part in that success, writing and singing many of its biggest hits and best songs.

Lennon began to record and perform outside the group in 1969, usually in the company of his wife, avant-garde artist Yoko Ono. The early Lennon-Ono records (and films and performance events) were experimental in nature, but as Lennon turned to recording as a solo performer, his work was more accessible to pop audiences, though his lyrical concerns were frequently political or scathingly personal. His first formal solo album was *John Lennon/Plastic Ono Band* in 1970, and he followed this with *Imagine* (1971), *Sometime in New York City* (1972), *Mind Games* (1973), *Walls and Bridges* (1974), and *Rock 'n' Roll* (1975). Most of his recordings sold well, with *Walls & Bridges* topping the charts along with its single, "Whatever Gets You through the Night."

Lennon, who had separated from Ono in 1973, was reconciled with her in 1975 and thereafter retired from music to raise their son Sean. He and Ono re-emerged with the album *Double Fantasy* in 1980, and had plans for further recordings and performances at the time he was assassinated. —*William Ruhlmann*

Two Virgins: Unfinished Music No. 1 / Nov. 11, 1968 / Apple ✦✦
Life with the Lions: Unfinished Music #2 / May 26, 1969 / Apple ✦✦
Live Peace in Toronto 1969 / Dec. 12, 1969 / Capitol ✦✦✦
Impromptu concert appearance, with Lennon singing a few rock 'n' roll oldies plus his then-new single, "Cold Turkey," backed by guitarist Eric Clapton. Also 17+ minutes of Yoko Ono screaming and singing over guitar feedback. —*William Ruhlmann*

Wedding Album / 1969 / Apple ✦✦
☆ **John Lennon/Plastic Ono Band** / Dec. 11, 1970 / Capitol ✦✦✦✦✦
A stark, harrowing set of songs in which Lennon recounts the horrors of his childhood ("Mother," "Working Class Hero"), the disillusionment of his adulthood ("I Found Out"), and his loss of faith in all idols ("God") including "Beatles." This album is one of rock's most personal—and most ambitious—statements. —*William Ruhlmann*

☆ **Imagine** / Sep. 9, 1971 / Capitol ✦✦✦✦✦
In addition to the justly revered title track (a No. 3 hit), this eclectic pop album also contains "Jealous Guy" (later a hit for Roxy Music) and

"Gimme Some Truth" (later adopted by such punk rockers as Generation X). — *William Ruhlmann*

Sometime in New York City / Jun. 12, 1972 / Capitol ✦

Mind Games / Nov. 2, 1973 / Capitol ✦✦✦
John Lennon retreated from the political tone of *Sometime in New York City* and returned to solo work here, managing a fitting follow-up to "Imagine" with the piano-based title track and also turning in one of his better ballads with "One Day (At a Time)." — *William Ruhlmann*

Walls and Bridges / Sep. 26, 1974 / Capitol ✦✦✦✦
Craftsmanlike pop-rock featuring the uptempo No. 1 hit "Whatever Gets You through the Night," its Top Ten follow-up, "No.9 Dream," and some lovely album tracks. — *William Ruhlmann*

Rock 'n' Roll / Feb. 17, 1975 / Capitol ✦✦✦

Shaved Fish / Oct. 24, 1975 / Capitol ✦✦✦✦
Although superseded by *The John Lennon Collection* (see below), this greatest-hits album is the only place to find such singles as "Cold Turkey" and "Happy Xmas (War Is Over)." — *William Ruhlmann*

Double Fantasy / Nov. 17, 1980 / Capitol ✦✦✦✦
On an album made shortly before his death, Lennon explores his retirement, his artistic rebirth, and his relationship with his family on such songs as "(Just Like) Starting Over," "Woman," and "Watching the Wheels," all of which were Top Ten hits. Lennon's songs are interspersed with surprisingly accessible contributions from Ono. — *William Ruhlmann*

★ **The John Lennon Collection** / Nov. 10, 1982 / Capitol ✦✦✦✦✦
Six of the seven Lennon tracks from *Double Fantasy*, plus nine of his best songs from 1969 to 1974, among them the singles "Give Peace a Chance," in its only album appearance, and "Instant Karma!" The CD version, released in 1989, adds four tracks, including the B-side single "Move Over Ms. L," making this album all the more necessary. — *William Ruhlmann*

Milk & Honey / Jan. 27, 1984 / Polydor ✦✦✦
Posthumous follow-up to *Double Fantasy*, featuring sometimes rough takes of perhaps unfinished songs that nevertheless sparkle with Lennon's wit and exuberance, among them the Top Five hit "Nobody Told Me." (Again, Ono's songs are interspersed with Lennon's contributions.) — *William Ruhlmann*

Live in New York City / Feb. 10, 1986 / Capitol ✦✦✦

Menlove Ave. / Nov. 3, 1986 / Capitol ✦✦✦

Imagine: John Lennon [O.S.T.] / Oct. 10, 1988 / Capitol ✦✦✦✦
A two-disc set containing a selection of Lennon's work with the Beatles and as a solo artist. This is the original soundtrack album. — *William Ruhlmann*

☆ **Lennon** / 1990 / Capitol ✦✦✦✦✦
Lennon is given a solid box-set treatment with this four-disc, 73-track collection. The set is so complete that there is essentially no need to go out and obtain any of his albums on disc. *Lennon* runs chronologically, from the Plastic Ono Band's "Give Peace a Chance," to "Grow Old with Me" from 1984's *Milk and Honey*. All the best stuff from *Live Peace in Toronto 1969* is here, as well as his live (with Elton John) versions of "I Saw Her Standing There" and "Lucy in the Sky with Diamonds." The book contains a generous collection of photos and lyrics to all of the songs. The A-to-Z color-coded index is overkill in lieu of any track information detailing where and when the songs were cut and who played on them. — *Rick Clark*

Let's Active

Power-Pop, Jangle-pop
Formed in 1981 by North Carolina musician/producer Mitch Easter, Let's Active was one of the premier bands of the Southern alternative-pop movement of the '80s. Easter is primarly known for his production of R.E.M.'s *Murmur* and *Reckoning*, yet that only scratches the surface of his work; at his Drive-In Studio, he produced numerous other bands during the decade. However, Easter's main project was Let's Active. Between 1983 and 1989, the band only released three albums and one EP, yet they showed a remarkable proficiency for ringing, melodic guitar pop as well as tangled neo-psychedelia. After their last album in 1988, the group split; Easter has concentrated on production work since then. — *Rick Clark*

Afoot / 1983 / IRS ✦✦✦✦
A six-song debut EP, featuring Mitch Easter's own brand of Southern power-pop. With hook-filled and instantly lovable songs, Easter proves to be a master of the three-minute form. — *Chris Woodstra*

Cypress / 1984 / IRS ✦✦✦✦
The band stretch out a bit on their first proper LP. While it is still every bit a jangly guitar-pop effort, Easter seems to be enjoying the powers of his studio, experimenting in different electronic sounds and neo-psychedelic

textures. "Waters Part," the failed single from the album, is still one of his finest moments as a songwriter. — *Chris Woodstra*

Big Plans for Everybody / 1986 / IRS ✦✦✦
Essentially a Mitch Easter solo project, *Big Plans for Everybody* moves into darker territory than the previous album. Though Easter's trademark bright production and quirky songwriting still stand out, the mood is decidedly melancholy. — *Chris Woodstra*

Every Dog Has His Day / Aug. 22, 1988 / IRS ✦✦✦
Every Dog Has His Day features some of Easter's strongest songs in a harder-edged setting. Almost completely ignored, this was the band's last effort before disbanding indefinitely. — *Chris Woodstra*

● **Cypress/Afoot** / 1989 / IRS ✦✦✦✦
This CD combines their first EP, *Afoot*, and their first album, *Cypress*. Featuring infectious hook-filled songs like "Every Word Means No" and "Waters Part," this perfect Southern power-pop is worth seeking out. — *Chris Woodstra*

Level 42

Synth-pop, New Wave, Pop-Rock
At the beginning of their career, Level 42 were a jazz-funk fusion band, following in the footsteps of such pioneers as Stanley Clarke. By the end of the '80s, they were a pop-R&B band with a number of hit singles to their credit. Featuring Mark King (bass, vocals), Phil Gould (drums), Boon Gould (guitar), and Mark Lindup (keyboards), the band formed in 1980. Before they released their first single, "Love Meeting Love," the band was pushed to add vocals to their music in order to give it a more commercial sound; they complied, with King becoming the lead singer. Released in 1981, their self-titled debut album was a slick soul-R&B collection that charted in the UK Top 20, resulting in the release of *The Early Tapes* by their former record label, Polydor. Level 42 had several minor hit singles before 1984's "The Sun Goes Down (Living It Up)" hit the British Top Ten. Released in late 1985, *World Machine* broke the band worldwide; "Lessons in Love" hit No. 1 in Britain and "Something About You" hit No. 7 in America. Their next two records, *Running in the Family* (1987) and *Staring at the Sun* (1988), were a big success in the UK, yet only made some headway in the US. Both of the Gould brothers left the band in late 1987; they were replaced by guitarist Alan Murphy and drummer Gary Husband. Murphy died of AIDS in 1991; he was replaced by the renowned fusion guitarist Allan Holdsworth for 1991's *Guaranteed*. — *Stephen Thomas Erlewine*

Level 42 / 1981 / Polydor ✦✦✦✦
The album was produced by label owner Andy Sojka. Highlights include "Love Meeting Love," "Wings of Love," "Love Games," "Turn It On," and "Starchild." — *Bil Carpenter*

Pursuit of Accidents / 1982 / Polydor ✦✦✦

True Colours / 1983 / Polydor ✦✦✦

● **Level Best** / 1989 / Polydor ✦✦✦✦
This hits CD draws heavily from *Running in the Family* (1987) and *World Machine* (1985) but offers a good introduction to this band. — *Scott Bultman*

Barbara Lewis

b. Feb. 9, 1943, South Lyon, MI
Vocals / Soul
Pop-soul doesn't get much better than Barbara Lewis, whose seductive, emotive croon took "Hello Stranger" to No. 3 in 1963. The Michigan native had been writing songs since the age of nine, and began recording as a teenager with producer Ollie McLaughlin, who'd also had a hand in the careers of Del Shannon, the Capitols, and Deon Jackson. Lewis wrote all of the songs on her debut LP (including "Hello Stranger"), and confidently handled harmony soul numbers (some with backing by the Dells) and more pop-savvy tunes, some of which, like "Hello Stranger," were driven by an organ and a bossa nova-like beat.

Follow-ups to "Hello Stranger" didn't sell nearly as well (although one of her singles, "Someday We're Gonna Love Again," was covered by the Searchers for a British Invasion hit). In the mid-'60s, she began doing some recordings in New York City, with assistance from producers like Bert Berns and Jerry Wexler, that employed more orchestral arrangements and pop-conscious material. The approach clicked, both commercially and artistically: "Baby I'm Yours" and "Make Me Your Baby" were both big hits, and both among the best mid-'60s girl-group style productions.

Lewis cut an album in the late '60s for Stax (on the Enterprise subsidiary) that, as one would expect, gave her sound a grittier approach, without compromising the smooth and poppy elements integral to the singer's appeal. It passed mostly unnoticed, though, and Lewis withdrew from the music business after a few other singles. The "beach music" scene of the Carolinas remains a bastion of appreciation for Lewis' records, which continue to enjoy popularity and airplay there decades after their original release. —*Richie Unterberger*

Snap Your Fingers / 1964 / Atlantic ✦✦✦
Not much. Lewis sings a variety of standards like "Twist and Shout" and even "Turn on Your Love Light." Nice music, but not great Barbara Lewis. —*Michael Erlewine*

Baby, I'm Yours / 1966 / Atlantic ✦✦✦✦
Here is a classic Barbara Lewis album with four tunes written by Lewis herself. "Baby, I'm Yours," and "Hello Stranger" we all know, but "Puppy Love," and "Think a Little Sugar" are also fine. The song "How Can I Say Goodbye" is wonderful. Most of these are available on compilations. —*Michael Erlewine*

It's Magic / 1966 / Atlantic ✦✦✦
An album of standards like "Yesterday" and "A Taste of Honey." Not the Lewis that most of us hunger for, although the cut "He's So Bad" is very good. —*Michael Erlewine*

Many Grooves of Barbara Lewis / 1969 / Stax ✦✦✦✦
Although this late-'60s album isn't nearly as well known as her poppier mid-'60s hits, this is excellent sweet soul that avoids slickness. Still working with producer Ollie McLaughlin, Lewis recorded this set of strong soul-pop in Chicago. The slightly updated, gutsier tone of the arrangements did nothing to obscure her characteristically smooth and assured delivery. The CD reissue adds three bonus tracks from singles. —*Richie Unterberger*

Hello Stranger / 1981 / Solid Smoke ✦✦✦✦
"Sixteen Smooth Sides By Detroit's Soulful Songstress" are featured on this compilation of singles and albums tracks, spanning 1962-68. Includes the No. 1 hit title track, as well as the girl-group-style Top Tenners "Make Me Your Baby" and "Baby I'm Yours," and the original version of "Someday We're Gonna Love Again" (which was a hit for the Searchers). Some of the most velvety soul ever waxed. —*Richie Unterberger*

★ **Hello Stranger: The Best of Barbara Lewis** / 1994 / Rhino ✦✦✦✦✦
At last! Twenty great Barbara Lewis songs in glorious remastered digital sound. In fact, the sound is so good it's like hearing these classic sides for the first time. The only significant omission is the song "On Bended Knee," but then again, I would have liked a two-disc compilation. Thank you Rhino! —*Michael Erlewine*

Gary Lewis (Gary Levital)

b. Jun. 31, 1946
Drums, Vocals / Pop-Rock
The son of comedian Jerry Lewis formed this American rock group in 1964. After landing a gig at Disneyland, they were immediately signed to Liberty Records and handed over to pop production genius Snuff Garrett. Utilizing the best songwriters and studio players available, Garrett fashioned five Top Five hits in a matter of 18 months (15 in the Hot 100 by 1969) around Lewis's meager abilities, sometimes augmenting his voice in the studio with backup singers doubling his part. Lewis pretty well held his own against the British Invasion, but the combination of his draft call in late 1966 and the rising tide of psychedelia put his days on the charts to an end. Still active on the oldies circuit, he fronts various backup bands under the name the Playboys. —*Cub Koda*

● **Legendary Masters Series** / 1990 / Capitol ✦✦✦✦
One of the most engaging pop acts of the mid-'60s, the Playboys benefited from strong songwriting (Al Kooper cowrote "This Diamond Ring") and studio personnel (courtesy of Leon Russell). It's still light, catchy pop with the enjoyable, unaffected vocals of Gary Lewis on top, and still fun. —*William Ruhlmann*

Greatest Hits [Curb] / 1994 / Curb ✦✦

Huey Lewis & The News

Pop-Rock
Before the formation of the News, Huey Lewis (born Hugh Cregg) had been part of the San Francisco band Clover from 1976 to 1980. During that time Clover (sans Lewis) backed up Elvis Costello on his debut *My Aim Is True*. Lewis also did session-sideman work on Nick Lowe's *Labour of Lust* and Dave Edmunds' *Repeat When Necessary*. Clover broke up in 1979 after bandleader John McFee split to join the Doobie Brothers. Lewis returned to a day gig and started jamming at a local Marin County bar called Uncle Charlie's. It was there that the nucleus of the News was formed out of visiting musicians, many of whom had previously backed up Van Morrison. The News' self-titled debut failed to sell, but "Do You Believe in Love?" went to No. 7. Their second album, *Picture This*, rose to No. 13 and produced a couple of moderate hits with "Hope You Love Me Like You Say You Do" (No. 36) and "Workin' for a Livin'" (No. 41). The next album, *Sports*, went multi-platinum and generated a number of hits. Between albums the News scored a No. 1 hit, "The Power of Love," from the movie *Back to the Future*. Their follow-up album, *Fore*

(No. 1), included five Top Ten hits: "Stuck with You," "Jacob's Ladder," "Hip to Be Square," and "Doing It All (For My Baby)." 1988's *Small World* marked the beginning of Lewis' commercial decline, which lasted until 1994, when The News became adult-contemporary favorites with their covers of classic soul songs. —*Rick Clark*

Huey Lewis & The News / 1980 / Chrysalis ✦✦
For most of their self-titled debut album, Huey Lewis & The News try to carve out their niche. While their basic idea is apparent—a cross between a driving bar band and catchy pop craftsmen—the group didn't write any songs to make their concept appealing. —*Stephen Thomas Erlewine*

Picture This / 1982 / Chrysalis ✦✦✦✦
Their second album broke through with the hits "Workin' for a Livin'" and "Do You Believe in Love?" —*Donna DiChario*

● **Sports** / 1983 / Chrysalis ✦✦✦✦
Their brand of spirited, no-frills rock 'n' roll features the hits "I Want a New Drug," "The Heart of Rock & Roll," and "Walkin' on a Thin Line," and helped sell more than seven million copies of this album. —*Donna DiChario*

Fore! / 1986 / Chrysalis ✦✦✦
More pop-rock featuring the hits "Stuck with You," "Jacob's Ladder," and "Hip to Be Square." —*Donna DiChario*

Small World / 1988 / Chrysalis ✦✦

Hard at Play / Jan. 1991 / EMI America ✦✦✦

● **The Heart of Rock & Roll: The Best of Huey Lewis & The News** / 1992 / Chrysalis ✦✦✦✦

Four Chords & Several Years Ago / 1994 / Elektra ✦✦

Jerry Lee Lewis

b. Sep. 29, 1935, Ferriday, LA
Piano, Vocals / Rock 'n' Roll, Rockabilly, Honky Tonk
Is there an early rock 'n' roller that has a crazier reputation than the Killer, Mister Jerry Lee Lewis? His exploits as a piano thumping egocentric wild man with an unquenchable thirst for living have become the fodder for numerous biographies, film documentaries, and a full-length Hollywood movie starring Dennis Quaid. Certainly few other artists came to the party with more ego and talent than he and lived to tell the tale. And certainly even fewer could successfully channel that energy into their music and prosper doing it as well as Jerry Lee. When he broke on the national scene in 1957 with his classic "Whole Lotta Shakin' Goin' On," he was every parents' worst nightmare perfectly realized; a long, blonde-haired Southerner who played the piano and sang with uncontrolled fury and abandon, while simultaneously reveling in his own sexuality. He was rock 'n' roll's first great wild man and also rock 'n' roll's first great eclectic. Ignoring all manner of musical boundaries is something that has not only allowed his music to have wide variety, but to survive the fads and fashions as well. Whether singing a melancholy country ballad, a lowdown blues or a blazing rocker, Lewis' wholesale commitment to the moment brings forth performances that are totally grounded in his personality and all singularly of one piece. Like the recordings of Hank Williams, Louis Armstrong and few others, Jerry Lee's early recorded work is one of the most amazing collections of American music in existence.

He was born to Elmo and Mamie Lewis on September 29, 1935, a breech baby, which has caused Lewis to always comment in interviews, "I was born feet first, been rockin' ever since." Though the family was dirt poor, there was enough money to be had to purchase a third-hand upright piano for the family's country shack in Ferriday, LA. Sharing piano lessons with his two cousins, Mickey Gilley and Jimmy Lee Swaggart, a ten-year-old Jerry Lee showed remarkable aptitude toward the instrument and made lightning quick progress. A visit from piano-playing older cousin Carl McVoy unlocked the secrets to the boogie-woogie styles he was hearing on the radio and across the tracks at Haney's Big House, owned by his uncle, Lee Calhoun and catering to Blacks exclusively. Lewis mixed that up with gospel and Country & Western and started coming up with his own mixture. He even mixed genres in the way he syncopated his rhythms on the piano; his left hand generally played a rock solid boogie pattern while his right played the high keys with much flamboyant filigree and showiness, equal parts gospel fervor and Liberace showmanship. By the time he was 14, by all family accounts, he was as good as he was ever going to get. Jerry Lee was already ready for prime time.

But his Mother Mamie had other plans for the young family prodigy. Not wanting to squander Jerry Lee's gifts on the sordid world of show business, she enrolled him in a bible college in Waxahatchie, TX, secure in the knowledge that her son would now be exclusively singing his songs to the Lord. But legend has it that the Killer tore into a boogie woogie rendition of "My God Is Real" at a church assembly that sent him packing the same night. The split personality of Jerry Lee, torn between the sacred and the profane (rock 'n' roll music), is something that has eaten away at him most of his adult life, causing untold aberrant personality changes over the years with no clear-cut answers to the problem. What is certain is that by the time a 21-year-old Jerry Lee showed up in Memphis on the doorstep of the Sun studios, he *had* been thrown out of bible college, been a complete failure as a sewing machine salesman, been turned down by most Nashville-based record companies *and* the "Louisiana Hayride," been married twice, in jail once and burned with the passion that *he* truly was the next big thing.

Sam Phillips was on vacation when he arrived, but his assistant Jack Clement put Roland Janes on guitar and J.M. Van Eaton on drums behind Jerry Lee, whose fluid left hand made a bass player superfluous. This little unit would become the core of Jerry Lee's recording band for almost the entire seven years he recorded at Sun. The first single, a hopped-up rendition of Ray Price's "Crazy Arms," sold in respectable enough quantities that Phillips kept bringing Lewis back in for more sessions, astounded by his prodigious memory for old songs and his penchant for rocking them up. A few days after his first single was released, Jerry Lee was in the Sun studios earning some Christmas money, playing backup piano on a Carl Perkins session that yielded the classics "Matchbox" and "Your True Love." At the tail end of the recording, Elvis Presley showed up, Clement turned on the tape machine, and the impromptu *Million Dollar Quartet* jam session ensued, with Perkins, Presley and Lewis all having the time of their lives.

With the release of his first single, the road beckoned and it was here that Jerry Lee's stage persona was developed. Discouraged because he couldn't dance around the stage strumming a guitar like Carl Perkins, he stood up in midsong, kicked back the piano stool and, as Carl has so saliently pointed out, "a new Jerry Lee Lewis was born." This new found stage confidence was not lost on Sam Phillips. While he loved the music of Carl Perkins and Johnny Cash, he saw neither artist as a true contender to Elvis' throne; with Jerry Lee he thought he had a real shot. For the first time in his very parsimonious life, Sam Phillips threw every dime of promotional capital he had into Jerry Lee's next single, and the gamble paid off a million times over. "Whole Lotta of Shakin' Goin' On" went to No. 1 on the country and the R&B charts, and was only held out of the top spot on the pop charts by Debbie Reynolds' "Tammy." Suddenly Jerry Lee was the hottest, newest, most exciting rock 'n' roller out there. His television appearances and stage shows were legendary for their manic energy, and his competitive nature to outdo anyone else on the bill led to the story—some say apocryphal—about how he once set his piano on fire at set's end to make it impossible for Chuck Berry to follow his act. Nobody messed with the Killer.

Jerry Lee's follow-up to "Shakin'" was another defining moment for his career, as well as the music's. "Great Balls of Fire" featured only piano and drums, but sounded huge with Phillips' production behind it. It got him into a rock 'n' roll movie (*Jamboree*) and his fame was spreading to such a degree that Johnny Cash and Carl Perkins left Sun to go to Columbia Records. His next single, "Breathless," had a promotional tie-in with Dick Clark's Saturday night "Bandstand" show, making it three hits in a row for the newcomer.

But Jerry Lee was sowing the seeds of his own destruction in record time. He sneaked off and married his 13-year-old cousin, Myra Gale Brown, the daughter of his bass playing uncle, J.W. Brown. With the Killer insisting that she accompany him on a debut tour of England, the British press got wind of the marriage and proceeded to crucify him in the press. The tour was canceled and Jerry Lee arrived back in the US to find his career in absolute disarray. His records were banned nationwide by radio stations and his booking price went from $10,000 a night to $250 in any honky tonk that would still have him. Undeterred, he kept right on doing what he had been doing, head unbowed and determined to make it back to the bigs, Jerry Lee Lewis style. It took him almost a dozen years to pull it off, but finally, with a sympathetic producer and a new record company willing to exact a truce with country disc jockeys, the Killer found a new groove, cutting one smash hit after another throughout the late '60s into the '70s. Still playing rock 'n' roll onstage whenever the mood struck him (which was often) while keeping all his releases pure country struck a creative bargain that suited Lewis well into the mid-'70s.

But while his career was soaring again, his personal life was falling apart. The next decade and a half saw several marriages fall apart (starting with his 13-year-long union with Myra), the deaths of his parents and oldest son, battles with the I.R.S. and bouts with alcohol and pills that frequently left him hospitalized. The Ferriday Fireball was nearing middle age and the raging fire seemed to be burned out.

But the mid-'80s saw another jumpstart to his career. A movie entitled *Great Balls of Fire* was about to be made of his life and Lewis was called in to sing the songs for the soundtrack. Showing everyone who was the real Killer, Jerry Lee sounded energetic enough to make you believe it was 1957 all over again with the pilot light of inspiration still burning bright. He also got a boost back to major label land with a one-song appearance on the soundtrack for *Dick Tracy*.

With box sets and compilations, documentaries, a bioflick and his induction into the Rock & Roll Hall of Fame all celebrating his legacy, Jerry Lee still continues to record and tour, delivering work that vacil-

lates from tepid to absolutely inspired. While his influence will continue to loom large until there's no one left to play rock 'n' roll piano anymore, the plain truth is that there's only *one* Jerry Lee Lewis and American music will never see another one like him. —*Cub Koda*

The Greatest Live Show on Earth / 1964 / Bear Family ✦✦✦✦
Combining two live albums originally issued in the '60s, Lewis proves that the onslaught of the British Invasion hadn't lowered his rocking quotient one single bit. Blazing performances. —*Cub Koda*

☆ **Live at the Star Club** / 1965 / Rhino ✦✦✦✦✦
The Killer at his storming best, dragging his backup group, the Nashville Teens, by the scruff of the neck through a blazing set that earmarks this recording as one of the finest live albums ever made. —*Cub Koda*

★ **18 Original Sun Greatest Hits** / 1984 / Rhino ✦✦✦✦✦
Solid single-disc collection of the records that got Lewis into the Rock & Roll Hall of Fame on the first ballot: "Whole Lotta Shakin' Goin' On," "Great Balls of Fire," "High School Confidential," and "Breathless" being merely the tip of the iceberg. —*Cub Koda*

☆ **Classic** / 1989 / Bear Family ✦✦✦✦✦
Eight-disc boxed set of Lewis' complete output for Sun Records. Along with Muddy Waters' Chess recordings, Louis Armstrong's *Hot Fives & Sevens*, and Hank Williams' undubbed MGM sides, this box comprises one of the finest bodies of American music ever recorded. —*Cub Koda*

★ **All Killer, No Filler: The Anthology** / May 18, 1993 / Rhino ✦✦✦✦✦
Excellent two-disc retrospective of Lewis' career, featuring all his rock and country hits. If the Bear Family box sets are too much for you to handle, this makes an indispensable alternative. —*Cub Koda*

Locust Years . . . and the Return to the Promised Land / 1994 / Bear Family ✦✦✦✦
Picking up where the eight-CD set *Classic* left off, the eight-CD box *The Locust Years . . . and the Return to the Promised Land* rivals its predecessor in quality. Tracing Jerry Lee Lewis' '60s career at Smash Records, the first two discs find the pianist trying to replicate his rock 'n' roll success; while the performances were good, it was clear he was out of touch with the times. During the third disc, he begins to concentrate on country music. The fourth, fifth, and sixth discs match his Sun recordings for consistently brilliant performances; several of the songs became big hits on the country charts, establishing him as a country star. The seventh disc chronicles an exciting unreleased show, while the eighth disc is an unexceptional interview. For dedicated Jerry Lee Lewis fans, *The Locust Years* is every bit as essential as *Classic*. —*Stephen Thomas Erlewine*

● **Killer Country** / 1995 / Mercury ✦✦✦✦
Killer Country is a well-chosen selection of Jerry Lee Lewis' biggest and best country hits from the '60s and '70s, which feature some of his finest performances. —*Stephen Thomas Erlewine*

Smiley Lewis

b. Jul. 5, 1913, DeQuincey, LA, **d.** Oct. 7, 1966, New Orleans, LA
Guitar, Vocals / R&B, New Orleans R&B
Dave Bartholomew has often been quoted to the effect that Smiley Lewis was a "bad luck singer," because he never sold more than 100,000 copies of his Imperial singles. In retrospect, Lewis was a lucky man in many respects—he enjoyed stellar support from New Orleans' ace sessioneers at Cosimo's, benefited from top-flight material and production (by Bartholomew), and left behind a legacy of marvelous Crescent City R&B. We're lucky he was there, that's for sure.

Born with the unwieldy handle of Overton Lemons, Lewis hit the Big Easy in his mid-teens, armed with a big, booming voice and some guitar skills. He played clubs in the French Quarter, often with pianist Tuts Washington (and sometimes billed as "Smiling" Lewis). By 1947, his following was strong enough to merit a session for DeLuxe Records, which issued his debut 78, "Here Comes Smiley." Nothing happened with that platter, but when Lewis signed with Imperial in 1950 (debuting with "Tee-Nah-Nah") things began to move.

As the New Orleans R&B sound developed rapidly during the early '50s, so did Lewis, as he rocked ever harder on "Lillie Mae," "Ain't Gonna Do It," and "Big Mamou." He scored his first national hit in 1952 with "The Bells Are Ringing," but enjoyed his biggest sales in 1955 with the exultant "I Hear You Knocking" (its immortal piano solo courtesy of Huey Smith). Here's where that alleged bad luck rears its head—pop chanteuse Gale Storm swiped his thunder for any pop crossover possibilities with her ludicrous whitewashed cover of the plaintive ballad.

But Storm wouldn't dare come near its roaring flip, the Joe Turnerish rocker "Bumpity Bump," or some of Smiley Lewis' other classic mid-'50s jumpers ("Down the Road," "Lost Weekend," "Real Gone Lover," "She's Got Me Hook, Line and Sinker," "Rootin' and Tootin'"). In front of the Crescent City's hottest players (saxists Lee Allen, Clarence Hall, and Herb Hardesty usually worked his dates), Lewis roared like a lion.

Strangely, Fats Domino fared better with some of Smiley Lewis' tunes than Lewis did ("Blue Monday" in particular). Similarly, Elvis Presley cleaned up the naughty "One Night" and hit big with it, but Lewis' original had already done well in 1956 (as had his melodic "Please Listen to Me"). His blistering "Shame, Shame, Shame" found its way onto the soundtrack of the steamy Hollywood potboiler *Baby Doll* in 1957 but failed to find entry to the R&B charts.

After a long and at least semi-profitable run at Imperial, Lewis moved over to Okeh in 1961 for one single, stopped at Dot in 1964 just long enough to make a solitary 45 (produced by Nashville deejay Bill "Hoss" Allen) and bowed out with an Allen Toussaint-produced remake of "The Bells Are Ringing" for Loma in 1965. By then, stomach cancer was eating the once-stout singer up. He died in the autumn of 1966, all but forgotten outside his New Orleans homebase.

The ensuing decades have rectified that miscarriage of justice, however. Smiley Lewis' place as one of the greatest New Orleans R&B artists of the 1950s is certainly assured. —*Bill Dahl*

● **The Best of** / 1992 / Capitol ✦✦✦✦
Smiley Lewis made several fabulous singles, had a booming, terrific voice, and received the same great backing and support that defined the city's R&B sound. But Lewis' records seldom made it outside New Orleans, even though they were frequently brilliant. This great 24-track anthology contains the four that did make it to the charts, among them the signature song "I Hear You Knocking." It shows Lewis doing first-rate novelty tracks, ballads, weepers, uptempo wailers and blues, and making wonderful recordings. The set also includes a thorough discography and good notes and is superbly mastered. It's magnificent, exuberant R&B, and deserved a much better national fate than it enjoyed. —*Ron Wynn*

☆ **Shame, Shame, Shame** / 1993 / Bear Family ✦✦✦✦✦
Booming-voiced Smiley may have never enjoyed his share of breaks (as his producer Dave Bartholomew never tires of pointing out), but he sure left behind a legacy of blistering 1950s New Orleans R&B. This four-disc boxed set contains every track Lewis cut for Imperial, along with a handful of obscurities issued on Okeh, Dot, and Loma not long before his untimely demise. If EMI's single disc retrospective isn't enough for you, this exhaustively annotated, beautifully presented package is the ultimate source. —*Bill Dahl*

Lightning Seeds

Pop-Rock
Seeds founder Ian Broudie played guitar in Liverpool bands like Big in Japan and Original Mirrors, but he made his name in the music business producing artists like Echo & the Bunnymen, Icicle Works, and the Fall. He collaborated with Wild Swans singer Paul Simpson under the moniker Care, releasing several singles. The Lightning Seeds are essentially a one-man band, with Broudie bringing in help when he needs it. The band's melodic pop has been compared to the Pet Shop Boys, but without the electronics. —*Steve Huey*

● **Cloudcuckooland** / 1989 / MCA ✦✦✦✦
Bouncy pop by Ian Broudie, producer of such groups as the Fall and Echo & the Bunnymen. —*David Szatmary*

Sense / Feb. 18, 1992 / MCA ✦✦✦
There's a certain school of distinctly British pop music characterized by a reserved, dignified demeanor and pretty, fragile melodies. The Lightning Seeds is one exponent of the genre that also includes such groups as Beautiful South and Trashcan Sinatras. The Seeds, mainly the one-man project of Liverpool artist-producer Ian Brodie, have more of a groove than their peers. Many of the songs tend to fall in the New Order camp, except that the vocals are more upfront than the rhythm tracks. —*Roch Parisien*

Jollification / 1994 / Trauma/Interscope ✦✦✦

Pure / Virgin ✦✦✦✦
Pure is an 18-track UK-only collection, covering the Lightning Seeds' biggest hits as well as some of their lesser known, though just as pleasing, songs. —*Chris Woodstra*

Bob Lind

Vocals / Singer-Songwriter, Pop, Folk-Rock
Bob Lind's "Elusive Butterfly" was one of the most successful one-shots of the mid-'60s folk-rock boom, reaching the Top Five in early 1966. He never came close to matching that early triumph, although other acts brought his songs to a wider audience with their covers of Lind compositions like "Cheryl's Going Home" (Blues Project), "Counting" (Marianne Faithfull), and "Mr. Zero" (Yardbirds' lead singer Keith Relf). The beauty of Jack Nitzsche's intricate production on Lind's two 1966 LPs, favoring acoustic guitars and pretty string arrangements, is admirable, but Lind himself hasn't worn that well. His songs are wordy and on the didactic side; his voice is nervous and lacks emotional range; his melodies are pretty, but not enormously so. —*Richie Unterberger*

● **The Best of Bob Lind** / Jun. 29, 1993 / EMI ✦✦✦✦
This 25-song compilation includes the entire contents of his two 1966 LPs, as well as a 1967 single and two previously unreleased tracks. This

period piece is highlighted by "Elusive Butterfly," the original versions of "Counting" and "Cheryl's Goin' Home," "Mr. Zero" (covered by Yardbird lead singer Keith Relf on a flop single), and the previously unreleased, gorgeous baroque rock song "English Afternoon." —*Richie Unterberger*

Little Eva

b. Jun. 29, 1943, Bell Haven, NC
Vocals / Girl Group, Brill Building Pop
Little Eva Narcissus Boyd was a babysitter for Carole King and Gerry Goffin when the songwriting team was inspired to write "Locomotion," a song based on a dance that Eva would do around the house. Eva also got to sing on their demo, which impressed Don Kirshner enough to release it as it was. One of the greatest girl-group hits, "Locomotion," hit No. 1 in 1962; the follow-up, "Keep Your Hands Off My Baby," was also written by Goffin-King. Almost as good as her debut, it reached the Top 20, and was even covered by the Beatles on stage in their early days (though they never recorded it in the studio). Unfortunately, Eva was then pigeonholed as a dance-craze singer and given inferior material. She never again reached the soulful heights of her first two singles; "Let's Turkey Trot" (1963) was her only other Top 20 hit. —*Richie Unterberger*

● **The Best of Little Eva** / 1988 / Murray Hill ✦✦✦✦
Fifteen songs, most cut for the Dimension label between 1962 and 1964. Includes all the hits and some pleasant girl-group flops in a more lightweight style than "Locomotion." —*Richie Unterberger*

The Loco-Motion / Feb. 27, 1996 / Rhino ✦✦✦
Some collectors will be glad to have some Little Eva available on CD domestically. At only ten cuts (and no liner notes), however, it's on the skimpy side, and "Let's Turkey Trot" is unexpectedly missing. The 15-song best-of on Murray Hill is considerably more extensive and well annotated (albeit getting harder to find). On the other hand, this Rhino comp does have seven songs not on the Murray Hill LP (including some obscure Goffin/King compositions), although some of these are covers of popular early '60s hits. —*Richie Unterberger*

Little Feat

Rock 'n' Roll, Blues-Rock
Little Feat was formed in 1970 when Frank Zappa encouraged his guitarist Lowell George to start his own band, after hearing George's original "Willin'." With Zappa bass player Roy Estrada in tow, George enlisted drummer Richie Hayward (formerly of Fraternity of Man) and keyboardist Billy Payne. The band's name came from Jimmy Carl Black's (of the Mothers of Invention) kidding about George's shoe size. Their first albums blended blues, country, and rock with gritty finesse. *Sailin' Shoes* (their second album) is loaded with fine songs and the rudest rock they ever committed to tape. With *Dixie Chicken* (considered by many to be Little Feat's best album), they added Kenny Gradney on bass and Sam Clayton on congas. The result was a New Orleans style of rhythmic gumbo and George's incredible slide guitar work. The title cut sums up many of the band's virtues, possessing a rubbery groove, off-kilter instrumental parts, and a classic, dryly humorous Lowell George tale. Subsequent albums increasingly sanded off the rough edges in favor of an eccentric fusion-like equivalent to the late-'70s Doobie Brothers.

Little Feat disbanded in April 1979 and Lowell George set out for a solo career, releasing the album *Thanks, I'll Eat It Here*. On June 29, 1979, George was found dead of a heart attack brought on from drug abuse.

In 1988 Little Feat reunited with former Pure Prairie League singer and guitarist Craig Fuller filling George's slot. Since then, the band has regained its status as a solid concert draw and has released several albums. —*Rick Clark*

Little Feat / 1971 / Warner Bros. ✦✦✦
Debut album finds Lowell George's songwriting, singing, and playing style in place on his signature song, "Willin'," as well as "Truck Stop Run" and "Crazy Captain Gunboat Willie." —*William Ruhlmann*

Sailin' Shoes / 1972 / Warner Bros. ✦✦✦✦
A near-peak of songwriting ("Easy to Slip," "Cold, Cold, Cold," "Sailin' Shoes") distinguishes this second album, on which the band finds a perfect second-line groove and Lowell George sings and plays with blues authority. —*William Ruhlmann*

★ **Dixie Chicken** / 1973 / Warner Bros. ✦✦✦✦✦
A reconfigured group adds greater depth to the percussion, along with a rhythm guitarist, who frees Lowell George to slide his way to heaven, and the songs—especially the title track, "Two Trains," and "Fat Man in the Bathtub"—are among George's best. —*William Ruhlmann*

Feats Don't Fail Me Now / 1974 / Warner Bros. ✦✦✦✦
Whereas earlier albums were carried by Lowell George, this one finds the band as a whole at a writing and performing peak, with Bill Payne and Paul Berrere especially standing out on such songs as "Rock and Roll Doctor," "Oh Atlanta," and "Skin It Back." —*William Ruhlmann*

The Last Record Album / 1975 / Warner Bros. ✦✦✦
From this point on, Lowell George's role in Little Feat seems to have diminished, with the group's direction increasingly left in the capable, if less inspired, hands of Bill Payne and Paul Barrere. The album does, however, contain two excellent George originals in "Down Below the Borderline" and "Long Distance Love." — *William Ruhlmann*

Time Loves a Hero / 1977 / Warner Bros. ✦✦✦
Lowell George's gradual disappearance from his own group continued here, with the album containing only one of his solo compositions, "Rocket in My Pocket," which wasn't one of his best. The title track and "Hi Holler," among other tracks, show Paul Barrere and Bill Payne to be talented substitutes, but this album, the original group's final studio effort, does not show them at their best. — *William Ruhlmann*

Waiting for Columbus / 1978 / Warner Bros. ✦✦✦✦
Excellent double-disc live album. — *William Ruhlmann*

Down on the Farm / 1979 / Warner Bros. ✦✦

Hoy-Hoy / 1981 / Warner Bros. ✦✦✦✦
Compilation of best songs and odds and ends makes a good wrap-up to the Lowell George years. — *William Ruhlmann*

Let It Roll / Jul. 1988 / Warner Bros. ✦✦✦

Representing the Mambo / 1989 / Warner Bros. ✦✦

Shake Me Up / Sep. 24, 1991 / Morgan Creek ✦✦

Ain't Had Enough Fun / 1995 / Zoo ✦✦✦

Live from Neon Park / Jun. 18, 1996 / ZOO ✦✦✦

Little Richard (Richard Wayne Penniman)

b. 1935
Piano, Vocals / R&B, Rock 'n' Roll, New Orleans R&B
Little Richard may or may not have been "the king of rock 'n' roll," as he eagerly proclaims to this day. But of all the major rock 'n' rollers of the 1950s, he certainly was the most flamboyant. Merging the fire of gospel with New Orleans R&B, he pounded the piano and wailed with gleeful abandon, brandishing a six-inch pompadour and mascara that were downright outlandish for the time—and more than a little threatening. Although he was only a hitmaker for a couple of years or so, his influence upon both the soul and British Invasion stars of the 1960s was vast, and he remains one of the yardsticks by which sheer rock 'n' roll outrageousness is measured.

Heavily steeped in gospel music while growing up in Georgia, when Little Richard began recording in the early '50s, he played unexceptional jump blues/R&B that owed a lot to his early inspirations Billy Wright and Roy Brown. In 1955, at Lloyd Price's suggestion, Richard sent a demo tape to Specialty Records, who were impressed enough to sign him and arrange a session for him in New Orleans. That session, however, didn't get off the ground until Richard began fooling around with a slightly obscene ditty during a break. With slightly cleaned-up lyrics, "Tutti Frutti" was the record that gave birth to Little Richard as we know him—the ecstatic trilling "woo!," the furious piano playing, the sax-driven, pedal-to-the-metal rhythm section. It was also his first hit, although, ridiculous as it now seems, Pat Boone's cover version outdid Richard's on the hit parade.

Pat Boone would also try to cover Richard's next hit, "Long Tall Sally," but by that time it was evident that audiences Black *and* White much preferred the real deal. In 1956 and 1957, Richard reeled off a string of classic hits—"Long Tall Sally," "Slippin' and Slidin'," "Jenny, Jenny," "Keep a Knockin'," "Good Golly, Miss Molly," "The Girl Can't Help It"—that remain the foundation of his fame. While Richard's inimitable mania was the key to his best records, he also owed a lot of his success to the gutsy playing of ace New Orleans session players like Lee Allen (tenor sax), Alvin Tyler (baritone sax), and especially Earl Palmer (drummer), who usually accompanied the singer in both New Orleans and Los Angeles studios. Richard's unforgettable appearances in early rock 'n' roll movies, especially *The Girl Can't Help It*, also did a lot to spread the rock 'n' roll gospel to the masses.

Little Richard was at the height of his commercial and artistic powers when he suddenly quit the business during an Australian tour in late 1957, enrolling in a bible college in Alabama shortly after returning to the States. Richard had actually been feeling the call of religion for a while before his announcement, but it was nonetheless a shock to both his fans and the industry. Specialty drew on unreleased sessions for a few more hard-rocking singles in the late '50s, but Richard virtually vanished from the public eye for a few years. When he did return to recording, it was as a gospel singer, cutting a few little-heard sacred sides for End, Mercury, and Atlantic in the early '60s.

By 1962, though, Richard had returned to rock 'n' roll, touring Britain to an enthusiastic reception. Among the groups that supported him on those jaunts were the Rolling Stones and the Beatles, whose vocals (Paul McCartney's especially) took a lot of inspiration from Richard's. In 1964, the Beatles cut a knockout version of "Long Tall Sally," with McCartney

on lead, that may have even outdone the original. It's been speculated that the success of the Beatles and other British Invaders who idolized Richard finally prompted the singer into making a full-scale comeback as an unapologetic rock 'n' roller. Hooking up with Specialty once again, he had a small hit in 1964 with "Bama Lama Bama Loo." These and other sides were respectable efforts in the mold of his classic '50s sides, but tastes had changed too much for Little Richard to climb the charts again. He spent the rest of the '60s in a continual unsuccessful comeback, recording for Vee-Jay (accompanied on some sides by Jimi Hendrix, who was briefly in Richard's band), OKeh, and Modern (for whom he even tried recording in Memphis with Stax session musicians).

It was the rock 'n' roll revival of the late '60s and early '70s, though, that really saved Richard's career, enabling him to play on the nostalgia circuit with great success (though he had one last small hit, "Freedom Blues," in 1970). Constant entertaining appearances on television talk shows seemed to ensure his continuing success as a living legend, yet by the late '70s he'd returned to the church again. Somewhat predictably, he'd eased back into rock and show business by the mid-'80s. Since then, he's maintained his profile with a role in *Down and Out in Beverly Hills*, and guest appearances on soundtracks, compilations, and children's rock records. At this point it's safe to assume that he never will get that much-hungered-for comeback hit, but he remains one of rock 'n' roll's most colorful icons, still capable of turning on the charm and charisma in his infrequent appearances in the limelight. —*Richie Unterberger*

★ **18 Greatest Hits** / 1985 / Rhino ✦✦✦✦✦
18 Greatest Hits is the definitive single-disc collection of Little Richard's Specialty singles, especially for listeners who only want the hits. Every one of Richard's biggest hits—"Tutti Frutti," "Long Tall Sally," "Slippin' and Slidin'," "Rip It Up," "Ready Teddy," "The Girl Can't Help It," "Lucille," "Send Me Some Lovin'," "Keep A-Knockin'," "Good Golly Miss Molly"—plus singles like "Heeby-Jeebies," "She's Got It," "Ooh! My Soul," "Miss Ann," "Kansas City/Hey Hey Hey," and "Bama Lama Bama Loo" that were bigger hits on the R&B charts than the pop charts. All of the singles are presented in chronological order and the disc simply rips it up from beginning to end. It's a definitive collection. —*Stephen Thomas Erlewine*

☆ **Specialty Box Set** / 1989 / Ace ✦✦✦✦✦
About a year after Ace Records released a six-disc box set of Little Richard's complete recordings for Specialty Records, Specialty released a condensed, three-disc version in the US, featuring all of his master takes plus assorted alternate takes, outtakes, demos and commercials. Out of the two sets, the three-disc *The Specialty Sessions* is the preferable of the two, because it is more judicious with its inclusion of alternate takes. Many of Little Richard's alternate takes are nearly identical to the released take, with the differences usually noticeable only to obsessive listeners. However, by using only the most interesting alternate takes—like the version of "Keep A-Knockin'" that contains the verse, "I'm drinkin' gin and you can't come in"—*The Specialty Sessions* manages to appeal to both completists and casual fans; the Ace set is only of interest to historians. Although a comprehensive box set can't replicate the exhilarating rush of any Little Richard singles compilation, it does illustrate the depth and breadth of his music and emphasize how timeless his music actually is. For fans that want more than just the obvious hits and for any serious rock 'n' roll fan, *The Specialty Sessions* is a necessary purchase. —*Stephen Thomas Erlewine*

The Formative Years 1951-53 / Jul. 1989 / Bear Family ✦✦✦✦
Early Richard, pre-"Tutti Frutti." —*Cub Koda*

★ **The Georgia Peach** / 1991 / Specialty ✦✦✦✦✦
Perhaps the greatest of Little Richard's greatest hits compilations, the 25-track *Georgia Peach* features all of his biggest hits in chronological order, as well as terrific singles that never were as big as "Tutti Frutti" and "Good Golly Miss Molly." On top of the sublime song selection and sound, the liner notes by compiler Billy Vera are splendid and insightful. —*Stephen Thomas Erlewine*

Shag on Down By the Union Hall / Feb. 13, 1996 / Specialty ✦✦✦✦
For those who want more classic Little Richard than a greatest-hits collection but aren't devoted enough to spring for the expensive box sets, this is an excellent anthology of 24 of his best lesser-known tracks. Most of it dates from his classic era at Specialty (1955-57), with alternate takes of a lot of his hits and some decent B-sides; there are also a few songs that he cut for the label during his 1964 comeback, including the minor hit "Bama Lama Bama Loo." —*Richie Unterberger*

Little Willie John (William Edgar John)

b. Nov. 15, 1937, Cullendale, AK, **d.** May 26, 1968, Walla Walla, WA
Vocals / Soul, R&B
He's never received the accolades given to the likes of Sam Cooke, Clyde McPhatter, and James Brown, but Little Willie John ranks as one of R&B's most influential performers. His muscular high timbre and enormous technical and emotional range belied his early age (his first hit came

when he was 18), but his mid-'50s work for Syd Nathan's King label would play a great part in the way soul music would sound. Everyone from Cooke, McPhatter, and Brown to Jackie Wilson, B.B. King, and Al Green has acknowledged his debt to this most overlooked of rock and soul pioneers. His debut recording, a smoking version of Titus Turner's "All around the World" from 1955, set the pattern for a remarkable string of hits: "Need Your Love So Bad," "Suffering with the Blues," "Fever," "Let Them Talk," and his last, "Sleep," from 1961. His version of "Fever" was copied note for note by Peggy Lee and Elvis Presley, both of whom had bigger hits with it; John's version, however, remains definitive. His second hit, "Need Your Love So Bad," contains one of the most intimate, tear-jerking vocals ever caught on tape.

John had a volatile temper, fueled by a taste for liquor and an insecurity regarding his slight height (5 ft 4 in). He was known to pack a gun and knife; in 1964, he stabbed a man and was sent to the Washington State penitentiary, where he died of pneumonia in 1968. James Brown recorded a tribute album to John that year, and his material has been recorded by scores of artists from the Beatles to Fleetwood Mac to the Blasters. Nevertheless, Little Willie John remains a stranger to most listeners and has never received the respect his talent deserves.

Little Willie John was one of the first artists featured in Rhino's King reissues series. *Fever* was issued late in 1993, and the 20-track anthology included such John releases as "Need Your Love So Bad," "Suffering with the Blues," and the title cut. —*John Floyd*

● **Fever: The Best of Little Willie John** / 1993 / Rhino ◆◆◆◆
Little Willie John had a commanding delivery, remarkable projection and a charismatic sound that was both instantly recognizable and unforgettable. His magical singles are contained on this superb 20-track anthology, arguably the best single-disc set of John material available. It includes his best-known song, "Fever" (Peggy Lee's cover version became a smash), plus such marvelous numbers such as "Home At Last," "Heartbreak (It's Hurtin' Me)" and "You Hurt Me." While John was a dynamic heartache talent, he could also do dance/novelty and double-entendre tunes such as "Let's Rock While The Rockin's Good" and "Leave My Kitten Alone." This anthology demonstrates why he's held in such high regard throughout the world of R&B and soul. —*Ron Wynn*

Live

Alternative Pop-Rock, Post-Grunge
With their muscular R.E.M. and U2 hybrid, Live straddles the line between alternative rock credibility and mainstream radio accessibility. When their first album was released, it was a moderate commercial success, made all the more impressive considering the reluctance of radio regarding alternative-oriented music. *Throwing Copper*, their second album, shot to the top of college charts when it was released in the spring of 1994, as well as receiving a substantial amount of mainstream sales and play on pop radio. In early 1995, the No. 1 album rock and modern rock single "Lightning Crashes" sent *Throwing Copper* into the pop Top Ten and by the summer, it had sold over four million copies. —*Stephen Thomas Erlewine*

Mental Jewelry / 1991 / Radioactive ◆◆◆◆
Live's debut album was an impressive set of righteous, hard-driving alternative rock; *Mental Jewelry* was in the vein of such college-radio favorites as U2, but was more vulnerable and less sanctimonious. —*Stephen Thomas Erlewine*

● **Throwing Copper** / 1994 / Radioactive ◆◆◆◆
Not only did Live's songwriting improve on their second album, *Throwing Copper*, but their sound was much stronger; their hooks were powerful and memorable, and their melodies were carefully crafted and catchy. The result was a major crossover hit, thanks to the singles "Selling the Drama," "I Alone," and "Lightning Crashes." —*Stephen Thomas Erlewine*

Lively Ones

Surf
One of the best of the many instrumental surf bands working the Southern Californian region in 1963, the Lively Ones' recordings were built around storming, reverb-drenched Fender guitars, embellished by occasional raunchy sax breaks. Originality was not the Lively Ones' forte: over a period of about 12 months, they ground out about five albums, filled out with many covers or retitled numbers based on other rock and R&B compositions. They had a couple of hits in the L.A. area in 1963 ("Surf Rider" and "Rik-A-Tik"), but their best moment was probably "Goofy Foot," whose staccato gunfire of riffs deservedly propelled the track onto several modern best-of-surf anthologies. They ranged far and wide for source material, giving the surf treatment to "Telstar," "Exodus," "Rawhide," and Cole Porter's "Night and Day." Even the overdone standards are arranged and executed with panache. One best-of compilation is all you need, but anyone who likes Dick Dale will dig the Lively Ones' similar sleek arrangements and prototypically twangy, classy surf guitar leads. —*Richie Unterberger*

Surf Rider / 1963 / Del Fi ◆◆◆

● **Hang Five!!! The Best of the Livelys** / 1995 / Del Fi ◆◆◆◆
A well-chosen 24-song retrospective, with six pages of informative liner notes by surf authority Domenic Priore. Includes "Goofy Foot," "Surf Rider," "Rik-A-Tik," and lots of other highlights from their Del-Fi releases, as well as a rare single they did for Smash. —*Richie Unterberger*

Loggins & Messina

Folk-Rock, Pop-Rock
Kenny Loggins and Jim Messina were the most successful pop-rock duo of the first half of the '70s. Loggins was a staff songwriter who had recently enjoyed success with a group of songs recorded by the Nitty Gritty Dirt Band when he came to the attention of Messina, a record producer and former member of Buffalo Springfield and Poco. Messina agreed to produce Loggins' first album, but somewhere along the way it became a duo effort that was released in 1972 under the title *Kenny Loggins with Jim Messina Sittin' In*. The album was a gold-seller that stayed in the charts more than two years.

In the next four years, Loggins & Messina released a series of gold or platinum albums, most of which hit the Top Ten. They were all played in a buoyant country-rock style with an accomplished band. *Loggins & Messina* (1972) featured the retro-rock hit "Your Mama Don't Dance." *Full Sail* (1973), *On Stage* (a double live album, 1974), and *Mother Lode* (1974) all hit the Top Ten. *So Fine* was an album of '50s cover songs. The pair's last new studio album, *Native Sons*, came out at the start of 1976.

Loggins & Messina split for two solo careers by the end of that year, their catalog completed by a greatest-hits album, *Best of Friends*, and a live record, *Finale*. —*William Ruhlmann*

● **The Best of Friends** / Nov. 1976 / Columbia ◆◆◆◆
Collects their biggest hits from "Your Mama Don't Dance" onward. —*Dan Heilman*

Kenny Loggins

b. Jan. 7, 1948, Everett, WA
Guitar, Keyboards, Vocals / Soft Rock, Pop-Rock
Singer, songwriter, and guitarist Kenny Loggins was born in Everett, WA, and moved to Los Angeles in his teens. He got a job as a staff writer and wrote four songs used on a Nitty Gritty Dirt Band album in 1970, among them the hit "House at Pooh Corner." This brought him to the attention of former Poco member Jim Messina, now a staff producer at CBS, who intended to produce Loggins' debut album. The two ended up in a duo, however, and Loggins & Messina made a series of successful albums during the '70s.

Loggins & Messina broke up in 1976, and Loggins went on to solo stardom with such million-selling albums as *Celebrate Me Home*, *Nightwatch* (which included the hit "Whenever I Call Your Friend"), and *Keep the Fire*, all in the cheerful, sensitive style he had displayed in Loggins & Messina. Loggins also became known as the king of the movie soundtrack song, scoring Top Ten hits with "I'm Alright" (from *Caddyshack*), "Footloose" (from *Footloose*), "Danger Zone" (from *Top Gun*), and "Nobody's Fool" (from *Caddyshack II*). His own albums sold less well (and came less frequently) throughout the '80s. —*William Ruhlmann*

Celebrate Me Home / Apr. 1977 / Columbia ◆◆◆

Nightwatch / Jun. 1978 / Columbia ◆◆◆

Keep the Fire / Oct. 1979 / Columbia ◆◆◆

● **Kenny Loggins Alive** / Sep. 1980 / Columbia ◆◆◆◆
This extended live effort arrived on the wings of Loggins' No. 7 hit "I'm Alright," from the movie soundtrack of *Caddyshack*. The concert version included here is much better, stripped of some of the cute studio tricks found on the single. Most of the material comes from previously released studio tracks, which are given faithful (but livelier) readings. —*Rick Clark*

High Adventure / Sep. 1982 / Columbia ◆◆◆◆
Loggins continued his successful string of hit albums with this release. A light mainstream rock duet with Journey lead-singer Steve Perry, titled "Don't Fight It," reached No. 17, while Loggins turned in a couple of MOR hits with "Heart to Heart" and "Welcome to Heartlight." As with all of his albums to this point, his sound is pleasant and well crafted. —*Rick Clark*

Lone Justice

Country-Rock, Roots-Rock
Lone Justice in its original form, ca. 1983, was a quartet based in Los Angeles and featuring singer Maria McKee (b. 1964), guitarist Ryan Hedgecock (b. ca. 1960), bassist Marvin Etzioni, and drummer Don Heffington. The group played in a country-rock style on their debut album, *Lone Justice* (1985). By the time of the second album, *Shelter* (1986), they had turned more toward mainstream rock and become a sextet, with only McKee and Hedgecock remaining from the original unit. Then Lone

Justice broke up, and McKee went on to a solo career. —*William Ruhl-mann*

● **Lone Justice** / 1985 / Geffen ✦✦✦✦
Maria McKee has one of those aching, little-girl voices (not unlike Stevie Nicks'), and it's heard to great effect on these country-rock tunes, especially Tom Petty and Mike Campbell's "Ways to Be Wicked." —*William Ruhlmann*

Shelter / 1986 / Geffen ✦✦✦

Long Ryders

Country-Rock, Roots-Rock
Although they played the same clubs as most of Los Angeles' "paisley underground" bands (i.e., Dream Syndicate, Rain Parade) and even featured Dream Syndicate leader Steve Wynn in an early lineup, the Long Ryders were actually more a roots-rock group strongly influenced by Gram Parsons. The group was founded by Kentucky native Sid Griffin, a Parsons devotee who moved to Los Angeles after hearing about that city's punk scene, with guitarist Stephen McCarthy, the only two members to remain throughout the group's tenure. The group's first rhythm section featured bassist Barry Shank and drummer Matt Roberts; they, along with Griffin, had previously been members of the Unclaimed. The band's 1983 debut EP, *10-5-60*, was a blend of punk attitude, '60s rock, and traditional country (Griffin played steel guitar, autoharp, and mandolin). Their first full-length album, the following year's *Native Sons*, was also arguably their best, and featured guest vocals from former Byrd Gene Clark. Subsequent albums failed to find an audience, and unhappy with their label's promotional efforts but unable to secure a release from their contract, the Long Ryders called it quits in 1987. McCarthy formed Gutterball and, along with Griffin, contributed to the 1993 Gram Parsons tribute album *Commemorativo*. Griffin, meanwhile, moved to London and formed the Coal Porters; today he works as a music critic and writer, foreshadowed by his definitive 1985 biography of (who else?) Gram Parsons. —*Steve Huey*

Native Sons / 1984 / Frontier ✦✦✦✦
This updates The Byrds and Gram Parsons. —*Robert Gordon*

● **State of Our Union** / 1985 / Island ✦✦✦✦
American country-tinged rock 'n' roll. —*Robert Gordon*

Los Lobos

Tex-Mex, Roots-Rock
Los Lobos were one of America's most distinctive and original bands of the '80s. They may have had a hit with "La Bamba" in 1987, yet that cover barely scratches the surface of their talents. Los Lobos are eclectic in the best sense of the word. While they draw equally from rock, Tex-Mex, country, folk, R&B, blues, and traditional Spanish and Mexican music, their music never sounds forced or self-conscious. Instead, all of their influences became one graceful, gritty sound. From their very first recordings their rich musicality was apparent; on nearly every subsequent record they have found ways to redefine and expand their sound, without ever straying from the musical traditions that form the heart and soul of the band. After releasing an independent EP in the late '70s and an EP in 1983, Los Lobos delivered their first major-label album, *How Will the Wolf Survive*, in 1984; it received an enormous amount of critical acclaim, as well as a dedicated following of fans. In the next four years, they released a marginally successful attempt to make their wildly eclectic sound palatable for a pop audience (*By the Light of the Moon*), a soundtrack of old Ritchie Valens songs that was a hit (*La Bamba*), and an album of traditional Mexican music (*La Pistola y El Corazon*). The band took two years off and returned with *The Neighborhood* in 1990; the album was a varied and powerful rock 'n' roll record that was better than anything they had released in six years. *Kiko*, released in 1992, brought the band into more experimental territory, without ever abandoning their graceful songwriting. Los Lobos released a career retrospective, *Just Another Band from East LA: A Collection*, in 1993. The following year, David Hidalgo and Louie Pereze released a side project called *Latin Playboys*, which also featured producers Mitchell Froom and Tchad Blake. In 1995, the group released a children's album called *Papa's Dream*. In the spring of 1996, Los Lobos released *Colossal Head*, the proper follow-up to *Kiko*. —*Stephen Thomas Erlewine*

...and a Time to Dance / 1983 / Slash ✦✦✦

● **How Will the Wolf Survive?** / 1984 / Slash ✦✦✦✦
A broader spectrum of music without a measure of the all-out joy of *... And a Time to Dance, How Will the Wolf Survive?* features at least two raveup rockers ("Don't Worry Baby" and "I Got Loaded"), an irresistible shuffle ("Evangeline"), two traditional Mexican numbers ("Seranata Norteña" and "Corrida No.1") and a stirring title tune. The album is well rounded and fully realized. —*Kit Kiefer*

By the Light of the Moon / 1987 / Slash ✦✦✦

La Bamba [O.S.T.] / Jun. 1987 / Slash ✦✦✦

La Pistola y El Corazon / Sep. 1988 / Slash ✦✦✦

The Neighborhood / 1990 / Slash ✦✦✦

Kiko / May 1992 / Slash ✦✦✦✦
With its highly textured layers of sound, *Kiko* sounds like nothing else Los Lobos has done. Although their sound is still based in roots music of all kinds (rock, folk, Mexican, country), the band has shaped it into a dense, impressionistic wall of sound that intensifies the emotions behind such carefully constructed and moving songs as "Two Janes," "Angels with Dirty Faces," and "Kiko and the Lavender Moon." It's certainly their most ambitious album, and it's arguably their best. —*Stephen Thomas Erlewine*

● **Just Another Band from East L.A.: A Collection** / Aug. 31, 1993 / Slash ✦✦✦✦
Just Another Band from East L.A.: A Collection is a splendid double-disc collection that draws an accurate picture of Los Lobos, one of the most musically versatile bands of the 1980s. Featuring all of the band's hits and best-known songs, as well as several rare and previously unreleased tracks, there isn't a weak spot among the compilation's forty-one songs. —*Stephen Thomas Erlewine*

Colossal Head / Mar. 19, 1996 / Warner Bros. ✦

Loud Family

Alternative Pop-Rock, Power-Pop
After dissolving Game Theory, Scott Miller formed Loud Family, releasing their album, *Plants and Birds and Rocks and Things*, on Alias Records. *Plants and Birds and Rocks and Things* received good reviews and maintained Miller's cult following, as did the EP, 1993's *Slouching Towards Liverpool*. In 1994, Loud Family released their second album, *The Tape of Only Linda*. The group's third album, *Interbabe Concern*, appeared in the late summer of 1996. —*Stephen Thomas Erlewine*

● **Plants and Birds and Rocks and Things** / 1992 / Alias ✦✦✦✦
Former Game Theory frontman Scott Miller returns with a new band and his classic style of power-pop. With a sound similar to the experimental *Lolita Nation*, Miller builds on his former band's strong points while leaving behind much of its excesses. *Plants and Birds and Rocks and Things* will be pleasantly familiar to old fans and will no doubt inspire newcomers to seek out Game Theory albums. —*Chris Woodstra*

Tape of Only Linda / 1994 / Alias ✦✦✦

Love

Psychedelic, Folk-Rock
One of the best West Coast folk-rock/psychedelic bands, Love may have also been the first widely acclaimed cult/underground group. During their brief heyday—lasting all of three albums—they drew from Byrdsish folk-rock, Stonesish hard rock, blues, jazz, flamenco, and even light orchestral pop to create a heady stew of their own. They were also one of the first integrated rock groups, led by genius singer-songwriter Arthur Lee, one of the most idiosyncratic and enigmatic talents of the 1960s. Stars in their native Los Angeles, and an early inspiration to the Doors, they perversely refused to tour until well past their peak. This ensured their failure to land a hit single or album, though in truth the band's vision may have been too elusive to attract mass success anyway.

Love was formed by Lee in in the mid-'60s in Los Angeles. Although only 20 at the time, Lee had already scuffled around the fringes of the rock and soul business for a couple of years. In addition to recording some flop singles with his own bands, he wrote and produced a single for Rosa Lee Brooks that Jimi Hendrix played on as session guitarist. Originally calling his outfit the Grass Roots, Lee changed the name to Love after another Los Angeles group called the Grass Roots began recording for Dunhill. Love's repertoire would be largely penned by Lee, with a few contributions by guitarist Bryan Maclean.

Inspired by British Invasion bands and local peers the Byrds, Love built up a strong following in hip L.A. clubs. Soon they were signed by Elektra, the noted folk label that was just starting to get its feet wet in rock (it had recorded material by early versions of the Byrds and the Lovin' Spoonful, and had just released the first LP by Paul Butterfield). Their self-titled debut album (1966) introduced their marriage of the Byrds and the Stones on a set of mostly original material, and contained a small hit, their punkish adaptation of Bacharach-David's "My Little Red Book." Love briefly expanded to a seven-piece for their second album, *Da Capo* (1967), which included their only Top 40 hit, the corkscrew-tempoed "7 and 7 Is." The first side was psychedelia at its best, with an eclectic palette encompassing furious jazz structures, gentle Spanish guitar interludes, and beautiful baroque pop with dream-like images ("She Comes in Colors"). It was also psychedelia at its most reckless, with the whole of side two taken up by a meandering 19-minute jam. It was still a great step forward, but by mid-'67, the band was threatening to disintegrate due to drugs and general disorganization.

The group was in such sad shape, apparently, that Elektra planned to record their third album with session men backing Lee (on his composi-

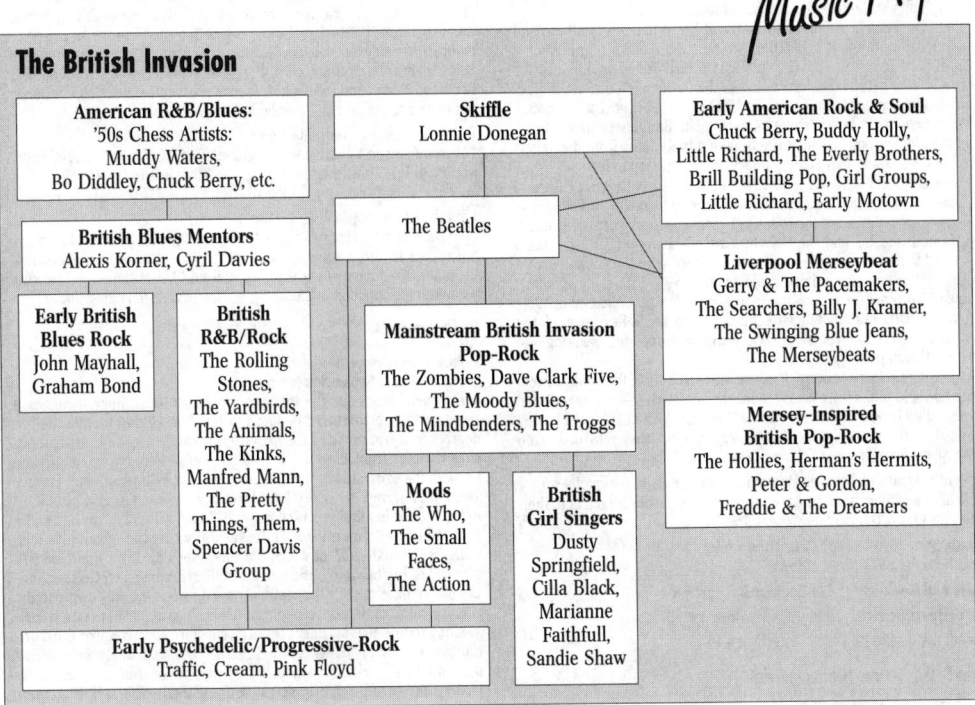

The British Invasion

American R&B/Blues:
'50s Chess Artists:
Muddy Waters,
Bo Diddley, Chuck Berry, etc.

Skiffle
Lonnie Donegan

Early American Rock & Soul
Chuck Berry, Buddy Holly,
Little Richard, The Everly Brothers,
Brill Building Pop, Girl Groups,
Little Richard, Early Motown

British Blues Mentors
Alexis Korner, Cyril Davies

The Beatles

Liverpool Merseybeat
Gerry & The Pacemakers,
The Searchers, Billy J. Kramer,
The Swinging Blue Jeans,
The Merseybeats

Early British Blues Rock
John Mayhall,
Graham Bond

British R&B/Rock
The Rolling Stones,
The Yardbirds,
The Animals,
The Kinks,
Manfred Mann,
The Pretty Things, Them,
Spencer Davis Group

Mainstream British Invasion Pop-Rock
The Zombies, Dave Clark Five,
The Moody Blues,
The Mindbenders, The Troggs

Mersey-Inspired British Pop-Rock
The Hollies, Herman's Hermits,
Peter & Gordon,
Freddie & The Dreamers

Mods
The Who,
The Small Faces,
The Action

British Girl Singers
Dusty Springfield,
Cilla Black,
Marianne Faithfull,
Sandie Shaw

Early Psychedelic/Progressive-Rock
Traffic, Cream, Pink Floyd

---

tions) or Maclean (on his compositions). Work on two tracks actually commenced in this fashion, but the shocked band pulled itself together to play their own material again, resulting in one of the finest rock albums of all time, *Forever Changes*. An exceptionally strong set of material graced by captivating lyrics and glistening, unobtrusive horn and string arrangements, it was not a commercial hit in the US (though it did pretty well in Britain), but remains an all-time favorite of many critics. Just at the point where they seemed poised to assert themselves as a top band, Love's first and best lineup was broken up in early 1968, at Arthur Lee's instigation. Several albums followed in the late '60s and early '70s which, though credited to Love, are in reality Arthur Lee and backup musicians—none of whom had skills on the level of Bryan Maclean or the other original Love men. Lee largely forsook folk-rock for hard rock, with unimpressive results, even when he was able to get Jimi Hendrix to play on one track. The problems ran deeper than unsympathetic accompaniment: Lee's songwriting muse had largely deserted him as well, and nothing on the post-*Forever Changes* albums competes with the early Elektra records.

Lee released a solo album in the early '70s, and then put another Love together for a last effort in 1974, but Love/Lee (the two had in effect become synonymous) ground to a halt in the mid-'70s. Lee's sporadically recorded and performed since then without coming up with anything resembling a unified full-length studio statement, though some scattered live and studio recordings have appeared, the most recent being a 1994 single on the tiny Distortions label. —*Richie Unterberger*

Love / 1966 / Elektra ✦✦✦✦
Their debut is both their hardest-rocking early album, and their most Byrds-influenced. Lee's songwriting muse hadn't fully developed at this stage, and in comparison with their second and third efforts, this is the least striking of the LPs featuring their classic lineup, with some similar-sounding folk-rock compositions and stock riffs. A few of the tracks are great, though: their punky rendition of Bacharach/David's "My Little Red Book" was a minor hit, "Signed D.C." and "Mushroom Clouds" were superbly moody ballads, and Bryan Maclean's "Softly to Me" served notice that Lee wasn't the only songwriter of note in the band. —*Richie Unterberger*

Da Capo / 1967 / Elektra ✦✦✦✦
Love broadened their scope into psychedelia on their sophomore effort, Lee's achingly melodic songwriting gifts reaching full flower. The six songs that comprised the first side of this album when it was first issued are a truly classic body of work, highlighted by the atomic blast of pre-punk rock "Seven and Seven Is" (their only hit single), the manic jazz

tempos of "Stephanie Knows Who," and the enchanting "She Comes in Colors," perhaps Lee's best composition (and reportedly the inspiration for the Rolling Stones' "She's a Rainbow"). It's only half a great album, though; the seventh and final track, "Revelation," is a tedious 19-minute jam that keeps *Da Capo* from attaining truly classic status. —*Richie Unterberger*

★ **Forever Changes** / 1967 / Elektra ✦✦✦✦
It wasn't a hit, but *Forever Changes* continues to regularly appear on critics' lists of the top ten rock albums of all time, and it had an enormously far-reaching and durable influence that went way beyond chart listings. The best fusion of folk-rock and psychedelia, it features Lee's trembling vocals, beautiful melodies, haunting orchestral arrangements, and inscrutable but poetic lyrics, all of which sound nearly as fresh and intriguing upon repeated plays. One of rock's most organic, flowing masterpieces, every song has a lingering, shimmering beauty, including the two penned by the band's other talented songwriter/guitarist/singer, Bryan Maclean. —*Richie Unterberger*

Four Sail / 1969 / Elektra ✦✦

Out Here / 1969 / One Way ✦✦

Love Live / **Studio** / 1982 / One Way ✦✦

● **Love Story 1966-1972** / 1995 / Rhino ✦✦✦✦
Double-CD box contains most of their classic first three albums (including the entirety of *Forever Changes*), all three non-LP tracks from their 1966-68 prime, and highlights of the better post-Bryan Maclean albums from the late '60s and early '70s. Great booklet of liner notes and photos, but considering that all of those first three albums remain easy to find, and that the post-*Forever Changes* material is far inferior to the early recordings, it's not an essential purchase. The absence of "Revelation" from *Da Capo* is no big deal, but a few tracks from the debut are missing, including one of the better ones, "Mushroom Clouds." —*Richie Unterberger*

Love & Rockets

Alternative Pop-Rock, Goth-Rock
Love & Rockets comprised guitarist/vocalist Daniel Ash, bassist/vocalist David J, and drummer Kevin Haskins, all former members of the pioneering goth band Bauhaus. However, the group didn't sound very similar to their first group. Instead, Love & Rockets emphasized the strains of psychedelia and glam rock that appeared underneath Bauhaus' gloomy drone, adding elements of pop songcraft, folk, and R&B, as well as cryptic, self-important lyrics. For most of the late '80s, the group had a devoted

cult following, resulting in a surprise Top Ten hit single, "So Alive," in 1989. During the early '90s, the group's audience steadily declined, although they still retained a number of loyal fans.

After Bauhaus broke up in 1983, David J recorded a solo album and collaborated with the Jazz Butcher, while Daniel Ash concentrated on a side project, Tones on Tail. Haskins soon joined Tones on Tail, but the group folded in 1984. Haskins and Ash then attempted to reunite Bauhaus. David J agreed to the project but the band's lead vocalist Peter Murphy refused. Instead of pursuing an incomplete Bauhaus reunion, Ash, J, and Haskins formed Love & Rockets, taking their name from the underground comic book written by Jaime and Gilbert Hernandez.

Love & Rockets released their first album, *Seventh Dream of Teenage Heaven*, in 1985; it received mixed reviews but it began to build their following. *Express*, released the following year, was more successful, charting in both the US and the UK On *Earth Sun Moon* (1987) the band retreated to more atmospheric musical territory, with the notable exception of the alternative/college radio hit "No New Tale to Tell," which helped to increase the group's fan base. *Love & Rockets*, released in 1989, broke the band into the mainstream, thanks to the T. Rex-inspired Top Ten single "So Alive." The album was nearly as successful, breaking into the Top 15 and going gold.

After the success of *Love & Rockets*, the members of the band concentrated on solo projects for nearly half a decade. Love & Rockets returned to recording in 1994 with *Hot Trip to Heaven*, which failed to make any inroads on the pop or alternative charts. In 1996, they returned again with *Sweet F.A.—Stephen Thomas Erlewine*

Seventh Dream of Teenage Heaven / 1985 / Beggars Banquet ✦✦✦
This album is filled with the dark, acoustic-driven work hinted at in their previous group, Bauhaus. —*Steve Aldrich*

● **Earth, Sun, Moon** / 1987 / Big Time ✦✦✦✦
Another solid LP. —*Steve Aldrich*

Love and Rockets / 1989 / Beggars Banquet ✦✦✦

Hot Trip to Heaven / 1994 / Warner Bros. ✦✦

Sweet F.A. / Mar. 19, 1996 / American ✦✦

Darlene Love (Darlene Wright)

b. Jul. 26, 1938
Vocals / R&B, Girl Group
Amazingly, Darlene Love, a superb vocalist, hasn't had much of a track record as a solo singer, at least not in terms of hits. Love was a founding member of the Blossoms in 1957. They did several sessions and were resident singers on the television show *Shindig*. Love sang lead vocals on "He's a Rebel," which was credited to the Crystals, and "Zip-A-Dee-Doo-Dah," which was issued as Bob B. Soxx and the Bluejeans. She cut six singles for Spector's Phillies label, with "Wait Till My Bobby Gets Back Home" the most successful. Love became busy as an actress, and reunited with Spector for the 1977 single "Lord, If You're a Woman." Love appeared in all three *Lethal Weapon* films, and was also in the Royal Shakespeare Company's co-production of Stephen King's *Carrie*. Her 1990 LP, *Paint Another Picture*, failed to chart in America. Love later toured as a background vocalist with Cher. She appeared briefly on the soap opera *Another World* in 1993. —*Ron Wynn*

Masters / 1981 / Phil Spector International ✦✦✦

● **The Best of Darlene Love** / 1992 / ABKCO ✦✦✦✦
A terrific compilation of Love's Phil Spector-produced hits, it includes "(Today I Met) the Boy I'm Gonna Marry," "Wait Till My Bobby Gets Back Home" and the hits she sang for the Crystals, "He's a Rebel" and "He's Sure the Boy I Love." —*AMG*

Loverboy

Hard Rock, Pop-Rock
With a string of three multi-platinum albums, Loverboy was one of the most successful mainstream hard rock groups of the early '80s. Comprised of vocalist Mike Reno, guitarist Paul Dean, bassist Scott Smith, keyboardist Doug Johnston, and drummer Matthew Frenette, the band formed in Toronto, Canada, in 1980 and immediately signed with CBS Records. Later that year, their Bruce Fairbairn-produced debut album appeared. Featuring the slick, hard-rocking singles "Turn Me Loose" and "The Kid Is Hot Tonite," the album went platinum in both Canada and America. Loverboy recorded the follow-up, *Get Lucky*, in 1981. Driven by the anthemic "Working for the Weekend," the Fairbairn-produced record was a major success in the US and Canada, yet it failed to gain an audience anywhere in Europe. Nevertheless, the band was a staple on AOR stations across North America, as well as a popular concert attraction. The band's good fortunes continued with the 1983 album *Keep It Up*. Again, Loverboy worked with Fairbairn, who kept their melodic yet tough sound intact; the album featured the hit single "Hot Girls In Love."

Loverboy's fortunes began to slip with 1985's *Lovin' Every Minute of It*, which was produced by Tom Allom (Judas Priest). Allom gave the

band a harder edge, which didn't prove as commercially successful as their past records; nevertheless, the band's fans managed to make the album go platinum. Fairbairn returned from working with Bon Jovi to produce 1987's *Wildside*, yet the combination didn't prove as potent as before. After an extensive two-year tour, the band returned to Canada. In 1989, their greatest-hits record, *Big Ones*, was released. The same year Reno and Dean announced plans to make solo records, which effectively put an end to the group. —*Stephen Thomas Erlewine*

Big Ones / 1989 / Columbia ✦✦✦✦
Loverboy's biggest and best hits include "Turn Me Loose," "Lovin' Every Minute of It," "This Could Be the Night," "Hot Girls in Love," "Heaven in Your Eyes," and "Working for the Weekend." —*AMG*

● **Loverboy Classics** / 1994 / Columbia ✦✦✦✦
Like *Big Ones*, *Loverboy Classics* doesn't contain all of the band's singles, but it does feature a greater selection of hits and album rock favorites, including Mike Reno's duet with Ann Wilson, "Almost Paradise," making it a better introduction to the group. —*Stephen Thomas Erlewine*

Lyle Lovett

b. Nov. 1, 1957, Houston, TX
Guitar, Vocals / Singer-Songwriter
Lyle Lovett represents the increasing diversity of country music as it recovers from a commercial slump in the '80s. Highly literate (he has degrees in journalism and German from Texas A&M), the Houston-born singer comes from the eclectic tradition of Western swing, as filtered through the work of such wry '70s songwriters as Guy Clark and Townes Van Zandt. Lovett has a dry but absurdly hilarious sense of humor, as expressed on his first recorded song, "If I Had a Boat." ("And if I had a pony, I'd ride him on my boat.") But he also writes bitingly of love relations, as in "God Will," in which the singer tells his lover that God will forgive her, but he won't, "and that's the difference between God and me." Despite some success in the country market and a Grammy award in the country category, it has been questionable since at least Lovett's second album, *Pontiac*, that his music could be categorized as country. But it's so multigeneric, with elements of folk, jazz, blues, and, lately, gospel, that it's hard to say exactly where it fits. At bottom, he's a singer-songwriter—and an amazingly imaginative one at that. —*William Ruhlmann*

Lyle Lovett / 1986 / Curb ✦✦✦✦
Lyle Lovett has an ironic overview of the world, expressed in songs he sings with the dead seriousness of the true comic. But he also has a finely defined sense of romantic troubles that sometimes isn't funny at all. Songs like "God Will" and "If I Were the Man You Wanted" mark him as one of the best new writers of the decade. —*William Ruhlmann*

★ **Pontiac** / 1987 / Curb ✦✦✦✦✦
Lovett's best overall collection of songs includes the gently absurd "If I Had a Boat," the subtly murderous "L.A. County," and the Henny Youngman-style "She's No Lady," among other gems. —*William Ruhlmann*

Lyle Lovett & His Large Band / 1989 / Curb ✦✦✦✦
On his third album, Lovett continues to explore a synthesis of country and big band. Included is his version of Tammy Wynette's country classic on "Stand by Your Man" and the bittersweet "I Married Her Just Because She Looks Like You." —*Rick Clark*

Joshua Judges Ruth / 1992 / Curb ✦✦✦✦
Lyle Lovett goes folk-gospel. To be fair, the country tag was never a comfortable fit for Lovett's eclectic musings. *Joshua Judges Ruth* distances him from the category without firmly boxing him into any new ones. There is a southern-fried gospel feel throughout much of the album, even if it's sometimes irreverent. "Church" best displays Lovett's surreal, dry wit, recounting a hunger-driven church rebellion complete with full gospel backing vocals. "She's Leaving Me," featuring guest vocals from Emmylou Harris, is the one sop offered to traditional country. Overall, though, the mood is somber bordering on bleak. Like the album cover and insert photos, *Joshua* deals in shades of gray and themes of loneliness and death. What one misses the most on this release is the infrequent surfacing of Lovett's weird, playful sense of humor. —*Roch Parisien*

I Love Everybody / 1994 / Curb ✦✦✦
A collection of odds and ends that Lyle Lovett has written over the years (some of the tunes date back to the late '70s), *I Love Everybody* doesn't have the self-conscious artistic importance of *Joshua Judges Ruth*, and it's all the better for it. Instead, Lovett offers a set of relaxed, casual songs, accentuating his infamous, off-kilter sense of humor ("Skinny Legs," "Penguins"). At the same time, the songs offer hints of Lovett's sly, subtle sense of menace, particularly "Creeps Like Me." —*Stephen Thomas Erlewine*

Road to Ensenada / Jun. 18, 1996 / Curb ✦✦✦✦
Since *Pontiac*, Lyle Lovett has been experimenting with different sounds, whether it was the big band posturing of *& His Large Band*, the gospel overtones of *Joshua Judges Ruth*, or the '70s singer-songwriter approach of *I Love Everybody*, his odds-and-ends collection. With *The*

Road to Ensenada, he hunkers down and produces his most straightforward album since *Pontiac.* As it happens, it is also his best record since that breakthrough album. Lovett strips the sound of the album down to the bare country essentials, allowing it to drift into western swing, country-rock, folk and honky tonk when necessary. He also decides to balance his weightier material ("Private Conversation," "Who Loves You Better," "It Ought to Be Easier," "I Can't Love You Anymore," "Christmas Morning") with fun, light-hearted numbers like "Don't Touch My Hat," "Fiona," and "That's Right (You're Not from Texas)," which are funny without being silly. In fact, *The Road to Ensenada* is the lightest album Lyle Lovett has ever made—the darkness that hung around the fringes of *Pontiac, Joshua Judges Ruth,* and *I Love Everybody* has drifted away, leaving his wry sense of humor and a newly found empathetic sentimentality. The combination of straight-forward instrumentation and lean, catchy, and incisive songwriting results in one of the best albums of his career—he's just as eclectic and off-handedly brilliant as he always been, but on *The Road to Ensenada* he's more focused and less flashy about his own talent than he's ever been. —*Stephen Thomas Erlewine*

Lene Lovich

b. Mar. 30, 1949, Detroit, MI
Saxophone, Vocals / New Wave

One of the more offbeat and memorable figures in new wave, Lene Lovich certainly drew much of her widely varied approach from her unconventional early experiences. Born of a Yugoslavian father and British mother, she spent much of her childhood in Detroit, MI. At age 13, she moved to Hull, England, with her mother. She ran away to London shortly thereafter, where she worked several odd jobs ranging from bingo caller to go-go dancer to street busker. Around this time, she developed an interest in art and theater, enrolling at the Central School of Art. She took up the saxophone and, after a brief stint in a soul-funk band (with future collaborator Les Chappell), Lovich wrote a string of songs for French disco star Cerrone. In 1978, Stiff Records signed her after hearing her first recording, a remake of "I Think We're Alone Now." She quickly became one of Stiff's brightest stars, headlining package tours and earning several UK hits over the next three years with the unforgettable "Lucky Number," "Say When," "Bird Song," and "New Toy." Unfortunately, her theatrical quirkiness didn't translate well into LP length and as new wave dissolved, she disappeared from the music scene. After an eight-year absence, she returned in 1990 with *March.* It failed to ignite any further interest and she again went into retirement. —*Chris Woodstra*

● **Stateless . . . Plus** / 1979 / Rhino ✦✦✦✦
Stateless, her aptly titled 1978 debut, is a new wave cult classic. Featuring her offbeat vocals and quirky synth-heavy production, this is her finest moment. Includes the great single, "Lucky Number." Now reissued on CD as *Stateless . . . Plus* with five extra tracks and extensive liner notes. —*Chris Woodstra*

Flex . . . plus / 1980 / Rhino ✦✦✦
Flex shows Lovich staying true to her unique sound, though it is somewhat watered down with super slick production. Now reissued on CD with six extra tracks as *Flex . . . Plus.* Includes the classic "New Toy" (written by Thomas Dolby). —*Chris Woodstra*

The Lovin' Spoonful

Folk-Rock, Pop-Rock

Right on the tails of the Beau Brummels and the Byrds, the Lovin' Spoonful were among the first American groups to challenge the domination of the British Invasion bands in the mid-'60s. Between mid-1965 and the end of 1967, the group was astonishingly successful, issuing one classic hit single after another, including "Do You Believe in Magic?," "You Didn't Have to Be So Nice," "Daydream," "Summer in the City," "Rain on the Roof," "Nashville Cats," and "Six O'Clock."

Like most of the folk-rockers, the Lovin' Spoonful were more pop and rock than folk, which didn't detract from their music at all. Much more than the Byrds, and even more than the Mamas & the Papas, the group exhibited a brand of unabashedly melodic, cheery, and good-time music, though their best single, "Summer in the City," was uncharacteristically riff-driven and hard-driving. More influenced by blues and jug bands than other folk-rock acts, their albums were spotty and their covers at times downright weak. As glorious as their singles were, the group lacked the depth and innovation of the Byrds, their chief competitors for the crown of best folk-rock band, and their legacy hasn't been canonized with nearly as much reverence as their West Coast counterparts.

Leader and principal songwriter John Sebastian was a young veteran of the Greenwich Village folk scene when he formed the band in 1965 with Zal Yanovsky, who'd already played primitive folk-rock of a sort with future members of the Mamas & the Papas in the Mugwumps. Sebastian already had some recording experience under his belt, playing harmonica (his father was a virtuoso classical harmonica player) on sessions by folkies like Tom Rush and Fred Neil. The Spoonful were

rounded out by Steve Boone on bass and Joe Butler on drums. After some tentative interest from Phil Spector (who considered producing them), they ended up signing with Kama Sutra. Sebastian's autoharp (which would also decorate several subsequent tracks) helped propel "Do You Believe in Magic" into the Top Ten in late 1965.

The Lovin' Spoonful were torn asunder by a drug bust in 1967. Boone and Yanovsky were arrested in California for marijuana possession, and evidently got out of trouble by turning in their source. This didn't sit well with the burgeoning counterculture, which called for a boycott of Spoonful product, although the effect on their sales may have been overestimated; most of the people who bought Spoonful records were average teenage Americans, not hippies. Yanovsky left the band in mid-1967, to be replaced by Jerry Yester, former producer of the Association.

The band had a few more mild hits, but couldn't survive the loss of John Sebastian, who effectively closed the chapter by leaving in 1968, although the group straggled on briefly under the helm of Butler. Sebastian went on to moderate success as a singer-songwriter in the 1970s. —*Richie Unterberger*

★ **Anthology** / 1990 / Rhino ✦✦✦✦✦
Unquestionably the finest collection of a major band that did much to launch American folk-rock in the mid-'60s. *Anthology* jams 26 cuts onto a single CD, including all of their hits and some of their strongest album tracks, drawing mostly from their 1965-66 prime. As for the more interesting non-smashes, these include the original version of John Sebastian's "Younger Girl," which was a hit in a more commercial version by the Critters; the minor 1967 hit "She Is Still a Mystery," a dreamily psychedelic number that holds its own with their other standards, but has somehow been forgotten by oldies radio; and "Good Time Music," recorded early in 1965 for an obscure Elektra sampler (and a small hit in a cover version by the Beau Brummels). The most overlooked find here is the instrumental "Lonely (Amy's Theme)," from the early Francis Ford Coppola film *You're a Big Boy Now,* a lushly orchestrated, melancholy tune featuring Sebastian's wistful harmonica. There are also little-known Sebastian originals, with vocals, from *You're a Big Boy Now* and Woody Allen's early screen venture *What's Up, Tiger Lily?* The accompanying booklet features comments from Sebastian himself about some of the group's most famous songs. —*Richie Unterberger*

Do You Believe in Magic/Hums / 1995 / Kama Sutra ✦✦✦✦
This 57-minute, 23-track CD reissues the Lovin' Spoonful's first album, *Do You Believe in Magic* (Nov. 1965), and its third, *Hums of the Lovin' Spoonful* (Nov. 1966). While it might have made more sense to pair *Magic* with its follow-up, *Daydream,* this disc presents the bulk of the Spoonful's well-known material—including "Do You Believe in Magic," "Did You Ever Have to Make Up Your Mind," "Rain on the Roof," "Nashville Cats," and "Summer in the City"—along with examples of John Sebastian's folk-country-blues-rock songwriting style, such as "Younger Girl," "Lovin' You," and "Coconut Grove," and showcases for guitarist Zally Yanovsky and drummer Joe Butler, who sings on a cover of Fred Neil's "The Other Side of This Life." A sleeve note reveals that the original multi-track tapes for the albums are lost, which explains why the sound, while good, does not exhibit the dramatic improvement that has become common on CD reissues of '60s music. —*William Ruhlmann*

Nick Lowe

b. Mar. 25, 1949, Suffolk, England
Guitar (Bass), Vocals / Rock 'n' Roll, Country-Rock, New Wave, Pop-Rock, Pub-Rock

After the seminal pub-rockers Brinsley Schwarz broke up in 1974, Nick Lowe let his love for pop music in all of its trashy, sleazy glory blossom. At a time when most artists were concerned about making art, he concentrated on returning to the days when rock 'n' roll was about nothing except love, sex, good times, and rock 'n' roll. The only thing was, Lowe paid tribute to classic rock and pop by twisting their conventions around; he took standard themes and melodies and turned them inside out with a wicked sense of humor. Lowe never sounded dated because at his heart he was a punk—his early records are ragged and raw, positively overflowing with energy. As his career moved into the '80s, he lost that reckless energy, but he always remained an outsider laughing at the mainstream.

Lowe moved to Stiff Records in 1976, Britain's first independent record label, after releasing several flop singles on Liberty/UA. The label's first record was his "So It Goes"/"Heart of the City" single; it cost 45 pounds to make. Lowe became the label's in-house producer and he was behind the boards for nearly every one of the label's singles during their early days; by the end of the decade, he had produced an impressive array of artists, including Elvis Costello, the Damned, Graham Parker, the Pretenders, and Dr. Feelgood. During this time he recorded his first solo album, 1978's *Jesus of Cool,* which was retitled *Pure Pop for Now People* in the US

By the time his debut was released, he had formed Rockpile with guitarist Dave Edmunds, drummer Terry Williams, and guitarist Billy Bremner; the band functioned as a touring band for Lowe and Edmunds, as well as providing support on their records. Lowe's next album, 1979's *Labour of Lust*, was recorded with Rockpile; it contained his only hit, "Cruel to Be Kind." After recording one album in 1980, Rockpile disbanded. Lowe began to experiment with country and Tex-Mex music on his '80s albums, without ever abandoning pop; the records were more polished, but they sold fewer copies than his earlier albums. However, he produced successful records by Carlene Carter, John Hiatt, the Fabulous Thunderbirds, and Paul Carrack during the decade.

While his days as a genuine musical force may be behind him, Lowe's albums have been consistently strong and when he's at the top of his form, he's an utterly original and inventive pop songwriter; his best songs make wading through his mediocre material worthwhile. — *Stephen Thomas Erlewine*

★ **Pure Pop for Now People** / 1978 / Columbia ✦✦✦✦✦
For his first solo album, *Pure Pop for Now People*, Nick Lowe completely abandoned the rootsy underpinnings of his work with Brinsley Schwarz and refashioned himself as a pop craftsman or, as the original British title put it, the *Jesus of Cool*. Lowe tries anything and everything on the record, from the sweet pop of "Tonight" to the blinding rock of "Heart of the City." It's a veritable tour de force of his songwriting talent, as well as his wit. Not only does he turn in a set of wildly eclectic pop songs, he writes lyrics that slyly and gleefully subvert and pervert rock 'n' roll tradition. *Pure Pop for Now People* sounds like '60s pop from an alternate universe, where hit singles are about actresses that are eaten by their pet dogs, castrating Castro, and grown men who write odes to teen idols. He also writes about the sleaziness of the music business itself with unrestrained joy. If Lowe's sense of humor wasn't so sharp and his melodies weren't so catchy, the amalgam of pop music and pop culture wouldn't have been so successful. However, he not only can write pop songs, he knows how to record them—each song sounds like an individual single and the cheap production means that the album sounds like it's coming out of tinny radio speakers. And that also means that it doesn't matter what sequence these songs are put in—the album is like a jukebox, where different musical styles can follow each other and it all makes perfect sense. — *Stephen Thomas Erlewine*

☆ **Labour of Lust** / 1979 / Demon ✦✦✦✦✦
The grooves are tighter here than before, mixing the roots-rock sensibilities of Rockpile with his love of a good pop hook. It contains several minor hits, including "Cruel to Be Kind." — *John Floyd*

Nick the Knife / 1982 / Demon ✦✦✦
Lowe's first album since the breakup of Rockpile was a casually rocking record that recalled his former band, which isn't surprising, considering that both Billy Bremner and Terry Williams provide instrumental support. — *Stephen Thomas Erlewine*

The Abominable Showman / 1983 / Demon ✦✦
On *The Abominable Showman*, Lowe's fascination with country music begins to assert itself on a collection of songs that only seems lighthearted. While songs like "We Want Action" and "Tanque Ray" are nothing more than solid pop-rockers, "Time Wounds All Heels," "Raging Eyes," "Wish You Were Here," and "(For Every Woman Who Ever Made a Fool of a Man There's a Woman Who Made a) Man of a Fool" are exceptionally well-written songs, full of subtle emotional power and catchy melodies. — *Stephen Thomas Erlewine*

Nick Lowe & His Cowboy Outfit / 1984 / Demon ✦✦✦
Thanks to a strong backing band, *Nick Lowe & His Cowboy Outfit* is his most musically satisfying album since *Labour of Lust*. Throughout the record, Lowe touches on all kinds of roots-rock, from Tex-Mex and three-chord garage rock to country and pop. And the great majority of the songs—from originals like the organ-driven rocker "Half a Boy and Half a Man" and the sly pop of "God's Gift to Women" to the excellent covers "You'll Never Get Me up in One of Those" and "Breakaway"—are simply irresistible. — *Stephen Thomas Erlewine*

The Rose of England / 1985 / Demon ✦✦✦✦
Lowe's second album with his Cowboy Outfit is an even better record than their previous collection. *The Rose of England* retains the band's low-key charm, but they now have a better set of songs to work with. Lowe's originals rank with his best material, and the covers, including Elvis Costello's "Indoor Fireworks" and John Hiatt's "She Don't Love Nobody," are perfectly suited to his style. — *Stephen Thomas Erlewine*

Pinker and Prouder Than Previous / 1988 / Demon ✦✦✦
Pinker and Prouder Than Previous is Nick Lowe's most relaxed and casual album to date, but it never sounds tossed off or careless. Instead, Lowe's subtle mastery of pop, rock, R&B, and country results in an unassuming and thoroughly enjoyable set of clever, well-written originals and fine covers. — *Stephen Thomas Erlewine*

● **Basher: The Best of Nick Lowe** / 1989 / Columbia ✦✦✦✦
A superb collection spanning Lowe's solo career, it has a smattering of Rockpile's sides tossed in. A fine introduction, but start with *Pure Pop for Now People*. — *John Floyd*

Party of One / 1990 / Upstart ✦✦
While Dave Edmunds' production makes *Party of One* Nick Lowe's sharpest-sounding record in years, his songwriting isn't as strong as it has been in the past. Only "(I Want to Build a) Jumbo Ark," "What's Shakin' on the Hill," and "I Don't Know Why You Keep Me On" rank with his best material. — *Stephen Thomas Erlewine*

The Wilderness Years / 1991 / Demon ✦✦✦✦
A wildly entertaining collection of outtakes, demos, and forgotten singles, *The Wilderness Years* captures Nick Lowe at the top of his form. Even seemingly slight songs like "Let's Go to the Disco" and "Bay City Rollers We Love You" are rough, melodic pop gems. The disc also contains some of Lowe's best performances, including the demo "Fool Too Long," the reckless single "Heart of the City," the "erstwhile Stiff advertising jingle" "I Love My Label," and a sublime version of Sandy Posey's "Born a Woman." The sheer quantity of brilliant material on *The Wilderness Years* makes it worthwhile even for Lowe's most casual fans. — *Stephen Thomas Erlewine*

The Impossible Bird / 1994 / Upstart ✦✦✦✦
Nick Lowe's best records have always been full of clever lyrics and undeniable pop craftsmanship; the exception is *The Impossible Bird*. For most of the 1980s, Lowe had been appropriating country and R&B influences, but *The Impossible Bird* is where he fully incorporates those styles into his songwriting. Lowe doesn't abandon his gift for melody; "Soulful Wind" and "12-Step Program (To Quit You Babe)" are as catchy as anything he's ever written. The difference is haunting songs like "The Beast in Me" and "Withered on the Vine," two rich, sad, introspective numbers that Lowe would never have put on previous albums. And that's what makes *The Impossible Bird* his best album since *Labour of Lust*—it's the most focused, mature, personal music of his career, without a single throwaway. — *Stephen Thomas Erlewine*

Lulu (Marie MacDonald McLaughlin Lawrie)

b. Nov. 3, 1948, Glascow, Scotland
Vocals / British Invasion, Pop-Rock, Girl Group
Most Americans first heard of Lulu when she soared to the top of the charts with the pop ballad "To Sir with Love," the theme to the film of the same name, in 1967. Actually, the Scottish singer—born Marie MacDonald McLaughlin Lawrie—had been a star in Britain since 1964, when she hit the Top Ten with a raucous version of "Shout." Lulu's mid-'60s recordings (which included a version of "Here Comes the Night" that preceded Them's hit rendition) were often surprisingly rowdy and R&B-influenced. Although she didn't match Dusty Springfield, her Brenda Lee-like rasp could be quite gutsy and soulful. Her career was headed in a determinedly middle-of-the-road direction by the late '60s, which saw her hosting a British variety show and marrying Bee Gee Maurice Gibb (they have since divorced). Recording intermittently ever since, she raised a few eyebrows by traveling to Muscle Shoals studios to record her 1970 album *New Routes*, and releasing a single of David Bowie tunes (which Bowie also played on and co-produced) in 1973. — *Richie Unterberger*

Something to Shout About / 1965 / Decca ✦✦✦

From Lulu . . . with Love / 1967 / Parrot ✦✦✦

Melody Fair / 1970 / Atlantic ✦✦✦
Since Lulu's most soulful qualities had usually been repressed or smothered by MOR-conscious material and production, this 1970 album seemed to have all the right ingredients for a blue-eyed soul triumph along the lines of Dusty Springfield's late-'60s LPs. The same label that midwifed those Springfield sessions was now doing the same for Lulu, matching her with backing by the Dixie Flyers, the Sweet Inspirations, and the Memphis Horns. Atlantic honchos Jerry Wexler, Tom Dowd, and Arif Mardin produced; the material included compositions by Gary Bonds, Lieber-Stoller, Randy Newman, and Bacharach-David. Yet the results, as is so often the case when the menu seems tasty, were rather underwhelming, the sums failing to add up to the parts. It's not at all bad, just unexciting. The songs aren't special enough, the arrangements never catch fire, and there are a couple ill-advised detours into cheery pop tunes by the Beatles and Bee Gees. But it's not all bad timing; Lulu herself never seemed to let it all hang out and belt as she had occasionally in the past, except for a few funky moments. — *Richie Unterberger*

Shout / 1983 / Decca ✦✦✦

● **From Crayons to Perfume: The Best of Lulu** / 1994 / Rhino ✦✦✦✦
By far the most wide-ranging retrospective of a singer who never found the consistently good material that her considerable talents deserved. Starting with her 1964 British hit cover of "Shout," it also includes the No. 1 single "To Sir with Love" and a few of her other British Top Ten hits from the '60s, including the nice '65 soul ballad "Leave a Little Love" and the chirpy 1967 Neil Diamond tune "The Boat That I Row" (the flipside of "To Sir with Love," which wasn't a hit at all in the UK). Unfortunately, it gives short shift to the raunchy R&B she recorded in the mid-'60s, but it does include the sadly neglected, moody "Dreary Nights and Rows"

(penned by "To Sir with Love" author Mark London) and the Top 40 orchestrated ballad "Best of Both Worlds," co-arranged by future Led Zepper John Paul Jones. You also get nifty covers of Tim Rose's "Morning Dew" and Nilsson's "Without Him," along with a few songs she recorded with Atlantic (some with the Dixie Flyers) that gave her more sympathetic soul material than she was accustomed to, including the hit "Oh Me Oh My." There's also her semi-legendary 1974 single "Watch That Man"/"The Man Who Sold the World," a double-sided 45 of David Bowie covers produced by Bowie, and the theme song to the James Bond film *The Man with the Golden Gun*. This 20-song compilation doesn't gather together all her fine material by any means, but it's the only one to cover most of her career. —*Richie Unterberger*

Luscious Jackson

Alternative Pop-Rock
With their dark hip-hop-influenced rock, Luscious Jackson recreates the dense, multicultural bohemian world of New York in a collage of sound, where Spanish guitars, jazzy keyboards, funky beats, and breathy vocals combine into one. Like The Beastie Boys, Luscious Jackson's eclectism doesn't acknowledge boundaries; instead, it takes freely from every kind of music, creating an amalgam that is distinctive and original. With their critically acclaimed 1993 debut EP, *In Search of Manny*, they earned a cult following; their first full-length album, 1994's *Natural Ingredients*, was even more eclectic and received terrific reviews. —*Stephen Thomas Erlewine*

● **In Search of Manny** / Oct. 11, 1993 / Grand Royal ✦✦✦✦
A darkly funky, atmospheric EP where hip-hop is used as a basis for the folk-tinged songs, which paint detailed, textured portraits of the New York bohemian slacker scene. An impressive debut from this New York quartet. —*Stephen Thomas Erlewine*

Natural Ingredients / 1994 / Capitol ✦✦✦✦
Luscious Jackson's first full-length album, *Natural Ingredients*, features a brighter, more open sound than *In Search of Manny*, without losing the funky, organic feel of the EP. Musically, the band continue to refine their hip-hop-influenced pop, adding stronger hooks and denser grooves. *Natural Ingredients* isn't as consistent or edgy as *In Search of Manny*, but the record fulfills their initial promise. —*Stephen Thomas Erlewine*

Lush

Alternative Pop-Rock, Shoegazing, Brit-Pop
Few bands live up to their names; Lush, however, does so in spades. Paced by Miki Berenyi's paper-thin voice (so thin you'll think she's on a respirator), Lush literally builds its music on a mountain of strummed guitars that approximates a rush of lava. Strong songwriting removes any tedium. —*John Dougan*

Gala / 1990 / 4AD ✦✦✦✦
A little of it goes a long way, but this is where Lush shines. By this time, their pop craft was developed enough to warrant repeated listenings. Fans of folkie-style guitar, albeit with a touch more volume, will love this. —*John Dougan*

● **Spooky** / 1992 / 4AD ✦✦✦✦
While Lush features fragile, dual-female vocals layered over hypnotic melodies, the group has always taken a minimalist approach to its music. The vocal tracks are just as likely to be wedded to fuzzy guitar riffs and pounding rhythms. Everything kind of blurs and merges together in an urgent, often disturbing mix that belies the vocal sweetness. There are exceptions. Lush softens its stance on several fragile acoustic tracks, notably "Tiny Smiles," "For Love," and "Monochrome." Then like a shattered mirror, "Superblast!" and "Laura" offer a harsher extreme, shards of glass splintering through the songs without mercy. While Lush's bittersweet soundscapes will never grace mainstream dance floors or Top 40 radio, *Spooky* does make fascinating listening under headphones in the dark. —*Roch Parisien*

Split / 1994 / Warner Bros. ✦✦✦✦
Featuring improved songwriting and catchier, more muscular hooks, *Split* rivals *Spooky* as Lush's best album. —*Stephen Thomas Erlewine*

Lovelife / Mar. 5, 1996 / Reprise/4AD ✦✦✦✦
Lovelife represents a major shift in style for Lush. Nearly abandoning the trancy melodies and droning guitars that were their trademark, the band has crafted an album full of sharp hooks and melodies, one that owes a great deal to the Britpop mania of 1995. From the circular melody of the opening "Ladykillers," it's clear that Lush had been influenced by the direct, jagged pop of Elastica, but they also have reached back into '60s pop. All of the ballads on *Lovelife* are rooted in the hazy dream-pop of the early '90s, but they are given stylish, mod arrangements complete with muted brass. Even more startling is the Nancy Sinatra/Lee Hazelwood pastiche of "Ciao!," an irresistible duet between Miki Berenyi and Pulp's Jarvis Cocker. *Lovelife* would have simply been an embarrassing attempt to seem fashionable if Lush hadn't succeeded in updating their sound. However, they have been able to recreate themselves as a pop

band and the result is their most direct—and arguably their most rewarding—album. —*Stephen Thomas Erlewine*

Frankie Lymon & The Teenagers

Doo Wop
Frankie Lymon (1942-1968) & the Teenagers were a New York doo-wop group consisting of Joe Negroni, Herman Santiago, Jimmy Merchant, and Sherman Garnes but centered around the extraordinary talents of their lead singer, 13-year-old Frankie Lymon. Lymon wrote their first big hit, "Why Do Fools Fall in Love?" His wise-beyond-his-years vocal and performing abilities not only made the Teenagers a group several notches above the competition but made Lymon the first Black teenage pop star. Though only together for a brief 18-month period, Lymon & The Teenagers exerted an enormous influence, spawning several "kid" vocal groups and providing initial inspiration to Berry Gordy to model his entire Motown production approach around Lymon's original vocal style. Inexplicably, the group split into two factions at the height of their success, and neither had a hit again. Lymon died from a drug overdose at age 26. Diana Ross, Smokey Robinson, Len Barry, and his principal protégé, Michael Jackson (whose early recordings with The Jackson 5 are virtual re-creations of the early Lymon sound, merely updated) all show the influence of Frankie Lymon & The Teenagers's groundbreaking work. —*Cub Koda*

★ **The Best of Frankie Lymon & The Teenagers** / 1990 / Rhino ✦✦✦✦✦
Frankie Lymon wrote "Why Do Fools Fall in Love?" at 13 and led his group, the Teenagers, to a brief stardom. They remain one of the finest examples of New York vocal group singing, and all of the essentials are on this album. —*Jeff Tamarkin*

Lynyrd Skynyrd

Southern Rock
From the time of their initial 1970 Sheffield, AL, demos to their tragic plane crash on Oct 20, 1977, the Jacksonville, FL, band Lynyrd Skynyrd fused the spirit of rock 'n' roll with the truth and lyrical directness of great country music. Lynyrd Skynyrd possessed a highly arranged approach to organizing their material. They also featured a powerful lead-guitar triumvirate in Allen Collins, Gary Rossington, and Ed King (later replaced by Steve Gaines), which augmented lead singer-songwriter Ronnie Van Zant's no-nonsense tales of the common man's exploits.
Skynyrd was discovered playing in an Atlanta club by Blood, Sweat & Tears-founder Al Kooper in 1972. Kooper signed them to his new Sounds of the South record label and released *Pronounced Leh-Nerd Skin-Nerd* (No. 27), which included the classic "Freebird" (No. 19-1975/No. 38-1977), one of the most requested songs in rock history.
The band, which drew heavily from the hard English blues-rock sound (Free, Cream, Stones), had the good fortune to have a fan in the Who's Pete Townshend, who requested that Skynyrd open for the 1973 *Quadrophenia* tour. As a result, the band developed a strong fan base early in their career.
"Sweet Home Alabama" (No. 8) from *Second Helping* (No. 12) was the band's biggest single. Other singles included "Saturday Night Special" (No. 27), "What's Your Name?" (No. 13), "Double Trouble" (No. 80), and "You Got That Right" (No. 69).
Survivors of the 1977 plane crash played in various amalgamations (Rossington-Collins Band, Allen Collins Band, etc.). Lynyrd Skynyrd reformed for a Tribute tour in 1987. After the tour, the reunited band began recording; they have since released a handful of albums. —*Rick Clark*

Pronounced Leh-Nerd Skin-Nerd / 1973 / MCA ✦✦✦✦
With the release of this debut album, Skynyrd was immediately recognized as one of the South's premier bands. The album's highlight is "Freebird," a song that, over time, has become one of the most requested rock songs in the history of radio. "Simple Man," "Gimmie Three Steps," and "Tuesday's Gone" are several other standards from this classic album. —*Rick Clark*

☆ **Second Helping** / 1974 / MCA ✦✦✦✦✦
The appropriately titled follow-up to their debut was equally impressive, containing their highest-charting hit, "Sweet Home Alabama." Unlike many albums, where the hit is the highlight, *Second Helping* is chock-full of great tunes like "Working for MCA," "Call Me the Breeze," "Don't Ask Me No Questions," and "Ballad of Curtis Loew." —*Rick Clark*

Nuthin' Fancy / 1975 / MCA ✦✦✦
Frazzled by too much endless roadwork and too little songwriting preparation, *Nuthin' Fancy* is a step down from its impressive predecessor. Nevertheless, "Saturday Night Special," the album's opener, is a classic rocker. Other standouts include the Free-style "On the Hunt," "Whiskey Rock-A-Roller," and "Am I Losin'." —*Rick Clark*

Gimme Back My Bullets / 1976 / MCA ✦✦✦
On their first production with the legendary Tom Dowd (Rod Stewart, Eric Clapton, Allman Brothers), Skynyrd sounds relatively uninspired,

even as they indignantly call for a return to platinum status with the Free-influenced title cut. Nevertheless, Van Zant's gift for plain-speaking lyrics and the band's undeniable chemistry help this record hold up better than many late-'70s AOR rock acts. —*Rick Clark*

One More from the Road / 1976 / MCA ✦✦✦

Street Survivors / 1977 / MCA ✦✦✦✦
The addition of lead guitarist and singer Steve Gaines goaded Ronnie Van Zant and the band into a dramatic rebirth. *Street Survivors* featured tighter songs, strong melodies, and an exciting element of vocal interplay between Van Zant and Gaines ("You Got That Right"). The contrast between Gaines' clean lead style, Collins' flash, and Rossington's thick-toned lyrical phrasing is something to behold. Without a doubt, it's Skynyrd's most cohesive body of work since *Second Helping.* —*Rick Clark*

Skynyrd's First and . . . Last / 1978 / MCA ✦✦✦

★ **Gold & Platinum** / 1980 / MCA ✦✦✦✦✦
Compiled by Gary Rossington and Allen Collins after their tragic 1977 plane crash, *Gold & Platinum* contains most of the band's essential tracks. It would've been nice if annotations had been included, but this is a good primer. —*Rick Clark*

Lynyrd Skynyrd 1991 / 1991 / Atlantic ✦✦

Lynyrd Skynyrd [Box Set] / 1991 / MCA ✦✦✦✦
This attractively packaged and well-chosen collection of the band's most popular tracks also includes early demos and other unreleased tracks. —*Rick Clark*

Kirsty MacColl

b. Oct. 10, 1959, London, England
Guitar, Vocals / Singer-Songwriter, Folk-Rock, Pop-Rock
Kirsty MacColl, daughter of folk singer-songwriter Ewan MacColl, began her own musical career while still in her teens, singing in a band called the Addix, and eventually signed to the legendary Stiff Records. Her first single, the modern girl-group gem, "They Don't Know," was released in 1979. Though it failed in the charts, it was later a major hit for Tracey Ullman. She switched to Polydor in the '80s and landed a UK Top 20 hit with the novelty song "There's a Guy Works Down the Chip Shop (Swears He's Elvis)." She followed the single with her first LP, *Desperate Character*, in 1981. In 1984, she married producer Steve Lillywhite and put her solo career on hold, raising their two children and working as a backup singer. MacColl returned in 1989 with a more mature effort, *Kite*, which reached the UK Top 20. Since then, she has released two more albums, *Electric Landlady* (1991) and *Titanic Days* (1993), displaying great talent and diversity and, above all, good pop sensibilities. —*Chris Woodstra*

Desperate Character / 1981 / Polydor ✦✦✦

Kite / 1989 / Charisma ✦✦✦
After nearly a decade's absence as solo performer, MacColl released the low-key *Kite*, a decidedly more mature effort. Her literate and sharp vocals are perfectly matched with lush, textured folk-pop arrangements. Johnny Marr contributes his distinctive guitar playing on several tracks. —*Chris Woodstra*

Electric Landlady / 1991 / Charisma ✦✦✦✦
MacColl is in peak form on the more experimental *Electric Landlady*. Playing with a different band on nearly every track, she effortlessly moves from the hip-hop of "Walking Down Madison," to the Latin-tinged "My Affair," to the Smiths' sound-alike "Children of the Revolution" (co-written by Smiths guitarist Johnny Marr). Overall, she builds on the folk-pop of her previous effort with much stronger material. Her lyrics have become more personal, mainly focusing on her relationship with and the recent death of her father. —*Chris Woodstra*

Essential Collection / 1993 / Stiff ✦✦✦✦
A fine collection of Kirsty MacColl's early singles for Stiff Records in the late '70s. She wrote effortlessly melodic three-minute pop singles that managed to recast the classic girl-group sound of the '60s into a style that was contemporary and timeless, much like how Rockpile energetically recast '50s and '60s rock 'n' roll. Not only were these singles some of the best she's ever written, the singles were among the best pop songs of the era, including the original version of Tracey Ullman's hit "They Don't Know" and the infectious "There's a Guy Works Down the Chip Shop (Swears He's Elvis)." —*Chris Woodstra*

Titanic Days / Oct. 5, 1993 / IRS ✦✦✦
MacColl delivers another brilliant album with 1993's *Titanic Days*. The arrangements have become more ambitious, as evident in the jazzy "Bad" and the heavily orchestrated "Soho Square." The lyrics are still sharp with biting commentary, this time backed by a more dance-oriented pop. —*Chris Woodstra*

● **Galore** / 1995 / IRS ✦✦✦
18-track compilation. The strength of these collected forces may just be

sufficient to overcome Kirsty MacColl's two fatal commercial "flaws": she spreads herself all over the musical map, and writes intelligent, often dryly humorous lyrics about life and relationships that never pander to chart sentimentality. MacColl oozes a pure, fresh-scrubbed, girl-next-door quality that belies the sophistication of her songwriting without ever resorting to vacant innocence. —*Roch Parisien*

Madness

New Wave, Ska-Revival, Pop-Rock
Along with the Specials, Madness were one of the leading bands of the ska-revival of the late '70s and early '80s. As their career progressed, Madness branched away from their trademark "nutty sound" and incorporated large elements of Motown, soul and British pop. Although the band managed one crossover American hit in 1983, the band remained a British phenomenon, influencing several successive generations of musicians and becoming one of the most beloved groups the country produced during the '80s.

The origins of Madness lie in a ska group known as Morris and the Minors,. By 1978, the band had changed their name to the Invaders and had added Graham "Suggs" McPherson, Mark Bedford, Chas Smash, and Dan Woodgate. Later in 1978, they changed their name to Madness, in homage to one of their favorite Prince Buster songs. The following year, Madness released their debut single, a tribute to Prince Buster entitled "The Prince," on Two-Tone. The song was a surprise success, reaching the British Top 20. Following its success, the band signed a record contract with Stiff Records and released another Prince Buster song, "One Step Beyond," which climbed to No. 7. Madness quickly recorded their debut album, also titled *One Step Beyond*, with producers Clive Langer and Alan Winstanley. Released toward the end of the year, the album peaked at No. 2 in Britain and it stayed on the charts for well over a year. At the beginning of 1980, the band's third single, "My Girl," peaked at No. 3. For the next three years, the group had a virtually uninterrupted run of 13 Top Ten singles, during which time they were one of the most popular bands in Britain, rivaled only by the Jam in terms of widespread popularity. Where the Jam appealed to teenagers and young adults, Madness had a broad fan base, reaching from children to the elderly. Which didn't mean their music was diluted—they continued to expand their sound, both musically and lyrically.

In the spring of 1980, Madness released *The Work Rest and Play* EP, which reached No. 6 on the strength of the EP's lead song, "Night Boat to Cairo." Also during the spring, *One Step Beyond* was released in the US, where it peaked at 128. Madness' second album, *Absolutely*, was released in the fall of 1980. The record peaked at No. 2 on the British charts, but it stalled at No. 146 in the US. Sire dropped the band after the commercial disappointment of *Absolutely*, leaving Madness without an American record contract for several years. Back in England, Madness continued to gain momentum, as the group began playing matinee shows on their tours so children under 16 years old could attend the concert. In the fall of 1981, the band released their third album, *Seven*, which peaked at No. 5. In January of 1982, Madness hit No. 4 with a cover of Labi Siffre's "It Must Be Love." In March, their streak of Top Ten hits was interrupted when "Cardiac Arrest" stalled at No. 14 on the charts. The band bounced back a few months later with "House of Fun," their first No. 1 single. That same month, the hits compilation, *Complete Madness*, reached No. 1.

Madness returned in the late summer of 1982 with *The Rise & Fall*, their full-fledged shift to British pop. Like their previous albums, it was a British hit, reaching the Top Ten, but it also contained the seeds of their brief American success with the Top Five British single "Our House." The single was released in America on the group's new label, Geffen, and it received heavy airplay from MTV. The music video television network had previously played the videos for "House of Fun," "It Must Be Love," and "Cardiac Arrest" when the band's albums were unreleased in the US, thereby setting the stage for "Our House" to become a massive hit. With "Our House," Madness had MTV exposure coincide with a record release for the first time, which sent the single into the American Top Ten in the summer of 1983. The success of the single brought the US compilation album, *Madness*, to no. 41. Madness managed one more American Top 40 hit that fall, when "It Must Be Love" peaked at No. 33.

At the end of 1983, Mike Barson—the band's key songwriter—left the group to settle down with his wife. Although Madness was able to stay near the top of the charts with their first post-Barson release, "Michael Caine," the band's fortunes began to decline over the course of 1984. Upon its release in the spring of 1984, *Keep Moving* hit No. six on the British charts; in America, the record reached No. 109. In June, the group released its final single for Stiff Records, "One Better Day," which peaked at No. 17. In the fall, Madness formed their own record label, Zarjazz, which was distributed through Virgin Records. Madness released "Yesterday's Men," their first recording on Zarjazz in September of 1985, nearly a year after the label's formation. The record peaked at No. 18 and its parent album, *Mad Not Mad*, reached No. 16 upon its October release. Their chart decline continued early in 1986, when their cover of Scritti

Politti's "Sweetest Girl" peaked at No. 35. For most of 1986, the group was quiet. In September, Madness announced they were disbanding. Two months later, their farewell single, "Waiting for the Ghost Train," was released, charting at No. 18.

After staying dormant for a year and a half, the group reunited at the beginning of 1988 as a quartet called the Madness, releasing its comeback single, "I Pronounce You," in March. The Madness featured Chris Foreman, Lee Thompson, Chas Smash, and Suggs, and was augmented by the Specials' keyboardist Jerry Dammers and Steve Nieve (keyboards) and Bruce Thomas (bass) of the Attractions. "I Pronounce You" reached No. 44 on the UK charts and its accompanying album stiffed upon its spring release. The group disbanded for a second time that fall.

In the summer of 1992, the original lineup of Madness reunited to perform two outdoor concerts at London's Finsbury Park. The group dubbed the event "Madstock" and released a recording of the shows on Go! Records. Madstock became an annual event for the next four years—every summer the band would reunite and headline an outdoor festival at Finsbury Park. Suggs launched a solo career in 1995 with *The Lone Ranger*, which performed respectably in the UK charts. In 1996, Madness played the final Madstock and announced they planned not to reunite for future concerts. —*Stephen Thomas Erlewine*

One Step Beyond / 1979 / Sire ✦✦✦✦
The band's debut shows the band in peak form. More than just the silly novelty act portrayed on the cover, Madness offers a lighthearted approach to ska with an irresistible dance beat. Includes the favorites, "One Step Beyond" and "Night Boat to Cairo." A landmark ska-revival album. —*Chris Woodstra*

Absolutely / Oct. 1980 / Sire ✦✦✦
Their early ska-influenced material, featuring such UK hits as "Baggy Trousers," "Embarrassment," and "Return of the Los Palmas 7." —*William Ruhlmann*

Seven / Sep. 1981 / Stiff ✦✦✦
Their "nutty sound" seems to fall to the background somewhat on this move toward more mature songwriting. Expanding beyond the limited scope of ska, this is a fine pop effort at times dabbling in more experimental sounds such as sitars and Arabic rhythms. Includes the splendid single "It Must Be Love." —*Chris Woodstra*

Rise & Fall / 1982 / Stiff ✦✦✦✦
Madness Present the Rise & Fall marks the band's most mature effort and artistic statement. Completely devoid of their early ska influence, they paint a picture of British life in the spirit of the Kinks' *Village Green Preservation Society*. Though it was never released in the US, several tracks were later placed on the compilation *Madness*, including "Our House," their biggest Stateside hit. —*Chris Woodstra*

★ Complete Madness / 1982 / Stiff ✦✦✦✦✦
A smartly assembled collection of their early singles. A good starting point for those interested in their self-described "nutty sound" ska/bluebeat. Pure fun. —*Chris Woodstra*

Madness / 1983 / Geffen ✦✦✦✦
A US compilation album released to coincide with the success of "Our House." It includes that hit, its follow-up, "It Must Be Love," and such UK successes as "Tomorrow's Just Another Day," "Shut Up," "House of Fun," and "Grey Day." —*William Ruhlmann*

Keep Moving / 1984 / Geffen ✦✦

Mad Not Mad / 1985 / Geffen ✦✦

Utter Madness / 1986 / Zarjazz ✦✦✦
Picking up where *Complete Madness* left off, this collection includes all of the key singles from 1982 to 1986. A good collection, though listeners will be better served by simply listening to *Rise and Fall* for a representation of this period. —*Chris Woodstra*

The Business / 1992 / Virgin ✦✦✦

Madness

b. Aug. 16, 1958, Rochester, MI
Vocals / Dance-Pop, Adult Contemporary, Pop-Rock, Club-Dance

After a star reaches a certain point, it's easy to forget what they became famous for and concentrate solely on their persona. Madonna is such a star. Madonna rocketed to stardom so quickly in 1984 that it obscured most of her musical virtues. Appreciating her music became even more difficult as the decade wore on, as discussing her lifestyle became more common than discussing her music. However, one of Madonna's greatest achievements is how she manipulated the media and the public with her music, her videos, her publicity, and her sexuality. Arguably, Madonna was the first female pop star to have complete control of her music and image.

Madonna moved from her native Michigan to New York in 1977, with dreams of becoming a ballet dancer. She studied with choreographer Alvin Ailey and modelled. In 1979, she became part of the Patrick Hernandez Revue, a disco outfit who had the hit "Born to Be Alive." She trav-

eled to Paris with Hernanadez; it was there that she met Dan Gilroy, who would soon become her boyfriend. Upon returning to New York, the pair formed the Breakfast Club, a pop/dance group. Madonna originally played drums for the band, but she soon became the lead singer. In 1980, she left the band and formed Emmy with her former boyfriend, drummer Stephen Bray. Soon, Bray and Madonna broke off from the group and began working on some dance/disco-oriented tracks. A demo tape of these tracks worked its way to Mark Kamins, a New York-based DJ/producer. Kamins directed the tape to Sire Records, who signed the singer during 1982.

Kamins produced Madonna's first single, "Everybody," which became a club and dance hit at the end of 1982; her second single, 1983's "Physical Attraction," was another club hit. In June of 1983, she had her third club hit with the bubbly "Holiday," which was written by Jellybean Benitez. Madonna's self-titled debut album was released in September of 1983; "Holiday" became her first Top 40 hit the following month. "Borderline" became her first Top Ten hit in March of 1984, beginning a remarkable string of 17 consecutive Top Ten hits. While "Lucky Star" was climbing to No. 4, Madonna began working on her first starring role in a feature film, Susan Seidelman's *Desperately Seeking Susan*.

Madonna's second album, the Niles Rodgers-produced *Like a Virgin*, was released at the end of 1984. The title track hit No. 1 in December, staying at the top of the charts for six weeks; it was the start of a whirlwind year for the singer. During 1985, Madonna became an international celebrity, selling millions of records on the strength of her stylish, sexy videos and forceful personality. After "Material Girl" became a No. 2 hit in March, Madonna began her first tour, supported by the Beastie Boys. "Crazy for You" became her second No. 1 single in May. *Desperately Seeking Susan* was released in July, becoming a box office hit; it also prompted a planned video release of *A Certain Sacrifice*, a low-budget erotic drama she filmed in 1979. *A Certain Sacrifice* wasn't the only embarrassing skeleton in the closet dragged into the light during the summer of 1985—both *Playboy* and *Penthouse* published nude photos of Madonna that she posed for in 1977. Nevertheless, her popularity continued unabated, with thousands of teenage girls adopting her sexy appearence, being dubbed "Madonna Wannabes." In August, she married actor Sean Penn; the couple had a rocky marriage that ended in 1989.

Madonna began collaborating with Patrick Leonard at the beginning of 1986; Leonard would co-write most of her biggest hits in the '80s, including "Live to Tell," which hit No. 1 in June of 1986. A more ambitious and accomplished record than her two previous albums, *True Blue* was released the following month, to both massive commercial success (it was a No. 1 in both the US and the UK, selling over five million copies in America alone) and critical acclaim. "Papa Don't Preach" became her fourth No. 1 hit in the US While her musical career was thriving, her film career took a savage hit with the November release of *Shanghai Surprise*. Starring Madonna and Sean Penn, the comedy received terrible reviews, which translated into disastrous box office returns.

At the beginning of 1987, she had her fifth No. 1 single with "Open Your Heart," the third No. 1 from *True Blue* alone. "La Isla Bonita," taken from the soundtrack of her third starring film, *Who's That Girl?*, was another Top Five hit, although the film itself was another box office bomb; the title track from the movie became her sixth No. 1 single. 1988 was a relatively quiet year for Madonna, as she spent the first half of the year acting in David Mamet's *Speed the Plow* on Broadway. In the meantime, she released the remix album *You Can Dance*. After withdrawing the divorce papers she filed at the beginning of 1988, she divorced Penn at the beginning of 1989.

Like a Prayer, released in the spring of 1989, was her most ambitious and far-reaching album, incorporating elements of pop, rock and dance. It was another No. 1 and launched the No. 1 title track and "Express Yourself," "Cherish," and "Keep It Together," three more Top Ten hits. In April 1990, she began her massive *Blonde Ambition* tour, which ran throughout the entire year. "Vogue" became a No. 1 hit in May, setting the stage for her co-starring role in Warren Beatty's *Dick Tracy;* it was her most successful film appearance since *Desperately Seeking Susan*. Madonna released a greatest hits album, *The Immaculate Collection*, at the end of the year. It featured two new songs, including the No. 1 single "Justify My Love," which sparked another controversy with its sexy video; the second new song, "Rescue Me," became the highest-debuting single by a female artist in US chart history, entering the charts at No. 15. *Truth or Dare*, a documentary of the *Blonde Ambition* tour, was released to positive reviews and strong ticket sales at the end of 1991.

Madonna returned to the charts in the summer of 1992 with the No. 1 "This Used to Be My Playground," a single featured in the film *A League of Their Own*, which featured the singer in a small part. Later that year, Madonna released *Sex*, an expensive, steel-bound soft-core pornography book that featured hundreds of erotic photographs of herself, several models, and other celebrities—including Isabella Rossellini, Big Daddy Kane, Naomi Campbell, and Vanilla Ice—as well as selected prose. *Sex* received wretched reviews and enormous negative publicity, yet that didn't stop the accompanying album, *Erotica*, from selling over two million copies. *Bedtime Stories*, released two years later, was a more sub-dued affair than *Erotica*. Initially, it didn't chart as impressively, prompt-ing some critics to label her a has-been, yet the album spawned her biggest hit, "Take a Bow," which spent seven weeks at No. 1. It also fea-tured the Björk-penned "Bedtime Stories," which became her first single not to make the Top 40; its follow up, "Human Nature," also failed to crack the Top 40. Nevertheless, *Bedtime Stories* marked her seventh album to go multi-platinum, ensuring her place as one of pop's most suc-cessful artists ever. — *Stephen Thomas Erlewine*

Madonna / 1983 / Sire ++++
Madonna's self-titled debut was one of the strongest dance records of the early '80s, featuring a state-of-the-art production and a handful of great songs. Although her voice was still quite thin at this point, Madonna pro-jected a powerful charisma, bringing slight material like "Everybody," "Physical Attraction," and "Burning Up" to life. However, it was on well-constructed pop songs like "Borderline," "Lucky Star," and "Holiday" that the record became truly impressive, as the material matched Madonna's performance. All three of the songs became hits and wrote the blueprint for dance-pop divas that dominated much of the remaining decade. — *Stephen Thomas Erlewine*

Like a Virgin / 1984 / Sire +++
With monster hits like "Material Girl," "Dress You Up," and the title track, this album exploits the traits that defined her then-budding persona. — *John Floyd*

True Blue / 1986 / Sire ++++
A staggering album from an artist known for hot singles, the hits include "Papa Don't Preach," "Open Your Heart," and "True Blue." "Live to Tell," her best, is also to be found here. — *John Floyd*

Who's That Girl / 1987 / Sire ++

You Can Dance / 1987 / Sire +++

☆ **Like a Prayer** / 1989 / Sire +++++
Out of all of Madonna's albums, *Like a Prayer* is her most explicit attempt at a major artistic statement. Even though it is apparent that she is trying to make a "serious" album, the kaleidoscopic variety of pop styles on *Like a Prayer* is quite dazzling. Ranging from the deep funk of "Express Yourself" and "Keep It Together," to the haunting "Oh Father" and "Like a Prayer," Madonna displays a commanding sense of songcraft, making this her best and most consistent album. — *Stephen Thomas Erlewine*

★ **The Immaculate Collection** / 1990 / Sire +++++
On the surface, the single-disc hits compilation *The Immaculate Collec-tion* appears to be a definitive retrospective of Madonna's heyday in the '80s. After all, it features 17 of Madonna's greatest hits, from "Holiday" and "Like a Virgin" to "Like a Prayer" and "Vogue." However, looks can be deceiving. It's true that *The Immaculate Collection* contains the bulk of Madonna's hits, but there are several big hits that aren't present, including "Angel," "Dress You Up," "True Blue," "Who's That Girl," and "Causing a Commotion." The songs that are included are frequently altered. Everything on the collection is remastered in Q-sound, which gives an exaggerated sense of stereo separation that often distorts the original intent of the recordings. Furthermore, several songs are faster than their original versions and some are faded out earlier than either their single or album versions, while others are segued together. In other words, while all the hits are present, they're simply not in their correct versions. Nevertheless, *The Immaculate Collection* remains a necessary purchase, because it captures everything Madonna is about and it proves that she was one of the finest singles artists of the '80s. Until the original single versions are compiled on another album, *The Immaculate Collec-tion* is the closest thing to a definitive retrospective. — *Stephen Thomas Erlewine*

Dick Tracy: "I'm Breathless" (Music from and Inspired by the Film) / 1990 / Sire ++

Erotica / Oct. 20, 1992 / Maverick +++

Bedtime Stories / 1994 / Maverick ++++
Perhaps Madonna correctly guessed that the public overdosed on the raw carnality of her book *Sex*. Perhaps she wanted to offer a more opti-mistic take on sex than the distant *Erotica*. Either way, *Bedtime Stories* is a warm album, with deep, gently pulsating grooves; the album's title isn't totally tongue-in-cheek. The best songs on the album ("Secret," "Inside of Me," "Sanctuary," "Bedtime Story," "Take a Bow") slowly work their mel-odies into the subconscious as the bass pulses. In that sense, it does offer an antidote to *Erotica*, which was filled with deep but cold grooves. The entire production of *Bedtime Stories* suggests that she wants listeners to acknowledge that her music isn't one-dimensional. She has succeeded with that goal, since *Bedtime Stories* offers her most humane and open music; it's even seductive. — *Stephen Thomas Erlewine*

Something to Remember / Nov. 7, 1995 / Maverick ++++
Something to Remember is Madonna's second greatest hits collection, compiling a selection of the singer's ballads. Several of her biggest hits

are included, including the No. 1's "Crazy for You," "Live to Tell," "This Used to Be My Playground," and "Take a Bow," as well as a handful of first-rate album tracks (a remixed "Love Don't Live Here Anymore," "Something to Remember," "Oh Father"), and three new tracks, most notably a version of Marvin Gaye's "I Want You" recorded with the Brit-ish trip-hop group Massive Attack. Only two tracks on the album overlap with *The Immaculate Collection*, and the disc also marks the first appearance of "This Used to Be My Playground" and "I'll Remember" on one of Madonna's albums. Throughout the album, Madonna proves that she's a terrific singer whose voice has improved over the years. Not one of the tracks is second-rate, and the best songs on *Something to Remem-ber* rank among the best pop music of the '80s and '90s. — *Stephen Tho-mas Erlewine*

Magnapop

Alternative Pop-Rock
This Athens, GA band creates high-energy punk-pop with catchy hooks and literate lyrics. Formed in 1987 by singer Linda Hopper, guitarist Ruthie Morris, drummer David McNair and bassist Shannon Mulvaney, the group recorded a demo album with their friend Michael Stipe in 1992, which was released on Caroline Records. In 1994 the group released their "official" debut, *Hot Boxing*, on Priority. *Hot Boxing* was produced by another of the band's friends, Bob Mould, and features a more streamlined, intense approach than the quirky, off-kilter demos. What makes Magnapop interesting (and different from many of the punk-pop bands out there) is the combination of Hopper's smooth, unhurried vocals and the furious lashings of Morris' guitar—it creates a tension that makes the group's songs all the more dramatic. An intelli-gent, underappreciated band. — *Heather Phares*

Magnapop / 1992 / Play It Again Sam ++++
This is a collection of demos and early singles produced by the band's friends, Michael Stipe and Bob Mould. *Magnapop* unveils the band as a punk-pop group with an arty bent, especially on songs like "Spill It" and "Favorite Writer." The cover of Big Star's "13" is a welcome addition to this good beginning. — *Heather Phares*

● **Hot Boxing** / 1994 / Priority ++++
On their official debut, Magnapop iron out the kinks of their sound and come out a tighter but slightly less interesting band for it. The group are at their best on "Lay It Down," "Piece of Cake," and "The Crush," where they mix punk-fueled energy and wistful lyrics. — *Heather Phares*

Rubbing Doesn't Help / May 21, 1996 / Priority +++

Magnetic Fields

Alternative Pop-Rock, Lo-Fi, Indie Rock
The Magnetic Fields are a bonafide band, but in most essential respects they are the project of studio wunderkind Stephin Merritt. Merritt writes, produces, and (lately) sings all of their material, as well as plays many of the instruments, concocting a sort of indie-pop synth-rock. While the Magnetic Fields may draw upon the electronic textures of vintage acts like ABBA, Kraftwerk, Roxy Music with Eno, Joy Division, and Gary Neu-man, Merritt's vision is far more pointed toward the alternative rock underground. His songs are also far warmer and more pure pop-oriented than the above reference points might lead you to believe, sounding at times like late-20th century equivalents to Phil Spector or Brian Wilson.

Merritt had been recording on his own four-track from a very young age, but didn't issue the first Magnetic Fields album until 1990, when he was well into his twenties. The first pair of discs featured the choirgirl vocals of Susan Amway, and are probably the most accessible offerings for general listeners wary of electro-rock.

On subsequent releases, Merritt handled the vocals himself in a deep croon not far removed from his European influences. The synth-pop quo-tient also became heavier, although Merritt has always taken care to mix in quite a few natural instruments with the electronic ones, often with the help of Claudia Gonson (percussion) and Sam Davol (cello, flute). The emphasis has always remained on the pop hooks and eccentric, romanti-cally reflective lyrics rather than the bedrock synthetic rhythms and tex-tures.

In addition to his work with Magnetic Fields, Merritt has involved himself in several side projects, the most notable being the 6ths' *Wasps Nests* album (1995). Merritt sang only one track himself on this disc, for which he acted as composer/producer/multi-instrumentalist, employing well-known alternative rock singers like Barbara Manning, Dean Ware-ham (Luna), Lou Barlow, Georgia Hubley (Yo La Tengo), Chris Knox, and Robert Scott (the Bats) to handle the lead vocals. — *Richie Unterberger*

Distant Plastic Trees / 1990 / Red Flame +++

The Wayward Bus / 1991 / Feel Good All Over ++++

Holiday / 1994 / Feel Good All Over ++++

The Charm of the Highway Strip / 1994 / Merge +++

● **The Wayward Bus/Distant Plastic Trees** / 1995 / Merge ++++

Get Lost / Oct. 24, 1995 / Merge ✦✦✦

The Main Ingredient

Soul, R&B
Originally formed in 1964 as the Poets, this New York soul group (Donald McPherson, Luther Simmons, Jr., and Tony Sylvester) recorded for Red Bird before changing their name in 1966. After McPherson's death in 1971, Cuba Gooding became the lead singer, and the band scored three Top 40 hits, including "Everybody Plays the Fool," which went to No. 3.

The Main Ingredient tried it again in 1986, with Cuba Gooding returning to his lead spot. They recorded for Zakia, but didn't get much response to "Do Me Right." They kept trying, cutting a song on Polydor in 1989. Longtime group member Luther Simmons, who had left in 1975 to become a stockbroker and then come back in 1980, returned to Wall Street and was replaced for this session by Jerome Jackson. —*Bil Carpenter & Stephen Thomas Erlewine*

A Quiet Storm / Apr. 1996 / RCA ✦✦✦✦
Be cautioned that this 20-track retrospective of material spanning the late '60s to the mid-'70s is not a best-of, although it does include some of their biggest hits ("Just Don't Want to Be Lonely," "Everybody Plays the Fool"). As the title indicates, this focuses on the mellow and romantic side of the group. As the Main Ingredient largely specialized in mellow and romantic songs, this ends up being close to something of a best-of anyway. The relentless soft-pillow ambience of the tracks can become wearisome; in this context, the easygoing "Everybody Plays the Fool" sounds more like a blitzkrieg than a "quiet storm." —*Richie Unterberger*

● The All-Time Greatest Hits / RCA ✦✦✦✦
It wasn't until 1971 that the Main Ingredient's fortunes changed; when Cuba Gooding replaced Donald McPherson, his engaging voice helped make them part of the "sweet" soul trend. Gooding's leads made "Spinning Around (I Must Be Falling in Love)" and "Everybody Plays the Fool" huge hits, as well as "Just Don't Want to Be Lonely" and "Happiness Is Just Around the Bend." These and several other hits are featured on this anthology covering their prime years on RCA. —*Ron Wynn*

The Mamas & The Papas

Folk-Rock, Pop-Rock
The leading California-based vocal group of the '60s, the Mamas & The Papas epitomized the ethos of mid- to late-'60s pop culture: live free, play free, and love free. Their music, built around radiant harmonies and a solid electric-folk foundation, was gorgeous on its own terms, but a major part of its appeal lay in the easygoing Southern California lifestyle it endorsed.

Founder and leader John Phillips came out of early rock roots and a partly successful folk career, as did Cass Elliott and Denny Doherty, while Phillips' wife Michelle was an ex-model who also sang. They got together out of several failed folk groups just as the music was going electric, pulled up stakes in New York and headed west, where they signed with Lou Adler and wowed the world with a song called "California Dreamin'."

Phillips was a pop poet with a commercial edge, and a good arranger. The group had enviable chart success, lived well, and indulged themselves lavishly yet retained credibility with the counterculture. But it all came apart in a couple of years, as the quartet's intertwining romantic entanglements, coupled with their chemical excesses (detailed in separate books by John and Michelle Phillips), strangled their ability to work. By 1971 they were a fond memory, although a reconstituted version of the quartet has done well on the oldies circuit in the late '80s and early '90s. —*Bruce Eder*

● 16 Greatest Hits / 1970 / MCA ✦✦✦✦
A great overview of the music from this group, one of the founders of the California sound in the late '60s. This is a good collection of their unforgettable electric folk-pop songs, including "Monday, Monday" and "California Dreamin'." (Originally released in August 1969 by Dunhill Records as *16 of Their Greatest Hits*, it was reissued on CD by MCA Records in 1986.) —*AMG*

Creeque Alley / 1991 / MCA ✦✦✦✦
They weren't the most important folk-rock group of the mid-'60s; the Byrds and others produced more enduring music. Yet the Mamas & The Papas were undoubtedly the most commercially successful folk-rock group of their time, racking up an astonishing nine Top 30 hits in little more than a year and a half. This 43-song double CD is by far the most comprehensive document of their legacy. It draws most heavily from their two 1966 albums (nine songs originate from their debut album *If You Can Believe Your Eyes and Ears* alone), when John Phillips' songwriting talent had yet to exhaust itself. Beyond the hits, the material is variable. Quite a few album tracks—especially "Got a Feelin'," "Straight Shooter," "Go Where You Wanna Go," "Once Was a Time I Thought," and their cover of Lennon/McCartney's "I Call Your Name"—were strong

enough to have been hits on their own steam. Their slowed-down, California-ized versions of rock oldies were more problematic. And there's no doubt that their later material is less spirited and memorable than their initial burst of glory. The set includes various late-'60s and '70s solo recordings by each of the group's members (including small hit singles by John Phillips and Cass Elliott). Perhaps the most intriguing rarities are from the members' pre-Mamas days. These include commercial folk by the Big Three (featuring Cass Elliott) and primitive pop-folk-rock by the Mugwumps (including Elliott, Denny Doherty, and future Lovin' Spoonful member Zal Yanovsky). —*Richie Unterberger*

Manfred Mann

Art-Rock/Progressive-Rock, British Invasion, Pop-Rock
An R&B band that only played pop to get on the charts, Manfred Mann ranked among the most adept British Invasion acts in both styles. South African-born keyboardist Manfred Mann was originally an aspiring jazz player, moving toward R&B when more blues-oriented sounds became in vogue in England in the early '60s. Original Manfred Mann singer Paul Jones was one of the best British Invasion singers, and his resonant vocals were the best feature of their early R&B sides, which had a slightly jazzier and smoother touch than the early work of the Rolling Stones and Animals. It was a couple covers of obscure girl group songs, "Do Wah Diddy Diddy" (the Exciters) and "Sha La La" (the Shirelles), that broke the group internationally—"Do Wah Diddy Diddy" reached No. 1 in the States, and "Sha La La" just missed the Top Ten. The Paul Jones lineup never duplicated this success, although "Come Tomorrow" and "Pretty Flamingo" were smaller hits. From 1964 to 1966, they took the approach of playing gutsy pop-rock on their singles (including the original version of "My Little Red Book") and soul and R&B on their albums, with occasional detours into jazz, Dylan (their cover of his then-unreleased "If You Gotta Go, Go Now" was a big British hit), and competent original material.

Jones left for a solo career and acting in 1966, and the group reformed around singer Mike D'Abo (Beatle friend Klaus Voormann was also in this aggregation on bass). Adopting an even more pop-oriented approach for the singles, with occasional psychedelic and progressive touches, the band ran off a string of Top Ten hits in their homeland until 1969, although the only one to hit the jackpot in the US was their cover of another unreleased Dylan song, "The Mighty Quinn."

Mann dissolved the D'Abo lineup in 1969 to form Manfred Mann Chapter Three with drummer Mike Hugg, who had been in the band since the beginning. The outfit's early jazz-rock efforts were interesting, but not very popular, and Manfred steered the ship back toward mainstream rock by forming yet another incarnation, Manfred Mann's Earth Band. The heavier, more synthesizer-oriented outfit made quite a few albums in the 1970s; 1976's *The Roaring Silence* made the Top Ten, and featured the no. 1 hit "Blinded by the Light" (Mann also made the Top 40 with another Springsteen cover, "Spirit in the Night"). Ironically, despite Mann's oft-proclaimed preferences for serious explorations of jazz, blues, and progressive music, it's his pop-rock recordings that hold up best, and for which he'll be remembered most. —*Richie Unterberger*

The Manfred Mann Album / 1964 / Ascot ✦✦✦
Manfred Mann's debut full-length US platter was probably their strongest, and indeed one of the stronger British Invasion albums of the very competitive year of 1964. Besides the smash "Do Wah Diddy Diddy," it contained a number of fine soul and R&B covers. Standouts were the versions of "Untie Me" and Ike & Tina Turner's "It's Gonna Work Out Fine," as well as the strong pounding Paul Jones original, "Without You." —*Richie Unterberger*

The Five Faces of Manfred Mann / 1965 / Ascot ✦✦✦

Soul of Mann / 1967 / See for Miles ✦✦✦

The Roaring Silence / 1976 / Warner Bros. ✦✦✦✦
A later edition of Mann's band, which had a '70s hit with Bruce Springsteen's "Blinded by the Light" (on this album). —*William Ruhlmann*

The R&B Years / 1982 / See for Miles ✦✦✦✦
The Manfreds always took great pains to point out that their true love was R&B and jazz, not the pop-rock they sang on their hit singles, although they should have realized that their fans dug both approaches. Anyway, this 20-song compilation is a good taste of their purer sounds, taken from LPs, EPs, and singles cut by the band during the Paul Jones era (1963-66). Look to EMI's fine *Best of Manfred Mann* CD for the big hits; this has covers of R&B and soul cuts by the likes of Willie Dixon, Muddy Waters, and Screamin' Jay Hawkins, as well as some more-than-competent group originals in the same vein. "I'm Your Kingpin," "Without You," and "Hubble Bubble (Toil and Trouble)" rank among the better early self-penned British R&B, and their cover of Ben E. King's "Groovin'" is a stormer. Although Manfred Mann weren't quite as fine R&B interpreters as fellow British Invaders the Stones, Yardbirds, and Animals, they were quite respectable, and this is a good complement to the more wide-ranging EMI anthology. —*Richie Unterberger*

● **Best of: The Definitive Collection** / 1992 / Capitol ✦✦✦✦
For a guy who claimed to be a jazz buff and to despise pop, Manfred Mann (the keyboard player) sure knew a pop hit when he heard one. And here they are, including "Do Wah Diddy Diddy" and "Pretty Flamingo." —*William Ruhlmann*

Chapter Two: The Best of the Fontana Years / 1994 / Fontana ✦✦✦
The departure of Paul Jones for a solo career in 1966 spelled major reorganization for Manfred and his troops, who recruited lead vocalist Mike D'Abo and bassist (and Beatle chum) Klaus Voormann. To the surprise of many, the new lineup rattled off seven Top Ten British hits in the next three years in a far less R&B-oriented style. Emphasizing harmonies and Manfred Mann's inventiveness as arranger and keyboardist (often employing the then-futuristic Mellotron), this represented the group's most commercial phase, with an upbeat approach that bordered on downright chipper. These 20 tracks include all the key singles from this time, as well as a few LP cuts. Frankly, this rather lightweight, prototypically cheery late-'60s British pop—sounding rather like a more commercial version of the *Odessey & Oracle*-era Zombies—hasn't aged nearly as well as their far gutsier Paul Jones-era recordings. Only one of these songs was a hit in the US, but it was a big one—their great 1968 arrangement of the then-unreleased Bob Dylan song "The Mighty Quinn." —*Richie Unterberger*

● **Best of the EMI Years** / Jan. 23, 1996 / Griffin ✦✦✦✦
This double-CD replaces EMI's *Best Of* anthology (1992) as the collection of choice for their British Invasion years due to its slightly more extensive length (34 tracks), including most of the tracks on the previous compilation. It has all of the British and American hits, as well as some standout B-sides and album tracks, some of which have been quite hard to come by on reissues. Classic British Invasion music by one of the most versatile bands of the era, comfortable with both straight pop-rock and jazz-tinged R&B. —*Richie Unterberger*

Manfred Mann Album/Five Faces of Manfred Mann / Feb. 20, 1996 / Capitol ✦✦✦✦
A CD reissue of their first two albums, with a few bonus tracks, most notably a previously unreleased version of "Sticks and Stones" and the instrumental "Mr. Anello," which was included on their UK debut LP, but left off its stateside counterpart. Very good British Invasion music, though most of the best songs are available on Griffin's *The Best of the EMI Years.* —*Richie Unterberger*

Manhattans

Soul, Urban, Doo Wop
A venerable soul quintet from New Jersey, whose career has spanned the dawn of soul and the death of disco, although they have steadfastly preferred ballads over the years. Led initially by George Smith, who died in 1970, the Manhattans first charted in 1965 with "I Wanna Be (Your Everything)." After a string of solid R&B sellers on Carnival and DeLuxe, Gerald Alston replaced the late Smith and the group moved to Columbia. In 1976 they struck pay dirt with the elegant platinum-selling ballad "Kiss and Say Goodbye," which topped both the pop and soul lists. Several more huge R&B hits preceded their uplifting 1980 gold record "Shining Star," and still more followed. —*Bill Dahl*

● **The Best of the Manhattans: Kiss and Say Goodbye** / Oct. 31, 1995 / Sony ✦✦✦✦

● **Dedicated to You: Golden Carnival Classics, Pt. 1** / Collectables ✦✦✦✦
The first of two superb volumes covering the Manhattans' early years on the Carnival label, the period many regard as their greatest. While they didn't come close to equaling the crossover/pop success they would enjoy with Columbia in their second incarnation, these were the pure soul works. The group featured both a glorious George "Smitty" Smith and young Blue Lovett, and their songs were produced solely with soul/R&B audiences in mind. There was little of the slick, polished orchestrations or smooth arrangements that were the hallmark of the Columbia hits. Instead, Smith's aching, soaring leads and the group's alternately mellow and frenzied harmonies were the high points. No matter what the sound quality, both this album and its counterpart are essential purchases for soul fans. —*Ron Wynn*

For You & Yours: Golden Carnival Classics, Pt. 2 / Collectables ✦✦✦✦
For many Manhattans fans, their earliest singles for Carnival were their greatest. These featured the wondrous George "Smitty" Smith, a young Blue Lovett, and some classic heartbreak and anguished soul singles, such as the divine "I Wanna Be (Your Everything)." These haven't been available on anthologies very often, and haven't been available anywhere since the early days of the Solid Smoke series. While Collectables' reissues sometimes leave a lot to be desired in the sound category, these songs are so good and so rare that any anthology featuring them has to get the highest recommendation, regardless of technical merit. This is the second of two volumes covering this era. —*Ron Wynn*

Barry Manilow

b. Jun. 17, 1946
Piano, Vocals / Adult Contemporary, Pop, Soft Rock
Although he has never earned the respect of critics or much of the public, Barry Manilow was one of the most successful recording artists of the '70s. Manilow began his pop music career by writing advertising jingles in the '60s; during this time, the Julliard-trained musician honed his pop instincts, as evidenced by the sheer number of successful advertisements he wrote. In 1972, he began accompanying Bette Midler on piano as she performed in New York City's gay bath houses. Manilow arranged her first two albums, which helped him earn a record contract with Bell. His self-titled first album was a flop, yet his second featured the No. 1 ballad "Mandy."

"Mandy" began a decade's worth of polished MOR hits for Manilow, which included the No. 1 singles "I Write the Songs" and "Looks Like We Made It," as well as Top Tens "Could It Be Magic," "Copacabana (At the Copa)" and "I Made It Through the Rain." Manilow also became a popular live act during this time. By the mid-'80s, he decided to broaden his musical horizons by making records of jazz and pop standards. At the end of the decade, the widow of Johnny Mercer invited him to set music to a number of the great songwriter's unpublished lyrics; some of the results appeared on *Showstoppers.* —*Stephen Thomas Erlewine*

● **Greatest Hits, Vol. 1** / Nov. 1978 / Arista ✦✦✦✦
Manilow has had a load of albums, but essentially he is a singles artist. This first *Greatest Hits* collection is the place to start, for those desiring an introduction to one of the most successful MOR singers of all time. Among the songs included in this collection are "Mandy," "Looks Like We Made It," "Can't Smile Without You," "Tryin' to Get the Feeling Again," and "Daybreak." —*Rick Clark*

● **Greatest Hits, Vol. 2** / Nov. 1983 / Arista ✦✦✦✦
Included is "Could It Be Magic," "This One's for You," "Weekend in New England," "Copacabana (At the Copa)," and "I Write the Songs." —*Rick Clark*

Greatest Hits, Vol. 3 / 1989 / Arista ✦✦✦✦
Vol. 3 isn't as consistently strong as the first two, since it consists mainly of his less successful tracks. This set contains "The Old Songs," "Memory," "Let's Hang On," "Somewhere Down the Road," "I Made It Through the Rain," and his Top Ten version of Ian Hunter's "Ships." —*Rick Clark*

Greatest Hits Box Set / 1992 / Arista ✦✦✦
For Barry Manilow fanatics, this lavish, expensive box set (which is filled with rarities) will be hard to live without, but more casual fans should stick with the *Greatest Hits* albums. —*Stephen Thomas Erlewine*

Aimee Mann

Bass, Guitar, Vocals / Singer-Songwriter, Pop-Rock
During the '80s, Aimee Man led the post-new wave pop group, Til Tuesday. After releasing three albums with the group, Mann broke up the band and embarked on a solo career. Her first solo album, *Whatever*, was a more introspective, folk-tinged effort than Til Tuesday's albums and received uniformly positive reviews upon its release in the summer of 1993. However, the album was only a small hit, spending only seven weeks on the American charts, where it peaked at 127. Nevertheless, *Whatever* rejuvenated her career—after its release, critics were praising her songwriting, as were peers like Elvis Costello, Difford & Tilbrook, and Andy Partridge.

Early in 1995, Mann had a modest hit with "That's Just What You Are," a song included on the soundtrack to the television series, *Melrose Place.* Following the success of the single, Mann was set to release her second solo album in the spring of 1995, but her record label, Imago, filed for bankruptcy before its release. She signed a contract with Reprise Records after Imago went under, but Imago prevented her from releasing any records. For most of 1995, Mann battled Imago in an attempt to free herself from the label, eventually winning her independence at the end of the year. After her dispute with Imago was settled, she signed with DGC Records. Mann's second album, *I'm with Stupid*, was released in England in the late fall of 1995 and in January of 1996 in America. Again, it was greeted with positive reviews, but weak sales. —*Stephen Thomas Erlewine*

● **Whatever** / May 11, 1993 / Imago ✦✦✦✦
Led by the instantly memorable power-pop of "I Should've Known," Aimee Mann's first solo album, *Whatever*, is a strong collection of pure pop singles and folk-tinged ballads, proving that she is a very talented songwriter with a gift for melody, as well as a fine lyricist. —*Stephen Thomas Erlewine*

I'm with Stupid / Nov. 1995 / Geffen ✦✦✦
From the opening of "Long Shot," with its rolling hip-hop-derived beat and its nonchalant profanity, it's clear that Aimee Mann is trying to appeal to a wider audience with her second solo album, *I'm with Stupid.* Taking her cues from Liz Phair and Beck, she adds alternative rock flour-

ishes to her music but she never abandons her love of the basic, three-minute pop single. Mann builds from the more pop-oriented songs on *Whatever*, incorporating her confessional singer-songwriter instincts into the pop songs while working with a more adventurous production and instrumentation. Occasionally, the fusion is a bit awkward, but the best moments on *I'm with Stupid*—the sighing "Choice in the Matter," the nearly perfect "That's Just What You Are," featuring backing vocals by Glenn Tilbrook, and the Bernard Butler collaboration "Sugarcoated"—surpass even the best moments on *Whatever*. However, *I'm with Stupid* falls short of matching Mann's debut for consistent song quality—there are several tracks that are pleasant, but simply don't lead anywhere. Nevertheless, the album confirms that she is a distinctive, talented songwriter. At her best, she is as capable of melding melody with intelligent lyrics as her idols Elvis Costello, Difford/Tillbrook, and Ray Davies. —*Stephen Thomas Erlewine*

The Marcels

Doo Wop
This Pittsburgh ensemble deserved a much better fate than being known primarily for a novelty-tinged cover of "Blue Moon." Baritone vocalist Richard F. Knauss teamed with Fred Johnson, Gene J. Bricker, Ron Mundy, and lead vocalist Cornelius Harp, an integrated ensemble. They named themselves after Harp's hairstyle, the marcel. The group did a string of covers as demo tapes that were sent to Colpix. The label's A&R director had them cut several oldies at RCA's New York studios in 1961, one of them being "Blue Moon." They used the bass intro arrangement from the Cadillacs' "Zoom" and the results were a huge hit. It eventually topped both the pop and R&B charts, and also was an international smash. The group eventually appeared in the film *Twist Around the Clock* with Dion and Chubby Checker. They eventually recorded an 18-cut LP for Colpix. Alan Johnson and Walt Maddox later replaced Knauss and Gene Bricker, making them an all-Black unit. The group did score another Top Ten pop single with "Heartaches," another cover of a pre-rock single. This peaked at No. 7 pop and No. 19 R&B in 1961. They continued recording on Kyra, Queen Bee, St. Clair, Rocky, and Monogram with varying lineups, but never again equaled their past success. —*Ron Wynn*

● **The Best of the Marcels** / 1990 / Rhino ✦✦✦✦
An outstanding vocal ensemble that is exceptional on nonsense/novelty tunes like "Blue Moon." —*Ron Wynn*

Marillion

Hard Rock, Art-Rock/Progressive-Rock
Marillion was one of the leading art-rock bands of the '80s, paying homage to the theatrical thrills of early Genesis before evolving into a more straightforward hard rock. Over the years, the group has been quite popular in the UK, peaking in 1985 with the *Misplaced Childhood* album, but has never been more than a cult act in the US; they continue to tour and record in the '90s, with a faithful cult of fans supporting their latest efforts. —*Stephen Thomas Erlewine*

Script for a Jester's Tear / 1983 / Capitol ✦✦✦✦
Their strong debut shows the influence of Peter Hammill, Pink Floyd, Rick Wakeman, Jethro Tull, and the much-ballyhooed resemblance to Genesis. —*Michael P. Dawson*

Fugazi / 1984 / Capitol ✦✦✦✦
Gut-wrenchingly powerful lyrics and dynamic prog-rock performance make this a classic! —*Michael P. Dawson*

Misplaced Childhood / 1985 / Capitol ✦✦✦✦
A masterpiece of articulate and emotional lyrics, it has exciting and colorful musical settings. The songs form a continuous album-length suite. —*Michael P. Dawson*

Clutching at Straws / Jun. 19, 1987 / Capitol ✦✦✦

The Thieving Magpie (la Gazza Ladra) / 1988 / Capitol ✦✦✦

Season's End / 1989 / Capitol ✦✦

● **Six of One, Half-dozen of the Other** / 1992 / IRS ✦✦✦✦
A fine collection of Marillion's best and most popular tracks, *Six of One, Half-Dozen of the Other* offers a good introduction to the art-rock group. —*Stephen Thomas Erlewine*

Martha & The Vandellas

Soul, Motown, Girl Group
One of Motown's finest female groups formed almost by accident. Martha Reeves had been in the Del-Phis and recorded solo for Checkmate, but in the early '60s was working as an A&R secretary at Motown, doing some background work on the side. She organized a group with Annette Beard and Rosalind Ashford in 1962. They roared into the spotlight with "Come and Get These Memories" in 1963, and Reeves' husky, alternately sensual and demure leads made them a hit attraction through 1967. They scored No. 1 R&B hits with "Heat Wave" and "Jimmy Mack" (both cross-

over Top Ten pop winners as well) and Top Ten R&B hits with "Quicksand," "Nowhere to Run," "My Baby Loves Me," "Honey Chile," and "I'm Ready for Love." Oddly, their finest song, "Dancing in the Streets," only reached No. 2. Beard departed in 1964, and was replaced by Betty Kelly, an ex-Velvelette. They disbanded from 1969 to 1971, then re-formed with Reeves and her sister Lois, plus Sandra Tilley. They split for good in 1972, as Martha Reeves went solo and Lois Reeves joined Quiet Elegance. Martha Reeves worked with various producers throughout the '70s, among them Richard Perry, and had only sporadic success recording for MCA, Arista, and Fantasy. She reunited with the Vandellas in 1989 and has continued performing with them ever since. She and original Vandellas Rosalind (Ashford) Holmes and Annette Beard recorded for Motorcity in England in 1989, and Lois Reeves also did a solo session with them, as did their brother Benny Reeves. —*Ron Wynn*

★ **Live Wire! The Singles (1962-1972)** / Sep. 7, 1993 / Motown ✦✦✦✦✦
This two-CD box set includes all of the top singles and many of the flip-sides that Martha Reeves and The Vandellas cut for Motown. All the hits are here, of course; the collector will be especially interested in the B-sides and non-hit singles, many of which employed the songwriting talents of Motown regulars like Holland-Dozier-Holland and Mickey Stevenson. There's also the rare single (featuring Gloria Williamson on lead vocals) cut by the Vells in 1962, before Reeves took top billing and the group changed their name. Eight of these cuts have never been released on album before. Among the non-hits, there isn't anything to match "Heat Wave" or "Dancing in the Street," but Reeves' astonishingly powerful voice never falters. She was arguably Motown's most talented female singer, but the label's investment in her seemed to flag as the decade progressed. The later material lacks the distinction of her classic period, though the 1970 album track "I Should Be Proud" is a little-known (if somewhat heavy-handed) protest against the Vietnam War. —*Richie Unterberger*

● **Milestones** / 1995 / Motown ✦✦✦✦
Featuring 18 of Martha & The Vandellas' biggest hits and finest songs, *Milestones* is an inexpensive introduction to one of Motown's best girl groups. —*Stephen Thomas Erlewine*

The Marvelettes

Soul, Motown, Girl Group
Probably the most pop-oriented of Motown's major female acts, the Marvelettes didn't project as strong an identity as the Supremes, Mary Wells, or Martha Reeves, but recorded quite a few hits, including Motown's first No. 1 single, "Please Mr. Postman" (1961). "Postman," as well as other chirpy early '60s hits like "Playboy," "Twistin' Postman," and "Beechwood 4-5789," were the label's purest girl group efforts. Featuring two strong lead singers, Gladys Horton and Wanda Young, the Marvelettes went through five different lineups, but maintained a high standard on their recordings. After a few years, they moved from girl group sounds to uptempo and midtempo numbers that were more characteristic of Motown's production line. They received no small help from Smokey Robinson, who produced and wrote many of their singles; Holland-Dozier-Holland, Berry Gordy, Mickey Stevenson, Marvin Gaye, and Ashford-Simpson also got involved with the songwriting and production at various points. After the mid-'60s, Wanda Young assumed most of the lead vocal duties, Gladys Horton departing from the group in the late '60s. While the Marvelettes didn't cut as many monster smashes as most of their Motown peers after the early '60s, they did periodically surface with classic hits like "Too Many Fish in the Sea," "Don't Mess with Bill," and "The Hunter Gets Captured by the Game." There were also plenty of fine minor hits and misses, like 1965's "I'll Keep Holding On," which is just as memorable as the well-known Motown chart-toppers of the era. The group quietly disbanded in the early '70s after several years without a major hit. —*Richie Unterberger*

Deliver: The Singles (1961-1971) / Sep. 7, 1993 / Motown ✦✦✦✦
Forty-one songs, featuring most of both the A-sides and B-sides, nine of which had never been issued on album before. The ace Motown songwriting and production stable was involved in virtually every one of these tracks, making for a surprisingly strong and consistent collection. Includes all the chart hits, as well as rarities like the Phil Spector-style single they released in 1963 as the Darnells. —*Richie Unterberger*

● **Motown Milestones** / Jul. 25, 1995 / Motown ✦✦✦✦
For those who don't want to invest in the two-CD *Deliver* anthology, this 20-song best-of is a good alternative. Contains all of their major pop hits, as well as some obscure low-charting singles. —*Richie Unterberger*

Barbara Mason

Vocals / Soul
An interesting minor soul performer, Mason initially focused on songwriting when she entered the music business in her teens. As a performer, though, she had a huge hit in 1965 with her self-penned "Yes, I'm Ready" (No. 5 pop, No. 2 R&B), a fetching soul-pop confection that spot-

lighted her high, girlish vocals. One of the first examples of the sweet, lush sound that came to be called Philly soul, she had modest success throughout the rest of the decade on the small Arctic label, reaching the pop Top 40 again in 1965 with "Sad, Sad Girl."

In the early and mid-'70s, Mason toughened her persona considerably, singing about sexual love and infidelity with a frankness that was uncommon for a female soul singer in songs like "Bed and Board," "From His Woman to You," and "Shackin' Up." Sweet soul continued to be her groove, and she continued to write some of her material. But the production, as it was throughout soul in the '70s, was more funk-oriented, and at times Mason would interrupt her singing to deliver some straight-talkin' raps about romance. Curtis Mayfield produced her on a cover of Mayfield's "Give Me Your Love," which restored her to the pop Top 40 and R&B Top Ten in 1973; "From His Woman to You" and "Shackin' Up" were also solid soul sellers in the mid-'70s. After leaving Buddah Records in 1975, she only dented the charts periodically, with "I Am Your Woman, She Is Your Wife" (1978), "Another Man" (1984), and a couple of other singles. —*Richie Unterberger*

● **The Very Best of Barbara Mason** / 1996 / Sequel ✦✦✦✦
Most of this 15-track comp deals with her 1972-75 stint on Buddah, ending with a few tracks from the late '70s and early '80s. Those who prefer '60s soul to '70s soul will prefer her early work, but at the time of its release this was the best CD compilation of her material available, including the hits "Give Me Your Love," "From His Woman to You," and "Shackin' Up." The version of "Yes I'm Ready" here, by the way, is not the 1965 original, but an early-'70s remake. —*Richie Unterberger*

Massive Attack

Alternative Pop-Rock, Club-Dance, Trip-Hop
Massive Attack was one of the pioneers of the British dance genre labelled "trip-hop," a dark, seductive combination of hip-hop beats, atmospheric reverb-laden guitars and samples, soul hooks, deep bass grooves, and ethereal melodies. Released in 1991, *Blue Lines* set the pace for much of the non-techno British dance of the decade, including that of Portishead and former Massive Attack member Tricky. Both of these acts managed to score more commercial success, including alternative hits in America, but much of their work builds on the concepts of Massive Attack. *Protection*, the group's second album, was a critical and underground hit in England during 1994, yet it made little impact in the US when it was released early in 1995. —*Stephen Thomas Erlewine*

● **Blue Lines** / 1991 / Virgin ✦✦✦✦
At the time of its 1991 release, *Blue Lines* was a startlingly fresh album. Before Massive Attack, few dance collectives attempted to fuse hip-hop rhythms with hypnotic, trance-like pop melodies and soul instrumentation. All of the album has a dark, muted quality, making the tracks blend together seamlessly. While that might mean the songs are indistinguishable from each other, Massive Attack offer enough subtle variations in the rhythms and arrangements to keep the record a mesmerising listen. —*Stephen Thomas Erlewine*

Protection / 1994 / Virgin ✦✦✦

No Protection / 1995 / Circa ✦✦✦✦
Protection was widely considered a disappointing follow-up to Massive Attack's groundbreaking debut, *Blue Lines*. Where their debut bent all of the conventional hip-hop, dub reggae, and soul rules, *Protection* essentially delivered more of the same. Perhaps that's the reason why Mad Professor's remix of the album, *No Protection*, was welcomed with open arms by both Massive Attack fans and critics. Mad Professor has returned the group to their experimental, cut-and-paste dub reggae and hip-hop roots. He has gutted the songs—twisting the melodies around and reassembling the vocal tracks, giving the songs deeper, fuller grooves and an eerily seductive atmosphere. In other words, he has made *Protection* into a more daring and fulfilling album with his remixes. —*Stephen Thomas Erlewine*

Material Issue

Alternative Pop-Rock, Power-Pop
Material Issue's music is a return to the classic power-pop formula: catchy, melodic songs driven by loud, jangly guitars and usually paying tribute to girls and teenage love. The inevitable Beatles/Big Star/Cheap Trick/Tom Petty comparisons sparked intense interest in the band from power-pop fans and critics, and the group's musical allegiances were further underscored when ex-Shoes member Jeff Murphy produced their first two records, and Cheap Trick's Rick Nielsen guested on 1994's *Freak City Soundtrack*. The group was formed in Chicago by vocalist/guitarist Jim Ellison, an early member of Green, and his friend Ted Ansani (bass); they located drummer Mike Zelenko through a want ad. They released a self-titled EP in 1987 and attracted some local attention through a 1989 single. Their 1991 debut for Mercury, *International Pop Overthrow*, was hailed as pure power-pop in all its glory and earned the band a fan base; several songs became hits on modern-rock radio. *Destination Universe*

tended to follow an identical formula and was not as well-received. *Freak City Soundtrack* utilized a more streamlined, '70s hard rock production and consolidated the group's standing as critics' darlings, but when the album failed to sell, Mercury dropped the group. Sadly, Ellison committed suicide on June 20, 1996, suffocating himself in his garage with carbon monoxide fumes from his moped. —*Steve Huey*

● **International Pop Overthrow** / 1991 / Mercury ✦✦✦✦
Produced by Jeff Murphy of the Shoes, this major-label debut contained some power-pop gems like "Renee Remains the Same," "Dianne," "Valerie Loves Me," and the title cut. Fans of Cheap Trick and early Who should love much of this. Also check out their self-titled EP, which preceded this album. —*Rick Clark*

Destination Universe / Mar. 1992 / Mercury ✦✦✦

Freak City Soundtrack / Mar. 8, 1994 / Mercury ✦✦✦
Energetic pop-rock abounds on Material Issue's third album. "Goin' Through Your Purse" kicks things off sounding like a garage punk version of "Ballroom Blitz"-era Sweet. The single, "Kim the Waitress," fuses Byrds-style 12-string guitars and electric sitar with rich vocal harmonies. Other highlights include "Funny Feeling" and "The Fan." —*Rick Clark*

Dave Matthews Band

Guitar, Vocals / Rock 'n' Roll
The South African vocalist/guitarist Dave Matthews formed the Dave Matthews band in Virginia in the early '90s. Featuring Matthews, Stefan Lessard, Leroi Moor, Boyd Tinsley, and Carter Beauford, the group's music presents a more pop-oriented version of The Grateful Dead, crossed with the worldbeat explorations of Paul Simon and Sting. The band built up a strong word-of-mouth following in the early '90s by touring the country constantly, concentrating on college campuses. In addition to amassing a sizable following, their self-released album *Remember Two Things* sold well for an independent release; soon, they were attracting the attention of majors. Signing with RCA, the Dave Matthews Band released their major-label debut, *Under the Table & Dreaming*, in the fall of 1994. By spring of 1995, the record had launched the hit single "What Would You Say" and sold over a million copies.

A year and a half after the release of *Under the Table & Dreaming*, the record had sold over four million copies in the US alone. In April of 1996, the Dave Matthews Band released *Crash*, which entered the charts at No. 2 and quickly went platinum. —*Stephen Thomas Erlewine*

Remember Two Things / 1993 / Bama Rags ✦✦✦

● **Under the Table & Dreaming** / Apr. 1994 / RCA ✦✦✦✦
On their major-label debut, *Under the Table & Dreaming*, the Dave Matthews Band is helped by the lean production of Steve Lillywhite, who manages to rein in the group's tendency to meander. The result is a set of eclectic pop-rock that is accentuated by bursts of instrumental virtuosity instead of being ruled by it. That also means that the Dave Matthews Band is capable of turning out pop songs, and as the hit single "What Would You Say" and "Ants Marching" illustrate, they have a flair for catchy hooks. —*Stephen Thomas Erlewine*

Crash / Apr. 1996 / RCA ✦✦✦
Under the Table and Dreaming, the Dave Matthews Band's first major label album, was their popular breakthrough, bringing their mildly eclectic sound to a mass audience. Although the group appeals to the same audience as Blues Traveler, Hootie & the Blowfish, and the Spin Doctors, the Dave Matthews Band has more influences than their peers. Fusing together folk-rock, worldbeat, jazz, and pop, the band is arguably the most musically adept of all their contemporaries. However, they have trouble coming up with engaging hooks, as their second album, *Crash*, proves. Although the band continues to get better—their musical crossbreeding is effortless and seamless—they often don't have an attractive frame for their skills. Strangely, the lack of memorable melodies doesn't particularly hurt the album—it actually emphasizes the band's instrumental talents. Nevertheless, since there's a lack of strong pop hooks, *Crash* is an album that will please fans, but not novices. —*Stephen Thomas Erlewine*

John Mayall

b. Nov. 29, 1933, Macclesfield, England
Organ, Guitar, Harmonica, Piano, Harmonium, Harpsichord, Keyboards, Tambourine, Ukulele, Vocals / Blues-Rock, British Blues
The elder statesman of British blues, it is Mayall's lot to be more renowned as a bandleader and mentor than as a performer in his own right. Throughout the '60s, his band, the Bluesbreakers, acted as a finishing school for the leading British blues-rock musicians of the era. Guitarists Eric Clapton, Peter Green, and Mick Taylor joined his band in a remarkable succession in the mid-'60s, honing their chops with Mayall before going on to join Cream, Fleetwood Mac, and the Rolling Stones, respectively. John McVie and Mick Fleetwood, Jack Bruce, Aynsley Dunbar, Dick Heckstall-Smith, Andy Fraser (of Free), John Almond, and Jon

Mark also played and recorded with Mayall for varying lengths of times in the '60s.

Mayall's personnel has tended to overshadow his own considerable abilities. Only an adequate singer, the multi-instrumentalist was adept in bringing out the best in his younger charges (Mayall himself was in his thirties by the time the Bluesbreakers began to make a name for themselves). Doing his best to provide a context in which they could play Chicago-style electric blues, Mayall was never complacent, writing most of his own material (which ranged from good to humdrum), revamping his lineup with unnerving regularity, and constantly experimenting within his basic blues format. Some of these experiments (with jazz-rock and an album on which he played all the instruments except drums) were forgettable; others, like his foray into acoustic music in the late '60s, were quite successful. Mayall's output has caught some flak from critics for paling next to the real African-American deal, but much of his vintage work—if weeded out selectively—is quite strong, especially his legendary 1966 LP with Eric Clapton, which both launched Clapton into stardom and kick-started the blues boom into full gear in England. Mayall had relocated to the US by the beginning of the 1970s, and although he's released numerous albums since and remained a prodigiously busy and reasonably popular live act, little of his post-1970 output is worthy of discussion. —Richie Unterberger

John Mayall Plays John Mayall / Mar. 26, 1965 / Decca ◆◆◆

★ **Bluesbreakers with Eric Clapton** / Jul. 1966 / Deram ◆◆◆◆◆
One of the seminal blues albums of the '60s with the Bluesbreakers, capturing Clapton on a series of blues standards, after the pop leanings of the Yardbirds and before the heavy indulgence of Cream. —William Ruhlmann

Raw Blues / Jan. 1967 / Deram ◆◆

A Hard Road / Feb. 17, 1967 / Deram ◆◆◆

Crusade / Sep. 1, 1967 / London ◆◆◆◆
The personnel changes in John Mayall's Bluesbreakers continued on his fourth album, and although Mayall had vowed not to, he had added two permanent horn players. Perhaps because he was putting out his second album within a year, Mayall wasn't able to fill up the record with his own compositions and turned to blues standards, which certainly didn't hurt the record overall. Mayall's heroes included Buddy Guy, Otis Rush, Freddie King, and Sonny Boy Williamson, and he did them proud. The album became his third straight UK Top Ten and, following the Bluesbreakers' first US tour in the summer of 1967, his first charting album in America. —William Ruhlmann

The Blues Alone / Nov. 1967 / Deram ◆◆◆

Bare Wires / Jun. 21, 1968 / Deram ◆◆◆

The Turning Point / 1969 / Deram ◆◆◆◆
Recorded just after Mick Taylor departed for the Stones, Mayall eliminated drums entirely on this live recording. With mostly acoustic guitars and John Almond on flutes and sax, Mayall and his band, as his typically overblown liner notes state, "explore seldom-used areas within the framework of low volume music." But it does work. The all-original material is flowing and melodic, with long jazzy grooves that don't lose sight of their bluesy underpinnings. Lyrically, Mayall stretches out a bit into social comment on "The Laws Must Change" on this fine, meditative mood album. —Richie Unterberger

Looking Back / Aug. 1969 / Deram ◆◆◆

Thru the Years / 1971 / Deram ◆◆◆◆
A grab bag of rare tracks over the '60s, some of which stand among Mayall's finest. His debut 1964 single "Crawling up a Hill" is one of his best originals; this comp also includes a couple of 1964-65 flipsides that were never otherwise issued in the US. The eight songs featuring Peter Green include some top-notch material that outpaces much of the only album recorded by the Green lineup (A Hard Road), particularly the Green originals "Missing You" and "Out of Reach," a great B-side with devastating, icy guitar lines and downbeat lyrics that ranks as one of the great lost blues-rock cuts of the '60s. The set is filled out with a few songs from the Mick Taylor era, the highlight being the vicious instrumental "Knockers Step Forward." Look for the CD reissue and not the early-'70s double US album of the same name, which includes a lot of superfluous material and omits the three 1964-65 songs from British 45s. —Richie Unterberger

Latest Edition / 1974 / Polydor ◆◆◆

Behind the Iron Curtain / 1985 / GNP ◆◆

Chicago Line / Aug. 1988 / Island ◆◆

A Sense of Place / Mar. 1990 / Island ◆◆◆

● **London Blues (1964-1969)** / 1992 / PolyGram ◆◆◆◆
Featuring 40 tracks over two discs, London Blues is an excellent collection of most of the best moments from Mayall and the Bluesbreakers' early recordings, a time when Eric Clapton, Peter Green, and Mick Taylor all passed through the band. —Stephen Thomas Erlewine

Room to Move (1969-1974) / 1992 / Polydor ◆◆◆◆
The majority of Mayall and the Bluesbreakers' best material from the early '70s is collected on this 29-track, double-disc set. Although Clapton appears on a couple of songs, the playing on Room to Move isn't as universally breathtaking as it is on London Blues, but the collection is thoroughly listenable, and it does feature many fine musicians. —Stephen Thomas Erlewine

Wake Up Call / 1993 / Jive/Novus ◆◆◆

Curtis Mayfield

b. Jun. 3, 1942, Chicago, IL
Guitar, Vocals / Soul, Funk, R&B
Perhaps because he didn't cross over to the pop audience as heavily as Motown's stars, it may be that the scope of Curtis Mayfield's talents and contributions have yet to be fully recognized. Judged merely by his records alone, the man's legacy is enormous. As the leader of the Impressions, he recorded some of the finest soul vocal group music of the 1960s. As a solo artist in the 1970s, he helped pioneer funk, and helped introduce hard-hitting urban commentary into soul music. "Gypsy Woman," "It's All Right," "People Get Ready," "Freddie's Dead," and "Superfly" are merely the most famous of his many hit records.

But Curtis Mayfield isn't just a singer. He wrote most of his material, at a time when that was not the norm for soul performers. He was among the first—if not the very first—to speak openly about African-American pride and community struggle in his compositions. As a songwriter and a producer, he was a key architect of Chicago soul, penning material and working on sessions by notable Windy City soulsters like Gene Chandler, Jerry Butler, Major Lance, and Billy Butler. In this sense, he can be compared to Smokey Robinson, who also managed to find time to write and produce many classics for other soul stars. Mayfield was also an excellent guitarist, and his rolling, Latin-influenced lines were highlights of the Impressions' recordings in the '60s. During the next decade, he would toughen up his guitar work and production, incorporating some of the best features of psychedelic rock and funk.

Mayfield began his career as an associate of Jerry Butler, with whom he formed the Impressions in the late '50s. After the Impressions had a big hit in 1958 with "For Your Precious Love," Butler, who had sung lead on the record, split to start a solo career. Mayfield, while keeping the Impressions together, continued to write for and tour with Butler before the Impressions got their first Top 20 hit in 1961, "Gypsy Woman."

Mayfield was heavily steeped in gospel music before he entered the pop arena, and gospel, as well as doo wop, influences would figure prominently in most of his '60s work. Mayfield wasn't a staunch traditionalist, however. He and the Impressions may have often worked the call-and-response gospel style, but his songs (romantic and otherwise) were often veiled or unveiled messages of Black pride, reflecting the increased confidence and self-determination of the African-American community. Musically he was an innovator as well, using arrangements that employed the punchy, blaring horns and Latin-influenced rhythms that came to be trademark flourishes of Chicago soul. As the staff producer for the OKeh label, Mayfield was also instrumental in lending his talents to the work of other Chi-town soul singers who went on to national success. With Mayfield singing lead and playing guitar, the Impressions had 14 Top 40 hits in the 1960s (five made the Top 20 in 1964 alone), and released some above-average albums during that period as well.

Given Mayfield's prodigious talents, it was perhaps inevitable that he would eventually leave the Impressions to begin a solo career, as he did in 1970. His first few singles boasted a harder, more funk-driven sound; singles like "(Don't Worry) If There's a Hell Below, We're All Gonna Go" found him confronting ghetto life with a realism that had rarely been heard on record. He really didn't hit his artistic or commercial stride as a solo artist, though, until Superfly, his soundtrack to a 1972 blaxploitation film. Drug deals, ghetto shootings, the death of young Black men before their time: all were described in penetrating detail. Yet Mayfield's irrepressible falsetto vocals, uplifting melodies, and fabulous funk-pop arrangements gave the oft-moralizing material a graceful strength that few others could have achieved. For all the glory of his past work, Superfly stands as his crowning achievement, not to mention a much-needed counterpoint to the sensationalistic portrayals of the film itself.

At this point Mayfield, along with Stevie Wonder and Marvin Gaye, was the foremost exponent of a new level of compelling auteurism in soul. His failure to maintain the standards of Superfly qualifies as one of the great disappointments in the history of Black popular music. Perhaps he'd simply reached his peak after a long climb, but the rest of his '70s work didn't match the musical brilliance and lyrical subtleties of Superfly, although he had a few large R&B hits in a much more conventional vein, such as "Kung Fu," "So in Love," and "Only You Babe."

Mayfield had a couple of hits in the early '80s, but the decade generally found his commercial fortunes in a steady downward spiral, despite some intermittent albums. On August 14, 1990, he became paralyzed from the neck down when a lighting rig fell on top of him at a concert in

Brooklyn, NY. In the mid-'90s, a couple of tribute albums consisting of Mayfield covers appeared, with contributions by such superstars as Eric Clapton, Bruce Springsteen, and Gladys Knight. These tributes are no substitute for the man himself, but they are an indication of the regard in which Mayfield is still held by his peers. —*Richie Unterberger*

☆ **Curtis** / Sep. 1970 / Ichiban ✦✦✦✦✦
A masterpiece, and still one of the greatest urban soul albums of all time. Curtis Mayfield stepped into the spotlight and immediately showed that he would have no trouble away from the Impressions. While he had done many transcendent singles with them, he'd never made a song as searing in its indictments or immediately compelling as "(Don't Worry) If There's a Hell Below We're All Gonna Go." That was just one of many classic tunes, which retain their impact 25 years later. Those who don't think there were great message songs before the hip-hop era should check this one out and then come up with better songs done by Public Enemy, Ice-T, Boogie Down Productions, or anyone else. —*Ron Wynn*

☆ **Superfly** / Jul. 1972 / Curtom ✦✦✦✦✦
Curtis Mayfield's talents as an all-around artist became evident in the 1970s. This was one of many inspirational soundtracks Mayfield composed for films that seldom matched his musical tapestry. *Superfly* was a misunderstood film, but there were no questions about the music; such songs as "Freddie's Dead," "Pusherman" and the title track brought home the impact and scourge of drugs with clarity and power. Mayfield's singing was consistently magnificent, and the production and arrangements were equally superb. —*Ron Wynn*

Of All Time: Classic Collection / 1990 / Curtom ✦✦✦✦
This anthology spotlights Curtis Mayfield's biggest hits as a solo star since 1970. It includes his first hit as a lead artist, "(Don't Worry) If There's a Hell Below We're All Gonna Go," plus "Superfly," "Freddie's Dead," "So in Love" and many other classics recorded for his Curtom label. Mayfield penned many masterful socio-political and protest tunes, but could also write poignant, expressive love songs. —*Ron Wynn*

★ **The Anthology 1961-1977** / 1992 / MCA ✦✦✦✦✦
An absolutely wonderful collection, it includes both the Impressions' '60s hits and Curtis Mayfield's early-'70s solo recordings on his Curtom label. All of the music on the two CDs (including "It's Alright," "People Get Ready," "Superfly," and "Freddie's Dead") is superb and the liner notes are excellent; it's the definitive Mayfield collection. —*AMG*

Living Legend / 1995 / Curtom ✦✦✦
Living Legend is a double-disc collection of some of Curtis Mayfield's finest solo material from the '70s, but it contains too much mediocre material to function as an effective introduction to the soul great. —*Stephen Thomas Erlewine*

People Get Ready: The Curtis Mayfield Story / Feb. 27, 1996 / Rhino ✦✦✦✦

Maze featuring Frankie Beverly

Soul, Funk, Urban
Frankie Beverly & Maze may be the ultimate Urban Contemporary group, though they're much more soulful and funky than many of their counterparts. They began in Philadelphia as the Butlers, and later became Raw Soul. They moved to San Francisco in the mid-'70s, and switched identities again to Maze. The lineup was lead singer Frankie Beverly, Wayne Thomas, Sam Porter, Robin Duke, Roame Lowry, McKinley Williams and Joe Provost. Ahaguna G. Sun later replaced Provost, and Sun was subsequently replaced by Billy "Shoes" Johnson. Ron Smith replaced Thomas, and Phillip Woo was added on keyboards in 1980. Though they've had only one No. 1 R&B hit in their long tenure ("Back in Stride" in 1985), Maze's popularity is unquestioned, especially as a live act. They recorded for Capitol from 1977 until 1989, when they moved to Warner Bros. and issued another smash LP in *Silky Soul*. Their most recent release was *Back to Basics* in 1993. —*Ron Wynn*

● **The Greatest Hits of Maze . . . Lifelines, Vol. 1** / Nov. 8, 1989 / Capitol ✦✦✦✦
When the Philadelphia band Raw Soul moved to San Francisco in the mid-'70s, they changed their name to Maze and made Frankie Beverly their lead singer. Beverly's personality and exuberance and their evolution into one of the tightest bands on the soul scene turned Maze into an institution. This collects formative hits from their years on Capitol, including "Golden Time of Day" and "Joy and Pain." It shows that they were both an enjoyable uptempo and funk band and a convincing ballad and love song ensemble. —*Ron Wynn*

Mazzy Star

Alternative Pop-Rock
If psychedelic music has a voice in '90s post-punk, Mazzy Star may be its strongest reincarnation. That doesn't necessarily mean that fans of the Jefferson Airplane and the Grateful Dead will find the band to their liking. Mazzy Star prefer the dark side of psychedelia, as exemplified by the

most distended tracks of the Doors and the Velvet Underground. Their fuzzy guitar workouts and plaintive folky compositions are often suffused in a dissociative ennui that is very much the 1990s, however much their textures may recall the drug-induced states of vintage psychedelia.

Although Mazzy Star are nominally a full band, they're basically the duo of guitarist David Roback and singer Hope Sandoval with backing musicians. Roback boasts a long history in the paisley underground, with the Rain Parade and Opal. He came across Sandoval after hearing a tape she had made as part of a folky duo, Going Home. (The Going Home album that Roback subsequently produced remains unissued, although its release has been rumored for some time.) Sandoval ended up replacing Kendra Smith on Opal's final tours. After Opal dissolved, Roback and Sandoval continued to work together as Mazzy Star, and released their first album for Rough Trade, *She Hangs Brightly*, in 1990.

Rough Trade's US branch went under shortly afterwards, but luckily Mazzy Star were picked up by Capitol, who kept the debut in print and issued their follow-up, 1993's *Tonight That I Might See*. There isn't much to differentiate the two albums, though that's not necessarily a criticism. Both share similar strengths and weaknesses: appealingly dreamy and atmospheric arrangements, rambling distorted guitar workouts, and lyrics that mix the haunting and the meaninglessly vague. *Tonight That I Might See* had been around for about a year before it suddenly got hot, reaching the Top 40, and spinning off a small hit single, "Fade into You." Even in the wake of this surprise success, Roback and Sandoval remained as enigmatic and aloof as their music, rarely submitting to interviews, and offering mysterious, unhelpful replies when journalists did manage to talk with them. —*Richie Unterberger*

She Hangs Brightly / 1990 / Capitol ✦✦✦

● **So Tonight That I Might See** / Sep. 27, 1993 / Capitol ✦✦✦✦
Treading a similar path as their debut, Mazzy Star generally succeed in their efforts to create an otherworldly, dream-state-like buzz with their lulling songs and layers of droning guitars. The duo offers a considerably warmer and more authentic persona on the pretty, acoustic-dominated songs than the droning trance-rock exercises. With its socially detached self-absorption, this CD is like a definitive soundtrack for the slacker elements of Generation X. —*Richie Unterberger*

MC5

Hard Rock, Proto-Punk
This Detroit rock 'n' roll band's musical and political stance helped sow the seeds of the British punk movement of the late '70s. Original members included Wayne Kramer (guitar), Rob Tyner (vocals), Bob Gaspar (drums), Pat Burrows (bass), and Fred "Sonic" Smith (guitar). They played around their native Detroit ca. 1966 as the Motor City Five. Both Gaspar and Burrows, who had shaped much of the band's early rhythmic drive, left before the band ever recorded and were replaced by Dennis Thompson (drums) and Michael Davis (bass). After two local singles went nowhere, manager John Sinclair (of the revolutionary White Panther Party) got them signed to Elektra, who recorded them live at Detroit's Grande Ballroom, where they enjoyed a fanatical local following. Troubles with the album's lyrical content (based in large part around the band's revolutionary sex, drugs, and rock 'n' roll rhetoric) and Sinclair's conviction on drug charges saw the band tone down its image for their second album, released on Atlantic. By the time their third album was released in 1971, the band was plagued by drugs and personal problems, and they broke up shortly thereafter. Though never commercially successful, the MC5 personified the Detroit high-energy sound and approach to rock 'n' roll, and their style lives on in the work of punk and alternative bands around the world. —*Cub Koda*

★ **Kick out the Jams** / 1969 / Elektra ✦✦✦✦✦
The band in full cry at the Grande Ballroom, 1968; one of the most exciting live albums ever recorded. Highlights include the title track (uncensored on CD), "Ramblin' Rose," and "Borderline." —*Cub Koda*

Back in the U.S.A. / 1970 / Rhino ✦✦✦✦
Their second album is not so wild but still exciting. Great original material is included, like "Shakin' Street" (featuring vocals by Fred "Sonic" Smith), "The American Ruse," "The Human Being Lawnmower," and "Looking at You," which featured some fiery lead-guitar work by Wayne Kramer. —*Rick Clark*

High Time / 1971 / Rhino ✦✦✦✦
Their last studio album, with "Sister Anne" and "Baby, Won't Ya" as principal highlights. —*Cub Koda*

Babes in Arms / 1983 / ROIR ✦✦✦

American Ruse / 1994 / Total Energy ✦✦

Paul McCartney

b. Jun. 18, 1942, Liverpool, England
Bass, Guitar, Piano, Keyboards, Vocals / Soft Rock, Pop-Rock
In the decade and a half after the demise of the Beatles in 1970, Paul

McCartney became one of the most successful figures in popular music. Though he had more trouble scoring hits after the mid-'80s, McCartney embarked on a triumphant world tour in 1989 and premiered his first classical work, *Paul McCartney's Liverpool Oratorio*, in 1991. He launched his third "New World" tour, commemorating the release of his *Off the Ground* album, in 1993.

Born in Liverpool, McCartney teamed with John Lennon and George Harrison in the '50s to form the nucleus of the Beatles, who scored unprecedented worldwide success in the '60s, much of it fueled by McCartney's melodic songs. The bass player and singer was a musical chameleon, equally capable of performing the most tender love song, the most schmaltzy show tune, or the most raucous rocker, on command. McCartney scored a film (*The Family Way*) in 1966 but otherwise restricted his musical activities to the group until the end of the '60s, when he launched his solo career with *McCartney*. In the early '70s, he formed a new group, Wings, and toured while recording frequently. Every new album hit the Top Ten, as did nearly every single. McCartney finally began to cool off in sales terms after the No. 1 album *Tug of War* in 1982, but artistically he continued to challenge himself, writing his own motion picture, *Give My Regards to Broad Street* (1984), and entering into a writing collaboration with Elvis Costello that resulted in hits for both of them. — *William Ruhlmann*

McCartney / Apr. 20, 1970 / Capitol ✦✦✦✦
McCartney's handmade solo debut has a rough-hewn, off hand quality that invites the listener into his highly melodic, sometimes whimsical musical imagination. The best songs include "That Would Be Something" (later revived by the Grateful Dead!), "Teddy Boy" (a Beatles outtake), and "Maybe I'm Amazed" (later a hit in a live 1977 version). — *William Ruhlmann*

Ram / May 17, 1971 / Capitol ✦✦✦
While lacking the polish of his later efforts, McCartney's second post-Beatles effort is brimming with melodies and intriguing ideas. Ultimately, it seems unfinished, but along the way one is treated to the delights of "Uncle Albert/Admiral Halsey" (a No. 1 hit), "Heart of the Country," and "Back Seat of My Car." — *William Ruhlmann*

Wild Life / Dec. 7, 1971 / Capitol ✦✦
The first album credited to Paul McCartney's group Wings is a collection of slight material (most of it written by Paul and Linda McCartney). Worst is the lyrically challenged "Bip Bop," which even comes with a reprise! This was the album that gave evidence to anyone who'd ever dismissed McCartney as a lightweight. (The CD version of the album added four non-LP singles tracks: "Oh Woman, Oh Why," which had been the B-side of McCartney's first solo single, "Another Day," and both sides of the single "Mary Had a Little Lamb"/"Little Woman Love.") — *William Ruhlmann*

Red Rose Speedway / 1973 / Capitol ✦✦
After the debacle of *Wild Life*, Paul McCartney spent 1972 rebuilding his reputation with a series of one-off singles, then released this, his fourth post-Beatles album, which restored his commercial fortunes by hitting No. 1 and spawning the No. 1 single "My Love." Like *Ram*, the album is awash in interesting musical ideas, most of which aren't finished off, and what sound like dummy lyrics that were never replaced with good ones. The only substantive song other than the single is the lead-off track, "Big Barn Bed." (The CD version adds three non-LP B-sides: "I Lie Around," "Country Dreamer," and "The Mess." The last, a live cut that was the B-side of "My Love," is the best uptempo rocker of McCartney's solo career up to this point.) — *William Ruhlmann*

Band on the Run / Dec. 5, 1973 / Capitol ✦✦✦✦
On his best post-Beatles album, McCartney uses his mastery of studio technique and gift for musical juxtaposition—from symphonic touches to hard rock to melodic acoustic music—in a wonderful collection of well-constructed songs, including the Top Ten hits "Helen Wheels," "Band on the Run," and "Jet." — *William Ruhlmann*

Venus & Mars / 1975 / Capitol ✦✦✦
A highly polished band album featuring the No. 1 hit "Listen to What the Man Said," as well as "Letting Go" and "Venus and Mars/Rock Show," which served to introduce the McCartney & Wings world tour of 1975-1976. — *William Ruhlmann*

Wings at the Speed of Sound / 1976 / Capitol ✦✦
Released the same month as the start of Paul McCartney's first post-Beatles tour of the US, this album stayed at No. 1 seven weeks and featured the No. 1 single "Silly Love Songs" and the Top Ten "Let 'Em In." Without the hoopla, it's actually a mediocre effort not helped by having other members of Wings contribute songs, although it contains one of those lost McCartney gems, the rocker "Beware My Love." (The CD contains three bonus tracks culled from non-LP singles: "Walking in the Park with Eloise," "Bridge on the River Suite," and "Sally G.") — *William Ruhlmann*

Wings over America / Dec. 11, 1976 / Capitol ✦✦✦

London Town / Mar. 31, 1978 / Capitol ✦✦
London Town found Wings once again reduced to the trio of the McCartneys and Denny Laine. It was typically successful, hitting No. 2 and selling a million copies, with the bouncy single "With a Little Luck" topping the charts and the follow-ups "I've Had Enough" and "London Town" making the Top 40. But the best tracks were "Deliver Your Children" and "Girlfriend," the latter discovered by Michael Jackson, who put it on his *Off the Wall* album the following year. (The CD contains the bonus track "Girls' School," which was a Top 40 single just prior to the album's release.) — *William Ruhlmann*

Wings Greatest / Nov. 22, 1978 / Capitol ✦✦✦✦
Most of McCartney & Wings' biggest hits, 1971-1978, among them the singles "Another Day," "Live and Let Die," "Junior's Farm," "Hi, Hi, Hi," and "Mull of Kintyre," which had not previously appeared on an album. — *William Ruhlmann*

Back to the Egg / 1979 / Capitol ✦✦

McCartney II / 1980 / Capitol ✦✦✦
Returning to an all-solo format, McCartney comes up with his best new studio album since *Band on the Run*, though ironically the album's hit is a live band version of "Coming Up," tossed in as a bonus. — *William Ruhlmann*

Tug of War / 1982 / Capitol ✦✦✦✦
McCartney turns to Beatles producer George Martin for a carefully constructed blockbuster album that features the No. 1 duet with Stevie Wonder, "Ebony and Ivory," and the Top Ten hit "Take It Away," plus McCartney's tribute to John Lennon, "Here Today." — *William Ruhlmann*

Pipes of Peace / 1983 / Capitol ✦✦
This was Paul McCartney's first new studio album, either as a member of the Beatles or as a solo artist, to miss the American Top Ten—ever—and this was despite the inclusion of the long-running No. 1 duet with Michael Jackson, "Say Say Say." Explicitly pitched as a follow-up to *Tug of War*, *Pipes of Peace* was not as carefully crafted as its predecessor, despite the presence of producer George Martin. But that doesn't explain the commercial disappointment. Hereafter, McCartney would struggle to maintain the mass audience he had previously taken for granted. — *William Ruhlmann*

Give My Regards to Broad Street / Jan. 1984 / Capitol ✦✦
McCartney's soundtrack to his poorly received feature film, this album contains rerecordings of Beatles songs and solo tunes, plus the hit single "No More Lonely Nights." — *William Ruhlmann*

Press to Play / Sep. 19, 1986 / Capitol ✦✦

● **All the Best [U.S.]** / 1987 / Capitol ✦✦✦✦
Unfortunately, this second greatest-hits collection repeats many of the tracks from the first. But it does add the singles "C Moon" and "Goodnight Tonight" (previously unavailable on an album) and some of the bigger '80s hits, such as "Say Say Say" and "No More Lonely Nights." — *William Ruhlmann*

Flowers in the Dirt / 1989 / Capitol ✦✦✦
A well-constructed comeback album on which McCartney collaborates with Elvis Costello for the Top 30 hit "My Brave Face," recalls his father on "Put It There," rocks out on "Figure of Eight," and turns in one of those lovely McCartney ballads on "This One." — *William Ruhlmann*

Tripping the Live Fantastic / Oct. 1990 / Capitol ✦✦

Choba B CCCP / 1991 / Capitol ✦✦

Liverpool Oratorio / 1991 / Angel ✦✦

Unplugged (The Official Bootleg) / May 1991 / Capitol ✦✦✦✦
A delightful acoustic performance in which McCartney resurrects some Beatles classics, some oldies, and some of his less well known solo songs in a live setting. — *William Ruhlmann*

Paul Is Live / Jan. 1, 1993 / Capitol ✦✦

Off the Ground / Feb. 1993 / Capitol ✦✦

James McCarty

b. Jul. 25, 1943, Liverpool, England
Guitar / Pop-Rock
James McCarty was one of the founding members of one of the seminal British Invasion groups, the Yardbirds. After leaving the group, he formed the progressive-rock outfit Renaissance with Yardbirds vocalist Keith Relf. McCarty left Renaissance in 1973; he wrote material for Dave Berry and Dave Clark, among others, before attempting to re-form Renaissance in 1976. Sadly, the band's plans were destroyed by Relf's death in 1976; the group continued as Illusion. In 1983, he joined former Yardbirds Chris Dreja and Paul Samwell-Smith as Box of Frogs. In the late '80s, McCarty launched his own solo album, which has produced four albums that meld his blues-rock heritage with new age philosophies and musical textures. — *Stephen Thomas Erlewine*

● **Out of the Dark** / 1994 / Higher Octave ✦✦✦✦
The are few modern albums that reflect the real spirit of the music in the 1960s. The haunting effect of something like Procol Harum's "A Whiter Shade of Pale" is hard to find today. James McCarty's has survived a long musical journey through the 1960s and beyond to the 1990s with his message quite intact. The whole album has an other- or future-world feel and yet no fussiness. There is real clarity here. The title cut is remarkable. —*Michael Erlewine*

Maria McKee

b. Aug. 17, 1964, Los Angeles, CA
Guitar, Vocals / Rock 'n' Roll, Country-Rock, Alternative Pop-Rock
While she was with Lone Justice, Maria McKee always showed promise; her gritty, soulful mix of R&B, rock, and country helped distinguish the band from the multitude of '80s roots rockers. When she released her first solo album in the late '80s, it suffered from the same problem as Lone Justice—lots of potential, but no delivery. However, 1993's *You Gotta Sin to Get Saved* showed McKee making good on her promise, with an album of impassioned rockers and ballads. Three years later, McKee released her third solo album, *Life Is Sweet*, an album that marked a depature from her roots-rock roots, a movement toward alternative and art-rock. —*Stephen Thomas Erlewine*

Maria McKee / 1989 / Geffen ✦✦✦
Three years after Lone Justice's last album, Maria McKee released her self-titled debut, which showed that her skills as a songwriter had grown considerably since her first band. Not only were her songs better, but McKee's singing had improved; while it was still a little thin, her voice had grown grittier and more soulful, which made her songs all the more convincing. Unfortunately, most of McKee's musical growth was obscured by Mitchell Froom's mushy overproduction. —*Stephen Thomas Erlewine*

● **You Gotta Sin to Get Saved** / Jun. 22, 1993 / Geffen ✦✦✦✦
A few years after an underappreciated solo album, former Lone Justice leader Maria McKee returns with *You Gotta Sin to Get Saved*, her best album yet. With Black Crowes and Jayhawks producer George Drakoulias at the helm, *You Gotta Sin to Get Saved* evokes the country-rock vibe of the early '70s (much like the aforementioned groups) without sounding like a studied replica. McKee sings a dynamic mix of originals and covers with conviction, making *You Gotta Sin to Get Saved* an album that demands repeated plays. —*Stephen Thomas Erlewine*

Life Is Sweet / Mar. 26, 1996 / Geffen ✦✦✦
For most of her career, Maria McKee has never deviated from country-rock, but *Life Is Sweet* is a bold departure from her trademark sound, taking her into new sonic territories. Although the loud, distorted guitars are the first noticeable change, it soon becomes apparent that the thing that makes the album sound so different is its latent progressive-rock influences. Throughout the album, McKee weaves complex, layered arrangements that interweave strings, guitars, and keyboards. Appropriately, her melodies are more convoluted than ever before, yet they never become too obtuse. Lyrically, she has become more cryptic and angry, but that is all part of the plan—*Life Is Sweet* is McKee's bid to be taken seriously as an artist. For some reason, that means she has constructed a hybrid of the prog-rock arrangements that dominate the first half of the album and the confessional songwriting that is prominent on the second. Fortunately, the results sound better than they read, primarily because beneath all of the bombastic arrangements, McKee has retained her keen sense of songcraft. Still, with its art-rock tendencies and naked ambition, *Life Is Sweet* may not appeal to fans that have become attached to McKee's country-rock. For those willing to accept her pretensions, it is a frustrating but rewarding album. —*Stephen Thomas Erlewine*

Sarah McLachlan

b. Jan. 28, 1968
Guitar, Piano, Vocals / Singer-Songwriter, Alternative Pop-Rock, Folk-Rock
Since her debut album in 1989, Sarah McLachlan's atmospheric folk-pop has gained a devoted following of fans, both in the US and UK Each record has shown McLachlan growing both as a songwriter and a musician. In 1994, she began to work her way into the mainstream with the album *Fumbling Towards Ecstasy* and the single "Possession." —*Stephen Thomas Erlewine*

Touch / 1989 / Arista ✦✦✦
On her debut effort, Maria McLachlan sets the stage for future greatness. While only in her early twenties, she shows insights beyond her years with highly personal and introspective lyrics. —*Chris Woodstra*

Solace / Sep. 10, 1991 / Arista ✦✦✦✦
With her second album, McLachlan shows a marked improvement in songwriting. Yearning lyrics flow perfectly with her 12-string guitar, a tight rhythm section, and strong Celtic influences. A fine folk-pop effort. —*Chris Woodstra*

Live EP / 1992 / Nettwerk ✦✦
● **Fumbling Towards Ecstasy** / Feb. 1, 1994 / Arista ✦✦✦✦
From the heavy dance beats of the opening single, "Possession," to the more delicate "Good Enough," McLachlan explores self-awareness and sensuality as well as a new world view in ways unrivaled by her previous efforts. Lush arrangements back her powerful vocals to build a highly rewarding album. —*Chris Woodstra*

The Freedom Sessions / 1995 / Nettwerk ✦✦✦
A nice companion piece to *Fumbling Towards Ecstasy*, *The Freedom Sessions* offers seven early versions of songs from that album in a more stripped-down form. Also included is a cover of Tom Waits' "Ol'55." —*Chris Woodstra*

Rarities, B-Sides, and Other Stuff / 1996 / Nettwerk ✦✦✦

Don McLean

b. Oct. 2, 1945, New Rochelle, NY
Guitar, Vocals / Folk, Singer-Songwriter
A singer-songwriter of a fiercely independent character, McLean dominated radio and record sales for weeks in 1971-1972 with his epic-length Buddy Hollyesque hit "American Pie." He could have gotten years more prominence by following it up and milking the sound; instead he wrote from a personal point of view, and achieved a level of respect more often associated with folksingers a good decade older than he is for valuing the past and himself more than chart action. —*Bruce Eder*

American Pie / Oct. 1971 / EMI America ✦✦✦✦
The album that made McLean famous. The title track is the only real rocker, but the rest is intelligently produced and at times quite haunting, if a little angst ridden. —*Bruce Eder*

Clyde McPhatter

b. Nov. 15, 1932, Durham, NC, d. Jun. 13, 1972, Teaneck, NJ
Vocals / R&B
Along with Ray Charles and Sam Cooke, Clyde McPhatter was one of the most influential and important vocalists to emerge in the '50s. His unusually high, muscular vocals brought gospel fervor and sexual passion to the early-'50s hits of Billy Ward's Dominoes, with whom McPhatter cut the showstopping "Have Mercy Baby" and "The Bells." Ahmet Ertegun signed him to Atlantic in 1953, after McPhatter and Ward parted company, and assembled the Drifters around his gorgeous soprano. His solo career began in 1955, while he was serving in the Army; "Treasure of Love," "Without Love," and "A Lover's Question" were his best solo hits. He had some minor success with Mercury in the '60s but died in obscurity in 1972. —*John Floyd*

★ **Deep Sea Ball: The Best of Clyde McPhatter** / 1991 / Atlantic ✦✦✦✦✦
This 19-track compilation contains all of the top hits that McPhatter scored between 1956 and 1959. He also charted singles on MGM and Mercury, but the bulk of his best-remembered work is here, including "A Lover's Question" and "Treasure of Love." —*William Ruhlmann*

Meat Puppets

Rock 'n' Roll, Alternative Pop-Rock, Hardcore Punk
Out of all of the bands that made SST Records a towering force in the American underground during the mid-'80s, the Meat Puppets lasted the longest, surviving where other bands fell apart. The Meat Puppets never had the dedicated following of Hüsker Dü or the Minutemen—two fellow SST bands that played the same circuit as the Puppets—but they were able to carve out a long career where other hardcore bands could not because they always drew from conventional hard rock as well as punk. Not only did they play hard, loud, and fast, but they also had elements of the blues-rock of ZZ Top, the ambling folk-rock of the Grateful Dead, and Neil Young's country-rock and hard rock. As they grew older, the band matured musically, developing an accomplished instrumental technique and moving closer to the traditional hard rock that was always underneath their punk; but they never quite abandoned their punk roots, even when they briefly broke into the mainstream in the early '90s.

The core of the Meat Puppets was Curt (guitar; b. January 10, 1959) and Cris Kirkwood (bass; b. October 22, 1960), a pair of brothers that were born and raised in Phoenix, AZ. As teenagers, the Kirkwoods played in local rock 'n' roll bands, primarily playing mainstream rock and hard rock. After graduating from a Jesuit prep school, the brothers formed the Meat Puppets in 1980 with drummer Derrick Bostrom. Unlike the Kirkwoods' earlier bands, the Meat Puppets were directly inspired by punk rock—they were so committed to keeping the music punk that they refused to rehearse.

A little over a year after their formation, the Meat Puppets released their first EP, *In a Car*, on World Imitation. At this point in their career, the band was at its noisiest, playing furious hardcore with avant-garde leanings. Greg Ginn, the lead guitarist for Black Flag and the head of SST Records, heard the record and offered the Meat Puppets a contract with

SST. In 1982, the band released their full-length eponymous debut album on SST, which continued in the experimental vein of their EP.

The Meat Puppets didn't develop their own distinctive voice until their second album, *Meat Puppets II*, which was released in 1984. On *Meat Puppets II*, the band created a fusion of punk and country that sounded unlike anything else in the American underground. With their second album and their constant touring, the Meat Puppets began to cultivate a dedicated cult following across the US that continued to grow throughout the rest of the decade. In 1985, the group released their third album, *Up on the Sun*, which earned them their first reviews in mainstream music publications. *Up on the Sun* also demonstrated that the band was beginning to streamline their sound, moving closer to traditional blues-rock, country-rock, and psychedelia. This shift toward conventional hard rock continued throughout the late '80s, as the band gradually sanded away their rougher, punk edges.

After releasing an EP called *Out My Way* in 1986, the Meat Puppets released two critically acclaimed albums—*Mirage* and *Huevos*—in 1987. By the release of *Mirage*, the Meat Puppets had established themselves as college radio stars, as well as popular attractions on the American underground circuit. *Monsters*, their final original album for SST Records, was released in 1989 and its heavy rock attack foreshadowed the approach the band would adopt in the following decade. The straightforward sound of *Monsters* wasn't greeted favorably by the band's cult following and the record stiffed at college radio.

Following the weak reception of *Monsters*, the Meat Puppets broke up, but their separation didn't last for long. In 1991, they re-formed and signed a major label deal with London Records. Before they recorded their first album for London, SST issued the compilation *No Strings Attached* in 1990. The following year, *Forbidden Places*, the group's major label debut, appeared in the stores. *Forbidden Places* was neither a commerical nor underground success, causing the Meat Puppets' career to stall for a short time.

For two years after the release of *Forbidden Places*, the Meat Puppets were relatively quiet, playing a couple of gigs every once in a while. In 1993, they re-emerged as an opening act on Nirvana's *In Utero* tour. Toward the end of the tour, Nirvana taped an appearance for *MTV Unplugged*, during which they covered three songs from *Meat Puppets II* with the Meat Puppets themselves. The exposure on *MTV Unplugged* helped set the stage for the commercial breakthrough of the band's second major label album, 1994's *Too High to Die*. Released around the same time as *MTV Unplugged* originally aired, *Too High to Die* didn't gather much attention at first, but after Kurt Cobain's suicide in April, the record and its first single, "Backwater," began to move. This was due to radio's acceptance of "Backwater," but also to MTV's constant airings of Nirvana's *Unplugged*. By the summer of 1994, "Backwater" was a genuine hit, climbing to no. 2 on the album rock charts and just missing the pop Top 40. None of the other singles from *Too High to Die* performed quite as well, but the album was a success, becoming the group's first gold album. The Meat Puppets released *No Joke!*, their follow-up to *Too High to Die*, in the fall of 1995. The album received mediocre reviews and little airplay and disappeared from the charts and radio a few months after its release. —*Stephen Thomas Erlewine*

Meat Puppets / 1982 / SST ✦✦✦

● **Meat Puppets II** / 1983 / SST ✦✦✦✦
More traditional songs, less noise, more great Curt Kirkwood guitar and vocals, this LP has been referred to as a seminal slice of country-punk, and who am I to argue. This record was a startling mini-masterpiece, primarily because their debut record hadn't prepared anyone for this sudden stylistic shift. And, in typical Meat Puppets fashion, they pulled it off without batting an eye, as if they'd been recording music like this for many years. One of the great rock records of the '80s. —*John Dougan*

Up on the Sun / 1985 / SST ✦✦✦✦
Moving even farther away from the dissonance of their debut, the Pups at this juncture were sounding more and more like a (gasp!) regular old rock band. But only a fool would consider their debut the best record of their career; clearly there was much more to this band than met the ear(s). *Up on the Sun* continues the postmodern country punk of *II* and offers up great greasy globs of guitar thanks to Curt Kirkwood's rapidly improving playing. There are some moments on this record that even leave rock behind in favor of folkie quietude, but for Meat Pups fans, they were turning into a formidable band unjustly ignored by the world. —*John Dougan*

Out My Way / 1986 / SST ✦✦✦✦

Huevos / 1987 / SST ✦✦✦✦
Punk ZZ Top wannabes. —*Robert Gordon*

Mirage / 1987 / SST ✦✦✦

Monsters / 1989 / SST ✦✦✦
I lump *Huevos* and *Monsters* together mainly because they are built around a similar "big rock" guitar sound. Kirkwood had been listening to a lot of ZZ Top at this point (not a bad thing to do, I might add!) and the

effect on the music of the Meat Puppets was obvious. Now playing Les Paul guitars and fancying a louder, more aggressive, fat, distorted wall of sound, the Pups sounded like world beaters on these two records. Old-time fans and purists were decidedly distraught when these records came out, for it sounded as though the Pups had simply decided to sound like just another country/blues-tinged hard rock band, but that was only true on the more mediocre songs; the reality was that the Pups were now diamond hard and air-tight. The proof of this is in songs like "Bad Love," "Sexy Music," and "I Can't Be Counted On" (from *Huevos*) and "Attacked by Monsters," "Meltdown," and "Party Til the World Obeys" (from *Monsters*). At this point (later borne out by Kurt Cobain during Nirvana's *Unplugged* gig), the Pups had become a tremendously influential American rock band. —*John Dougan*

No Strings Attached / 1990 / SST ✦✦✦

Forbidden Places / 1991 / London ✦✦✦

Too High to Die / 1994 / London ✦✦✦✦
Still crazy after all these years, the Pups sound in fine fettle on this appropriately named recording, but a touch of sameness is starting to creep in, making *Too High* probably the least essential of the band's later recordings. Being a laidback rock band can be cool, but it can also mean that falling into a rut is easier than taking on new challenges. But if the history of the Meat Puppets teaches us anything, it's that this band is capable of surprises—and plenty of them! —*John Dougan*

No Joke! / Oct. 3, 1995 / London ✦✦

Meat Loaf

Hard Rock, Pop-Rock
A rock singer (born Marvin Lee Aday) with a full, dramatic voice; also an actor who shot to fame with the multi-platinum album *Bat out of Hell* in 1977. After everybody had written him off as a has-been, Meat Loaf rocketed back to the top of the charts in 1993 with *Bat out of Hell II: Back into Hell*, which became a multi-platinum hit. —*William Ruhlmann*

● **Bat out of Hell** / 1978 / Epic ✦✦✦✦
Meat Loaf's powerful, passionate voice serves as the messenger for Jim Steinman's over-the-top rock songs, which treat teenage angst in practically Wagnerian terms, while Todd Rundgren provides a clean, well-articulated Wall of Sound production in this kitsch masterpiece, which includes "Two Out of Three Ain't Bad" and "Paradise by the Dashboard Light." —*William Ruhlmann*

Hits out of Hell / 1984 / Epic ✦✦✦
Since Meat Loaf's *Bat out of Hell* album is vastly better than its follow-ups, *Dead Ringer* and *Midnight at the Lost and Found*, the idea of doing a hits compilation culling familiar tracks from the three albums is not really a good one. But the second and third albums did feature UK hits, and *Hits* does contain the four key tracks from *Bat*—the title track, "Two Out of Three Ain't Bad," "You Took the Words Right out of My Mouth," and "Paradise by the Dashboard Light." A few tracks from *Dead Ringer*, notably "Read 'Em and Weep" and "I'm Gonna Love Her for Both of Us," are in the same spirit, but the songs from *Midnight* are simply inferior. —*William Ruhlmann*

Bat out of Hell II: Back into Hell / 1993 / MCA ✦✦✦✦
Although Meat Loaf has made several albums since *Bat out of Hell* (most of them never released in the US), *Bat out of Hell II: Back into Hell* is an explicit sequel to that milestone of '70s pop culture. Reprising the formula of the original nearly to the letter, *Back into Hell* is bombastic and has too much detail, thanks to the pseudo-operatic splendor of Jim Steinman's grandly cinematic songs. From the arrangements to the length of the tracks, everything on the album is overstated; even the album version of the hit single, "I Would Do Anything for Love (But I Won't Do That)," is twelve minutes long. Yet that's precisely the point of this album, and is also why it works so well. No other rock 'n' roller besides Meat Loaf could pull off the humor and theatricality of *Back into Hell* and make it seem real. In that sense, it's a worthy successor to the original. —*Stephen Thomas Erlewine*

Joe Meek

Pop-Rock
Not an artist in the traditional sense of the term—he couldn't play or sing at all—producer Joe Meek has nonetheless been belatedly recognized as an important, even inimitable, figure of early British rock 'n' roll. Like Phil Spector, Meek developed idiosyncratic production techniques that, much more than the artists he worked with, stamped a vision of mad genius on his recordings. In Meek's case, this usually amounted to super-compressed sound, wavering sped-up vocals, ghostly backing violins and choruses, spooky echo and reverb, ticky-tack varispeed piano, and all manners of Halloween and outer-space sound effects. The recordings were all the more remarkable for being produced not in a state-of-the-art studio, but in Meek's own bedroom-sized facility, located over a shop within the flat he rented. Meek couldn't rightly be compared to Phil

Spector—he favored gawky, dippy teen-idol fare for gawky, dippy teen idols, not the gutsy soul and R&B-infused Wall of Sound. But he was a trailblazer in his own right—even before Spector, he set up shop as rock 'n' roll's very first independent producer of note, making recordings on his own terms and leasing them to labels for distribution. In the US, he only scored big with the Tornados' "Telstar" (the first British rock 'n' roll record to top the American charts, a year before the Beatles) and the Honeycombs' "Have I the Right." In the UK, he produced scores of records, many of them flops, and many others hits, for the Tornados, Honeycombs, Screaming Lord Sutch, John Leyton, Heinz, the Outlaws (featuring Ritchie Blackmore for a time), and many more. Highly prized by some collectors, these range from brilliant to insufferably insipid, though, as none other than Jello Biafra noted in the book *Incredibly Strange Music Volume 2*, "you can tell a Joe Meek record a mile away."

Meek's business and production methods may have been ahead of his time, but his actual musical tastes actually started to run behind the times with the advent of the self-contained groups of the British Invasion. He actually recorded a few respectable efforts in the R&B/mod vein, but his career was in a severe spiral by the time his life ended in tragic circumstances in early 1967, when he shot his landlady and himself. The existing CD compilations of his work don't actually do him justice; it's better to seek out the greatest hits collections of the artists mentioned above. John Repsch's book *The Legendary Joe Meek* (published in the UK only) is a good biography of this fascinating figure. —*Richie Unterberger*

Joe Meek Story, Vol. 1 / 1991 / Line ✦✦✦
Although one can hear the genesis of some of Meek's unique methods on this 20-track collection of 1960 releases, the material and performances are fairly insufferable, exhibit A in the lameness of much pre-Beatle British rock. Includes the super-rare (and silly) science fiction EP about intelligent life in outer space that he created with then-futuristic sound effects and tape manipulation under the moniker "The Blue Men." —*Richie Unterberger*

Joe Meek Story: The Pye Years / 1991 / Sequel ✦✦✦
48-track double CD of Meek productions released on the British Pye label between 1960 and 1966 give a surprisingly scattershot and fragmented overview of his work, with an overabundance of weak early '60s-type teen idol and instrumental fare, despite some strong tracks by the Honeycombs, Riot Squad, and Glenda Collins. —*Richie Unterberger*

● **It's Hard to Believe: The Amazing World of Joe Meek** / Oct. 1995 / Razor & Tie ✦✦✦✦
Twenty of Meek's most notable hit singles and misses from 1960 to 1966. Includes his biggest hit productions (the Tornados' "Telstar," the Honeycombs' "Have I the Right," Heinz' "Just like Eddie," Mike Berry's "Tribute to Buddy Holly," John Leyton's "Johnny Remember Me"). Just as intriguing, though, are the more obscure items, some of which are hard or impossible to find on other compilations. Among these are the wild horror-rock of Screaming Lord Sutch's "Til the Following Night," the super-creepy Moontrekkers instrumental "Night of the Vampire," the soul-pop of the Riot Squad (with Mitch Mitchell on drums), brassy femme pop by Glenda Collins, and a couple of excerpts from *I Hear a New World*, his bizarre outer-space opus. There are many other interesting Meek discs out there for those who want to go further, but this is an excellent introduction. —*Richie Unterberger*

Megadeth

Thrash, Heavy Metal
Megadeth formed in 1983 after Dave Mustaine left Metallica and moved to Los Angeles, where he met bassist Dave Ellefson. With guitarist Chris Poland and Gar Samuelson, they landed a contract with Combat Records, releasing their debut album in 1985. They became the first thrash band signed to Capitol Records. The next two albums on that label did extremely well, putting them among the top thrash bands with Metallica, Slayer, and Anthrax. Their music was very tight and the lyrics showed depth and intelligence. As far as Megadeth's impact on the world of heavy metal, they've lasted through many personnel changes and substance-abuse problems, while many other metal bands have since come and gone. —*John Book*

Killing Is My Business ... and Business Is Good! / 1985 / Combat ✦✦✦

● **Peace Sells ... But Who's Buying?** / 1986 / Capitol ✦✦✦✦
From the politics of war to the politics of the environment, Megadeth covered them all on an album that brought them from cult status to the eyes and ears of the mainstream. *Peace Sells ... But Who's Buying?* is considered to be one of the best thrash albums of the '80s. —*John Book*

So Far, So Good ... So What! / 1988 / Capitol ✦✦✦

Rust in Peace / Sep. 24, 1990 / Capitol ✦✦✦✦
After kicking drugs, Dave Mustaine returned with yet another new drummer and guitarist with *Rust in Peace*, a stronger collection than *So Far, So Good*, featuring some of Megadeth's most intricately constructed song riffs to date. —*Stephen Thomas Erlewine*

Countdown to Extinction / 1992 / Capitol ✦✦✦✦
Countdown to Extinction is proof that good ol' thrash can still survive in the '90s. Included are strongly written songs, wonderfully executed playing from the entire band, and believable lyrics ranging from suicide ("Skin O' My Teeth") to the destruction of civilization as we know it ("Ashes in Your Mouth"). It's arguably the band's best since their *Peace Sells ... But Who's Buying?*—*John Book*

Youthanasia / 1994 / Capitol ✦✦✦

Hidden Treasures / Jul. 18, 1995 / Capitol ✦✦

The Mekons

Alternative Pop-Rock, Post-Punk
More than any band that came out of late-'70s England, the Mekons (the name taken from the popular low-tech British sci-fi show *Dr. Who*) have perhaps the most devoted fans of any band even remotely connected to punk rock. And why not? After 16 years together, this band, with an ever-shifting lineup (only Jon Langford and Tom Greenhaigh remain from the original lineup), has produced some of the best rock 'n' roll on the planet; be it amateurish rock-noise, cool synth-driven pop, guitar rave-ups, or post-modern Country & Western, the Mekons have done it all and done it with style, grace, and a ribald sense of humor.

Emerging from the same Leeds University "scene" that begat the Gang of Four, the Mekons weren't as overtly political as their Marxist-inspired brethren, but their punk-rock pedigree and unsubtle anti-Thatcher and Reaganisms did set them apart from the post-punk world's innumerable careerists and posers. Their early recordings were exceedingly low-fi affairs that valued emotion and energy over anything that remotely resembled musical proficiency. Songs like "Never Been in a Riot" and "32 Weeks" sound as if the band entered the studio, arbitrarily decided who was going to play what, and started the tapes rolling. It was fun, challenging and anarchic—principles to which the band has clung, musical genre notwithstanding, since their inception.

From the time of their debut album, *The Quality of Mercy Is Not Strnen*, the Mekons had turned into a slightly more accomplished post-punk band, who, like their pals in the Gang of Four, wielded trebly guitars and shouted vocals over semi-funky rhythms tracks. The songs lacked focus, but this was a bizarre record that, for all of its oddly ingratiating music, offered little insight as to who was making it. This remained true for a couple of years or so as the band (basically Langford, Greenhaigh, Kevin Lycett and whoever else they could rope into a session) made one exciting, enigmatic and extremely difficult-to-find record after another.

In 1985, after it seemed the earth had swallowed them whole, the Mekons released the startling *Fear & Whiskey*, a ragged country album influenced by the ghosts of Hank Williams and Gram Parsons that was unlike anything they'd ever recorded. Thus began the second coming of the Mekons, who finally began to reach an underground/alternative rock audience that had missed them the first time around. Soon they began touring more frequently, putting on clamorous, exciting shows. Talented new members jumped on board, like violinist Susie Honeyman and singer Sally Timms, and even former Pretty Thing Dick Taylor was a Mekon for a while; records started coming out with more frequency and, despite considerable trouble from major labels that sent them back to the indies, could be found in nearly any record store. In the interim between *Fear & Whiskey* and their most recent record, *Retreat from Memphis*, the Mekons have continually reinvented themselves: sodden country band, wiseass folk-rock band, cranked-up guitar band, trouble-making punk band; whatever the scenario, what has remained consistent throughout the Mekons' existence has been great, great music. —*John Dougan*

The Quality of Mercy Is Not Strnen / 1979 / Caroline ✦✦✦

Fear & Whiskey / 1985 / Sin ✦✦✦✦
A startling, unexpected record that sounds as wonderful now as it did when it was released. *Fear & Whiskey* uses American country music as its foundation, and the Mekons (ever the playful band) screw around with the genre, alternating between an honest-to-God reverence and flat-out parody. Don't expect sharply executed singing and playing; that's never been the Mekons' style. Instead, plan on a rambling, sodden opus of cowpunk with Hank Williams' ghost lurking in the shadows. In 1989, *Fear & Whiskey* was issued on CD by the Minneapolis-based indie label Twin/Tone with extra material and retitled *Original Sin*. —*John Dougan*

Edge of the World / 1986 / Sin ✦✦✦✦
Hot on the heels of *Fear* came this terrific follow-up that mined the same cowpunk terrain as its predecessor. The new members (Timms, et al) sound fully integrated into the lineup, and the manic intensity doesn't let up for an instant. It's a party, but a very weird one indeed. —*John Dougan*

Honky Tonkin' / 1987 / Loud ✦✦✦✦
Finally, nearly a decade after the first Mekons release and after years of purchasing high-priced English imports, one of America's coolest indie labels manages to unleash the mighty Mekons domestically. The won-

derful *Honky-Tonkin'* marks the Mekons' last overt country/cowpunk record as they slowly shifted into more guitar-oriented rock. Its title taken from the classic Hank Williams song, this is slightly less essential than *Fear* or *Edge*, but with songs as great as "If They Hang You" and the goofy "Sympathy for the Mekons," you most certainly need it as you build your Mekons collection. —*John Dougan*

New York / 1987 / Combat ✦✦✦✦
You know a band is great when they release odds and ends that are better than most other bands' painstakingly rendered studio efforts. *New York* is a shambling ode to life on the road that features live tracks, band commentary (including snoring), and a ratty version of the Band's "The Shape I'm In." Upon its release, I thought *New York* the province of Mekons fanatics, that the casual fan or curious would tire of its casual attitude, lack of focus, and its audio-verite documentary approach. Now I think that if you like the Mekons, there is no good reason not to possess this recording. Originally released on cassette, *New York* was reissued on CD by ROIR/Important in 1990. —*John Dougan*

So Good It Hurts / 1988 / Twin/Tone ✦✦✦

● **The Mekons Rock 'n' Roll** / 1989 / A&M ✦✦✦✦
Asking a Mekons fan to select a favorite Mekons record is crazy—there isn't one, there are many. But, if the situation were such that a choice had to be made, this might be the record. Loud, unruly guitars, pissed-off vocals—the Mekons have made an unregenerate, unapologetic punk rock record. This is a dark record, one that comfortably negotiates the dark recesses of rock 'n' roll. They rip the messianic aspirations of U2's Bono ("Blow Your Tuneless Trumpet") and sing a tale of substance abuse that is both cautionary and parodic ("Cocaine Lil"), all the while cranking up a sonic tarpit of guitar noise. Bands this far on in a career, generally speaking, don't make records this good. But *The Mekons Rock 'n' Roll* is one of those cathartic records that only righteously indignant, justifiably pissed-off, grizzled veterans could make. Sadly, and perhaps unsurprisingly, it sold next to nothing and precipitated the band's departure from A&M, who didn't want to release another record like this one. —*John Dougan*

Curse of the Mekons / 1991 / Blast First ✦✦✦✦
It's amazing that as down and out as the Mekons were at this point, they could manage to summon up the emotional wherewithal to make a record as excellent as *Curse*, but they did. The title most definitely reflects the band's mindset at this time, but this is not the music of self-pity and despair ("We're right in all we distrust" yelps Greenhaigh on the title track); in fact, if it weren't for *Rock 'n' Roll*, this might be the Mekons' finest moment. Politically charged songs despairing about communism and capitalism, a return to C&W (Sally Timms' passionate reading of John Anderson's "Wild and Blue"), and a dig at America's status as the world's only post-Cold War superpower ("100% Song"). Heady stuff, and not all happy, but remarkably assured and very rewarding. —*John Dougan*

The Mekons Story / 1993 / CNT ✦✦

I Love Mekons / 1993 / Quarterstick ✦✦✦✦
A series of rancorous disagreements with the high and mighty at Warner Bros. subsidiary Loud forced the Mekons into an unanticipated two years of silence that nearly scuttled this record and ended the band's career. Eventually, Warner relented (they had maintained the record was not good enough to release), and the increasingly restless Mekons fans were able to judge for themselves that this was another terrific Mekons record. More traditionally rock-oriented and less prone to stylistic leaps than before, *I Love Mekons* is a strong, confident record that should have placed the Mekons at the forefront of the growing "alternative rock" market. It didn't, but often there's no accounting for taste. —*John Dougan*

Retreat from Memphis / 1994 / Quarterstick ✦✦✦

John Cougar Mellencamp (John Mellencamp)

b. Oct. 7, 1951, Seymour, IN
Guitar, Vocals / Rock 'n' Roll, Pop-Rock
Indiana-native John Mellencamp is the American small-town boy who made good, selling millions of records while wresting artistic control from the record label and, all along, never disowning his heartland roots. Unlike Springsteen, who has been lionized as a practically flawless all-American rocker for most of his career, Mellencamp seems utterly human, bull-headed, idealistic and preachy, indulgent, and very capable of sticking his foot in his mouth. In 1971 Mellencamp formed a glam rock band called Trash. It basically went nowhere but his admiration for David Bowie's music led him to the artist's manager, Tony DeFries of MainMan Mgmt. DeFries landed Mellencamp a deal at MCA. When the album *Chestnut Street Incident* was released, Mellencamp discovered his last name had been changed to Cougar, courtesy of DeFries. That event is the beginning of a series of humiliating record-biz miscalculations that (not unlike Tom Petty) caused Mellencamp to cut an image as a regular guy out to beat the system. In 1982 Mellencamp (as John Cougar) scored the rock equivalent of winning a state lottery by selling five

million copies of *American Fool* (No. 1), which produced two huge hits, "Jack and Diane" (No. 4) and "Hurts So Good" (No. 1). Like anyone from the underbelly of the American middle class who wins big, Mellencamp underwent a running battle, trying to figure out how to stay sane while hanging onto the jackpot and trying to figure out why the gnawing vacuum deep inside him wouldn't go away. Ever since then, Mellencamp's albums have been public airings of the American Dream come true, undergoing an initiation through the Book of Lamentations. (In 1983 he added Mellencamp back to his name. In 1991 Mellencamp dispensed with the Cougar moniker altogether.) Mellencamp's sound, while firmly rooted in rock, became increasingly earthy and acoustic until 1991's *Whenever We Wanted*, which was musically a return to a harder-edged sound.

Despite releasing a series of remarkably consistent records, Mellencamp had been in a bit of a commercial rut since 1989's *Big Daddy*. With its sinewy cover of Van Morrison's "Wild Night," 1994's *Dance Naked* put a halt to that decline; the duet with Me'Shell NdegeOcello was his biggest hit in years, appealing to a multitude of radio formats. —*Rick Clark*

American Fool / 1982 / Mercury ✦✦✦
One of the biggest albums in 1982, *American Fool* established Mellencamp (then known as John Cougar) as a major star. His fatalistic ode, "Jack and Diane," and the radio rock sleaze-fest "Hurts So Good" were major hits. Even though Mellencamp was occasionally a clumsy lyricist, his small-town punk image, believable intentions, and rhythm-guitar-heavy rock were embraced by millions throughout the American heartland. —*Rick Clark*

Uh-Huh / 1983 / Mercury ✦✦✦✦
After the mega-platinum *American Fool*, Mellencamp roughened up his sound and began adopting a more topical stance with hits like "The Authority Song," "Pink Houses," and the Stones-sounding "Crumblin' Down." —*Rick Clark*

● **Scarecrow** / 1985 / Mercury ✦✦✦✦
Recorded at his home studio in Indiana, *Scarecrow* reflected Mellencamp's concern over the plight of the American farmer. The title track is one of the most fully realized statements of purpose in his artistic career. However, there are times when Mellencamp bludgeons the listener with heavy-handed polemics that lack focus. On the plus side, *Scarecrow* was loaded with great rock-radio singles like "Lonely Ol' Night," "R.O.C.K. in the USA," "Rumbleseat," and "Small Town." The raw noisy production did a good job of enhancing the sparks in Mellencamp's excellent band. —*Rick Clark*

The Lonesome Jubilee / 1987 / Mercury ✦✦✦✦
Here Mellencamp infused his heartland rock with a strong dose of acoustic and country instrumentation in the form of fiddle, accordion, hammer dulcimer, dobro, banjo, and pedal steel. Thematically, he attempted to flesh out the big statements that dominated his previous album *Scarecrow*. In spite of the fact that Mellencamp's admonishments (with almost biblical undertones) are delivered with the proselytizing earnestness of the recently converted, *Jubilee*'s spirited performances and memorable melodies make this one of his best efforts. Highlights include "Check It Out," "Paper in Fire," "Rooty Toot Toot," and "Cherry Bomb." —*Rick Clark*

Big Daddy / 1989 / Mercury ✦✦✦
Mellencamp went deeper into acoustic-dominated rock with *Big Daddy*, an album where his focus was fine-tuned through smaller, personalized settings and stories. As a result, *Big Daddy* contained some of Mellencamp's best material, with tracks like "Jackie Brown," "Mansions in Heaven," "Void in My Heart," and "Sometimes a Great Notion." *Big Daddy* is his most subdued album (except for such tracks as his remake of the Hombres' "Let It Out (Let It All Hang Out)," "Martha Say," and his no. 15 hit whinefest "Pop Singer"). This was Mellencamp's first self-produced effort. The sounds are great but sometimes his vocals are buried way too deeply into the mix ("Mansions in Heaven") to be clearly intelligible. —*Rick Clark*

Whenever We Wanted / 1991 / Mercury ✦✦✦

Human Wheels / 1993 / Mercury ✦✦✦✦
Arguably Mellencamp's best album to date, *Human Wheels* is a dark, somber portrait of America. Mellencamp's lyrics have been broody for years now, but on *Human Wheels* the music matches his words—the dark R&B and rock sounds as anguished as his voice. At one time, he would have sung "What If I Came Knocking" seductively, but here he sounds as if nothing would change if she answered the door. *Human Wheels* might not have the hit singles of *Scarecrow* and *The Lonesome Jubilee* or the punch of *Whenever We Wanted*, but it's more consistent and moving than any of those albums. —*Stephen Thomas Erlewine*

Dance Naked / 1994 / Mercury ✦✦✦

Harold Melvin &The Blue Notes

Soul, Doo-Wop, Philly Soul
Starting out in 1954 in Philadelphia as a doo-wop group with Harold Melvin as lead singer, the Blue Notes first recorded for the New York-

based Josie label two years later. They debuted on the R&B charts in 1960 on the Value label with "My Hero." A 1965 release, "Get Out," with a lead vocal by John Atkins, also charted R&B Top 40 on Landa. But it was not until 1972, when drummer Teddy Pendergrass took over lead vocal chores and the group came under the wing of Kenny Gamble and Leon Huff and their Philadelphia International label, that Harold Melvin & The Blue Notes became consistent chart-makers.

Pendergrass' vocals smoldered with sensuality. Combined with the smooth group harmonies that had always been a Blue Note trademark, Gamble and Huff's superior writing, and lush productions, the superb TSOP house band records, such as "I Miss You," "If You Don't Know Me by Now," and "The Love I Lost" were staples on both Black and White radio from 1972 to 1975. Pendergrass went solo in 1975 and the Blue Notes' glory days came to an end. Recording subsequently for a number of labels (including ABC, Source, MCA, and Philly World), Harold Melvin & The Blue Notes hit the R&B charts another ten times, often with lead vocals by Sharon Paige. Three of those 45s permeated the Top 20, one of which (1977's "Reaching for the World") reached as high as no. 6. The latter was the only one of the Blue Notes' post-Pendergrass recordings to break the Pop Hot 100. —*Rob Bowman*

★ **The Best of Harold Melvin & The Blue Notes** / Feb. 28, 1995 / Epic/ Legacy ✦✦✦✦✦
Although the ten-track disc is criminally brief, *The Best of Harold Melvin & The Bluenotes* contains most of their biggest hits and offers a good portrait of one of the finest soul groups of the '70s. —*Stephen Thomas Erlewine*

Members

New Wave, Ska-Revival
Formed in Surrey, England, in the summer of 1977, the Members were among the new wave of British bands jumping on the punk bandwagon. The band—composed of Nicky Tesco (vocals), Jean-Marie Caroll (guitar), Gary Baker (guitar), Adrian Lillywhite (drums) and Chris Payne (bass)—was among the first to successfully blend reggae rhythms with punk's attitude and aggression. Stiff Records saw some promise in the band and signed them early in 1978, releasing their first single, "Solitary Confinement." The success of the single led to their signing with Virgin Records in 1979. Their Virgin debut single, "Sound of the Suburbs," made it into the British Top 20 but subsequent singles failed to match its success. After replacing Baker with Nigel Bennett, they recorded their first LP, *Live at the Chelsea Nightclub*, which also made a brief appearance in the lower reaches of the UK charts. Around this time, the two-Tone movement was stealing much of their limelight and their popularity began to fade. After one more album for Virgin in 1980, *1980 The Choice Is Yours*, they were dropped by the label. After a brief layoff, they returned in 1982 with *Uprhythm, Downbeat* (released in 1983 in the UK as *Going West*), broadening their sound with horns and a more serious attitude. "Working Girl" from the album became a cult classic in the US through MTV exposure but mainsteam acceptance eluded them on both sides of the Atlantic. The band called it quits the following year. —*Chris Woodstra*

● **At the 1980 Chelsea Night Club** / 1979 / Caroline ✦✦✦✦
The only Members album worth owning, *Chelsea Nightclub* plays into the band's strengths and is loaded with their strongest songwriting (e.g. "Stand up and Spit," "Off-Shore Banking Business"). —*John Dougan*

1980 The Choice Is Yours / 1980 / Virgin ✦✦

Uprhythm, Downbeat / 1982 / Arista ✦✦✦
After the flop of *1980 The Choice Is Yours*, the band took two years off to regroup and change strategies; the resulting *Uprhythm, Downbeat* (retitled *Going West* and released a year later in the UK) shows a more serious band (now a seven piece with a horn section) with a fuller sound. Their punk edges have been smoothed over, leaving a slick reggae-funk-pop sound. While it fit nicely with the new wave era, it hasn't dated very well. Only the classic "Working Girl" leaves a lasting impression. —*Chris Woodstra*

● **Sound of the Suburbs: A Collection of the Members' Finest Moments** / 1995 / Caroline ✦✦✦✦
True to its subtitle, this 18-track collection compiles the finest moments of the band's two-year stay at Virgin Records (1979-1980). While this period was the strongest for the band, it would have been nice to include a track or two from their final album, *Uprhythm, Downbeat*, such as the near-hit "Working Girl." —*Chris Woodstra*

Men at Work

New Wave, Pop-Rock
The Australian band Men at Work might still be a sensation relegated to the down under if it weren't for MTV's constant airing of their humorously oddball videos in America's heartland and FM radio's awareness that it was in dire need of some fresh faces. Men at Work's bar-band, Police-like pop-rock did have its share of hooks, particularly the sax line on their No. 1 international debut hit "Who Can It Be Now?" Their next

single, "Down Under," went No. 1 as well. Both of those tracks came from *Business as Usual*, which was No. 1 in 1982.

Their follow-up, *Cargo*, produced two more big hits with "Overkill" and the topical "It's a Mistake." A two-year layoff effectively killed the band's momentum. —*Rick Clark*

● **Business as Usual** / 1981 / Columbia ✦✦✦✦
Their smash debut contains "Who Can It Be Now" and "Down Under." —*Dan Heilman*

Cargo / 1983 / Columbia ✦✦✦✦
Men at Work's follow-up to their smash hit debut is a more varied collection, anchored by the fine ballad "Overkill" and the satiric "It's a Mistake." —*Stephen Thomas Erlewine*

Two Hearts / 1985 / Columbia ✦✦

Contraband: The Best Of / Mar. 26, 1996 / Sony/Legacy ✦✦✦✦
Men at Work's records were always somewhat uneven affairs. Certainly, the singles were the highlights, but they had a handful of first-rate album tracks that made the records necessary for dedicated fans, even if the overall album was inconsistent. *Contraband: The Best of Men at Work* does a terrific job of consolidating all of their highlights onto one disc. From hits like "Who Can It Be Now?," "Down Under," "Overkill," and "It's a Mistake" to slightly neglected album tracks like "Be Good Johnny," *Contraband* has every great track from the Australian new wave band. For most fans, it will be the only disc they need. —*Stephen Thomas Erlewine*

Men Without Hats

New Wave, Pop-Rock
The new wave synth-pop collective Men without Hats was formed in 1980 by brothers Ivan and Stefan Doroschuk. Ivan was the leader of the group, writing the majority of the songs and providing the lead vocals; Stefan was the guitarist, and the other members changed frequently throughout the course of their career. The group independently released their debut EP, *Folk of the '80s*, in 1980; it was reissued the following year by Stiff in Britain.

During 1982, the band consisted of Ivan, Stefan, and keyboardist Colin Doroschuk, along with drummer Allan McCarthy; this is the lineup that recorded Men without Hats' 1982 debut album *Rhythm of Youth*. Taken from their debut, the single "The Safety Dance" became a major hit, peaking on the American charts at No. 3 in 1983. Driven by an insistent three-chord synthesizer riff, the song was one of the biggest synth-pop hits of the new wave era. The group wasn't able to exploit its success, however. *Folk of the '80s (Part III)* stalled at No. 127 on the charts in America and made even less of an impact in other parts of the world. Thanks to the minor hit title track, 1987's *Pop Goes the World* was a bigger success, yet it didn't recapture the audience their first album had gained. Released two years later, *The Adventures of Women & Men without Hats in the 21st Century* failed to chart, as did its follow-up, 1991's *Sideways*. The two albums' lack of success effectively put an end to Men without Hats' career. —*Stephen Thomas Erlewine*

Rhythm of Youth / 1982 / Backstreet ✦✦✦✦
Men without Hats' debut album *Rhythm of Youth* was a set of catchy, appealing synth-pop. Although the material on the album was wildly inconsistent, the group's energy was infectious, making up for the weaker songs. And when the band managed to write a solid melody—such as the hit single "The Safety Dance"—the results were quite memorable. —*Stephen Thomas Erlewine*

Folk of the '80s (Pt. III) / 1984 / MCA ✦✦✦

Pop Goes the World / 1987 / Mercury ✦✦✦

● **Collection** / Feb. 20, 1996 / Oglio ✦✦✦✦

Natalie Merchant

b. Oct. 26, 1963, Jamestown, NY
Piano, Vocals / Singer-Songwriter, Pop-Rock
Natalie Merchant was the lead singer for 10,000 Maniacs from their inception in the early '80s to her departure in early 1994. Merchant began a solo career the following year, releasing her solo debut, *Tiger Lily*, in the summer of 1995. —*Stephen Thomas Erlewine*

Tigerlily / 1995 / Elektra ✦✦✦✦
Tigerlily, Natalie Merchant's first solo record, does sound different than 10,000 Maniacs. Instead of relying strictly on jangly folk-rock, Merchant continues opening her music up as she did on *Our Time in Eden*, her last album with the Maniacs. From the understated groove of "Carnival" to the rolling "San Andreas Fault," the added emphasis on rhythmic texture works, creating an intimate but not exclusive atmosphere that holds throughout the record, even when her occasionally sophomoric, sentimental poetry threatens to sink the album in the weight of its own preciousness (as in "River," her tribute to the late actor River Phoenix). —*Stephen Thomas Erlewine*

Mercury Rev

Alternative Pop-Rock, Psychedelic, Indie Rock
Considering that the band's leader, guitarist Jonathan Donahue, spent a short time with the Flaming Lips, it's not surprising that Mercury Rev's music is a splendid, scattershot amalgam of psychedelia, pop, experimental noise, rock, free-form jazz, and movie soundtracks. What is surprising is that Donahue's songs are the band's most pop-oriented material, consolidating all of their colorful sonic rush into a three-minute blast. Vocalist David Baker's songs are more languid and less dependent on structure. It doesn't matter if it is a three-minute or a 12-minute song—it is always impossible to tell where Mercury Rev is coming from and where they are going.

After releasing two acclaimed albums in 1991 and 1993, Baker left the band acrimoniously and pursued a solo career. After releasing the "Everlasting Arm" single in 1994, Mercury Rev returned with *See You on the Other Side*, their first full-length album without Baker, in the summer of 1995. —*Stephen Thomas Erlewine*

Yerself Is Steam / 1991 / Columbia ✦✦✦✦
One of the most original debuts in years, Mercury Rev's *Yerself Is Steam* could be classified as '70s art-rock played with '90s postmodern sensibilities, but the band refuses to stay in one place. Instead of the self-absorbed excesses of Pink Floyd, there are elements of psychedelia, punk, free jazz, and warped pop. *Yerself Is Steam* only hints at the band's potential. Columbia's CD reissue includes the Velvet Underground pop of "Car Wash Hair" as a bonus track. —*Stephen Thomas Erlewine*

● **Boces** / Jun. 1, 1993 / Columbia ✦✦✦✦
Boces, Mercury Rev's second album, is an even stronger affair than their first, showcasing the possibilities of their truly mind-bending neo-psychedelic guitar rock. All of their flights into the netherworld are fascinating; even the 11-minute songs seem too short. —*Stephen Thomas Erlewine*

See You on the Other Side / 1995 / Columbia ✦✦✦

The Merry-Go-Round

Pop-Rock
Like the Left Banke, the Merry-Go-Round were teen pop-rock prodigies who combined British Invasion pop melodies with baroque-pop studio polish. The L.A. group, dominated by singer and songwriter Emmitt Rhodes, had a couple huge local hits, "Live" and "You're a Very Lovely Woman," but achieved little national success before disbanding in 1969. A Paul McCartney soundalike and lookalike, Rhodes was blatantly influenced by McCartney's *Magical Mystery Tour*-era compositions, as one listen to "Pardon Me" (a ringer for "Fool on the Hill") will attest. Rhodes achieved modest commercial and critical recognition with his solo recordings in the early '70s. —*Richie Unterberger*

● **Best of the Merry-go-round** / 1985 / Rhino ✦✦✦✦
Fourteen-song compilation of songs from their sole album, plus a few rare singles. Highlights include "Live," "Come Ride," "Time Will Show the Wiser" (covered by Fairport Convention on their first album), and especially the gorgeous, haunting string ballad "You're a Very Lovely Woman." Solid, melodic late-'60s pop-rock with sophisticated arrangements, though it's sometimes lightweight. —*Richie Unterberger*

The Merseybeats

British Invasion
The Merseybeats were one of the better Liverpool bands of the British Invasion, scoring several large and minor hits in the UK, although they made no impact whatsoever in America. Friends of the Who (with whom they shared management for a time) and the Beatles, the band leaned toward mid-tempo harmony numbers, with the occasional ballads and ravers thrown in. Not nearly as distinguished as top-line British Invasion pop-rockers like the Hollies and the Searchers, the Merseybeats did have classy taste in cover material, recording Bacharach-David's "Wishin N' Hopin'" (a hit in the US for Dusty Springfield), reaching the UK Top 40 with "I Stand Accused" (covered by Elvis Costello), and releasing covers of "Mr. Moonlight" and "Fortune Teller" before the Beatles and the Stones recorded their more famous versions. Like many of the original Liverpool bands, they were crippled by a lack of songwriting talent. After breaking up in 1966, members Tony Crane and Billy Kinsley formed the Merseys, who landed a huge British hit with "Sorrow" (covered by David Bowie on *Pin Ups*) the same year. —*Richie Unterberger*

The Merseybeats / 1964 / Fontana ✦✦✦
A very well-programmed 18-song collection representing the band's good and bad sides. The former includes crisp pop-rock ditties like "Don't Turn Around," "Last Night," and "It's Love That Really Counts," while the latter is mostly an over-reliance on show tunes. —*Bruce Eder*

● **Beat & Ballads** / 1982 / Edsel ✦✦✦✦
All of their British hits, and indeed most of the A- and B-sides they cut between 1963 and 1965—"I Think of You," "Don't Turn Around," "Wishin

'N' Hopin'," "I Stand Accused." Also includes the 1964 single "Last Night," which flopped, but is one of the best obscure British Invasion pop-rockers. —*Richie Unterberger*

The Merton Parkas

Power-Pop, Mod-revival
The Merton Parkas, taking their name from their home in South London (Merton) and the classic mod-wear (the parka), are another footnote in the British mod-revival of the late '70s (which itself was merely a footnote in music history). Formed by brothers Mick Talbot (keyboards) and Danny Talbot (vocals) along with Neil Wurrel (bass) and Simon Smith (drums) in 1978, they became one of the first third-wave mod-revivalists to release an album, *Face in the Crowd*, which featured the hit single "You Need Wheels." While many of the movement's followers took a more serious approach, the Merton Parkas tapped into the novelty side of the genre, becoming something of a mod version of Madness, though less innovative (and less interesting). Mick Talbot later teamed up with Paul Weller to form the Style Council in 1983. —*Chris Woodstra*

● **Face in the Crowd** / 1979 / Beggars Banquet ✦✦✦✦
The band's sole LP, while certainly flawed, offers a lightweight, novelty approach to the Jam-inspired mod-revival. A little too derivative to be taken seriously, but there are some fun songs nonetheless such as the UK hit "You Need Wheels," "Plastic Smile," and the title track. —*Chris Woodstra*

Metallica

Thrash, Heavy Metal
Metallica was easily the best, most influential heavy metal band of the '80s, responsible for bringing the music back to earth. Instead of playing the usual rock star games of metal stars of the early '80s, the band looked and talked like they were from the street. Metallica expanded the limits of thrash, using speed and volume not for their own sake, but to enhance their intricately structured compositions. The release of 1983's *Kill 'Em All* marked the beginning of the legitimization of heavy metal's underground, bringing new complexity and depth to thrash metal. With each album, the band's playing and writing improved; James Hetfield developed a signature rhythm playing that matched his growl, while lead guitarist Kirk Hammett became one of the most copied guitarists in metal. Lars Ulrich's thunderous, yet complex, drumming clicked in perfectly with Cliff Burton's innovative bass playing.

After releasing their masterpiece *Master of Puppets* in 1986, tragedy struck the band when their tour bus crashed while traveling in Sweden, killing Burton. When the band decided to continue, Jason Newsted was chosen to replace Burton; two years later, the band released the conceptually ambitious . . . *And Justice for All*, which hit the Top Ten without any radio play and very little support from MTV. But Metallica completely crossed over into the mainstream with 1991's *Metallica*, which found the band trading in their long compositions for more concise song structures; it resulted in a No. 1 album that sold over seven million copies in the US alone. The band launched a long, long tour which kept them on the road for nearly two years. By the '90s, Metallica had changed the rules for all heavy metal bands; they were the leaders of the genre, respected not only by headbangers, but by mainstream record buyers and critics. No other heavy metal band has ever been able to pull off such a trick.

However, the group lost some members of their core audience with their long-awaited follow-up to *Metallica*, 1996's *Load*. For *Load*, the band decided to move toward alternative rock in terms of image—they cut their hair and had their picture taken by Anton Corbijn. Although the album was a hit upon its summer release—entering the charts at No. 1 and selling three million copies within two months—certain members of their audience complained about the shift in image, as well as the group's decision to headline the sixth Lollapalooza. —*Stephen Thomas Erlewine*

☆ **Kill 'Em All** / 1983 / Elektra ✦✦✦✦✦
The true birth of thrash. On *Kill 'Em All*, Metallica fuses the tight, controlled riffing of N.W.O.B.H.M. bands like Judas Priest, Iron Maiden, and Diamond Head with the velocity of Motörhead and punk and hardcore bands. James Hetfield's technical rhythm guitar style drives most of the album, especially on classic tracks like "The Four Horsemen," "Jump in the Fire," and "Seek and Destroy." Unlike later releases, there isn't much variation (apart from a lyrical bass solo from Cliff Burton), but the band's jaw-dropping power makes up for it. An Elektra reissue added the cover songs "Blitzkrieg" and "Am I Evil?" from the European *Creeping Death* EP, which have since been deleted but are worth tracking down. —*Steve Huey*

Ride the Lightning / 1984 / Elektra ✦✦✦✦
An incredibly ambitious follow-up, *Ride the Lightning* finds Metallica aggressively expanding their compositional technique and range of expression. The material ranges from blasts of fury ("Fight Fire with Fire") to tight, concise groove-rockers ("For Whom the Bell Tolls,"

"Escape") to the extended title track, but perhaps the strongest single song is the slow, haunting, partially acoustic suicide lament "Fade to Black," which also illustrates the band's move away from traditional metal theatrics toward more serious fare. While it is a transitional album, *Ride the Lightning*'s experiments push the boundaries of metal in consistently intriguing ways. —*Steve Huey*

★ **Master of Puppets** / 1986 / Elektra ♦♦♦♦♦
Without question Metallica's finest album, and that says something. The extended, progressive compositions (eight songs in just under one hour) vary enough in texture, tempo, and mood to hold interest throughout; taken as a whole, the album is a masterpiece, and the first half in particular is absolutely flawless. The subject matter is fairly cohesive; in general, *Master of Puppets* addresses the misuse of power in various ways. Even though it follows much the same pacing as *Ride the Lightning*, *Master* is more focused, and the band sounds more in control of its innovations. It stands as one of the best heavy metal albums ever recorded; some critics have called it *the* best. —*Steve Huey*

Garage Days Re-Revisited / 1987 / Elektra ♦♦♦

. . . And Justice for All / 1988 / Elektra ♦♦♦♦
The first thing a listener will notice about . . . *And Justice for All* isn't the ever-growing sophistication of Metallica's compositions or the chilling, apocalyptic lyrics—it's the terrible production, which unfortunately overshadows some of the band's brilliance. The guitars buzz thinly, the drums click more than pound, and Newsted's bass is nearly inaudible. That said, . . . *And Justice for All* is Metallica's most complex, ambitious work; every song is an expanded suite, with none clocking in at under five minutes. While not as consistently focused as *Master of Puppets*, the best moments here are at least its equal. Based on Dalton Trumbo's anti-war novel *Johnny Got His Gun*, "One" is a tour de force and possibly the band's best song, combining spooky arpeggios, an oddly haunting melody, and a structure building up to the pummeling "machine-gun" section and wild guitar solo that close the track. The abundance of good material here makes the poor sound that much more frustrating. —*Steve Huey*

Metallica / 1991 / Elektra ♦♦♦♦
Longtime fans may call this one a sellout but that's hardly the case. Instead, the group has increased the bottom end of their sound and keeps the riff-per-song limit down to about two. This may keep *Metallica* from alienating staunch metal-haters, but it's the quality of the songs—hits such as "Enter Sandman" and the ballad "Nothing Else Matters," but also "Holier Than Thou"—that has made this their most successful (and best) album to date. —*John Floyd*

Live Shit . . . Binge and Purge / 1993 / Elektra ♦♦♦

Load / Jun. 1996 / Elektra ♦♦♦

Meters

Soul, Funk, R&B, New Orleans R&B
The top instrumental band in New Orleans during the late '60s and much of the '70s, both on their own and as a session crew (formed in 1966). Keyboardist Art Neville, guitarist Leo Nocentelli, bassist George Porter Jr., and drummer Zigaboo Modeliste played on numerous sessions for producer Allen Toussaint before they climbed the R&B charts themselves in 1969 with "Sophisticated Cissy" and "Cissy Strut" on the Josie label. They remained with Josie into the early '70s, issuing more funky hit instrumentals such as "Look-Ka-Py-Py" and "Chicken Strut" before spending the mid-'70s with the major labels Reprise and Warner. The quartet went their separate ways in 1977 but sometimes re-form for the New Orleans Jazz & Heritage Festival. —*Bill Dahl*

Look-Ka-Py-Py / 1970 / Rounder ♦♦♦♦
The Meters' great 1960s singles anticipated the coming of funk. They made short, catchy tunes and scored occasional hits, particularly the single "Look-Ka-Py-Py," one of 12 outstanding tunes on this CD. These were the ultimate party/dance records, and they also showed the link between traditional African rhythms, New Orleans shuffle, second line sounds, soul, and funk. Marvelous rhythm music at its hottest. —*Ron Wynn*

Good Old Funky Music / 1990 / Rounder ♦♦♦

● **Funkify Your Life** / Feb. 28, 1995 / Rhino ♦♦♦♦
Two discs of the Meters is a lot to ask of most casual fans, yet for the devoted few, *Funkify Your Life* is essential. Featuring tracks from both their Josie and Warner years, the double-disc set captures some of the rawest New Orleans funk recorded in the Crescent City. —*Stephen Thomas Erlewine*

George Michael

b. Jun. 26, 1963, Watford, England
Guitar, Vocals / Dance-Pop, Adult Contemporary, Pop-Rock
Yorgos Kyriatou Panayioutou (George Michael) achieved fame in the duo Wham! in his native UK in 1982. Through 1986, he and his partner, Andrew Ridgeley, scored hit after hit in a variety of styles from rap to uptempo pop to slow ballads. As songwriter and lead singer, Michael gradually overshadowed the group, and by the time they split, he was ready for a massively successful solo career. This began with the 1987 album *Faith*, which featured a series of chart-topping hit singles and sold more than seven million copies. That Michael had not achieved a similar critical success was evident from the title of his follow-up album, *Listen Without Prejudice*—Vol. 1, which, though it sold a million copies, included two Top Ten hits, and hit No. 2, must be considered a major commercial disappointment. With *Vol. 2* apparently shelved, Michael contributed several songs to the charity album *Red Hot + Dance* in 1992, and one of them, "Too Funky," reached the Top 20.

After the failure of *Listen without Prejudice*, Michael engaged in a bitter legal battle with his record company, accusing them of not properly promoting the album and asking them to release him from his contract; he stated that he would refuse to release any records if he lost the lawsuit. He lost. After losing an appeal, Michael bought his way out his Columbia contract and signed with the music division of Dreamworks, a fledgling entertainment corporation founded by Steven Spielberg, Jeffrey Katzenberg, and David Geffen. In 1996, he released *Older*. —*William Ruhlmann*

★ **Faith** / 1987 / Columbia ♦♦♦♦♦
George Michael certainly looked like the biggest pop star to emerge in the second half of the '80s when he released this debut album after his years in Wham! It wasn't just that the record topped the charts for 12 weeks and sold seven million copies and that six of its nine tracks were Top Ten hits (four No. 1s, a No. 2, and a No. 3); it was that Michael, who wrote, arranged, and produced, seemed to have a broad understanding of all aspects of pop, from the rockabilly of the title track and the heartfelt ballad "Father Figure" to the R&B dance grooves of "I Want Your Sex" (indeed, the album also got to No. 2 on the Black charts). —*William Ruhlmann*

Listen without Prejudice, Vol. 1 / 1990 / Columbia ♦♦♦♦
Michael's follow-up to the massive success of *Faith* found him turning inward, trying to gain critical acclaim as well as sales. *Listen without Prejudice* is not an entirely successful effort; Michael has cut back on the effortless hooks and melodies that crammed not only *Faith* but also his singles with Wham!, and his socially conscious lyrics tend to be heavy-handed. But the highlights—the light, Beatlesque harmonies of "Heal the Pain," the plodding No. 1 "Praying for Time," "Waiting for That Day," and the Top Ten "Freedom '90"—make a case for his talents as a pop craftsman. —*Stephen Thomas Erlewine*

Older / Apr. 1996 / DreamWorks ♦♦♦

Lee Michaels

Piano, Vocals / Psychedelic, Pop-Rock
One of the most interesting second-division California psychedelic musicians, keyboardist Lee Michaels was one of the most soulful White vocalists of the late '60s and early '70s. Between 1968 and 1972, he released half a dozen accomplished albums on A&M that encompassed baroque psychedelic pop and gritty White, sometimes gospelish R&B with equal facility. A capable songwriter, Michaels was blessed with an astonishing upper range, occasionally letting loose some thrilling funky wails; for a time he played, live and in the studio, with the mammoth drummer "Frosty" as his only accompanist. In 1971, he landed a surprise Top Ten single with "Do You Know What I Mean," one of the best and funkiest AM hits of the early '70s, but Michaels was really much more of an album-oriented artist. His albums for Columbia in the mid-'70s were both commercial and critical disappointments, and he's rarely performed or recorded since. —*Richie Unterberger*

Carnival of Life / 1968 / A&M ♦♦♦
A strong, cheerful debut, awash in the Summer of Love vibe, but featuring tight songs and arrangements. Although Lee played fewer instruments himself here than he would on his subsequent work, it introduces his organ/piano/harpsichord blend, heard to best effect on the uplifting opening track, "Hello." —*Richie Unterberger*

Recital / 1968 / A&M ♦♦♦
Michaels produced his second album himself and took over all the keyboard chores (he had played only sporadically on his first LP), accompanied by top-flight L.A. session players. Quite similar in sound and direction to his debut, it does show him expanding his songwriting horizons on tracks like "Grocery Soldier" and "The War." —*Richie Unterberger*

Lee Michaels / 1969 / A&M ♦♦♦♦
An abrupt but fairly successful change in direction, Lee's third album was recorded in a mere seven hours with drummer Frosty as his sole sideman, and is basically a reflection of his live set at the time. Far bluesier than his first two albums, side one is a 20-minute medley; side two features his superb interpretation of "Stormy Monday" and one of his best good-time numbers, "Heighty Hi." Some superb organ playing and thrilling high vocal trills, although Frosty's drum solo on the 20-minute track is tough to sit through. —*Richie Unterberger*

Fifth / 1971 / A&M ✦✦✦

Michaels went for a sparse, heavily soul- and gospel-influenced approach on this album, which includes his only big hit, "Do You Know What I Mean." For that matter, it also includes his only small hit, "Can I Get a Witness." But it's not among his best efforts, due to the similar arrangements and compositions, most of which echo the clanky piano-organ approach of "Do You Know I Mean?" less effectively. —*Richie Unterberger*

● **The Collection** / 1992 / Rhino ✦✦✦✦

Good 18-track overview of his A&M work, drawing from all six of the albums he released between 1968 and 1972. Includes "Do You Know What I Mean," "Stormy Monday," "Heighty Hi," "Hello," "The War," and "Carnival of Life," as well as the 1969 non-LP B-side "Goodbye, Goodbye," and his only Top 40 single besides "Do You Know What I Mean," a cover of "Can I Get a Witness." —*Richie Unterberger*

Mickey & Sylvia

R&B, Rock 'n' Roll

Although this duo is primarily remembered as a one-hit act—for "Love Is Strange," which reached No. 11 in 1957—they actually recorded quite a few exciting hybrids of R&B and rock 'n' roll in the mid- and late '50s. Playing on countless '50s sessions for various labels (especially Atlantic and Okeh), Mickey Baker was one of the greatest guitar players of early rock 'n' roll. With his partner (and former guitar student) Sylvia Robinson, he got to stretch out a bit from his usual role, with some trailblazing piercing, lean and bluesy leads. Vocally, Mickey & Sylvia had an engagingly playful, occasionally sly 'n' sassy repartee that makes up in charm what it might lack in smoke and firepower. Their recordings were inconsistent, but at their best they offered a fetching blend of blues, Bo Diddley, calypso, and doo wop.

After "Love Is Strange," whose devastating licks inspired countless guitarists, the duo notched a couple more substantial R&B hits. But although they recorded as late as 1965, they never approached the Top 20 again. Mickey Baker recorded as a solo artist and enjoyed a fairly successful career as an expatriate sessionman in France. Sylvia Robinson unexpectedly re-emerged with the No. 3 pre-disco hit "Pillow Talk" in 1973, and cofounded the pioneering rap label Sugar Hill in the late '70s. —*Richie Unterberger*

Love Is Strange / 1990 / Bear Family ✦✦✦

This two-CD, 60-song (!) set includes many alternate takes and a fair amount of previously unreleased material, spanning 1955 to 1964. A lot of the obscurities are in the close harmony, doo wop vein, and are disappointingly short on verbal sparring and scorching Baker guitar. Lovingly packaged, but everyone except hardcore specialists should stick with the RCA compilation. —*Richie Unterberger*

● **"Love Is Strange" & Other Hits** / 1990 / RCA ✦✦✦✦

Unless you're a major R&B collector, it's likely you've never heard anything by this duo besides "Love Is Strange," their only major hit (and a great one). With 20 cuts from 1956-60, this disc reissues the bulk of their most interesting work. "Love Is Strange" will remain their most memorable tune after you've heard this, but on the whole, this is way-above-average '50s R&B/rock. If you're hungering for more great solos like the ones in "Love Is Strange," you'll find some here, especially in "There Oughta Be a Law" and the instrumental "Shake It Up," although Baker's virtuosity doesn't dominate most of the songs. Some of these tunes are routine doo wop, but a little over half the material is pretty strong, ranging from the calypso-box they're best remembered for to ballads to straightahead R&B shouters, with King Curtis on sax. —*Richie Unterberger*

The Willow Sessions / 1995 / Sequel ✦✦✦

Midnight Oil

Alternative Pop-Rock

An Australian quintet formed in 1978 and led by singer Peter Garrett. Other members: Peter Gifford, bass (replaced by Bones Hillman in 1987); Martin Rotsey, guitar; James Moginie, guitar and keyboards; and Rob Hirst, drums. The group came up playing for the surf crowd in Sydney bars but always had a serious, political side. Its first three albums, *Midnight Oil* (1978), *Head Injuries* (1979), and *Place without a Postcard* (1981), were released only in Australia. (They appeared in the US in 1990.) Midnight Oil's first two US releases, *10, 9, 8, 7, 6, 5, 4, 3, 2, 1* (1983) and *Red Sails in the Sunset* (1985) had only modest sales, but *Diesel and Dust* (1988) was a major hit, selling a million copies and featuring the Top 20 hit "Beds Are Burning." *Blue Sky Mining* went gold in 1990, and Midnight Oil released an album of concert recordings dating from 1982 to 1990, *Scream in Blue Live*, in 1992. —*William Ruhlmann*

Midnight Oil / 1978 / Columbia ✦✦

Generally speaking, Midnight Oil records pre-*10,9,8,7,6,5,4,3,2,1* are the sound of a band honing its skills, trying to find itself, and succeeding infrequently. Their debut is worth mentioning only because it's a virtu-

ally worthless record. In fact, the leap they made between their first release and their great mid-'80s output is all the more astounding. Sounding clumsy and unsure of themselves, the Oil's debut sounds like a record they were told to make rather than one they wanted to make. —*John Dougan*

Head Injuries / 1979 / Columbia ✦✦✦✦

Fortunately the same was not true on their second release, *Head Injuries* (great title). From start to finish this is a stoked and smokin' piece of punk-inspired hard rock with Garrett wailing away as though his life depended on it. Furious, relentless, chocked to the brim with solid songs and fierce playing, *Head Injuries* is hands-down the best of the Oil's early output. —*John Dougan*

Bird Noises / 1980 / Columbia ✦✦✦

On this four-song EP, Midnight Oil tried some musical variations after two albums of hard rock. "Let's rock," declared Peter Garrett at the outset of "No Time for Games" (a lament for the loss of childhood in the modern world), but the music in fact was restrained, and the group tried acoustic instruments and a moody instrumental for an intriguing change of pace from their usual style. (Originally released in November 1980 in Australia on Powderworks Records, *Bird Noises* was released in 1990 in the US on Columbia Records as Columbia 46136.) —*William Ruhlmann*

Place Without a Postcard / 1981 / Columbia ✦✦✦

Place without a Postcard, produced by the usually reliable Glyn Johns, is so-so, but a real letdown after the intensity of *Head Injuries*. The songs are very good and at its best, it hints at the consistency that was to mark the rest of their recorded work, but it never coalesces into a whole. Even after repeated plays, this album is too much of a mess to recommend unequivocally. —*John Dougan*

10, 9, 8, 7, 6, 5, 4, 3, 2, 1 / 1983 / Columbia ✦✦✦✦

Midnight Oil's first album to have a full-scale production, this album effectively brings out the band's driving rock sound, Peter Garrett's impassioned vocals, and the band's forthright political standpoint. —*William Ruhlmann*

Red Sails in the Sunset / 1984 / Columbia ✦✦✦✦

Midnight Oil's second international release found them ambitiously taking on a variety of lyrical causes in a variety of musical styles. Their basic approach, with its martial rhythms, chanted vocals, and guitar textures, served as a jumping-off place, but they always sounded more assured when they stuck to that, rather than trying other things. And the unrelentingly judgmental tone of the lyrics, sung with dead seriousness by Peter Garrett, tended to douse the album's potential enjoyment, too. It's hard to dance when you're being lectured to. It wasn't much of a surprise when Garrett decided to run for the Australian Senate shortly after this album's release. (Originally released on CBS Records Australia in 1984, *Red Sails in the Sunset* was released on Columbia Records in the US in July 1985.) —*William Ruhlmann*

Species Deceases / 1985 / Columbia ✦✦✦

● **Diesel & Dust** / Aug. 1987 / Columbia ✦✦✦✦

A thematic album dealing with the plight of Aborigines in Australia, *Diesel and Dust* contains Midnight Oil's most focused and compelling music. Its single most impressive song, "The Dead Heart," works powerfully, both as agit-pop and as moving rock music. Also included is the anthemic hit single "Beds Are Burning." (Originally released by CBS Records Australia in August 1987, *Diesel and Dust* was released on Columbia Records in the US in January 1988.) —*William Ruhlmann*

Blue Sky Mining / 1990 / Columbia ✦✦✦

Diesel & Dust, only with less aggression. It's still a solid record. —*John Dougan*

Scream in Blue Live / May 5, 1992 / Columbia ✦✦

Earth and Sun and Moon / Apr. 1993 / Columbia ✦✦✦✦

After the slightly uninspired *Blue Sky Mining*, Midnight Oil sound revitalized on *Earth & Sun & Moon*. Their most melodic, nearly Beatlesque effort is arguably their best yet. Unfortunately, the album was generally overlooked. —*Chris Woodstra*

Steve Miller

b. Oct. 5, 1943, Milwaukee, WI

Guitar, Vocals / Blues-Rock, Psychedelic, Pop-Rock

Steve Miller's career has encompassed two distinct stages: one of the top San Francisco blues-rockers during the late '60s and early '70s, and one of the top-selling pop-rock acts of the mid-to-late '70s and early '80s with hits like "The Joker," "Fly Like an Eagle," "Rock'n Me," and "Abracadabra." Miller was turned on to music by his father, who worked as a pathologist but knew stars like Charles Mingus and Les Paul, whom he brought home as guests; Paul taught the young Miller some guitar chords and let him sit in on a session. Miller formed a blues band, the Marksmen Combo, at age 12 with friend Boz Scaggs, later a star in his own right; the two teamed up again at the University of Wisconsin in a group called the Ardells, later the Fabulous Night Trains. Miller moved to

Chicago in 1964 to get involved in the local blues scene, teaming with Barry Goldberg for two years. He then moved to San Francisco, and formed the first incarnation of the Steve Miller Blues Band, featuring guitarist James "Curly" Cooke, bassist Lonnie Turner, and drummer Tim Davis. The band built a local following through a series of free concerts and backed Chuck Berry in 1967 at a Fillmore date later released as a live album. Scaggs moved to San Francisco later that year and replaced Cooke in time to play the Monterey Pop Festival; it was the first of many personnel changes. Capitol signed the group as the Steve Miller Band following the festival.

The band flew to London to record *Children of the Future*, which was praised by critics and received some airplay on FM radio. It established Miller's early style as a blues-rocker influenced but not overpowered by psychedelia. The follow-up, *Sailor*, has been hailed as perhaps Miller's best early effort; it reached No. 24 on the *Billboard* album charts and consolidated Miller's fan base. A series of high-quality albums with similar chart placements followed; while Miller remained a popular artist, pop radio failed to pick up on any of his material at this time, even though tracks like "Space Cowboy" and "Brave New World" had become FM rock staples. 1971's *Rock Love* broke Miller's streak with a weak band lineup and poor material, and Miller followed it with the spotty *Recall the Beginning . . . A Journey from Eden*. Things began to look even worse for Miller when he broke his neck in a car accident and subsequently developed hepatitis, which put him out of commission for most of 1972 and early 1973.

Miller spent his recuperation time reinventing himself as a blues-influenced pop-rocker, writing compact, melodic, catchy songs. This approach was introduced on his 1973 LP *The Joker* and was an instant success, with the album going platinum and the title track hitting No. 1 on the pop charts. Now an established star, Miller elected to take three years off. He purchased a farm and built his own recording studio, at which he crafted the wildly successful albums *Fly Like an Eagle* and *Book of Dreams* at approximately the same time. *Eagle* was released in 1976 and eclipsed its predecessor in terms of quality and sales (over four million copies) in spite of the long down time in between. It also gave Miller his second No. 1 hit with "Rock'n Me," plus several other singles. *Book of Dreams* was almost as successful, selling over three million copies and producing several hits as well. All of the hits from Miller's first three pop-oriented albums were collected on *Greatest Hits 1974-1978*, which to date has sold over six million copies and remains a perennially popular catalog item. Miller again took some time off, not returning again until late 1981 with the disappointing *Circle of Love*. Just six months later, though, Miller rebounded with *Abracadabra;* the title track gave him his third No. 1 single and proved to be his last major commercial success. A box set covering most of Miller's career was compiled by the artist himself in 1994. — *Steve Huey*

Children of the Future / 1968 / Capitol ✦✦✦✦
Recorded in England with producer Glyn Johns (the Who, the Faces), this debut effort presented Miller as someone who was not only immersed in the blues but also fascinated with sound effects and sequencing, not unlike the Moody Blues or Pink Floyd. As a whole, this album flows nicely. Among the album's many highlights are "Baby's Callin' Me Home" (written by Boz Scaggs), "Stepping Stone," "Roll with It," "Junior Saw It Happen," and the spacey Mellotron-heavy ballad "In My First Mind." — *Rick Clark*

Sailor / 1968 / Capitol ✦✦✦✦
Less than six months after *Children of the Future*, Miller's solid follow-up proved that he wasn't a flash in the pan. Like its predecessor, *Sailor* dabbled in neat segues and effects, but to a lesser degree. Miller shines on the gently acoustic "Quicksilver Girl" and haunting "Dear Mary." *Sailor* has a couple of great rockers with "Living in the USA." (Miller's first hit at No. 94) and "Dime a Dance Romance," penned by soon-to-be-departing member Boz Scaggs. — *Rick Clark*

Your Saving Grace / 1969 / Capitol ✦✦✦

Brave New World / 1969 / Capitol ✦✦✦✦
From the anthemic opening title cut, accelerating to the crash-and-burn closer, "My Dark Hour" (featuring Paul McCartney ghosting on drums, bass, and vocals under the pseudonym of Paul Ramon), *Brave New World* is a tour de force. Other standout tracks include Miller's atmospheric "Seasons," "Kow Kow," and "Space Cowboy," an FM rock classic. — *Rick Clark*

Number Five / 1970 / Capitol ✦✦✦

● **Anthology** / 1972 / Capitol ✦✦✦✦
This is a smartly assembled best-of collection that provides a good introduction to Miller's work up to this point. Those interested in digging deeper than this should check out *Brave New World, Sailor, Children of the Future*, and *Your Saving Grace*, in that order. — *Rick Clark*

Recall the Beginning: A Journey From Eden / 1972 / Capitol ✦✦✦

The Joker / 1973 / Capitol ✦✦✦
While not as strong as some of his earlier work, *The Joker*'s title cut (built

from a simple guitar riff) was Miller's first huge No. 1 single. "Sugar Babe" and "Something to Believe In" were also highlights. Miller's focus on basic catchy material laid the groundwork for his incredibly successful late-'70s albums. — *Rick Clark*

Fly Like an Eagle / 1976 / Capitol ✦✦✦✦
In his effort to create the ultimate playable album, Miller re-incorporated his interest in spacey sound effects and neat segues and synthesized them with a batch of tightly crafted light pop-rock tunes. The result generated a load of seamless hits like "Take the Money and Run," "Rock N' Me," and the title track. — *Rick Clark*

Book of Dreams / 1977 / Capitol ✦✦✦✦
Recorded at the same time as *Fly Like an Eagle*, this album repeated the same formula, with the same big results. Hits included "Jet Airliner" (a slight reworking of an old R&B tune by Paul Pena), "Jungle Love," and "Swingtown." — *Rick Clark*

★ **Greatest Hits 1974-1978** / 1978 / Capitol ✦✦✦✦✦
This collection remains, to this day, Miller's most consistent-selling catalog item. It includes all of the hit singles and important album tracks from his biggest albums. — *Rick Clark*

Circle of Love / 1981 / Capitol ✦✦✦

Abracadabra / 1982 / Capitol ✦✦✦

Living in the 20th Century / Dec. 15, 1987 / Capitol ✦✦

Born 2B Blue / 1988 / Capitol ✦✦✦

The Best of Steve Miller (1968-1973) / 1990 / Capitol ✦✦✦✦
Some duplication with *Anthology*, but this is a better initiation to the early days, including some cuts from *The Joker*. — *John Floyd*

Wide River / Jun. 8, 1993 / Polydor ✦✦

Steve Miller Band [Box Set] / Jul. 26, 1994 / Capitol ✦✦✦✦
This is one case where the project would have, more than likely, been better served if it was compiled without the help of the artist. This three-disc set is broken down into pre-"Joker" (vol. 1), post-"Joker" (vol. 2), and "Blues" (vol. 3). While Miller aced Vol. 2's song selection, and the third disc is enjoyably playable, it's obvious he holds much of his earlier work in disregard. It's hard to justify why he would perform horrible editing jobs and fade-outs on some of his best early work. Why didn't Miller just include *Anthology*, with a couple of extra cuts, as Disc One? The set does feature great sound and the liner notes and the pictures in the booklet are first-rate. — *Rick Clark*

Garnet Mimms

b. Nov. 26, 1937, Ashland, WV
Piano, Vocals / Soul, R&B
With his backing band the Enchanters in the early '60s, Garnet Mimms cut several fine, underrated R&B singles, including the hit "Cry Baby." After the Enchanters fell apart in 1964, Mimms pursued a solo career that merged a sophisticated R&B backing with his gospel-influenced singing. He made many terrific records that never hit the charts; it wasn't until 1977 that he had another hit, "What It Is." But in the '60s, Mimms made many records that should have been hits; they remain criminally unheard, but fans of '60s soul and R&B should seek them out. — *Stephen Thomas Erlewine*

Cry Baby / Sep. 20, 1963 / United Artists ✦✦✦✦
Mimms' debut album was a well-above-average effort for soul LPs of the era. Besides the title smash, it featured solid material that married Garnet's gospel feel with uptown New York soul production; "Anytime You Want Me," "Wanting You," and "Baby Don't You Weep" were some of his finest songs. It's been reissued in its entirety, along with 14 other cuts, on the British CD *Cry Baby/Warm & Soulful;* most of the songs are on the domestic compilation *The Best of Garnet Mimms*. — *Richie Unterberger*

● **The Best of Garnet Mimms/Crybaby** / 1993 / EMI ✦✦✦✦
Excellent compilation of this early soul singer, whose influence extended beyond his one big hit, the 1963 title track. Emerging from a gospel background and obscure doo-wop groups, Mimms invested the increasingly sophisticated R&B sound of the mid-'60s with both emotion and supple pipes. He never hit the top ten after "Cry Baby," but rang off a string of minor hits like "Baby Don't You Weep," "For Your Precious Love," "It Was Easier to Hurt Her," and "I'll Take Good Care of You." Grittier than Motown, but not as down-home as Stax, Mimms married his vocals to the uptown production values and pop songwriting savvy of his producer Jerry Ragavoy to produce some of the more memorable early soul recordings. This 25-track anthology, covering his recordings for United Artists between 1963 and 1966, is unerringly consistent. It features all of his hit singles, highlights from the three albums he released during this period, and the original versions of "My Baby" (later one of Janis Joplin's signature tunes) and "Anytime You Want Me" (covered by the Who on a B-side in 1965). — *Richie Unterberger*

Cry Baby/Warm & Soulful / 1995 / Beat Goes On ✦✦✦✦
This 26-track compilation of Mimms' work between 1963 and 1966

(including his entire '63 debut LP) is roughly equal in merit to the US *The Best of Garnet Mimms* compilation. Each focuses upon the singer's prime; each largely duplicates the other's track selection; and each has some songs that are not on the other. The most notable item here that isn't on the American compilation is "It Won't Hurt (Half as Much)," which was also recorded by Them in the mid-'60s. The US anthology, however, rates a slight edge: it's easier to locate (in North America, that is), and has the crucial track "My Baby" (covered by Janis Joplin), which is missing from this British comp. —*Richie Unterberger*

Ministry
....
Industrial, Alternative Pop-Rock, Heavy Metal

When Ministry released their first EP in 1981, it seemed impossible that the band would become one of the biggest industrial terrorists of the late '80s and '90s. On their first album and EP, the band was a synth-funk duo, more similar to the Human League than Einstürzende Neubauten. Yet lead singer/guitarist Al Jourgensen was smart enough to abandon that sound and begin constructing a terrifying new form of dance music. Using heavy guitar, synthesizers, samples, distorted vocals, massive drums, noise, and tape effects, Ministry created some of the first industrial dance records to cross over to a mass audience. And it wasn't because Jourgensen diluted the power of the music. Although the band sometimes approached conventional song structures that were simply fueled by jack-hammer guitars, the real reason Ministry appealed to heavy metal fans as much as the alternative crowd is because of how the band looked. Instead of the faceless, abrasive drone of KMFDM or Skinny Puppy, Ministry acted like rock stars, dressing in leather and sunglasses, playing a relentlessly heavy guitar rock that happened to have a dance beat and synthesizers. After years of slowly building a large fan base, the band completed their cross over into the mainstream with 1992's *Psalm 69;* the album's success confirmed that Ministry was one of the most popular hard rock and industrial bands of the early '90s. —*Stephen Thomas Erlewine*

Twelve Inch Singles (1981-1984) / 1987 / Wax Trax! ♦♦♦

● **The Land of Rape and Honey** / 1988 / Sire ♦♦♦♦
Considered to be one of Ministry's best albums, this is the one that crossed them over from the industrial-alternative scene into the heavy metal crowds. It's very heavy and enjoyable from start to finish. —*John Book*

In Case You Didn't Feel Like Showing Up (Live) / Sep. 4, 1990 / Sire ♦♦

Psalm 69: The Way to Succeed & The Way to Suck Eggs / 1992 / Sire ♦♦♦♦
Although this is Ministry's most accessible album, it is not a sellout. Al Jourgensen and company never let the intensity up, with the machine-like grind of the rhythm section constantly driving the same sixteenth-note rhythms again and again. "Just One Fix" is the best track on a remarkable, intense album, which also includes the single "Jesus Built My Hotrod." —*Stephen Thomas Erlewine*

Filth Pig / 1995 / Sire ♦♦

Minor Threat
....
Hardcore Punk

Minor Threat was the definitive Washington, DC, hardcore band, writing the rules for straight-edged, hardcore punk rockers. Led by Ian MacKaye, the band was one of the first to reject drugs and alcohol, leading a call for self-awareness, as well as having a fiercely intelligent political bent to their music. Each of their songs were short, sharp, and lethal, made all the more frightening by MacKaye's raging vocals. Minor Threat wouldn't have been half as invigorating and powerful as they were if they didn't have his literate, intelligent lyrics; they were simple, direct, and vicious, much like the band's music. After two years of recording, the band broke up in 1983; MacKaye went on to form the more successful—but no less uncompromising—Fugazi, yet Minor Threat remains his most influential band. —*Stephen Thomas Erlewine*

★ **Complete Discography** / 1988 / Dischord ♦♦♦♦♦
Everything the seminal hardcore band Minor Threat ever recorded is collected on this single disc; it's the ultimate statement of straight-edged, razor-sharp early-'80s hardcore. —*Stephen Thomas Erlewine*

Minutemen
....
Alternative Pop-Rock, Hardcore Punk

More than any other hardcore band, the Minutemen epitomized the free-thinking independent ideals that formed the core of punk-alternative music. Wildy eclectic and politically revolutionary, the Minutemen never stayed in one place too long—they moved from punk to free jazz to funk to folk at a blinding speed. And they toured and recorded at blinding speed—during the early '80s, they were constantly on the road, turning out records whenever they had a chance. Like their peers Black Flag,

Hüsker Dü, R.E.M., Sonic Youth, and the Meat Puppets, the Minutemen built a large, dedicated cult following throughout the US through their relentless touring. Like their fellow American indie bands, the trio was poised to break into the world of major labels in 1986, if it weren't for the tragic death of guitarist/vocalist D. Boon in December of 1985. Even though bassist Mike Watt and drummer George Hurley carried on with fIREHOSE in the late '80s, the legacy of the Minutemen overshadowed the new band in the late '80s and early '90s, as the San Pedro trio influenced several generations of musicians.

D. Boon and Mike Watt began playing music when they were teenagers in the mid-'70s, covering '70s hard rock standards. After they graduated from high school in 1976, they heard their first punk rock records, which marked a significant change in their musical development. Once Boon and Watt heard punk, they began writing their own songs and decided to form their first full-fledged rock 'n' roll band. In 1980, the pair assembled a quartet called the Reactionaries, which featured drummer Frank Tonche and a second guitarist. Within a few months, their second guitarist left and the band changed their name to the Minutemen, since most of their songs were not much longer than a minute in duration. They recorded one single with Tonche before he was replaced by George Hurley. After Hurley joined the band, the Minutemen recorded *Paranoid Time*, their first EP; the record was released on SST Records in 1981. From the start, the band was eclectic and political, but they didn't find their voice until their first full-length album, 1981's *The Punch Line*.

Following the release of *The Punch Line*, the Minutemen embarked on a punishing touring schedule, driving across America and playing any city where they could get a gig. They were recording frequently, too. All of their major records appeared on SST Records, but they also issued selected tracks and EPs for other independent labels, beginning with 1982's *Bean-Spill* EP, which appeared on Thermidor Records. The band's second full-length album, 1983's *What Makes a Man Start Fires?*, earned them considerable critical acclaim throughout the underground and alternative press, as well as mentions in selected mainstream publications. Later in 1983, they released their third album, *Buzz or Howl Under the Influence of Heat.*

By the end of 1983, the Minutemen had become one of the most popular bands in the American underground, a status they only built upon during 1984. That year, they delivered the double album *Double Nickels on the Dime*. The length of the album was a response to Hüsker Dü's 1984 double album *Zen Arcade*, but the expanded length gave the group an opportunity to stretch out and showcase their increasing musical depth and vision. *Double Nickels on the Dime* was a considerable underground hit, earning substantial college radio play and critical praise; many critics named it one of the best albums of the year. Also in 1984, the band released a collection of outtakes and unreleased material called *The Politics of Time* on New Alliance Records.

Throughout 1985, the Minutemen churned out recordings, beginning with the *Tour-Spiel* EP on Reflex Records. It was followed by the cassette-only retrospective *My First Bells*, which was released on SST. After *My First Bells*, the group issued another EP, *Project Mersh*, which featured covers of "commercial" arena rock bands like Steppenwolf plus several long original "spiels." Around the same time, the group recorded the *Minuteflag* EP, a one-off collaboration with Black Flag. Finally, the Minutemen released the full-length follow-up to *Double Nickels on the Dime*, *3-Way Tie (For Last)*, toward the end of the year. Like its predecessor, *3-Way Tie (For Last)* received overwhelming positive reviews, including notices in mainstream publications.

In December of 1985, D. Boon and his girlfriend were driving home from a concert when they suffered a fatal automobile accident. For the first part of 1986, Mike Watt and George Hurley were trying to decide whether they would continue playing music. During this time, the live *Ballot Result* was compiled and released. After a few months, both Watt and Hurley had decided to quit music when they were convinced to continue playing by a passionate Minutemen fan and guitarist called Ed Crawford. Watt, Hurley, and Crawford formed fIREHOSE in 1986 and later in the year, the new band released their debut album, *Ragin', Full-On.* fIREHOSE toured and recorded for the next seven years, signing with the major label Columbia in 1991. —*Stephen Thomas Erlewine*

Paranoid Time / 1980 / SST ♦♦♦

Punch Line / 1981 / SST ♦♦♦
With lyrics that sound lifted from William Carlos Williams' poetry, this is a hit of punk rock unlike anything else available at the time. With dense, compact songs (18, and the record isn't even 30 minutes long) that spin off into the stratosphere in their jagged, funky way, it's an exhilarating, totally original record—one that alleged alternative rockers of today probably would never think of making. A bold indication of the great music that was to come. —*John Dougan*

Buzz or Howl under the Influence of Heat / 1983 / SST ♦♦♦♦
Not wasting an instant, the Minutemen recorded *Buzz or Howl* in a near-improvisatory frenzy. The arrangements seem looser and the lyrics more

Beat-inspired in their harsh, epigramatic imagism ("Dreams Are Free, Motherfucker"). With only eight tracks, this record began a larger critical examination of the Minutemen due to its dazzling music. The racket and wailing kicked up by Boon, Watt and Hurley was indisputably great—and original. It was clear from this recording that it was only a matter of time (the next record to be exact) before the Minutemen exploded with a major work(s). —*John Dougan*

What Makes a Man Start Fires? / 1983 / SST ✦✦✦✦
At the time this record was released, nothing in punk rock (or in any kind of rock, for that matter) sounded like the Minutemen. And although their earlier EPs and singles had provided glimpses at what kind of band they were, *What Makes a Man . . .* was an amazingly confident display of talent proving that this was one of the best young bands in America, and that punk rock (or in this instance, hardcore) could no longer be defined simply as yowling guitar rant. On this record, Boon's guitar is all over the place, as Hurley and Mike Watt begin to assert themselves as punk rock's greatest rhythm section. As usual, brevity is the soul of the Minutemen's wit, but unlike earlier recordings, the songs here are more expansive and complex. —*John Dougan*

★ **Double Nickels on the Dime** / 1984 / SST ✦✦✦✦✦
Today it seems hard to believe that a record as amazing as this was released the same month as Hüsker Dü's *Zen Arcade*, and it seemed that many critics at the time were knee-deep in either record. An astonishing record, *Double Nickels* remains the Minutemen's finest moment. It was on this record that the music, political activism, and band chemistry coalesced into a forceful document of rage during the height of the Reagan Administration's marketable "me-first" jingoism. Boon's guitar sputters, clanks, and cajoles, while Watt and Hurley explode in rhythmic splendor. The songs, now more explicitly political, question US covert military operations in Central America and challenge accepted approaches to American political history, as well as the crassness and narcissism of popular culture and the business machinations of corporate rock 'n' roll. Daring, justifiably pissed-off and accusatory, this is a benchmark work of the era that hasn't lost an ounce of power since the day it was released. In fact, it gets better with age. —*John Dougan*

Politics of Time / 1984 / SST ✦✦✦

My First Bells / 1985 / SST ✦✦✦✦
A superb collection of all Minutemen recordings from their first EP (*Paranoid Time*) up to and including *What Makes a Man Start Fires*. Rather than going crazy looking for those hard-to-find bits of vinyl, here's the whole shootin' match from 1980-83 in one spot. Cheap at twice the price. —*John Dougan*

Project: Mersh / 1985 / SST ✦✦✦✦
"Mersh" is San Pedro slang for commercial, and as the hilarious cover art by D. Boon indicates, the Minutemen were a long way from establishing any kind of toehold in the commercial rock marketplace. But that didn't slow them down from recording, nor did it force them to reevaluate what they had done up to this point. The Minutemen were true punk rockers, and commercial success (and I'm talking huge mega-unit-selling success here, not simply making a solid middle-class life for oneself) was treated more as an accident, not as an aspiration. *Mersh* is only a six-song EP, but it sated the appetites of hungry Minutemen fans awaiting the first full-length record in the wake of *Double Nickels*. This proved that there was plenty more good stuff on the way, especially in Mike Watt's "Take out Test" and Boon's incredible "The Cheerleaders" and "King of the Hill." Added bonus is a hilarious run-through of Steppenwolf's "Hey, Lawdy Mama." —*John Dougan*

3-Way Tie (For Last) / Oct. 1985 / SST ✦✦✦✦
D. Boon's death in December 1985 was one of rock's most tragic occurrences. And, a decade later, I find that it still affects the way I listen to this, the "final" Minutemen record. Boon was hitting his stride here; the songs were emphatic, smart and marked by his increasing sociopolitical awareness. Boon did not suffer fools gladly, and this record (as does the best of the Minutemen) retains a strong sense of moral indignation (listen to "The Price of Paradise" and "The Big Stick"). One fact that shouldn't be lost in eulogizing over Boon was the significant role Mike Watt was playing in the band. This hadn't happened overnight, but with each successive record Watt's confidence as a bass player and songwriter was growing, and by the time of *3-Way Tie*, his skills were in full flower—so much so that one side of the record is called Side D., the other Side Mike. Dense and driving, this is a bittersweet moment closing an excellent band's career. —*John Dougan*

Post-Mersh, Vol. 1 (Punch Line/What Makes a Man Start Fires) / 1987 / SST ✦✦✦✦

Post-Mersh, Vol. 2 (Buzz or Howl under the Influence of Heat / 1987 / SST ✦✦✦✦

Ballot Result / 1987 / SST ✦✦✦

Post-Mersh, Vol. 3 / 1989 / SST ✦✦✦✦

The Misfits

Hardcore Punk
Long before Danzig (the band) sold tons of records and showed up with regularity on MTV, Glenn Danzig (the guy) sang for the Misfits. Crawling out of the swamps of New Jersey in the late '70s, the Misfits were part of the early hardcore scene populating New York's trend-setting underground rock Bowery hangout, CBGB's. But while other bands favored skinheads and Doc Martens boots, Danzig and pals drew their look from early goth-punks like the Damned's Dave Vanian. Playing tuneful, ferocious speed-punk, Danzig's big baritone bellowed lyrics that sounded torn from '50s and '60s grade-Z gore flicks (e.g. "Mommy, Can I Go Out and Kill Tonight?," "Vampira," "Last Caress"). As scary as they tried to be, there was always something cartoonish about the Misfits, and that made their horror-punk less shocking and more tastelessly funny (and sometimes just tasteless). Still, they were a potent rock band, capable of some thunderously good music. Some would argue that the Misfits are an underappreciated band, but with Glenn Danzig now so successful, he's probably having the last laugh. Danzig split up the Misfits in 1983 and then formed the gloomier, more ghoulish (and not nearly as good) Samhain. Danzig (the band) debuted in 1988. —*John Dougan*

Walk among Us / 1982 / Ruby ✦✦✦✦
With imagery lifted from sci-fi flicks and gory horror films, Glenn Danzig and Co. sound all revved up and ready to go on their debut record. With Ramones-influenced punk that occasionally veers into speedy, unintelligible hardcore, this is a ferocious, relentless record that makes no apologies for its capacity to alienate listeners. Ugly, unrepentantly nasty, and essential. Issued on CD in 1988. —*John Dougan*

Earth A.D. / 1983 / Plan 9/Caroline ✦✦✦

Legacy of Brutality / 1985 / Plan 9/Caroline ✦✦✦

● **Misfits** / 1986 / Plan 9/Caroline ✦✦✦✦
Purists may disagree, but for the benighted, this is the best place to start. A 20-track anthology that gives you the most Misfits for your money. Everything that made the Misfits great is here, including the odd remix, alternate take and re-edited version. The band is loud and defiant, as is Danzig, whose considerable vocal chops are well displayed here. The perfect music for an evening of headbanging or watching gore films. —*John Dougan*

Die Die My Darling / 1987 / Plan 9/Caroline ✦✦✦✦

The Misfits Box Set / Feb. 27, 1996 / Caroline ✦✦✦✦
The Misfits' self-titled box set is designed for the collector, not the casual fan. Featuring a selection of tracks from their five official albums, the set is full of rarities, including the entire *Static Age* album, plus 30 other rarities, ranging from outtakes to alternate takes. Of course, this means that *The Misfits Box Set* won't be of interest to anyone but the diehard fans, but for those fans, it's an indispensable, rare treasure. —*Stephen Thomas Erlewine*

Mission of Burma

Punk, Post-Punk
Of all the punk-inspired bands that came out of Boston in the early '80s, none were better than Mission of Burma. Arty without being too pretentious, capable of writing gripping songs and playing with ferocious intensity, guitarist Roger Miller, bassist Clint Conley, drummer Peter Prescott, and tapehead Martin Swope galvanized the city's alternative rock scene.

Burma's music is vintage early-'80s post-punk: jittery rhythms, odd shifts in time, declamatory vocals; an aural assault similarly employed by bands such as the Gang of Four, Mekons and Pere Ubu—Burma's peers as well as their influences. Also, conspicuously present in the mix was the proto-punk of the Stooges and Velvet Underground, bands that inspired Burma's darker songwriting impulses and tendencies toward longish, repetitive jams capable of boring holes into your skull. What Burma added was a sonic texture through the use of extreme volume. Roger Miller's guitar enveloped the band in thick, distorted cascading chords, erupting into squealing solos and (intentional) squalls of feedback. With Prescott and Conley furiously bashing in support, the band's sound was extremely physical (ask anyone who saw them live) to the point of leaving you feeling slightly bruised, battered, but extremely happy.

After releasing an explosive single ("Academy Fight Song," still one of punk rock's greatest songs) on Boston's then-hippest indie label Ace of Hearts, Burma released two excellent records in just over a year: the *Signals, Calls and Marches* EP and their only full-length studio album, *VS.* The former was poppier, but in a breathtakingly intense way; the latter dark and ominous, lacking in riff-heavy punch, but still delivering a wicked blast of aural chaos. Unbeknownst to fans, this was the beginning of the end. The massive volume, a key element in Burma's sound, had taken its toll on the band members, especially Miller, who developed a severe case of tinnitus that hastened the band's demise. (Always the trooper, Miller played the band's final tour wearing a protective headset used on shooting ranges to prevent his ears from absorbing more punishment.) After a bittersweet farewell tour in 1983, the shows were released as a live LP entitled *The Horrible Truth About Burma*, an occasionally thrilling example of their considerable stage prowess.

Miller has since gone on to a career as a solo artist and with his non-touring band Birdsongs of the Mesozoic. Prescott formed the wonderful Volcano Suns, who released a half-dozen records all worth checking out, before starting a new band, Kustomized, with ex-Bullet Lavolta singer Yukki Gipe. Clint Conley produced the first Yo La Tengo record and then left the music business. He now reportedly works as a television producer in New Jersey. —*John Dougan*

The Horrible Truth About Burma [EP] / 1985 / Ace of Hearts ✦✦

● **Mission of Burma** / 1988 / Rykodisc ✦✦✦✦
A stunning, long (80 minutes) career overview of this magnificent band that includes all of *Signal Calls and Marches, VS.* and the single "Academy Fight Song." Only two tracks from *Horrible Truth* are here, and recent converts will want to find the original album to hear Burma's sonic madness in its entirety. Very simply a great release from a great band, whose best moments have served as inspiration for hundreds of younger bands. —*John Dougan*

Let There Be Burma / 1990 / Taang! ✦✦✦

Mission UK

Alternative Pop-Rock, Goth-Rock
Derided by critics as pompous, melodramatic, and bombastic, the Mission, as they were known in their native UK (their name had to be changed in America owing to a Philadelphia R&B band with the same moniker), nonetheless attracted a core audience of goth-rock fans and continues to record today. The Mission was formed in 1986 by guitarist/singer Wayne Hussey and bassist Craig Adams, who both left the Sisters of Mercy to do so. (Hussey had also played with the Walkie Talkies and Dead or Alive.) The two recruited Artery guitarist Simon Hinkler and former Red Lorry Yellow Lorry drummer Mick Brown and called themselves the Sisterhood, to which Sisters of Mercy leader Andrew Eldritch objected strenuously. The Mission released two successful independent singles in the UK and signed to Mercury in 1986. The group soon completed its debut album, *God's Own Medicine*, which critics lambasted as ponderous and derivative of Led Zeppelin and Yes, but the album produced several UK hits anyway. The band toured extensively in the UK and America; Adams had to return home from the latter after suffering from exhaustion. Produced by Led Zeppelin bassist John Paul Jones, *Children* widened the band's audience, reaching No. 2 on the UK album charts. 1990's *Carved in Sand* shed some of the Mission's Zep fascination for more refined songwriting. Hinkler left the band midway through the supporting tour and was eventually replaced permanently by Paul Etchells. Meanwhile, several Mission members backed Slade members Noddy Holder and Jim Lea on the Christmas charity single "Merry Xmas Everybody." By 1992, Hussey was the only original member left; following the 1994 *Sum and Substance* retrospective, he recorded the album *Neverland* with a new Mission lineup. —*Steve Huey*

● **God's Own Medicine** / 1986 / Mercury ✦✦✦✦
The debut by ex-Sisters of Mercy members engages in puffy synth-heavy pomp rock. Regardless, this effort produced a handful of British hits. "Bridges Burning" is an overwrought highlight. —*Rick Clark*

Grains of Sand / 1990 / Mercury ✦✦✦✦
This continues what "God's Own Medicine" started, with weaker songs, except for "Hands Across the Ocean" (one of their best). Maybe XTC member Andy Partridge's production was the difference. —*Rick Clark*

The Misunderstood

Psychedelic, Garage Rock
Of the thousands of US garage bands that struggled in the 1960s without achieving international success, the Misunderstood were not only among the very best, but among the very few to progress beyond basic garage sounds to music that has been (belatedly) recognized as nearly as accomplished and innovative as that of the British Invasion bands that touched off the garage explosion in the first place. Formed in Riverside, CA, in 1963, the group began as a basic R&B/rock combo in the tradition of the Stones and Animals. After the addition of steel guitarist Glenn Campbell, they rapidly moved toward a proto-psychedelic sound with guitar feedback, sustain, Middle Eastern influences, and exploratory song structures that strongly echoed the Yardbirds. With the encouragement of local expatriate British radio announcer John Ravenscroft (who would shortly become one of Britain's most influential DJs as John Peel, a designation he holds to this day), the band moved to England in 1966 in an attempt to find a sympathetic audience. The group cut six songs (a few of which were issued as extremely rare singles) that found them anticipating the early innovations of groups like Pink Floyd and Jimi Hendrix. The group were praised by the British press and up-and-coming acts like

Pink Floyd and the Move, but were hounded by US draft authorities and internal problems, and disbanded in confusion around early 1967. Campbell kept the Misunderstood name alive briefly with a couple unimpressive singles before forming Juicy Lucy, who had a small British hit with a cover of "Who Do You Love?" The group's other guitarist, Tony Hill (actually a Britishman who joined the band after they arrived in England), joined High Tide, who recorded some progressive-rock albums. The Misunderstood finally gained some measure of the respect due them with a well-packaged reissue of their best material in the early '80s. —*Richie Unterberger*

● **Before the Dream Faded** / 1982 / Cherry Red ✦✦✦✦
One of the great lost '60s albums. Side one includes all six of the tracks they recorded in England in 1966, with magnificent guitar work and nervy, ambitious (if a bit overtly cosmic) songwriting that combines some of the best aspects of the Jeff Beck-era Yardbirds and Syd Barrett's Pink Floyd. Remember that Pink Floyd and Hendrix had yet to record when these sides were waxed; they aren't derivations, but genuinely innovative and groundbreaking performances. Side two contains seven pre-psychedelic demos from their US garage days in the mid-'60s that, while not nearly as important as their 1966 work, are solid, crunching R&B-soaked rock in the tradition of their chief British influences. —*Richie Unterberger*

Golden Glass / 1984 / Cherry Red ✦✦✦
Only Glenn Campbell remains from the original lineup on this album of 1969 material. Competent blues-rock, with some commendable steel guitar work by Campbell, is nonetheless a pale shadow of the group's psychedelic recordings. Instead of picking this up, be on the lookout for a three-song EP (also called *Golden Glass*) that includes wild psychedelic covers of "Shake Your Money Maker" and "I'm Not Talkin'" by the original lineup in early 1966, and the eight-minute 1969 track "Golden Glass," which is probably the best cut from the last version of the band. —*Richie Unterberger*

Joni Mitchell

b. Nov. 7, 1943, Fort MacLeod, Canada
Guitar, Piano, Keyboards, Vocals / Singer-Songwriter, Folk-Rock
One of the most important artists to emerge from the singer-songwriter era of the early '70s. Mitchell first gained notice as a songwriter when her "Both Sides Now" was a hit by Judy Collins in 1968. That same year, Mitchell released her debut album, *Joni Mitchell*. It was followed by *Clouds* in 1969 and *Ladies of the Canyon* in 1970, the latter containing the much-covered songs "Big Yellow Taxi" and "Woodstock." *Blue*, her 1971 album, was her first to hit the Top 20 and has now sold over a million copies. *For the Roses* in 1972 was Mitchell's first gold album and included her first Top 40 hit, "You Turn Me on, I'm a Radio."

Mitchell's 1974 album, *Court and Spark*, was a commercial breakthrough, producing two hit singles, selling a million copies, and being nominated for several Grammys. She followed it with a live album, *Miles of Aisles*, that duplicated its success. From the mid-'70s on, Mitchell's work became more complicated and less folk/pop-oriented. *Hejira*, for example, paired her acoustic guitar with the bass improvisations of Jaco Pastorius, and *Don Juan's Reckless Daughter* contained an impressionistic side-long song. Her most experimental album was *Mingus* (1979), which found her setting lyrics to the last tunes written by jazz composer Charles Mingus, at his request. The live *Shadows and Light* (1980), recorded with jazz guitarist Pat Metheny, also leaned in this direction.

Since 1982, Mitchell has adopted a slightly more accessible approach in a series of albums that take into consideration contemporary pop sounds. They have gained critical respect and sold moderately well. —*William Ruhlmann*

Joni Mitchell / Mar. 1968 / Reprise ✦✦✦
David Crosby produced this debut album, on which Mitchell sings in a formal, restrained manner and writes in a wordy, poetic style, which is nevertheless touching on such songs as "I Had a King" and "Michael from Mountains." —*William Ruhlmann*

Clouds / May 1969 / Reprise ✦✦✦
Contains Mitchell's version of "Both Sides Now," as well as the exuberant "Chelsea Morning" and such vulnerable love songs as "I Don't Know Where I Stand." Grammy Award-winner for best folk performance. —*William Ruhlmann*

Ladies of the Canyon / Apr. 1970 / Reprise ✦✦✦✦
Contains several Mitchell standards, including "For Free," "Big Yellow Taxi," "Woodstock," and "The Circle Game." —*William Ruhlmann*

☆ **Blue** / Jun. 1971 / Reprise ✦✦✦✦✦
An extraordinarily revealing study in romance and dependency that begins with the girlish infatuation of "All I Want" and ends with the downcast but determined "The Last Time I Saw Richard." The spare music is dominated by Mitchell's newly expressive singing and her guitar and dulcimer work. —*William Ruhlmann*

For the Roses / Nov. 1972 / Asylum ✦✦✦✦
Mitchell rails against the music industry and defends the position of the artist in isolation, at the same time moving toward more of a pop sound, notably on the Top 25 hit "You Turn Me on, I'm a Radio." — *William Ruhlmann*

★ **Court and Spark** / Jan. 1974 / Asylum ✦✦✦✦✦
Mitchell's commercial peak came with this polished collection, which features the backup of a clutch of jazz-oriented session aces. "Help Me" was a Top Ten hit, and "Free Man in Paris" reached No.22. — *William Ruhlmann*

Miles of Aisles / Nov. 1974 / Asylum ✦✦✦
The Hissing of Summer Lawns / Nov. 1975 / Asylum ✦✦✦✦
Mitchell turned her back on stardom with this admirable, idiosyncratic effort. — *Dan Heilman*

Hejira / Nov. 1976 / Asylum ✦✦✦
Spare recordings prominently featuring the bass of Jaco Pastorius. Mitchell sings of life on the road, literally and figuratively. — *William Ruhlmann*

Don Juan's Reckless Daughter / Dec. 1977 / Asylum ✦✦
Mingus / Jun. 1979 / Asylum ✦✦✦
Mitchell sets lyrics to Charles Mingus' last melodies in collaboration with the composer and a Who's Who of jazz musicians. — *William Ruhlmann*

Shadows and Light / Sep. 1980 / Warner Bros. ✦✦
On her second live album, Mitchell fronted a band that included fusion-jazz stars Pat Metheny, Lyle Mays, Michael Brecker, and Jaco Pastorius, who gave considerable validity to the jazzy compositions she had been writing over the last five years. — *William Ruhlmann*

Wild Things Run Fast / Oct. 1982 / Geffen ✦✦✦
On her first new studio album of original material in five years and her debut for Geffen Records, Joni Mitchell achieved more of a balance between her pop abilities and her jazz aspirations, meanwhile rediscovering a more direct, emotional lyric approach. The result was her best album since the mid-'70s. — *William Ruhlmann*

Dog Eat Dog / Oct. 1985 / Geffen ✦✦
Chalk Mark in a Rain Storm / Mar. 1988 / Geffen ✦✦✦
Turbulent Indigo / 1994 / Warner Bros. ✦✦✦

Moby Grape
....
Rock 'n' Roll, Country-Rock, Psychedelic, Folk-Rock
One of the best '60s San Francisco bands, Moby Grape were also one of the most versatile. Although they are most often identified with the psychedelic scene, their specialty was combining all sorts of roots music—folk, blues, country, and classic rock 'n' roll—with some Summer of Love vibes and multilayered, triple-guitar arrangements. All of those elements only truly coalesced, however, for their 1967 debut LP. Although subsequent albums had more good moments than many listeners are aware of, a combination of personal problems and bad management effectively killed off the group by the end of the '60s.

Many San Francisco bands of the era were assembled by recent immigrants to the area, but Moby Grape had even more tenuous roots in the region than most when they formed. Matthew Katz, who managed the Jefferson Airplane in their early days, helped put together Moby Grape around Skip Spence. Spence, a legendarily colorful Canadian native whose first instrument was the guitar, had played drums in the Airplane's first lineup at the instigation of Marty Balin. Spence left the Airplane after their first album, and reverted to his natural guitarist and songwriting role for the Grape (the Airplane had already recorded some of his compositions). Guitarist Jerry Miller and drummer Don Stevenson were recruited from the Northwest bar band the Frantics; guitarist Peter Lewis had played in Southern California surf bands like the Cornells; and bassist Bob Moseley had also played with outfits from Southern California.

The group's relative unfamiliarity with each other may have sown seeds for their future problems, but they jelled surprisingly quickly, with all five members contributing more or less equally to the songwriting on their self-titled debut (1967). *Moby Grape* remains their signature statement, though the folk-rock and country-rock worked better than the boogies; "Omaha," "Sittin' by the Window," "Changes," and "Lazy Me" are some of their best songs. Columbia Records, though, damaged the band's credibility with over-hype, releasing no less than five singles from the LP simultaneously. Worse, three members of the group were caught consorting with underage girls. Though charges were eventually dropped, the legal hassles, combined with an increasingly strained relationship with manager Katz, sapped the band's drive.

Moby Grape's follow-up, the double LP *Wow*, was one of the most disappointing records of the '60s, in light of the high expectations fostered by the debut. The studio half of the package had much more erratic songwriting than the first recording, and the group members didn't blend their instrumental and vocal skills nearly as well. The "bonus" disc was

almost a total waste, consisting of bad jams. Spence departed while the album was being recorded in New York in 1968, as a result of a famous incident in which he entered the studio with a fire axe, apparently intending to use it on Stevenson. Committed to New York's Bellevue Hospital, he did re-emerge to record a wonderful acid-folk solo album at the end of 1968, but that would be his only notable post-Grape project; he struggles with mental illness to this day.

Another unexpected blow was dealt when Moseley, despite his membership in a band that emerged from the Haight-Ashbury psychedelic scene, joined the Marine Corps at the beginning of 1969. The band did struggle on and release a couple more albums during that year, and the best tracks from these (particularly the earlier one, *Moby Grape '69*) proved they could still deliver the goods, though usually in a more subdued, countrified fashion than their earliest material. The group broke up at the end of the '60s, although they would periodically reunite for nearly unheard albums over the next two decades, in lineups featuring varying original members. Their problems were exacerbated by Matthew Katz, who owns the Moby Grape name, and has sometimes prevented the original members from using the name when they worked together. — *Richie Unterberger*

Moby Grape / Jun. 1967 / San Francisco Sound ✦✦✦✦
Some consider this 1967 debut to be the most impressive of the San Francisco rock revolution. Not a wasted moment. — *Jeff Tamarkin*

Wow/Grape Jam / 1968 / San Francisco Sound ✦✦✦
● **Vintage: The Very Best of Moby Grape** / May 11, 1993 / Columbia/Legacy ✦✦✦✦
It's hard to imagine a better-produced package of Moby Grape's work than this two-disc, 48-track condensation of their best late-'60s recordings. The first disc of this set centers around their entire 1967 self-titled debut LP (included in its entirety), which mixed blues, country, and folk influences with hard-charging psychedelic rock 'n' roll. The result was one of the Summer of Love's more enduring works. The second disc boils their wildly inconsistent 1968-69 material down to a fairly strong and coherent selection. While it doesn't match the peak of the group's initial burst, it features some strong folk and country-rock originals that wear much better in the absence of the bloated jams and half-baked hard rock that could make their albums a chore to sit through. Each disc includes interesting demos, outtakes, and live performances that round out the legacy of this prodigiously talented but ill-fated band, which was overcome by internal strife and label/management difficulties after their promising debut. — *Richie Unterberger*

The Mojos
....
British Invasion
Known mostly in the States for doing the original version of "Everything's Alright," The Mojos were one of the best Liverpool groups of the British Invasion. Besides "Everything's Alright," they never scored any other British hits of note, though a couple squeezed into their Top 30. At times, they could be pretty wimpy, with jerky vocals and material that would have been at home with Gerry & The Pacemakers. But at other times, with their electric keyboard-driven sound, they echo the much tougher Manfred Mann. Way below the Beatles and even the Searchers in terms of quality, they were, except for the Swinging Blue Jeans and maybe the Merseybeats, the best of the rest in their home city. — *Richie Unterberger*

● **Working** / 1982 / Edsel ✦✦✦✦
This compilation includes 16 tracks recorded by the group between 1963 and 1965, taken from rare singles and their sole EP. This stuff isn't exactly timeless, but it has a giddy Merseybeat enthusiasm that remains infectious. Comes with a detailed history of the band. — *Richie Unterberger*

The Monkees
....
Pop-Rock
Formed primarily for the purpose of starring in a television series, the Monkees were on one hand a cynically manufactured group, devised to cash in on the early Beatles' success by applying the most superficial aspects of the British Invasion formula to capture a preteen audience. On the other hand, they weren't devoid of musical talent, and at their best managed to craft some enduring pop-rock hits. "I'm a Believer," "Last Train to Clarksville," "A Little Bit Me, A Little Bit You," "Pleasant Valley Sunday," "Stepping Stone," "Take a Giant Step," "Valleri," "Words"—all were pleasantly jangling, harmony rock numbers with hooks big enough for a meat locker, and all were huge hits in 1966-68. Scorned at their peak by hipsters for not playing on many of their own records, the group gained some belated critical respect for their catchy, good-time brand of pop. It would be foolish to pretend, however, that they were a band of serious significance, despite the occasional genuinely serious artistic aspirations of the members. The Monkees were the brainchild of television producers Bert Schneider and Bob Rafelson, who decided to

emulate the zany, madcap humor of the Beatles' *A Hard Day's Night* for the small screen. In September 1965, they placed in ad in *Variety* for four "folk & rock musicians" to appear in a TV series. Over 400 applied for the job, including Stephen Stills and Harry Nilsson, but as it turned out only one of the four winners, guitarist and songwriter Michael Nesmith, actually saw the ad. Mickey Dolenz (who would play drums), Davy Jones (who would sing), and Peter Tork (bass) found out about the opportunity from other sources. Nesmith and Tork had experience in the folk scene; Dolenz and Jones were primarily actors (although Nesmith and Jones had already made some obscure solo recordings).

From the outset, it was made clear that the Monkees were hired to be television actors first, and musicians a distant second. There would be original material generated for them to sing in the series, mostly by professional songwriters like Tommy Boyce, Bobby Hart, Carole King, Gerry Goffin, and Neil Diamond. There would be records, as well—had to be, with that kind of weekly exposure, to promote the tunes—but the group wouldn't do much more than sing, although the series would give the impression that they played their own instruments.

The TV show was a big hit with young audiences between 1966 and 1968, with slapstick comedy, super-fast editing, and thin plots that could be banded together by almost surreal humor. It wasn't *A Hard Day's Night*, but it was, in its way, innovative relative to the conventions of television at the time. The irony was that, by the time the series debuted in September 1966, the Beatles themselves had just released *Revolver,* and had evolved way beyond their moptop phase into psychedelia.

Also in September 1966, their debut single "Last Train to Clarksville" became their first big hit, reaching No. 1, as did the follow-up, "I'm a Believer." They were quickly one of the most popular acts in the business, yet they were not allowed to play anything on most of their first records, only to sing; the instruments would be handled by session players. This was particularly hard for Mike Nesmith, a serious musician and songwriter, to swallow, although he did manage to place a few of his own tunes on their records from the start.

Eventually the Monkees revealed that they didn't play on most of their own records, and Nesmith in particular incited the group to wrest control of their recordings. Partly to deflect criticism of the group as nothing more than puppets, and partly to effect control over their musical destiny (some of their early recordings had been packaged and released without their consent), the Monkees did indeed play and write much of the music on their third album, *Headquarters* (1967), with a lot of help from producer Chip Douglas. It didn't prove the band to be hidden geniuses, in fact sounding not much different from their previous releases, but as a hard-won victory to establish their own identity, it was a major point of pride. They would continue, however, to rely upon industry songwriters for the rest of their hit singles, and frequently employ session musicians throughout the rest of their career.

Despite the questions surrounding their musical competence, the Monkees did tour before live audiences. They made their own contribution to rock history by enlisting Jimi Hendrix, then barely known in the US, as an opening act for a 1967 tour; Hendrix lasted only a few shows before everyone agreed that the combination was a mismatch (to put it mildly). But the Monkees were always a lot hipper personally than many assumed from their bubblegum packaging. Their albums are strewn with rather ambitious, even mildly psychedelic cuts, some rather successful ("Porpoise Song," Nesmith's "Circle Sky"), some absolutely awful. In 1968, they gained their freak credentials with the movie *Head,* a messy, indulgent, occasionally inspired piece of drug-addled weirdness that was co-written and co-produced by Jack Nicholson (before he had broken through to stardom with *Easy Rider*).

By 1968, the Monkee phenomenon was drawing to a close. The show's final episode aired in March 1968, and *Head,* released in November, was not a commercial success, confusing the teenyboppers and confounding the critics (not many people saw it to begin with in any case). Surprisingly, it was not Nesmith, but Tork who was the first to leave the group, at the end of 1968. They carried on as a trio, releasing a couple of fairly dismal albums in 1969, as well as producing a little-seen TV special. By the end of the '60s, Nesmith—who had established his credentials as a songwriter with "Different Drum," which was taken into the Top 20 by Linda Ronstadt and the Stone Poneys—was also gone, to start a lengthy solo career that finally allowed him to stretch out as a serious artist. That left only Dolenz and Jones, who fulfilled the Monkees contract with the pointless *Changes* in 1970.

When enough years separated the music from the hype, the Monkees underwent a critical rehab of sorts, as listeners fondly remembered their singles as classy, well-executed, fun pop-rock. That led to a predictable clamor for a reunion, especially after their albums were reissued and surprisingly swift sales in the mid-'80s, and their series was rerun on MTV. Nesmith was having none of it; by this time he was a respected and hugely successful music video mogul with his Pacific Arts company. The other three did reunite to tour and record a predictably horrendous album, *Pool It!* (Nesmith did join them once onstage in 1989). Rhino has treated the Monkee catalog with a respect usually accorded for Charlie

Parker outtakes, reissuing all of their original albums on CD with added unreleased/rare bonus tracks, and even assembling a box set. —*Richie Unterberger*

The Monkees / Oct. 1966 / Rhino ✦✦✦
The Monkees did virtually nothing besides sing lead vocals on their full-length debut; poor Peter Tork didn't even get to do that, his contribution being limited to one of the six guitar parts on "Papa Gene's Blues." Given that it wasn't a project of high integrity, it wasn't bad—in fact, much of this is reasonably gutsy pop-rock, including their TV theme song, the hits "Last Train to Clarksville" and "Take a Giant Step," and various decent songs by top Brill Building tunesmiths like Goffin/King, Boyce/Hart, and David Gates. Nesmith was allowed one composition ("Papa Gene's Blues") that indicated his country-rock direction. The CD reissue includes unremarkable bonus tracks of alternate versions of the Monkees theme and a couple of songs that would turn up on subsequent LPs. —*Richie Unterberger*

More of the Monkees / Jan. 10, 1967 / Rhino ✦✦✦
Second album, same as the first, virtually: a huge single ("I'm a Believer"/ "Steppin' Stone"), a couple of token Mike Nesmith songs (including "Mary, Mary," previously recorded by the Paul Butterfield Blues Band and a rap hit for Run-D.M.C. in 1988), tunes by Boyce/Hart, Goffin/King, Neil Diamond, Jeff Barry, Neil Sedaka, and Carole Bayer; no participation from the group other than lead vocals. The band was quite upset at their lack of input at the time, but it's relatively decent (if quite harmless) pop-rock, featuring one of their best album tracks, "She." Like all of the Rhino CD reissues, it adds marginally interesting bonus tracks of unreleased alternate versions, including an early take of "I'm a Believer." —*Richie Unterberger*

Headquarters / May 22, 1967 / Rhino ✦✦✦
For their third album, the Monkees were determined to wrest control of the creative process, and with producer Chip Douglas functioning as frequent bassist and auxiliary member, they were indeed able to play most of the instruments and write much of the material. It would be nice to report that the result far exceeded previous efforts and established the group as visionary artists, but in fact this was, again, pleasantly inoffensive pop-rock. There was more of a country flavor and a sense of personal involvement, though the group still tapped songwriting pros like Boyce/Hart and Mann/Weil for about half the songs. Standouts included Nesmith's "You Just May Be The One," one of his best Monkee tunes, and Tork's "For Pete's Sake," which became the show's closing theme. The CD reissue includes six unreleased tracks and alternate takes, a couple of which (Nilsson's "All of Your Toys" and Nesmith's "The Girl I Knew Somewhere") rank among their finest. —*Richie Unterberger*

Pisces, Aquarius, Capricorn & Jones Ltd. / Nov. 14, 1967 / Rhino ✦✦✦✦
One of their better efforts, featuring the double-sided hit "Pleasant Valley Sunday"/"Words," and some of their best album tracks, like "She Hangs Out," "Star Collector," and "Cuddly Toy," the last of which was one of the first Nilsson songs to be covered by a major artist. As usual, some of the country-rockers and half-baked psychedelic tunes are tedious, though a couple tracks are notable for featuring some of the first uses of a Moog synthesizer on a rock record. The CD reissue adds some previously unissued alternate mixes, as well as the killer soulful B-side "Goin' Down," which ranks as one of their very best tracks despite its obscurity. —*Richie Unterberger*

The Birds, the Bees & the Monkees / Apr. 22, 1968 / Rhino ✦✦

Head / Dec. 1, 1968 / Rhino ✦✦✦✦
Like the film from which it came, the soundtrack to *Head* was far from a masterpiece, but had some inspired moments. These include the spacy "Porpoise Song," written by Gerry Goffin and Carole King; the tough-rocking "Circle Sky," probably the best song Mike Nesmith wrote for the group; "Can You Dig It," one of Peter Tork's best contributions; and "As We Go Along" and "Daddy's Song," little-known songs by Carole King and Nilsson, respectively. As a listening experience, it's made more difficult by the juxtaposition of music and dialogue from the film. The CD reissue adds bonus unissued jingles and alternate takes, highlighted by a live version of "Circle Sky." —*Richie Unterberger*

Instant Replay / Feb. 15, 1969 / Rhino ✦✦

The Monkees Present / Oct. 1969 / Rhino ✦✦

Changes / Jun. 1970 / Rhino ✦

Missing Links / 1987 / Rhino ✦✦✦
A fine selection of rarities and oddities that every Monkee maniac with more than a passing interest should own. —*Jeff Tamarkin*

Missing Links 2 / 1990 / Rhino ✦✦✦
Nineteen rare and unreleased tracks that, like the rest of the Monkees' output, ranges from excellent to insufferable, with plenty of mediocre material between. The highlights are the sprightly pop-rocker "All the King's Horses" (a 1966 Mike Nesmith original) and alternate versions of two of the group's best singles, "Words" and "Valleri." These alternate

takes aren't exactly better, but they are definitely different and less elaborately produced. Most of the rest is either lightweight 1966 pop-rock or weedy 1968 Mike Nesmith country-rock tunes that foreshadow his solo work; several cuts are alternate versions of songs that were hardly notable efforts in the first place. An exception is the live 1968 recording of the unusually forceful Nesmith original "Circle Sky," which was featured in their movie *Head* (although a studio version was substituted on the actual soundtrack album). Odds and ends like an instrumental banjo piece by Peter Tork and a Spanish Christmas carol are pleasant but inessential. A thoughtfully compiled CD, it nonetheless really gives this group more respect than they're due by treating these artifacts with such importance. —*Richie Unterberger*

Listen to the Band / 1991 / Rhino ++++
A four-CD boxed set that includes every Monkees track a fan could want, and much more. Excessive, but a collector's dream. —*Jeff Tamarkin*

● **Greatest Hits** / Nov. 1995 / Rhino ++++
Twenty-song collection includes all of their big chart hits, as well as key album tracks like "(Theme From) the Monkees" and "Mary, Mary," and the ace B-side "Goin' Down." The slightly more extensive Arista anthology still has the edge, due to the inclusion of two good cuts ("Take a Giant Step" and "She") that are somehow omitted from this Rhino compilation. On the other hand, if you're still in the market for just one Monkees album, this will do just fine. Good, extensive liner notes, though the last two songs (from 1987 singles that only featured Dolenz and Tork) are a waste. —*Richie Unterberger*

Missing Links 3 / Mar. 26, 1996 / Rhino +++

The Monks

Rock 'n' Roll, Garage Rock
One of the strangest stories in rock history, the Monks were formed in the early '60s by American G.I.s stationed in Germany. After their discharge, the group stayed on in Germany as the Torquays, a standard "beat" band. After changing their name to the M onks in the mid-'60s they changed their music, attitude, and appearance radically. Gone were standard oldie covers, replaced by furious, minimalistic original material that anticipated the blunt, harsh commentary of the punk era. Their insistent rhythms recalled martial beats and polkas as much as garage rock, and the weirdness quotient was heightened by electric banjo, berserk organ runs, and occasional bursts of feedback guitar. To prove that they meant business, the Monks shaved the top of their heads and performed their songs—crude diatribes about the Vietnam war, dehumanized society, and love/hate affairs with girls—in actual monks' clothing. This was pretty strong stuff for 1966 Germany, and their shocking repertoire and attire were received with more confusion than hostility or warm praise. Well-known in Germany as a live act, their sole album and several singles didn't take off and were never released in the US, it was rumored, because the lyrical content was deemed too shocking. They disbanded in confusion around 1967, but their album—one of the most oddball constructions in all of rock—gained a cult following among collectors, and has ironically made them much more popular and influential on an international level than they were during their lifetime. Bassist Eddie Shaw's 1994 autobiography, *Black Monk Time*, is a fascinating narrative of the Monks' stranger-than-fiction story. —*Richie Unterberger*

● **Black Monk Time** / 1966 / Repertoire ++++
The Monks' only album is packed with angst anthems on the order of "Shut Up," "I Hate You," "Complication," and "Drunken Maria." The CD reissue adds their two later non-LP singles, making it a complete document of the Monks' entire recorded legacy. —*Richie Unterberger*

Chris Montez

b. Jan. 17, 1943
Vocals / Rock 'n' Roll
One of the leading rockers in the Los Angeles Hispanic community after the tragic death of Ritchie Valens, Chris Montez later mellowed out under the tutelage of Herb Alpert and tallied several MOR-style hits. His first smash was on Monogram in 1962, "Let's Dance." It was a grinding rocker with roller-rink organ. Montez changed his attitude after signing with A&M. With Alpert producing, Montez adopted an easygoing approach on "Call Me," "The More I See You," and "Time after Time," all solid sellers in 1966. The formula quickly faded, however, and his final chart entry came the following year with "Because of You." —*Bill Dahl*

● **All-Time Greatest Hits** / 1991 / DCC ++++
Montez began as a Ritchie Valens-style rocker and reemerged as a crooner of pop ballads in the mid-'60s. He excelled at both styles, each of which is amply documented here. —*Jeff Tamarkin*

Moody Blues

Art-Rock/Progressive-Rock, British Invasion, Pop-Rock
Formed in Birmingham, England, as an R&B quintet in 1963, the Moody

Blues originally consisted of Denny Laine (guitar), Mike Pinder (piano), Ray Thomas (harmonica), Graeme Edge (drums), and Clint Warwick (bass). The band emerged in 1965 with a soulful cover of an American R&B number called "Go Now," which topped the charts in both the UK and the US. They toured with the Beatles and seemed poised for stardom, but none of their subsequent records made any impact. The quintet soon returned to playing the ballroom circuit, discovering at the same time that their management had filched much of their prior earnings. Amid these crises, Laine—who, after a furtive solo career and a tour with Ginger Baker, became Paul McCartney's lead guitarist in Wings—and Warwick were voted out of the group. In their places came Justin Hayward (guitar) and John Lodge (bass).

The Moody Blues 1966 records were heavily influenced by the Beatles, very upbeat, and unsuccessful. But in 1967 they were asked to record a stereo demonstration record with a major production budget, and came up with *Days of Future Passed.* Built around the concept of a day represented by rock songs, which were bridged by sweeping orchestral passages, this record yielded two major hits, "Tuesday Afternoon" and "Nights in White Satin," of which the latter became their signature tune. The Moodies established themselves as the pop mystics of the Summer of Love, their music blossoming on a series of impeccably produced albums in pseudo-classical glory, driven by Pinder's lush Mellotron orchestrations, Hayward's and Lodge's multilayered guitars, Thomas's flute, and a great beat from Graeme Edge, when he wasn't reciting overblown poetry. Although many critics looked down on them, the band was very popular with college-age listeners and broadened the spectrum of rock sounds, thus paving the way for such art-rock outfits as King Crimson, Yes, and Emerson, Lake & Palmer.

In 1973, after seven albums, the Moodies decided to take a five-year hiatus devoted to solo projects. Pinder exited permanently following the 1978 comeback album, Octave, and was replaced by ex-Yes keyboard player Patrick Moraz. At this point, they became less interesting—Hayward could be relied on for passionate love songs, Lodge for driving but predictable rockers, and Thomas for his mysticism, which sounded woefully out of place in the '80s, but except for an occasional hit like 1986's nostagia-laden "In Your Wildest Dreams" (itself a look back at their own history), little of the new material stood out. The Moodies were reduced to an arena oldies act. —*Bruce Eder*

The Magnificent Moodies / 1965 / Polydor +++

Days of Future Passed / 1967 / Polydor ++++
The reconstituted Moody Blues, with Justin Hayward and John Lodge established on guitar, bass, and vocals, venture into progressive-rock territory with The London Festival Orchestra and have their first major success, both with the album and the singles "Nights in White Satin" and "Tuesday Afternoon." The material seems pretentious but really rocks pretty hard, and the orchestral interludes, courtesy of the late Peter Knight, have an epic sweep that still dazzles the ear. In 1967, a lot of people hungry for something to put on the turntable after *Sgt. Pepper* turned to this, and turned it into an international hit with good reason. —*Bruce Eder*

In Search of the Lost Chord / 1968 / Polydor +++
The Moody Blues discover drugs and mysticism as a basis for songwriting, and come up with a compelling psychedelic album, filled with songs about Dr. Timothy Leary and the astral plane and other psychedelic-era concerns, all resplendent in sweeping choruses and an elegant mix of conventional rock instruments augmented by flutes, sitars, tablas, cellos, and electronic orchestrations. Beautiful and elegant. —*Bruce Eder*

On the Threshold of a Dream / 1969 / Polydor ++++
Mysticism gives way to science-fiction on this album, which abandons Indian sitars and tablas in favor of more traditional sounding orchestrations, and also rocks a little harder in spots than their previous records. —*Bruce Eder*

To Our Children's Children's Children / 1969 / Polydor +++
The Moody Blues' most personal album was also, oddly enough, the poorest seller among their psychedelic period releases, taking longer to go gold. The material here dwells on time, space, and distance, with a curious mood of loneliness on several of the songs. The last of the band's "studio"-based albums, it has a very lush, rich sound, although the group avoids extended suites of the kind on their previous two albums. And Hayward's "Gypsy" and "Watching and Waiting" are among the best songs in their history. —*Bruce Eder*

Question of Balance / 1970 / Polydor +++

● **Every Good Boy Deserves Favour** / 1971 / Polydor ++++
The most well realized of the band's psychedelic era albums, filled with gorgeous melodies, superbly crafted songs, and a dazzling array of keyboard and guitar pyrotechnics—"Emily's Song," "Nice to Be Here," and "My Song" are among the best work the group has ever done, and "The Story in Your Eyes" is the best rock number they've ever cut, with a riveting beat and the kind of insights one expected more out of George Harrison at his best. —*Bruce Eder*

Seventh Sojourn / 1972 / Polydor ✦✦✦
The group's hardest rocking album, and one that closed their psychedelic period. The songs generally lack the rich Mellotron orchestrations of the earlier records, and most of the songs are built around John Lodge's and Graeme Edge's driving rhythm section—"New Horizons" was the most romantic number the band had debuted since "Nights in White Satin," while "I'm Just a Singer in a Rock 'n Roll Band" showed the sudden emergence of John Lodge as a major songwriter in the group. —*Bruce Eder*

This Is the Moody Blues / 1974 / Polydor ✦✦✦✦
A double CD best-of covering the group's 1967-1972 period, its tapes recompiled and remastered for the compact disc reissue. The selection is reasonably complete, although it leaves out one excellent number for every two that are included, and the individual CDs are probably a better investment. The new liner notes by John Tracy are also thoughtful and informative. —*Bruce Eder*

In the Beginning / 1975 / Deram ✦✦✦

Caught Live + Five / 1977 / PolyGram ✦✦✦

Octave / 1978 / Polydor ✦✦✦

Long Distance Voyager / 1981 / Polydor ✦✦✦
The group's biggest-selling album of the '80s also marked a turning point in their fortunes, where they began losing even the mainstream critics. The music has drive, and is extremely well played and produced (this was the only album the band ever got to do at their own, custom-designed Threshold Studios), but also seemed very dated in its time, with a '60s sensibility that was out of place. —*Bruce Eder*

The Present / 1983 / Polydor ✦✦

● **Voices in the Sky: Best of the Moody Blues** / 1985 / Polydor ✦✦✦✦
A good sampling of the Moody Blues' greatest hits from the 1960s and '70s; it's fine for those who only want the hits. —*Stephen Thomas Erlewine*

The Other Side of Life / 1986 / Polydor ✦✦✦

Prelude / 1987 / Polydor ✦✦✦

Greatest Hits / 1989 / Polydor ✦✦✦✦
All of the Moody Blues' best songs and biggest hits from the 1980s are collected on *Greatest Hits;* it's the most mainstream pop-oriented material the band has ever recorded. —*Stephen Thomas Erlewine*

A Night at Red Rocks with the Colorado . . . / 1993 / Polydor ✦✦✦

Time Traveller / 1994 / PolyGram ✦✦✦✦
When the Moody Blues were due for the box set treatment, it would have been uncharacteristic for the production to be lacking in overstated grandiosity. On that count, this four-CD retrospective does not disappoint, including the bulk of their most famous work (from their 1967-72 albums), lots from their later records and side projects, and a few rarities. There's not a great deal of reason for anyone but fanatics to fork out for this package; the albums (which were specifically programmed to work as separate entities) remain readily available, there's too much late stuff and Hayward/Blue Jays tracks, and there's nothing from the Denny Laine era. The three non-LP 1967 cuts that open the set are available on the double import LP *A Dream* (still possible to find), an album that also has the additional 1967 B-side "Really Haven't Got the Time," which somehow doesn't make it onto *Time Traveller*. As consolation, the liner notes are pretty good and extensive, and the first printings of the set include a bonus disc of a 1992 concert with The Colorado Symphony Orchestra. —*Richie Unterberger*

Moonglows

R&B, Doo Wop
Among the most seminal R&B and doo wop groups of all time, the Moonglows' lineup featured some of the genre's greatest pure singers. The original lineup from Louisville included Bobby Lester, Harvey Fuqua, Alexander Graves, and Prentiss Barnes, with guitarist Billy Johnson. They were originally called the Crazy Sounds, but were renamed by disc jockey Alan Freed as the Moonglows. The group also cut some recordings as the Moonlighters. Their first major hit was the No. 1 R&B gem "Sincerely" for Chess in 1954, which reached No. 20 on the pop charts. They enjoyed five more Top Ten R&B hits on Chess from 1955 to 1958, among them "Most of All," "We Go Together," "See Saw," and "Please Send Me Someone to Love," as well as "Ten Commandments of Love." Fuqua, the nephew of Charlie Fuqua of the Ink Spots, left in 1958. He recorded "Ten Commandments of Love" as Harvey & The Moonglows with Marvin Gaye, Reese Palmner, James Knowland, and Chester Simmons before founding his own label, Tri-Phi. Fuqua created and produced the Spinners in 1961 and wrote and produced for Motown until the early '70s. The Moonglows disbanded in the '60s, then reunited in 1972 with Fuqua, Lester, Graves, Doc Williams, and Chuck Lewis. They recorded for RCA and a reworked version of "Sincerely" eventually charted, but wasn't a major hit. —*Ron Wynn*

● **Blue Velvet/The Ultimate Collection** / 1993 / Chess ✦✦✦✦
Few rivaled the Moonglows in musical sophistication, inventiveness or flair. They could sing gorgeous heartache ballads, rollicking uptempo rhythm tunes, creditable period-piece novelty numbers, wonderful pop covers or shattering originals. This two-disc set contains 44 outstanding numbers, with every major Moonglows anthem and several others that weren't big hits but deserved to be, such as "Penny Arcade" and "Love Is a River." This collection updates and expands the *Greatest Sides* single LP release briefly available when Sugar Hill had the Chess catalog in the 1970s. It wisely restricts material to the era when they were at their best, the 1950s, and includes an excellent booklet. —*Ron Wynn*

Gary Moore

b. Apr. 4, 1952, Belfast, Ireland
Guitar / Blues-Rock, Hard Rock
Belfast native Gary Moore first achieved renown as the lead guitarist of hard rockers Thin Lizzy. Moore's first band, Skid Row, featured bassist Brendan Shields, drummer Noel Bridgeman, and singer Phil Lynott, who left to form Thin Lizzy while Moore remained to pursue a record deal with the help of Fleetwood Mac guitarist Peter Green. Skid Row recorded three albums before Moore left for a solo career, releasing his first album, *Grinding Stone*, in 1973. Lynott then invited Moore to join Thin Lizzy as a replacement for guitarist Eric Bell; Moore stayed for a short time before leaving to pursue session work, which he has continued off and on throughout his career. Moore joined the fusion outfit Colosseum II in 1975 and rejoined Thin Lizzy in 1977 as a full-time member, appearing on their 1979 album *Black Rose*. In the middle of a 1979 American tour, Moore left Thin Lizzy again to form the unsuccessful G-Force; his single "Parisienne Walkways," from the solo LP *Back on the Streets*, became a UK hit that May.

Moore recorded a series of moderately successful albums during the 1980s and had popular UK numbers with "Empty Rooms" in 1985 and a collaboration with Lynott, "Out in the Fields." 1989's *After the War* showed the influence of Celtic music, but Moore's breakthrough came with the following year's *Still Got the Blues*. Toning down the hard rock feel of many of his previous recordings, Moore mixed traditional blues standards with a sprinkling of originals and delivered a superb performance vocally and instrumentally, and the album became a critical and commercial success. Moore followed his surprise success with *After Hours*, which featured guest spots from B.B. King and Albert Collins and solidified Moore's reputation as a blues-rocker of note. Moore recorded a side project called BBM in 1994 with former Cream rhythm section Jack Bruce and Ginger Baker, and in 1995, he released a tribute album to his idol, Peter Green, composed entirely of Green originals played on a guitar Green had given him years ago. —*Steve Huey*

● **Still Got the Blues** / 1990 / Charisma ✦✦✦✦
Relieved from the pressures of having to record a hit single, he cuts loose on some blues standards as well as some newer material. Moore plays better than ever, spitting out an endless stream of fiery licks that are both technically impressive and soulful. It's no wonder *Still Got the Blues* was his biggest hit. —*David Jehnzen*

After Hours / 1992 / Charisma ✦✦✦✦
Not wanting to leave a good thing behind, Moore reprises *Still Got the Blues* on its follow-up, *After Hours*. While his playing is just as impressive, the album feels a little calculated. Nevertheless, Moore's gutsy, impassioned playing makes the similarity easy to ignore. —*David Jehnzen*

Blues for Greeny / 1995 / Charisma ✦✦✦

Ballads & Blues 1982-1994 / Mar. 21, 1995 / Charisma ✦✦✦✦

Alanis Morissette

b. Jun. 1, 1974, Ottawa, Canada
Vocals / Dance-Pop, Alternative Pop-Rock, Pop-Rock
Alanis Morissette was one of the most unlikely stars of the mid-'90s. A former child actress turned dance-pop diva, Morissette transformed herself into a confessional alternative singer-songwriter, in the vein of Liz Phair and Tori Amos. However, she added enough pop sensibility, slight hip-hop flourishes and marketing savvy to that formula to become a superstar with her third album, *Jagged Little Pill*.

In her childhood, Morissette began playing piano and writing songs. At the age of ten, she joined the cast of *You Can't Do That on Television*, a children's TV program. Using money that she earned on the show, Morissette recorded an independent single, "Fate Stay with Me," which was released when she was ten. After leaving the show, she continued to act, but she concentrated on a musical career, signing a music publishing contract when she was 14. The publishing contract led to a record deal with MCA/Canada. In 1991, she moved to Toronto and released her debut album, *Alanis*.

Alanis was a collection of pop-oriented dance numbers and ballads that was successful in Canada, selling over 100,000 copies, and leading to a Juno Award for Most Promising Female Artist. However, no other country paid any attention to the record. In 1992, she released *Now Is the Time*, an album that closely resembled her debut. Like its predecessor, it was a success in Canada, even if it sold half of what *Alanis* did. Following the release *Now Is the Time*, Morissette relocated to Los Angeles, where she met Glen Ballard in early 1994. Ballard had previously written Michael Jackson's hit "Man in the Mirror," produced Wilson Phillips' debut album, and worked with David Hasselhoff. Despite the duo's mainstream pop pedigree, they decided to pursue an edgier, alternative rock-oriented direction. The result was *Jagged Little Pill*, which was released on Maverick Records, Madonna's label.

On the strength of the single "You Oughta Know," *Jagged Little Pill* gained attention upon its release in the summer of 1995. Soon, the single received heavy airplay from both alternative radio and MTV, sending the album into the Top Ten and multi-platinum status. The second and third single from *Jagged Little Pill*, "Hand in My Pocket" and "All I Really Want," kept the album in the Top Ten. In early 1996, she was nominated for six Grammys. Shortly after the nominations, Morissette released her fourth single, "Ironic," which proved to be another crossover success. Morissette won several Grammy awards in 1996, including Album of the Year and Record of the Year. *— Stephen Thomas Erlewine*

● **Jagged Little Pill** / 1995 / Maverick ✦✦✦✦

Alanis Morissette knows the pain of love—you can tell from the caterwauling single "You Oughta Know." Over a grinding alterna-funk groove, Morissette rails against her ex-lover who's left her for someone "older" than her and wonders "is she perverted like me?" Morissette doesn't understand why she's been left alone, since he said he would "hold me until you died, until you died/But you're still alive!" Every song on *Jagged Little Pill* reads exactly like that—it sounds like the writings of a dejected college sophomore, so perhaps it isn't surprising that the majority of *Jagged Little Pill* was written when she was 19 years old. In that sense, it is a pseudo-concept album where a confused teenager, inspired by Liz Phair, begins to grow up, learning about sex, relationships, drugs, and life in general. Morissette doesn't have a great, or even good voice—it's herky-jerky, making the octave jumps of Sinead O'Connor but without the sense of pitch. Her lyrics are too personal to connect with universal truths—when she tells one ex-boyfriend "You took me out to wine dine 69 me / But didn't hear a damn word I said . . . Now that I'm Miss Thing / Now that I'm a zillionaire / You scan the credits for your name / And wonder why it's not there," it's hard to gather much sympathy for her. And, despite the presence of superstar musicians like Benmont Tench, Flea, and Dave Navarro, the album sounds like the work of studio hacks. It's enjoyable in small doses, yet her music is merely a vehicle for her hackneyed prose. *— Stephen Thomas Erlewine*

Van Morrison

b. Aug. 31, 1945, Belfast, Ireland

Guitar, Harmonica, Keyboards, Saxophone, Vocals / Singer-Songwriter, Adult Contemporary, Soft Rock, Folk-Rock, Pop-Rock, Blue-Eyed Soul, Jazz-Rock

Van Morrison is one of the most critically acclaimed pop music singer-songwriters to have emerged in the 1960s. His bluesy voice and jazzy sense of improvisation have resulted in a three-decade career full of outstanding albums and concert performances. Morrison's father was a fan of American music, and he grew up listening to records by Leadbelly, Woody Guthrie, Jelly Roll Morton, and Jimmy Rodgers, among others, spanning the genres of blues, folk, jazz, and country. As a teen, Morrison took up guitar and saxophone and played in a series of local bands, culminating in the formation of Them, an R&B quintet, in 1964. Signed to Decca Records (now controlled by PolyGram), Them released two albums, *Them* (issued as *The Angry Young Them* in the US) and *Them Again* and scored Top Ten hits in the UK with "Baby Please Don't Go" and "Here Comes the Night" in 1965. In the US, Them also charted with two Morrison-composed songs, "Gloria" (which became a rock standard) and "Mystic Eyes." But the group disbanded in 1966.

Morrison signed to Bang Records, a label set up by songwriter Bert Berns, who had written "Here Comes the Night," and in March 1967, recorded eight tracks in New York intended for single release. The first result of the session was "Brown-Eyed Girl," which became a US Top Ten hit, prompting Bang to release the singles session as Morrison's first solo album, *Blowin' Your Mind!* (Jul. 1967), though Morrison had not approved the release, the title, or the trendy psychedelic cover. Nevertheless, Morrison returned to the studio in the fall and cut eight more songs for Bang, which took five of them, culled five from the previous album, and released the deceptively titled *The Best of Van Morrison* (Nov. 1967). With that, Morrison negotiated to get off the label, a process made easier by the sudden death of Berns in December 1967. Morrison agreed to turn over his next ten compositions to Bang, but submitted a tape of unusable off-the-cuff improvisations finally released in 1994 on *Payin' Dues*. (The Bang material has been reissued endlessly, the most complete version being Epic/Legacy's 1991 *Bang Masters*.) Morrison then signed to

Warner Bros. Records and recorded *Astral Weeks* (Nov. 1968), which failed to chart but seems to have made every critic's all-time Top Ten list ever since. Living in Woodstock, NY, and later in Marin County, CA, with his wife Janet Planet, Morrison adopted a more commercial country-pop sound, and his second Warner Bros. album, *Moondance* (Feb. 1970), was more of a sales success, spawning a Top 40 hit in "Come Running" and eventually selling over a million copies. Its follow-up, *His Band and the Street Choir* (Oct. 1970), featured chart singles in "Domino" (which hit the Top Ten), "Blue Money," and "Call Me Up in Dreamland." Completing a trilogy of country-pop successes, *Tupelo Honey* (Oct. 1971) produced chart singles in the title song and "Wild Night" and eventually went gold. Morrison took a more soul-oriented approach on *Saint Dominic's Preview* (Jul. 1972), characterized by the album's first single, "Jackie Wilson Said (I'm in Heaven When You Smile)."

Hard Nose the Highway (Jul. 1973), released around the time of the breakup of his marriage, found a more introspective Morrison crooning such material as *Sesame Street* puppet Kermit the Frog's "[It isn't easy bein'] Green," but he bounced back with a powerful double live album, *It's Too Late to Stop Now* (Feb. 1974), then made his most reflective album since *Astral Weeks* in *Veedon Fleece* (Oct. 1974) before disappearing from record stores for two and a half years, reportedly due to writer's block. He returned with *A Period of Transition* (Mar. 1977), an R&B-tinged effort that paired him with Dr. John. More assured was *Wavelength* (Sep. 1978), whose title track was his biggest chart single in more than six years. *Into the Music* (Aug. 1979) explicitly looked back on earlier styles and revealed an increasing religious interest, while the pastoral *Common One* (Sep. 1980) was filled with references to English poets.

Morrison's albums of the 1980s and '90s largely repeated the musical styles and spiritual lyric themes he had developed in the 1970s, though they frequently contained moving performances. In 1984, Morrison switched from Warner Bros. Records to PolyGram, which had been distributing his albums outside the US since 1979 on its Mercury label. He recorded with the Chieftains on the traditional album *Irish Heartbeat* (Jun. 1988), a change of pace. In 1990, he experienced a career resurgence when Mercury/PolyGram released *The Best of Van Morrison*, which quickly became his biggest seller, at two million copies and counting. In his concert performances of the 1990s, Morrison increasingly relied on a band led by British jazz organist Georgie Fame and introduced guest singers, among them his daughter Shana. A typical performance was captured on *A Night in San Francisco* (Jun. 1994). Morrison also continued to release new albums almost annually: *Days like This* (Jun. 1995) was his 22nd studio album of new, mostly original material in 28 years. *— William Ruhlmann*

☆ **Astral Weeks** / Nov. 1968 / Warner Bros. ✦✦✦✦✦

Astral Weeks is generally considered one of the best albums in pop music history. In the 1978 book *Rock Critics' Choice*, compiled by Paul Gambaccini, it was ranked fourth on a list of "the all-time greatest rock albums chosen by the world's top DJs and critics." In 1985, it ranked second on the *New Musical Express*'s "all-time Top 100 LPs" list. In 1987, *Rolling Stone* magazine placed it seventh on a list of "the 100 best albums of the last 20 years." In 1995, *MOJO* magazine put it at No. 2 in a list of the "greatest albums ever made." For all that renown, *Astral Weeks* is anything but an archetypal rock 'n' roll album: In fact, it isn't a rock 'n' roll album at all. Employing a mixture of folk, blues, jazz, and classical music, Van Morrison spins out a series of extended ruminations on his Belfast upbringing, including the remarkable character "Madame George" and the climactic epiphany experienced on "Cyprus Avenue." Accompanying himself on acoustic guitar, Morrison sings in his elastic, bluesy voice, accompanied by a jazz rhythm section (Jay Berliner, guitar, Richard Davis, bass, Connie Kay, drums), plus reeds (John Payne) and vibes (Warren Smith, Jr.), with a string quartet overdubbed. An emotional outpouring cast in delicate musical structures, *Astral Weeks* has a unique musical power. Unlike any record before or since, it nevertheless encompasses the passion and tenderness that have always mixed in the best post war popular music, easily justifying the critics' raves. *— William Ruhlmann*

☆ **Moondance** / Feb. 1970 / Warner Bros. ✦✦✦✦✦

After *Astral Weeks*, Morrison switched gears for *Moondance*, a flawless collection of more accessible R&B-rooted material, which drew from easygoing swing ("These Dreams"), upbeat shuffles ("Come Running"), gospel-influenced song structures like "Crazy Love," and "Caravan," the latter a celebration of radio that didn't pander to that medium's more self-congratulatory nature. The jazzy title cut is a classic, as is "Into the Mystic," a song that essentially encapsulated Morrison's artistic bent. *Moondance*'s tasteful production imbued the music with a timeless quality. *—Rick Clark*

His Band & Street Choir / Oct. 1970 / Warner Bros. ✦✦✦✦

It is a noticeable step down from the amazing *Moondance*, primarily in the sense that some of the material and performances lack Morrison's characteristic edge. Nevertheless, Morrison's immersion into R&B helped produce his highest-charting track, "Domino" (No. 9), as well as two lesser hits, "Blue Money" and "Call Me up in Dreamland." —*Rick Clark*

Tupelo Honey / Oct. 1971 / Warner Bros. ✦✦✦✦
The pastoral *Tupelo Honey* is another fine Morrison album, which ranges from the R&B rock of "Wild Night" to the folky gospel of the title cut, a heavenly love letter. —*Rick Clark*

Saint Dominic's Preview / 1972 / Warner Bros. ✦✦✦✦
Rarely has there ever been so joyous a rocker as "Jackie Wilson Said (I'm in Heaven When You Smile)," with its brilliantly arranged cascading horn lines. That's just one of many delights found here. From the inspirational title cut's tale of resolve to the primally prayerful "Listen to the Lion," *Saint Dominic's Preview* stands as one of Morrison's finest albums. This is one of the few Warner reissues that actually was given a fine remastering for CD. —*Rick Clark*

Hard Nose the Highway / Aug. 1973 / Warner Bros. ✦✦✦
It's Too Late to Stop Now / Jan. 1974 / Warner Bros. ✦✦✦✦
This dynamic double-disc set finds Morrison covering everything from his early work with Them, through *Astral Weeks,* to his early-'70s Warner hits and album tracks. Morrison is in great vocal form, and the band, The Caledonia Soul Orchestra, is exceptionally hot. Any fan of Morrison's should own this one. —*Rick Clark*

Veedon Fleece / Feb. 1974 / Warner Bros. ✦✦✦✦
His most willfully introspective album since *Astral Weeks, Veedon Fleece* (written in Ireland) is almost a classic, full of delicately rendered reflections and more open-ended vocal excursions. Morrison runs out of steam slightly during the second half of the proceedings, but not enough to keep this from being a pretty magical album. Highlights are "You Don't Pull No Punches but You Don't Push the River," "Fair Play," "Linden Arden Stole the Highlights," "Streets of Arklow," and "Comfort You." —*Rick Clark*

A Period of Transition / 1977 / Warner Bros. ✦✦✦
Wavelength / 1978 / Warner Bros. ✦✦✦
The self-produced *Wavelength* marked an improvement over *A Period of Transition,* producing a near-hit with the title cut. Other highlights included "Santa Fe," co-written with Jackie DeShannon. —*Rick Clark*

Into the Music / 1979 / Warner Bros. ✦✦✦✦
Five years after Van's last great album (*Veedon Fleece*), he returns with one of his finest albums, *Into the Music,* which fuses the earthly with the spiritual. Highlights include "Bright Side of the Road," "Full Force Gale," "Angelou," and a version of "It's All in the Game." Not the first place to go to discover Morrison, it's a masterful album nonetheless. —*Rick Clark*

Common One / 1980 / Warner Bros. ✦✦✦
Van Morrison's most meditative album since *Veedon Fleece, Common One* paints a pastoral portrait dominated by such extended pieces as "Summertime in England" and "When the Heart Is Open," each of which was more than 15 minutes long. The result can be soothing, but also enervating. —*William Ruhlmann*

Beautiful Vision / 1982 / Warner Bros. ✦✦✦
Beautiful Vision improved upon its meandering predecessor, *Common One,* first by having some stronger melodies, and second by having a song as mystically upbeat as "Cleaning Windows." —*Rick Clark*

The Inarticulate Speech of the Heart / Mar. 1983 / Warner Bros. ✦✦✦
Van Morrison's final album for Warner Bros. Records was one of his more uncompromising efforts, including the two-part instrumental title track and "Rave On, John Donne," a spoken tribute to one of Morrison's influences. —*William Ruhlmann*

A Sense of Wonder / 1985 / Mercury ✦✦✦
Live at the Grand Opera House Belfast / 1985 / Polydor ✦✦✦✦
Not as fiery as *It's Too Late to Stop Now,* it's still an enjoyable set, featuring "It's All in the Game," "Cleaning Windows," and other tracks from this period. —*Rick Clark*

No Guru, No Method, No Teacher / Jul. 1986 / Mercury ✦✦✦
Poetic Champions Compose / 1987 / Mercury ✦✦✦✦
The hypnotic string arpeggios and rolling rhythms of "The Mystery," the gentle exhortation of "Did Ye Get Healed," and even reverberant cocktail-jazz instrumentals like "Spanish Steps" help make the meditative *Poetic Champions Compose* one of Morrison's better albums during the '80s. —*Rick Clark*

Irish Heartbeat / 1988 / Mercury ✦✦✦✦
Although still purposeful, Van Morrison's '80s albums were becoming repetitive when he took a break for this collaboration with the Chieftains on traditional Irish songs. The result takes him back to his earliest days and finds him singing with renewed conviction. This album should appeal to all fans of Irish music as well as Morrison lovers. —*William Ruhlmann*

Avalon Sunset / 1989 / Polydor ✦✦✦✦
Avalon Sunset's evocative melodies and almost prayful sentiments make this one of Morrison's finest albums during the '80s. Some might

find this album's rich orchestration a little too close to easy listening, but repeated listenings reveal it adds a quiet dignified elegance and atmospheric unity to the proceedings, not unlike the strings on Marvin Gaye's transcendent *What's Going On.* "I'm Tired Joey Boy," "Orangefield," "Have I Told You Lately?," "I'd Love to Write Another Love Song," and the supplicatory "When Will I Learn to Live in God?" are among the many highlights. *Avalon Sunset* is the mature, timeless work of an artist beyond fashion. —*Rick Clark*

★ **The Best of Van Morrison** / Jan. 1990 / Mercury ✦✦✦✦✦
This is a strong collection of many of Van Morrison's best songs. Of particular note is the inclusion of "Wonderful Remark," previously only available on *The King of Comedy* soundtrack. That alone makes this worth having. Many of the key Them tracks are here ("Gloria," "Here Comes the Night"), as is Morrison's classic "Brown-Eyed Girl." Even though it's a strong sampler, it fails to draw a complete-enough picture of the depth of his work. Sonically, this CD is quite impressive. —*Rick Clark*

Enlightenment / Feb. 1990 / Mercury ✦✦✦
Hymns to the Silence / 1991 / Polydor ✦✦✦
The Bang Masters / 1991 / Epic ✦✦✦✦
With excellent sound and packaging of Morrison's work at Bert Bern's Bang label, the tracks range from the morose "T.B. Sheets," to his pop standard "Brown Eyed Girl." This is a must for fans who want to go deeper than just obtaining his obviously classic albums. —*Rick Clark*

The Best of Van Morrison, Vol. 2 / 1993 / PolyGram ✦✦✦✦
Unlike *Volume One*'s dependence on his early Warner Bros. catalog, this collection exclusively features his later Polygram work and pre-Warners sides with his old band Them. While not as strong, there are some wonderful tracks, such as "When Will I Ever Learn to Live in God?," "Coney Island," "Enlightenment," "Hymns to the Silence," and "The Mystery." —*Rick Clark*

Too Long in Exile / Jun. 8, 1993 / Polydor ✦✦
A Night in San Francisco / 1994 / Polydor ✦✦✦
Payin' Dues / 1994 / Charly ✦✦✦
A most fascinating double disc. The first contains the tracks found on *Bang Masters;* the bonus CD contains 31 previously unreleased acoustic ditties. The word ditties is a description, not a value judgment. According to one account, Morrison cut these purely out of necessity to fulfill his Bang contract, delivering the most unusable material possible. All of the cuts are between 45 and 90 seconds, divided between the inane (numerous nonsensical variations on "La Bamba," "Twist and Shout," and "Hang on Sloopy") and the viciously uncommercial ("The Big Royalty Check," "Ring Worm," "Blow in Your Nose"), along with a few silly variations on "Madame George." Along with Lou Reed's *Metal Machine Music,* this ranks as the least commercial music ever recorded by a major rock artist, and the nastiest spit in the eye of commercial expectations and contractual obligations. It's much more listenable than *Metal Machine Music,* though, and funnier. If you haven't picked up the *Bang Masters* collection, the addition of this off-the-wall material (which may never find release in the US) makes *Payin' Dues* a recommended alternative. —*Richie Unterberger*

Days Like This / 1995 / Polydor ✦✦
How Long Has This Been Going On? / 1995 / Polygram ✦✦

Morrissey

b. May 22, 1959, Manchester, England
Vocals / Alternative Pop-Rock
With the Smiths, singer-songwriter Morrissey established himself as a post-punk hero, becoming the spokesman for millions of disaffected teenagers and young adults with his literate, biting, and sensitive lyrics and dramatic vocals. After the band broke up in 1987, he pursued a solo career, releasing his first album the following year. While he released several excellent singles in the late '80s, he ultimately began to sink into his persona without producing enough quality songs. After 1991's self-absorbed *Kill Uncle,* many critics considered him as a has-been, with his best work in the past. Thanks to the explosive, Mick Ronson-produced *Your Arsenal,* Morrissey regained his credibility; it was almost universally acclaimed as one of the best albums of the year and many said it was his best work since the Smiths' masterpiece *The Queen Is Dead.* His fan base continued to grow, both in size and devotion. With 1994's *Vauxhall and I,* he even had a hit single ("The More You Ignore Me, the Closer I Get") scrape the Top 50 singles chart in America, which would have been unthinkable when "Hand in Glove" was released a decade earlier. —*Stephen Thomas Erlewine*

Viva Hate / 1988 / Sire ✦✦✦✦
Morrissey pairs with Stephen Street for an album very much in the mold of his Smiths work, i.e., melodic rock dominated by jangly guitar serving as a musical bed for the singer's idiosyncratic lyrical interests and uncon-

cerned delivery on such songs as "Everyday Is like Sunday" and "Hairdresser on Fire." —*William Ruhlmann*

Bona Drag / 1990 / Sire ✦✦✦✦
This collection of less than successful singles somehow plays nicely in the context of an album. As in the case of the Smiths, many found the *Hatful of Hollow* collection to be a favorite; the same formula works again here. It's far preferable to *Kill Uncle*, the proper album that followed. —*Steve Aldrich*

Kill Uncle / 1991 / Sire ✦✦
Clive Langer and Alan Winstanley provide a pop production dominated by keyboards for this typically catchy collection, with typically off-kilter songs like "(I'm) the End of the Family Line." —*William Ruhlmann*

● **Your Arsenal** / 1992 / Sire ✦✦✦✦
Nothing could prepare you for the shock of this album. From the opening shot, this is the most overt rock 'n' roll of Morrissey's career. The inspired choosing of Mick Ronson as producer solidifies the link to the '70s glam influences here. And Morrissey serves up his best material since *The Queen Is Dead. Your Arsenal* cannot be viewed as anything less than a major comeback. —*Steve Aldrich*

Vauxhall and I / 1994 / Sire ✦✦✦✦
While it isn't a gutsy rock 'n' roll record like *Your Arsenal, Vauxhall and I* is equally impressive. Filled with carefully constructed guitar-pop gems, the album contains some of Morrissey's best material since the Smiths. Out of all of his solo albums, *Vauxhall and I* sounds the most like his former band, yet the textured, ringing guitar on this record is an extension of his past, not a replication of it. In fact, with songs like "Now My Heart Is Full" and "Hold on to Your Friends," Morrissey sounds more comfortable and peaceful than he ever has. And "The More You Ignore Me, The Closer I Get," "Speedway," and "Spring-Heeled Jim" prove that he hasn't lost his vicious wit. —*Stephen Thomas Erlewine*

World of Morrissey / 1995 / Sire ✦✦✦

Southpaw Grammar / Aug. 1995 / Reprise ✦✦

Mother Love Bone

Hard Rock, Heavy Metal
When other Seattle bands were releasing singles and EPs of hard garage grunge, Mother Love Bone had their sights set on the arenas, making a grandiose heavy metal that recalled Zeppelin and Aerosmith with a slight punk fervor; in a sense, the band was a response to Guns N' Roses' sleazy guitar boogie. Considering that guitarist Stone Gossard and bassist Jeff Ament formed the rhythmic core of the Stooges-soaked Green River, it was a little strange that the band played it so safe, but that was mainly due to the lead vocalist, Andrew Wood. Wood was a modern-day hippie, preaching love and understanding, as well as a healthy dose of sex. Most of the hooks came from Gossard and Ament, but Wood was the focal point. The band was set to make their stab at the big time with 1990's *Apple*, but Wood died of a heroin overdose before it was released; the *Temple of the Dog* album, featuring Gossard, Ament, Soundgarden's Matt Cameron and Chris Cornell, and vocalist Eddie Vedder, was released as a tribute to him.

Gossard and Ament went on to form Pearl Jam, which took many of the hard rock elements of Mother Love Bone, except it was rawer and more honest. Also, Pearl Jam had a distinctive lead vocalist and lyricist in Eddie Vedder, who easily eclipsed the macho posturings of Wood. —*Stephen Thomas Erlewine*

● **Stardog Champion** / 1990 / Stardog ✦✦✦✦
Released after the phenomenal success of Pearl Jam, *Mother Love Bone* collects everything Mother Love Bone ever released. Their resurrection of the epic hard rock of the 1970s was quite good, but also derivative. While Wood was a fine singer, he wasn't a very original vocalist and often sounded very similar to Robert Plant. *Mother Love Bone* is the definitive collection of the band, and worth the time of fans of Pearl Jam and the Seattle scene. —*Stephen Thomas Erlewine*

Mötley Crüe

Hard Rock, Heavy Metal, Hair Metal
As far as commercial appeal goes, Mötley Crüe was one of the top heavy metal bands in the '80s, exploiting every trend in metal and hard rock without seeming crass or opportunistic. *Shout at the Devil* had them embracing a theatrical, Kiss-styled Satanism; *Theater of Pain* saw them ride the line between glam and pop-metal; *Girls Girls Girls* had them toughening up their image with leather and harder guitars, reaching for a street credibility; *Dr. Feelgood* had them sharpening the guitars of the previous album while adding a pop sensibility that took them straight to the top of the charts. Throughout their changes, the Crüe remained joyously sleazy and stupid, with their Zeppelin/Aerosmith-based hard rock making them high school favorites across the country. After the success of *Dr. Feelgood*, singer Vince Neil was fired from the band. When the band re-emerged in 1994 with their new vocalist John Corabi, they had

changed their image again, falling somewhere between Ministry, Stone Temple Pilots, and Soundgarden in an attempt to recapture the new alternative metal audience. *Mötley Crüe*, the new lineup's first album, was a commercial disappointment, spending ten weeks on the charts and only going gold. —*Stephen Thomas Erlewine*

Too Fast for Love / 1981 / Elektra ✦✦✦

Shout at the Devil / 1983 / Elektra ✦✦✦

Theater of Pain / 1985 / Elektra ✦✦✦✦
Powered by a sneering remake of Brownsville Station's "Smokin' in the Boy's Room" and the classic power ballad "Home Sweet Home," *Theater of Pain* was Mötley Crüe's biggest hit up to that point, even if the rest of the album wasn't as strong as its hit singles. —*Stephen Thomas Erlewine*

Girls, Girls, Girls / 1987 / Elektra ✦✦✦✦
With *Girls, Girls, Girls*, Mötley Crüe toughens up their music as well as their image, turning in an album of greasy, sleazy hard-rock boogie that, at its best, rivals Aerosmith. —*Stephen Thomas Erlewine*

Dr. Feelgood / 1989 / Elektra ✦✦✦✦
Producer Bob Rock gives the Crüe a high-gloss, corporate rock sheen, eliminating most of the band's self-indulgent tendencies. Thanks to a detox program, the Crüe itself sounds tighter, giving *Dr. Feelgood* a mindless but strong catchiness. *Dr. Feelgood*'s four Top 40 hits—the title track, the ballad "Without You," the driving "Kickstart My Heart," and caustic "Don't Go Away Mad (Just Go Away)"—form the heart of the album, but solid album tracks like "S.O.S. (Same Old Situation)" help make *Dr. Feelgood* arguably the band's best album. — *Stephen Thomas Erlewine*

● **Decade of Decadence** / 1991 / Elektra ✦✦✦✦
This is a collection of some of their hits and the best of their album material. —*John Book*

Mötley Crüe / 1994 / Elektra ✦✦

Motörhead

Hard Rock, Thrash, Heavy Metal, British Metal
English metal band Motörhead formed in 1975. Led by bassist Ian "Lemmy" Kilmister, the band was originally named Bastard but soon changed to Motörhead (American slang for speed freak), a name that suited their style of playing very well. Along with guitarist Larry Wallis and drummer Lucas Fox, Lemmy and the boys brought the concept of the power trio to new heights, using the bass almost as a lead instrument behind a wall of noise emanating from the other two instruments. They attracted a huge following in England during the late-'70s punk-rock era with their combination of breakneck speed and deafening volume. Though Lemmy remains as the only original member (having revamped the lineup several times over), and their style hasn't progressed much in almost 20 years, their hardcore fans wouldn't have it any other way. —*Cub Koda*

Overkill / 1979 / Roadrunner ✦✦✦✦
Motörhead's second album followed the same pattern as the first—it was a relentless collection of fast, loud, and simple heavy metal—but the songwriting was more melodic and consistent than the debut. —*Stephen Thomas Erlewine*

Bomber / 1979 / Roadrunner ✦✦✦✦
By the time of Motörhead's third album *Bomber*, it was clear that the band had one basic sound and nothing else. However, that didn't mean the group was boring—the lethal attack of their buzzing guitars and Lemmy's hoarse vocals never became tedious because of the immediacy of the group's sound, as well as their talent for coming up with memorable riffs and tightly written songs. *Bomber* sounded no different than Motörhead's two previous albums, but the group had lost none of its impact and the album featured "Dead Men Tell No Tales," one of their finest songs. —*Stephen Thomas Erlewine*

Ace of Spades / 1980 / Roadrunner ✦✦✦✦
The forefathers of thrash on one of their better-known albums, *Ace of Spades* features guitarist "Fast" Eddie Clark, who later left and formed Fastway. Highlights include "(We Are) The Road Crew" and the title track. —*John Book*

Iron Fist / 1982 / Roadrunner ✦✦✦

★ **No Remorse** / 1984 / Roadrunner ✦✦✦✦✦
No Remorse is a solid collection (in spite of the omission of the band's Chiswick recordings), consisting of key album, EP, and single tracks. Included are Motörhead standards like "Killed by Death" and "Please Don't Touch." Unfortunately, this Roadrunner reissue of the 1984 release omits "Leaving Here" and "Louie Louie." Overall, *No Remorse* is a great intro to the band's earlier thrash sound. —*Rick Clark*

Orgasmatron / 1986 / Sinclair ✦✦✦✦
For *Orgasmatron*, Motörhead enlisted producer Bill Laswell, who assisted the band in achieving a dense wall of sound, which sounded a little too compressed. Highlights include "Built for Speed," "Deaf For-

ever," and the title track, an incredible aural sludgefest that borders on psychedelic. —*Rick Clark*

1916 / 1991 / WTG ◆◆◆◆
Produced by Pete Solley and Ed Stasium, *1916* is Motörhead's most diverse effort, including humorous sendups like "Ramones" (a tribute to the New York speed punkers) and "Angel City" (a love letter to Los Angeles), as well as grim topics, like the dying World War I soldier's perspective in the title track. Motörhead manages to cover all this territory without ever losing their basic sonic integrity. All in all, *1916* is arguably this band's finest release thus far. —*Rick Clark*

Motors

Rock 'n' Roll, New Wave, Power-Pop
After several years in England's pub-rock scene, ex-Duck Deluxe members Nick Garvey and Andy McMaster formed the Motors in 1977 with vocalist Bram Tchaikovsky and drummer Ricky Slaughter. Their first album was a splendid piece of guitar-driven pop-rock highlighted by the single "Dancing the Night Away." *Approved by* was the album that earned them the UK hits "Airport" and "Forget About You"; the record saw the band's songwriting improving with forceful melodies and invigorating performances. After that record, the Motors split up; Garvey and McMaster used the band's name for the 1980 album *Tenement Steps*, which didn't equal the spark of their first two records. —*Stephen Thomas Erlewine*

Motors 1 / 1977 / Virgin ◆◆◆
Their debut features a reworked version of pub-rock with an edgier punk feel. Includes the catchy single "Dancing the Night Away," the high point of the album. —*Chris Woodstra*

Approved by the Motors / 1978 / Virgin ◆◆◆◆
Their second album shows a marked improvement over the debut, with a stronger melodic base and catchier songs including the British hits "Airport" and "Forget About You." The CD version adds three bonus tracks. —*Chris Woodstra*

Tenement Steps / 1980 / Virgin ◆◆
The band, now reduced to Nick Garvey and Andy McMaster, is a little too ambitious and overproduced. While not their best album, it does include one of their finest songs, "Love and Loneliness," making it worthwhile for those who liked the first two albums. Essential for collectors if only for the uniquely shaped sleeve. —*Chris Woodstra*

● **Airport: The Motors' Greatest Hits** / 1995 / Caroline ◆◆◆◆
A solid collection of the band's best moments, *Airport* provides a good introduction for the uninitiated, drawing from the brilliant first two albums and the lesser *Tenement Steps*. —*Chris Woodstra*

Mott the Hoople

Rock 'n' Roll, Hard Rock
Originally a Herefordshire, England, band named Silence, Mott the Hoople was signed to Island in 1969 by A&R man Guy Stevens, who suggested that they change their name (inspired by a Willard Manus novel) and dump their lead singer, Stan Tippens, in their search for a stronger identity. Tippens was made road manager (he later worked for the Pretenders), and Ian Hunter (an engineering apprentice) was brought in to sing and play piano. Stevens, in turn, became the band's manager and producer. Between 1969 and 1972, Mott cut four albums, two of which contained some great rock 'n' roll. Nevertheless, the band's future looked bleak, due to diminishing sales with each release. A happenstance pairing with ascending glam rock star David Bowie caused a fortuitous turn of events, which culminated in a new record deal (Columbia) and sound. The result of their collaboration was the Bowie-produced *All the Young Dudes*, a blatant glam sendup. The title cut became Mott's first hit, and in the time one could say the words "image makeover," Mott was camping it up, teetering around the stage in makeup and cartoonish platform shoes. Their follow-up effort, *Mott*, was the band's finest artistic statement, loosely addressing the travails of rock "stardom." After that, Mott began to lose its focus, and the departure of lead singer-songwriter Ian Hunter hastened the band's demise. They eventually broke up in 1976. Hunter later enjoyed a moderately successful cult following with his solo career. As a songwriter, he scored some substantial hits with artists like Great White ("Once Bitten Twice Shy") and Barry Manilow ("Ships"). —*Rick Clark*

Mott the Hoople / 1969 / Atlantic ◆◆◆◆
Mott the Hoople, with its hard-rock variation of Dylan's *Blonde on Blonde* sound, stands as one of the band's better efforts. This debut sported some fine originals, particularly "Backsliding Fearlessly" and "Rock and Roll Queen," as well as some unusual (but hip) song covers, like Sonny Bono's "Laugh at Me" and Doug Sahm's "At the Crossroads." The Kinks' garage-riff standard "You Really Got Me" gets a high-octane instrumental treatment. Only on the middle section of the lengthy "Half Moon Bay" does *Mott the Hoople* lose momentum. The fidelity on this

disc (and *Brain Capers*) rivals the sound of a good vinyl import version. —*Rick Clark*

Brain Capers / 1971 / Atlantic ◆◆◆◆
After a couple of fairly dismal efforts, Mott rebounded with one of the great lost hard rock albums of the '70s. Released with practically no fanfare whatsoever, *Brain Capers* sank without a trace. Certainly, in the decade that produced Styx and Journey, *Brain Capers* (from the audaciously titled "Death May Be Your Santa Claus," to the closing "The Wheel of the Quivering Meat Conception") convincingly drew a line in the sand, revealing most everything called "rock" to be a fraud. Some of this was due, in part, to the return of Guy Stevens at the production helm. Among the album's highlights are versions of Dion's "Your Own Backyard," The Youngbloods' "Darkness Darkness," and Ian Hunter's powerful "The Journey," "Sweet Angeline," and the previously mentioned "Death . . .". —*Rick Clark*

All the Young Dudes / 1972 / Columbia ◆◆◆◆
Just as Mott was about to pack it in due to their amazing lack of public acceptance, David Bowie entered the picture, and with the recording of a few cannily conceived songs, containing strong gay allusions (Bowie's "All the Young Dudes" and "Sucker" and "One of the Boys"), Mott went from potential has-beens to avatars of the glam rock movement. The Bowie-produced album contained a version of Lou Reed's "Sweet Jane" and Mick Ralphs' "Ready for Love," one of his finest bits of writing to date. As on many albums of that genre, the production sounds stiff and dry. Nevertheless, Mott makes the proceedings rock fairly convincingly. —*Rick Clark*

☆ **Mott** / 1973 / Columbia ◆◆◆◆◆
Regarded by many to be their finest album, this self-produced effort was a loosely conceived concept album about the ups and downs of rock 'n' roll success. *Mott* contained two UK hits with "All the Way from Memphis" and "Honaloochie Boogie." Other highlights were "The Ballad of Mott the Hoople," "Whizz Kid," "Violence," and "Drivin' Sister." The sound of this reissue is a little on the muddy side. Nevertheless, of their Columbia-period albums, this is the one to get. —*Rick Clark*

★ **The Ballad of Mott: A Retrospective** / 1993 / Columbia ◆◆◆◆◆
Mott the Hoople were punks without realizing it. Combining a heavy-metal roar with the sneering hipster stance of 1965 Bob Dylan, Mott the Hoople made some of the best, most original rock 'n' roll of the early '70s. This two-disc set chronicles their Columbia recordings, with four tracks from their early Atlantic albums thrown in for good measure. Because of David Bowie's production of *All the Young Dudes* and their stage costumes, Mott was tossed into the glam-rock scene, but their music was often wittier and meaner than other glam-rock bands. This made the group an enormous element in the punk/new wave movement. Although it isn't definitive because it doesn't contain enough material from *Mott the Hoople* or *Brain Capers*, *The Ballad of Mott* is all the Mott most people will need. Nearly all of the songs from their two classic Columbia albums, *All the Young Dudes* and *Mott*, are included, as is a generous selection of tracks from *The Hoople* and a number of B-sides and unreleased tracks. While the band didn't receive much attention at the time, their music still sounds vital over 20 years later. —*Stephen Thomas Erlewine*

Backsliding Fearlessly: The Early Years / 1994 / Rhino ◆◆◆◆
A compilation of 16 songs from their first four albums, covering their strongest material from the records pre-dating their *All the Young Dudes* breakthrough. This shows the band casting about, sometimes wildly, for an identity. The earliest tunes (including a cover of Sonny Bono's "Laugh at Me") are perhaps the most blatant imitations of Dylan's *Blonde on Blonde* period ever attempted. Subsequent efforts found them getting into boogie and hard rock, with a few Stones riffs copied here and there. The gut-stomping "Death May Be Your Santa Claus" is a highlight, and Ian Hunter's piano-based ballad "When My Mind's Gone" hints at the more complex psychological territory he'd explore during Mott's prime. This isn't bad and is often interesting, but it is neither very similar to Mott's best work, nor nearly as good as Mott's best stuff. Weirdest cut: a cover of Melanie's "Lay Down." But where is their instrumental version of "You Really Got Me"? —*Richie Unterberger*

Bob Mould

b. 1961
Guitar, Vocals / Singer-Songwriter, Alternative Pop-Rock
Guitarist/singer-songwriter Bob Mould was initially a member of Hüsker Dü, one of the most influential American bands of the '80s. Hüsker Dü was a post-hardcore punk band that helped define the sound and ideals of alternative rock.

After Hüsker Dü broke up, Bob Mould signed a solo contract with Virgin Records in 1988. The following year, he released his first solo album, *Workbook*, which represented a major shift in sonic direction. *Workbook* was an introspective collection, featuring keyboards, acoustic guitars, and even strings. The album received excellent reviews and spent 14 weeks on the charts, peaking at 127; "See a Little Light" became a Top Ten modern rock hit. Mould returned to loud, guitar-driven rock on his second solo album, 1990's *Black Sheets of Rain.* Featuring the Top Ten modern rock hit "It's Too Late," *Black Sheets of Rain* received mixed reviews.

Frustrated with the business operations of major record labels, Mould left Virgin after the release of *Black Sheets of Rain;* they would later release a compilation of the two albums, *Poison Years.* Mould then formed an independent record company, SOL (Singles Only Label), which released 45s from new, developing bands as well as cult bands. In 1992, he formed a new trio, Sugar, with bassist David Barbe and drummer Malcolm Travis; the band signed with Rykodisc in the US, Creation in the UK.

Sugar's first album, *Copper Blue,* was released in the fall of 1992 to enthusiastic reviews and it became Mould's most successful project to date. *Copper Blue* nearly went gold and spawned several alternative radio and MTV hits, including "Helpless" and "If I Can't Change Your Mind." In the spring of 1993, Sugar released the mini-LP *Beaster,* a more abrasive collection than *Copper Blue* that was recorded at the same sessions.

Around the time of the release of *Beaster,* Mould was forced out of the closet by various gay publications, with hopes that he would embrace their political cause; he rejected their requests.

Mould wrote the material for the second Sugar album during 1993. The band began recording in the spring of 1994, but the sessions ground to a halt and the tapes were erased. Mould decided to give the album one more try and it was recorded quickly late that spring. The album, *File Under: Easy Listening,* appeared in the fall of 1994. Although it received good reviews and was moderately successful commercially, it didn't match the performance of *Copper Blue.*

In the spring of 1995, it was announced that Sugar was on hiatus. *Besides,* a collection of rarities and B-sides, was released that summer. By the fall, Mould had broken up the band and begun to work on a third album entirely by himself. Mould played all of the instruments on his self-titled third album, which was released in the spring of 1995. —*Stephen Thomas Erlewine*

● **Workbook** / 1989 / Virgin ✦✦✦✦
Mould takes a less raucous, more coherent approach than on his Hüsker Dü work for this solo debut, which combines somewhat pessimistic lyrics with majestic guitar parts matched to a prominent cello. —*William Ruhlmann*

Black Sheets of Rain / May 1990 / Virgin ✦✦✦
A scalding, monolithic collection of soul-baring lyrics and primal guitars, *Black Sheets of Rain* is extremely powerful musically, but is also slightly monotonous. Nevertheless, the record features several inspired songs from Mould, including the catchy single "It's Too Late." —*Stephen Thomas Erlewine*

Poison Years / 1994 / Virgin ✦✦✦

Bob Mould / Apr. 30, 1996 / Rykodisc ✦✦✦✦
As he was promoting the last Sugar album, *File Under: Easy Listening,* Bob Mould hinted that he was tired of working with a band and was fascinated by the simple, four-track recordings of Sebadoh and Guided by Voices. So, it didn't come as a complete surprise when he disbanded Sugar a year after the release of *FU:EL* and began working on a record by himself. *Bob Mould,* his third solo album, was recorded entirely by Mould, but it doesn't sound like a lo-fi project—it doesn't have the professional production of Sugar's records, but it has all their sonic detail. What has changed is the details themselves. *Bob Mould* may not surge on waves of loud guitars like Hüsker Dü or Sugar, but Mould is reaching into new territory, using distortion as a coloring device and exploring trancier melodies. And Mould sounds revitalized throughout the album—although it is clear that this isn't a collection of first takes, his obsession with making the album entirely on his own makes the music fierce and alive. Mould may be heading further into singer-songwriter territory with each album he releases, but he keeps his music away from stodginess by continually changing his approach and delving into new sonic territories. It also doesn't hurt that his increasingly bitter lyrics are gut-wrenchingly provocative and his melodies are consistently engaging. —*Stephen Thomas Erlewine*

The Move

Art-Rock/Progressive-Rock, Pop-Rock
The Move were the best and most important British group of the late '60s that never made a significant dent in the American market. Through the band's several phases (which were sometimes dictated more by image than musical direction), their chief asset was guitarist and songwriter Roy Wood, who combined a knack for Beatlesque pop with a peculiarly British, and occasionally morbid, sense of humor. On their final albums (with considerable input from Jeff Lynne), the band became artier and more ambitious, hinting at the orchestral rock that Wood and Lynne would devise for the Electric Light Orchestra. The Move, however,

always placed more emphasis on the pop than the art, and never lost sight of their hardcore rock 'n' roll roots.

Formed in the mid-'60s, the Move were so named because the five musicians from the original lineups were moving from established Birmingham groups into a new band. Most of the Move, in fact, had previously recorded flop singles in average, unremarkable British Invasion styles as members of other outfits. Taken under the wing of manager Tony Secunda, the group moved to London and crafted an explosive act, heavily influenced by the Who, which found them destroying televisions on stage. The Move's early singles were also heavily influenced by mod pop in their chunky chords and oddball character sketches, although Roy Wood's songs were much poppier and bouncier than those of Pete Townshend.

With Wood handling all of the writing, the group's first four singles ("Night of Fear," "I Can Hear the Grass Grow," "Flowers in the Rain," and "Fire Brigade") all made the British Top Ten in 1967-68. Despite the strength of the music (and a solid debut album in 1968), management and press gave more attention to their flamboyant stage antics, clothes, and outrageous publicity stunts. The most famous of these—a publicity mailing for "Flowers in the Rain" picturing British Prime Minister Harold Wilson in an embarrassing state of undress—backfired badly when the band lost royalties from the single in a subsequent libel suit.

Bassist Ace Kefford (never an essential part of the band except for image purposes) left the Move in 1968. After a couple of less successful singles, they topped the British charts for the only time in 1969 with one of their best songs, "Blackberry Way," a kind of black-humored flipside to "Penny Lane." Guitarist Trevor Burton, who had moved to bass after Kefford left, split himself just after "Blackberry Way." Rick Price was brought in to replace Burton, and the group's second album, *Shazam* (1970), was one of their best, allowing them to stretch out in more progressive and experimental directions than they could within the format of hit singles. After a misguided venture into the cabaret circuit, singer Carl Wayne left, leaving the lead vocal chores primarily in the hands of Roy Wood.

The rapid succession of personnel changes would have stopped most bands in their tracks, but the Move, if anything, became a more interesting group in the early '70s. This was due primarily to the replacement of Wayne by Jeff Lynne, previously with the cutesy but interesting pop-rock group the Idle Race. Lynne would be the only member of the Move other than Wood to contribute notable songs and help shape the band's vision. On *Looking On* (1971) and *Message from the Country* (1972), Lynne's cheerier pop inclinations would effectively counterpoint Wood's darker and more ironic compositions, in the manner of great rock collaborations like Lennon-McCartney and Stills-Young. Their best work from this period, though, is actually contained on their singles, several of which ("Brontosaurus," "California Man," and "Tonight") were British hits.

The Move remained unknown in the US (where they had barely toured), and concentrated primarily on studio work after Lynne joined. Their arrangements became denser and more ambitious, particularly as Wood developed proficiency on a number of common and exotic instruments. As a result of their increasing fascination with orchestral rock, Wood, Lynne, and drummer Bev Bevan discontinued the Move in the early '70s to form the Electric Light Orchestra. ELO's remake of one of the Move's final singles, "Do Ya" (which had scraped the bottom of the US charts in 1972), would become a hit in 1977. By that time, though, Wood was long gone from ELO—in 1972 he left to pursue a career as a leader of Wizzard and as a solo artist. And for all ELO's massive worldwide success, they never matched the intriguing blend of pop and experimentation that characterized the best work of the Move. —*Richie Unterberger*

The Move / 1968 / Repertoire ✦✦✦✦
The Move's debut album was a solid effort of mod-pop-psychedelia, boasting a number of fine Roy Wood compositions: the British hits "Flowers in the Rain" and "Flower Brigade," the original version of "Cherry Blossom Clinic," and the lesser-known but equally worthy "Yellow Rainbow" and "Walk Upon the Water." The three routine covers (of Eddie Cochran, the Coasters, and Moby Grape) that pad the album dilute it only slightly. The German CD reissue adds seven bonus tracks from late-'60s singles, but if you can live with vinyl, you should still seek out the A&M double LP compilation *The Best of the Move,* which has the entire debut album and even more of their late-'60s and early-'70s 45s. —*Richie Unterberger*

Something Else from the Move / 1968 / Regal Zonophone ✦✦✦
When the Move were reaching the peak of their popularity after a burst of fine psychedelic-tinged power-pop singles, they issued this rather odd live five-song, 12-inch EP consisting entirely of covers. If nothing else, it proves The Move were a dynamic live act with an eclectic range, to say the least, as they cover tunes by the Byrds, Love, Eddie Cochran, Jerry Lee Lewis, and Spooky Tooth on this set. They really burn it up, in fact, on The Byrds' "So You Want to Be a Rock and Roll Star" and Love's "Stephanie Knows Who," with spinning and frenetic guitar work. The rest of the set is more routine, coming off more as a tribute to some of their idiosyncratic favorites. —*Richie Unterberger*

☆ **Shazam** / 1970 / A&M ✦✦✦✦✦
The single most accomplished album to be recorded by any of the Birmingham rock bands (which include the Moody Blues), *Shazam* is sort of *Sgt. Pepper* with an attitude, a mixture of expansive progressive-rock worthy of the Beatles and high energy music honed by years of playing loud on stage. The rendition of Tom Paxton's "The Last Thing on My Mind" pushes these guys simultaneously into Byrds and Jimi Hendrix territory, while "Beautiful Daughter" is one of the most unabashedly pretty records of this era, and "Cherry Blossom Clinic Revisited" is defiantly strange. The album only exists as an import from Japan, paired up on one CD with the earlier *Flowers in the Rain* album (all songs in print domestically or a better German version filled out with five live tracks from London's Marquee Club, off of the super-rare *Something Else* EP). —*Bruce Eder*

Looking On / 1971 / Capitol ✦✦

Message from the Country / 1971 / One Way ✦✦✦

Best of the Move / 1974 / A&M ✦✦✦✦
Really the best of the group's early period, ranging from delightfully trippy ("Here We Go Round the Lemon Tree," "Flowers in the Rain") to downright weird ("Zing Went the Strings of My Heart," "Night of Fear") singles and album sides that helped establish the group's reputation for eccentricity. —*Bruce Eder*

Black Country Rock / 1993 / Gold Standard ✦✦✦
This quasi-legal compilation of 26 BBC performances from the late 1960s, in reasonable to excellent fidelity, shows the Move's astonishing versatility and range of influences. Ten of these are live-in-the-studio runthroughs of original material, including most of their early British hits—"Night of Fear," "Fire Brigade," "Flowers in the Rain," "I Can Hear The Grass Grow," and "Blackberry Way." More interesting from a historical perspective are the 16 covers, showing an eclectic range that must have been the equal of any major group of the time—the Byrds, Simon & Garfunkel, Tim Rose, Love, Jerry Lee Lewis, Eddie Cochran, Neil Diamond, Jackie Wilson, Janis Joplin, Johnny Cash, Moby Grape, and the Beach Boys all come in for the Move's accomplished chunky rock, harmony-laden treatment. The covers of the Byrds' "Goin' Back" and Paul Simon's "Sounds of Silence" are particularly nifty. It's not recommended to anyone except serious fans, but that small audience could hardly wish for a better collection of rarities from the group's salad days. —*Richie Unterberger*

BBC Sessions / 1994 / Band of Joy ✦✦✦
This is exactly the same (in content and fidelity) as the quasi-legal *Black Country Rock* compilation on Gold Standard, with the notable omission of one of the best songs, a cover of Simon & Garfunkel's "The Sounds of Silence." —*Richie Unterberger*

★ **Great Move! The Best of the Move** / Jun. 15, 1994 / EMI ✦✦✦✦✦
The title is really a misnomer; it includes much of the best of the Move, but can hardly stake a claim as a definitive collection, as it only covers their final years in the early '70s. Which isn't to say it isn't good. This is basically a spruced-up version of their final album, *Message from the Country* (1971), with the addition of five bonus tracks from early-'70s singles. *Message from the Country* itself was an erratic affair, alternating between lumbering forays into hard rock, revivalist roots rock and country, and some of Roy Wood and Jeff Lynne's most inspired Beatlesque progressive compositions. The singles, most of which were previously issued on the *Split Ends* compilation, include some of their most memorable moments. "Tonight" (a British hit) is Roy Wood at his most tuneful, wistful, and folk-rockish; "Chinatown," though not quite as good (and not quite as big a British hit), is in much the same vein; and "Do Ya," redone with much more success by ELO, is one of their catchiest all-out rockers. Wood also gets into heavy sounds on the Top Ten British hit "California Man." Includes informative liner notes by respected rock critic Ira Robbins. —*Richie Unterberger*

Mu

Art-Rock/Progressive-Rock, Psychedelic
This intriguing early '70s Southern Californian group featured the talents of singer-songwriter Merrell Fankhauser (who was also at the helm of cult classics in the '60s by Fapardokly and HMS Bounty) and Jeff Cotton, previously slide guitarist with Captain Beefheart. Their sole album (from 1971) is a gem of the late hippie era, combining the fractured blues-based tangents of Beefheart with the loose flow and stoned lyricism of bands like the late '60s Grateful Dead. After a couple more singles, Mu moved to Maui and cut a fair amount of unreleased material before breaking up around 1974. Their eponymous album, as well as a lot of their unreleased material, was reissued in the 1980s. —*Richie Unterberger*

● **Mu** / 1971 / Reckless ✦✦✦✦
One of the best overlooked albums of the early '70s. Daring rhythms and song structures that build off the blues without following the standard three-chord/12-bar progressions, occasional modal jazzy sax by Cotton,

and great slide guitar combine to form one of the most unclassifiable recordings of the time, with a high-spirited lightness that avoids the heavy excesses that sometimes burdened late-period psychedelia. —*Richie Unterberger*

End of an Era / 1988 / Reckless ✦✦✦
Seventeen songs recorded after their relocation to Maui in 1974. More subdued and acoustic than the *Mu* LP, but still worthwhile, with Crosby, Stills, & Nash-like harmonies, melancholy melodies, and almost prototypically hippie-ish lyrics about visitations from other planets, searches for lost lands, mystical love, and the like. —*Richie Unterberger*

Mudhoney

Alternative Pop-Rock, Grunge
With their fuzzed-out guitars and Mark Arm's straining vocals, Mudhoney defined '80s and '90s grunge rock. In fact, their 1988 debut single "Touch Me, I'm Sick" is the definitive grunge song—an obnoxious, dirty song driven by massively distorted guitars and a screaming vocal. It was a terrific, invigorating song that the band rewrote on each album that followed, but that's alright because Mudhoney only has one other song—a slow, sludgy Stooges grind. But their limitations are ultimately endearing; the band is a punk band, not like a '70s or '80s group, but like a '60s garage band, kicking out the same three chords with an unbridled enthusiasm. Leave the serious themes to Nirvana, Pearl Jam, Soundgarden, and Alice in Chains—Mudhoney takes the same themes but makes them sleazy and trashy, like the Russ Meyers film they named themselves after. Their records are inconsistent but when they are good, they are great. —*Stephen Thomas Erlewine*

● **Superfuzz Bigmuff (& Early Singles)** / 1988 / Sub Pop ✦✦✦✦
Combining the band's first EP with a handful of early singles, this disc showcases Mudhoney at their most furious and fine. *Superfuzz Bigmuff* keeps the overextended riffing and hyper-vocalizing down to a minimum, focusing on maximum-torque, metallic garage raunch. —*John Dougan & Meredith Erlewine*

Mudhoney / Jul. 1989 / Sub Pop ✦✦✦

Every Good Boy Deserves Fudge / 1991 / Sub Pop ✦✦✦✦
It's no great stylistic breakthrough, but what Mudhoney record is? Instead, it's another solid album of fuzzed-out three-chord garage rockers. Song, it's their most consistent album. —*Stephen Thomas Erlewine*

Piece of Cake / Oct. 1992 / Reprise ✦✦✦

Five Dollar Bob's Mock Cooter Stew / 1993 / Reprise ✦✦✦

My Brother the Cow / 1995 / Reprise ✦✦✦✦
Mudhoney doesn't have an expansive musical vocabulary, they're all about grunge. Naturally, they don't abandon it now that it's no longer hip—they just keep going and going. In fact, they make it harsher and nastier, stripping melody off of the songs. The guitar hooks growl, occasionally sinking their teeth in, and Mark Arm has never sounded quite so pissed off. *My Brother the Cow* isn't much for songs—it's nearly all sneering attitude—yet the sound is positively galvanizing. —*Stephen Thomas Erlewine*

Mumps

New Wave
The Mumps were one of the most obscure, but distinctive, New York bands of the late '70s, performing an absurdly theatrical fusion of pop, punk, and glam rock. Led by vocalist Lance Loud, the group's music was an affectionate satire of '70s kitsch culture, predating the similar obsessions of the B-52's by a number of years. The Mumps rocked as hard as the New York Dolls, while writing clever pop hooks that updated trashy garage and bubblegum singles of the '70s. Although they never even earned a large underground following, the group was a favorite of many punk rockers of the era (including the Ramones, Blondie, the New York Dolls, X, Television, the Cramps, Devo, and the Go-Go's), as well as '80s alternative rockers like R.E.M., Game Theory, and Sparks. In addition to Lance Loud, the core lineup of the Mumps also featured keyboardist Kristiann Hoffman, guitarist Rob Duprey, bassist Kevin Kiely, and drummer Paul Rutner. Over the years, the lineup changed slightly, with Loud, Hoffman, and Duprey remaining the constant members in each incarnation of the band. The Mumps only released two singles while they were active in the late '70s, but in 1994 Eggbert Records released a CD called *Fatal Charm* that compiled everything the band ever recorded, including outtakes, alternate takes, and live rehearsals. *Fatal Charms* proves that the Mumps' music remains vibrant, creative, and intoxicatingly bizzare nearly 20 years after it was recorded. —*Stephen Thomas Erlewine*

Fatal Charm / 1994 / Eggbert ✦✦✦✦

Peter Murphy

b. Jul. 11, 1957, Northhampton, England
Vocals / Alternative Pop-Rock, Goth-Rock
Despite having a successful solo career as a cult artist, vocalist Peter Mur-

phy remains best known as the lead vocalist for Bauhaus, the pioneering post-punk goth-rock band of the early '80s. After disbanding Bauhaus in 1983, Murphy formed Dali's Car with former Japan member, Mick Karn. Dali's Car only released one album, *The Waking Hour*, in 1984. Following its release, the duo broke up and Murphy hesitatingly began a solo career with a cover of Magazine's "The Light Pours out of Me," which was featured on a 1985 Beggars Banquet compilation called *The State of Things*. In 1986, he released his first full-fledged solo album, *Should the World Fail to Fall Apart*, which featured a number of guest artists, including former Bauhaus member Daniel Ash. Two years later, Murphy released his second solo album, *Love Hysteria*. Like its predecessor, *Love Hysteria* received lukewarm reviews but sold well to his dedicated fan base.

With 1990's *Deep*, Murphy had a surprise hit—the first single from the record, the Bowie-esque "Cuts You Up," became the American modern rock hit of the year, spending seven weeks at the top of the US charts and crossing over to AOR radio and the pop charts, where it peaked at No. 55. Following its success, *Deep* reached No. 44 on the album charts. Murphy wasn't able to sustain that success with his next album, 1992's *Holy Smoke*, which only reached 108 on the charts, despite the No. two modern rock hit, "The Sweetest Drop."

In 1995, Murphy issued *Cascade*, which was greeted with weak reviews. The album failed to chart in either America or Britain. —*Stephen Thomas Erlewine*

Should the World Fail to Fall / 1986 / Beggars Banquet ♦♦

Love Hysteria / 1988 / Beggars Banquet ♦♦♦

● **Deep** / 1990 / Beggars Banquet ♦♦♦♦
This contains Murphy's dramatic alternative rock hit "Cuts You Up." Forceful grooves and thick (somewhat dissonant) arrangements and production propel material reminiscent of David Bowie's work with Brian Eno. —*Rick Clark*

Holy Smoke / Apr. 14, 1992 / Beggars Banquet ♦♦♦

Cascade / 1995 / Beggars Banquet ♦♦

Music Machine

Psychedelic, Garage Rock
Most famous for "Talk Talk," a Top 20 single from 1966 that was one of the most manic '60s garage-punk hits, the Music Machine had much more depth and songwriting talent than the typical one-hit wonders of the day. Lead singer and songwriter Sean Bonniwell's strangled lyrics and dark, verbose vision paced the group's wiry psychedelic guitar lines and ominous, minor-key Farfisa organ. Only one album was released with the original lineup, and the group's ferocious energy was diluted on subsequent recordings. Despite chalking up only one more minor hit single ("The People in Me"), the Music Machine recorded quite a few excellent, imaginatively produced singles and album tracks that found them exploring the darker side of psychedelia with compelling intensity and imagination. —*Richie Unterberger*

(Turn On) the Music Machine / 1966 / Performance ♦♦♦
The Music Machine's debut would have been a lot better if they'd let Sean Bonniwell write all of the songs. Yet it was, as was often the case at the time, divided between fine Bonniwell originals and dispensable covers of current rock hits. Which means that, side by side with excellent Bonniwell originals like "Talk Talk," "The People in Me," and "Trouble," you'll find lukewarm covers of Neil Diamond's "Cherry Cherry," the Beatles' "Taxman," and "96 Tears" (though the slow, moody reading of "Hey Joe" is nice). Most of the Bonniwell songs were issued in much better company on the Rhino anthology, although one good one, the typically tortuous "Wrong," is only available on this album. —*Richie Unterberger*

Bonniwell Music Machine / 1968 / Warner Bros. ♦♦♦

● **Best of the Music Machine** / 1984 / Rhino ♦♦♦♦
Besides "Talk Talk" and "The People in Me," this features the best cuts from their first LP, some fine non-LP singles that rank among the best obscure gems of the psychedelic era, and some decent previously unissued cuts. The package is enhanced by detailed liner notes by Sean Bonniwell. —*Richie Unterberger*

● **Beyond the Garage** / 1995 / Sundazed ♦♦♦♦
Although the material the Music Machine recorded for Warner Bros. (released under the name Bonniwell Music Machine) is little known, it's almost up to the high standards of their Original Sound sides. It's also been extremely hard to find, until this excellent 20-track reissue. This contains the entire contents of the 1968 *Bonniwell Music Machine* album (some of which had actually been released on the Music Machine's 1967 singles for Original Sound), plus various rare singles and a couple of unreleased tunes. Though a bit erratic, the best of this is thrilling stuff, as exciting as experimental garage rock ever got. "Bottom of the Soul," "The Eagle Never Hunts the Fly," "Talk Me Down," and "Double Yellow Line" all count among their toughest pop-psych punkers.

Tracks like "Tin Can Beach," "The Trap," and "Discrepancy" also show songwriter and lead singer Sean Bonniwell expanding from the pounding guitar-organ prototype into more eclectic, but equally compelling, directions with touches of folk and orchestration. Inventive studio arrangements and lyrical wordplay are constants throughout. You won't find Bonniwell's name mentioned in many standard rock reference books, but this CD further bolsters his credentials as one of the most underappreciated innovators of late-'60s rock. —*Richie Unterberger*

My Bloody Valentine

Alternative Pop-Rock, Shoegazing
My Bloody Valentine is ear-splittingly loud, constructing their records with layers of sound and noise. It may sound unlistenable at first, but the sheer sonics of the band are beautiful and shimmering, with the vocals only adding another texture to the overall sound; underneath the white noise, the band plays simple, melodic pop. Comparisons to the Jesus and Mary Chain or Sonic Youth may be inevitable, but My Bloody Valentine is much more atmospheric than either band; their distorted noise is not confrontational or aggressive, it is rolling sheets of gorgeous dissonance. After several years of independent label releases, the band released the monolithic *Loveless* in 1991 which increased their cult dramatically. Although they haven't released a record since *Loveless*, their fan base has not diminished. —*Stephen Thomas Erlewine*

This Is Your Bloody Valentine / 1985 / Tycoon ♦♦♦

Ecstasy / 1987 / Lazy ♦♦♦

Isn't Anything / 1988 / Creation/Sire ♦♦♦♦
The first of My Bloody Valentine's two landmark albums, *Isn't Anything* combines delicate, brittle melodies and big guitars. "Lose My Breath" and "No More Sorry" highlight Belinda Butcher's understated but charismatic voice, while guitars take the spotlight on "Cupid Come." Songs like "Sue Is Fine" and the seminal "Feed Me with Your Kiss" point towards the band's future sound of fuzzed-out, multi-tracked guitars and blissful male-female vocal harmonies. An underrated and surprisingly accessible album. —*Heather Phares*

Ecstasy & Wine / 1989 / Lazy ♦♦♦

Glider / 1989 / Sire ♦♦♦♦

★ **Loveless** / 1991 / Sire ♦♦♦♦♦
One of the best and most influential albums in '90s alternative rock, *Loveless* puts the band's innovative sonic style over lyrical substance. And the sonic styles of *Loveless* change constantly: Drums bludgeon the listener's ears and fade into nothingness; guitars whine like chainsaws and hum like cellos. The intricate mix of feedback, guitar washes and dreamy harmonies on songs like "Til Here Knows When" and "Blown a Wish" is awe-inspiring; though it takes My Bloody Valentine many years of work to complete their albums, it's easy to understand why when the results are this breathtaking. —*Heather Phares*

Rick Nelson (Eric Hilliard Nelson)

b. May 8, 1940, Teaneck, NJ, **d.** Dec. 31, 1985, Dekalb, TX
Guitar, Vocals / Rock 'n' Roll, Country-Rock, Pop-Rock, Teen Idol
Rick Nelson made it a little safer for "respectable" American teenagers to rock. When 16-year-old Ricky cut his debut single in 1957—a timid cover of Fats Domino's "I'm Walkin,'" allegedly on a dare from his girlfriend—the sneering image of Elvis Presley was still taboo in many households. Nelson, the nonthreatening, cleancut youth, commanded the perfect vehicle for spreading his rocking message—his family's beloved TV sitcom, "The Adventures of Ozzie and Harriet."

With a genuine passion for Sun-style rockabilly and the searing lead-guitar work of Joe Maphis initially and later the brilliantly inventive James Burton (from "Believe What You Say" on), Ricky signed with Imperial later in 1957. He waxed one incendiary rocker after another, including "Stood Up," "Waitin' in School," and "It's Late." He introduced them via those TV airwaves, thus ensuring gold record status well into the '60s.

As the demand for unrelenting rock 'n' roll slowly faded, Ricky's sound softened as well, with smoother material such as "Never Be Anyone Else But You" in 1959 and his 1961 chart-topper "Travelin' Man." A much-publicized name switch to Rick on his 21st birthday reflected that maturity.

But Nelson never forgot his roots, not even during the lean mid-'60s on Decca, when he ran dry of fresh material and revived too many old Tin Pan Alley standards that should have stayed buried. But triumphantly to the top in 1972 with the introspective Garden Party, Rick Nelson proved emphatically that he was more than just another teen-idol hunk, right up to his fatal plane crash on New Year's Eve of 1985. Like his idols at Sun, this kid was born to rock—and showed America that it was no sin. —*Bill Dahl*

Hey Pretty Baby / 1986 / Rockstar ♦♦♦
If you're looking for Imperial-era material that's not on the EMI best-of compilation CDs, this 16-track British import offers a good selection.

Much of this is not present on those domestic CDs, and the collection emphasizes his more rocking side, with James Burton frequently contributing his tasty licks. But it doesn't compare with the best of his vintage material, though it's pleasant enough (and quite innocuous); most listeners will be content to pick up the greatest-hits comps and leave it at that. —*Richie Unterberger*

★ **Legendary Masters** / 1990 / EMI America ✦✦✦✦✦
Legendary Masters compiles all of the hits Ricky Nelson released for Imperial Records in the late '50s, including "Be-Bop Baby," "Stood Up," "Lonesome Town," "It's Late," "Poor Little Fool," "Sweeter Than You," "Just a Little Too Much," "Never Be Anyone Else but You," and "Believe What You Say." A few essential items are missing—such as the Verve sides "A Teenager's Romance" and "I'm Walking"—and it would have been nice if the disc had extended into the early '60s, so songs like "Travelin' Man" and "Mary Lou" could have been included. —*Stephen Thomas Erlewine*

Best of 1963-1975 / 1990 / MCA ✦✦✦
No longer Rockin' Ricky, but Responsible Rick, his Decca output was wildly inconsistent. The early efforts like "Fools Rush In" and "String Along" still feature guitarist James Burton prominently. —*Bill Dahl*

Best of Rick Nelson, Vol. 2 / 1991 / Capitol ✦✦✦✦
Focusing primarily on Rick's early-'60s material for Imperial, this 27-cut disc is not quite as rocking as Vol. 1, but still offers plenty of worthy moments. It includes all of his massive, midtempo teen idol ballad hits of the era: "Young World," "A Wonder like You," "Teenage Idol," "It's Up to You," and the No. 1 hit "Travelin' Man." Teen ballads they might have been, but James Burton's masterful guitar licks and Nelson's assured, committed delivery placed them leagues above other teen-idol hits of the period. Of more interest to serious fans are the inclusion of several minor hit singles and covers of R&B tunes. And of course, there's the first-class rockabilly hit "Hello Mary Lou" (penned by Gene Pitney), perhaps his best recording of the decade. His surprisingly raucous cover of "Summertime" features, amazingly, the same bass line used as a hook on the Blues Magoos' psych-pop-garage hit "We Ain't Got Anything Yet" years later. The pleasures of this CD are modest but consistent. —*Richie Unterberger*

Rockin' with Ricky / 1996 / Ace ✦✦✦✦
Originally released as an LP in 1984, the CD version of this collection of Nelson's hardest-rocking early material doubles in length to include a whopping 32 tracks (on one disc) from the late '50s and early '60s. This has most of his uptempo smashes, a la "Be-Bop Baby," "Waitin' in School," and "Believe What You Say," with a host of LP tracks, many of them covers of songs made famous by Elvis, Carl Perkins, Roy Orbison, and the like. The two volumes of greatest hits on EMI are more well-rounded, and on the whole better, retrospectives of his classic era. This is pretty good proof that he could rock respectably, though, with some good cuts that are hard to find on reissues, like "You're So Fine" and "Poor Loser." —*Richie Unterberger*

Stay Young: The Epic Recordings / Epic ✦✦✦
Stay Young is an entertaining overview of Rick Nelson's country-tinged years at Epic, proving that he recorded plenty of worthwhile material in the '70s. —*Stephen Thomas Erlewine*

Michael Nesmith

b. Dec. 30, 1943, Houston, TX
Guitar / Country-Rock, Singer-Songwriter, Folk-Rock
You'll get very little argument that Michael Nesmith's songs are the highlights of the Monkees' catalog. If given a chance on his own, Nesmith might have beat Gram Parsons in a race to invent country-rock. When he ceased to be "Monkee Mike," Nesmith created rootsy country music, unaffected by the often cynical approach of numerous contemporaries. Nesmith's stature as an outside producer grew, and he eventually shed much of the country influence of his writing before ultimately shelving his musical career entirely. What remains is a sizable body of solo work that too few have investigated. Now that it is readily available again, it would be well worth the effort to check out. —*Steve Aldrich*

Mike Nesmith Presents the Wichita Train Whistle Sings / 1968 / Dot ✦✦
With this record, Nesmith's momentum builds as this album is even better than the first. While the single from this album didn't do as well as his previous hit, it was a better song and kicks off the album nicely. Also, steel player extraordinaire, "Red" Rhodes, is beginning to take a more dominant role in the sound of the band. Of special interest are Nesmith's third go at recording "Listen to the Band," a fine cover of Patsy Cline's "I Fall to Pieces," and his renewed interest in Latin rhythms. —*Jim Worbois*

Magnetic South / 1970 / Pacific Arts ✦✦✦✦
This fine collection not only features Nesmith originals (and his first solo hit) but one of the most interesting versions of "Beyond the Blue Horizon" ever committed to vinyl. For nearly six minutes we follow a day in

the life of the singer, from the minute he wakes in the morning and goes off to work on his tractor, until the time he returns at day's end. Also, at least two of the Nesmith originals were songs from his Monkee days, but the Monkee versions of these songs would not be heard until the issue of the *Missing Links* series nearly 20 years later. —*Jim Worbois*

Nevada Fighter / 1971 / Pacific Arts ✦✦✦

Tantamount to Treason / 1972 / Pacific Arts ✦✦✦

And the Hits Just Keep on Comin' / 1972 / RCA ✦✦✦✦
If you don't own this record, there is a huge hole in your collection. Nesmith's own version of "Different Drum" (a song which introduced Linda Ronstadt to many of us back in 1968 and which most of us had only heard Nesmith do as a speeded up, mumbled "audition" on an old Monkees episode) may be the key to lure you in, but every song is a gem. This is easily some of Nesmith's finest work as both a songwriter and an artist. Also, between Nesmith and Red Rhodes, the sound is so full that it's easy to forget that a full band wasn't used in creating this record. —*Jim Worbois*

Pretty Much Your Standard Ranch Stash / 1973 / Pacific Arts ✦✦✦✦
Despite the comment inside the cover that "After two or three months this album may lose potency although some of the aroma may linger," this record holds up some 20 years later as one of Nesmith's finest. He continues to mix originals and a nice selection of covers as before but somehow this record feels more "comfortable" than his previous efforts. This seems to be, in part, due to the strong musical bond between Nesmith and steel player Red Rhodes. If the "Buy This Record" inducement on the front cover doesn't make this a must for your collection, one listen to the music inside will! —*Jim Worbois*

The Prison / 1974 / Rio ✦✦

From a Radio Engine to the Photon Wing / 1977 / Pacific Arts ✦✦

Live at Palais / 1978 / Pacific Arts ✦✦

Infinite Rider on the Big Dogma / 1979 / Pacific Arts ✦✦✦

Newer Stuff / 1989 / Rhino ✦✦✦
This compilation of later solo material is often glossy and overreaching but still quite impressive. —*Jeff Tamarkin*

● **The Older Stuff: Best of Michael Nesmith (1970-1973)** / 1991 / Rhino ✦✦✦✦
Post-Monkees country-oriented material is proof that at least one member of the "pre-fab four" possessed genuine musical talent. —*Jeff Tamarkin*

Tropical Campfires / 1992 / Rio ✦✦✦

● **Complete** / 1993 / Pacific Arts ✦✦✦✦
All of Michael Nesmith and the First National Band's three albums are collected on this superb two-disc set. —*Stephen Thomas Erlewine*

The Neville Brothers

Soul, Funk, R&B, New Orleans R&B
After more than two decades of performing together and alone, the Nevilles returned to their home turf, New Orleans, in 1977. The music they began making was grounded in that city's rhythms and folklore. Individually, the first Neville to get on record was Art, who joined the Hawketts and scored with "Mardi Gras Mambo" (1955) and on his own with "Cha Dooky Do" (1958). Then Aaron made his mark with "Over You" (1960) and the anthemic "Tell It Like It Is" (1966). The details of how Art, Aaron, Charles, and Cyril passed through the Meters, the Wild Tchoupitoulas, and other outfits to form their family band would defy a genealogist, and their less-than-successful debut on Capitol suggested that it was hardly worth the trouble. But then came *Fiyo on the Bayou* on A&M in 1981. Since then, the brothers have gone from strength to strength, plundering their New Orleans heritage and combining it with an eclectic mix of material to produce music that is virtually without category. Exposure in the band has finally enabled Aaron Neville to gain recognition as one of the truly great, eccentric voices in Black music. *Rolling Stone* and then Linda Ronstadt offered their seals of approval, with the result that the brothers are now both funky and chic. —*Colin Escott*

Fiyo on the Bayou / Apr. 1981 / A&M ✦✦✦✦
A brilliant updating of the New Orleans R&B sound to include strains of Cajun, rock, and reggae on standards ranging from "Hey Pocky Way" to "The Ten Commandments of Love" and "Sitting in Limbo." —*William Ruhlmann*

Neville-Ization / Jun. 1984 / Black Top ✦✦✦✦
It took Black Top Records two years to put this record out after the Neville Brothers recorded it live at Tipitina's in New Orleans in September, 1982, and one reason may be that it presents a mediocre, going-through-the-motions set. At their best, The Nevilles achieve a transcendent musical mixture, and even at the level of mere professionalism they're an impressive unit, but this just isn't the live album of which they are capable. —*William Ruhlmann*

★ **Treacherous: A History of the Neville Brothers 19** / 1986 / Rhino
✦✦✦✦✦
The music of the Neville Brothers was more a matter of rumor than documentation to most record buyers outside the New Orleans area until 1986, when Rhino Records finally gathered together their various solo and group records dating back 30 years and presented their story coherently on this two-disc set. Suddenly, it all makes sense, and the Nevilles' mixture of styles emerges as a singular American genre unto itself. This record is a revelation. — *William Ruhlmann*

Uptown / Mar. 1987 / EMI America ✦✦

Yellow Moon / 1989 / A&M ✦✦✦✦
The Neville Brothers made a bid for pop-rock stardom with this well-produced album for A&M, their first under a new pact with the label inked in the late '80s. It was certainly as solid as any they cut for A&M; the vocals were both nicely arranged and expertly performed, the arrangements were basically solid, and the selections were intelligently picked and sequenced. The album charted and remained there for many weeks, while the Nevilles toured and generated lots of interest. It didn't become a hit, but it did respectably and represents perhaps their finest overall pop LP. — *Ron Wynn*

Brother's Keeper / 1990 / A&M ✦✦✦

Treacherous Too!: History of / 1991 / Rhino ✦✦✦✦
Okay, there's no such thing as secondhand revelation, but the Neville Brothers had more than enough stray tracks from their decades of local music-making around New Orleans to justify this second, single-disc follow-up to Rhino's first Nevilles history. There's more of an emphasis on novelty material here, but once again you can hear the roots of the Nevilles' cross-genre appeal in pop, R&B, and soul music dating back to the 1950s. Since most of these songs were recorded as singles, they have an immediate surface appeal, but repeated listenings also bring out the sounds of the tight session bands (including members of the Meters) who backed the Nevilles up. Actually, it's only the five 1980s tracks from just-okay albums like *Neville-ization* and *Uptown* that keep this collection from classic status, not the older stuff. — *William Ruhlmann*

Live on Planet Earth / Apr. 19, 1994 / A&M ✦✦✦

Aaron Neville

b. Jan. 24, 1941, New Orleans, LA
Vocals / Soul, R&B, Adult Contemporary, Pop-Rock
Although Neville is often compared to singer Sam Cooke in terms of sheer vocal refinement, he has a voice and style uniquely his own. Today he is well known as part of the New Orleans sound of the Neville Brothers. Yet, aside from the 1967 No. 1 R&B hit "Tell It Like It Is," few have heard his incredible early solo recordings. Many of the first recordings of Aaron Neville, in the early and mid-'60s, were arranged, produced, and often written by the brilliant Allen Toussaint—another talent only now being really appreciated. Most of these sides were cut for the Minit (and later) Parlo labels. Songs like "She Took You for a Ride" and "You Think You're So Smart" on Parlo are masterpieces. While his more recent work, including that with Linda Ronstadt, makes for pleasant listening, it lacks the sheer persuasion of his early songs. Aaron has re-recorded his early work often, and it is important to hear the originals. The early sides of Aaron Neville are just waiting to be heard.

Aaron Neville has been venturing more into other waters besides R&B. 1993's *The Grand Tour* included a remake of a George Jones song that got Neville a little country attention, and he announced plans in 1994 to do a complete country album. He was also one of several R&B artists who teamed with country stars for the *Rhythm, Country and Blues* session. Neville was paired with Trisha Yearwood, and the duo also performed together in a benefit concert for the LP held in Los Angeles in April 1994. The LP made history by debuting in the Top Ten on the pop, R&B, and country charts. — *Michael Erlewine and Ron Wynn*

Greatest Hits / 1957 / Curb ✦✦✦

● **Tell It Like It Is** / 1967 / Curb ✦✦✦✦
Eleven of Neville's best Parlo cuts, including those mentioned above, are included on one CD. His biggest solo smash from 1966, plus more songs in the same style. Sublime stuff. — *Bill Dahl*

Like It 'Tis / Oct. 14, 1967 / EMI America ✦✦✦
An excellent vinyl compilation of Neville's early-'60s Allen Toussaint-produced Minit singles, this includes the amusingly macabre 1960 rocker "Over You." — *Bill Dahl*

Orchid in the Storm / Dec. 1986 / Rhino ✦✦✦✦
Aaron Neville's wondrous singing on this poorly distributed EP was overlooked by many still unaware of his stunning falsetto. But Neville covered doo-wop, soul, and even country on this project, singing with a soaring conviction and poignancy that made it a delightful, though short, set. Rhino has thankfully reissued it on CD. It's actually closer to representing Neville's real style than his recent much-hyped, overproduced pop records. — *Ron Wynn*

Show Me the Way / Aug. 1989 / Charly ✦✦✦

Warm Your Heart / 1991 / A&M ✦✦✦
This new set finds Neville's wavering vocals as elegant as ever on a ballad-oriented program. — *Bill Dahl*

My Greatest Gift / 1991 / Rounder ✦✦✦

Aaron Neville's Soulful Christmas / Oct. 5, 1993 / A&M ✦✦✦

● **Tell It Like It Is: Golden Classics** / Collectables ✦✦✦✦
One of many collections covering Aaron Neville's superb early R&B and soul classics. The burly Neville, whose delicate, feathery voice stands in vivid contrast to his muscular body, made great heartache ballads, uptempo wailers, and brilliantly sung originals for tiny New Orleans labels, often not even getting widespread soul airplay. Now that's he's hot property, the domestic anthologies are coming out left and right. This one is as good as any other, although for my money the import labels have still done a better job on early Neville than the American companies. — *Ron Wynn*

New Colony Six

Garage Rock, Pop-Rock
Chicago's New Colony Six originally emerged as a tough, British Invasion-styled outfit prominently featuring Farfisa organ and a novel (at the time) Lesley guitar. Scoring a huge local hit with "I Confess," their early recordings—exemplified by their 1966 debut album, *Breakthrough*—featured first-class original material that gave the sound of Them and the Yardbirds a more commercial, American garage-based, vocal harmony approach. The rest of the '60s saw the band gradually abandoning their roots for middle-of-the-road pop with horns and strings. Continuing to rack up major local hits and minor national ones, they finally cracked the US Top 30 with "Love You So Much" (1968) and "Things I'd Like to Say" (1969). — *Richie Unterberger*

Breakthrough / 1966 / Sentar ✦✦✦✦
Breakthrough was one of the very finest American garage LPs, fusing Midwestern guitar-organ pop with the raunch of British Invasion groups, and stressing well-written original material. It is also extremely rare, and extremely expensive should you locate an original copy. But take heart—ten of the 12 tracks have been reissued on Sundazed's *At the River's Edge* CD. The two other songs are routine, dispensable covers of the Yardbirds' "Mr. You're a Better Man than I" and the McCoys' "Hang On Sloopy," so you shouldn't fret about their absence from your collection. — *Richie Unterberger*

Colonized! The Best of New Colony Six / 1993 / Rhino ✦✦

● **At the River's Edge** / 1993 / Sundazed ✦✦✦✦
Twenty-two tracks, including all of the worthwhile songs from their classic *Breakthrough* album, a non-LP single, and most of their second album, *Colonization*. The only New Colony Six package worth owning. — *Richie Unterberger*

New Edition

Urban, Pop-Rock
When Maurice Starr assembled New Edition in the early '80s, he never could have guessed that the group would produce some of the biggest, most influential urban R&B stars of the following decade. At the time of their first record, Bobby Brown, Ralph Tresvant, Ricky Bell, Mike Bivins, and Ronald Davoe were barely in their teens, yet they had impressive voices and a natural charisma that sent them to the charts with their first single, "Candy Girl." Their second album was even bigger, featuring the No. 2 single "Cool It Now." New Edition's songs were either light funk or sweet ballads, yet they followed their formula well, even if much of it seems quaint now, especially compared to their groundbreaking solo work.

Brown left the band after their third album, being replaced by Johnny Gill. The band released two more albums before splitting. After the group was finished, they each became successful as solo artists in the late '80s.

New Edition reunited in 1996, releasing a new album in the fall of that year. — *Stephen Thomas Erlewine*

Candy Girl / 1983 / Warlock ✦✦✦✦
When Maurice Starr uncovered the talents of a Roxbury vocal group in the early '80s, he envisioned a second Jackson 5. That was the direction he took New Edition in in its early days, and this album includes such overt Jackson 5 ripoffs as "Candy Girl" and the title track. None of the toughness or street touches that emerged on their later material were evident on this slick, pop-oriented session. Ralph Tresvant, Ronald DeVoe, Michael Bivins, Ricky Bell and Bobby Brown were all aged 13 to 15 when this was released. — *Ron Wynn*

New Edition / 1984 / MCA ✦✦✦✦
Maurice Starr's vision peaked with this second album by New Edition. They were now thoroughly Jackson 5 clones and were reaping similar commercial dividends thanks to the teen angst cuts "Cool It Now" and

"Mr. Telephone Man." They earned their first platinum album, one Top Ten hit and another Top 20 pop single (both songs topped the R&B charts) and were among the hottest acts in either pop or R&B during this stretch. — *Ron Wynn*

All for Love / 1985 / MCA ✦✦✦

Under the Blue Moon / 1986 / MCA ✦✦✦

Heart Break / 1989 / MCA ✦✦✦

● **Greatest Hits, Vol. 1** / 1991 / MCA ✦✦✦✦

For anyone who missed New Edition in either its Jackson 5 imitation phase or final days as a funkier, more aggressive urban contemporary vocal group with a slight dance influence, this collection contains examples of both incarnations. Kiddie-pop hits such as "Candy Girl," "Cool It Now" and "Mr. Telephone Man" are included, along with their final hits "If It Isn't Love," "Can You Stand the Rain" and the appropriately titled "Is This the End." This anthology shows how dominant New Edition was during the 1980s and early '90s. — *Ron Wynn*

New Order

Dance-Pop, Synth-pop, Alternative Pop-Rock, New Wave, Post-Punk, Club-Dance

Of all of the synth-based post-punk bands that emerged in the '80s, New Order is the most important. After Ian Curtis hung himself, the remaining members of Joy Division—Bernard Sumner, Peter Hook, and Stephen Morris—picked up the pieces and formed New Order, adding keyboardist Gillian Gilbert. While the group alleviated some of Curtis' most morbid tendencies, their music still was serious; the band also adhered to pop melodies and structure more frequently than Joy Division. New Order exploited synthesizers and electronics to their fullest, creating a detached, yet strangely human soundscape that managed to convey the emotional alienation of the Thatcher and Reagan era. The band was also not afraid to use disco as the basic rhythm in their music, laying the groundwork for the house scene in the UK at the end of the decade, as well as the cold, detached synth-dance pop that dominated the charts in America and the UK for most of the beginning of the decade. In the UK, New Order were stars, yet they never developed anything larger than a cult following in America.

After 1991's *Technique*, the band members concentrated on solo projects (Sumner in Electronic, Hook in Revenge, Gilbert and Morris in the Other Two), fueling rumors that they had broken up. In 1993, they returned with *Republic*, which earned them their first genuine hit single in America, "Regret." After a tension-filled tour, the members resumed their solo projects, again sparking rumors of the band's split. — *Stephen Thomas Erlewine*

Movement / 1981 / Factory ✦✦✦

New Order's debut album *Movement* bridges the gap between the dance-rock the group would later develop and Joy Division's languid, morbid drone. *Movement* pointed the way toward New Order's future by featuring more synthesizers than any of Joy Division's records, as well as more accessible hooks and melodies. — *Stephen Thomas Erlewine*

Power Corruption and Lies / 1983 / Qwest ✦✦✦✦

Synthesized dance music at moderate tempos, plus calmly sung, distanced lyrics, makes for an entrancing effect. — *William Ruhlmann*

Low Life / 1985 / Qwest ✦✦✦✦

New Order's messages are no less dire here, but the tempos are faster, the singing more engaged, and the melodies more distinct. In fact, "Love Vigilantes" is positively catchy. — *William Ruhlmann*

Brotherhood / 1986 / Qwest ✦✦✦✦

Brotherhood reapeated the formula of *Low-Life*, but instead of being a mere retread of its predecessor, the new album was a refinement of the innovations of the previous album, as the group's songwriting became tighter and more accessible, as the single "Bizarre Love Triangle" proved. — *Stephen Thomas Erlewine*

★ **Substance** / 1987 / Qwest ✦✦✦✦✦

A collection of New Order singles—some of their best work—little of which had previously turned up on albums or in the US — *William Ruhlmann*

Technique / 1989 / Qwest ✦✦✦✦

Technique expands New Order's trademark sound by adding elements of dense acid house rhythms, the occasional acoustic guitar, and a greater reliance on pop melody. All of the subtle experimentation made *Technique* one of their most intriguing and successful records. — *Stephen Thomas Erlewine*

Republic / May 11, 1993 / Qwest ✦✦✦

★ **Best of New Order** / 1995 / Qwest ✦✦✦✦✦

Instead of presenting New Order as a progressive dance band as *Substance* did, *(The Best Of) New Order* showcases New Order the pop band, condensing their hit singles onto one disc. A couple of remixes are thrown in (Shep Pettibone takes over "Blue Monday"), but it is still a con-

cise explanation of why the group was one of the most important of the '80s. — *Stephen Thomas Erlewine*

The New York Dolls

Rock 'n' Roll, Hard Rock, Proto-Punk

The New York Dolls created punk rock before there was a term for it. Building on the Rolling Stones' dirty rock 'n' roll, Mick Jagger's androgeny, girl group pop, the glam rock of David Bowie and T. Rex, and the Stooges' anarchic noise, the New York Dolls created a new form of hard rock that presaged both punk rock and heavy metal. Their drug-fueled, shambolic performances influenced a generation of musicians in New York and London, who all went on to form punk bands. And although they self-destructed quickly, the band's two albums remained two of the most popular cult records in rock 'n' roll history.

All of the members of the New York Dolls played in New York bands before they formed in late 1971. Guitarists Johnny Thunders and Rick Rivets, bassist Arthur Kane and drummer Billy Murcia were joined by vocalist David Johansen. Early in 1972, Rivets was replaced by Syl Sylvian and the group began playing regularly in lower Manhattan, particularly at the Mercer Arts Center. Within a few months, they had earned a dedicated cult following, but record companies were afraid of signing the band because of their cross-dressing and blatant vulgarity.

Late in 1972, the New York Dolls embarked on their first tour of England. During the tour, drummer Murcia died after mixing drugs and alcohol. He was replaced by Jerry Nolan. After Nolan joined the band, the Dolls finally secured a record contract with Mercury Records. Todd Rundgren—whose sophisticated pop seemed at odds with the band's crash and burn rock 'n' roll—produced the band's eponymous debut, which appeared in the summer of 1973. The record received overwhelmingly positive reviews, but it didn't stir the interest of the general public—the album peaked at No. 116 on the US charts. The band's follow-up, *Too Much Too Soon*, was produced by the legendary girl group producer George "Shadow" Morton. Although the sound of the record was relatively streamlined, the album was another commercial failure, only reaching No. 167 upon its early summer 1974 release.

Following the disappointing sales of their two albums, Mercury Records dropped the New York Dolls. No other record labels were interested in the band, so they decided to hire a new manager, the British Malcolm McLaren, who would soon become famous for managing the Sex Pistols. With the Dolls, McLaren began developing his skill for turning shock into invaluable publicity. Although he made it work for the Pistols just a year later, all of his strategies backfired for the Dolls. McLaren made the band dress completely in red leather and perform in front of the USSR's flag—all of which meant to symbolize the Dolls' alleged communist allegiance. The new approach only made record labels more reluctant to sign the band and members soon began leaving the group.

By the middle of 1975, Thunders and Nolan left the Dolls. The remaining members, Johansen and Sylvain, fired McLaren and assembled a new lineup of the band. For the next two years, the duo led a variety of different incarnations of the band, to no success. In 1977, Johansen and Sylvain decided to break up the band permanently. Over the next two decades, various outtakes collections, live albums, and compilations were released by a variety of labels and the New York Dolls' two original studio albums never went out of print.

Upon the Dolls' break up, David Johansen began a solo career that would eventually metamorphose into his lounge-singing alter-ego Buster Poindexter in the mid-'80s. Syl Sylvain played with Johansen for two years before he left to pursue his own solo career. Johnny Thunders formed the Heartbreakers with Jerry Nolan after they left the group in 1975. Over the next decade, the Heartbreakers would perform sporadically and Thunders would record the occasional solo album. On April 23, 1991, Thunders—who was one of the more notorious drug abusers in rock 'n' roll history—died of a heroin overdose. Nolan performed at a tribute concert for Thunders later in 1991; a few months later, he died of a stroke at the age of 40. — *Stephen Thomas Erlewine*

★ **New York Dolls** / 1973 / Mercury ✦✦✦✦✦

There are hints of girl group pop and more than a hint of the Rolling Stones, but *The New York Dolls* doesn't really sound like anything that came before it. It's hard rock with a self-conscious wit, a celebration of camp and kitsch that retains a menacing, malevolent edge. The New York Dolls play as if they can barely keep the music from falling apart and David Johansen sings and screams like a man possessed. *The New York Dolls* is a noisy, reckless album that rocks and rolls with a vengance. The Dolls rework old Chuck Berry and Stones riffs, playing them with a sloppy, violent glee. "Personality Crisis," "Looking for a Kiss," and "Trash" strut with confidence, while "Vietnamese Baby" and "Frankenstein" sound otherworldly, working the same frightening drone over and over again. *The New York Dolls* was the definitive proto-punk album, even more than anything the Stooges released. It plunders history while celebrating it, creating a sleazy urban mythology along the way. — *Stephen Thomas Erlewine*

☆ **Too Much, Too Soon** / 1974 / Mercury ✦✦✦✦✦
Their second (and last) album mixes well-chosen soul/R&B covers with a slew of striking Johnny Thunders-David Johansen originals. It's good enough to make their early demise even more regrettable. —*John Floyd*

Rock & Roll / 1994 / Mercury ✦✦✦✦
Rock & Roll contains all of the original material from the Dolls' two classic albums and adds a couple of outtakes and rarities. So why isn't it as much fun as *New York Dolls* or *Too Much Too Soon?* For starters, the Dolls' versions of "Pills," "Stranded in the Jungle," "Don't Start Me Talkin'," and "(There's Gonna Be A) Showdown" weren't filler, they were essential to the overall feeling of the albums. And that brings us to the main problem of *Rock & Roll*—it isn't sequenced in an inviting manner. Instead of showcasing the New York Dolls in all of their trashy glory, the disc manages to make them sound rather tedious, which is something their proper albums certainly aren't. Nevertheless, there's plenty of fine music here, and hardcore fans will want the rarities. But the original albums remain the best way to hear the Dolls. — *Stephen Thomas Erlewine*

Randy Newman

b. Nov. 28, 1943, New Orleans, LA
Piano / Singer-Songwriter, Brill Building Pop
Randy Newman, nephew of Lionel and Alfred Newman (Hollywood composers and arrangers), was already steeped in a rich creative environment when he chose to pursue music as a career. Newman's first attempt as a solo artist was the 1961 Dot single "Golden Gridiron Boy," which was produced by Pat Boone. Even though the record went nowhere, Newman embarked on a successful songwriting career, with songs cut by the Fleetwoods, Jerry Butler, Cilla Black, Judy Collins, Manfred Mann, Nilsson, and Three Dog Night, among others. Since 1968, when he released his self-titled Warner Bros. debut, Newman has employed a seductive blend of ragtime, rolling Fats Domino-style rock 'n' roll, blues, and classic Hollywood cinema-style melodies (with a touch of Stephen Foster), which has been effective in luring the listener into the twisted mindsets of the characters that populate many of his songs. Newman often sang from the protagonist's point of view, he rarely wasted time moralizing his position. In 1978, Newman's tongue-in-cheek acerbity produced a hit with "Short People" (No. 2), off of *Little Criminals* (No. 9), but it also rankled many, who thought the single was mean-spirited. Even Newman's fans began to wonder about the literalness of his sentiment with the 1979 album *Born Again* (No. 41), which mercilessly skewered each of the protagonists represented.
In 1981 Newman did the soundtrack for the movie *Ragtime*, beginning a successful career in film scoring. Newman has continued to sporadically release solo albums that are many cuts above the average release. — *Rick Clark*

Randy Newman / 1968 / Reprise ✦✦✦✦
"Randy Newman creates something new under the sun," read the banner on the back of Newman's debut album, but it wasn't so much that as that, in keeping with the intended irony of the statement, Newman was intent upon taking cliches and using them to satirize social conventions, a popular parlor game in the late '60s. Thus, we have "Love Story" (predating the sappy book/movie of the same title), in which the lovers retire to Florida and pass away, "So Long Dad," in which a son squares things with his old man, and "Davy the Fat Boy," in which an affectionate friend exploits the title character. But there were also songs like "Living without You" and "I Think It's Gonna Rain Today," which were so painfully lonely you wished they weren't so sincere. Taken together, this was an audacious first album by a major, if extremely quirky, talent. — *William Ruhlmann*

★ **12 Songs** / 1970 / Reprise ✦✦✦✦✦
Randy Newman's droll humor and ability to render ludicrous settings (through the eyes of protagonists who were obviously not playing with full decks) made *12 Songs* an instant classic to the handful of people lucky enough to hear it. The bare-bones production, along with assistance from guitarist Ry Cooder, gave the record a homey immediacy. Highlights are hard to single out but "Mama Told Me Not to Come" (later a hit for Three Dog Night), "Yellow Man," "Lucinda," and "Uncle Bob's Midnight Blues" are great. —*Rick Clark*

Randy Newman Live / 1971 / Reprise ✦✦✦

☆ **Sail Away** / 1972 / Reprise ✦✦✦✦✦
Sail Away was Newman's first synthesis of his satirical writing and his impressive orchestral arrangement skills. The result was one of his very best albums. The title cut was a brilliantly twisted take on slaves coming on a ship from Africa, set to a score that owed much to Stephen Foster. "Burn On," Newman's sentimental-sounding ode to the polluted Cuyahoga River (in Cleveland, OH), and his perverse "You Can Leave Your Hat On" are among the many great songs to be found on *Sail Away*. —*Rick Clark*

☆ **Good Old Boys** / 1974 / Reprise ✦✦✦✦✦
On *Good Old Boys*, Newman increasingly focused his obsessions on the South, but his slant seemed to be rooted more in Steppin' Fetchit and Shirley Temple *Little Rebel* Hollywood films than in reality. As distorted as viewing things through that particular lens may be, the South in *Good Old Boys* is undeniably poignant. "Louisiana 1927" is an affecting account of a spring flood, while "Marie" (a love song from a drunk) is one of the most touching songs written in popular music. The grand, sweeping melodies and arrangements are quite simply beautiful. Newman's sloppy, soulful mumble and understated piano keep this great record from tumbling into drippy sentimentality. —*Rick Clark*

Little Criminals / 1977 / Reprise ✦✦✦

Born Again / 1979 / Reprise ✦✦✦

Trouble in Paradise / 1983 / Reprise ✦✦✦✦
After the mean-spirited 1979 release *Born Again,* Newman regrouped and released *Trouble in Paradise*, an album that employed more lyrical subtlety and was more successful at skewering its terminally character-disordered targets ("Christmas in Capetown," "Song for the Dead," "My Life Is Good"). "The Blues," a dryly humorous duet with Paul Simon, was a moderate hit at No. 51. "I Love L.A." failed to chart, in spite of extensive exposure. Musically, Newman downplayed the timeless feel of his best work in favor of a trendier, clean West Coast-pop sound. As a result, this effort doesn't age so well. *Trouble in Paradise* may not be Newman's best work, but fans will enjoy it. —*Rick Clark*

● **Retrospect** / 1983 / WEA ✦✦✦✦
To date, Warner Bros. in the US has not released a compilation of Randy Newman's best work, but the UK division has, and here it is. From "Political Science" to "God's Song," these 16 songs should show any listener the depth of Randy Newman's talent as a songwriter and provide some big horse laughs along the way. —*William Ruhlmann*

Land of Dreams / 1988 / Reprise ✦✦✦✦

Faust / Sep. 19, 1995 / Reprise ✦✦

Olivia Newton-John

b. Sep. 26, 1948, Cambridge, England
Vocals / Pop-Rock
Olivia Newton-John ranks at No. 12 in chart researcher Joel Whitburn's ranking of the most successful singles artists of the '70s. The biggest of her 15 Top Ten hits, "Physical," came in the '80s, when it spent ten weeks at No. 1. Born in Cambridge, England, but raised in Australia, she returned to her native country after winning a talent contest and spent several years struggling before she scored a Top Ten UK hit in 1971 with a cover of Bob Dylan's "If Not for You." But it was not until 1973 that Newton-John made her real American breakthrough with the first of five straight gold-selling Top Ten hits, "Let Me Be There." She scored two No. 1 albums in 1974 and 1975 with *If You Love Me, Let Me Know* and *Have You Never Been Mellow.* (Newton-John's simultaneous success on the country charts and her winning of Grammy and Country Music Association awards in country categories were controversial in Nashville.)
Newton-John's career cooled in 1976 and 1977, but in 1978 she appeared in the film version of the retro-'50s musical *Grease*, which not only added to her hit total but also moved her image from sweetness and innocence to a more aggressive posture. She capitalized on the change and on the disco wave for songs like the sexually provocative "Physical," and enjoyed a new vogue as a dance-pop singer in the early '80s. Her last Top Ten hit, "Twist of Fate" was in 1984, also the year Newton-John married actor Matt Lattanzi. She has since released the gold-selling *Soul Kiss* in 1985, *The Rumour* in 1988, and released *Warm and Tender* (1989), an album of children's lullabies. —*William Ruhlmann*

● **Back to Basics** / 1992 / Geffen ✦✦✦✦
An artist well-defined by her hit singles, Olivia Newton-John has had a stylistically varied career, as is illustrated on *Back to Basics: The Essential Collection 1971-1992*, a set that ranges from her teary ballad "I Honestly Love You" to that bouncy paean to getting horizontal, "Physical." Fans may quibble that such hits as "Let Me Be There" and "Make a Move on Me" are not included, but Newton-John's two greatest-hits albums are out of print, and this is the only collection to combine both her good-girl and bad-girl personae. —*William Ruhlmann*

Nico (Christa Paffgen)

b. Oct. 16, 1938, **d.** Jul. 18, 1988
Harmonium, Vocals / Art-Rock/Progressive-Rock, Experimental, Euro-Dance
One of the most fascinating figures of rock's fringes, Nico hobnobbed, worked, and was romantically linked with an incredible assortment of the most legendary entertainers of the 1960s. The paradox of her career was that she herself never attained the fame of her peers, pursuing a distinctly individualistic and uncompromising musical career that was uncommercial, but wholly admirable and influential. Nico first rose to

fame as a European supermodel, also landing a bit part in Fellini's *La Dolce Vita* film and giving birth to a son by Alain Delon. In 1965, she attracted the attention of Rolling Stones manager Andrew Loog Oldham, who gave her a chance to record for his Immediate label, though the resulting single, which also featured Brian Jones and Jimmy Page on guitars, flopped. Shortly afterwards, she moved to New York, where Andy Warhol installed her as a vestigial presence and occasional lead singer for the Velvet Underground. The band never really accepted her as a bonafide member, and she departed in 1967, but not before contributing unforgettable deadpan vocals to three of the songs on their classic 1967 debut album.

Nico embarked on a solo career, recording folk-rock flavored songs for her debut *Chelsea Girl* album with assistance from Jackson Browne, Lou Reed, and John Cale. Her 1969 follow-up, *The Marble Index*, was a dramatic departure that unveiled her doom-laden, gothic persona, produced by Cale and prominently featuring her deep vocals, impenetrable lyrics, and ghostly harmonium. Her subsequent 1970s albums explored much the same territory, with assistance from Cale and influential art-rockers like Eno and Phil Manzanera. Her career fell into disarray during the rest of the '70s and the '80s, as she struggled with a massive drug habit and tangled personal life. She released several live albums on various labels, but the ill-planned *Drama of Exile* and the more successful *Camera Obscura* were her only coherent studio efforts until she died of a cerebral hemorrhage in Ibiza in 1988.

The original goth-rocker, Nico's albums are demanding and bleak, but map a unique and starkly powerful vision that has become more influential with age. An intimate of Bob Dylan, Jackson Browne, the Velvets, the Stones, Jim Morrison, Iggy Pop, and others, her fascinating story is recounted in the biography *Nico: The Life & Lies of an Icon*, by Richard Witts, published in Great Britain by Virgin books; *The End*, by James Young, is a seedy look at her drug-addled final years by a member of her touring band. — *Richie Unterberger*

● **Chelsea Girl** / 1968 / Polydor ◆◆◆◆
Nico's distanced, German-accented voice is presented over austere strings and, in one case, electric guitar on a series of songs reminiscent of her work with the Velvet Underground and written by Velvets John Cale and Lou Reed. Other songs (some unrecorded elsewhere) were written by a young Jackson Browne. — *William Ruhlmann*

The Marble Index / 1969 / Elektra ◆◆◆
The quirky, orchestrated folk-rock of Nico's 1968 debut album *Chelsea Girl* in no way prepared listeners for the stark, almost avant-garde flavor of her 1969 follow-up, *The Marble Index*. Produced by former Velvet Underground partner John Cale, the chanteuse presented an uncompromisingly bleak, gothic soundscape on her second album. Dominated by spare harmonium and Nico's deep, brooding vocals, this album unveiled her singularly morose songwriting (her first record featured none of her compositions). Owing more to European classical and folk music than rock, it found little favor with 1969 audiences. But like the work of the Velvet Underground, it proved to be quite influential in the long run on a future generation of black-clad goth-rockers. The 1991 reissue of this recording adds two previously unreleased songs, "Roses in the Snow" and "Nibelungen." — *Richie Unterberger*

Desert Shore / 1971 / Reprise ◆◆◆◆
John Cale produces, arranges, and plays almost all the instruments on this atmospheric collection of songs well suited to Nico's droning delivery. — *William Ruhlmann*

The End / 1974 / Island ◆◆◆
The most remote and Teutonic of Nico's studio albums features Roxy Music guitarist Phil Manzanera, Brian Eno on synthesizer, and John Cale (who also produced) on a dozen instruments. After five Nico originals, it concludes with chilling readings of The Doors' "The End" and "Das Lied Der Deutschen." — *Richie Unterberger*

Peel Sessions / 1988 / Dutch East India ◆◆◆

Night Ranger

Hard Rock, Pop-Rock, Heavy Metal, Hair Metal, Arena Rock
Featuring ex-Ozzy Osbourne guitarist Brad Gillis and former Montrose keyboardist Alan Fitzgerald, Night Ranger was one of the most popular mainstream hard rock bands of the mid-'80s. The group formed in the early '80s in San Francisco; in addition to Gillis and Fitzgerald, the members included Jack Blades (vocals, bass), Jeff Watson (guitar), and Kelly Keagy (drums). After a few local gigs, promoter Bill Graham managed to get them supporting slots on Judas Priest, Santana, and Doobie Brothers concerts. Night Ranger's first album, *Dawn Patrol* (1982), reached No. 38 on the US charts, yet it was 1983's *Midnight Madness* that established the band as a commercial force. Featuring the AOR hit "(You Can Still) Rock in America" and the No. 5 single "Sister Christian," the record peaked at No. 15 and sold over a million copies. 1985's *7 Wishes* was just as successful, reaching No.10 on the charts. Night Ranger's audience began to diminish after 1987's *Big Life*. Fitzgerald left the following year

and the band released their last album, *Man in Motion*, which failed to go gold or spawn any Top 40 singles. Night Ranger broke up the next year. Jack Blades joined the supergroup Damn Yankees, which also featured Ted Nugent and Tommy Shaw. — *Stephen Thomas Erlewine*

● **Night Ranger's Greatest Hits** / 1989 / Camel ◆◆◆◆
Night Ranger's albums were usually hit-or-miss affairs. Without exception, the strongest songs on the records were the singles, which combined their hard rock crunch with pop hooks. *Greatest Hits* collects all of their Top 40 singles, including "Sister Christian," "When You Close Your Eyes," and "Sentimental Street," as well as lesser hits "(You Can Still) Rock in America" and "Sing Me Away" and album rock radio hits like "Restless Kind" and "Eddie's Comin' Out Tonight," making it a definitive compilation. — *Stephen Thomas Erlewine*

Harry Nilsson

b. Jun. 15, 1941, Brooklyn, NY, **d.** Jan. 15, 1994, Agoura Hills, CA
Piano, Vocals / Singer-Songwriter, Pop-Rock
Though he is best known as a singer, Harry Nilsson first gained recognition as a songwriter in the mid-'60s, when his songs were recorded by the Ronettes, the Modern Folk Quartet, and the Monkees. By the time Three Dog Night took his "One" into the Top Five, Nilsson had released two albums of his own on RCA. Neither of them was a hit, but Nilsson did score with his cover of Fred Neil's "Everybody's Talkin'" when it was used as the theme song of the film *Midnight Cowboy*. Nilsson wrote his own film and television scores and in 1970 made an album of songs written by Randy Newman. His career was not helped by his disinclination to undertake live appearances.

Nevertheless, Nilsson broke commercially with his late-1971 album, *Nilsson Schmilsson*, which contained his version of Badfinger's "Without You," a No. 1 hit, and his own novelty number, "Coconut," which also hit the Top Ten. Son of Schmilsson, another appealing collection, was successful the following year. Nilsson's next album was a collection of standards sung against an orchestra conducted by noted '50s arranger Gordon Jenkins, *A Little Touch of Schmilsson in the Night*.

Nilsson had always been a favorite of the Beatles (he was sometimes rumored to be joining the group), and he engaged in projects with Ringo Starr (a film called *Son of Dracula*) and John Lennon (who produced Nilsson's Pussy Cats) in the mid-'70s. After Lennon's murder, Nilsson became an outspoken advocate of gun control and devoted much of his time to the cause. In the early '90s, he was exhibiting his art in galleries and starting a comeback in music. Unfortunately, his comeback never materialized—Nilsson died of a heart attack in early 1994. — *William Ruhlmann*

Pandemonium Shadow Show / 1967 / RCA ◆◆◆◆
It's no wonder that Nilsson was taken up by members of the Beatles after they heard this album, which demonstrated that the singer understood better than most the eclectic whimsy that had given birth to *Sgt. Pepper's Lonely Hearts Club Band*. Contains the bittersweet "1941" and "Cuddly Toy," which was covered by the Monkees. — *William Ruhlmann*

Aerial Ballet / 1968 / RCA ◆◆◆◆
Nilsson's second effort is on the lightweight side; the tunes are always clever, but often cloying, sounding at times like a rock album for little kids (which he would indeed produce shortly afterwards with *The Point*). The influence of Tin Pan Alley and the lighter elements of Lennon-McCartney hover over the piano-dominated compositions, which could often use a little more guts. When he does reach for a little more complexity and melancholy, he comes up with some of his strongest material: his effervescent interpretation of Fred Neil's "Everybody's Talkin'" (which became a Top Ten hit), "One" (a smash for Three Dog Night), and a couple of more obscure gems in the pensive and melodic "Don't Leave Me" and "Together." — *Richie Unterberger*

Nilsson Sings Newman / Feb. 1970 / RCA ◆◆◆◆
Nilsson turns out to be a wonderful interpreter of the work of Randy Newman, his light voice making Newman's satiric humor even drier than when the composer himself sang the songs. — *William Ruhlmann*

Aerial Pandemonium Ballet / 1971 / RCA ◆◆◆

Nilsson Schmilsson / Nov. 1971 / RCA ◆◆◆◆
Nilsson's most successful album was a bouncy Richard Perry production, whose catchy songs were deepened by the singer's puckish humor. Contains the hits "Without You," "Jump into the Fire," and "Coconut." — *William Ruhlmann*

Son of Schmilsson / Jul. 1972 / RCA ◆◆◆◆
The humor is starting to take over on this follow-up, but the songs are still entertaining, and the session players, including "George Harrysong" and "Richie Snare," make for a great backup band. Contains the hits "Spaceman" and "Remember (Christmas)," as well as the ultimate put-down song, "You're Breaking My Heart." — *William Ruhlmann*

A Little Touch of Schmilsson in the Night / 1973 / RCA ◆◆

Pussy Cats / Aug. 19, 1974 / RCA ◆◆◆

● **All-Time Greatest Hits** / 1978 / RCA ✦✦✦✦
Nilsson's albums tended to hang together well, but that didn't keep him from throwing off singles, at least in the late '60s and early '70s. This collection contains all ten of his chart singles (including "Everybody's Talkin'"), plus his version of his song "One," which was a hit for Three Dog Night. — *William Ruhlmann*

Personal Best: The Harry Nilsson Anthology / Feb. 28, 1995 / RCA ✦✦✦✦
Spanning two discs, *Personal Best: The Harry Nilsson Anthology* is a comprehensive overview of Nilsson's varied career, including all of the hits and many significant album tracks, yet it offers too much material for the casual fan, who would be better served by *All-Time Greatest Hits*. — *Stephen Thomas Erlewine*

Nine Inch Nails

Industrial, Alternative Pop-Rock, Club-Dance
Nine Inch Nails, the one-man band of Trent Reznor, brought industrial music to the masses with 1989's *Pretty Hate Machine*. With its electronic rush, incessant beats, and distorted guitars, the album appeared to be like much industrial music on the surface, yet Reznor wrote pop songs, not the soundtrack to a personal horror movie. NIN's scarred, harsh soundscapes were bleak enough, yet Reznor's lyrics rise the despair and self-loathing to new heights; at times, his relentless darkness can veer dangerously close to self-parody.

Pretty Hate Machine wasn't a hit when it was released; it charted in 1990 and stayed on the charts for years afterward. By the time Reznor assembled a band for the first Lollapalooza tour in 1991, the group had a sizable following that only grew with NIN's ferocious performances on the tour. Legal troubles with his record company delayed the release of a second album; in 1992, he released a stop-gap EP, *Broken*, that was harder and more abrasive than the debut, yet still conformed to conventional song structures; it debuted in the *Billboard* Top Ten. With their second full-length album, Reznor showed his true roots—'70s progressive-rock. *The Downward Spiral* was promoted as a concept album, a cohesive piece of work; it also featured ex-King Crimson guitarist Adrian Belew. Still, NIN is able to straddle two seemingly opposing genres easily, gaining alternative and mainstream hard rock fans alike; whether he likes it or not, Trent Reznor is the man that made industrial palatable for pop fans. — *Stephen Thomas Erlewine*

Pretty Hate Machine / 1989 / TVT ✦✦✦✦✦
The reason *Pretty Hate Machine* gained a huge cult following is that Trent Reznor didn't make an industrial album in the strict sense of the term; his songs are pop songs played in an industrial style. Meanwhile, he constructs a towering monument of angst and hatred in his lyrics, perfect for legions of alienated adolescents. As Reznor says, "I'd rather die than give you control," and he proves it throughout *Pretty Hate Machine*. Full of hooks, beats, and abrasive noise, this album gave a generation of adolescents a martyr as well as a great way to vent anger. — *Stephen Thomas Erlewine*

Broken / 1992 / Interscope ✦✦✦✦✦
After the unexpected success of *Pretty Hate Machine*, Trent Reznor found himself unable to enjoy it. Instead, he became embroiled in an ugly lawsuit with his record company, which prevented him from releasing any new material for three years. Although *Broken* is only an EP, the wait was more than worth it. Those who fell in love with the pseudo-industrial *Pretty Hate Machine* will likely be alienated by the raging, angry assault of *Broken*. Instead of blaming everyone else for his troubles, Reznor turns his anger inward. "Wish" and "Happiness in Slavery" are busier, angrier, and noisier than anything on *Pretty;* the songs still have hooks, but the hooks are the noise. The anger on *Broken* is real, not feigned, and for those who can stomach undiluted rage, it is a masterpiece. (Note: There are two bonus tracks at 98 and 99 that equal the other six songs.) — *Stephen Thomas Erlewine*

Fixed / Nov. 1992 / Interscope ✦✦✦
Even more than *Broken*, the limited-edition *Fixed* EP sounds like an attempt by Reznor to whittle down the size of his audience. The remixes on *Fixed* totally distort all of the original meanings and intents of the original versions on *Broken;* it's the closest Reznor has come to pure industrial music. While the remixes completely rearrange the songs, *Fixed* is additional proof that NIN is not a flash in the pan. A bold artistic move, and not for the faint of heart. — *Stephen Thomas Erlewine*

The Downward Spiral / 1994 / Interscope ✦✦✦
Although Trent Reznor designed *The Downward Spiral* as a concept album about despair and anger, these are familiar themes for Nine Inch Nails; it's up to the music to carry the album. And it does carry the album, featuring harder guitars and more brutal beats. However, the songwriting has slipped and the aggression sounds forced. — *Stephen Thomas Erlewine*

Further Down the Spiral / 1995 / Nothing/Interscope ✦✦

Nirvana

Alternative Pop-Rock, Grunge
With one album, Nirvana changed rock 'n' roll. Before "Smells like Teen Spirit" and *Nevermind* were released in 1991, alternative and post-punk rock had never been considered profitable or commercial. Nirvana changed the record industry's conception of what was mainstream, as well as the public's. *Nevermind* marked a shift in the mainstream, when punk rock finally reclaimed the rock 'n' roll mainstream for itself. Other post-punk bands that crossed over into the mainstream had done so slowly; by the time U2 and R.E.M. became superstars in 1987, their audiences were large enough to guarantee them a hit album. Besides, neither band had as much raw guitars and naked angst as Nirvana; they were as close to a punk band as possible in the '90s.

Nirvana combined strands of rock from all eras into one explosive burst of rage. Combining the melodic pop of the Beatles, the '70s sludge of Black Sabbath, and the spiky song structure of the Pixies with the fierce indie ethics of the American indie underground of the '80s, the band came up with a signature pop-punk that was distinctly their own.

Bleach, their 1989 debut, made the band underground darlings and led to a major-label contract. In 1990, Dave Grohl became Nirvana's permanent drummer, teaming with bassist Chris Novoselic to form the fiercest rhythm section in rock. Guitarist/vocalist Kurt Cobain's new songs surpassed anything on their debut; his songs were stunning, concise bursts of melody and rage, that occasionally spilled over into haunting, folk-styled acoustic ballads.

Nevermind wasn't expected to sell over 100,000 copies; by early 1992, the album was the top-selling record in the country. However, the band's personal fortunes weren't as smooth. During 1992, Cobain developed a debilitating heroin habit that strained relations with the rest of the band. By the beginning of 1993, Cobain admitted that he had just detoxed from heroin, which he claimed he used to fight a chronic stomach problem. Nirvana released their third album, *In Utero*, in September of 1993; the album debuted at No. 1 and soon went double platinum. The band launched a US tour in October; all of the articles about the band portrayed a happier, calmer Cobain.

Those images began to unravel in March of 1994, when he overdosed on champagne and tranquilizers while on vacation in Rome. For all of March, rumors were flying about Nirvana's future. All of the rumors stopped on April 8, when Cobain's body was discovered at his home in Seattle; he had died three days earlier of a self-inflicted gunshot wound.

Since his death, Cobain has been equally revered and reviled; he wasn't universally mourned because he wasn't universally loved. Even after *Nevermind*, Nirvana's music was too raw for many listeners. But that doesn't mean that Cobain was not gifted or that his music was not important. Nirvana proved to both the record companies and the public that post-punk music and culture had a prominent place in mainstream culture. More importantly, the band made some undeniably great music. — *Stephen Thomas Erlewine*

☆ **Bleach** / 1989 / Sub Pop ✦✦✦✦✦
At the time, *Bleach* was a stellar piece of Seattle sludge, state-of-the-art indie-rock. Although it still stands as one of the best albums in the Sub Pop catalog, it pales next to their other work. *Bleach* is clearly a debut album; there is a fair amount of filler, and the band sometimes collapses into a sub-Sabbath murk, but "School," "Love Buzz," "Blew," and "Negative Creep" are outstanding, furious rockers, and the gorgeous, Beatlesque ballad "About a Girl" signals the heights the band would reach on their next album. — *Stephen Thomas Erlewine*

★ **Nevermind** / 1991 / DGC ✦✦✦✦✦
If "Smells like Teen Spirit" was the only good song on *Nevermind*, the album wouldn't have inspired the popular revolution that it did. Although the "Louie Louie"-meets-the-Pixies teen angst of "Teen Spirit" is what crossed Nirvana over, what made the album so remarkable was the quantum leap in Kurt Cobain's songwriting. The throttling punk rockers "Breed" and "Territorial Pissings" demolish anything on *Bleach*, and the haunting "Something in the Way" and "Polly" show Cobain's full range. Even better are "In Bloom," "Drain You," "On a Plain," and "Lithium," which fully combine both the melodicism and the sonic roar that Nirvana does so well. And the record wouldn't sound half as good as it does without Dave Grohl, who pushes every song to the limit. — *Stephen Thomas Erlewine*

Incesticide / Dec. 1992 / DGC ✦✦✦✦
More than anyone else, Nirvana itself was caught completely off guard by the overwhelming success of *Nevermind*. While Cobain wondered what do next, the band put out *Incesticide*, a collection of B-sides, live performances, outtakes, demos, and "rare" singles. The first half of the album is terrific, but after "Beeswax" the entire enterprise collapses into half-baked ideas and outtakes that deserved to stay that way. The first half is filled with BBC sessions previously only available on the Japanese import *Hormoaning*, the B-sides "Been a Son" and "Son of a Gun," and a Sub Pop single. The price of the CD is justified by the first two tracks, the

"Dive"/"Sliver" single, which was released just before *Nevermind* was recorded. *—Stephen Thomas Erlewine*

☆ **In Utero** / 1993 / DGC ✦✦✦✦✦
Despite all of the pre-release rumors predicting a noisy all-out sonic assault, *In Utero* is not an alienating alternative rock monster. Instead, *In Utero* retains all of the melodic splendor of *Nevermind*, injecting it with a raw roar louder and harder than anything on *Bleach*. However, Kurt Cobain remains a pop songwriter, and the melodies don't get buried under Steve Albini's sonic assault, as "Heart-Shaped Box" and "Penny-royal Tea" prove. The songs are among Cobain's best, making *In Utero* a successful follow-up to a landmark, groundbreaking album. *—Stephen Thomas Erlewine*

☆ **MTV Unplugged in New York** / 1994 / DGC ✦✦✦✦✦
Sadly, *MTV Unplugged* stands as Nirvana's last album. While it's an album of covers and old songs, it ranks as one of the band's most cohesive records. Instead of relying on the trio's overpowering sonic force, *Unplugged* concentrates on Kurt Cobain's subtly shaded songwriting and Nirvana's deceptively simple musical power. Every version of their previously recorded songs, with the possible exception of "On a Plain," dramatically improves the original, and the covers reveal more about Cobain than he intended. By the time Nirvana close with a wrenching, spine-chilling version of Leadbelly's "Where Did You Sleep Last Night?" the emotional complexity of Nirvana's music is clear. It's also clear that they could have made even greater music. *—Stephen Thomas Erlewine*

NRBQ (New Rhythm & Blues Quintet)

Rock 'n' Roll
Formed in 1967 in Florida as New Rhythm & Blues Quintet, the original lineup included pianist Terry Adams, guitarist Steve Ferguson, bassist Joey Stampinato, vocalist Frank Gadler, and drummer Tom Staley. After recording two albums for Columbia (including one with Carl Perkins), which went nowhere, guitarist Al Anderson joined in 1971, replacing Ferguson. Gadler left in 1972; Staley was replaced by drummer Tom Ardolino in 1974.

This versatile and witty quartet is at home with everything from atonal jazz to rockabilly to country swing to pop jangle to roadhouse R&B. But they don't always give eclecticism a good name; although there's something worth hearing on each of their albums, NRBQ's humor is often corny, and their penchant for indulging their every artistic whim means that even their best albums are padded with silly hokum. They've been doing the same stuff for nearly 30 years and have amassed a fanatical cult following. And at times, NRBQ can sound like the greatest rock band in the world.

After two decades without any lineup shakeups, Anderson left the band after the release of their 1994 album, *Message for Our Mess-Age*, to pursue a career writing country songs; he toured as Carlene Carter's guitarist immediately after his departure. NRBQ replaced Anderson with Stampinato's brother, Johnny. *—Cub Koda and John Floyd*

NRBQ / 1969 / Columbia ✦✦✦
The Q's debut is as succinct a summation of what this band was about than perhaps anything they've released since. After opening the record with a storming version of Eddie Cochran's "C'mon Everybody," they take a breath and leap headlong into a raucous version of Sun Ra's "Number 9." Add to that a songwriting collaboration between Terry Adams and jazz composer Carla Bley, and the great guitar playing of Steve Ferguson (really great on "Stomp"), and you've got the makings of a tremendously important record by a furiously eclectic and always wonderful band. *—John Dougan*

Scraps / 1972 / Polydor ✦✦✦
Scraps/Workshop / 1976 / Annuit ✦✦✦✦
When vinyl was still the prevailing form of sound reproduction, these two long-lost records were rereleased in this fantastic double set, which is probably out of print, but (assuming it hasn't been issued on CD) is worth ferreting out. Both records feature the debut of Al Anderson's superb guitar, and (trivia buffs take note) *Scraps* is the only time in the band's history they were a quintet with lead vocalist Frank Gadler (who's very good). Both records are chock full of classic Q: "Howard Johnson's Got His Hojo Working on Me," "C'Mon If You're Comin'," "Get That Gasoline," and "Magnet." Also making these records indispensable is Joey Spampinato's best-ever Beatles impression "It's Not So Hard," maybe the best pop song The Q ever recorded. Buyers note: parts of *Workshop*, along with an assortment of outtakes, was issued by Rounder in 1986 as an album entitled *RC Cola & a Moon Pie*. *—John Dougan*

All Hopped Up / 1977 / Rounder ✦✦✦
● **NRBQ at Yankee Stadium** / 1978 / Mercury ✦✦✦✦
More than just NRBQ's best record, but one of the great records of the '70s (maybe ever!). This album contains the strongest batch of new Q songs on one record, many of them the best and most memorable songs in the band's long and storied career. Starting with Terry Adams' herky-jerky "Green Lights" to the rollicking "I Want You Bad," the band has

rarely sounded better. The record's gem, however, is an Al Anderson song left over from their previous record (*All Hopped Up on Red Rooster*), "Ridin' In My Car." A song about lost love and blown chances, it has Al's characteristic wry sensibility and (non-fatal) heartache, all wrapped up in an ebullient pop package driven by Terry Adams' melodic keyboard riffing and Tom Ardolino's amazingly assertive drumming. *Yankee Stadium* should have been a huge album, but Mercury booted it and never capitalized on the band's fanatical support base. Caveat emptor: when this record was issued by Mercury on CD just a couple of years back, they inexplicably left off "Ridin' In My Car." As to whether that idiotic oversight has been rectified, I haven't a clue. *—John Dougan*

Kick Me Hard / 1979 / Rounder ✦✦✦✦
This is a decent mix of tough rockers and cheesy pop. *—John Floyd*

Tiddlywinks / 1980 / Rounder ✦✦✦✦
After being unceremoniously dumped by Mercury after *Yankee Stadium*, NRBQ returned to that warm embrace of Rounder and recorded a string of fine records that started with *Kick Me Hard*. This lineup was to remain intact for nearly 20 years, but here, fairly early on, the synchronicity among the quartet was apparent; it was if they'd been playing together forever, and the music excelled as a result. The songwriting was getting better too: Al, Terry and Joey were dividing the chores but never losing the group's cohesiveness. At times, Terry's songs would be a little too goofy, and Joey's heartfelt pop might dip into saccharine sweetness now and again, but never so much so that it becomes a huge problem. Of these two excellent records, *Kick Me Hard* lives up to its title, especially during the bluesy organ workout "Don't You Know" and the riff-happy "All Night Long" (great solo by Al). *Tiddlywinks* is carried by "Me And the Boys" (later to be recorded by Bonnie Raitt) and Al's beautiful "Never Take the Place of You." *—John Dougan*

Grooves in Orbit / 1983 / Bearsville ✦✦✦
Back to a major label, NRBQ came up with a solid record that, again, didn't significantly increase their audience, even though many musicians (Elvis Costello, Bonnie Raitt) were singing their praises. Although very good, *Grooves* is not significantly better (actually it's not any better) than *Kick Me Hard* or *Tiddlywinks*. Both sides end with a whimper rather than a bang, and it seems that the band was developing an overreliance on recycling material (their cover of Johnny Cash's "Get Rhythm" shows up on *Yankee Stadium*). Still, the crucial stuff ("Rain at The Drive-In" and "Smackeroo") fit the bill. *—John Dougan*

Tap Dancin' Bats / 1983 / Rounder ✦✦✦
She Sings, They Play / 1985 / Rounder ✦✦✦
God Bless Us All / 1987 / Rounder ✦✦✦
Wild Weekend / 1989 / Virgin ✦✦
● **Peek-A-Boo: Best of NRBQ (1969-1989)** / 1990 / Rhino ✦✦✦✦
A two-CD set that does a great job of hitting the band's high spots, without sacrificing any of the freewheeling stylistic leaps or engaging lunacy that has made NRBQ one of America's longest-lived bands. If you're interested in a career overview and little more, this is the ideal release. However, it is my considered opinion that anyone who loves this stuff (and to emphatically use a double negative, there's nothing not to love) will have their appetite whetted for more. Not a slow spot, ill-chosen track or bad decision among the 35 songs, this is as great a statement for NRBQ as one of the best rock bands America has ever produced. Few bands, genre notwithstanding, have been able to effortlessly recombine styles, be so defiantly off-the-wall, and rock like all get-out for so long and still sound so good. God bless them all. *—John Dougan*

Stay with We: The Best of NRBQ / 1993 / Columbia ✦✦✦
Featuring 24 songs including eight unreleased tracks, *Stay With We* is the definitive compilation of NRBQ's early years at Columbia. *—Stephen Thomas Erlewine*

Message for the Mess Age / 1994 / Forward ✦✦✦

Ted Nugent

b. Dec. 13, 1948, Detroit, MI
Guitar / Hard Rock, Heavy Metal, Arena Rock
Nugent started in a local Detroit teen band, the Lourds, and formed the Amboy Dukes in late 1965 or early 1966. He scored his first hit with "Journey to the Center of Your Mind" in 1968. Several albums using the Amboy Dukes tag followed, with the personnel changing with almost every album. Nugent went solo in 1975, marking his greatest success to date with one album after another in the charts; he put his solo career on hold to become a member of the group Damn Yankees in 1990. He resumed his solo career in 1995 with *Spirit of the Wild*. A powerful, high-decibel guitarist, Nugent's energy more than makes up for whatever subtleties he lacks. *—Cub Koda*

Free for All / 1976 / Epic ✦✦✦✦
Ted Nugent's career kicked into gear with his second solo album, *Free-for-All*, which was a collection of storming hard rockers sung by Meat

Loaf, who had yet to establish himself as a star in his own right. —*Stephen Thomas Erlewine*

Cat Scratch Fever / 1977 / Epic ✦✦✦✦
Driven by a set of hard-driving, catchy riffs and numerous gut-wrenching solos, *Cat Scratch Fever* remains Ted Nugent's best studio album. —*Stephen Thomas Erlewine*

Weekend Warrior / 1978 / Epic ✦✦✦

Double Live Gonzo / 1978 / Epic ✦✦✦✦
This is the ultimate document of Nugent's mountain-man persona. —*Dan Heilman*

● **Great Gonzo: The Best of Ted Nugent** / 1981 / Epic ✦✦✦✦
Featuring all of his hard-rock standards from the '70s, this album is a better collection than *Out of Control*, since there isn't a bit of filler. —*Stephen Thomas Erlewine*

● **Ted Nugent and the Amboy Dukes** / 1987 / DCC ✦✦✦✦
Featuring the psychedelic classic "Journey to the Center of the Mind," as well as several other similar-sounding acid rockers, *Ted Nugent and the Amboy Dukes* is the best record Nugent made with his first band. —*Stephen Thomas Erlewine*

Out of Control / Jun. 22, 1993 / Epic ✦✦✦✦
Out of Control is two CDs of prime Nugent, covering his days with the Amboy Dukes as well as his lengthy solo career. —*AMG*

Spirit of the Wild / 1995 / Atlantic ✦✦✦✦
Spirit of the Wild ranks as one of Ted Nugent's finest moments because it cuts away the filler and keeps the wildman's tendency for indulgence in check. A fair amount of the material does concern itself with the wilderness, which fits right in with his '90s reinvention as a conservative family-values spokesman. That doesn't mean that it's a tame record—it means that Nugent sounds committed again, since that passion for hunting and family flows throughout his performance. —*Stephen Thomas Erlewine*

Gary Numan (Gary Webb)

b. 1958
Synthesizer, Vocals / Synth-pop, Electronic, New Wave, New Romantic
Gary Numan managed to incorporate the electronic innovations of Kraftwerk, Brian Eno, and David Bowie into pop music, creating some of the first synth-pop hits of the new wave era. Numan originally performed under the name Tubeway Army, which had a chart-topping British single with "Are 'Friends' Electric?" The first record he released under his own name, 1979's *Pleasure Principle*, featured the international hit "Cars"; the single hit No. 1 in the UK and reached the US Top Ten. Throughout the early '80s, Numan was one of the most popular artists in the UK, amassing several Top Ten hits and two No. 1 albums. Around 1983, his career began to slip, as each record became indistinguishable from the other. Even as he fell out of the Top Ten, Numan held on to his die hard fans. He continued to record into the '90s. —*Stephen Thomas Erlewine*

Tubeway Army / Nov. 1978 / Beggars Banquet ✦✦✦

Replicas / 1979 / Atco ✦✦✦✦
On *Replicas*, Gary Numan took top billing over Tubeway Army, which was appropriate, considering that Numan's synthesizers were now the dominant instruments in the band's music. The new direction was successful, both artistically and commercially, with the cold, catchy single "Are 'Friends' Electric?" reaching the top of the UK charts. —*Stephen Thomas Erlewine*

● **The Pleasure Principle** / Sep. 1979 / Arista ✦✦✦✦
Gary Numan perfected his combination of Kraftwerk-influenced synth-drone and pop melodies on *The Pleasure Principle*, the first album he released under his own name. —*Stephen Thomas Erlewine*

Telekon / 1980 / Atco ✦✦✦✦
After the synthesized triumph of *The Pleasure Principle*, Gary Numan brought some guitars back into his sound on *Telekon*. Unlike *Tubeway Army*, which was dominated by guitars, the instrument is used to flesh out the keyboard-created textures on *Telekon*, which makes the album one of his most intriguing and creative records. —*Stephen Thomas Erlewine*

I, Assassin / 1982 / Atco ✦✦✦✦
Although it showcases his trademark sound to a fine effect, the repetitive, formulaic songwriting of *I, Assassin* suggests that Gary Numan had hit a brick wall with his robotic, synthesized pop. —*Stephen Thomas Erlewine*

Laura Nyro

b. Oct. 18, 1947, Bronx, NY
Piano, Vocals / Singer-Songwriter
While Laura Nyro remains best known for providing hit material for a number of late-'60s acts, it's a mystery why she never had a smash or her

own. Essential college-dorm-room listening for the era, and often bagged as a sort of East Coast answer to Joni Mitchell, in reality Nyro was in a class by herself. Nyro's songs were steeped in classic R&B and framed in stark settings, her vocal gymnastics often accompanied only by her own piano work. Any doubts as to where her music came from were erased by the album *Gonna Take a Miracle;* a brilliant collection of soul covers recorded with the resurrected LaBelle. It was also one of the first albums of all-outside material by a major rock-era songwriter. In the '70s Nyro became more reclusive, releasing only the occasional album, letting us in on a bit of her home life. Even now, the promise of new Laura Nyro material is still cause for much hope. —*Steve Aldrich*

More Than a New Discovery / 1967 / Verve/Forecast ✦✦✦

● **Eli and the 13th Confession** / 1968 / Columbia ✦✦✦✦
The hits (for others) keep coming—"Sweet Blindness," "Eli's Comin'," and "Stoned Soul Picnic" are all here, sung by their author—but Nyro not only proves herself a powerful singer in her own right, comfortable in styles from jazz to gospel/R&B to stark balladry, she also begins to turn to a more introspective, personal writing and singing that no one will be able to replicate. —*William Ruhlmann*

New York Tendaberry / 1969 / Columbia ✦✦✦✦
A stunning musical journey through love, loss, religion, and eroticism, by turns passionate, inspired, and suicidal, this is Nyro's most accomplished, most idiosyncratic record, and one of the greatest singer-songwriter works ever made. Using a wide vocal range and her often delicate piano work with deftly added instrumental touches, Nyro creates an aural landscape that spans the extremes of human emotion. It's not listed as her "pick" album only because it's not the place to start; rather, it's the logical conclusion of her musical development. —*William Ruhlmann*

Gonna Take a Miracle / 1971 / Columbia ✦✦✦✦
A joyous change of pace, this album presents inspired readings of pop/R&B hits of the '60s, songs like "Jimmy Mack" and "Nowhere to Run," produced by creamy-smooth soul producers Gamble & Huff and sung rapturously by Nyro, with gorgeous backing by Patti LaBelle, Sarah Dash, and Nona Hendryx. —*William Ruhlmann*

The First Songs / 1973 / Columbia ✦✦✦

Smile / 1976 / Columbia ✦✦✦

Season of Lights . . . Laura Nyro in Concert / 1977 / Columbia ✦✦

Mother's Spiritual / 1984 / Columbia ✦✦

Live at the Bottom Line / 1990 / Cypress ✦✦✦

Walk the Dog & Lite the Lite (Run the Dog Darling Lite Delite) / Aug. 17, 1993 / Columbia ✦✦✦

Oasis

Rock 'n' Roll, Alternative Pop-Rock, Brit-Pop
Oasis shot from obscurity to stardom in 1994, and became one of Britain's most popular and critically acclaimed bands of the decade; along with Blur and Suede, they are responsible for returning British guitar-pop to the top of the charts. Led by guitarist/songwriter Noel Gallagher, the Manchester quintet adopts the rough, thuggish image of the Stones and the Who, crosses it with Beatlesque melodies and hooks, adds distinctly British lyrical themes and song structures like those of the Jam and the Kinks, and ties it all together with a massive, loud guitar roar, as well as a defiant sneer that draws equally from the Sex Pistols' rebelliousness and the Stone Roses' cocksure arrogance. Gallagher's songs frequently rework previous hits from T. Rex ("Cigarettes and Alcohol" borrows the riff from "Bang a Gong") to Wham! ("Fade Away" takes the melody from "Freedom"), yet the group always puts the hooks in different settings, updating past hits for a new era.

Originally, the group was formed by schoolmates Liam Gallagher (vocals), Paul "Bonehead" Arthurs (guitar), Paul McGuigan (bass), and Tony McCarroll (drums). After spending several years as the guitar technician for the Stone Roses-inspired group the Inspiral Carpets, Noel Gallagher returned to Manchester to find that his brother had formed a band. Noel agreed to join the band if he could have complete control of the group, including contributing all the songs; the rest of the band agreed and under the new name Oasis, they began a year of rehearsing.

After playing a handful of small club gigs, the band cornered Alan McGee, the head of Creation Records, and forced him to listen to their demo. Impressed, he signed the band. The group released their first single, "Supersonic," in the spring of 1994; it edged its way into the charts on the back of positive reviews. With a melody adapted from "I'd Like to Teach the World to Sing," "Shakermaker" became a bigger hit in the early summer. Released a month before their debut album, the soaring ballad "Live Forever" became a major hit in England. The group's first record, *Definitely Maybe*, became the fastest-selling debut in British history, entering the charts at No. 1. Oasis mania continued throughout 1994, as the group began playing larger theaters and each new single outperformed the last. However, tensions in the group began to build—Liam and Noel refused to do joint interviews because they always fought—and Noel briefly left the band at the end of a difficult fall American tour; he rejoined and the band headed back to England. As "Supersonic" began to climb the US rock and modern rock charts, the non-LP, string-laden "Whatever" hit No. 2 over the British Christmas season.

At the beginning of 1995, the group concentrated on America, promoting the single "Live Forever." The song became a major hit on MTV, album rock, and modern rock radio stations, peaking at No. 2, and *Definitely Maybe* went gold in the US. Returning to England after a sold-out American tour, the group recorded a new single, "Some Might Say." On the eve of its release, drummer Tony McCarroll parted ways with the band, with Alan White taking his place. "Some Might Say" entered the charts at No. 1 upon its May release; its success led to all of their previous singles re-entering the indie charts. Oasis spent the rest of the summer completing their second album, *(What's the Story) Morning Glory?*, which was released in October 1995. Upon its release, the album shot to No. 1 in England, becoming the fastest-selling in the UK since Michael Jackson's *Bad*. —*Stephen Thomas Erlewine*

● **Definitely Maybe** / Aug. 1994 / Epic ◆◆◆◆
Definitely Maybe manages to encapsulate much of the best of British rock 'n' roll, from the Beatles to the Stone Roses, in the space of 11 songs. Their sound is louder and more guitar-oriented than any British band since the Sex Pistols, and the band is blessed with the excellent songwriting of Noel Gallagher. Gallagher writes perfect pop songs, offering a platform for his brother Liam's brash, snarling vocals. Not only does the band have melodies, but they have the capability to work a groove with more dexterity than most post-punk groups. But what makes *Definitely Maybe* so intoxicating is that it already resembles a greatest hits album. From the swirling rush of "Rock 'n' Roll Star," through the sinewy "Shakermaker," to the heartbreaking "Live Forever," each song sounds like an instant classic. —*Stephen Thomas Erlewine*

(What's the Story) Morning Glory / Oct. 3, 1995 / Epic ◆◆◆◆
If *Definitely Maybe* was an unintentional concept album about wanting to be a rock 'n' roll star, *(What's the Story) Morning Glory* is what happens after the dreams come true. Oasis turns in a relatively introspective second record, filled with big, gorgeous ballads instead of ripping rockers. Unlike *Definitely Maybe*, the production on *Morning Glory* is varied enough to handle the range of emotions; instead of drowning everything with amplifiers turned up to 12, there are strings, keyboards, and harmonicas. This expanded production helps give Noel Gallagher's sweeping melodies an emotional resonance that he occasionally can't convey lyrically. However, that is far from a fatal flaw; Gallagher's lyrics work best in fragments, where the images catch in your mind and grow, thanks to the music. Gallagher may be guilty of some borrowing, or even plagiarism—a track called "Step Out" had to be pulled at the last minute because it sounded too similar to Stevie Wonder's "Uptight"—but he uses the familiar riffs as building blocks. This is where Gallagher's genius lies: he's a thief and doesn't have many original thoughts, but as a pop-rock melodist he's pretty much without peer. Likewise, as musicians, Oasis members are hardly innovators, yet they have a majestic grandeur in their sound that makes ballads like "Wonderwall" or rockers like "Some Might Say" positively transcendent. Alan White does add authority to the rhythm section, but the most noticeable change is in Liam Gallagher. His voice sneered throughout *Definitely Maybe*, but on *Morning Glory* his singing has become more textured and skillful. He gives the lyric in the raging title track a hint of regret, is sympathetic on "Wonderwall," defiant on "Some Might Say," and humorous on "She's Electric," a bawdy rewrite of "Digsy's Diner." It might not have the immediate impact of *Definitely Maybe*, but *Morning Glory* is just as exciting and compulsively listenable. —*Stephen Thomas Erlewine*

Billy Ocean

b. 1950, Trinidad
Vocals / Soul, Adult Contemporary, Pop-Rock
Born in Trinidad, Billy Ocean emigrated to the UK as a child. He worked as a tailor while pursuing music on the side in the '60s, then broke through with the Motown-flavored "Love Really Hurts Without You," which hit No. 3 in the UK in 1976. Ocean continued to have UK hits through the end of the '70s but didn't achieve mass success in the US until 1984, when "Caribbean Queen (No More Love on the Run)" became a No. 1 hit, the first of seven Top Ten hits over the next four years. —*William Ruhlmann*

● **Greatest Hits** / 1989 / Jive ◆◆◆◆
Contains his cool '80s disco hits "Caribbean Queen" and "Get Outta My Dreams, Get Into My Car" and piano-based ballads like "There'll Be Sad Songs (To Make You Cry)." —*Bil Carpenter*

Sinéad O'Connor

b. 1967, Dublin, Ireland
Guitar, Keyboards, Vocals / Alternative Pop-Rock
From Dublin, Ireland, Sinéad O'Connor came onto the music scene in

1987 with a powerful image of a woman who could express great sensitivity while not losing any qualities of inner strength. In public, O'Connor's seemingly audacious pronouncements about the state of the world around her may have put off those unaccustomed to a woman so forthright with her feelings; nevertheless, it's that courageousness that has endeared her to millions of fans. O'Connor's second album, *I Do Not Want What I Haven't Got*, was a worldwide hit. Musically, O'Connor draws from hard synth-rock, Celtic folk, and funk. Her dramatic alto explores sound in much the same way Peter Gabriel applies varied tonal dynamics.

After the success of *I Do Not Want What I Haven't Got*, O'Connor seemed a bit directionless. Two years later, she released an album of big-band covers, *Am I Not Your Girl?*, a strange record that was a commercial disappointment. Even worse, the singer suffered a tidal wave of bad publicity when she tore a photo of the Pope on "Saturday Night Live," saying "Fight the real enemy." For the next year, O'Connor laid low, recording a new album that was released in the fall of 1994. —*Rick Clark*

The Lion and the Cobra / 1987 / Ensign ◆◆◆◆
The Lion and the Cobra was an impressive showcase for this Dubliner's vocal and writing skills. On this self-produced effort, O'Connor incorporates bits of hard rock, folk, synth-pop, and light funk onto standout tracks like "I Want Your (Hands on Me)," "Jerusalem," and "Mandinka," a wonderful synth-rocker. —*Rick Clark*

● **I Do Not Want What I Haven't Got** / 1990 / Ensign ◆◆◆◆
O'Connor's debut might have been a strong showing, but her follow-up, *I Do Not Want What I Haven't Got*, was a stunner. Her songwriting skills were much more incisive and, vocally, O'Connor exhibited a greater range of interpretive skills. Highlights include "The Emperor's New Clothes," "I Am Stretched on Your Grave," "Jump in the River," "Black Boys on Mopeds," and the international hit "Nothing Compares 2 U," which was penned by Prince. —*Rick Clark*

Am I Not Your Girl? / 1992 / Ensign ◆◆

Universal Mother / 1994 / Ensign ◆◆◆

Offspring

Hard Rock, Alternative Pop-Rock, Punk Revival
Offspring's metal-inflected punk became a popular sensation in 1994, selling over four million copies on an independent record label. While the group's credentials and approach follows the indie-rock tradition of the '80s, sonically they sound more like an edgy, hard-driving heavy metal band, with their precise, pulsing power chords and Brian "Dexter" Holland's flat vocals. Featuring Holland, guitarist Kevin "Noodles" Wasserman, bassist Greg Kriesel, and drummer Ron Welty, the Offspring released their second album, *Ignition*, in 1993. It was an underground hit, setting the stage for the across-the-board success of 1994's *Smash*. The Nirvana-soundalike "Come Out and Play," the first single from the album, became an MTV hit in the summer of 1994, which paved the way to radio success. The band was played on both alternative and album rock stations, confirming their broad-based appeal. "Self Esteem," the second single, followed the same soft verse/loud chorus formula and stayed on the charts nearly twice as long as "Come Out and Play." The group got offers from major labels, yet they chose to stay with Epitaph. While they were able to play arenas in the US, their success didn't translate in foreign countries. Nevertheless, the band's popularity continued to grow in America, as "Gotta Get Away" became another radio/MTV hit in the beginning of 1995. The Offspring recorded a version of the Damned's "Smash It Up" for the *Batman Forever* soundtrack in the summer of that year; it kept the band on the charts as they worked on their third album. —*Stephen Thomas Erlewine*

Offspring / 1989 / Nemesis ◆◆◆

Ignition / 1993 / Epitaph ◆◆◆

● **Smash** / 1994 / Epitaph ◆◆◆◆
The Offspring's second album for Epitaph did the impossible: it landed in the Top Five, unheard of for independent records. The Offspring crossed over due to the raucous, Eastern-tinged single "Come Out and Play (Keep 'em Separated)," which stopped and started just like Nirvana, only without the Seattle trio's recklessness. The record stayed in the charts because The Offspring sounded relentlessly heavy, no matter how much the band claimed to be punk. Their tempos are slower than traditional hardcore, and their attack is as heavy as Metallica's. But they acted like they were punk, with odes to no "Self Esteem" and singing about fighting in school. Nothing on the album matches the incessant catchiness of the singles, but *Smash* is a solid record, filled with enough heavy riffs to keep most teenagers happy. —*Stephen Thomas Erlewine*

Ohio Express

Bubblegum
Ohio Express and 1910 Fruitgum Co. were two of the leading late-'60s bubblegum rock groups. Under the aegis of producers Jerry Kasenetz

and Jeff Katz, both of these rather anonymous bands surfaced repeatedly on the late-'60s pop charts for Buddah Records, spearheading the bubble-gum rock craze. With Joey Levine taking the vocals on their early hits, Ohio Express roared up in 1968 with "Yummy Yummy Yummy" and "Chewy Chewy," a pair of million-sellers. Future 10CC leader Graham Gouldman fronted Express on their final chart bow in 1969, "Sausalito (Is the Place to Go)."

At the same time, another Kasenetz-Katz discovery, New Jersey's 1910 Fruitgum Co., was bubbling over with the obnoxiously catchy "Simon Says," "1-2-3, Red Light," and "Indian Giver," another goldrecord triumvirate. Like their labelmates, their mercurial chart run was history before 1969 was over. — *Bill Dahl*

● **Golden Classics** / 1994 / Collectables ◆◆◆◆

The Ohio Players

Soul, Funk

Originally formed in 1959 as an instrumental R&B group, Ohio Untouchables (as they were then known) provided backup on Falcons' records. After the Untouchables broke up, two of the members (Clarence "Satch" Satchell and Marshall "Rock" Jones) formed a new outfit called the Ohio Players and began working as the house band at Compass Records. In the early '70s, the Ohio Players had a steady stream of funky, sexual hit singles, including the No. 1 songs "Fire" and "Love Roller-coaster." As the decade progressed, their sound gradually transformed into a throbbing disco pulse and their sales slowly tapered off. — *Stephen Thomas Erlewine*

Pain / 1972 / Westbound ◆◆◆

Pleasure / 1973 / Westbound ◆◆◆

Climax / 1974 / Westbound ◆◆◆

Fire / 1974 / Mercury ◆◆◆◆
The Ohio Players peaked as a funk band with this record, which became their lone No. 1 pop hit. The title track was a No. 1 pop and R&B single, while "I Want to Be Free" was perhaps their best non-dance or novelty hit. The horn charts were catchy and energetic, guitarist Leroy Sugarfoot Bonner was in his prime, and the vocals were silly but hypnotic. — *Ron Wynn*

Skin Tight / 1974 / Mercury ◆◆◆◆
This earned the Ohio Players their first gold album, as well as a No. 2 R&B single with the title cut. The group was honing its punchy funk arrangements and exuberant vocal style, and "Skin Tight" was the first song since "Funky Worm" to earn both R&B and pop attention. It was also their debut album on Mercury, and it did so well that their old label Westbound rushed out a compilation of old cuts called *Climax*. — *Ron Wynn*

Honey / 1975 / Mercury ◆◆◆◆
A huge hit album and their second most successful LP ever, Honey peaked at the No. 2 spot on the R&B charts, although it didn't generate any pop action (none of their albums ever crossed over). The album cover, with its photo of a gorgeous woman having hot honey poured on her, wouldn't even make it to the drawing board today, and it generated a firestorm in the mid-'70s when it turned out that one of the women in the photo shoot got burned. Many think the title track was a hit, but it was actually the single "Sweet, Sticky Thing" that cemented the LP's hit status. That and "Love Rollercoaster" were R&B chart toppers; "Honey" didn't even chart. — *Ron Wynn*

★ **Ohio Players Gold** / 1976 / Mercury ◆◆◆◆◆
A strong overview of their biggest hits and best moments, including "Fire," "Fopp," "Skin Tight," and the shattering "Love Rollercoaster." — *Stephen Thomas Erlewine*

Angel / 1977 / Mercury ◆◆

Funk on Fire: The Mercury Anthology / 1995 / Mercury Funk Essentials ◆◆◆◆

The O'Jays

Soul, R&B, Urban, Philly Soul

Perhaps the reigning vocal group of the '70s and '80s, the O'Jays began in Canton as the Triumphs in 1958. The original lineup was Eddie Levert, Walter Williams, William Powell, Bobby Massey, and Bill Isles. They recorded as the Mascots for King in 1961 and were renamed by Cleveland disc jockey Eddie O'Jay. Isles departed in 1965 and Massey left in 1971 to become a producer, making the group a trio. They got their first chart single in 1963 for Imperial, for whom they recorded until 1967. The O'Jays' first major hit was "I'll Be Sweeter Tomorrow (Than I Was Today)" for Bell in 1967, which reached No. 8 on the R&B charts. They continued on Bell and Neptune until they attained stardom in 1972 on Philadelphia International. "Back Stabbers" was the first of eight No. 1 R&B hits they would get on the label from 1972-1987. Others included "Love Train," "Give the People What They Want," "I Love Music," "Livin' for the Week-end," "Message to Our Music," "Use Ta Be My Girl," "Darlin' Darlin' Baby

(Sweet, Tender, Love)," and "Lovin' You." They also had eight other Top Ten R&B hits and four other Top Ten pop smashes, while "Love Train" also topped the pop charts in 1973. They moved to EMI in 1987 and continued recording. Their most recent release was *Heartbreaker* in 1993. — *Ron Wynn*

O'Jays in Philadelphia / 1969 / Philadelphia International ◆◆◆◆
The O'Jays' first album with the Gamble-Huff production team was a landmark for all parties involved. A respected but journeyman soul outfit since the early '60s, the singers benefited immensely from distinctive, innovative production; in the O'Jays, Gamble and Huff found what may have been the best vehicle for framing their lush arrangements. Gamble and Huff wrote most of the material; Thom Bell handled about half the arrangements. There weren't any monster hits, but the result was considerably above the average late-'60s soul album, with strong songs and propulsive strings and brass that clearly blueprinted the Philadelphia soul sound. — *Richie Unterberger*

☆ **Back Stabbers** / 1972 / Philadelphia International ◆◆◆◆◆
Although you could lean toward *Ship Ahoy*, it would be hard to argue with the general assessment that this is their greatest album. Certainly no other single in 1973 was as transcendent and definitive as "Love Train," without question their greatest track. "Back Stabbers" isn't far behind; the message, harmonies, Eddie Levert's lead, and the group's refrains are all testimonies to soul's glory, and Gamble and Huff were in peak form. There were other good songs on the record, like "Listen to the Clock on the Wall" and "Shiftless, Shady, Jealous Kind of People," but they were completely blown away by "Love Train" and "Back Stabbers." — *Ron Wynn*

Ship Ahoy / 1973 / Philadelphia International ◆◆◆◆
The "other" O'Jays album masterpiece, *Ship Ahoy* combined shattering message tracks and stunning love songs in a fashion matched only by Curtis Mayfield's finest material. From the album cover showing a slave ship to the memorable title song and incredible "For the Love of Money," Gamble and Huff addressed every social ill from envy to racism to greed. Eddie Levert's leads were consistently magnificent, as were the harmonies, production, and arrangements. "Put Your Hands Together" and "You Got Your Hooks in Me" would be good album cuts, but on *Ship Ahoy* they were merely icing on the cake. — *Ron Wynn*

Survival / 1975 / Philadelphia International ◆◆◆◆
The O'Jays followed the spectacular *Back Stabbers* and *Ship Ahoy* with the good, but not on the same level, *Survival*. It was unrealistic to expect masterpieces every time out, and the LP included many strong ballads and good message tracks. But while it may not have been as epic in its performances and compositions, it was certainly the other albums' equal in sales strength. The group had two No. 1 R&B hits in 1975, "Give the People What They Want" and "I Love Music (Part 1)." In addition, the title track made the charts as the B-side to "Let Me Make Love to You," another rousing ballad. — *Ron Wynn*

Family Reunion / 1975 / Philadelphia International ◆◆◆

★ **Collector's Item** / 1977 / Philadelphia International ◆◆◆◆◆
After enjoying an impressive string of gold and platinum albums, the O'Jays had this collection of their biggest hits on Philadelphia International released in 1978. There was no way to lose with such songs as "Back Stabbers," "Love Train," "For the Love of Money," and "I Love Music." Unfortunately, Philadelphia International haphazardly sequenced the collection, ignoring chronological and stylistic considerations and just sticking tracks on the two sides without any attention to pacing. That gaffe aside, it's a worthy anthology for the casual listener, although the hardcore fan should look elsewhere. — *Ron Wynn*

So Full of Love / 1978 / Philadelphia International ◆◆◆

● **Greatest Hits** / 1984 / Philadelphia International ◆◆◆◆
When the O'Jays left Columbia for EMI, the company promptly issued this greatest hits package, although they opted to put fewer tracks on it than on the 1978 *Collector's Item*. So, the logical question would be, why would anyone want it? Probably because they've made *Collector's Item* extremely difficult to locate, and also because this mid-'80s release had better mastering of such seminal O'Jays items as "Love Train" and "For the Love of Money." While it has gaping holes as a single-disc anthology, this release provides an acceptable overview of the group's Epic/Philadelphia International/TSOP material. — *Ron Wynn*

● **Love Train: The Best of the O'Jays** / Aug. 9, 1994 / Epic/Legacy ◆◆◆
All of the band's monster 1972-76 Philadelphia International hits are here, as well as a couple of small ones. The essay by Robert Palmer is good, but at a mere ten tracks, the selection is unaccountably skimpy. — *Richie Unterberger*

● **Give the People What They Want** / 1995 / Epic/Legacy ◆◆◆
Give the People What They Want collects 11 of the O'Jays' politically oriented songs, including the hit title song and "Ship Ahoy." Since most of these tracks were not singles, it's a good supplement to an O'Jays' greatest-hits collection. — *Stephen Thomas Erlewine*

Let Me Make Love to You / Jan. 24, 1995 / Epic/Legacy ✦✦✦
Like *Give the People What They Want, Let Me Make Love to You* is a concept compilation, collecting ten of the O'Jays' most underappreciated love ballads, including the title track, which was a minor hit, "Stairway to Heaven," and "Listen to the Clock on the Wall." Again, the disc is not a hits collection, but a sampling of some of the group's finest album tracks and forgotten singles, and in that context, it's very enjoyable. — *Stephen Thomas Erlewine*

In Bed with the O'Jays: Greatest Love Songs / Aug. 20, 1996 / Capitol ✦✦✦✦
In Bed with the O'Jays: Greatest Love Songs is the first compilation to draw from songs the O'Jays recorded for both Philadelphia International and EMI. That doesn't mean it's a comprehensive collection, however. As the title implies, *In Bed with the O'Jays* draws strictly from the group's romantic ballads, ignoring such hit singles and groundbreaking songs as "Back Stabbers," "Love Train," and "For the Love of Money." Instead, this disc is nothing but quiet storm and smooth grooves. As a compilation of the latter half of the group's career and their romantic material, *In Bed with the O'Jays* is excellent, since it contains everything from 1976's "Darlin' Darlin' Baby (Sweet, Tender, Love)" to 1987's "Lovin' You." If you're not expecting to hear their more political and funky material, *In Bed* will not disappoint. — *Stephen Thomas Erlewine*

The Only Ones

Punk, New Wave, Power-Pop
Led by the raffish and slightly scuzzy romance-obsessed Peter Perrett, the Only Ones were one of the punk era's most underrated bands. Not as confrontational as the Sex Pistols, as politically indulgent as the Clash, or as stripped down as the Ramones, the Only Ones played not-so-fast guitar rock that sounded deeply indebted to the New York Dolls and other mid-'70s proto-punks. Singing his intelligently crafted pop songs in a semituneful whine of a voice and backed by a band that effectively combined youthful exuberance with gracefully aging veterans (nonpunk drummer Mike Kellie had done time with early-'70s clod-rockers Spooky Tooth, bassist Alan Mair was nearly 40!), Perrett was an astute chronicler of the vagaries of modern, dysfunctional love. Despite a career that lasted from 1978-1981 and one certifiable "hit" song to their credit (the brilliant "Another Girl, Another Planet"), the Only Ones became the archetypal contenders that never broke big, despite assurances from fans and critics that they couldn't miss.

Although they split up in 1981 after only three records, the Only Ones, due in large part to "Another Girl, Another Planet," became more influential than one would have guessed. Listen to Paul Westerberg and you'll hear more than a little Peter Perrett (in fact, the Replacements covered "Another Girl"); look at the number of Only Ones releases over the past decade (a half-dozen at least) and you soon realize that a significant cult surrounding the band grew after their breakup. Ironically, it was the posthumous release of the sessions for John Peel's BBC show that, more than any of the proper studio releases, accurately displayed the muscle and smarts of this fine band. There have been many rumors surrounding Perrett's life after the Only Ones, many of them involving an alleged heroin addiction. In 1996, he re-emerged with a solo album. — *John Dougan*

The Only Ones / Apr. 1978 / CBS ✦✦✦✦
"Another Girl, Another Planet" is here, but then again, it surfaces on a number of Only Ones records. The best of their studio releases, this record is a tuneful anomaly of mid-'70s rock that stands in stark contrast to the prevailing punk zeitgeist. Still, the band (even the old guys) play with an infectious enthusiasm, and, Perrett, despite his tendency toward adenoidal Dylanesque vocals, is particularly winning. — *John Dougan*

● **Special View** / 1979 / Epic ✦✦✦✦
In America, Epic couldn't decide whether or not to release any Only Ones recordings, so they came up with this halfway measure: a sampler. *Special View* took the strongest tracks from their debut, added tracks from their so-so second album, *Even Serpents Shine*, and the result was (surprise) a great record. All these years later, *Special View* is as good a sampler of early Only Ones as anyone could have hoped for and should be considered an important purchase, although I think it's no longer in print. — *John Dougan*

Peel Sessions / 1989 / Dutch East India ✦✦✦✦
Frankly, one could argue an eloquent case either way as to why *Special View* or the *Peel Sessions* are the most important Only Ones recordings. I tend to recommend the *Peel Sessions*, because it's rougher, a little meaner, and the Only Ones were in the midst of their 15 minutes of fame as a rock band; plus, there's a swagger here that's missing on other recordings. — *John Dougan*

Live / 1989 / Edsel ✦✦

Opal

Alternative Pop-Rock, Psychedelic
The neo-psychedelic group Opal formed in the mid-'80s, featuring former Rain Parade guitarist David Roback and former Dream Syndicate bassist Kendra Smith. Initially, the group was called Clay Allison, yet the group dropped the name after one single; Roback, Smith, and drummer Keith Mitchell released the remaining Clay Allison tracks underneath their own name in 1984, on the *Fell from the Sun* EP. After its release, the group adopted the name Opal and released an EP, *Northern Line*, in 1985. *Happy Nightmare Baby*, their first full-length album, followed in 1987. Smith left the group during the *Happy Nightmare* tour, effectively putting an end to the band. Roback continued with vocalist Hope Sandoval; the group then metamorphosed into Mazzy Star. — *Stephen Thomas Erlewine*

Orb

Ambient, Techno, Trance
Originating from Dr. Alex Paterson's ambient-house sets at a popular London chill-out club with Jimmy Cauty of the KLF, the Orb resurrected slower, more soulful, electronic rhythms (reminiscent of Pink Floyd and Tangerine Dream) on their debut LP, *The Orb's Adventures Beyond the Ultraworld*. With partner Kris Weston (aka Thrash), Paterson gained an audience with "Little Fluffy Clouds." A welcome turn for frenzied club-kids worn out by years of harsh techno, The Orb's live dates featured amazing light shows, visuals, and a relaxed, positive vibe rarely found in previous electronic circles. *U.F.Orb*, released in 1992, continued the Orb's popularity. As the ambient-house genre began to take off, though, the duo were grounded by legal trouble with their label, Big Life, and spent almost two years trying to sever ties with the company.

The Orb finally reemerged in 1994 with the EP *Pomme Fritz* and an album the following year, *Orbvs Terrarvm*. While ambient-house has spawned legions of imitators, including many new-age bandwagon-jumpers, the Orb moves on, restless to explore new vistas of sound and rhythm. — *John Bush*

● **The Adventures Beyond Ultraworld** / 1991 / Big Life ✦✦✦✦
The Orb's first full-length album expands on the strengths of their debut EP, resulting in one of the most compulsively listenable techno albums ever recorded. — *Stephen Thomas Erlewine*

U.F.Orb / Mar. 1992 / Big Life ✦✦✦✦
So far, the Orb hasn't made an album better than *U.F.Orb*, a hypnotic series of trance-inducing rhythms and interweaving synths that never grows boring, even at its 74-minute length. — *Stephen Thomas Erlewine*

Live 93 / 1993 / Island ✦✦✦✦
Although the thought of an Orb live album may raise some eyebrows, the resulting two-CD set is amazing, a complete representation of the group in concert and living proof that techno is indeed a live, as well as recorded, art form. Besides, the consistent Pink Floyd jokes on the record (as well as the brilliant cover art) are hilarious. — *Stephen Thomas Erlewine*

Pomme Fritz / 1994 / Island Red ✦✦

Orbvs Terrarvm / Apr. 4, 1995 / Island ✦✦✦

Roy Orbison

b. Apr. 23, 1936, Vernon, TX, d. Dec. 6, 1988, Hendersonville, TN
Guitar, Vocals / Rock 'n' Roll, Rockabilly, Pop, Pop-Rock
Although he shared the same rockabilly roots as Carl Perkins, Johnny Cash, and Elvis Presley, Roy Orbison went on to pioneer an entirely different brand of country/pop-based rock 'n' roll in the early '60s. What he lacked in charisma and photogenic looks, Orbison made up for in spades with his quavering operatic voice and melodramatic narratives of unrequited love and yearning. In the process, he established rock 'n' roll archetypes of the underdog and the hopelessly romantic loser. These were not only amplified by peers such as Del Shannon and Gene Pitney, but also influenced future generations of roots rockers such as Bruce Springsteen and Chris Isaak, as well as current country stars the Mavericks.

Orbison made his first widely distributed recordings for Sun Records in 1956. He was a capable rockabilly singer and had a small national hit with his first Sun single, "Ooby Dooby." But even then, Orbison was far more comfortable as a ballad singer than as a hepped-up rockabilly jive cat. Other Sun singles met with no success, and by the late '50s, he was concentrating primarily on building a career as a songwriter, his biggest early success being "Claudette" (recorded by the Everly Brothers).

After a brief, unsuccessful stint with RCA, Orbison finally found his voice with Monument Records, scoring a No. 2 hit in 1960 with "Only the Lonely." This established the Roy Orbison persona for good: a brooding rockaballad of failed love with a sweet, haunting melody, enhanced by his Caruso-like vocal trills at the song's emotional climax. These and his subsequent Monument hits also boasted innovative, quasisymphonic production, with Orbison's voice and guitar backed by surging strings, ominous drum rolls, and heavenly choirs of backup vocalists.

Between 1960 and 1965, Orbison would have 15 Top 40 hits for Monument, including such nail-biting minidramas as "Running Scared,"

"Crying," "In Dreams," and "It's Over." Not just a singer of tear-jerking ballads, he was also capable of effecting a tough, bluesy swagger on "Dream Baby," "Candy Man," and "Mean Woman Blues." In fact, his biggest and best hit was also his hardest-rocking: "Oh, Pretty Woman" soared to No. 1 in late 1964, at the peak of the British Invasion.

It seemed at that time that Roy was well-equipped to survive the British onslaught of the mid-'60s. He had even toured with the Beatles in Britain in 1963, and John Lennon has admitted trying to emulate Orbison when writing the Beatles' first British chart-topper, "Please Please Me." But Orbison's fortunes declined rapidly after he left Monument for MGM in 1965. It would be easy to say that the major label couldn't replicate the unique production values of the classic Monument singles, but that's only part of the story. Orbison, after all, was still writing most of his material, and his early MGM records were produced in a style that closely approximated the Monument era. The harder truth to face was that his songs were sounding to start like lesser variations of themselves, and that contemporary trends in rock and soul were making him sound outdated.

Orbison, like many early rock greats, could always depend on large overseas audiences to pay the bills. The two decades between the mid-'60s and mid-'80s were undeniably tough ones for him, though, both personally and professionally. A late-'60s stab at acting failed miserably. In 1966, his wife died in a motorcycle accident; a couple of years later, his house burned down, two of his sons perishing in the flames. Periodic comeback attempts with desultory albums in the 1970s came to naught.

Orbison's return to the public eye came about through unexpected circumstances. In the mid-'80s, David Lynch's *Blue Velvet* film prominently featured "In Dreams" on its soundtrack. That led to the singer making an entire album of re-recordings of hits, with T-Bone Burnett acting as producer. The record was no subsitute for the originals, but it did help restore him to prominence within the industry. Shortly afterward, he joined George Harrison, Bob Dylan, Tom Petty, and Jeff Lynne in the Traveling Wilburys. Their successful album set the stage for Orbison's best album in over 20 years, *Mystery Girl*, which emulated the sound of his classic 1960s work without sounding hackneyed. By the time it reached the charts in early 1989, however, Orbison was dead, claimed by a heart attack in December 1988. —*Richie Unterberger*

Crying / 1962 / Sony ♦♦

There Is Only One / 1965 / PolyGram ♦♦

Fastest Guitar Alive / 1968 / Columbia Special Products ♦♦

All-Time Greatest Hits of Roy Orbison / 1976 / Monument ♦♦♦♦
All-Time Greatest Hits of Roy Orbison is an essential collection. It rounds up 20 of the Big O's best '60s recordings, with some fine album tracks thrown in. —*John Floyd*

★ **For the Lonely: 18 Greatest Hits** / 1988 / Rhino ♦♦♦♦♦
This compilation offers the usual Monument hits along with a few Sun tunes. Buyers beware: The vinyl version contains more cuts than the CD. —*John Floyd*

The Legendary Roy Orbison / 1988 / Sony ♦♦♦♦
While the Rhino set *For the Lonely: 18 Greatest Hits*, is the most essential single-disc release of Orbison's work, *The Legendary Roy Orbison* tries to flesh out the picture considerably with a four-disc, 75-track boxed set. It may be overkill for some, and certain tracks feel like pointless inclusions, but fans who want more than just a hits collection should like this set. The enclosed booklet contains a wealth of photos and the annotation is informative. —*Rick Clark*

The Classic Roy Orbison (1965-1968) / 1989 / Rhino ♦♦♦
The hits dried up when Orbison left the Monument label for MGM in 1965. The 14 recordings here, taken from singles and LP tracks, feature arrangements and production not far removed from his classic Monument era. The singing is wonderful, but stacked up against his classic hits, a lot is missing. Lacking the ace songwriting of his best work, there's lots of midtempo, melodramatic rock balladry here, but somehow nothing nearly as gripping as his best compositions. —*Richie Unterberger*

Mystery Girl / 1989 / Virgin ♦♦♦♦
Roy's comeback is remarkable in that every song, from "You Got It" to "She's a Mystery to Me" to "The Only One," proves that the formula of his '60s stuff is still vital 30 years later. —*John Floyd*

The Sun Years 1956-58 / Apr. 1989 / Bear Family ♦♦♦♦
It contains Orbison's complete Sun output, featuring many undubbed recordings and the pile-driving "Domino." —*John Floyd*

Orchestral Manoeuvres in the Dark

Synth-Pop, New Wave, Club-Dance, New Romantic
Featuring core members Paul Humphreys and Andy McCluskey, the Liverpudlian synth-pop group Orchestral Manoeuvers in the Dark formed in the late '70s. Humphreys and McCluskey began performing together in school, playing in the bands VCL XI, Hitlerz Underpantz, and the Id. After the Id split in 1978, McCluskey was with Dalek I Love You for a

brief time. Once he left Dalek, he joined with Humphreys and Paul Collister to form Orchestral Manoeuvres in the Dark. The group released their first single, "Electricity," on Factory Records; the record led to a contract with the Virgin subsidiary DinDisc. Using their record advance, McCluskey and Humphreys built a studio, which allowed them to replace their four-track recorded with drummer Malcolm Holmes (formerly of the Id) and Dave Hughes (formerly of Dalek I Love You).

In 1980, the group released their self-titled debut album, which featured the UK Top Ten single "Enola Gay." *Organisation* appeared the same year; Hughes was replaced by Martin Cooper after its release. The band's next few albums—*Architecture and Morality* (1981), *Dazzle Ships* (1983), *Junk Culture* (1984)—found the band experimenting with their sound, resulting in several UK hit singles. Recorded with two new members, Graham and Neil Weir, *Crush*, their most pop-oriented album, found more success in America than in Britain, as the single "So in Love" hit No. 26 on the charts. "If You Leave," taken from the *Pretty in Pink* soundtrack, was their biggest American hit, climbing to No. 4 in 1986. *The Pacific Age* was released the same year, yet America was the only country where it was popular. Shortly after its release, the Weir brothers left the band, followed by Holmes, Cooper, and Humphreys. McCluskey continued on, releasing *Sugar Task* in 1991; in the meantime, Humphreys formed the Listening Pool. —*Stephen Thomas Erlewine*

● **The Best of O.M.D.** / 1988 / A&M ♦♦♦♦

The Originals

Soul, Motown
Detroit soul vocal group. Led by Freddie Gorman, the Originals took the R&B world by storm in 1969, although they had worked at Motown for years as invaluable background vocalists. Gorman recorded as a solo for Berry Gordy in 1961 and co-wrote "Please Mr. Postman" for the Marvelettes, and the Originals cut a version of Leadbelly's "Goodnight Irene" for Gordy's Soul subsidiary in 66 with ex-Falcon Joe Stubbs as lead. But Stubbs had split to form 100 Proof Aged in Soul by the time the quartet waxed the beautiful doo wop throwback "Baby I'm for Real," an R&B chart-topper in 1969 that was co-written and lushly produced by Marvin Gaye. The same combination also produced "The Bells," another major hit in 1970. Former solo act Ty Hunter joined the group in 1971, and the Originals continued to chart into the next decade. —*Bill Dahl*

● **Motown Superstar Series, Vol. 10** / 1976 / Motown ♦♦♦♦
The Detroit-based Originals began singing in 1966, with tenor vocalists Crathman Spencer and Henry Dixon, bassist Freddie Gorman, and baritone Walter Gaines. Marvin Gaye helped bring them to Motown and later wrote or co-wrote three of their singles, including the anthemic "Baby, I'm for Real." That single, their other major hit, "The Bells," and the third Gaye single, "We Can Make It Baby," are among the tunes on this anthology. They weren't a great group, but their two hits are as gripping and wonderfully produced and arranged as any Motown material. —*Ron Wynn*

The Orioles

R&B, Doo Wop
Led by Sonny Til, the Orioles were the first African American vocal group to sing music directly for a Black audience. Through their early recordings—which were made in the late '40s and early '50s—the band laid the groundwork for R&B vocal groups and doo wop. The Orioles fused traditional pop songs with gospel sensibilities and arranged blues and gospel material with smooth harmonies, designed to appeal to the broadest audience possible.

Based in Baltimore, the Orioles consisted of lead vocalist Sonny Til (born Earlington Carl Tilghman, Aug. 18, 1928; d. Dec. 9, 1981), Alexander Sharp (tenor vocals), George Nelson (baritone vocals), Johnny Reed (bass vocals), and guitarist Tommy Gaither. Originally called the Vibranaires, the group formed when its members were teenagers. They came to the attention of Deborah Chessler, a local merchant whoalso wrote songs; she would write many of the group's subsequent hits. Chessler became the band's manager and was able to get the Vibranaires a spot on Arthur Godfrey's "Talent Scouts" TV show. Although the group lost to pianist George Shearing, they caught the eye of Jerry Blaine, a New York record company executive, while they were in town for the program.

Jerry Blaine signed the group to his newly created It's a Natural record label and had the band cut "It's Too Soon to Know," a ballad written by Chessler. After they signed their deal with It's a Natural, the band changed its name to the Orioles. In the late summer of 1948, "It's Too Soon to Know" was released on It's a Natural. Shortly after the single's release Blaine complained about the name of his new label, so he re-released the song on Jubilee Records, a record label he had previously used to release Yiddish comedy records. "It's Too Soon to Know" became a No. 1 R&B hit and crossed over to No. 13 on the pop charts. At the time of its release, no African American group had managed to cross over to the pop charts with what was then known as a "race" record. The Orioles immediately followed the success of their debut single with the seasonal "(It's Gonna Be a) Lonely Christmas," which reached the R&B Top Ten at the end of 1948.

"Tell Me So" became the Orioles' second No. 1 R&B hit in the spring of 1949, beginning a streak of six hit R&B singles that year. In addition to "Tell Me So," the group charted with "A Kiss and a Rose" (No. 12, late summer), "I Challenge Your Kiss (No. 11, fall)," "Forgive and Forget" (No. 5, fall), a re-released "(It's Gonna Be a) Lonely Christmas" (No. 5, winter), and the B-side of "Lonely Christmas," "What Are You Doing New Year's Eve" (No. 9, winter).

Following their peak year of 1949, the group ran into tragedy. In 1950, Gaither, Nelson, and Reed were in an automobile accident that killed Gaither and severely injured the other two members; Nelson quit the group later that year. As Reed recovered from the accident, the group found replacements for Gaither and Nelson, finally settling on guitarist Ralph Williams and vocalist Gregory Carroll. The new lineup of the band had its first hit in 1952, when "Baby Please Don't Go" reached No. 8 on the R&B charts. The following year, the group had their biggest hit with "Crying in the Chapel." Released in the summer of 1963, "Crying in the Chapel" spent five weeks on the R&B charts and reached No. 11 on the pop charts, eventually going gold; Elvis Presley had a hit with the song 12 years later. Toward the end of the year, the group had another Top Ten R&B hit with "In the Mission of St. Augustine." The single would turn out to be their last hit.

In 1954, the Orioles began to splinter, as Sharp and Reed left to join the Ink Spots. Sonny Til assembled a new lineup, but the group didn't gain much attention. Til continued to lead various incarnations of the Orioles, performing concerts and re-recording the group's old hits, until his death in 1981. George Nelson died sometime in 1959 and Alexander Sharp died in the early '70s.

In 1995, 40 years after the original lineup of the group disbanded, the Orioles were inducted into the Rock & Roll Hall of Fame. — *Stephen Thomas Erlewine*

Jubilee Sides / 1993 / Bear Family ♦♦♦♦
This exhaustive six-CD box set shows you all the reasons why the Orioles, led by smooth-as-silk vocalist Sonny Til, were one of the most pivotal, if not the most important, of all the early Black vocal groups. The group's honey-smooth harmonies perfectly frame Til's soaring, sexy vocals against the simplest of backgrounds on their earliest sides, while later sessions with full orchestras surprisingly do little to intrude, with interesting results. With typical Bear Family completeness, this rounds up everything the group cut for Natural-Jubilee from two different tenures with the label. — *Cub Koda*

★ **Sing Their Greatest Hits** / Collectables ♦♦♦♦♦
This Orioles hit package is about equal to any other that's available, but pales next to the Bear Family boxed set. The now defunct Murray Hill also had a great Orioles box several years ago. Save your money and grab the Bear Family recording if you want the real story on the Orioles. — *Ron Wynn*

Ozzy Osbourne (John Osbourne)

b. Dec. 3, 1948, Birmingham, England
Vocals / Hard Rock, Heavy Metal
Ozzy Osbourne has been ridiculed over the years, yet he has had an immeasurable effect on heavy metal, while he was in Black Sabbath and as a solo artist. Osbourne doesn't have a great voice—it's thin and it doesn't have much range—yet he has a good ear and great dramatic flair. Over the course of his career, his band has featured some of the most innovative and distinctive guitarists in hard rock, including the late Randy Rhoads. As a showman, Osbourne's instincts are nearly as impeccable; his live shows have been overwrought spectacles with gore and glitz that have endeared him to adolescents around the world. Indeed, Osbourne has managed to establish himself as an international superstar, capable of selling millions of records with each album and packing arenas across the world, capturing new fans with each release.

Ozzy Osbourne began his professional career with Black Sabbath, who released their first album in 1970. Throughout the '70s, the group carved out a distinctive brand of slow, gloomy heavy metal that became the essence of metal for many listeners. Osbourne left the band in 1979, embarking on a solo career. Supported by a band featuring ex-Uriah Heep drummer Lee Kerslake, former Rainbow bassist Bob Daisley, and ex-Quiet Riot guitarist Randy Rhoads, the singer recorded *Blizzard of Ozz;* the group would adopt the album's title as their name. Released in 1981, *Blizzard of Ozz* had some of the same ingredients of Black Sabbath—the lyrics focused on the occult, and the guitars were loud and heavy—yet he was supported by a group that was more technically proficient and capable of varying the standard metal formulas. The record hit No. 7 on the UK charts; it peaked at No. 21 in the US, staying on the charts for over two years and going platinum. Before the band began their first US tour in 1981, Kerslake and Daisley left the band; they were replaced by former Pat Travers Band drummer Tommy Aldridge and ex-

Quiet Riot bassist Rudy Sarzo. This is the group that recorded Osbourne's second album, *Diary of a Madman;* the album charted at No. 16 in the US and also became a platinum seller. Following its release, Daisley returned to the group and Aldridge left; former Rainbow keyboardist Don Airey was added to the lineup at this time, as well.

During Osbourne's 1982 tour, guitarist Randy Rhoads died in a bizarre plane accident, leaving a gaping hole in Osbourne's band, since Rhoads essentially determined the musical direction of the group. He was replaced by Brad Gillis, a former member of Night Ranger. Gillis' first record with Osbourne was *Speak of the Devil,* a live album of Black Sabbath material released to combat Sabbath's live album, *Live at Last.* After the release of *Speak of the Devil,* Osbourne reshaped the lineup of his band, adding guitarist Jake E. Lee. The new group recorded *Bark at the Moon,* which repeated the success of the first two records. For the rest of the decade, Osbourne's band continued to change, yet the only lineup changes that mattered were the guitarists. Lee left the band in 1987 and was replaced by Zakk Wylde, who led Osbourne's group into the '90s. Even as Osbourne approached his 50th birthday, he remained one of the biggest stars in heavy metal. — *Stephen Thomas Erlewine*

Blizzard of Ozz / 1981 / Jet ♦♦♦♦
Osbourne's solo debut not only re-established him as a viable attraction, it also introduced the ample talents of guitarist Randy Rhoads, whose classically influenced style had a huge impact on rock guitar in the '80s. Say what you will about Ozzy Osbourne, but the music here is simply great: Osbourne-Rhoads collaborations like "Crazy Train," "Mr. Crowley," and "Revelation (Mother Earth)" still stand today as all-time heavy-metal classics. — *Steve Huey*

Diary of a Madman / 1981 / Jet ♦♦♦♦
The follow-up was rushed, and it shows: Rhoads didn't even have time to lay down a real solo on "Little Dolls" (the solo used was intended only as a guide). Even so, his classical training manifests itself even more, and the compositions generally increase in sophistication (especially the epic title track). One wonders how much the Osbourne-Rhoads combination would have accomplished had Rhoads not been killed in a plane crash five months after this recording. — *Steve Huey*

Speak of the Devil / 1982 / Jet ♦♦♦
A live album recorded from Osbourne's 1982 tour, it features powerful new versions of Black Sabbath classics. It caused a minor controversy, since Sabbath (with Ronnie James Dio as vocalist) released their first live album (*Live Evil*) at the same time, also with early Black Sabbath material. Osbourne's band at the time featured drummer Tommy Aldridge (now with House of Lords), Night Ranger guitarist Brad Gillis, and bassist Rudy Sarzo, later a member of Whitesnake. (Sarzo was also a founding member of Quiet Riot, an early incarnation of which featured a young guitarist named Randy Rhoads.) — *John Book*

● **Tribute** / 1987 / Epic ♦♦♦♦
This live double album, released five years after Randy Rhoads' death, showcases a hard-rock guitarist whose all-around ability was arguably second only to Eddie Van Halen. Osbourne leads his best band lineup through the entire *Blizzard* repertoire, plus a few *Diary* and Sabbath numbers. Of special note are Rhoads' unaccompanied solos, leaving no doubts about his virtuosity, and the studio outtakes of his short solo piece, "Dee." Rhoads' entire output is essential for guitar freaks, but he sounds even better live than in the studio. — *Steve Huey*

No More Tears / 1991 / Epic ♦♦♦♦
While looking for fresh inspiration, Osbourne started writing songs with Motörhead's Lemmy Kilmister, the kind of collaboration metal fans dream about. As a result, the songs on *No More Tears* are more compact, the sound denser, the musical payoffs more immediate. And not that Osbourne's mellowing in old age or anything, but *No More Tears* contains two of his best ballads—"Mama, I'm Coming Home" and "Time After Time." — *Brian Mansfield*

Ozzmosis / Oct. 24, 1995 / Epic ♦♦

The Palace Brothers

Alternative Pop-Rock, Indie Rock, Alternative Country-Rock
Known alternately as Palace, Palace Songs, and the Palace Brothers, this outfit is the project of guitarist/vocalist Will Oldham. The Palace Brothers takes the harsher side of country and folk and reworks it into devastatingly spare, intense indie-rock. Oldham's voice whimpers and whines like a centegenarian, and the simplicity and effortlessness of the songs suggest that they are timeless. While the Palace Brothers are definitely a high concept group, the music speaks for itself. — *Heather Phares*

There Is No-One What Will Take Care of You / Jun. 14, 1993 / Drag City ♦♦♦
The name says it all. Dramatic, desperate country-indie rock that focuses on the dark side of life. — *Heather Phares*

● **Palace Brothers [EP]** / 1994 / Drag City ♦♦♦♦
Oldham's second EP is even more spartan and gaunt-sounding than Palace's debut. Strumming away on an acoustic guitar, his feeble voice

barely topping a whisper, Oldham croaks out tunes of quiet despair like "Pushkin" and "I Am a Cinematographer." —*Heather Phares*

Viva Last Blues / 1995 / Drag City ✦✦✦
Viva Last Blues continues Oldham and company's trend of spare acoustic tunes with sad, world-weary themes. Palace seems to be refining and honing both their playing and songwriting skills with each album. —*Heather Phares*

Arise Therefore / Apr. 1996 / Drag City ✦✦✦✦
Once again Will Oldham emerges out of the murky, Midwestern haze with another helping of lovely, low-key musings on his fourth full-length album, *Arise Therefore*, this time recorded under the name Palace Music (previously the Palace Brothers, Palace Songs, or just plain Palace). Much quieter than last year's *Viva Last Blues*, and less Appalachian in its folk-spirit than Palace's earlier music, the songs on *Arise Therefore* shift and moan with breathy cracks and shivers, Oldham's meandering, poet-speak vocals and guitar accompanied by Ned's bass, David Grubbs' piano, and (surprise!) a Maya Tone drum machine. The lyrics (included for the first time) are beautiful in their stark, pale honesty as often as they are indecipherable. "I watch things painted on public walls, now but I see other things as well, behind but right fuck in front of my spirit is how the real road's laid out in a line," he sings on "Kid of Harith." Don't ask for an interpretation: it will come with time, or it won't. —*Kurt Wolff*

Robert Palmer

b. Jan. 19, 1949
Vocals / Pop-Rock
British singer (and occasional songwriter), with a strong taste for R&B, Caribbean, New Orleans, and other rhythmic styles. He made a series of well-received albums in the '70s but finally broke through commercially in the '80s, singing in the Duran Duran side-project band Power Station and later on his own. —*William Ruhlmann*

Sneakin' Sally Through the Alley / 1974 / Island ✦✦✦✦
On his debut solo album, Palmer employs members of the Meters and Little Feat for a musical gumbo enriched by his husky, percussive voice. —*William Ruhlmann*

Pressure Drop / 1976 / Island ✦✦✦✦
Palmer's own songs (especially the silky "Give Me an Inch" and "Work to Make It Work") and the backing of Little Feat help make this a worthy followup to *Sally*. —*William Ruhlmann*

Some People Can Do What They Like / 1976 / Island ✦✦✦✦
Palmer's "Keep in Touch," "Man Smart, Woman Smarter," and "Spanish Moon" (the latter by Little Feat's Lowell George) pace *Some People Can Do What They Like*, another terrific collection. —*William Ruhlmann*

Double Fun / 1978 / Island ✦✦✦

Secrets / 1979 / Island ✦✦✦✦
Palmer scores his biggest hit single of the '70s with the uptempo rocker "Bad Case of Loving You (Doctor, Doctor)" on an album that also includes a wonderful version of Todd Rundgren's ballad "Can We Still Be Friends." —*William Ruhlmann*

Clues / 1980 / Island ✦✦✦

Maybe It's Live / 1982 / Island ✦✦

Pride / 1983 / Island ✦✦

Riptide / Nov. 1985 / Island ✦✦✦✦
Palmer's commercial breakthrough, much of it in the hard rock style of his one-shot band Power Station, featuring the hits "Discipline of Love," "Addicted to Love" (a No. 1 hit), "Hyperactive," and "I Didn't Mean to Turn You On." —*William Ruhlmann*

Heavy Nova / Jun. 1988 / EMI America ✦✦

● **Addictions, Vol. 1** / 1989 / Island ✦✦✦✦
Thirteen-track compilation containing Palmer's biggest hits, not only the ones on Island but also the Power Station singles and "Simply Irresistible," from Palmer's first EMI album. —*William Ruhlmann*

Don't Explain / 1990 / EMI America ✦✦

Addictions, Vol. 2 / May 5, 1992 / Island ✦✦✦
Apart from "I Didn't Mean to Turn You On," there are no big hits, only album tracks and failed singles, all of which are quite good. Unfortunately, the majority of the material has been remixed, remade, or has new vocal tracks; the album may sound great, but it isn't an accurate retrospective. —*Stephen Thomas Erlewine*

Pantera

Heavy Metal
Pantera's massively brutal, aggressive, jagged heavy metal earned them a large cult following in the early '90s. During the early '80s, the band explored several different styles of hard rock; sometimes they sounded like Kiss and Aerosmith, other times like Def Leppard. After several

years of struggling, the band changed their tune in 1988, becoming rougher and harder, much like Metallica. Guitarist Diamond Darrell (aka "Dimebag") rejected an offer to join Megadeth, concentrating on Pantera's new direction. The change in style proved successful; 1992's *Vulgar Display of Power* became an underground metal hit, eventually scaling *Billboard*'s Top 50. When their new album *Far Beyond Driven* was released in 1994, the band debuted at No. 1. Some chart-watchers were surprised, but anyone that followed their rise from obscurity to *Vulgar Display of Power* knew that Pantera was one of the most popular metal bands of the early '90s. *Great Southern Trendkill* was released in May 1996. —*Stephen Thomas Erlewine*

Cowboys from Hell / 1990 / East West ✦✦✦✦
Technical thrash from Texas, this is the album that put them in the spotlight and opened the door for thrash bands who were a little different. —*John Book*

● **Vulgar Display of Power** / 1992 / East West ✦✦✦✦
A burning, disemboweling collection of brutal riffs, pulverizing speed, and hoarse, shouted vocals, *Vulgar Display of Power* is the record that established Pantera as the most vicious and popular heavy metal band of the early '90s. —*Stephen Thomas Erlewine*

Far Beyond Driven / 1994 / East West ✦✦✦

Great Southern Trendkill / May 1996 / Atlantic ✦✦✦

Graham Parker

b. Nov. 15, 1950
Guitar, Vocals / Rock 'n' Roll, New Wave, Pop-Rock, Pub-Rock
Graham Parker is the quintessential angry young man; his early albums are full of righteous passion, vicious sarcasm, and great, powerful rock 'n' roll. Graham Parker is also the quintessential bitter old man; while the occasional good song pops up here and there, his later albums are weighed down by petty anger, disgust, and frustration. But when he was at the top of his form in the late '70s, Parker was a singer-songwriter like no other. Backed by his superb band the Rumour, he turned out a series of clever, concise songs that bristled with energy; his songs drew heavily from R&B, rock 'n' roll, and rockabilly without ever sounding dated. Parker's music sounded vital because of his unrestrained passion, as well as the way his lyrics and song structures redefined and subverted the traditions of the '50s and '60s.

Howlin' Wind, his 1976 debut album, earned him scores of lavish critical praise, as did its follow-up, *Heat Treatment*, released the same year. In 1977, he formed the Rumour and released the inconsistent, but occasionally exceptional *Stick to Me*. Parker left Mercury in 1978, leading to his classic attack on the record label, "Mercury Poisoning"; the company rushed out a live album to fulfill his contract. With 1979's *Squeezing Out Sparks* in 1979, Parker had made his finest record; again, he received an overwhelming amount of critical acclaim but no sales.

After *Squeezing Out Sparks*, Parker began to sink into his own cynicism as he tried to refashion his sound for the mainstream marketplace; he had only one hit from the four albums he released between 1980 and 1985—"Wake Up (Next to You)" in 1985. Following that minor chart success, his songs became more direct, as shown by 1988's *Mona Lisa's Sister*, the best thing he had released in years. It began a string of strong albums that were sometimes undone by his own relentless pessimism. By this time, the anger that fueled his early records had turned into mere bitterness. However, when Parker can keep his sniping to a minimum, he is as good as he has ever been. —*Stephen Thomas Erlewine*

☆ **Howlin' Wind** / Jul. 1976 / Mercury ✦✦✦✦✦
Parker comes across as both tough-minded and optimistic (maybe the word is "determined") on his debut album, on which he sings with conviction against the cohesive backing of the Rumour. —*William Ruhlmann*

Heat Treatment / Oct. 1976 / Mercury ✦✦✦✦
Essentially *Howlin' Wind, Vol. 2*, as Parker and the Rumour demonstrate that their initial burst of high-quality songs can extend to a second album, in the same year as their debut. —*William Ruhlmann*

Stick to Me / Oct. 1977 / Mercury ✦✦✦✦
Graham Parker and the Rumour's third new studio album to be released in 18 months finds the bandleader running short of top-flight material; "Thunder and Rain" and "Watch the Moon Come Down" are up to his usual standards, but songs like "The Heat in Harlem" find him dangerously out of his depth. As a result, although fiercely played, this star-crossed release (it had to be re-recorded when the first version suffered technical problems) is a cut below Parker's first two albums. —*William Ruhlmann*

The Parkerilla/Live / 1978 / Mercury ✦✦

☆ **Squeezing Out Sparks** / Mar. 1979 / Arista ✦✦✦✦✦
Older and more bitter, Parker unleashes his deeper demons, and the Rumour just plays harder. Parker's best album, and one of the best albums of the decade. —*William Ruhlmann*

The Up Escalator / May 1980 / Arista ✦✦✦✦
On his last album with the Rumour, Parker goes for mainstream rock success, employing the widescreen production style of Jimmy Iovine and such guests as Bruce Springsteen. It didn't sell, but it was a great try. — *William Ruhlmann*

Another Grey Area / Mar. 1982 / Razor & Tie ✦✦✦✦
Parker begins to make his peace with human imperfection (though he can still be sharp-tongued) and starts to look for love ("It's All Worth Nothing Alone"), backed by a smooth session band and a clean Jack Douglas production, which cool his usual fire without putting it out. — *William Ruhlmann*

The Real Macaw / Jul. 1983 / Razor & Tie ✦✦✦

Steady Nerves / Mar. 1985 / Elektra ✦✦✦
Graham Parker moves to his third record label (following stints at Mercury and Arista), forms a backup band called The Shot (again led by guitarist Brinsley Schwarz), and continues alternately arguing with existence ("Break Them Down") and praising his romantic life ("Wake Up [Next to You]"). — *William Ruhlmann*

Mona Lisa's Sister / Apr. 1988 / RCA ✦✦

Live! Alone in America / Jul. 1989 / RCA ✦✦✦

Human Soul / Jan. 1990 / RCA ✦✦

Struck by Lightning / Feb. 1991 / RCA ✦✦✦

Burning Questions / Jul. 20, 1992 / Capitol ✦✦

● **Passion Is No Ordinary Word: The Graham Parker Anthology 1976-1991** / Sep. 21, 1993 / Rhino ✦✦✦✦
With its smart song selection and entertaining liner notes, *Passion Is No Ordinary Word* is an excellent two-CD anthology covering Parker's entire career, complete with such rarities as "Mercury Poisoning" and "I Want You Back (Alive)" among such signature songs as "White Honey" and "You Can't Be Too Strong." A terrific introduction to Parker's career. — *Stephen Thomas Erlewine*

12 Haunted Episodes / 1995 / Razor & Tie ✦✦✦

Live from New York, NY / Aug. 20, 1996 / Razor & Tie ✦✦

Robert Parker

b. Oct. 14, 1930, Crescent City, LA
Saxophone, Vocals / Soul, R&B
Parker's dance raver "Barefootin'" was one of the biggest hits to come out of New Orleans during the mid-'60s. Parker played sessions as a saxophonist back in 1949 with the legendary pianist Professor Longhair, and his 1959 solo debut for Ron, "All Night Long," was a scorching two-part instrumental. But Parker's underutilized vocal talents suddenly emerged in 1966, when his highly infectious "Barefootin'" became a giant hit on tiny Nola. Only one other Parker single, "Tip Toe," charted the next year, but Parker remains a popular attraction in his hometown. — *Bill Dahl*

● **Barefootin'** / 1966 / Collectables ✦✦✦✦
Originally issued in 1987 on vinyl by England's Charly, this collection includes Parker's main claim to fame, the 1966 R&B and pop dance smash "Barefootin'"; its flip side, "Let's Go Baby (Where the Action Is)"; both sides of a 1969 single Parker cut for Silver Fox; and a number of '70s recordings the erstwhile sax player waxed for Sansu Enterprises. Much of the CD, including the title cut, is infectious New Orleans R&B of a high caliber, but other tracks find Parker attempting to cut mainstream funk and disco, usually with less-than-inspiring results. If possible, find the Charly release, because Collectables, in their typically shoddy manner, do not bother to provide songwriting credits, let alone track credits or liner notes. A good policy is to buy Collectables only if there is no other anthology of the same material issued anywhere else in the world, no matter what the price difference. — *Rob Bowman*

Parliament

Soul, Funk, R&B
Parliament started as a doo wop group centered around a barbershop owned and operated by George Clinton in New Jersey in the late '50s. One 45 was released on the APT label before Clinton and company headed off to Detroit. Updating their sound to reflect the innovations of Motown, Parliament had a No. 3 R&B/No. 20 pop hit with "(I Wanna) Testify" for Revilot in 1967. Leaving Revilot before the group's contract had legally expired, Clinton lost the right to the name for a few years.
Putting his backup band up front, Clinton signed with Detroit's Westbound label and called the group Funkadelic. By 1971 Clinton regained title to the original name, while still recording as Funkadelic as well. Parliament's records tended to be more R&B dance-oriented, while Funkadelic leaned toward the psychedelic side of rock 'n' roll.
Parliament was signed first to Invictus and then to Casablanca. In the mid-and late '70s, they were at the forefront of funk music, playing crazed shows that included spaceships landing on stage and articulated

Clinton's acid-tinged funk cosmology, where the pro-funk and anti-funk forces battled it out. Characters such as Sir Nose D'Void of Funk were routinely forced to give up the funk and dance at the end of Parliament's concerts. Hits included "Up for the Down Stroke," "Chocolate City," "Tear the Roof Off the Sucker (Give Up the Funk)," and "Flash Light." Group members included Fuzzy Haskins, Bernie Worrell, Bootsy Collins, Fred Wesley, Maceo Parker, Eddie Hazel, Gary Shider, and Michael Hampton. Offshoots included the P-Funk All-Stars, Bootsy's Rubber Band, the Brides of Funkenstein, Fred Wesley & the Horny Horns, and Parlet. — *Rob Bowman*

Osmium / 1970 / Invictus ✦✦

Up for the Down Stroke / 1974 / Casablanca ✦✦✦✦
The first album by Clinton's revamped Parliament remains a perfect introduction, although its best songs are on their *Greatest Hits*. — *John Floyd*

Chocolate City / 1975 / Casablanca ✦✦✦
The title track was a masterpiece, one of George Clinton's satirical triumphs. Whether you think it was a political work or not, everything clicked—the production, comic lead vocals, lyrics, and arrangements. The remainder of the album wasn't quite that strong, but was still excellent. It mixed every Clinton element: chaotic jamming, quirky outlook, hilarious vocals, and that sense of the casually absurd that Clinton championed. — *Ron Wynn*

Clones of Dr. Funkenstein / 1976 / Casablanca ✦✦✦✦
George Clinton had his otherworldly, controlled, chaotic vision well in gear for this album. He milked the Frankenstein notion, creating a mad scientist and sonically documenting his warped funk notions. Clinton got instrumental assistance from a crack corps that included keyboardist Bernie Worrell, saxophonist Maceo Parker, and trombonist Fred Wesley, plus numerous vocalists, guitarists, and instrumentalists. The album went gold, although it wasn't as inspired or successful as *Mothership Connection*. But such songs as "Dr. Funkenstein," "I've Been Watching You (Move Your Sexy Body)," and "Everything Is on the One" are quintessential Parliament jams. — *Ron Wynn*

☆ **Mothership Connection** / 1976 / Casablanca ✦✦✦✦✦
This was *the* Parliament masterpiece. It mixed creative and clever satirical takeoffs on James Brown, Sly Stone, and classic black radio with the kind of loose, inventive improvising seldom heard in R&B or soul circles. The narratives were swift and humorous and the music crackling, fast-moving and progressive. The title cut, "Tear the Roof Off the Sucker (Give Up the Funk)," and others marked the beginning of Clinton and Parliament/Funkadelic's evolution into national celebrities. — *Ron Wynn*

☆ **Funkentelechy Vs the Placebo Syndrome** / 1977 / Casablanca ✦✦✦✦✦
Funkentelechy Vs the Placebo Syndrome offers an even better introduction to the group than the singles collection, by presenting the most intelligible and rhythmically unstoppable glimpse into Clinton's P-Funk world. — *John Floyd*

Live: P-Funk Earth Tour / 1977 / Casablanca ✦✦✦

Motor Booty Affair / 1978 / Casablanca ✦✦✦

Gloryhallastoopid / 1979 / Casablanca ✦✦✦

Trombipulation / 1980 / Casablanca ✦✦

Greatest Hits (The Bomb) / 1984 / Casablanca ✦✦✦✦
This is a solid if scanty assortment of their best singles. — *John Floyd*

☆ **Tear the Roof Off** / May 18, 1993 / Casablanca ✦✦✦✦✦
Two discs of the hardest funk ever recorded, *Tear the Roof Off* is essential for both the casual fan and the hardcore collector. In addition to the presence of the full-length versions of all their hits, several 12-inch mixes make their first appearances on CD here. Without the music on *Tear the Roof Off*, contemporary music would not sound as it does today. — *AMG*

Live 1972-1993 / 1994 / Aem ✦✦

★ **The Best of Parliament: Give Up the Funk** / 1995 / Mercury Funk Essentials ✦✦✦✦✦
The Best of Parliament supplements *Greatest Hits (The Bomb)* by offering a better selection of tracks, as well as more songs. — *Stephen Thomas Erlewine*

Alan Parsons Project

Art-Rock/Progressive-Rock, Pop-Rock
Engineer/producer Alan Parsons and his colleague, songwriter-lyricist Eric Woolfson, formed the Alan Parsons Project in 1975. Throughout their career, the Alan Parsons Project has recorded concept albums, with a revolving cast of session musicians. *Eye in the Sky* was their greatest success; the title track charted in the Top Ten on the pop charts, and the album went platinum. Although they haven't been able to repeat that success, the group has maintained a devoted cult audience. — *AMG*

Tales of Mystery & Imagination / 1975 / Mercury ✦✦✦✦
This "project," led by former Beatles engineer Alan Parsons, was recorded at Abbey Road and featured a session group including Terry

Sylvester and Arthur Brown (he of the "Crazy World"). It made its first and best album by interpreting the ominous poems and stories of Edgar Allan Poe. Heavy on synthesized keyboards and dramatic choral parts, it's rock soundtrack music minus the film. The group went on to make a series of similar follow-ups, notably including *I Robot* and *Eye in the Sky*, but this is the place to start. — *William Ruhlmann*

I Robot / Jun. 1977 / Arista ✦✦✦✦
The Alan Parsons Project was established as a top record-seller with *I, Robot*, their second album. Musically, the record continued the ideas of their debut. Thematically, the record was an exploration of the science-fiction concept of a world run by machines and mechanized human beings, particularly robots. — *David Jehnzen*

Pyramid / Jun. 1978 / Arista ✦✦✦

Eve / Sep. 1979 / Arista ✦✦
Eve continued the Alan Parsons Project's string of best-selling albums, peaking at No. 13 and going gold. Musically, it reiterated the group's first three records, while thematically it explored the "perplexing nature" of women. Although the concept is certainly intriguing, Parsons' lyrical outlook is rather cold, opening him to charges of misogyny. — *David Jehnzen*

The Turn of a Friendly Card / Nov. 1980 / Arista ✦✦✦✦
The Turn of a Friendly Card was the Alan Parson Project's second straight No. 13 album, but it proved more successful than either *Pyramid* or *Eve*, going platinum and spending over a year on the charts. Musically, the group had matured, offering intricate, carefully crafted pop songs that were exacting in detail. Thematically, the record seemed to be their slightest effort to date, as it superficially explored the medieval ramifications of a card game. Dig a little deeper, however, and the record reveals itself to be a rumination about destiny versus the choice of self-determination. It features the hit "Games People Play." — *David Jehnzen*

Eye in the Sky / Jun. 1982 / Arista ✦✦✦✦
Eye in the Sky was the Alan Parsons Project's most successful record, peaking at No. 7 and going platinum as the title track hit No. 3. Musically, it expanded the ideas of *Turn of a Friendly Card*, adding some softer edges and lusher textures; despite its hit single, the album worked better as a whole, not as a series of songs. Thematically, it was a snapshot of an Orwellian future, ruled by the all-seeing "Eye in the Sky," who watches over its populace with a calm, menacing glee. — *David Jehnzen*

● **The Best of the Alan Parsons Project** / 1983 / Arista ✦✦✦✦
Although the Alan Parsons Project is a quintessential album-rock act, their most effective statements were made on singles, and this collection features their best songs, including "Eye in the Sky" and "Games People Play." — *Stephen Thomas Erlewine*

Ammonia Avenue / Feb. 1984 / Arista ✦✦✦

Vulture Culture / Mar. 1985 / Arista ✦✦

Stereotomy / Nov. 1985 / Arista ✦✦

Gaudi / 1987 / Arista ✦✦

The Best of the Alan Parsons Project, Vol. 2 / 1988 / Arista ✦✦✦✦
The Alan Parsons Project didn't have as many hits between 1983 and 1988 as they did between 1976 and 1983, so the task of compiling a second volume of greatest hits was somewhat difficult. Instead of conquering this problem head on, the compilers ignore it, choosing a selection of album tracks from the group's first six albums as well as adding the hit "Don't Answer Me" and several tracks from *Stereotomy, Vulture Culture,* and *Ammonia Avenue*. It's an effective sampler of some of their more ponderous work. — *David Jehnzen*

The Instrumental Works / 1988 / Arista ✦✦

Gram Parsons (Cecil Ingram Connor)

b. Nov. 5, 1946, Winterhaven, FL, d. Sep. 19, 1973, Joshua Tree, CA
Guitar, Vocals / Country-Rock
Gram Parsons is the father of country-rock. With the International Submarine Band, the Byrds, and the Flying Burrito Brothers, Parsons pioneered the concept of a rock band playing country music, and as a solo artist he moved even further into country music, blending the two genres to the point that they became indistinguishable from each other. While he was alive, Parsons was a cult figure that never sold many records, but influenced countless fellow musicians, from the Rolling Stones to the Byrds. In the years since his death, his stature has only grown, as numerous rock and country artists build on his small but enormously influential body of work.

Parsons was the grandson of John Snivley, who owned about one-third of all the citrus fields in Florida. Snivley's daughter married Coon Dog Connor. As a child, Gram Parsons learned how to play the piano at the age of nine, the same year he saw Elvis Presley perform at his school; following that performance, he decided to become a musician. When Parsons was 12, his father committed suicide. After Connor's death, Parsons and his mother moved in with her parents in Winter Haven, FL; a

year after the move, his mother married Robert Parsons, who adopted Gram, and the boy legally changed his name to Gram Parsons.

At the age of 14, Parsons began playing in the local rock 'n' roll band the Pacers, which evolved into the Legends. During their time together, the Legends featured Jim Stafford and Kent Lavoie, who would later come to fame under the name Lobo. In 1963, Parsons formed a folk group called the Shilos who performed throughout Florida and wound up cutting two singles for Columbia Records. In 1965, Parsons graduated from high school; on the same day he graduated, his mother died of alcohol poisoning. Following his graduation, Parsons enrolled at Harvard, where he studied theology. Parsons only stayed one semester at Harvard and while he was there, he spent more time playing music than attending classes. During this time he formed the International Submarine Band with guitarist John Nuese, bassist Ian Dunlop, and drummer Mickey Gauvin. After he dropped out of college, he moved to New York with the International Submarine Band in 1966. The group spent a year in New York, developing a heavily country-influenced rock 'n' roll sound and cutting two unsuccessful singles for Columbia. The band relocated to Los Angeles in 1967, where they secured a record contract with Lee Hazelwood's LHI record label. The group's debut album, *Safe at Home*, was released in early 1968, but by the time it appeared in the stores, the group had already disbanded. Around the time the International Submarine Band dissolved, Parsons met Chris Hillman, the bassist for the Byrds. At that time, the Byrds were rebuilding their lineup and Hillman recommended to the band's leader, Roger McGuinn, that Parsons join the band. By the spring of 1968, Parsons had become a member of the Byrds and he was largely responsible for the group's shift towards country music with their album *Sweetheart of the Rodeo*. Originally, the album was going to feature Parsons' lead vocals, but he was still contractually obligated to LHI, so his voice had to be stripped from the record.

Gram Parsons only spent a few months with the Byrds, leaving the band in the fall of 1968 because he refused to accompany them on a tour of South Africa, allegedly because he opposed apartheid. Chris Hillman left the band shortly after him, and the duo formed the Flying Burrito Brothers in late 1968. Parsons and Hillman enlisted pedal steel guitarist "Sneaky" Pete Kleinow and bassist Chris Ethridge to complete the band's lineup and recorded their debut album with a series of session drummers. *The Gilded Palace of Sin*, the Flying Burrito Brothers' debut album, was released in 1969. Although the album only sold a few thousand copies, the group gathered a dedicated cult following, which was mainly composed of musicians, including the Rolling Stones. In fact, by the time the album was released, Parsons had begun hanging around the Rolling Stones frequently and became close friends with Keith Richards. Prior to his time with the Stones, Parsons had experimented with drugs and alcohol, but in 1969 he dove deep into substance abuse, which he supported with his huge trust fund.

Parsons recorded a second album with the Flying Burrito Brothers, but by the time the record—entitled *Burrito Deluxe*—appeared in the spring of 1970, he had left the band. Shortly after leaving the group, he recorded a handful of songs with producer Terry Melcher, but he never completed the album. Following these sessions, Parsons entered a holding pattern where he acted the role of being a rock star instead of actually playing music. He spent much of his time either hanging out with the Stones or ingesting large amounts of drugs and alcohol; frequently, he did a combination of the two. In 1971, he toured with the Rolling Stones in England, attending the recording of the band's *Exile on Main Street*, and it appeared that he would sign with the band's record label. Instead, he headed back to Los Angeles late in 1971, spending the rest of the year and the first half of 1972 writing material for an impending solo album. In 1972, he met Emmylou Harris through Chris Hillman and asked her to join his backing band; she accepted.

By the summer of 1972, he was prepared to enter the studio to record his first solo album. Parsons had assembled a band—which included Harris, guitarist James Burton, bassist Rick Grech, Barry Tashian, and Glen D. Hardin, and Ronnie Tutt—and had asked Merle Haggard to produce the album. After meeting Parsons, Haggard turned the offer down, so Parsons chose Haggard's engineer, Hugh Davis, as the album's producer. The resulting album, *G.P.*, was released late in 1972 to good reviews but poor sales.

Following the release of *G.P.*, Parsons embarked on a small tour with his backing band, the Fallen Angels. After the tour was completed, they entered the studio to record his second album, *Grievous Angel*. The album was completed toward the end of the summer. A few weeks after the sessions, Parsons went on a vacation near the Joshua Tree National Monument in California. He spent most of his time there consuming drugs and alcohol. On September 19, 1973, he overdosed on morphine and tequila and was rushed to the Yucca Valley Hospital—he was pronounced dead on arrival. According to the funeral plans, his body was to be flown back to New Orleans for a burial. However, Parsons' road manager, Paul Kaufman, stole the body after the funeral and carried it back out to the desert, where he cremated it. Kaufman revealed that the cremation had been Parsons' wish. Kaufman could not be convicted for stealing the body, but he was arrested for stealing and burning the coffin.

In the two decades following Gram Parsons' death, his legacy continued to grow, as both country and rock musicians built on the music he left behind. Everyone from Emmylou Harris to Elvis Costello has covered his songs, and his influence could still be heard well into the '90s. —*Stephen Thomas Erlewine*

Gram Parsons Int Sub Band (Safe at Home) / 1967 / Shiloh ✦✦✦
Safe at Home represents some of Gram Parsons' earliest recordings as a part of the International Submarine Band. Arguably the first country-rock album, this more than hints at Parsons' greatness to come. This charming document is essential listening. —*Chris Woodstra*

★ **G.P./Grievous Angel** / 1973 / Reprise ✦✦✦✦✦
Parson's two best albums appear on one compact disc. Seeking to synthesize his own ideas with those of classic country and rock, Parsons hired Merle Haggard's recording engineer (he had approached Haggard himself about producing) and members of Elvis Presley's band, including pianist Glen D. Hardin and guitarist James Burton. The result had its roots in everything but sounded like nothing else. Parson's songs were the musings of a wounded soul, and his taste in others' material ran from Harlan Howard to the J. Geils Band. On *Grievous Angel*, Emmylou Harris emerges from the background to provide an angelic foil for Parsons' lost folkie voice. —*Brian Mansfield*

Sleepless Nights / 1976 / A&M ✦✦✦
Sleepless Nights is a collection of unreleased Gram Parsons material recorded while he was in the Flying Burrito Brothers. Most of the material are covers, yet the selection demonstrates how Parsons closed the gap between rock and country. —*Stephen Thomas Erlewine*

Gram Parsons & the Fallen Angels / 1981 / Sierra ✦✦✦✦
A good live document of Parsons' last tour, recorded at radio station WLIR in New York. —*Kenneth M. Cassidy*

Warm Evenings, Pale Mornings, Bottled Blues / 1992 / Raven ✦✦✦✦
Although all of Parsons' albums are essential, this import-only collection provides an excellent sampling of his entire career including his stints with the Shilos, the International Submarine Band, the Byrds (complete with Parsons' vocals restored), the Flying Burrito Brothers, and the solo years.
—*Chris Woodstra*

Cosmic American Music / Jul. 18, 1995 / Sundown ✦✦
Cosmic American is a collection of demos made in various homes and hotel rooms in 1972. In an informal, sing-along environment, Parsons works through embryonic versions of songs and old favorites with friends Emmylou Harris, Barry Tashian, and Ric Grech (among others)—several songs never making it to the studio. Though the quality of the recordings can be off-putting to the casual fan, those who count themselves among GP's ever-growing cult will find this intimate look a compulsive listen. —*Chris Woodstra*

Les Paul (Lester William Poifus, Hot Rod Red, Rhubarb Red)

b. Jun. 9, 1915, Waukseha, WI
Guitar / Swing, Pop
The history of recorded music would have been different, much different, if it were not for the pioneering efforts of guitarist and inventor Les Paul. He started as a country musician, working radio spots in the early '30s as Rhubarb Red. Bitten by the jazz bug early on, he formed the Les Paul Trio in 1936, working for bandleader Fred Waring through the end of the decade. By the '40s, he was experimenting with guitars and recording gear. He was among the first to build a solid-body electric and certainly the first to popularize the idea; his Gibson Les Paul models of the '50s are now all highly sought-after collector's items. He was the first to pioneer multitrack recording and overdubbing, the use of tape echo, phase shifting, etc., changed the sound of popular music forever, most notably on the recordings made in the early '50s with his wife, vocalist Mary Ford. Paul is a consummate player, arranger, engineer, and entertainer; his inventions are only part of what makes him one of the giants of American music. —*Cub Koda*

The Legend and the Legacy / 1991 / Capitol ✦✦✦✦
Beautiful four-CD boxed set of all of Paul and Ford's best Capitol recordings, with the bonus of numerous unissued songs and a track-by-track commentary by Paul in the accompanying booklet. A must-have. —*Cub Koda*

★ **The Best of the Capitol Masters** / 1992 / Capitol ✦✦✦✦✦
A good single-disc distillation of the highlights of Les Paul's epic four-disc box set, *The Legend and the Legacy, Best of the Capitol Masters* is all most casual fans will need to own. —*Stephen Thomas Erlewine*

Pavement

Alternative Pop-Rock, Lo-Fi, Indie Rock
With their fractured songs, unexpected blasts of feedback, laconic vocals,

cryptic lyrics, and defiant low-fidelity, Pavement is one of the most influential and distinctive bands to emerge from the American underground in the '90s. For several years before their first full-length album, the group had been releasing a series of singles and EPs on small, obscure labels. During this period, Pavement was essentially a studio project featuring guitarists/vocalists Stephen Malkmus and Scott Kannberg.

By the time of Pavement's first album, 1992's *Slanted & Enchanted*, Malkmus and Kannberg had added drummer Gary Young to the lineup. *Slanted & Enchanted* took the world of rock criticism by storm; before the album was even available promotionally, critics were lavishly praising it. Initially, the band's following was based more on the press instead of word of mouth, but soon word began to spread on the street as well as in the magazines. During 1992, a permanent lineup of Pavement was established, as the group added bassist Mark Ibold and percussionist Bob Nastanovich.

Before Pavement recorded their second album, the band kicked Gary Young out of the group, due to his erratic behavior and performances; he was replaced by Steve West. Pavement's second album, 1994's *Crooked Rain, Crooked Rain*, saw the band toning down its extreme sonics for a laidback record that emphasized songs over sound. The album helped the band consolidate its position as alternative stars and critic's darlings, as well as expanding their cult; they charted in the lower reaches of *Billboard's* Top 200 Album chart and had an alternative rock hit with "Cut Your Hair."

The following year, Pavement released their third album, sprawling *Wowee Zowee*, which debuted higher than *Crooked Rain* in the charts without the benefit of an alternative radio or MTV hit single on the level of "Cut Your Hair." In the summer of 1995, the group toured with Lollapalooza. —*Stephen Thomas Erlewine*

★ **Slanted & Enchanted** / May 1992 / Matador ✦✦✦✦✦
Slanted and Enchanted is like listening to a college radio station that you can barely tune in—melodies are interrupted by shards of white noise, only to have several "sha-la-la's" bring it back into focus. —*Stephen Thomas Erlewine*

Watery, Domestic / Nov. 1992 / Matador ✦✦✦

Westing (by Musket & Sextant) / 1993 / Drag City ✦✦✦
A collection of all of Pavement's low-fidelity early singles and EPs, which feature considerably less melody than *Slanted & Enchanted*. It's nice to have this rare material on one CD, although the music is defiantly anti-CD. Those who boarded the train with the acclaimed *Slanted & Enchanted* should catch up on what they've missed. —*Stephen Thomas Erlewine*

Crooked Rain, Crooked Rain / Feb. 1994 / Matador ✦✦✦✦
Although it's much calmer than the critically acclaimed *Slanted & Enchanted, Crooked Rain, Crooked Rain* shares the same spirit of the band's debut—it's a messy, impossibly catchy catalog of pop music and culture. On their second full-length album, Pavement have abandoned much of the lo-fi squalor of their earlier work, opting for a laidback, subdued sound that borders on country-rock and jazz-rock at times, and pure pop and rock 'n' roll at others. In other words, it's more accessible than *Slanted & Enchanted* but just as distinctive and original. Ultimately, *Crooked Rain, Crooked Rain* revamps rock history and reinvents it for the slacker generation. —*Stephen Thomas Erlewine*

Wowee Zowee / Apr. 1995 / Matador ✦✦✦✦
With its vast array of musical styles, *Wowee Zowee* isn't as accessible as *Crooked Rain, Crooked Rain* or as immediate as the bracing, noisy pop of *Slanted & Enchanted*. Pavement never abandon their warped pop aesthetic, they simply expand it, incorporating elements of folk-rock, English music-hall, soul, jazz, and country, as well as adding asides to such contemporaries as Suede ("We Dance"), Ween ("Brinx Job"), and Stereolab ("Half a Canyon"). Alternating between majestic epics like "Grounded" and ragged narratives like "Rattled by the Rush" and "Father to a Sister of Thought," to song fragments like "Brinx Job" and the punkish "Serpentine Pad," the record might seem disjointed at first. After repeated listens, the songs play off each other, creating a dense collage of '90s rock 'n' roll that recasts past and present into one rich, kaleidoscopic, and blissfully cryptic world view. —*Stephen Thomas Erlewine*

Freda Payne

b. Sep. 19, 1945, Detroit, MI
Vocals / Soul
A Detroit soul/jazz/pop vocalist. Multitalented and beautiful, Payne crashed the soul and pop playlists in 1970 with a series of powerful sides for Holland-Dozier-Holland's Invictus imprint. Payne's early musical experience was quite varied, and she debuted on the jazz-oriented Impulse! label in 1965. Her 1970 blockbuster, "Band of Gold," made her a pop star with its strident message and insistent bassline, and she encored with "Deeper & Deeper." The controversial antiwar anthem "Bring the Boys Home" proved her biggest R&B seller the next year. Payne hosted a TV gabfest during the '80s. —*Bill Dahl*

● **Greatest Hits** / 1991 / HDH ✦✦✦✦
Payne, an old childhood friend of Holland and Dozier, had already
worked with Pearl Bailey, Duke Ellington, and Quincy Jones when she
signed to Hot Wax/Invictus. Her biggest claim to fame was the No. 3 hit
"Band of Gold," which eventually sold more than five million copies.
Interestingly, Payne was reluctant to do the song. She garnered some
moderate successes with the follow-up singles, "Deeper and Deeper" and
"Cherish What Is Dear to You," but her heartfelt plea to end the Vietnam
War, "Bring the Boys Home," hit a nerve with the public and became a
No. 12 hit. —*Rick Clark*

Pearl Jam

Hard Rock, Alternative Pop-Rock, Grunge
Pearl Jam rose from the ashes of Mother Love Bone to become the most
popular American rock 'n' roll band of the early '90s. After vocalist
Andrew Wood overdosed on heroin, guitarist Stone Gossard and bassist
Jeff Ament assembled a new band, bringing in Mike McCready on lead
guitar, Dave Krusen on drums, and vocalist Eddie Vedder. Naming themselves Pearl Jam, the band recorded their debut album, *Ten*, in the beginning of 1991. *Ten* didn't begin selling in significant numbers until early
1992, after Nirvana made mainstream rock radio receptive to alternative
rock acts. Soon, Pearl Jam outsold Nirvana, which wasn't surprising.
Pearl Jam fused the riff-heavy stadium rock of the '70s with the grit and
anger of '80s post-punk, without ever neglecting hooks and choruses;
"Jeremy," "Evenflow," and "Alive" fit perfectly into album-rock radio stations that were looking for new blood.
    Krusen left the band shortly after the release of *Ten;* he was replaced
by Dave Abbruzzese. Pearl Jam's audience continued to grow during
1992, thanks to a series of radio and MTV hits, as well as a successful
appearance on the second Lollapalooza tour. Despite their status as rock
'n' roll superstars, the band refused to succumb to the accepted conventions of the music industry. The group refused to release any videos or
singles from their second album, 1993's *Vs.* Nevertheless, it was another
multi-platinum success, debuting at No. 1 and selling nearly a million
copies in its first week of release. On their spring 1994 American tour,
the band decided not to play the conventional stadiums, choosing to play
smaller arenas, including several shows on college campuses.
    Pearl Jam cancelled their 1994 summer tour, claiming they could not
keep ticket prices below $20 because Ticketmaster was pressuring pro-
moters to charge a higher price. The band took Ticketmaster to the judi-
cial department for unfair business practices. As the band fought Ticketmaster, they recorded a new album in the spring and summer of 1994.
After the record was completed, the group fired Dave Abbruzzese,
replacing him with former Red Hot Chili Peppers and Eleven drummer
Jack Irons.
    Vitalogy, the band's third album, appeared at the end of 1994. For the
first two weeks, it was available as a limited vinyl release, but the record
charted in the Top 60. Once *Vitalogy* was available on CD and cassette,
the album shot to the top of the charts and became multi-platinum. Pearl
Jam continued to battle Ticketmaster in 1995, but the Justice Department
eventually ruled in favor of the ticket agency. In early 1995, the band
recorded an album with Neil Young. Vedder toured with his experimental project Hovercraft in the spring of 1994 as Stone Gossard founded an
independent record company. Mad Season, Mike McCready's side -
project with Layne Staley of Alice in Chains, released their first album,
Above, in the spring of 1995. Comprised entirely of Neil Young songs,
Mirror Ball appeared in the summer under Young's name; although the
individual members of the band were credited, the name Pearl Jam did
not appear on the cover due to legal complications. Pearl Jam released a
single culled from the sessions, *Mirkin Ball*, in the fall of 1995.
    In late summer of 1996, Pearl Jam released their fourth album, *No
Code*. —*Stephen Thomas Erlewine*

★ **Ten** / 1992 / Epic Associated ✦✦✦✦✦
The first Seattle band to hit the big time after Nirvana, Pearl Jam was not
anyone's pick to be successful. Yet Pearl Jam's brand of hard rock made
them more accessible than any other Seattle band, including Nirvana.
Pearl Jam's music is not as confused as Mudhoney, as melodic as Nirvana, as menacing as Alice in Chains, or as bloated as Soundgarden. *Ten*
is remarkably clearheaded and clean, and very politically correct—a perfect soundtrack for the 1990s. The muscular, melodic blend of "Jeremy,"
"Alive," and "Evenflow" brought Pearl Jam crossover success, helping *Ten*
climb into the Top Ten and sell over nine million copies. —*Stephen Thomas Erlewine*

Vs. / 1993 / Epic Associated ✦✦✦
On the first listen, it appears that Pearl Jam's second album has no songs
as instantly stunning as the best songs on *Ten*, but after a couple of plays,
Vs. reveals its strengths. Instead of copying *Ten*'s signature clear, dark
hard rock, *Vs.* is rawer and more open, with a number of different textures. From the pulverizing assault of "Go," "Animal," and "Leash" to the
folkier, more reflective "Daughter," "Elderly Woman Behind the Counter
in a Small Town," and "Indifference," Pearl Jam proves that their initial

success was no fluke. Occasionally, the band falls into treacherous politically correct waters (the silly "Glorified G" and the meandering
"W.M.A."), but for most of the album, Pearl Jam locks hold, and the best
results are riveting. —*Stephen Thomas Erlewine*

Vitalogy / 1994 / Epic Associated ✦✦✦✦
Thanks to its stripped-down, lean production, *Vitalogy* stands as Pearl
Jam's most original and uncompromising album. While it isn't a concept
album, *Vitalogy* sounds like one. Death and despair shroud the album,
rendering even the explosive celebration of vinyl "Spin the Black Circle"
somewhat muted. But that black cloud works to Pearl Jam's advantage,
injecting a nervous tension to brittle rockers like "Last Exit" and "Not for
You," and especially introspective ballads like "Corduroy" and "Better
Man." In between the straight rock numbers and the searching slow
songs, Pearl Jam contributes their strangest music—the mantra-funk of
"Aye Davanita," the sub-Tom Waits accordion romp of "Bugs," and the
chilling sonic collage "Hey Foxymophandlemama, That's Me." Pearl Jam
are at their best when they're fighting, whether it's Ticketmaster, fame, or
their own personal demons. —*Stephen Thomas Erlewine*

No Code / Aug. 27, 1996 / Sony ✦✦✦

Ann Peebles

b. Apr. 27, 1947, St. Louis, MO
Vocals / Soul
Ann Peebles was the queen of Willie Mitchell's Memphis-based Hi
Records roster during the '70s, when Al Green was its undisputed king.
Sung in a voice as bittersweet as it is riveting, her always-dramatic
recordings include one undisputed masterpiece, "I Can't Stand the Rain,"
cited as a favorite by John Lennon and most recently covered by Tina
Turner. Other covers abound—Robert Palmer took "I'm Gonna Tear Your
Playhouse Down," and Bette Midler claimed "Breakin' Up Somebody's
Home." Backed by the brilliant Hi rhythm section and flawlessly produced by Mitchell, Peebles sang and wrote (often in partnership with
husband Don Bryant) of the feminine perspective on the darker side of
love—sometimes untrusting love, but love, for better or worse. Her work
represents, with elegance and grit, some of the best of Memphis soul.
    After a long absence from recording, Ann Peebles returned to the
wars with the CD *Full Time Love* in 1992 for Bullseye/Rounder. While it
didn't get much exposure or recognition in urban circles, it was a wonderfully sung and well-produced attempt at giving Peebles some contemporary tweaking without losing her gritty qualities. —*Christine Ohlman
and Ron Wynn*

Part Time Love / 1971 / The Right Stuff ✦✦✦✦
The title track was a masterpiece, and everything else on this dynamic
early '70s soul session is a jewel. Ann Peebles may have been the most
overlooked great soul singer, male or female, who emerged in the '70s. Hi
couldn't strike crossover gold twice, and Al Green was becoming a
superstar. But Peebles deserved a better fate than obscurity, as this collection of soul wailers and weepers proves. —*Ron Wynn*

I Can't Stand the Rain / 1974 / The Right Stuff ✦✦✦
The title song was an instant classic, and its lyrics are among the most
moving and gripping in soul annals. This was Ann Peebles' finest album
for Hi Records, and it should have been a massive success. Instead, while
it's celebrated in Europe and now considered an anthem, it floundered
and barely scraped the pop charts, although the single was her biggest
R&B hit. —*Ron Wynn*

● **Ann Peebles' Greatest Hits** / MCA ✦✦✦✦
Backed by the vaunted Hi rhythm section and produced by Willie Mitch-
ell, this includes her original "Come to Mama" and "I Can't Stand the
Rain." These are classics of the '70s Memphis soul idiom. —*Bill Dahl*

Teddy Pendergrass

b. Mar. 26, 1950
Drums, Vocals / Soul, Urban, Club-Dance
In 1970, Pendergrass joined Harold Melvin and the Blue Notes as their
drummer and lead vocalist; he sang on all of the group's Top 40 hits. Pendergrass left the group in 1976 and scored eight Hot 100 hits before he
was in an auto accident that left him partially paralyzed. He made a
comeback two years later with *Heaven Only Knows*, which did not fare
all that well commercially despite "Hold Me," a Top 50 duet with a young
Whitney Houston. Subsequent albums also did not sell particularly well.
—*Stephen Thomas Erlewine*

● **Greatest Hits** / 1987 / Philadelphia International ✦✦✦✦
This collection covers Pendergrass' run of big hits from the Philadelphia
International era, including "I Don't Love You Anymore," "Close the
Door," and "Turn Off the Lights." —*Ron Wynn*

Penguins

Doo Wop
Best known for their hit single "Earth Angel," the doo wop quartet the

Penguins were never able to replicate the success of their only Top 40 hit, but the song became a rock 'n' roll classic. The Penguins formed in 1954, when the members—Cleveland Duncan (lead vocal), Curtis Williams (tenor vocal), Dexter Tisby (baritone vocal), and Bruce Tate (tenor vocal)—were all attending Fremont High School in Los Angeles, CA. Although he wasn't the lead singer, Curtis Williams was the leader of the group. He learned "Earth Angel" from vocalist Jesse Belvin—some sources claim that Williams wrote the song alone, others say he co-wrote the song with Belvin, while others claim Gaynel Hodge, a member of the doo wop group the Turks, wrote the song with the duo (in fact, Hodge won a lawsuit filed in 1956 that gave them a co-writing credit)—and had the Penguins sing the song.

Around 1954, the Penguins signed with the local Los Angeles independent label Dootone Records. The group's first single was going to be the uptempo "Hey, Senorita," and the ballad "Earth Angel" was going to be the B-side. Upon the release of the single in the latter half of 1954, Los Angeles radio stations were receiving more requests for "Earth Angel" than "Hey, Senorita" and the song soon became the record's A-side. By the beginning of 1955, the single had scaled the national charts, spending three weeks at the top of the R&B charts and peaking at No. 8 on the pop charts.

For the next few years, the Penguins continued to record singles for Dootone Records. Shortly after the success of "Earth Angel," Tate left the group and Randolph Jones became their baritone vocalist. Around 1956, the Penguins left Dootone Records and signed with Mercury Records. After cutting some sides for Mercury, the group moved to Atlantic Records, where they had their second and final hit, "Pledge of Love," which climbed to No. 15 on the R&B charts in the summer of 1957. That same year, the group released their only album, *The Cool, Cool, Penguins*.

By 1959, the group had returned to their hometown of Los Angeles; shortly after their relocation, they broke up. Over the next four decades, Cleveland Duncan led various incarnations of the Penguins through reunion tours and re-recordings of their hits. In 1963, Duncan, Tisby, and two new members recorded "Memories of El Monte," a song future Mothers of Invention members Frank Zappa and Ray Collins wrote specifically for the group; the single failed to make any impact. Duncan went back to leading new incarnations of the Penguins, while Tisby briefly joined the Coasters. — *Stephen Thomas Erlewine*

● **Authentic Golden Hits** / 1993 / Juke Box Treasures ✦✦✦✦
At long last, a well-thought-out compilation that gathers up all of the group's best sides for Dootone Records, including the original versions of the classics "Earth Angel" and "Hey, Senorita" in their original, unedited form. — *Cub Koda*

● **Best of the Mercury Years** / Jul. 1996 / Polygram ✦✦✦✦
The Best of the Mercury Years not only includes all of the Penguins' hit singles (most notably, of course, "Earth Angel"), but also a number of singles that missed the charts, album tracks, B-sides, and rarities. For some casual fans, this in-depth presentation might prove to be a bit too much, but this single-disc collection remains the definitive compilation on the seminal doo wop group. — *Stephen Thomas Erlewine*

Earth Angel / Ace ✦✦✦
A 21-track anthology from the Dootone label, it's a deeper look at the group's '50s sides and style, built around the title track that sold five million copies worldwide. (Import) — *Hank Davis*

Michael Penn

Guitar, Vocals / Singer-Songwriter, Pop-Rock
Michael Penn was one of the best singer-songwriters to emerge in the late '80s, capable of melding Beatlesque pop melodies with wordplay that rivals Elvis Costello. *March*, in 1989, was critically acclaimed and had a surprise hit single with "No Myth." Although his second album, 1992's *Free-for-All*, didn't have a hit on the size of "No Myth," it displayed his folk roots alongside his pop sensibilities. — *Stephen Thomas Erlewine*

● **March** / 1989 / RCA ✦✦✦✦
A solid debut album, it includes the hit "No Myth." — *Kenneth M. Cassidy*

Free-for-All / 1992 / RCA ✦✦✦
Free-for-All, Michael Penn's second album, isn't as immediately accessible as *March*, but his cryptic lyrics and twisting melodies will work their way into your memory if given some time. — *Stephen Thomas Erlewine*

Pere Ubu

Alternative Pop-Rock, Post-Punk
Named for the French absurdist play by Alfred Jarry, Pere Ubu is one of the most important and long-lived bands of the punk/new wave era. The group was organized in Cleveland in September 1975 by David Thomas (vocals) and fellow rock journalist Peter Laughner (guitar, bass) for the purpose of recording the apocalyptic single "30 Seconds Over Tokyo." By the spring of 1976, Pere Ubu had recorded a second single, "Final Solution," and traveled to New York, where they gained exposure. The band

was then reorganized, minus Laughner, who died the following year. Mercury/PolyGram Records signed Pere Ubu and issued their debut album, *The Modern Dance*, on its short-lived Blank Records label in February 1978. The album's combination of uncompromising rock, featuring odd noises, and Thomas' high-pitched singing earned the group critical hosannas and commercial indifference beyond a loyal cult, a situation that would continue for the rest of their existence. That existence has been fitful. Pere Ubu was dropped by PolyGram and signed by Chrysalis, which released *Dub Housing* (1978) and *New Picnic Time* (1979), after which the group split again. But they were back to release *The Art of Walking* in 1980 on Rough Trade. *Song of the Bailing Man* (1981) was the last album before another lengthy split in 1982. Pere Ubu reformed in 1987 with a lineup of Thomas, original member Allen Ravenstine (synthesizer), original member Scott Krauss (drums), Tony Maimone (bass), who had first joined in 1976, and two new members, Jim Jones (guitar) and Chris Cutler (drums). The group then released a series of slightly more commercially accessible albums: *The Tenement Year* (1987), *Cloudland* (1989), and *Worlds in Collision* (1991), reverting to its more abrasive style on *Story of My Life* (1993) and *Ray Gun Suitcase* (1995). As of 1995, Pere Ubu's lineup consisted of Thomas, Jones, Michele Temple, Robert Wheeler, and Scott Benedict. In 1996, Pere Ubu prepared a boxed set retrospective. — *William Ruhlmann*

The Modern Dance / 1978 / Blank ✦✦✦✦
Aggressive punk rock, punctuated by found sounds and noises and topped by Thomas' remarkably affecting near-falsetto shriek. It's not easy listening, but it's powerful and daring, and has lost none of its impact since release. — *William Ruhlmann*

New Picnic Time / 1979 / Rough Trade ✦✦✦✦
The last album from the late '70s version of Ubu is extreme dada, with a beat (sometimes). — *Myles Boisen*

Art of Walking / 1980 / Rough Trade ✦✦✦
An early-'80s recording with guitarist Mayo Thompson, this is a buoyant and groovy accompaniment to Thomas' surrealism. — *Myles Boisen*

390 Degrees of Simulated Stereo (Live) / 1981 / Rough Trade ✦✦

Song of the Bailing Man / 1982 / Rough Trade ✦✦✦

★ **Terminal Tower** / 1985 / Twin/Tone ✦✦✦✦✦
The songs on *Terminal Tower*, many of them taken from Pere Ubu's first singles, demonstrate what helped make them one of the most original and challenging bands of the American new wave of the '70s. Be warned that songs like "30 Seconds Over Tokyo" and "Final Solution" will have a polarizing effect on the listener: either this on-the-edge rock is just what you've been looking for, or it isn't. — *William Ruhlmann*

The Tenement Year / 1988 / Enigma ✦✦✦✦
Since the re-formed version of Pere Ubu reins in (slightly) the group's more extreme tendencies, this album, which nevertheless presents David Thomas' unique vision and the band's somewhat off-kilter approach to rock more or less intact, may be the place for neophytes to get their feet wet with a highly unusual group. This one should give you the idea—then you're on your own. — *William Ruhlmann*

Cloudland / 1989 / Fontana ✦✦✦✦
David Thomas returns to his favorite boyhood themes, with his new pop band in tow. — *Myles Boisen*

One Man Drives / 1989 / Rough Trade ✦✦

Worlds in Collision / 1991 / Fontana ✦✦✦

Story of My Life / 1993 / Imago ✦✦✦

Ray Gun Suitcase / 1995 / Cooking Vinyl ✦✦✦

Datapanik in the Year Zero [Box] / Aug. 27, 1996 / DGC ✦✦✦✦
Pere Ubu's troubles with record companies are legendary within certain underground rock circles. In perhaps the most bizarre turn of events, the group's collected works of 1978-1982—after being out of print for nearly a decade—were reissued by Geffen as a five-disc box set, *Datapanik in the Year Zero*. Named after the group's 1978 EP, the set is arranged chronologically and occasionally substitutes live versions for studio tracks, but that hardly matters—nearly every song the band recorded during the five-year time span is included. In addition to the official Pere Ubu material, the box includes a disc of rare singles from early incarnations of Ubu and other Cleveland-area punk rockers like Rocket from the Tombs, 15-60-75, and Mirrors, which were released on David Thomas' independent record label. With this much material, it's safe to say that the set is a definitive retrospective and its worth is increased because most of this material hasn't been widely available on CD, so collectors won't feel like they've paid a lot of money for a handful of rarities. However, if you're simply interested in Pere Ubu, consider the set carefully before investing. Pere Ubu was indeed one of the most innovative and challenging bands of their era, which means that their music is an acquired taste. However, those willing to invest in the box will find a wealth of inventive, hard-edged avant-garde rock 'n' roll. — *Stephen Thomas Erlewine*

Carl Perkins (Carl Lee Perkins)

b. Apr. 9, 1932, Lake City, TN
Guitar, Vocals / Rock 'n' Roll, Rockabilly

While some ill-informed revisionist writers of rock history would like to dismiss Carl Perkins as a rockabilly artist who became a one-hit wonder at the dawn of rock 'n' roll's early years, a deeper look at his music and career reveals much more. A quick look at his songwriting portfolio shows that he has composed "Daddy Sang Bass" for Johnny Cash, "I Was So Wrong" for Patsy Cline, and "Let Me Tell You About Love" for the Judds, big hits and classics all. His influence as the quintessential rockabilly artist has played a big part in the development of every generation of rocker to come down the pike since, from the Beatles' George Harrison to the Stray Cats' Brian Setzer to a myriad of others in the country field as well. His guitar style is the other twin peak—along with that of Elvis' lead man Scotty Moore—of rockabilly's instrumental center, so pervasive that modern-day players automatically gravitate toward it when called upon to deliver the style, not even realizing that they're playing Carl Perkins licks, sometimes note for note. As a singer, his interpretation of country ballads is every bit as fine as his better-known rockers. And within the framework of the best of his music is a strong sense of family and roots, all of which trace straight back to Perkins' humble beginnings.

He was born to sharecroppers Buck and Louise Perkins (misspelled on his birth certificate as "Perkings") and was soon out in the fields picking cotton and living in a shack with his parents, older brother Jay, and younger brother Clayton. Working alongside African Americans in the field every day, it's not at all surprising that when Carl was gifted with a secondhand guitar, he went to a local sharecropper for lessons, learning firsthand the boogie rhythm that he would later build a career on. By his teens, Carl was playing electric guitar and had recruited his brothers Jay on rhythm guitar and Clayton on string bass to become his first band. The Perkins Brothers Band, featuring both Carl and Jay on lead vocals, quickly established themselves as the hottest band in the get-hot-or-go-home cut-throat Jackson, TN, honky tonk circuit. It was here that Carl started composing his first songs with an eye toward the future. Watching the dance floor at all times for a reaction, he kept reshaping these loosely structured songs until he had a completed composition, which would then be finally put to paper. Carl was already sending demos to New York record companies, who kept rejecting him, sometimes explaining that this strange new hybrid of country with a Black rhythm fit no current commercial trend. But once Perkins heard Elvis on the radio, he not only knew what to call it, but knew that there was a record company person who finally understood it and was also willing to gamble in promoting it. That man was Sam Phillips and the record company was Sun Records, and that's exactly where Perkins headed in 1954 to get an audition.

It was here, at his first Sun audition, that the structure of the Perkins Brothers Band changed forever. Phillips didn't show the least bit of interest in Jay's Ernest Tubb-styled vocals, but flipped over Carl's singing and guitar playing. A scant four months later, he had issued the first Carl Perkins record, "Movie Magg" and "Turn Around," both sides written by the artist. By his second session, he had added W.S. Holland—a friend of Clayton's—to the band playing drums, a relatively new innovation to country music at the time. Phillips was still channeling Perkins in a strictly hillbilly vein, feeling that two artists doing the same type of music (in this case, Elvis and rockabilly) would cancel each other out. But after Elvis' contract was sold to RCA Victor in December, Carl was encouraged to finally let his rocking soul come up for air at his next Sun session. And rock he did with a double-whammy blast that proved to be his ticket to the bigs. The chance overhearing of a conversation at a dance one night between two teenagers coupled with a song suggestion from label mate Johnny Cash, Perkins approached Phillips with a new song he had written called "Blue Suede Shoes." After cutting two sides that Phillips planned on releasing as a single by the Perkins Brothers Band, Perkins laid down three takes each of "Blue Suede Shoes" and another rocker, "Honey Don't." A month later, Phillips decided to shelve the two country sides and go with the rockers as Carl's next single. Three months later, "Blue Suede Shoes," a tune that borrowed stylistically from pop, country, and R&B music, is sitting at the top of all charts, the first record to accomplish such a feat while becoming Sun's first million-seller in the bargain.

Ready to cash in on a national basis, Carl and the boys headed up to New York for the first time to appear on the "Perry Como Show." While enroute, their car rammed the back of a poultry truck, putting Carl and his brother Jay in the hospital with a cracked skull and broken neck, respectively. While in traction, Carl saw Presley performing his song on the "Dorsey Brothers Stage Show," his moment of fame and recognition snatched away from him. Perkins shrugged his shoulders and went back to the road and the Sun studios, trying to pick up where he left off.

The follow-ups to "Shoes" were, in many ways, superior to his initial hit, but each succeeding Sun single held diminishing sales, and it wasn't until the British Invasion and the subsequent rockabilly revival in the early '70s that the general public got to truly savor classics like "Boppin'

the Blues," "Matchbox," "Everybody's Trying to Be My Baby," "Your True Love," "Dixie Fried," "Put Your Cat Clothes On," and "All Mama's Children." While labelmates Johnny Cash and Jerry Lee Lewis (who played piano on "Matchbox") were scoring hit after hit, Perkins was becoming disillusioned with his fate, fueled by his increasing dependence on alcohol and the death of brother Jay to cancer. He kept plugging along, and when Johnny Cash left Sun to go to Columbia in 1958, Perkins followed him over. The royalty rate was better, and Perkins had no shortage of great songs to record, but Columbia's Nashville watch-the-clock production methods killed any of the spontaneity that was the charm of the Sun records. By the early '60s, after being dropped by Columbia and moving over to Decca with little success, Perkins was back playing the honky tonks and contemplating getting out of the business altogether. A call from a booking agent in 1964 offering a tour of England changed all of that. Temporarily swearing off the bottle, Perkins was greeted in Britain as a conquering hero, playing to sold-out audiences and being particularly lauded by a young beat group on the top of the charts named the Beatles. George Harrison had cut his musical teeth on Perkins' Sun recordings (as had most British guitarists), and the Fab Four ended up recording more tunes by him than any other artist except themselves. The British tour, not only rejuvenated his outlook, but suddenly made him realize that he had gone—through no maneuvering of his own—from has-been to legend in a country he had never played in before. Upon his return to the States, he hooked up with old friend and former labelmate Johnny Cash and was a regular fixture of his road show for the next ten years, bringing his battle with alcohol to an end. The '80s dawned with Perkins going on his own with a new band consisting of his sons backing him. His election to the Rock & Roll Hall of Fame in the mid-'80s was no less than his due. While battles with throat cancer and other ailments have curtailed his work load in the '90s, Carl Perkins continues to write, record, and perform, still grateful to be a part of the music business, while being totally secure in the fact that his place in the history books is assured. —*Cub Koda*

★ **Original Sun Greatest Hits** / 1986 / Rhino ✦✦✦✦✦
Essential, primal rockabilly, including "Everybody's Trying to Be My Baby," "Matchbox," "Honey Don't," "Boppin' the Blues," "Glad All Over," and the original "Blue Suede Shoes." —*Hank Davis*

Honky Tonk Gal / Apr. 1989 / Rounder ✦✦✦
Quirky, obscure, and offbeat, this is a much deeper look into Perkins' Sun period, with emphasis on hillbilly roots. —*Hank Davis*

The Jive After Five: Best of Carl Perkins (1958-1978) / 1990 / Rhino ✦✦✦✦
His later CBS work, much of which is excellent. —*Hank Davis*

The Classic / Feb. 1990 / Bear Family ✦✦✦✦
Simply the most comprehensive collection imaginable; included are all of his essential Sun tracks and alternate takes on five discs. All the 1958-1962 CBS sides are here, plus his 1963-1964 Decca sessions. It is indispensable for the serious fan and completist. —*Hank Davis*

Restless: The Columbia Recordings / May 12, 1992 / Columbia ✦✦✦

The Persuaders

Soul

This group made a pair of marvelous heartache ballads in 1971, but have the unfortunate legacy of having their finest cuts turned into pop hits via covers. Lead singer Douglas Scott, whose nickname appropriately was "Smokey," Willie Holland, James Barnes, and Charles Stodghill formed in New York in 1969. They signed with Atlantic in the early '70s and had their lone R&B chart topper in 1971, the shattering classic "Thin Line Between Love & Hate." It was also their only single. The follow-up was nearly as strong; "Love's Gonna Pack Up (And Walk Out)" reached No. 8 on the R&B charts, but had no crossover appeal. They continued on Win & Lose until 1973, then moved to Atco, where "Some Guys Have All the Luck" was a No. 7 R&B single in 1973. It was their final hit, though they kept recording until the late '70s, doing their last session for Calla. Besides the Pretenders redoing "Thin Line Between Love & Hate," Rod Stewart had a Top Ten pop hit with his version of "Some Guys Have All the Luck" in 1984. —*Ron Wynn*

● **Thin Line Between Love & Hate** / 1974 / Collectables ✦✦✦✦
A gritty soul unit, adept at tragic encounter tunes. The title song is a soul anthem. —*Ron Wynn*

Pet Shop Boys

Dance-Pop, Disco, Pop-Rock, Club-Dance

With their detached, intellectual, and often very funny lyrics and relentlessly hip, melodic, synth-driven disco, Neil Tennant and Chris Lowe were one of the most commercially successful groups in America and England in the late '80s, scoring a consistent string of hit singles through 1991. Through four albums and several singles, the Pet Shop Boys explored every dance trend from disco to house, creating beautifully lush, haunting soundscapes with their synthesizers and drum machines.

By the time *Very* was released in 1993, the popular audience had shifted away from dance-pop, and they had difficulty receiving mainstream airplay and MTV wouldn't air their videos. However, the duo continued to sell respectably while they continued to expand and redefine their music. —*Stephen Thomas Erlewine*

Please / 1986 / EMI America ✦✦✦
A collection of immaculately crafted and seamlessly produced synthe-sized dance-pop, the Pet Shop Boys' debut album *Please* sketches out the basic elements of the duo's sound. At first listen, most of the songs come off as mere excuses for the dance floor, driven by cold, melodic keyboard riffs and pulsing drum machines. However, the songcraft that the beats support is surprisingly strong, featuring catchy melodies that appear slight because of Neil Tennant's thin voice. Tennant's lyrics were still in their formative stages, with half of the record failing to transcend the formulaic constraints of dance-pop. The songs that do break free—the crass "Opportunities (Let's Make Lots of Money)," the lulling "Suburbia," and the hypnotic "West End Girls"—are not only classic dance singles, they're classic pop singles. —*Stephen Thomas Erlewine*

Disco / Oct. 1986 / EMI America ✦✦

Actually / Jun. 1987 / EMI America ✦✦✦✦
With their second album *Actually*, the Pet Shop Boys perfected their melodic, detatched dance-pop. Where most of *Please* was dominated by the beats, the rhythms on *Actually* are part of a series of intricate arrangements that create a glamorous but disposable backdrop for Neil Tennant's tales of isolation, boredom, money, and loneliness. Not only are the arrangements more accomplished, but the songs themselves are more striking, incorporating a strong sense of melody, as evidenced by "What Have I Done to Deserve This?," a duet with Dusty Springfield. Tennant's lyrics are clever and direct, chronicling the life and times of urban, lonely, and bored yuppies of the late '80s. And the fact that dance-pop is considered a disposable medium by most mainstream critics and listeners only increases the reserved emotional undercurrent of *Actually*, as well as its irony. —*Stephen Thomas Erlewine*

Introspective / Apr. 1988 / EMI America ✦✦✦

Behavior / 1990 / EMI America ✦✦✦✦
Behavior was a retreat from the deep dance textures of *Introspective*, as it picked up on the carefully constructed pop of *Actually*. In fact, *Behavior* functions as the Pet Shop Boys' bid for mainstream credibility, as much of the album relies more on pop craft than rhythmic variations. Although it's a subtle maneuver, it would have been rather disastrous if the results weren't so captivating. Tennant takes this approach seriously, singing the lyrics instead of speaking them. That doesn't necessarily give the album added emotional baggage—all of the distance and detachment in the duo's music is not a hindrance, it's part of the concept—but it does result in an ambitious and breathtaking pop album, which manages to include everything from the spiteful "How Can You Expect to Be Taken Seriously?" to the wistful "Being Boring." —*Stephen Thomas Erlewine*

★ **Discography: The Complete Singles Collection** / 1991 / EMI America ✦✦✦✦✦
Most of the Pet Shop Boys' albums are well-crafted and thoroughly intriguing in their own right, but dance-pop is a medium that is driven by hit singles. *Discography* collects all the duo's numerous hit singles, including a handful of non-album tracks, in their original seven-inch single mix, which occasionally varies from the album version, particularly in the case of the *Introspective* material. Presented chronologically, the singles not only demonstrate the band's increasing musical sophistication, they illustrate what fine songwriters Tennant and Lowe are. These 19 songs form one of the most consistent and innovative bodies of work of its era. Some of the production techniques have dated slightly, but the music has remained impressive. —*Stephen Thomas Erlewine*

Very / 1993 / ERG ✦✦✦✦
Because they work in a field that isn't usually taken seriously, the Pet Shop Boys are often ignored in the rock world. But make no mistake—they are one of the most talented pop outfits working today, witty and melodic with a fine sense of flair. *Very* is one of their best records, expertly weaving between the tongue-in-cheek humor of "I Wouldn't Normally Do This Kind of Thing," the quietly shocking "Can You Forgive Her?" and the bizarrely moving cover of the Village People's "Go West." Alternately happy and melancholy, *Very* is the Pet Shop Boys at their finest. —*Stephen Thomas Erlewine*

Disco 2 / 1994 / Capitol ✦✦

Alternative / 1995 / EMI ✦✦✦✦
Alternative is a double-disc set of the Pet Shop Boys' B-sides. Far from being a superfluous collection, the album contains a wealth of prime material, including several tracks that surpass those the duo put on their albums. Consequently, the set is worthwhile not only for hardcore fans, but for listeners with a passing interest in the group. —*Stephen Thomas Erlewine*

Peter & Gordon

British Invasion
In June 1964, Peter & Gordon became the very first British Invasion act after the Beatles to take the No. 1 spot on the American charts with "A World Without Love." That hit, and their subsequent successes, were due as much or more to their important connections as to their talent. Peter Asher was the older brother of Jane Asher, Paul McCartney's girlfriend for much of the 1960s. This no doubt gave Asher and Gordon Waller access to Lennon-McCartney compositions that were unrecorded by the Beatles, such as "A World Without Love" and three of their other biggest hits, "Nobody I Know," "I Don't Want to See You Again," and "Woman" (the last of which was written by McCartney under a pseudonym). But Peter & Gordon were significant talents in their own right, a sort of Everly Brothers-styled duo for the folk-rock of the mid-'60s. In fact, when Gene Clark first approached Jim McGuinn in 1964 about working together in a group that would eventually evolve into the Byrds, he suggested that they could form a Peter & Gordon-styled act.

Asher and Waller had been singing together since their days at Westminster School for Boys, a private school in London. "A World Without Love" was their biggest and best hit, one that sounded very much like the Beatles' more pop-oriented originals. Their other two 1964 hits, "Nobody I Know" and "I Don't Want to See You Again," were pleasant but less distinguished. Sounding like McCartney-dominated Beatle rejects (which, in fact, they were), the production employed a softer, more acoustic feel than the hits by the Beatles and other early British Invasion guitar bands. "I Don't Want to See You Again" used strings, as would several of the duo's subsequent hits, which became increasingly middle-of-the-road in their pop orientation.

Some scattered folky B-sides showed that Asher and Waller may have been capable of developing into decent songwriters, but like many of the less-talented British Invaders, their lack of songwriting acumen and ability to move with the times would eventually work against them. They did continue to hit the charts for a couple of years, with updates of the oldies "True Love Ways" (Buddy Holly) and "To Know You Is to Love You" (a variation of the Teddy Bears' "To Know Her Is to Love Her"). There was also a Top Ten cover of Del Shannon's "I Go to Pieces," and the brassy, McCartney-penned "Woman." The overtly cute and British novelty "Lady Godiva," though, became their last big hit in late 1966.

After Peter & Gordon broke up in 1968, Asher became an enormously successful producer, first as the director of A&R at the Beatles' Apple Records (where he worked on James Taylor's first album). He relocated to Los Angeles in the 1970s and became one of the principal architects of mellow Californian rock, producing Taylor and Linda Ronstadt. —*Richie Unterberger*

● **Best of Peter & Gordon** / 1991 / Rhino ✦✦✦✦
This duo synthesized Beatles and Everly Brothers harmonies into a wonderfully seamless string of mid-'60s British Invasion lite-pop hits. The popular songs are all contained here, with great sound and well-rendered liner notes. —*Rick Clark*

Tom Petty & the Heartbreakers

Rock 'n' Roll
Since 1976, Tom Petty & the Heartbreakers have been one of America's finest rock 'n' roll bands, combining the ringing guitars of the Byrds with the gritty rhythmic drive of the Rolling Stones. Petty's tales of American losers and dreamers were simple and direct, but emotionally charged. The Heartbreakers were a lean, tight band that could handle hard rock 'n' roll and melodic pop equally well. The group gained critical attention and solid sales with their first album, but 1979's *Damn the Torpedoes* was their commercial breakthrough, selling over two million copies; it couldn't have come at a better time, since Petty filed for bankruptcy before its release.

During the '80s, Petty sold consistently well, as he expanded his sound with the release of each album. In 1989, he released his first solo album, *Full Moon Fever*, which became his biggest hit yet. That momentum carried over into the next Heartbreakers release, 1991's *Into the Great Wide Open*, which went platinum. As they were preparing their next album, the group released a greatest hits album in 1993, which contained the hit single, "Mary Jane's Last Dance." *Greatest Hits* was the last album the group released on MCA Records. In 1994, Petty began a new contract with Warner Bros., releasing *Wildflowers* toward the end of that year; *Wildflowers* became another multi-platinum success for him. In 1995, MCA Records released a five-disc box set called *Playback*. In the summer of 1996, Petty & the Heartbreakers released *Songs and Music from She's the One*. —*Stephen Thomas Erlewine*

Tom Petty & the Heartbreakers / 1976 / Gone Gator ✦✦✦
Originally released on Denny Cordell's Shelter label, the 1976 self-titled debut was a real sleeper until the single "Breakdown" became Petty's first hit almost a year and a half later. This album's release coincided

with the advent of the punk and new wave movements. The lean, edgy production and arrangements only enhanced that perception, in spite of the fact the the songs clearly drew inspiration from the Byrds and '60s Anglo-rock. Among the highlights are the gritty riff-rocker "Strangered in the Night" (which features Dwight Twilley), "American Girl" (a song so shamelessly influenced by the Byrds that even Roger McGuinn covered it), "Hometown Blues" (later covered by Rosanne Cash), and "The Wild One, Forever." — *Rick Clark*

You're Gonna Get It! / 1978 / Gone Gator ✦✦✦

☆ **Damn the Torpedoes** / 1979 / MCA ✦✦✦✦✦
Petty switched producers to Jimmy Iovine, and together they created the masterful *Damn the Torpedoes*. For once, Petty's voice was up front in the mix, giving him much more character. The band never sounded so full or punchy before this. *Torpedoes* opens with a seamless string of great rockers, "Refugee," "Here Comes My Girl," and "Even the Losers." Other highlights include "Century City" and "Don't Do Me Like That." — *Rick Clark*

Hard Promises / 1981 / MCA ✦✦✦✦
Pre-album publicity made much of the fact that Petty was taking issue with his record label (MCA) over gouging his fans with a list-price increase on this album. Petty won, reinforcing the notion that he was a principled people's artist. The aptly titled *Hard Promises* became another platinum hit. Even though *Hard Promises* is a slight step down from its predecessor, there is plenty of strong material. "The Waiting," one of Petty's finest songs, is the stylistic epitome of his Byrds fixation. Other standouts include the rockers "Kings Road," "A Thing About You," and the darkly humorous "Something Big." — *Rick Clark*

Long After Dark / 1982 / MCA ✦✦
The highlights of this album, "Straight into Darkness," "Change of Heart," "Deliver Me," and "You Got Lucky," may be some of Petty's best, but much of *Long After Dark* suffers from weak melodies and flat-sounding production. — *Rick Clark*

Pack Up the Plantation: Live! / 1985 / MCA ✦✦

Southern Accents / 1985 / MCA ✦✦✦

Let Me Up (I've Had Enough) / 1987 / MCA ✦✦✦
After the failed *Southern Accents*, Petty and company return to a fairly straightahead collection of rock 'n' roll. Except for a handful of strong tunes like the free-associative rocker (co-written with Dylan) "Jammin' Me," "Runaway Trains," and "My Life/Your World," much of this album feels like the product of an uninspired band. — *Rick Clark*

Full Moon Fever / 1989 / MCA ✦✦✦✦
Recorded as a casual side project, Petty's first solo album possessed more flashes of brilliance than most of his albums put together. It also produced four hits: "Free Fallin'," "A Face in the Crowd," "Runnin' Down a Dream," and "I Won't Back Down." Another highlight was a great remake of the Byrds' "I'll Feel a Whole Lot Better." Petty ought to moonlight more often. — *Rick Clark*

Into the Great Wide Open / 1991 / MCA ✦✦✦
This is Petty's first Heartbreakers album after his multi-platinum solo effort, *Full Moon Fever*. The band sounds a little more lively than on the previous two efforts, and the material is generally better than much of their previous two studio albums. However, *Full Moon Fever* is a stronger album, overall. — *Rick Clark*

★ **Greatest Hits** / 1993 / MCA ✦✦✦✦✦
All of Petty's biggest hits collected, along with two new tracks—the excellent "Mary Jane's Last Dance" and a cover of Thunderclap Newman's "Something in the Air"—on one essential disc. Everything from "American Girl" to "Free Fallin'" is included, with 16 tracks proving that Petty is one of the best rockers of the past 15 years. — *Stephen Thomas Erlewine*

Wildflowers / 1994 / Warner Bros. ✦✦✦✦
Under the guidance of producer Rick Rubin, Tom Petty turns in a stripped-down, subtle record with *Wildflowers*. Coming after two albums of Jeff Lynne-directed bombast, the very sound of the record is refreshing; Petty sounds relaxed and confident. Most of the songs are small gems, but a few are a little too laidback, almost reaching the point of carelessness. Nevertheless, the finest songs here ("Wildflowers," "You Don't Know How It Feels," "It's Good to Be King," and several others) match the quality of his best material, making *Wildflowers* one of Petty's most distinctive and best albums. — *Stephen Thomas Erlewine*

Playback / 1995 / MCA ✦✦✦✦
The first question roosting in the brain while cracking open *Playback* is: how many artists in rock 'n' roll can really justify a six-CD compilation? Despite these initial misgivings, *Playback* works. The impressive box has not been thrown together haphazardly, nor does it try to overpower on bulk alone. MCA did a brilliant job of compiling and sequencing here. The material is grouped logically; nothing sounds superfluous, and it's entirely possible to spend the better part of a day combing through the content—including an exhaustive 75-page booklet—without a hint of impatience or monotony setting in. Slipped from elegant, slim-line cardboard sleeves, the first three discs capture the best of Petty's Shelter and

MCA work, from 1976's eponymous debut to 1993's *Greatest Hits*. Disc four features 15 single B-sides, but the real find for Petty-ophiles is the remaining two discs of previously unreleased material, going back to demos of Heartbreaker-precursors Mudcrutch, right up to an early-'90s session where Petty felt re-energized after hearing Nirvana for the first time. Much of this material is eminently interesting and listenable. — *Roch Parisien*

Songs and Music from She's the One / Aug. 1996 / Warner Bros. ✦✦✦

Pezband

Rock 'n' Roll, Power-Pop
Hailing from the same state as Cheap Trick (Illinois), the Pezband were a mostly fine, occasionally wonderful, power-pop band that specialized in hook-filled hard rock with sweet multi-part harmonies. Led by the strong, blues-influenced singing of Mimi (a guy) Betinis and the rampaging Jeff Beck-influenced guitar playing of Tommy Gawenda, the Pezzers' first LP (released in 1977) was not as hard and heavy as Cheap Trick, nor did it exhibit the berserk panache of their fellow Illini. But that all changed with their second LP, *Laughing in the Dark*, which contained a high quotient of good-to-great songs, excellent production by Jesse Hood Jackson, and a wonderful lack of the smugness and calculation that was slowly infiltrating every power-pop band in America. A huge public reaction, however, was not forthcoming. The band had its supporters (like most of the editorial staff of *Trouser Press*), but power-pop/hard rock from Illinois was dominated by Cheap Trick, and everybody else had to find a place in the pecking order. For bands like the Pezband, that meant far less coverage than they deserved. There was also another issue: the band didn't deliver another record as good as *Laughing*, nor could they recapture the excitement and messy mania of their live show (forever preserved on an excellent pair of EPs, *Too Old, Too Soon* and *Thirty Seconds Over Schaumburg*) in the studio. Hence, the rest of their recorded output is serviceable, but only hints at what the band was truly capable of doing. It's too bad, because they were such unpretentious, likable guys. By the early '80s, the Pezband had virtually vanished from the music scene, but a Chicago-based independent label (in 1994!) released some outtakes and other previously unreleased material, and the word is that Mimi Betinis is putting the band back together. Cautious optimism is suggested. — *John Dougan*

● **Laughing in the Dark** / 1978 / Radar ✦✦✦✦
Without a doubt, the best Pezband record available. Side one offers an especially strong trio of rock-pop songs ("Love Goes Underground," "I'm Leavin'," and "Stop! Wait a Minute"). Sadly, many other bands got more press, and this record was lost in the shuffle. The good news is that if you found it in a used record store (assuming there still are a few in your neighborhood), you could probably get it for $2. Some may dismiss it as formulaic, and that might be true, but no one ever said that formula couldn't be fun. — *John Dougan*

Too Old, Too Soon Live at Dingwalls / 1978 / Passport ✦✦✦
A great four-track live EP recorded at the much-missed club Dingwalls in London. Side one features rough and ready versions of "Stop! Wait a Minute" and "Lovesmith"; Side two features a manic "Not Fade Away" and a thoroughly great romp through the Swinging Blue Jeans' "Hippy Hippy Shake." Power-pop with the accent on power. — *John Dougan*

Thirty Seconds Over Schaumburg / 1978 / PVC ✦✦✦✦
The title is a tongue-in-cheek reference to the Chicago suburb from whence they came. The music is loud, ferocious, and wonderful. Tommy Gawenda is a little out of control here (too many multichorus solos), but after all is said and done, this record proves what a great live band the Pezband were. Extra point for a rippin' version of Jeff Beck's "Blue Wind" and its neat segue into the Yardbirds' "Stroll On." — *John Dougan*

Liz Phair

b. Apr. 17, 1967
Guitar, Vocals / Singer-Songwriter, Alternative Pop-Rock, Lo-Fi
For several years, singer-songwriter Liz Phair recorded home-made tapes under the name Girlysound; one of the cassettes reached Matador Records, which offered her a contract. Phair's first album, the double-length *Exile in Guyville*, was released in the early spring of 1993; by the end of the year, it was topping nearly every critic's poll in America. During the course of the year, Phair became the figurehead for the new movement of female artists, particularly those in alternative rock. Combining elements of both traditional singer-songwriters and alternative rockers, Phair stands as an original; although her roots are identifiable, nothing in her music sounds derivative.

Whip-Smart, Phair's 1994 follow-up to *Exile in Guyville*, was a commercial success, debuting at No. 27, but it received mixed reviews. "Supernova," the first single pulled from the album, was a Top Ten alternative radio hit. In the summer of 1995, Phair released *Juvenelia*, an EP that featured the first commercial release of selected *Girlysound* material. — *Stephen Thomas Erlewine*

★ **Exile in Guyville** / 1993 / Matador ✦✦✦✦✦

Liz Phair's stunningly accomplished and ambitious debut album *Exile in Guyville* is loosely based on the Rolling Stones' classic *Exile on Main Street*, retelling that album's weary tales of love and sex from a female perspective. While there is some anger here ("Fuck and Run"), there are also love songs ("Never Said"), lust songs ("Flower"), haunting character sketches ("Canary" and "Explain It to Me"), and exceptional narratives ("Divorce Song," "Stratford-on-Guy," and "Help Me Mary"). While her lyrics are literate without being pretentious, what makes the album so impressive is her musical diversity; from rock 'n' roll to folk, from experimental rock to just a piano and a voice, *Exile in Guyville* is an endlessly inventive album that only gets better with repeated plays. *— Stephen Thomas Erlewine*

Whip-Smart / 1994 / Matador ✦✦✦

Expectations ran extremely high for Phair's follow-up to *Exile in Guyville*, one of the most critically acclaimed debut albums of all time. If there are flaws in this generally first-rate follow-up, they mostly arise in comparison with *Guyville*, a record of such unexpected impact that most anything Phair could have done may have been found lacking. She continues to explore sex and relationships with exhilarating frankness and celebration, employing her much-touted profanity to a conversational rather than a sensational effect. The sound is somewhat more produced, though still pretty basic, and the compositions are by and large tuneful and lyrically intriguing. It's not, after all is said and done, quite as striking as *Guyville;* like many sophomore efforts, it mines similar territory without making huge strides forward. Several songs are reprised from her widely circulated *Girlysound* demo tapes, and in some instances the more heavily produced, self-consciously ingenious arrangements here suffer in comparison to their blueprints. The title track, one of the highlights of those tapes, comes off as particularly gimmicky in its new incarnation, with the addition of all manner of superfluous animal noises. There's no question that Phair is a major songwriter and artist, but this album is more a solidification of her talents than a breakthrough statement. *— Richie Unterberger*

Girlysound / Bootleg ✦✦✦✦

Before signing to Matador Records, Phair recorded a wealth of home demos that were only circulated, primarily to acquaintances, on cassette. In fact, it was a tape of this material that brought Phair to the attention of Matador in the first place. Featuring just Liz and her low-volume electric guitar, with layers of overdubs enabling Liz to harmonize with herself, this collection of over 20 low-fidelity, intensely personal songs has circulated among literally thousands of Phair fans, making this one of the most popular and sought-after alternative-rock bootlegs of all time. A few of the tracks found their way onto her first couple of albums in drastically reworked versions, including "Stratford-on-Guy," "Flower," "Johnny Sunshine," "Whip-Smart," "Never Said," "Shane," and "Chopsticks." These stripped-down versions aren't necessarily better than (although "Whip-Smart" sounds much less tongue-in-cheek and more effective in its original incarnation), but they are fascinating to hear in such barebones arrangements. The substantial majority of these have not been released by Phair, and while some are clearly tentative drafts or awkward, half-baked efforts, others are as tuneful and provoking as anything on her official albums. Phair is arguably a more powerful performer when stripped to her essentials of voice and guitar, and this tape is as vital to her legacy as her Matador discs. *— Richie Unterberger*

Sam Phillips

Vocals / Pop-Rock

Sam Phillips the singer, not the former head of Sun Records, is a California-based singer-songwriter, whose 1987 debut album, *The Turning* (released under her given name of Leslie Phillips), was a contemporary Christian recording issued by Myrrh and produced by fellow Christian and then-future husband T-Bone Burnette. He also handled the boards for Phillips' three secular albums, which have garnered considerable critical praise. *— William Ruhlmann*

The Indescribable Wow / 1988 / Virgin ✦✦✦✦

T-Bone Burnette surrounds Phillips' voice, which has both a little-girl bounce and a teenage ache in it, with neo-'60s pop arrangements on songs whose lyrics are often more serious than the inevitably cute-sounding production. But that only means that, once the music has seduced you, the words surprise you. *— William Ruhlmann*

Cruel Inventions / 1991 / Virgin ✦✦✦

● **Martinis & Bikinis** / 1994 / Virgin ✦✦✦✦

Sam Phillips' third album is a remarkably rich and varied set of Beatlesque pop, distinguished by her exceptional songwriting. *— Stephen Thomas Erlewine*

Omnipop / Aug. 20, 1996 / Virgin ✦✦✦

Martinis & Bikinis was an edgy, catchy pop-rock album that expanded Sam Phillips' sonic palette without losing sight of her melodic, layered songwriting. With *Omnipop (It's Only a Fleshwound Lambcomp)*, the

follow-up to *Martinis & Bikinis*, Phillips concentrates on creating soundscapes that are vaguely experimental and layered with effects and synthesizers, sounding unlike much of her catalog. The problem is that the soundscapes hide a lack of substance within the songs themselves. Much of the lyrics are underdeveloped and cliched, while the music itself doesn't have the punch or hooks of her previous three albums. And that makes *Omnipop* a muddled, ineffective affair. A few songs sink in after repeated listens, but the album on the whole is a failed—albeit honorable—experiment. *— Stephen Thomas Erlewine*

Phish

Rock 'n' Roll, Fusion, Neo-Psychedelia

During the early '90s, Phish emerged as the heirs to the Grateful Dead's throne. Although their music is somewhat similar to the Dead's—it's an eclectic, free-form rock 'n' roll encompassing folk, jazz, country, bluegrass, and pop—the group adheres more to a jazz tradition than a folk tradition of improvisation and they have a looser, goofier attitude. After all, their drummer regularly plays a vacuum cleaner during their concerts. Phish's main claim as the inheritors to the Dead's legacy is their approach to their musical career. The band didn't concentrate on albums, they dedicated themselves to live improvisation. Within a few years of their 1988 debut album, Phish had become an institution in certain sections of America, particularly college campuses. And their in-concert popularity didn't translate to record sales—by the middle of the '90s, Phish was able to pack stadiums, but none of their albums had gone gold. Nevertheless, the band was one of the most popular American groups of the '90s, cultivating legions of dedicated fans that followed the band from show to show and bought countless numbers of bootleg recordings.

Guitarist/vocalist Trey Anastasio, drummer Jon Fishman, and guitarist Jeff Holdsworth formed the band in late 1983 while attending the University of Vermont. After meeting and jamming in their dormitory, the trio posted flyers across campus, recruiting a bassist. Mike Gordon answered the advertisement and he was soon added to the original lineup. The group began practicing regularly and they soon assembled a demo tape. In the fall of 1984, Phish began performing off-campus concerts. At this stage in their career, the band was augmented by percussionist Marc Daubert and, occasionally, a vocalist called the Dude of Life. Soon, the group was playing concerts on nearby campuses, including Goddard College's Springfest in 1985. Page McConnell organized the Springfest at Goddard and he became a fan of the band. Later in the year, after Anastasio and Fishman spent the summer busking in Europe, McConnell convinced the group to add him as a keyboardist in late 1985. Shortly after McConnell joined Phish, Holdsworth left the group. In the fall of 1986, Anastasio and Fishman transferred to Goddard College. For most of 1987, the band attended college and played gigs regularly.

Early in 1988, Phish recorded *Junta*, which they sold at their shows as a cassette-only release. In 1989, the group played their first tour outside of New England, traveling through the Southeast. Phish also recorded their second album, *Lawn Boy*, in 1989, although the album wasn't released until the fall of 1990; the record was released on the independent record label Absolute A-Go-Go, a subsidiary of Rough Trade. Throughout early 1991, Phish toured America. During the summer, they recorded their third album, as well as a set of sessions with their old friend, the Dude of Life. Late in August, Rough Trade collapsed, taking Absolute A-Go-Go with it. Phish was left without a record contract but they were soon signed by Elektra Records. In February of 1992, *A Picture of Nectar* was released by Elektra. After its release, the group embarked on an extensive national tour, which was followed by their first European tour, during which they opened for the Violent Femmes. In the summer of 1992, Phish played a handful of shows on the first H.O.R.D.E. tour. Also that summer, Elektra reissued *Lawn Boy* and *Junta*.

Rift, the band's fourth album and the first they recorded with a producer, appeared in February 1993. During Phish's 1993 tour, the group sold tickets that were specifically designed for fans taping the concert. *Hoist*, the band's fifth album, was released in 1994. "Down with Disease," one of the songs on *Hoist*, became the band's first video and it received some airplay on MTV. *Hoist* sold better than the group's previous albums, which was an indication of how large the group's fan base had gotten. In the fall of 1994, *Crimes of the Mind*, the album Phish recorded with the Dude of Life in 1991, was released on Elektra Records. In the summer of 1995, the band released the double-live album, *A Live One*. In early 1996, Trey Anastasio released a free-form jazz side-project called *Surrender to the Air*. During the spring of 1996, Phish completed their sixth album, which was produced by Steve Lillywhite and released in the fall of that year. *— Stephen Thomas Erlewine*

Junta / 1988 / Elektra ✦✦✦✦

Phish's debut album is a bit long-winded and unfocused, yet it establishes their dedication to musical exploration effectively. *— David Jehnzen*

Lawn Boy / 1991 / Elektra ✦✦✦

A Picture of Nectar / Aug. 1991 / Elektra ✦✦✦✦
A wildly eclectic album in the vein of the Grateful Dead, *A Picture of Nectar* is the best studio example of Phish's genre-jumping good-time rock 'n' roll. —*David Jehnzen*

Rift / 1993 / Elektra ✦✦

Hoist / 1994 / Elektra ✦✦✦

● **A Live One** / 1995 / Elektra ✦✦✦✦
Phish's strength has always been its live shows, and *A Live One* shows why. Given the opportunity, they take their songs in every direction, winding through several different sounds within the course of a song. *A Live One* also features seven previously unreleased songs, making it worthwhile listening for even casual fans. Then again, most fans of Phish will want to hear everything the group has ever played. —*Stephen Thomas Erlewine*

Wilson Pickett

b. Mar. 18, 1941, Prattville, AL
Vocals / Soul, R&B
The Wicked Pickett, as he dubbed himself, first achieved a measure of success as the apopletic lead tenor on the Falcons' "I Found a Love" in 1962. Fleeting success followed (his original of "If You Need Me" was scooped up by Solomon Burke), before he signed with Atlantic Records in 1964. After a couple of false starts, he was shipped down to Memphis and came back with "In the Midnight Hour." It was followed by similarly compelling entries such as "Don't Fight It," "634-5789," "Mustang Sally," and a hysterical revival of Chris Kenner's mid-tempo shuffle, "Land of 1000 Dances." Scouring old albums, one will also notice that Pickett never lost his feel for a slow ballad, despite his reputation as the prince of the dance floor. Some have charged that Pickett went on to reduce spontaneous emotion to a cliché, and most of his later records certainly reinforce that notion, but at his considerable best, Pickett was an immensely compelling performer at any tempo. The hit movie *The Commitments* hinted broadly at the esteem in which vintage Pickett is held. Sampled at his best, he was a titan. —*Colin Escott*

In the Midnight Hour / 1965 / Atlantic ✦✦✦

The Exciting Wilson Pickett / 1966 / Atlantic ✦✦✦✦
Less of a hodgepodge than his debut *In the Midnight Hour* album, Pickett's second LP established—if there had been any doubt—his stature as a major '60s soul man. The 12 tracks include his monster hits "634-5789," "Ninety-Nine and a Half (Won't Do)," "In The Midnight Hour," and "Land Of 1000 Dances" (the last of which was his first Top Ten pop hit). Collectors will be more interested in the non-hit cuts, which are of nearly an equal level. These include covers of the R&B standards "Something You Got," "Mercy Mercy," and "Barefootin'"; several original tunes written in collaboration with Memphis soul greats Steve Cropper, Eddie Floyd, and David Porter; and Bobby Womack's "She's So Good to Me." It all adds up to one of the most consistent 1960s soul albums. The CD reissue of this 1966 record features detailed liner notes and session documentation. —*Richie Unterberger*

The Wicked Pickett / 1966 / Atlantic ✦✦✦✦
A fabulous album, done when Pickett was in the midst of his best period at Atlantic. It had everything—great songs, wonderful production and arrangements, and a hungry, galvanizing Wilson Pickett hollering, screaming, shouting, and soaring on anything he covered, from ballads to uptempo dance and mid-tempo wailers. It also has been deleted at present. —*Ron Wynn*

The Sound of Wilson Pickett / 1967 / Atlantic ✦✦✦✦
A masterpiece, perhaps his finest '60s album. This wasn't a hits collection, but a batch of great singles. His version of "Funky Broadway" may still be the best; it was certainly the most swaggering and posturing, punctuated by his screams and jubilant cries. Pickett was all over the R&B charts in 1967, and this was one of three albums Atlantic issued on him that year. Each one was a classic. —*Ron Wynn*

I'm in Love / 1968 / Atlantic ✦✦✦

Midnight Mover / 1968 / Atlantic ✦✦✦

A Man and a Half: The Best of Wilson Pickett / 1992 / Rhino ✦✦✦✦
This tribute to the soulful career of the Wicked One is simply one of the most fabulous compilation reissues of 1992. From the fire-breathing kickoff of "I Found a Love," Pickett's debut recording with the Falcons, through all the great Atlantic hits, this two-disc set spotlights some of the greatest singing ever recorded. Songs like "In the Midnight Hour," "Mustang Sally," and "Land of 1000 Dances" helped define '60s soul music. Great liner notes by Leo Sacks and equally great photos. A must for your collection. —*Christine Ohlman*

★ **The Very Best of Wilson Pickett** / 1993 / Rhino ✦✦✦✦✦
Although the double-disc set *A Man and a Half* is necessary for serious soul fans, *The Very Best of Wilson Pickett* should satiate the needs of any casual fan. Featuring 16 of his biggest Atlantic hits—including "In the Midnight Hour," "634-5789 (Soulsville, USA)," "Land of 1000 Dances,"

"Mustang Sally," "Funky Broadway," "She's Looking Good," and "I'm a Midnight Mover"—*The Very Best of Wilson Pickett* contains all of his truly essential items, making it both an excellent introduction and the closest thing possible to a definitive single-disc retrospective. —*Stephen Thomas Erlewine*

Pink Floyd

Vocals / Art-Rock/Progressive-Rock, Psychedelic
Practically from its inception in 1965, Pink Floyd was on the cutting edge of psychedelic rock experimentalism, utilizing feedback, sound effects, light shows, unorthodox lyrical themes, and spacey productions. It was band member Syd Barrett (b. Jan. 6, 1946) who gave the band its moniker, inspired by Georgia bluesmen Pink Anderson and Floyd Council. Barrett's trippy songwriting on their debut album, *The Piper at the Gates of Dawn* (UK No. 6), set the band even further apart from most bands of the time. Barrett, however, left the band due to psychological deterioration encouraged by drug abuse, leaving bassist Roger Waters (b. Sep. 9, 1944) to take over the songwriting duties.
The band's sonic explorations achieved focus with 1973's seamless *Dark Side of the Moon* (No. 1), an album that firmly placed them in the big time. Follow-up albums *Wish You Were Here* (No. 1), *Animals* (No. 3), *The Wall* (No. 1), and *The Final Cut* (No. 6) enjoyed phenomenal success.
Waters revealed an increasingly vitriolic spirit in his conceptual themes as he addressed the breakdown of individual dignity in the face of a perceived Orwellian post-World War II social order.
It should be said that guitarist Dave Gilmour's (b. Mar. 6, 1946) soaring guitar work and songwriting contributions to *The Wall's* "Comfortably Numb" gave him a high profile in the band. After *The Final Cut*, Waters and the band acrimoniously split up in 1983, leaving them to pursue various solo efforts, with moderate success.
Gilmour re-formed Pink Floyd in 1987 with drummer Nick Mason (b. Jan. 27, 1945) and keyboardist Rick Wright (b. Jul. 28, 1945), releasing *A Momentary Lapse of Reason* (No. 3), which sparked a flurry of lawsuits between Waters and the band over the ownership of the name. While the album lacks the thematic bite of Waters' input, the band's sound is intact. The new Pink Floyd's success continued in 1994, when *The Division Bell* topped the charts upon its release. —*Rick Clark*

☆ **The Piper at the Gates of Dawn** / Aug. 5, 1967 / Capitol ✦✦✦✦✦
The debut album combines long, group-written, largely instrumental compositions with shorter, whimsical, eclectic pop songs written by lead singer and guitarist Syd Barrett (his only full-length album appearance with the group). A wonderful evocation of the distinctly British take on '60s psychedelic music. (Note: Avoid the out-of-print LP version *Pink Floyd*, Tower 5093, which abridges the original UK album.) —*William Ruhlmann*

Tonite Let's All Make Love in London / 1968 / CBS ✦✦✦

A Saucerful of Secrets / Jun. 29, 1968 / Capitol ✦✦✦
A transitional album on which the band moved from Barrett's relatively concise and vivid songs to spacey, ethereal material with lengthy instrumental passages. Barrett's influence is still felt (he actually did manage to contribute one track, the jovial "Jugband Blues"), and much of the material retains a gentle, fairy-tale ambience. "Remember a Day" and "See Saw" are highlights; on "Set the Controls for the Heart of the Sun," "Let There Be More Light," and the lengthy instrumental title track, the band begin to map out the dark and repetitive pulses that would characterize their next few records. —*Richie Unterberger*

More / Jul. 1969 / Capitol ✦✦

Ummagumma / Nov. 1969 / Capitol ✦✦✦
A two-disc set, the first disc containing a definitive live set, the second experimental contributions from each of the band members. —*William Ruhlmann*

Atom Heart Mother / Oct. 1970 / Capitol ✦✦✦
Pink Floyd started to stretch out its long numbers here, with the orchestrated title track taking up an entire side of the album. Still not as focused as they would be, the group nevertheless was beginning to show the musical ambition that would lead to their later successes. —*William Ruhlmann*

Relics / May 1971 / Barclay ✦✦✦✦
A singles collection from the Syd Barrett era, containing the British hits "Arnold Layne" and "See Emily Play," among other psychedelic nuggets. —*William Ruhlmann*

Meddle / Oct. 30, 1971 / Capitol ✦✦✦✦
With *Meddle*, Pink Floyd instrumentally arrived at an airy ensemble sound, which would eventually find full flower on their 1973 classic *Dark Side of the Moon*. This approach is particularly evident on "Echoes," a periodically languorous jam that takes up one-half of the album. Nevertheless, there are enough sonic concepts and pleasant melodies at work on this album to make it worthwhile to the Floyd fan looking to dig deeper than *Dark Side of the Moon* or *The Wall*. —*Rick Clark*

Obscured by Clouds / Jun. 1972 / Capitol ✦✦
Like *More, Obscured by Clouds* was a soundtrack album Pink Floyd threw together quickly for a film by Barbet Schroeder. Songs like "Free Four" show Roger Waters developing the songwriting skill that would catapult Pink Floyd to mass stardom with its next new release, *Dark Side of the Moon.* — *William Ruhlmann*

★ **Dark Side of the Moon** / Mar. 24, 1973 / Capitol ✦✦✦✦✦
Pink Floyd's instrumental prowess and mastery of sound effects, married for the first time to bassist Roger Waters' lyrics about madness, "Time," "Money," and other concerns make for the most impressive mood music of the decade (and sales of 25 million copies so far). — *William Ruhlmann*

☆ **Wish You Were Here** / Sep. 12, 1975 / Columbia ✦✦✦✦✦
A concept album paying tribute to Syd Barrett ("Shine on You Crazy Diamond") and lambasting the music industry ("Have a Cigar"). — *William Ruhlmann*

Animals / Oct. 2, 1977 / Columbia ✦✦✦
Consisting of heavily reworked songs that had long been a part of Pink Floyd's live repertoire and were now given an Orwellian overview, *Animals* found Pink Floyd acting as the mouthpiece for Roger Waters' increasingly vitriolic takes on modern life. The result was one of its less successful later efforts. — *William Ruhlmann*

☆ **The Wall** / Nov. 1979 / Columbia ✦✦✦✦✦
This is Roger Waters' two-disc meditation on the travails of a rock star, whose unhappy life causes him to build a psychological barrier between himself and the rest of the world. Contains the No. 1 hit "Another Brick in the Wall (Part 2)" and the concert favorite "Comfortably Numb" (co-written by David Gilmour). — *William Ruhlmann*

Collection of Great Dance Songs / Nov. 1981 / Columbia ✦✦

Works / 1983 / Capitol ✦✦

The Final Cut / Apr. 1983 / Columbia ✦✦✦
A Roger Waters solo album in all but name, containing the composer's response to Britain's Falklands War in the form of a massive condemnation of war and government. — *William Ruhlmann*

A Momentary Lapse of Reason / 1987 / Columbia ✦✦
A David Gilmour solo album in all but name, featuring the kind of atmospheric instrumental music and Gilmour guitar sound typical of the Floyd before the now-departed Roger Waters took over but lacking Waters' unifying vision and lyrical ability. — *William Ruhlmann*

Delicate Sound of Thunder / Jan. 2, 1988 / Columbia ✦✦

The Division Bell / 1994 / Columbia ✦✦

Pulse / 1995 / Columbia ✦✦

Gene Pitney

b. Feb. 17, 1941, Hartford, CT
Vocals / Pop, Pop-Rock, Teen Idol, Brill Building Pop
One of the most interesting and difficult-to-categorize singers in '60s pop, Gene Pitney had a long run of hits distinguished by his pained, one-of-a-kind melodramatic wail. Pitney is sometimes characterized (or dismissed) as a shallow teen-idol type prone to operatic ballads. It's true that some of his biggest hits—"Town Without Pity," "Only Love Can Break a Heart," "I'm Gonna Be Strong," "It Hurts to Be in Love," and "Twenty Four Hours from Tulsa"—are archetypes of adolescent or just-post-adolescent agony, characterized by longing and not a little self-pity.

But Pitney was not just an archetype of his style—he was one of the best at his style, and indeed one of the few (along with Roy Orbison) who could pull it off convincingly. Also (like Orbison), he had more range than he's generally given credit for, making forays into tough pop-rock, country, and even borderline rockabilly. Other than Dionne Warwick, he was the best interpreter of Bacharach-David's early compositions. Although he didn't pen much of his material, he was a composer of note, writing "He's a Rebel" for the Crystals and "Hello Mary Lou" for Rick Nelson. He was also something of a closet hipster—he was the first American artist to cover a Jagger-Richards song ("That Girl Belongs to Yesterday," which was a British hit before the Rolling Stones had ever entered the US Top 100), contributed to an actual Rolling Stones session in early 1964 (during which they recorded "Not Fade Away"), had a brief fling with a teenage Marianne Faithfull, and recorded songs by Randy Newman and Al Kooper long before those musicians became famous.

Pitney broke into music as a songwriter in his late teens, getting his first taste of success when Rick Nelson had a hit with "Hello Mary Lou" in 1961. That same year, Pitney had a small hit with his first single, "(I Wanna Love My Life Away)," a self-penned demo on which he sang and played every instrument—an extraordinary feat for 1961. Another 1961 single, Goffin-King's "Every Breath I Take," was produced by Phil Spector and is one of the very first examples of his pull-out-the-stops Wall of Sound productions. Pitney didn't really find his metier, however, until late-1961's "Town Without Pity," which became his first Top 20 entry. For the next four years, Pitney was one of the most successful solo male

vocalists in America, reeling off over a dozen more Top 40 hits. While lovelorn angst was his stock-in-trade, some of the singles were fairly innovative—"Half Heaven-Half Heartache" and "(The Man Who Shot) Liberty Valance" were crossover country-pop before that term existed; "Mecca" was one of the few big pop-rock hits to bear the influence of Middle Eastern music (albeit in a superficial fashion); and "Last Chance to Turn Around" was a hard-boiled tough-luck tale worthy of a top-notch B-movie thriller.

Pitney withstood the initial onslaught of the British Invasion fairly well, scoring Top Ten hits in 1964 with "It Hurts to Be in Love" and "I'm Gonna Be Strong." By 1966, though, he was in serious trouble stateside. Ironically, by this time he was a much bigger star in Britain, making the UK Top Ten six times in 1965-66. He could also depend on a faithful international audience throughout Europe, and frequently recorded in Italian and Spanish for overseas markets. In 1966, he became one of the first artists to reach success with Randy Newman compositions, taking "Nobody Needs Your Love" and "Just One Smile" into the British Top Ten.

Pitney entered the US Top 20 one last time in 1968 with "She's a Heartbreaker," a rather forced updating of his trademark sound. That was basically it for his career as a significant recording artist, although he remains a big concert draw on the overseas nostalgia circuit. In 1989, he made No. 1 in the UK again by duetting with Mark Almond on a remake of one of his '60s singles, "Something's Gotten Hold of My Heart." — *Richie Unterberger*

● **Anthology 1961-1968** / 1986 / Rhino ✦✦✦
The voice still sounds surreal, like no one else in pop music, and this collection of hits exudes class. Emotional, pained, stunning. Pitney is a master—rock's Caruso. — *Jeff Tamarkin*

More Greatest Hits / 1995 / Varese Sarabande ✦✦✦
A worthy supplement to *Anthology;* in fact, it's almost as good. Has a lot of minor hits, some ("I Must Be Seeing Things," "Backstage") ranking among his best; "Nobody Needs Your Love," an early Randy Newman composition that was a No. 2 hit in England in 1966; Pitney's versions of his compositions "Hello Mary Lou" and "Today's Teardrops," much better known via their interpretations by Rick Nelson and Roy Orbison, respectively; and interesting album tracks and flop singles. All cuts are from the '60s, except the 1989 version of "Something's Gotten Hold of My Heart," performed as a duet with Marc Almond. — *Richie Unterberger*

The Pixies

Alternative Pop-Rock
With their jagged, roaring guitars and undeniable pop melodies, the Pixies were arguably the best American alternative rock band of the late '80s. Many critics accused the band of being pretentious, amateurish college students just wanting to make noise, and some of that criticism is rather accurate; their records are filled with squealing guitar noise that could only be made by enthusiastic, inexperienced musicians and rabid rock fans. But the band was able to meld punk and post-punk indie guitar rock, classic pop, surf rock, and stadium-sized riffs with singer/guitarist Black Francis' (born Charles Thompson) bizarre, fragmented lyrics about space, religion, sex, mutilation, and pop culture; while the meaning of his lyrics may have been impenetrable, the music was direct and forceful. The Pixies' busy, brief songs, extreme dynamics and subversion of conventional song structures were very influential on many bands of the '90s; Nirvana, in particular, cited them as one of their favorite bands, admitting that "Smells Like Teen Spirit" was a Pixies rip-off.

By the time of their last album, 1991's *Trompe le Monde,* the band was increasingly becoming a solo project for Black Francis; bassist/vocalist Kim Deal barely sang on the record and was reportedly angry that she wasn't allowed any space for her songs on the last two albums. After a tension-filled final tour opening U2's 1992 Zoo TV stadium extravaganza, Black Francis informed the band in early 1993 that they were officially broken up. He inverted his stage name to Frank Black and released his first solo album three months later. Lead guitarist Joey Santiago played with Black; drummer David Lovering joined Cracker. At the time, Deal was already at work on the Breeders' second album, which became a much bigger commercial success than any Pixies record. — *Stephen Thomas Erlewine*

Come on Pilgrim / 1987 / 4AD/Elektra ✦✦✦
The band's first mini-album is actually some of the demos that the group gave to 4AD. The label was so impressed by the group's potential that it released eight of the demos (paid for by Black Francis' dad). It's easy to see why they were impressed; *Come on Pilgrim* contains some of the group's best material, from the eerie opener "Caribou" to the propulsive pop of the final track, "Levitate Me." Not one of the eight tracks on *Come on Pilgrim* is a ringer; "I've Been Tired," "Nimrod's Son," and "Ed Is Dead" also prove that the Pixies' debut is one of their finest efforts. — *Heather Phares*

☆ **Surfer Rosa** / 1988 / 4AD/Elektra ✦✦✦✦✦
Surfer Rosa is one of the seminal art-punk albums of the '80s. It mixes thrashy guitars, boy-girl harmonies and strange lyrics in a way that still

sounds fresh and innovative. Joey Santiago's prickly guitar work, Black Francis' psychotic shriek of a voice, Kim Deal's steady bass and luminous vocals, and David Lovering's formidable drumming unite in some blazing punk and unique pop. "Bone Machine," "Broken Face," "Oh My Golly!" and "Vamos" zip along at a fearsome rate, taking no prisoners. But the Pixies' beauty is as apparent on *Surfer Rosa*. Tracks like Deal's "Gigantic" and Francis' "Where Is My Mind" provide refreshing contrasts to the rest of the album's incandescent energy. —*Heather Phares*

★ **Doolittle** / 1989 / 4AD/Elektra ✦✦✦✦✦
The group's third album (and their first for Elektra) continues the Pixies' winning break. With Gil Norton producing, the band's raw edge is smoothed and streamlined into something too clever to be just punk but too edgy and neurotic to be simply pop. Driving surf tunes like "Debaser" and "Wave of Mutilation" coexist with raw, disturbing tracks like "Dead," "Tame," and "Gouge Away." But as always, the Pixies exhibit their schizophrenic pop sensibilities and also produce melodic and catchy tunes like "Here Comes Your Man" and "La La Love You." —*Heather Phares*

Bossanova / 1990 / 4AD/Elektra ✦✦✦✦
The Pixies' fourth album dives deeper into the group's twin fascinations of surf pop and science fiction. Much of the hyperkinetic punk energy of the first three albums is missing, resulting in a kinder, gentler, but no less iconoclastic band. "Is She Weird," "Rock Music," "Allison," and "All Over the World" are some of the album's highlights, as well as "Havalina," which shows off Deal's glorious voice. —*Heather Phares*

Trompe le Monde / 1991 / 4AD/Elektra ✦✦✦
The band's final album is not so much a return to their early, aggressive sound as it is a fusion of their raw energy and eccentricity. It's both arty and rousing, especially on fun tracks like "Subbacultcha," "Palace of the Brine," "D Equals RxT," and "U-Mass." Beautiful and offbeat songs like "Bird Dream of the Olympus Mons," "The Navajo Know," and "Letter to Memphis" confirm that the Pixies were and are one of the most individual talents in alternative music. —*Heather Phares*

Pizzicato Five

Alternative Pop-Rock, Club-Dance
Truly an alternative '90s band for postmoderns, Japan's Pizzicato Five cuts up and deconstructs detritus from American pop with imagination and humor. Sound engineers Yashuaru Konishi and K-Taro Takanami compile, sample, and edit scraps from various critically ignored schools of pre-1980 pop, including disco, spy soundtracks, Bacharach-David pop, bossa nova, and easy listening; Maki Nomiya often lays her chanteuse English/Japanese vocals on top. After over a dozen albums in Japan, they were introduced to the US audience in 1994 via Matador's *Made in USA* compilation. Too kitschy for many listeners (both mainstream and alternative), there's no denying that Pizzicato Five go about their business with fun and intelligence. —*Richie Unterberger*

● **Made in USA** / 1994 / Matador ✦✦✦✦
Although it's not billed as such, the group's stateside debut is a compilation of tracks from their 15 or so albums. You need a taste for irreverent sampling and ironic deconstruction of lightweight pop idioms to dig this. But within that narrow field, Pizzicato Five are as good as it gets. They devise fare that's both funky and funny, made more human than most such projects by Maki Nomiya's fetching vocals. —*Richie Unterberger*

The Sound of Music by Pizzicato Five / Oct. 31, 1995 / Atlantic ✦✦✦✦

Robert Plant

b. Aug. 20, 1948
Harmonica, Vocals / Hard Rock, Pop-Rock
British hard rock/heavy metal singer Robert Plant had released a couple of singles and worked with a number of bands before he hooked up with Jimmy Page's New Yardbirds, subsequently renamed Led Zeppelin, around the time of his 20th birthday in 1968. For the next 12 years, Plant was one of the biggest rock stars on the planet. He gradually developed as a singer, branching out into other styles within Zeppelin's hard-rock framework, and he blossomed as a songwriter.

Plant launched a solo career in 1982 with the album *Pictures at Eleven*, a gold-selling hit. He did even better the following year with *Principle of Moments*. It sold a million copies, included the Top 20 hit "Big Log," and led to his first post-Zeppelin concert tour. Surprisingly, Plant then organized a one-off mini-album, *The Honeydrippers, Vol. 1*, recording some rock oldies with a superstar pickup band. He faced greater consumer resistance with his third solo album, *Shaken 'n' Stirred*, perhaps because joint appearances with Page led an audience to desire for a Zeppelin reunion. To an extent, Plant fed that desire with *Now & Zen*, which sampled Zeppelin tracks and featured Page. It was another million-seller. Plant's 1990 follow-up, *Manic Nirvana*, went gold. —*William Ruhlmann*

Pictures at Eleven / 1982 / Swan Song ✦✦✦✦
The directions in which Plant seemed to be heading in the later Zeppelin

records—toward lighter, more melodic music, tempered with sometimes odd rhythms—are continued on his first solo album, which finds him singing more and screaming less. It wasn't Led Zeppelin, but then, that was the whole point. —*William Ruhlmann*

● **Principle of Moments** / 1983 / Es Paranza ✦✦✦✦
Plant reinvents rock and pop oldies in much the way Led Zeppelin did old blues songs. "Other Arms" recasts "Lay Down Your Arms," as Plant declares, "I'm not a prisoner of the big parade," while "In the Mood" retools an old pop theme. The playing is propulsive (thanks to guest drummer Phil Collins) and Plant's singing unusually supple. —*William Ruhlmann*

Shaken 'n' Stirred / 1985 / Es Paranza ✦✦✦
Robert Plant continued to expand the horizons of his music with his third album, *Shaken 'n' Stirred*, adding elements of worldbeat to his increasingly atmospheric and synth-driven pop-rock. Although the experimentation is admirable, and occasionally successful, the best tracks on the album are straightforward numbers like "Little by Little." —*Stephen Thomas Erlewine*

Now & Zen / 1989 / Es Paranza ✦✦✦
Robert Plant hires a new band, prominently featuring keyboardist Phil Johnstone, and also adds a backup singer for a fuller sound. At the same time, the appearance of Jimmy Page on "Tall Cool One," a Top 25 hit, casts a glance back at Plant's Led Zeppelin days. —*William Ruhlmann*

Manic Nirvana / 1990 / Es Paranza ✦✦

Fate of Nations / May 27, 1993 / Es Paranza ✦✦✦

The Platters

R&B, Pop, Doo Wop
The Platters started out as a Los Angeles-based Black doo wop group with little identity of their own to make them stand out from the pack. They started out making their first records for Federal, a subsidiary of Cincinnati's King Records. These early sides don't sound *anything* like the better-known sides that would eventually emerge from this group, instead merely aping the current R&B trends and styles of the day. What changed their fortunes can be reduced down to one very important name, their mentor, manager, producer, songwriter and vocal coach, Buck Ram. Ram took what many would say was a run of the mill R&B doo wop vocal group and turned them into stars and one of the most enduring and lucrative groups of all time. By 1954, Ram was already running a talent agency in Los Angeles—writing and arranging for publisher Mills Music, managing the Three Suns—a pop group with some success—and working with his protégés, the Penguins. The Platters seemed like a good addition to his stable.

After getting them out of their Federal contract, Ram placed them with the burgeoning national independent label Mercury Records (at the same time he brought over the Penguins following their success with "Earth Angel," automatically getting them into pop markets through the label's distribution contacts alone. The Ram started honing in on the group's strengths and weaknesses. The first thing he did was put the lead vocal stature squarely on the shoulders of lead tenor Tony Williams. Williams' emoting power was turned up full blast with the group (now augmented with Zola Taylor from Shirley Gunter and the Queens) working as very well structured vocal support framing his every note. With Ram's pop songwriting classics as its musical palette, the group quickly became a pop and R&B success, eventually earning the distinction of being the first Black act of the era to top the pop charts. Considered the most romantic of all the doo wop groups (i.e., the ultimate in "make out music"), hit after hit came tumbling forth in a seemingly effortless manner: "Only You," "The Great Pretender," "My Prayer," "Twilight Time," "Smoke Gets in Your Eyes," "Harbor Lights," establishing the Platters as the classiest of all.

Williams struck out on his own in 1961 and, by decades' end, the group had disbanded with various members starting up their own version of the Platters. This bit of franchising now extends into the present day, with an estimated 125 sanctioned versions of 'the original Platters' out on the oldies show circuit. —*Cub Koda*

The Very Best of the Platters / 1991 / Mercury ✦✦✦✦
The Platters' 12 biggest hits are featured on this brief, but solid, collection; it's fine for those who don't want to spend the money on the double-disc set. —*Stephen Thomas Erlewine*

★ **The Magic Touch: An Anthology** / 1991 / Mercury ✦✦✦✦✦
Double-disc set of all their best sides, including "The Great Pretender," "Smoke Gets in Your Eyes," "Only You," "Harbor Lights," and the title track. Great annotation and impeccable sound. All compilations should be done this well. —*Cub Koda*

Plimsouls

New Wave, Power-Pop
With their sharp guitar hooks, memorably sweet melodies, and raggedly

beautiful harmonies, the Plimsouls made music that invigorated power-pop in the early '80s. Led by Peter Case's strong songwriting, the group only released two albums and an EP before breaking up in 1983, yet their records sound fresh and exciting more than a decade after their split. —*Stephen Thomas Erlewine*

● **The Plimsouls . . . Plus** / 1981 / Rhino ✦✦✦✦
Now reissued as *Plimsouls . . . Plus* with bonus tracks from the *Zero Hour* EP, the band's first album showcases their blend of power-pop and gritty Southern soul. Hook-laden and filled with raw energy, this is a lost masterpiece that shouldn't be missed this time around. —*Chris Woodstra*

Everywhere at Once / 1983 / Geffen ✦✦✦✦
The second album retains all of the fiery spirit of the debut with a smoother production. This album holds up much better than many others of the period. Includes the infectious "A Million Miles Away." —*Chris Woodstra*

Poco

Rock 'n' Roll, Country-Rock
Founded by Jim Messina and Richie Furay during the dying days of Buffalo Springfield, with Randy Meisner (who dropped out shortly before the recording of their first album), Rusty Young, and George Grantham, the band built a solid reputation in Los Angeles as an innovative country-rock ensemble. Their first album, *Pickin' Up the Pieces*, was one of the strongest debut records of its era, a blend of country and western influences, Beatlesque harmonies, and mainstream rock, all within one cover. They began developing a major national reputation with the release of their second album, *Poco*, at the same time that the group's membership entered what proved to be a virtually constant state of flux. By the mid-'70s, the band had become an established fixture in the middle reaches of the national charts, but Messina and Furay were long gone. The band continued recording well into the late '70s on MCA after leaving Epic, and their following was strong enough to justify a posthumous live album from Epic at the same time. The original quintet, which never did get to record, finally went into the studio under the auspices of RCA in the late '80s. —*Bruce Eder*

Pickin' Up the Pieces / 1969 / Epic ✦✦✦✦
Their debut album, which is as accomplished as anything by Buffalo Springfield, also recalls the Beatles and the Byrds in its musical orientation. —*Bruce Eder*

Poco / May 6, 1970 / Epic ✦✦✦
Their still-fresh, and very Beatlesque, album is a fine continuation from the early Buffalo Springfield. —*Bruce Eder*

From the Inside / 1971 / Epic ✦✦

Deliverin' / Jan. 13, 1971 / Epic ✦✦✦

A Good Feelin' to Know / Oct. 25, 1972 / Epic ✦✦✦

Crazy Eyes / 1973 / Epic ✦✦✦

Seven / 1974 / Epic ✦✦

The Very Best of Poco / Sep. 1975 / Epic ✦✦✦✦
A well-chosen double LP compilation (now on one CD) chronicling Poco's Epic Records period, 1969-1974. —*William Ruhlmann*

Crazy Loving: Best of Poco 1975-1982 / 1989 / MCA ✦✦✦
In the wake of Poco's success with *Legacy*, MCA Records resurrected their 1982 best of, *Backtracks*, added tracks to fill it out to respectable CD length, threw in some liner notes, and reissued it under a new title. It's not Poco's best period, but this is a good selection that will satisfy most casual listeners. —*William Ruhlmann*

● **The Forgotten Trail (1969-1974)** / 1990 / Epic ✦✦✦✦
This definitive two-CD collection is full of wonderful moments and great songs, so it is the obvious starting point. —*Bruce Eder*

The Pogues (Pogue Mahone)

Alternative Pop-Rock, British Folk
The Pogues combined traditional folk of all stripes (with an emphasis on Irish folk) with rock muscle, producing some of the most original and remarkable music of the '80s. Originally known as Pogue Mahone (Gaelic for "kiss my ass"), the group (Shane MacGowan, vocalist and songwriter; Philip Chevron, guitar; Spider Stacy, tin whistle; Andrew Ranken, drums; James Fearnley, accordion; Darryl Hunt, bass; Jem Finer, banjo; Terry Woods, mandolin) formed in 1982. The Elvis Costello-produced *Rum Sodomy & the Lash* proved MacGowan was a gifted songwriter and earned the band several UK hits. Original bassist Caitlin O'Riordan left the band in 1985 and married Costello; she was replaced by Hunt. The Pogues signed to Island, releasing *If I Should Fall from Grace with God*, arguably their best album, in 1988. MacGowan's health began to deteriorate due to drug use, culminating in a breakdown in the fall of 1990; Joe Strummer toured with the band after his departure.

MacGowan resurfaced on a one-off Christmas single with Nick Cave; he formed a new band late in 1993. The Pogues continued with Spider

Stacy on lead vocals, releasing a new album in 1993; it received a luke-warm critical and commercial reception. By the beginning of 1994, there were rumors that the band had decided to call it quits. —*Stephen Thomas Erlewine*

Red Roses for Me / 1984 / Enigma ✦✦✦
The Pogues' debut was hampered by an unfocused production, which lets the band run loose over the traditional numbers but gives Shane MacGowan's originals a careening power that belies the fact that he was still finding a distinctive voice. —*Stephen Thomas Erlewine*

Rum Sodomy & the Lash / 1985 / MCA ✦✦✦✦
A triumph, produced by Elvis Costello. Shane MacGowan has never sounded so intense, nor has the band played with such authority. A classic melding of punk era-defined sensibilities and the magic of Celtic traditionalism. Features a stirring version of Eric Bogle's classic "And the Band Played Waltzing Matilda." —*John Dougan*

● **If I Should Fall from Grace with God** / 1987 / Island ✦✦✦✦
The Pogues' third album is another fiery, eclectic meld of traditional Celtic music and rock played with punk venom. The band can barely keep up with the breakneck pace of songs like "Bottle of Smoke," which is what makes the album so appealing. Overall, this album has more of a rock spirit than *Rum Sodomy & the Lash*, and MacGowan's songs show significant strides in quality. —*Stephen Thomas Erlewine*

Peace and Love / 1989 / Island ✦✦✦

Hell's Ditch / 1990 / Island ✦✦✦

Yeah Yeah Yeah Yeah / 1990 / Island ✦✦

Essential Pogues / 1991 / Island ✦✦✦✦
Essential Pogues doesn't cover *Red Roses for Me* or *Rum Sodomy & the Lash*, so it isn't a definitive collection. However, it does capture the majority of the highlights from their Island albums and functions as a good introduction to the band. One complaint: the tedious extended remix of "Yeah Yeah Yeah Yeah" was included instead of the punchy, energetic original single. —*Stephen Thomas Erlewine*

Waiting for Herb / 1993 / Chameleon ✦✦

Pogues Mahone / Oct. 1995 / WEA ✦✦✦

The Pointer Sisters

Soul, Urban, Pop-Rock
Versatile Ruth, Anita, June, and Bonnie Pointer regularly scored pop and soul hits throughout the '70s and '80s in a chameleonlike variety of styles. Formed in Oakland, they had their first successes for Blue Thumb Records blending funky rhythms with a novel nostalgic attitude (beginning with their 1973 revival of Allen Toussaint's "Yes We Can Can"), leading up to their first No. 1 R&B item in 1975, "How Long (Betcha' Got a Chick on the Side)."

Bonnie signed with Motown in 1978 and kicked off her own string of R&B hits with "Free Me from My Freedom/Tie Me to a Tree (Handcuff Me)." (Jun. and Anita also tried the solo route during the '80s, without leaving the fold.)

By 1979, when the remaining trio covered Bruce Springsteen's "Fire," the Pointer Sisters were headed in a more contemporary direction on the Planet label, and "He's So Shy" (1980), "Slow Hand" (1981), "Automatic," and the anthemic "Jump (For My Love)" (the last two both 1984) were savvy ditties that blazed trails across the R&B and pop charts.

The Pointer Sisters enjoyed renewed exposure and recognition in 1994. They teamed with Clint Black on "Chain of Fools," one of several projects teaming R&B and country acts for the release *Rhythm, Country and Blues* and also issued a new release on RCA. —*Bill Dahl*

● **The Best of the Pointer Sisters** / 1976 / RCA ✦✦✦✦
An excellent companion to their *Greatest Hits* collection, with the emphasis on their early work with Richard Perry's Planet label. The focal points, however, were the hits—"He's So Shy," "Slow Hand," "Fire," and the girl-groupish ditty "Should I Do It." —*John Lowe*

● **Greatest Hits** / 1982 / Planet ✦✦✦✦
A good anthology covering their '70s and '80s hits. There are now at least six Pointer Sisters anthologies, covering all of the Blue Thumb, Planet, and RCA material. This one was issued on vinyl and can't match the digital sound quality of some later Pointer Sisters releases, but has more than enough hit material to satisfy even their hardcore fans. —*Ron Wynn*

● **Jump: Best of the Pointer Sisters** / 1989 / RCA ✦✦✦✦
Jump covers their hits for the Planet record label. They had moved beyond their camp-novelty origins and away from their country flirtation, and were comfortable making exuberantly sung, conservatively produced, soul-tinged pop. During this period, they scored a number of crossover smashes, including "Jump," "He's So Shy," "Automatic," and "Slow Hand"; all of their 1980s hits are included on this album. —*Ron Wynn*

Very Best of the Pointer Sisters: Fire / Jun. 1996 / RCA ✦✦✦✦
Over the course of two CDs, *The Very Best of the Pointer Sisters: Fire* run through every one of the group's biggest hits of the '70s, from their first hit "Yes We Can" through "Fire," and stopping just after their 1983-1984 peak of popularity with "Automatic," "Jump (For My Love)," "I'm So Excited," and "Neutron Dance." Two discs is too much material for anyone but devoted fans, but this is the most complete retrospective available about the Pointer Sisters, and it's hard to imagine that there will ever be another compilation quite so thorough. *— Stephen Thomas Erlewine*

Poison

Hard Rock, Pop-Rock, Heavy Metal, Hair Metal
A hard-rock quartet consisting of singer Bret Michaels, guitarist C.C. Deville, bassist Bobby Dall, and drummer Rikki Rockett, Poison was formed in Harrisburg, PA, in 1983, though the band members relocated to Los Angeles early on, where their highly visual approach (drummer Rockett was also a hairdresser who advised them on clothes, hair, and makeup) made them favorites in the city's glam-rock underground. C.C. Deville left the band in early 1992.
　Deville's replacement, Richie Kotsen, appeared on 1993's *Native Tongue*, an attempt to become a grittier, serious rock band; he was fired during the subsequent tour. *— William Ruhlmann*

Look What the Cat Dragged In / 1986 / Capitol ✦✦✦

● **Open Up & Say . . . Ahh!** / 1988 / Capitol ✦✦✦✦
This, the group's most popular album, presents its taste for straightforward hard rock ("Nothin' but a Good Time"), for acoustic ballads ("Every Rose Has Its Thorn"), and for its roots in simple pop-rock ("Your Mama Don't Dance"). *— William Ruhlmann*

Flesh & Blood / 1990 / Capitol ✦✦✦✦
On their third album, vocalist Bret Michaels puts in his best performance. "Unskinny Bop" and the anthemic "Something to Believe In" were both Top Ten hits. *— John Book*

Swallow This Live / 1991 / Capitol ✦✦✦

Native Tongue / Feb. 8, 1993 / Capitol ✦✦

The Police

New Wave, Pop-Rock
In 1977, Sting (a British ex-schoolteacher born Gordon Sumner) and Stewart Copeland (a young drummer from the US) met up with guitarist Andy Summers (of Soft Machine), and the three formed the final lineup of the Police—the rock group that would later take the early '80s by storm. The band's debut album, *Outlandos d'Amour*, which sported jazz and reggae rhythms in a pop-rock format, was released in 1978. The album, with such classic songs as "Roxanne," was popular with college radio, marking the beginning of the Police's ascent to fame. The follow-up, *Regatta de Blanc*, was released the next year; with its bouncy, lively songs, it hit No. 1 in the UK for four weeks. *Zenyatta Mondatta*, released in 1980, achieved the same success on the UK charts and became the band's first album to place into the US Top Ten. *Ghost in the Machine* was a success as well, and in 1983 *Synchronicity* was released and went multi-platinum. It was No. 1 on the US charts for 12 weeks, winning three Grammy Awards, including Song of the Year for the single "Every Breath You Take." In 1985 the three band members split to pursue solo careers. Apart from reuniting in 1986 to record a new version of "Don't Stand So Close to Me" for their stellar compilation *Every Breath You Take: The Singles*, the band has remained inactive. *— Iotis Erlewine*

Outlandos d'Amour / Nov. 1978 / A&M ✦✦✦✦
The Police's first album, although fairly rough, is still an impressive first effort. Although "Can't Stand Losing You" was their first hit (it made the Top 50), the best-known track on this album is definitely "Roxanne," still a favorite among college-radio stations. The influence of the punk era on this album is evident, as is bass player Sting's jazz background. A great deal of fun. *— Iotis Erlewine*

Regatta de Blanc / 1979 / A&M ✦✦✦
The very title, *Regatta de Blanc* (rough French for "White reggae"), describes the style of the Police's second album. This speedy mix of reggae and mainstream rock spawned two No. 1 UK hits with "Message in a Bottle" and "Walking on the Moon." The reggae influence is most noticeable in the rhythms, especially on the tracks "Bring on the Night," "Walking on the Moon," and "The Bed's Too Big Without You." *— Iotis Erlewine*

Zenyatta Mondatta / 1980 / A&M ✦✦✦✦
This album, although a bit rough around the edges, marks a transitional point in the band's career. "Don't Stand So Close to Me" became a No. 1 hit on the UK charts, and the band edged further into the mainstream. The sound became more pop oriented on this album, with songs like "De Do Do Do, De Da Da Da" and "Canary in a Coalmine," although they retained their unique sense of rhythm. For a good introduction to early Police, this album is a wise choice. *— Iotis Erlewine*

Ghost in the Machine / 1981 / A&M ✦✦✦
One of the Police's best songs, "Every Little Thing She Does Is Magic," is featured on this album, but as a whole, *Ghost in the Machine* is bland. Besides being poorly mixed (the music overpowers the vocals), the songs lack the musical simplicity and direction that is so appealing in the earlier albums. *— Iotis Erlewine*

Synchronicity / 1983 / A&M ✦✦✦
A departure from early Police, this album completed the band's transition into mainstream pop while, at the same time, becoming more musically refined. *Synchronicity* had the complexity of *Ghost in the Machine* without the boredom. The Police get louder and angrier, making this a stronger, more driving album. *Synchronicity* contains some of the band's most well-known work: "Every Breath You Take," which went to No. 1 on both the US and the UK charts; "Wrapped Around Your Finger"; and "King of Pain." The pinnacle of the band's career, it went multi-platinum and secured the Police's claim to the title of "rock gods" in the early '80s. With the exception of Andy Summers' "Mother," there is not a bad song on the album. The CD contains the bonus track "Murder by Numbers." *— Iotis Erlewine*

Every Breath You Take: The Singles / 1986 / A&M ✦✦✦✦
A collection of singles from the five Police albums, this provides a consistent sampling of some of the Police's best work, from "Roxanne" to "Every Breath You Take." It's a good overview of the band's work and an excellent place to get an introduction to their music. This also includes a 1986 remake of "Don't Stand So Close to Me," featuring all three members of the band. *— Iotis Erlewine*

Message in a Box / 1993 / A&M ✦✦✦✦
All of the studio recordings the trio made during their short career (except for a couple of foreign-language recordings, remixes, and live tracks) are collected together on the four-disc *Message in a Box*. There are enough rarities in this attractive, sonically impressive package to justify its purchase for hardcore fans; for anyone who doesn't own any Police, it is an easy way to have the entire collection at once, but casual fans will be more satisfied by *Every Breath You Take: The Singles*. *— Stephen Thomas Erlewine*

Live / 1995 / A&M ✦✦

★ **Every Breath You Take: The Classics** / Sep. 12, 1995 / A&M ✦✦✦✦✦
Every Breath You Take: The Classics improves on the previous *Every Breath You Take: The Singles* by adding the original version of "Don't Stand So Close to Me," as well as a handful of other songs that aren't on its predecessor; the extra songs make *The Classics* the preferable collection. *— Stephen Thomas Erlewine*

Iggy Pop　(James Newell Osterberg)

b. 1947
Vocals / Hard Rock, Proto-Punk
After the disbandment of the proto-punk group the Stooges, vocalist Iggy Pop (born James Osterberg) embarked on a solo career that flirted with the mainstream while keeping his fiery punk spirit alive. Pop laid low for a couple of years following the breakup of the Stooges, resurfacing in 1977 with two David Bowie-produced albums, *The Idiot* and *Lust for Life*. These records expanded his trademark full-throttle rock 'n' roll, incorporating a more pop-oriented approach that increased his audience; *The Idiot* remains his highest-charting album, peaking at No. 72 in America.
　However, Pop soon returned to straightforward, raging hard rock with the double-punch of *TV Eye Live* (1978) and 1979's *New Values*, which was recorded with former Stooges guitarist James Williamson. Although he kept changing his backing band, both 1980's *Soldier* and 1981's *Party* followed the same blueprint as *New Values*. Released in 1982, the Chris Stein-produced *Zombie Birdhouse* (which appeared on Stein's private label, Animal) was the most varied collection Pop had created since *Lust for Life*.
　After the release of *Zombie Birdhouse*, Pop took some time off, reappearing four years later with the Bowie-produced *Blah Blah Blah;* the record became his highest-charting album since *The Idiot*. He followed it in 1989 with *Instinct*, another return to basic hard rock. Released the following year on Virgin Records, the Don Was-produced *Brick by Brick* was his most accessible and commercially successful album, producing his first Top 40 hit, "Candy." Pop began an acting career during the next few years, appearing in John Waters' *Cry Baby*. Pop's first album since *Brick by Brick* was *American Caesar* (1993), which was yet another return to punky hard rock. *— Stephen Thomas Erlewine*

The Idiot / 1977 / Virgin ✦✦✦✦
Although it appears that producer David Bowie directed the proceedings a bit too carefully, remaking Iggy Pop entirely in his own image, *The Idiot* proves that Pop was equally responsible for the menacing electronic music. *The Idiot* was an effective reinvention on the part of Iggy Pop partially because it removed him completely from the primal heavy-guitar grind of the Stooges. A different musical direction in itself would

be meaningless if Pop and Bowie hadn't produced a set of songs that supported the new, synth-driven style. "Funtime" is essentially a sleazy, mid-tempo rocker that is re-energized by its context, but most of the album explores the various subtexts within the bleak, keyboard-dominated soundscapes. Pop's lyrics are some of his best, as he faithfully recreates the hedonistic underworld of jet-setting "Nightclubbing," with both humor and rage. Several of the songs—including "Funtime," "China Girl," and "Nightclubbing"—have become post-punk standards, but that doesn't remove the jarring, disturbing sound of the record. In its own quiet way, *The Idiot* is as discomforting as *Fun House*. —*Stephen Thomas Erlewine*

● **Lust for Life** / 1977 / Virgin ◆◆◆◆
The pounding drums that open *Lust for Life* instantly signal that the album is a brighter, harder-rocking affair than *The Idiot*. While black humor was an undercurrent throughout *The Idiot*, it is brought to the front on *Lust for Life*, both musically and lyrically. Using the title track as a template, the record not only rocks, it swings and it swings hard. Bowie wrote most of the music for the record, and it reflects his musical ambition, careening from the hard rock of the title track to the strutting piano of "The Passenger," the jaunty ironic sing-along of "Success," to the stylized R&B of "Tonight." While Iggy Pop spent most of the decade trying to escape the pop leanings of *Lust for Life*, he never made a better record. —*Stephen Thomas Erlewine*

TV Eye / 1978 / RCA ◆

New Values / 1979 / Arista ◆◆◆

Soldier / 1980 / Arista ◆◆◆

Party / 1981 / Arista ◆◆

Zombie Birdhouse / 1982 / IRS ◆◆

Choice Cuts / 1984 / RCA ◆◆◆◆
Following the success of David Bowie's version of "China Girl," RCA assembled *Choice Cuts*, a compilation of Iggy Pop's two albums for the label. Actually, "compilation" is a misleading word: Side one of *Choice Cuts* features side one of *The Idiot*, while side two features side one of *Lust for Life*. It effectively illustrates the differences between the record and includes most of the prime material from each collection, yet the two albums are necessary listens in their entireties, making *Choice Cuts* an engaging but useless compilation. —*Stephen Thomas Erlewine*

Blah Blah Blah / 1986 / A&M ◆◆◆

Instinct / 1988 / A&M ◆◆
Instinct suggested that Iggy Pop had run out of ideas. *Brick by Brick* put an end to that speculation. While it's easily the most mainstream record Pop has ever recorded, it rivals his two Bowie-produced 1977 albums in terms of sheer accomplishment. Under the direction of producer Don Was, Pop twists through a number of styles, recorded with an ever-shifting assembly of studio musicians like David Lindley and Waddy Wachtel, members of Guns N' Roses, John Hiatt, John Mellencamp's drummer Kenny Aronoff, and the B-52's singer Kate Pierson. Pop's duet with Pierson on the pure pop of "Candy" is the highlight, yet the record also features Pop at his toughest ("Home," "Butt Town," "I Won't Crap Out," "Pussy Power") and his most sensitive ("Moonlight Lady"). Although there was potential for a slick, mainstream sell-out with *Brick by Brick*, Was has helped Pop turn in a well-crafted and thoroughly enjoyable album. And with Pop, a consistent album is a rare occurence. —*Stephen Thomas Erlewine*

American Caesar / 1993 / Virgin ◆◆◆

Naughty Little Doggie / 1996 / Virgin ◆◆

Porno for Pyros

Alternative Pop-Rock
Perry Farrell's post-Jane's Addiction band, Porno for Pyros, followed the same path as his previous band, combining art-rock, punk, heavy metal, and funk into one shrieking whole. On their self-titled 1993 debut, Farrell's pretensions got out of hand at times, resulting in some ridiculously self-absorbed conceptual pieces sitting next to some straightforward rockers and pop songs; it sold well at first, but soon slipped down the charts. While he prepared new Porno material in 1994, Farrell returned to the organization of Lollapalooza—the traveling rock festival he conceived—for the first time since 1992. The band released *Good Gods Urge* in 1996. —*Stephen Thomas Erlewine*

Porno for Pyros / 1993 / Warner Bros. ◆◆◆

● **Good Gods Urge** / Jun. 1996 / Warner Bros. ◆◆◆◆

Portishead

Alternative Pop-Rock, Trip-Hop
Led by keyboardist Geoff Barrow, the British group Portishead combined hip-hop rhythms and samples, jazzy melodic textures, and pop-

rock instrumentation into a alluringly dark, atmospheric sound, distinguished by the seductive vocals of Beth Gibbons. The group's 1994 debut album, *Dummy*, earned glowing reviews, landing on many critics' year-end Top Ten lists. *Dummy* crossed over into the mainstream in both America and Britain in late 1994, thanks to the hit single "Sour Times." —*Stephen Thomas Erlewine*

Dummy / 1994 / PolyGram ◆◆◆◆
Dummy plays like a romantic film noir, filled with reverb, sighing strings, dark erotic arrangements, and the doomed, sighing vocals of Beth Gibbons. —*Stephen Thomas Erlewine*

The Posies

Alternative Pop-Rock, Power-Pop
One of the major '90s power-pop revivalist groups, Seattle's Posies combine the genre's standard influences (Big Star, Raspberries, etc.) with Hollies-like harmonies, roaring guitars, and odd lyrics about mundane, everyday concerns. Their first record, 1988's *Failure*, featured founding guitarists/vocalists Jonathan Auer and sometime Sub Pop producer Ken Stringfellow and fit squarely into the "slacker" trend. Geffen Records signed them, and they filled out the lineup with Dave Fox and Mike Musberger for *Dear 23*. The 1993 Don Fleming-produced *Frosting on the Beater* (an allusion to masturbation) broke the band in the college radio market and was a critical success as well. *Amazing Disgrace* in 1996 consolidated the Posies' position as critics' darlings with even wider acclaim. —*Steve Huey*

Failure / 1988 / Pop Llama ◆◆◆

● **Dear 23** / 1990 / DGC ◆◆◆◆
From the Move-influenced "My Big Mouth," to the delicate, wistful "Everyone Moves Away," through tracks that would do Badfinger or Big Star proud, like "Apology," "Golden Blunders," and "Suddenly Mary," *Dear 23* is Anglo-pop-rock heaven. John Leckie's larger-than-life production might be a little overwhelming at times, but overall it highlights this band's gorgeous harmonies and arrangements to great effect. —*Rick Clark*

Frosting on the Beater / Apr. 27, 1993 / DGC ◆◆◆

Amazing Disgrace / May 14, 1996 / DGC ◆◆
On their fourth album, the Posies sound like a bunch of high school kids desperately trying to fit into the in-crowd, not realizing that the cool kids have already abandoned last year's fashions for something hipper. At the height of grunge, the Posies were stuck in power-pop territory. They began to move toward loud guitars on their third album, *Frosting on the Beater*, but they didn't embrace grunge until *Amazing Disgrace*, which appeared nearly four years after grunge peaked in popularity. That in itself wouldn't be so bad if the group didn't sound so wimpy. The Posies try to prove how hard they are by throwing the word "fuck" randomly into the lyrics. Furthermore, their ability to craft a sly, catchy hook has greatly diminished—the best songs here can't match the ones on their two previous albums. And to top it off, they offer a saccharine tribute to one of the great songwriters of the '80s, ex-Hüsker Dü drummer Grant Hart, without ever demonstrating an understanding of the man's music. It's clear from the bland textures of *Amazing Disgrace* that they never will, either. —*Stephen Thomas Erlewine*

Duffy Power

b. Sep. 9, 1941
Harmonica, Vocals / Blues-Rock, British Invasion
Power is a lost figure of the '60s who drifted into the inner circle of British blues after a middling career as a teen idol in the early '60s. He recorded one of the first Beatle covers (on an early 1963 single of "I Saw Her Standing There"), and never experienced acclaim as a commercial pop singer or blues vocalist. But he recorded some fine, little-known blues-cum-R&B/rock sides in the '60s, some of which featured present and future members of the Graham Bond Organisation, Cream, and Pentangle. The pleasures of Power are subtle and not easily captured in print. He doesn't have the best voice, and will never be mistaken for a Steve Winwood or Eric Burdon. But his original material is strong, his arrangements imaginative, and his performance sincere; he's grounded in the blues, but doesn't fall into shopworn clichés, bringing a lot of himself and the innovations of British '60s rock into the picture. —*Richie Unterberger*

Blues Power / 1992 / See For Miles ◆◆◆◆
Most of the recordings on *Blues Power* were originally released on Power's self-titled album on the tiny UK Spark label in 1969. Duffy says in the liner notes of this reissue that the album was never intended for release, and that these sessions were acoustic demos for an LP that never got produced with the arrangements he had envisioned. That may be so, but it's still a worthy document of this underrated British bluesman at his most bare-boned and haunting. With just his guitar and harmonica, Power runs through both moody originals and covers of R&B/blues standards (with the Beatles' "Fixing a Hole" thrown in) that are rearranged

and drastically stripped down. This reissue includes the 15 tracks from the 1969 release, a couple more from the same sessions that were issued on the extremely obscure *Firepoint* compilation album, and three from the mid-'60s (also included on the *Little Boy Blue* reissue) that also explore acoustic moods, forming a picture of Power's most intimate work. — *Richie Unterberger*

● **Little Boy Blue** / 1992 / Edsel ✦✦✦✦
His best recordings, as noteworthy for the players on the album as Power himself. Laid down sometime in the mid-'60s, Power (who sings and plays occasional guitar and harp) is backed by a rotating ensemble including, at various points, John McLaughlin and Jack Bruce (before they gained fame), as well as future Pentangle members Danny Thompson and Terry Cox. Neither as rock-oriented as the Stones nor as strictly revivalist as Alexis Korner (with whom Power played for a time), this is one of the best British blues recordings, cutting straight down the middle between gutbucket blues and soulful R&B. Divided equally between Power originals and R&B/blues covers, the material and performances are spare, powerful, and as consistent as any '60s British blues album. Unfortunately, these sessions were unissued for several years, surfacing briefly under the title *Innovations* in 1970 on the British Transatlantic label. This reissue on another tiny British label is equally obscure, but should not be missed by fans of '60s British R&B. — *Richie Unterberger*

Just Say Blue / 1995 / Retro ✦✦✦✦
While not up to the level of the other vintage Power compilations available (*Little Boy Blue* and *Blues Power*), this is a worthwhile supplement to those CDs, featuring 21 tracks of rare and unreleased material cut by the singer from 1965 to 1971. The first half, focusing on his 1965-67 output, is the more interesting portion by a considerable margin, as much for the jazz-blues-R&B fusion of the arrangements (featuring contributions from Jack Bruce, John McLaughlin, Ginger Baker, and Pentangle's Danny Thompson and Terry Cox) as Power's singing. The early-'70s songs that make up the remainder of the disc have a more pedestrian blues-rock feel, but there are some good, inspired moments, with cameos by Rod Argent, Thompson, Cox, and Alexis Korner. — *Richie Unterberger*

Prefab Sprout

Pop-Rock
Prefab Sprout, the vision of Newcastle singer-songwriter Paddy McAloon, garnered critical approval for its intelligent, quirky lyrics, jazzy pop often performed with synths and acoustic backing, and beautiful female harmony vocals. McAloon formed the band in 1982 with brother Martin on bass, plus drummer Neil Conti; early fan Wendy Smith joined on vocals and guitar following the recording of the "Lions in My Own Garden" single, which got the band signed to the Kitchenware label. Their debut, *Swoon*, was a showcase for Paddy's literate lyrics and found a fan in producer/synth whiz Thomas Dolby, who remixed a single and produced their next album, *Two Wheels Good* (titled *Steve McQueen* everywhere except the US). The 1988 *From Langley Park to Memphis* incorporated bits of lounge music and show tunes, with mixed results, and featured appearances from Stevie Wonder and Pete Townshend. While the band took a bit of time to get its bearings, a collection of songs originally intended as the follow-up to *Two Wheels Good* called *Protest Songs* was released. Prefab Sprout returned in 1990 with *Jordan: The Comeback*, which explored McAloon's fascinations with religion and American cultural icons such as Elvis Presley and was hailed as perhaps the band's greatest work. However, it failed to sell well, and Prefab Sprout has been silent since. — *Steve Huey*

Swoon / 1984 / Epic ✦✦✦
Their full-length album debut is rough around the edges, but shows the band reaching beyond the tired and clichéd. — *Scott Bultman*

Two Wheels Good / 1985 / Epic ✦✦✦✦
A strong album debut of atmospheric, breathy, and clever pop music, it features Thomas Dolby's tight production. Earthy and ethereal at the same time, the album was released overseas as *Steve McQueen*, but with a different name for the US version due to protests from the actor's estate. — *Scott Bultman*

From Langley Park to Memphis / 1988 / Epic ✦✦✦✦
A good but inconsistent record, it includes shining tracks like "The Golden Calf," "Cars and Girls," and "I Remember That." Paddy McAloon begins to explore his fixation with pop icons like Elvis and Springsteen. A must for fans. — *Scott Bultman*

Jordan: The Comeback / 1990 / Epic ✦✦✦✦
A stunning masterwork with 19 tracks (over 70 minutes) tied together by recurrent themes of God and Elvis, this one is stylistically all over the map—gospel, soul, rock, and pop. The pop songwriting has acknowledged influences from Jimmy Webb and Paul McCartney. — *Scott Bultman*

● **A Life of Surprises: The Best of Prefab Sprout** / 1992 / Epic ✦✦✦✦
This hits package offers a well-chosen set and two previously unreleased tracks, "The Sound of Crying" and "If You Don't Love Me." The 16 tracks

draw more selections from the *From Langley Park to Memphis* LP than the other albums, but this is a good single-disc introduction to Prefab Sprout's music. — *Scott Bultman*

Elvis Presley (Elvis Aron Presley)

b. Jan. 8, 1935, Tupelo, MS, **d.** Aug. 16, 1977, Memphis, TN
Rock 'n' Roll, Rockabilly, Pop, Pop-Rock
Elvis Presley was the defining figure of rock 'n' roll music. He is the biggest record seller in history. During his lifetime, especially in the 1950s, he was the focal point for the emergence of rock 'n' roll culture, and he made some of the genre's seminal recordings. Since his death, he has become a pervasive American icon.

Elvis Presley did not invent rock 'n' roll. In fact, as an artist who did not write songs and whose abilities as an instrumentalist were only rudimentary, he was essentially a transitional performer, bridging the gap between pre-rock singers such as Dean Martin, whom he openly admired, and later rock stars such as the Beatles. But by fusing the existing entertainment industry to the emerging genres of country and blues, he helped turn a hybrid into a national phenomenon. He was the foremost popularizer of rock 'n' roll, and the name "Elvis" became synonymous with the music itself.

Presley grew up in Memphis, TN. He first recorded for the local Sun Records label, owned by Sam Phillips, which issued his initial singles, "That's All Right (Mama)"/"Blue Moon of Kentucky" (Jul. 1954), "Good Rockin' Tonight"/"I Don't Care If the Sun Don't Shine" (Sep. 1954), and "Milkcow Blues Boogie"/"You're a Heartbreaker" (Jan. 1955), before reaching the Top Ten of the country charts with "Baby, Let's Play House"/"I'm Left, You're Right, She's Gone" (Apr. 1955).

Both sides of Presley's fifth Sun single, "Mystery Train"/"I Forgot to Remember to Forget" (Aug. 1955) also reached the country charts, with the latter hitting No. 1. In November 1955, Phillips sold Presley's contract to RCA Victor Records, along with his master tapes. Presley would record for RCA Victor from then on. (The Sun material is available on the *The Sun Sessions* CD [1987] [RCA Victor 6414].)

Starting with "Heartbreak Hotel" (Jan. 1956), Elvis Presley dominated the popular music of the second half of the 1950s. That single topped the pop charts as did "I Want You, I Need You, I Love You" (May), "Hound Dog"/"Don't Be Cruel" (Jul.), and "Love Me Tender" (Sept.), and the albums *Elvis Presley* (Mar.) and *Elvis* (Oct.), all in 1956 alone. "Love Me Tender" was the title song of Presley's first motion picture, which opened in November.

The following year was more of the same, as Presley went to No. 1 with "Too Much" (Jan. 1957), "All Shook Up" (Mar.), "(Let Me Be Your) Teddy Bear" (Jun.), and "Jailhouse Rock" (Sept.), and the albums *Loving You*, the soundtrack to his second movie (Jul.) and *Elvis' Christmas Album* (Nov.).

Drafted by the Army, Presley entered the service in March 1958, which slowed down his hit-making slightly, but he still managed to reach the top of the charts with "Don't" (Jan.), "Hard Headed Woman" (Jun.), and "A Big Hunk o' Love" (Jun. 1959), and stay in the movie theaters with *King Creole* (Jun. 1958), all work done before his induction.

Presley's return to civilian status in March 1960 was marked by a renewed flurry of success with the No. 1 singles "Stuck on You" (Mar.), "It's Now or Never" (Jul.), and "Are You Lonesome Tonight" (Nov. 1960), and the soundtrack album *G.I. Blues* (Oct.). Such recordings found him moving more to the ballad material, as his rebellious '50s image gave way to a more conventional star persona in the '60s. But his "comeback" continued into 1961, as he topped the charts with "Surrender" (Feb.) and the albums *Something for Everybody* (Jun.) and *Blue Hawaii* (Oct.).

After 1961, Presley gave up performing live and concentrated almost exclusively on making movies and recording soundtracks. His records continued to sell, if at a slightly less frantic pace. "Good Luck Charm" (Feb. 1962) and the soundtrack to *Roustabout* (Nov. 1964) went to No. 1, and Presley was a frequent visitor in the Top Ten, but especially after the US arrival of the Beatles in February 1964, the King of Rock 'n' Roll began to seem a figure from an earlier time. His records disappeared from the Top Ten after "Crying in the Chapel" (Apr. 1965), which had been recorded back in October 1960, and the *Harum Scarum* soundtrack (Oct. 1965).

Presley turned his career around with a second comeback launched by a TV special broadcast in December 1968. The centerpiece of the show was a performance in the round in which Presley performed many of his '50s hits with the original backing musicians, wearing a black leather suit and evoking the rebellious image of old. A soundtrack album drawn from the "comeback special," *Elvis* (Dec. 1968), returned him to the Top Ten.

Presley began to take greater care with his recordings, returning to Memphis to make records not intended for movie soundtracks. The result was his first Top Ten single in four years, "In the Ghetto" (Apr. 1969) and the gold album *From Elvis in Memphis* (May 1969). Presley gave up acting in favor of a return to live work, starting in Las Vegas in

July 1969. His next single, "Suspicious Minds" (Aug. 1969), was his first chart topper since 1962.

Presley's '70s career as a live performer followed a similar pattern to his '60s career as a singing movie star—early success followed by a gradual decline. He reached the Top Ten with "Don't Cry Daddy" (Nov. 1969), "The Wonder of You" (May 1970), and "Burning Love" (Aug. 1972), and topped the charts with the TV soundtrack album *Aloha from Hawaii Via Satellite* (Feb. 1973), but gradually the releases became less considered and there were more live recordings. Presley's health declined and his weight increased, and his death in August 1977 has been blamed on a number of factors, including the excessive ingestion of prescription drugs, though the official cause of death was heart failure.

Since his death, Presley has gone beyond legend to become a cultural stereotype, with dozens, if not hundreds, of professional imitators curling their lips and slurring their words in tribute to him, and the lunatic fringe continually reporting sightings of him in convenience stores. His home, Graceland, has become something of a national shrine. Meanwhile, RCA Victor has reissued his work in a dizzying variety of configurations, gradually coming to give it the respect and consideration it deserves. *— William Ruhlmann*

☆ **Elvis Presley** / Mar. 1956 / RCA ✦✦✦✦✦
While RCA had the material, they opted to play it safe and combine five Sun outtakes with seven new recordings and release the Hillbilly Cat's first album. This is a great way to begin a career! The best material here is on a par with the Sun singles. While "Blue Suede Shoes" is a cultural cornerstone of sorts, hearing Elvis' version of Clyde McPhatter's "Money Honey" is still, after four decades, revelatory. *—Neal Umphred*

☆ **Elvis** / Oct. 1956 / RCA ✦✦✦✦✦
Almost any number of the '50s could have claimed this as their best album. While there are some excellent rhythm numbers ("Rip It Up," "Paralyzed," and the too-country "When My Blue Moon Turns to Gold Again"), the album's standout is the panting "Love Me." *—Neal Umphred*

Elvis' Golden Records, Vol. 1 / Mar. 1958 / RCA ✦✦✦✦
This is the greatest-hits album by which all greatest-hits albums should be measured. Fourteen sides sold umpteen bejillion records in the previous two years. The only discrepancy is the inclusion of "That's When Your Heartaches Begin," which failed to reached the Top 40 as the flip of "All Shook Up," at the expense of "I Was the One," "My Baby Left Me," and "Playing for Keeps," each much bigger hits. *—Neal Umphred*

50,000,000 Elvis Fans Can't Be Wrong: Elvis' Golden Records, Vol. 2 / 1960 / RCA ✦✦✦✦
The beginner is pointed toward the first two gold-record sets, which contain the hits that make up oldies fare, and the not so well-known, such as—in the case of this second volume—the smoldering "One Night" and the rousing "I Need Your Love Tonight." *—Neal Umphred*

☆ **His Hand in Mine** / Dec. 1960 / RCA ✦✦✦✦✦
Presley cut several good gospel albums over the course of his career, most of them overblown affairs. This one's easily his best; stripped-down arrangements with Elvis passionately involved every note of the way. *—Cub Koda*

Elvis' Golden Records, Vol. 3 / Sep. 1964 / RCA ✦✦✦✦
This third package of gold captures most of the hits from 1960-1962 and is a marvelous album, a model in selection and programming. The songs are all excellent; Elvis was in a period that is always overlooked by fans, critics, and biographers; the band often cooked; and the production and engineering were flawless. Much of what Elvis achieved here on songs like "(Marie's the Name) His Latest Flame" and "Little Sister" has not been duplicated elsewhere in the field of rock 'n' roll, although the influences are sprouting up in contemporary country. *—Neal Umphred*

How Great Thou Art / Mar. 1967 / RCA ✦✦✦✦
Between 1966 and 1968, Elvis recorded just enough studio material to fill one complete secular album and *How Great Thou Art*, a far more polite (and slightly surreal) reading of traditional religious material than the previous outing, a half-dozen years earlier. The performances throughout are superb, the sound impeccable; this actually beat *Sgt. Pepper* as the Best Engineered Album of 1967 in the Grammys! This album is also much closer to mainstream gospel and may not be so immediately accessible to the unconverted; don't let that steer you away from an otherwise great record. *—Neal Umphred*

☆ **NBC TV Special** / Dec. 1968 / RCA ✦✦✦✦✦
After years of making abysmal movies, Presley appeared before a live audience, scared to death. That he more than rose to the challenge is evidenced here, a masterly performance highlighted by the jam-session segment with DJ Fontana and Scotty Moore, where Presley plays electric guitar and knocks out drop-dead versions of "Baby, What You Want Me to Do" and "Tiger Man." *—Cub Koda*

☆ **From Elvis in Memphis** / May 1969 / RCA ✦✦✦✦✦
Presley returned to Memphis, recording 30-odd songs in Chips Moman's America Sound Studios in 1969, leading to his artistic and commercial resurgence ("In the Ghetto" and "Suspicious Minds") and what may be

his single greatest album, *From Elvis in Memphis*. The first track opens with Elvis' hoarsely shouting, "I had to leave town for a little while . . . " and then announces—in no uncertain terms—that he's back. A brilliant selection of material, Elvis sings like his life depended on it. (It didn't; his career did.) The musicians (all regulars from Chips Moman's American Sound Studios) cook, and the overdubbed horns and background vocals are among the most appropriate ever used on a White singer's record. *—Neal Umphred*

From Memphis to Vegas / From Vegas to Memphis / Nov. 1969 / RCA ✦✦✦✦
One-half of the imponderably titled *From Memphis to Vegas / From Vegas to Memphis*, (later issued as a separate album, *Elvis in Person at the International Hotel*) captures Elvis from the summer of 1969 while the exhilaration of conquest was still evident. It's a nice compromise between mere entertainment and the revelatory: the first few songs are old hits to pull you in; the second side opens with a roaring medley of "Mystery Train" and Rufus Thomas' "Tiger Man" and leads to a staggering seven-minute "Suspicious Minds." The studio album, ten tracks from the previous Memphis sessions, are a letdown and, even at the time of release, the two-fer concept seemed ill-conceived. Had the best of the rest of the Memphis material been collected on a single album and titled *Suspicious Minds*, it's possible this album could have leapt to No. 1 and outsold the first. *—Neal Umphred*

Worldwide 50 Gold Award Hits, Vol. 1 / Aug. 1970 / RCA ✦✦✦✦
A combination of the two four-LP *Worldwide* boxes, this two-CD set contains each of the 50 sides that RCA credits with accumulated worldwide sales in excess of one million copies! And in chronological order of release in mono! One can either trace the obvious decline of the artist into entertainer, or marvel at how good the bad stuff sounds in context. Million-selling B-sides and EPs that most assuredly had topped the seven-digit figure but were routinely ignored by most compilations are also included. If all you want in your collection from Elvis is the most obvious hits, this is the one to go with. *—Neal Umphred*

In Person at the International Hotel Las Vegas / Nov. 1970 / RCA ✦✦✦✦
When Elvis and the Colonel decided it was time to start appearing live again, they assembled a crackerjack band (featuring guitarist James Burton) and took on Vegas full bore. Easily the King's best live album, the highlights on *In Person (At the International Hotel, Las Vegas, NV)* include "Johnny B. Goode," the "My Babe/Mystery Train/Tiger Man" medley, and "Suspicious Minds." *—Cub Koda*

That's the Way It Is / Dec. 1970 / RCA ✦✦✦✦
Returning to the more familiar haunts of Nashville in 1970, Elvis & Co. recorded three-dozen tracks, the best of which are on a par with the Memphis recordings from the preceding year. From these, two albums emerged, both flawed, both excellent. *That's the Way It Is*, purporting to be the soundtrack from the documentary of the same name, contains eight of those sides, with Elvis at his most delicious ease. The live recordings are negligible and sink the album's basic level *except* for Elvis' magnificent "I Just Can't Help Believin'." *—Neal Umphred*

Elvis Country / Jan. 1971 / RCA ✦✦✦✦
Elvis Country was the second album from the June 1970 sessions. It is Elvis' best single album from the '70s and one of his very best ever. Every performance has something to offer; one can argue about the outstanding selection, although one tends away from the pleading of "I Really Don't Want to Know" to the raving "(I Washed My Hands in) Muddy Water." Even "Snowbird" is sung with passion! *—Neal Umphred*

He Touched Me / Apr. 1972 / RCA ✦✦✦✦
As if to make up for not recording in the studio for all those Hollywood years, Elvis took the first few years of his comeback dead seriously. As it stands, *He Touched Me* blends the earthiness of the 1960 gospel album with a bit of the preternatural churchiness of the 1966 recordings. This is a fine record, and you don't need to be a Christian to dig this music. *—Neal Umphred*

☆ **Reconsider Baby** / 1985 / RCA ✦✦✦✦✦
A 12-song, budget-priced compilation of Elvis' most notable blues sides for the label. A good place to start digging Elvis' commitment to the music—always returning to it right up through the '70s like an old friend, whenever he needed a quick fix of the *real* thing—as he takes on everything from R&B slices like Tommy Tucker's "High Heel Sneakers" to Percy Mayfield's "Stranger in My Own Home Town." Major highlights on this collection are Elvis playing acoustic rhythm guitar and driving the band through a take of the Lowell Fulson title track, blistering versions of two Arthur Crudup songs, an unreleased Sun recording of Lonnie Johnson's "Tomorrow Night," and the R-rated take of Smiley Lewis' "One Night (of Sin)." *—Cub Koda*

★ **Top Ten Hits** / 1987 / RCA ✦✦✦✦✦
The one definitive collection to own, 38 essential tracks are spread over two CDs. Think of any of Elvis' biggest chartbusters, they're all here. *—Hank Davis & Cub Koda*

The Number One Hits / 1987 / RCA ✦✦✦✦
Number One Hits contains 18 No. 1 records from the charts of *Billboard*, who somehow didn't rank "Crying in the Chapel," "In the Ghetto," "Burning Love," and "Way Down" as chart-toppers, although other national surveys did. In fact, according to RCA, every copy of "Way Down" was sold out within days after Presley's death, not just here but all over the planet, and somehow, amazingly, it didn't even make the magazine's Top Ten! — *Neal Umphred*

☆ **The Memphis Record** / 1987 / RCA ✦✦✦✦✦
Coming hot off the heels of his breakthrough NBC special in 1968, Presley returned to Memphis to record for the first time in 12 years and laid down 20 tracks in the space of four days. He was hot, he was inspired, and it's all here. — *Cub Koda*

★ **The Complete Sun Sessions** / 1987 / RCA ✦✦✦✦✦
The place where rock 'n' roll begins. "That's All Right," "Baby, Let's Play House," "Mystery Train," "Milkcow Blues Boogie," and "Good Rockin' Tonight," plus fascinating outtakes like "When It Rains, It Really Pours." The cornerstone of any rock 'n' roll collection, and great notes by Peter Guralnick too. — *Cub Koda*

☆ **Million Dollar Quartet** / 1990 / RCA ✦✦✦✦✦
For years available only as a poor-fidelity bootleg, this is Elvis jamming in the Sun studios with Carl Perkins, Jerry Lee Lewis, and others on a set of primarily gospel and hillbilly material. Loose as a goose, with a true jam-session spirit to it, it offers a fascinating glimpse of one of the few times Presley let his true musical soul come up for air with somebody (Sam Phillips) there to record it. — *Cub Koda*

☆ **The King of Rock 'n' Roll: The Complete 50s Masters** / 1992 / RCA ✦✦✦✦✦
A casual Elvis fan wanting to assemble a decent overview of the King's '50s sides could probably sweat it down to the *Sun Sessions* CD and volume one of the *Top Ten Hits* compilation. But for those of you who take your '50s Presley seriously, *The King of Rock 'n' Roll—The Complete 50s Masters* is absolutely essential. For the hardcore Elvis fan, the booklet and CD graphics for this five-disc set provide incentive enough to justify its purchase. The liner notes by Presley expert Peter Guralnick are passionate, contagious in their enthusiasm, and filled with a real sense of history, time, and place. The treasure-trove of unpublished photos, session information, and Elvis memorabilia accompanying the booklet text is no less inspiring. But it's the music (140 tracks in all) that's the real meat and potatoes of this set. Every studio track cut during the '50s—the seminal Sun sides, the early RCA hits, movie soundtracks, alternates, live performances, rarities (including both sides of the long-lost acetate he cut for his mother back in 1953)—it's all here in one gorgeous package. Soundwise, this box makes any of the previous issues of this material pale by comparison, the proper (nonreverbed) inclusion of the Sun masters being a particular treat. This is no mere rehash of what's been around a dozen times before—there's a lot of thought and care behind this package, and no serious fan of American rock 'n' roll should consider a collection complete without it. — *Cub Koda*

☆ **From Nashville to Memphis: The Essential 60's Masters** / 1993 / RCA ✦✦✦✦✦
Continues the tradition of first-quality sound remastering and packaging. Much of Elvis' '60s work is arguably not as essential as the '50s stuff, but this meticulous five-disc, 130-track set makes an impressive case for the defense. A thick booklet contains riveting liner notes, full-color photos, complete discography and session listings; a sheet of RCA album-cover stamps tops off the set. — *Roch Parisien*

Amazing Grace: His Greatest Sacred Songs / 1994 / RCA ✦✦✦
Elvis recorded quite a bit of gospel over the course of his career, and this two-CD, 55-song collection has the bulk of it. Most of this is drawn from his three gospel LPs (*His Hand in Mine*, 1960; *How Great Thou Art*, 1967; *He Touched Me*, 1972), as well as a 1957 EP. Presley was undoubtedly heavily influenced by gospel (at times he indicated regret at not having chosen to become a gospel singer), and this material has played pretty well with critics. Elvis sings with skill and reasonable commitment, and the backing musicians include such Elvis/Nashville standbys as Scotty Moore, Hank Garland, Floyd Cramer, Charlie McCoy, Pete Drake, the Jordanaires, and James Burton. At the same time, let's have a reality check here. Rock- and pop-oriented fans are going to find this two-and-a-half hour set tough going, unless they have a taste for spirituals as well. Things get a little more accessible when the tempos brighten, but often it's on the sedate side. For both collectors and listeners, highlights of the collection are five previously unreleased tracks from 1972. Recorded with only Charlie Hodges on piano and J.D. Sumner & the Stamps on backing vocals, they present Presley's gospel at its sparsest and most spontaneous. — *Richie Unterberger*

Command Performances: The Essential '60s Masters II / 1995 / RCA ✦✦✦
Elvis Presley's 1960s film soundtracks are renowned as the repository of his most frivolous (many would say ridiculous) material. This 62-song, double CD draws from no less than 26 of those screen vehicles to present the "best" of these performances; the idea is to complement the first volume of *Essential 60's Masters*, which focused on his non-soundtrack recordings from the decade and doesn't include any of the cuts from this collection. The goal of this package may have been to boil away the dross (as big as this is, there's a LOT of stuff they left off). But if anything, it perhaps inadvertently demonstrates just how lousy most of those recordings were; even this selective, chronologically programmed set feels way too long and could have probably been cut in length to a single CD without too much loss. That's not to say that what's here is entirely negligible. There are some classic singles ("Return to Sender," "Can't Help Falling in Love"), fair rockers ("What'd I Say," "Little Egypt"), and more than a few cuts that are transcendentally great/awful in their mindless silliness ("Rock-a-Hula Baby," "Viva Las Vegas," "Do the Clam"), songs that are archetypes, for better or worse, of the kitschiest facet of Presley's myth. But much of the rest is just unremarkable, or even bad: stupid novelties ("Poison Ivy League"), drab ballads, and many mediocre rock tunes. This doesn't include such legendarily idiotic songs as "No Room to Rhumba in a Sports Car," "Yoga Is as Yoga Does," and "Fort Lauderdale Chamber of Commerce"; you can find those on the original soundtracks, or a famous out-of-print bootleg, the aptly titled *Elvis' Greatest Shit*. — *Richie Unterberger*

☆ **Walk a Mile in My Shoes: The Essential '70s Masters** / Oct. 10, 1995 / RCA ✦✦✦✦✦
In most conventional rock criticism, Elvis Presley's '70s records are considered his weakest, as they were recorded while he was falling deeper into drug addiction. However, as Dave Marsh argues in the liner notes of *Walk a Mile in My Shoes: The Essential '70s Masters*, the music on the five-CD box set is among the most personal and adventurous of Elvis' career, even if the individual albums don't always reflect that diversity. By cutting away all of the dross that accumulated over the decade and sequencing the songs in a logical, entertaining manner, *Walk a Mile in My Shoes* supports the argument. On the first two discs, all of the singles Presley released during the '70s are presented, and while there are couple of weak numbers, the music stands as an impressive continuation of his artistry. — *Stephen Thomas Erlewine*

Elvis Presley '56 / Mar. 5, 1996 / RCA ✦✦✦✦
Sure the music on here's great. How could it not be? It has 22 of his hottest tracks from his first year at RCA, including not only the hits "Heartbreak Hotel," "Hound Dog," "Don't Be Cruel," and "Too Much," but such noted early rockers as "My Baby Left Me," "Blue Suede Shoes," "Money Honey," and "So Glad You're Mine." From a collector's viewpoint, though, you have to wonder whether it was really necessary. The only previously unreleased item is a sparser earlier take of "Heartbreak Hotel." Everything else has been widely available (even on CD) for years, and it's a good bet that many of the Elvis fans who buy this already have virtually all of the contents on the *King of Rock 'n' Roll* box set. — *Richie Unterberger*

Essential Elvis, Vol. 4: 100 Years from Now / Jul. 1996 / RCA ✦✦✦✦
This is the fourth installment in RCA's *Essential Elvis* series. The previous three volumes were all comprehensive box sets, but *100 Years from Now* is a single-disc collection that focuses on a very specific time frame—namely, the sessions Elvis cut in Nashville during 1970 and 1971. With the addition of some between-song narration, the music from these sessions would later become the *Elvis Country* album. All of the *Elvis Country* record is presented on *100 Years from Now* in its original form—sans narration, without overdubs and in full running time. There are also the standard rarities and previously unreleased song. Even with the newly discovered material, what is special about this set is the original *Elvis Country* album, which represents his last great album, and sounds even better in its original, uncut version. — *Stephen Thomas Erlewine*

Billy Preston

b. Sep. 9, 1946, Houston, TX
Piano, Keyboards, Vocals / Soul, R&B
It's advantageous to get an early start on your chosen career, but Billy Preston took the concept to extremes. By age ten, he was playing keyboards with gospel diva Mahalia Jackson, and two years later, in 1958, he was featured in Hollywood's film bio of W.C. Handy, *St. Louis Blues*, as young Handy himself. Preston was a prodigy on organ and piano, recording during the early '60s for Vee-Jay and touring with Little Richard. He was a loose-limbed regular on the mid-'60s ABC-TV "Shindig" series, proving his talent as both vocalist and pianist, and he built an enviable reputation as a session musician, even backing the Beatles on their *Let It Be* album. That impressive Beatles connection led to Preston's big break as a solo artist with his own Apple album, but it was his early-'70s soul smashes "Outa-Space" and the high-flying vocal "Will It Go Round in Circles" for A&M that put him on the permanent musical map. Sporting a humongous Afro and an omnipresent gap-toothed grin, Preston

showed that his enduring gospel roots were never far removed from his joyous approach, less so now than ever. —*Bill Dahl*

Most Exciting Organ Ever / 1965 / Vee-Jay ✦✦✦✦
The hyperbole of the title aside, Preston did produce some flamboyant organ solos and keyboard work throughout this album. His use of bass pedals, dazzling intervals, octave jumps, phrases, and chordal maneuvers were impressive. This hasn't been reissued by Vee-Jay, and certainly should be if the label hasn't lost the masters. It's another side of Preston, one that became lost as he gained more and more popularity in the '70s as a singer. —*Ron Wynn*

Wildest Organ in Town! / 1966 / Capitol ✦✦✦

That's the Way God Planned It / 1969 / Apple ✦✦✦✦
A great bit of gospel-soul in the title cut, and otherwise a fine record that didn't make Billy Preston a huge star but alerted everyone that he was more than just a talented keyboard player backing the Beatles. This was one of two albums Preston did on the Beatles' Apple label, and while nothing made the charts, it was a good introduction for those unaware of Preston's multiple skills. —*Ron Wynn*

● **The Best of Billy Preston** / 1988 / A&M ✦✦✦✦
It contains several fun pop hits, including "Will It Go Round in Circles" and "Outa-Space." —*Dan Heilman*

The Pretenders

Rock 'n' Roll, New Wave, Pop-Rock
Over the years, the Pretenders have become a vehicle for guitarist/vocalist Chrissie Hynde's songwriting, yet it was a full-fledged band when it was formed in the late '70s. With their initial records, the group crossed the bridge between punk-new wave and Top 40 pop more than any other band, recording a series of hard, spiky singles that were also melodic and immediately accessible. Hynde was an invigorating, sexy singer that bended the traditional male roles of rock 'n' roll to her own liking, while guitarist James Honeyman-Scott created a sonic palate filled with suspended chords, effects pedals, and syncopated rhythms that proved remarkably influential over the next two decades. After Honeyman-Scott's death, the Pretenders became a more straightforward rock band, yet Hynde's semi-autobiographical songwriting and bracing determination meant that the group never became just another rock band, even when their music became smoother and more pop-oriented.

Originally from Akron, OH, Hynde moved to England in the early '70s, when she was in her twenties. British rock journalist Nick Kent helped her begin writing for the *New Musical Express;* she wrote for the newspaper during the mid-'70s. She also worked in Malcolm McLaren's Sex boutique before she began performing. After playing with Chris Spedding, she joined Jack Rabbit; she quickly left the band and formed the Berk Brothers.

In 1978, Hynde formed the Pretenders, which eventually consisted of Honeyman-Scott, bassist Pete Farndon, and drummer Martin Chambers. Later in the year, they recorded a version of Ray Davies' "Stop Your Sobbing," produced by Nick Lowe. The single made it into the British Top 20 in early 1979, supported by positive reviews. "Kid" and "Brass in Pocket," the group's next two singles, also were successful. Their self-titled debut album was released in early 1980 and eventually climbed to No. 1 in the UK. The Pretenders were nearly as successful in America, with the album reaching the Top Ten and "Brass in Pocket" reaching No. 14.

During an American tour in 1980, Hynde met Ray Davies and the two fell in love. Following a spring 1981 EP, *Extended Play*, the group released their second album, *Pretenders II*. Although it fared well on the charts, it repeated the musical ideas of their debut. In June 1982, Pete Farndon was kicked out of the band, due to his drug abuse. A mere two days later, on June 16, James Honeyman-Scott was found dead of an overdose of heroin and cocaine. Pregnant with Davies' child, Hynde went into seclusion following Honeyman-Scott's death. In 1983, two months after Hynde gave birth, Farndon also died of a drug overdose.

Hynde regrouped the Pretenders at the end of 1983, adding guitarist Robbie McIntosh and bassist Malcolm Foster; the reconstituted band released "2000 Miles" in time for Christmas. The new Pretenders released *Learning to Crawl* early in 1984 to positive reviews and commercial success. Hynde married Jim Kerr, the lead vocalist of Simple Minds, in May 1984, effectively ending her romance with Ray Davies.

Apart from a performance at Live Aid, the only musical activity from the Pretenders during 1985 was Hynde's appearance on UB40's version of "I Got You Babe." Hynde assembled another version of the Pretenders for 1986's *Get Close*. Only McIntosh and herself remained from *Learning to Crawl*—the rest of the album was recorded with session musicians. *Get Close* showed the Pretenders moving closer to MOR territory, with the bouncy single "Don't Get Me Wrong" making its way into the American Top Ten in 1987. Hynde recorded another duet with UB40 in 1988, the old Dusty Springfield song, "Breakfast in Bed."

Hynde's marriage to Kerr fell apart in 1990, and the Pretenders recorded *Packed!*, which failed to ignite the charts in either America or Britain. She was relatively quiet for the next few years, re-emerging in

1994 with *Last of the Independents*, which was hailed as a comeback by some quarters of the press. The album did return the Pretenders to the Top 40 with the ballad "I'll Stand by You." In the fall of 1995, the Pretenders released the live album, *Isle of View*. —*Stephen Thomas Erlewine*

★ **Pretenders** / 1980 / Sire ✦✦✦✦✦
Chrissie Hynde's tough-girl persona, allied with the aggressive onslaught of Pete Farndon, James Honeyman-Scott, and Martin Chambers, makes this the top debut album of its year and prime evidence of the enlivening influence punk had on mainstream rock. —*William Ruhlmann*

Pretenders II / Aug. 1981 / Sire ✦✦✦✦
A well-named follow-up, since this album successfully repeats the formula of the debut, from its punky leadoff track, "The Adultress," to its catchy pop-rock single, "Talk of the Town," and even to its Kinks cover, "I Go to Sleep." But if you liked the first one . . . —*William Ruhlmann*

☆ **Learning to Crawl** / 1984 / Sire ✦✦✦✦✦
Half the band is dead, Chrissie Hynde has taken time off to have a baby, and the world has changed. The Pretenders are now a front for Hynde, solo artist, an adult rock singer-songwriter and, on such songs as "Middle of the Road," "Back on the Chain Gang," and "My City Was Mine," a damn good one too. —*William Ruhlmann*

Get Close / 1986 / Sire ✦✦✦
By now, Hynde is writing songs to her child and taking on social issues. But the chiming guitars are gorgeous, and Hynde's caught-in-the-throat voice has never been more expressive. —*William Ruhlmann*

☆ **The Singles** / 1987 / Sire ✦✦✦✦✦
Although the singles-only format makes the Pretenders sound more pop-oriented than they were, especially in the beginning, this album essentially addresses the legacy of punk in the ten years after its peak, tracing a heritage back to mid-'60s Merseybeat and forward to a more rock-based pop music. It also makes the case for Chrissie Hynde as a major artist. —*William Ruhlmann*

Packed! / May 1990 / Sire ✦✦

Last of the Independents / 1994 / Sire ✦✦✦

Isle of View / Oct. 24, 1995 / Warner Bros. ✦✦

Pretty Things

Rock 'n' Roll, Art-Rock/Progressive-Rock, British Invasion
Of all the original British Invasion groups, perhaps none is as underappreciated in the US as the Pretty Things. Featuring the hoarse vocals of Mick Jagger-lookalike Phil May and the stinging leads of guitarist Dick Taylor (who actually played in early versions of the Rolling Stones with Jagger and Keith Richards), the Pretties recorded a clutch of raunchy R&B rockers in the mid-'60s that offer a punkier, rawer version of the early Stones' sound. Their first two albums, as well as a brace of fine major and minor British hits (of which "Don't Bring Me Down" and "Honey I Need" were the biggest), feature first-rate original material and covers, and remain the group's most exciting and influential recordings. Unfortunately, the band remained virtually unknown to American audiences, most of whom would first hear "Don't Bring Me Down" on David Bowie's *Pin Ups* album (which also included a version of the Pretties' "Rosalyn").

After their initial run of success, the group took a sharp left turn into psychedelia with the orchestrated album *Emotions* (1967), impressive singles that owed more to Pink Floyd than Bo Diddley and, most significantly, *S.F. Sorrow* (1968). The first rock opera, *S.F. Sorrow* was a major influence upon Pete Townshend, who released his much more successful opera, *Tommy*, with the Who the following year. Founding member Taylor left shortly after *S.F. Sorrow*, and the group continued to record progressive-rock and hard rock with less impressive results through the mid-'70s, although *Parachute* (1970) was named by *Rolling Stone* as album of the year. The group reunites sporadically for occasional gigs and recordings in their early R&B vein. —*Richie Unterberger*

Pretty Things / 1965 / Fontana ✦✦✦✦
The Pretty Things' debut was one of the prime cuts of early British R&B, featuring such definitively raunchy exponents of the genre as "Roadrunner," "Big City," "Mama, Keep Your Big Mouth Shut," "Pretty Thing," and "Honey I Need." A couple of weak jams prevent the album from ranking as a true classic. It differs slightly from the US version of the record, which took off four tracks and substituted four others. Most of the songs from both versions of the LP are on the *Get a Buzz* compilation. —*Richie Unterberger*

Get the Picture? / Dec. 1965 / Fontana ✦✦✦
The group's second album wasn't quite as powerful as the first, and showed them starting to shift their emphasis to more original material, with a more pronounced soul influence and tentative stabs at folk-rock. It's got plenty of good stuff, however, and "Can't Stand the Pain," "You'll Never Do It Babe," "I Want Your Love," and "London Town" are all among their best early songs. Most (but not all) of the better tracks

appear on the *Get a Buzz* compilation; all of the LP's cuts have been reissued at one time or another. *—Richie Unterberger*

Emotions / 1967 / Fontana ♦♦♦
In accordance with their label's (and not the band's) wishes, the Pretties were teamed with a middle-aged orchestra directed by Reg Tilsley on this album, which saw the Phil May-Dick Taylor songwriting team making an effort to move beyond R&B knockoffs into more sophisticated territory. Sometimes the arrangements (dubbed onto tracks without much involvement from the group) worked; more often, they were an unnecessary hindrance. An interesting failure, it contained some genuinely top-rank originals that saw the group expanding their vision into social observation and tentative psychedelia, including "My Time," "The Sun," and especially the moody, folk-rockish "Death of a Socialite." *—Richie Unterberger*

Parachute / 1970 / Rare Earth ♦♦♦
The last Pretty Things album to explore interesting territory, this progressive-rock is grounded by some solid harmonies and riffs, but is ultimately not nearly as compelling as its *Rolling Stone* Album of the Year award would suggest. *—Richie Unterberger*

Electric Banana / 1991 / Repertoire ♦♦

● **Get a Buzz: The Best of the Fontana Years** / 1992 / Fontana ♦♦♦♦
It's missing a few good tracks, but this is a good retrospective of their British Invasion-era work, running through the 1967 *Emotions* LP. Includes all their major singles—"Rosalyn," "Don't Bring Me Down," "Honey I Need," "Midnight to Six Man," "Come See Me." *—Richie Unterberger*

On Air / 1992 / Band of Joy ♦♦

Lloyd Price

b. Mar. 9, 1933, Kenner, LA
Vocals / R&B, Rock 'n' Roll, New Orleans R&B
Having taken New Orleans by storm in 1952 with his often-covered No. 1 R&B hit "Lawdy Miss Clawdy" and a raft of sizzling encores, Lloyd Price yearned for new horizons in 1958, when he signed with ABC-Paramount Records. Price wanted to be a pop star, and it didn't take him long to achieve his goal. Price's pleading style worked brilliantly on his initial New Orleans sides for Specialty Records, resulting in a string of 1952-1953 R&B hits, but his later ABC output left the second-line rhythms behind in favor of prominent female choruses and giant supper-club-style horn sections. His socko reading of the old Crescent City chant "Stagger Lee" deservedly topped the R&B and pop lists in 1958, and he followed it with the utterly pop-styled "Personality" and "I'm Gonna Get Married," another pair of R&B No. 1 hits that sported no hint of Price's New Orleans roots. As the '60s dawned, Price insisted on interpreting a variety of Tin Pan Alley standards on his albums, although "Come into My Heart" and "Lady Luck," both hits, swung with a brassy, R&B-based drive. Price formed his own Double-L logo in 1963, issuing hits by Wilson Pickett and one for himself—a Vegas-oriented treatment of "Misty." Price seemed to prefer the business end of show biz after that rather than focusing on his singing career. *—Bill Dahl*

● **Greatest Hits [MCA]** / 1982 / MCA ♦♦♦♦
Price wasn't content with R&B fame; he yearned for pop acceptance too. He got plenty at ABC-Paramount from 1957 to 1960 (the time frame this 18-song retro addresses). Creating a brassy, accessible sound, Price hit huge with his rock 'n' roll rendition of "Stagger Lee" (here in two versions—original and "American Bandstand"-sanitized) and went all the way pop with the undeniably catchy "Personality." Innovative arrangements and Price's earnest vocals greatly distinguish "Have You Ever Had the Blues?," "Lady Luck," "Three Little Pigs," and "Where Were You (On Our Wedding Day)?," and there's a previously unissued "That's Love" to up the ante. *—Bill Dahl*

★ **Lawdy!** / 1991 / Specialty ♦♦♦♦♦
Twenty-five stellar 1952-1956 examples of why Lloyd Price ranks with the greatest R&B performers ever to emerge from the Crescent City. Beginning with his debut smash "Lawdy Miss Clawdy," Price wails the rocking "Mailman Blues," "Where You At?," "Rock 'n' Roll Dance," and "Baby Please Come Home" in front of fat sax cushions, rolling pianos, and steamy rhythm sections. *—Bill Dahl*

Heavy Dreams, Vol. 2 / 1993 / Specialty ♦♦♦♦
No discernible artistic dropoff on Specialty's encore Price retrospective, distinguished by his classics "Oooh-Oooh-Oooh," "Tell Me Pretty Baby," "Ain't It a Shame?" (not Fats Domino's hit), "Country Boy Rock," and "Why" (he'd later recut the latter for ABC-Paramount). *—Bill Dahl*

● **Lloyd Price Sings His Big Ten** / Feb. 8, 1994 / Capitol/Curb ♦♦♦♦
Like all standard Curb anthologies, this is too skimpy, numbering ten tracks. It does, however, include all of Price's major hits—"Stagger Lee," "Personality," "I'm Gonna Get Married," "Where Were You (On Our Wedding Day)?," "Lady Luck." And in its favor, it also includes the most famous of his pre-ABC hits, "Lawdy Miss Clawdy." *—Richie Unterberger*

Primal Scream

House Music, Rock 'n' Roll, Alternative Pop-Rock, Techno
Primal Scream might be the greatest charlatans of the '90s. With their third album, *Screamadelica*, the band was hailed as great musical innovators, dragging rock 'n' roll kicking and screaming into the drug-soaked dance club scene of the early '90s. As it turns out, the record was merely a means to an end—Primal Scream just wants to be rock stars and they don't care what they actually sound like, as long as they get there.

On their first two albums, the band recycled '60s and early '70s guitar pop and hard rock to some acclaim in the UK, but it was 1991's *Screamadelica* that established Primal Scream as major stars in England and earned them a cult following in America. *Screamadelica* took the classic early '70s rock of the Stones and the Faces and submerged it in techno and house dance music, creating a blissed-out, colorful pseudo-psychedelic extravaganza. It was a distinctive, innovative album, but Primal Scream's actual contribution to the sound of the record is questionable. What carried the album was its admittedly amazing production, mainly provided by Andrew Weatherall; there were few songs that could actually be attributed to the group and those that could were blatantly derivative.

Primal Scream's true roots appeared on their follow-up album, 1994's *Give Out but Don't Give Up*, which saw the band accentuating the classic rock currents that ran beneath their music and refashioning themselves as retro-rockers like the Black Crowes. Of course, that may again be the work of their producers—R&B veteran Tom Dowd, George Clinton, and Black Crowes mastermind George Drakoulias—but either way, the band lost many of its fans in the dance world while gaining a new audience of rockers. *—Stephen Thomas Erlewine*

Sonic Flower Groove / 1987 / Elevation ♦♦

Primal Scream / 1989 / Mercenary ♦♦

● **Screamadelica** / Oct. 8, 1991 / Sire ♦♦♦♦
Screamadelica is an impressive, innovative album that seamlessly combines classic rock with the throbbing beat of the dance club. While it doesn't contain any concise pop songs besides "Movin' on Up," the album is remarkably consistent and proved that it was possible to inject some true grit into the highly stylized world of techno, house, and rave. *—Stephen Thomas Erlewine*

Give Out but Don't Give Up / Sep. 1993 / Sire ♦♦♦

Primus

Alternative Pop-Rock, Funk Metal, Alternative Metal
Primus is all about Les Claypool; there isn't a moment on any of their other records where his bass isn't the main focal point of the music, with his vocals acting as a bizarre sideshow. Which isn't to deny guitarist Larry LaLonde or drummer Tim "Herb" Alexander any credit—no drummer could weave in and around Claypool's convoluted patterns as effortlessly as Alexander and few guitarists would as willingly push the spotlight away like LaLonde, so he can produce a never-ending spiral of avant-noise. All of this means that they are miles away from being another punk-funk combo like the Red Hot Chili Peppers; Claypool may slap and pop his bass, but there is little funk in the rhythm he and Alexander lay down. Instead, they're a post-punk Rush spiked with the sensibility and humor of Frank Zappa. Primus doesn't want to make you dance, they want to play music; songs are secondary to showcasing their instrumental prowess.

Primus' music is willfully weird and experimental, yet it's not alienating; the band was able to turn their goofy weirdness into pop stardom. At first, the band was strictly an underground phenomenon but in the years between their third and fourth albums, their cult grew rapidly. The 1991 *Sailing the Seas of Cheese* went gold shortly before the release of *Pork Soda*. By the time of the album's 1993 release, Primus had enough devoted fans to make *Pork Soda* debut in the Top Ten. After touring for a year—including a headlining spot on 1993's Lollapalooza—Claypool revived his Prawn Song record label in 1994 and released a reunion record by Primus' original lineup under the name Sausage. In the summer of 1995, Primus released their fifth album, *Tales from the Punch Bowl*. It was another success, going gold before the end of the year. In the summer of 1996, Primus announced they were parting ways with their drummer, Tim Alexander. *—Stephen Thomas Erlewine*

Suck on This / Jan. 1990 / Caroline ♦♦♦

Frizzle Fry / Feb. 1990 / Caroline ♦♦♦

● **Sailing the Seas of Cheese** / 1991 / Interscope ♦♦♦♦
The band's major-label debut features an appearance by Tom Waits on "Tommy the Cat" (originally found on *Suck on This*). Guitarist Larry Lalonde, formerly with Possessed and Blind Illusion, shows his death-metal roots on some of the songs on this album. *—John Book*

Pork Soda / 1993 / Interscope ♦♦♦♦
Apart from the bizarre murder tale "My Name Is Mud," few tracks on *Pork Soda* rival "Tommy the Cat" or "Jerry Was a Race Car Driver";

another troubling sign of a lack of songwriting ideas is that one track, "The Pressman," was originally released on *Suck on This*. However, the overall quality of the playing is so good that it almost doesn't matter that the songs are frequently simplistic and occasionally awful. Primus continue to improve as musicians, so *Pork Soda* is hardly a terrible album—in fact, it's their best, most consistent effort to date, even though it would benefit from some editing. —*Stephen Thomas Erlewine*

Tales from the Punch Bowl / 1995 / Interscope ✦✦

Prince (Prince Rogers Nelson)

Bass, Guitar, Drums, Keyboards, Vocals / Soul, Funk, Rock 'n' Roll, Urban, Pop-Rock, Club-Dance, Neo-Psychedelia

Few artists have created a body of work as rich and varied as Prince. During the '80s, he emerged as one of the most singular talents of the rock 'n' roll era, capable of seamlessly tying together pop, funk, folk, and rock. Not only did he release a series of groundbreaking albums, he toured frequently, produced albums and wrote songs for many other artists, and recorded hundreds of songs that still lie unreleased in his vaults. With each album he has released, Prince has shown remarkable stylistic growth and musical diversity, constantly experimenting with different sounds, textures, and genres. Occasionally, his music can be maddeningly inconsistent because of this eclecticism, but his experiments frequently succeed; no other contemporary artist can blend so many diverse styles into a cohesive whole.

Prince's first two albums were solid, if unremarkable, late '70s funk-pop. With 1980's *Dirty Mind*, he recorded his first masterpiece, a one-man tour de force of sex and music; it was hard-funk, catchy Beatlesque melodies, sweet soul ballads, and rocking guitar-pop, all at once. The follow-up, *Controversy*, was more of the same, but *1999* was brilliant. The album was a monster hit, selling over three million copies, but it was still nothing compared to 1984's *Purple Rain*.

Purple Rain made Prince a superstar; it sold over ten million copies in the US and spent 24 weeks at No. 1. Partially recorded with his touring band the Revolution, the record featured the most pop-oriented music he has ever made. Instead of continuing in this accessible direction, he veered off into the bizarre psycho-psychedelia of *Around the World in a Day* (1985), which nevertheless sold over two million copies. In 1986, he released the even stranger *Parade*, which was in its own way was as ambitious and intricate as any art-rock of the '60s; however, art-rock was ever grounded with a hit as brilliant as the spare funk of "Kiss."

By 1987, Prince's ambitions were growing by leaps and bounds, resulting in the sprawling masterpiece *Sign o' the Times*. Prince was set to release the hard funk of the *Black Album* by the end of the year, yet he withdrew it just before its release, deciding it was too dark and immoral. Instead, he released the confused *Lovesexy* in 1988, which was a commercial disaster. With the soundtrack to 1989's *Batman* he returned to the top of the charts, even if the album was essentially a recap of everything he had done before. The following year he released *Graffiti Bridge*, the sequel to *Purple Rain*, which turned out to be a considerable commercial disappointment.

In 1991, Prince formed the New Power Generation, the most versatile and talented band he has ever assembled. With their first album, *Diamonds and Pearls*, Prince reasserted his mastery of contemporary R&B; it was his biggest hit since 1985. The following year, he released his 12th album, which was titled with a cryptic symbol; in 1993, Prince legally changed his name to the symbol. In 1994, he independently released "The Most Beautiful Girl in the World" single, which became his biggest hit in years. Late in the summer of 1994, he released *Come* under the name of Prince; the record was a moderate success, going gold.

After *Come*, Prince agreed to release the *Black Album* officially in November 1994. In early 1995, he immersed himself in another legal battle with Warner, as the record company refused to release the *Gold Experience*. By the end of the summer, the disputes had been resolved and the album was released in the fall. In the summer of 1996, Prince released *Chaos & Disorder*, which reportedly was his last album of original material for Warner Bros. Records. —*Stephen Thomas Erlewine*

For You / 1978 / Warner Bros. ✦✦
Prince's debut is a fairly conventional blend of erotic funk, highlighted by the horny "Soft and Wet" and subverted by too much mediocre material. —*John Floyd*

Prince / 1979 / Warner Bros. ✦✦✦

☆ Dirty Mind / 1980 / Warner Bros. ✦✦✦✦✦
This delirious, hard-on masterpiece is dedicated to the joy of sex. The guitars are revved up a few notches, the funk has more muscle, and the songs make explicit just how unique (and sometimes twisted) Prince's vision can be. —*John Floyd*

Controversy / 1981 / Warner Bros. ✦✦✦
Synthesizers move to the forefront and, though the sound is riveting and while "Do Me, Baby" and the title cut are among his best, this is a tad short on decent songs. —*John Floyd*

☆ 1999 / 1982 / Warner Bros. ✦✦✦✦✦
This double-album mingling of politics and sex features Prince's sturdiest dance grooves and his first crossover hits ("Little Red Corvette," "Delirious," and the title track). This album is a near-masterpiece. —*John Floyd*

☆ Purple Rain / 1984 / Warner Bros. ✦✦✦✦✦
Upon its release, the soundtrack from Prince's big-screen debut sounded as if his artistry had blossomed fully. Today it remains essential for the singles, like "When Doves Cry" and "Let's Go Crazy." Elsewhere, it retreads familiar ground. —*John Floyd*

Around the World in a Day / 1985 / Paisley Park ✦✦✦
Prince got his first negative reviews when this album was originally issued. Cries of rip-off and imitator were leveled his way, while defenders rushed into the fray. The album was hardly the flop it's been perceived as. While it did reflect Prince's love of the Beatles' psychedelic period, it also topped the charts for three weeks and ultimately yielded the hits "Pop Life" and "Raspberry Beret." But Prince would return to a harder, funkier sound the next time out, and the album seems a logical end to a direction he began with *Purple Rain*. —*Ron Wynn*

Parade (Music from the Motion Picture *Under the Cherry Moon*) / 1986 / Paisley Park ✦✦✦
Another soundtrack that boasts some strong singles ("Kiss," "Mountains," and "Anotherloverholenyohead") and some dreary, neo-psychedelic filler. —*John Floyd*

☆ Sign o' the Times / 1987 / Paisley Park ✦✦✦✦✦
This two-disc, one-man-band romp through everything he does best goes from galvanizing grooves (one of which was recorded with the Revolution) to some slinky smoochers, which show for the first time sympathy and genuine affection for his romantic objects. This is Prince's greatest album. —*John Floyd*

Black Album / 1987 / Warner Bros. ✦✦✦
Recorded in 1987 but shelved until 1994 in favor of *Lovesexy*, the *Black Album* is a sinister funk-fest, long on the boogie but short on anything really remarkable. —*John Floyd*

Lovesexy / Feb. 1988 / Paisley Park ✦✦✦

Batman / 1989 / Paisley Park ✦✦✦

Graffiti Bridge / Aug. 21, 1990 / Paisley Park ✦✦✦

Diamonds and Pearls / 1991 / Paisley Park ✦✦✦
Out of nowhere, Prince suddenly regathers his strengths, assembles the New Power Generation, the best band of his career, and shimmies and strolls through his best album since *Times*. An eclectic yet seamless attestation of Prince's vitality in the '90s. —*John Floyd*

Love Symbol Album / Oct. 13, 1992 / Paisley Park ✦✦✦✦
The New Power Generation is the most talented and versatile band Prince has ever fronted, and they fulfill their potential on *Symbol*. Although the NPG factored heavily on *Diamonds and Pearls*, it still sounded like a solo Prince album. *Symbol* sounds like a band performing together, working off of each other's strengths and weaknesses. Opening with the dance smash "My Name Is Prince" and the deep funk of "Sexy M.F.," *Symbol* has Prince's best dance tracks since the *Black Album*. But Prince wasn't content; he decided to run the gamut of modern pop/R&B/dance, and the music is uniformly accomplished and excellent. Unfortunately, he also decided to make a "rock soap opera," so the music is saddled with ridiculous lyrics and annoying sound bridges by Kirstie Alley. However, *Symbol* has some of the finest, most inventive music of Prince's career. —*Stephen Thomas Erlewine*

★ The Hits 1 / 1993 / Paisley Park ✦✦✦✦✦
The primary fault with Prince's two-part *Hits* collection is that both volumes are missing some important singles and are sequenced incoherently, thereby failing to give an accurate impression of his astonishing musical growth. However, they do contain enough necessary items to illustrate why he was one of the most influential and gifted musicians of the '80s, as well as providing a reasonable introduction and compilation for casual fans. *Hits 1* contains a good cross-section of his biggest hits—"When Doves Cry" (presented in an edited version), "When You Were Mine," "Let's Go Crazy," "1999," "Sign o' the Times," "Alphabet Street," "Diamonds and Pearls," "7"—plus new items like "Pink Cashmere" and "Nothing Compares 2 U" (a Prince song that Sinéad O'Connor took to No. 1), which are nearly as good as the familiar tracks. However, it provides an incomplete portrait, making *Hits 2* a necessary purchase. —*Stephen Thomas Erlewine*

★ The Hits 2 / 1993 / Paisley Park ✦✦✦✦✦
Like *Hits 1*, *Hits 2* presents an illogically sequenced cross-section of some of Prince's biggest hits and most notorious songs, including "Dirty Mind," "I Wanna Be Your Lover," "Head," "Delirious," "Little Red Corvette," "I Would Die 4 U," "Raspberry Beret," "Kiss," "U Got the Look," "Cream," and "Purple Rain." Two new tracks, "Peach" and "The Pope," are included among the 18 cuts and while they don't match the rest of the songs (or the new cuts on *Hits 1*), they are nevertheless enjoyable. On the

whole, *Hits 2* is a slightly stronger collection than its predecessor, but it still gives a rather incomplete portrait—if you buy *Hits 2*, you need to buy *Hits 1*. —*Stephen Thomas Erlewine*

The Hits/B-Sides / 1993 / Paisley Park ++++
While it isn't a truly comprehensive set, Prince's singles collection does contain most of his biggest hits. The two volumes are available separately or packaged together with a third disc of B-sides; apart from the glorious "Erotic City," the flip sides are only of interest to devoted fans. —*Stephen Thomas Erlewine*

Come / 1994 / Warner Bros. ++

Gold Experience / Oct. 1995 / Warner Bros./NPG ++++
Prince changed his name to an unpronounceable symbol in 1993, but it wasn't until 1995 that he actually released a record credited to that symbol. During those two years, he released a greatest-hits collection, an official version of his much-bootlegged *Black Album*, and a final Prince album, the lackluster *Come*. Throughout 1994, he pressured Warner to release another album, *Gold Experience*, but the company refused and he staged a public protest in the media, calling himself a slave to the label. By the summer of 1995, the artist and the company had made amends, and the record was released in the fall. In a way, *Gold Experience* lives up to the manufactured hype created while it languished on the shelf. More of a creative rebirth than a change in direction, the record finds Prince and the New Power Generation running through a typically dazzling array of musical styles, subtly twisting new sounds out of familiar forms. Much like the *Love Symbol Album*, it follows a loose concept, interweaving a variety of pop, funk, rock, soul, and jazz styles into a vague story. Song for song, *Gold Experience* is slightly stronger than its predecessor, as Prince's melodies are more immediate, especially on the Philly soul tribute "The Most Beautiful Girl in the World" and the pure pop of "Dolphin." Also, the band's performance is lively and confident, bringing an effortless virtuosity to funk workouts ("P Control") and fuzzed-out rockers ("Endorphinmachine"), as well as ballads like "Eye Hate U." *Gold Experience* is somewhat weighed down by interludes that attempt to further the story but wind up interrupting the flow of the music, yet that doesn't stop the album from being Prince's most satisfying effort since *Sign o' the Times*. —*Stephen Thomas Erlewine*

Chaos & Disorder / Jul. 1996 / Warner Bros. +++

P.J. Proby (James Marcus Smith)

b. Nov. 6, 1938, Houston, TX
Vocals / British Invasion
Like the Walker Brothers, he wasn't British, he sang more ballads than rock 'n' roll, and he was far more successful in the UK than the States. Texan P.J. Proby was pretty hot stuff in England for a time, as much—indeed, probably more—for his then-risqué stage act, which saw him incorporate split pants into it after they (he claimed) accidentally ripped during a performance. Artistically, this is a case when the taste of the British listening public could be called into question. Proby sang in a pinched facsimile of Elvis and Gene Pitney that grew increasingly pained as it approached the upper register. A few of his hits were MOR ballads like "Somewhere" and "Maria," but he did manage an infectious Merseyish rocker on his first (and biggest) British smash, "Hold Me." In the US, he is most remembered for recording the Lennon-McCartney composition "That Means a Lot" in 1965 (which the Beatles themselves didn't release at the time), and his sole Top 40 US hit (from 1967), the Cajun-flavored "Nicki Hoeky." —*Richie Unterberger*

● **Legendary P.J. Proby at His Very Best: Vol. 2** / 1987 / See For Miles ++++
Oddly, this is a better compilation than *Vol. 1*, which focused more on his ballads; this is oriented toward his rock and soul recordings. Includes "Hold Me," "Nicki Hoeky," the 1964 British Top 20 single "Together," and "Just Call and I'll Be There" (also recorded by Francoise Hardy in French), where Proby sounds like the loser in a Gene Pitney soundalike contest. Spanning from 1964 to 1968, most of the rest consists of rock and soul covers that range from passable to horrid. —*Richie Unterberger*

Procol Harum

Art-Rock/Progressive-Rock, Psychedelic
Formed in 1967, Procol Harum incorporated a weighty classicism into their sound, with occasional traces of R&B and rock 'n' roll. This British group was originally formed around the core of lyricist Keith Reid and singer-songwriter Gary Brooker, who hailed from the R&B club band the Paramounts. Their first collaboration, the stately "A Whiter Shade of Pale," was loosely built off of Bach's "Air on a G String." A band was formed (named after Reid's cat), and in short order, Procol Harum had a record deal and an international hit on their hands. Part of the success of the band's sound was due to Matthew Fisher's stately organ work and Robin Trower's lyrical blues-based lead-guitar playing, which appeared on Procol's second and third albums, *Shine on Brightly* and *A Salty Dog*. In spite of further lineup changes (eventually incorporating most of the

Paramounts), Procol Harum enjoyed even greater chart success during the early '70s, particularly *Live in Concert with the Edmonton Symphony Orchestra* (No. 5). By this time, the band seemed to be trading on its past glories, with flashes of their earlier brilliance briefly resurfacing on their 1974 release *Exotic Birds and Fruit* (No. 86). Procol Harum eventually broke up in 1977, after the spotty *Something Magic*. —*Rick Clark*

Procul Harum / 1967 / Deram ++++
Their spectacular debut showed remarkable songwriting and became a late-'60s classic, due to the immense popularity of "A Whiter Shade of Pale," which made their reputation. —*Cub Koda & Dan Heilman*

Shine on Brightly / 1968 / A&M ++++
Procol's ambitious sophomore effort expanded upon their symphonic-style rock, particularly the 18-plus-minute conceptual opus "In Held 'Twas in I." The title track was another highlight. —*Rick Clark*

A Salty Dog / 1969 / A&M ++++
Procol's synthesis of blues and grand, classically inspired melodies reached an apex on their third album. The tasteful production featured sweeping orchestrations, subtle sound effects, and dynamic arrangements. *A Salty Dog* became one of Procol's signature numbers. —*Rick Clark*

Home / 1970 / A&M +++

Procol Harum Live: In Concert with the Edmonton Symphony Orchestra & the Da Camera Sin / 1972 / A&M +++

The Best of Procol Harum / 1973 / A&M ++++
A fine wrap-up of the band's 1967-73 output, it documents their most creative era. —*Dan Heilman*

Exotic Birds & Fruit / 1974 / Chrysalis +++

● **Classics, Vol. 17** / 1987 / A&M ++++
This best-of collection covers the hits, plus a decent collection of album tracks. —*Rick Clark*

The Psychedelic Furs

Alternative Pop-Rock, New Wave
The Psychedelic Furs, whose name belies their punk-influenced music, were formed in England in 1977 by brothers Richard Butler (vocals) and Tim Butler (bass), along with saxophone player Duncan Kilburn and guitarist Roger Morris. By the time they released their self-titled debut album in 1980, the group had become a sextet, adding guitarist John Ashton and drummer Vince Ely. That album, featuring Butler's hoarse voice (the tone of which suggested John Lydon without the sneer) was a bigger hit in England, where it reached the Top 20, than in the US.

Talk Talk Talk (1981) did better, reaching the US Top 100 and producing two British singles-chart entries, one of which was "Pretty in Pink," later also a hit in the US when a new version was used as the title song of a film. *Forever Now* (1982) saw the band reduced to a quartet with the departure of Kilburn and Morris. The rest moved to the US, turned to producer Todd Rundgren, and scored a US Top 50 hit with "Love My Way." Ely then left, and the remaining trio of the two Butlers and Ashton made *Mirror Moves* (1984), the biggest Psychedelic Furs hit yet.

The film *Pretty in Pink* helped spread their name further before the release of their next album, *Midnight to Midnight* (1986), which consequently got to No. 12 in the UK and the Top 30 in the US. *World Outside* (1991) also failed to find an audience. The Psychedelic Furs then folded up shop, and Richard Butler launched a new group, Love Spit Love. —*William Ruhlmann*

The Psychedelic Furs [1st LP] / 1980 / Columbia ++++
This auspicious debut finds the sextet turning out thick, noisy rock (especially in the saxophone-guitar combination) through which Richard Butler's voice cuts like a buzz saw. Best track: "Imitation of Christ." (The UK version of *The Psychedelic Furs* differed from the US version and was released earlier, in February 1980.) —*William Ruhlmann*

Talk Talk Talk / Jun. 1981 / Columbia ++++
An even better follow-up makes explicit the Furs' connection to The Velvet Underground (their name comes from the Velvets' song "Venus in Furs"). Their strongest overall collection, this includes the original (superior) version of "Pretty in Pink," "Dumb Waiters," and the definitive Psychedelic Furs song, "Into You Like a Train." —*William Ruhlmann*

Forever Now / 1982 / Columbia +++
Actually, Todd Rundgren's much-vaunted clean, sharp production style has very little effect on the Furs' sound, which is still pretty noisy and still dominated by Butler's hoarse, slightly scornful voice on such songs as "Love My Way," "President Gas," and the title track. —*William Ruhlmann*

Mirror Moves / 1984 / Columbia +++
On *Mirror Moves*, the Psychedelic Furs began to move toward a slicker, accessible pop-rock sound. By and large, the extra gloss works, as the group turns in a set of catchy rockers that manages to incorporate some mainstream concessions into their signature sound without losing their

personality. It may not be as exciting as their first four records, but they pull off the streamlined pop on *Mirror Moves* with considerable panache. —*Stephen Thomas Erlewine*

Midnight to Midnight / 1987 / Columbia ✦✦✦

● **All of This and Nothing** / 1988 / Columbia ✦✦✦✦
Not a perfect Furs compilation, but this 12-track look back does contain the notable tracks from the albums *Mirror Moves* and *Midnight to Midnight*, plus some of the necessary ones from the albums listed above and a good new song, "All That Money Wants." —*William Ruhlmann*

Book of Days / 1989 / Columbia ✦✦

World Outside / 1991 / Columbia ✦✦✦

B-Sides & Lost Grooves / 1994 / Columbia/Legacy ✦✦✦

Public Image Limited (PiL)

Alternative Pop-Rock, Experimental, Post-Punk
Public Image Ltd. originally was a quartet led by singer John Lydon (formerly Johnny Rotten, b. Jan. 31, 1956) and guitarist Keith Levene, who had been a member of the Clash in one of its early lineups. The band was filled out by bassist Jah Wobble (born John Wordle) and drummer Jim Walker. It was formed in the wake of the 1978 breakup of Lydon's former group, the Sex Pistols. For the most part, it devoted itself to droning, slow-tempo, bass-heavy noise rock, overlaid by Lydon's distinctive, vituperative rant.

The group's debut single, "Public Image," was more of an uptempo pop-rock song, however, and it hit the UK Top Ten upon its release in October 1978. The group itself debuted on Christmas Day, shortly after the release of its first album, *Public Image*. Neither the single nor the album was released in the US.

Metal Box, the band's second UK album, came in the form of three 12-inch, 45-rpm discs in a film cannister. It was released in the US in 1980 as the double album *Second Edition*. (By this time, PiL was a trio consisting of Lydon, Levene, and Wobble.) The third album, not released in the US, was the live *Paris in the Spring* (1980). Lydon and Levene, plus hired musicians, made up the group by the time of *Flowers of Romance* (1981), the much-acclaimed fourth album, which reached No. 11 in the UK.

In 1983, PiL scored its biggest UK hit, when "This Is Not a Love Song" reached No. 5. By this time, however, Levene had left, and the name from here on would simply be a vehicle for John Lydon. A second live album, *Live in Tokyo*, appeared in England in 1983.

The next year saw the release of *This Is What You Want . . . This Is What You Get*, only PiL's third album to be released in the US, though it now had six albums out. It marked the start of Lydon's move toward a more accessible dance-rock style, a direction that would be pursued further in *Album* (1986, also called *Cassette* or *Compact Disc*, depending on the format), notably on the hit "Rise," as well as on *Happy?* (1987) and *9* (1989). In 1990, PiL released the compilation album *The Greatest Hits, So Far*, and in 1991 came the new album, *That What Is Not*.

After completing his memoirs in late 1993, Lydon decided to put an end to PiL and pursue a solo career. —*William Ruhlmann*

Public Image Ltd / Dec. 1978 / Warner Bros. ✦✦✦

Second Edition / Jul. 1980 / Warner Bros. ✦✦✦✦
A two-disc deconstruction of traditional rock music, its tempos steady but slow, its bass track mixed high as in a reggae dub album, and Lydon's droning voice, with its scornful lyrics, wafting in the back. It is what PiL called it at the time, "anti-rock 'n' roll," and it's fascinating. —*William Ruhlmann*

Flowers of Romance / 1981 / Warner Bros. ✦✦✦

This Is What You Want . . . This Is What You Get / 1984 / Virgin ✦✦✦✦
Lydon adds keyboards, horns, and even a violin, double-tracks his vocals, and writes shorter songs with faster tempos. *This Is What You Want . . . This Is What You Get* doesn't quite add up to a pop album, but you can dance to it. Contains the UK hit "This Is Not a Love Song." —*William Ruhlmann*

Album/Compact Disc/Cassette / 1986 / Elektra ✦✦✦✦
Hot guitars and 4/4 time signatures make this sound more like a hard-rock album than anything Lydon's done since the Sex Pistols. And the hit single "Rise" is actually a catchy number, believe it or not. —*William Ruhlmann*

Happy? / 1987 / Virgin ✦✦✦✦
Continuing with the deceptively pop-oriented studio sheen of *Album*, *Happy?* is a set of outwardly friendly material, which reveals its fractured melodies and concepts upon closer inspection. Song for song, *Happy?* isn't quite as strong as *Album*, but it continues its predecessor's sound to a fine effect. —*Stephen Thomas Erlewine*

9 / 1989 / Virgin ✦✦✦

● **The Greatest Hits So Far** / 1990 / Virgin ✦✦✦✦
Fourteen tracks, recorded between 1978 and 1990, that trace PiL from the punk energy of the first single, "Public Image" (not previously

released in the US), through the anti-rock of "Death Disco" and "Flowers of Romance" to the almost-pop of "This Is Not a Love Song" and "Rise" and the best of the late-'80s material. —*William Ruhlmann*

That What Is Not / 1992 / Virgin ✦✦

Pulp

Alternative Pop-Rock, Brit-Pop
Most bands hit the big time immediately and fade away, or they build a dedicated following and slowly climb their way to the top. Pulp didn't follow either route. For the first 12 years of their existence, Pulp languished in near total obscurity, releasing a handful of albums and singles in the '80s to barely any attention. At the turn of the decade, the group began to gain an audience, sparking a remarkable turn of events that made the band one of the most popular British groups of the '90s. By the time Pulp became famous, the band had gone through different incarnations and changes in style, covering nearly every indie-rock touchstone from punk to dance. Pulp's signature sound is a fusion of David Bowie and Roxy Music's glam rock, disco, new wave, acid house, Euro pop, and British indie rock. The group's cheap synthesizers and sweeping melodies reflect the lyrical obsessions of lead vocalist Jarvis Cocker, who alternates between sex and sharp, funny portraits of working class misfits. Out of secondhand pop, Pulp fashioned a distinctive, stylish sound that made camp into something grand and glamourous and retained a palpable sense of gritty reality.

Jarvis Cocker formed Pulp in 1978, when he was 15 years old. Originally called Arabicus Pulp, the first lineup consisted of schoolmates of his. After a year, the band's name was truncated to Pulp. While they were in school, Pulp performed a handful of gigs. The band recorded a demo sometime in 1980-81, giving the tape to John Peel at one of his traveling shows. Peel liked the tape and invited the band to appear on his show. Pulp had their first Peel Session in November 1981. Instead of leading to record deals and pop stardom, Pulp's appearance on Peel led nowhere. Discouraged by the band's lack of success, every member but Cocker left the band in 1982 to go to university. Cocker assembled a new lineup the following year, which featured eight members, including keyboardist Simon Hinkler, who would later join the Mission. In this incarnation, Pulp had pronounced folky overtones, as well as new wave underpinnings. The group landed their first record contract, releasing their debut album, *It*, in 1984. *It* didn't make much of an impact, either critically or commercially, and the band fell apart again. After the second incarnation of Pulp disintegrated, Cocker formed another version of the band, with guitarist/violinist Russell Senior, who became Cocker's first full-fledged collaborator. Cocker and Senior added drummer Magnus Doyle and bassist Peter Mansell to the group, as well as Tim Allcard, who did nothing but read poetry. Musically, Pulp backed away from the folky inclinations of *It*, adding keyboardist Candida Doyle in 1985, which led to a darker sound; shortly after her arrival, Allcard left the group. In 1985, Pulp released a series of singles on Fire Records. Just as their fortunes were looking up, Jarvis became injured severely. As he was trying to impress a girl, he fell 30 feet out of a window, injuring his pelvis, foot, and wrist. For two months, he was confined to a wheelchair, but he performed concerts anyway.

Released in 1986, Pulp's second album, *Freaks*, was a dense, dark affair. Following its release, the band split during the filming of the video for "They Suffocate at Night." All of the members except Cocker and Senior left the group. For a year, the band was dormant, but Candida Doyle returned in 1987, with drummer Nick Banks and bassist Steven Havenhand joining shortly afterward. Havenhand was soon replaced by Anthony Genn, who was soon replaced by Steve Mackey. Although the group had a stable lineup, they weren't gaining much of a following. In 1988, Jarvis Cocker moved to London with Mackey and began studying filmmaking at St. Martin's College. While he was studying, Pulp was offered the chance to record another album. The resulting album, *Separations*, was recorded in 1989 and reflected Cocker's newfound obsession with acid house but also boasted some full-fledged pop songs. *Separations* was released nearly three years after it was completed. Cocker was prepared to stake out a career in film when a single from the album, "My Legendary Girlfriend," was released. *NME* named the song Single of the Week in 1991, and Pulp's career suddenly took off.

In early 1992, Pulp left Fire Records for Gift and began releasing a series of singles that consolidated the success of "My Legendary Girlfriend." In particular, "Babies" earned the band a great deal of attention. "Babies" led to a contract with Island Records, their first major-label deal. Island released *PulpIntro*, a compilation of the Gift singles, as the band recorded its major-label debut, *His 'n' Hers*. Upon its spring 1994 release, *His 'n' Hers* earned positive reviews and became an unexpected success, reaching the British Top Ten; it was also nominated for the 1994 Mercury Award. For the rest of 1994 and the early part of 1995, Jarvis Cocker suddenly became omnipresent on British TV. He hosted Top of the Pops, mocking every one of the acts appearing on the program. He appeared on *Pop Quiz* drunk, but still managed to ridicule the host and the show and lead his team to victory. These TV appearances became legendary, making Cocker somewhat of a national hero, as well as a sex symbol.

No matter how popular Jarvis Cocker had become, the band didn't break into the big time until they released "Common People." The single became a massive hit upon its May 1995 release, debuting at No. 2 on the UK charts. In July, Pulp accepted a last-minute headlining slot at the Glastonbury festival when the Stone Roses had to cancel. Pulp's set was rapturously received, launching the band into genuine superstar status in England and conveniently setting the stage for their forthcoming album, *Different Class*. During the recording of the album, guitarist Mark Webber—the president of Pulp's fan club—became a full-time member of the group. The first record to feature Webber was the double A-sided single, "Mis-shapes" and "Sorted for E's and Wizz," which was released in August, two months before *Different Class*. The single became a No. 2 hit, despite a major tabloid controversy over the lyrics to *Sorted*. *Different Class* arrived in late October to rave reviews throughout the British press. The album entered the charts at No. 1, going gold within its first week and platinum within the second. At the end of the year, *Different Class* topped many best-of-the-year lists. In February 1996, *Different Class* was released in the US to positive reviews. —*Stephen Thomas Erlewine*

It / 1983 / Red Rhino ✦✦

Freaks / 1986 / Fire ✦✦

Separations / 1992 / Razor & Tie ✦✦✦

PulpIntro—The Gift Recordings / 1993 / Island ✦✦✦✦
All of the singles Pulp recorded for Gift Records, including both the A- and B-sides, are collected on *PulpIntro: The Gift Recordings*. From the opening track "Space," it's clear that Pulp's confidence and talents have grown considerably, even from the relatively accomplished *Separations*. Now, the band has created a signature sound that relies heavily on cheap, synthesized sounds as well as tight pop melodies and a theatrical attack that nearly approximates the art-rock of Roxy Music and David Bowie. However, Pulp is too concerned with earthly pleasures to really recall Roxy or Bowie. Furthermore, the band's knack for creating terrific pop singles prevents them from being too pretentious as the singles "O.U.," "Razzamatazz," and, particularly, "Babies," illustrates. And even though it's just a collection of singles, *PulpIntro* holds together as well as *Separations*, if not better. —*Stephen Thomas Erlewine*

His 'n' Hers / 1994 / Island ✦✦✦✦
Jarvis Cocker's update on Bryan Ferry's lounge lizard persona works because he recognizes the sleaziness beneath the style. Instead of chronicling the lives and times of jet-setting club-hoppers, Cocker sneaks into the closet of his girlfriend to watch her sister have sex, reveals a fetish for pink gloves among other things, and remembers the first time. Pulp's fake, synthetic backdrop sounds like it was constructed on bargain Casio keyboards, adding an extra layer of seaminess to Cocker's songs. That sense of cheap, faux-glamour is essential to the success of *His 'n' Hers*, Pulp's commercial and artistic breakthrough. It's the sound of a poor man giving up everything he has so he can act out his expensive, elegant fantasies. He may never get there, but the approximation of glamour is more appealing and compelling than the reality, which is what gives *His 'n' Hers* a grand tragic romanticism. —*Stephen Thomas Erlewine*

Masters of the Universe / 1994 / Fire ✦✦

● **Different Class** / Oct. 30, 1995 / Island ✦✦✦✦
After years of obscurity, Pulp shot to stardom in Britain with 1994's *His 'n' Hers*. By the time *Different Class* was released at the end of October 1995, the band, particularly lead singer Jarvis Cocker, were genuine British superstars, with two No. 2 singles and a triumphant last-minute performance at Glastonbury under their belts, as well as one tabloid scandal. On the heels of such excitement, anticipation for *Different Class* ran high, and not only does it deliver, it blows away all their previous albums, including the fine *His 'n' Hers*. Pulp doesn't stray from their signature formula at all—it's still grandly theatrical, synth-spiked pop with new wave and disco flourishes, but they have mastered it here. Not only are the melodies and hooks significantly catchier and more immediate, the music explores more territory. From the faux-showtune romp of the anthemic opener "Mis-Shapes" and the glitzy, gaudy stomp of "Disco 2000" (complete with a nicked riff from Laura Branigan's "Gloria") to the aching ballad "Underwear" and the startling sexual menace of "I Spy," Pulp construct a diverse, appealing album around the same basic sound. Similarly, Jarvis Cocker's lyrics take two themes, sex and social class, and explore a number of different avenues in bitingly clever ways. As well as perfectly capturing the behavior of his characters, Cocker grasps the nuances of language, creating a dense portrait of suburban and working-class life. All of his sex songs are compassionate, while the subtle satire of "Sorted for E's & Wizz" is affectionate, the best moment on the album is the hit single "Common People," about a rich girl who gets off by slumming with the lower class. Coming from Cocker, who made secondhand clothes and music glamourous, the song is undeniably affecting and exciting, much like *Different Class* itself. —*Stephen Thomas Erlewine*

Countdown / Mar. 1996 / Nectar Masters/Fire ✦✦✦✦
A double-disc collection released to cash in on Pulp's massive success with *Different Class*, *Countdown* might be a rip-off compilation, but it does offer an effective introduction to Pulp's '80s catalog. Since their recordings on Fire were decidedly uneven, *Countdown* does distill all the highlights a casual fan could want to hear. Beginning with the latest track, the 1990 single "Countdown," and working its way backward, the compilation's sequencing eases newer fans into both the band's more experimental and folkier work. Even though all of Pulp's best material from this era is included, they lacked the pop sense that they developed in the early '90s, which could make this rough sailing for some recent fans. For those who want to dig deeper, there is plenty of fascinating material here. —*Stephen Thomas Erlewine*

Pure Prairie League

Country-Rock
For a short time, Pure Prairie League was one of America's best country-rock bands, but personnel shifts ultimately destroyed its early promise. The group was formed in 1971 by vocalists/guitarists Craig Lee Fuller (the band's main songwriter) and George Ed Powell, steel guitarist John Call, bassist Jim Lanham, and drummer Jim Caughlin, and recorded their self-titled debut album just a year later. Its fusion of laid-back singer-songwriter-styled rock and country earned critical praise, but much of the group departed, leaving only Fuller, Powell, and several session musicians. Even so, *Bustin' Out* proved to be an unqualified success, featuring the innovative addition of string arrangements by David Bowie guitarist Mick Ronson. Unfortunately, Fuller left in 1975, leaving the group without a strong songwriter or leader. Powell carried on with guitarist Larry Goshorn, bassist Mike Reilly, and pianist Michael Connor for several albums, none of which were as commercially or artistically successful as *Bustin' Out*. The group did enjoy a brief resurgence in 1980 with the Top Ten single "Let Me Love You Tonight," featuring future country star Vince Gill on lead vocals, but finally called it quits in 1983. Fuller has since joined Little Feat. —*Steve Huey*

● **Bustin' Out** / 1972 / RCA ✦✦✦✦
Bustin' Out was this band's most distinctive album, featuring very bright, thin-sounding acoustic guitars and dramatic string arrangements, courtesy of David Bowie's lead player Mick Ronson. "Amie" became a standard of sorts for the college coffeehouse crowd. Other highlights include "Jazzman," "Early Morning Riser," "Boulder Skies," "Call Me Tell Me," and "Angel," a song originally recorded on J.D. Blackfoot's *The Ultimate Prophecy*. —*Rick Clark*

Pure Prairie League / 1972 / RCA ✦✦✦✦
For all those who think the Eagles are the be-all and end-all of country-rock, you owe it to yourself to search out this album. Any track here (or on the follow-up, *Bustin' Out*) holds up as well, if not better than, anything by the Eagles. This album also proves that Craig Fuller is a grossly underrated songwriter. A country-rock must! —*Jim Worbois*

Two Lane Highway / 1975 / RCA ✦✦✦

Amie & Other Hits / 1981 / RCA ✦✦✦✦
This best-of collection contains all the hits and most of the essential album cuts, including a healthy sampling from *Bustin' Out*. —*Rick Clark*

● **Best of Pure Prairie League** / 1995 / Mercury Nashville ✦✦✦✦
Containing most of their hits and key album tracks, *Best of Pure Prairie League* provides an effective introduction to the country-rock group. —*Sara Sytsma*

James and Bobby Purify

Soul
James (b. May 12, 1944) and Bobby (b. Sep. 2, 1939) of this Southern soul duo are not actually brothers but cousins. James Purify and Robert Lee Dickey joined forces for some classic Southern soul duets during the mid-'60s. Producer Papa Don Schroeder brought the soulful Floridians to Muscle Shoals in 1966 to record at Rick Hall's Fame studios, and the result was the gorgeous mid-tempo "I'm Your Puppet." The Dan Penn-Spooner Oldham ballad proved their biggest hit for the Bell label, although "Let Love Come Between Us" and their revival of the Five Dutones' "Shake a Tail Feather" also made some major noise in 1967. When Bobby mutinied, James went it alone for a while before recruiting a new Bobby (Ben Moore), and they picked up right where the old duo left off. —*Bill Dahl*

● **Best of James Purify** / 1985 / Arista ✦✦✦✦
The Purify cousins made decent, occasionally excellent confessional soul tunes for Bell from 1966 to 1968, the best of them being "I'm Your Puppet," "Shake a Tail Feather," and "Let Love Come Between Us." While some compared them to Sam & Dave, they were actually more like Mel & Tim, since they didn't have songs anywhere as transcendent as those Isaac Hayes and David Porter were giving Sam & Dave. —*Ron Wynn*

Pussy Galore

Alternative Pop-Rock, Indie Rock
You either loved them or loathed them (some did both) but it was difficult to ignore the bawling, intentionally crude, anti-musicianship
coughed up by Pussy Galore. A bunch of scuzzy-looking juveniles from
Washington DC—their name coming from Honor Blackman's character
in the James Bond film *Goldfinger*—and led by a young punk-rockin'
bohemian hipster wannabe named Jon Spencer, Pussy Galore created an
unholy metallic ruckus that was part serious avant-garde noise wail, part
bullshit pose. Considering their limited skills, narcissistic tendencies, and
drug-cult mythologizing, there is a sizable body of work from this band.
The problem is that it's mostly hit-and-miss, which is a polite way of saying a little Pussy Galore goes a long way.

A serious discussion of Pussy Galore's musical attributes must thoroughly ignore technical ability; they have none. Spencer and guitarists
(no bass) Julia Cafritz and Neil Hagerty locked horns in a badly played
riff-fest with ex-Sonic Youth drummer Bob Bert sounding as if he's dropping pots and pans on the floor. Surprisingly, with all of their hip attitude
and condescending, arty indifference, Pussy Galore was capable of creating some great trash rock. However, I would argue that these moments
were accidental, the byproduct of doing something long enough and
eventually getting it right.

Really the only difference between good Pussy Galore music and bad
is that the latter is boring and the former is not—that is unless you have
an extremely high tolerance for low-rent nihilism. At their noisiest and
most frantic (e.g., the two fine EPs, *Groovy Hate Fuck* and *Sugarshit
Sharp*) there is a messy ebullience to this muck that undercuts their normal snotty, calculatedly offensive shtick. And they did have a sense of
humor as they proved on their 1986 cassette-only release, a track-by-
track cover of the Rolling Stones' classic *Exile on Main Street*. This
release is not recommended to Stones fans. Still, for a band that no one
predicted would have a long life, Pussy Galore has turned out many
interesting side projects and bands since their demise in 1990. Spencer
went on to form Boss Hog, and the more recent and much better Jon
Spencer Blues Explosion, while also adding his distinctively smartass
touch to recent recordings by the Gibson Bros; while Neil Hagerty joined
forces with Jennifer Herrema and formed Royal Trux. —*John Dougan*

Sugarshit Sharp / 1988 / Caroline ✦✦✦✦
Both of these records *Groovy Hate Fuck* and *Sugarshit Sharp* come
highly recommended if only because, as EPs, filler is kept to a minimum.
Groovy Hate Fuck lives up to its title: it's a mess of a record thrown
together by a bunch of bored kids who want to be as offensive as possible. On that level it's a near total success. Don't be shocked by the song
titles (e.g., "Cunt Tease," "You Look Like a Jew," "Dead Meat"), simply
enjoy the violent, sonic chaos they whip up. It's very energetic. *Sugarshit
Sharp* is even better. Side one is a cover of Einstürzende Neubauten's "Yu
Gung," side two is more death-grunge rendered with a maximum of
noise and minimum of panache. But at under 30 minutes, it's free of a lot
of arty-farty jerking around. —*John Dougan*

● **Corpse Love: The Firstyear** / Feb. 14, 1992 / Caroline ✦✦✦✦
With the exception of *Corpse Love*, a pretty good career anthology, I recommend all of Pussy Galore's full-length records with this caveat: Not a
one of them is strong all the way through. All have their moments (especially *Right Now!*) but after a while (a short while) you'll be able to anticipate every one of their moves, and the cacophonous anti-rock thrash
and bash becomes samey sounding. Freaks for this stuff will want all
three records, but as trashy noise rock goes, there are better bands, and
certainly plenty who are less patronizing to their audiences. —*John Dougan*

Pylon

New Wave
Let it be known that R.E.M. wasn't the only great band to come from the
college town of Athens, GA; Pylon emerged in the early '80s as one of the
best bands from this arty, exciting scene. True, their success never came
close to that of R.E.M. (or the B-52s for that matter), but they approached
post-punk dance music in a unique manner and recorded some exciting
music. Slightly more avant-garde than the B-52s, and more willing to
take risks, Pylon featured the ecstatic whoopin' and hollerin' of lead
singer Vanessa Briscoe-Hay (formerly Vanessa Ellison). Helped by the
sturdy rhythm section of drummer Curtis Crowe and bassist Michael
Lachowski and the scratchy, forceful guitar of Randy Bewley, Pylon created bizarre song shards that were giddy, surreal, and propulsive.

Despite good word-of-mouth, numerous critical huzzahs, and the hip
production pals Chris Stamey and Gene Holder (of the dB's), Pylon called
it quits after LP number two (*Chomp*) in 1983. Ironically, there seemed to
be plenty of bands appropriating Pylon's jittery, art-dance rock, but none
were doing it with their panache and spirit. After a layoff of about six
years, the band reunited to promote a great anthology entitled *Hits* in
1989. Enjoying playing together after such a long time, Pylon released a

new LP, *Chain*, in 1990, that enhanced their reputation as an influential
cult band but did little to expand their cult audience. Pylon may not sell
huge amounts of records, but they are still stars, regardless of how much
they were overshadowed by their peers. —*John Dougan*

● **Hits** / 1989 / DB ✦✦✦✦
While searching out the two Pylon LPs *Gyrate* and *Chomp* is recommended, a better place to start would be this anthology, which includes
practically everything they recorded. It's dance music with an arty tinge,
but it's never cold, off-putting, or less than groove-filled. In fact, Pylon
proved to be a better band than the more lauded B-52s. But that's an
argument you'll want to start after you've heard this record. —*John Dougan*

Chain / 1990 / Dog Gone ✦✦✦
The reformed Pylon acquit themselves nicely on *Chain*, but never deliver
a knockout blow. Stylistically speaking, there are no big changes here,
but the exuberance and emotion carry even the most rote workouts.
—*John Dougan*

Queen

Hard Rock, Art-Rock/Progressive-Rock, Pop-Rock
Queen was a quartet that combined elements of hard rock, heavy metal,
and art-rock, adding other styles along the way for an often majestic
sound that also contained a distinct element of campy humor. The group
was formed in England in 1971 by singer Freddie Mercury (born Frederick Bulsara, Sep. 5, 1946, d. Nov 24, 1991); guitarist Brian May (b. Jul. 19,
1947); bassist John Deacon (b. Aug. 19, 1951); and drummer Roger Taylor
(b. Jul. 26, 1949). They released their first album, *Queen*, in 1973, and it
first reached the charts in the US (going gold in 1977). It wasn't until the
following year that Queen broke through in its native country, getting a
Top Ten with "The Seven Seas of Rhye" and reaching the album chart
with *Queen II*. *Sheer Heart Attack*, later the same year, was a substantial
hit on both sides of the Atlantic (a No. 2 UK hit with "Killer Queen," No.
12 in the US).

The biggest of Queen's early albums, however, was *A Night at the
Opera* (1975), which topped the UK chart, made the Top 5 in the US, and
included the gold-selling single "Bohemian Rhapsody," the longest-running UK No. 1 in 18 years (in 1992, bolstered by an appearance in the
film *Wayne's World*, it would be a hit all over again in the US). *A Day at
the Races* (1976) was also a substantial hit, though it couldn't match its
predecessor.

Queen turned to a harder rock approach for 1977's *News of the World*,
which included the Top 5 hit "We Are the Champions," still a sporting-
event favorite. *Jazz* (1978) and *Live Killers* (1979) were successful, if less
substantial albums, but Queen took a sharp stylistic turn for *The Game*
in 1980 and was rewarded with two uncharacteristic No. 1 hits, the rockabilly-tinged "Crazy Little Thing Called Love" and the disco-rock
"Another One Bites the Dust."

Though Queen scored gold in the US with the subsequent releases
Hot Space (1982) and *The Works* (1984), the group was in a gradual commercial decline throughout the '80s. It returned to gold-selling status
with *Innuendo* in 1991, but singer Freddie Mercury died of AIDS in
November of that year. That set off a sales bonanza in Europe and, belatedly, in the US, with a giant benefit concert held in Mercury's honor at
Wembley Stadium in England in April 1992. Posthumous releases began
to appear, with a boxed set promised. —*William Ruhlmann*

Queen / Sep. 1973 / Hollywood ✦✦✦

Queen II / Apr. 1974 / Hollywood ✦✦✦

Sheer Heart Attack / Nov. 1974 / Hollywood ✦✦✦✦
An effective demonstration of the range of Queen's musical tastes, from
the guitar pyrotechnics of "Brighton Rock" to the vocal histrionics of
"Killer Queen" and the on-the-road diary "Now I'm Here." —*William
Ruhlmann*

☆ **A Night at the Opera** / Dec. 1975 / Hollywood ✦✦✦✦✦
In case there was any doubt that Queen was devoted to over-the-top
effects, this massively overdubbed combination of hard rock and opera,
paced by May's monster guitar riffs and Mercury's million-voiced choir
and emotive solo singing, should have erased it. Contains "Death on Two
Legs," "You're My Best Friend," and, of course, "Bohemian Rhapsody."
—*William Ruhlmann*

A Day at the Races / Dec. 1976 / Hollywood ✦✦✦
A Day at the Races was the inevitable second-best follow-up to *A Night
at the Opera*, the album that made Queen a superstar act. The group's
patented brand of hard rock and melodic overstatement was in place on
such songs as "Tie Your Mother Down" and "Somebody to Love" (the two
hit singles), so that anyone who loved the previous album would at least
like this one. —*William Ruhlmann*

News of the World / Nov. 1977 / Hollywood ✦✦✦
In the balance between Queen's operatic tendencies and its desire to rock
out, the rock side once again gained an upper hand on this release. Not
that the bombast lessened, but songs like "We Will Rock You" were actu-

ally dry runs for the stripped-down approach of *The Game,* and even "We Are the Champions" was a ballad. Well, almost. — *William Ruhlmann*

Jazz / Nov. 1978 / Hollywood ✦✦✦✦
Despite its commercial success, Queen's albums were hit-and-miss affairs, with every step forward (*News of the World*) seemingly followed by a misstep (*Jazz*). What they meant by the title has never been clear, and the single "Bicycle Race"/"Fat-Bottomed Girls," although it became a minor hit on career momentum, is not among the group's more memorable efforts. After this, it was time for a new direction, and happily, Queen found it with *The Game.* — *William Ruhlmann*

The Game / Jul. 1980 / Hollywood ✦✦✦✦
The basic elements of Queen's approach, from May's heavy guitar to Mercury's vocal army, were in attendance here, but the album owes its success to its novelties, especially "Another One Bites the Dust" and "Crazy Little Thing Called Love." — *William Ruhlmann*

Flash Gordon / Dec. 1980 / Hollywood ✦✦
★ **Greatest Hits** / Oct. 1981 / Elektra ✦✦✦✦✦
They may not have started out that way, but by 1981 Queen definitely was perceived as a singles act. This record gathers their biggest US/UK hits, 1973-1981, including the collaboration with David Bowie, "Under Pressure." Not to be confused with the 1992 Hollywood Records (61625) release also called *Greatest Hits,* which isn't as good but has the advantage of being in print. — *William Ruhlmann*

Hot Space / May 1982 / Hollywood ✦✦✦
The Works / Feb. 1984 / Hollywood ✦✦
A Kind of Magic / Jun. 1986 / Hollywood ✦✦
The Miracle / May 1989 / Hollywood ✦✦
Innuendo / Feb. 1991 / Hollywood ✦✦
● **Greatest Hits** / 1992 / Hollywood ✦✦✦✦
This is going to take a little explaining. In 1981, when it was contracted to Elektra Records in the US, Queen released an album called *Greatest Hits* (Elektra 564), which contained 14 songs that chronicled singles from 1973 to 1981. In 1990, Hollywood Records acquired CD rights to Queen's catalog, by which time the Elektra *Greatest Hits* had gone out of print on vinyl. Hollywood released *Classic Queen,* a compilation that covered Queen's hits from 1982 to its demise in 1991, with a few older songs thrown in. Then it released this album, its version of *Greatest Hits,* which is a 15-track album that deletes the songs from the first *Greatest Hits* that appeared on *Classic Queen* (among them Queen's biggest hit, "Bohemian Rhapsody") and adds a few tracks from the 1973-1982 era that did not appear on the original release. The Elektra *Greatest Hits* LP had a superior selection, but it's gone now, so you're stuck with this. (New fans don't seem to have minded, as this new *Greatest Hits* sold better than the first one.) — *William Ruhlmann*

Classic Queen / Mar. 10, 1992 / Hollywood ✦✦✦✦
Essentially, this 17-album is a second-volume Queen's *Greatest Hits,* picking up the story from that album's 1981 release and taking it to the end of Queen's career. But the album also contains a few tracks—"Bohemian Rhapsody," "Keep Yourself Alive," and "Under Pressure"—that appeared on that first set, as well as a couple—"Stone Cold Crazy" and "Tie Your Mother Down"—from the same era. The remaining 12 tracks, culled from *The Works, A Kind of Magic, The Miracle,* and *Innuendo,* represent songs that were not big hits in the US Nevertheless, with a resurgence of interest in Queen and the second coming of "Bohemian Rhapsody," courtesy of *Wayne's World,* this album returned Queen to platinum status and the US Top 5 for the first time since the early '80s. — *William Ruhlmann*

Made in Heaven / Nov. 7, 1995 / Parlophone ✦✦

Queensrÿche

Hard Rock, Art-Rock/Progressive-Rock, Heavy Metal
During the early '80s, Queensrÿche was a standard heavy-metal band, sounding like a cross between Iron Maiden and Judas Priest. In the middle of the decade, the band shifted to a more progressive sound, adding elements of '70s art-rock, particularly Pink Floyd, to their music. Queensrÿche came into their own on 1988's *Operation Mindcrime,* a concept album about a media-dominated future. With *Empire* two years later, the band crossed over into the mainstream with the hit "Silent Lucidity." Four years later, the band returned with *Promised Land;* the album went gold with little radio support and minimal airplay on MTV, proving that the group had not lost their devoted fans. — *Stephen Thomas Erlewine*

Queensrÿche / 1983 / EMI America ✦✦
The Warning / 1984 / EMI America ✦✦✦
Operation Mindcrime / 1988 / EMI America ✦✦✦✦
Seattle's best-kept secret is let out of the box with a concept album that brought comparisons to Pink Floyd and the Who. Fantastic lyrics with a great story line, powerful playing by the band, and powerful vocals by

Geoff Tate made them finally noticed by fans a year after its release. — *John Book*

● **Empire** / 1990 / EMI America ✦✦✦✦
This band knows what they want and how to get it. Masterfully produced (recorded digitally), this is the album that made the band international superstars. — *John Book*

Promised Land / 1994 / EMI America ✦✦✦

? & the Mysterians

Garage Rock
Originally formed in Flint, MI, in 1962, this group took its name from the obscure science-fiction movie *The Mysterians.* They recorded the anthemic "96 Tears" for the local Spanish music label Pa-Go-Go in 1966. It was immediately picked up for national consumption by Cameo-Parkway, going on to be one of the most covered garage band classics of the '60s. Lead singer Question Mark (real name listed as both Rudy Martinez and Reeto Rodriguez) continues to front a version of the band on oldies package shows across the US. — *Cub Koda*

● **96 Tears** / 1966 / Cameo ✦✦✦✦
A true garage band classic, featuring the title track and 11 others straight from the band's set list. — *Cub Koda*

96 Tears Forever / 1985 / ROIR ✦✦✦✦
This is a band that definitely got by on attitude, as this collection of lesser tracks shows. — *Dan Heilman*

Quicksilver Messenger Service

Psychedelic
The band that became Quicksilver Messenger Service originally was conceived as a rock vehicle for folk singer-songwriter Dino Valenti (b. Nov. 7, 1943), author of "Get Together." Living in San Francisco, Valenti had found guitarist John Cipollina (b. Aug. 24, 1943, d. May 29, 1989) and singer Jim Murray. Valenti's friend David Freiberg (b. Aug. 24, 1938) joined on bass, and the group was completed by the addition of drummer Greg Elmore (b. Sep. 4, 1946) and guitarist Gary Duncan (b. Sep. 4, 1946). As the band was being put together, Valenti was imprisoned on a drug charge and he didn't rejoin Quicksilver until later.

They debuted at the end of 1965 and played around the Bay Area and then the West Coast for the next two years, building up a large following but resisting offers to record that had been taken up by such San Francisco acid rock colleagues as Jefferson Airplane and the Grateful Dead. Quicksilver finally signed to Capitol toward the end of 1967 and recorded their self-titled debut album in 1968 (by this time, Murray had left). *Happy Trails,* the 1969 follow-up, was recorded live. After its release, Duncan left the band and was replaced for *Shady Grove* (1970) by British session pianist Nicky Hopkins. By the time of its release, however, Duncan had returned, along with Valenti, making the group a sextet.

This version of Quicksilver, prominently featuring Valenti's songs and lead vocals, lasted only a year, during which two albums, *Just for Love* and *What About Me,* were recorded. Cipollina, Freiberg, and Hopkins then left, and the remaining trio of Valenti, Duncan, and Elmore hired replacements and cut another couple of albums before disbanding. There was a reunion in 1975, resulting in a new album and a tour, and in 1986, Duncan revived the Quicksilver name for an album that also featured Freiberg on background vocals. — *William Ruhlmann*

Quicksilver Messenger Service / May 1968 / Capitol ✦✦✦✦
The band's debut effort was a little more restrained and folky than some listeners had expected, given their reputation for stretching out in concert. While some prefer the mostly live *Happy Trails,* this is inarguably their strongest set of studio material, with the accent on melodic folk-rockers. Highlights include their cover of folksinger Hamilton Camp's "Pride of Man," probably their best studio track; "Light Your Windows," probably the group's best original composition; and founding member Dino Valenti's "Dino's Song" (Valenti himself was in jail when the album was recorded). "Gold and Silver" is their best instrumental jam, and the 12-minute "The Fool" reflects some of the best and worst traits of the psychedelic era. — *Richie Unterberger*

Happy Trails / Mar. 1969 / Capitol ✦✦✦✦
Quicksilver was heard at its best on this partially live album, which contained a 25-minute version of Bo Diddley's "Who Do You Love." — *William Ruhlmann*

Shady Grove / Dec. 1969 / One Way ✦✦✦✦
Even though the opening title track featured all the elements that made Quicksilver one of the great Bay Area bands (particularly John Cipollina's vibrato-laden lead guitar), *Shady Grove* was a transitional album. The addition of pianist Nicky Hopkins (Rolling Stones, Steve Miller) gave the band more colors to work with. One of Quicksilver's better albums, *Shady Grove* shines brightest on tracks like "Joseph's Coat," the dazzling Hopkins keyboard instrumental showcase "Edward (The Mad Shirt

Grinder)," and the title cut. The sound on this disc isn't particularly good. —*Rick Clark*

Just for Love / Aug. 1970 / One Way ✦✦✦

What About Me / Dec. 1970 / One Way ✦✦✦

Maiden of the Cancer Moon / 1983 / Psycho ✦✦✦

Peace by Piece / Jul. 1986 / Capitol ✦

● **Sons of Mercury (1968-75)** / 1991 / Rhino ✦✦✦✦
This thorough two-disc best-of contains Quicksilver's most familiar material from its various lineups, plus some rarities. The only thing keeping this from being essential is the exclusion of the complete live version of "Who Do You Love," over a single edited version. —*William Ruhlmann*

Radiohead

Alternative Pop-Rock, Brit-Pop
Radiohead's combination of British pop sensibilities and noisy, Pixies-derived post-punk managed to cross into the mainstream while keeping a fair amount of alternative credibility. Consisting of vocalist Thom E. Yorke, Johnny and Colin Greenwood, Ed O'Brien, and Phil Selway, the Oxford-based group were relative unknowns in their homeland when the brooding single "Creep" became an American hit in 1993. "Creep" carried their debut album, *Pablo Honey,* into the charts, as well as into gold-record status; soon, the single also became a hit in Britain. However, the group wasn't able to produce any successful follow-up singles, and the record disappeared from the charts by the end of the year. Radiohead delivered their second album, *The Bends,* in spring of 1995. Although it received positive reviews and sold well upon its British release, the record was still-born in America. After a couple of months, radio and MTV began playing "Fake Plastic Trees," making the single an alternative hit and pushing *The Bends* into the charts. —*Stephen Thomas Erlewine*

Pablo Honey / 1993 / Capitol ✦✦✦
Oxford, England's, Radiohead often wear their cleverness on their collective sleeve for debut release *Pablo Honey.* There is great potential here. Thom Yorke has a great singing voice that ranges from moody angst to soaring falsetto. It's hard to define the music, which displays both good pop sense and a sometimes skillful use of controlled noise. British singles such as "Creep" (an ode to self-loathing) and band anthem "Anyone Can Play Guitar" are marvy and essential. "Blow Out" closes *Pablo Honey* in full accordance with all truth-in-advertising legislation. —*Roch Parisien*

● **The Bends** / 1995 / Capitol ✦✦✦✦
With one stroke, Radiohead casts off the albatross of their obsession-inducing hit "Creep" and, at the same time, fights off the dreaded sophomore jinx. *The Bends* is a work of remarkable, fragile, but sinewy beauty. Producer John Leckie perfectly balances Thom Yorke's pivotal choirboy vocals, Jon Greenwood and Ed O'Brian's distorted, Nirvana-ish guitar thrusts, and the flexible Colin Greenwood/Phil Selway rhythm axis. —*Roch Parisien*

Rage Against the Machine

Alternative Pop-Rock, Alternative Metal
On the strength of their fiercely political debut album, Rage Against the Machine became an alternative-rock sensation in 1993. Combining a technically advanced post-punk guitar roar with an amateurish stab at hip-hop, the band's sound is polarizing: you believe either they're the most uncompromising rockers on earth or they're whining, simplistic hypocrites (after all, how many revolutionaries sign to Sony). Either way, with their fiery, militant rock, the band managed to gain more fans than most stridently political bands, as well as earning a considerable amount of critical acclaim for their abrasive sound.

After nearly three years of delays, Rage Against the Machine's second album, *Evil Empire,* was released in the spring of 1996. It entered the US charts at No. 1 and quickly went platinum. —*Stephen Thomas Erlewine*

● **Rage Against the Machine** / Nov. 3, 1992 / Epic ✦✦✦✦
Rage Against the Machine's debut album is overflowing with barely contained anger that comes across better in the scalding music than the half-baked, clichéd lyrics. —*Stephen Thomas Erlewine*

Evil Empire / Apr. 1996 / Epic ✦✦✦✦
Rage Against the Machine spent four years making their second album, *Evil Empire.* As the title suggests, their rage and contempt for the "fascist" capitalist system in America hasn't declined in the nearly half-decade they were away. Their musical approach didn't change, either. Lead vocalist Zach De La Rocha is caught halfway between the militant raps of Chuck D and the fanatical ravings of a street preacher, shouting out his simplistic, libertarian slogans over the sonically dense assault of the band. Since the band did not perform together much after 1993, there isn't a collective advance in their musicianship. Nevertheless, guitarist Tom Morello demonstrates an impressive palette of sound, creating new

textures in heavy metal, which is quite difficult. Even with Morello's studied virtuosity, the band sounds leaden, lacking the dexterity to fully execute their metal/hip-hop fusion—they don't get into a groove, they simply pound. But that happens to fit the hysterical ravings of De La Rocha. Though his dedication to decidedly left-wing politics is admirable, his arhythmic phrasing and grating shouting cancel out any message he is trying to make. And that means *Evil Empire* succeeds only on the level of a sonic assault. —*Stephen Thomas Erlewine*

Rain Parade

Alternative Pop-Rock, Power-Pop, Paisley Underground
Formed in Los Angeles in the early '80s, Rain Parade was one of the major bands of the psychedelic revival of the mid-'80s, a movement that was called the "paisley underground" by some critics. Initially led by David Roback (vocals, guitar, percussion), the group also featured his brother Steve (vocals, bass), Matthew Piucci (vocals, guitar, sitar), Eddie Kalwa (drums), and Will Glenn (keyboards, violin). Rain Parade's self-released debut single, "What She's Done to Your Mind," led to a contract with Enigma Records. Released in 1983, their first album, *Emergency 3rd Rail Power Trip,* received positive reviews and became a hit on college radio; the record gained enough attention to earn them a contract with Island Records. Before they could make the transition to Island, Dave Roback left the band to form Opal; he was replaced by John Thoman. Around the same time, drummer Mark Marcum replaced Eddie Kalwa; this new lineup recorded the 1985 live album, *Beyond the Sunset.* The following year, Rain Parade released their major label debut, *Crashing Dream,* yet it failed to recapture the audience *Emergency 3rd Rail Power Trip* had gained them. Two years later, the band released their last album, *Explosions in a Glass Palace.* —*Stephen Thomas Erlewine*

● **Emergency 3rd Rail Power Trip** / 1983 / Restless ✦✦✦✦
A popular band among the West Coast paisley underground movement during the early '80s, they drew inspiration from '60s California 12-string pop, as well as from the Velvet Underground. Pleasantly trippy, in a sleepwalking kind of way, the highlights are: "1 Hr 1/2 Ago," "What She's Done to Your Mind?," and "This Can't Be Today." —*Rick Clark*

Raincoats

Post-Punk
The Raincoats were one of the most experimental bands that immediately followed the initial burst of punk rock in the late '70s. With their minimalistic approach to guitar-driven folk-rock, the band developed a distinctive, jagged sound, punctuated by a shrill violin. The Raincoats were also one of the first all-female post-punk bands, which wasn't common in the late '70s and early '80s. When they were recording, the band gained a small cult following in their native England and an even smaller audience in America; they broke up in 1984. Nearly ten years later, the band became a hip name in alternative rock, thanks to Kurt Cobain's mention of the group in the liner notes to a Nirvana album. Geffen picked up the rights to the Raincoats' catalog and reissued their albums in late 1993 and 1994. The band reunited and toured with Nirvana in the UK before heading out on their own tour of the US in 1994. —*Stephen Thomas Erlewine*

● **The Raincoats** / 1980 / DGC ✦✦✦✦
Picking the "best" Raincoats is more an intellectual exercise than it is a work of thoughtful criticism. So, to make it easy for the benighted, all three studio releases are absolutely essential. Their live cassette is wonderful, but I wouldn't start there. Better yet, start with their debut, a soaring, daring, avant-garde-influenced folk-punk record. Don't let the words "avant-garde" scare you off; the Raincoats are not harsh or unapproachable. In fact, this music, even at its most dissonant, is stunning and captivating. There's a great cover of the Kinks' "Lola" that's so skewed and obtuse, I'm sure Ray Davies never dreamed it could sound this way. Reissued by Geffen on CD with extra tracks in 1995. —*John Dougan*

Odyshape / 1981 / DGC ✦✦✦✦
It was the late Kurt Cobain (with some help from labelmates Sonic Youth) that initiated Geffen's reissue of the Raincoats' catalog. And listening to *Odyshape,* it's easy to see why Cobain loved them so. There's an emotional directness about these songs that hooks you from the start. Mostly you hear about emotions and situations, sometimes indirectly, almost as if you are eavesdropping on a conversation. Then it hits you: it's almost like you're talking to old friends. That's the way the Raincoats' music worked: it's deceptively simple, but extremely complicated. Also, as on this record, it makes demands of the listener. But songs like "Red Shoes" and "Dancing in My Head" say this far more eloquently. Reissued by Geffen with extra tracks, 1995. —*John Dougan*

Kitchen Tapes / 1983 / ROIR ✦✦✦✦
Rough, loose-limbed, warm, exciting and everything you'd expect from the Raincoats onstage. Bolstered by the heavy percussion of Richard Dudanski and Derek Godard, this recording pulsates, while the band

dances around the beat tossing in shards of guitar, vocals, and violin. Excellent liner essay by Greil Marcus. *—John Dougan*

Moving / 1984 / DGC ✦✦✦✦
What a wonderful cacophony of sounds! The Raincoats' last record (until their reunion EP of 1995) is a triumph of excitement and intensity equaling that of their previous studio work. Some of these songs are from the live tape and are in sharper (and I'd say better) form here. Yet another important record by one of the most important bands of the post-punk era. Reissued by Geffen with extra tracks in 1995. *—John Dougan*

Looking in the Shadows / 1996 / DGC ✦✦

Bonnie Raitt

b. Nov. 8, 1949, Cleveland, OH

Guitar, Vocals / Modern Electric Blues, Modern Acoustic Blues, Blues-Rock, Singer-Songwriter, Pop-Rock
In 1989, Bonnie Raitt, singer-songwriter and guitarist, finally hit major success, after almost 20 years of performing, with the aptly titled *Nick of Time*. The album came at a time when the market was ready for something earthy, and fortunately Capitol Records, who had just signed Raitt, had the foresight to encourage her love of sexy folk-blues, R&B, and intelligently thoughtful sentiment. Raitt, who has always championed quality songwriters like John Prine, John Hiatt, Terry Adams, Jackson Browne, and Jerry Williams, is quite an accomplished songwriter herself, penning songs for *Nick of Time* that equal anything she has covered.

Before Raitt's late-'80s success, she had enjoyed a few moderate successes and a respectable cult following. By 1986, with the release of Nine Lives, Raitt's career seemed to be stagnating, and Warner Bros. (her label of 15 years) cut her loose.

Raitt's soulful guitar playing, particularly slide, has sadly been overlooked. Lesser male guitar players have graced the covers of major music magazines. Hopefully, her time of recognition in that area will arrive as well. *—Rick Clark*

Bonnie Raitt / 1971 / Warner Bros. ✦✦✦
By the time Raitt recorded this impressive self-titled debut, she had developed quite a set of blues chops playing with artists like Mississippi Fred McDowell, Howlin' Wolf, and other blues greats. In fact, she enlisted Chicago-bluesmen Junior Wells and A.C. Reed to aid in the proceedings, which are relaxed and earthy. *—Rick Clark*

● **Give It Up** / Sep. 1972 / Warner Bros. ✦✦✦✦
Raitt's sophomore release is a classic. Of all the albums from her days with Warner, this is the one that put forth her folky singer-songwriter sensitivities with her love for country-blues. *Give It Up*, which took 13 years to go gold, showcased an intelligent song selection, with tracks by Jackson Browne ("Under the Falling Sky"), Eric Kaz ("Love Has No Pride"), and Joel Zoss ("Been Too Long at the Fair"). Her self-penned "Love Me Like a Man" highlighted her impressive guitar technique. *—Rick Clark*

Takin' My Time / 1973 / Warner Bros. ✦✦✦✦
Raitt continued her streak of quality albums with *Takin' My Time*. Like her previous efforts, Raitt drew from the cream of the songwriting crop. Randy Newman's "Guilty" and Jackson Browne's "I Thought I Was a Child" are highlights. *—Rick Clark*

Streetlights / 1974 / Warner Bros. ✦✦✦

Homeplate / 1975 / Warner Bros. ✦✦✦

Sweet Forgiveness / Apr. 1977 / Warner Bros. ✦✦

The Glow / 1979 / Warner Bros. ✦✦✦

Green Light / 1982 / Warner Bros. ✦✦✦✦
Raitt dumps the slick stuff and goes for the grit with this energetic set, featuring her band, which included keyboardist Ian MacLagan (whose credits included the Stones and Faces). Raitt's sensitive electric slide-guitar work was finally up front in the mix. It's one of her very best albums. Raitt does spirited versions of NRBQ's "Green Light" and "Me and the Boys." Other standouts include the wreckless rockers "Willya Wontcha" and "I Can't Help Myself." "River of Tears" is a powerful track that Raitt has dedicated to the memory of Little Feat's Lowell George in shows over the years. *—Rick Clark*

Nine Lives / 1986 / Warner Bros. ✦✦✦

● **Nick of Time** / Mar. 1989 / Capitol ✦✦✦✦
Few comebacks have been as celebrated as Raitt's multi-platinum hit *Nick of Time*, an album that included some of her strongest performances as a musician and singer. The determined "I Will Not Be Denied" seemed to say it all. Her poignant self-penned title cut revealed Raitt as a mature songwriter, on the level of the best writers whose work she had covered. She dug deep with some solid roadhouse R&B in "Love Letter," "Road's My Middle Name," and "Real Man." Her playful version of John Hiatt's "Thing Called Love" was another highlight. All in all, this is a very seamless album. Highly recommended. *—Rick Clark*

The Bonnie Raitt Collection / 1990 / Warner Bros. ✦✦✦✦
A good (not great) sampler of Raitt's years at Warner, it's also a good starting place. *—Rick Clark*

Luck of the Draw / Jun. 1991 / Capitol ✦✦✦✦
Raitt followed *Nick of Time* with *Luck of the Draw*, another great album. Among the album's many highlights are "I Can't Make You Love Me" and a duet with Delbert McClinton on "Good Man, Good Woman." *—Rick Clark*

Longing in Their Hearts / Mar. 14, 1994 / Capitol ✦✦✦✦
On the follow-up to the follow-up (and another million-selling No. 1 hit), Bonnie Raitt contributes more than her usual share of original songs, writing four songs herself and setting a lyric of her husband's to music for a fifth. Elsewhere, she draws on such strong writers as Richard Thompson and Paul Brady, all for a collection devoted to devotion. Song after song expresses passion, usually with happy results—this is not the album of a woman with the blues. Even when she's dressing down a parent in her own "Circle Dance," Raitt offers forgiveness and understanding. There, and in other songs, the object of her emotions rarely seems to be perfect, but she takes that in and loves him, anyway. Co-producer Don Was provides a detailed production in which single elements—an accordion, a harmony vocal by Levon Helm or David Crosby—effectively color arrangements and complement Raitt's always soulful singing. *— William Ruhlmann*

Road Tested / Nov. 7, 1995 / Capitol ✦✦✦✦

The Ramones

Punk
The Ramones are the first punk rock band. There were other bands, such as the Stooges and the New York Dolls, that came before them and set the stage and aesthetic for punk, and bands that immediately followed, such as the Sex Pistols, that made the latent violence of the music more explicit, but the Ramones crystallized the musical ideals of the genre. By cutting rock 'n' roll down to its bare essentials—four chords, a simple, catchy melody, and irresistably inane lyrics—speeding up the tempo considerably, the Ramones created something that was rooted in early '60s, pre-Beatles rock 'n' roll and pop but sounded revolutionary. Since their breakthrough was theoretical as well as musical, they comfortably became the leaders of the emerging New York punk rock scene. While their peers such as Patti Smith, Television, Talking Heads, and Richard Hell all were more intellectual and self-consciously artistic than the Ramones, they nevertheless appealed to the same mentality because of how they turned rock conventions inside out and celebrated kitschy pop culture with stylized stupidity. The band's first four albums set the blueprint for punk, especially American punk and hardcore, for the next two decades. And the Ramones themselves were major figures for the next two decades, playing essentially the same music without changing their style much at all. Although some punk diehards—including several of their peers—would have claimed the band's long career wound up undercutting the ideals the band originally stood for, the Ramones always celebrated not just the punk aesthetic, but the music itself.

Based in the Forest Hills section of Queens, NY, the Ramones formed in 1974. Originally, the band was a trio consisting of Joey Ramone (vocals, drums; born Jeffrey Hyman, May 19, 1952), Johnny Ramone (guitar; born John Cummings, Oct. 8, 1951), and Dee Dee Ramone (bass; born Douglas Colvin, Sep. 18, 1952), with Tommy Ramone (born Tom Erdelyi, Jan. 29, 1952) acting as the group's manager. All of the group's members adopted the last name "Ramone" and dressed in torn blue jeans and leather jackets, in homage to '50s greaser rockers. The group played their first concert on March 30, 1974, at New York's Performance Studio. Two months after the show, Joey switched to vocals and Tommy became the band's drummer. By the end of the summer, the Ramones earned a residency at CBGB's. For the next year, they played regularly at the nightclub, earning a dedicated cult following and inspiring several other artists to form bands with simliar ideals. All of the Ramones sets clocked in at about 20 minutes, featuring an unrelenting barrage of short, barely two-minute songs. By the end of 1975, the Ramones secured a recording contract with Sire; discounting Patti Smith, they were the first New York punk band to sign a contract.

Early in 1976, the Ramones recorded their debut album for just over $6,000. The resulting album, *Ramones*, was released in the spring, gained some critical attention, and managed to climb to 111 on US album charts. On July 4, the band made their debut appearance in the UK, where their records were becoming a big influence on a new generation of bands. Throughout 1976, the Ramones toured constantly, inaugurating nearly 20 years of relentless touring. By the end of the year, the group released their second album, *Ramones Leave Home*. While the album just scraped the US charts, it became a genuine hit in England in the spring of 1977, peaking at No. 48. By the summer of 1977, the Sex Pistols and the Ramones were seen as the two key bands in the punk rock revolution, but where the Pistols imploded, the Ramones kept on rolling.

Following the UK Top 40 hit "Sheena Is a Punk Rocker," the Ramones released their third album, *Rocket to Russia*, in the fall of 1977.

Tommy Ramone left the band in the spring of 1977, although he produced the group's subsequent album. He was replaced by former Voidoid Marc Bee, who immediately changed his name to Marky Ramone. With their new drummer in place, the Ramones recorded their fourth album, *Road to Ruin*, which was released in the fall. *Road to Ruin* marked the band's first significant attempt to change their sound—not only were there stronger bubblegum, girl group, surf, and '60s pop influences on the music, it was the first of their albums to run over a half hour. Although their sound was more accessible, it didn't gain the band a noticeably larger following. Neither did *Rock N' Roll High School*, the 1979 Roger Corman film in which the Ramones had a pivotal part. The soundtrack to *Rock N' Roll High School* and the UK-only live album *It's Alive* were the band's only releases of 1979. For most of the year, they were in the studio recording their fifth album with legendary '60s pop producer Phil Spector. The title song to the Corman movie was the first track released from the sessions, although the soundtrack album did feature a number of older Ramones songs remixed by Spector. *End of the Century*, the Spector-produced Ramones album, finally appeared in January 1980 to mixed reviews. Despite the lukewarm reception to the album, the record's cover of the Ronettes' "Baby I Love You" became their only Top Ten British hit; in America, none of the singles made an impact, although the record became their biggest hit, peaking at No. 44.

The Ramones continued their attempts at crossover success with their sixth album, *Pleasant Dreams*, which was released in 1981. Featuring a production by former Hollies and 10cc member Graham Gouldman, the record was a commercial disappointment in both America and England. The band was relatively quiet during 1982, spending most of their time touring. In the spring of 1983, the band returned with *Subterranean Jungle*, which was produced by Ritchie Cordell and Glen Koltkin, the heads of the American indie label Beserkley Records. Not only did *Subterranean Jungle* fail to gain the band the larger audience they desired, it continued the erosion of the band's diehard fan base, as well as their decline in the eyes of many rock critics. Following the album's release, Marky Ramone left the band; he was replaced by Richard Beau, a former member of the Velveteens, who changed his name to Richie Ramone.

With 1984's *Too Tough to Die*, the Ramones delivered a belated response to America's burgeoning hardcore punk scene that was largely produced by Tommy Erdelyi. The album helped restore their artistic reputation, as did the 1985 single, "Bonzo Goes to Bitburg," an attack on President Ronald Reagan's 1985 visit to Germany. Instead of continuing with the sound of *Too Tough to Die*, the Ramones began pursuing a more streamlined, stylized, and conventional take on their songwriting formula with 1986's *Animal Boy*. This was a direction the group followed for the remaining ten years of their career. Following the release of 1987's *Halfway to Sanity*, Richie Ramone left the band and Marky Ramone rejoined the group. In 1988, the career retrospective *Ramones Mania* appeared. In 1989, the Ramones contributed the theme song to the Stephen King movie *Pet Sematary*, and the track was included on *Brain Drain*, which was released in the summer of that year. After its release, the group's bassist, Dee Dee Ramone, left the band to pursue a career as a rapper called Dee Dee King; after his debut rap recording failed miserably, he formed the band Chinese Dragons. Dee Dee was replaced by C.J. Ramone (born Christopher John Ward).

In the early '90s, the Ramones sobered up, with both Joey and Marky undergoing treatment for alcoholism. The band returned to recording in 1992, first releasing the live *Loco Live* and then *Mondo Bizarro*, their first studio album in three years. *Mondo Bizarro* turned out to be a commercial failure, as did their 1994 covers album, *Acid Eaters*.

Following the release of *Acid Eaters*, the mainstream guitar-rock audience in America finally embraced punk rock, in the form of young bands like Green Day and Offspring. Sensing that the climate may have been right for the crossover success they had desired for so many years, the Ramones immediately followed *Acid Eaters* with *Adios Amigos*, claiming that unless the new album sold in substantial numbers, the band would call it quits after a final farewell tour. *Adios Amigos* only spent two weeks in the charts. Nevertheless, the Ramones embarked on a long farewell tour that ran throughout the rest of 1995. The band was set to split in the beginning of 1996 when they were offered a slot on the sixth Lollapalooza festival. The Ramones toured with the festival that summer. Following the completion of the tour, the Ramones parted ways, 20 years after the release of their first album. —*Stephen Thomas Erlewine*

☆ **The Ramones** / 1976 / Sire ♦♦♦♦♦

With the three-chord assault of "Blitzkrieg Bop," *The Ramones* begins at a blinding speed and never once over the course of its 14 songs does it let up. *The Ramones* is all about speed, hooks, stupidity, and simplicity. The songs are imaginative reductions of early rock 'n' roll, girl group pop, and surf-rock. Not only is the music only boiled down to its essentials, but the Ramones offer a twisted, comical take on pop culture with their lyrics, whether it's the horror schlock of "I Don't Wanna Go Down to the Basement," the drug deals of "53rd and 3rd," the gleeful violence of "Beat on

the Brat" or the maniacal stupidity of "Now I Wanna Sniff Some Glue." And the cover of Chris Montez's "Let's Dance" isn't a throwaway—with its single-minded beat and lyrics, it encapsulates everything the group loves about pre-Beatles rock 'n' roll. They don't alter the structure, or the intent, of the song, they simply make it louder and faster. And that's the key to all of the Ramones' music—it's simple rock 'n' roll, played simply, loud, and very, very fast. None of the songs clock in at any longer than two and half minutes and most are considerably shorter. In comparison to some of the music the album inspired, *The Ramones* sounds a little tame—it's a little too clean and compared to their insanely fast live albums, it even sounds a little slow—but there's no denying that it still sounds brilliantly fresh and intoxicatingly fun. —*Stephen Thomas Erlewine*

The Ramones Leave Home / 1977 / Sire ♦♦♦♦

The disappointing second album was still hipper than, well, Peter Frampton or something. —*Jeff Tamarkin*

☆ **Rocket to Russia** / Nov. 1977 / Sire ♦♦♦♦♦

The Ramones provided the blueprint and *Leave Home* duplicated it with lesser results, but the Ramones' third album, *Rocket to Russia*, perfected it. *Rocket to Russia* boasts a cleaner production than its predecessors, which only gives the Ramones' music more force. It helps that the group wrote its finest set of songs for the album. From the mindless opening of "Cretin Hop" and "Rockaway Beach" to the urban surf-rock of "Sheena Is a Punk Rocker" and ridiculous anthem "Teenage Lobotomy," the songs are teeming with irresistibly catchy hooks; even their choice of covers, "Do You Want to Dance?" and "Surfin' Bird," provide more hooks than usual. The Ramones also branch out slightly, adding ballads to the mix. Even with these (relatively) slower songs, the speed of the album never decreases. However, the abundance of hooks and slight variety in tempos makes *Rocket to Russia* the Ramones' most listenable and enjoyable album—it doesn't have the revolutionary impact of *The Ramones*, but it's a better album and one of the finest records of the late '70s. —*Stephen Thomas Erlewine*

It's Alive / 1979 / Sire ♦♦♦

End of the Century / 1980 / Sire ♦♦♦

The Ramones as produced by Phil Spector. Not a disaster but not all it should've been. —*Jeff Tamarkin*

Pleasant Dreams / 1981 / Sire ♦♦♦

The group reportedly wasn't happy with this Graham Gouldman-produced album, but it holds up well—one of their more solid '80s releases. —*Jeff Tamarkin*

Subterranean Jungle / 1983 / Sire ♦♦♦

On *Subterranean Jungle* the Ramones returned to their basic formula after the heavy-handed pop experiments of *End of the Century* and the heavy *Pleasant Dreams*. While they've slowed the tempo down slightly, the record remains an infectious slice of powerful rock 'n' roll. —*Stephen Thomas Erlewine*

Too Tough to Die / 1984 / Sire ♦♦♦♦

With the Ramones' original drummer Tommy Erdelyi producing, the group returns to simple, scathing punk rock on *Too Tough to Die*. The group takes the big guitar riffs of *Subterranean Jungle* and makes them shorter and heavier. The Ramones rhythms are back up to jackhammer speed and the songs are down to short, terse statements. The results read like a reaction to hardcore punk, but the Ramones are more melodic than any hardcore band, as well as smarter than most. Apart from the occasional foray into pop, such as the surprisingly effective Dave Stewart-produced "Howling at the Moon," the album is a sterling set of lethal punk. The last great record they would ever make. —*Stephen Thomas Erlewine*

Animal Boy / 1986 / Sire ♦♦♦

The Ramones get d-u-m-b again and score with a back-to-basics roaring set. —*Jeff Tamarkin*

Halfway to Sanity / 1987 / Sire ♦♦

Ramones Mania / 1989 / Sire ♦♦♦♦

The best of the Ramones, or, how to pack 30 songs onto one CD—not all of their "hits" but a crash course in stripped-down genius. —*Jeff Tamarkin*

Brain Drain / 1989 / Sire ♦♦

★ **All the Stuff & More, Vol. 1** / 1990 / Sire ♦♦♦♦♦

The first two albums, *Ramones* and *Leave Home*, condensed onto one CD, plus bonus tracks. —*Jeff Tamarkin*

☆ **All the Stuff & More, Vol. 2** / 1990 / Sire ♦♦♦♦♦

The third and fourth albums, *Rocket to Russia* and *Road to Ruin*, combined the present Ramones at their peak on one CD plus bonus tracks. —*Jeff Tamarkin*

Loco Live / 1991 / Sire ♦♦

Mondo Bizarro / 1992 / Radioactive ♦♦

Acid Eaters / 1994 / Radioactive ♦♦

Adios Amigos / 1995 / Radioactive ✦✦✦
Greatest Hits Live / Jun. 18, 1996 / MCA ✦✦✦

Rancid

Alternative Pop-Rock, Alternative Metal, Punk Revival, Third Wave Ska-Revival

Rancid is a punk revivalist band that came to national attention in late 1994 with their second album, *Let's Go*. Comprised of Tim Armstrong, Lars Frederiksen, Matt Freeman, and Brett Reed, Rancid reworks the sound of 1977, sounding like an updated version of the Clash's roar. —*Stephen Thomas Erlewine*

Let's Go / 1994 / Epitaph ✦✦✦✦
Whatever Rancid lacks in innovation, it makes up with sheer energy. The group rushes through *Let's Go* with an invigorating recklessness, sounding like a less-serious, party-ready version of the Clash. It's almost impossible to understand what vocalist Tim Armstrong sings at any given moment, yet there is no great meaning in what Rancid says—the message is in the buzzing guitars and speeding rhythms. It doesn't hurt that the band can throw out the occasional memorable hook or melody, like the single "Salvation," as well. —*Stephen Thomas Erlewine*

● **And Out Come the Wolves** / Oct. 1995 / Epitaph ✦✦✦✦
In the wake of the Offspring's success, Rancid became a hot band, earning a dedicated cult and sparking a major-label bidding war. After flirting with a handful of major labels, the band decided to stick with Epitaph and returned with *And Out Come the Wolves*. While the title is a veiled reference to the attention the band gained, the album doesn't mark an isolationist retreat into didactic, defiantly underground punk rock. Instead, Rancid develop their own identity on the record, which ironically makes them more accessible. Although they continue to draw heavily from the Clash and the Specials—and their roots in the ska-punk band Operation Ivy are quite clear throughout the record—the band plays with such energy and conviction, it's easy to forgive their derivativeness. On the whole, *And Out Come the Wolves* is a little too long to make a major impact, but individual tracks are classic moments of revivalist punk, including the skittering 2-Tone tribute "Time Bomb." —*Stephen Thomas Erlewine*

The Rascals

Pop-Rock, Blue-Eyed Soul

The Rascals, along with the Righteous Brothers, Mitch Ryder, and precious few others, were the pinnacle of '60s blue-eyed soul. The Rascals' talents, however, would have to rate above their rivals, if for nothing else than the simple fact that they, unlike many other blue-eyed soulsters, penned much of their own material. They also proved more adept at changing with the fast-moving times, drawing much of their inspiration from British Invasion bands, psychedelic rock, gospel, and even a bit of jazz and Latin music. They were at their best on classic singles like "Good Lovin,'" "How Can I Be Sure," "Groovin,'" and "People Got to Be Free." When they tried to stretch their talents beyond the impositions of the three-minute 45, they couldn't pull it off, a failure which—along with crucial personnel losses—effectively finished the band as a major force by the 1970s.

The roots of the Rascals were in New York-area twist and bar bands. Keyboardist/singer Felix Cavaliere, the guiding force of the group, had played with Joey Dee & the Starliters, where he met Canadian guitarist Gene Cornish and singer Eddie Brigati. Eddie would split the lead vocals with Cavaliere and also write much of the band's material with him. With the addition of drummer Dino Dinelli, they became the Rascals. Over their objections, manager Sid Bernstein (who had promoted the famous Beatles concerts at Carnegie Hall and Shea Stadium) dubbed them the Young Rascals, although the "Young" was permanently dropped from the billing in a couple of years.

After a small hit with "I Ain't Gonna Eat out My Heart Anymore" in 1965, the group hit No. 1 with "Good Lovin,'" a cover of an R&B tune by the Olympics, in 1966. This was the model for the Rascals' early sound: a mixture of hard R&B and British Invasion energy, with tight harmony vocals and arrangements highlighting Cavaliere's Hammond organ. After several smaller hits in the same vein, the group began to mature at a rapid rate in 1967, particularly as songwriters. "Groovin,'" "Beautiful Morning," "It's Wonderful," and "How Can I Be Sure?" married increasingly introspective and philosophical lyrics to increasingly sophisticated arrangements and production, without watering down the band's most soulful qualities. They were also big hits, providing some of the era's most satisfying blends of commercial and artistic appeal.

In 1968, almost as if to prove they could shake 'em down as hard as any soul revue, the Rascals made No. 1 with one of their best songs, "People Got to Be Free." An infectious summons to unity and tolerance in the midst of a very turbulent year for American society, it also reflected the Rascals' own integrationist goals. Not only did they blend White and

Black in their music; they also, unlike many acts of the time, refused to tour on bills that weren't integrated as well.

"People Got to Be Free," surprisingly, was the group's last Top 20 hit, although they would have several other small chart entries over the next few years, often in a more explicitly gospel-influenced style. The problem wasn't bad timing or shifting commercial taste; the problem was the material itself, which wasn't up to the level of their best smashes. More worrisome were their increasingly ambitious albums, which found Cavaliere in particular trying to expand into jazz, instrumentals, and Eastern philosophy. Not that this *couldn't* have worked well, but it *didn't*. They had never been an album-oriented group, but unlike other some other great mid-'60s bands, they were unable to satisfactorily expand their talents into full-length formats.

A more serious problem was the departure of Brigati, the band's primary lyricist, in 1970. Cornish was also gone a year later, although Cavaliere and Dinelli kept the Rascals going a little longer with other musicians. The band broke up in 1972, with none of the members going on to notable commercial or artistic success on their own, though Cavaliere remained the most active. —*Richie Unterberger*

Anthology (1965-1972) / 1992 / Rhino ✦✦✦✦
Anthology is the most comprehensive overview of one of the greatest bands of the '60s. All 18 of their hits as well as important album cuts (including tracks from their Columbia releases) are here on this double-disc, 44-track set. —*Rick Clark*

● **Very Best of the Rascals** / 1994 / Rhino/Atlantic ✦✦✦✦
Although Rhino issued a deluxe two-CD set covering the Rascals a few years ago, this single disc set contains enough essential songs for you to get the point. The Rascals, along with the Righteous Brothers, defined blue-eyed soul singing, making records that were as churchy, earthy, and convincing as anything that came out of the South or Motown in the '60s, backed by tight, anthemic arrangements and excellent combo playing. The 16 cuts include their first hit, "I Ain't Gonna Eat Out My Heart Anymore," and continues on into their flirtation with psychedelia in 1970. The only quibble is their failure to include "Look Around," a sociopolitical cut from the *Freedom Suite* album that's just a cut below "People Got to Be Free" or "A Ray of Hope." —*Ron Wynn*

The Raspberries

Power-Pop, Pop-Rock

Led by Eric Carmen (b. Aug. 11, 1949), the Raspberries, from Cleveland, OH, brought out their exuberant Beatles-style Anglo-pop and matching outfits at a time in the early '70s when art-rock, concept albums, and serious "statements" were being heralded. It was a time when pop for pop's sake was decidedly uncool. Capitol Records accentuated the band's teenybopper appeal by marketing their self-titled debut with a raspberry-scented scratch-and-sniff sticker on the cover. The band's dynamic first single, "Go All the Way" (No. 5), was a huge hit.

Carmen's tenor had the range of Paul McCartney, and he had the goods to write a handful of truly great guitar-pop hits. Lead guitarist Wally Bryson, who filled out their sound with a Beatles-meets-Free crunch, also contributed some solid material. Unfortunately, the public increasingly cooled off on the band, unwilling to buy into harder-rocking single releases like "I'm a Rocker," "Ecstascy," and the truly amazing "Tonight."

Drummer Jim Bonfanti (b. Dec. 17, 1948) and bassist Dave Smalley (b. Jul. 10, 1949) left in 1973, frustrated over the group's image problems. They were replaced by drummer Michael McBride and bassist Scott McCarl.

The 1973 follow-up effort, *Starting Over*, documented the dreams and frustrations of wanting to be pop stars. The track "Overnight Sensation (Hit Record)" went to No. 18, but the album ended up being one of the great lost pop albums of the '70s. The group disbanded shortly afterward, and Eric Carmen went on to pursue a sporadically successful solo career that resembled Barry Manilow more than rock 'n' roll. —*Rick Clark*

Raspberries / 1972 / Capitol ✦✦✦✦
An excellent first effort, highlighted by "Go All the Way," "Don't Want to Say Goodbye," "I Saw the Light," and "Come Around and See Me." At the time, audiences thought they heard echoes of Paul McCartney's work with the Beatles, and they weren't far wrong, in terms of what the group was capable of. —*Bruce Eder*

Fresh / Dec. 1972 / Capitol ✦✦✦✦
The second best of the four albums issued by the band, with "I Wanna Be with You," "If You Change Your Mind," and "Drivin' Around" as highlights amid some overall incredibly superb rock craftsmanship. The band's sound overall is more confident, and more powerful. —*Bruce Eder*

Side Three / 1973 / Capitol ✦✦✦
One of the group's most accomplished album, almost Beatles-like in its richness, romanticism, cleverness, and even its packaging, which is one of the few "novelty" jacket designs (it's shaped like a basket of . . . you

guessed it) that works. The band was at its peak and it showed in "Ecstacy" and "Last Dance," among numerous others. —*Bruce Eder*

Starting Over / 1974 / Capitol ✦✦✦
The band's last album is something of a disappointment, much louder and punchier than their previous work but lacking the elegance that characterized their overall sound. None of the songs is bad, and some are quite good, but they sound like they're going through the motions at this point, and they did break up soon after. —*Bruce Eder*

★ **Capitol Collectors Series** / 1991 / Capitol ✦✦✦✦✦
Twenty songs covering an entire cross-section of the group's history, with more superb notes, and this time superb sound as well. Short of having the second and third albums, the best the group has to offer. —*Bruce Eder*

Greatest Hits / Aug. 1, 1995 / Capitol ✦✦✦✦

Power Pop, Vol. 1 / 1996 / RPM ✦✦✦✦
Featuring the hit singles "Go All the Way," "Don't Want to Say Goodbye," "I Wanna Be with You," and "Let's Pretend," *Power Pop, Vol. 1* combines the Raspberries' first two albums—*Raspberries* and *Fresh Raspberries*—onto one CD. —*Stephen Thomas Erlewine*

Power Pop, Vol. 2 / 1996 / RPM ✦✦✦✦
Featuring the hit singles "Tonight," "I'm a Rocker" and "Overnight Sensation (Hit Record)," *Power Pop, Vol. 2* combines the Raspberries' last two albums—*Side Three* and *Starting Over*—on one CD. —*Stephen Thomas Erlewine*

Ratt

Hard Rock, Heavy Metal, Hair Metal
Ratt's brash, melodic heavy metal made the Los Angeles quintet one of the most popular rock acts of the mid-'80s. The group had its origins in the '70s group Mickey Ratt, which had evolved into Ratt by 1983; at that time the band featured vocalist Stephen Pearcy, guitarist Robbin Crosby, guitarist Warren D. Martini, bassist Juan Croucier, and drummer Bobby Blotzer. The band released their self-titled first album independently in 1983, which led to a major label contract with Atlantic Records. Their first album under this deal, 1984's *Out of the Cellar*, was a major success, reaching the American Top Ten and selling over three million copies. "Round and Round," the first single drawn from the album, hit No. 12, proving the band had pop crossover potential. While their second album, 1985's *Invasion of Your Privacy*, didn't reach the multi-platinum figures of *Out of the Cellar*, it also reached the Top Ten and sold over a million copies. By that time, the band could sell out concerts across the country and were a staple on MTV and AOR radio. Both *Dancin' Undercover* (1986) and *Reach for the Sky* (1988) continued the band's platinum streak, and their audience had only slipped slightly by the time of their final album, 1990's *Detonator*. In 1992, Pearcy left Ratt to form his own band; his departure effectively put an end to the group. —*Stephen Thomas Erlewine*

Out of the Cellar / 1984 / Atlantic ✦✦✦✦
The first album by Los Angeles' Ratt brought them instant success and a number of memorable hits. The cover featured actress Tawny Kitaen. —*John Book*

Invasion of Your Privacy / 1985 / Atlantic ✦✦✦✦
They may have been influenced by Aerosmith but at this stage Ratt were recording songs that were powerful as well as masterful hits. This album also showed they were a lot more than a hit-making machine. —*John Book*

Dancin' Undercover / 1986 / Atlantic ✦✦✦

● **Ratt & Roll 8191** / 1991 / Atlantic ✦✦✦✦
A greatest-hits package, it has the best of Ratt's impressive ten-year career. —*John Book*

Lou Rawls

b. Dec. 11, 1935, Chicago, IL
Vocals / Soul, R&B, Pop-Rock, Philly Soul
When Chicago-born Lou Rawls croons a soulful love song, his deep-hued pipes rumble with simmering passion. Rawls did the usual gospel apprenticeship before breaking out on a landmark jazz album with pianist Les McCann's trio for Capitol that launched his secular career. But it took Rawls a while to establish himself as a soul artist—perhaps he was perceived as a little too sophisticated and jazzy (although his uncredited responses on Sam Cooke's "Bring It on Home to Me" certainly proved he could wail). "Love Is a Hurtin' Thing" instantly changed that notion when it topped the R&B charts in 1966, and the unyielding "Dead End Street" and "Your Good Thing (Is About to End)" perpetuated his success.

After memorably delivering Bobby Hebb's powerful "A Natural Man" in 1971, Rawls joined forces with Philadelphia producers Kenny Gamble and Leon Huff in 1976, emerging with the silky "You'll Never Find Another Love Like Mine," another gigantic R&B and pop smash tailormade for nattily sweeping across the classiest disco dance floors. The

disco era's long gone now, but Rawls maintains elegantly. He's still as cool as cool can be. —*Bill Dahl*

Lou Rawls Sings/Les McCann Plays Stormy Monday / 1962 / Capitol ✦✦✦✦
This reissue spotlights the Lou Rawls/Les McCann highly popular souljazz duo in the '60s team in peak form. Rawls sang gritty blues and R&B, while McCann added funky keyboard solos and accompaniment. The album was an early indicator that McCann would be a steady, consistent seller working the same territory as Ramsey Lewis. This 1990 reissue included three bonus cuts. —*Ron Wynn*

● **Stormy Monday** / Feb. 5, 1962 Feb. 2, + 19 / Blue Note ✦✦✦✦
Lou Rawls has enjoyed success in almost every musical arena, from traditional gospel to R&B, soul, pop, and blues. This was his strictest jazz material, as he received excellent backing from the Les McCann trio. McCann, himself a pretty fair singer, played funky keyboards and fronted the trio, while Rawls did shouting stompers and blues, mellow ballads, standards, and pre-rock pop, with the bulk of this material being blues and ballads. —*Ron Wynn*

Spotlight on Lou Rawls / Jan. 23, 1996 / Capitol ✦✦✦

● **The Best of Lou Rawls** / Capitol ✦✦✦✦
A nice collection of Rawls' Capitol singles, which include his No. 1 hit "Love Is a Hurtin' Thing" and many other fine chart singles, all produced by David Axelrod. Rawls got in a groove during his Capitol years, singing songs that had a soul feel but a jazz and blues base. In some ways, he's never made better songs than his late-'60s and early-'70s stint at Capitol. —*Ron Wynn*

The Records

New Wave, Power-Pop
The Records are probably best remembered for their cult classic and minor hit, "Starry Eyes"—a near-perfect song that defined British powerpop in the '70s. And while they never quite matched the success of that record, their high-quality output from 1979 to 1982 has not only held up better than most of the era with its timeless appeal, but has also served as a blueprint for the various waves of British and American power-pop since then. Some have gone as far as to call them the "British Big Star," which is probably a fair comparison—within their genre, they're seen as giants, yet the general public has missed them for the most part.

The band was formed around 1977, when pub-rockers Kursaal Flyers broke up. The drummer from the band, Will Birch, and vocalist/guitarist John Wicks, who had joined the Kursaals in the last stages, began writing together, inspired by the pure-pop tradition of the Raspberries, Badfinger, and Big Star. By 1978, they had completed the group by adding bassist Phil Brown and guitarist Huw Gower. After a series of live gigs, they released their debut, "Starry Eyes," on the independent Record Company label in November the same year. They received some valuable early exposure on the Stiff label's "Be Stiff" tour, which lead to their signing with Virgin Records.

Wicks and Birch continued to churn out should-have-been-hit pop classics over the next three years and three albums—1979's *Shades in Bed* (released in a slightly modified form as *The Records* in the US), 1980's *Crashes* (which found Jude Cole replacing Gower) and 1982's *Music on Both Sides* (which replaced Cole with Dave Whelan and added another vocalist, Chris Gent). Aside from a minor hit with "Starry Eyes" in the US, their efforts were criminally unrewarded. The band broke up in 1982, though they reformed temporarily in 1990 to contribute a track to a Brian Wilson tribute album. Birch went on to become a notable music critic and historian; he also compiled several CD reissues, including *Naughty Rhythms: The Best of Pub Rock*. Wicks began a solo career in the mid-'90s, appearing on the *Yellow Pills, Vol. 3* collection with a song co-written with Birch, "Her Stars Are My Stars"—a pop gem that picks up right where they left off. "Starry Eyes" continues to be a cult pop classic—still heavily requested on alternative radio retro shows. —*Chris Woodstra*

The Records / 1979 / Virgin ✦✦✦✦
Virtually every song here is a catchy guitar-driven pop song with sweet harmonies, from the single "Starry Eyes" through "Teenarama" and "Another Star." The album includes a bonus record containing the Records' versions of such oldies as the Kinks' "See My Friends" and Spirit's "1984." —*William Ruhlmann*

Crashes / 1980 / Virgin ✦✦✦
The Records' second album is just as tuneful and nearly as catchy as its predecessor, though none of the songs have the punch of "Starry Eyes." "Girl in the Golden Disc" and "Hearts Will Be Broken" are the highlights. Unfortunately, the band's take on the brilliant "Hearts in Her Eyes" (a song written by Will Birch and covered more successfully by the reunited Searchers the previous year) is lackluster and somewhat of a letdown. —*Chris Woodstra*

Music on Both Sides / 1982 / Virgin ✦✦✦
With a tighter, harder-rocking five-man lineup, the Records returned with *Music on Both Sides*. Despite the usual strong material courtesy of the John Wicks/Will Birch partnership, the album failed to make an impact. This would be their last album. —*Chris Woodstra*

● **Smashes Crashes and Near Misses** / 1988 / Virgin ✦✦✦✦
The Records may not have been great innovators but they undeniably made some of the best singles of the era. *Smashes Crashes and Near Misses*, a 20-track collection, is the definitive proof of the band's generally overlooked brilliance. Anyone interested in power-pop should start here. —*Chris Woodstra*

Paying for the Summer of Love / 1990 / Skyclad ✦✦
A collection of demos recorded prior to the first album, *Paying for the Summer of Love* provides an interesting look at the songs in their formative stages, but only true fans need to seek this one out. —*Chris Woodstra*

The Red Hot Chili Peppers

Alternative Pop-Rock, Funk Metal
A quartet with varying personnel, anchored by lead singer Anthony Kiedis and bassist Flea (born Michael Balzary), the Red Hot Chili Peppers play a hybrid rock, incorporating punk, funk, rap, and metal. Though the mixture was ahead of its time when the group was first organized in the early '80s in Los Angeles, the music industry has since caught up to it, which earns the group the right to call itself the forerunner of an approach now adopted by such acts as Living Colour and Faith No More, and also means the Peppers themselves have finally hit the big time. In 1988, guitarist Hillel Slovak died of an overdose and the band reorganized, with John Frusciante on guitar and Chad Smith on drums. This lineup scored a commercial breakthrough with *Mother's Milk*, which went gold after its release in 1989. They ascended to real star status with the release of *Blood Sugar Sex Magik*, which sold two million copies and included the Top Ten hit "Under the Bridge." In mid-1992, Frusciante left the group and was replaced by Arik Marshall.
Marshall was replaced by Jesse Tobias in 1993. Tobias' tenure with the group was extremely brief; after a couple of months, he was replaced by ex-Jane's Addiction guitarist Dave Navarro. —*William Ruhlmann*

Red Hot Chili Peppers / 1984 / EMI America ✦✦✦✦
The Red Hot Chili Peppers' debut album sketched out their funk-metal hybrid quite effectively, especially on the warped deep groove of "True Men Don't Kill Coyotes." Even though their fusion of heavy guitars and slapping bass was audacious, their first effort didn't quite gel into a cohesive album. —*Stephen Thomas Erlewine*

Freaky Styley / 1985 / EMI America ✦✦✦✦
Under the guiding hand of George Clinton, the Red Hot Chili Peppers turned in a nastier, funkier album their second time around with *Freaky Styley*. It also didn't hurt that it was the first album the group recorded with Hillel Slovak; he was performing with What Is This at the time the debut was recorded. Even though Slovak and Clinton help make the music more exciting, their contributions didn't necessarily mean that *Freaky Styley* was more coherent than the debut—it just meant that it was more compelling —*Stephen Thomas Erlewine*

The Uplift Mofo Party Plan / 1987 / EMI America ✦✦✦
Mother's Milk / 1989 / EMI America ✦✦✦✦
While *Mother's Milk* is not their most adventurous or best release, it's a good album, which expanded the Red Hot's cult. Mainstream listeners were attracted to the band in large part because of their cover of Stevie Wonder's "Higher Ground," the best song on *Mother's Milk*. Other highlights include "Knock Me Down," "Taste the Pain," "Nobody Weird Like Me," and "Sexy Mexican Maid." —*Meredith Erlewine & Stephen Thomas Erlewine*

Blood Sugar Sex Magik / 1991 / Warner Bros. ✦✦✦✦
It isn't just that the world has finally come around to the Peppers' funk-rock mixture, it's that, with the help of producer Rick Rubin, they've found a focus and that, as musicians, they've reached a sufficient level of competence to execute their ideas. The result is their best album, containing the hit "Under the Bridge." —*William Ruhlmann*

● **What Hits!?** / 1992 / EMI America ✦✦✦✦
A sampling of tracks from the band's ten-year career, it includes the hit "Under the Bridge," plus "Higher Ground" and "Fight Like a Brave." —*AMG*

One Hot Minute / Sep. 12, 1995 / Warner Bros. ✦✦✦

Red House Painters

Alternative Pop-Rock
With their slow, atmospheric alternative folk-rock, Red House Painters have earned considerable critical acclaim and a cult following. Prolific to a fault, the band released their first EP late in 1992, following it with two albums the next year. On each record, leader Mark Kostelich's introspective melancholia is detailed over a moody soundscape that is occasion-

ally interrupted with bursts of distorted guitar. At their best, Red House Painters are hypnotic; at their worst, they are boring. Since they are still developing their style, it's understandable that they occasionally fall into their own mire; fortunately, they are often more mesmerizing than dull. —*Stephen Thomas Erlewine*

Down Colorful Hill / 1992 / 4AD ✦✦✦✦
Red House Painters / May 25, 1993 / 4AD ✦✦✦✦
A slow, stark mood piece, with its folk-pop roots in the somber meditations of Nick Drake, Love's *Forever Changes*, and fellow San Franciscans American Music Club, *Red House Painters* will either mesmerize or act as a cure for insomnia, depending on your mood. —*Stephen Thomas Erlewine*

Red House Painters [untitled] / Sep. 1993 / 4AD ✦✦✦
● **Ocean Beach** / 1995 / 4AD ✦✦✦✦
Red House Painters has always been Mark Kozlik's project, but *Ocean Beach* represents the first record that is almost entirely a solo project. Not that that distinction has made a great change in the music—*Ocean Beach* is a spare, gentle, nearly painfully introspective folk-rock album that draws more from Simon & Garfunkel than Bob Dylan. Kozlik's reigns the droning experimental tendencies of the group's first full-length album, yet he is more generous with his melodies and arrangements than the band's second untitled record. While Red House Painters remains very arty and self-conscious, *Ocean Beach* shows the singer-songwriter breaking out of his shell ever so slightly, bringing more fully developed songs and melodies with him. —*Stephen Thomas Erlewine*

Songs for a Blue Guitar / 1996 / Supreme ✦✦✦

Leon Redbone

Guitar, Vocals / Folk
Leon Redbone got his start in Toronto at the start of the '70s, then (as now) performing songs primarily of the teens, '20s, and '30s and accompanying his affectionate crooning baritone (which some found funny, either intentionally or unintentionally) with simple, syncopated guitar-playing. Folk stars such as Maria Muldaur and Bob Dylan spread the word, and Redbone eventually signed to Warner Bros., for whom he recorded three albums (*On the Tracks* (1976), *Double Time* (1977), and *Champagne Charlie* (1978)), whose sales were increased by his appearances on the TV show "Saturday Night Live." His recordings from 1981-on were infrequent and on small labels, but he made a good living as the voice (on and off screen) in many TV commercials. —*William Ruhlmann*

● **On the Track** / 1976 / Warner Bros. ✦✦✦✦
Debut album contains a typical collection of campy oldies ("Ain't Misbehavin'," "Lulu's Back in Town"), accompanied by a varied cast including folky Don McLean and jazz stars Milt Hinton and Ralph McDonald. —*William Ruhlmann*

Leon Redbone Live / 1985 / Pair ✦✦✦✦
A live setting is just about ideal for a performer like Redbone, and he does not disappoint on this two-record set, which features "Diddy Wah Diddy," "Champagne Charlie," and other favorites. —*William Ruhlmann*

Red to Blue / 1985 / August ✦✦✦
Redbone's best overall album veers from country to jazz to folk to blues. Backup includes members of Vince Giordano's old-time jazz band, Dr. John, David Bromberg, and the Roches on songs ranging from "Lovesick Blues" to Bob Dylan's "Living the Blues," and with two Redbone originals, as well. —*William Ruhlmann*

Up a Lazy River / 1992 / Private Music ✦✦✦

Otis Redding

b. Sep. 9, 1941, Dawson, GA, **d.** Dec. 10, 1967, Madison, WI
Vocals / Soul
We are left to guess the direction Otis Redding's music would have taken had he lived. His last hit, the gently affecting "Dock of the Bay," pointed away from the impassioned soul ballads with which he'd made his name and strayed further yet from the Little Richard imitations with which he'd begun his career. Like many others during the mid-'60s, Redding discovered what was special about his music in Memphis. He had been recording sporadically and unsuccessfully for three or four years when he arrived at Stax and cut "These Arms of Mine." It gave us everything we could expect from him for the next few years: the almost exaggeratedly impassioned vocals couched in the sparse elegance of the Stax/Volt rhythm and horn sections. Wrenching ballads such as "I've Been Loving You" and "That's How Strong My Love Is" were judiciously mixed with uptempo stomps like "Mr. Pitiful" and "Respect." The individual albums inevitably contain some duds, but Redding rarely fired blanks on his singles. Redding's appearance at the Monterey Pop Festival and on the West Coast club circuit was beginning to spread word of his music beyond the traditional confines of the R&B market when he was tragically killed in a plane crash in December 1967. —*Colin Escott*

Pain in My Heart / 1964 / Atco ✦✦✦✦
Redding's first release. Includes the title track, a deep-soul gem, plus "These Arms of Mine" and "Security." —*Christine Ohlman*

The Great Otis Redding Sings Soul Ballads / 1965 / Atco ✦✦✦✦
Redding's second album includes "Mr. Pitiful," "That's How Strong My Love Is," "Chained and Bound." He moves out of the country-soul genre into his own stompin' thing. —*Christine Ohlman*

☆ **Otis Blue** / 1966 / Atco ✦✦✦✦✦
Pretty essential if you can only afford individual albums. Three Sam Cooke covers, including "Shake" and "A Change Is Gonna Come" are included, as well as "I've Been Loving You Too Long," "Satisfaction," and the original version of "Respect." —*Christine Ohlman*

☆ **The Dictionary of Soul** / 1966 / Atco ✦✦✦✦✦
If you can only afford one Redding album, start here. Includes "Try a Little Tenderness," "My Lover's Prayer," "Fa-Fa-Fa-Fa-Fa (Sad Song)." One of the best album covers ever! —*Christine Ohlman*

The Soul Album / 1966 / Atco ✦✦✦

King and Queen / 1967 / Atco ✦✦✦✦
Eleven duets by the undisputed ruler and his consort Carla Thomas. Includes "Tramp" and "Lovey Dovey." Sweet and soulful! —*Christine Ohlman*

Live in Europe / 1967 / Atco ✦✦✦

In Person at the Whisky a Go Go / 1968 / Rhino ✦✦✦✦
Redding captured live in 1966, at the peak of his form! —*Christine Ohlman*

The Dock of the Bay / 1968 / Atco ✦✦✦✦
Includes the posthumously released classic title track plus the great "Ole Man Trouble." —*Christine Ohlman*

The Immortal Otis Redding / 1968 / Atco ✦✦✦

Love Man / 1969 / Rhino ✦✦✦

Tell the Truth / 1970 / Rhino ✦✦✦

The Otis Redding Story / 1989 / Atlantic ✦✦✦✦
A few previously unissued tracks, plus *all* the hits, from "These Arms of Mine" (1962) through "Dock of the Bay" (1967). A magnificent tribute to a magnificent career. It's a little expensive but it'll completely rock your soul! —*Christine Ohlman*

Remember Me / 1992 / Stax ✦✦✦

Good to Me: Live at the Whiskey A Go Go, Vol. 2 / 1993 / Stax ✦✦✦

★ **The Very Best of Otis Redding** / 1993 / Rhino ✦✦✦✦✦
For a single-disc collection, *The Very Best of Otis Redding* is unbeatable. All of his biggest hits are here—it's a dynamite album, essential for any lover of soul. —*Stephen Thomas Erlewine*

☆ **Otis! The Definitive Otis Redding** / 1993 / Rhino ✦✦✦✦✦
Although it includes the same studio tracks, *Otis!* supplants the previous, excellent *Otis Redding Story* by adding improved liner notes and sound, as well as a fourth disc of prime live material gathered from various performances. —*Stephen Thomas Erlewine*

☆ **The Very Best of Otis Redding, Vol. 2** / 1995 / Rhino ✦✦✦✦✦
The Very Best of Otis Redding did its job so well that its sequel is a little unsatisfactory. Although *The Very Best of Otis Redding, Vol. 2* has several of essential songs—"That's What My Heart Needs," "Security," "Chained and Bound," "Hard to Handle"—the bulk of this 16-track collection consists of solid but unremarkable covers and strong album tracks. If you want to dig a little deeper than *The Very Best of Otis Redding*, skip this volume and head straight for the original albums or one of the box sets. —*Stephen Thomas Erlewine*

Lou Reed

b. Mar. 2, 1942, Freeport, Long Island, NY
Guitar, Vocals / Rock 'n' Roll, Singer-Songwriter, Proto-Punk
The career of Lou Reed defies capsule summarization. Like David Bowie (whom Reed directly inspired in many ways), he has made over his image many times, mutating from theatrical glam rocker to scary-looking junkie to avant-garde noiseman to straight rock 'n' roller to yer average guy. A firmer grasp of rock's earthier qualities has ensured a more consistent career path than Bowie's, particularly in his latter years. Yet his catalog is extremely inconsistent, in both quality and stylistic orientation. Liking one Lou Reed LP, or several, or all of the ones he did in a particular era, is no guarantee that you'll like all of them, or even most of them.

Few would deny Reed's immense importance and considerable achievements, however. As has often been written, he expanded the vocabulary of rock 'n' roll lyrics into the previously forbidden territory of kinky sex, drug use (and abuse), decadence, transvestites, homosexuality, and suicidal depression. As has been pointed out less often, he remained (and remains) committed to using rock 'n' roll as a forum for literary, mature expression well into middle age, without growing lyrically soft or

musically complacent. By and large, he's taken on these challenging duties with uncompromising honesty and a high degree of realism. For these reasons, he's often cited as punk's most important ancestor. It's often overlooked, though, that he's equally skilled at celebrating romantic joy, and rock 'n' roll itself, as he is at depicting harrowing urban realities.

Although Reed achieved his greatest success as a solo artist, his most enduring accomplishments were as the leader of the Velvet Underground in the 1960s. If Reed had never made any solo records, his work as the principal lead singer and songwriter for the Velvets would have still ensured his stature as one of the greatest rock visionaries of all time. The Velvet Underground are discussed at great length in many other sources, but it's sufficient to note that the four studio albums they recorded with Reed at the helm are essential listening, as is much of their live and extraneous material. "Heroin," "Sister Ray," "Sweet Jane," "Rock and Roll," "Venus in Furs," "All Tomorrow's Parties," "What Goes On," and "Lisa Says" are just the most famous classics that Reed wrote and sang for the group. As innovative as the Velvets were at breaking lyrical and instrumental taboos with their crunching experimental rock, they were unappreciated in their lifetime. Five years of little commercial success was undoubtedly a factor in Reed leaving the group he had founded in August 1970, just before the release of their most accessible effort, *Loaded.*

Although Reed's songs and streetwise, sing-speak vocals dominated the Velvet, he was perhaps more reliant upon his talented collaborators than he realized, or is even willing to admit to this day. The most talented of these associates was John Cale, who was apparently fired by Reed in 1968, after the Velvets' second album (although the pair have worked together on various other projects since then). Reed has a reputation of being a difficult man to work with for an extended period, and that has made it difficult for his extensive solo oeuvre to compete with the standards of brilliance set by the Velvets. Nowhere was this more apparent than on his self-titled solo debut from 1971, recorded after he'd taken an extended hiatus from music, moving back to his parents' suburban Long Island home at one point. *Lou Reed* mostly consisted of flaccid versions of songs dating back to the Velvets days, and he could have really used the group to punch them up, as the many outtake versions of these tunes that he actually recorded with the Velvet Underground (some of which didn't surface until about 25 years later) prove.

Reed got a shot in the arm (no distasteful pun intended) when David Bowie and Mick Ronson produced his second album, *Transformer*. A more energetic set that betrayed the influence of glam rock, it also included his sole Top 20 hit, "Walk on the Wild Side," and other good songs like "Vicious" and "Satellite of Love." It also made him a star in Britain, which was quick to appreciate the influence Reed had exerted on Bowie and other glam rockers. Reed went into more serious territory on *Berlin* (1973), its sweet orchestral production coating lyrical messages of despair and suicide. In some ways Reed's most ambitious and impressive solo effort, it was accorded a vituperative reception by critics in no mood for a nonstop bummer (however elegantly executed). Unbelievably, in retrospect, it made the Top Ten in Britain, though it flopped stateside.

Having been given a cold shoulder for some of his most serious (if chilling) work, Reed apparently decided he was going to give the public what it wanted. He had guitarists Steve Hunter and Dick Wagner (who had already played on *Berlin*) give his music a pop-metal, more radio-friendly sheen. More disturbingly, he decided to play up to the cartoon junkie role that some of his audience seemed eager to assign to him. Onstage, that meant shocking bleached hair, painted fingernails, and simulated drug injections. On record, it led to some of his most careless performances. One of these, the 1974 album *Sally Can't Dance*, was also his most commercially successful, reaching the Top Ten, thus confirming both Reed's and the audience's worst instincts. As if to prove he could still be as uncompromising as anyone, he unleashed the double album *Metal Machine Music*, a nonstop assault of unlistenable electronic noise. Opinions remain divided as to whether it was an artistic statement, a contract quota-filler, or a slap at the face of the public.

While Reed has never behaved as outrageously (in public and in the studio) as he did in the mid-'70s, there's been plenty of excitement in the past two decades. When he decided to play it relatively straight, sincere, and hard-nosed, he could produce affecting work in the spirit of his best vintage material (parts of *Coney Island Baby* and *Street Hassle*). At other points, he seemed not to be putting too much effort into any aspect of his songs (*Rock & Roll Heart*). With 1978's *Take No Prisoners*, he delivered one of the weirdest concert albums of all time, more of a comedy monologue (which not too many people laughed hard at) than a musical document. Reed had always been an enigma, but no one questioned the serious intent of his work with the Velvet Underground. As a soloist, it was getting impossible to tell when he was serious, or whether he even wished to be taken seriously anymore.

At the end of the 1970s, *The Bells* set the tone for most of his future work. Reed would settle down; he would play it straight; he would address serious, adult concerns, including heterosexual romance, with sincerity. Not a bad idea, but though the albums that followed were much more consistent in tone, they remained erratic in quality and, worse, could occasionally be quite boring. The recruitment of Robert Quine as lead guitarist helped, and *The Blue Mask* (1982) and *New Sensations* (1984) were fairly successful, although in retrospect they didn't deserve the raves they received from some critics at the time. Quine, however, would also find Reed too difficult to work with for an extended period.

(1989) *New York*, heralded both a commercial and critical renaissance for Reed, and in truth it was his best work in quite some time, although it didn't break any major stylistic ground. Reed works best when faced with a challenge, which arrived when he collaborated with former partner John Cale in 1990 on a song cycle for the recently deceased Andy Warhol. In both its recorded and stage incarnations, this was the most experimental work that Reed had devised in quite some time. (1992) *Magic and Loss*, returned him to the more familiar straight rock territory of *New York*, again to critical raves. The reformation of the Velvet Underground for a 1993 European live tour could not be considered an unqualified success, however. European audiences were thrilled to see the legends in person, but critical reaction to the shows was mixed, and critical reaction to the live record was tepid. More distressingly, old conflicts reared their head within the band once again, and the reunion ended before it had a chance to get to America. Cale and Reed at this point seem determined never to work with each other again. (The death of Velvet Underground guitarist Sterling Morrison in 1995 seemed to permanently nix prospects of more VU projects.) Reed's solo work ultimately cannot stack up to his Velvet output, despite its many highlights. As distinctive as his street-talk vocals and basic rock melodies are, they've become more formulaic with time, and their limitations more apparent. Still, most would have to concede that with the exception of Neil Young, no other star that rose to fame in the 1960s has continued to push himself so diligently into creating work that is meaningful and contemporary. If that means he relies on stock musical and lyrical ideas at times (as Young does), it also means he's proved that rock can remain relevant to listeners other than hormone-crazed teenagers. —*Richie Unterberger*

Lou Reed / 1972 / RCA ✦✦✦

Transformer / 1972 / RCA ✦✦✦✦
Produced by David Bowie and Mick Ronson, *Transformer* has a lushness and beauty to its production and arrangements that Reed's material had never before received. The hit single "Walk on the Wild Side" was a fluke brought about by the actions of one fill-in disc jockey at the BBC. The song chronicles several personages from Andy Warhol's Factory retinue, including speed-freaks and transvestites alike; it is boggling to this day that it got by AM radio programmers. Other Reed classics such as "Vicious" and "Satellite of Love" get similar treatment. —*Rob Bowman*

Berlin / 1973 / RCA ✦✦✦
Relations between Bowie and Reed had been strained during the recording of *Transformer*, so for his third solo album, Reed hired Canadian studio whiz Bob Ezrin. Ezrin and Reed concocted a brilliant album-length concept loosely constructed around the song "Berlin," from Reed's first solo album. Reed, of course, wrote the basic songs (several stemming back to demos recorded but not released by the Velvet Underground), and Ezrin and Allan MacMillan wrote orchestral arrangements for each track. Recording in London, Ezrin assembled a dream band including Jack Bruce, Steve Winwood, Aynsley Dunbar, and two relatively unknown guitar heroes, Steve Hunter and Dick Wagner, while Reed's writing and singing has never been better. A number of reactionary writers thought that orchestration automatically meant somehow compromising one's authenticity, while others found the level of depression and vitriol in the story more than they wanted to bear. —*Rob Bowman*

Rock & Roll Animal / 1974 / RCA ✦✦✦

Sally Can't Dance / 1974 / RCA ✦✦✦

Lou Reed Live / 1975 / RCA ✦✦✦

Metal Machine Music / 1975 / RCA Victor ✦
A double-record of galvanizing white noise, *Metal Machine Music* gained instant notoriety when it was released, inspiring reams of rock criticism speculating whether the album was a serious attempt at avant-garde music or not. Considering that the record was a relentless series of layered, overlapping loops of guitar feedback, it probably was intended as a mammoth "fuck you" not only to the fans he acquired with *Sally Can't Dance*, but to his dedicated followers, critics, and record company. Regardless of Reed's intentions, *Metal Machine Music* is the most uncompromising work he ever released, featuring no lyrics, no hooks, no songs, no melodic themes—there's nothing but endless layers of noise. It's not necessarily unlistenable—in the two decades since its release, the atonal guitar experiments of Sonic Youth and their offspring have made *Metal Machine Music* sound downright conventional. It is boring, however. There is no variation in the processed noise, making the record's four sides unbearably tedious. —*Stephen Thomas Erlewine*

Coney Island Baby / Feb. 1976 / RCA ✦✦✦✦
Coney Island Baby was an album of renewal for Reed. The year 1974 had witnessed one of his worst albums ever in *Sally Can't Dance*, and, early in 1975, in reaction to a career spinning out of control, he had released the lyricless sonic feedback assault of *Metal Machine Music*. *Coney Island Baby* was a return to peak songwriting form. The title track reflected Reed's early love of doo wop. It is probably the grandest love song of his career. "Kicks" is a rather frightening internal study of a diseased mind that eventually turns to murder. As with most of Reed's writing in the '60s and '70s, he draws no conclusion; he simply paints a picture. —*Rob Bowman*

Rock & Roll Heart / Nov. 1976 / Arista ✦✦

Walk on the Wild Side: The Best of Lou Reed / 1977 / RCA ✦✦✦✦

Live: Take No Prisoners / 1978 / Arista ✦

Street Hassle / 1978 / Arista ✦✦✦
Reed's second album for Arista has a few weak spots, but most of it, including the 11-minute title song, is unmitigated brilliance. The sound is rather odd as Reed began experimenting with Manfred Schunke's binaural recording process. Some tracks on the album are part live and part studio while others are near totally live or totally studio. *Street Hassle* includes Reed's tongue-in-cheek take on racial stereotypes, "I Wanna Be Black," and a quite strange reinterpretation of the Velvet Underground's "Real Good Time Together." —*Rob Bowman*

The Bells / 1979 / Direct Disk ✦✦✦

Growing Up in Public / 1980 / Arista ✦✦

Rock & Roll Diary / 1980 / Arista ✦✦✦

The Blue Mask / 1982 / RCA ✦✦✦✦
Reed took nearly two years off at the end of the '70s to dry out and clean up. When he did return to recording, it was with a vengeance. In an odd quirk of fate, Reed had re-signed with RCA and he had also gone back to a lineup of two guitars, a bass, and drums. *The Blue Mask* sounds immaculate. The guts of Reed's sound are still present in no uncertain terms, but there is also a richness to the finished mix that is striking. The bass player, Fernando Saunders, became Reed's right-hand man for the next several years, and guitarist Robert Quine was Reed's ideal foil for this and the subsequent *Legendary Hearts*. The result was Reed's best album since *Berlin*. His songwriting had taken a quantum leap since his cleaning up. The maturity was inspiring, as was the breadth of the material. —*Rob Bowman*

Legendary Hearts / 1983 / RCA ✦✦✦✦
Continuing with Quine and Saunders, coupled with a different drummer in Fred Maher, Reed delivered his second superb album in a row. This was a more subdued affair than *The Blue Mask* but the writing was no less impressive. —*Rob Bowman*

Live in Italy / 1984 / RCA ✦✦✦✦

New Sensations / 1984 / RCA ✦✦✦✦
After a few challenging (and critically acclaimed) albums, Reed dispensed with densely literate (and dissonant) excursions into the dark side of the human psyche and delivered a solid, upbeat (and at times humorous) collection of accessible rock 'n' roll. Reed celebrated love ("I Love You Suzanne"), poked fun at power-plays between the genders ("My Red Joystick"), and, as the title track suggested, generally looked forward with optimism. Reed's dirty-electric rhythm, Fernando Saunders' elastic bass work, and Fred Maher's forceful drumming provide a solid bed of ragged but tight ensemble work behind Reed's dry narratives. —*Rick Clark*

Mistrial / 1986 / RCA ✦✦✦

New York / 1989 / Sire ✦✦✦✦
Reed's first album in three years hailed another peak in his recording career. In the past he had always painted pictures of any given social situation. Positive or negative, he had never stated a point of view. On *New York*, he rails. Sporting a new band, including bass virtuoso Rob Wasserman and Reed's brother-in-law, guitarist Mike Rathke, Reed indicts everyone from slum lords to polluters. *New York* contains, perhaps, his finest writing. —*Rob Bowman*

Songs for Drella / Jul. 1990 / Sire ✦✦✦✦
Reed and Cale's tribute to Andy Warhol brings out the best in both of them. It's a spare collection, the only instruments Reed's guitar and Cale's keyboards and viola. The songs trace Warhol's life in a witty, conversational way that evokes his spirit far better than any biographical work of the artist yet attempted. —*William Ruhlmann*

Magic and Loss / 1992 / Sire ✦✦✦

Between Thought and Expression: The Lou Reed Anthology / 1992 / RCA ✦✦✦
Over the course of 45 songs on three CDs or cassettes, *Between Thought and Expression* chronicles the first 16 years of Lou Reed's solo work, from his debut, self-titled album that followed his 1970 departure from the Velvet Underground through the RCA and Arista years that culmi-

nated in 1986's *Mistrial*. On the way, the anthology delivers stellar moments from Reed's David Bowie-produced *Transformer* period, several pieces from the hauntingly doom-laden *Berlin*, and the '70s guitar anthem "Sweet Jane" from *Rock & Roll Animal*. The set includes five previously unreleased tracks, one non-LP B-side, and two soundtrack-only numbers. The tracks were selected and remastered for Reed's participation, and the refurbished sound is a revelation, particularly on the early material. — *Roch Parisien*

Set the Twilight Reeling / Feb. 20, 1996 / Warner Bros. ✦✦

● **Different Times: Lou Reed in the '70s** / May 1996 / RCA ✦✦✦✦

Reed is very much an album-oriented artist, and those who think they may develop a serious interest in his work are better advised to seek individual titles than compilations. If you just want some of his best songs around the house, though, this is a well-chosen, economic 17-track survey of his best material from his best period as a solo act (the early to mid-'70s). Drawing most heavily from the *Transformer* and *Berlin* albums, this has his most famous/notorious early solo works ("Walk on the Wild Side," "Vicious," "Satellite of Love," "Caroline Says"); some inferior but notably different remakes of songs he recorded with the Velvet Underground ("Lisa Says," "I Can't Stand It," "Sweet Jane"); and other high points like "Kill Your Sons" and "Coney Island Baby." — *Richie Unterberger*

R.E.M.

Alternative Pop-Rock, Jangle Pop

R.E.M., along with their English counterparts the Smiths, mark the point when post-punk turned into alternative rock. When their first single, "Radio Free Europe," was released in 1981, it created a massive buzz in the American underground that continued to grow through the release of their first full-length album, 1983's *Murmur*. What made R.E.M. so different from other guitar-driven pop bands of their time was the subtlety of their influences; although they were clearly influenced by punk, they didn't sound like any punk group. Instead, Peter Buck's arpeggiated rhythm guitar recalled the Byrds and the Velvet Underground, while Mike Mills was reminiscent of the melodic bass lines of the Beach Boys and the Beatles. But the band was never a retro-group or pop revivalists—Bill Berry's strong drumming and Michael Stipe's mumbled vocals and abstract lyrics place them squarely into the post-punk era. While their influences are discernable, the clean, atmospheric folk-rock of their early records are clearly their own.

Murmur was adored by critics, as well as earning legions of listeners in the college rock underground. Even with Stipe's inaudible, cryptic lyrics, the band's guitar pop was highly melodic and accessible, yet it didn't fit into the strict confines of AOR or Top 40 radio; consequently, it stayed in the American underground, gaining an enormous following over the years, as well as countless imitators. Yet, R.E.M. continued to improve with each record, continually expanding their fan base through constant touring and uniformly excellent albums. By the time they had their first hit single in 1987—the Top Ten "The One I Love"—their underground fans were devoted enough not to be scared off by the success; besides, R.E.M. had not compromised their music in order to sell records.

During the late '80s, the band became genuine rock stars, selling out arenas across the world. Stipe was becoming the focal point for many of the new fans, as well as the press, but R.E.M. had always functioned as a band, not as a backing group and a singer. Their albums were always the result of a collaborative effort between their members, which is the reason they continued to be musically inventive in the '90s.

Although the band didn't tour at all in the first half of the '90s, they were at the height of their popularity, releasing three multi-platinum albums and scoring several Top 40 hits; in addition to their commercial success, countless bands cited R.E.M. not only as a musical influence but as an ideological model. After releasing the lush pop of *Out of Time* in 1991 and the haunting acoustic melancholia of *Automatic for the People* in 1992, R.E.M. returned to loud rock 'n' roll in 1994 with the *Monster* album. Following its release, the group embarked on their first world-wide tour since 1989. — *Stephen Thomas Erlewine*

Chronic Town / 1982 / IRS ✦✦✦

R.E.M.'s debut EP *Chronic Town* expanded the catchy, jangling pop of their first single, "Radio Free Europe," by making it murkier, but no less melodic or memorable. Stipe may mumble the lyrics throughout the record, but that doesn't detract from the quiet grace of "Gardening at Night" and "Carnival of Sorts (Box Cars)," or the ringing guitars of "Stumble." — *Stephen Thomas Erlewine*

☆ **Murmur** / 1983 / IRS ✦✦✦✦✦

All of R.E.M.'s imitators base their homages on this strange, eerie album. Out of all of their albums, none have the mood this one has—it's the aural equivalent of the creeping kudzu on the cover. The music belongs to no time—the guitars and rhythms may have their roots in 1960s pop and folk, but the vocals couldn't have been produced before 1977 and the punk-rock movement. — *Stephen Thomas Erlewine*

☆ **Reckoning** / 1984 / IRS ✦✦✦✦✦

The guitar still rings and chimes, the vocals still mumble, but the rhythm section is brought toward the front of the mix and the sound is brighter. While the mood has changed (it isn't out of time like *Murmur*), the songs are better—nothing on *Murmur* had the power of "(Don't Go Back to) Rockville" and "So. Central Rain." — *Stephen Thomas Erlewine*

Fables of the Reconstruction / 1985 / IRS ✦✦✦✦

Fables of the Reconstruction is R.E.M.'s most folk-oriented record, but it never strays from the band's highly developed pop sensibilities, as "Can't Get There from Here," "Green Grow the Rushes," and "Driver 8" prove. — *Stephen Thomas Erlewine*

Life's Rich Pageant / 1986 / IRS ✦✦✦✦

This is not R.E.M.'s most successful album, but it captures the band at an important crossroads. The ringing guitars of *Murmur* and *Reckoning* remain ("Fall on Me," "Flowers of Guatemala," "What If We Give It Away?"), but the bombastic directness of their next two albums is anticipated with tracks like "Just a Touch," "Begin the Begin," and their cover of "Superman." An important transitional album. — *Stephen Thomas Erlewine*

Dead Letter Office / 1987 / IRS ✦✦✦

For the fans: a collection of B-sides and outtakes, including a drunken cover of Roger Miller's "King of the Road" and three Lou Reed songs. An entertaining album that will leave the unconverted scratching their heads and the fans delighted. The CD version includes their fine 1982 debut EP *Chronic Town*. — *Stephen Thomas Erlewine*

☆ **Document** / 1987 / IRS ✦✦✦✦✦

The breakthrough. R.E.M.'s first Top Ten (and Top 40) single, "The One I Love," is included, as is the anthem "It's the End of the World As We Know It (And I Feel Fine)." Those two songs illustrate the difference in the band—loud guitars, driving rhythms, and clear (or at least clearer) vocals. "It's the End of the World" may be unintelligible, but Stipe's vocals are audible throughout the album, even though the lyrics are murky. — *Stephen Thomas Erlewine*

● **Eponymous** / 1988 / IRS ✦✦✦✦

Basically a singles collection from R.E.M.'s first five albums, *Eponymous* gives the listener a sense of R.E.M.'s change from a folk-rock band to a rock band. The songs are intelligently selected, distilling most of the best moments from their first five albums for I.R.S. Included is the original single of "Radio Free Europe," different mixes of "Gardening at Night" (where it's actually possible to hear the vocal) and "Finest Worksong," and the previously unreleased (and unspectacular) "Romance." (Note: An import collection, *The Best of R.E.M.*, doesn't have the rarities, but has 16 songs, including the remainder of *Eponymous*, plus many other important songs from their I.R.S. years. Worth the couple of extra dollars for the beginner.) — *Stephen Thomas Erlewine*

Green / 1988 / Warner Bros. ✦✦✦

Green is R.E.M.'s most disjointed and strange recording. Alternating between eerie acoustic numbers and all-out guitar rave-ups, there is no cohesion here. Nevertheless, there is some good material: the goofy "Stand," the veiled confessions of "Hairshirt" and "World Leader Pretend," the guitar workout of "Turn You Inside Out," the mocking "Pop Song 89," and the charming untitled 11th track. — *Stephen Thomas Erlewine*

Out of Time / 1991 / Warner Bros. ✦✦✦

In contrast to the directness of *Green* and *Document*, this may seem like a return to the abstractness of the early years, but that isn't the case. *Out of Time* is among R.E.M.'s best work—a mature, balanced, graceful collection of pop songs quite different from *Murmur* and *Reckoning*. Buck, Berry, and Mills switch instruments frequently, keeping the music fresh and exciting. — *Stephen Thomas Erlewine*

☆ **Automatic for the People** / Jul. 1992 / Warner Bros. ✦✦✦✦✦

After electing not to support the success of *Out of Time* with a tour, R.E.M. promised a hard, driving guitar-rock album by the end of the next year. Fortunately, R.E.M. delivered *Automatic for the People*, a beautifully sad album that is anything but hard rock 'n' roll. A dark, brooding meditation on loss of all sorts, *Automatic for the People* is arguably R.E.M.'s finest moment. Largely acoustic, with lush string arrangements by John Paul Jones, *Automatic for the People* is sorrowful and nostalgic without being crass, shallow, or pandering. Whether it's the adolescent memories of "Nightswimming" and "Find the River," the celebrity deaths of "Monty Got a Raw Deal" and "Man on the Moon," or the consolations of "Everybody Hurts" and "Sweetness Follows," R.E.M. never falls into false sentiment. — *Stephen Thomas Erlewine*

Monster / 1994 / Warner Bros. ✦✦✦

Monster is indeed R.E.M.'s long-promised "rock" album; it just doesn't rock in the way one might expect. Instead of R.E.M.'s trademark anthemic bashers, *Monster* offers a set of murky sludge, powered by the heavily distorted and delayed guitar of Peter Buck. Stipe's vocals have been pushed to the back of the mix, along with Bill Berry's drums, which accentuates the muscular pulse of Buck's chords. From the androgynous sleaze of "Crush with Eyeliner" to the subtle, Eastern-tinged menace of "You," most of the album sounds dense, dirty and grimy, which makes the punchy guitars of "What's the Frequency, Kenneth?" and the warped soul of "Tongue" all the more distinctive. *Monster* doesn't have the conceptual unity or consistently brilliant songwriting of *Automatic*, but it does offer a wide range of sonic textures that have never been heard on an R.E.M. album before. *— Stephen Thomas Erlewine*

The Rembrandts

Pop-Rock

Even though they became best known for recording "I'll Be There for You," the theme song to the smash NBC sitcom "Friends," the Rembrandts were actually rather successful back in 1991 with their self-titled debut album, which produced a Top 20 hit in "Just the Way It Is, Baby." The duo of songwriter Danny Wilde and Phil Solem, both originally in the Los Angeles band Great Buildings, forged a Beatle-tinged brand of pop-rock with ringing guitars and fresh harmonies that found favor with radio programmers across the country, as well as "Friends" co-producer Kevin Bright. The Rembrandts were invited to record a theme song for the show, which they completed in three days; after the show became a hit, radio demand for a full-length version was overwhelming, and one was added to 1995's *LP* at the last minute. While the song was an instant radio smash, topping *Billboard's* airplay chart for eight weeks, it wasn't released as a single until four months later in September, which makes its overall chart peak of No. 17 somewhat deceptive. *LP*, meanwhile, went platinum. *— Steve Huey*

● **The Rembrandts** / 1990 / Atco ✦✦✦✦
This promising debut contains "Just the Way It Is," which was a minor hit. *— Dan Heilman*

Untitled / 1992 / Atco ✦✦✦

LP / 1995 / East West ✦✦✦
Most of the merits of the Rembrandts' third album, *LP*, were overshadowed by the massive success of "I'll Be There for You," the infectious theme from the Generation X hit sitcom "Friends." Included on *LP* at the last minute—the first pressings didn't list the song on the album cover—"I'll Be There for You" received saturation radio airplay, topping the adult contemporary charts, yet it was never released as a single, forcing fans of the song to buy the entire album to own the song. While the Monkees guitar riffs and layered harmonies are not entirely representative of the Rembrandts—it makes them out to be a bubblegum band—the record is filled with smart, hook-laden guitar pop that won't disappoint old Rembrandts fans or listeners attracted by the hit. *— Stephen Thomas Erlewine*

Renaissance

Art-Rock/Progressive-Rock

The history of Renaissance is essentially the history of two separate groups, rather similar to the two phases of the Moody Blues or the Drifters. The original group was founded in 1969 by ex-Yardbirds members Keith Relf and Jim McCarty as a sort of progressive folk-rock band, who recorded two albums (of which only the first, self-titled LP came out in America, on Elektra Records) but never quite made it, despite some success on England's campus circuit.

The band went through several membership changes, with Relf and his sister Jane (who later fronted the very Renaissance-like Illusion) exiting and McCarty all but gone after 1971. The new lineup formed around the core of bassist Jon Camp, keyboard player John Tout, and Terry Sullivan on drums, with Annie Haslam, an aspiring singer with operatic training and a three-octave range.

Their first album in this incarnation, *Prologue*, released in 1972, was considerably more ambitious than the original band's work, with extended instrumental passages and soaring vocals by Haslam. Their breakthrough came with their next record, *Ashes Are Burning*, issued in 1973, which introduced guitarist Mick Dunford to the line-up and featured some searing electric licks by guest axeman Andy Powell. Their next record, *Turn of the Cards*, released by Sire Records, had a much more ornate songwriting style and was awash in lyrics that alternated between the topical and the mystical.

The group's ambitions, by now, were growing faster than its audience, which was concentrated on America's East Coast, especially in New York and Philadelphia—*Scheherazade* (1975) was built around a 20-minute extended suite for rock group and orchestra that dazzled the fans but made no new converts. A live album recorded at a New York concert date reprised their earlier material, including the "Scheherazade" suite, but covered little new ground and showed the group in a somewhat lethargic manner. The band's next two albums, *Novella* and *A Song for All Seasons*, failed to find new listeners, and as the 1970s closed out, the group was running headlong into the punk and new wave booms that made them seem increasingly anachronistic and doomed to cult status. Their 1980s' albums were released with less than global or even national fan-

fare, and the group split up in the early '80s amid reported personality conflicts between members. During 1995, however, both Haslam and Dunford made attempts to revive the Renaissance name in different incarnations, and Jane Relf and the other surviving members of the original band were reportedly planning to launch their own "Renaissance" revival which, if nothing else, may keep the courts and some trademark attorneys busy for a little while. *— Bruce Eder*

Renaissance / 1969 / Elektra ✦✦✦
The original group's debut album was a then-groundbreaking meld of progressive-rock with classical and jazz influences. The album is a little clunky by today's standards, and far druggier than the later group in its ambience (cofounders Keith Relf and Jim McCarty were the heavily psychedelic half of the final lineup of the Yardbirds, which made them anathema to Jimmy Page), but vocalist Jane Relf had a striking individual style and the classical influence was unique for its time. *— Bruce Eder*

Prologue / 1972 / One Way ✦✦✦✦
The debut of Renaissance Mark II, featuring Annie Haslam on lead vocals and John Tout on keyboards, is a solid meld of classical and rock, most of the material built around long, highly developed instrumental lines and Haslam's soaring three-octave range. Nineteenth-century European classical influences (especially Chopin) abound, in a mix of electric and acoustic rock. Reissued on CD by One Way Records in the '90s. *— Bruce Eder*

Ashes Are Burning / 1973 / One Way ✦✦✦
With electric guitarist Andy Powell sitting in on the title track, Renaissance delivered its best, and first fully formed album, mixing Russian, French, and Indian influences in musical settings that are both lively and elegant. The title track is one of the few lengthy progressive-rock pieces of the era that holds up, and the rest of the material runs the gamut from folk to Impressionist, all of it hauntingly beautiful and enlivening. Reissued in 1993 by One Way Records, with excellent sound. *— Bruce Eder*

Turn of the Cards / 1974 / Sire ✦✦✦

Scheherazade & Other Stories / 1975 / Repertoire ✦✦✦✦
The group's most ambitious album is slightly disappointing because the material in the title track seems somewhat repetitive and the orchestra is mixed a little too far down. The rest of the material is livelier and, in some ways, more impressive and memorable. *— Bruce Eder*

Illusion / 1976 / Island ✦✦✦
The group's second album is more polished in its sound, but the record never found an audience because it has never remained in print for very long or been very easy to find. The classical influence is more pronounced, and Jane Relf stretches out further in her vocalizing, as the original group evolved somewhat in the direction of Renaissance Mark II. *— Bruce Eder*

Live at Carnegie Hall / 1976 / Sire ✦✦

Novella / 1977 / Sire ✦✦

A Song for All Seasons / 1978 / Sire ✦✦

In the Beginning / 1978 / Capitol ✦✦✦

● **Tales of 1001 Nights, Vol. 1** / 1990 / Sire ✦✦✦✦
An intelligently programmed collection of highlights from their Sire years. *— Bruce Eder*

Tales of 1001 Nights, Vol. 2 / Mar. 27, 1990 / Sire ✦✦✦✦
Less satisfying than the first volume with fewer memorable melodies, although it's worth a listen. *— Bruce Eder*

REO Speedwagon

Pop-Rock, Arena Rock

REO Speedwagon may not have been the most talented arena-rock band of the '70s, but they were almost certainly worked harder than any other group on the same circuit. In 1971, they released their first album of competent hard rock, but they didn't chart until 1974 with *Ridin' the Storm Out*. That album was recorded with temporary vocalist Michael Murphey, who would later have some solo success of his own; regular vocalist/rhythm guitarist Kevin Cronin rejoined the band in 1975. The first album released after Cronin rejoined REO was only moderately successful, but 1977's *REO Speedwagon Live/You Get What You Play For* began a string of gold and platinum albums, culminating with the 1980 album *Hi-Infidelity*, which sold over seven million copies in America. Although their style had shifted to a slick, mainstream AOR rock and they were known for power ballads, their hits didn't stop coming until 1990, when the band's support dropped off sharply; their 1991 album didn't even chart. However, the band remains a solid touring attraction, and they continue to release albums into the '90s. *— Stephen Thomas Erlewine*

R.E.O. 2 / 1972 / Epic ✦✦✦

Ridin' the Storm Out / 1973 / Epic ✦✦✦✦
REO Speedwagon began to come into its own with its third album, *Ridin' the Storm Out*. Over the years, the record became a platinum-seller, but it originally charted at No. 171, due to the strength of their

series of opening shows for more successful rock acts. While the group still had elements of their bar-band boogie, they began to streamline their approach on this album. Although it only resulted in one minor hit, with the title track scraping the bottom of the singles charts, the record was one of their most consistent efforts. —*Stephen Thomas Erlewine*

Live: You Get What You Play For / 1977 / Epic ♦♦♦

You Can Tune a Piano but You Can't Tuna Fish / 1978 / Epic ♦♦♦♦
You Can Tune a Piano, but You Can't Tuna Fish was REO Speedwagon's biggest hit of the '70s, featuring the singles "Roll with the Changes" and "Time for Me to Fly." —*AMG*

Decade of Rock & Roll '70-'80 / 1980 / Epic ♦♦♦♦
This is a well-chosen recap of REO's dues-paying years. —*Dan Heilman*

Hi-Infidelity / 1982 / Epic ♦♦♦♦
The band's breakthrough album with the masses. Heavy on the syrupy ballad formula that brought them success. —*Cub Koda*

Wheels Are Turnin' / 1984 / Epic ♦♦♦

● **The Hits** / 1988 / Epic ♦♦♦♦
This collects their chart hits and some old favorites. —*Dan Heilman*

Second Decade of Rock & Roll / 1991 / Epic ♦♦♦
Second Decade of Rock & Roll isn't as strong a compilation as *The Hits*, lacking the focused concentration of the previous compilation, but it does contain a fair amount of highlights from REO Speedwagon's '80s albums. —*AMG*

The Replacements

Rock 'n' Roll, Alternative Pop-Rock
The Replacements initially formed in 1979, when Paul Westerberg joined the a garage-punk band formed by brothers Bob (guitar) and Tommy Stinson (bass) and Chris Mars (drummer). Originally, the band was called the Impediments, but they changed their name to the Replacements after being banned from a local club for disorderly behavior. In their early days, they sounded quite similar to Hüsker Dü, the leaders of the Minneapolis punk scene. However, the Replacements were wilder and looser than the Hüskers and quickly became notorious for their drunken, chaotic gigs. After the band built up a sizable local following, the Minneapolis label Twin/Tone signed them.

Sorry Ma, Forgot to Take Out the Trash, a sloppy hardcore collection, was released in 1981 but failed to make much of an impact on the national scene. It was followed the next year by the *Stink* EP, which followed the same pattern as the debut. It was the band's third album, 1983's *Hootenanny*, that first garnered the band attention and helped build their fan base. On *Hootenanny*, the group started playing around with other genres, adding elements of pop, straightforward rock 'n' roll, country, and folk.

Hootenanny set the stage for *Let It Be*, the band's critical and artistic breakthrough. Released in 1984, *Let It Be* showed that the band had successfully expanded their musical reach and that Westerberg had grown considerably as a songwriter; he was now capable of pop like "I Will Dare," full-throttle rock 'n' roll, and introspective ballads like "Answering Machine." Critics and fellow musicians were quick to praise the band, and they developed a large underground following. The buzz was large enough to convince Sire to sign the band in 1985.

The Replacements' first major-label album, *Tim*, was scheduled to be produced by Westerberg's idol, Alex Chilton, but the sessions fell through; the album was produced by former Ramone Tommy Erdelyi. Upon its release in 1985, *Tim* garnered rave reviews that equalled those for *Let It Be*. Though the band was poised for a popular breakthrough, they were unsure about making the leap into the mainstream. As a result, they never let themselves live up to their full potential. The Replacements landed a spot on "Saturday Night Live," but they were roaring drunk throughout their performances and Westerberg said "fuck" on the air. Their concerts had became notorious for such drunken, sloppy behavior. Frequently, the band was barely able to stand up, let alone play, and when they did play, they often didn't finish their songs. The Replacements also refused to make accessible videos—the video for "Bastards of Young" featured nothing but a stereo system, playing the song—thereby cutting themselves off from the mass exposure MTV could have granted them.

After the tour for *Tim*, Bob Stinson was fired from the band, allegedly for his drug and alcohol addictions. The Replacements recorded their next album as a trio in Memphis, TN, with former Big Star producer Jim Dickinson. The resulting album, *Pleased to Meet Me*, was more streamlined than their previous recordings. Again, the reviews were uniformly excellent upon its spring 1987 release, but the band didn't earn many new fans. During the tour for *Pleased to Meet Me*, guitarist Slim Dunlap filled the vacant lead-guitarist spot and he became a full-time member after the tour.

Two years later, the band returned in the spring of 1989 with *Don't Tell a Soul*, the Replacements' last bid for a mainstream audience. The band had cleaned up, admitting that their years of drug and alcohol

abuse were behind them, and were now willing to play the promotional game. *Don't Tell a Soul* boasted a polished, radio-ready production and the group shot MTV-friendly videos, beginning with the single "I'll Be You." Initially, the approach worked—"I'll Be You" became a No. 1 album-rock track, crossing over to No. 51 on the pop charts. However, *Don't Tell a Soul* never really took off—it only sold around 300,000 copies and failed to establish the band as a major commercial force. Furthermore, a tour supporting Tom Petty & the Heartbreakers was poorly received, causing tensions within the group.

Defeated from the lackluster performance of *Don't Tell a Soul*, Westerberg planned on recording a solo album, but Sire rejected the idea. Consequently, the next Replacements album, *All Shook Down*, was a solo Westerberg record in all but name. Recorded with a cast of session musicians as well as the band, *All Shook Down* was a stripped-down, largely acoustic affair that hinted at the turmoil within the band. Mars left shortly after its fall 1990 release, claiming that Westerberg had assumed control of the band; he would launch a solo career two years later. The Replacements toured in support of *All Shook Down*, with Steve Foley, formerly of the Minneapolis-based Things Fall Down, as their new drummer. Neither the tour nor the album were successful, and the Replacements quietly disbanded in the summer of 1991.

Stinson formed Bash & Pop the following year; in 1995, he formed a new band called Perfect. Dunlap released a solo album in 1993. Bob Stinson died February 15, 1995 from a drug overdose. Westerberg began a solo career slowly, releasing two songs on the *Singles* ("Dyslexic Heart," "Waiting for Somebody") soundtrack in 1992; he also scored the film. He released his debut solo album, *14 Songs*, in the summer of 1993 to mixed reviews. Paul Westerberg's second solo album, *Eventually*, was released in the spring of 1996. —*Stephen Thomas Erlewine*

Sorry Ma, Forgot to Take Out the Trash / 1981 / Twin/Tone ♦♦

The Replacements Stink / 1982 / Twin/Tone ♦♦♦

Hootenanny / 1983 / Twin/Tone ♦♦♦
A hodgepodge of hard rock, country, punk—everything. It's patchy, but "Color Me Impressed," "Willpower," and "Within Your Reach" are among their best. —*John Floyd*

☆ **Let It Be** / 1984 / Twin/Tone ♦♦♦♦♦
This is where they realized their potential and consolidated their diversity into a masterpiece that screams, cries, comforts, and antagonizes. Highlights include "Unsatisfied," one of Westerberg's finest songs and vocal performances, as well as the reckless swinging "I Will Dare," and the playful "Androgynous." —*John Floyd*

★ **Tim** / 1985 / Sire ♦♦♦♦♦
Their major-label debut isn't a great leap forward, but their raggedness is retained, and Westerberg contributes anthems of rebellion and insecurity, like "Bastards of Young" and "Hold My Life." Also included is a hard-rockin' nod to alternative radio (with Alex Chilton), "Left of the Dial." —*John Floyd*

The Shit Hits the Fans / 1985 / Twin/Tone ♦

Pleased to Meet Me / 1987 / Sire ♦♦♦♦
Pared down to a trio, the band offers a complex set of ballads and guitar blazers and continues its examination of the effects of rock stardom. Producer Jim Dickinson (Big Star) gives the group a pile-driver sound, like a boombox with the volume up to ten. "Alex Chilton," a hard-rocking ode to Big Star's founder; "Can't Hardly Wait," with its great Memphis groove and Box Tops-style horn and string parts; and the haunting "Skyway" are among this album's highlights. —*John Floyd*

Don't Tell a Soul / 1989 / Sire ♦♦♦

All Shook Down / 1990 / Sire ♦♦♦♦
More a Westerberg solo album than a band effort, this is a delicate, acoustic-based set, which finds him finally facing the perils of adulthood. But don't worry, he hasn't become a Jackson Browne-ian simp. —*John Floyd*

Paul Revere & the Raiders

Rock 'n' Roll, Pop-Rock
With their Revolutionary War costumes and upbeat attitude, Paul Revere & the Raiders were one of the more entertaining rock 'n' roll bands of the mid-'60s. They began in the late '50s as a more hard-edged outfit, and after the mid-'70s, they evolved into a musical-comedy lounge act. The group was put together by keyboard player Paul Revere (b. Paul Revere Dick, Jan. 7, 1938, Harvard, NE) and singer/saxophonist Mark Lindsay (b. Mar. 9, 1942, Eugene, OR) in Caldwell, ID, and scored a Top 40 hit with the instrumental "Like, Long Hair" in 1961. They eventually based themselves in Portland, OR, where they competed on the lively Northwest circuit with acts like the Wailers and the Kingsmen and earned a recording contract with Columbia Records in 1963 on the strength of their recording of "Louie, Louie." (The Kingsmen, however, beat them out for a hit with the song.) But it wasn't until the summer of 1965, when they were chosen as the house band on the afternoon TV show "Where the Action

Is," that Paul Revere and the Raiders really took off, with Lindsay becoming a teenage heartthrob. ("Featuring Mark Lindsay" was added to their name.) In 1966 and 1967, they enjoyed four Top Ten hits—"Kicks," "Hungry," "Good Thing," and "Him or Me—What's It Gonna Be?"—and four Top Ten, gold-selling albums—*Just Like Us!, Midnight Ride, The Spirit of '67,* and *Greatest Hits.* Their good-time style became less fashionable in the late '60s, though they continued to reach the Top 40. After a temporary name change to simply "Raiders" in 1970, they scored their sole No. 1 hit with the gold single "Indian Reservation (The Lament of the Cherokee Reservation Indian)" in 1971. But in the early '70s, they made a transition to more of a Las Vegas-style live show and Revere's gags began to dominate the act. Lindsay left in early 1975, though he has occasionally reunited with the group onstage and on record. —*William Ruhlmann*

Legend of Paul Revere / 1990 / Columbia/Legacy ✦✦✦✦
This two-CD anthology, with 55 songs, may be a lot more Raiders than the average fan would want. But go for it and be amazed at how consistently strong this rocking band from the Great Northwest was. Includes all the hits. —*Jeff Tamarkin*

● **The Essential Ride '63-'67** / 1995 / Columbia/Legacy ✦✦✦✦
A much more sensible buy than the double-CD *Legend of Paul Revere,* this 20-track compilation focuses on their toughest (and therefore best) early material. Has all the big early hits, and about half the songs weren't on *Legend,* most notably their fine pre-Monkees version of "Steppin' Stone." Note that the version of "Hungry" here is an alternate take, good or bad news depending on whether you have the original hit rendition already. —*Richie Unterberger*

Rock & Roll / ✦✦✦

Rezillos

Punk, New Wave
One of Scotland's great punk bands, the Rezillos came on like gangbusters with a hip attitude, a revved-up band (featuring soon-to-be Human Leaguer Jo Callis) and the remarkable pipes of Ms. Fay Fife. With a flair for garish '60s pop-art artifacts (something I'm positive influenced the B-52s), the Rezillos were decidedly less serious than their punk contemporaries, but their debut album *Can't Stand the Rezillos* is a cheesy classic. —*John Dougan*

● **Can't Stand the Rezillos** / 1978 / Sire ✦✦✦✦
Wild, untempered, poppish punk. One of the best outcomes of the new wave era. —*David Szatmary*

Emitt Rhodes

Keyboards, Vocals / Singer-Songwriter, Pop-Rock
Hawthorne, California, native Emitt Rhodes made his first mark in the music world in 1967 as the leader of the baroque-pop band the Merry-Go-Round. The band achieved some marginal success with the Rhodes-penned "Live," and "You're a Very Lovely Woman," recording one album of *Magical Mystery Tour*-inspired pop. When the band broke up in 1969, Rhodes set up a home studio in his parents' garage and began his solo career, engineering and playing all instruments himself. The strength of his initial demos, now showing a strong Paul McCartney influence, helped him get signed to ABC/Dunhill. His critically acclaimed, self-titled debut managed to break into the Top 40 in 1971, but pressure from his record company forced him to rush-release a follow-up, *Mirror,* the same year. *Mirror* was predictably a lesser effort, barely charting. By the time of the third album, 1973's *Farewell to Paradise,* Rhodes was running into legal problems with ABC, since he was unable to fulfill his contract, which demanded he deliver a new album every six months. Disillusioned, he retired from the performing side of the business, working instead as an engineer and studio operator for Elektra/Asylum. Though he hasn't released an album since *Farewell to Paradise,* he continues to write and demo new songs. —*Chris Woodstra*

Emitt Rhodes / 1970 / One Way ✦✦✦✦
Rhodes turns in a fine performance, much in the style of Paul McCartney's first solo album. Like McCartney, Rhodes wrote all the songs, played all the instruments and recorded the album at home. There the comparison ends. Songs like "With My Face on the Floor" and "She's Such a Beauty" are the kinds of songs that pop into your head 20 years later and get you as excited as the first time you heard them. —*Jim Worbois*

The American Dream / 1971 / A&M ✦✦✦

Mirror / 1972 / Dunhill ✦✦✦

● **Listen, Listen: The Best of Emitt Rhodes** / 1995 / Varese Sarabande ✦✦✦✦
Listen, Listen is an extensive, 21-track overview of Rhodes' commercially underappreciated career. A chronological collection, the disc begins with his work with the Merry-Go-Round (six tracks—nearly all of the band's finest moments), covers his solo years with highlights from the three

albums as well as a rare single from 1972 ("Tame the Lion"), and ends with a track from a 1980 aborted solo album. —*Chris Woodstra*

Cliff Richard (Harry Webb)

Rock 'n' Roll, Pop, Pop-Rock, Teen Idol
Britain's answer to Elvis Presley, Richard (born Harry Webb) dominated the pre-Beatles British pop scene in the late '50s and early '60s. An accomplished singer with a genuine feel for the music, Richard's artistic legacy is nonetheless meager, as he was quickly steered toward a middle-of-the-road pop direction. Several of his late '50s recordings, however, were genuinely exciting Presley-esque rockers—especially his first hit, "Move It" (1958)—and gave British teenagers their first taste of genuine homegrown rock 'n' roll talent. Backed by the Shadows—clean-cut instrumental virtuosos who became legends of their own—Richard embarked on a truly awesome string of hit singles in Britain, scoring no less than 43 Top 20 hits between 1958 and 1969. One of these, although it was by no means one of the more successful, was an actual Mick Jagger/Keith Richards composition (the ballad "Blue Turns to Grey").

In his homeland, Richard's popularity was diminished only slightly by the rise of the Beatles, but in his prime, he had a much rougher time in the US, hitting the Top 40 only twice (with "Living Doll" in 1959 and "It's All in the Game" in 1963). Richard belatedly cracked the US Top Ten in 1976 with "Devil Woman," and racked up a few other hits ("We Don't Talk Anymore," "Dreaming," "A Little in Love") in a mainstream pop-rock style. He remains an institution in Britain, where he is one of the nation's most popular all-around entertainers of all time. —*Richie Unterberger*

● **20 Rock N'Roll Hits** / 1979 / EMI ✦✦✦✦
Concentrating mostly on his 1958-59 material, this has Richard's most untamed recordings (bearing in mind that they're still pretty polished compared to most US rockabilly). Includes his first brace of hits—"Move It," "High Class Baby," "Mean Streak," and "Never Mind"—along with the megasmash "Livin' Doll," which pointed the way toward the pop-ballad path he would follow in the '60s. —*Richie Unterberger*

Cliff Richard & the Shadows / 1984 / EMI ✦✦✦✦
Cliff Richard & the Shadows rock out like nobody's business on this classic live album (arguably rock's first authorized and professionally recorded concert album). Recorded in February 1959 at EMI in front of 500 screaming fans, the sound is raw and raunchy by British standards of the time. —*Bruce Eder*

Lionel Richie

b. Jun. 20, 1949, Tuskegee, AL
Keyboards, Vocals / Urban, Pop
After he left the Commodores in 1981, Lionel Richie became one of the most successful solo artists of the early '80s, earning a string of 13 Top Ten hits between 1981 and 1987, including five No. 1 singles ("Endless Love," "Truly," "All Night Long (All Night)," "Hello," "Say You, Say Me"). Between 1986 and 1992 he didn't release any new material, but in 1996 he re-emerged with a new album that sold well, although not up to the standards he set a decade earlier. —*Stephen Thomas Erlewine*

Lionel Richie / 1982 / Motown ✦✦✦✦
Lionel Richie was perhaps the dominant songwriter and performer of the early '80s. His overwhelmingly sentimental love tunes were massive crossover hits, and he turned awkwardness into an art form. This was his first big album, and it peaked at No. 3 on the pop album chart, eventually selling over four million copies and staying on the charts for 140 weeks. —*Ron Wynn*

Can't Slow Down / 1983 / Motown ✦✦✦✦
The Lionel Richie gravy train was in full throttle on this second big hit album, which eventually sold over eight million copies. Richie earned the 1984 Grammy for Album of the Year, and such tunes as "Hello," "Running with the Night," "Stuck on You," and "Love Will Find a Way" were all over the R&B, pop, and even country airwaves. —*Ron Wynn*

Dancing on the Ceiling / 1986 / Motown ✦✦

● **Back to Front** / 1992 / Motown ✦✦✦✦
Back to Front is an ideal greatest-hits collection from Lionel Richie, featuring all of his biggest hits, including "All Night Long," "Truly," and "Say You, Say Me." It's the ideal place to start listening to Richie, as well as the most consistent, enjoyable record he ever released. —*Stephen Thomas Erlewine*

Louder Than Words / Apr. 1996 / Mercury ✦✦✦

Jonathan Richman & the Modern Lovers

b. 1951, Boston, MA
Guitar, Vocals / Rock 'n' Roll, Pop-Rock, Proto-Punk
Jonathan Richman is a certifiable rock weirdo. In 1971 he and the Modern Lovers cut some demos for Warner Bros. (produced by John Cale) that funneled the influence of the Velvet Underground into the twisted

vision of a high-school geek. Those demos were finally released in 1976, but everything he's done since then has pushed the parameters of cuteness into theme albums (*Jonathan Goes Country*, etc.), amplifying Richman's lighthearted approach. —*John Floyd & Cub Koda*

☆ **Modern Lovers** / 1976 / Rhino ◆◆◆◆◆
This is a reissue of the 1971 John Cale-produced demos that unknowingly precipitated what would eventually become punk rock. As he states on "Roadrunner," he's in love with the modern world but also with girls. His odes to a lack of love make for a cogent debut. —*John Floyd*

Jonathan Richman & the Modern Lovers / Jan. 1977 / Beserkley ◆◆◆◆
Richman's second collection of Modern Lovers, over which he was billed (eventually, the group name would be dropped) had a lighter rock 'n' roll sound than the first. In fact, as often as not, Richman played acoustic guitar. And his lyrical concerns had similarly lightened up, to the point of childlike whimsy on such songs as "Hey There Little Insect" and "Here Come the Martian Martians." But the focus was still Richman's unabashed vocalizing (the word "sings" is put in quotes on the back cover), giving the whole album an amateurish charm. —*William Ruhlmann*

Rock 'n' Roll with the Modern Lovers / Feb. 1977 / Rhino ◆◆◆◆
Richman branches out to Japanese music, a "South American Folk Song," and even "Egyptian Reggae" (the last earning him a UK Top 5 hit), but the real highlight on this album is the ode to a totaled car, "Dodge Veg-O-Matic." —*William Ruhlmann*

The Original Modern Lovers / 1981 / Bomp! ◆◆◆◆
There's a good deal of confusion about when the demos on this album were recorded; the liner notes claim that they were made in 1972, before John Cale produced the tracks that eventually composed their official debut release (although it has been reported that the Cale sessions date from 1971). Anyway, the fidelity on these cuts (produced by Kim Fowley) is less than optimal, but the performances are probably the best that the original lineup managed to lay down during their haphazard existence, and the truest to the band's vision. Includes fiery takes of many of their best songs ("Roadrunner," "Astral Plane," "I'm Straight," "I Wanna Sleep"), and some Richman originals that are not to be found anywhere else. —*Richie Unterberger*

Rockin' & Romance / 1985 / Twin/Tone ◆◆◆◆
While it is generally true that many of Richman's post-1980 albums are all but interchangeable, with their earnest naive cheerfulness, this stands as one of the best, if you like his schtick and need to make a choice. The production is sparse, accentuating the acoustic guitar and the doo wop harmonies (both male and female), with light but purposeful drums. Jonathan covers his usual terrain here: juvenilia ("My Jeans," "The U.F.O. Man," "Chewing Gum Wrapper"), cultural heroes ("Vincent Van Gogh," "Walter Johnson"), and optimistic paeans to the simple pleasures of life ("The Beach"). Heart-warming and melodic stuff that might well sound insipid in the hands of others. —*Richie Unterberger*

● **Beserkley Years** / 1987 / Rhino ◆◆◆◆
After the first Modern Lovers album, Richman's records were enjoyable but fairly spotty. Thankfully, *Beserkley Years* collects the best moments from his '70s records, when his cutesiness was endearing, not irritating. With "Roadrunner," "Pablo Picasso," "Here Come the Martian Martians," "Important in Your Life," "Ice Cream Man," and "Dodge Veg-O-Matic" forming its core, this collection is a definitive portrait of his goofy, catchy minimalist pop and rock. —*Stephen Thomas Erlewine*

Modern Lovers 88 / 1988 / Rounder ◆◆◆
One of his better '80s efforts, and certainly one of the most basic, performed in an acoustic trio format. It's nonetheless quite rocking, with heavy debts to doo wop and Bo Diddley rhythms, and a jolly (though not sappy) summertime campfire feel. Some of his best uptempo tunes are here, including "I Love Hot Nights," "California Desert Party," and "Gail Loves Me." —*Richie Unterberger*

Precise Modern Lovers Order / 1994 / Rounder ◆◆◆
Live material recorded in various locations, circa 1971-1973 (the exact dates have become muddied with time). The fidelity and performances are fairly funky—this is essentially a high-quality bootleg—but the band (augmented by original guitarist John Felice on the earliest cuts) attacks the material with a fair amount of élan. Includes most of their best songs—"Roadrunner," "Girlfriend," "She Cracked," "I'm Straight," "Pablo Picasso"—as well as rarities like "The Mixer," "Womanhood," "Dance with Me," and a cover of the Velvet Underground obscurity "Foggy Notion." —*Richie Unterberger*

Ride

Alternative Pop-Rock, Shoegazing
With their first records, Ride created a unique wall of sound that relied on massive, trembling distortion in the vein of My Bloody Valentine but with a simpler, more direct melodic approach. The band's shatteringly loud, droning neo-psychedelia was dubbed "shoegazing" by the British

press, because they stared at the stage while they performed. Along with their initial influence, My Bloody Valentine, Ride stood apart from the shoegazing pack, primarily because of their keen sense of songcraft and dynamics. For a while, the band was proclaimed the last great hope of British rock, but they fell from the spotlight nearly as quickly as they entered it.

Ride was formed in Oxfordshire, England, in 1988 by guitarist/vocalist Andy Bell, vocalist/guitarist Mark Gardener, bassist Stephan Queralt and drummer Loz Colbert when the group were still in their late teens. The band soon earned a dedicated following through their blisteringly loud, intense live shows. Creation Records signed the band in 1989, and the group released their self-titled debut EP later in the year. Not only did the British music critics welcome the arrival of *The Ride EP*, but the public did too—the EP climbed into the lower reaches of the UK charts.

Play, Ride's second EP, appeared in the spring of 1990 and surpassed the success of its predecessor, entering the Top 40 upon its release. Ride continued to gain new fans and quickly became darlings of the UK press. *Nowhere*, the group's first album, was released at the end of the year and became a significant hit in England, peaking at No. 14. The band's third EP, *Fall*, was released in the summer of 1991 and became a Top 20 hit in the UK Ride released their second album, *Going Blank Again*, in the spring of 1992. *Going Blank Again* was successful, particularly in the UK where its first single, "Leave Them All Behind," went into the Top Ten, but didn't increase their audience dramatically. That lack of a breakthrough success caused tensions within the band, especially between Bell and Gardner. After completing a frustrating American tour, the band nearly broke up but decided to take an extended break. It would be two years before Ride re-emerged with their third album, *Carnival of Light*.

Carnival of Light represented a major shift toward conventional psychedelic rock, and it turned out to be a commercial misstep. Not only did their diehard following dislike the record, but the band failed to pick up a new batch of fans with their stylistic makeover. Wounded from a lack of sales and critical respect, the band moved to the studio in the summer of 1995 to record their fourth album, *Tarantula*. Tensions between Bell and Gardner escalated throughout the recorded sessions. After *Tarantula* was completed in August 1995, Gardner left the band; Bell followed immediately afterward. Ride announced its disbandment in January 1996. The album was released in March 1996. — *Stephen Thomas Erlewine*

● **Nowhere** / 1990 / Sire ◆◆◆◆
Rackety, reverberant, psychedelic drone-rock from Oxford, England. Fans of hypnotic detached singing against numbing waves of dissonance should find this somewhat interesting, particularly the throbbing "Polar Bear," the lumbering yet airy "Vapour Trail," the fairly accessible "Taste," and the reckless "Here and Now." The title cut is an effective fusing of early Pink Floyd sonic freakout and industrial noise sludge. —*Rick Clark*

Smile / Jan. 1990 / Sire ◆◆◆◆
Their first two EPs from Britain's Creation label appear on one American collection. Sonically, it is muddier than *Nowhere* (if that can be possible), but the tuneful crash-and-burn of "Like a Daydream" is one of their best. —*Rick Clark*

Going Blank Again / Oct. 1991 / Sire ◆◆◆

Carnival of Light / 1994 / Sire ◆◆◆
A thoroughly impressive, assured set of swirling guitar psychedelia that recalls classic British pop without ever sounding dated. —*Stephen Thomas Erlewine*

Tarantula / Mar. 12, 1996 / Sire ◆◆◆

The Righteous Brothers

Pop-Rock, Brill Building Pop, Blue-Eyed Soul
They weren't brothers, but Bill Medley and Bobby Hatfield (both born in 1941) were most definitely righteous, defining (and perhaps even inspiring) the term "blue-eyed soul" in the mid-'60s. The White, Southern California duo were an established journeyman doo wop/R&B act before an association with Phil Spector produced one of the most memorable hits of the 1960s, "You've Lost That Lovin' Feelin'." The collaboration soon fell apart, though, and while the singers had some other excellent hit singles in a similar style, they proved unable to sustain their momentum after just a year or two at the top.

When Medley and Hatfield combined forces in 1962, they emerged from regional groups the Paramours and the Variations; in fact, they kept the Paramours billing for their first single. By 1963, they were calling themselves the Righteous Brothers, Medley taking the low parts with his smoky baritone, Hatfield taking the higher tenor and falsetto lines. For the next couple of years they did quite a few energetic R&B tunes on the Moonglow label that bore similarity to the gospel/soul/rock style of Ray Charles, copping their greatest success with "Little Latin Lupe Lu," which became a garage band favorite covered by Mitch Ryder, the Kingsmen, and others. Even on the Moonglow recordings, Bill Medley acted as producer and principal songwriter, but the duo wouldn't break out nationally until they put themselves at the services of Phil Spector. Spector gave the wall-of-sound treatment to "You've Lost That Lovin' Feelin.'" a grandiose ballad penned by himself, Barry Mann, and Cynthia Weil. At nearly four minutes, the song was pushing the limits of what could be played on radio in the mid-'60s, and some listeners thought they were hearing a 45 single played at 33 rpm due to Medley's low, blurry lead vocal. No matter; the song had a power that couldn't be denied, and went all the way to No. 1.

The Righteous Brothers had three more big hits in 1965 on Spector's Philles label ("Just Once in My Life," "Unchained Melody," and "Ebb Tide"), all employing similar dense orchestral arrangements and swelling vocal crescendos. Yet the Righteous Brothers-Spector partnership wasn't a smooth one, and by 1966 the duo had left Philles for a lucrative deal with Verve. Medley, already an experienced hand in the producer's booth, reclaimed the producer's chair, and the Righteous Brothers had another No. 1 hit with their first Verve outing, "(You're My) Soul and Inspiration." Its success must have been a particularly bitter blow for Spector, given that Medley successfully emulated the wall-of-sound orchestral ambience of the Righteous Brothers' Philles singles down to the smallest detail, even employing the same Mann-Weil writing team that had contributed to "You've Lost That Lovin' Feelin.'"

It's a bit of a mystery as to why the Righteous Brothers never came close to duplicating that success during the rest of their tenure at Verve. But they would only have a couple of other Top 40 hits in the 1960s ("He" and "Go Ahead and Cry," both in 1966), even with the aid of occasional compositions by the formidable Goffin-King team. In 1968 Medley left for a solo career; Hatfield, the less talented of the pair (at least from a songwriting and production standpoint), kept the Righteous Brothers going with Jimmy Walker (who had been in the Knickerbockers).

Medley had a couple of small hits in the late '60s as a solo act, but unsurprisingly neither "brother" was worth half as much on their own as they were together. In 1974 they reunited and had a No. 3 hit with "Rock and Roll Heaven," a tribute to dead rock stars that some found tacky. A couple of smaller hits followed before Medley retired from performing for five years in 1976; they've toured the oldies circuit off and on in the 1980s and 1990s. —Richie Unterberger

★ **Anthology 1962-1974** / 1989 / Rhino ✦✦✦✦✦
For some listeners, a double-disc of the Righteous Brothers might seem like overkill, but Anthology 1962-1974 should silence most skeptics. Over the course of the two discs, it becomes clear that the duo were the finest blue-eyed soul singers of their era. Not only do the hits ("Little Latin Lupe Lu," "You've Lost That Lovin' Feeling," "Unchained Melody," "Ebb Tide," "(You're My) Soul and Inspiration," "Rock and Roll Heaven") retain their power, there are numerous forgotten gems, like the harder-rocking "Justine" and an excellent version of "This Little Girl of Mine." For listeners who want to dig a little deeper into the Righteous Brothers' music than the hits, they'll be generously rewarded by Anthology. —Stephen Thomas Erlewine

Live 1967 / Live Gold ✦✦✦

Billy Lee Riley

b. 1933
Bass, Guitar, Harmonica, Drums, Vocals / Rockabilly
Billy Lee Riley is a rockabilly singer and multi-instrumentalist. An alumni of Sun Records, he was one of the most crazed, unabashed rockers that label had to offer—in the company of Jerry Lee Lewis, Carl Perkins, and Sonny Burgess, that's saying a lot. Proficient at harmonica, guitar, bass, and drums, Riley contributed as a sideman to many a classic Sun session, and his combo the Little Green Men (most notably guitarist Roland Janes and drummer J.M. Van Eaton) in time became the Sun house band. Riley recorded for a number of labels in a variety of styles, especially effective with blues. Though never commercially successful, Riley's Sun recordings of "Flying Saucer Rock 'n' Roll" and "Red Hot" (both covered in wooden renditions by Robert Gordon) remain landmarks of the genre. —Cub Koda

● **Classic Recordings, 1956-1960** / Jul. 1990 / Bear Family ✦✦✦✦
All the classic Sun sides, plus later Memphis recordings in a brilliant two-CD set. Raw rockin' at its finest. —Cub Koda

Johnny Rivers (John Ramistella)

b. Nov. 7, 1942
Guitar, Vocals / Pop-Rock
Johnny Rivers, intent on getting a break in the music business, left his Baton Rouge home for New York and Nashville. DJ Alan Freed suggested the name change to Rivers, since he originated from the Delta South. After a series of movies and song cuts and a stint with Louie Prima, Rivers gained attention on the Los Angeles club scene, particularly at the Whiskey a Go-Go, where he recorded his debut, Johnny Rivers at the Whiskey a Go-Go, for Imperial Records. Versions of Chuck Berry's

"Memphis" and "Maybellene" hit, launching a series of live hit singles that reflect his tendency to draw from the blues and old rock 'n' roll. Rivers scored with "Secret Agent Man," capitalizing on the then-current fascination with foreign espionage. After that he increasingly turned his attentions to a lusher MOR formula with the No. 1 "Poor Side of Town," "Baby I Need Your Lovin,'" "The Tracks of My Tears," and the haunting "Summer Rain." During the '70s, Rivers had a comeback with several remakes of old rock hits, as well as a hit with the romantic "Swayin' to the Music (Slow Dancin')." Besides his artistry, Rivers displayed good commercial instincts by discovering and signing the 5th Dimension and assisting the career of writer Jimmy Webb. Rivers continues to perform, sounding like he hasn't aged a day since his biggest hits. —Rick Clark

Last Boogie in Paris / 1974 / Varese Sarabande ✦✦
● **The Best of Johnny Rivers** / 1987 / EMI America ✦✦✦✦
A fine single-disc collection, Best of Johnny Rivers features most of his biggest hits, making it a good purchase for those who don't want the definitive double-disc set. —Stephen Thomas Erlewine

Anthology / 1991 / Rhino ✦✦✦✦
One of the great interpretive singers in rock 'n' roll. Rivers made every song his own, and this two-CD package is proof that he rarely faltered. —Jeff Tamarkin

Changes/Rewind / 1993 / Capitol ✦✦✦✦
Johnny Rivers took a dramatic step during the late '60s, embracing adult standards and recording several Jimmy Webb compositions. These were solemn, literate tales of woe, anguish, and turmoil requiring lyric interpretation and careful vocal pacing. They were also heavily produced numbers with string sections and background vocalists. The change didn't hurt Rivers' career; indeed, it won him new critical attention as a serious ballad stylist and landed him some hits. This single-disc collection covers 23 songs from two LPs, Changes and Rewind. Besides the big hit covers "Tracks of My Tears" and "Baby, I Need Your Loving," there is arguably his greatest ballad, "Poor Side of Town." While not everything worked, this material showed another side of Johnny Rivers and expanded his popularity. —Ron Wynn

The Rivieras

Rock 'n' Roll
A South Bend, IN, rock 'n' roll band, the Rivieras' one big hit was one of the last great gasps of pure American rock 'n' roll before the British Invasion took over the charts. Original members Otto Nuss (organ), Doug Gean (bass), Marty "Bo" Fortson (vocals and guitar), Joe Pennell (guitar), and Paul Dennert (drums) were local teen ballroom heroes. They recorded a supercharged version of the Joe Jones R&B semi-hit "California Sun" featuring a powerful drum intro and the now-famous signature guitar and organ riff. The song became a hit in the midst of the first flush of Beatlemania, only nudged out of the No. 1 spot on the national charts by "I Want to Hold Your Hand." Although several equally fine 45s and two albums followed, the band's relatively young ages, coupled with numerous personnel changes caused by the draft and the changing musical climate, caused the band to break up by 1966. Nuss, Gean, and Fortson reunited the Rivieras in the mid '80s, recording and doing local shows, sounding as great as ever. Though their time in the spotlight was brief, their one big hit continues to define for future generations everything that's pulsatingly great about American teen-band rock 'n' roll. —Cub Koda

● **California Sun** / 1964 / Sonet ✦✦✦✦
Import reissue of their first album. —Cub Koda

Campus Party / 1965 / Riviera ✦✦✦✦
Second album; classic frat-band sound. Out of print and impossibly rare but worth the search at any cost. —Cub Koda

The Rivingtons

R&B, Doo Wop
The Rivingtons were a West Coast vocal group featuring Al Frazier, Carl White, John "Sonny" Harris, and Turner "Rocky" Wilson, Jr. Though they are best known for their string of early-'60s novelties, the Rivingtons in reality had a rich tradition of doo wop in their background, going back to their original recordings for Federal as the Lamplighters in 1953. They did extensive backup group work throughout the '50s between their own stray releases under a number of different names; the Sharps (singing on the original "Little Bitty Pretty One" and "Over and Over" by Thurston Harris), the Tenderfoots, the Rebels (they do all the backups on the Duane Eddy hits), the Four After Fives, the Crenshaws. They even sang backup on Paul Anka's first record, credited as the Jacks! In 1962 they became the Rivingtons and hit pay dirt with their first record, the self-penned "Pa Pa Ooh Mow Mow," one of the truly great rock 'n' roll songs to make a virtue of sheer gibberish. They hit the charts again a year later with "The Bird's the Word," capitalizing on a current West Coast dance fad that teenagers were doing to "Pa Pa Ooh Mow Mow." A landlocked surf-teen combo from Minnesota called the Trashmen combined the two

songs, revved up the beat to warp factor nine, and scored a massive hit with "Surfin' Bird." Despite no further chart success, their place in rock 'n' roll history (both for the classic performances they recorded and for being the inspiration behind one of the great noise-rock anthems of all time) is assured. *—Cub Koda*

● **The Liberty Years** / 1991 / EMI America ✦✦✦✦
An excellent 23-track CD with detailed notes and great sound, featuring both sides of all their original-issue 45s (including the insane follow-up "Mama Ooh Mow Mow") plus all the tracks from their lone Liberty album, *Doin' the Bird.* *—Cub Koda*

Robbie Robertson

b. Jul. 1943
Guitar, Vocals / Singer-Songwriter, Pop-Rock
The chief songwriter and lead guitarist of the Band, Robertson dissolved the group in late 1976. He then acted in and produced *Carny*, wrote and/or chose the music for the soundtracks of Martin Scorsese's *Raging Bull, King of Comedy*, and *The Color of Money*, and in 1987 released his first solo album. Relatively inactive in the late '80s, Robertson's second solo album, *Storyville*, was not released until 1991. Three years after the release of *Storyville*, Robertson released *Music for the Native Americans.* *—Rob Bowman*

● **Robbie Robertson** / 1987 / Geffen ✦✦✦✦
Robbie Robertson's first solo album, released 11 years after the Band called it quits at *The Last Waltz*, found the singer/guitarist mining radically new territory. Hiring Daniel Lanois as co-producer, Robertson crafted an album that owed very little to the Band's roots-Americana sound. Instead, Robertson opted for a quirky, enigmatic modern approach, using drum programs, the stick, and guest musicians such as U2, Peter Gabriel, and Bill Dillon. If the album had a weakness, it was in the vocal department. Robertson had only sung lead on a couple of songs with the Band. His reedy ghost of a voice can be quite effective but wears a bit thin over the course of a whole album. Ultimately that is a minor complaint, as the songwriting, arrangements, playing, and sound-painting are superb. Highlights: "Broken Arrow" and "Somewhere Down the Crazy River." *—Rob Bowman*

Storyville / 1991 / Geffen ✦✦✦
Music for the Native Americans / 1994 / Capitol ✦✦✦

Smokey Robinson & the Miracles (William Robinson)

Soul, R&B, Urban, Motown
Bob Dylan called him "America's greatest living poet." Certainly, he was—and is—one of America's greatest living voices; he has brought his thrilling high tenor to a wide variety of material, most of it marked by his innate good taste. Smokey Robinson's association with Motown-founder Berry Gordy goes back to the late '50s, when Gordy produced and co-wrote the singles that the Miracles recorded for Chess and Roulette. Subsequently, the Miracles were one of the first acts to record for Tamla—and one of the first to break; "Shop Around" was a hit in 1960 and was followed by 38 more before Robinson quit the group in 1972. He also wrote for other acts (including "The Way You Do the Things You Do" and "My Girl" for the Temptations and "My Guy" and "Two Lovers" for Mary Wells).

Perhaps Robinson's masterpiece was "Tracks of My Tears," which he recorded with the Miracles. Its success was all the more surprising because the group had largely confined themselves to dance-oriented novelties before then. Robinson's contributions to Motown as an artist, writer, and producer were rewarded with a vice presidency, although the group's momentum was sagging. Their career was temporarily bolstered in 1970 when "Tears of a Clown" (cut three years earlier) became their first No. 1 pop hit. Robinson went solo two years later, and his solo albums trace the journey of a man who peaked early in life but has never lost the creative spark. *—Colin Escott*

Cookin' with the Miracles / Nov. 1962 / Motown ✦✦✦

★ **Anthology** / 1973 / Motown ✦✦✦✦✦
Detroit vocal group the Miracles were a fixture at Motown from day one. Driven by Robinson's superior writing and smooth, silky falsetto, the Miracles placed a stunning 48 singles on the Billboard charts, 39 of those with Smokey in tow. Virtually all of them are included on this collection. Songs such as "Ooh Baby Baby," "The Tracks of My Tears," and "The Tears of a Clown" define much that was good about the '60s. The 1995 double-CD reissue is digitally remastered and includes virtually the same tracks, adding a couple previously unreleased songs and extensive liner notes. *—Rob Bowman*

☆ **A Quiet Storm** / Mar. 1975 / Motown ✦✦✦✦✦
The landmark artistic release of Smokey Robinson's solo career. This album didn't equal the sales of his '80s LPs, but was extremely influential. Robinson linked the songs conceptually and produced the album with almost no breaks between selections. *A Quiet Storm* was as influen-

tial as Marvin Gaye's *What's Going On* or Isaac Hayes' *Hot Buttered Soul.* It also spawned the rise of a new sound—soul aimed at an adult audience. Many radio stations aired various unedited cuts from this LP late at night or after dark. Soon an entire format was developed that emphasized adult ballads and played album cuts as much as, if not more than, edited singles. This format was called "Quiet Storm." *—Ron Wynn*

Where There's Smoke . . . / May 1979 / Motown ✦✦✦
Warm Thoughts / Feb. 1980 / Motown ✦✦✦
Being with You / Feb. 1981 / Motown ✦✦✦
Whatever Makes You Happy: More of the Best . . . / 1993 / Rhino ✦✦✦✦
Solid compilation of 18 of the most interesting non-hits from Smokey's (and Motown's) golden era. Culled from 11 albums, this is an intelligent and consistent overview of Robinson's relatively unknown tunes. These cuts show the stylistic evolution of Motown as surely as any greatest-hits collection, moving from bluesy, raucous R&B to assembly-line soul to songs reflecting the lyrical and instrumental innovations of the psychedelic era. Robinson's peerless soul songwriting and the Miracles' smooth harmonies remained constant no matter what the era, making this a much more fluid set than you might expect. Ultimately, the songs don't boast hooks quite as memorable as their classic hit singles, despite their similarities in structure and production. The early-'60s tracks are perhaps the record's most interesting, displaying a gritty, almost salacious approach that had yet to be toned down by slicker production values. Dominated by Robinson originals, this collection also includes scattered covers of "Money" and hits by the Temptations and Supremes, as well as the original version of "From Head to Toe," later covered by Elvis Costello. *—Richie Unterberger*

☆ **Thirty-Fifth Anniversary Box** / 1994 / Motown ✦✦✦✦✦
This four-CD boxed set covers every essential track that Smokey Robinson and the Miracles ever recorded, and then some—at least a dozen never previously anthologized tracks are included here, among them the original single versions of "Way Over There" (unavailable elsewhere) and "Shop Around" (which had already been released locally in Detriot when Berry Gordy decided one night to get a session together, punch up the rhythm, and lay down a new version, which became the hit). Even better is the remastering, which runs circles around any previous edition of the Miracles' work, and the annotation—including an essay by Claudette Robinson—that gives credit to all of the participants, including the backup musicians who were seldom if ever mentioned during Motown's heyday. The Smokey Robinson & the Miracles *Anthology* is a fine collection, but this set is the definitive history, and irreplaceable for anyone who genuinely loves the group. *—Bruce Eder*

Tom Robinson

Bass, Vocals / Rock 'n' Roll, New Wave
Although his career had pretty much flamed out by the start of the '80s, there were few punk-era major label performers as intensely controversial as Tom Robinson. Cutting his teeth with folk-rockers Cafe Society (who released a Ray Davies-produced record on the head Kinks' Konk label in 1975), Robinson roared into the spotlight in 1978 with a great single ("2-4-6-8 Motorway") and a much-ballyhooed contract with EMI. What was remarkable about this was that Robinson was the kind of politically conscious, confrontational performer that major labels generally ignored: he was openly gay and sang about it ("Glad to be Gay"), vociferous in his hatred for then-British Prime Minister Margaret Thatcher, helped form Rock Against Racism, and generally spoke in favor of any leftist political tract that would embarrass the ruling ultra-conservative Tory government. His debut album, 1978's *Power in the Darkness*, was an occasionally stunning piece of punk/hard rock agit-prop that, along with being ferociously direct, was politicized rock that focused more on songs than slogans.

However, by the release of the second album, the Todd Rundgren-produced *TRB Two*, the songs were getting weaker and Robinson began sounding like a boring idealogue. Similarly the band, even terrific guitarist Danny Kustow, sounds as if on automatic pilot. By the end of the '70s, Robinson had been dropped by EMI and signed to maverick major IRS as a solo act. In a wise move, he ditched the hard-rock polemics of the TRB for a more sophisticated pop-rock sound, but found his audience dwindling. A brief period of silence ended with him, somewhat surprisingly, signing with Geffen and releasing *Hope and Glory*, a politically tinged, but mostly mainstream rock record that featured a cover of that decidedly non-punk song, Steely Dan's "Rikki Don't Lose That Number," with Robinson deftly exploring the song's homoerotic subtext. Still, it wasn't enough to resuscitate his career and for the remainder of the decade Robinson released English-only albums that tried the patience of even longtime fans.

As to his current whereabouts, Robinson is rumored to be married to a woman (!) and raising a family in England. He's still writing songs and occasionally performing, but it can be safely assumed that whatever he's doing, it's light years away from the radical energy and excitement of *Power in the Darkness.* —*John Dougan*

● **Power in the Darkness** / 1978 / Capitol ✦✦✦✦
This is angry British political punk at its best. —*David Szatmary*

TRB Two / 1979 / Harvest ✦✦✦

Hope and Glory / 1984 / Geffen ✦✦✦

Rockpile

Rock 'n' Roll, New Wave, Pop-Rock, Pub-Rock
During the late '70s, Rockpile was the touring band for both Dave Edmunds and Nick Lowe. Like Edmunds, the band was passionate about traditional rock 'n' roll. Like Lowe, the band played with a reckless, trashy abandon. Driven by the powerful rhythm section of drummer Terry Williams and Lowe's bass, guitarists Billy Bremner and Edmunds were free to spit out crushing rock, blues, rockabilly, and country licks. With their fierce live energy and unpretentious rock 'n' roll, the band fit easily into the post-punk new wave at the end of the decade.
Although they only released one album as a group—1980's *Seconds of Pleasure*—the band provided support for most of the albums Lowe and Edmunds recorded in the late '70s. After the rushed release of *Seconds of Pleasure*, the band toured one last time before splitting apart, largely due to mismanagement. All of the members continued to occasionally collaborate with each other throughout the '80s. —*Stephen Thomas Erlewine*

Seconds of Pleasure / 1980 / Columbia ✦✦✦✦
Rockpile's only proper album is an inspired collection of old-fashioned rock 'n' roll, which sounds vital because of the band's unrelenting energy and Nick Lowe's consistently inventive songwriting. The CD includes the bonus EP of Everly Brothers covers that was included in the album's original pressing. —*Stephen Thomas Erlewine*

Tommy Roe

b. May 9, 1942
Guitar, Vocals / Rock 'n' Roll, Pop-Rock, Bubblegum
Widely perceived as one of the archetypal bubblegum artists of the late '60s, Tommy Roe cut some pretty decent rockers along the way, especially early in his career—many displaying some pretty prominent Buddy Holly roots. In fact, Roe's initial pop smash, 1962's chart-topping "Sheila," was quite reminiscent of Holly's "Peggy Sue," utilizing a very similar throbbing drum beat and Roe's hiccuping vocal. The singer had previously cut the song for the smaller Judd label before remaking it in superior form for ABC-Paramount. The infectious "Everybody"—another hot item the next year—was waxed in Muscle Shoals at Rick Hall's Fame studios, normally an R&B-oriented facility (it's not widely known that Roe wrote songs for the Tams, a raw-edged soul group from his Atlanta hometown).
Once Roe veered off on his squeaky-clean bubblegum tangent, he stuck with it for the rest of the decade. His lighthearted "Sweet Pea" and "Hooray for Hazel" burned up the charts in 1966, and he was still at it three years later when he waxed his biggest hit, "Dizzy," and "Jam Up Jelly Tight." —*Bill Dahl*

● **Greatest Hits** / 1993 / MCA ✦✦✦✦
Supplants previous anthologies as the best Roe collection available. Eighteen songs spanning 1962 to 1971, including all the big singles, with thorough liner notes. —*Richie Unterberger*

Greatest Hits / 1994 / Curb ✦✦
There's an identically titled CD on MCA, issued around the same time. The Curb disc has many of the same songs, but considerably less in total (only ten in all). Since the MCA anthology also has much better liner notes, you'd be foolish to pick up this one instead. —*Richie Unterberger*

The Rolling Stones

Group / Rock 'n' Roll, Hard Rock, British Invasion, Pop-Rock, British Blues
The Rolling Stones are the definitive rock 'n' roll band and, by now, the longest-lived rock 'n' roll band to remain consistently popular throughout their (30-year) career. The group came together in London, where singer Mick Jagger (b. Jul. 26, 1943) and guitarist Keith Richards (b. Dec. 18, 1943), who had been grade school classmates, joined with guitarist Brian Jones (b. Feb. 28, 1942, d. Jul. 3, 1969) and a rhythm section then consisting of pianist Ian Stewart, bassist Dick Taylor, and drummer Mick Avory (later of the Kinks) at a debut show at the Marquee on July 12, 1962. Taylor was replaced soon after by Bill Wyman (b. Oct. 24, 1936), and Avory eventually gave way to jazz drummer Charlie Watts (b. Jun. 2, 1941).
The Rolling Stones played an eight-month residency at the Crawdaddy Club in 1963, during which they signed a management contract with Andrew "Loog" Oldham (who demoted Ian Stewart to road manager) and a recording contract with Decca. The group was devoted to playing Chicago blues and its offshoots, notably the rock 'n' roll of Chuck

Berry, and its early records were either covers of such music or extremely derivative originals. The Stones' first single, for example, was a cover of Berry's "Come On." It was followed by "I Wanna Be Your Man," a song written for the Stones by John Lennon and Paul McCartney.
The Stones' first really successful single, however, was a version of Buddy Holly's "Not Fade Away," which reached No. 3 in England and became their first American chart entry. Their next five UK singles all hit No. 1, and by 1965 they had established themselves as second only to the Beatles as the most popular British rock group, a position they held until the Beatles broke up.
The important factor setting the Stones apart from their lesser competition was that they successfully moved from being a blues-rock cover band to being a band that performed primarily original pop-rock material with a blues base. Jagger and Richards turned into a songwriting team as early as 1964, and by 1965 such Stones hits as "The Last Time" and "(I Can't Get No) Satisfaction" were scoring on both sides of the Atlantic.
The Stones toured extensively in the mid-'60s, with their success partially attributable to frontman Mick Jagger, who became the most prominent lead singer in rock. They followed many of the trends of the '60s as the decade wore on, and their involvement with drugs curtailed their ability to play in the US after 1966. By that time, like the Beatles and others, their musical horizons had expanded to include a variety of eclectic styles. Unlike the Beatles, however, the Stones were never really comfortable with psychedelia, and after their 1967 *Sgt. Pepper* knock-off, *Their Satanic Majesties Request*, they returned to a more basic hard-rock style on the single "Jumpin' Jack Flash" and the album *Beggars Banquet.*
In 1969, the Stones re-emerged as a concert attraction after firing Brian Jones (who died shortly after) and hiring guitarist Mick Taylor (b. Jan. 17, 1948), who in turn was replaced by Ron Wood (b. Jun. 1, 1947) in 1976. They released the single "Honky Tonk Women" and the album *Let It Bleed* and embarked on an American concert tour that culminated in the disastrous Altamont Festival. Despite that debacle, after the Beatles' split the following year, the Stones were undisputed in their claim to being "the greatest rock 'n' roll band in the world."
In the '70s, the Stones toured every three years and released a series of million-selling, chart-topping albums, despite guitarist Keith Richards' descent into heroin addiction. The drug problem came to a head when Richards was arrested in Toronto in 1977. He subsequently cleaned up, however, and took a more active role in the Stones' creative efforts, resulting in improved albums in the late '70s and early '80s.
The band played a world tour 1981-1982 and continued actively into the mid-'80s, but when Jagger made a solo album in 1985 and then refused to tour behind the Stones' 1986 *Dirty Work* album, their long career together seemed to be over. Richards reluctantly began work on a solo album and publicly voiced his anger. Jagger released a second solo album in 1987 and toured Japan in 1988, but by the time of the release of Richards' solo album, *Talk Is Cheap*, the Stones were in discussions about a reunion. A new album, *Steel Wheels*, was recorded and released in 1989, accompanied by another world tour lasting into 1990.
Bill Wyman left the group for good after the *Steel Wheels* tour. For a couple of years, the Stones had no bassist; they signed a multi-million dollar deal with Virgin Records in 1992 as a four-piece. After all four members released solo records in 1992 and 1993, the band began auditioning bassists during rehearsals for their new album. Released in the summer of 1994, *Voodoo Lounge* was recorded with former Miles Davis and Sting bassist Darryl Jones; after the album's release, he was named as Wyman's permanent replacement. —*William Ruhlmann*

The Rolling Stones (England's Newest Hitmakers) / May 30, 1964 / ABKCO ✦✦✦✦
The group's debut album, a bit bluesier and more acoustically textured than the sound they later became famous for, with the influence of Slim Harpo and Muddy Waters getting equal time with Chuck Berry and Bo Diddley. "Carol," "King Bee," and "Route 66" are just a few of the indispensable highlights. —*Bruce Eder*

☆ **12 X 5** / Oct. 17, 1964 / ABKCO ✦✦✦✦✦
A much more rock-oriented album than their debut, *12 X 5* is the album that solidified the group's Chuck Berry and Bo Diddley-based sound, and on which guitarists Keith Richards and Brian Jones first flexed their muscles. —*Bruce Eder*

The Rolling Stones Now! / Apr. 1965 / ABKCO ✦✦✦✦
This album is a louder blues record, moving toward rock, with Mick Jagger beginning to stretch out as a vocalist and the band hardening its sound. "Everybody Needs Somebody to Love" and "Mona" are among the best parts of a near-perfect record. —*Bruce Eder*

Out of Our Heads / Aug. 1965 / ABKCO ✦✦✦✦
The first of the American patchwork albums, assembled from sessions on two continents and some London concerts, and it all works—"Satisfaction" was the hit, but "I'm Alright" was a concert favorite for years. —*Bruce Eder*

December's Children / Dec. 1965 / ABKCO ✦✦✦✦
A much more artful release, compiled from various singles and album sessions. The blues material is subservient to rock numbers like "Get Off of My Cloud" and elegant R&B such as "You Better Move On." —*Bruce Eder*

Big Hits High Tide and Green Grass / Mar. 1966 / ABKCO ✦✦✦✦
A concise collection of the group's early hits, with no surprises. —*Bruce Eder*

☆ **Aftermath** / Jun. 1966 / ABKCO ✦✦✦✦✦
The group's most accomplished studio record of the '60s, and the first to feature all Jagger-Richards originals. The sound also expands here to embrace the mild psychedelic/Eastern sound of "Paint It Black," and the barrier-bursting ten-minute-plus "Goin' Home," highlighted by Jones's workout on blues harp. —*Bruce Eder*

Got Live If You Want It / Nov. 4, 1966 / ABKCO ✦✦

☆ **Between the Buttons** / Jan. 1967 / ABKCO ✦✦✦✦✦
A spaced-out, trippy mix of psychedelia, vaudeville, and Dylan homages that has worn well despite the inclusion of two hits ("Let's Spend the Night Together" and "Ruby Tuesday") that had nothing to do with the rest of it. A self-conscious album, and very theatrical. —*Bruce Eder*

Flowers / Jun. 1967 / ABKCO ✦✦

Their Satanic Majesties Request / Nov. 1967 / ABKCO ✦✦✦
Underrated psychedelic venture by the Stones, who seem to lack confidence in their abilities and material (and lacked a producer at the time as well). The dross is balanced out by a couple of minor hits ("2000 Light Years from Home," "She's a Rainbow") and a couple of brilliant album tracks ("2000 Man" and "Citadel"). —*Bruce Eder*

☆ **Beggars Banquet** / Nov. 1968 / ABKCO ✦✦✦✦✦
The group's newly matured sound came together on this album, a mixture of blues and politics that proved almost too controversial to release at the time. "Salt of the Earth," "Parachute Woman," "Street Fighting Man," and "Jigsaw Puzzle" make it worthwhile. —*Bruce Eder*

☆ **Let It Bleed** / Nov. 28, 1969 / ABKCO ✦✦✦✦✦
A coda to the Brian Jones era, and the start of the Mick Taylor era, with a dazzling collection of numbers ("Gimme Shelter," "Midnight Rambler," "Love in Vain," "You Can't Always Get What You Want," "Let It Bleed," etc.), most of which figured prominently in the group's subsequent tour. —*Bruce Eder*

Get Yer Ya-Ya's Out / Sep. 4, 1970 / ABKCO ✦✦✦✦
This live album, released largely to counteract the effect of the bootleg *Liver Than You'll Ever Be*, captured the new-era Stones in their top form, doing all of the key material from their preceding pair of albums. —*Bruce Eder*

☆ **Sticky Fingers** / Apr. 23, 1971 / Virgin ✦✦✦✦✦
A ballsy, bluesy masterpiece made up of leftovers and works in progress from the preceding two years, including "Wild Horses," "Brown Sugar," and "Sister Morphine." —*Bruce Eder*

● **Hot Rocks 1964-1971** / Jan. 1972 / ABKCO ✦✦✦✦
This import double-disc anthology contains their biggest hits on London, as well as many of their most popular album tracks. A stereo version of "Satisfaction" is the highlight, and worth the price, even though the US mono version is also pretty cool. —*Bruce Eder*

☆ **Exile on Main Street** / May 12, 1972 / Virgin ✦✦✦✦✦
Originally rock's most musically successful double album, this epic collection has aged magnificently. Includes the hit "Tumbling Dice," as well as "Rocks Off," "Happy," "Rip This Joint," and "Sweet Virginia." —*Bruce Eder*

● **More Hot Rocks (Big Hits and Fazed Cookies)** / Nov. 1972 / ABKCO ✦✦✦✦
Highlighted by a unique stereo edition of "It's All Over Now." Often thought of as secondary, this anthology is really a lot more interesting than *Hot Rocks*. —*Bruce Eder*

Goats Head Soup / Aug. 31, 1973 / Virgin ✦✦✦
Compared to the monumental *Exile on Main Street*, *Goats Head Soup* is bound to sound inferior, and it does. Nevertheless, the album doesn't deserve its bad reputation. It might be careless and decadent, but that excess is quite intoxicating, as the nasty rocker "Star Star" and the finely crafted ballad "Angie" prove. —*Stephen Thomas Erlewine*

It's Only Rock and Roll / Oct. 18, 1974 / Virgin ✦✦✦
It's uneven, but at times *It's Only Rock and Roll* catches fire. The songs and performances are stronger than those on *Goats Head Soup;* the tossed-off numbers sound effortless, not careless. Throughout, the Stones wear their title as the "World's Greatest Rock & Roll Band" with a defiant smirk, which makes the bitter cynicism of "If You Can't Rock Me" and the title track all the more striking, and the reggae experimentation of "Luxury," the aching beauty of "Time Waits for No One," and the agreeable filler of "Dance Little Sister" and "Short and Curlies" all the more enjoyable. —*Stephen Thomas Erlewine*

Metamorphosis / Jun. 1975 / ABKCO ✦✦

Black & Blue / Apr. 20, 1976 / Virgin ✦✦✦
Ron Wood's first album with the Stones finds the band working through a number of reggae- and funk-tinged numbers, trying to expand their sound. Consequently, songs are sacrificed for grooves; only the ballads "Memory Motel" and "Fool to Cry" are fully developed, but the grooves that dominate the album are strong enough to make the record successful. —*Stephen Thomas Erlewine*

☆ **Some Girls** / Jun. 9, 1978 / Virgin ✦✦✦✦✦
A nasty, hard-rocking album, *Some Girls* finds the Stones turning out an effortlessly brilliant and eclectic set of material, encompassing the disco pulse of "Miss You," the sleazy snarl of "When the Whip Comes Down," the campy country of "Far Away Eyes," the moving ballad "Beast of Burden," and Richards' best outlaw song, "Before They Make Me Run." —*Stephen Thomas Erlewine*

Emotional Rescue / Jun. 23, 1980 / Virgin ✦✦✦
While it isn't a great album, *Emotional Rescue* is good. The Stones made a set of skillfully crafted pop-rock, which embraces disco and new wave to a greater extent than *Some Girls*. When *Emotional Rescue* is on, as on "She's So Cold," "Where the Boys Go," "Send It To Me," and the hypnotic, pulsing title track, it is damn good. —*Stephen Thomas Erlewine*

Tattoo You / Aug. 30, 1981 / Virgin ✦✦✦✦
Tattoo You remains the Stones' last great album. While the rockers on side one provide some sparks, the heart of the album lies in the second side, with the gorgeous ballads "Worried About You" and "Waiting on a Friend." —*Stephen Thomas Erlewine*

Undercover / Nov. 7, 1983 / Virgin ✦✦✦
A glorious return to form, with topical politics, sex, and decadence all colliding to create some memorable sparks. In addition to the title track, "She Was Hot" was also a hit and managed to create a fair amount of controversy with its subject matter and the accompanying video clip. —*Bruce Eder*

Dirty Work / 1986 / Virgin ✦✦✦

☆ **Singles Collection: The London Years** / 1989 / ABKCO ✦✦✦✦✦
The best individual collection of their classic hits ever assembled, for sound and content. —*Bruce Eder*

Steel Wheels / 1989 / Virgin ✦✦✦

Voodoo Lounge / 1994 / Capitol ✦✦✦

Stripped / Nov. 14, 1995 / Virgin ✦✦✦

Henry Rollins

Vocals / Spoken Word, Alternative Pop-Rock
In the '90s, Henry Rollins emerged as a post-punk renaissance man, without the self-conscious trappings that plagued such '80s artists as David Byrne. Since Black Flag's break-up in 1986, Rollins has been relentlessly busy, recording albums with the Rollins Band, writing books and poetry, performing spoken-word tours, writing a magazine column in *Details*, acting in several movies, and, most surprisingly, appearing on MTV as an occasional VJ. All the while, he has kept his artistic integrity, becoming a kind of father figure for many alternative bands of the '90s.

The Rollins Band's records are uncompromising, intense, cathartic fusions of hard rock, funk, post-punk noise, and jazz experimentalism, with Rollins shouting angry, biting self-examinations and accusations over the grind. On his spoken-word albums, he is remarkably more relaxed, showcasing a hilariously self-deprecating sense of humor that is often absent in his music. —*Stephen Thomas Erlewine*

Hot Animal Machine / 1987 / Texas Hotel ✦✦✦✦
A good solo effort, raw and powerful. This CD includes the EP *Drive by Shootings*. —*John Dougan*

Do It / 1988 / Texas Hotel ✦✦✦

Life Time / 1988 / Texas Hotel ✦✦✦

Hard Volume / 1989 / Texas Hotel ✦✦✦

Turned On / 1990 / Quarterstick ✦✦✦

● **The End of Silence** / 1992 / Imago ✦✦✦✦
Intense is the only word that can describe Henry Rollins, and his band is the most intense unit recording today. *The End of Silence* is arguably the Rollins Band's best effort to date, full of angry, abrasive hardcore-jazz fusion, highlighted by the crushing "Low Self Opinion." —*Stephen Thomas Erlewine*

Deep Throat / Feb. 1992 / Quarterstick ✦✦✦✦
All of Rollins' early spoken-word releases are gathered in the reasonably priced six-disc box set *Deep Throat*. As with each of his spoken albums, Rollins is incisive, moving, self-effacing, and very funny; it's worth the price of the discs. —*Stephen Thomas Erlewine*

● **Rollins: The Boxed Life** / 1993 / Imago ✦✦✦✦
Rollins' spoken-word records are comedy records, more like Lenny Bruce or Richard Pryor than Andrew Dice Clay or Eddie Murphy. Under-

neath all the laughter there are some serious themes; the humor is drawn from pain. But the main reason to hear *The Boxed Life* (or any of Rollins' spoken-word records) is that he's a superb storyteller with a wicked sense of humor. Some of the topics are squeamish (animal testing, safe sex, depression) and there is a generous helping of profanity, but it is genuinely funny and moving. —*Stephen Thomas Erlewine*

Weight / Apr. 12, 1994 / Imago ✦✦✦✦
The latest effort from the Rollins Band is able to mix the musicians' love for jazz with a blindingly direct hard-rock assault, making a twisted form of metal-jazz. Rollins' lyrics have also begun to move away from his relentless self-examination, adding a touch of the self-effacing humor that distinguishes his spoken records. The new lyrical dimension adds depth to the band's music, making *Weight* the most impressive album they have released to date. —*Stephen Thomas Erlewine*

Romantics

Power-Pop, Pop-Rock
In the early '80s, the Romantics were a terrific rock band, joyously tearing through loose, infectious power-pop gems like the classic "What I Like About You." After two albums of energetic pop-rock, the band shifted its direction to a slicker, more radio-friendly pop; the change of style worked, resulting in the hit singles "Talking in Your Sleep" and "One in a Million" in 1983. Surprisingly, their drummer Jimmy Marinos left after their success; the band recorded one more album in 1985 before breaking up.

In the early '90s, "What I Like About You" began appearing in TV commercials, leading the band to reunite. They have recorded one EP and have toured several times since re-forming. —*Stephen Thomas Erlewine*

The Romantics / Feb. 1980 / Epic ✦✦✦✦
The cover, featuring the four members decked out in identical red leather outfits with the de rigueur skinny ties, leaves no doubt as to the album's content. This is your basic artifact of the era—lusty, girl-crazed, teen anthems sung to hard-driving, punchy power-pop. "What I Like About You" was the hit, but any of these songs could have been hits. It's easy to dismiss this band, but few albums provide this much guilty pleasure. —*Chris Woodstra*

National Breakout / Dec. 1980 / Epic ✦✦✦
Their sophomore effort follows much of the same formula of the debut. Unfortunately, none of the songs had the instantly endearing catchiness of "What I Like About You" and the album failed to live up to the optimistic title's promise. —*Chris Woodstra*

Strictly Personal / Oct. 1981 / Epic ✦✦✦
Strictly Personal, the Romantics' commercial breakthrough, loses much of the innocence (and fun) of the first two albums, with its slicker production. "Talking in Your Sleep" and "One in a Million" both broke the Top Ten, but the album offers little else. —*Chris Woodstra*

Rhythm Romance / 1985 / Nemperor ✦✦

● **What I Like About You (& Other Romantic Hits)** / 1990 / Nemperor ✦✦✦✦
The title track was their finest hour, but there are a couple of other hits here too. —*Dan Heilman*

Romeo Void

New Wave
A post-punk quintet formed in San Francisco in 1979, consisting of singer Debora Iyall (b. 1956), bassist Frank Zincavage, guitarist Peter Woods, drummer Jay Derrah (replaced by John Stench and then Larry Carter), and saxophone player Ben Bossi. They released several albums on 415 Records (distributed by CBS) from 1981 to 1984. Iyall then left for a solo career. —*William Ruhlmann*

It's a Condition / Mar. 1981 / 415 ✦✦✦

Benefactor / 1982 / Columbia ✦✦✦

Instincts / 1984 / Columbia ✦✦✦

● **Warm, in Your Coat** / May 2, 1992 / Columbia/Legacy ✦✦✦✦

The Ronettes

Girl Group
Before Phil Spector took them under his wing in the early '60s, the Ronettes had already recorded several singles and were regionally successful. But the Spector-produced records are what everyone remembers and for a good reason—they featured some of his biggest, best productions along with equally impressive songs. Beneath his monumental wall of sound, lead vocalist Ronnie Bennett, who would later marry Spector, sang songs of teenage love in a plain, girlish voice; "Be My Baby," the group's first and biggest hit, was the pinnacle of the group's talent, as well as being one of the producer's finest moments. None of their following singles (including "Baby, I Love You," "(The Best Part of)

Breaking Up," and "Walking in the Rain") were quite as successful commercially, although they were nearly as strong artistically. While Spector was inactive in the mid-'60s, the Ronettes were also inactive; together they re-emerged in 1969, to a small commercial reception. After Ronnie divorced Spector in 1973, she formed a new version of the Ronettes that lasted for three years; after the group disbanded, she launched a solo career. —*Stephen Thomas Erlewine*

The Ronettes: The Early Years / 1965 / Rhino ✦✦✦✦
The early Ronettes songs weren't as immaculately produced or as evocative as Phil Spector's productions. Their sound was more generic and resembled other girl groups like the Shirelles or Chiffons. They recorded for Colpix and Dimension during 1961 and 1962, with Ronnie Bennett doing most of the leads, while her sister Estelle and cousin Nedra added soothing harmonies and backgrounds. At times, as on "My Guiding Angel" or "You Bet I Would," they came close to the appealing mix of innocence and earnestness that characterized their later (and greatest) tracks. But despite getting material from such songwriters as Jackie DeShannon and Carole King, many of these cuts were more serviceable than classic. Still, this is the foundation for the sound that exploded in the mid-'60s. —*Ron Wynn*

★ **The Best of the Ronettes** / 1992 / ABKCO ✦✦✦✦✦
For a couple of years, the Ronettes made music that was as moving and unforgettable as any made during the rock era. Their voices merged sensuality, longing, anguish, and sentimentality, with Ronnie Spector's angelic leads framed by Phil Spector's sweeping production, the lyrics of Ellie Greenwich, Jeff Barry, Barry Mann, Cynthia Weil, Spector, and others. While such songs as "Walking in the Rain," "Be My Baby," "Baby, I Love You," and "(The Best Part of) Breaking Up" may seem hopelessly naive and possibly sexist in today's cynical world, they're still classic love poems. Ronnie Spector's voice retains its allure and appeal, and the 18 tracks on this CD will never become dated. —*Ron Wynn*

Linda Ronstadt

b. Jul. 15, 1946, Tucson, AZ
Vocals / Country-Rock, Adult Contemporary, Pop, Soft Rock, Folk-Rock, Pop-Rock
With roots in the Los Angeles country and folk-rock scenes, Linda Ronstadt became one of the most popular interpretive singers of the '70s, earning a string of platinum-selling albums and Top 40 singles. Throughout the '70s, her laidback pop never lost sight of her folky roots, yet as she moved into the '80s, she began to change her sound with the times, adding new wave influences. After a brief flirtation with pre-rock pop, Ronstadt settled into a pattern of adult contemporary pop and Latin albums, sustaining her popularity in both fields.

While Ronstadt was a student at Arizona State University, she met guitarist Bob Kimmel. The duo moved to Los Angeles, where guitarist/songwriter Kenny Edwards joined the pair. Calling themselves the Stone Poneys, the group became a leading attraction on California's folk circuit, recording their first album in 1967. The band's second album, *Evergreen, Vol. 2*, featured the Top 20 hit "Different Drum." After recording one more album with the group, Ronstadt left for a solo career at the end of 1968.

Ronstadt's first two solo albums—*Hand Sown Home Grown* (1969) and *Silk Purse* (1970)—accentuated her country roots, featuring several honky tonk numbers. Released in 1971, her self-titled third album was a pivotal record in her career. Featuring a group of session musicians that would later form the Eagles, the album was a softer, more laidback variation of the country-rock she had been recording. With the inclusion of songs from singer-songwriters like Jackson Browne, Neil Young, and Eric Anderson, *Linda Ronstadt* had folk-rock connections as well. *Don't Cry Now*, released in 1973, followed the same formula to greater success, yet it was 1974's *Heart Like a Wheel* that perfected the sound, making Ronstadt a star. Featuring the hit covers "You're No Good," "When Will I Be Loved," and "It Doesn't Matter Anymore," *Heart Like a Wheel* reached No. 1 and sold over two million copies.

Released in the fall of 1975, *Prisoner in Disguise* followed the same pattern as *Heart Like a Wheel* and was nearly as successful. *Hasten Down the Wind*, released in 1976, suggested a holding pattern, even if it charted higher than *Prisoner in Disguise*. *Simple Dreams* (1977) expanded the formula by adding a more rock-oriented supporting band. The record became the singer's biggest hit, staying on the top of the charts for five weeks and selling over three million copies. With *Living in the USA* (1978) Ronstadt began experimenting with new wave, recording Elvis Costello's "Alison"; the album was another No. 1 hit. On 1980's *Mad Love*, she made a full-fledged new wave record, recording three Costello songs and adopting a synth-laden sound. While the album was a commercial success, it signalled that her patented formula was beginning to run out of steam. That suspicion was confirmed with 1982's *Get Closer*, her first album since *Heart Like a Wheel* to fail to go platinum.

Sensing it was time to change direction, Ronstadt starred in the Broadway production of Gilbert and Sullivan's *Pirates of Penzance*, as well as the accompanying movie. *Pirates of Penzance* led the singer to a collaboration with Nelson Riddle, who arranged and conducted her 1983 collection of pop standards, *What's New.* While it received lukewarm reviews, it was a considerable hit, reaching No. 3 on the charts and selling over two million copies. Ronstadt's next two albums—*Lush Life* (1984) and *For Sentimental Reasons* (1986)—were also albums of pre-rock standards recorded with Riddle.

At the end of 1986, Ronstadt returned to contemporary pop, recording "Somewhere Out There," the theme to the animated *An American Tail,* with James Ingram; the single became a No. 2 hit. She also returned to her country roots in 1987, recording the *Trio* album with Dolly Parton and Emmylou Harris. That same year, Ronstadt recorded *Canciones de mi Padre,* a set of traditional Mexican songs that became a surprise hit. Two years later, she recorded *Cry like a Rainstorm—Howl Like the Wind,* her first pop album since 1982's *Get Closer.* Featuring four duets with Aaron Neville, including the No. 2 hit "Don't Know Much," the album sold over two million copies. Ronstadt returned to traditional Mexican and Spanish material with *Mas Canciones* (1991) and *Frenesi* (1992). She returned to pop with 1994's *Winter Light,* which failed to generate a hit single, as did 1995's *Feels Like Home.* —*Stephen Thomas Erlewine*

Hand Sown Home Grown / 1969 / Capitol ✦✦

Silk Purse / 1970 / Capitol ✦✦✦
While it followed the same musical approach of the debut, *Silk Purse* was an improvement on *Hand Sown Home Grown,* featuring more confident vocals from Linda Ronstadt and a stronger selection of songs, including "Lovesick Blues" and "Long Long Time." —*Stephen Thomas Erlewine*

Linda Ronstadt / 1971 / Capitol ✦✦✦
Linda Ronstadt's self-titled third album captured the singer moving away from the rootsier charms of her first two albums, toward a more polished take on country-rock. Supported by the Eagles throughout the record, Ronstadt turns in a strong performance, aided by a fine selection of material, including "Rock Me on the Water," "Crazy Arms," "I Still Miss Someone," and "I Fall to Pieces." —*Stephen Thomas Erlewine*

Don't Cry Now / 1973 / Asylum ✦✦✦

Different Drum / 1974 / Capitol ✦✦✦✦
Different Drum collects the highlights of Linda Ronstadt's first three solo albums, adding five Stone Poneys tracks, including the hit "Different Drum," for good measure. It misses some fine tracks from her solo records, but the album remains a fine introduction to her early years. —*Stephen Thomas Erlewine*

☆ **Heart Like a Wheel** / 1974 / Capitol ✦✦✦✦✦
Ronstadt's breakthrough album, and her most perfectly realized. Solid from top to bottom, featuring the title track, "When Will I Be Loved?," "Desperado," and "You're No Good." Essential. —*Cub Koda*

Prisoner in Disguise / 1975 / Asylum ✦✦✦✦
Linda Ronstadt followed the commercial and critical breakthrough success of *Heart Like a Wheel* with *Prisoner in Disguise,* a record that essentially repeated the formula of its predecessor. While it lacked the consistency of *Heart Like a Wheel,* it was thoroughly enjoyable, highlighted by sturdy remakes of the Motown classics "Tracks of My Tears" and "Heat Wave." —*Stephen Thomas Erlewine*

● **Greatest Hits, Vol. 1** / 1976 / Asylum ✦✦✦✦
A concise collection of her chart successes. —*Dan Heilman*

Hasten Down the Wind / 1976 / Asylum ✦✦✦

Simple Dreams / 1977 / Asylum ✦✦✦✦
Featuring a broader array of styles than any previous Linda Ronstadt record, *Simple Dreams* reconfirms her substantial talents as an interpretive singer. Ronstadt sings Dolly Parton ("I Never Will Marry") with the same conviction as the Rolling Stones ("Tumbling Dice"), and she manages to update Roy Orbison ("Blue Bayou") and direct attention to the caustic, fledgling singer-songwriter Warren Zevon ("Poor Poor Pitiful Me" and "Carmelita"). The consistently adventurous material and Ronstadt's powerful performance makes the record rival *Heart Like a Wheel* in sheer overall quality. —*Stephen Thomas Erlewine*

Living in the U.S.A. / 1978 / Asylum ✦✦✦

Greatest Hits, Vol. 2 / 1980 / Asylum ✦✦✦✦
Next dozen hits, more formulaic, but bigger on the charts. —*Cub Koda*

Mad Love / 1980 / Asylum ✦✦

Get Closer / 1982 / Asylum ✦✦

What's New / 1983 / Asylum ✦✦✦

Canciones de Mi Padre / 1987 / Asylum ✦✦✦

Cry Like a Rainstorm—Howl Like the Wind / 1989 / Asylum ✦✦✦

Diana Ross (Diane Earle)

b. Mar. 26, 1944, Detroit, MI
Vocals / Soul, Disco, Urban, Pop-Rock, Club-Dance
As a solo artist, Diana Ross is one of the most successful female singers

of the rock era. If you factor in her work as the lead singer of the Supremes in the 1960s, she may be *the* most successful. With her friends Mary Wilson, Florence Ballard, and Barbara Martin, Ross formed The Primettes vocal quartet in 1959. In 1960, they were signed to local Motown Records, changing their name to the Supremes in 1961. Martin then left, and the group continued as a trio. Over the next eight years, The Supremes (renamed "Diana Ross and the Supremes" in 1967, when Cindy Birdsong replaced Ballard) scored 12 No. 1 pop hits. After the last one, "Someday We'll Be Together" (Oct. 1969), Ross launched a solo career.

Motown initially paired her with writer/producers Nickolas Ashford and Valerie Simpson, who gave her four Top 40 pop hits, including the No. 1 "Ain't No Mountain High Enough" (Jul. 1970).

Ross branched out into acting, starring in a film biography of Billie Holiday, *Lady Sings the Blues* (Nov. 1972). The soundtrack went to No. 1, and Ross was nominated for an Academy Award.

She returned to record-making with the Top Ten album *Touch Me in the Morning* (Jun. 1973) and its chart-topping title song. This was followed by a duet album with Marvin Gaye, *Diana & Marvin* (Oct. 1973), that produced three chart hits. Ross acted in her second movie, *Mahogany* (Oct. 1975), and it brought her another chart-topping single in the theme song, "Do You Know Where You're Going To." That and her next No. 1, the disco-oriented "Love Hangover" (Mar. 1976), were featured on her second album to be titled simply *Diana Ross* (Feb. 1976), which rose into the Top Ten.

Ross' third film role came in *The Wiz* (Oct. 1978). *The Boss* (May 1979) was a gold-selling album, followed by the platinum-selling *Diana* (May 1980) (the second of her solo albums with that name, though the other, a 1971 TV soundtrack, had an exclamation mark). It featured the No. 1 single "Upside Down" and the Top Ten hit "I'm Coming Out."

Ross scored a third Top Ten hit in 1980 singing the title theme from the movie *It's My Turn.* She then scored the biggest hit of her career with another movie theme, duetting with Lionel Richie on "Endless Love" (Jun.e 1981). It was her last big hit on Motown; after more than 20 years, she decamped for RCA. She was rewarded immediately with a million-selling album, titled after her remake of the old Frankie Lymon And The Teenagers hit, "Why Do Fools Fall in Love," which became her next Top Ten hit. The album also included the Top Ten hit "Mirror, Mirror."

Silk Electric (Oct. 1982) was a gold-seller, featuring the Top Ten hit "Muscles," written and produced by Michael Jackson, and *Swept Away* (Sep. 1984) was another successful album, containing the hit "Missing You," but Ross had trouble selling records in the second half of the 1980s. By 1989, she had returned to Motown, and by 1993 was turning more to pop standards, notably on the concert album *Diana Ross Live: The Lady Sings . . . Jazz & Blues, Stolen Moments* (Apr. 1993). Motown released a four-CD/cassette boxed set retrospecive, *Forever Diana* (Oct. 1993), and the singer published her autobiography in 1994. —*William Ruhlmann*

Diana Ross / May 1970 / Motown ✦✦✦✦
This remains arguably her finest solo work at Motown and perhaps her best ever; it was certainly among her most stunning. Everyone who doubted whether Diana Ross could sustain a career outside the Supremes found out immediately that she would be a star. The single "Reach Out and Touch (Somebody's Hand)" remains a staple in her shows, and is still her finest message track. —*Ron Wynn*

Lady Sings the Blues / Dec. 1971 / Motown ✦✦✦

Diana / May 1980 / Motown ✦✦✦

★ **Anthology** / Sep. 28, 1995 / Motown ✦✦✦✦✦
The double-disc set *Anthology* contains all of Diana Ross' solo hits for Motown Records, from "Ain't No Mountain High Enough" to "Endless Love." It's a comprehensive collection, featuring all of her biggest hits plus many important album tracks and smaller hit singles. Since it doesn't delve too deeply into obscurities and contains all of Ross' most popular songs, *Anthology* is the definitive career compilation for fans who want more than just the standard cuts but are unwilling to explore the original albums or invest in the box set. —*Stephen Thomas Erlewine*

David Lee Roth

b. Oct. 10, 1955, Bloomington, IN
Vocals / Hard Rock, Pop-Rock, Heavy Metal
With Van Halen, vocalist David Lee Roth raised the role of a heavy metal frontman to a performance art. After the band's commercial breakthrough with the *1984* album, Roth released *Crazy from the Heat,* a 1985 EP that displayed his blatant pop roots, covering everything from the Beach Boys to Louis Prima. With two hit singles, *Crazy from the Heat* confirmed Roth's solo commercial potential, prompting his decision to leave Van Halen in June of 1985.

For his first full-length album, 1986's *Eat 'em & Smile,* Roth hired guitarist Steve Vai and bassist Billy Sheehan for a grossly exaggerated take on heavy arena rock. It was a mammoth hit, as was the more pop-oriented follow-up, *Skyscraper.* After *Skyscraper,* Vai and Sheehan left to form their own bands (the Steve Vai Band and Mr. Big, respectively).

Roth put together a new band for 1991's *A Little Ain't Enough,* which was his first album not to go platinum. Sensing that it was time for a change, he tried to refashion himself as a slick hard-rock singer-songwriter with 1994's *Your Filthy Little Mouth,* but it resulted in his least successful album yet. — *Stephen Thomas Erlewine*

Crazy from the Heat / 1985 / Warner Bros. ✦✦✦✦
For his first solo effort, Roth stripped away the gonzo guitars that are Van Halen's trademark and accentuated his lounge-lizard-as-rock-star persona, resulting in an EP that succeeds because of that persona, not because the music is anything special. Certainly, he doesn't add anything to "California Girls" and "Just a Gigolo/I Ain't Got Nobody" other than his joking, over-the-top vocals. Then again, that's all he needs to do. — *Stephen Thomas Erlewine*

● **Eat 'em & Smile** / 1986 / Warner Bros. ✦✦✦✦
This flamboyant frontman is flanked by bassist Billy Sheehan and guitar-shredder Steve Vai, blazing the solo trail with these big and bawdy rockers, like "Goin' Crazy!" — *Donna DiChario*

Skyscraper / 1988 / Warner Bros. ✦✦✦

A Little Ain't Enough / Apr. 1991 / Warner Bros. ✦✦

Your Filthy Little Mouth / Mar. 8, 1994 / Warner Bros. ✦✦

Roxette

Pop-Rock
It's tempting to write Roxette off as nothing more than a shallow pop-rock band, but their shameless hooks are precisely what makes them so enjoyable. Roxette has a knack for writing extremely catchy and simple hooks and melodies that are sweet but not saccharine; it's radio-friendly pop, but the hooks don't wear thin with repeated plays. The duo of guitarist Per Gessle and vocalist Marie Fredriksson released an album in 1986 that didn't display much of their talents, but the infectious follow-up, 1988's *Look Sharp!* brought them to the top of the charts in America and England; 1991's *Joyride* was almost equally successful. After a couple of years off, Roxette returned with a new album in 1994. — *Stephen Thomas Erlewine*

Look Sharp! / 1988 / EMI America ✦✦✦✦
A fun, dynamic debut, it features the hit singles "The Look," "Dressed for Success," "Listen to Your Heart," and "Dangerous." — *Dan Heilman*

Joyride / 1991 / EMI America ✦✦✦

Tourism (Songs from Studios, Stages, Hotelrooms & Other Strange Places) / 1992 / EMI America ✦✦✦

Crash! Boom! Bang! / 1994 / EMI America ✦✦

● **Don't Bore Us . . . Get to the Chorus: Greatest Hits Vol. 1** / Nov. 1995 / EMI ✦✦✦✦
Roxette provided artificial pop thrills of the highest order, crafting a series of international hit singles that were as sweet as sugar and nearly as synthetic as plastic. However, that synthetic element is what made their hits so infectious—they were carefully crafted, as if by a machine, filled with catchy hooks and memorable melodies. As *Don't Bore Us . . . Get to the Chorus* proves, they didn't turn out winning singles at a rapid clip—there's a fair amount of dreck here—but when they were on, they produced some first-rate pop singles, particularly "The Look" and "Joyride." — *Stephen Thomas Erlewine*

Roxy Music

Art-Rock/Progressive-Rock, Glam Rock, Pop-Rock, Proto-Punk
Roxy Music scored enormous success in its native England in the '70s, first as a leader of the glam-rock movement and later for its sophisticated sound. The group was formed in London in 1971 around lead singer Bryan Ferry (b. Sep. 26, 1945). Personnel came and went until the group solidified by the time of its 1972 debut album with a lineup of Ferry, reed player Andy Mackay (b. Jul. 23, 1946), guitarist Phil Manzanera (b. Jan. 31, 1951), keyboardist Brian Eno (b. May 15, 1948), and drummer Paul Thompson (b. May 13, 1951). The band's original bassist, Graham Simpson, left during the album sessions and was replaced initially by Rik Kenton, though the group employed a series of bassists throughout its career.
   Roxy Music was a Top Ten UK hit in the summer of 1972, spinning off the Top Ten single, "Virginia Plain." *For Your Pleasure* (1973) did even better, getting to No. 4. Eno had left the band by the time it made its third album, *Stranded* (going on to an extensive career as a solo artist and record producer), and was replaced by Eddie Jobson (b. Apr. 28, 1955), who played violin and keyboards. *Stranded* was another UK hit, going to No. 1, and it was followed by *Country Life,* Roxy Music's first album to sell in even modest numbers in the US *Siren* (1975) contained the American Top 30 hit "Love Is the Drug" (No. 2 in the UK).
   At the point of American commercial breakthrough, however, Roxy Music disbanded, with Ferry, Mackay, Manzanera, and Jobson going off to solo careers. The group re-formed in 1978, minus Jobson, and recorded *Manifesto* (1979), after which Thompson left. The remaining trio released *Flesh and Blood* and *Avalon* (the latter was Roxy's only US gold album),

albums made in a smooth, melodic art-rock style before the group folded again in 1983. — *William Ruhlmann*

Roxy Music / 1972 / Reprise ✦✦✦

☆ **For Your Pleasure** / 1973 / Reprise ✦✦✦✦✦
For Your Pleasure, Roxy's schizophrenic second album, vacillates between campy rockers like "Do the Strand" and "Editions of You" (both UK hits) and creepy mood pieces like "In Every Dream Home a Heartache" (an ode to an inflatable sex doll) and the title cut, which showcases lead singer Bryan Ferry's ghoulish croon over an instrumental track that would work well on "Twin Peaks." — *Rick Clark*

Stranded / 1973 / Reprise ✦✦✦✦
On *Stranded,* their first album without sound-manipulator Brian Eno, Roxy affected a more sophisticated, self-absorbed stance with elegant numbers like "A Song for Europe" and "Psalm." Roxy's penchant for fine oddball pop-rockers continued with "Street Life" (a No. 9 UK hit), "Amazona," and the soaring "Serenade." — *Rick Clark*

★ **Country Life** / 1974 / Reprise ✦✦✦✦✦
Arguably their best album, *Country Life's* everything-and-the-kitchen-sink art-rock production and steely dissonance reached a pinnacle with tracks like the "The Thrill of It All," "All I Want Is You," and "Casanova." "Out of the Blue," one of their finest songs, showcased Eddie Jobson on a powerfully phase-shifted violin solo. The beautifully unsettling "Bitter-Sweet" reflected Bryan Ferry's flirtation with Germanic melodicism and fascist imagery. — *Rick Clark*

☆ **Siren** / 1975 / Reprise ✦✦✦✦✦
Siren provided Roxy Music with their first international hit, the coolly funky "Love Is the Drug" (No. 30). Except for "Sentimental Fool," "Both Ends Burning," and "Whirlwind," most of this album fails to deliver the power or memorable melodies of either *Country Life* or *Stranded.* — *Rick Clark*

Manifesto / 1979 / Reprise ✦✦✦
After a four-year layoff, Roxy shed their aggressively dense rock sound and returned with a more streamlined (but still weird) danceable pop. Detractors claimed that the band had lost their edge, but *Manifesto* introduced Roxy Music to a new audience looking for a sophisticated alternative to generic late-'70s disco. Highlights include "Angel Eyes," "Dance Away," and the title cut. — *Rick Clark*

Flesh + Blood / 1980 / Reprise ✦✦
Flesh + Blood finds Roxy making a further transition away from dissonant arrangements. The sleepwalking delivery of "In the Midnight Hour" is oddly fascinating, as is the discoish streamlining of the Byrds' classic "Eight Miles High." Nevertheless, many of the originals lack any memorable qualities. — *Rick Clark*

☆ **Avalon** / 1982 / Reprise ✦✦✦✦✦
From the beautifully longing romanticism of Bryan Ferry's melodies to the dreamy soundscapes rendered by Rhett Davies, Roxy Music, and Bob Clearmountain, *Avalon* is fashion-plate cool, yet somehow exudes a weird, intoxicating kind of detached soulfulness that makes this one of the most elegant-sounding releases ever committed to disc. — *Rick Clark*

Atlantic Years (1973-1980) / 1983 / Atco ✦✦✦✦
Atlantic Years (1973-1980) provides the cream of *Flesh + Blood* and *Manifesto* (as well as a couple of key tracks from Roxy's earlier work on Reprise). Overall it lacks the substance of their original 1977 Atco *Greatest Hits* package, which was an essential showcase for their earlier work. — *Rick Clark*

Street Life: 20 Greatest Hits / 1986 / Reprise ✦✦✦✦
This compilation is a more general (not entirely satisfactory) overview of Roxy tracks and Bryan Ferry's urbane dance-pop hits. — *Rick Clark*

Thrill of It All / 1995 / ✦✦✦✦
Album-rock artists like Roxy Music always make a difficult subject for comprehensive, multi-disc box sets. Frequently, their albums were designed as a cohesive whole and the idea of individual singles never really entered the picture at all. Roxy Music was slightly different than the average art/prog-rock band—not only did they make albums, they also made singles. And that is one of the reasons why the four-disc set *The Thrill of It All* is successful. Roxy's songs stand as individual works, and they make sense outside of their original sense, even if they make more sense *within* their original context. Thankfully, the majority of each of their major albums are reproduced on the first three discs of this collection, leaving the fourth disc for non-LP singles, remixes, and B-sides. Most of this material has not been available on CD before, making *The Thril of it All* essential for collectors. Nevertheless, it's a helpful guide to Roxy's career for casual fans—it contains all of the essential songs and shows why the group was one of the seminal bands of the '70s. — *Stephen Thomas Erlewine*

The Rubinoos

New Wave, Power-Pop
For a brief moment, San Francisco's the Rubinoos seemed to be the last

hope for pure pop music, carrying on the tradition of the Raspberries. The band was formed in 1973 by teenage friends Jon Rubin (vocals, guitar) and Tommy Dunbar (guitar, keyboards, vocals) along with Royse Adler (bass) and Donn Spindt (drums) but it wasn't until 1977 that they made their recording debut for Beserkley Records. The single, a cover of Tommy James' "I Think We're Alone Now," made an appearance in the lower reaches of the US charts, giving the indie label their first hit. The same year, their self-titled debut LP received rave reviews all around but failed commercially. *Back to the Drawing Board (1979)*, another solid collection of bouncy pop songs, again went ignored despite its classic single "I Wanna Be Your Boyfriend." The band effectively broke up the following year. Rubin and Dunbar returned in 1983, using the band name one more time for the Todd Rundgren-produced *Party of Two* EP. "If I Had You Back" from the EP saw some airplay on MTV but it failed to ignite enough interest for the band to go on. They reunited in the late '80s, and have since issued collections of lost recordings from the early '80s though new recordings have yet to be released. *—Chris Woodstra*

● **The Rubinoos** / 1977 / Beserkley ✦✦✦✦
This little gem is a celebration of pop music. There's no other way to describe this record. Catchy tunes with a touch of tongue-in-cheek, mixed with exuberance and joy make this record as much fun as when it was first released. *—Jim Worbois*

Back to the Drawing Board / Jan. 1979 / Beserkley ✦✦✦
Overall, this is not quite as strong a record as the first one but still, not to be missed. There are some fine original tunes on this record and one quite interesting cover, "Hold Me," taken from *Three Faces of Eve. —Jim Worbois*

Party of Two / 1983 / Warner Bros. ✦✦
Basement Tapes: Studio Demos Circa 1980-1981 / 1994 / One Way ✦✦✦
Basement Tapes is a collection of studio demos from 1980 to 1981 for an album that never happened. And while it lacks the polish of production, the material stands up against their released output. The track-by-track comments by the band members are a nice touch. *—Chris Woodstra*

Garage Sale / 1994 / Big Deal ✦✦✦
A nice companion piece to One Way's *Basement Tapes, Garage Sale* collects previously unreleased demos, alternate takes, and other oddities ranging from their earliest recordings in 1973 (at age 15) through 1985—complete with track-by-track commentary. This provides an interesting look at a band with no shortage of great material. Essential for fans. *—Chris Woodstra*

Rufus & Chaka Khan

Soul, Funk
Rufus was one of the most commercially successful funk bands of the mid-'70s, primarily because lead vocalist Chaka Khan was a dynamic singer, capable of making even the band's pedestrian material seem interesting. Their self-titled debut album suffered from a lack of strong single material, but the follow-up featured Stevie Wonder's "Tell Me Something Good," which he wrote specifically for the band after hearing Khan sing; it became a No. 3 hit single. After that song, the hits kept coming until the end of the '70s. Chaka Khan began a solo career that eventually eclipsed Rufus' success in 1978, continuing to record with the band until 1983; the group fell apart shortly after her departure. *—Stephen Thomas Erlewine*

Rufusized / 1974 / MCA ✦✦✦✦
With the addition of guitarist/songwriter Tony Maiden, Rufus delivers one of their best albums. It features the hits "Once You Get Started" and "Please Pardon Me (You Remind Me of a Friend)." *—Rick Clark*

● **Rags to Rufus** / 1974 / MCA ✦✦✦✦
From the hard-funk opener of "You Got the Love" to the Stevie Wonder-penned "Tell Me Something Good," *Rags to Rufus* is a fine showcase for Chaka Khan's amazing vocals. *—Rick Clark*

Rufus Featuring Chaka Khan / 1975 / MCA ✦✦✦
Ask Rufus / 1977 / MCA ✦✦✦

Todd Rundgren

b. Jun. 22, 1948, Upper Darby, PA
Guitar, Keyboards, Vocals / Pop-Rock
Over the course of his lengthy career, Todd Rundgren (b. Jun. 22, 1948) has created some of popular music's finer moments, as well as some of its most frustrating. He has proved to be a master of great pop melodies (with influences from the Beatles to Philly Soul) and heartfelt lyrical sentiment, while also releasing albums of tedious prog-rock that only a diehard fan could care about. At times Rundgren's productions seemed to have existed independently of the music, rather than enhancing it; nevertheless, Rundgren is an influential Renaissance man in the history of rock. His first taste of success came with the psychedelic pop-rock group Nazz, in 1967. "Hello, It's Me" (No. 71/No. 66) charted twice, while the

heavily phased riff-rocker "Open My Eyes" became a signature tune of sorts. Rundgren left Nazz (future Cheap Trick guitarist Rick Nielsen was his replacement) and pursued a solo career with the 1970 debut *Runt. Something/Anything*, Rundgren's third album, was his finest showcase as a songwriter. It was during this time that Rundgren began making a name for himself as an innovative producer. Over the years he has worked on projects for Badfinger, New York Dolls, Foghat, Patti Smith, Cheap Trick, XTC, Meat Loaf, and others. In 1974 Rundgren formed Utopia, a quartet that helped fulfill his prog-rock tendencies. By the late '70s, Rundgren was actively exploring the medium of rock video, opening his own computer video studio in Woodstock, NY. He continues to produce various artists and to release solo albums that enjoy a solid cult success. *—Rick Clark*

Runt / Sep. 1970 / Bearsville ✦✦✦✦
Runt, Todd Rundgren's debut, might have been a little uneven, but its homemade production, spirited arrangements, and great tunes, like "We Gotta Get You a Woman" and "I'm in the Clique," made this one of the most appealing albums of his career. *—Rick Clark*

Runt: Ballad of Todd Rundgren / Jun. 1971 / Rhino ✦✦✦
Rundgren's sophomore release didn't contain the flashes of brilliance found on *Runt*, but "Be Nice to Me," "Parole," and "Remember Me" are standouts on this relatively low-key effort. *—Rick Clark*

★ **Something/Anything?** / Feb. 1972 / Bearsville ✦✦✦✦✦
From beginning to end, *Something/Anything?* is Rundgren's best album, featuring the hit singles "I Saw the Light," and "Hello, It's Me." There are also a load of gems like "It Wouldn't Have Made Any Difference," "Wolfman Jack," and "Couldn't I Just Tell You?," one of the finest power-pop tracks ever cut. Rundgren plays every instrument and sings all the parts on three-fourths of this self-produced release. Even though Rundgren had flashes of brilliance after *Something/Anything?*, he never came up with an album with performances and material as consistently satisfying. *—Rick Clark*

A Wizard a True Star / Mar. 1973 / Bearsville ✦✦✦✦
Rundgren's keen sense for writing tight pop songs is almost nowhere to be found on this over-the-top production job. That's not to say that *A Wizard a True Star* doesn't have its virtues. Rundgren's take on *Peter Pan's* "Never Never Land" is otherworldly, and his Philly-soul medley is quite fine. "International Feel" and "Just One Victory" are other standout tracks. *—Rick Clark*

Todd Rundgren's Utopia / Oct. 1974 / Bearsville ✦✦
Initiation / May 1975 / Bearsville ✦✦✦
Another Live / Oct. 1975 / Bearsville ✦✦
Faithful / Apr. 1976 / Bearsville ✦✦✦
RA / Feb. 1977 / Bearsville ✦✦✦
Back to the Bars / 1978 / Bearsville ✦✦✦
Hermit of Mink Hollow / Apr. 1978 / Bearsville ✦✦✦✦
By the release of this album, Rundgren had ditched the homemade charm of *Something/Anything?* for a warbly hard rock/pop sound. Tracks like "Determination," "Out of Control," "You Cried Wolf," and "Fade Away" best exemplify that approach. "Can We Still Be Friends?" became a No. 29 hit. *—Rick Clark*

Adventures in Utopia / Jan. 1980 / Bearsville ✦✦✦
Deface the Music / Oct. 1980 / Bearsville ✦✦✦
Healing / Feb. 1981 / Rhino ✦✦
Swing to the Right / Mar. 1982 / Bearsville ✦✦
The Ever Popular Tortured Artist Effect / Jan. 1983 / Rhino ✦✦✦✦
This album, one of Rundgren's best do-it-yourself efforts of the '80s, contains his No. 63 hit "Bang the Drum All Day" and a swell remake of the Small Faces' "Tin Soldier." *—Rick Clark*

A Cappella / Sep. 1985 / Rhino ✦✦
● **Anthology (1968-1985)** / 1989 / Rhino ✦✦✦✦
Anthology is a fairly comprehensive overview of Rundgren's entire career, starting with "Open My Eyes" by Nazz, and including "Something to Fall Back On," from Rundgren's 1985 solo album *A Cappella.* All of his radio hits are included, as well as many important album tracks. Nevertheless, there are several key tracks missing, like "Wolfman Jack," "International Feel/Never Never Land," and Nazz's "Forget All About It" and "Hang on Paul." Like all of Rundgren's reissues on Rhino, *Anthology* has been given a first-class remastering job. *—Rick Clark*

Nearly Human / May 1989 / Warner Bros. ✦✦✦
Second Wind / Jan. 1991 / Warner Bros. ✦✦
The Best of Todd Rundgren / 1994 / Rhino ✦✦✦✦

Rush

Hard Rock, Art-Rock/Progressive-Rock
Inspired by Cream, Led Zeppelin, and Jimi Hendrix, the Toronto, Canada,

power trio Rush formed in 1969, comprising guitarist Alex Lifeson (b. Aug. 27, 1953), bassist Geddy Lee (b. Jul. 29, 1953), and original drummer John Rutsey—later replaced by Neil Peart (b. Sep. 12, 1952). Their first few albums were rather pedestrian hard rock, but the addition of Peart in 1974 prodded the group into a more complicated, heavy art-rock mode: King Crimson and Yes meet Led Zeppelin.

"The Trees," metaphorically addressing the Quebec secessionist movement (off of 1978's No. 47 *Hemispheres*) became a controversial rock-radio hit. The 1980 album *Permanent Waves* (No. 4), containing two substantial AOR hits with "Freewill" and "Spirit of the Radio" (No. 51), marked the beginning of a golden period for the band, which peaked with the No. 3 follow-up *Moving Pictures*.

Rush briefly flirted with a more synthesized sound, sublimating the band's natural interplay. Fortunately, recent albums indicate Rush is back in top form with *Presto* and *Roll the Bones*. —*Rick Clark*

Rush / 1974 / Mercury ✦✦

Caress of Steel / 1975 / Mercury ✦✦

Fly by Night / 1975 / Mercury ✦✦

All the World's a Stage / 1976 / Mercury ✦✦✦

2112 / 1976 / Mercury ✦✦✦✦
This is Rush's first successful stab at a concept album. Like many of Rush's albums during the '70s, this one deals with a futuristic scenario where an individual triumphs over an impersonalized high-tech society. —*Rick Clark*

A Farewell to Kings / 1977 / Mercury ✦✦✦

Archives / 1978 / Mercury ✦✦✦

Hemispheres / 1978 / Mercury ✦✦✦

Permanent Waves / 1980 / Mercury ✦✦✦✦
The cumulative effect of endless tours and obvious growth with each studio effort, Rush hit it big with this effort, delivering with their best material to date. "Spirit of the Radio," "Freewill," and "Entre Nous" were big FM rock hits. "Jacob's Ladder" was another highlight. —*Rick Clark*

★ **Moving Pictures** / 1981 / Mercury ✦✦✦✦✦
On *Moving Pictures*, Rush's aggressive prog-rock hit a zenith, with challenging playing that never became formless or devoid of good melodic integrity. The trio's active ensemble work reached new levels of interplay. "Tom Sawyer," "Limelight," "Red Barchetta," and the instrumental "YYZ" are standouts. —*Rick Clark*

Exit Stage Left / 1981 / Mercury ✦✦✦✦
A good live collection, it's possibly the best of their three such releases. —*Rick Clark*

Signals / 1982 / Mercury ✦✦✦✦
This is the third in a trio of great albums. "Digital Man" and "Analog Kid" are powerful riff-rockers. "New World Man" was a No. 21 hit, and "Subdivisions" was an FM rock favorite. The soundstage lacks some of the ambience found on *Moving Pictures*, but the performances still pack quite a punch. —*Rick Clark*

Grace Under Pressure / 1984 / Mercury ✦✦

Power Windows / 1985 / Mercury ✦✦✦

Hold Your Fire / 1987 / Mercury ✦✦✦

A Show of Hands / Jan. 2, 1988 / Mercury ✦✦✦

Presto / 1989 / Atlantic ✦✦✦✦
Presto, Rush's 13th album of new studio material, and their first for Atlantic, showed this Canadian trio coming out from under a succession of bloodless-sounding techno-excursions (*Grace Under Pressure, Hold Your Fire*) and going for a much more open, accessible sound. From beginning to end, the arrangements reflect more straightahead rock playing than on any of their other albums. *Presto* contains some of Neil Peart's best lyrics, and along with *Moving Pictures*, smartly presents many of Rush's virtues in their best light. —*Rick Clark*

● **Chronicles** / 1991 / Mercury ✦✦✦✦
Anyone wanting an essential overview of this Canadian band's prog-rock work should start here. All of their FM rock hits and most of the important album tracks are here. —*Rick Clark*

Roll the Bones / 1991 / Atlantic ✦✦✦

Counterparts / 1993 / Atlantic ✦✦

Leon Russell

b. Apr. 2, 1941, Lawton, OK
Piano, Vocals / Singer-Songwriter, Pop-Rock
Leon Russell has had a widely varied career as an artist, a songwriter, a record-label owner, a producer, and an in-demand session sideman. As part of Phil Spector's "Wall of Sound" wrecking crew, Russell played on hits by the Crystals. He also played on Herb Alpert's *Taste of Honey* and the Byrds' *Mr. Tambourine Man* and played and arranged tracks for Gary Lewis & the Playboys. Russell also toured with Delaney & Bonnie

and briefly with Paul Revere & the Raiders when Revere was drafted. Russell organized Joe Cocker's Mad Dogs & Englishmen tour, which led him to tours with Bob Dylan, Eric Clapton, and the Rolling Stones, and a performance at George Harrison's Concert for Bangladesh.

In 1970 Russell formed Shelter Records with English record producer Denny Cordell. The label eventually released albums by Willis Alan Ramsey, Dwight Twilley, and Phoebe Snow, among others. In October 1971, the Carpenters had a huge hit with Russell's "Superstar." (Years later, another composition, "This Masquerade," became a career-making hit for George Benson.)

All of this visibility set the stage for Russell's lucrative solo career, which fused gospel, blues, country, rock, and light jazz behind his quirky warble of a voice. Russell had seven Top 40 albums, with 1972's *Carney* peaking at No. 2 for four weeks. "Tightrope" (No. 11), "Lady Blue" (No. 14), and a double-sided single remake of Hank Williams' "Roll in My Sweet Baby's Arms"/"I'm So Lonesome I Could Cry" (No. 78) are a few of Russell's hits. In 1992, he released a comeback effort, *Anything Can Happen*. —*Rick Clark*

Leon Russell / 1970 / Capitol ✦✦✦✦
Russell's self-titled debut features his strongest set of songs and performances, with tracks like "A Song for You," "Dixie Lullaby," "Shoot Out at the Plantation," and "Delta Lady," which became one of Joe Cocker's early signature songs. The CD includes a brief version of Dylan's "Masters of War." —*Rick Clark*

And the Shelter People / 1971 / DCC ✦✦✦✦
Released hot on the heels of his Mad Dogs & Englishmen tour with Joe Cocker, Russell released this spirited outing, which included covers of tunes by George Harrison ("Beware of Darkness") and Dylan ("It's a Hard Rain Gonna Fall," "It Takes a Lot to Laugh, It Takes a Train to Cry") and some fine originals: "Alcatraz," "Home Sweet Oklahoma," "Stranger in a Strange Land" (an FM hit), and the title cut. The CD includes three bonus versions of Dylan tunes. —*Rick Clark*

Asylum Choir II / 1971 / Capitol ✦✦

Carney / 1972 / Capitol ✦✦✦
Carney became Russell's highest charting album with the aid of the oddball No. 11 hit "Tight Rope." Also included is "This Masquerade," a song that later became an international hit for George Benson. "If the Shoe Fits" is a great putdown of pop-star sycophants. Other highlights include "Manhattan Island Serenade" and "Cajun Love Song." —*Rick Clark*

Hank Wilson's Back / 1973 / Capitol ✦✦✦

Leon Live / 1973 / DCC ✦✦✦

● **Best of Leon Russell** / 1976 / DCC ✦✦✦✦
This is a straightforward hits and key-album-tracks collection, including "Lady Blue," "Tightrope," "A Song for You," "This Masquerade," and "Stranger in a Strange Land," among others. —*Rick Clark*

Anything Can Happen / Sep. 1992 / Virgin ✦✦✦

Rutles

Pop-Rock
Originally broadcast on network TV in 1978, ex-Monty Python member Eric Idle's satire of the Beatles legend was one of the very few successful rock parodies; only Spinal Tap, perhaps, has outdone it. One of the key elements of this mock "rockumentary" was the brilliantly executed "soundtrack" by Python associates and ex-Bonzo Dog Band member Neil Innes (he also played the character loosely based upon John Lennon in the film itself). As an actual peer of the group in the '60s (the Bonzos even appeared in the *Magical Mystery Tour* film), Innes was well qualified to satirize the Fab Four phenomenon in song. With the exception of Idle, each of the four "Rutles" played their own instruments on the recording in addition to acting in the film. —*Richie Unterberger*

● **The Rutles** / 1978 / Rhino ✦✦✦✦
Neil Innes delivered catchy, harmony-laden tunes that deftly and lovingly parody every phase of the moptops' career, from their Hamburg/Cavern Club days through "Get Back" (here retitled "Get Up and Go"). In between are fully realized send-ups of "If I Fell," "I Want to Hold Your Hand," "Penny Lane," "Lucy in the Sky," "I Am the Walrus," "All You Need Is Love," and more. "Ouch!," their hilarious mockery of "Help!," is perhaps the album's highlight. The 1990 CD reissue adds six very worthwhile "bonus tracks" that were used in the special but were unavailable on the original 1978 Warner album, making for 20 cuts in all. —*Richie Unterberger*

Mitch Ryder (William Levise)

b. Feb. 26, 1945, Hamtrack, MI
Rock 'n' Roll
Mitch Ryder & the Detroit Wheels blended the Motown-soul sound with over-revved Midwestern rock 'n' roll. Mitch Ryder's (born William Levise) gutsy soul shouting and superhuman screams were some of the most electrifying sounds to charge AM radio in the mid-'60s, landing some-

where between the Rascals' Felix Cavaliere and Wilson Pickett. The Wheels sported two strong lead guitarists in Joe Cubert and Jim McCarty (later in Cactus and Detroit), and they were pushed along by one of the great unsung rock drummers of all time, John ("Johnny Bee") Badanjek.

It was producer Bob Crewe who signed the band to his New Voice label, releasing a string of high-octane raveups in "Jenny Take a Ride" (No. 10), "Little Latin Lupe Lu" (No. 17), "Devil with a Blue Dress On/Good Golly Miss Molly" (No. 4), "Sock It to Me Baby!" (No. 6), and "Too Many Fish in the Sea" (No. 24). In spite of all the hits and visibility, Mitch Ryder & the Detroit Wheels were victims of the era, making loads of money for Crewe and New Voice, but ending up broke. — *Rick Clark*

Take a Ride / 1966 / New Voice ✦✦✦✦
The debut album of Ryder & the Wheels, fresh from the teenage ballroom circuit in Detroit, where they held court in earlier days as Billy Lee & the Rivieras. One of the defining moments in the history of Motor City music, *Take a Ride* is the sound of poor White kids claiming the music as theirs, too, while infusing it with the manic energy of the color-blind dreams of anybody who ever wanted to be somebody. Built entirely around their stage act, this album captures a band in full cry at the peak of their powers. This is what they mean when they say the words "high-energy Motor City rock 'n' roll." — *Cub Koda*

Breakout . . . !!! / 1966 / New Voice ✦✦✦✦
Ryder & the Wheels' second album, featuring the classic "Devil with a Blue Dress On/Good Golly, Miss Molly" workout, continues the pattern of their debut; strong renditions of R&B classics, chopped and channeled and revved up to maximum torque. With the use of the original two-track master, the sound of it fairly sparkles. — *Cub Koda*

Sock It to Me / 1967 / New Voice ✦✦✦✦
Ryder's last album with the Detroit Wheels before going solo finds the material reverting to producer Bob Crewe's readymades, no match for the authentic R&B found on the first two albums, but still strutted out with typical Detroit-like flair. Three bonus tracks and the use of the original stereo masters makes this a must-have for serious Mitch Ryder collectors. — *Cub Koda*

● **Rev-Up; The Best of Mitch Ryder & the Detroit Wheels** / 1990 / Rhino ✦✦✦✦
Perhaps the most raucous White soul band of the '60s, Ryder & the Detroit Wheels scored a series of hits, 1966-1968, by souping up rock and R&B ravers to fever pitch. This is hard party music. — *William Ruhlmann*

Sade (Helen Folsade Adu)

Vocals / Urban, Adult Contemporary, Pop
Sade's smooth, silky jazz-tinged pop-oriented R&B earned several hits and a large following in the mid-'80s. Borrowing the spirit, if not the sophisticated sound, of her idols Billie Holiday and Nina Simone, her music was lush and stylish, helped considerably by her talented supporting band. After her 1988 album, *Stronger Than Pride*, Sade disappeared for several years, reappearing in 1992 with *Love Deluxe*, which returned her to the spotlight, selling over a million copies in the first few months after it was released. — *Stephen Thomas Erlewine*

● **Best of Sade** / 1994 / Epic ✦✦✦✦
It's easy to dismiss Sade as makeout music for Calvin Klein Obsession models, but the group created an impressive body of work over the course of a decade, a series of moody singles with cool jazz passion and the kick of good R&B. All the hits are here, of course, from "Smooth Operator" to "No Ordinary Love." — *Eddie Huffman*

Saint Etienne

Alternative Pop-Rock, Club-Dance
Formed by UK rock journalist Bob Stanley and Pete Wiggs in late 1988, Saint Etienne became one of the leading British dance-pop bands of the early '90s, combining elements of house, techno, pop, disco, and hip-hop in a melodic, hypnotically rhythmic music that not only was popular in dance clubs, but also had crossover appeal. Considering their detached, intellectual approach to pop, it's not surprising that the group has experienced its greatest success in Europe—particularly in England—and has only been a cult band in America. After a series of female singers, Sarah Cracknell became their permanent lead vocalist during the recording of their debut album, 1991's *Fox Base Alpha*. — *Stephen Thomas Erlewine*

Foxbase Alpha / Jan. 14, 1992 / Warner Bros. ✦✦✦✦

So Tough / 1993 / Warner Bros. ✦✦✦✦
British duo Bob Stanley and Pete Wiggs deserve recognition as the genius pop Svengalis of their generation. Eerie, dreamy, moody, hypnotic, all those clichéd terms don't disguise the fact that under the name Saint Etienne, they craft superb, digital aural candy on *So Tough*. While delicately applied Prophet, Roland, Moog, and Emax sampler synths comprise the duo's main stock in trade, their key weapon is Sarah Cracknell's waifish vocals. — *Roch Parisien*

Tiger Bay / 1994 / Warner Bros. ✦✦✦

● **Too Young to Die** / Nov. 1995 / Heavenly ✦✦✦✦
Although their albums were considerably more consistent than most dance-pop acts, Saint Etienne's high points were always their singles. Released prior to a quiet, lengthy hiatus, *Too Young to Die* collects all of their singles, from their debut disco cover of Neil Young's "Only Love Can Break Your Heart" to their last, "He's on the Phone," providing a thoroughly entertaining chronicle of the group's career. Much of the music sounds somewhat dated—which is always a problem with dance music—but Saint Etienne was essentially a very good Euro-pop band, revelling in kitsch and style in equal measure. At their best—"Only Love Can Break Your Heart," "You're in a Bad Way," "Join Our Club," "Who Do You Think You Are," among others—they found the heart in nightclubbing. The quality of the music dips slightly in the latter half of the album, but there is plenty prime pop throughout the disc. (Initial pressings came with a bonus disc of remixes, all of which are worthwhile for dedicated fans.) — *Stephen Thomas Erlewine*

Sam & Dave

Soul
Perhaps no act epitomized soul music as the secularization of gospel more than Sam & Dave. The original pairing of Sam Moore and Dave Prater met in Florida in 1961, and they recorded unsuccessfully for several years before being signed to Atlantic Records in 1965. Atlantic persuaded their Memphis affiliate Stax Records to produce them, and in December that year the writing and production team of Isaac Hayes and David Porter delivered the crisply soulful "You Don't Know Like I Know." Hayes and Porter became the "eminences grises" behind Sam & Dave, much as Holland-Dozier-Holland pulled the strings behind the Supremes. They wrote, they produced—and the result was a string of hits, including "Soul Man," "Hold on I'm Coming," and "I Thank You," songs that survive as the very epitome of Southern soul. Certainly, Sam & Dave's hits are among the most soulful ever to crack the Hot 100. Their albums often bore the hallmarks of hasty execution, though. The dissolution of the partnership between Stax and Atlantic virtually sealed the fate of Sam & Dave; there were a few more hits (and, later, a revival of interest thanks to the Blues Brothers), but the glory days were over.

Sam Moore's solo career was reinvigorated by his participation in the *Rhythm, Country & Blues* project in 1994. The CD, which paired country and R&B artists in various duets, teamed Moore with Conway Twitty in what turned out to be one of Twitty's last sessions. They did "Rainy Night in Georgia." Rhino issued *Sam & Dave: Sweat 'n' Soul*, a two-disc anthology of their greatest recordings, in 1993. — *Colin Escott*

☆ **Sweat 'n' Soul** / 1993 / Rhino/Atlantic ✦✦✦✦✦
Sam Moore and Dave Prater were the ultimate soul duo; one a high-voiced wailer, the other a low-toned blaster. They came together in the mid-'60s to form a superb duo, singing tunes penned by soul's finest writing tandem, Isaac Hayes and David Porter. They made a host of great singles before ego battles broke them apart. This 50-cut, two-disc anthology not only has every song of significance, but plenty of obscure worthwhile items, like a "Stay in School" promo, some overlooked material done with the Dixie Flyers, and a couple of numbers cut by Moore as a solo act in the early '70s. The sound quality, annotation, and song sequencing are as outstanding as the songs themselves. — *Ron Wynn*

★ **The Very Best of Sam & Dave** / 1995 / Rhino ✦✦✦✦✦
The Very Best of Sam & Dave contains all of Sam & Dave's Top 40 hits, including "You Don't Know Like I Know," "Hold On! I'm Comin,'" "Said I Wasn't Gonna Tell Nobody," "You Got Me Hummin'," "When Something Is Wrong with My Baby," "Soothe Me," "Soul Man," and "I Thank You," plus a handful of essential album tracks and B-sides like "I Can't Stand Up For Falling Down." It's an expertly compiled, concise collection that contains everything you need to know. If you need to dig deeper, the double-disc *Sweat 'n' Soul* is essential, but most casual fans will be completely satisfied by *The Very Best of Sam & Dave*. — *Stephen Thomas Erlewine*

Carlos Santana (Devadip Carlos Santana)

b. Jul. 20, 1947, Autlan de Navarro, Mexico
Guitar / Rock 'n' Roll, Blues, Rock, Fusion, Psychedelic
Santana is the name of a band that has successfully married elements of blues, rock, and Latin music and enjoyed international acclaim for more than two decades. It is also the name of the guitarist, Carlos Santana, who has led that band and made other recordings over the same period of time. In its original manifestation, the Santana Blues Band was a group of equals, with Carlos named as leader only because of a musicians-union requirement that such a designation be made. The group was formed in San Francisco in the mid-'60s and first gained recognition in the same dance halls that hosted the psychedelic rock groups of the era, although, with its Latin and African roots, Santana never quite fit in with the psychedelic sound. The group came under the direction of pro-

moter Bill Graham and had already scored a contract with Columbia when it appeared at the Woodstock Festival in August 1969. Personnel at that time, in addition to Carlos, included Gregg Rolie (vocals and keyboards), Dave Brown (bass), Mike Shrieve (drums), Armando Peraza (percussion and vocals), and Mike Carabello and Jose Areas (percussion).

Santana, the debut album, was a massive success, including the No. 4 hit "Evil Ways." *Abraxas* (1970) did even better, topping the charts for six weeks and featuring the hits "Black Magic Woman" and "Oye Como Va." For *Santana III* (1971), the group expanded to a septet with the addition of guitarist Neal Schon, though an additional six sidemen were listed in the album credits. This album was No. 1 for five weeks.

Guitarist Santana released a live duet album with drummer and vocalist Buddy Miles (later a member of Santana) in 1972; then came the fourth Santana Band album, *Caravanserai*, on which different musician credits were listed for each track, none of them including bassist Dave Brown or percussionist Mike Carabello. The album was a Top Ten hit. Carlos released another duet album in 1973 with guitarist John McLaughlin (the two shared a guru), followed by *Welcome*, credited to "The New Santana Band," its only remaining original members being Santana, Mike Shrieve, Armando Peraza, and Jose Areas (Rolie and Schon had decamped to found Journey).

In subsequent years, "Santana" for the most part referred to Carlos and a band of hired musicians playing in the established Santana style, while the leader also made occasional solo albums that varied the style somewhat. In 1992, Santana ended his long association with Columbia and signed to Polydor, which set up a custom label for him, calling for him to sign his own new acts. — *William Ruhlmann*

Santana / Aug. 1969 / Columbia ✦✦✦✦
A brilliant combination of rock with Latin and African influences, prominently featuring the organ playing and husky vocals of Gregg Rolie; the energetic, precise drumming of Mike Shrieve; and, especially, the soaring, immediately identifiable guitar sound of Carlos Santana. Justifiably a massive hit and the prototype for an assembly line of similar records. Contains "Evil Ways" and "Soul Sacrifice." — *William Ruhlmann*

☆ **Abraxas** / Sep. 1970 / Columbia ✦✦✦✦✦
Excellent continuation of the first album, with songwriting credits to four of the six band members, plus a terrific version of Tito Puentes's "Oye Como Va." The hit was a cover of the Fleetwood Mac song "Black Magic Woman." — *William Ruhlmann*

Santana III / Sep. 1971 / Columbia ✦✦✦✦
Completes a trilogy of tightly constructed, exciting band albums filled with percolating, multirhythmic percussion and fiery guitar work. The last album that is the work of the Woodstock-era Santana band. — *William Ruhlmann*

Carlos Santana & Buddy Miles! Live! / Jun. 1972 / Columbia ✦✦

Caravanserai / Oct. 1972 / Columbia ✦✦✦✦
On *Caravanserai*, individual personnel credits were included for each song, suggesting changes in the band's lineup. But perhaps more significant than the personnel shifts was the changed musical direction of the band. The album cover depicted a desert scene complete with camels, and the opening track was called "Eternal Caravan of Reincarnation," which should give some indication of the global and spiritual concerns addressed in the music. Tempos were slower, there were more instrumentals, and the overall sound had little of the fiery Latin-rock feel of previous Santana efforts. The result was an album with no hit singles and a fall-off in sales, although *Caravanserai* still made the Top Ten and sold a million copies. — *William Ruhlmann*

Love Devotion Surrender / 1973 / Columbia ✦✦✦

Welcome / Nov. 1973 / Columbia ✦✦✦
On the group's fifth album, "The New Santana Band," as it was called, was an octet. Musically, the album was something of a companion piece to Carlos Santana's duet album with John McLaughlin, *Love Devotion Surrender*, even including a song by that title and, like the earlier record, containing compositions by McLaughlin and John Coltrane. In addition to the jazz influences, there was also a new blues sound courtesy of Leon Thomas, a smooth-voiced singer in the Joe Williams tradition. The record was musically adventurous, but as Santana continued to diverge from its Latin-rock roots, its popularity eroded. — *William Ruhlmann*

Lotus / May 1974 / Columbia ✦✦✦✦
Recorded in Japan in July 1973, this massive live album, originally on three LPs and now on two compact discs, was available outside the US in 1974, but held back from domestic release until long into the CD age. It features the same "New Santana Band" that recorded *Welcome* and combines that group's jazz and spiritual influences with performances of earlier Latin-rock favorites like "Oye Como Va." — *William Ruhlmann*

● **Greatest Hits** / Jul. 1974 / Columbia ✦✦✦✦
This ten-song sampler presents the best of Santana, 1969-71, the period of its greatest popularity. The hits include "Black Magic Woman," "Evil Ways," "Everybody's Everything," and "Oye Como Va." But note that this is a bare minimum of prime Santana. Not only does the sampler choose

from only Santana's first three albums, but it leaves out such seminal numbers as "Nobody to Depend On" and "Soul Sacrifice." Those looking for a more extensive overview should consider *Viva Santana!* — *William Ruhlmann*

Illuminations / Sep. 1974 / Columbia ✦✦

Borboletta / Oct. 1974 / Columbia ✦✦✦
Borboletta was the first new Santana band studio album in 11 months and the group's sixth overall. Once again, individual credits were listed for each song. The main problem was that the band seemed to be coasting; Carlos turned in the usual complement of high-pitched lead guitar work, and the percussionists pounded away, but the Santana sound had long since taken over from any individual composition, and the records were starting to sound alike. That, in turn, started to make them inessential; *Borboletta* spent less time in the charts than any previous Santana album. — *William Ruhlmann*

Amigos / Mar. 1976 / Columbia ✦✦✦✦
By the release of *Amigos*, the Santana band's seventh album, only Carlos Santana and David Brown remained from the band that conquered Woodstock, and only Carlos had been in the band continuously since. Meanwhile, the group had made some effort to arrest its commercial slide, hiring an outside producer, David Rubinson, and taking a tighter, more uptempo, and more vocal approach to its music. The overt jazz influences were replaced by strains of R&B/funk and Mexican folk music. The result was an album more dynamic than any since *Santana III* in 1971. "Let It Shine" (No. 77), an R&B-tinged tune, became the group's first chart single in four years, and the album returned Santana to Top Ten status. — *William Ruhlmann*

Festival / Jan. 1977 / Columbia ✦✦✦

Moonflower / Oct. 1977 / Columbia ✦✦✦

Inner Secrets / Oct. 1978 / Columbia ✦✦

Oneness: Silver Dreams Golden Realities / Mar. 1979 / Columbia ✦✦✦

Marathon / Sep. 1979 / Columbia ✦✦

The Swing of Delight / Aug. 1980 / Columbia ✦✦

Zebop! / Apr. 1981 / Columbia ✦✦

Shango / Aug. 1982 / Columbia ✦✦

Havana Moon / Apr. 1983 / Columbia ✦✦✦

Beyond Appearances / Feb. 1985 / Columbia ✦✦

Freedom / Feb. 1987 / Columbia ✦✦✦

Blues for Salvador / Oct. 1987 / Columbia ✦✦✦✦
On previous "solo" albums, Carlos Santana had made noticeable stylistic changes and worked with jazz, pop, and even country musicians. On this, his fourth Carlos Santana release, the line between a "solo" and a "group" project is blurred; this record is really a catchall of Santana band outtakes and stray tracks. For example, included are an instrumental version of "Deeper, Dig Deeper" from *Freedom* and an alternate take of "Hannibal" from *Zebop!*, as well as "Now That You Know" from the group's 1985 tour. Given the variety of material, the album is somewhat less focused than most Santana band albums, but there are individual tracks that are impressive, notably "Trane," which features Tony Williams on drums. (*Blues for Salvador* won the Grammy Award for Best Rock Instrumental Performance.) — *William Ruhlmann*

Viva Santana! / Aug. 1988 / Columbia ✦✦✦✦
A lovingly assembled two-disc retrospective set that collects the best of the Santana band, along with many interesting rarities. — *William Ruhlmann*

Spirits Dancing in the Flesh / Jun. 1990 / Columbia ✦✦✦

Milagro / 1992 / Polydor ✦✦✦

Sacred Fire: Santana Live in South America / Oct. 19, 1993 / Polydor ✦✦

Dance of the Rainbow Serpent / 1995 / Columbia ✦✦✦

Joe Satriani

b. Jul. 15, 1957, Carle Place, NY
Guitar, Drums / Hard Rock, Fusion, Pop-Rock
Joe Satriani was one of the best, most influential rock guitarists of the late '80s, equally capable of fast flights of blinding technique as well as sweet, lyrical passages. What also separates Satriani from most technically gifted guitar virtuosos is that he treats a song as a song, not as an excuse to shred. For these reasons, he appeals not only to guitarists, but also to many rock fans who have never touched the instrument—his breakthrough 1987 album, *Surfing with the Alien*, was the first rock instrumental album in years to chart in the Top 30 on *Billboard's* Top 200 Albums. Since then, he has added vocals to his records; while his voice can't compare to his guitar, it added another dimension to an artist that was already more versatile than the majority of contemporary musi-

cians. Before Satriani became a recording star, he taught guitar in San Francisco; several of his students became famous, influential guitarists in their own right, before he even recorded his first album in 1988. Metallica's Kirk Hammett was the first of his students to hit the big time, followed by Steve Vai and Larry LaLonde of Primus. —*Stephen Thomas Erlewine*

Not of This Earth / 1986 / Combat ✦✦✦

● **Surfing with the Alien** / 1987 / Combat ✦✦✦✦
Hard-hitting, intense, and foot-to-the-floor guitar playing, it's all instrumental. —*Paul Kohler*

Flying in a Blue Dream / Feb. 1990 / Combat ✦✦✦

The Extremist / Jul. 1992 / Combat ✦✦✦

Time Machine / 1993 / Combat ✦✦✦✦
Satriani has proven to be one of the most technically gifted and influential guitarists of the '90s, and the two-disc *Time Machine* compiles his long out-of-print first EP with several live tracks, making it a good showcase for his considerable talents. —*Stephen Thomas Erlewine*

Joe Satriani / Oct. 1995 / Relativity ✦✦✦

Savage Rose

Art-Rock/Progressive-Rock
One of the most well-known rock groups from Continental Europe, Denmark's Savage Rose recorded a wealth of intriguing and eclectic progressive-rock in the late '60s and '70s. In their early work, one hears faint echoes of the Airplane, Doors, Pink Floyd, and other psychedelic heavyweights, combined with classical, jazz, and Danish-Euro folk elements. Their arrangements rely heavily on an incandescent, watery organ that sounds like nothing so much as psychedelic aquarium music. The most striking aspect of the band's sound, however, was the vocals of lead singer Annisette. Her childish, wispy, and sensual phrasing can suddenly break into jarring, almost histrionic wailing, like a Janis Joplin with Yoko Ono-isms, and eerily foreshadows Kate Bush's style.

Stars in their native land, Savage Rose also achieved a bit of underground success abroad, and several of their albums were released in North America. Between 1968 and 1978, the group released nine albums, moving from vaguely psychedelic rock and the heavily gospel-influenced *Refugee* to the nearly classical ballet score *Dodens Triumf* and the folky, nearly all-Danish *Solen Var Ogsa Din* (their first eight albums were sung entirely in English). Always a radical band—the Black Panthers even invited the group to play at a benefit for Bobby Seale after hearing one of Savage Rose's records—they took the extremely radical step of ending their professional and recording career around 1980 in order to use their music to support revolutionary causes. Although they actually continued to make music and perform, they were only heard at benefits and free concerts (actually playing in Lebanese hospitals, schools, and refugee camps at the PLO's invitation). They continue to perform to this day, and have actually been back in the studio to record in recent years. —*Richie Unterberger*

● **Savage Rose** / 1968 / Polydor ✦✦✦✦
Their debut is their lightest and most charming effort. Waltzing melodies give way to thunder-of-doom bass runs, and the storybookish lyrics have a forlorn, yearning quality. With its oddly hollow sound, one is never really sure whether the tone is supposed to be playful or ominous. —*Richie Unterberger*

In the Plain / 1969 / Polydor ✦✦✦
The band takes a more aggressive and soul-oriented approach on their second album, but the material isn't as strong, and much of the ethereal ambience that made their first LP special is lost. It does include the terrific, rollicking "Evening's Child," as well as the pre-doom and gloom workout "A Trial in Our Native Town." —*Richie Unterberger*

Travelin' / 1969 / Polydor ✦✦✦
More excursions into soul-rock territory dominate one of their less distinguished albums. Highlights include the more serene and melodic cuts ("Travelin'," "Sailing Away") and the shockingly titled (for 1969) "My Family Was Gay," with its rather straightforward hints of incest. —*Richie Unterberger*

Your Daily Gift / 1970 / Gregar ✦✦✦
Their most well-known album, singled out for praise by critic Greil Marcus in his anthology *Stranded*. About half of this is fairly undistinguished heavy progressive-psychedelic rock, but the other half ranks among their most fragile and best material—the group were always better when they waxed reflective than when they tried to rock out. The lengthy, bittersweet, melancholy title track (complete with weepy European sidewalk cafe accordion) is one of their finest moments. —*Richie Unterberger*

Refugee / 1971 / Gregar ✦✦✦
Their most gospel and soul-influenced recording. Recalls Janis Joplin's more generic solo recordings, albeit with a more subdued feel. —*Richie Unterberger*

Dodens Triumf / 1972 / Polydor ✦✦✦✦
An unheralded landmark in art-rock, this features Savage Rose keyboardist Thomas Koppel's score for a ballet by Flemming Flindt (the title translates to *Triumph of Death*). Nearly entirely instrumental (one song features Annisette on vocals), this is one of the finest classically influenced rock records. Moody and melancholy, at times almost doomy, yet always melodic, this 40-minute selection of haunting pieces prominently features the group's unique underwater organ sound, and makes for compelling listening. —*Richie Unterberger*

Babylon / 1972 / Polydor ✦✦✦
With contributions by noted jazz saxophonist Ben Webster and the American gospel quintet the Stars of Faith, this is their most R&B-influenced recording, at times achieving a churchy, old-time New Orleans-like feel. —*Richie Unterberger*

Wild Child / 1973 / Polydor ✦✦✦
One of their better efforts. The R&B influence retreats in favor of a tender, melodic approach emphasizing the organ, piano, and accordions on a strong set that favors their European folk influences. —*Richie Unterberger*

Sole Var Ogsa Din / 1978 / Sonet ✦✦✦
A welcome return to their lightest and wispiest styles, with clear, instrumental textures that are almost like sonic waterfalls. Their enigmatic, moody song structures and melodies remain, with the most histrionic edges of Annisette's vocals toned down. As all but two of the songs are in their native Danish, this can perhaps be considered their most personal effort as well. —*Richie Unterberger*

Boz Scaggs (William Royce Scaggs)

b. Jun. 8, 1944, Ohio
Guitar, Vocals / Soft Rock, Pop-Rock
Boz Scaggs got his start in 1959, playing with Steve Miller in the Dallas band, the Marksmen. It was Miller who taught Scaggs guitar. Scaggs and Miller eventually formed the Steve Miller Band, with Scaggs leaving after their classic second album, *Sailor*. *Rolling Stone* editor Jann Wenner helped Scaggs secure a solo artist deal with Atlantic. Scaggs' self-titled debut failed to sell in spite of critical praise and the presence of sidemen like Duane Allman on the album. A deal with Columbia in 1970 was more fruitful, with each of Scaggs' albums selling in increasing numbers. In 1976 Scaggs achieved stardom, thanks to the elegant urban pop of *Silk Degrees*. Over the next five years, he released a string of R&B-influenced pop hits. In recent years, Scaggs' output has been very sporadic, as he became a restaurant owner in San Francisco. —*Rick Clark*

Boz Scaggs / 1969 / Atlantic ✦✦✦✦
Produced by Jann Wenner and featuring crack accompaniment by the Muscle Shoals house band, Scaggs' solo debut is a near-masterwork, mingling the pathos and heartbreak of vintage honky tonk with the celebration and release of Southern soul. The highlights of the album also flaunt its diversity: "Loan Me a Dime," an extended blues dirge, which features some of Duane Allman's finest work, and "Waiting on a Train," Scaggs' marvelous revamping of Jimmie Rodgers' classic hobo song. —*John Floyd*

Moments / 1971 / Columbia ✦✦✦

My Time / 1972 / Columbia ✦✦✦✦
Scaggs' last rock 'n' roll gasp, the ballads that would become his trademark are already surfacing, but you need this one for "Full-Lock Power Slide" and "Dinah Flo," two scorching rockers that give this album the muscle it needs. —*John Floyd*

Silk Degrees / Feb. 1976 / Columbia ✦✦✦✦
Scaggs reached his commercial peak with this elegant collection of soulful urban pop, thanks to hits like the ultrasmooth disco of "Lowdown," the revved-up "Lido Shuffle," and "We're All Alone," Scaggs' finest ballad. —*Rick Clark*

● **Hits!** / Nov. 1980 / Columbia ✦✦✦✦
In spite of the inclusion of "Dinah Flo," *Hits!* primarily focuses on Scaggs' '80s pop hits like "Lowdown," "Jojo," "Break Down Dead Ahead" and "Look What You've Done to Me." —*Bil Carpenter*

Other Roads / 1988 / Columbia ✦✦

Some Change / Apr. 5, 1994 / Virgin ✦✦✦✦
This album has a nice organic feel to it that many of Scaggs' more commercially successful albums lacked. Scaggs plays a lot more guitar here, and his singing has a relaxed soulfulness. This is one of his very best albums. —*Rick Clark*

Scorpions

Heavy Metal
A German metal band formed in 1970 by Rudolf and Michael Schenker, the Scorpions also included vocalist Klaus Meine, bassist Lothar Heimberg, and drummer Wolfgang Dziony. The original lineup stayed intact for three years, until Michael quit in 1973 to join UFO. The band broke

up briefly and was re-formed at the end of the same year by Rudy Schenker with Meine, guitarist Uli Roth, bassist Francis Buchholz, and drummer Jorgen Rosenthal (replaced in 1975 by Rudy Lenners). Lenners was replaced in 1977 by Herman Rarebell. Roth left to form Electric Sun in 1978, replaced by Matthias Jabs, the two of them in and out of the band during the '80s. Undoubtedly the biggest group to come out of Germany, the Scorpions have survived in a genre not noted for longevity, cutting several classic sides along the way. — *Cub Koda*

Fly to the Rainbow / 1974 / RCA ✦✦✦

In Trance / 1975 / RCA ✦✦✦✦
Still rockin' hard in the '70s. This one features "Robot Man," "Dark Lady in Trance" and "Top of the Bill." — *Cub Koda*

Virgin Killers / 1976 / RCA ✦✦✦✦
Features the title track, "Hell Cat," "Backstage Queen," "Polar Night" and "Yellow Raven." — *Cub Koda*

Tokyo Tapes / 1978 / RCA ✦✦✦

Lovedrive / 1979 / Mercury ✦✦✦✦
Well-written songs and powerful singing from Klaus Meine are some of the reasons given for calling *Lovedrive* one of the best Scorpions ever. Rudolf Schenker and Matthais Jabs provide many of this album's highlights, with lots of great guitar. — *John Book*

Blackout / 1982 / Mercury ✦✦✦✦
The band experiments with pop smarts in a few of the songs, while retaining the solid hard-rock sound they have molded over the years. *Blackout* provided this German band with their first major hit, "No One Like You" (No. 65). — *John Book*

Love at First Sting / 1984 / Mercury ✦✦✦✦
Love at First Sting was the Scorpions' US commercial breakthrough, thanks to the single "Rock You Like a Hurricane." — *Sara Sytsma*

● **The Best of Rockers 'n' Ballads** / 1989 / Mercury ✦✦✦✦
This good collection spotlights the band's best tracks from the '80s, including "Rock You Like a Hurricane," "Rhythm of Love," "No One Like You," and "Still Loving You." — *AMG*

Crazy World / 1990 / Mercury ✦✦✦✦
Crazy World featured the Scorpions' biggest (and best) hit single, the reflective ballad "Wind of Change," which was the highlight on one of the band's most consistent, accomplished albums. — *Stephen Thomas Erlewine*

Live Bites 1988-95 / Apr. 18, 1995 / Mercury ✦✦

Pure Instinct / May 21, 1996 / Atlantic ✦✦

Gil Scott-Heron

b. Apr. 1, 1949, Chicago, IL
Piano / Fusion
Pianist, composer, and poet Gil Scott-Heron has had a prime influence on contemporary African-American popular music. He attended Lincoln and Johns Hopkins University and wrote two novels, highly popular among Black college students, *The Vulture* and *The Nigger Factory*. He began working with musician Brian Jackson on putting music to his oral narratives and monologs. His 1972 release, *Small Talk at 125th and Lenox*, attracted underground attention, while the follow-up, *Pieces of a Man*, was a major hit. Throughout the '70s and early '80s, Heron's commentaries on racism, injustice, and inequality, with side trips on jazz, romance, and family life, were very popular among jazz fans with leftwing views as well as rock, R&B, and pop audiences. Although disputes with Arista over artistic direction and production control have resulted in very few Scott-Heron recordings in recent years, he continues to tour and give interviews. — *Ron Wynn*

The Revolution Will Not Be Televised / 1975 / Bluebird ✦✦✦✦
The poem "The Revolution Will Not Be Televised" was perhaps Gil Scott-Heron's first major hit. It wasn't on any charts, but its searing message resounded on college campuses across the nation. This was the centerpiece for an album that also included several crackling protest pieces such as "Pieces of a Man," "Home Is Where the Hatred Is" and "Save the Children," plus the poignant "Lady Day and John Coltrane." The guest list of jazz participants included Ron Carter and Hubert Laws. — *Ron Wynn*

From South Africa to South Carolina / 1975 / Arista ✦✦✦

Winter in America / Sep. 4, 1975 Mar. + 19 / Strata East ✦✦✦

● **Best of Gil Scott-Heron** / 1984 / Arista ✦✦✦✦
An exemplary firebrand poet whose raps and lyrics influenced the entire hip-hop generation, yet who has said his own influence was jazz. — *Ron Wynn*

Screaming Trees

Hard Rock, Alternative Pop-Rock, Psychedelic, Grunge
Putting their post-punk guitar noise within traditional hard-rock song structure, the Screaming Trees crafted a new form of psychedelia. Instead

of the long, spacey trips of the late '60s, the band took the sonic explorations of indie guitar bands and used it for a mind-altering journey instead of expressions of aggression. Their late '80s releases on SST are raw, on the level of the label's other groups but trading angst for a drug-inspired mysticism that is too realistic and gritty for the Screaming Trees to be called hippies. When the band signed to a major label in the early '90s, some of the rough edges in their sound were smoothed out, yet they continued to produce some fine hard rock, incorporating more traditional rock styles (like the country-tinged "Dollar Bill") that kept the band's sound from growing stale. — *Stephen Thomas Erlewine*

Even If and Especially When / 1987 / SST ✦✦✦✦
The Screaming Trees were still trying to define their style on their second album, *Even If and Especially When*, but that makes it one of their most intriguing and exciting efforts. — *Stephen Thomas Erlewine*

Invisible Lantern / 1988 / SST ✦✦✦

Buzz Factory / 1989 / SST ✦✦✦

Uncle Anesthesia / 1991 / Epic ✦✦✦✦
Major-label bucks don't detract from their punch. — *Robert Gordon*

● **Anthology: SST Years** / 1991 / SST ✦✦✦✦
A scalding collection of their finest moments from the late '80s. — *Stephen Thomas Erlewine*

Sweet Oblivion / Mar. 1992 / Epic ✦✦✦

Dust / Jun. 25, 1996 / Epic ✦✦✦✦
In many ways, the Screaming Trees missed their opportunity. They released *Sweet Oblivion* just as grunge began to capture national attention and they didn't tour the album extensively, which meant nearly all of their fellow Seattle bands became superstars while they stood to the side. After four years, they returned with *Dust*, their second major-label album, and by that point, the band's sound was too idiosyncratic for alternative radio. Which is unfortunate, because *Dust* is the band's strongest album. Sure, the rough edges that fueled albums like *Uncle Anesthesia* are gone, but in its place is a rustic hard-rock, equally informed by heavy metal and folk. The influence of Mark Lanegan's haunting solo albums is apparent in both the sound and emotional tone of the record, but this is hardly a solo project—the rest of the band has added a gritty weight to Lanegan's spare prose. The Screaming Trees sound tighter than they ever have and their melodies and hooks are stronger and more memorable, making *Dust* their most consistently impressive record. — *Stephen Thomas Erlewine*

Seals & Crofts

Singer-Songwriter, Soft Rock, Pop-Rock
One of the 1970s' most successful soft-rock acts, the duo of Jim Seals and Dash Crofts met while playing with singer Dean Beard in 1958. That year, Beard was invited to join the Champs (of "Tequila" fame), and Seals and Crofts tagged along, remaining with the group until 1965. The two then bounced from the Mushrooms to the Dawnbreakers before deciding to strike out on their own as a duo in 1969. Seals played guitar, saxophone, and fiddle, while Crofts handled drums, mandolin, keyboards, and guitar. From 1972 to 1976, the duo had a string of five gold albums for Warner Bros., with an additional greatest-hits compilation certified double platinum. Their hit singles from this period include "Summer Breeze," "Diamond Girl," "We May Never Pass This Way (Again)," and "Get Closer"; all except the third mentioned reached No. 6 on the *Billboard* charts. The group became embroiled in controversy in 1974 due to the title track of their *Unborn Child* album, an anti-abortion song written from the fetus's point of view; the album was a critical failure, while the single flopped and outraged abortion advocates, who held demonstrations at many of the group's shows.

By 1976, Seals & Crofts' appeal began to decline; their albums failed to sell as well, and they scored their last Top 40 hit in 1978 with "You're the Love." Warner dropped them shortly after their 1980 LP *The Longest Road*, but by this time, both Seals and Crofts were more interested in devoting themselves fully to the Baha'i religion they had converted to back in 1969. The two have reunited occasionally at Baha'i gatherings, and for a short 1991-1992 tour; Crofts has lived in several different countries, while Seals moved to a Costa Rican coffee farm in 1980. During the '80s, Seals' brother Dan became a prominent country singer after leaving the duo England Dan and John Ford Coley. — *Steve Huey*

● **Greatest Hits** / 1975 / Warner Bros. ✦✦✦✦
This album has all their hits, including "Summer Breeze," "Hummingbird," "We May Never Pass This Way (Again)," "Diamond Girl," and "When I Meet Them." — *Dan Heilman*

The Searchers

British Invasion, Power-Pop, Pop-Rock
Founded in 1957 by John McNally (guitar/vocals), the Searchers were originally one of thousands of skiffle groups formed in the wake of Lonnie Donegan's success with "Rock Island Line." The Searchers' immediate

competitors included bands such as the Wreckers and the Confederates, both led by Michael Pender (guitar/vocals), and the Martinis, led by Tony Jackson (guitar/vocals). By 1959, McNally and Pender were working together as a duet; later in the year, Jackson joined as the lead vocalist. After drummer Norman McGarry left the Searchers, he was replaced by Chris Crummy, who quickly renamed himself Chris Curtis. Other changes were in the works as Jackson built and learned to play a customized bass guitar. Learning his new job on the four-stringed instrument proved too difficult to permit him to continue singing lead, and McNally and Pender brought in a fifth member, Johnny Sandon (born Billy Beck). Johnny Sandon & the Searchers lasted from 1960 through February 1962, and were extremely popular on the dance hall and club circuit in Liverpool. Sandon cut out for a career on his own, with another band called the Remo Four in early 1962.

Meanwhile, the Searchers, now a quartet with Jackson once again lead singer, became one of the top acts on the Liverpool band scene, playing textured renditions of American R&B, rock 'n' roll, country, soul, and rockabilly. The group was signed to Pye Records in mid-1963 and their first single, a cover of the Drifters' "Sweets for My Sweet," was released in August 1963, hitting No. 1 on the British charts. While the Beatles quickly outdistanced all comers, the Searchers did, indeed, go to the top of the charts with two of their next three singles, "Needles and Pins" and "Don't Throw Your Love Away." Another record, "Sugar and Spice," written by their producer Tony Hatch under the pseudonym Fred Nightingale, stalled at the No. 2 spot. Over the next nine months, the band staked out a sound that was one of the most distinctive in a rock scene crawling with hundreds of bands. Their music was built around the sound of a crisply played 12-string guitar, coupled with strong lead vocals and carefully, sometimes exquisitely arranged harmonies, so that they could credibly cover American R&B standards like "Love Potion No. 9" or Phil Spector-based girl-group pop like "Be My Baby." Their 1964 singles included a venture into folk-rock before the genre had been "invented" in the press, in the form of a cover of Malvina Reynolds' "What Have They Done to the Rain." Interestingly, their 12-string guitar sound would become a key ingredient in the success of the Byrds, who even took the riff from "Needles and Pins" and transformed it into the main riff of "Feel a Whole Lot Better."

In July 1964, with the group riding the upper reaches of the British charts, and with their third album in nine months in release, it was announced that Tony Jackson was leaving the Searchers to form his own band, and would be replaced by Frank Allen, who had been playing bass with Cliff Bennett & the Rebel Rousers. The turning point for the band came in 1965, as the British and international fascination with the Liverpool sound faded away. The Searchers began casting their net wider for material to cover, in addition to coming up with one original hit, the Curtis/Pender-authored "He's Got No Love." By the beginning of 1966, the group's string of chart hits seemed to have run out, and Chris Curtis exited in early 1966, claiming to have become exhausted from the group's constant touring. The Searchers, with Johnny Blunt on drums, continued working and had their last hit, "Have You Ever Loved Somebody," which barely cracked the Top 50 in October 1966. The group continued working, however, playing clubs and cabarets in England and Europe. Blunt exited at the end of the 1960s, but was replaced by Billy Adamson, and this lineup of the Searchers continued intact until the mid-1980s, working for 35 weeks a year throughout Europe with an occasional US visit. Although they played as part of Richard Nader's "Rock 'n' Roll Revival" shows, they never became an "oldies" act, always adding new material, including originals and covers of work by songwriters such as Neil Young to their sets, and in 1972, the band cut an album for British RCA.

At the end of the 1970s, their recording fortunes were revived once again as Seymour Stein, the head of Sire Records, signed the Searchers for two albums. Those records, *The Searchers* and *Love's Melodies*, were the best work the group ever did, highlighted by achingly beautiful yet vibrant and forceful playing and singing, and an unerring array of memorable hooks and melodies. Those two albums were followed by a series of tracks recorded for their original label, Pye Records, in the early 1980s. The group held their audience well into the 1980s, playing before crowds as large as 15,000 along one US tour. In 1985, after playing together for 26 years, Pender and McNally split up, with McNally continuing to lead The Searchers (with Adamson and Allen, with Spencer James added on second guitar and vocals), while Pender formed Mike Pender's Searchers, consisting of Chris Black (guitar, vocals), Barry Cowell (bass, vocals), and Steve Carlyle (drums, vocals). Both groups have toured extensively and the Searchers under McNally have recorded on occasion. *—Bruce Eder*

Sugar & Spice / 1963 / Castle ♦♦♦

Meet the Searchers / 1963 / Castle ♦♦

It's the Searchers / 1964 / Castle ♦♦♦♦

Perhaps the best studio album by a band that is really best represented by greatest-hit collections. This 1964 LP includes the classic hits "Needles and Pins" and "Don't Throw Your Love Away." It also features some of

their best LP cuts, on which they applied their famed harmonies to American material that was both strong and obscure. The best of these covers are Bacharach-David's "This Empty Space" (originally by Dionne Warwick), the Jackie DeShannon-penned "Can't Help Forgiving You," the Drifters' "I Count the Tears," the folkish "Sea of Heartbreak," and "Where Have You Been" (which was also part of the Beatles' repertoire during their Hamburg days). The harder-rocking songs don't lend themselves as well to the group's talents, which always (with some notable exceptions) lay more in the folk-rock and Merseybeat direction than R&B/rockabilly. *—Richie Unterberger*

Take Me for What I'm Worth / 1965 / PRT ♦♦

The Searchers / 1979 / Castle ♦♦♦♦

Love's Melodies / 1981 / Sire ♦♦♦♦

These two albums (*The Searchers* and *Loves Melodies*) represent the Searchers at their peak as a recording outfit, having maintained their original mid-'60s emphasis on excellent harmonies and crisply played guitars but also absorbed lessons from such '70s pub-rockers as Brinsley Schwarz and roots-rock expert Dave Edmunds. The material is some of the most beautiful recorded anywhere in this era, and anyone lucky enough to spot a copy of either of these records—neither of which has yet shown up on CD—should grab them. *—Bruce Eder*

● **Greatest Hits** / 1985 / Rhino ♦♦♦♦

The best American best-of on the band, and the most desirable for those on a budget, with superior sound to the *Silver Searchers* collection. *—Bruce Eder*

30th Anniversary Collection / 1992 / Sequel ♦♦♦♦

Although it's missing one or two fairly strong tracks, this three-CD, 84-song set is a pretty definitive collection of the group's best '60s material, for those who want to go beyond the greatest hits. Besides including all of their key A- and B-sides, it has an entire disc of their best '60s album tracks. The rarities disc includes foreign-language versions, outtakes, mid-'60s BBC performances, and solo discs by Tony Jackson and Chris Curtis. Highlights here include an alternate take of "Someday We're Gonna Love Again," a BBC version of "Blowin' in the Wind," and the previously unreleased "Once Upon a Time" (recorded by Dusty Springfield). The package includes liner notes, discography, and a family tree. *—Richie Unterberger*

Sebadoh

Alternative Pop-Rock, Lo-Fi, Indie Rock

After leaving Dinosaur Jr., Lou Barlow formed Sebadoh. Instead of working like a traditional rock band and collaborating on each song, Sebadoh acts as a backing band for the material of each individual band member. Consequently, their albums can be a little schizophrenic, covering all kinds of indie guitar-rock from R.E.M.-style pop to Dinosaur-style melancholy and Sonic Youth sonic explosions, all recorded in ragged low-fidelity. Fortunately, each member is a talented songwriter, managing to wear their influences without sounding exactly like any of them; they are one of the most unique bands of the early '90s. Sebadoh's artistic breadth makes them critical and cult favorites; their jagged playing and oblique songwriting guarantees that they will never cross over into the mainstream, but that has never seemed a concern of the band. *—Stephen Thomas Erlewine*

Freed Weed / 1990 / Positive ♦♦♦

Weed Forestin / 1990 / Homestead ♦♦

The press release to this LP boasted that it, unlike their debut, "was actually recorded with the knowledge that it would be released." Apparently Lou Barlow and Eric Gaffney had a pretty clear crystal ball; the music was taped in 1986 and 1987, but didn't actually come out on vinyl until 1990. Sebadoh's first LP, *The Freed Man*, boasts some of the most deliberately awful fidelity of all time (against some stiff competition); this is somewhat, but only somewhat, more hi-fi. Barlow's gifts are often in evidence: his appealing voice, sensitive wit, and knack for affected burned-out acid-folk. Alas, the merits are often buried beneath hiss and tomfoolery, as if he wasn't convinced his music was any good on its own terms, and so tried to pretend it was a big joke. The LP has since been reissued (along with most of *The Freed Man*) on the CD *Freed Weed.* *—Richie Unterberger*

● **III** / 1991 / Homestead ♦♦♦♦

Smash Your Head on the Punk Rock / 1992 / Sub Pop ♦♦♦

Bubble & Scrape / 1993 / Sub Pop ♦♦♦♦

Bakesale / 1994 / Sub Pop ♦♦♦♦

With *Bakesale*, Sebadoh has trimmed down to Lou Barlow, Jason Loewenstein, and Bob Fay, with Barlow and Loewenstein taking on the lion's share of the songwriting. Maybe the change in personnel was needed, because *Bakesale* is their most accessible, concise work to date. Without the noise that usually envelops their records, the solid, unconventional pop songwriting of Barlow and Loewenstein shines through brightly. *—Stephen Thomas Erlewine*

Harmacy / Aug. 20, 1996 / Sub Pop ✦✦✦✦
Part of Sebadoh's charm is that their records are inconsistent, flipping wildly between sonic extremes and musical genres. In a sense, *Harmacy* is no different than its predecessors, but there are some crucial differences that makes it their most accessible effort. Previously, that title was held by 1994's *Bakesale*, but between that record and *Harmacy*, Lou Barlow had a Top 40 hit with the Folk Implosion's "Natural One." Although nothing on *Harmacy* sounds much like the hip-hop hybrid of "Natural One," its success did have an effect on Barlow, leading him toward straightforward song structures and cleaner productions. Instead of diluting the impact of Sebadoh's music, the clearer production strengthens it. Barlow's sighing melodies and jangling indie rock become more resonant, and his batch of songs are among his best. Jason Loewenstein, Sebadoh's other main songwriter, suffers at the hands of cleaner production. Loewenstein sticks closer to the band's hardcore punk roots than Barlow, so his songs could use the extra layer of murk that cheap productions lend recordings. It also doesn't help that he tends to sink into faceless indie noise-rock. When Loewenstein takes a stab at pop melodies, such as "Can't Give Up," his songs are memorable but on the whole uneven. If it weren't for Lowenstein's erratic songwriting, *Harmacy* might rank as Sebadoh's masterpiece, but as it stands it's just another very fine and sometimes frustrating record. — *Stephen Thomas Erlewine*

John Sebastian

b. Mar. 17, 1944, New York, NY
Harmonica, Vocals / Singer-Songwriter, Folk-Rock, Pop-Rock
Born in New York City, the son of a classical harmonica player, John Sebastian grew up in the Greenwich Village coffeehouses and was a popular sideman to various folk artists prior to forming the folk-rock band the Lovin' Spoonful, for which he served as lead singer and songwriter in the mid-'60s. When the Spoonful broke up, Sebastian went solo, appearing at the Woodstock Festival in 1969 and releasing the Top 20 *John B. Sebastian* album in 1970. Subsequent efforts were less successful, but in 1976 Sebastian scored a No. 1 hit with "Welcome Back," the theme song from the TV series *Welcome Back, Kotter*. Sebastian continues to tour and play on occasional sessions; he released his first album since the '70s in 1993. — *William Ruhlmann*

John B. Sebastian / 1970 / MGM ✦✦✦✦
A strong debut solo album spotlighting Sebastian's warm voice and optimistic, melodic folk-pop songwriting. — *William Ruhlmann*

Cheapo Cheapo Production Presents / 1971 / Reprise ✦✦✦✦
Cheapo Cheapo Production Presents is an exuberant solo appearance at which Sebastian's humor and wit are at their apex. A wide variety of songs, from old folk-blues standards to Spoonful favorites. Makes you wish you'd been there. — *William Ruhlmann*

● **The Best of John Sebastian** / 1989 / Rhino ✦✦✦✦
A 16-track selection from Sebastian's solo albums from 1970 to 1976, including the hit "Welcome Back." — *William Ruhlmann*

Tar Beach / 1993 / Shanachie ✦✦✦

Jon Secada

Vocals / Urban, Latin Pop, Adult Contemporary, Pop, Club-Dance
With only one album, Jon Secada became one of the biggest adult contemporary artist of the '90s, selling over six million albums worldwide. Secada's smooth mix of R&B, pop, and Latin music appealed to a number of different audiences. What separates him from the overly slick sound of most adult contemporary artists are his considerable songwriting skills; he's able to write sweet ballads that rarely seem contrived. As well as becoming a huge pop star, Secada is one of the hottest Latin artists recording in the '90s; his Spanish-language album *Otro Dia Mas Sin Verte* was *Billboard*'s No. 1 Latin album in 1992 and won a Grammy for Best Latin Pop album. — *Stephen Thomas Erlewine*

● **Jon Secada** / 1992 / SBK ✦✦✦✦
Secada, formerly a backup singer for Gloria Estefan, provides an impressive mix of appealing Top Ten dance singles and powerful ballads in his English album debut. Notable cuts from this self-titled album include "Just Another Day" and "Angel," both of which have accompanying Spanish versions on the release, with Estefan and Secada collaborating on their lyrical content. Estefan also provides background vocals on "Otro Dia Mas Sin Verte," the Spanish version of "Just Another Day." If these titles are any indication of his future work, Secada will definitely be an impact artist to look for in coming years. — *Ashley S. Battel*

Heart, Soul & a Voice / May 24, 1994 / SBK ✦✦✦

Si Te Vas / Jun. 28, 1994 / EMI Latin ✦✦✦

Amor / Oct. 10, 1995 / EMI Latin/SBK ✦✦✦

Secret Affair

Power-Pop, Mod-Revival
Secret Affair, consisting of Ian Page (vocals, trumpet, piano, organ), David

Cairns (guitar, backing vocals), Dennis Smith (bass, backing vocals), and Seb Shelton (drums), formed in 1978. Taking their inspiration from the Jam, the group was quickly seen as one of the shining stars of the mod-revival movement of the late '70s. They received their most important early exposure by supporting the Jam on small-scale tours in England and followed with several mod package tours with bands such as the Purple Hearts. Their first single, "Time for Action," was the perfect youth anthem for the time and certainly one of the most memorable and successful of the movement. The band released its first album, *Glory Boys*, late in 1979 on their own label, I-Spy (distributed by Arista in the UK and Sire in the US). Both the album and their subsequent singles charted but by the time 1980's *Behind Closed Doors* was released, the revival was dissolving and they were too firmly rooted in the movement to change their arrogant stance. The band began to break up when drummer Seb Shelton left in 1980. They held on until 1982, releasing one more album, *Business as Usual*, to an uninterested public; the members went their separate ways shortly after its release. — *Chris Woodstra*

Glory Boys / 1979 / Sire ✦✦✦✦
Glory Boys clearly placed Secret Affair at the top of the mod-revival's third wave. The songs are top notch, building on rather than ripping off the Jam's sound—a refreshing change from the second- and third-rate soundalikes the revival usually produced. Ian Page's arrogant, self-important lyrics are a little too much in places, but overall, this was a promising debut. — *Chris Woodstra*

Behind Closed Doors / Nov. 1980 / I Spy ✦✦✦

Business as Usual / 1982 / Arista ✦✦

● **Glory Boys/Behind Closed Doors** / 1995 / Arista ✦✦✦✦
As far as mod-revival bands go, Secret Affair were probably the purest—a textbook example of all that was good (and bad) about the revival. They could write concise pop songs, but in the end their arrogance and inflexibility doomed them. *Glory Boys*, the band's first album, was one of the finest albums produced by the revival, and the single, "Time for Action," served as a perfect youth anthem. By 1980's *Behind Closed Doors* (the second album), the band seemed to place a little too much importance on the fad, staying in character even after it was clearly out of style—at the end of their career, they were verging on the point of parody. As an artifact, this two-fer is quite fun to revisit. As a portrait of the band, this is both the starting and the ending point. — *Chris Woodstra*

Neil Sedaka

b. Mar. 13, 1939, Brooklyn, NY
Piano, Vocals / Pop, Pop-Rock, Brill Building Pop
An excellent songwriter, Sedaka came from a doo wop background (working with an early version of the Tokens). He sharpened his skills with Juilliard training and enjoyed much success with a number of pre-Beatles-era hits. Though the British Invasion stopped the flow of hits, he re-entered the charts in the mid-'70s with a string of chart-toppers that extended into the following decade. A major influence on Elton John, Sedaka continues performing today. — *Cub Koda*

● **All-Time Greatest Hits** / 1975 / RCA ✦✦✦✦
Includes "Calendar Girl," "Happy Birthday, Sweet Sixteen," "Breaking Up Is Hard to Do," and other sprightly pop numbers. — *Dan Heilman*

● **Laughter in the Rain: The Best of Neil Sedaka, 1974-1980** / 1994 / Varese Sarabande ✦✦✦✦
His biggest and best work for MCA and Elektra are represented in this set, with "Laughter in the Rain," "Bad Blood," "Love in the Shadows," and his reconstruction of "Breaking Up Is Hard to Do" being the highlights. — *John Lowe*

The Seeds

Psychedelic, Garage Rock
The Seeds (formed in 1965 in Southern California) produced five albums of magically limited garage-psychedelia extolling the virtues of sex and drugs and drugs and sex. Sky Saxon, the band's self-absorbed singer-songwriter, evidently understood arrested development quite well, making the Seeds' records a pretty enjoyable '60s punk sleazefest.
The urgent trashola snarl (and corny "Rawhide"-style backup vocals) of "Pushin' Too Hard" (No. 36) helped give them their only hit. "Can't Seem to Make You Mine," probably their best song, was later affectionately covered by Alex Chilton as the B-side of his "Bangkok" single. Both of those songs can be found on their self-titled debut. Even though subsequent albums recycled the basic formula of the Seeds, their second album, *A Web of Sound*, is worth checking out. — *Rick Clark*

The Seeds / 1966 / GNP ✦✦✦✦
Punk sneers, cheesy organ, and an attitude. A garage-band classic. — *Bruce Eder*

Web of Sound / 1966 / GNP ✦✦✦
A more ambitious but less successful venture into teenage rages and lusts. — *Bruce Eder*

● **Evil Hoodoo** / 1988 / Edsel ✦✦✦✦
The only serious attempt at a best-of Seeds retrospective features 16 songs culled from their half-dozen or so '60s albums. Besides "Pushin' Too Hard," it features their sole other hit single of any magnitude ("Can't Seem to Make You Mine"), as well as other fairly well-remembered cuts like "The Wind Blows Your Hair," "Tripmaker," "Falling Off the Edge of My Mind," "Mr. Farmer," and "Up in Her Room." Non-converts to the Sky Saxon legend may be excused for wondering what all the fuss is about: even distilled to 16 cuts, the melodies and arrangements are almost interminably monotonous. Comes with an extensive group history by rock archivist Brian Hogg. —*Richie Unterberger*

The Seekers
Pop, Folk-Rock
During the mid-'60s, Australia's Seekers scored several pop hits featuring their rich, folky harmonies and British Invasion leanings. The band was formed in 1963 and featured Athol Guy (standup bass), Bruce Woodley (vocals, guitar), Keith Potger (vocals, guitar), and Judith Durham (vocals), who replaced original vocalist Ken Ray before the group achieved popularity. After the Seekers appeared on TV, producer and songwriter Tom Springfield offered his services. The Seekers broke through in the US and UK in 1965 with the hits "I'll Never Find Another You" and "A World of Our Own." Bruce Woodley formed a short songwriting partnership with Paul Simon, which produced the Cyrkle hit "Red Rubber Ball." (1967) "Georgy Girl" was their biggest American hit, peaking at No. 2, but the group had little further success and broke up in 1990. Woodley became a TV jingle writer, while Guy served in the Victoria parliament. Potger put together the New Seekers in 1970 with a completely different lineup and had some success, but a full-fledged Seekers reunion did not occur until Judith Durham was involved in a serious car accident in 1990. After recovering, she got the original group back together and toured Australia and New Zealand; they played several shows in the UK in 1994. —*Steve Huey*

Come the Day / 1966 / Columbia ✦✦✦✦
Their best album, with their biggest hit and the Simon-Woodley songs. Also includes a killer rendition of Tom Paxton's "The Last Thing on My Mind." The US title is *Georgy Girl*. —*Bruce Eder*

● **Capitol Collectors Series** / 1992 / Capitol ✦✦✦✦
The Seekers' rich folky harmonies, fronted by the clear alto of Judith Durham, are given an excellent presentation on this 23-song anthology. All of their Capitol hits are here, including "Georgy Girl," "A World of Our Own," "Come the Day," and "I'll Never Find Another You." Typical of *Capitol Collectors Series* reissues, this set contains ample annotation, track info, and photos. —*Rick Clark*

The Seekers / EMI ✦✦✦✦
A compilation featuring over one hour of hits and key album tracks on this British import. Completely comprehensive, with the best sound ever. —*Bruce Eder*

Bob Seger
b. May 6, 1945, Dearborn, MI
Guitar, Piano, Vocals / Rock 'n' Roll, Pop-Rock
At his best, Detroit rocker Bob Seger has produced some incredibly clearheaded music speaking to and about the working class's fleeting joys, shortchanged dreams, and grinding existence. Many of the people who populate Seger's material possess some kind of resolve and dignity. Seger grew up as one of these people, and he's never really forgotten it. Musically, Seger's influences range from Chuck Berry to Creedence Clearwater Revival, the Rolling Stones, and Bob Dylan to Bruce Springsteen and the Eagles, all merged together in a Heartland rock stew. Seger's first hit was the 1969 heavy soulful stomper "Ramblin' Gamblin' Man" (No. 17). For years after that, he consistently landed regional Top Ten hits that never saw the light of day anywhere else in the country. That was until the release of 1976's *Live Bullet*, a great concert album that encapsulated Seger's career to that point with an impassioned delivery. It became his first million-seller, charting at No. 34. His next two studio efforts, *Night Moves* (No. 8) and *Stranger in Town* (No. 4), were artistic highlights. By this time, Seger had become a major arena attraction. He stumbled on the mediocre *Against the Wind*, reducing once-effective sentiment to hack wordplay, but he regained his focus on *The Distance*. His latest effort, *The Fire Inside*, is solid but fails to mine any new territory. Blessed with a voice that could sing the phone book and sound great, Seger has even scored hits with his most pedestrian work. Nevertheless, he has created a body of work that, at its best, celebrates the spirit of rock in the face of mortality with a hard-won wisdom. —*Rick Clark*

66-67 / 1967 / KWR ✦✦✦✦
Unless you grew up in Michigan in the mid-'60s, you probably have no idea that Seger's roots extend further than his bar band/road band/singer-songwriter/arena star experiences. Way back before the '70s, he

was one of many talented Michigan garage rockers, releasing several stomping singles in the style. Some were quite popular regionally, but none made it nationally; all were far raunchier in execution than anything he's done since. Perhaps he prefers to keep it in the closet, but these sides have proven very hard to come by; this compilation, almost certainly unauthorized, gathers together a dozen of them. And it's good stuff: the sub-"Subterranean Homesick Blues" of "Persecution Smith," the local hit "East Side Story" (a mini-drama that sounds like Springsteen as a '60s punk), the satirical "Sock It to Me Santa" and "Ballad of the Yellow Beret," the storming, twisting "Vagrant Winter," and hints of the '70s singer-songwriter in "Heavy Music" and "Looking Back." Fans of tough '60s rock, indeed, will probably find this superior to most or all of his subsequent work, although fans of his more famous post-1970 recordings may feel a little lost. This LP is virtually impossible to locate these days; it's time for the official reissue of this material, as it can hold its head high next to top-flight Michigan rock of the time by Mitch Ryder, the Rationals, and others. —*Richie Unterberger*

Ramblin' Gamblin' Man / 1968 / Capitol ✦✦✦✦
The title track on Seger's Capitol debut is one of the all-time-great rock 'n' roll stompers with its bone-crunching two- and four-drum groove and gospel-choir backup. Other highlights include the incredibly hard-rocking antiwar track "2 + 2 Equals ?," and "Down Home," a rude harmonica-driven rocker that sports an absolutely addled rhythm section. In spite of some cornball psychedelic-period mixes, *Ramblin' Gamblin' Man*, with its reckless over-the-top delivery, is Seger's hardest-rocking album. Throughout many of these tracks, Seger wails like a banshee. Seger's later rock hits sound absolutely tame next to this stuff. —*Rick Clark*

Smokin' O.P.'s / 1973 / Capitol ✦✦✦

Beautiful Loser / 1975 / Capitol ✦✦✦✦
After several years of relative obscurity, Seger emerged with this rather reflective effort. The hard-rocking "Katmandu," however, was a substantial hit in the Midwest. —*Rick Clark*

Live Bullet / 1976 / Capitol ✦✦✦✦
A blistering live show from Cobo Hall, containing raucous versions of early material like "Nutbush City Limits" and "Get Out of Denver" as highlights. —*Cub Koda*

★ **Night Moves** / 1976 / Capitol ✦✦✦✦✦
Seger's breakthrough album, a classic of blue-collar rock, features such standouts as the wistful "Mainstreet," the no-frills rock of "Rock and Roll Never Forgets," and the title track, a reflective coming-of-age masterpiece. Throughout, Seger believably details the characters in his songs with compassion. —*Rick Clark*

Stranger in Town / 1978 / Capitol ✦✦✦✦
It's not quite as strong as *Night Moves*, but *Stranger in Town* continues Seger's streak of great songwriting and performance. Highlights include the relentless rockers "Hollywood Nights" and "Feel Like a Number." Seger's facility with the ballads "Still the Same" and "We've Got Tonight" produced substantial hits. —*Rick Clark*

Against the Wind / 1980 / Capitol ✦✦✦
Against the Wind became Seger's first No. 1 album, producing the hits and key album rock-radio tracks, "Fire Lake," "You'll Accomp'ny Me," "The Horizontal Bop," and the No. 5 title cut. However, after two fine albums, Seger's lyrical abilities and melodic skills began to reveal a cookie-cutter sameness. His singing still had plenty of passion. —*Rick Clark*

Nine Tonight / 1981 / Capitol ✦✦✦

The Distance / 1982 / Capitol ✦✦✦✦
The Distance was a strong rebound after the spotty *Against the Wind*, featuring his rocking Chuck Berry-like auto-worker's tribute, "Makin' Thunderbirds," the resolute rock anthem "Even Now," and a fine version of Rodney Crowell's "Shame on the Moon." —*Rick Clark*

● **Greatest Hits** / 1994 / Capitol ✦✦✦✦
For over 20 years, Bob Seger has been one of the best mainstream rock 'n' rollers in America, developing a distinctive body of honest, hard-rocking songs. More songs than can be put on this single-disc set, unfortunately. While many of Seger's trademarks are here—"Turn the Page," "Old Time Rock 'n' Roll," "Night Moves"—there is no "Rock and Roll Never Forgets," "Katmandu," "Shame on the Moon," or any of his pulverizing early records, when he was as tough as fellow Michigan rockers the MC5 and the Stooges; this is one time when a double-disc set would have held enough quality material. Nevertheless, what is here is fine and contains enough first-rate material to satisfy most fans. —*Stephen Thomas Erlewine*

It's a Mystery / Oct. 24, 1995 / Capitol ✦✦✦

Selecter
New Wave, Ska-Revival
Despite being the band that got the least press during the ska-revival of

the early '80s, and despite only recording one undeniably fine record, Selecter deserved better than they got. Hailing from Coventry, England, the same hometown as ska pals the Specials, Selecter's secret weapon was lead singer Pauline Black, arguably the best lead singer of the ska-revival, who gave the jumpy and jittery songs an edge that veered into haunting drama. Although they got off to a roaring start with their debut record, 1980's *Too Much Pressure*, the second record, *Celebrate the Bullet*, was a strained follow-up that led to the band's rapid demise.

Black spent some time singing solo and eventually rejoined guitarist Neol Davis in a Selecter reunion in the early '90s that has seen them become dance-club favorites. According to those attending recent Selecter shows, the vibe is strong and the music great. However, don't expect a recording renaissance any time soon. — *John Dougan*

● **Too Much Pressure** / May 1980 / 2 Tone/Chrysalis ✦✦✦✦
At the time of its release, *Too Much Pressure* was relegated to second-class status behind the debut records by Madness and the Specials. Now it's easy to see that this record was the equal to the Specials record, and (I realize I'm getting into trouble here) better than the first (and second) Madness records. Pauline Black is the key, and she makes songs like "On My Radio" and the title track classic chunks of Caribbean-influenced pop rather than mere stylistic mimicry. Much better that the weak second record, *Celebrate the Bullet*, or the 1989 anthology, *Selected Selecter Selections.* — *John Dougan*

Celebrate the Bullet / Mar. 1981 / 2 Tone/Chrysalis ✦✦

Selected Selecter Selections / 1989 / 2 Tone/Chrysalis ✦✦✦✦
It features the greatest hits from their two studio albums. — *David Szatmary*

Selena (Selena Quintanilla)

d. Apr. 30, 1995
Vocals / Latin Pop, Pop-Rock, Latin Continuum, Tejano
The tragic shooting death of talented, young Tejano singer Selena spawned a reaction within the Latino community that can be compared to the reactions to the deaths of Elvis Presley and John Lennon. An enormously popular singer in Latino communities across North America, her emotionally charged music crossed cultural boundaries to touch the lives of young and old alike. A flamboyant, sexy stage performer, sometimes hailed as the Latina Madonna, Selena was nonetheless considered a role model, for off-stage she was gentle, trusting and family-oriented, active in antidrug campaigns and AIDS-awareness programs.

Selena was born to Mexican-American parents in Lake Jackson, TX. Many years before her birth, her father, Abraham, had been a member of Los Dinos. When Selena began performing at age ten, her father became her manager and Los Dinos became her backing band. In 1983, she made her recording debut after appearing on the popular radio show of Los Angeles deejay Johnnie Canales. While Selena grew up understanding Spanish, English was her first language. Her first records were recorded in Spanish, and she sang the words phonetically. After her music began to catch on, she began learning Spanish formally and by the time of her death was fluent in the language.

In the '80s, Selena married Los Dinos' lead guitarist Chris Perez. Other group members included her brother, Abraham Quintanilla III, who played bass and penned many of her songs, and her sister Suzette, the drummer. By 1987, she was named Female Vocalist of the Year and Performer of the Year at the Tejano Music Awards. Two years later she contracted with EMI Latin and in 1990, she and Los Dinos released their eponymous debut album. Later that year she released a "best of" album, *Personal Best*, featuring some of her hottest singles, and she also released *Ven Conmigo*. In 1991 the title track of the latter became the first Tejano record to go gold. Selena also released two more albums, including one of Cumbia music, *Baila Esta Cumbia*. She won her first Grammy in 1993 for Best Mexican American Performance for her album *Selena Live*. She also released an album of love songs, *Quiero.* Later that year, she also opened Selena Etc, a clothing manufacturing business. In 1994, she made her feature film debut in *Don Juan DeMarco*, in which she played a singer. Later that year, she and her band embarked upon a tour of New York, Los Angeles, Argentina, and Puerto Rico. *Amor Prohibido* was released in 1994; the title track won a Grammy and went gold. In 1995 Selena began preparing to make her breakthrough into the American pop mainstream.

In the spring of that year she was working on her first English-language album, when she went to a motel room in Corpus Christi, TX, to fire 34-year-old Yolanda Saldivar, the woman who managed Selena's boutique in San Antonio and the founder of the Selena fan club. A few days before the confrontation, Selena's father had unearthed paperwork proving that Saldivar had been embezzling from the fan club. Selena and Saldivar argued and as the singer left, she was fatally shot in the back with a .38 revolver. Selena didn't die right away and managed to stagger into the lobby where she named Saldivar as the killer. An hour later, Selena died in a local hospital. It was a death that rocked the entire

Latino music industry. Saldivar was convicted for the murder of Selena in November 1995, and sentenced to at least 30 years in prison.

A special service was held in the Los Angeles Coliseum where she was to give a concert. Less than a month later, Texas governor, George W. Bush declared April 16 "Selena Day," to honor her contribution toward popularizing Tejano music and for the good works she did for Latino communities. *Dreaming of You*, her final album, was released posthumously in the early summer. It became the first Tejano album to reach No. 1 in America and was double platinum by the end of the year. — *Sandra Brennan*

Entre a mi Mundo / 1992 / EMI Latin ✦✦✦

Live / May 4, 1993 / EMI Latin ✦✦✦✦
Selena's *Live* offers proof that she was an energetic, exciting live performer. The vocalist runs through many of her most popular numbers in front of an enthusiastic audience. The album captures some of that energy and shows why she was so popular. — *Stephen Thomas Erlewine*

12 Super Exitos / 1994 / EMI Latin ✦✦✦✦
Selena's greatest Tejano hits are collected on *12 Super Exitos*, providing a good introduction to the vocalist. — *Stephen Thomas Erlewine*

● **Amor Prohibido** / Mar. 13, 1994 / EMI Latin ✦✦✦✦
Amor Prohibido was Selena's biggest album before her crossover attempt, *Dreaming of You*. While the album is slightly uneven, she was a dynamic, charismatic singer and is able to pull across the weaker material. Indeed, the record is her strongest album and shows why she was the biggest Tejano star of the '90s. — *Stephen Thomas Erlewine*

★ **Dreaming of You** / 1995 / EMI Latin ✦✦✦✦✦
Most of America first learned of Selena because of her tragic murder; accordingly, the posthumous *Dreaming of You* was the first record they ever heard. While it isn't her best—*Amor Prohibido* is a more consistent release—it was an effective introduction and showed why she was so beloved by Tejano fans. The English tracks on the album are no different than her Spanish songs. Selena was essentially a singer much like her idol Madonna. She was able to sing ballads and dance-pop convincingly. *Dreaming of You* would have been a stronger album if she had lived, but it still stands as a powerful—and touching—testament to her talents. — *Stephen Thomas Erlewine*

The Sex Pistols

Punk
The Sex Pistols may have only been together for two years in the late '70s, but they changed the face of popular music. Through their raw, nihilistic singles and violent performances, the band revolutionized the idea of what rock 'n' roll could be. In England, the group was considered dangerous to the very fabric of society and were banned across the country; in America, they didn't have the same impact, but countless bands in both countries were inspired by the sheer sonic force of their music, while countless others were inspired by their independent, do-it-yourself ethics. Even if they didn't release any singles by themselves, there was an implicit independence in the way they played their music and handled their career. The band gave birth to the massive independent music underground in England and America that would soon include bands that didn't have a direct musical connection to the Sex Pistols' initial three-minute blasts of rage, but couldn't have existed without those singles.

Guitarist Steve Jones and drummer Paul Cook were regulars at a boutique owned by their manager, Malcolm McLaren; bassist Glen Matlock worked at the store. Vocalist John Lydon, who would later perform as Johnny Rotten, met the rest of the group at the shop and was asked to join the band. While the band played simple rock 'n' roll loudly and abrasively, Rotten arrogantly sang of anarchy, abortion, violence, fascism, and apathy; without Rotten, the band wouldn't have been threatening to England's government—he provided the band's conceptual direction, calculated to be as confrontational and threatening as possible. The publicity caused by their caustic first single "Anarchy in the UK" caused the band to be dropped by their record label, EMI. Matlock was fired before their next single "God Save the Queen," which was released on Virgin; it was banned by the BBC. Matlock's replacement was Sid Vicious, a street tough who, unlike the rest of the band, couldn't play his instrument.

After releasing one album in 1977, the band headed over to the US for a tour in January of 1978; it lasted 14 days. Rotten left the band after their show at San Francisco's Winterland Ballroom on January 14, heading back to New York; he would form Public Image Limited later that year. McLaren tried to continue the band, but Cook and Jones soon turned against him. In the two decades following the Sex Pistols' implosion, an endless stream of outtakes, demos, repackagings, and live shows were released on a variety of labels, which only helped their cult grow.

In 1996, to celebrate their impending 20th anniversary, the Sex Pistols reunited, with original bassist Glen Matlock taking the place of the deceased Sid Vicious. The band embarked on an international tour in

June 1996, releasing the *Filthy Lucre Live* album the following month. —*Stephen Thomas Erlewine*

★ **Never Mind the Bollocks** / Oct. 1977 / Warner Bros. ✦✦✦✦✦
While mostly accurate, dismissing *Never Mind the Bollocks* as merely a series of loud, ragged, mid-tempo rockers with a harsh, grating vocalist and not much melody would be a terrible error. Already anthemic songs are rendered positively transcendent by Johnny Rotten's rabid, foaming delivery. His bitterly sarcastic attacks on pretentious affectation and the very foundations of British society were all carried out in the most confrontational, impolite manner possible. Most imitators of the Pistols' angry nihilism missed the point: underneath the shock tactics and theatrical negativity were social critiques carefully designed for maximum impact. *Never Mind the Bollocks* perfectly articulated the frustration, rage, and dissatisfaction of the British working class with the establishment, a spirit quick to translate itself to strictly rock 'n' roll terms. The Pistols paved the way for countless other bands to make similarly rebellious statements, but arguably none were as daring or effective. It's easy to see how the band's roaring energy, overwhelmingly snotty attitude, and Rotten's furious ranting sparked a musical revolution, and those qualities haven't diminished one bit over time. *Never Mind the Bollocks* is simply one of the greatest, most inspiring rock records of all time. —*Steve Huey*

The Great Rock & Roll Swindle / 1979 / Warner Bros. ✦✦✦✦
A wildly inconsistent but often entertaining collection, the soundtrack to the Pistols' pseudo-documentary contains great music, wacked-out novelties, and flat-out tripe in approximately equal proportions. Some formative recordings are included—mostly covers like "(I'm Not Your) Stepping Stone," plus a demo of "Anarchy in the UK" that somehow manages to top the version on *Never Mind the Bollocks* in terms of raw rage and sheer power. "I Wanna Be Me" and a veiled chronicle of the band's breakup, "Silly Thing," are also necessary items. Devoted fans will enjoy the Black Arabs' disco medley of Pistols hits, a French version of "Anarchy in the UK" complete with accordion, two tracks sung by loony Edward Tudor-Pole (later of Tenpole Tudor), and Sid Vicious' awful but strangely appropriate reading of Frank Sinatra's "My Way." —*Steve Huey*

Flogging a Dead Horse / 1980 / Virgin ✦✦✦✦

Chaos / Feb. 27, 1996 / Restless ✦✦

Filthy Lucre Live / Jul. 1996 / Virgin ✦✦✦

Shadows of Knight

Garage Rock
"The Stones, Animals, and Yardbirds took the Chicago blues and gave it an English interpretation. We've taken the English version of the blues and re-added a Chicago touch." The Shadows of Knight's self-description was fairly accurate. Although this mid-'60s garage band from the Windy City did not match the excellence of either their British or African-American idols, the teen energy of their recordings remains enjoyable, if not overwhelmingly original. The group took a tamer version of Them's classic "Gloria" into the American Top Ten in 1966, and also took a Yardbirdized version of Bo Diddley's "Oh Yeah" into the Top 40 the same year. Their patchy albums contained a few exciting R&B covers in the Yardbirds/Stones style and a few decent originals in the same vein. The group's original lineup splintered quickly, and the Shadows faded in the late '60s after briefly pursuing a more commercial pop sound. —*Richie Unterberger*

Gee-El-O-Are-I-Ay / 1985 / Edsel ✦✦✦✦
Boils the Shadows' legacy down to 16 essential tracks. Contains "Gloria," "Oh Yeah," and the flop singles "Bad Little Woman" and "I'm Gonna Make You Mine," as well as the better tracks from their first two LPs, including the impressive originals "Light Bulb Blues" and "Gospel Zone." —*Richie Unterberger*

Raw 'n' Alive at the Cellar, Chicago 1966! / 1992 / Sundazed ✦✦✦

● **Dark Sides: The Best of Shadows of the Knight** / 1994 / Rhino ✦✦✦✦
More easily available to North Americans than the British Edsel best-of, but not necessarily an improvement. Adds some tracks from both the original lineup and their unimpressive, more pop-oriented singles from the late '60s, and has more comprehensive liner notes, but also omits a few decent covers that are on the UK compilation, particularly their smoking, over-the-top version of "I Just Want to Make Love to You." —*Richie Unterberger*

The Shaggs

Alternative Pop-Rock
In 1969 the Shaggs, comprising three sisters, Dorothy, Betty, and Helen Wiggin, entered a Revere, MA, recording studio under the encouragement and financial support of their father, Austin Wiggin. The recording engineer, upon hearing the band, tactfully suggested that they weren't ready to be a recording unit, but their father insisted on catching the band on tape "while they were hot." The result of this session, their first

album, was called *Philosophy of the World*. Their follow-up effort, the appropriately titled *Shaggs' Own Thing*, actually reflects some growth in the area of technical facility.

Depending on your point of view, this is the most hilarious-sounding mishmash of ineptitude ever committed to CD, or it's an unconscious musical realization of everything great naive American art desires to be, believably innocent. Either way, you'll either love them or hate them. —*Rick Clark*

● **Philosophy of the World** / 1969 / Rounder ✦✦✦✦
This release compiles the Wiggins sisters' (otherwise known as the Shaggs) two releases *Philosophy of the World* and *Shaggs' Own Thing*. Anyone with unconventional tastes interested in taking a harrowing trip into the twilight zone of naive Americana pop should check this out. —*Rick Clark*

The Shangri-Las

Rock 'n' Roll, Girl Group, Brill Building Pop
Along with the Shirelles and the Ronettes, the Shangri-Las were the greatest girl group; if judged solely on the basis of attitude, they were the greatest of them all. They combined an innocent adolescent charm with more than a hint of darkness, singing about dead bikers, teenage runaways, and doomed love affairs as well as ebullient high-school crushes. These could be delivered with either infectious, hand-clapping harmonies or melodramatic, almost operatic recitatives that were contrived but utterly effective. Tying it all together in the studio was Shadow Morton, a mad genius of a producer that may have been second in eccentric imagination only to Phil Spector in the mid-'60s.

Originally the Shangri-Las were comprised of two pairs of sisters from Queens, NY (identical twins Marge and Mary Ann Ganser and siblings Mary and Betty Weiss). They had already recorded a couple of obscure singles when they were hired by George "Shadow" Morton to demo a song he had recently written, "Remember (Walkin' in the Sand)." The haunting ballad, with its doomy "Moonlight Sonata"-like piano riffs, wailing lead vocal, and thunderous background harmonies seguing into an a cappella chorus backed by nothing except handclaps and seagull cries, made the Top Five in late 1964. It also began their association with Jerry Leiber and Mike Stoller's Red Bird label, which would handle the group for the bulk of their career.

The quality of Morton's work with the Shangri-Las on Red Bird (with assistance from Jeff Barry and Artie Butler) was remarkable considering that he had virtually no prior experience in the music business. The group's material, so over the top emotionally that it sometimes bordered on camp, was lightened by the first-class production, which embroidered the tracks with punchy brass, weeping strings, and plenty of imaginative sound effects. Nowhere was this more apparent than on "Leader of the Pack," with its periodic motorcycle roars and crescendo of crashing glass. The death-rock classic became the Shangri-Las' signature tune, reaching No. 1.

Several smaller hits followed in 1965 and 1966, many of them excellent. "Give Him a Great Big Kiss" proved they could handle more conventionally, bubbly girl-group fare well; "I Can Never Go Home Anymore," a runaway tale that took their patented pathos to the extreme, would be their third and final Top Ten hit. These all show up on oldies collections, but lots of listeners remain unaware of the other fine singles in their catalog, like the moody "Out in the Streets," the dense orchestral swamp of "He Cried" (which cuts Jay & the Americans' original, "She Cried," to pieces), and another teen death tale, "Give Us Your Blessings." Some of their best songs, in fact, were B-sides; "Dressed in Black," yet another teen death drama, had a marvelously hushed and damned atmosphere, and "Paradise" was co-written by a young Harry Nilsson. Their most unusual single of all was "Past, Present and Future," which didn't feature a single sung note, presenting a somber spoken monologue and occasional spoken background chants over a classical piano track. It was too unconventional to rise above the middle of the charts, especially given that the narrative could quite possibly be construed as recollections of an assault-rape victim.

Unlike some girl groups, the Shangri-Las were dynamic onstage performers, choreographing their dance steps to their lyrics and wearing skin-tight leather pants and boots that were quite daring for the time. Their real lives, however, were not without elements of drama themselves. Their constant personnel changes baffle historians; sometimes they are pictured as a trio, and sometimes one of the members in the photos is clearly not one of the Weiss or Ganser sisters. Worse, the Red Bird label ran into serious organizational difficulties in the mid-'60s, and wound down its operations in 1966. The group moved to Mercury for a couple of dispirited singles, but had split by the end of the 1960s. Shadow Morton went on to an interesting, erratic career that included involvement with Janis Ian, the New York Dolls, and Mott the Hoople. Mary Ann Ganser died of encephalitis in 1971.

Even today, the Shangri-Las' history remains somewhat murky and mysterious; the original members have rarely reunited for oldies shows or talked to the press. The situation was exacerbated by frustratingly sub-standard reissues of their Red Bird work, which made it impossible to collect all of their fine sides without buying numerous packages, many of which boasted shockingly shoddy sound quality. Happily, the situation was rectified in the mid-'90s with excellent, comprehensive compilations of the Red Bird material in both the UK and US. —*Richie Unterberger*

● **Golden Hits of the Shangri-Las** / 1984 / PolyGram ✦✦✦✦
It includes all the eerie three-minute melodramas from one of the all-time-great girl groups: "Leader of the Pack," "I Can Never Go Home Any-more," "Past, Present, and Future." —*George Bedard*

● **Myrmidons of Melodrama** / 1994 / RPM ✦✦✦✦
Until the release of this import, there had never been a truly satisfactory Shangri-Las anthology; in fact, the group had been subject to worse piecemeal mangling than almost any other significant act of the 1960s. This 33-track production finally sets the record straight, including all of the significant A-sides, B-sides, and album tracks they recorded for Red Bird between 1964 and 1966, as well as an earlier single for a different label and four radio commercials. Includes every one of their hits, but anyone who likes those will be enchanted by quite a few of their more obscure numbers here; "Dressed in Black," "Paradise," "It's Easier to Cry," "Never Again," and "Heaven Knows" are all first-class (if sometimes mor-dant). Not everything is up to that level, but enough is to make a case for them as one of the very best girl groups, and the good sound and thor-ough liner notes are significant bonuses. It may be more extensive and expensive than some fans wish, but don't settle for the numerous skimpy, rip-off domestic compilations, all of which manage to leave off some key tunes; this is the definitive document. —*Richie Unterberger*

Best of Shangri-Las / Jun. 18, 1996 / Polygram ✦✦✦✦
This 25-song best of actually covers most of their discography, contain-ing all of the chart singles, and notable misses and B-sides like "Paradise" and "Dressed in Black." An excellent package, but the British *Myrmidons of Melodrama* (on RPM) is just a bit better, assembling a few more of their Red Bird tracks, including a couple of pretty notable ones ("It's Eas-ier to Cry" and "The Boy") that this domestic anthology omits. The Mer-cury CD does have their rare (but unexceptional) final two singles, which don't appear on *Myrmidons of Melodrama*. —*Richie Unterberger*

At Their Best / Collectables ✦✦✦✦

Del Shannon (Charles Westover)

b. Dec. 30, 1934, Coopersville, MI, d. Feb. 8, 1990, Santa Clarita, CA
Guitar, Vocals / Rock 'n' Roll, Teen Idol
One of the best and most original rockers of the early '60s, Del Shannon was also one of the least typical. Although classified at times as a teen idol, he favored brooding themes of abandonment, loss, and rejection. In some respects he looked forward to the British Invasion with his fre-quent use of minor chords and his ability to write most of his own mate-rial. In fact, Shannon was able to keep going strong for a year or two into the British Invasion, and never stopped trying to play original music, though his commercial prospects pretty much died after the mid-'60s.

Born Charles Westover, Shannon happened upon a gripping series of minor chords while playing with his band in Battle Creek, MI. The chords would form the basis for his 1961 debut single, "Runaway," one of the greatest hits of the early '60s, with its unforgettable riffs, Shannon's amazing vocal range (which often glided off into a powerful falsetto), and the creepy, futuristic organ solo in the middle. It made No. 1, and the sim-ilar follow-up, "Hats Off to Larry," also made the Top Ten.

Shannon had intermittent minor hits over the next couple of years ("Little Town Flirt" was the biggest), but was even more successful in England, where he was huge. On one of his European tours in 1963, he played some shows with the Beatles, who had just scored their first big British hits. Shannon, impressed by what he heard, would become the first American artist to cover a Beatles song when he recorded "From Me to You" for a 1963 single (although it would give him only a very small hit). Shannon's melodic style had some similarities with the burgeoning pop-rock wing of the British Invasion, and in 1965 Peter & Gordon would cover a Shannon composition, "I Go to Pieces," for a Top Ten hit.

Del got into the Top Ten with a late-1964 single, "Keep Searchin'," that was one of his best and hardest-rocking outings. But after the similar "Stranger in Town" (No. 30, 1965), he wouldn't enter the Top 40 again for nearly a couple of decades. A switch to a bigger label (Liberty) didn't bring the expected commercial results, although he was continuing to release quality singles. Part of the problem was that some of these were a bit too eager to recycle some of his stock minor-keyed riffs, as good as his prototype was. A brief association with producer Andrew Loog Oldham (also manager/producer of the Rolling Stones) found him continuing to evolve, developing a more baroque, orchestrated pop-rock sound and employing British session musicians such as Nicky Hopkins. Much to Shannon's frustration, Liberty decided not to release the album that resulted from the collaboration (some of the material appeared on sin-

gles, and much of the rest of the sessions would eventually be issued for the collector market).

By the late '60s, Shannon was devoting much of his energy to produc-ing other artists, most notably Smith and Brian Hyland. Shannon was a perennially popular artist on the oldies circuit (particularly in Europe, where he had an especially devoted audience), and was always up for a comeback attempt on record. Sessions with Jeff Lynne and Dave Edmunds in the '70s didn't amount to much, but an early '80s album pro-duced by Tom Petty (and featuring members of the Heartbreakers as backing musicians) got him into the Top 40 again with a cover of "Sea of Love." He was working on another comeback album with Jeff Lynne, and was sometimes rumored as a replacement for Roy Orbison in the Travel-ing Wilburys, when he unexpectedly killed himself on February 8, 1990, while on antidepressant drugs. —*Richie Unterberger*

Little Town Flirt / 1963 / Rhino ✦✦✦

The Vintage Years / 1975 / Sire ✦✦✦✦
A very strong 28-track compilation of his best '60s work. Most fans will want to stick with *Greatest Hits*, but this more extensive (though out-of-print) overview goes deeper without much filler. Major advantages are its inclusion of material from both the earlier and later part of the decade (with emphasis on pre-1966 sides), and extensive liner notes by Greg Shaw. —*Richie Unterberger*

I Go to Pieces / 1990 / Edsel ✦✦✦✦
A British import and an indispensable complement to the Rhino hits package. Sixteen important tracks, capturing Shannon's sound at its most achingly beautiful. —*Bruce Eder*

★ **Greatest Hits** / 1990 / Rhino ✦✦✦✦✦
An almost-perfect collection of his best tracks from the US catalog. The gaps can (and should) be filled by his album *I Go to Pieces*. —*Bruce Eder*

Sandie Shaw (Sandra Goodrich)

b. Feb. 26, 1947, Dagenham, Essex
Vocals / British Invasion, Girl Group
British singer Sandie Shaw had a string of girl group-styled singles in the mid-'60s before she retired in the early '70s. Shaw was discovered by pop singer Adam Faith in 1963, who led her to his manager, Eve Taylor; she released her debut single, "As Long as You're Happy," the following year. It didn't hit the charts, yet her next record, "(There's) Always Something There to Remind Me," hit No. 1 in the UK; the single hit No. 52 in the US, yet Shaw was never as big a star in the States as she was in the UK. For the next three years, she had a string of hits—most of them written by her producer Chris Andrews—that kept her at the top of the charts. In 1967, Taylor began to move Shaw into cabaret territory; the approach proved a success when the Bill Martin/Phil Coulter song "Puppet on a String" hit No. 1. She recorded one more Coulter song, "Tonight in Tokyo," before returning to Chris Andrews. However, none of her further work with Andrews resulted in hit singles. Released in early 1969, her English version of the French "Monsieur Dupont" managed to crack the Top 20; it would turn out to be her last hit.

In 1970, Shaw tried to become a family entertainer, yet those plans were scuttled by a failed marriage and scandalous rumors that circulated in the British newspapers. She subsequently retired for the rest of the '70s. Shaw returned to recording in the early '80s when BEF, a Heaven 17 side project, prompted her to record "Anyone Who Had a Heart," an old Cilla Black hit. The Smiths' lead singer Morrissey began championing her in interviews, as well, which led her to record a version of the band's "Hand in Glove" supported by the Smiths themselves; the single briefly appeared on the UK charts. Shaw recorded a version of Lloyd Cole's "Are You Ready to Be Heartbroken?" in 1986; like "Hand in Glove," it scraped the bottom of the pop charts. In 1988, she recorded an entire album, *Hello Angel;* although it featured songs by the Smiths and the Jesus and Mary Chain, it failed to make a large impression on the pop charts. —*Stephen Thomas Erlewine*

● **64/67 Complete Sandie Shaw Set** / 1994 / Sequel ✦✦✦✦
A double-disc set that features all of her big hits as well as all of her minor ones, this provides the definitive portrait of the British girl-group vocalist. —*Stephen Thomas Erlewine*

Nothing Less Than Brilliant: The Best Of / 1995 / Virgin ✦✦✦✦
Most of Sandie Shaw's biggest hits are included on *Nothing Less Than Brilliant*, but the collection tries to balance her '60s hits with her '80s comeback, which makes the disc somewhat inconsistent. Nevertheless, it is a good career portrait, featuring many of her finest moments. —*Stephen Thomas Erlewine*

Collection / Castle ✦✦✦✦
Collection is an effective overview of Sandie Shaw's entire career, from her early hits to her '80s collaborations with the Smiths. It covers more ground than the double-disc *Complete* but it doesn't have quite as much prime material. —*Stephen Thomas Erlewine*

Jules Shear

b. Mar. 7, 1952, Pittsburgh, PA
Guitar, Vocals / Singer-Songwriter, Pop-Rock
Though he's never been able to record a hit of his own, singer-songwriter Jules Shear has recorded several albums of highly accessible, hit-worthy material, and as a testament to his abilities, he's penned hits for others including "All Through The Night" for Cyndi Lauper and "If She Knew What She Wants" for the Bangles.

Born in Pittsburgh, Shear began writing songs as a teenager. He relocated to Los Angeles in the mid-'70s, joining his first band, a typically laidback combo called the Funky Kings. The band released one album for Arista in 1976. While "Slow Dancing" from the album (written by Jack Tempchin) would later be hit for Johnny Rivers, the three Shear songs were clearly the highlights of the album. Shear left the following year to form his own group, Jules & the Polar Bears, who released two critically acclaimed, though commercially overlooked, albums for Columbia. When a third album was rejected by the label, Shear forged on as a solo artist.

Signing on to EMI-America, he released two solo albums, 1983's *Watch Dog* and 1985's *Eternal Return;* both received critical praise but few sales. Once again, he was dropped by his label and unable to secure another deal. Shear then formed the Reckless Sleepers with the Cars' Elliot Easton. In 1988, without Easton, the Reckless Sleepers released their sole album for IRS, *Big Boss Sounds;* it failed to make much impact though "If We Never Meet Again" from the album was later covered by Roger McGuinn. In contrast to the Reckless Sleepers' hard-rock tendencies, Shear teamed up with the Church's Marty Wilson-Piper for an all acoustic, Dylan-esque album, *The Third Party,* in 1989. The album ultimately led to a spot on MTV, hosting the first 13 episodes of *Unplugged*—he left when the show switched to the single-artist format. Since then, Shear has released the two strongest albums of his career, 1992's *The Great Puzzle* and 1995's *Healing Bones. —Chris Woodstra*

Watch Dog / 1983 / EMI ✦✦✦✦
His first solo album following the breakup of the Polar Bears, *Watch Dog* features a new-found maturity in songwriting with an eclectic mix of styles from ultrasmooth pop to R&B-inflected rockers. Shear sounds much more comfortable on his own, even under Todd Rundgren's heavy-handed production. Highlights includes "All Through The Night" (a hit for Cyndi Lauper), "Whispering Your Name," and the more experimental, Brian Wilson-inspired "Longest Drink." Another unjustified commercial sleeper. —*Chris Woodstra*

Eternal Return / 1985 / EMI America ✦✦✦
Seemingly unfazed by *Watch Dog's* failure, Shear again produces a slick pop delight in *Eternal Return.* Shear explores a more soulful side in songs like "Steady" and the yearning "You're Not Around" while perfecting his hook-laden melodies. Despite being perfectly in line with the mid-'80s sound, this one also slipped through the cracks. The Bangles would later find a hit in the lead-off track, "If She Knew What She Wants." —*Chris Woodstra*

Demo-Itis / 1987 / Enigma ✦✦
Of interest mainly to fans, this collection of demos shows Shear's true talent, free of the often smothering-production that plagued his previous albums. In addition to early versions of old favorites, several songs that never made it on the LPs appear for the first time. —*Chris Woodstra*

The Third Party / 1989 / IRS ✦✦✦
Shear sings his songs with no more accompaniment than the acoustic guitar of Marty Wilson-Piper of the Church. The results are stark but impressive. — *William Ruhlmann*

The Great Puzzle / 1992 / Polydor ✦✦✦✦
Full-band production gives a pop sheen to Shear's excellent songs, notably the ballad "We Were Only Making Love." — *William Ruhlmann*

● **Horse of a Different Color (1976-1989)** / 1994 / Razor & Tie ✦✦✦✦
This retrospective covers everything from Shear's work with Funky Kings, Jules & the Polar Bears, and Reckless Sleepers to his solo work. Of particular note is the beautiful Byrds-like "If We Never Meet Again" and "If She Knew What She Wants," later recorded by the Bangles. —*Rick Clark*

Healing Bones / 1994 / PolyGram ✦✦✦
While Shear's albums are always packed with craftsmanlike songwriting, the production and arrangements often end up dating them. What sets *The Healing Bones* apart from most of his back catalog is a certain timelessness of the sound. The songs are definitely among his finest. Includes a cover of The Walker Brothers' classic "The Sun Ain't Gonna Shine Anymore." —*Chris Woodstra*

The Shirelles

Girl Group, Brill Building Pop
The Shirelles were instrumental in defining the girl-group sound and were one of the style's most successful acts between 1960 and 1963,

when they placed six singles in the Top Ten. Bridging doo wop and uptown New York pop-soul, the group projected a beguiling mixture of tenderness and innocence that was grounded in R&B as much as pop-rock. Forming as high school classmates in New Jersey, the Shirelles came under the wing of manager Florence Goldberg, who also ran the Scepter label. Many of their classic early sides featured innovative, occasionally string-laden production by Luther Dixon, who also penned several of their greatest songs. Top Brill Building songwriters like Goffin-King, Bacharach-David, and Van McCoy also supplied the group with material. "Will You Love Me Tomorrow," "Baby It's You," "Foolish Little Girl," "Soldier Boy," "Dedicated to the One I Love," and "Mama Said" were their biggest hits, but they also cut a number of delightful less-famous sides, including "Boys," which (like "Baby It's You") was covered by the Beatles on their first LP. After mid-1963, the Shirelles were unable to dent the Top 40, although they recorded some excellent songs, including the original version of "Sha La La" (covered for a hit by Manfred Mann). The group recorded well into the '70s, updating their sound into a more soul-oriented mode that was lacking in comparison. —*Richie Unterberger*

Baby It's You / 1962 / Sundazed ✦✦✦

A Shirelles & King Curtis Give a Twist Party / 1962 / Sundazed ✦✦✦

★ **Anthology (1959-1967)** / 1988 / Rhino ✦✦✦✦✦
One of the most consistently excellent and diverse of the '60s girl groups, the Shirelles were a hit-making machine. "Soldier Boy," "Dedicated to the One I Love," "Will You Still Love Me Tomorrow?," and 13 others can be found here. —*Jeff Tamarkin*

Lost & Found / 1994 / Ace ✦✦

Shirley & Lee

R&B, New Orleans R&B
Shirley Goodman's (b. Jun. 19, 1936) screechy vocals and Leonard Lee's (b. Jun. 29, 1936—d. Oct. 23, 1976) bluesy retorts added up to R&B gold during the '50s for the young Crescent City duo. The teenagers' debut on Aladdin, the Dave Bartholomew-produced "I'm Gone," was a major R&B hit in 1952. Shirley & Lee caught fire in 1955-1956 with three rocking smashes: "Feel So Good," the R&B chart-topping "Let the Good Times Roll," and "I Feel Good," all written by Lee. The pair stayed on Aladdin into 1959 before moving to Warwick and re-doing "Let the Good Times Roll." The "Sweethearts of the Blues" broke up after a few 1962-1963 singles for Imperial. In 1974 Goodman returned under the sobriquet of Shirley & Company with a No. 1 R&B smash, the discofied "Shame, Shame, Shame," for producer Sylvia Robinson on the Vibration logo. —*Bill Dahl*

● **Legendary Masters** / EMI America ✦✦✦✦
The "Sweethearts of the Blues" in all their glory, it includes "Let the Good Times Roll" and more. —*Dan Heilman*

Michelle Shocked

b. Feb. 24, 1962, Dallas, TX
Guitar, Vocals / Urban-Folk, Singer-Songwriter, Alternative Pop-Rock, Folk-Rock
According to her own, undoubtedly semifictional account, Michelle Shocked was born in Dallas, TX, in 1962, where she spent her early childhood traveling around army bases. In 1977, she ran away from her Mormon fundamentalist mother to live with her father who introduced her to country bluesmen Big Bill Broonzy and Leadbelly as well as contemporary songwriters Guy Clark and Randy Newman. She spent the next several years exploring the folk underground, spending the early '80s in Austin, where she began honing her own songwriting skills. Shocked left Texas in 1983, traveled throughout the US and became an activist in the squatters movement.

In 1986, while volunteering at the Kerrville Folk Festival, English producer Pete Lawrence was impressed by her campfire-side playing and recorded her on his Sony Walkman. The recordings surfaced in the fall of that year as *The Texas Campfire Tapes* on Cooking Vinyl Records and became a surprise hit in England, eventually topping the independent charts. The success led to her signing with Mercury Records in 1988. *Short Sharp Shocked,* produced by Pete Anderson in 1988, displayed even more talent, combining the informal, tradition-rooted folkiness of *The Texas Campfire Tapes* with a strong post-modern feminist perspective and punk attitude. The album quickly earned her respect among the alternative community and critics. In an unexpected move, Shocked returned in 1989 with *Captain Swing,* a '40s-style big-band swing outing that shocked her fans initially but had no shortage of strong material. In 1992, she took something of a step back with *Arkansas Traveler,* a rootsy collection of songs based on the blackface minstrelsy that covered all forms of early American, homegrown music. In 1993, Mercury finally became fed up with her confusing style jumping and refused to release her proposed gospel album. She then left on a solo tour, selling her newly recorded, independently produced (with Tony Berg) *Kind Hearted*

Woman. Late in 1995, Shocked began legal action against Mercury Records.

By 1996, Shocked was released from Mercury and embarked on the First Annual Underground Test Site Tour, with Fianchna O'Braonain. Another independent release, *Artists Make Lousy Slaves*, was sold at the shows. *—Chris Woodstra*

The Texas Campfire Tapes / 1986 / Mercury ✦✦✦
Her debut, recorded live around a campfire on a Walkman, is a wildly overrated but interesting introduction to her talents. *—John Dougan*

★ **Short Sharp Shocked** / 1988 / Mercury ✦✦✦✦✦
With the great miss-you song "Anchorage," this is Shocked's strongest record from start to finish. Rich and evocative, there's hardly a clinker in the bunch. Special credit to Pete Anderson for a sympathetic production job. *—John Dougan*

Captain Swing / 1989 / Mercury ✦✦✦
Whoa, stop right there. Read the title. This is swing music like your parents listened to. That's right, Goodman, Herman, the lot. Includes "On the Greener Side." *—John Dougan*

Arkansas Traveler / Oct. 1991 / Mercury ✦✦✦✦
Part three of the trilogy that began with *Short Sharp Shocked*, *Arkansas Traveler* focuses this time on American-roots music of the South, mainly rural blues and country; according to her theory in the album's liner notes, all of these songs are based on the legacy of blackface minstrels. Recorded with a mobile studio at various nonconventional locations around the country, it features an amazing array of guest musicians, including Pops Staples, Doc Watson, and Gatemouth Brown. Those who were put off by the unexpected direction of *Captain Swing* will certainly welcome this return to form—her best since *Short Sharp Shocked.* *—Chris Woodstra*

Kind Hearted Woman / 1994 / ✦✦✦

Artists Make Lousy Slaves / 1996 / Independent ✦✦✦

Shoes

Power-Pop

It may not have been the hip thing to do at the time but Shoes carried on the pure pop traditions of the Beatles and the Raspberries during the late '70s and early '80s with a charming innocence and execution unmatched by the more derivative bands lumped into the category "power-pop."

Shoes was formed in Zion, IL, in 1975 by Jeff Murphy, John Murphy, Gary Klebe, and Skip Meyer—the Murphys and Klebe all sharing songwriting duties. After one self-made and extremely limited album (only 300 were pressed), 1975's *Un Dans Versalles*, and the unreleased *Bazooka* (1976), they recorded their true debut for national consumption, *Black Vinyl Shoes*, in Jeff Murphy's living room and released it on their own label, Black Vinyl Records. Though it was barely distributed, enough critics and key people heard the record to start a word-of-mouth buzz. Eventually, Greg Shaw, the head of Bomp! Records, heard the record and arranged for the band to release one single, the brilliant "Tommorrow Night"/"Okay," on his label. A contract with Elektra Records soon followed. Elektra released the group's next three power-pop albums: *Present Tense* (1979), *Tongue Twister* (1981), and *Boomerang* (1982). Despite the instantly accessible, catchy quality of the songs, they were unable to achieve mainstream success; among specialists however, these albums, along with the debut, stand as the high points of the era.

Elektra dropped Shoes after the release of *Boomerang*, and Meyer left the band. The remaining three retreated back to the home studio, returning with *Silhouette* in 1984, a more subtle, keyboard-oriented album released only in Europe. They disappeared for the next five years and popped up again in 1989 with *Stolen Wishes* on their reactivated Black Vinyl Records. Since then, Shoes have remained more or less active, releasing two more albums—*Propeller* (1994) and the live *Fret Buzz* (1995)—as well as producing other like-minded bands for release on Black Vinyl. The collective efforts of Shoes in the mid-'90s led to a power-pop revival in indie-rock circles in the US. *—Chris Woodstra*

Black Vinyl Shoes / 1977 / Black Vinyl ✦✦✦✦
A homemade demo that became their first national release, this is a dazzling collection of pop songs driven by thick sheets of guitar and warm, emotive singing. *—John Dougan*

Present Tense / 1979 / Elektra ✦✦✦✦
Their major-label debut suffers from a bit of overwhelming post-production, but there isn't enough interference to ruin this great collection of tunes. The CD version is a two-fer that combines *Present Tense* with *Tongue Twister.* *—John Dougan*

Tongue Twister / 1981 / Elektra ✦✦✦
After a short stint at Bomp!, the Shoes were snapped up by Elektra for their major-label debut. The songs are good, the sound is right, but something is missing. Maybe it's because they were saddled with a co-pro-

ducer. Still, not to be missed. On the CD issue, *Tongue Twister* has been combined with *Present Tense.* *—Jim Worbois*

Boomerang/Shoes on Ice / May 1982 / Black Vinyl ✦✦✦✦
In an early interview, the Beatles were asked why they chose their name, to which Paul McCartney replied, "for all you know, we might have been called the Shoes." Fortunately, there *is* a band called the Shoes, and this is one of the finest pop albums ever made. Back on their own territory and producing their own records, this is the album that *Tongue Twister* should have been. It stands as one of their best. A live EP, *Shoes on Ice*, which came with the initial pressing of the album, has now been added to the CD version. *—Jim Worbois*

Silhouette / 1984 / Black Vinyl ✦✦✦
Now reduced to a three-piece (John Murphy, Jeff Murphy, and Gary Klebe), the band recorded their fifth album independently in their home studio in Illinois. A pleasant, though unexceptional album, *Silhouette* is a softer, more keyboard-dominated effort. Without an American outlet (they left Elektra prior to recording), this album was only available in Europe until the band's own label, Black Vinyl, reissued it in the late '80s. *—Chris Woodstra*

● **Shoes Best** / 1987 / Black Vinyl ✦✦✦✦
A 22-song compilation, this is a wonderfully comprehensive overview of this wonderful band. Good liner notes by former *Trouser Press* head honcho Ira Robbins. *—John Dougan*

Stolen Wishes / 1989 / Black Vinyl ✦✦
The Shoes still sound good and they obviously still enjoy what they are doing, but the tunes on *Stolen Wishes* don't stand up to some of their earlier work. Still, the Shoes never released a bad album, so you won't be out anything if you take a chance on this one. *—Jim Worbois*

Propeller / 1994 / Black Vinyl ✦✦

Fret Buzz / 1995 / Black Vinyl ✦✦✦

Shonen Knife

Alternative Pop-Rock

At their best, the Japanese punk-pop band Shonen Knife is an irresistible delight, combining sweet Beatlesque pop with buzzing Ramones power chords, singing about the schlockiest things pop culture has churned out. At their worst, the band's cuteness seems contrived, as if they were using their fractured English and obsession about Barbie Dolls, ice cream, and Hello Kitty as a deliberately cloying, cutesy marketing ploy. Even worse, at times it seems that their fans are not laughing with the band, they're laughing *at* their fascination with American kitsch culture and their bad English. Nevertheless, when taken on a strictly musical level, Shonen Knife's best records are truly intoxicating, rocking hard with a melody you can hum for days. *—Stephen Thomas Erlewine*

Pretty Little Baka Guy / Live In / 1986 / Rockville ✦✦✦✦
The CD reissue of this album adds eight live tracks (some that go as far back as 1982, when they were barely teens!) and makes this hands-down the best Shonen Knife record available. On *Baka Guy*, their pop-culture obsessions are clearly and humorously articulated ("I Wanna Eat Choco Bars" and "Ice Cream City"), and the record includes the best song ever about public bath houses, "Public Bath." Too often, cute, condescending terminology is used to describe Shonen Knife as though they were candy-floss teddy bears instead of a rock band. So, let's get one thing straight: this is a great rock 'n' roll record by one of Japan's great rock 'n' roll bands. *—John Dougan*

Shonen Knife / 1990 / Positive ✦✦✦✦
A superb collection of material previously available only in Japan on the albums *Burning Farm* and *Yama No Attchan*, covering Shonen Knife's early career from 1983 to 1985. The purist in me has become increasingly disappointed with Shonen Knife's records, as they sound more and more like generic alternative rock. On these recordings there's a nearly palpable sense of joy that comes with the discovery that you've mastered four chords, can keep a steady beat, and are now considered a band. Also, this material is unforced, almost carefree, and has little of the calculation that's creeping into their more recent work. Very simply, fabulous pop music. *—John Dougan*

712 / 1991 / Rockville ✦✦✦✦
"Good morning Shonen Knife freaks!" is the cry that opens *712*, Shonen Knife's last indisputably great record. The playing and songwriting has matured here, but not to the point where it begins to sound sterile or overly sophisticated. Of course, what would a Shonen Knife record be without a few goofy tributes to junk culture, as in "Fruit Loop Dreams" and "Expo '90"? There's a surprising cover of John Lennon's "Luck of the Irish" with vocal help from Redd Kross' Jeff MacDonald. Note: The song "Blue Oyster Cult" is not a tribute to the band; it's about food poisoning from eating raw oysters. *—John Dougan*

● **Let's Knife** / 1993 / Capitol ✦✦✦✦
Song titles "Twist Barbie," "Flying Jelly Attack," and "I Am a Cat" offer an accurate snapshot of this Japanese band . . . then there's the environmen-

tal anthem (?) "Bear Up Bison": "He has a right to live though he's ill ill ill-shaped/He's on the way to extinction/We only want what's best for him/Bear up bison never say die!" There's something fascinating about having Western culture thrown back at us in this quirky, unpretentious manner, and Shonen Knife are well on their way to becoming a cult favorite—for those who "get" it. —*Roch Parisien*

Rock Animals / 1994 / Virgin ++

Birds & the B-Sides / Mar. 5, 1996 / Virgin +++

The Silver Jews

Alternative Pop-Rock, Indie Rock
Not quite a side project, but not quite a full band, the Silver Jews are a "sister band" of the wonderfully sprawling, beyond-diverse group Pavement. And what a sister: the Jews' leader, D.C. Berman, is joined by Pavement's guitarist/vocalist Steven Malkmus and percussionist Bob Nastanovich, creating a sound that's definitely homespun, sometimes lighthearted, and other times emotional. Countrified ballads rest comfortably alongside experimental noise-fests on the group's two releases, 1993's *The Arizona Record* EP and 1994's *Starlite Walker*. Not surprisingly, *The Arizona Record* is a more rackety, unkempt affair than the full-length *Starlite Walker*, which was recorded in an actual studio in Tennessee. —*Heather Phares*

The Arizona Record [EP] / 1993 / Drag City +++
D.C. Berman, Stephen Malkmus, and Bob Nastanovich recorded this EP on a Walkman, and it sure shows. About as lo-fi, avant-garde, and willfully experimental as you can get on a shoestring budget, it sounds like it was lots of fun to record. While it's not essential listening, it gives a sense of history to the group's other recordings. —*Heather Phares*

● **Starlite Walker** / 1994 / Drag City ++++
Starlite Walker was recorded in an actual studio in Tennessee and contains lots of gorgeous pop songs penned by Berman and Malkmus. The album has an appealingly off-handed, laidback feel that gives simple but eloquent songs like "New Orleans," "Trains Across the Sea," and "Advice to the Graduate" an added intimacy and resonance. Aside from a couple of instrumentals, *Starlite Walker* is filled with enjoyable, folky-countrified pop that improves with each listen. —*Heather Phares*

Simon & Garfunkel

Folk-Rock
The most successful folk-rock duo of the 1960s, Paul Simon and Art Garfunkel crafted a series of memorable hit albums and singles featuring their choirboy harmonies, ringing acoustic and electric guitars, and Simon's acute, finely wrought songwriting. The pair always inhabited the more polished end of the folk-rock spectrum and were sometimes criticized for a certain collegiate sterility. Many also feel that Simon, as both a singer and songwriter, didn't truly blossom until he began his own hugely successful solo career in the 1970s. But the best of S&G's work can stand among Simon's best material, and the duo did progress musically over the course of their five albums, moving from basic folk-rock productions into Latin rhythms and gospel-influenced arrangements that foreshadowed Simon's eclecticism on his solo albums.

Simon & Garfunkel's recording history actually predated their first mid-'60s hit by almost a decade. Childhood friends while growing up together in Forest Hills, NY, they began making records in 1957, performing (and often writing their own material) in something of a juvenile Everly Brothers style. Calling themselves Tom and Jerry, their first single, "Hey Schoolgirl," actually made the Top 50, but a series of follow-ups went nowhere. The duo split up, and Simon continued to struggle to make it in the music business as a songwriter and occasional performer, sometimes using the names of Jerry Landis or Tico & the Triumphs.

By the early '60s, both Simon and Garfunkel were coming under the influence of folk music. When they reteamed, it was as a folk duo, though Simon's pop roots would serve the act well in their material's synthesis of folk and pop influences. Signing to Columbia, they recorded an initially unsuccessful acoustic debut (as Simon & Garfunkel, not Tom and Jerry) in 1964, *Wednesday Morning, 3 A.M.* They again went their separate ways, Simon moving to England, where he played the folk circuit and recorded an obscure solo album.

The Simon & Garfunkel story might have ended there, except for a brainstorm of their producer, Tom Wilson (who also produced several of Bob Dylan's early albums). Folk-rock was taking off in 1965, and Wilson, who had helped Dylan electrify his sound, took the strongest track from S&G's debut, "Sounds of Silence," and embellished it with electric guitars, bass, and drums. It got to No. 1 in early 1966, giving the duo the impetus to reunite and make a serious go at a recording career, Simon returning from the UK to the US. In 1966 and 1967 they were regular visitors to the pop charts with some of the best folk-rock of the era, including "Homeward Bound," "I Am a Rock," and "A Hazy Shade of Winter."

Simon & Garfunkel's early albums were erratic, but they steadily improved as Simon sharpened his songwriting and as the duo became more comfortable and adventurous in the studio. Their execution was so clean and tasteful that it cost them some hipness points during the psychedelic era, which was a bit silly. They were far from the raunchiest thing going, but managed to pull off the nifty feat of appealing to varying segments of the pop and rock audience—and various age groups, not just limited to adolescents—without compromising their music. *Parsley, Sage, Rosemary & Thyme* (late 1966) was their first really consistent album; *Bookends* (1968), which actually blended previously released singles with some new material, reflected their growing maturity. One of its songs, "Mrs. Robinson," became one of the biggest singles of the late '60s after it was prominently featured in one of the best films of the period, *The Graduate* (which also had other Simon & Garfunkel songs on the soundtrack).

It was unsurprising, in retrospect, that the duo's partnership began to weaken in the late '60s. They had known each other most of their lives, and been performing together for over a decade. Simon began to feel constrained by the limits of working with the same collaborator; Garfunkel, who wrote virtually none of the material, felt overshadowed by the songwriting talents of Simon, though Garfunkel's high tenor was crucial to their appeal. They started to record some of their contributions separately in the studio, and barely played live at all in 1969, as Garfunkel began to pursue an acting career.

Their final studio album, *Bridge Over Troubled Waters*, was an enormous hit, topping the charts for ten weeks and containing four hit singles (the title track, "The Boxer," "Cecilia," and "El Condor Pasa"). It was certainly their most musically ambitious, with "Bridge Over Troubled Waters" and "The Boxer" employing thundering drums and tasteful orchestration, and "Cecilia" marking one of Simon's first forays into South American rhythms. It also caught the confused, reflective character of the times better than almost any other popular release of 1970.

That would be their last album of new material. Although they didn't necessarily intend to break up at the time, the break from recording eventually became permanent, as Simon began a solo career that brought him as much success as the S&G outings, and Garfunkel pursued simultaneous acting and recording careers. They did reunite in 1975 for a Top Ten single, "My Little Town," and have periodically performed together since, without ever coming close to generating albums of new material. A 1981 concert in New York's Central Park attracted half a million fans and was commemorated with a live album; they also toured in the early '80s, but a planned studio album was canceled due to artistic differences. —*Richie Unterberger*

Wednesday Morning 3 A.M. / Oct. 1964 / Columbia ++
The Sounds of Silence / Jan. 1966 / Columbia +++
The sudden, if belated, success of the folk-rock version of "The Sounds of Silence" as a single called for an immediate accompanying album, so Simon & Garfunkel, who had more or less disbanded after the commercial failure of *Wednesday Morning 3 A.M.*, quickly reformed and recut many of the songs Simon had recorded in England for his *Paul Simon Songbook* solo album (issued only in the UK at the time). The album did not contain the follow-up hit to "The Sounds of Silence," "Homeward Bound," but it did contain the follow-up to that, "I Am a Rock," as well as Simon's musical rewrite of Edward Arlington Robinson's poem "Richard Cory" and other songs that aspired to poetry with an earnestness that made up for their preciousness. Still, this was a rushed album (S&G would never rush again), and it shows. —*William Ruhlmann*

Parsley, Sage, Rosemary & Thyme / Sep. 1966 / Columbia ++++
A far more considered album than the rushed *Sounds of Silence*, *PSR&T* features "Homeward Bound" and S&G's fourth hit single, "The Dangling Conversation" (their first not to be a big hit), plus a slew of memorable album tracks: "Scarborough Fair/Canticle," which became a single in the wake of its appearance in the film *The Graduate;* "The 59th Street Bridge Song (Feelin' Groovy)," which became a hit for Harpers Bizarre; and "For Emily, Whenever I May Find Her," a showcase for Garfunkel's heavenly voice, among other songs. —*William Ruhlmann*

Bookends / Mar. 1968 / Columbia ++++
A conceptual album about friendship and old age, *Bookends* was one of the best and most ambitious records of the 1960s. Album tracks like "America" and "Old Friends" have become S&G standards, and the LP also contains four hit singles: "Mrs. Robinson," "A Hazy Shade of Winter," "Fakin' It," and "At the Zoo" (the last two redone from their single versions.) —*William Ruhlmann*

☆ **Bridge Over Troubled Water** / Feb. 1970 / Columbia +++++
The massive commercial success of *Bridge Over Troubled Water*—it topped the charts for 10 weeks, won the Grammy Award for Album of the Year, included four hit singles, and has sold more than five million copies in the US—tends to exaggerate its significance in the Simon & Garfunkel catalog. Actually, it's a step down from the masterpiece of *Bookends*, containing some filler, such as the comic if slight "Baby Driver" and the pleasant if inessential live cover of the Everly Brothers' "Bye Bye Love"; it also lacks the previous album's musical and thematic unity. Still, one is admittedly splitting hairs when talking about an

album that contains such classics as the title song and "The Boxer," as well as such notable tunes as "Cecilia," "El Condor Pasa," and "So Long, Frank Lloyd Wright." This is Simon & Garfunkel's most popular album because it legitimately spoke to its audience, and much of it continues to set standards in thoughtful pop music decades later. — *William Ruhlmann*

● **Greatest Hits** / Jun. 1972 / Columbia ✦✦✦✦
Nothing much more than what it says, although the live tracks are interesting. — *Bruce Eder*

☆ **Collected Works** / 1981 / Columbia ✦✦✦✦✦
The three-disc box set *Collected Works* contains all of Simon & Garfunkel's studio albums, from *Wednesday Morning 3 A.M.* to *Bridge Over Troubled Water.* Though this is too much material for casual fans, any serious fan of Simon & Garfunkel or folk-rock will need to acquire the set, simply because it presents the albums in their best-ever sound. The duo did record a handful of tracks that didn't make the set—and if Columbia was assembling a true "collected works" compilation, they would have to be included—but the genuinely essential material is present, making it a good buy for the budget-conscious. — *Stephen Thomas Erlewine*

Concert in Central Park / Feb. 1982 / Warner Bros. ✦✦✦✦
Simon & Garfunkel reunited on September 19, 1981, to perform a free concert in Central Park, New York City. This two-record set presents some of the duo's biggest hits in a live context and also allows listeners a chance to hear what many Simon solo numbers could sound like in S&G mode. — *William Ruhlmann*

Carly Simon

b. Jun. 25, 1945, New York, NY
Guitar, Piano, Keyboards, Vocals / Singer-Songwriter, Adult Contemporary, Soft Rock, Pop-Rock
Simon, who possesses an airy, somewhat unsteady alto, was one of the more popular female artists of the '70s, presenting a blend of singer-songwriter introspection and slick pop-smarts. After working with her sisters in a music group, the Simon Sisters, and experiencing a false solo-artist start in 1966, Simon's career took a turn for the better with her self-titled debut. It produced hits in "That's the Way I've Always Heard It Should Be." *Anticipation,* her second album, went gold and produced another hit with its title track. With her third effort, *No Secrets,* Simon linked up with producer Richard Perry, resulting in a No. 1 album that included her politely snotty putdown hit, "You're So Vain." The followup, *Hotcakes,* was practically a duet album with then-husband James Taylor (they split in 1982).

Simon has continued to enjoy periodic chart success in recent years. Her hits include "Nobody Does It Better," "The Right Thing to Do," "Haven't Got Time for the Pain," "You Belong to Me," "Jesse," and "Coming Around Again." — *Rick Clark*

● **The Best of Carly Simon** / Nov. 1975 / Elektra ✦✦✦✦
Good collection from Simon's most popular period, including "Anticipation," "That's the Way I've Always Heard It Should Be," and "You're So Vain." — *Cub Koda*

Paul Simon (Paul Frederick Simon)

b. Oct. 13, 1941, Newark, NJ
Guitar, Vocals / Singer-Songwriter, Pop-Rock
In a career dating back to the '50s, Paul Simon has established himself among the best and most popular songwriters of the rock era. Growing up in Queens, NY, Simon befriended schoolmate Art Garfunkel, who had an angelic tenor voice, and the two teamed up as Tom and Jerry, taking the names of the cartoon characters. In the winter of 1957-58, they scored a chart hit with "Hey Schoolgirl"; both were 16 years old.

Simon continued to try to score hits in the late '50s and early '60s, reaching the charts briefly in 1962 in the group Tico and the Triumphs with "Motorcycle" and under the name Jerry Landis in 1963 with "The Lone Teen Ranger." He and Garfunkel teamed up again as a folk duo in Greenwich Village, signed to Columbia Records, and released *Wednesday Morning 3 A.M.* (Oct. 1964). The album flopped initially, but Simon, who had been spending a lot of time in England, was picked up as a solo artist by CBS [UK] and recorded *The Paul Simon Songbook,* released only in Great Britain in the spring of 1965. In the wake of the folk-rock trend prevalent that year, producer Tom Wilson took the acoustic track "The Sounds of Silence" from the *Wednesday Morning* album, over-dubbed electric guitar, bass, and drums, and released the result as a single in October 1965, a full year after the album's release. It took off and hit No. 1, establishing Simon & Garfunkel.

For the next five years, they were one of the most successful acts in pop music. Simon wrote the songs, and the two harmonized on a series of hit singles and albums. They split up in 1970, after the release of their most popular album, *Bridge Over Troubled Water.* Simon returned to solo work with *Paul Simon* (Jan. 1972), which could not hope to match

the success of *Bridge,* but which did sell a million copies and feature the reggae-tinged Top Ten single "Mother and Child Reunion." *There Goes Rhymin' Simon* (May 1973) was another million-seller, containing the hits "Kodachrome" and "Loves Me Like a Rock." After a 1974 live album, Simon released *Still Crazy After All These Years* (Oct. 1975), which topped the charts, won the Grammy for Album of the Year, and included the No. 1 hit "50 Ways to Leave Your Lover."

Simon took his time following this success, though he did release a greatest hits album featuring a new hit, "Slip Slidin' Away," and contributed to a remake of "What a Wonderful World" with Garfunkel and James Taylor. Moving to Warner Bros. Records, he wrote and starred in the film *One Trick Pony* (Aug. 1980), the soundtrack of which contained the Top Ten hit "Late in the Evening."

Another three years passed before Simon returned with *Hearts & Bones* (Oct. 1983), which did not match his usual level of commercial success. Simon experimented with songwriting styles and became interested in South African music, resulting in *Graceland* (Aug. 1986), which became his biggest selling solo album and won him another Album of the Year Grammy. Four years later, he delivered *The Rhythm of the Saints* (Oct. 1990), which did for Brazilian music what *Graceland* had done for South African music and was another multi-platinum seller. Simon played a free concert in Central Park in August 1991 (ten years after Simon and Garfunkel had done one) and released a live album from the show. In 1993, Warner Bros. released a boxed set retrospective on Simon's career, and he undertook a tour that featured Garfunkel on their old hits, as well as covering other aspects of his career. — *William Ruhlmann*

☆ **Paul Simon** / 1972 / Warner Bros. ✦✦✦✦✦
Backing away from the heavy production of the last Simon and Garfunkel album, Paul Simon's first solo outing is a quiet affair based around acoustic guitar. "Mother and Child Reunion," a successful experiment with reggae, is included, as is "Me and Julio Down by the Schoolyard"; the great Stephane Grappelli guests on "Hobo's Blues." Many of Simon's finest songs are found here. — *Stephen Thomas Erlewine*

There Goes Rhymin' Simon / May 1973 / Warner Bros. ✦✦✦✦
Simon listened to R&B when he was growing up, and he returns to those roots on *Rhymin' Simon.* At times, the results are true R&B and even gospel ("Loves Me like a Rock" was recorded with the Dixie Hummingbirds), but mostly there is a lot of beautiful, sophisticated pop shaded with blues ("St. Judy's Comet" and "Something So Right.") Not as fully realized as *Paul Simon,* but there is much rewarding listening to be found. — *Stephen Thomas Erlewine*

Live Rhymin' / Feb. 1974 / Warner Bros. ✦✦✦

Still Crazy After All These Years / Oct. 1975 / Warner Bros. ✦✦✦✦
Replacing the guitar with the piano as the primary instrument, Simon produced a quiet, introspective Grammy-winning album centering around lost love. Simon reunites with Garfunkel on "My Little Town," a track that sounds nothing like old S&G songs. *Still Crazy* doesn't really resemble Simon's two previous albums; it is a serious, somber album with none of the light touches present on *Paul Simon* and *Rhymin' Simon.* — *Stephen Thomas Erlewine*

One Trick Pony [O.S.T.] / Aug. 1980 / Warner Bros. ✦✦✦
This is usually categorized as a regular Paul Simon album, although its songs were featured in the Simon-written-and-starring film of the same name. Featuring New York session aces like Steve Gadd, Richard Tee, Tony Levin, and Eric Gale, the music has a contemporary jazz feel, and typical of a Simon album there are some extraordinary lyrics. "Late in the Evening" was the hit, but that's only the beginning. — *William Ruhlmann*

Hearts & Bones / Oct. 1983 / Warner Bros. ✦✦✦✦
An understated set of introspective folk-rock that contains some of Simon's finest, most literate songs. — *Stephen Thomas Erlewine*

☆ **Graceland** / Aug. 1986 / Warner Bros. ✦✦✦✦✦
Graceland is immediately accessible because the music is exotic yet familiar. As Simon says in the liner notes, he was drawn to South African music because it sounded "like '50s rock 'n' roll out of the Atlantic Records school of simple three-chord pop." Simon put his own melodies and lyrics to South African rhythms and chords, producing a remarkable hybrid. The songs are some of his best, recovering from a ten-year dry spell. Los Lobos guests on "All Around the World." *Graceland* is not only Simon's best album but an all-time classic rock 'n' roll album. — *Stephen Thomas Erlewine*

● **Negotiations & Love Songs 1971-1986** / Oct. 1988 / Warner Bros. ✦✦✦✦
A good sampler of Paul Simon's personal favorites and hits. Many of his frequent changes in style are captured here, as are the highlights of the *One Trick Pony* and *Hearts & Bones* albums. — *Stephen Thomas Erlewine*

Rhythm of the Saints / Oct. 1990 / Warner Bros. ✦✦✦✦
Simon moved from Africa to Brazil and produced an album that resembles *Graceland*, but is harder to grasp. The songs are more oblique than *Graceland*'s and the music is harder to absorb in one listen. After a couple of repeat listenings, the album begins to take shape, and melodies emerge under the heavy percussion. It's necessary to put some time into this album, but the results are well worth it. *— Stephen Thomas Erlewine*

Paul Simon's Concert in the Park, August 15, 1991 / Nov. 1991 / Warner Bros. ✦✦✦✦
Simon plays all the favorites from his African and Brazilian albums and recasts some old favorites in these settings. Sometimes the results are thought-provoking ("Bridge Over Troubled Water" and "Sound of Silence"), sometimes severely faulted ("Kodachrome" and "Cecilia"), but the album is immensely entertaining and listenable. *— Stephen Thomas Erlewine*

1964-1993 / Sep. 28, 1993 / Warner Bros. ✦✦✦
Simon's box set contains a great deal of fine music, including all of his hits, as well as a smattering of rare and unreleased material. However, he has already released two other fine compilations, and *1964-1990* treads the same ground as those. It also draws too heavily on *Graceland* and *The Rhythm of the Saints*, devoting an entire disc to these two albums, while shortchanging his work with Simon & Garfunkel. Collectors will also be frustrated by the small amount of rarities, as well as the poorly executed packaging. There's no denying that the music here is great, but this box could have been much more than what it is. *— Stephen Thomas Erlewine*

Simple Minds

Alternative Pop-Rock, Pop-Rock
Simple Minds was conceived in 1977 out of the remains of the Glasgow, Scotland, band Johnny & the Self-Abusers. Their initial albums were rather dissonant, moody, synth-heavy dance-music excursions that enjoyed increasing popularity in the British Isles, due to the band's incessant touring. The 1982 album *New Gold Dream* spent a year on the British charts and produced three hit singles; the follow-up, *Sparkle in the Rain*, was a No. 1 hit in England. In 1984, lead singer Jim Kerr's marriage to Chrissie Hynde of the Pretenders became a pop-media event.

Nevertheless, it wasn't until the band recorded a nonoriginal track, "Don't You Forget about Me," for the 1985 brat-pack film *The Breakfast Club* that the group began making a big impression in the US. During that time, Simple Minds played at the historic Live Aid benefit in Philadelphia. Their next album, *Once Upon a Time*, featured a clean, radio-friendly production by Bob Clearmountain and Jimmy Iovine and generated a few Top 40 hits.

Subsequent efforts have included a fine live album and a couple of dramatically produced studio releases that continue the band's hopeful humanitarian themes. *— Rick Clark*

New Gold Dream / 1982 / A&M ✦✦✦✦
New Gold Dream was the first effort (after many spotty earlier releases) to exhibit a focused collection of strong songs. The material, overall, is a coolly elegant style of synth-rich dance-pop. Among the album's highlights are "Promised You a Miracle," "Glittering Prize," and the title song. *— Rick Clark*

Sparkle in the Rain / 1984 / A&M ✦✦✦✦
On *Sparkle in the Rain*, Simple Minds assembled the best songs of their career and brought in producer Steve Lillywhite (XTC, Psychedelic Furs, U2) to help articulate their vision. The result was the best album of their career, thus far. Lillywhite's sweeping cinematic soundscapes perfectly suited grand songs like "WaterFront," "Book of Brilliant Things," "Up on the Catwalk," "East of Easter," and a version of Lou Reed's "Street Hassle." "Kick Inside of Me" rocks harder than anything the band has ever done. Highly recommended! *— Rick Clark*

Once Upon a Time / 1985 / A&M ✦✦✦✦
On the wings of the popular 1985 *Breakfast Club* soundtrack hit, Simple Minds enlisted in-demand producers Jimmy Iovine and Bob Clearmountain and released the ready-made-for-American-FM-radio *Once Upon a Time*. In spite of the fact that this album generated three hits with "Alive & Kicking" (No. 3), "Sanctify Yourself" (No. 14), and "All the Things She Said" (No. 28), Simple Minds had lost the inspirational edge they had attained on *Sparkle in the Rain*. *— Rick Clark*

Live in the City of Light / 1987 / A&M ✦✦✦

● **Glittering Prize** / 1993 / A&M ✦✦✦✦
Glittering Prize falls short of being a true anthology of Simple Minds, eliminating many key tracks (not even "Glittering Prize," the song the album is named after, is included) and giving too much weight to the band's later years (an inexplicable three tracks from 1991's *Real Life* are included). Still, all the mid-'80s hits are here, including "(Don't You) Forget About Me," making its first appearance on a Simple Minds album, which will be enough for most casual fans. *— Stephen Thomas Erlewine*

Simply Red

Adult Contemporary, Pop-Rock, Club-Dance, Blue-Eyed Soul
The British soul-pop band Simply Red was formed in 1984 by singer Mick "Red" Hucknall (born Michael James Hucknall, Jun. 8, 1960, Manchester, England) with three ex-members of Durutti Column, Tony Bowers (b. Oct. 31, 1952) (bass), Chris Joyce (b. Oct. 11, 1957, Manchester, England) (drums), and Tim Kellett (b. Jul. 23, 1964, Knaresborough, England) (brass, keyboards), plus Sylvan Richardson (guitar) and Fritz McIntyre (b. Sep. 2, 1956, Birmingham, England) (keyboards).

The group signed to Elektra Records and released *Picture Book* (Oct. 1985), which featured "Money's Too Tight (To Mention)," a Top 40 cover of a 1982 R&B chart single by the Valentine Brothers, and "Holding Back the Years," a Hucknall original that topped the US charts, caused the album to go platinum, and made the group one of the major successes of 1986. *Men and Women* (Mar. 1987), which featured two collaborations between Hucknall and soul songwriter Lamont Dozier, was less popular, though it generated the Top 40 hit "The Right Thing." (In the UK, "Infidelity" and a cover of Cole Porter's "Ev'ry Time We Say Goodbye" also made the Top 40.) Richardson left in 1987 and was replaced by guitarist Aziz Ibrahim, who was replaced by Heitor T.P. (b. Brazil). The third album, *A New Flame* (Feb. 1989), went gold due to the cover of the 1972 Harold Melvin and the Blue Notes hit "If You Don't Know Me by Now" that hit No. 1 and became a gold single. (In the UK, "It's Only Love" and "A New Flame" also made the Top 40.) By the time of the fourth album, *Stars* (Sep. 1991), Bowers and Joyce had left, with Shaun Ward joining on bass and Gota on drums, and saxophonist Ian Kirkham had become a permanent member. *Stars* was a relative commercial disappointment in the US (though it spawned Top 40 hits in "Something Got Me Started" and "Stars" and eventually went gold), but it became a major success elsewhere, especially in the UK, where it was the bestselling album of 1991, topped the charts for 19 weeks, and spawned the Top Ten hits "Stars" and "For Your Babies" and the Top 40 hits "Something Got Me Started," "Thrill Me," and "Your Mirror." Worldwide, it had sold 8.5 million copies by the second quarter of 1993. Ward and Gota were gone by the release of Simply Red's fifth album, *Life* (Oct. 1995), leaving a lineup of Hucknall, McIntyre, Heitor T.P., Kirkham, and backup singer Dee Johnson. The album again proved more of a success at home than in America, topping charts all over Europe, as did its lead-off single, "Fairground," while spending only three months in the US charts. *— William Ruhlmann*

● **Picture Book** / 1985 / Elektra ✦✦✦✦
The band finds a steady R&B groove reminiscent of '60s Stax house band the MG's, and, as with the MG's, it's all in the service of a big-voiced soul singer, in this case a British redhead. Features the US No. 1 "Holding Back the Years" and the UK Top 20 "Money's Too Tight (To Mention)." *— William Ruhlmann*

Men & Women / 1987 / Elektra ✦✦✦

A New Flame / 1989 / Elektra ✦✦✦✦
Although Hucknall tries to resurrect soul in his own original songs, he's most successful at evoking the past, notably on Simply Red's second No. 1, a remake of the Harold Melvin and the Blue Notes classic "If You Don't Know Me by Now." *— William Ruhlmann*

Stars / Sep. 30, 1991 / East West ✦✦✦✦
Although it didn't have a single as strong as "Holding Back the Years" or "If You Don't Know Me by Now," *Stars* was Simply Red's best album since its debut. It was smoother and more polished than their previous work, while Mick Hucknall was singing better than ever and his songwriting was improving. *— Stephen Thomas Erlewine*

Life / Oct. 24, 1995 / East West ✦✦✦

Siouxsie & the Banshees

Punk, Alternative Pop-Rock, Post-Punk
One of the first UK punk bands inspired directly by the Sex Pistols, Siouxsie & the Banshees fashioned their own dark, confrontational brand of rock, becoming one of the first goth bands. Led by the cold, detached vocals of singer Siouxsie Sioux, the band's music was abrasive but not fast; it was a wall of terror and darkness. On stage she frequently flirted with Nazi symbols, causing quite a controversy in Britain; despite the onstage imagery, the band's music was gathering quite a following in the UK.

After their first few albums, the band began softening its harsh sound, wandering into pop territory; in 1983, the group had a UK hit with its sublime version of the Beatles' "Dear Prudence." Siouxie's voice had become warmer and more accessible, which helped the band become more commercially successful. All the while, the band has never lost their creative edge, exploring new territory with each new album. *— Stephen Thomas Erlewine*

The Scream / 1978 / Geffen ✦✦✦✦
By waiting until punk essentially had blown over to sign a contract, the Banshees had a clear field for their harsh-rock attack, and plenty of time

to prepare it. The result is this fierce debut, which fulfills the promise of punk and suggests (unlike most of its progenitors) that it has a future. — *William Ruhlmann*

● **Once Upon a Time: The Singles** / 1981 / Geffen ✦✦✦✦
This compilation of UK singles (some appearing on an album for the first time) emphasizes the more pop sound of Siouxsie & the Banshees. Still not easy listening, though. — *William Ruhlmann*

Juju / Aug. 1981 / Geffen ✦✦✦

Hyaena / 1984 / Geffen ✦✦✦
Siouxsie & the Banshees' first album to benefit from a major-label push in the US (and make the charts) finds them taking a more melodic, expressive approach and even covering the Beatles' "Dear Prudence." Old fans howled, but there were a lot of new fans. — *William Ruhlmann*

Through the Looking Glass / 1987 / Geffen ✦✦✦
Well-selected album of rock and pop cover songs, including everything from Sparks' "This Town Ain't Big Enough for Both of Us" to "Strange Fruit." — *William Ruhlmann*

● **Twice Upon a Time: The Singles** / Oct. 13, 1992 / Geffen ✦✦✦✦
A good collection of singles, *Twice Upon a Time* picks up where *Once Upon a Time* left off, 1981 to 1993, their most mainstream period. The albums from this time span may be too ambitious for some, but the singles shouldn't be missed. This is probably the best introduction to the band. — *Chris Woodstra*

The Sir Douglas Quintet

Rock 'n' Roll, Tex-Mex
Texas always had its own brand of rock 'n' roll—a little bit o' country, a little bit o' blues, with a heapin' helpin' o' hot sauce poured over the top. Doug Sahm was no stranger to the studio when he formed the Sir Douglas Quintet in 1964; he'd been at it since the age of six, and already possessed an encyclopedic knowledge and innate understanding of those local flavors when the band cut its first big hit, "She's About a Mover."

The ingredient that set the Quintet apart was Tex-Mex, that curious, joyous, irresistible, danceable, festive feast that married the jumpy Mexican *conjunto* to good ol' rock 'n' roll. With Augie Meyers on the organ and a rhythm section that couldn't stop cookin', Sir Doug Sahm let it be known that good-time music was alive and kickin' in San Antone.

After the Quintet itself dissolved, Sahm cut numerous solo albums and collaborations, spreading the Tex-Mex influence. In the late '80s he and Meyers teamed up with two of their mentors, Freddy Fender and Flaco Jimenez, to form the Texas Tornados, keeping that high and happy sound alive. — *Jeff Tamarkin*

● **Best of Sir Douglas Quintet** / 1980 / Takoma ✦✦✦✦
Contains the hits "She's About a Mover" and "Mendocino." Not to be confused with the similarly titled albums on Tribe, Crazy Cajun, and Mercury. — *William Ruhlmann*

Sir Doug's Recording Trip: The Mercury Years / 1988 / Edsel ✦✦✦✦
An incredible 30-song sampling of his Quintet and solo years, it features most of the hits, some rare delicacies, and an educational set of notes by Ed Ward. — *John Floyd*

● **The Best of Doug Sahm & Sir Douglas Quintet** / 1990 / PolyGram ✦✦✦✦
This is not as thorough as *Sir Doug's Recording Trip*, but it's easier to find and gives you 22 essential tracks in sterling digital fidelity. — *John Floyd*

Sister Sledge

Soul, Disco, Club-Dance
Sisters Debra, Joan, Kim, and Kathie began recording as Sisters Sledge for Money back in 1971. They also did numerous sessions before dropping the "s" from their first name. They collaborated with Chic for some seminal dance-soul hits in the late '70s and early '80s. Sister Sledge enjoyed two No. 1 R&B hits and two other Top Ten singles from 1979 to 1981, as well as Top Ten pop hits. Both "He's the Greatest Dancer" and "We Are Family" were international smashes, with the Pittsburgh Pirates adopting "We Are Family" as their theme song during their world championship season in 1979. "Got to Love Somebody" and "All American Girls" were also major hits. The group began producing its own singles in 1981, but ran into tough sledding in the wake of the antidisco backlash. They began on Atco in 1974, and remained on Cotillion from 1976 to 1983. They moved to Atlantic in 1985, but were unable to regain their former glory. Kathy Sledge issued her own LP on Epic, *Heart*, in 1992. — *Ron Wynn*

We Are Family / 1979 / Rhino ✦✦✦✦
The Sledge sisters floundered in search of a format for several years before Atlantic gave them, almost in desperation, to the Chic production team. This 1979 album ended eight years of frustration and was their greatest triumph. The title track became the theme song for the world-champion Pittsburgh Pirates baseball team, while Nile Rodgers' splintering guitar and Bernard Edwards' steady bass, plus the duo's production

genius, garnered two huge hits for Sister Sledge in "We Are Family" and "He's the Greatest Dancer." — *Ron Wynn*

● **The Best of Sister Sledge (1973-1985)** / 1992 / Rhino ✦✦✦✦
Containing seven of their eight Hot 100 hits plus a host of lesser-known tracks, *Best of Sister Sledge (1973-1985)* is the definitive Sister Sledge collection. — *AMG*

Sisters of Mercy

Alternative Pop-Rock, Goth-Rock
One of England's leading goth bands of the 1980s, the Sisters of Mercy play a slow, gloomy, ponderous hybrid of metal and psychedelia, often incorporating dance beats; the one constant in the band's career has been deep-voiced singer Andrew Eldritch. (There is some disagreement as to whether the group took its name from an order of Catholic nuns or from the Leonard Cohen song of the same name.) Eldritch originally formed the band in 1980 with guitarist Gary Marx and recorded its first single with a drum machine dubbed Doktor Avalanche. Guitarist Ben Gunn and bassist Craig Adams were added to make live gigs feasible, and the Sisters built a reputation through several singles and EPs. Gunn left the band in 1983 and was replaced by Wayne Hussey. The Sisters of Mercy recorded their first full-length album, *First & Last & Always*, in 1985, but two years later internal dissent had split them apart. Marx left to form Ghost Dance, and Adams and Hussey departed shortly thereafter. A legal dispute ensued over the rights to the name Sisters of Mercy; Adams and Hussey attempted to use the name Sisterhood, but Eldritch released an EP under the name to prevent its usage, and the two finally settled on the Mission. Eldritch chiefly utilized a corps of temporary sidemen from this point on (although former Gun Club bassist Patricia Morrison was an official member of the group for a short time) and rebounded with his two biggest-selling American LPs, *Floodland* and *Vision Thing*. He is currently the group's only member. — *Steve Huey*

First & Last & Always / 1985 / Elektra ✦✦✦
Sisters of Mercy's first full-length album didn't quite have the powerful musical vision of their early EPs, but its gloom was more focused, making it an impressive debut album. — *Stephen Thomas Erlewine*

Floodland / 1987 / Elektra ✦✦✦✦
Sisters of Mercy's second album was a monolithic slab of goth-rock, featuring a more ambitious and accomplished musical scope than the debut, along with better lyrics. — *Stephen Thomas Erlewine*

Vision Thing / 1990 / Elektra ✦✦✦✦
Guitar-based pop fueled by the bright-sounding sensibilities of ex-Generation X axeman Tony James. — *David Szatmary*

● **Some Girls Wander by Mistake** / 1992 / Elektra ✦✦✦✦
Collecting a No. of their better singles, *Some Girls Wander by Mistake* offers a good introduction to the Sisters of Mercy. — *AMG*

Skid Row

Hard Rock, Heavy Metal, Hair Metal
Before alternative music crossed over into the mainstream, Skid Row was one of the top heavy-metal bands of the '90s, pounding out a radio-friendly mix of Bon Jovi, Aerosmith, and Led Zeppelin. On the strength of the "18 and Life" and "I Remember You" singles, their 1989 debut album sold over three million copies. The 1991 follow-up, *Slave to the Grind*, sold a million copies and hit No. 1. Later that year, the band began a quick fall from the limelight. The success of Nirvana (who, ironically, were called Skid Row in an earlier incarnation) changed the rules of hard rock, making Skid Row seem irrelevant. In 1995, they released their third album, *Subhuman Race*. — *Stephen Thomas Erlewine*

Skid Row / 1989 / Atlantic ✦✦✦

● **Slave to the Grind** / 1991 / Atlantic ✦✦✦✦
Skid Row's impressive second album has some great rockers, a nice ballad or two, even a heavy venture into thrash. It was one of the best metal albums of 1991. — *John Book*

B-side Ourselves / 1992 / Atlantic ✦✦✦

Subhuman Race / 1995 / WEA ✦✦✦✦
Skid Row waited out the grunge storm and returned in 1995 with *Subhuman Race*, their strongest and most vicious record to date. Abandoning most of the pop-metal posturing of their early hit albums, Skid Row strips back their music to the basics—roaring guitars and Sebastian Bach's shriek. It wasn't a hit on the size of *Slave to the Grind*, yet it made an impressive showing, climbing into the Top 40. — *Stephen Thomas Erlewine*

Skinny Puppy

Industrial, Alternative Pop-Rock
Skinny Puppy was one of the pioneers of industrial music, cultivating a scalding mix of electronics, samples, found sounds, and beats. All of their albums are thunderously menacing experimentations with dance and

synthesizers, creating a consistent body of dense, dark music that owes a debt to the nightmarish vision of Cabaret Voltaire and Throbbing Gristle. Skinny Puppy were primarily responsible for popularizing the cut-and-paste techniques of those '70s electronic forefathers during the late '80s; Ministry and Nine Inch Nails picked up much of their sonic terrorism from Skinny Puppy's early records. After industrial music had worked its way into the mainstream in the early '90s, Skinny Puppy landed their first major-label contract with American Records. — *Stephen Thomas Erlewine*

Bites / 1985 / Nettwerk ✦✦✦

Mind: The Perpetual Intercourse / 1986 / Nettwerk ✦✦

Cleanse Fold & Manipulate / 1987 / Nettwerk ✦✦✦✦
While it doesn't deviate from their previous lyrical territory, the music is more intense and scary; for the first time, Skinny Puppy has made an album that actually *sounds* frightening. — *Stephen Thomas Erlewine*

Vivi Sect VI / Jul. 1988 / Nettwerk ✦✦✦✦
Vivi Sect VI is the first explicitly political Skinny Puppy album, which adds some depth to their standard throbbing, gloomy industrial dance-rock. — *Stephen Thomas Erlewine*

Rabies / 1989 / Nettwerk ✦✦✦

● **12 Inch Anthology** / 1990 / Nettwerk ✦✦✦✦
Featuring both sides of four 12-inch singles from 1985 to 1989, *12-Inch Anthology* offers a good introduction to Skinny Puppy's psycho-terrorist dance music. — *Stephen Thomas Erlewine*

Too Dark Park / 1990 / Nettwerk ✦✦✦✦
Skinny Puppy's first studio of the 1990s is a thicker, more layered and bass-heavy record than their previous work, which makes it one of the most interesting albums they have released. — *Stephen Thomas Erlewine*

The Process / Feb. 27, 1996 / Warner Bros. ✦✦

Skyliners

Doo Wop, R&B
This Pittsburgh vocal group made a magnificent heartache ballad in 1959, "Since I Don't Have You." It remains among R&B's ultimate agonizing triumphs, and Chuck Jackson later did an equally gripping version. Jimmy Beaumont was the lead vocalist, with Janet Vogel, Wally Lester, Joe VerScharen, and Jackie Taylor. Beaumont, Taylor, and Lester had been in the Crescents, while Vogel and VerScharen were alumni of the El Rios. Their follow-up, "This I Swear," was a creditable effort that peaked at No. 20 on the R&B charts, but few remember it. Oddly, "Since I Don't Have You" only reached No. 3 on the R&B side and No. 12 on the pop charts. But it's certainly one song for whom the numbers really don't come close to telling the story. The Skyliners had two chart singles on Calico and then had one other song reach the R&B Top 40 in 1965, "The Loser," for Jubilee. — *Ron Wynn*

● **Skyliner's Greatest Hits** / Original Sound ✦✦✦✦

Since I Don't Have You / Ace ✦✦✦✦
The Skyliners were among the more dramatic, theatrical White doo wop groups. Their hit "Since I Don't Have You" has been covered by numerous performers, and it's among the 21 singles featured on this Ace anthology, covering numbers recorded for Calico and Laurie. Jimmy Beaumont's tremendous leads distinguished "I Swear," "It Happened Today," and the title track, among others. It's no surprise that such flamboyant performers as Patti LaBelle and Chuck Jackson are big Skyliners fans. — *Ron Wynn*

Slave

Soul, Funk, Disco
Arguably the hottest of the '70s Ohio funk bands, Slave had a great run in the late '70s and early '80s. Trumpeter Steve Washington formed the group in Dayton in 1975. Vocalist Floyd Miller teamed with Tom Lockett, Jr., Charles Bradley, Mark Adams, Mark Hicks, Danny Webster, Orion Wilhoite, and Tim Dozier. Vocalists Steve Arrington and Starleana Young came aboard in 1978, with Arrington ultimately becoming lead vocalist. Their first big hit was the thumping single "Slide" in 1977 for Cotillion, where they remained until 1984. Their best tracks were lyrically simple and at times silly, but the arrangements and rhythms were intense and hypnotic. Other Top Ten R&B hits were "Just a Touch of Love" in 1979, "Watching You" in 1980, and "Snap Shot" in 1981. Young, Washington, and Lockett departed to form Aurra in 1979. Arrington himself left in the early '80s. They added Charles C. Carter, Delburt Taylor, Sam Carter, Kevin Johnson, and Roger Parker as replacements and continued on, though much less successfully, into the late '80s. They moved to Atlantic for one LP in 1984, then switched to the Atlanta-based Ichiban in 1986 for singles and LPs that were just a shade of the former vibrant Slave sound. Their most recent release was *The Funk Strikes Back* in 1992. Rhino issued *Stellar Funk: Best of Slave*, a first-rate anthology of their finest cuts, in 1994. — *Ron Wynn*

● **Stellar Funk: Best of Slave** / 1994 / Rhino ✦✦✦✦
Slave's music was straight, simple funk: prominent bass lines, catchy phrases, and either comical or throwaway lyrics. This excellent 15-track anthology contains Slave's finest hits, each with a captivating, thudding bass riff: "Slide," "Just a Touch of Love," and "Watching You," among others. There are also five Steve Arrington numbers, among them his best dance cut ("Weak at the Knees") and topical tune ("Feel So Real"). Although not as acclaimed as Parliament/Funkadelic or Earth, Wind And Fire, this CD shows that Slave deserves recognition for its ability to keep the funk with style and verve. — *Ron Wynn*

Slayer

Thrash, Heavy Metal
Slayer formed in Los Angeles in 1982, featuring bassist/vocalist Tom Araya, guitarists Jeff Hanneman and Kerry King, and drummer Dave Lombardo. They got their start when one of their songs was featured on the *Metal Massacre III* compilation. Soon after that, they were signed to Metal Blade Records. In their early years, the band wore a great deal of eye makeup and took an over-the-top, often self-parodying approach to their lyrics, which addressed evil, death, Satan, graphic mutilation, and their corollaries. The band usually wore upside-down crosses and incorporated an inverted pentagram into its logo. Many in metal circles considered them a joke at the time, but they found a small following among metal listeners looking for something new, different, and extreme. *Hell Awaits*, their second album, was released to much excitement among their fans and showed strong improvement, but their sound was still somewhat murky. The band caught the attention of Def Jam owner and producer Rick Rubin, who at that time was known primarily for working with hip-hop artists. Rubin signed them to his label and took a raw, stripped-down approach to their third studio album. CBS refused to distribute the record due to what they perceived as advocacy of Satanism, giving the band wide publicity; Geffen eventually stepped in and took over. The record, *Reign in Blood*, was not only the band's finest moment, but perhaps the entire speed-metal genre's finest moment, winning over legions of new fans and becoming an instant classic.

Reign established Slayer as the fastest and most graphically extreme band in metal, but the band didn't want themselves pigeonholed, so for their next album, *South of Heaven*, they slowed things down and attempted a more refined approach, which did not prove quite as popular. *Seasons in the Abyss* brought them back a bit, combining the approaches of their last two albums. After their 1991 live album, Lombardo left the band to form Grip Inc. with former Overkill guitarist Bobby Gustafson. Slayer regrouped, hiring ex-Forbidden drummer Paul Bostaph. (1994) *Divine Intervention* was released to glowing reviews and debuted in *Billboard's* Top Ten.

Slayer's jarring, disturbing style is not only a very effective way of expressing their ideas, but it has also proved highly influential. The band is one of the major inspirations behind the burgeoning underground phenomenon of death metal, which takes Slayer-esque songwriting and subject matter to an even more extreme realm, both sonically and lyrically. Slayer is one of the few truly unique metal bands, and they continue to prove their worth, relevance, and originality today. — *Steve Huey*

Show No Mercy / 1984 / Metal Blade ✦✦

Hell Awaits / 1985 / Metal Blade ✦✦✦

★ **Reign in Blood** / 1986 / Def American ✦✦✦✦✦
Slayer's masterpiece opens and closes with two longer, now-standard tracks, "Angel of Death" and "Raining Blood." Sandwiched in between are eight short (all under three minutes), very fast bursts of aggression that change tempo or feel without warning, keeping the listener off balance and producing a very wild, disjointed, barely controlled effect. The short songs prevent the extreme graphic violence and paranoia in the lyrics from descending into self-parody. This is simply Slayer's best music, and it proved hugely influential in the evolution of the death-metal style. Along with Metallica's *Master of Puppets*, *Reign in Blood* is the pinnacle of thrash. — *Steve Huey*

South of Heaven / 1988 / Def American ✦✦

Seasons in the Abyss / 1990 / Def American ✦✦✦
Slayer bounces back here, alternating between pounding speed and more mid-tempo grooves. Their music continues in a more refined direction, and it works better than on *South of Heaven*. The band doesn't turn to the supernatural quite as much for its subject matter, preferring to examine real topics like war, murder, and human weakness from the traditional dark, dramatic Slayer viewpoint, but their music is so effective that the mood is much the same. This is probably their most accessible album, but it doesn't compromise a bit. — *Steve Huey*

Decade of Aggression: Live / 1991 / Def American ✦✦✦

Divine Intervention / 1994 / American ✦✦✦✦
Slayer sounds revitalized on *Divine Intervention*, with a raw sound and a rhythmic spark provided by new drummer Paul Bostaph. They continue in a more political direction lyrically, and the vocals are better than

ever. The band hasn't sounded this fierce, nor has the music been this visceral, since *Reign in Blood*. Slayer shows that they remain a vital and creative force, something that very few metal bands have been able to do in the post-Nirvana '90s. —*Steve Huey*

Undisputed Attitude / Jun. 1996 / American ✦✦

Percy Sledge

b. Nov. 25, 1941, Leighton, AL
Vocals / Soul
"When a Man Loves a Woman" existed long before Michael Bolton ever came on the scene—it's hard to believe that anyone could be unaware of Percy Sledge's original version of the song. As the first Southern soul recording to top both the R&B and pop charts in 1966, the emotionally supercharged ballad was a groundbreaker, and Sledge's remarkably anguished performance ranks as an unrivaled masterpiece of the soul genre. Sledge often seems to teeter on the verge of tears on his best Atlantic label releases of the late '60s. A product of the musically fertile area around Muscle Shoals, AL, Sledge recorded "When a Man Loves a Woman" and the equally moving follow-ups "It Tears Me Up," "Out of Left Field," and "Take Time to Know Her" with the same session aces that played on most Muscle Shoals classics of the period. By the turn of the decade, Sledge's well had run dry, although he's recorded off and on ever since. —*Bill Dahl*

★ **It Tears Me Up** / 1992 / Rhino ✦✦✦✦✦
This stunning compilation from the vaults of Atlantic Records spotlights the voice that gave us the original version of "When a Man Loves a Woman." Lesser-known hits like "It Tears Me Up," "Take Time to Know Her," and "Warm and Tender Love" are equally wonderful, and all are included in this must-have package. Great liner notes by Dave Marsh. Soul music just doesn't get any more heart-wrenching than this. Absolutely essential! —*Christine Ohlman*

Sleeper

Alternative Pop-Rock, Brit-Pop
Louise Wener (vocals, guitar); Jon Stewart (guitar); Andy Maclure (drums); Diid Osman (bass). Wener and Stewart met while studying politics at school in Manchester, England. Relocating to London, the two recruited Osman and Maclure and began playing Wener's original songs. The group made its debut in 1993, which led to a series of positive reviews in the British music weeklies. By November 1993, the group had released an independent single ("Alice in Vain"). In February 1994, the band released "Swallow," which charted in the Top 100; the following May, "Delicious" was released and became a No. 1 independent single. During May, Sleeper supported Blur on the London band's enormously successful *Parklife* tour. In February 1995, Sleeper released their debut album *Smart*, which entered the UK album chart at No. 5 and the independent chart at No. 1; it would be certified a silver album in four months. *Smart* was released in the US in March to positive reviews, yet it failed to duplicate the band's British commercial success.
   In the late spring of 1996, Sleeper released their second album, *The It Girl*. Again, the album was a major hit in the UK, yet it barely made an impact in the US. —*Stephen Thomas Erlewine*

Smart / 1995 / Arista ✦✦✦✦
"Inbetweener" is an intoxicating single. Fuzz guitars, light harmonies, sing-song melodies and hooks keep piling up until the whole thing collapses in a heap after three minutes. Unfortunately, there's nothing that matches it on *Smart*, Sleeper's debut album. Occasionally, Louise Wener comes up with a memorable hook, melody, or lyric, but can never quite pull them together into something as well-crafted (and sexy) as "Inbetweener." Still, the flashes of inspiration scattered across *Smart* prove Sleeper has potential—which they have already fulfilled once, with the single. —*Stephen Thomas Erlewine*

● **The It Girl** / Jun. 18, 1996 / Arista ✦✦✦✦
Although it lacks a standout track on the level of *Smart*'s "Inbetweener," Sleeper's second album, *The It Girl*, is a stronger effort, suggesting that lead singer-songwriter Louise Wener could develop into a distinctive talent. Certainly, her melodies and hooks are uniformly better this time around, ranging from the bouncy "Sale of the Century" to the sighing melancholy of "What Do I Do Now?" Wener's lyrics continue to be underdeveloped and simplisitic, but her hooks usually make that tendency easy to ignore. What would have made *The It Girl* an even stronger album is a clearer, more focused production. Although the sound of the album changes subtly throughout the course of the record, the overall effect is numbingly similar. The rhythm section lacks drive and the guitars lack balls—they blend together into one dull grind. Out of all of Stephen Street's productions, this is the most undistinguished. Occasionally, the song is strong enough to compensate for the flat production, and ultimately, Sleeper albums will not only improve according to the development of Louise Wener's songwriting, but also as the band finds the right producer. —*Stephen Thomas Erlewine*

The Slits

Punk, Post-Punk
Along with the Raincoats and Liliput, the Slits are one of the most significant female punk-rock bands of the late '70s. Not only did they bravely (or foolishly, you be the judge) leap into the fray with little, if any, musical ability (on their debut tour with the Clash, Mick Jones used to tune their guitars for them), but through sheer emotion and desire created some great music, especially when they began working with veteran reggae producer Dennis Bovell, setting the stage for a future generation of riot grrrls. Tthe Slits formed in 1976 when 14-year-old Ari Upp (sometimes Arri Up) ran into her friend Palmolive at a Patti Smith gig in London. The latter suggested the former consider becoming the lead singer for a new all-girl punk band. Upp agreed on the spot, and the Slits, with borrowed equipment and knowledge of two, maybe three chords, were a reality. They made some crude recordings (so crude that they make early Mekons recordings sound like 64-track by comparison) that were never widely circulated, and it wasn't until they nabbed the opening spot on the Clash's "White Riot" tour of England in 1977 that the Slits became a part of the punk pantheon. Despite this sudden notoriety, little was recorded by the Slits in the early days, save for a couple of sessions of John Peel's BBC radio show. These recordings place the Slits firmly in the punk-rock aesthetic of blaring guitars and braying vocals. But it's not generic-sounding rant: Upp's voice bounces along, alternately hiccuping and bellowing to the stiff rhythms; the songs are meditations on alienation, but there is a satiric, tongue-in-cheek quality to them instead of strident preachiness.
   It wasn't until 1979 that the Slits made their first proper record under the watchful, supportive eyes and ears of reggae vet Dennis Bovell. By the time *Cut* was released, the raging guitars were replaced by subtle reggae riddims, the band was now a trio (Palmolive had been replaced by new drummer Budgie, soon to join Siouxsie & the Banshees), and there was a stylistic suppleness that the Slits had heretofore never displayed. Upp's voice still warbled uncertain of the key, but for a band that had been playing their instruments for less than two years, this is a remarkably confident record. It was two years before a second record was released (*Return of the Giant Slits*), which was denser, darker, and full of surprises. But the Slits, due primarily to their interest in incorporating other forms of ethnic music into their mix, were leaping beyond what was commonly accepted as punk rock, and as a result, were no longer seen as a punk band. I'm sure this didn't distress them in the least, as they were more interested in expanding the barriers of punk rock rather than simply adhering to "rules" that claimed all punk bands must bash out simplistic guitar rant. By the close of 1981, Ari Upp was singing in Adrian Sherwood's dub-funk aggregation the New Age Steppers, and the Slits had become both legendary and somewhat notorious. Though much derided in their short existence, what the Slits achieved and what they meant to succeeding generations of young female rockers cannot be underestimated. —*John Dougan*

● **Cut** / 1979 / Antilles ✦✦✦✦
Almost as well known for its cover (the three Slits are half-naked and covered in mud) as it was for the music, *Cut* is an ebullient piece of post-punk mastery that finds the Slits' interest in Caribbean and African rhythms smoothly incorporated into their harsher, punk-rock stylings. Ari Upp's wandering voice (a touch like Yoko Ono) might be initially off-putting, but not so much so that it makes listening to the record difficult. Six tracks are revamped from earlier Peel sessions and sound better for the extra effort (especially "New Town" and "Love and Romance"). With its goofy charm, gleeful swing and sway, and subtle yet compelling libertarian feminism (get up and do it girls!), this is one of the best records of the era. —*John Dougan*

Return of the Giant Slits / 1981 / CBS ✦✦✦
The Peel Sessions / 1989 / Dutch East India ✦✦✦✦
This seven-track disc contains all of the material recorded at two sessions for John Peel's BBC radio show. It's vintage early Slits, lots of crashing and bashing, but with a touch of the sophistication and Caribbean influence that was to follow about a year later on *Cut*. Not just for completists, this is a valuable addition to any serious collection of the music of the punk era, and an interesting document of a young band's growth. —*John Dougan*

P.F. Sloan

Guitar, Vocals / Singer-Songwriter, Folk-Rock
He was there at the dawn of surf music, he was crowned king of the West Coast protest folkies, and he created some of the great American pop records of the '60s, yet today, the name P.F. Sloan is scarcely remembered outside of a circle of collectors and other period enthusiasts. Teamed early with Steve Barri, Sloan had a lasting partner. The duo cashed in on the surf craze as the Fantastic Baggies, and Sloan has claimed to be involved with countless more surf productions. Sloan and Barri wrote and produced hits for the likes of the Turtles and Johnny Rivers, and may best be remembered for Barry McGuire's "Eve of Destruction." Sloan's

own albums for Dunhill were based on the kind of material he had given McGuire, and despite being dismissed by the "serious" protest-folk community of the day, they stand as excellent on their own merits.

Sloan's attempt to shift away from the West Coast folk-rock he largely created was reflected with the R&B-tinged album *Measure for Pleasure*, and following another album in the early '70s, he was gone. In spite of the occasional live gig and rumors of a comeback, it appears that P.F. Sloan will remain forever connected with his '60s work, his behind-the-scenes efforts overshadowing the fine music under his own name. —*Steve Aldrich*

The Best of P.F. Sloan (1965-1966) / 1986 / Rhino ✦✦✦✦
While One Way's *Anthology* has a wider range, it may be that many listeners will prefer this 14-song collection, as it focuses exclusively on tracks from Sloan's first two LPs. This means you get nothing but sub-Dylanesque folk-rock, but after all, that's what most people value most by Sloan. The tracks are universally strong, including his most famous tunes ("Eve of Destruction," "The Sins of a Family," "Take Me for What I'm Worth") and lesser-known, equally worthy ones like "Lollipop Train," "From a Distance," "Here's Where You Belong," and "I Get Out of Breath." —*Richie Unterberger*

P.F. Sloan/The Grass Roots / 1988 / Big Beat ✦✦✦
While this isn't as solid as the other P.F. Sloan collections, the concept is interesting, combining some of his most famous solo performances with five songs that were credited to the Grass Roots in the mid-'60s, but were for most intents and purposes Sloan performances. You can avoid this confusing approach by getting the Grass Roots' *Where Were You When I Needed You?* CD and Sloan's first two LPs. But those original Sloan albums are pretty hard to come by these days, meaning that our choices are largely limited to relatively pathwork compilations such as these. —*Richie Unterberger*

● Anthology / 1993 / One Way ✦✦✦✦
A well-compiled 18-track anthology featuring Sloan's overlooked recording career. This is essential folk-rock in the singer-songwriter tradition. Included is his wonderful version of "Eve of Destruction," which was written by Sloan and popularized by Barry McGuire. —*Chris Woodstra*

Sly & the Family Stone

Soul, Funk, R&B, Pop-Rock
Sylvester Stewart came charging out of the psychedelic environs of San Francisco in 1967 with a band—and a sound—that made good on the communal spirit most acid-scorched bands only talked about. The Family Stone was rock's first fully integrated group: men and women, Black and White, they refused to play the music business game of racial and sexual segregation, mixing rock and R&B until, as critic Dave Marsh pointed out, "you couldn't find where one began and the other left off."

Songs such as "Everyday People" explained Stone's desire to mix everything up, while "I Want to Take You Higher" and "Dance to the Music" made explicit the community of the Family Stone. But Stone's optimism began to sour in the wake of Dr. Martin Luther King's assassination and the return of segregation, and his music took on a chilling tone. The dizzy glee of "Hot Fun in the Summertime" gave way to the scathing "Thank You (Falettinme Be Mice Elf Agin)" and *There's a Riot Goin' On*. Eventually, his career bogged down under a shroud of drug problems. But Sly Stone's stamp is as indelibly placed on pop music as James Brown's, and his influence can be heard and felt in the work of Kool and the Gang, Prince, George Clinton, and dozens of others. —*John Floyd*

Whole New Thing / 1967 / Epic ✦✦✦

Dance to the Music / 1968 / Epic ✦✦✦
Sly's second album reached the lower echelons of *Billboard*'s album charts due to the quintessential psychedelic, soul single, "Dance to the Music." The rest of the album is uneven, early, and tentative, with the full funk being a little further around the bend. —*Rob Bowman*

Life / 1968 / Epic ✦✦✦✦
The Family Stone's third album was a step forward with a harder drum sound, sharper horn lines, and more focused writing. Despite these developments, *Life* failed to yield a hit single ("Plastic Jim," "Life," and "M'Lady" were all fine candidates). —*Rob Bowman*

☆ Stand! / 1969 / Epic ✦✦✦✦✦
The album on which Sly's integrationist vision paid big dividends. Four of the record's seven songs, including "I Want to Take You Higher" and "Everyday People," charted as singles. The group contained Blacks and Whites, men and women; voices and instruments careened off one another in one apocalyptic vision of community. At the time, such an album seemed to be the clarion call of a new day. Brilliant. —*Rob Bowman*

★ Greatest Hits / 1970 / Epic ✦✦✦✦✦
This greatest-hits package was released as a stopgap while Sly was taking two years to record *There's a Riot Goin' On*. It's what you would expect from a greatest-hits package, with the addition of two newly

recorded monster-hit singles, "Hot Fun in the Summertime" and "Thank You (Falettinme Be Mice Elf Agin)." —*Rob Bowman*

☆ There's a Riot Goin' On / 1971 / Epic ✦✦✦✦✦
Sly gets darker and funkier. By *Riot*, Sly was a bona fide superstar. His personal behavior became more erratic, and his songwriting became more eclectic and adventurous. There is no precedent for such a record; songs were conceived from the rhythm up, and often left in sparse, naked, seemingly semifinished form. Sly's earlier hit, "Thank You (Falettinme Be Mice Elf Agin)" is slowed down, turned inside out, and retitled "Thank You for Talkin' to Me Africa." The result is an extremely personal stab at exorcism that takes the listener through the new reality of Black and White America in the early '70s. Mesmerizing. The album's most accessible songs, "Family Affair" and "Runnin' Away," were R&B and pop hit singles, the former reaching the No. 1 spot on both charts. —*Rob Bowman*

☆ Fresh / 1973 / Epic ✦✦✦✦✦
Stripped down and funky, minus thumb-popping bass whiz Larry Graham (who had left to found Graham Central Station), Sly turned in a fine album. One Top Ten R&B hit resulted with "If You Want Me to Stay," while two other songs, "Frisky" and "If It Were Left up to Me," also received substantial airplay on Black radio. In the wake of Sly's politics on *Riot* and his increasingly erratic personal and concert behavior, most pop-radio programmers seemed to grow leery of the Family Stone. The first single, "If You Want Me to Stay," reached No. 12 pop, but it was to be the last Sly Stone record to receive any significant pop success. —*Rob Bowman*

Small Talk / 1974 / Epic ✦✦

★ Anthology / 1981 / Epic ✦✦✦✦✦
This repeats some cuts from *Greatest Hits* but also includes highlights from *Riot* and *Fresh*. But you should hear those albums in their entirety. —*John Floyd*

Precious Stone: In the Studio / 1994 / Ace ✦✦✦

The Small Faces

British Invasion, Pop-Rock, Mod
The Small Faces were the best English band never to hit it big in America. On this side of the Atlantic, all anybody remembers them for is their sole stateside hit, "Itchycoo Park"—but in England, the Small Faces were one of the most extraordinary and successful bands of the mid-'60s; their music remains some of the most valuable and enjoyable of the era.

Lead singer/guitarist Steve Marriott's formal background was on the stage; as a young teenager, he'd auditioned and won the part of the Artful Dodger in the Lionel Bart musical *Oliver!*. Marriott was earning his living at a music shop when he made the acquaintance of Ronnie Lane (bass, backing vocals), who had formed a band called the Pioneers, which included drummer Kenney Jones. Lane invited Marriott to jam with the Pioneers at a show they were playing at a local club—the gig was a disaster, but out of that show the group decided to turn their talents toward American R&B. The band—with Marriott now installed permanently and Jimmy Winston recruited on organ—cast its lot with a faction of British youth known as the Mods, stylish posers who, among their other attributes, affected a dandified look and a fanatical love of American R&B. The quartet, now christened the Small Faces ("face" being a piece of Mod slang for a fashion leader), began making a name for themselves on stage, sparked by the group's no-holds-barred performance style.

The quartet was signed by manager Don Arden and brought to Decca/London to record. The band's debut single, "What'cha Gonna Do About It," was released in August 1965 and reached No. 14 on the charts; a second single, "I've Got Mine," failed to chart when released in November. Soon after its recording, Winston exited the lineup; he was replaced by Ian McLagen (organ/guitar/vocals). The group returned to the charts in February 1966 with "Sha-La-La-La-Lee," which rose to No. 3 in England. Three months later, they were back at No. 10 with "Hey Girl," and heralded this new single release with their first album, *Small Faces*. "All or Nothing" marked their first chart-topping entry, and its follow-up, "My Mind's Eye," followed it nearly as high. On the surface, nothing could possibly have seemed wrong for the band. Keeping up the standard of songwriting and recording that they were maintaining was difficult, however, and they were increasingly unhappy with Arden. At the end of 1966, the band severed their ties with him and eventually moved under the wing of Rolling Stones manager/producer Andrew "Loog" Oldham. Oldham signed the group as clients; by the middle of the 1967 he had gotten them moved over to his new Immediate Records label.

With the shift in management and label, the group suddenly found themselves with a drastically reduced touring schedule and vastly increased time available in the studio. Their sound immediately became looser. They remained a top-flight R&B-driven band, but a much wider array of sounds and instruments began figuring in their music. Their first Immediate album, entitled *Small Faces* (known in the US as *There Are but Four Small Faces*), was issued in mid-1967, and was an instant hit. In

August of the year, they released "Itchycoo Park," a lilting, lyrical idyll to the Summer of Love that captured the hearts of listeners on both sides of the Atlantic. The band had bigger aspirations than doing more hit singles and set to work across five months during 1968 in at least four different studios recording what proved to be their magnum opus, *Ogden's Nut Gone Flake*. The group's fortunes didn't equal the artistic success of the album. In June 1968, to announce the release of the album, Immediate took out an ad in the music trade papers that included a parody of the Lord's Prayer managed to offend several million people before an apology from the band was issued. And Immediate, over the objections of Marriott, chose to release the song "Lazy Sunday"—which he'd recorded as a joke—as a single, and its rise to No. 2 on the British charts did nothing to ease his unhappiness.

Already, the group was showing serious signs of strain. A tour of Australia ended with complaints from the authorities concerning the band's behavior, and there were reports of late arrivals (or no-shows) by the band at their English gigs. "The Universal," a single released in the summer of 1968, was to have been Marriott's most serious effort in that vein in over a year; it subsequently failed to crack the Top 20, and much of his interest in continuing with the band seemed to falter. The end came soon after, on New Year's Day, 1969, when Marriott suddenly left the stage while the band was jamming to "Lazy Sunday" during a show at the Alexandria Palace; he later called Peter Frampton, a guitarist from the Herd, and the two began mapping plans for a band of their own called Humble Pie.

The Small Faces did carry on into 1969, but it wasn't the same. With Marriott gone, they needed a replacement singer and lead guitarist, and found them in Rod Stewart and Ron Wood. They carried on under the name the Small Faces briefly, before dropping the "Small" and going on to greater glory as the Faces. During the mid-1970s the Small Faces reunited (without Ronnie Lane) for two albums, *Playmates* and *78 in the Shade*, that attracted a lot of press attention but nothing resembling the chart action of their earlier releases. Lane recorded with Pete Townshend, amongst others, before contracting multiple sclerosis, which ended his career as a musician (he later organized the A.R.M.S. benefit concerts to raise money for research into a cure for the disease). Jones subsequently joined the Who, replacing Keith Moon after the latter's sudden death in 1978, and did a couple of tours and a pair of albums with the band. Steve Marriott always seemed poised for a comeback, and in 1991 it looked as though he was going to finally pull it off—alas, he died in his sleep when fire swept his home in England, tragically just a couple of days after beginning work on a new album in America with his former bandmate Peter Frampton. — *Bruce Eder*

Small Faces / 1966 / PolyGram ✦✦✦✦
The group's debut album is a rip-roaring R&B showcase, built on the interplay of Steve Marriott's loud, mourning, soul-shouting voice and the grinding sound of his guitar and Ian McLagan's organ. Especially not to be missed by anyone who likes the early Rolling Stones or the Who in their early R&B period. — *Bruce Eder*

From the Beginning / 1967 / PolyGram ✦✦✦
☆ **There Are but Four Small Faces** / 1967 / Sony ✦✦✦✦✦
The band's first album for Andrew "Loog" Oldham's Immediate label originally appeared in two different forms in England (where it was known as *Small Faces*) and America, and the two song lineups have been combined on an early-'90s American Sony Music reissue. The music here is much more fully developed and experimental than their preceding album, still largely R&B-based (apart from the delightfully trippy "Itchycoo Park," the band's sole American hit) but with lots of unusual sounds and recording techniques being attempted. — *Bruce Eder*

☆ **Ogden's Nut Gone Flake** / 1968 / Sony ✦✦✦✦✦
The best album the Small Faces ever released and one of the great records of the late '60s, a kind of Cockney *Sgt. Pepper*, with tough, grinding rock numbers, blues shouts, and psychedelia all mixing together into one brilliant whole. A vital addition to any record or CD collection, and also a promotional one—a promotional ad taken out in the British music trades at the time managed to blaspheme several religions at once. Alas, Steve Marriott decided to call it quits with the group less than six months after this record was released. — *Bruce Eder*

Autumn Stone / 1969 / Immediate ✦✦✦
★ **25 Greatest Hits** / 1992 / Repertoire ✦✦✦✦✦
Featuring all of their big British hits from "What'cha Gonna Do About It" to "The Universal," as well as worthy obscurities like "Donkey Rides a Penny a Glass," *25 Greatest Hits* is the best Small Faces compilation available, even if the tracks aren't presented in chronological order. — *Stephen Thomas Erlewine*

The Immediate Years / Jan. 1996 / Charly ✦✦✦
The Definitive Anthology of the Small Faces / Feb. 1996 / Repertoire ✦✦✦✦

All or Nothing / 199 / CBS ✦✦✦✦
The best collection to date of odd outtakes, obscure B-sides, and other rarities, remastered for superior sound and reconfigured so that, among other advantages, the live tracks from *The Autumn Stone* are assembled together in sequence. Also contains lots of alternate takes, instrumental backing tracks etc. — *Bruce Eder*

Smashing Pumpkins

Alternative Pop-Rock
Smashing Pumpkins played the indie-rock game, although they didn't quite fit in with the rest of the crowd. Out of his affection for '70s stadium and progressive-rock, guitarist/vocalist Billy Corgan fashioned a distinctive, layered sound for the band, dripping with distortion, thick hooks, and airy melodies. Unlike most alternative bands, Smashing Pumpkins don't try to disguise their pretensions or their roots; they are an album rock band, in the tradition of Queen and Black Sabbath. Where most alternative bands use guitar for sonic texture, they use it as a lead instrument in intricate compositions. Smashing Pumpkins rose to success through the alternative scene instead of AOR for two reasons. First, their music was too detailed, creative, and different to fit easily into the conservative hard-rock radio formats of the pre-Nirvana '90s. Secondly, Corgan's lyrics are definitely post-punk, celebrating self-proclaimed geeks and detailing depression and angst. Their mammoth guitars and fragility made them alternative superstars with their 1991 debut *Gish*. When they honed their riffs and Corgan tightened his songwriting for the follow-up, 1993's major-label debut *Siamese Dream*, the band crossed over into the mainstream. After all, most of their new fans didn't pay attention to the lyrics of "Cherub Rock" or "Today"—they just liked the way those guitars sounded. — *Stephen Thomas Erlewine*

Gish / 1991 / Caroline ✦✦✦✦
A fine debut album that follows a simple structural philosophy: fast songs good, slow songs not so good. Snazzy sound courtesy of hip independent producer Butch Vig. — *John Dougan*

Lull / 1992 / Caroline ✦✦✦
● **Siamese Dream** / 1993 / Virgin ✦✦✦✦
Dense with detail and texture, Smashing Pumpkins' breakthrough second album is a highly personal, ambitious record that unfolds after a few plays. *Siamese Dream* expands on all the promise of *Gish*, offering more pop melodies, heavy-metal riffs, bombastic progressive instrumental sections, and punk angst. Apart from the succinct "Today," the music is so dense and insular that it requires some patience for it to make sense, but given some time, *Siamese Dream* becomes addictive. — *Stephen Thomas Erlewine*

Pisces Iscariot / 1994 / Capitol ✦✦✦
Mellon Collie and the Infinite Sadness / Oct. 24, 1995 / Virgin ✦✦✦✦
Smashing Pumpkins didn't shy away from making the follow-up to the grand, intricate *Siamese Dream*. With *Mellon Collie and the Infinite Sadness*, the band turns in one of the most ambitious and indulgent albums in rock history. Lasting over two hours and featuring 28 songs, the album is certainly a challenging listen. To Billy Corgan's credit, it's a rewarding and compelling one as well. Although the artistic scope of the album is immense, the Smashing Pumpkins flourish in such an overblown setting. Corgan's songwriting has never been limited by conventional notions of what a rock band can do, even if it is clear that he draws inspiration from scores of '70s heavy-metal and art-rock bands. Instead of copying the sounds of his favorite records, he expands on their ideas, making the gentle piano of the title track and the sighing "1979" sit comfortably against the volcanic rush of "Jellybelly" and "Zero." In between those two extremes lay an array of musical styles, drawing from rock, pop, folk, and classical. Some of the songs don't work as well as others, but *Mellon Collie* never seems to drag. Occasionally they fall flat on their face, but over the entire album, the Smashing Pumpkins prove that they are one of the more creative and consistent bands of the '90s. — *Stephen Thomas Erlewine*

Huey Piano Smith

b. Jan. 26, 1934, New Orleans, LA
Piano / R&B, New Orleans R&B
At one time a madcap vocalist and underrated pianist, Huey "Piano" Smith was a star in New Orleans during the '50s. He sang with Earl King from 1951 to 1954, then recorded with Guitar Slim in the early '50s. He did several sessions and also led the Clowns, whose roster at one point included Bobby Marchan. Smith's biggest hit wasn't the song he's best known for, "Rocking Pneumonia and the Boogie Woogie Flu," but "Don't You Just Know It," which was his only Top Ten pop and R&B hit. It reached No. 4 R&B and No. 9 pop in 1958, a year after "Rocking Pneumonia" peaked at No. 5 R&B. Smith kept going until he became a Jehovah's Witness and left the music business. — *Ron Wynn*

● **Rock & Roll Revival** / Jan. 1991 / Ace ✦✦✦✦
A terrific 16-track collection of Huey "Piano" Smith & the Clowns' biggest hits and best material, including "Rocking Pneumonia" and "Don't You Just Know It," plus a couple of fine previously unreleased tracks. —*Stephen Thomas Erlewine*

Patti Smith

b. Dec. 30, 1946
Vocals / Rock 'n' Roll, Proto-Punk
Patti Smith is a poet and rock singer who first gained notice when reading her poetry at gatherings in New York City in the early '70s. By 1974 Smith had edged toward music by reading with the backup of electric guitarist and rock critic Lenny Kaye, notably on her independent-label single, "Piss Factory." By 1975 Smith had organized a band that was playing in such clubs as the punk birthplace in New York, CBGB's, and she earned a contract with Arista Records. This resulted in the release of *Horses*, a critically acclaimed album that featured her songs, sometimes melded to dramatic readings, and such rock oldies as "Land of 1,000 Dances." *Radio Ethiopia* was both mainstream-rock-oriented and more experimental, depending on which track you played. With 1978's *Easter*, Smith was definitely moving in a more commercial direction, especially by pairing with Bruce Springsteen for the hit single "Because the Night." That marked the high point of Smith's rock career. *Wave* (1979) found her waving goodbye; she married ex-MC5 guitarist Fred "Sonic" Smith and retired from the music business. Her return came with the promising 1988 album *Dream of Life*, but she was not back to full-time duty. —*William Ruhlmann*

★ **Horses** / Nov. 1975 / Arista ✦✦✦✦✦
One of the more successful matings of poetry and rock, this landmark changed the role of women in rock and paved the way for rock without excess. —*Jeff Tamarkin*

Radio Ethiopia / Oct. 1976 / Arista ✦✦✦
Her disjointed second album takes the focus off of Smith's words and shifts it to her excellent band. Intelligent rock 'n' roll, minus a bit of the edge. —*Jeff Tamarkin*

Easter / Mar. 1978 / Arista ✦✦✦✦
Although it contained the hit cover of Springsteen's "Because the Night," Smith's writing was weaker on this third album. The group burns though. —*Jeff Tamarkin*

Wave / May 1979 / Arista ✦✦✦
The Todd Rundgren-produced final album by the PSG is unfocused and over-produced. Smith was smart to quit while she was ahead. —*Jeff Tamarkin*

Dream of Life / Jun. 1988 / Arista ✦✦✦

Gone Again / Jun. 18, 1996 / Arista ✦✦✦

Warren Smith

b. Feb. 7, 1933, **d.** Jan. 31, 1980
Vocals / Traditional Country, Rockabilly
For sheer, heartfelt vocalizing abilities, of all the folks who stood in front of the microphone at Sun studio, Warren Smith may have been the most talented. Equally adept at storming rockabilly and the most gut-wrenching of country ballads, Smith always sang from the heart, without giving in to phony rasping or histrionics. Though typecast as strictly a rocker, Smith left Sun and achieved minor success in the '60s as a country singer, his first love. —*Cub Koda*

The Classic Recordings 1956-59 / 1992 / Bear Family ✦✦✦✦
Smith's entire output (31 tracks in all) for Sun Records. Includes the rockabilly classics "Rock & Roll Ruby," "Ubangi Stomp," and "Miss Froggie," as well as heartfelt country performances on "The Darkest Cloud," "I'd Rather Be Safe Than Sorry," and "Goodbye Mr. Love." No Sun collection can really be considered complete without adding this one to the list. —*Cub Koda*

● **Uranium Rock: Best Of** / 1995 / AVI ✦✦✦✦

The Smithereens

Rock 'n' Roll
Pat DiNizio (vocals, guitar), Jim Babjak (guitar), Mike Mesaros (bass), and Dennis Diken (drums) make up the Smithereens, formed in New Jersey in 1980 when DiNizio answered an ad placed by the three others. The band plays in a '60s British Invasion rock 'n' roll style, DiNizio's songs overtly evoking that era. The Smithereens gigged around the New York area and recorded a couple of EPs on small labels in the early '80s, then scored a record contract with the independent Enigma, which issued *Especially for You* in 1986. It stayed on the charts nearly a year. Its follow-up, *Green Thoughts* (1988), also showed staying power in the charts, producing the AOR radio hit "Only a Memory." The Smithereens reached the pop Top 40 with "A Girl Like You" from their third album, *11*, in 1989. A fourth album, *Blow Up*, stirred college and AOR radio interest for the track "Top of the Pops" in 1991, but it was less of a sales success. The group's fifth album, *A Date with the Smithereens* (1994), didn't gain much attention at either radio or retail. The band released a greatest-hits collection the following year. —*William Ruhlmann*

Beauty & Sadness / 1983 / Enigma ✦✦✦

Especially for You / 1986 / Enigma ✦✦✦✦
On *Especially for You*, the Smithereens achieved a near-perfect blend of exuberant rockers and moody excursions. Don Dixon's production captured the band's exciting chemistry, while keeping lead singer Pat DiNizio up front in the mix, on this, their best album. "Behind the Wall of Sleep" and "Blood and Roses" were big college-music favorites, helping pave the way for greater success. Other highlights included "Strangers When We Meet," "Time and Time Again," "Groovy Tuesday," and "Alone at Midnight." —*Rick Clark*

Green Thoughts / 1988 / Capitol ✦✦✦✦
The follow-up to *Especially for You* was another impressive batch of power-pop rockers. "Only a Memory" and "House We Used to Live In" were FM rock hits. Again, Dixon's production demonstrated his empathy for the band's sound. Other highlights included "Something New," "Drown in My Own Tears," and the title track. —*Rick Clark*

11 / 1990 / Capitol ✦✦✦
On *11*, the Smithereens employed alternative hard-rock producer Ed Stasium (Cavedogs, Living Colour) to beef up their sound. The result was a thick guitar-riff-heavy sound. The approach helped "A Girl Like You" become a big rock and MTV hit but, taken as a whole, *11* lacked the dynamics and natural soundstage that made their earlier work so fresh sounding. "Yesterday Girl," "Baby Be Good," and "A Girl Like You" are highlights, though. —*Rick Clark*

Blow Up / 1991 / Capitol ✦✦✦

Date with the Smithereens / Apr. 26, 1994 / RCA ✦✦✦

Attack of the Smithereens / 1995 / Capitol ✦✦✦✦
At first glance, a Smithereens rarities compilation might seem like an odd release. After all, the band never had more than one gold album and none of their singles cracked the Top 30. That doesn't mean the band didn't have fans, however, nor does it mean that their music was undistinctive, as *Attack of the Smithereens* proves. Filled with B-sides, demos, rare singles, and live tracks, the collection has a loose charm and freewheeling energy that their proper albums occasionally lacked. Much of this material is as good as anything the group released, making it a necessary purchase for most fans. Even casual fans will find something to cherish. —*Stephen Thomas Erlewine*

● **Blown to Smithereens: The Best of the Smithereens** / Apr. 4, 1995 / Capitol ✦✦✦✦
Collecting together all the hits and highlights from the Smithereens' Capitol albums, *Blown to Smithereens* contains all of their finest hard-rocking pop gems. —*Stephen Thomas Erlewine*

The Smiths

Alternative Pop-Rock
At the beginning of the '80s, both the British pop and independent charts were filled with synth-pop, goth-rock, and lightweight new wave. In this climate, the Smiths' first single, "Hand in Glove," caused a quiet revolution. With their first album and singles, the Smiths led rock 'n' roll into a new era, where songs were again of the utmost importance, guitars replaced synthesizers as the prominent instrument on the pop and indie charts, and where lyrics were unabashedly personal and poetic; in short, they helped post-punk become alternative rock. In their native England, the band were superstars; each of their albums hit the Top Ten. America never warmed to their distinctly British sensibility, yet they did earn a sizable cult following across the US. Ten years after the release of their first album, their influence is still substantial; from the Stone Roses to Suede, the Smiths were the root of nearly every significant development in British music since 1984.

At its core, the Smiths' music was pure guitar-based pop-rock, recalling hooks and textures from the '60s. While their music was rooted in British pop, it also borrowed significantly from the energy and independence of punk; it never sounded dated or derivative. Morrissey's yearning voice and literate lyrics complimented Johnny Marr's understated, textured guitar to the point where the two were inseparable. Marr had a skill for writing melodic hooks that sounded simple and direct, yet were incredibly complex web of interweaving guitar lines. But Morrissey was the focal point of the band. Some critics accused him of being tuneless, yet he was a great vocalist, effortlessly conveying the exaggerated angst and self-deprecating humor of his words with unusual, unexpected pitches and phrasing. Morrissey's introspective lyrics strongly connected with disaffected youth around the world, yet they aren't adolescent; beneath his grandly dramatic vocals, there is genuine emotion, humor, melancholy, and compassion.

The songwriting team of Morrissey and Marr was remarkably inventive and prolific; during their brief four-year career, the Smiths released four proper albums, several non-LP singles and B-sides, and two singles compilations. All of their material was remarkably consistent, proving the band's mastery of pop songwriting.

the Smiths broke up in early fall of 1987, just before the release of their fourth and final album, *Strangeways Here We Come*. Bassist Andy Rourke and drummer Mike Joyce supported Sinead O'Connor for a time; Joyce eventually joined the reunited Buzzcocks. Marr went on to work with The Pretenders, The The, and Electronic. Morrissey began a solo career that proved just as popular as the Smiths'. — *Stephen Thomas Erlewine*

☆ **The Smiths** / 1984 / Sire ✦✦✦✦✦
The Smiths make ear-pleasing, catchy pop-rock, and it seduces the listener into paying attention to Morrissey's dead pan lyrics, which are deliberately self-pitying, sometimes caustic, and usually funny. "Reel Around the Fountain" is a classic, and the album also contains the UK singles "Hand in Glove" and "What Difference Does It Make?" — *William Ruhlmann*

☆ **Hatful of Hollow** / 1984 / Sire ✦✦✦✦✦
A collection of singles, B-sides, and BBC radio sessions, *Hatful of Hollow* shows how rapidly the Smiths were evolving. Containing some of their best songs—"William, It Was Really Nothing," "How Soon Is Now?," "This Charming Man," "Hand in Glove," "Reel Around the Fountain," "Please, Please, Please, Let Me Get What I Want"—the album is a more exciting and effective record than their debut album. — *Stephen Thomas Erlewine*

Meat Is Murder / 1985 / Sire ✦✦✦
The Smiths' second album isn't a great leap forward, but it does contain some fine guitar-pop, including "The Headmaster Ritual," "Rusholme Ruffians," and "That Joke Isn't Funny Anymore." The American version included the pulsating "How Soon Is Now?," which doesn't fit the mood of the rest of the album. — *Stephen Thomas Erlewine*

☆ **The Queen Is Dead** / 1986 / Sire ✦✦✦✦✦
The Queen is Dead is the Smiths' masterpiece, boasting an amazingly accomplished set of songs, including the surrealistic humor of the title track, the lilting "The Boy with the Thorn in His Side," the deceptively sunny pop of "Cemetry Gates," the nasty "Bigmouth Strikes Again," and the gorgeous "There Is a Light That Never Goes Out." Morrissey's lyrics have never been better and Marr's hooks are among his best. — *Stephen Thomas Erlewine*

Louder Than Bombs / 1987 / Sire ✦✦✦✦
The Smiths' second singles and B-sides collection is every bit as essential as the first, containing such brilliant songs as "Panic," "London," "You Just Haven't Earned It Yet, Baby," and "Is It Really So Strange?" There's a bit of duplication with *Hatful of Hollow*, but the music on *Louder Than Bombs* was some of the most vital and timeless pop music of the 1980s. — *Stephen Thomas Erlewine*

Strangeways Here We Come / 1987 / Sire ✦✦✦✦
While there are some fine songs here, *Strangeways Here We Come* is ultimately a disappointing final effort from the Smiths. Nevertheless, the album's best songs—"Stop Me if You've Heard This One Before," "I Won't Share You," "Last Night I Dreamt That Somebody Loved Me," "Girlfriend in a Coma"—are among the best the band recorded. — *Stephen Thomas Erlewine*

Rank / 1988 / Sire ✦✦

The Best, Vol. 1 / 1992 / Sire ✦✦

The Best, Vol. 2 / Dec. 8, 1992 / Sire ✦✦

★ **Singles** / 1995 / Reprise ✦✦✦✦✦
The *Best of the Smiths* collections didn't work since they didn't have a sense of history and distorted the underlying sense of urgency that helped make the Smiths important. *Singles* simply collects all of the singles from one of the greatest singles bands since the Beatles. It's essential and influential guitar-pop, presented in a way that makes sense and is endlessly listenable. — *Stephen Thomas Erlewine*

Smog

Alternative Pop-Rock, Indie Rock

One of the gloomiest bands since the demise of Joy Divison, Smog is the project of guitarist/vocalist/keyboardist Bill Callahan, who is occasionally joined by guitarist/vocalist Cynthia Dall and a host of drummers and cellists. From the first, Smog has been an unusual band, mixing grim subject matter and instrumentations with a punk-indie aesthetic. The intensely emotional and claustrophobic result is catalogued on the group's two full-length albums and the *Burning Kingdom* EP. While often difficult and probably not everyday listening, Smog is oddly dramatic and affecting. It won't cheer you up, but it will provoke a reaction. — *Heather Phares*

Julius Caesar / 1993 / Drag City ✦✦✦
The debut album from Bill Callahan, Cynthia Dall, and company is rife with downbeat and occasionally poignant indie pop that mixes clangy guitars with strings and synthesizers for a unique, evocative sound. One

of the standout tracks is "Your Wedding," as bitter and complex a jealousy song as you're likely to hear. — *Heather Phares*

Burning Kingdom / 1994 / Drag City ✦✦✦
Four vignettes of concentrated sadness, *Burning Kingdom* has to be one of the darkest-sounding EPs released in recent memory. Particularly effective is the haunting "Reneé Died," which pits Dall's frail voice against brittle acoustic guitars. — *Heather Phares*

● **Wild Love** / 1995 / Drag City ✦✦✦✦
The group's second full-length album is slightly less melancholy than *Burning Kingdom* and even manages some pitch-black humor in tracks like "Prince Alone in the Studio," "Be Hit," and "Sweet Smog Children." But some of the most poignant songs Callahan has written appear on *Wild Love*, including "Bathysphere," "The Candle," "Limited Capacity," and the luminous, empathetic "It's Rough." "Goldfish Bowl" is one of the catchiest numbers on *Wild Love*, which is Smog's finest work to date. — *Heather Phares*

Kicking a Couple Around [EP] / Apr. 1996 / Drag City ✦✦✦✦
This four-song EP contains some of Smog's finest, most heartbreaking songs. *Kicking a Couple Around* is perhaps Smog's most intimate-sounding release, featuring singer-songwriter Bill Callahan on guitar backed with some understated percussion. This restrained, minimal sound is a perfect foil for Callahan's warm, empathetic voice and eloquent lyrics: "I'm trying to learn your language / It's like a fly learning how to bark," from "Back in School" and "Just a few well-placed words / And their wandering hearts are gone" from "I Break Horses" tell sad stories in a short time. *Kicking a Couple Around* is Smog's most affecting, accessible release yet, and a must for both fans and those curious about the band. — *Heather Phares*

The Smoke

British Invasion, Psychedelic

More than any other band, the Smoke epitomized the groove of Swinging London. Their sound fell somewhere between mod and the Beatles—their instrumental attack was somewhat Who/Small Faces-like, yet they delighted in cheerful vocals and infectious harmonies and melodies. Only slightly popular on their home turf, and unknown in the US, their biggest success was in Germany (oddly enough, for such a British-sounding group). *It's Smoke Time*, their only album, was issued in Germany in 1967 and is one of the most cheerful records ever made, though not at all wimpy. "My Friend Jack," with its crushing reverb feedback, was a big hit in Germany, and on its way to becoming a hit in the UK when it was banned by British radio for supposed drug references. The Smoke issued several rare singles, some of them quite good, after the album before disbanding. — *Richie Unterberger*

My Friend Jack [1974 reissue] / 1974 / Gull ✦✦✦

● **It's Smoke Time** / 1994 / Repertoire ✦✦✦✦
Besides "My Friend Jack," other highlights of the group's only album (all but one of whose tracks were group originals) include the beautiful mid-tempo ballad "Waterfall" and the bee-humming guitars and lilting backup vocals on "You Can't Catch Me." The German CD reissue adds fourteen additional cuts, including non-LP singles, a single issued in 1965 by the Shots (an earlier version of the group), a single puzzlingly issued under the alias the Chords Five, and an interesting alternate take of "My Friend Jack." A lot of these tracks pale in comparison to the 12 from the original album, but "Have Some More Tea" is a great Who-ish number, and "Sydney Gill" is a good stab at a more progressive mood. — *Richie Unterberger*

Sneakers

Power-Pop

While the Sneakers never made much of an impact when they were together, the band marks the first appearance of several seminal figures of the alternative-pop scene of the early '80s. Chris Stamey, Mitch Easter, and Will Rigby formed the core of the Sneakers, writing well-crafted, guitar-driven pop rockers; their self-titled debut EP was engineered by Don Dixon, who went on to be a successful producer, as well as a solo artist. After one excellent full-length album, the Sneakers broke up. Stamey and Rigby went on to form the dB's, one of the '80s best American guitar-pop bands; Easter led Let's Active, as well as becoming a record producer (including R.E.M.'s first two albums). However, the Sneakers are more than historical curiosity; although they didn't record very much, their album and EP contain some of the finest power-pop of the late '70s. — *Stephen Thomas Erlewine*

In the Red / 1978 / CAR ✦✦✦

● **Racket** / 1993 / East Side Digital ✦✦✦✦
This disc contains selections from the Sneakers' unfinished third record, *Wig Cleaner*, as well as all the original compositions from *In the Red* and the band's first release, *Carnivorous No.1*. While all of the songs were written in the late '70s, some of the recordings were done as recently as

1992. Songs like "Some Kinda Fool" and "Story of a Girl" exude an effortless sophistication of chord structure and melody. Lovers of quirky guitar pop-rock (read: early dB's fans) should have this one. —*Rick Clark*

The Soft Boys

Alternative Pop-Rock, Post-Punk
While they were together, the Soft Boys recorded three discs of blissful post-punk weirdness, fueled by the winding guitar of Kimberly Rew and the warped vision of Robyn Hitchcock. Rew joined the band after an independent EP, in time for the recording of their full-length debut, *A Can of Bees*. But the focal point of the band was singer/guitarist Hitchcock, a bizarrely gifted pop songwriter with an affection for Syd Barett and John Lennon. Hitchcock melded the psychedelic guitars of *Revolver*-era Beatles with the sheer dementia of Barrett, creating a stripped-down guitar rock unlike anything else in the post-punk world. And the Soft Boys were assuredly inspired by punk—both their raw sound and lyrical obsessions were outgrowths of the punk era. Their time together was brief—about three years—yet their music has inspired a cult of devoted fans. Hitchcock went on to a successful cult career as a singer-songwriter; Rew formed Katrina & the Waves, where he earned a surprising amount of pop success. —*Stephen Thomas Erlewine*

A Can of Bees / 1979 / Rykodisc ✦✦✦
The Soft Boys' debut album *A Can of Bees* was an uneven but impressive debut featuring a set of catchy, warped pop songs driven by the ringing guitar riffs of Kimberly Rew and Robyn Hitchcock. —*Stephen Thomas Erlewine*

★ Underwater Moonlight / 1980 / Rykodisc ✦✦✦✦
Wry, savage humor permeates this near-virtuoso album. Extraordinarily well played, especially the guitars. —*Bruce Eder*

Invisible Hits / 1983 / Rykodisc ✦✦✦
A collection of outtakes and singles recorded in 1978 and 1979 but released in 1983, *Invisible Hits* isn't an inferior collection to *A Can of Bees* and *Underwater Moonlight*. Instead, it illustrates the creativity and the distinctiveness of their guitar-pop and contains a couple of their classics, including "Have a Heart, Betty (I'm Not Fireproof)," "Let Me Put It Next to You," and "Blues in the Dark." —*Stephen Thomas Erlewine*

1976-81 / 1994 / Rykodisc ✦✦✦
Along with several classic album tracks, the double-disc collection *1976-81* is filled with rarities and live tracks, making it more appealing to the collector than the neophyte. —*Stephen Thomas Erlewine*

Soft Cell

Dance-Pop, New Wave, New Romantic
Like the traditional synthesizer-driven dance-pop of the early '80s, Soft Cell was detached from their material, yet they were not cold. Instead, the duo of vocalist Marc Almond and keyboardist David Ball was warm and human; they were joyfully sleazy, celebrating kinky sex and trashing pop standards. Their finest moment came with a single from their first album, *Non-Stop Erotic Cabaret*, in 1981. "Tainted Love" represents everything Soft Cell wanted to achieve and it was an enormous success, spending nearly a year on the *Billboard* singles charts. After that, the duo occasionally recaptured some of the spark of that single (their cover of "Where Did our Love Go?," in particular) but more frequently slipped into self-parody; they broke up in 1984. —*Stephen Thomas Erlewine*

● Memorabilia: Singles / 1991 / Mercury ✦✦✦
Although it doesn't contain a couple of key tracks, including the 12-inch version of "Tainted Love/Where Did Our Love Go," *Memorabilia* is the best Soft Cell collection available. —*Stephen Thomas Erlewine*

Soft Machine

Art-Rock/Progressive-Rock, Psychedelic, Early Jazz Rock
Soft Machine were never a commercial enterprise, and indeed still remain unknown even to many listeners that came of age during the late '60s, when the group was at their peak. In their own way, however, they were one of the more influential bands of their era, and certainly one of the *most* influential underground ones. One of the original British psychedelic groups, they were also instrumental in the birth of both progressive-rock and jazz-rock. They were also the central foundation of the family tree of the "Canterbury school" of British progressive-rock acts, a movement that also included Caravan, Gong, Matching Mole, and National Health, not to mention the distinguished solo careers of founding members Robert Wyatt and Kevin Ayers.

Considering their well-known experimental and avant-garde leanings, the roots of Soft Machine were in some respects surprisingly conventional. In the mid-'60s, Wyatt sang and drummed with the Wilde Flowers, a Canterbury group that played more or less conventional pop and soul covers of the day. Future Soft Machine members Ayers and Hugh Hopper would also pass through the Wilde Flowers, whose original material began to reflect an odd sensibility, cultivated by their highly educated backgrounds and a passion for improvised jazz. In 1966, Wyatt teamed up with bassist/singer Ayers, keyboardist Mike Ratledge, and Australian guitarist Daevid Allen to form the first lineup of Soft Machine.

This incarnation of the group, along with Pink Floyd and Tomorrow, the very first underground psychedelic bands in Britain and quickly became well-loved in the burgeoning London psychedelic underground. Their first recordings (many of which only surfaced years later on compilations of 1967 demos) were by far their most pop-oriented, which doesn't mean they weren't exciting or devoid of experimental elements. Surreal wordplay and unusually (for rock) complex instrumental interplay gave an innovative edge to their ebullient early psychedelic outings. They only managed to cut one (very good) single, though, which flopped. Allen, the weirdest of a colorful group of characters, had to leave the band when he was refused re-entry into the UK after a stint in France, due to the expiration of his visa.

The remaining trio recorded their first proper album in 1968. The considerable melodic elements and vocal harmonies of their 1967 recordings were now giving way to more challenging, artier postures that sought—sometimes successfully, sometimes not—to meld the energy of psychedelic rock with the improvisational pulse of jazz. Soft Machine was taken on by Jimi Hendrix's management, leading to grueling stints supporting the Jimi Hendrix Experience on their 1968 American tours. Because of this, the group at this point were probably more well-known in the US than their homeland. In fact, their debut LP was only issued, oddly, in the States. For a couple of months in 1968, strangely enough, Soft Machine became a quartet again with the addition of future Police guitarist Andy Summers, although that didn't work out, and they soon reverted to a trio. The punishing tours took their toll on the group, and Ayers had left by the end of 1968, to be replaced by Wyatt's old chum Hugh Hopper.

Their second album, *Vol. 2* (1969), further submerged the band's pop elements in favor of extended jazzy compositions, with an increasingly lesser reliance on lyrics and vocals. Ratledge's fuzzy, buzzy organ and Wyatt's pummeling, imaginative drumming and scat vocals paced the band on material that became increasingly whimsical and surrealistic, if increasingly inaccessible to the pop-rock audience. For their third album, they went even further in these directions, expanding to a seven-piece by adding a horn section. This record virtually dispensed with vocals and conventional rock songs entirely, and is considered a landmark by both progressive-rock and jazz-rock aficionados, though it was too oblique for many rock listeners.

Soft Machine couldn't afford to continue to support a seven-member lineup, scaled back to a quartet for their fourth album, retaining Elton Dean on sax. Wyatt had left by the end of 1971, briefly leading the similar Matching Mole, and then establishing a long-running solo career. In doing so he was following the path of Kevin Ayers, who already had several solo albums to his credit by the early '70s; Daevid Allen, for his part, had become a principal of Gong, one of the most prominent and enigmatic '70s progressive-rock bands.

For most intents and purposes, Wyatt's departure spelled the end of Soft Machine's reign as an important band. Although Soft Machine were always a collaborative effort, Wyatt's humor, humanism, and soulful raspy vocals could not be replaced. Ratledge and Hopper kept the group going with other musicians, though by now they were an instrumental fusion group with little vestiges of their former playfulness. Hopper left in 1973, and Ratledge, the last original member, was gone by 1976. Other lineups continued to play under the Soft Machine name, amazingly, until the 1990s, but these were Soft Machine in name only. —*Richie Unterberger*

Live at the Proms 1970 / 1988 / Reckless ✦✦✦

● Vols. 1 & 2 / Sep. 1989 / Big Beat ✦✦✦✦
A combination of their first two studio albums onto one CD. Their first (originally titled *The Soft Machine*, from 1968), recorded with the trio of Wyatt, Ratledge, and Ayers, combines goofy humor, psychedelia, and some free jazz into an erratic but invigorating brew that was comparable to little else in the late-'60s rock world. Ayers had left to be replaced by Hugh Hopper for 1969's *Vol. 2*, which took a definite spin toward jazz and increasingly surrealistic material, stringing together whimsical bits and pieces for side-long suites. Not as pop-oriented as their initial 1967 recordings or as jazz-oriented as their final albums with Wyatt, the material compiled here is perhaps the best representation of Soft Machine's accomplishments. —*Richie Unterberger*

Jet-Propelled Photograph / Charly ✦✦✦✦
The latest available CD version of a title that has been repackaged and retitled several times over the last 20 years. Recorded in London in April 1967 and produced by the legendary Giorgio Gomelsky, these nine demos feature the original Soft Machine lineup of Robert Wyatt, Kevin Ayers, Mike Ratledge, and Daevid Allen. Although not intended for release, these rough but accomplished performances show the band at their most pop- and song-oriented. Not far removed from Syd Barrett-era

Pink Floyd, the jazzy chord changes, unpredictable bursts of scat singing, glib free-association lyrics, ominous buzzing organ, and Robert Wyatt's soulful rasp convey the freewheeling abandon and giddy high spirits that characterized the best early British psychedelia. For similar but more elaborately produced relics from the Daevid Allen lineup, check for the three tracks on the hard-to-find triple LP *Triple Echo*. —*Richie Unterberger*

Sonic Youth

Alternative Pop-Rock, Experimental, Indie Rock
When Sonic Youth began as a downtown New York band in the early '80s, they rejected most traditional rock 'n' roll formalities such as Western tuning and song structure. With screwdrivers randomly stuck into their guitar necks, the quartet created discordant, droning, mantralike songs, which were quietly forceful. As they matured, their material became more accessible and the songs more conventional, even as they retained their discordance. By the early '90s, Sonic Youth was approaching mainstream acceptance.

The band (Kim Gordon, bass and vocal; Thurston Moore, guitar and vocal; Lee Ranaldo, guitar; Steve Shelley, drums) had several releases before their sound crystallized. *Sonic Youth, Confusion Is Sex, Kill Yr Idols*, and *Sonic Death* document a band learning to express their complex ideas. These releases are often coarse and brash, sometimes unlistenable, and frequently startling in their power.

The band's cult following continued to grow throughout the late '80s, culminating in a major-label contract with Geffen Records. The corporate machine helped them develop a still-larger following. After their Geffen debut, 1990's *Goo*, Sonic Youth rested for two years. Their past indicates that a pause to regroup is usually followed by a burst of new creativity.

The band re-emerged with *Dirty*, their most direct stab at traditional pop-rock songwriting. The album was more successful than any of their past efforts, making the band popular with MTV-weaned adolescents. Naturally, Sonic Youth responded with a change in direction. *Experimental Jet Set, Trash & No Star* (1994) was their calmest record, yet it was more abstract than either of their major-label releases; it had an instant alternative radio/MTV hit with "Bull in the Heather." After headlining the fifth Lollapalooza package tour in the summer of 1995, Sonic Youth released *Washing Machine*, their tenth album of original material, in the fall. —*Robert Gordon*

Confusion Is Sex / 1983 / SST ✦✦

Bad Moon Rising / 1985 / DGC ✦✦✦

EVOL / 1986 / SST ✦✦✦✦
EVOL ("love" spelled backward) is composed of catchy rhythms and melodies, even some hooks; however, a menacing darkness remained, even dominated. Vocals were split pretty evenly between Gordon and Moore. *EVOL* remains a high point for the band, with provocative songs that force us, even after punk, to question what was commonplace in pop. Featured are "Green Light" and "Expressway to Yr Skull." —*Robert Gordon*

☆ **Sister** / 1987 / SST ✦✦✦✦✦
Sister found them largely embracing the rock aesthetic, though with little sacrifice to their own code. The album retains its menace and punkish attitude while totally rocking out. It's sort of the other side of the *EVOL* coin. They achieve a similar end, but instead of using spacious and brooding songs, they play hard, succinct, and tight. The CD features the bonus track "Master Dik." —*Robert Gordon*

★ **Daydream Nation** / 1988 / DGC ✦✦✦✦✦
Daydream Nation is a double album that warrants its indulgences; if the songs run long, they're worth it. When "Total Trash" devolves into a furious jam, its cacophony is beautiful, surpassed only by the surprise return to structure. The appeal of the "Teenage Riot" single brought the band a greater audience, and, if it seems to compromise their stance, in the context of the album it makes perfect sense. —*Robert Gordon*

Goo / 1990 / DGC ✦✦✦
Though *Goo* is not a sellout, it didn't advance the band in the leaps their previous few albums had. Mostly it sounds like *Daydream Nation* rehashed. Included are "Tunic," "Dirty Boots," and "Kool Thing." —*Robert Gordon*

Dirty / 1992 / DGC ✦✦✦✦
Sonic Youth could never sell out, no matter how hard they tried. Their sound—a jarring barrage of distorted guitars and feedback—is entirely too singular and avant-garde to ever completely cross over. However, *Dirty* is the closest Sonic Youth has ever come to the mainstream, and it is their most accessible album to date. "100%" is nearly a pop single, complete with hooks and an identifiable song structure. But Sonic Youth hasn't lost their edge, as Kim Gordon's tracks in particular prove. —*Stephen Thomas Erlewine*

Experimental Jet Set, Trash & No Star / 1994 / DGC ✦✦
Opening with their first acoustic number ever, *Experimental Jet Set, Trash & No Star* is Sonic Youth's calmest record to date. While the band's sound is different, their ideas aren't—they're essentially repeating *Sister*. There are a couple of interesting tracks, but most of the album is surprisingly boring. —*Stephen Thomas Erlewine*

Screaming Fields of Sonic Love / 1995 / DGC ✦✦✦
Sonic Youth isn't really a singles band, nor a band that works best taken as individual songs, so the idea of a compilation seems a little half-hearted. And, *Screaming Fields of Sonic Love* is a bit haphazard. —*Stephen Thomas Erlewine*

Made in USA / Feb. 28, 1995 / Rhino ✦✦

Washing Machine / Oct. 1995 / DGC ✦✦✦✦
After the regressive, low-key *Experimental Jet Set, Trash & No Star*, Sonic Youth appeared to be floundering somewhat, but *Washing Machine* erased any notion that the band had run out of things to say. Easily their most adventurous, challenging and best record since *Daydream Nation*, the album finds Sonic Youth returning to the fearless exploration of their SST records, but the group has found a way to work that into tighter song structures. Although the songs are more immediate than most of the material on their earlier records, the sound here is warm and open, making *Washing Machine* their most mature and welcoming record to date. It's not a commercial record, nor is it a pop record, but *Washing Machine* encompasses everything that made Sonic Youth innovators and shows that they can continue to grow, finding new paths inside their signature sound. —*Stephen Thomas Erlewine*

The Sonics

Rock 'n' Roll, Garage Rock
A rock 'n' roll band from Tacoma, WA, the Sonics' original members were Gerry Roslie (lead singer and piano/organ), Andy Parypa (guitar), Larry Parypa (bass), Bob Bennett (drums), and Rob Lind (saxophone). Forming in the wake of the early-'60s success of local favorites the Kingsmen and the Wailers (whose Etiquette label they recorded for), the Sonics combined the classic Northwest-area teen-band raunch with early English-band grit (particularly influenced by the Kinks), relentless rhythmic drive, and unabashed '50s-style blues-shouting for a combination that still makes their brand of rock 'n' roll perhaps the raunchiest ever captured on wax. Lead singer Gerry Roslie was no less than a White Little Richard, whose harrowing soul-screams were startling even to the Northwest teen audience, who liked their music powerful and driving with little regard for commercial subtleties. With hit after hit on the local charts (and influencing every local band that ever took the stage), the band inexplicably was never able to break out nationally, leaving their sound largely undiluted for mass consumption. Breaking up in the late '60s (after one ill-fated album attempt to water down their style for national attention), the Sonics continue today to be revered by '60s collectors the world over for their unique brand of rock 'n' roll raunch. —*Cub Koda*

● **Here Are the Ultimate Sonics** / 1991 / Etiquette ✦✦✦✦
Combining all the tracks from their first two Etiquette albums, three tracks from the label's Christmas album, live tracks, and an alternate take of "The Witch," this compilation more than lives up to its title. The definitive overview. —*Cub Koda*

Sonny & Cher

Folk-Rock, Pop-Rock
Sonny & Cher proved one of the magical musical combinations of the '60s, with their wisecracking repartee providing counterpoint to a series of adoring hit duets. Sonny Bono (b. Feb. 16, 1935) started out at Los Angeles-based Specialty Records as a songwriter in the late '50s. While working sessions with legendary producer Phil Spector, Bono met and married background singer Cher (born Cherilyn Lapierre, May 20, 1946) and formed a duet with his new wife. Neither was blessed with an outstanding vocal range, but no matter—they went gold in 1965 with the pop-chart topper "I Got You Babe" on Atco and did well with "Baby Don't Go" on Reprise. At the same time, both enjoyed success separately—Sonny with "Laugh at Me" for Atco, Cher with "All I Really Want to Do" and "Bang Bang (My Baby Shot Me Down)" on Imperial. "The Beat Goes On" in 1967 and "All I Ever Need Is You" four years later presaged the pair's anointment as popular TV variety-hour hosts from 1971 to 1974 (the year they were divorced). Since then, Cher has gone on to megastardom on record and on the silver screen. Sonny, meanwhile, was elected mayor of Palm Springs, CA. —*Bill Dahl*

● **The Beat Goes On: The Best of Sonny & Cher** / 1975 / Atco ✦✦✦✦
They were the ultimate "hip luv" couple of the '60s and their many hits are still fun to listen to. "I Got You Babe," "Laugh at Me," and the title track are three of the 21 original recordings included on this definitive collection. —*Jeff Tamarkin*

All I Ever Need: The Kapp/MCA Anthology / Jan. 1996 / MCA ✦✦✦✦

The Sorrows

British Invasion

One of the most overlooked bands of the British Invasion, the Sorrows offered a tough brand of R&B-infused rock that recalled the Pretty Things (though not as R&B-oriented) and the Kinks (though not as pop-oriented). Their biggest British hit, "Take a Heart," stopped just outside the UK Top 20; several other fine mid-'60s singles met with either slim or a total lack of success. With the rich, gritty vocals of Don Fardon, taut raunchy guitars, and good material (both self-penned and from outside writers), they rank as one of the better British bands of their era, and certainly among the very best never to achieve success of any kind in the US. After their sole LP (also titled "Take a Heart"), they issued a couple impressive singles with psychedelic and Dylan-esque overtones, and had somehow relocated to Italy in the late '60s, where they played out their string of material in a much more progressive (and less distinctive) vein. Don Fardon had a Top 20 hit in America with a pre-Raiders version of "Indian Reservation" in 1968. *—Richie Unterberger*

● **The Sorrows** / 1991 / Sequel ◆◆◆◆
The best reissue of the *Take a Heart* album (which has also been reissued in other configurations). Includes all the tracks from the LP, all the important non-LP singles, a couple unissued tracks, and Don Fardon's version of "Indian Reservation." *—Richie Unterberger*

Soul Asylum

Rock 'n' Roll, Alternative Pop-Rock, Pop-Rock

Initially, Soul Asylum didn't sound that much different from their Minneapolis peers Hüsker Dü and the Replacements, churning out fast, spirited punk rockers. Even at that stage, there were hints of musical diversity, from folk and country to straight-ahead pop, beneath the roar. As the band's career progressed, the songwriting of lead vocalist/guitarist Dave Pirner became sharper, relying on conventional, melodic song structure instead of aimless, raging sound; guitarist Dan Murphy's writing was equally good. After they signed to A&M in 1988, Soul Asylum hit their artistic stride, releasing two excellent albums that suffered from poor promotion on the label's part; the label dropped the band after their *And the Horse They Rode On* album.

Soul Asylum's last chance for success was 1992's *Grave Dancer's Union*, an album that was more accessible than their previous albums without compromising their artistic integrity. Amazingly, the band *did* hit the big time, thanks to the folky ballad "Runaway Train." The band became superstars, touring the world for nearly two years and going platinum several times over; they even performed at the White House. For a band that seemed destined to the same fate as their long-gone Minneapolis contemporaries, their success was nothing short of a miracle. Soul Asylum's commercial success continued with *Let Your Dim Light Shine*, their 1995 follow-up to *Grave Dancer's Union*. *—Stephen Thomas Erlewine*

Say What You Will / 1984 / Twin/Tone ◆◆◆

While You Were Out / 1986 / Twin/Tone ◆◆◆

Made to Be Broken / 1986 / Twin/Tone ◆◆

Time's Incinerator / 1986 / Twin/Tone ◆◆◆

Clam Dip and Other Delights / Jan. 1988 / Twin/Tone ◆◆◆◆
A great EP with a hysterical cover parody of Herb Alpert's sexy *Whipped Cream and Other Delights* album cover, this shows Soul Asylum growing up but not growing old. Starting with the huge thudding riff of "Just Plain Evil," this adds the triumphantly poppy "Chains" and the funky "Take It to the Root," which originally appeared on *Time's Incinerator*. Oddly, what was originally intended as a minor release turned out to be a major work in Soul Asylum's early career. *—John Dougan*

● **Hang Time** / Feb. 1988 / A&M ◆◆◆◆
More riff-heavy than usual, with considerable help from producer Lenny Kaye, *Hang Time* turned out to be the best of Soul Asylum's early records. The guitars of Pirner and Dan Murphy synchronize into a sonic wad of incredible power, while the songs (especially "Cartoon," "Some Time to Return," and "Beggars and Choosers") showed that Pirner had become a first-rate songwriter. Clever without being glib, and heartfelt without resorting to clichés, Pirner was doing something that eluded many of his peers: dealing with the transition from youth to adulthood and all the inherent conflicts that arise during this time. They would become superstars later, but this record should have done the trick. *—John Dougan*

And the Horse They Rode On / 1990 / A&M ◆◆◆◆

Grave Dancers Union / May 1992 / Columbia ◆◆◆
Soul Asylum's first Columbia release, *Grave Dancers Union*, is a significant step down from *And the Horse They Rode On*. From the start of the album, it's clear that Dave Pirner has been somewhat lost with the band's lack of success. Soul Asylum frequently sounds like a band that has lost their footing, grabbing onto anything they can. Pirner currently writes

big, rootsy ballads and Stones/Replacements-style rockers instead of the songs typical of their earlier, punky material. The addition of strings and the synths/horns on "The Sun Maid" sounds forced. Still, the crunching "99%" and wistful "Runaway Train" prove that Pirner can write a killer song when needed. *—Stephen Thomas Erlewine*

Let Your Dim Light Shine / 1995 / Columbia ◆◆

Soul II Soul

Soul, House Music, Urban, Club-Dance

Led by producer/vocalist/songwriter DJ Jazzie B, Soul II Soul were one of the most innovative R&B/dance outfits of the late '80s, creating a seductive, deep R&B that borrowed from Philly soul, disco, reggae, and '80s hip-hop. Originally featuring Jazzie B, producer/arranger Nellee Hooper, and instrumentalist Philip "Daddae" Harvey, the musical collective came together in the late '80s. The group had a residency at the Africa Centre in Covent Garden, which led to a record contract with 10, a subsidiary of Virgin. Two singles, "Fairplay" and "Feel Free," began to attract attention both in clubs and in the press.

Featuring the vocals of Caron Wheeler, Soul II Soul's third single "Keep on Movin,'" reached the UK Top Five in March 1989. Released in the summer of 1989, "Back to Life" also featured Wheeler and became another Top Ten hit. Soul II Soul released their debut album, *Club Classics, Vol. 1*, shortly afterward. The album was released in America under the title *Keep on Movin';* both "Keep on Movin'" and "Get a Life" became substantial hits, propelling the album to double-platinum status.

Wheeler left the group before the recording of the group's second album, *Vol. 2: 1990*—A New Decade. The album debuted at No. 1 in the UK, yet it caught the group in a holding pattern. Hooper soon left the collective, leaving Jazzie B. to soldier on alone. Hooper went on to work with several of the most influential and popular acts of the early '90s, including Massive Attack (*Blue Lines*), Björk (*Debut* and *Post*), Madonna (*Bedtime Stories*), and U2 ("Hold Me, Thrill Me, Kiss Me, Kill Me"). In 1992, Soul II Soul released *Vol. 3: Just Right*, to both lukewarm reviews and sales. The group's fourth album of original material was scheduled for release in the fall of 1995. *—Stephen Thomas Erlewine*

● **Keep on Movin'** / 1988 / Virgin ◆◆◆◆
The group's debut (originally titled *Club Classics, Vol. 1* in Europe) contains their finest single, "Keep on Movin,'" and "Back to Life" but is padded by stilted raps and plodding beat fodder. *—John Floyd*

Vol. 2: 1990—A New Decade / 1990 / Virgin ◆◆◆◆
A better album but a deceptive one: even the best songs here don't intoxicate as thoroughly as "Keep on Movin,'" but within the context of the album, each plays a vital part. In other words, this is a genuine *album*, and not just a pastiche of singles. *—John Floyd*

Vol. 3: Just Right / 1992 / Virgin ◆◆

Vol. 5: Believe / 1995 / Virgin ◆◆◆

Soundgarden

Alternative Pop-Rock, Heavy Metal, Grunge

Soundgarden was responsible for making true, gutsy heavy metal hip in the American underground of the late '80s. Fueled by the primal, sub-Sabbath riffing of guitarist Kim Thayil and the shrieking wail of vocalist Chris Cornell, Soundgarden offers a revamped, post-punk take on heavy metal. While they never dispense with the traditions of metal—pummelling riffs, long solos, machismo—they add a significant amount of angst and irony. Their songs are always more intricate than the average Black Sabbath number, yet never as detailed as a Led Zeppelin.

Soundgarden worked its way into the mainstream through a series of late '80s independent releases, culminating in a major-label deal with A&M; their first major-label album, *Louder Than Love*, was released in 1989. Before Nirvana exploded down the doors for alternative rockers in general and Seattle bands in particular in 1991, Soundgarden had earned a following that was larger than any other Seattle band; with songs like "Big Dumb Sex" and "Hands All Over" they appealed both to the riff-hungry heavy metal-fans as well as the cool, detached alternative-rock fans. But their real mainstream breakthrough didn't come until 1994, when the band released the critically acclaimed *Superunknown*. The album expanded their primal metal into a variety of new musical territory without ever losing sight of the core of their music—their overpowering riffs. It established Soundgarden as one of the most popular rock bands of the early '90s, selling over three million copies.

Soundgarden released *Down on the Upside*, their follow-up to *Superunknown*, in the spring of 1996; the album entered the charts at No. 2. Following its release, the group toured with the sixth Lollapalooza. *—Stephen Thomas Erlewine*

Ultramega OK / 1989 / SST ◆◆◆◆
A noticeable improvement from their EPs, Soundgarden's first full-length release is an impressive mixture of slow Zeppelin/Sabbath-style riffs updated for a new generation with even more murkiness. Cornell's vocals can be irritatingly overblown, and the band can be unfocused (as

on their cover of Howlin' Wolf's "Smokestack Lightning"), but the whole thing sounds fresh. —*Stephen Thomas Erlewine*

Louder Than Love / 1990 / A&M ✦✦✦
The first major-label release from Soundgarden is a step down from the independent *Ultramega OK*, as Thayil's guitar drowns in the murkiness of the production that Cornell tries to bellow through. It's uneven, but there are some staple Soundgarden songs that are among their best, including "Full on Kevin's Mom," "Hands All Over," "Ugly Truth," and the extraordinarily stupid "Big Dumb Sex." —*Stephen Thomas Erlewine*

Screaming Life / **Fopp** / 1990 / Sub Pop ✦✦✦

Badmotorfinger / 1991 / A&M ✦✦✦✦
Soundgarden's most accessible and accomplished album captures the band stretching out and successfully experimenting. Unlike those on *Louder Than Love*, the songs have varied tempos and textures, along with memorable riffs. With Cornell singing better than he ever has on a Soundgarden album, the band delivered a set of songs that now stands as their signature statement. —*Stephen Thomas Erlewine*

● **Superunknown** / Mar. 8, 1994 / A&M ✦✦✦✦
Superunknown expands on the bottomless heavy metal of *Badmotorfinger* by adding touches of psychedelia and pop to Soundgarden's signature sludge. The result is the band's best album, full of powerful, expertly crafted hard rock that improves with repeated listens. —*Stephen Thomas Erlewine*

Down on the Upside / May 21, 1996 / A&M ✦✦✦

Spandau Ballet

New Wave, Pop-Rock, New Romantic
After recording two albums in the early '80s of new romantic synth-pop that resulted in only one great single ("To Cut a Long Story Short"), Spandau Ballet abruptly changed their style to a smooth, soul-influenced pop sound. The change in direction resulted in their biggest success, with the international hit "True" and its accompanying album. After another album in the same vein didn't sell, they changed their direction again, becoming an arena-rock outfit; the new records failed miserably. By 1989, the band combined *all* of their previous incarnations into one faceless album. At that time, the acting careers of guitarist Gary Kemp and bassist Martin Kemp took off, earning a substantial amount of critical acclaim for their roles in the English gangster film *The Krays*. —*Stephen Thomas Erlewine*

● **The Singles Collection** / 1985 / Chrysalis ✦✦✦✦
Traces the group's development from the melodramatic, "new-romantic" dance-pop style of "To Cut a Long Story Short" to the lush ballad "True." Spandau Ballet always went in for big effects, but they became more subtle as they went along. —*William Ruhlmann*

The Specials

New Wave, Ska-Revival
True innovators of the punk era, the Specials began the British ska-revival craze, combining the highly danceable ska and rocksteady beat with punk's energy and attitude, and taking on a more focused and informed political and social stance than their predecessors. The band was formed in Coventry in 1977 as The Coventry Automatics and later the Special A.K.A. by songwriter/keyboardist Jerry Dammers with Terry Hall (vocals), Lynval Golding (guitar, vocals), Neville Staples (vocals, percussion), Roddy Radiation (guitar), Sir Horace Gentleman (bass), and John Bradbury (drums). An opening slot for the Clash stirred up interest with the major labels, but Dammers instead opted to start his own 2-Tone label, named for its multiracial agenda and after the two-tone tonic suits favored by the like-minded mods of the '60s. The Dammers-designed logos, based in '60s pop art with black and white checks, gave the label an instantly identifiable look. Dammers' eye for detail and authenticity also led to the band adopting '60s-period rude-boy outfits (porkpie hats, tonic and mohair suits, and loafers). The band released the "Gangsters" single which reached the UK Top Ten. Soon after, hordes of bands and fans followed in the same tradition and the movement was in full swing. Over the next several months, 2-Tone enjoyed hits by similar-sounding bands, such as Madness, the (English) Beat, and the Selecter. Late in 1979, the band released its self-titled debut album, produced by Elvis Costello. They followed with several 2-Tone package tours and a live EP, *Too Much Too Young* (confusingly credited to Special A.K.A.). The title track, a pro-contraception song, was banned by the BBC but reached the No. 1 spot in the UK. At this time, the band switched musical directions, releasing album number two, *More Specials*, with a new neo-lounge persona. Signs indicated that the movement was fading and 2-Tone began to experience financial troubles. The Specials released the timely "Ghost Town" single in 1981 amid race-related unemployment riots in Brixton and Liverpool. The single jumped to No. 1, but the band was falling apart. Hall, Staples, and Golding left to form Fun Boy Three, leaving the band without its trademark voice. Dammers held on, reverting back to the old name, Special A.K.A., and enlisting a new vocalist,

Stan Campbell. After several years in the studio, they returned with *In the Studio* in 1984. The album managed a few hits with "Racist Friend" and "Free Nelson Mandela" but the album stiffed. Dammers dissolved the unit, pursuing political causes such as Artists Against Apartheid. —*Chris Woodstra*

★ **The Specials** / Nov. 1979 / 2 Tone/Chrysalis ✦✦✦✦✦
The Specials' self-titled debut sparked the Two-Tone movement in the late '70s. With well-chosen ska classics and Prince Buster-inspired originals, the band mixed political and social activism and blended punk's intensity with an infectious dance beat. This is essential listening. Produced by Elvis Costello. —*Chris Woodstra*

More Specials / Oct. 1980 / 2 Tone/Chrysalis ✦✦✦✦
Losing some of their ska roots, the band moves directionlessly into a neo-lounge act. Still in full force is the biting social commentary only in a slightly skewed environment. While somewhat of a disappointment after the brilliant debut, with time *More Specials* can be nearly as rewarding. —*Chris Woodstra*

In the Studio / 1984 / 2 Tone/Chrysalis ✦✦✦
When Hall, Staples, and Golding left to become Fun Boy Three, Jerry Dammers decided to continue with the addition of vocalist Stan Campbell. Nearly three years in the making, *In the Studio* lacks any hint of ska, and Campbell's vocals, while good, lack the tension needed for the overtly political direction of the band. The highpoints, "Racist Friend" and the anthem "Free Nelson Mandela" can be found on the *Singles Collection*, so only completists need bother. —*Chris Woodstra*

☆ **The Singles Collection** / Sep. 1991 / 2 Tone/Chrysalis ✦✦✦✦✦
All of the essential singles from their three albums are present on this 15-track collection. Not only the perfect starting point for the curious, the inclusion of B-sides and rarities—like an inspired cover of Dylan's "Maggie's Farm"—makes this essential for fans. —*Chris Woodstra*

Coventry Automatics AKA The Specials: Dawning Of a New Era / 1994 / Receiver ✦✦
The first incarnation of the Specials, a six-piece band called the Automatics, recorded a batch of demos in London in 1978, hoping to obtain a major recording deal; *Dawning of a New Era* presents them for the first time. As is the case with most demos, these recordings have a limited audience, but diehard fans will thrill to the early, rawer versions of their favorites along with songs that never made it to actual albums. —*Chris Woodstra*

Phil Spector

b. Dec. 26, 1940, Bronx, NY
Vocals / Rock 'n' Roll, Pop-Rock, Brill Building Pop
Strictly speaking, Phil Spector doesn't belong in this section—he's a musician, yes, but he very rarely released records under his name. However, as a producer—and, to a significant extent, songwriter, label owner, and session player—he's influenced the course of rock 'n' roll more than have all but a handful of performers. The "Wall of Sound" that he perfected in the early '60s opened unlimited possibilities for arrangements and sound construction in rock and pop, and his brilliant talents imprinted the discs that he produced with an artistic vision that was much more attributable to him than the talented performers with whom he worked.

Spector entered the record business in 1958 as songwriter, guitarist, and backup singer for the L.A. group the Teddy Bears, who landed a left-field No. 1 with their first release, "To Know Him Is to Love Him." The Teddy Bears couldn't follow their hit up and soon disbanded, but Spector almost immediately moved to New York and became a songwriter and producer. After producing a few hits, he founded his own label, Philles, and ran off a series of brilliant smashes, primarily with girl groups the Crystals and the Ronettes.

To an extent that had never been imagined in rock 'n' roll, Spector pumped his records full of orchestration—strings, horns, rattling percussion—that coalesced into teenage symphonies, never overwhelming the material or the passionate vocals. Often called a mad genius because of his eccentric and temperamental behavior, Spector's idiosyncrasies were almost always validated by the artistic and commercial results of his sessions, which combined dozens of instruments and innovative production techniques into end products that only he could combine into works of art. His influence was immense, not only in the dozens of imitation Wall of Sound productions (some very accurate and worthy, it must be added) that flooded the market between 1962 and 1965, but as an inspiration to Brian Wilson of the Beach Boys, Rolling Stones producer Andrew Loog Oldham, and others.

Spector was hip to the British Invasion before it had even reached the US, befriending the Beatles and Rolling Stones, but had nearly as much trouble as the rest of the industry in maintaining his success. Self-contained bands were writing more adventurous material and finding more adventurous sounds, and Spector's teen operas were becoming out of fashion, although he enjoyed a lot of success with blue-eyed soul duo the

Righteous Brothers in the mid-'60s. After the failure of Ike & Tina Turner's 1966 single "River Deep, Mountain High"—which he always considered among his greatest achievements, blaming a vengeful US music industry for its poor sales (although it was a big hit in Britain)—he retired to his L.A. mansion, marrying Ronnie Spector, lead singer of the Ronettes.

Spector re-emerged in the late '60s, and was hired by the Beatles to do post-production on their controversial *Let It Be* album; critics and Paul McCartney himself found his work faulty, although it must be pointed out that the material he was given to work with didn't rank among The Beatles' best work. He then produced George Harrison and John Lennon's first solo albums. Though these were artistic triumphs, they were hardly Spector productions in the classic sense, owing much more of their success to the talents of the performers than the producer. For the past couple of decades, he's been active only sporadically, producing isolated albums by Dion, Leonard Cohen, and the Ramones. Today he's one of rock's most legendary recluses, rarely appearing in public, but his accomplishments cast a shadow over all performers and producers who aspire to create works of art in the studio. —*Richie Unterberger*

Early Productions 1958-1961 / 1983 / Rhino ♦♦♦
A sampling of Spector's earliest work, generally more pop-oriented, sappy, and far less distinguished than his early and mid-'60s classics. The Teddy Bears' "To Know Him Is to Love Him," Gene Pitney's "Every Breath I Take," the Paris Sisters' "I Love How You Love Me," and Curtis Lee's "Pretty Little Angel Eyes" are fine hits that reveal much of the talent that would fully blossom on his Philles singles. The other tracks, including rarities by the Ducanes, Kell Osborne, and Spector's Three, suffer from weak songwriting, and would be downright dispensable if not for their historical significance. —*Richie Unterberger*

★ **Back to Mono (1958-1969)** / 1991 / ABKCO ♦♦♦♦♦
If you look hard enough, you can find decent one-album samplers of Phil Spector's greatest recordings, but this four-disc boxed set (three sets of singles and the entire *A Christmas Gift for You* on the fourth) is the jewel of Spector's legacy. Aside from his sporadic '70s productions, *Back to Mono* contains everything you'd ever want by rock's supreme romantic: early productions with Curtis Lee, Ben E. King, and Gene Pitney; the girl-group effervescence of the Ronettes, the Crystals, and Darlene Love; the soul innovations of the Righteous Brothers and the Checkmates; and his notorious sessions with Ike and Tina Turner. Throughout the set, Spector's artistic vision (which has influenced dozens of producers and hundreds of performers) shines like the smile on a lover's lips. This is one of the greatest and most fully realized boxed sets ever issued. —*John Floyd*

Skip Spence

b. Apr. 18, 1946, Windsor, Canada
Guitar, Drums / Singer-Songwriter, Psychedelic, Folk-Rock
Like a rough, more obscure American counterpart to Syd Barrett, Skip Spence was one of the late '60s' most colorful acid casualties. The original Jefferson Airplane drummer (although he was a guitarist who had never played drums before joining the group), Spence left after their first album to join Moby Grape. Like every member of that legendary band, he was a strong presence on their first album, playing guitar, singing, and writing "Omaha," one of the LP's best songs. The group ran into rough times in 1968, and Spence had the roughest time, flipping out and (according to varying accounts) running amok in a record studio with a fire axe, ending up committed to New York's Bellevue Hospital. Upon his release, Spence cut an acid-charred classic, *Oar*, in 1969. Though released on a major label (Columbia), this was reportedly one of the lowest-selling items in its catalog and is hence one of the most valued psychedelic collector items. Much rawer and more homespun than the early Grape records, it features Spence on all (mostly acoustic) guitars, percussion, and vocals. With an overriding blues influence and doses of country, gospel, and acid freakout thrown in, this sounds something like Mississippi Fred McDowell imbued with the spirit of Haight-Ashbury 1967. It also featured great cryptic, punning lyrics and wonderful wraithlike vocals that range from a low Fred Neil with gravel hoarseness to a barely there-high wail. Sadly, it was his only solo recording; more sadly, mental illness continues to prevent Spence from reaching a fully functional state to this day, although he periodically plays music, sometimes with former members of the Grape. —*Richie Unterberger*

● **Oar** / 1969 / Sony ♦♦♦♦
The tight, charging S.F. rock of the Grape in no way prepares the listener for the spaced-out, rural ambience here. Drug-addled, yes, but also inspirational, warm, and haunting, like a charred but charming survivor of the Summer of Love. The CD reissue of this premier acid-folk album adds a few previously unreleased loose jams. —*Richie Unterberger*

Jon Spencer

Guitar, Vocals / Alternative Pop-Rock, Indie Rock
After a long and semisuccessful tenure as leader of scuzz-rock heroes

Pussy Galore, Jon Spencer took his anti-rock vision and hooked up with guitarist Judah Bauer and drummer Russell Simins to create the scuzz-blues trio the Jon Spencer Blues Explosion. Postmodern to the core, this is an ironic name; little of what this band plays resembles standard blues. There is, however, a blues feel to what they play, meaning that in many instances they appropriate aspects of the blues (very often clichés) and incorporate them into their anarchic, noisy sound. Not part of alternarock's commercial establishment, Spencer has also managed to sharply divide critics who tend to see him as either inspired showman or mendacious con man (frankly, he's both). He is, however, gaining popularity and critical respect, and, as of this writing, seems poised for greater success.

As with Royal Trux, the other band to emerge after the breakup of Pussy Galore, the Blues Explosion's earliest recordings are virtually incomprehensible (and impossible to find). The bass-less mix is awash in distorted guitars, precious little backbeat, and howled vocals. In its favor is the music's exciting, improvisatory feel; also true is that it's frequently incoherent and careless and doesn't hold up well to repeated listenings. It was with the band's 1992 self-titled release that the band began to write semicoherent songs; Spencer adopted an imitation, blues vocal style, and the band riffed wildly and crashed around him in a bluesy sort of way. It was mostly fun, but it also seemed like a bit of a put-on, and more than a little smug.

The Blues Explosion's "breakthrough" came (as it did for Royal Trux) when they began to sound like a '70s rock band. With the release of *Extra Width* in 1993, Spencer and Co. actually got some air time on MTV's alternarock show *120 Minutes* with the video for the song "Afro." The most noticeable change was the new emphasis on tight songs, funky backbeats, and loads of catchy riffs and hooks. As for Spencer, he was now singing like a grade-Z Elvis impersonator, but in turn lost some of the condescending attitude. Live, the band was (and remains) quite a show, generating the kind of sweat and excitement that became anathema to many punk and post-punk bands. The most recent release, *Orange*, which is even more accessible than *Extra Width*, has netted the band even more fans, and it seems likely that Spencer may see his greatest commercial success with this admittedly odd group. Still, there is a compelling argument to be made that despite his hip credentials, Spencer is more style than substance. Love him or loathe him (and it's easy to do both), he's a force to reckoned with. —*John Dougan*

The Jon Spencer Blues Explosion / Apr. 24, 1992 / Caroline ♦♦♦

Extra Width / 1993 / Matador ♦♦♦♦
Much more accessible than the aforementioned record, but in no way does its accessibility detract from the record's adventurousness. *Extra Width* is a crankin' piece of bluesoid ranting, with Spencer working up one hysterical performance after another. "Afro" is as funky as all get-out and sounds like an old Curtis Mayfield tune. Similarly, "Soul Letter" is a hefty chunk of riff-muck, as is the noisy bliss of "Soul Typecast." The playing is energetic and unhinged, and Spencer drives the engine with his whoopin' and hollerin'. Plenty of noticeably '70s production techniques add to the atmosphere, contributing significantly to what may be Spencer's best record. —*John Dougan*

● **Orange** / 1994 / Matador ♦♦♦♦
By this juncture, you either love Spencer enough to listen to every record, or you've heard plenty and are decidedly uninterested. Still, *Orange* mines the same territory as *Extra Width*, and that may not be enough. At times, even during *Orange*'s best tracks ("Bell Bottoms"), the thin, retro-'70s worshipping sounds phoned-in and lacking in real emotional commitment. As with a lot of junk-rock, sometimes it can be appreciated for simply being junk, and that's fine. But I'm willing to bet that Spencer's core fans like the idea of the blues more than the reality. In other words, they don't mind the pose, nor do they mind the facade. In Jon Spencer's world, image is everything. —*John Dougan*

Spinanes

Alternative Pop-Rock
In alternative rock, as in any other genre, it's hard to stand out from a crowded field. When the Spinanes emerged in the early '90s, they got a couple legs up on the competition to be different. Taking the power-trio format one stage further, they created a full-bodied rock sound with just two members, guitarist/singer Rebecca Gates and drummer Scott Plouf. They also were one of the first sub-pop bands that did *not* subscribe to a grungy metallic sound, although they rocked pretty hard.

Beyond these striking characteristics, however, the Spinanes' music isn't far off the beaten path of standard college-radio alternative fare, with its droning guitar textures, occasional harmonies, and measured vocals that avoid both slickness and extreme emotion. They're wise enough to realize the limits of their format, and their second album, *Strand* (1996), expands their instrumental, production, and songwriting ranges in enough interesting ways to make the group worth keeping an eye on. —*Richie Unterberger*

Manos / 1993 / Sub Pop ♦♦♦
While singer/guitarist Rebecca Gates and drummer Scott Plouf are the

only musicians on their debut album, the approach isn't minimalist à la Mecca Normal or some such band. They're a full-bodied rock group that happens to only have two members. That oddity factor aside, this is accomplished but fairly standard alternative pop-rock, a bit on the downbeat side at times and not diverse enough to keep the interest level from dragging over the course of a full-length record. *—Richie Unterberger*

● **Strand** / Feb. 27, 1996 / Sub Pop ✦✦✦✦
Although Gates and Plouf still play almost everything on their second outing, they make things more interesting by fooling around with a greater variety of instruments (adding more keyboards particularly) and getting outside guest vocalists to harmonize on a few songs. The songwriting (now handled by Gates exclusively) gets more penetrating as well, and the production is more imaginative (but does not approach slickness). At their most morose they recall "sadcore" groups like Low and Spain, but the Spinanes have more diversity than those acts. *—Richie Unterberger*

The Spinners

Soul, Philly Soul
There are plenty of Philly-soul groups that were as good as the Spinners, but none of them were better. They never cut anything as searing as the O'Jays' "For the Love of Money"; Teddy Pendergrass brought more eroticism to the hits of the Blue Notes; and they never matched the breathy, helium croon of the Stylistics' Russell Tompkins. What the Spinners and producer Thom Bell did was consolidate the best elements of Philly soul into a hit-making machine that could be as topical ("Ghetto Child"), romantic ("Could It Be I'm Falling in Love"), and blistering ("I'm Coming Home") as anything Gamble and Huff ever whipped up for Eddie LeVert and Teddy Pendergrass. And Spinners lead vocalist Philippe Wynne had a voice that damn near outflanked anyone for versatility and sheer gospel slow-burn; think of him as soul's answer to Claude Jeter, with the mental imbalance of James Carr.

The group didn't last as long as their slick-soul contemporaries: Wynne left the fold in 1977 and they never found a suitable replacement. (Wynne died of a heart attack in 1984 while performing in San Francisco.) Most of their work is still in print, and urban stations regularly program the hits from the Spinners' glory years. If you think pure soul singing died in the '60s (and some people do), a session with the Spinners should change your mind. *—John Floyd*

Mighty Love / Jan. 1974 / Atlantic ✦✦✦✦
Phillippe Wynne's twisting, soulful, frequently captivating voice was at its finest on this 1974 album. The title track was a smash in edited single form, and the extended album version contains marvelous Wynne adlibs and exchanges nicely contrasted by the group's harmonizing. The album contains many other fine songs, like "Ain't No Price on Happiness" and "I'm Coming Home," and was their second Atlantic release. It equaled the gold-selling pace of its predecessor and cemented the Spinners' status as R&B stars. *—Ron Wynn*

Dancin' and Lovin' / 1979 / Rhino ✦✦✦

☆ **One of a Kind Love Affair** / 1991 / Atlantic ✦✦✦✦✦
Spanning from their first single, 1961's "That's What Girls Are Made For," to their last charting single more than 20 years later, *One of a Kind Love Affair* is the definitive Spinners collection. The bulk of the two-CD compilation is the group's work with Thom Bell during the mid-'70s, easily the best work they ever recorded and arguably the finest Philly soul singles. All of the Spinners' major hits are here, as are excellent, informative liner notes (including complete personnel and discography). *—Stephen Thomas Erlewine*

★ **Very Best of** / 1993 / Rhino ✦✦✦✦✦
Very Best of the Spinners contains all of the group's essential hits, from "It's a Shame" and "I'll Be Around" to "The Rubberband Man" and "Working My Way Back to You/Forgive Me, Girl." A few hits are missing, but the serious fan can find those on the double disc set *One of a Kind Love Affair*. For the casual fan who only wants the biggest hits, *Very Best of the Spinners* is a necessary purchase. In a concise 16 tracks, it makes a convincing case that the group was the greatest soul vocal group of the '70s. *—Stephen Thomas Erlewine*

Split Enz

New Wave
Best known for their early '80s new wave pop hits, particularly "I Got You," Split Enz—after surviving a dizzying array of image and personnel changes and a full decade without any recognition outside of their homeland—became the first New Zealand band to achieve worldwide success. Although they never reached superstar status outside Australia and New Zealand, the band developed a strong international cult following that continued to thrive over a decade after their breakup. Split Enz's output always seemed slightly outside of the times and often frustratingly obscure, but in the end, they left behind a body of work that was always interesting and often reached pure pop brilliance. The group was

founded in 1972 in Auckland, New Zealand, by Brian Timothy Finn and Phil Judd. Initially, the band was a light acoustic combo called Split Ends and consisting of Judd (guitar, vocals), Finn (vocals, piano), Miles Golding (violin), Mike Howard (flute), and Mike Chunn (bass). Finn and Judd were the main songwriting force of the band's early years. Judd drew his inspiration from a wild variety of often nonmusical sources while Finn's tastes leaned toward the British pop of the Beatles, the Kinks, and the Move. In a creative rush that lasted several months, the two bashed out songs on acoustic guitars—Judd working out the basic song with lyrics and Finn providing the melodies. Miles Golding came from a classical background and pushed the band into complex, neo-classical structures and arrangements. The result was an eclectic mix of styles that was quite original though not very commercial. After months of rehearsals, the group went into the studio to record their first single, "For You"/"Split Ends," in February 1973. After the single was released, the band launched a small tour; upon its completion, Golding left the group to study in London. At Chunn's urging, the band went for a new, electric sound, adding Geoff Chunn on drums, Wally Wilkinson on guitar, and saxophonist Rob Gillies, who was only a part-time member. After the new lineup was in place, Judd refused to tour, claiming their music was too complex for stage presentation; he stayed behind to write and record new material while the rest of the band toured, although he would later re-join the live lineup. The group made an appearance on the televised New Zealand talent contest, *New Faces*—though they finished second to last, it gave them some crucial early exposure. In 1974, keyboardist Tony (Eddie) Rayner was added to the band and they changed their name to Split Enz. Following the name change, the group embarked on a series of radio-sponsored "Buck-a-Head" shows—rather than play the more traditional pub circuit, they played theaters, which seemed more suited to the band's style. The group's shows took on a theatrical tone, as band members wore wild, colorful costumes and sported a variety of odd hairdos. Finn acted as master of ceremonies, giving odd spoken soliloquies. Judd made the occasional appearances as did costume designer and spoons soloist Noel Crombie. By the fall of 1974, Crombie was added as a full-time member on percussion. Before the tour was completed, Geoff Chunn was replaced by Paul Crowther and Rob Gillies left the group.

In March 1975, the group traveled to Australia—at this time, all members except Judd switched to using their middle names. Mistakenly billed as "New Zealand's raunchiest rock 'n' roll band," the band struggled for nine months but eventually earned a small cult following and secured a contract with Mushroom Records. Their debut album, *Mental Notes*, was recorded in two weeks. While their inexperience in the studio combined with an unsympathetic producer led to a less-than-satisfying result in the band's eyes, the album encapsulated the band at its artiest and most ambitious. The album made a brief appearance on both the Australian and New Zealand charts. By November 1975 Wilkinson was fired and Gillies rejoined.

Split Enz had caught the attention of Roxy Music's Phil Manzanera, who offered to help the band with their next album; they arranged to meet them in England to redo *Mental Notes*. Before leaving, they recorded a new single, "Late Last Night." Despite the complex song-structure, the single showed the band moving toward a pop direction; nevertheless, it failed to have much impact. "Late Last Night" was accompanied by a video clip, which was an uncommon practice in 1976; the band would continue to make conceptual clips from that point on. In April 1976, Split Enz joined up with Manzanera in England and signed to Chrysalis for worldwide distribution. While the recordings went well, they found it impossible to secure live work in Britain without an agent. The band rehearsed constantly, although the songwriting partnership of Judd and Finn had dried up and no new songs were being written. *Second Thoughts*, essentially a reworked *Mental Notes*, was released toward the end of 1976 (it was released internationally as *Mental Notes*). Before the band supported the album with a US tour in early 1977, Crowther was replaced on drums by Mal Green. Judd, fed up with uninterested audiences and the demands of promotion, left the band during the tour and Chunn left two months later. The band returned to England to regroup—they replaced Judd with Tim's younger brother Neil and recruited bassist Nigel Griggs.

Tim Finn assumed leadership of the new incarnation of Split Enz, and the group began to move away from its arty, theatrical tendencies on their next LP, 1977's *Dizrhythmia*. In Australia, the album went gold and the single "My Mistake" became their first Top 20 hit. In England, the group fared far worse. In the wake of the punk explosion, Split Enz seemed slightly out of touch. Though their odd looks and new, leaner material wasn't so far removed from post-punk styles, their earlier reputation seemed more in line with the progressive-rock the punks sought to destroy. However, they did manage to keep a small cult following within the UK.

By early 1978, Split Enz had been dropped by Chrysalis and, unable to get gigs, were forced to go on the dole. They continued writing new material at a feverish pace and rehearsing constantly. Gillies was fired, and Judd rejoined but he found himself unable to fit into the new direction of the band and left the group shortly thereafter; he later found limited success as the leader of the Swingers and as a solo artist. The New Zealand Arts Council came to the band's aid with a $5,000 grant. A studio in Luton was booked, and the band knocked off 28 songs in under five days. These sessions, known as the "Rootin' Tootin' Luton Tapes," displayed a newfound edge and considerable commercial potential. Around the same time, they recorded a new single with producer David Tickle—a straight-ahead rocker called "I See Red"—which charted respectably in Australia. Split Enz returned to Australia to make their next album, 1978's *Frenzy*, re-recording many songs from the Luton tapes. However, the final product paled in comparison to the demos—the high energy of the original tapes simply wasn't captured and many of the best songs were left on the demos. Many of the Luton recordings would later resurface on the A&M version of *Frenzy*, released in North America in 1981.

The band teamed up again with David Tickle for their next album, *True Colours* in 1979. The album lacked the excesses of their previous albums and showcased their new pure-pop direction. With Neil Finn's seductive "I Got You," the band finally broke through—the single and album hit No. 1 in Australia and New Zealand, eventually selling 200,000 albums in Australia, the equivalent of one in every ten homes in that country. The success led to an international deal with A&M Records. *True Colours* performed well in the UK and the US and went platinum in Canada. The band quickly recorded a follow-up during a mid-year break in touring. The result—called *Corroborree* in Australia and *Waiata* internationaly—was released in April 1981. The record was somewhat disappointing, seeming to follow the same formula as its predecessor but with decidedly lesser material. The album failed to match the success of *True Colours*, but it did manage two hit singles, "One Step Ahead" and "History Never Repeats." On their subsequent North American tour, Split Enz were billed equally with Tom Petty & the Heartbreakers, which stands as a testament to the band's growing popularity. Mal Green left the band to work on solo projects and Crombie took over on drums.

By late 1981, after many months of intensive touring, the band retreated to the studio to record their most personal and creatively satisfying album to date, *Time & Tide*. Released in 1982, it immediately topped the Australian and New Zealand charts. The advent of MTV and the channel's commitment to new wave acts helped the band's growing cult status in America—both "Dirty Creature" and "Six Months in a Leaky Boat" (as well as earlier videos) saw heavy airplay on the channel—but the album failed to see much chart action.

Early in 1983, Tim Finn took a break from Split Enz to work on a solo album, *Escapade*. The album was a big success in Australasia, spawning several hit singles including the Top Ten "Fraction Too Much Friction." For all of its success, though, the album distracted Finn, delaying the follow-up to *Time & Tide* and effectively ending the momentum Split Enz had built over the previous three albums. *Conflicting Emotions* was finally finished by the fall of 1983. Prior to this album, Finn had been the primary contributor, but for this effort, he was overshadowed by brother Neil, who had written a considerable majority of songs for the first time. The album, while predictably successful in Australia/New Zealand, saw a delayed release in the States and failed to make much impact. A new drummer, Paul Hester, was added, demoting Crombie to percussion. Before work was begun on the next album, Tim Finn announced that he was leaving the band. With Neil Finn as the leader, the band carried on for one more album—1984's *See Ya Round*, an uneven album which was released only in Australia, New Zealand, and Canada. Neil decided to fold the band following a farewell tour, *Enz with a Bang!*, for which Tim rejoined the group.

Neil and Paul Hester went on to form the internationally successful Crowded House, Tim continued a sporadic solo career, joining Crowded House for the *Woodface* album in 1991. Nigel Griggs, Noel Crombie, and Phil Judd formed Schnell Fenster, releasing two albums before disbanding, and Eddie Rayner has done session work and formed his own combo, the Makers. Tim and Neil Finn reunited for a Finn Brothers album in 1995. Split Enz remains an institution in their homeland, frequently re-forming for one-off reunion gigs. In 1996, the New Zealand Symphony Orchestra performed a tribute to Split Enz—the resulting album, *ENZSO*, spent several weeks in the Australian and New Zealand Top Ten. —*Chris Woodstra*

Mental Notes [Mushroom] / 1975 / Mushroom ✦✦✦✦
The first proper Enz album features the band at its eccentric best. *Mental Notes* is completely noncommercial art-rock filled with ambitious arrangements and slightly disturbing themes courtesy of the Phil Judd/Tim Finn songwriting partnership. Finn's bittersweet crooning perfectly compliments Judd's madman persona on tracks like "Stranger Than Fiction." Although the album would be repackaged, renamed, and re-recorded in years to come, the band would never again produce anything like it. —*Chris Woodstra*

Second Thoughts / 1976 / Mushroom ✦✦✦
After *Mental Notes* failed commercially, the band left for England to rework the tracks with Roxy Music's Phil Manzanera producing. *Second Thoughts* is an eccentric album filled with the theatrics that gained the

band its early notoriety. Mainly new versions of old songs, the album adds some new tracks such as the brilliant "Late Last Night" and "Woman Who Loves You." Released in America and the UK as *Mental Notes* with a modified cover. —*Chris Woodstra*

Dizrhythmia / Oct. 1977 / Mushroom ✦✦✦
With Tim Finn's leadership and brother Neil replacing founding member Phil Judd, the band makes a move into the mainstream. While the eccentricity is still evident, the album shines with a melodic pop sensibility. Contains the classics "Bold as Brass," "Charlie," and "Crosswords." —*Chris Woodstra*

Frenzy [Australian] / 1978 / Mushroom ✦✦✦
Although often thought of as a transitional album, *Frenzy* shows the band in top form. Produced in England on a diminished budget, the album showcases pure pop with a hungry edge. "I See Red," added after the initial pressing, became a moderate hit in Australia and New Zealand, allowing the band the financial freedom to follow up with the blockbuster *True Colours* in 1980. Stripped down of the earlier excesses, the album more than hints at greatness to come in the '80s. The album was reissued in the US in 1981, dropping half of the tracks and adding songs from the legendary "Rootin' Tootin' Luton Tapes" recorded in 1978. —*Chris Woodstra*

True Colours / 1979 / A&M ✦✦✦✦
This New Zealand band's most cohesive pop statement was their most successful American release. On these clever pop songs with synthesizer textures, Neil Finn comes into his own as a writer in his brother's band. —*Scott Bultman*

Beginning of the Ends / 1979 / Mushroom ✦✦✦✦
A compilation of demos from 1972-1975. This Australian-only release shows the band in its eccentric formative years before a recording contract. Light acoustic arrangements of songs appearing on later albums coupled with long-forgotten gems make this a favorite among die-hard fans. Not the most representative picture of the band, but an interesting one. —*Chris Woodstra*

Beginning of the Enz / 1980 / Chrysalis ✦✦
Waiata (Corroboree) / May 1981 / A&M ✦✦✦
Also titled *Corroboree* (in Australia and New Zealand), this follow-up to the successful *True Colours* album offers more Neil Finn-penned gems like "One Step Ahead" and "History Never Repeats," although the music is less edgy, with more emphasis on pleasant synth-pop. It includes three instrumentals: "Iris," "Ships," and "Albert of India." —*Scott Bultman*

Time & Tide / 1982 / A&M ✦✦✦✦
Time & Tide is the band's creative high point and most fully realized effort. Combining beautiful melodies with introverted, soul-searching lyrics, the album gives listeners new insights into the band. Both Tim and Neil Finn reach new peaks in their songwriting. Includes the hits "Dirty Creature" and "Six Months in a Leaky Boat." —*Chris Woodstra*

Conflicting Emotions / 1983 / A&M ✦✦✦
Less focused than *Time & Tide*, *Conflicting Emotions* is still a high point for the band. With Tim Finn stepping back and Neil Finn playing a more dominant role in the songwriting, the album is both dark and beautiful. Neil Finn's strong sense of melody builds on heavy rhythms and direct playing to produce a solid, if not exceptional album. Highlights include "Message to My Girl" and "Bullet Brain and Cactus Head." Note to collectors: The first pressing in New Zealand came with a bonus 12-inch single with two new songs: "Kia Kaha" and "Parasite." —*Chris Woodstra*

Enz of an Era / 1983 / Mushroom ✦✦✦✦
A solid collection of the singles from *Second Thoughts* (1976) to *Time and Tide* (1982). Although not all of the singles are present, all of the hits from that period are covered. *Enz of an Era* is most notable for inclusion of the rare "Another Great Divide" but it has been superceded by more current (and more easily found) collections. —*Chris Woodstra*

See Ya Round / 1984 / Mushroom ✦✦
With Tim Finn departing for a solo career, Neil Finn takes charge of the aging band for their final studio album. While not living up to the band's previous brilliance, songs such as "Years Go By," "One Mouth Is Fed," and an early version of "I Walk Away" are delightful Finn compositions. Side two features songs written by each of the remaining members. Released only in Australia, New Zealand, and Canada. —*Chris Woodstra*

Living Enz / 1985 / Mushroom ✦✦✦
● **History Never Repeats: The Best of Split Enz** / 1987 / A&M ✦✦✦✦
All the best songs from their American albums (A&M new wave period 1979-1983) are here, although many other great songs can be found on their import CDs. A good place to get acquainted with the band; the fans already have the albums. —*Scott Bultman*

1973-1979: Oddz & Enz / 1993 / Mushroom ✦✦✦
This Australian-only box set covers the band's more experimental beginnings (1973-1979). From the light acoustic demos of *Beginning of the Enz* and the art-rock of *Mental Notes*, to the edgy-pop of *Frenzy*, the listener gets a strong sense of the band's pre-popularity evolution. With over an

hour of non-LP tracks on the bonus disc and improved sound quality, this is essential for fans. —*Chris Woodstra*

1980-1984: Rear Entz / 1993 / Mushroom ♦♦♦
This Australian-only box set covers the period of the band's peak in popularity (1980-1984). Beginning with *True Colours* and ending with their swansong, *See Ya Round*, it shows the band in perfect pop form. While this is too ambitious for the casual fan, the devoted will find this essential for considerably improved sound and the bonus disc of previously unreleased tracks. —*Chris Woodstra*

Anniversary / 1994 / Mushroom ♦♦

● **Best Of Split Enz** / 1994 / Chrysalis ♦♦♦♦
Chrysalis Records handled the band's non-Australia/New Zealand releases from 1976 to 1977—an extremely low point in terms of sales. Not surprisingly, *Best of Split Enz* focuses a little too heavily on this early period to truly give the casual listener a representative collection of the band. The big A&M hits ("I Got You," "One Step Ahead") are covered adequately, but this was clearly an attempt to cash in on Crowded House's success in Europe the year before. —*Chris Woodstra*

Spongetones

Power-Pop
One of the most underrated power-pop bands of the '80s, the Spongetones released several albums of effortlessly melodic, catchy guitar-pop that captured the feel of '60s British Invasion pop with remarkable accuracy and feeling. While they never received much critical or commercial attention, their music has aged much better than most power-pop from the era; the band continues to record and perform in the '90s. —*Chris Woodstra*

Beat Music / 1982 / Ripete ♦♦♦
Beat Music, the Spongetones' debut album, features some of their finest music, drawing heavily on the Beatles, Dave Clark Five, and the Hollies without shame. And while this is certainly derivative stuff, it's a nostalgia trip so well executed and so enjoyable. *Beat Music* and its follow-up, *Torn Apart*, have been combined on a single disc, *Beat & Torn*. —*Chris Woodstra*

Where-Ever Land / 1984 / Triapore ♦♦

● **Oh Yeah!** / 1991 / Black Vinyl ♦♦♦♦
The Spongetones return after a long absence with 1991's *Oh Yeah!* They effectively pick up where they left off in the '80s with their infectious Beatlesque power-pop. Easily their best songwriting and a good place to get acquainted with the band. —*Chris Woodstra*

Beat & Torn / 1994 / Black Vinyl ♦♦♦♦
Now combined on one CD, *Beat Music* and *Torn Apart* represent the band's earliest recordings and some of their finest. Southern power-pop at its best. —*Chris Woodstra*

Textural Drone Thing / 1995 / Black Vinyl ♦♦♦
Textural Drone Thing may not reach the heights of its predecessor, *Oh Yeah!*, but that's tough competition. The approach is considerably more subtle, and it lacks the band's usual immediacy, but with melodies like these, it's well worth the effort. —*Chris Woodstra*

Dusty Springfield (Mary O'Brien)

b. Apr. 16, 1939, London, England
Vocals / Soul, Pop-Rock, Girl Group
Born Mary O'Brien before changing her name professionally, Dusty Springfield first emerged during the early '60s as one-third of the British folk-pop trio the Springfields, which also included her brother Tom. They had several hits, including "Island of Dreams" and "Silver Thread and Golden Needles," and the latter topped the US charts a year before the Beatles' first records.
In 1963, the Springfields split up, with Tom going off to produce the Seekers. Dusty made herself over vocally, evolving from a folk alto into a powerful White soul singer, capable of credibly covering Motown material (she dueted with Martha Reeves on TV's *Ready, Steady, Go* without embarrassing herself at all) and belting out British pop numbers with seismic intensity. "I Only Want to Be with You," "Stay Awhile," "Wishin' and Hopin'," and "24 Hours from Tulsa" were just a few of her successes, and all were heavily played in either England or America. In 1969, Springfield recorded *Dusty in Memphis*, a landmark White soul album done at Stax studios, which received critical raves and is something of a legendary record.
Since the early '70s, Springfield has recorded and made infrequent appearances, but none of her work since the Memphis album has been taken up by the public. She remains a respected and much-loved figure from British rock's heyday, however, even 30 years later. —*Bruce Eder*

Dusty / 1964 / Philips ♦♦♦
Not quite as good as her first American LP, but a good mix of R&B/soul covers and orchestrated pop-rock in the manner of early Dionne Warwick. Standouts include the cover of Bacharach-David's "I Just Don't

Know What to Do with Myself" (a British hit), "All Cried Out," and the epic ballad "Summer Is Over," which foreshadows the style she'd use on her later hit "You Don't Have to Say You Love Me." —*Richie Unterberger*

Stay Awhile/I Only Want to Be with You / 1964 / Philips ♦♦♦♦
Her most rock 'n' roll-oriented album, and one of the finest solo rock albums of the mid-'60s. Besides the two hit title tracks, Dusty covers various American soul and pop tunes that usually rank at least equal to the originals, in some cases totally outclassing them. In particular, she improves upon "24 Hours from Tulsa," "Anyone Who Had a Heart," "You Don't Own Me," and "When the Lovelight Starts Shining Through Her Eyes." The production is the most credible approximation of the Phil Spector wall of sound ever managed in the UK, with full brass and strings, soulful female backup choruses, and pounding piano and drums. Also includes a first-rate Springfield original, "Somethin' Special." —*Richie Unterberger*

Ooooooweeee!!! / 1965 / Philips ♦♦♦
No hits here (though "Losing You" made the British Top Ten), and a couple of pointless repeats from the first album. Still, it's another solid set of exuberant, soulful girl group-style British Invasion pop. "Losing You," "Once Upon a Time," and "He's Got Something" remain some of her most unjustly overlooked performances. —*Richie Unterberger*

Ev'rything's Coming Up Dusty / 1965 / Beat Goes On ♦♦♦
Dusty started to lean in a somewhat less R&B and somewhat more pop direction on this album, with covers of "La Bamba" and Anthony Newley's "Who Can I Turn To?" Still, it has good interpretations of songs by Goffin-King, Jerry Ragovoy, Randy Newman, Bacharach-David, and the Zombies' Rod Argent, highlighted by "Oh No! Not My Baby" and Newman's "I've Been Wrong Before." —*Richie Unterberger*

Golden Hits / 1966 / Philips ♦♦♦♦
A fair representation of her mid-'60s hits, with major gaps. The imported CDs are preferable. —*Bruce Eder*

★ **Dusty in Memphis** / 1969 / Rhino ♦♦♦♦♦
Sometimes memories distort or inflate the quality of recordings deemed legendary, but in the case of *Dusty in Memphis*, the years have only strengthen, its reputation. The idea of taking England's reigning female soul queen to the home of the music she had mastered was an inspired one. The Jerry Wexler/Tom Dowd/Arif Mardin production and engineering team picked mostly perfect songs, and those that weren't so great were salvaged by Springfield's marvelous delivery and technique. This set has definitive numbers in "So Much Love," "Son of a Preacher Man," "Breakfast in Bed," "Just One Smile," "I Don't Want to Hear About It Anymore" and "Just a Little Lovin'," and offers exquisite mastering, informative notes, and an unreleased version of "What Do You Do When Love Dies." It's truly a disc deserving of its classic status. —*Ron Wynn*

A Brand New Me / 1970 / Rhino ♦♦♦♦
While it's not quite as uniformly excellent as *Dusty in Memphis*, *A Brand New Me* comes close to recapturing its predecessor's magic and is easily one of Springfield's best albums. —*Stephen Thomas Erlewine*

● **The Silver Collection** / Jan. 1988 / Philips ♦♦♦♦
Twenty-four songs, encompassing her British and American chart history for the '60s. Superb sound. —*Bruce Eder*

Sounds of the 60's / 1989 / Pickwick ♦♦♦
Intelligently assembled Springfield compilations have proven to be a surprisingly elusive concept, if you want to go beyond the big hits. There's lots of good stuff on this 24-track survey of her 1960s work: some (not all) of her big early hits, and some superb mid-'60s LP-only covers like "Oh No Not My Baby" and "Anyone Who Had a Heart." These are interspersed with less-impressive items from later in the decade, and chronologically and stylistically it jumps all over the place. So it's not bad, but doesn't really satisfy either the collector or the listener who just wants the greatest hits. —*Richie Unterberger*

Something Special / 1996 / Mercury ♦♦♦♦
A 48-song, double-CD set of rarities and album tracks, including eight previously unreleased cuts and plenty of songs that had rarely or never been on album before. Sure, this is primarily for Springfield fans, and not the first (or second) anthology recommended to casual listeners. But quite a bit of this is on par, or nearly on par, with her best work. What's more, the bulk of it dates from her '60s prime, although there are about a dozen mediocre numbers from the late '70s/early '80s on which her voice still cuts it, but the material and production don't. Big Dusty Springfield fans will already have some or all of the songs taken from albums, but about half of this is very hard or impossible to find elsewhere, and much of it is very good. Highlights include the title track (one of her best girl group-style numbers); a 1965 Italian-language single in the "You Don't Have to Say You Love Me" ballad style; soulful mid-'60s B-sides like "I'm Gonna Leave You" and "I'll Love You for a While"; and the strange 1968 outtake "Don't Speak of Love," based on a classical piece by Wagner. —*Richie Unterberger*

Rick Springfield

b. Aug. 23, 1949, Sydney, Australia
Guitar, Keyboards, Vocals / Power-Pop, Pop-Rock

Before he became a soap star, Rick Springfield was a rock star in his native Australia. After scoring several hits with his band Zoot in the early '70s, he went solo and tried to make the big time in America. Springfield released several power-pop albums to no success; he then decided to become a TV actor, landing a role on *General Hospital*. While he was acting on the soap opera, he gained a strong following, which led him to revive his singing career in the early '80s. This time, his records were more successful—"Jessie's Girl," his first single since returning to music, hit No. 1. Several other Top Ten hits followed, before his career started to slip in the mid-'80s; despite his diminished sales, he continued recording and acting through the rest of the decade. *—Stephen Thomas Erlewine*

Comic Book Heroes / 1974 / Columbia ◆◆◆

Springfield grew considerably as a writer between his first record and *Comic Book Heroes*. Although he is still doing some sensitive singer-songwriter material, it no longer sounds as awkward. In fact, a couple tracks, like "Weep No More," are very memorable. On the other hand, "Misty Water Woman" sounds like an overly melodramatic attempt at being Elton John. Still, the good stuff makes it worth owning. *—Jim Worbois*

● **Working Class Dog** / 1981 / RCA ◆◆◆◆

Forget that Rick Springfield was a soap star for a moment and listen to his music, because he made some of the finest guitar-driven mainstream pop-rock of the early '80s. *Working Class Dog* is his finest moment, filled with expertly crafted pop songs, highlighted by the massive hit "Jessie's Girl." *—Stephen Thomas Erlewine*

Success Hasn't Spoiled Me Yet / 1982 / RCA ◆◆◆◆

Rick Springfield's follow-up to his commercial breakthrough *Working Class Dog* wasn't quite as consistent, but it contained a number of solid power-pop tracks, including "Calling All Girls," "What Kind of Fool Am I," "How Do You Talk to Girls," "The American Girl," and the Top Ten hit "Don't Talk to Strangers." *—Stephen Thomas Erlewine*

Living in Oz / 1983 / RCA ◆◆◆

Hard to Hold / 1984 / RCA ◆◆

Tao / 1985 / RCA ◆◆◆

Rock of Life / 1988 / RCA ◆◆

Greatest Hits / 1989 / RCA ◆◆◆◆

A good collection, it includes Springfield's greatest hits. *—David Jehnzen*

Bruce Springsteen

b. Sep. 23, 1949, Freehold, NJ
Guitar, Vocals / Rock 'n' Roll, Singer-Songwriter

When Bruce Springsteen finally broke through to national recognition in the fall of 1975 after a decade of trying, critics hailed him as the savior of rock 'n' roll, the single artist who brought together all the exuberance of '50s rock and the thoughtfulness of '60s rock, molded into a '70s style. He rocked as hard as Jerry Lee Lewis, his lyrics were as complicated as Bob Dylan's, and his concerts were near-religious celebrations of all that was best in the music. One critic became so enamored that he quit reviewing to become Springsteen's manager.

But the hosannas, when piped through the publicity machine of a major record company, were perceived as hype by a significant part of the public as well as the mainstream media—Springsteen landed on the covers of *Time* and *Newsweek*, but both magazines were covering the phenomenon, not the music. Springsteen's album, *Born to Run*, became a hit, and he jumped to arena status as a live act, but as many people were turned off by the press campaign as turned on by the records and shows.

Two decades later, however, Springsteen remained an established star who could look back on a career that had produced one of the bestselling albums of all time, sold-out stadium shows, Grammy Awards and an Oscar, and a group of imitators who constituted their own subgenre of popular music. If he no longer seemed divine, he remained popular enough for his *Greatest Hits* album to enter the charts at No. 1, and he had won over many of those skeptics from 1975.

Growing up in southern New Jersey, Springsteen turned to rock 'n' roll as a teenager and played in a series of bands from the mid-'60s on, varying in style from garage rock to power trio blues-rock. By the early '70s, he was trying his hand at being a folky singer-songwriter in Greenwich Village. But when he was signed to Columbia Records in 1972, he brought into the studio many of the New Jersey-based musicians with whom he'd played over the years.

The result was *Greetings from Asbury Park NJ* (Jan. 1973), which went unnoticed upon initial release, though Manfred Mann's Earth Band would turn its lead-off track, "Blinded by the Light," into a No. 1 hit four years later. *The Wild, the Innocent and the E Street Shuffle* (Nov. 1973)

also failed to sell, despite some rave reviews. (Both albums have since gone platinum.)

The following year, Springsteen revised his backup group—dubbed "The E Street Band"—settling on a lineup that included saxophone player Clarence Clemons, second guitarist "Miami" Steve Van Zandt, organist Danny Federici, pianist Roy Bittan, bassist Gary Tallent, and drummer Max Weinberg. With this unit he barnstormed the country while working on his third and last chance with Columbia. By the time *Born to Run* (Aug. 1975) was released, the critics and a significant cult audience were with him, and the title song became a Top 40 hit while the album reached the Top Ten.

What Springsteen needed to do in the wake of the hype, of course, was to play and record more to consolidate his position. He was prevented at least from the latter by a former manager, who kept him in court during the next couple of years. Meanwhile, the musical world changed. Part of the reason critics had welcomed Springsteen so enthusiastically in 1975 was that he seemed a return to basic rock 'n' roll values in a world of soft rock, heavy metal, and art-rock.

By the time Springsteen returned with his fourth album, *Darkness at the Edge of Town* (May 1978), however, the punk/new wave movement had outflanked him, pushing him from the vanguard to the mainstream. Similar-sounding heartland rockers such as Bob Seger had appeared, so that Springsteen sounded less like an innovator than a member of an established genre.

Nevertheless, he set about winning fans with an album that found lost children of his early albums stuck in factory jobs, still longing for some escape. The album was a hit, though it did not match the success of *Born to Run*. Springsteen returned with the double album *The River* (Oct. 1980), which topped the charts and featured his first Top Ten hit, "Hungry Heart."

Nobody was calling him a hype anymore, but Springsteen retreated from his expanding success, next recording the low-key album *Nebraska* (Sep. 1982), a virtual demo tape-on-vinyl. (Springsteen did not tour to promote the album, and in the interim E Street Band guitarist Van Zandt amicably left the group for a solo career, to be replaced by Nils Lofgren.)

But then came *Born in the USA* (Jun. 1984) and a two-year international tour. The album threw off seven hit singles and sold over ten million copies, putting Springsteen in the pop heavens with Michael Jackson and Prince. After touring for more than a year, he released a five-LP/three-CD concert album, *Bruce Springsteen & the E Street Band/Live 1975-1985* (Sep. 1986), which topped the charts.

Characteristically, Springsteen returned with a more introverted effort, *Tunnel of Love* (Oct. 1987), which presaged his divorce from his first wife. (He married a second time to singer Patti Scialfa, who had joined the E Street Band.)

After another marathon tour, Springsteen gave the E Street Band notice in November 1989, breaking up a celebrated unit that had stayed together 15 years. In March 1992, he simultaneously released *Human Touch* and *Lucky Town*, and though the albums premiered near the top of the charts, they were less successful with fans than previous albums. In the fall, Springsteen taped an "MTV Unplugged" segment (though he plugged in after one song), and the performance was released as an album in Europe in 1993.

Springsteen continued to tour until July 1993. In the fall, he wrote and recorded "Streets of Philadelphia" for the soundtrack to the film *Philadelphia*, which concerned a lawyer dying of AIDS. The song became a Top Ten hit in 1994, winning the Academy Award for Best Song and cleaning up in the Grammys the following year. At the same time, Springsteen had readied his *Greatest Hits* album (Mar. 1995), reassembling the E Street Band to record a few new tracks. The album was an immediate best-seller. *—William Ruhlmann*

Greetings from Asbury Park NJ / Jan. 5, 1973 / Columbia ◆◆◆◆

The songs, laced with Dylanistic wordplay, are gorgeous street vignettes fused with romance, idealism, and a true sense of wonder. *—John Floyd*

☆ **The Wild, the Innocent and the E Street Shuffle** / Sep. 11, 1973 / Columbia ◆◆◆◆◆

The Wild, the Innocent & the E Street Shuffle is a subtle masterpiece. The grooves are tougher, revealing the R&B heart that *Greetings from Asbury Park* stifled, and the songs are long enough to let him develop his characters and their situations. *—John Floyd*

☆ **Born to Run** / Aug. 25, 1975 / Columbia ◆◆◆◆◆

A bombastic masterpiece, his breakthrough is a testament not only to the sound of Phil Spector's '60s hits, but to the romanticism, the longing, and the determination of those hits. The title cut and "Thunder Road" are anthems that deserve that status. *—John Floyd*

Darkness on the Edge of Town / Jun. 2, 1978 / Columbia ◆◆◆◆

On this, the flip side of *Born to Run*, the idealism of those characters turns into stark terror once they hit adulthood. This is where Springsteen's reputation as a working-class mouthpiece is based, but there's much more here than that. *—John Floyd*

☆ **The River** / Oct. 10, 1980 / Columbia ✦✦✦✦✦
In many ways his best album, it balances the dashed dreams of *Darkness on the Edge of Town* with the hope of *Born to Run*, but it trades the Spectorian wallop for a taut, frat-rock sound that is alternately wiry, delicate, and full-blown. —*John Floyd*

☆ **Nebraska** / Sep. 20, 1982 / Columbia ✦✦✦✦✦
A set of acoustic demos, it offers ravaged tales of despair, defeat, and defiance. —*John Floyd*

★ **Born in the U.S.A.** / Jun. 4, 1984 / Columbia ✦✦✦✦✦
The album that pushed him into superstar status ironically examines the dirty underbelly of America in both political and domestic terms. The big, catchy, hard-slamming rock 'n' roll that carries the lyrics only adds to the irony. —*John Floyd*

Live 1975-1985 / Nov. 4, 1986 / Columbia ✦✦✦✦
A career-defining three-disc live collection, it is among the three or four greatest boxed sets ever issued. —*John Floyd*

☆ **Tunnel of Love** / Oct. 9, 1987 / Columbia ✦✦✦✦✦
A moody and dark inquiry, it asks why people fall in love, why they get married, why they lose faith in the people closest to them, and why they even bother. Required listening for anyone contemplating the altar. —*John Floyd*

Human Touch / Mar. 31, 1992 / Columbia ✦✦
His first proper recording without the E Street Band, Springsteen continues the conversation started on *Tunnel of Love* through the pleading urgency of "Soul Driver" and the forthright admissions on "Real World." Musically, the set balances E Street retreads ("Roll of the Dice," "All or Nothin' at All") with taut soul grooves and slashing hard rock, emphasizing Springsteen's astonishing guitar playing. —*John Floyd*

Lucky Town / Mar. 31, 1992 / Columbia ✦✦✦
Because they failed to repeat the massive success of *Born in the USA*, and because they eschewed the working-class posturing of his most famous work, many critics claimed *Human Touch* and *Lucky Town* offered proof that Springsteen had lost his creative foothold. Nothing could be further from the truth. Rather than letting a cast of desolate losers and struggling optimists do his talking, Springsteen forced *himself* to do it. They're both strikingly personal and confessional albums that analyze the difficulties of making commitments and the necessity of making those commitments. *Lucky Town*, recorded chiefly by Springsteen, with occasional assistance from E Street keyboardist Roy Bittan, is the thematic antithesis of Dylan's *Blood on the Tracks*, an album devoted to the requisiteness of love and romance and how empty lives are without that love and romance. *Lucky Town* offers living proof that Bruce Springsteen's grappling with domestic bliss and superstardom is just as enlightening as his struggle to attain them. —*John Floyd*

In Concert/MTV Plugged / Apr. 1993 / Columbia ✦✦✦

Greatest Hits / Feb. 28, 1995 / Columbia ✦✦✦
Compiling a "Greatest Hits" of Bruce Springsteen should be an easy task, yet *Greatest Hits* manages to miss the mark. Nothing from his first two albums is included and the set includes such non-hits like "Atlantic City" and "The River" instead of hits like "Cover Me," "Tunnel of Love," and "Fade Away." In fact, a good portion of his hits are missing, as are important album tracks like "Backstreets," "Rosalita," and "Candy's Room," making this neither a straight hits collection nor a compilation of his best tracks. What's left is some of his biggest hits and best songs ("Born to Run," "Glory Days," "The River"), but not all of them, as well as four new tracks, the best of which is an outtake from the *Born in the USA* sessions ("Murder Inc.") Aside from "Murder Inc.," the new tracks follow the synth-laden adult-contemporary direction Springsteen began pursuing with "Streets of Philadelphia," only without the lyricism or melody. So, it's a mixed bag, drawing an incomplete portrait of one of the prime rockers of the '70s and '80s. Casual fans would be better served by *Born in the USA*, which encompasses all of Springsteen's sides. —*Stephen Thomas Erlewine*

The Ghost of Tom Joad / Nov. 21, 1995 / Columbia ✦✦

Squeeze

New Wave, Pop-Rock

Squeeze is a British pop-rock quintet that serves as a forum for the songs of its lead singer Glenn Tilbrook (b. Aug. 31, 1957) and his partner, guitarist Chris Difford. The duo formed Squeeze in 1974 with keyboardist Jools Holland (b. Jan. 24, 1958), whose bubbly personality made him a natural frontman, bassist Harry Kakouli (replaced by John Bentley after the first album), and drummer Gilson Lavis (b. Jun. 27, 1951). They reached the UK Top 20 in 1978 with the single "Take Me I'm Yours," but really broke through the following year, when their second album, *Cool for Cats*, produced two UK Top Ten hits in the title track and the Difford-sung "Up the Junction." *Argybargy*, their third album, was a moderate success in 1980 (and their first US chart entry), but their next milestone came in 1981 with *East Side Story*, an album for which Holland was

replaced by former Ace lead singer Paul Carrack (b. Apr. 22, 1951), who sang lead on "Tempted," Squeeze's first US chart single. The album, which hit the UK Top 20, also featured a No. 4 British hit, "Labelled with Love." As it turned out, Carrack left after the one album, replaced by Don Snow (b. Jan. 13, 1957) for *Sweets for a Stranger*, after which Squeeze disbanded. They re-formed in 1985 with Tilbrook, Difford, Holland, and Lavis, plus Keith Wilkinson on bass, to release *Cosi Fan Tutti Frutti* and then, in 1987, *Babylon and On*, which featured "Hourglass," a Top 20 hit on both sides of the Atlantic. *Frank* came out in 1989, followed in 1990 with the live album *A Round and a Bout*, which finished Squeeze's contract with A&M. They then signed to Warner Bros. and released *Play* in 1991.

After the sluggish sales of *Play*, Warner dropped the band; they resigned with A&M soon afterward. Gilson Lavis left the band before they recorded 1993's *Some Fantastic Place*, leaving Difford and Tilbrook as the band's only original members. In late 1995, Squeeze released *Ridiculous*. —*William Ruhlmann*

U.K. Squeeze / 1978 / A&M ✦✦

Cool for Cats / 1979 / A&M ✦✦✦✦
The band's second album shows a great leap in songwriting skills. While an emphasis on English themes can leave most Americans bewildered, the catchy pop melodies crossed with a pub-rock sensibility are simply irresistible. Highlights include "Cool for Cats" and "Up the Junction," a pure pop classic. —*Chris Woodstra*

☆ **Argybargy** / 1980 / A&M ✦✦✦✦✦
Upbeat, cleverly crafted pop-rock with decidedly British themes. Tilbrook's guitar work and Jools Holland's keyboards shine as Squeeze moves from being pub-rockers to critics' darlings. —*Scott Bultman*

East Side Story / 1981 / A&M ✦✦✦✦
Their US breakthrough album featured the hit "Tempted," sung and written by Paul Carrack (of the '70s band Ace), who was Squeeze's keyboardist for this one album. This is the album that sparked the comparisons of Difford/Tilbrook to Lennon/McCartney. A broader pop style with classical overtones and a country influence courtesy of producers Elvis Costello and Dave Edmunds. —*Scott Bultman*

Sweets from a Stranger / 1982 / A&M ✦✦
Still riding high on the success of *East Side Story*, Squeeze continues to write perky, upbeat tunes, but with the blue-eyed soul influence of the quickly departed Paul Carrack, they begin their move away from their classic sound. The hit "Black Coffee in Bed" sounds amazingly like a Paul Carrack song, perhaps an attempt to duplicate the success of Carrack's "Tempted." —*Scott Bultman*

★ **Singles 45's & Under** / 1982 / A&M ✦✦✦✦✦
This consists of twelve early Squeeze singles and one non-album track ("Annie Get Your Gun"). This is classic Squeeze, the songs that made them. Includes "Tempted," "Black Coffee in Bed," and "Another Nail for My Heart." —*Scott Bultman*

Cosi Fan Tutti Frutti / 1985 / A&M ✦✦✦
After *Sweets from a Stranger* and the Difford/Tilbrook solo effort, this re-formed Squeeze (with Jools Holland returning on keyboards) makes a move in another direction, with a less-overt soul influence, and high pop-craft and experimentation. Laurie Latham's technicolor/cinerama production makes this their most glossy album. Keith Wilkinson takes over on bass. —*Scott Bultman*

Babylon and On / 1987 / A&M ✦✦
Yet another step back to their classic sound, this time rewarded with minor chart success. Squeeze regains their drive and perkiness, firing on all cylinders. Includes the US Top 20 "Hourglass." —*Scott Bultman*

Frank / 1989 / A&M ✦✦
Along with the return of keyboardist Jools Holland comes an attempt to return to the classic Squeeze sound. "If It's Love" and "She Doesn't Have to Shave" more than make up for the blandness of the previous album with their memorable hooks and irresistible melodies, but much of the material unfortunately misses the mark. —*Chris Woodstra*

A Round & A Bout (Live) / 1990 / IRS ✦✦

Play / 1991 / Reprise ✦✦✦
This unfortunately overlooked album finds the songwriting team of Difford and Tilbrook still in strong form through a 12-track song cycle. Now a four-piece band, there is less dependence on keyboards and a focus on more acoustic arrangements. A considerably more subdued mood but no less rewarding on repeated listening. —*Chris Woodstra*

Some Fantastic Place / Sep. 14, 1993 / A&M ✦✦✦

Ridiculous / 1995 / A&M ✦✦✦
After nearly 20 years of recording, it would be easy to write Squeeze off as spent creative force—certainly their most recent albums have seemed like somewhat forced attempts to recapture the glory days of *Cool for Cats*, *Argybargy*, and *East Side Story*. With *Ridiculous*, Difford and Tillbrook (the only original members left and still the band's primary songwriters) seem content to have passed the Brit-pop torch on, and, as a

result, this effortless album is also one of their most enjoyable in recent years. Ridiculous isn't an embarrassing attempt to rewrite previous hits, but rather, a natural progression executed with a dignified maturity rather than resignation. "This Summer" and "Electric Trains," though not candidates for the top of the charts at this point, certainly rank among their finest singles. —Chris Woodstra

Piccadilly Collection / Aug. 20, 1996 / A&M ✦✦✦

Squire
....

Power-Pop, Mod-Revival

Though they never received the recognition they deserved, Squire was one of the earliest and finest mod-revival bands of the late '70s. Like the founders of the revival, the Jam, Squire were able to transcend the limits of the genre with their high-quality blend of pop smarts and songcraft, which drew equal parts from punk spirit and '60s sensibilities.

The band formed in Guildford, England, around 1977 as a covers band consisting of Enzo Esposito (vocals/bass), Steve Baker (guitar) and Ross Di'Landa (drums). In June 1978, songwriter/guitarist Anthony Meynell joined just prior to a high profile gig opening for the Jam. The addition of Meynell changed the band's focus to producing original material, and by 1979, they had released their first single for ROK Records, "Get Ready to Go." While the single gained them some airplay, their biggest break came with the newly termed mod-revival movement and their appearance on the legendary *Mods Mayday* album, which featured two new songs by the band. Ian Page of Secret Affair (one of Squire's mod peers) had just started his own I-Spy label and signed the band on the merits of their appearance on *Mods Mayday*. The signing led to some personnel changes. First, Di'Landa was replaced by Kevin Meynell, then Baker quit without replacement. In 1979, Squire released two wonderful singles for I-Spy: "Walking Down the Kings Road" and "The Face of Youth Today." Out of the two singles, only "Walking Down the Kings Road" charted. In 1980, Squire switched record labels, signing with another independent, Stage One Records. The band's first release on Stage One was "My Mind Goes Round in Circles" which, like its predecessors, barely made an impact on the charts. Frustrated by a lack of success, the band essentially dissolved when the last original member, Esposito, left.

Anthony Meynell decided to give it another try when he started his own label, Hi-Lo, in 1981. The first release was *Hits from 3000 Years Ago*, a collection of demos and leftovers from the original Squire lineup. He reactivated the band, adding Jon Bicknell on bass, and releasing a new single, "No Time for Tomorrow," in 1982. Though they were still virtually unknown in their homeland, America had begun picking up on *Hits from 3000 Years Ago*. Delayed by a short promotional tour in the States, their first proper album, *Get Smart*, was finally released late in 1983. They never made the breakthrough into the mainstream, but the album and its follow-up EP, *September Gurls*, (the title track was a cover of the Big Star classic) in 1984 became cult classics in American power-pop circles. Squire began preparation for their next album, *Smash*, but decided to call it quits before its completion. —Chris Woodstra

● **Big Smashes** / 1992 / Tangerine ✦✦✦✦
Big Smashes is a 24-track best of that compiles the band's mod-revival singles from the '70s and the more power-pop-oriented material from their Hi-Lo albums. As an introduction to this unfairly overlooked band, there is no better place to begin. These are truly lost classics that deserve discovery. —Chris Woodstra

Get Ready to Go! / 1995 / Tangerine ✦✦✦
A nice companion to the *Big Smashes* collection, *Get Ready* focuses on the early work of the original lineup from their mod days. This release supplants *Hits from 3000 Years Ago* by picking the highlights (most of the album) and combining their first single, the brilliant "Get Ready Go," with B-sides, previously unreleased material, a track from the *Odd Bods, Mods and Sods* compilation, and a track from a fan club release. —Chris Woodstra

SRC
....

Hard Rock, Psychedelic

Along with the Stooges, MC5, and the Amboy Dukes, SRC were local heroes of the Michigan rock scene in the late '60s and early '70s, although in terms of national success, they were relegated to the second division populated by such bands as the Frost and the Rationals. Led by the Quackenbush brothers Gary and Glenn, the Ann Arbor group evolved out of The Fugitives, adding lead singer Scott Richardson from fellow garage band the Chosen Few. SRC recorded three erratic albums for Capitol that blended Motor City crunch with sustain-laden psychedelic guitar, pompous bursts of organ, spacy lyrics, and unexpectedly wispy, vulnerable vocals, throwing in some pretty ballads and harmonies to temper the hard-rock excess. —Richie Unterberger

Traveller's Tale / 1970 / Capitol ✦✦✦
SRC's final album was recorded after the departure of guitarists Gary Quackenbush and Steve Lyman, Ray Goodman assuming all the guitar

chores. Despite the shakeup, the sound hardly changed at all, perhaps becoming a bit more progressive minded. The organ-guitar duels and alternation of concise hard rock with lengthy progressive passages also remained intact. If this album came out today, you'd swear it was a satire of the progressive-rock era, some of it is so prototypical. But these guys were serious about what they did, and impressive, in their own way. The CD reissue includes a non-LP B-side from the same era, "My Fortune's Coming True." —Richie Unterberger

● **The Revenge of the Quackenbush Brothers** / 1987 / Bam Caruso ✦✦✦✦
Good selection of key cuts from all three albums; "Daystar," "Marionette," and "Black Sheep" are first-rate hard psychedelia. One Way has reissued all of the original albums, as well as some unissued material, but this is the best and most judicious selection. Comes with detailed group history. —Richie Unterberger

Chris Stamey
....

Bass, Guitar, Vocals / Power-Pop, Experimental, Jangle-Pop

Chris Stamey might not be a household name, but among the cult of melodic guitar pop-rock fans, he's a major player. Stamey played with the seminal North Carolina '70s pop band the Sneakers and was a founding member of the dB's. After the dB's fell apart, Chris Stamey recorded an album with fellow dB Peter Holsapple; after that album, Stamey released his first solo record in 1991. —Rick Clark

Instant Excitement / 1984 / Coyote ✦✦✦

It's Alright / 1987 / A&M ✦✦✦✦
With the help of Alex Chilton, Richard Lloyd, Mitch Easter, Marshall Crenshaw, and others, Stamey presented a cohesive body of fine poprock songs, most notably "Cara Lee," "Incredible Happiness," "27 Years in a Single Day," and "The Seduction." —Rick Clark

● **Fireworks** / 1991 / Rhino ✦✦✦✦
Fireworks, the album that A&M allegedly rejected, surfaced on Rhino's new artist imprint RNA. While it is arguably his best solo album, the overly reverberant production and thin sounds steal the thunder from this album. Another problem comes in the lyric department. Stamey's earnest lyrics are often too arty, while failing to communicate any real enhancing art. Nevertheless, Stamey delivers some beautiful melodies and songs like "The Company of Light," "Something Came Over Me," "Glorious Delusion," and "On the Radio (For Ray Davies)" are wonderful listens. —Rick Clark

Wonderful Life / 1992 / East Side Digital ✦✦✦
This playful disc includes Stamey's 1982 solo effort, *It's a Wonderful Life* and 1984's *Instant Excitement*. Stamey experiments with percussion, triggering other types of instrumental sounds—something he calls the Groovegate System. All in all this disc feels like an idea scrapbook more than a polished release. —Rick Clark

Robust Beauty / 1995 / East Side Digital ✦✦

The Standells
....

Garage Rock

A '60s Los Angeles-based rock group, the Standells had the greasy garage-band sound down to perfection, and their pounding ode to Boston's "Dirty Water" was a huge hit in 1966. Prior to hitting national playlists, the band had recorded for MGM and Liberty and appeared in the 1964 movie *Get Yourself a College Girl*. Signed to Capitol's Tower subsidiary, drummer (former Mouseketeer) Dick Dodd's snarling vocal and pounding backbeat made "Dirty Water" (produced by Ed Cobb of the Four Preps, who were about as far opposed to the Standells' approach as could possibly be) their top-seller. Three subsequent 1966-1967 Standells singles also charted, but the quartet fell apart before the end of the decade. —Bill Dahl

Dirty Water / 1966 / Sundazed ✦✦✦

Why Pick on Me / 1966 / Sundazed ✦✦✦

Hot Ones / 1966 / Sundazed ✦✦

Try It / 1967 / Sundazed ✦✦

Anthology of Legendary Recordings, Vol. 1 / 1981 / AVI ✦✦✦✦
There have been various best-of compilations since this vinyl-only one came out in the early '80s, the one on Rhino being the easiest to acquire. There's nothing particularly wrong with this one, though; the 16 tracks include all of the big hits, and some good LP tracks like "All Fall Down" and "Trip to Paradise," as well as good liner notes. —Richie Unterberger

● **The Best of the Standells** / 1984 / Rhino ✦✦✦✦
Most '60s punk bands could barely fill an album side with decent material. This 18-song compilation is a tribute to the vitality of the Standells' raunch-and-roll attack, including not only their one hit ("Dirty Water") but salacious essentials ranging from the swaggering "Sometimes Good Guys Don't Wear White" to the horny wail of "Barracuda." —John Floyd

Ringo Starr (Richard Starkey)

b. Jul. 7, 1940, Dingle, Liverpool, England
Drums, Vocals / Pop-Rock
Ringo Starr, born Richard Starkey, was the drummer in the Beatles from 1962 to 1970 and thus one of the most famous musicians of the '60s. Though the least prominent member of the quartet, he distinguished himself as an occasional singer of good-natured material and as an actor. Upon the group's split, Starr went solo with two novelty projects: the first, an album called *Sentimental Journey* found him covering pre-rock standards, and the second, *Beaucoups of Blues*, was a country music collection.

Starr then scored Top Ten hits with two nonalbum singles, "It Don't Come Easy" in 1971 and "Back Off Boogaloo" in 1972. In 1973 he paired with producer Richard Perry and, with assistance from the three other ex-Beatles, made *Ringo*, which featured two No. 1 hits, "Photograph" and "You're Sixteen." "Oh My My," a Top Ten hit, was also included. Almost as successful was the 1974 follow-up, *Goodnight Vienna*, which featured the hits "Only You" and "No No Song."

Starr continued to release albums through 1981, though with diminishing success. His 1983 album *Old Wave* did not find a US distributor. Starr was also suffering from the excesses of his lifestyle, but by the late '80s he had cleaned up, and in 1989 he toured with his "All-Starr Band." In 1992, he signed to Private Music and released a new studio album, *Time Takes Time.* — *William Ruhlmann*

Sentimental Journey / Apr. 24, 1970 / Capitol ✦✦✦
A trip down memory lane—Ringo does the '40s. —*Jeff Tamarkin*

Beacoups of Blues / Sep. 28, 1970 / Capitol ✦✦✦✦
More sentimental nostalgia while Ringo decided whether life after Beatles existed. —*Jeff Tamarkin*

● **Ringo** / Nov. 2, 1973 / Capitol ✦✦✦✦
One of the great Beatle solo albums, and the only one to feature a little help from all three ex-friends in the band. Starr's apex. The 1991 CD reissue of *Ringo* contains three bonus tracks, the hit single "It Don't Come Easy," the autobiographical B-side "Early 1970," and "Down and Out." —*Jeff Tamarkin*

Goodnight Vienna / Nov. 18, 1974 / Capitol ✦✦✦
Even with John Lennon, Elton John, and a couple of bonafide hits, little here holds up. —*Jeff Tamarkin*

● **Blast from Your Past** / Nov. 20, 1975 / Capitol ✦✦✦✦
A formidable collection, including a couple of the more venerable hits. —*Jeff Tamarkin*

Ringo's Rotogravure / Sep. 27, 1976 / Atlantic ✦✦✦

Ringo the 4th / Sep. 26, 1977 / Atlantic ✦✦

Bad Boy / Apr. 21, 1978 / Portrait ✦✦

Stop & Smell the Roses / Oct. 27, 1981 / The Right Stuff/Capitol ✦✦✦

Old Wave / Jun. 16, 1983 / Right Stuff/Capitol ✦✦

Starr Struck: Best of, Vol. 2 / 1989 / Rhino ✦✦✦
For Beatles loyalists only—leftovers and losers only. —*Jeff Tamarkin*

All-Starr Band / 1990 / Rykodisc ✦✦✦
"Soundtrack" from the 1989 tour, with contributions from not only Starr, but Joe Walsh, Billy Preston, and others. —*Jeff Tamarkin*

Time Takes Time / May 1992 / Private Music ✦✦✦✦
A sober, reflective Ringo Starr returns, after a near-decade's absence, with a solid set of songs that could have been the work of, well, a Beatle. —*Jeff Tamarkin*

Live From Montreux, Vol. 2 / 1994 / Rykodisc ✦✦✦

Steely Dan

Soft Rock, Pop-Rock, Jazz-Rock
If most art-rock bands borrowed from the European folk and classical-music traditions for their attempts at heightened hybrids of rock, Steely Dan (formed in 1972) drew inspiration from American jazz, big band, and R&B artists like Charlie Parker, Stan Kenton, and Ray Charles, as well as Brill Building pop, to arrive at their sophisticated rock mutations. To say that Steely Dan was a rock band made about as much sense as saying Gentle Giant was a rock band. True, they employed rock instrumentation and various production values, but rock 'n' roll was clearly not the bottom line in their artistic vision. Built around Donald Fagen (b. Jan. 10, 1948) and Walter Becker (b. Feb. 20, 1950), Steely Dan was more a studio vehicle for their songwriting and arrangement concepts than a real live touring unit. In fact, as Steely Dan shed members, Becker and Fagen merely plugged the holes by incorporating more session sidemen, as opposed to maintaining a band.

Thematically, Becker and Fagen relished exploring the fetishes, twisted logic, and misadventures of society's losers and misfits, with a blackly humorous, cryptic lyric style. Sonically, Steely Dan's albums have earned them raves from practically ever corner of the audiophile world.

Their 1973 debut, *Can't Buy a Thrill* (No. 17), presented a six-piece band (with a handful of sidemen), sounding like a sophisticated alternative to fellow ABC labelmates Three Dog Night on tracks like "Midnight Cruiser," "Kings," and "Dirty Work." That album produced Steely Dan's first two hits, "Do It Again" (No. 6) and "Reeling in the Years" (No. 11).

By the time of their fifth album, the 1977 platinum *Aja* (No. 3), Becker and Fagen had fine-tuned their spare grooves, quirky melodies, and mildly dissonant jazz chordal clusters into a peculiarly seamless pop sound that was embraced by practically every radio format outside of country music. Sophisticated hits like "FM (No Static at All)" (No. 22), "Deacon Blues" (No. 19), "Peg" (No. 11), and "Josie" (No. 26) were among the many songs that became required soundtracks for every fern bar in the country. Becker and Fagen disengaged Steely Dan indefinitely after the 1981 release *Gaucho* (No. 9), which included the classy title cut and hits "Hey Nineteen" (No. 10) and "Time Out of Mind" (No. 22).

Since then Becker has produced other artists, like China Crisis, and Fagen released a successful solo album, *The Nightfly* (No. 11), which produced a hit with "I.G.Y. (What a Beautiful World)" (No. 26). Fagen has also recorded "Century's End" for the movie *Bright Lights, Big City.*

Becker produced Fagen's second solo album, 1993's *Kamakiriad;* the collaboration led to a Steely Dan reunion, which has resulted in two successful tours but no recordings to date. —*Rick Clark*

Can't Buy a Thrill / 1972 / MCA ✦✦✦
The Steely Dan that appeared on this debut was basically a sophisticated perversion of the sound forged by fellow-ABC-labelmates Three Dog Night. Check out "Dirty Work," "Kings," and "Midnight Cruiser," and say that it isn't true. It's certainly one of the best debuts by any group to emerge from the '70s. *Can't Buy a Thrill* also produced two classic hits with the dirty Latin-influenced groove of "Do It Again" and the edgy shuffle "Reelin' in the Years." —*Rick Clark*

☆ **Countdown to Ecstasy** / 1973 / MCA ✦✦✦✦✦
Compared to their debut, *Countdown to Ecstasy* was a commercial failure (rocketing up and down the charts in three weeks) once it became apparent that this wasn't *Reelin' in the Years, Part 2.* The melodies and arrangements were more subtle and the lyrics a little more impenetrable. Nevertheless, this is the album that initially hooked many hardcore Dan fans. "Show Biz Kids" and "My Old School" became moderate hits. Other standouts include the jazzy rocker "Bodhisattva" and "King of the World." —*Rick Clark*

☆ **Pretzel Logic** / 1974 / MCA ✦✦✦✦✦
On *Pretzel Logic*, Steely Dan most successfully synthesized their love for jazz into their dense pop-rock sound. The grooves were funky ("Night by Night," "Monkey in Your Soul") and the arrangements sophisticated ("Parker's Band," "Through with Buzz"). "Rikki Don't Lose That Number," featuring an incredibly lyrical guitar solo by Jeff Baxter, became Dan's biggest hit at No. 4. The title track and "Any Major Dude Will Tell You" are more highlights. —*Rick Clark*

☆ **Katy Lied** / 1975 / MCA ✦✦✦✦✦
With its appealing melodies and oddball themes, this was a strong successor to *Pretzel Logic.* By this time, Steely Dan was Becker and Fagen, aided by an army of Los Angeles's "A"-list session stars—Hugh McCracken, Larry Carlton, Jeff Porcaro, Hal Blaine, Michael McDonald, and more. Sonically, *Katy Lied*'s super-clean mix pointed the way to the elegantly shrink-wrapped sound of their later work. Among the standout tracks are "Black Friday," "Daddy Don't Live in That New York City No More," "Chain Lightning," and "Throw Back the Little Ones," featuring an expressive closing piano improvisation by Michael Omartian. —*Rick Clark*

The Royal Scam / 1976 / MCA ✦✦✦
With *The Royal Scam*, Steely Dan delivered a rather cluttered, abrasive-sounding collection of tracks, which were further undermined by weaker melodies. If fusion ever found a home in disco, "Kid Charlemagne" was it. Smugly humorous tracks like "Haitian Divorce," "Green Earrings," and the fetish sendup, "The Fez," are some of *Scam*'s highlights. —*Rick Clark*

Aja / 1977 / MCA ✦✦✦✦
During the late '70s, *Aja* became required soundtrack music for fern bars throughout the country whose owners desired an upscale ambience. This was due to precision-crafted jazz-fusion pop-rock tracks like "Deacon Blues," "Josie," "Peg," and the title track, which featured a wonderfully musical drum solo by Steve Gadd. —*Rick Clark*

Gaucho / 1980 / MCA ✦✦✦
Three years after *Aja*, Becker and Fagen returned with the obsessively streamlined *Gaucho.* This impeccably recorded set contained two fine hits, "Hey Nineteen" and "Time out of Mind." "Babylon Sisters" was another memorable highlight, while the title track sported one of the most entrancingly convoluted melodies of their career. However, "Glamour Profession," with its sophisticated disco feel, seemed tailor-made for the perpetual happy hour. —*Rick Clark*

★ **A Decade of Steely Dan** / 1985 / MCA ✦✦✦✦✦
This collection features many of Dan's high spots, but it's hardly definitive. Nevertheless, this is the place to go if you are only budgeting for a
single disc. —*Cub Koda*

Gold (Expanded Edition) / 1991 / MCA ✦✦✦✦
Now expanded past its original length, this companion to *Decade* fea-
tures newly remastered versions of tracks like "FM (No Static at All),"
Donald Fagen's "Century's End," and previously unreleased live work.
—*Rick Clark*

Citizen Steely Dan / 1993 / MCA ✦✦✦
Collecting all of Steely Dan's albums in chronological order, plus all of
their two or three B-sides and one demo in a four-CD box, *Citizen Steely
Dan* is only worthwhile for the fan replacing their old records. The
remastering on the box is exactly the same as the newly upgraded CDs,
and everything but the demo is available on other discs. —*Stephen Thomas Erlewine*

Alive in America / Oct. 17, 1995 / Giant ✦✦

Steppenwolf

Hard Rock, Psychedelic, Acid Rock
Led by John Kay (born Joachim Krauledat, April 12, 1944), Steppenwolf's
blazing biker anthem "Born to Be Wild" roared out of speakers everywhere in the fiery summer of 1968, John Kay's threatening rasp sounding a mesmerizing call to arms to the counterculture movement rapidly
sprouting up nationwide. German immigrant Kay got his professional
start in a bluesy Toronto band called Sparrow, recording for Columbia in
1966. After Sparrow disbanded, Kay relocated to the West Coast and
formed Steppenwolf, named after the Herman Hesse novel. "Born to Be
Wild," their third single on ABC-Dunhill, was immortalized on the
soundtrack of Dennis Hopper's underground film classic *Easy Rider*. The
song's reference to "heavy metal thunder" finally gave an assignable
name to an emerging genre. Steppenwolf's second monster hit that year,
the psychedelic "Magic Carpet Ride," and the follow-ups "Rock Me,"
"Move Over," and "Hey Lawdy Mama" further established the band's
credibility on the hard-rock circuit. By the early '70s, Steppenwolf ran out
of steam and disbanded. Kay continued to record solo, as other members
put together ersatz versions of the band for touring purposes. During the
mid '80s Kay re-formed his own version of Steppenwolf, grinding out his
hits (and some new songs) at oldies shows. Nevertheless, they'll be
remembered for generations to come for creating one of the ultimate gas
'n' go rock anthems of all time. —*Bill Dahl & Cub Koda*

Early Steppenwolf / 1969 / MCA ✦✦✦

● **16 Greatest Hits** / 1973 / MCA ✦✦✦✦
Just what the name implies; "Born to Be Wild," "Magic Carpet Ride,"
"The Pusher," and "Rock Me" are just some of the highlights. Everything
you're going to want to hear in one neat little package. —*Cub Koda*

Born to Be Wild: A Retrospective / 1991 / MCA ✦✦✦✦
A double-disc collection of Steppenwolf's lengthy career, *Born to Be
Wild: A Retrospective* includes more music than anyone but hardcore
fans need, but the song selection and packaging are superb, making it
essential for those devoted fans. —*Stephen Thomas Erlewine*

Stereolab

*Alternative Pop-Rock, Experimental, Post-Rock/Experimental, Indie
Rock*
One of the most distinctive bands making music today, Stereolab formed
when songwriter/guitarist/keyboardist Tim Gane dissolved his previous
group McCarthy and met songwriter/vocalist Laetitia Sadier. Together,
along with Mary Hanson (vocals, moog), Duncan Brown (bass), Andy
Ramsay (drums), and Sean O'Hagan (keyboards), the band makes music
that alternates between swirling and ethereal and harsh and atonal; the
title of one of their songs, "John Cage Bubblegum," sums up their aesthetic. The mix of heavy, droning keyboards, Sadier's and Hanson's mellifluous vocals, and the group's socialist leanings make for some cutting-
edge space-age bachelor pad music. —*Heather Phares*

Switched On / 1992 / Slumberland ✦✦✦
Stereolab's musical vision was nearly full-formed on their debut album,
Switched On. Driven by calm vocals, light pop melodies, and droning
keyboards and guitars, the simple production keeps the record edgy.
—*Stephen Thomas Erlewine*

Peng! / 1992 / WEA ✦✦✦
Peng! is the band's debut full-length album, on which Stereolab continue
to develop their unique approach to experimental pop music. "Super
Falling Star," "Peng! 33," "K-Stars," "The Seeming and the Meaning," and
"Surrealchemist" are just some of the album's standout tracks, combining dreamy harmonies and swirling keyboards with dissonant guitars
and Marxist lyrics. —*Heather Phares*

The Groop Played "Space Age Bachelor Pad Music" / 1993 / Too
Pure/American ✦✦✦

Music Map

British Punk

| Pub-Rock | Early '70s American Proto-Punk |

1st Generation British Punk
The Sex Pistols, The Clash, The Jam, The Damned,
Generation X, The Buzzcocks

Second Generation British Punk
The Adverts, The Undertones, X-Ray Spex, The Vibrators

| **Early British New Wave** Elvis Costello, Nick Lowe, Tom Robinson | **Arty British Punk/ New Wave** Wire, Joy Division, The Fall, Magazine, Siouxsie & The Banshees |

● **Transient Random Noise Bursts with Announcements** / Aug. 1993 /
Elektra ✦✦✦✦
Stereolab's major-label debut is also one of their finest and most experimental releases. More emphasis is placed on instrumentals and instrumental breaks on *Transient Random-Noise Bursts*. The 15-minute
"Jenny Ondioline" and noisy cuts like "Our Trinitone Blast" and "Ana-
logue Rock" showcase Stereolab's experimental tendencies, while tracks
like "Tone Burst," "Pack Your Romantic Mind," and "Lock Group Lullaby" show that the group is just as capable of creating beautiful, if offbeat pop songs as it is adept at bringing the noise. The group's most varied and characteristic recording. —*Heather Phares*

Mars Audiac Quintet / 1994 / Elektra ✦✦✦✦
The band's fourth album tones down their avant-garde edge, concentrating instead on Sadier's and Hansen's vocal interplay, as well as song
structures. A beautiful, if less challenging album, *Mars Audiac Quintet*
features plenty of bouncy, dreamy tunes like "Three-Dee Melodie," "Des
Étoiles Électroniques," "Ping Pong," "Seven Longers Later," and "Fiery
Yellow." *Mars Audiac Quintet* is a good starting point for Stereolab novices, as it gives an appealing but accurate introduction to the group's distinct and innovative sound. —*Heather Phares*

Refried Ectoplasm (Switched on Volume 2) / 1995 / Duophonic
✦✦✦✦

Music for the Amorphous Body Center / Apr. 1995 / Duophonic
✦✦✦✦
Recorded especially for an art exhibit, *Music for the Amorphous Body
Center* expands on Stereolab's trademark guitar-and-organ drone by
adding strings. With the subtle, lush strings as support, the group's easy
listening and '60s pop inclinations become more pronounced, making
the overlapping textures of "Pop Quiz" swirl magnificently. Such small
adjustments make the EP quite wonderful; it proves that there are hidden variations in Stereolab's music that don't quite come to the forefront
immediately. —*Stephen Thomas Erlewine*

Emperor Tomato Ketchup / Apr. 1996 / Elektra ✦✦✦✦
Stereolab was poised for a breakthrough release with *Emperor Tomato
Ketchup*, their fourth full-length album. Not only was their influence
becoming apparent throughout alternative rock, but *Mars Audiac Quintet* and *Music for the Amorphous Body Center* indicated they were moving closer to distinct pop melodies. The group certainly hasn't backed
away from pop melodies on *Emperor Tomato Ketchup*, but just as their
hooks are becoming catchier, they bring in more avant-garde and experimental influence, as well. Consequently, the album is Stereolab's most
complex, multi-layered record. It lacks the raw, amateurish textures of
their early singles, but the music is far more ambitious, melding electronic drones and sing-song melodies with string sections, slight hip-hop
and dub influences, and scores of interweaving counter melodies. Even
when Stereolab appears to be creating a one-chord trance, there is a lot
going on beneath the surface. Furthermore, the group's love for easy listening and pop melodies means that the music never feels cold or inaccessible. In fact, pop singles like "Cybele's Reverie" and "The Noise of
Carpet" help ease listeners into the group's more experimental tendencies. Because of all its textures, *Emperor Tomato Ketchup* isn't as immediately accessible as *Mars Audiac Quintet*, but it is a rich, rewarding listen. —*Stephen Thomas Erlewine*

Cat Stevens (Steve Georgiou)

b. Jul. 21, 1947, London, England
Synthesizer, Guitar, Piano, Keyboards, Vocals / Singer-Songwriter, Soft Rock, Pop-Rock

Cat Stevens was the son of a Greek father and a Swedish mother. Stevens became interested in folk and rock 'n' roll in his teens and scored his first UK hit, "I Love My Dog," before he turned 20. Stevens reached the singles charts four more times, getting to No. 2 with "Matthew and Son" and releasing the similarly titled Top Ten album before he contracted tuberculosis in 1968 and was forced to retire from music. He re-emerged with a new, mature style in 1970 with the album *Mona Bone Jakon* and hit the UK Top Ten with "Lady D'Arbanville." But it was his late 1970 follow-up, *Tea for the Tillerman,* that made him an international success. The album hit the Top Ten and went gold in the US, producing the hit "Wild World." *Teaser & the Firecat,* released in 1971, did even better, including the hits "Peace Train" and "Morning Has Broken." Stevens became so successful as an albums artist that, even though his next couple of albums did not generate big hit singles, they were still big sellers: *Catch Bull at Four* (1972) went to No. 1 and *Foreigner* (1973) reached No. 3. Stevens' 1974 album *Buddha & the Chocolate Box,* which included the No. 10 hit "Oh Very Young," reached No. 2. Stevens' records were gradually less successful during the second half of the '70s. In 1979, he became a Muslim, adopted the name Yusef Islam, and retired from music. He was not heard from for another ten years, until he shocked admirers at the end of the '80s by supporting the death sentence ordered by the Ayatollah Khomeini against novelist Salman Rushdie for writing the book *The Satanic Verses.* Some "classic rock" radio stations discontinued playing him as a result, though his music remains popular. *—William Ruhlmann*

Matthew & Son / 1967 / Deram ✦✦✦

Released in the late winter of 1967, 19-year-old Cat Stevens' debut album, *Matthew & Son,* contained his breakthrough UK hits "I Love My Dog" (No. 28) and the title song (No. 2), and spawned a third, "I'm Gonna Get Me A Gun" (No. 6). (The Tremeloes took a cover of the album's "Here Comes My Baby" to UK No. 4.) While it is a precocious effort (Stevens wrote all the songs) and the material is undeniably catchy, it's also wildly overproduced, with gimmicky arrangements typical of the mid-'60s British pop sound around the time of *Sgt. Pepper.* This is especially noticeable, heard in the context of Stevens' later, less-produced, more meaningful efforts. *—William Ruhlmann*

New Masters / 1967 / Deram ✦✦

Mona Bone Jakon / Jul. 1970 / A&M ✦✦✦

☆ **Tea for the Tillerman** / Nov. 1970 / A&M ✦✦✦✦✦

Tea for the Tillerman is like a musical collection of children's tales by Stevens. The delicacy of the arrangements, Paul Samwell-Smith's brilliant otherworldly production, and Stevens' entrancing melodies and images easily make this his best work. "Wild World" was a huge hit, but emotive tracks like "Father and Son," "Where Do the Children Play?," and the haunting "Into White" and "Sad Lisa" make this a must-own for fans of singer-songwriter pop. *—Rick Clark*

Teaser & the Firecat / Oct. 1971 / A&M ✦✦✦✦

The follow-up to *Tea for the Tillerman* was almost as impressive. Sonically, less energy was put into creating empty real soundscapes, with more emphasis on tighter song constructions and immediacy. The result paid off with three international hits, "Peace Train," "Moonshadow," and "Morning Has Broken." Other highlights included "Tuesday's Dead," "The Wind," "Bitter Blue," and "Ruby Love." After *Tea for the Tillerman,* this is the one to get. *—Rick Clark*

Catch Bull at Four / Oct. 1972 / A&M ✦✦✦✦

Catch Bull at Four was Stevens' commercial peak, holding the No. 1 spot for three weeks. Much of the reason for this was probably public anticipation that this would be as smoothly appealing as his previous two outings. With this album, Stevens' melodies became more ornate and his delivery became a little gruffer. Overall, it is one of his better albums with "Eighteenth Avenue," "Sitting," and "Can't Keep It In" as highlights. *—Rick Clark*

Buddha & the Chocolate Box / Apr. 1974 / A&M ✦✦✦

● **Greatest Hits** / Jun. 1975 / A&M ✦✦✦✦

This is the most popular best-of collection. It has his biggest hits and a couple of important album tracks. The CD version is just a straight reissue of the original LP release, therefore utilizing only about half of the time available on disc. *—Rick Clark*

Footsteps in the Dark: Greatest Hits, Vol. 2 / Nov. 1984 / A&M ✦✦✦✦

Classics, Vol. 24 / 1987 / A&M ✦✦✦✦

After several collections, there has yet to be a definitive representation of Stevens' work. Half of his Top 40 hits (like "Wild World," "Another Saturday Night," "Two Fine People," "The Hurt," and "Ready") are missing. On the plus side, some nice album cuts like "The Wind" and "18th Avenue" and highlights from the movie *Harold and Maude* are here. *—Rick Clark*

Al Stewart

b. Sep. 5, 1945, Glasgow, England
Guitar, Keyboards, Vocals / Singer-Songwriter, Folk-Rock

Glasgow native Al Stewart began his career playing guitar in Tony Blackburn's band the Sabres, and moved from there to the London folk club scene. After an unsuccessful single on Decca, "The Elf" (which featured Jimmy Page on guitar), Stewart signed with CBS and released a series of albums largely consisting of introspective, confessional love songs beginning in 1967. *Love Chronicles* was the only one to be released in the US, and the autobiographical title track, which detailed Stewart's romantic involvements, attracted a bit of attention for the singer's use of the word "fucking" in a song with supposed artistic credibility. On 1973's *Past, Present and Future,* Stewart switched gears, exploring his fascination with historical tales, and was rewarded with his first US chart album. *Modern Times* was even more successful, and *Year of the Cat* was an unqualified hit, selling over a million copies and spawning the Top Ten title single. *Time Passages* duplicated both feats, but Stewart's creativity dried up soon afterward, and difficulties over his contract and change of labels prevented him from releasing any new material until 1984. *Russians & Americans* was highly political, but sales were disappointing. Even so, Stewart has recorded and toured sporadically in the late '80s and '90s while devoting time to his hobby of wine collecting. *—Steve Huey*

Bedsitter Images / 1967 / Epic ✦✦

Love Chronicles / 1969 / Epic ✦✦✦

Zero She Flies / 1970 / Epic ✦✦✦

Orange / 1972 / Beat Goes On ✦✦✦

Past, Present & Future / 1973 / Arista ✦✦✦

On *Past, Present & Future,* Al Stewart began to reach his artistic fruition, as he crafted a lush, winding song cycle about the writings of Nostradamus, highlighted by the majestic "Nostradamus." *—Daevid Jehnzen*

Modern Times / 1975 / Rhino ✦✦✦✦

Stewart's airy (sometimes sentimental) obsessions with the passage of time take on a special resonance on this outing. Highlights include "Carol," "Apple Cider Re-Constitution," "Dark and Rolling Sea," and "The Modern Times." *—Rick Clark*

Year of the Cat / 1976 / Arista ✦✦✦✦

Stewart's calm delivery gives his songs a reserved, tasteful sense of understatement, especially on the title track, one of those "mysterious woman" songs, which captivated listeners and turned the album into a million-seller. *—William Ruhlmann*

Time Passages / 1978 / Arista ✦✦✦✦

A return to Stewart's historical themes lyrically, though it's still the overall smoothness of his music that connected with another million listeners. *—William Ruhlmann*

24 Carrots / 1980 / Razor & Tie ✦✦✦

Live Indian Summer / 1981 / Arista ✦✦

Russians & Americans / 1984 / Passport ✦✦

Out of all his grandly ambitious albums, *Russians & Americans* is among the most problematic, since he takes an actual political position, which tends to hurt the flow of the music. *—Daevid Jehnzen*

● **The Best of Al Stewart** / 1988 / Arista ✦✦✦✦

All of Al Stewart's stateside hits are available here, as well as most of the best cuts from the hit albums *Year of the Cat* and *Time Passages.* Not a comprehensive overview of his career, it's still the best sampler available. *—Rick Clark*

Last Days of the Century / 1988 / Enigma ✦✦

Rhymes in Rooms / 1992 / Mesa Blue Moon ✦✦✦

Dave Stewart/Spiritual Cowboys

b. Sep. 9, 1952, Sunderland, England
Piano / Pop-Rock

Dave Stewart was the musical mastermind of Eurythmics, but on his solo recordings with the Spiritual Cowboys, he made more atmospheric, guitar-based albums that became minor hits in the UK in the early '90s. Stewart also has written several soundtracks and produced many artists, including Bob Dylan and Mick Jagger. *—Stephen Thomas Erlewine*

Lily Was Here / 1989 / Anxious ✦✦✦

The soundtrack to a fairly unknown film, *Lily Was Here* was Dave Stewart's first solo effort. It's an atmospheric, subdued effort, highlighted by a revamped "Here Comes the Rain Again," with Annie Lennox on lead vocals, and a handful of tracks featuring saxophonist Candy Dulfer. *—Sara Sytsma*

● **Dave Stewart & Spiritual Cowboys** / 1990 / Arista ✦✦✦✦

Dave Stewart's first album with the Spiritual Cowboys is a fine collection of atmospheric pop-rock. *—AMG*

Honest / 1991 / Arista ✦✦✦
Dave Stewart's second album with the Spiritual Cowboys expanded the musical ideas of their debut, although it was slightly less focused and pop-oriented than its predecessor. —*Sara Sytsma*

Greetings from the Gutter / 1995 / East West ✦✦✦
Greetings from the Gutter is Dave Stewart's first official solo album and it's his most mainstream album to date, featuring several concise pop songs, as well as a handful of more complex, involved pieces. —*Sara Sytsma*

Rod Stewart

b. Jan. 10, 1945, London, England
Vocals / Rock 'n' Roll, Adult Contemporary, Pop-Rock
Rod Stewart may have began his career as a respected singer, but he lost much of that respect as he got older. While he has recorded some terrible albums—and he would admit that freely—Stewart was once rock 'n' roll's best interpretive singer, as well as an accomplished songwriter, creating a combination of folk, rock, blues, and country that sounded like no other folk-rock or country-rock. Instead of finding the folk in rock, he found how folk rocked like hell on its own. After he became successful, he began to lose the rootsier elements of his music, yet he remained a superb singer. Soon, Stewart abandoned the thought of blazing his own artistic path, choosing to follow pop trends.

Stewart began his musical career after spending some time as an apprentice with the Brentford Football Club, touring Europe with folksinger Wizz Jones in the early '60s; during this time he was deported from Spain for vagrancy. When he returned to England in 1963, he joined the Birmingham-based R&B group Jimmy Powell and the Five Dimensions, as a vocalist and harmonica player. The band toured the UK and recorded one single for Pye Records, which featured Stewart on blues harp. After moving back to London, he joined Long John Baldry's band, the Hoochie Coochie Men. The group recorded a single in 1964, "Good Morning Little Schoolgirl," which failed to chart and soon afterward the group became Steampacket.

During the summer of 1965, the group supported the Rolling Stones and the Walker Brothers on a UK tour, as well as recording an album that remained unreleased until 1970. Early in 1966, Steampacket disbanded and Stewart became a member of the blues-rock combo Shotgun Express, which released one single before splitting. Rod Stewart then joined the Jeff Beck Group at the end of 1966.

With the Jeff Beck Group, Rod Stewart began his climb to stardom. Stewart and the former Yardbird guitarist pioneered the heavy blues-rock team of a virtuoso guitarist and a dynamic, sexy lead vocalist which became the standard blueprint for heavy metal. *Truth*, the band's debut album, was released in the fall of 1968, becoming a hit in both America and Britain. The Jeff Beck Group toured both countries several times in 1968 and 1969, gaining a dedicated following. In the summer of 1969, they released their second album, *Beck-Ola*, which became another hit record in both the US and UK However, the group fell apart in the fall.

After rejecting an offer to join the American rock group Cactus, Stewart and Jeff Beck Group bassist Ron Wood joined the Small Faces, replacing the departed vocalist/guitarist Steve Marriott. With Wood switching over to guitar, the group shortened their name to the Faces and recorded their debut album, *First Step*. During this time, Stewart had also signed a solo contract, releasing his first album, *An Old Raincoat Won't Let You Down* (re-titled *The Rod Stewart Album* for its American release), at the end of 1969; the record failed to chart in the UK, yet it made it to No. 139 on the US charts. On the album, Stewart's folk roots meshed with his R&B and rock influences, creating a distinctive, stripped-down acoustic-based rock 'n' roll that signaled he was a creative force in his own right.

The Faces released *First Step* in the spring of 1970. The album was a departure both from the R&B/pop direction of the Small Faces and the heavy blues of the Jeff Beck Group; instead, the group became a boisterous, boozy, and sloppy Stones-inspired rock 'n' roll band. The album fared better in the UK than it did in the US, yet the group built a devoted following on both continents with their reckless, messy live shows. Stewart released his second solo album, *Gasoline Alley*, in the fall of 1970, supporting it with an American tour.

1971 proved to be the pivotal year in Stewart's career. At the beginning of the year, the Faces released their second album, *Long Player*, which became a bigger hit than *First Step*, yet his third solo album, *Every Picture Tells a Story*, made Rod Stewart a household name, reaching No. 1 in both America and Britain. "Reason to Believe" was the first single from the album, becoming a minor hit in both countries, but when DJs began playing the B-side, "Maggie May," the single became a No. 1 hit in both the UK and US for five weeks in September. The Faces released their third album, *A Nod Is as Good as a Wink... To a Blind Horse*, a couple of months later. Thanks to the success of *Every Picture Tells a Story*, the album was a Top Ten hit in both countries; it also launched the single "Stay with Me," which became the band's only Top 40 hit in the US. The following year, the Faces began a lengthy spring tour. During

the tour, tensions grew within the band as Stewart's solo career increased in popularity. That summer, Stewart released his fourth solo album, *Never a Dull Moment*, which nearly replicated the success of *Every Picture Tells a Story*, peaking at No. 2 in the US and No. 1 in the UK In the spring of 1973, The Faces released their final album, *Ooh La La*. Stewart expressed his disdain for the record in the press, yet it hit No. 1 in the UK and No. 21 in the US After releasing the "Pool Hall Richard" single in the beginning of 1974, the band went on tour; it would prove to be their last. Stewart released *Smiler* in the fall of 1975. *Smiler* followed the same formula as his previous four albums—and it also became a hit—yet it showed signs that the formula was wearing thin. In March of 1975, he began a love affair with Swedish actress Britt Ekland; the romance, along with a bitter fight with UK tax collectors, prompted him to apply for US citizenship. *Atlantic Crossing*, released in the summer of 1975, made the singer's relocation explicit. Recorded with producer Tom Dowd and the Muscle Shoals rhythm section, the album removed much of the singer's folk roots and accentuated his pop appeal. At the end of the year, Stewart left the Faces and the band finally called it quits.

Recorded in Los Angeles with a group of studio musicians, 1976's *A Night on the Town* continued Stewart's move to slicker pop territory and proved quite successful, becoming his first platinum album; it featured the hit single "Tonight's the Night," which was No. 1 in the US for eight weeks. *Foot Loose and Fancy Free*, released the following year, followed the same artistic pattern as *A Night on the Town* while surpassing its commercial performance, selling over three million copies. Stewart incorporated some disco to his musical formula for 1978's *Blondes Have More Fun*. Supported by the No. 1 single "Da Ya Think I'm Sexy?," the record became Stewart's first No. 1 album since *Every Picture Tells a Story*, selling over four million records. By this time, Stewart was notorious for his jet-set lifestyle, particularly the series of actresses and models he dated.

With 1981's *Tonight I'm Yours*, Stewart began adding elements of new wave and synth-pop to his formula, resulting in another platinum album. Soon afterward, his career hit a slump—his next four albums sounded forced and he only scored three Top Ten hits between 1982 and 1988; out of those four albums, only 1983's *Camouflage* went gold. Stewart rebounded with 1988's *Out of Order*, recorded with Duran Duran's Andy Taylor and Chic's Bernard Edwards. His version of Tom Waits' "Downtown Train," taken from the 1989 four-disc box set *Storyteller*, became his biggest hit since "Da Ya Think I'm Sexy?" *Vagabond Heart* (1991) reflected a more mature and reflective Rod Stewart and continued his comeback streak. Stewart reunited with Ron Wood to record an *MTV Unplugged* concert in 1993; the accompanying album launched the Top Ten hit single, "Have I Told You Lately." *Unplugged* also returned Stewart to a more acoustic-based sound, reminiscent of his early-'70s albums. On his 1995 album, *A Spanner in the Works*, the singer explored a more polished version of this sound, scoring another hit with Tom Petty's "Leave Virginia Alone." —*Stephen Thomas Erlewine*

The Rod Stewart Album / 1969 / Mercury ✦✦✦✦
This interesting, if spotty, hodgepodge of delicate folk ballads and blazing rave-ups is highlighted by "An Old Overcoat Won't Ever Let You Down." —*John Floyd*

☆ **Gasoline Alley** / 1970 / Mercury ✦✦✦✦✦
Gasoline Alley follows the same formula of Rod Stewart's first album, intercutting contemporary covers with slightly older rock 'n' roll and folk classics and originals written in the same vein. The difference is in execution. Stewart sounds more confident, claiming Elton John's "Country Comfort," the Small Faces' "My Way of Giving," and the Rolling Stones' version of "It's All Over Now" with a ragged, laddish charm. Like its predecessor, nearly all of *Gasoline Alley* is played on acoustic instruments—Stewart treats rock 'n' roll songs like folk songs, reinterpreting them in individual, unpredictable ways. For instance, "It's All Over Now" becomes a shambling, loose-limbed ramble instead of a tight R&B/blues groove, and "Cut Across Shorty" is based around a howling, mid-eastern violin instead of a rockabilly riff. Of course, being a rocker at heart, Stewart doesn't let these songs become limp acoustic numbers—these rock harder than any fuzz-guitar workout. The drums crash and bang, the acoustic guitars are pounded with a vengance—it's a wild, careening sound that is positively joyous with its abandon. And on the slow songs, Stewart is nuanced and affecting—his interpretation of Bob Dylan's "Only a Hobo" is one of the finest Dylan covers, while the original title track is a vivid, loving tribute to his adolescence. And that spirit is carried throughout *Gasoline Alley*. It's an album that celebrates tradition while moving it into the present and never once does it disown the past. —*Stephen Thomas Erlewine*

★ **Every Picture Tells a Story** / 1971 / Mercury ✦✦✦✦✦
Achieving the same variety as the debut, Stewart's title cut and "Maggie May," plus his covers of vintage Temptations, Arthur Crudup, and Tim Hardin material, flaunt the versatility and savvy of his vision. A grand statement by a major player. —*John Floyd*

☆ **Never a Dull Moment** / 1972 / Mercury ✦✦✦✦✦
This repeats the formula of *Every Picture Tells a Story,* but the originals, with the exception of the beautiful "Italian Girls," are just slightly below par. Still worthwhile, though. —*John Floyd*

Smiler / 1974 / Mercury ✦✦

Atlantic Crossing / 1975 / Warner Bros. ✦✦✦✦
Atlantic Crossing wasn't simply the moment when Rod Stewart left Britain for the greener pasture of America, it was the moment when he accepted his role as a full-fledged, jet-setting superstar. Stewart abandoned the formula of his first five solo records, as well as most of his folk-rock and hard rock undercurrents, trading them for a professionally polished, rock and soul-inflected pop, courtesy of Muscle Shoals' musicians and producer Tom Dowd. The glossy production doesn't obscure or trivialize Stewart's talents—coming after the tired *Smiler,* the slickness actually accentuated his strength as an interpretive singer. "The fast half" suffers from a couple of weak tracks, but "Three Time Loser" and "Stone Cold Sober" catch fire, and "the slow half" is generally excellent, but Stewart's heart-wrenching rendition of Danny Whitten's "I Don't Want to Talk About It" ranks as one of his finest performances. —*Stephen Thomas Erlewine*

A Night on the Town / 1976 / Warner Bros. ✦✦✦✦
After bouncing back to life with *Atlantic Crossing,* Rod Stewart crafted his most self-consciously ambitious record with *A Night on the Town.* The centerpiece of the album, "The Killing of Georgie (Part I and II)," was a long, winding Dylan-esque tale of the murder of one of Stewart's gay friends and was one of his better songs of the mid-'70s. Even if "The Killing of Georgie" was the conscious artistic focal point of *A Night on the Town,* the true masterpiece of the album was an eloquent rendition of Cat Stevens' "The First Cut Is the Deepest." Apart from the flawed political platitudes of "Trade Winds," the rest of the album was filled with competent, professional pop-rock, highlighted by the No. 1 hit "Tonight's the Night (Gonna Be Alright)," a ballad where the gallant Rod relieves a teenager of her virginity. And, again, the "Slow Half" was more convincing than the frequently perfunctory "Fast Half." —*Stephen Thomas Erlewine*

Foot Loose & Fancy Free / 1977 / Warner Bros. ✦✦

Blondes Have More Fun / 1978 / Warner Bros. ✦✦✦

Greatest Hits / 1979 / Warner Bros. ✦✦✦✦
Even though it has a couple of flaws—particularly the appearance of "Maggie May," which doesn't quite fit in with the rest of the material—*Greatest Hits* is an enjoyable sampler of Rod Stewart's first four Warner albums, including most of the hits but not necessarily all of his greatest performances. —*Stephen Thomas Erlewine*

Foolish Behaviour / 1980 / Warner Bros. ✦✦

Tonight I'm Yours / 1981 / Warner Bros. ✦✦✦✦
This lacks the muscle of the early stuff but remains Stewart's last burst of creativity. This is the last time he sounds like he cares. —*John Floyd*

Body Wishes / 1983 / Warner Bros. ✦

Camouflage / 1984 / Warner Bros. ✦✦

Rod Stewart / 1986 / Warner Bros. ✦

Out of Order / 1988 / Warner Bros. ✦✦✦

Storyteller: Complete Anthology / 1989 / Warner Bros. ✦✦✦✦
This 4-disc set contains most of the essentials (but not enough material from the Faces) and all the late-'70s and '80s hits for those who care. It should've been better. —*John Floyd*

Downtown Train (Selections from the Storyteller Anthology) / Mar. 6, 1990 / Warner Bros. ✦✦✦

Vagabond Heart / Mar. 26, 1991 / Warner Bros. ✦✦✦

The Mercury Anthology / 1992 / Mercury ✦✦✦✦
A two-disc anthology of Rod Stewart's early Mercury recordings, which, in conjunction with the albums he recorded with the Faces, are inarguably his finest (nothing from the Faces records is included). Most of the highlights of his terrific first four albums are here—"Maggie May," "You Wear It Well," "Handbags and Gladrags," "Gasoline Alley"—as well as selections from the lukewarm *Smiler,* a live album recorded with the Faces, and a couple of rare B-sides. —*Stephen Thomas Erlewine*

Unplugged . . . and Seated / May 25, 1993 / Warner Bros. ✦✦✦

Spanner in the Works / 1995 / Warner Bros. ✦✦✦

Stiff Little Fingers

Punk
A taut, explosive Belfast-based punk band, Stiff Little Fingers (named after a Vibrators song) had the dubious distinction of being referred to as the "Irish Clash." What must have seemed like a compliment at the time did little to help their career, only because it made comparisons between the two bands inevitable. Granted, there were many similarities: Both bands debuted playing revved-up late-'70s punk rock, both were politi-

cally inclined, featured pissed-off lead singers, a love for reggae, and a near-palpable sense of isolation and desperation. But as we all know, the Clash offered complexity, panache, and a consistently breathtaking body of work. Stiff Little Fingers, on the other hand, were simply a very good punk rock band. With sandpaper-throated frontman Jake Burns leading the way, SLF did release an auspicious, if badly produced, debut album, *Inflammable Material,* that featured the band's two best songs, "Alternative Ulster" and "Suspect Device." Both were passionate, ferocious songs dealing with the harsh, deadly realities of growing up in the middle of two decades of Northern Ireland's violence. These songs thrust SLF into the limelight and got them loads of enthusiastic press, which led to a contract with the decidedly anti-punk Chrysalis label in 1980. After that, SLF released a handful of pretty good records (including a terrific live album, *Hanx),* but their unregenerate fast and loud punk style started to sound stale. In 1982, the band released their most non-punk record (*Now Then . . .*), which was greeted by general apathy. In a musical rut, dogged by the facile Clash comparisons, and with punk rock running out of steam, Burns pulled the plug on SLF.

Sadly, the band's breakup lasted only five years. After a string of forgettable solo singles and a stint as a BBC Radio producer, Burns, hoping to cash in on punk nostalgia, reformed SLF (with another aging punk rocker, ex-Jam bassist Bruce Foxton) in 1987 and released a bunch of lousy (mostly live) records for the rest of the decade. —*John Dougan*

● **Inflammable Materials** / 1979 / Restless ✦✦✦✦
With "Alternative Ulster" and "Suspect Device" leading the way, this is a compelling, raging record that derives most of its style from the Sex Pistols and simply cranks up the personal political issues a notch or two. There is a so-so version of Bob Marley's "Johnny Was" (call it the obligatory reggae cover), but that doesn't hamper the enjoyment, nor does it detract from the record's overwhelming power. Issued on CD by Restless Retro in 1990. —*John Dougan*

Hanx / 1980 / Restless ✦✦✦

All the Best / 1983 / One Way ✦✦✦✦
The best anthology of SLF available. A 30-track chronological overview that's as articulate an argument for SLF's greatness as anything else they released. A perfect way to hear their development from the early punk days to their more "mature" punk-pop period just prior to their breakup: Jake Burns goes from shouter to singer, hooks and riffs replace simple walls of distorted guitars, the reggae influence becomes stronger and is played with greater dexterity; all and all, you simply can't go wrong here. —*John Dougan*

Sting (Gordon Sumner)

b. Oct. 2, 1951
Bass, Guitar, Vocals / Adult Contemporary, Pop-Rock
Sting launched his musical career as the lead singer of the successful rock band the Police. After the Police split in 1984, the English singer-songwriter and bassist embarked upon a successful solo career. Sting's solo works focus less on achieving pop success, instead voicing his political views and concerns. His 1985 debut album, *Dream of the Blue Turtles,* is heavily jazz-influenced and boasts a number of jazz musicians, including Branford Marsalis. This album, while it contained lyrical references to turbulent Soviet-American relations and the British coal-miners strike, still managed to sell two million copies. The *Dream* tour resulted in a two-disc live album, *Bring on the Night,* which featured some new live renditions of Police songs. In 1987, Sting released a second solo album, *Nothing like the Sun . . . ,* which was very politically based as well. One of the most powerful songs on the album was "They Dance Alone," an outright criticism of the regime of Chilean General Augusto Pinochet. *The Soul Cages,* released in 1991, deals with the death of Sting's mother and father and veers away from political issues. It was a more introspective work, although rather gloomy, dealing with the ideas of death and loss. In addition to his music, Sting has also appeared in a number of movies and plays, including *The Bride* and *The Threepenny Opera.* Sting has used his status as a well-known performer to lend assistance to many worthy organizations, including Band Aid, Live Aid, Special Olympics, Greenpeace, Amnesty International, and the Rainforest Foundation. Sting has made a significant contribution, not only to the music world but to the rest of the world as well. —*Iotis Erlewine*

The Dream of the Blue Turtles / 1985 / A&M ✦✦✦✦
Sting's early jazz experience was very evident on his solo debut album. Kenny Kirkland (piano), Omar Hakim (drums), Darryl Jones (bass), and Branford Marsalis (sax) contributed greatly to the jazz "feel" of the songs. This captures some of the energy and exuberance of the early Police, like *Regatta de Blanc,* but also maintains some of the somber, serious tone of *Synchronicity.* Sting's first album is his most impressive, boasting such songs as "Love Is the Seventh Wave," "Fortress Around Your Heart," "Children's Crusade," and "Moon over Bourbon Street." —*Iotis Erlewine*

Bring on the Night / 1986 / A&M ✦✦✦

Nothing like the Sun / 1987 / A&M ✦✦✦✦
This album is more somber than *Dream of the Blue Turtles* and light on the jazz influences, focusing more on Brazilian and Hispanic rhythms. Not as lively and concise as *Dream* due to the heavy, political lyrics (on such songs as "They Dance Alone" and "Fragile"), this is a good album, nevertheless. Along with Sting's own songs, the album includes a cover of Hendrix's "Little Wing." This album includes guests Mark Knopfler, Eric Clapton, the Gil Evans Band, former Police bandmember Andy Summers (who plays on "Lazarus Heart"), and, once again, Branford Marsalis featured on sax. — *Iotis Erlewine*

The Soul Cages / 1991 / A&M ✦✦✦
This long-awaited album followed the death of Sting's father, which may explain the melancholy, pained tone of these songs. The focus here is very much on death and dying, making the album a bit of a downer and hard to listen to in a single sitting. Although the material may not be as good overall as Sting's previous work, the song "All This Time" is definitely one of his best. — *Iotis Erlewine*

● **Ten Summoner's Tales** / Mar. 9, 1993 / A&M ✦✦✦✦
Ten Summoner's Tales is the most song-oriented, lighthearted collection Sting has delivered since his solo debut. Sting's songs remain densely literate, although the melodies aren't; they are devoid of the jazz pretensions of *Nothing Like the Sun* and the oppressive seriousness of *The Soul Cages*. When he doesn't get carried away by his own cleverness, Sting can deliver the goods with some terrific pop songs ("If I Ever Lose My Faith in You," "Epilogue [Nothin' 'Bout Me]," and "Seven Days"). Those songs help make *Ten Summoner's Tales* one of his strongest solo releases. — *Stephen Thomas Erlewine*

Fields of Gold: Best of Sting 1984-1994 / Nov. 8, 1994 / A&M ✦✦✦
This collection eliminates a lot of the more pretentiously "sophisticated" album tracks. The legion of Sting fans who consider the previous sentence heresy already own 12 out of 14 tracks; two new songs are included: "When We Dance" and "This Cowboy Song." — *Roch Parisien*

Mercury Falling / Mar. 12, 1996 / A&M ✦✦✦

Stone Poneys

Folk-Rock, Pop-Rock
Before becoming a solo act, Linda Ronstadt was the lead singer of the Stone Poneys, an L.A.-based trio with an acoustic, folkish sound and strong original material. The band's focal point and greatest asset was Ronstadt's clear, powerful vocals. Originally recording in a coffeehouse folk style not far removed from Peter, Paul & Mary, the group rocked up their sound slightly and scored a Top 20 hit with "Different Drum," written by Mike Nesmith of the Monkees, in 1967. — *Richie Unterberger*

● **Stone Poneys Featuring Linda Ronstadt** / 1967 / Capitol ✦✦✦✦
It doesn't have "Different Drum," but the first Stone Poneys album is their folkiest and best, dominated by close harmonies and strong original material by the group's guitarists, Bob Kimmel and Ken Edwards. — *Richie Unterberger*

Evergreen, Vol. 2 / 1967 / Capitol ✦✦✦
Evergreen, Vol. 2 wasn't as strong as their debut album, but it did contain their only hit, "Different Drum," as well as several other pleasant songs in a similar vein. — *Stephen Thomas Erlewine*

Stone Poneys & Friends, Vol. 3 / 1968 / Capitol ✦✦✦
The Stone Poneys broke up during the recording of their final album, leaving Ronstadt to finish the work with various sessionmen (hence the billing "Stone Poneys & Friends"). It's a solid effort, though, of decent if muted Californian folk-rock, with a laid-back (but not offensively so), carefully produced feel. Certainly the material is varied, with selections from the Stone Poneys, Mike Nesmith, and Laura Nyro, and occasional intimations of the country-rock direction that Ronstadt would frequently pursue during the '70s. The inclusion of three Tim Buckley songs serves as evidence that Ronstadt was hipper than some of her detractors have made her out to be. — *Richie Unterberger*

Stone Roses

Alternative Pop-Rock, Brit-Pop
Meshing '60s-styled guitar-pop with an understated '80s dance beat, the Stone Roses defined the British guitar-pop scene of the late '80s and early '90s. After their eponymous 1989 debut album became an English sensation, countless other groups in the same vein became popular, including the Charlatans (UK), Inspiral Carpets, and Happy Mondays. However, the band was never able to capitalize on the promise of their first album, waiting five years before they released their second record and slowly discintigrating in the year and a half after its release.

The Stone Roses emerged from the remains of English Rose, a Manchester-based band formed by schoolmates John Squire (guitar) and Ian Brown (vocals). In 1985, the Stone Roses officially formed, as Squire and Brown added drummer Reni (b. Alan John Wren), guitarist Andy Couzens, and bassist Pete Garner. The group began playing warehouses around Manchester, cultivating a dedicated following rather quickly. Around this time, the group was a cross between classic British '60s guitar-pop and heavy metal, with touches of goth-rock. Couzens left the group in 1987, followed shortly afterward by Garner. Garner was replaced by Mani (b. Gary Mounfield) and the group recorded their first single, "So Young," which was released to little attention by Thin Line Records. At the end of 1987, the Stone Roses released their second single, "Sally Cinnamon," which pointed the way toward the band's hook-laden, ringing guitar-pop. By the fall of 1988, the band secured a contract with Silvertone Records and released "Elephant Stone," a single that set the band's catchy neo-psychedelic guitar-pop in stone.

Shortly after the release of "Elephant Stone," the Stone Roses' bandwagon took off in earnest. In early 1989, the group was playing sold-out gigs across Manchester and London. In May, the Stone Roses released their eponymous debut album, which demonstrated not only a predilection for '60s guitar hooks, but also a contemporary dance-club and acid-house rhythmic sensibility. *The Stone Roses* received rave reviews and soon, a crop of similar-sounding bands appeared in the UK. By the end of the summer, the Stone Roses were perceived as leading a wave of bands that fused rock 'n' roll and acid house culture. "She Bangs the Drums," the third single pulled from the debut, became the group's first Top 40 single at the end of the summer. In November, the group had their first Top Ten hit when "Fool's Gold" climbed to No. 8. By the end of the year, band had moved from selling out clubs to selling out large theaters in the UK.

For the first half of 1990, re-releases of the band's earlier singles clogged the charts. The group returned in July 1990 with the single "One Love," which entered the charts at No. 4. Prior to the release of "One Love," the Stone Roses organized their own festival at Spike Island in Widnes. The concert drew over 30,000 people and would prove to be their last concert in England for five years. After Spike Island, the Stone Roses became embroiled in a vicious legal battle with Silvertone Records. The group wanted to leave the label but Silvertone took out a court injunction against the group, preventing them from releasing any new material. For the next two years, the band fought Silvertone Records while they allegedly prepared the follow-up to their debut album. However, the Stone Roses did next to nothing as the court case rolled on. In the meantime, several major record labels began negotiating with the band in secret. In March of 1991, the lawsuit went to court. Two months later, the Stone Roses won their case against Silvertone and signed a multi-million deal with Geffen Records.

For the next three years, the Stone Roses worked sporadically on their second album, leaving behind scores of uncompleted tapes. During these years, the group kept a low-profile in the press but that wasn't to preserve the mystique—they simply weren't doing much of anything besides watching football. Finally, in the spring of 1994, Geffen demanded that the group finish the album and the band complied, completing the record, titled *Second Coming*, in the fall. "Love Spreads," the Stone Roses' comeback single, was debuted on Radio One in early November. The single received a lukewarm reaction and entered the charts at No. 2, not the expected No. 1. *Second Coming* received mixed reviews and only spent a few weeks in the Top Ten. The Stone Roses planned an international tour in early 1995 to support the album, but the plans kept unravelling at the last minute. Before they could set out on tour, Reni left the band, leaving the group without a drummer. He was replaced by Robbie Maddix, who had previously played in Rebel MC. After Maddix joined the band, they embarked on a short American tour at the conclusion of which John Squire broke his collarbone in a bike accident. Squire's accident forced them to cancel a headlining spot at the 25th Glastonbury Festival, which would have been their first concert in the UK in five years. As Squire recuperated, the Stone Roses continued to sink in popularity and respect—even their peers, the Charlatans and former Happy Mondays vocalist Shaun Ryder (who had a new band, Black Grape), made unexpectedly triumphant comebacks. The Stone Roses, however, were ridiculed in the press, and their singles failed to become big hits.

The Stone Roses added a keyboardist to the lineup prior to their UK tour at the end of 1995—it was the first British tour since 1990. John Squire announced that he was leaving the band he founded in order to form a new, more active band. The Stone Roses announced their intention to carry on with a new guitarist. — *Stephen Thomas Erlewine*

★ **The Stone Roses** / 1989 / Silvertone ✦✦✦✦✦
Since the Stone Roses were the nominal leaders of Britain's "Madchester" scene—an indie-rock phenomenon that fused guitar-pop with drug-fueled rave and dance culture—it's rather ironic that their eponymous debut only hints at dance music. What made the Stone Roses important was how they welcomed dance and pop together, treating it as if it were the same beast. Equally important was the Roses' cool, detached arrogance which was personified by Ian Brown's nonchalant vocals. Brown's effortless malevolence is brought to life with songs that equal both his sentiments and his voice—"I Wanna Be Adored," with its creeping bass line and waves of cool guitar hooks, doesn't demand adoration, it just

expects it. Similarly, Brown can claim "I Am the Resurrection" and lay back, as if there were no room for debate. But the key to *The Stone Roses* is John Squire's layers of simple, exceedingly catchy hooks and how the rhythm section of Reni and Mani always imply dance rhythms without overtly going into the disco. On "She Bangs the Drums" and "Elephant Stone" the hooks wind into the rhythm inseparably—the '60s hooks and the rolling beats manage to convey the colorful, neo-psychedelic world of acid house. Squire's riffs are bright and catchy, recalling the British Invasion while suggesting the future with their phased, echoey effects. *The Stone Roses* was a two-fold revolution—it brought dance music to an audience that was previously obsessed with droning guitars, while it revived the concept of classic pop songwriting, and the repercussions of its achievement could be heard throughout the '90s, even if the Stone Roses could never match this level of achievement ever again. —*Stephen Thomas Erlewine*

Turns into Stone / Oct. 27, 1992 / Silvertone ✦✦✦

Second Coming / Dec. 1994 / Geffen ✦✦✦

The Complete Stone Roses / 1995 / Silvertone ✦✦✦✦
The title's a bit of a misnomer. *The Complete Stone Roses* concentrates on the band's first album, compiling the A- and B-sides of the group's hits from "Elephant Stone" to "One Love." In addition to the familiar material, the disc includes rare, early singles like "So Young" and "Sally Cinnamon" for the first time on compact disc, giving their classic material some context. The loud guitars of "So Young" are clearly the work of a hesitant band, while "Sally Cinnamon" is the first indication of John Squire's gift for ringing, melodic guitar hooks. However, their inclusion—as well as the appearance of the B-sides, which lack the consistent brilliance of "I Wanna Be Adored," "She Bangs the Drums," "Elephant Stone," "Waterfall," etc.—make *The Complete Stone Roses* a flawed introduction to the band. Nevertheless, there's a fair amount of classic pop here and the rarities are necessary for dedicated fans. —*Stephen Thomas Erlewine*

Stone Temple Pilots

Hard Rock, Alternative Pop-Rock, Grunge
Stone Temple Pilots were able to make alternative rock into stadium rock; naturally, they became the most critically despised band of their era. Accused by many critics of being nothing more than rip-off artists, pilfering from Pearl Jam, Soundgarden, and Alice in Chains, the band nevertheless became major stars in 1993. And the influences of those bands *are* apparent in their music, but Stone Temple Pilots do manage to change things around a bit. STP are more concerned with tight song structure and riffs than punk rage. Their closest antecedents are not the Sex Pistols or Hüsker Dü; instead the band resembles arena rock acts from the '70s—it's popular hard rock that sounds good on the radio and in concert. No matter what the critics might say, Stone Temple Pilots have undeniably catchy riffs and production; there's a reason why over three million people bought their debut album, *Core*, and why their second album, *Purple*, shot to No. 1 when it was released.

Following the success of *Purple* and its accompanying tour, the band took some time off, during which the group's lead singer, Scott Weiland, developed a heroin addiction. In the spring of 1995, he was arrested for possession of heroin and cocaine, and he was sentenced to a rehabilitation program. Following his completion of the program, Stone Temple Pilots recorded their third album. Released in the spring of 1996, *Tiny Music... Songs from the Vatican Giftshop*, entered the charts at No. 4. Shortly after its release, Stone Temple Pilots announced that Weiland had relapsed and had entered a drug rehabilitation facility, thereby canceling the group's plans for a summer tour. Weiland's drug problems and the group's inability to support *Tiny Music* with a tour meant that the album couldn't replicate the success of its predecessors—by the end of the summer, it had fallen out of the Top 50 and had stalled at platinum, which was considerably less than what the group's two previous albums achieved. —*Stephen Thomas Erlewine*

Core / 1992 / Atlantic ✦✦✦✦
While the Stone Temple Pilots may not be sincere alternative rockers, they do know how to write a killer riff, which is why their debut album sold nearly as many copies as Pearl Jam. Admittedly, STP can sound like either Pearl Jam ("Plush"), Alice in Chains ("Sex Type Thing" and "Wicked Garden"), Soundgarden ("Dead & Bloated"), or even R.E.M. ("Creep"), depending on their mood, but their hooks are undeniably catchy, making the songs much better than they have any right to be. In fact, Stone Temple Pilots appear to be the hard rock arena act for the 1990s, and that's a compliment. —*Stephen Thomas Erlewine*

● **Purple** / 1994 / Atlantic ✦✦✦✦
Stone Temple Pilots may have topped the charts with *Core*, yet it was with *Purple* that they established their across-the-boards popularity. Trimming back the excesses of their debut, *Purple* is a lean, throttling piece of post-alternative hard rock. STP doesn't rely simply on riffs, although there is a fair share of killer hooks; the band writes songs,

where the melodies and chords intertwine, becoming inseparable. From the brooding ballad "The Big Empty" to the simple, pounding, fuzzy riffs of "Vasoline," the group has improved in every facet—their songs are stronger and their playing is more convincing and powerful. Best of all is "Interstate Love Song." Clocking in at under three minutes, the record became one of the biggest album rock hits ever, spending 15 weeks at the top of the charts, and deservedly so—with its carefully measured dynamics and memorable melody, it's a showcase for everything that's good about hard rock. —*Stephen Thomas Erlewine*

Tiny Music... Songs from the Vatican Gift Shop / Mar. 26, 1996 / Atlantic ✦✦✦✦
Purple established that Stone Temple Pilots were not one-album wonders but *Tiny Music... Songs from the Vatican Gift Shop* illustrates that the band isn't content with resting on its laurels. Without abandoning their trademark hard rock, STP have added a new array of sounds that add depth to their immediately accessible hooks. Dean DeLeo layers his guitar tracks to create distinctive, multi-textured sounds that make his riffs more powerful. Though there are hints of grunge scattered throughout the album, what makes *Tiny Music* impressive is how the band brings in elements of psychedelia, trancy shoegazing, jangle-pop, and other forms of melodic alternative guitar-pop. By accentuating their pop tendencies in both their riffs and melodies, they are able to slip in a number of creative arrangements which manage to expand their musical repertoire significantly. Although the lyrics are nearly as ambitious as the music, they simply don't have the same weight. But with a band like Stone Temple Pilots, the music is what matters and *Tiny Music* showcases the band at their most tuneful and creative. —*Stephen Thomas Erlewine*

The Stooges

Hard Rock, Proto-Punk
This Detroit rock 'n' roll band was formed in 1967 as the Psychedelic Stooges with lead singer Iggy Pop (born James Newell Osterberg, 1947; original stage name was Iggy Stooge, the Iggy appellation coming from his drumming tenure with local teen band The Iguanas). The group also included Ron Asheton (guitar), Scott Asheton (drums), and Dave Alexander (bass). If local favorites the MC5 struck fear into the hearts of Motor City parents with their manifesto of sex, drugs, rock 'n' roll, and politics, they looked normal in comparison to the stage antics of Iggy & the Stooges. Violent interaction with members of the audience (both verbal and physical), vomiting, and self-mutilation with beer bottles were some of the more predictable aspects of their live presentation, while the music itself was simplistic and angry one- to three-chord grunge-rock, with lyrics ranging from teenage disorientation to animal lust. Two excellent albums for Elektra followed (they were signed the same night as The MC5), but the drug lifestyle of the band caused its breakup in the early '70s. They re-formed with James Williamson on guitar and Asheton moving over to bass for the next album in 1973, but disbanded again a year later. Working with David Bowie, Iggy cut two good solo albums in the mid-'70s, when bands like the Sex Pistols defined him as "The Godfather of Punk." He has kept recording and touring to his hardcore cult following up to the present time, with small acting roles in *The Color of Money* and *Cry Baby* as well. —*Cub Koda*

The Stooges / 1969 / Elektra ✦✦✦✦
Debut album; the true birth of punk rock. —*Cub Koda*

☆ **Fun House** / 1970 / Elektra ✦✦✦✦✦
Fun House is the quintessential Stooges album, the one where the music constantly sounds as if it were falling apart. Most of the songs on *Fun House* essentially recycle the same riff, but the key to the record isn't the songs, it's the sound. Where John Cale gave *The Stooges* a sound that was a bit too clean, *Fun House* sounds completely unproduced. Instruments bleed all over the place, Ron Asheton bangs out impossibly primitive riffs, Scott Asheton and Dave Alexander pound out brutal, simple rhythms, and Iggy Pop screams incoherent babble. *Fun House* only has seven songs, but it plays as one long piece—the violent swagger of "Down on the Street" morphs into the open wound of "T.V. Eye" and the dark dirge of "Dirt" before it all comes crashing down in the atonal climax of "L.A. Blues." At the time of its release, no other record sounded quite so raw, amateurish, and noisy—the Velvet Underground may have explored the avant-garde with the white noise experiments on their first two albums, but the Stooges sound as if they are leaving any artistic pretentions behind and are simply celebrating the sound of feedback, shouts, and crashing drums. —*Stephen Thomas Erlewine*

★ **Raw Power** / 1973 / Columbia ✦✦✦✦✦
The Stooges broke up after Elektra Records dropped them following the release of *Fun House*. Upon the urging of David Bowie, the group re-formed with a new guitarist, James Williamson, and proceeded to record *Raw Power*. Many Stooges fans have continually debated the merits of the group's third and final album, claiming that Bowie diluted the sound of the record by mixing the bass almost entirely out of the final version and not giving the guitars enough power. Even though there is some

truth to these allegations, *Raw Power* remains a definitive Stooges album—the group positively seethes with energy. The cleaner production and performances don't hurt the band. Instead, they give Iggy Pop a clearer, more direct platform for his scary posturing. Being able to hear everything on the record gives it a lethal force, though fans of *Fun House* will miss the murk. Nevertheless, *Raw Power* is the group's most accessible effort, and many of the Stooges imitators that followed in the '80s and '90s basically reworked the sound of this album, making it just slightly grungier. —*Stephen Thomas Erlewine*

Metallic K O / 1976 / Skydog ✦✦✦✦
The last Stooges live show; scary as hell. Bootleg import. Worth the search. —*Cub Koda*

The Stranglers

Rock 'n' Roll, Punk
The Stranglers—Hugh Cornwell (b. Aug. 28, 1949), guitarist, vocalist; Jean Jacques Burnel, bassist, vocalist; Dave Greenfield, keyboard player; and Jet Black, drummer—are one of the longest-lived bands associated with the British punk explosion of the '70s, but they were never really a punk group. Formed in Guildford in 1975, the group adopted a spare sound reminiscent of the Doors. They were categorized as punk because they came up at the same time as the punk originators and because their demeanor was angry and threatening.

The Stranglers broke through in 1977, scoring three Top Ten hits, "Peaches," "Something Better Change," and "No More Heroes," and two Top Ten albums, *IV Rattus Norvegicus* and *No More Heroes*. The group never achieved commercial success in the US but did well consistently in the UK. They gradually evolved from the hard-edged style to a more mainstream rock sound. —*William Ruhlmann*

No More Heroes / 1977 / A&M ✦✦✦✦
Rattus is hardly a punk rock classic but still is a pretty good chunk of art punk. Hugh Cornwell's testosterone level is very high here and the macho preening gets a bit much, but it's still an enjoyable bit of noise that holds up better than I'm sure anyone would have guessed at the time. Still, it's odd to think of this as a part of the punk rock era; with the exception of the fast and sloppy production by Martin Rushent, and the short songs, there's not much that's overtly punk about it. *Heroes* on the other hand is faster, nastier, and better. At this point the Stranglers were on top of their game and the ferocity and anger that suffuses these records would never be repeated. —*John Dougan*

Live (X Cert) / 1979 / IRS ✦✦✦
● **Greatest Hits 1977-1990** / 1990 / Epic ✦✦✦✦
Despite its rather cheeky title, this is a good place to sample the entire Stranglers output. From the squalor of the late-'70s material, to the smoothed out glopam pop of songs like "Skin Deep" and other mid- to late-'80s neo-goth-rock, this is a solid anthology that values substance over style and exhaustive track selection. Trust me, a well-edited Stranglers anthology is the only way to enjoy them; they recorded way too much dross to spend time searching out all of their plentiful, marginal records. —*John Dougan*

Strawberry Alarm Clock

Psychedelic
Strawberry Alarm Clock were a psychedelic bubblegum band of the mid-'60s, reaching the top of the charts with "Incense and Peppermints" at the height of the flower power era. Originally called the Sixpence, The Californian group consisted of Ed King (lead guitar), Lee Freeman (rhythm guitar), Gary Lovetro (bass), Mark Weitz (organ), and Randy Seol (drums). On the band's debut single, "Incense and Peppermints," lead vocals were sung by Greg Munford, a 16-year-old friend of the band. Before recording their debut album, the band added George Bunnell, who also played bass; more importantly, Bunnell became the group's main songwriter. In the summer of 1967, the Strawberry Alarm Clock contributed music to the film *Psych-Out*, as well as appearing in it. Gary Lovetro left the band before they recorded their second album, *Wake Up It's Tomorrow*, which also appeared in 1967. Between 1968's *The World in a Seashell* and 1969's *Good Morning Starshine* the band went through lineup changes; as of *Good Morning Starshine* the band featured King on bass, Weitz, guitarist Jimmy Pitman, and drummer Gene Gunnels. By this time, the Strawberry Alarm Clock had lost much of its audience. They managed to keep performing until 1971, when the band finally broke up. Ed King went on to join Lynyrd Skynyrd; several of the former members of Strawberry Alarm Clock reunited in the '80s to perform at oldies tours. —*Stephen Thomas Erlewine*

● **Strawberries Mean Love** / 1992 / Big Beat ✦✦✦✦
For a little more money, this 21-track CD compilation is a better deal than its American counterpart (One Way's *Anthology*), offering a slightly more extensive selection and extensive liner notes, and including almost all of the cuts contained on *Anthology*. Drawn from their four albums (with the accent, properly, on the first two), it also has a clutch of non-LP

singles. "Incense and Peppermints" and the small follow-up hit, "Tomorrow," are by far the best things on here; much of the rest is trendy period pop/psychedelia, sounding at various times like a bush league Doors, or a *really* spaced out Association, with a bit of garage raunch tossed in on the B-side of "Incense" ("The Birdman of Alkatrash"). The two hits were included on Rhino's *Nuggets* compilations, which might be a better context in which to appreciate the group's fairly minimal contributions to psychedelia. —*Richie Unterberger*

● **Anthology** / 1993 / One Way ✦✦✦✦

The Strawbs

Art-Rock/Progressive-Rock, Folk-Rock, British Folk
Originally a folk and bluegrass trio formed by Dave Cousins, with Sandy Denny as lead singer, the Strawbs evolved into an acoustic folk quartet and later into a progressive-rock quintet, complete with electric keyboards and an epic/classical orientation. The exits of bassist John Ford and drummer Richard Hudson in the early '70s led to a toughening of the group's sound but also a weaker songwriting contingent. Their return, and Cousins' hookup with guitarist Brian Willoughby, made them musically if not commercially viable again in the '80s and '90s. —*Bruce Eder*

Sandy Denny & the Strawbs / 1968 / Hannibal ✦✦✦✦
Acoustic folk and bluegrass. Mostly a showcase for Denny, plus a few clues to the group's future evolution. —*Bruce Eder*

Strawbs / 1969 / A&M ✦✦✦
Dragonfly / 1970 / A&M ✦✦✦
Just a Collection of Antiques and Curio / 1970 / A&M ✦✦
A live recording from Queen Elizabeth Hall. The still-acoustic ensemble pulls their sound together in a series of long jams, but keyboardist Rick Wakeman's solo just doesn't fit. (Japanese import). —*Bruce Eder*

Grave New World / 1972 / A&M ✦✦✦✦
Fulfillment! singer-songwriter Dave Cousins finds a space somewhere between Bob Dylan and John Bunyan, Hudson and Ford come up with some superb hooks, and the electric sound is powerful and majestic. Powerful and sincere, if a little too serious and downbeat. —*Bruce Eder*

Bursting at the Seams / 1973 / A&M ✦✦✦✦
A magnum opus: romantic, mystical, electrifying, and it rocks with a defiant smile. "Down by the Sea" is as fine a piece of progressive-rock as was ever produced. —*Bruce Eder*

Hero & Heroine / 1973 / A&M ✦✦✦
The group's last great album, filled with mysticism and sexuality but lacking melodic subtlety. Loud, but with less richness of expression. —*Bruce Eder*

Strawbs by Choice / 1974 / A&M ✦✦✦
Ghosts / 1975 / A&M ✦✦
Best of Strawbs / 1978 / A&M ✦✦✦
Preserves Uncanned / 1991 / Road Goes On Forever ✦✦✦✦
A double CD of 38 previously unreleased songs (one is unlisted on the sleeve) dating from 1966-68, prior to the recording of their proper debut album. Most of these are demos, and many would surface (sometimes in altered form) on future Strawbs and Dave Cousins albums, although quite a few were never officially rerecorded. Its appeal isn't just limited to Strawbs specialists—it's good, versatile (if slightly derivative) late-'60s British folk-rock, recalling Fairport Convention and (to a lesser degree) Pentangle in its eclecticism, though the Strawbs were no match for the Fairports in the vocal department. Most of the songs are Cousins originals, including tuneful, almost poppy harmony numbers and wordy tracts that take their lyrical cues from Bob Dylan and Ray Davies; the traditional folk tunes and bluegrass instrumentals, though indicative of the group's multi-faceted talents, are less interesting. Self-penned compositions like "October to May," "Martin Luther King's Dream," "Where Is the Dream of Your Youth," and "The Man Who Called Himself Jesus" are among the best (not to mention most lyrically ambitious) songs Cousins has ever done; "All I Need Is You" and the Beatles-ish "And You Need Me" are among the poppiest. Good sound quality, and detailed liner notes by Cousins himself. —*Richie Unterberger*

● **A Choice Selection of Strawbs** / 1993 / A&M ✦✦✦✦
Very few of the UK group's albums have been released in CD format, and this comprehensive, 74-minute collection goes a long way to sating the resultant thirst. While there are elements of the Strawbs' mellotron-based sound that make *A Choice Selection* sound dated at times, the material survives better than many of the group's "progressive-minded" contemporaries. The Strawbs' roots went back to folk and bluegrass, and leader David Cousins never let instrumental virtuosity get in the way of a good song and well-turned lyric. —*Roch Parisien*

The Stray Cats

Rockabilly, New Wave
This US rock trio consists of Brian Setzer (b. 1960), standup bass slapper

Lee Rock (born Lee Drucher), and drummer Slim Jim Phantom (born James McDonnell). It was formed in 1979 in the midst of the punk/new wave scene, playing retro-rockabilly style. Emigrating to England shortly thereafter, they caught on quickly with a music scene that was always interested in the "next big thing," and their top-notch production by Dave Edmunds quickly moved them into the charts. Visual image and European success augered well for their return to the US just in time to mine the early motherlode of MTV video-land. By the mid-'80s, after much success, the gimmick had worn off, and the band broke up by late 1984. They regrouped in the '90s after various solo projects had fizzled, with their style relatively unchanged. — *Cub Koda*

● **The Best of Stray Cats: Rock This Town** / 1990 / EMI America ✦✦✦✦
Best of the Stray Cats—Rock This Town is a nice, solid compilation, featuring the title track, "Stray Cat Strut," and others. — *Cub Koda*

Nolan Strong & the Diablos

R&B
This early Detroit R&B vocal group formed in 1950, originally featuring Nolan Strong, Juan Guiterriec, Willie Hunter, Quentin Eubanks, and Bob "Chico" Edwards on guitar. Strong was blessed with a beautiful high tenor voice (and even higher falsetto) and writing and arranging skills far surpassing those of most doo-wop groups of the era. What makes his recordings (with and without the Diablos) so special is that we're hearing the Motown sound in its embryonic form. Nolan was the original Smokey Robinson, the original Michael Jackson, years before either of them stood before a microphone at Motown. Recording his entire career for the tiny independent Fortune (Detroit's first Black R&B label), Strong's influence on Smokey and the early Motown stable of talent was unmistakable. As late as the early '60s, Berry Gordy tried to buy Nolan's contract from Fortune and install him as head arranger and producer but to no avail. (The job went instead to Robinson.) Incredibly handsome with a strong stage presence, Strong came close to the big time on several occasions (when his "Mind Over Matter" started to break nationally, Gordy recruited the Temptations to cover it under the name the Pirates, the only time in the history of Motown that this was done), but his erratic temperament and lifestyle ensured that it was not to be. The genius of one of the greatest and yet most underappreciated artists in the history of pop music lives on in the 20-odd years of recordings Strong did in a tiny, crudely equipped studio situated in the back of a record shop. The original sound of the Motor City, indeed. — *Cub Koda*

● **Fortune of Hits, Vol. 1** / 1961 / Fortune ✦✦✦✦
All the early hits, and the perfect place to start. — *Cub Koda*

Fortune of Hits, Vol. 2 / 1962 / Fortune ✦✦✦✦
Included is "Daddy Rocking Strong," "Adios My Dearest Love," "Danny Boy" (pre-Jackie Wilson), "Mambo of Love," and for all you R&B Christmas collectors, Nolan Strong's falsetto is put to good use on The Diablos' version of "White Christmas." — *Roundup Newsletter*

Daddy Rock / 1963 / Fortune ✦✦✦

The Style Council

Pop-Rock
Guitarist/vocalist Paul Weller broke up the Jam, the most popular British band of the early '80s, at the height of their success in 1982 because he was dissatisfied with their musical direction. Weller wanted to incorporate more elements of soul, R&B, and jazz into his songwriting, which is something he felt his punk-oriented bandmates were incapable of performing. In order to pursue this musical direction, he teamed up in 1983 with keyboardist Mick Talbot, a former member of the mod revival band the Merton Parkas. Together, Weller and Talbot became the Style Council—other musicians were added according to what kind of music the duo were performing. With the Style Council, the underlying intellectual pretensions that ran throughout Weller's music came to the forefront. Although the music was rooted in American R&B, it was performed slickly—complete with layers of synthesizers and drum machines—and filtered through European styles and attitudes. Weller's lyrics were typically earnest, yet his leftist political leanings became more pronounced. His scathing criticisms of racism, unemployment, Margaret Thatcher, and sexism sat uneasily beside his burgeoning obsession with high culture. As his pretensions increased, the number of hits the Style Council had decreased; by the end of the decade, the group was barely able to crack the British Top 40 and Weller had turned from a hero into a has-been.

Released in March of 1983, the Style Council's first single "Speak like a Child" became an immediate hit, reaching No. 4 on the British charts. Three months later, "The Money-Go-Round" peaked at No. 11 on the charts as the group was recording an EP, *Paris*, which appeared in August; the EP reached No. three. "Solid Bond in Your Heart" became another hit in November, peaking at No. 11.

The Style Council released their first full-length album, *Cafe Bleu*, in March of 1984; two months later, a resequenced version of the record, re-

titled *My Ever Changing Moods*, was released in America. *Cafe Bleu* was Weller's most stylistically ambitious album to date, drawing from jazz, soul, rap, and pop. While it was musically all over the map, it was their most successful album, peaking at No. 5 in the UK and No. 56 in the US "My Ever Changing Moods" became their first US hit, peaking at No. 29. In the summer of 1985, the Style Council had another UK Top Ten hit with "The Walls Come Tumbling Down." The single was taken from *Our Favorite Shops*, which reached No. 1 on the UK charts; the record was released as *Internationalists* in the US The live album, *Home and Abroad*, was released in the spring of 1986; it peaked at No. 8.

The Style Council had its last Top Ten single with "It Didn't Matter" in January of 1987. *The Cost of Loving*, an album that featured a heavy emphasis on jazz-inspired soul, followed in February. Although it received unfavorable reviews, the record peaked at No. 2 in the UK That spring, "Waiting" became the group's first single not to crack the British Top 40, signaling that their popularity was rapidly declining. In July of 1988, the Style Council released their last album, *Confessions of a Pop Group*, which featured Weller's most self-important and pompous music—the second side featured a ten-minute orchestral suite called "The Gardener of Eden." The record charted fairly well, reaching No. 15 in the UK, but it received terrible reviews. In March of 1989, the Style Council released a compilation, *The Singular Adventures of the Style Council*, which reached No. 3 on the charts. Later that year, Weller delivered a new Style Council album, which reflected his infatuation with house and club music, to Polydor. Polydor rejected the album and dropped both the Style Council and Weller from the label. Paul Weller and Mick Talbot officially broke up the Style Council in 1990. In 1991, Weller launched a solo career which would return him to favor in the mid-'90s. — *Stephen Thomas Erlewine*

Introducing the Style Council / 1983 / Polydor ✦✦✦✦
A solid EP collection of the band's initial British singles, it includes the ersatz soul of "Long Hot Summer," the bubbling pop of "Speak like a Child," and "Money-Go-Round," a fine British-funk manifesto. — *John Floyd*

Cafe Bleu / 1984 / Polydor ✦✦✦✦
Style Council's first proper album *Cafe Bleu* was one of their better efforts, but it indicated the group's fatal flaw—a tendency to be too eclectic and overambitious. Amidst the lazy jazz instrumentals, many of them courtesy of Mick Talbot, Paul Weller inserted several solid soul-tinged pop songs, including "My Ever Changing Moods," "Headstart for Happiness," "You're the Best Thing," and "Here's One that Got Away." However, that doesn't excuse the rap experiment, "A Gospel." The album was later released with a slightly different running order as *My Ever Changing Moods* in the US. — *Stephen Thomas Erlewine*

Our Favourite Shop / 1985 / Polydor ✦✦✦✦
Our Favourite Shop, the Style Council's second proper album, was still quite eclectic, but it didn't seem as schizophrenically diverse as *Cafe Bleu*. Weller had been able to incorporate his soul and jazz experiments into his songwriting, writing the fine "Walls Come Tumbling Down," "Come to Milton Keys," "Boy Who Cried Wolf," and "Down in the Seine," which were some of his best songs for the Style Council. The occasional misguided experiment remained—the stiff funk of "The Internationalists" and the self-righteous "The Stand Up Comic's Instructions" were particularly embarrassing—but the record was more cohesive and stronger than the debut. In America, the album was released without "Our Favourite Shop" and retitled *Internationalists*. — *Stephen Thomas Erlewine*

Home & Abroad / 1986 / Geffen ✦✦

Cost of Loving / 1987 / Polydor ✦✦

Confessions of a Pop Group / 1988 / Polydor ✦
If *The Cost of Loving* was a thoroughly mediocre affair, *Confessions of a Pop Group* was flat-out bad, without a single like "It Didn't Matter" to redeem its indulgences. Throughout the album, Weller engages in some of his most pretentious and mean-spirited lyrics but they are no match for the music he's written, which ranges from self-important jazz-pop fusions to an orchestral suite that finishes the album. The result was bad enough to leave him without a record contract in the UK, where he was considered a god just eight years earlier. — *Stephen Thomas Erlewine*

● **The Singular Adventures of the Style Council** / 1989 / Polydor ✦✦✦✦
An adequate hits collection, it skims the cream from their otherwise disappointing albums and includes "You're the Best Thing," the closest they've ever come to a US hit. — *John Floyd*

Here's Some That Got Away / Feb. 22, 1994 / Polydor ✦✦✦
Since the Style Council's albums were either inconsistent or downright boring, the idea of a B-sides and rarities collection isn't exactly enticing. However, this album is surprisingly enjoyable, proving that Paul Weller was at his best when he wasn't trying to make serious, self-important music. — *Stephen Thomas Erlewine*

Style Council Collection / Mar. 1996 / Polydor ✦✦✦

Not a strict greatest hits, *The Style Council Collection* balances some of the group's biggest singles with some relatively obscure album tracks. Like the band itself, the album loses steam toward the end, but the best songs here—"My Ever-Changing Moods," in particular—prove that, contrary to popular belief, the Style Council wasn't a complete waste of Paul Weller's time and that he did explore some new territory with the group. —*Stephen Thomas Erlewine*

The Stylistics

Soul

One of the sweetest soul groups hailing from Philly, with an incredible run of soul smashes from 1971 to 1975. The fragile falsetto of Russell Thompkins, Jr. (b. Mar. 21, 1951) and sumptuous production of Thom Bell added up to serious long-term success for the Stylistics. The quintet debuted on the charts in 1971 with "You're a Big Girl Now" and proceeded to set the soul and pop markets ablaze with "You Are Everything," "Betcha by Golly Wow," "I'm Stone in Love with You," "Break Up to Make Up"—all ballads—and the untypical rocker "Rockin' Roll Baby" on Avco. Although they left the label in 1976, the hits rolled on for another decade, albeit not on so lofty a scale. —*Bill Dahl*

The Stylistics / 1971 / Avco Embassy ✦✦✦

Round 2 / 1972 / Amherst ✦✦✦✦

The Russell Tompkins, Jr. legend began to grow in the early '70s with this superb album. His version of "You'll Never Get To Heaven If You Break My Heart" inspired fantasies from women that probably surpassed what Dionne Warwick generated in men, while "Break Up To Make Up" and "I'm Stone In Love With You" were instant anthems and are still among the great 1970s love ballads. —*Ron Wynn*

Love Hits / 1974 / Amherst ✦✦✦✦

Another anthology, this one covering the beautiful love songs and romantic ballads that were The Stylistics' specialty. These are all magnificent, some of the finest sentimental soul that's ever been recorded. But it's also been issued before, and Amherst's mastering isn't anything to write home about, especially the way they tend to wash out Russell Tompkins, Jr's high notes. —*Ron Wynn*

Let's Put It All Together / 1974 / Avco Embassy ✦✦✦

Heavy / 1974 / Avco Embassy ✦✦✦

● **The Best of the Stylistics** / 1975 / Amherst ✦✦✦✦

Any of their collections are good, but this features their biggest and best hits, including "I'm Stone in Love with You," "Rockin' Roll Baby," "Betcha by Golly Wow," and "You Make Me Feel Brand New." —*Cub Koda*

● **Very Best of the Stylistics** / 1983 / H&L ✦✦✦✦

This is one of many collections that gather their hit singles; "Make Up To Break Up," "You Are Everything," "Rock and Roll Baby" and many others are landmark numbers, even if thematic variety and stylistic diversity weren't Stylistics traits. —*Ron Wynn*

Styx

Hard Rock, Art-Rock/Progressive-Rock, Pop-Rock, Arena Rock

Styx were one of the biggest art-rock bands of the late '70s, capable of producing monster hits with their stadium rock, power ballads, and concept albums. More than any other art-rock band, Styx was able to cross over into the pop charts, scoring hits with "Babe," "Lady," "Come Sail Away," "Too Much Time on My Hands," and "Don't Let It End." Never one for subtlety, their ballads featured sweeping, over-arranged guitars and keyboards while their rockers were long and detailed, with several different sections and gargantuan guitar solos. When MTV rolled around in the early '80s, the hits stopped coming; they broke up in 1984. Six years later, they reunited and released *Edge of the Century;* the record featured "Show Me the Way," which became popular as a Gulf War anthem. The band went on hiatus a couple of years after the album's release. —*Stephen Thomas Erlewine*

Styx II / 1973 / RCA ✦✦✦

Man of Miracles / 1974 / RCA ✦✦

Crystal Ball / 1976 / A&M ✦✦✦

The Grand Illusion / 1977 / A&M ✦✦✦✦

With *The Grand Illusion*, Styx catapulted to Top Ten and multi-platinum status, thanks to the hit single, "Come Sail Away." Although the group's sound was still based in art-rock, the best moments on the record occur when they fit majestic pomp into the constraints of a pop song like "Fooling Yourself (The Angry Young Man)" or "Come Sail Away." —*Stephen Thomas Erlewine*

Pieces of Eight / 1978 / A&M ✦✦✦✦

Pieces of Eight continued Styx's winning streak, selling over three million copies over the years. Styx was savvy enough to make their art-rock appear like arena rock, as the "Blue Collar Man (Long Nights)" single indicates, as well as the hit "Renegade." —*Stephen Thomas Erlewine*

Cornerstone / 1979 / A&M ✦✦✦✦

"Babe" became Styx's first No. 1 single and its accompanying album, *Cornerstone*, saw the band expanding their pop accessibility without dispensing the art-rock traditions that made them famous. —*Stephen Thomas Erlewine*

Paradise Theater / 1980 / A&M ✦✦✦✦

Paradise Theater was Styx's masterpiece, filled with conceptually ambitious songs as well as concise pop singles, like the driving hard rocker "Too Much Time on My Hands" and the power ballad "The Best of Times." It perfectly encapsulates both the band's progressive side and their catchy, hard rock leanings. —*Daevid Jehnzen*

Kilroy Was Here / 1983 / A&M ✦✦✦

Classics, Vol. 15 / 1987 / A&M ✦✦✦✦

This best-of collection amply covers this group's primary radio hits and key album cuts. Included are "Babe," "Best of Times," "Too Much Time on My Hands," "Mr. Roboto," "Don't Let it End," "Blue Collar Man (Long Nights)," "Come Sail Away," "Crystal Ball," and "Grand Illusion." —*Rick Clark*

Edge of the Century / 1990 / A&M ✦✦

● **Greatest Hits** / 1995 / A&M ✦✦✦✦

Replacing the band's volume in A&M's *Classics* series, *Greatest Hits* collects all Styx's major chart and radio hits, from "Lady" to "Show Me the Way." Although they were a definitive album rock band, creating records that were meant to be listened to as a whole, their finest moments were always their singles, making *Greatest Hits* the only Styx disc many fans will need to own. —*Stephen Thomas Erlewine*

Greatest Hits Part II / Jun. 1996 / A&M ✦✦✦

Suede

Alternative Pop-Rock, Brit-Pop

Like many English bands that receive massive praise from the British press, Suede were dismissed as mere hype by most listeners before they had even released a record. However, this was one time that the press were right. Suede might not be entirely original, yet their sweaty, sensual mix of the decadent elegance of '70s glam rock and the tortured angst of the post-punk British rock of the '80s makes them one of the most exciting English guitar bands of the '90s. Bernard Butler's guitar combines the crunch of Mick Ronson with the innovative, intricate rhythms and textures of Johnny Marr; Bret Anderson's exaggerated accent can be grating to some ears, yet it fits the grandly theatrical ballads "So Young" and "Stay Together," as well as throttling rockers like "Metal Mickey" and "Animal Nitrate." Anderson's impressionistic lyrics can be a little precious, but the band's musical ability saves him from his pretensions.

Suede's 1993 debut was a huge hit in the UK, but they only gained a small cult in the US. As the band was recording their follow-up in 1994, an obscure American jazz-pop singer that called herself Suede forced the band to change their name to the London Suede in the US; in the rest of the world, they've been able to retain their name.

Before Suede released their follow-up to their debut in the fall of 1994, guitarist Bernard Butler left the band in a bitter creative dispute. The remaining members completed the album, entitled *DogManStar*, and released it in 1994. It became another UK success, but failed to gain them a larger audience in the US. Suede replaced Butler a few months after his departure with Richard Oakes. Suede released their third album, *Coming Up*, in 1996. —*Stephen Thomas Erlewine*

● **Suede** / Apr. 1993 / Nude/Columbia ✦✦✦✦

It's not often that an album can live up to its pre-release hype, but Suede's debut album is one of those rare occasions. A uniquely original amalgam of glam-rock and post-punk pop, *Suede* takes the snarling guitars of early-'70s rock and sets them to the pop smarts of The Smiths. Although he is a fine singer, there is no doubt that Brett Anderson's grandly theatrical vocals are an acquired taste, but the strength of their material warrants such indulgences. It's been a while since a rock 'n' roll band has captured adolescent sexual yearnings so well. —*Stephen Thomas Erlewine*

Dog Man Star / Oct. 25, 1994 / Nude/Columbia ✦✦✦✦

Recorded as guitarist Bernard Butler's relationship with songwriting partner Brett Anderson was fraying, *Dog Man Star* is a sweeping, cinematic triumph of a second album. While some of the youthful energy of "The Drowners" and "Metal Mickey" remain (particularly on the crunching "This Hollywood Life"), most of *Dog Man Star* finds Suede creating grand, lush, seething soundscapes. Occasionally boosted by dramatic strings, the songs are the best Butler and Anderson have ever written; from the sleazy, muscular pulse of "We Are the Pigs" through the aching ballad "The Wild Ones" to the finale "Still Life," the entire album fulfills the potential of Suede's debut. —*Stephen Thomas Erlewine*

Sugar

Alternative Pop-Rock

After two solo albums, ex-Hüsker Dü guitarist/vocalist Bob Mould formed Sugar in 1992, with bassist David Barbe and drummer Malcolm Travis; the band signed with Rykodisc in the US, Creation in the UK. Sugar's first album, *Copper Blue*, was released in the fall of 1992 to enthusiastic reviews and it became Mould's most successful project to date. *Copper Blue* nearly went gold and spawned several alternative radio and MTV hits. In the spring of 1993, Sugar released the mini-LP *Beaster*, a more abrasive collection than *Copper Blue* that was recorded at the same sessions.

Around the time of the release of *Beaster*, Mould was forced out of the closet by various gay publications, with hopes that he would embrace their political cause; he rejected their requests.

Mould wrote the material for the second Sugar album during 1993. The band began recording in the spring of 1994, but the sessions grounded to a halt and the tapes were erased. Mould decided to give the album one more try and it was recorded quickly late that spring. The album, *File Under: Easy Listening*, appeared in the fall of 1994. Although it received good reviews and was moderately successful commercially, it didn't match the performance of *Copper Blue*. In the spring of 1995, it was announced that Sugar was on hiatus. *Besides*, a collection of rarities and B-sides, was released that summer. By the fall, Mould had broken up the band and begun to work on a third album entirely by himself. Mould played all of the instruments on his self-titled third album, which was released in the spring of 1995. — *Stephen Thomas Erlewine*

● **Copper Blue** / 1992 / Rykodisc ✦✦✦✦
Featuring some of Mould's best songwriting, Sugar's debut album is a stunning piece of hook-laden punk-pop, highlighted by the '60s-style "If I Can't Change Your Mind," the loud guitars of "Man on the Moon," and the tongue-in-cheek Pixies tribute, "A Good Idea." — *Stephen Thomas Erlewine*

Beaster / 1993 / Rykodisc ✦✦✦

File Under: Easy Listening / 1994 / Rykodisc ✦✦✦✦
Given Bob Mould's reputation for searing electric rock 'n' roll, it may be easy to think that the title is ironic, and it is to a certain extent. But beneath the loud guitars lay the friendliest, most relaxed pop songs Mould has ever written. "Your Favorite Thing" and "Can't Help You Anymore" are two of Mould's most direct, pop-oriented songs, driven by instantly memorable melodies and hooks; they are also the most conventional songs on the record. The best moments come when Sugar push the boundaries a bit, whether it's on the country-rock of "Believe What You're Saying," the swirling "What You Want it To Be" and "Company Book," the searching ballad "Panama City Motel," or "Explode and Make Up," which bristles even at its most delicate moments. Mould throws in one classic spite-fueled rocker, "Granny Cool," but the record's finest moment is "Gee Angel," a powerhouse melodic scorcher. — *Stephen Thomas Erlewine*

Besides / 1995 / Rykodisc ✦✦✦

Sugarcubes

Alternative Pop-Rock
The Sugarcubes were the biggest group ever to emerge from Iceland, which helps explain their off-kilter sense of melody. Their 1988 debut, *Life's Too Good*, attracted terrific reviews and became a college radio hit, but they never were able to recapture that sense of excitement.

According to group legend, the Sugarcubes formed on June 8, 1986, the day that vocalist Björk (born Björk Gudmundsdottir, 1966, Reykjavik, Iceland) gave birth to her son. Prior to that day, the members of the group had been a variety of Icelandic bands. Björk had the longest career out of any of the members. When she was 11 years old, the vocalist had recorded a children's album. In her late teens, she joined the Icelandic hard-rock band Theyer, which also featured future Sugarcubes drummer Siggi Baldursson. Theyer's most prominent international moment came in 1982, when they recorded with Youth and Jaz Coleman of Killing Joke. At the same time Theyer was popular within Iceland, Einar Orn Benediktsson and Bragi Olafsson formed a punk band called Purrkur Pillnikk, who released records on Benediktsson's own label, Gramm.

By 1984, Björk, Benediktsson, and Baldursson had joined forces, forming KUKL with keyboardist Einar Mellax. KUKL—which means witch in Icelandic—was a noisy, artsy post-punk band that released several singles on the independent British record label Crass. In 1986, KUKL evolved into the Sugarcubes, adding Björk's then-husband Thor Jonson on guitar and Olafsson on bass.

In late 1987, the band signed to One Little Indian in the UK, Elektra Records in the US. The Sugarcubes released their debut album, *Life's Too Good*, in 1988 to critical acclaim in both the UK and the US. "Birthday," the first single from the album, became an indie hit in Britain and a college radio hit in America. In particular, Björk received a heap of praise, which began tensions between her and Benediktsson. By the time the group recorded their second album, Thor had divorced Björk and married Magga Ornolfsdottir, who became the group's keyboardist after Einar Mellax left. Furthermore, Olaffson divorced his wife—who hap-

pened to be the twin sister of Baldursson's wife—and married Benediktsson, making their union the first openly gay marriage in pop music.

Here Today, Tomorrow, Next Week!, the Sugarcubes' second album, was released in 1989. The album, featuring a greater vocal contribution by Benediktsson, was criticized in many of the record's reviews, which were noticably more tepid than those for *Life's Too Good*. After the release of *Here Today, Tomorrow, Next Week!*, the band embarked on a lengthy international tour. At the conclusion of the tour in late 1990, the band members pursued their own individual interests. *Stick Around for Joy*, the band's third album, was released in 1992; before the record appeared, a collection of remixes called *It's It* was released in Europe. *Stick Around for Joy* received better reviews than *Life's Too Good*, but the album failed to yield a hit single. Following its release, the Sugarcubes disbanded. In 1993, Björk launched a critically acclaimed and commercially successful solo career that is based in dance music. — *Stephen Thomas Erlewine*

● **Life's Too Good** / 1988 / Elektra ✦✦✦✦
With strong songs built around Björk Gudmundsdottir's piercing, striking voice, this record lived up to all the advance hype. This is the perfect introduction to the Cubes. — *John Dougan*

Here Today, Tomorrow, Next Week! / 1989 / Elektra ✦✦✦

Stick Around for Joy / 1992 / Elektra ✦✦✦

Donna Summer

b. Dec. 31, 1948, Boston
Vocals / Disco, Urban, Pop-Rock, Club-Dance
Born Donna Gaines, to a church-going family in the Mission Hill section of Boston, Summer took her name from Helmut Sommer, whom she married while living in Munich, Germany, as a member of a traveling cast of *Hair*. Italian electro-pop arranger Giorgio Moroder met her, and in 1975 they recorded "Love to Love You Baby," a 16-minute, riff-driven update of Jane Birkin and Serge Gainsbourg's version of "Je t'aime . . . moi non plus." But Summer, as it turned out, had a sturdiness quite different from Birkin's short bursts of this and that, and a flair for kitschy show tunes and overproduced slickness, both of which ideally complimented the transparent impersonality of Moroder's electronic rhythms. She and Moroder created entire subgenres of disco, and there was no stopping them until Summer stopped herself.

Beginning with 1980's *The Wanderer* (except for the title song) she began to sing exactly the kind of pop-rock material her daring impressionism had fought against. She tried to become a pop singer; and when, as in *She Works Hard for the Money*, she drew upon gospel styles, she was listened to. But during the '70s, she wasn't merely listened to, she was a leader. Today Summer tries to catch up, sadly, with a generation whose greatest aesthetic achievement was to catch up with her. — *Michael Freedberg*

● **The Donna Summer Anthology (Chronicles Series)** / Sep. 21, 1993 / Casablanca ✦✦✦✦
A double-disc set that collects all of Summer's biggest hits and finest moments, it's the definitive anthology. — *AMG*

★ **Endless Summer: The Very Best Of** / 1995 / Casablanca ✦✦✦✦✦
A condensed, more concise collection than *Anthology*, it has greater historical depth than previous collections and all the major hits are represented here. — *John Lowe*

The Sundays

Alternative Pop-Rock
Building on the jangly guitar-pop of the Smiths and the trance-like dream-pop of bands like the Cocteau Twins, the Sundays cultivated a dedicated following in indie-rock circles, both in their native England and in America, in the early '90s. Although the sales of their first two albums were strong, the band never crossed over into the mainstream, as so many observers and critics predicted they would.

The Sundays formed in the summer of 1987 in London, England. Originally, the group consisted of vocalist Harriet Wheeler, who had previously sung with a band called Jim Jiminee, and guitarist David Gavurin. After the duo had written several songs, they added a rhythm section, featuring bassist Paul Brindley and drummer Patrick Hannan. In August of 1988, the Sundays performed their first concert, playing at the Falcoln "Vertigo Club" in Camden, London. The concert generated good word-of-mouth within the industry and the group were the target of a record label bidding war. By the end of the year, the band had signed to Rough Trade; they would sign a deal with DGC Records for American distribution within a year.

"Can't Be Sure," the Sundays' first single, appeared in January of 1989 and entered the UK charts at No. 45. The group took a year to record their first album, *Reading, Writing, Arithmetic*. The debut was released in early 1990 to very postive critical notices and unexpectedly entered the UK charts at No. 4. Upon its American release later in the year, the album became a modern rock hit, peaking at No. 39. Its success in the US was largely due to heavy radio and MTV airplay for the single, "Here's Where the Story Ends." The single wound up topping the modern rock charts in America. The Sundays spent the rest of 1990 successfully touring America, Europe, and Japan.

During 1991, Rough Trade collapsed due to financial mismanagement. After the label went out of business, the Sundays signed a deal with Parlophone Records in the UK; *Reading Writing & Arithmetic* went out of print in England and it would not go back in print until 1996. Even considering the setback of Rough Trade's implosion, the Sundays took a long time to write and record their second album. They finally delivered the follow-up to *Reading Writing & Arithmetic* in the fall of 1992. The resulting album, entitled *Blind*, was greeted with mixed reviews but it was an immediate hit in the US and UK In America, "Love" became a No. 2 modern rock hit and "Goodbye" peaked at No. 11. Although *Blind* was initially successful, it didn't have they staying power of the debut and dropped off the charts by the summer of 1993. The Sundays supported the album with an international tour.

After the release of *Blind*, the Sundays were quiet for the next several years. The only sign of the band was the use of their cover of the Rolling Stones' "Wild Horses" in an American TV commercial in 1994. — *Stephen Thomas Erlewine*

● **Reading Writing & Arithmetic** / 1990 / DGC ✦✦✦✦
The Sundays' debut album built on the layered, ringing guitar hooks and unconventional pop melodies of the Smiths, adding more ethereal vocals and a stronger backbeat. As evidenced by the lilting, melancholy single "Here's Where the Story Ends," it was a winning combination, making this a thoroughly engaging debut. — *Stephen Thomas Erlewine*

Blind / 1992 / DGC ✦✦✦

Superchunk

Alternative Pop-Rock, Indie Rock
In the big-business world of '90s alternative rock, Superchunk remains a staunchly independent guitar-rock band. When their record label, Matador, signed a major-label distribution deal, the band refused to be a part of the deal; with their next record, they switched labels to their privately owned Merge label. All the while, the band continues to gain more fans. Superchunk's stripped-down, speedy punk rock is proudly low-fidelity, yet their songs are well-written, packed with hooks and raw, energetic rocking. Although their singles and albums show little stylistic variation, they rock so hard the similiarity hardly matters. — *Stephen Thomas Erlewine*

No Pocky for Kitty / 1992 / Matador ✦✦✦✦
After a series of blistering singles, Superchunk released *No Pocky for Kitty*, which confirmed their status as one of the best and most diverse punk rock groups of the early '90s. — *Stephen Thomas Erlewine*

● **Tossing Seeds (singles 89-91)** / 1992 / Merge ✦✦✦✦
Featuring the classic '90s anti-anthem "Slack Motherfucker," *Tossing Seeds (singles 89-91)* is a superb collection of early non-LP singles by one of the best indie guitar bands of the early '90s. — *Stephen Thomas Erlewine*

On the Mouth / 1993 / Matador ✦✦✦✦
On the Mouth is one of Superchunk's best albums, not because it offers anything different than their previous work, but because the band's songwriting is at a peak, which make songs like "The Question Is How Fast" sound fresh and exciting, not empty exercises in punk nostalgia. — *Stephen Thomas Erlewine*

Foolish / Dec. 1993 / Merge ✦✦✦

Incidental Music / Jun. 20, 1995 / Merge ✦✦✦✦
Singles are the most effective forum for Superchunk's music, which makes *Incidental Music (singles 92-94)* one of their most consistent records. It might not have a single song as definitive as "Slack Motherfucker," but this collection of non-LP singles is filled with some of their finest moments. — *Stephen Thomas Erlewine*

Here's Where the Strings Come In / Sep. 19, 1995 / Merge ✦✦✦

Supergrass

Alternative Pop-Rock, Brit-Pop
Like many other British bands of the '90s, Supergrass' musical roots lie in the infectiously catchy punk-pop of the Buzzcocks and the Jam, as well as the post-punk pop of Madness and the traditional British pop of the Kinks and Small Faces. Perhaps because of their age—two of the trio were still in their teens when they recorded their debut single—the band also brings in elements of decidedly un-hip groups like Elton John, as well as classic rockers like David Bowie, the Beatles, and the Rolling Stones. With an exuberant, youthful enthusiasm, Supergrass tied all of their influences together in new surprising ways, where a Buzzcocks riff could slam into three-part harmonies out of "Crocodile Rock," or have a galloping music hall rhythm stutter like the best moments of the Who. Consisting of guitarist/vocalist Gaz Coombes, bassist Mickey Quinn, and

drummer Danny Goffey, Supergrass released their first single, the semi-autobiographical "Caught by the Fuzz," in the summer of 1994 on the indie label Backbeat; Parlophone signed the band and reissued the single in the fall of the year. "Caught by the Fuzz" generated a significant amount of buzz, including praise from Blur and Elastica. "Mansize Rooster," the group's second single, was released in the spring of 1995; it made it into the pop charts, as did "Lenny," which was released right before their debut album, *I Should Coco*.

Released in May, 1995, *I Should Coco* received glowing reviews in the UK press and debuted in the Top Ten. The band's popularity continued to grow, leading to the No. 2 double-A-sided single, "Alright"/"Time." Staying in the top three for nearly a month, the single pushed the album to No. 1. *I Should Coco* was released in the US three months later and a buzz began to build there, as "Caught by the Fuzz" began receiving MTV and radio play. — *Stephen Thomas Erlewine*

● **I Should Coco** / 1995 / Parlophone ✦✦✦✦
Tearing by at a breakneck speed, *I Should Coco* is a spectacularly eclectic debut by Supergrass, a trio barely out of their teens. Sure, the unbridled energy of the album illustrates that the band is young, yet what really illustrates the youth of the band is how they borrow from their predecessors. Supergrass treat the Buzzcocks, the Beatles, Elton John, David Bowie, Blur, and Madness as if they were all the same thing—they don't make any distinction between what is cool and what isn't, they just throw everything together. Consequently, the jittery "Caught by the Fuzz" slams next to the music-hall rave-up "Mansize Rooster" and the trippy psychedelia of "Sofa of My Lethargy," or the heavy stomp of "Lenny" or the bonafide teen anthem "Alright." *I Should Coco* is the sound of adolescence, but performed with a surprising musical versatility that makes the record's exuberant energy all the more infectious. — *Stephen Thomas Erlewine*

Supertramp

Art-Rock/Progressive-Rock, Pop-Rock
Once upon a time in 1969, a young Dutch millionaire by the name of Stanley August Miesegaes gave his acquaintance, vocalist and keyboardist Roger Davies a "genuine opportunity" to form his own band; he could form the band of his dreams and Miesegaes would pay for it. After placing an ad in *Melody Maker*, Davies assembled Supertramp. Supertramp released two long-winded progressive-rock albums before Miesegaes withdrew his support. With no money or fan base to speak of, the band was forced to redesign their sound. Coming up with a more pop-oriented form of progressive-rock, the band had a hit with their third album, *Crime of the Century*. Throughout the decade, Supertramp had a number of best-selling albums, culminating in their 1979 masterpiece, *Breakfast in America*. *Breakfast in America* marked their first album that tipped the scale completely in favor of pop songs; on the strength of the hit singles "Goodbye Stranger," "Logical Song," and "Take the Long Way Home" it sold over 18 million copies worldwide. After that album, Supertramp continued to develop a more R&B-flavored style; the change in direction was successful on 1982's *Famous Last Words*, but they soon ran out of hits. The band continued to record and tour into the '90s. — *Stephen Thomas Erlewine*

Supertramp / 1970 / A&M ✦✦

Indelibly Stamped / 1971 / A&M ✦✦

Crime of the Century / 1974 / A&M ✦✦✦✦
With *Crime of the Century*, Supertramp established themselves as one of the handful of progressive-rock acts that could sell albums and have hit singles. Stripping away the long-winded excesses of their first two albums, *Crime of the Century* featured tighter, more melodic songs, as evidenced by the singles "Bloody Well Right" and "Dreamer." — *Stephen Thomas Erlewine*

Crisis? What Crisis? / 1975 / A&M ✦✦✦

Even in the Quietest Moments / 1977 / A&M ✦✦✦✦
Like *Crisis? What Crisis?*, *Even in the Quietest Moments* is a jumbled affair, alternating between long, unfocused sections and relatively concise pop songs. — *Stephen Thomas Erlewine*

● **Breakfast in America** / 1979 / A&M ✦✦✦✦
With *Breakfast in America*, Supertramp had a genuine blockbuster hit, topping the charts for four weeks in the US and selling millions of copies worldwide; by the 1990s, the album had sold over 18 million units across the world. Although their previous records had some popular success, they never even hinted at the massive sales of *Breakfast in America*. Then again, Supertramp's earlier records weren't as pop-oriented as *Breakfast*. The majority of the album consisted of tightly written, catchy, well-constructed pop songs, like the hits "The Logical Song," "Take the Long Way Home," and "Goodbye Stranger." Supertramp still have a tendency to indulge themselves occasionally, but *Breakfast in America* had very few weak moments. It was clearly their high-water mark. — *Stephen Thomas Erlewine*

Paris / 1980 / A&M ✦✦

...famous last words.../ 1982 / A&M ✦✦✦

Brother Where You Bound / 1985 / A&M ✦✦

● **Classics, Vol. 9** / 1987 / A&M ✦✦✦✦
This is a fairly good sampler of this band's bigger radio tracks as well as key album numbers. Included are "Bloody Well Right," "Ain't Nobody but Me," "The Logical Song," "Give a Little Bit," "It's Raining Again," "Good-bye Stranger," "Take the Long Way Home,"and "Dreamer." Unfortunately, "Even in the Quietest Moments" is curiously omitted. —*AMG*

The Supremes

Soul, Motown, Girl Group
The most successful Black performers of the 1960s, the Supremes for a time rivaled even the Beatles in terms of red-hot commercial appeal, reeling off five No. 1 singles in a row at one point. Critical revisionism has tended to undervalue the Supremes' accomplishments, categorizing their work as more lightweight than the best soul stars' (or even the best Motown stars), and viewing them as a tool for Berry Gordy's crossover aspirations. There's no question that there was about as much pop as soul in the Supremes' hits, that even some of their biggest hits could sound formulaic, and that they were probably the Black performers who were most successful at infiltrating the tastes and TVs of middle America. This shouldn't diminish either their extraordinary achievements or their fine music, the best of which renders the pop vs. soul question moot with its excellence.

The Supremes were not an overnight success story, although it might have seemed that way when they began topping the charts with sure-fire regularity. The trio that would become famous as the Supremes—Diana Ross, Mary Wilson, and Florence Ballard—met in the late '50s in Detroit's Brewster housing project. Originally known as the Primettes, they were a quartet (Barbara Martin was the fourth member) when they made their first single for the Lupine label in 1960. By the time they debuted for Motown in 1961, they had been renamed the Supremes; Barbara Martin reduced them to a trio when she left after their first single.

The Supremes' first Motown recordings were much more girl-group-oriented than their later hits. Additionally, not all of them featured Diana Ross on lead vocals; Flo Ballard, considered to have as good or better a voice, also sang lead. Through a lengthy series of flops, Berry Gordy remained confident that the group would eventually prove to be one of Motown's biggest. By the time they finally did get their first Top 40 hit, "When the Lovelight Starts Shining Through His Eyes," in late 1963, Ross had taken over the lead singing for good.

Ross was not the most talented female singer at Motown; Martha Reeves and Gladys Knight in particular had superior talents. What she did have, however, was the most purely pop appeal. Gordy's patience and attention paid off in mid-1964, when "Where Did Our Love Go" went to No. 1. Written by Holland-Dozier-Holland, it established the prototype for their run of five consecutive No. 1 hits in 1964-65 (also including "Baby Love," "Stop! In the Name of Love," "Come See About Me," and "Back in My Arms Again"). Ross' cooing vocals would front the Supremes' decorative backup vocals, put over on TV and live performance with highly stylized choreography and visual style. Holland-Dozier-Holland would write and produce all of the Supremes' hits through the end of 1967.

Not all of the Supremes' singles went to No. 1 after 1965, but they usually did awfully well, and were written and produced with enough variety (but enough of a characteristic sound) to ensure continual interest. The chart-topping and uncharacteristically tough) "You Keep Me Hangin' On" was the best of their mid-period hits. Behind the scenes, there were some problems brewing, although these only came to light long after the event. Other Motown stars (most notably Martha Reeves) resented what they perceived as the inordinate attention lavished upon Ross by Gordy, at the expense of other artists on the label. The other Supremes themselves felt increasingly pushed to the background. In mid-1967, as a result of what was deemed increasingly unprofessional behavior, Ballard was replaced by Cindy Birdsong (from Patti LaBelle and the Bluebelles). Ballard become one of rock's greatest tragedies, eventually ending up on welfare and dying in 1976.

After Ballard's exit, the group would be billed as Diana Ross & the Supremes, fueling speculation that Ross was being groomed for a solo career. The Supremes had a big year in 1967, even incorporating some mild psychedelic influences into "Reflections." Holland-Dozier-Holland, however, left Motown around this time, and the quality of the Supremes' records suffered accordingly (as did the Motown organization as a whole). The Supremes were still superstars, but as a unit, they were disintegrating; it's been reported that Wilson and Birdsong didn't even sing on their final hits, a couple of which ("Love Child" and "Someday We'll Be Together") were among their best.

In November 1969, Ross' imminent departure for a solo career was announced, although she played a few more dates with them, the last in Las Vegas in January 1970. Jean Terrell replaced Ross, and the group continued through 1977, with some more personnel changes (although Mary

Wilson was always involved). Some of the early Ross-less singles were fine records, particularly "Stoned Love," "Nathan Jones," and the Supremes-Four Tops duet "River Deep—Mountain High." Few groups have been able to rise to the occasion after the loss of their figurehead, though, and the Supremes proved no exception, rarely making the charts after 1972. It is the Diana Ross-led era of the 1960s for which they'll be remembered. —*Richie Unterberger*

★ **Greatest Hits** / Aug. 1967 / Motown ✦✦✦✦✦
Although all of these 20 songs were credited to the Supremes when they were released between 1963 and 1967, this album marked the first LP on which the group was billed as "Diana Ross and the Supremes." However you credit it, this out-of-print double-LP contains the bulk of the best of the Supremes, no less than 10 No. 1 hits from "Where Did Our Love Go" to "The Happening," and thus some of the most popular music of the 1960s. Ross and the Supremes, together and separately, continued to score afterwards, but this was their peak. —*William Ruhlmann*

★ **Anthology** / May 1974 / Motown ✦✦✦✦✦
When it was released in 1974, Motown's Diana Ross and the Supremes *Anthology* was the most comprehensive compilation yet issued on one of the '60s most popular groups. A 35-track triple-LP, it superseded the 1967 double-LP *Greatest Hits*, including 17 of that album's 20 tracks, as well as the 1969 *Greatest Hits, Volume 3*, all of which was repeated. All 27 of the Supremes' R&B hits between 1962 and 1969 were featured, as well as 28 of their 30 pop chart entries. That represented a formidable chunk of the decade's biggest hits, among them the chart toppers "Where Did Our Love Go," "Baby Love " "Come See About Me," "Stop! In the Name of Love," "Back in My Arms Again," "I Hear a Symphony," "You Can't Hurry Love," "You Keep Me Hangin' On," "Love Is Here and Now You're Gone," "The Happening," "Love Child," and "Someday We'll Be Together." The lengthy album also found space for some of the group's musical experiments devoting a five-song side, dubbed "Versatile Stylists," to material culled from the albums *A Bit of Liverpool, The Supremes Sing Country Western & Pop, We Remember Sam Cooke, The Supremes Sing Rodgers & Hart,* and *Diana Ross and the Supremes Sing and Perform "Funny Girl."* They made for an interesting interlude, but the heart of the matter remained the Supremes' brilliant interpretations of the Holland-Dozier-Holland hits of the mid-'60s, which were all here. (The Diana Ross and the Supremes *Anthology* [Motown 794] was released as a triple-LP containing 35 songs in May 1974. In August 1986, Motown issued a 50-song double-CD under the same title [Motown 6198]. Nine years later, the label again revamped the *Anthology* idea for a 52-track double-CD [Motown 0511] released on September 28, 1995.) —*William Ruhlmann*

70's Greatest Hits & Rare Classics / Motown ✦✦✦

The Surfaris

Surf
Glendora, CA, surf group remembered for "Wipe Out," the No. 2 1963 hit that ranks as one of the great rock instrumentals, featuring a classic up-and-down guitar riff and a classic solo drum-roll break, both of which were emulated by millions (the number is no exaggeration) of beginning rock 'n' rollers. They recorded an astonishing number of albums (about half a dozen) and singles in the mid-'60s; the "Wipe Out" follow-up, "Point Panic," was the only one to struggle up to the middle of the charts. The Surfaris were not extraordinary, but they were more talented than the typical one-shot surf group; drummer Ron Wilson was praised by session stickman extraordinaire Hal Blaine, and his uninhibited splashing style sounds like a direct ancestor to Keith Moon. He also took the lead vocals on the group's occasional passable Beach Boy imitations. —*Richie Unterberger*

● **Wipe Out! The Best of the Surfaris** / 1994 / Varese Sarabande ✦✦✦✦
Decent 18-track distillation of their 1962-65 work, including several album tracks and non-LP singles. "Wipe Out" is by far the best cut, of course, but the instrumentals, packed with reverbed guitars, honking saxes, and high-end drums aplenty, usually have an admirably sleek power. Two of the vocal surf tunes were co-written by Gary Usher, who also worked with the Beach Boys during this time. —*Richie Unterberger*

Surfaris Stomp / Jul. 4, 1995 / Varese Saraband ✦✦✦
Aside from the significant drawback of missing "Wipe Out," this second anthology of the Surfaris' best work is just as good as the other Varese Sarabande compilation, *The Best of the Surfaris* (which doesn't duplicate any of the tracks here). Largely taken from rare singles and albums that the group recorded for Decca between 1963 and 1965, it also has a few previously unreleased cuts, some dating from their initial session (the same one that produced "Wipe Out"). If you like *The Best of the Surfaris*, you can't go wrong by adding this one to your collection as well—it's packed with haunting reverb, Ron Wilson's nonstop drum fills rank among the best stickwork of the pre-Keith Moon era, and one of the three vocal cuts is one of the most obscure Brian Wilson compositions

ever released ("My Buddy Seat," co-written with Gary Usher). —*Richie Unterberger*

Billy Swan

b. May 12, 1942, Cape Giradeau, MS
Guitar, Keyboards, Vocals / Rock 'n' Roll, Country-Rock
One of rock's more interesting fringe characters, Billy Swan had been in the music business for more than a decade before he landed a surprise No. 1 neo-rockabilly hit in 1974 with "I Can Help." His composition "Lover Please" was a hit for Clyde McPhatter in the early '60s, and he spent the rest of the decade as a combination roadie, engineer's assistant, and songwriter, penning material for Conway Twitty, Waylon Jennings, and Mel Tillis. He played with Kris Kristofferson, Kinky Friedman, and Billy Joe Shaver in the '70s before the success of "I Can Help," whose swirling organ and classic '50s rockabilly arrangement anchored one of the best hit singles of the mid-'70s. Swan recorded a few albums as a solo act that were well received by critics, but he never hit the Top 40 again. Too eclectic to be characterized as a '50s revivalist, he actually mixed country, soul, and pop into his sound more frequently than out-and-out rockabilly. After a few years, Swan returned to Kristofferson's band, where he stayed until 1992. —*Richie Unterberger*

● **Billy Swan's Best** / 1993 / Red Baron ✦✦✦✦
Listeners expecting tuneful updated rockabilly along the lines of "I Can Help" (which leads off this collection) may be disappointed by this CD. There's nothing as instantly compelling as the big hit (only "Vanessa" approaches its energy), much of the material lies closer to country than rock, and there are a few tame covers of '50s oldies. Nonetheless, Swan ranks among the more interesting country-pop-rock hybrids, as you could guess from the song title "(You Just) Woman Handled My Mind," and his thin, wavering voice is oddly memorable. Most of the material on this best-of is written by Swan, with occasional assistance from notables Guy Clark, Buddy Emmons, and Kris Kristofferson. —*Richie Unterberger*

Sweet

Rock 'n' Roll, Glam Rock, Pop-Rock, Bubblegum
In some ways, the Sweet epitomized all the tacky hubris and garish silliness of the early '70s. Fusing bubblegum melodies with crunching, fuzzy guitars, the band looked like a heavy metal-band, but were as tame as any pop group. It was a dichotomy that served them well, as they racked up a number of hits in both the UK and the US. Most of those hits were written by Nicky Chinn and Mike Chapman, a pair of British songwriters had a way with silly, simple, and catchy hooks. Chinn and Chapman and Sweet were smart enough to latch on to the British glam-rock fad, building a safer, radio-friendly, and teen-oriented version of Queen, T. Rex, and Gary Glitter. By the end of the '70s, the group's time at the top of the charts had expired, but their hit singles lived on not only as cultural artifacts, but also as the predecessors for the pop-metal of the '80s.

Originally, the Sweet were called the Sweetshop and consisted of Brian Connolly (vocals), Mick Tucker (vocals, drums), Frank Torpey (guitar), and Steve Priest (bass). In 1970, the group truncated their name to Sweet and signed a record contract with Fontana/EMI, releasing four unsuccessful singles. Following the failure of the four singles, Torpey left the group and was replaced by Andy Scott. The new lineup of Sweet signed to RCA Records in 1971, where they were placed under the direction of songwriters Chinn and Chapman, who wrote a number of light bubblegum-pop songs for the group, the first of which, "Funny Funny" reached No. 13 on the UK charts. Following "Funny Funny," the duo wrote five more Top 40 hits for the group—including "Little Willy" and "Wig-Wam Bam"—which were all lightweight bubblegum numbers loaded with double entendres. During this time, Sweet were writing their own B-sides and album tracks. All of the group's compositions were harder than Chinn and Chapman's songs, featuring crunching hard-rock guitars. Consequently, the duo decided to write tougher songs for the group. "Blockbuster," the first result of Chinn and Chapman's neo-glam rock approach, was the biggest hit Sweet ever had in the UK, reaching No. 1 on the charts in early 1973 and eventually going platinum. For the next two years, Sweet continued to chart with Chinn and Chapman compositions, including the Top Ten hits "Hell Raiser," "Ballroom Blitz," "Teenage Rampage," and "The Six Teens."

By the summer of 1974, the members of Sweet had grown tired of the control Chinn and Chapman exerted over their career and decided to record without the duo. The resulting album, *Sweet Fanny Adams*, reached No. 27 in the UK, but it yielded no hits. In the spring of 1975, Sweet had their first self-penned hit with "Fox on the Run," which reached the Top Ten in both the UK and the US "Fox on the Run" appeared on the collection *Desolation Boulevard* in America, its release helped "Ballroom Blitz" reach the Top Ten in the summer of 1975. *Strung Up*, released in the fall of 1975, continued the group's move toward album-oriented rock. For the rest of the decade, the group continued to churn out albums, which were all less successful than their predecessor. Sweet bounced back into the charts in 1978 with "Love Is like Oxygen,"

but the single proved to be their last gasp—they never reached the Top Ten again, neither in the US or the UK.

Connolly left the band after "Love Is like Oxygen" and the group replaced him with keyboardist Gary Moberley. The group cared on for three more years, releasing three more albums that all achieved little success. After several years of little success or attention, Sweet broke up in 1982. In the decade following their breakup, Sweet reunited on various occasions. In 1985, a dance-club medley of their hits called "It's the Sweet Mix" became a British Top 50 hit and following the single's success, the group re-formed for a tour that proved to be less anticipated than expected. Later in the decade, Scott toured as part of the group Paddy Goes to Holyhead. In 1989, Scott and Tucker re-formed Sweet to record a live album at London's Marquee Club. —*Stephen Thomas Erlewine*

Desolation Boulevard / 1974 / Capitol ✦✦✦✦
This surprisingly solid hard rock record features "Ballroom Blitz." —*Dan Heilman*

● **The Best of Sweet** / Mar. 1, 1993 / Capitol ✦✦✦✦
Nobody played rock 'n' roll trashier or dumber than Sweet, and their best moments shine on this terrific 16-track compilation. Every one of their hits were powered by an irresistibly stupid melody, big dumb guitars, and, on occasion, a whining synthesizer. It was glitter-rock for teens at its best, without the dark sensuality of T. Rex. Even today, Sweet's best songs—"Ballroom Blitz," "Little Willy," "Blockbuster," "Teenage Rampage," and the nearly perfect "Fox on the Run"—still sound gloriously trashy. —*Stephen Thomas Erlewine*

Matthew Sweet

Guitar / Alternative Pop-Rock, Power-Pop
For the most of the '80s, Matthew Sweet played guitar with Oh-OK and Lloyd Cole; he released his first solo album, *Inside*, in 1986. Both *Inside* and 1989's *Earth* showed promise, drawing equally from the jangly guitar pop of the Byrds and Big Star and the Southern pop of R.E.M. and the dB's. But it wasn't until 1992's *Girlfriend* that Sweet came into his own artistically. Where his other albums were good, *Girlfriend* was exceptional, full of raging guitars (courtesy of Richard Lloyd and Robert Quine) and aching melodies; it expertly fused the Beatles, Big Star, and Neil Young into one distinctive, melodic style. The album was critically acclaimed, as well as relatively commercially successful; Sweet had a minor hit with the title track and he earned many fans. *Altered Beast*, released the following year, was sloppier yet it expanded his cult and helped him inch his way into the mainstream. —*Stephen Thomas Erlewine*

Inside / 1986 / Columbia ✦✦
Earth / 1989 / A&M ✦✦✦

● **Girlfriend** / 1991 / Zoo ✦✦✦✦
Matthew Sweet's third album is a remarkable artistic breakthrough. Grounded in the guitar-pop of the Beatles, Big Star, Byrds, R.E.M., and Neil Young, *Girlfriend* melds all of Sweet's influences into one majestic, wrenching sound that encompasses both the gentle country-rock of "Winona" and the winding guitars of the title track and "Divine Intervention." Sweet's music might have recognizable roots, but *Girlfriend* never sounds derivative; thanks to his exceptional songwriting, the album is a fresh, original interpretation of a classic sound. —*Stephen Thomas Erlewine*

Altered Beast / Feb. 1993 / Zoo ✦✦✦✦
Compared to the concise songwriting of *Girlfriend*, *Altered Beast* is all over the place, both emotionally and musically. Ranging from piercing guitar rave-ups ("Dinosaur Act") to gorgeous country-rock ("Time Capsule"), the album not only covers all sides of Sweet's musical personality, but pastes them together haphazardly. Consequently, it takes a bit of time for all of it to make sense, but after a few listens, it falls together, and its best moments equal *Girlfriend*. —*Stephen Thomas Erlewine*

Son of Altered Beast / Mar. 15, 1994 / Zoo ✦✦✦
Collecting several B-sides and outtakes, *Son of Altered Beast* is actually more consistent and enjoyable than the full-length *Altered Beast*. —*Stephen Thomas Erlewine*

100% Fun / Mar. 14, 1995 / Zoo ✦✦✦✦
Clocking in at 45 minutes, Matthew Sweet's third record of guitar-dominated, hook-laden power-pop runs through its 12 songs at a classic speed, piling up songs that lovingly conform to the three-minute pop tradition. Richard Lloyd's gnarled guitars save Sweet's melodies and harmonies from being saccharine or sappy. Behind Sweet's bright hooks lies something darker—the self-loathing of "Sick of Myself" and the mental manipulation of "We're the Same" aren't evident from the sound of the record, which obliterates any hidden meanings with its chiming guitars and driving rhythms. It might not have the consistent barrage of great songs like *Girlfriend*, yet it tames the wilder impulses of *Altered Beast* into an album that rocks its worries away without ever getting rid of them. —*Stephen Thomas Erlewine*

Rachel Sweet

b. 1963, Akron, OH
Vocals / New Wave, Pop-Rock
After a couple of failed singles as a teenage country singer, the diminutive Sweet plugged her big voice into the burgeoning punk movement after being signed to Stiff Records. Along with Lene Lovich, she was one of the early women recording for the label, with a succession of great records that garnered much critical acclaim but failed to catch on in the marketplace. She dropped out of sight for a few years, then came back working for director John Waters both on and off the screen (*Hairspray, Cry Baby*) and has recently turned up working on cable's Comedy Channel. — *Cub Koda*

Protect the Innocent / 1980 / Rhino ✦✦✦✦
Sweet's second and most perfectly realized album features "Take Good Care of Me" and a slam-bang version of "Baby, Let's Play House." Out of print, but it's worth the search. — *Cub Koda*

● **Fool Around: The Best of Rachel Sweet** / 1992 / Rhino ✦✦✦✦
A solid best-of collection showcasing Sweet's dazzling vocal capabilities. — *Cub Koda*

Swingers

New Wave
After leaving Split Enz, guitarist/singer-songwriter Phil Judd left behind his previous arty pretensions in favor of a straight-forward punky three piece, with Dwayne "Bones" Hillman (bass) and Buster Stiggs (drums). The band, formed in 1978, received favorable reviews and a great deal of early exposure playing support slots for established Aussie bands (including Split Enz) through the late '70s. In 1980, Stiggs left and was replaced by Ian "Killjoy" Gilroy. 1981's *Practical Jokers* LP (released by Mushroom Records) became an instant hit in their homeland with the infectious "Counting the Beat" reaching the No. 1 spot. Resequenced and edited, the album saw an American release under the title *Counting the Beat* in 1982 on Backstreet Records. The title track, "It Ain't What You Dance," and the newly added single, "One Good Reason (Gimme Love)," seemed to fit perfectly into the new wave and found a fair amount of exposure on the then-infant MTV. A major role in the cult film *Starstruck* had the band poised for a major breakthrough. Judd instead opted to dissolve the band in favor of a solo career. Hillman later found success as a member of Midnight Oil. Judd released one poorly received solo album and two more with ex-Split Enz bandmates as Schnell Fenster; he now keeps a low profile, dividing his time between painting and composing music for films. — *Chris Woodstra*

● **Practical Jokers** / 1979 / Mushroom ✦✦✦✦
For *Practical Jokers*, his first post-Enz project, Judd left his arty leanings behind in favor of a tight blend of mid-'60s pop, punk, and new wave, resulting in a fine collection of fractured, eccentric pop songs. With the exception of "Ayatollah," which instantly dates the album, it remains just as fresh and enjoyable 15 years after its release. The quirky "Counting the Beat" became a hit single in Australia/New Zealand. — *Chris Woodstra*

Counting the Beat / 1982 / Backstreet ✦✦✦✦
In an attempt to capitalize on US interest in the band generated by their appearance in the cult film *Starstruck*, Backstreet Records resequenced the *Practical Jokers* album, adding "One Good Reason (Gimme Love)" from the film. Unfortunately, it failed to make much of an impact in the US and quickly disappeared. — *Chris Woodstra*

Swinging Blue Jeans

British Invasion
Although they're only remembered today for their 1964 hit "Hippy Hippy Shake," The Swinging Blue Jeans were actually one of the strongest of the Liverpool bands from the '60s British Invasion. "Hippy Hippy Shake"—a cover of an obscure '50s rocker that was actually done much better by the Beatles on tapes of their BBC performances—was their only Top 30 entry in the US But the band enjoyed some other major and minor hits in the UK, including a top-notch Merseyization of Betty Everett's (and later Linda Ronstadt's) "You're No Good," which they took into the British Top Five in 1964. They also wrote some catchy and energetic, if slightly sappy, originals in the purest Merseybeat style. While it doesn't add up to an enduring legacy, there's a lot to be said for the naive energy of the best of their early tunes. — *Richie Unterberger*

● **Hippy Hippy Shake: the Definitive Collection** / May 4, 1993 / Capitol ✦✦✦✦
All of their UK and US hits are included on this compilation. Highlights are "You're No Good," "Hippy Hippy Shake," and their fine (pre-Who) cover of Johnny Kidd's "Shakin' All Over," though even for the Anglophile, about half of this CD is forgettable, especially the dreary post-1966 stuff. This anthology includes several non-LP/rare singles and unreleased songs. — *Richie Unterberger*

David Sylvian

Guitar, Keyboards, Vocals / Art-Rock/Progressive-Rock
An alternative-rock vocal stylist from the band Japan, Sylvian's solo efforts include work with progressive sidemen such as Robert Fripp (King Crimson), Bill Nelson (Be Bop Deluxe), and Holger Czukay (Can). He draws his style from '70s art-rock fixtures like Roxy Music and David Bowie, with a spark from the experimental electronic movement of the '80s. — *AMG*

Gone to Earth / 1986 / Virgin ✦✦✦
Sylvian is joined by guitarists Robert Fripp and Bill Nelson on this 68-minute CD, which features tracks of Sylvian's trademark vocals and instrumentals. These dreamy, atmospheric works have nice musical support from Steve Nye, Kenny Wheeler, and Mel Collins. — *Scott Bultman*

● **Secrets of the Beehive** / 1987 / Virgin ✦✦✦✦
A consistent mood is sustained throughout this one. Sylvian is joined by Ryuichi Sakamoto, David Torn, Mark Isham, ex-Japan drummer Steve Jansen, and others. It includes a vocal version of the Sylvian/Sakamoto cut "Forbidden Colours" from the *Merry Christmas, Mr. Lawrence* soundtrack. — *Scott Bultman*

Plight & Premonition / 1988 / Venture ✦✦✦✦
This is a collaboration between David Sylvian, frontman for Japan, and Holger Czukay, the bassist for Can. — *Michael P. Dawson*

Flux and Mutability / 1989 / Venture ✦✦✦

Talk Talk

Synth-pop, New Wave, New Romantic
Talk Talk began their career as a synth-pop new wave band, but as the years moved on, the group refashioned themselves as an art-rock outfit, recording albums that flirted with the ambient, textural experimentations of Brian Eno. Formed in England in 1981, Talk Talk comprised Mark Hollis (vocals), Simon Brenner (keyboards), Paul Webb (bass), and Lee Harris (drums). They were quickly signed to EMI, Duran Duran's record label. Like Duran Duran, Talk Talk looked pretty and sounded slick, enabling them to fit in with the "new romantic" pop movement of the early '80s. After scoring a couple of hits—"Talk Talk" and "Today"—and touring with Duran Duran, the group took a year off to regroup. Hollis reorganized the lineup during the recording of the group's second album, 1984's *It's My Life*. While it was slightly more experimental than their previous album, it still followed pop structures. *The Colour of Spring*, released two years later, completed the group's transition to an art-rock group. Appearing in 1988, *Spirit of Eden* was Talk Talk's most experimental record, which proved to be a commercial disaster—it led to EMI dropping the band. Talk Talk then signed with Polydor Records, releasing *Laughing Stock* in 1991. — *Stephen Thomas Erlewine*

The Party's Over / 1982 / EMI America ✦✦✦

It's My Life / 1984 / EMI America ✦✦✦✦
The follow-up is more polished, less like Duran Duran and more like Roxy Music. It features the hit title track. — *Scott Bultman*

The Colour of Spring / 1986 / EMI America ✦✦✦✦
Talk Talk begins their move away from light pop into more adventurous ground. The results are hit-and-miss, but several good tracks like "Life's What You Make It" are worthwhile. — *Scott Bultman*

Spirit of Eden / 1988 / EMI America ✦✦✦
Moody and atmospheric, *Spirit Of Eden* was a three hundred and sixty degree turn away from Talk Talk's predecessor *Colour of Spring*. What was once dismissed as free-form ramblings, *Spirit of Eden* is now considered a forerunner of today's ambient movement. While the songs tend to flow into and out of one another, repeated listenings will reward one with an emotional ride not often found in music these days. Throughout the album, lyrics deal with dark passions, addiction, and desire, while the music ebbs and flows in an oft-times reassuring manner. Difficult, but well worth the listening experience. — *James Chrispell*

● **The Natural History: The Very Best of Talk Talk** / 1990 / EMI America ✦✦✦✦
A collection of the best material from their first four albums, plus two live tracks; all their hits are here, like "It's My Life," "Such a Shame," and "Life's What You Make It." — *Scott Bultman*

Laughing Stock / 1991 / Polydor ✦✦✦
This hauntingly beautiful dissonance is almost like free-form jazz. Not pop music, to be sure, but interesting atmospheric instrumentals. This is the culmination of the direction they were taking on their previous two albums. — *Scott Bultman*

Talking Heads

New Wave, Pop-rock
At the start of their career, Talking Heads were all nervous energy, detached emotion, and subdued minimalism. When they released their

last album about twelve years later, the band had recorded everything from art-funk to polyrhythmic worldbeat explorations and simple, melodic guitar-pop. Between their first album in 1977 and their last in 1988, Talking Heads became one of the most critically acclaimed bands of the '80s, while managing to earn several pop hits. While some of their music can seem too self-consciously experimental, clever, and intellectual for its own good, at their best, Talking Heads represents everything good about art-school punks.

And they were literally art-school punks. Guitarist/vocalist David Byrne, drummer Chris Franz, and bassist Tina Weymouth met at the Rhode Island School of Design in the early '70s; they decided to move to New York in 1974 to concentrate on making music. The next year, the band won a spot opening for the Ramones at the seminal New York punk club, CBGB's. In 1976, keyboardist Jerry Harrison, a former member of Modern Lovers, was added to the lineup. By 1977, the band had signed to Sire Records and released its first album, *Talking Heads '77*. It received a considerable amount of acclaim for its stripped-down rock 'n' roll, particularly Byrne's geeky, overly intellectual lyrics and uncomfortable, jerky vocals.

For their next album, 1978's *More Songs About Buildings and Food*, the band worked with producer Brian Eno, recording a set of carefully constructed, arty pop songs, distinguished by extensive experimenting with combined acoustic and electronic instruments, as well as touches of surprisingly credible funk. On their next album, the Eno-produced *Fear of Music*, Talking Heads began to rely heavily on their rhythm section, adding flourishes of African-styled polyrhythms. This approach came to a full fruition with 1980's *Remain in Light*, which was again produced by Eno. Talking Heads added several sidemen, including a horn section, leaving them free to explore their dense amalgam of African percussion, funk bass and keyboards, pop songs, and electronics.

After a long tour, the band concentrated on solo projects for a couple of years. By the time of 1983's *Speaking in Tongues*, the band had severed their ties with Brian Eno; the result was an album that still relied on the rhythmic innovations of *Remain in Light*, except within a more rigid pop-song structure. After its release, Talking Heads embarked on another extensive tour, which would turn out to be their last; it's captured in the Jonathan Demme-directed concert film, *Stop Making Sense*. After releasing the straightforward pop album *Little Creatures* in 1985, Byrne directed his first movie, *True Stories* the following year; the band's next album featured songs from the film. Two years later, Talking Heads released *Naked*, which marked a return to their worldbeat explorations, although it sometimes suffered from Byrne's lyrical pretensions.

After its release, Talking Heads were put on "hiatus;" Byrne pursued some solo projects, as did Harrison; Franz and Weymouth continued with their side project, the Tom Tom Club. In 1991, the band issued an announcement that they had broken up. *— Stephen Thomas Erlewine*

☆ **Talking Heads '77** / Sep. 16, 1977 / Sire ✦✦✦✦✦
This edgy set of weird, funk-like rockers introduced David Byrne's skewed world outlook. "Pull Me Up" and "New Feeling" are the standouts. *—John Floyd*

☆ **More Songs about Buildings & Food** / Jul. 14, 1978 / Sire ✦✦✦✦✦
Producer Brian Eno added muscle and flair to the group's arty funk-rock, making this a dense and beautiful set. *—John Floyd*

Fear of Music / Aug. 3, 1979 / Sire ✦✦✦✦
A weird, dance-worthy album was made creepy by Byrne's paranoid vision and Eno's dense production. But "Life during Wartime" is one hell of a single. *—John Floyd*

☆ **Remain in Light** / Oct. 8, 1980 / Sire ✦✦✦✦✦
Song structure shimmies out the window as Eno and the band flex their Afro-funk muscles. It works as both brain music and dance music. *—John Floyd*

The Name of This Band Is Talking Heads / Mar. 24, 1982 / Sire ✦✦✦

Speaking in Tongues / Jun. 1, 1983 / Sire ✦✦✦✦
A pulsating mix of the heavy funk *Remain in Light* and song structures that hark back to *More Songs About Buildings & Food*. It contains the hit "Burning Down the House" and the hypnotic "This Must Be the place." *—John Floyd*

Stop Making Sense / 1984 / Sire ✦✦✦

Little Creatures / Jun. 10, 1985 / Sire ✦✦✦✦
Musically, this is a return to spare production and simple melodies, but this is also Byrne's most coherent and mature set of songs. *—John Floyd*

True Stories / 1986 / Sire ✦✦

Naked / Mar. 1988 / Fly ✦✦

● **Popular Favorites, 1984-1992: Sand in the Vaseline** / Oct. 13, 1992 / Sire ✦✦✦✦
Featuring material from every Talking Heads album except the live *The Name of This Band is Talking Heads*, *Sand in the Vaseline* is a terrific double-disc retrospective of the band's long and varied career. Featuring all of their hit singles and trademark songs—"Psycho Killer," "Take Me to

the River," "Burning Down the House," "And She Was," "Once In a Lifetime," "Swamp," "Memories Can't Wait," "Crosseyed and Painless," "Road to Nowhere," "(Nothing But) Flowers," "Life During Wartime"—the set also includes five previously unreleased tracks. *—Stephen Thomas Erlewine*

Tall Dwarfs

Alternative Pop-rock
Formed in the early '80s by ex-Toy Love members Alex Bathgate and Chris Knox, the Tall Dwarfs were one of the most influential bands to emerge from New Zealand's independent scene of the '80s. Arguably the first low-fi band in indierock, the Tall Dwarfs' albums were made at home on a four-track tape recorder. While the group's songs were highly melodic, the fidelity of their recordings always twisted their most accessible material into something otherworldly.

The group's first record, the *Three Songs EP*, was released in 1981; two years later, the group released its first full-length album, *Canned Music*. Since they were all recorded with the same equipment, their recordings are more or less interchangeable; surprisingly, the quality of their material was remarkably high as well. The Tall Dwarfs stopped recording around 1988 when Chris Knox began a solo career. Even in New Zealand their original recordings are rare; *Hello Cruel World* collects the highlights of their career on one disc. *—Stephen Thomas Erlewine*

● **Hello Cruel World** / 1987 / Positive ✦✦✦✦
The band's U.S.? debut, *Hello Cruel World*, collects their legendary and most influential early recordings from 1981 to 1984—with selections from the ultra-rare *Three Songs* EP (1981), *Louis Loves His Daily Dip* EP (1982), *Canned Music* (1983), and *Slugbucket Hairybreath Monster* EP (1984). An excellent introduction to a truly unique and innovative band. *—Chris Woodstra*

Howard Tate

b. 1938, Macon, GA
Vocals / Soul
Highly regarded by soul music cultists, and virtually unknown by anybody else, Howard Tate had some minor success with the Verve label in the late '60s. The singer brought a lot of blues and gospel to his phrasing, but what made him palatable to the modern R&B (and, to a lesser degree, pop) audience was the Northeast soul production of Jerry Ragovoy, who also wrote much of Tate's material. Howard made the R&B Top 20 three times in the late '60s (with "Ain't Nobody Home," "Stop," and "Look at Granny Run Run"). However, he's most famous to rock audiences as the original performer of "Get It While You Can," which became one of Janis Joplin's signature tunes.

Before establishing himself as a solo performer, Tate sang with the Gainors, a North Philadelphia doo wop group that also included future soul star Garnet Mimms. In the early '60s, he was the vocal frontman for Bill Doggett, the organist famous for the instrumental hit "Honky Tonk." Jerry Ragovoy was urged to check out Tate by a member of the Enchanters, Garnet Mimms' backup singers. He recorded about ten singles with Tate between 1966 and 1969, the first for the small Utopia label, the rest for Verve.

Tate moved on to Lloyd Price's Turntable label, for which he recorded a few singles in the late '60s and early '70s. From there he chalked up a short stint with Atlantic, which saw a few other 45s and a critically well-received album, but again little commercial success. A final 1974 single for Epic was his swan song. Always somewhat of a mysterious figure, he hasn't been seen since the early '80s. His music has received its greatest exposure via cover versions: Jimi Hendrix and Hugh Masekela did "Stop," Ry Cooder and rappers Brand Nubian covered "Look at Granny Run Run," and B.B. King recorded "Ain't Nobody Home."and rappers Brand Nubian sampled "Look at Granny Run Run." And of course Joplin (who also raided the Ragovoy catalog for "Try (Just a Little Bit Harder)," "Cry Baby," and "My Baby") did "Get It While You Can" in a manner closely derived from Tate's interpretation. *—Richie Unterberger*

● **Get It While You Can: Legendary Sessions** / 1995 / Mercury ✦✦✦✦
Tate's entire Verve output, condensed into a tidy 17-track compilation, including all of his late '60s singles for the label, and one previously unreleased track. Solid period soul with a slight eclectic bent for the blues, gospel, and some pop influences. *—Richie Unterberger*

James Taylor

b. Mar. 12, 1948
Guitar, Vocals / Singer-Songwriter, Adult Contemporary, Soft Rock
When people use the term "singer-songwriter" (often with the word "sensitive"), in praise or in criticism, it's James Taylor that they're thinking of. Yet in a career now extending over a quarter-century, Taylor's biggest hits have come with his cover versions of other people's songs. Go figure. Taylor grew up in Massachusetts and North Carolina, forming the band the Flying Machine with guitarist Danny Kortchmar in 1967. He was signed

as a solo artist by Apple in 1968 and released his debut album, *James Taylor*, in 1969. But it was his 1970 album, *Sweet Baby James*, with its understated autobiographical hit, "Fire and Rain," that was his commercial breakthrough. *Mud Slide Slim and the Blue Horizon* went to No. 2 in 1971 and contained the No.1 single, "You've Got a Friend," written by Carole King. Taylor scored his next big hit with a remake of Marvin Gaye's "How Sweet It Is (To Be Loved by you)" in 1975, and hit again in 1977 with Jimmy Jones' "Handy Man." He has recorded with Simon & Garfunkel, his ex-wife Carly Simon, and J.D. Souther, and he continues to release gold-selling albums every few years. — *William Ruhlmann*

James Taylor / Dec. 6, 1968 / Capitol ✦✦✦✦
A lovely debut album, beautifully produced by Peter Asher. It features Taylor's sometimes dour sentiments sung in his compelling but quiet voice. "Something in the Way She Moves," "Carolina in My Mind," and "Rainy Day Man." — *William Ruhlmann*

☆ **Sweet Baby James** / Feb. 1970 / Warner Bros. ✦✦✦✦✦
The heart of Taylor's appeal is that you can take him two ways. On the one hand, his music, including that warm voice, is soothing; its minor key melodies and restrained playing draw in the listener. On the other hand, his world view, especially on such songs as "Fire and Rain," reflects the pessimism and desperation of the '60s hangover that was the early '70s. Either way, this is impressive stuff. — *William Ruhlmann*

Mud Slide Slim and the Blue Horizon / Apr. 1971 / Warner Bros. ✦✦✦✦
The changeover here—and it's the big changeover in Taylor's work—is that he is trying to jettison the past ("Don't come to me with your sorrows anymore" is the album's opening line) and look to a hopeful future. That he doesn't quite succeed makes the album itself a success. You need a little darkness to make the light stand out. — *William Ruhlmann*

One Man Dog / Nov. 1972 / Warner Bros. ✦✦✦

Walking Man / Jun. 1974 / Warner Bros. ✦✦✦

Gorilla / May 1975 / Warner Bros. ✦✦✦

In the Pocket / Jun. 1976 / Warner Bros. ✦✦✦✦

● **Greatest Hits** / Nov. 1976 / Warner Bros. ✦✦✦✦
Pretty great. Be warned, however, that the versions of "Something in the Way She Moves" and "Carolina in My Mind" are re-recordings. — *William Ruhlmann*

JT / Jun. 1977 / Columbia ✦✦✦✦
The bad news is that by the time he switched to Columbia, Taylor had made the transition to craftsmanlike pop music, abandoning the shadows of his earlier work. The good news is that the Columbia work is so well crafted, you are forced to acknowledge what a good singer Taylor is. If the songs are less thoughtful, they are no less appealing as music. This is the best of six Columbia studio albums so far, but they're all of a piece. Good, easy listening. — *William Ruhlmann*

Flag / May 1979 / Columbia ✦✦✦✦
James Taylor followed his double-platinum Columbia Records label debut *JT* with this hodgepodge of a record. There are pointless covers of the Beatles' "Day Tripper" and The Drifters' "Up on the Roof" (No. 7 Adult Contemporary, No. 28 Pop), a remake of Taylor's own "Rainy Day Man," songs written for the failed Broadway musical *Working,* and a few inconsequential new Taylor compositions. The usual brain trust (producer Peter Asher) and the usual backup team (Danny Kortchmar, Dan Grolnick, Leland Sklar, Russ Kunkel) were on board, but the cruise was a snooze. — *William Ruhlmann*

Dad Loves His Work / Mar. 1981 / Columbia ✦✦✦
James Taylor bounced back from the spotty *Flag* with this all-original album led by his collaboration with J.D. Souther on "Her Town Too" (No. 11 Pop, No. 5 Adult Contemporary), his biggest pop hit since "Handy Man" and biggest non-cover hit since his first, "Fire and Rain," in 1970. Also included were "Hard Times" (No. 72 Pop, No. 23 Adult Contemporary) and "Summer's Here" (No. 25 Adult Contemporary), not to mention the unusually impassioned "Stand And Fight." After simmering this long, there wasn't much hope Taylor would ever come to a boil, but that track indicated he could at least heat up now and then. — *William Ruhlmann*

That's Why I'm Here / Oct. 1985 / Columbia ✦✦✦
Taylor took four and a half years off from record-making in the early 1980s, returning with *That's Why I'm Here*, which suggested he had found his long-term niche with Baby Boomer fans now permanently tuned to soft-rock radio—this was Taylor's first record to spawn three Top Ten adult contemporary hits, with the title track, "Only One," and a cover of Buddy Holly's "Everyday." But those boomers just don't go to the record store as often as their children, and the album failed to go gold and was his lowest-charting effort since his debut. If, in the title song, he had reconciled himself to the notion that he was here to sing "Fire and Rain" at summer concerts, that also meant he was settling for a complacent position in which his new material was virtually irrelevant, and that being the case, why should people buy it? — *William Ruhlmann*

Never Die Young / Jan. 1988 / Columbia ✦✦
While his aging contemporaries took a variety of tacks to keep up with changing fashions, from adopting more synthesized, percussive production styles to assembling an orchestra and singing standards, James Taylor just kept playing a summer concert tour each year and periodically putting out another collection of similar-sounding songs. *Never Die Young* was unusual only in that there was no big oldies cover from the '50s or '60s—every song was written or co-written by Taylor—but otherwise it addressed the same audience in much the same terms as he always had. The title song and "Baby Boom Baby" (both Adult Contemporary hits) referred to the passage of time, and the rest floated on a sea of yuppie contentment. "I work hard to see that you remember my name," he sang, and that work seemed to consist of reminding his listeners why they had liked him in the first place. — *William Ruhlmann*

● **Classic Songs** / 1990 / CBS ✦✦✦✦
Classic Songs is the only compilation to feature the original versions of all of James Taylor's classics. Unfortunately, it's only available in Europe, yet it remains the best collection of his work to date. — *Sara Sytsma*

New Moon Shine / Sep. 24, 1991 / Columbia ✦✦✦

Live / Aug. 10, 1993 / Columbia ✦✦✦

Johnnie Taylor

b. May 5, 1938, Crawfordsville, AK
Vocals / Soul
Aptly dubbed the "Philosopher of Soul" by the Stax publicity department, Johnnie Taylor set the ladies' hearts aflutter during the early '70s with his tender brand of Memphis soul. Taylor wasn't always the sincere crooner he developed into. A Sam Cooke protégé who took over with the Soul Stirrers when Cooke went secular, and who retained a hint of his mentor's mellifluous delivery, Taylor took the same pop route via Cooke's SAR label in 1961. Once he got on the Stax label in 1966, the vocalist forged a sublime blues/soul synthesis with a series of absolutely gorgeous efforts. But there was nothing subtle about Taylor's first No. 1 in 1968: "Who's Making Love" was an uncompromising treatise on cheating lovers, with storming brass and slashing guitar. The follow-ups "Take Care of Your Homework" and "Jody's Got Your Girl and Gone" pounded the same message home from different angles. As the decade turned, though, Taylor perceptibly mellowed, turning increasingly to ballads for inspiration. By the time he went platinum with the horribly repetitive "Disco Lady" in 1976, the rough edges that made his early work so absorbing were smoothed away, although his recent Malaco output sometimes manages to suggest Taylor's glory years. —*Bill Dahl*

● **Johnnie Taylor Chronicle** / 1977 / Stax ✦✦✦✦
The definitive Johnnie Taylor retrospective/anthology package. It contains every major Stax hit, some album cuts, and an extensive set of liner notes from Robert Palmer. While the soul hardcore had already purchased it on vinyl, anyone who missed it that time around should immediately rush and get the CD. If you love soul, you can't be without it. —*Ron Wynn*

● **Best Of: Rated X-Traordinaire** / Mar. 12, 1996 / Columbia/Legacy ✦✦✦✦
The 16-track *Rated X-Traordinaire* sets out to rescue the reputation of the Johnnie Taylor of 1976-1980, the period that began with his biggest smash, "Disco Lady," but that found him, so the conventional wisdom goes, a Southern soul man set adrift on the disco wave. Annotator Kalamu ya Salaam argues that "Disco Lady" is not a disco song, and backs this up by noting that the track actually was played by members of Parliament-Funkadelic. True enough, though that only applies to Taylor's debut Columbia album, *Eargasm.* Elsewhere, Taylor did drift, from Muscle Shoals tracks that updated his Stax Memphis sound to tracks that sounded like Marvin Gaye. The early years, 1976 and 1977, were more accomplished than the later ones, and that's where compilation producer Leo Sacks concurs, with 12 of the 16 tracks coming from then. In so doing, he ignores R&B chart singles like "Keep on Dancing" and "Ever Ready," but he satisfies the "best of" title. — *William Ruhlmann*

Tears for Fears

New Wave, Pop-rock
Childhood friends Curt Smith (b. Jun. 24, 1961) and Roland Orzabal (b. Aug. 22, 1961) first worked together in 1980 with the ska-pop quintet Graduate, which produced an oddball British single "Elvis Should Play Ska." After the demise of Graduate, the twosome began recording demos of some of Orzabal's morose synth-pop tunes, "Suffer the Children" and "Pale Shelter," which eventually become part of *The Hurting,* their debut release as Tears for Fears (the name was inspired by primal scream therapy psychologist Arthur Janov).

Their 1985 sophomore release, *Songs from the Big Chair,* became a worldwide success, containing several huge hits in "Shout" (No. 1),

"Everybody Wants to Rule the World" (No. 1), "Head over Heels" (No. 3), and "Mother's Talk" (No. 27).

Perfectionism delayed their over-reaching third album, *The Seeds of Love*, by four years. One of the album's highlights was the addition of soulful American singer Oleta Adams, whom Orzabal and Smith discovered singing in a Kansas City hotel lounge. That album's hits included "Sowing the Seeds of Love," "Woman in Chains," and "Advice for the Young at Heart."

Before the recording of their fourth album, Smith and Orzabal had a falling out, leaving Orzabal as the only member of Tears for Fears; he released *Elemental* in 1993 to respectable sales. In October 1995, the Orzbal led band released *Raoul & the Kings of Spain* to a luke-warm reception. Curt Smith released a solo album, *Soul on Board* in, 1993.
—*Rick Clark*

The Hurting / 1983 / Mercury ✦✦✦✦
Roland Orzabal and Curt Smith's debut featured the morose synth-pop hits "Pale Shelter" and "Mad World." —*Scott Bultman*

Songs from the Big Chair / 1985 / Mercury ✦✦✦✦
Their best album is a good mix of synthesizers and traditional instruments. It includes the hits "Shout," "Head over Heels," and "Everybody Wants to Rule the World." —*Kenneth M. Cassidy*

The Seeds of Love / 1989 / Fontana ✦✦✦

● **Tears Fall Down (The Hits 1982-1992)** / 1992 / Fontana ✦✦✦✦
All of this duo's hits (plus some other key tracks) are included, from throughout their career. It's a perfect overview and (essentially) the only disc to have. This anthology includes "Pale Shelter," "Shout," "Everybody Wants to Rule the World," "Head over Heels", and "Sowing the Seeds of Love," among others. —*Rick Clark*

Elemental / Jun. 22, 1993 / Mercury ✦✦

Raoul & The King of Spain / Oct. 10, 1995 / Epic ✦✦

Saturnine Martial & Lunatic / Aug. 1996 / Polygram ✦✦✦

Teenage Fanclub

Alternative Pop-rock, Power-Pop, Pop-rock
Although their music may not be particularly innovative, Teenage Fanclub are great synthesizers of pop music, tying together everything from the Beach Boys and Big Star to Sonic Youth, Neil Young, and Madonna. On their earlier records, they leaned toward loud guitar pop, drenched in dissonance. Starting with 1991's *Bandwagonesque*, the band toned down the noise and reached deeper into their melodic gifts; the result was a brilliant homage to Big Star's chiming guitars and Neil Young's lazy melodies. The record earned them substantial critical praise—*Spin* named it the record of the year—as well as some critical scorn. While the album helped the band gain a cult following in America, it made them stars in England. Two years later, they delivered *Thirteen*, which showed the band incorporating their influences into their own signature sound instead of just paying homage to them. While it wasn't as big a success as *Bandwagonesque*, it showed that Teenage Fanclub hadn't lost their gift for loud, lush guitar pop. —*Stephen Thomas Erlewine*

Catholic Education / 1990 / Matador ✦✦

● **Bandwagonesque** / 1991 / DGC ✦✦✦✦
Much cleaner than the debut, this is a slice of Big Star worship that never fails to deliver the goods. Although it gets bogged down in obviousness from time to time, Teenage Fanclub prove they are a fine pop band, loaded with ringing guitars and breathtaking choruses. —*John Dougan*

Thirteen / 1993 / DGC ✦✦✦✦
Opening with the snarling T. Rex-meets-Nirvana guitar of "Hang On," which soon melts away into a sea of gorgeous Beatlesque harmonies, *Thirteen* marks a shedding of the Big Star devotions that made *Bandwagonesque* so delicious, but that doesn't make it any less enjoyable. Instead of concentrating on one band, Teenage Fanclub pillages through all of the pages of pop history, producing a layered, infectious slice of guitar pop that only gets better with repeated listenings. —*Stephen Thomas Erlewine*

Deep Fried Fanclub / 1995 / Paperhouse/Fire ✦✦

Grand Prix / 1995 / DGC ✦✦✦✦
Grand Prix returns Teenage Fanclub to the more concise pop structures of *Bandwagonesque* while keeping much of the ambitious arrangements of *Thirteen*. Their writing has gotten tighter, with catchier, simpler hooks, making the record their most cohesive statement. —*Stephen Thomas Erlewine*

Television

Punk, Proto-Punk
Television were one of the most creative bands to emerge from New York's punk scene of the mid-'70s, creating an influential new guitar vocabulary. While guitarists Tom Verlaine and Richard Lloyd liked to jam, they didn't follow the accepted rock structures for improvisa-

tion—they removed the blues while retaining the raw energy of garage rock, adding complex, lyrical solo lines that recalled both jazz and rock. With its angular rhythms and fluid leads, Television's music always went in unconventional directions, laying the groundwork for many of the guitar-based post-punk pop groups of the late '70s and '80s.

In the early '70s, Television began as The neon Boys, a group featuring guitarist/vocalist Tom Verlaine, drummer Billy Ficca, and bassist Richard Hell. At the end of 1973, the group reunited under the name Television, adding rhythm guitarist Richard Lloyd. The following year, the band made its live debut at New York's Townhouse theater and began to build up an underground following. Soon, their fan base was large enough that Verlaine was able to persuade CBGB's to begin featuring live bands on a regular basis; the club would become an important venue for punk and new wave bands. That year, Verlaine played guitar on Patti Smith's first single, "Hey Joe"/"Piss Factory," as well as writing a book of poetry with the singer.

Television recorded a demo tape for Island Records with Brian Eno in 1975, yet the label decided not to sign the band. Hell left the band after the recording of the demo tape, forming the Heartbreakers with former New York Doll guitarist Johnny Thunders; the following year, he began a solo career supported by the Voidoids, releasing a debut album, *Blank Generation*, in 1977. Hell was replaced by ex-Blondie bassist Fred Smith and Television recorded "Little Johnny Jewel," releasing it on their own Ork record label. "Little Johnny Jewel" became an underground hit, attracting the attention of major record labels. In 1976, the band released a British EP on Stiff Records, which expanded their reputation. They signed with Elektra Records and began recording their debut album.

Marquee Moon, the group's first album, was released in early 1977 to great critical acclaim, yet it failed to attract a wide audience in America; in the UK, it reached No. 28 on the charts, launching the Top 40 singles "Prove It" and "Foxhole." Television supported Blondie on the group's 1977 tour, but the shows didn't increase the group's following significantly.

Television released its second album, *Adventure*, in the spring of 1978. While its American sales were better than those of *Marquee Moon*, the record didn't make the charts; in Britain, it became a Top Ten hit. Months later, the group suddenly broke up, largely due to tensions between the two guitarists. Smith rejoined Blondie, while Verlaine and Lloyd both pursued solo careers; Lloyd also played on John Doe's first solo album, as well as joining Matthew Sweet's supporting band with the 1991 album, *Girlfriend*.

Nearly 14 years after their breakup, Television re-formed in late 1991, recording a new album for Capitol Records. The reunited band began their comeback with a performance at England's Glastonbury summer festival in 1992, releasing *Television* a couple months later. The album received good reviews, as did the tour that followed, yet the reunion was short-lived—the group disbanded again in early 1993. —*Stephen Thomas Erlewine*

★ **Marquee Moon** / 1977 / Elektra ✦✦✦✦✦
Marquee Moon is a revolutionary album, but it's a subtle, understated revolution. Without question, it is a guitar-rock album—it's astonishing to hear the interplay between Tom Verlaine and Richard Lloyd—but it is a guitar-rock album unlike any other. Where their predecessors in the New York punk scene, most notably the Velvet Underground, had fused blues structures with avant-garde flourishes, Television completely strips away any sense of swing or groove, even when they are playing standard three chord changes. *Marquee Moon* is composed entirely of tense garage rockers that spiral into heady intellectual territory, which is achieved through the group's long, interweaving instrumental sections, not through Tom Verlaine's words. That alone made *Marquee Moon* a trailblazing album—it's impossible to imagine post-punk soundscapes without it. Of course, it wouldn't have had such an impact if Verlaine hadn't written an excellent set of songs that conveyed a fractured urban mythology unlike any of his contemporaries. From the nervy opener "See No Evil" to the majestic title track, there is simply not a bad song on the entire record. And what has kept *Marquee Moon* fresh over the years is how Television fleshes out Verlaine's poetry into sweeping sonic epics. —*Stephen Thomas Erlewine*

Adventure / 1978 / Elektra ✦✦✦✦
This is a subdued set in both sound and content, but the songs sport stronger melodies, and "Glory" anticipates R.E.M.'s sound. —*John Floyd*

Blow Up / 1982 / ROIR ✦✦✦

Television / Sep. 28, 1992 / Capitol ✦✦✦

The Temptations

Soul, R&B, Motown
The early history of the Temptations parallels that of the Supremes. The Tempts started as the Primes, the Supremes as the Primettes. They joined Motown at roughly the same time and broke through at the same time. That the Temptations had a more thorough grounding in the R&B tradition, though, is a fact evident in their work. They employed the clas-

sic gospel-group formula: a light tenor against a gutbucket rasp, with flashes of falsetto for emphasis. The Temptations had the benefit of the writing and production skills of Norman Whitfield and Smokey Robinson, who crafted songs for them such as "The Way You Do the Things You Do" and "My Girl."

With a classic lineup that included David Ruffin and Eddie Kendricks, the Temptations were the hottest R&B group during the ten-year period between 1965 and 1975. Ruffin left in 1968, the year the group experimented with psychedelia ("Cloud Nine" and later "Psychedelic Shack"); Kendricks quit in 1971. Increasingly, they fell under the spell of Norman Whitfield's preoccupations and grandiose productions, although Whitfield rose to the occasion magnificently in 1972 with "Papa Was a Rolling Stone." It was the group's last No. 1 pop hit, and in 1976 the group left Motown for a brief stint with Atlantic before returning to the fold. They continue to record and score R&B hits, but most people associate them with their golden period. — *Colin Escott*

★ **Anthology** / Feb. 1973 / Motown ✦✦✦✦✦
The double-disc/triple-LP set *Anthology* is a comprehensive collection that features all of the Temptations' major hit singles, as well as the best of the group's lesser-known hit singles and album tracks. For fans wanting a more extensive compilation than a single-disc greatest hits collection, but unwilling to invest in the multi-disc box set *Emperors of Soul*, *Anthology* is the ideal purchase. — *Stephen Thomas Erlewine*

● **All the Million-Sellers** / 1982 / Motown ✦✦✦✦
An excellent anthology, even though the Temptations had many great tunes that weren't big sellers. But it does contain almost every major hit, and they're well-mastered versions. The original Temptations anthology is probably still preferable, but this ranks as one of their better specialty reissues. — *Ron Wynn*

25th Anniversary / 1986 / Motown ✦✦✦

Hum Along and Dance: More of the Best (1963-1974) / 1993 / Rhino ✦✦✦
This 18-track compilation contains Temptations B-sides, non-hit cuts, and obscure sides recorded from 1963-1974. It includes such sumptuous ballads as "What Love Has Joined Together" and "Gonna Keep On Trying Till I Win Your Love," plus uptempo wailers and an occasional dud ("Stop The War Now"). The early tracks show the group evolving from its doo-wop roots into soul's premier group. While the cuts on this disc aren't the ones that made the Temptations popular music institutions, they're still a vital part of their legacy. — *Ron Wynn*

Emperors Of Soul / 1994 / Motown ✦✦✦✦
The Temptations were unquestionably one of Motown's greatest groups, recording a large number of classic singles. They were also one of the handful of Motown groups that were able to successfully make the transition from the '60s to the '70s, giving them a sizable amount of quality material from both decades. *Emperors of Soul*, a lavishly produced five-CD box set, draws from the Temptations' entire career, treating all aspects of it with equal respect. For the dedicated fan, the box set is a treasure—the sound is great and there are numerous rarities. However, for most listeners, it is simply too much music, featuring too many unfamiliar songs. — *Stephen Thomas Erlewine*

One By One: Best of Their Solo Years / Mar. 19, 1996 / Motown ✦✦✦
☆ **Anthology [1995]** / Motown ✦✦✦✦✦
There were three versions of this collection (first released in 1973) that provided an overview of their career at Motown. The second (1986) collection was an update that featured digitally remastered sound and some later hits that were not featured in the earlier incarnation, like "Shakey Ground," (1975), "Power," (1980), and the excellent "Treat Her like a Lady." (1983). Unfortunately, the updated 1995 collection (like the previously two incarnations) omits many fine tracks recorded and released before their 1964 breakthrough, like "I Want a Love I Can See" (1962) and "Check Yourself" (1963). Even so, *Anthology* is a conciser, less-expensive alternative to the box-set *Emperors of Soul*. — *John Lowe*

10,000 Maniacs

Alternative Pop-rock, Folk-Rock

10,000 Maniacs (named after the low-budget horror movie *2,000 Maniacs*) was formed in Jamestown, NY, in 1981 by singer Natalie Merchant and guitarist John Lombardo. Other members of the sextet were Robert Buck (guitar), Steven Gustafson (bass), Dennis Drew (keyboards), and Jerry Ausugstyniak (drums). The group gigged extensively and recorded independently before signing with Elektra and making *The Wishing Chair* in 1985. Cofounder Lombardo left the band in 1986, and they continued as a quintet, releasing the second album, *In My Tribe*, in 1987. This album broke into the charts, where it stayed 77 weeks, peaking at No. 37. *Blind Man's Zoo*, the 1989 follow-up, hit No. 13 and went gold.

After 1992's *Our Time in Eden* had finished its run on the charts, Natalie Merchant announced that she was leaving for a solo career. *MTV Unplugged* was released a few months after her departure. The remaining 10,000 Maniacs decided to continue performing, adding the folk-rock

duo John & Mary. Merchant released her first solo album, *Tiger Lily*, in the summer of 1995. — *William Ruhlmann*

The Wishing Chair / 1985 / Elektra ✦✦✦
Put simply, 10,000 Maniacs sound a lot like Fairport Convention with Sandy Denny, so it's appropriate that Fairport's original producer, Joe Boyd, was brought in to handle their major-label debut. The result is a gentle folk/rock record that highlights the haunting voice of Natalie Merchant. — *William Ruhlmann*

● **In My Tribe** / 1987 / Elektra ✦✦✦✦
The band's breakthrough album and creative high point, *In My Tribe* offers a survey in social concerns including child abuse ("What's the Matter Here"), illiteracy ("Cherry Tree"), war ("Gun Shy"), and the environment ("Campfire Song")—all tackled subtly and tastefully without too much preaching or pretension and in believable, real-life situations. Producer Peter Asher, whose credits include James Taylor and Linda Ronstadt, provides the perfect sheen—the group's pleasant folk-pop lends itself nicely to the '70s-styled singer-songwriter production. In the end, the album proves powerful not for the ideas (they've been covered before) but rather for the graceful execution and pure listenability. *In My Tribe* has served as one of the soundtracks for P.C. living and was required listening on college campuses in the late '80s. — *Chris Woodstra*

Blind Man's Zoo / 1989 / Elektra ✦✦✦
After the success of *In My Tribe*, it would be expected that hordes of bands would take a stab at the market with their own second-rate versions of the album—it's disappointing that 10,000 Maniacs would be one of them, churning out not only *In My Tribe, Pt. 2*, but an inferior copy at that. It's not that the album is bad, but in handling the issues (there's no shortage of them), Merchant has become more direct and obvious. For all of its earnestness and good-intentioned teachings, *Blind Man's Zoo* ultimately fails in its heavy-handed and generally uninteresting approach. — *Chris Woodstra*

Hope Chest: The Fredonia Recordings 1982-1983 / 1990 / Elektra ✦✦
Hope Chest collects the ultra-rare early recordings of the band—the *Human Conflict Number 5* EP from 1982 and *Secrets of the I Ching* from 1983—remastered and resequenced presumably for easier listening. While the songs are predictably unfocused and full of underdeveloped (though ambitious) ideas, these recordings give an interesting picture of the band's formative years. — *Chris Woodstra*

Our Time in Eden / Sep. 29, 1992 / Elektra ✦✦✦✦
On their last album, *Our Time In Eden*, 10,000 Maniacs experiment with their trademark sound without ever losing sight of the gentle, melodic folk-rock that has gained them legions of fans. They wind up with their best album since *In My Tribe*, highlighted by the rolling "These Are Days" and the horn-spiked "Candy Everybody Wants." — *Stephen Thomas Erlewine*

MTV Unplugged / 1993 / Elektra ✦✦

Ten Years After

Blues-Rock

Ten Years After is a British blues-rock quartet consisting of Alvin Lee (b. Dec.19, 1944), guitar and vocals; Chick Churchill (b. Jan. 2, 1949), keyboards; Leo Lyons (b. Nov. 30, 1944) bass; and Ric Lee (b. Oct. 20, 1945), drums. The group was formed in 1967 and signed to Decca in England. Its first album was not a success, but its second, the live *Undead* containing "I'm Going Home," a six-minute blues workout by the fleet-fingered Alvin hit the charts on both sides of the Atlantic. *Stonedhenge* hit the UK Top Ten in early 1969. Ten Years After's US breakthrough came as a result of its appearance at Woodstock, at which it played a nine-minute version of "I'm Going Home." Its next album, *Ssssh*, reached the US Top 20, and *Cricklewood Green*, containing the hit single "Love Like a Man," reached No. 14. *Watt* completed the group's Decca contract, after which it signed with Columbia and moved in a more mainstream pop direction, typified by the gold-selling 1971 album *A Space in Time* and its Top 40 single "I'd Love to Change the World." Subsequent efforts in that direction were less successful, however, and Ten Years After split up after the release of *Positive Vibrations* in 1974. They reunited in 1988 for concerts in Europe and recorded their first new album in 15 years, *About Time*, in 1989. — *William Ruhlmann*

Undead / 1968 / Deram ✦✦✦✦
A live album from a group best experienced live, including some amazing guitar playing at phenomenal speeds from Alvin Lee. — *William Ruhlmann*

Greatest Hits / 1977 / Deram ✦✦✦✦
The group's 1968-1970 best, including the hit "Love like a Man" and the Woodstock version of "I'm Going Home." — *William Ruhlmann*

● **Essential** / 1991 / Chrysalis ✦✦✦✦
While it doesn't include all of their prime material, *Essential* features enough of their best songs to make it a fine introduction. — *AMG*

Tenpole Tudor

New Wave, Pub-Rock

Tenpole Tudor was one of the strangest and silliest groups on Stiff Records, a label that was known for its oddballs. Led by Eddie Tudor (born Edward Tudor-Pole), a former actor that could barely carry a tune, the group played a mixture of punk, roots-rock, pop, and British dance-hall music, developing a thoroughly entertaining and ridiculous style. Tudor formed the band in 1974 with guitarist Bob Kingston, bassist Dick Crippen, and drummer Gary Long. Before recording the band's first album, Tudor appeared in the Sex Pistols' movie *The Great Rock 'N' Roll Swindle*, singing "Who Killed Bambi." After releasing a single on Korova records, the group joined the Stiff Roster, releasing "Three Bells in a Row." Tenpole Tudor released their debut album, *Eddie, Old Bob, Dick & Gary* in 1981; it sold well, launching two minor singles in addition to "Three Bells in a Row"—"Wunderbar" and "Swords of a Thousand Men." That same year, the group released their second album, *Let the Four Winds Blow*, which also performed well. The following year, Eddie Tudor broke up Tenpole Tudor; while he led a cajun-inspired version of Tenpole Tudor, the rest of the band became the Tudors. After the new incarnation of Tenpole Tudor failed, Tudor left Stiff Records and began performing in jazz and swing bands, as well as returning to acting; he has since concentrated on acting, although he has assembled new versions of Tenpole Tudor since. — *Stephen Thomas Erlewine*

● **Eddie, Old Bob, Dick & Gary** / 1981 / Stiff ✦✦✦✦

Let the Four Winds Blow / 1981 / Stiff ✦✦✦

Tesla

Hard Rock, Heavy Metal

With their first album, *Mechanical Resonance*, Tesla quickly established themselves as one of the better hard rock/heavy metal bands of the late '80s. Although they weren't utterly original, the band was tight and showed an ability for crafting melodic, driving riffs. What made Tesla different from other metal bands with pop inclinations was the fact that their music was grounded in gritty, bluesy hard rock instead of slick arena rock.

Although their debut climbed all the way to No. 32 on the *Billboard* charts, their second album, 1989's *The Great Radio Controversy*, was an even greater success, scoring a Top Ten hit with the ballad "Love Song." Their follow-up album, *Five Man Acoustical Jam*, showed that the band didn't need overdriven amplifiers in order to play; it also showed that they had a fondness for sentimental hippie oldies, as their hit version of "Signs" proved. The record also turned out to be their biggest hit, reaching No. 12 on the charts. While its follow-up, *Psychotic Supper*, wasn't as commercially successful, it captured Tesla branching into new musical territories; it proved that the band hadn't lost its creative spark. — *Stephen Thomas Erlewine*

Mechanical Resonance / 1986 / Geffen ✦✦✦✦

The Great Radio Controversy / 1989 / Geffen ✦✦✦✦
More use of acoustic instruments make this a treat. It features the Top Ten hit "Love Song," as well as "The Way It Is" and "Heaven's Trail (No Way Out)." — *John Book*

Five Man Acoustical Jam / 1990 / Geffen ✦✦✦

Psychotic Supper / 1991 / Geffen ✦✦✦

Bust a Nut / 1994 / Geffen ✦✦

● **Time's Makin' Changes: The Best of Tesla** / 1995 / Geffen ✦✦✦✦
Tesla's greatest hits and most popular album rock cuts are collected on *Time's Makin' Changes: The Best of Tesla*. In addition to hits like "Signs," "The Way It Is," and "Love Song," the compilation includes a new song, "Steppin' Over," which isn't paritcularly distinctive. Nevertheless, the record remains the one to get for casual fans—it has all the hits, in one place, after all. — *Stephen Thomas Erlewine*

Joe Tex (Joe Arrington, Jr.)

b. Aug. 8, 1933, Rogers, TX, d. Aug. 13, 1982, Navasota, TX
Vocals / Soul, Funk

Often pausing in the middle of a ballad for a brief but sincere secular sermon on the inherent value of true love or the hazards of cheating, Joe Tex was one of the Southern soul genre's most enduring performers—and one of its most versatile. With a stage surname reflecting his home state, Tex first entered a recording studio in 1955 for King, singing some potent R&B before trying his luck in New Orleans with Ace. Tex joined forces with Nashville producer Buddy Killen (who formed the Dial logo to market the singer's output) and finally scaled the soul playlists in 1965 with his smash "Hold What You've Got." The prototypical Tex track, loaded with sound advice and down home homilies.

That's not to say that Tex didn't record some hard-driving uptempo soul during the mid-'60s—"A Sweet Woman like You," "S.Y.S.L.J.F.M. (The

Letter Song)," and "Show Me" all sizzle, while the hilarious "Skinny Legs and All," another major R&B and pop hit, accurately testifies to Tex's live charisma. With his microphone-stand acrobatics a longtime trademark, Tex's winning streak endured into the next decade with the grunting "I Gotcha," his biggest crossover success in 1972. He eked out another smash in the midst of disco fever with "Ain't Gonna Bump No More (With No Big Fat Woman)," his ebullient sense of humor still intact. Tex died in 1982. — *Bill Dahl*

● **I Believe I'm Gonna Make It** / 1988 / Rhino ✦✦✦✦
First-rate country/soul, sung with the just the right blend of whimsy, worry, and relief. Joe Tex was routinely turning out excellent cuts throughout the mid-'60s, but it wasn't until his novelty/disco tunes of the mid-'70s that he finally attained any widespread recognition. Sadly, none of his great Dial albums are currently in print. — *Ron Wynn*

Show Me: The Hits . . . & More / 1992 / Ichiban ✦✦✦✦
While he could spin a mean yarn, Tex was also a mournful, moving vocalist whose convincing delivery on country/soul ballads was sorely underrated. This 18-track collection includes some of Tex's biggest hits, fine covers of "Dark End of the Street" and "You're Right," plus several Tex originals such as "I Want to Do Everything for You," "Same Old Soup," and "King Thaddeus." While there are some notable and surprising exclusions, it's a representative Tex collection, but isn't as complete as Rhino's single-disc anthology from 1988. — *Ron Wynn*

The The

Alternative Pop-Rock

The The is essentially the solo project of Londoner Matt Johnson. Johnson released a solo album, *Burning Blue Soul*, in the early '80s which sketched out The The's sound—atmospheric, experimental songs that rely more on sound than song. With the first official The The album, 1983's *Soul Mining*, Johnson expanded his sound somewhat, concentrating more on songwriting while retaining the hollow, haunting ambience of his sound. With 1986's *Infected*, he began recording with studio musicians; this allowed him to embellish his music with several different styles, particularly dance. On The The's next album, 1989's *Mind Bomb* former Smiths guitarist Johnny Marr joined the band, which helped Johnson to present his music more clearly. With each release, The The became more direct; 1993's *Dusk* was their most straightforward album yet. Even though Johnson has strayed slightly from his spare, experimental roots, he remains an ambitious artist that has always satisfied and challenged his cult. — *Stephen Thomas Erlewine*

Burning Blue Soul / 1981 / 4AD ✦✦✦✦

Soul Mining / 1983 / Epic ✦✦✦

Infected / 1986 / Epic ✦✦✦✦
Infected is such a leap forward from *Soul Mining* that the album hardly seems like the work of the same band. Instead of the light, agreeable dance-pop of the previous album, *Infected* draws a dense, dark sonic landscape that accurately conveys the alienation and despair Matt Johnson sings about. — *Stephen Thomas Erlewine*

● **Mind Bomb** / 1989 / Epic ✦✦✦✦
With the addition of former Smiths guitarist Johnny Marr, The The attempted their most ambitious album yet with *Mind Bomb*. Instead of the darkly polished dance-pop stylings of *Infected*, *Mind Bomb* opens up the music to reveal a slow, winding textured world of sound that celebrates its rough edges instead of hiding them. It's serious, dance-influenced rock of the highest order. — *Stephen Thomas Erlewine*

Dusk / Jan. 5, 1993 / Epic ✦✦✦✦

Hanky Panky / 1995 / 550 Music/Epic ✦✦

Thee Midniters

Rock 'n' Roll, Garage Rock

Indisputably the greatest Latino rock band of the '60s, Thee Midniters took their inspiration from both the British Invasion sound of the Rolling Stones and the more traditional R&B that they were weaned on in their native Los Angeles. Hugely popular in east Los Angeles, the group, featuring both guitars and horns, had a local hit (and a small national one) with their storming version of "Land of a Thousand Dances" in 1965. Much of their repertoire featured driving, slightly punkish rock/R&B, yet lead singer Willie Garcia also had a heartbreaking delivery on slow and steamy ballads. In the manner of other local phenomenons like the Rationals (from Detroit), they were equally talented at whipping up a storm with uptempo numbers and offering smoldering, romantic soul tunes. After a few albums and an interesting detour into social consciousness with the single "Chicano Power," the group split in the early '70s, though their legacy is felt in later popular Latino L.A. rock acts like Los Lobos. — *Richie Unterberger*

Unlimited / 1967 / Whittier ✦✦✦

● **Best of Thee Midniters** / 1983 / Rhino ✦✦✦✦
An excellent compilation of 14 of their best songs, including "Land of a Thousand Dances" and "Chicano Power." They make a fair Latino Rolling Stones on "Empty Heart," "Everybody Needs Somebody," and "Whittier Blvd." (a thinly disguised reworking of the Stones' "2120 South Michigan Ave."); "That's All," "Dreaming Casually," and "Sad Girl" are exceptional slow R&B ballads; and "Jump, Jive and Harmonize" is a tough garage-punk original. —*Richie Unterberger*

Them

Rock 'n' Roll, British Invasion, British Blues
Not strictly a British group, but packaged as part of the British Invasion, Them forged their hard-nosed R&B sound in Belfast, Ireland, moving to England in 1964 after landing a deal with Decca Records. The band's simmering sound was dominated by boiling organ riffs, lean guitars, and the tough vocals of lead singer Van Morrison, whose recordings with Them rank among the very best performances of the British Invasion. Morrison also wrote top-notch original material for the outfit, whose lineup changed numerous times over the course of their brief existence. As a hit-making act, their résumé was brief—"Here Comes the Night" and "Baby Please Don't Go" were Top Ten hits in England, "Mystic Eyes" and "Here Comes the Night" made the Top 40 in the US—but their influence was considerable, reaching bands like the Doors, who Them played with during a residency in Los Angeles just before Van Morrison quit the band in 1966. Their most influential song of all, the classic three-chord stormer "Gloria," was actually a B-side, although the Shadows of Knight had a hit in the US with a faithful, tamer cover version.

Morrison has recalled his days with Them with some bitterness, noting that the heart of the original group was torn out by image-conscious record company politics, and that session men (including Jimmy Page, who played a scorching solo on "Baby Please Don't Go") often replaced members on recordings. That may be, but whether the records are faithful to the original Them sound or not, they were usually great—in addition to hits, Them released a couple fine albums and several flop singles that mixed fine Morrison compositions with hot R&B and soul covers, as well as a few songs written for them by producers like Bert Berns (who penned "Here Comes the Night"). After Morrison left the group, Them splintered into the Belfast Gypsies, who released a decent album that (except for the vocals) approximated Them's early records, and a psychedelic outfit that kept the name Them, releasing four fairly weak LPs with little resemblance to the tough sounds of their mid-'60s heyday.

Them's legacy is disgracefully underrepresented on CD; no major British Invasion act has been worse served by reissues in the digital age. Almost everything they recorded under Morrison's leadership is worth hearing, and a double CD compiling all several dozen of their songs from 1964 to 1966 would have little filler. For the time being, their output is scattered among some skimpy CD collections and various out-of-print LPs. —*Richie Unterberger*

Them [Parrot] / Apr. 1965 / Parrot ✦✦✦✦✦
Them Again / Apr. 1966 / Parrot ✦✦✦
Backtrackin' / 1974 / London ✦✦✦

● **Them Featuring Van Morrison [CD]** / 1987 / London ✦✦✦✦
Not to be confused with the identically titled Parrot Records release, which is an out-of-print 20-track double-LP set, this is a 13-track single CD set and a US reissue of the Decca UK LP from 1982. It would have been less confusing if they had called it *Them's Greatest Hits*, since it is primarily a singles compilation. But then, only four of Them's singles were hits, either in the UK or the US—"Baby, Please Don't Go," "Gloria," "Here Comes the Night," and "Mystic Eyes," all included here. Also featured are such non-charting singles as "Don't Start Crying Now," "One More Time," "(It Won't Hurt) Half As Much," and "Richard Cory." This is not the ideal Them compilation, but this is the one in print on CD that contains Them's most familiar material, so it will stand as the pick among their releases unless PolyGram, which owns the catalog, decides to do the kind of thorough retrospective the group deserves. —*William Ruhlmann*

They Might Be Giants

Alternative Pop-Rock
This Brooklyn-based duo, made up of John Flansburgh and John Linell, gives a new twist to pop music. Their lyrics (which are often funny and always offbeat) are accompanied by Flansburgh's guitar and Linell's accordion, giving their songs a unique sound. Full of puns, wisecracks, and thesaurus-dependent lyrics, TMBG's music is always entertaining. —*Iotis Erlewine*

They Might Be Giants / 1986 / Restless ✦✦✦✦
TMBG's debut album. The album includes a few good songs, such as "Don't Let's Start," "Put Your Hand Inside the Puppet Head," and "I Hope That I Get Old Before I Die." Overall, the album is too rough and tedious,

featuring TMBG's trademark "under three-minute" songs. —*Iotis Erlewine*

● **Lincoln** / 1989 / Restless ✦✦✦✦
TMBG's most entertaining album lets you have fun with the songs without trying to ferret out any deeper meaning in the bizarre lyrics. Here, TMBG reaches a good balance between goofy lyrics and listenable music. The songs won't spark any deep intellectual conversations, but you might just enjoy yourself. —*Iotis Erlewine*

Flood / 1990 / Elektra ✦✦✦
Musically, this is their best album, but in their attempt to put meaning into their lyrics, they have lost sight of TMBG's most appealing quality—the fun. *Flood* features a cover of "Istanbul (Not Constantinople)," written by J. Kennedy And N. Simon. There are a few outstanding songs, such as "Birdhouse in Your Soul" and "Particle Man." —*Iotis Erlewine*

Miscellaneous T / 1991 / Bar/None ✦✦✦
This album is a collection of TMBG's B-sides that includes several previously unreleased songs. For die-hard fans only. —*Iotis Erlewine*

Apollo 18 / 1992 / Elektra ✦✦✦
John Henry / 1994 / Elektra ✦✦

Thin Lizzy

Hard Rock, Heavy Metal
Despite a huge hit single in the mid-'70s ("The Boys Are Back in Town") and becoming a popular act with hard-rock/heavy-metal fans, Thin Lizzy are still, in the pantheon of '70s rock bands, underappreciated. Formed in the late '60s by Irish singer-songwriter/bassist Phil Lynott, Lizzy, though not the first band to do so, combined romanticized working-class sentiments with their ferocious, twin-lead guitar attack. As the band's creative force, Lynott was a more insightful and intelligent writer than many of his ilk, preferring slice-of-life working-class dramas of love and hate influenced by Bob Dylan, Bruce Springsteen, and virtually all of the Irish literary tradition. Also, as a Black man, Lynott was an anomaly in the nearly all-White world of hard rock, and as such imbued much of his work with a sense of alienation; he was the outsider, the romantic guy from the other side of the tracks, a self-styled poet of the lovelorn and downtrodden. His sweeping vision and writerly impulses at times gave way to pretentious songs aspiring to clichéd notions of literary significance, but Lynott's limitless charisma made even the most misguided moments worth hearing.

After a few early records that hinted at the band's potential, Lizzy released *Fighting* in 1975, and the band (Lynott, guitarists Brian Robertson and Scott Gorham, and drummer Brian Downey) had molded itself into a pretty tight recording and performing unit. Lynott's thick, soulful vocals were the perfect vehicle for his tightly written melodic lines. Gorham and Robertson generally played lead lines in harmonic tandem, while Downey (a great drummer who had equal amounts of power and style) drove the engine. Lizzy's big break came with their next album, *Jailbreak*, and the record's first single, "The Boys Are Back in Town." A paean to the joys of working-class guys letting loose, the song resembled similar odes by Bruce Springsteen, with the exception of the Who-like power chords in the chorus. With the support of radio and every frat boy in America, "Boys" became a huge hit, enough of a hit as to ensure record contracts and media attention for the next decade ("Boys" is now used in beer advertising).

Never the toast of critics (the majority writing in the '70s hated hard rock and heavy metal), Lizzy toured relentlessly, building an unassailable reputation as a terrific live band, despite the lead guitar spot becoming a revolving door (Eric Bell, Gary Moore, Brian Robertson, Snowy White, and John Sykes all stood next to Scott Gorham). The records came fast and furious, and despite attempts to repeat the formula that worked like a charm with "Boys," Lynott began writing more ambitious songs and wrapping them up in vaguely articulated concept albums. The large fan base the band had built as a result of "Boys" turned into a smaller, yet still enthusiastic bunch of hard rockers. Adding insult to injury was the rise of punk rock, which Lynott vigorously supported, but made Lizzy look too traditional and too much like tired old rock stars.

By the mid-'80s, resembling the dinosaur that punk rock wanted to annihilate, Thin Lizzy called it a career. Lynott recorded solo records that more explicitly examined issues of class and race, published a now out-of-print book of poetry, and sadly, became a victim of his longtime abuse of heroin, cocaine, and alcohol, dying in 1986 at age 35. As the mega-popular alternative rock bands of the mid-'90s appropriate numerous musical messages from their '70s forebears, it's hoped that the work of Phil Lynott and Thin Lizzy will been seen for the influential rock 'n' roll it is. —*John Dougan*

Jailbreak / 1976 / Mercury ✦✦✦✦
Purely and simply a great rock 'n' roll record. "Boys" is here in all its rabble-rousing glory, but better yet is the title track. Robertson and Gorham sound inspired, and Lynott's solid singing is made better by the sharp

melodies he's written. Perhaps a greatest hits compilation is a better place for the uninitiated to start, but *Jailbreak* is a keeper. —*John Dougan*

Johnny the Fox / 1976 / Mercury ♦♦♦
Hot on the heels of *Jailbreak* came *Johnny the Fox*, which was a thematically linked group of songs that (fortunately) worked individually or as a concept record. The band sounds looser and funkier here (Lynott was sucker for a James Brown-style rhythmic kick), and that pays off big time. Not essential, but by no means a waste of time. —*John Dougan*

Bad Reputation / 1977 / Mercury ♦♦♦
Although this record had an obvious attempt at a hit single ("Dancing in the Moonlight"), it also had the relentlessly propulsive title track and a half-dozen or so great songs that showed a band hitting its stride, comfortable with its place in the world and not losing one bit of power. Lizzy's third great record in a row. —*John Dougan*

Live & Dangerous / 1978 / Warner Bros. ♦♦♦♦
Some prefer the 1983 set *Life* (and it's very good), but I like this (albeit studio-enhanced) live record, which has as strong a selection of Lizzy fare in one place as one is likely to find. Along with the live standards ("Boys," "Cowboy Song," "Jailbreak," and "Dancing in the Moonlight"), there are some great semi-obscurities (Bob Seger's "Rosalie" and the macho "The Rocker"). Loud, proud, and chock-full of dazzling guitar solos, this is a hard-rock dream come true. Proof positive that in the arena rock sweepstakes, few bands were better onstage than Thin Lizzy. —*John Dougan*

● **Dedication: The Very Best of Thin Lizzy** / 1991 / Mercury ♦♦♦♦
A good, if somewhat brief look at all the high spots, featuring great guitar from fretmeisters Gary Moore, Eric Bell, John Sykes, and others. —*Cub Koda*

Peel Sessions / 1995 / Strange Fruit/Dutch East ♦♦♦♦
Better than the too-short, but still okay *Dedication* greatest hits compilation released by Mercury in 1991, *The Peel Sessions* features raw and wild versions of great Lizzy songs that provide an historical overview of the band's development. For what it's worth, this is the only Peel session release with liner notes written by John Peel himself. —*John Dougan*

Thirteenth Floor Elevators

Psychedelic, Garage Rock
Featuring the yelping vocals and visionary, occasionally demented lyrics of Roky Erickson, the Thirteenth Floor Elevators were one of the original acid bands. Formed in Texas in the mid-'60s, the Elevators started as a garage-rock outfit, scoring their one and only modest national hit with "You're Gonna Miss Me." While Erickson's loopy persona, along with Tommy Hall's odd "jug" percussion, was the band's most distinguishing feature, several members of the group's original lineup contributed strong material to their albums. Although these inconsistent efforts sometimes wander off into a cloudy haze, they also include sturdy folk-rock tunes and driving psychedelic rockers. Trips to San Francisco established the group as up-and-coming underground favorites, but Erickson's drug problems led to the singer's commission to a state mental hospital in the late '60s, an ordeal from which he has never fully recovered. The band was really only at full power for a couple of albums, although all of their releases for the legendary International Artists label—produced by, of all people, Kenny Rogers' brother Leland—are revered among psychedelic collectors. Live recordings and outtakes of the Elevators continue to surface, though a cogent domestic compilation of the best of these erratic pioneers' work remains overdue. —*Richie Unterberger*

● **Thirteenth Floor Elevators** / 1966 / International Artists ♦♦♦♦
Their first album is their best, although their second (*Easter Everywhere*) also had some good material. Besides "You're Gonna Miss Me," includes "Fire Engine," "Tried to Hide," "Roller Coaster," and Erickson's best composition, the gentle folk-rocker "Splash 1." —*Richie Unterberger*

Easter Everywhere / 1967 / Collectables ♦♦♦
Basically an extension of the sound of their first album, but more overtly trippy, with material that is not quite as strong. "She Lives (in a Time of Her Own)" is probably the best cut; the rustic folk mood on "Dust" and "I Had to Tell You" is a good change of pace. —*Richie Unterberger*

Bull of the Woods / 1968 / Decal ♦♦♦
Guitarist Stacy Sutherland wrote most of the songs on the band's final studio album, as Roky was largely absent due to drugs and problems with the law. Decent psychedelic rock—pretty straight-ahead and disciplined for the genre, actually—that doesn't match the inspired heights of their previous material. The closing "May the Circle Be Unbroken," with its wads and wads of reverb, may be the strangest thing the band ever cut. —*Richie Unterberger*

Live at the Avalon, 1966 / 1978 / Lysergic ♦♦♦

Fire in My Bones / 1985 / Texas Archive ♦♦♦
The best collection of previously unreleased Elevators. Side one has six songs from an early 1966 live Dallas TV broadcast, including "You're Gonna Miss Me" and "Fire Engine," as well as covers of hits by the Kinks, Them, and Chuck Berry. Side two has alternate versions of four songs

from the first LP that are more uninhibited in spots than the official versions, as well as the previously unreleased song "Fire in My Bones" and a live jam. —*Richie Unterberger*

Elevator Tracks / 1987 / Texas Archive ♦♦♦

Original Sound of / 1988 / 13th Hour ♦♦
The outtake barrel starts to run thin on yet another collection of unreleased material. Side one has different (but not too different) studio versions of songs from the first LP, and side two is a fair-quality tape of five songs from a club gig in Austin in 1966. —*Richie Unterberger*

● **Best of the Thirteenth Floor Elevators** / 1994 / Eva ♦♦♦♦
Finally, a best-of compilation for one of the most popular cult psychedelic groups of all time. The 22 tracks draw most heavily upon the first LP, with choice bits from the second and third, as well as some material Roky Erickson cut with his pre-Elevators group The Spades. —*Richie Unterberger*

.38 Special

Southern Rock
This hard-touring Jacksonville-based band (formed 1975) featured lead singer Donnie Van Zant, brother of Lynyrd Skynyrd's lead singer Ronnie Van Zant. .38 Special delivered a brand of Southern pop-rock that wasn't quite so hard-hitting as Skynyrd's, while showcasing an Allman Brothers-like lineup, with two lead guitarists and two drummers. They also charted more hits than either of those bands. Their most popular hits included "Caught up in Loosely," "Hold on Loosely," "Back Where You Belong," "Like No Other Night," "Second Chance," "If I'd Been the One," and "Rockin' into the Night." —*Rick Clark*

Wild Eyed & Live / 1978 / A&M ♦♦♦

● **Flashback: Best of .38 Special** / 1987 / A&M ♦♦♦♦
An excellent retrospective, featuring all the hits. The last commercial flowering of Southern rock. —*Cub Koda*

This Mortal Coil

Alternative Pop-Rock
This Mortal Coil is the brainchild of 4AD's president, Ivo Watts. It's not really a band, it's a way for Watts to explore different musical territory and cover his favorite artists, including Syd Barrett, Alex Chilton, Talking Heads, Tim Buckley, and Gene Clark. Over the years, the lineup has featured various stars from the record label's roster including Kim Deal, Tanya Donelly, Heidi Berry, and Robin Guthrie and Elizabeth Fraser from the Cocteau Twins. Like most 4AD bands, This Mortal Coil is atmospheric, sometimes dreamy, other times haunting. Watts has said that 1991's *Blood* is the last album the outfit will release. —*Stephen Thomas Erlewine*

It'll End in Tears / 1984 / 4AD ♦♦♦
Features the Cocteau Twins' Elizabeth Fraser singing Tim Buckley's "Song to the Siren," Gordon Sharp singing Rema-Rema's "Fond Affections," and Howard Devoto singing Alex Chilton's "Holocaust." Lisa Gerrard and Brendan Perry of Dead Can Dance are also included on this first collection of covers from 4AD. —*Heather Phares*

Filigree & Shadow / 1986 / 4AD ♦♦♦♦
The second album of This Mortal Coil interpretations includes the vocalist, Jean, doing a version of Van Morrison's "Come Here My Love," and Deidre and Louise Rutkowski singing Tim Buckley's "Morning Glory." Other songs include David Byrne's "Drugs," and Gene Clark's "Strength of Strings." —*Heather Phares*

● **Blood** / 1991 / 4AD ♦♦♦♦
The final This Mortal Coil album includes some of the project's finest moments, including a cover of the Byrds' "I Come and Stand at Every Door" by Louise and Deidre Rutkowski, Syd Barrett's "Late Night" sung by Caroline Crawley of Shellyan Orphan, a cover of Gene Clark's "With Tomorrow," and a standout performance of Chris Bell's "You and Your Sister" by The Breeders' Kim Deal and Belly's Tanya Donelly. —*Heather Phares*

1983-1991 / 1993 / 4AD ♦♦♦
All three of This Mortal Coil's albums packaged in an expensive slipcase, along with a disc of the original versions of the songs they covered. Fans of 4AD bands like Throwing Muses, the Cocteau Twins, and Dead Can Dance will thoroughly enjoy This Mortal Coil's lush, haunting music; some members of these bands play on various tracks on the box, including a standout duet between Kim Deal and Tanya Donelly on Chris Bell's "You and Your Sister." Although the packaging is beautiful, there are no liner notes. —*Stephen Thomas Erlewine*

Carla Thomas

b. Dec. 21, 1942, Memphis, TN
Vocals / Soul
In the glorious decade and a half of sound that was Stax in the '60s and

early '70s, Carla Thomas was the Queen of Memphis Soul. She was born in Memphis in 1942, and 18 years later she recorded a duet with her father Rufus Thomas, giving the fledgling Satellite label its first taste of success with the regional hit "'Cause I Love You." As her 18th birthday drew nigh, she cut her first solo single, the teen ballad "Gee Whiz (Look at His Eyes)." Written a few years earlier and rejected by Vee-Jay in Chicago, it gave Satellite its first national hit, breaking the Top Ten mark on both the R&B and pop charts. Shortly thereafter Satellite became Stax, and Carla proceeded to claw her way onto the national charts another 22 times with immortal slices of soul as her answer song to Sam Cooke, "I'll Bring It on Home to You," as well as "Let Me Be Good to You," "B-A-B-Y," "Tramp" (with Otis Redding), and "I Like What You're Doing to Me." Carla released six solo albums and, with Otis Redding, one duet album on Stax between 1961 and 1971. —*Rob Bowman*

Gee Whiz / 1961 / Atlantic ◆◆◆
Carla Thomas' first album was typical fare for the R&B market of the time, combining two chart entries (the title song and "A Love of My Own") with covers of recent chart hits (the Drifters' "Fools Fall in Love" and "Dance with Me," the Five Satins' "To the Aisle"), standards ("The Masquerade Is Over"), and a handful of originals. This was the first album produced by the then-fledgling Stax label and the unique Stax sound was not yet manifest. —*Rob Bowman*

Carla / 1966 / Atlantic ◆◆◆◆
Paired with Stax writing whiz-kids Isaac Hayes and David Porter, Thomas had her greatest chart run, beginning with the hit "B-A-B-Y" and continuing with "Let Me Be Good to You." Both of those appear here, alongside evocative slabs of country-soul in covers of Hank Williams' "I'm So Lonesome I Could Cry" and Patsy Cline's "I Fall to Pieces." For good measure, Thomas also tries her hand at the blues with covers of Howlin' Wolf's "Little Red Rooster" and Jimmy Reed's "Baby What You Want Me to Do?" —*Rob Bowman*

Comfort Me / 1966 / Atlantic ◆◆◆◆
A collection of twelve tracks recorded over a year and a half, *Comfort Me* showcases Thomas in the midst of the developed Stax sound. Backed by Booker T. and the MG's and the Mar-Key horns, Thomas turns in fine covers of Baby Washington's "Move on Drifter," the Marvelettes' "Forever," the Shirelles' "Will You Love Me Tomorrow?," the Everly Brothers' "Let It Be Me," Jackie DeShannon's "What the World Needs Now," the Toys' "Lover's Concerto," and Barbara Mason's "Yes I'm Ready," coupled with a number of efforts by Thomas herself, Steve Cropper, and Eddie Floyd. The highlight is the Cropper-Floyd title cut, with utterly gorgeous backing by Gladys Knight and the Pips. —*Rob Bowman*

Hidden Gems / 1992 / Stax ◆◆◆
Twenty outtakes recorded for Stax between 1960 and 1968, a number of which are gems. In fact, it is really surprising just how good the unreleased Stax stuff was in the '60s. "Loneliness," "Sweet Sensation," and "It Ain't No Easy Thing" all could have been superb singles. —*Rob Bowman*

● **Gee Whiz: The Best of Carla Thomas** / 1994 / Rhino ◆◆◆◆
A sterling collection, it includes all of Carla Thomas' biggest hits and best material. —*AMG*

Sugar / 1994 / Stax ◆◆◆
A collection of odds and ends from the late '60s and early '70s, including some obscure Stax singles, duets with Pervis Staples and Johnnie Taylor, and three live numbers from the *Wattstax* soundtrack. It's not the first (or second) Carla Thomas collection you should pick up, but it's solid material. Donny Hathaway and Chips Moman each produced a couple of the singles spotlighted here (A-sides and B-sides are included), adding moderately ambitious variations on the standard Stax sound. —*Richie Unterberger*

Irma Thomas

b. Feb. 18, 1941
Vocals / Soul, New Orleans R&B
Radiating an outgoing joy that's inevitably at the heart of her infectious vocal delivery, Irma Thomas has no rivals as the Soul Queen of New Orleans. Working at a Crescent City nightery as a waitress in 1959, Thomas sat in one night with Tommy Ridgely's band and made such a favorable impression that the veteran bandleader hustled her into the studio shortly thereafter to wax her first hit for the Ron label, the driving "Don't Mess with My Man." She joined forces with producer Allen Toussaint to make some of her most moving outings for Minit Records during the early '60s, notably "It's Raining," "Ruler of My Heart," and "Cry On," before venturing to the West Coast, where she cut both her biggest seller, the lushly produced "Wish Someone Would Care," and her best-known song, the original "Time Is on My Side"—and she's still bitter enough about the Rolling Stones' cover stealing her thunder to discourage requests for the tune. The highly adaptable chanteuse also made some sizzling soul at Rich Hall's Muscle Shoals studio for Chess in the summer of 1967 before cooling off for a while during the '70s. But she's back now, as radiant as ever—and for convincing proof, listen to her buoyant 1990

concert performance on Rounder, *Live! Simply the Best*. Now that's truth in packaging!
Irma Thomas finally fulfilled a lifelong ambition in 1994 by recording her first gospel release. *Walk Around Heaven* was as magnificently sung and emotionally convincing as any of her classic New Orleans soul cuts. —*Bill Dahl*

Time Is on My Side [Kent] / 1983 / Kent ◆◆◆◆
Solid 16-song compilation of material from the mid-'60s. Most of this is duplicated by the more extensive CD compilations of the same era on EMI and Razor & Tie. But it's not entirely superfluous; five of the songs don't appear on either of the other collections. Those tracks are worth hearing, particularly the gutsy soul-pop concoction "Baby Don't Look Down," one of Randy Newman's earliest compositions. —*Richie Unterberger*

Ruler of Hearts / 1989 / Charly ◆◆◆
Sides from her early-'60s Minit sessions. The most New Orleans R&B-influenced of Thomas' early work, it includes "Cry On," "It's Raining," and "Ruler Of My Heart," as well as lesser-known but equally moving cuts like "Two Winters Long" and "It's Too Soon to Know." —*Richie Unterberger*

★ **Time Is on My Side (The Best of Irma Thomas), Vol. 1** / 1992 / EMI America ◆◆◆◆◆
Twenty-three sides representing the cream of Irma Thomas' brilliant Minit/Liberty years (1961-1966), when her reputation as "The Soul Queen of New Orleans" was built. Virtually all her best-known tunes are here—"Wish Someone Would Care," "Ruler of My Heart," "It's Raining," and "Time Is on My Side" (covered note-for-note by the Stones). Beautiful singing from one of the first ladies of soul music. Essential. —*Christine Ohlman*

Sweet Soul Queen of New Orleans: The Irma Thomas Collection / 1996 / Razor & Tie ◆◆◆◆
Twenty three-track collection of early and mid-'60s sides largely duplicates the material on EMI's *Time Is on My Side* collection, with some additions and subtractions. The EMI set has a very slight edge, though for most listeners either compilation will do the job. It's too bad somebody doesn't take the plunge and issue an 80-minute CD documenting this era; as it is, serious Irma fans will need to get each best-of, as each contains tracks not on the other. —*Richie Unterberger*

Rufus Thomas

b. Mar. 26, 1917, Casey, MS
Vocals / Soul, R&B
Few of rock 'n' roll's founding figures are as likable as Rufus Thomas. From the 1940s onward, he has personified Memphis music; his small but witty cameo role in Jim Jarmusch's *Mystery Train*, a film that satirizes and enshrines the city's role in popular culture, was entirely appropriate. As a recording artist, he wasn't a major innovator, but he could always be depended upon for some good, silly, and/or outrageous fun with his soul dance tunes. He was one of the few rock or soul stars to reach his commercial and artistic peak in middle age, and was a crucial mentor to many important Memphis blues, rock, and soul musicians.
Thomas was already a professional entertainer in the mid-'30s, when he was a comedian with the Rabbit Foot Minstrels. He recorded music as early as 1941, but really made his mark on the Memphis music scene as a deejay on WDIA, one of the few Black-owned stations of the era (his broadcasts could be heard from the '40s through the mid-'70s). He also ran talent shows on Memphis' famous Beale Street that helped showcase the emerging skills of such influential figures as B.B. King, Bobby Bland, Junior Parker, Ike Turner, and Roscoe Gordon.
Thomas had his first success as a recording artist in 1953 with "Bear Cat," a funny answer record to Big Mama Thornton's "Hound Dog." It made No. 3 on the R&B charts, giving Sun Records its first national hit, though some of the sweetness went out of the triumph after Sun owner Sam Phillips lost a lawsuit for plagiarizing the original Jerry Leiber/Mike Stoller tune. Thomas, strangely, would make only one other record for Sun, and recorded only sporadically throughout the rest of the 1950s.
Thomas and his daughter Carla would become the first stars for the Stax label, for whom they recorded a duet in 1959, "'Cause I Love You" (when the company was still known as Satellite). In the '60s, Carla would become one of Stax's biggest stars. On his own, Rufus wasn't as successful as his daughter, but issued a steady stream of decent dance/novelty singles.
These were not deep or emotional statements, or meant to be. Vaguely prefiguring elements of funk, the accent was on the stripped-down groove and Rufus' good-time vocals, which didn't take himself or anything seriously. The biggest by far was "Walking the Dog," which made the Top Ten in 1963, and was covered by the Rolling Stones on their first album.
Thomas hit his commercial peak in the early '70s, when "Do the Funky Chicken," "(Do the) Push and Pull," and "The Breakdown" all made the R&B Top Five. As the song titles themselves make clear, funk

was now driving his sound rather than blues or soul. Thomas drew upon his vaudeville background to put them over onstage with fancy footwork that displayed remarkable agility for a man well into his 50s. The collapse of the Stax label in the mid-'70s meant the end of his career, basically, as it did for many other artists with the company. —*Richie Unterberger*

● **Do the Funky Somethin': Best Of** / Apr. 1996 / Rhino ♦♦♦♦
Overdue career-spanning collection of his best material, centering around his Stax hits from the '60s and early '70s. The whole "dog" series of novelty dance songs from 1963-64 is here, as well as the hit "Jump Back" and a clutch of Stax singles that weren't hits, but became pretty well-known anyway, like "Sister's Got a Boyfriend" and "Sophisticated Sissy." There are also the early-'70s funk dance hits "Do the Funky Chicken," "(Do the) Push and Pull," "The Breakdown," and "Do the Funky Penguin," a couple of '60s duets with his daughter Carla, and his 1953 blues single "Bear Cat (the Answer to Hound Dog)," the first hit on Sun Records. A few other compilations have gone into specific phases of his career in greater depth, but this is certainly the best overview of a man who offered some of the funkiest and funniest Memphis soul around. —*Richie Unterberger*

Richard Thompson

b. Apr. 3, 1949, London, England
Dulcimer, Guitar, Mandolin, Vocals / Singer-Songwriter, Folk-Rock, British Folk

Richard Thompson is among the most admired guitarists and songwriters in folk-rock music, and in the 1980s and '90s, he moved from a fervent cult following to broader exposure while maintaining critical accolades for his biting guitar work and sardonic songs. He was a founding member of Fairport Convention, the most important British folk-rock group to emerge in the 1960s, and he recorded five albums with them—*Fairport Convention* (Jun. 1968), *What We Did on Our Holidays* (Jan. 1969), *Unhalfbricking* (Jul. 1969), *Liege and Lief* (Dec. 1969), and *Full House* (Jul. 1970). Quitting the group in January 1971, he made his debut solo album, *Henry the Human Fly* (Jun. 1972), before forming a duo with his wife, Linda. The Thompsons released six albums—*I Want to See the Bright Lights Tonight* (Apr. 1974), *Hokey Pokey* (Mar. 1975), *Pour Down like Silver* (Nov. 1975), *First Light* (Nov. 1978), *Sunnyvista* (1979), and *Shoot Out the Lights* (1982), before breaking up personally and professionally. In 1981, Thompson had made a second solo album of instrumentals, *Strict Tempo!;* with 1983's *Hand of Kindness*, his first charting album, he relaunched his solo career. (Five years later, Joel Sonnier took "Tear-Stained Letter," from the album, into the Country Top Ten.) Thompson followed with an acoustic live album, *Small Town Romance* (1984). He had recorded primarily for Island Records or his friend and producer Joe Boyd's Hannibal/Carthage labels, and his albums had been distributed inconsistently in the US With *Across a Crowded Room* (Feb. 1985), he moved to Polydor, a major. The album spent more than three months in the US charts. Polydor seems to have expected better sales than that, however, and after *Daring Adventures* (Oct. 1986), Thompson left for Capitol Records, for which he has made *Amnesia* (Oct. 1988), *Rumor and Sigh* (May 1991), *Mirror Blue* (Feb. 1994), and *You? Me? Us?* (Apr. 1996). Thompson's earlier work has been reissued extensively by Hannibal Records through Rykodisc, including a three-disc retrospective, *Watching the Dark* (Apr. 1993). *Beat the Retreat* (Oct. 1994), a tribute album featuring Thompson's songs performed by R.E.M., Bob Mould, Bonnie Raitt, Los Lobos, and David Byrne, among others, offered further testimony to the high regard in which Thompson is held. —*William Ruhlmann*

Henry the Human Fly / 1972 / Hannibal ♦♦♦♦
Supposedly the worst-selling album in the history of Warner Bros. Records (now available through Hannibal), this was Richard Thompson's debut solo album after a couple of years of playing sessions that followed his departure from Fairport Convention in 1970. It's a dry run for his six duet albums with his wife, Linda, who is credited here under her maiden name, Linda Peters, and features some terrific folk songs, notably "Nobody's Wedding." —*William Ruhlmann*

Hokey Pokey / 1974 / Hannibal ♦♦♦
Richard and Linda Thompson's second album (not released in the US until 1983) was a somewhat lighter one than their debut, *I Want to See the Bright Lights Tonight*, from earlier in 1974, but with tracks like "The Sun Never Shines on the Poor," not much. "I'll Regret It All in the Morning" and especially "A Heart Needs a Home" were classics. —*William Ruhlmann*

☆ **I Want to See the Bright Lights Tonight** / Apr. 1974 / Hannibal ♦♦♦♦♦
The debut album by the duo of Richard and Linda Thompson picked up from where Richard had left off in Fairport Convention. Casting his wife in the role of Sandy Denny (a part she carried off beautifully), Richard mixed rock and blues elements with traditional British folk music to striking effect. But where Fairport had employed some actual traditional songs and used the dark tone of some folk music sparingly, Richard

plunged in on his original songs, painting portraits of drunks and beggars for whom religion provides the salvation to be found in death. Linda's moving voice made songs like "Withered and Died" and "The Great Valerio" as compelling as they were mournful, but Richard could be terrifying: He began the devil's lullaby "The End of the Rainbow," "I feel for you, you little horror," and went on to inform the infant, "There's nothing to grow up for anymore." The album was uncompromising and riveting. It seemed like a set of songs unearthed from the Dark Ages, and argued that those times had never really left. (Originally released in the UK in Apr. 1974 as Island 9266, *I Want to See the Bright Lights Tonight* was released in the US in 1976 as one of the two LPs that made up *Richard Thompson Live! (More or Less)*. It was reissued in 1983 as Carthage 4407 and in 1991 as Hannibal/Rykodisc 4407. —*William Ruhlmann*

Pour Down Like Silver / 1975 / Hannibal ♦♦♦♦
The third Richard and Linda Thompson album (and the first to be released in the US) features "For Shame of Doing Wrong," "Beat the Retreat," and "Dimming of the Day/Dargai," all doomy Richard Thompson songs, the last with an extensive guitar coda. But there's also the rollicking "Jet Plane in a Rocking Chair." The couple appeared on the album cover in mufti, indicative of their dedication to the Sufi sect of Islam, which would consume their attention for the next few years, such that they didn't release another new album until 1978. —*William Ruhlmann*

Guitar, Vocal / May 1976 / Hannibal ♦♦
First Light / 1978 / Hannibal ♦♦♦
Richard and Linda Thompson returned to action with this, their fourth duo album, after three years away from music. It was not one of their best albums, although it did include the impressive "Don't Let a Thief Steal into Your Heart" and the title track. —*William Ruhlmann*

Sunnyvista / 1979 / Hannibal ♦♦♦
Richard and Linda Thompson's fifth album was more of a pop record than previous releases (although Chrysalis, their label, didn't see fit to release it in the US after *First Light* failed to sell, and it didn't appear domestically until it was picked up by Hannibal in 1983). Many Fairport Conventioneers guested, but the songwriting was not up to Richard Thompson's usual standard. —*William Ruhlmann*

Strict Tempo! / 1981 / Hannibal ♦♦
★ **Shoot out the Lights** / 1982 / Hannibal ♦♦♦♦♦
One of the most mesmerizing recordings ever committed to tape by a husband/wife team, *Shoot out the Lights* is the sound of a marriage falling apart—particularly Richard and Linda Thompson's. Linda's beautifully world-weary alto and Richard's indignant quaver deliver some monumental performances on tracks like "The Wall of Death," "Don't Renege on Our Love," "Did She Jump or Was She Pushed?," "Walking on a Wire," and "Just the Motion." The title track features some incredible lead-guitar playing by Richard. It's indispensible for any comprehensive rock collection, particularly fans of folk-rock. —*Rick Clark*

Hand of Kindness / Jul. 1983 / Hannibal ♦♦♦♦
It was too big a coincidence for most listeners that Richard Thompson's first solo album after his breakup with his wife and musical partner Linda Thompson was full of painful, sometimes venomous songs about romance gone wrong; the assumption (denied by Thompson) was that this was his divorce album. Whether or not that was the case, heartache gave Thompson a focus for some of the most accomplished songwriting of his career, beginning with "Tear-Stained Letter" ("And just when I thought I could learn to forget her / Right through the door came a Tear-Stained Letter"), covered by Joel Sonnier for a Top Ten Country single in 1988, and continuing with the heart-wrenching "How I Wanted To" and "A Poisoned Heart and a Twisted Memory." With his typically authoritative six-string work driving the folk-rock music (played by a band anchored by members of Fairport Convention), which could be surprisingly jaunty given the subject matter, Thompson turned in his finest solo effort and, in the estimation of many critics including this one, one of the best rock albums of 1983. —*William Ruhlmann*

Small Town Romance / 1984 / Hannibal ♦♦♦
Across a Crowded Room / Feb. 1985 / Polydor ♦♦♦♦
After *Hand of Kindness* earned critical kudos and broke into the charts on the tiny Hannibal label, Polydor signed Richard Thompson with hopes of a commercial breakthrough. His first major-label solo album, *Across a Crowded Room* was very much in the style of *Hand of Kindness*. He was not through expressing anger about love gone wrong; the lead-off track, "When the Spell Is Broken," plunged right back in, with Thompson intoning, "Can't cry if you don't know how." In "You Don't Say," backup singers Christine Collister and Clive Gregson filled the verses with criticisms made by a woman scorned. "Do you mean she still cares?" asked Thompson in the chorus. And so it went, as love was equated with spying ("Love in a Faithless Country") and violence ("She Twists the Knife Again"). Thompson's worldview had always been dire, and so it remained ("Walking Through a Wasted Land"). But his romantic venom gave his disdain energy, and the musical combination of blues-rock and Scots-Irish folk was compelling on its own. *Across a Crowded*

Room was a worthy successor to *Hand of Kindness* and even threatened to make the Top 100 bestsellers list, though that turned out to be an aberration. — *William Ruhlmann*

Daring Adventures / Mar. 1986 / Polydor ✦✦✦
Richard Thompson's second Polydor album contained some terrific and varied songs, from the raucous "A Bone Through Her Nose" to the mournful "Missie How You Let Me Down" and "Al Bowlly's in Heaven." Good as it was, it didn't establish Thompson as a big seller, and Polydor dropped him. — *William Ruhlmann*

Amnesia / 1988 / Capitol ✦✦✦✦
Here Thompson has really redefined himself, taking the more pop sound of *Dangerous Adventures* further. Again produced by Mitchell Froom, this record smokes with the concert favorite "Turning of the Tide," "The Reckless Kind," and the bittersweet "Waltzing for Dreamers." — *Richard Meyer*

Rumor and Sigh / May 1991 / Capitol ✦✦✦✦
Richard Thompson's second Capitol Records outing and second collaboration with producer Mitchell Froom was a lengthy 14-track opus that gave a thorough airing to his usual concerns—twisted love, crime, death, drinking. Somehow, all of this had come to seem a little less and a little more derivative, both of earlier Thompson and of Bob Dylan. Compare a lyric like "I ask you what's wrong, and you say, / I'm all yours / I ask who your friend is, / And you say, Santa Claus" (Thompson's "I Plead"), for example, with "Well, I go to pet your monkey / I get a face full of claws / I ask who's in the fireplace / And you tell me Santa Claus" (Dylan's "On the Road Again"). "Psycho Street," meanwhile, sounds like the kind of weird recitals John Cale used to cook up for the Velvet Underground. The trio of songs that open the album, "Read About Love," "I Feel So Good," and "I Misunderstood," are worthy additions to Thompson's repertoire of witty doomed love songs, and "1952 Vincent Black Lightning" is a timeless death ballad, but not all of the album reaches that standard, and with a running time over an hour, it just goes on too long. Froom abets Thompson's more extreme tendencies rather than reining them in, so it's no surprise *Rumor and Sigh* became his first major-label solo album to miss the charts. — *William Ruhlmann*

Watching the Dark / May 11, 1993 / Hannibal ✦✦✦✦
A sprawling three-disc compilation tracing Richard Thompson's career from his beginnings with Fairport Convention, through his days with his ex-wife Linda, to his recent solo recordings, *Watching the Dark* is a treasure for longtime fans as well as those who want an introduction to his distinctive English folk-rock. Instead of being assembled chronologically, each disc contains three separate eras, which helps illustrate how consistently rich his music has been through the years. Nearly half of the tracks are rare or unreleased; instead of betraying Thompson's gifts, the song selection helps convey the breadth and scope of his talents. Although the material might be skewed toward hardcore fans, anyone unfamiliar with Thompson will realize why he is one of the most revered (and, unfortunately, unknown) songwriters and guitarists of his era by listening to *Watching the Dark*. — *Stephen Thomas Erlewine*

Mirror Blue / Feb. 8, 1994 / Capitol ✦✦
In many ways, *Mirror Blue* is Thompson's pop radio record, with shorter songs and a crisp, slick production. While that may put some fans off, the songs prove to be another set of rich, detailed stories; even the supposed toss-offs are bright, catchy, and memorable. In fact, the best moments of *Mirror Blue* equal the best of *Rumor and Sigh*—it's hard to equal the subtle power of "Mingus Eyes" or "Mascara Tears," and the closing song, "Taking My Business Elsewhere," is one of the best things he has ever written. — *Stephen Thomas Erlewine*

You? Me? Us? / Apr. 16, 1996 / Capitol ✦✦✦
On the surface, *You? Me? Us?* appears to be a major statement from Richard Thompson. Spread out over two discs, the budget-priced album features 19 tracks, separated into an electric ("Voltage Enhanced") disc and an acoustic ("Nude") disc, which each run around 40 minutes; "Razor Dance" and "Hide It Away" appear on both discs. Despite its appearance, *You? Me? Us?* isn't one of Thompson's major works. What sinks the album isn't the songs—as always, Thompson has written a handful of gems—but Mitchell Froom's production. Froom's gauzy, pseudo-experimental approach masks the songs in an impenetrable haze, which neither Thompson's guitar or voice can cut through. There is no texture to the album's sound—it is mushy and colorless, which cuts away at the heart of Thompson's direct, emotional songs. If the songs on *You? Me? Us?* were given the simple, direct production they deserve, it would have been a completely different, more compelling experience. As it stands, it's a wildly uneven and unengaging listen, like the majority of the Froom-produced Thompson records. — *Stephen Thomas Erlewine*

George Thorogood & the Destroyers

Guitar, Vocals / Rock 'n' roll, Blues-Rock, Boogie Rock
A Delaware-based blues band formed in 1973 and led by guitarist/singer George Thorogood, who brings a rough-voiced enthusiasm to the music

of John Lee Hooker, Elmore James, and others. The group scored five gold albums in 1980–1988. — *William Ruhlmann*

George Thorogood & the Destroyers / 1977 / Rounder ✦✦✦✦
Contains Thorogood's crowd-pleasing rendition of John Lee Hooker's "One Bourbon, One Scotch, One Beer." Its basic approach—heavy on Thorogood's bluesy guitar playing—serves as the prototype for every Destroyers record that followed. — *William Ruhlmann*

Move It on Over / 1978 / Rounder ✦✦✦

More George Thorogood & the Destroyers / 1980 / Rounder ✦✦

Bad to the Bone / 1982 / EMI America ✦✦✦✦
Though songs such as "Back to Wentzville" are credited to G. Thorogood, he'd be the first to admit that they are proudly derivative of Chuck Berry and his other mentors. The title track, another Thorogood copyright, has become ubiquitous in *Terminator 2* and the *Problem Child* movies and elsewhere, but it's still terrific. — *William Ruhlmann*

● **The Baddest of George Thorogood and the Destroyers** / 1992 / EMI America ✦✦✦✦
The aptly titled *The Baddest of George Thorogood and the Destroyers* offers a dozen tracks that cleanse the church of rock 'n' roll of all but its most basic elements: guitar, bass, drums, and a pile of Chuck Berry, Bo Diddley, and Rolling Stone licks. Delaware's George Thorogood has never quite captured his wildman live presence in the studio, but having all his best material gathered on one disc—including "Bad to the Bone," "Move It on Over," and "One Bourbon, One Scotch, One Beer"—makes for a great party. Steve Morse's liner notes are brief but, like the songs, get right to the point . . . cut to the bone, you might say. — *Roch Parisien*

Haircut / 1993 / EMI America ✦✦

Three Dog Night

Pop-Rock
At a time when rock elitists deemed Top 40 radio decidedly uncool, the slick multivocal blend of soulful pop-rock of Three Dog Night (formed 1968) made 21 trips to the charts from 1969 to 1975.
    The centerpiece of Three Dog Night's sound was the band's trio of lead singers: Danny Hutton (b. Sep. 10, 1946), Chuck Negron (b. Jun. 8, 1942), and Cory Wells (b. Feb. 5, 1944). Composed of seasoned players, the band displayed quite a bit of proficiency musically, even though their lurching, soulful dance rhythms occasionally sounded awkward.
    Since the band lacked any real songwriting resource from within, they were smart enough to look outside for material and had the good taste to plug into some of the era's best songwriters. While Three Dog Night's versions of the material may not have been definitive, they opened the door to the mass market's awareness of talented writers like Steve Winwood, Harry Nilsson, Robbie Robertson, Randy Newman, Hoyt Axton, Neil Young, Laura Nyro, and many others. Elton John and Bernie Taupin had their first US success with Three Dog Night's cover of "Lady Samantha." — *Rick Clark*

● **The Best of Three Dog Night** / 1983 / MCA ✦✦✦✦
This collection contains all of Three Dog Night's hits, plus a few key album tracks. Among the tracks included are "One," "Easy to Be Hard," "Eli's Coming," "Mama Told Me Not to Come," "Joy to the World," "Black & White," "Shambala," "An Old-Fashioned Love Song," "Never Been to Spain," and "Celebrate." — *Rick Clark*

Celebrate: The Three Dog Night Story, 1965-1975 / 1993 / MCA ✦✦✦✦
A comprehensive double-disc anthology, *Celebrate* is necessary for devoted fans of Three Dog Night, but most listeners will be content with *The Best of Three Dog Night*, which features all of the hits on a single disc. — *AMG*

Throwing Muses

Alternative Pop-Rock
One of the quietly great college bands from the 1980s, Throwing Muses was formed in 1983 by guitarist/vocalist Kristin Hersh and her half-sister guitarist/vocalist Tanya Donelly (now of Belly) with a few friends from high school. In 1986 the group's debut album was put out by the prestigious British label 4AD; Throwing Muses were the first American band to be released on that label. Throwing Muses' angular, anguished, mercurial sound had much to do with Hersh's mental illness (she suffered from a form of bipolarity that caused her to hallucinate), especially on the early albums like *House Tornado*. 1991's *The Real Ramona* marked a break from the heaviness of the previous albums, with lots of shimmery pop gems penned both by Hersh and Donelly, who contributed at least one song an album throughout her stay in the band. Creative tensions between the two songwriters rose until Donelly left in 1992 to play with the Breeders and ultimately form Belly. That year Hersh reformed the Muses with drummer David Narcizo and released the band's fourth album, *Red Heaven*. After that, Hersh released a solo album and toured extensively, leaving fans to wonder about the status of the Muses. In

1995, however, Hersh and the rest of the Muses (Narcizo and bassist Bernard Georges) released *University,* one of the band's most cohesive and accessible efforts; *University* was followed by *Limbo* in 1996. Though Throwing Muses have had little commercial success throughout their career, they have released some of the most challenging and genuine music of recent years—and hopefully will continue to do so. —*Heather Phares*

Throwing Muses / 1986 / 4AD ✦✦✦✦
The band's eponymous first album is a startling, uncompromising collection of musings from Hersh and Donelly. Songs like "Hate My Way," "Call Me," and "Vicky's Box" feature mercurial dynamic and meter shifts. Hersh's guitar playing and voice are particularly dramatic; both swing from delicate melodicism to shrill atonality, especially on "Rabbits Dying" and "Delicate Cutters." Tanya Donelly contributes an ethereally beautiful love song in "Green." While this is not the most accessible album in the Muses' repertoire, it is an emotionally powerful and genuine one. —*Heather Phares*

Chains Changed [EP] / 1987 / 4AD ✦✦✦
The Fat Skier [EP] / 1988 / 4AD/Sire ✦✦✦
House Tornado / 1988 / 4AD/Sire ✦✦✦
House Tornado is a more melodic take on Throwing Muses' challenging style. Hersh's vocals are commanding and varied. But the Muses' pop side surfaces more on this album than on their previous work, particularly on tracks like "Juno," "Run Letter," and on Donelly's "Giant." Like their debut, this album is an acquired taste, but an ultimately rewarding one. —*Heather Phares*

Hunkpapa / 1990 / 4AD/Sire ✦✦
On the group's third full-length album and their second for Sire, Throwing Muses display a rare creative lull. Many of the songs are just not as powerful as their prior material, but the album is not a total loss. The wild, desolate "Bea" and explosive "Mania" are two of Hersh's finest songs, and Donelly's "Dragonhead" and "Angel" show her growing prowess as a songwriter. —*Heather Phares*

● **The Real Ramona** / 1991 / 4AD/Sire ✦✦✦✦
The Real Ramona is the Muses' finest pop moment. Hersh's material is some of her most melodic and accessible, yet it retains her unflinching honesty and emotional pull. "Counting Backwards," "Ellen West," "Hook in Her Head," and "Red Shoes" are both catchy and riveting works of songwriting. "Graffiti" and "Two-Step" are two of Hersh's most appealing pop snippets, and Donelly contributes two of the best songs she's ever written, the gleeful and giddy "Not Too Soon" and "Honeychain." Simply put, *The Real Ramona* is a great starting point for new Muses fans. —*Heather Phares*

Red Heaven / 1992 / 4AD/Sire ✦✦✦
The Muses' fourth album is their first as a trio, with Tanya Donelly exiting and original bassist Leslie Langston replacing Fred Abong. The material is more rock-oriented than on the Muses' lighter and more abstract material, especially on "Furious," "Firepile," and "Dio," on which Hersh duets with Bob Mould. "Summer St." is one of Hersh's most endearing songs, and tunes like "Carnival Wig" and "Earl" maintain her reputation as an inventive and thoughtful songwriter. —*Heather Phares*

University / 1995 / Sire/Reprise ✦✦✦✦
University, the group's most recent album, sees Hersh, drummer David Narcizo, and new bassist Bernard Georges grow into writing and playing material for a trio. The result is some of the group's most buoyant punk-pop music, with "Bright Yellow Gun," "Start," and "Shimmer" being the chief examples. The delicate melodies of "That's All You Wanted" and "Crabtown" and the intensity of "Fever Few" show that Hersh has not lost her creative edge. Another good introduction to the Muses' work, especially their post-Donelly material. —*Heather Phares*

Limbo / 1996 / Rykodisc ✦✦✦✦
Throwing Muses' album *Limbo* is their first on their self-owned record label, Throwing Music. Though it should be a celebration of the band's liberation from a major label that was a major disappointment, it's a strangely anticlimactic record. While a solid, well-written affair, it lacks the shimmery spark of the group's best material. The opening three songs—"Buzz," "Ruthie's Knocking," and "Freeloader"—get *Limbo* off to a propulsive start. But on the whole, the album suffers from similar rhythms and progressions on each song. *Limbo* is also poorly sequenced, with most of the louder songs on the first half, and the slower, quieter songs sinking to the end of the album. The result isn't so much limbo as it is déjà vu—it's ironic that a band that started out as wildly mercurial is now edging towards predictability. There are moments worthy of vintage Throwing Muses on *Limbo,* however. "Tango" and "Serene" are subtly edgy, "Night Driving" is a dreamy ballad, and "Shark" closes the album on a malevolent note. *Limbo* is a Throwing Muses album, after all. But for that to mean something so predictably peculiar is somewhat disappointing. —*Heather Phares*

'Til Tuesday

New Wave, Pop-Rock
Aimee Mann was the lead singer and bass player in the Boston-based 'Til Tuesday, which scored a Top Ten hit with "Voices Carry" and a gold-selling album of the same name in 1985. The rest of the group was Michael Hausmann, drums; Robert Holmes, guitar; and Joey Pesce, keyboards. The group recorded two more albums but broke up after *Everything's Different Now* in 1988. —*William Ruhlmann*

Voices Carry / 1985 / Epic ✦✦✦✦
'Til Tuesday showed a lot of promise with this debut album, which focused on Aimee Mann's emotive singing, notably on the title track. —*William Ruhlmann*

Welcome Home / 1986 / Epic ✦✦✦
● **Everything's Different Now** / 1988 / Epic ✦✦✦✦
Til Tuesday's final album is their best record, showcasing Aimee Mann's emergence as a songwriter capable of impeccably crafted guitar-pop gems. —*Stephen Thomas Erlewine*

Time

Funk, Urban
From their origins as Prince's first pet project to their self-produced funk-rock oeuvre, the Time has been a fascinating and outrageous congregation. Vocalist Morris Day infused his cocky, swaggering personality into dance hits that would make Rufus Thomas envious and, unlike most of the competition, the band managed to do something unique with Prince's genre-busting innovations. Time broke up in the late '80s, with Day going on to a somewhat disastrous solo career, Jesse Johnson crafting two dazzling solo albums, and Jimmy Jam and Terry Lewis becoming one of the most successful production teams this side of Gamble-Huff, working with everyone from Full Force and Janet Jackson to the S.O.S. Band and Human League. The group re-formed in 1990 and released the excellent *Pandemonium.* —*John Floyd*

The Time / 1981 / Warner Bros. ✦✦✦
● **What Time Is It?** / 1982 / Warner Bros. ✦✦✦✦
After a tentative debut, the Time bounced back with one of 1982's best dance albums, full of hilarious stompers and braggadocio ballads. —*John Floyd*

Ice Cream Castle / 1984 / Warner Bros. ✦✦✦✦
Ice Cream Castle finds the band stepping out of Prince's purple shadow and discovering their own personality. The relentless "Jungle Love" is their best song. —*John Floyd*

Pandemonium / 1990 / Paisley Park ✦✦

Toad the Wet Sprocket

Folk-Rock, Pop-Rock
Toad the Wet Sprocket's second-generation, R.E.M.-derived guitar-pop made them stars in 1992, with the gentle, highly melodic *Fear.* Although they released two albums before their commercial breakthrough, they hadn't yet developed a signature style; with *Fear* the band's songwriting improved and their sound developed into a graceful, folk-rock that incorporated the band's influences instead of mimicking them. Both radio and MTV played the singles "All I Want" and "Walk on the Ocean" constantly, making the album a hit. In 1994, the band released *Dulcinea,* which was a hit upon its release, thanks to the single, "Fall Down." —*Sara Sytsma*

Bread & Circus / 1989 / Columbia ✦✦✦
Pale / 1990 / Columbia ✦✦✦✦
Pale improved on the formula Toad the Wet Sprocket sketched out on their debut, *Bread and Circus,* since the band contributed a set of stronger songs with catchier melodies. —*Sara Sytsma*

● **Fear** / 1991 / Columbia ✦✦✦✦
Since their first release, *Bread and Circus,* Toad has grown dramatically as players and song crafters. *Fear* is the pleasant result of these developments. It contains the Top 40/alternative hit single "All I Want"; the opening track, "Walk on the Ocean," is another highlight. —*Rick Clark*

Dulcinea / 1994 / Columbia ✦✦✦
In Light Syrup / Oct. 24, 1995 / Columbia ✦✦✦

Tommy Tutone

New Wave, Power-Pop, Pop-Rock
Tommy Tutone were an early-'80s power-pop band led by vocalist Tommy Heath and guitarist Jim Keller. The group's first single, 1980's "Angel Say No," scraped the bottom of the American Top 40, yet it was 1981's "867-5309/Jenny" that sent the group to the top of the charts. Peaking in early 1982, the single hit No. 4 and went gold. Tommy Tutone was never able to duplicate that success and the band broke up after the release of their third album, 1983's *National Emotion.* —*Stephen Thomas Erlewine*

Tommy Tutone / 1980 / Columbia ✦✦✦✦
Main songwriters Jim Keller and Tom Heath show a rare talent for writing catchy hooks and memorable melodies on this fine debut. Despite a considerable promotional push from Columbia and no shortage of quality material, this record lacked the extra something needed to distinguish it from the masses of similar sounding bands of the time. The single, "Angel Say No," was a minor US hit. —*Chris Woodstra*

● **Tommy Tutone 2** / 1981 / Columbia ✦✦✦✦
The band's breakthrough features the unforgettable "867-5309/Jenny" and its lesser follow-up, "Which Man Are You," along with a batch of similar sounding originals. *Tommy Tutone 2* is consistently fun, hard-driving, working-class power-pop that was unfortunately overshadowed by the smash hit single. —*Chris Woodstra*

National Emotion / 1983 / Columbia ✦✦✦

Tomorrow

Psychedelic
In the early days of British psychedelia, three bands were consistently cited as first-generation figureheads of the London-based underground sound: Pink Floyd, the Soft Machine, and Tomorrow. Pink Floyd became superstars, and the Soft Machine, influential cult legends, but Tomorrow is mostly remembered (if at all) for featuring Steve Howe as their lead guitarist in his pre-Yes days. That's a pity, as Tomorrow were nearly the equal of the two more celebrated outfits. With the early Floyd and Softs, they shared a propensity for flower-power whimsy. Though they were less recklessly innovative and imaginative, their songwriting was accomplished, with adroit harmonies, psychedelic guitar work, and adventurous structures and tempo changes. They never succumbed to mindless indulgence or jamming; indeed, their tracks were rather short and tightly woven in comparison with most psychedelic bands. A couple of singles (especially "My White Bicycle") were underground favorites, but the group only managed to record one album before breaking up in 1968. Lead singer Keith West, even before the breakup, had a No. 2 British hit with "Excerpt from a Teenage Opera," which helped inspire Pete Townshend's *Tommy*. Drummer Twink joined the Pretty Things and, later, the Pink Fairies. —*Richie Unterberger*

● **Tomorrow** / 1968 / Decal ✦✦✦✦
Tomorrow's sole album was a solid effort, with quite a few first-rate tracks. "My White Bicycle" was one of the first songs to prominently feature backwards guitar phasing, "Real Life Permanent Dream" has engaging English harmonies and sitar riffs, "Revolution" is an infectious hippie anthem, and "Now Your Time Has Come" features intricate riffing from Steve Howe. "Hallucinations," with its irresistible melody, gentle harmonies, and affectingly trippy lyrics, was perhaps their best track. The more self-conscious English whimsy—populated by jolly little dwarfs, Auntie Mary's dress shop, colonels, and the like—is less successful, although the band's craftsmanship is strong enough to avoid embarrassment. The 1986 reissue of this album features detailed liner notes and the worthy B-side "Claremont Lake," though unfortunately West's sappy but influential "Excerpt from a Teenage Opera" was deleted. —*Richie Unterberger*

Tony! Toni! Tone!

Urban
Brothers Dwayne and Raphael Wiggins and cousin Timothy Christian have proven themselves durable guardians of the soul and funk tradition, while also infusing their music with enough contemporary devices to remain popular. This Oakland trio scored a No. 1 R&B hit right out of the box in 1988 with "Little Walter," a song that generated some criticism from gospel audiences for its use of the melody from "Wade in the Water." But they've since been able to keep things going on their own, as their LPs, *The Revival* in 1990 and *Sons of Soul* in 1993, have also been enormously successful. —*Ron Wynn*

Who? / Jan. 1988 / Wing ✦✦✦

The Revival / 1990 / Wing ✦✦✦✦
The trio followed their fine debut album with an even more polished and better produced second effort. "Feels Good" was an uptempo, hook-laden hit, while "It Never Rains in Southern California" was a nicely sung, elegantly arranged, and tightly performed ballad, and a sign that they were real craftsmen rather than trendy followers. "The Blues" expressed their love for vintage music, while "Whatever You Want" was another style tune that displayed genuine style and compositional depth. —*Ron Wynn*

● **Sons of Soul** / 1993 / PolyGram 3145 ✦✦✦✦
With their third album, Tony! Toni! Tone! received their greatest chart success, without compromising their music; it was still the finely crafted, highly eclectic and funky pop-soul that distinguished their first two albums, while the band's songwriting and playing had improved. The result was the band's most successful album yet, both commercially and successfully. —*Stephen Thomas Erlewine*

Tornados

Instrumental Rock
A fascinating footnote in '60s rock, the Tornados topped the charts in both Britain and the US in 1962 with their instrumental classic "Telstar." Inspired by the American satellite, this haunting, otherworldly tune—with its inimitable piercing clavioline, harp-like glissandos, outerspace sound effects, and mysterious wordless chanting near the end—was probably Joe Meek's finest production. It was also the first British rock 'n' roll record to top the charts in the US, beating the Beatles by a full year.

The Tornados were actually a group of British sessionmen that Meek had been using on his independently produced recordings. Quite a few Meek-produced singles followed in the next few years, all employing piercing organ and mysterious percolating percussion, sounding like nothing so much as pre-psychedelic roller-rink music. None of them came close to matching the majestic "Telstar"; in fact, they were usually pretty thin and gimmicky, although tracks like "Ridin' the Wind," "Love and Fury," and "Blue, Blue, Blue Beat" fascinate with their spectral, shimmering organs. The Tornados never entered the US Top 40 again, though they had more Top 20 hits at home in 1963 with "Globetrotter," "Ice Cream Man," and "Robot." Bassist Heinz Burt departed in 1963 for brief stardom as a Meek-produced solo vocalist. —*Richie Unterberger*

Away from It All / 1963 / Castle ✦✦

● **Telstar: The Original Sixties Hits of the Tornados** / 1994 / Music Club ✦✦✦✦
All you could possibly want to hear: both sides of the nine singles they cut for Decca between 1962 and 1964, along with the small US hit "Ridin' the Wind" and a cut from a soundtrack LP. A fun, if slight, document of one of the most distinctive instrumental rock groups of the early '60s, with thorough liner notes. —*Richie Unterberger*

Toto

Soft Rock, Pop-Rock
Formed in 1978, Toto immediately became favorites on FM rock and pop formats with their million-selling mainstream rocker "Hold the Line," followed by the mildly funky "Georgy Porgy." Their sound, honed from years of session work, had a steely precision that, while sounding impressive, seemed bloodless. Nevertheless, their fourth album, *Toto IV* (1983), became the biggest album of their career, earning six Grammy awards. During this time, Toto continued doing session work for many artists, in a sense defining much of the sound of radio during the mid-'80s. —*Rick Clark*

Toto IV / Apr. 1982 / Columbia ✦✦✦✦
This is the album that cleaned up at the 1982 Grammys. Most of *Toto IV* is a seamless collection of precision-crafted hard rockers and power ballads. The album contains five hits, the biggest being "Africa," "Rosanna," and "I Won't Hold You Back." —*Rick Clark*

● **Past to Present 1977-1990** / Sep. 1990 / Columbia ✦✦✦✦
Toto's compilation is to be recommended in that it contains all four of the group's Top-Ten hit singles—"Hold the Line," "Rosanna," "Africa," and "I Won't Hold You Back." It also contains four more of Toto's 14 pop chart singles—"Georgy Porgy," "99," "I'll Be over You," and "Pamela." But that means it leaves out six chart entries, including the Top 40 hits "Make Believe," "Stranger in Town," and "Without Your Love." In their place are an album track from the most recent album, *The Seventh One*, and four newly recorded songs co-written and sung by the group's fourth lead vocalist, Jean-Michel Byron, who is more soulful than his predecessors, but no more memorable. As such, this is not the ideal Toto best-of and earns its "pick" designation over Toto IV only by virtue of its inclusion of the group's first hit, "Hold the Line." —*William Ruhlmann*

Allen Toussaint

b. 1938
Piano, Vocals / R&B, New Orleans R&B
His inherently funky piano work heavily influenced by his Crescent City forefathers—Professor Longhair, Huey "Piano" Smith, and Fats Domino—and with a heavy dose of Ray Charles, a young visionary named Allen Toussaint almost singlehandedly fashioned a fresh, vital New Orleans R&B sound for the early '60s. Earning a vaunted reputation as a session pianist, Toussaint debuted on vinyl in 1958 with an obscure RCA album whimsically billed as "A. Tousan." When Joe Banashak inaugurated his Minit label in 1960, Toussaint joined the firm as A&R man and quickly proved himself the ultimate behind-the-scenes wizard on the New Orleans scene. During the early-to mid-'60s, Toussaint tirelessly wrote, arranged, produced, and played on hits by Ernie K-Doe, Irma Thomas, Jessie Hill, Chris Kenner, Barbara George, Lee Dorsey, Benny Spellman, the Showmen, and many more, his rolling keyboards vital to the charm of virtually all of them. After unleashing the Meters on the world, Toussaint finally began to step out as a front man in 1970, although his

low-key vocals have never achieved quite the same level of success as his previous productions for others. His brilliant compositions have been covered by everyone from Herb Alpert & the Tijuana Brass to Robert Palmer and Bonnie Raitt. Allen Toussaint's stature as a New Orleans musical giant endures.

Allen Toussaint found a new audience in 1994 when he joined country legend Chet Atkins for an updated rendition of "Southern Nights" on the CD *Rhythm, Country and Blues. —Bill Dahl*

Toussaint / 1971 / Scepter ◆◆◆
New Orleans production and performing wizard Allen Toussaint launched his solo career with this early-'70s release. But for some strange reason, the same performer who's written and produced marvelous material for Irma Thomas, Lee Dorsey, Chocolate Milk, and General Johnson among others, was never able to score the same success working as a lead act. There was nothing on this album even in the same arena as his classic R&B tunes, and throughout Toussaint's run of solo releases, only the song "Southern Nights," which Glen Campbell made a hit, could be even mentioned in the same sentence with Toussaint classics like "Ride Your Pony" or "It Will Stand." —*Ron Wynn*

● **Allen Tousaint Collection** / 1991 / Reprise ◆◆◆◆
A representative cross-section of the legendary New Orleans piano man's solo output—uneven but interesting. —*Bill Dahl*

The Complete "Tousan" Sessions / 1992 / Bear Family ◆◆◆◆
A compilation of instrumentals from 1958 and 1959 featuring Toussaint at the top of his form, *The Complete "Tousan" Sessions* is a wonderful portrait of the seminal New Orleans pianist; it's also the first time this material has ever been available on CD. —*Stephen Thomas Erlewine*

Pete Townshend

b. May 19, 1945, London, England
Guitar / Rock 'n' roll
Pete Townshend was the guitarist and songwriter for the Who from 1964 to 1982. Best-known for his conceptual works, he wrote *Tommy* and *Quadrophenia* for the group. Townshend made his first, tentative solo album, *Who Came First*, in 1972. Dedicated to his guru, Meher Baba, the album continued themes pursued in the previous Who album, *Who's Next*, and contained material from an abortive conceptual work, *Lifehouse*. The album sold modestly. In 1976, Townshend made a duo album, *Rough Mix*, with Ronnie Lane, formerly the bassist in the Small Faces.

Townshend's first full-fledged solo effort, however, was *Empty Glass* (1980), which sold half a million copies, reached the Top Five, and featured the Top Ten hit "Let My Love Open the Door," as well as the minor hits "A Little Is Enough" and "Rough Boys." Townshend followed this in 1982 with *All the Best Cowboys Have Chinese Eyes.*

Following the demise of the Who, Townshend released *Scoop*, a two-disc collection of demos, in 1983 (a second volume appeared in 1987). In 1985 he returned to thematic efforts with the album *White City—A Novel*, which included the Top 30 single "Face the Face." In the same year, Townshend published a book of short stories, *Horse's Neck*. As part of the *White City* project, Townshend appeared in an accompanying film, for which he organized a band called Pete Townshend's Deep End. The unit played only a few gigs, but one was videotaped and recorded, resulting in the 1986 album *Pete Townshend's Deep End Live!* In 1989, Townshend released an album based on Ted Hughes' children's story, *The Iron Man*. The record featured guest vocals by John Lee Hooker and Nina Simone, as well as two tracks featuring the three surviving members of the Who. Simultaneous with the album's release, Townshend embarked on a reunion tour with the Who.

Although the reunion tour was successful, it didn't help *The Iron Man* at all. Four years later, Townshend delivered *Psychoderelict* to mixed reviews and lukewarm sales. By that time, he had successfully reinvented himself as a Broadway tunesmith—the Broadway production of *The Who's Tommy* had become a runaway hit, earning Townshend a Tony and prompting him to pursue more stage musicals. —*William Ruhlmann*

Who Came First / 1972 / Rykodisc ◆◆◆
Pete Townshend's first solo album was a homespun, charming forum for low-key, personal songs that weren't deemed suitable for the Who, as well as spiritual paeans (direct and indirect) to his spiritual guru, Meher Baba. Who fans will be immediately attracted by the presence of a couple of songs from the aborted Who concept album *Lifehouse* (much of which ended up on *Who's Next*), "Pure & Easy" and "Let's See Action." The Who did eventually release their own versions of both those songs. But Townshend's own versions aren't the highlights of this record, which shows a folkier and gentler side to the Who's chief muse than his albums with the group. "Sheraton Gibson" is a neat tune about rock 'n' roll road life, and "Time Is Passing" takes very subtle inspiration from Baba. Most of the rest of the album contains some of the most unusual pieces Townshend has released: his acoustic cover of Jim Reeves' "There's a Heartache Following Me" (recorded because it was one of Baba's favorite tunes), "Evolution" (which is actually pretty much a solo track by his buddy Ronnie

Lane of the Faces), "Parvardigar" (adapted from Baba's Universal Prayer), and "Content" (a philosophical poem by Maud Kennedy that Townshend put to music). The 1993 reissue of this LP for compact disc fleshes out the program considerably with six previously unreleased tracks, including Townshend's demo of the Who single "The Seeker." The other bonus cuts are by no means filler; meditative and melancholy originals, they're just as strong as the tracks on the original release. —*Richie Unterberger*

Rough Mix / 1977 / Atco ◆◆◆
Pete Townshend and Ronnie Lane rock it up, with some good melodies thrown in. Tops among Townshend's non-Who projects. —*Bruce Eder*

★ **Empty Glass** / 1980 / Atco ◆◆◆◆◆
A bright, energetic rock album, tightly played and sung in a manner equalling the best Who albums. —*Bruce Eder*

All the Best Cowboys Have Chinese Eyes / 1982 / Atco ◆◆◆
Pete Townshend followed his pop breakthrough *Empty Glass* with *All the Best Cowboys Have Chinese Eyes*, his most ambitious and difficult album. Abandoning conventional pop structures, Townshend creates a long, twisting soundscapes with intricate, synth-based arrangements and dense poetry. For some, the self-conscious poetry and obtuse, winding melody lines are nearly impenetrable, but the album features some of his most intriguing and beautiful work, including the cascading "The Sea Refuses No River" and "Uniforms." —*Stephen Thomas Erlewine*

Scoop / 1983 / Atco ◆◆◆◆
Townshend's first batch of Who demos. Not viscerally exciting, but musically intriguing. —*Bruce Eder*

White City: A Novel / 1985 / Atco ◆◆◆
After the experimental *All the Best Cowboys Have Chinese Eyes*, Pete Townshend returned to a more traditional form of concept album with *White City*. Built around a loose narrative concerning urban despair, the album doesn't work very well conceptually, yet a handful of the individual songs are among his finest solo work, including the punchy "Face the Face" and the anthemic "Give Blood." —*Stephen Thomas Erlewine*

Pete Townshend's Deep End Live! / 1986 / Atco ◆◆◆◆
An energetic live album featuring a handful of R&B classics (including "Barefootin' "), a few Who chestnuts, and some of his best solo work, *Pete Townshend's Deep End Live!* is the tightest rock 'n' roll record he released as a solo artist. —*Stephen Thomas Erlewine*

Another Scoop / 1987 / Atco ◆◆◆◆
The second batch of Who demos, with better songs than the first. Some surprises for the serious fan. —*Bruce Eder*

The Iron Man: A Musical / 1989 / Atlantic ◆◆

Psychoderelict / Jun. 15, 1993 / Atlantic ◆◆

Coolwalkingsmoothtalkingstraightsmokingfirestoking: Best Of / Apr. 1996 / Atlantic ◆◆◆◆
Despite some unnecessary problems, *coolwalkingsmoothtalkingstraightsmokingfirestoking: The Best of Pete Townshend* is a good sampling of Townshend's biggest solo hits, as well as some of the songwriter's personal favorites. One of the major problems of the collection is Townshend's inability to leave the original mixes alone—for instance, there are two versions of "Let My Love Open the Door" and neither of them is the original version. Furthermore, some tracks have longer mixes, others are shorter, and occasionally the mixes are significantly different from the album. Even with these problems, the album provides a good idea of the arc of Townshend's solo career, making it an adequate starting point for neophytes. For dedicated fans, it's a very frustrating release—not only is it baited with the unreleased *Psychoderelict* outtake "Uneasy Street" and the "E. Cola mix" of "Let My Love Open the Door," the remixes and edits are awkward for those intimately familiar with the tracks. Which means *The Best of Pete Townshend* is best as a sampler, not as a definitive retrospective. —*Stephen Thomas Erlewine*

Traffic

Art-Rock/Progressive-Rock, Psychedelic, Pop-Rock
Among all the bands to emerge from England in the '60s, Traffic is one of the few who have aged gracefully.

At the time of Traffic's inception in 1967, former Spencer Davis bandmate Stevie Winwood (b. May 12, 1948) was its most noted member, but with the release of their debut, *Mr. Fantasy*, it became clear that this was truly a band of four equally creative multi-instrumentalists. Their initial efforts fused an ecumenical range of musical genres through a fairly psychedelic sensibility, most of it among the best examples of that approach to late-'60s pop-rock. Guitarist and vocalist Dave Mason (b. May 10, 1947) penned some particularly strong material on those first Traffic albums, especially "Feelin' Alright," a song that was later popularized by Joe Cocker, Three Dog Night, and many others.

After many instances of quitting the band over creative differences (the remaining three were resistant to his obvious pop tendencies), Mason left for good after 1971's *Welcome to the Canteen* (No. 26), a live album. By then, he had already earned a gold album for his 1970 debut, *Alone Together* (No. 22).

After their second self-titled album, Traffic parted ways when Winwood joined the short-lived supergroup, Blind Faith. After Blind Faith's demise, Winwood began a solo effort, tentatively titled *Mad Shadows*. As the project developed, Winwood increasingly sought the input of Chris Wood and Jim Capaldi. The result was the funkier, earthier *John Barleycorn Must Die* (No. 5).

Traffic's studio follow-up, *The Low Spark of High Heeled Boys* (No. 7), incorporated a spacier, improvisational sound. The title cut became an FM rock-radio standard. Several more albums followed, and the band parted ways in 1974.

Wood died on July 12, 1983, of liver failure. Capaldi and Dave Mason have experienced sporadically successful solo careers. Winwood, on the other hand, has had a long and profitable string of releases.

When Winwood's solo career began to sag in 1994, he re-formed with Capaldi; Mason didn't participate, choosing to stay in Fleetwood Mac. While the album proved a commercial disappointment, the reunited Traffic tour was successful, although neither proved exciting. *— Rick Clark*

☆ **Mr. Fantasy** / Jan. 1967 / Island ✦✦✦✦✦
Produced by Jimmy Miller (Rolling Stones, Spooky Tooth, Blind Faith), *Mr. Fantasy* is sonically decked out in *Sgt. Pepper*-period psychedelic splendor. Although much music of the period sounds quite dated, *Mr. Fantasy* and the self-titled follow-up have aged gracefully. This is in no small part due to Dave Mason's refined pop sensibilities. Even though he occasionally gets lost in a sea of sitars ("Utterly Simple"), Mason gives the material much of the form and restraint that latter-period Traffic, at times, desperately needed. Even Winwood turns in some of the tightest pop-song constructions in his career, thanks to Jim Capaldi and Chris Wood's co-writing input. The band's almost whimsical approach to integrating its eclectic influences keeps the material sounding fresh, too. Traffic's hodgepodge of psychedelia always sounds like the product of a band that really plays together rather than existing as a studio concoction. Check out "Coloured Rain" or the title cut for an example. *— Rick Clark*

★ **Traffic** / Feb. 1968 / Island ✦✦✦✦✦
It's songs like "Feelin' Alright," "Pearly Queen," "You Can All Join In," "Vagabond Virgin," and "40,000 Headmen" that make Traffic's self-titled second effort a classic. Although not quite as trippy as their debut, most of the sonic observations mentioned for *Mr. Fantasy* apply here. *— Rick Clark*

Last Exit / Jan. 1969 / Island ✦✦✦

John Barleycorn Must Die / Jan. 1970 / Island ✦✦✦✦
Upon the demise of the short-lived supergroup project Blind Faith, Stevie Winwood began work on a solo album entitled *Mad Shadows*. As the project developed, it evolved into a Traffic reunion of sorts, as Winwood brought in Wood and Capaldi. The result, *John Barleycorn Must Die*, became an instant success, with its lengthy funky, R&B, jazz, and folk explorations. The playing is top-notch throughout, with Wood blowing some inspired sax, Capaldi laying down the trademark fluid percussion grooves, and Winwood's Hammond B3 and piano work in peak form. "Glad," "Freedom Rider," "Empty Pages," and the title cut are the highlights. *— Rick Clark*

The Low Spark of High Heeled Boys / Jan. 1971 / Island ✦✦✦
Opening with the pastoral "Hidden Treasure," *Low Spark* flows effortlessly, almost lazily, to the last song, "Rainmaker." The band does shake things up a little with "Rock & Roll Stew" and "Light Up or Leave Me Alone." The title cut, at over 12 minutes of spacey jamming, is one of Traffic's most well-known FM hits. *— Rick Clark*

Welcome to the Canteen / Feb. 1971 / Island ✦✦✦

Shoot out at the Fantasy Factory / 1973 / Island ✦✦✦
The title cut has its moments, but the augmentation of Muscle Shoals studio heavies Barry Beckett, Roger Hawkins, and David Hood ultimately turned down most of the remaining sparks in search of the eternal groove. *— Rick Clark*

When the Eagle Flies / 1974 / Asylum ✦✦

Smiling Phases / 1991 / Island ✦✦✦✦
Island remastered the tracks included in this double-disc anthology, and the difference is remarkable. Except for a few curious omissions, this is absolutely essential. *— Rick Clark*

Far from Home / May 3, 1994 / Virgin America ✦✦✦✦

Trammps

Soul, Disco
Disco's most soulful vocal group began in the '60s as the Volcanos, and were also called the Moods. Gene Faith was the original lead vocalist, with Earl Young, Jimmy Ellis, guitarist Dennis Harris, keyboardist Ron Kersey, organist John Hart, bassist Stanley Wade, and drummer Michael

Thomas. But by the time they'd gone through various identities and emerged as the Trammps in the mid-'70s, the lineup featured lead vocalist Ellis, Harold and Stanley Wade, Robert Upchurch, and Young. A snappy revival of Judy Garland's '40s tune "Zing Went the Strings of My Heart" was their first chart single, reaching No. 17 on the R&B list in 1972. Despite their well-deserved reputation and boisterous, jubilant harmonies and sound, the Trammps were never huge commercial successes even during disco's heyday. Indeed, they had only three R&B Top Ten hits from 1972 through 1978, and such wonderful records as "Soul Bones," "Ninety-Nine and a Half," and "I Feel Like I've Been Livin' (On the Dark Side of the Moon)" stiffed on the charts though they were beloved by club audiences and R&B fans alike. Their only huge hit was "Disco Inferno" in 1977, which was a No. 9 R&B single in 1977 and was also featured in *Saturday Night Fever*. Yet it missed the pop Top Ten, peaking at No. 11. But The Trammps' prowess can't be measured by chart popularity; Jimmy Ellis' booming, joyous vocals brilliantly championed the celebratory fervor and atmosphere that made disco both beloved and hated among music fans. *— Ron Wynn*

● **The Best of the Trammps** / 1978 / Atlantic ✦✦✦✦
A good collection of the band's best tracks, including the monolithic "Disco Inferno" and "Disco Party." *— Stephen Thomas Erlewine*

Translator

New Wave
Translator was formed in Los Angeles in 1979 by Steven Barton (guitar, vocals), Robert Darlington (guitar, vocals), Larry Dekker (bass), and David Scheff (drums). They moved to San Francisco in 1980, where they signed to Howie Klein's 415 Records and released their debut album, *Heartbeats and Triggers*, in 1982. It was followed by *No Time like Now* (1983), *Translator* (1985), and *Evening of the Harvest* (1986). But despite favorable critical notices, Translator failed to attract a mass audience, and the group broke up in 1986. A decade later, when their first CD compilation, *Everywhere That We Were . . . The Best of Translator*, was released, they had begun to seem like one of the precursors to alternative rock. *— William Ruhlmann*

Translation / 1995 / Oglio ✦✦✦✦
Translator's *Translation* is a set of infectious new-wave pop. Although it's slightly inconsistent, it does contain the gem "Everywhere That I'm Not." *— Stephen Thomas Erlewine*

● **Everywhere That We Were: Best Of** / Mar. 26, 1996 / Columbia/Legacy ✦✦✦✦
In the mid-'80s, Translator, with its short, peppy songs, catchy guitar riffs, and strong harmonies, provided by its two in-house songwriters, Steven Barton and Robert Darlington, sounded like a pleasant throwback to *Beatles 65*. Despite such strong and immediately memorable material as Barton's "Everywhere That I'm Not" and Darlington's "Everywhere," both found on their debut album *Heartbeats and Triggers* and repeated here, the group never broke through, but ten years later this 17-track, one-hour compilation demonstrates that they were just as much ahead of their time as after it. Catchy pop-rock has perennial appeal, and if it's too late for Translatormania, *Everywhere That We Were* demonstrates that it was being made as well in the '80s as it is now. *— William Ruhlmann*

The Trashmen

Rock 'n' roll, Surf, Garage Rock
A Minneapolis rock 'n' roll band, they evolved from a group Jim Thaxter & The Travelers, recording one single under that name ("Sally Jo"/ "Cyclone"). The group comprises Tony Andreason (lead guitar), Dan Winslow (guitar/ vocals), Bob Reed (bass), and Steve Wahrer (drums/vocals). Unfairly depicted as a novelty act, the Trashmen were in actuality a top-notch rock 'n' roll combo, enormously popular on the teen-club circuit, playing primarily surf music to a landlocked Minnesota audience. Drummer Steve Wahrer combined two songs by the Rivingtons ("The Bird's the Word" and "Pa Pa Ooh Mow Mow"), added freakish vocal effects and a pounding rhythm to the mix, and, by early 1964, the group was in the Top Ten nationwide with "Surfin' Bird." Though the group continued to release great follow-up singles and an excellent album, their moment in the sun had come and gone; they disbanded by late 1967/ early 1968. They re-formed in the mid-'80s and continued to play locally until Wahrer's death. The Trashmen are revered by '60s collectors as one of the great American teen-band combos of all time, their lone hit exemplifying wild, unabashed rock 'n' roll at its most demented, bare-bones-basic, lone-E-chord finest. *— Cub Koda*

Surfin' Bird / 1964 / Sundazed ✦✦✦✦
The only album released by the group during their lifetime actually outstrips most of the Southern California-based competition, due to the ferocious grit of the playing and a vaguely demented, go-for-broke recklessness. A good mix of instrumentals and vocals, though nothing else is on the level of the title cut; the CD reissue adds demos of "Surfin' Bird" and "Bird Dance Beat," and a couple of rare singles. *— Richie Unterberger*

- **Best of the Trashmen** / 1992 / Sundazed ✦✦✦✦
The original *Surfin' Bird* album, plus all the original Garrett singles from that period. The perfect primer set. —*Cub Koda*
The Great Lost Trashmen Album! / 1994 / Sundazed ✦✦✦✦
Fine unreleased studio recordings. —*Cub Koda*
Live Bird '65-'67 / Sundazed ✦✦✦

The Tremeloes

British Invasion, Pop-Rock
Quartet most famous for being picked for a contract by England's Decca Records in early 1962 in place of the Beatles. They actually started long before the Beatles, but it wasn't until after the Liverpool quartet hit that they saw any success in England or America. Their biggest British success was a version of the Contours' "Do You Love Me," but the hottest number on their first album was a searing (by British standards) rendition of "I Want Candy," later popularized by the Strangeloves, whose Bo Diddley-based beat Bob Porter and company handled with admirable style. Poole later faded into obscurity, while the Tremeloes achieved success on their own. —*Bruce Eder*
Here Come the Tremeloes / 1967 / CBS ✦✦✦✦✦
A pleasant, upbeat collection with a jovial mood, but nothing as impressive as their Brian Poole-era "I Want Candy." (Out of print.) —*Bruce Eder*
- **Best of the Tremeloes** / 1992 / Rhino ✦✦✦✦✦
A generous twenty-track collection of the band's finest moments, it includes all of their US hits. —*AMG*

The Treniers

R&B, Jump Blues
Featuring twin brothers Cliff and Claude Trenier, the Treniers helped link swing music to rock 'n' roll with their brand of hot jump blues in the late '40s and early '50s. To the latter-day listener, their early '50s singles can sound closer to swing than rock; indeed, Cliff and Claude had once sung with the Jimmie Lunceford Orchestra. The group did anticipate some crucial elements of rock 'n' roll, though, with their solid, thumping beats, their squealing saxophone solos, and their song titles, such as "Rocking on Sunday Night," "Rockin' Is Our Business," and "It Rocks! It Rolls! It Swings!" The Treniers' brand of swing-cum-R&B was undoubtedly an influence on Bill Haley, who saw them when both acts were playing summer shows at Wildwood, NJ. Their best work was recorded for OKeh in the early '50s; by the middle of the decade, their sound was more R&B-oriented. Like many early R&B pioneers, they were unable to find success in the rock 'n' roll era, though they appeared in a few of the first rock 'n' roll films. —*Richie Unterberger*
- **They Rock! They Roll! They Swing!: The Best of the Treniers** / 1995 / Epic/Legacy ✦✦✦✦
This 20-track compilation has all of their key early- and mid-'50s OKeh singles (only one of which, "Go! Go! Go!," was actually an R&B hit), five previously unreleased songs, and their 1953 version of Bill Haley's "Rock-a-Beatin' Boogie," which must rank as one of the first (if not the very first) covers of a White rock song by a Black artist. —*Richie Unterberger*

T. Rex

Rock 'n' Roll, Glam Rock, Proto-Punk
Initially a British folk-rock combo called Tyrannosaurus Rex, T. Rex was the primary force in glam rock, thanks to the creative direction of guitarist/vocalist Marc Bolan (b. Marc Feld). Bolan created a deliberately trashy form of rock 'n' roll that was proud of its own disposability. T. Rex's music borrowed the underlying sexuality of early rock 'n' roll, adding dirty, simple grooves and fat, distorted guitars, as well as an overarching folkie/hippie spirituality that always came through the clearest on ballads. While most of his peers concentrated on making cohesive albums, Bolan kept the idea of a three-minute pop single alive in the early '70s. In Britain, he became a superstar, sparking a period of "T. Rextacy" among the pop audience with a series of Top Ten hits, including four No. 1 singles. Over in America, the group only had one major hit—the Top Ten "Bang a Gong (Get It On)"—before disappearing from the charts in 1973. T. Rex's popularity in the UK didn't begin to waver until 1975, yet they retained a devoted following until Marc Bolan's death in 1977. Over the next two decades, Bolan emerged as a cult figure and the music of T. Rex has proven quite influential on hard rock, punk, new wave, and alternative rock.

Following a career as a teenage model, Marc Bolan began performing music professionally in 1965, releasing his first single, "The Wizard," on Decca Records. Bolan joined the psychedelic folk-rock combo John's Children in 1967, appearing on three unsuccessful singles before the group disbanded later that year. Following the breakup, he formed the folk duo Tyrannosaurus Rex with percussionist Steve Peregrine Took. The duo landed a record deal with a subsidiary of EMI in February 1968, recording their debut album with producer Tony Visconti. "Debora," the

group's first single, peaked at No. 34 in May of that year, and their debut album, *My People Were Fair and Had Sky in Their Hair, but Now They're Content to Wear Stars on Their Brow*, reached No. 15 shortly afterward. The duo released their second album, *Prophets, Seers and Sages, the Angels of the Ages*, in November of 1968.

By this time, Tyrannosaurus Rex was building a sizable underground following, which helped Bolan's book of poetry, *The Warlock of Love*, enter the British best-seller charts. In the summer of 1969, the duo released their third album, *Unicorn*, as well as the single "King of the Rumbling Sprires," the first Tyrannosaurus Rex song to feature an electric guitar. Following an unsuccessful American tour that fall, Took left the band and was replaced by Mickey Finn. The new duo's third single did not chart, yet their first album, 1970's *A Beard of Stars*, reached No. 21.

The turning point in Bolan's career came in October of 1970, when he shortened the group's name to T. Rex and released "Ride a White Swan," a fuzz-drenched single driven by a rolling backbeat. "Ride a White Swan" became a major hit in the UK, climbing all the way to No. 2. The band's next album, *T. Rex*, peaked at No. 13 and stayed on the charts for six months. Encouraged by the results, Bolan expanded T. Rex to a full band, adding bassist Steve Currie and drummer Bill Legend (b. Bill Fifield). The new lineup recorded "Hot Love," which spent six weeks at No. 1 in early 1971. That summer, T. Rex released "Get It On" (retitled "Bang a Gong (Get It On)" in the US), which became their second straight UK No. 1; the single would go on to be their biggest international hit, reaching No. 10 in the US in 1972. *Electric Warrior*, the first album recorded by the full band, was released in the fall of 1971; it was No. 1 for six weeks in Britain and cracked America's Top 40.

By now, "T. Rextacy" was in full swing in England, as the band had captured the imaginations of both teenagers and the media with its sequined, heavily made-up appearance; the image of Marc Bolan in a top hat, feather boa, and platform shoes, performing "Get It On" on the BBC became as famous as his music. At the beginning of 1972, T. Rex signed with EMI, setting up a distribution deal for Bolan's own T. Rex Wax Co. record label. "Telegram Sam," the group's first EMI single, became their third No. 1 single. "Metal Guru" also hit No. 1, spending four weeks at the top of the chart. *The Slider*, released in the summer of 1972, shot to No. 1 upon its release, allegedly selling 100,000 copies in four days; the album was also T. Rex's most successful American release, reaching No. 17. Appearing in the spring of 1973, *Tanx* was another Top Five hit for T. Rex; the singles "20th Century Boy" and "The Groover" soon followed it to the upper ranks of the charts. However, those singles would prove to be the band's last two Top Ten hits. In the summer of 1973, rhythm guitarist Jack Green joined the band, as did three backup vocalists, including the American soul singer Gloria Jones; Jones would soon become Bolan's girlfriend. At the beginning of 1974, drummer Bill Legend left the group and was replaced by Davy Lutton, as Jones became the group's keyboardist.

In early 1974, the single "Teenage Dream" was the first record to be released under the name Marc Bolan and T. Rex. The following album, *Zinc Alloy and the Hidden Riders of Tomorrow*, was the last Bolan recorded with Tony Visconti. Throughout the year, T. Rex's popularity rapidly declined; "Teenage Dream" hit No. 13 early in the year, but by the time "Zip Gun Boogie" was released in November, it could only reach No. 41. Finn and Green left the group at the end of the year, while keyboardist Dino Dins joined. The decline of T. Rex's popularity was confirmed when 1975's *Bolan's Zip Gun* failed to chart. Bolan took the rest of the year off, returning in the spring of 1976 with *Futuristic Dragon*, which peaked at No. 50. Released in the summer of 1976, "I Love to Boogie," a disco-flavored three-chord thumper, became Bolan's last Top 20 hit.

Bolan released *Dandy in the Underworld* in the spring of 1977; it was a modest hit, peaking at No. 26. While "The Soul of My Suit" reached No. 42 on the charts, T. Rex's next two singles failed to chart. Sensing it was time for a change of direction, Bolan began expanding his horizons in August. In addition to contributing a weekly column for *Record Mirror*, he hosted his own variety television show, called *Marc*. Featuring guest appearances by artists like David Bowie and Generation X, *Marc* helped restore Bolan's hip image. Signing with RCA Records, the guitarist formed a new band with bassist Herbie Flowers and drummer Tony Newman, yet he never was able to record with the group. While driving home from a London club with Bolan, Gloria Jones lost control of her car, smashing into a tree. Marc Bolan, riding in the passenger's seat of the car, was killed instantly.

While T. Rex's music was intended to be disposable, it has proven surprisingly influential over the years. Hard-rock and heavy-metal bands borrowed the group's image, as well as the pounding insistence of their guitars. Punk bands may have discarded the high heels, feather boas, and top hats, yet they adhered to the simple three-chord structures and pop aesthetics that made the band popular. —*Stephen Thomas Erlewine*

T Rex / 1970 / Fly ✦✦✦
★ **Electric Warrior** / 1971 / Reprise ✦✦✦✦✦
Kicking off with the fat guitars of "Mambo Sun," *Electric Warrior* winds through all of Marc Bolan's obsessions, from sleazy teenage rock 'n' roll

to spacy mysticism. "Bang a Gong (Get It On)" was the well-deserved hit, full of lust and flamboyance, but it's by no means the only good thing here. With the trashy blues stomps of "Jeepster" and "Lean Woman Blues" sitting next to the space-age rock of "Monolith" and "Planet Queen," *Electric Warrior* has nothing but teenage kicks; it's glam rock at its absolute best. Without question, the definitive, classic T. Rex. — *Stephen Thomas Erlewine*

☆ **The Slider** / Jan. 1972 / Relativity ♦♦♦♦♦
Surprisingly, *The Slider* was T. Rex's highest-charting record, without the benefit of a hit single. Even without a hit, the record was a gas, powered by the killer riffs of "Baby Strange," "Buick Makane," and "Telegram Sam." *The Slider* offers nothing new—it's still the same trashy glam-rock that made *Electric Warrior* and *Tanx* sublime—but that's why it's special. No one else could get away with "Metal Guru," "Baby Boomerang," and "Chariot Choogle" without seeming like a fool. Bolan does it with style and grace, and with a wink. It's tremendous fun and the last great record he would ever make. — *Stephen Thomas Erlewine*

Tanx / Feb. 1973 / Relativity ♦♦♦♦
Although the songs are not quite as well-constructed as those on *Electric Warrior*, *Tanx* still finds Bolan and T. Rex in top form, storming through a set of songs that kick hard, like "Country Honey," swing, like "Mad Donna," and sigh, like "Brokenhearted Blues." It's prime T. Rex and a terrific record. — *Stephen Thomas Erlewine*

Zinc Alloy & the Hidden Riders / 1974 / Combat ♦♦
Coming after a series of well-constructed and best-selling albums, *Zinc Alloy & the Hidden Riders of Tomorrow* was a bit of a disappointment, with a good majority of the material seeming forced and incomplete, but the swaggering "Venus Loon" and "Teenage Dream" make up for the weaker moments. — *Stephen Thomas Erlewine*

Zip Gun / 1975 / EMI ♦♦
Bolan's Zip Gun was an improvement over the stilted, over-produced *Zinc Alloy*, featuring a relatively stripped-back production and a number of tight rockers, including "Light of Love" and "Token of My Love." — *Stephen Thomas Erlewine*

Futuristic Dragon / 1976 / Relativity ♦♦♦

Dandy in the Underworld / 1977 / Relativity ♦♦♦

20th Century Boy / 1985 / Relativity ♦♦♦

Essential Collection / 1991 / Relativity ♦♦
T. Rex is worthy of a great box set, but *The Essential Collection* isn't it. Bypassing all of Bolan's earlier folk work, the set has no cohesion—it's just a bunch of tracks piled together haphazardly. "Jeepster," not "Bang a Gong (Get It On)," is the only track from *Electric Warrior* to make the box, leaving their best record woefully underrepresented; instead, the box concentrates on the spottier records from the mid-'70s. Ultimately, *The Essential Collection* does a disservice to T. Rex. — *Stephen Thomas Erlewine*

Definitive Tyrannosaurus Rex / 1994 / Sequel ♦♦♦♦
Featuring over 20 tracks of prime Tyrannosaurus Rex material, *The Definitive Tyrannosaurus Rex* is indeed the definitive portrait of Marc Bolan's early years. — *Stephen Thomas Erlewine*

Tricky

b. 1964
Vocals / Alternative Pop-Rock, Trip-Hop
An inventive, colorful musician, Tricky began recording with the seminal hip-hop/techno outfit Massive Attack in 1990. In 1992, he discovered vocalist Martine and started recording tracks with her, and formed the group Tricky. Their sound is both hard-hitting and surprisingly ethereal, mixing the chatting rap style of Tricky with Martine's smooth yet slightly abrasive singing. Tricky samples Smashing Pumpkins, covers Public Enemy songs, and yet still remains entirely unique from the groups it is compared with, such as Massive Attack and Portishead. — *Heather Phares*

● **Maxinquaye** / 1995 / 4th & Broadway/Durban Poison ♦♦♦♦
Though he hates the label of trip-hop, Tricky's debut album *Maxinquaye* is one of the finest that the genre has to offer. "Ponderosa," "Suffocated Love," and "Pumpkin" are disturbing and beautiful, with ominous background noises and Martine's soaring vocals, while tracks like the group's cover of "Black Steel" show off their harder side. A striking debut, Tricky's *Maxinquaye* is only the beginning for this innovative artist. — *Heather Phares*

Nearly God / Apr. 29, 1996 / Fourth & Broadway/Durban Poison ♦♦♦♦
Nearly God is Tricky's unofficial second album—he calls it a collection of brilliant, incomplete demos. When Tricky signed his contract with Island, it allowed him to release an album a year under a different name and *Nearly God* is the first of these efforts. Tricky recorded the record with a diverse cast of collaborators—in addition to his partner Martina, there's Terry Hall, Björk, Neneh Cherry, Cath Coffey, Dedi Madden, and Alison Moyet (Damon Albarn pulled his track just before the album's release).

Building on the ghostly, dark soundscapes of Tricky's debut, *Maxinquaye*, *Nearly God* narrows the focus of his first record by making the music slower, hazier, and more disturbing. It's not as coherent as *Maxinquaye*, but that's part of its appeal. *Nearly God* is a haunting, fractured, surreal nightmare that doesn't always make sense, but never fails to make an impact. Certain collaborators work better than others—Tricky understands the eeriness of Terry Hall's voice, but he does nothing to tame Alison Moyet's inappropriate bluesy shrieking—but the overall effect of the album is quietly devastating. It gets under your skin and stays there. It's a brilliantly evocative nightmare. — *Stephen Thomas Erlewine*

Grassroots EP / Aug. 1996 / Ffrr ♦♦♦

The Troggs

British Invasion
Remembered chiefly as proto-punkers who reached the top of the charts with the "caveman rock" of "Wild Thing" (1966), the Troggs were also adept at crafting power-pop and ballads. Hearkening back to a somewhat simpler, more basic British Invasion approach as psychedelia began to explode in the late '60s, the group also reached the Top Five with their flower-power ballad "Love Is All Around" in 1968. While more popular in their native England than the US, the band also fashioned memorable, insistently riffing hit singles like "With a Girl like You," "Night of the Long Grass," and the notoriously salacious "I Can't Control Myself" between 1966 and 1968. Paced by Reg Presley's lusting vocals, the group—which composed most of their own material—could crunch with the best of them, but were also capable of quite a bit more range and melodic invention than they've been given credit for.

Hailing from the relatively unknown British town of Andover, the Troggs hooked up with manager/producer Larry Page (who was involved in the Kinks' early affairs) in the mid-'60s. After a flop debut single, they were fortunate enough to come across a demo of Chip Taylor's "Wild Thing" (which had already been unsuccessfully recorded by the Wild Ones). In the hands of the Troggs, "Wild Thing"—with its grungy chords and off-the-wall ocarina solo—became a primeval three-chord monster, famous not only in its original hit Troggs version, but in its psychedelic revamping by Jimi Hendrix, who used it to close his famous set at the 1967 Monterey Pop Festival.

"Wild Thing" made No. 1 in the States, but the Troggs' momentum there was impeded by a strange legal dispute that saw their early records simultaneously released on two different labels. Nor did it help that the band didn't tour the US for a couple of years. As a consequence, the fine follow-up singles "With a Girl like You" and "I Can't Control Myself" didn't do as well as they might have. In Britain, it was a different story—they were smashes, although "I Can't Control Myself" had such an open-hearted lust that it encountered resistance from conservative radio programmers all over the globe.

The Troggs tempered their image on subsequent ballads, which utilized a sort of pre-"power ballad" approach. These weren't bad, and a few of them were British hits, but they weren't as fine as the initial blast of singles that established the band's image. "Love Is All Around," which restored them to the American Top Ten in 1968, was their finest effort in this vein. It was also their final big hit on either side of the Atlantic.

But the Troggs would keep going for a long, long time. In a sense they were handicapped by their image—they were not intellectuals, certainly, but they weren't dumb either. They wrote most of their songs, and their albums were reasonably accomplished, if hardly up to the level of the Kinks or Traffic, containing some nifty surprises like the gothic ballad "Cousin Jane," or the tongue-in-cheek psychedelia of "Maybe the Madman." By 1970, though, they were struggling. They continued to release a stream of singles, most of which had a straightforward simplicity that was out of step with the progressive-rock of the time, all of which flopped, though some were fairly good.

The Troggs' image as lunkheads couldn't have been helped by the notorious *Troggs Tapes*, a 12-minute studio argument that was captured on tape while the band was unaware. The *Spinal Tap*-like dialog helped keep their cult alive, though, and as punk gained momentum in the mid-'70s, they gained belated appreciation as an important influence on bands like the Ramones and (earlier) the MC5. They found enough live work (sometimes on the punk/new-wave circuit) to keep going, although their intermittent records generally came to naught. In 1992, they rose to their highest profile in ages when three members of R.E.M., which had covered "Love Is All Around," backed the Troggs on the comeback album *Athens Andover*. — *Richie Unterberger*

● **The Best of the Troggs** / 1988 / PolyGram ♦♦♦♦
"Wild Thing" is the hit, but there's lots of good, raunchy rock here. — *Dan Heilman*

Archeology (1967-1977) / 1992 / Fontana ♦♦♦♦
A double-CD, 52-track box set that proves there was a lot more to the Troggs than "Wild Thing" and "Love Is All Around." This archetypally primitive British Invasion quartet scored many hits in the UK that barely

dented the charts in the US, like "With a Girl Like You," "Night of the Long Grass," and the notoriously racy "I Can't Control Myself." They're all here, along with notable album cuts, B-sides, and worldwide post-1968 flops. Primitive they may have been, but the Troggs—who wrote most of their own material—did not lack a flair for hard pop hooks, and could display a surprising delicacy in their ballads. Several of their obscure singles and album tracks are equal in worth to their hits, like the gothic but pretty "Cousin Jane," and the witty light psychedelia of "Maybe the Madman" and "Purple Shades." Some of the '70s hard rockers and glammish novelties are unimpressive, and 52 songs are arguably excessive. But there are a fair number of obscure gems to be found on this well-annotated package. —*Richie Unterberger*

Doris Troy

Vocals, Vocals (Background) / Soul

Surely one of the most talented one-hit wonders of the rock era, Doris Troy hit the Top Ten with "Just One Look" in 1963, but also recorded many other fine pop-soul sides for Atlantic between 1963 and 1965. Unlike many soul performers of the time, Troy wrote most of her own material (under the pseudonym Payne), and had already written for other artists, and sung backup with Dionne and Dee Dee Warwick and Cissy Houston on New York soul records, before striking out on her own. More melodically ambitious and stylistically eclectic than many of her peers, her Atlantic sides blend elements of gospel, girl group, blues, and pop into a rich New York soul sound. Troy never reached the charts again after "Just One Look," but was more appreciated in England, where she toured occasionally, and where the Hollies covered her "What'cha Gonna Do About It" on their first album. Moving to Britain, she recorded an album for Apple in 1970 with assistance from George Harrison and Billy Preston. In the early '70s, she sang backup vocals for British rock groups, as well as recording a couple more albums. In the '80s, she starred in *Mama I Want to Sing*, a musical based on her life story. —*Richie Unterberger*

Doris Troy / 1970 / Capitol ♦♦♦

● **Just One Look: The Best of Doris Troy** / 1994 / Ichiban Soul Classics ♦♦♦♦

This 21-track anthology of her 1963-65 Atlantic sides is as comprehensive as one could ask for. It includes all of her singles, her rare album, three cuts only issued on British singles, and her rare 1965 single for the Calla label, "I'll Do Anything (He Wants Me to Do)." Besides "Just One Look," there are quite a few other downright excellent lost gems here: "What'cha Gonna Do About It," the bluesy "Draw Me Closer," the driving "You'd Better Stop" (with a fierce guitar break that sounds like a young Jimmy Page), and the soulful wall of sound on "I'll Do Anything." "How My Heart Aches" is a special standout that ranks among the very finest wrenching, melancholy soul ever waxed. Much more than a collector's item, this proves Troy to be a genuinely overlooked major talent. —*Richie Unterberger*

Ike Turner

Guitar, Piano, Vocals / Soul, R&B, Soul Blues

It is arguably true that Ike Turner would have never amounted to more than a footnote of rock history if he hadn't joined forces with Tina Turner in 1960. But as a solo artist, he's an important footnote. In 1951, he made a lasting contribution to the music by playing piano on Jackie Brenston's "Rocket 88," which is often cited as one of the very first rock 'n' roll records. That session was one of the first blues/R&B/rock 'n' roll dates produced at Sun Studios in Memphis; Turner learned guitar shortly afterwards, and backed up other R&B artists at Sun in the early '50s. Throughout the decade, the guitarist and piano player was a prolific session player, contributing to records by blues legends Elmore James, Howlin' Wolf, and Otis Rush.

Ike also backed a host of obscure R&B artists in his early years, occasionally issuing discs under his name. Not much of a singer, both his own records and the ones he contributed to and/or produced often showcased his stinging, bluesy licks, and the best of his solo outings tended to be his instrumentals. He continued to put out the occasional solo session and work with other artists after he hooked up with Tina, sometimes under the name Ike Turner's Kings of Rhythm. His career has lurched along in obscurity since he broke up with Tina in the mid-'70s, though he remains active. —*Richie Unterberger*

● **I Like Ike! The Best of Ike Turner** / 1994 / Rhino ♦♦♦♦

Eighteen songs spotlighting Turner's work as a bandleader, guitarist, and solo artist from 1951 to 1972, concentrating heavily on his work in the 1950s and early '60s. Leading off with Jackie Brenston's classic "Rocket 88," it includes rare singles featuring Turner by Dennis Binder, the Sly Fox, Willie King, and others, along with rare Turner solo recordings, some under the pseudonym Icky Renrut, and a 1958 45 with Tina, then known as Annie Mae Bullock, on backing vocals. These singers are usu-

ally journeymen, frankly, and the material is rather standard-issue R&B. —*Richie Unterberger*

1958-1959 / Paula ♦♦♦♦

Ever the hustler, Ike Turner found himself picking up some extra money on a road trip through Chicago recording for Cobra Records both as a bandleader and sideman. After contributing the sparkle to several Otis Rush classics and some early Buddy Guy sides, Turner also recorded a handful of sides, scant few of them seeing release until now. This CD collects them all up, including surviving alternate versions and is a delightful fly on the wall invite to a 1950s Chicago blues session. —*Cub Koda*

Ike and Tina Turner

Soul, R&B

There was a time when the Ike and Tina Turner Revue was one of the hottest, most durable, and potentially most explosive of all R&B ensembles. Fronted by Tina, with one of the rawest, most sensual, and impossibly dynamic voices in Black music, the Ike and Tina Revue was an ensemble that dripped musical discipline while manifesting nearly unbearable tension, eventually giving way to wave upon wave of catharsis.

Their story is a long and convoluted one. Ike was born in 1931 in Clarksdale, MS; Tina was born Annie Mae Bullock in 1938 in Nutbush, TN. They met in 1959 in East St. Louis, where Ike's Kings of Rhythm were the reigning patriarchs of the local R&B scene. Up to that point, Ike had been a DJ on WROX in Clarksdale, a talent scout and producer for Modern Records (waxing sides for the likes of B.B. King, Rosco Gordon, Elmore James, and Junior Parker), and a recording artist, his Kings of Rhythm appearing in one guise or another on Chess, Modern, King, Cobra, Artistic, and Stevens. Their most famous record, *Rocket 88*, appeared under the moniker "Jackie Brenston with his Delta Cats" in 1951. It played an integral part in jump-starting the rock 'n' roll revolution.

Once Tina joined the Kings of Rhythm, life changed for all concerned. They recorded a demo of "A Fool in Love" in late 1959; by the autumn of 1960 the record was a No. 2 R&B hit on Sue Records. "I Idolize You," "It's Gonna Work Out Fine," "Poor Fool," and "Tra La La La La" all quickly followed, giving the Revue five Top Ten R&B hits in two and a half years. All told, from 1960 to 1975 Ike and Tina Turner placed 25 records on the R&B charts for nine separate record companies. —*Rob Bowman*

River Deep & Mountain High / 1966 / A&M ♦♦♦♦

These sessions, recorded in 1966, were produced by Phil Spector. Spector's production chops and Tina's voice were a match made in heaven. Tina possesses one of the strongest voices ever committed to wax; Spector envelops it in the grandest version of his Wall of Sound that he ever conceived. Besides the title track, Spector cut the Turners redoing their first three chart hits, "A Fool in Love," "I Idolize You," and "It's Gonna Work Out Fine." Although it's a sacrilege to say so, these versions are better than the originals. Finally, Turner's performance of the obscure Holland-Dozier-Holland ditty "A Love like Yours" bowls me over with every listen. —*Rob Bowman*

Workin' Together / 1970 / Liberty ♦♦♦

● **Proud Mary: The Best of Ike & Tina Turner** / Mar. 18, 1991 / EMI America ♦♦♦♦

Proud Mary: The Best of Ike & Tina Turner is a fine 23-track collection that looks at the Turners' career at the beginning and the end. Their early-'60s hits on Juggy Murray's Sue label are included, as are their early- and mid-'70s successes on Liberty and United Artists. The mid- and late-'60s recordings for Kent, Loma, Modern, Innis, Blue Thumb, and Minit are not here, unfortunately. Superior liner notes round out a fine package. —*Rob Bowman*

Tina Turner (Annie Mae Bullock)

b. Nov. 26, 1938, Nutbush, TN

Vocals / Soul, R&B, Pop-Rock

The woman who taught the world how to dance in high heels, Tina Turner has never been less than electrifying. Her full-throated rasp, full of low-note rumblings and soulful shrieks, is one of the most distinctive in any field of music, and her overtly sexual stage presence is nothing short of mesmerizing. The early part of her career, with then-husband Ike Turner, has been well documented but she really hit her stride and found a whole new audience with the coming of the MTV generation, her solo career bringing her the acclaim that had been long overdue. —*Cub Koda*

● **Private Dancer** / Nov. 16, 1984 / Capitol ♦♦♦♦

The one that won her a pile of awards, and rightly so, because it's simply her finest solo album. Using a multitude of producers and cut in a variety of locations, *Private Dancer* still sounds amazingly unified. Includes the title cut, "What's Love Got to Do with It," "Let's Stay Together," "Better Be Good to Me," and a blistering Jeff Beck solo on "Steel Claw." —*Cub Koda*

Break Every Rule / 1986 / Capitol ♦♦♦

Tina Live in Europe / 1988 / Capitol ✦✦

Foreign Affair / Sep. 13, 1989 / Capitol ✦✦✦

Simply the Best / 1991 / Capitol ✦✦✦✦

A solid greatest-hits collection culled from her solo Capitol albums. Includes "Typical Male," "Steamy Windows" (written and produced by Tony Joe White), "I Can't Stand the Rain," and a duet with Rod Stewart on "It Takes Two." —*Cub Koda*

What's Love Got to Do with It / Jun. 15, 1993 / Capitol ✦✦✦

Collected Recordings—Sixties to Nineties / 1994 / Capitol ✦✦✦

The Turtles

Folk-Rock, Pop-Rock

The Turtles were a pop-rock quintet 1963-69, with varying personnel, though always featuring lead singer Howard Kaylan (b. Jun 22, 1945) and backup/harmony singer Mark Volman (b. Apr 19, 1944). Other original members were guitarists Al Nichol (b. Mar 31, 1945) and Jim Tucker, and bassist Chuck Portz (b. Nov 8, 1945). They began life as a surf band called the Crossfires, but by the time of their debut album on White Whale Records, they'd become a folk-rock group singing Bob Dylan songs including their first hit, "It Ain't Me Babe." More characteristic of their style, however, was the sweet pop hit "You Baby" of 1966. The Turtles topped the charts with "Happy Together" in 1967 and scored several more romantic pop hits before they split up at the end of the '60s, after which Kaylan and Volman hooked up with Frank Zappa in the Mothers, then performed on their own as Flo And Eddie. Today, they continue to perform under that name and as the Turtles. —*William Ruhlmann*

It Ain't Me Babe / 1965 / Rhino ✦✦✦✦

The Turtles' first album presents them as a folk-rock group covering a lot of Dylan and P.F. Sloan material. They also found "It Was a Very Good Year" on a Kingston Trio album and cut it. Frank Sinatra heard their version and had one of his bigger hits with it, but their version is good, too. —*William Ruhlmann*

You Baby / 1966 / Rhino ✦✦✦

Happy Together / 1967 / Rhino ✦✦✦✦

The Turtles's best studio album includes the title hit, "She'd Rather Be with Me," "Guide for the Married Man," and then-unknown Warren Zevon's "Like the Seasons," among other songs. —*William Ruhlmann*

Wooden Head / 1970 / Rhino ✦✦✦

● **20 Greatest Hits** / 1983 / Rhino ✦✦✦✦

A witty and underrated band, the Turtles compiled this fine set themselves. —*Dan Heilman*

20/20

Power-Pop

20/20 was formed in Tulsa, Oklahoma, by high school friends Steve Allen (guitar, vocals) and Ron Flynt (bass, vocals). They relocated to Los Angeles in 1977, adding Mike Gallo on drums, and began playing local clubs. Greg Shaw, the head of Bomp! Records, was impressed with their highly charged power-pop and signed them to his label in 1978. The resulting single, "Under the Freeway," created enough interest in the band to secure a deal with Portrait Records. They added keyboardist Chris Sylgali and recorded their first LP, *20/20*. "Cheri" from the album saw some minor regional success but the album was virtually ignored apart from critical acclaim. The follow-up, *Look Out!* (1981), was equally strong but again failed. The band was dropped by Portrait in 1982 and effectively disbanded. They returned in 1983 with the independently released *Sex Trap*, but by this time, their sound was out of style and the band finally called it quits. A revived interest in the genre in the '90s inspired the band to reunite, contributing a few new songs to Big Deal's *Yellow Pills* compilations and recording a new album, *House Tornado*, for the fall of 1995. —*Chris Woodstra*

● **20/20** / 1979 / Portrait ✦✦✦✦

Released during the initial power-pop craze of the late '70s, the band's self-titled debut quickly stood out among the masses with its consistent quality, strict adherence to the melodic three-minute form, and tight, driving rhythm. Though the sales didn't reflect the strength of the album, songs like "Cheri" and "Yellow Pills" are considered classics of the period, the latter becoming the title for the premier power-pop fanzine, still in existence today. —*Chris Woodstra*

Look Out! / Jun. 1981 / Portrait ✦✦✦✦

An equally strong follow-up, *Look Out!*, is a pure pop artifact with its teen anthems discussing the "nuclear boys in the nuclear world," obsessing over girls (the haunting "Girl like You"), and telling the tale of a bizarre alien love affair (the silly "Alien"). *Look Out!* and *20/20* have been reissued as a two-fer CD on Oglio in 1995—an essential part of any power-pop collection. —*Chris Woodstra*

Sex Trap / 1982 / Teldec ✦✦

4 Day Tornado / 1995 / Oglio ✦✦✦

Dwight Twilley

b. Jun. 6, 1951, Tulsa, OK
Keyboards, Vocals / Power-Pop

Dwight Twilley fused rockabilly, mid-'60s Anglo-pop, and Byrdsy jangle into a distinctly reverberant sound. In 1976 Twilley and his partner Phil Seymour released the exceptional No. 16 Anglo-rockabilly hit "I'm on Fire" on Denny Cordell's Shelter label. Unfortunately, Shelter's lack of organization delayed the release of Twilley's debut album, *Sincerely*, by over a year. In spite of glowing reviews concerning the album's rich melodicism and sparkling production, *Sincerely* sank without a trace.

After the follow-up, *Twilley Don't Mind*, Twilley jumped ship for Arista, releasing a self-titled album. In spite of some brilliant power-pop ("Alone in My Room," "It Takes a Lotta Love"), problems arose at the label, and Twilley jumped again to EMI, releasing *Scuba Divers*. It was on his next album that he scored his next hit, "Girls." —*Rick Clark*

Sincerely / 1976 / DCC ✦✦✦✦

From the opening Anglo-pop-rock-meets-rockabilly blast of the Top 20 hit single "I'm on Fire," through breezy jangle-rock numbers like "You're So Warm," "Just like the Sun," and "England," to the dirge-like psychedelia of the title song, *Sincerely* is Twilley's finest album. It's a must-own for fans of guitar pop-rock. The CD includes four bonus tracks. —*Rick Clark*

Twilley Don't Mind / 1977 / DCC ✦✦✦

Twilley drops the ball slightly on this second album, in spite of good tracks like "Looking for the Magic," "Here She Come," "Sleeping," and the title cut. —*Rick Clark*

Twilley / 1979 / Arista ✦✦✦✦

This self-titled third album rivals Twilley's debut as his best album with super tracks like "Alone in My Room," "It Takes a Lot of Love," "Darlin'," and "I Want to Make Love to You." As of this printing, this fine pop-rock album has yet to see a CD release. If you like Twilley's other albums, then this is worth the search. —*Rick Clark*

Scuba Divers / 1982 / EMI ✦✦✦✦

1982's *Scuba Divers* continues the band's fine pop tradition though the material is not quite up to the standards of its predecessors. —*AMG*

Jungle / 1984 / EMI ✦✦✦✦

Twilley makes an unexpected return to the charts with the Top 20 single "Girls"; an equally enjoyable album. —*AMG*

The Great Lost Twilley Album / Apr. 1993 / Shelter ✦✦✦

This collection of unreleased tracks from 1974 to 1980 will please fans. Good songs, but the uninitiated should go to the first or third albums. —*Rick Clark*

● **XXI** / Mar. 19, 1996 / The Right Stuff ✦✦✦✦

Despite critical raves at the time and the undeniable high quality of the songs, the Dwight Twilley Band never quite achieved the success they so sorely deserved. *XXI* collects the finer moments of the band's brief recording career, which only ran from 1976 to 1978, as well as highlights from Twilley's solo work, beginning from 1979 to late 1995. This 21-track compilation includes a good sampling of album favorites, the hits ("I'm On Fire" and "Girls"—both peaked at No. 16), some lost should-have-been hits ("Shark" and "Somebody to Love"), a never-before-released song from an aborted 1994 album and a newly recorded track, "That Thing You Do." For fans, the rarities and song-by-song commentary by Twilley make *XXI* an essential addition. For those unfamiliar with Twilley and company's perfect pop, there is no better place to start. —*Chris Woodstra*

Twisted Sister

Hard Rock, Heavy Metal

Long Island metal band featuring lead singer Dee Snider, with guitarists Jay French and Eddie Ojeda, bassist Mark "The Animal" Mendoza (formerly of the Dictators), and drummer A.J. Pero. Their original purpose was to be the antithesis of disco, creating a bizarre, outrageous look for themselves with frizzy hair and heavy makeup. Musically, they played simple, melodic metal with consciously provocative lyrics and oft-repeated choruses. The group got a major push from MTV in 1984, as their image attracted the attention of teenage boys throughout the country. Their adolescent anthems "We're Not Gonna Take It" and "I Wanna Rock" pushed *Stay Hungry*'s sales into the double-platinum range. This proved to be the peak of their success, and they disbanded in 1987 when their label decided they had run out of ideas. Snider then formed Desperado. —*Steve Huey*

You Can't Stop Rock 'n' Roll / 1983 / Atlantic ✦✦✦

Stay Hungry / 1984 / Atlantic ✦✦✦✦

Hard-hitting aggressively progressive metal, this set includes "The Price," "I Wanna Rock," and "We're Not Gonna Take It." —*Bil Carpenter*

Come out & Play / 1985 / Atlantic ✦✦✦

● **Big Hits and Nasty Cuts: Best of Twisted Sister** / 1992 / Atlantic ◆◆◆◆

All of the highlights of Twisted Sister's long career are included on this collection. —*AMG*

U2

Alternative Pop-Rock, Pop-Rock, Post-Punk

In 1976, four Dublin schoolboys started the band that, under the name U2, would dominate rock music in the late '80s. Consisting of lead singer Bono (b. Paul Hewson, May 10, 1960), guitarist The Edge (b. David Evans, Aug. 8, 1961), bassist Adam Clayton (b. Mar. 13, 1960), and percussionist Larry Mullen, Jr. (b. Oct. 31, 1961), U2 has helped to open up the doors for many other Irish bands.

U2 started out as a Dublin pub band and began earning recognition after the band won a talent contest sponsored by Guinness in 1979. This led to the Irish release of a three-track EP, *U2-3,* that topped the charts in Ireland and won them quite a following. They were signed by the Island label in 1980 and released their debut album, *Boy,* later that year. Unfortunately, *Boy* and the band's 1981 follow-up, *October,* did not gain much recognition outside of Ireland (where the band was playing sold-out concerts). It was not until the 1983 release of the critically acclaimed album, *War,* that U2 began to get a taste of success. *War* was the band's major breakthrough in the US, going platinum although the first two albums had never made it into the Top 40. *Under a Blood Red Sky,* a live concert album from the *War* tour, was released in 1983, followed by *The Unforgettable Fire* in 1984; both went platinum in the States as well.

With the release of *The Joshua Tree* (1987), U2 became one of the world's leading rock bands. Entering at No. 1 on the UK charts, *The Joshua Tree* went platinum within 48 hours. The album also spent nine weeks at No. 1 on the US charts, and "With or Without You" became the band's first No. 1 single in America, followed by "I Still Haven't Found What I'm Looking For." As the new rock sensation, U2 appeared on the covers of *Time, Musician,* and *Rolling Stone* and won two awards at the 1988 Grammy Awards, including Album of the Year. In 1988 the band went on to release a full-length concert film, *Rattle and Hum,* and an album of the same name.

Achtung Baby, released in late 1991, proved to be quite a departure from their previous work. Darker and more atmospheric than their other albums, it proved to be not only successful commercially and artistically, but it preserved their image of being on the cutting edge. After the release of *Achtung Baby,* U2 embarked on a major world tour, called *Zoo TV,* that featured state-of-the-art video images. During the tour, they recorded *Zooropa,* which was released in 1993; it was even more experimental and darker than their previous album. Naturally, it was a worldwide hit, even if it didn't have any hit singles as big as "One" or "Mysterious Ways."

U2 could arguably be called the greatest rock band of the '80s. Out of sheer determination (or cockiness), they have avoided the musical ruts that stardom can produce and have gone out of their way to experiment with new sounds and musical ideas. It is this musical growth and exploration that make U2 a great band. —*Iotis Erlewine*

Boy / 1980 / Island ◆◆◆◆

The inexperience of the band, not yet at its musical peak, is compensated for by its raw power. The songs on *Boy* are full of teen angst and rebellion, a result of the influence of punk bands like the Virgin Prunes. In spite of the roughness of this album, its simplicity and directness are very appealing. Including "I Will Follow" and "Out of Control," this album is a good example of U2's early work; so far, the band has been unable to match the sheer energy of *Boy.* —*Iotis Erlewine*

October / 1981 / Island ◆◆◆

U2's second album lost a lot of the fire and momentum that was in *Boy.* The band is better musically on this album, but it lacks spontaneity and seems a little too rehearsed. *October* incorporates Christian religious symbolism, apparent in songs like "Gloria" and "Rejoice." The album has some great songs (such as the minor UK hit "Gloria" and the melancholy "Tomorrow") but as a whole is a rather weak follow-up. —*Iotis Erlewine*

☆ **War** / 1983 / Island ◆◆◆◆◆

This album was a major turning point for U2—the band went from being a minor Irish band to being a world-renowned rock group. *War* retains some of the anger that is found on *Boy,* but it is more subtle and mature. This album features some of U2's best-known songs—"New Year's Day," "Sunday Bloody Sunday," "Seconds," and "Two Hearts Beat as One." In spite of all the protest, aggression, and outrage in these songs, the album ends with the optimistic "40," a song that sets the uplifting words of Psalm 40 to music. With such spectacular songs and emotion, *War* is a must for any fan of rock music. —*Iotis Erlewine*

Under a Blood Red Sky / 1983 / Island ◆◆◆

This is a great concert album from U2's *War* tour, most of which was recorded during their concert at the Red Rocks Festival in Colorado. The album includes "11 O'Clock Tick Tock" and "Party Girl" (which previously were available only as singles) and intense performances of "New

Year's Day" and "Sunday Bloody Sunday." *Under a Blood Red Sky* captures some of the power and charisma that make U2 such a great live band. —*Iotis Erlewine*

The Unforgettable Fire / 1984 / Island ◆◆◆

After *War,* this was U2's second No. 1 album in the UK (No. 12 in the US), and it features two of the band's better-known songs, "Pride" and "Bad." Ironically, even in spite of its relative success, this remains one of U2's "forgotten" albums. The quality of the songs may play a part in this—either the songs are outstanding or they are not even worth mentioning. It is this kind of inconsistency that causes this album to be so frequently overlooked. —*Iotis Erlewine*

Wide Awake in America / 1985 / Island ◆◆

★ **The Joshua Tree** / 1987 / Island ◆◆◆◆◆

The Joshua Tree is the album that won the US (and the rest of the world) over. Before this release, the band had met with considerable success but nothing like what was to follow *The Joshua Tree.* This album moved away from the loud anger of *War* and focused on a more subtle, refined sound. The wistful, searching quality of this album captures U2 at a transition, as the band attempts to rediscover themselves. Including such songs as "With or Without You," "I Still Haven't Found What I'm Looking For," "Where the Streets Have No Name," "In God's Country," and "Running to Stand Still," this album is among U2's best works. —*Iotis Erlewine*

Rattle & Hum / 1988 / Island ◆◆◆

U2's ego manifests itself. Billed as U2's "exploration of America," this album was a grave disappointment. There are, however, some excellent tracks, such as "When Love Comes to Town" (featuring B.B. King), "All I Want Is You," "Desire," and "Angel of Harlem." —*Iotis Erlewine*

☆ **Achtung Baby** / 1991 / Island ◆◆◆◆◆

This album was a big change in style for U2—it's the band's only album to date that you can dance to. On this album, the group drops some of the pretentiousness of the last few albums and stops taking itself so seriously, and the result is very impressive. Although some of the lyrics are downright laughable, *Achtung Baby* is more direct and honest than some of the previous, preachier albums. Promoted as U2's "dark, trashy" album, this is, as far as I'm concerned, the most sophisticated work the band has yet created. The songs on this album (like the powerful "One" and "Love Is Blindness") revolve around human emotion instead of politics. I highly recommend *Achtung Baby*—it may be a shock the first time you hear it, but the more you listen, the better it gets. —*Iotis Erlewine*

Zooropa / May 1993 / Island ◆◆◆◆

After their successful artistic renewal with 1991's *Achtung Baby,* U2 mounted a staggering world tour filled with glitz, empty slogans, mammoth TV screens, and stunning music. Originally intended as an EP, *Zooropa* was recorded in a short break in their European tour. Instead of sounding like a pure piece of product, *Zooropa* is a complex album that takes the sonic experimentations of *Achtung Baby* even further—listen to the grinding "Numb" for proof. Some of the songwriting isn't as fully developed as it could have been, but the album creates a terrifically claustrophobic atmosphere that comes to an incredible close with "The Wanderer," where Johnny Cash's lead vocal sounds completely natural among the ominous synthesizers. —*Stephen Thomas Erlewine*

UB40

Reggae, Adult Contemporary, Pop-Rock

Named after a British unemployment benefit form, pop-reggae band UB40 was formed in a welfare line in 1978, and its multiracial lineup reflected the working-class community its members came from. The band consolidated its street credibility with political topics appealing to dissatisfied youth and got a boost from fans of the waning 2-Tone ska-revival movement. Brothers Robin (lead guitar) and Ali Campbell (guitar, lead vocals) formed the centerpiece of the group, which also included bassist Earl Falconer, keyboardist Mickey Virtue, saxophonist Brian Travers, drummer Jim Brown, percussionist Norman Hassan, and toaster Terence "Astro" Wilson. The band purchased its first instruments with compensation money Ali Campbell received after a bar fight, even though few of the members knew how to play them. But by the end of the year, the group was invited to tour with the Pretenders. Their "Food For Thought" single reached the UK Top Ten in 1980, beginning a long streak of chart appearances. *Signing Off* and *Present Arms* were big sellers in Britain, if not America, and addressed the political issues of the day in songs like "One in Ten," a Top Ten hit blasting Margaret Thatcher for the country's unemployment rate. 1983's *Labour of Love,* an album of reggae cover songs, gave the group its first chart album in America and first No. UK hit with Neil Diamond's "Red Red Wine." Several albums of original material sold well in the UK, but only respectably in the US, where the group's biggest hit was a Top 30 cover of Sonny and Cher's "I Got You Babe" featuring the Pretenders' Chrissie Hynde.

In 1988, the group performed "Red Red Wine" at a Nelson Mandela tribute concert, and a Phoenix radio station trotted the single out for a second go-round. Listener response was far more enthusiastic, and "Red Red Wine" re-entered the charts and went all the way to the top. Finally having hit on a way to conquer the lucrative American market, UB40 responded with another covers album, *Labour of Love II*, which produced Top Ten singles with versions of the Temptations' "The Way You Do the Things You Do" and Al Green's "Here I Am (Come and Take Me)." The group scored a huge hit in America with Elvis Presley's "Can't Help Falling In Love," which was initially featured in the Sharon Stone film *Sliver* and spent seven weeks at No.1. By this time, UB40 had largely abandoned its trademark left-wing politics and was concentrating more on perfecting its reggae oldies covers than its original material; however, the gimmick has thus far resulted in huge sales figures in both the US and UK, with *Promises and Lies* reaching No. 6 and No. 1, respectively. —*Steve Huey*

Best of UB40 (1980-1983) / 1983 / A&M ♦♦♦

● **Labour of Love** / Sep. 1983 / A&M ♦♦♦♦
Long stars in England, UB40 finally found Stateside success (and that belatedly) by recording an album of their favorite Jamaican cover tunes. One of these, "Red Red Wine," finally took off in the US in 1988 and went to No. 1. —*William Ruhlmann*

Geffery Morgan / 1984 / A&M ♦♦♦♦
UB40 was faced with following up the surprisingly successful covers album *Labour of Love* (which had topped the UK chart and become their US chart debut) with this album of original material. Their own songs were good, but no match for what then seemed a one-of-a-kind collection. "If It Happens Again," which went to No. 9 in Britain, sounded like a song by the English Beat, while the second single, "Riddle Me" (No. 59), was a deeper reggae groove tune. It was a good set, but without a classic like "Red Red Wine" suffered from a certain anonymity, especially in the US. —*William Ruhlmann*

Little Baggaridim / 1985 / A&M ♦♦♦
UB40 scored their first Top 30 hit in the US with a cover of Sonny And Cher's "I Got You, Babe," set to a reggae beat and sung with the Pretenders' Chrissie Hynde, heard on this mini-album. —*William Ruhlmann*

Rat in the Kitchen / 1986 / A&M ♦♦♦♦
In the UK, UB40 were major stars, and this album was their sixth Top Ten hit, featuring the singles "Sing Your Own Song" (No. 5), "All I Want To Do" (No. 41), and "Rat in the Kitchen" (No. 12). In the US, the group remained a developing act with a modest following, only able to score a hit by covering a previous hit like "I Got You, Babe." *Rat in the Kitchen* did nothing to change that, although it was, as usual, a tuneful collection of reggae. —*William Ruhlmann*

UB40 CCCP: Live in moscow / Oct. 1987 / A&M ♦♦

Labour of Love II / 1989 / Virgin ♦♦

Promises and Lies / 1993 / Virgin ♦♦

The Best Of UB40, Vol. 2 / Oct. 1995 / Virgin ♦♦♦♦
UB40's tepid reggae-pop cross-over had enough edge in its early years to justify an initial compilation, but *The Best of Volume Two* stretches the concept considerably. A paltry ten tracks in which the group confuses rhythmic reworkings of "The Way You Do the Things You Do," "Superstition," and "Can't Help Falling in Love" with originality. —*Roch Parisien*

UK

Art-Rock/Progressive-Rock
Featuring members of Yes, King Crimson, Roxy Music, and Soft Machine, UK was one of the most prominent progressive-rock supergroups of the late '70s. Various members of UK—guitarist Allan Holdsworth, keyboardist/violinist Eddie Jobson, bassist/vocalist John Wetton, and drummer Bill Bruford—had all played together in their previous bands, but when the group formed in 1977, it was the first time all of the musicians had played together. Although the lineup was unstable—Holdsworth and Bruford left after one album, with former Frank Zappa drummer Terry Bozzio replacing Bruford—and the group was short-lived, the band maintained a dedicated cult following years after their early '80s breakup.

Prior to the formation of UK, Bill Bruford and John Wetton had recently played together in King Crimson and Allan Holdsworth had played guitar on Bruford's debut album, 1978's *Feels Good to Me*. Shortly after the recording of *Feels Good to Me*, Bruford, Holdsworth, and Wetton formed UK, adding former Roxy Music member Eddie Jobson to the lineup.

UK released their eponymous debut in 1978, and the album captured the attention of progressive-rock and jazz-fusion fans, as did the record's supporting tour. At the conclusion of the tour, Holdsworth and Bruford left the group to form Bruford, leaving keyboardist Jobson as the band's leader. UK didn't hire another guitarist, but they did have Terry Bozzio replace Bruford. The new lineup of UK released *Danger Money* in 1979 and followed the album with a tour. Once the tour was completed, the group broke up. The posthumous live album *Night After Night* was released shortly afterward. Following the disbandment of UK, Eddie Jobson became a member of Jethro Tull, Terry Bozzio formed Missing Persons, and John Wetton formed Asia with fellow progressive-rock stars Steve Howe, Carl Palmer, and Geoffrey Downes. —*Stephen Thomas Erlewine*

● **UK** / 1978 / EG ♦♦♦♦
An impressive debut album, it features Allan Holdsworth, John Wetton, Bill Bruford, and Eddie Jobson. —*Paul Kohler*

Danger Money / 1979 / EG ♦♦♦

Night After Night / 1979 / EG ♦♦♦

Tracey Ullman

Vocals / New Wave, Pop-Rock
Before she became a famous TV comedienne, Tracy Ullman recorded two albums in the early '80s that effortlessly recalled the classic girl group sound of the '60s. Ullman covered everything from Doris Day ("Move over Darling") to Blondie ("[I'm Always Touched by Your] Presence, Dear"), finding the underlying connections between classic pop songs of all eras. *You Broke My Heart in 17 Places*, her debut album, was a hit in the UK and she even managed to have a Top Ten hit in America with a version of Kirsty MacColl's "They Don't Know." Although it had some fine numbers, the follow-up *You Caught Me Out* wasn't as successful, prompting Ullman to return to television. By the end of the '80s, her comedy show, *The Tracy Ullman Show*, was one of the most critically acclaimed television shows in America; she hasn't recorded any music since. —*Stephen Thomas Erlewine*

You Broke My Heart in 17 Places / 1983 / Stiff ♦♦♦♦
Ullman's first album, recorded in the middle of the new-wave and synth-pop movements, provided a refreshing break with its retro girl group sound. Includes her only US hit, "They Don't Know" (written by Kirsty MacColl) as well as carefully chosen obscure oldies. One of the great lost classics. —*Chris Woodstra*

You Caught Me Out / 1984 / Repertoire ♦♦♦
The second album follows the same formula as the first—a well-chosen collection of covers from obscure oldies to contemporary favorites (Madness' "My Girl"—retitled here as "My Guy") and even another stab at a Kirsty MacColl song ("Terry")—all done in the classic '60s girl group sound. Though it failed to produce the smash hits of the debut, "My Guy" and "Sunglasses" were minor hits in the UK, and the album is nearly as much fun. Repertoire has released a CD version with six bonus tracks. —*Chris Woodstra*

● **The Best of Tracey Ullman** / 1991 / Rhino ♦♦♦♦
This 20-track compilation provides an extensive look at the nearly forgotten singing career of this now famous actress. Combining the entire first LP, *You Broke My Heart in 17 Places*, the highlights from her second effort *You Caught Me Out*, and well-chosen B-sides, it more than lives up to its name. Although this material was recorded in the early '80s, lovers of the classic '60s-girl-group sound will find these retro-gems a familiar delight. —*Chris Woodstra*

Ultravox

New Wave, Pop-Rock
Ultravox (or Ultravox!—as it was called at first) had two separate identities and styles of music during its existence. Formed in London in 1974, it was originally intended as a platform for singer John Foxx (born Dennis Leigh) and included guitarist Stevie Shears, keyboardist and violinist Billy Currie, bassist Chris Cross, and drummer Warren Cann. With this lineup, the group recorded its debut album, *Ultravox!* (1977), produced by Brian Eno and Steve Lillywhite during the height of the punk/new-wave movement. A second album, *Ha! Ha! Ha!* (1977), was released only in the UK A third, *Systems of Romance* (1978), marked the last appearance of Foxx, who went solo, and of guitarist Robin Simon, who had replaced Shears. The remaining trio enlisted singer/guitarist Midge Ure, formerly of the teenybop band ilk, and recorded *Vienna* (1980), which marked a sharp turn toward synthesizer pop and helped give birth to the British "new romantic" movement of the early '80s. The album was Ultravox's first to chart; the title track went to No. 2 and "All Stood Still" reached the Top Ten. There followed a series of successful albums in the UK: *Rage in Eden* (1981), *Quartet* (1982), *Monument—The Soundtrack* (1983), *Lament* (1984), and *U-Vox* (1986). *The Collection* (1984) was a hits album. Of these, only *Quartet* made any significant inroads in the US Ultravox split in mid-1987, when Ure decided to turn his full attention to his solo career. —*William Ruhlmann*

Ultravox / 1977 / Island ♦♦♦

Vienna / 1980 / Chrysalis ♦♦♦♦
The new Ultravox, under Midge Ure, has a dreamy, ethereal sound heard at its best on its debut album, which features the title song, "All Stood Still," "Passing Strangers," and "Sleepwalk," all UK hits. —*William Ruhlmann*

● **The Collection** / 1984 / Chrysalis ✦✦✦✦
Ultravox's UK hit singles during the Midge Ure era. —*William Ruhl-mann*

Rare, Vol. 1 / 1994 / Chrysalis ✦✦

Uncle Tupelo

Alternative Country-Rock
Uncle Tupelo's skillful updating of country and folk for the post-punk era made the band one of the best of the early '90s. Beginning with their first independent record in 1990, the band played direct, hardcore country, injecting it with the loud fervor of punk. Over the course of four albums, the overt punk elements of their music became less dominant, as the group's fascination with country came to the forefront. By the time of their major label debut in 1993, Uncle Tupelo had developed a familiar, yet distinct, sound that had traces of the Flying Burrito Brothers, Neil Young, and Hank Williams; their music was based in tradition, yet it didn't sound nostalgic—their conviction and passion made it sound vital and contemporary. Unfortunately, the band broke up the following year; the group's two songwriters—Jay Farrar and Jeff Tweedy—each had formed new bands by the end of the year. —*Stephen Thomas Erlewine*

No Depression / 1990 / Gasatanka ✦✦✦

March 16-20, 1992 / 1992 / Gasatanka ✦✦✦✦
A remarkably accomplished set of contemporary country-rock. —*Stephen Thomas Erlewine*

● **Anodyne** / May 1993 / Sire ✦✦✦✦
Uncle Tupelo's other albums are impressive, but their final record, *Anodyne*, is a brilliant reinterpretation of traditional country, folk, and country-rock. Filled with excellent songs, it sounds both contemporary and timeless. —*Stephen Thomas Erlewine*

Undertones

Punk, New Wave
There are those who would disagree vehemently, but in my estimation the Undertones were Ireland's best rock band—ever. Roaring out of the Northern Ireland city of Derry in 1976, the Undertones fused speedy, loud Ramones-inspired walls of guitar racket with irresistible '60s pop hooks, with just a touch of mid-'70s glam rock for good measure. With the singular tenor vocals of frontman Feargal Sharkey making them instantaneously recognizable, Undertones songs tended to eschew punk vitriol for songs about teenage love, girls, snotty cousins, and summertime—life's simple joys (and pains). No more succinct a summation of their style, wit, and power can be found than on their out-of-print debut EP *Teenage Kicks*, released in 1978 on the Belfast indie label Good Vibrations. A record of startling ebullience, the songs (many of which showed up on their eponymous debut album) sound as exhilarating today as they did nearly 20 years ago. However, the Undertones did not go into creative stasis with their winning punk-pop and simply replicate a proven formula over and over. As they grew as musicians, so did their albums change, incorporating some of the Tamla/Motown soul music they loved as kids. As a live band, they were tremendous; just ask anyone who saw them opening for the Clash in the late '70s. Sadly, the Undertones' story ended far too quickly. Growing up meant too much change too fast, and by the time they released their mediocre fourth album, restlessness and "musical differences" were splitting them apart. Sharkey went off to a short-lived solo career, while the guitar-playing O'Neill brothers put together the politically charged That Petrol Emotion. In the late '80s, there were whispers of a reunion which didn't occur, much to the relief of those who preferred the Undertones' legacy to remain unsullied. —*John Dougan*

★ **The Undertones** / 1979 / Rykodisc ✦✦✦✦✦
An absolutely essential purchase. One of the best albums of the punk era, or any era. Song after song is infused with a liberating joy and intensity that only a handful of rock records at the time equaled. A crucial record, the 'Tones' debut shows how influential '70s commercial pop was on the growing punk community, who embraced it and then tore it all to hell. A record that hasn't lost its luster after hundreds of plays and nearly two decades. Reissued on CD with seven bonus tracks by Rykodisc in 1994. —*John Dougan*

Hypnotised / 1980 / Rykodisc ✦✦✦✦
It's ridiculous to not encourage you to purchase the first three Undertones records, because they are such wonderful distillations of all that makes rock 'n' roll great. *Hypnotised* picks up where the debut leaves off, but adds a slightly more sarcastic touch to some of the songs, especially the witty "My Perfect Cousin" and the goofy "More Songs About Chocolate and Girls" (a not-so-subtle parody of the title of Talking Heads' second LP *More Songs About Buildings and Food*). Reissued on CD with five bonus tracks by Rykodisc in 1994. —*John Dougan*

Positive Touch / 1981 / Rykodisc ✦✦✦

The Very Best of the Undertones / 1994 / Rykodisc ✦✦✦✦
The Very Best of the Undertones collects the cream of the catalog. The group's earliest high-energy teenage anthems (themes of doubt, deceit, yearning, and infatuation) give way, over the course of 25 songs, to the sublime intimacy of "Wednesday Week" and "Julie Ocean," and then the sophisticated, Tamla/Motown layering of "Soul Seven." Group members discuss each track in the informative liner notes. Start here, fall in love, then go find the individual albums! —*Roch Parisien*

Unrest

Alternative Pop-Rock, Indie Rock
Unrest formed in the early 1980s and was originally conceived as an artsy-hardcore act. In this incarnation, the Washington, DC, group released many singles and seven inches, but did not gain their definitive, ultra-melodic and catchy sound until bassist/songwriter/vocalist Bridget Cross joined in 1990. In 1992 the band released their first full-length album, *Imperial f.f.r.r.*, which featured the closely intertwined, harmonic playing of Cross and guitarist/songwriter/vocalist Mark Robinson. More singles and EPs followed, culminating in the release of 1993's more experimental *Perfect Teeth*. After a few more singles, the group broke up in early 1994, with Robinson and Cross forming the group Air Miami after the split. —*Heather Phares*

Imperial f.f.r.r. / Jul. 14, 1992 / Number Six ✦✦✦✦
Imperial is Unrest's full-length debut. It fleshes out the pop promise of their early singles, and expands on their pop and experimental background as well. "I Do Believe You Are Blushing," "Cherry Cream On," "Suki," "Isabel," and "June" are still some of the band's best songs, mixing high-energy guitars and subjects like girls and death to infectious effect. A near-perfect album of indie-pop. —*Heather Phares*

Isabel Bishop [EP] / 1993 / 4AD/TeenBeat ✦✦✦✦

● **Perfect Teeth** / 1993 / 4AD/Warner Bros. ✦✦✦✦
The band's final and best album is both jangly and lush, and covers many styles of pop music. "Angel, I'll Walk You Home" is filled with pristine vocal harmonies, while "Cath Carroll" is flashy, thrashy punk-pop. "Light Brigade" is both wistful and triumphant. "Breather x.o.x.o" is majestically melancholy, and "West Coast Love Affair" is breezy and tongue-in-cheek. Unrest's experimental and pop leanings come together with terrific success on *Perfect Teeth*, making it a high point in the band's too-brief recording career. —*Heather Phares*

Fuck Pussy Galore and All Her Friends / 1994 / Matador ✦✦✦

Urge Overkill

Rock 'n' roll, Alternative Pop-Rock
Unlike most alternative-rock bands, Urge Overkill set out to be rock stars. They found an image—stylish, hip swingers with impeccable taste in fashion, music, and women—and made music that suited that persona. Picking up their Les Pauls and turning up their Marshall stacks, Urge Overkill made rock 'n' roll that was full of instantly memorable choruses, guitar solos, loud and catchy guitars, and a powerful backbeat; in short, music that *rocked*. Of course, it took them a couple of albums before they got that good. Initially, they were another Steve Albini-produced, buzzing guitar band from Chicago. With their second album, *Americruiser*, they began to write actual songs. By 1991's *Supersonic Storybook* album, the band's lineup was set in stone—Nash Kato on guitar and vocals, "Eddie" King Roeser on bass, guitar, and vocals, and drummer Blackie Onassis—and Urge released their first consistent album; it had stadium-sized riffs played with punkish aggression. Before they made the jump to the major labels, they released their most varied and diverse recording, the *Stull* EP. And with 1993's *Saturation*, Urge finally perfected the glamorous, powerful rock 'n' roll that they always wanted to record. While it didn't make them the superstars they wanted to be, it sold well and had a minor hit with "Sister Havana." —*Stephen Thomas Erlewine*

Americruiser/Jesus Urge Superstar / 1990 / Touch & Go ✦✦✦

The Supersonic Storybook / 1991 / Touch & Go ✦✦✦✦
With the addition of drummer Blackie Onassis, Urge Overkill shapes up into a killer rock 'n' roll combo. It also doesn't hurt that the songs are the finest they have written to date. Although the production is a little flat, there's no denying the force of the best tracks. "The Candidate" boasts a huge, stadium-size riff, "The Kids Are Insane" is a frenzied, frenetic rocker, "Today Is Blackie's Birthday" is gleefully stupid, and the band is surprisingly sexy on the old soul song "Emmaline." Things bog down a bit on the second side, but Urge is starting to sound like the rock stars they always knew they were. —*Stephen Thomas Erlewine*

Stull [EP] / 1992 / Touch & Go ✦✦✦✦
It's not the full-throttle rock masterpiece that *Supersonic Storybook* suggested, but the *Stull EP* is almost as remarkable. Opening with a straight cover of Neil Diamond's "Girl, You'll Be a Woman Soon" (which fits Urge Overkill's image perfectly), the EP is an atmospheric guitar workout.

While "Stitches" is a salute to their punk roots, the most impressive moments come during the stylish kiss-off to indie-rock "Goodbye to Guyville" and "Stull," with its sly, laidback groove. As the richness of *Stull* proves, Urge's vision was too large for the independents, and it was time to move on. — *Stephen Thomas Erlewine*

● **Saturation** / Jun. 8, 1993 / DGC ✦✦✦✦
When they hit the major labels, Urge Overkill followed through on their promise with the blistering *Saturation*. It's stadium rock by clever post-punkers who are smart enough to not let their carefully crafted image interfere with the music. Every one of the twelve songs is a killer, from the outlandish menace of "Stalker" to the moving ballad "Back on Me," as well as the tongue-in-cheek "Woman 2 Woman" and the radio hit "Sister Havana." — *Stephen Thomas Erlewine*

Exit the Dragon / Oct. 1995 / DGC ✦✦✦✦
Sonically falling somewhere between *Supersonic Storybook* and *Stull*, *Exit the Dragon* is a dark, lean album, the flipside of *Saturation*'s glossy celebration of '70s rock 'n' roll excess and easily Urge Overkill's most haunting collection of songs. It kicks off with "Jaywalking," a terse, powerful rocker lamenting "all the evil in this world," which sets the album's tone. *Exit the Dragon* is dominated by Eddie "King" Roeser, with Nash Kato on only six of the 14 songs. As usual, Roeser's songs are more claustrophobic than Kato's, particularly the clenched riffs of "The Break" and the slow crawl of "Tin Foil." Although Kato contributes the flat-out rocker "Need Some Air," many of his songs are nearly as dark as Roeser's, whether it's the acoustic "View of the Rain" (previously released as "Take a Walk" on the *No Alternative* compilation), the skipping pop of "Somebody Else's Body," the power-pop of "Monopoly," or the soaring closer "Digital Black Epilogue," a duet with an uncredited female soul singer. But the heart of the record is Blackie Onassis' "The Mistake," an eerie tale of a drug overdose that helps *Exit the Dragon* take the form of a loose concept album about a rock 'n' roll band beset by troubles on the road. While the subject is ripe for parody, Urge Overkill performs *Exit the Dragon* without much irony at all. Instead of being a fatal misstep, this choice proves that Urge is a tight, powerful rock 'n' roll band blessed with first-rate songwriters, capable of more emotions than many listeners might have expected. — *Stephen Thomas Erlewine*

Uriah Heep

Hard Rock, Art-Rock/Progressive-Rock, Heavy Metal
Uriah Heep's by-the-books progressive heavy metal made the British band one of the most popular hard-rock groups of the early '70s. Formed by vocalist David Byron and guitarist Mick Box in the late '60s, the group went through an astonishing number of members over the next two decades—nearly 30 different musicians passed through the band over the years. Byron and Box were members of the mid-'60s rock band called the Stalkers; once that band broke up, the duo formed another group called Spice. Spice would eventually turn into Uriah Heep in the late '60s, once Ken Hensley (guitar, keyboards, vocals) and bassist Paul Newton joined the pair. Former Spice drummer Alex Napier was the band's drummer for a brief time; he was quickly replaced by Nigel Olsson.

Uriah Heep released their debut album *Very 'eavy, Very 'umble* (called *Uriah Heep* in the US) in 1970. After its release, Keith Baker became the group's drummer; he recorded *Salisbury*, the group's second album, before deciding he couldn't keep up with the band's extensive touring and was replaced by Ian Clarke. Featuring a 16-minute title track recorded with a 26-piece orchestra, *Salisbury* showcased the band's more progressive tendencies. Later that year, Ian Clarke was replaced by Lee Kerslake and Mark Clarke replaced Newton; Mark Clarke quickly left the band and Gary Thain became the group's bassist. This lineup of Uriah Heep was its most stable and popular; beginning with 1972's *Demons and Wizards*, they released five albums between 1972 and 1975.

After 1975, the band's popularity began to slip. Byron left the band in 1977 and was replaced by John Lawton, yet the group's fortunes kept declining right into the early '80s. However, Uriah Heep soldiers on, continuing to release albums in the '90s. — *Stephen Thomas Erlewine*

Very 'umble Very 'eavy / 1970 / Mercury ✦✦✦

Salisbury / 1971 / Mercury ✦✦✦

Look at Yourself / 1971 / Mercury ✦✦✦✦
Look at Yourself was the beginning of Uriah Heep's commercial fortunes, as it became the first of their albums to hit the UK charts. Musically, it compromised the boogie of their debut with the sweeping ambitions of *Salisbury*. — *Daevid Jehnzen*

Demons & Wizards / Jan. 1972 / Mercury ✦✦✦✦
As the fanciful title suggests, Uriah Heep began to delve deeper and deeper into mystical lyricism on their fourth album, which was supported by their spacy but earthy guitar rock. — *Daevid Jehnzen*

Magician's Birthday / Feb. 1972 / Mercury ✦✦✦✦
Magician's Birthday continued to expand the mystical concerns of *Demons & Wizards*, and it was nearly as successful, thanks to the group's knack for heavy guitars. — *Daevid Jehnzen*

Wonderworld / 1974 / Roadrunner ✦✦✦

● **The Best of Uriah Heep** / 1976 / Mercury ✦✦✦✦
Collecting the best moments of their sometimes inconsistent albums, *The Best of Uriah Heep* is an effective introduction to the band. — *Daevid Jehnzen*

A Time of Revelation / 1996 / Essential! ✦✦✦✦
A Time of Revelation is a four-disc box set spanning Uriah Heep's entire career. The bulk of the set draws from the Heep's '70s heyday, including album tracks, live cuts, and previously unavailable on disc rarities. For the die-hard collector, the set is a must-have for its obscure items, but the set is too much for casual fans, even those that want more than a simple greatest hits collection. After all, Uriah Heep were an album rock band that tailored individual albums, which means their songs often make more sense in the context of their original albums, not on compilations like these. — *Stephen Thomas Erlewine*

King Uszniewicz & His Uszniewicztones

Novelty, Rock 'n' roll
A hilariously inept Detroit bowling-alley/lounge band fronted by Ernie "King" Uszniewicz (b. 1945) from 1969 to 1979. The crudest tenor saxophonist in the history of rock 'n' roll, King Uszniewicz (pronounced "you-snev-vitch") & the U-Tones had only one single, issued on a local label during the '70s. Dubbed by one critic as "the worst oldies band I ever heard in my life," they played with a bludgeoning energy, oblivious to the fact that they were woefully shy in the talent department. However, when the group's first album showed up on several college-radio playlists in 1989, they earned a minor cult following among both record collectors and young alternative-music fans. — *Stephen Thomas Erlewine*

Teenage Dance Party / Norton ✦✦✦

● **Twistin' and Bowlin'** / Norton ✦✦✦✦
Subtitled "just when you thought it was safe to go back into the bowling alley," and more than living up to all that implies. Drunken, out-of-control versions of "Way Down Yonder in New Orleans," "Peppermint Twist," and Johnny Mathis' "Chances Are" are among the numerous highlights. Scary. — *Stephen Thomas Erlewine*

Doin' the Woo-Hoo / Norton ✦✦✦✦
More oldies-band mayhem. "At the Hop," "G.T.O.," "Love Letters in the Sand," the title cut, and King Uszniewicz's wife, Arlene, belting out "It's My Party" are just a few of the standout tracks. Extremely potent stuff. — *Stephen Thomas Erlewine*

Utopia

Art-Rock/Progressive-Rock, Pop-Rock
Utopia is a rock quartet that theoretically features equal participation by its members, although singer and guitarist Todd Rundgren (b. Jun 22, 1948), who formed the band, is a recognized solo star and frequently dominates the group. The first two albums found them billed as Todd Rundgren's Utopia, a six-piece unit. But as of the third album, *Ra*, Utopia was a four-piece unit, including Rundgren, Roger Powell, John Wilcox, and Kasim Sulton, and that lineup was still in place as of 1986, which is the last time they released new material. — *William Ruhlmann*

Todd Rundgren's Utopia / Oct. 1974 / Bearsville ✦✦

RA / Feb. 1977 / Bearsville ✦✦

Oops! Wrong Planet / Sep. 1977 / Bearsville ✦✦✦

Adventures in Utopia / Jan. 1980 / Bearsville ✦✦✦

Deface the Music / Oct. 1980 / Bearsville ✦✦✦

Swing to the Right / Mar. 1982 / Bearsville ✦✦

Utopia / Sep. 1982 / Rhino ✦✦

POV / Jan. 1985 / Food For Thought ✦✦

● **Anthology** / 1989 / Rhino ✦✦✦✦
Annotator Bud Scoppa calls this "the definitive Utopia album," which is fair enough. Utopia's ten albums tended to be uneven affairs, with the first three, *Todd Rundgren's Utopia, Another Live*, and *RA*, very much in a fusion/progressive style that could be somewhat opaque. *Deface the Music* was an overt pastiche of the Beatles, but the other six albums also bore the influence of pop's master group, as the four band members shared songwriting and lead vocal duties in a series of commercial-sounding ballads and rockers, only three of which became charting singles. *Anthology* rescues those tracks and several others from *Oblivion* (one of their ironic album titles) and even gives a taste of the band's early space-rock tendencies. A good companion to the Todd Rundgren *Anthology* released simultaneously by Rhino. — *William Ruhlmann*

Steve Vai

Hard Rock, Fusion, Heavy Metal
Vai was a pupil of Joe Satriani as a teenager and studied at the Berkley School of Music before moving to Los Angeles at age 19. He was a huge

fan of Frank Zappa's and joined Zappa's band after proving that he knew most of the repertoire and could transcribe orchestral pieces by ear. Zappa credited him on albums as the "stunt guitarist." He released the self-produced *Flex-Able* in 1984, combining his Zappa and Satriani influences, and went on to play with Alcatrazz, David Lee Roth, and Whitesnake. Vai released his finest solo effort, the varied *Passion and Warfare*, in 1990. He then formed a backing group called VAI featuring vocalist Devin Townsend for *Sex & Religion* before recording the solo *Alien Love Secrets.* Vai is considered to be one of rock's top instrumentalists. *—Steve Huey*

Flex-able / 1984 / Akashic ◆◆◆◆
The self-released solo album from this former Zappa guitarist, featuring Zappa-influenced vocals, was recorded by Vai at home on an eight-track machine. The CD offers extra material from the *Flex-able* sessions originally released as a 10-inch EP. *—Paul Kohler*

● **Passion & Warfare** / Sep. 1990 / Relativity ◆◆◆◆
One of the most creative, musical, and mystical guitar albums ever made, it is a must-have. *—Paul Kohler*

Sex & Religion / Jul. 27, 1993 / Relativity ◆◆

Alien Love Secrets / 1995 / Relativity ◆◆◆

Fire Garden / 1996 / Epic ◆◆◆◆

Ritchie Valens

b. May 13, 1941, Pacoima, CA, **d.** Feb. 3, 1959, Clear Lake, IA
Guitar, Vocals / Rock 'n' roll
Valens will forever be known primarily as one of the two rock stars (along with the Big Bopper) who perished with Buddy Holly when their private plane crashed in the midst of a Midwest tour in 1959. At the time, Valens had established himself as one of the most promising young talents in rock 'n' roll, just missing the top of the charts with his ballad "Donna," and recording a pioneering blend of rock and Latin music with its almost equally popular flipside, "La Bamba." More than almost any other rock star who died prematurely, it's difficult to assess his unrealized potential; he was only 17 at the time of his death, and had just barely begun to make records.

The first Hispanic rock star, Valens grew up in Los Angeles suburbs, and was playing guitar by the time he was in junior high school. Inspired by Little Richard and rockabilly performers, he was discovered by producer Bob Keane in 1958. Keane signed the guitarist to his Del-Fi label, and they soon had a sizable hit with the brash "Come on Let's Go," which made No. 42. It was the pensive, almost awkward "Donna" that got him to No. 2 in early 1959. More innovative was the flipside, "La Bamba," sung entirely in Spanish, and featuring some fierce guitar work, as well as the thick sound of the Danelectro bass, which gave the instrument more electric presence than it had ever previously enjoyed on a rock 'n' roll disc.

Valens only had about two albums worth of material in the can, as well as some lo-fi live tapes of a gig at a local junior high, before his death; undoubtedly some or many of these were demos or unfinished tracks. A few other singers emulated Valens' Mexican-American brand of rock in the following years, most notably Chan Romero (originator of "Hippy Hippy Shake," who also recorded for Del-Fi and used some of the same musicians that had backed Valens) and Chris Montez. In the 1980s and 1990s, L.A. Latino rock band Los Lobos were often cited for reflecting Valens' influence. The 1987 film *La Bamba* (whose soundtrack featured Los Lobos) gave his story the Hollywood treatment, exposing his legacy to millions even as it introduced the usual distortions and factual errors in its dramatization of his brief life. *—Richie Unterberger*

In Concert at Pacioma Jr. High / 1960 / Rhino ◆◆◆

The Best of Ritchie Valens / 1986 / Rhino ◆◆◆◆
The virtually complete recording legacy of an all-too-brief career. *—Bruce Eder*

The Ritchie Valens Story / Jun. 15, 1993 / Del Fi ◆◆

● **The Very Best of Ritchie Valens** / 1995 / Del Fi ◆◆◆◆
There have been a few best-of packages for Valens over the last 20 years, and you're not necessarily better off with this one if you've picked up a collection in the past. As of the mid-'90s, though, this is the best anthology available. The 22 tracks cover all the important bases, including the few hits, several covers, and the best cuts from the remainder of his meager discography. *—Richie Unterberger*

Luther Vandross

b. Apr. 20, 1951, **d.** , New York, NY
Vocals / Soul, Urban, Club-Dance
In R&B music, Luther Vandross ranked with Prince, Stevie Wonder, and Michael Jackson as one of the most successful singer-songwriters and producers of the '80s. Amazingly, unlike those peers, Vandross for the most part did not cross over to widespread pop appeal, a situation that finally began to change at the end of the '80s and the start of the '90s.

Born in New York City, Vandross has an elastic tenor that made him a natural for backup singing and commercial work in the '70s, when he became a top session vocalist. In 1975, Vandross worked with David Bowie on the latter's *Young Americans* album, even co-writing (with Bowie and John Lennon) the No. 1 hit "Fame." In the second half of the '70s, he recorded under a variety of guises, cutting two albums for Cotillion under the name "Luther," recording with the session groups Roundtree and Change, and singing on hits by Chic.

In 1981, Vandross signed with Epic and released his debut album *Never Too Much,* which topped the R&B chart and sold a million copies. The title track was also an R&B No. 1 hit single and reached the pop Top 40. Vandross went on to produce albums for Aretha Franklin and other female singers, while maintaining his own career through the '80s. His albums *Forever, for Always, for Love* (1982), *Busy Body* (1983), *The Night I Fell in Love* (1985), *Give Me the Reason* (1986), and *Any Love* (1988) were all million-sellers that spawned major R&B hits, but Vandross' pop success was spotty until 1989, when Epic released *The Best of Luther Vandross . . . The Best of Love,* a double-pocket greatest-hits album containing the new track "Here and Now," which became Vandross' first Top Ten pop hit. That proved his breakthrough, and Vandross' next album, *Power of Love* (1991), another million-seller, featured two pop hits, "Power of Love/Love Power" and "Don't Want to Be a Fool."

Things basically went smooth for Luther Vandross on the commercial front in the early '90s, though not so smoothly behind the scenes. He toured with Anita Baker in 1990 and En Vogue in 1993, and on both tours there were disputes that eventually went public. Vandross issued *Never Let Me Go* in 1993, and while it did well, it wasn't quite the commercial powerhouse of his past releases. *—William Ruhlmann*

Never Too Much / 1981 / Epic ◆◆◆◆
The auspicious debut, demonstrating Vandross' gorgeous vocal arrangements and his lush, romantic singing on the No.1 R&B smash "Never Too Much" and the Top Ten "Don't You Know That?," plus the tour de force version of "A House Is Not a Home." *—William Ruhlmann*

Forever for Always for Love / 1982 / Epic ◆◆◆

Busy Body / 1983 / Epic ◆◆◆

The Night I Fell in Love / 1985 / Epic ◆◆◆◆
A wonderful version of Stevie Wonder's "Creepin'" almost gets lost on another hit-filled collection, which includes the Top Five R&B smashes "'Til My Baby Comes Home" and "It's Over Now." *—William Ruhlmann*

Give Me the Reason / 1986 / Epic ◆◆◆

Any Love / 1988 / Epic ◆◆◆◆
There were some who felt that Vandross suffered a slight slump when this album only reached the platinum level after two consecutive double-platinum winners. But "Here and Now" was a huge smash, and by now the pop crowd was fully aware of Vandross' vocal charms and allure. "She Won't Talk to Me" was a bit on the posturing side, but still managed to do decently, while there were also fine album cuts like "I Wonder" and "Are You Gonna Love Me." *—Ron Wynn*

★ **The Best of Luther Vandross** / 1989 / Epic ◆◆◆◆◆
By the time this way-overdue double-record hits collection came out, Vandross had done many more R&B singles than could fit on it, so *The Best of Luther Vandross . . . The Best of Love* is inadequate to encompass him. It does, however, contain "Here and Now," which broke Vandross through to the pop Top Ten long after most people had given up hope that he'd ever cross over. *—William Ruhlmann*

Greatest Hits 1981-1995 / Jan. 1996 / Epic ◆◆◆◆

Van Halen

Hard Rock, Pop-Rock, Heavy Metal
Van Halen was one of the most popular American hard-rock/heavy metal-bands to emerge in the '70s, primarily distinguished by the fleet fingers of guitarist Eddie Van Halen. Actually, Eddie and his brother Alex, who played the drums, were born in the Netherlands, though they moved to California as children, as did bassist Michael Anthony and singer David Lee Roth. They formed the group in Pasadena in 1974 and worked their way up the Southern California club circuit, signing with Warner Bros. in 1977. Their debut album, *Van Halen,* released in 1978, went gold in three months, platinum in eight. Every album since has sold at least a million copies.

The group hit a popular peak in 1984 with *1984,* which sold four million copies in its first year of release, and its No.1 single, "Jump," after which Roth left the band for a solo career. He was replaced by Sammy Hagar, and the success has continued, with four successive chart-topping albums to date. *—William Ruhlmann*

★ **Van Halen** / 1978 / Warner Bros. ◆◆◆◆◆
The prototype: Eddie Van Halen proves the hand is quicker than the ear, while David Lee Roth plays the role of outrageous frontman to perfection. Includes "You Really Got Me" and "Runnin' with the Devil." *—William Ruhlmann*

Van Halen II / 1979 / Warner Bros. ✦✦✦✦
Van Halen's second album sounded identical to their debut, yet it lacked the consistent songwriting of the first album. "Dance the Night Away" was a Top 20 hit and "Beautiful Girls" became one of their AOR staples, but most of the album sounded rushed and incomplete. —*Stephen Thomas Erlewine*

Women & Children First / 1980 / Warner Bros. ✦✦✦✦
Women and Children First expanded the musical range of Van Halen, as Eddie Van Halen increased his bag of tricks, flipping out bizarre noises and lightning-fast licks as mere asides. David Lee Roth used Eddie's aural jokes as a platform for lyrical jokes. In a whirlwind performance, Roth acted more like a comedian than a lead singer, and while that may be annoying on occasion, it certainly kept the record interesting. —*Stephen Thomas Erlewine*

Fair Warning / 1981 / Warner Bros. ✦✦✦
Perhaps as a reaction to David Lee Roth's unhinged performance on *Women & Children First*, *Fair Warning* was dominated by Eddie Van Halen, who has rarely played better than he has here, filling the record with imaginative sonic textures. However, sonic textures don't necessarily make for great songs, and that's the main problem with *Fair Warning*. Eddie's guitar has as much personality as Diamond Dave's strutting vocals, and given the right context could carry an album as effectively as Roth did with *Women & Children First*, but the songs do not provide a consistently strong support for his playing. Still, few guitarists match his power or his grace, and his performance is quite compelling. —*Stephen Thomas Erlewine*

Diver Down / 1982 / Warner Bros. ✦✦✦
Although it went platinum, *Fair Warning* didn't match the multi-platinum standards of Van Halen's first three records, so the group revamped their sound slightly for the follow-up, *Diver Down*. Adding the slightest hints of synthesizers and streamlining both the guitar indulgences of Eddie Van Halen and the vocal excesses of David Lee Roth, the album contained some of the group's most pop-oriented performances—and they were all in the guise of covers. "(Oh) Pretty Woman" and "Dancing in the Street" had the traditional mechanical Van Halen rhythmic pulse, as well as concise solos from Eddie and restrained vocals from Diamond Dave, which helped them become the hits they were designed to be. If they were offset by more original material like "Hang 'Em High," the concessions would have been acceptable, but the rest of *Diver Down* is filled with covers, including "Big Bad Bill," "Where Have All the Good Times Gone," and a closing "Happy Trails." All of the songs are professionally performed, and the music features more ideas than most previous Van Halen albums, but the lack of strong original material makes *Diver Down* less of an accomplishment than it appears. —*Stephen Thomas Erlewine*

☆ **1984** / 1984 / Warner Bros. ✦✦✦✦✦
Adding synthesizers to the mix, Van Halen turned pop while retaining much of its hard-rock propulsion, resulting in a quantum leap in sales. Includes "Jump," "I'll Wait," "Panama," and "Hot for Teacher." —*William Ruhlmann*

5150 / 1986 / Warner Bros. ✦✦✦
Van Halen proves it can survive in the post-Roth era, as Eddie continues to burn up the fretboard and Sammy Hagar turns out to fit into the group's style just fine. Includes "Why Can't This Be Love," "Dreams," and "Love Walks In." —*William Ruhlmann*

OU812 / 1988 / Warner Bros. ✦✦✦
Van Halen broke open the pop innovations of *5150* with *OU812*, their second album with Sammy Hagar. On *OU812*, Hagar's direct approach is fully incorporated into the group, as the band churns out straight-ahead heavy rockers like "Black and Blue" and pulsing power ballads like "Feels So Good." Under Eddie's direction, the group adds a couple of stylistic quirks—from the chicken-picking of "Finish What You Started" and the Hawaiian flourishes of "Cabo Wabo" to the driving, jazz-inflected metallic "Mine All Mine"—which make *OU812* one of the band's most intriguing and rewarding albums. —*Stephen Thomas Erlewine*

For Unlawful Carnal Knowledge / 1991 / Warner Bros. ✦✦
The smirking title indicates the true nature of *For Unlawful Carnal Knowledge*, Van Halen's third album with Sammy Hagar. Backing away from the diversity of *OU812*, the band turns in some of the most basic, straightforward rock 'n' roll of their career. At times, *F.U.C.K.* recalls the sleek hard rock of Hagar's early-'80s albums, and it's undeniable that his limited vocal power had a great deal to do with the obvious nature of most of this music. While the band is still tight and professional—and Eddie's guitar-work remains impressive—the songwriting is, by and large, undistinguished, with the anthemic "Right Now" standing out as the most memorable song of the batch, mainly because of its incessant chorus. —*Stephen Thomas Erlewine*

Van Halen Live: Right Here, Right Now / 1993 / Warner Bros. ✦✦
Balance / 1995 / Warner Bros. ✦✦

Vapors

New Wave, Power-Pop, Mod-revival
Led by vocalist/guitarist Dave Fenton, the Vapors were a short-lived new-wave guitar group that is best known for the spiky pop single "Turning Japanese." Fenton formed the first version of the Vapors in 1978, yet he was the only member to survive that lineup; in 1979, former Ellery Bops members Ed Bazalgette (lead guitar) and Howard Smith (drums) joined the band and bassist Steve Smith came aboard shortly afterward. One of the band's first concerts was seen by the Jam's Bruce Foxton, who asked them to perform on his group's *Setting Sons* tour. Before long, the Vapors were managed by Foxton and John Weller, the manager of the Jam, as well as the father of the group's leader, Paul Weller.

The Vapors signed to United Artists, releasing their first single, "Prisoners," at the end of 1979; it failed to chart. "Turning Japanese," the band's second single, became a major hit, reaching No. 3 on the UK charts in March of 1980. *New Clear Days*, the band's debut album, was released two months later, which didn't sell as well as the single. In 1981, the Vapors released the more ambitious *Magnets*, yet it received lukewarm reviews and poor sales; the group disbanded shortly after its release. —*Stephen Thomas Erlewine*

New Clear Days / Jun. 1980 / United Artists ✦✦✦✦
It's easy to dismiss this band as a one-hit wonder—surely the album has nothing quite as infectious as the single, "Turning Japanese." *New Clear Days* is, however, a fine example of punchy Brit-pop in the vein of the Jam that holds up better than most albums from the period. —*Chris Woodstra*

Magnets / 1981 / Liberty ✦✦✦
David Fenton was obviously growing tired of being written off as lightweight after "Turning Japanese" and responded with the more ambitious and mature *Magnets*. Here he explores the darker side of life, discussing the Kennedy assasination ("Magnets"), police harrassment ("Civic Hall"), and even cult leader/mass murder Rev. Jim Jones ("Jimmy Jones," the failed single). Musically the band is more sophisticated, taking the occasional misstep in the arrangements by adding an annoying synthesizer in songs like "Spiders." Virtually ignored by both critics and the buying public, this is a strong follow-up that deserved a better fate. —*Chris Woodstra*

● **Anthology** / 1995 / One Way ✦✦✦✦
A somewhat misleading title, *Anthology* is a straight reissue of *New Clear Days* with four songs from *Magnets* tacked on to the end. Since the band only made two albums it would have been nice to release both as a two-fer—or at least add some rare tracks to the anthology. Minor complaints aside, this is probably all the Vapors most people will ever need. —*Chris Woodstra*

Stevie Ray Vaughan

b. Oct. 3, 1954, Dallas, TX, d. Aug. 27, 1990, East Troy, WI
Guitar / Modern Electric Blues, Blues-Rock
Stevie Ray Vaughan was the most impressive blues guitarist to appear in the '80s, which made his death in a helicopter crash at the start of the '90s all the more tragic. Vaughan grew up in Dallas, the younger brother of Jimmie Vaughan (co-founder of the Fabulous Thunderbirds). Stevie began playing in clubs at 12, and by 17 had dropped out of high school and moved to Austin, TX. There followed years of struggling until April 23, 1982, when Vaughan and his group, Double Trouble, played a private audition for the Rolling Stones in New York. The gig led to an invitation to appear at the Montreux Jazz Festival, at which Vaughan was seen by David Bowie, who hired him to play guitar on his *Let's Dance* album, and Jackson Browne, who offered the free use of his recording studio. Vaughan took up that offer after being signed by legendary talent scout John Hammond to Epic, recording his debut album, *Texas Flood*, in the fall of 1982.

The release of the album led to a wave of recognition that included gold albums, Grammy awards, and other accolades over the next seven years. In 1987, Vaughan took time out to go through a rehabilitation program to overcome alcohol and drug addiction, and he wrote about the experience on his final studio album, *In Step* (1989). In the last year of his life, he embarked on a co-headlining tour with Jeff Beck and recorded a duo album with his brother. He had just finished a jam with Eric Clapton and Robert Cray at a show at Alpine Valley in East Troy, WI, when he was killed. In 1991 Epic released the posthumous *The Sky Is Crying*, assembled by Jimmie Vaughan. —*William Ruhlmann*

Texas Flood / 1983 / Epic ✦✦✦
A late-arriving star, Vaughan did not make his first album until the age of 28. By that time he had become a seasoned player, so this doesn't really sound like a debut album; rather, it sounds like a blues guitar master at the top of his form. —*William Ruhlmann*

Couldn't Stand the Weather / 1984 / Epic ✦✦✦✦
Vaughan does not ease up on this second set, even taking on Jimi Hendrix in a rendition of "Voodoo Chile (Slight Return)," and handling it beautifully. — *William Ruhlmann*

Soul to Soul / 1985 / Epic ✦✦✦✦

Live Alive / Jul. 1986 / Epic ✦✦✦

In Step / 1989 / Epic ✦✦✦✦
Vaughan sounds just as fierce sober as he did before, and he is beginning to bloom as a songwriter, a fact most notable on the driving "The House Is Rockin'" and the confessional "Wall of Denial." — *William Ruhlmann*

The Sky Is Crying / 1991 / Epic ✦✦✦✦
The posthumously released *The Sky Is Crying,* assembled out of tracks recorded between 1984 and 1989, is a lovingly assembled tribute to Vaughan's brilliance as a guitarist. Arguably this is Vaughan's finest album. The first-rate playing is unforced and natural in execution. On the songs, from his impeccable version of Hendrix's "Little Wing" to the hard blues shuffle of "Empty Arms," Vaughan's execution is unforced and his phrasing is relaxed. The release contains great liner notes and track information. Fans of hard blues-rock should check this one out. — *Rick Clark*

In the Beginning / Oct. 6, 1992 / Epic ✦✦

★ **Greatest Hits** / Nov. 21, 1995 / Epic ✦✦✦✦✦
Stevie Ray Vaughan was a great guitarist, but he had trouble making consistent albums. *Greatest Hits* rectifies that problem by collecting all of his best-known tracks, from "Pride and Joy" to "Crossfire." Not only is it a terrific introduction, it's his most consistent album, demonstrating exactly why he was one of the most important guitarists of the '80s. — *Stephen Thomas Erlewine*

Bobby Vee

b. Apr. 30, 1943, Fargo, ND
Vocals / Pop-Rock, Teen Idol, Brill Building Pop
Bobby Vee enjoyed his greatest success in the early '60s, with five Top Ten singles, including the classic, "Take Good Care of My Baby." Vee's vocal style was similar to that of his hero, Buddy Holly. Ironically, Vee's break came when he filled in for Holly the day after his death in a plane crash. Like those of many of his contemporaries, his career went into a tailspin with the arrival of the British Invasion in 1964. He did score one more Top Ten single in 1967 with "Come Back When You Grow Up." — *Kenneth M. Cassidy*

● **Legendary Masters** / 1990 / EMI America ✦✦✦✦
The most complete collection of Vee's recordings includes "Take Good Care of My Baby," "Rubber Ball," and "The Night Has a Thousand Eyes." — *Kenneth M. Cassidy*

Greatest Hits / 1994 / Curb ✦✦✦
Ten of his biggest hits, including "Take Good Care of My Baby," "Run to Him," and "Come Back When You Grow Up," for those of you who are in a rush and have no time for nuances like liner notes and low-charting singles. These *are* all original recordings, though the minimal packaging and liner notes on Curb's *Greatest Hits* series might lead you to suspect otherwise. — *Richie Unterberger*

Suzanne Vega

b. Aug. 12, 1959, Santa Monica, CA
Guitar, Vocals / Singer-Songwriter
Vega was born in Santa Monica, CA, and moved to New York City at age two. She attended the High School of Performing Arts, then Barnard College. Vega was still at Barnard when she began attracting attention in Greenwich Village folk clubs and was featured on several issues of the songwriters' magazine/record album *The CooP* (later *The Fast Folk Musical Magazine*) in 1982. She was signed to A&M Records in 1984 and released her first album, *Suzanne Vega* in 1985. It was a critical success and a moderate seller. Vega's second album, *Solitude Standing,* featured "Luka," a song about child abuse that became a surprise hit single in 1987. The album itself went gold. Vega took three years to release the follow-up, *Days of Open Hand* (1990), which was a commercial disappointment, though a few months later a couple of British DJs, under the name D.N.A., put out a dance version of her a cappella song "Tom's Diner" from the album *Solitude Standing,* and it became a hit.
On her next album, 1992's *99.9 Degrees F.,* Vega experimented with the dance rhythms that made "Tom's Diner" a hit; although the result was interesting, it didn't give her any hits. — *William Ruhlmann*

Suzanne Vega / May 1985 / A&M ✦✦✦✦
Vega's most consistent collection of songs spotlights her hushed, restrained singing style and the spare, precise backup produced by Lenny Kaye. But it's those songs, "Small Blue Thing," "Undertow," "Marlene on the Wall," with their brittle imagery (things are always frozen, flat, or cracking) and restraint, that let you know there's a big new talent here. — *William Ruhlmann*

● **Solitude Standing** / Apr. 1987 / A&M ✦✦✦✦
The usual sophomore jinx is that, since you don't have enough time while promoting your first album to write enough songs for your second, you make up the difference by using older songs that didn't make it before, which makes your second album inconsistent and disappointing. The songs on *Solitude Standing,* Suzanne Vega's second album, had years listed beside them on the lyric sheet, so you could see that some of them dated back to 1978. But that bold admission heralded the album's triumph—that its diversity was what made it so good. Partially, that was because the old songs were the equal of anything on the first album—it was just that tunes like the a cappella slice-of-life "Tom's Diner" and the warmly romantic "Gypsy" wouldn't have fit thematically on the austere, self-absorbed-yet-distanced debut. ("Calypso," on the other hand, would have fit perfectly.) On *Solitude Standing,* they became part of an album of story songs set in a variety of musical contexts. The first album, consisting of songs Vega had developed as a solo acoustic performer, essentially retained those arrangements with a little extra instrumentation here and there for color. But many of the songs on *Solitude Standing* had band arrangements; in fact, members of Vega's touring band often were credited with co-writing the music. The group played elegant folk/pop-rock, and the album had a sparkling sound. Vega had developed more as a singer without losing the focused intonation that had made her debut compelling. Those elements helped make "Luka," a character song about domestic abuse, a fluke hit, and all that was wrong with that was that Vega was never going to be a singles act and that she might be considered a one-hit wonder in industry terms when that became apparent. In the interim, the hit did what hits do: It sold records and helped Vega gain exposure. Not so much noticed at the time was that, based on the newer songs, Vega was making a transition to a less personal, more externalized songwriting approach that was sketchier and more dependent on her music. For the moment, however, *Solitude Standing* seemed like an artistic development for her, and it clearly moved more units than the debut, and that's what you look for in a second album from the standpoint of career building. — *William Ruhlmann*

Days of Open Hand / Apr. 1990 / A&M ✦✦

99.9 Degrees F. / Sep. 8, 1992 / A&M ✦✦✦

The Velvet Underground

Rock 'n' roll, Proto-Punk
Few rock groups can claim to have broken so much new territory, and maintain such consistent brilliance on record, as the Velvet Underground during their brief lifespan. It was the group's lot to be ahead of, or at least out of step with, their time. The mid-to-late '60s was an era of explosive growth and experimentation in rock, but the Velvets' innovations—which blended the energy of rock with the sonic adventurism of the avant-garde, and introduced a new degree of social realism and sexual kinkiness into rock lyrics—were too abrasive for the mainstream to handle. During their time, the group experienced little commercial success; though they were hugely appreciated by a cult audience and some critics, the larger public treated them with indifference or, occasionally, scorn. The Velvets' music was too important to languish in obscurity, though; their cult only grew larger and larger in the years following their demise, and continues to mushroom today. By the 1980s, they were acknowledged not just as one of the most important rock bands of the '60s, but one of the best of all time, and one whose immense significance cannot be measured by their relatively modest sales.

Historians often hail the group for their incalculable influence upon the punk and new wave of subsequent years, and while the Velvets were undoubtedly a key touchstone of the movements, to focus upon these elements of their vision is to only get part of the story. The group were uncompromising in their music and lyrics, to be sure, sometimes espousing a bleakness and primitivism that would inspire alienated singers and songwriters of future generations. But their colorful and oft-grim soundscapes were firmly grounded in strong, well-constructed songs that could be as humanistic and compassionate as they were outrageous and confrontational. The member most responsible for these qualities was guitarist, singer, and songwriter Lou Reed, whose sing-speak vocals and gripping narratives have come to define street-savvy rock 'n' roll.

Reed loved rock 'n' roll from an early age, and even recorded a doo-wop-type single as a Long Island teenager in the late '50s (as a member of the Shades). By the early '60s, he was also getting into avant-garde jazz and serious poetry, coming under the influence of author Delmore Schwartz while studying at Syracuse University. After graduation, he set his sights considerably lower, churning out tunes for exploitation rock albums as a staff songwriter for Pickwick Records in New York City. Reed did learn some useful things about production at Pickwick, and it was while working there that he met John Cale, a classically trained Welshman who had moved to America to study and perform "serious" music. Cale, who had performed with John Cage and LaMonte Young, found himself increasingly attracted to rock 'n' roll; Reed, for his part, was interested in the avant-garde as well as pop. Reed and Cale were both interested in fusing the avant-garde with rock 'n' roll, and had found the ideal partners for making the vision (a very radical one for the mid-'60s) work; their synergy would be the crucial axis of the Velvet Underground's early work.

Reed and Cale (who would play bass, viola, and organ) would need to assemble a full band, making tentative steps along this direction by performing together in the Primitives (which also included experimental filmmaker Tony Conrad and avant-garde sculptor Walter DeMaria) to promote a bizarre Reed-penned Pickwick single ("The Ostrich"). By 1965, the group was a quartet called the Velvet Underground, including Reed, Cale, guitarist Sterling Morrison (an old friend of Reed's), and drummer Angus MacLise. MacLise quit before the band's first paying gig, claiming that accepting money for art was a sellout; the Velvets quickly recruited drummer Maureen Tucker, a sister of one of Morrison's friends.

Even at this point, the Velvets were well on their way to developing something quite different. Their original material, principally penned and sung by Reed, dealt with the hard urban realities of Manhattan, describing drug use, sadomasochism, and decadence in cool, unapologetic detail in "Heroin," "I'm Waiting for the Man," "Venus in Furs," and "All Tomorrow's Parties." These were wedded to basic, hard-nosed rock riffs, toughened by Tucker's metronome beats, the oddly tuned, rumbling guitars, and Cale's occasional viola scrapes. It was an uncommercial blend to say the least, but the Velvets got an unexpected benefactor when artist and all-around pop-art icon Andy Warhol caught the band at a club around the end of 1965. Warhol quickly assumed management of the group, incorporating them into his mixed-media/performance-art ensemble, the Exploding Plastic Inevitable. By spring 1966, Warhol was producing their debut album.

Warhol was also responsible for embellishing the quartet with Nico, a mysterious European model/chanteuse with a deep voice whom the band accepted rather reluctantly, viewing her spectral presence as rather ornamental. Reed remained the principal lead vocalist, but Nico did sing three of the best songs on the group's debut, often known as "the banana album" because of its distinctive Warhol-designed cover. Recognized today as one of the core classic albums of rock, it featured an extraordinarily strong set of songs, highlighted by "Heroin," "All Tomorrow's Parties," "Venus in Furs," "I'll Be Your Mirror," "Femme Fatale," "Black Angel's Death Song," and "Sunday Morning." The sensational drug-and-sex items (especially "Heroin") got most of the ink, but the more conventional numbers showed Reed to be a songwriter capable of considerable melodicism, sensitivity, and almost naked introspection.

The album's release was not without complications, though. First, it wasn't issued until nearly a year after it was finished, due to record-company politics and other factors. The group's association with Warhol and the Exploding Plastic Inevitable had already assured them of a high (if notorious media) profile, but the music was simply too daring to fit onto commercial radio; "underground" rock radio was barely getting started at this point, and in any case may well have overlooked the record at a time when psychedelic music was approaching its peak. The album only reached No. 171 in the charts, and that's as high as any of their LPs would get upon original release. Those who heard it, however, were often mightily impressed; Brian Eno once said that even though hardly anyone bought the Velvets records at the time they appeared, almost everyone who did formed their own bands.

A cult reputation wasn't enough to guarantee a stable livelihood for a band in the '60s, and by 1967 the Velvets were fighting problems within their own ranks. Nico, never considered an essential member by the rest of the band, left or was fired sometime during the year, going on to a fascinating career of her own. The association with Warhol weakened, as the artist was unable to devote as much attention to the band as he had the previous year. Embittered by the lukewarm reception of their album in their native New York, the Velvets concentrated on touring cities throughout the rest of the country. Amidst this tense atmosphere, the second album, *White Light/White Heat*, was recorded in late 1967.

Each of the albums the group released while Reed led the band was an unexpected departure from all of their other LPs. *White Light/White Heat* was probably the most radical, focusing almost exclusively on their noisiest arrangements, overamped guitars, and most willfully abrasive songs. The 17-minute "Sister Ray" was their most extreme (and successful) effort in this vein. Unsurprisingly, the album failed to catch on commercially, topping out at No. 199.

By the summer of 1968, the band had a much graver problem on its hands than commercial success (or the lack of it). A rift developed between Reed and Cale, the most creative forces in the band and, as one could expect, two temperamental egos. Reed presented the rest of the band with an ultimatum, declaring that he would leave the group unless Cale was sacked. Morrison and Tucker reluctantly sided with Lou, and Doug Yule was recruited to take Cale's place.

The group's self-titled third album (1969) was an even more radical left turn than *White Light/White Heat*. The volume and violence had nearly vanished; the record featured far more conventional rock arrangements that were sometimes so restrained it seems as though they were

making an almost deliberate attempt to avoid waking the neighbors. Yet the sound was nonetheless effective for that; the record contains some of Reed's most personal and striking compositions, numbers like "Pale Blue Eyes" and "Candy Says" ranking among his most romantic, although cuts like "What Goes On" proved they could still rock out convincingly (though in a less experimental fashion than they had with Cale). The approach may have confused listeners and critics, but by this time their label (MGM/Verve) was putting little promotional resources behind the band anyway.

Even in the absence of Cale, the Velvets were still capable of generating compelling heat onstage, as *Live 1969* (not released until the mid-'70s) confirms. MGM was by now in the midst of an infamous "purge" of its supposedly drug-related rock acts, and the Velvets were setting their sights elsewhere. Nevertheless, they recorded about an album's worth of additional material for the label after the third LP, although it remains unclear whether this was intended for a fourth album or not. Many of the songs, though, were excellent, serving as a bridge between *The Velvet Underground* and 1970's *Loaded;* a lot of it was officially released in the 1980s and 1990s.

The beginning of the 1970s seemed to herald considerable promise for the group, as they signed to Atlantic, but at this point the personnel problems that had always dogged them finally became overwhelming. Tucker had to sit out *Loaded* due to pregnancy, replaced by Yule's brother Billy. Doug Yule, according to some accounts, began angling for more power in the band. Unexpectedly, after a lengthy residency at New York's famous Max's Kansas City club, Reed quit the band near the end of the summer of 1970, moving back to his parents' Long Island home for several months before beginning his solo career, just before the release of *Loaded*, his final studio album with the Velvets.

Loaded was by far the group's most conventional rock album, and the most accessible one for mainstream listeners. "Rock and Roll" and "Sweet Jane" in particular were two of Reed's most anthemic, jubilant tunes, and ones that became rock standards in the '70s. But the group's power was somewhat diluted by the absence of Tucker, and by the decision to have Doug Yule handle some of the lead vocals. Due to Reed's departure, though, the group couldn't capitalize on any momentum it might have generated. Unwisely, the band decided to continue, though Morrison and Tucker left shortly afterwards. That left Doug Yule at the helm of an act that was the Velvet Underground in name only, and the 1973 album that was billed to the group (*Squeeze*) is best forgotten, and not considered as a true Velvets release.

With Reed, Cale, and Nico establishing important solo careers of their own, and such important figures as David Bowie, Brian Eno, and Patti Smith making no bones about their debts to the band, the Velvet Underground simply became more and more popular as the years passed. In the 1980s, the original albums were reissued, along with a couple of important collections of outtakes. Hoping to rewrite the rules one last time, Reed, Cale, Morrison, and Tucker attempted to defy the odds against successful rock reunions by reforming in the early '90s (Nico had died in 1988). A European tour, and a live album, was completed in 1993 to mixed reviews; before a planned American jaunt could start, Reed and Cale (who have feuded constantly over the past few decades) fell out yet again, bringing the reunion to a sad close. Sterling Morrison's death from illness in 1995 seems to have permanently iced any prospect of more projects under the Velvet Underground name, although a few of the surviving members played together when they were inducted into the Rock and Roll Hall of Fame. By that time, an impressive five-CD box set (containing all four of the studio albums issued when Reed was in the band, as well as a lot of other material) was available to enshrine the group's legacy for the ages. *—Richie Unterberger*

☆ **The Velvet Underground & Nico** / Jan. 1967 / Verve ✦✦✦✦✦
Nominally produced by Andy Warhol, *The Velvet Underground & Nico* is one of the most important and influential albums of all time. The only record the group recorded with Nico, the disc includes the seminal "Heroin," "I'm Waiting for the Man," and "Venus in Furs." As with the finest films and books, each song provides a window into a world that most will otherwise not have experienced. "Heroin" is probably the finest example of this, with the rush and subsequent down of the drug masterfully conveyed via Tucker's unorthodox drum style (simply involving padded beaters on a bass drum turned on its side), continuous changes in tempo, different musicians playing in different tempos at the same time, and Cale's shrieking viola-induced feedback at the end. In terms of sound the whole album is wide ranging, moving from the melodic beauty of "Femme Fatale" to the intense cacophony of "European Son." *—Rob Bowman*

☆ **White Light/White Heat** / 1967 / Verve ✦✦✦✦✦
By the time of *White Light/White Heat*, Nico had departed to embark upon a solo career. The Velvets, now also minus Warhol, concocted an extraordinarily abrasive, tension-filled album, full of mind-numbing feedback and incessant drones. The playing and production on this album herald a punk aesthetic eight years ahead of the fact. Standout

tracks include the sidelong improvisatory "Sister Ray" and the John Cale-narrated, Lou Reed-written "The Gift." —*Rob Bowman*

☆ **The Velvet Underground** / 1969 / Verve ◆◆◆◆◆
In an unexpected, abrupt departure from the ferocity of their first two albums, the Velvets' third album is a muted, folk-rockish, even warm affair. The impression is almost of a band deliberately turning down to create a restrained, haunting ambience, but it suffers not in the least for the loss of volume: "Pale Blue Eyes," "I'm Set Free," and "Candy Says" are some of Reed's greatest songs, "Some Kinda Love" will satisfy those looking for the requisite Velvet kinkiness, and "Beginning to see The Light" and "What Goes On" prove that the group can handle straightforward, charging rockers masterfully. —*Richie Unterberger*

☆ **Loaded** / 1970 / Warner Bros. ◆◆◆◆◆
Recorded in the summer of 1970 while the band was playing a summer-long residency at Max's Kansas City in New York. Feeling increasingly disaffected, Reed walked out after the last gig at Max's, never to return. The album was remixed and edited without him, much to his later chagrin. Whatever imperfections may have consequently occurred, *Loaded* remains an absolute must. The Velvets were now playing stripped-down rock 'n' roll and Reed was writing such enduring classics as "Sweet Jane" and "Rock & Roll," as well as the underrated "New Age," "Train Round the Bend," and "Oh! Sweet Nuthin'." —*Rob Bowman*

Live at Max's Kansas City / 1972 / Cotillion ◆◆◆
Literally recorded the last night Lou Reed ever played with the Velvet Underground, at New York's Max's Kansas City, we have this album due to the foresight of Warhol acolyte and employee Brigid Polk, who happened to bring her cassette recorder to document that evening. The sound is a little one-dimensional, and you can hear Jim Carroll ask for Tylenol and others order drinks over the course of the record, but the recording is nonetheless fascinating. Brigid's tape was about an hour and a half long. Cotillion released just under half of it. The sound of the group is a little different, because Doug Yule's brother Billy was temporarily replacing drummer Maureen Tucker, since the latter was pregnant with her first child. —*Rob Bowman*

☆ **1969: Velvet Underground Live** / 1974 / Mercury ◆◆◆◆◆
Originally a double album and released in two volumes with added songs on CD, *1969: Velvet Underground Live* is a stunning document of the Reed, Yule, Morrison, Tucker edition of the Velvets at their pinnacle. Recorded privately in Texas and San Francisco, the Velvets play extended, intensely driven, and out-and-out versions of songs from their first three albums as well as then-unreleased material such as "Ocean," "Real Good Time Together," and "Sweet Bonnie Brown." —*Rob Bowman*

☆ **Vu** / 1985 / Verve ◆◆◆◆◆
Composed principally of songs that would have appeared on the Velvets' unreleased fourth MGM album, this is only slightly less impressive than their first three LPs, striking a balance between the searing pre-punk of their first two efforts and the calm eloquence of the third. "Lisa Says," "Ocean," and "Stephanie Says" are some of Reed's greatest ballads; "I Can't Stand It" is one of the Velvets' toughest and best conventional hard rock songs. Some of the other tunes are slight (if engaging) in comparison with the Velvets' prime work. Many of the tracks were rerecorded by Reed on his early solo albums, and in every instance, the Velvets' versions are better. —*Richie Unterberger*

Another View / 1986 / Verve ◆◆◆
Polygram finally started to scrape the bottom of the barrel with this grab bag of outtakes from 1967 to 1969, most of which don't approach the magnificence of most of the Velvets' studio output. It's never less than interesting, though, and certainly worth perusal by Velvets fans. Especially noteworthy are a gloriously tough version of "We're Gonna Have a Good Time Together" (one of their best simple rock tunes), the grinding instrumental "Guess I'm Falling In Love," and an early version of "Rock and Roll." —*Richie Unterberger*

● **Best of the Velvet Underground** / 1989 / Verve ◆◆◆◆
The Best of the Velvet Underground: Words and Music of Lou Reed is a 15-track summary of the Velvets' career, borrowing heavily from the debut (six tracks) and featuring "Sweet Jane" and "Rock & Roll," licensed from Atlantic. —*William Ruhlmann*

Live MCMXCIII / 1993 / Warner Bros. ◆◆
☆ **Peel Slowly and See** / 1995 / Polydor ◆◆◆◆◆
Does this five-CD box set feature an abundance of essential material? Certainly. It has all four of the studio albums released by the Lou Reed-led lineup, and a wealth of previously unreleased goodies. Is it an essential purchase? That depends on your level of fanaticism. Most serious Velvets fans have all four of the core studio albums already (although the third, self-titled LP is presented in its muffled, so-called "closet" mix), and will be most interested in the previously unavailable recordings, which do hold considerable fascination. The entire first disc is devoted to a drummer-less 1965 rehearsal tape in John Cale's loft, with radically different, almost folky run-throughs of some of the most important songs from their classic debut ("Venus in Furs," "I'm Waiting for the Man," "All

Tomorrow's Parties," "Heroin"), as well as a song that only made it onto Nico's first LP ("Wrap Your Troubles in Dreams"), and one which makes its first appearance anywhere (the Dylanesque "Prominent Men"). "Venus in Furs" (with Cale on vocals) and "All Tomorrow's Parties" sound particularly different here, almost like English folk ballads. Other big bonuses include no less than seven outtakes from *Loaded*, featuring excellent, high-spirited versions of "Ocean," "Satellite of Love," and other songs re-done by Reed on his early solo albums, though the versions here are considerably better. Then there are several early 1967 demos (in lo-fi but listenable quality) of songs that never got recorded by the Velvets otherwise, some very good. And there are sundry other unreleased live and studio items, highlighted by a scorching live 1967 "Guess I'm Falling in Love" and the 1969 demo "Countess from Hong Kong." There are also highlights from *VU* and *Another View*, longer versions of *Loaded*'s "Sweet Jane" and "New Age" that restore fragments edited out in the final mix, and an 80-page booklet. The thing is, though, that virtually everyone who's interested in this material has already bought the four studio albums, sometimes several times over. A separate release of the two discs or so of truly new material would have been welcomed by the many fans who aren't interested in paying for a five-CD box of stuff when they already have well over half of it. But as a friend of mine is fond of saying, that eats into profit margins real fast. —*Richie Unterberger*

The Ventures

Rock 'n' roll, Instrumental Rock, Surf
From Tacoma, WA, the Ventures formed in 1959, originally named the Versatones. The early lineup consisted of Don Wilson (b. 1937), rhythm guitar; Bob Bogle (b. 1937), lead guitar; Nokie Edwards (b. 1939), bass; and Howie Johnson, drums. They pressed a twangy, rocked-up version of Johnny Smith's "Walk Don't Run" on their own Blue Horizon label, which was later picked up by Dolton Records. It became a No. 2 hit in 1960. Bogle and Edwards switched instruments and Mel Taylor replaced Johnson on drums in 1963. More hit singles featuring their cleanly played but rockin' style followed, but the band wisely entered the album market early on, and it was there they found their true format placing 37 chart entries and more than 50 albums between 1960 and the mid '70s.
The Ventures are the biggest-selling instrumental group of all time, but their influence extends far beyond mere record sales. With their solid-body Fender guitars (later switching to Mosrite Ventures models) and matching suits, their album covers defined what a rock 'n' roll combo should look like. Likewise, their sound was so popular that they released several successful instructional albums in the *Play with the Ventures* series that many later rock stars cut their teeth on. Because they played instrumentals, they were among the first American bands to break big in Japan (no language barrier), eventually honored as the first foreign members of that country's Conservatory of Music for selling over 40 million records. Edwards left and was replaced for a while by Jerry McGee, but he returned in 1972, restoring the early '60s lineup, which has endured to the present day. They continued to tour and record, sounding better than ever, their place in rock 'n' roll guitar history assured. —*Cub Koda*

Ventures Play Telstar & the Lonely Bull / 1962 / Liberty ◆◆

Ventures in Space / 1963 / Dolton ◆◆◆
Few listeners need to dig deeper than a greatest hits collection for the Ventures, but this early effort is an arguable exception. The group embellished their trademark sleek guitar instrumentals with creepy, then-futuristic production effects, sounding at times like a mix of surf music and the incidental music to *Star Trek*. The ghostly, theremin-like sounds on several tracks are actually produced by top session player Red Rhodes on steel guitar. The British instrumental group the Tornados (of "Telstar" fame) did this kind of stuff better, if you're looking for this kind of thing. The CD reissue combines this album and the 1962 LP *The Ventures Play Telstar*—The Lonely Bull and Others. —*Richie Unterberger*

The Ventures on Stage / 1965 / Dolton ◆◆◆◆
Explosive live recordings from Japan, England, and the US, with a hot greatest-hits medley and a wild "Driving Guitars" being among the highlights. *The Ventures on Stage Around the World* is out of print but worth any search. —*Cub Koda*

★ **Walk, Don't Run: The Best of the Ventures** / 1990 / EMI America ◆◆◆◆◆
A perfect 29-track CD compilation, with great notes and superlative sound. All the hits, from "Walk Don't Run" to "Hawaii Five-O." Important album sides, plus interviews and radio spots. A perfect introduction. —*Cub Koda*

Live In Japan '65 / 1995 / ◆◆◆◆
Originally released in Japan as a double album, this live set was unavailable in the US until 1995. So cleanly recorded (the drums are especially crisp) that one is tempted to believe these tracks might have actually been laid down in the studios, it has a speedy, frenetic, well-executed

edge that makes this worth checking out by Ventures fans. 78 minutes of material, including most of their big '60s hits, covers of then-contemporary surf and British Invasion tunes, and surprises like "The Pink Panther Theme" and a 10-minute version of Duke Ellington's "Caravan." —*Richie Unterberger*

Vibrators

Punk

One of the great myths in rock 'n' roll is that only serious, dedicated musicians can make great records; a philosophical tract dictating that great rock 'n' roll is not the province of bandwagon jumpers, poseurs, fakes, and commercially minded trend groupies. The reality is that great rock 'n' roll can be made by anyone, even accidentally. Case in point, the Vibrators. If you saw a photograph of this "punk" band a few months before they signed a label deal with Columbia in 1976, you would have seen long hair and bell-bottom trousers—they were bloody hippies! But by the time they released their debut LP, *Pure Mania*, they had short hair, fake leopard-skin pants, safety pins, cheap sunglasses, all the accoutrements a good born-again punk band needed. Did that make them inherently bad? Not really, a tad disingenuous perhaps, but no worse than a punk band (e.g., Generation X) that professed to being real punks all the while secretly harboring the desire of being as commercially viable as the dinosaur bands they purportedly loathed.

Although the existence of *Pure Mania* is a good illustration of accidental inspiration, it also proves that moments like this can happen once in a dross-filled career. Such was the case with the Vibrators who went on to record nearly a dozen records over a 15-year period, none of them worth mentioning. *Pure Mania*, on the other hand, remains as good now as it did when it was released. This is due to the fact that the band simply adapted a formula that eschewed the rage and fury of the Sex Pistols and Clash for the relative accessibility of the Ramones and the Damned. So, while the Pistols sang "No Future," *Pure Mania* is jumpstarted by a track called "Into the Future." Even the songs about emotional desolation ("No Heart") are more catchy than frightening or ominous. Sure, *Pure Mania* is a fake through and through, but hating it for that reason alone makes you the boring old fart. Besides, the speedy guitars, irresistible hooks, and snappy songs are infectious. —*John Dougan*

Pure Mania / 1977 / Columbia ◆◆◆◆
Don't be fooled into thinking that, based on *Pure Mania*, The Vibrators released everything else of merit. They didn't. But this is a fine, funny fake of a record from the squalling "Into the Future . . . " to the softcore fantasy "Whips and Furs" to the tongue-in-cheek sexism of "I Need a Slave." Punky pop, not punk rage. Not inspirational, but what did you expect from a bunch of poseurs? —*John Dougan*

● **The Power of Money: The Best of the Vibrators** / Dec. 1991 / Continuum ◆◆◆◆
By taking the best moments from the Vibrators' debut *Pure Mania*, as well as their inconsistent follow-ups, *Power of Money* winds up as a fine collection of their energetically melodic punk rock. —*Stephen Thomas Erlewine*

Gene Vincent (Vincent Eugene Craddock)

b. Feb. 11, 1935, Norfolk, VA, **d.** Oct. 12, 1971, Los Angeles, CA
Vocals / Rock 'n' roll, Rockabilly

Gene Vincent only had one really big hit, "Be Bop a Lula," which epitomized rockabilly at its prime in 1956 with its sharp guitar breaks, spare snare drums, fluttering echo, and Vincent's breathless, sexy vocals. Yet his place as one of the great early rock 'n' roll singers is secure, backed up by a wealth of fine smaller hits and non-hits that rate among the best rockabilly of all time. The leather-clad, limping, greasy-haired singer was also one of rock's original bad boys, lionized by romanticists of past and present generations attracted to his primitive, sometimes savage style and indomitable spirit.

Vincent was bucking the odds by entering professional music in the first place. As a 20-year-old in the Navy, he suffered a severe motorcycle accident that almost resulted in the amputation of his leg, and left him with a permanent limp and considerable chronic pain for the rest of his life. After the accident he began to concentrate on building a musical career, playing with country bands around the Norfolk, Virginia, area. Demos cut at a local radio station, fronting a band assembled around Gene by his management, landed Gene Vincent and the Blue Caps a contract at Capitol, which hoped they'd found competition for Elvis Presley.

Indeed it had, as by this time Vincent had plunged into all-out rockabilly, capable of both fast-paced exuberance and whispery, almost sensitive ballads. The Blue Caps were one of the greatest rock bands of the '50s, anchored at first by the stunning silvery, faster-than-light guitar leads of Cliff Gallup. The slap-back echo of "Be Bop a Lula," combined with Gene's swooping vocals, led many to mistake the singer for Elvis when the record first hit the airwaves in mid-1956, on its way to the Top Ten. The Elvis comparison wasn't entirely fair—Vincent had a gentler,

less melodramatic style, capable of both whipping up a storm or winding down to a hush.

Brilliant follow-ups like "Race with the Devil," "Bluejean Bop," and "B-I-Bickey, Bi, Bo-Bo-Go" failed to click in nearly as big a way, although these too were emblematic of rockabilly at its most exuberant and powerful. By the end of 1956, the Blue Caps were beginning to undergo the first of constant personnel changes that would continue throughout the '50s, the most crucial loss being the departure of Gallup. The 35 or so tracks he cut with the band—many of which showed up only on albums or B-sides—were unquestionably Vincent's greatest work, as his subsequent recordings would never again capture their pristine clarity and uninhibited spontaneity.

Vincent had his second and final Top 20 hit in 1957 with "Lotta Lovin'," which reflected his increasingly tamer approach to production and vocals, the wildness and live atmosphere toned down in favor of poppier material, more subdued guitars, and conventional-sounding backup singers. He recorded often for Capitol throughout the rest of the '50s, and it's unfair to dismiss those sides out of hand; they were respectable, occasionally exciting rockabilly, only a marked disappointment in comparison with his earliest work. His act was captured for posterity in one of the best scenes of one of the first Hollywood films to feature rock and roll stars, *The Girl Can't Help It*.

Live Vincent continued to rock the house with reckless intensity and showmanship, and he became particularly popular overseas. A 1960 tour of Britain, though, brought tragedy when his friend Eddie Cochran, who shared the bill on Gene's UK shows, died in a car accident that Gene was also involved in, though Vincent survived. By the early '60s, his recordings had become much more sporadic and lower in quality, and his chief audience was in Europe, particularly in England (where he lived for a while) and France.

His Capitol contract expired in 1963, and he spent the rest of his life recording for several other labels, none of which got him close to that comeback hit. Vincent never stopped trying to resurrect his career, appearing at a 1969 Toronto rock festival on the same bill as John Lennon, though his medical, drinking, and marital problems were making his life a mess, and diminishing his stage presence as well. He died at the age of 36 from a ruptured stomach ulcer, one of rock's first mythic figures. —*Richie Unterberger*

The Capitol Years 1956-63 / 1987 / Charly ◆◆◆◆
While Vincent recorded a fair number of overlooked gems during his prime, he also cut a greater number of uninspired tracks. This lavishly packaged and exhaustively annotated ten-album set inadvertently charts the rapidly plummeting quality of his recordings, even as it unearths worthy obscurities. It does manage to gather all of his classic 1956 sessions with guitarist Cliff Gallup in the same place, but Gene's subsequent efforts could have easily been boiled down to a supplementary disc or two. —*Richie Unterberger*

★ **Capitol Collectors Series** / 1990 / Capitol ◆◆◆◆◆
Breathless, unintelligible, and spirited rockabilly at its non-Sun best, this 21-track compilation covers Vincent's Capitol recordings (including "Be Bop a Lula," "Race with the Devil," and "Lotta Lovin'") in admirable form. —*Hank Davis & Stephen Thomas Erlewine*

Greatest Hits / 1993 / Curb ◆◆

Gene Vincent Box Set / 1994 / EMI ◆◆◆◆
Six CDs containing the complete Capitol and EMI-Columbia recordings by Vincent, from 1956 through 1964. The 151 tracks may seem excessive, but the sound glitters, and since most of the post-1962 material was never issued in the US, this stuff could be revelatory to serious fans. And the booklet is filled with detailed notes, sessionographies, and great photos. —*Bruce Eder*

Violent Femmes

Alternative Pop-Rock, New Wave

With their geeky, nervous folk-pop, the Violent Femmes became one of the '80s' biggest cult bands. The new-wave group features Gordon Gano (vocals, guitar, songwriter), Brian Ritchie (bass), and Victor DeLorenzo (drums). The Femmes formed in the early '80s in Milwaukee, WI. In 1982, they released their self-titled debut, which has approached neo-classic status in some circles. Their following albums weren't as popular or consistent, yet each one has a few good songs. —*Michael Anne Erlewine*

★ **Violent Femmes** / 1983 / Slash ◆◆◆◆◆
One of the leading albums in alternative rock. On their first album (by far their best) the Violent Femmes began their professional career with a style that proves both entertaining and distinctive. Includes "Blister in the Sun," "Add It Up," and "Gone Daddy Gone." —*Meredith Erlewine*

Hallowed Ground / 1985 / Slash ◆◆◆
Though mistaken for a parody when it was released, *Hallowed Ground* features Gordon Gano's serious Christian convictions. The teenage angst is pushed aside on this more mature effort based, for the most part, in

traditional American folk—of course, it's slightly skewed. —*Chris Woodstra*

Blind Leading the Naked / 1986 / Slash ✦✦✦✦
A more mainstream effort courtesy of producer Jerry Harrison (Talking Heads). Gano returns to his troubled teen persona and the band rocks harder than on the previous two releases. A nice cover of the T-Rex classic "Children of the Revolution" and the yearning "I Held Her in My Arms," complete with a horn section. —*Chris Woodstra*

3 / 1989 / Slash ✦✦
The fourth album finds the band in somewhat of a rut creatively. Fans of the band's early days will appreciate the slightly stripped-back acoustic production but without much energy, the album falls flat in most places. Only the single "Nightmares" and the confessional "See My Ships" leave any lasting impression. —*Chris Woodstra*

Debacle: The First Decade / 1991 / Slash ✦✦✦✦
This album is a compilation of all of their best recordings. Even though it contains a variety of the Femmes' changes in style, it doesn't live up to the standards of their first release. Still, enough highlights are covered to make this album the only other Violent Femmes album you'll need. —*Meredith Erlewine*

Why Do Birds Sing? / 1991 / Reprise ✦✦✦
After a several year absence, the Femmes make a comeback of sorts with the charming *Why Do Birds Sing?* Returning to their street-busking roots, the band plays stripped-back acoustic songs as a three piece. Though they can't fight the fact that they have grown up, the songs show that they can still have fun. —*Chris Woodstra*

Add It Up (1981-1993) / 1993 / Warner Bros. ✦✦✦✦
Although it isn't as comprehensive as it seems, *Add It Up* is a good collection of most of the Violent Femmes' best tracks. —*AMG*

New Times / 1994 / Elektra ✦✦

Tom Waits

b. Dec. 7, 1949, Pomona, CA
Organ, Guitar, Piano, Harmonium, Vocals / Singer-Songwriter, Experimental
In the 1970s, Tom Waits combined a lyrical focus on desperate, lowlife characters with a persona that seemed to embody the same lifestyle, which he sang about in a raspy, gravelly voice. From the '80s on, his work became increasingly theatrical as he moved into acting and composing. Growing up in Southern California, Waits attracted the attention of manager Herb Cohen, who also handled Frank Zappa, and was signed by him at the beginning of the 1970s, resulting in the material later released as *The Early Years* and *The Early Years, Vol. 2*. His formal recording debut came with *Closing Time* (1973) on Asylum Records, an album that contained "Ol' 55," which was covered by labelmates the Eagles on their *On the Border* album. Waits attracted critical approbrium and a cult audience for his subsequent albums, *The Heart of Saturday Night* (1974), the two-LP live set *Nighthawks at the Diner* (1975), *Small Change* (1976), *Foreign Affairs* (1977), *Blue Valentine* (1978), and *Heart Attack and Vine* (1980). His music and persona proved highly cinematic, and starting in 1978 he launched parallel careers as an actor and as a composer of movie music. He wrote songs for and appeared in *Paradise Alley* (1978), wrote the title song for *On the Nickel* (1980), and was hired by director Francis Coppola to write the music for *One from the Heart* (1982), which earned him an Academy Award nomination. While working on that project, Waits met and married playwright Kathleen Brennan, with whom he later collaborated. Moving to Island Records, Waits made *Swordfishtrombones* (1983), which found him experimenting with horns and percussion and using unusual recording techniques. The same year, he appeared in Coppola's *Rumble Fish* and *The Outsiders*, and in 1984, he appeared in the director's *The Cotton Club*. In 1985, he released *Rain Dogs*. In 1986, he appeared in *Down by Law* and made his theatrical debut with Chicago's Steppenwolf Theatre in *Frank's Wild Years*, a musical play he had written with Brennan. An album based on the play was released in 1987, the same year Waits appeared in the films *Candy Mountain* and *Ironweed*. In 1988, he released a third album and soundtrack album depicting one of his concerts, *Big Time*. In 1989, he appeared in the films *Bearskin: An Urban Fairytale, Cold Feet,* and *Wait Until Spring*. In 1991, he appeared in the films *Quee's Logic, The Fisher King,* and *At Play in the Fields of the Lord*. In 1992, he scored the film *Night on Earth*, released the album *Bone Machine*, which won a Grammy Award for Best Alternative Music Album, and appeared in the films *Deadfall* and *Bram Stoker's Dracula*. In 1993, he released *The Black Rider*, the recording of a musical he had co-written with Beat novelist William Burroughs for opera director Robert Wilson in 1990, and appeared in the film *Short Cuts*. —*William Ruhlmann*

● **Closing Time** / 1973 / Asylum ✦✦✦✦
Tom Waits' debut album was a minor-key masterpiece filled with songs of late-night loneliness. Within the apparently narrow range of the cocktail bar pianistics and muttered vocals, Waits and producer Jerry Yester managed a surprisingly broad collection of styles, from the jazzy "Virginia Avenue" to the uptempo funk of "Ice Cream Man" and from the acoustic guitar folkiness of "I Hope That I Don't Fall in Love with You" to the saloon song "Midnight Lullaby," which would have been a perfect addition to the repertoires of Frank Sinatra or Tony Bennett. Waits' entire musical approach was stylized, of course, and at times derivative—"Lonely" borrowed a little too much from Randy Newman's "I Think It's Going to Rain Today"—and his lovelorn lyrics could be sentimental without being penetrating. But he also had a gift for gently rolling pop melodies, and he could come up with striking, original scenarios, as on the best songs, "Ol' 55" and "Martha," which Yester discreetly augmented with strings. *Closing Time* announced the arrival of a talented songwriter whose self-conscious melancholy could be surprisingly moving. —*William Ruhlmann*

The Heart of Saturday Night / 1974 / Asylum ✦✦✦
If *Closing Time*, Tom Waits' debut album, consisted of love songs set in a late-night world of bars and neon signs, its follow-up, *The Heart of Saturday Night*, largely dispensed with the romance in favor of poetic depictions of the same setting. On "Diamonds on My Windshield" and "The Ghosts of Saturday Night," Waits didn't even sing, instead reciting his verse rhythmically against bass and drums like a Beat hipster. Musically, the album contained the same mixture of folk, blues, and jazz as its predecessor, with producer Bones Howe occasionally bringing in an orchestra to underscore the loping melodies. Waits' songs were sometimes sketchier in addition to being more impersonal, but "(Looking For) The Heart of Saturday Night" and "Semi Suite" were the equal of anything on *Closing Time*. Still, with lines such as ". . . the clouds are like headlines / Upon a new front page sky" and references to "a 24-hour moon" and "champagne stars," Waits' imagery was beginning to get florid, and in material this stylized, the danger of self-parody was always present. —*William Ruhlmann*

Nighthawks at the Diner / Oct. 1975 / Asylum ✦✦✦
For his third album, Tom Waits set up a nightclub in the studio, invited an audience, and cut a 70-minute, two-LP set of new songs. It was an appropriate format for compositions that dealt even more graphically and, for the first time, humorously, with Waits' late-night world of bars and diners. The love lyrics of his debut album had long since given way to a comic lonely guy stance glimpsed in "Emotional Weather Report" and "Better off Without a Wife." But what really mattered was the elaborate scene-setting of songs like the six-and-a-half-minute "Spare Parts," the seven-and-a-half-minute "Putnam County," and especially the 11-minute "Nighthawk Postcards" that were essentially poetry recitations with jazz backing. Waits was a colorful tour guide of midnight L.A., raving over a swinging rhythm section of Jim Hughart (bass) and Bill Goodwin (drums), with Pete Christlieb wailing away on tenor sax between paragraphs and Mike Melvoin trading off with Waits on piano runs. You could call it overdone, but then, this kind of material made its impact through an accumulation of miscellaneous detail, and who was to say how much was too much? —*William Ruhlmann*

● **Small Change** / Oct. 1976 / Asylum ✦✦✦✦
The fourth release in Tom Waits' series of skid-row travelogues, *Small Change* proved to be the archetypal album of his '70s work. A jazz trio comprising tenor sax player Lew Tabackin, bassist Jim Hughart, and drummer Shelly Manne, plus an occasional string section, backed Waits and his piano on songs steeped in whiskey and atmosphere in which he alternately sang in his broken-beaned drunk's voice (now deeper and overtly influenced by Louis Armstrong) and recited jazzy poetry. It was as if Waits was determined to combine the Humphrey Bogart and Dooley Wilson characters from *Casablanca* with a dash of *On the Road's* Dean Moriarty to illuminate a dark world of bars and all-night diners. Of course, he'd been in that world before, but in songs like "The Piano Has Been Drinking" and "Bad Liver and a Broken Heart," Waits gave it its clearest expression. *Small Change* is not Tom Waits' best album. It is, like most of the albums he made in the '70s, uneven, probably because he was putting out one a year and didn't have time to come up with enough first-rate material. But it is the most obvious and characteristic of his albums for Asylum Records. If you like it, you also will like the ones before and after it; otherwise, you're not Tom Waits' kind of listener. —*William Ruhlmann*

Foreign Affairs / Sep. 1977 / Asylum ✦✦✦
Tom Waits gave one side of his fifth album to his more structured, bluesy ballads and the other to his jazz raps. On side one, you got his duet with Bette Midler on the singles-bar dialogue "I Never Talk to Strangers" and his take on his Beat predecessors, Jack Kerouac and Neal Cassidy, on "Jack Neal." On side two, you found the extended observations of "Potter's Field" and "Burma Shave." Waits' voice was becoming ever more gravelly, but his basic musical approach remained the same, and he had attracted a steady cult audience that enjoyed his verbal flights and boozy philosopher persona, even as critics began to complain that he was repeating himself. By the way, that's Waits' then-girlfriend, the then-unknown Rickie Lee Jones, on the cover with him. —*William Ruhlmann*

Blue Valentine / Oct. 1978 / Asylum ✦✦✦

Two welcome changes in style made *Blue Valentine* a fresh listening experience for Tom Waits fans. First, Waits had altered the instrumentation, bringing in electric guitar and keyboards and largely dispensing with the strings for a more blues-oriented, hard-edged sound. Second, though his worldview remained fixed on the lowlifes of the late night, he had expanded beyond the musings of the bar-stool philosopher who previously had acted as the first-person character of most of his songs. When Waits did use the "I," it was to write a "Christmas Card from a Hooker in Minneapolis," not the figure most listeners had associated with the singer himself. The result was a broadening of subject matter, a narrative discipline that made most of the tunes story songs, and a coherent framing for Waits' typically colorful and intriguing imagery. These were not radical reinventions, but Waits had followed such a rigidly stylized approach on his previous albums that for anyone who had followed him so far, the course correction was big news. *— William Ruhlmann*

Heartattack and Vine / Sep. 1980 / Asylum ✦✦✦

Heart Attack and Vine, Tom Waits' first album in two years and his last of seven for Asylum Records, was a transitional album, with tracks like the rhythm-heavy title song and "Til the Money Runs Out" foreshadowing the sonic experiments of the Island albums, while piano-with-orchestra tracks like "Saving All My Love for You" and "On the Nickel" (written as a motion-picture title tune) harked back to Waits' Randy Newman-influenced early days. It was just as well that Waits never entirely gave up on the ballad material; "Jersey Girl," a Drifters-style song, was a winner, and it was appropriated by Bruce Springsteen on his 1981 tour. Also, at least at this point, the rougher tunes all tended to sound the same. *— William Ruhlmann*

☆ **Swordfishtrombones** / Sep. 1983 / Island ✦✦✦✦✦

Between the release of *Heartattack and Vine* in 1980 and *Swordfishtrombones* in 1983, Tom Waits got rid of his manager, his producer, and his record company. And he drastically altered a musical approach that had become as dependable as it was unexciting. *Swordfishtrombones* had none of the strings and much less of the piano work that Waits' previous albums had employed; instead, the dominant sounds on the record were low-pitched horns, bass instruments, and percussion, set in spare, close-miked arrangements (most of them by Waits) that sometimes were better described as "soundscapes." Lyrically, Waits' tales of the drunken and the lovelorn had been replaced by surreal accounts of people who burned down their homes and of Australian towns bypassed by the railroad—a world (not just a neighborhood) of misfits now had his attention. The music could be primitive, moving to odd time signatures, while Waits alternately howled and wheezed in his gravelly bass voice. He seemed to have moved on from Hoagy Carmichael and Louis Armstrong to Kurt Weill and Howlin' Wolf (as impersonated by Captain Beefheart). Waits seems to have had trouble interesting a record label in the album, which was cut 13 months before it was released, but when it appeared rock critics predictably raved: After all, it sounded weird and it didn't have a chance of selling. Actually, it did make the bottom of the bestseller charts, like most of Waits' albums, and, now that he was with a label based in Europe, even charted there. Artistically, *Swordfishtrombones* marked an evolution of which Waits had not seemed capable (though there were hints of this sound on his last two Asylum albums), and in career terms it reinvented him. *— William Ruhlmann*

Anthology of Tom Waits / 1985 / Asylum ✦✦✦✦

Anthology collects most of the key tracks from Waits' Asylum years, except for *Nighthawks at the Diner*. *—Rick Clark*

★ **Rain Dogs** / Aug. 1985 / Island ✦✦✦✦✦

With its jarring rhythms and unusual instrumentation-marimba, accordion, various percussion—as well as its frequently surreal lyrics, *Rain Dogs* was very much a follow-up to *Swordfishtrombones*, which is to say that it sounded for the most part like the Threepenny Opera being sung by Howlin' Wolf. The chief musical difference was the introduction of guitarist Marc Ribot, who added his noisy leads to the general cacophony. But *Rain Dogs* was sprawling where its predecessor had been focused: Waits' lyrics here sometimes were imaginative to the point of obscurity, seemingly chosen to fit the rhythms rather than for sense. In the course of 19 tracks and 54 minutes, Waits sometimes went back to the more conventional music of his earlier records, which seemed like a retreat, though such tracks as the catchy "Hang Down Your Head," "Time," and especially "Downtown Train" (frequently covered and finally turned into a Top Ten hit by Rod Stewart five years later) provided some relief as well as variety. *Rain Dogs* could not surprise as *Swordfishtrombones* had, and in his attempt to continue in the direction suggested by that album, Waits occasionally bordered on the chaotic (which may only be to say that, like most of his records, this one was uneven). But much of the music matched the earlier album, and there was so much of it that that was enough to qualify *Rain Dogs* as one of Waits' better albums. *— William Ruhlmann*

The Asylum Years / Oct. 1986 / Asylum ✦✦✦✦

The second British Tom Waits compilation was a more extensive look at the 1973-1980 Asylum Records catalog than the first, *Bounced Checks* from 1981 (fourteen tracks vs. ten), but it was another idiosyncratic selection. Waits' stellar first two albums were better represented, with three strong tracks drawn from *The Heart of Saturday Night* and two from *Closing Time*, but "Ol' 55" was ignored again, and nothing was included from the third album, *Nighthawks at the Diner*, which is the favorite of many Waits fans. Three tracks were repeated from *Bounced Checks* —"Burma Shave," "I Never Talk to Strangers," a duet with Bette Midler, and "Tom Traubert's Blues"—and they were worthy, but where was "Jersey Girl"? The choices from the later albums were spotty: Why use Waits' questionable cover of "Somewhere" from *West Side Story* and leave out a brilliant story song like "Romeo Is Bleeding"? The overall unevenness of the Asylum albums cries out for a well-chosen compilation. After three attempts in the US and UK, it still hasn't been assembled. *— William Ruhlmann*

Frank's Wild Years / Aug. 1987 / Island ✦✦✦✦

Tom Waits wrote a song called "Frank's Wild Years" for his 1983 *Swordfishtrombones* album, then used the title (minus its apostrophe) for a musical play he wrote with his wife, Kathleen Brennan, and toured with in 1986. The *Franks Wild Years* album, drawn from the show, is subtitled, "un operachi romantico in two acts," though the songs themselves do not carry the plot. Rather, this is just the third installment in Waits' eccentric series of Island Records albums in which he seems most inspired by German art song and carnival music, presenting songs in spare, stripped-down arrangements consisting of instruments like marimba, baritone horn, and pump organ and singing in a strained voice that has been artificially compressed and distorted. The songs themselves often are conventional romantic vignettes, or would be minus the oddities of instrumentation, arrangement, and performance. For example, "Innocent When You Dream," a song of disappointment in love and friendship, has a winning melody, but it is played in a seesaw arrangement of pump organ, bass, violin, and piano, and Waits sings it like an enraged drunk. (He points up the arbitrary nature of the arrangements by repeating "Straight to the Top," done as a demented rhumba in Act I, as a Vegas-style Frank Sinatra swing tune in Act II.) The result on record may not be theatrical, exactly, but it certainly is affected. It also has the quality of an inside joke that listeners are not being let in on. *— William Ruhlmann*

Big Time / Sep. 1988 / Island ✦✦✦

The Early Years / Jul. 1991 / Bizarre/Straight ✦✦✦✦

This is an album of early demos recorded by a 21-year-old Tom Waits in 1971, two years before the release of his first album, *Closing Time*, and issued on the record label owned by his ex-manager. Waits accompanies himself on piano or guitar and sings in an unaffected nasal tenor. (One track, "Ice Cream Man," is given a full-band treatment.) Several of these songs, notably "Ice Cream Man," "Virginia Ave.," "Midnight Lullabye," and "Little Trip to Heaven," turned up on his later albums, but the overall level of writing and performance is well below Waits' usual standard. Clearly, his better early material was chosen for his Asylum albums. Hardcore fans will want to hear this album, of course, but others need not bother. *— William Ruhlmann*

Night on Earth / Apr. 1992 / Island ✦✦

☆ **Bone Machine** / Aug. 1992 / Island ✦✦✦✦✦

Tom Waits' first album in seven years not to be made as part of a theater or film project, *Bone Machine* marked an even more minimalist musical approach than that Waits had adopted in the early '80s. Largely missing were the horns, marimbas, and pump organs that had given the music the flavor of German art song, but Waits had replaced them only with an increased use of percussion, much of an unorthodox nature. The loud, miscellaneous baps and blats came from such Waits inventions as the "conundrum," about which he said, "[I]t looks like a big iron crucifix, and there are a lot of different things that we hang off of it. Crowbars, Tijuana sabers, and found metal objects that I like the sound of." Waits also liked the sound of his own voice distorted and compressed, and he liked loose arrangements with lots of space in the mix. Once you got past the production style, if you did, you would discover that the songs frequently concerned death, murder, and despair. Song titles included "Earth Dies Screaming," "Murder in the Red Barn," and "Dirt in the Ground" (as in, "We're all gonna be . . ."). Frequently, the lyrics were abstract even though they were full of detail, but the mood clearly was ominous. All of which is to say that *Bone Machine* was anything but an easy listen. If you did listen carefully, however, you realized that, like most Waits albums, it was uneven—songs like "Who Are You" and "I Don't Wanna Grow Up" were as well-written as anything he had ever done, but others seemed like tossed-off fragments of ideas rather than fully realized compositions. Maybe it was just as well, then, that he threw up so much interference. Still, it seemed that Waits had been confusing art with artifice for a long time by now. *— William Ruhlmann*

The Early Years, Vol. 2 / Feb. 1993 / Bizarre/Straight ✦✦✦✦
Like its predecessor, *The Early Years, Vol. 2* consists of demos recorded by Tom Waits in 1971, two years before he released his debut album, *Closing Time.* "Hope I Don't Fall in Love with You," "Ol' 55," "Grapefruit Moon," and "Old Shoes" later turned up on that album, while "Shiver Me Timbers," "Diamonds on My Windshield," and "Please Call Me Baby" appeared on Waits' second album, *The Heart of Saturday Night,* in 1974. The release of the two *Early Years* albums demonstrates that Waits' better early material made it onto his regular releases—the previously unreleased stuff, while interesting, is not as good. And since Waits' albums were not overproduced, the main difference between these versions and the familiar ones is that the familiar ones are better. Still, Waits fans will enjoy hearing, for example, "Ol' 55" performed in a higher key and with an acoustic guitar backing. —*William Ruhlmann*

The Black Rider / Nov. 2, 1993 / Island ✦✦

Walker Brothers

Pop, British Invasion, Soft Rock, Pop-Rock
They weren't British, they weren't brothers, and their real names weren't Walker, but Californians Scott Engel, John Maus, and Gary Leeds were briefly huge stars in England (and small ones in their native land) at the peak of the British Invasion. Engel and Maus were playing together in Hollywood when drummer Leeds suggested they form a trio and try to make it in England. And they did—with surprising swiftness, they hit the top of the British charts with "Make It Easy on Yourself" in 1965. "The Sun Ain't Gonna Shine Any More" repeated the feat the following year, and the group also had UK hits with "My Ship Is Coming In," "(Baby) You Don't Have to Tell Me," "Another Tear Falls," and others. For a few months they experienced frenzied adulation almost on the level of the Beatles and Stones, though in the US (where they rarely performed), only "Make It Easy on Yourself" and "The Sun Ain't Gonna Shine Any More" entered the Top 20.

While the Walkers looked the part of British Invaders with their shaggy mop-tops, in fact they were far more pop than rock. Nor did they play on most of their records. With producer Johnny Franz and veteran British arrangers like Ivor Raymonde (who also worked with Dusty Springfield) and Reg Guest, they favored orchestrated ballads that were a studied attempt to emulate the success of another brother act who weren't really brothers—the Righteous Brothers. Not as soulful as the Righteous Brothers, lead singer Scott Walker's deep croon wasn't chopped liver by any means, although it betrayed strong debts to non-rock vocalists like Tony Bennett and Frank Sinatra. While their biggest hits were covers of songs by American pop songwriting teams like Bacharach-David and Mann-Weill, Scott (and occasionally John Walker) could write strong, brooding originals in a more personal, less over-blown style when given the chance.

In the intensely competitive days of 1967, the Walkers' brand of pop suddenly become passé, and the group disbanded in the face of diminishing success and Scott's increasingly fruitful solo career. Scott ran off a series of Top Ten British solo albums in the late '60s, which have attracted a sizable cult with their idiosyncratic marriage of Scott's brooding, insular songs and ornate orchestral arrangements. Gary Walker released a few singles and an album with his group The Rain in a much harder rocking guitar-oriented format. The Walkers reunited for a while in the mid-'70s, which produced a final British hit ("No Regrets") but disappointing music. Much of the Walkers' story is retold in the biography *Scott Walker: A Deep Shade of Blue,* published only in Britain. —*Richie Unterberger*

Introducing the Walker Brothers / 1965 / Smash ✦✦✦

No Regrets / 1975 / GTO ✦✦✦

Nite Flights / 1978 / GTO ✦✦✦
Nite Flights was another mixed effort by the reunited Walker Brothers, but it had a side of original Scott Walker compositions that were his best in years, particularly the haunting "The Electrician," which attracted praise from Brian Eno and David Bowie and reinvigorated Scott's solo career. —*Stephen Thomas Erlewine*

● **After The Lights Go Out: The Best Of 1965-1967** / 1990 / Fontana ✦✦✦✦
Twenty of their best songs, including all of their hit singles. On original compositions like "Mrs. Murphy," "Archangel," "Orpheus," and "Deadlier Than the Male," Scott Walker unveils the disturbed visions that would characterize his solo work, and John Walker's "Saddest Night in The World" and "I Can't Let It Happen to You" display a solid writing talent that he was sadly unable to develop into a solo career of his own. —*Richie Unterberger*

● **Anthology** / 1995 / One Way ✦✦✦✦
Although it contains the Walker Brothers' big hits from the '60s, *Anthology* is basically a resequenced version of the group's first album, adding a couple of bonus tracks. Nevertheless, it's a serviceable introduction to the group. —*Stephen Thomas Erlewine*

Junior Walker & the All-Stars

b. 1942, Blytheville, AR
Saxophone, Vocals / Soul, Motown
Of all the great musicians who played on scores of Motown records, none of them got label credit, much less a chance to bask in the spotlight. The lone exception was Junior Walker (born Audrey Dewalt), whose tenor sax wailings were made up of equal parts Illinois Jacquet high-note shrieks, Coleman Hawkins growls, and pure Midwest soul. Never much of a vocalist, Walker nonetheless scored hits with his rough-grained chops, though the sax solos remained the definite focal point. Highly influential on the Tom Scott/David Sanborn crowd, Walker should be close to the top of any list of rrock 'n' roll's great tenor saxophonists. —*Cub Koda*

● **Greatest Hits** / 1982 / Motown ✦✦✦✦
All the hits, including "Shotgun," "What Does It Take to Win Your Love," and "Roadrunner." The definitive package. —*Cub Koda*

Nothing but Soul: The Singles / 1994 / Motown ✦✦✦✦
This 40-song double CD includes virtually every Walker track of significance, and then some. Walker is a great player and hits a great groove, but that groove can get tiring over the course of several dozen tracks, especially the similar-sounding early instrumental cuts. Also, the post-'60s selections that take up much of disc two are hampered by material that is inferior to the best output of his '60s heyday. Excellent package and liner notes, but most listeners should be satisfied with the single-disc *Greatest Hits,* leaving this one for the collectors and specialists. —*Richie Unterberger*

Scott Walker (Noel Scott Engel)

b. Jan. 9, 1944, Hamilton, OH
Vocals / Pop, Soft Rock, Pop-Rock, Experimental
One of the most enigmatic figures in rock history, Scott Walker was known as Scotty Engel when he cut obscure, flop records in the late '50s and early '60s in the teen-idol vein. He then hooked up with John Maus and Gary Leeds to form the Walker Brothers. They weren't named Walker, they weren't brothers, and they weren't English, but they nevertheless became a part of the British Invasion after moving to the UK in 1965. They enjoyed a couple years of massive success there (and a couple hits in the US) in a Righteous Brothers vein. As their full-throated lead singer and principal songwriter, Scott was the dominant artistic force in the group, which split in 1967.

While remaining virtually unknown in his homeland, Scott launched a hugely successful solo career in Britain with a unique blend of orchestrated, almost MOR arrangements with idiosyncratic and morose lyrics. At the height of psychedelia, Walker openly looked to crooners like Sinatra, Jack Jones, and Tony Bennett for inspiration, and to Jacques Brel for much of his material. None of those balladeers, however, would have sung about the oddball subjects—prostitutes, transvestites, suicidal brooders, plagues, and Joseph Stalin—that populated Walker's songs. His first four albums hit the Top Ten in the UK—his second, in fact, reached No. 1 in 1968, in the midst of the hippie era. By the time of 1969's *Scott 4,* the singer was writing all of his material. Although this was perhaps his finest album, it was a commercial disappointment, and unfortunately discouraged him from relying entirely upon his own material on subsequent releases.

The 1970s were a frustrating period for Walker, pocked with increasingly sporadic releases and a largely unsuccessful reunion with his "brothers" in the middle of the decade. His work on the Walkers' final album in 1978 prompted admiration from David Bowie and Brian Eno. After a long period of hibernation, he emerged with an album in 1984, *Climate of Hunter,* which drew critical raves for a minimalistic, trance-like ambience that showed him keeping abreast of cutting-edge '80s rock trends. This notoriously reclusive figure, who has rarely been interviewed or even seen in public since his days of stardom, emerged from hibernation in 1995 with a new album, *Tilt.* He was a substantial, if largely overlooked, influence upon the vocal style of David Bowie and Bryan Ferry. A biography, *Scott Walker: A Deep Shade of Blue,* was published by Virgin in the UK in 1994. —*Richie Unterberger*

Scott / 1967 / Fontana ✦✦✦✦
Scott Walker's success as a teen-idol singer of Spectorish ballads with the Walker Brothers in no way prepared listeners for the mordant, despairing lyrics of his solo debut. To compound the surprise, he does his best to imitate the vocal girth of Tony Bennett and Frank Sinatra on this mix of original tunes and covers, which also features sweeping, bloated orchestral arrangements. It was hardly rock, and pop of a most oddball sort, but it found a surprisingly large audience—in Britain, anyway, where it reached the Top Three in 1967. Poke behind the velvet curtain of the languid MOR arrangements, and one finds a surprisingly literate existentialist at the helm of these proceedings. His lyrical nuances were probably lost on his audience of predominately teenage girls, though they've earned him a small cult audience that endures to this day. Besides pre-

senting three of his own compositions, Walker covers tunes by Weill/ Mann, Tim Hardin, and Andre and Dory Previn on this album, as well as three songs by his favorite writer, Jacques Brel. Highlights include his exquisitely anguished rendition of Brel's classic "Amsterdam" and his dramatic cover of the early-'60s Timi Yuro pop ballad "The Big Hurt." —*Richie Unterberger*

Scott 2 / 1968 / Philips ✦✦✦✦
Although Walker's second album was his biggest commercial success, actually reaching No.1 in Britain, it was not his greatest artistic triumph. His taste remains eclectic, encompassing Bacharach/David, Tim Hardin, and, of course, his main man Jacques Brel (who is covered three times on this album). And his own songwriting efforts hold their own in this esteemed company. "The Girls from the Streets" and "Plastic Palace People" show an uncommonly ambitious lyricist cloaked behind the over-the-top, schmaltzy orchestral arrangements, one more interested in examining the seamy underside of glamour and romance than celebrating its glitter. The Brel tune "Next" must have lifted a few teenage mums' eyebrows with its not-so-hidden hints of homosexuality and abuse. Another Brel tune, "The Girl and The Dogs," is less controversial, but hardly less nasty in its jaded view of romance. Some of the material is not nearly as memorable, however, and the over-the-top show ballad production can get overbearing. The album included his first Top 20 UK hit, "Jackie." —*Richie Unterberger*

Scott 3 / 1969 / Philips ✦✦✦
Scott Walker's final British Top Ten album was the first to be dominated by his own songwriting. Ten of the thirteen tunes on this 1969 LP are originals; the remaining three, naturally, were written by one of his chief inspirations, Jacques Brel. There are some interesting moments here. "Big Louise" talks about a hefty prostitute with shocking explicitness for a pop star album of the era. "Copenhagen" (like much of Walker's '60s work) foreshadows David Bowie. "No Last Tango" is a particularly vicious Brel song. "30 Century Man" is an uncommonly folkish and focused tune for Walker. "We Came Through" is an oddball cavalry charge featuring one of his occasional forays into Ennio Morricone spaghetti-Western-like production. The tension between Walker's dense, foreboding lyrics and orchestral production is unusual, to say the least. But too often, it's too difficult to penetrate Walker's insights through Wally Scott's string-drenched production. It shrouds the lyrics in a fog that's often too syrupy to justify the effort needed to fight through it. —*Richie Unterberger*

Scott 4 / 1969 / Philips ✦✦✦✦
Walker dropped out of the British Top Ten with his fourth album, but the result was probably his finest '60s LP. While the tension between the bloated production and his introspective, ambitious lyrics remains, much of the over-the-top bombast of the orchestral arrangements has been reined in, leaving a relatively stripped-down approach that complements his songs rather than smothering them. This is the first Walker album to feature entirely original material, and his songwriting is more lucid and cutting. Several of the tracks stand among his finest. "The Seventh Seal," based upon the classic film by Ingmar Bergman, features remarkably ambitious (and relatively successful) lyrics set against a haunting Ennio Morricone-style arrangement. "The Old Man's Back Again" also echoes Morricone, and tackles no less ambitious a lyrical palette; "dedicated to the neo-Stalinist regime," the "old man" of this song was supposedly Joseph Stalin. "Hero of the War" is also one of Walker's better vignettes, serenading his war hero with a cryptic mix of tribute and irony. Other songs show engaging folk, country, and soul influences that were largely buried on his previous solo albums. —*Richie Unterberger*

Climate of Hunter / 1984 / Virgin ✦✦

● **Boy Child: Best of 1967-1970** / 1992 / Fontana ✦✦✦✦
This collection of "Scott's best self-composed songs" features 20 Walker originals from his 1967-70 heyday. While he covered some interesting material on his albums during this period, paying tribute to Jacques Brel with special devotion and frequency, his original compositions are his most enduring achievements. Besides such highlights as "Big Louise," "We Came Through," "The Seventh Seal," "Plastic Palace People," and "The Old Man's Back Again," it includes half a dozen songs that were not included on the four other solo albums that Fontana UK has reissued on CD. Some of those cuts are very strong, especially "The Rope and the Colt," a dramatic Western ballad with an arrangement that would do Ennio Morricone proud; the positively eloquent despair of the ennui-ridden "Time Operator"; and "The Plague," a representative sampling of Walker's taste for the disquieting and bizarre. This is a recommended starting point for those interested in checking out this singularly strange '60s phenomenon, who was a relatively unacknowledged and undetected, but nonetheless substantial, influence on David Bowie and other fashionably decadent British singers. —*Richie Unterberger*

No Regrets: Best of Scott Walker & Walker Brothers / 1992 / Fontana ✦✦✦✦
Including both of the Walker Brothers' big hits ("The Sun Ain't Gonna Shine Any More," "Make It Easy on Yourself") and material from Scott

Walker's solo albums, *No Regrets: The Best of the Walker Brothers* is the best introduction to Walker's more pop-oriented music. —*Stephen Thomas Erlewine*

Tilt / 1995 / Fontana ✦✦
Tilt, Scott Walker's first album in eleven years, is a dense, impenetrable record, bleak in its outlook and approach. Walker has dispensed with conventional pop songwriting—actually, he's dispensed with pop altogether. *Tilt* is nearly operatic, with long, twisting melody lines, no verses and no choruses. Lyrically, the record is just as inaccessible, with obscure literary references and winding, oblique prose. There's no escaping that the record is some sort of an accomplishment—very few pop musicians have ever attempted a record of this scope, one that is free-form in structure but with carefully considered arrangements. Nevertheless, it's hard to like the album because very little of it ever sinks in, and it's hard to appreciate it because it takes its pretensions so seriously. It's arguably the most inaccessible, difficult album ever recorded. —*Stephen Thomas Erlewine*

Joe Walsh

b. Nov. 20, 1947, Wichita, KS
Guitar / Rock 'n' roll
After coming to national fame as the leader of The James Gang, Walsh's skewed humor and bluesy guitar chops have forged a nice solo career for him. Walsh's solo debut *Barnstorm* displayed him as not only an innovative guitarist but a competent keyboardist and a songwriter with much scope. Walsh's second solo effort, *The Smoker You Drink, the Player You Get*, perfectly suited the tastes of FM-rock programmers and firmly established his career. "Rocky Mountain Way" and "Meadows" are hits off that album. Walsh also produced some outside projects, including Dan Fogelberg's first hit album, *Souvenirs*.

The Eagles enlisted Walsh as a replacement for Bernie Leadon in December of 1975. Their next studio album, *Hotel California*, heavily featured Walsh's playing, particularly on "Life in the Fast Lane" and "Hotel California." Walsh played on their live album and *The Long Run*, the band's swan song.

All along, Walsh has continued his solo efforts, scoring big in 1978 with *But Seriously Folks...*, an album that brings his goofy humor to the forefront, with the hit "Life's Been Good." "All Night Long," a track from the *Urban Cowboy* soundtrack, continued Walsh's string of success. During the '80s, Walsh has had sporadic success.

In addition to Dan Fogelberg, Walsh has produced other artists, including Spirit's Jay Ferguson, and Ringo Starr (working as bandleader on Starr's late-'80s/early-'90s tours). In 1994, Walsh joined the reunited Eagles for their *Hell Freezes Over* tour. —*Cub Koda and Rick Clark*

Barnstorm / 1972 / Mobile Fidelity ✦✦✦✦
Even though he had developed quite a rep as the lead guitarist for The James Gang, Joe Walsh's debut (under the band moniker Barnstorm) was an impressive showcase for his songwriting and arranging. Produced by Bill Szymczyk, *Barnstorm* exudes a thick, textured sound. Some of Walsh's most distinctive guitar sounds are found here. Sonically, *Barnstorm* is shown to fine effect on this Mobile Fidelity reissue. (Currently, there isn't a regular domestic disc available.) Highlights include "Here We Go," "Mother Says," and "Turn to Stone." —*Rick Clark*

The Smoker You Drink, the Player You Get / 1973 / MCA ✦✦✦✦
On Walsh's second outing, he fused the dynamics and textures of *Barnstorm*, mixed in a few well-crafted tunes, perfect for FM radio, and scored his highest charting album. *Smoker's* centerpiece was the plodding "Rocky Mountain Way," a perfect vehicle for his soaring slidework and squirrelly tenor strangle. "Meadows" was also a substantial FM hit. Other highlights are "Days Gone By" and "Happy Ways." —*Rick Clark*

● **The Best of Joe Walsh** / 1978 / MCA ✦✦✦✦
Featuring the biggest James Gang hits and early solo hits. —*Cub Koda*

But Seriously Folks / 1978 / Asylum ✦✦✦✦
This is his biggest solo success, featuring the hit "Life's Been Good." —*Cub Koda*

● **Look What I Did!: The Joe Walsh Anthology** / May 23, 1995 / MCA ✦✦✦✦
A double-disc set that draws from all of the phases of Joe Walsh's career, with the notable exception of The Eagles, *Look What I Did!* features almost every worthwhile song the guitarist ever recorded, even though it does contain pure dreck like "I.L.B.T.s," which is also known as "I Love Big Tits." —*David Jehnzen*

War

Soul, Funk, Pop-Rock
Freewheeling War mixed rock, jazz, and soul influences into a spicy stew throughout the '70s, resulting in a series of R&B and pop hits sporting funky melodies and politically aware messages. Born in Long Beach in 1969, the large combo initially served as rocker Eric Burdon's group, backing the ex-Animal on his 1970 million-seller "Spill the Wine." Bid-

ding Burdon adieu, the band signed with United Artists in 1971 and enjoyed its first smash the next year with "Slippin' into Darkness." Tapping into a sizzling, horn-fueled rock/soul synthesis, "The World Is a Ghetto," "The Cisco Kid," and "Why Can't We Be Friends?" all went gold during the mid-'70s. Despite numerous personnel and label changes, War remained eminent throughout the '80s.

In the early '90s, War experienced a revival, partially due to the fact that all of their albums were reissued. But the group was also acknowledged as a primary influence on contemporary R&B and hip-hop. War released a new album in 1994 to capitalize on their newfound popularity. —*Bill Dahl*

Eric Burdon Declares War / 1970 / Rhino ✦✦✦
The debut effort by Eric Burdon & War was an erratic effort that hinted at more potential than it actually delivered. Three of the five tunes are meandering blues-jazz-psychedelic jams, two of which, "Tobacco Road" and "Blues For Memphis Slim," chug along for nearly 15 minutes. These showcase the then-unknown War's funky fusion and Burdon's still-impressive vocals, but suffer from a lack of focus and substance. "Spill the Wine," on the other hand, is inarguably the greatest moment of the Burdon-fronted lineup. Not only was this goofy funk shaggy-dog story one of the most truly inspired off-the-wall hit singles of all time, it was War's first smash—and Eric Burdon's last. The odd closing track, a short piece of avant-garde sentimentality called "You're No Stranger," was deleted from rereleases of this album for years due to legal complications, but was restored for its CD reissue. —*Richie Unterberger*

The Black-Man's Burdon / 1970 / Rhino ✦✦✦✦
Burdon's second and final album with War was a double set that could have benefited from quite a bit of judicious editing. Composed mostly of sprawling psychedelic funk jams, it does find War mapping out much of the jazz/Latin/soul grooves that, cut down to much more economical song structures, would shortly bring them success on their own. Highlights include the soulful vamps "Pretty Colors" and "They Can't Take Away Our Music"; the 13-minute "Paint It Black" medley is the height of their eccentricity, and not one, but two covers of "Nights in White Satin" are absurd low points. —*Richie Unterberger*

War / Jan. 1971 / Rhino ✦✦
All Day Music / Feb. 1971 / Rhino ✦✦✦✦
A great War album, the first where all their influences meshed. They blended gospel-tinged soul, funk, Afro-Latin, and light jazz, with enthusiastic group vocals and interplay, plus just the right amount of instrumental support and occasional solos by Lee Oskar on harmonica, Lonnie Jordan on keyboards, and Charles Miller on saxophone and flute. It also contained the fantastic "Slippin' into Darkness," one of their best-arranged and performed numbers. —*Ron Wynn*

The World Is a Ghetto / 1972 / Rhino ✦✦✦✦
War hit its peak with this 1972 album, the only one they ever released that topped the pop charts. The title track was a triumphant blend of great exchanges and unison vocals, plus concise and spirited musical contributions all around. It also contained the delightful "Cisco Kid" and elaborate "City, Country, City," plus the curious "Beetles in the Bog." Harmonica player Lee Oskar and percussionist Papa Dee Allen were at their best, as were keyboardist Lonnie Jordan and saxophonist/flutist Charles Miller. —*Ron Wynn*

Deliver the Word / 1973 / Rhino ✦✦✦
War Live / 1973 / Rhino ✦✦
Why Can't We Be Friends / 1975 / Rhino ✦✦✦✦
War returned with a vengeance and new material in the mid-'70s, as the title hit was both a pop and R&B Top Ten smash and "Low Rider" did even better, topping the soul surveys and peaking at No. 7 pop. More importantly, they were once more a carefree, loose, jamming band. Unfortunately, it was the last definitive War album, as ego and production battles would soon undermine their success. —*Ron Wynn*

★ **Greatest Hits** / 1976 / United Artists ✦✦✦✦✦
If you can find this collection (only available on vinyl), get it. *Greatest Hits* truly lives up to the title, with tracks like "Summer," "All Day Music," "Cisco Kid," "Slippin' into Darkness," "The World Is a Ghetto," and more. —*Rick Clark*

★ **The Best of War & More** / 1991 / Rhino/Avenue ✦✦✦✦✦
It's not a perfect compilation by any means, but *Best of War & More* is the pick for that original vinyl. But search for that original vinyl, because it was definitive. —*Stephen Thomas Erlewine*

● **Anthology** / Oct. 18, 1994 / Rhino/Avenue ✦✦✦✦
A two-disc set collecting the highlights from War's long, prolific career, *Anthology* is the definitive retrospective of the seminal funk band, containing all of their hits as well as most of their best album tracks. —*Stephen Thomas Erlewine*

The Best of War & More, Vol. 2 / Sep. 3, 1996 / Rhino ✦✦✦✦
Since Avenue botched War's *The Best of... and More* by neglecting to put on hit singles like "The World Is a Ghetto" and "Gypsy

Music Map

┌───┐
│   **American Punk**   │
│   │
│ **'60s Proto-Punk Groups**   │
│ The Velvet Underground, The Stooges, The MC5│
│   │
│ **Early '70s Proto-Punk Groups**   │
│ The Modern Lovers, The New York Dolls   │
│   │
│ **CBGB's Groups**   **Ohio Groups**│
│ The Patti Smith Group, The   Pere Ubu, Devo │
│ Ramones, Television, Blondie,   │
│ Richard Hell & The Voidoids,   │
│ Talking Heads, The Heartbreakers   │
│   │
│ **California Punk**   **New York No Wave** │
│ The Avengers,   Suicide, Lydia Lunch,│
│ X, The Dils,   James Chance,   │
│ The Germs   Glenn Branca   │
└───┘

Man"—although there was plenty of room for both songs, among others—the company needed to assemble a second compilation to take care of all the leftover singles and songs that didn't make the first volume. But they managed to botch *The Best of War... And More, Vol. 2* as well. Sure, "The World Is a Ghetto," "Gypsy Man," "L.A. Sunshine," "Good, Good Feelin'," and several other R&B hit singles made the cut this time around, but the album is baited by an unnecessary remix of "Spill the Wine" by Junior Vasquez, plus selections from their latter-day albums (such as "Peace Sign") that could have been replaced by more first-rate album tracks in the vein of the killer "Don't Let No One Got You Down." Still, if you want to supplement the first *Best of* collection, *Vol. 2* is necessary. However, if you're going to spring for just two discs of War, you might as well go with the comprehensive double-disc collection, *Anthology.* —*Stephen Thomas Erlewine*

Billy Ward

b. Sep. 19, 1921, Los Angeles, CA
Piano / R&B
The ultra-strict disciplinarian and bandleader of a seminal R&B group, Billy Ward ruled over the Dominoes in a tight-fisted manner. He attempted to regulate everything from onstage harmonies to offstage lifestyles. The group's ranks at one time included Clyde McPhatter and Jackie Wilson, but Ward's insistence on dictatorial control resulted in both of them soon bolting for solo status. The group remained active until the early '60s and scored ten Top Ten R&B hits and two colossal No. 1 singles during its heyday from 1951 to 1957. "Sixty Minute Man" in 1951 was the ultimate innuendo hit, while "Have Mercy Baby" was a landmark uptempo stomper. Each topped the R&B charts for more than two months. All their hits were on either Federal or King, except for their final one, a cover of "Star Dust" in 1957 for Liberty that reached No. 5 R&B and No. 12 pop. —*Ron Wynn*

★ **Sixty Minute Men: The Best of Billy Ward & His Dominoes** / 1993 / Rhino ✦✦✦✦✦
Billy Ward was neither a flamboyant vocalist nor a great instrumentalist; his success came directly from his ability to spot and nurture talent. Unfortunately, Ward was also a taskmaster and couldn't hold onto singers very long after discovering and recruiting them for his groups. But for a short period in the 1950s, Ward and the Dominoes ruled R&B by featuring two of its premier vocalists, Clyde McPhatter and Jackie Wilson. Neither stayed long, but were in the band enough time to make some seminal hits, included in this 20-cut anthology. Ironically, the song the group is remembered for the most featured bass vocalist Bill Brown doing the lead on the title track. —*Ron Wynn*

Jennifer Warnes

b. Mar. 3, 1947, Seattle, WA
Keyboards, Vocals / Country-Rock, Adult Contemporary, Pop
Over the last 25 years, Jennifer Warnes has enjoyed a widely varied career, including performing the lead female role in the Los Angeles production of *Hair*, appearing as a regular on the '60s hit show "The Smoth-

ers Brothers Comedy Hour," scoring hits as a country-rock/pop singer ("Right Time of the Night," "I Know a Heartache When I See One"), winning a Grammy for her duet with Joe Cocker on their version of "Up Where We Belong" from the movie *An Officer and a Gentleman*, and garnering critical acclaim for her solo interpretations of Leonard Cohen's songs on the album *Famous Blue Raincoat*. In 1987 Warnes was featured on Roy Orbison's TV special, and she also landed a No. 1 hit duet with former Righteous Brother Bill Medley on "(I've Had) the Time of My Life" from the film *Dirty Dancing. —Rick Clark*

I can Remember / 1968 / Parrot ✦✦

See Me / 1969 / Parrot ✦✦✦

The Best of Jennifer Warren / 1982 / Arista ✦✦✦✦✦

● **Famous Blue Raincoat** / Jan. 1987 / Private Music ✦✦✦✦
Leonard Cohen's material never received a more elegant treatment than the one Jennifer Warnes gave him on *Famous Blue Raincoat*. Warnes is supported by an impressive cast of sidemen, including Stevie Ray Vaughan. The quality of this recording is first-rate. Among the many great songs found here is a powerful version of "Joan of Arc," "Song of Bernadette," "Coming Back to You," and "Came So Far for Beauty" are other highlights. —*Rick Clark*

Dionne Warwick

b. Dec. 12, 1940, East Orange, NJ
Vocals / Soul, Pop, Brill Building pop
The magically melodic voice of Dionne Warwick and the sophisticated pop compositions of Burt Bacharach and Hal David were the proverbial match made in heaven. Warwick proved the prolific songwriting team's favorite interpreter, scaling the pop and soul charts time and again with her soaring renditions of their memorable songs.

Warwick hailed from a musical brood with a strong gospel heritage, and her sister Dee Dee scored a few hits of her own. Dionne's sultry pipes stood out, even on the highly competitive background vocal scene in New York, and she got a chance to step out front in 1963, hitting big on Scepter with the uptown soul classic "Don't Make Me Over."

Under the expert tutelage of Bacharach and David, who doubled as her producers, Warwick's sound soon became smoother and more accessible to pop programming—a formula that resulted in the massive acceptance of her "Walk On By," "I Say a Little Prayer," "This Girl's in Love with You," and a slew of others.

Strangely, Warwick never made it to the top of the pop charts until she broke away from her mentors, traveling to Philadelphia to record the R&B-oriented "Then Came You" with the Spinners in 1974. As elegant and tasteful as ever, Dionne Warwick's breathy vocals still haven't gone out of style—she's managed to remain contemporary while never jeopardizing her appeal. —*Bill Dahl*

Greatest Hits 79-90 / 1989 / Arista ✦✦✦
This collection gathered the great hits from Dionne Warwick's rebirth on Arista. Barry Manilow wisely recast her doing sophisticated pop, moving her into adult contemporary love ballads and away from straight soul and R&B. It was an inspired move, and returned her to the top of the charts frequently in the late '70s and '80s. But while the songs were good, the collection didn't fare so well on the charts. —*Ron Wynn*

★ **The Dionne Warwick Collection: Her All-Time Greatest Hits** / 1989 / Rhino ✦✦✦✦✦
The finest collection of Warwick material compiled by anyone, this excellent set gathered every Warwick gem and smartly remastered them. It's a definitive CD, containing several landmark releases featuring the collaborative compositions of Burt Bacharach and Hal David. These songs underscored Warwick's ability to embody her pop tunes with a soulful, but also light and innocent, quality. It also has excellent liner notes and intelligent sequencing. This is by far the set to get if you want a comprehensive presentation of Warwick's pop-soul greatness. —*Ron Wynn*

Hidden Gems: Best of Dionne Warwick, Vol. 2 / 1992 / Rhino ✦✦✦✦
A fine collection of rarities and forgotten singles from Warwick's heyday with Bacharach/David; it's a good supplement to Rhino's *Dionne Warwick Collection. —Stephen Thomas Erlewine*

From the Vaults / Oct. 1995 / Soul Classics ✦✦✦
An anthology of 24 fairly obscure tracks, drawn from Warwick's 1963-66 albums and B-sides. Although it has the look of something that would appeal primarily to serious fans and collectors, this is hardly any less satisfying than the greatest hits collections covering the same era. It's also just as good as Rhino's *Hidden Gems*, another anthology of little-known Warwick recordings from the '60s; what's more, it doesn't repeat any selections from that previous compilation. The first half of the CD (covering 1962-64) shows Dionne at her most girl groupish and soulful, with arrangements that often recall those of her labelmates, the Shirelles (who in fact recorded their own versions of a few of these songs). "It's Love That Really Counts" and "Get Rid of Him" are highlights; "Mr. Heartbreak" is a wrenching, stately ballad, easily up to the standard of her hits of the period. The last half of the program covers material from

1965 and 1966, all of which (like most of the songs she sang in the late '60s) was penned by Bacharach-David. These show her going in a smoother, adult pop-oriented direction, and while I prefer the somewhat gutsier earlier sides, there are some good tunes that are impossible to come by otherwise, except on long-out-of-print LPs. —*Richie Unterberger*

Was (Not Was)

Urban, Alternative Pop-Rock, Pop-Rock
Was (Not Was) plays contemporary R&B dance music, with lyrics that range from the satiric to the bizarre. The group is led by Detroit-natives David Weiss (David Was), who plays flute and writes those lyrics, and Don Fagenson (Don Was), who plays bass and writes music, but the group is fronted by singers Harry Bowens and Sweet Pea Atkinson. Was (Not Was) first gained notice for a dance single called "Wheel Me Out" in 1980. Their first album, *Was (Not Was)* (1981), did not reach the charts, but its follow-up, *Born to Laugh at Tornados* (1983), did. Then little was heard from the group for five years. They returned in 1988 with *What Up, Dog?*, which featured the No.16 hit "Spy in the House of Love" and the No. 7 hit "Walk the Dinosaur." (During this period, Don Was had become a prominent record producer, handling the board for Bonnie Raitt's Grammy-winning *Nick of Time*, among many other mainstream pop records.) The fourth Was (Not Was) album, *Are You Okay?*, appeared in 1990.

Are You Okay? wasn't as commercially successful as the previous *What Up, Dog?* After the album's release, Don Was continued to pursue his production career, which began to increase tensions between him and David. In 1993, Was (Not Was) officially parted ways. —*William Ruhlmann*

Born to Laugh at Tornados / 1983 / Geffen ✦✦✦

● **What Up, Dog?** / 1988 / Chrysalis ✦✦✦✦
The guests are fewer (though Frank Sinatra, Jr., sings one song), but the oddities go on, with "11 MPH," a review of the JFK assassination, and "Dad I'm in Jail," a proud rant by David Was. Also included: the hits "Spy in the House of Love" and "Walk the Dinosaur." —*William Ruhlmann*

Are You Okay? / 1990 / Chrysalis ✦✦✦

Roger Waters

b. Sep. 6, 1944
Bass / Art-Rock/Progressive-Rock, Pop-Rock
Roger Waters was the bassist for Pink Floyd from 1965 to 1983. Waters assumed an increasingly dominant position in the band, writing all lyrics in addition to some of the music as of *The Dark Side of the Moon* (1973) and singing most of the lead vocals on *The Wall* (1979). Waters issued his debut solo album, *The Pros and Cons of Hitch Hiking*, in 1984. In the mid-'80s, he engaged in a protracted legal battle, arguing that the other members of Pink Floyd could not continue using the name without him in the band; he lost. In 1987, Waters released his second album, *Radio K.A.O.S.*, and in 1990 he staged a concert version of *The Wall* in Berlin. In 1992 he released his third album, *Amused to Death. —William Ruhlmann*

Music from "The Body" / 1970 / Restless ✦✦✦

The Pros & Cons of Hitch-Hiking / 1984 / Columbia ✦✦✦✦
The loose framing device of this album is a series of daydreams experienced while waking up. Eric Clapton contributes guitar, but he can't provide enough musical interest to sustain Roger Waters' lyric-heavy ruminations. —*William Ruhlmann*

Radio K.A.O.S. / 1987 / Columbia ✦✦✦✦
There's more story than can be effectively told on this concept album dealing with radio, computers, and the threat of nuclear war, but many of the songs are up to Waters's Pink Floyd ever did. —*William Ruhlmann*

The Wall in Berlin 1990 / 1990 / Mercury ✦✦✦

● **Amused to Death** / Sep. 1, 1992 / Columbia ✦✦✦✦
Yet another installment in Waters' lectures about the horrors of war and man's inhumanity to man, *Amused to Death* is helped considerably by the presence of Jeff Beck, who contributes some brilliant, free-form guitar to the meandering songs. Waters himself is in fine form, spitting out bitter, sarcastic lyrics over his slow, grandiose instrumental backdrops. While he could have fleshed out the melodies a little bit more, his execution is what matters, and his performance on *Amused to Death* is the liveliest of any of his solo records. —*Stephen Thomas Erlewine*

Jimmy Webb

Piano, Keyboards, Vocals / Singer-Songwriter, Pop-Rock
Even if you never have heard a Jimmy Webb album, you have at least heard his songs. During the late '60s and early '70s, Webb was writing a series of hits for the Fifth Dimension, Glen Campbell, Richard Harris, and Cher, including "Wichita Lineman" and "By the Time I Get to Phoenix;" both songs have become pop standards. His first hit was the Fifth

Dimension's "Up, Up and Away," which was eventually used in TWA television commercials.

After having many different artists record his songs successfully, Webb officially launched a solo career in 1970; a collection of his demos had been released against his will in 1968. Although his debut album, *Words and Music*, earned mixed reviews, it helped him gain a sizable cult following. While he recorded a series of overlooked albums in the '70s, other artists continued to record his songs, including Art Garfunkel, Judy Collins, Joe Cocker, and Lowell George. During the '80s, he concentrated on scoring films and television shows, releasing only one album. In 1993, he returned to the studio to record his first album since 1982; produced by Linda Rondstadt, *Suspending Disbelief* earned good reviews, but poor sales, which seems to be Webb's curse. Even though he has never has had success with his own recordings, Jimmy Webb remains one of the best-loved and most-recorded songwriters of his generation. —*Stephen Thomas Erlewine*

Jim Webb Sings Jim Webb / 1968 / Epic ♦♦

Words & Music / Feb. 1970 / Reprise ♦♦♦
Words and Music marked Webb's official debut as a singer of his own songs. Though the second side's experiments (a suite in three movements and a song cycle/medley linking "Let It Be Me," "Never My Love," and "I Wanna Be Free") are a little too ambitious for comfort, side one features the concise, well-crafted pop (such as "P.F. Sloan" and "Love Song") that would feature heavily on later releases. —*Chris Woodstra*

And So On / 1971 / Reprise ♦♦♦
Webb's second album stripped down the excesses of its predecessor for a more consistently enjoyable set, featuring the haunting "Met Her on a Plane" (later covered by Ian Matthews) as well as the equally powerful "If Ships Were Made to Sail," "One Lady," and "All My Love's Laughter." —*Chris Woodstra*

El Mirage / 1977 / Atlantic ♦♦♦♦
Produced by George Martin, *El Mirage* is one of Webb's strongest albums. As always, the songs are perfectly constructed but this time sung with more confidence than ever before. Highlights include "If You See Me Getting Smaller" and "Christian No." —*Chris Woodstra*

Angel Heart / 1982 / Sony ♦♦

Suspending Disbelief / 1993 / Elektra ♦♦♦
After a several year absence, Webb returns with one of his most polished efforts to date. His hook-filled melodies are instantly endearing, while he sings a love song to his sports car and remembers a meeting with Elvis. His voice, never one of his strong points in the past, has aged particularly well. —*Chris Woodstra*

● **Archive** / 1993 / WEA ♦♦♦♦
Archive is an excellent 20-track (UK import only) overview of Webb's criminally overlooked career as a performer from 1970 to 1977, his most productive period. While he is best remembered as the composer of hits for others, this collection offers proof that he was equally adept at interpreting his own songs—oftentimes bringing more emotion to them. —*Chris Woodstra*

Ween

Alternative Pop-Rock, Indie Rock
Utterly bizarre. That's the best way to describe Ween, a duo going by the names Dean Ween (guitars) and Gene Ween (vocals). The Ween school of songwriting consists of taking lots of hallucinogens and then writing songs from the weird visions that pop into their heads. Ween began in 1985, when the then-high school-mired Ween boys met and started recording themselves. 1989's *God Ween Satan* reveals the band in all their adolescent glory, with over 20 songs and snippets crammed into a disc that can barely contain them; 1994's *Chocolate and Cheese* shows that the brothers Ween actually can play their instruments, and play them well; the album ranges from creepy ditties about childhood diseases to Prince send-ups. These albums, and everything in between, are definitely an acquired taste, but a yummy one at that. —*Heather Phares*

GodWeenSatan: The Oneness / 1990 / Twin/Tone ♦♦♦♦
A crank phone call of epic proportions, this 20-plus song strong debut is filled with plenty of inanity, insanity, and obscenity. Stylistically, the group veers off in all directions. The helium-laced pop of "Don't Laugh, I Love You," the stomp of "Old Queen Cole," and the delicate ballad "Squelch the Little Weasel" make this a crazy, unfocused collection of gross fun. —*Heather Phares*

The Pod / 1991 / Shimmy Disc ♦♦♦
The Pod continues the wackiness and effrontery that the Ween brothers started on *GodWeenSatan*. However, the tone of the album is more sluggish and off-kilter, perhaps from the severe case of mononucleosis the group had when they recorded this. "Dr. Rock" and "Pollo Asado" are two standouts on this bizarre and somewhat inaccessible album. —*Heather Phares*

Pure Guava / 1992 / Elektra ♦♦♦♦
The band's third album finds them moving in a more pop direction. Tunes like "Push the Little Daisies," "Springtheme" and "Don't Get Too Close to My Fantasy," though certainly bizarre, are catchy and fun to listen to. However, the Ween boys don't forget to be disgusting, as song titles like "Reggaejunkiejew" and "Flies on my Dick" subtly hint. —*Heather Phares*

● **Chocolate & Cheese** / 1994 / Elektra ♦♦♦♦
Chocolate & Cheese is the group's fourth and most accomplished album yet, focusing their gonzo sensibilities into a collection of hummable tunes. "Take Me Away" and "Tear for Eddie" are clever parodies of classic rock, while "Roses Are Free" and "Freedom of '76" pay homage to Prince and '70s soul, respectively. The touching Mexican ballad "Buenos Tardes Amigo" and the downright creepy "Spinal Meningitis Got Me Down" show that Ween's smirks are still firmly on their faces, even if they are creating increasingly memorable tunes. *Chocolate & Cheese* is a good beginning point for novices to the crazy world of Dean and Gene Ween. —*Heather Phares*

12 Golden Country Greats / Jul. 1996 / Elektra ♦♦♦

Weezer

Alternative Pop-Rock
Led by guitarist/vocalist/songwriter Rivers Cuomo, Weezer mixed the off-kilter punk-pop of the Pixies with a new-wave pop sensibility and arena rock beat, becoming one of the surprise success stories of 1994. Cuomo was still in college when their self-titled debut record came out in the summer of 1994. Produced by Ric Ocasek, the record shot to popularity once MTV began playing the incessant "Undone (The Sweater Song)" heavily. The band followed through with another hit single, "Buddy Holly," at the end of the year. In the spring of 1995, the album had gone platinum; the band's third single, "Say It Ain't So," became their third straight modern rock hit in the summer of 1995. —*Stephen Thomas Erlewine*

● **Weezer** / 1994 / DGC ♦♦♦♦
Falling between the warped pop of the Pixies and the straight-ahead thump of arena rock, Weezer's debut album offers embarrassingly pleasurable pop thrills. Weezer is unabashedly pop. Songs like "Buddy Holly," "Undone—The Sweater Song," "In the Garage," "The World Has Turned and Left Me Here," and "Surf Wax America" are filled with strong, simple guitar hooks and relentlessly catchy melodies. What makes the band so enjoyable is their charming geekiness; instead of singing about despair, they sing about love, which is kind of refreshing in the gloom-drenched world of '90s guitar-pop. —*Stephen Thomas Erlewine*

Paul Weller

b. May 25, 1958, Woking, England
Guitar, Vocals / Pop-Rock
After disbanding the Style Council, former Jam leader Paul Weller went solo, making a series of soul-inspired pop-rock records. While his self-titled 1992 debut was a return to form, it was the following year's *Wild Wood* (not released in the US until 1994) that showed he was still a vital songwriter and artist. Like the rest of Weller's work, the album was a hit in nearly every country except the US. —*Stephen Thomas Erlewine*

Paul Weller / 1992 / London ♦♦♦♦
Weller's voice has matured into a deep, soulful, resonant instrument, in keeping with his new inward-looking material. He's obviously come to terms with being an effective chronicler of his own feelings rather than being the spokesperson of a generation. His ease with this role makes *Paul Weller* a comfortable—if not groundbreaking—listening experience all around. —*Roch Parisien*

● **Wildwood** / 1993 / PolyGram ♦♦♦♦
Paul Weller signaled that the songwriter had returned to form, but *Wildwood* is the album that reestablished him as a British superstar. And for good reason, too. Expanding the tight, stripped-down soul and R&B-inflected pop of his debut, Weller adds a relaxed, laidback approach that recalls the better moments of Traffic. Throughout the record, Weller's songwriting is concise and soulful, giving the musicians a solid foundation for their instrumental excursions, which never become boring and indulgent. —*Stephen Thomas Erlewine*

Live Wood / 1994 / Go! Discs ♦♦♦

Stanley Road / 1995 / Go! Discs ♦♦♦
In many ways, *Stanley Road* is *Wild Wood*—Part Two, a continuation of the laidback, soul-inflected rock that dominated his previous albums. Named after the street where he grew up, *Stanley Road* could be seen as a return to Paul Weller's roots, yet his roots were in the Who and the Kinks, not in Traffic. (At this point, the sound of the Jam matters little in what his music sounds like.) Weller's music has always had R&B roots—the major difference with both *Wild Wood* and *Stanley Road* is

how much he and his band stretch out. *Stanley Road* in particular features more jamming than any of his previous work. That doesn't mean he has neglected his songwriting—a handful of Weller classics are scattered throughout the album. Unfortunately, too much of it is spent on drawn-out grooves that are self-conscious about their own authenticity. Still, he has the good sense to revive Dr. John's "I Walk on Gilded Splinters" and invite his disciple Noel Gallagher (Oasis) along to jam. *—Stephen Thomas Erlewine*

Mary Wells

b. May 13, 1943, Detroit, MI, **d.** Jul. 26, 1992, Los Angeles, CA
Vocals / Soul, Motown, Girl Group

Time and legions of other soul superstars have obscured the fact that for a brief moment, Mary Wells was Motown's biggest star. She came to the attention of Berry Gordy as a 17-year-old, hawking a song she'd written for Jackie Wilson; that song, "Bye Bye Baby," became her first Motown hit in 1961. The full-throated approach of that single was quickly toned down in favor of a pop-soul sound. Few other soul singers managed to be as shy and sexy at the same time as Wells (Barbara Lewis is the only other that springs to mind), and the soft-voiced singer found a perfect match with the emerging Motown production team, especially Smokey Robinson. Smokey wrote and produced her biggest Motown hits—"Two Lovers," "You Beat Me to the Punch," and "The One Who Really Loves You" all made the Top Ten in the early '60s, and "My Guy" hit the No. 1 spot in mid-1964, at the very height of Beatlemania.

Mary turned 21 years old as "My Guy" was rising to the top of the charts, and left Motown almost immediately afterward for a reported advance of several hundred thousand dollars from 20th Century Fox. The circumstances remain cloudy 30 years later, but Wells and her husband-manager felt Motown wasn't coming through with enough money for its new superstar; she was also lured by the prospect of movie roles through 20th Century Fox (which never materialized). It's been rumored that Wells was being groomed for the sort of plans that were subsequently lavished upon Diana Ross; more nefariously, it's also been rumored that Motown quietly discouraged radio stations from playing Wells' subsequent releases. What is certain is that Wells never remotely approached the success of her Motown years, entering the pop Top 40 only once (although she had some R&B hits). Motown, for its part, took care throughout the rest of the '60s not to lose its big stars to larger labels.

Wells' departure from Motown was so dramatic and unsuccessful that it's tended to overshadow the quality of her later work, which has almost always been dismissed as trivial by critics. True, it didn't match the quality of her Motown recordings—Smokey Robinson could not be replaced. But her '60s singles for 20th Century Fox, Atco, and Jubilee were solid pop-soul on which her vocal talents remained undiminished. She wrote and produced a lot of her late '60s and early '70s sessions with her second husband, guitarist Cecil Womack (brother of Bobby), and these found her exploring a somewhat earthier groove than her more widely known pop efforts. She had trouble landing recording deals in the '70s and '80s, and succumbed to throat cancer in 1992. *—Richie Unterberger*

Greatest Hits / Apr. 15, 1964 / Motown ✦✦✦✦
Since Mary Wells left Motown in 1964, this 12-song compilation, released at the time, contains all her successful singles for the label, from "Bye Bye Baby" to "My Guy," with the exception of "I Don't Want to Take a Chance." As such, it is just about all the Mary Wells anyone reasonably needs. *—William Ruhlmann*

Complete Jubilee Sessions / 1993 / Sequel ✦✦✦✦
More proof that Wells still had what it took after leaving Motown. This 26-song collection assembles everything she recorded for the Jubilee label in the late '60s and early '70s: her 1968 LP *Servin' Up Some Soul*, a couple non-LP B-sides, and the entirety of a scrapped follow-up album (although some of the songs from that unreleased LP appeared on singles, seven were unreleased before this reissue). This is Wells' gutsiest period, with the majority of the material penned by her and husband Cecil Womack, who provides some excellent bluesy guitar licks. Wells is in top voice on both the fairly strong originals and a variety of well-done covers. The earlier *Servin' Up Some Soul* sessions have the edge over the later, slicker tracks, but almost all of it is well worth hearing. *—Richie Unterberger*

★ **Looking Back 1961-1964** / Sep. 7, 1993 / Motown ✦✦✦✦✦
This two-CD, 43-track box set is the most comprehensive retrospective of Motown's biggest female star before Diana Ross. Although her first hit, "Bye Bye Baby," presented Wells as a blues belter, she quickly settled into a sly and sassy groove. Subsequent hits like "You Beat Me to the Punch," "Two Lovers," and "My Guy" (all included here) made the most of her shy, seductive voice by teaming her with some great songs and production by Smokey Robinson. Though many of these tunes were relegated to B-sides, album tracks, or even the can (11 were previously unreleased), the material—written by Motown stalwarts like Berry Gordy, Holland-Dozier-Holland, and Mickey Stevenson when Smokey was unavail-

able—is not far below the hits in quality. This is as much a testimony to Motown's overflow of prolific talent as Wells, but doesn't detract from the consistency of this set, which includes her duets with Marvin Gaye. Includes a comprehensive essay in the photo-packed booklet, although the mysterious absence of the excellent "Was It Worth It" is a notable loss. *—Richie Unterberger*

Ain't It the Truth: The Best of Mary Wells 1964-1982 / 1994 / Varese Sarabande ✦✦✦
It doesn't have anything from her 1965-67 years with Atco (those tracks are compiled on a separate collection), but otherwise this does a good job of assembling the highlights of her post-Motown career. The focus is on her handful of minor mid-'60s hits for 20th Century Fox (which were conscious or half-conscious attempts to emulate her Motown sound) and her grittier 1968-70 recordings for Jubilee (which she co-wrote and co-produced with guitarist and husband/producer Cecil Womack). A couple of unimpressive tracks from her 1981 Epic album round out the collection; Wells is in fine form throughout. *—Richie Unterberger*

Dear Lover: The Atco Sessions / 1995 / Ichiban Soul Classics ✦✦✦
In his autobiography, Jerry Wexler characterized Wells' tenure with Atlantic from 1965-67 as a failure for all parties concerned, but he's being too harsh. Commercially, it was certainly a fallow period; only the title track (a Top Ten R&B hit) paid off. But actually, her Atco singles were solid mid-'60s soul, usually recorded in Chicago and bearing the influence of that city's noted soul producer, Carl Davis (who produced some of these tracks). This collection includes both sides of all four of her Atco singles, five covers from her sole Atco LP, and a couple of decent previously unreleased tracks. *—Richie Unterberger*

Never, Never Leave Me/The 20th Century Sides / Feb. 1996 / Soul Classics ✦✦✦
If Wells' brief stint with 20th Century had been a total misdirected failure, it would be easier to dismiss. It wasn't, though. Wells continued to deliver pop-flavored soul in just as good a voice as ever, and in fact had a few small hits. The problem is not so much approach as quality. Her material, though not bad, lacked the special magic of her best Motown classics; the production was somewhat thinner as well. This 18-track anthology assembles her best 20th Century performances, including her singles, songs from her first 20th Century LP, and three previously unreleased songs. Though it's principally of interest to Wells fans, it's better than you might expect, worth hearing for the pleasure of Wells' voice if not the average material. *—Richie Unterberger*

Paul Westerberg

b. Dec. 31, 1960, Minneapolis, MN
Guitar, Piano, Vocals / Rock 'n' roll, Alternative Pop-Rock

After disbanding the Replacements in 1991, singer-songwriter Paul Westerberg resurfaced the following year with two songs on the *Singles* soundtrack. A year later, Westerberg released his first solo album, *14 Songs*, in the summer of 1993. Although the record received generally positive reviews and spawned the modern rock hit, "World Class Fad," the album failed to break the songwriter into the mainstream. Three years later, Westerberg released his second solo album, *Eventually*. Like *14 Songs* and the entire Replacements catalog before it, *Eventually* received good reviews but failed to become a commercial success. *—Stephen Thomas Erlewine*

● **14 Songs** / Jun. 15, 1993 / Sire ✦✦✦✦
Westerberg's first solo album since the breakup of the Replacements is a strong yet incoherent collection of songs from one of the most influential songwriters of the 1980s. Falling somewhere between the sound of *All Shook Down* and the songwriting of *Tim*, *14 Songs* is a more mature effort from Westerberg, sounding like the optimistic brother of the last Replacements album. It's not as raw as *Let It Be* or *Tim* or as consistent as *Pleased to Meet Me*, but it is a solid collection of expertly crafted rock and pop songs. *—Stephen Thomas Erlewine*

Eventually / Apr. 1996 / Reprise ✦✦✦

Wham!

Pop-Rock

Wham! was a UK pop-dance duo formed in 1981 by George Michael (born Yorgos Panayiotou, Jun. 26, 1963) and Andrew Ridgeley (b. Jun. 25, 1963). Combining light soul music with slow, romantic ballads, they first hit the UK charts in the fall of 1982 with "Young Guns (Go for It)." It hit No. 3, the first of ten UK Top Ten hits for the duo. The first Wham! album, *Fantastic*, topped the UK charts in 1983. The group broke through in the US the following year with "Wake Me up Before You Go-Go," the first of three straight No. 1 hits. The second of those chart-toppers was "Careless Whisper," billed as "featuring George Michael," the first sign that Michael, who sang lead and wrote the songs, was emerging as a solo entity. Nevertheless, Wham! continued through 1986, finishing their career at Wembley Stadium in England, after which Michael went on to a successful solo career. *—William Ruhlmann*

● **Make It Big** / 1984 / Columbia ✦✦✦✦
George Michael demonstrates a thorough knowledge of danceable pop, from the '60s-ish "Wake Me up Before You Go-Go" to the tear-jerking ballad "Careless Whisper." Also includes "Everything She Wants" and "Freedom." — *William Ruhlmann*

Music from the Edge of Heaven / 1986 / Columbia ✦✦✦

Barry White

b. Sep. 12, 1944, Galveston, TX
Keyboards, Vocals / Soul, Disco, Urban, Club-Dance
Barry White has been involved in the popular music industry since age 11, when he played piano on Jesse Belvin's hit single "Goodnight My Love." He recorded with the Upfronts for Lumntone in 1960, then as a lead vocalist for Atlantic in 1964 and for Downey and Veep in 1965 under the name of Barry Lee. He was an A&R man for Mustang/Bronco Records in 1966 and 1967. White formed the female trio Love Unlimited in 1969, and also became leader of the 40-piece Love Unlimited Orchestra. His solo career was revitalized in the early '70s as his formidable, deep, captivating bass, coupled with pseudo-sophisticated strings and elaborate productions, helped him rack up five No. 1 hits and seven other Top Ten R&B hits from 1973 until 1978 for 20th Century Records. He also scored five Top Ten pop singles and one No. 1 in that same stretch. "I'm Gonna Love You a Little More Baby" started the string in 1973, and his final Top Ten R&B single was "Your Sweetness Is My Weakness," which peaked at No. 2 in 1978. White continued recording for United Gold, 20th Century again, United Gold, and A&M. He scored a mild comeback by being one of the featured vocalists on Quincy Jones' single "The Garden" in 1989 and continues recording for A&M in the '90s. *The Icon Is Love* (1994) marked White's return as a potent commercial force. — *Ron Wynn*

Greatest Hits, Vol. 1 / 1975 / Casablanca ✦✦✦✦
Before a definitive multi-disc boxed set was issued in the 1990s, there were two single-album volumes of Barry White hits released by Casablanca in the 1970s. The first edition was the best, with sweeping versions of such disco classics as "Can't Get Enough of Your Love, Babe" and "You're the First, the Last, My Everything." White's productions and arrangements were never as intricate as they seemed, but his booming baritone and romantic dialogue sounded convincing when underscored by the lush backgrounds. If you only want a little Barry White, this is the album to grab. — *Ron Wynn*

Greatest Hits, Vol. 2 / 1981 / Casablanca ✦✦✦✦
This second set of Barry White hits isn't quite as impressive or essential as its predecessor. White's arrangements and compositions grew stale as the 1970s wore on, and he recycled the romantic dialogue and exploited the robust baritone until he became a caricature of himself. Put this one in the "for fans only" category. — *Ron Wynn*

Just for You / 1992 / Casablanca ✦✦✦✦
A three-disc box set containing more music than anyone but the most devoted fan could want. — *Stephen Thomas Erlewine*

★ **All Time Greatest Hits** / 1995 / Mercury ✦✦✦✦✦
Condensing the best moments from the two *Greatest Hits* collections onto one disc, *All Time Greatest Hits* is the deep-voiced disco crooner's one essential album. — *Stephen Thomas Erlewine*

Whitesnake

Hard Rock, Heavy Metal, Hair Metal
After recording two solo albums, former Deep Purple vocalist David Coverdale formed Whitesnake around 1977. In the glut of hard-rock and heavy-metal bands of the late '70s, their first albums got somewhat lost in the shuffle, although they were fairly popular in Europe and Japan. During 1982, Coverdale took some time off, so he could take care of his sick daughter. When he re-emerged with a new version of Whitesnake in 1984, the band sounded revitalized and energetic. *Slide It In* may have relied on Led Zeppelin and Deep Purple's old tricks, but the band had a knack for writing hooks; the record became their first platinum album. Three years later, Whitesnake released an eponymous album that was even better. Portions of the album were blatantly derivative—"Still of the Night" was a dead ringer for early Zeppelin—but the group could write powerful, heavy rockers like "Here I Go Again" that were driven as much by melody as riffs, as well as hit power ballads like "Is This Love." *Whitesnake* was an enormous international success, selling over six million copies in the US alone.

Before they recorded their follow-up, 1989's *Slip of the Tongue*, Coverdale again assembled a completely new version of the band, featuring guitar virtuoso Steve Vai. Although the record went platinum, it was a considerable disappointment after the across-the-boards success of *Whitesnake*. Coverdale put Whitesnake on hiatus after that album. In 1993, he released a collaboration with former Led Zeppelin guitarist Jimmy Page that was surprisingly lackluster. The following year, Whitesnake released a greatest hits album and it seemed likely that Coverdale

was going to form a new version of the band. — *Stephen Thomas Erlewine*

Slide It In / 1984 / Geffen ✦✦✦✦
With its combination of stadium-sized hard-rock riffing and solid commercial melodies, *Slide It In* laid the groundwork for the blockbuster follow-up *Whitesnake*. Nevertheless, the album is rawer and cruder than their subsequent pop hit and is more representative of the band's metal roots. — *Stephen Thomas Erlewine*

Whitesnake / 1987 / Geffen ✦✦✦✦
After slugging it out in the British hard-rock market for almost ten years, Whitesnake achieved platinum success with this highly crafted mainstream AOR. It includes the No. 1 "Here I Go Again," "Is This Love?" (No. 2), and the Led Zeppelin rip "Still of the Night." — *AMG*

● **Whitesnake's Greatest Hits** / 1994 / Geffen ✦✦✦✦
All of the best moments from Whitesnake's late-'80s glory days collected on one disc. — *Stephen Thomas Erlewine*

The Who

Rock 'n' roll, Hard Rock, British Invasion, Pop-Rock
Founded in the early '60s by Pete Townshend, John Entwistle, and Roger Daltrey (with Keith Moon coming along slightly later), the Who were originally a fairly conventional R&B-based outfit, with Townshend and Daltrey sharing guitar chores, Enwistle on bass, and Doug Sanden (later replaced by Keith Moon) on drums. Early on, however, they fell under the influence of Johnny Kidd & the Pirates, a British band that pioneered a lean, muscular sound built around a single guitar and a rhythm section of bass and drums (most British bands of the period also featured a rhythm guitar very prominently) behind a lone singer. Kidd had originally with "Shakin' All Over," a number that the Who would adopt into their repertoire. Daltrey gave up the guitar to concentrate on singing, Townshend turned his rhythm guitar into a lead instrument, and the band emerged with a powerful, sweaty brand of R&B, all very Memphis-influenced ("Green Onions" was long part of their stage act) and louder than anything that London audiences were used to. They quickly became favorites of the R&B-loving mods, and by 1964 were ready to cut their first single, a quickie rewrite of "Got Love If You Want It" entitled "I'm the Face" ("face" being a key part of mod slang) under the temporary name the High Numbers.

It was around this time that Pete Townshend discovered two key talents. As a songwriter, Townshend showed a remarkable capacity for writing anthem-like songs, which, if not exactly Top 40 material, were certainly memorable to their core audience and just different enough to get airplay. "My Generation" was the first and most important of these, and while his songwriting would broaden in coming years to embrace longer thematic canvases (including the so-called rock opera), it was songs like "My Generation," "The Magic Bus," and the epic-length "Won't Get Fooled Again" that would make the most lasting impact on rock 'n' roll. Townshend's other major talent was in the area of destruction—by accident one night, he shattered the neck of his guitar during a performance, and the crowd seemed to appreciate it. Gradually guitar smashing became a trademark of the band's sets, an effective but extremely expensive publicity vehicle.

Meanwhile, Roger Daltrey emerged as one of the most powerful singers of his generation, a soul-shouter whose voice could be heard even above Townshend's ringing power-chords and Keith Moon's flamboyant drumming. They built their reputations gradually in the US during the mid-'60s, emerging as one of the better acts at the Monterey Pop Festival (alongside Jimi Hendrix), but it was their rock opera, *Tommy*, that finally transformed the group into a major international rock act.

Tommy's pretensions aside, the passions and seemingly allegorical search for truth behind the story of the deaf, dumb, and blind boy seemed to strike a chord with a generation of teenagers and college students who were searching for something different and more genuine in their own lives—the opera's clear rejection of drugs (which echoed Townshend's own philosophy) was conveniently ignored, and the sky seemed to be the limit for the band for the ten years after *Tommy*'s release.

A live album followed, reminding audiences of the group's R&B roots, and after a false start on a film project, in 1971 the Who released *Who's Next*, which was probably their strongest individual album. Very little that they did afterward was quite as successful artistically as this brilliant compendium of religious musings, idealism at high volume, and revolutionary anthems, but it didn't matter. *Quadrophenia* was too vague a subject for Americans who were unfamiliar with its mod-culture roots, *Who by Numbers* seemed slight after the records that had preceded it; and *Who Are You* showed a certain softening of the edges, but the audiences kept buying albums and, even more important, kept going to concerts. Then in 1978, shortly after the release of *Who Are You*, Keith Moon died, and that was pretty much it for the Who. Their work became softer and less urgent (a process that might have been hastened also by Pete Townshend's progressive hearing loss), and while the audiences still bought tickets, their music no longer seemed very important. What little musical capital the group still possessed in the late '80s was squandered on one-too-many farewell tours. —*Bruce Eder*

The Who Sings My Generation / 1965 / MCA ✦✦✦✦
The group's debut album is more R&B-oriented than their subsequent records, but it's honest and direct. Includes covers of James Brown material amid the Beatlesque originals such as "The Kids Are Alright." —*Bruce Eder*

A Quick One (Happy Jack) / 1966 / MCA ✦✦✦✦
The group's second album is a transitional work, containing a rudimentary rock opera ("A Quick One") and a bizarre collection of originals by Roger Daltrey and Keith Moon as well as the expected Pete Townshend and John Entwistle. The flashes of brilliance make up for the defects in the writing, and Entwistle's "Boris the Spider" and "Whiskey Man" are among the best songs he has ever written. The 1995 CD reissue adds ten bonus tracks: some 1966-67 B-sides, their UK-only 1966 *Ready Steady Who!* EP, an acoustic version of "Happy Jack," and a previously unreleased cover of the Everly Brothers' "Man with the Money." —*Bruce Eder*

☆ **The Who Sell Out** / 1967 / MCA ✦✦✦✦
Arguably rock's first important concept album and infinitely more effective and humorous than *Tommy* or *Quadrophenia*, this is a full-length tribute to Britain's pirate radio stations, complete with commercials by the band. "I Can See for Miles" was the hit off of the record, but the material ranges from the ethereal "Sunrise" to the proto-*Tommy* mini-opera "Rael." Funny as well as scintillating. The 1995 CD reissue has over half a dozen interesting outtakes from the time of the sessions, as well as unused commercials, the B-side "Someone's Coming," and an alternate version of "Mary Anne with the Shaky Hand." —*Bruce Eder*

Tommy / 1969 / MCA ✦✦✦✦
The original rock opera. The material hasn't worn well as a conceptual creation, but the individual songs still have an energy that is refreshing. Keith Moon's nasty sense of humor stands out. —*Bruce Eder*

☆ **Live at Leeds** / 1970 / MCA ✦✦✦✦✦
A loud, raunchy concert showcase for the group, with surprisingly little material from *Tommy*. The group's R&B roots are showcased here far better than on their post-*My Generation* studio albums, and the only problem for some listeners is the lack of the sophisticated studio sound they'd developed on previous releases. The 1995 CD reissue doubles the length of the original LP, with plenty of additional material from the same performance, including versions of some more of their early singles and unexpected items like "Tattoo" and the R&B standard "Fortune Teller." —*Bruce Eder*

★ **Meaty, Beaty, Big & Bouncy** / 1971 / MCA ✦✦✦✦✦
The first halfway-decent retrospective on the group, covering their American singles as of 1972, including "I Can See for Miles," "My Generation," "The Magic Bus," "The Seeker," and a lot of other material that subsequently became staples of FM radio. —*Bruce Eder*

★ **Who's Next** / 1971 / MCA ✦✦✦✦✦
The group's magnum opus, a rich, expressive, loud piece of hard rock that summed up the first six years of the band's history. "Won't Get Fooled Again" became a major radio anthem and "Behind Blue Eyes" unexpectedly became a favorite Pete Townshend number as well. Roger Daltrey never sang better, and John Entwistle's bass achieved new heights of prominence, while Keith Moon turned in an explosive performance on drums. —*Bruce Eder*

Quadrophenia / 1973 / MCA ✦✦✦✦
The group's second rock opera wasn't nearly the success that *Tommy* had been, but it proved more fertile in other media—"Love Reign o'er Me" was a moderate success as a single but precious little else seemed to register with the public. Ironically, this is a finely produced album, with a sound that is both hard and lush, and Roger Daltrey seemed to achieve a larger-than-life performance as the embattled mod Jimmy. —*Bruce Eder*

Odds & Sods / 1974 / MCA ✦✦✦

The Who by Numbers / 1975 / MCA ✦✦✦
The Who by Numbers functions as Pete Townshend's confessional singer-songwriter album, as he chronicles his problems with alcohol ("However Much I Booze"), women ("Dreaming from the Waist" and "They Are All in Love"), and life in general. However, his introspective musings are rendered ineffective by Roger Daltrey's bluster and the cloying, lightweight filler of "Squeeze Box." In addition, Townshend's songs tend to be underdeveloped, relying on verbosity instead of melodicism, with only the simple power of "Slip Kid," the grace of "Blue Red and Gray," and John Entwistle's heavy rocker "Success Story" making much of an impact. —*Stephen Thomas Erlewine*

Who Are You / 1978 / MCA ✦✦✦
The final worthwhile album by the band, a somewhat arch collection of pretentious rock anthems and failed concepts surrounding a powerful title track whose video clip marked Keith Moon's final public appearance with the band. —*Bruce Eder*

The Kids Are Alright / 1979 / MCA ✦✦✦✦
Soundtrack to a dazzling video portrait of the band, better in many ways than any of the hits collections out of the group for the surprises and odd takes that it contains. —*Bruce Eder*

Face Dances / 1981 / MCA ✦✦✦
Without Keith Moon, the Who may have lacked the restless firepower that distinguished their earlier albums, but *Face Dances* had some of Pete Townshend's best, most incisive compositions since *Quadrophenia*. "Don't Let Go the Coat" was one of his better odes to the Meher Baba, "You Better You Bet" was a driving rocker, as was the rueful "Cache Cache," while "How Can You Do It Alone" was a solid ballad. While Townshend's songs were graceful and introspective, Roger Daltrey delivered them without any subtlety, rendering their power impotent. —*Stephen Thomas Erlewine*

It's Hard / 1982 / MCA ✦✦
Driven by Pete Townshend's arching musical ambitions, *It's Hard* was an undistinguished final effort from the Who. Featuring layers of synthesizers and long-winded, twisting song structures, the album featured few memorable melodies and little energy, with only the anthemic "Athena" and the terse "Eminence Front" making a lasting impression. —*Stephen Thomas Erlewine*

Who's Missing / 1985 / MCA ✦✦✦

Two's Missing / 1987 / MCA ✦✦✦

Thirty Years of Maximum R&B / 1994 / MCA ✦✦✦
One of the more overblown recent box sets, this four-CD collection does include all of their big hits and the lion's share of their key album tracks. Previously unreleased rarities include some interesting selections (the '60s outtakes "Early Morning Cold Taxi" and "Melancholia"), but these bits and pieces, which include some live versions, commercials, Keith Moon sketches, and the like, are mostly inessential. The post-Keith Moon cuts that bring us up to the present are out of the league of the body of the Who's work. As most of the Who's '60s and '70s albums are very strong, cohesive works in and of themselves, this can't be recommended as either a starting point or a necessary addition. —*Richie Unterberger*

● **My Generation: Very Best of the Who** / Aug. 27, 1996 / MCA ✦✦✦✦
The Who have issued more greatest hits collections than any other major artist, releasing a vast array of compilations while they were together and in the years following their breakup. Released in 1996, *My Generation: The Very Best of the Who* was intended to be the definitive single-disc collection, replacing all the others that preceded it. While it is a very good collection, it just misses being a definitive sampler. Essentially, *My Generation* is a replica of *Who's Better, Who's Best* that adds four tracks that were missing from the previous compilation, including the seminal post-Tommy single "The Seeker" and the original single mix of "Magic Bus." *My Generation* isn't strictly a singles collection, since it contains such album rock staples as "Baba O'Riley" and the full-length version of "Won't Get Fooled Again." It also spans the group's entire career, so it has a bit of a scattershot feel to it—"You Better You Bet" sounds a little odd next to tense early singles like "Substitute" and "I Can See For Miles." The career-spanning approach doesn't make for a cohesive collection as *Meaty, Beaty, Big and Bouncy*, but it does mean that *My Generation* is an excellent—even necessary—introduction. There's a lot more in the Who's catalog that needs to be heard, but *My Generation* does boil down the most essential items (even though the abominable "Squeeze Box" is included) to a fine single-disc set. —*Stephen Thomas Erlewine*

Andre Williams

b. 1936
Vocals / R&B

Singer, songwriter, arranger, producer, and one of the mightiest talents to emerge from Detroit's pre-Motown era, Andre Williams started recording in 1957 for the tiny Fortune label, with his group, The Five Dollars (aka The Don Juans), and as a solo artist. Employing his stop-time "wavy gravy" beat and hitting the charts with oddball spoken-word numbers like "Bacon Fat," "The Greasy Chicken," and "Jail Bait," Williams was the original rapper before there was ever a name for it. Moving to Chicago in the early '60s, he wrote "Shake a Tail Feather" for the 5 Du-Tones and "Twine Time" for Alvin Cash, produced albums for Bobby Blue Bland, and scored national hits of his own for Chess with "Cadillac Jack," "Girdle Up," and "Humpin', Bumpin' & Thumpin." He continues to record and produce other artists sporadically, still keeping abreast of the times, still "Mr. Rhythm," the original rappin' man. —*Cub Koda*

● **Jail Bait** / Fortune ✦✦✦✦
Good, but not complete, overview of Andre's Fortune period. —*Cub Koda*

Larry Williams

b. May 10, 1935, New Orleans, LA, d. Jan. 7, 1980, Los Angeles, CA
Piano, Vocals / R&B, Rock 'n' roll

A rough, rowdy rock 'n' roll singer, Larry Williams had several hits in the late '50s, several of which—"Bony Maronie," "Dizzy, Miss Lizzy," "Short Fat Fannie," "Bad Boy," "She Said Yeah"—became genuine rock 'n' roll classics and were recorded by British Invasion groups; John Lennon, in particular, was a fan of Williams, recording several of his songs over the course of his career.

As a child in New Orleans, Williams learned how to play piano. When he was a teenager, he and his family moved to Oakland, CA, where he joined a local R&B group called the Lemon Drops. In 1954, when he was 19 years old, Williams went back to New Orleans for a visit. During his trip, he met Lloyd Price, who was recording for Specialty Records. Price hired the teenager as his valet and introduced him to Robert "Bumps" Blackwell, the label's house producer. Soon, the label's owner, Art Rupe, signed Williams to a recording contract.

Just after Specialty signed Larry Williams, Specialty lost Little Richard, who had been their biggest star and guaranteed hitmaker. Little Richard decided to abandon rock 'n' roll for the ministry shortly after Williams cut his first single, a cover of Price's "Just Because," with Richard's backing band; "Just Because" peaked at No. 11 on the R&B charts in the spring of 1957. After Richard left the label, the label put all of its energy into making Williams a star, giving him an image makeover and a set of material—ranging from hard R&B, rock 'n' roll, to ballads—that was quite similar to Richard's hits.

Williams' first post-Little Richard single was the raucous "Short Fat Fannie," which shot to No. 1 on the R&B charts and No. 5 on the pop charts in the summer of 1957. It was followed in the fall by "Bony Maronie," which hit No. 4 on the R&B charts and No. 14 on the pop charts. Williams wasn't able to maintain that momentum, however. "You Bug Me, Baby" and "Dizzy Miss Lizzy," his next two singles, missed the R&B charts but became minor pop hits in late 1957 and early 1958. Despite the relative failure of these singles, Williams' records became popular import items in Britain; the Beatles would cover both sides of the "Dizzy Miss Lizzy" single (the B-side was "Slow Down") in the mid-'60s. However, Williams' commercial fortunes in America continued to decline, despite Specialty's release of a constant stream of singles and one full-length album.

In 1959, Williams was arrested for selling narcotics, which caused Specialty to drop him from the record label. During the '60s, he drifted through a number of labels, recording songs for Chess, Mercury, Island, and Decca. By the mid-'60s, he had hooked up Johnny "Guitar" Watson and the duo cut several sides for OKeh Records in the mid- and late '60s, including the Top 40 R&B hits "Mercy, Mercy, Mercy" (spring 1967) and "Nobody," which was recorded with Kaleidoscope (early 1968). Williams also became a house producer for OKeh Records in 1966, although very few of his productions became hits.

Between 1968 and and 1978, Williams was inactive, recording nothing and performing very little. In 1978, he released a funk album, *That's Larry Williams*, for Fantasy Records that sold poorly and received bad reviews. In 1980, Larry Williams was found dead in his Los Angeles home; he died of a gunshot wound to his head. The medical examiners called the death a suicide, but rumors persisted for years after his death that he was murdered because of his involvement in drugs, crime, and—allegedly—prostitution.

A compilation of Larry Williams' biggest hits and best-known songs entitled *Bad Boy* was released on Specialty records in 1989. —*Stephen Thomas Erlewine*

Unreleased Larry Williams / 1986 / Specialty ◆◆◆

★ **Bad Boy** / 1989 / Specialty ◆◆◆◆◆
Vintage (1957-1958) rock from this Little Richard soundalike, it features backing from hot New Orleans and Los Angeles sidemen. This is an excellent 23-track collection with informative notes. —*Hank Davis*

Maurice Williams & the Zodiacs

R&B, Doo-Wop
Although Maurice Williams & the Zodiacs only had one big hit, the song became one of the classic singles in the history of rock 'n' roll and R&B. The song, "Stay," was a No. 1 hit upon its release in 1960. Williams and the Zodiacs' career didn't prove to be as popular as the song itself. They only had two more minor pop hits before they disappeared from the charts, but over the course of the next three decades, "Stay" remained one of the most popular songs of the era and it was played constantly on oldies radio station. "Stay" was covered by numerous other artists and has enjoyed a few revivals in mass popularity, most notably when it was featured in the hit 1987 film, *Dirty Dancing*.

Before he formed the Zodiacs, Maurice Williams sang with a number of different doo wop and R&B vocal groups, beginning with the Royal Charms in the early '50s. In 1955, he formed the Gladiolas with Earl Gainey, Willie Jones, William Massey, and Norman Wade. The Gladiolas signed to Excello and recorded "Little Darlin'," which reached No. 11 on the R&B charts, No. 41 pop in the spring of 1957. The single's ascension on the pop charts was undercut by a cover of the song by the White Cana-

dian vocal group, the Diamonds. After a financial dispute, Williams lost the rights to the name the Gladolias in 1959.

Maurice Williams formed the Zodiacs in 1960, recruiting Wiley Bennett, Albert Hill, Henry Gaston, Little Willie Morrow, and Charley Thomas. The group released their first single, "Stay," on Herald records in the summer of 1960. The song worked its way up the charts, peaking at No. 3 on the R&B charts and No. 1 on the pop charts. After the single charted nationally, the Zodiacs constantly toured America, playing revues with artists like James Brown. The group released a follow-up single titled "I Remember" at the end of the year, but it didn't make it past No. 86 on the pop charts and didn't appear on the R&B charts at all. Neither did "Come Along," which was released in the spring of 1961 and only climbed to No. 83 on the pop charts.

Maurice Williams and the Zodiacs continued to release singles until the late '60s, but none of the records received any attention. Throughout the '70s and '80s, Williams led various incarnations of the Zodiacs on oldies tours, primarily on the Beach Music circuit on the US East Coast. —*Stephen Thomas Erlewine*

● **Best of Maurice & the Zodiacs** / 1989 / Relic ◆◆◆◆
"Little Darlin'," a minor 1957 R&B chart hit . . . the perfect summertime soundtrack—piano and guitar-driven boogie shuffles, and loads of falsetto yelps and throaty pleas of love and devotion. —*John Floyd, Rock & Roll Disc*

Vanessa Williams

b. Mar. 18, 1963, Buffalo, NY
Vocals / Dance-Pop, Urban, Adult Contemporary
When Vanessa Williams lost her Miss America crown in 1984, it seemed like her career was over. Actually, the truth was quite different. Four years later, she re-emerged as an urban R&B vocalist with *The Right Stuff*, which featured the Top Ten hit "Dreamin'." Her next album was an even bigger success, thanks to the smash hit "Saving the Best for Last"; it confirmed her status as one of urban R&B's most popular vocalists. —*Stephen Thomas Erlewine*

The Right Stuff / Feb. 1988 / Wing ◆◆◆◆
The disc is evenly divided between dance-floor fodder and AOR fluff, and it ain't half bad. Despite the fact that Williams works with six producers and eight songwriters, the disc has a consistent feel, and while Vanessa doesn't have a voice suited to belting out raunchy R&B, she's smart enough to stay within her limitations and let her personality take up the slack. —*J. Poet*

● **The Comfort Zone** / 1991 / Wing ◆◆◆◆
Former Miss America Vanessa Williams retained the momentum from her hit debut release *The Right Stuff* with this prototype urban contemporary album. She used different producers, arrangers, and songwriters on almost every track, and nicely balanced the menu between dance-oriented uptempo numbers, like the title track and "Running Back to You," with syrupy but extremely popular ballads like "Save the Best for Last" and "Just for Tonight." While far from being soulful, Williams' voice had enough earnestness and conviction to make the love songs seem sincere and not be buried in the mix on the rhythm cuts. —*Ron Wynn*

Sweetest Days / 1995 / Wing ◆◆◆

Chuck Willis

b. Jan. 31, 1928, Atlanta, GA, **d.** Apr. 10, 1958, Atlanta, GA
Vocals / R&B
There were two distinct sides to Chuck Willis. In addition to being a convincing blues shouter, the Atlanta-born Willis harbored a vulnerable blues balladeer side. In addition, he was a masterful songwriter who penned some of the most distinctive R&B numbers of the 1950s. We can't grant him principal credit for his 1957 smash adaptation of "C.C. Rider," an irresistible update of a classic folk-blues, but Willis did write such gems as "I Feel So Bad" (later covered by Elvis Presley, Little Milton, and Otis Rush), the anguished ballads "Don't Deceive Me (Please Don't Go)" and "It's Too Late" (the latter attracting covers by Buddy Holly, Charlie Rich, and Otis Redding), and his swan song, "Hang Up My Rock and Roll Shoes." Harold Willis (he adopted Chuck as a stage handle) received his early training singing at YMCA-sponsored "Teenage Canteens" in Atlanta and fronting the combos of local bandleaders Roy Mays and Red McAllister. Powerful deejay Zenas "Daddy" Sears took an interest in the young vocalist's career, hooking him up with Columbia Records in 1951. After a solitary single for the major firm, Willis was shuttled over to its recently reactivated OKeh R&B subsidiary. In 1952, he crashed the national R&B lists for OKeh with a typically plaintive ballad, "My Story," swiftly encoring on the hit parade with a gentle cover of Fats Domino's "Goin' to the River" and his own "Don't Deceive Me" the next year and "You're Still My Baby" and the surging Latin-beat "I Feel So Bad" in 1954. Willis also penned a heart-tugging chart-topper for Ruth Brown that year, "Oh What a Dream." Willis moved over to Atlantic Records in 1956 and immediately enjoyed another round of hits with "It's Too Late" and "Jua-

nita." Atlantic strove mightily to cross Willis over into pop territory, inserting an exotic steel guitar at one session and chirpy choirs on several more. The strategy eventually worked when his 1957 revival of the ancient "C.C. Rider" proved the perfect number to do the "Stroll" to; *American Bandstand* gave the track a big push, and Willis had his first R&B No. 1 hit as well as a huge pop seller (Gene "Daddy G" Barge's magnificent sax solo likely aided its ascent).

Barge returned for Willis's similar follow-up, "Betty and Dupree," which also did well for him. But the turban-wearing crooner's time was growing short—he had long suffered from ulcers prior to his 1958 death from peritonitis. Much has been made of the ironic title of his last hit, the touching "What Am I Living For," but it was no more a clue to his impending demise than its flip, the joyous "Hang Up My Rock and Roll Shoes." Both tracks became massive hits upon the singer's death, and his posthumous roll continued with "My Life" and a powerful "Keep A-Driving" later that year.

Willis's cousin, Robert "Chick" Willis, who began his career as a backup singer for Chuck, remains active nationally. —*Bill Dahl*

Let's Jump Tonight! The Best of Chuck Willis 1951-56 / 1994 / Epic/ Legacy ◆◆◆◆
Before his brief turn as a rock 'n' roll star with Atlantic, Willis cut a lot of material for Okeh in much more of an R&B/jump blues vein. This 26-cut collection includes all of his early and mid-'50s R&B hits—"My Story," "Goin' to the River," "Don't Deceive Me," "You're Still My Baby," and his most famous number from this period, "I Feel So Bad" (revived by Elvis Presley, among others). The influence of Joe Turner, Charles Brown, early Lloyd Price, and similar performers is strongly felt; Willis could shout competently, but was much better on the emotional R&B ballads. Not as strong or distinctive as his Atlantic material, this includes several cuts that were previously unreleased or previously unavailable in the US —*Richie Unterberger*

★ **Stroll On: The Chuck Willis Collection** / 1994 / Razor & Tie ◆◆◆◆◆
All 25 of the versatile Atlanta-bred singer's Atlantic Records sides, presented beautifully (every R&B reissue on CD should be packaged so well, with plenty of brilliant stereo). Willis really hit his stride at Atlantic, doing the Stroll with his easy-going "C.C. Rider" and "Betty and Dupree" (both boasting darting sax breaks from Gene Barge), baring his tender soul on a devotional "What Am I Living For," and taking R&B into fresh directions with a jumping "Kansas City Woman," the relentless "Keep A-Drivin'," and a buoyant "Hang Up My Rock and Roll Shoes." —*Bill Dahl*

Jackie Wilson

b. Jun. 9, 1934, Detroit, MI, **d.** Jan. 21, 1984, Mount Holly, NJ
Vocals / Soul, R&B
In terms of range, vocal gymnastics, and showmanship—not to mention the ability to simply belt out a song—nobody could match Jackie Wilson. Graduating from Billy Ward's Dominoes, he signed with the Brunswick label and began his career performing songs co-written by fellow Detroiter Berry Gordy, later the founder of Motown. These included "To Be Loved," "Lonely Teardrops," and "Reet Petite." Wilson trod the line between R&B and pop, often favoring the latter where he could use his astonishing range to good effect. His records were frequently characterized by a surfeit of brass and *Tonight Show* arrangements. Fans contend that Jackie Wilson was incapable of making a bad record, but his output remains a mixed bag to most ears. The best is among the most thrilling music to emerge from the late '50s and early '60s.

Wilson's career entered the doldrums as the British invaded, and it took a new producer, Carl Davis, to revitalize him. Davis produced the timeless soul classics "Whispers" (1966) and "Higher and Higher" (1967), and Wilson was still charting on a regular—if somewhat lowly—basis when he collapsed onstage in 1975. He lived in a coma for another eight-and-a-half years. —*Colin Escott*

Mr. Excitement / 1992 / Rhino ◆◆◆◆
A three-CD box from the experts of reissue at Rhino, *Mr. Excitement* takes Wilson's career from his first sides with Billy Ward and the Dominoes in 1956 through his final recordings in the early '70s. The former Detroit boxer hit either the R&B or pop chart over 50 times, making him the 26th most successful R&B artist, in chart terms at least. Every one of those recordings is contained in this set, including such classics as "Reet Petite," "Lonely Teardrops," and "(Your Love Keeps Lifting Me) Higher and Higher." Wilson had an explosive falsetto and a downright weird sense of phrasing that made him utterly unique. Some of his productions were a little overwrought but even in the most extreme cases, that voice was a gift from God. Seminal. —*Rob Bowman*

★ **The Very Best of Jackie Wilson** / 1993 / Ace ◆◆◆◆◆
The Very Best of Jackie Wilson is a terrific single-disc collection, containing all of Wilson's biggest hits, including "Reet Petite," "Lonely Teardrops," "Doggin' Around," "Higher and Higher," and "Baby Work Out," among others. —*Stephen Thomas Erlewine*

Jesse Winchester

b. May 17, 1944, Shreveport, LA
Guitar, Keyboards, Vocals / Folk, Singer-Songwriter
The country-folk singer-songwriter Jesse Winchester first gained notice for his debut album, *Jesse Winchester* (1970), produced by the Band's Robbie Robertson. It featured such songs as "The Brand New Tennessee Waltz" and "Yankee Lady," which were covered by a wide range of performers. The subtext of his appeal, however (and of songs like "Yankee Lady"), was that Winchester was an American living in Canada to avoid the draft. Born in Shreveport, LA, he had grown up in Memphis and attended Williams College, from which he graduated in 1966. While studying in Germany in 1967, he received his draft notice and moved to Montreal.

Winchester's second album, *Third Down 110 to Go*, was released in 1972 and got into the charts briefly, but he was hindered by his inability to play in the US. In 1973 Winchester became a Canadian citizen. He released more records, but it wasn't until 1977, when President Jimmy Carter instituted an amnesty for draft resisters, that Winchester was able to appear in the US. His appearances made his next album, *Nothing but a Breeze*, his biggest-seller yet. *A Touch on the Rainy Side* (1978) was a more moderate success, while *Talk Memphis* (1981) featured the Top 40 hit "Say What." This was his last album for seven years, until the independent Sugar Hill label issued *Humour Me* (1988). Winchester continues to tour. —*William Ruhlmann*

Jesse Winchester / 1970 / Rhino ◆◆◆◆
Jesse Winchester first gained notice as a protégé of the Band's Robbie Robertson, who produced and played guitar on his debut album and brought along bandmate Levon Helm to play drums and mandolin. The album had much of the rustic Southern charm and rollicking country-rock of the Band. Winchester's other immediate appeal was a certain sense of mystery. A Southern American expatriate living in Canada, he was unable to appear in the US to promote the album, which was released in a fold-out LP jacket that featured the same sepia-toned portrait (which looked like one of those austere Matthew Brady photos from the Civil War era) on each of its four sides. Winchester emphasized the dichotomy between his southern origins and his northern exile in songs like "Snow" (which Robertson co-wrote), "The Brand New Tennessee Waltz" ("I've a sadness too sad to be true"), and "Yankee Lady." *Jesse Winchester* was timely: It spoke to a disaffected American generation that sympathized with Winchester's pacifism. But it was also timeless: The songs revealed a powerful writing talent (recognized by the numerous artists who covered them), and Winchester's gentle vocals made a wonderful vehicle for delivering them. (Originally released by Ampex in 1970, *Jesse Winchester* was reissued by Bearsville Records in 1976 and again in 1988 by Rhino/Bearsville). —*William Ruhlmann*

Third Down, 110 to Go / 1972 / Bearsville ◆◆◆◆
If Jesse Winchester's debut album was an auspicious introduction to a powerful new songwriting talent, his two-and-a-half-years-in-the-making follow-up was in some ways even more impressive. Without the influence of Robbie Robertson, Winchester, who produced most of the album himself (three tracks were handled by Todd Rundgren), gave it a homemade feel, using small collections of acoustic instruments, an appropriate setting for a group of short, intimate songs that expressed a deliberately positive worldview set against an acknowledgment of desperate times. Winchester found hope in religion and domesticity, but the key to his stance was a kind of good-humored accommodation. "If the wheel is fixed," he sang, "I would still take a chance. If we're skating on thin ice, then we might as well dance." The album was littered with such examples of aphoristic folk wisdom, adding up to a portrait of a man, cut off from his very deep roots and yet determined to maintain his dignity with grace and even occasionally a goofy sense of humor. —*William Ruhlmann*

Let the Rough Side Drag / 1976 / Bearsville ◆◆◆
At his best, Jesse Winchester is an inspired songwriter with a unique worldview. But even at less than his best, he is a craftsman, capable of turning out an album's worth of well-written songs like those here that, now and then, suggest his personal viewpoint. The title track, another of Winchester's reflections on the importance of persevering under difficult circumstances, and "Damned If You Do," which suggests that you might as well follow your heart because you're in trouble either way, are up to his usual standard. But even slight songs like "Everybody Knows But Me" are clever and enjoyable, and overall, *Let the Rough Side Drag*, with its accomplished mixture of country and R&B, was Winchester's most accessible album so far, even if it was his least ambitious. —*William Ruhlmann*

Humour Me / 1988 / Sugar Hill ◆◆◆
● **The Best of Jesse Winchester** / 1989 / Rhino ◆◆◆◆
Jesse Winchester wrote and recorded more than enough great songs for Bearsville to fill a single-disc compilation, which means that some of them were bound to be left off. The trick was to balance the material

from the brilliant first two albums with a careful selection from the subsequent five albums, each of which had its virtues. This 14-track album chooses four from *Jesse Winchester*, including the essential "Yankee Lady," "Biloxi," and "The Brand New Tennessee Waltz," and three from its follow-up, *Third Down, 110 to Go*. There are three from *Learn to Love It*, one each from *Nothing but a Breeze* and *A Touch on the Rainy Side*, and two from *Talk Memphis*. Lesser material such as "Tell Me Why You Like Roosevelt" and "Rhumba Man" could have been excised in favor of more from *Third Down*, but the selection is good enough to give a reasonable representation of Winchester's seven Bearsville albums, which contain some of the most impressive songwriting of the '70s. — *William Ruhlmann*

Johnny Winter

b. Feb. 23, 1944, Leland, MS
Guitar, Vocals / Blues-Rock
Blues guitarist Winter became a major star in the late '60s and early '70s. Since that time he's confirmed his reputation in the blues by working with Muddy Waters and continuing to play in the style, despite musical fashion. Born in Leland, MS, Winter formed his first band at 14 with his brother Edgar in Beaumont, TX, and spent his youth in recording studios cutting regional singles and in bars playing the blues. His discovery on a national level came via an article in *Rolling Stone* in 1968, which led to a management contract with New York club owner Steve Paul and a record deal with Columbia. His debut album (there are numerous albums of juvenilia), *Johnny Winter*, reached the charts in 1969. Starting out with a trio, Winter later formed a band with former members of the McCoys, including second guitarist Rick Derringer. It was called Johnny Winter And. He achieved a sales peak in 1971 with the gold-selling *Live/Johnny Winter And*. He returned in 1973 with *Still Alive and Well*, his highest-charting album. His albums became more overtly blues-oriented in the late '70s and he also produced several albums for Muddy Waters. In the '80s he switched to the blues label Alligator for three albums, and has since recorded for the labels MCA and Virgin. — *William Ruhlmann*

Johnny Winter / 1969 / Columbia ✦✦✦✦
Winter's stunning debut features his fiery blues playing in both electric and acoustic settings, with backup that includes Willie Dixon. — *William Ruhlmann*

● Second Winter / 1969 / Columbia ✦✦✦✦
Winter leans more toward mainstream rock 'n' roll, though the guitar playing remains fierce. Originally a *three-sided LP, this now makes a long CD*. — *William Ruhlmann*

Johnny Winter and . . . / 1970 / Columbia ✦✦✦✦

Johnny Winter and . . . Live / 1971 / Columbia ✦✦✦
Winter and his new band turn out hard-rock versions of "Jumpin' Jack Flash," "Johnny B. Goode," and other rock 'n' roll favorites. — *William Ruhlmann*

Nothin' but the Blues / 1977 / Blue Sky ✦✦✦✦
After a long period making rock records, Winter fronts the Muddy Waters band (with Waters singing) on this Chicago blues workout. He sounds happier than ever before. — *William Ruhlmann*

Birds Can't Row Boats / 1988 / Relix ✦✦✦✦
Aside from "Ice Cube" (a 1959 instrumental), these tracks date from 1965 to 1968. Many are previously unissued or only available on rare 45s. Those accustomed to his more famous recordings are in for a jolt, as this shows Johnny in several unexpected settings: grinding Texas psychpunk, the British Invasion-cum-folk-rock garage single "Gone for Bad," blue-eyed R&B/soul, an Everly Brothers cover, a *Highway 61*-era Dylan imitation, and even a shit-kickin' C&W tune. There are also some straight, predominantly acoustic blues numbers. — *Richie Unterberger*

A Rock N' Roll Collection / 1994 / Columbia/Legacy ✦✦✦✦
A two-CD survey of Winter's recordings for Columbia between 1969 and 1979, the era of his greatest commercial success. This collects many of his most popular tracks, though it doesn't do much to argue a case for artistic diversity. Includes two otherwise unavailable songs: an alternate take of "30 Days," and a previously unreleased 1973 cover of Robert Johnson's "Come on in My Kitchen." — *Richie Unterberger*

Steve Winwood

b. May 12, 1948, Birmingham, England
Guitar, Keyboards, Vocals / Pop-Rock
singer-songwriter, keyboardist, and guitarist Steve Winwood was a well-known musician long before he finally embarked on a solo career in the second half of the '70s. Born in Birmingham, England, Winwood joined the Spencer Davis Group with his older brother Muff when he was only 15 years old. His was the soulful, Ray Charles-like voice on such hits as "Gimme Some Lovin'" and "I'm a Man," songs he also co-wrote. In 1967 he formed Traffic, which he led, with time off for the supergroup Blind Faith in 1969, until 1974. Winwood finally released his first solo album in

1977 and, in 1981 had his first million-seller with his second album, *Arc of a Diver. Talking Back to the Night* (1982) was not as much of a success, and Winwood spent four years preparing *Back in the High Life* (1986), which sold three million copies. *Roll with It* (1988) went to No. 1, but *Refugees of the Heart* (1990) was not up to his usual standard.

After the relative failure of *Refugees of the Heart*, Winwood and Jim Capaldi re-formed Traffic in 1994; although their record and tour were well-received, the reunion wasn't as successful as expected. — *William Ruhlmann*

Steve Winwood / Jun. 1977 / Island ✦✦✦

Arc of a Diver / Jan. 1981 / Island ✦✦✦✦
Utterly unencumbered by the baggage of his long years in the music business, Winwood reinvents himself as a completely contemporary artist on this outstanding album, leading off with his best solo song, "While You See a Chance." Winwood also plays all the instruments. — *William Ruhlmann*

Talking Back to the Night / Aug. 1982 / Island ✦✦✦

● Back in the High Life / Jun. 1986 / Island ✦✦✦✦
Turning to involved percussion tracks and horns, Winwood turns another musical corner on this sophisticated album, which contains echoes of everything from gospel to Caribbean music. Contains the No. 1 hit "Higher Love." — *William Ruhlmann*

Chronicles / Nov. 1987 / Island ✦✦✦✦
This isn't an adequate compilation of the years 1977-1986, but it does manage to gather some of the better songs of the period. — *William Ruhlmann*

Roll with It / Jun. 1988 / Virgin ✦✦✦

Refugees of the Heart / Nov. 1990 / Virgin ✦✦✦

The Finer Things / 1995 / Island ✦✦✦✦
Steve Winwood has led a long and varied career, recording everything from straight R&B and jazz-flavored rock to folk and pop. Over the course of four discs, *The Finer Things* chronicles the entirety of his career, beginning with the Spencer Davis Group, through Traffic and Blind Faith, right until his successful solo career. It includes all of the hits and many of his finest album tracks, yet the overall approach is rather exhausting—the rarities are rarely illuminating, they're just there for the sake of being there. Nevertheless, it is a worthwhile purchase for anyone wanting a comprehensive picture of Winwood in all of his various guises. — *Stephen Thomas Erlewine*

Wire

Punk, Alternative Pop-Rock, Post-Punk
Wire's brief, fractured songs and minimalistic sound made them the artiest of all punk bands, as well as one of the most influential. Unlike most other punk bands, their stripped-down approach was not an attempt to get back to rock's roots; it was cutting the music to its raw nerve, so nothing extraneous was left. On their 1977 debut, *Pink Flag*, Wire managed to tear through 21 songs in under 40 minutes. Although they never managed to match that album's accomplishment, they recorded two other excellent albums before breaking up in late 1979.

Wire was quiet for several years. They returned to recording in 1986 with the *Snakedrill* EP, quickly following it with 1987's full-length *The Ideal Copy*. Amazingly, Wire's capabilities were still intact; the only concession the group made was adding synthesizers to their music, which they managed to work in quite well. However, after *The Ideal Copy*, the band began to slip, as they were attempting to incorporate synths and samplers to a greater degree; their experimental tendencies began to overshadow their musical sense. Eventually, the band shortened their name to Wir; their first release in this new incarnation was 1991's *The First Letter*. — *Stephen Thomas Erlewine*

☆ Pink Flag / Dec. 1977 / Restless ✦✦✦✦✦
Wire's debut effort, *Pink Flag*, was one of the strongest releases of the late-'70s British punk scene, mixing the aggressive punch of the Sex Pistols with the humor and brevity of the Ramones. *Pink Flag* packed 21 tracks into the space of 37 minutes; twelve of the tracks were under a minute and a half. ("Field Day for the Sundays" clocked in at just 28 seconds.) Somehow none of these tracks felt short; Wire merely made their point and moved on to the next idea. — *Rick Clark*

Chairs Missing / Aug. 1978 / Restless ✦✦✦✦
In *Chair's Missing*, Wire stretched out into longer pieces and artier production. Not as impressive as *Pink Flag*, the album does contain some standout tracks with "Outdoor Miner," "French Film Blurred," "I Am the Fly," and "Question of Degree." — *Rick Clark*

154 / 1979 / Restless ✦✦✦✦
154 integrated more keyboards and slowed the pace down a bit, but Wire didn't lose any of the eccentric edge. They just kept getting stranger. If *Ummagumma*-period Pink Floyd, early King Crimson, and the Moody Blues at their musically most cosmic were filtered through the punk movement, you'd get an idea what a peculiar album *154* is. Call it psyche-

delic punk. Among the highlights are "Two People in a Room," "The 15th," "Map Ref. 41ø N 93ø W," "The Other Window," "Single K.O.," and "40 Versions." —*Rick Clark*

● **On Returning (1977-1979)** / 1989 / Restless ✦✦✦✦
This magnificent 31-song overview collects highlights from *Pink Flag*, and many of the best songs from the two follow-ups, plus some interesting rarities. —*John Floyd*

Bill Withers

b. Jul. 4, 1938, Slab Fork, WV
Vocals / Soul, Urban
It was a chance 1970 meeting with the legendary Booker T. Jones (of Stax's Booker T. & the MG's) that opened the door for Bill Withers into the world of pop success. At the time of their meeting, Withers was working in a factory that built toilet seats for jet airplanes. Jones, impressed with Withers's demos, helped secure a deal with Sussex Records. Withers' Jones-produced debut, *Just As I Am*, was a classic of folky acoustic-guitar-driven soul, complemented by Withers's earthy vocal delivery and largely autobiographical tales. His next few albums capitalized on that sound, but as the late '70s came around, Withers gravitated toward a sophisticated urban R&B sound, sometimes collaborating with groups like the Crusaders. —*Rick Clark*

● **Lean on Me: The Best of Bill Withers** / Aug. 9, 1994 / Columbia ✦✦✦✦
Eighteen tracks, from the early '70s to the mid-'80s, including his early Top Ten singles, but also minor hits like "Grandma's Hands," "Kissing My Love," and "Lovely Day." Those who admire songs like "Lean on Me" and "Ain't No Sunshine" are advised to approach this best-of with caution; from the mid-'70s onward, Withers forsook his folky singer-songwriter soul for more anonymous, slick MOR soul and urban contemporary. His early sound was far more distinctive, and his early-'70s Sussex albums are recommended alternatives to this compilation. —*Richie Unterberger*

Womack & Womack

Soul, R&B, Urban
Cecil Womack (b. 1947) and his wife, Linda (b. 1952), had a long history before the release of their first duo album in 1983. Cecil was one of the gospel-singing Womack brothers who became the Valentinos and toured with Sam Cooke in the early '60s; Linda was Cooke's daughter. Both Womacks were successful songwriters for such performers as Teddy Pendergrass, Wilson Pickett, and Aretha Franklin prior to hooking up as a performing team. The focus is on songwriting in their collaboration; they began with *Love Wars*, which featured the Top 40 R&B hit "Baby I'm Scared of You." *Radio M.U.S.I.C. Man* (1985) contains unfinished Sam Cooke songs completed by the duo. It was followed by *Conscience* in 1988 and *Family Spirit* in 1991. —*William Ruhlmann*

● **Love Wars** / 1983 / Elektra ✦✦✦✦
Womack And Womack are steeped in the early-'60s style of Cecil's Valentinos and Linda's father, Sam Cooke, but they have updated the style. Nevertheless, this is contemporary soul likely to be embraced by fans of Cooke, Otis Redding, and others of the genre. —*William Ruhlmann*

Radio M.U.S.I.C. Man / 1985 / Elektra ✦✦✦

Conscience / Jun. 13, 1988 / Island ✦✦✦

Family Spirit / 1991 / RCA ✦✦✦

Bobby Womack

b. Mar. 4, 1944, Cleveland, OH
Guitar, Vocals / Soul, R&B
Few careers in American popular music have been as consistently productive and influential as that of singer-songwriter and guitarist Bobby Womack. Sam Cooke, for whom Womack played guitar, financed his first recordings in the early '60s. With his brothers as The Valentinos, he cut two R&B classics, "It's All Over Now" (later a hit for the Stones) and "Lookin' for a Love" (a mega-hit for J. Geils). the Valentinos' combination of shouting lead vocals and blues/gospel harmonies predated late-'60s soul music.

Womack knew and championed Jimi Hendrix early on, befriending him during a 1962 soul package tour. Womack's lean, groundbreaking guitar work, so similar in flavor to that of his contemporary Curtis Mayfield, influenced Hendrix. Later, Hendrix would return the favor by popularizing the wah-wah—an effect Womack would use to chilling effect on Sly Stone's *There's a Riot Goin' On* album and its smash single, "Family Affair" (he doubled here on bass). That's also Womack's guitar on Wilson Pickett's "Funky Broadway" and on Aretha Franklin's *Lady Soul* album.

In fact, Womack himself was one of the legendary "wild" soul men, friend and partying companion of Wilson Pickett, for whom he wrote "Midnight Mover" and "I'm in Love." He even scored a movie, *Across 110th Street*, which came out at the same time as the landmark blaxploitation film *Shaft*. Womack's singing career resumed in the '70s; James Taylor covered his No. 1 R&B hit, "Woman's Got to Have It." He made a

stunning 1981 comeback with the No. 1 R&B album *The Poet* and reunited with old Memphis studio friends and producer Chips Moman on 1986's *Womagic*.

Bobby Womack's career is far from over. Look for more greatness from this soulful, innovative musician and singer. P.S.: He belongs in the Rock & Roll Hall of Fame! —*Christine Ohlman*

Greatest Hits / 1974 / Liberty ✦✦✦✦
Includes his great remake of the Valentinos hit "Lookin' for a Love," as well as his other chart hits—"That's the Way I Fell About Cha," "Harry Hippy," and "Nobody Wants You When You're Down and Out." —*Christine Ohlman*

● **Midnight Mover** / Feb. 1993 / EMI ✦✦✦✦
Spanning the length of his influential career, *Midnight Mover* features two discs of one of the major figures of contemporary soul and R&B, covering all of his hits and best moments. It is essential for any R&B collection. —*AMG*

Only Survivor: The MCA Years / Mar. 26, 1996 / MCA ✦✦✦

Stevie Wonder (Steveland Morris)

b. May 13, 1950, Saginaw, MI
Piano, Vocals / Soul, Funk, Urban, Motown, Pop-Rock
When Stevie Wonder began recording in 1963, he was only 13 years old. Even then, his talent was evident, although there was no sign of how deep it was. After all, the music was the work of a startlingly gifted child; it was all exuberant flash, with few complexities. Soon, Wonder would go far beyond the infectious energy of "Fingertips (Part 2)." In two years, he became one of Motown's finest artists, recording a series of brilliant singles for a solid nine years, the overwhelming majority of which he wrote himself. During this time, his albums were like other Motown albums—a combination of killer singles and pleasant filler, only Wonder was allowed to record the occasional number that reflected his increasing social consciousness, like his hit version of Bob Dylan's "Blowin' in the Wind." By the end of the '60s, he was not only hitting the charts with his own records, but writing material for many other Motown artists, including the Spinners' "It's a Shame" and co-writing "The Tears of a Clown" with Smokey Robinson.

With his creativity growing by leaps and bounds, Wonder soon felt limited by Motown's strict production and publishing contracts. When his record contract expired in 1971, Wonder recorded two full albums by himself and used them as a bargaining tool during contract negotiations with Motown. The record label gave him total artistic control of his albums, as well as the rights to his own songs. Soon afterward, the two albums—*Where I'm Coming From* and *Music of My Mind*—were released.

Music of My Mind, especially, helped usher in a new era of soul/R&B. Along with Sly Stone and Marvin Gaye, Wonder was responsible for making soul and R&B albums not just collections of singles, but cohesive artistic statements, where artists could extend their music beyond the confines of a three-minute hit single. With his next two albums, *Talking Book* and *Innervisions*, Wonder's music became richly complex and inventive; in addition to his musical innovations, Wonder's lyrics addressed social and racial issues as eloquently and incisively as any other pop songwriter. Wonder sustained his creative peak through 1974's *Fulfillingness' First Finale* and 1976's *Songs in the Key of Life*.

Three years later, he released the ambitious and bewildering *Journey Through the Secret Life of Plants*, which received terrible reviews upon its release. Wonder released the more straightforward *Hotter than July* in 1980; the album received substantially better reviews and became his first platinum album. However, he wasn't able to sustain that momentum for the rest of the decade. Although his records sold well and he scored the occasional hit—including the smash hit ballad "I Just Called to Say I Love You"—his albums weren't as focused as they were a decade earlier. By the '90s, he was still an immensely respected musician, but his music was no longer on the cutting edge. —*Stephen Thomas Erlewine*

The 12 Year Old Genius / May 31, 1963 / Motown ✦✦✦

Greatest Hits / Mar. 1968 / Motown ✦✦✦✦
When it was released, Stevie Wonder's first hits collection, a 12-track disc tracing his work from 1963 to 1967, served a common function of compilations: it gathered together stray, disparate pieces, from "Fingertips—Pt. 2" to "I Was Made to Love Her," and focused attention on the artist. Wonder had a spotty singles record: five Top Ten hits, but only two of them in succession, over the four and a half years, but *Greatest Hits* made him seem like a consistent hitmaker with an astounding range, from those early harmonica instrumentals to soulful wailers like "Uptight (Everything's Alright)" and even oddball ballads like "A Place in the Sun." By now this set has long since been eclipsed, notably by the *Looking Back* album, but as a demonstration of Wonder's early promise, it is notable. —*William Ruhlmann*

Signed, Sealed & Delivered / Aug. 7, 1970 / Motown ✦✦✦

Where I'm Coming From / Apr. 12, 1971 / Motown ✦✦✦✦
Released one month before Stevie Wonder's 21st birthday, *Where I'm Coming From* is really his first adult album, and although it was not a massive hit, it anticipated the musical approach of his commercial breakthrough, *Talking Book*, by a year and a half. The lovely "Never Dreamed You'd Leave in Summer," as the B-side to a cover of the Beatles' "We Can Work It Out," has become a Wonder standard, and the album's real hit, "If You Really Love Me" (No. 8 pop, No. 4 R&B), marked the first rewards of his alliance with then-wife Syreeta Wright. Elsewhere, Wonder, who produced and composed all the tracks, introduced the funky keyboard style that would take him through the next few years, as well as the social concerns that would absorb him later on. This album was a shot across the bow, fair warning that a major, nearly mature talent had arrived. — *William Ruhlmann*

Greatest Hits, Vol. 2 / Oct. 1971 / Motown ✦✦✦

Music of My Mind / Mar. 1972 / Motown ✦✦✦✦
When Wonder turned 21 he renegotiated his Motown contract; the key issue was control. Stevie Wonder had a vision that veered far away from that of the Motown hit-making machine. Influenced by the work of Isaac Hayes in 1969 and 1970 and label-mate Marvin Gaye in 1971, Wonder was no longer content with putting out albums that were a collection of two or three hit singles plus filler; he wanted to record full-length albums that had an integrity unto themselves. *Music of My Mind* was the first such effort. Wonder produced, wrote the songs, and played the majority of the instruments. At the time it was a revelation. Compared with Wonder's subsequent efforts, it pales just slightly. — *Rob Bowman*

☆ **Talking Book** / Nov. 1972 / Motown ✦✦✦✦✦
Talking Book is the album that crystallized Wonder as the self-contained singer-songwriter. "Superstition" and "You Are the Sunshine of My Life" were both No.1 singles. The rest of the album maintains an equally torrid level. — *Rob Bowman*

☆ **Innervisions** / Aug. 1973 / Motown ✦✦✦✦✦
For my money, Stevie Wonder's finest moment. Three massive hits, "Higher Ground," "Living for the City," and "Don't You Worry 'Bout a Thing," were drawn from the album. "Golden Lady" and "He's Misstra Know-It-All" could have been equally successful. From the titles alone, one can see that Wonder had developed a social conscience and, as many other singer-songwriters of the time were doing, he politicized his music. Intelligent lyrics that one can boogie to—what more could one want from popular music? — *Rob Bowman*

Fulfillingness' First Finale / Jul. 1974 / Motown ✦✦✦✦
The funky "Boogie on, Reggae Woman" and "You Haven't Done Nothin'" are the high points of this record. Much of the rest of the album is centered around the electric piano, a sound ubiquitous in Black music in the early '70s. Wonder occasionally gets a little syrupy on the nonhit material, although his phrasing is so fine that one tends to be forgiving. —*Rob Bowman*

Songs in the Key of Life / Sep. 1976 / Motown ✦✦✦✦
Wonder the auteur began to get out of hand with this sprawling double album plus four-song-EP set. Much is maudlin, cloying, and pretentious; yet great songs, such as "Sir Duke," rear their heads at various junctures throughout the set. —*Rob Bowman*

★ **Looking Back** / Dec. 1977 / Motown ✦✦✦✦✦
Between 1963 and the end of 1971, Little Stevie Wonder placed 25 songs on *Billboard's* charts. Twenty-four of those, including such radio staples as "Fingertips—Pt. 2," "Uptight (Everything's Alright)," "I Was Made to Love Her," "For Once in My Life," "My Cherie Amour," and "Signed, Sealed, Delivered, I'm Yours" appear on *Looking Back*. Wonder's recordings in the '60s stand apart from most Motown acts partially because he was paired with producers and writers who very rarely worked with the Temptations, Supremes, et al. In the beginning Wonder was often produced by Clarence Paul and/or William Stevenson; during the golden years Henry Cosby was usually manning the controls. Then in 1970 Wonder started producing himself, beginning with "Signed, Sealed, Delivered." Most of Wonder's singles were written by Wonder himself in tandem with a variety of others, or by Ron Miller. The hits alternated between stomping barnburners and mid-tempo, understated ballads. —*Rob Bowman*

Journey Through the Secret Life of Plants / Oct. 1979 / Motown ✦✦✦

Hotter Than July / Sep. 1980 / Motown ✦✦✦✦
Hotter Than July was Wonder's real follow-up to *Songs in the Key of Life*, even if it took him the then-unconscionably long four years to release it. Wonder had been perhaps the most accomplished and successful pop artist of the years 1972-1977, but his absence had cooled him off commercially, and this album demonstrated that, artistically, he was also past his peak. Individual moments suggested his earlier triumphs, and Wonder remained a remarkably facile singer/player/composer, but he had lost his ability to amaze his listeners. The album's biggest single was "Master Blaster (Jammin')" (No. 5 pop, No. 1 R&B), an adequate but unremarkable reggae number, but the standout track was "Happy Birthday," the

theme song for the ultimately successful campaign to make Dr. Martin Luther King, Jr.'s, birthday a national holiday. —*William Ruhlmann*

★ **Original Musiquarium I** / May 1982 / Motown ✦✦✦✦✦
Most of Wonder's chart hits from 1972 through 1982 (although why "You Haven't Done Nothin'" is not here I will never know) are included on *Stevie Wonder's Original Musiquarium I*, plus three newly written and recorded tunes. Simply put, some of the finest Black music made in the '70s. Essential. —*Rob Bowman*

In Square Circle / 1985 / Motown ✦✦✦

Characters / Nov. 1987 / Motown ✦✦✦

Jungle Fever / May 28, 1991 / Motown ✦✦✦

Conversation Peace / 1995 / Motown ✦✦✦

Natural Wonder / 1995 / Motown ✦✦✦

Brenton Wood

b. Jun. 26, 1941, Shreveport, LA
Vocals / Soul
Wood's quirky rhythmic sense and happy-go-lucky vocal delivery clicked with R&B and pop audiences in 1967, when "The Oogum Boogum Song" and "Gimme Little Sign" both proved potent hits. Born in Shreveport, LA, Wood moved west to San Pedro and found inspiration in the mellifluous styles of Sam Cooke and Jesse Belvin. He formed a vocal group called the Quotations while attending college, before signing with Double Shot Records and hooking up with producers Joe Hooven and Hal Winn. After making it three hits in a row with "Baby You Got It," Wood only notched a couple more minor chart items for the label in 1968. —*Bill Dahl*

● **Brenton Wood's 18 Best** / 1991 / Original Sound ✦✦✦✦
Probably the best collection of Brenton Wood, one of the few voices that rival Sam Cooke's in both quality and content. This collection of 18 songs includes all the hits and shows what a great singer this underappreciated artist is. Songs like "Gimme Little Sign," "Oogum Boogum," and "Baby You Got it" most of us know. But lesser known songs like "I'm the One Who Knows," "Catch You on the Rebound," and "Two Time Loser" make for some great listening. —*Michael Erlewine*

Roy Wood

b. Nov. 8, 1946, Birmingham, England
Bass, Guitar, Horn, Keyboards, Vocals, Wind, Multi-Instruments / Rock 'n' roll, Art-Rock/Progressive-Rock, Pop-Rock
Roy Wood, born Ulysses Adrian Wood in Birmingham, England, has long been regarded as one of the most important, if eccentric, rock musicians to have come out of that city, primarily for his role as the leader/cofounder of both the Move and the Electric Light Orchestra.

Wood took up the guitar in his early teens and the first "successful" band of which he was a member was Gerry Levene and the Avengers, which actually got to record a single. They broke up in mid-1964, and Wood joined Mike Sheridan and the Nightriders. During this period, Wood attended the Moseley College of Art, from which he was expelled in 1964. That same year, he organized the Move, with Bev Bevan (drums), Carl Wayne (lead vocals), Ace Kefford (bass), and Trevor Burton (guitar). The band was fortunate enough to land a residency at London's Marquee Club, where they began to build an enthusiastic following. Wood contributed most of the songs and eventually many of the vocals to the Move. Their single "Night of Fear" rose to No. 2 on the UK charts in early 1967. The group evolved over the ensuing three years, eventually becoming a quartet. Later, the group added guitarist Jeff Lynne and passed through psychedelic, progressive, and heavy metal phases. Albums such as *Shazam*, *Message from the Country*, and *Looking On*, were popular in England but virtually unknown in America. Their sound embraced everything from old time rock 'n' roll, including Duane Eddy and even some doo wop influences, but also displayed Beatles-style harmonies and lyrical complexity.

By 1971, Wood had developed ideas and ambitions that were too wide to be embraced by any one band, and proposed the formation of an offshoot of the Move called the Electric Light Orchestra. The group's eponymous debut was released on the Harvest label in England to strong critical approval and decent sales—indeed, the new band seemed to attract more serious attention than the Move had been getting. Originally ELO and the Move were to have existed side-by-side, but ELO supplanted the Move, and the latter ceased to exist. Wood exited soon after, leaving ELO in the hands of Lynne and Bevan, while Wood went off to form Wizzard.

Wizzard's first single, "Ballpark Incident," combined the Move's hard rock with a texture reminiscent of Phil Spector's "wall of sound" productions, and rose to No. 6 on the British charts. In April of 1973, Wizzard reached No. 1 with "See My Baby Jive." Unfortunately, the band's first album, *Wizzard's Brew*, didn't fare nearly as well, being a highly experimental body of work. The group's fortunes, even as a singles band, faltered after this, partly because of Wood's decision to continue recording and releasing records under his own name in addition to his work with Wizzard. His Phil Spector-ish "I Wish It Could Be Christmas Everyday" reached No. 4 in England in 1973, and "Forever" made it to No. 8 the same year. The Wizzard albums *See My Baby Jive* and *Eddie & the Falcons* were both critical and commercial failures, and the unsuccessful release of the latter led to the demise of the group. Meanwhile, Wood's own solo albums, *Boulders* (1970) and *Mustard* (1975), were too idiosyncratic to achieve major followings.

The Roy Wood Story (Harvest), released in 1976, summed up his career with EMI Records, and performed well as a best-of. His subsequent records, *On the Road* (1979) and *Starting Up* (1987), failed to achieve anything like the success of his early-'70s work, and since then Wood has become one of the more elusive active musicians of his generation, although he has continued to record into the 1990s. —*Bruce Eder*

Boulders / 1973 / United Artists ◆◆◆◆
Wood's solo albums are a mixed lot, mostly thanks to the sheer diversity of sound that he's comfortable dealing with. *Boulders* is his best solo work to date, a strangely offbeat, hard-rocking yet progressive, lush yet minimalist-sounding work that encompasses all of Wood's influences, from Duane Eddy to the Beatles to classical music's late-19th-century Romanticism. —*Bruce Eder*

● **The Roy Wood Years 1971-73: You Can Dance The Rock 'N Roll** / EMI/Harvest ◆◆◆◆
The finest compilation of Wood's work to date, drawing on his closing years with The Move, his sole album with ELO, the biggest hits of Wizzard, and Wood's official solo albums and singles. —*Bruce Eder*

Link Wray

b. 1930
Guitar / Rock 'n' roll, Instrumental Rock
Up until Link Wray's groundbreaking instrumental "Rumble" (1958), White guitarists in the main either took the jazz route or tried their best to emulate some form of the Chet Atkins/Merle Travis style. Link changed all that. With the pioneering use of distortion, tremolo, and feedback, plus an unabashed attack that owed much to soul-blues, Wray created a style that was years ahead of its time. Creating one great instrumental after another on primarily chordal themes (making him the godfather of the now-common power chord), his music contained the groundbreaking roots of heavy metal, ten years before it came into being. A seminal influence on Pete Townshend, Jeff Beck, and others, Wray continues to record sporadically, sounding wilder and crazier than ever, giving the lie to the cliché of being "too old to rock 'n' roll." —*Cub Koda*

Link Wray & the Wraymen / 1960 / Edsel ◆◆◆
Walkin' with Link / Apr. 1992 / Epic ◆◆◆◆
An excellent 20-track compendium of Wray's tenure with Columbia-Epic back in the late '50s and early '60s. Nasty, searing guitar instrumentals like the title cut, "Ramble," "Rawhide," "Comanche," and "Radar" make this an indispensable part of any Link collection. —*Cub Koda*

★ **Rumble! The Best of Link Wray** / May 18, 1993 / Rhino ◆◆◆◆◆
Finally, a multi-label Link Wray collection spanning his lengthy career is available. Starting, appropriately enough, with "Rumble," *Rumble! The Best of Link Wray* illustrates through its 20 tracks (15 on cassette) that Wray was indeed one of the pioneering guitarists of rock 'n' roll, expanding the sonic possibilites of the instrument with a variety of effects. All of the tracks feature some truly warped, genius-caliber fretboard work from Wray, and a few also feature his equally demented vocals. *Rumble! The Best of Link Wray* is the definitive Wray collection. —*Stephen Thomas Erlewine*

Mr. Guitar / 1995 / Norton ◆◆◆◆
While Link cut great records in the late '50s and early '60s, he reached his peak during his stay with the Swan label in the early and mid-'60s. This double-CD, 63-song set documents this period with as much thoroughness as anyone is likely to attempt, including great singles like "Jack the Ripper," "Mr. Guitar," "Ace of Spades," and "The Fat Back," where Link let loose with his dirtiest and most groundbreaking fuzz tones. Including quite a few rarities and tracks that were never previously released in the US, as well as a good number of vocal performances (which were never Wray's forte), this is perhaps too exhaustive for the average fan. A single-disc distillation of his best Swan sides would be absolutely killer, but this is still one of the greatest collections of instrumental rock out there, despite its unevenness. —*Richie Unterberger*

Guitar Preacher: The Polydor Years / 1995 / Polydor ◆◆◆
Missing Links, Vols. 1-3 / Ace ◆◆◆◆
A brilliant three-volume set of rare recordings. —*Cub Koda*

Wreckless Eric

Rock 'n' roll, New Wave, Pub-Rock
Wreckless Eric's music wasn't much more than simple, basic rock 'n' roll

played with an energetic abandon, but at his best, he made pop singles that were immediately gripping and surprisingly timeless. During the late '70s, he recorded several minor punk/new-wave classics on Stiff Records, including "Whole Wide World" and "Semaphore Signals," which sound fresh and exciting a decade and a half after they were recorded. Those two songs, benefited from the brilliant pop sense of Nick Lowe, who produced the single and provided instrumental support for Eric's snarling vocals. After Lowe left Stiff, Wreckless Eric was left without a strong producer and bandleader, making his music much more inconsistent, yet still highly enjoyable. During the '80s, his sound was polished up slightly, which removed much of the crackling energy of his early records. Now, he lives in France and continues to tour and record, playing for a small cult of fans in Europe. —*Stephen Thomas Erlewine*

Wreckless Eric / 1978 / Stiff ◆◆◆
A wonderful collection of sloppy, snarling rock 'n' roll that nearly makes good on the promise of "Whole Wide World." —*Stephen Thomas Erlewine*

Wonderful World of Wreckless Eric / Nov. 1978 / Stiff ◆◆◆
Wreckless Eric's second album is a tighter, more pop-oriented collection that still has a vital, ragged edge. —*Stephen Thomas Erlewine*

● **The Whole Wide World** / 1979 / Stiff ◆◆◆◆
Taking the best moments from Wreckless Eric's first two exciting but spotty albums, *Whole Wide World* contains everything you need to know about this forgotten but charming punk/new-wave rocker. —*Stephen Thomas Erlewine*

Big Smash / 1980 / Stiff ◆◆◆◆
Le Beat Group Electrique / 1989 / New Rose ◆◆◆◆
This overlooked comeback effort was an unheralded triumph for Eric, on which he fronted a guitar-bass-drums trio (he also plays his usual cheesy organ) on a stripped-down set of strong songs with a live production feel. With his strangled, yearning vocals, basic melodic hooks, and songs about messed-up relationships, Wreckless recalls some of Lou Reed and Syd Barrett's better solo work, as he makes his confusion a cause for infectious celebration instead of gloomy moping. —*Richie Unterberger*

Betty Wright

b. Dec. 21, 1953, Miami, FL
Vocals / Soul
A consistently strong presence on the Miami music scene throughout the '70s and '80s, Betty Wright was just 15 when she cut the Top 40 "Girls Can't Do What the Guys Do." A child gospel star who switched to R&B at age 13, she put the Miami scene on the map in 1971 with the No. 6 hit "Clean Up Woman," notable for its prominent guitar riff and Wright's swaggering lead vocal. She won a Grammy in 1974 for "Where Is the Love?" (not to be confused with the Roberta Flack/Donny Hathaway tune of the same name). She collaborated with Stevie Wonder in 1981 on the Epic hit "What Are You Gonna Do with It?" —*Christine Ohlman*

● **The Best of Betty Wright** / 1992 / Rhino ◆◆◆◆
An excellent collection, covering the years between 1968 and 1978; it's 20 tracks of Betty Wright at her best. —*Stephen Thomas Erlewine*

Charles Wright

Guitar, Vocals / Soul, Funk
Charles Wright headed one of the late '60s and early '70s great funk groups, the Watts 103rd Street Band. Wright, who was born in Clarksdale, MS, was a singer, pianist, guitarist, and leader of the eight-member band, recruited from Watts in Los Angeles. They were originally known as the Soul Runners. Bill Cosby helped get the band off the ground by giving them appearances at his gigs. They began recording for Keyman in 1967, then moved to Warner Bros. in 1969. While "Do Your Thing" and "Till You Get Enough" were Top 20 R&B hits, their finest selection was "Express Yourself," a song that expressed the urge for freedom as adroitly as the Isley Brothers' "It's Your Thing" had in the '60s. It has also been among the most sampled funk tracks for hip-hop and rap groups. "Your Love (Means Everything to Me)" was their final R&B hit in 1971, peaking at No. 9 R&B and No. 12 pop. The group's best ballad, "Love Land," did better pop-wise than among R&B fans, many of whom saw it as a bit soft. They continued recording for Dunhill in 1973 before disbanding. Drummer James Gadson and guitarist Al McKay, who later joined Earth, Wind and Fire, were among the instrumental corps of the Watts 103rd Street Rhythm Band. —*Ron Wynn*

● **Express Yourself: The Best Of** / 1993 / Warner Bros. ◆◆◆◆
A definitive, 16-track collection of Charles Wright's best material. —*Stephen Thomas Erlewine*

O.V. Wright

b. Oct. 9, 1939, Leno, TX, **d.** Nov. 16, 1980
Vocals / Soul
A truly incendiary deep-soul performer. O.V. Wright's melismatic vocals

and Willie Mitchell's vaunted Hi Rhythm Section combined to make classic Memphis soul during the early '70s. Overton Vertis Wright learned his trade on the gospel circuit with the Sunset Travelers before going secular in 1964 with the passionate ballad "That's How Strong My Love Is" for Goldwax in Memphis. Otis Redding liked the song so much that he covered it, killing any chance of Wright's version hitting. Since Wright was already under contract to Houston-based Peacock as a gospel act, owner Don Robey demanded his return, and from then on, Wright appeared on Robey's Backbeat subsidiary. Wright's sanctified sound oozes sweet soul on the spine-chilling "You're Gonna Make Me Cry," a 1965 smash, but it took Memphis producer Willie Mitchell to wring the best consistently from Wright. Utilizing Mitchell's surging house rhythm section, Wright's early-'70s Backbeat singles "Ace of Spades," "A Nickel and a Nail," and "I Can't Take It" rank among the very best Southern soul of their era. No disco bandwagon for O. V. Wright—he kept right on pouring out his emotions through the '70s, convincing his faithful that "I'd Rather Be (Blind, Crippled & Crazy)," that he was "Into Something (Can't Shake Loose)." Unfortunately, he apparently was—drugs have often been cited as causing Wright's downfall; the soul great died at only 41 years of age in 1980. —Bill Dahl

● The Soul of O.V. Wright / 1992 / MCA ✦✦✦✦
O.V. Wright epitomized gospel-based soul singing. He screamed, roared, belted, hollered, and wailed, proclaiming his need for love. His songs were simple; they were often anguished remembrances of lost loves or pleas that this time things might be different. Occasionally, he did an uptempo dance or novelty number, but Wright was at his best on slow burners. This collection of 1960s and '70s material for Don Robey's Back Beat label includes evocative ballads, lightweight but enjoyable numbers, and songs that returned him to his gospel days. While several foreign anthologies spotlighting Wright have been issued, this 18-track CD stands as the most complete domestic reissue package currently available. —Ron Wynn

X

Punk, Alternative Pop-Rock
X was a Los Angeles-based punk-rock band of the '80s. It was an outstanding critical success, especially in its first years of record making, but it never broke through to the kind of record sales necessary to sustain a band on a national level. X was formed in the winter of 1977-1978 by singer and bassist John Doe (b. Feb. 24, 1954), guitarist Billy Zoom (b. Feb. 20, late 1940s), singer Exene Cervenka (b. Feb. 1, 1956), and D.J. Bonebrake (b. Dec 8., 1955).

Over the next couple of years, they rose to the top of a punk rock scene that had begun to emerge just as the ones in New York and London were fading away. The group signed to the local Slash label and released their debut album, *Los Angeles* (produced by Ray Manzarek of the Doors), in 1980. The album, with its driving rock, led by Zoom's Chuck Berry-influenced guitar, and the co-lead vocals of Cervenka and Doe on a series of poetic, socially conscious lyrics, was a critical success and sold well for an album on a small label. *Wild Gift* (1981) did even better, even reaching the national charts. Inevitably, X then signed to a major label, Elektra, and went from being a big fish in a small pond to the opposite. Their third album, *Under the Big Black Sun* (1982), was well received, but *More Fun in the New World* (1983) and *Ain't Love Grand* (1985) failed to expand their audience or to excite critics the way earlier records had done. Billy Zoom left X in late 1985 and was replaced by former Blasters guitarist Dave Alvin, who had played with Cervenka and Doe in a country-rock spin-off band, the Knitters. Tony Gilkyson, formerly of Lone Justice, was added as a second guitarist in March 1986. This quintet recorded *See How We Are* (1987) (though Alvin had quit for a solo career before it was released); it was considered a critical comeback but its sales were unimpressive. X released a double live album in 1988, then announced a hiatus. Both Cervenka and Doe made solo albums during the next five years.

X reunited in 1993, releasing the *Hey Zeus!* album and touring the country; although the album received respectable reviews, it didn't sell very many copies. —William Ruhlmann

Los Angeles / 1980 / Slash ✦✦✦✦
Although classified as punk because of their simple hard-rock sound and caustic lyrics ("The World's a Mess; It's in My Kiss"), X always had more of a rockabilly edge, courtesy of former Gene Vincent guitarist Billy Zoom, and were always funnier than the punk label implies, which may be why they were a cut above their competition. —William Ruhlmann

Wild Gift / May 1981 / Slash ✦✦✦✦
As with many groups, X had more good songs in their repertoire than could fit on their debut, and their second album presents the rest. Appropriately, the two albums have been packaged together on a single CD. —William Ruhlmann

Under the Big Black Sun / Jul. 1982 / Elektra ✦✦✦✦
Unlike many groups, X responded to the pressure to write a new body of material after their initial burst of songs by coming up with the goods,

especially "The Hungry Wolf" and "Riding with Mary." —William Ruhlmann

More Fun in the New World / 1983 / Elektra ✦✦✦✦
More Fun in the New World is essentially a continuation of the sound X began to fashion on *Under the Big Black Sun*. While the musical direction of the album isn't as focused as its predecessor, the songwriting is just as accomplished, featuring highlights like "The New World," "Breathless," and "I Must Not Think Bad Thoughts." —Stephen Thomas Erlewine

Ain't Love Grand! / 1985 / Elektra ✦✦

See How We Are / 1987 / Elektra ✦✦✦✦
X had moved toward becoming more of a mainstream hard-rock act by the time of their last studio album and, given how good the song "4th of July" is, it's a shame its writer, Dave Alvin, didn't stay with the band long enough to contribute more. —William Ruhlmann

Live at the Whiskey a Go-Go / 1988 / Elektra ✦✦✦

★ Los Angeles/Wild Gift / Sep. 20, 1988 / Slash ✦✦✦✦✦
X's two first two albums, *Los Angeles* and *Wild Gift*, which are generally considered their two best records, are combined on this single compact disc. —Stephen Thomas Erlewine

Hey Zeus! / Jun. 8, 1993 / Big Life ✦✦

Unclogged / 1995 / ✦✦✦

X-Ray Spex

Punk
One of the great English punk bands of the late '70s, there is only one thing wrong with the careers of X-Ray Spex and lead singer Poly Styrene—they didn't record enough music. Formed in 1976 by school friends Marion Elliot (Styrene) and Susan Whitby (saxophonist Lora Logic), X-Ray Spex exploded onto the punk scene with one of the era's great singles, the feminist punk rallying cry "Oh Bondage, Up Yours." With Logic's sax stating the melody semi-tunefully and Jak Airport's guitar laying down a wash of distorted chords, Poly's vocal, especially on the chorus, is a marvel. Along with the early Sex Pistols and Clash singles, this was one of punk rock's great moments.

So, too, was X-Ray Spex's debut LP *Germ Free Adolescents*, which was great in spite of "Oh Bondage" not being on it (a situation that would be rectified with the 1993 CD reissue). Lora Logic was gone (to form Essential Logic), but her replacement, Rudi Thompson, played in as rudimentary a fashion, but stayed in tune a little more. The songs were guitar-driven punk-pop that combined outrage and aggression with a sense of alienation and disenfranchisement about rampant commerciality and an increasingly sterile and artificial world. Poly's songs were more likely to be about drowning in a sea of corporate-designed consumer fantasies than straight-out attacks against the government. This didn't mean the songs were any less political; they simply attacked the zeitgeist from a different vantage point.

Tragically, there was no second X-Ray Spex record. But there was Poly Styrene's only full-length solo record, *Translucence*. Abandoning completely the loud guitars of X-Ray Spex, *Translucence* is quiet and jazzy in a way that anticipates the work of Ben Watt and Tracey Thorn in *Everything but the Girl*. It's a bit of a shock coming after *Germ Free Adolescents*, but it's a beautiful album, and her singing, though not as exciting and unhinged, is frequently stunning. Consistent with her career up to this point, Poly Styrene dropped out of music entirely shortly after the release of *Translucence* and joined a London-based Hare Krishna sect. She emerged from "retirement" in 1986 with a wonderful EP titled *Gods and Goddesses*. Although rumored to be preparing another LP, she's been pretty quiet for the last decade. —John Dougan

● Germ Free Adolescents / Nov. 1978 / Blue Plate ✦✦✦✦
The CD adds "Oh Bondage, Up Yours," making this one of the five great punk records made. The excitement here is contagious, the songs smart and captivating, the playing energetic if occasionally sloppy. In other words, brilliant. Buy it today. —John Dougan

XTC

Alternative Pop-Rock, New Wave, Pop-Rock
XTC was one of the smartest—and catchiest—British pop bands to emerge from the punk and new-wave explosion of the late '70s. From the tense, jerky riffs of their early singles to the lushly arranged, meticulous pop of their later albums, XTC's music has always been driven by the hook-laden songwriting of guitarist Andy Partridge and bassist Colin Moulding. While popular success has eluded them in both Britain and America, the group has developed a devoted cult following in both countries that remains loyal nearly 20 years after their first records.

Partridge, Moulding, and drummer Terry Chambers formed the first version of the band around 1976, calling themselves Star Park. As punk rock took off in 1977, the group changed their name to Helium Kidz and added former King Crimson keyboardist Barry Andrews. After being turned down by CBS Records, the band changed their name to XTC and secured a record contract with Virgin; they released their first EP, *3-D*, in October of 1977. *White Music*, the band's first full-length album, was recorded in a week and released by the end of the year. Critics praised the angular yet melodic pop, and the album reached No. 38 in the UK charts. However, none of the singles released from the album charted (including "This Is Pop"), nor did "Are You Receiving Me?," the teaser single for their second album, *Go 2* (1978).

After returning from a brief US tour, Andrews quit the band; he would eventually form The League of Gentlemen with Robert Fripp, as well as pursue a solo career. Guitarist David Gregory was added to the lineup after Andrews' departure and the group recorded their first charting single, "Life Begins at the Hop." XTC released their third album, the calmer, more pop-oriented *Drums and Wires*, that summer; the record climbed to No. 37 on the charts, thanks to the hit single "Making Plans for Nigel."

XTC continued to smooth out their edges on 1980's *Black Sea*, bringing in elements of mid-'60s Beatles and Kinks to their guitar-driven pop; thanks to the singles "Generals and Majors" and "Towers of London," the album was the group's most successful American album, peaking at No. 41 while reaching No. 16 on the British charts. Released the following year, *English Settlement* featured more complex arrangements, as well as more intellectual lyrics, particularly from Andy Partridge. Nevertheless, the album was XTC's biggest success in the UK, reaching No. 5 on the album charts and launching the Top Ten single, "Senses Working Overtime." While on tour in March of 1982, Partridge collapsed while on stage, suffering from exhaustion. Less than a month later, he collapsed again with a stomach ulcer. The band canceled the tour after his second collapse, prompting Chambers to leave the group. In November, Partridge announced that XTC would never play live again, concentrating on recording instead; he also blamed his collapses on stage fright. As the band completed their new album, a compilation called *Waxworks—Some Singles (1977-1982)* was released at the end of the year.

Mummer, the first album the studio-bound XTC recorded, appeared in the summer of 1983. XTC refused to tour for the record, which caused some tension between the band and Virgin, and was presumably the reason why "Love on a Farmboy's Wages" didn't make it past No. 50 on the charts. Recording under the name the Three Wise Men, the group released the holiday single "Thanks for Christmas" at the end of the year.

Released in the fall of 1984, *The Big Express* essentially followed the same pattern as *Mummer*, yet it charted higher in the UK XTC released a psychedelic parody album, *25 O'Clock*, under the name the Dukes of Stratosphear in 1985. After a difficult recording session with producer Todd Rundgren, the pastoral *Skylarking* appeared in the fall of 1986. Upon its release the album was hailed as a masterwork by critics, even though the band were claiming they were dissatisfied with the production. *Skylarking* was a bigger hit in the US than it was in the UK, spending over six months on the charts and peaking at No. 70.

XTC recorded another Dukes of Stratosphear album, *Psonic Psunspot*, in 1987; the two Stratosphear albums were collected on one disc the following year. *Oranges and Lemons* (1989) reworked the psychedelia of the Stratosphear side-project, leaving out much of the loopy humor and replacing it with a Ray Davies-inspired nostalgia. The album was a minor hit in both Britain and America, reaching No. 28 and No. 44, respectively; "Mayor of Simpleton" became XTC's only charting US single, reaching No. 72. Three years later, the group released *Nonsuch*, an album that recalled both *Pet Sounds* and *Revolver*. Like every XTC record, its critical acclaim was greater than its sales—the album dropped out of the British charts after two weeks. In America, *Nonsuch* was more successful, reaching No. 97 and staying on the charts for 11 weeks.

XTC's lack of commercial success isn't because their music isn't accessible—their bright, occasionally melancholic, melodies flow with more grace than most—it has more to do with the group constantly being out of step with the times. However, the band has left behind a remarkably rich and varied series of albums that make a convincing argument that XTC is the great lost pop band. *—Stephen Thomas Erlewine*

White Music / Jan. 1978 / Geffen ✦✦✦
XTC's first full album shows the band going full throttle in true punk spirit. More dissonant than their latter period, the young band shines with directionless energy and a good sense of humor. Highlights include the catchy singles "This Is Pop" and "Radios in Motion" as well as a jumpy version of "All Along the Watchtower." Their first release, *3D EP*, has been appended to the CD version. *—Chris Woodstra*

Go 2 / Feb. 1978 / Geffen ✦✦
The band's second album, *Go 2*, continues in the same high energy vein as *White Music* with slightly less memorable results. *—Chris Woodstra*

Drums & Wires / 1979 / Geffen ✦✦✦✦
By the release of the Steve Lillywhite-produced *Drums and Wires*, XTC had developed a unique sound that integrated (and plundered) late-'70s new wave, '60s-style pop, and psychedelia. The album produced XTC's first big British hit, "Making Plans for Nigel" (No 17 UK). *—Rick Clark*

Black Sea / 1980 / Geffen ✦✦✦✦
On *Black Sea*, again produced by Steve Lillywhite, XTC turned influences (like the Beatles and Beach Boys) inside out with agitated rhythms and mildly dissonant instrumental voicings. *Black Sea* generated four moderate British hit singles. One of them, "Towers of London," features a marvelously twisted Badfinger-style guitar hook set against a wonderfully gallumping bass line. "Respectable Street" is another standout on this, one of their best albums. *—Rick Clark*

● **Waxworks: Some Singles 1977-1982** / 1982 / Geffen ✦✦✦✦
This is a smartly assembled collection of the band's better early tracks. *—Rick Clark*

Beeswax: Some B-Sides 1977-1982 / 1982 / Virgin ✦✦✦

English Settlement / Mar. 1982 / Geffen ✦✦✦✦
English Settlement, a double-album set, heightened XTC's stateside visibility with the track "Senses Working Overtime." Unfortunately, the album lacked the consistency of *Black Sea*, primarily because of the flat-sounding production, which seemed to steal the impact of the music. *—Rick Clark*

Mummer / 1983 / Geffen ✦✦✦
With a couple of exceptions, *Mummer* is a relaxed lat-sounding affair. Andy Partridge manages to get a little venom out with the acidic "Funk Pop 'a Roll." Other highlights are Colin Moulding's "Love on a Farmboy's Wages" (No. 50 UK), "Wonderland," and "Great Fire." *—Rick Clark*

The Big Express / 1984 / Geffen ✦✦✦
Following up the relatively somnolent *Mummer*, *The Big Express* was a return to the playful upbeat pop-rock of some of XTC's previous works. "The Everyday Story of a Small Town" is a highlight, as well as "All You Pretty Girls." *—Rick Clark*

Compact XTC: The Singles 1978-85 / 1985 / Virgin ✦✦✦✦
Taking the *Waxworks* collection one step further, this 18-track disc collects all of the pre-*Skylarking* singles. A nice place for beginners to start. *—Chris Woodstra*

★ **Skylarking** / 1986 / Geffen ✦✦✦✦✦
With *Skylarking*, XTC addressed coming-of-age issues like marriage ("Big Day"), supporting a family ("Earn Enough for Us"), and the existence of a loving God ("Dear God"), while clothing them with performances that suggested XTC hadn't lost the capacity for childlike wonder. Todd Rundgren's production of *Skylarking* is one of his best, bathing the album in a pleasantly trippy soundstage. Other highlights include "The Meeting Place" and "Grass." *—Rick Clark*

Oranges & Lemons / 1989 / Geffen ✦✦✦✦
Compared to their best work, *Oranges & Lemons* is a little uneven—a case of a double album that would have made a great single release if XTC had pared it down. *Oranges & Lemons* did produce two big alternative pop-rock hits, "The Mayor of Simpleton" and "King for a Day." Other highlights include the optimistic "The Loving" and "Pink Thing." *—Rick Clark*

Explode Together (The Dub Experiments '78-'80) / 1990 / Virgin ✦✦
Between 1978 and 1980, Andy Partridge experimented with the power of the studio—the results were the puzzling releases of *Go+* (an EP of dub remixes of the *Go 2* album) and *Take Away/Lure of the Salvage* (an electronic collage based on the *Drums and Wires* album and credited under the name Mr. Partridge). *Explode Together* combines the two unusual projects. This is purely experimental music for the curious completists only. *—Chris Woodstra*

Rag 'N' Bone Buffet / 1990 / Geffen ✦✦✦
This is a collection of B-sides, live performances, and alternative versions culled from throughout their career. Among the oddities contained here is a cleaned-up-for-radio version of "Respectable Street," from *Black Sea*. Among the live recordings are "Another Satellite," taken from a BBC broadcast, and a great version of "Scissor Man," originally on *Drums and Wires*. Also included are various solo recordings by bandmates Andy Partridge and Colin Moulding. All in all, *Rag 'N' Bone Buffet* is a desirable item for any XTC fan looking to round out their collection of this band's work. *—Rick Clark*

Nonsuch / Oct. 1992 / Geffen ✦✦✦✦
Nonsuch, produced by Gus Dudgeon (Elton John, Bowie), trims the excesses found on *Oranges and Lemons* and recalls the pastoral refinement of *Skylarking* and the rocky edge found on *The Big Express*. Andy Partridge's "The Ballad of Peter Pumpkinhead," "The Disappointed," and "Crocodile" are highlights, as are Colin Moulding's "Books Are Burning" and "Bungalow." It's one of their better albums. *—Rick Clark*

Drums And Wireless: BBC Live / 1994 / Virgin ✦✦✦

The Yardbirds
....
Group / Rock 'n' roll, Blues-Rock, British Invasion, Psychedelic, British Blues

The Yardbirds are mostly known to the casual rock fan as the starting point for three of the greatest British rock guitarists—Eric Clapton, Jeff Beck, and Jimmy Page. Undoubtedly these three figures did much to shape the group's sound, but throughout their career, the Yardbirds were very much a unit, albeit a rather unstable one. And they were truly one of the great rock bands—one whose contributions went far beyond the scope of their half dozen or so mid-'60s hits ("For Your Love," "Heart Full of Soul," "Shapes of Things," "I'm a Man," "Over Under Sideways Down," "Happenings Ten Years Time Ago"). Not content to limit themselves to the R&B and blues covers they concentrated upon initially, they quickly branched out into moody, increasingly experimental pop-rock. The innnovations of Clapton, Beck, and Page redefined the role of the guitar in rock music, breaking immense ground in the use of feedback, distortion, and amplification with finesse and breathtaking virtuosity. With the arguable exception of the Byrds, they did more than any other outfit to pioneer psychedelia, with an eclectic, risk-taking approach that laid the groundwork for much of the hard rock and progressive-rock from the late '60s to the present.

No one could have predicted the band's metamorphosis from their humble beginnings in the early '60s in the London suburbs as the Metropolis Blues Quartet. By 1963, they were calling themselves the Yardbirds, with a lineup featuring Keith Relf (vocals), Paul Samwell-Smith (bass), Chris Dreja (rhythm guitar), Jim McCarty (drums), and Anthony "Top" Topham (lead guitar). The 16-year-old Topham was only to last for a very short time, pressured to leave by his family. His replacement was an art-college classmate of Relf's, Eric Clapton, nicknamed "Slowhand."

The Yardbirds quickly made a name for themselves in London's rapidly exploding R&B circuit, taking over the Rolling Stones' residency at the famed Crawdaddy club. The band took a similar guitar-based, frenetic approach to classic blues/R&B as the Stones, and for their first few years they were managed by Giorgio Gomelsky, a colorful figure who had acted as a mentor and informal manager for the Rolling Stones in that band's early days.

The Yardbirds made their first recordings as a backup band for Chicago blues great Sonny Boy Williamson, and little of their future greatness is evident in these sides, in which they were still developing their basic chops. (Some tapes of these live shows were issued after the group had become international stars; the material has been reissued ad infinitum since then.) But they really didn't find their footing until 1964, when they stretched out from straight R&B rehash into extended, frantic guitar-harmonica instrumental passages. Calling these ad hoc jams "rave ups," the Yardbirds were basically making the blues their own by applying a fiercer, heavily amplified electric base. Taking some cues from improvisational jazz by inserting their own impassioned solos, they would turn their source material inside out and sideways, heightening the restless tension by building the tempo and heated exchange of instrumental riffs to a feverish climax, adroitly cooling off and switching to a lower gear just at the point where the energy seemed uncontrollable. The live 1964 album *Five Live Yardbirds* is the best document of their early years, consisting entirely of reckless interpretations of US R&B/blues numbers, and displaying the increasing confidence and imagination of Clapton's guitar work.

As much they might have preferred to stay close to the American blues and R&B that had inspired them (at least at first), the Yardbirds made efforts to crack the pop market from the beginning. A couple of fine studio singles of R&B covers were recorded with Clapton that gave the band's sound a slight polish without sacrificing its power. The commercial impact was modest in the UK and nonexistent in the States, however, and the group decided to change direction radically on their third single. Turning away from their blues roots entirely, "For Your Love" was penned by British pop-rock songwriter Graham Gouldman, and introduced many of the traits that would characterize the Yardbirds' work over the next two years. The melodies were strange (by pop standards) combinations of minor chords; the tempos slowed, speeded up, or ground to a halt unpredictably; the harmonies were droning, almost Gregorian; the arrangements were, by the standards of the time, downright weird, though retaining enough pop appeal to generate chart action. "For Your Love" featured a harpsichord, bongos, and a menacing Keith Relf vocal; it would reach No. 2 in Britain, and No. 6 in the States.

For all its brilliance, "For Your Love" precipitated a major crisis in the band. Eric Clapton wanted to stick close to the blues, and for that matter didn't like "For Your Love," barely playing on the record. Shortly afterward, around the beginning of 1965, he left the band, opting to join John Mayall's Bluesbreakers a bit later in order to keep playing blues guitar. Clapton's spot was first offered to Jimmy Page, then one of the hottest session players in Britain; Page turned it down, figuring he could make a lot more money by staying where he was. He did, however, recommend another guitarist, Jeff Beck, then playing with an obscure band called the Tridents, as well as having worked a few sessions himself.

While Beck's stint with the band lasted only about 18 months, in this period he did more to influence the sound of '60s rock guitar than anyone except Jimi Hendrix. Clapton saw the group's decision to record

adventurous pop like "For Your Love" as a sellout of their purist blues ethic. Beck, on the other hand, saw such material as a challenge that offered room for unprecedented experimentation. Not that he wasn't a capable R&B player as well—on tracks like "The Train Kept A-Rollin'" and "I'm Not Talking," he coaxed a sinister sustain from his instrument by bending the notes and using fuzz and other types of distorted amplification. The Middle Eastern influence extended to his work on all of their material, including his first single with the band, "Heart Full of Soul," which (like "For Your Love") was written by Gouldman. After initial attempts to record the song with a sitar had failed, Beck saved the day by emulating the instrument's exotic twang with fuzz riffs of his own. It became their second Transatlantic Top Ten hit; the similar "Evil-Hearted You," again penned by Gouldman, gave them another big British hit later in 1965.

The chief criticism that could be levied against the band at this point was their shortage of quality original material, a gap addressed by "Still I'm Sad," a haunting group composition based around a Gregorian chant and Beck's sinewy, wicked guitar riffs. In the US, it was coupled with "I'm a Man," a rehaul of the Bo Diddley classic that built to an almost avant-garde climax, Beck scraping the strings of the guitar for a purely percussive effect; it became a Top 20 hit in the US in early 1966. Beck's guitar pyrotechnics came to fruition with "Shapes of Things," which (along with the Byrds' "Eight Miles High") can justifiably be classified as the first psychedelic rock classic. The group had already moved into social comment with a superb album track, "Mr. You're a Better Man than I"; on "Shapes of Things" they did so more succinctly, with Beck's explosively warped solo and feedback propelling the single near the US Top Ten. At this point the group were as innovative as any in rock 'n' roll, building their résumé with the similar hit follow-up to "Shapes of Things," "Over Under Sideways Down."

But the Yardbirds could not claim to be nearly as consistent as peers like the Beatles, Rolling Stones, and Kinks. 1966's *Roger the Engineer* was their first (and, in fact, only) studio album composed entirely of original material, and highlighted the group's erratic quality, bouncing between derivative blues-rockers and numbers incorporating monks-of-doom chants, Oriental dance rhythms, and good old guitar raveups, sometimes in the same track. Its highlights, however, were truly thrilling; even when the experiments weren't wholly successful, they served as proof that the band were second to none in their appetite for taking risks previously unheard of within rock.

Yet at the same time, the group's cohesiveness began to unravel when bassist Samwell-Smith—who had shouldered most of the production responsibilities as well—left the band in mid-1966. Jimmy Page, by this time fed up with session work, eagerly joined on bass. It quickly became apparent that Page had more to offer, and the group unexpectedly reorganized, Dreja switching from rhythm guitar to bass, and Page assuming dual lead guitar duties with Beck.

It was a dream lineup that was, like the best dreams, too good to be true, or at least to last long. Only one single was recorded with the Beck/Page lineup, "Happenings Ten Years Time Ago," which—with its astral guitar leads, muffled explosions, eerie harmonies, and enigmatic lyrics—was psychedelia at its pinnacle. But not at its most commercial—in comparison with previous Yardbirds singles, it fared poorly on the charts, reaching only No. 30 in the States. Around this time, the group (Page and Beck in tow) made a memorable appearance in Michaelangelo Antonioni's film classic *Blow Up*, playing a reworked version of "The Train Kept-A-Rollin'" (retitled "Stroll On"). But in late 1966, Beck—who had become increasingly unreliable, not turning up for shows and suffering from nervous exhaustion—left the band, emerging the following year as the leader of the Jeff Beck Group.

The remaining Yardbirds were determined to continue as a quartet, but in hindsight it was Beck's departure that began to burn out a band that had already survived the loss of a couple important original members. Also to blame was their mysterious failure to summon original material on the order of their classic 1965-66 tracks. More to blame than anyone, however, was Mickey Most (Donovan, Herman's Hermits, Lulu, the Animals), who assumed the producer's chair in 1967, and matched the group with inappropriately lightweight pop tunes. The band's unbridled experimentalism would simmer in isolated moments on some B-sides and album tracks, like "Puzzles," the psychedelic U.F.O. instrumental "Glimpses," and the acoustic "White Summer," which would serve as a blueprint for Page's acoustic excursions with Led Zeppelin. "Little Games," "Ha Ha Said the Clown," and "Ten Little Indians" were all low-charting singles for the group in 1967, but were travesties compared to the magnificence of their previous hits, trading in fury and invention for sappy singalong pop. The 1967 *Little Games* album (issued in the US only) was little better, suffering from both hasty, anemic production and weak material.

The Yardbirds continued to be an exciting concert act, concentrating most of their energies upon the US, having been virtually left for dead in their native Britain. The B-side of their final single, the Page-penned "Think About It," was the best track of the entire Jimmy Page era, showing they were still capable of delivering intriguing, energic psychedelia. It was too little too late—the group were truly on the wane by 1968, as an artistic rift developed within the ranks. To overgeneralize somewhat, Relf and McCarty wanted to pursue more acoustic, melodic music; Page especially wanted to rock hard and loud. A live album was recorded in New York in early 1968, but scrapped; overdubbed with unbelievably cheesy crowd noises, it was briefly released in 1971 after Page had become a superstar in Led Zeppelin, but was withdrawn in a matter of days (it has since been heavily bootlegged). By this time the group was going through the motions, leaving Page holding the bag after a final show in mid-1968. Relf and McCarty formed the first incarnation of Renaissance. Page fulfilled existing contracts by assembling a "New Yardbirds" that, as many know, would soon change their name to Led Zeppelin.

It took years for the rock community to truly comprehend the Yardbirds' significance; younger listeners were led to the recordings in search of the roots of Clapton, Beck, and Page, each of whom had become a superstar by the end of the 1960s. Their wonderful catalog, however, has been subject to more exploitation than any other group of the '60s; dozens, if not hundreds, of cheesy packages of early material are generated throughout the world on a seemingly monthly basis. Fortunately, the best of the reissues cited below (on Rhino, Sony, Edsel and EMI) are packaged with great intelligence, enabling both collectors and new listeners to acquire all of their classic output with a minimum of fuss and repetition. —*Richie Unterberger*

Five Live Yardbirds / Dec. 1964 / Rhino ✦✦✦✦
Recorded live at London's Marquee Club, *Five Live Yardbirds* is the best document of Eric Clapton's work with the band. Tracks like "Too Much Monkey Business," "Got Love If You Want It," and "Smokestack Lightning" were good representations of the Yardbirds's "rave-ups," which were open-ended improvisations that helped lay the groundwork for groups like Cream and the Jimi Hendrix Experience. —*Rick Clark*

Roger the Engineer / 1966 / Edsel ✦✦✦✦
Roger the Engineer is a classic Yardbirds studio album, thanks to tracks like "Lost Woman," "Over Under Sideways Down," "What Do You Want?," "Psycho Daisies," and "Ever Since the World Began." Not available in the States, this British import (on Edsel) is the best-sounding Yardbirds CD by a long shot and a must-own for fans of this band. —*Rick Clark*

★ **Greatest Hits, Vol. 1: 1964-1966** / 1986 / Rhino ✦✦✦✦✦
Sonically, these tracks fail to match the brilliance and warmth of the original vinyl pressings, but *Greatest Hits* has more punch. "For Your Love" is an exception, with the record version sounding extremely compressed. Of the various Yardbird collections that exist, this is still the most intelligently chosen, even though it lacks key tracks from *Roger the Engineer*. —*Rick Clark*

On Air / 1991 / Band Of Joy ✦✦✦

Vol. 1: Smokestack Lightning / 1991 / Sony ✦✦✦✦
This double-disc set focuses on tracks from *For Your Love* and *Having a Rave-Up with the Yardbirds*. Included are live tracks recorded at the Crawdaddy Club while touring with Sonny Boy Williamson. Most of these tracks on *Smokestack Lightning* (as well as *Blues, Backtracks*) were mastered off safety tapes, as opposed to the original masters, since EMI England has possession of them. Considering that EMI won't release the masters to anyone, this is a respectable sound—though not as good as the first vinyl pressings. —*Rick Clark*

Vol. 2: Blues, Backtracks and Shapes of Things / 1991 / Sony ✦✦✦✦
Another double-disc set, this covers some later hits (including the classic future-rock of "Shapes of Things"), *Roger the Engineer* outtakes, and various other oddities. The sound on some of the outtakes is pretty respectable, considering that some of them were taken from the original acetates. —*Rick Clark*

The Yardbirds Little Games Sessions & More / 1992 / EMI America ✦✦✦

Yaz

Dance-Pop, Synth-Pop, New Wave
Yaz was the American name taken by Yazoo, a British duo made up of former Depeche Mode synthesizer player Vince Clarke and singer Alison Moyet (b. Jun. 18, 1961). The two stayed together only about a year and a half (1982-1983), but that was long enough to score four British hit singles and two top-selling albums. Moyet then went solo and Clarke eventually formed another successful duo, Erasure. —*William Ruhlmann*

Upstairs at Eric's / 1982 / Sire ✦✦✦✦
Yaz's music is spare, striking electronic backup contrasted with full-throated, emotional singing, but one shouldn't discount some remarkable songwriting, especially the hits "Don't Go," "Only You," and "Situation." —*William Ruhlmann*

● **You & Me Both** / 1983 / Sire ✦✦✦✦
Perhaps a more consistent collection overall than the first album, this

one demonstrates that the duo was anything but played out. While both have gone on to successful careers, you can't help regretting that this is the end of Yaz. —*William Ruhlmann*

Yello

Art-Rock/Progressive-Rock, Club-Dance
This group from Switzerland is a picture of professionalism, although none of the members are trained musicians. Boris Blank, Dieter Meier, and Carlos Peron do not go overboard trying to be innovative and original, but that is certainly the outcome. They have created a distinctive and bright listening style, unusual and very simplistic, not based on traditional harmony or pretensions. Their rich, unique sound and strong emphasis on modern synthesizer technology make this group one of the most significant in contemporary music history. —*Vladimir Bogdanov*

Stella / 1985 / Mercury ✦✦✦✦
This is one of their disco-oriented albums; it includes "Desire" and "Sometimes." —*Vladimir Bogdanov*

One Second / 1987 / Mercury ✦✦✦
This album offers a great variety of styles, effects, textures, and rhythms. It includes the songs "The Rhythm Divine" and "The Secret Fazida." —*Vladimir Bogdanov*

Flag / 1988 / Mercury ✦✦✦✦
This is Yello's most dynamic album, with excellent composition. Picking highlights would be difficult, since the songs segue, and the album just begs to be listened to as a whole. —*Vladimir Bogdanov*

● **Essential** / 1992 / Smash ✦✦✦✦
This good compilation will satisfy fans of their infamous "Oh Yeah." —*AMG*

Yes

Art-Rock/Progressive-Rock, Pop-Rock
Yes is, without a doubt, the definitive English progressive-rock band, purveyors of cosmic lyrics, virtuoso playing, and vast musical tapestries topped off with heart-stoppingly gorgeous melodies and sealed with a rock 'n' roll kick. Yes was formed in London in 1968 by singer Jon Anderson and bassist Chris Squire, both owners of high, clear tenor voices that blend seamlessly in the band's trademark harmonies. The history of Yes is one of constant changes in personnel, but the group's most celebrated lineup came about when founding members Anderson, Squire, and drummer Bill Bruford, plus guitarist Steve Howe (who had enlisted in 1970), were joined in 1971 by keyboard whiz Rick Wakeman. Thus constituted, the band cut its signature tune, "Roundabout" (from the fourth Yes album, *Fragile*), not to mention the sumptuously symphonic magnum opus *Close to the Edge*. A further series of comings and goings led to a disastrous 1980 lineup (documented on "Drama") in which Squire was the only remaining original member. After a three-year hiatus, a revamped Yes (Anderson, Squire, original keyboardist Tony Kaye, long-time drummer Alan White, and South African guitarist Trevor Rabin) emerged in 1983 with a streamlined, commercialized sound, topping the charts with "Owner of a Lonely Heart." Anderson split in 1988, teaming up with some old cohorts as Anderson Bruford Wakeman Howe—essentially a rival version of Yes! The two bands joined forces in 1991 as an eight-man "mega-Yes," combining their separately recorded efforts on *Union*. —*Michael P. Dawson*

Yes / Oct. 15, 1969 / Atlantic ✦✦✦

Time and a Word / Nov. 2, 1970 / Atlantic ✦✦✦

The Yes Album / Mar. 19, 1971 / Atlantic ✦✦✦✦
This is the album that first gave shape to the established Yes sound, built around science-fiction concepts, folk melodies, and soaring organ, guitar, and vocal showpieces. "Your Move" actually got some airplay as a single, and "Starship Troopers" became a much-loved part of the band's set. —*Bruce Eder*

★ **Fragile** / Jan. 4, 1972 / Atlantic ✦✦✦✦✦
The breakthrough album for the band, in which the science-fiction and fantasy elements of the songs became dominant and the addition of Rick Wakeman on organ added a larger-than-life element to the group's sound. Ironically, the album was a patchwork job, hastily assembled to help cover the cost of Wakeman's expanded array of instruments, but the short form of "Roundabout" clicked on AM radio, album buyers liked the long version, plus the rest of the material they found, and the band was made. —*Bruce Eder*

☆ **Close to the Edge** / Sep. 13, 1972 / Atlantic ✦✦✦✦✦
The group's sound broke more boundaries here, as sidelong suites allowed Jon Anderson even more opportunity for vocal acrobatics and Wakeman an even bigger canvas on which to paint his electronic-synthesizer swirls and organ arpeggios. The poetry also had a peculiarly hypnotic quality, which overcame its relatively obscure passages. —*Bruce Eder*

Yessongs / May 4, 1973 / Atlantic ✦✦✦
The best live album to emerge from the entire art-rock scene, a compendium of blazing performances covering the previous three studio albums by the group and the accompanying solo career of Rick Wakeman. Some of the performances are superior to their studio originals, although "And You and I" is something of a disappointment next to the version on *Close to the Edge*. —*Bruce Eder*

Tales from Topographic Oceans / Jan. 9, 1974 / Atlantic ✦
This was where the Yes spell began to break, partly due to the excesses inherent in a double album containing one long song per side. Jon Anderson's fascination with Eastern religions swelled to mammoth proportions here, and while individual parts of this album are gorgeous and fascinating, the piece as a whole proved overwhelming to many critics. —*AMG*

Relayer / Dec. 5, 1974 / Atlantic ✦✦✦

Yesterdays / Feb. 27, 1975 / Atlantic ✦✦✦

Yesshows / Nov. 24, 1980 / Arista ✦✦✦

Classic Yes / Nov. 30, 1981 / Atlantic ✦✦✦✦
Classic Yes collects the group's biggest radio hits, which were frequently their most accessible and catchy songs. Nevertheless, Yes made albums, not singles, in the '70s, so these songs make more sense in their original context than they do on this compilation. —*Stephen Thomas Erlewine*

90125 / Nov. 7, 1983 / Atlantic ✦✦✦✦
A ridiculously successful "comeback" album with a slightly different membership. For completists. —*Bruce Eder*

Big Generator / Sep. 17, 1987 / Atlantic ✦✦

Yesyears / 1991 / Atlantic ✦✦✦✦
This four-CD set is sonically so far superior to the individual CDs by the group that on this basis alone it is worth owning. Unfortunately, there are important songs that didn't get the remastering treatment, and they are missed. —*Bruce Eder*

● **The Very Best of Yes** / 1993 / Atlantic ✦✦✦✦
The very best of Yes is hard to stick on merely one disc; this set includes tracks from each era of the band. Not essential, it's still a decent sampler. —*Rick Clark*

Yo La Tengo

Alternative Pop-Rock
Those who claim that rock critics are little more than frustrated musicians have evidently spent little time listening to former critic Ira Kaplan's great band Yo La Tengo. Coming out of the Hoboken, NJ, scene (sourcepoint: the very hip club Maxwell's) in the mid-'80s, Yo La Tengo (Spanish for "I've got it"; Kaplan took the expression in honor of a Latin ballplayer for his beloved New York Mets) is an extreme band in the sense that they ran the gamut from harsh, coruscating walls of feedback to supple, endearing folk-derived pop. But, despite the disparate nature of the two genres, Kaplan and his creative partner and wife Georgia Hubley make the two work seamlessly, and by doing so have created a large and excellent body of work that stands in stark contrast to the careerists and manipulators that glut the "alternative" landscape. As a former critic and compulsive record collector, Kaplan's influence on the band is one that prides eclecticism and unpredictability over career moves that would firmly ensconce Yo La Tengo in the profitable alternative rock sweepstakes. Because they are slippery and somewhat undefinable (which is a big part of their charm), Yo La Tengo will probably never be MTV's next-big-thing, nor will they have Soundgarden-like sales figures. And, if pressed, I bet Kaplan and Hubley wouldn't care all that much. Instead, they soldier on, recording great music for those whose taste for pop music runs the gamut from the Velvet Underground and Sonic Youth to the Holy Modal Rounders and NRBQ. —*John Dougan*

Ride the Tiger / 1986 / Coyote/Twintone ✦✦✦✦
A fine debut that shows off this band's smarts and style. Not as aggressive in the noise department as some later releases, this is still a confident and assured record. As usual, Kaplan comes up with a cool, if fairly obscure cover or two (here it's Ray Davies's "Big Sky") as well as loading up the record with some fine originals. The presence of ex-Mission of Burma bassist Clint Conley as producer adds a touch of professionalism that doesn't detract from the album's cheery and insistent low-fi charm. —*John Dougan*

● **President Yo La Tengo/New Wave Hot Dogs** / 1989 / Twin/Tone ✦✦✦✦
Two records now available as a single CD, these really show off Yo La Tengo's ability to create musical extremes. *New Wave Hot Dogs* has the firm pop sense and strong songwriting of the debut, but *President Yo La Tengo* offers up a little more free-form skronk in the ten-minute live version of "The Evil That Men Do," a gloriously squalling, over-the-top crash and bash session that proves how liberating and fun sonic dissonance can be. Just in case you don't like that sort of thing, "Evil" also shows up as a straight-ahead folk-rock track. This is a great collection of material

that, as well as anything else they have recorded, gets to the heart of what makes this band tick. —*John Dougan*

Fakebook / 1990 / Bar/None ✦✦✦✦
Recommending *Fakebook* as the best place to begin a relationship with Yo La Tengo is slightly disingenuous, mainly because Yo La Tengo has never made another record like it, and perhaps never will. So, as completely wonderful as this record is (and believe me, it is), it's an accurate representation of one side of Yo La Tengo, and assuming that everything sounds like *Fakebook* might be disappointing. A collection of cover songs that lean towards the idiosyncratic (e.g., Peter Stampfel, Daniel Johnston, Jad Fair), *Fakebook* is warm, low-key, and lovely, with heartfelt singing and playing that never flags after hundreds of replays. It's impossible to imagine playing this record and not smiling and singing along. A big bonus is a great version of the Flamin' Groovies "You Tore Me Down." —*John Dougan*

May I Sing with Me / 1992 / Alias ✦✦✦

Painful / 1993 / Matador ✦✦✦✦
Yo La Tengo has released several fine albums before, but only *Painful* encapsulates their folky guitar experimentalism perfectly. Alternating between dreamy Velvet Underground-style ballads and raving, Sonic Youth guitar squalls, *Painful* also finds the group improving their songwriting skills immeasurably. Before, they relied on soundscapes; now, the sound fleshes out their songs, from the trance-like "Nowhere Near" to the dense "From a Motel 6" and the two versions of "Big Day Coming," which cover both ends of the spectrum. A subtly addicting album. —*Stephen Thomas Erlewine*

Electr-O-Pura / 1995 / Matador ✦✦✦

Neil Young

b. Nov. 12, 1945, Toronto, Canada
Guitar, Piano, Ukulele, Vocals / Rock 'n' Roll, Country-Rock, Singer-Songwriter, Hard Rock, Folk-Rock
With the exception only of Bob Dylan, Neil Young is the most acclaimed and accomplished singer-songwriter of his generation. Born in Toronto, Young learned to play ukelele and then guitar in his teens, and played in a variety of groups. He moved to Los Angeles with his friend, bassist Bruce Palmer, and hooked up with Stephen Stills, Richie Furay, and Dewey Martin to form Buffalo Springfield in 1966. After the Springfield split in 1968, Young went solo, releasing his first album, *Neil Young*, an acoustic effort with strings, in January 1969. Characteristically, Young followed it only four months later with the hard rock *Everybody Knows This Is Nowhere*, backed by the electric three-piece band Crazy Horse; it became his first gold-selling album. Young joined Crosby, Stills & Nash in June 1969, and combined solo and group careers until the band split the following summer. His third solo album, *After the Gold Rush* (Aug. 1970), reached the Top Ten and included his first Top 40 hit, "Only Love Can Break Your Heart." But Young's commercial peak came early in 1972, when he released the No. 1, three-million-selling album *Harvest*, which contained the chart-topping gold single "Heart of Gold."

Instead of following up such success, Young worked on the documentary film *Journey Through the Past* (and its accompanying soundtrack album) for the rest of the year, then launched a concert tour in early 1973, by which time Crazy Horse's guitarist Danny Whitten had died of a heroin overdose. The tour was a ragged affair chronicled on the live album *Time Fades Away*. After it, Young recorded (but did not release) *Tonight's the Night*, which memorialized Whitten and Bruce Berry, a Young roadie who had also overdosed.

Young's first new studio album in 18 months, *On the Beach*, was released in the summer of 1974. Much of it was acoustic, and it expressed dire sentiments. He finally put out *Tonight's the Night* in the summer of 1975, and the hard-rocking *Zuma* the following autumn. In the spring of 1976, Young toured with Stephen Stills, and the two recorded the duo album *Long May You Run*. Young's next solo album was 1977's *American Stars 'n' Bars*, made up of studio tracks dating back three years. In the fall of 1977, he released *Decade*, a three-album (later two-CD) career retrospective. *Comes a Time*, Young's most country-folk-oriented album since *Harvest*, was released in 1978 and, like *Harvest*, reached the Top Ten. In 1979 Young launched a tour with Crazy Horse under the banner Rust Never Sleeps, including a critically acclaimed album of the same name and, eventually, a tour film and a live album called *Live Rust*.

Young spent the better part of the '80s veering from one musical style to another, as his commercial fortunes declined. He turned to electronic music on *Trans*, to rockabilly on *Everybody's Rockin'*, to country on *Old Ways*, and to horn-backed R&B on *This Note's for You*. In 1989, however, Young returned to his more familiar folk and rock styles for *Freedom*, and was rewarded with critical hosannas and his first gold album in a decade. The hard-rocking *Ragged Glory* was even more rapturously received, topping the *Village Voice* critic's poll for Best Album of 1990. In late 1991, Young issued a double live album, *Weld*, as well as *Arc*, an album of instrumental guitar feedback. He was said to be working on a boxed-set retrospective follow-up to *Decade*.

In 1992, Young was being hailed as "the Godfather of Grunge," as dozens of new rock 'n' roll bands from Pearl Jam to the Jayhawks were claiming him as an influence. Naturally, Young backed away from the hard, overdriven rock of *Weld* and *Ragged Glory*, releasing the quiet *Harvest Moon*, the sequel to his country-rock landmark, *Harvest*. In 1993, he released a live album *(Unplugged)* while he worked on his long-awaited box set; he released another album recorded with Crazy Horse, *Sleeps With Angels*, in late summer of 1994. The following summer Young released *Mirror Ball*, which was recorded with Pearl Jam. — *William Ruhlmann*

Neil Young / Jan. 1969 / Reprise ✦✦✦
Neil Young's debut solo album, after three records with Buffalo Springfield, found him in a quiet moods, his songs frequently backed only by acoustic guitar strings arranged by Jack Nitzsche. There were instrumentals and a long, Dylanish ballad called "The Last Trip to Tulsa," while the most memorable song was "The Loner." Young failed to attract an audience with this approach. *Neil Young* was his only solo album to miss the charts, and he immediately turned around and produced a rock album. *Everybody Knows This Is Nowhere*, which appeared within three months and established him as a solo star. — *William Ruhlmann*

☆ **Everybody Knows This Is Nowhere** / May 1969 / Reprise ✦✦✦✦
Young's breakthrough album is also the first one to feature the backup of Crazy Horse for a seminal rock session that produced Young favorites "Cinnamon Girl," "Down by the River," and "Cowgirl in the Sand." — *William Ruhlmann*

☆ **After the Gold Rush** / Aug. 1970 / Reprise ✦✦✦✦✦
The years have only been kind to what sounded like Young's best album when it was released. It's a mixture of his folky ("Tell Me Why"), country ("Oh, Lonesome Me"), and hard-rocking ("Southern Man") selves, and there's also that mystical title track, which remains Neil Young's definitive statement of purpose. — *William Ruhlmann*

Harvest / Feb. 1972 / Reprise ✦✦✦✦
Uneven, yes, perhaps due to the overambitiousness of the orchestral pieces, but this album, Young's biggest seller, still contains "Heart of Gold," the rocker "Alabama," and such telling ballads as "Old Man." — *William Ruhlmann*

Journey through the Past / Nov. 1972 / Reprise ✦✦
Neil Young's unexpected followup to the million-selling *Harvest* was this two-LP soundtrack to his rarely seen film. It contains performances by Buffalo Springfield and Crosby, Stills, Nash and Young, plus Young himself, all previously familiar, except for one minor new Young song, "Soldier." — *William Ruhlmann*

Time Fades Away / Oct. 1973 / Reprise ✦✦✦
The beginning of Young's mid-'70s descent into decadence, this is part of a trilogy including *Tonight's the Night* and *On the Beach* that explores drug addiction, desperation, and determination, and the subject matter isn't only expressed in the lyrics, it's in the roughly played music and the strained vocals. The most gripping music of Young's career. — *William Ruhlmann*

☆ **On the Beach** / Jul. 1974 / Reprise ✦✦✦✦✦
Part three of the doom trilogy was actually the second to be released, as Young began to dig himself out of the depression of the previous year, noting that "Sooner or later, it all gets real" but also fearing that he's "just pissing in the wind." — *William Ruhlmann*

☆ **Tonight's the Night** / Jun. 1975 / Reprise ✦✦✦✦✦
This belatedly released masterpiece (part two of the trilogy) is one of the scariest records ever released. It names names and spares no one in its depiction of the ravages of the druggy life of rock 'n' roll. Least of all spared is the author, who often sounds like he's about to nod out himself. Probably the best album Neil Young will ever make, and not listed as his pick only because it's not the place to start. — *William Ruhlmann*

Zuma / Nov. 1975 / Reprise ✦✦✦✦
"Don't cry no tears around me," Young declares, trying for the second album in a row (after *On the Beach*) to put the past behind him and take on new topics and directions. And so he does, though by calling on other aspects of his past. Crazy Horse is back, with Frank Sampedro replacing Danny Whitten, and Young even includes "Through My Sails," a track from an abortive Crosby, Stills, Nash and Young session. But the highlight is "Cortez the Killer," Young's best guitar workout since *Everybody Knows This is Nowhere*. — *William Ruhlmann*

Long May You Run / Aug. 1976 / Reprise ✦✦
American Stars & Bars / Jun. 1977 / Reprise ✦✦✦
★ **Decade** / Oct. 1977 / Reprise ✦✦✦✦✦
A 3-LP/2-CD retrospective with material dating back to Buffalo Springfield (some of it unreleased) and including such previously non-LP gems as "Sugar Mountain." As a best-of, it's idiosyncratic, but as a rarities album, it's invaluable. — *William Ruhlmann*

Comes a Time / Oct. 1978 / Reprise ✦✦✦✦
From the reflective opener "Goin' Back," to the airy remake of Ian & Sylvia's "Four Strong Winds," *Comes a Time* is Young's most delicately (and oddly) atmospheric album. The album's dreamy country-folk music frames Young's homey discourses on "Peace of Mind," the "Field of Opportunity," and the "Human Highway." The collective effect is a lulling optimism, even when his mind at times seems to be bangin' on one cylinder merely dishing out alien-sounding toss-offs clothed in plain-speak. Overall, *Comes a Time* is a strangely entrancing high point in Young's willfully erratic career. — *Rick Clark*

☆ **Rust Never Sleeps** / Jun. 1979 / Reprise ✦✦✦✦✦
Like the album that followed it, *Live Rust*, this is a live album. The difference is that this is a single album containing all-new material. The songs are among Young's best ever. — *William Ruhlmann*

Live Rust / Nov. 1979 / Reprise ✦✦✦✦
This two-record set is a live album culled from Neil Young's 1979 tour with Crazy Horse and a de facto soundtrack album to his concert movie, *Rust Never Sleeps*. Its 16 songs chronicle his career from early efforts like "Sugar Mountain" and "The Loner" to recent compositions heard on the *Rust Never Sleeps* album from five months before (with which there is some overlap). — *William Ruhlmann*

Hawks & Doves / Nov. 1980 / Reprise ✦✦✦

Re-ac-tor / Nov. 1981 / Reprise ✦✦
The news that Neil Young is recording with Crazy Horse usually means that fans are in for a superior, rocking effort. Not this time. Young could have written the songs in an afternoon (one consists of the repeated lines, "Got mashed potato / Ain't got no t-bone") and recorded them that night. Raggedness is what one looks for in a Neil Young/Crazy Horse release, but not toss-offs. This is mere product. — *William Ruhlmann*

Trans / Jan. 1983 / Geffen ✦✦

Everybody's Rockin' / Aug. 1983 / Geffen ✦✦

Old Ways / Aug. 1985 / Geffen ✦✦✦

This Note's for You / Apr. 1988 / Reprise ✦✦✦

Eldorado / 1989 / Reprise ✦✦✦

Freedom / Oct. 1989 / Reprise ✦✦✦✦
"Rockin' in the Free World" represents a renewal of Young's commitment to his artistic vision and to his audience, and, as with all his best work, it recognizes the worst while it hopes for the best. A stunning return to form for an artist who seemed to have wandered too far from his original promise ever to find his way back. — *William Ruhlmann*

☆ **Ragged Glory** / Sep. 1990 / Reprise ✦✦✦✦✦
Young is reunited with Crazy Horse for an album of noisy guitar rock that sounds perfect when played right after *Everybody Knows This Is Nowhere*, and that's a high recommendation. — *William Ruhlmann*

Weld / Oct. 1991 / Reprise ✦✦✦✦
With the double-disc *Weld*, Neil Young closes the door on his return to overamplified guitar grunge. Recorded at various tour stops during the Gulf War in 1991, *Weld* is full of anger, patriotism, optimism, and confusion, perfectly capturing the atmosphere of the time. Although there is a heavy political undertow on *Weld*, the main reason to listen to it is that it rocks like a demon. Neil Young has never released such a towering monument of noise before, and the sheer rage and volume of *Weld* are overpowering. Live albums are rarely this good or this relevant. (Note: The first editions of *Weld* featured *Arc*, a 35-minute aural collage of feedback recorded throughout the tour. Although the premise sounds frightening, *Arc* is a surprisingly accessible, enjoyable listen. It was later issued separately as an EP.) — *Stephen Thomas Erlewine*

Harvest Moon / Nov. 3, 1992 / Reprise ✦✦✦

Lucky Thirteen / 1993 / Geffen ✦✦✦

Unplugged / Jun. 15, 1993 / Reprise ✦✦✦✦
Like Paul McCartney's, Neil Young's *Unplugged* seems to be an attempt to thwart bootleggers by releasing the material before they get a chance. Young's album doesn't offer any revelations, it's just a solid, thoroughly enjoyable concert. Acoustic performances of "Mr. Soul," "World On a String," "Like a Hurricane," and especially the synthesized "Transformer Man" are essential for the serious Young collector. Fans of *Harvest, After the Gold Rush, Comes A Time*, and *Harvest Moon* will find that this is the live Neil Young they need in their collection; hardcore fans will realize that this is the acoustic equivalent of the stunning *Weld*. — *Stephen Thomas Erlewine*

Sleeps with Angels / Aug. 16, 1994 / Reprise ✦✦✦✦
Reportedly spurred by the death of Kurt Cobain (who quoted Young's line, "It's better to burn out than to fade away," in his suicide note), Young turns in an unusually low-key, elegiac effort, its songs worrying about depression, lack of communication, and drive-by shootings, its music (despite the presence of Crazy Horse) slow and meditative (except for the funny change-of-pace rocker "Piece Of Crap"). The result is not as gloomy as *Tonight's The Night* (in which Young seemed past the point of caring

and even managed a certain gallows humor), but extremely mournful, with only glimmers of hope. — *William Ruhlmann*

Mirror Ball / 1995 / Reprise ♦♦♦
Broken Arrow / Jul. 2, 1996 / Reprise ♦♦♦

Young-Holt Unlimited

Soul, Soul Jazz
In the mid-'60s, bassist Eldee Young and drummer Isaac "Red" Holt, who had done time for about a dozen years as Ramsey Lewis' rhythm section, split to form their own act. As the Young Holt Trio they had a quick Top 20 R&B hit with the infectiously silly "Wack Wack," after which they changed their name to Young-Holt Unlimited. On most of their material, they cut an invigorating soul-jazz groove that explored the territory between Jimmy Smith and Junior Walker, with dour bass, Ray Charles-inspired keyboards, faint scat vocals, and a live party ambience. When they tightened up and added some funky rhythms, they had a left-field smash with the instrumental "Soulful Strut," which went to No.3 in 1969. —*Richie Unterberger*

● **Wack Wack** / 1986 / Kent ♦♦♦♦
Sixteen late-'60s tracks, taken from various LPs and singles. An enjoyable if minor collection of this forgotten group, whose excursions into jazz-soul work much better than their attempts to milk the "Soulful Strut" groove on lesser follow-ups. Includes "Wack Wack," "Soulful Strut," and a surprisingly successful reworking of Donovan's "Mellow Yellow" into a cool jazz-funk jive number. —*Richie Unterberger*

The Best of Young Holt Unlimited / 1995 / Brunswick ♦♦♦♦
Twelve of their most famous cuts, including the hits "Soulful Strut" and "Wack Wack," a live medley, and some neat obscurities (like "Give It Up" and the propulsive "Dig Her Walk"). It's not quite as comprehensive, however, as the 16-track British import *Wack Wack* (on Kent), which is still the better collection to pick up if you can find it. The only song here that's not on *Wack Wack* is their version of "Light My Fire." —*Richie Unterberger*

The Youngbloods

Folk-Rock
The Youngbloods could not be considered a major '60s band, but they were capable of offering some mighty pleasurable folk-rock in the late '60s, and produced a few great tunes along the way. One of the better groups to emerge from the East Coast in the mid-'60s, they would temper their blues and jugband influences with gentle California psychedelia, particularly after they moved to the San Francisco Bay area. For most listeners, they're identified almost exclusively with their Top Ten hit "Get Together," but they managed several respectable albums as well, all under the leadership of singer-songwriter Jesse Colin Young.

Young got his start on the folk circuits of Boston and New York, and had already cut a couple of solo albums before forming the Youngbloods. John Sebastian was one of the supporting musicians on Young's second LP, and comparisons between the two—and between the Youngbloods and the Lovin' Spoonful—are inevitable. Both groups offered good-timey folk-rock with much stronger jugband influences than West Coast rivals like the Byrds, though the Youngbloods made greater use of electric keyboards than the Spoonful, courtesy of the enigmatically named Lowell "Banana" Levinger. The Youngbloods didn't craft nearly as many brilliant singles as the Lovin' Spoonful, but (unlike the Spoonful) endured well into the hippie/psychedelic era.

While Young was always the focal point of the band, their first two albums also had songwriting contributions from guitarist Jerry Corbitt. Produced by Felix Pappalardi (who also worked with Cream), these records (*The Youngbloods* and *Earth Music*) were engaging and mature, if inconsistent, folk-rock. Corbitt's "Grizzly Bear" was a small hit, as was "Get Together," a Dino Valenti song that had previously been recorded by the Jefferson Airplane. The Youngbloods' slow, soulful interpretation of "Get Together" was definitive, but it wouldn't reach the Top Ten until it was re-released in 1969, after the song had been used in a television public service ad.

By that time, Corbitt had left, and the Youngbloods, reduced to a trio, were living in Marin County, CA. 1969's *Elephant Mountain* was produced by, of all people, Charlie Daniels. Reflecting the mellowing influence of San Francisco psychedelia, it was their best effort, featuring some of Young's best songs. They released a few more albums in the early '70s (some live), but on these the mellow California rock sound that had served them well on *Elephant Mountain* had begun to turn limpid and wimpy. The group broke up in 1972, and Jesse Colin Young had a long and moderately successful career as a solo singer-songwriter. —*Richie Unterberger*

The Youngbloods / 1967 / Edsel ♦♦♦♦
The New York quartet came off as a mini-Lovin' Spoonful on their engaging debut, with a deeper touch of melancholy and more prominent electric keyboards. As with the Spoonful, they would have been better off

leaving the blues alone, but the rest of the material is good, highlighted by "Get Together" and the achingly tuneful "All Over the World (La-La)." —*Richie Unterberger*

Earth Music / 1967 / Edsel ♦♦♦
Elephant Mountain / 1969 / RCA ♦♦♦♦
By the time they made this album, the group had relocated to Northern California from New York and guitarist Jerry Corbitt had departed, leaving the songwriting chores almost exclusively in the hands of Jesse Colin Young. The mellower, more psychedelic sound reflected the group's new surroundings, and despite some weak moments, it remains their strongest and most cohesive LP. Young's acoustic love song "Sunlight" is his best original composition, and the Youngbloods' best track besides "Get Together"; "Darkness, Darkness" and "Smug" are also outstanding. —*Richie Unterberger*

● **The Best of the Youngbloods** / 1970 / RCA ♦♦♦♦
It's a bit short at ten songs, but this collection offers a nice overview of this '60s band's growth from good-time ragtimers to laidback jammers. —*Jeff Tamarkin*

Frank Zappa (Francis Vincent Zappa)

b. Dec. 21 1940, Baltimore, MD, d. Dec. 4, 1993, Los Angeles, CA
Guitar / Rock 'n' roll, Hard Rock, Fusion, Art-Rock/Progressive-Rock, Early Jazz Rock, Experimental
Frank Zappa was one of the most accomplished composers of the rock era; his music combines an understanding of and appreciation for such contemporary classical figures as Stravinsky, Stockhausen, and Varese with an affection for late-'50s doo wop rock 'n' roll and a facility for the guitar-heavy rock that dominated pop in the '70s. But Zappa was also a satirist whose reserves of scorn seemed bottomless and whose wicked sense of humor and absurdity have delighted his numerous fans, even when his lyrics crossed over the broadest bounds of taste. Finally, Zappa was perhaps the most prolific record-maker of his time, turning out massive amounts of music on his own Barking Pumpkin label and through distribution deals with Rykodisc and Rhino after long, unhappy associations with industry giants like Warner Bros. and the now-defunct MGM.

Zappa became interested in music early and pursued his studies in school, up through a six-month stint at Chaffey College in Alta Loma, CA. He scored a couple of low-budget films and used the money to buy a low-budget recording studio. In 1964, he joined a local band called the Soul Giants, which, over the course of the next two years, evolved into the Mothers, who played songs written by Zappa. The band was signed to the Verve division of MGM by producer Tom Wilson in 1966 and recorded its first album, a two-LP set called *Freak Out!*, which introduced Zappa's interests in both serious music and pop as well as his scathing wit. (Verve insisted on adding "of Invention" to the band's name.)

Subsequent albums extended the musical and lyrical themes of the debut, and they came frequently. Three albums, for example, hit the charts in 1968: *We're Only in It for the Money*, a Mothers album that made fun of hippies and *Sgt. Pepper*; *Lumpy Gravy*, a Zappa solo album recorded with an orchestra; and *Cruising with Ruben & the Jets*, on which the Mothers played neo-doo-wop. Toward the end of the '60s, Zappa expanded the Mothers lineup, turning more toward instrumental jazz-rock, much of which displayed his technically accomplished guitar playing. But by the end of the decade, he had broken up the band.

In 1970, however, Zappa reassembled a new edition of the Mothers, featuring former Turtles lead singers Mark Volman and Howard Kaylan as frontmen. The lineup moved the group more in the direction of X-rated comedy, notably on the album *Fillmore East June 1971*, but it was short-lived: during a performance at the Rainbow Theatre in London, Zappa was pushed from the stage by a demented fan and seriously injured.

While he recovered, Zappa released several albums, then he re-formed the Mothers with himself as lead singer and made pop-rock albums, such as *Over-nite Sensation*, which were among his best-selling records ever. By the end of the '70s, Zappa was recording on his own labels, distributed in some cases by the majors, and he had attracted a consistent cult following for both his humor and his complex music. (Zappa's band, in fact, became a training ground for high-quality rock musicians, much as Miles Davis' was for jazz players.)

In the '80s, Zappa gained the rights to his old albums and began to reissue them, at first on his own and then through the pioneering Rykodisc CD label. He wrote his autobiography and embarked on a world tour in 1988. That was the end of his live performing, except for such isolated appearances as one in Czechoslovakia at the invitation of its post-Communist president, Zappa fan Vaclav Havel.

In late 1991, it was confirmed that Zappa was seriously ill with cancer. Nevertheless, his schedule of album releases continued to be rapid. Zappa died in December of 1993. —*William Ruhlmann*

Freak Out / Jul. 1966 / Rykodisc ♦♦♦♦
Once an LP, now an hour-long CD, but still featuring the Mothers' opening salvo to the world, playing what is often melodic '60s pop-rock with

doo wop influences. But the lyrics in songs like "Who Are the Brain Police?" and "Trouble Every Day" mark composer Frank Zappa as having a social conscience and a wickedly satiric sense of humor. — *William Ruhlmann*

Absolutely Free / May 26, 1967 / Rykodisc ✦✦✦✦
The satire gets even sharper on such songs as "Plastic People" and "Status Back Baby," while the references are often only local to the band's Los Angeles environs (and, increasingly, part of a private, absurdist language), and the music gets increasingly complicated. — *William Ruhlmann*

★ **We're Only in It for the Money** / Jan. 1968 / Verve ✦✦✦✦✦
A simultaneous condemnation of the straights and the hippies, its songs segue as on *Sgt. Pepper* and, with verbal asides included, a sound collage that was the original Mothers' highest-charting album. — *William Ruhlmann*

Lumpy Gravy / Mar. 1968 / Verve ✦✦✦✦
Initially commissioned by Capitol Records when the Mothers of Invention were signed to Verve, *Lumpy Gravy* was Frank Zappa's first solo album, one on which he continued his tape experiments and employed an orchestra along with members of the Mothers. Snatches of conversation and sound collages make up the bulk of it, so that it is the most exploratory (but not the most accomplished) album Zappa made in the 1960s. — *William Ruhlmann*

Cruising with Ruben and the Jets / Oct. 1968 / Rykodisc ✦✦✦

Uncle Meat / Apr. 1969 / Rykodisc ✦✦✦✦
A sprawling, largely instrumental soundtrack to a movie that was never finished, including everything from the pop tune "The Air" to the extended "King Kong," complete with variations. — *William Ruhlmann*

Burnt Weenie Sandwich / Jun. 1969 / Barking Pumpkin ✦✦✦✦✦

Hot Rats / Oct. 10, 1969 / Rykodisc ✦✦✦✦
Zappa disbanded the original Mothers group in 1969 and cut this solo album, most of which consists of well-organized jazz-rock instrumentals such as "Peaches En Regalia," one of his most appealing compositions. Captain Beefheart provides a guest vocal on "Willie the Pimp," which also features violin by Jean-Luc Ponty. — *William Ruhlmann*

Weasels Ripped My Flesh / Aug. 1970 / Rykodisc ✦✦✦✦
An album of live material recorded from 1967 to 1969 and featuring an expanded lineup with horn section. Highlights include Sugar Cane Harris's violin work on Little Richard's "Directly from My Heart to You" and Zappa's vocal on "My Guitar Wants to Kill Your Mama." — *William Ruhlmann*

Fillmore East: June 1971 / Aug. 1971 / Rykodisc ✦✦✦

Waka/Jawaka / Jul. 5, 1972 / Rykodisc ✦✦✦

The Grand Wazoo / Nov. 1972 / Rykodisc ✦✦✦✦
Frank Zappa continued to experiment with an expanded musical unit on this largely instrumental album, which took a big band approach, prominently featuring reeds and horns. — *William Ruhlmann*

☆ **Over-Nite Sensation** / Sep. 1973 / Barking Pumpkin ✦✦✦✦✦
This is actually Zappa's first new studio album of vocal music in three years, and it finds him with another edition of Mothers (from this point, Mothers group albums and Zappa solo albums become indistinguishable), this time taking the lead vocals himself and writing a new set of catchy, satiric rock-pop songs like "Camarillo Brillo" and "Montana." — *William Ruhlmann*

☆ **Apostrophe** / Mar. 1974 / Barking Pumpkin ✦✦✦✦✦
Zappa's only gold-selling Top Ten album, featuring the satiric "Don't Eat the Yellow Snow," along with other parodic songs in the same style as *Over-Nite Sensation*. — *William Ruhlmann*

One Size Fits All / Jun. 25, 1975 / Rykodisc ✦✦✦

Bongo Fury / Oct. 2, 1975 / Rykodisc ✦✦✦

Zappa in New York / Mar. 3, 1978 / Barking Pumpkin ✦✦✦✦

Joe's Garage: Acts 1-3 / 1979 / Rykodisc ✦✦✦✦
As part of its contract to reissue vintage Frank Zappa material, Rykodisc reissued the two parts of *Joe's Garage*, originally released in 1979, on a double-CD in 1987. The album is a concept piece about a future time when music is illegal. In it, Zappa continued his fascination with ethnic stereotypes ("Catholic Girls") and bathroom activities ("Why Does It Hurt When I Pee?"). But he wasn't able to use it to fulfill a satisfying dramatic function. — *William Ruhlmann*

Sleep Dirt / Jan. 19, 1979 / Barking Pumpkin ✦✦✦

Orchestral Favorites / May 4, 1979 / Rykodisc ✦✦✦

Tinsel Town Rebellion / May 17, 1981 / Rykodisc ✦✦✦

You Are What You Is / Sep. 1981 / Barking Pumpkin ✦✦✦✦✦
1981 proved to be another prolific year for Frank Zappa as, counting his three LPs of guitar solos and his two-LP set *Tinsel Town Rebellion*, along with this two-LP set, he released seven LPs' worth of material during the

year, just as he had in 1979. The sarcasm was running heavy on this studio album, with Zappa taking off especially on the beauty/fashion industry in songs like "I'm a Beautiful Guy," "Beauty Knows No Pain," and "Charlie's Enormous Mouth" (the last based on a then-current TV commercial for perfume). Elsewhere, Zappa skewered punk ("Mudd Club"), the hesitant ("The Meek Shall Inherit Nothing"), the stupid ("Dumb All Over"), the religious ("Heavenly Bank Account"), and the depressed ("Suicide Chump") for good measure. — *William Ruhlmann*

Ship Arriving Too Late to Save a Drowning Witch / May 1982 / FZ/ Rykodisc ✦✦✦

Them or Us / Oct. 1984 / Rykodisc ✦✦✦

Thing-Fish / Nov. 1984 / Rykodisc ✦✦✦

Shut up 'n Play Yer Guitar / Sep. 1, 1986 / Rykodisc ✦✦✦✦
This is the first of three albums of guitar solos by Frank Zappa released simultaneously by his mail-order record company, Barking Pumpkin, and subsequently released to retail by Rykodisc on September, 1, 1986, as part of a two-CD set, also called *Shut up 'n Play Yer Guitar*. The tracks were recorded, mostly in concert, in 1979 and 1980, and they demonstrate Zappa's mastery of the electric guitar, establishing him as the peer of the other guitar heroes of his generation. — *William Ruhlmann*

Shut up 'n Play Yer Guitar Some More / Sep. 1, 1986 / Barking Pumpkin ✦✦✦✦
This is the second of three albums of guitar solos by Frank Zappa released simultaneously by his mail-order record company, Barking Pumpkin, and subsequently released to retail by Rykodisc on September 1, 1986, as part of a two-CD set called *Shut up 'n Play Yer Guitar*. This one features "Variations On the Carlos Santana Secret Chord Progression," which should be useful to guitar students everywhere. — *William Ruhlmann*

Jazz from Hell / Nov. 15, 1986 / Rykodisc ✦✦✦✦
This is an album of jazz-rock-oriented instrumental music that, with the exception of the track "St. Etienne," was recorded on the Synclavier music synthesizer. As an expression of Frank Zappa's more popular music styles, it ranks in execution with such albums as *Hot Rats*. It is the winner of a Grammy award for Best Rock Instrumental Performance (Orchestra Group or Soloist). — *William Ruhlmann*

London Symphony Orchestra 2 / 1987 / Rykodisc ✦✦✦

● **You Can't Do That on Stage Anymore, Vol. 1** / May 16, 1988 / Rykodisc ✦✦✦✦
This two-LP set provides a curtain-raiser on the massive *You Can't Do That on Stage Anymore* series and is typical of the approach of the series in that it jumps from one time and band and location to another, leading off, for example, with a version of "Plastic People" recorded by the Mothers of Invention in 1969 and moving immediately to a version of "The Torture Never Stops" by Frank Zappa's band in 1977. Some of Zappa's more entertaining numbers are here, such as "Montana," "King Kong" (a short version from 1982), and "Cosmic Debris," but, as with most of the series, the jumping around gives the album an unfocused feel. — *William Ruhlmann*

Broadway the Hardway / Oct. 1988 / Rykodisc ✦✦✦✦
A live album culled from Zappa's final world tour of 1988. It features his comments on Elvis Presley ("Elvis Has Just Left the Building"), televangelists ("Jesus Thinks You're a Jerk"), and other objects of political scorn. — *William Ruhlmann*

Frank Zappa Meets the Mothers of Prevention / May 1990 / Rykodisc ✦✦✦

The Best Band You Never Heard in Your Life / Apr. 1991 / Barking Pumpkin ✦✦✦✦
This is the second album that Frank Zappa culled from live performances on his final 1988 world tour, the first being *Broadway the Hard Way*. That release contained newly written material; this one, in contrast, contains, as Zappa puts it in his liner notes, "big-band arrangements of concert favorites and obscure album cuts, along with deranged versions of cover tunes and a few premiere recordings." In practice, that means you have the opportunity to hear Zappa treatments of such surprising songs as "Ring of Fire," "I Left My Heart In San Francisco," "Bolero," "Purple Haze," and "Stairway To Heaven." In other words, even for an idiosyncratic artist, this is an idiosyncratic album. (The title derives from Zappa's note that the band "self-destructed" before most of the US could hear it play.) — *William Ruhlmann*

Make a Jazz Noise Here / Jun. 1991 / Barking Pumpkin ✦✦✦

Beat the Boots! [Box] / Jul. 7, 1991 / Rhino ✦✦✦

● **Zappa: The Yellow Shark** / 1993 / Barking Pumpkin ✦✦✦✦
Released only a month before Frank Zappa's death, *The Yellow Shark* is an album of orchestral treatments of Zappa's compositions done by the 25-piece Ensemble Modern orchestra, conducted by Peter Rundel. It features vintage material like "Dog Breath Variations" as well as more recent work, played with more sensitivity and verve than previous

orchestras have brought to Zappa's music. Hence, the "pick" notation should alert fans who want to hear the orchestral Zappa—this is the best executed and most varied of the albums Zappa devoted to his "serious" music. — *William Ruhlmann*

● **Strictly Commercial: The Best of Frank Zappa** / Aug. 22, 1995 / Rykodisc ✦✦✦✦

For all of his many attributes, one thing Frank Zappa most certainly was not is commercial. Presumably, the title of this collection is ironic. *Strictly Commercial: The Best of Frank Zappa* is a compilation not of the composer's hits—he only broke the Top 40 on one occasion, with "Valley Girl"—but rather, a collection of his best-known material, from "Don't Eat the Yellow Snow" to "Sexual Harrassment in the Workplace." Zappa's albums often function as individual works, but the disc offers an intelligent selection of songs, serving as an introduction to the maverick musician. — *Stephen Thomas Erlewine*

Lost Episodes / Feb. 27, 1996 / Rykodisc ✦✦✦✦

A 30-track compilation of rarities, spanning much of his career, but in the main confined to the 1960s and early '70s (some date from as early as the late '50s!). Much of it's previously unreleased, or extremely hard to locate. It's not just a collection of fan-oriented odds and ends, though. The material, for one thing, is extremely diverse, ranging from collaborations with Captain Beefheart and primitive teenage garage recordings to comic dialog to progressive instrumentals and orchestral pieces. The pre-*Freak Out* stuff in particular is revelatory, in the sense that it finds Zappa's sophisticated compositional and arrangement skills in full bloom years before he made his proper debut. There's also good old rock 'n' roll, in an early version of "Any Way the Wind Blows," and an early '60s take of "Fountain of Love" with explosive fuzz bass. The cuts range in duration from 11 seconds to 11 minutes, often connected by amusing bits of spoken patter or nifty instrumental links. The effect is somewhat like *Uncle Meat* or *Lumpy Gravy*, meaning that those who appreciate that period of Zappa's evolution will find an immediate affinity with this anthology. —*Richie Unterberger*

Warren Zevon

b. Jan. 24, 1947, Chicago, IL

Bass, Guitar, Keyboards, Vocals / Rock 'n' roll, Singer-Songwriter

How did a guy with such a wickedly black sense of humor and a love for tough rock 'n' roll get to be a '70s Los Angeles songwriting pro? By tempering that dark streak with some evocative and personal ballads, which surveyed the trappings of the Los Angeles lifestyle. Even at his worst, Zevon was always better than the Eagles, and with less sexism to boot. —*John Floyd*

Warren Zevon / 1976 / Asylum ✦✦✦✦

A beautiful and ambitious debut, it paints a gloomy and cryptic portrait of Hollywood's casualties through gripping songs like "Carmelita," "I'll Sleep When I'm Dead," and "Mohammed's Radio." —*John Floyd*

Excitable Boy / 1978 / Asylum ✦✦✦✦

A disappointing followup, Zevon's sensitivity is sacrificed for mere weirdness. Nevertheless, there's some fine music here. —*John Floyd*

Bad Luck Streak in Dancing School / 1980 / Asylum ✦✦

Stand in the Fire / 1981 / Asylum ✦✦✦

The Envoy / 1982 / Asylum ✦✦✦

● **A Quiet Normal Life: The Best of Warren Zevon** / 1986 / Asylum ✦✦✦✦

This is an adequate but skimpy best-of. —*John Floyd*

Sentimental Hygiene / 1987 / Virgin ✦✦✦✦

Warren Zevon returned in 1987 with his first new album in five years, *Sentimental Hygiene*. Featuring musical support by R.E.M., Zevon's songs take on a tough but melodic edge and the songs comprise his most consistent and impressive set since *Excitable Boy*. —*Stephen Thomas Erlewine*

Transverse City / 1989 / Virgin ✦✦✦

Mr. Bad Example / 1991 / Giant ✦✦

Learning to Flinch / 1993 / Warner Bros. ✦✦✦

Zombies

British Invasion, Psychedelic, Pop-Rock

Aside from the Beatles and perhaps the Beach Boys, no mid-'60s rock group wrote melodies as gorgeous as those of the Zombies. Dominated by Colin Blunstone's breathy vocals, choral backup harmonies, and Rod Argent's shining jazz- and classical-influenced organ and piano, the band sounded utterly unique for their era. Indeed, their material—penned by either Argent or guitarist Chris White, with unexpected shifts from major to minor keys—was perhaps too adventurous for the singles market. To this day, they're known primarily for their three big hit singles, "She's Not There" (1964), "Tell Her No" (1965), and "Time of the Season" (1969).

Most listeners remain unaware that the group maintained a remarkably high quality of work for several years.

The Zombies formed in the London suburb of St. Albans in the early '60s, and actually didn't entertain serious professional ambitions until they won a local contest, the prize being an opportunity to record a demo for consideration at major labels. Argent's composition "She's Not There" got them a deal with Decca, and the song ended up being their debut release. It was a remarkably confident and original first-time effort, with a great minor melody and the organ, harmonies, and urgent, almost neurotic vocals that would typify much of their work. It did well enough in Britain (making the Top 20), but did even better in the States, where it went to No. 2.

In fact the group would experience a lot more success across the waters than they did at home throughout their career. In early 1965, another piece of classic British Invasion pop, "Tell Her No," went into the Top Ten. Yet that was as much Top 40 success as the group would have for several years.

The tragedy was that throughout 1965 and 1966, the Zombies released a string of equally fine, intricately arranged singles that flopped commercially, at a time in which chart success on 45s was a lot more important to sustain a band's livelihood than it would be a few years down the road. "Remember When I Loved Her," "I Want You Back Again," "Indication," "She's Coming Home," "Whenever You're Ready," "Gotta Get a Hold of Myself," "I Must Move," "Remember You," "Just out of Reach," "How We Were Before"—all are lost classics, some relegated to B-sides, that went virtually unheard, all showing the group eager to try new ideas and expand their approaches. What's worse, the lack of a big single denied the group opportunities to record albums—only one LP, rushed out to capitalize on the success of "She's Not There," would appear before 1968.

Their failure to achieve more widespread success is a bit mystifying, perhaps explained by a few factors. While undeniably pop-based, their original compositions and arrangements were in some senses too adventurous for the radio. "Indication," for instance, winds down with a lengthy, torturous swirl of bitter organ solos and wordless, windblown vocals; "Remember When I Loved Her," despite its beautiful melody, has downbeat lyrics that are almost morbid; "I Want You Back Again" is arranged like a jazz waltz, with the sorts of sudden stops, tempo shifts, and lengthy minor organ solos found in a lot of their tunes. The group were also, perhaps unfairly, saddled with a somewhat square image; much was made of their formidable scholastic record, and they most definitely did not align themselves with the R&B-based school of British bands, preferring more subtle and tuneful territory.

By 1967, the group hadn't had a hit for quite some time, and reckoned it was time to pack it in. Their Decca contract expired early in the year, and the Zombies signed with CBS for one last album, knowing before the sessions it was to be their last. A limited budget precluded the use of many session musicians, which actually worked to the band's advantage, as they became among the first to utilize the then-novel Mellotron to emulate strings and horns.

Odessey and Oracle, the group's only cohesive full-length platter (the first album was largely pasted together from singles and covers). A near-masterpiece of pop/psychedelia, it showed the group reaching new levels of sophistication in composition and performance, finally branching out beyond strictly romantic themes into more varied lyrical territory. The album passed virtually unnoticed in Britain, and was only released in the States after some lobbying from Al Kooper. By this time it was 1968, and the group had split for good.

The Zombies had been defunct for some time when one of the tracks from *Odessey*, "Time of the Season," was released as a single, almost as an afterthought. It took off in early 1969 to become their biggest hit, but the members resisted temptations to reform, leading to a couple of bizarre tours in the late '60s by bogus "Zombies" with no relation to the original group. By this time, Rod Argent was already recording as the leader of Argent, which went in a harder rock direction than the Zombies. After a spell as an insurance clerk, Blunstone had some success (more in Britain than America) in the early '70s as a solo vocalist, with material that often amounted to soft-rock variations on the Zombies sound.

Much more influential than their commercial success would indicate, echoes of the Zombies' innovations can be heard in the Doors, the Byrds, the Left Banke, the Kinks, and many others. After a long period during which most of their work was out of print, virtually all of their recordings have been restored to availability on CD. —*Richie Unterberger*

Odessey & Oracle / 1968 / Rhino ✦✦✦✦

A psychedelic effort whose best song, "Time of the Season," became a monster hit with a sultry, soulful sound not replicated elsewhere on the album. —*Bruce Eder*

Time of the Zombies / 1973 / Epic ✦✦✦

Live on the BBC / 1985 / Rhino ✦✦✦

Best & the Rest of the Zombies / 1986 / Back-Trac ✦✦✦

★ **Singles A's & B's** / 1990 / See For Miles ✦✦✦✦✦

While "She's Not There" and "Tell Her No" are the only well-remembered mid-'60s Zombies singles, they recorded quite a few great non-hit 45s as well during this period. This outstanding collection (now available on CD) features all 22 of the sides they released on singles between 1964-67, and shows the group to be among the most superbly inventive pop-rock composers of their era, exploring moody minor-key melodies more than anyone before or since. Colin Blunstone's delicate, neurotic vocals and Rod Argent's biting electric keyboards pace the band on this set, which features the two big hits and such great lost classics as "Remember When I Loved Her," "I Want You Back Again," "I Must Move," "Indication," and "Gotta Get a Hold of Myself." Essential British Invasion music. —*Richie Unterberger*

ZZ Top

Group / Rock 'n' Roll, Blues-Rock, Hard Rock, Boogie Rock

This sturdy American blues-rock trio from Texas consists of Billy Gibbons (guitar), Dusty Hill (bass), and Frank Beard (drums). They were formed in 1970 in and around Houston from rival bands the Moving Sidewalks (Gibbons) and the American Blues (Hill and Beard). Their first two albums reflected the strong blues roots and Texas humor of the band. Their third album (*Tres Hombres*) gained them national attention with hit "La Grange," a signature riff tune to this day, based on John Lee Hooker's "Boogie Chillen." Their success continued unabated throughout the '70s, culminating with the year-and-a-half-long Worldwide Texas Tour.

Exhausted from the overwhelming work load, they took a three-year break, then switched labels and returned to form with *Deguello* and *El Loco*, both harbingers of what was to come. By their next album, *Eliminator*, and its worldwide smash follow-up, *Afterburner*, they had successfully harnessed the potential of synthesizers to their patented grungy blues-groove, giving their material a more contemporary edge while retaining their patented Texas style. Now sporting long beards, golf hats, and boiler suits, they met the emerging video age head-on, reducing their "message" to simple iconography. Becoming even more popular in the long run, they moved with the times while simultaneously bucking every trend that crossed their path. As genuine roots musicians, they have few peers; Gibbons is one of America's finest blues guitarists working in the arena of rock idiom—both influenced by the originators of the form and British blues-rock guitarists like Peter Green—while Hill and Beard provide the ultimate rhythm section support. The only rock 'n' roll group that's out there with its original members still aboard after 20-plus years, ZZ Top's music is always instantly recognizable, eminently powerful, profoundly soulful, and 100% American in derivation. They have continued to support the blues through various means, perhaps the most visible when they were given a piece of wood from Muddy Waters' shack in Clarksdale, MS. The group members had it made into a guitar, dubbed the "Muddywood," then sent it out on tour to raise money for the Delta Blues Museum. ZZ Top's support and link to the blues remains as rock solid as the music they play. —*Cub Koda*

ZZ Top's First Album / 1970 / Warner Bros. ✦✦✦

Rio Grande Mud / 1972 / Warner Bros. ✦✦✦

Tres Hombres / 1973 / Warner Bros. ✦✦✦✦

Constant touring and favorable radio exposure made *Tres Hombres* ZZ's first hit album, thanks in no small part to "La Grange," an ode to a whorehouse. By this album, Billy Gibbons had practically perfected his distinctively dirty electric-guitar sound. His riffs and chordal voicings were also more memorable. Highlights included "Beer Drinkers & Hell Raisers," "Precious & Grace," "Waitin' for the Bus," and "Jesus Just Left Chicago." —*Rick Clark*

Fandango / 1975 / Warner Bros. ✦✦✦

★ **The Best of ZZ Top** / 1977 / Warner Bros. ✦✦✦✦✦

The sound may be a little muddy, but this anthology is still the best representation of ZZ's early work. It contains classic rude, riff-heavy bluesrockers like "Just Got Paid," "Jesus Just Left Chicago," "Heard It on the X," "Tush," and "La Grange." —*Rick Clark*

Deguello / 1979 / Warner Bros. ✦✦✦✦

Deguello was ZZ's best album from their pre-robotic blues-rock period—the last reminder of what a tough ensemble this trio could be. It was the first time they infused their lunkhead approach to fast cars, kinky girls, and partying with some bizarre humor. Their version of Sam & Dave's "I Thank You" (No. 34) became their first Top 40 hit in five years. Other highlights included the oddball "Manic Mechanic," a riproaring version of Elmore James's "Dust My Broom," the funky boogie of "Cheap Sunglasses," and "Fool for Your Stockings," a down-and-dirty fetish blues. —*Rick Clark*

El Loco / 1981 / Warner Bros. ✦✦✦

Eliminator / 1983 / Warner Bros. ✦✦✦✦

Hardcore fans might have cried "sellout," but ZZ's introduction of a streamlined synth-heavy sound (and three slickly produced T&A videos)

turned this trio from potential blues-rock has-beens to multi-platinum purveyors of space boogie. Most of this album became a staple on album rock radio, with "Gimme All Your Lovin'" (No. 37), "Sharp Dressed Man" (No. 56), and "Legs" (No. 8) becoming the primary hits. —*Rick Clark*

Afterburner / 1985 / Warner Bros. ✦✦✦

Recycler / 1990 / Warner Bros. ✦✦✦

● **Greatest Hits** / 1992 / Warner Bros. ✦✦✦✦

An 18-song compilation, it features the greatest hits of ZZ Top's MTV era, including "Gimme All Your Lovin'," "Sharp Dressed Man," "Tush," "Pearl Necklace," "Cheap Sunglasses," "Sleeping Bag," "Rough Boy," and a remixed version of "Legs." It's a good, fun collection that should have been sequenced better and, unfortunately, omits a few good songs. —*AMG*

Antenna / 1994 / RCA ✦✦✦

One Foot in the Blues / 1994 / Warner Bros. ✦✦

Various Artists

'70s Teen Idols / Rhino ✦✦✦✦✦

A fun collection of the lightweight pin-up stars of the '70s. *Yesterday's Heroes: '70s Teen Idols* is the perfect compliment to Rhino's *Have a Nice Day* series. It's some serious fun. —*AMG*

18 Soul Hits from the '60s / 1996 / JCI ✦✦✦

There are better and more extensive '60s soul collections around, but sticking just to the contents at hand, this is first-rate stuff by any measure. Includes major hits by James Brown, Wilson Pickett, the Isley Brothers, Sam & Dave, Otis Redding, Carla Thomas, and Johnnie Taylor, as well as big singles by minor performers like the Capitols, Archie Bell, Fontella Bass, Don Covay, Robert Parker, and James & Bobby Purify. —*Richie Unterberger*

AK-47 / Mushroom ✦✦✦✦

AK-47 is probably the best compilation of New Zealand's entries for punk rock and new wave of the late '70s. While most of this material was released on small independent labels like Ripper, Propeller, Flying Nun, and Mushroom and never saw any exposure outside of New Zealand, the quality of the songs and raw energy behind them should appeal to genre specialists and certainly deserves discovery. Included are rarities from the brilliant yet underrated Swingers, Suburban Reptiles, and Toy Love, among others. —*Chris Woodstra*

● **Acid Visions: Best of Texas Punk/Psychedelic, Vol. 1** / Collectables ✦✦✦✦✦

One of the very best '60s garage compilations, a high compliment given the thousands of competitors, and the very best Texas '60s garage anthology. With the possible exception of California, Texas was home to more fine obscure garage records than any other state, and these 14 cuts are among the finest. Roy Head delivers a fine Johnny Winter tune, "Easy Lovin' Girl," and Winter himself sings a prime slice of folk-rock-acidpunk, "Birds Can't Row Boats" (this version, incidentally, is much better than the one found on the early Winter compilation of the same name). The other names are totally obscure, and some of the tracks weren't even released until the 1980s. But the Things and the Bad Roads come through with fine pop-punk numbers, and A-440's "Torture," Satori's "Time Machine," and the Pandas' "Walk" have been belatedly recognized as some of the best garage psychedelia ever, combining sharp melodic hooks and songwriting with out-and-out dementia. —*Richie Unterberger*

The Adventures of Priscilla Queen of the Desert / 1994 / Mother ✦✦✦✦✦

An irresistible set of disco classics (some available in their original, rare 12-inch mixes), the soundtrack to the drag queen epic *Priscilla, Queen of the Desert* is a thoroughly engaging album, ranking as one of the best disco compilations available. —*Stephen Thomas Erlewine*

Another Saturday Night: Classic Recordings From the Louisiana Bayous / 1990 / Ace (UK) ✦✦✦

Southern Louisiana is home to the fascinating hybrid of music known as swamp pop, which mixes ingredients from rock, country, rockabilly, blues, soul, and Cajun into its own idiosyncratic brew. It's rarely achieved much popularity outside its region; the flip side of that is its enduring popularity in its own backyard, despite the increasing homogenization of American pop. This compiles 20 tracks (most from the '60s and early '70s) that illustrate the style, ranging from swamp pop-influenced straightahead rock to cuts that almost fall in the mainstream of Cajun music. They're quite obscure; Cookie and His Cupcakes and Tommy McLain are the best known names, but still ones that are barely known unless you're deeply into the genre. The records chosen for the anthology are good-natured and swinging, yet this is more of a folklore document than a set of exciting pop-rock tunes. Pleasant but not memorable. —*Richie Unterberger*

☆ **Atlantic R&B**—1947-1974 / 1991 / Atlantic ✦✦✦✦✦
Along with Specialty, Aladdin, Chess, Sun, and a few other labels, Atlantic paved the way for rock 'n' roll. Started by Ahmet Ertegun and Herb Abramson in 1947, Atlantic brought meticulous recording techniques—usually reserved only for jazz sessions—to R&B. They assembled a revolving cast of crack studio musicians. This seven-disc set (eight CDs on the box set) is a perfect collection of all the best singles from Atlantic Records. —*John Floyd*

Atlantic Sisters of Soul / 1992 / Rhino ✦✦✦✦✦
A fine collection of lesser-known female soul artists on Atlantic, including artists that aren't normally associated with the label, like Mary Wells and the Pointer Sisters. All of the songs were recorded in the late '60s and early '70s, and only three of its 23 tracks scratched the R&B Top 20, although most of the tracks were good enough to be hits. While the songs may not be familiar, their sweet sound is, making the disc a worthwhile purchase for fans of early-'70s soul. —*Stephen Thomas Erlewine*

★ **Back to Mono (1958-1969)** / 1991 / ABKCO ✦✦✦✦✦
If you look hard enough, you can find decent one-album samplers of Phil Spector's greatest recordings, but this four-disc box set (three sets of singles and the entire *A Christmas Gift for You* on the fourth) is the jewel of Spector's legacy. Aside from his sporadic '70s productions, *Back to Mono* contains everything you'd ever want by rock's supreme romantic: early productions with Curtis Lee, Ben E. King, and Gene Pitney; the girl group effervescence of the Ronettes, the Crystals, and Darlene Love; the soul innovations of the Righteous Brothers and the Checkmates; and his notorious sessions with Ike and Tina Turner. Throughout the set, Spector's artistic vision (which has influenced dozens of producers and hundreds of performers) shines like the smile on a lover's lips. This is one of the greatest and most fully realized boxw sets ever issued. —*John Floyd*

☆ **Beach Classics: All Original Recordings** / 1987 / Dcc ✦✦✦✦✦
A terrific 20-song collection of surf hits from the early '60s, including the classics "Miserlou," "California Sun," and "Surfin' Bird," as well as many forgotten gems. Not only is the song selection first rate, but the sound is as good as it could be, considering that the original master tapes were probably not well preserved. —*Stephen Thomas Erlewine*

Beatle Originals (Original Versions of the Songs the Beatles Made Famous) / 1986 / Rhino ✦✦✦✦✦
A pretty neat concept for a record: 13 of the *original* versions of the more obscure songs covered by the Beatles on their early albums. The biggest hits that the group interpreted—early Motown songs, Chuck Berry rockers, "Twist and Shout," "Long Tall Sally," "Chains," "Baby It's You"—are not here, on the reasonable grounds that the originals are easily available, and most likely in the collection of many Beatle fans already. Instead it has the less-traveled original tracks by Larry Williams and Carl Perkins (three songs apiece), Little Richard's "Kansas City/Hey Hey Hey," Buddy Holly's "Words of Love," Arthur Alexander's "Anna," the Shirelles' "Boys," and Buck Owens' "Act Naturally." The most noteworthy items are the two tracks which even collectors found difficult to locate: the Donays' girl group single "Devil in His Heart," and Dr. Feelgood's "Mr. Moonlight." The material is classic in its own right: equally important, it gives Beatle fans the opportunity to hear original versions that were virtually inaccessible for years, compare them to the (usually great) renditions by the Beatles, and appreciate the well-rounded scope of their influences. Unfortunately, it does not include the prototype versions of "A Taste of Honey" and "Till There Was You," on the debatable premise that they were too pop-oriented to warrant interest. —*Richie Unterberger*

The Best of Ace Records: The Pop Hits, Vol. 1 / 1992 / Scotti Bros. ✦✦✦
In the late '50s and early '60s, Ace was one of the most successful New Orleans-based rock 'n' roll labels, recording hits by Huey Smith, Frankie Ford, and Jimmy Clanton. This 14-song compilation isn't the best way to hear the Ace catalog, though. Ford and Smith, both of whom have tracks here, are better represented by full compilations of their work; Ford's magnificent "Sea Cruise" is here, but Smith's only big hit, "Don't You Just Know It," is strangely missing in favor of a couple much less renowned tracks. Clanton recorded some nice hits in the teen idol style ("Just a Dream," "Venus in Blue Jeans," and "Go, Jimmy, Go"), all of which are here. But these sound misplaced next to Ford and Smith, and the other Clanton cuts are weak. There's also a rare early single by Joe Tex, "Charlie Brown Got Expelled," an answer record to the Coasters' "Charlie Brown." —*Richie Unterberger*

Best of Ace Records, Vol. 2: R&B Hits / 1993 / Scotti Bros. ✦✦✦✦
Scotti Brothers' two volumes of highlights from Ace Records' roster are the best available sampler of the label's late-'50s/early-'60s R&B and pop hits, featuring such stars as Huey "Piano" Smith, Frankie Ford, Joe Tex, and Jimmy Clanton. Both volumes have detailed liner notes and great songs; both are essential for comprehensive rock and R&B collections. —*Stephen Thomas Erlewine*

☆ **The Best of Chess R&B, Vol. 1** / MCA ✦✦✦✦✦
This Chess R&B anthology came out initially in a pair of double-album

sets. Then it was reissued on two CDs, with each disc covering one of the albums, although they left some tracks off each volume due to programming restrictions. This covers the first double album and includes cuts from the Moonglows, some early Miracles, Etta James, Sugar Pie Desanto, Jan Bradley, Billy Stewart, and Little Milton. —*Ron Wynn*

☆ **The Best of Chess R&B, Vol. 2** / MCA ✦✦✦✦✦
The second Chess CD covers the second double album and features later R&B cuts from Billy Stewart, Mitty Collier, the Dells, Jackie Ross, Etta James, the Ramsey Lewis Trio, and the Radiants. The stylistic lines are blurred a bit here, since some of these artists were also featured on the *Best of Chess* soul anthology that had been previously issued. —*Ron Wynn*

☆ **The Best of Chess Rhythm & Blues** / Chess ✦✦✦✦✦
A good various-artists collection from the great Chicago R&B label, it includes Fontella Bass' "Rescue Me," Billy Stewart's "Summertime," Jan Bradley's "Mama Didn't Lie," and an early Smokey Robinson & the Miracles effort, "Bad Girl." —*Dan Heilman*

☆ **The Best of Chess Rock & Roll** / Chess ✦✦✦✦✦
Over two separate volumes, *Best of Chess Rock & Roll* gives a good portrait of the seminal record label's massive contributions to rock 'n' roll. Not only are landmarks like Chuck Berry's "Johnny B. Goode" and Bo Diddley's "Bo Diddley" covered, cult favorites like the Moonglows and the Students are also featured. With "Johnny B. Goode," "Maybelline," "Who Do You Love," "Ain't Got No Home," "Rocket 88," and "Susie Q" all on the first volume, it is one of the most essential single-disc rock collections ever assembled; the second volume is nearly as important, with "Book of Love," "High Heel Sneakers," "No Particular Place to Go," "Ten Commandments of Love," and "Road Runner" among the featured tracks. —*Stephen Thomas Erlewine*

The Best of Chess Vocal Groups / Chess ✦✦✦✦✦
Rounding out the trilogy of Chess sampler albums, this one features "Long Lonely Nights" by Lee Andrews & the Hearts, the highly influential "Every Day of the Week" by the Students, and the Southern soul of the Knight Brothers "Temptation 'Bout to Get Me." —*Cub Koda*

☆ **Best of Excello Records, Vol. 1** / 1991 / Rhino ✦✦✦✦✦
The Nashville-based Excello label specialized in obscure blues, R&B, and rock 'n' roll from the '50s and early '60s. This first volume of *Sound of the Swamp (The Best of Excello Records)* covers the best from Crowley, LA, producer Jay Miller's blues, rockabilly, and swamp-pop sides. —*John Floyd*

★ **The Best of New Orleans Rhythm & Blues, Vol. 1** / 1988 / Rhino ✦✦✦✦✦
Some of the greatest music ever, period—The Meters, Clarence Henry, Lloyd Price, etc. Endless groovin'. —*Jeff Tamarkin*

The Best of Sue Records / Collectables ✦✦✦✦✦
Find out why Sue Records was one of New Orleans' greatest and most revered R&B/soul labels, and the early home to such artists as Aaron Neville and Ike & Tina Turner. —*John Floyd*

Beyond the Wall of Sound / Roxy ✦✦✦
Like its sister compilation *Lookin' for Boys*, this is the finest anthology of obscure girl group singles. *Lookin' for Boys* has the edge for its slightly stronger track selection, but this features several cuts that are almost as great as the best classics of the genre, especially the rarities by Diane Renay ("Watch Out Sally"), Shelley Fabares ("He Don't Love Me"), and Shirley Matthews ("Big Town Boy"). —*Richie Unterberger*

Billboard Top Dance Hits: 1976 / 1976 / Rhino ✦✦✦✦✦
Covering the disco years in detail, Rhino's five-volume *Billboard Top Dance Hits* series is a worthwhile budget retrospective. It isn't as complete or definitive as the label's *Disco Years* series, but it features several tracks that didn't make that series, as well as songs that aren't easily available on other compilations, making it necessary for disco fans. Ten of the top dance hits for each year from 1976 to 1980 are featured on each disc, including such hits as "You Should Be Dancing," "Love Hangover," "Ring My Bell," "You Make Me Feel (Mighty Real)," "Funkytown," "Got to Give It Up," and "Call Me" in their original single form. Unlike the other *Billboard* series, *Top Dance Hits* actually has liner notes about the songs, not trivia about a particular year. —*Stephen Thomas Erlewine*

☆ **Billboard Top Hits: 1980** / 1992 / Rhino ✦✦✦✦✦
When Rhino's *Billboard Top Hits* series hit the 1980s, the collection began to lose a little steam. From 1980 through 1985, the discs are representative of the pop mainstream, although there were the usual major artists missing. Still, the discs contained plenty of one-hit wonders and classic singles like "Bette Davis Eyes," "Jessie's Girl," "Down Under," "Maneater," and "Centerfold," with the highest concentration of good singles on the 1983 volume. As the series approached the end of the decade, the problem of licensing reared its ugly head; not only were major artists like Madonna, Prince, Phil Collins, and Guns N' Roses unavailable, but smaller artists like Rick Astley, Roxette, Poison, and Michael Damien also don't appear. Although there are a couple of enjoyable period pieces, like

Donny Osmond's "Soldier of Love," the bulk of the tracks can't cover the absence of "Never Gonna Give You Up," "Every Rose Has Its Thorn," and "The Look." Perhaps these should have waited a couple of years. *—Stephen Thomas Erlewine*

☆ **Billboard Top R&B Hits: 1955** / 1989 / Rhino ♦♦♦♦♦
Despite its faults, Rhino's *Billboard Top R&B Hits* is one of the finest retrospectives of R&B from 1955 to 1974 ever assembled. The song selection was sometimes puzzling, the liner notes nonexistent, and each disc only had ten tracks, frequently lasting under half an hour. However, the 20-disc series featured most of the major artists and singles of each individual year, as well as providing a rough sketch of the evolution from R&B to soul to disco. For beginners, such an affordable introduction was invaluable; for collectors, the brevity may have been frustrating, but they couldn't argue with the fidelity or the fact that many of these songs were appearing on disc for the first time. Legends like Clyde McPhatter, Little Richard, Jackie Wilson, James Brown, Ben E. King, Brook Benton, Marvin Gaye, Temptations, Supremes, Aretha Franklin, Smokey Robinson, Isley Brothers, Sly Stone, and Curtis Mayfield are featured. The series is currently out of print, but can still be found in cut-out bins. *—Stephen Thomas Erlewine*

☆ **Billboard Top Rock & Roll Hits: 1955** / 1988 / Rhino ♦♦♦♦♦
Despite its many faults, Rhino's *Billboard Top Rock & Roll Hits* is as good an introduction to the consistently diverse music as possible. It's marred by a confusing song selection, poor liner notes, and brevity, as well as the omission of several important pop, rock, and album-rock artists. However, the series isn't attempting to be comprehensive. Instead, it offers a view of the popular mainstream for each year from 1955 to 1974 at an affordable price. With Elvis, Chuck Berry, Fats Domino, Jerry Lee Lewis, the Everly Brothers, Buddy Holly, and Carl Perkins on the initial '50s volumes, the discs are essential. As the series moves into the '60s, the discs remain remarkably consistent, featuring several Phil Spector hits, the Beach Boys, Dion, and the Kingsmen. It's only in the mid-'60s that the series begins to represent only radio hits, instead of portraying what was really happening during the era. Nevertheless, the 20 discs remain enjoyable listening. *—Stephen Thomas Erlewine*

☆ **Billboard Top Rock & Roll Hits: 1975** / 1991 / Rhino ♦♦♦♦♦
Rhino ended its *Billboard Top Rock & Roll Hits* series with the 1974 volume, replacing it with the *Billboard Top Hits* series beginning with the year 1975. It has the same faults and attributes as the *Rock & Roll* series; the only difference is the fact that it merges R&B hits with the pop singles. Since the late '70s were filled with cheerfully disposable pop singles, each volume differs greatly in quality; the 1978 and 1979 discs are the most consistent, with several soft-rock and disco hits on each album. Rhino's *Have a Nice Day* and *Disco Years* series cover this era in greater detail, with more hits and novelty items on both series; however, these are concise, fun snapshots of a particularly embarrassing and enjoyable moment in pop history. *—Stephen Thomas Erlewine*

Birth of Soul / 1996 / Kent ♦♦♦♦♦
An ingenious mix of 28 pivotal tracks from 1957-1965, mostly from the early '60s, that helped lay the groundwork for soul music. Some heavy-duty collectors may have wished these were all rarities, rather than a blend of hits and rarities. But it must be said that several of the hits here don't turn up on many compilations, like the ones by Inez & Charlie Foxx ("Mockingbird"), the Tams ("Hey Girl Don't Bother Me"), Joe Henderson ("Snap Your Fingers"), Bobby Bland ("Ain't Nothing You Can Do"), and the Marvelows ("I Do"). And there are plenty of nifty collector items as well: outtakes by Otis Redding and Wiliam Bell, "answer" records by Thelma Kilgore and Gloria Lynne, and early Southern soul by Jimmy Hughes. A special treat is the rabble-rousing city soul of Derek Martin's "Daddy Rollin' Stone," which became one of the Who's most obscure tracks when they covered it on the B-side of their second British 45 in 1965. The compilation may fall between the cracks of general soul listeners and soul specialists. But if you don't have most of the tracks yet, it's a good survey of early soul, with an all-encompassing diversity that includes many regional styles and embraces both "down-home" and "uptown" productions. *—Richie Unterberger*

Blackbox: Wax Trax! Records: The First 13 Years / 1994 / Wax Trax! ♦♦♦♦♦
Wax Trax is the defining industrial music label; *Blackbox* is the definitive statement on their accomplishment. More than any other label, they defined the corrosive guitars, synths, distorted vocals, and jackhammer beats that came to define industrial. Ministry, KMFDM, and Trent Reznor all recorded for them. *Blackbox* gathers nearly every worthwhile song to emerge from the Chicago label, including many rare singles, and provides an excellent introduction and summary of the most cutting-edge dance music of the 1980s and '90s. *—Stephen Thomas Erlewine*

☆ **Brief History of Ambient, Vol. 1** / Feb. 22, 1994 / Virgin ♦♦♦♦♦
Although it seemed to arrive out of nowhere in the early '90s, ambient music actually has a long and varied history, leading back to Brian Eno and Kraftwerk's electronic experiments in the 1970s right up to Aphex Twin's textural techno soundscapes. As an introduction and history lesson, the two-disc *A Brief History of Ambient Music* can't be beat; it shows that the latest techno trend has roots that most fans wouldn't even realize existed. *—Stephen Thomas Erlewine*

Brill Building Sound / 1993 / Era ♦♦♦♦♦
Although Phil Spector's songs weren't available due to licensing restrictions, the four-CD box set *The Brill Building Sound* remains an important and entertaining collection, featuring many of the songs that made the Brill Building a pop music institution in the early '60s. *—Stephen Thomas Erlewine*

★ **The British Invasion: History of British Rock, Vols. 1-9** / 1991 / Rhino ♦♦♦♦♦
Imagine nine CDs (available separately or in a box) of those classic AM radio hits of the '60s, all of them from England, most of them as fresh-sounding and exciting as they were more than two decades ago. Now imagine that these nine CDs are devoid of Beatles (except for one early track), Stones, Who, early Animals, Dave Clark Five, and Herman's Hermits (all due to licensing problems), but that you won't miss them, and you'll get an idea of just how much quality pop-rock 'n' roll came out of the UK in those several years. Included are the Kinks, Zombies, Hollies, Small Faces, Yardbirds, Manfred Mann, Them, Donovan, Peter and Gordon, Bee Gees, Cream, and much more. *—Jeff Tamarkin*

British R & B Explosion: '62-'68, Vol. 1 / See For Miles ♦♦♦
There really isn't any thread tying this 20-track compilation together, other than the fact that all of them originally appeared on Decca Records. It does offer the British Invasion collector a convenient way to gather up some loose ends, including rare early singles by Rod Stewart and Joe Cocker, three Graham Bond rarities that only appeared on an EP and a compilation, obscure 45s by cult artists Graham Gouldman, Duffy Power, and Zoot Money, and garage-cum-R&B cuts by Blues by Five, the Fairies, and others. The problem is, most of it's fairly humdrum: the really good selections (by the Fairies and Them) are easily available elsewhere, and much of the rest is pedestrian, even strained, British R&B. The top find is Tony Knight's "I Feel So Blue," which is not exactly R&B, but sounds like a Joe Meek production with its hyperventilating tempo and brilliant nervous guitar line. *—Richie Unterberger*

The Brunswick Years, Vol. 1 / 1995 / Brunswick ♦♦♦
In the 1960s and early 1970s, the Brunswick label recorded some of the best soul to come out of Chicago. This two-disc, 40-song collection would have ranked higher if the organization was a little less scattered. The cuts by Jackie Wilson, Gene Chandler, Tyrone Davis, Young-Holt Unlimited, and the Chi-Lites are mostly good, but are better heard in the context of those artists' own compilations. Collectors will welcome the presence of rarer items by Barbara Acklin, Billy Butler, the Artistics, Otis Leavill, and Erma Franklin (Aretha's sister), though these tracks are pleasant period fare, not obscure classics. This isn't a bad anthology for those who prefer their vintage soul on the sweet side, but it's probably only worthwhile for specialists. *—Richie Unterberger*

● **Bubblegum Classics, Vol. 1 & 2** / 1995 / Varese Vintage ♦♦♦♦♦
Although they're missing a few key tracks (notably the Archies' hits and Kasenetz-Katz's "Quick Joey Small"), these are the best collections of late-'60s and early-'70s bubblegum hits ever assembled, including most of the major hits and a fair number of enticing rarities. In their favor, they encompass not just the most infantile, pre-teen smashes of the genre (1910 Fruitgum Co., Tommy Roe, Bobby Sherman), but also quite a few cuts that could just as easily be classified as enjoyable, highly polished mainstream pop-rock (the Monkees, Tommy James, the Cuff Links, Keith, the Five Americans, the Flying Machine). Running at 20 tracks each, they're maybe a bit much all at once, but they're the best overview of a significant chapter in rock history. *—Richie Unterberger*

Carnival Time: The Best of Ric Records, Vol. 1 / 1988 / Rounder ♦♦♦♦♦
Stomping, romping good, time numbers are the menu on this 14-track anthology issued in 1988. Such artists as Joe Jones, Al Johnson, Johnny Adams, and Edgar Blanchard were hit acts in New Orleans at the time, but made raw music intended for only for the R&B faithful. While an occasional number like Adams' "I Won't Cry" or Jones' "You Talk Too Much" got a little pop attention, most, like Blanchard's hot "Let's Get It" and Tommy Ridgley's "She's Got What It Takes," didn't move anyone who didn't already have the soul spirit, and that's what made them great. *—Ron Wynn*

Casablanca Records Story / 1994 / Casablanca/Mercury ♦♦♦♦
Even though it includes four discs, *The Casablanca Records Story* ignores the record label's biggest success, Kiss. But that doesn't matter; Kiss didn't fit into the rest of the label's roster. Driven by the massive success of Donna Summer, Casablanca was arguably the definitive disco label in the late '70s, scoring a string of hit singles that have become classics of the era. Featuring four discs of original single versions and 12-inch mixes, *The Casablanca Records Story* features most of the best music the label released, even though it probably could have been more effectively compiled on two or three discs. Nevertheless, there is plenty of fine,

even seminal, music here, which makes it essential for serious disco collectors. *—Stephen Thomas Erlewine*

Chartbusters: The Best of Beserkley, 1975-1978 / Rhino ✦✦✦✦✦
Beserkley never scored any chart hits, but they were one of the best American independent record labels of the late '70s and early '80s, featuring such cult favorites as Jonathan Richman and Greg Kihn. *Best of the Beserkley Years* gathers up some the label's best stripped-down rock 'n' roll, offering a good picture of their music. *—Stephen Thomas Erlewine*

Cheatin': From a Woman's Point of View / 1995 / Ichiban/Soul Classics ✦✦✦
Nifty collection of soul tunes which, just as the title says, deal with cheatin' lovers. Most of these date from the late '60s and early '70s, and while one of these was a Top Ten pop hit (Betty Wright's "Clean Up Woman"), the majority were much bigger on the R&B charts. These include little-anthologized Top Ten R&B hits by Dee Dee Warwick, the Soul Children, and Barbara Moon. There are also pretty well-known soul classics by Laura Lee ("Dirty Man") and Ann Peebles ("Part Time Love"), one of Gladys Knight's more obscure Motown hits ("I Don't Want to Do Wrong"), and little-heard numbers by Irma Thomas, the Emotions, and Margie Joseph. Shirley Murdock and Millie Jackson offer tracks from the past decade, in contrast to the rest of the set. On the whole, this functions as an excuse to pick up some decent, off-the-beaten-path soul. *—Richie Unterberger*

☆ Chess Rhythm & Roll / 1994 / Chess ✦✦✦✦✦
A four-disc set chronicling the more rockin' sides in this landmark label's catalog. Here we have the landmark early recordings by Chuck Berry, Bo Diddley, the Moonglows, the Flamingos, marvelous one-shot hit artists like the Monotones ("Book of Love"), Dale Hawkins ("Susie-Q"), the Sensations ("Let Me In"), as well as seminal soul sides from Etta James, Billy Stewart, and Tommy Tucker's original "High Heel Sneakers." Essential doesn't even begin to describe this box; music from a landmark label that changed the world. *—Cub Koda*

Classic, Funk Vol. 1 / Feb. 1996 / React/PolyGram ✦✦✦
Collectors will find little they don't have on this 12-track compilation, which sticks to popular cuts by George Clinton, Parliament, the O'Jays, Kool & the Gang, Ohio Players, the Average White Band, James Brown, and James Brown-associated projects from the early '70s. It's certainly alright as a taster for those who want to start with prime funk before investigating deeper, or those who just want a little of the style in their library. *—Richie Unterberger*

Classic Rock: 1968 / 1987 / Time-Life ✦✦✦✦
24 tracks of some of the year's biggest hits, including "I Thank You" by Sam & Dave, "The Dock of the Bay" by Otis Redding, and "Cry like a Baby" by the Box Tops. For a straight-up, no-nonsense basic-hits compilation, it's hard to find anything wrong with this one. *—Cub Koda*

Colpix Dimension Story / 1994 / Rhino ✦✦✦
In the first half of the 1960s, Colpix and Dimension were record label offshoots of Columbia Pictures; Colpix tended toward teen idols, while Dimension was mainly an outlet for the compositions of the Gerry Goffin/Carole King songwriting team. This 40-song double CD includes all the major hits on the labels by the Marcels, James Darren, Shelley Fabares, Paul Petersen, Little Eva, the Cookies, and Carole King herself, as well as quite a few rarities. Although the compilers have done a thorough job, the jumble of disparate styles—sappy teen-idol pop, rhythm and blues, girl groups, soul, even a garage band—makes for tough end-to-end listening. Several of the sides by Darren and Petersen are unbearably cloying; the ones by Fabares, Teddy Randazzo, and Sandy Stewart are barely any better. The hits by Little Eva and the Cookies, on the other hand, are great, dynamic girl group performances. And some of the rarities are pretty cool—Carole King's odd, almost folk-rockish flop single "He's a Bad Boy," Earl-Jean's original version of "I'm into Something Good" (covered for a hit by Herman's Hermits), The Girlfriends' "My One and Only, Jimmy Boy" (the best Wall of Sound girl group record not produced by Phil Spector), the little-anthologized Top Ten soul hit "Hey Girl" by Freddie Scott, rare sides by Lou Christie and Duane Eddy, a silly Beatle parody by Sonny Curtis, and extremely rare (if not terribly good) singles by David Jones and Michael Nesmith before they joined the Monkees. *—Richie Unterberger*

☆ The Complete Stax-Volt Singles 1959-1968 / 1991 / Atlantic ✦✦✦✦✦
This 244-track, nine-disc box set includes *all* of the 45 rpm A-sides ever released (as well as a few choice B-sides) on these legendary Memphis labels, during and preceding their association with Atlantic Records. Even though Stax/Volt continued to release more strong sides after 1968, with Isaac Hayes ("Shaft") and the Staple Singers, many consider that their classic sound is the one represented here. The consistently great songs and performances found on this collection, by artists like Otis Redding, Carla Thomas, Sam & Dave, Booker T. & the MG's, Eddie Floyd and many more, are a testament to Stax/Volt's vision. The tracks (remastered from the original mono masters on specially modified equipment) sound

amazingly warm and full. Included is a booklet with extensively detailed liner notes and a generous selection of photos. For anyone who has the change to part with for a box set of this size, this is absolutely essential, provided you are a serious lover of gritty soul music. *—Rick Clark*

The Complete Stax-Volt Soul Singles, Vol. 2, 1968-1971 / 1993 / Stax ✦✦✦✦✦
Massive nine-CD deluxe box set containing all 216 singles released by the seminal soul label. During their first four years after leaving Atlantic's distribution wing, Stax had some of the biggest soul hits (and stars) of the day, and they're all here, with deluxe packaging and superb sound. This is a perfect companion to the Atlantic Stax box set. *—Cub Koda*

Conmemorativo: A Tribute to Gram Parsons / 1993 / Rhino ✦✦✦✦✦
Conmemortivo is a scattered, yet enjoyable, tribute to Gram Parsons, the legendary father of country-rock. As with most tribute records, the results are a mixed bag; some bands play the songs as straight rock without any trace of country, but the best moments capture the spirit, if not the exact sound, of Parsons' originals. Bob Mould and Vic Chesnutt's mournful rendition of "Hickory Wind" is a particular highlight. *—Stephen Thomas Erlewine*

Cowabunga! The Surf Box / 1996 / Rhino ✦✦✦✦✦
Massive, though not quite definitive, four-CD, 82-track box set of surf music. The first three discs are devoted to material from the genre's '60s prime, and the fourth devoted to revivalists from 1977 to 1995. Most listeners are still better off with the several excellent single-disc surf compilations available (the best of which, like this one, are on Rhino). If your interest runs very deep, this should satisfy, placing most of the emphasis on instrumentals rather than vocals (though significant efforts in the latter vein by the Beach Boys, Jan & Dean, and others are included). It has most of the big hits, and quite a few of the ones which were principally popular in Southern California, as well as some neat rarities that are hard to find anywhere, like the Illusions' storming "Jezebel," the Surfmen's "Paradise Cove," the Latin-surf hybrid of Dave Myers' "Moment of Truth," the Sandals' "Theme from Endless Summer," and the Sunrays' pale Beach Boys xerox, "I Live for the Sun." The fourth disc of modern-day revivalists, alas, was probably unnecessary in the minds of everyone except the compilers; it's the first three that really deal with the heart of the matter, with voluminous annotation in the 66-page booklet. *—Richie Unterberger*

Creole Kings of New Orleans / 1992 / Specialty ✦✦✦✦
Creole Kings of New Orleans is a splendid 26-track sampler of Specialty Records' numerous R&B legends, including Professor Longhair, Percy Mayfield, Lloyd Price, Joe Liggins, and Guitar Slim. Although only a couple of big hits are included, the material is consistently strong, making the disc an excellent purchase. *—Stephen Thomas Erlewine*

Creole Kings of New Orleans, Vol. 2 / 1993 / Specialty ✦✦✦
25 New Orleans R&B/rock/blues sides from the '50s, taken from the vaults of Specialty, Ebb, and Regal Records. There aren't any big hits here (though some did well on the R&B charts), and despite the presence of names like Lloyd Price, Professor Longhair, Guitar Slim, Clifton Chenier, and Larry Williams, there are several other vintage Crescent City R&B collections that you should pick up before getting to this one. It's generic, but quite acceptable. Its appeal will primarily lie in the R&B collector crowd, due to obscure tracks by the above-mentioned names (including Price's follow-up singles to his famous "Lawdy Miss Clawdy") and unknowns like Willie Johnson, Roy Montrell, and Ernest Kador (who became Ernie K-Doe of "Mother-in-Law" fame). There are also curious demos of "Good Golly Miss Molly" (by Bumps Blackwell) and "All Around the World" (Li'l Millet), which are much more renowned via the Little Richard versions. *—Richie Unterberger*

☆ Crescent City Soul: The Sound of New Orleans / Apr. 2, 1996 / EMI ✦✦✦✦✦
The new king of the hill as far as retrospectives of early New Orleans R&B/rock go. This four-CD, 119-song box has hits by all of the major artists, and hits and misses by most of the important minor ones as well. The standards for inclusion are flexible and reasonable: Although New Orleans residents usually carry the day, important records that were recorded in New Orleans by nonnatives are also featured. Fats Domino, Little Richard, Irma Thomas, Lee Dorsey, Smiley Lewis, Chris Kenner, Barbara George, Ernie K-Doe, Clarence "Frogman" Henry, Lloyd Price, Aaron Neville, Professor Longhair, Shirley & Lee, and Dr. John are all here, as are one-shots and regional figures like the Showmen, Earl King, Benny Spellman, Dave Bartholomew, and the Spiders. There are plenty of hits, but also plenty of fine songs that most listeners won't be aware of: the original versions of "My Ding-a-Ling" (two of them!), "I'm Gonna Be a Wheel Someday," and "One Night," for instance, which were covered for huge smashes by Fats Domino, Chuck Berry, and Elvis Presley. It's not perfect: the absence of Frankie Ford's "Sea Cruise" is absolutely inexcusable, and the omission of hits like "Blueberry Hill," "Ya Ya," and "Rocking Pneumonia" only slightly less mystifying. It's still the best chunk of New Orleans rock/R&B in one place, with more than enough variety to make the lengthy set a pleasure all the way through. *—Richie Unterberger*

★ **D.I.Y.: Anarchy in the UK: UK Punk I (1976-77)** / Jan. 19, 1993 / Rhino +++++

With the exception of the Clash, who could not be included because of licensing obstacles, this 19-song collection includes all of the major originators of British punk music. The Sex Pistols are here, of course, with somewhat rawer demo versions of "Anarchy in the UK" and "God Save the Queen" that have previously appeared on various quasi-legitimate albums. Otherwise, you get the major singles from a posse of leading bands of the movement, including the Damned, the Saints, the Jam, and the Buzzcocks. Cult acts of nearly equal importance, like X-Ray Spex, the Adverts, the Only Ones, Generation X, and Wire, also weigh in with trailblazing singles like "Orgasm Addict" and "One Chord Wonders." Major punk fans and collectors won't find anything here that they don't already have. But for those who didn't pick up everything the first time around, or weren't even around the first time around, it's as ideal an introduction as can be imagined to a sound that totally realigned rock with its emphasis on brittle guitars, amphetamine rhythms, and socially charged songwriting. The booklet includes a lengthy, informative essay by Jon Savage, author of the British punk history *England's Dreaming*. *—Richie Unterberger*

★ **D.I.Y.: Blank Generation: The New York Scene (1975-78)** / 1993 / Rhino +++++

— *Blank Generation*—is actually where the story begins. It was the mid-'70s rumblings of Patti Smith and the Ramones emanating from NYC's famed C.B.G.B.'s club that served as the catalyst for what followed. The Ramones debut album, released in May 1976, lit a match to the dry tinder of England's alienated youth and set the pace for the Sex Pistols and the Damned. . *—Roch Parisien*

★ **D.I.Y.: Come out and Play: American Power Pop . . .** / 1993 / Rhino +++++

Come Out and Play, the first of two discs of American power-pop in the *D.I.Y.* series, is a terrific 19-track collection of heavyweights such as Cheap Trick, Flamin' Groovies, Chris Stamey, and Chris Bell, as well as more obscure bands like Fotomaker, Pezband, and the Diodes. It's essential for fans of power-pop or anyone who loves a good melody. *—Stephen Thomas Erlewine*

D.I.Y.: Mass. Ave.: The Boston Scene (1979-83) / 1993 / Rhino +++++

Out of all of the volumes in the *D.I.Y.* series, *Mass. Ave*—The Boston Scene (1975-1983) is probably the weakest, but by no means does that mean it's worthless; it does chronicle its scene very well, but Boston's punk/new wave scene was not as strong as New York's or Los Angeles'. The CD is full of wonderful moments, including Mission of Burma, the Lyres, a demo from the Cars, Willie Alexander, and Human Sexual Response among its 19 tracks. It's definitely worth purchasing for punk and new wave aficionados. *—Stephen Thomas Erlewine*

D.I.Y.: Shake It Up: American Power Pop 2 . . . / 1993 / Rhino +++++

Shake It Up!, *D.I.Y.*'s second volume of American power-pop, is slightly less consistent than the first, but it's still full of wonderful music, making it just as essential as the first volume. Includes the Shoes, Chris Stamey & the DB's, Pearl Harbor & the Explosions, the Plimsouls, and the Romantics' infectious "What I Like About You." *—Stephen Thomas Erlewine*

★ **D.I.Y.: Teenage Kicks: UK Pop (1976-79)** / Jan. 19, 1993 / Rhino +++++

Disc three (*Teenage Kicks*) and its companion volume number four, (*Starry Eyes*) capture the evolution from the early Stiff Records sound of Nick Lowe and Wreckless Eric, to hard, crystalline gems from Ireland's the Undertones and the comic-book hyberbole of Scotland's the Rezillos. Many performers charted in England but went virtually ignored in North America. Early tracks from longer-lived names like XTC, Squeeze, and Joe Jackson are also included. Back in New York City, *Blank Generation* offers period essentials from Television, Richard Hell & the Voidoids, the Dictators, Blondie, Dead Boys, and the Heartbreakers, in addition to Smith and the Ramones. *—Roch Parisien*

☆ **D.I.Y.: The Modern World: UK Punk 2 (1977-78)** / 1993 / Rhino +++++

Disc two—This Is the Modern World—chronicles the splintering of the initial punk wave into different factions and styles: Mod-inspired workouts from the Jam, working-class anthems by 999 and Sham 69, the progressive tendencies of Magazine and the Fall, emerging psychedelia from the Soft Boys, and powerful politics from Ireland's Stiff Little Fingers. *—Roch Parisien*

D.I.Y.: We're Desperate: The L.A. Scene (1976-79) / 1993 / Rhino +++++

Twenty-one tracks of raw Los Angeles punk form *We're Desperate*—The L.A. Scene (1976-79), another solid installment in Rhino's *D.I.Y.* punk/new wave series. Although it isn't a front-to-back blowout like the New York volume, *We're Desperate* is a disc all punk and new wave fans will want to add to their collection, considering that the original versions of

all of the singles have been included. The CDs feature such bands as the Germs, the Dickies, the Weirdos, the Plugz, the Zippers, the Motels, and X, Los Angeles' quintessential punk band. *—Stephen Thomas Erlewine*

The Del-Fi & Donna Story / Ace +++

In the late 1950s and early 1960s, Del-Fi was an interesting, eclectic Los Angeles-based independent rock label, recording surf, rockabilly, R&B, and pop, occasionally landing a national hit. Precisely because of that eclecticism, though, a survey disc of notable tracks from the Del-Fi vaults isn't the smoothest listen. This 31-disc compilation does include good sides by Ritchie Valens, Chan Romero (famous for "Hippy Hippy Shake"), Ron Holden (who had a one-shot with the New Orleans R&B-like "Love You So") teen idol Johnny Crawford, and surf combo the Lively Ones. Serious collectors will also appreciate the CD availability of rare sides by Dick Dale, Rene Hall (who played guitar on Valens' classic "La Bamba"), a pre-Bread David Gates, and other unknown tracks in the surf, R&B, and instrumental vein. Valens, Romero, Crawford, and the Lively Ones are better appreciated in the context of their own best-of compilations, however. *—Richie Unterberger*

☆ **The Disco Years, Vol. 1: Turn the Beat Around** / 1990 / Rhino +++++

A comprehensive series featuring many of the greatest disco songs ever recorded, Rhino's five-volume *Disco Years* set accurately chronicles the pop music sensation of the mid-'70s. The first two volumes are the places to start; the other three are necessary for devoted disco fans and pop music historians. *—Stephen Thomas Erlewine*

Don't It Sound Good: The Great Atlantic Vocal Groups / 1995 / Rhino/Collectors' Choice Music +++++

Fifty doo wop cuts from the Atlantic vaults on this double CD, all but one from the 1950s. Divided between hits and rarities, there's no getting around the fact that, due to the factors of both familiarity and quality, the hits are far more interesting to the noncollector. There are quite a few of those here by both the Drifters and the Clovers, as well as the Robins' "Smokey Joe's Cafe," the Chords' "Sh-Boom," and the Cardinals' "Wheel of Fortune." After that, it's collector territory, with outfits like the Diamonds (no relation to the White group that had a hit with "Little Darlin' "), the Regals, the Pearls, the Raiders, the Royal Jokers, the Sensations, and others. Characteristically well-done vocal arrangements don't disguise the truth that the material is not as memorable as the hits. Nevertheless, doo wop fans will certainly dig this, as the Atlantic imprint ensured a basic standard of quality. Available by mail-order only, from Collectors' Choice Music (P.O. Box 838, Itasca, IL 60143-0838, 800-923-1122). *—Richie Unterberger*

☆ **Doo Wop Box** / 1994 / Rhino +++++

Rhino's four-disc collection *The Doo Wop Box* may not contain every classic doo wop single ever recorded, but it comes damn close. Featuring a hundred tracks, superb sound, and amazingly detailed liner notes, the set is one of the best various-artist box sets ever assembled; although these four discs will be all the doo wop some listeners will ever need, hopefully the set will make most listeners want to investigate the genre even further. *—Stephen Thomas Erlewine*

Electric Sugar Cube Flashbacks, Vols. 1-4 / AIP +++

In comparison to US bands, obscure British groups of the mid- and late '60s have been ill-served by compilations; there are dozens of Pebbles volumes, and hundreds of American garage-rock compilations in the same vein, but comparatively few for their British counterparts. There are some, however, and the *Electric Sugar Cube Flashbacks* series is probably the best of them, spotlighting rare early British R&B, "beat," and psychedelic recordings from impossibly rare 45s, many of which were never released in the States. The British bands tended to be somewhat more accomplished, tuneful, and imaginative in their lyrics and arrangements than their American counterparts; those looking for obscure music in the classic British '60s R&B/rock and power-pop style should check these out, with the awareness that they're generally more crudely performed, written, and produced than the material by the British Invasion giants we know and love. As is the case with all AIP series, the volumes tend to get worse as the series progresses; Vol. 1, if you can find it, is by far the best. *—Richie Unterberger*

Electric Sugar Cube Flashbacks / AIP +++++

When AIP upgrades its catalog to CD, there's a lot of confusion; the same title is usually kept as the vinyl edition, but the tracks are taken from various volumes of a series, and lots of previously uncompiled bonus tracks are tacked on. The CD version of *Electric Sugar Cube Flashbacks* draws from a few volumes of the multi-LP series of British '60s psychedelic rarities that went under that name, especially Vol. 4. About a dozen of the cuts, though (over half the CD), didn't appear on any of the vinyl compilations. There are a few moderately well-known groups among the 21 tracks (the Smoke, Family) and rarities by big-time artists (the Dave Clark Five, Sweet). But mostly these are no-names who caught the lightning for a track or two on hopelessly obscure singles. Not everything here's great, but a lot of it's good, or better than that, fusing melodic crunch with experimentation better than virtually any other subgenre of rock. Highlights are the contributions by the Smoke, Big Boy Pete, Andy

Ellison, Svensk, and Mike Stuart Span (represented by a rare BBC version of their glorious flop single, "Children of Tomorrow"). —*Richie Unterberger*

Elpee's Worth of Productions / 1992 / Rhino ✦✦✦✦✦
Essentially a scrapbook of Rundgren's productions with artists like Patti Smith, Meatloaf, New York Dolls, Grand Funk Railroad, Pursuit of Happiness, XTC, and more. The diversity of artists makes a nice case for Rundgren's wide range of taste, but many of the selections seem odd choices, considering that better material existed on those albums. —*Rick Clark*

English Freakbeat, Vols. 1-5 / AIP ✦✦✦
Like its cousin series *Electric Sugar Cube Flashbacks*, this focuses on way-obscure British "beat," R&B, and early psychedelia, circa 1964-1968. There are some great cuts to be found on these, as well as super-rare singles by groups that featured future stars like Steve Howe, Mick Ronson, and Graham Gouldman, and even famous never-weres like Pete Best. They're very uneven anthologies, though, more so than the *Electric Sugar Cube Flashbacks* volumes; one gets the feeling that the tracks were sometimes selected as much or more for their rarity than their actual musical value. —*Richie Unterberger*

Faster & Louder: Hardcore Punk, Vol. 2 / 1993 / Rhino ✦✦✦
Considered unimaginably over-the-top and atonal at the time, the early sounds of hard core punk don't sound nearly as noisy 15 years later. Dare we say, they even sound a bit poppy and tightly conceived in comparison with the uncompromisingly bleak, rushed, and amelodic sounds of today's underground hard core groups. That's not to take away from the undeniable influence and power of first-generation hard core. *Faster & Louder: Hardcore Punk, Vol. 2* does a good job of assembling some of the most enduring and accessible moments of the genre's genesis. This 17-song compilation includes the first singles by Hüsker Dü and X, who went on to transcend hard core's limitations pretty rapidly. It also includes seminal tracks by Agent Orange and Wire, as well as influential bands with smaller cults like the Wipers, the Dils, and Zero Boys, down to nearly forgotten acts (Dys, Stranglehold). The bleakest and most vicious strand of early hard core is represented by Fear, the Germs, and the Subhumans. Not a bad package for those who want to sample the genre's highlights and limit its representation in their collection to this fairly small and manageable dose. —*Richie Unterberger*

Fire/Fury Records Story / 1993 / Warner Brothers ✦✦✦✦✦
A fine two-disc compilation of the seminal blues label, it includes many groundbreaking artists. —*AMG*

Flight to Lowland's Paradise: The Netherlands, Part 1 & 2 / Moxie ✦✦✦✦✦
Pebbles Vol. 15: The Netherlands remains the best compilation of mid-'60s Dutch beat-punk, but these two anthologies, issued in the US in the mid-'80s, are nearly on the same level. Each volume has 16 tracks demonstrating the uniquely brooding Dutch take on British Invasion R&B and mod, with songs by both well-known acts on the scene (the Outsiders, Les Baroques, the Motions, Cuby & the Blizzards) and total unknowns. Good stuff, not mere rare novelties. —*Richie Unterberger*

☆ **Frat Rock** / 1991 / Rhino ✦✦✦✦✦
Rhino's *Frat Rock* series is an excellent overview of '60s rock 'n' roll and R&B party anthems like the Kingsmen's "Louie Louie," "Double Shot of My Baby's Love" (Swinging Medallions), "La La La La La" (Blendells), "Shout" (Isley Brothers), "Do You Love Me?" (the Contours), and "Mony Mony" (Tommy James & the Shondells). —*John Floyd*

Frat Rock: More of the '70s / 1995 / Rhino ✦✦✦
Like the first volume of *Frat Rock: The '70s, More of the '70s* functions more as a sampler of album-rock hits than frat-house rock, but it still contains a number of good songs, including Golden Earring's "Radar Love," Deep Purple's "Smoke on the Water," the Kinks' "Sleepwalker," Joe Walsh's "Life's Been Good," Foghat's "Slow Ride," Bad Company's "Can't Get Enough," and Gary Glitter's anthemic "Rock and Roll, Part 2." —*Stephen Thomas Erlewine*

Frat Rock: The '80s / 1995 / Rhino ✦✦✦
The '70s editions of the *Frat Rock* series concentrated on album-rock crossover hits. *Frat Rock: The '80s* is more schizophrenic. Most of the disc concentrates on new wave hits like Madness' "Our House," Adam Ant's "Goody Two Shoes," Devo's "Whip It," Stray Cats' "Rock This Town," and Tommy Tutone's "867-5309/Jenny Jenny," but it also has album-rock tracks like the J. Geils Band's "Centerfold" and Top 40 cuts like Robert Palmer's "Addicted to Love," Glenn Frey's "The Heat Is On," and Poison's "Nothin' but a Good Time." —*Stephen Thomas Erlewine*

Frat Rock: The '70s / 1995 / Rhino ✦✦✦
A fun, but haphazard, collection of album-rock rave-ups from the '70s, this disc contains highlights like Alice Cooper's "School's Out," Grand Funk Railroad's "We're an American Band," Foreigner's "Hot Blooded," and The Knack's "My Sharona." —*Stephen Thomas Erlewine*

Funky Broadway Stax Revue Live at the 5/4 Ballroom / 1992 / Stax ✦✦✦✦✦
Nearly an hour of previously unreleased Stax soul recorded at a Los Angeles venue in August 1965, including cuts by Booker T. & the MGs, Carla Thomas, Rufus Thomas, William Bell, and the Mar-Keys; a couple of relatively little-known Stax vocal groups, the Mad Lads and the Astors, round out the program. This isn't just of interest to soul completists. Good live mid-'60s soul records, in decent fidelity, are fairly rare items. This is genuinely galvanizing stuff, with a rawer, more party-oriented feel than the classic Stax studio sides of the same era. Especially good are Booker T. & the MGs, who really burn through classics like "Green Onions" and "Soul Twist," and Rufus Thomas, who clowns his way through a nine-minute version of "Do the Dog." —*Richie Unterberger*

Funky Stuff: The Best of Funk Essentials / May 18, 1993 / PolyGram ✦✦✦✦✦
This terrific compilation of the highlights of Mercury's *Funk Essentials* series (which includes individual titles by Parliament, the Bar-Kays, Cameo, and Con Funk Shun) also includes songs from artists that don't have their own CDs. It's essential for anyone curious about the funk. —*AMG*

Get Down Tonight: Best of T.K. Records / 1990 / Rhino ✦✦✦✦
A fine collection of the best tracks from the seminal '70s disco label, including tracks by KC & the Sunshine Band, George McCrae, Gwen McCrae, Betty Wright, Latimore, and Little Beaver. —*Stephen Thomas Erlewine*

Get with the Beat: Mar-Vel' Masters / 1989 / Rykodisc ✦✦✦
Based near Chicago, the Mar Vel' label recorded lots of regional roots music during the 1950s and early '60s. Although they recorded some R&B and rockabilly, this compilation of 27 cuts by 19 artists—none of whom achieved any national fame whatsoever—leans toward hillbilly, country boogie, and country swing. Though these rarities have their merits, they aren't nearly as good as the classic material by stars mining the same territory. —*Richie Unterberger*

Girls In The Garage, Vols. 1-6 / Romulan ✦✦✦
Even more than most rock 'n' roll styles, garage rock is thought of as a primarily male terrain, especially given the macho posturing adopted by most of its proponents. *Girls In The Garage* proves that there were also quite a few female groups mining similar territory in the mid-'60s. The compilers have gone far and wide to assemble dozens of doggoned rare singles to fill out these anthologies, and if they don't exactly place among the very top rank of the hundreds of '60s garage-rock collections, there's a fair amount of decent stuff to be found here. There simply weren't a lot of females with guitars forming their own groups in the '60s, and so a lot of this material isn't "garage" in the classic sense; a fair amount is raw girl group-style stuff, novelties, or classic garage bands that happened to feature a female singer. Which isn't a drawback, as the collections have more variety than you'll find on your average garage comp. Good liner notes too, although Romulan seems to have resorted to filling out the volumes with some unmemorable, even inept tracks due to the scarcity of source material to choose from. —*Richie Unterberger*

★ **Golden Age of American Rock 'n' Roll** / Ace (UK) ✦✦✦✦
For many years, Original Sound's *Oldies But Goodies* series was acknowledged as the best source for catching up on the many great early rock 'n' roll hits by artists who had only one (or two, or three, or even a few more) classics to offer. Ace's *Golden Age of American Rock 'n' Roll* series, however, has surpassed *Oldies But Goodies* as the series of choice in the CD age. Even at an import price, they offer better value (with 30 songs each!); they use the best possible available source tapes for remastering; they also offer lengthy, intelligent liner notes and some photos, where Original Sound has historically offered none. Most important, they offer a wealth of great hits from rock 'n' roll's first decade as a widespread phenomenon (1954-63), some of which are very difficult to find on other recordings, CD or not. There are some huge hits represented, but an equal amount of attention is paid to lower-charting items that have fallen out of rotation at oldies stations, as well as some slight/regional hits that you might not have heard even if you grew up during the era. Vol.1 , like each installment, reflects the incredible diversity and excitement of rock's first decade: doo wop, primitive rockabilly, girl groups, instrumental rock, proto-soul, pop-rock, and more, ranging from famous one-shots (the Jaynetts' "Sally Go Round the Roses," the Penguins' "Earth Angel") to semiforgotten treasures like the Fendermen's "Mule Skinner Blues" and Toni Fisher's "The Big Hurt." —*Richie Unterberger*

★ **The Golden Age of American Rock 'n' Roll, Vol. 2** / 1993 / Ace ✦✦✦✦✦
No volume of the *Golden Age of American Rock 'n' Roll* series is more essential than any other one. As all have a good range of styles, and a mix of big and small hits, none is particularly recommended more than others; all are worth acquiring if you want to build a serious rock 'n' roll collection. Vol 2.has plenty of classics (the Silhouettes' "Get a Job," Maurice Williams' "Stay," Lonnie Mack's "Memphis," the Rivieras' "California

Sun," Link Wray's "Rumble") to go along with some neat one-shots (the Bell-Notes' "I've Had It," Barbara George's "I Know," Harold Dorman's "Mountain of Love"). Just as interesting are the minor hits, like the Eternals' ridiculous "Rockin' in the Jungle" (uptempo doo wop with side-splitting bird calls) and the Gladiolas' original version of "Little Darlin' " (covered with much bigger success by the Diamonds). —*Richie Unterberger*

★ **The Golden Age of American Rock 'n' Roll, Vol. 3** / 1994 / Ace ✦✦✦✦✦
More good, classic stuff. Everyone will have different favorites according to their tastes, which is an advantage of having such a diverse collection on CD—you can skip around as you like. The roll call here includes many classic one-shots, by Wilbert Harrison ("Kansas City"), Bill Parsons ("The All American Boy," sung by Bobby Bare, although Parsons got the label credit), the Teddy Bears ("To Know Him Is to Love Him,") Phil Spector's first classic), the Turbans ("When You Dance"), Skip & Flip ("It Was I"), the Olympics ("Western Movies"), and the Castells ("Sacred"). —*Richie Unterberger*

★ **The Golden Age of American Rock 'n' Roll, Vol. 4** / 1994 / Ace ✦✦✦✦✦
Another reliably well-packaged collection of major and minor pre-Beatle rock hits. Besides the hits by stars like Dion, Gary US Bonds, Jan & Dean, and Buddy Knox, you have plenty of one-shots by the likes of the Edsels ("Rama Lama Ding Dong"), Little Caesar & the Romans ("Those Oldies But Goodies"), Barbara Lynn ("You'll Lose a Good Thing"), and Ray Sharpe (the classic R&B/jump rocker "Linda Lu"). The further the series goes, the deeper it gets into the lower rungs of the charts, so even rock scholars may not have previously heard cuts by the likes of Nat Kendrick, Nappy Brown, or the Royaltones. Others you may have only heard once or twice, like the ones by Tommy Facenda, the Rip Chords, and Billy & Lillie. —*Richie Unterberger*

★ **The Golden Age of American Rock 'n' Roll, Vol. 5** / 1995 / Ace ✦✦✦✦✦
It's been said before, but it bears repeating: much of the history (and soul) of early rock 'n' roll resides not only in the recordings of giants like Elvis, Little Richard, Chuck Berry, and Buddy Holly, but in the literally hundreds of acts who managed to produce one or two great singles, in an incredible variety of styles. You can't claim to have a comprehensive rock 'n' roll collection without seeking them out, and you'll have a surprising amount of fun doing so. The fifth volume of the *Golden Age of American Rock'n'Roll* series shows no signs of flagging in its mission to document these important sounds. Big hits by stars (Freddie Cannon, Jan & Dean, Gene Chandler); huge one-shot hits like Dale & Grace's "I'm Leaving It Up to You," Johnnie & Joe's "Over the Mountain, Across the Sea," and Jimmy McCracklin's "The Walk"; treasured cult classics by the Showmen ("It Will Stand") and Eddie Fontaine ("Nothin' Shakin'," covered by the Beatles on *Live at the BBC*); all are here, and more. —*Richie Unterberger*

Golden Groups / 1993 / Specialty ✦✦✦✦✦
Originally compiled and issued on Relic Records as part of their superlative label-by-label Golden Groups series, this boasts the addition of eight bonus tracks and improved remastering quality. Featuring such wild West Coast gems as the Pentagons' "Silly Dilly," Tony Allen's "Night Owl," not to mention early recordings by Clydie King and Darlene Love (as part of her first group, the Echoes), this makes a wonderful companion volume to *Hardcore Doo Wop: In the Hallway*—Under the Streetlamp. —*Cub Koda*

Got a Good Thing Going / 1996 / Sequel ✦✦✦✦✦
Subtitled "25 R&B Radio Hits of the 60s," Billy Vera compiled this with the intention of giving listeners some prime soul singles that weren't huge hits, but also not selected simply on the basis of obscurity. Besides J.J. Jackson's "But It's All Right" and Freddie Scott's "Hey Girl," however, you'd be hard-pressed to recognize any of these, unless you listened to soul stations all the time in the '60s. The attention to quality over rarity, however, has resulted in one of the finest anthologies of semi-obscure and very obscure '60s soul that you're likely to come across, with lots of diversity, ranging from gospel-tinged shouters to uptown New York productions to exquisite ballads. Almost all of this is very good, and some of it's a lot better than that—the original version of "You're No Good" by Dee Dee Warwick (covered by Betty Everett in the '60s and Linda Ronstadt in the '70s) is a stunner. Little Buster has a fine Sam Cooke soundalike, Jimmy Ricks has a deep croon that sounds like a 45 playing at 33 RPM, Mary Wells offers an overlooked bluesy cut from the late '60s, and Valerie Simpson and Nick Ashford are heard on a rare 1965 single attributed simply to Valerie and Nick. And the mysterious Mighty Hannibal's "Hymn No. 5" is a must-hear for any '60s soul-rock fan, its creepy gospel-soul moan offering one of the best understated protests against the Vietnam War ever recorded. —*Richie Unterberger*

☆ **Grandson of Frat Rock** / 1991 / Rhino ✦✦✦✦✦
Rhino's *Frat Rock* series is an excellent overview of '60s rock 'n' roll and R&B party anthems like the Kingsmen's "Louie Louie," "Double Shot of My Baby's Love" (Swinging Medallions), "La La La La La" (Blendells),

"Shout" (Isley Brothers), "Do You Love Me?" (the Contours), and "Mony Mony" (Tommy James & the Shondells). —*John Floyd*

Growin' Up Too Fast: The Girl Group Anthology / 1996 / Mercury ✦✦✦
A two-CD, 50-song collection of girl group hits and misses originally released on the MGM, Smash, Philips, Fontana, 20th Century Fox, and Mercury labels in the early and mid-'60s. It's nice to have some of these rarities easily available in state-of-the-art fidelity, but it's not one of the best girl group compilations around, in terms of either thematic coherence or consistent quality. The hits by the Shangri-Las, Lesley Gore, Dusty Springfield, the Angels, and the Royalettes are good to great, but are better heard in the context of their own compilations. Much of the rest—by obscure singers like Ginny Arnell, the Pixies Three, and Beverly Washburn—is pleasant but rather forgettable. There are some really neat one-shots and lost classics here, though, like Diane Renay's Top Ten hit, "Navy Blue," and her flop follow-up, "Watch Out, Sally!," is one of the toughest White girl group records ever. Also cool are the Secrets' "The Boy Next Door" (an Angels soundalike) and the two songs by Sadina, which are among the best unknown wall-of-sound-type productions ever. —*Richie Unterberger*

☆ **Hardcore Doo-Wop: In the Hallway**—Under the Street Lamp / 1993 / Specialty ✦✦✦✦✦
This compact disc collects 25 doo wop collector's classics from a variety of small West Coast R&B labels who dabbled in the genre. The California version of the streetcorner vocal group phenomena had stronger leanings toward bluesier harmonies and vocal performances bordering on madness. As best exemplified here by groups like Arthur Lee Maye & the Crowns and Byron "Slick" Gipson & the Sliders, the West Coast doo wop movement definitely had a sound all its own. —*Cub Koda*

Harlem Shuffle: 60s Soul Classics / Charly ✦✦✦✦✦
A perfect selection (and disc order) of lesser-known but essential soul hits, including the Barbara Lewis hits "Hello Stranger," "Make Me Your Baby," and "Baby I'm Yours," plus "Oogum Boogum Song" and "Gimme Little Sign" by Brenton Wood, and "Get On Up and Get Away" by the Esquires. Twenty one classic sides in all, every one a delight. An import but worth the trouble to find. —*Michael Erlewine*

Here Come the Girls: British Girl Singers of the '60s, Vol. 1 / 1990 / Sequel ✦✦✦✦✦
The British girl group scene wasn't nearly as vital as the American one, but there were still quite a few fun recordings produced in the style during the mid-'60s. This compilation is a good overview of lesser-known highlights of a subgenre that is nearly unknown in the US The emphasis is not on groups, but solo singers in the girl group style; Petula Clark was the only one of these 24 performers to reach stardom Stateside, and only a couple of others (Sandie Shaw, the Honeycombs) became even moderately well known. In fact, most of these singles flopped in the UK as well. There's still a good amount of sass and sub-New York soul/pop-rock production to be found in the tracks by the Breakaways, Antoinette, Val McKenna, and others. Notable highlights include Sarah Jane's "Listen People" (a ringer for Marianne Faithfull's mid-'60s sound) and Julie Grant's splendidly sultry, operatic "Come to Me." —*Richie Unterberger*

The History of Cadence Records, Vols. 1-2 / Apr. 1996 / Varese Vintage ✦✦✦✦
When checking out these two recently released volumes of hits from Archie Bleyer's Cadence Records, one has to ask that hardest to ask of all questions: Is this the way the '50s and early '60s *really* were? Could there actually have been a time when a wild, distorted guitar instrumental like "Rumble" by Link Wray and His Ray Men was being heard on AM transistor radios nationwide right next to pop fluff like "Lollipop" by the Chordettes? Could Julius LaRosa ("Eh, Cumpari") and Andy Williams ("Butterfly") turn out to be the Michael Boltons of their day, while the Everly Brothers racked up one classic after another at exactly the same time? Compilations like these give you a much more informed outlook as to the renegade spirit of rock 'n' roll (and how weirdly it was originally perceived) when you think of the early seminal sides that made it to the national level having to wade through the pop murk of tunes like Archie Bleyer's "The Naughty Lady of Shady Lane" and "Hernando's Hideaway." If the notion of Chuck Berry's "Maybellene" being kept out of the No. 1 spot on the charts by Bill Hayes' "The Ballad of Davy Crockett" (the mid-'50s equivalent of the Barney phenomena and heard here in an alternate version, minus the jew's harp ding-ding-a-ding after every chorus), just think of it as the historical percursor to somebody 40 years from now writing about the alternative music movement of the '90s and having to explain Garth Brooks. Cadence was by no means strictly a rock 'n' roll label; that simply wasn't Archie Bleyer's style, even if Don and Phil were keeping the doors open for a lot of years. But as a barometer of pop tastes of the period, these two volumes go a long way to setting the historical record straight and, in the bargain, sounding a lot like radio really was back in those days. —*Cub Koda*

History of Dot Records, Vol. 1: Young Love / Jun. 1996 / Varese Sarabande ✦✦✦✦✦

The two volumes of *The History of Dot Records* are a lot like the two-volume *Best of Cadence Records* Varese Sarabande released, with pop junk sitting next to rock 'n' roll killers and the occasional R&B classic. If pop music's not your thing, you might have a *real* rough time hacking through Tab Hunter giving Sonny James' "Young Love" on *Vol. 1* new meaning to the phrase "stiff and White," but among the poppier offerings from the Fontane Sisters, Gale Storm, the Hilltoppers, Billy Vaughn, and the ubiquitous Pat Boone, you get Robin Luke's Buddy Holly-ish smash "Susie Darlin'" (the first rock 'n' roll hit from Hawaii!) and Sonny Knight's R&B smoothie "Confidential," Robin Ward's classic girl sound single "Wonderful Summer," and the jazzy Mills Brothers' novelty, "Cab Driver." *—Cub Koda*

History of Dot Records, Vol. 2: Come Go with Me / Jun. 1996 / Varese Sarabande ✦✦✦✦✦

The two volumes of *The History of Dot Records* are a lot like the two-volume *Best of Cadence Records* Varese Sarabande released, with pop junk sitting next to rock 'n' roll killers and the occasional R&B classic. *Vol. 2* has way more rock 'n' roll on it than the first volume, with the roadhouse Texas stomp of "Henrietta" by Jimmy Dee and the Offbeats, "Sugar Shack" by Jimmy Gilmer and the Fireballs, Sanford Clark's (with Al Casey on guitar) "The Fool," Arthur Alexander's blueprint for the Beatles number "Anna (Go to Him)," and the Dell-Vikings' excellent title song being all counted up in the mix. I'm figuring this series has to go to another volume at least (where's "Wipe Out" by the Surfaris, "Pipeline" by the Chantays, "Boss" by the Rumblers, "Does Your Chewing Gum Lose It Flavor" by Lonnie Donegan, "Speedy Gonzalez" by Pat Boone, and the rockabilly nutzo classic "Love Me" by the Phantom?), and you wouldn't get any argument out of me if it did. Another good little series that should see expansion sooner than Major League Baseball. *—Cub Koda*

☆ **Hitsville USA: The Motown Singles Collection 1959-1971** / 1992 / Motown ✦✦✦✦✦

A terrific four-disc box set that features many of Motown's greatest hits in superb sound. While nearly every song is a gem, this is one of the few box sets that isn't comprehensive enough. If anything, it could have used another disc to fit in some more material, particularly more songs by the Supremes. Nevertheless, what is here is transcendent. *—Stephen Thomas Erlewine*

Hitsville USA, Vol. 2: The Motown Singles Collection (1972-1992) / Oct. 19, 1993 / Motown ✦✦✦

Where the first *Hitsville* box suffered from not featuring enough material, the sequel suffers from having too many tracks. During the 1970s, the label lost its distinctive sound, although the hits continued to come for a number of years. Unfortunately, as the years progress, the hits become fewer and less distinctive—they follow the trends, instead of setting them. Perhaps this could have been a successful two-CD set, but at four discs, there aren't enough gems to justify the hefty price ticket. *—Stephen Thomas Erlewine*

In Yo' Face! (The History of Funk), Vol. 1 / 1993 / Rhino ✦✦✦✦✦

Funk fans eagerly anticipated Rhino's five-part series, thinking that they would get something equivalent to the label's wonderful 1970s soul line. While the final results are good, things are not quite as rosy as earlier reports indicated. The most disappointing thing was the decision to settle for single versions of tracks rather than extended ones. This was how the songs sounded on radio, but the results are truncated versions of "Sex Machine" and "Keep On Truckin'," rather than the glorious full cuts with complete musical interludes. Otherwise, most song choices are great, especially the JB's, Funkadelic, and Lyn Collins. *—Ron Wynn*

In Yo' Face! (The History of Funk), Vol. 2 / 1993 / Rhino ✦✦✦✦✦

Vol.2 of Rhino's funk series offers 15 more mostly strong cuts, although it is disappointing to hear edited versions of great anthems. The marvelous trumpet solo and additional chorus from the O'Jays' "For the Love of Money" has been trimmed, and although they don't tell you, only part of B.T. Express' "Do It ('Til You're Satisfied" is included. There's still plenty of wonderful funk, including classics by Sly & the Family Stone, James Brown, Kool & the Gang, Rufus, Parliament, AWB, and the Temptations. *—Ron Wynn*

In Yo' Face! (The History of Funk), Vol. 3 / 1993 / Rhino ✦✦✦✦

By the third volume of Rhino's generally solid funk series, it has become apparent who did and did not permit their songs to be licensed. Once more there are songs from James Brown, Sly & the Family Stone, Parliament, Funkadelic, the O'Jays, and AWB, and it's great that George McRae's delightful "I Get Lifted" made the cut, as well as Graham Central Station's "The Jam." Cameo's "Funk Funk" reveals how close to Parliament they were early in their career, while the Brothers Johnson, Kool and the Gang in their great pre-J.T. Taylor phase, and one-hit wonders Wild Cherry complete the disc. *—Ron Wynn*

In Yo' Face! (The History of Funk), Vol. 4 / 1993 / Rhino ✦✦✦✦✦

Familiar names comprise the bulk of the fourth volume in Rhino's funk series. There are more tracks by James Brown, Sly & the Family Stone, and AWB, plus numbers from repeat entries the Isley Brothers, Earth, Wind & Fire, Kool & the Gang, and Graham Central Station. But new acts offer prototype funk on some smoking numbers such as Slave's "Slide," the Bar-Kays' "Shake Your Rump to the Funk," Brick's "Dazz," and George Duke's "Reach For It." Bootsy's "The Pinocchio Theory" was a classic, and the same is true for Marvin Gaye's "Got to Give It Up, Part 1." Only Brass Construction's "L-O-V-E-U" falls below the standard. *—Ron Wynn*

In Yo' Face! (The History of Funk), Vol. 5 / Rhino ✦✦✦✦✦

Another solid installment in the *In Yo' Face* series, the fifth volume contains essential tracks from Parliament, Con Funk Shun, Rick James, Zapp, and Cameo. *—AMG*

It's Bigger than the Both of Us—N.Z. Singles 1979-82 / 1989 / Festival ✦✦✦✦

It's Bigger than the Both of Us offers two discs worth of rare singles and stray tracks from New Zealand's often overlooked underground from 1979 to 1981. Featuring some legendary tracks from the Clean, Toy Love, Tall Dwarves, and the Swingers, this is essential listening for anyone interested in the development of New Zealand rock. *—Chris Woodstra*

● **It's Hard to Believe: The Amazing World of Jor Meek** / Oct. 1995 / Razor & Tie ✦✦✦✦✦

Twenty of Meek's most notable hit singles and misses from 1960 to 1966. Includes his biggest hit productions (the Tornados' "Telstar," the Honeycombs' "Have I the Right," Heinz's "Just like Eddie," Mike Berry's "Tribute to Buddy Holly," John Leyton's "Johnny Remember Me"). Just as intriguing, though, are the more obscure items, some of which are hard or impossible to find on other compilations. Among these are the wild horror-rock of Screaming Lord Sutch's "'Til the Following Night," the supercreepy Moontrekkers instrumental "Night of the Vampire," the soul-pop of the Riot Squad (with Mitch Mitchell on drums), brassy femme pop by Glenda Collins, and a couple of excerpts from *I Hear a New World*, his bizarre outer-space opus. There are many other interesting Meek discs out there for those who want to go further, but this is an excellent introduction. *—Richie Unterberger*

Jungle Exotica / Strip ✦✦✦✦✦

For every big early rock star, or even one-hit wonder, there were plenty of hopelessly obscure rock 'n' roll singles with no chance of making it big in the marketplace. This didn't stop a lot of people from trying to find the right gimmick. Sometimes that gimmick would involve downright nutty marriages of raw rock 'n' roll with "jungle" rhythms and chants, striptease bump-and-grind cheapness, silly Middle Eastern and Chinese melodies (and accents), and horror movie sound effects and screams. That's what you'll find on this amazing compilation, which has 32 tracks, and nearly 70 minutes, of early rock 'n' roll at its most ridiculously sublime. There's not a star or even a recognizable name in sight on this CD, which rescues impossibly rare singles—known only to the hardest of the hardcore collectors—from oblivion. This is not "exotica" in the Martin Denny easy-listening sense of the term. These are early rock 'n' roll novelties that are, without exaggeration, breathtakingly frantic and absurd. The "jungle" culture adopted by a lot of the performers came not from real jungles, but from the jungle as it was pictured in Hollywood movies. As such, the chest-beating ape mating calls and bird noises decorating many of these tracks—not to mention phrases like the fake Chinese "Ah, so!" (which was used as the title for *two* separate songs) or the Bela Lugosi-intoned "come with me to the casbah"—skirt stereotypes that, in later times, would be called politically incorrect. Nonetheless, these cuts are so infectiously silly, and the primeval rock 'n' roll/R&B guitar-and-sax riffing so hot, that you'll have a hard time not laughing at and enjoying this, no matter what your worldview is. *—Richie Unterberger*

Kill Rock Stars / 1991 / KK ✦✦✦✦✦

Excellent modern-day punk rock collection of various cutting-edge artists, including Nirvana and riot grrrls Bikini Kill. Alternative-rock fans will find much to savor here. (Lois, leading a duo cheekily named Courtney Love, acoustic folk-pop "Don't Mix the Colors" is particularly noteworthy). *—Stephen Thomas Erlewine*

Live Stiffs / Edsel ✦✦✦✦✦

Recorded on the first "Live Stiffs" tour in the late '70s, this record contains some fine performances by Elvis Costello, Nick Lowe, and Graham Parker. *—AMG*

Living in Oblivion, Vol. 1 / 1993 / Capitol ✦✦✦✦✦

A somewhat haphazardly assembled retrospective of '80s pop, *Living in Oblivion* contains not only classic new wave cuts, but also features several MTV hits from the mid-'80s and radio hits from the end of the decade. While there are some great songs on every volume, each disc is wildly inconsistent; only the first disc is somewhat coherent. Nevertheless, *Living in Oblivion* captures the fractured mainstream of the decade quite well and manages to include some classic pop songs along the way. —*Stephen Thomas Erlewine*

Lookin' for Boys / 198? / Roxy ✦✦✦✦

Quite simply, this is the best compilation of little-known early- to mid-'60s girl group singles ever assembled, and proof that quite a few songs never get to be hits for reasons that have nothing to do with their quality. A couple of these (the Girlfriends' "Jimmy Boy" and Earl-Jean's original version of "I'm into Something Good") were small hits, but by and large these were flops. What's amazing is how meticulously produced and tuneful they were; in 1963, the industry was dazzled by Phil Spector's success, and employed quite a few producers and performers that emulated the master very well. Great melodies, harmonies, and Wall-of-Sound Jr. production on most of these, and noted songwriter Ellie Greenwich's dramatic "You Don't Know" is one of the finest obscure mid-'60s rock 'n' roll singles of any genre. —*Richie Unterberger*

Max Weinberg Presents: Let There Be Drums, Vols. 1-3 / 1994 / ✦✦✦✦✦

Weinberg was the drummer for Bruce Springsteen's E Street Band for many years, and assembled this series as a retrospective of some of the greatest drum playing to be heard on rock 'n' roll records. Sometimes that means actually drummers with solos, like Sandy Nelson, Preston Epps, and Cozy Cole; sometimes that means hits that feature classic brief drum solos, like the Ventures' "Walk, Don't Run" and the Surfaris' "Wipe Out." Most often, though, it means classic hits that owe a lot of their strength to the rhythm, from Little Richard to the Edgar Winter Group. Vol. 1 covers the '50s, Vol. 2 the '60s, Vol. 3 the '70s; Weinberg provides extensive liner notes throughout, illuminating the many types of drum styles heard on these early rockabilly, soul, British Invasion, progressive-rock, funk, and even folk-rock records. For those who don't pay special attention to the drums, it's more of a collection of great vintage rock classics with an assortment of great beats. —*Richie Unterberger*

Metal Age: The Roots of Metal / 1992 / Rhino ✦✦✦✦✦

Actually, *Roots of Metal* comes closer to representing the heyday of heavy metal. From Status Quo to Motörhead, all kinds of '70s arena hard rock and metal are covered; over the course of the disc, it becomes clear that metal does *not* all sound the same—there's quite a difference between the thuggish Wishbone Ash, the melodic Cheap Trick, snarling Runaways, and the bloated blues of Beck, Bogert, and Appice. Some of it holds up surprisingly well and some of it is embarrassing, but there's no question that it captures its era particularly well. —*Stephen Thomas Erlewine*

Mods Mayday '79 / 1979 / Dojo ✦✦✦✦

Since the British music market was flooded with mod-revivalists in the late '70s, the only effective way to promote the bands was through package tours—several like-minded (and like-sounding) bands playing short sets on the same night. *Mods Mayday '79* is a classic collection which compiles the highlights of one of these tours. Most of the second-wave revivalists—bands who received their inspiration directly from the Jam's early albums—are represented: Secret Affair, Beggar, Small Hours, the Mods, Squire, and the Merton Parkas. The one glaring omission is the Lambrettas, who were unable to attend the tour due to contractual obligations. Nevertheless, this provides the best look at the genre and is the only place to hear some of the bands who, despite their derivative nature, wrote some excellent pop songs that hold up pretty well even when removed from their context. —*Chris Woodstra*

Monterey International Pop Festival Box Set / Jun. 1967 / Rhino ✦✦✦✦

A sumptuous, four-CD box set with all the deluxe trimmings celebrating the granddaddy of all outdoor rock concerts. With legendary performances by Otis Redding, the Who, Jimi Hendrix, Janis Joplin, the Byrds, and Paul Butterfield all taken from the mobile-unit multitrack masters (not to mention an album-sized booklet that'll knock your eyes out), this box evokes a sound and an era the way few (if any) retrospectives of like material ever do. Important music from a turning point in rock's history. —*Cub Koda*

More Gumbo Stew / 1993 / Ace ✦✦✦✦✦

The second batch of material from the vaults of Harold Battiste's AFO label is actually a stronger collection than the first (*Gumbo Stew*), although over half of it was previously unissued. Most of it's good early '60s New Orleans R&B, with genuine highlights like Prince La La's "Need You" (a futuristic foreshadowing of the sort of voodoo rock that Dr. John would play in the late '60s), a couple rambunctious performances by the young Dr. John himself ("The Fix" sounds like the early Animals as played on a department-store-quality organ), and the Dr. John-penned "World of Dreams," sung in heart-tugging fashion by Tami Lynn. Also includes tracks by Barbara George, Alvin Robinson, Eddie Bo, and Johnny Adams (a live 1960 performance), as well as Lee Dorsey's smash "Ya Ya" (not recorded at AFO, but included because AFO chief Harold Battiste says he produced it). If you've already got the best New Orleans R&B anthologies and want more of the same, you should make this one of your next stops. —*Richie Unterberger*

Motown's Blue Evolution / Feb. 1996 / Motown ✦✦✦

From the beginning, Motown was almost exclusively devoted to soul. But they did have a few blues-oriented artists on their roster, especially in the early 1960s. Truthfully, though, this 20-track compilation isn't exactly a blues anthology. It's more like a collection of soul cuts with a bluesy feeling, by performers who had substantial or deep roots in pure blues. Mable John (Little Willie's sister) and Sammy Ward, for instance, sing R&B/soul with some bluesy shadings; jump blues veteran Amos Milburn sings modified earthy R&B, married to Motown's embryonic production machine; Earl King has a slight New Orleans flavor to his previously unreleased performances. The unknown Arthur Adams sings blues-soul crossover; Luther Allison comes by far the closest to real blues and is the only one of the artists whose selections date from the 1970s. You can quibble about the accuracy of the compilation's theme, but it's not a bad excuse to get some interesting Motown performances out of the vaults and onto CD, though it's not truly top-drawer blues or soul. Only one of these was even a modest hit (Sammy Ward's 1960 single "Who's the Fool"), and seven tracks were previously unreleased (King and Adams never even got to officially release anything on Motown), so even seasoned Motown collectors will find much of interest here. —*Richie Unterberger*

The Muscle Shoals Sound / Rhino ✦✦✦✦✦

In a series of nondescript studios in tiny towns tucked in the corner of northwest Alabama, a small band of musicians, singers, and producers sculpted a sound that revolutionized rhythm and blues in the 1960s. Dubbed the "Muscle Shoals Sound" after one of those towns, this region gave birth to the grittiest and funkiest Southern soul music of the era. The 18-song compilation *The Muscle Shoals Sound* presents a cross-section of some of the most influential grooves laid down in these studios during its golden decade (1962-1972). Besides hits by soul giants like Otis Redding, Aretha Franklin, and Wilson Pickett, it includes influential sides by lesser stars like Percy Sledge ("When a Man Loves a Woman"), Etta James ("Tell Mama"), Arthur Conley ("Sweet Soul Music"), and Clarence Carter ("Patches"). It also includes the very first hit cut in the region, Arthur Alexander's "You Better Move On." Behind the scenes, songwriters and musicians like Spooner Oldham, Dan Penn, and Duane Allman were equally important in crafting a style distinguished by rock-solid rhythms and passionate performances. With thorough liner notes about the songs, performers, and musicians, this is a fine introduction to the "deep soul" music that was envied by such heavyweights as the Rolling Stones. —*Richie Unterberger*

The Music Never Stopped: Roots of the Grateful Dead / Nov. 1995 / Shanachie ✦✦✦✦

An interesting concept: a compilation of the original versions of 17 songs frequently covered by the Grateful Dead in concert. Thoughtfully assembled, it showcases several aspects of their eclectic roots, encompassing jugband folk, country & western, Appalachian mountain music, country blues, '50s Chicago electric blues, R&B, Dylan, Guthrie, Holly, Berry, and more. Some of the recordings are very famous (Dylan's "It's All Over Now, Baby Blue," Holly's "Not Fade Away"); others are downright obscure (Obray Ramsey's "Rain and Snow," the rare original version of "Morning Dew" by little-known Canadian folkie Bonnie Dobson). If you're a Dead fan, this is a valuable, very listenable collection of some of their key influences. It may seem churlish to point this out to Deadheads, but if you're *not* a Dead fan, you'll find this to be a first-rate collection of roots music that's much more enjoyable than hearing the Dead's interpretations of the same tunes. —*Richie Unterberger*

☆ Naughty Rhythms: The Best of Pub Rock / Apr. 1996 / EMI Premier ✦✦✦✦✦

Pub rock is the frequently forgotten forefather of punk rock, although on the surface the two genres don't appear to have much in common. Punk rock was about revolution and pub rock was about tradition, at least superficially. But place pub rock in its proper context, and it was nearly as revolutionary as punk. In the early '70s, rock 'n' roll was dominated by heavy metal, art-rock, and blues-rock, all genres that required skill. The simple, laidback three-chord shuffles of pub rock—ranging from straightahead rock 'n' roll, to country and blues-rock—didn't require much skill, but it was a working class, do-it-yourself movement that took rock 'n' roll back to its roots, which is essentially what punk rock did. Furthermore, pub rock bands established a circuit of nightclubs within England, which is where all the original punk bands played. *Naughty Rhythms: The Best of Pub Rock* is the first comprehensive collection of the scene, featuring every major pub-rock band, as well as nearly every minor band. Compiled by former Kursaal Flyer Will Birch with Paul Bradshaw, the double-disc set effectively traces the development of the genre, from its country-rock roots with Brinsley Schwarz to the pounding, proto-punk of Eddie & the Hot Rods. In between, there are 34 other songs that cover all the aspects of pub rock, from the relaxed acoustic rock of Eggs Over Easy and the Stonesy groove of Ducks Deluxe and Dr. Feelgood to the commercial gloss of Ace and the eccentric rock of Kilburn and the High Roads. The double-disc set provides all the worthwhile songs from almost every band featured on the collection, with the notable exception of Brinsley Schwarz, who were already represented with five tracks. *Naughty Rhythms* is the definitive document of pub rock, and for most listeners, it will be all they need to know. —*Stephen Thomas Erlewine*

No Alternative / 1993 / Arista ✦✦✦✦✦
A mixture of B-sides, outtakes, live tracks, and newly recorded songs, *No Alternative* is the most successful benefit album of 1993, both commercially and artistically. Exceptional songs from Nirvana, Bob Mould, Barbara Manning, Overkill, Smashing Pumpkins, American Music Club, and Pavement enhance fine outtakes from Buffalo Tom and Matthew Sweet, strengthen Uncle Tupelo and Soul Asylum's strong covers, and make the weak live tracks from the Beastie Boys, Sonic Youth, and the Breeders tolerable. However, nothing can save the Goo Goo Dolls' atrocious pop-metal take on the Rolling Stones' "Bitch." Still, that's only one song out of 19, making *No Alternative* a worthy purchase. —*Stephen Thomas Erlewine*

☆ **Nuggets, Vol. 1: The Hits** / 198_ / Rhino ✦✦✦✦✦
A straightforward collection of garage-punk chart successes, including "Psychotic Reaction," "Dirty Water," "Nobody but Me," and "I Had Too Much to Dream Last Night." —*Bruce Eder*

Nuggets, Vol. 2 / 198_ / Rhino ✦✦✦
A top-notch collection of some of rock's spacier singles, B-sides, and odd tracks. —*Bruce Eder*

Nuggets, Vol. 3: Psychedilic / 198_ / Rhino ✦✦✦
A good assembly of spaced-out works. —*Bruce Eder*

Nuggets, Vol. 4: Pop, Pt. 2 / 1984 / Rhino ✦✦✦
Most of the acts here take their cues from the lightest aspects of the Beatles. More often than not, the results are pretty infectious. Highlights include the E-Types, the Royal Guardsmen, and the Palace Guard, which featured future Merry-Go-Round leader Emmitt Rhodes. —*Richie Unterberger*

Nuggets, Vol. 5: Pop, Pt. 3 / 1985 / Rhino ✦✦✦
A little sappier than the previous "pop" installments of this series. Highlighted by obscure, minor hit singles by the Strawberry Alarm Clock, the Knickerbockers, the Association, and the Lovin' Spoonful. —*Richie Unterberger*

Nuggets, Vol. 6: Punk, Pt. 2 / 1985 / Rhino ✦✦✦✦✦
Includes a lot of the greatest regional garage hits of the mid-'60s: the Brogues, We the People, the Unrelated Segments, the Chocolate Watch Band, and Mouse & the Traps all weigh in with strong cuts. Also includes worthy observations by Captain Beefheart ("Diddy Wah Diddy") and minor but exciting hits by the Shadows of Knight ("Oh Yeah") and the Electric Prunes (the psychedelic classic "Get Me to the World on Time"). —*Richie Unterberger*

Nuggets, Vol. 7: Early San Francisco / 1985 / Rhino ✦✦✦✦✦
A fine collection of pre-Summer of Love rarities from the mid-'60s. Besides hits by the Beau Brummels and We Five, it features rarities by tThe Vejtables, the Great Society (featuring a pre-Jefferson Airplane Grace Slick), and Country Joe & the Fish. —*Richie Unterberger*

Nuggets, Vol. 8: The Northwest / 198_ / Rhino ✦✦✦
The Northwest was renowned for some of the rawest, most R&B-grounded garage bands of the '60s. While the region wasn't as studded with riches as Texas and California, this comp has strong cuts by the Sonics and national hits by the Kingsmen and Paul Revere & the Raiders, as well as decent folk-rock psychedelia by the Daily Flash. —*Richie Unterberger*

Nuggets, Vol. 9: Acid Rock / 198_ / Rhino ✦✦✦
Switching to a decidedly heavier mode, this comp includes hits by Love, the Byrds, Steppenwolf, Iron Butterfly, the Chambers Brothers, Vanilla Fudge, and the Strawberry Alarm Clock, as well as worthy lighter, slightly obscure offerings by the Grass Roots, the Monkees, and the Young Rascals. —*Richie Unterberger*

Nuggets, Vol. 10: Folk Rock / 198_ / Rhino ✦✦
One of the weakest offerings in the series, with oft-anthologized hits by the Byrds, Turtles, Scott McKenzie, and Barry McGuire. The nonhit cuts tend toward the lightest, poppiest facets of folk-rock. An exception is the powerful acoustic, original version of "Dazed and Confused" by Jake Holmes, which was transformed into heavy metal by Led Zeppelin. —*Richie Unterberger*

Nuggets, Vol. 11: Pop, Pt. 4 / 198_ / Rhino ✦✦✦
Solid collection of slightly psychedelic-influenced, progressive '60s pop. Fine hits by the Left Banke, Fever Tree, and the Grass Roots, neat tracks by the Blues Project, Lee Michaels, and Gene Clark, worthy obscurities by the Magicians, Montage (a Left Banke spinoff), the Critters, and Keith. —*Richie Unterberger*

Nuggets, Vol. 12: Punk, Pt. 3 / 198_ / Rhino ✦✦✦
Decent offering of strong cuts by some of the most esteemed regional garage bands of the '60s. The hits by the Hombres, the Syndicate of Sound, and Paul Revere are actually outdone by the tracks from Mouse & the Traps, the Remains, the Unrelated Segments, Kenny & the Kasuals,

and the Lollipop Shoppe. Includes the hit "Shape of Things to Come," performed by Max Frost & the Troopers in the psychedelic exploitation film *Wild in the Streets.* —*Richie Unterberger*

Oh Yeah!: the Best of Dunwich Records / 1992 / Sundazed ✦✦✦✦✦
Dunwich Records was to '60s garage bands what Sun was to rockabilly. This CD features a generous sampling of the best of Chicago's teen scene of that period. Great sound and liner info, too. —*Cub Koda*

The Okeh Rhythm & Blues / Apr. 1, 1993 / Columbia ✦✦✦✦✦
A fine three-disc box, it features most of the greatest hits from the seminal R&B label. —*AMG*

Oldies but Goodies, Vol. 1 / Original Sound ✦✦✦
Oldies but Goodies was the first rock 'n' roll anthology, setting the standards for various artists anthologies when it was originally issued in the early '60s. Over the years, the series has held up well in many respects; although there isn't a unifying theme to any of the albums, the music is first rate, full of popular singles that form the basis of oldies radio stations. However, when the series made its transition to compact disc in 1987, it wasn't nearly as successful. Taken on their own terms, the fidelity of these 14 discs is quite bad, with muffled, distorted sound on almost every song; compared to CD reissues by other labels, the discs sound positively atrocious. If bad sound doesn't stand in your way, there's plenty of good music to be found on these CDs; the original records remain fine items. —*Stephen Thomas Erlewine*

One Hit Wonders: The 60s, Vol. 1 / Rhino ✦✦✦✦✦
So what if Barry & the Tamerlanes and Jimmy Soul never had another hit? The dozen tracks here by them and others like them will hold up long after a bigger star's music has faded. —*Jeff Tamarkin*

One Hit Wonders: The 60s, Vol. 2 / Rhino ✦✦✦✦✦
This stuff is too much fun! The Hombres, Soul Survivors, and more are a sure thing every time. —*Jeff Tamarkin*

Pebbles, Vol. 8: Southern California 1 / 1996 / AIP ✦✦✦✦✦
Southern California, and specifically the Los Angeles area, was one of the most active hotbeds of '60s garage punk, both because of its huge size and its flourishing musical and youth culture. Not all Los Angeles garage rock was great, and this 25-song compilation (much of which has appeared on previous vinyl garage anthologies, *Pebbles* included) is a good way to ferret out some of the better rare singles of the genre. Terry Randall's protest rocker "S.O.S," the Rumors' "Louie Louie" ripoff "Hold Me Now," Byron & the Mortals' organ-driven "Do You Believe Me," the Dovers' Byrds-meets-the-Zombies "She's Not Just Anybody"—all are among the best garage classics. Most of the rest is pretty good, if a bit generic at times. Lots of informative liner notes, too. —*Richie Unterberger*

Pebbles, Vols. 1-28 / ✦✦✦✦✦
In the early '70s, the *Nuggets* compilation reawakened listeners to the sounds of mid-'60s garage rock. As much of a revelation as that double album was at the time, it only focused on the tip of the iceberg of garage rock. Behind those forgotten hits and semihits lurked hundreds, if not thousands, of regional hits and flops from the same era, most even rawer and cruder. In the late '70s, the *Pebbles* compilations came along to fill in the gap and then some. Each volume gathered 15-20 obscure 45s—originally issued on tiny labels, and remastered right from the excruciatingly rare original vinyl—of prime mid-'60s garage rock. Sometimes a track by a relatively well-known performer would show up, but by and large these acts were unknown to anyone but collectors and those who happened to have lived in the areas where the bands played. More than any other factor, these compilations were responsible for the resurgence of interest in garage rock, which remains high among collectors to this day. The lyrical attitudes of the bands immortalized on *Pebbles* by and large have to do with cheating girls, adolescent rebellion, and high times. At times downright juvenile and sexist, the lyrics aren't the main attraction so much as the sound and stance, which anticipates the outrage of punk rock, but tempers it with tough British Invasion-inspired melodies, harmonies, and hooks, as well as fuzz-toned guitars, Farfisa organs, and wildly manic songwriting and performances. There are a lot of great unknown songs on *Pebbles*, way too many to cite in a brief review, from all over North America, most from 1965-67. There are also a fair number of generic tunes that have little to recommend beyond an excess of energy, which can make listening to an entire volume at once as much a challenge as a joy. Listeners approaching this series for the first time should search for the first ten volumes; after this initial burst, the well ran increasingly dry, and the later volumes can be a chore. Most of the individual installments don't have themes, but those looking for a concentration of certain items should check out *Vol. 3* (psychedelia) and *Vol. 6* (British R&B/mod); *Vol. 4*, devoted to surf, is actually the weakest of the early volumes. Of special interest among the later volumes are installments devoted to obscurities from the European continent. More wideranging in style than the typical volume covering US garage, these include albums devoted to '60s rarities from Holland, Sweden, Denmark,

and Switzerland; though wildly uneven, they contain some surprisingly strong material. —*Richie Unterberger*

☆ **Phat Trax, Vols. 1-5** / 1994 / Rhino ✦✦✦✦✦
Rhino's five-volume chronicle of '70s and '80s funk eclipses their *In Yo' Face* series simply by including more rarities and 12-inch mixes than its predecessor. The grooves on this series laid the groundwork for much of the hip-hop and R&B of the '80s and '90s, which makes it essential listening. —*Stephen Thomas Erlewine*

Punk You, Vol. 1 / 1995 / EMI ✦✦✦✦✦
No compilation that omits cuts by the Sex Pistols, Clash, and the Jam (to name just the most obvious examples) can claim to be a comprehensive survey of early punk. However, this 17-song collection does have notable songs (usually the most famous/notorious) by the Damned, Generation X, the Buzzcocks, X-Ray Spex, Siouxsie & the Banshees, Wire, Tom Robinson, Stiff Little Fingers, and 999, among others. That makes it a useful enough disc for someone who isn't concerned with building a massive punk collection, although the emphasis is almost totally upon British bands. —*Richie Unterberger*

Rare Surf, Vol. 3 / Feb. 27, 1996 / AVI ✦✦✦
Kudos to AVI for bringing another great volume of classic surf sounds to compact disc. This time it's a regular battle of the bands pitting Johnny Fortune vs. Johnny Barakat and the Vestalls with no clear- cut winner. For Mister Fortune's half of this 24-track compilation, it's the reish of his legendary *Soul Surfer* album, while Johnny & the Vestalls' 12 tracks run from raw demos to their scant few singles, all of it imbued with a teenage drive that's hard to beat. This is the real stuff right here. —*Cub Koda*

Rarest Rockabilly & Hillbilly Boogie: The Best . . . / Ace ✦✦✦✦✦
This is actually two earlier vinyl compilations on one compact disc, 28 tracks in all, hence the overlong title. The first compilation features artists incredibly obscure, playing music with a delightful, homespun crudity to all of it that's home, grown rock 'n' roll in a most embryonic stage. The second features more name-brand artists, the majority of them from the Starday catalog, and offers classic '50s sides from Sonny Fisher, Sleepy LaBeef, and a very young George Jones. —*Cub Koda*

Rebel Rousers: Southern Rock Classics / Jan. 24, 1992 / Rhino ✦✦✦✦✦
An audio tour of some of the genre's best moments, featuring seminal tracks by Lynyrd Skynyrd, the Allman Brothers Band, the Outlaws, the Marshall Tucker Band, and .38 Special. Interesting to compare these sides with the early-'90s vogue in country music. —*Cub Koda*

The Red Bird Story / 1991 / Charly ✦✦✦✦✦
Red Bird was a great label in the mid-'60s, releasing some excellent soul-pop hybrids and some of the greatest girl group records of all time, especially those by the Shangri-Las and the Dixie Cups. This four-CD, 96-track compilation is a frustratingly mixed attempt to enshrine its legacy. There are lots of great sides here: all the Shangri-Las and Dixie Cups hits, many of their rarities, one-shots by the Ad Libs, Jelly Beans, Butterflies, and Tradewinds, and cool rarities by Bessie Banks, Dee Dee Warwick, Evie Sands, Ellie Greenwich, the Soul Brothers, Cathy Saint, Linda Jones, and Andy Kim. But the programming is unnervingly jumpy and haphazard, the liner notes surprisingly fuzzy (no information whatsoever is given about many of the lesser-known artists), and, in the absence of master tapes, some of the cuts were obviously taken from records. And for all its length, it's not even a complete collection of Red Bird's output; some songs that were excluded had even surfaced on previous Charly vinyl anthologies. There's still a lot of great music here, but the execution could have been a lot better. —*Richie Unterberger*

Red Hot & Blue: A Tribute to Cole Porter / 1990 / Chrysalis ✦✦✦✦✦
These new recordings of Cole Porter songs (released in 1990) benefit AIDS research. Artists include U2, the Neville Brothers, Fine Young Cannibals, K.D. Lang, and Annie Lennox. The songs, recorded in a wide variety of styles, reaffirm what a great, timeless writer Porter was. —*Kenneth M. Cassidy*

Reservoir Dogs / 1992 / MCA ✦✦✦✦✦
Only five songs here were featured prominently in Quentin Tarantino's rousing crime film ("Little Green Bag," "Hooked On a Feeling," "I Gotcha," "Stuck in the Middle with You," and "Coconut"), but they include Steven Wright's introductions from the film (separately indexed, thankfully), as well as Tarantino's infamous interpretation of the meaning of Madonna's "Like a Virgin" and Harvey Keitel's monologue on how to rob a jewelry store. In total, that's about 15 to 20 minutes of material. Padding out the rest of the disc are three new songs—"Fool for Love" is very good, "Harvest Moon" passable, and "Magic Carpet Ride" is abominable. After this, the disc has passed the half-hour mark by two minutes. The amount of music you'll actually want to listen to makes it even shorter, but it is a soundtrack you'll want to return to. —*Stephen Thomas Erlewine*

The Return of the Del-Fi & Donna Story / 1994 / Del-Fi ✦✦✦
Like the first volume (*The Del-Fi & Donna Story*), this has 30-odd cuts from the late- '50s to early- '60s heyday of Del-Fi, the Los Angeles-based

indie noted for recording Ritchie Valens, Johnny Crawford, and various one-shot artists. The music isn't as strong as the previous disc, but it does go further into the vaults for rarer items (some of which were previously unreleased), although as a whole it's kind of a mish-mash of styles. There are reasonably interesting numbers by the likes of Preston Epps, Ron Holden, Chan Romero (including some of his unreleased demos), doo woppers the Pentagons, the Addrisi Brothers, and a few instrumental acts, though nothing that would appeal to those without a very deep interest in early rock 'n' roll. —*Richie Unterberger*

☆ **Rock Instrumental Classics, Vol. 1: The '50s** / 1994 / Rhino ✦✦✦✦✦
Rhino begins yet another concept line with 18 tasty instrumentals from the rock era. It's the first of a five-volume set devoted to this genre, and they certainly picked the right era to launch it. From Duane Eddy's shuddering guitar riffs and Link Wray's rumbling licks to Lee Allen's honking sax lines and bleating phrases, Dave "Baby" Cortez's distorted organ and Ernie Fields' swing-boogie, this anthology shows how early rock 'n' roll emerged through the union of seemingly disparate musical elements. Besides big-band jazz and shouting blues, there were also bits of rockabilly, pop, novelty tunes, and country, reworked and presented in short, captivating ditties. —*Ron Wynn*

☆ **Rock Instrumental Classics, Vol. 2: The '60s** / Rhino ✦✦✦✦✦
The second release in Rhino's rock instrumentals series moves into the 1960s, again presenting a wide array of material. There's jazz-tinged fare by pianist Ray Bryant, roadhouse blues-boogie from Lonnie Mack, the Ventures' signature surf tune, "Walk Don't Run," and another Duane Eddy floor-shaker, "Because They're Young." This collection also shows that the novelty and silly tunes weren't quite as inspired in the 1960s; neither the Fireballs' "Bulldog" nor the T-Bones' "No Matter What Shape (Your Stomach's In)" will ever make anyone forget the Coasters. There are several interesting gimmick and period-piece oddities, from Mason Williams' "Classical Gas" to Jorgen Ingmann's "Apache" and (Ghost) Riders in the Sky" by the Ramroads. It's shorter than the first volume and has a bit more fluff, but is still quite valuable. —*Ron Wynn*

Rock Instrumental Classics, Vol. 3: The '70s / 1971 / Rhino ✦✦✦✦
Rhino's third rock instrumentals volume covers the '70s, a period that found disco, funk, and fusion joining the formula alongside one-shot concept works and the usual novelty numbers. The 18 cuts include stomping club-funk from B.T. Express and Brass Construction, King Curtis' updated honking sax cover of Led Zeppelin's "Whole Lotta Love," very stylized material from the Electric Light Orchestra and Deodato, and memorable outings by Billy Preston, Edgar Winter, and AWB. Gary Glitter, Edgar Winter, the Chakachas, Rhinoceros, and Van McCoy offer lighter pop variations, and "Sun Goddess" was a musically adventurous excursion into fusion by Earth, Wind and Fire. —*Ron Wynn*

☆ **Rock Instrumental Classics, Vol. 4: Soul** / 1962 / Rhino ✦✦✦✦
While the material on volume four of Rhino's rock instrumentals set chronologically preceded what was on the third volume, no soul, R&B, or even soul-jazz and funk fan should mind these 18 genuine classics, including two superb numbers from Booker T. and the MGs, seminal tracks by the Mar-Keys, Bar-Kays, and Cannonball Adderley, and great Latin tunes from Ray Barretto and Mongo Santamaria. There's absolutely no fluff, and the presence on CD of rare cuts like the Young Holt Trio's "Wack Wack" and Alvin Cash & the Crawlers' "Twine Time" is most welcome. —*Ron Wynn*

☆ **+ Rock Instrumental Classics, Vol. 5: Surf** / 1961 / Rhino ✦✦✦✦✦
Rhino closes its five-volume rock instrumentals series with an 18-track outing devoted to surf guitar. This fast-paced, prickly, and frequently exciting form may not be among the most diversified structurally, but it does offer some surging playing from its practitioners. They range from founding father Dick Dale to its most popular bands, the Surfaris, Belairs, Ventures, and Chantays. While not particularly a hard-core surf collection, this disc certainly outlines its virtues, and the tunes were long enough to display guitar proficiency, but short enough to prevent self-indulgence and repetition. —*Ron Wynn*

☆ **Rock This Town: Rockabilly Hits, Vol. 2** / 1991 / Rhino ✦✦✦✦✦
The second volume of this anthology is just as satisfying through the first ten tracks, when it suddenly veers toward contemporary interpreters. —*Bill Dahl*

Rock of the 80's / Priority ✦✦✦✦✦
Like Priority's *'70s Greatest Rock Hits* series, the 15-volume *Rock of the '80s* offers a haphazard, yet enjoyable, presentation of hit singles and one-hit wonders from each year of the decade. While the '70s discs are loosely arranged according to theme, the '80s discs just feature ten songs, regardless of when they were released or what they are about. Nevertheless, the series features a nice cross-section of songs and the sound is good, even if there are no liner notes. Despite its flaws, the series remains a good sampler of '80s pop hits. —*Stephen Thomas Erlewine*

Rockabilly in Memphis: 1954-1968 / 1954-1968 / Smithsonian ✦✦✦✦✦
Many superb rockabilly acts never got their day in the sun, and the genre

has not received the documentation it merits. This 18-cut anthology goes a long way towards straightening out this problem; it includes cuts from such neglected performers as Ray Harris, Sonny Burgess, Carl Mann, Malcolm Yelvington, and Ray Smith. Robert Gordon's notes detail exactly how the intersection of Southern Black and White cultures resulted in rockabilly, a genuine hybrid that shared characteristics of both. While such selections as Johnny Cash's "I Walk the Line" and Roy Orbison's "Ooby Dooby" have been reissued to death, hearing them one more time is not much to ask for the chance to get Carl McVoy's version of "You Are My Sunshine." —*Ron Wynn*

Rockin' in the Farmhouse: Original Rockabilly and Chicken Bop, Vol. 2 / 1992 / Sundazed ◆◆◆◆◆
Rockin' in the Farmhouse—Original Rockabilly and Chicken Bop—Vol. 2 is an excellent 20-track compilation featuring the best of the Roulette label's rarest rockabilly tracks. Highlights include Don "Red" Roberts' "Only One," Jimmy Isle's "Goin' Wild," Jimmy Lloyd's "Rocket in My Pocket," and five chaotic unissued tracks by The Rock-A-Teens. —*Cub Koda*

☆ **Roots of British Rock** / Sire ◆◆◆◆◆
Easily the most comprehensive early British rock collection ever assembled, and all the more amazing since it is a US release. From Tommy Steele in 1956 to the Tornados in 1962, there are few major stones left unturned on this jewel of a two-record set. An honest look at what was popular in Britain before the Beatles. A vital addition to any oldies collection. —*Bruce Eder*

San Francisco Nights / 1991 / Rhino ◆◆◆◆◆
Probably the most interesting and accessible collection of its kind ever to come from America, more substantial than many European collections. Featuring the obvious and the weird, including the Beau Brummels, the Charlatans, the Vegetables, and the Mystery Trend. —*Bruce Eder*

The Scepter Records Story / May 26, 1992 / Capricorn ◆◆◆◆◆
During the '50s and early '60s, NYC-based Scepter Records and its subsidiary Wand were part of a group of independents whose artists churned out hit after hit, defining the sound of the day and shaping the sound of the future. The Shirelles, Dionne Warwick, and the Isley Brothers all got their start there; if you love tough, pre-soul-era records like "Will You Still Love Me Tomorrow," "Twist and Shout," and "Walk On By," then this is for you. The label's roster also included singers Chuck Jackson, Maxine Brown, and Tommy Hunt; instrumentalist King Curtis; proto-pop/country artists B. J. Thomas and Ronnie Milsap; and punksters Kingsmen. That's right—"Louie Louie" is here, along with lots of other truly great music. Even though the three discs could have been condensed to a killer two, this box gets high marks. —*Christine Ohlman*

Shakin' Fit! / 1992 / Candy ◆◆◆◆◆
1960s soul music wasn't just Motown, earnest gospel-filled ballads, and dancefloor rabble-rousers. There were also quite a few soul performers who treated the music as fun, first and foremost, taking a somewhat looser and goofier approach than the stars that had long careers. This 29-track CD is a good document of soul music as pure fun, by singers who never had a hit (Don & Dewey are the only marginally recognizable names here), and who owed stronger debts to the honking R&B music of the '50s than most other soul performers. Some of these are downright funny novelties (the Five Du-Tones' "The Chicken Astronaut," Emanual Laskey's "Welfare Cheese"); a great deal of these are novelty-tinged dance tunes that verge on silly, in the best sense of the word ("The Frog," "Skin the Cat," "Sticky Pig Feet," "The Cow," "The Chicken Scratch"). This could have done with some decent liner notes (there are virtually none), but it's a good deal for soul fans looking for some totally overlooked and fun-filled rarities. —*Richie Unterberger*

Slow Jams: The 60s, Vols. 1 & 2 / The Right Stuff ◆◆◆
There aren't many surprises on these collections of romantic soul ballads from the '60s: lots of fine songs, virtually all of them big hits, nothing obscure in the least. For the general fan who just wants a decently programmed set, it does the job, with cuts by such greats as Percy Sledge, Aretha Franklin, Otis Redding, Dionne Warwick, the Temptations, James Brown, Smokey Robinson, and one-shots like Doris Troy and Barbara Mason, along with good liner notes from soul expert David Nathan. —*Richie Unterberger*

Slow Jams: The 70s, Vols. 1-3 / The Right Stuff ◆◆◆
The *Slow Jams* compilations of romantic soul ballads are obviously not designed for the ravenous collector: there are only ten tracks per disc, the liner notes are informative but basic, and most of the selections are well-known hits. But if you just want some basic highlights of lush '70s soul, or you're giving this to someone with a short attention span, the series does a respectable job. Hits by stars like Al Green, the Stylistics, the Isleys, the O'Jays, and Barry White are mixed with cuts by lesser-known singers like Sylvia, Norman Connors, and Major Harris. —*Richie Unterberger*

Smooth Grooves: A Sensual Collection, Vol. 5 / 1996 / Rhino ◆◆◆
The *Smooth Grooves* series is an exceptional collection of neglected soul and urban R&B singles. Concentrating on the early '80s and late '70s, the

selections of the series are lush and seductive, drawing from Philly soul and disco in equal measures. *Smooth Grooves, Vol. 5* features selections by the Spinners, Teddy Pendergrass, Grover Washington, Jr., the Manhattans, and Earth, Wind & Fire. —*Stephen Thomas Erlewine*

Smooth Grooves: A Sensual Collection, Vol. 6 / 1996 / Rhino ◆◆◆
The *Smooth Grooves* series is an exceptional collection of neglected soul and urban R&B singles. Concentrating on the early '80s and late '70s, the selections of the series are lush and seductive, drawing from Philly soul and disco in equal measures. *Smooth Grooves, Vol. 6* features selections by the Bobby Womack, the Persauders, Debra Laws, the O'Jays, Shirley Murdock, and a duet with Phyllis Hyman and Michael Henderson. —*Stephen Thomas Erlewine*

Smooth Grooves: A Sensual Collection, Vol. 7 / 1996 / Rhino ◆◆◆
The *Smooth Grooves* series is an exceptional collection of neglected soul and urban R&B singles. Concentrating on the early '80s and late '70s, the selections of the series are lush and seductive, drawing from Philly soul and disco in equal measures. *Smooth Grooves, Vol. 7* features selections by Ready for the World, Betty Wright, Force MD's, A Taste of Honey, Klymaxx, and Stacy Lattisaw. —*Stephen Thomas Erlewine*

Songs by Richard Thompson / 1994 / Capitol ◆◆◆
One of the better tribute albums of 1994, *Beat the Retreat* manages to capture not only the dark grace of Richard Thompson, but also his spirit. R.E.M.'s faithful reading of "Wall of Death" is full of beautiful melancholy, while Bob Mould's galloping take on "Turning of the Tide" pays homage to Thompson's breathtaking instrumental skills simply by making the song his own. Most of *Beat the Retreat* works in the same way. The artists' love for the material never shadows their appreciation for Thompson's individuality. Hence, the songs are never replications of the original versions; they are interpretations, which is much more effective. —*Stephen Thomas Erlewine*

Songs of Protest / 1991 / Rhino ◆◆◆
Of course there are too many noteworthy songs of protest to fit onto one collection, even (or especially) if you're limiting youself to the '60s, as Rhino does on this compilation. Still, it does a good job of mixing monster hits by Barry McGuire, Sonny Bono, Dion, the Kingston Trio, the Temptations, and Edwin Starr with more obscure cuts. Country Joe's "I-Feel-Like-I'm-Fixin'-to-Die Rag" is here, as well as Sonny Bono's self-pitying "Laugh at Me," the pre-electric Donovan's cover of Buffy Saint-Marie's "Universal Soldier," and Manfred Mann's fine, overlooked cover of Dylan's "With God on Our Side." The most hard-to-find songs span the opposite ends of the spectrum. "It's Good News Week," a 1966 hit for the Jonathan King-led group Hedgehoppers Anonymous, is a lightweight catalog of social ills that retains considerable period charm. Far more earnest is Phil Ochs' "I Ain't Marchin' Anymore," represented here by the non-LP, electric folk-rock version released as a single in 1966. Although it made no commercial impact, it holds up to the best protest anthems of the era, both musically and lyrically. —*Richie Unterberger*

☆ **Soul Hits of the 70s: Didn't It Blow Your Mind, Vol. 1** / 1991 / Rhino ◆◆◆◆◆
This 15-volume set was released in 1991 and is a veritable Comstock Lode of overlooked hits from an era most rock fans have yet to discover. By offering the best recordings by the likes of the O'Jays, the Blue Notes, the Chi-Lites, and many others, *Soul Hits* gives the listener a feel for just how vital Black pop and disco was in an era when rock was starting to sag. But the inclusion of dozens of forgotten one-shot hits makes each volume a history lesson in the continued innovation and sheer joy of R&B, proving that Blacks didn't stop making great music after Muddy Waters and Sly Stone bit the dust. —*John Floyd*

Soul Shots, Vol. 1: We Got More Soul (Dance Party) / 1987 / Rhino ◆◆◆◆◆
The 11-volume *Soul Shots* series, originally issued on vinyl in the late '80s, are the best general overview compilations of soul music. They've since been condensed into a four-CD series which reprises some of the highlights from the records and adds some new tracks. As many of the songs from the original 11-volume set didn't make it onto the CDs, the vinyl editions, which are still easy to find, are still recommended, and even necessary, for the soul connoisseur. *Vol. 1*, with the focus on raucous uptempo numbers, has a characteristic mix of stars (James Brown, Jackie Wilson) with important minor figures (Jackie Lee, J.J. Jackson, Dyke & the Blazers, Robert Parker). With thorough liner notes, these compilations are great ways to catch up on a lot of the best one- and two-shot artists of the soul era. —*Richie Unterberger*

Soul Shots, Vol. 2: The "In" Crowd / 1987 / Rhino ◆◆◆◆◆
"Sweet soul" is not slow ballads, but light-hearted, pop-oriented soul, with the accent on pleasant (often high) vocal arrangements. Not as critically respected as dance soul, deep soul, Motown, or some other subgenres, there were nonetheless many fine cuts recorded in this style during soul's heyday. This compilation has a lot of good ones, including Brenton Wood's "Gimme Little Sign," Deon Jackson's "Love Makes the World Go Round," the Esquires' "Get On Up," the Larks' "The Jerk,"

Bobby Hebb's "Sunny," and several other lesser-known cuts. —*Richie Unterberger*

Soul Shots, Vol. 3: Soul Twist (Soul Instrumentals) / 1987 / Rhino ✦✦✦✦✦

More than other mid- and late-'60s pop styles, soul lent itself well to instrumentals, both party tunes and slower romantic stuff. This volume has big hits by most of the major soul instrumental stars (Booker T. & the MG's, the Mar-Keys, King Curtis, the Bar-Kays, Young-Holt Unlimited, Ramsey Lewis, Hugh Masekela), as well as one-shots like Cliff Nobles ("The Horse") and cuts by Alvin Cash and the Viscounts that rarely get played on oldies radio. —*Richie Unterberger*

Soul Shots, Vol. 4: Tell Mama (Screamin' Soul Sisters) / 1987 / Rhino ✦✦✦✦✦

One of the best volumes of the series, assembling some of soul's most emotional and expressive female performers. Running from Motown imitations to novelties to pop-soul to raw deep soul to blues-soul, it has outstanding cuts by Etta James, Koko Taylor, Maxine Brown, Fontella Bass, Barbara George, Gloria Jones, and Shirley Ellis. Lorraine Ellison, Linda Jones, and Patti Drew are names only known to serious soul fans, but their tracks are just as fine as the ones by more famous names, and the two selections by Aretha Franklin are among her more obscure ("Lee Cross," from her Columbia era, and the 1968 B-side "You Send Me"). —*Richie Unterberger*

Soul Shots, Vol. 5: La-La Means I Love You / 1987 / Rhino ✦✦✦✦

Another good mixture of stars and one-shots, different regions, and different styles. This has cuts by the Impressions, James Carr, Lou Rawls, and Aaron Neville, Philly soul by the Delfonics and Eddie Holman, girl group soul by Barbara Mason, blue-eyed soul by Thee Midniters, New York soul by Garnett Mimms, and eccentric soul by Billy Stewart. All cuts are first-rate slow-tempo smoochers. —*Richie Unterberger*

Soul Shots, Vol. 6: Blue-Eyed Soul / 1988 / Rhino ✦✦✦✦

There weren't a great deal of White performers who sang and wrote soul with authentic conviction—most knew better than to try—but there were a few who not only pulled it off, but did it well, sometimes even crossing over into the Black audience. This LP has many of the more notable blue-eyed soul performers: the Rascals, Tony Joe White, Roy Head, Bill Deal, the Soul Survivors—as well as interesting obscurities in the style by the likes of Bob Kuban and Dean Parrish, and cuts in a blue-eyed soul vein by performers not strictly associated with the style, like P.J. Proby, Billy Joe Royal, Lonnie Mack, and Wayne Cochran. It's missing major blue-eyed soulsters like the Righteous Brothers, John Fred, and the Box Tops, but those performers have good anthologies of their own. —*Richie Unterberger*

Soul Shots, Vol. 7: Urban Blues / 1988 / Rhino ✦✦✦✦✦

Another interesting subgenre that doesn't get a lot of critical attention: city blues bearing heavy soul influences. Every one of the performers on this compilation was a blues or soul performer of significance. B.B. King, Junior Wells, Albert King, Buddy Guy, and Otis Rush are bluesmen represented by some of their most soul-soaked cuts; Little Junior Parker, Bobby Bland, Little Milton, and Lowell Fulsom worked the territory between soul, R&B, and blues; Tommy Tucker and Little Johnny Taylor were R&B singers who had hits with heavy blues influences, rounding out the several perspectives of this anthology. —*Richie Unterberger*

Soul Shots, Vol. 8: Sweet Soul Sisters / 1988 / Rhino ✦✦✦✦✦

They may be sweet in that they sing about love and have a lot of pop appeal, but the female soul singers on this anthology are measurably earthier and heavier than the male "sweet" soul singers spotlighted on *Vol. 2* of this series. Jan Bradley, the Jewels, and Betty Everett fall close to the girl group sound; the Sweet Inspirations, led by Cissy Houston (mother of Whitney), take it to the most gospel-flavored extreme. Barbara Acklin and Brenda & the Tabulations are among the better-known minor female soul stars; there are also obscure singers like Jackie Ross, Patti Drew, and the Flirtations, whose hit "Nothing but a Heartache" was one of the best soul one-shots of the '60s. For many listeners, the highlight will be Gloria Jones' original version of "Tainted Love," emasculated into a synth-pop hit much later by Soft Cell. Jones' rendition isn't exactly sweet soul, but a storming dance number that ranks as one of the great hits-that-never-were of the '60s. —*Richie Unterberger*

Soul Shots, Vol. 9: More Dance Party / 1988 / Rhino ✦✦✦✦✦

As *Soul Shots* volumes go, this is populated with more obscure performers/songs than usual, enhancing its appeal for collectors without decreasing in accessibility whatsoever. Etta James, Ike & Tina Turner, and Johnnie Taylor are stars, of course; there are also thrilling one-shots by the Capitols ("Cool Jerk"), the Parliaments ("I Wanna Testify," with a lineup including George Clinton), and the Marvelows ("I Do"). Jamo Thomas' "I Spy (For the FBI)" is one of soul's finer novelties, and the compilation also includes the rare original versions of the standards "Shake a Tail Feather" (by the Five Du-Tones) and "Mustang Sally" (by Sir Mack Rice). —*Richie Unterberger*

Soul Shots, Vol. 10: More Sweet Soul / 1988 / Rhino ✦✦✦✦✦

At least as good, and perhaps better than, the original "Sweet Soul" volume. This has classic hits by Tyrone Davis, Major Lance, James Carr, the Impressions, and the Dells, as well as lesser-known selections by the O'Jays and Eddie Floyd, and hard-to-find items by the likes of the Radiants, Tony Clarke, Bobby Moore, and the Poets. The Showmen's "39-21-46," featuring future Chairmen of the Board lead singer General Johnson, is one of early soul's most genuinely eccentric moments. —*Richie Unterberger*

Soul Shots, Vol. 11: More Ballads / 1988 / Rhino ✦✦✦✦✦

For the soul fan looking to dig a little deeper than established classics, this is probably more exciting than the previous ballad collection in this series. McKinley Mitchell, Spyder Turner, Betty Harris, Jimmy Holiday—they're all names known primarily to collectors, and they're all represented here. So are stars like the Impressions, Chuck Jackson, the Dells, and O.V. Wright, but the tracks are not among their famous hits. Especially interesting are the original versions of "Get It While You Can" (by Howard Tate), later covered by Janis Joplin, and "You Can Make It If You Try" (by Gene Allison), covered by the Rolling Stones on their first album. Other highlights are Jay Wiggins' "Sad Girl," one of the most haunting soul ballads ever, and Gloria Walker's "Talking About My Baby," one of the most deliciously bitchy and spiteful female soul performances, despite the fact that it rips off Etta James' "I'd Rather Go Blind." —*Richie Unterberger*

☆ **Soul Train: Hall of Fame** / 1974-1991 / Rhino ✦✦✦✦✦

"Soul Train," the longest-running weekly syndicated program in television, gave Black artists and dancers a forum when there was no interest from the major networks. This fine three-disc boxed set celebrates the show's two decades and serves as a good overview for how contemporary black pop has changed during its run. The opening disc is by far the most diverse; during the mid-'70s, there was still room for Southern soul and blues, stylish pop, funk, and vocal groups. The second disc mirrors the turn toward more sophisticated production, a less soulful sound, and the coming of disco. The final CD begins with light soul and pop-tinged fare, then slides into rap, hip-hop and new jack swing. Most of these songs are available elsewhere, but this collection gives listeners a consistently entertaining tour. Rhino deserves bonus points for using all original versions throughout. —*Ron Wynn*

Sound of the Seventies: 1974 / 1990 / Time-Life ✦✦✦✦✦

A solid, 20-track collection of hits that serve the memory of the year well. Includes Al Wilson's "Show and Tell," Eric Clapton's "I Shot the Sheriff," Elton John's "Bennie and the Jets," Lynyrd Skynyrd's "Sweet Home Alabama," and Brownsville Station's "Smokin' in the Boy's Room." —*Cub Koda*

Space Daze 2000 / Jan. 30, 1996 / Cleopatra ✦✦✦✦✦

The sequel to *Space Daze, Space Daze 2000* is an excellent sampling of ambient music. Drawing from both techno and rock, the collection features groundbreaking tracks from Brian Eno, Kraftwerk, and David Bowie, as well as tracks from artists like Future Sound of London and Spiral Realms that popularized ambient in the '90s. It's a perfect introduction to a sometimes challenging music. —*Stephen Thomas Erlewine*

The Specialty Story / 1994 / Specialty ✦✦✦✦✦

Label-owner Art Rupe was a business man who knew the Black jukebox industry and what made it tick when he started his Specialty label in the late-'40s. This sumptuous five-disc box set contains a bevy of highlights from this seminal R&B/rock 'n' roll label. Over the years, Rupe recorded a bit of everything; early big-band jump (the Liggins brothers), down-home blues and zydeco (Guitar Slim, Frankie Lee Sims, Clifton Chenier), gospel (early Sam Cooke and the Soul Stirrers), and doo wop (the Pentagons, Jesse Belvin). But with the discovery of the label's biggest star, Little Richard, in 1955, here is where the real story of rock 'n' roll begins. A box set that no lover of the real thing can be without. —*Cub Koda*

Stax Presents . . . Sweet Soul Music / 1988 / Stax ✦✦✦

Stax is usually thought of as the gritty alternative to pop-soul, but in their later years it recorded a fair quantity of "sweet" soul more akin to Motown and Gamble-Huff than Otis Redding and Wilson Pickett. This has 13 Stax productions from the late '60s and early '70s, sung by smooth (and obscure) male groups like the Limitations, the Epsilons, the Lords, the Newcomers, and Fat Larry's Band; the Dramatics and (to a lesser degree) the Mad Lads and the Temprees are the only easily recognizable names to casual soul fans. It's okay, but primarily for collectors. It's pleasantly produced and harmonized, but nothing jumps out as a lost classic, and there are better discs of late-period sweet soul around. —*Richie Unterberger*

The Stax Soul Sisters / 1988 / Stax ✦✦✦

Fourteen cuts of female-sung soul, cut for the Stax label between the late '60s and mid-'70s. It's fair material that will largely appeal to collectors, not being near the top echelon of either soul music or Stax recordings. Carla Thomas, Barbara Lewis, Carla Thomas, Inez Foxx, and Mavis Staples are all represented by little-known tracks; second- or third-division singers like Linda Lyndell, Veda Brown, Mabel John, and Margie Joseph fill out the rest of the disc. The ears only really perk up for Jean Knight's sassy "Mr. Big Stuff," a 1971 No. 2 hit that's available on various other compilations. —*Richie Unterberger*

Stax/Volt Revue, Vol. 3: Live in Europe—Hit the Road Stax / 1992 / Stax ✦✦✦✦✦
Seventy-two minutes of early 1967 performances from the European tour of the Stax/Volt Revue, recorded in London and Paris, with cuts by Booker T. & the MG's, Carla Thomas, Otis Redding, Eddie Floyd, and the Mar-Keys. Not released until 1992, none of these tracks were included on four previous albums of material from the tour. It's certainly up to the level of those other recordings, in both performance and sound quality, Booker T. & the MG's coming off as especially tight. —*Richie Unterberger*

The Stiff Records Box Set / 1992 / Rhino ✦✦✦✦✦
Stiff Records was the first independent record label in England, partially responsible for starting the punk and new wave revolution of the late '70s. Under the guidance of house producer Nick Lowe, Stiff turned out an enormous number of seminal punk and new wave singles in their first years, including classic tracks by the Damned, Elvis Costello, Graham Parker, the Adverts, Ian Dury, and Lowe himself. But what really gave the label its wild, original flavor were minor artists like Ian Dury, Wreckless Eric, Tenpole Tudor, the Yachts, Lene Lovich, Rachel Sweet, and Mickey Jupp, who turned out a series of raw pop gems that were everything good rock 'n' roll singles should be—catchy, energetic, and memorable. Over 100 of Stiff's finest tracks are collected on this wonderful four-disc box set. While most of these songs weren't hits, they are classic rock 'n' roll. The first three discs are excellent; the fourth disc contains some bright moments, but by that time, their artists were pretty much spent. However, the box remains one of the most compulsively listenable sets ever assembled, providing the definitive retrospective of arguably the most important and influential British record label of the late '70s. —*Stephen Thomas Erlewine*

The Sue Records Story / 1994 / EMI ✦✦✦
An extensive 100-song four-CD document of this label from the Big Apple, it includes hits, B-sides, and rarities by Ike & Tina Turner, Baby Washington, Barbara George, the Soul Sisters, Eddie and Ernie, and more. —*Rick Clark*

Sun & Surf, Cars & Guitars / 1994 / Del-Fi ✦✦✦
Another Del-Fi compilation that mixes up a bunch of rarities into a blender, spitting it out as "Sun, Surf, Cars & Guitars," an umbrella that doesn't leave much out when you're talking early rock 'n' roll. The lack of liner notes adds to the slapped-together feel, but it's a decent pastiche of material that found a home on the Los Angeles label in the early half of the '60s, though a good deal of the cuts by the Lively Ones, Bobby Fuller, the Centurions, and others can be found on other Del-Fi comps. As far as enticing collectibles go, the "Twist and Shout" ripoff by the American Four tops the list, as it features a pre-Love Arthur Lee as lead vocalist. There are also three hot-rod instrumentals by the Darts with Glen Campbell on guitar, a Buddy Hollyish number by Dick Dale, and future Beach Boy Bruce Johnston's "Do the Surfer Stomp." —*Richie Unterberger*

☆ **The Sun Records Story** / Rhino ✦✦✦✦✦
Landmark '50s recordings from Memphis by Presley, Cash, Orbison, Jerry Lee Lewis, Carl Perkins, and others. —*Hank Davis*

☆ **The Sun Story** / 1994 / Rhino ✦✦✦✦✦
There have been a lot of Sun compilations over the years; this three-CD, 74-song compilation strikes the medium ground between abridged single-disc highlights and overkill ten-album box sets. What this means is that you get virtually all the key sides of this vastly influential blues, country, and rockabilly label, including the biggest Sun hits cut by Elvis, Carl Perkins, Jerry Lee Lewis, Johnny Cash, Charlie Rich, and Roy Orbison. There's also a lot of the pioneering electric blues cut by label head Sam Phillips before he made rockabilly Sun's focus, including sides by Howlin' Wolf, B.B. King, Rufus Thomas, Junior Parker, and James Cotton. Then there are the interesting small hits and flops by minor rockabilly figures like Warren Smith, Billy Lee Riley, Malcolm Yelvington, Onie Wheeler, and Carl Mann. There aren't any previously unreleased songs, so the Sun specialist most likely already has everything here; it's a better buy for the avid, knowledgeable fan who isn't a completist. —*Richie Unterberger*

☆ **Super Hits of the '70s: Have a Nice Day, Vols. 1-4** / 1990 / Rhino ✦✦✦✦✦
The definitive collection of AM hits from an FM decade. —*Jeff Tamarkin*

☆ **Super Hits of the '70s: Have a Nice Day, Vol. 2** / Feb. 1990 / Rhino ✦✦✦✦✦
This is where it gets silly—"My Baby Loves Lovin'," "Spirit in the Sky," "Everything Is Beautiful." Pass the smiley-face buttons, please. —*Jeff Tamarkin*

☆ **Super Hits of the '70s: Have a Nice Day, Vol. 3** / Rhino ✦✦✦✦✦
What a weird decade—did we really buy all those Bobby Sherman and Melanie records? —*Jeff Tamarkin*

☆ **Super Hits of the '70s: Have a Nice Day, Vol. 5** / Rhino ✦✦✦✦✦
"Chick a Boom," "Me and You and a Dog Named Boo," "When You're Hot You're Hot." And Nixon in the White House?! Say it was all a bad dream. —*Jeff Tamarkin*

☆ **Super Hits of the '70s: Have a Nice Day, Vol. 6** / Jun. 1990 / Rhino ✦✦✦✦✦
It just gets sillier, folks—by this time (1970-1971), "Signs" and "Gimme Dat Ding" were the best the Top 40 had to offer. No wonder Grand Funk got so huge! —*Jeff Tamarkin*

Super Hits of the '70s: Have a Nice Day, Vol. 8 / Aug. 1990 / Rhino ✦✦✦✦✦
Did Gilbert O'Sullivan really exist? Did Sammy Davis, Jr., really sing "Candy Man?" Be a believer with this best of 1972. —*Jeff Tamarkin*

Super Hits of the '70s: Have a Nice Day, Vol. 9 / Sep. 1990 / Rhino ✦✦✦✦✦
"Brandy," "Popcorn," and "Frankenstein." And those were the good ones. —*Jeff Tamarkin*

☆ **Super Hits of the '70s: Have a Nice Day, Vol. 10** / Oct. 1990 / Rhino ✦✦✦✦✦
Even the '70s were realizing it was no '60s—"It Never Rains in Southern California," "Brother Louie," "Dead Skunk." Get a life, all of you. —*Jeff Tamarkin*

Super Hits of the '70s: Have a Nice Day, Vol. 12 / Dec. 1990 / Rhino ✦✦✦✦✦
A fun volume, featuring "The Streak," "Rock and Roll, Hoochie Koo," and "Jim Dandy," for starters. But then again, there's "Seasons in the Sun." —*Jeff Tamarkin*

☆ **Super Hits of the '70s: Have a Nice Day, Vol. 13** / 1990 / Rhino ✦✦✦✦✦
"Billy Don't Be a Hero," "The Night Chicago Died," "Beach Baby." If 1974 isn't a contender for rock's most inane year, I don't know what is. —*Jeff Tamarkin*

Super Hits of the '70s: Have a Nice Day, Vol. 14 / Rhino ✦✦✦✦✦
Yes, "Kung Fu Fighting" really was a hit. So were "Chevy Van" and "Jackie Blue." Don't believe us? Here's proof. —*Jeff Tamarkin*

Super Hits of the '70s: Have a Nice Day, Vol. 15 / 1990 / Rhino ✦✦✦✦✦
Yeah, 1975-1976: "Convoy," "Rocky," "Run Joey Run," "I'm Not Lisa." No wonder punk rock was around the corner. —*Jeff Tamarkin*

Super Hits of the '70s: Have a Nice Day, Vol. 16 / 1993 / Rhino ✦✦✦✦✦
Vol. 16 contains the most cream here, mainly because 1970-72 was the peak for this kind of post-bubblegum ear candy. "Vehicle" by the Ides Of March remains a summer cruising classic; Blues Image's "Ride Captain Ride" and Tin Tin's "Toast and Marmalade for Tea" maintain a deliciously off-center psychedelic edge. —*Roch Parisien*

Super Hits of the '70s: Have a Nice Day, Vol. 17 / 1993 / Rhino ✦✦✦✦✦
Vol. 17, covering primarily 1973-75, offers the exuberant "Dancing in the Moonlight" (King Harvest), the sassy "Smokin' in the Boy's Room" (Brownsville Station), and the poignant-but-tuff "Love Hurts" (Nazareth) but also gets into serious cringe territory with "Theme from the Rockford Files" (urrk) and Morris Albert's "Feelings." —*Roch Parisien*

Super Hits of the '70s: Have a Nice Day, Vol. 18 / 1993 / Rhino ✦✦✦✦✦
By *Vol. 18*, we're getting into diminishing returns. It spends most of its time locked in 1976—a year mostly memorable for songs you will not want to be reminded of. Anyone for "Afternoon Delight" by Starland Vocal Band, "Moonlight Feels Right" by Starbuck, and "I'd Really Love to See You Tonight" by England Dan and John Ford Coley? Still, even the cheesiest stuff here evokes all kinds of memories, tastes, and smells. —*Roch Parisien*

Surf & Drag, Vol. 1 / 1989 / Sundazed ✦✦✦✦✦
All the great surf and hot-rod sides from the Challenge label. Features Gary Usher, the Four Speeds, the Knickerbockers, Jan and Dean, the Royal Coachmen, Donna Loren, and the Rhythm Rockers. Powerful genre material—this is as good as it gets. —*Cub Koda*

Surf & Drag, Vol. 2 / 1993 / Sundazed ✦✦✦✦
Featuring more rare tracks from the second tier of surf and hot-rod performers, this volume is no less potent than the first. Highlights include the original version of "She Rides with Me" by Paul Petersen, "Bustin' Surfboards" by the Tornadoes, and "GeeTO Tiger" by the Tigers. —*Cub Koda*

Sweet Relief: Benefit for Victoria Williams / Jul. 6, 1993 / Thirsty Ear/Chaos Rec ✦✦✦✦✦
The shear breadth and diversity of artists gathered for this benefit project is a tribute to the affection with which Victoria Williams is held by her peers. It conveniently also makes for heady listening for any fan of contemporary music. The hard brittle edges of Soul Asylum ("Summer of

Drugs") and Buffalo Tom ("Merry Go Round") stand shoulder to shoulder with the country-folk of Lucinda Williams ("Main Road") and Maria McKee (an inspired and riveting "Opelousas—Sweet Relief"). *Sweet Relief* offers a unique opportunity to introduce yourself to an enduring songwriter while savouring some of the day's most intriguing musicians. How sweet it is! —*Roch Parisien*

Taste of Doo-Wop, Vol. 2 / 1993 / Vee-Jay ✦✦✦✦✦
The second Vee-Jay various-artists anthology showcasing diverse doo wop hits takes the same formula as its predecessor, featuring strong songs by more obscure acts rather than huge hits from established greats. the Kool Gents (a group that once included Dee Clark), the Prodigals, the Hi-Liters, and the El Dorados, plus set one holdovers the Magnificents, 5 Echoes, and Impressions, are on hand providing 25 more examples of marvelous harmony singing, jump cuts, and swooning romantic ballads. —*Ron Wynn*

Teen Beat, Vol. 1 / 1993 / Ace ✦✦✦
Thirty instrumentals from the late '50s and early '60s, the era when instrumental rock was at its peak. Most of these were hits, though a few of them didn't make the Top 20, and some didn't even make the Top 100. Hence the selections are often more obscure than what you'll find on Rhino's *Rock Instrumentals* series. The Rhino series, however, remains not only a much better introduction to this nifty genre, but considerably higher in overall quality. The best songs on *Teen Beat* are often on the Rhino series as well (the Ventures' "Walk Don't Run," Preston Epps' "Bongo Rock," Link Wray's "Rumble"); the lesser-known ones, though a boon to collectors, simply aren't as good or imaginative. It's a serviceable supplement, though, if you're looking for more of the style, and the best cuts are certainly dynamite. —*Richie Unterberger*

Teen Beat, Vol. 2 / 1994 / Ace ✦✦✦
This digs way deeper into the cobwebs of history than the first volume of the series. Although a few of these were big hits, over half of the 30 tracks didn't even make it into the Top 100. That doesn't mean they should be dismissed. But in the case of these selections at least, they're simply not nearly as memorable as the best early rock 'n' roll instrumentals, whether hits or flops. There are some nifty highlights, like two raw, bluesy 1961 cuts by a young Roy Buchanan, uncommonly rocking items by Chet Atkins, and the early Danelectro bass workout by the Fireballs ("Carioca"). But a lot of these are standard-issue three-chord instrumentals by no-names like the Atmospheres, or forgettable flop follow-ups by one-hit wonders like Dave Cortez, Floyd Cramer, and the Champs. The energy level is always high, but that in itself isn't a high recommendation, although devotees of instrumental rock will certainly find a lot of cuts here that are hard to locate on CD. —*Richie Unterberger*

Teen Beat, Vol. 3 / 1996 / Ace ✦✦✦
Devoted wholly to rock instrumentals of the late '50s and early '60s, this 30-track disc is a good investment for collectors looking for hits in the genre that didn't crack the Top 20 (and hence don't get played on oldies radio today) or missed the charts entirely. A couple smashes ("Wipe Out," "Pipeline") slip through, but otherwise there's a variety of forgotten hot wordless platters here, like the Astronauts' "Baja" (some of the best instrumental surf to originate outside out of California), the New Orleans-cum-Philly R&B of saxophonist Lee Allen, the creepy organ of the Wailers' "Mau Mau," the minimalist rockabilly of the Rock-a-Teens' "Woo-Hoo," the Ramrods' wacky adaptation of "Ghost Riders in the Sky," and the hard guitar of Duane Eddy associate Al Casey. When all's said and done, though, these aren't as good as the most famous vintage instrumental hits—stick with the more prominent compilations unless you're deeply into the sound. —*Richie Unterberger*

Texas Music, Vol. 3: Garage Bands & Psychedelia / 1994 / Rhino ✦✦✦
Texas arguably produced the most manic and raunchiest garage rock of any state during the 1960s. While seasoned collectors will find little on this 18-song compilation that they don't already have, it's a decent intro to some of the Lone Star State's shining moments. Long renowned as a melting pot of sounds, Texas groups often flavored their records with R&B, blues, and Tex-Mex, which means that in addition to classic garage sides by the Bobby Fuller Four, the Thirteenth Floor Elevators, Kenny & the Kasuals, and Mouse & the Traps, you get blues-rock (Steve Miller, Johnny Winter), blue-eyed soul (Roy Head's "Treat Her Right"), Tex-Mex-flavored rock (Sam the Sham & the Pharoahs and the Sir Douglas Quintet), and the all-out weirdness of the Legendary Stardust Cowboy ("Paralyzed"). There are also garage singles by the Chessmen, Scotty McKay, and Nobody's Children that were largely rare in their day, though they've appeared on easy-to-find garage compilations. The real find is the Ron-Dels' (featuring Delbert McClinton) "If You Really Want Me To, I'll Go," a country-flavored beat ballad strongly reminiscent of the Beatles' similar material from 1964 and 1965. —*Richie Unterberger*

That'll Flat Git It!, Vol. 1 / 1992 / Bear Family ✦✦✦✦✦
Thirty one tracks of '50s rockabilly-rock 'n' roll tracks culled from the vaults of RCA Victor. Highlights include Joe Clay's "Sixteen Chicks," Joey Castle's "That Ain't Nothin' but Right," and Ric Cartey's ultra-primitive "Heart Throb." —*Cub Koda*

That'll Flat Git It!, Vol. 2: Rockabilly From . . . / 1992 / Bear Family ✦✦✦✦
This is a sterling collection of obscure rockabilly from the vaults of Decca Records. Both hard-core and casual rockabilly fans will find much to treasure in this wonderful package. —*AMG*

That'll Flat Git It!, Vol. 3: Rockabilly From . . . / 1992 / Bear Family ✦✦✦✦✦
More raw rockabilly and country bop, this time from the vaults of Capitol Records. While the label had Gene Vincent and Esquerita, a quick listen to these will reveal rockabilly sounds with the accent on the 'billy. Skeets McDonald's "You Oughta See Grandma Rock" goes a long way toward defining the compilation's strengths, and Tommy Sands, long thought of as a teen idol singing pop mush, stokes the fires here with "The Worryin' Kind" and "Playin' the Field." While Ferlin Husky masquerading as Simon Crum on "Bop Cat Bop," the Rio Rockers' "Mexicali Baby," and Bobby Lee Trammell's "You Mostest Girl" show the length and breadth of the genre, perhaps the most fascinating earful of all is the Louvin Brothers testing the waters of rockabilly with "Red Hen Hop" and "Cash on the Barrelhead." —*Cub Koda*

☆ **There's a Riot Goin'** / 1991 / Rhino ✦✦✦✦✦
Sure, you can spend a lot of dough buying CD reissues of all the bands Leiber and Stoller wrote songs for. And while that would give you a great record collection (especially of Drifters and Coasters material), you might want to start with this indispensable 18-track collection. All the big hits are here, as are the songs that show off Leiber and Stoller's melodramatic way with a song ("I Who Have Nothing") and their deft comic touch ("Charlie Brown"). The essence of Leiber and Stoller's genius is here, and I'm willing to wager you'll recognize nearly every one of these songs as soon as they start. Memory can be a wonderful thing. —*John Dougan*

This Is Mod, Vol. 1: The Rarities 1979-1981 / 1995 / Anagram ✦✦✦
The British mod revival may have been a fad, driven by fashion and most of the time too derivative, but it did produce some fun singles. Since many of the bands that jumped on the bandwagon only released singles or poorly distributed albums for independent labels, much of this music has been hopelessly lost over the years; *This Is Mod, Vol. 1* collects many of the admittedly third-rate (though enjoyable) revival bands for the first time on CD. In 21 tracks, this disc provides the nearly complete recorded output of the Circles, the Amber Squad, the Cigarettes, the Deadbeats, the Letters, the Nips, the Odds, and the Sussed (whose novelty record, "I've Got Me Parka," takes a fun look at the fad)—with each band receiving detailed biographical sketches. For specialists and fetishists, this disc is essential. For most, it's simply excessive. —*Chris Woodstra*

This Is Mod, Vol. 2: More Rarities 1979-81 / 1996 / Anagram ✦✦✦✦
The second volume of the *This Is Mod* series covers more mod revivalists: the Killermeters, the Exits, the V.I.P.'s, the Crooks, the Same, Teenage Filmstars, Terry Tonik, and the Purple Hearts. Only the Purple Hearts came close to being major contenders, but all provide a fascinating look at the short-lived genre. —*Chris Woodstra*

This Is Merseybeat / 1989 / Edsel ✦✦✦
At the outset of Beatlemania in July 1963, the tiny UK Oriole label went to Liverpool with a mobile sound unit to record unsigned local beat groups for a pair of compilation LPs (combined onto this reissue). Only a couple of them (the Nomads, who soon became the Mojos, and the Merseybeats) achieved any British hits. A full 24 of these 28 tunes are covers of US R&B/rock/pop standards. In comparison to the originals they sound pale—the vocals are often especially twee—and the four originals are derivative and unexceptional, a bit cloddish even. This comp illustrates that the Beatles were more a unique product of the Mersey sound than a representative one. —*Richie Unterberger*

Totally Wired / Oct. 1995 / Razor & Tie ✦✦✦✦
As the 1970s turned into the 1980s, the first explosion of punk had run its course, and what we now call "post-punk" or "alternative rock" had yet to really coagulate. In the meantime, there were many bands who took their unconventional attitude from the punk era, but sought a more musically diverse format. *Totally Wired* was an 18-song compilation of bands that were staples of college radio during the time, although they were virtually ignored (or scorned) by the mainstream. Featured are key cuts by bands like Gang of Four, the Fall, the Raincoats, the Slits, Joy Division, Bauhaus, Magazine, Au Pairs, and Pylon, as well as even more cultish acts like Delta 5, the Mo-Dettes, and Bush Tetras. Those who followed this fragmented scene at the time won't find much here they're not already familiar with or own. But for others it's a pretty useful intro to acts that embodied an era which has yet to generate much historical commentary or preservation. —*Richie Unterberger*

☆ **The Two Tone Compilation: Checkered Past** / Nov. 16, 1993 / Chrysalis ✦✦✦✦✦
An essential double-disc set, it provides all the greatest tracks from the seminal ska-revival record label, including classic singles by the Specials and the English Beat. —*AMG*

Ugly Things, Vols. 1-3 / Raven ✦✦✦
US and UK audiences were totally unaware at the time, but Australia was home to a thriving garage-punk scene in the mid-'60s. The scope and output of these groups were limited by the country's population, which was only about 15 million or somewhat less, after all. But there was a surprisingly large number of fine singles, some of which measured up to the manic, over-the-top R&B-derived energy of anything coming from Texas, California, or London. *Vol. 1* is by far the best of the series, and indeed, one of the best '60s garage compilations ever, filled with good hooks, screams, and crunching riffs. *Vol. 2* and *3* aren't nearly as good, peppered with undistinguished covers and unmemorable tracks, although some excellent ones do surface, including some from neighboring New Zealand; the best of these two LPs should have been combined into one. Raven has put out a best-of compilation CD from the *Ugly Things* series that draws from all of the volumes and adds some other cuts. —*Richie Unterberger*

Ultimate Girl Groups / Goldmine ✦✦✦✦✦
One of the best compilations of obscure girl group singles from the mid-'60s. And we are talking obscure; Diane Renay is the only artist on this 27-track compilation who had a hit of any sort. These actually fall much closer to girl group soul than girl group pop-rock, the influence of Motown being particularly prevalent. These aren't meant as criticisms; these are mostly infectious, well-produced tracks, some of which, like Judy Hughes' "Fine, Fine, Fine," could have been big hits. —*Richie Unterberger*

VH1: The Big '80s / 1996 / Rhino ✦✦✦✦
Drawn from the VH1 music video series *The Big '80s*, this single-disc compilation offers a good portrait of the sound of early MTV, even if it doesn't follow any strict generic guidlines. New wavers like Squeeze ("Tempted"), the Go-Go's ("We Got the Beat"), and Gary Numan ("Cars") line up with '70s leftovers like Steve Miller ("Abracadabra") and ABBA's Frida ("I Know There's Something Going On"), as well as pop-metal bands (Night Ranger's "Sister Christian") and power-pop one-hit wonders (Tommy Tutone's "867-5309"). Much of this has appeared on other, more coherent collections, but this has a couple of items that show up on many '80s compilations (most notably the Frida track) and it does sound remarkably similar to what MTV actually sounded like in 1983 and 1984. —*Stephen Thomas Erlewine*

The Vee-Jay Story: 1953-1993 / 1993 / Vee-Jay ✦✦✦✦✦
This definitive three-disc retrospective documents this seminal R&B and blues record label. —*AMG*

Wax 'Em Down / Revell ✦✦✦✦✦
Cool compilation of rare surf tunes, not too hard to find despite appearing on a tiny reissue label. Divided about equally between instrumentals and vocals; the instrumentals, usually featuring magnificent reverb-soaked guitar lines, certainly have the edge. Only a couple of recognizable names here: the Original Surfaris' "Surfari" is the B-side of their well-known "Bombora," and Sandy Nelson's "Casbah" is a great lost treasure, with searing guitar by well-known session player and producer Richie Polodor. Also includes a first-rate surf novelty in Frank Sinatra, Jr.'s "Beach Girls & the Monster" (included in both vocal and instrumental versions). —*Richie Unterberger*

We Got a Party: Best of Ron Records, Vol. 1 / 1988 / Rounder ✦✦✦✦✦
There's something for R&B, blues, and soul fans of all persuasions on this anthology spotlighting various New Orleans artists who recorded for the Ron label in the late '50s and early '60s. There were celebrities, like pianist Professor Longhair and the sultry soul queen Irma Thomas, country-rockabilly singers like Warren Lee, novelty specialist Chris Kenner, and shouters such as Bobby Mitchell. The 14 tracks on the CD are all good; most are wonderful, even if most of the singers never attained any recognition outside Crescent City R&B circles. —*Ron Wynn*

Wild Surf! / 1996 / Del-Fi ✦✦✦
In the early and mid-1960s, Del-Fi recorded a good deal of surf music. This compilation brings together 24 tracks recorded by acts whose impact was strictly regional, including the Lively Ones, the Centurions, Dave Myers, the Sentinals, the Impacts, the Surfman, the Original Surfaris (not the "Wipe Out" guys), the Pharos, and the Gonzos. Some of the best tunes have shown up on surf compilations (like Rhino's *Surf Box*). But if your interest in surf runs deeper than the usual greatest-hits collections, this is one of the more solid secondary anthologies out there, many of the tracks exhibiting a distinct Latin influence in the melodies and rhythms. —*Richie Unterberger*

Wild Things: Wild Kiwi Garage 1966-1969 / 1991 / Flying Nun ✦✦✦✦✦
New Zealand, a tiny country with a population less than the metropolitan San Francisco Bay Area, nevertheless had a fairly prolific and interesting garage-beat scene in the mid-'60s. This collects 16 singles that, with one or two exceptions, were obscure even in the land of their release. Like the bands from neighboring Australia, the Kiwis compensated for their isolation with crude mania, and this has some ferocious sub-Stones pounders from the likes of the La De Da's, Chants R&B, and the Bluestars. An above-average garage collection, well worth checking out by '60s aficionados. —*Richie Unterberger*

Wild Wild Young Women / Rounder ✦✦✦✦✦
Rockabilly was largely a male domain; except for Wanda Jackson and Brenda Lee, no female rockabilly singers made a notable national impact. But there were a few other women rockabilly vocalists making some good records, and this is the best basic collection of them. Janis Martin, known as "the female Elvis," checks in with three cuts, including "My Boy Elvis"; the Davis Sisters (one of whom was Skeeter Davis) and Rose Maddox are represented by some mid-'50s sides which illustrate rockabilly's close links to country boogie. The Collins Kids recorded some of the most hyper-tempo rockabilly of any sort, and Sparkle Moore, from Nebraska, had a great over-the-top, swooping delivery. You also get some even more obscure, but also worthy, cuts from the Nettles Sisters, Jean Chapel, Joan King, Linda and the Epics, and Alvadean Coker. More sides are available on single-artist compilations by some of these acts, particularly the Collins Kids, the Davis Sisters, Janis Martin, and Rose Maddox, but the compilers have done a good job of selecting first-rate tracks for a general overview. —*Richie Unterberger*

The Wildest from Specialty / 1994 / Specialty ✦✦✦
Excellent 25-track compilation featuring '50s sides that appeared on the Specialty label. Highlights include Jerry Byrne's "Lights Out" and "Carry On" (both featuring a young Dr. John on piano), Bob "Froggy" Landers' surreal "Cherokee Dance," Don and Dewey's original take of "Justine," the Pentagons' "It's Spring Again" and Roddy Jackson's "Moose on the Loose." From the label that brought you Little Richard, this is piano poundin', shack shakin', borderline-nuts first-generation rock 'n' roll. For once, a compilation that truly reflects its title. —*Cub Koda*

Yellow Pills, Vol. 1 / 1994 / Big Deal ✦✦✦✦✦
A dynamic power-pop collection featuring new and old tracks by some of the leading groups of the last ten years, including Dwight Twilley, the Shoes, the Rubinoos, and Tommy Keene. The music on *Yellow Pills* is strong enough to convert casual fans into hard-core power-pop fanatics. —*Stephen Thomas Erlewine*

RAP

The most popular and influential form of African-American pop music of the 1980s and 1990s, rap is also one of the most controversial styles of the rock era. And not just among the guardians of cultural taste and purity that have always been counted among rock 'n' roll's chief enemies—Black, White, rock, and soul audiences continue to fiercely debate the musical and social merits of rap, whose most radical innovations subverted many of the musical and cultural tenets upon which rock was built. Antecedents of rap are easy to find in rock and other kinds of music. Music is often used to tell a story, often with spoken rhymes over instruments and rhythms. Talking blues, spoken passages of sanctified prose in gospel, and numerous hits that call out slogans and rhymes, from Bo Diddley's "Say Man" and Shirley Ellis' "The Name Game" to Jerry Reed's "When You're Hot, You're Hot." More direct paths leading to rap, though, can be found in a few of the trends of the late '60s and '70s. In R&B music, funk and disco stripped soul down to its most basic rhythms, forgoing much of the instrumentation and vocals habitually used as embellishments. James Brown in particular is often cited as a forefather in his use of stream-of-consciousness raps over elemental funk backup, and he (as well as other funk giants) has been sampled by modern-day rappers on innumerable occasions

Two much more overlooked influences originated from outside of the R&B and rock mainstream. The Last Poets, Gil Scott-Heron, and Jayne Cortez set highly politicized tales of African-American and urban life against percussive jazz tracks in the early '70s. In reggae, the use of DJs, or "toasters," to rap over basic instrumental backing tracks when they took their mobile sound systems to dances became widespread. New York City, particularly Brooklyn and (more importantly in terms of rap's birth) the Bronx, was home to a large Jamaican community. Jamaican DJs (DJ Kool Herc has been credited as the first) mixed sounds from several turntables, devices that would become a rap trademark. Although mixing from large sound systems began to be employed at New York house parties in the 1970s, it didn't really emerge as a recorded sound until the Sugarhill Gang's "Rapper's Delight" in 1979. While many critics and listeners shrugged the song aside as a fluke novelty hit, the early rap sound—usually composed of slangy, boastful spoken rhymes over basic bass and percussion grooves—continued to spread in the early '80s, due in large part to the efforts of the Sugarhill label itself. Grandmaster Flash's hard-hitting 1982 single, "The Message," really stands as rap's watershed mark, with a massive impact belied by its relatively modest peak on the pop charts. No longer could rap be ignored as a frivolous microgenre; here was straight-up social commentary, reporting from the front lines of the ghetto with more immediacy than almost any newspaper or television broadcast.

From its inception, rap endured a lot of hostility from listeners—many, but not all, White—who found the music too harsh, monotonous, and lacking in traditional melodic values. However, millions of others—often, though not always, young African-Americans from underprivileged inner-city backgrounds—found an immediate connection with the style. Here was poetry of the street, directly reflecting and addressing the day-to-day reality of the ghetto in a confrontational fashion not found in any other music or medium. What's more, you could dance to it, rhyme to it, bring it most anywhere on increasingly ubiquitous portable cassette players (dubbed "ghetto blasters"), and, in the best rock 'n' roll tradition, form your own band without much in the way of formal training. The basic workouts of early rappers like Kurtis Blow and the Fat Boys (eventually referred to as "old school" rap) can sound a bit tame today,

although the productions of veterans like Afrika Bambaataa and Keith LeBlanc have lost none of their luster.

Many were still expecting the music to peter out before Run-D.M.C. came along. Rap was, and to a large degree still is, a singles-oriented medium, but these men from Queens proved that rappers could maintain interest and diversity over the course of entire full-length albums. Combining hard beats and innovative production with material that emphasized positive social activism without ignoring the cruel realities of urban life, they found as much favor with the critics as the street. Among the first rap groups to climb the pop charts in a big way, they also were among the first to make big inroads into the White and Middle-American audiences when they teamed up with Aerosmith's Stephen Tyler and Joe Perry for the hit single "Walk This Way." The mid- and late '80s saw rap continuing to explode in popularity, with the ascendancy of superstars like LL Cool J and Hammer (the latter is often accused of providing a safe rap-pop alternative). Although most early rap productions originated in New York City and its environs, the music took hold as a national phenomenon, with strong scenes developing in other East Coast cities like Philadelphia, as well as West Coast strongholds in Los Angeles and Oakland. Production techniques became increasingly sophisticated; electronics, stop-on-a-dime editing, and—most importantly—sampling from previously recorded sources became prominent. The increased emphasis on electronic beats led to the popularization of the term "hip-hop," a designation which is by now used more or less interchangeably with rap. The Beastie Boys, obnoxious white ex-punks from New York, brought rap further into the Middle-American mainstream with their vastly popular hybrids of hip-hop, hard rock, and in-your-face braggadocio. While rap had always forthrightly dealt with urban struggle, the late '80s saw the emergence of a more militant strain of the music. Sometimes dubbed "gangsta-rap," the hotbed of this school was found in the disadvantaged neighborhoods of South Central Los Angeles, although performers like Philadelphia's Schoolly D proved that the genre was not specific to the area. Boogie Down Productions laid down a prototype that was taken to more extreme measures by N.W.A., who reported on the crime, sex, and violence of the ghetto with an explicit verve that some viewed as verging on celebration rather than journalism. Enormously controversial, and enormously popular with record buyers, several N.W.A. members went on to stardom as solo acts, including Ice Cube, Eazy-E, and Dr. Dre. The most popular and controversial of the militant rappers, the New York-based Public Enemy, were perhaps the most political as well. Their brand of activism, like that of Malcolm X's two decades earlier, made a lot of people, including liberals, pretty uncomfortable, with their emphasis upon black nationalism and careless anti-Semitic, homophobic, and sexist references

Groups such as Public Enemy ignited an ongoing debate in the media. Activist-oriented critics and audiences found a lot to praise in their music. At the same time, they could not let the xenophobic tendencies of these acts pass unnoticed, or ignore the frequent quasi-celebration in much rap music of misogyny, drugs, and violence, and the status to be gained in the urban community by the practice thereof. Passionate advocates of civil liberties and free speech wondered, sometimes aloud, whether rappers were taking those privileges too far.

It's a conundrum that remains unresolved as of this writing in 1995. The apolitical, over-the-top explicit sexual boasting of 2 Live Crew seemed too comically overdrawn to really inspire serious controversy. Some government authorities felt otherwise, subjecting the

Miami-based Luther Campbell, the leader of the group, to serious legal pressure and harassment. First Amendment champions found themselves in the awkward position of defending his and other rappers' rights to spew content that they found morally reprehensible. Newly emerging gangsta rappers like Snoop Doggy Dogg, Slick Rick, and 2Pac not only take the violent subject matter of their lyrics to new extremes (and to the top of the charts), but have been accused of enacting their scenarios in real life, landing in jail for manslaughter or fighting similarly grave charges. These performers often unrepentantly contend they are only reporting things as they happen in the 'hood, of a culture that not only shoots people, but is being shot *at*. Many critics find their line between art and reality too thin, and are loath to see them spreading their gospel from the top of the charts (2Pac's 1995 album "Me Against the World" debuted at No. 1 even as he was serving a prison sentence), or serve as role models for international youth. Gangsta rap may have gotten a lot of the headlines in recent years, but the field of rap as a whole remains diverse and not as dominated by the shoot-'em-out minidramas of gangsta rap, as many would have you believe. De La Soul took rap and hip-hop productions to new heights with their 1989 debut *Three Feet High & Rising*, an almost psychedelic mélange of sampling and editing of a wildly eclectic pool of sources that would do Frank Zappa proud. Their humorous and cheerful vibe inspired a mini-school of "Afrocentric" acts, most notably the the Jungle Brothers and A Tribe Called Quest. Arrested Development, Digable Planets, and Digital Underground also pursued playful, heavily jazz- and funk-oriented paths to immense success and high critical praise. The world of rap is a highly macho (some would say sexist) environment, but some female performers arose to provide a much-needed counterpoint from various perspectives: the saucy (the various Roxannes), the pop

(Salt-N-Pepa), and the feminist (Queen Latifah). It is a measure of rap's huge influence that the style has infiltrated mainstream soul and rock as well. Producer Teddy Riley gave urban-contemporary performers like Bobby Brown a vaguely hip edge with his brand of "New Jack Swing;" White alternative rockers like G. Love, Bobby Sichran, and most notably Beck devised a strange hybrid of rap, blues, and rock. Vanilla Ice proved that whitebread pop-rap could top the charts, though he was unable to sustain his success

More than most genres, rap/hip-hop has become a culture with its own sub-genres and buzzwords that can seem almost impenetrable to the novice. Despite this proliferation of schools of production and performance, many rap records can appear virtually indistinguishable from each other to the new listener. And there's no getting around the fact that a lot of them are—the market is saturated with repetitive beats and monotonously uncompromising slices of urban street life, to the point that they've lost a lot of both their musical novelty and shock value. Rap music has lost none of its momentum—or its capacity to inspire outrage in society as a whole—as we head into the last half of the 1990s. Scenes continue to proliferate, not just on the coasts, but in Atlanta, Houston, and such unlikely locales as Paris (home of leading French rapper MC Solaar). It may appeal more to inner-city adolescents than anyone else, but gangsta rap may be bigger than anything else in R&B music commercially, and there are more multiplatinum rap/hip-hop acts than you can count. Shinehead, Shabba Ranks, and less-heralded performers like Sister Carol have fused reggae and rap. And the jazz and rap worlds are being brought closer together than ever through the efforts of Gang Starr and their leader Guru, US3, and the landmark *Stolen Moments: Red, Hot + Cool* compilation, which united many of the top names of hip-hop and jazz. —*Jimmy James*

Arabian Prince

Rap

A founding member of the Compton, CA, rap group Niggaz with Attitudes (N.W.A.), he found the going tough when he departed the group for a solo career in 1988. His debut *Brother Arab* on Orpheus scraped the bottom of the R&B and pop charts in 1989. —*Ron Wynn*

Brother Arab / Sep. 1989 / Orpheus ✦✦✦

● **Tha Underworld** / 1992 / EMI America ✦✦✦✦
Arabian Prince doesn't discuss anything that hasn't been talked about numerous times by other gangsta types. But his commentaries on drugs, violence, sex, and such are done in such a deadpan, yet defiant and angry manner, that you're hooked even while being disgusted by a litany of hopelessness and injustice. —*Ron Wynn*

Arrested Development

Rap, Urban

One of the major success stories of 1992, Arrested Development is a progressive rap collective fusing soul, blues, hip-hop, and Sly and the Family Stone-influenced funk with political, socially conscious lyrics. The group was founded in the late '80s by rapper Speech (born Todd Thomas) and DJ Headliner (born Timothy Barnwell), who met while attending the Art Institute of Atlanta. The two formed a gangsta-rap outfit called Disciples of Lyrical Rebellion and later became Secret Society. After hearing Public Enemy, the two decided to make the transition to a more positive, Afrocentric viewpoint, and gradually picked up members such as dancers Montsho Eshe and Aerle Taree (the latter is Speech's cousin), percussionist Rasa Don, singer Dionne Farris, and spiritual adviser and theorist Baba Oje. Arrested Development's debut album took its title from the amount of time it took the group to secure a record contract; *Three Years, Five Months and Two Days in the Life of. . .* produced the hit "Tennessee," a spiritual track inspired by the deaths of Speech's brother and grandmother and partially based on summer visits to the latter's home in Ripley, Tennessee, as a child. The album garnered rave reviews and sold over four million copies, while "Tennessee" went gold and hit the Top Ten; its two follow-ups, "People Everyday" (a rewrite of Sly's "Everyday People") and "Mr. Wendal" did likewise. Accolades poured in; Arrested Development won Grammys for Best Rap Album by a Duo or Group and Best New Artist (the first rap act to do so) and were named *Rolling Stone's* Band of the Year.

The band played on the 1993 Lollapalooza tour, released an *Unplugged* album, and also contributed "Revolution" to Spike Lee's *Malcolm X*. However, there was dissension; Farris, whose vocals were a big part of "Tennessee"'s success, left the group for a solo career, and Speech shook up the lineup, switching Headliner to a co-rapping slot and replacing him with DJ Kwesi Asuo, also adding bassist Foley, singer Nadirah, and dancer Ajile. Their second album, *Zingalamaduni* (Swahili for "beehive of culture"), was released in 1994; while some re-

views hailed it as a major work, overall response was ambivalent. Speech, who writes a column on racial issues for his mother's newspaper, the *Milwaukee Community Journal*, and occasionally lectures on his political views, was criticized for allowing his politics to become heavy-handed, while he himself was portrayed as a control freak unable to work with others after Farris' departure. Those rumors were lent credence in 1996 when, contrary to Speech's assertion that the group would be around for ten or twelve years, Arrested Development broke up. Speech recorded a solo album, which failed to make an impact. —*Steve Huey*

● **Three Years, Five Months & Two Days in the Life of. . .** / 1992 / Chrysalis ✦✦✦✦
A crew that became one of 1992's sensations by infusing hip-hop with blues on their debut, *Three Years, Five Months & Two Days in the Life of. . .*, especially on the single "Tennessee." —*Ron Wynn*

Unplugged / 1993 / Chrysalis ✦✦

Zingalamaduni / 1994 / Chrysalis ✦✦✦

Afrika Bambaataa

Vocals / Rap, Urban

Some call him the godfather of rap; others put him in the category of genre creator. Bronx DJ Afrika Bambaataa's record "Planet Rock," co-written by John Robie and produced by Arthur Baker, was the seminal presentation of scratching, electronic additions, high-tech beats, cutting rhythms, and highly processed vocals. The single, and its followers like "Looking for the Perfect Beat" and "Renegades of Funk," opened the door for the '80s electro-funk movement. Later, his collaboration with James Brown on "Unity" and vocals with John Lydon on "World Destruction" furthered the link between hip-hop, funk, soul, and rock. He's done work as a member of the group Shango, but it's as a producer, compositional force, rapper, and father figure that Afrika Bambaataa rules in the hip-hop nation. —*Ron Wynn*

☆ **Looking for the Perfect Beat** / 1982 / Tommy Boy ✦✦✦✦✦
Producer Arthur Baker proved the star on this seminal 1982 album, adding what were then state-of-the art studio effects and mixing gimmicks to balance often repetitive rhythms. This was a milestone, despite limited rap skills by 1990s standards. —*Ron Wynn*

Unity / 1984 / Tommy Boy ✦✦✦✦

★ **Planet Rock** / 1986 / Tommy Boy ✦✦✦✦✦
All the important 12-inchers from 1982-1984 are here, including "Planet Rock" and "Looking for the Perfect Beat," and three previously unreleased tracks (with Soulsonic Force). —*John Floyd*

Beware (The Funk Is Everywhere) / 1986 / Tommy Boy ✦✦✦✦
Another stunning assortment of singles are included, with heavier beats, thicker rhythms, and a blistering cover of The MC5's "Kick Out the Jams." —*John Floyd*

The Light / 1988 / EMI America ✦✦
Diverse personalities and styles are the hook for this 1988 album, which isn't a Bambaataa project, but a group effort with some Bambaataa involvement. The guest list ranges from Boy George to George Clinton, Yellowman, UB40, and Bootsy Collins, with Bambaataa offering a brief, rather formulaic rap on UB40's "Reckless" and "Shout It Out." This was a mildly entertaining effort, but so varied that there was no cohesion or unified focus. *—Ron Wynn*

1990-2000: The Decade of Darkness / Jun. 1991 / EMI America ✦✦✦
After several lackluster albums, Bambaataa came back with a record that explored modern-day dance trends without losing his signature sound. Fueled by righteous social commentary throughout the songs, the record showed that he wasn't creatively spent. It wasn't as innovative as his groundbreaking singles from the early '80s, but it was far from being an embarrassment. *— Stephen Thomas Erlewine*

Don't Stop . . . Planet Rock [The Remix EP] / 1992 / Tommy Boy ✦✦
An updated EP takes the by-now-ancient "Planet Rock" beat and runs it through the 1990s hip-hop production machine. The results aren't all that successful, even though the sound is now contemporary. But its hook was old-school, as was its charm. The newer version lacks bite. *—Ron Wynn*

Rob Base

Vocals / Rap
A New York-based DJ who caused a stir with his clipped cadences and straightahead raps contrasted by choruses lifted from classic soul songs, notably Frankie Beverly and Maze's "Joy and Pain," which he neglected to credit. He had a partner, DJ E-Z Rock, on his first release, *It Takes Two*. He did the second on his own, and continued his formula from the first release, this time using as his base (no pun intended) music from Edwin Starr, Marvin Gaye and Tammi Terrell, and Native American rockers Redbone. *—Ron Wynn*

● **It Takes Two** / 1988 / Profile ✦✦✦✦
This wildly successful debut album from 1988 contains the excellent title cut and "Joy and Pain," which lifts from The Maze hit of the same name. Base is joined by DJ E-Z Rock. *—John Floyd*

The Incredible Base / 1989 / Profile ✦✦✦

The Beastie Boys

Rap, Alternative Pop-Rock, Hardcore Punk
When they were terrorizing America in 1987 with *Licensed to Ill*, nobody imagined that seven years later the Beastie Boys would still be recording, let alone be respected and release a series of consistently creative albums. But that is what happened. The Beasties have managed to tie together the two largest underground musical movements of the '80s—hip-hop and punk/post-punk—into one wildly eclectic mix, borrowing from any genre they can get their hands on.

Originally, the Beastie Boys were a hardcore New York punk band in the early '80s, releasing a couple of weak EPs before becoming infatuated with the burgeoning rap underground. By that time, the Beastie Boys were three—Adam Yauch (MCA), Mike Diamond (Mike D), and Adam Horovitz (Ad-Rock). The trio hooked up with Rick Rubin, one of the cofounders of Def Jam Records, who produced the group's first full-length album, *Licensed to Ill*, which was released in late 1986. A brutal and hysterical amalgam of hard rock, hip-hop, and satiric macho posturing, *Licensed to Ill* followed the footsteps of Run-DMC's groundbreaking commercial breakthrough *Raising Hell*, becoming the first rap album to reach No.1; it eventually sold over four million copies and scored a No. 7 single with "(You Gotta) Fight for Your Right (To Party)."

After a tour that wallowed in its own decadence, the group became embroiled in a vicious fight with Def Jam that prevented them from releasing new material for a couple of years. In 1989, the Beastie Boys reappeared on Capitol Records with *Paul's Boutique*, an album that was radically different from their debut. Although it was a commercial failure, it was a surreal, brilliantly inventive record that foreshadowed many hip trends of the early '90s.

After another three-year absence, the Beastie Boys emerged with *Check Your Head* in 1992. They returned to playing live instruments, creating a sloppy, inspired album that featured equal doses of Stax soul, hardcore punk, '70s funk, reggae, and '90s hip-hop beats. It was as bold of a departure from *Paul's Boutique* as that album was from *Licensed to Ill*, except this time, it sold. The Beastie Boys emerged as cultural icons for the new alternative audience, which continued with their follow-up, 1994's *Ill Communication*, a record that refined the innovations of *Check Your Head*. *—Stephen Thomas Erlewine*

☆ **Licensed to Ill** / 1986 / Def Jam ✦✦✦✦✦
The impact of this album in 1987 was about as subtle as a brick through a window. It was the first No. 1 hip-hop album, selling four million copies, and the first album from a White rap group. From the opening kick of John Bonham's drums (taken from "When the Levee Breaks"), the

Beasties proceed to steal from every record they can get their hands on and rhyme about an absurd array of macho fantasies. Sure, it's obnoxious—but it's an act, and an insanely humorous one at that; no other rappers brag about being thrown out of White Castle, drinking Budweiser, or having "more rhymes than Phyllis Diller." Even if some of it sounds dated today, the sheer force of the music and the whiny rhymes still make this worth hearing. *—Stephen Thomas Erlewine*

★ **Paul's Boutique** / 1989 / Capitol ✦✦✦✦✦
Endlessly complex and relentlessly innovative, *Paul's Boutique* is the Beastie Boys' masterpiece. It's very dense, with samples from nearly every genre of music and clever, literate, absurd lyrics dropping references from Jack Kerouac to *Dragnet*; *Paul's Boutique* is a virtual catalog of pop culture, deeply rooted in the 1970s. As rappers, The Beasties have grown immeasurably, writing lyrics that are both smart-assed and smart. Musically, the album is much richer than *Ill*, covering everything from funk and pop to country and hip-hop, with several layers of samples and beats on each track. *Paul's Boutique* is a brilliant, visionary album, and hasn't aged a day since its release. *—Stephen Thomas Erlewine*

☆ **Check Your Head** / 1992 / Capitol ✦✦✦✦✦
Check Your Head returned The Beastie Boys to the spotlight, although in the most unlikely manner possible. Refashioning themselves as a loose and gritty groove band, The Beasties picked up their instruments again and made an album of dirty Stax and New Orleans funk, tripped-out reggae, hard hip-hop, blistering hardcore punk, and scores of pop culture references and jokes. In its own way, *Check Your Head* is as trailblazing as *Paul's Boutique*; with its inspired amateurishness, it acknowledges no boundaries or limitations, creating a post-post-punk world where Eddie Harris, Bob Dylan, Cheap Trick, Groove Holmes, Spoonie Gee, and Biz Markie exist together as one music. And, strange as it may sound, it works. *—Stephen Thomas Erlewine*

Some Old Bullshit / 1994 / Grand Royal/Capitol ✦✦

Ill Communication / May 23, 1994 / Grand Royal/Capitol ✦✦✦✦
More of a refinement and restatement of *Check Your Head* than a bold departure, *Ill Communication* still finds the Beastie Boys in prime form, adding more elements of jazz to their dense, surrealistic sound. From the scores of wah-wah guitars to the short hardcore punk songs, *Ill Communication* is firmly entrenched in '70s worship without ever sounding like it's recycled. It may offer the same thing as *Check Your Head*, but *Ill Communication* never sounds formulaic or tired. *—Stephen Thomas Erlewine*

Root Down EP / May 23, 1995 / Grand Royal/Capitol ✦✦

The In Sound from Way Out / Apr. 2, 1996 / Grand Royal/Capitol ✦✦✦
Originally released through the Beasties' French fan club, *The In Sound from Way Out* is a collection of the group's funky instrumentals from *Check Your Head* and *Ill Communication*, with a couple of new tracks thrown in. The Beasties have a flair for loose, gritty funk and soul-jazz and the stuttering, greasy keyboards of Money Mark give the music an extra edge—he helps make the music sound as authentic as anything from the early '70s. Fans of the band's dynamic wordplay might find *The In Sound from Way Out* a disappointment, but anyone that grooved on the wildly eclectic fusions of *Check Your Head* and *Ill Communication* will find the album endlessly enjoyable. *—Stephen Thomas Erlewine*

Big Daddy Kane

Vocals / Rap
Brooklynite Big Daddy Kane (born Antonio Hardy; KANE is an acronym for King Asiatic Nobody's Equal) has been able to nicely balance his image as the ultimate hipster with the requisite solemnity and air of indignation and anger necessary to creditably deliver messages of Afrocentric awareness and Muslim reverence. He's done alternately inspirational, prophetical, ridiculous, and scandalous raps over his career, and has also managed to include duets with the maestro of love, Barry White, and legendary comedian Rudy Ray Moore, aka Dolemite, who laid waste to Kane in a dozens (insult-swapping) classic.

Big Daddy Kane has been a high profile figure the past couple of years. Not only has he appeared in such films as *Posse* and *Gunmen*, but he also posed in Madonna's controversial photo book, *Sex*, and issued a defiant disc, *Looks like a Job for Big Daddy Kane*, that offered no apologies for past actions and ridiculed unnamed individuals he claimed were fronting as gangsters.*—Ron Wynn*

● **Long Live the Kane** / 1988 / Cold Chillin' ✦✦✦✦
Kane's debut was his hottest. *—Dan Heilman*

It's a Big Daddy Thing / 1989 / Cold Chillin' ✦✦✦✦
A good application of funk sentiments and influence within hip-hop, particularly "I Get the Job Done." But Kane also veers into homophobic and sexist territory, notably on "Pimpin' Ain't Easy." *—Ron Wynn*

Taste of Chocolate / 1990 / Cold Chillin' ✦✦✦
Worth the purchase price for the exchange between Kane and Rudy Ray Moore (*Dolemite*), longtime champion of the underground Black comic circuit. Moore lays waste to Kane with relish. *—Ron Wynn*

Prince of Darkness / 1991 / Cold Chillin' ✦✦

Looks Like a Job for Big Daddy / May 25, 1993 / Cold Chillin' ✦✦✦

Looks like a Job for Big Daddy Kane was a solid comeback record by Kane, bringing him back to the harder beats of his earlier albums. His rapping hasn't lost its spark, and the music is sparse and funky. However, it doesn't have the same flair or innovation of *Long Live the Kane* and *It's a Big Daddy Thing*, and it fell off the charts quickly. *—Stephen Thomas Erlewine*

Black Sheep

Rap

Bronx rapper Andre "Dres" Titus and William "Mista Lawnge" McLean scored a big hit with the debut *A Wolf in Sheep's Clothing* for Mercury in 1991. The disc went gold, with the single "The Choice Is Yours" scoring on the R&B charts and getting extensive pop exposure as well. The follow-up, *Non-Fiction*, had less of an impact. *—Ron Wynn*

● **A Wolf in Sheep's Clothing** / 1991 / Mercury ✦✦✦✦

Bronx rappers Black Sheep scored with the single "Choice Is Yours," a song featuring the catch phrase "you can get with this or you can get with that." But while this hit and "Strobelite Honey" were more satirical, the album also included the biting "Black With N.V. (No Vision)" and "To Whom It May Concern," message tracks that harshly criticized successful blacks who turned their backs on the inner city. *—Ron Wynn*

Non-Fiction / 1994 / Mercury ✦✦✦

The follow-up to 1991's massive debut, *Non-Fiction* is a troubled sophomore album; it has a few good moments, but it can't compare to the raw immediacy of *A Wolf in Sheep's Clothing.* Dres' raps are just as solid, but the mostly R&B-influenced backing is flat and unexciting. "Without a Doubt," however, is as house-rockin' a cut as any on the debut. *—John Bush*

Kurtis Blow

b. Aug. 9, 1959, New York City, NY
Keyboards, Vocals / Rap

Arguably rap's first crossover star, at least from a chart standpoint, New Yorker Blow emerged in the early '80s. He began doing both social protest/Afrocentric material and boasting and posturing material, though not to the degree that has since become commonplace. His landmark recording, "The Breaks," was an eye-opener for its time in terms of pace, verbal dexterity, and its rhythm track. Blow was also a big-time producer at one point, using the likes of Bob Dylan and George Clinton in guest stints and incorporating bits from television shows and cartoons in his production. Blow was finally overhauled by New School producers and rappers in the late '80s, and his early work now sounds quite dated by comparison. *—Ron Wynn*

Kurtis Blow / 1980 / Mercury ✦✦✦✦

Kurtis Blow exploded onto the fledgling rap scene with "The Breaks," still one of the rawest, most hypnotic bits of rhythm and oral narrative ever issued. Blow's defiant, posturing rap, punctuated by drums that seemed to signify an invading army, surprised, shocked, and amazed listeners totally unprepared for anything so stark in 1980. An edited version only got mild pop response, but the complete single was a huge hit among Black and club audiences. The song was so definitive that it rendered everything else on the LP irrelevant, even the good second single "Hard Times." *—Ron Wynn*

Deuce / 1981 / Mercury ✦✦✦✦

Things cooled quickly for Kurtis Blow following the success of "The Breaks" in 1980. He was unable to get any single from this record on the charts, even though "Rockin'" and "It's Gettin' Hot" were well produced and competently delivered. But rap was still far from being a mainstream phenomenon, and this album did very poorly commercially. *—Ron Wynn*

Party Time? / 1983 / Mercury ✦✦✦✦

An ahead-of-its time collaboration between Kurtis Blow and EU, which was really a five-song EP rather than a full-length album. Rap met go-go in a rousing, nicely performed set that deserved more attention, but didn't generate much action. *—Ron Wynn*

Ego Trip / 1984 / Mercury ✦✦✦

Kurtis Blow briefly returned to the spotlight with the single "Basketball" from this LP. His brand of sparse, electro-funk rap was fading, and it was clear that Blow's skills were in production rather than performance. "Eight Million Stories" was a decent cut inspired by the old "Naked City" television series, while "Fallin' In Love Again" was among his better romantic efforts, but Blow's albums were always erratic propositions, and this one proved no different. *—Ron Wynn*

America / 1985 / Mercury ✦✦✦

Consistent rap beats with poignant social commentary. *—Bil Carpenter*

Kingdom Blow / 1986 / Mercury ✦✦

★ **Best of Kurtis Blow** / 1994 / Mercury ✦✦✦✦✦

While he made many groundbreaking singles, Kurtis Blow was never a consistent album artist, making this best-of collection his definitive artistic statement. Throughout the early '80s, Blow helped define what rap could do, and these tracks confirm his status as one of hip-hop's legendary acts. *—Stephen Thomas Erlewine*

Bone Thugs N Harmony

Rap, Hip-hop, G-Funk

The Cleveland-based hardcore rap collective Bone Thugs N Harmony was one of Eazy-E's last production efforts before his death in March 1995. Featuring Krayzie Bone, Layzie Bone, Bizzy Bone, Wish Bone, and Flesh-N-Bone, the group released their first EP, *Creepin on Ah Come Up,* in June of 1994. It sold over three million copies and had a crossover hit single with "Thuggish-Ruggish-Bone." *—Stephen Thomas Erlewine*

Creepin on Ah Come Up / 1994 / Ruthless ✦✦✦✦

Bone Thugs N Harmony came out of nowhere and scored a double-platinum hit with the *Creepin on Ah Come Up* EP, which is more notable for the group's hard-edged gangsta stance than the music, which is standard hardcore hip-hop. *—Stephen Thomas Erlewine*

E. 1999 Eternal / Jul. 25, 1995 / Ruthless ✦✦✦✦

E. 1999 Eternal fulfills the promise of Bone Thugs N Harmony's debut EP, expanding the hip-hop/soul fusions of *Creepin' on Ah Come Up.* It doesn't necessarily break new ground, but the group comes up with a surprising number of strong songs. The album sags a bit toward the end, but most of *E. 1999 Eternal* provides undiluted gangsta soul thrills. *—Stephen Thomas Erlewine*

Boo-Yaa T.R.I.B.E.

Rap

The six sons of a Samoan-descended Baptist minister comprising Los Angeles' Boo-Yaa T.R.I.B.E. have never had their brand of gangsta rap criticized as a commercial pose, as all members have been in prison at one time or another for producing and selling drugs and/or gun running. Brother Robert Devoux's death in a shooting provided the impetus for the formation of the Boo-Yaa T.R.I.B.E., which takes its name from a slang term for discharging a shotgun, by lead rapper Ganxsta Ridd, Ganxsta OMB, EKA, Rosco, Don-L, and the Godfather. The sextet moved to Tokyo to live with a sumo wrestler cousin and escape L.A.'s gang warfare; they performed as a dance-oriented rap outfit in Japan during the late '80s. Encouraged by their success, they returned to Los Angeles to pursue a record contract and were signed by Island. The aggressive, slamming *New Funky Nation* was released in 1990. After a four-year layoff, the T.R.I.B.E. returned with *Doomsday,* an album in similar style which contained rebukes of rappers posing as genuine gangstas for profit. *—Steve Huey*

● **New Funky Nation** / 1990 / Fourth & Broadway ✦✦✦✦

Boo-Yaa T.R.I.B.E. came onto the scene in top form with *New Funky Nation,* a hard-bitten collection of surly, edgy raps delivered over music supplied by an equally animated live band. This is one of the more underpublicized album statements done in 1990. *—Ron Wynn*

Doomsday / 1995 / Bullet Proof/Music For Nations ✦✦✦✦

Occupation Hazardous / Nov. 7, 1995 / First Kut Records ✦✦✦

Rumors of a Dead Man / Hollywood ✦✦✦

Boogie Down Productions

Rap, Gangsta Rap

Formed in 1986 by Laurence Krisna Parker and Scott Sterling, Boogie Down Productions quickly became one of the most influential and important hip-hop groups. Parker adopted the name KRS-One (an acronym for Knowledge Reigns Supreme Over Almost Every One) and Sterling became DJ Scott LaRock. They released an independent single, "Crack Attack," in 1986. BDP's groundbreaking 1987 debut, *Criminal Minded,* full of blunt, matter-of-fact tales of life on the mean streets, was a prototype for gangsta-rap. As the album was building to a massive underground success, LaRock was shot to death in the South Bronx as he tried to settle an argument. Instead of calling it quits, KRS-One continued BDP with his brother Kenny Parker and D-Nice as DJs and released *By All Means Necessary* the following year. KRS-One began calling himself "the Teacher," promoting self-awareness and education in his rhymes. He began touring colleges on the lecture circuit around 1989, and some of his writings appeared in the *New York Times.* It became evident that KRS-One had taken his role as the Teacher too far on 1990's *Edutainment,* where most tracks were lectures pasted over lackluster beats.

KRS-One obliterated all concerns that he sold out on 1992's *Sex and Violence,* where he sounds angrier and stronger than he has in years. However, the album wasn't the commercial blockbuster it could have been. The following year, KRS-One released his first solo album, *Return of the Boom Bap*, which was even better; many hip-hop critics equated it with the seminal *By All Means Necessary*. But by early 1994, it had already dropped off the R&B and hip-hop charts. — *Stephen Thomas Erlewine*

★ **Criminal Minded** / 1987 / Sugar Hill ✦✦✦✦✦
Classic early "gangsta" rap work. *Criminal Minded* was the only time the contributions of DJ Scott LaRock (Scott Sterling) were featured on a Boo-gie Down Productions recording, as he was murdered shortly after this was issued. The toughest, hardest-hitting BDP effort. — *Ron Wynn*

☆ **By All Means Necessary** / 1988 / Jive ✦✦✦✦✦
Boogie Down Productions' first album since the death of Scott LaRock finds KRS-One keeping his hardcore, proto-gangsta stance and strength-ening it with socially conscious rhymes. All the while, the beats and sam-ples are richer than the first record, creating a dense urban landscape for KRS-One's fiercely intelligent raps. — *Stephen Thomas Erlewine*

Ghetto Music: The Blueprint of Hip Hop / 1989 / Jive ✦✦✦✦
On BDP's third album, KRS-One strips the beat down to the basics, con-centrating his efforts on his rhymes. KRS-One has called himself the Teacher, and teach he does on *Ghetto Music*. From hip-hop to heritage, there isn't a single subject that slips by him. Sadly, *Ghetto Music* would prove to be the last time he would be able to completely capture the imagination of the hip-hop audience; it remains one of BDP's finest efforts. — *Stephen Thomas Erlewine*

Edutainment / 1990 / Jive ✦✦
Some speculated Kris Parker (KRS-One) might be getting a bit soft with this one, despite the lengthy expositions on the impact of poverty, drugs, and violence on his life. Parker emphasized a "humanist" tone on most of the material. — *Ron Wynn*

Live Hardcore Worldwide / 1991 / Jive ✦✦✦

Sex and Violence / 1992 / Jive ✦✦✦
KRS-One demolishes any idea he's losing his clout or anger. *Sex and Vio-lence* is his most chilling, slashing, and effective overall statement since *Criminal Minded*. — *Ron Wynn*

Brand New Heavies

Rap, Urban, Club/Dance
Another of the "acid-jazz" groups that have emerged during the '80s and '90s, the Brand New Heavies have attracted substantial attention on both sides of the Atlantic for their sometimes clever, sometimes cool mix of quasi-sophisticated vocals, jazz backing, and samples. The Lon-don band began in the mid-'80s with drummer/keyboardist Jan Kincaid, percussionist/guitarist Lascelles, guitarist Simon Bartholomew, bassist/keyboardist Andrew Levy, saxophonist Mike Smith, trumpeter Paul Dias, saxophonist/keyboardist Jim Wellman, and vocalist Jay Ella Ruth. They were active on what was then called the "rare groove" circuit, playing funk and soul. They became the Brand New Heavies in the late '80s, cutting the single "Got to Give" for the Cooltempo label. They switched to the Acid Jazz label and style in 1990. Their 1991 debut for Delicious Vinyl/Island did moderately well, but they gained even more exposure (despite generating lackluster sales) with *Heavy Rhyme Expe-rience: Vol 1*, a 1992 record that paired them with several hip-hop groups and big-name rappers. The guest list included Main Source, Gang Starr, Grand Puba, Master Ace, Kool G. Rap, Black Sheep, Ed O.G., Tiger, The Pharcyde, and Jamalski. Vocalist N'Dea Davenport was a con-tributor to *Jazzmatazz*, a similar all-star jazz/hip-hop set produced by Gang Starr's Guru. Brand New Heavies released their third album, *Brother Sister*, in 1994. — *Ron Wynn*

The Brand New Heavies / 1991 / Delicious Vinyl ✦✦✦✦
Brand New Heavies' debut album finds them trying to weld classic soul vocals and instrumentals, as well as jazz, to contemporary hip-hop. While it isn't entirely successful, the moments that it does work make the album worth listening to. — *Stephen Thomas Erlewine*

● **Heavy Rhyme Experience, Vol. 1** / 1992 / Atlantic ✦✦✦✦
Between their debut and full-fledged second album, Brand New Heavies released an album of collaborations with some of the brightest stars in hip-hop, such as Gang Starr, Grand Puba, and Main Source. *Heavy Rhyme Experience: Vol. 1* actually works better than their debut, since the rappers bring a gritty street credibility to the group's lush R&B; at its best, the album stands as a splendid fusion of jazz, soul, and hip-hop. — *Stephen Thomas Erlewine*

Brother Sister / 1994 / Delicious Vinyl ✦✦✦

Excursions . . . Remixes and Rare Grooves / 1995 / Capitol ✦✦

Brand Nubian

Rap
Picking up on the so-called "daisy age" sound of De La Soul, Brand Nubian's cool, funky sound serves as a platform for the group's declara-tions of Islamic faith and for the teachings of the Five Percent Nation. The group's original lineup was composed of lead rapper Maxwell

"Grand Puba" Dixon (formerly of the Masters of Ceremony), Lorenzo "Lord Jamar" Dechelaus, Derrick "Sadat X" Murphy, and his cousin DJ Alamo. Following the group's acclaimed 1990 debut, *One for All*, Grand Puba departed for a solo career, taking DJ Alamo with him. The remain-ing members added DJ Sincere and have continued to record albums detailing their religious beliefs and promoting self-reliance and peace. — *Steve Huey*

● **One for All** / 1990 / Elektra ✦✦✦✦
These post-De La Soul, daisy-age rappers are here to wrap their Islamic-slanted lyrics around challenging, clever, and hard-hitting beats and samples. — *John Floyd*

In God We Trust / 1993 / Elektra ✦✦✦✦

Bushwick Bill

Vocals / Rap, Gangsta Rap
A one-time member of Houston's the Geto Boys, Bushwick Bill created a stir with his 1992 release *Little Big Man*. It was an unvarnished, some-times frightening release, with details about the shooting incident that cost him an eye, along with the customary sexism, violent imagery, and outlandish inner-city narratives that have long been the group's stock-in-trade. — *Ron Wynn*

Little Big Man / 1992 / Priority ✦✦✦
Bushwick Bill went solo and made an effective debut album, chronicling the shooting incident that cost him an eye in graphic detail. While the Geto Boys were more disgusting than incisive, he actually turned in some coherent message tracks, notably "Letter From KKK" and "Stop Lying." Of course, it wouldn't have been a Bushwick Bill disc without some disgusting tracks, and "Ever So Clear" and "Call Me Crazy" cer-tainly fit that description. — *Ron Wynn*

● **Phantom of the Rapra** / 1995 / Rap-A-Lot ✦✦✦✦
Although Bushwick Bill changed his name before the release of *Phan-tom of the Rapra* (to the absurd Dr. Wolfgang Von Bushwickin The Bar-barian Mother-Funky Stay High Dollar Billstir), he hasn't changed his musical style at all for his second solo album. Throughout the record, Bushwick runs through his standard lyrical targets over his standard musical backdrops. That doesn't mean *Phantom of the Rapra* is a tedious listen. By now, Bushwick Bill is a skilled professional and he knows how to entertain. And that's what the record is, even if he does bring politics into the fray every once in a while. Bushwick's taste for comic book vio-lence and horror films overshadows his social commentary, as well as his latent misogynist tendencies. But that affection for the theatrical and the bizarre is what makes *Phantom of the Rapra* such enjoyable, volatile entertainment. Unlike his imitators, Bushwick knows exactly how to sat-isfy fans of ridiculously violent hardcore rap. — *Stephen Thomas Erlewine*

Luther Campbell

Vocals / Rap
The founder/creator of 2 Live Crew, owner of Luke Records and former concert promoter, Luther Campbell at one time was arguably the nation's most controversial hip-hop figure. Campbell formed the Miami-based quartet in 1987 and they were the centerpiece of a national campaign against allegedly obscene lyrics. He was embroiled in a trial pitting him against then-Florida attorney general Jack Thomp-son. Campbell later became a solo artist, issuing his own discs as Luke featuring 2 Live Crew. He released *Banned in the USA.*, a parody of Bruce Springsteen's "Born in the USA," and *I Got S—t on My Mind*. Campbell also published an autobiography and revamped 2 Live Crew, adding fresh members. They issued *Back at Your Ass for the Nine-4*, which peaked at No. 9 on the R&B chart in 1994. Campbell also won a Supreme Court decision which ruled that his parody of Roy Orbison's "Oh, Pretty Woman" didn't violate the copyright held by Acuff-Rose. Campbell launched the career of R&B vocalists H-Town, issuing their debut LP. — *Ron Wynn*

● **Banned in the U.S.A.** / 1990 / Luke ✦✦✦✦
A decent parody of Bruce Springsteen's "Born in the USA." helped turn the debut by 2 Live Crew founder Luther Campbell into a mini-event. Campbell didn't show any great rapping or rhyming skills on the micro-phone, but did speak frankly about those he considered fake "gangstas" in between the constant sexual innuendos, invitations, admonitions and declarations. — *Ron Wynn*

I Got Shit on My Mind / 1992 / Luke ✦✦
Luther Campbell, 2 Live Crew founder, impresario and overlord, took the microphone for a second session of his impressions on various sub-jects, mostly sexual and occasionally political. But where his debut had the novelty factor of hearing The Crew's head man out front, the second time around was much less entertaining and a lot more tiresome. — *Ron Wynn*

Candyman

Vocals / Rap

Los Angeles rapper Candyman was featured backing Tone-Loc before he earned his own solo stint. His 1990 debut *Ain't No Shame in My Game* scored a Top Ten pop hit with "Knockin' Boots." The following year, he followed that with another less successful LP for Epic, *Playtime Is Over*. His most recent release was *I Thought U Knew* for I.R.S. in 1993, which also failed to click. *—Ron Wynn*

● **Ain't No Shame in My Game** / 1990 / Epic ✦✦✦✦
Although this scored a huge crossover hit with "I Got a Man," the rest of the record didn't prove if the single was a fluke or not; the jury was still out. *—Ron Wynn*

Playtime Is Over / 1991 / Epic ✦✦✦
A decent follow-up, but it lines up in the pop/gimmick camp despite occasionally interesting raps and production. *—Ron Wynn*

I Thought U Knew / Jun. 29, 1993 / IRS ✦✦
The third Candyman CD, his first for I.R.S., lacked either the pop charm of his debut or the leering insolence of the follow-up. *—Ron Wynn*

Neneh Cherry

b. Mar. 10, 1964, Stockholm, Sweden
Vocals / Dance-Pop

A one-time member of Rip Rig + Panic and of the punk group the Slits, she had a massive 1989 hit with "Buffalo Stance," which masterfully balanced hip-hop sensibilities with the crisp, accessible bounce of high-tech R&B. Cherry is also the stepdaughter of jazz trumpeter Don Cherry. After several years of inactivity, Cherry returned in 1992 with the critically acclaimed *Home Brew;* although it failed to capture the same sales as her debut, it proved that she remained artistically innovative.*—John Floyd*

Raw Like Sushi / 1989 / Virgin ✦✦✦✦
Cherry's wonderful debut, produced by British dance master Bomb The Bass, offers a brash, sassy portrait of a contemporary feminist, unwilling to take shit from a lip-flapping homeboy and confident enough to tackle thorny issues, both political and sexual. *—John Floyd*

● **Homebrew** / 1992 / Virgin ✦✦✦✦
Despite the absence of a knockout single like "Buffalo Stance," *Homebrew* is a stronger album than *Raw Like Sushi.* On *Homebrew,* Cherry's melding of hip-hop and R&B is so complete that no seams show; it doesn't belong to either genre, but stands on its own. It takes a couple of plays before it starts to sink in, but after some time, even Michael Stipe's rap on "Trout" seems completely natural. *—Stephen Thomas Erlewine*

Chubb Rock

Vocals / Rap, Hip-hop, Urban

Weighing in at 250 pounds, Chubb Rock (born Richard Simpson) often evokes images of a hip-hop Barry White (whom he dueted with on *And the Winner Is . . .*). Chubb Rock had a group while he was a teenager in New York but started his career in earnest after he dropped out of college. After three singles from his first album went nowhere, his second album *And the Winner Is . . .* was released to greater commercial and critical acclaim, thanks to a remixed single version of "Caught Up" that was released prior to the album. *—Stephen Thomas Erlewine*

Chubb Rock / 1988 / Champ ✦✦✦

Featuring Hitman Howie Tee / 1988 / Select ✦✦✦
Interesting, entertaining raps, witty quips, and good samples from disco and funk works. *—Ron Wynn*

● **And the Winner Is . . .** / 1989 / Select ✦✦✦✦
Sharp humor with first-rate samples and production, plus insightful commentary on ghetto violence and the ignorance of the National Academy of Recording Arts and Sciences. *—Ron Wynn*

The One / 1991 / Select ✦✦✦
Rock still raps hard, but uneven production and mixes sometimes slow the momentum. *—Ron Wynn*

I Gotta Get Mine Yo / 1992 / Select ✦✦

Coolio

Vocals / Rap

Coolio (born Artis Ivey) is a native of Compton, CA, yet his variation of the P-Funk-inspired rap of Dr. Dre is calmer, less violent, and funnier. Recorded with his DJ Bryan "Wino" Dobbs, Coolio's 1994 debut album, *It Takes a Thief,* was a smash hit, selling over a million records and featuring the No. 3 single, "Fantastic Voyage." *—Stephen Thomas Erlewine*

It Takes a Thief / 1994 / Tommy Boy ✦✦✦
Just when it looked like rap would completely succumb to the violent hyperbole and mean-spirited "realness" of gangsta rap, new blood entered the scene in 1994 to nudge the genre back toward friendlier turf.

That new blood included Nas, Craig Mack, and Coolio, whose *It Takes a Thief* starts with the easy-rolling funk of Lakeside's "Fantastic Voyage" and goes from there, infusing rap with a much-needed sense of humor and the promise of good times. While Coolio is no simp—"County Line" playfully explores the hassles of welfare, while some tracks dip into gangsta territory—he manages to make rap a cool, inclusive journey. *—Eddie Huffman*

● **Gangsta's Paradise** / Nov. 21, 1995 / Tommy Boy ✦✦✦✦
Most of Coolio's hit debut *It Takes a Thief* was fairly upbeat material, but the appearance of the stark single "Gangsta's Paradise" in the summer of 1995 signaled a change in the rapper's music. Driven by an ominously deep bass line and slashing strings, the creeping, threatening funk of "Gangsta's Paradise" was the most chilling thing Coolio had recorded to date, but the menace didn't come at the expense of his considerable talent for immediate, catchy hooks. Consequently, the single shot to the top of the charts and hovered in the Top Ten for many weeks. The album followed shortly afterwards, and it didn't fail to deliver on the promise of the single. Not only did Coolio expand his sound, but his songwriting skills improved, as *Gangsta's Paradise* has very few weak moments. Alternating between slow, funky grooves and elastic, party-ready anthems, *Gangsta's Paradise* is proof that Coolio is one of the most exciting and interesting hip-hop artists of the mid-'90s. *—Stephen Thomas Erlewine*

Cypress Hill

Rap, Hip-hop

With their lazily menacing hip-hop, Cypress Hill became one of the biggest hip-hop groups of the early '90s. Powered by the slow, stoned production of DJ Muggs, the group's self-titled debut album became a sleeper sensation in 1991. B-Real's whiny vocals were balanced by the more straightforward rapping of Sen Dog, yet both of their lyrics were severely warped, whether they were telling surreal gangsta tales or celebrating marijuana. With its deliberate bass and beats, Cypress Hill's music sounded stoned—it was one of the most unique, creative sounds to hit hip-hop since The Bomb Squad. While preparing the group's second album, DJ Muggs produced a number of best-selling acts, including House of Pain and Funkdoobiest. All the while, the group earned notoriety for continuing to campaign for the legalization of marijuana.

Cypress Hill's second album, 1993's *Black Sunday*, was an even bigger hit than their debut, selling over a million copies and earning a crossover hit with "Insane in the Brain." *—Stephen Thomas Erlewine*

★ **Cypress Hill** / 1991 / Ruffhouse ✦✦✦✦✦
With its slow, heavily stoned funk, surrealistic gangsta fantasies and whining delivery, *Cypress Hill* was a landmark hip-hop album of the early '90s, ushering in an era of marijuana and lazy funk. But it wasn't all good times—"How I Could Just Kill a Man" and "Hand on the Glock" were positively terrifying when delivered in their slow, blunted fashion. *—Stephen Thomas Erlewine*

Black Sunday / 1993 / Columbia ✦✦✦✦
It doesn't matter if *Black Sunday* follows the same formula as *Cypress Hill,* because it does so in such an intoxicating, convincing manner. Bolstered by the splendid singles "We Ain't Goin' Out Like That," "When the Sh— Goes Down," and "Insane in the Brain," *Black Sunday* is a surreal, stoned vision of contemporary hip-hop culture that is as funny as it is frightening. *—Stephen Thomas Erlewine*

Cypress Hill III: Temples of Boom / 1995 / Columbia ✦✦✦

Unreleased & Revamped / Aug. 1996 / Sony ✦✦

Da Brat

Vocals / Rap, Urban

Da Brat (born Shawntae Harris) was discovered by producer Jermaine Dupri after winning an amateur rap contest at a Kris Kross concert in Chicago. Dupri masterminded Da Brat's 1994 million-selling hard-edged, funky debut effort, *Funkdafied. —Stephen Thomas Erlewine*

● **Funkdafied** / 1994 / So So Def/Chaos ✦✦✦✦

Da Lench Mob

Rap

Ice Cube produced this West Coast rap trio's 1992 project *Guerillas in Tha Mist.* It featured T-Bone, J-Dee, and Shorty and the title track proved an R&B and rap hit, with a video loosely modeled on the film *Predator* that included an appearance by Cube. *—Ron Wynn*

● **Guerillas in Tha Mist** / 1992 / Atco ✦✦✦✦
Not surprisingly, Da Lench Mob has some similarities to their mentor and producer Ice Cube. Da Lench Mob elaborate Cube's hardcore fantasies with their group sound and contribute their own dose of scathing politics and controversy. Gangsta-rap fans should take note, if they haven't already. *—AMG*

Plant Of Da Apes / 1994 / Priority ✦✦✦
With the same aggressive style as partner Ice Cube, Da Lench Mob criticizes White society for the ills of the country. Preaching that Blacks must help themselves, the group has some laid-back rhythms that contrast with their lyrics, but somehow it works. —*John Bush*

Das EFX

Rap, Hip-hop
With their first album, Das EFX caused a minor revolution based on their speedy, quick-tongued stuttering; it helped that they backed their rhymes with thick, funky tracks. The album was a major success, scoring a Top 40 pop single and going gold. On their second LP, *Straight Up Sewaside*, the duo of Drayz and Skoob Effect slightly altered their approach. They downplayed the high speed stuttering, though they continued with the intense rhyming and confrontational themes that made their debut so memorable. —*AMG*

● **Dead Serious** / 1992 / East West ✦✦✦✦
Their raps are often lightweight, but this album has made an immediate and substantial impact in the hip-hop community. —*Ron Wynn*

Straight Up Sewaside / 1993 / East West ✦✦✦
It may not be as revolutionary or immediately memorable as the twisting rhymes of *Dead Serious*, but the harder-edged styles of *Straight Up Sewaside* have enough slamming rhythms and rhymes to satisfy most fans. —*Stephen Thomas Erlewine*

Hold It Down / Oct. 1995 / East West ✦✦✦
Although the duo tries very hard, there isn't much on *Hold It Down*, Das EFX's third album, that makes it very different from their previous records. The production is a bit leaner and their delivery is a bit harder, yet that doesn't disguise the fact that the beats aren't as strong as their earlier albums, nor are their raps as exciting and inventive. Nevertheless, there are some strong moments on *Hold It Down*, and it should please fans of the duo, even if it doesn't appeal to the same large audience that embraced their debut. —*Stephen Thomas Erlewine*

De La Soul

Rap
This trio of Long Island rappers consists of Posdnous (born Kelvin Mercer), Trugoy (born David Jolicoeur), and Mase. Their albums are lyrically keen and idiomatically diverse, sampling cuts from both The Coasters and the Turtles (the latter got them in some legal hot water), while espousing viewpoints that put them in the Afrocentric pocket yet don't wed them to any hard-and-fast religious or political position. Some have called them hip-hop's first hippies; more to the point, they're among rap's sharpest and savviest performers.

De La Soul answered detractors who claimed they lacked edge with *Buhloone Mind State* in 1993. It was their answer to gangsta rappers who had called them irrelevant, as they skewered that idiom for its obsessiveness with hardness and posturing.

In 1996, the trio released their fourth album, *Stakes Is High*. —*Ron Wynn*

★ **Three Feet High & Rising** / 1989 / Tommy Boy ✦✦✦✦✦
A remarkable debut that runs the gamut from absurdity ("Jenifa Taught Me" and "Plug Tunin'") to hard-hitting social commentary ("Ghetto Thang" and "Say No Go"), and also contains the hit "Me Myself and I." De La Soul's inventiveness shines—not many rappers would be able to pull funky beats from Steely Dan and Turtles tracks. Throughout the album, a mock game show is interspersed between the songs, giving the entire recording a bizarre, humorous feel. *Three Feet High & Rising* would be incoherent if it wasn't for the sizable rhyming and musical talents of the trio. —*Stephen Thomas Erlewine*

De La Soul Is Dead / 1991 / Tommy Boy ✦✦✦✦
The title and cover (a picture of a broken pot of daisies) illustrate that De La Soul wishes to debunk their myth and shed the attention their debut album earned them. For the most part, the songs on the album are considerably less lighthearted than the ones on the debut, but are no less impressive—"Millie Pulled a Pistol on Santa" is one of the most chilling tales of child abuse ever recorded. *De La Soul Is Dead* is not easy to assimilate on the first listen, but the rewards are great. —*Stephen Thomas Erlewine*

Buhloone Mindstate / 1993 / Tommy Boy ✦✦✦

Stakes Is High / 1996 / Tommy Boy ✦✦✦
Although De La Soul's albums are consistently critically acclaimed, ever since their 1989 debut, *3 Feet High & Rising*, the trio has had trouble recapturing a broad-based audience. Even though their audience has shrunk, their desire to expand and deepen their music hasn't, as *Stakes Is High*, their fourth album, illustrates. De La Soul consciously rejects all of the hip-hop trends of the mid-'90s on *Stakes Is High*, eschewing G-funk and Wu-Tang-inspired soundscapes for a jazzier, more soulful version of their trademark eclecticism. By this point, the trio's sound isn't as surpris-

ing or exciting as it was on *3 Feet High*, but the increased maturity and subtle variations on the sound makes *Stakes Is High* an impressive effort from one of hip-hop's most restless bands. —*Leo Stanley*

Willie Dee

Vocals / Rap
William "Willie Dee" Dennis was an original member of the Houston rap ensemble The Geto Boys. Willie Dee's 1990 debut *Controversy* certainly started some with the track "F— Rodney King," a no-holds-barred attack on King for purportedly selling out when he made his famous "can't we all just get along?" comment. Dee followed that with *I'm Going Out like a Soldier*. —*Ron Wynn*

● **Controversy** / 1992 / Priority ✦✦✦✦
Former Geto Boy Willie Dee started his own controversy when he lit into Rodney King on this album. "F— Rodney King" was a blistering indictment and denunciation, depicting King as a sellout, traitor, and collaborator for asking his now-famous "Can't we all just get along" question during the Los Angeles riots. Unfortunately, the rage Dee felt toward King or America in general wasn't effectively communicated, either on that cut or the rest of the album. The raps were unfocused, the beats predictable and the rhymes seldom catchy or inventive. —*Ron Wynn*

Digable Planets

Rap, Urban, Hip-hop
One of the hottest hip-hop jazz groups to emerge in the '90s, Digable Planets combined a witty, loose rapping style similiar to the old "beat" poetry with improvisational backing to score a commercial and aesthetic success with their debut CD, *Reaching: A New Refutation of Time & Space*. *Reaching* proved to be both a critical and commercial success. Its follow-up, 1994's more street-oriented *Blowout Comb,* didn't achieve as many sales, yet it confirmed the group's status as one of hip-hop's most praised bands. —*Ron Wynn*

● **Reachin': A New Refutation . . .** / 1993 / Pendulum ✦✦✦✦
Digable Planets' debut album was one of the more successful fusions of jazz and rap, blending the two genres into a funky, seamless, stylish sound, without losing the integrity of jazz or hip-hop street credibility. —*Stephen Thomas Erlewine*

Blowout Comb / 1994 / Pendulum ✦✦✦✦
Digable Planets set the hip-hop world on its ear with their jazz-inflected debut, *Reachin'.* Their follow-up, *Blowout Comb*, not only offers a deeper exploration of their jazz roots, but also more politicized and harder-edged lyrics than their debut, even if it lacks a single song as impressive as "Rebirth of Slick (Cool Like Dat)." —*Stephen Thomas Erlewine*

Digital Underground

Rap, Hip-hop
Nearly every rap posse from the '80s and '90s has borrowed from George Clinton's mountain of P-Funk, but this Bay Area conglomerate (led by rappers Shock-G and Humpty Hump) have mutated Clinton's boogie into the heaviest funk-fueled sound in rap. And their sense of humor is always dead on target.

Digital Underground wasn't able to replicate the commercial success of their 1990 debut *Sex Packets*, yet their music has remained consistently strong, even if it all sounds a bit similar. —*John Floyd*

★ **Sex Packets** / Jan. 1990 / Tommy Boy ✦✦✦✦✦
With their debut album *Sex Packets*, Digital Underground kick-started the Parliament/Funkadelic obsessions that dominated the hip-hop world of the early '90s. Digital Underground create a full-length tribute to George Clinton's warped fantasy world, taking both the elastic bass lines and the goofy, surreal sense of humor and adopting it to their own purposes. With their ridiculous sense of humor and endless, loping synth-laced grooves, the two hit singles, "The Humpty Dance" and "Doowutchyalike," seem to tell the whole story, but that's not the case. Within the album tracks of *Sex Packets* are jazzy experiments, hardcore funk and loads of innovative rhymes and grooves that set the pace for much of the music that followed. Furthermore, the Underground has a good-natured, welcoming sense of humor that infuses everything on *Sex Packets*, particularly the tongue-in-cheek sci-fi mini-opera that comprises the title track. Although they made some musical innovations on their two subsequent albums, the Digital Underground never made an album as consistently engaging as their debut. —*Stephen Thomas Erlewine*

This Is an EP Release / Feb. 1990 / Tommy Boy ✦✦✦
Two decent remixes from their debut pad this half-hour mini opus. The new stuff ("Same Song," "Nuttin' Nis Funky") attests to the Underground's devotion to the funk and to their staying power. —*John Floyd*

Sons of the P / 1991 / Tommy Boy ✦✦✦✦
Their devotion to brother George Clinton mutates into a full-blown sort-of concept album. No truly great singles, but as a whole, this is their best album. —*John Floyd*

The Body Hat Syndrome / 1993 / Tommy Boy ✦✦✦
With their third album, Digital Underground doesn't change their style much, but that isn't bad. Instead, *The Body-Hat Syndrome* is an endearing mess of P-Funk-inspired hip-hop, with enough good humor and beats to satisfy their fans. — *Stephen Thomas Erlewine*

Future Rhythm / Jun. 1996 / Radikal ✦✦

Disposable Heroes of the Hiphoprisy

Rap, Urban
Michael Franti's deep and defiant tones were the lure for this short-lived group that didn't bill itself a rap band. Franti's resemblance in style, tone, and timbre to Gil Scott-Heron, plus his willingness to tackle targets ranging from television to fellow rappers, won them immediate attention. There were charges that The Disposable Heroes of Hiphoprisy were themselves engaging in hypocrisy by not identifying with rappers, yet cashing in on the genre's popularity. They issued only one album before disbanding. — *Ron Wynn*

● **Hypocrisy Is the Greatest Luxury** / 1992 / 4th & Broadway ✦✦✦✦
Hard-hitting political rap that is excellent on the rhetoric and lyrics but a bit weak on the grooves; it's closer to Gil Scott-Heron than Public Enemy. —*AMG*

DJ Jazzy Jeff & The Fresh Prince

Rap
If you're looking for bubblegum rap, these guys are your best bet. The Prince spins his teen-suburban tales in a pleasant, if facile fashion, and Jeff isn't bad on the turntable. Don't look for anything gritty or street-smart: when Jeff boasts that he can beat Mike Tyson, that's about as menacing as it gets. The Fresh Prince starred in the early-'90s TV sitcom, **Fresh Prince of Bel Air.**
Will Smith, the "Fresh Prince" part of the team, has greatly expanded his horizons in the '90s. He appeared in the films *Independence Day, Six Degrees of Separation*, and *Bad Boys* and also tried to expand his hip-hop horizons enough to offset the talk that his raps had become hopelessly white bread and irrelevant. *Homebase* in 1991 included "Dog Is a Dog" and the Top Ten pop hit "Summertime," with Smith's rap done in a leaner, harder fashion, even if the lyrics were pretty much family hour. But by *Code Red* in 1993 it seemed Smith had made peace with his image and was back to laidback, pop-oriented material such as "Boom! Shake the Room," "I Wanna Rock," and "Can't Wait to Be with You," which had a guest stint from Christopher Williams. —*John Floyd*

Rock the House / 1987 / Jive ✦✦✦
A ten-song work originally issued on Pop Art Records and later picked up by Jive. Containing the hit "Girls Ain't Nothing But Trouble," which launched them as the kings of teen/clean rap, it had maximum crossover appeal yet retained a large following among the core hip-hop audience. —*Ron Wynn*

● **He's the D.J. I'm the Rapper** / 1988 / Jive ✦✦✦✦
Their commercial breakthrough contains their No.12 hit, "Parents Just Don't Understand," and other good-time raps. —*Dan Heilman*

And in This Corner . . . / 1989 / Jive ✦✦✦
More wit and whim from Jeff and The Prince, this time with assistance from saxes, flutes, and trumpets. Though not as commercially successful as its predecessors, it's actually a more faithful rap work. —*Ron Wynn*

Homebase / 1991 / Jive ✦✦✦✦
After enduring a temporary sales slump, DJ Jazzy Jeff & The Fresh Prince roared back with *Homebase*. They scored a huge pop and R&B hit with "Summertime," using Kool & The Gang's "Summer Madness" single for the music base while Will Smith rapped about romantic hopes and community barbeques. He landed another Top 20 single with "Ring My Bell," this time reworking Anita Ward's oldie while offering his own double-entendre take. Undoubtedly helped by the success of his television show, this album returned the duo to platinum status, even as Smith showed once more (protests to the contrary notwithstanding) that he was an accomplished pop rapper. —*Ron Wynn*

Code Red / Oct. 12, 1993 / Jive ✦✦✦
After years of proclaiming that he wouldn't do gangsta rap, The Fresh Prince finally succumbs to a harder-edged style on *Code Red*. And, surprisingly, he pulls it off well, thanks to sharp production and his endearing personality. —*Stephen Thomas Erlewine*

DJ Quik

Vocals / Rap
From references to Compton's Tree Top Piru Bloods in his songs to dropping the "c" from Quik because it stands for "Crips," DJ Quik (born David Blake) leaves little doubt about either the authenticity of his gangsta rap or which side he's on. Quik grew up in Compton as a gang member; he left that life for music, but still remains true to his roots and old connections. In 1991, when he was 20, Quik recorded his debut

album, *Quik Is the Name;* it and its follow-up, *Way 2 Fonky*, went gold. Dissatisfied with his life and his musical direction, Quik signed with Death Row Records and made CEO Marion "Suge" Knight his manager. The results were Quik's best album, 1995's *Safe + Sound*, which draws heavily on the influence of Parliament-Funkadelic. —*Steve Huey*

● **Quik Is the Name** / 1991 / Profile ✦✦✦✦
DJ Quik was 20 years old when he came roaring out of the chute in 1991 with the single "Tonite." It was a mild hit, while "Quik's Groove," "Born and Raised in Compton" and "Deep" were more appropriate for establishing Quik as another in the line of hard West Coast rappers. While overdosing on the sexist references, Quik's furious pace and flippant style signaled that he could be a force. —*Ron Wynn*

Way 2 Fonky / 1992 / Profile ✦✦✦✦
DJ Quik proved his mettle with "Jus Lyke Compton," a definitive bit of regional touting that proclaimed West Coast rap the style setter and all others followers. Whether or not you bought the line, you were hooked by the rap. Nothing else on the disc matched this single's intensity and wit, but it helped him earn a second straight gold LP. —*Ron Wynn*

Safe + Sound / Feb. 21, 1995 / Profile ✦✦✦
Caught up with extolling his sexiness and success with women, DJ Quik raps about little else on his third album. The lyrics are funny though, and his G-funk grooves do help things. —*John Bush*

The D.O.C.

Rap, G-Funk
After the release of his debut album, the career of Texas-born rapper the D.O.C. was shattered by a car crash that almost took his life. Although he could no longer rap like he used to, his former producer Dr. Dre featured the rapper on his groundbreaking album *The Chronic*, which built on the foundation laid by the D.O.C.'s *No One Can Do It Better;* he was also featured on Snoop Doggy Dogg's *Doggystyle*. The D.O.C. returned in early 1996 with *Helter Skelter*, his first album in nearly seven years. The album received mixed reviews and failed to earn a large audience. —*Stephen Thomas Erlewine*

★ **No One Can Do It Better** / 1989 / Ruthless ✦✦✦✦✦
This Texas-born rapper hooks up with Dr. Dre of N.W.A. fame to make an effective effort fusing funk, hip-hop, soul, and reggae, along with some tough, taut commentary and raps. Guest spots from Eazy-E, Miche'le, and MC Ren. —*Ron Wynn*

Helter Skelter / 1996 / Giant ✦✦✦

Domino

Rap
Domino's *Sweet Potato Pie* was a pop and R&B hit from his self-titled debut LP. The album was issued in December 1993. Three years later, Domino delivered his second album, *Physical Funk*, which failed to become as successful as its predecessor. —*Ron Wynn*

● **Domino** / 1993 / Mocity Music ✦✦✦✦
Rapper Domino's scattershot/stuttering rhyming (a near flawless imitation of early DAS EFX) yielded a hit with "Getto Jam," and is the hook for his CD. "Do You Qualify" offers a comic (if not comical) spin on a tale of mistaken identity and consensual sex, while "Money Is Everything" and "Sweet Potato Pie" give Domino's insights into materialism and sexual conquest, and "Raincoat" is his safe sex lecture. He's not really a gangsta, satirist or protester; Domino's songs are delivered in a deadpan, half-sung, half-spoken fashion; he's aided by tight production from DJ Battlecat and smart samples. —*Ron Wynn*

Physical Funk / Apr. 1996 / Outburst ✦✦✦✦

Dr. Dre

Keyboards, Vocals / Rap, G-Funk
Hip-hop's reigning star and sales giant Andre "Dr. Dre" Young was a member of World Class Wreckin' Cru along with DJ Antoine "Yella" Carraby. They left to join Eric "Eazy-E" Wright, Lorenzo "M.C. Ren" Patterson and Oshea "Ice Cube" Jackson in creating N.W.A. Their 1989 album *Straight Outta Compton* shocked many observers with its vulgarity and sexism, but it shot them to the top, becoming a double platinum record. N.W.A. stayed in the spotlight a couple of years, then splintered due to internal strife and the defection of Ice Cube and Eazy-E. Eazy-E, Ice Cube, and Dr. Dre also had a falling out over fiscal matters involving their former label Ruthless Records and ex-agent Jerry Heller. Dre emerged as the head of his own organization and a solo star as a rapper/producer in 1993; his protégé Snoop Doggy Dogg became an equally huge star, rapping in a lower-key, off-rhythm fashion. Dre's commanding, brusque, and menacing cadences, coupled with his adoption of Parliament/Funkadelic and classic funk beats, made *The Chronic* a rap juggernaut. —*Ron Wynn*

★ **The Chronic** / 1993 / Death Row ✦✦✦✦✦
With its deeply funky George Clinton-inspired grooves, whining synthesizers, female backing vocals, and romantic gangsta tales, *The Chronic*
redefined hip-hop for the 1990s. Dr. Dre's genius lies in keeping the funk
loose but concise, creating perfect singles like "Down Wit Dre Day," "Let
Me Ride," and "Nuthin' But A 'G' Thang." For all his musical genius, Dr.
Dre remains an unspectacular rapper, which makes Snoop Doggy Dogg
all the more remarkable. Snoop raps as much as Dre throughout *The
Chronic,* and his surreally menacing drawl shows the reality behind the
stylized portraits of sex and violence. —*Stephen Thomas Erlewine*

First Round Knockout / May 21, 1996 / Triple X ✦✦

Eazy-E

b. Sep. 7, 1963, d. Mar. 26, 1995
Vocals / Rap
After leaving N.W.A., rapper Eazy-E led a career that was filled with controversy and was successful commercially, even if it never matched the
creativity of his previous band. Eazy-E began his solo career in 1988
with *Eazy-Duz-It;* it was his only full-length album. Eazy-E left N.W.A.
after the 1991's *Niggaz4Life* hit the top of the charts. The breakup of
N.W.A. was bitter, and Eazy earned the wrath of Dr. Dre. Dre and Eazy
carried out their feud on record throughout the early '90s. Even though
he released several hit EPs, Eazy's career was in decline when he
announced he was suffering from AIDS in early March of 1995; he only
learned that he had the disease in the previous month. Three weeks
later, the rapper died on March 26, 1995—he was 31 years old.
—*Stephen Thomas Erlewine*

Eazy-Duz-It / 1988 / Ruthless ✦✦✦✦
Eazy-E's debut has something to offend just about everyone, regardless
of leftist or rightist leanings or vehemence regarding issues of feminism.
But at its best, *Eazy-Duz-It* is a fiery piece of hip-hop menace, marred
only by E's incessant whine of a voice and his rampant sexism. Play at
your own risk. —*John Floyd*

5150 Home 4 Tha Sick / 1992 / Priority ✦✦
Eazy-E issued this ill-conceived, stiffly rapped EP, which generated some
quick response and then disappeared. —*Ron Wynn*

It's on (Dr. Dre 187um) Killa / 1993 / Ruthless ✦✦✦
Eazy-E fired back in the unending war of words with former N.W.A. comrade Dr. Dre on the EP *It's On (Dr. Dre 187um) Killa.* At the time of the
EP's release, Eazy-E had already lost credibility in hip-hop circles for
appearing at Republican fund-raisers and supporting one of the officers
involved in the Rodney King incident. Thus, his charges that Dre is a
fraud lack consistency and weight; in addition, his raps sound tired
throughout the disc. Where Eazy-E was once cocky, funny and often
intriguing, he now sounds merely bitter. Besides the usual sexist and sexual posturing, he even reprises N.W.A.'s debut single "Boyz in Tha Hood"
again. The song was once an entertaining manifesto, but now it's just
dated, "G" mix and all. —*Ron Wynn*

Temporary Insanity / Feb. 1993 / Priority ✦✦✦

Str8 Off Tha Streetz / 1995 / Ruthless ✦✦

● **Eternal E** / Dec. 1995 / Ruthless/Priority ✦✦✦

Eightball & MJG

Rap
Eightball & MJG are a hardcore rap duo from Tennessee. They released
their first album, *Comin' Out Hard,* in 1993 but didn't hit the big time
until 1995, when they debuted in the pop Top Ten with *On Top of the
World.* —*Stephen Thomas Erlewine*

Comin' out Hard / Aug. 1, 1993 / Suave ✦✦✦
Eightball & MJG's first record, *Comin' Out Hard,* was a muddled affair of
standard gangsta hip-hop that only hinted at the scarily accomplished
rappers they would later become. —*Stephen Thomas Erlewine*

● **On the Outside Looking In** / 1994 / Suave ✦✦✦✦
Eightball & MJG made some significant strides forward on their second
collection *On the Outside Looking In.* Featuring improved production
skills and tighter rapping, the album suggested that the Southern duo
had the potential to break nationally. —*Stephen Thomas Erlewine*

EPMD

Rap
Long Island rappers Erick Sermon and Parrish Smith (EPMD stands for
Erick & Parrish Making Dollars) have confounded some observers by
achieving monumental success despite utilizing minimal production
and rapping skills. The deadpan, almost mushmouth, rapping style and
simplistic insertion of samples and snippets throughout their three
albums notwithstanding, such cuts as "You Gots to Chill" and "Rampage" have been hits. The duo are also accomplished producers and pre-

side over The Hit Squad, a combination of rap acts including Redman,
K-Solo, and DAS EFX.
Sermon and Smith were unable to reconcile artistic differences and
personality conflicts and dissolved their formerly successful partnership
in 1993. Sermon issued his own CD, *No Pressure,* later that same year.
—*Ron Wynn*

★ **Strictly Business** / 1988 / Priority ✦✦✦✦✦
In reality a collection of singles, EPMD's debut turns some clever samples (Steve Miller, Kool & The Gang, Bob Marley, Otis Redding) into an
overpowering funk assault. "You Gots to Chill" is a classic. —*John Floyd*

Unfinished Business / 1989 / Priority ✦✦✦✦
Although this doesn't hit as hard as their debut, it does contain some
good jabs at the quiet-storm, Black upwardly mobile crowd and also
some slams at their detractors. —*Ron Wynn*

Business As Usual / 1991 / Def Jam ✦✦✦
A little to the processed side production-wise, but it boasts one good collaboration with LL Cool J on "Rampage." —*Ron Wynn*

Business Never Personal / Jul. 28, 1992 / Ral ✦✦✦✦
EPMD's terse, thick-tongued rapping style was back on point with their
fourth album. Although behind-the-scenes turmoil finally split Erick Sermon and Parrish Smith up, they were together and cooking on this 1992
record. They scored their final signature single with "Crossover," a dead-
on commentary directed at rappers putting pop hopes ahead of hip-hop
values. "Headbanger" and "Can't Hear Nothing But The Music" were
other sterling tracks from their last great album. —*Ron Wynn*

Eric B & Rakim

Rap, Hip-hop
The Queens, NY, duo has the distinction of being the first of dozens of
ensembles to construct a sound around James Brown samples. The
rapid-fire boasts of Rakim and Eric B's inventive turntable techniques
make their entire catalog worth investigating.
This once formidable duo, whose biting, sullen style was among the
tightest and most influential during the '80s, called it quits in
1993.—*John Floyd*

Microphone Fiend / 1982 / UNI ✦✦

★ **Paid in Full** / 1987 / 4th & Broadway ✦✦✦✦✦
Their debut contains new mixes of early singles ("I Ain't No Joke," "Eric
B. Is President") and adds some prime stuff, including the monumental
"Paid in Full," which became a heavily sampled item in the late '80s.
—*John Floyd*

Just a Beat / 1988 / UNI ✦✦

☆ **Follow the Leader** / 1988 / UNI ✦✦✦✦✦
On their second album, Eric B. & Rakim deliver an album that expands
on the power of their debut. Taking a cue from the Coldcut remix of
"Paid in Full" that became a hit after the release of *Paid in Full, Follow
the Leader* has a looser, wilder beat than its predecessor. Eric B. uses the
spare, James Brown-influenced grooves that dominated *Paid in Full* as a
starting point, adding all kinds of production flourishes that flesh out the
funk without watering it down. Not only are Eric B.'s musical accomplishments impressive, but so are Rakim's rhymes, which are more
detailed and complex than before, even if his subject matter didn't
change much. In short, *Follow the Leader* is the second hip-hop classic
Eric B. & Rakim delivered in a row—it captures the duo at the top of their
game. —*Leo Stanley*

Let the Rhythm Hit 'Em / 1990 / MCA ✦✦✦
This subdued set works its magic more subtly, but the title is no joke.
—*John Floyd*

Don't Sweat the Technique / 1992 / MCA ✦✦✦✦
While it doesn't match their trailblazing work of the late '80s, *Don't
Sweat the Technique* is a solid effort from this influential duo. —*Stephen
Thomas Erlewine*

Eric B. / 1995 / Nine ✦✦

The Fat Boys

Rap
One of early rap's most successful acts, the Fat Boys parlayed a combined weight of over 750 pounds into a novelty act that sustained them
through several albums and hit singles. Originally known as the Disco
3, Brooklynites Mark "Prince Markie Dee" Morales, Damon "Kool Rock-
ski" Wimbley, and Darren "Buff the Human Beat Box" Robinson won a
talent contest at Radio City Music Hall in 1983, thanks in part to Robinson's talent for using his mouth to improvise hip-hop rhythms and
sound effects. The trio changed their name and recorded good-time
party anthems and songs humorously exploiting their weight; their first
few records were produced by Kurtis Blow and feature fusions of hip-
hop with reggae and rock. The Fat Boys hit their commercial peak with
1987's platinum LP *Crushin',* a collection of entertaining party tunes

that included a hit collaboration with the Beach Boys, "Wipeout." The group took the opportunity to star in the comedy film *Disorderlies* that year. *Coming Back Hard Again* essentially repeated the formula of *Crushin';* the cover this time was "The Twist (Yo' Twist)," which featured backing from Chubby Checker. However, audience tastes were changing, and the Fat Boys' gimmicky novelty act was quickly becoming passé. The group tried to expand their artistic and street credibility with the ill-advised "rap opera" *On and On,* which promptly stiffed and prefaced the group's breakup. Prince Markie Dee recorded a solo album in 1992 and has gone on to a successful R&B songwriting/producing career. Darren Robinson died of a heart attack in December 1995. *—Steve Huey*

Fat Boys / 1984 / Sutra ✦✦✦✦
This rotund rap trio's heft and Darren Robinson's verbal skills were the hooks that helped The Fat Boys land a gold record with their self-titled debut album. Even the lack of a standout single couldn't prevent the album from being a steady seller or limit the group's popularity. Such singles as "Human Beat Box" and "Jail House Rap" helped them quickly build a solid following that they retained until the end of the decade. *—Ron Wynn*

Crushin' / 1987 / PolyGram ✦✦✦✦
The Fat Boys enjoyed their biggest year in 1987. Their film *Disorderlies* proved much more resilient than anticipated, and this LP earned their only platinum certification, while becoming the lone Fat Boys album to make the pop Top Ten (peaking at No. 8). They also landed a Top 20 single with a version of "Wipeout." *—Ron Wynn*

Coming Back Hard Again / 1988 / Tin Pan Apple ✦✦✦
The last Fat Boys LP to make any noise, this sixth Sutra release proved their second most successful album, peaking at 33 and earning them their last gold record. It piggybacked on the success of "Louie Louie," their last chart single. They did try to adjust to changing audience demands, cutting "Rock the House, Y'all" and "Powerlord," but The Fat Boys' strength remained novelty numbers and weight-based raps like "Big Daddy" and "Pig Feet," which had lost almost all their popularity by this time. *—Ron Wynn*

● **Greatest Hits** / Jul. 1, 1991 / Unidisc ✦✦✦✦

Doug E. Fresh & The Get Fresh Crew

Rap
New Yorker Doug E. Fresh (born Doug E. Davis) got his initial notoriety for being the "human beatbox," able to approximate and imitate a rhythm machine. He had a string of hit singles with his then partner Ricky Dee in the early and mid-'80s, notably "The Show (Oh, My God)" in 1985, which included guest stints from jazz veteran trumpeter Jimmy Owens and synthesizer player Bernard Wright. Fresh had a long absence from the scene after 1988's *The World's Greatest Entertainer* and has just resurfaced with a new release on a small independent label. *—Ron Wynn*

Oh, My God! / 1986 / Reality ✦✦✦✦
Zany rhymes, slashing beats, with bits and pieces of everything from reggae to gospel to funk. *—Ron Wynn*

● **The World's Greatest Entertainer** / 1988 / Reality ✦✦✦✦
With the exception of the monster hit "Keep Risin' to the Top," Fresh trimmed the religious zealotry and increased the lyrical and rhythmic potency. *—Ron Wynn*

Doin' What I Gotta Do / Apr. 27, 1992 / Bust It ✦✦
Play / Nov. 1995 / Gee Street Independent ✦✦✦
Greatest Hits, Vol. 1 / Aug. 1996 / BUS ✦✦✦✦
Greatest Hits, Vol. 1 collects all of Doug E. Fresh's biggest hit singles—including "La Di Da Di," "Keep Risin' to the Top," and "The Show"—adding a couple of new tracks produced by Sean "Puffy" Combs for good measure. It's a concise and entertaining retrospective that sums up his career very well. *—Stephen Thomas Erlewine*

Fu-Schnickens

Rap
This Brooklyn rap trio has been among the better humor-oriented hiphop groups. They devised their name by combining the abbreviations FU (For Unity) with Schnicken, a term they invented designed to convey coalition. Their 1992 debut *F.U.—Don't Take It Personal* on Jive didn't yield any big hits. But the group hit paydirt when they collaborated with NBA star Shaquille O'Neal on the single "What's up Doc." It got them widespread visibility and exposure, making their follow-up album eagerly anticipated. *—Ron Wynn*

F.U.—Don't Take It Personal / Feb. 25, 1992 / Jive ✦✦✦✦
What makes the Fu-Schnickens' debut album special isn't their beats, but their verbal facility. Not only are they blindingly fast, but their lyrics are clever and inventive; the excitement of their rhyming makes the rote backing tracks invigorating. *—Stephen Thomas Erlewine*

What's up Doc / Jun. 8, 1993 / Jive ✦✦✦
● **Greatest Hits** / Dec. 1995 / Jive ✦✦✦✦

Fugees

Rap
Wyclef Jean ("Clef") and Prakazrel Michel ("Pras") are producers/MCs of Haitian descent who joined with rapper/singer Lauryn Hill to form The Fugees. Their 1994 debut, *Blunted on Reality,* combined reggae, rock, and funk with their ragga-tinged delivery. The Fugees released their second album, *The Score,* in early 1996. *The Score* became the surprise hip-hop hit of the year, reaching No. 1 on the pop charts and selling over four million copies within its first four months of release. *—John Bush*

Blunted on Reality / 1994 / Ruffhouse ✦✦✦
● **The Score** / Feb. 1996 / RuffHouse ✦✦✦✦
An open, yet funky, collage of hip-hop, soul, blues, jazz, and reggae, the Fugees' second album, *The Score,* is a great step forward for the New York trio. On their debut, the group had sketched out a pattern similar to the multi-ethnic, edgy music on *The Score,* but they didn't deliver it with the authority that they do here. The Fugees cover Bob Marley's "No Woman, No Cry" and Roberta Flack's "Killing Me Softly," which gives an idea of their range, as well as their intent to carry on the soul/R&B tradition. They pull it off with a surprising amount of style and innovation—with its intelligent, gritty lyrics and brave eclecticism, *The Score* simply sounds like few rap records of the mid-'90s. *—Stephen Thomas Erlewine*

Full Force

Rap
A Brooklyn production and songwriting sextet, Full Force became quite prominent in the mid- and late '80s. Brian and Paul Anthony George teamed with their cousins Gerry Charles, Junior Clark, and Curt Bedeau. At one point they were producing sessions for Lisa Lisa, UTFO, and Roxanne Shanté, and even worked with James Brown. They recorded a number of LPs for Columbia as performers, and scored five Top Ten R&B hits recording with Lisa Lisa & Cult Jam, the biggest being "All Cried Out" in 1986. It peaked at No. 3 R&B and No. 8 pop. Their most recent effort was *Don't Sleep!* in 1992, which paired them with longtime James Brown Revue contributor Bobby Byrd. *—Ron Wynn*

Full Force / 1985 / Columbia ✦✦✦
Although they were among the hottest production and performance combos on the scene in the mid- and late '80s, Full Force was never able to translate that magic to their own albums. This 1986 debut included the mildly entertaining "Alice, I Want You Just for Me!," but was mostly either uneventful love tunes, haphazard novelty pieces or unfocused and formulaic quasi-raps. *—Ron Wynn*

● **Get Ready 1 Time** / 1986 / Columbia ✦✦✦✦
The second Full Force release was a little better than the first, but still far from the levels they were scoring with Lisa Lisa & Cult Jam. Once more, they were unable to get any breakout or chart singles, and while songs like "Body Heavenly" and "Old Flames Never Die" may have contained potentially catchy lyrics, they lacked defined vocals, attractive arrangements, or interesting production. *—Ron Wynn*

Guess Who's Comin' to the Crib? / 1987 / Columbia ✦✦✦✦
Full Force's third album did only marginally better than the first two; it peaked a little higher on the low end of the pop albums chart. They tried everything in their creative arsenal, from the bittersweet sentiments of "Love Is for Suckers (Like Me and You)" to the naughty double-entendre notions expressed on "Low Blow Brenda" and even a traditional soul number, "Take Care of Homework." Nothing clicked, and it probably didn't help matters that the album included the justifiable but shrill diatribe "Black Radio." *—Ron Wynn*

Smoove / 1989 / Columbia ✦✦✦
Don't Sleep! / Aug. 31, 1992 / Capitol ✦✦
Full Force tried a comeback in 1992, teaming with longtime James Brown confidant and vocal partner Bobby Byrd on *Don't Sleep!* All it did was show that a lot of folks evidently thought that Full Force was in retirement, as the album failed to get even a cursory glance from urban contemporary radio, and hip-hop/rap audiences weren't interested in 1980s legends. This was their first release for Capitol; there hasn't been another thus far. *—Ron Wynn*

Funkdoobiest

Rap
Thanks to the production efforts of DJ Muggs from Cypress Hill, Funkdoobiest became a hot cult item in 1993 with their critically acclaimed debut album. *—Stephen Thomas Erlewine*

● **Which Doobie U B?** / May 4, 1993 / Epic ✦✦✦✦
Thanks to producer DJ Muggs, Funkdoobiest has the same spaced-out funk as Cypress Hill and House of Pain, but with an engaging, surrealistic point of view that keeps their album original. —*Stephen Thomas Erlewine*

Brothas Doobie / 1995 / Immortal/Epic ✦✦✦
A more laid-back album than their first, *Brothas Doobie* also deals with a few social problems, an improvement over the debut's continuous self-praising. —*John Bush*

Warren G

Vocals / Rap, Club/Dance, G-Funk
Born Warren Griffin III, Warren G exploded out of the burgeoning Long Beach rap scene in 1994 with the smash single "Regulate," a duet with longtime friend Nate Dogg, and its accompanying album, *Regulate... G Funk Era*. G grew up in Long Beach listening to his parents' extensive collection of jazz, soul, and funk records, also frequently hanging out at the local V.I.P. record store. As a teenager, he and his friends Nate Dogg and future superstar Snoop Dogg formed a rap group called 213, after their area code. Unfortunately, all had brushes with the law and spent time in jail, which motivated them to get jobs, also working on their music as a side note. Eventually, the V.I.P. record store allowed the trio to practice and record in a back room. It was here that Snoop cut the demo "Super Duper Snooper," which G played for his half-brother, Dr. Dre, at a party. Dre invited all three to his studio and wound up collaborating with Snoop on *The Chronic;* while G also made several contributions, he opted to develop his talents mostly outside of Dre's shadow. He honed his musical skills while producing such artists as MC Breed and 2Pac. A break came when his vocal collaboration with Mista Grimm, "Indo Smoke," appeared on the *Poetic Justice* soundtrack. Soon after that, G recorded his debut album for Def Jam. "Regulate" appeared on the *Above the Rim* soundtrack and was released as a single. It quickly became a massive hit, peaking at No. 2 on the *Billboard* charts and pushing the album up to the same position. —*Steve Huey*

● **Regulate... G Funk Era** / 1994 / Def Jam ✦✦✦✦
Dr. Dre's little brother Warren G proved that he was a talent in his own right with his debut record, *Regulate... G Funk Era*. With his music's slow, bass-heavy grooves and layers of synthesizers, Warren G sounds slightly similar to his older brother, but his album is more relaxed. That doesn't mean he's soft. In fact, his casual mix of singing and speaking is often more evocative than Dre's standard thundering beats and whining keyboards. Plus, Warren G's sly, direct lyrics manage to convey the tragedy of the ghetto. —*Stephen Thomas Erlewine*

Gang Starr

Rap
These Brooklyn rappers are near the top among hip-hop artists influenced by and interested in jazz. In 1989, jazz and Black-pop publicist Elliot Horne placed a poem he wrote with them, and the group used it as the foundation for the song "Jazz Music" on their debut *No More Mr. Nice Guy*. That track was later included on the soundtrack for Spike Lee's *Mo' Better Blues*. The group has also used saxophonist and **"Tonight Show"** bandleader Branford Marsalis and included acoustic as well as electric instruments on their follow-up release *Step in the Arena*. They've also discussed the jazz/rap connection in such magazines as *The Source* and *The Wire*. They did make a big gaffe on one cut though, crediting Dizzy Gillespie with playing the saxophone rather than the trumpet. Both Gang Starr and their main man Guru have been in the limelight in 1993 and 1994. Guru teamed with old and new jazz types Donald Byrd, Roy Ayers, and Ronnie Foster, as well as vocalist N'Dea Davenport, and other guest stars for the session *Jazzmatazz*. He later did some New York club dates with some of the same musicians. Gang Starr issued *Hard to Earn* in March of 1994; it debuted on the *Billboard* R&B charts at No. 2.—*Ron Wynn*

No More Mr. Nice Guy / 1989 / EMI America ✦✦✦

Step in the Arena / 1991 / Chrysalis ✦✦✦

● **Daily Operation** / 1992 / Chrysalis ✦✦✦✦
Arguably the best example of the hip-hop/jazz coalition, Gang Starr's latest continues the trailblazing path. —*Ron Wynn*

Hard to Earn / Mar. 8, 1994 / Chrysalis ✦✦✦✦
Although they were pioneers in the hip-hop/jazz movement, Gang Starr is still primarily a rap group. They reaffirm that on their newest venture, a 17-track set that's much more on the hard-hitting hip-hop tip than a restating of their jazz connections. The disc also offers more evidence that Guru is among rap's finest wordsmiths and verbal improvisers; whether moving over a midtempo groove, doing autobiographical sketches, criticizing other rappers, or just describing his environment and feelings, Guru's tone and voice are an effective mix of striking and reflective. *Hard To Earn* ranks as one of 1994's outstanding rap albums. —*Ron Wynn*

Geto Boys

Rap, Gangsta Rap
Houston's Geto Boys have at times rivaled Public Enemy, 2 Live Crew, and Ice-T for their ability to generate controversial publicity. Among the most outrageous, outlandish, and frequently offensive gangsta-rap crews, they have released songs that include violent and perverse subject matter that some may find distasteful. They also had problems with stores refusing to stock their albums, and in some cases even labels refusing to distribute them. After scoring a crossover success with "Mind Playing Tricks on Me," on 1991's *We Can't Be Stopped*, the group slowly lost its audience, as well as its will to work with each other. Shortly after the appearance of 1993's *Till Death Do Us Part*, the members parted ways and each rapper—Scarface, Willie Dee, and Bushwick Bill—all experienced solo success. In 1996, the group reunited and released *The Resurrection*, which received the group's best reviews to date. —*Ron Wynn*

Grip It! On That Level / 1990 / Def American ✦✦✦✦
The Geto Boys hit the national spotlight with this debut, which disgusted many, frightened a few others, and won them a niche in hip-hop's growing "gangsta" constituency. From the sheer repulsiveness of "Let a Ho Be a Ho" and "Do It Like a G.O." to the frightening nihilism of "Mind of a Lunatic" and "Life in the Fast Lane," this was one group definitely uninterested in pop/mainstream approval. The rapping ranged from surly to sleazy, the beats were sometimes popping, sometimes slashing, and even the most loyal fan would have a tough time finding something good to say about "Trigga Happy Nigga" or "Scarface." —*Ron Wynn*

We Can't Be Stopped / 1991 / Rap-A-Lot ✦✦✦✦
It contains their best song, the disturbing "Mind Playing Tricks on Me." —*Dan Heilman*

● **Geto Boys: The Best Uncut Dope** / 1992 / Rap-A-Lot ✦✦✦✦
With various members opting for solo projects and the group disintegrating, Rap-A-Lot Records primed the pump one last time with what was essentially a greatest hits CD. It wasn't totally a retrospective because it included "Damn It Feels Good to Be a Gangsta," the ultimate genre definition piece and the last significant Geto Boys composition. "And My Word," "Actions Speak Louder Than Words" and "The Unseen" were other fresh jams that joined the Geto Boys anthems "Mind Playing Tricks on Me," "Assassins," "Scarface," and "Mind of a Lunatic," among others. The old/new menu made this the one to grab if one Geto Boys CD is all you need. —*Ron Wynn*

Till Death Do Us Part / 1993 / Rap-A-Lot ✦✦✦
The Geto Boys' last album finds them expanding on the success of "Mind Playing Tricks on Me" with "Six Feet Deep," but more frequently, it keeps to their standard, grotesque gangsta rap with "Murder Ave." and "This Dick's for You." On these tracks, the whole shock formula seems like a worn-out trick and points the way to their eventual disbanding. —*Stephen Thomas Erlewine*

The Resurrection / Apr. 2, 1996 / Rap-A-Lot/Noo Trybe ✦✦✦✦
After spending nearly five years apart, the Geto Boys reunited in 1996 and released *The Resurrection*. Since they were more notorious for their lyrical violence than their music—only 1991's "We Can't Be Stopped," with its stunning single "Mind Playing Tricks on Me," showed the band experimenting musically—it comes as a surprise that *The Resurrection* is such a strong album. Although the band never deviates from their standard blood-guts-sex lyrical routine, they have a greater sense of humor throughout the album. More importantly, they perform with energy and their backing tracks are vigorous and funky. As a result, *The Resurrection* outstrips every other Geto Boys record in every sense—it is the leanest, meanest, and funkiest thing they've ever recorded. —*Stephen Thomas Erlewine*

Grand Puba

Vocals / Rap
The lead rapper for Brand Nubian came out roaring on his own with *Reel to Reel* in 1992. It contained everything from unrelenting Nation of Islam propaganda to one number that seemed like an updated "My Ding-a-Ling" with its shameless touting of Puba's sexual prowess. But overall, it showed he had the skills to flourish on his own. —*Ron Wynn*

● **Reel to Reel** / 1992 / Elektra ✦✦✦✦
Grand Puba's first solo album is an angry, righteous record, which is saved by his lyrical inventiveness, not his rhetoric. —*Stephen Thomas Erlewine*

2000 / 1995 / Elektra ✦✦✦
Grand Puba's second solo album continues his groundbreaking fusion of jazz and hip-hop, adding a harder, street-oriented edge for *2000*. The production saves the album, even when the songs are weak. —*Stephen Thomas Erlewine*

Grandmaster Flash (Joseph Saddler)

Rap, Hip-hop

Grandmaster Flash (born Joseph Saddler, January 1, 1958) and The Furious Five (Cowboy, Keith Wiggins; Melle Mel, Melvin Glover; Kidd Creole, Danny Glover; Mr. Ness, Eddie Morris; and Rahiem, Guy Williams) were the most important group in the early days of rap music and, in fact, developed certain crucial aspects of the genre. Saddler was the DJ, providing the musical bed by manipulating records on turntables, scratching them, repeating particular instrumental sections, and thus creating new music out of collages of existing recordings. The most important such work was the single "The Adventures of Grandmaster Flash on the Wheels of Steel," released in 1981.

Most of the group's records, however, featured the interlocking raps of the five rappers, and the most significant of these was "The Message" (1982), led primarily by Melle Mel, which turned away from the party subjects of many current rap records to focus on urban social issues.

The group had split by 1984, with Melle Mel going off on his own. It later re-formed in 1987.

Grandmaster Flash resurfaced in the public consciousness in late 1993, thanks to interviews done in *Rolling Stone* and *The Source* and Rhino reissues featuring such legendary tracks as "White Lines" and "Grandmaster Flash on the Wheels of Steel." — *William Ruhlmann*

The Message / 1982 / Sugar Hill ◆◆◆◆
Grandmaster Flash & The Furious Five merged the Afrocentric consciousness expressed by such early rappers as Gil Scott-Heron and The Last Poets with b-boy production to create "The Message," an all-time rap anthem. It was the focal point of this LP, which also included "It's Nasty" and "Scorpio," two other strong cuts that might have been winners on their own. Unfortunately, rather than a starting point, this album proved to be their ultimate peak. — *Ron Wynn*

The Source / 1986 / Elektra ◆◆◆
Grandmaster Flash's follow-up to *The Message* was his first minus The Furious Five. Things weren't the same from a compositional or performance standpoint, as his raps seemed weaker and his rhymes almost devoid of crispness, humor or insight. Only "Ms. Thang" and "Street Scene" offered any hint of the incisiveness or vision depicted in "The Message." — *Ron Wynn*

Da Bop Boom Bang / 1987 / Elektra ◆◆
The fire was gone and the imagination and flair diminished on this 1987 album. Grandmaster Flash sounded too tired on such cuts as "Big Black Caddy," "Get Yours" and "U Know What Time It Is" to recapture the spirit and bristling intensity that made "The Message" an anthem. Sadly, he was more effective doing nonsense like "Them Jeans." — *Ron Wynn*

★ **Message from Beat Street: The Best of** / 1994 / Rhino ◆◆◆◆◆
Grandmaster Flash was one of the most important, groundbreaking rap artists of the early '80s, and all of his most important records—with and without Melle Mel and the Furious Five—are collected on this essential 11-track disc, which includes the classic tracks "The Message" and "White Lines (Don't Don't Do It)." — *Stephen Thomas Erlewine*

Adventures Of: More of the Best / Jul. 1996 / Rhino ◆◆◆◆
Although most of Grandmaster Flash's best, biggest, and most groundbreaking work was compiled on *Message from Beat Street: The Best of, The Adventures of Grandmaster Flash: More of the Best* is necessary for any comprehensive rap collection. The rest of Grandmaster Flash's most important singles, many of which have not appeared on compact disc before, are corralled onto this single disc. On the whole, the album concentrates on the group's latter-day efforts for Elektra Records, but the cream of the album is the handful of singles for Sugarhill, including the pioneering "The Adventures of Grandmaster Flash on the Wheels of Steel," which presents the group at its freshest and most innovative. Some of the Elektra recordings are a little rote and by-the-book, but the Sugarhill songs help make this an essential purchase. — *Stephen Thomas Erlewine*

Gravediggaz

Rap

Gravediggaz's violent mixture of hardcore gangsta-rap and heavy metal was labeled "horrorcore" by some in the press. The whole incident is somewhat ironic, considering the heritage of the group. The mastermind of the group, The Undertaker, is better known as Stetsasonic's Prince Paul (born Paul Huston), who has produced De La Soul among other "alternative" hip-hop groups. The other members include The Rzarector (Prince Rakeem of Wu-Tang Clan), The Grym Reaper (Poetic), and The Gatekeeper (Fruitkwan; born Arnold Hamilton). Gravediggaz's 1994 debut album *Six Feet Deep* was a minor hit, breaking the Top 40 of the pop album charts and containing the single "Diary of a Madman." — *Stephen Thomas Erlewine*

● **6 Feet Deep** / 1994 / Gee Street ◆◆◆◆
Horrorcore, a rather suspect variation of gangsta rap, didn't make the

expected waves in the hip-hop world. Gravediggaz, however, are more intelligent than their image conveys. *6 Feet Deep* is an all-star effort including Prince Paul, MC Serch, Biz Markie, Masta Ace, and Vernon Reid. Obviously the dominant theme, death is tackled with good results on "Defective Trip" and "1-800 Suicide." Big beats and jazzy samples carry the raps well. — *John Bush*

Guru

Vocals / Rap

The main cog behind Gang Starr, rapper/composer Guru stepped out on his own in 1994 with the album *Jazzmatazz*. He enlisted support from the hip-hop and jazz communities, getting everyone from Roy Ayers and Donald Byrd to N'Dea Davenport of the Brand New Heavies. Guru later did selected club dates with some of the *Jazzmatazz* personnel, before returning to straighter hip-hop on Gang Starr's *Hard to Earn*. — *Ron Wynn*

● **Jazzmatazz, Vol. 1** / 1993 / Chrysalis ◆◆◆◆
Gang Starr's Guru has put together the best hip-hop/jazz outing issued yet, at least on these shores. Instead of merely wedding rap to recycled jazz samples, Guru and a cast of jazz, fusion, and R&B stars actually converge performance-wise, with the jazz musicians playing and the rappers and vocalists singing fresh material. The results are never less than enjoyable, and occasionally inspirational. Guru's deadpan rap style works, as do N'Dea Davenport's sultry vocals, and Roy Ayers, Donald Byrd, and Lonnie Liston Smith sound more convincing doing these songs than they have on any recent release of their own. — *Ron Wynn*

Jazzmatazz Vol. II: The New Reality / Jul. 18, 1995 / Chrysalis ◆◆◆
Featuring the likes of Ramsey Lewis, Branford Marsalis, Jamiroquai, Donald Byrd and others, this is former Gang Starr artist Guru's second foray into a fusion of jazz and hip-hop. — *Jonathan Ball*

Hammer

Vocals / Rap

Considered the ultimate success story or consummate fraud, Oakland's MC Hammer, a one-time jack-of-all-trades for the Oakland Athletics baseball team, dominated the charts in 1990 with *Please Hammer Don't Hurt 'Em*. The single "U Can't Touch This," despite a feeble rap and recycle job on Rick James' "Superfreak," was a crossover smash. Hammer puts on a fine show as far as dancing, sound, light effects, and production. But from a technical standpoint, everything, from his rhymes to his enunciation, qualifies as the ultimate in "wack" (weak) performance. He does have great taste in songs, picking choice items from Marvin Gaye, B.B. King, The Chi-Lites, and Prince, among others. He's since dropped the MC from his name.

After staying in the limelight as a race horse owner and Evander Holyfield's promoter, Hammer returned to the rap wars in 1994 with *The Funky Headhunter*. It featured a leaner, harder sound, with assistance and material provided by gangsta-rap producers, and featured Hammer sporting a more street look. He previewed the new style on Arsenio Hall's show early in the year, then issued the CD in March. It debuted at No. 2 on *Billboard's* R&B charts, then dipped the next week to six. Skeptics voiced their doubts about the new Hammer, especially in the hip-hop press. — *Ron Wynn*

Let's Get It Started / 1988 / Capitol ◆◆◆
MC Hammer's debut established him as a hip-hop superstar, with energetic dance tracks under its pop-tinged choruses, highlighted by the single "Turn This Mutha Out." — *Stephen Thomas Erlewine*

● **Please Hammer, Don't Hurt 'Em** / 1990 / Capitol ◆◆◆◆
MC Hammer's second album stands as the pinnacle of pop-rap crossover, with "U Can't Touch This," "Have You Seen Her," and "Pray" forming its core. Hammer relied on pop choruses as much as hip-hop beats, which helped the album sell over ten million copies and stay on the top of the charts for 21 weeks. — *Stephen Thomas Erlewine*

Too Legit to Quit / 1991 / Capitol ◆◆◆
Hammer responded to hip-hop credibility charges by dropping the "MC" and releasing *Too Legit to Quit*, an album recorded with a live band. Although it sold over three million copies and had a hit in the title track and "This Is the Way We Roll," the results were more well-intentioned than successful. — *Stephen Thomas Erlewine*

The Funky Headhunter / Mar. 1, 1994 / Giant ◆◆◆◆
The former MC Hammer resurfaced with a new musical identity and rap approach on this 1994 album. Getting help from new school producers and debuting a video on *The Arsenio Hall Show*, Hammer's sound was leaner, his rapping tougher and more fluid, and his subject harder and less humorous. The results seemed to have worked; *Funky Headhunter* peaked at No. 2 on the R&B list, went gold and remained in the Top 30 midway through the year. — *Ron Wynn*

Inside Out / Sep. 12, 1995 / Giant ◆◆

Heavy D & The Boyz

Rap, Hip-hop, Urban

Jamaican-born Heavy D (born Dwight Myers) sports a 260-pound frame but can move and dance with agility and verve. He wisely chose sensitivity, rather than obesity or verbosity, as his framework, and many of his lyrics emphasize his search for a mate of similar qualities. He's also done good cover songs and penned cultural awareness tunes and tributes to Black women. Heavy D has managed perhaps the ultimate balancing act. He's remained a positive figure with close ties to his mother and is arguably the most admired male rap figure among African-American feminists. At the same time he's been willing to take chances musically, never embracing hardcore gangsta-rap, but yet able to incorporate snatches of pop, R&B, reggae, and funk into his music without being assaulted with cries of sellout. He's even survived the tragic death of longtime friend and original Boyz member Troy Dixon, aka T-Roy, in 1990. *Blue Funk* in 1993 is a recent release. —*Ron Wynn*

Living Large / 1987 / Uptown ✦✦✦

This offers his first hit, a smartly done remake of "Mr. Big Stuff," plus charming romantic entries, though he sometimes overdoes the "overweight lover" routine. —*Ron Wynn*

Big Tyme / 1989 / Uptown ✦✦✦✦

Heavy D's breakthrough is his best album. —*Dan Heilman*

● **Peaceful Journey** / 1991 / Uptown ✦✦✦✦

A continuation of the fine direction cemented in *Big Tyme*, this includes a first-rate rendition of The O'Jays/Third World hit "Now That We Found Love," plus strong message and romance cuts. —*Ron Wynn*

Blue Funk / 1993 / Uptown ✦✦✦

Although it didn't have a big hit, *Blue Funk* was another solid album of pop-oriented, R&B-tinged rap from Heavy D. —*AMG*

Nuttin But Love / 1994 / Uptown ✦✦✦✦

House of Pain

Rap

This Irish rap ensemble headed by former Rhythm Syndicate member Everlast vaulted into national stardom in 1992 with "Jump Around" from their self-titled debut LP. After weathering criticism about their hip-hop integrity, they returned in 1994 with the harder, funkier *Same as It Ever Was*. —*Ron Wynn*

● **House of Pain** / 1992 / Tommy Boy ✦✦✦✦

It would be hard for nearly anyone to top the explosive, insanely catchy "Jump Around," so it's no great surprise to find that House of Pain isn't up to the task. At times, HOP come close to duplicating the intoxicating power of their slamming single, but for the most part, their debut album is a repetitive circle of similar beats, misogyny, racism, and posturing lyrics. But the perfection of "Jump Around" almost makes up for the numerous faults. —*Stephen Thomas Erlewine*

Same as It Ever Was / 1994 / Tommy Boy ✦✦✦✦

House of Pain's second album finds the group getting harder, adding elements of jazz and dirty, street-oriented funk to their sound. *Same as It Ever Was* may not have a hit the size of "Jump Around"—and it may be plagued by misogynist lyrics—but it's a more focused, impressive effort. —*Stephen Thomas Erlewine*

Ice Cube

Vocals / Rap, Gangsta Rap

Through his detailed, unflinching lyrical stance and his inventive phrasing, this former N.W.A. writer and rapper has become the finest mouthpiece gangsta-rap has produced. His posse, The Lynch Mob, construct sonic backdrops that kick with the force of the best Public Enemy. Ice Cube is a controversial but major figure in contemporary pop, and has an acting career with films, including 1991's *Boyz n the Hood*.

Ice Cube has arguably become rap's most controversial and widely known figure in the '90s. He's topped R&B, pop, and rap charts with his releases *AmeriKKKa's Most Wanted*, *The Predator*, and *Lethal Injection*. Cube has been the cover boy for every magazine from *Vibe* to *The Source*, and also joined the Nation of Islam. He currently ranks alongside Ice-T as perhaps the most feared personality in rap circles.

Whispers abounded that marriage and his decision to join the Nation of Islam were responsible for Ice Cube's weakest CD as a solo act. *Lethal Injection* went platinum, but the rage was more unfocused, the rhymes less fluid and thoughtful and the rapping less striking than on any other Ice Cube session. While his interviews sounded just as fierce, the speculation abounds that Ice Cube may have peaked as a creative force in hip-hop. —*John Floyd*

☆ **AmeriKKKa's Most Wanted** / 1990 / Priority ✦✦✦✦✦

Cube gets some production help from Public Enemy's Bomb Squad and comes up with a stark and gripping portrait of life in America's inner cit-

ies. If you can get past the sexism, you'll find this debut to be one of rap's most unflinching bursts of rhythmic and political fury. —*John Floyd*

Kill at Will / 1990 / Priority ✦✦✦✦

A few remixes from the debut bog this one down, but the title track, which examines the emotional facets of gangland murder with brutal nakedness and accuracy, is Cube's best moment. —*John Floyd*

★ **Death Certificate** / 1991 / Priority ✦✦✦✦✦

Death Certificate is even harder and angrier than *AmeriKKKa's Most Wanted*, which is both a good and a bad thing, depending on your politics. If you're inclined to see Ice Cube as a spokesman and social commentator, *Death Certificate* will support your claims—it continues the sharp insights and unflinching looks at contemporary urban lifestyles that his solo debut only hinted at; in short, it's hardcore without any gangsta posturing. If you're inclined to see Ice Cube as a bigoted, misogynistic rabble-rouser, *Death Certificate* will also support your claims—"No Vaseline" contains explicit anti-Semitic taunts directed at his former manager, there are homophobic slurs scattered throughout the album and women frequently are either bitches or whores. However, if you look beyond the surface—no matter what political viewpoint you happen to have—you will find that Cube's rhymes do promote self-awareness and education. In short, they are some of the most incisive raps about life as a young African-American man since the advent of Public Enemy. Considering this, it's not surprising that *Death Certificate* bears the mark of Public Enemy's dense, abrasive soundscapes—it's a funkier, noisier and more musically effective album than *AmeriKKKa's Most Wanted*. Ice Cube had never before created a statement of purpose as coherent and incendiary as *Death Certificate* and, sadly, he never did again. —*Leo Stanley*

The Predator / 1992 / Priority ✦✦✦

Although Ice Cube makes a lot of noise throughout *The Predator*, he never actually says anything. For the most part, *The Predator* is Ice Cube by the numbers, spouting his standard line about women, police, drugs, and gangsters. The album doesn't sound weak at all; it's full of strong beats and muscular rhymes. Das EFX invigorate "Check Yo Self," "Wicked" is a classic single, and the light '70s groove of "It Was a Good Day" proves that Ice Cube doesn't need hardcore beats to succeed. If Ice Cube hadn't just blustered grandiosely, *The Predator* might have ranked among his previous efforts. —*Stephen Thomas Erlewine*

Lethal Injection / 1993 / Scarface ✦✦

Bootlegs & B-Sides / 1994 / Priority ✦✦✦

It's nothing but a collection of remixes and flip-sides, but Ice Cube's *Bootlegs & B-Sides* proves that he has always remained in step with the times and, more importantly, often set the standards for hip-hop. In fact, the record almost functions as an alternate best-of; none of the original single versions are included, but the material is so strong, it doesn't matter—these songs are essential listening, no matter what mix they are heard in. —*Stephen Thomas Erlewine*

Ice-T

Vocals / Rap, Gangsta Rap

Ice-T (born Tracy Morrow) has proven to be one of hip-hop's most articulate and intelligent stars, as well as one of its most frustrating. At his best, the rapper has written some of the best portraits of ghetto life and gangsters, as well as some of the best social commentary hip-hop has produced. Just as often, he can slip into sexism and gratuitous violence, but even then his rhymes are clever and biting. Ice-T's best recordings have always been made in conjunction with strong collaborators, whether it's The Bomb Squad or Jello Biafra. With his music, Ice-T has made a conscious effort to win the vast audience of White male adolescents, as his frequent excursions with his heavy metal band Body Count show. All the while, he has withstood a constant barrage of criticism and controversy to become a respected figure not only in the music press, but the mainstream media as well.

Although he was one of the leading figures of California hip-hop in the '80s, Ice-T was born in Newark, NJ. When he was a child, he moved from his native Newark to California after his parents died in an auto accident. While he was in high school, he became obsessed with rap while he went to Crenshaw High School in South Central Los Angeles. Ice-T took his name from Iceberg Slim, a pimp that wrote novels and poetry. Ice-T used to memorize lines of Iceberg Slim's poetry, reciting them for friends and classmates. After he left high school, he recorded several undistinguished 12-inch singles in the early '80s. He also appeared in the low-budget hip-hop films *Rappin',* *Breakin',* and *Breakin' II: Electric Boogaloo* as he was trying to establish a career.

Ice-T finally landed a major label record deal with Sire Records in 1987, releasing his debut album, *Rhyme Pays.* On the record, he is supported by DJ Aladdin and producer Afrika Islam, who helped create the rolling, spare beats and samples that provided a backdrop for the rapper's charismatic rhymes, which were mainly party-oriented; the record wound up going gold. That same year, he recorded the theme song for

Dennis Hopper's *Colors*, a film about inner-city life in Los Angeles. The song—also called "Colors"—was stronger—both lyrically and musically—and more incisive than anything he had previously released. Ice-T formed his own record label, Rhyme Syndicate (which was distributed through Sire/Warner) in 1988, and released *Power*. *Power* was a more assured and impressive record, earning him strong reviews and his second gold record. Released in 1989, *The Iceberg / Freedom of Speech . . . Just Watch What You Say* established him as a true hip-hop superstar by matching excellent abrasive music with fierce, intelligent narratives and political commentaries, especially about hip-hop censorship.

Two years later, Ice-T began an acting career, starring in the updated blaxploitation film *New Jack City;* he also recorded "New Jack Hustler" for the film. "New Jack Hustler" became one of the centerpieces of 1991's *O.G.: Original Gangster*, which became his most successful album to date. *O.G.* also featured a metal track called "Body Count" recorded with Ice-T's band of the same name. Ice-T took the band out on tour that summer, as he performed on the first Lollapalooza tour. The tour setup increased his appeal with both alternative music fans and middle class teenagers. The following year, the rapper decided to release an entire album with the band, also called *Body Count*.

Body Count proved to be a major turning point in Ice-T's career. On the basis of the track "Cop Killer"—where he sang from the point-of-view of a police murderer—the record ignited a national controversy; it was protested by the NRA, police activist groups, and the offices of Time-Warner. The record company initially supported Ice-T, yet they refused to release his new rap album, *Home Invasion*, on the basis of the record cover. Ice-T and the label parted ways by the end of the year. *Home Invasion* was released on Priority Records in the spring of 1993 to lukewarm reviews and sales. Somewhere along the way, Ice-T had begun to lose most of his original hip-hop audience; now he appealed primarily to suburban White teens. In 1994, he wrote a book and released the second Body Count album, *Born Dead*, which failed to stir up the same controversy as the first record—indeed, it failed to gain much attention of any sort. Nevertheless, Body Count was successful in clubs and Ice-T continued to tour with the band.

In the summer of 1996, Ice-T released his first rap album since 1993, *Return of the Real*. The album was greeted by mixed reviews and it failed to live up to commercial expectations. —*Stephen Thomas Erlewine*

Rhyme Pays / 1987 / Sire ♦♦

Power / 1988 / Sire ♦♦♦♦
His second release is a quantum-leap improvement over his debut—better samples, a more pronounced and developed rapping style, and smarter material. Ice-T does marvelous homage to Curtis Mayfield with an excellent adaptation of "I'm Your Pusherman" from the vintage *Superfly* soundtrack. —*Ron Wynn*

☆ **The Iceberg/Freedom of Speech . . . Just Watch What You Say** / 1989 / Sire ♦♦♦♦♦
The Iceberg: Freedom of Speech . . . Just Watch What You Say is a brutal, occasionally brilliant condemnation of censorship, drug use, and societal injustice, marred only by a few conflicting ideals and his own sexism. —*John Floyd*

★ **O.G. Original Gangster** / 1991 / Sire ♦♦♦♦♦
T's masterpiece is an ambitious, sprawling examination of gangsta-rap culture that confronts all the relevant issues and even offers a few alternatives and solutions. It's also Ice-T's most musically visceral outburst. —*John Floyd*

Body Count / 1992 / Sire ♦♦♦
Ice-T's excursion into heavy metal brought him a firestorm of controversy, but the album is actually a tepid collection of '80s-style arena metal that never sounds dangerous. Frequently, it's hard to tell if Ice takes this stuff seriously; tracks like "Body Count" and "Cop Killer" are invigorating stabs at social criticism, but most of the album is filled with stupid attempts at being threatening, like "KKK Bitch" and "Mama's Gotta Die Tonight." Maybe the humor was intentional, but too frequently the record sounded embarrassing. After "Cop Killer" was pulled from the album, it was replaced with a version of "The Iceberg" recorded with Jello Biafra. —*Stephen Thomas Erlewine*

Home Invasion / 1993 / Priority ♦♦♦

The Classic Collection / May 4, 1993 / Rhino ♦♦

Last Temptation of Ice/Home Invasion / 1995 / Virgin/Rhyme Syndicate ♦♦♦

Return of the Real / Jun. 1996 / Priority ♦♦♦

Montell Jordan

Vocals / Rap, Urban
Montell Jordan began singing in his hometown of Los Angeles in talent shows, church choirs, and later nightclubs. After graduating from Pep-

perdine University, he spent seven years looking for a record deal, finally getting an opportunity through Paul Stewart, the president of PMP Records. Jordan and Stewart flew to New York, where Jordan sang for Russell Simmons and was promptly signed to a contract. For his first album, Jordan heavily sampled B.B. King tracks (the first to do so), and took his lyrical inspiration from the more positive sides of life in his native South Central Los Angeles in an attempt to balance the negative pictures coming out of most SoCal gangsta rap. Jordan was rewarded with a massive No. 1 smash in the party anthem "This Is How We Do It," which sold over one million copies. —*Steve Huey*

This Is How We Do It / 1995 / PMP/RAL ♦♦♦
Montell Jordan was blessed with a strong set of producers for his debut album, *This Is How We Do It*. Working with material that is essentially sub-par, the production team turns in seamless performances, creating hooks and melodies from the deep bass and beats. Jordan's skills as a rapper are fine—he does nothing particularly noteworthy, yet he certainly does not ruin the tracks. It was just the sort of competent R&B that hits the chart, and it did hit the charts, becoming a No. 1 R&B album. —*Stephen Thomas Erlewine*

● **More to Tell** / Aug. 27, 1996 / Def Jam ♦♦♦♦

Jungle Brothers
....
Rap, Hip-hop
An endlessly funky New York trio, Jungle Brothers have collaborated with like minds such as De La Soul and A Tribe Called Quest. Their love of James Brown goes deeper than mere sampling.

Although the Jungle Brothers have received an enormous amount of critical acclaim, they have not yet been able to score a commercial success as large as either De La or Tribe. —*John Floyd*

● **Straight out the Jungle** / 1988 / Warlock ♦♦♦♦
The trio's debut is powered by muscular funk riffs underpinned by an Afrocentric sensibility and a sharp sense of humor. —*John Floyd*

Done by the Forces of Nature / 1989 / Warner Brothers ♦♦♦♦
By injecting some vocal delicacy and some clever samples into their moderately militant message, they made a second album that elaborates on their own winning formula. —*John Floyd*

J. Beez Wit the Remedy / Jun. 22, 1993 / Warner Brothers ♦♦♦
Nearly four years after *Done by the Forces of Nature*, the Jungle Brothers return with a hazy, funky album, filled with their brand of literate hip-hop. Although they've made some stylistic progressions since the last record, it wasn't enough to be a completely groundbreaking release, nor was it commercial enough to break them out of their critically acclaimed/cult status. Instead, it was another solid, inventive album that didn't receive the attention it deserved. —*Stephen Thomas Erlewine*

Kid 'N Play
....
Rap
They've recorded several decent albums with the aid of producer Hurby Luv Bug, but this duo is best known for their starring roles in the *House Party* film series.

The *House Party* movies helped Kid 'n Play's infectious pop-flavored hip-hop to cross over into the mainstream without losing much street credibility. —*John Floyd*

● **2 Hype** / 1988 / Select ♦♦♦♦
A solid debut with snatches of house, dance, and go-go. Despite minimal rapping abilities, the duo quickly captured a chunk of the hip-hop audience. —*Ron Wynn*

Kid 'n Play's Fun House / 1990 / Select ♦♦♦
One of two releases from the twosome in 1990, this one has new cuts with funkier, looser foundations and more ambitious adult lyrics and rapping style. —*Ron Wynn*

House Party [O.S.T.] / 1990 / Motown ♦♦♦
Not strictly, or even mainly, their album, it does contain the singles "Funhouse" and "Kid vs. Play (The Battle)." Its prime importance was as the soundtrack from an extremely successful film of the same name, which launched the duo into cinematic stardom. —*Ron Wynn*

Kool Moe Dee
....
Vocals / Rap
One old-school rapper who's managed to thrive mixing it up with new-school types, Kool Moe Dee was a member of Harlem trio The Treacherous Three in the early '80s and was spotted by music veteran and producer Bobby Robinson. The trio eventually split from Robinson and joined rival Sugarhill Records, then disbanded when their contract expired. Dee hooked up with producer Teddy Riley, now the king of New Jack Swing efforts, and hit instant gold with the single "Go See the Doctor," an amazing safe-sex story that combines a cautionary message with a frenetic hypnotic beat. Since then, Dee has had a lengthy, disturbing sexist slant. He engaged fellow rapper LL Cool J in a continuing bat-

tle of words that was interesting for a while but degenerated into a stock formula. *—Ron Wynn*

I'm Kool Moe Dee / 1986 / Jive ✦✦✦
A commanding debut, especially the smashing tune "Go See the Doctor," one of the best and most pointed cautionary sex songs ever. *—Ron Wynn*

How Ya Like Me Now / 1987 / Jive ✦✦✦✦
The title track was a big smash, and it marked the beginning of the lengthy Kool Moe Dee vs. LL Cool J rap war. The second hit "Wild, Wild West" was also a masterpiece; the album's greatness overcomes its forays into sexism on "Stupid." *—Ron Wynn*

The Best / 1987 / Jive ✦✦✦✦
The value of this compilation has been diminished by the release of a superior 1993 hits package. This contains several of Kool Moe Dee's big records from the early '80s, and is a blueprint for his rise and the emergence of the Kool Moe Dee/LL Cool J rivalry. *—Ron Wynn*

★ **Greatest Hits** / 1989 / Sequel ✦✦✦✦✦
As much as any single performer, Kool Moe Dee epitomized rap's rise from an East Coast underground genre to a national youth sound, and has been unceasing in his demands for respect and recognition. Dee was also among the first able to bring social significance to his material without being pedantic, and his songs (with the exception of "They Want Money") weren't littered with sexist and misogynistic rhetoric. This 15-song collection covers his biggest recordings, from novelty-type fare ("The Wild Wild West" and "Whosgotdaflava") to the safe sex number "Go See the Doctor," cultural battle cries like "Rise 'N' Shine" and "No Respect," and his "war" with LL Cool J that peaked with "Death Blow" and "How Ya Like Me Now." *—Ron Wynn*

Knowledge Is King / 1989 / Jive ✦✦✦
Another brilliant hit with "They Want Money," though he expands a disturbing anti-female line. But it's balanced by a stirring anti-drug, Afrocentric philosophy and a rap methodology that puts him near the top among hip-hop purists. *—Ron Wynn*

Funke Funke Wisdom / 1991 / Jive ✦✦✦
The single "Rise 'n' Shine" was a summit meeting of rap theorists, with Dee joined by Chuck D from Public Enemy and KRS-One. Unfortunately, an overreliance on sexual posturing and macho imagery have begun to set in, weighing down an otherwise notable effort. *—Ron Wynn*

● **Jive Collection Series, Vol. 2** / 1995 / Jive ✦✦✦✦
Kool Moe Dee's installment of the *Jive Collection Series* contains all of the rapper's groundbreaking singles from the early '80s, plus a selection of lesser-known album tracks and singles. The album isn't as consistently entertaining as his previous *Greatest Hits* compilation, but *Jive Collection Series* remains a good introduction to his pioneering career. *—Stephen Thomas Erlewine*

Kriss Kross (Kris Kross)

Rap
Thirteen-year-old rappers Chris "Daddy Mack" Smith and Chris "Mack Daddy" Kelly became the pop sensations of 1992 as Kris Kross. The two were discovered at an Atlanta mall in 1991 by then-19-year-old producer Jermaine Dupri, who took them under his wing and came up with the gimmick of having the duo wear all of their clothing backwards, lending more significance to their name. Thanks in part to savvy marketing, "Jump," which sampled the Jackson 5's "I Want You Back," became the fastest-selling single in 15 years, staying at No. 1 for eight weeks on the *Billboard* charts and pushing the sales of their debut album, *Totally Krossed Out*, past four million. Another gold single followed in "Warm It Up," and Kris Kross toured Europe with Michael Jackson and appeared on innumerable teen-oriented TV shows.

By their follow-up album, 1993's *Da Bomb*, the boys had hit puberty, and their voices were deeper; they tried to affect a tougher, more hardcore sound and image, with less success. "Alright" was their third single to go gold or better, but *Da Bomb* failed to even go platinum by the end of the year. Kris Kross took some time off and returned in 1996 with *Young, Rich and Dangerous*, which featured the gold-selling rap ballad "Tonite's Tha Night." *—Steve Huey*

● **Totally Krossed Out** / 1992 / Ruffhouse ✦✦✦✦
The hottest rap duo of the summer of 1992, thanks to their penchant for wearing their clothes backward and the single "Jump," which crossed over to pop and R&B markets. *—Ron Wynn*

Da Bomb / 1993 / Ruffhouse ✦✦✦
Young, Rich and Dangerous / Jan. 1996 / Ruffhouse/Columbia ✦✦✦
Ever since their first massive hit single "Jump," Kriss Kross has had a difficult time shaking the novelty tag bestowed upon them. They have literally grown up in public—the Kriss Kross of 1996 is a lot different than the Kriss Kross of 1992. For starters, the group is tougher and harder, flirting with gangsta rap and G-Funk, and they have become more imaginative, fluent rappers. That doesn't necessarily mean *Young, Rich and*

Dangerous, the duo's third album, is more enjoyable than their previous releases—it just means they're trying harder. Parts of the album click, but much of the music sounds generic or underdeveloped, which makes *Young, Rich and Dangerous* nothing more than an admirable, but failed, effort. *—Stephen Thomas Erlewine*

KRS-One

Vocals / Rap
KRS-One (born Laurence Krisna Parker) was the leader of Boogie Down Productions, one of the most influential hardcore hip-hop outfits of the '80s. At the height of his career—roughly 1987-1990—KRS-One was known for his furiously political and socially-conscious raps, which is the source of his nickname, "The Teacher." Around the time of 1990's *Edutainment*, BDP's audience began to slip, as many fans thought his raps were becoming preachy. In response, KRS-One began to re-establish his street credibility with harder, sparer beats and raps. BDP's 1992 *Sex and Violence* was the first sign that he was taking a harder approach, one that wasn't nearly as concerned with teaching. KRS-One's first solo album, 1993's *Return of the Boom Bap*, was an extension of the more direct approach of *Sex and Violence*, yet it didn't halt his commercial decline. *—Stephen Thomas Erlewine*

Return of the Boom Bap / Sep. 28, 1993 / Jive ✦✦
● **KRS-One** / Nov. 7, 1995 / Jive ✦✦✦✦
For his second solo album, KRS-One worked with a variety of younger hip-hop talents, perhaps in an attempt to resuscitate his street credibility and his commercial standing. Featuring appearances by Das EFX, Mad Lion, Fat Joe, and Channel Live, *KRS-One* is loaded with fresh talent of the first rank and they help spark The Teacher into giving an inspired performance. The album also showcases a bit fuller production than *Return of the Boom Bap*, but that doesn't mean he has sold out—it just means he's continuing to experiment, which is one of the reasons KRS-One remained a vital artist nearly a decade after his first record. *—Stephen Thomas Erlewine*

L'Trimm

Rap
Miami-based female rappers Tigra and Bunny D. were 18 years old when they scored a mild hit, "Cars That Go Boom," in 1988. For a brief period their CD *Grab It!* stayed on the charts after Atlantic leased it from Time-X, but they were unable to get another single to maintain the momentum, and kiddie-pop gradually lost its audience. *—Ron Wynn*

● **Grab It!** / 1988 / Atlantic ✦✦✦✦
Miami teen rappers L'Trimm enjoyed a little pop mileage with "Cars That Go Boom," a single reflecting the days when hip-hop was less serious and novelty/comic tunes could still get sizable audiences. The duo sounded cute and eager, but when they tried to show they could also handle more "adult" material, the credibility gap nearly swallowed them. *—Ron Wynn*

LL Cool J (James Smith)

b. Jan. 14, 1968
Vocals / Rap, Hip-hop
The importance of LL Cool J (born James Smith, his moniker stands for Ladies Love Cool James) in rap cannot be exaggerated. By fusing the beatbox minimalism of Run-DMC with the b-boy snarl of his defiant lyrics, LL Cool J pushed the music into new terrain, opening the door for numerous hip-hop contenders and becoming a superstar in the process.

Since the across-the-board success of *Mama Said Knock You Out*, LL Cool J's had trouble reclimbing the mountain from which he once stood tall. He predicted *14 Shots to the Dome* would be the ticket, and it did respectably, but lacked either the resonance or the power of *Mama Said*. *—John Floyd*

☆ **Radio** / 1985 / Def Jam ✦✦✦✦✦
LL Cool J's debut, produced by Rick Rubin, is a brilliant mix of hardcore street anthems ("I Can't Live Without My Radio," "Rock the Bells") and updated twists on the dozens ("That's a Lie"), with a couple of ballads thrown in. *—John Floyd*

Bigger and Deffer / 1987 / Def Jam ✦✦
On his second album, LL Cool J's ego goes to his head, resulting in a weak album of mild beats and inflated bragging, which is only partially saved by his first successful ballad, the syrupy "I Need Love." *—Stephen Thomas Erlewine*

Walking with a Panther / 1989 / Def Jam ✦✦✦✦
A sprawling follow-up to his stinko second album, it's his most ambitious. LL Cool J not only regroups the strengths that made his debut a winner, but shows a musical expansion of his art that bodes well for the future. Includes "I'm That Type of Guy," "Going Back to Cali," and "Big Ole Butt." *—John Floyd*

Music Map

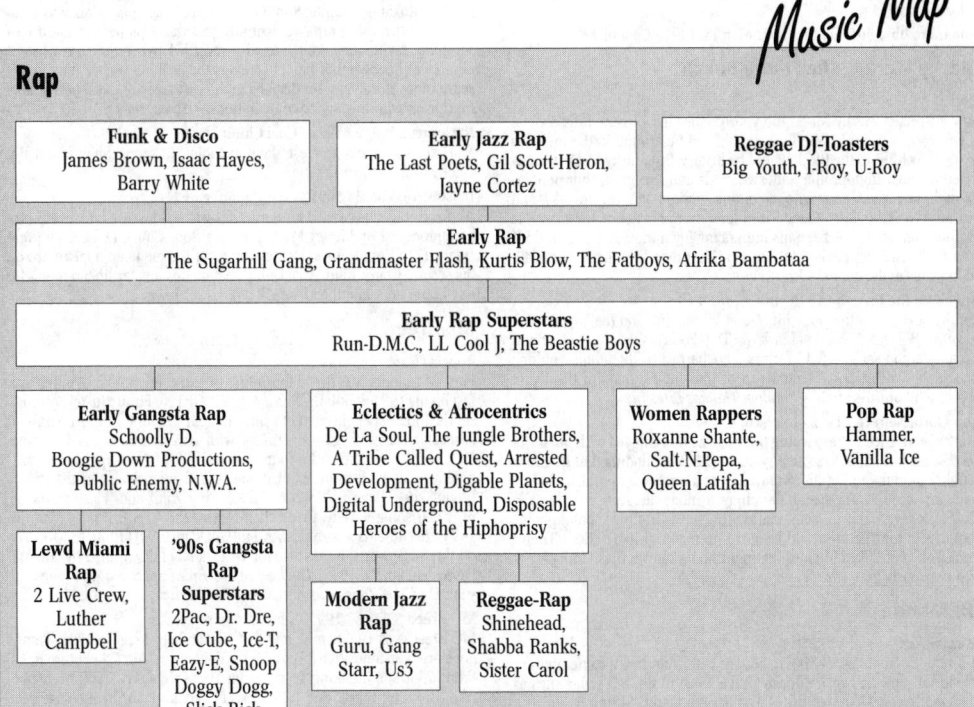

Rap

Funk & Disco	Early Jazz Rap	Reggae DJ-Toasters
James Brown, Isaac Hayes, Barry White	The Last Poets, Gil Scott-Heron, Jayne Cortez	Big Youth, I-Roy, U-Roy

Early Rap
The Sugarhill Gang, Grandmaster Flash, Kurtis Blow, The Fatboys, Afrika Bambataa

Early Rap Superstars
Run-D.M.C., LL Cool J, The Beastie Boys

Early Gangsta Rap	Eclectics & Afrocentrics	Women Rappers	Pop Rap
Schoolly D, Boogie Down Productions, Public Enemy, N.W.A.	De La Soul, The Jungle Brothers, A Tribe Called Quest, Arrested Development, Digable Planets, Digital Underground, Disposable Heroes of the Hiphoprisy	Roxanne Shante, Salt-N-Pepa, Queen Latifah	Hammer, Vanilla Ice

Lewd Miami Rap	'90s Gangsta Rap Superstars	Modern Jazz Rap	Reggae-Rap
2 Live Crew, Luther Campbell	2Pac, Dr. Dre, Ice Cube, Ice-T, Eazy-E, Snoop Doggy Dogg, Slick Rick	Guru, Gang Starr, Us3	Shinehead, Shabba Ranks, Sister Carol

★ **Mama Said Knock You Out** / 1990 / Def Jam ✦✦✦✦✦
The future Cool J 1990-style. He's mixing house and hip-hop into his minimalist backdrops, and he's finally come up with some decent love songs. With "The Boomin' System," he's created yet another essential rap anthem. Includes "Around the Way Girl," "6 Minutes of Pleasure," "Jingling Baby," and the title track. —*John Floyd*

14 Shots to the Dome / 1993 / CBS ✦✦✦
It's not the tour de force of *Mama Said Knock You Out*, but *14 Shots to the Dome* is a solid effort, finding LL Cool J maturing gracefully and strongly, without selling out. *14 Shots* may not have sold as well as *Mama*, but at least half of the album ranks with his best work. —*Stephen Thomas Erlewine*

Mr. Smith / Nov. 1995 / Def Jam ✦✦

The Luniz

Rap
The Luniz are a rap duo out of Oakland consisting of Yukmouth and Knumskull, two friends who have known each other since junior high. Originally calling themselves Luni Tunz, the two gained fame after six years together when they appeared on Dru Down's *Explicit Game* album. Their debut album, *Operation Stackola*, was released in 1995 and knocked Michael Jackson's *HIStory* off the top of the R&B charts on the strength of the hit single "I Got 5 on It," which featured guest vocals by Michael Marshall of the Timex Social Club. The Luniz' lyrics take novel, comic approaches to sex, drugs, and everyday occurrences. —*Steve Huey*

● **Operation Stackola** / Jul. 4, 1995 / Noo Trybe ✦✦✦✦

Craig Mack

Vocals / Rap
Under the guidance of producer Sean "Puffy" Combs, the Long Island native and former EPMD roadie Craig Mack became a sensation in 1994 with the pop-friendly hip-hop of his debut album *Project: Funk Da World* and the Top Ten single "Flava in Ya Ear." —*Stephen Thomas Erlewine*

Project: Funk Da World / 1994 / Arista ✦✦✦✦
Mack uses Dr. Dre's album-tested formula of syrupy P-Funk beats, but makes it his own with his rigorous delivery. Dancehall rhythms also surface, and he tackles issues (like Black tradition) that Dre and Snoop

wouldn't touch. In all, this LP isn't the stuff of a revolution, but Mack sure knows his way around a good groove. —*John Bush*

Mantronix

Rap, Hip-hop
Combining rap, funk, pop, reggae, and electronics, Mantronix was one of the most innovative hip-hop groups of the mid-'80s. Formed in 1984, the New York group comprised DJ/keyboardist Mantronik (born Curtis Khalee) and rapper MC Tee (born Tooure Embden). Mantronix's demo tape gained the attention of William Socolov, the head of the independent record label Sleeping Bag. The group released their first single, "Fresh Is the Word," in 1985; it was a big hit on the street and in the clubs, as was their debut album, *Mantronix*. The duo enhanced their reputation by producing Joyce Sims and 12.41. However, their second record, 1986's *Music Madness*, showed them in a holding pattern; soon afterward, their audience began to shrink and by the beginning of the '90s they had faded away. —*Stephen Thomas Erlewine*

● **The Album** / 1985 / Sleeping Bag ✦✦✦✦
Mantronix's finest album remains this intriguing mid-'80s debut, when Curtis "Mantronix" Kahleel and rapper MC Tee scored with what was then an imaginative and unusual mix of dance and hip-hop production styles and sensibility with soul and R&B vocals. They weren't house, or rap, or urban contemporary, but a wonderful hybrid of all these and more, including touches of dancehall reggae and even pop and funk. The album had two fine singles in "Bassline" and "Ladies" and made Mantronix a hot property. —*Ron Wynn*

This Should Move Ya / 1987 / Capitol ✦✦✦
Mantronix switched labels in the late '80s, moving from the independent Sleeping Bag to the major label Capitol. Although the lineup had now changed, with Bryce Luvah and D.J.D. on board rather than MC Tee, the group had another strong single in "Got to Have Your Love," and Capitol was providing Curtis "Mantronix" Kahleel with a bigger push and sharper production and sound. But the underground spirit that permeated Mantronix's Sleeping Bag albums was missing, as was the quirky air that marked their past singles. —*Ron Wynn*

In Full Effect / 1988 / Capitol ✦✦✦
This is the final album featuring rapper MC Tee. This album skirted the lower regions of the pop charts and had a less abrasive, smoother sound, although the patented dance/hip-hop/urban contemporary fusion hadn't been affected. But overall, it wasn't quite as risky or spirited as their

Sleeping Bag records, which may have been the reason Tee departed. *—Ron Wynn*

The Incredible Sound Machine / Mar. 18, 1991 / Capitol ✦✦

Marky Mark & The Funky Bunch

Rap

Few suspected Marky Mark, the younger brother of New Kids on The Block vocalist Donnie Wahlberg, would still be around in the mid-'90s while New Kids on the Block would be history. But Marky Mark has survived through high-profile underwear ads and low-grade, but popular enough, pop-rap. He's even overcome a homophobic controversy, and scored a No. 1 hit with "Good Vibrations" from his debut *Music for the People;* that single has been his high point. Even though the second LP, *You Gotta Believe,* peaked at number 14, it didn't duplicate the platinum status of the debut. *—Ron Wynn*

● **Music for the People** / 1991 / Interscope ✦✦✦
On the strength of the No. 1 hit "Good Vibrations" and the Top Ten follow-up "Wildside," Marky Mark & The Funky Bunch's first album became a pop sensation. Unfortunately, the rest of the album couldn't match the catchy, pop-oriented rap of the singles, making the entire record a hit-or-miss affair. *— Stephen Thomas Erlewine*

You Gotta Believe / 1992 / Interscope ✦✦✦
Marky Mark tried to keep riding the wave he had enjoyed with *Music for the People,* but failed to score any pop or R&B hit, finding that it's much tougher to find another hit to scavenge or maintain a gimmick the second time around. He eventually enjoyed moderate success with "You Gotta Believe," but a combination of some ill-timed homophobic remarks in an interview and rather limp material like " 'Bout Time I Funk You" and "I Run Rhymes" extinguished whatever fires Marky Mark had previously lit. *—Ron Wynn*

Biz Markie

Vocals / Rap

A productive member of Marley Marl's posse, Markie is a contemporary master of comedic rap. He doesn't have much to say, but songs such as "Picking Boogers" are worthy of The Fat Boys, and "Spring Again" is a classic summer single. Biz Markie managed to dodge a potential career-ending bullet when a controversy involving a sample from Gilbert O'Sullivan's "Alone Again Naturally" was resolved. Markie had allegedly used the sample without permission, triggering a lawsuit. He gave his own spin to the controversy with the 1993 release *All Samples Cleared.* *—John Floyd*

Goin' Off / Feb. 23, 1988 / Cold Chillin' ✦✦✦✦
Biz Markie's debut album introduced his absurdly comical and extremely inventive musical style. While he talked about "Pickin' Boogers," hanging out at "Albee Square Mall," and made music with his mouth, The Biz never kept the music similar, with Marley Marl's production covering all of the bases, concentrating on a deeply funky R&B/dance beat. It was a funny, surrealistic minor masterpiece. *— Stephen Thomas Erlewine*

The Diabolical Biz Markie: The Biz Never Sleeps / Oct. 10, 1989 / Cold Chillin' ✦✦✦✦
Biz Markie's madcap humor was effectively utilized on this release. Markie relied on puns, quips, bad jokes and his disjointed rap style, creating material quite different from the hard-edged fare that now rules hip-hop. Some of it was funny, some of it stupid, but none of it vicious or offensive. The album contained the hits "Just a Friend" and "Spring Again." *—Ron Wynn*

I Need a Haircut / Aug. 27, 1991 / Cold Chillin' ✦✦✦
While others rap about gang strife, inner-city turmoil, their proficiency on the mike or their sexual prowess, Biz Markie discussed bad haircuts and other such weighty matters on this release. This might be what the Coasters would sound like if they had grown up during the rap era. Sadly, there aren't many people on the '90s hip-hop scene interested in absurdist humor. *—Ron Wynn*

All Samples Cleared / 1993 / Cold Chillin' ✦✦
Biz Markie made sure he had permission for every sample featured on this album. Unfortunately, it seemed that the effort to get clearances took its toll on the creative process. The bizarre humor that made his earlier releases so entertaining was less evident, as Markie now strained for results and mostly came up short. *—Ron Wynn*

● **Biz's Baddest Beats** / Jul. 1, 1994 / Cold Chillin' ✦✦✦✦
Biz's Baddest Beats collects all of Biz Markie's hit singles, making the album a good introduction to his bizarrely humorous hip-hop. *— Stephen Thomas Erlewine*

Marley Marl

Vocals / Rap, Hip-hop

One of old school rap's first superproducers, Marley Marl (b. Marlon Wil-

liams) has worked with such artists as MC Shan, Big Daddy Kane, Biz Markie, Roxanne Shanté, Kool G Rap, and Master Ace. Marl was credited with increasing rap's accessibility and was a pioneer in the use of sampling techniques. Marl has also recorded two rather inconsistent albums of his own, but he only creates the backing tracks; the records serve more as vehicles for displaying the vast array of guest performers Marl from whom wangled contributions. *—Steve Huey*

● **In Control, Vol. 1** / 1988 / Cold Chillin' ✦✦✦✦
Marl shows off his greatest stars, including Roxanne Shanté and Big Daddy Kane. *—Dan Heilman*

In Control, Vol. 2 / 1991 / Cold Chillin' ✦✦✦
Although the date carried his name, this was a showcase for various rappers produced by Marley Marl. Everyone from Chuck D, LL Cool J and Heavy D to Chubb Rock, Def Jef and King Tee made an appearance on his second Cold Chillin' CD. Unfortunately this all-star lineup didn't hit any home runs, and the LP struck out. *—Ron Wynn*

MC Breed

Vocals / Rap

Flint, MI, rapper MC Breed (born Eric Breed) came out hard, tough and fast on his 1991 debut *MC Breed & DFC.* "Ain't No Future in Yo' Frontin' " set the tone for a collection of confrontational, at times almost paranoid Afrocentric and/or gangsta tracks with occasional reggae flavoring. DFC were nowhere to be found on the 1992 follow-up *20 Below.* It opted to be even more explicit, angry and offensive than the debut, though such tracks as "Little Child Running Wild" and "Flash's Groove" provided some variety. Breed then issued *The New Breed* for Wrap in 1993. He came back strong with *Funkafied* in 1994, hitting the Top Ten on the R&B charts. It was also for Wrap, a label distributed by Atlanta-based Ichiban. In 1995, *The Best of MC Breed* appeared; the following year, *Da Hood Tapes* was released. *—Ron Wynn*

MC Breed & DFC / 1991 / Ichiban ✦✦✦✦
MC Breed was 19 when he and DFC made their debut in 1991. Things got started on a positive front with the defiant cut "Ain't No Future in Yo' Frontin'," a tough-talking, nicely rapped, and rhymed assault on hypocrisy. "Black for Black" and "I Will Excel" were also worthy message cuts, while "Get Loose" and "Job Corp" added more good material. It was a solid but low-selling first album. *—Ron Wynn*

● **20 Below** / 1992 / Wrap/Ichiban ✦✦✦✦
MC Breed came out even harder and more combative on his second CD than he did on his debut. "Jealous Pimp" and "Ain't to Be F— With" set the agenda squarely in gangsta territory, although he hedged his bets with "Life of a Flintstone" and "Whenever You Want Me." But apparently, audiences were also unsure as to whether MC Breed wanted to brandish a gun or hang out with Bugs Bunny. *—Ron Wynn*

The New Breed / 1993 / Wrap/Ichiban ✦✦✦
MC Breed was alone and rapping with fire and fury on this album. He continued changing his image to that of seasoned, prophetic gangsta commentator, rather than alternating between hard and light material. Breed's raps weren't always fluid, but his rhymes were frequently compelling. *—Ron Wynn*

Funkafied / Jun. 7, 1994 / Wrap/Ichiban ✦✦✦

● **Best of MC Breed** / Oct. 1995 / Wrap ✦✦✦✦

Da Hood Tapes / Apr. 1996 / Ichiban ✦✦✦

MC Lyte

Vocals / Rap

Though she's turned a bit in the pop direction on her latest release, Brooklyn rapper MC Lyte has done some inventive, distinctive material on her two prior releases. She's provided some of the better comebacks and put-downs aimed at out-of-control male egos and libidos, and she's also quite funny. It's to be hoped that the pop tinges on *Act like you Know* are merely an alternative, rather than a primary, direction. MC Lyte responded to fans questioning her direction on *Ain't No Other,* her 1993 album. This marked a return to the tough-talking, fat beats, and no-nonsense persona that had characterized her most successful material. *—Ron Wynn*

Lyte as a Rock / 1988 / First Priority ✦✦✦
The debut from this femme rapper thrusts a middle finger toward the sexism of the male-dominated rap turf, through clever rhymes and a sharp sense of humor, ensuring that her feminism never exhausts and always enlightens. *—John Floyd*

● **Eyes on This** / 1989 / First Priority ✦✦✦✦
This expands on the promise of her debut, both musically (the samples are more dense) and lyrically (witness "Shut the Eff Up! (Hoe)" and the winningly arty "Cuppucino"). *—John Floyd*

Ain't No Other / 1993 / First Priority ✦✦✦

Bad As I Wanna B / Aug. 27, 1996 / Elektra/Asylum ✦✦✦

MC Ren

Vocals / Rap

MC Ren (born Lorenzo Patterson) joined the list of N.W.A. members gone solo in 1992 with *Kizz My Black Azz.* It peaked at No. 12 and eventually went platinum despite being unplayable on even the most underground radio station. The follow-up *Shock of the Hour* briefly topped the pop charts, but didn't have lasting power. On both releases, Ren has showed facility and fluidity as a rapper, but the rhymes haven't been anything special, or the beats. MC Ren's third solo album, *The Villain in Black,* appeared in the spring of 1996; it disappeared from the charts shortly after its release. — *Ron Wynn*

Kizz My Black Azz / Jun. 30, 1992 / Priority ✦✦✦
It would be easier to dismiss MC Ren's obsessively violent and sexist lyrics if his music wasn't so tight and menacing. Taken on purely musical terms, *Kizz My Black Azz* is thrilling; when it's analyzed more deeply, the simplistic, disturbing lyrics unravel the achievements of the music. However, the production and beats are so deeply funky that they almost lift Ren's debut solo EP out of the swamp of violent, misogynist gangstas. Almost. — *Stephen Thomas Erlewine*

● **Shock of the Hour** / 1993 / Ruthless ✦✦✦✦
MC Ren's debut LP is uneven, but presents a lyrical vision when it's not spewing out familiar sexist clichés about women. Ren highlights American hypocrisy with a vengeance, and the title track foresees the nation's end in an apocalyptic fury, enabling Black people to finally achieve justice. Both this tune and "Attack on Babylon" come closest to presenting a coherent, effective philosophy. Another provocative track is "Same Old S," a song that strips away any pretense of glamour around the gangsta lifestyle and outlines the brutality, paranoia, and violence at its core. These tracks display MC Ren's potential as a hip-hop theorist; the others just fill out the CD. — *Ron Wynn*

The Villain in Black / Apr. 1996 / Relativity ✦✦
MC Ren's solo career has suffered from an over-reliance on gangsta rap clichés, and his second full-length album, *Da Villain in Black,* is no exception. Working with Above the Law's Cold 1987um, Ren has constructed an album that doesn't deviate from clichéd G-funk grooves. Furthermore, Ren hasn't come up with lyrics to match his first two solo records, let alone Dre, Ice Cube, or Eazy-E. Relying on profanity instead of insight, the half-hearted raps sadly fit the unimaginative music perfectly. — *Stephen Thomas Erlewine*

MC Serch

Vocals / Rap

MC Serch (born Michael Berrin) was half of the White rap duo 3rd Bass, still the most insightful and "authentic" of the Caucasian hip-hoppers. When 3rd Bass disbanded, Serch began rapping on his own. He had a sizable solo hit with "Here It Comes" from his 1992 release *Return of the Product* on Def Jam. — *Ron Wynn*

Return of the Product / 1992 / Def Jam ✦✦✦✦
MC Serch's first album after the breakup of 3rd Bass was a stripped-down, surprisingly melodic album that suffers from a lack of sharp production. Even so, Serch's skillful rhymes overcome most of the weaknesses of the record. — *Stephen Thomas Erlewine*

Monie Love

Vocals / Rap, Urban, Club/Dance

London-born Simone Wilson, aka Monie Love, was featured on Queen Latifah's single "Ladies First" while a teen. Her CDs as a leader have been erratic, often suggesting more than they delivered, though they've usually contained at least one strong single. After *Down to Earth,* Love issued *In a Word or 2* in 1993. — *Ron Wynn*

Down to Earth / 1990 / Warner Brothers ✦✦✦
The mood moves through vibrant, concerned, bemused, and resigned. Nice samples and good production. — *Ron Wynn*

● **In a Word or 2** / 1993 / Warner Brothers ✦✦✦✦
Monie Love's second CD was more ambitious, taking a harder, less pop tone and approach. She spoke frankly and with clarity about such topics as promiscuity and self-esteem, while her rapping was more focused, her beats starker and more forceful, and the rhymes less gimmicky. — *Ron Wynn*

Nas

Vocals / Rap

Long Island rapper Nas, born Nasir Jones, immersed himself in hip-hop and street culture at age nine, the fruits of which can be heard on his 1994 debut, *Illmatic.* Nas got his big break when former 3rd Bass rapper MC Serch included his "Half Time" on the soundtrack of the film *Zebrahead,* which led to a deal with Serch's production company. *Illmatic* was released on Columbia in 1994 and attracted attention for its

depiction of ghetto life and Nas' refusal to include much of the misogyny and violence of standard gangsta rap, not to mention his admiration of Michael Jackson and the Jackson 5.

Nas' second album, *It Was Written,* was an immediate hit upon its release in the summer of 1996, entering the charts at No. 1, which far eclipsed the No. 12 peak of *Illmatic.* — *Steve Huey*

● **Illmatic** / 1994 / Columbia ✦✦✦✦

It Was Written / 1996 / Columbia ✦✦✦✦
For his second album, *It Was Written,* Nas hired a bunch of hip-hop's biggest producers—including Dr. Dre, DJ Premier, Stretch, and Trackmasters—to help him create the musical bed for his daring, groundbreaking rhymes. Although that rhyme style isn't as startling on *It Was Written* as it was on his debut, *Illmatic,* Nas has deepened his talents, creating a complex series of rhymes that not only flow, but manage to tell coherent stories as well. Furthermore, Nas often concentrates on creating vignettes about life in the ghetto that never are apolitical or ambivalent. This time around, the production is more detailed and elaborate, which gives the music a wider appeal. Sometimes this is a detriment—Nas sounds better when he tries to keep it at street-level—but usually, Nas' lyrical force cuts through the commercial sheen. Combined with the spare but deep grooves, his rhymes have a resonance unmatched by most of his mid-'90s contemporaries. No matter how deep his lyrics are, his grooves are just as deep, and that bottomless funk and spare beats are what makes *It Was Written* so compulsively listenable. — *Leo Stanley*

Naughty by Nature

Rap, Gangsta Rap

One of the finest new rap posses received some help from Queen Latifah on their 1991 debut and landed a huge hit with the naggingly incessant "O.P.P."

Naughty by Nature scored another huge hit with their next release. *19 Naughty III* featured "Hip Hop Hooray," which rivaled "O.P.P." as a crossover smash and national catchphrase in 1993. — *John Floyd*

● **Naughty by Nature** / 1991 / Tommy Boy ✦✦✦✦
This leering trio's first single, "O.P.P.," dominated the airwaves in the fall of 1991 on the strength of its home-truth bedroom message and its butt-hugging beat. Fans of the single will find plenty more in NBN's rollicking debut album. — *John Floyd*

19 Naughty III / 1993 / Tommy Boy ✦✦✦✦
With its slamming beats and infectious hooks (exemplified by the hit single "Hip Hop Hooray"), *19 Naughty III,* Naughty by Nature's second album, proves that they're not a one-hit-wonder group. Although the music is terrific, the lyrical posturing and misogyny can grow tiresome. — *Stephen Thomas Erlewine*

Poverty's Paradise / 1995 / Tommy Boy ✦✦✦
For their third album, Naughty by Nature do little to truly change their style. Some of the beats are a little slower and funkier, some of the rhymes are more dexterous, some of the rhythms are a little more complex—yet nothing distinguishes *Poverty's Paradise* from the group's two previous, and superior, records. — *Stephen Thomas Erlewine*

Clap Yo Hands / 1995 / Tommy Boy ✦✦✦

The Notorious B.I.G.

Vocals / Rap, G-Funk

The Brooklyn-born rapper the Notorious B.I.G. (born Chris Wallace) first gained attention for his work on Mary J. Blige's "What's the 411?" When he delivered his debut album, *Ready to Die,* in 1994, it became one of the most popular hip-hop releases of the year. In June of 1995, his single "One More Chance" debuted at No. 5 in the pop singles chart, tying Michael Jackson's "Scream/Childhood" as the highest-debuting single of all time. — *Stephen Thomas Erlewine*

● **Ready to Die** / 1994 / Arista ✦✦✦✦
With the galvanizing deep funk of *Ready to Die,* the Notorious B.I.G. scores one of the most impressive rap debuts since Dr. Dre's seminal *The Chronic.* While *Ready to Die* takes its throbbing bass grooves from that P-Funk-saturated album, the Notorious B.I.G. writes more acute and evocative lyrics, as well as being a more skillful rapper. — *Stephen Thomas Erlewine*

N.W.A.

Rap, Gangsta Rap

This Compton, CA, ensemble once held the title of "most controversial rap act," but in recent years others have surfaced to share some of the heat. The original posse, including Ice Cube, Eazy-E, Arabian Prince, MC Ren, and the D.O.C., made their first release in 1987. *N.W.A. and the Posse* was mainly a party/fun record but cuts like "Boyz 'N' the Hood" and "Dope Man" should have been a warning to alert ears of what was coming. Anyone who missed the debut was certainly caught by surprise when the 1988 follow-up, *Straight Outta Compton,* came along. The stark, brutal depictions of gang strife and urban warfare, the coarse, obscene language and the complete amoral tone, plus the anti-authority number "F°°k tha Police" earned N.W.A. scorn from middle-class types of all colors and also attempts from the FBI to get retailers not to stock it. Since that high point, N.W.A. has really become less an entity and more an amalgam of solo acts. Ice Cube, Eazy-E, Arabian Prince, D.O.C., and MC Ren have all done separate projects; Cube has not only left the group but has engaged in bitter, heated public feuds with them; and D.O.C. suffered a near-fatal car crash that took him out of circulation for quite some time. The EP *100 Miles and Runnin'* (1990) was half-hearted, and the group's 1991 release *Niggaz4Life* elicited some controversy but nothing close to past albums. Amidst gargantuan clashes of egos, N.W.A. dissolved the following year, leaving behind an enormously influential body of work. —*Ron Wynn*

N.W.A. and the Posse / 1987 / Priority ✦✦✦✦
This is a hodgepodge of early singles from N.W.A. and some of their Compton contemporaries (including D.O.C.). The highlights are N.W.A.'s "Boyz 'N the Hood" and "Dope Man." —*John Floyd*

★ **Straight Outta Compton** / 1989 / Priority ✦✦✦✦✦
This is a scalding, relentless, and always jolting look at life in the ghettos of South Central Los Angeles. You may not agree with their relish of violence or the rampant sexism, but this series of inflammatory and bruising vignettes is a visceral landmark on a par with the MC5 or the Sex Pistols. —*John Floyd*

100 Miles & Runnin' / 1990 / Priority ✦✦
Niggaz4life / 1991 / Priority ✦✦✦
This is where N.W.A. went off the deep end and became a self-parody. Their tales of urban horror have no reality anymore and simply aren't dangerous or menacing. But that was all that was expected of them; the majority of N.W.A.'s audience was always White, and suburban kids glommed onto the silly fantasies of *Niggaz4life* by the thousands, rocketing the album to the upper reaches of the charts. While the tracks sound great (Dr. Dre is unquestionably the only talent left), there is nothing here. —*Stephen Thomas Erlewine*

Greatest Hits / 1996 / Ruthless ✦✦✦✦
N.W.A.'s career isn't necessarily one that lends itself well to anthologies. Though they had important singles, especially in the underground hip-hop community in the late '80s, they never received any support from radio or MTV, which meant they never had any official "hits." Instead, their albums were more important, popular and influential than singles, even if individual tracks—"F°°k tha Police," "Straight Outta Compton," "Gangsta Gangsta," "Express Yourself"—became the focus of attention. And, if you notice, all those songs were from *Straight Outta Compton,* the only good album the group ever made. *Greatest Hits* does include all of the high points from that album (the title track is present in a previously unavailable remix), plus a scattershot sampling of raw early singles and the highlights from *100 Miles & Runnin'* and *Niggaz4Life.* It's nice to have the good tracks isolated from the group's latter-day efforts, but *Greatest Hits* is unnecessary—all you need is *Straight Outta Compton.* —*Stephen Thomas Erlewine*

Ol' Dirty Bastard

Vocals / Rap
A member of the Brooklyn hip-hop congregation the Wu-Tang Clan, Ol' Dirty Bastard released his first solo album in the spring of 1995, after the Clan imploded. Produced by fellow Wu-Tang member Prince Rakeem, Ol' Dirty Bastard's *Return to the 36 Chambers* sounds identical to the Clan's 1993 debut album, *Enter the Wu-Tang (36 Chambers).* —*Stephen Thomas Erlewine*

● **Return to the 36 Chambers** / Mar. 28, 1995 / Elektra ✦✦✦✦
On a break from the Wu-Tang Clan, Ol' Dirty Bastard hands in a defiantly vulgar record, *Return to the 36 Chambers.* Choosing not to stray from the hardcore style of the Clan, Ol' Dirty Bastard keeps the sound and makes it looser lyrically. Nothing on the record stands out as an equal to *Enter the 36 Chambers,* but the good times keep flowing, and "Brooklyn Zoo" is one of the classics of 1995. —*Stephen Thomas Erlewine*

Onyx

Rap
The hip-hop trio Onyx ushered in a new development in 1993; rap in the mosh pit. Their shouting, in-your-face brand of high volume rapping didn't sit well with everyone, but their debut CD *Bacdafucup* included a huge crossover smash with "Slam." —*Ron Wynn*

● **Bacdafucup** / 1993 / Ral ✦✦✦✦
With their simple, brutal production and shouted rhymes, Onyx's debut album was a menacing, threatening record, relying more on sheer aggression than musical competence. Still, that aggression could produce undeniably classic tracks, like their breakthrough single, "Slam." —*Stephen Thomas Erlewine*

Paris

Vocals / Rap
This San Francisco rapper debuted in 1990 with *The Devil Made Me Do It* for Tommy Boy, then moved to the independent Scarface label with *Sleeping with the Enemy* in 1992. His fiercely Afrocentric themes were reminiscent of The Last Poets or Gil Scott-Heron, but didn't generate as much response as anticipated. They did cause lots of controversy in other circles however, leading to allegations of "reverse" racism. —*Ron Wynn*

The Devil Made Me Do It / 1990 / Tommy Boy ✦✦✦
San Francisco rapper Paris' debut album featured several angry, Afrocentric numbers (the CD included four selections that didn't make it onto the vinyl LP, and two that weren't on the cassette). There was little here designed to make anyone feel good, and it was Paris, not Sister Souljah, who effectively described racism's impact on the psyche of oppressed people with his composition "Hate That Hate Made." —*Ron Wynn*

● **Sleeping with the Enemy** / 1993 / Scarface ✦✦✦✦
It took several months and a change of record labels before it was released, but Paris' *Sleeping with the Enemy* was the most incendiary political hip-hop album released since Ice Cube's *Death Certificate* in 1991. Paris' production may rely on beats that have been done before, but in no way does that detract from the strength of his militant rhymes or the controlled, vicious anger of the music. —*Stephen Thomas Erlewine*

Guerrilla Funk / 1994 / Scarface ✦✦✦✦
Guerrilla Funk wasn't quite as scathing as the previous *Sleeping with the Enemy,* but that's only relative. Paris hasn't tempered his rage at all, he's just expanded his range, adding more societal issues to his hit list. In addition, the music hasn't lost any of its potency, making *Guerrilla Funk* a worthy contender for one of the most incendiary hip-hop albums of the '90s. —*Stephen Thomas Erlewine*

The Pharcyde

Rap
The Pharcyde are a rap quartet from South Central Los Angeles consisting of MCs/producers Tre "Slimkid" Hardson, Derrick "Fatlip" Stewart, Imani Wilcox, and Romye "Booty Brown" Robinson. Hardson, Wilcox, and Robinson were all dancers and choreographers who met on the Los Angeles underground club circuit in the late '80s, worked together for a while, and served a stint as dancers on *In Living Color.* Stewart, meanwhile, performed at local clubs and eventually hooked up with the others in 1990. Under the tutelage of Reggie Andrews, a local high school music teacher, the group learned about the music industry and the process of recording an album. They landed a deal with Delicious Vinyl in 1991, and a year later released their eccentric, influential debut album, *Bizarre Ride II the Pharcyde,* which went gold. After a successful spot on Lollapalooza's second stage in 1994, the group released its second album, *LabCabinCalifornia,* which was calmer than their first but no less warped. —*Steve Huey*

● **Bizarre Ride to the Pharcyde** / 1992 / Atlantic ✦✦✦✦
A wild ride through The Pharcyde's warped, surrealistic world, their first album is filled with uneasy and absurd humor, as well as skewered, funky production. It's by no means a consistent record, but the depth of their vision (beneath their humor lie some serious themes) makes it a rewarding record. —*Stephen Thomas Erlewine*

LabCabinCalifornia / Nov. 28, 1995 / Delicious Vinyl ✦✦✦

PM Dawn

Rap, Urban
Comprised of brothers Prince B (Attrell Cordes) and DJ Minute Mix (Jarrett Cordes), the early '90s group PM Dawn straddled the gap between hip-hop and smooth '70s-style soul, creating an innovative urban R&B that owed as much to pop as it did to rhythm and blues. The brothers recorded their debut single, "Ode to a Forgetful Mind," in 1988. PM Dawn didn't release a full-length album until 1991. The record, *Of the Heart, of the Soul and of the Cross: The Utopian Experience,* was an immediate hit, thanks to the single "Set Adrift on Memory's Bliss," which sampled Spandau Ballet's new wave hit "True." Both the album and the single received glowing reviews, as did the 1993 follow-up *The Bliss Album?,* which featured the hit singles "I'd Die Without You" and "Looking Through Patient Eyes." —*Stephen Thomas Erlewine*

★ **Of the Heart, of the Soul and of the Cross . . .** / 1991 / Gee Street ✦✦✦✦✦
Of the Heart, of the Soul and of the Cross: The Utopian Experience is a standout release, sandwiching psychedelic tinges, political/social discourse, and invigorating raps and production. Includes the hit "Set Adrift on Memory's Bliss." —*Ron Wynn*

The Bliss Album? / 1993 / Gee Street ✦✦✦✦
It's inaccurate to label PM Dawn a hip-hop band, since their sensibility lies with smooth ballads and mellow soul; they only use hip-hop to underscore their songs. In many ways, *The Bliss Album?* is a more focused album than their debut, containing such brilliant ballads as "I'd Die Without You" and "Looking Through Patient Eyes." When Prince B tries to go harder, as on "Plastic," the results are well-intentioned, but seriously flawed—they don't have the strength or power to pull off hardcore material. But when they stick to their pop-friendly R&B, PM Dawn is often quite remarkable; *The Bliss Album?* was the rare second album to expand on, rather than duplicate, the achievements of the debut.
— Stephen Thomas Erlewine

Jesus Wept / Oct. 3, 1995 / Gee Street ✦✦✦✦
With their third album, *Jesus Wept*, PM Dawn doesn't necessarily make a great leap forward. Instead, they make some great refinements. Prince B's lyrics are just as trippy and cryptic as ever, but they appear more focused, offering a poetic, spiritual worldview that is supported by the lovely, layered music. Using artists like Prince, Stevie Wonder, Marvin Gaye, and the Beatles as starting points, Prince B creates a unique world assembled equally from soul, pop, hip-hop, and psychedelia. As individual pieces, the songs might not always make much sense, but taken as a whole, they create a singular world that is rich in lush melodies and sumptuous arrangements. Occasionally, PM Dawn's ambition gets the best of them and the results sound self-indulgent, not transcendent. However, those moments are few and far between on *Jesus Wept,* the group's best album. *— Stephen Thomas Erlewine*

Positive K

Rap
Positive K's debut LP *Da Skills Dat Pay Da Bills* on Island landed a hit with the single "I Got a Man." The CD was a mix of sexual one-upmanship and Afrocentric, Islamic rhetoric that retained a sense of humor even in the midst of the propaganda. *— Ron Wynn*

● **The Skills Dat Pay Da Bills** / 1992 / Island ✦✦✦✦
Positive K scored one of 1992's few non-political rap hits with the amusing "I Got a Man," a song exploring all the shadings of the age-old game of sexual pursuit. The remaining cuts ranged from predictable Afrocentric and gangsta posturing to decent pop-flavored ditties and boasts. *— Ron Wynn*

Prime Minister Pete Nice & Daddy Rich

Rap
The original lineup for the rap ensemble 3rd Bass featured White rappers Pete Nice (born Pete Nash), MC Serch, and DJ Richie Rich (born Richard Lawson), the group's lone African-American. When Serch split in 1992, Nice and Rich tried it as a duo. Their 1993 debut *Dust to Dust* failed to equal the success of 3rd Bass. *— Ron Wynn*

Dust to Dust / Apr. 27, 1993 / Def Jam ✦✦✦✦
When 3rd Bass disbanded, Prime Minister Pete Nice and Daddy Rich tried to regroup with this 1993 album. It contained some competent message tracks and hard-edged commentary, but failed to recapture the niche or audience 3rd Bass had previously enjoyed. *— Ron Wynn*

Professor Griff

Vocals / Rap
Professor Griff (born Richard Griffin), was the minister of information for Public Enemy until June of 1989. He gave a controversial interview to the *Washington Post* that included comments deemed anti-Semitic by many. In the ensuing furor, Chuck D eventually fired him from Public Enemy and even briefly disbanded the group, only to re-form them. Griff formed his own band, The Asiatic Disciples. The results have been mixed, the slant predictably Islamic and Afrocentric. *— Ron Wynn*

● **Pawns in the Game** / 1990 / Luke ✦✦✦✦
A respectable showing from Griff, it came in the face of negative expectations. *— Dan Heilman*

Kao's II Wiz-7-Dome / 1991 / Luke ✦✦✦
Professor Griff tried again with this 1991 release on Luther Campbell's Luke label. But like his previous effort, Griff failed to realize that advocacy alone, regardless of the justness of his message, couldn't overcome pedestrian production, unconvincing rhymes and a stiff, leaden rap style. Rather than threatening, the net effect was boring. *— Ron Wynn*

Public Enemy

Rap, Hip-hop
Without question, the most talked-about rap group ever and among the most controversial and publicized bands of its day in any genre. Carlton Ridenour, a Long Island college student and former radio disc jockey, has parlayed a booming voice, congenial yet forceful personality, and the articulation skills necessary to cogently present often inflammatory viewpoints into a hugely successful performance, marketing, and prose-lytizing empire. As Chuck D, Ridenour is Public Enemy's theorist, lyricist, and head rapper. He's quoted constantly, seen on television around the world, and idolized by legions of Black and White youth. Through five albums, Public Enemy has served as the hip-hop vanguard, rapping about issues of race, rage, and inequality without lapsing (too often) into vicious sexism or homophobia, though they've been tagged with charges of anti-Semitism. They did eventually cut loose former minister of information Professor Griff, following a flap about comments he made in an interview, but the group has been able to ride out storms over lyric content and maintain their popularity without any stylistic compromise. Hank Shocklee, Terminator X, Flavor Flav, and the rest of The Bomb Squad and crew also deserve praise, especially Shocklee and Terminator X, whose dynamite production keeps things anchored through hard-hitting, rapid-fire snippets and impressive studio techniques. Flav's absurdist raps and onstage antics provide some welcome levity and comic relief.

After laying low for nearly three years, the reaction was swift and mostly unfavorable when Public Enemy's first new full-length album since *Apocalypse '91* was unveiled in 1994. Not only did *Rolling Stone* and *The Source* give *Muse Sick 'N' Hour Mess Age* bad reviews, but the album sold poorly, disappearing from the charts quickly. In the summer of 1995, Chuck D announced that Public Enemy was retiring from live performances, giving the members time to pursue other studio projects. *— Ron Wynn*

Yo! Bum Rush the Show / 1987 / Def Jam ✦✦✦✦
When their debut was released in 1987, very few rap groups even approached Public Enemy's musical or political stance. Listening to the first album now, it's surprising how few of the songs are actually political—the sheer force of the sound fools the listener into thinking Chuck D is saying more than he actually is. Still, "Megablast," "Public Enemy No. 1," and "Miuzi Weighs a Ton" carry a small amount of political rhetoric. Much sparer than later releases, the album is carried over the top by Chuck D's bulldozer roar. *— Stephen Thomas Erlewine*

★ **It Takes a Nation of Millions to Hold Us Back** / 1988 / Def Jam ✦✦✦✦✦
Arguably the best hip-hop album ever made, *It Takes a Nation of Millions to Hold Us Back* was a huge leap forward not only for Public Enemy, but for all of hip-hop. PE's signature sound—a barrage of found sounds, densely woven samples, and noisy tape loops—was evident for the first time, courtesy of The Bomb Squad. Chuck D's lyrics, full of revolutionary rhetoric yet managing to avoid being hysterical, matched the aural onslaught. The group's political stance would be meaningless if the music didn't put it over the top throughout, and that does happen on "Black Steel in the Hour of Chaos," "Night of the Living Baseheads," "Rebel Without a Pause," "Don't Believe the Hype," and "Bring the Noise," in particular. There isn't a weak moment on the album. A landmark recording. *— Stephen Thomas Erlewine*

☆ **Fear of a Black Planet** / 1990 / Def Jam ✦✦✦✦✦
Nothing could quite match the pure, concentrated fury of *It Takes a Nation of Millions . . .* , and Public Enemy wisely didn't try to replicate it on their third album. *Fear of a Black Planet* is much more experimental than its predecessor, boasting an impressive array of textures from pseudo-reggae to crushing hip-hop. Chuck D's phrasing and vocalization have matured; he even sounds seductive on "Pollywanacraka." The basic theme of *Fear of a Black Planet* is an exploration of American racism, concentrating on interracial relationships and White injustice. The relative lack of heavy beats and the wall of rage caused some to cry sellout, but *Fear* is hardly that. *— Stephen Thomas Erlewine*

☆ **Apocalypse '91 . . . The Enemy Strikes Black** / 1991 / Def Jam ✦✦✦✦✦
In response to the accusations that *Fear of a Black Planet* was a sellout, Public Enemy lashed out with *Apocalypse '91 . . . The Enemy Strikes Black,* an album of hard, noisy funk, much closer to *Millions* than to *Fear.* Having dealt with White racism on their previous album, Public Enemy set their sights on correcting problems in the Black community. On "1 Million Bottlebags," "Nighttrain," "Shut 'Em Down," and "By the Time I Get to Arizona," Chuck D offers some of his hardest-hitting rhymes, matched to equally hard rhythm tracks. Public Enemy even offers solutions on a few tracks, a rarity in the rap world. Although the Imperial Grand Ministers of Funk have replaced The Bomb Squad (who are listed as executive producers) as the main production team, Public Enemy's sound didn't change drastically. *— Stephen Thomas Erlewine*

Greatest Misses / Sep. 15, 1992 / Def Jam ✦✦
For the first time in their career, Public Enemy sound unsure of the direction of their music. *Greatest Misses* is half original tracks and half remixes, and consequently sounds muddled. Public Enemy sound like they're treading water throughout the new songs; none of them are particularly bad, but unlike all of their previous material, none of it is groundbreaking. None of the remixes are awful, but they are neither revelatory nor insightful and often miss the original intent of the song. *— Stephen Thomas Erlewine*

Muse Sick 'N' Hour Mess Age / 1994 / Def Jam ✦✦

Queen Latifah

b. Mar. 18, 1970, Newark, New Jersey
Vocals / Rap, Hip-hop
Although Queen Latifah was certainly not the first female rapper, she was the first to bring a feminist consciousness to the genre's political agenda with her groundbreaking 1989 debut, *All Hail the Queen* and its single "Ladies First." Latifah (an Arabic word translating as "delicate" or "sensitive") was born Dana Owens in Newark, NJ, and served a stint as a human beatbox in the group Ladies Fresh. She recorded a single, "Wrath of My Madness," in 1988 and later released *All Hail the Queen* to strongly favorable reviews; the album showcased her versatility on material ranging from soul, dub reggae and dance to straight hip-hop, and established a tough, no-nonsense, intelligent persona. *Nature of a Sista* expanded on that role with some more personal material, but *Black Reign* became her most popular album, probably boosted by Latifah's increased visibility as a cast member of the Fox sitcom "Living Single." The album was dedicated to her late brother, who was killed in a motorcycle accident in 1992, and produced the hit single "U.N.I.T.Y.," which won a Grammy for Best Rap Solo Performance. In addition to *Living Single*, Latifah has also appeared in the films *Jungle Fever, Juice*, and *House Party 2. — Steve Huey*

● **All Hail the Queen** / 1989 / Tommy Boy ✦✦✦✦
Her genius is two-fold. She preaches Afrocentrism through clever, versatile, and educated raps, and they're coming from a clever, versatile, and educated feminist. The whole shebang is funky beyond belief. *—John Floyd*

Nature of a Sista' / 1991 / Tommy Boy ✦✦✦
Her feminism becomes even more focused on this follow-up. With an equally diverse and creative set list, Latifah is becoming the female voice in a male-dominated genre. *—John Floyd*

Black Reign / Nov. 16, 1993 / Motown ✦✦✦✦
Black Reign marked Latifah's move to Motown, and was also a return to the tough-talking, lyrically frank, frequently controversial material that established her as arguably the finest female rapper. "Coochie Bang" and "Weekend Love" were harsh and explicit attacks on would-be hit-and-run lovers, while "Just Another Day" and "I Can't Understand" examined the continuing inequities plaguing inner-city youth, and "Superstar" took a pointedly unglamorous view of her situation and the perils of hip-hop supremacy. *—Ron Wynn*

The Real Roxanne

Vocals / Rap
Following the massive success of UTFO's "Roxanne, Roxanne" single in late 1984 and early 1985, over 100 answer records appeared, and several female rappers adopted the Roxanne alias; The Real Roxanne (born Adelaida Martinez) was perhaps the most talented of the bunch and really only had to contend with Roxanne Shanté for the title. It took her until 1988 to release an album, by which time the Roxanne fad had run its course; still, the self-titled release packed a wallop thanks to producers Jam Master Jay, Howie Tee, and Full Force, plus the Real Roxanne's own forceful, sassy personality. *—Steve Huey*

The Real Roxanne / 1988 / Select ✦✦✦✦
With the aid ofJam Master Jay, Howie Tee, and Full Force, this Puerto Rican whipped up a stunning debut that highlights her inimitable skills as a rapper and lyricist, as well as her band's way with the funk. *—John Floyd*

Redman

Vocals / Rap
New Jersey rapper Redman made his initial impact with *Whut? Thee Album* in 1992. He blended reggae and funk influences with topical commentary and displayed a terse, though fluid rap style that was sometimes satirical, sometimes tough, and sometimes silly. Redman returned in 1994 with his second album, *Dare Iz a Darkside*, which was a harder album than his debut. *—Ron Wynn*

● **Whut? Thee Album** / Sep. 22, 1992 / Chaos ✦✦✦✦
Redman's debut album is a minor masterpiece, fueled by the thick, P-Funk-influenced production of Erick Sermon. Redman's rhyming is forceful and intelligent, and he's never afraid to lighten his rhetoric with humor. Plus, the deeply funky grooves forming the core of the album never grow tiresome or repetitive. *—Stephen Thomas Erlewine*

Dare Iz a Darkside / 1994 / Ral ✦✦✦

Pete Rock & C.L. Smooth

Rap
Mt. Vernon, New Yorkers Pete Rock, a producer and disc jockey, and rapper C.L. Smooth emerged in 1992 as both a powerhouse performance

duo and as prolific producers. Their album *Mecca & the Soul Brother* was a solid hit, notably the cuts "They Reminisce Over You (T.R.O.Y.)" and "Straighten It Out." They later collaborated with Mary J. Blige for a remix of her song "Reminisce" that effectively merged the two tracks in a re-edited hit. Their next album, *The Main Ingredient*, appeared in 1994. They've also done many productions for both hip-hop acts and Urban Contemporary artists like Johnny Gill. *—Ron Wynn*

All Souled Out / 1991 / Elektra ✦✦✦✦
This strong debut release combines jazz and hip-hop to impressive effect. *—AMG*

● **Mecca & the Soul Brother** / 1992 / Asylum ✦✦✦✦
C.L. Smooth's clever raps and Pete Rock's snazzy production put this duo into the hip-hop big time with their second album. There were tremendous message cuts and attractive general material, and it was simply an excellent album on every level. It includes the hit single "They Reminisce Over You (T.R.O.Y.)." *—Ron Wynn*

The Main Ingredient / 1994 / Elektra ✦✦✦
Pete Rock & C.L. Smooth's sequel to the groundbreaking *Mecca & the Soul Brother* wasn't quite as focused or innovative as its predecessor, but *The Main Ingredient* included several first-rate tracks, making the album a succcessful follow-up. *—Stephen Thomas Erlewine*

Run-D.M.C.

Rap, Hip-hop
More than any other hip-hop group, Run-D.M.C. is responsible for the sound and style of the music. As the first hardcore rap outfit, the trio set the sound and style for the next decade of rap. With its spare beats and excursions into heavy metal samples, the trio was tougher and more menacing than its predecessors Grandmaster Flash and Whodini. In the process, it opened the door for both the politicized rap of Public Enemy and Boogie Down Productions, as well as the hedonistic gangsta fantasies of N.W.A. At the same time, Run-D.M.C. helped move rap from a singles-oriented genre to an album-oriented one—they were the first hip-hop artists to construct full-fledged albums, not just a collection with two singles and a bunch of filler. By the end of the '80s, Run-D.M.C. had been overtaken by the groups they had spawned, but they continued to perform to a dedicated following well into the '90s.

All three members of Run-D.M.C. were natives of the middle-class New York borough Hollis, Queens. Run (born Joseph Simmons, November 14, 1964) was the brother of Russell Simmons, who formed the hip-hop management company Rush Productions in the early '80s; by the mid-'80s, Russell had formed the pioneering rap label Def Jam with Rick Rubin. Russell encouraged his brother Joey and his friend, Darryl McDaniel (b. May 31, 1964), to form a rap duo. The pair of friends did just that, adopting the names Run and D.M.C. respectively. After they graduated from high school in 1982, the pair enlisted their friend, Jason Mizell (b. January 21, 1965), to scratch turntables; Mizell adopted the stage name Jam Master Jay.

In 1983, Run-D.M.C. released its first single, "It's Like That"/"Sucker M.C.'s," on Profile Records. The single sounded like no other rap at the time—it was spare, blunt and skillful, with hard beats and powerful, literate, daring vocals, where Run and D.M.C.'s vocals overlapped as they finished each other's lines. It was the first "new school" hip-hop recording. "It's like That" became a Top 20 R&B hit, as did the group's second single, "Hard Times"/"Jam Master Jay." Two other hit R&B singles followed in early 1984—"Rock Box" and "30 Days"—before the group's eponymous debut appeared.

By the time of their second album, 1985's *King of Rock*, Run-D.M.C. had become the most popular and influential rappers in America, already spawning a number of imitators. As the *King of Rock* title suggests, the group was breaking down the barriers between rock 'n' roll and rap, rapping over heavy metal records and thick, dense drum loops. Besides releasing the *King of Rock* album and scoring the R&B hits "King of Rock, "You Talk Too Much" and "Can You Rock It like This" in 1985, the group also appeared in the rap movie *Krush Groove*, which also featured Kurtis Blow, the Beastie Boys, and the Fat Boys.

Run-D.M.C.'s fusion of rock and rap broke into the mainstream with their third album, 1986's *Raising Hell*. The album was preceded by the Top Ten R&B single "My Adidas," which set the stage for the group's biggest hit single, a cover of Aerosmith's "Walk This Way." Recorded with Aerosmith's Steven Tyler and Joe Perry, "Walk This Way" was the first hip-hop record to appeal to both rockers and rappers, as evidenced by its peak position of No. 4 on the pop charts. In the wake of the success of "Walk This Way," *Raising Hell* became the first rap album to reach No. 1 on the R&B charts, to chart in the pop Top Ten, and the first to go platinum, and Run-D.M.C. was the first rap act to receive airplay on MTV—they were the first rappers to cross over into the pop mainstream. *Raising Hell* also spawned the hit singles "You Be Illin'" and "It's Tricky." Run-D.M.C. spent most of 1987 recording *Tougher than Leather*, their follow-up to *Raising Hell*. *Tougher than Leather* was accompanied by a movie of the same name. Starring Run-D.M.C., the film was an affectionate parody of '70s Blaxploitation films. Although Run-D.M.C. had been at the height of their popularity when they were recording and filming *Tougher than Leather*, by the time the project was released, the rap world had changed. Most of the hip-hop audience wanted to hear hardcore political rappers like Public Enemy, not crossover artists like Run-D.M.C. Consequently, the film bombed and the album only went platinum, failing to spawn any significant hit singles. Two years after *Tougher than Leather*, Run-D.M.C. returned with *Back from Hell*, which became their first album not to go platinum. Following its release, both Run and D.M.C. experienced problems as Daniels suffered a bout of alcoholism and Simmons was accused of rape. After Daniels sobered up and the charges against Simmons were dismissed, both of the rappers became born-again Christians, touting their religious conversion on the 1993 album, *Down with the King*. Featuring guest appearances and production assistance from artists as diverse as Public Enemy, EPMD, Naughty by Nature, A Tribe Called Quest, Neneh Cherry, Pete Rock, and KRS-One, *Down with the King* became the comeback Run-D.M.C. needed. The title track became a Top Ten R&B hit and the album went gold, peaking at number 21. Although they were no longer hip-hop innovators, the success of *Down with the King* proved that Run-D.M.C. were still respected pioneers. — *Stephen Thomas Erlewine*

☆ **Run-D.M.C.** / 1984 / Profile ✦✦✦✦✦
Their album debut features all the early singles, including "It's like That" and "Rock Box," which stripped rap down to the bare essentials and introduced slews of innovations, lyrically and musically. — *John Floyd*

☆ **King of Rock** / 1985 / Profile ✦✦✦✦✦
Run-D.M.C. scored their first platinum LP and roared into pop consciousness with this 1985 LP. Such cuts as "King of Rock," "Rock the House" and "Can You Rock It like This" were definitive, and their tough tone, clipped style and posturing attitudes set the hip-hop agenda for several years. — *Ron Wynn*

☆ **Raising Hell** / 1986 / Profile ✦✦✦✦✦
The collaboration with Steven Tyler and Joe Perry on "Walk This Way" made this the most successful rap album of its time, but the blistering title track, the pulsating "You Be Illin'," kept it in the Top Ten. It is a masterful and important release, not just for rap but for modern music. — *John Floyd*

Tougher Than Leather / 1988 / Profile ✦✦✦
After the epic *Raising Hell*, it was almost a drop in the bucket for Run-D.M.C. to get only a platinum LP for *Tougher Than Leather*. It included the mild hit "Mary Mary," but was also an indication that all was not well with the trio creatively. There was an ominous quality to "I'm Not Going Out Like That," and such cuts as "Miss Elaine" and "Beats to the Rhyme" signaled that their run to the top was in its final stages. — *Ron Wynn*

Back from Hell / 1990 / Profile ✦✦✦

★ **Together Forever: Greatest Hits 1983-1991** / 1991 / Profile ✦✦✦✦✦
For the most part, all of Run-D.M.C.'s most important singles and biggest hits are included on *Together Forever: Greatest Hits 1983-1991*. That alone makes the compilation a necessary purchase. However, that doesn't mean that it is a perfectly assembled collection. Instead of presenting the singles in chronological order, the sequencing skips back and forth—for example, it opens with "Sucker M.C.'s," jumps ahead to "Walk This Way," jumps further ahead to "Together Forever," then slams back to "King of Rock." Still, *Together Forever* has 18 of the groundbreaking group's essential items, from "It's Like That" and "Hard Times" to "It's Tricky" and "Run's House," which makes it an ideal introduction and an enjoyable retrospective. It's just not the definitive collection it could have been. — *Stephen Thomas Erlewine*

Down with the King / May 4, 1993 / Profile ✦✦✦
After 1990's lackluster *Back from Hell*, most fans thought that Run-D.M.C. were no longer capable of delivering a solid record. *Down with the King* proved those doubters wrong. Although it didn't burn up the charts like *Raising Hell* and was not as innovative as their first album, *Down with the King* showed that they remained strong and talented; it also didn't hurt that the production was provided by several of the 1990s' most talented artists, including Public Enemy, Pete Rock, Naughty by Nature, and Q-Tip. — *Stephen Thomas Erlewine*

Salt-N-Pepa
Rap, Urban
Queens, NY, rappers Sandy Denton, Cheryl James, and DJ Dee Dee Roper have been prime female stars since 1986, when *Hot, Cool & Vicious*, with its single smash "Push It," made them stars. The duo has been able to shift gears at will, sometimes being naughty, other times nice, letting the beat propel their rhymes on one song, and then slicing their exchanges off it on the next. They've done numbers with feminist viewpoints, then turned around and echoed the conventional wisdom regarding male/female relationships in another number. But contradictions aside, they're among the tightest, most accomplished rap outfits active, and their records have held up well. Salt-N-Pepa made the pop

big time with *Very Necessary* in 1993. The huge hit "Whatta Man" teamed them with En Vogue. They also did commercials for the NBA and various products, while finding themselves the rap act of choice for the upper class. At the same time, they recaptured the Black audience that they'd previously lost with their more lightweight material like *A Salt with a Deadly Pepa*. The group also took more control over their image and production, wresting the reins from longtime producer Hurby Astor. — *Ron Wynn*

Hot, Cool & Vicious / 1987 / London ✦✦✦✦
One of the earliest female rap groups, they hit the big leagues with this debut that includes the pulsating "Push It" and the salacious "Tramp." — *John Floyd*

A Salt with a Deadly Pepa / 1988 / London ✦✦✦
A concept album musically, if not lyrically, this one fleshes out one terrific single, "Shake Your Thing," with a sharpening of the trio's sensibilities and talents. — *John Floyd*

A Blitz of Hits: The Hits Remixed / 1990 / London ✦✦

● **Blacks' Magic** / 1990 / London ✦✦✦✦
Another concept album, this time the themes celebrate Black education and awareness, with some concise feminism included. — *John Floyd*

Very Necessary / 1993 / PolyGram ✦✦✦✦
Driven by the ferociously sexy "Shoop," Salt-N-Pepa's latest album matches the drive of that hit as well as the best of their earlier classics, making it one of the best albums of their successful career. — *AMG*

Scarface
Vocals / Rap, Gangsta Rap
Brad "Scarface Akshen" Jordan was an original member of the Houston rap group the Geto Boys. He became the latest Geto Boy to go solo with *Mr. Scarface Is Back* in 1991. *The Diary* and *The World is Yours* followed in 1993 and 1995, the former featuring Ice Cube on one track. His albums have had some impact, but other than Bushwick Bill, most of the Geto Boys did better together than apart. — *Ron Wynn*

● **Mr. Scarface Is Back** / 1991 / Rap-A-Lot ✦✦✦
Scarface became the latest Geto Boy to try it solo with this 1991 album. He created a memorable message track in "A Minute to Pray and a Second to Die," a song that should have been a crossover sensation. Few gangsta numbers have more vividly and effectively chronicled the litany of hopelessness and violence plaguing the nation's inner cities. Other cuts, like "Body Snatcher," "Born Killer" and "Diary of a Madman," were less compelling and more chilling. — *Ron Wynn*

The Diary / 1993 / Rap-A-Lot ✦✦✦✦
Scarface's debut album after the break-up of his controversial band, the Geto Boys, *The Diary* is just that—a journal of the trials of inner-city life. Related with his rhythmic, deep-voiced delivery, this gangsta album has some of the deepest, darkest beats around, and one track with guest Ice Cube. — *John Bush*

The World Is Yours / 1995 / Rap-A-Lot ✦✦✦
The second album from former Geto Boy Scarface didn't contain any single cut as moving or hypnotic as "A Minute to Pray and a Second to Die," but it proved even more popular. It also was an indication that the Geto Boys were kaput, as everyone continued cutting solo albums, and talk of a proposed new Geto Boys album went from probable to possible to the back burner. — *Ron Wynn*

Schoolly D
Vocals / Rap
Opinion has been widely mixed about the merits of Philadelphia rapper Jesse B. Weaver, Jr., aka Schoolly D. Long before the debate about gangsta-rap lyrics became an easy way to get national newsprint, there was outrage over Schoolly D's explicit and undiluted narratives on inner-city strife. *Saturday Night* in 1987 and *Smoke Some Kill* in 1988 had city officials openly endorsing removal of the albums from record stores. He has continued in the same vein. Schoolly D's rather lackluster rapping style and repetitive material doesn't place him in the forefront of hip-hop creators, but he does merit mention (or blame, depending on your perspective) for being an early gangsta proponent. — *Ron Wynn*

Schoolly D / 1986 / Jive ✦✦

Saturday Night / 1987 / Jive ✦✦✦✦
Philadelphia rapper Schoolly D functions better as an absurdist commentator exploring the netherworld of inner city chaos than as a political philosopher or Afrocentric advocate. This 1987 album was among his best, precisely because he chose to be bizarre rather than prophetic and kept things freewheeling instead of didactic. — *Ron Wynn*

● **The Adventures of Schoolly D** / 1987 / Rykodisc ✦✦✦✦
This collects his early singles, cut before his bad-ass rep subverted whatever creativity he had left. — *John Floyd*

Smoke Some Kill / 1988 / Jive ✦✦

Am I Black Enough for You? / 1991 / Jive ✦✦✦
While Schoolly D's attempts to present Afrocentric philosophy and call for self-determination were commendable, he failed to present them in either a musically satisfying or lyrically convincing manner. This album did little beyond rip White society for its ills and injustices in a fashion merging the worst excesses of rambling propaganda and irrational nationalism. *—Ron Wynn*

How a Blackman Feels / Oct. 14, 1991 / Capitol ✦✦

Welcome to America / 1994 / Ruffhouse ✦✦✦
Schoolly D returns with a spare, dark attempt to recapture the gangsta audience he helped create back in the 1980s; it helps that the record contains the best music he has ever recorded, although the best moments can't hide the fact that Schoolly D doesn't have the lyrical grace of the rappers that followed his footsteps. *—Stephen Thomas Erlewine*

● **Jive Collection Series, Vol. 3** / 1995 / Jive ✦✦✦✦
According to the charts, Schoolly D never had any official hits, but a number of singles were underground sensations during the early '80s. *Jive Collection Series* compiles the bulk of these singles and throws in a handful of album tracks and lesser-known singles for good measure. The result is not only an ideal introduction to his music, but also a definitive retrospective of his glory days, when he was still a respected rapper within the hip-hop community. *—Stephen Thomas Erlewine*

Gangster's Story / Aug. 1996 / CTRA ✦✦✦✦
Gangster's Story functions as an excellent introduction to Schoolly D, one of the first gangsta rappers of the '80s. Although the production on the album has dated poorly and some of the songs sound tame compared to what came later, *Gangster's Story* showcases what Schoolly D was all about, both for better and for worse. It's not the kind of disc that will convert listeners to gangsta rap, but historians and aficionados will find it a useful collection. *—Stephen Thomas Erlewine*

Roxanne Shanté

Vocals / Rap
Roxanne Shanté (born Lolita Goodeh) was walking outside a New York housing project called the Queensbridge when she heard three men talking about how the trio U.T.F.O. had cancelled their appearance at a show they were promoting. Gooden offered to make a rap record that would get back at U.T.F.O., who'd previously recorded "Roxanne, Roxanne," a song about a woman too stuck up to notice them. The three, Tyrone Williams, disc jockey Mister Magic, and producer Marley Marl, took her up on the idea, with Marl producing "Roxanne's Revenge." The song was confrontational, sneering, boastful, and even borderline obscene, and it spawned 102 additional answer records. Since then, she's had two albums. The original "Roxanne's Revenge" was issued by Pop Art. Eventually U.T.F.O. threatened to sue Shanté for using their B-side as the musical foundation. She settled with them and recut the song with a different, though related, track.
Roxanne Shanté's fortunes have been thin since the heyday of the "Roxanne, Roxanne" rush. She did share a No. 1 R&B and a Top Ten pop hit with Rick James in 1986, "Loosey's Rap," but has otherwise found the going tough. *—Ron Wynn*

Bad Sister / 1989 / Cold Chillin' ✦✦✦✦
Her debut album doesn't quite live up to the promise of her early singles, which can be found on various rap compilations. *—Dan Heilman*

● **Greatest Hits** / 1995 / Cold Chillin' ✦✦✦✦

Shinehead

Vocals / Rap
Though born in London, Shinehead (born Carl Aiken) was raised in both Jamaica and the Bronx. His divided residences were reflected in his knowledge of reggae, rock, and rap, all of which he incorporated into his debut *Unity* for Elektra in 1988. Neither it nor the 1990 follow-up, *The Real Rock*, were able to generate much momentum, but they were forerunners to the hip-hop/reggae convergence later exploited by Shabba Ranks, the Mad Cobra and others. *—Ron Wynn*

● **Unity** / 1988 / Elektra ✦✦✦✦
A promising, original album. *—Dan Heilman*

The Real Rock / 1990 / Elektra ✦✦✦✦
Fine follow-up to *Unity*, with Shinehead sandwiching together melodies from classic R&B with rock and reggae inflection, and adding his own wild originals as well. *—Ron Wynn*

Sidewalk University / 1992 / Elektra ✦✦

Toddin' / 1995 / Elektra ✦✦

Sir Mix-A-Lot

Vocals / Rap
Sir Mix-A-Lot put Seattle on the rap map in the late '80s with catchy, comedic dramas drenched in b-boy culture and punctuated by his whiny vocals. Sir Mix-A-Lot vaulted into the spotlight and into controversy with the single "Baby Got Back." Not only was it an enormous pop and R&B hit, it triggered a backlash against what was widely viewed as both sexist and racist lyrics from Mix-A-Lot in his celebration of rear ends and putdown of women who lacked them. It helped make the *Mack Daddy* album one of 1992's biggest. *—John Floyd*

Swass / 1988 / Def American ✦✦✦
Sir Mix-A-Lot's debut album fluctuated between heavy bass tracks reminiscent of 2 Live Crew and heavy metal/rap fusions, like a heavier version of Run-D.M.C. At this point, he hadn't perfected his goofy, almost satiric, take on gangsta rap, although some tracks pointed the way toward his finest album, 1992's *Mack Daddy*. *—Stephen Thomas Erlewine*

Seminar / Mar. 1988 / Def American ✦✦✦

● **Mack Daddy** / Apr. 1991 / Def American ✦✦✦✦
Sir Mix-A-Lot scored a huge sleeper hit with his ridiculous paean to large buttocks, "Baby Got Back," in the summer of 1992. For those who want it, the rest of *Mack Daddy* offers more of the same—skeletal raps verging on parody. Sir Mix-A-Lot can barely rap, and his lyrics are full of posturing tales that never have a dose of reality. But this is the element that makes *Mack Daddy* fun, because Sir Mix-A-Lot tries so hard and sounds so silly. *—Stephen Thomas Erlewine*

Chief Booty Knocka / 1994 / Rhyme Cartel ✦✦✦

Return of the Bumpasaurus / Aug. 27, 1996 / Warner Brothers ✦✦✦
Sir Mix-A-Lot tries to return to the glory days of "Baby Got Back" with the salacious *Return of the Bumpasaurus*. Unfortunately, he lost the absurd sense of humor that distinguished *Mack Daddy*, nor has he developed a sense of funk that would make the lack of humor forgivable. It's slightly better than its predecessor *Chief Booty Knocka*, but *Return of the Bumpasaurus* does nothing to dispel the suspicion that Sir Mix-A-Lot is past his peak. *—Leo Stanley*

Sister Souljah

Vocals / Rap
Then-presidential candidate Bill Clinton helped turned a little-known rapper Sister Souljah briefly into a celebrity when he attacked her album *360 Degrees of Power*. During an interview Souljah called for African Americans to stop destroying their own property and turn their efforts on the White power brokers instead. Clinton accused her of appealing to hatred and urging Blacks to randomly target and kill Whites. The resulting controversy didn't sell many copies of her record, but did get her onto numerous talk shows and into many general interest magazines. She was eventually dropped by Epic when the record bombed. *—Ron Wynn*

● **360 Degrees of Power** / Jan. 1992 / Epic ✦✦✦✦
Seldom has something so mundane generated more controversy. Candidate Bill Clinton garnered some cheap positive publicity when he attacked Sister Souljah for allegedly encouraging African-Americans to blindly strike against Whites. If he had actually heard the CD, he would have known that Sister Souljah's raps and rhymes were so unappealing and delivered so flatly that few hip-hoppers, let alone any adults, would be paying much attention after the first few minutes. *—Ron Wynn*

Skee-Lo

Vocals / Rap
Skee-Lo is an anomaly in the rap world of the '90s: instead of spinning violent gangsta tales or extolling the virtues of marijuana, Skee's songs are profanity-free, good-time stories with a self-deprecating sense of humor. Skee-Lo was born in Poughkeepsie, NY, and moved to Riverside, CA, at age nine. He was turned on to rap by Kurtis Blow records, admiring their down-to-earth quality. His "I Wish" single, with a video that parodied *Forrest Gump*, became a huge hit on radio and MTV during the summer of 1995, and his identically titled debut album was released shortly thereafter. *—Steve Huey*

● **I Wish** / Jun. 27, 1995 / Sunshine/Scotti Bros. ✦✦✦✦

Slick Rick (Ricky Walters)

b. London, England
Vocals / Rap
Born in London and raised in the Bronx, Slick Rick carved himself a niche with his debut album *The Great Adventures of Slick Rick*, with a sly, drawling delivery and detailed and inventive storybook raps. The onetime partner of Doug E. Fresh, Slick Rick eventually wound up in jail following a shooting incident, and has been charged with attempted murder. *—John Floyd & Ron Wynn*

★ **The Great Adventures of Slick Rick** / 1989 / Def Jam ✦✦✦✦✦
Slick Rick first gained an audience by rapping on Doug E. Fresh's "La-Di-Da-Di" and "The Show," two songs that established him as a talent upon their release in 1985. It may have taken him three years to deliver his

full-length debut, but when *The Great Adventures of Slick Rick* arrived in 1988, it was a classic. What makes *The Great Adventures of Slick Rick* such a stunning achievement isn't necessarily the music—in retrospect, it's strong, but unexceptional, street funk—but Rick's rhyming. His style was fluid, but filled with odd cadences and an idiosyncratic phrasing. Furthermore, his storytelling technique is unparalleled, filled with detail and dramatic momentum; his skewed, slightly cartoonish viewpoint is nearly as influential. Unfortunately, his rampant misogyny and cool, amoralistic outlook became equally influential on '90s hip-hop. Even though Slick Rick released a series of mediocre follow-ups and spent an extended stay in prison, his failure to live up to the potential of *The Great Adventures* doesn't dilute the impact of the album at all. Years after its release, it still sounds fresh. —*Stephen Thomas Erlewine*

The Ruler's Back / 1991 / Def Jam ✦✦✦✦
A fine follow-up from a troubled soul. —*Ron Wynn*

Behind Bars / 1994 / Def Jam ✦✦

Snoop Doggy Dogg

Vocals / Rap, G-Funk
Rap's reigning superstar, Snoop Doggy Dogg, made his debut on Dr. Dre's *The Chronic*. His laconic, low-volume rap style struck a nerve with hip-hop audiences and his debut release, *Doggystyle*, became the first album ever by a new artist to make its initial entry onto the pop albums chart at No. 1. The album had sold over four million copies by the midpoint of 1994, and also generated plenty of controversy for its sexist and homophobic tendencies and explicit language. The record did shine the spotlight on some neglected acts and music from the '70s, notably the Dramatics, who appeared in one of Dogg's videos and backed him on one single. —*Ron Wynn*

Doggystyle / 1993 / Interscope ✦✦✦✦
Snoop Doggy Dogg's debut entered the charts at No. 1, and it has proven popular even though there's little departure musically or productionwise from Dr. Dre's release. *Doggystyle* features more of Dogg's partdrawl, part-spoken word narratives, but expresses a vision more paranoid than confident. Throughout the disc, Snoop has nightmares about being killed, and spends most of his time either defaming women or getting out of conflicts. The single "Who Am I (What's My Name)" uses nearly the same samples and bass lines as "Dre Day," and only Snoop's lean, almost casual sneers and rejoinders differentiate it from Dre's prior recording. He also throws a few darts at Eazy-E, but otherwise, this is prototype gangsta rap with Snoop's signature style as its major hook. —*Ron Wynn*

Snow

Vocals / Rap, Club/Dance
Canadian rapper Snow scored one of 1993's biggest hits with his single "The Informer." His patois-laced song soared up the pop and R&B charts, even though only hardcore reggae listeners could understand it without a lyric translation sheet. The album *12 Inches of Snow* also did well, with the second single, "Girl I've Been Hurt," becoming a hit. —*Ron Wynn*

● **12 Inches of Snow** / 1993 / East West ✦✦✦✦
Canadian dancehall rapper Snow became a celebrity when his single "Informer" soared to the top of the charts in 1993. The song shattered the myth that pop audiences wouldn't embrace any tune whose lyrics weren't in pristine English; when his video was released, it included a translation at the bottom. Unfortunately, the rest of this album was pleasant, instantly forgettable pop/reggae delivered in a manner that made Shabba Ranks sound like U-Roy. —*Ron Wynn*

Murder Love / 1995 / Elektra ✦✦✦
Snow's follow-up to his multimillion-selling debut isn't a departure from his pop-oriented dancehall, yet he doesn't have the songs to pull off another crossover hit. —*Stephen Thomas Erlewine*

Spice 1

Rap
Too $hort discovered rapper Spice 1, who was born in Texas before moving to California. His self-titled debut was as vivid and fatalistic a gangsta album as possible, and his hard-edged, angry, and pessimistic rapping style and tone only added to the despair emanating from the disc. He followed it with an even more bitter and nihilistic release, *187 He Wrote*, in 1993, complete with simulated gunfire. —*Ron Wynn*

Let It Be Known / 1988 / Triad ✦✦

Spice 1 / May 12, 1992 / Jive ✦✦✦
The sheer vulgarity, anger, coarseness, sexism, and horror unveiled, celebrated, and presented on Oakland rapper Spice 1's debut release can be frustrating and saddening. But more importantly, it should not be ignored. Spice 1 has done what "gangsta" rap's detractors should want; he's stripped away even the slightest veneer of glamour around the

atmosphere of casual violence, sexual exploitation, and drug selling he examines. His style, an appropriate mix of irony, disdain, acceptance, and confusion, never succumbs to the situation or seeks to justify or downplay the sense of impending doom. —*Ron Wynn*

● **187 He Wrote** / Sep. 28, 1993 / Jive ✦✦✦✦
Spice 1 continues his bleak, stripped-down version of gangsta rap with *187 He Wrote*, an album that can be harrowing and appalling. Throughout the record, the spare, funky production keeps the music engaging, making the disturbing lyrics cut even deeper. —*Stephen Thomas Erlewine*

AmeriKKKa's Nightmare / 1995 / Jive ✦✦✦

Full Metal Jacket / Nov. 7, 1995 / Jive ✦✦✦

1990 Sick / Dec. 1995 / Jive ✦✦✦
Spice 1 doesn't change his style much on *1990 Sick*, his third album. Building from a solid West Coast hip-hop base, Spice 1 adds raggamuffin and dancehall flourishes, which makes him distinctive as an MC. Much of the record suffers from unimaginative production and standard musical ideas, but Spice 1 is an engaging rapper—he is talented enough to disguise the weaknesses in the music with his verbal skills. —*Stephen Thomas Erlewine*

Stetsasonic

Rap, Hip-hop
One of the first rap groups to use a live band, Brooklyn's Stetsasonic formed in 1981 and were also among the first to promote a positive Black consciousness that found its ultimate expression in the so-called daisy-age sounds of De La Soul and the Jungle Brothers. The group consisted of DJs "Prince Paul" Huston and Leonard "Wise" Nelson, keyboardist/drummer/DJ Marvin "DBC" Nemley, and rappers Glenn "Daddy-O" Bolton, Martin "Delite" Wright, and Bobby "Fruitkwan" Simmons. Daddy-O and Delite founded the group as the Stetson Brothers, after the hat company, and began performing in New York hip-hop clubs, picking up other members along the way. Their debut, *On Fire*, was released in 1986, but it was the follow-up, *In Full Gear*, that brought them critical acclaim and an R&B hit, "Sally."

1991's *Blood, Sweat & No Tears* was considered by many to be their best and most diverse album, but Daddy-O decided that they had run out of ideas and broke up the band. He went on to work with Mary J. Blige, Queen Latifah, Big Daddy Kane, and the Red Hot Chili Peppers as a producer and remixer. Meanwhile, Prince Paul had already established himself as a producer through his work with De La Soul and Fine Young Cannibals, and later worked with Fruitkwan in the Gravediggaz. —*Steve Huey*

On Fire / 1986 / Tommy Boy ✦✦✦
There weren't many bands utilizing a hip-hop format in the mid-'80s, making Stetsasonic quite unique on the pop front in 1986. While their subject matter was invariably light and their raps now hopelessly tame and effete, they were groundbreaking at the time and retain a certain charm. —*Ron Wynn*

● **In Full Gear** / 1988 / Tommy Boy ✦✦✦✦
They're not "the world's only hip-hop band" anymore, but this sevenpiece group (real drums even!) paved the way. Their second disc documents their innovative best, culminating in the anthemic "Talkin' All That Jazz." —*John Floyd*

Blood, Sweat & No Tears / 1991 / Tommy Boy ✦✦✦

The Sugarhill Gang

Rap, Hip-hop
The Sugarhill Gang—Master Gee (born Guy O'Brien, 1963), Wonder Mike (born Michael Wright, 1958), and Big Bank Hank (born Henry Jackson, 1958)—were the first group to record rap music, releasing the popular single "Rapper's Delight" in 1979. —*William Ruhlmann*

● **Rapper's Delight: Hip Hop Remix** / 1980 / Sugar Hill ✦✦✦✦
The Sugarhill Gang's 1979 hit "Rapper's Delight" is arguably the first true rap song to gain widespread recognition and, as such, the progenitor of one of the major musical genres of the '80s. No wonder it doesn't sound dated yet. —*William Ruhlmann*

The Sugarhill Gang / 1980 / Sugar Hill ✦✦✦✦

8th Wonder / 1992 / Sugar Hill ✦✦✦
The Sugarhill Gang enjoyed its final moments in the spotlight with this 1982 LP. They scored two moderate hits with the title cut and "Apache," while continuing the old-school approach that initially gained mainstream attention and exposure for rap. —*Ron Wynn*

The Best of the Sugarhill Gang / Oct. 1995 / Sequel ✦✦✦

● **Best of the Sugarhill Gang** / Jul. 1996 / Rhino ✦✦✦✦
Sugarhill Gang's biggest hits are collected on this single-disc compilation. In addition to "Rapper's Delight"—the first rap single to reach the pop Top Ten—the group's seven other R&B hits are included on the disc,

plus three other singles that never made the charts. All of the songs are presented in their original 12-inch versions. Not all of the material is first-rate—in retrospect, the group's old-school groove tended to be a little simplistic, monotonous, and too polished, while their rhymes were frequently stilted and sometimes just outright silly—but this music, especially "Rapper's Delight," is important historically.

Most casual fans of old-school hip-hop will be content with purchasing "Rapper's Delight" on a various artists collection, but for those wanting to dig deeper into the trio's history, *The Best of Sugarhill Gang* is a definitive retrospective. —*Stephen Thomas Erlewine*

Terminator X & the Valley of the Jeep Beats

(Norman Rogers)

Vocals / Rap

Best known as the innovative DJ of Public Enemy, Terminator X (born Norman Rogers) also pursued a secondary solo career beginning in 1991. His debut, *Terminator X and the Valley of the Jeep Beets*, was not a radical departure from his work with PE and consisted largely of dance tracks, although there were some vocal contributions from Andrew 13 and Sister Souljah. Prior to the release of his second solo album in 1994, Terminator X suffered two broken legs in a motorcycle accident, but has since recovered. —*Steve Huey*

● **Terminator X & the Valley of the Jeep Beats** / 1991 / Ral ◆◆◆◆
Public Enemy's turntable whiz takes center stage on a debut that spans the gamut of contemporary Black pop, from scalding hip-hop to reggae. —*John Floyd*

Terminator X and the Godfathers of Threatt / 1994 / Rush ◆◆

3rd Bass

Rap

Along with the Beastie Boys, 3rd Bass stand as the rare White hip-hop act that's actually won respect and credibility among the rap hardcore. Pete Nice, one-time English major at Columbia whose radio program "Top of the Hip-hop" was unceremoniously canceled by the purportedly progressive WKCR-FM, teamed with MC Serch to offer devastating putdowns of the hip-hop lifestyle and worldview. They have since disbanded, but their two albums were definitive, if at times uneven. —*Ron Wynn*

● **The Cactus Album** / 1989 / Def Jam ◆◆◆◆
With their first album, 3rd Bass turned in a surrealistically funky record of uproarious jokes, cutting social criticism, and eclectic music, drawing from Stax and Blood, Sweat & Tears. —*Stephen Thomas Erlewine*

Derelicts of Dialect / 1991 / Def Jam ◆◆◆
After countless false starts and an EP/remix filler, 3rd Bass finally issued their second album. It was an impressive statement, with a devastating attack on Vanilla Ice via the cut "Pop Goes the Weasel." —*Ron Wynn*

Tim Dog

Vocals

Bronx rapper Tim Dog (born Tim Blair) fired fresh shots in the long-simmering hip-hop coastal warfare with his 1991 album *Penicillin on Wax*. His single "F— Compton" triggered answers and comebacks in West and East Coast circles, and helped his album become an underground sensation, though not a major hit. Tim Dog's alternately leering and fiery tone, with his confrontational diatribes and cutting beats were even more vigorous on the follow-up *Do or Die* in 1993. —*Ron Wynn*

● **Penicillin on Wax** / Nov. 12, 1991 / Ruffhouse ◆◆◆◆
Driven by the furious "F— Compton," Tim Dog's debut album offered some of the hardest gangsta rap of 1991, as well as some of the worst; the best moments make *Penicillin on Wax* worthwhile. —*Stephen Thomas Erlewine*

Do or Die / 1993 / Ruffhouse ◆◆◆
Tim Dog fired more shots in the constant East vs. West Coast war. His second CD was just as defiant and disrespectful as his debut. Dog once more refused to moderate his chip-on-the-shoulder attitude, the results sometimes being mildly amusing and extremely offensive on other occasions. —*Ron Wynn*

TLC

Hip-hop, Urban

Comprised of Tionne "T-Boz" Watkins, Rozonda "Chilli" Thomas, and Lisa "Left Eye" Lopes, the Atlanta, Georgia-based hip-hop trio TLC released their first album, *Ooooooh . . . On the TLC Tip*, in early 1992 to immediate success. Masterminded by the successful R&B producer/singer Pebbles, the group had three consecutive Top Ten hits in 1992, including "Ain't 2 Proud 2 Beg," "What About Your Friends," and "Baby-Baby-Baby." Shortly before the release of their second album, Lopes was arrested for burning down the house of her boyfriend, Andre Rison, a

member of the Atlanta Falcons. Lopes' arrest didn't affect the sales of their second album, 1994's *CrazySexyCool*, which featured three No. 1 one singles and sold over four million copies. —*Stephen Thomas Erlewine*

Ooooooohhh . . . On the TLC Tip / 1992 / La Face ◆◆◆
TLC's debut album was a well-produced but inconsistent effort, with the three hit singles—"Ain't 2 Proud 2 Beg," "Baby-Baby-Baby," and "What About Your Friends"—being the catchiest and most memorable songs on the album. —*Sara Sytsma*

● **CrazySexyCool** / 1994 / LaFace ◆◆◆◆
On their second album, TLC downplays their overt rap connections, recording a smooth, seductive collection of contemporary soul reminiscent of both Philly soul and Prince, powered by new jack and hip-hop beats. Lisa Lopes contributes the occasional rap, but the majority of *CrazySexyCool* belongs to Tionne Watkins and Rozonda Thomas. While they're not the most accomplished vocalists—they have a tendency to be just slightly off-key—the material they sing is consistently strong. As the cover of Prince's "If I Was Your Girlfriend" indicates, TLC favors erotic, mid-tempo funk. Yet the group removes any of the psychosexual complexities of Prince's material, leaving a batch of sexy material that just sounds good, especially the hit singles. Both "Creep" and "Red Light Special" have a deep groove that accentuates the slinky hooks, but it's "Waterfalls," with its gently insistent horns and guitar lines and instantly memorable chorus, that ranks as one of the classic R&B songs of the '90s. —*Stephen Thomas Erlewine*

Tone-Loc

Vocals / Rap

Tone-Loc (born Tony Smith) soared from obscurity into pop stardom in 1989 when his hoarse voice and unmistakable delivery made the song "Wild Thing" (using a sample from Van Halen's "Jamie's Cryin'") a massive hit. The song was co-written by Marvin Young, better known as Young MC, as was the second single smash "Funky Cold Medina." The album *Loc-ed After Dark* became the second rap release to top the pop charts. Tone-Loc expanded his horizons into acting in 1992 and 1993, appearing a few times on the Fox sitcom *Roc*. He was also in the films *Posse* and *Ace Ventura: Pet Detective*. —*Ron Wynn*

● **Loc-ed After Dark** / 1989 / Delicious Vinyl ◆◆◆◆
An engaging debut, it contains both "Wild Thing" and "Funky Cold Medina." —*Dan Heilman*

Cool Hand Loc / 1992 / Delicious Vinyl ◆◆◆
Tone-Loc's second album didn't generate the pop appeal or quiet the rumblings and disdain he had earned from the hardcore audience for his double-platinum smash *Loc-ed After Dark*. In fact, things were so commercially uneventful that Loc began putting more energy into acting, securing television and film roles with relish. —*Ron Wynn*

Too $hort

Rap

Oakland rapper ,Todd Shaw, has become a huge star without getting any pop airplay or crossover support. He's mined the mack (pimp) routine effectively, turning out albums routinely loaded with plenty of X-rated sexual escapades and commentary or variations on a day in the life of a player/pimp. He did score one classic sociopolitical number, his take on "The Ghetto," and has also done a good anticensorship bit with Ice Cube on "Ain't Nothin' but a Word to Me."

Too $hort's eighth release *Get in Where You Fit In* had plenty of pimping, explicit language and commentary on players. The unrepentant $hort maintained he had no plans to moderate his language to accomodate those who protested that his lyrics demeaned African-American women. He also established headquarters in Atlanta, building a studio and home there. —*Ron Wynn*

Life Is . . . Too $hort / 1988 / Jive ◆◆◆◆
Essential, bawdy, and often offensive and troubling. —*Ron Wynn*

Born to Mack / 1989 / Jive ◆◆◆
A breakout release. —*Ron Wynn*

● **Short Dog's in the House** / 1990 / Jive ◆◆◆◆
A tremendous combination of outrage, anger, and morbid outlook. —*Ron Wynn*

Shorty the Pimp / Jul. 14, 1992 / Jive ◆◆◆

Get in Where You Fit In / 1993 / Jive ◆◆
Although he tries to cop part of the P-Funk inspired gangsta rap, Too $hort sounds lost and dated on this album, which is overlong, sample-reliant, grotesquely misogynist, and musically muddled. —*AMG*

Greatest Hits, Vol. 1: The Player Years, 1983-1988 / 1993 / In-A-Minute ◆◆◆◆
If you've never read the collected works of Chester Himes or Iceberg Slim, simply run through this Too $hort anthology and you'll have the general idea. Although never an inventive rapper or clever composer of

rhymes, Too $hort was smart enough to find his niche and stick to it. Most people who continually mined the pimp arena quickly become merely tedious; Too $hort became both tedious and profitable. *—Ron Wynn*

Cocktails / 1995 / Jive ♦♦

Gettin' It (Album Number Ten) / Jun. 18, 1996 / Dangerous ♦♦♦

A Tribe Called Quest

Rap

The junior part of the Native Tongues—the prolific Afrocentric family from New York that also includes the Jungle Brothers and De La Soul—this foursome displayed intriguing subject variety on their debut, covering everything from social ills to the adventures of a shaggy dog and problems with lice. Their second effort, *The Low End Theory*, reflected through arrangements and sensibility the influence of an emerging jazz/rap stylistic coalition, and yielded a huge hit in "Scenario." A Tribe Called Quest modified their jazz ties with *Midnight Marauders* in 1993. Though it still had an improvisational undergirding, the raps were tougher, the production tighter and the beats more unpredictable and varied. In the summer of 1996, the group released their third album, *Beats, Rhymes and Life*. *—Ron Wynn*

People's Instinctive Travels and the Paths of Rhythm / 1990 / Jive ♦♦♦

People's Instinctive Travels and the Paths of Rhythm is a brilliant concept with jazzy edges and tense, biting narratives. It's a visionary release blending the improvisatory force of jazz with the technological wizardry and verbal inventiveness of hip-hop. *—Ron Wynn*

★ **The Low End Theory** / 1991 / Jive ♦♦♦♦♦

A Tribe Called Quest came into their own with their second album, *The Low End Theory*. Where their debut only hinted at the group's musical depths, *The Low End Theory* explodes all expectations—it's the first album that successfully fuses jazz and hip-hop together. Not only does the music ebb and flow like the best soul-jazz and hard bop (partially due to the presence of bassist Ron Carter), so do the rhymes of Q-Tip and Phife, as evidenced by such hit singles as "Check the Rhime" and "Award Tour." Furthermore, the album doesn't feel forced or pretentious—it flows naturally, as the rhythms and rhymes play off of each other. Others tried to replicate its sound and Tribe tried desperately to duplicate its magic, but *The Low End Theory* stands not only as the group's finest moment, but the pinnacle of the jazz/hip-hop fusion. *—Stephen Thomas Erlewine*

Midnight Marauders / 1993 / Jive ♦♦♦♦

Midnight Marauders was an intriguing and smartly paced collection that ranged from descriptive verbal essays on city life to confrontational taunts, comic expositions, denunciations, and even quasi-religious theorizing. While their celebrated hip-hop/jazz roots were often evident, the group also utilized fusion, urban contemporary, Afro-Latin and funk samples, and Q-Tip's rap style could be cool and deadpan, reflective, analytical, and satirical, or disgusted and angry. There was precious little "gangsta" posturing or sexist rhetoric, and such numbers as "Sucka Nigga," "God Lives Through," "Electric Relaxation," and "Award Tour" were cleverly delivered and brilliantly composed. *—Ron Wynn*

Beats, Rhymes and Life / Jul. 1996 / Jive ♦♦♦♦

With their fourth album *Beats, Rhymes and Life*, A Tribe Called Quest manages to be one of the few hip-hop acts to successfully age by pushing both their music and their lyrics in new directions. Stylistically, the record is closest to its immediate predecessor, *Midnight Marauders*, in the sense that the group's jazz-rap fusion is downplayed and the beat stays surprisingly hard throughout the album. What distinguishes *Beats, Rhymes and Life* from *Marauders* is a deeper sense not only of eclecticism, but of spirituality and maturity. Shortly before the album was written and recorded, Q-Tip converted to Islam and the religion's ideals are an undercurrent in nearly every track on the album. But what really stands out is Tip's unease with the transience of the youth-oriented hip-hop scene and his own urges to settle down. Unlike most rappers, he confronts these feelings in the music, by writing lyrics and helping to create music that illustrates the contradictions of growing old with hip-hop. And by tackling the issue head-on, A Tribe Called Quest sound fresh and suggest that it is possible to sustain a career in rap as you approach a full decade of recording, after all. *—Leo Stanley*

2 Live Crew

Rap, Hip-hop

This Florida rap band was organized, supervised, and conceived by Luther Campbell, a promoter, record label owner, and rapper, as an updated version of oldtime X-rated party performers. Campbell's production consists of heavy doses of booming synthesized bass, scratching effects, samples, and explicit sex raps and leers. From their beginnings in 1986, the notoriety of Campbell and the group grew in direct proportion to the lewdness of the material. As their songs attained more

national prominence, Campbell has become part of a national controversy involving censorship and lyrics. He's issued two solo records.

2 Live Crew hasn't found the going quite as smooth in the '90s. They've continued recording for Luke Records, but haven't scored as much success with such releases as *Move Somethin'* and *Sports Weekend*. Founder Luther Campbell issued both clean and dirty versions in an effort to defuse criticism, but 2 Live Crew's detractors have moved on to gangsta-rap and the group's most recent releases have been almost ignored. They resurfaced in 1994 as The New 2 Live Crew, releasing *Back at Your Ass for the Nine 4*. It did well briefly, peaking at No. 9 on the R&B chart. But their brand of X-rated humor seemed almost tame compared to the mix of explicit sex and violence available on more hardcore gangsta-rap sessions, while the Jamaican toasters like Shabba Ranks or The Mad Cobra outdistanced them in creative lewdness. *—Ron Wynn*

2 Live Crew Is What We Are / 1986 / Luke ♦♦♦

The record that launched the whole phenomenon. If the puerile language and vulgarity had been allowed to run its course without censorship attempts, this lunacy might have ended right here. The production does provide good examples of Miami "bass" music. *—Ron Wynn*

Move Somethin' / 1987 / Luke ♦♦♦

Luther Campbell hits on the ingenious idea of issuing clean and dirty versions simultaneously in an ill-fated attempt to take censorship heat off. The clean version lacks guts; the dirty version lacks taste. *—Ron Wynn*

As Nasty as They Wanna Be / 1989 / Luke ♦♦♦♦

Not only did it cause all the legal controversies, but *As Nasty as They Wanna Be* is the quintessential 2 Live Crew album, in all their tasteless, bass-driven glory. *—AMG*

Banned in the USA / 1990 / Atlantic ♦♦♦

This offers an interesting, if somewhat perverse version of Springsteen's "Born in the USA" as the title track and underlying theme. The rest is an erratic, meandering blend of X-rated sexual comments and quasi-political rhetoric. *—Ron Wynn*

Sports Weekend: As Nasty as They Wanna Be, Pt. 2 / 1991 / Luke ♦♦

● **Greatest Hits** / 1992 / Luke ♦♦♦♦

Full of the low-minded humor that made this Miami outfit notorious throughout the country, *Greatest Hits* does contain the best material 2 Live Crew ever recorded; it is all the 2 Live Crew most will ever need to hear. *—Stephen Thomas Erlewine*

Back at Your Ass for the Nine-4 / Feb. 8, 1994 / Luke ♦♦

2Pac (Tupac Shakur)

Rap

Rapper Tupac Amaru Shakur threatened to supplant Luther Campbell and Ice-T as the most demonized figure in hip-hop. The former Digital Underground member became a solo performer with *2Pacalypse Now*, then his status soared following a critically acclaimed performance in *Juice*. His follow-up album also earned a hit with "Keep Your Head Up." But Shakur generated much more negative publicity for several incidents, one of which earned him a criminal record. He was convicted of assault for attacking the Hughes brothers, who'd fired him from the film *Menace II Society*. He was also awaiting trials on other charges stemming from various incidents. This hadn't stopped his acting career; there were appearances in the films *Poetic Justice* with Janet Jackson and *Above the Rim*.

While he was serving his jail sentence for sexual battery in early 1995, 2Pac released *Me Against the World*, which entered the US charts at No. 1 and spawned the Top 10 pop single, "Dear Mama." 2Pac was released from prison in the summer of 1995. In early 1996, he released *All Eyez On Me*, the first double-disc set of newly recorded material in hip-hop history. It entered the charts at No. 1. Shakur died in September 1996 of gunshot wounds. *—Ron Wynn*

2Pacalypse Now / 1992 / Interscope ♦♦♦

Few expected former Digital Underground member Tupac Amaru Shakur to become hip-hop enemy number one when he made his solo debut with this 1992 album. Songs like "Crooked Ass Nigga" and "Tha' Lunatic" might have hinted that storm clouds were on the horizon, but there were also excellent advocacy numbers like "Words of Wisdom" and "Young Black Male." This didn't make him a celebrity, but it put Tupac Shakur on the road to stardom. *—Ron Wynn*

Strictly 4 My N.I.G.G.A.Z. / 1993 / Atlantic ♦♦♦♦

Tupac Shakur not only became a crossover acting and singing success with this release, but found himself on police blotters coast-to-coast and the designated demon of anti-rap forces nationwide. This disc yielded a couple of hits, with the fiery message track "Keep Your Head Up" particularly outstanding. Unfortunately, several ugly personal incidents, among them a public physical fight with film directors the Hughes brothers, allegations of violent attacks on an off-duty police officer, and sexual misconduct threatened to derail a promising multimedia career. —*Ron Wynn*

● **Me Against the World** / Mar. 14, 1995 / Interscope ✦✦✦✦
Released just after 2Pac began serving a jail sentence for sexual assault, *Me Against the World* became a No. 1 hit and it's fairly easy to see why—the record is impeccably produced, with rumbling, funky bass and rhythms that flow throughout the entire album. 2Pac's rhymes are so considered and graceful that it's hard to believe the same man was imprisoned. —*David Jehnzen*

All Eyez On Me / Feb. 13, 1996 / Death Row ✦✦✦✦
As the first double-disc collection of original rap material released, 2Pac's first post-prison album, *All Eyez on Me*, would have been notable, even if the rapper didn't deliver the musical goods. However, he has made a messy, sprawling album that illustrates his talents quite effectively. Certainly, the album could have been trimmed down to one disc, but his ambition is admirable at a time when even the big hip-hop artists play it safe. Even with the abundance of mediocre and unfinished material, there are enough prime tracks—from the G-Funk update of the Dr. Dre duet "California Love" to his smooth soul experiments—to make the record an engaging, fascinating listen, even if it doesn't have the consistency of *Me Against the World*. —*Stephen Thomas Erlewine*

Ultramagnetic MC's

Rap
Arising from the Boogie Down Bronx in the mid-'80s as a far-flung hip-hop trio with a heap of new ideas to try out, Ultramagnetic's Kool Keith, Ced Gee, and DJ Moe Love occupy something of a singular place in the old-school pantheon. Combining funk-heavy tracks with jeep-rocking beats and obscure lyrical references, the UMCs have a list of firsts to their credit: the first group to employ a sampler as an instrument, the first to feature extensive use of live instrumentation . . . the first to feature a former psychiatric patient (Keith) on the mic. Early singles like "Something Else" and "Space Groove" were block party staples and created waves in the underground, eventually landing the group on the disco-dominated Next Plateau label, where they released their underappreciated debut. The following years found the group shuffling from label to label, releasing albums on Mercury and Wild Pitch before splitting to pursue various projects. A reunion project is in the works. —*Sean Cooper*

Critical Beatdown / 1988 / Next Plateau ✦✦✦✦
Another one for the unfortunately crowded "waaaay too far ahead of its time to be commercially successful" file, the UMCs' debut was loaded with deep, crushing breakbeats and musical ideas only recently being excavated by hip-hop. Keith's rhymes are a wonderfully confused lot, and DJ Moe Love's turntable niceties round out an all-time classic. —*Sean Cooper*

Funk Your Head Up / 1992 / Mercury ✦✦✦

The Four Horsemen / Aug. 10, 1993 / Wild Pitch ✦✦✦✦
Back on track and on yet another label. The last album by the group before Keith would head off on his solo Doctor Octagon tangent. —*Sean Cooper*

● **Basement Tapes: 1984-1990** / 1995 / Tuff City ✦✦✦✦

Us3

Rap, Hip-hop, Jazz
Jazz/hip-hop fusion collective Us3 scored a major hit in 1994 with "Cantaloop (Flip Fantasia)," a song that displayed the group's fondness for sampling classic recordings on the Blue Note label (in this case, Herbie Hancock's "Cantaloupe Island"). The group was founded in London in 1991 when concert promoter and jazz writer Geoff Wilkinson met Mel Simpson, who was writing music for television shows and ad jingles and had once played keyboards with John Mayall. The two produced an independent single, "Where Will We Be in the 21st Century?," which sold less than 250 copies. In 1992, their song "The Band That Played the Boogie" attracted the attention of Blue Note owner Capitol Records, which gave Simpson and Wilkinson free rein to sample anything over the catalog. The two immediately went to work, hiring several musicians and rappers Kobie Powell and Rahsaan Kelly, with Tukka Yoot joining later. The sessions resulted in the hit "Cantaloop" and the album *Hand on the Torch*. The group toured Japan and Europe, gradually weaning itself away from using samples in a live setting, and played a well-received show at the 1993 Montreux Jazz Festival. *Hand on the Torch* was ignored by most jazz publications, but was chosen Album of the Year by Japan's *Swing Journal*, and the group were named Jazz Musicians of the Year by Britain's *Independent*. —*Steve Huey*

● **Hand on the Torch** / 1993 / Blue Note ✦✦✦✦
Hip-hop/jazzers Us3 have forged the most elaborate union between the styles since the early days of Gang Starr and A Tribe Called Quest. Blue Note's vast catalog gives them a huge advantage over several similar

groups in terms of source material, and classic sounds by Art Blakey, Horace Silver and Herbie Hancock provide zest and fiber to their narratives. Indeed, when things falter, it's because the raps aren't always that creative. They are serviceable and sometimes catchy, but too often delivered without the snazzy touches or distinctive skills that make Quest and Gang Starr's material top-notch. But when words and music mesh, as on "Cantaloop" or "The Darkside," Us3 show how effectively hip-hop and jazz can blend. —*Ron Wynn*

U.T.F.O.

Rap
Doctor Ice, the Kangol Kid, and the Educated Rapper (later joined by Mix-Master Ice) formed the Brooklyn group Untouchable Force Organization (U.T.F.O.) by dreaming up a tune about a gorgeous woman oblivious to their charms and appeals. "Roxanne, Roxanne" dominated the airwaves for much of 1984 and 1985, yielding eventually over 100 answer versions. Their first albums included the hit single plus "Roxanne Part 2" and "The Real Roxanne." The group's popularity and influence waned as the Roxanne fad peaked, and subsequent releases had limited appeal. —*Ron Wynn*

● **UTFO** / 1985 / Elektra ✦✦✦✦
The Brooklyn production/performance combo U.T.F.O. shot to fame in the mid-'80s with their story about "Roxanne, Roxanne." It generated a flood of answer songs, started the careers of both Roxanne Shanté and the Real Roxanne, and for a moment put U.T.F.O. in the thick of hip-hop and urban contemporary music. Unfortunately, they really weren't that gifted, as they showed on such singles as "Bite It," "Beats and Rhymes," and "Lisa Lips." They're now rightly regarded as novelty/one-hit wonders. —*Ron Wynn*

Skeezer Pleezer / 1986 / Elektra ✦✦✦
Reality began to set in for U.T.F.O. with their second album in 1986. They got a little buzz from the single "We Work Hard," but were essentially already in stylistic retreat as the gimmick tag they picked up for the success of "Roxanne, Roxanne" was proving difficult to shake. It didn't help that songs like "Bad Luck Barry" and "House Will Rock" didn't exactly inspire generations of aspiring rappers. —*Ron Wynn*

Lethal / 1987 / Select ✦✦

Doin' It! / 1989 / Select ✦✦

Bag It & Bone It / 1990 / Jive ✦✦

Vanilla Ice

Vocals / Rap
With his hit single "Ice Ice Baby" and its accompanying album, *To the Extreme*, Vanilla Ice became the second White rapper to top the charts. Unlike the Beastie Boys, he didn't have any street credibility, so the Miami-born rapper decided to invent some of his own, claiming he had a seriously violent gangster past. Nevertheless, "Ice Ice Baby" became a No. 1 hit late in 1990, thanks to the pulsating bass riff from David Bowie and Queen's "Under Pressure." *To the Extreme* also went to the top of the charts, spending 16 weeks at No. 1 and selling over seven million copies. Ice began filming a feature film, *Cool as Ice*, in the spring of 1990, but by the time the film came out in the fall, his star had fallen dramatically; *To the Extreme* was at No. 1 longer than the soundtrack to *Cool as Ice* was on the charts.

Sensing that his time had passed, Vanilla Ice took a couple years off, re-emerging in 1994 with *Mind Blowin'.* Dispensing with the pop-rap formula of his debut, the rapper adopted the lazy, rolling funk of Cypress Hill, as well that trio's obsession with pot. The album was a commercial disaster, disappearing from sight immediately after its release. —*Stephen Thomas Erlewine*

● **To the Extreme** / 1990 / SBK ✦✦✦✦
On the strength of the incessantly catchy single "Ice Ice Baby," *To the Extreme* was an enormous success, holding the No. 1 slot for 16 weeks and selling over seven million copies in America. Apart from that single and a cover of Wild Cherry's "Play That Funky Music," the album was unmemorable, with limp beats and tepid rhymes. —*Stephen Thomas Erlewine*

Extremely Live / Mar. 1991 / SBK ✦

Mind Blowin' / 1994 / SBK ✦✦

Whodini

Rap, Hip-hop
Coming out of the fertile early-'80s New York rap scene, Whodini was one of the first rap groups to add a straight R&B twist to their music, thus laying the groundwork for the New Jack Swing movement. The group consisted of rappers Jalil Hutchins and John "Ecstasy" Fletcher, adding legendary DJ Drew "Grandmaster Dee" Carter, known for being able to scratch records with nearly every part of his body, in 1986. Whodini made its name with good-humored songs like "Magic's Wand"

(the first rap song to feature an accompanying video), "The Haunted House of Funk" (a rewrite of "Monster Mash"), and "Freaks Come out at Night," and their live shows were the first rap concerts to feature official dancers (U.T.F.O. members Dr. Ice and Kangol Kid). Following 1987's *Open Sesame*, Whodini went on hiatus due to problems with their record company, as well as to concentrate on new families. The group attempted a comeback in 1991 with *Bag-a-Trix* without much success, in spite of receiving their due as rap innovators. —*Steve Huey*

Whodini / 1983 / Jive ✦✦✦
More singers than straight rappers, Jali Hutchins and Ecstasy made a successful conversion to hip-hop, scoring two hits on their debut with "Rap Attack" and "The Haunted House of Funk," a reworking of "The Monster Mash." —*Ron Wynn*

Escape / 1984 / Jive ✦✦✦✦
Their best release, containing "Friends," "Freaks Come out at Night," and "Big Mouth." Memorable tunes and state-of-the-art (for that time) production. —*Ron Wynn*

Back in Black / 1986 / Jive ✦✦✦
Signs of stagnation and decay are evident, though the cut "Funky Beat" forestalled the decline for a short while. —*Ron Wynn*

Open Sesame / 1987 / Jive ✦✦
★ **Greatest Hits** / 1990 / Jive ✦✦✦✦✦
A worthwhile compilation that shows what all the fuss was about regarding this unit in the early '80s. —*Ron Wynn*

Bag-a-Trix / 1991 / MCA ✦✦
● **Jive Collection Series, Vol. 1** / 1995 / Jive ✦✦✦✦
Whodini's installment of the *Jive Collection Series* contains all of the group's groundbreaking singles from the early '80s, plus a selection of lesser-known album tracks and singles, making it an ideal introduction to the group. —*Stephen Thomas Erlewine*

Wreckx-N-Effect

Rap, New Jack R&B
Wreckx-N-Effect earned a huge crossover smash with the single "Rump Shaker" off their 1992 album *Hard or Smooth.* The accompanying video with its array of shapely women following the directions of the lead singer generated nearly as much heat as Sir Mix-A-Lot's "Baby Got Back." It also helped the group secure a platinum certification, something it hardly seemed they'd earn from their Motown debut *Wreckx-N-Effect* in 1990. Markell Riley, brother of super producer Teddy Riley, was part of the rap ensemble along with Aquil Davidson and Brandon Mitchell; Mitchell was killed in a 1990 shooting. —*Ron Wynn*

● **Wreckx-N-Effect** / 1991 / Atlantic ✦✦✦✦
A striking mix of go-go funk and New Jack Swing is highlighted by "New Jack Swing," an anthem for the new beat. Produced by Teddy Riley, who created that new beat with Guy. —*John Floyd*

Hard or Smooth / 1992 / MCA ✦✦✦✦
Although nothing else on *Hard or Smooth* compares to the monster groove of "Rump Shaker," the rest of the album offers enough beats to satisfy most fans of the hit singles. —*AMG*

Wu-Tang Clan

Rap
When the Wu-Tang Clan appeared in 1993, the release of their debut album *Enter the 36 Chambers* sent shock waves throughout the hip-hop community. With their sparse, dark funk and bracingly violent martial arts imagery, the group immediately attracted a following. However, the band self-destructed within a year of their record's release, with rappers Method Man and Ol' Dirty Bastard going on to solo success in their own right. —*Stephen Thomas Erlewine*

★ **Enter the Wu-Tang (36 Chambers)** / Nov. 1993 / Loud ✦✦✦✦
The Wu-Tang Clan's debut album *Enter the Wu-Tang (36 Chambers)* wasn't an across-the-board blockbuster like Dr. Dre's *The Chronic,* the other seminal hip-hop record of the early '90s, but its impact was just as widespread. Where Dr. Dre was loose, hedonistic and funky, the Wu-Tang was tense, scary and funny. *Enter the Wu-Tang* is a series of intense, surrealistic soundscapes that draws equally from pop culture, martial arts, and gangsta traditions. Other hardcore gangstas simply boasted about their hardness—the Wu-Tang clan boasted, but they supported their inventive rhymes with stripped-down samples and lean, menacing beats that evoked their gritty, urban surroundings more effectively than their words. And that's what makes *Enter the Wu-Tang* so effective—the group's unique lyrical obsessions and the distinctive, innovative production techniques of Prince Rakeem. After releasing this pioneering debut, all the members pursued solo careers that explored various elements of *Enter the Wu-Tang* in more depth—and, occasionally, with more effective results—but this contains the roots of everything that followed. —*Stephen Thomas Erlewine*

Yo Yo

Vocals / Rap
Yolanda Whitaker has been among the most sophisticated and unpredictable female rappers around. She doesn't take an overtly feminist tack but urges young women to show sexual restraint and use their minds as well as their bodies. She's released two records as a leader. Yo Yo came out less embracing and more confrontational on *You Better Ask Somebody,* her 1993 album. There was little compromise in her rapping, or the record's mood. Where before she'd sometimes seemed conciliatory, this time she was stark and combative, particularly in her demands for respect. —*Ron Wynn*

Make Way for the Motherlode / 1991 / East West ✦✦✦✦
Intelligent, forceful, and affirmative rap from a woman whose cadence, tone, and delivery are as hard as any man on either coast and anywhere in-between. —*Ron Wynn*

● **Black Pearl [uncensored]** / 1992 / East West ✦✦✦✦
Yo Yo's positive (but not simplistic or naive) messages regarding female sexuality, self-esteem and achievement were grounded in hard raps and thudding beats on this album, a complete and effective production. Unfortunately, it seemed that only cutesy material like "You Can't Play With My Yo-Yo" from her first release could get the widespread support and attention necessary for a hit. —*Ron Wynn*

Young MC

Rap
Intelligent and middle-class, rapper Marvin Young earned a degree in economics from USC, where he met Michael Ross and Matt Dike, cofounders of the fledgling Delicious Vinyl rap label. He made his debut as Young MC on the single "I Let 'Em Know." In 1989, Young collaborated with Tone Loc on "Wild Thing," the first Top Ten pop hit for a Black rapper, and the follow-up smash "Funky Cold Medina." Young MC stepped out on his own later in the year with the Top Ten smash "Bust a Move," a good-natured examination of romantic successes and failures spiced by his sense of humor and quick-tongued rapping. The song won a Grammy for Best Rap Performance, and its strong pop appeal helped the attendant album *Stone Cold Rhymin'* go platinum. The follow-up, "Principal's Office," was a humorous, everyday high school tale resembling a Chuck Berry plot and also climbed into the Top 40.

Following Young MC's success, he split acrimoniously from Delicious Vinyl, citing restrictions on his work and unwanted tinkering with his album; the label sued him for breach of contract and eventually settled out of court. Young signed with Capitol and released *Brainstorm* in 1991, expanding into message tracks promoting personal responsibility. The album didn't fare as well, and by 1993, audience tastes had shifted toward harder-edged hip-hop, rendering *What's the Flavor?* a flop. —*Steve Huey*

Brainstorm / 1989 / Capitol ✦✦✦
● **Stone Cold Rhymin'** / 1989 / Delicious Vinyl ✦✦✦✦
Young MC's first album was a major hit, featuring pop-rap crossover classics like "Bust a Move" and "Principal's Office." With his friendly, clever rhyming and a warm, funky production dominating the album, *Stone Cold Rhymin'* was not only Young MC's most popular album, but also his best. —*Stephen Thomas Erlewine*

What's the Flavor? / Jun. 7, 1993 / Capitol ✦✦✦
On his third album, Young MC was trying to recapture his audience, adding elements of jazz-rap—thanks to the production of A Tribe Called Quest's Ali Shaheed—to his pop-oriented style. While it didn't rocket him back to the top of the charts, the results were agreeable and likeable, with only a couple of embarrassing tracks. —*Stephen Thomas Erlewine*

Various Artists

Big Phat Ones of Hip Hop, Vol. 1 / 1995 / BOXtunes ✦✦✦✦✦
Big Phat Ones of Hip Hop, Vol. 1 is a collection of big hip-hop hits from the mid '90s, as presented by the Box video network. It's one of the best collections of rap singles of its era, featuring hits by Coolio, Warren G., Salt 'n' Pepa, Notorious B.I.G., and R. Kelly. —*Stephen Thomas Erlewine*

☆ **Def Jam Classics, Vol. 1** / 1991 / Def Jam ✦✦✦✦✦
A useful overview of the seminal rap label, it includes their best artists and some sumptuous rarities. —*John Floyd*

☆ **Def Jam Music Group**—Ten Year Anniversary / 1995 / Def Jam ✦✦✦✦✦
In the '80s, Def Jam Records became the leading rap and hip-hop label in America. Featuring a roster filled with superstars—including Public Enemy, LL Cool J, the Beastie Boys, Slick Rick, and EPMD—Def Jam released many of the most innovative and groundbreaking records of the late '80s, and as the four-CD box *Ten Year Anniversary* proves, the music has lost none of its impact over the years. Over the course of the four discs, the set runs through a number of hip-hop classics, including "I Can't Live Without My Radio," "Fight the Power," "(You Gotta) Fight for

Your Right (To Party)," "Slam," "Don't Believe the Hype," "Rock the Bells," "Regulate," "Crossover," and over 50 other tracks. The one (minor) drawback of the set is the fact that it isn't sequenced chronologically; nevertheless, each disc in the box is compulsively listenable. In sheer musical terms, *Ten Year Anniversary* is one of the best box sets ever compiled and is essential to any popular music collection. — *Stephen Thomas Erlewine*

Electric Funk, Pt. 3 / 1994 / Rhino ✦✦✦
Electro-funk, bass music, and early rap are among the styles featured on the third volume of Rhino's electric funk series. Unlike '70s funk, which was horn-based and soul-tinged, '80s funk was electric, synthesized, and dance/disco-influenced. "All Night" by Trinere and "The Party Has Begun" by Free Style feature sizzling rhythm tracks with light Afro-Latin tinges and prominent bass lines, while the vocals are exuberant if less than distinguished. There's also some interesting foundation rap from Grandmaster Flash & Melle Mel on "White Lines (Don't Do It)," still among the better anti drug tracks, and "Surgery" from the Wrecking Cru, with a much less menacing and fiery-sounding Dr. Dre doing the rap. — *Ron Wynn*

☆ **Hip Hop Greats: Classic Raps** / Rhino ✦✦✦✦✦
A decent overview of rap's salad days, it includes the Sugarhill Gang's "Rapper's Delight," Grandmaster Flash's best singles ("White Lines," "The Message"), plus "Jam on It" from Newcleus. A nice place to start your education. — *John Floyd*

☆ **Hip Hop Heritage, Vol. 1** / 1987 / Jive ✦✦✦✦✦
Pioneering cuts from Grandmaster Flash, Spoonie Gee, and others. — *Ron Wynn*

Rap Beat from the Street / K-Tel ✦✦✦✦✦
A solid collection of some of 1991's harder-edged hip-hop without any profanity or overt political messages. That doesn't mean the music is lacking, as Public Enemy's "Shut 'Em Down," Cypress Hill's "The Phuncky Feel One," and the Geto Boys' incredible "Mind Playing Tricks on Me" prove. — *Stephen Thomas Erlewine*

Rap's Biggest Hits / 1990 / K-Tel ✦✦✦✦✦
A strong collection of some of hip-hop's biggest and most important singles from 1986-1989, including Tone Loc, Public Enemy, Run D.M.C., and Rob Base & D.J. E-Z Rock. A good introduction to hip-hop. — *Stephen Thomas Erlewine*

Rap's Most Wanted / 1991 / K-Tel ✦✦✦✦✦
Riding on the strength of Biz Markie's "Just a Friend," Candyman's "Knockin' Boots," Eric B. & Rakim's "Let the Rhythm Hit 'Em," and LL Cool J's "Around the Way Girl," *Rap's Most Wanted* is a very good collection of hip-hop's pop crossovers in the early '90s. — *Stephen Thomas Erlewine*

Rap: Today's Greatest Hits / 1993 / K-Tel ✦✦✦✦✦
A good collection of some of the best mainstream hip-hop of the early '90s, including Eric B. & Rakim's terrific "Don't Sweat the Technique," Snap's "Rhythm Is a Dancer," "Fakin' the Funk" by Main Source, and Digital Underground's "No Nose Job." It's by no means a complete picture of hip-hop in 1992, but it is a thoroughly enjoyable singles collection. — *Stephen Thomas Erlewine*

Rapmasters, Vol. 1: Best of the Jam / Priority ✦✦✦✦✦
This is an ambitious and exhaustive historical survey of rap from the early days up to yesterday. The categorical divisions of each volume don't mean much, and each one contains at least four songs that are essential to any rap collection. Mix 'em, match 'em, or buy them all. — *John Floyd*

Straight from the Basement of Kooley High / Def Jam ✦✦✦✦
This rambling, wildly erratic session contained enough mildly amusing elements for a good record, but lacked coherence and focus. It seemed like a work in progress, and the raps fluctuated from being clever to silly to boring. The same held true for the production and rhymes. — *Ron Wynn*

Street Jams: Back 2 the Old Skool, Vol. 1 / Aug. 20, 1996 / Rhino ✦✦✦✦✦
The *Back 2 the Old Skool* volumes of Rhino's *Street Jams* series concentrate on late-'70s and early-'80s funk, always presented in their full-length versions. Where the *Hip-Hop from the Top* and *Street Funk* edi-

tions are more closely related to hip-hop, these songs provided the basis for many hip-hop records, either as the source for samples or as the scratched grooves. *Street Jams: Back 2 the Old Skool, Vol. 1* features songs by Bootsy Collins, Dazz, Fatback, and several other artists. Rhino has presented these songs on other collections—most notably *Phat Trax*—before, but *Back 2 the Old Skool* remains an entertaining and informative listen. — *Leo Stanley*

Street Jams: Back 2 the Old Skool, Vol. 2 / Aug. 20, 1996 / Rhino ✦✦✦✦✦
Street Jams: Back 2 the Old Skool, Vol. 2 features songs by Funkadelic, Slave, Zapp, Mtume, and several other artists. — *Leo Stanley*

Street Jams: Back 2 the Old Skool, Vol. 3 / Aug. 20, 1996 / Rhino ✦✦✦✦✦
Street Jams: Back 2 the Old Skool, Vol. 3 features songs by Bootsy Collins, Chic, Mtume, Zapp, and several other artists. — *Leo Stanley*

Street Jams: Electric Funk 1 / 1992 / Rhino ✦✦✦
An excellent collection of 12 inch mixes of influential dance records from the early '80s, it's essential for any funk, rap, and dance collection. —*AMG*

Street Jams: Electric Funk 2 / 1992 / Rhino ✦✦✦
An excellent collection of 12" mixes of influential dance records from the early '80s, it's essential for any funk, rap, and dance collection. — *AMG*

Street Jams: Hip Hop from the Top, Pt. 1 / 1992 / Rhino ✦✦✦
A terrific collection of groundbreaking rap from the early '80s, *Street Jams: Hip-Hop from the Top* is essential for any comprehensive rap or funk collection. — *AMG*

Street Jams: Hip Hop from the Top, Pt. 2 / 1992 / Rhino ✦✦✦
A terrific collection of groundbreaking rap from the early '80s, *Street Jams: Hip-Hop from the Top* is essential for any comprehensive rap or funk collection. — *AMG*

Street Jams: Hip Hop from the Top, Part 3 / 1994 / Rhino ✦✦✦
As rap became more of a commercial property in the 1980s, the artists' major lyrical intention often seemed to be staking out territorial rights and proclaiming their superiority at the mike. Doug E. Fresh & the Get Fresh Crew, the Furious Five, the Boogie Boys, Kurtis Blow, and Marley Marl featuring MC Shan all do some variation on these themes on this 12-song anthology. "Romeo (Part 1)" by the Real Roxanne featuring Howie Tee is a putdown of the male romantic predator, while Whodini's "Freaks Come Out at Night" was one of the prime pop-rap hits of its day. While most of these cuts now sound simplistic and old, they were quite influential in helping cement rap's popularity, and Run-D.M.C.'s "Here We Go (The Funhouse)" remains a favorite among hip-hop historians. — *Ron Wynn*

Street Jams: Hip Hop from the Top, Part 4 / 1994 / Rhino ✦✦✦
The fourth volume of Rhino's hip-hop history series includes Dana Dane's stream-of-consciousness/dream raps, the silliness of the Fat Boys and Spyder D, early and pivotal work by Run-D.M.C., and sassy, confrontational material from Roxanne Shanté. At this stage, rap still sounds less strident and more novelty/comical, not addressing any issues beyond the verbal skills of individual disc jockeys. The production hasn't progressed that much either; the bulk of the tracks feature a straight, primary beat with some scratching and a rapper performing over it; even the verbal styles are slower. — *Ron Wynn*

Tommy Boy's Greatest Hits / Tommy Boy ✦✦✦✦✦
This is an excellent overview of '80s-era hits from the pioneering hip-hop label. It includes the finest work of Arthur Baker, Afrika Bambaataa, and many others. — *John Floyd*

☆ **West Coast Rap: The First Dynasty, Vol. 1** / 1992 / Rhino ✦✦✦✦✦
Rhino's *West Coast Rap* is an excellent collection of groundbreaking rap from the early and mid-'80s. —*AMG*

☆ **West Coast Rap: The First Dynasty, Vol. 2** / 1992 / Rhino ✦✦✦✦✦
Rhino's *West Coast Rap* is an excellent collection of groundbreaking rap from the early and mid-'80s. —*AMG*

☆ **West Coast Rap: The First Dynasty, Vol. 3** / 1992 / Rhino ✦✦✦✦✦
Rhino's *West Coast Rap* is an excellent collection of groundbreaking rap from the early and mid-'80s. —*AMG*

BLUES

To paraphrase the incomparable Delta blues performer Robert Johnson, "The blues is a low-down aching chill; if you ain't never had 'em, I hope you never will." Blues is the most emotional, gut-wrenching style of 20th-century American secular music. It evolved in the deep South shortly before the turn of the century from the spirituals, work songs, and country-dance instrumentals sung or performed by African Americans. This music has long exhibited strong regional as well as racial characteristics. Consider, for example, the light, ragtime-influenced music of Blind Boy Fuller in contrast to Texas Alexander's moaning, which sounds close to an old field holler. But not all blues are sorrowful and low-down—witness the "hokum" blues of Tampa Red and Georgia Tom, Frankie Jaxon, and others. They are laced with clever double-entendres as well as such salacious food metaphors as "hot nuts" and "jelly roll."

The blues have always kept up-to-date. The classic Chicago blues sound of Muddy Waters, Howlin' Wolf, and Little Walter is the perfect example of this. It is basically the Mississippi Delta blues sound, amplified and adapted for a Northern audience of southside Chicago immigrants who themselves had moved up from the mid South.

When Charlie Christian, T-Bone Walker, and others began experimenting with electric guitars in the mid- to late '30s, many of the popular blues singers like Big Bill Broonzy were right with them. Ultimately, this resulted in the commercial success of B. B. King and other similar urban blues legends, beginning in the early '50s.

In the '90s it is perfectly clear that this music and its 12-bar musical form has influenced not only most of our contemporary popular music but many musicians from outside the United States. This is particularly true in Europe and Great Britain, where rock stars ranging from Eric Clapton to U2 have long acknowledged their debt to the blues. In the middle of this latest blues boom, which has been partially fueled by the new wave of CDs, we are fortunate to have an immense range of blues. In 1968 I never thought I'd live to see a convenient way to have all of Sleepy John Estes' Victor and Decca 78s or a comprehensive retrospective of the Trumpet and Chess selections of Sonny Boy Williamson #2. With so much wonderful blues material around, the Hokum Boys summed it up well: "You can't get enough of that." —*Kip Lornell*

Johnny Adams

b. Jan. 5, 1932, New Orleans, LA
Vocals / Soul, R&B, Soul Blues
Renowned around his Crescent City homebase as "the Tan Canary" for his extraordinary set of soulfully soaring pipes, veteran R&B vocalist Johnny Adams has tackled an exceptionally wide variety of material for Rounder in recent years—elegantly rendered tribute albums to legendary songwriters Doc Pomus and Percy Mayfield preceded forays into mellow, jazzier pastures. But then, Adams was never particularly into the parade-beat grooves that traditionally define the New Orleans R&B sound, preferring to deliver sophisticated soul ballads draped in strings.

Adams sang gospel professionally before crossing over to the secular world in 1959. Songwriter Dorothy LaBostrie—the woman responsible for cleaning up the bawdy lyrics of Little Richard's "Tutti Frutti" enough for worldwide consumption—convinced her neighbor Adams to sing her tasty ballad "I Won't Cry." The track, produced by a teenaged Mac Rebennack, was released on Joe Ruffino's Ric logo, and Adams was on his way. He waxed some outstanding follow-ups for Ric, notably "A Losing Battle" (the Rebennack-penned gem proved Adams' first national R&B hit in 1962) and "Life Is a Struggle."

After a prolonged dry spell, Adams resurfaced in 1968 with an impassioned R&B revival of Jimmy Heap's country standard "Release Me" for Shelby Singleton's SSS imprint that blossomed into a national hit. Even more arresting was Adams' magnificent 1969 country-soul classic "Reconsider Me," his lone leap into the R&B Top Ten; in it, he swoops effortlessly up to a death-defying falsetto range to drive his anguished message home with fervor.

Despite several worthy SSS follow-ups ("I Can't Be All Bad" was another sizable seller), Adams never traversed those lofty commercial heights again (particularly disappointing was a short stay at Atlantic). But he's found a new extended recording life at Rounder—his 1984 set, *From the Heart*, proved to the world that this Tan Canary can still chirp like a champ. —*Bill Dahl*

From the Heart / 1984 / Rounder ✦✦✦✦
First-class production by Scott Billington, a delicious Crescent City combo led by longtime cohort Walter "Wolfman" Washington on guitar and Red Tyler on tenor sax, and Adams' perennially luxurious pipes tab this as one of his finest contemporary outings. Nice song selection: the pens of Tony Joe White, Percy Mayfield, Sam Cooke, and Doc Pomus

were all tapped Adams unfurls his "mouth trombone" on Mayfield's "We Don't See Eye to Eye." —*Bill Dahl*

● **Reconsider Me** / 1987 / Charly ✦✦✦✦
This 22-song British compilation is the only place to find a decent cross-section of Adams' SSS sides, including his two biggest hits, the stately "Release Me" and the truly stunning "Reconsider Me." Not all of Adams' late-'60s waxings were ballads; "South Side of Soul Street" is a sizzling upbeat workout. But it's as a balladeer that Adams has always excelled; some of his finest soul senders are to be found right here. —*Bill Dahl*

● **I Won't Cry** / 1991 / Rounder ✦✦✦✦
Even on his earliest singles, Adams already had developed a velvety crooning style seemingly at odds with most of his raucous hometown. This 14-track collection of Adams' 1959-63 work for Ric Records contains some stunning stuff, most of it in the big-voiced ballad mode (with an occasional nod to Ray Charles). "I Won't Cry," "A Losing Battle," and "Lonely Drifter" capture Adams' tender, mellifluous delivery beautifully. —*Bill Dahl*

Luther Allison

b. Aug. 17, 1939, Mayflower, AR
Guitar, Harmonica, Vocals / R&B, Modern Electric Blues, Chicago Blues
An American-born guitarist, singer and songwriter who's lived in France since 1980, Luther Allison has been the man to book at blues festivals in the mid-'90s. Allison's comeback into the mainstream was ushered in by a recording contract with an American record company, Alligator Records in 1994.

Born August 17, 1939, in Widener, AR, Allison was the fourteenth of 15 children, the son of cotton farmers. His parents moved to Chicago when he was in his early teens.

It was while living with his family on Chicago's West Side that Allison had his first awareness of wanting to become a full-time bluesman, and he played bass behind guitarist Jimmy Dawkins. When he was 18 years old, Allison's brother showed him basic chords and notes on the guitar, and he made rapid progress after that. Allison went on to "blues college" by sitting in with some of the most legendary names in blues in Chicago's local venues: Muddy Waters, Elmore James, and Howlin' Wolf among them.

His first chance to record came with Bob Koester's then-tiny Delmark Record label, and his first album, *Love Me Mama*, was released in 1969. But like anyone else with a record out on a small label, it was up to him to go out and promote it, and he did, putting in stellar, show-stopping performances at the Ann Arbor Blues festivals in 1969, 1970, and 1971. After that, people began to pay attention to Luther Allison, and in 1972 he signed with Motown Records.

Although his Motown albums allowed him to tour Japan and new venues in Europe, the recordings didn't sell well. Allison stayed busy in Europe through the rest of the 1970s and 1980s, and recorded *Love Me Papa* for the French Black & Blue label in 1977. He eventually settled outside of Paris in 1984, since France and Germany were such major markets for him. At home in the US, Allison continued to perform sporadically.

Now in his mid-50s, Allison continues to delight club and festival audiences around the world with his lengthy, sweat-drenched, high energy shows, complete with dazzling guitar playing and inspired, soulful vocals. —*Richard Skelly*

Luther's Blues / 1973 / Gordy ✦✦✦✦
Luther's Blues is where Luther Allison began to come into his own, developing a fluid, gutsy style full of soulful string bending. There are still a few weak spots, but the album remains an effective slice of contemporary Chicago blues. —*Thom Owens*

● **Love Me Papa** / Dec. 13, 1977 / Evidence ✦✦✦✦
Luther Allison is the blues' proverbial little boy with the curl; when he's good, he's great. When he's bad, he's awful. Allison was on throughout most of the nine tracks (three bonus cuts) on this 1977 date recently reissued by Evidence on CD, playing with the ferocity, direction, and inventiveness that is often missing from his more uneven efforts. His covers of Little Walter Jacobs' "Last Night" and "Blues with a Feeling" are not reverential or respectful but are launching pads for high-octane, barreling riffs, snappy phrases, and exciting solos. His vocals are not always that keen, but Allison at least stretches them out and adds verbal embellishments, yells, and shouts of encouragement. —*Ron Wynn*

Serious / 1987 / Blind Pig ✦✦✦✦
Serious marks the beginning of Luther Allison's late-'80s/early-'90s hot streak. The more streamlined, rock-oriented approach actually is a benefit, since it gives Allison a shot of energy that makes his guitar simply burn all the way through the record. —*Thom Owens*

Soul Fixin' Man / 1994 / Alligator ✦✦✦✦
This venture, recorded in Memphis, is Allison's finest session since his days at Delmark. He blends blues, soul/R&B, and even occasional funk, and his guitar playing is alternately flashy and refined, sometimes explosive, sometimes carefully measured. His vocals are powerful, convincing, and earnest on all 12 selections. Luther Allison finally gives American blues fans the definitive portrait they wanted. —*Ron Wynn*

Blue Streak / Oct. 1995 / Alligator ✦✦✦✦
Luther Allison's run of winning contemporary blues albums continues with *Blue Streak*, a typically enjoyable set of hot guitar playing and impassioned singing, hampered only slightly by occasionally perfunctory songwriting. —*Thom Owens*

The Motown Years 1972–1976 / Feb. 1996 / Motown ✦✦✦
Allison's reign as Motown's only bluesman saw the guitarist offer competently executed, but basically unmemorable, blues with some soul and rock influences. This 17-track compilation includes selections from all three of the LPs he issued on the label (drawing most heavily from his second, *Luther's Blues*), and adds a previously unreleased live cut from the 1972 Ann Arbor Blues Festival. Pop influences can be heard in the occasional wah-wah guitar and brass-conscious production; Berry Gordy even co-wrote one of the tracks ("Someone Pretty Baby"), and Randy Brecker arranged the horns on Allison's final Motown full-length. —*Richie Unterberger*

Hand Me Down My Moonshine / Inakustik ✦✦✦

Billy Boy Arnold

b. Sep. 16, 1935, Chicago, IL
Harmonica, Vocals / Electric Chicago Blues
Talk about a comeback! After too many years away from the studio, Chicago harpist Billy Boy Arnold has returned to action in a big way with two fine albums for Alligator: 1993's *Back Where I Belong* and 1995's *Eldorado Cadillac*. Retaining his youthful demeanor despite more than four decades of blues experience, Arnold's wailing harp and sturdy vocals remain in top-flight shape following the lengthy recording layoff.

Born in Chicago rather than in Mississippi (as many of his musical forefathers were), young Billy Boy gravitated right to the source in 1948. He summoned up the courage to knock on the front door of his idol, harmonica great John Lee "Sonny Boy" Williamson, who resided nearby. Sonny Boy kindly gave the lad a couple of harp lessons, but their relationship was quickly severed when Williamson was tragically murdered. Still in his teens, Arnold cut his debut 78 for the extremely obscure Cool logo in 1952. "Hello Stranger" went nowhere but gave him his nickname when its label unexpectedly read "Billy Boy Arnold." Arnold made an auspicious connection when he joined forces with Bo

Diddley and played on the shave-and-a-haircut-beat specialist's two-sided 1955 debut smash "Bo Diddley"/"I'm a Man" for Checker. That led, in a roundabout way, to Billy Boy's signing with rival Vee-Jay Records (the harpist mistakenly believed Leonard Chess didn't like him). Arnold's "I Wish You Would," utilizing that familiar Bo Diddley beat, sold well and inspired a later famous cover by the Yardbirds. That renowned British blues-rock group also took a liking to another Arnold classic on Vee-Jay, "I Ain't Got You." Other Vee-Jay standouts by Arnold included "Prisoner's Plea" and "Rockinitis," but by 1958, his tenure at the logo was over.

Other than an excellent Samuel Charters-produced 1963 album for Prestige, *More Blues on the South Side*, Arnold's profile diminished over the years in his hometown (though European audiences enjoyed him regularly). Fortunately, that's changed: *Back Where I Belong* restored this Chicago harp master to prominence, and *Eldorado Cadillac* drove him into the winner's circle a second time. —*Bill Dahl*

More Blues on the South Side / 1964 / Prestige ✦✦✦✦
Over half a decade away from the studio didn't hinder Arnold one bit on this 1963 session. His still-youthful vocals, strong harp, and imaginative songs are very effectively spotlighted, backed by a mean little Chicago combo anchored by guitarist Mighty Joe Young and pianist Lafayette Leake. The CD reissue adds a previously unreleased instrumental, "Playing with the Blues." —*Bill Dahl*

● **I Wish You Would** / 1980 / Charly ✦✦✦✦
The harpist's indispensable dozen 1955-1957 waxings for Vee-Jay, including the classic "I Wish You Would" and its blues-soaked flip "I Was Fooled" (stinging guitar by Jody Williams), the often-covered (but never bettered, except maybe by Jimmy Reed) "I Ain't Got You," and the vicious "Don't Stay Out All Night" and "You've Got Me Wrong." Also included are a pair of rarities Arnold cut for Chess prior to his exit as Diddley's sideman; "Sweet on You Baby" and "You Got to Love Me" feature big bad Bo on guitar and the ever-dynamic Jerome Green shakin' the maracas. —*Bill Dahl*

Back Where I Belong / 1993 / Alligator ✦✦✦✦
Indeed he is. Recorded in Los Angeles with a crew of young acolytes offering spot-on backing (guitarists Zach Zunis and Rick Holmstrom acquit themselves well), Arnold eases back into harness with a remake of "I Wish You Would" before exposing some fine new originals (the Chuck Berry-styled rocker "Move on Down the Road" is a stomping standout) and an homage to his old mentor Sonny Boy (a romping "Shake the Boogie"). —*Bill Dahl*

Going to Chicago / 1995 / Testament ✦✦✦

Eldorado Cadillac / 1995 / Alligator ✦✦✦✦
This time around, Arnold recorded in his hometown with another gang of well-seasoned players behind him (guitar duties were ably handled by ex-Muddy Waters bandsman Bob Margolin and the versatile James Wheeler), retaining the same high standards set by his previous offering. Seven impressive new originals are joined by solid covers of Roosevelt Sykes' downbeat "Sunny Road" and Ray Charles' streetwise "It Should Have Been Me." —*Bill Dahl*

Kokomo Arnold (James "Kokomo" Arnold)

b. Feb. 15, 1901, Lovejoys Station, GA, **d.** Nov. 8, 1968, Chicago, IL
Guitar, Vocals / Blues, Acoustic Blues
A popular recording artist of the '30s, James "Kokomo" Arnold was a left-handed bottleneck guitarist who usually recorded solo, occasionally with piano accompaniment. His first Chicago session (Decca, 1934) produced the widely covered "Milk Cow Blues" and "Old Original Kokomo Blues" (the model for Robert Johnson's "Sweet Home Chicago"), as well as the first appearance on record of the classic "I believe I'll dust my broom" line (in "Sagefield Woman Blues"). Critic Hugues Panassi wrote, "Arnold is one of the greatest blues singers ever recorded." Arnold continued to play for a few years in Chicago after his last session (1938) but later took a job in a steel mill, disillusioned with the music business. Interviewed by two Frenchmen in 1959, Arnold said, "I'm finished with music and that mad way of life." —*Jim O'Neal*

★ **Bottleneck Guitar of the '30s** / Yazoo ✦✦✦✦✦
Bottleneck Guitar of the '30s collects all of Kokomo Arnold's classic tracks from the '30s, including the classic "Milk Cow Blues." It's an essential item for a blues library—within these sides lay the groundwork for the Delta and Chicago blues to come, from Robert Johnson to Elmore James. —*Thom Owens*

Marcia Ball

b. 1950
Piano, Vocals / Modern Electric Blues, Piano Blues, Modern Electric Texas Blues
Pianist, singer, and songwriter Marcia Ball is a living example of how east Texas blues meets southwest Louisiana swamp rock. Ball was born March 20, 1949, in Orange, TX, but grew up across the border in Vinton, LA. Her piano style, which mixes equal parts boogie woogie with zydeco

Blues Styles

CLASSIC FEMALE BLUES — The earliest recorded form of the blues. This genre features female vocalists singing material with close connections to pop music of the period (mid '20s to early '30s) and primarily jazz backings. Main proponents: Mamie Smith, Bessie Smith, Ma Rainey, Lucille Bogan, and Victoria Spivey.

DELTA BLUES — Also known as Mississippi blues, this is the earliest guitar-dominated music to make it onto record. Consisting of performers working primarily in a solo, self-accompanied context, it also embraces the now-familiar string-band/small-combo format, both precursors to the modern-day blues band. Main proponents: Charlie Patton, Robert Johnson, and Son House.

COUNTRY-BLUES — A term that delineates the depth and breadth of the first flowering of guitar-driven blues, embracing all regional styles and variations (Piedmont, Atlanta, early Chicago, ragtime, folk, songster, etc.). Primarily acoustic guitarists, some country-blues performers later switched to electric guitars without changing their style. Major proponents: Henry Thomas, Skip James, Barbecue Bob, Leadbelly, Mississippi John Hurt, Lonnie Johnson, Blind Blake, and Tommy Johnson.

MEMPHIS BLUES — A strain of country-blues all its own, the Memphis style gives us the rise of two distinct forms, the jug band (humorous, jazz-style blues played on homemade instruments) and the separation of guitarists into solo (lead) and rhythm, a tradition that is now part-and-parcel of all modern-day blues bands. The later, post-WWII electric version of this genre featured explosive guitar work, thunderous drumming, and declamatory vocals. Main proponents: Cannon's Jug Stompers, Furry Lewis, Memphis Minnie, and the early recordings of B.B. King and Howlin' Wolf.

TEXAS BLUES — A subgenre earmarked by a more relaxed, swinging feel than other styles of blues. The earlier, acoustic version embraced both songster and country-blues traditions, while the post-war electric style featured jazzy, single-string soloing over predominately horn-driven backing. Main proponents: Blind Lemon Jefferson, Lightnin' Hopkins, Clarence "Gatemouth" Brown, and T-Bone Walker.

CHICAGO BLUES — Delta blues fully amplified and put into a small-band context. Later permutations of the style took their cue from the lead guitar work of B.B. King and T-Bone Walker. Main proponents: Muddy Waters, Howlin' Wolf, Little Walter, Big Walter Horton, Jimmy Rogers, Elmore James, Jimmy Reed, Otis Rush, Magic Sam, and Buddy Guy.

JUMP BLUES — Uptempo, jazz-tinged blues, usually featuring a vocalist in front of a large, horn-driven orchestra with less reliance on guitar work than other styles. Main proponents: Amos Milburn, Johnny Otis, Roy Brown, Wynonie Harris, and Big Joe Turner.

NEW ORLEANS BLUES — Primarily (but not exclusively) piano- and horn-driven, this genre strain is enlivened by Caribbean rhythms, party atmosphere, and the "second-line" strut of the Dixieland music so indigenous to the area. Main proponents: Professor Longhair, Guitar Slim, and Snooks Eaglin.

WEST COAST BLUES — More piano-based and jazz-influenced than anything else, the West Coast style (California in particular) also embraces post-war Texas guitar expatriates and jump-blues practitioners. Main proponents: Charles Brown, Pee Wee Crayton, Lowell Fulson, and Percy Mayfield.

PIANO BLUES — A genre that runs through the entire history of the music itself, this embraces everything from ragtime, barrelhouse, boogie-woogie, and smooth West Coast jazz stylings to the hard-rocking rhythms of Chicago blues. Main proponents: Big Maceo Merriweather, Leroy Carr, Sunnyland Slim, Roosevelt Sykes, Albert Ammons, and Otis Spann.

LOUISIANA BLUES — A looser, more laidback and percussive version of the Jimmy Reed side of the Chicago style. Production techniques on most of the recordings utilize massive amounts of echo, giving the performances a "doomy" sound and feel. Main proponents: Slim Harpo, Lightnin' Slim, and Lazy Lester.

R&B/SOUL BLUES — A more modern form, this fuses elements of African American popular music (the rhythm and blues strain of the '50s and the Southern soul style of the mid-'60s) into a wholly urban blues amalgam of its own.

MODERN ACOUSTIC BLUES — Newer artists reviving the older, more country-derived styles of blues. Main proponents: John Hammond, Rory Block, John Cephas, Taj Mahal, and the earlier recordings of Bonnie Raitt.

MODERN ELECTRIC BLUES — An eclectic mixture, this genre replicates older styles of urban blues while simultaneously recasting them in contemporary fashion. Main proponents: Stevie Ray Vaughan, the Fabulous Thunderbirds, Robert Cray, and Roomful of Blues.

BRITISH BLUES — More than a mere geographical distinction, the British style pays strict adherence to replicating American blues genres, with an admiration for its originators bordering on reverence. Main proponents: Alexis Korner, John Mayall, and the early recordings of Fleetwood Mac and the Rolling Stones.

— Cub Koda

and Louisiana swamp rock, is best exemplified on her series of excellent recordings for the Rounder label. They include *Soulful Dress* (1984), *Hot Tamale Baby* (1986), *Gatorhythms* (1989) and *Blue House* (1994).

Although best a splendid piano player and a more than adequate vocalist, "the songwriting process is the most fulfilling part of the whole deal for me," she said in a 1994 interview, "so I always keep my ears and eyes open for things I might hear or see . . . . I like my songs to go back to blues in some fashion." As much a student of the music as she is a player, some of Ball's albums include covers of material by O.V. Wright, Dr. John, Joe Ely, Clifton Chenier, and Shirley and Lee.

Ball, who's established herself as an important player in the club scenes in both New Orleans and Austin, continues to work at festivals and clubs throughout the US, Canada, and Europe. *—Richard Skelly*

Soulful Dress / 1984 / Rounder ✦✦✦

Hot Tamale Baby / 1986 / Rounder ✦✦✦✦

Marcia Ball solidifies the favorable impression made with her debut Rounder effort with this rousing second outing. She dedicated it to the late King of Zydeco, Clifton Chenier, and is backed by a fine band of veteran pros that include saxophonist Alvin Tyler. Ball rips through Booker T. Jones' soul gem "Never Like This Before" and Chenier's title composition, while also demonstrating her own facility with R&B on "That's Enough of That Stuff" and "Love's Spell." She comes close, but doesn't quite hit the mark on O.V. Wright's "I'm Gonna Forget About You," turning in a more than acceptable rendition that still doesn't approach the original. But other than that one misstep, which she compensates for with a charged version of "I Don't Know," Marcia Ball proves that her debut was no fluke. *—Ron Wynn*

● **Gator Rhythms** / 1989 / Rounder ✦✦✦✦

Marcia Ball explores R&B and honky-tonk country on this album, keeping her blues chops in order while expanding her repertoire. She includes a pair of tunes by country vocalist Lee Roy Parnell, "What's a Girl to Do" and "Red Hot," doing both in a feisty, attacking fashion. She also is challenging and upbeat on Dr. John's "How You Carry On" and "Find Another Fool." Her third Rounder album is her most entertaining and dynamic, and Ball becomes less of an interpreter and more of an individualist. *—Ron Wynn*

Barbecue Bob (Robert Hicks)

b. Sep. 11, 1902, Walnut Grove, GA, **d.** Oct. 21, 1931, Lithonia, GA
Guitar, Vocals / Acoustic Country Blues

Barbecue Bob may be a familiar name to some blues fans today because at least two young White musicians have adopted the name, but back in the '20s the original Barbecue Bob (Robert Hicks) was a big name on the Black "race-records" scene. Recording for Columbia from 1927 to 1930, Hicks was the most popular of the Atlanta blues guitarists of his time, and Columbia's best-selling bluesman. But Barbecue Bob died of pneumonia at the age of 29, and some of his contemporaries like Blind Willie McTell are much better known to modern-day audiences. Most of Bob's recordings were solo outings featuring rhythmic 12-string bottleneck-guitar work and original lyrical themes. In historian Stephen Calt's opinion, "For sheer musical verve and punch, Hicks easily rivals Charley Patton." *—Jim O'Neal*

● **Chocolate to the Bone** / Yazoo ✦✦✦✦

Fourteen selections from popular '20s Atlanta 12-string slide artist Robert Hicks, aka Barbecue Bob. A fine American collection, with good sound quality. —*Barry Lee Pearson*

Complete Recorded Works, Vols. 1-3 / Document ✦✦✦
Over the course of three CDs, Document Records compiled every note Barbecue Bob recorded in the late '20s. The first volume covers everything he cut between March 25, 1927 and April 13, 1928; the second, April 21, 1928 to November 3, 1929; the third November 6, 1929 to December 8, 1930. In between the first song on the set—which has been issued as individual volumes—and the last song, there is some incredible country blues; there was a reason why he was among the most popular bluesmen of his time. Although there is too much music here for anyone but dedicated country blues fans to be able to digest and the sound quality isn't terrific (which isn't surprising, considering that the series had to be mastered from 78s), Document's *Complete Recorded Works in Chronological Order* is an excellent historical document that contains music that still sounds fresh and vital decades after it was recorded. —*Thom Owens*

Roosevelt "Booba" Barnes

b. Sep. 25, 1936, Longwood, MS, **d.** Apr. 2, 1996
Guitar, Vocals / Blues, Electric Delta Blues
Booba Barnes and his Playboys band rocked the hardest of all the juke-joint combos in the Mississippi delta during the '80s, and after the release of his debut album (*The Heartbroken Man*, 1990), "Booba" took his act and his band north to Chicago, following the trail of his idols Howlin' Wolf and Little Milton. In a *Guitar Player* review, Jas Obrecht called Barnes "a wonderfully idiosyncratic guitar player and an extraordinary vocalist by any standard." —*Jim O'Neal*

● **The Heartbroken Man** / 1990 / Rooster Blues ✦✦✦✦
Featured is a no-frills recording of hair-raising modern Delta blues. —*Jas Obrecht*

Carey Bell

b. Nov. 14, 1936, Macon, MS
Bass, Guitar, Harmonica, Drums, Vocals / Electric Chicago Blues
His place on the honor roll of Chicago blues harpists long ago assured, Carey Bell has truly come into his own during the last few years as a bandleader with terrific discs for Alligator and Blind Pig. He learned his distinctive harmonica riffs from the Windy City's very best (both Walters—Little *and* Big—as well as Sonny Boy Williamson No.2), adding his own signature effects for good measure (an other-worldly moan immediately identifies many of his more memorable harp rides).

Bell served invaluable early-'70s stints in the bands of Muddy Waters and Willie Dixon, touring extensively and recording with both legends. Alligator Records has been responsible for much of Bell's best recorded work as a leader, beginning with a joint venture with Horton back in 1972. Four cuts by Bell on the first batch of Alligator's *Living Chicago Blues* anthologies in 1978 preceded his participation in the 1990 harmonica summit meeting *Harp Attack!*, which brought him into the studio with fellow greats James Cotton, Junior Wells, and Billy Branch. His recent solo set for Alligator, *Deep Down*, rates as his finest album to date. Bell has sired a passel of blues-playing progeny; best-known of the brood is mercurial guitarist Lurrie Bell. —*Bill Dahl*

Harp Attack! / 1990 / Alligator ✦✦✦✦
Four of Chicago's preeminent blues harpists—Bell, James Cotton, Junior Wells, and relative newcomer Billy Branch—gathered in a downtown studio to wax this historic summit meeting. Bell's vocal showcases include two originals, "Hit Man" and "Second Hand Man," and a Muddy Waters cover, "My Eyes Keep Me in Trouble." —*Bill Dahl*

Mellow Down Easy / 1991 / Blind Pig ✦✦✦✦
The harpist hooked up with a young Maryland-based band called Tough Luck for this disc, certainly one of his better outings. The traditional mindset of the combo pushed Bell back to his roots, whether on the originals "Just like You" and the Horton homage "Big Walter Strut" or revivals of Muddy Waters' "Short Dress Woman" and "Walking Thru the Park" and the classic Little Walter title cut. —*Bill Dahl*

● **Deep Down** / 1995 / Alligator ✦✦✦✦
More than a quarter century after he cut his debut album, Bell recently made his finest disc to date. Boasting superior material and musicianship (guitarists Carl Weathersby and Lurrie Bell and pianist Lucky Peterson are all stellar) and a goosed-up energy level that frequently reaches incendiary heights, the disc captures Bell outdoing himself vocally on the ribald "Let Me Stir in Your Pot" and a suitably loose "When I Get Drunk" and instrumentally on the torrid "Jawbreaker." For a closer, Bell settled on the atmospheric Horton classic "Easy"; he does it full justice. —*Bill Dahl*

Last Night / 1995 / One Way ✦✦✦
Nothing flashy or outrageous here, just a meat-and-potatoes session produced by Al Smith that satisfyingly showcases Bell's charms. Once again, there are hearty tributes to Little Walter ("Last Night") and Muddy Waters ("She's 19 Years Old"), but there's some original stuff too, backed

by a combo that boasted a daunting collective experience level: Taylor and Perkins return, along with bassist David Myers and drummer Willie "Big Eyes" Smith. —*Bill Dahl*

Tab Benoit

b. Nov. 17, 1967
Guitar, Vocals / Electric Louisiana Blues
Guitarist, singer and songwriter Tab Benoit makes his home south of New Orleans in Houma, LA. Born November 17, 1967, he's one of a handful of bright rising stars on the modern blues scene. Since the release of his first album for Justice, Benoit has taken his brand of Cajun-influenced blues all over the US, Canada and Europe. *Nice and Warm*, his debut album for Houston-based Justice Records, prompted some critics to say he's reminiscent, at times, of three blues guitar gods: Albert King, Albert Collins and Jimi Hendrix.
—*Richard Skelly*

● **Nice and Warm** / 1992 / Justice ✦✦✦✦
Tab Benoit's debut album *Nice & Warm* is a startingly fresh debut. The guitarist has a gutsy, fuel-injected style that adds real spice to his swampy blues. Benoit draws equally from the Louisiana and Texas traditions and *Nice & Warm* proves it; not only does he carry on the tradition, he offers a fresh take on it as well. —*Thom Owens*

What I Live For / 1994 / Justice ✦✦✦

Standing on the Bank / 1995 / Justice ✦✦✦

Buster Benton

b. Jul. 19, 1932, Texarkana, AR
Guitar
An underrated, entertaining guitarist and vocalist whose style hugs the line between blues, R&B and soul, Buster Benton sang in a gospel choir while growing up in Texarkana, Arkansas. He started playing guitar after moving to Toledo in 1952, and then relocated to Chicago in the late '50s. There Benton formed a band and began recording for Melloway, Twinight and Alteen. He played with Willie Dixon several years, and also owned the Stardust Lounge. Ralph Bass produced many Benton recordings for Jewel in the '70s, and he scored a regional hit with "Spider in My Stew." He's remained active into the '90s, recording for Blue Phoenix and Ichiban. —*Ron Wynn*

● **Spider in My Stew** / 1978 / Ronn ✦✦✦✦
Without a doubt, this album, originally released on Ronn in 1979, stands as the best place to begin an in-depth examination of Benton's legacy. "Spider in My Stew," obviously, is here, along with the wonderful Cooke-influenced R&B outing "Lonesome for a Dime"; an irresistibly funky "Sweet 94" (Ron Scott's gurgly electric saxophone gives this cut and several others a unique feel); a driving "Funny About My Money"; and the mournful minor-key blues "Sorry." Ronn has beefed the CD program up still further with three additions: the doomy, Bobby Bland-styled "Money Is the Name of the Game," a shuffling "Dangerous Woman," and Benton's happy-go-lucky cover of David Dee's "Going Fishin'." —*Bill Dahl*

Blues at the Top / Nov. 22, 1983-May 2, 1985 / Evidence ✦✦✦✦
A compilation of the two albums Benton made for the French Black & Blue label in 1983 and 1985, this 15-song collection rates with his best. Two separate bands are involved, and the sound changes with them: backed by harpist Billy Branch's Sons of Blues, Benton exercises his R&B-laced chops, while the older hands behind him on "Honey Bee," "The Hawk Is Coming," and "Hole in My Head" (guitarist Johnny Littlejohn, pianist Lovie, drummer Odie Payne) assure that the grooves stay more in the mainstream. —*Bill Dahl*

Big Maybelle (Maybelle Smith)

b. May 1, 1924, Jackson, TN, **d.** Jan. 23, 1972, Cleveland, OH
Vocals / R&B, Electric Jump Blues
Her mountainous stature matching the sheer soulful power of her massive vocal talent, Big Maybelle was one of the premier R&B chanteuses of the 1950s. Her deep, gravelly voice was as singular as her recorded output for Okeh and Savoy, which ranged from down-in-the-alley blues to pop-slanted ballads. Alleged drug addiction leveled the mighty belter at the premature age of 47, but Maybelle packed a lot of living into her shortened lifespan.

Gospel music was an important element in Maybelle's intense vocal style, but the church wasn't big enough to hold her talent. She debuted on wax with pianist Christine Chatman's combo on Decca in 1944 before signing with Cincinnati's King Records in 1947 for three singles of her own backed by trumpeter Hot Lips Page's band.

Producer Fred Mendelsohn discovered Smith in the Queen City, rechristened her Big Maybelle, and signed her to Columbia's Okeh R&B subsidiary in 1952. Her first Okeh platter, "Gabbin' Blues," swiftly hit, climbing to the upper reaches of the R&B charts. "Way Back Home" and "My Country Man" made it a 1953 hat trick for Maybelle and Okeh. In

1955, she cut "Whole Lotta Shakin' Goin' On" a full two years before Louisiana piano pumper Jerry Lee Lewis got his hands and feet on it. Mendelsohn soon brought her over to Savoy. Maybelle rocked harder than ever at Savoy, her "Ring Dang Dilly," "That's a Pretty Good Love," and "Tell Me Who" benefitting from blistering backing by New York's top sessioneers.

Maybelle persevered throughout the '60s, recording for Brunswick, Scepter (her "Yesterday's Kisses" found her coping admirably with the uptown soul sound), Chess, Rojac (source of "96 Tears"), and other labels. But the good years were long gone when she slipped into a diabetic coma and passed away in a Cleveland hospital in 1972. —*Bill Dahl*

● **The Complete Okeh Sessions 1952-'55** / 1994 / Epic/Legacy ✦✦✦✦
Maybelle's entire Okeh output—26 tracks—including her three R&B chart items, "Whole Lotta Shakin' Goin' On," and the risque slow blues "I'm Getting 'Long Alright." "Gabbin' Blues," her 1952 Okeh debut smash, is a humorous dialog between Maybelle and gossiping rival Rosemarie McCoy, the tune's co-writer. Maybelle was no mere copyist; her sandpapery vocals stood in sharp contrast to the many interchangeable thrushes then populating the R&B world. Great support from New York session wizards such as tenor saxist Sam "The Man" Taylor and guitarist Mickey Baker throughout. —*Bill Dahl*

Candy / 1994 / Savoy Jazz ✦✦✦✦
The belter moved over to Newark, NJ-based Savoy midway through the decade and continued to prosper: "Candy," "Ramblin' Blues," and the intense "Blues Early, Early" rate with her finest cuts. "Ring Dang Dilly" and "Tell Me Who" rock with the seemingly effortless swing peculiar to New York's R&B scene at the time, thanks to the presence of saxists Warren Lucky and Jerome Richardson and guitarists Baker and Kenny Burrell, among others. —*Bill Dahl*

The Big Three Trio

Group / Acoustic Chicago Blues
For the legendary Willie Dixon, the Big Three Trio was an important launching pad for a fantastic career. Pianist Leonard "Baby Doo" Caston and guitarist Bernardo Dennis (replaced after a year by Ollie Crawford) joined upright bassist Dixon to form the popular trio in 1946. Caston was just out of the service (where he'd played on USO tours during World War II); Dixon had been a conscientious objector. Dixon had previously worked with Caston in the Five Breezes and with Dennis in the Four Jumps of Jive.

Sharing vocal (they specialized in three-part harmonies) and writing duties democratically, the trio signed with Jim Bulleit's Bullet imprint in 1946 for a solitary session before making a giant jump in stature to Columbia Records in 1947. Their polished, pop-oriented presentation resulted in one national hit, "You Sure Look Good to Me," in 1948, and a slew of other releases that stretched into 1952.

Caston split at the end of 1952, effectively breaking up the trio. But Dixon's destiny was at Chess Records, where he was already making inroads as a session bassist and songwriter. Pretty soon, he'd be recognized as one of the most prolific and invaluable figures on the Windy City scene. —*Bill Dahl*

I Feel Like Steppin' Out / 1986 / Dr. Horse ✦✦✦

● **The Big Three Trio** / 1990 / Columbia ✦✦✦✦
The only domestic compilation celebrating this trio's accomplishments is a 21-track affair containing Dixon's "dozens" diatribe "Signifying Monkey," the catchy "Tell That Woman" (later covered by Peter, Paul & Mary as "Big Boat Up the River"), and several crackling instrumentals ("Big 3 Boogie," "Hard Notch Boogie Beat") that show what fine musicianship this triumvirate purveyed. Points off, though, for not including their only legit hit, "You Sure Look Good to Me." —*Bill Dahl*

Elvin Bishop

b. Oct. 21, 1942, Glendale, CA
Guitar, Vocals / Blues-Rock, Southern Rock, Contemporary Electric Blues
Elvin Bishop was born in Glendale, CA, on October 21, 1942. He grew up on a farm in Iowa with no electricity and no running water. His family moved to Oklahoma when he was ten. Raised in an all-White community, he had no exposure to Blacks or their music except though the radio, where he would listen to sounds from far away Mexico and blues stations in Shreveport, LA. In particular, the piercing sound of Jimmy Reed's harmonica got his attention.

In the early '60s he met and teamed up with Paul Butterfield to become the core of the Butterfield Blues Band. Bishop helped to create and played on the first several Butterfield albums. (The Pigboy Crabshaw is Bishop's countrified persona referred to in the title of the third Butterfield album.)

When he left the Butterfield band after the *In My Own Dream* album (1968), Bishop settled in the San Francisco area, where he appeared often at the Fillmore with artists like Eric Clapton, B.B. King, and Jimi

Hendrix. He recorded for Epic (four albums) and later signed with Capricorn in 1974. His recording of "Traveling Shoes" (from the album *Let It Flow*) hit the charts, but he scored big with the lovely tune "Fooled Around and Fell in Love" (from his album *Struttin' My Stuff*) in 1976. He was (and is) famous for having fun on stage (putting on a great show) and letting the good times roll. Over the next few years the Elvin Bishop Group dissolved. He released his album *Best Of* in 1979, and was not heard from much until he signed with Alligator in 1988.

Bishop then released *Big Fun* (1988) and *Don't Let the Bossman Get You Down* (1991), which were well received. He also participated in Alligator's 1992 20th Anniversary cross-country tour. His latest release is *Ace in the Hole* (1995). Over the years, Bishop has graced the albums of many great bluesmen including Clifton Chenier and John Lee Hooker. He toured with B.B. King in 1995. Bishop is known for his sense of humor, his unique style of slide guitar, and fusion of blues, gospel, R&B, and country flavors. He lives with his wife and family in the San Francisco area, is a prodigious gardener, and continues to play dates in the US and abroad. —*Michael Erlewine*

Let It Flow / May 1974 / Capricorn ✦✦✦✦
For his fourth album, Elvin Bishop organized a new backup group and switched to Capricorn Records. Capricorn was known as the standard bearer of the Southern rock movement—the Allman Brothers Band, The Marshall Tucker Band, etc.—and Bishop was able to emphasize the country/blues aspects of his persona and his music in the move from Marin County, California, to Macon, Georgia. The guest artists included the Allmans' Dickey Betts, Marshall Tucker's Toy Caldwell, Charlie Daniels, and Sly Stone, and Bishop turned in one of his best sets of songs, including "Travelin' Shoes" (with its Allmans-like twin lead guitar work), which became his first charting single, just as the album was his first to make the Top 100 LPs. —*William Ruhlmann*

Juke Joint Jump / Apr. 1975 / Capricorn ✦✦✦

The Best of Elvin Bishop: Crabshaw Rising / Sep. 1975 / Epic ✦✦✦
In his first manifestation as a band leader (1969-1972), Elvin Bishop lived in Marin County, CA, and performed under the auspices of promoter Bill Graham. Not surprisingly, the three albums he cut in that period, two for Graham's Fillmore label and the third for its parent, Epic, fit into the soul-blues-rock style of post-psychedelic San Francisco, even to the point of featuring an extended instrumental, "Hogbottom," on which Bishop takes Carlos Santana's place fronting the Santana percussion section. This ten-track compilation selects from the albums *The Elvin Bishop Group*, *Feel It!*, and *Rock My Soul*, effectively summarizing this phase in Bishop's career. Long out of print, it was superseded in 1994 by the 18-track CD *The Best of Elvin Bishop: Tulsa Shuffle*, which contained nine of its selections. Then, oddly enough, it was reissued in 1996! —*William Ruhlmann*

Struttin' My Stuff / Dec. 1975 / Capricorn ✦✦✦

Hog Heaven / 1978 / Capricorn ✦✦✦

Big Fun / 1988 / Alligator ✦✦✦

Don't Let the Bossman Get You Down! / 1991 / Alligator ✦✦✦✦
On *Don't Let the Bossman Get You Down*, Bishop projects a good-natured, humorous persona in the extended spoken-word sections of his songs, but still finds time to play a lot of tasty blues guitar. —*William Ruhlmann*

● **Sure Feels Good: The Best of Elvin Bishop** / 1992 / PolyGram ✦✦✦✦
A fine collection of the blues-rock guitarist's best moments, which covers more material than the earlier compilation, *Best of Elvin Bishop/Crabshaw Rising*. —*Stephen Thomas Erlewine*

Best of Elvin Bishop: Tulsa Shuffle / May 10, 1994 / Epic/Legacy ✦✦✦✦
This 18-track compilation selects from the albums *The Elvin Bishop Group*, *Feel It!*, and *Rock My Soul*. The only thing wrong with it is that it would be easy to make the mistake of thinking that it covers all of his solo career rather than only the first four years, especially because there have now been four different albums released with the title *The Best of Elvin Bishop*. —*William Ruhlmann*

Ace in the Hole / 1995 / Alligator ✦✦✦

Scrapper Blackwell (Francis Blackwell)

b. Feb. 21, 1903, Syracuse, NC, d. Oct. 7, 1962, Indianapolis, IN
Guitar, Vocals / Acoustic Chicago Blues
Scrapper Blackwell was best known for his work with pianist Leroy Carr during the early and mid-'30s, but he also recorded many solo sides between 1928 and 1935. A distinctive stylist whose work was closer to jazz than blues, Blackwell was an accomplished player with a technique, built around single-note picking, that anticipated the electric blues of the 1940s and 1950s. He abandoned music for more than 20 years after Carr's death in 1935, but re-emerged at the end of the 1950s

and began his career anew, before his life was taken in an apparent robbery attempt.

Francis Hillman "Scrapper" Blackwell was born and raised in Syracuse, NC. By the time he was a teenager, Blackwell was working as a part-time musician. By most accounts, as an adult Blackwell had a withdrawn personality, although he had an exceptionally good working relationship with Nashville-born pianist Leroy Carr, whom he met in Indianapolis in the mid-'20s. They made a natural team, for Carr's piano playing emphasized the bass, and liberated Blackwell to explore the treble strings of his instrument to the fullest. Carr and Blackwell performed together throughout the Midwest and parts of the South, including Louisville, St. Louis, Cincinnati, and Nashville, and were notably successful. With Blackwell's help, Carr became one of the top blues stars of the early '30s, and the two recorded well over 100 sides together between 1928 and 1935. Carr's heavy drinking and a nephritis condition caused his death in Indianapolis on April 29, 1935. After the Carr's death, Blackwell continued working long enough to cut a tribute to his late partner. His withdrawn personality didn't lend itself to an extended solo career, and he gave up the music business before the end of the 1930s.

At the end of the 1950s, with the folk/blues revival gradually coming into full swing, he was rediscovered living in Indianapolis, and prevailed upon to resume playing and recording. This he did, for the Prestige/Bluesville label, with at least one album's worth of material that showed his singing and playing unmarred by age or other abuse. Blackwell appeared ready to resume his career without missing a beat. In 1962, however, soon after finishing his work on his first Prestige/Bluesville long-playe, Blackwell was shot to death in a back alley in Indianapolis, the victim of a mugging. The crime was never solved.

Scrapper Blackwell was one of the most important guitar players of the 1920s and early '30s, with a clean, dazzlingly articulate style that anticipated the prominent solo work that would emerge in Chicago as electric blues in the 1940s and 1950s. His "string-snapping" solos transcend musical genres and defy the limitations of his period. Although Blackwell's recordings were done on acoustic guitar, the playing on virtually every extant track is—and this is no joke—electrifying in its clarity and intensity. Along with Tampa Red, Blackwell was one of a handful of pre-war blues guitarists whose work should be known by every kid who thinks it all started with Chuck Berry or even Muddy Waters. —*Bruce Eder*

★ **Virtuoso Guitar 1925-1934** / 1991 / Yazoo ✦✦✦✦✦
It's for recordings like this that a lot of blues guitar fans started listening to the music in the first place. The definitive Blackwell collection to date, featuring not only his best extant solo sides, but also his work in association with Leroy Carr, Black Bottom McPhail, and Tommy Bradley. The 14 songs here all have something to offer in the playing—and generally the singing as well—that will give the listener pause: a run, an arpeggio, a solo passage that makes you say, "Whoa, what was that?" The sound is surprisingly good, and one only wishes there were more than 14 songs here, although it's hard to imagine anything that could follow the last track, Leroy Carr's "Barrelhouse Woman No. 2." —*Bruce Eder*

Bobby "Blue" Bland

b. Jan. 27, 1930, Rosemont, TN
Vocals / Soul, R&B, Soul Blues, Electric Texas Blues, Electric R&B
Bobby Bland earned his enduring blues superstar status the hard way: without a guitar, harmonica, or any other instrument to fall back upon. All Bland had to offer was his magnificent voice, a tremendously powerful instrument in his early heyday, injected with charisma and melisma to spare. Just ask his legion of female fans, who deem him a sex symbol to this day.

For all his promise, Bland's musical career ignited slowly. He was a founding member of the Beale Streeters, the fabled Memphis aggregation that also included B.B. King and Johnny Ace. Singles for Chess in 1951 (produced by Sam Phillips) and Modern the next year bombed, but that didn't stop local deejay David Mattis from cutting Bland on a couple of 1952 singles for his fledgling Duke logo.

Bland's tormented crying style was still pretty rough around the edges before he entered the Army in late 1952. But his progress upon his 1955 return was remarkable; with saxist Bill Harvey's band (featuring guitarist Roy Gaines and trumpeter Joe Scott) providing sizzling support, Bland's assured vocal on the swaggering "It's My Life Baby" sounds like the work of a new man. By now, Duke was headed by hard-boiled Houston entrepreneur Don Robey, who provided top-flight bands for his artists. Scott soon became Bland's mentor, patiently teaching him the intricacies of phrasing when singing sophisticated fare (by 1962, Bland was credibly crooning "Blue Moon," a long way from Beale Street).

Most of Bland's savage Texas blues sides during the mid-to-late '50s featured the slashing guitar of Clarence Hollimon, notably "I Smell Trouble," "I Don't Believe," "Don't Want No Woman," "You Got Me

(Where You Want Me)," and the torrid "Loan a Helping Hand" and "Teach Me (How to Love You)." But the insistent guitar riffs guiding Bland's first national hit, 1957's driving "Farther up the Road," were contributed by Pat Hare, another vicious picker who would eventually die in prison after murdering his girlfriend and a cop. Later, Wayne Bennett took over on guitar, his elegant fretwork prominent on Bland's Duke waxings throughout much of the '60s.

The gospel underpinnings inherent in Bland's powerhouse delivery were never more apparent than on the 1958 outing "Little Boy Blue," a vocal tour de force that wrings every ounce of emotion out of the grinding ballad. Scott steered his charge into smoother material as the decade turned—the seminal mixtures of blues, R&B, and primordial soul "I Pity the Fool," the Brook Benton-penned "I'll Take Care of You," and "Two Steps from the Blues" were tremendously influential to a legion of up-and-coming southern soulsters.

Scott's blazing brass arrangements upped the excitement ante on Bland's frantic rockers "Turn on Your Love Light" in 1961 and "Yield Not to Temptation" the next year, but the vocalist was learning his lessons so well that he sounded just as conversant on soulful R&B rhumbas (1963's "Call on Me") and polished ballads ("That's the Way Love Is," "Share Your Love with Me") as with an after-hours blues revival of T-Bone Walker's "Stormy Monday Blues" that proved a most unlikely pop hit for him in 1962. With "Ain't Nothing You Can Do," "Ain't Doing Too Bad," and "Poverty," Bland rolled through the mid-'60s, his superstar status diminishing not a whit.

In 1973, Robey sold his labels to ABC Records, and Bland was part of the deal. Without Scott and his familiar surroundings to lean on, Bland's releases grew less consistent artistically, though *His California Album* in 1973 and *Dreamer* the next year boasted some nice moments (there was even an album's worth of country standards). The singer reteamed with his old pal B.B. King for a couple of mid-'70s albums that broke no new ground but further heightened Bland's profile, while his solo work for MCA teetered closer and closer to MOR (Bland has often expressed his admiration for ultra-mellow pop singer Perry Como).

Since the mid-'80s, Bland has recorded for Jackson, MS's Malaco Records. His pipes undeniably reflect the ravages of time, and those phlegm-flecked "snorts" he habitually emits become annoying in large doses. But Bobby "Blue" Bland endures as a blues superstar of the loftiest order. —*Bill Dahl*

Blues Consolidated / May 1958 / Duke ✦✦✦✦
An album split between Bland and his Blues Consolidated touring partner Junior Parker, featuring great early-'50s sides by these two Houston-based performers. —*Cub Koda & Hank Davis*

☆ **Two Steps from the Blues** / 1962 / Duke ✦✦✦✦✦
Including classics like "Don't Cry No More," "I Pity the Fool," and "Little Boy Blue," this early-'60s set captures Bland where his sound had just fully matured into a horn-punctuated blend of blues, gospel, and early soul. All 12 of the songs are included on MCA's *Duke Recordings* series, though, making this unnecessary if you're building a complete collection of Bland on CD. —*Richie Unterberger*

Call on Me / 1963 / MCA ✦✦✦✦
A near-perfect collection of early-'60s sides documents the man at his best. —*Hank Davis*

Touch of the Blues / 1968 / Duke ✦✦✦✦
During his Duke tenure, Bobby "Blue" Bland's rich, creamy voice was at its stark, dramatic peak. Like his other label releases, even when he got overly sentimental or just plain corny material, or the songs were overarranged, Bland's smashing leads made everything work. —*Ron Wynn*

★ **The Best of Bobby Blue Bland** / 1972 / MCA ✦✦✦✦✦
Excellent compilation of the sides that made the legend. Includes "Call on Me," "Farther up the Road," "I Pity the Fool," and "Turn on Your Love Light." —*Cub Koda*

His California Album / 1973 / MCA ✦✦✦
And his first for ABC-Dunhill in 1973 after more than two decades with Duke (Robey's still represented, though, under his songwriting alias of Deadric Malone, on four cuts, including the album's biggest hit, "This Time I'm Gone for Good"). Producer Steve Barri contemporized Bland by having him cover Leon Russell's "Help Me Make It Through the Day," Luther Ingram's "(If Loving You Is Wrong) I Don't Want to Be Right," and Gladys Knight & the Pips' "I've Got to Use My Imagination." —*Bill Dahl*

Together for the First Time . . . Live / 1974 / MCA ✦✦✦

☆ **The Best of Bobby Blue Bland, Vol. 2** / 198X / MCA ✦✦✦✦✦
Features the classics "It's My Life Baby," "Queen for a Day," and "Two Steps from the Blues." —*Cub Koda*

The 3b Blues Boy—the Blues Years: 1952-59 / 1991 / Ace ✦✦✦
25-track compilation of bluesy material that Bland recorded for Duke between 1952 and 1959. Bland had previously released a few sides for Chess and Modern in the early '50s, but these sides represent the era in which he began to find his voice. It still catches him at a relatively early stage in his development, concentrating on jump blues-oriented mate-

rial, sometimes with horn sections, showing the considerable influence of B.B. King. There's some sharp guitar on these sides (including some by Roy Gaines, who also played with Chuck Willis and Hound Dog Thornton), and the vocals are full and confident, if a bit overripe. But neophytes should begin with his early and mid-'60s sides, when his blend of blues and soul reached a much higher level of maturity. —Richie Unterberger

The Voice: Duke Recordings 1959-69 / 1991 / Ace ✦✦✦✦
A 26-track compilation of Duke sides from Bland's peak decade (1959-1969). MCA's two-volume The Duke Recordings covers this period in greater depth, and will be more readily available to most North American consumers. On its own terms, though, it's an excellent collection. Contains most of his biggest R&B hits ("Turn on Your Love Light," "Stormy Monday Blues," "Call on Me," "Ain't Nothing You Can Do"), as well as some cuts that didn't make it onto The Duke Recordings. —Richie Unterberger

★ **I Pity the Fool/The Duke Recordings, Vol. 1** / 1992 / MCA ✦✦✦✦✦
Everything the young Bland waxed for Duke between 1952 and the 1960 date that produced "Cry, Cry, Cry" and the R&B-laced "Don't Cry No More." From 1955 on, this is uniformly seminal stuff, Bland's vocal confidence growing by the session and buttressed by the consistently innovative riffs and solos of guitarists Clarence Hollimon, Wayne Bennett (he's amazing on a torrid "You Did Me Wrong"), Roy Gaines, and Pat Hare. "Farther Up the Road," the exotic ballad "Hold Me Tenderly," "Little Boy Blue," and the title track are but few of the two-disc collection's many standouts. No blues fan should be minus this set! —Bill Dahl

Years of Tears / 1993 / Malaco ✦✦✦✦
Perhaps no artist has flourished at Malaco more than Bobby "Blue" Bland. Bland's animated, raw voice, though not as wide-ranging, still has a character and quality unmatched in blues, soul or vintage R&B. This CD is his finest for the label since Members Only. The opening number "Somewhere Between Right & Wrong" has a simmering track, Bland's mournful, explosive leads, tasty organ, tight drumming, and on-the-money lyrics from composers Johnny Barranco and Jackson. It sets the stage for nine additional country-tinged and bluesy soul tunes, including three from Frederick Knight, who also produced his compositions. It's not his Duke material, but it's close enough to satisfy. —Ron Wynn

☆ **Turn on Your Love Light/The Duke Recordings, Vol. 2** / 1994 / MCA ✦✦✦✦✦
Picking up right where the first volume left off and continuing into 1964, this two-disc compilation (50 tracks!) showcases one of Bland's most appealing periods at Duke. Joe Scott was experimenting boldly with his protegé's repertoire, his brass-powered arrangements urging Bland to increased heights of incendiary energy on "Turn on Your Love Light" and "Yield Not to Temptation" (driven by future James Brown drummer Jabo Starks' funky traps) and advanced sophistication levels for the honey-smooth "Share Your Love with Me" and "That's the Way Love Is." Bennett's crackling blues licks invest "Stormy Monday Blues," "The Feeling Is Gone," and "Black Night" with T-Bone-derived tradition, while Bland handles Charlie Rich's "Who Will the Next Fool Be" with just the right amount of bluesy resignation. —Bill Dahl

Touch of the Blues/Spotlighting The Man / Mobile Fidelity ✦✦✦✦
Two of Bland's better albums for Duke coupled on one great-sounding CD. Both LPs were issued originally in 1969 but contained tracks from as far back as his 1967 Top Ten R&B hit "That Did It" and its immediate follow-up, "Touch of the Blues." Bland never turned his back on the style that brought him to prominence (he digs into Charles Brown's "Driftin' Blues" aggressively, Bennett providing luscious chording behind him), even if his stately reading of Joe Turner's "Chains of Love" is sweetened considerably by strings. On the other hand, the husky singer's unwise whack at Anthony Newley's Broadway showstopper "Who Can I Turn To" is about as far removed from blues tradition as is imaginable. —Bill Dahl

Blind Blake (Arthur Phelps)

b. 189?, Jacksonville, FL, d. 1933
Guitar, Vocals / Acoustic Country Blues, Piedmont Blues
What happened to Blind Blake? His disappearance in 1932 from the Chicago blues scene, where he was undisputed king of the string and recorded 81 solo sides for Paramount, is one of the unresolved mysteries of early blues. Similarly mysterious is Blake's prodigious fingerstyle guitar technique, which has plank spankers to this day asking: "How the hell did he do that!?"

Like many early blues recording artists, Blake was regionally well-known, if not legendary, before he began making records. His peregrinations through the Southeast and Midwest were those of the itinerant songster; his repertoire included everything from blues to rags to music hall novelties. On Paramount records he broke out in 1926 with his debut release, a finger-buster called "West Coast Blues." Through the late '20s he performed and recorded with banjoists Papa Charlie Jackson and Gus Cannon, chanteuses Ma Rainey and Ida Cox, pianist Char-

lie Spand and a host of others as first-call guitar on Paramount's studio A-team. His best playing, however, was reserved for solo outings like "Diddie-Wah-Diddie" or "Police Dog Blues." On these he spun off guitar variations so dense they were dubbed "piano sounding" by his label. The hot licks framed lyrics often laced with suggestive double entendre. His hypermetabolic instrumentals were full of diffident spoken asides in an accent that gave credence to his supposed Southern seaboard origins.

Blake spent part of 1930 and 1931 touring with the vaudeville show "Happy-Go-Lucky" and returned to the Paramount studios in Grafton, WI, for his final session in 1932. His subsequent whereabouts, including rumors of his murder or death by mishap, have never been substantiated. It's commonly supposed that, as the Depression knocked the bottom out of the race record industry, Blake simply moved back to the South so beloved in his song lyrics, and died there soon after.

Blake's influence, especially in the folk/blues revival, was pervasive. His brilliant playing was touted by guitar godfathers like Josh White and Gary Davis; his songs covered by contemporary acousticians including Dave Van Ronk, Leon Redbone and Ry Cooder. On guitar, he's still the one to beat . . . probably always will be. As he says himself, "Here's somethin' gonna make you feel good!" —Steve James

★ **Ragtime Guitar's Foremost Fingerpicker** / 1984 / Yazoo ✦✦✦✦✦
Ragtime Guitar's Foremost Fingerpicker contains a total of 28 prime tracks from Blind Blake. Alternating between solo acoustic numbers and songs recorded with a string band, the set demonstrates how exceptionally gifted the guitarist was—he's playing arrangements and rhythms that several subsequent generations were never able to completely figure out. Blind Blake was one of the finest acoustic guitarists of the '20s and '30s and this is the definitive compilation. —Thom Owens

Rory Block
....

Guitar, Vocals / Modern Acoustic Blues
Rory Block is one of the brightest stars among a galaxy of modern-day country-blues interpreters. Rory's superb renderings of classic songs by Robert Johnson, Tommy Johnson, Charley Patton, and others display her deep passion and instinct for historic preservation, but seldom are her covers mere mimics. With its body-pounds, potent bass-string snaps, and precision rhythms, her fierce acoustic-guitar attack recalls the great Willie Brown. Rory's originals are often as strong as her covers, a standout being the title track from Mama's Blues. Her urgent, soulful voice is in a class of its own. As Taj Mahal says, "She's very simply the best there is." —Jas Obrecht

High Heeled Blues / 1982 / Rounder ✦✦✦✦
This was the most blues-oriented release of the three sessions Block issued in 1989 for Rounder; it was also the most concentrated and successful. There were none of the experimental or tentative qualities that sometimes marred the other two dates; Block was in command from the opening moments of her cover of "Walkin' Blues" to the final bars of "Uncloudy Day." Her voice had fire, soul and grit, and she never sounded maudlin or unconvincing, whether doing "Hilarity Rag" or "Devil Got My Man." Her playing was also dynamic and focused, and John Sebastian obviously made a good production partner, as Block got back on track after making records that contained some good cuts but weren't as consistent. —Ron Wynn

Rhinestones and Steel Strings / 1984 / Rounder ✦✦✦✦
Guitarist/vocalist Rory Block's mix of traditional blues covers, originals, satirical and folk/country material was featured on this album mixing mid-'80s and early-'90s tracks. Her versions of Robert Wilkins' "No Way for Me to Get Along" and Rev. Gary Davis' "Sit Down on the Banks" were among the high points, as well as Block's "Dr. Make It Right" and "I Might Find a Way." For the most part, the songs were nicely performed and varied between upbeat and somber themes. Block's vocals were frequently outstanding and never less than convincing, while her playing was strong and steady. —Ron Wynn

● **Best Blues and Originals** / 1988 / Rounder ✦✦✦✦
Best Blues and Originals collects the highlights from Rory Block's '80s albums for Rounder, saving a bunch of fine tracks from otherwise spotty releases. It's a nice overview and, consequently, a solid introduction to her catalog. —Thom Owens

Mama's Blues / 1991 / Rounder ✦✦✦

Ain't I a Woman / 1992 / Rounder ✦✦✦✦
Rory Block's 11th album marked both a personal and professional milestone. Now a thoroughly experienced singer, Block sounded much more confident and assured doing traditional blues tunes. Her performance on the title cut was both assertive and definitive, while she also displayed her customary versatility, doing country and folk-flavored numbers such as "Silver Wings" and "Rolling Log" in addition to a stunning gospel number, "Walk in Jerusalem." Block's vocals and guitar work have blossomed, toughened, and greatly improved over her career, and were in prime form here. —Ron Wynn

Michael Bloomfield

b. Jul. 28, 1943, Chicago, IL, **d.** Feb. 15, 1981

Guitar / Electric Chicago Blues, Blues-Rock

Michael Bloomfield was born July 28, 1943, in Chicago, IL. An indifferent student and self-described social outcast, Bloomfield immersed himself in the multicultural music world that existed in Chicago in the 1950s.

He got his first guitar at age 13. Initially attracted to rock 'n' roll, Bloomfield soon discovered the electric blues indigenous to Chicago. At the age of 14 he began to visit blues clubs on Chicago's South Side in search of his new heroes: players such as Muddy Waters, Otis Spann, Howlin' Wolf, and Magic Sam. Not content with viewing the scene from the audience, Bloomfield was known to leap onto the stage, asking if he could sit in as he simultaneously plugged in his guitar and began playing riffs.

Bloomfield was quickly accepted on the South Side, as much for his ability as for the audiences' appreciation of the novelty of seeing a young White player where few Whites were seen. Bloomfield soon discovered a group of like-minded outcasts. Young White players such as Paul Butterfield, Nick Gravenites, Charlie Musselwhite, and Elvin Bishop were also establishing themselves as fans who could hold their own with established bluesmen.

In addition to playing with the established stars of the day, Bloomfield began to search out older, forgotten bluesmen, playing and recording with Sleepy John Estes, Yank Rachell ,Little Brother Montgomery, and Big Joe Williams, among others. By this time he was managing a Chicago folk music club, the Fickle Pickle, and often hired older acoustic blues players for the Tuesday night blues sessions. Bloomfield's guitar work as a session player caught the ear of legendary CBS producer and talent scout John Hammond, Sr., who flew to Chicago and immediately signed him to a recording contract. However CBS was unsure of exactly how to promote their new artist, declining to release any of the tracks recorded by Bloomfield's band, which included harp player Charlie Musselwhite.

With a contract but not much else, Bloomfield returned to playing clubs around Chicago until he was approached by Paul Rothchild, the producer of the Paul Butterfield Blues Band albums. Bloomfield was recruited to play slide guitar and piano on early recordings (later released as *The Lost Elektra Sessions*) which were rejected for not fully capturing the sound of the band. Although more competitors than friends, the addition of Bloomfield to the Butterfield Band provided Paul Butterfield with a musician of equal caliber—Paul and Michael inspired and challenged each other as they traded riffs and musical ideas.

In between recording sessions with the Butterfield Band, Bloomfield backed up Bob Dylan on the classic *Highway 61 Revisited* album, and appeared with him at the Newport Folk Festival in 1965. Declining an offer from Dylan to join his touring band, Bloomfield and the Butterfield Band returned to the studio; with the addition of pianist Mark Naftalin they finally captured their live sound on vinyl.

The first two Butterfield Blues Band albums, the Dylan sessions, and the live appearances by the Butterfield Band firmly established Bloomfield as one of the most talented and influential guitar players in America. The second album featured the Bloomfield composition "East-West" which ushered in an era of long instrumental psychedelic improvisations.

Bloomfield left the Butterfield Blues Band in early 1967 ostensibly to give original guitarist Elvin Bishop, in Mike's words, "a little space". Undoubtedly he had also become uncomfortable with Paul Butterfield's position as bandleader and was anxious to lead his own band.

That band, the Electric Flag, included Bloomfield's old friends from Chicago, organist Barry Goldberg and singer-songwriter Nick Gravenites, as well as bass player Harvey Brooks and drummer Buddy Miles. The band was well received at its official debut at the Monterey Pop Festival but quickly fell apart due to drugs, egos, and poor management.

Bloomfield, weary of the road, suffering from insomnia, and uncomfortable in the role of guitar superstar, returned to San Francisco to score movies, produce other artists, and play studio sessions. One of those sessions was a day of jamming in the studio with keyboardist Al Kooper, who had previously worked with Bloomfield on the 1965 Dylan sessions.

Super Session, the resultant release, with Bloomfield on side one and guitarist Stephen Stills on side two, once again thrust Bloomfield into the spotlight.

Although *Super Session* was the most successful recording of his career, Bloomfield considered it to be a "scam," more of an excuse to sell records than a pursuit of musical goals. After a follow-up live album, he "retired" to San Francisco and lowered his visibility.

In the '70s, Bloomfield played gigs in the San Francisco area and infrequently toured as Bloomfield and Friends, a group which usually included Mark Naftalin and Nick Gravenites. Bloomfield also occasion-

ally helped out friends by lending his name to recording projects and business propositions, such as the ill-fated Electric Flag reunion in 1974 and the KGB album in 1976. In the mid-'70s Bloomfield recorded a number of albums with a more traditional blues focus for smaller record labels.

By the late '70s, Bloomfield's continuing drug and health problems caused erratic behavior and missed gigs, alienating a number of his old associates. Michael Bloomfield was found dead in his car of a drug overdose in San Francisco, CA, on February 15, 1981.

Nick Gravenites remembers Michael Bloomfield this way: "I thought he was a huge giant of a person. I think the totality of his character is the thing that impressed me most. People forget how charismatic he was. I think it was the totality of his character I was impressed with, not only his musical ability but also his intellect, his sense of humor, his compassion, his generosity, all those things that make up a human being. And those are my fondest memories, of character.

"Michael's friends, the ones that were closest to him, really loved the guy. And they did it for a lot of reasons. He helped them live their lives, make something out of their lives in many ways, very profoundly. I can still think in terms of those major, those big terms, when I think about Michael." —*Jan Mark Wolkin*

● **Super Session** / 1968 / Columbia ✦✦✦✦
Al Kooper was the mastermind behind this appropriately named album, one side of which features his "spontaneous" studio collaboration with Mike Bloomfield and the other a session with Stephen Stills. The recordings have an off-the-cuff energy that displays the inventiveness of the two guitarists to best advantage. The best-selling recording of Bloomfield's career, it inspired the follow-up *The Live Adventures of Mike Bloomfield and Al Kooper.* —*Jeff Tamarkin*

It's Not Killing Me / 1969 / Columbia ✦✦
Let's see. For his first solo album, take a brilliant young guitarist who can barely sing and put the emphasis on . . . his vocals. Well, somebody thought it was a good idea. Too bad they were wrong. There are just a few examples of that B.B. King-inflected guitar style among the rock and country-flavored throwaways. —*Cary Wolfson*

The Live Adventures of Mike Bloomfield and Al Kooper / 1969 / Columbia ✦✦
Recorded over three nights in 1968 at the Fillmore Auditorium in San Francisco, the follow-up to the acclaimed *Super Session* has its moments, but is mostly long on '60s noodly grooviness and lacking in focus and inspiration. It's notable (sort of) for Bloomfield's singing debut. —*Cary Wolfson*

Triumverate / 1973 / Columbia ✦✦✦
In 1973 someone at Columbia evidently decided to try to recoup some of the investment the label had made in Bloomfield and John Hammond—they were thrown into a recording studio along with Dr. John, who had recently scored a hit with "Right Place, Wrong Time." It probably sounded like a good idea at the time, but the results were uninspired. Pass by this CD and pick up any one of their solo recordings instead. —*Jan Mark Wolkin*

Try It Before You Buy It / 1975 / One Way ✦✦
Try It Before You Buy It is one of Michael Bloomfield's neglected albums, and there's a reason why—although there's some very fine playing scattered throughout the album, the performances are uneven and unfocused. Furthermore, the album leans too close to a straight rock 'n' roll direction for blues purists. If you dig hard, there are some rewards on *Try It Before You Buy It*, but on the whole, it's one that should be left on the shelf. —*Thom Owens*

Living in the Fast Lane / 1980 / AJK ✦✦✦
Michael Bloomfield was a pioneer in blues-rock, one of the performers who found a way to maintain his own sound while paying tribute to the blues greats that created the music he idolized. The ten tracks presented on *Living in the Fast Lane* weren't as vital as his earlier material, but were done with the same intensity and passion that marked all his numbers. They were backed on several cuts by Duke Tito and The Marin Country Playboys, while on "When I Get Home," the Singers of The Church of God in Christ joined lead vocalist Roger Troy for a rousing, spirit-filled performance that was the album's high point. —*Ron Wynn*

● **Don't Say That I Ain't Your Man** / 1994 / Sony ✦✦✦✦
Fifteen tracks covering the pioneering blues-rock guitarist's '60s work, which was by far his best and most influential. Bloomfield worked with a bunch of bands during the decade, and the compilation flits rather hurriedly from his contributions to the Paul Butterfield Blues Band and Electric Flag to his collaborations with Al Kooper and some late-'60s solo tracks (none of his groundbreaking mid-'60s work with Dylan is here). Collectors will be interested in the first five songs, which date from previously unreleased sessions produced by John Hammond in late 1964 and early 1965. Featuring Charlie Musselwhite on harmonica, this pre-Butterfield Blues Band outfit plays convincingly, but the material is standard-issue, and Bloomfield's vocals are thin and weak (they didn't

improve much over time). As befits Bloomfield's considerable but erratic talent, this is an interesting but erratic compilation; seek out the first two Paul Butterfield albums for a more cohesive showcase of his skills. *—Richie Unterberger*

I'm With You Always / Demon ✦✦✦
This release, recorded at McCabe's Guitar Shop in Santa Monica, CA, in 1977, captures a superb live show, with Bloomfield in top form as he performs before an appreciative audience in an intimate setting. Michael's singing is spirited and his guitar playing is precise and inventive as he plays favorite songs from his repertoire. Highlights include solo acoustic performances of two songs written by Shelton Brooks in the early 1900s, a piano/guitar duet demonstrating the rapport he had with pianist Mark Naftalin, and hot performances by Bloomfield, Naftalin and a rhythm section of Buddy Helm on drums and Buell Neidlinger on bass. Bloomfield shows what he had been doing all those years out of the spotlight—refining his technique and researching the music he loved. *—Jan Mark Wolkin*

The Root of Blues / Laserlight ✦✦✦
A budget-label reissue of the instructional blues LP released by *Guitar Player* magazine in 1976, this CD includes most of the songs but omits Michael's spoken passages about each track. Bloomfield pays tribute to his influences and favorites: acoustic and electric, solo and with a band. Standout tracks include "Death in My Family," played in the style of Guitar Slim, "WDIA," a tribute to B.B. King, "City Girl," dedicated to T-Bone Walker, and an acoustic version of "Kansas City," played, in Bloomfield's words, "in a style I would call 'Travis Picking'," after Merle Travis. It seems an anomaly to use a modern style for such an old song, but the method of syncopated contrapuntal fingerpicking is well suited to the song because the key of E has so many open strings." *—Jan Mark Wolkin*

Juke Boy Bonner

b. Mar. 22, 1932, Bellville, TX, d. Jun. 29, 1978, Houston, TX
Guitar, Harmonica, Vocals / Electric Texas Blues
One-man bands weren't any too common on the postwar blues scene. Joe Hill Louis and Dr. Ross come to mind as greats who plied their trade all by their lonesome—and so did Juke Boy Bonner, a Texan whose talent never really earned him much in the way of tangible reward.

Born into impoverished circumstances in the Lone Star State during the Depression, Weldon Bonner took up the guitar in his teens. He caught a break in 1947 in Houston, winning a talent contest that led to a spot on a local radio outlet. He journeyed to Oakland in 1956, cutting his debut single for Bob Geddins's Irma imprint ("Rock with Me Baby"/ "Well Baby") with Lafayette "Thing" Thomas supplying the lead guitar. Goldband Records boss Eddie Shuler was next to take a chance in 1960; Bonner recorded for him in Lake Charles, LA, with Katie Webster on piano, but once again, nothing happened career-wise.

Troubled by stomach problems during the '60s, Bonner utilized his hospital downtime to write poems that he later turned into songs. He cut his best work during the late '60s for Arhoolie Records, accompanying himself on both guitar and racked harmonica as he weaved extremely personal tales of his rough life in Houston. A few European tours ensued, but they didn't really lead to much. Toward the end of his life, he toiled in a chicken processing plant to make ends meet. Bonner died of cirrhosis of the liver in 1978. *—Bill Dahl*

● **Life Gave Me a Dirty Deal** / 1969 / Arhoolie ✦✦✦✦
Likely the most consistent and affecting collection you'll encounter by this singular Texas bluesman, whose strikingly personal approach was stunningly captured by Arhoolie's Chris Strachwitz during the late '60s in Houston. Twenty-three utter originals include "Stay off Lyons Avenue," "Struggle Here in Houston," "I Got My Passport," and the title track. Bonner sang movingly of his painfully impoverished existence for Arhoolie, and the results still resound triumphantly today. *—Bill Dahl*

☆ **The Struggle** / 1981 / Arhoolie ✦✦✦✦✦
Recorded in extreme stereo, with drums on one channel and Bonner's guitar on the other, this is Juke Boy Bonner's most cohesive album. Great songwriting and performances throughout. *—Cub Koda*

Roy Book Binder

b. Oct. 5, 1941, New York City, NY
Guitar / Modern Acoustic Blues
An often stirring folk/blues guitarist and vocalist, Roy Book Binder's been playing country blues since the mid-'60s, when he began recording for Blue Goose. Greatly influenced by Rev. Gary Davis and Pink Anderson, Book Binder played in East Coast coffeehouses in the early '60s, then began accompanying Rev. Davis on tours in the mid-'60s. He also played with Larry Johnson, Arthur "Big Boy" Crudup, and Homesick James. Besides constant concerts and tours, Book Binder's made additional recordings for Blue Goose, Adelphi, and Rounder. *—Ron Wynn and Stephen Thomas Erlewine*

Bookeroo! / 1988 / Rounder ✦✦✦

● **The Hillbilly Blues Cats** / 1992 / Rounder ✦✦✦✦
Roy Book Binder and his Hillbilly Blues Cats band expertly convey the urgency of vintage blues by performing them with a brash rockabilly attitude. They cover classic songs in a manner that's neither reverential nor disrespectful, putting their own spin on such numbers as Blind Willie McTell's "Statesboro Blues" or Happy Traum's "Mississippi John." Book Binder's vocals are joyous, exuberant and sometimes comical, while his trio provides stomping backgrounds and harmonies. Although Book Binder and the band can't improve upon the originals, they do nothing to detract from an appreciation of them. *—Ron Wynn*

James Booker (James Carroll Booker III)

b. Dec. 17, 1939, d. Nov. 8, 1983
Piano / R&B, Blues, Piano Blues, Acoustic New Orleans Blues, Boogie-Woogie
Certainly one of the most flamboyant New Orleans pianists in recent memory, James Carroll Booker III was a major influence on the local rhythm and blues scene in the '50s and '60s. Booker's training included classical instruction until age 12, by which time he had already begun to gain recognition as a blues and gospel organist on radio station WMRY every Sunday. By the time he was out of high school he had recorded on several occasions, including his own first release, "Doing the Hambone" in 1953. In 1960 he made the national charts with "Gonzo," an organ instrumental, and over the course of the next two decades played and recorded with artists as varied as Lloyd Price, Aretha Franklin, Ringo Starr, the Doobie Brothers, and B.B. King. In 1967 he was convicted of possession of heroin and served a one-year sentence at Angola Penitentiary (referred to as the "Ponderosa"), which took the momentum out of an otherwise promising career. The rediscovery of "roots" music by college students during the '70s (focusing primarily on "Fess"—Professor Longhair) provided the opportunity for a comeback by 1974, with numerous engagements at local clubs like Tipitina's, the Maple Leaf, and Snug Harbor.

Booker's left hand was simply phenomenal, often a problem for bass players who found themselves running for cover in an attempt to stay out of the way; with it he successfully amalgamated the jazz and rhythm and blues idioms of New Orleans, adding more than a touch of gospel for good measure. His playing was also highly improvisational, reinventing a progression (usually his own) so that a single piece would evolve into a medley of itself. In addition, he had a plaintive and searing vocal style that was equally comfortable with gospel, jazz standards, blues, or popular songs. Despite his personal eccentricities, Booker had the respect of New Orleans' best musicians, and elements of his influence are still very much apparent in the playing of pianists like Henry Butler and Harry Connick, Jr. *—Bruce Boyd Raeburn*

New Orleans Piano Wizard: Live! / Nov. 27, 1977 / Rounder ✦✦✦✦
Why so much of what pianist/vocalist James Booker recorded in the 1970s didn't surface until the '90s is a mystery, but that's secondary compared to the greatness routinely presented on this CD. It contains nine Booker selections that he performed at the 1977 Boogie Woogie and Ragtime Piano Contest held in Zurich. His relentless, driving style, ability to switch from a hard-hitting tune to a light, soft one without skipping a beat, and wild mix of sizzling keyboard licks and bemused, manic vocals is uniformly impressive. It's a bit short for a CD at 37 minutes, but it has so much flamboyant music and singing that it shouldn't be missed. *—Ron Wynn*

Resurrection of the Bayou Maharajah / 1977-1982 / Rounder ✦✦✦✦
Pianist/vocalist James Booker was a wondrous player and a rollicking, unpredictable performer. This collection of late-'70s and early-'80s tracks feature amazing chordal forays, splintering riffs, barrelhouse, boogie-woogie, and second-line-tinged R&B solos. Booker rambles, cajoles, exaggerates, mocks,and soars while punctuating his wry singing with astonishing keyboard maneuvers. There is nothing here that isn't first-rate. While Booker's demise was a tragedy, this and other sessions that he left behind are the ultimate tribute to his greatness. *—Ron Wynn*

★ **Classified** / Oct. 18, 1982+Oct. 20, 1982 / Rounder ✦✦✦✦✦
While there has suddenly been a flood of CDs featuring masterful New Orleans keyboard wizard and vocalist James Booker, his best release arguably remains *Classified*. The 12-track set, recently issued on CD, was a landmark album, as Booker displayed every facet of his distinctive style. He did uptempo blues, quasi-classical, rock and R&B, making them all sound easy while performing frequently awesome keyboard feats. His "Professor Longhair Medley: Bald Head/Tipitina" pays homage to a legend while also demonstrating how much farther Booker's pianistic skills had developed. While his vocals sometimes aren't the equal of his brilliant playing, they're never less than effective and are sometimes almost frightening in their intensity. *—Ron Wynn*

King of the New Orleans Keyboard / Junco Partner ✦✦✦✦
Spectacular date by a great New Orleans pianist whose personal difficulties prevented him from both long life and sustained career achievement. Booker was cited as inspiration by everyone from Dr. John to

Harry Connick, Jr., and played with an array of performers, from Lloyd Price to Aretha Franklin, B.B. King, Ringo Starr, and the Doobie Brothers. He seamlessly fused a blues base, jazz touches, and R&B/gospel feeling, and this was among his best (and few) recordings. —*Ron Wynn*

Eddie Boyd (Edward Riley Boyd)

b. Nov. 25, 1914, Stovall, MS, d. Jul. 13, 1994
Piano, Vocals / Chicago Blues, Piano Blues

Few postwar blues standards have retained the universal appeal of Eddie Boyd's "Five Long Years." Cut in 1951, Boyd's masterpiece has attracted faithful covers by B.B. King, Muddy Waters, Jimmy Reed, Buddy Guy, and too many other bluesmen to recount here. But Boyd's discography is filled with evocative compositions, often full of after-hours ambience.

Like so many Chicago blues stalwarts, Boyd hailed from the fertile Mississippi Delta. The segregationist policies that had a stranglehold on much of the South didn't appeal to the youngster, so he migrated to Memphis. In 1941 Boyd settled in Chicago, falling in with the "Bluebird beat" crowd that recorded for producer Lester Melrose. Melrose produced Boyd's own 1947 recording debut for RCA as well; the pianist stayed with Victor through 1949.

Boyd reportedly paid for the date that produced "Five Long Years" himself, peddling the track to JOB Records (where the stolid blues topped the R&B charts during 1952). Powerful deejay Al Benson signed Boyd to a contract with his Parrot imprint and promptly sold the pact to Chess, inaugurating a stormy few years with Chicago's top blues outlet. There he waxed "24 Hours" and "Third Degree," both huge R&B hits in 1953, and a host of other Chicago blues gems. But Boyd and Leonard Chess were often at loggerheads, so it was on to Narvel "Cadillac Baby" Eatmon's Bea & Baby imprint in 1959 for eight solid sides with Robert Jr. Lockwood on guitar and to a slew of lesser labels after that.

Sick of the discrimination he perceived toward African-Americans in this country, Boyd became enamored of Europe during his tour with the 1965 American Folk Blues Festival, so he moved to Belgium. Boyd cut prolifically during the late '60s, including two LPs for producer Mike Vernon. In the early '70s, he settled in Helsinki, Finland, where he played often and lived comfortably until his death. —*Bill Dahl*

7936 South Rhodes / 1968 / Epic ✦✦✦
Recorded in London in January 1968 with three members of the early lineup of Fleetwood Mac (the one that played blues, not pop-rock): Peter Green (guitar), John McVie (bass), and Mick Fleetwood (drums). It's an adequate setting for Boyd's straight Chicago piano blues, going heavier on the slow-to-mid-tempo numbers than the high-spirited ones, though Green is a far more sympathetic accompanist than the rhythm section. —*Richie Unterberger*

● **Third Degree** / 1993 / Charly ✦✦✦✦
Amazingly, the only comprehensive overview of Boyd's 1951-1959 Chess stint available on CD. Both "Third Degree" and "24 Hours" are aboard this 20-track compilation, along with the lesser-known standouts "I Got the Blues," "Nothing but Trouble," and "Cool Kind Treatment." Boyd's sturdy, concise piano work and darkly introspective vocals were brilliantly captured on tape by Leonard Chess, even if the two weren't exactly the best of pals. —*Bill Dahl*

Five Long Years / EVI ✦✦✦✦
One of the first and best of Boyd's many overseas recordings, cut while he was in the midst of that auspicious 1965 American Folk Blues Festival tour of Europe. While the caravan was ensconced in London, young producer Mike Vernon spirited Boyd and a rhythm section (guitarist Buddy Guy, bassist Jimmie Lee Robinson, and drummer Fred Below) off to the studio, where Boyd ran through some of his classics ("I'm Comin' Home," "24 Hours," the title track) and a few less familiar items while alternating between piano and organ. —*Bill Dahl*

Tiny Bradshaw

b. Sep. 23, 1905, Youngstown, OH, d. Nov. 26, 1958, Cincinnati, OH
Piano, Drums, Vocals / Electric Jump Blues

Tiny Bradshaw was one of the most prominent bandleaders of the '30s and '40s, who led groups of essentially jazz-trained musicians into the developing (and more commercial) field that came to be known as rhythm and blues. A vocalist with other bands early in his career, Bradshaw formed his own band in 1934 and kept it going through the early '50s, enjoying five *Billboard* hits (and also recording the original "Train Kept A-Rollin'") with King Records (where he was a labelmate to many of the other leading jump blues performers of the era). Bradshaw's band produced such saxophone stars as Sonny Stitt, Red Prysock, and Sil Austin; among the vocalists to record with the group were Roy Brown, Arthur Prysock, Lonnie Johnson, and Tiny Kennedy. —*Jim O'Neal*

Great Composer / 1959 / King ✦✦✦
Domestic CD collection that duplicates one of the popular jump blues bandleader's early albums from the King catalog. —*Bill Dahl*

● **Breaking Up the House** / Charly ✦✦✦✦
Sixteen of Tiny Bradshaw's biggest and hardest-swinging King label waxings from 1950-52, notably "The Train Kept A-Rollin'," "Well, Oh Well," "Two Dry Bones on the Pantry Shelf," "Walkin' the Chalk Line," and the jiving title item. Unfortunately, the torrid big band-styled instrumental arrangements that also defined Bradshaw's output are nowhere to be found on this collection. —*Bill Dahl*

Billy Branch (William Earl Branch)

b. Oct. 3, 1951, Great Lakes, IL
Harmonica, Vocals / Modern Electric Blues, Chicago Blues

If blues harmonica has a longterm future on the Chicago circuit, Billy Branch will likely play a leading role in shaping its direction. Educator as well as musician, Branch has led the Sons of Blues, his skin-tight quartet, since the late '70s. Despite numerous personnel changes, the SOBs have never wavered in their dedication to pure, unadulterated Chicago blues. —*Bill Dahl*

Harp Attack! / 1990 / Alligator ✦✦✦✦
Four of the Windy City's undisputed harmonica masters in the same studio, trading solos and vocals with good-natured abandon. Billy's showcases are the apt original "New Kid on the Block" and a deft cover of Little Walter's "Who." —*Bill Dahl*

● **The Blues Keep Following Me Around** / 1995 / Verve ✦✦✦✦
Branch and Carl Weathersby ventured down to Maurice, LA, to cut this impressive disc with a home-grown rhythm section, but only Branch's name appears on its front. Certainly the harpist is the star of the show, growling covers of dusties by Sonny Boy Williamson, Willie Dixon, and Howlin' Wolf. Nevertheless, guitarist Weathersby provides two of the set's highlights, passionately singing his own "Should Have Been Gone" and "Should Have Known Better." —*Bill Dahl*

Billy Branch and Hubert Sumlin / Wolf ✦✦✦✦
This disc is a fine portrait of Chicago blues—past and present. Award-winning harpist Billy Branch and legendary giant of the famed Howlin' Wolf Band, Hubert Sumlin, here join hands with some of the finest contemporary musicians in the Windy City—among them: Willie Kent, John Primer, Johnny B. Moore, and Carl Weathersby. Sumlin offers two superb band tracks as well as five acoustic duets with guitarist John Primer. In addition, there are four Billy Branch numbers that recast the work of Jimmy Rogers, Jimmy Reed, and Little Walter without ever becoming slavish. The dual-guitar work of Johnny B. Moore and John Primer is exceptional. —*Larry Hoffman*

Hadda Brooks

Piano, Vocals / Piano Blues

In the mid-to-late '40s, Black popular music began to mutate from swing jazz and boogie-woogie into the sort of rhythm and blues that helped lay the foundation for rock 'n' roll. Singer and pianist Hadda Brooks was one of the many figures who were significant in aiding that transition, although she's largely forgotten today. While her torch song delivery was rooted in the big-band era, her boogie-woogie piano looked forward to jump blues and R&B. Ironically, the same qualities that made her briefly successful—her elegant vocals and jazzy arrangements—left her ill-equipped to compete when harder-driving forms of rhythm and blues, and then early rock 'n' roll, began to dominate the marketplace in the early '50s. —*Richie Unterberger*

● **That's My Desire** / 1994 / Virgin ✦✦✦✦
Twenty-five tracks from her prime, recorded for Modern in the 1940s and 1950s, including her hits "That's My Desire" and "Out of the Blue," as well as "Anytime, Anyplace, Anywhere." While Brooks was an important figure of the L.A. 1940s R&B scene, latter-day listeners may find this rather tame. Vocally she owed much more to pop-jazz stylings than gritty R&B influences. Her most durable and influential performances were her instrumental ones at the piano bench, especially on the pounding "Swingin' the Boogie," which leads off this collection. —*Richie Unterberger*

Lonnie Brooks

b. Dec. 18, 1933, Dubuisson, LA
Guitar, Vocals / Modern Electric Blues

Having forged a unique Louisiana/Chicago blues synthesis unlike anyone else's on the competitive Windy City scene, charismatic guitarist Lonnie Brooks has long reigned as one of the town's top bluesmen. A masterful showman, the good-natured Brooks puts on a show equal to his recordings (and that's saying a lot, considering there's four decades of wax to choose from).

Born Lee Baker, Jr., in Louisiana, Lonnie didn't play guitar seriously until he was in his early 20s and living in Port Arthur, TX. Rapidly assimilating the licks of B.B. King and Long John Hunter, he landed a gig with zydeco pioneer Clifton Chenier before inaugurating his own recording career in 1957 with the influential swamp-pop ballad "Family

Rules" for Goldband Records. The young rock 'n' roller—then billed as Guitar Junior—enjoyed more regional success on Goldband with the rocking dance number "The Crawl." Mercury also issued two 45s by Guitar Junior.

When Sam Cooke offerred the young rocker a chance to accompany him to Chicago, he gladly accepted. But two problems faced him once he arrived: there was another Guitar Junior in town (precipitating the birth of Lonnie Brooks), and the bayou blues that so enthralled Gulf Coast crowds didn't cut it up north. Scattered session work and a series of R&B-oriented 45s for Midas, USA, Chirrup, and Chess ensued during the '60s, as Lonnie learned a new style of blues.

By the late '70s, Brooks was gaining a deserved reputation as an exceptionally dynamic Chicago bluesman with a fresh perspective. He cut four outstanding sides for Alligator's first batch of *Living Chicago Blues* anthologies in 1978 that quickly led to his own 'Gator debut LP, *Bayou Lightning*, the next year. Five more albums of his own for the label and extensive touring have cemented Brooks' standing as a Chicago blues giant. —*Bill Dahl*

● **Bayou Lightning** / 1979 / Alligator ✦✦✦✦
All the promise that Lonnie Brooks possessed was realized on this album, his finest and most consistent to date. The churning bayou groove of "Voodoo Daddy," a soul-steeped "Watch What You Got," a bone-chilling remake of Junior Parker's "In the Dark," rollicking covers of Tommy Tucker's "Alimony" and Brooks' own "Figure Head," and the swaggering originals "You Know What My Body Needs" and "Watchdog" are among the set's many incendiary highlights. —*Bill Dahl*

Turn on the Night / 1981 / Alligator ✦✦✦

Hot Shot / 1983 / Alligator ✦✦✦✦
A return to rollicking good-time form, boasting the roaring "Don't Take Advantage of Me" and "I Want All My Money Back," relentless rocking revivals of Otis Blackwell's "Back Trail" and J.B. Lenoir's "One More Shot," and a faithful remake of Lonnie Brooks' own "Family Rules" from the Guitar Junior era. —*Bill Dahl*

The Crawl / 1984 / Charly ✦✦✦✦
Lonnie Brooks' pervasive 1950s bayou blues roots, laid bare and rocking hard. "Family Rules" was highly influential to the blossoming swamp-pop movement soon sweeping southern Louisiana; "The Crawl," "I Got It Made (When I Marry Shirley Mae)," "Roll, Roll, Roll," and "Knocks Me Out" (the latter one of his Mercury singles) drive with youthful abandon. The youngster's ears were wide-open—he even covered Harlan Howard's country ditty "Pick Me Up on Your Way Down," investing it with serious swamp angst. —*Bill Dahl*

Live at Pepper's 1968 / 1985 / Black Top ✦✦✦

Wound up Tight / 1986 / Alligator ✦✦✦
More energetic efforts with a decidedly rocked-up edge. Johnny Winter, long an ardent admirer of Brooks back to the Guitar Junior days, drops by with a passel of fiery guitar licks for the title track and "Got Lucky Last Night." —*Bill Dahl*

Big Bill Broonzy (William Lee Conley Broonzy)

b. Jun. 26, 1893, Scott, MS, d. Aug. 15, 1958, Chicago, IL
Guitar, Mandolin, Violin, Vocals / Acoustic Country Blues
In terms of his musical skill, the sheer size of his repertoire, the length and variety of his career and his influence on contemporaries and musicians who would follow, Big Bill Broonzy is among a select few of the most important figures in recorded blues history. Among his hundreds of titles are standards like "All by Myself" and "Key to the Highway." In this country he was instrumental in the growth of the Chicago Blues sound, and his travels abroad rank him as one of the leading blues ambassadors.

Literally born on the banks of the Mississippi, he was one of a family of 17. He learned to fiddle on a homemade instrument. Taught by his uncle, he was performing by age ten at social functions and in church. After brief stints on the pulpit and in the Army, he moved to Chicago, where he switched his attention from violin to guitar, playing with elders like Papa Charlie Jackson. Broonzy began his recording career with Paramount in 1927. In the early '30s he waxed some brilliant blues and hokum and worked Chicago and the road with great players like pianist Black Bob, guitarist Bill Weldon, and Memphis Minnie.

During the Depression Big Bill Broonzy continued full steam ahead, doing some acrobatic label-hopping (Paramount to Bluebird to Columbia to Okeh!). In addition to solo efforts, he contributed his muscular guitar licks to recordings by Bumble Bee Slim, John Lee (Sonny Boy) Williamson, and others who were forging a powerful new Chicago sound.

In 1938, Broonzy was at Carnegie Hall (ostensibly filling in for the fallen Robert Johnson) for John Hammond's revolutionary Spirituals to Swing Series. The following year he appeared with Benny Goodman and Louis Armstrong in George Seldes' film production *Swingin' the Dream*. After his initial brush with the East Coast cognoscenti, however,

Broonzy spent a good part of the early '40s barnstorming the South with Lil Green's road show or kicking back in Chicago with Memphis Slim.

He continued alternating stints in Chicago and New York with coast-to-coast road work until 1951, when live performances and recording dates overseas earned him considerable notoriety in Europe and led to worldwide touring. Back in the States he recorded for Chess, Columbia, and Folkways, working with a spectrum of artists from Blind John Davis to Pete Seeger. In 1955 *Big Bill Blues*, his life as told to Danish writer Yannick Bruynoghe, was published.

In 1957, after one more British tour, the pace began to catch up with Broonzy. He spent the last year of his life in and out of hospitals and succumbed to cancer in 1958. He survives though; not only in his music, but in the remembrances of people who knew him... from Muddy Waters to Studs Terkel. A gentle giant they say, tough enough to survive the blues world but not so tough he wouldn't give a struggling young musician the shirt off his back. His music, of course, is absolutely basic to the blues experience. —*Steve James*

Big Bill Broonzy Sings Folk Songs / 1962 / Smithsonian/Folkways ✦✦✦✦
Big Bill Broonzy was a narrative genius; someone who could take lyrics, situations, and themes and make them resonate with pain, sadness, anger, or joy. This 11-song set takes a slightly different tack. It's a compilation with Broonzy doing his renditions of well-known (some obscure) folk songs. From the woeful laments of "Backwater Blues" and "Tell Me Who" to the assertive strains of "This Train" and "I Don't Want No Woman (To Try to Be My Boss)," Broonzy puts his own stamp on every number, even shopworn items like "John Henry" and "Bill Bailey." —*Ron Wynn*

Big Bill Broonzy and Washboard Sam / 1962 / MCA ✦✦✦

★ **The Young Big Bill Broonzy (1928-35)** / 1968 / Yazoo ✦✦✦✦✦
The young Bill Broonzy was as far removed from his later folk blues posturings as you could imagine. If you're only familiar with his later work, these early sides will come as quite a jolt. Big Bill whips off some fleet-fingered single note leads and his rhythmic drive is never less than spot on. Great stuff. —*Cub Koda*

☆ **Do That Guitar Rag (1928-1935)** / 1973 / Yazoo ✦✦✦✦✦
This is a marvelous little companion piece to *Young Big Bill Broonzy (1928-35)* on Yazoo. Broonzy's ragtime guitar picking is textbook in its scope, and his vocals are as warm as can be. Dubbed from old 78s, the ultra high quality of the music make any audiophile nitpicking a moot point indeed. Broonzy at his youngest and full of pep. —*Cub Koda*

★ **Good Time Tonight** / 1990 / Columbia/Legacy ✦✦✦✦✦
If you're following the 30-plus year career of Bill Broonzy and already have the two early compilations available on Yazoo, here's where you go next. These are basically ensemble works covering the time frame between 1930 to 1940 and Broonzy sounds very comfortable in the company of Blind John Davis and Joshua Altheimer. The 20 tracks compiled here (culled from various Vocalion, ARC, and Columbia sessions) sound pretty great, benefitting mightily from modern sound restoration devices. —*Cub Koda*

☆ **Blues in the Mississippi Night** / 1990 / Rykodisc ✦✦✦✦✦
Writer, producer, and historian Alan Lomax managed something truly unique in 1946. He not only brought together pianist Memphis Slim, guitarist Big Bill Broonzy, and harmonica player Sonny Boy Williamson together for a concert, but managed to get them to talk frankly and specifically about their experiences in the segregated Deep South. At this time, few people outside the region really knew what was happening there, and even fewer who lived under the system ever discussed it openly. The anecdotes and incidents described are shocking and disgusting; they were even more shocking when aired in 1946. The complete version appears here in all its hard-hitting glory. —*Ron Wynn*

Buster Brown

b. Aug. 15, 1911, Georgia, d. Jan. 31, 1976, Brooklyn, NY
Harmonica, Vocals / R&B, Electric Blues, Electric Harmonica Blues
Whooping blues harpists nearing the age of 50 with No. 1 R&B hits to their credit were predictably scarce in 1959. Nevertheless, that's the happy predicament Buster Brown found himself in when his infectious "Fannie Mae" paced the charts. Even more amazingly, the driving number made serious inroads on the pop airwaves as well.

The Georgian, whose harp style was clearly influenced by Sonny Terry, had never made a professional recording (there was a 1943 Library of Congress session that laid unissued at the time) before Fire Records boss Bobby Robinson brought the short, stockily built Brown into a New York studio in June of 1959 to wax "Fannie Mae."

Brown's reign as an unlikely star was short-lived. He managed minor follow-up hits on Fire with a rather ragged 1960 revival of Louis Jordan's "Is You Is or Is You Ain't My Baby" and his 1962 farewell bow, the effervescent rocker "Sugar Babe." A subsequent 1964 stop at Chicago's

Checker Records produced a glistening update of the old blues "Craw-lin' Kingsnake" that sank without a trace. —*Bill Dahl*

● **The New King of the Blues** / 1959 / Collectables ✦✦✦✦
Best of the Fire sessions, including No. 1 hit "Fannie Mae" and "Is You Is or Is You Ain't My Baby?" —*Barry Lee Pearson*

Raise a Ruckus Tonight / 1976 / DJM ✦✦✦✦
Twenty-one Fire Records masters by the whooping harmonica ace, including his classic "Fannie Mae" (in crystal-clear stereo), the irresistible "Sugar Babe," and a load of similar stompers that should have been hits but weren't—"Good News," "Doctor Brown," the previously unissued "No More," and "Lost in a Dream." Even at something other than 12-bar fare; "Blueberry Hill," "St. Louis Blues," and the Moonglows' "Sincerely" definitely didn't suit Brown's raucous, untutored approach. —*Bill Dahl*

Charles Brown

b. Sep. 13, 1922, Texas City, TX
Piano, Vocals / R&B, Electric West Coast Blues, Acoustic West Coast Blues, West Coast Blues
How many blues artists remain at the absolute top of their game after more than a half century of performing? One immediately leaps to mind: Charles Brown. His incredible piano skills and laidback vocal delivery remain every bit as mesmerizing today as they were way back in 1945, when his groundbreaking waxing of "Drifting Blues" with gui-tarist Johnny Moore's Three Blazers invented an entirely new blues genre for sophisticated postwar revelers—an ultra-mellow, jazz-inflected sound perfect for sipping a late-night libation in some hip after-hours joint. Brown's smooth trio format was tremendously influ-ential to a host of high-profile disciples—Ray Charles, Amos Milburn, and Floyd Dixon, for starters.

Classically trained on the ivories, Brown earned a degree in chemistry before moving to Los Angeles in 1943. He soon hooked up with the Blazers (Moore and bassist Eddie Williams), who modeled themselves after Nat "King" Cole's trio but retained a bluesier tone within their ballad-heavy repertoire. With Brown installed as their vocalist and pianist, the Blazers' "Drifting Blues" for Philo Records remained on *Billboard*'s R&B charts for 23 weeks, peaking at No. 2. Follow-ups for Exclusive and Modern (including "Sunny Road," "So Long," "New Orleans Blues," and their immortal 1947 Yuletide classic "Merry Christ-mas Baby") kept the Blazers around the top of the R&B listings from 1946 through 1948, until Brown opted to go solo.

If anything, Brown was even more successful on his own. Signing with Eddie Mesner's Aladdin logo, he visited the R&B Top Ten no less than ten times from 1949 to 1952, retaining his mournful, sparsely arranged sound for the smashes "Get Yourself Another Fool," the chart-topping "Trouble Blues" and "Black Night," and "Hard Times." Despite a 1956 jaunt to New Orleans to record with the Cosimo's studio band, Brown's mellow approach failed to make the transition to rock's brasher rhythms, and he soon faded from national prominence.

Occasionally recording without causing much of a stir during the '60s and '70s, Brown began to regroup by the mid-'80s. *One More for the Road*, a set cut in 1986, announced to anyone within earshot that Brown's talents hadn't diminished at all while he was gone. Bonnie Raitt took an encouraging interest in Brown's comeback bid, bringing him on tour with her as her opening act. His recording career took off too, with a series of albums for Bullseye Blues, and more recently, a disc for Verve.

Today touring extensively with a terrific combo in tow headed by guitarist Danny Caron, Charles Brown is finally receiving at least a por-tion of the recognition he's deserved for so long as a genuine rhythm and blues pioneer. —*Bill Dahl*

One More for the Road / 1986 / Alligator ✦✦✦

All My Life / 1990 / Bullseye Blues ✦✦✦✦
By far Brown's best contemporary effort (and the set that really got his recording career back in high gear), kicked off by Dr. John and Ruth Brown certainly didn't hurt the set's chances, but it's the eternally suave pianist and his excellent road band (especially guitarist Danny Caron and saxist Clifford Solomon) that make this such a delightful collection. —*Bill Dahl*

Someone to Love / 1992 / Bullseye Blues ✦✦✦

★ **Driftin' Blues: The Best of Charles Brown** / 1992 / EMI America ✦✦✦✦✦
If your budget only allows the acquisition of a single CD of Brown's Alad-din material, let it be this one. It sports most of the truly important hits that inspired so many West Coasters—"Driftin' Blues," "Black Night," "Trouble Blues," and many others. —*Bill Dahl*

☆ **The Complete Aladdin Recordings of Charles Brown** / 1994 / Mosaic ✦✦✦✦✦
Every single brilliant side—some 109 in all—that this elegant, tremen-dously influential pianist cut for the Mesner brothers' Philo and Aladdin

imprints from 1945 to 1956 is housed in this lavishly produced five-disc boxed set. Mosaic's customary attention to detail is evident in the packag-ing and the sound; Brown's brilliance makes the entire box a delight, from his earliest sessions with the Three Blazers through his hitmaking run as a solo star during the late '40s and early '50s. The genesis of the entire West Coast "club blues" style resides in this box; its expense is well worth it. —*Bill Dahl*

Snuff Dippin' Mama / 1995 / Night Train ✦✦✦✦
Even with the above box, you won't own all of Brown's seminal work. In 1946, he and the Blazers landed at Exclusive Records, which is the era that this collection examines via 19 fine sides including the jivey "Juke Box Lil" and "C.O.D.," a mournful "Sunny Road," and the jazzy "B-Sharp You'll See." Guitarist Johnny Moore and bassist Eddie Williams were indeed sharp in smooth support. —*Bill Dahl*

Clarence "Gatemouth" Brown

b. Apr. 18, 1924, Vinton, LA
Bass, Guitar, Mandolin, Violin, Drums, Vocals / Country, Texas Blues
Whatever you do, don't refer to multi-instrumentalist Clarence "Gate-mouth" Brown as a bluesman, although his imprimatur on the develop-ment of Texas blues is enormous. You're liable to get him riled. If you must pigeonhole the legend, just call him an eclectic Texas musical master whose interests encompass virtually every roots genre imagin-able.

Tagged with the "Gatemouth" handle by a high school instructor who accused Brown of having a "voice like a gate," Brown has used it to his advantage throughout his illustrious career. (His guitar-wielding brother, James "Widemouth" Brown, recorded "Boogie Woogie Night-hawk" for Jax in 1951.)

In 1947, Gate's impromptu fill-in for an ailing T-Bone Walker at Hous-ton entrepreneur Don Robey's Bronze Peacock nightclub convinced Robey to assume control of Brown's career. After two singles for Alad-din stiffed, Robey inaugurated his own Peacock label in 1949 to show-case Gate's blistering riffs, which proved influential to a legion of Hous-ton string-benders (Albert Collins, Johnny Copeland, Johnny "Guitar" Watson, Cal Green, and many more have pledged allegiance to Brown's riffs). Brown broke new ground often—even in the '50s, he insisted on sawing his fiddle at live performances, although Robey wasn't inter-ested in capturing Gate's violin talent until "Just Before Dawn" (his final Peacock platter in 1959).

When Gate began to rebuild his career in the '70s, he was determined to do things his way. Country, jazz, even calypso now played a promi-nent role in his concerts; he's as likely to launch into an oldtime fiddle hoedown as a swinging guitar blues. He turned up on *Hee Haw* with pickin' and grinnin' pal Roy Clark after they cut a sizzling 1979 duet album for MCA, *Makin' Music*. Acclaimed discs for Rounder, Alligator and Verve over the last 15 years have proven that Gatemouth Brown is a steadfastly unclassifiable American original. —*Bill Dahl*

Just Got Lucky / Mar. 1973-Jul. 1, 1977 / Evidence ✦✦✦✦
More goodies from the same French 1973 dates (originally issued on Black & Blue). Lots of Jordan covers, along with Brown's own "Here Am I" and "Long Way Home," three Peacock remakes, and a sizzling revival of Bill Doggett's "Honey Boy." The last three titles date from a 1977 ses-sion, again cut in France, and are all Brown originals. —*Bill Dahl*

Makin' Music [Roy Clark] / 1979 / MCA ✦✦✦✦
Surround two of the most versatile guitar pickers on the planet in a stu-dio with a cadre of world-class sidemen and what do you get? This irre-sistible duet album by Gate and Roy Clark, first out on MCA. Good vibes abound as the fun-loving pair blast out "Caldonia," "Take the 'A' Train," "The Drifter," "Justice Blues," and more, trading licks, vocals, and quips with a jam session-oriented looseness. —*Bill Dahl*

San Antonio Ballbuster / 1982 / Red Lightnin' ✦✦✦✦
Considering how sub-par the sound quality is on this disc (it's a CD reproduction of an old Red Lightnin' bootleg), it wouldn't rate a recom-mendation if the material therein were otherwise available. But many of these Peacock masters aren't obtainable anywhere else—the stunning 1953 instrumental "Boogie Uproar," storming rockers "Win with Me Baby," "You Got Money," and "Just Got Lucky," and the after-hours hit "I've Been Mistreated," for starters. So until something better comes along . . . —*Bill Dahl*

Alright Again! / 1982 / Rounder ✦✦✦✦
One of the most satisfying contemporary Brown discs of all for the dis-cerning blues fan. Nothing but swinging, horn-abetted blues adorn this album, as Gate pays tribute to an influence and a protege by covering T-Bone Walker's "Strollin' with Bones" and Albert Collins' "Frosty." Brown jauntily revives Junior Parker's "I Feel Alright Again" and Percy May-field's "Give Me Time to Explain," while his own numbers—a funky "Dollar Got the Blues," the luxurious blues "Sometimes I Slip"—are truly brilliant. —*Bill Dahl*

One More Mile / 1983 / Rounder ✦✦✦

★ **The Original Peacock Recordings** / 1984 / Rounder ✦✦✦✦✦
Only 12 songs long, this collection remains the best place to begin appreciating why so many young Texas blues guitarists fell in love with Gatemouth Brown's style (until MCA decides to compile the ultimate Brown package, anyway). Listen to the way his blazing axe darts and weaves through trombonist Pluma Davis' jazzy horn chart on 1954's "Okie Dokie Stomp," or the stratospheric licks drenching "Dirty Work at the Crossroads." Brown proves that a violin can adapt marvelously to the blues (in the right hands, anyway) on "Just Before Dawn," and blows a little atmospheric harp on "Gate's Salty Blues." —*Bill Dahl*

Pressure Cooker / 1987 / Alligator ✦✦✦✦
Before Gate was able to rebuild a following stateside, he frequently toured Europe. He recorded the contents of this inexorably swinging set in France in 1973 with all-star backing by keyboardists Milt Buckner and Jay McShann, saxists Arnett Cobb and Hal Singer, among others. Brown indulges his passion for Louis Jordan by ripping through "Ain't That Just like a Woman" and "Ain't Nobody Here but Us Chickens" and exhibits his immaculate fretwork on the torrid title item. —*Bill Dahl*

Standing My Ground / 1989 / Alligator ✦✦✦✦
A delightfully eclectic program spotlighting nearly all of Gate's musical leanings—blues, jazz, country, even a hearty taste of "Louisiana Zydeco"—and a revealing glimpse of his multi-instrumental abilities: he plays guitar, violin, drums, and piano! There's a tender remake of the Chuck Willis R&B ballad and a funk-tinged update of "Got My Mojo Working," but everything else is from Brown's own pen. —*Bill Dahl*

No Looking Back / 1992 / Alligator ✦✦✦

Man / 1995 / Verve ✦✦✦

Long Way Home / 1996 / Verve ✦✦

J. T. Brown

b. Apr. 2, 1918, d. Nov. 24, 1969
Tenor Saxophone, Vocals / Chicago Blues, Electric Blues
Saxophonist J.T. Brown was a honking, stomping soloist whose licks embellished recordings by numerous blues musicians from Little Brother Montgomery to Roosevelt Sykes, Elmore James, Muddy Waters, Howlin' Wolf, and Willie Dixon. His braying, bleating sound was also featured on his own recordings for Harlem and United. Brown's early years were spent touring and playing with various medicine and minstrel shows. He moved to Chicago from Mississippi in the mid-'40s, and played on RCA sessions for Washboard Sam, Eddie Boyd, and Memphis Jimmy Clarke. He also frequently worked with Jump Jackson, whom he introduced to producer Lester Melrose. Brown began cutting his own dates in 1950 and continued through the mid-'50s. —*Ron Wynn*

● **Rockin' with J T** / 1984 / Krazy Kat ✦✦✦✦
Chicago jump blues, wailing stuff from the late '40s and early '50s. —*Bill Dahl*

Windy City Boogie / Pearl ✦✦✦✦
Inexplicably still unavailable on CD, this LP showcases Brown's hearty vocals and "nanny goat horn" in a bandleading role. With frequent cohort Little Brother Montgomery deftly tinkling the ivories, Brown delivers "Blackjack Blues" and "When I Was a Lad." Storming boogie instrumentals were an integral part of Brown's repertoire; this set (spanning 1951-1956) boasts a host of stellar houserockers. —*Bill Dahl*

Nappy Brown (Napoleon Brown)

b. Oct. 12, 1929, Charlotte, NC
Vocals / R&B, Electric Jump Blues
Nobody sounded much like Nappy Brown during the mid-'50s. Exotically rolling his consonants with sing-song impunity (allegedly, Savoy Records boss Herman Lubinsky thought Brown was singing in Yiddish), bellowing the blues with gospel-inspired ferocity, Brown rode rock 'n' roll's first wave for a few glorious years before his records stopped selling. But a dozen years ago or thereabouts, Brown seemingly rose from the dead to stage a comeback. Now he's ensconced once again as a venerable blues veteran who'll stop at nothing (including rolling around the stage in sexual simulation) to enthrall his audience.

Nappy Brown was fronting a spiritual aggregation, the Heavenly Lights, who were signed to Savoy Records when Lubinsky convinced the leather-lunged shouter to cross the secular line in 1954. Brown brought hellfire intensity to his blues-soaked Savoy debut, "Is It True," but it was "Don't Be Angry" the next year that caused his fortunes to skyrocket. The sizzling rocker sported loads of Brown's unique vocal gimmicks and a hair-raising tenor sax solo by Sam "The Man" Taylor, becoming his first national smash. Novelty-tinged upbeat items such as "Little by Little" and "Piddily Patter Patter" defined Nappy's output, but his throat-busting turn on the 1957 blues "The Right Time" (borrowed by Ray Charles in short order!) remains a highlight of Brown's early heyday. After decades away from the limelight, Brown resurfaced in 1984 with a very credible album for Landslide Records, *Tore Up*, with guitar-

ist Tinsley Ellis' band, the Heartfixers. Since then he's recorded a fine set for Black Top (*Something Gonna Jump Out the Bushes*) with Anson Funderburgh, Ronnie Earl, and Earl King sharing guitar duties, and some not-so-fine CDs for other logos. —*Bill Dahl*

★ **Don't Be Angry!** / 1985 / Savoy ✦✦✦✦✦
Rolling his consonants like a crazed cantor, shouter Nappy Brown brought a gospel-imbued fervor to his rocking mid-'50s R&B that few of his peers could match. Backed by some of New York's finest sessioneers, Brown roars 16 of his best early Savoy sides on this essential purchase. "Don't Be Angry," "Just a Little Love," "Open Up That Door," and "Bye Bye Baby" rate with his hottest jump efforts, "I Cried like a Baby" and "It's Really You" are hair-raising blues, and "Little by Little" rides a bouncy, pop-accessible groove. Now where's volume two?? —*Bill Dahl*

Something Gonna Jump out the Bushes / 1988 / Black Top ✦✦✦✦
Ultra-solid support from guitarists Anson Funderburgh, Eugene Ross, Ronnie Earl, and Earl King and Black Top's superb house horn section make this Dallas-cut set Brown's best contemporary album to date. His lusty shouting style works well on covers of the Dominoes' "Have Mercy Baby," the "5" Royales' title track, a pair of Earl King-penned numbers, and Robert Ward's "Your Love Is Real." —*Bill Dahl*

Tore Up / 1989 / Alligator ✦✦✦
After too many years during which he was missing and presumed forever lost in action, Brown returned to prominence with this very credible album, cut with backing by guitarist Tinsley Ellis and the Heartfixers and originally issued on the tiny Landslide logo. He reprises his salacious blues "Lemon Squeezin' Daddy" and rolls his R's like the good old days on dusties by Little Walter, the Midnighters, Howlin' Wolf, and even Bob Dylan and the Allmans. —*Bill Dahl*

Roy Brown

b. Sep. 10, 1925, New Orleans, LA, d. May 25, 1981, San Fernando, CA
Piano, Vocals / R&B, Rock 'n' Roll, Electric Jump Blues
When you draw up a short list of the R&B pioneers who exerted a primary influence on the development of rock 'n' roll, respectfully place singer Roy Brown's name near its very top. His seminal 1947 DeLuxe Records waxing of "Good Rockin' Tonight" was immediately ridden to the peak of the R&B charts by shouter Wynonie Harris and subsequently covered by Elvis Presley, Ricky Nelson, Jerry Lee Lewis, and many more early rock icons (even Pat Boone!). In addition, Brown's melismatically pleading, gospel-steeped delivery impacted the vocal styles of B.B. King, Bobby Bland, and Little Richard (among a plethora of important singers). Clearly, Roy Brown was an innovator—and from 1948-1951, an R&B star whose wild output directly presaged rock's rise.

As a teenager, Bing Crosby was Brown's favorite singer—but a nine-month stint at a Shreveport, LA nightclub exposed him to the blues for the first time. He conjured up "Good Rockin' Tonight" while fronting a band in Galveston, TX. Ironically, Harris wanted no part of the song when Brown first tried to hand it to him. Though Brown's original waxing was a solid hit, Harris's cover beat him out for top chart honors. Brown didn't have to wait long to dominate the R&B lists himself. He scored 15 hits from mid-1948 to late 1951 for DeLuxe, ranging from the emotionally wracked crying blues "Hard Luck Blues" (his biggest seller of all in 1950) to the party-time rockers "Rockin' at Midnight," "Boogie at Midnight," "Miss Fanny Brown," and "Cadillac Baby." Strangely, his sales slumped badly from 1952 on, even though his sides for Cincinnati's King Records rate among his hottest houserockers.

Brown was unable to cash in on the rock 'n' roll idiom he helped to invent, though he briefly rejuvenated his commercial fortunes at Imperial Records in 1957. Working with New Orleans producer Dave Bartholomew, then riding high with Fats Domino, Brown returned to the charts with the original version of "Let the Four Winds Blow" (later a hit for Fats) and cut the sizzling sax-powered rockers "Diddy-Y-Diddy-O," "Saturday Night," and "Ain't Gonna Do It."

After a long dry spell, Brown's acclaimed performance as part of Johnny Otis' troupe at the 1970 Monterey Jazz Festival and a 1973 LP for ABC-BluesWay began to rebuild his long-lost momentum. But it came too late—Brown died of a heart attack in 1981 at age 56, his role as a crucial link between postwar R&B and rock's initial rise still underappreciated by the masses. —*Bill Dahl*

★ **Good Rocking Tonight: The Best of Roy Brown** / 1994 / Rhino ✦✦✦✦✦
An unassailable 18-cut cross-section of the monstrously popular and influential New Orleans jump blues shouter's sides for the DeLuxe, King, and Imperial labels that spans 1947-57 and takes in his seminal "Good Rocking Tonight" (where it all began!), "Rockin' at Midnight," "Boogie at Midnight," and "Love Don't Love Nobody," the almost unbearably tortured "Hard Luck Blues," and the unbelievably raunchy two-parter "Butcher Pete." Looking for the origins of rock? Here they are! —*Bill Dahl*

The Complete Imperial Recordings / Oct. 1995 / Capitol ✦✦✦
In the mid-'50s Brown, like many other early R&B pioneers, was a bit lost at sea amid the rock 'n' roll explosion. From 1956 to 1958, he recorded these 20 tracks for Imperial under the direction of legendary New Orleans R&B producer Dave Bartholomew. Brown and Bartholomew were attempting to update Brown's jump blues/R&B hybrid with a lot of Fats Domino-type Crescent City influence on these sides. The results weren't bad, but with Bartholomew co-writing most of the tunes and using local musicians like saxophonist Lee Allen, Brown sounded more like a journeyman New Orleans R&B singer than an innovative, bluesy forefather of rock 'n' roll. There were a couple of commercial successes: his cover of Buddy Knox's "Party Doll" made the R&B Top 20, and "Let the Four Winds Blow" actually made the pop Top 40, although Fats Domino would have much greater success with the same song when he covered it a few years later. Diluted by occasional pop and rock influences, as well as a substandard variation of "Good Rockin' Tonight," this compilation shouldn't be the first Brown on your shelf. But for those who want to go a little further, it's packaged very well, with thorough liner notes and seven previously unissued cuts. —*Richie Unterberger*

Bob Brozman

b. Mar. 8, 1954
Guitar, Ukulele / Blues, Acoustic Country Blues, Electric Blues, Folk, Hawaiian
Multi-instrumentalist, historian, and educator Bob Brozman was born in New York on March 8, 1954. His uncle, Barney Josephson, was a prominent clubowner who ran Cafe Society in Greenwich Village, one of the first places in New York, or anywhere, where Black and White musicians played on stage together.

Brozman studied music and ethnomusicology at Washington University in St. Louis. Brozman is not only a master of classic blues from the '20s and '30s, but a competent performer of early jazz and ragtime. In the mid-'70s, while still in college, he would make trips South to find, interview, and play with the older blues artists from the 1920s and '30s whom he admired.

Brozman recorded several fine albums in the early and mid-'80s for the Kicking Mule and Rounder labels, and though they may not have been reissued on compact disc, for students of early, vintage blues and vintage guitar aficionados, they're well worth digging out of the vinyl shops. Brozman's albums include *Blue Hula Stomp* (1981) and *Snapping the Strings* (1983), both for the California-based Kicking Mule label. In 1985 he recorded *Hello Central, Give Me Dr. Jazz* for the Massachusetts-based Rounder label and followed up in 1988 with *Devil's Slide*. For die-hard blues fans who seek an album devoid of any of the other genres Brozman so easily interprets (like ragtime and calypso), the one to get is *A Truckload of Blues*, a 1992 Rounder release. —*Richard Skelly*

● **Devil's Slide** / 1988 / Rounder ✦✦✦✦
Blues, Hawaiian, calypso, hot jazz—slide-wizard Bob can do it all with startling authenticity and humor. This CD compilation has five cuts from his *Hello Central* album to boot. —*Myles Boisen*

A Truckload of Blues / 1992 / Rounder ✦✦✦✦
Guitarist Bob Brozman's long-awaited all-blues album covers similar territory as others who have turned in heartfelt treatments of traditional and Delta blues tunes. But the difference between Brozman and many of his predecessors is that he has fun doing these songs. He's wise enough to understand that there are only so many ways one can sing "Old Dog Blues" or "Kitchen Man," and that many of the great veterans really enjoyed what they sang. Brozman is also a technical marvel, particularly on bottleneck. But just as his vocals aren't simply replications, he doesn't merely whip out licks and display flash; there's thought in the soloing, creativity in the riffs and plenty of heart in the grooves. Brozman emerges with one of the better and more memorable repertory projects, one that seems more like his take on traditional blues rather than one more museum piece. —*Ron Wynn*

Roy Buchanan

b. Sep. 23, 1939, Ozark, AL, **d.** Aug. 14, 1988
Guitar / Blues-Rock
Buchanan's reputation as a hot-shot guitarist extends back to the beginnings of rock 'n' roll itself. On the road and recording with Dale Hawkins by his teens, Buchanan became the law of the land around the Washington, D.C., area by the mid-to-late '60s. His use of the Fender Telecaster, using high harmonic squeals in place of feedback and distortion, was part and parcel of rock guitar's vocabulary by the early '70s. A reluctant legend, Buchanan later became more unfocused as his career waned, but his unique stylings remain etched into his best records.

Sadly, when Buchanan seemed on the verge of a comeback in 1986, he hung himself in a police cell after he was arrested on a drunk-driving charge. He left behind a number of records which testify that he was a

consummate guitarist, capable of tones and techniques that other guitarists only dream of. —*Cub Koda*

Roy Buchanan / Aug. 1972 / Polydor ✦✦✦✦
His debut album, with a skunk-hot stage band. Buchanan's guitar sizzles on tracks like "Haunted House," "Sweet Dreams," and "The Messiah Will Come Again." —*Cub Koda*

Second Album / 1973 / Polydor ✦✦✦
More blues-based than his debut, with great stretched-out jams showcasing some of his best playing. —*Cub Koda*

That's What I Am Here For / Feb. 1974 / Polydor ✦✦✦
Excellent blues-rock guitar, it includes the riveting Hendrix tribute "Hey Joe." —*David Szatmary*

Live Stock / Aug. 1975 / Polydor ✦✦✦✦
Brilliant live blues-rock guitar by the legend who turned down a spot in the Rolling Stones. A must for guitar-hero fans. —*David Szatmary*

Hot Wires / 1987 / Alligator ✦✦✦
Another stinging effort. —*David Szatmary*

● **Sweet Dreams: The Anthology** / 1992 / Polydor ✦✦✦✦
Over two CDs, *Sweet Dreams* collects the finest moments from Buchanan's '70s albums, including nine unreleased tracks; as a career retrospective, it's the finest collection available. —*Stephen Thomas Erlewine*

Guitar on Fire: Atlantic Sessions / 1993 / Rhino ✦✦✦

George "Mojo" Buford

b. Nov. 10, 1929, Hernando, MS
Harmonica / Electric Chicago Blues
When Muddy Waters deemed a harp player talented enough to follow Little Walter and James Cotton into his peerless combo, he must have been someone special. Mojo Buford spent several stints in the employ of the Chicago blues legend, and was his harpist of choice in the final edition of the Waters band.

George Buford left Mississippi for Memphis while still young, learning his early blues lessons there. He relocated to Chicago in 1952, eventually forming a band called the Savage Boys that mutated into the Muddy Waters Jr. Band (no, they weren't fronted by a Waters imitator; they subbed for their mighty sponsor at local clubs when he was on the road). Buford played with Muddy as early as 1959, but a 1962 uprooting to Minneapolis to front his own combo and cut a couple of solid but extremely obscure LPs for Vernon and Folk-Art removed him from the Windy City scene for a while. Buford returned to Muddy's combo in 1967 for a year, put in a longer stint with Waters during the early '70s, and came back for the last time after Jerry Portnoy exited with the rest of his mates to form the Legendary Blues Band. Buford has recorded as a bandleader for Mr. Blues (later reissued on Rooster Blues) and the British JSP logo, never drifting far from his enduring Chicago blues roots. —*Bill Dahl*

● **Mojo Buford's Blues Summit** / 1981 / Rooster Blues ✦✦✦✦
Buford in the company of guitarists Little Smokey Smothers, Pee Wee Madison, Sammy Lawhorn, and Sonny Rogers, with a rhythm section pounding it out like crazy. —*Cub Koda*

Bumble Bee Slim (Amos Easton)

b. May 7, 1905, Brunswick, GA, **d.** 1968, Los Angeles, CA
Guitar, Vocals / Acoustic Country Blues
Popular and prolific, Bumble Bee Slim parlayed a familiar but rudimentary style into one of the earliest flowerings of the Chicago style. Much of what he performed he adapted from the groundbreaking duo Leroy Carr and Scrapper Blackwell—Slim built on Carr's laconic, relaxed vocal style and Blackwell's guitar technique. During the mid-'30s Bumble Bee Slim recorded a number of sides for a variety of labels, including Bluebird, Vocalion, and Decca, becoming one of the most-recorded bluesmen of the decade. —*Cub Koda and Stephen Thomas Erlewine*

● **1931-1937** / Document ✦✦✦✦
A solid 18-track import compilation of all his best sides. —*Cub Koda*

George "Wild Child" Butler

b. Oct. 1, 1936, Autaugville, AL
Guitar, Harmonica, Vocals / Electric Chicago Blues
From all accounts, George Butler was indeed a "wild child." But he found time between the youthful shenanigans that inspired his mom to bestow his descriptive nickname to learn some harp basics at age 12. He was gigging professionally as a bandleader by the late '50s, but Butler's recording career didn't blossom until he moved to Chicago in 1966 and signed with Shreveport, LA-based Jewel Records (his sidemen on these sessions included bassist Willie Dixon and guitarist Jimmy Dawkins).

The harpist didn't have much luck in the recording wars—his 1969 Mercury album sank with little trace, while a 1976 LP for T.K., *Funky Butt Lover*, did equally little for his fortunes (it was later reissued in slightly altered form on Rooster Blues as *Lickin' Gravy*). Around 1981, Butler moved up north to Ontario, Canada, and continued his career. A decade later, he cut the first of two albums for British producer Mike Vernon; *These Mean Old Blues* was an engaging set of original material cut in London. *Stranger,* the fruits of another English session, emerged in 1994. —*Bill Dahl*

● **Open Up Baby** / 1984 / Charly ✦✦✦✦
Solid collection of Butler's best sides for the Jewel label. —*Cub Koda*

These Mean Old Blues / 1992 / Bullseye Blues ✦✦✦✦
The combination of veteran southern blues harpist Wild Child Butler and a British band works surprisingly well on this solid collection produced by the eminently experienced Mike Vernon. Another major plus: everything here is an original composition, all the better to properly spotlight Butler's down-home vocal phrasing and meat-and-potatoes harmonica style. —*Bill Dahl*

Paul Butterfield

b. Dec. 17, 1942, Chicago, IL, **d.** May 4, 1987, N. Hollywood, CA
Flute, Guitar, Harmonica, Vocals / Electric Chicago Blues, Blues-Rock
Butterfield grew up in Chicago's Hyde Park, and according to his brother Peter, "There was a lot of music around." Butterfield was culturally sophisticated. His father was a well-known attorney in the Hyde Park area, and his mother was an artist—a painter. Butterfield took flute lessons from an early age and by the time he reached high school, was studying with the first-chair flautist of the Chicago Symphony. He was exposed to both classical music and jazz from an early age. Butterfield ran track in high school and was offered a running scholarship to Brown University, which he had to refuse after a serious knee injury. From that point onward, he turned toward the music scene around him. He began learning the guitar and harmonica.

Butterfield met singer Nick Gravenites and started hanging around outside of the Chicago blues clubs, listening. He and Gravenites began to play together at various campuses—Ann Arbor, University of Wisconsin, and the University of Chicago. His parents sent him off to the University of Illinois, but he would put in a short academic week, choosing to play and hang out at the blues clubs. Soon he wasn't attending school at all. When this was discovered by his parents, he then dropped out of college and turned to music full time.

Butterfield practiced long hours by himself—just playing all the time. His brother Peter writes, "It was a very solitary effort. It was all internal, like he had a particular sound he wanted to get and he just worked to get it."

In the meantime, Elvin Bishop had come from Oklahoma to the University of Illinois on a scholarship and had discovered the various blues venues for himself. Elvin remembers, "One day I was walking around the neighborhood and I saw a guy sitting on a porch drinking a quart of beer—White people that were interested in blues were very few and far between at that time. But this guy was singing some blues and singing it good. It was Butterfield. We gravitated together real quick and started playing parties around the neighborhood, you know, just acoustic. He was playing more guitar than harp when I first met him. But in about six months, he became serious about the harp. And he seemed to get about as good as he ever got in that six months. He was just a natural genius. And this was in 1960 or 1961."

Butterfield and Bishop began going down to the clubs, sitting in, and playing with all the great Black blues players—musicians like Otis Rush, Magic Sam, Howlin' Wolf, Junior Wells, Little Walter, and especially Muddy Waters. They often were the only Whites there, but were soon accepted because of their sincerity, their sheer ability, and the protection of players like Muddy Waters, who befriended them.

An important event in the history of introducing blues to White America came in 1963 when Big John's, a club located on Chicago's White North Side, invited Butterfield to bring his band there and play on a regular basis. After accepting the gig, Butterfield and Bishop set about putting such a band together. They pulled Jerome Arnold (bass) and Sam Lay (drums) from Howlin' Wolf's band (with whom they had worked for the past six years!), by offering them more money. Butterfield and Bishop (the core team), Arnold, and Lay were all about the same age, and these four became the Butterfield Blues Band. They had been around for a long time and knew the Chicago blues scene and its repertoire cold. This new racially mixed band opened at Big John's, was very successful, and made the first great step to opening up the blues scene to White America.

When the new group thought about making an album, they looked around for a lead guitarist. Michael Bloomfield, who was known to Butterfield from his appearances at Big John's, joined the band early in 1965. Bloomfield, somewhat cool at first to Butterfield's commanding manner, warmed to the group as Butterfield warmed to his guitar playing. It took a while for Bloomfield to fit in, but by the summer of that year, the band was cookin'. Mark Naftalin, another music student who

studied keyboards, joined the band as the first album was being recorded. These six, then, became the Paul Butterfield Blues Band.

The first two Butterfield Blues albums are essential from an historical perspective. While *East-West,* the second album, with its Eastern influence and extended solos set the tone for psychedelic rockers, it was that incredible first album that alerted the music scene to what was coming. Although it has been perhaps over-emphasized in recent years, it is important to point out that the release of *The Paul Butterfield Blues Band* on Elektra in 1965 had a huge effect on the White music culture of the time. Used to hearing blues covered by groups like the Rolling Stones, that first album had an enormous impact on young (and primarily White) rock players. Here is no deferential imitation of Black music by Whites, but a racially mixed hard-driving blues album that, in a word, rocked. It was a signal to White players to stop making respectful tributes to Black music, and just play it. In a flash the image of blues as old-time music was gone. Modern Chicago style urban blues was out of the closet and introduced to mainstream White audiences, who loved it. The Butterfield band appeared at the Newport Folk Festival late in 1965 to rave reviews.

Perhaps the next major event in the Butterfield band came when drummer Sam Lay became ill late in 1965. Jazz drummer Billy Davenport was called in and soon became a permanent member of the group. Davenport was to become a key element in the development of the second Butterfield Blues Band album, *East-West,* and in particular the extended solo of the same name.

Fueled by Bloomfield's infatuation with Eastern music and Indian ragas at the time and aided by Davenport's jazz-driven sophistication on drums, there arose in the group a new music form that was to greatly affect rock music—the extended solo. There is little question that here is the root of psychedelic (acid) rock—a genuine fusion between East and West. Those first two albums served as a wakeup call to an entire generation of White would-be blues musicians. Speaking as one who was on the scene, that first Butterfield album stopped us in our tracks and we were never the same afterward. It changed our lives.

Released in 1967, *The Butterfield Blues Band; The Resurrection of Pigboy Crabshaw,* is the last that preserves any of the pure blues direction of the original group. By this time, Bloomfield had left to create his own group, the Electric Flag, and, with the addition of a horn section (including a young David Sandborn), the band drifted more toward an R&B sound. Mark Naftalin left the group soon after this album and the Butterfield band took on other forms.

Aside from these first three albums, later Butterfield material somehow misses the mark. He never lost his ferocity or integrity, but the synergy of that first group was special. There has been some discussion in the literature about the personal transformation of Butterfield as his various bands developed. It is said that he went from being a self-centered bandleader (shouting orders to his crew a la Howlin' Wolf) to a more democratic style of leadership, providing his group with musical freedom (like Muddy Waters). For what it's worth, it is clear that the best music is in those first two (maybe three) albums. Subsequent albums, although also interesting, have not gotten as much attention then or now from reviewers.

When I knew Butterfield (during the first three albums), he was always intense, somewhat remote, and even, on occasion, downright unfriendly. Although not much interested in other people, he was a compelling musician and a great harp player. Bloomfield and Naftalin, also great players, were just the opposite—always interested in the other guy. They went out of their way to inquire about you, even if you were a nobody. Naftalin, well known around the San Francisco Bay Area, continues to this day to support blues projects and festivals (Marin County Blues Festival, etc.) in the San Francisco Bay area.

After Bloomfield and Naftalin left the group, Butterfield spun off on his own more and more. The next two albums, *In My Own Dream* (1968) and *Keep on Moving* (1969) moved still farther away from the blues roots until in 1972, Butterfield dissolved the group, forming the group Better Days. This new group recorded two albums, *Paul Butterfield's Better Days* and *It All Comes Back.* After that, Butterfield faded into the general rock scene, with an occasional appearance here and there, as in the documentary *The Last Waltz* (1976)—a farewell concert from The Band. The albums *Put It in Your Ear* (1976) and *North South* (1981) were attempts to make a comeback, but both failed. Paul Butterfield died of a drug-related heart failure in 1987.

Even to this day, Butterfield remains one of the few White harmonica players to develop his own style (another is William Clarke)—one respected by Black players. Butterfield has no real imitators. Like most Chicago-style amplified harmonica players, Butterfield played the instrument like a horn—a trumpet. Although he sometimes used a chromatic harmonica, Butterfield mostly played the standard Hohner Marine Band in the standard cross position. Remember, he was left handed and held the harp in his left hand, but in the standard position with the low notes facing to the left. He tended to play single notes rather than bursts of chords. His harp playing is always intense, understated, concise, and serious—only Big Walter Horton has a better sense of note selection.

The effect of the Butterfield Blues Band on aspiring White blues musicians was enormous, and the impact of the band on live audiences was stunning. Butterfield the performer was always intense, serious, and definitive—no doubt about this guy. Blues purists sometimes like to quibble about Butterfield's voice and singing style, but the moment he picked up a harmonica, that was it. He is one of the finest harp players, period.

Butterfield and the six members of the original Paul Butterfield Blues Band made a huge contribution to modern music, turning a whole generation of White music lovers onto the blues as something other than a quaint piece of music history. The musical repercussions of the second Butterfield album, *East-West*, continue to echo through the music scene even today!

We would like to thank *Blues Access* magazine for permission to use the quotes by Peter Butterfield and Elvin Bishop from the excellent article by Tom Ellis. —*Michael Erlewine*

☆ **Paul Butterfield Blues Band** / 1965 / Elektra ♦♦♦♦♦
Butterfield's unique amplified harmonica style is already present on this classic first album—a wakeup call for a generation of young White players used to hearing blues filtered through covers by groups like the Rolling Stones or as a part of music history. Here was a racially mixed group of brilliant young players that rocked—an historic album. Great guitar from Michael Bloomfield and Elvin Bishop. With Mark Naftalin (organ), Jerome Arnold (bass), and Sam Lay (drums). —*Michael Erlewine*

★ **East-West** / 1966 / Elektra ♦♦♦♦♦
The second Butterfield album had an even greater effect on music history, paving the way for experimentation that is still being explored today. This came in the form of an extended blues-rock solo (some 13 minutes)—a real fusion of jazz and blues inspired by the Indian raga. This groundbreaking instrumental was the first of its kind and marks the root from which the acid rock tradition emerged. —*Jeff Tarmarkin and Michael Erlewine*

The Resurrection of Pigboy Crabshaw / 1968 / Elektra ♦♦♦♦
In his third album, Butterfield adds a horn section and the direction of the group has started to veer away from straight Chicago-style blues toward a sound more influenced by R&B. By this time, Bloomfield has left the group and Elvin Bishop (aka Pigboy Crabshaw) takes over on lead guitar. A lot of great tunes here, like "Driftin' and Driftin'." —*Michael Erlewine*

An Offer You Can't Refuse / 1972 / Red Lightnin' ♦♦♦
This album released on the Red Lightnin' label in 1972 consists of one side of Big Walter Horton and one of very early Paul Butterfield (1963) (See: Big Walter Horton). Contains six tracks with Butterfield, Smokey Smothers on guitar, Jerome Arnold on bass, and Sam Lay on drums. This was recorded at Big John's, the North Side Chicago club where the Butterfield Band first played in 1963—some two years before the material on the first Paul Butterfield Blues Band album, which was released in 1965. The six tracks include two instrumentals, "Got My Mojo Working" and the Butterfield-authored tune "Loaded." Although this is very early Butterfield, the harp playing is excellent and already in his own unique style. The singing is a little rough and heavy sounding. Butterfield fans will want to find this rare vinyl for musical and historical reasons. —*Michael Erlewine*

The Original Lost Elektra Sessions / 1995 / Rhino ♦♦♦♦
All but one of these 19 tracks were recorded in December, 1964, as Butterfield's projected first LP; the results were scrapped and replaced by their official self-titled debut, cut a few months later. With both Bloomfield and Bishop already in tow, these sessions rank among the earliest blues-rock ever laid down. Extremely similar in feel to the first album, it's perhaps a bit rawer in production and performance, but not appreciably worse or different than what ended up on the actual debut LP. Dedicated primarily to electric Chicago blues standards, Butterfield fans will find this well worth acquiring, as most of the selections were never officially recorded by the first lineup (although different renditions of five tracks showed up on the first album and the *What's Shakin'* compilation). —*Richie Unterberger*

Strawberry Jam / 1995 / Winner ♦♦♦
These nine cuts are from various live performances of the Paul Butterfield Blues Band during their heyday in the middle-to-late '60s. This album was put together by Mark Naftalin, who played keyboards on those first few incredible Butterfield albums. Don't look for the clearest sound (it's adequate) because these are live tunes recorded at clubs, often with minimal equipment. It is the music that is in focus here—a window into that incredible band at a time when they were hot. Those of us who were on the scene at the time know that, although the original Butterfield albums are great, the band was a total knockout when heard live. Featuring Butterfield's harmonica, here are glimpses into that time and music. Most of the tunes have appeared elsewhere, but the extended instrumental "Strawberry Jam" (written by Naftalin) is unique to this

album—worth hearing. It features great guitar by Elvin Bishop. —*Michael Erlewine*

East-West Live / Sep. 1996 / Winner ♦♦♦♦
The tune "East-West" from the second Butterfield Blues Band album of the same name made music history. It is arguably the first extended rock solo, a fusing of blues-rock with Eastern scales and tone. Here is the root of psychedelic—acid rock. Now, thanks to Mark Naftalin (the original Butterfield keyboardist), we have three live recordings of "East-West" recorded in 1966-1967 that capture the origin and development of this classic tune. The first example (some 12 minutes) was taped prior to the edited studio version; the second (16 minutes) and third (28 minutes) were recorded after the album cut. There is some great music (and music history) here. —*Michael Erlewine*

Eddie C. Campbell

b. May 6, 1939, Duncan, MS
Guitar, Vocals / Modern Electric Blues
Happily, Eddie C. Campbell is currently back in Chicago after spending a decade entrenched in Europe. His shimmering West Side-styled guitar style and unusually introspective songwriting have been a breath of fresh air on the Windy City circuit, reuniting the veteran bluesman with fans he left behind in 1984.

Campbell left rural Mississippi for the bright lights of Chicago at age ten, sneaking a peek at Muddy Waters at the 1125 Club soon after he arrived and jamming with his idol when he was only 12. He fell in with some West Side youngbloods—Luther Allison, Magic Sam—and honed a guitar attack rooted deep in the ringing style. Campbell paid his sideman dues on the bandstand with everyone from Howlin' Wolf and Little Walter to Little Johnny Taylor and Jimmy Reed. Koko Taylor recommended Eddie to Willie Dixon, who hired him as a Chicago Blues All-Star in 1976.

Campbell cut his own debut album, the rousing *King of the Jungle*, in 1977 for Steve Wisner's short-lived Mr. Blues logo (now available on Rooster Blues, it includes the guitarist's lighthearted Yuletide perennial "Santa's Been Messin' with the Kid"). But he split the country for calmer European climates, recording a nice 1984 album with a Dutch group, *Let's Pick It!*, that first came out on Black Magic and now adorns the Evidence catalog.

When Eddie C. finally returned stateside for the birth of his son, he made up for lost time by gigging steadily around Chicago and making a comeback album for Blind Pig, *That's When I Know*, that contained some very distinctive originals. Hopefully, he'll stay put for a while. —*Bill Dahl*

● **King of the Jungle** / 1977 / Rooster Blues ♦♦♦♦
Flamboyant West Side-styled guitarist's debut album, first issued on the short-lived Mr. Blues logo, remains his best, with its slashing guitar,and lowdown vocals beautifully presented on covers of material by Magic Sam, Muddy Waters, Percy Mayfield, Willie Mabo, and his own Yuletide perennial "Santa's Messin' with the Kid." Great band, too: harpist Carey Bell, pianist Lafayette Leake, bassist Bob Stroger, and drummer Clifton James. —*Bill Dahl*

Let's Pick It! / Oct. 1984 / Evidence ♦♦♦♦
Recorded while Eddie Campbell was on a European sojourn that lasted a decade or so, this disc, cut back in 1984 for Black Magic with an overseas combo, is a very convincing effort mixing Campbell's own "Cold and Hungry," "Dream," and "Messin' with My Pride" with songs by Albert King, Jimmy Reed, Jimmie Lee Robinson, and Magic Sam. —*Bill Dahl*

That's When I Know / 1994 / Blind Pig ♦♦♦♦
During that long decade away from home, Eddie C's skills as a unique blues songwriter certainly blossomed. His triumphant homecoming set contains some highly distinctive material—a homespun "Sister Taught Me Guitar," the incandescent title track, a forceful "Sleep," "Busted," and a decidedly mystical "Son of Sons." —*Bill Dahl*

Cannon's Jug Stompers (Gus Cannon)

Banjo, Guitar, Piano, Kazoo, Vocals, Jug / Acoustic Memphis Blues
Gus Cannon was the best known of all the jugband musicians and a seminal figure on the Memphis blues scene. His recollections have also provided us with much of our knowledge of the earliest days of the blues in the Mississippi Delta. Cannon led his Jug Stompers on banjo and jug in a historic series of dates for the Victor label in 1928-1930. The ensemble usually included a second banjoist or guitarist, one of whom often doubled on kazoo, and the legendary Noah Lewis on harmonica. The jug-band style enjoyed a revival during the folk boom of the '50s and '60s, resulting in an ultra-rare Gus Cannon album on Stax, of all labels, after his "Walk Right In" became the nation's best-selling record for the Rooftop Singers in 1963. Cannon's Victor output was also a favorite source of early blues material for the Grateful Dead. —*Jim O'Neal*

● **The Complete Recordings** / Yazoo ✦✦✦✦
This innocent and exuberant Memphis good-time blues was the inspiration for '50s British skiffle and Greenwich Village folkies alike. —*Mark A. Humphrey*

Leroy Carr

b. Mar. 27, 1905, Nashville, TN, d. Apr. 29, 1935, Indianapolis, IN
Piano, Vocals / Blues, Piano Blues
The term "urban blues" is usually applied to post-World War II blues-band music, but one of the forefathers of the genre in its pre-electric format was pianist Leroy Carr. Teamed with the exemplary guitarist Scrapper Blackwell in Indianapolis, Carr became one of the top blues stars of his day, composing and recording almost 200 sides during his short lifetime, including such classics as "How Long, How Long," "Prison Bound Blues," "When the Sun Goes Down," and "Blues Before Sunrise." His blues were expressive and evocative, recorded with only piano and guitar; yet as author Sam Charters has noted, Carr was "a city man" whose singing was never as rough or intense as the country bluesmen's. As reissue producer Francis Smith put it, "He, perhaps more than any other single artist, was responsible for transforming the rural blues patterns of the '20s into the more city-oriented blues of the '30s."

Born in Nashville, Leroy Carr moved to Indianapolis as a child. While he was still in his teens, he taught himself how to play piano. Carr quit school in his mid-teens, heading out for a life on the road. For the next few years he played piano at various parties and dances in the Midwest and South. Carr wandered back toward Indianapolis, where he met guitarist Scrapper Blackwell in 1928. The duo began performing, and shortly afterward they were recording for Vocalion, releasing "How Long, How Long Blues" before the year was finished. The song was an instant, surprise hit. For the next seven years Carr and Blackwell recorded a number of classic songs for Vocalion, which would make Carr one of the most popular blues musicians in America.

While his professional career was successful, his personal life was spinning out of control, as he sank deeper and deeper into alcoholism. His addiction eventually cut his life short—he died in April 1935. Carr left behind an enormous blues catalog, and his influence could be heard throughout successive generations of blues musicians, as evidenced by artists like T-Bone Walker, Otis Spann, and Champion Jack Dupree. —*Jim O'Neal and Stephen Thomas Erlewine*

★ **Blues Before Sunrise** / 1962 / Portrait ✦✦✦✦✦
Despite minimal sound quality, this reissue contains some prime Leroy Carr/Scrapper Blackwell material. They were arguably the greatest piano and guitar duo to emerge in the late '20s and early '30s. You can find these tracks on other import collections, but this was among the first reissues available on a domestic label. —*Ron Wynn*

Singin' the Blues / 1973 / Biograph ✦✦✦✦
This is late period Carr, superb material done in 1934. It's hard to believe, considering the depth of his piano playing and the vocal quality, that by the end of the next year, Carr's career would be finished. The sound quality is good enough to convey the range and might in Carr's piano fills and delivery. —*Ron Wynn*

☆ **Naptown Blues (1929-1934)** / 1988 / Yazoo ✦✦✦✦✦
A seminal piano/guitar duo, Leroy Carr was among the most influential early blues singer/pianists, and Scrapper Blackwell was a remarkably fluid guitarist. —*Mark A. Humphrey*

Bo Carter (Armenter Chatmon)

b. Mar. 21, 1893, Bolton, MS, d. Sep. 21, 1964, Memphis, TN
Banjo, Bass, Clarinet, Guitar, Vocals / Acoustic Delta Blues
Bo Carter (Armenter "Bo" Chatmon) had an unequaled capacity for creating sexual metaphors in his songs, specializing in such ribald imagery as "Banana in Your Fruit Basket," "Pin in Your Cushion," and "Your Biscuits Are Big Enough for Me." One of the most popular bluesmen of the '30s, he recorded enough material for several reissue albums, and he was quite an original guitar picker, or else three of those albums wouldn't have been released by Yazoo. (Carter employed a number of different keys and tunings on his records, most of which were solo vocal and guitar performances.) Carter's facility extended beyond the risqué business to more serious blues themes, and he was also the first to record the standard "Corrine Corrina" (1928). Bo and his brothers Lonnie and Sam Chatmon also recorded as members of the Mississippi Sheiks with singer/guitarist Walter Vinson. —*Jim O'Neal*

● **Greatest Hits, 1930-1940** / Feb. 1970 / Yazoo ✦✦✦✦
With mostly solo selections by Carter, plus a couple of Mississippi Sheiks songs, this album features very fine and distinctive country-blues guitar playing and singing. Most of the songs are of the double-entendre variety—a possible reason why he's not as well known as he deserves to be, since some blues researchers did not deem his material worthy. As with most Yazoo releases, the liner notes include various guitar tunings and

chord progressions for each song—fascinating for guitarists. —*George Bedard*

Banana in Your Fruit Basket / 1978 / Yazoo ✦✦✦✦
Some of Carter's best double-entendre material, including the salacious "I Got Ants in My Pants." —*Cub Koda*

John Cephas with Phil Wiggins

b. Sep. 4, 1930
Guitar, Harmonica, Vocals / Modern Acoustic Blues
Piedmont blues specialists John Cephas (guitar) and Phil Wiggins (harmonica) are two of a handful of blues musicians who've benefited from the renewed interest in acoustic music in recent years. Cephas has been praised by the *New York Times* and other important media as "one of the outstanding exponents of the Piedmont style guitar."

Both were born in Washington, D.C., though Wiggins is 25 years younger than his guitar-playing partner. Both sing well, and their albums are a mix of standard classic blues as well as their own originals. Along with John Jackson from Virginia, they are some of the names that come to mind when we think of Piedmont blues. The Piedmont region (a geological term referring to foothills) includes the hills between the Appalachian mountains and the Atlantic Coastal plain that run from northern Virginia to Florida. Piedmont blues refers to a blues sub-genre that is characteristic of performers from Virginia, the Carolinas, Florida, and Georgia. Piedmont blues performers include Peg Leg Howell, Pink Anderson, Jackson, Blind Blake and Willie Walker.

The duo's albums include several critically acclaimed releases for Marimac Recordings, Flying Fish Records, and most recently, *Cool Down* for the Chicago-based Alligator Records. The pair's Flying Fish releases from the 1980s include *Dog Days of August, Guitar Man* and *Flip, Flop and Fly*. All are great examples of state-of-the-art, acoustic Piedmont blues. They remain a popular festival act, and can be seen throughout the summer months at most US blues festivals. —*Richard Skelly*

● **Dog Days of August** / 1986 / Flying Fish ✦✦✦✦
Handy Award-winning acoustic guitar and harmonica Piedmont blues. Includes ballads "John Henry," "Staggerlee," and ten original compositions. —*Barry Lee Pearson*

Guitar Man / 1987 / Flying Fish ✦✦✦✦
Their second Handy Award winner includes slide guitar, Piedmont finger-picking, and wonderful harmonica. —*Barry Lee Pearson*

Walking Blues / 1988 / Marimac ✦✦✦✦
A fine assortment of Piedmont blues, ragtime, and country. Includes "Walking Blues." —*Barry Lee Pearson*

Sam Chatmon

b. Jan. 10, 1897, Boltmon, MS, d. Feb. 2, 1983, Hollandale, MS
Guitar, Vocals / Acoustic Country Blues
A product of the prodigious Chatmon family that included not only Lonnie of the famous Mississippi Sheiks but also the prolific Bo Carter and several other blues-playing brothers, Sam Chatmon survived to be hailed as a modern-day blues guru when he began performing and recording again in the '60s. Sam continued brother Bo's tradition of sly double-entendre blues to entertain a new generation of aficionados, but he also showed a more serious side on songs like the title track of the early Arhoolie anthology *I Have to Paint My Face*.

Chatmon began playing music as a child, occasionally with his family's string band, as well as the Mississippi Sheiks. Sam launched his own solo career in the early '30s. While he performed and recorded as a solo act, he would still record with the Mississippi Sheiks and with his brother Lonnie. Throughout the '30s, Sam travelled throughout the South, playing with a variety of minstrel and medicine shows. He stopped travelling in the early '40s, making himself a home in Hollandale, Mississippi, where he worked on plantations.

For the next two decades, Sam Chatmon was essentially retired from music and only worked on the plantations. When the blues revival arrived in the late '50s, he managed to capitalize on the genre's resurgent popularity. In 1960, he signed a contract with Arhoolie and he recorded a number of songs for the label. Throughout the '60s and '70s, he recorded for a variety of labels, as well as playing clubs and blues and folk festivals across America. Chatmon was an active performer and recording artist until his death in 1983. —*Jim O'Neal & Stephen Thomas Erlewine*

● **Sam Chatmon's Advice** / 1979 / Rounder ✦✦✦✦
Outstanding blues and double-entendre delights. —*Ron Wynn*

William Clarke

b. Mar. 29, 1951, Inglewood, CA
Harmonica, Vocals / Modern Electric Blues
I have had the very good fortune to hear great Chicago harp (harmon-

ica) players like Little Walter, Junior Wells, Big Walter Horton, and others playing live in the clubs of Chicago. Those days are gone, and I had given up hope of ever hearing a new voice on amplified blues harp. Then came William Clarke. Technically, Clarke is a master of both the cross and chromatic harps. He takes blues on the chromatic up to and well beyond where Little Walter left it years ago. But far more important than the technique is the music. Clarke plays straightahead blues that is music to the ears, and it rocks.

William Clarke was born March 29, 1951, in Inglewood, CA, and became turned onto blues during the 1960s, oddly enough by hearing covers of blues tunes by groups like the Rolling Stones. Although he had played some guitar and drums, Clarke started playing the harmonica in 1967. He states that his main early influences were Big Walter Horton, James Cotton, Junior Wells, and Sonny Boy Williamson II. In mid-1968 Clarke began listening to jazz organists such as Jack McDuff, Jimmy McGriff, Shirley Scott, and Richard "Groove" Holmes.

Clarke recorded a number of albums before releasing his first CD. They are *Hittin' Heavy* (Good Time, 1978), *Blues from Los Angeles* (1980), *Can't You Hear Me Calling* (Watch Dog, 1983), *Rockin' the Boat* (Riviera, 1985), and *Tip of the Top* (Satch, 1987—nominated for a Handy award). He won the 1991 Handy award for blues song of the year, "Must Be Jelly," and has also received six W.C. Handy Award nominations.

Clarke writes most of his own songs, and many of them are real ear catchers. He has a working-class background, and songs like "Gambling for my Bread" and "Pawnshop Bound" are right on the money—just great tunes.

William Clarke (along with Big Walter Horton and Paul Butterfield) has an almost impeccable sense of which notes to play. There are a lot of players out there who basically play what's on the records of the great Chicago artists. Nothing wrong with this, but no news there either. Clarke is an original. Having heard him play live a number of times, I can testify that here is the real thing—an extension of the classic Chicago-style amplified harp tradition into the present. Just listen to those first two Alligator albums—it's all on the CDs.

Harmonica recording artist Charlie Musselwhite says that Clarke is his "favorite living harp player—no doubt about it." I am in total agreement with Musselwhite. While most great players are either dead or on the decline, Clarke is available and cookin' right now. He's been playing about 200 gigs a year. Check him out. —*Michael Erlewine*

Can't You Hear Me Calling / 1983 / Rivera ✦✦✦
Can't You Hear Me Calling only gives a glimmer of what's to come from this new genius of the blues, but it is enjoyable nonetheless. —*Cub Koda*

Tip of the Top / 1987 / Satch ✦✦✦
Tip of the Top is a loose tribute to William Clarke's mentor, George Harmonica Smith, who taught Clarke many of his tricks. Clarke plays a selection of tracks that were staples in Smith's catalog (including a version of "Hard Times," which features Smith himself), as well as newer songs written in the same style. But what really makes *Tip of the Top* notable is how William Clarke begins to develop his distinctive, idiosyncratic sound on the record. Unlike his debut *Can't You Hear Me Calling*, *Tip of the Top* explores some new sounds, which would come to fruition in his next few albums. —*Thom Owens*

Rockin' the Boat / 1988 / Rivera ✦✦✦✦
Recorded live in 1987, this features Clarke and his regular working band on a wide variety of material showcasing his formidable talents as a vocalist and harmonica man extraordinaire. —*Cub Koda*

★ **Blowin' Like Hell** / 1990 / Alligator ✦✦✦✦✦
The title says it all. William Clarke cooks on this one, his first CD. And these are new sounds. Songs like "Lollipop Mama," "Gambling for My Bread," and "Lonesome Bedroom Blues" (all written by Clarke) are just great tunes. "Must Be Jelly" won Clarke a W.C. Handy Award for blues song of the year in 1991. I find myself humming them. Clarke's timing and music are right on the money. With the great Alex Schultz on lead guitar. There is no doubt that Clarke is one of the few modern bluesmen who are exploring and extending the amplified blues harp tradition without violating any of its principles. No one plays chromatic blues harp with this kind of passion and sheer conviction. Hear for yourself. —*Michael Erlewine*

☆ **Serious Intentions** / 1992 / Alligator ✦✦✦✦✦
His follow-up to *Blowin' Like Hell* burns with a ferocious intensity, particularly for his groundbreaking work on chromatic harp and his ability to cover all styles with remarkable elan. Again, he wrote most of the songs, and "Pawnshop Bound," "Trying to Stretch My Money," and "With a Tear in My Eye" are real songs. Instrumentals like "Chasin' the Gator" feature Clarke with Alex Schulz on lead guitar. —*Cub Koda and Michael Erlewine*

Groove Time / 1994 / Alligator ✦✦✦✦
Here is Clarke, hot again. This time he has added a horn section on some cuts for this recording. No problem. Alex Schultz is there on lead guitar to make sure that this album rocks. Clarke once again writes most of the songs—all 15 fat tracks. By this time, his Alligator albums have a style

and feel (all his own) that one looks forward to. Plenty of high-impact amplified chromatic harmonica here of the push-the-band-hard variety that Clarke does so well, plus some tasty acoustic thrown in too. —*Michael Erlewine*

The Hard Way / 1996 / Alligator ✦✦✦✦
His fourth CD from Alligator is his jazziest and bluesiest recording to date. Clarke has written half of the compositions and put his own sound and style on those he did not write. Highlights include "The Boss" (inspired by saxophonist Willis Jackson,) which is a fast jump that finds chromatic harp riffing along with a horn section—some interesting ideas. Other tracks are the Benny Motensong "Moten Swing," "My Mind Is Working Overtime," (a Latin-tinged tune written by Clarke), and "Letter from Home." —*Michael Erlewine*

Francis Clay

b. Nov. 16, 1923
Drums
Drummer Francis Clay was born in Rock Island, IL, on November 16, 1923. Learning music from his family, Clay was playing some guitar and entering amateur contests at the age of five. But it was drums that fascinated him and he would create his own drum set from things around the house. He turned professional when he was 15 years old. In 1941 Clay formed his first band—Francis Clay and His Syncopated Rhythm playing behind acts like Gypsy Rose Lee, in circuses, on riverboats, etc. This lasted until around 1944. He returned to his home in 1946 and ran a booking office, recording studio, and taught drums. Around 1947 Clay was playing with George "Harmonica" Smith in Chicago. In the early '50s he toured with jazz organist Jack McDuff.

In 1957, Clay took a fill-in job with Muddy Waters and, since he had only played jazz, had no idea how to play the blues. Muddy Waters taught him and in several days they had the thing together. Waters asked him to stay on and Clay was there for the next four years.

In 1962, Clay left Muddy Waters and formed a band with James Cotton, which lasted about a year. Clay then worked with Otis Rush, Buddy Guy, Bobby Fields, and others. In 1965, Clay rejoined Muddy Waters for a stint of almost two years.

In the late '60s, Clay worked and recorded with a number of artists including James Cotton, Muddy Waters, Lightnin' Hopkins, John Lee Hooker, Big Mama Thornton, Victoria Spivey, George "Harmonica" Smith, Shakey Jake Harris, Sunnyland Slim and others. Due to knee problems, Clay has not done much playing in recent years. Francis Clay has been called "the definitive Muddy Waters drummer." He resides in San Francisco. —*Michael Erlewine*

Albert Collins (Al Collins)

b. Oct. 3, 1932, Leona, TX, **d.** Nov. 24, 1993, Las Vegas, NV
Guitar, Vocals / R&B, Spoken Word, Electric Texas Blues, Bop, Ballads, Post-Bop
Albert Collins, "The Master of The Telecaster," "The Iceman," and "The Razor Blade" was robbed of his best years as a blues performer by a bout with liver cancer that ended with his premature death on November 24, 1993. He was just 61 years old. The highly influential, totally original Collins, like the late John Campbell, was on the cusp of a much wider worldwide following via his deal with Virgin Records' Pointblank subsidiary. However, unlike Campbell, Collins had performed for many more years, in obscurity, before finally finding a following in the mid-'80s.

Collins was born October 1, 1932, in Leona, TX. His family moved to Houston when he was seven. Growing up in the city's Third Ward, Collins started out taking keyboard lessons. His idol when he was a teen was Hammond B-3 organist Jimmy McGriff. But by the time he was 18 years old, he switched to guitar. Collins began performing in local clubs, going after his own style, characterized by his use of minor tunings and a capo, by the mid-'50s. It was also at this point that he began his "guitar walks" through the audience, which made him wildly popular with the younger White audiences he played for years later in the 1980s. He led a ten-piece band, the Rhythm Rockers, and cut his first single in 1958 for the Houston-based Kangaroo label, "The Freeze." The single was followed by a slew of other instrumental singles with catchy titles, including "Sno-Cone," "Icy Blue" and "Don't Lose Your Cool." All of these singles brought Collins a regional following. After recording "De-Frost" for Hall-Way Records of Beaumont, TX, he hit it big in 1962 with "Frosty," a million-selling single. The tune quickly became part of his ongoing repertoire, and was still part of his live shows more than 30 years later, in the mid-'80s. Collins' percussive, ringing guitar style became his trademark, as he would use his right hand to pluck the strings. Blues-rock guitarist Jimi Hendrix cited Collins as an influence in any number of interviews he gave.

Through the rest of the 1960s, Collins continued to work day jobs while pursuing his music with short regional tours and on weekends. He recorded for other small Texas labels, including Great Scott, Brylen and TFC. In 1968, Canned Heat's Bob "The Bear" Hite took Collins to California, where he was immediately signed to Imperial Records. By later 1968 and 1969, the '60s blues revival was still going on, and Collins got wider exposure opening for groups like the Allman Brothers at the Fillmore West in San Francisco.

He recorded three albums for the Imperial label before jumping to Tumbleweed Records. The label folded in 1973. Despite the fact that he didn't record much through the 1970s and into the early '80s, he had gotten sufficient airplay around the US with his singles to be able to continue touring. His big break came about in 1977, when he was signed to the Chicago-based Alligator Records, and he released his brilliant debut for the label in 1978, *Ice Pickin'.* Collins recorded six more albums for the label, culminating in 1986's *Cold Snap,* on which organist Jimmy McGriff performs. It was at Alligator Records that Collins began to realize that he could sing adequately, and working with his wife Gwynn, he co-wrote many of his classic songs, including items like "Mastercharge" and "Conversation with Collins."

An album he recorded with fellow guitarists Robert Cray and Johnny "Clyde" Copeland for Alligator in 1987, *Showdown!* brought a Grammy award for all three musicians. His *Cold Snap,* released in 1986, was nominated for a Grammy award.

In 1989, Collins signed with the Pointblank subsidiary of major label Virgin Records, and his debut, *Iceman,* was released in 1991. The label released *Collins Mix* in 1993, posthumously. Other compact-disc reissues of his early recordings were produced by other record companies who saw Collins' newfound popularity on the festival and theater circuit, and they include *The Complete Imperial Recordings* on EMI Records (1991) and *Truckin' with Albert Collins.*

Although he'd spent far too much time in the 1970s without recording, Collins could sense that the blues were coming back stronger in the mid-'80s, with interest in Stevie Ray Vaughan at an all-time high. Collins enjoyed some media celebrity in the last few years of his life, via concert appearances at Carnegie Hall, on "Late Night with David Letterman," in the Touchstone film, *Adventures in Babysitting,* and in a classy Seagram's Wine Cooler commercial with Bruce Willis. The blues revival that Collins, Vaughan, and the Fabulous Thunderbirds helped bring about in the mid-'80s has continued into the mid-'90s. But sadly, Collins has not been able to take part in the on-going evolution of the music. *—Richard Skelly*

Truckin' with Albert Collins / 1969 / MCA ✦✦✦✦
Truckin' with Albert Collins is a 1969 Blue Thumb reissue of *The Cool Sound of Albert Collins,* which was originally released on TCF Hall Records in 1965. These are the earliest recordings that Collins made and already his trademark sound is in place—his leads are stinging, piercing and direct. The album features a set of blistering instrumentals (with the exception of the vocal "Dyin' Flu") that would eventually become his signature tunes, including "Frosty" and "Frostbite." Collins doesn't just stick to blues, he adds elements of surf, rock, jazz, and R&B. These songs may not have been hits at the time, but they helped establish his reputation as the Master of the Telecaster. *— Thom Owens*

★ **Ice Pickin'** / 1978 / Alligator ✦✦✦✦✦
Ice Pickin' is the album that brought Albert Collins directly back into the limelight, and for good reason, too. The record captures the wild, unrestrained side of his playing that had never quite been documented before. Though his singing doesn't quite have the fire or power of his playing, the album doesn't suffer at all because of that—he simply burns throughout the album. *Ice Pickin'* was his first release for Alligator Records and it set the pace for all the albums that followed. No matter how much he tried, Collins never completely regained the pure energy that made *Ice Pickin'* such a revelation. *— Thom Owens*

Frostbite / 1980 / Alligator ✦✦✦
Frozen Alive! / 1981 / Alligator ✦✦✦
Cold Snap / 1986 / Alligator ✦✦✦
Showdown / 1987 / Alligator ✦✦✦

★ **The Complete Imperial Recordings** / 1991 / EMI ✦✦✦✦✦
Texan Albert Collins was in the very first rank of post-war blues guitarists. This two-CD set is a reissue of all 36 sides he cut for Imperial from 1968 to 1970—representing this artist's second major recording stint. Instrumentals comprise roughly three-fourths of the material. They frame his distinctive guitar-work with a tight ensemble of organ, bass, and drums, adding at times a piano and/or second guitar, punctuated by a horn section. About ten of these tunes are as great as anything Collins ever did. They are riddled with the biting, incisive, dramatic, and economical playing that made him a legend. There are also some outstanding vocals. Although this set is not without its clinkers, it is a solid package and a must for any Collins fan. *—Larry Hoffman*

Collins Mix (The Best Of) / Oct. 5, 1993 / Point Blank ✦✦✦✦
This provided fresh looks at 11 Collins classics, among them such epic numbers as "Don't Lose Your Cool," "Frosty," "Honey Hush" and "Tired Man." There were slow, wailing ballads with blistering solos, electrifying

uptempo wailers with a great horn section answering Collins' phrases with their own bleats, and first-rate mastering and production. Guest stars included B.B. King, Branford Marsalis, Kim Wilson, and Gary Moore, while Collins injected vitality into numbers he'd already made standards years ago. This set is a wonderful tribute to an incredible guitarist and musician. *—Ron Wynn*

Live 92/93 / Sep. 12, 1995 / Point Blank ✦✦✦

Johnny Copeland

b. 1938, Homer, LA
Guitar, Vocals / R&B, Electric Texas Blues
Considering the amount of time he's spent steadily rolling from gig to gig, Houston-native Johnny "Clyde" Copeland's rise to prominence in the blues world in recent years isn't all that surprising. In the last few years, he's earned some well-deserved breaks: a contract with the PolyGram/Verve label has put his 1990s recordings into the hands of thousands of blues lovers around the world. It's not that Copeland's talent has changed all that much since he recorded for Rounder Records in the 1980s; it's just that major companies are again beginning to see the potential of great, hardworking blues musicians like Copeland. Unfortunately, Copeland has been forced to slow down in 1995-96 by heart-related complications, but as of this writing, Copeland had received a left ventricular assist device (L-VAD) for his heart and was continuing to perform shows within a two-hour drive of his home in northern New Jersey.

Copeland has recorded seven albums for Rounder Records, beginning in 1981, including *Copeland Special, Make My Home Where I Hang My Hat, Texas Twister, Bringing It All Back Home, When the Rain Starts a Fallin', Ain't Nothing but a Party* (live, nominated for a Grammy), and *Boom Boom,* and he won a Grammy award in 1986 for his efforts on an Alligator album, *Showdown!* with Robert Cray and the late Albert Collins.

Although Copeland has a booming, shouting voice and is a powerful guitarist and live performer, what most people don't realize is just how clever a songwriter he is. His more recent releases for the PolyGram/Verve/Gitanes label, including *Flyin' High* (1993) and *Catch Up with the Blues,* provide ample evidence of this on "Life's Rainbow (Nature Song)" (from the latter album) and "Circumstances" (from the former album). *—Richard Skelly*

● **Copeland Special** / 1977 / Rounder ✦✦✦✦
This immaculate collection put the veteran Houston axeman among the blues elite; it features searing guitar and soulful vocals. *—Bill Dahl*

Make My Home Where I Hang My Hat / 1982 / Rounder ✦✦✦
This second Rounder Records album has its share of incendiary moments. *—Bill Dahl*

Texas Twister / 1983 / Rounder ✦✦✦✦
Johnny Copeland's tenure on Rounder Records was mostly productive. He made several albums that ranged from decent to very good, increased his audience and name recognition and got better recording facilities and company support than at most times in his career. The 15 numbers on this anthology cover four Rounder sessions, and include competent renditions of familiar numbers. But what makes things special are the final three selections; these were part of Copeland's superb and unjustly underrated *Bringing It Back Home* album, recorded in Africa, which matched Texas shuffle licks with swaying, riveting African rhythms. *—Ron Wynn*

I'll Be Around / 1984 / Mr. R&B ✦✦✦✦
Exceptional collection of Copeland's primordial work. *—Bill Dahl*

Showdown [A Collins and R Cray] / 1985 / Alligator ✦✦✦✦
A summit meeting between Texas guitar veterans Collins and Johnny Copeland and newcomer Robert Cray, the set is scorching all the way. *—Bill Dahl*

Down on Bending Knee / 1985 / Mr. R&B ✦✦✦✦
This second volume of his early sides is equally impressive. *—Bill Dahl*

Bringin' It All Back Home / 1986 / Rounder ✦✦✦✦
Imaginative hybrid of blues and African idioms. *—Bill Dahl*

Ain't Nothing But a Party [Live] / 1988 / Rounder ✦✦✦

Collection, Vol. 1 / 1988 / Collectables ✦✦✦
These early 1960-1968 Houston sides are obscure but satisfying. *—Bill Dahl*

James Cotton

b. Jul. 1, 1935, Tunica, MS
Guitar, Harmonica, Drums, Vocals / Electric Chicago Blues
At his high-energy 1970s peak as a bandleader, James Cotton was a bouncing, sweaty, whirling dervish of a bluesman, roaring his vocals and all but sucking the reeds right out of his defenseless little harmonicas with his prodigious lungpower. Due to throat problems, Cotton's

vocals are no longer what they used to be, but he remains a masterful instrumentalist.

Cotton had some gargantuan shoes to fill when he stepped into Little Walter's slot as Muddy Waters' harp ace in 1954, but for the next dozen years, the young Mississippian filled the integral role beside Chicago's blues king with power and precision. Of course, Cotton prepared for such a career move for a long time, having learned how to wail on harp from none other than Sonny Boy Williamson himself.

Cotton was only a child when he first heard Williamson's fabled radio broadcasts for *King Biscuit Time* over KFFA out of Helena, AR. When he was a teenager, Cotton was ready to unleash a sound of his own. Gigging with area notables Joe Willie Wilkins and Willie Nix, Cotton built a sterling reputation around West Memphis, following in his mentor's footsteps by landing his own radio show in 1952 over KWEM. Sam Phillips, whose Sun label was still a fledgling operation, invited Cotton to record for him, and two singles commenced: "Straighten Up Baby" in 1953 and "Cotton Crop Blues" the next year.

When Waters rolled through Memphis minus his latest harpist, Cotton hired on with the legend and came to Chicago. Unfortunately for the youngster, Chess Records insisted on using Little Walter on the great majority of Waters' waxings until 1958, when Cotton blew behind Waters on "She's Nineteen Years Old" and "Close to You."

By 1966, Cotton was primed to make it on his own. Waxings for Vanguard, Prestige, and Loma preceded his official full-length album debut for Verve Records in 1967. His own unit then included fleet-fingered guitarist Luther Tucker and hard-hitting drummer Sam Lay. Throwing a touch of soul into his eponymous debut set, Cotton ventured into the burgeoning blues-rock field as he remained with Verve through the end of the decade.

In 1974, Cotton signed with Buddah and released *100% Cotton*, one of his most relentless LPs, with Matt "Guitar" Murphy sizzlingly backing him up. A decade later, Alligator issued another standout Cotton LP, *High Compression*, that was split evenly between traditional-style Chicago blues and funkier, horn-driven material. *Harp Attack!*, a 1990 summit meeting on Alligator, paired Cotton with three exalted peers: Wells, Carey Bell, and comparative newcomer Billy Branch. Antone's Records was responsible for a pair of gems: a live 1988 set reuniting the harpist with Murphy and Tucker and a stellar 1991 studio project, *Mighty Long Time*.

Cotton still commands a huge following, even though serious throat problems have tragically robbed him of his once-ferocious roar. —*Bill Dahl*

Chicago/ the Blues/ Today!, Vol. 2 / 1964 / Vanguard ✦✦✦✦
Classic compilation, also starring Otis Rush and Homesick James. —*Bill Dahl*

Live and on the Move / 1966 / One Way ✦✦✦

100% Cotton / Mar. 1974 / One Way ✦✦✦✦
The ebullient, roly-poly Chicago harp wizard was at his zenith in 1974, when this cooking album was issued on Buddah. Matt "Guitar" Murphy matched Cotton note for zealous note back then, leading to fireworks aplenty on the non-stop "Boogie Thing," a driving "How Long Can a Fool Go Wrong," and the fastest "Rocket 88" you'll ever take a spin in. —*Bill Dahl*

● **High Compression** / 1984 / Alligator ✦✦✦✦
This is the best contemporary Cotton album gracing the shelves today, thanks to its ingenious formatting: half the set places Cotton in a traditional setting beside guitarist Magic Slim and pianist Pinetop Perkins, and a solid rhythm section; the other half pairs him with a contemporary combo featuring guitarist Michael Coleman's swift licks and a three-piece horn section. Both combinations click on all burners. Includes scorching theme song, "Superharp." —*Bill Dahl*

Live at Antone's / 1988 / Antone's ✦✦✦✦
Reuniting Cotton with his former guitarists Matt Murphy and Luther Tucker, pianist Pinetop Perkins, and Muddy Waters' ex-rhythm section (bassist Calvin Jones and drummer Willie Smith) looks like a great idea on paper, and it worked equally well in the flesh, when this set was cut live at Antone's Night Club in Austin, TX. —*Bill Dahl*

Harp Attack! / 1990 / Alligator ✦✦✦✦
Four Chicago harmonica greats, one eminently solid album. Teamed with Junior Wells, Billy Branch, and Carey Bell, Cotton sings Willie Love's Delta classic "Little Car Blues" and Charles Brown's "Black Night" and plays along with his cohorts on most of the rest of the set. —*Bill Dahl*

Mighty Long Time / 1991 / Antone's ✦✦✦✦
Although the titles are all familiar (most of them a little too much so), Cotton and his all-star cohorts (guitarists Jimmie Vaughan, Matt Murphy, Luther Tucker, Hubert Sumlin, and Wayne Bennett, the omnipresent Perkins on keys) pull the whole thing off beautifully. Cotton's cover of Wolf's "Moanin' at Midnight" is remarkably eerie in its own right, and he romps through Muddy Waters' "Blow Wind Blow" and "Sugar Sweet" with joyous alacrity. —*Bill Dahl*

● **Best of the Verve Years** / 1995 / Verve ✦✦✦✦
Taken from the high-energy harpist's first three albums for Verve following his split from Muddy Waters (including the entirety of his fine eponymous 1967 debut), this 20-track anthology is a fine spot to begin any serious Cotton collection. In those days, Cotton was into soul as well as blues—witness his raucous versions of "Knock on Wood" and "Turn on Your Lovelight," backed by a large horn complement. Compiler Dick Shurman has chosen judiciously from his uneven pair of Verve follow-ups, making for a very consistent compilation. —*Bill Dahl*

Ida Cox

b. Feb. 25, 1896, Toccoa, GA, **d.** Nov. 10, 1967, Knoxville, TN
Vocals / Blues, Classic Female Blues
One of the finest classic blues singers of the 1920s, Ida Cox was singing in theaters by the time she was 14. She recorded regularly during 1923-29 (her "Wild Woman Don't Have the Blues" and "Death Letter Blues" are her best-known songs). Although she was off record during much of the 1930s, Cox was able to continue working and in 1939 she sang at Cafe Society, appeared at John Hammond's "Spirituals to Swing" concert and made some new records. Ida Cox toured with shows until a 1944 stroke pushed her into retirement; she came back for an impressive final recording in 1961. —*Scott Yanow and Stephen Thomas Erlewine*

★ **Blues for Rampart Street** / 1961 / Riverside ✦✦✦✦✦
With Coleman Hawkins. This is latter-period Cox, with jazz all-stars. Some of her best tunes. —*Michael G. Nastos*

Wild Women Don't Have the Blues / 1961 / Rosetta ✦✦✦✦
Ida Cox's *Wild Women Don't Have the Blues* was recorded at the end of her career. Surprisingly, Cox's voice hadn't faded away—she could belt out a song with nearly as much power as she did in her early career. In fact, *Wild Women Don't Have the Blues* ranks as one of her finest albums. Not only is Cox in fine voice, the support Coleman Hawkins and his small group lends is strong and sympathetic, making this album one to treasure. —*Thom Owens*

Robert Cray

b. Aug. 1, 1953, Columbus, GA
Guitar, Vocals / Modern Electric Blues, Blues
Tin-eared critics have frequently damned him as a yuppie blues wannabe whose slickly soulful offerings bear scant resemblance to the real downhome item. In reality, Robert Cray is one of a precious few young (at this stage, that translates to under 50 years of age) blues artists with the talent and vision to successfully usher the idiom into the 21st century without resorting either to slavish imitation or simply playing rock while passing it off as blues. Just as importantly, his immensely popular records helped immeasurably to jump-start the contemporary blues boom that still holds sway to this day.

Blessed with a soulful voice that sometimes recalls '60s-great O.V. Wright and a concise lead guitar approach that never wastes notes, Cray's rise to international fame was indeed a heartwarming one. For a guy whose 1980 debut album for Tomato, *Who's Been Talkin'*, proved an instantaneous cutout, his ascendancy was amazingly swift—in 1986 his breakthrough *Strong Persuader* album for Mercury (containing "Smoking Gun") won him a Grammy and shot his asking price for a night's work skyward.

Unlike too many of his peers, Cray continues to experiment within his two presiding genres, blues and soul. Sets such as *Midnight Stroll, I Was Warned* and *Shame + a Sin* for Mercury show that the "bluenatics" (as he amusedly labels his purist detractors) have nothing to fear and plenty to anticipate from this innovative, laudably accessible guitarist. —*Bill Dahl*

Who's Been Talkin' / 1980 / Atlantic ✦✦✦✦
The Pacific Northwest-based blues savior's first album in 1980 boded well for his immediate future. Unfurling a sterling vocal delivery equally conversant with blues and soul, Cray offers fine remakes of the Willie Dixon-penned title tune, O.V. Wright's deep soul romp "I'm Gonna Forget About You," and Freddy King's "The Welfare (Turns Its Back on You)," along with his own "Nice as a Fool Can Be" and "That's What I'll Do." —*Bill Dahl*

☆ **Bad Influence** / 1983 / HighTone ✦✦✦✦✦
One of Cray's best albums ever, and the one that etched him into the consciousness of blues aficionados prior to his mainstream explosion. Produced beautifully by Bruce Bromberg and Dennis Walker, the set sports some gorgeous originals ("Phone Booth," "Bad Influence," "So Many Women, So Little Time") and two well-chosen covers, Johnny "Guitar" Watson's "Don't Touch Me" and Eddie Floyd's Stax-era "Got to Make a Comeback." Few albums portend greatness the way this one did. —*Bill Dahl*

False Accusations / 1985 / HighTone ✦✦✦✦
If its predecessor hadn't been so powerful, this collection might have

been a little more striking in its own right. As it is, a solid if not over-whelming album sporting the memorable "Playin' in the Dirt" and "I've Slipped Her Mind." —*Bill Dahl*

Showdown [A Collins and J Copeland] / 1985 / Alligator ✦✦✦✦
Cray found himself in some pretty intimidating company for this Grammy-winning blues guitar summit meeting, but he wasn't deterred, holding his own alongside his idol Albert Collins and Texas great Johnny Copeland. Cray's delivery of Muddy Waters' rhumba-rocking "She's into Something" was one of the set's many highlights. —*Bill Dahl*

★ **Strong Persuader** / 1986 / Mercury ✦✦✦✦✦
The set that made Cray a pop star, despite its enduring blues base. Cray's smoldering stance on "Smoking Gun" and "Right Next Door" rendered him the first sex symbol to emerge from the blues field in decades, but it was his innovative expansion of the genre itself that makes this album a genuine 1980s classic. "Nothing but a Woman" boasts an irresistible groove pushed by the Memphis Horns and some metaphorically inspired lyrics, while "I Wonder" and "Guess I Showed Her" sizzle with sensuality. —*Bill Dahl*

Don't Be Afraid of the Dark / 1988 / Mercury ✦✦
A followup to *Strong Persuader,* this suffers from weak songs, but is worthwhile for fans. —*John Floyd*

Too Many Cooks / 1990 / Tomato ✦✦✦✦
Too Many Cooks is a reissue of Robert Cray's first album, *Who's Been Talking.* —*AMG*

Midnight Stroll / Jun. 1990 / Mercury ✦✦✦
Cray went into a more soul-slanted direction for this solid collection, coarsening his vocal cords for "The Forecast (Calls for Pain)" and the rest of the set. —*Bill Dahl*

I Was Warned / Apr. 1992 / Mercury ✦✦✦

Shame + a Sin / Oct. 5, 1993 / Mercury ✦✦✦✦
This time, Cray veered back toward the blues (most convincingly, too), even covering Albert King's "You're Gonna Need Me" and bemoaning paying taxes on the humorous "1040 Blues." Unlike his previous efforts, Cray produced this one himself. Also, longtime bassist Richard Cousins was history, replaced by Karl Sevareid. —*Bill Dahl*

Some Rainy Morning / 1995 / Mercury ✦✦✦
Typically well-produced and well-played outing—mostly originals, with smoldering covers of Syl Johnson's "Steppin' Out" and Wilson Pickett's "Jealous Love" for good measure. Cray's crisp, concise guitar work and subtly soulful vocals remain honed to a sharp edge. —*Bill Dahl*

Pee Wee Crayton

b. Dec. 18, 1914, Rockdale, TX, d. Jun. 25, 1985, Los Angeles, CA
Guitar, Vocals / R&B, Electric West Coast Blues, West Coast Blues
Although he was certainly inexorably influenced by the pioneering electric guitar conception of T-Bone Walker (what axe-handler wasn't during the immediate postwar era?), Pee Wee Crayton brought enough daring innovation to his playing to avoid being labeled as a mere T-Bone imitator. Crayton's recorded output for Modern, Imperial, and Vee-Jay contains plenty of dazzling, marvelously imaginative guitar work, especially on stunning instrumentals such as "Texas Hop," "Pee Wee's Boogie," and "Poppa Stoppa," all far more aggressive performances than Walker usually indulged in. —*Bill Dahl*

● **Blues After Hours** / 1993 / P-Vine ✦✦✦✦
Regrettably, this is the only compact disc available of Crayton's brilliant early sides for Modern—and it's a genuine, make no mistake. But it's worth it (until Pointblank sees fit to anoint us with a domestic collection, anyway)—its 19 sides include the essential instrumentals "Blues After Hours" and "Texas Hop," along with a variety of fine vocal efforts by this California blues guitar mainstay of the late '40s and early '50s. —*Bill Dahl*

● **The Complete Aladdin and Imperial Recordings** / 1996 / Capitol ✦✦✦✦
Crayton was fading fast commercially by the time he cut these sides in the 1950s, though his vocal and instrumental skills, particularly his stinging guitar, were undimmed. Aside from two 1951 tracks cut for Aladdin in 1951, this 20-song compilation is devoted to his mid-'50s hitch with Imperial. The label had him record in New Orleans with Dave Bartholomew and other local musicians, giving many of these sides a hybrid jump blues/New Orleans R&B feel (Imperial would use the same approach with Roy Brown around this time). It's not his very best work, but even at its slightest this is pleasant. It's most effective, however, when the Crescent City touches are muted in favor of slicing straight-ahead blues riffing, as on the instrumental "Blues Before Dawn." Another obscure cut, "Do Unto Others," is nothing less than a revelation, boasting a light-years-ahead-of-its-time opening riff that sounds almost identical—we kid you not—to the blast of notes that opens the Beatles' "Revolution," cut nearly 15 years later. —*Richie Unterberger*

Arthur "Big Boy" Crudup

b. Aug. 24, 1905, Forest, MS, d. Mar. 28, 1974, Nassawadox, VA
Guitar, Vocals / R&B, Electric Blues, Electric Delta Blues, Acoustic Delta Blues
Arthur Crudup may well have been Elvis Presley's favorite bluesman. The swivel-hipped rock god recorded no less than three of Big Boy's Victor classics during his rockabilly heyday—"That's All Right Mama" (Elvis' Sun debut in 1954), "So Glad You're Mine," and "My Baby Left Me." Often lost in all the hubbub surrounding Presley's classic covers are Crudup's own contributions to the blues lexicon. He didn't sound much like anyone else, and that makes him an innovator, albeit a rather rudimentary guitarist (he didn't even pick up the instrument until he was 30 years old).

Around 1940, Crudup migrated to Chicago from Mississippi. By September of 1941, he had landed a record contract with RCA/Victor Records. Crudup pierced the uppermost reaches of the R&B lists during the mid-'40s with "Rock Me Mama," "Who's Been Foolin' You," "Keep Your Arms Around Me," "So Glad You're Mine," and "Ethel Mae." He cut the original "That's All Right" in 1946 backed by his usual rhythm section of bassist Ransom Knowling and drummer Judge Riley, but it wasn't a national hit at the time. Crudup remained a loyal and prolific employee of Victor until 1954, when a lack of tangible rewards for his efforts soured Crudup on Nipper (he had already cut singles in 1952 for Trumpet disguised as Elmer James and for Checker as Percy Lee Crudup).

In 1961, Crudup surfaced after a long layoff with an album for Fire. Another lengthy hiatus preceded Delmark boss Bob Koester's following the tip of Big Joe Williams to track down the elusive legend. Happily, the guitarist's sound hadn't been dimmed by Father Time: his late-'60s work for Delmark rang true as he was reunited with Knowling (Willie Dixon also handled bass duties on some of his sides). Finally, Crudup began to make some decent money, playing various blues and folk festivals for appreciative crowds for a few years prior to his 1974 death. —*Bill Dahl*

That's All Right Mama [Relic] / 1961 / Relic ✦✦✦

★ **That's All Right Mama** / 1991 / RCA ✦✦✦✦✦
This may not have been where rock 'n' roll all started, but it's very likely where Elvis Presley's knowledge of blues began: 22 tracks dating from 1941 to 1954 by the guitarist whose "That's All Right" proved Presley's ticket to Sun Records stardom. Crudup was fairly limited on guitar—his accompaniment is rudimentary at best—but his songs were uncommonly sturdy (Elvis also covered "So Glad You're Mine" and "My Baby Left Me," both here in their original incarnations) and his vocals strong. —*Bill Dahl*

Meets the Master Blues Bassists / 1994 / Delmark ✦✦✦

Cyril Davies

b. 1932, Denham, Buckinghamshire, England, d. Jan. 7, 1964, England
Harmonica, Vocals / Electric British Blues, British Blues
The Cyril Davies R&B All-Stars were, after the Rolling Stones, the best British blues band of the early '60s—and if they'd gotten to stay together a little longer under Davies, they might even have given Mick Jagger, Brian Jones, and company a real run for their money. This regrettably short-lived blues band was assembled by harpist/singer Cyril Davies (1932-1964) in 1963, after his exit from Blues Incorporated. The group's original lineup featured Davies on harp and vocals, Bernie Watson on guitar, Nicky Hopkins on piano, Ricky Brown playing bass, and Carlo Little on the drums; all four had been recruited from the ranks of Screamin' Lord Sutch's Savages. This quintet recorded an initial single, "Country Line Special," driven by Davies' wailing harp and vocals, that was sufficiently authentic to get it placed alongside the British releases of songs by Muddy Waters, Howlin' Wolf, and the rest of the Chess Record luminaries in England's Pye Records catalog.

Watson and Brown went their separate ways during the summer of 1963, and Jeff Bradford and Cliff Barton came in on guitar and bass, respectively, with Long John Baldry—another Blues Incorporated alumnus—occasionally sitting in on vocals. Their second single, "Preachin' the Blues," was released in September to modest but promising success, and for a time it looked as if Davies and company were going to be a major force on the burgeoning R&B scene. But Davies collapsed late in 1963 and was diagnosed as suffering from acute leukemia; he died in January of 1964. —*Bruce Eder*

The Legendary Cyril Davies / 1957 / Folklore ✦✦✦
Early acoustic sides by Davies and Korner, reissued in 1970 on the Folklore label. The two hadn't found their way yet, and while the playing is raw and interesting, the work is a little too unfinished to be truly representative of either artist. The Marquee Club album is more representative. —*Bruce Eder*

● **R&B from the Marquee** / 1962 / Decca ✦✦✦✦
The most important of Blues Incorporated's albums, this record features Davies all over it, and is his one reasonably representative album. He

may be the best thing here, his blues harp the most accomplished and authentic-sounding instrument, and his vocals are quite convincing and natural as well. —*Bruce Eder*

Blind John Davis

b. Dec. 7, 1913, Hattiesburg, MS, **d.** Oct. 12, 1985, Chicago, IL
Piano, Vocals / Piano Blues
The piano work of John Davis was featured on blues records by the score during the '30s and '40s. His accompaniments to Tampa Red, Sonny Boy Williamson, Big Bill Broonzy, and others brought him fame as a blues musician, but like his piano compatriot Little Brother Montgomery, Davis did not care to be typecast as such and often expressed a preference for the sweet, sentimental favorites he played in countless piano lounges. But as with Montgomery, most of Davis' own recording opportunities came from blues companies, and he never failed to acquit himself well when it came to blues and boogie-woogie. He was the first pianist to do a European blues tour (with Broonzy in 1952), returning to the continent frequently as a solo act during the '70s and '80s. With blues-piano appreciation in Europe being what it is and has been, it's not surprising that most of the albums of Blind John Davis were recorded there and not in Chicago, his home from the age of two until his death. —*Jim O'Neal*

● **Stompin' on a Saturday Night** / 1978 / Alligator ✦✦✦✦
Solid blues piano. Excellent phrasing and rhythms. —*Ron Wynn*

Rev. Gary Davis

b. Apr. 30, 1896, Laurens, SC, **d.** May 5, 1972, Hammonton, NJ
Guitar, Vocals / Acoustic Country Blues, Gospel, Piedmont Blues
In his prime, which is to say the late '20s, the Reverend Gary Davis was one of the two most renowned practitioners of the East Coast school of ragtime guitar; 35 years later, despite two decades spent playing on the streets of Harlem in New York, he was still one of the giants in his field, playing before thousands of people at a time, and an inspiration to dozens of modern guitarist/singers including Bob Dylan, Taj Mahal, Donovan, Jorma Kaukonen, David Bromberg, and Ry Cooder, who studied with Davis.

Davis was partially blind at birth and lost what little sight he had before he was an adult. He was self-taught on the guitar, beginning at age six, and by the time he was in his 20s he had one of the most advanced guitar techniques of anyone in blues—his only peers among ragtime-based players were Blind Arthur Blake, Blind Lemon Jefferson, and Blind Willie Johnson. Davis himself was a major influence on Blind Boy Fuller.

Davis' influences included gospel, marches, ragtime, jazz, and minstrel hokum, and he integrated them in a style that was his own. In 1911, when Davis was a still teenager, the family moved to Greenville, SC, and he fell under the influence of such local guitar virtuosi as Willie Walker, Sam Brooks, and Baby Brooks. Davis moved to Durham in the mid-'20s, by which time he was a full-time street musician, and celebrated not only for the diversity of styles that his playing embraced, but for his skills with the guitar, already virtually unmatched in the blues field.

Davis went into the recording studio for the first time in the '30s with the backing of a local businessman. He cut a mixture of blues and spirituals for the American Record Company label, but there was never an equitable agreement about payment for the recordings, and after these sessions, it was 19 years before he entered the studio again. During that period, he went through many changes. Like many other street buskers, Davisintersersed gospel songs amid his blues and ragtime numbers, to make it harder for the police to interrupt him. He began taking the gospel material more seriously, and in 1937 he became an ordained minister. After that he usually refused to perform any blues.

Davis moved to New York in the early '40s and began preaching and playing on street corners in Harlem. He recorded again at the end of the 1940s, with a pair of gospel songs, but it wasn't until the mid-'50s that a real following for his work began developing anew. His music, all of it now of a spiritual nature, began showing up on labels such as Stinson, Folkways, and Riverside, where he recorded seven songs in early 1956. Davis was "rediscovered" by the folk revival movement, and after some initial reticence, he agreed to perform as part of the budding folk music revival, appearing at the Newport Folk Festival, where his raspy-voiced sung sermons, most notably his transcendant "Samson and Delilah (If I Had My Way)"—a song most closely associated with Blind Willie Johnson—and "Twelve Gates to the City," were highlights of the proceedings for several years. He recorded a live album for Vanguard at one such concert, as well as appearing on several Newport live anthology collections. He was the subject of two television documentaries, one in 1967 and one in 1970.

Davis became one of the most popular players on the folk revival and blues revival scenes, playing before large and enthusiastic audiences—most of the songs that he performed were spirituals, but they

weren't that far removed from the blues that he'd recorded in the 1930s, and his guitar technique was intact. Davis' skills as a player, on the jumbo Gibson acoustic models that he favored, were undiminished, and he was a startling figure to hear, picking and strumming complicated rhythms and countermelodies. Davis became a teacher during this period, and his students included some very prominent White guitar players, including David Bromberg and the Jefferson Airplane's Jorma Kaukonen (who later recorded Davis' "I'll Be Alright" on his acclaimed solo album *Quah!*) The Reverend Gary Davis left behind a fairly large body of modern (i.e., post-World War II) recordings, taking the revival of his career in stride as a way of carrying the message of the gospel to a new generation. He even recorded anew some of his blues and ragtime standards in the studio, for the benefit of his students. —*Bruce Eder*

Pure Religion and Bad Company / 1957 / Smithsonian/Folkways ✦✦✦✦
Moses Asch became the first producer to record Davis in a full-length album release, showcasing his dazzling guitar style more fully than ever before. —*Bruce Eder*

At Newport / 1959 / Vanguard ✦✦✦✦
One of the finest single artist albums to come out of Newport, not quite in the league of Muddy Waters' performance but a superb introduction to the range of his repertory, from ragtime and novelty tunes to gospel numbers. —*Bruce Eder*

☆ **1935-1949** / 1960 / Yazoo ✦✦✦✦✦
Davis' first recordings, encompassing his short-lived 1930s studio career and a pair of sides from after the war. The 1930s material is the real article, Davis in his prime as a singer and player. —*Bruce Eder*

Say No to the Devil / 1961 / Bluesville ✦✦✦✦
Say No to the Devil is Rev. Gary Daviss third Bluesville album. Davis was in fine form throughout the session, playing some startlingly intricate 12-string guitar licks, blowing some rootsy harp, and singing with conviction. Between the songs, Davis tells some rambling stories, which are just as gripping and fascinating as the music itself. —*Thom Owens*

Gospel, Blues & Street Songs / Jul. 1961 / Riverside ✦✦✦✦
Eight of Davis' best-known gospel songs, cut in 1956 in New York, and among the most glowing sides of his career. Paired up with seven tracks cut by Pink Anderson for Riverside in 1950. —*Bruce Eder*

Blues and Ragtime / 1993 / Shanachie ✦✦✦✦
The Rev. Gary Davis forsook his gospel calling for a little while between 1962 and 1966 to set down formal studio versions of many of his most important blues and ragtime repertory. Some of the material here runs over ten minutes, as Davis lays out his best playing and singing voice. The booklet includes a fairly detailed biography as well as musical annotation. —*Bruce Eder*

★ **Complete Early Recordings** / 1994 / Yazoo ✦✦✦✦✦
Complete Early Recordings collects the highlights of Rev. Gary Davis' work from the late '30s, presented in an intelligent and wisely sequenced fashion. This is country blues at its purest and finest, and a necessary addition to nearly any blues collection. —*Thom Owens*

Jimmy Dawkins

b. Oct. 24, 1936
Guitar, Vocals / Modern Electric Blues, Chicago Blues
Chicago guitarist Jimmy Dawkins would just as soon leave his longtime nickname "Fast Fingers" behind. It was always something of a stylistic misnomer anyway; Dawkins' West Side-styled guitar slashes and surges, but seldom burns with incendiary speed. Dawkins' blues are generally of the brooding, introspective variety—he doesn't engage in flashy pyrotechnics or outrageous showmanship.

It took a long time for Dawkins to progress from West Side fixture to nationally known recording artist. He rode a Greyhound bus out of Mississippi in 1955, dressed warm to ward off the Windy City's infamous chill factor. Only trouble was, he arrived on a sweltering July day! Harpist Billy Boy Arnold offered the newcomer encouragement, and he eventually carved out a niche on the competitive West Side scene (his peers included Magic Sam and Luther Allison).

Sam introduced Dawkins to Delmark Records boss Bob Koester. *Fast Fingers,* Dawkins' 1969 debut LP for Delmark—still his best album to date—was a taut, uncompromising piece of work that won the Grand Prix du Disque de Jazz from the Hot Club of France in 1971 as the year's top album. Andrew "Big Voice" Odom shared the singing and Otis Rush the second guitar duties on Dawkins' 1971 encore *All for Business.* But after his Delmark LP *Blisterstring,* Dawkins' subsequent recordings lacked intensity until 1992's oddly titled *Kant Sheck Dees Bluze* for Chicago's Earwig Records. Since then, Dawkins has waxed a pair of discs for Ichiban and continues to tour extensively. —*Bill Dahl*

● **Fast Fingers** / 1969 / Delmark ✦✦✦✦
Still his toughest and most satisfying album to date, and still criminally not available on CD. Dawkins burst onto the blues scene with this album

at the dawn of the '70s, his slashing, angular guitar lines and reserved vocal style beautifully captured throughout the set. —*Bill Dahl*

Tribute to Orange / Nov. 30, 1971-Nov. 2, 1974 / Black & Blue ✦✦✦

All for Business / 1973 / Delmark ✦✦✦
This time around (1971), Dawkins handed the majority of the vocal duties to Andrew "Big Voice" Odom and concentrated on his guitar (actually, he had some potent help in that department, too: Otis Rush was on second guitar). A generally solid but not overly enthralling set, with two bonus cuts and an alternate take of "Moon Man" added to the CD version. —*Bill Dahl*

Kant Sheck Dees Bluze / Jun. 1991 / Earwig ✦✦✦✦
Incredibly weird title (many of the songs sport equally bizarre spellings), but a major step back in the right direction for the guitarist, whose dirty, distorted tone won't thrill the purists. —*Bill Dahl*

B Phur Real / 1995 / Wild Dog/Ichiban ✦✦✦
Here we go again with the off-the-wall spellings ... more listenable modern work from the Chicago guitarist, who's found his groove again after quite a few years of less than enthralling releases. —*Bill Dahl*

Paul deLay

b. Jan. 31, 1952, Portland, OR
Harmonica / Modern Electric Blues
Paul deLay was born in Portland, OR, on January 31, 1952, but grew up in Milwaukie, OR—a suburb of Portland. He grew up listening to classical, big band jazz, Dixieland, barrelhouse piano, and barbershop quartets. He came to blues through rock and the various blues covers of British artists. When he discovered Chess records and the original blues recordings, he had found his vocation.

DeLay joined the band Brown Sugar in 1970, and the band played a combination of blues, soul, and R&B. They stayed together for about ten years working the local scene. In 1979, deLay formed his own four-piece Chicago-style blues band. This became the Paul deLay Band. DeLay took Paul Butterfield as his model early on but says of his playing, "I guess, more or less, what I've ended up sounding like is a combination between Big Walter, George Smith, Sonny Boy II, and Toots Thielemans. In 1990, deLay was arrested on cocaine-related charges and spent three years in federal prison. In the early '90s the band released two CDs, *The Other One* (1991) and *Paulzilla* (1992).

While deLay was serving time, his band teamed up with singer Linda Hornbuckle, calling themselves the "No Delay Band" and waited for Paul to return. Upon his release, they reformed as the "Paul deLay Band" and are releasing their first post-prison album, *Ocean of Tears*, in September 1996. The main (long-standing) members of the deLay band include Peter Dammann (lead guitar), Louis Pain (keyboards), and Dan Fincher(sax).

DeLay has an excellent voice—an apologist-style singer in the manner of Bobby Bland and Junior Parker. As a harp player, he is superb. Not just another White guy playing the records of other bluesmen, deLay is expert on both the standard Marine Band Hohner and the chromatic. He (along with William Clarke) has taken the blues chromatic to new heights. DeLay has received a number of awards, including a Handy Award nomination, and appeared at many blues and jazz festivals. —*Michael Erlewine*

Teasin' / 1982 / Criminal ✦✦
The deLay band's first recording gave birth to Criminal Records. —*Michael Erlewine*

American Voodoo / 1984 / Criminal ✦✦✦
The standout album from the early material, this second deLay album reached No. 2 on the Italian blues charts. Worth seeking out. —*Michael Erlewine*

The Blue One / 1985 / Criminal ✦✦
Six tunes with the earlier band, including "Something's Got a Hold on Me." —*Michael Erlewine*

Burnin' / 1988 / Criminal ✦✦✦✦
Reached No. 20 on the *Living Blues* chart. This album was the debut of guitarist Peter Dammann. Includes hornwork by ex-Mayall sax player Chris Mercer. —*Michael Erlewine*

The Other One / 1990 / Criminal ✦✦✦
All 11 songs written by deLay plus plenty of fine harp playing. With Peter Dammann on guitar and Louis Pain on keyboards. —*Michael Erlewine*

The Best of Paul deLay: You're Fired / 1990 / Red Lightnin' ✦✦✦✦
A collection of deLay material released by the British label Red Lightnin' in May of 1990. —*Michael Erlewine*

Paulzilla / 1992 / Criminal ✦✦✦✦
Declared the album of the year by the Cascades Blues Association, this was completed just days before deLay's three-year visit to the pen. DeLay wrote most of the songs and there is plenty of first-rate chromatic harp playing here. With Peter Dammann on guitar and Louis Pain on keyboards. —*Michael Erlewine*

● **Take It from the Turnaround** / 1996 / Evidence ✦✦✦✦
Combining the best of two albums (1991's *Just This One* and 1992's *Paulzilla*) on one CD, *Take It from the Turnaround* heralds the arrival of a harp player who's been a certified blues legend in his native region of Portland, OR. DeLay blows with authenticity and a full command of his instrument and way more than a hint of reckless abandon. Traditional blues, even by modern bar-band standards, this ain't, but the high creative level of deLay's songwriting on numbers like "Second Hand Smoke," "Merry Way" and the heartfelt "Just This One" heralds the arrival of a new way of looking at things and bodes well for future recordings. As a parenthetical note, the liner notes that accompany this release are superlative, telling deLay's story in a way that's both horrifying and inspiring. The man has lived a life in the blues and not only lived to tell the tale, but has triumphed over the worst elements of a road musician has to suffer through. —*Cub Koda*

Ocean of Tears / Sep. 1996 / Evidence ✦✦✦✦
This features deLay, after he was released from prison, with his original band doing ten tunes, all written by deLay, either by himself or as coauthor. Features the title cut "Ocean of Tears," "What Went Wrong" and a duet with Linda Hornbuckle, "Maybe Our Luck Will Change." —*Michael Erlewine*

Floyd Dixon

b. Feb. 8, 1929, Marshall, TX
Piano, Vocals / R&B, Electric West Coast Blues, Acoustic West Coast Blues, West Coast Blues
Floyd Dixon was an unabashed admirer of Charles Brown's mellow "club blues" sound, but he added a more energetic, aggressive jump blues edge to his sound during the early '50s—a formula that made the L.A.-based pianist an R&B star.

Like so many of his postwar California contemporaries a Texas emigre, Dixon hit the City of Angels at age 13. Influenced by Louis Jordan and Amos Milburn along with Brown, Dixon was swept up in the late '40s R&B boom, recording for Supreme in 1947 and signing with Modern Records in 1949. He nudged into the R&B Top Ten with "Dallas Blues" and just missed similar lofty stature with "Mississippi Blues" later in 1949. After cutting prolifically for Modern, he switched over to Eddie Mesner's Aladdin logo and hit in 1950 with "Sad Journey Blues" (also issued on Peacock), "Telephone Blues" the next year (backed by Johnny Moore's Three Blazers, the same crew that catapulted Charles Brown to stardom), and the mournful "Call Operator 210" in 1952.

But there was a playfully ribald side to Dixon, too. The double-entendre "Red Cherries," a storming "Wine, Wine, Wine," and the two-sided 1951 live waxing "Too Much Jelly Roll" (penned by a young Jerry Leiber and Mike Stoller) and "Baby, Let's Go Down to the Woods" showcased his more raucous leanings. The hits ceased, but Dixon's West Coast R&B odyssey continued with dates for Specialty in 1953, Atlantic's Cat subsidiary in 1954 (where he waxed the rollicking "Hey Bartender," likely his best-known tune thanks to covers by Koko Taylor and the execrable Blues Brothers), Ebb (where he challenged Little Richard's galvanic energy levels on the torrid "Oooh Little Girl" in 1957), and Checker.

The self-proclaimed "Mr. Magnificent" is still at it today. His career should enjoy an upcoming renaissance, thanks to an upcoming release on Alligator Records. —*Bill Dahl*

Opportunity Blues / 1976 / Route 66 ✦✦✦✦
Vinyl-only examination of the pianist's early sides for several West Coast R&B indies that spans 1948-1961. Dixon's ballad style was quite reminiscent of Charles Brown's but his jump blues leanings—here typified by "Wine, Wine, Wine" and "Real Lovin' Mama"—were all his own. —*Bill Dahl*

Houston Jump / 1979 / Route 66 ✦✦✦✦
Another cross-section of Dixon's 1947-1960 output that hasn't made the jump to the digital age as of yet. Surveys a wide array of labels, including a 1954 date for Atlantic's short-lived Cat subsidiary that produced "Roll Baby Roll" and "Is It True." —*Bill Dahl*

● **His Complete Aladdin Recordings** / 1996 / Capitol ✦✦✦✦
It's a matter of opinion as to whether Dixon's Aladdin output was his peak; many would give his Specialty sides (available on the *Marshall Texas Is My Home* compilation) the nod. Still, his late '40s and early '50s work for the label included some of his most popular and best tracks, such as "Wine, Wine, Wine," "Call Operator 210," "Tired, Broke and Busted," "Let's Dance," "Telephone Blues," and "Too Much Jelly Roll" (the last of which was one of Leiber-Stoller's first recorded compositions). This two-CD, 48-track compilation is geared more toward the completist collector than the average fan, especially with the inclusion of five Sonny Parker sides (which Dixon now says he didn't play on, despite some reports to the contrary) and about ten songs that feature Mari Jones on vocals. The best stuff is jump blues at its best, though, with good guitar work by Johnny and Oscar Moore (the latter of whom had played with Nat King Cole), Dixon's fine piano playing, and witty, knowing vocals and lyrics. —*Richie Unterberger*

Marshall Texas Is My Home / Specialty ✦✦✦✦
Dixon landed at Art Rupe's Specialty label in 1953, his music jumping harder than ever. These 22 tracks rate with his best; the collection is full of rarities and previously unissued items, many featuring the wailing tenor sax of Carlos Bermudez in lusty support of the pianist. By 1957, when he momentarily paused at Ebb Records, Dixon could do a pretty fair breathless imitation of Little Richard, as the scorching "Oooh Little Girl" definitively proves. Also includes Dixon's best-known number, the often-covered rocker "Hey Bartender" (first out on Atlantic's Cat subsidiary in 1954). —*Bill Dahl*

Willie Dixon

b. Jul. 1, 1915, Vicksburg, MS, **d.** Jan. 29, 1992, Burbank, CA
Bass, Guitar, Vocals / Electric Chicago Blues, Acoustic Chicago Blues
Willie Dixon's life and work were virtually an embodiment of the progress of the blues, from an accidental creation of the descendants of freed slaves to a recognized and vital part of America's musical heritage. That Dixon was one of the first professional blues songwriters to benefit from his work in a serious, material way—and that he had to fight to do it—also made him an important symbol of the injustice that still informs the music industry, even at the end of this century. A producer, songwriter, bassist, and singer, he helped Muddy Waters, Howlin' Wolf, Little Walter, and others find their most commercially successful voices.

By the time he was a teenager, Dixon was writing songs and selling copies to local bands. He also studied music with a local carpenter, Theo Phelps, who taught him about harmony singing. Dixon, a bass, later joined a group organized by Phelps, the Union Jubilee Singers. Dixon eventually made his way to Chicago, where he won the Illinois State Golden Gloves Heavyweight Championship. He might've been a successful boxer, but he turned to music instead, thanks to Leonard "Baby Doo" Caston, a guitarist who had seen Dixon at the gym where he worked out. The two formed a duo, performing on street corners, and later Dixon took up the bass as an instrument. They later formed a group, the Five Breezes, who recorded for the Bluebird label. The group's success was halted, however, when Dixon refused induction into the armed forces as a conscientious objector and was put in jail. He was freed after a year, and formed another group, the Four Jumps of Jive. In 1945, however, Dixon was back working with Caston in a group called the Big Three Trio, with guitarist Bernardo Dennis (later replaced by Ollie Crawford).

During this period Dixon would occasionally appear as a bassist at late-night jam sessions featuring members of the growing blues community, including Muddy Waters. Later on when the Chess brothers—who owned a club where Dixon occasionally played—began a new record label, Aristocrat (later Chess), they hired him, initially as a bassist on a 1948 session for Robert Nighthawk. The Chess brothers liked Dixon's playing and his skills as a songwriter and arranger, and during the next two years he worked regularly for the Chess brothers. He got to record some of his own material, but Dixon was seldom featured as an artist at these sessions.

Dixon's real recognition as a songwriter began with Muddy Waters' recording of "Hoochie Coochie Man." The success of that single, "Evil" by Howlin' Wolf, and "My Babe" by Little Walter saw Dixon established as Chess' most reliable tunesmith, and the Chess brothers continually pushed Dixon's songs on their artists. In addition to writing songs, Dixon continued as bassist and recording manager of many of the Chess label's recording sessions, including those by Lowell Fulson, Bo Diddley, and Otis Rush. Dixon's remuneration for all of this work, including the songwriting, was minimal—he was barely able to support his rapidly growing family on the $100 a week that the Chess brothers were giving him, and a short stint with the rival Cobra label at the end of the '50s didn't help him much.

During the mid-'60s, Chess gradually phased out Dixon's bass work, in favor of electric bass, thus reducing his presence at many of the sessions. At the same time, a European concert promoter named Horst Lippmann had begun a series of shows called the American Folk-Blues Festival, for which he would bring some of the top blues players in America over to tour the continent. Dixon ended up organizing the musical side of these shows for the first decade or more, recording on his own as well as earning a good deal more money than he was seeing from his work for Chess. At the same time, he began to see a growing interest in his songwriting from the British rock bands that he saw while in London—his music was getting covered regularly by artists like the Rolling Stones and the Yardbirds, and when he visited England, he even found himself cajoled into presenting his newest songs to their managements. Back at Chess, Howlin' Wolf and Muddy Waters continued to perform Dixon's songs, as did newer artists such as Koko Taylor, who had her own hit with "Wang Dang Doodle." Gradually, however, after the mid-'60s, Dixon saw his relationship with Chess Records come to a halt.

By the end of the 1960s, Dixon was eager to try his hand as a performer again, a career that had been interrupted when he'd gone to

work for Chess as a producer. He recorded an album of his best-known songs, *I Am the Blues*, and organized a touring band, the Chicago Blues All-Stars, to play concerts in Europe. Suddenly, in his 50s, he began making a major name for himself on stage for the first time in his career. Around this time, Dixon began to have grave doubts about the nature of the songwriting contract that he had with Chess' publishing arm, Arc Music. He was seeing precious little money from songwriting, despite the recording of hit versions of such Dixon songs as "Spoonful" by Cream. He had never seen as much money as he was entitled to as a songwriter, but during the 1970s he began to understand just how much money he'd been deprived of.

Arc Music had sued Led Zeppelin for copyright infringement over "Bring It on Home" on *Led Zeppelin II*, saying that it was Dixon's song, and won a settlement that Dixon never saw any part of until his manager did an audit of Arc's accounts. Dixon and Muddy Waters would later file suit against Arc Music to recover royalties and the ownership of their copyrights. Additionally, many years later Dixon brought suit against Led Zeppelin for copyright infringement over "Whole Lotta Love" and its resemblance to Dixon's "You Need Love." Both cases resulted in out-of-court settlements that were generous to the songwriter.

The 1980s saw Dixon as the last survivor of the Chess blues stable, and he began working with various organizations to help secure song copyrights on behalf of blues songwriters who, like himself, had been deprived of revenue during previous decades. In 1988, Dixon became the first producer/songwriter to be honored with a box-set collection, when MCA Records released *Willie Dixon: The Chess Box*, which included several rare Dixon sides as well as the most famous recordings of his songs by Chess' stars. The next year Dixon published *I Am the Blues* (Da Capo Press), his autobiography, written in association with Don Snowden.

Dixon continued performing and was called in as a producer on movie soundtracks such as *Gingerale Afternoon* and *La Bamba*, producing the work of his old stablemate Bo Diddley. By that time, Dixon was regarded as something of an elder statesman, composer, and spokesperson of American blues. Dixon suffered from increasingly poor health and lost a leg to diabetes. He died peacefully in his sleep early in 1992. —*Bruce Eder*

Willie's Blues / 1959 / Bluesville ✦✦✦
I Am the Blues / 1970 / Mobile Fidelity ✦✦✦
★ **The Chess Box** / 1989 / MCA/Chess ✦✦✦✦✦
There are a few holes in this collection, but not many. As it is, the material is virtually a best-of-Chess collection, featuring some of the best tracks in the respective outputs of Muddy Waters, Howlin' Wolf, Little Walter, Sonny Boy Williamson, Bo Diddley, Lowell Fulson, Koko Taylor et al. —*Bruce Eder*

The Original Wang Dang Doodle / 1995 / MCA/Chess ✦✦✦✦
This is a good collection of hard-to-find and previously unreleased Dixon sides, although there are several Chess tracks that were left off that would have made it much more valuable. The title track is especially worthwhile, as is "Tail Dragger," but it is also easy to see from this collection why Dixon was never quite a star in his own right as a performer—he has a good voice, but not a very memorable or powerful one, compared with Muddy Waters, Howlin' Wolf et al. —*Bruce Eder*

Chris Duarte

Guitar, Vocals / Modern Electric Blues
Austin-based guitarist, songwriter and singer Chris Duarte is such a promising young upstart in the world of modern blues that he's already being compared with the late Stevie Ray Vaughan. It's heady stuff for the 32-year-old musician, who plays a rhythmic style of Texas blues-rock that is at times reminiscent of Vaughan's sound, and at other times reminiscent of Johnny Winter. The truth is, Duarte has his own sound that draws on elements of jazz, blues and rock 'n' roll. Although he is humbled by the comparisons with the late Vaughan, the San Antonio-raised musician began playing out in clubs there when he was 15 years old.

After Duarte moved to Austin when he was 16, he began taking his guitar playing much more seriously, and at that time, Vaughan was still around playing in Austin-area clubs. Duarte was one of those lucky few thousand who got to see Vaughan at the Continental Club before the late guitarist got his first break with David Bowie. After a short stint in an Austin jazz band, Duarte joined Bobby Mack and Night Train, and began getting heavily into blues at that point. He traveled all over Texas with that band before a big break came his way in 1994, when New York-based Silvertone Records released his critically praised debut album, *Texas Sugar/Strat Magik*. —*Richard Skelly*

● **Texas Sugar Strat Magic** / 1994 / Silvertone ✦✦✦✦
Guitarist Chris Duarte's *Texas Sugar Strat Magik* is an impressive debut album, showcasing his fiery, Stevie Ray Vaughan-derived blues-rock. As

a songwriter, Duarte is still developing—he fails to come up with any memorable songs, although he does contribute several competent, unexceptional genre pieces—but as an instrumentalist, he's first-rate, spitting out solos with a blistering intensity or laying back with gentle, lyrical phrases. And that's what makes *Texas Sugar Strat Magik* a successful record—it's simply a great album, full of exceptional playing. —*Stephen Thomas Erlewine*

Champion Jack Dupree

b. Jul. 4, 1910, New Orleans, LA, **d.** Jan. 21, 1992, Hanover, Germany
Guitar, Piano, Drums, Vocals / Piano Blues
A formidable contender in the ring before he shifted his focus to pounding the piano, Champion Jack Dupree often injected his lyrics with a rowdy sense of down-home humor. But there was nothing lighthearted about his rock-solid way with a boogie; when he shouted "Shake Baby Shake," the entire room had no choice but to acquiesce.

Dupree was notoriously vague about his beginnings, claiming in some interviews that his parents died in a fire set by the Ku Klux Klan, at other times saying that the blaze was accidental. Whatever the circumstances of the conflagration, Dupree grew up in New Orleans' Colored Waifs' Home for Boys (Louis Armstrong also spent his formative years there). Learning his trade from barrelhouse 88s ace Willie "Drive 'em Down" Hall, Dupree left the Crescent City in 1930 for Chicago and then Detroit. By 1935 he was boxing professionally in Indianapolis, battling in an estimated 107 bouts.

In 1940 Dupree made his recording debut for Chicago A&R man extraordinaire Lester Melrose and Okeh Records. Dupree's 1940-41 output for the Columbia subsidiary exhibited a strong New Orleans tinge despite the Chicago surroundings; his driving "Junker's Blues" was later cleaned up as Fats Domino's 1949 debut, "The Fat Man." After a stretch in the Navy during World War II (he was a Japanese POW for two years), Dupree decided tickling the 88s beat pugilism any old day. He spent most of his time in New York and quickly became a prolific recording artist, cutting for Continental, Joe Davis, Alert, Apollo, and Red Robin (where he cut a blasting "Shim Sham Shimmy" in 1953), often in the company of Brownie McGhee. Contracts meant little—Dupree masqueraded as Brother Blues on Abbey, Lightnin' Jr. on Empire, and the truly imaginative Meat Head Johnson for Gotham and Apex.

King Records corralled Dupree in 1953 and held onto him through 1955 (the year he enjoyed his only R&B chart hit, the relaxed "Walking the Blues"). Dupree's King output rates with his very best—the romping "Mail Order Woman," "Let the Doorbell Ring," and "Big Leg Emma's" contrasting with the rural "Me and My Mule" (Dupree's vocal on the latter emphasizing a harelip speech impediment for politically incorrect pseudo-comic effect).

After a year on RCA's Groove and Vik subsidiaries, Dupree made a masterpiece LP for Atlantic. *Blues from the Gutter* is a magnificent testament to Dupree's barrelhouse background, boasting marvelous readings of "Stack-O-Lee," "Junker's Blues," and "Frankie and Johnny" beside the risque "Nasty Boogie."

Dupree was one of the first bluesmen to leave his native country for a less racially polarized European existence in 1959. He lived in a variety of countries, continuing to record prolifically for Storyville, British Decca (with John Mayall and Eric Clapton lending a hand at a 1966 date), and many other firms.

Perhaps sensing his own mortality, Dupree returned to New Orleans in 1990 for his first visit in 36 years. While there, he played the Jazz & Heritage Festival and laid down a zesty album for Bullseye Blues, *Back Home in New Orleans*. Two more albums of new material were captured by the company the next year, before the pianist's death in January 1992. —*Bill Dahl*

★ **Blues from the Gutter** / 1958 / Atlantic ◆◆◆◆◆
The 1958 masterwork album of Dupree's long and prolific career. Cut in New York (in stereo!) with a blasting band that included saxist Pete Brown and guitarist Larry Dale, the Jerry Wexler-produced Atlantic collection provides eloquent testimony to Dupree's eternal place in the New Orleans blues and barrelhouse firmament. There's some decidedly down-in-the-alley subject matter—"Can't Kick t'Habit," "T.B. Blues," a revival of "Junker's Blues"—along with the stomping "Nasty Boogie" and treatments of the ancient themes "Stack-O-Lee" and "Frankie and Johnny." —*Bill Dahl*

Sings the Blues / 1961 / King ◆◆◆◆
A domestic no-frills collection of Champion Jack Dupree's aforementioned King label material, albeit containing fewer tracks and little in the way of annotation—but you can't argue with the wonderful music therein! —*Bill Dahl*

Blues for Everybody / 1990 / Charly ◆◆◆◆
Although Dupree seldom paused at any one label for very long, the piano pounder did hang around at Cincinnati-based King Records from 1951 to 1955—long enough to wax the 20 sides comprising this set and a few more that regrettably aren't aboard. By this time, Dupree was a sea-

soned R&B artist, storming through "Let the Doorbell Ring" and "Mail Order Woman" and emphasizing his speech impediment on "Harelip Blues" (one of those not-for-the-politically- correct numbers). Most of these tracks were done in New York; sidemen include guitarist Mickey Baker and saxist Willis Jackson. —*Bill Dahl*

Back Home in New Orleans / 1990 / Bullseye Blues ◆◆◆◆
By far the best of Dupree's three albums for Bullseye Blues, this collection was cut during the pianist's first trip home to the Crescent City in 36 long years. With his longtime accompanist Kenn Lending on guitar, Dupree sounds happy to be back in his old stomping grounds throughout the atmospheric set. —*Bill Dahl*

New Orleans Barrelhouse Boogie (The Complete Champion Jack Dupree) / 1993 / Columbia/Legacy ◆◆◆◆
The New Orleans barrelhouse boogie piano specialist's earliest sides for Okeh, dating from 1940-1941 and in a few cases sporting some fairly groundbreaking electric guitar runs by Jesse Ellery. Dupree rocks the house like it's a decade later on two takes of "Cabbage Greens" and "Dupree Shake Dance," while his drug-oriented "Junker Blues" was later cleaned up a bit by a chubby newcomer named Fats Domino for his debut hit 78 "The Fat Man." —*Bill Dahl*

Snooks Eaglin

b. Jan. 21, 1936, New Orleans, LA
Guitar, Vocals / Acoustic New Orleans Blues, Electric New Orleans Blues, Electric New Orleans
When they refer to consistently amazing guitarist Snooks Eaglin as a human jukebox in his New Orleans hometown, they're not dissing him in the slightest. The blind Eaglin is a beloved figure in the Crescent City, not only for his gritty, Ray Charles-inspired vocal delivery and wholly imaginative approach to the guitar, but for the seemingly infinite storehouse of oldies that he's liable to pull out on stage at any second (often confounding his bemused band in the process!).

Born Ford Eaglin, Jr., and blind since very early childhood due to glaucoma and a brain tumor, the lad (named after radio character Baby Snooks, who shared his mischievous ways) picked up the guitar at age six and commenced to mastering every style imaginable. Gospel, blues, jazz—young Snooks Eaglin could play it all. He spent time with a Crescent City band, the Flamingoes, whose members also included pianist Allen Toussaint, played around town as Little Ray Charles, and recorded for Chess as accompanist to Sugar Boy Crawford before going it alone on the streets of the French Quarter.

His earliest recordings in 1958 for Folkways presented Eaglin as a solo acoustic folk-blues artist with an extremely eclectic repertoire. His dazzling finger-picking was nothing short of astonishing, but Eaglin really wanted to be making R&B with a band. Imperial Records producer Dave Bartholomew granted him the opportunity in 1960, and the results were sensational. Eaglin's fluid, twisting lead guitar on the utterly infectious "Yours Truly" (a Bartholomew composition first waxed by Pee Wee Crayton) and its sequel "Cover Girl" was unique on the New Orleans R&B front, while his brokenhearted cries on "Don't Slam That Door" and "That Certain Door" were positively mesmerizing. Eaglin stuck with Imperial through 1963, when the firm closed up shop in New Orleans, without ever gaining national exposure.

There followed a dry period for the guitarist, but he came back first as accompanist to Professor Longhair (who was in the midst of a rather remarkable comeback bid himself) and then on his own. Eaglin has reasserted his brilliance in recent years with a series of magnificent albums for hometown Black Top Records (notably his last two, *Teasin' You* and *Soul's Edge*). —*Bill Dahl*

Country Boy Down in New Orleans / 1958 / Arhoolie ◆◆◆◆
Country Boy Down in New Orleans collects 23 tracks Snooks Eaglin recorded in the '50s. During this time, he was a street musician, playing with just one guitar or as a one-man band. On these tracks, he is accompanied by a couple of washboard players and a harpist. As expected, the sound is stripped-down, but it is exciting. Eaglin's early repertoire included a broad variety of blues, folk, and gospel songs and all of these genres are covered thoroughly on this delightful single disc. It may not be the ripping electric blues of his best-known records, but it is just as enjoyable. —*Thom Owens*

That's All Right / 1961 / Prestige ◆◆◆
Recorded during the time in which Eaglin was doubling as a blues/folk singer and a commercial R&B artist (for Imperial). He addresses the acoustic folk and blues side of his repertoire, performing everything solo on six and 12-string guitars. Time will probably judge these not to be as interesting as his full-band New Orleans R&B recordings. But this is warm, good-natured acoustic blues, with interpretations of traditional tunes, early blues by Robert Johnson, and then-recent R&B hits by Ray Charles, Arthur Crudup, and Amos Milburn. —*Richie Unterberger*

Baby, You Can Get Your Gun / 1987 / Black Top ◆◆◆◆
The first of the masterful guitarist's amazing series of albums for Black

Top is an earthly delight; his unpredictable guitar weaves and darts through supple rhythms provided by New Orleans vets Smokey Johnson on drums and Erving Charles, Jr. on bass (David Lastie is on sax). Few artists boast Eaglin's "human jukebox" capabilities; his vast knowledge of eclectic numbers takes in the Four Blazes' "Mary Jo," Tommy Ridgley's "Lavinia," and the Ventures' version of "Perfidia." *—Bill Dahl*

☆ **Teasin' You** / 1992 / Black Top ✦✦✦✦✦
The best of Eaglin's terrific series of Black Top efforts so far—song selection is absolutely unassailable (lots of savage New Orleans covers, from Lloyd Price and Professor Longhair to Willie Tee and Earl King), the band simmers and sizzles with spicy second-line fire (bassist George Porter, Jr. and drummer Herman Ernest III are a formidable pair indeed), and Eaglin's churchy, commanding vocals and blistering guitar work are nothing short of mind-boggling throughout the entire disc. *—Bill Dahl*

Soul's Edge / 1995 / Black Top ✦✦✦✦
Give this New Orleans master enough studio time, and he'll redo the history of post-war R&B his own way. Here he lays his mind to Joe Simon's powerhouse soul ballad "Nine Pound Steel," the Midnighters' "Let's Go, Let's Go, Let's Go," even Bill Haley & the Comets' "Skinny Minnie" and the Five Keys' loopy "Ling Ting Tong," giving each the singular treatment that he's always brought to his recordings. Porter and Ernest return to lay down their immaculate grooves, and Fred Kemp blows sturdy sax on Eaglin's parade-beat "I Went to the Mardi Gras." *—Bill Dahl*

● **Complete Imperial Recordings** / Oct. 24, 1995 / Capitol ✦✦✦✦
These days, Eaglin is apt to be classified as a blues singer with considerable New Orleans R&B influences. This collection of his early-'60s recordings for the Imperial label would be much more appropriately categorized as exactly the opposite. Produced by Dave Bartholomew (who also wrote over half of the material), the thrust of these recordings is most definitely in the classic-'50s/early-'60s New Orleans R&B mold, though Eaglin's vocal delivery may be bluesier than some other practitioners of the sound. It doesn't suffer for this in the least; it's solid stuff betraying the influence of Guitar Slim and Ray Charles (though Eaglin's style is sometimes compared to the latter, it isn't extremely similar, with sparer arrangements and a distinct Creole vocal slur). This compiles 26 tracks (seven previously unreleased) that he cut between 1960 and 1963, none of which were hits, perhaps because the commercial peak of classic New Orleans R&B had already passed. But it's well worth looking into if you like records from the same period by the likes of Bartholomew, Lee Dorsey, and the early Nevilles. *—Richie Unterberger*

Ronnie Earl & The Broadcasters

b. Mar. 10, 1953, New York City, NY
Guitar / R&B, Modern Electric Blues
Guitarist Ronnie Earl (born Ronald Horvath) was born March 10, 1953, in New York City, but later moved to Boston. In 1975, while attending a Muddy Waters concert, he was so moved by what he heard that he decided to learn the guitar and dedicate himself to mastering the blues tradition. He was soon playing in clubs in and around the Boston area as well as backing various blues artists on tour. He claims that his main influences were T-Bone Walker, B.B. King, Magic Sam, and Robert Jr. Lockwood. In 1980 he replaced Duke Robillard in Roomful of Blues and worked with that band for eight years, helping to take the band to national acclaim.

In the 1980s he recorded three solo albums with his band, the Broadcasters, that were very well received: *Smokin'* (Black Top, 1987), *They Call Me Mr. Earl* (Black Top, 1984), and *I Like It When It Rains* (Antone's, 1990). Earl left Roomful of Blues in 1988 and continues to perform and record. His intense guitar style, somewhat in the style of T-Bone Walker, has made him one of the most respected young players in the business—much in demand as a backup musician for recording dates. *—Michael Erlewine*

Surrounded by Love / May 1991 / Black Top ✦✦✦
Ronnie Earl recorded *Surrounded by Love* with a new version of the Broadcasters. The most notable factor of the new lineup is the reappearance of Sugar Ray Norcia, the finest vocalist/harpist Earl ever recorded with. The band sounds tight and energetic, especially on the three tracks they cut with Robert Jr. Lockwood. Parts of the album are a little slow, but the album is very entertaining, even with its minor flaws. *—Thom Owens*

● **Test of Time** / Black Top ✦✦✦✦
Test of Time collects the highlights from Ronnie Earl's six Black Top albums. The 18-song compilation showcases one of the finest blues guitarists of the '80s, picking nearly all of his best material, which happens to include duets with Robert Jr. Lockwood and Hubert Sumlin. The album is an excellent introduction to Earl, as well as his most consistently entertaining release. *—Thom Owens*

Tinsley Ellis and The Heartfixers

Guitar, Vocals / Modern Electric Blues
A fiery guitarist and talented songwriter, Tinsley Ellis plays a unique

blend of Memphis R&B, Southwest blues, and urban funk. Born in Atlanta, GA, Ellis was raised in South Florida and got his first guitar around age seven. Primary influences for Ellis include Elmore James, B.B. King, Freddie King, and Gatemouth Brown. While attending Emory University in Atlanta, Ellis worked in a few local bands, including the Alley Cats along with Preston Hubbard, who became a bassist for the Fabulous Thunderbirds. In the early '80s, Ellis and harpman Bob Nelson founded the Heartfixers, a rather eclectic club band that played blues, rockabilly, R&B, and early rock. They became popular on the Southeast club circuit and by 1986 had recorded four albums. Early on, Ellis was compared to Johnny Winter and Stevie Ray Vaughan, but though he had a healthy following in his region, his name was largely unknown to the mainstream. He left the Heartfixers in 1987 and began recording as a solo artist. Though recorded for Landslide, his debut, *Georgia Blue,* was distributed by Alligator Records the following year to good response. Subsequent albums, all for Alligator, include *Trouble Time* (1992) and *Storm Warning* (1994). A tireless live performer, Tinsley and his eponymous band tour constantly and log over 200 performances per year. *—Sandra Brennan*

Cool on It / Jan. 91, 1986 / Alligator ✦✦✦✦
High-energy roadhouse-rock and blues-rock with the Heartfixers. *—Niles J. Frantz*

● **Fanning of the Flames** / 1989 / Alligator ✦✦✦✦
Fanning of the Flames is an erratic but impressive set from Tinsley Ellis. While his basic sound is indebted to Stevie Ray Vaughan, the guitarist borrows from every other major blues artist. Furthermore, he has a tendency to overplay his licks, giving the album a feeling of unfocused fury. However, that sound can be overwhelming—his technique is impressive, even if he doesn't know when to rein it in. As a consequence, *Fanning of the Flames* is of interest only to guitar fans, not general listeners, but for guitar fans, there's plenty of music to treasure here. *—Thom Owens*

Sleepy John Estes (John Adams Estes)

b. Jan. 25, 1899, Ripley, TN, **d.** Jun. 5, 1977, Brownville, TN
Guitar, Vocals / Acoustic Country Blues
Big Bill Broonzy called John Estes' style of singing "crying" the blues because of its overt emotional quality. Actually his vocal style harks back to his tenure as a work-gang leader for a railroad maintenance crew, where his vocal improvisations and keen, cutting voice set the pace for work activities. Nicknamed "Sleepy" John Estes, supposedly because of his ability to sleep standing up, he teamed with mandolinist Yank Rachell and harmonica player Hammie Nixon to play the houseparty circuit in and around Brownsville in the early '20s. Forty years later, the same team reunited to record for Delmark and play the festival circuit. Never an outstanding guitarist, Estes relied on his expressive voice to carry his music, and the recordings he made from 1929 on have enormous appeal and remain remarkably accessible today.

Despite the fact that he played to mixed Black and White audiences in string band, jug band, or medicine show format, his music retains a distinct ethnicity and has a particularly plaintive sound. Astonishingly, he recorded during six decades for Victor, Decca, Bluebird, Ora Nelle, Sun, Delmark, and others. Over the course of his career, his music remained simple yet powerful, and despite his sojourns to Memphis or Chicago he retained a traditional down-home sound. Some of his songs are deeply personal statements about his community and life, such as "Lawyer Clark" or "Floating Bridge." Other compositions have universal appeal ("Drop Down Mama" or "Someday Baby") and went on to become mainstays in the repertoires of countless musicians. One of the true masters of his idiom, he lived in poverty, yet was somehow capable of turning his experiences and the conditions of his life into compelling art. *—Barry Lee Pearson*

The Legend of Sleepy John Estes / 1962 / Delmark ✦✦✦✦
The best of his Delmark rediscovery recordings. *—Barry Lee Pearson*

★ **Sleepy John Estes 1929-1940: I Ain't Gonna Be Worried No More** / 1992 / Yazoo ✦✦✦✦✦
I Ain't Gonna Be Worried No More compiles 23 songs Sleepy John Estes recorded between 1929 and 1941, capturing the bluesman at the height of his creative powers. Unlike many Delta bluesmen of his era, Estes worked with a full jug band, which gave his music a greater variety of textures. His music swings, with a loose, relaxed feel that isn't heard on many Delta blues records. Furthermore, his songs are inventive, featuring pseudo-autobiographical lyrics loaded with evocative imagery. Nearly all of his best material is included on *I Ain't Gonna Be Worried No More*, making it as close to a definitive retrospective of Estes' music as possible. *—Thom Owens*

Frank Frost (Frank Otis Frost)

b. Apr. 15, 1936, Augusta, AR
Organ, Guitar, Harmonica, Piano, Vocals / R&B, Electric Delta Blues
The atmospheric juke joint blues of Frank Frost remain steeped in

unadulterated Delta funk. But his ongoing musical journey has taken him well outside his Mississippi homebase. He moved to St. Louis in 1951, learning how to blow harp first from Little Willie Foster and then from the legendary Sonny Boy Williamson, who took him on the road—as a guitar player—from 1956 to 1959. Drummer Sam Carr, a longtime Frost ally, was also part of the equation, having enticed Frost to front his combo in 1954 before hooking up with Sonny Boy.

Leaving Williamson's employ in 1959, Frost and Carr settled in Lula, MS. Guitarist Jack Johnson came aboard in 1962 after sitting in with the pair at the Savoy Theatre in Clarksdale. The three meshed perfectly—enough to interest Memphis producer Sam Phillips in a short-lived back-to-the-blues campaign that same year. *Hey Boss Man!*, issued on Sun's Phillips International subsidiary as by Frank Frost and the Nighthawks, was a wonderful collection of uncompromising Southern blues (albeit totally out of step with the marketplace at the time).

Elvis Presley's ex-guitarist Scotty Moore produced Frost's next sessions in Nashville in 1966 for Jewel Records. Augmented by session bassist Chip Young, the trio's tight down-home ensemble work was once again seamless. "My Back Scratcher," Frost's takeoff on Slim Harpo's "Baby Scratch My Back," even dented the R&B charts on Shreveport-based Jewel for three weeks.

Chicago blues fan Michael Frank sought out Frost in 1975. He located Frost, Johnson, and Carr playing inside Johnson's Clarksdale tavern, the Black Fox. Mesmerized by their sound, Frost soon formed his own record label, Earwig, to capture their raw, charismatic brand of blues. 1979's *Rockin' the Juke Joint Down*, billed as by the Jelly Roll Kings (after one of the standout songs on that old Phillips International LP), showcased the trio's multi-faceted approach—echoes of R&B, soul, even Johnny & the Hurricanes permeate their Delta-based attack.

In the years since, Frost has waxed his own Earwig album (1988's *Midnight Prowler*) and appeared on Atlantic's 1992 *Deep Blues* soundtrack—an acclaimed film that reinforced the fact that blues still thrives deep in its birthplace. —*Bill Dahl*

● **Hey Boss Man** / 196_ / Phillips ✦✦✦✦
One of the last great blues recordings produced by the legendary Sam Phillips. Frost and his Mississippi cohorts Jack Johnson and Sam Carr played Southern juke joint blues rough and ready in the classic mold, with plenty of dynamic interplay and nasty, lowdown grooves. —*Bill Dahl*

Ride with Your Daddy Tonight / 1985 / Charly ✦✦✦✦
Frost's best sides for the Jewel label. Some of the most down-home '60s blues ever recorded. —*Cub Koda*

Jelly Roll Blues / 1991 / Paula ✦✦✦✦
Same band, different producer: this time it was Elvis Presley's legendary guitarist, Scotty Moore, behind the glass as Frost and his pals dished out the lowdown sounds during the mid-'60s for Stan Lewis' Jewel logo. "My Back Scratcher" owes a stylistic debt to Slim Harpo but feels mighty good all the same. The entire 13-song disc reeks of steamy juke-joint ambience. —*Bill Dahl*

Rockin' the Juke Joint Down (as Jelly Roll Kings) / 1993 / Earwig ✦✦✦✦
Michael Frank inaugurated his Earwig imprint with this 1979 album reteaming Frost, Johnson, and Carr in all their glory. Frank was mesmerized by the trio's almost telepathic musical interplay, a trait captured vividly by the album itself. This trio's repertoire was varied—the no-holds-barred "Slop Jar Blues" is offset by the bubbly instrumental "Sunshine Twist." Frost and Johnson share vocal duties. —*Bill Dahl*

Blind Boy Fuller

b. 1908, Wadesboro, NC, **d.** Feb. 13, 1941, Durham, NC
Guitar, Vocals / Acoustic Country Blues, Piedmont Blues
Unlike blues artists like Big Bill or Memphis Minnie, who recorded extensively over three or four decades, Blind Boy Fuller recorded his substantial body of work over a short, six-year span. Nevertheless, he was one of the most recorded artists of his time and by far the most popular and influential Piedmont blues player of all time. Fuller could play in multiple styles: slide, ragtime, pop, and blues were all enhanced by his National steel guitar. Fuller worked with some fine sidemen, including Davis, Sonny Terry, and washboard player Bull City Red. Initially discovered and promoted by Carolina entrepreneur H.B. Long, Fuller recorded for ARC and Decca. He also served as a conduit to recording sessions, steering fellow blues musicians to the studio.

In spite of Fuller's recorded output, most of his musical life was spent as a street musician and house party favorite, and he possessed the skills to reinterpret and cover the hits of other artists as well. In this sense, he was a synthesizer of styles, parallel in many ways to Robert Johnson, his contemporary who died three years earlier. Like Johnson, Fuller lived fast and died young in 1942, only 33 years old. Fuller was a fine, expressive vocalist and a masterful guitar player best remembered for his uptempo ragtime hits "Rag Mama Rag," "Trucking My Blues Away," and "Step It Up and Go." At the same time he was capable of

deeper material, and his versions of "Lost Lover Blues" or "Mamie" are as deep as most Delta blues. Because of his popularity, he may have been overexposed on records, yet most of his songs remained close to tradition and much of his repertoire and style is kept alive by North Carolina and Virginia artists today. —*Barry Lee Pearson*

★ **Truckin' My Blues Away** / 1978 / Yazoo ✦✦✦✦✦
Piedmont blues at its best, with fine guitar work from this popular and influential bluesman. —*Barry Lee Pearson*

East Coast Piedmont Style / Aug. 1991 / Columbia/Legacy ✦✦✦✦
A very good 20-cut roots and blues collection with Sonny Terry, Gary Davis, and Bull City Red. —*Barry Lee Pearson*

Jesse Fuller

b. Mar. 12, 1896, Jonesboro, GA, **d.** Jan. 29, 1976, Oakland, CA
Guitar, Harmonica, Kazoo, Vocals / Acoustic Country Blues, Acoustic West Coast Blues
Equipped with a bandful of instruments operated by various parts of his anatomy, Bay Area-legend Jesse Fuller was a folk-music favorite in the '50s and '60s. His infectious rhythm and gentle charm graced old folk tunes, spirituals, and blues alike. One of his inventions was a home-made, foot-operated instrument called the "footdella" or "fotdella." Naturally, Fuller never needed other accompanists to back his one-man show. His best-known songs include "San Francisco Bay Blues" and "Beat It on Down the Line" (the first one covered by Janis Joplin, the second by The Grateful Dead).

Born and raised in Georgia, Jesse Fuller began playing guitar when he was a child, although he didn't pursue the instrument seriously. In his early '20s, Fuller wandered around the southern and western regions of the United States, eventually settling down in Los Angeles. While he was in Southern California, he worked as a film extra, appearing in *The Thief of Bagdad, East of Suez, Hearts in Dixie*, and *End of the World*. After spending a few years in Los Angeles, Fuller moved to San Francisco. While he worked various odd jobs around the Bay Area, he played on street corners and at parties.

Jesse's musical career didn't properly begin until the early '50s, when he decided to become a professional musician—he was 55 years old at the time. Performing as a one man band, he began to get spots on local television shows and nightclubs. However, Fuller's career didn't take off until 1954, when he wrote "San Francisco Bay Blues." The song helped him land a record contract with the independent Cavalier label, and in 1955 he recorded his first album, *Folk Blues: Working on the Railroad with Jesse Fuller*. The album was a success and soon he was making records for a variety of labels, including Good Time Jazz and Prestige.

In the late '50s and early '60s, Jesse Fuller became one of the key figures of the blues revival, helping bring the music to a new, younger audience. Throughout the '60s and '70s, he toured America and Europe, appearing at numerous blues and folk festivals, as well as countless coffeehouse gigs across the US. Fuller continued performing and recording until his death in 1976. —*Jim O'Neal and Stephen Thomas Erlewine*

Jazz, Folk Songs, Spirituals and Blues / Apr. 1958 / Good Time Jazz ✦✦✦✦
Jesse Fuller was among the greatest one-man bands in blues history. The title of this 1958 date adequately described the session's musical width and depth; Fuller handled everything from old spirituals such as "I'm Going to Meet My Loving Mother" to the rollicking "Memphis Boogie" and "Fingerbuster" and the concluding "Hesitation Blues." As sole performer, melodic, rhythmic and performing focus, Fuller's energy never wanes through the CD's 11 numbers. He nicely conveys the varying moods, themes and sentiments, knowing which lyrics to emphasize, when to intensify the pace and when to lower his voice and let the music make the point. —*Ron Wynn*

Favorites / 1965 / Prestige ✦✦✦
Jesse Fuller's *Favorites* is a highly enjoyable collection of the singer's favorite blues standards. Performing everything as a solo piece, he runs through classics like "Key to the Highway," "The Midnight Special," and "Brownskin Gal" with humor and warmth. It's a small, but entertaining gem. —*Thom Owens*

Frisco Bound / 1968 / Arhoolie ✦✦✦✦
A one-man band with guitar, harmonica, kazoo, and "footdella" bass, these are some of his first recordings, ca. 1955. Innocent echoes of turn-of-the-century rural America. —*Mark A. Humphrey*

● **San Francisco Bay Blues** / 1988 / Good Time Jazz ✦✦✦✦
Fuller's hit and more includes no misses. —*Mark A. Humphrey*

Lowell Fulson

b. Mar. 31, 1921, Tulsa, OK
Guitar, Vocals / R&B, Electric West Coast Blues, Acoustic West Coast Blues, West Coast Blues
Lowell Fulson has recorded every shade of blues imaginable. Polished urban blues, rustic two-guitar duets with his younger brother Martin,

funk-tinged grooves that pierced the mid-'60s charts, even an unwise cover of the Beatles' "Why Don't We Do It in the Road!" Clearly, the veteran guitarist, who's been at it now for more than half a century, isn't afraid to experiment. Perhaps that's why his last couple of discs for Rounder are so vital and satisfying—and why he's been an innovator for so long.

Exposed to the western swing of Bob Wills as well as indigenous blues while growing up in Oklahoma, Fulson joined up with singer Texas Alexander for a few months in 1940, touring the Lone Star state with the veteran bluesman. Fulson was drafted in 1943. The Navy let him go in 1945; after a few months back in Oklahoma, he was off to Oakland, CA, where he made his first 78s for fledgling producer Bob Geddins. Soon enough, Fulson was fronting his own band and cutting a stack of platters for Big Town, Gilt Edge, Trilon, and Down Town (where he hit big in 1948 with "Three O'Clock Blues," later covered by B.B. King).

Swing Time Records prexy Jack Lauderdale snapped up Fulson in 1948, and the hits really began to flow: the immortal "Every Day I Have the Blues" (an adaptation of Memphis Slim's "Nobody Loves Me"), "Blue Shadows," the two-sided holiday perennial "Lonesome Christmas," and a groovy mid-tempo instrumental "Low Society Blues" that really hammers home how tremendously important pianist Lloyd Glenn and alto saxist Earl Brown were to Fulson's maturing sound (all charted in 1950!).

Fulson toured extensively from then on, his band stocked for a time with dazzling pianist Ray Charles (who later covered Lowell's "Sinner's Prayer" for Atlantic) and saxist Stanley Turrentine. After a one-off session in New Orleans in 1953 for Aladdin, Fulson inked a long-term pact with Chess in 1954. His first single for the label was the classic "Reconsider Baby," cut in Dallas under Stan Lewis's supervision with a sax section that included David "Fathead" Newman on tenor and Leroy Cooper on baritone.

The relentless mid-tempo blues proved a massive hit and perennial cover item—even Elvis Presley cut it in 1960, right after he got out of the Army. But apart from "Loving You," the guitarist's subsequent Checker output failed to find widespread favor with the public. Baffling, since Fulson's crisp, concise guitar work and sturdy vocals were as effective as ever. Most of his Checker sessions were held in Chicago and L.A. (the latter his home from the turn of the '50s).

Fulson stayed with Checker into 1962, but a change of labels worked wonders when he jumped over to Los Angeles-based Kent Records. 1965's driving "Black Nights" became his first smash in a decade, and "Tramp," a loping, funk-injected workout co-written by Fulson and Jimmy McCracklin, did even better, restoring the guitarist to R&B stardom, gaining plenty of pop spins, and inspiring a playful Stax cover by Otis Redding and Carla Thomas only a few months later that outsold Fulson's original.

A couple of lesser follow-up hits for Kent ensued before the guitarist was reunited with Stan Lewis at Jewel Records. That's where he took a crack at that Beatles number, though most of his outings for the label were considerably closer to the blues bone. Fulson has never been absent for long on disc; 1992's *Hold On* and its 1995 follow-up *Them Update Blues*, both for Ron Levy's Bullseye Blues logo, are among his most recent efforts, both quite solid.

Few bluesmen have managed to remain contemporary the way Lowell Fulson has for more than five decades. And fewer still will make such a massive contribution to the idiom. —*Bill Dahl*

Lowell Fulson (Early Recordings) / 1975 / Arhoolie ✦✦✦
Mostly the country blues roots of the Oklahoma-born guitarist. The first ten tracks, duets with brother Martin on second guitar, are worlds apart from the swinging horn-powered R&B efforts that Fulson is famous for. The last four numbers, though, revert to that attractive format—especially the scorching instrumental closer "Lowell Jumps One." —*Bill Dahl*

Everyday I Have the Blues / 1984 / Night Train ✦✦✦✦
The first of two extremely solid compilations of the guitarist's late-'40s/early-'50s output for Jack Lauderdale's Los Angeles-based Swing Time imprint. You'll need 'em both, since the essentials are spread across 'em about evenly—Fulson's smashes "Every Day," "Lonesome Christmas," and "Blue Shadows" regally inhabit this 20-cut disc. —*Bill Dahl*

San Francisco Blues / 1988 / Black Lion ✦✦✦✦
Guitarist and vocalist Lowell Fulson helped establish his reputation with a string of fine songs for the Swingtime label in the late '40s and early '50s. Fulson showed he could belt out hard-hitting blues, do sentimental ballads, double-entendre novelty pieces or irony-filled laments, and also play riveting solos. This '92 CD reissue collects 16 early Fulson numbers, all original compositions, and features Fulson leading a group with Lloyd Glenn, King Solomon or Rufus J. Russell on piano, Ralph Hamilton, Billy Hadnott or Floyd Montgomery on bass, and Bob Harvey or Asal Carson on drums. —*Ron Wynn*

Tramp/Soul / 1991 / Flair ✦✦✦✦
The veteran guitarist's two best mid-'60s albums for Kent Records on one

packed-to-the-gills CD. Fulson cannily made the leap into soul-slanted grooves while at Kent, scoring a major R&B smash with "Tramp." Also aboard is Fulson's classic "Black Nights," "Talkin' Woman" (later revived most memorably by Albert Collins as "Honey Hush"), and a fine version of Smokey Hogg's enduring "Too Many Drivers." —*Bill Dahl*

Hold On / May 1992 / Bullseye Blues ✦✦✦✦
Nothing dated about this fine album, produced by organist Ron Levy—Fulson sounds at once both contemporary and timeless, slashing through a mostly original set with Jimmy McCracklin helping out on piano and the sax section including Bobby Forte and Edgar Synigal. —*Bill Dahl*

Reconsider Baby / 1993 / Charly ✦✦✦✦
A more in-depth assessment of Fulson's Chess years (20 titles), minus a few of the most important sides nestled on *Hung Down Head* but boasting a few others of nearly equal import: "Lonely Hours," "Rollin' Blues," "Don't Drive Me Baby," and especially the insane 1957 rocker "Rock This Morning," where Fulson does his best Little Richard imitation as Eddie Chamblee blows up a tenor sax hurricane. —*Bill Dahl*

Them Updated Blues / 1995 / Bullseye Blues ✦✦✦
A half century after he made his debut waxings, Fulson is still going strong—and not as some museum piece, either. Still a vital blues artist who refuses to rest on his massive laurels, Fulson's latest is a fine addition to his vast discography, comprised mostly of fresh originals and featuring his customary biting guitar and insinuating vocals. —*Bill Dahl*

Sinner's Prayer / 1995 / Night Train ✦✦✦✦
Twenty more Swing Time essentials, notably Lowell Fulson's original reading of the mournful "Sinner's Prayer" (soon revived by his one-time band pianist Ray Charles), the exultant instrumental "Low Society" (featuring Earl Brown's sturdy alto sax), and one of Fulson's wildest rockers, "Upstairs." —*Bill Dahl*

★ **Hung Down Head** / MCA/Chess ✦✦✦✦✦
The most indispensable collection in Fulson's vast discography. He was hitting on all burners during the mid-'50s when he was with Chess, waxing the immortal "Reconsider Baby," swinging gems like "Check Yourself," "Do Me Right," and "Trouble, Trouble," and the supremely doomy "Tollin' Bells," here in many truncated false takes before he and the band finally jell. —*Bill Dahl*

Rory Gallagher

b. Mar. 2, 1949, Ballyshannon, Ireland, **d.** Jun. 14, 1995
Guitar, Vocals / Blues-Rock, British Blues

For a career that was cut short by illness and a premature death, guitarist, singer, and songwriter Rory Gallagher sure accomplished a lot in the blues music world. Although Gallagher didn't tour the US nearly enough, spending most of his time in Europe, he was known for his no-holds-barred, marathon live shows at clubs and theaters around the United States.

Gallagher was born in Ballyshannon, County Donegal, Irish Republic on March 2, 1949. He passed away from complications owing to liver transplant surgery on June 14, 1995, at age 46. Shortly after his birth, his family moved to Cork City in the south, and at age nine, he became fascinated with American blues and folk singers he heard on the radio. An avid record collector, he had a wide range of influences including Leadbelly, Buddy Guy, Freddie King, Albert King, Muddy Waters, and John Lee Hooker. Gallagher would always try to mix some simple country blues songs onto his recordings.

Some of Gallagher's best work on record isn't under his own name, it's stuff he recorded with Muddy Waters on *The London Sessions* (Chess, 1972) and with Albert King on *Live* (RCA/Utopia). Gallagher made his last US tours in 1985 and 1991, and he has admitted in interviews that he's always been a guitarist who feeds off the instant reaction and feedback a live audience can provide. —*Richard Skelly*

Rory Gallagher / 1971 / Atlantic ✦✦✦
Rory Gallagher's eponymous debut is an entertaining, but relatively undistinguished collection of blues-rock, highlighted by his flash slide guitar. —*Thom Owens*

Live in Europe/Stage Struck / 1972 / IRS ✦✦✦
The live album *Live in Europe/Stage Struck* captures Rory Gallagher at his finest, as he tears his way through many of his very best songs. Though the performance quality is a little uneven, there are gems scattered throughout the record, including smoking versions of "Messin' with the Kid" and "Laundromat." —*Thom Owens*

Tattoo / 1973 / Castle ✦✦✦
Rory Gallagher forges a distinctive style on *Tattoo*, one of his strongest albums. Working with a tight quartet, he's given a solid foundation for his terrific solos—it's especially exciting to hear him supported by a piano. All of the players deliver with conviction and studied passion, which makes the record an exciting listen. —*Thom Owens*

Irish Tour '74 / 1974 / IRS ✦✦✦✦
With *Irish Tour '74*, Rory Gallagher hit his highwater mark. Recorded live on his successful 1973 tour, Gallagher displays a remarkable empathy with his band, as they both churn out crunching riffs and fluid, soulful solos. Many of his best songs are included on the set and far eclipse the studio versions. *—Thom Owens*

Calling Card / 1976 / IRS ✦✦✦✦
Following the excellent live set *Irish Tour '74*, Rory Gallagher delivered his best studio album, *Calling Card*. The record captures the dynamic interplay between the guitarist and his band—they burn with a roaring intensity. It also doesn't hurt that the songs are the best batch that Gallagher ever came up with for a record. The combination of top-notch performances and first-rate songs equals the hardest-edged and most rewarding studio set the guitarist ever cut. *—Thom Owens*

● **Edged in Blue** / 1992 / Edsel ✦✦✦✦
Edged in Blue is a solid, if not exactly definitive, retrospective of Rory Gallagher's career that offers a fine introduction to the British blues star. *—Thom Owens*

Jazz Gillum (William McKinley Gillum)

b. Sep. 11, 1904, Indianola, MS, **d.** Mar. 29, 1966, Chicago, IL
Harmonica / Chicago Blues, Blues, Urban
Next to John Lee "Sonny Boy" Williamson, no harmonica player was as popular or as much in demand on recording sessions during the '30s as Jazz Gillum. His high, reedy sound meshed perfectly on dozens of hokum sides on the Bluebird label, both as a sideman and as a leader.

Born in Indianola, MS, (B.B. King's birthplace as well) in 1904, Gillum was evidently teaching himself how to play harmonica by the tender age of six. After running away from home in 1911 to live with relatives in Charleston, MS, Jazz spent the next dozen or so years working a day job and spending his weekends playing for tips on local street corners. When he visited Chicago in 1923, he found the environment very much to his liking and put down roots there.

There he met guitarist Big Bill Broonzy, and the two of them started working club dates around the city as a duo. By 1934 Gillum started popping up on recording dates for ARC and later Bluebird, RCA Victor's budget label. This association would prove to be a lasting one, as Chicago producer Lester Melrose frequently called on Gillum as a sideman—as well as cutting sides on his own—as part of the 'Bluebird beat' house band. His career seemed to screech to a halt when the label folded in the late '40s, and aside from a Memphis Slim session in 1961, he seems to have been largely inactive throughout the '50s until his death from a gunshot wound as a result of an argument in 1966. *—Cub Koda*

● **Roll Dem Bones 1938-49** / Wolf ✦✦✦✦
Best selection of Gillum sides available. Not a bad one in this bunch. *—Cub Koda*

Lloyd Glenn

b. Nov. 21, 1909, San Antonio, TX, **d.** May 23, 1985, Los Angeles, CA
Piano / Piano Blues
As a integral behind-the-scenes fixture on the L.A. postwar blues scene, pianist/arranger/A&R man Lloyd Glenn had few equals. His rolling ivories anchored many of Lowell Fulson's best waxings for Swing Time and Checker, and he scored his own major hits on Swing Time with the imaginative instrumentals "Old Time Shuffle Blues" in 1950 and "Chica Boo" the next year. Glenn was already an experienced musician when he left the Lone Star state for sunny California in 1942. His early sessions there included backing T-Bone Walker at the 1947 Capitol date that produced the guitarist's immortal "Call It Stormy Monday." Glenn recorded for the first time under his own name the same year for Imperial with his band, the Joymakers, which included guitarist Gene Phillips, saxist Marshall Royal, and singer Geraldine Carter.

Massively constructed guitarist Tiny Webb introduced Glenn to Swing Time owner Jack Lauderdale in 1949, inaugurating a five-year stint for Glenn as A&R man at the label. After Swing Time's demise, the pianist moved to Aladdin Records, issuing more catchy instrumentals for Eddie Mesner's label through 1959. There was also an isolated session for Imperial in 1962 that produced "Twistville" and "Young Date." The pianist remained active into the 1980s, often touring as Big Joe Turner's accompanist. *—Bill Dahl*

Honky Tonk Train / 1983 / Night Train ✦✦✦✦
In addition to waxing his own bouncy instrumentals during his late-'40s/early-'50s stay at Swing Time Records (an unissued take of "Old Time Shuffle," one of his own hits, graces this disc), pianist Lloyd Glenn also arranged and played behind several of the label's veteran vocalists—explaining the presence of exceptional blues outings by Joe Pullum and Jesse Thomas. *—Bill Dahl*

● **Chica Boo** / 1988 / Night Train ✦✦✦✦
Quite a bit of duplication between this 18-song collection and Night Train's previous disc. But since this one contains both of his hits—"Old

Time Shuffle" and "Chica Boo"—it wins hands down. Pullum and Thomas are back as guest vocalists on these 1947-1952 waxings. This is lightly swinging West Coast blues with an elegant, understated edge. *—Bill Dahl*

Guitar Slim (Eddie Jones)

b. Dec. 10, 1926, Greenwood, MS, **d.** Feb. 7, 1959, New York City, NY
Guitar, Vocals / Electric New Orleans Blues
No 1950s blues guitarist even came close to equalling the flamboyant Guitar Slim in the showmanship department. Armed with an estimated 350 feet of cord between his axe and his amp, Slim would confidently stride onstage wearing a garishly hued suit of red, blue, or green—with his hair usually dyed to match! It's rare to find a blues guitarist hailing from Texas or Louisiana who doesn't cite Slim as one of his principal influences; Buddy Guy, Earl King, Guitar Shorty, Albert Collins, Chick Willis, and plenty more have enthusiastically testified to Slim's enduring sway.

Born Eddie Jones in Mississippi, Slim didn't have long to make such an indelible impression. He turned up in New Orleans in 1950, influenced by the atomic guitar energy of Gatemouth Brown. But Slim's ringing, distorted guitar tone and gospel-enriched vocal style were his alone. He debuted on wax in 1951 with a mediocre session for Imperial that barely hinted at what would soon follow. A 1952 date for Bullet produced the impassioned "Feelin' Sad," later covered by Ray Charles (who would arrange and play piano on Slim's breakthrough hit the next year).

With the emergence of the stunning "The Things That I Used to Do" on Art Rupe's Specialty logo, Slim's star rocketed to blazing ascendancy nationwide. Combining a swampy ambience with a churchy arrangement, the New Orleans-cut track was a monster hit, pacing the R&B charts for an amazing 14 weeks in 1954. Strangely, although he waxed several stunning follow-ups for Specialty in the same tortured vein—"The Story of My Life," "Something to Remember You By," "Sufferin' Mind"—as well as the blistering rockers "Well I Done Got Over It," "Letter to My Girlfriend," and "Quicksand," Slim never charted again.

The guitar wizard switched over to Atlantic Records in 1956. Gradually, his waxings became tamer, though "It Hurts to Love Someone" and "If I Should Lose You" summoned up the old fire. But Slim's lifestyle was as wild as his guitar work. Excessive drinking and life in the fast lane took its inevitable toll over the years, and he died in 1959 at age 32. Only in recent years has his monumental influence on the blues lexicon begun to be fully recognized and appreciated.

Incidentally, one of his sons bills himself as Guitar Slim, Jr. around the New Orleans circuit, his repertoire heavily peppered with his dad's material. *—Bill Dahl*

Atco Sessions / Jul. 1988 / Atlantic ✦✦✦
Sometimes a bit subdued compared to his bone-chilling output for Specialty, these 1956-1958 sides for Atco still possess considerable charm, especially the tough "It Hurts to Love Someone" and "If I Should Lose You," which conjure up the same hellfire and brimstone intensity as Slim's earlier work. *—Bill Dahl*

★ **Sufferin' Mind** / 1991 / Specialty ✦✦✦✦✦
His guitar fraught with manic high-end distortion and his vocals fried over church-fired intensity, Eddie "Guitar Slim" Jones influenced a boatload of disciples while enjoying the rewards that came with his 1954 R&B chart-topper "The Things That I Used to Do." This 26-song survey of Slim's seminal 1953-1955 Specialty catalog rates with the best New Orleans blues ever cut—besides the often-imitated but never-duplicated smash, his "Story of My Life," "Sufferin' Mind," and "Something to Remember You By" are overwhelming in their ringing back-alley fury. Slim could rock, too: "Well I Done Got Over It," "Quicksand," "Certainly All," and the raucous introduction "Guitar Slim" drive with blistering power (saxist Joe Tillman was a worthy foil for the flamboyant guitarist in the solo department). *—Bill Dahl*

Buddy Guy

b. Jul. 30, 1936, Lettsworth, LA
Guitar, Vocals / Electric Chicago Blues
He's Chicago's blues king today, ruling his domain just as his idol and mentor Muddy Waters did before him. Yet there was a time, and not all that long ago either, when Buddy Guy couldn't even negotiate a decent record deal. Times sure have changed for the better—Guy just racked up another Grammy for his last studio album, *Slippin' In* (his third in three tries for the Silvertone label). His latest disc, a sizzling live collection recorded with G.E. Smith's horn-powered Saturday Night Live Band at his own spacious Chicago venue, Buddy Guy's Legends, threatens to make it four for four. Eric Clapton unabashedly calls Buddy Guy his favorite blues axeman, and so do a great many adoring fans worldwide.

High-energy guitar histrionics and boundless onstage energy have always been Guy trademarks, along with a tortured vocal style that's nearly as distinctive as his incendiary rapid-fire fretwork. He's come a long way from his beginnings on the 1950s Baton Rouge blues scene—at his first gigs with bandleader "Big Poppa" John Tilley, the young guitarist had to chug a stomach-jolting concoction of Dr. Tichenor's antiseptic and wine to ward off an advanced case of stage fright. But by the time he joined harpist Raful Neal's band, Guy had conquered his nervousness.

Guy journeyed to Chicago in 1957, ready to take the town by storm. But times were tough initially, until he turned up the juice as a showman (much as another of his early idols, Guitar Slim, had back home). It didn't take long after that for the new kid in town to establish himself. He hung with the city's blues elite: Freddy King, Muddy Waters, Otis Rush, and Magic Sam, who introduced Buddy Guy to Cobra Records boss Eli Toscano. Two searing 1958 singles for Cobra's Artistic subsidiary were the result: "This Is the End" and "Try to Quit You Baby" exhibited more than a trace of B.B. King influence, while "You Sure Can't Do" was an unabashed homage to Guitar Slim. Willie Dixon produced the sides.

When Cobra folded, Guy wisely followed Rush over to Chess. With the issue of his first Chess single in 1960, Guy was no longer aurally indebted to anybody. "First Time I Met the Blues" and its follow-up, "Broken Hearted Blues," were fiery, tortured slow blues brilliantly showcasing Guy's whammy-bar-enriched guitar and shrieking, hell-hound-on-his-trail vocals.

Although he's often complained that Leonard Chess wouldn't allow him to turn up his guitar loud enough, the claim doesn't wash: Guy's 1960-1967 Chess catalog remains his most satisfying body of work. A shuffling "Let Me Love You Baby," the impassioned downbeat items "Ten Years Ago," "Stone Crazy," "My Time After Awhile," and "Leave My Girl Alone," and a bouncy "No Lie" rate with the hottest blues waxings of the '60s. While at Chess, Guy worked long and hard as a session guitarist, getting his licks in on sides by Waters, Howlin' Wolf, Little Walter, Sonny Boy Williamson, and Koko Taylor (on her hit "Wang Dang Doodle").

Upon leaving Chess in 1967, Guy signed with Vanguard. His first LP for the label, *A Man and the Blues*, followed in the same immaculate vein as his Chess work and contained the rocking "Mary Had a Little Lamb," but *This Is Buddy Guy* and *Hold That Plane!* proved somewhat less consistent. Guy and harpist Junior Wells had long palled around Chicago (Guy supplied the guitar work on Wells' seminal 1965 Delmark set *Hoodoo Man Blues*, initially billed as "Friendly Chap" because of his Chess contract); they recorded together for Blue Thumb in 1969 as *Buddy and the Juniors* (pianist Junior Mance being the other Junior) and Atlantic in 1970 (sessions co-produced by Eric Clapton and Tom Dowd) and 1972 for the solid album *Buddy Guy & Junior Wells Play the Blues*. Buddy and Junior toured together throughout the '70s, their playful repartee immortalized by *Drinkin' TNT 'n' Smokin' Dynamite*, a live set cut at the 1974 Montreux Jazz Festival.

Guy's reputation among rock guitar gods such as Eric Clapton, Jimi Hendrix, and Stevie Ray Vaughan was unsurpassed, but prior to his Grammy-winning 1991 Silvertone disc *Damn Right, I've Got the Blues*, he amazingly hadn't issued a domestic album in a decade. That's when the Buddy Guy bandwagon really picked up steam—he began selling out auditoriums and turning up on network television (David Letterman, Jay Leno, etc.). *Feels Like Rain*, his 1993 encore, was a huge letdown artistically, unless one enjoys the twisted concept of having one of the world's top bluesmen duet with country hat act Travis Tritt and hopelessly overwrought rock singer Paul Rodgers. By comparison, 1994's *Slippin' In*, produced by Eddie Kramer, was a major step back in the right direction, with no hideous duets and a preponderance of genuine blues excursions.

A Buddy Guy concert can sometimes be a frustrating experience. He'll be in the middle of something downright hair-raising, only to break it off abruptly in mid-song, or he'll ignore his own massive songbook in order to offer imitations of Clapton, Vaughan, and Hendrix. But Guy, whose club remains the most successful blues joint in Chicago (you'll likely find him sitting at the bar whenever he's in town), is without a doubt the Windy City's reigning blues artist—and he rules benevolently. —*Bill Dahl*

I Left My Blues in San Francisco / 1967 / MCA/Chess ✦✦✦
A late-'60s Chess LP that included several standout efforts from Guy's early catalog—"Leave My Girl Alone," "Every Girl I See," and the searing "Mother-in-Law Blues." —*Bill Dahl*

A Man and His Blues / 1968 / Vanguard ✦✦✦✦
The guitarist's first album away from Chess—and to be truthful, it sounds as though it could have been cut at 2120 S. Michigan, with Guy's deliciously understated guitar work and a tight combo anchored by three saxes and pianist Otis Spann laying down tough grooves on the vicious "Mary Had a Little Lamb," "I Can't Quit the Blues," and an exultant cover of Mercy Dee's "One Room Country Shack." —*Bill Dahl*

Buddy Guy and Junior Wells Play the Blues / 1972 / Rhino ✦✦✦

I Was Walkin' through the Woods / 1974 / MCA/Chess ✦✦✦✦
Ten of the mercurial guitarist's best recordings ever for Chess, cut during

his early-'60s peak. "First Time I Met the Blues" and "Broken Hearted Blues" are harrowing downbeat blues of enormous power, Guy's shrieks and tremolo-rich guitar bursts boasting an intensity level he's only achieved intermittently ever since. Even better, they're here in stereo—unlike virtually every other Chess collection to follow. —*Bill Dahl*

Live in Montreux / Jul. 9, 1977 / Evidence ✦✦✦

Pleading the Blues / Oct. 1979 / Evidence ✦✦✦
Recorded on Halloween night in 1979, this pairs up Wells and Guy in a fashion that hasn't been heard since *Hoodoo Man Blues*, their first, and best collaboration. Solid backing by the Philip Guy band (Buddy's brother) makes this album a rare treat. —*Cub Koda*

Alone and Acoustic / 1991 / Alligator ✦✦✦

Damn Right I've Got the Blues / 1991 / Silvertone ✦✦✦✦
Grammy-winning comeback set that brought Guy back to prominence after a long studio hiatus. Too many clichéd cover choices—"Five Long Years," "Mustang Sally," "Black Night," "There Is Something on Your Mind"—to earn unreserved recommendation, but Guy's frenetic guitar histrionics ably cut through the superstar-heavy proceedings (Eric Clapton, Jeff Beck, and Mark Knopfler all turn up) on the snarling title cut and a handful of others. —*Bill Dahl*

☆ **The Complete Chess Studio Sessions** / 1992 / MCA/Chess ✦✦✦✦✦
Here's everything that fleet-fingered Buddy Guy waxed for Chess from 1960 to 1966, including numerous unissued-at-the-time masters, offering the most in-depth peek at his formative years imaginable. Stone Chicago blues classics ("Ten Years Ago," "My Time After Awhile," "Let Me Love You Baby," "Stone Crazy"), rockin' oddities ("American Bandstand," "$100 Bill," "Slop Around"), even a cut that features guitarist Lacy Gibson's vocal rather than Guy's ("My Love Is Real")—some 47 sizzling songs in all. —*Bill Dahl*

● **The Very Best of Buddy Guy** / 1992 / Rhino ✦✦✦✦
Credible attempt to digitally summarize Guy's entire pre-Silvertone career on a single 18-song disc. Encompasses the guitarist's 1957 demo "The Way You Been Treating Me," two killer Cobras, four of his hottest Chess sides, a couple notable Vanguards, a pair of alluring Atlantics, and three tremendously unsubtle 1981 items from Guy's days with the British JSP label. —*Bill Dahl*

Feels Like Rain / 1993 / Jive/Novus ✦✦✦

Slippin' In / 1994 / Silvertone ✦✦✦✦
Now this is more like it: no sign of any superfluous duets, and far fewer hoary standards to contend with (only the Z.Z. Hill title track, in fact). Lots of high-energy guitar fireworks and vocal intensity from the perpetually eager-to-please blues superstar, as he drives through well-chosen numbers first rendered by Bobby Bland, Jimmy Reed, Charles Brown, and Fenton Robinson and Guy's own impassioned "Cities Need Help" and "Little Dab-A-Doo." —*Bill Dahl*

Southern Blues 1957-63 / 1994 / Paula ✦✦✦

Live—The Real Deal / 1996 / Silvertone ✦✦✦✦
As close as Buddy Guy's ever likely to come to recapturing the long-lost Chess sound. Cut live at his popular Chicago nightspot, Buddy Guy's Legends, with guitarist G.E. Smith's horn-leavened Saturday Night Live Band and pianist Johnnie Johnson in lush support, Guy revisits his roots on sumptuous readings of "I've Got My Eyes on You," "Ain't That Lovin' You," "My Time After Awhile," and "First Time I Met the Blues." No outrageous rock-based solos or Cream/Hendrix/Stevie Ray homages; this is the Buddy Guy album that purists have salivated for the last quarter century or so. —*Bill Dahl*

John Hammond, Jr. (John Paul Hammond)

b. Nov. 13, 1942, New York City, NY
Guitar, Harmonica, Vocals / R&B, Modern Acoustic Blues, Blues-Rock
With a career that now spans in excess of three decades, John Hammond is one of a handful of White blues musicians who was on the scene at the beginning of the first blues renaissance of the mid-'60s. That revival, brought on by renewed interest in folk music around the US, brought about career boosts for many of the great classic blues players, including Mississippi John Hurt, Rev. Gary Davis and Skip James. Some critics have described Hammond as a White Robert Johnson, and Hammond does justice to classic blues by combining powerful guitar and harmonica playing with expressive vocals and a dignified stage presence. Within the first decade of his career as a performer, Hammond began crafting a niche for himself that is completely his own: the solo guitar man, harmonica slung in a rack around his neck, reinterpreting classic blues songs from the 1930s, '40s and '50s. Yet, as several of his mid-'90s recordings for the Pointblank label demonstrate, he's also a capable bandleader who plays wonderful electric guitar. This guitar-playing and ensemble work can be heard on *Found True Love* and *Got Love If You Want It*, both for the Pointblank/Virgin label. —*Richard Skelly*

Big City Blues / 1964 / Vanguard ✦✦✦✦
Hammond's second effort was one of the first electric White blues recordings, and one of the very first that could be said to be blues-rock. Covering a variety of Chess Records classics and electrifying some older tunes, the playing, featuring Hammond, Billy Butler, and James Spruill on electric guitar, is first-rate. But Hammond's vocals are overly mannered and overwrought, and although he would improve, these flaws would keep him from rising to the top rank of White bluesmen. —*Richie Unterberger*

Country Blues / 1964 / Vanguard ✦✦✦✦
Although Hammond had already recorded electric material, he went back to a solo acoustic format for his fourth album, accompanying himself on guitar and harmonica on faithful interpretations of standards by Robert Johnson, Blind Willie McTell, John Lee Hooker, Sleepy John Estes, Jimmy Reed, Willie Dixon, and Bo Diddley. If it sounds a bit unimaginative and routine today, one has to remember that the general listening audience was much less aware of these artists and songs in the mid-'60s. Hammond did a commendable job of rendering them here, with fine guitar work and vocals that were a considerable improvement over his earliest efforts. —*Richie Unterberger*

I Can Tell / 1967 / Atlantic ✦✦✦✦
I Can Tell boasts an all-star backing band of rock 'n' roll stars, featuring everyone from Bill Wyman to Robbie Robertson. Hammond leads the band through a set of Chicago blues standards, reaching deep into the catalogs of Willie Dixon, Elmore James, Howlin' Wolf, and many others. Although the performances can occasionally sound too studied, the album is by and large unadulterated delight—the affection Hammond and his band have for the material is quite clear. The CD reissue includes four cuts from his 1970 album, *Southern Fried*, which feature Duane Allman on slide guitar. —*Thom Owens*

Live / 1983 / Rounder ✦✦✦✦
John Hammond has dealt with issues of authenticity and origin, both musical and personal, and moved beyond them. This 18-song session, recorded live in 1983 and recently reissued on CD, may have been his definitive session. It was certainly a masterpiece, with Hammond doing confident, thoroughly distinctive versions of signature Delta and Chicago blues classics by Robert Johnson, Muddy Waters, Willie Dixon, Son House and others. While "Dust My Broom," "Drop Down Mama," "Wang Dang Doodle" and all the rest have certainly been done to death, Hammond's spirited vocals, riveting guitar work on acoustic or bottleneck and his overall charismatic performances made them seem like fresh discoveries. —*Ron Wynn*

● **The Best of John Hammond** / 1989 / Vanguard ✦✦✦✦
The best early works of this folk-blues artist. Acoustic and essential. —*Michael G. Nastos*

Got Love If You Want It / 1992 / Charisma ✦✦✦
In many ways, *Got Love If You Want It* is standard-issue John Hammond, Jr. The album is filled with covers by great bluesmen like Son House and Slim Harpo, as well as rock 'n' rollers like Chuck Berry. The difference is ability—Hammond is a professional and is able to pull off convincing performances of these warhorses. Backed by Little Charlie and the Nightcats—who have rarely sounded better, incidentally—Hammond tears through these songs with passion, which makes even the oldest songs sound rather fresh. —*Thom Owens*

W.C. Handy

b. Nov. 16, 1873, Muscle Shoals, AL, **d.** Mar. 28, 1958
Piano, Bandleader / Early American Blues
Often referred to as the "father of the blues," William Christopher Handy was born on November 16, 1873, in Muscle Shoals, AL. He studied music early on, starting with the cornet in a brass band, working with a vocal quartet, and eventually playing throughout the South in minstrel and tent shows. It was during his many travels that he began to notate the music he heard, including Delta blues. He would adapt these tunes and sounds to his own performance, in this way popularizing the music he heard, the blues in particular. He was the first to add flatted thirds and sevenths (so-called "blue notes") to published compositions.

He became music director of Mahara's Minstrels in 1896, a group that played rags, popular dance numbers, and even some light classical compositions. They toured the South in the late 1800s and early 1900s. He recorded in New York in 1917 with his Memphis Orchestra.

Handy was the first to compose and publish a tune with the word "blues" in it, "Memphis Blues" in 1912. He composed and published many classic blues tunes including "St. Louis Blues," "Beale Street Blues," "Ole Miss," and "Yellow Dog Blues." Handy's foray into writing and publishing blues songs inspired other writers, including Perry Bradford, the author of "Crazy Blues"—the first blues song ever recorded (1920).

Handy moved himself and his Memphis Orchestra to New York in 1917, started the Handy Record Company (a failure) in 1922, and recorded with his own band until 1923. Throughout the later 1920s and

1930s Handy, who had developed eye problems, was forced to work less. Still, he continued working with many orchestras. He was on recording sessions with Red Allen and Jelly Roll Morton. His autobiography *Father of the Blues* was written in 1938, the same year that he was given a tribute concert in Carnegie Hall. In his later years, Handy was not very active. He died on March 28, 1958. The movie *St. Louis Blues* was released in 1958, starring Nat King Cole. It is not considered to be very reflective of the facts of Handy's life. A legend in Memphis, Handy has a park named after him there containing a statue of himself. The W.C. Handy Award is the most prestigious honor currently awarded to blues artists. Handy, along with Duke Ellington, appears on a US postage stamp.

Although no one person is the father of the blues, and Handy was not by temperament or cultivation what we might call a bluesman, W.C. Handy did much to popularize and publicize what had been until that time a very personal and local phenomenon. Handy helped to broadcast the blues form to the world. —*Michael Erlewine*

Slim Harpo (James Moore)

b. Jan. 11, 1924, Lobdell, LA, **d.** Jan. 31, 1970, Baton Rouge, LA
Guitar, Harmonica, Vocals / Electric Louisiana Blues
In the large stable of blues talent that Crowley, LA, producer Jay Miller recorded for the Nashville-based Excello label, no one enjoyed more mainstream success than Slim Harpo. Just a shade behind Lightnin' Slim in local popularity, Harpo played both guitar and neck-rack harmonica in a more down-home approximation of Jimmy Reed, with a few discernible, and distinctive, differences. Slim's music was certainly more laid-back than Reed's, if such a notion was possible. But the rhythm was insistent and overall, Harpo was more adaptable than Reed or most other bluesmen. His material not only made the national charts, but also proved to be quite adaptable for White artists on both sides of the Atlantic, including the Rolling Stones, Yardbirds, Kinks, Dave Edmunds with Love Sculpture, Van Morrison with Them, Sun rockabilly Warren Smith, Hank Williams, Jr., and the Fabulous Thunderbirds.

A people-pleasing club entertainer, he certainly wasn't above working rock 'n' roll rhythms into his music, along with hard-stressed, country & western vocal inflections. Several of his best tunes were co-written with his wife, Lovelle, and show a fine hand for song construction, appearing to have arrived at the studio pretty well formed. His harmonica playing was driving and straightforward, full of surprising melodicism, while his vocals were perhaps best described by writer Peter Guralnick as "if a Black country and western singer or a White rhythm and blues singer were attempting to impersonate a member of the opposite genre." And here perhaps was Harpo's true genius, and what has allowed his music to have a wider currency. By the time his first single became a Southern jukebox favorite, his songs were beiong adapted and played by White musicians left and right. Here was good-time Saturday night blues that could be sung by elements of the Caucasian persuasion with a straight face. Nothing resembling the emotional investment of a Howlin' Wolf or a Muddy Waters was required; it all came natural and easy, and its influence has stood the test of time.

He was born James Moore just outside of Baton Rouge, LA. After his parents died, he dropped out of school to work every juke joint, street corner, picnic and house rent party that came his way. By this time he had acquired the alias of Harmonica Slim, which he used until his first record was released. It was fellow bluesman Lightnin' Slim who first steered him to local record man J.D. Miller. The producer used him as accompanist to Hopkins on a half dozen sides before recording him on his own. When it came time to release his first single ("I'm a King Bee"), Miller informed him that there was another Harmonica Slim recording on the West Coast, and a new name was needed before the record could come out. Moore's wife took the slang word for harmonica, added an 'o' to the end of it, and a new stage name was the result, one that would stay with Slim Harpo the rest of his career.

Harpo's first record became a double-sided R&B hit, spawning numerous follow-ups on the "King Bee" theme, but even bigger was "Rainin' in My Heart," which made the *Billboard* Top 40 pop charts in the summer of 1961. It was another perfect distillation of Harpo's across-the-board appeal, and was immediately adapted by country, Cajun, and rock 'n' roll musicians; anybody could play it and sound good doing it. In the wake of the Rolling Stones covering "I'm a King Bee" on their first album, Slim had the biggest hit of his career in 1966 with "Baby, Scratch My Back." Harpo described it "as an attempt at rock 'n' roll for me," and its appearance in *Billboard*'s Top 20 pop charts prompted the dance-oriented follow-ups "Tip on In" and "Tee-Ni-Nee-Ni-Nu," both R&B charters. For the first time in his career, Harpo appeared in such far-flung locales as Los Angeles and New York City. Flush with success, he contacted Lightnin' Slim, who was now residing outside of Detroit, MI. The two reunited and formed a band, touring together as a sort of blues mini-package to appreciative White rock audiences until the end of the decade. The new year beckoned with a tour of Europe (his first ever) all firmed up, and a recording session scheduled when he arrived in London. Unexplainably, Harpo—who had never been plagued with any ailments stronger than a common cold—suddenly succumbed to a heart attack on January 31, 1970. —*Cub Koda*

Rainin' in My Heart / 1961 / Excello ✦✦✦✦
The original 12-song Excello album with the addition of six extra tracks, all of which were originally issued as singles only. With the exception of "Dream Girl," "My Home Is a Prison" and "What a Dream," everything on here also appears on the AVI double disc collection. —*AMG*

Shake Your Hips / 1986 / Flyright ✦✦✦✦
The second installment in Ace's overview of Harpo's swamp blues career, spanning 1962-1966 and including all four of the harpist's rare 1962 sides for Imperial (cut during a brief rift with his producer J.D. Miller). More rarities and unissued gems, including a tracks that exhibit soul tendencies (a genre that Harpo took to surprisingly well). —*Bill Dahl*

★ **Scratch My Back: The Best of Slim Harpo** / 1989 / Rhino ✦✦✦✦✦
All the hits, including the original "I'm a King Bee," "Baby, Scratch My Back," "Got Love If You Want It," "Shake Your Hips," "Rainin' in My Heart," "Tip on In," and "Strange Love." A best-of that really is, with topflight sound as a bonus. —*Cub Koda*

☆ **Hip Shakin': The Excello Collection** / 1995 / AVI-Excello ✦✦✦✦✦
A shapely two-disc retrospective, *Hip Shakin'* is the definitive Slim Harpo package. Collecting all of his hits ("I'm a King Bee," "Got Love If You Want It," "Baby, Scratch My Back") along with other defining moments from his stay with the label, this 44-track compilation also includes three live recordings from a 1961 fraternity dance. —*AMG*

The Scratch: Rare and Unissued / Feb. 1996 / AVI-Excello ✦✦✦✦
A 25-track single disc comp loaded with previously unissued sides and alternate takes (the title track is an interesting variant of his hit, "Baby, Scratch My Back"), making it the perfect companion volume to the above. This also has the added bonus of more (and even wilder) live recordings from the infamous 1961 frat party dance in Alabama. Dodgy sound on the live sides, but performances too great to leave in the can either way. —*AMG*

Wynonie Harris

b. Aug. 24, 1915, Omaha, NE, **d.** Jun. 14, 1969, Los Angeles, CA
Drums, Vocals / R&B, Electric Jump Blues, Jump Blues
No blues shouter embodied the rollicking good times that he sang of quite like raucous shouter Wynonie Harris. "Mr. Blues," as he was not-so-humbly known, joyously related risque tales of sex, booze, and endless parties in his trademark raspy voice over some of the jumpingest horn-powered combos of the postwar era.

Those wanton ways eventually caught up with Harris, but not before he scored a raft of R&B smashes from 1946 to 1952. Few records made a stronger seismic impact than Harris' 1948 chart-topper "Good Rockin' Tonight." Ironically, Harris shooed away its composer, Roy Brown, when he first tried to hand it to the singer; only when Brown's original version took off did Wynonie cover the romping number. With Hal "Cornbread" Singer on wailing tenor sax and a rocking, socking backbeat, the record provided an easily followed blueprint for the imminent rise of rock 'n' roll a few years later (and gave Elvis Presley something to place on the A side of his second Sun single). —*Bill Dahl*

★ **Bloodshot Eyes: The Best of** / 1993 / King/Rhino ✦✦✦✦✦
Wynonie Harris was a hard-living, rousing R&B shouter who made some of the most sexually explicit songs in modern popular music history. Harris didn't leave much to the imagination, but he also possessed a booming voice with wonderful tone and range, and the comedic skill to execute these tunes without becoming raunchy. There are many hilarious cuts on this 18-track anthology, among them "I Like My Baby's Pudding," "Grandma Plays the Numbers" and "Good Morning Judge." Harris roars, struts and wails over equally feverish arrangements, and earns a draw with Joe Turner on "Battle of the Blues." These songs give a good portrait of a delightful, often spectacular vocalist who could be both provocative and compelling. —*Ron Wynn*

Everybody Boogie! / 1996 / Delmark ✦✦✦✦
This is one marvelous collection of 1945 recordings made for Apollo Records with Harris' powerhouse vocals backed by jump blues bands led by jazz greats Illinois Jacquet, Oscar Pettiford, and Jack McVea. No real honking and bar walking going on here; quite the opposite, as the Pettiford sides have bop lines creeping in throughout. But Harris seems oblivious to it all as tracks like "Time to Change Your Town," "Here Come the Blues," "Stuff You Gotta Watch," and "Somebody Changed the Lock on My Door" are on an equal par for sheer bravado and intensity with the best of his later work for King. A welcome compilation. —*Cub Koda*

Wilbert Harrison

b. Jan. 5, 1929, Charlotte, NC, **d.** Oct. 26, 1994
Guitar, Piano, Drums, Vocals / Soul, R&B, Rock 'n' Roll
Perceived by casual oldies fans as a two-hit wonder (his 1959 chart-top-

per "Kansas City" and a heartwarming "Let's Work Together" a full decade later), Wilbert Harrison actually left behind a varied body of work that blended an intriguing melange of musical idioms into something quite distinctive.

Harrison waxed his driving "Kansas City" for Harlem entrepreneur Bobby Robinson in 1959. With a barbed-wire guitar solo by Wild Jimmy Spruill igniting Harrison's no-frills piano and clenched vocal, "Kansas City" paced both the R&B and pop charts soon after its issue on Fury Records (not bad for a $40 session). —*Bill Dahl*

Listen to My Song / 1954-1957 / Savoy ✦✦✦✦
Harrison's first label association of any endurance commenced when he signed with Herman Lubinsky's Savoy logo in 1954 for a two-year stretch. Top New York sessioneers like saxophonist Mickey Baker and Kenny Burrell and saxists Buddy Lucas and Budd Johnson help out on these 16 Savoy tracks (still unavailable on CD). He liked that C&W; Terry Fell's "Don't Drop It" is a tremendously catchy hillbilly tune given an R&B flavor by the young singer. —*Bill Dahl*

● **Kansas City** / 1991 / Relic ✦✦✦✦
Finally, paydirt! Harrison smashed the charts in 1959 with his massive hit "Kansas City" for Bobby Robinson's Fury logo. Here we have 22 fine sides from the Fury hookup, some in stereo and many with Wild Jimmy Spruill on lead guitar. "Cheatin' Baby," "C.C. Rider," "1960," and the inevitable sequel "Goodbye Kansas City" are prime examples of Harrison's slightly off-kilter approach to his craft, while his infectious "Let's Stick Together" developed into the more worldly "Let's Work Together" toward the end of the decade. —*Bill Dahl*

Ted Hawkins

b. 1936, Biloxi, MS, **d.** Jan. 1, 1995
Guitar, Vocals / Soul, Modern Acoustic Blues, Singer-Songwriter
Overseas, he was a genuine hero, performing to thousands. But on his L.A. hometurf, sand-blown Venice Beach served as Ted Hawkins' makeshift stage. He'd deliver his magnificent melange of soul, blues, folk, gospel, and a touch of country all by his lonesome, with only an acoustic guitar for company. Passersby would pause to marvel at Hawkins' melismatic vocals, dropping a few coins or a greenback into his tip jar on the way by.

That was the way Ted Hawkins kept body and soul together until 1994, when DGC/Geffen Records issued *The Next Hundred Years*, his breakthrough album. Suddenly, Hawkins was poised on the precipice of stardom. And then, just after Christmas that same year, in a bout of cruel irony, he died of a stroke. —*Bill Dahl*

Watch Your Step / 1982 / Rounder ✦✦✦
Songs from Venice Beach / 1985 / Evidence ✦✦✦✦
Blending every form of roots music imaginable into his own singular soulful stew, the incomparable Ted Hawkins stuck mostly to R&B covers on this splendid 1985 solo outing—songs by Sam Cooke (his idol), Jerry Butler, Bobby Bland, the Temptations, and Garnet Mimms receive gorgeous readings by the acoustic guitarist. But even though he only contributed one original, the touching "Ladder of Success," to the set, Hawkins wasn't content to remain in one genre—his commanding revival of Webb Pierce's hillbilly weeper "There Stands the Glass" ranks with the disc's very best moments (of which there are many). —*Bill Dahl*

● **Happy Hour** / 1987 / Rounder ✦✦✦✦
Guitarist/vocalist Ted Hawkins' second Rounder record enhanced his reputation. *Happy Hour* features Hawkins' memorable compositions, plus a wonderful version of Curtis Mayfield's "Gypsy Woman." Hawkins' vocals were even more gritty and striking, as was his acoustic guitar backing and chording. He teamed with his wife Elizabeth on "Don't Make Me Explain It," "My Last Goodbye" and "California Song," and with guitarist Night Train Clemons on "Gypsy Woman" and "You Pushed My Head Away." Hawkins blended soul and urban blues stylings with country and rural blues inflections and rhythms, making another first-rate release. —*Ron Wynn*

The Next Hundred Years / 1994 / DGC ✦✦✦
The former L.A. street musician's major label breakthrough was in a great many ways a far weaker outing than what came before, largely due to a plodding band unwisely inserted behind Hawkins that tends to distract from rather than enhance his impassioned vocals and rich acoustic guitar strumming. Mostly originals ("There Stands the Glass" returns, as does "Ladder of Success") that would have sounded so much better in an intimate solo context. —*Bill Dahl*

Z. Z. Hill (Arzell Hill)

b. Sep. 30, 1935, Naples, TX, **d.** Apr. 27, 1984, Dallas, TX
Vocals / Soul, R&B, Soul Blues
Texas-born singer Z.Z. Hill managed to resuscitate both his own semi-flagging career and the entire genre at large when he signed on at Jackson, MS', Malaco Records in 1980 and began growling his way through

some of the most uncompromising blues to be unleashed on Black radio stations in many a moon.

His impressive 1982 Malaco album *Down Home Blues* remained on *Billboard*'s soul album charts for nearly two years, an extraordinary run for such a blatantly bluesy LP. His songs "Down Home Blues" and "Somebody Else Is Steppin' In" have graduated into the ranks of legitimate blues standards (and there haven't been many of those over the last couple of decades).

Hill's vocal grit was never more effective than on his blues-soaked Malaco output. From 1980 until 1984, when he died suddenly of a heart attack, Z.Z. bravely led a personal back-to-the-blues campaign that doubtless helped to fuel the current contemporary blues boom. It's a shame he couldn't stick around to see it blossom. *—Bill Dahl*

Let's Make a Deal / 1978 / Columbia ◆◆◆
One of the most commercial of Hill's albums, this disco-tinged release included the minor hits "This Time They Told the Truth" and "Love Is So Good When You're Stealing It." *—Richie Unterberger*

The Mark of Z.Z. Hill / 1979 / Columbia ◆◆◆
Hill's second and final Columbia LP was essentially a continuation of the first. On both, Hill sounds like a journeyman Southern soul singer embellished with period disco/mainstream R&B production, which neither added to the quality of the music nor made it unlistenable. *—Richie Unterberger*

Z.Z. Hill / 1981 / Malaco ◆◆◆◆
The initial step in Hill's amazing rebirth as a contemporary blues star, courtesy of Jackson, MS', Malaco Records and producers Tommy Couch and Wolf Stephenson. The vicious blues outings "Bump and Grind" and "Blue Monday" were the first salvos fired by Hill at the blues market, though much of the set—"Please Don't Make Me (Do Something Bad to You)," "I'm So Lonesome I Could Cry"—was solidly in the Southern soul vein. *—Bill Dahl*

The Rhythm and The Blues / 1982 / Malaco ◆◆◆◆
Led by Hill's second immediate standard—the Denise LaSalle-penned "Someone Else Is Steppin' In"—Hill's third Malaco album was another consistent effort, if not quite the blockbuster that his previous effort was. Hill again dipped into the Little Johnny Taylor songbook for a humorous slow blues, "Open House at My House," while relying on talented songwriters George Jackson and Frank Johnson for most of his tailor-made material. *—Bill Dahl*

☆ **Down Home** / 1982 / Malaco ◆◆◆◆◆
One of the very few classic blues albums of the 1980s. Hill revitalized the genre among African-American listeners with his "Down Home Blues," which earned instant standard status. But the entire album is tremendously consistent, with the percolating R&B workouts "Givin' It Up for Your Love" and "Right Arm for Your Love" contrasting with an intimate "Cheatin' in the Next Room" and the straightahead blues "Everybody Knows About My Good Thing" and "When It Rains It Pours." *—Bill Dahl*

I'm a Blues Man / 1983 / Malaco ◆◆◆◆
Fueled by more impressive material from the pens of Jackson, Johnson, and LaSalle, Hill was in an amazing groove during the years prior to his untimely demise, and the crack Malaco house band was certainly up to the task. Just like the title track ably demonstrated, Z.Z. Hill had indeed rechristened himself as a blues man of the first order. *—Bill Dahl*

★ **In Memorium (1935-1984)** / 1985 / Malaco ◆◆◆◆◆
Most of the highlights of Hill's glorious blues-singing stint at Malaco, although the individual albums possess more than their share of worthwhile moments that aren't here. But with hallowed titles like "Down Home Blues," "Someone Else Is Slippin' In," and "Everybody Knows About My Good Thing," this stunning collection neatly summarizes Hill's heartwarming rise to blues power. *—Bill Dahl*

The Down Home Soul of Z.Z. Hill / 1992 / Kent ◆◆◆◆
Before Hill made his sensational 1980s comeback as a blues growler, he sang a slightly sweeter brand of West Coast soul during the mid-'60s at Kent. Under saxist Maxwell Davis' supervision, Hill waxed a series of magnificent R&B ballads—"Happiness Is All I Need," "I Need Someone (to Love Me)"—that should have hit but inexplicably didn't. Gathered on one 22-track import disc, they sound terrific in retrospect. *—Bill Dahl*

The Complete Hill Records Collection/United Artists Recordings 1972-1975 / 1996 / Capitol ◆◆◆◆
The gritty singer made three albums for United Artists (mostly under his brother Matt's supervision) from 1972 to 1975, and they were an idiomatically mixed bag. All three LPs are housed in their entirety on this two-disc set, its selections ranging from the deep soul sincerity of "I've Got to Get You Back" and "Your Love Makes Me Feel Good" and the country-soul hybrids "You're Killing You (Slowly But Surely)" and "Country Love" to the funky Lamont Dozier-produced "I Created a Monster" and an Allen Toussaint-supervised "I Keep on Lovin' You." *—Bill Dahl*

Love Is So Good When You're Stealing It / 1996 / Ichiban Soul Classics ◆◆◆

Dave Hole

Guitar, Vocals
Slide guitarist Dave Hole played 20 years in remote western Australian towns before making *Short Fuse Blues*, an album he financed, produced and recorded with his band, Short Fuse, in three days around 1990. He then hawked the album during club performances. On a whim he sent a copy to *Guitar Player* magazine in the US. The editor listened to it, liked it, wrote a praise-filled article hailing him as the newest guitar wizard and comparing him to such greats as Stevie Ray Vaughan and Albert King. He then helped Hole land a distribution deal with Alligator Records.

As a performer, Hole is noted for his energetic, high-volume rock 'n' roll/blues music and unusual playing style. Though left-handed, Hole plays right-handed guitar and instead of fretting the usual way, developed a technique to compensate for a finger injury in which he places his fingers over the top of the neck. He also uses a pick for a slide and when playing normally utilizes finger picking. *—Sandra Brennan*

Short Fuse Blues / 1992 / Alligator ◆◆◆
Dave Hole's American debut album is a stunning display of slide guitar pyrotechnics. Hole runs through a dizzying array of licks and solos, pulling out a variety of different tones and textures from his guitar. He can play it straight and greasy or spooky, tough, and gritty or subtle and melodic—his technique is quite impressive. Although the songs themselves are occasionally weak, *Short Fuse Blues* is essentially a guitar record, so the songs don't matter as much as the playing. And the playing is superb throughout. *—Thom Owens*

● **Working Overtime** / 1993 / Alligator ◆◆◆◆
Hole's second disc features nine original compositions and covers of Muddy Waters and Big Bill Broonzy, rendered in a vocal and guitar style somewhat similar to Johnny Winter's best blues work but with an edge of youthful vigor. "Biting slide guitar work" is an understatement. Hole can also play the thoughtful Roy Buchanan card on the likes of "Berwick Road." *—Roch Parisien*

Steel on Steel / 1995 / Alligator ◆◆◆
With his third album, *Steel on Steel*, Dave Hole turns in another set of ready-made originals and covers, all highlighted by his sizzling slide guitar work. *—Stephen Thomas Erlewine*

The Holmes Brothers

Group / Soul, R&B, Modern Electric Blues
The Holmes Brothers' unique synthesis of gospel-inflected blues harmonies, accompanied by good drumming and rhythm-based guitar playing, gives them a down-home rural feeling that no other touring blues group can duplicate.

Brothers Sherman and Wendell Holmes, along with drummer Popsy Dixo, (the falsetto voice), are the group's core members, although they occasionally tour with extra musicians. All three harmonize well together. The Holmes Brothers are so versatile, they're booked solid every summer at folk, blues, gospel, and jazz festivals, as they play a style of music that is a gumbo of church tunes, blue, and soul. Although people like Bo Diddley and especially Jimmy Reed were early influences on Wendell and Sherman, gospel music also played an important role in their respective upbringings.

Although they'd been performing in Harlem for years, the Holmes Brothers—originally from Christchurch, VA—have only recently become international blues touring stars. Thanks to a fair deal at Rounder Records, the group has released three recordings for that label, beginning with a 1989 release, *In the Spirit*. When this album made waves and got them off and running on the festival and club circuit around the US and Europe, they followed it up two years later with *That's Where It's At* (1991) and then *Soul Street* (1993).

The group's career has been aided by the interest of people like Peter Gabriel, who recruited them for his WOMAD (world music) Festivals in England and who also recorded them in a gospel context on the album *Jubilation*, for his Real World subsidiary of Virgin Records in 1992. *—Richard Skelly*

In the Spirit / 1990 / Rounder ◆◆◆◆
The Holmes Brothers' voices are too potent, their harmonies too smashing, and their love of vintage sounds too immense for them to be content with producer-dominated, softer urban contemporary sounds. This set includes some riveting gospel tunes like "None But the Righteous" and "Up Above My Head," plus a credible (if a little lengthy) version of "When Something Is Wrong with My Baby" and the tighter, hard-hitting tunes "Please Don't Hurt Me," "Ask Me No Questions" and "The Final Round." If straighahead, rousing shared leads and booming harmonies interest you, the Holmes Brothers do it the way they used to throughout the South in the '60s and '70s. *—Ron Wynn*

Where It's At / 1991 / Rounder ◆◆◆◆
Their second release contains 11 more wonderful tunes that easily move from surging R&B to rousing blues with an occasional venture

into gospel or country. They cover "Drown in My Own Tears" and "High Heel Sneakers" and have the requisite qualities for each one down pat, as well as "Never Let Me Go," "The Love You Save" and "I Saw the Light." But their own numbers, like "I've Been a Loser" and the title track, are even better, displaying a contemporary sensibility and classic style and sound. *—Ron Wynn*

● **Soul Street** / 1993 / Rounder ✦✦✦✦
This album continues the Holmes Brothers' tradition of doing tremendous covers ("You're Gonna Make Me Cry," "Down in Virginia" and "Fannie Mae"), and authentic originals ("I Won't Hurt You Anymore," "Dashboard Bar") and adding gospel ("Walk in the Light") and honky-tonk ("There Goes My Everything") to their blend. There's little to criticize about the Holmes Brothers; their sound, vocals, and harmonies aren't laid-back or restrained, and everything they sing is done with exuberance and integrity. It may not be commercially viable, but it's musically sound. *—Ron Wynn*

Earl Hooker (Earl Zebedee Hooker)

b. Jan. 15, 1930, Clarksdale, MS, d. Apr. 21, 1970, Chicago, IL
Guitar, Vocals / Electric Chicago Blues
If there was a more immaculate slide guitarist residing in Chicago during the 1950s and '60s than Earl Hooker, his name has yet to surface. Boasting a fretboard touch so smooth and clean that every note rang as clear and precise as a bell, Hooker was an endlessly inventive axeman who would likely have been a star had his modest vocal abilities matched his instrumental prowess and had he not been dogged by tuberculosis (it killed him at age 41).
Born in the Mississippi Delta, Hooker arrived in Chicago as a child. There he was influenced by another slide wizard, veteran Robert Nighthawk. But Hooker never remained still for long. He ran away from home at age 13, journeying to Mississippi. After another stint in Chicago, he rambled back to the Delta again, playing with Ike Turner and Sonny Boy Williamson. Hooker made his first recordings in 1952 and 1953 for Rockin', King, and Sun. At the latter, he recorded some terrific sides with pianist Pinetop Perkins (Sam Phillips inexplicably sat on Hooker's blazing rendition of "The Hucklebuck").
Back in Chicago, Hooker's dazzling dexterity was intermittently showcased on singles for Argo, C.J., and Bea & Baby during the mid-to-late '50s before he joined forces with producer Mel London (owner of the Chief and Age logos) in 1959. For the next four years, he recorded both as sideman and leader for the producer, backing Junior Wells, Lillian Offitt, Ricky Allen, and A.C. Reed and cutting his own sizzling instrumentals ("Blue Guitar," "Blues in D-Natural"). He also contributed pungent slide work to Muddy Waters' Chess waxing "You Shook Me." Opportunities to record grew sparse after Age folded, but Hooker made some tantalizing sides for Sauk City, WI's, Cuca Records from 1964 to 1968 (several featuring steel guitar virtuoso Freddie Roulette).
Hooker's amazing prowess (he even managed to make the dreaded wah-wah pedal a viable blues tool) finally drew increased attention during the late '60s. He cut LPs for Arhoolie, ABC-BluesWay, and Blue Thumb that didn't equal what he'd done at Age, but they did serve to introduce Hooker to an audience outside Chicago and wherever his frequent travels deposited him. But tuberculosis halted his wandering ways permanently in 1970. *—Bill Dahl*

Two Bugs and a Roach / 1966 / Arhoolie ✦✦✦✦
A nice representative sample from Chicago's unsung master of the electric guitar, it includes the title track, "Anna Lee," and the atmospheric instrumental, "Off the Hook." *—Bruce Lee Pearson*

● **Blue Guitar** / 1981 / Paula/Flyright ✦✦✦✦
The slide guitar wizard's immaculate fretwork was never captured more imaginatively than during his early-'60s stay with Mel London's Age/Chief labels. Twenty-one fascinating tracks from that period include Hooker's savage instrumentals "Blue Guitar," "Off the Hook," "The Leading Brand," "Blues in D Natural," and "How Long Can This Go On," along with tracks by A.C. Reed, Lillian Offitt, and Harold Tidwell that cast Hooker as a standout sideman. *—Bill Dahl*

Play Your Guitar, Mr. Hooker / 1985 / Black Top ✦✦✦
1964-1967 output by the guitarist that was largely done for the tiny Cuca logo of Sauk City, WI. The normally tight-lipped Hooker proves that he could sing on this romping version of "Swear to Tell the Truth," while A.C. Reed, Little Tommy, Frank Clark, and Muddy Waters, Jr. help out behind the mike elsewhere. A pair of live cuts from 1968 find Hooker stretching out in amazing fashion. *—Bill Dahl*

John Lee Hooker

b. Aug. 17, 1920, Clarksdale, MS
Guitar, Vocals / R&B, Electric Delta Blues, Acoustic Delta Blues
He's beloved worldwide as the king of the endless boogie, a genuine blues superstar whose droning, hypnotic one-chord grooves are at once

both ultra-primitive and timeless. But John Lee Hooker has recorded in a great many more styles than that over a career that stretches back more than half a century.
The Hook is a Mississippi native who became the top gent on the Detroit blues circuit in the years following World War II. The seeds for his eerily mournful guitar sound were planted by his stepfather, Will Moore, while Hooker was in his teens. Hooker had been singing spirituals before that, but the blues took hold and simply wouldn't let go. Overnight visitors left their mark on the youth, too—legends like Blind Lemon Jefferson, Charlie Patton, and Blind Blake, who all knew Moore.
Hooker heard Memphis calling while he was still in his teens, but he couldn't gain much of a foothold there. So he relocated to Cincinnati for a seven-year stretch before making the big move to the Motor City in 1943. Jobs were plentiful, but Hooker drifted away from day gigs in favor of playing his unique free-form brand of blues. A burgeoning club scene along Hastings Street didn't hurt his chances any.
In 1948, the aspiring bluesman hooked up with entrepreneur Bernie Besman, who helped him hammer out his solo debut sides, "Sally Mae" and its seminal flip, "Boogie Chillen." This was blues as primitive as anything then on the market; Hooker's dark, ruminative vocals were backed only by his own ringing, heavily amplified guitar and insistently pounding foot. Their efforts were quickly rewarded. Los Angeles-based Modern Records issued the sides and "Boogie Chillen"—a colorful, unique travelogue of Detroit's blues scene—made an improbable jaunt to the very peak of the R&B charts.
Modern released several more major hits by the Boogie Man after that: "Hobo Blues" and its raw-as-an-open wound flip, "Hoogie Boogie"; "Crawling King Snake Blues" (all three 1949 smashes), and the unusual 1951 chart-topper "I'm in the Mood," where Hooker overdubbed his voice three times in a crude early attempt at multi-tracking.
But Hooker never, ever let something as meaningless as a contract stop him for making recordings for other labels. His early catalog is stretched across a roadmap of diskeries so complex that it's nearly impossible to fully comprehend (a vast array of recording aliases don't make things any easier).
Along with Modern, Hooker recorded for King (as the geographically challenged Texas Slim), Regent (as Delta John, a far more accurate handle), Savoy (as the wonderfully surreal Birmingham Sam and his Magic Guitar), Danceland (as the downright delicious Little Pork Chops), Staff (as Johnny Williams), Sensation (for whom he scored a national hit in 1950 with "Huckle Up, Baby"), Gotham, Regal, Swing Time, Federal, Gone (as John Lee Booker), Chess, Acorn (as the Boogie Man), Chance, DeLuxe (as Johnny Lee), JVB, Chart, and Specialty before finally settling down at Vee-Jay in 1955 under his own name. Hooker became the point man for the growing Detroit blues scene during this incredibly prolific period, recruiting guitarist Eddie Kirkland as his frequent duet partner while still recording for Modern.
Once tied in with Vee-Jay, the rough-and-tumble sound of Hooker's solo and duet waxings was adapted to a band format. Hooker had recorded with various combos along the way before, but never with sidemen as versatile and sympathetic as guitarist Eddie Taylor and harpist Jimmy Reed, who backed him at his initial Vee-Jay date that produced "Time Is Marching" and the superfluous sequel "Mambo Chillun."
Taylor stuck around for a 1956 session that elicited two genuine Hooker classics, "Baby Lee" and "Dimples," and he was still deftly anchoring the rhythm section (Hooker's sense of timing was his and his alone, demanding big-eared sidemen) when the Boogie Man finally made it back to the R&B charts in 1958 with "I Love You Honey."
Vee-Jay presented Hooker in quite an array of settings during the early '60s. His grinding, tough blues "No Shoes" proved a surprisingly sizable hit in 1960, while the storming "Boom Boom," his top seller for the label in 1962 (it even cracked the pop airwaves), was an infectious R&B dance number benefiting from the reported presence of some of Motown's house musicians. But there were also acoustic outings aimed squarely at the blossoming folk-blues crowd, as well as some attempts at up-to-date R&B that featured highly intrusive female background vocals (allegedly by the Vandellas) and utterly unyielding structures that hemmed Hooker in unmercifully.
British blues bands such as the Animals and Yardbirds idolized Hooker during the early '60s; Eric Burdon's boys cut a credible 1964 cover of "Boom Boom" that outsold Hooker's original on the American pop charts. Hooker visited Europe in 1962 under the auspices of the first American Folk Blues Festival, leaving behind the popular waxings "Let's Make It" and "Shake It Baby" for foreign consumption.
Back home, Hooker cranked out gems for Vee-Jay through 1964 ("Big Legs, Tight Skirt," one of his last offerings on the logo, was also one of his best), before undergoing another extended round of label-hopping (except this time, he was waxing whole LPs instead of scattered 78s). Verve-Folkways, Impulse, Chess, and BluesWay all enticed him into recording for them in 1965-66 alone! His reputation among hip rock cognoscenti in the States and abroad was growing exponentially, espe-

cially after he teamed up with blues-rockers Canned Heat for the massively selling album *Hooker 'n' Heat* in 1970.

Eventually, though, the endless boogie formula grew incredibly stagnant. Much of Hooker's 1970s output found him laying back while plodding rock-rooted rhythm sections assumed much of the work load. A cameo in the 1980 movie *The Blues Brothers* was welcome, if far too short.

But Hooker wasn't through—not by a long shot. With the expert help of slide guitarist extraordinaire/producer Roy Rogers, the Hook waxed *The Healer*, an album that marked the first of his guest star-loaded albums (Carlos Santana, Bonnie Raitt, and Robert Cray were among the luminaries to cameo on the disc, which picked up a Grammy).

Major labels were just beginning to take notice of the growing demand for blues records, and Pointblank snapped Hooker up, releasing *Mr. Lucky* (this time teaming Hooker with everyone from Albert Collins and John Hammond to Van Morrison and Keith Richards). Once again, Hooker was resting on his laurels by allowing his guests to wrest much of the spotlight away from him on his own album, but by then, he'd earned it. Another Pointblank set, *Boom Boom*, soon followed.

Happily, Hooker is now enjoying the good life. He's in semi-retirement, splitting his relaxation time between several houses he's acquired up and down the California coast. Baseball also takes up much of his interest during the summer months; he's an inveterate Dodger fan. When the right offer comes along, though, he takes it, as that amusing TV commercial for Pepsi indicates.

The King of the Boogie is also one of the last living links to the prewar blues tradition. He's a true original. —*Bill Dahl*

Everybody's Blues / 1950-1954 / Specialty ✦✦✦

House of the Blues / 1960 / MCA/Chess ✦✦✦✦
Verbatim CD reissue of a 1959 Chess album that collected 1951-1954 efforts by the Hook. Some important titles here: an ominous "Leave My Wife Alone," the stark "Sugar Mama" and "Ramblin' by Myself," and with Eddie Kirkland on second guitar, "Louise" and "High Priced Woman." —*Bill Dahl*

The Country Blues of John Lee Hooker / Jan. 1960 / Riverside ✦✦✦
Hooker was still churning out R&B-influenced electric blues with a rhythm section for Vee-Jay when he recorded this, his first LP packaged for the folk/traditional blues market. He plays nothing but acoustic guitar, and seems to have selected a repertoire with old-school country blues in mind. It's unimpressive only within the context of Hooker's body of work; in comparison with other solo outings, the guitar sounds thin, and the approach restrained. —*Richie Unterberger*

Plays and Sings the Blues / 1961 / MCA/Chess ✦✦✦✦
A 1961 Chess album restored to digital print by MCA that's filled with 1951-1952 gems from the Hook's heyday. Chess originally bought "Mad Man Blues" and "Hey Boogie" from the Gone label; the rest first came out on Chess during Hooker's frenzied early days of recording, when his platters turned up on nearly every R&B indie label existant at the time. —*Bill Dahl*

Dont Turn Me from Your Door / 1963 / Atlantic ✦✦✦

John Lee Hooker at Newport / 1964 / Vee-Jay ✦✦✦✦
Arguably his finest live date, this was John Lee Hooker minus the self-congratulatory mugging now an almost mandatory part of his sets. Instead, there's just lean, straight, defiant Hooker vocals and minimal, but effective backing. —*Ron Wynn*

The Real Folk Blues / 1966 / MCA/Chess ✦✦✦
Although the great majority of the albums in Chess' *Real Folk Blues* series were vintage compilations, this disc was cut in 1966 with longtime cohort Eddie Burns on second guitar and an uncredited band behind him. Not exactly essential in Hooker's personal pantheon, but decent nonetheless. —*Bill Dahl*

Simply the Truth / 1969 / Bluesway ✦✦✦

That's Where It's At! / 1969 / Stax ✦✦✦
A characteristic solo outing with moody compositions and that doomy one-electric-guitar-and-stomping-foot ambience. One of his sparer and more menacing post-'50s outings, highlighted by "Two White Horses" and a seven-minute "Feel So Bad," which features extended verbal sparring with an unidentified male partner. —*Richie Unterberger*

Hooker 'n' Heat / 1971 / EMI America ✦✦✦
Probably no other White blues band took John Lee Hooker's boogie rhythms and made a career out of it as much as Canned Heat. It was certainly inevitable that the two forces would unite for a joint recording project and this double CD package (recorded in 1970 and originally a double album) is the delightful result. Canned Heat certainly knew what they were going after, as Hooker brandishes a mean guitar tone that hadn't surfaced since his early Detroit recordings. Surprisingly, Canned Heat hangs back a bit as over half the material are riveting solo recordings, with the full band only coming in as support on the second half. Compare this with most of his '70s recordings for Bluesway (now MCA)

and you'll quickly realize that these sides contain some of his most cohesive work with a band, ever. —*Cub Koda*

The Healer / 1989 / Chameleon ✦✦
The Healer was a major comeback for John Lee Hooker. Featuring a wide array of guest stars, including Bonnie Raitt, Keith Richards, Johnnie Johnson, and Los Lobos, *The Healer* captured widespread media attention because of all the superstar musicians involved in its production. Unfortunately, that long guest list is what makes the album a fairly unengaging listen. Certainly there are moments where it clicks, but that's usually when the music doesn't greatly expand on his stripped-down boogie. The other moments are professional, but not exciting. It's a pleasant listen, but never quite an engaging one. —*Thom Owens*

★ **The Ultimate Collection (1948-1990)** / 1991 / Rhino ✦✦✦✦✦
The single best place to begin appreciating the Boogie Man's incredible contributions to the blues lexicon, since it surveys a wide cross-section of labels and eras. Disc one contains "Boogie Chillen," "Sally Mae," "Huckle Up Baby," "I'm in the Mood," "Dimples," and "It Serves Me Right." The second spottier CD sports "Boom Boom," "One Bourbon, One Scotch, One Beer," a snarling "I'm Bad like Jesse James," and an utterly superfluous finale with Bonnie Raitt from a Showtime TV program. At only 31 songs, it could unequivocally be longer, but this anthology serves as a convenient spot for the neophyte to delve into Hookerology. —*Bill Dahl*

More Real Folk Blues: The Missing Album / Sep. 10, 1991 / MCA/Chess ✦✦✦

The Best of John Lee Hooker 1965-1974 / 1992 / MCA ✦✦✦
MCA's *The Best of John Lee Hooker* has a misleading title. All of the 16 selections are taken from his recordings for ABC, which were made at the end of the '60s and beginning of the '70s. During this time, his producers were experimenting with his sound, adding contemporary sonic touches like funk rhythms and wah-wah pedals. Needless to say, this sound didn't sit particularly well with Hooker's lean, haunting blues. However, these songs do take the best material from generally poor albums—anyone who wants to sample his ABC material should turn here first and they'll realize that they don't need to explore much further. —*Thom Owens*

Graveyard Blues / 1992 / Specialty ✦✦✦✦
At the beginning of his career, Hooker's sides were leased to several different labels. This 20-song anthology of material from the late '40s and early '50s was originally released on the Sensation and Specialty labels; while the track listings indicate a timespan of 1948-50, the liner notes say that much of it was recorded in 1954. Doesn't anyone proofread these things? Anyway, this was mostly recorded solo, and boasts his characteristic spooky electric minimalist boogie sound. *The Legendary Modern Recordings*, covering the same era, is a better place to start for this kind of thing due to its stronger content. If you want more of the same, though, this (and Capitol's *Alternative Boogie*) is the next stop. —*Richie Unterberger*

On Vee-Jay 1955-1958 / 1993 / Vee-Jay ✦✦✦✦
Some of Hooker's finest recordings with a band were also some of his first recordings with a band. The unpredictable guitarist seemed to mesh well with guitarist Eddie Taylor, harpist Jimmy Reed, and the rest of the sidemen he was given on his 1955-58 Vee-Jay output. Includes the classic "Baby Lee" and "Dimples," along with 20 more that crackle with electricity. —*Bill Dahl*

★ **The Legendary Modern Recordings 1948-1954** / 1994 / Virgin ✦✦✦✦✦
From the beginning of his career, Hooker recorded prolifically, sometimes for several labels at once, sometimes under a number of pseudonyms. That makes his discography a bit difficult for the collector to sort out, but if you want just one document of his early years, this is the anthology of choice, containing 24 sides from 1948 to 1954 that were issued on the Modern label. These, more than any other, are the recordings that did the most to establish the Hooker prototype—the overamplified electric guitar, the moody boogies, the stomping foot rhythms, performed without a rhythm section (some sides feature accompaniment by Eddie Kirkland on second guitar). Contains his two most massive early hits, "Boogie Chillen" and "I'm in the Mood," as well as his oft-covered "Crawling Kingsnake." This one can get a bit similar-sounding over the course of two dozen tracks, but little other post-war electric blues can match the stark power here. —*Richie Unterberger*

☆ **The Early Years** / 1994 / Tomato ✦✦✦✦✦
Hooker's voluminous output for Vee-Jay Records is scattered across numerous compilations. This double CD contains 31 songs spanning the mid-'50s to the mid-'60s, and is probably the most extensive and satisfying retrospective of his Vee-Jay work (at least domestically). That's not to say it's perfectly assembled; Tomato, as usual, declines to include trimmings like songwriter credits, although Pete Welding's liner notes do (unlike most Tomato releases) provide dates and discuss the sessions in some detail. Hooker's Vee-Jay material was in most ways the most commercially minded of his early efforts, often employing a rhythm section

and R&B-influenced arrangements, and occasionally using horns. It's sometimes been said that this approach diluted Hooker's strengths, but one listen to this collection refutes that notion soundly. This is by and large prime Hooker, with some of his best (and best-selling) songs, like "Boom Boom," "Dimples," "I'm So Excited," and "One Bourbon, One Scotch, One Beer." Hooker may have sometimes sounded a bit ill at ease with a band, but he usually worked with backing musicians very well. Non-purists will find these tracks to be some of his most accessible and dynamic performances. —*Richie Unterberger*

Chill Out / 1995 / Pointblank ✦✦
Chill Out isn't the superstar blowout of John Lee Hooker's late-'80s albums, yet it retains that flavor. Featuring some extended soloing from Carlos Santana, *Chill Out* is filled with long blues workouts, all captured in pristine, state-of-the-art technology. Nothing on the disc captures the raw vitality of Hooker's prime material—it's all relaxed blues-rock jams. The clean, sterile production doesn't help the basically directionless music. Certainly nothing on *Chill Out* is outright bad; in fact, most of it is pleasant, yet few of the songs on the album warrant repeated listens. —*Stephen Thomas Erlewine*

★ **Very Best Of** / Apr. 25, 1995 / Rhino ✦✦✦✦✦
The Very Best of John Lee Hooker provides a definitive introduction to the seminal bluesman, presenting over 15 classic tracks in their original hit versions. —*Stephen Thomas Erlewine*

Alternative Boogie: Early Studio Recordings 1948-1952 / Oct. 24, 1995 / Capitol ✦✦✦✦
A whopping three CDs, and 56 songs, from Hooker's early sessions that were unreleased at the time, although they were available for a while in the early 1970s on some United Artists LPs. Like his more widely known material of the period, it mostly features Hooker unaccompanied, though he's aided by piano and second guitarists on a few tracks. Some of these are alternates of songs that were released in different versions, or embryonic renditions of compositions that evolved into somewhat different shapes. Especially interesting are early versions of his big hit "I'm in the Mood." It's too much at once, though, and too unvarying in approach, for anyone but Hooker specialists. General fans are advised to stick with *The Legendary Modern Recordings*, which has 24 more renowned, and somewhat more accomplished, tracks from the same era. It's certainly a well-done package, though, containing a 38-page insert with detailed liner notes and session information. —*Richie Unterberger*

The Best of Hooker 'n' Heat / 1996 / EMI ✦✦✦
These ten songs were originally released as part of a 1971 album (on Liberty 35002); this reissue, despite the lack of historical liner notes, isn't exactly short value, clocking in at 56 minutes. Canned Heat gets top billing, but really it's Hooker's show, as he sings all the tracks and takes all the songwriting credits for the material, which includes remakes of classics like "Dimples," "Boogie Chillen," "Burning Hell," and "Bottle Up and Go." With Hooker fronting a White blues-rock-boogie group, this doesn't offer the optimum circumstances to hear the man. But it's not bad either, Canned Heat playing with spirit and relative economy, although the 11-minute "Boogie Chillen" is excessive. —*Richie Unterberger*

Lightnin' Hopkins (Sam Hopkins)

b. Mar. 15, 1912, Centerville, TX, d. Jan. 30, 1982, Houston, TX
Organ, Guitar, Piano, Vocals / Electric Texas Blues, Acoustic Texas Blues
Sam Hopkins was a Texas country bluesman of the highest caliber whose career began in the 1920s and stretched all the way into the 1980s. Along the way, Hopkins watched the genre change remarkably, but he never appreciably altered his mournful Lone Star sound, which translated onto both acoustic and electric guitar. Hopkins's nimble dexterity made intricate boogie riffs seem easy, and his fascinating penchant for improvising lyrics to fit whatever situation might arise made him a beloved blues troubadour.

Hopkins's brothers John Henry and Joel were also talented bluesmen, but it was Sam that became a star. In 1920, he met the legendary Blind Lemon Jefferson at a social function, and even got a chance to play with him. Later, Hopkins served as Jefferson's guide. In his teens, Hopkins began working with another pre-war great, singer Texas Alexander, who was his cousin. A mid-'30s stretch in Houston's County Prison Farm for the young guitarist interrupted their partnership for a time, but when he was freed, Hopkins hooked back up with the older bluesman.

The pair was dishing out their lowdown brand of blues in Houston's Third Ward in 1946 when talent scout Lola Anne Cullum came across them. She had already engineered a pact with Los Angeles-based Aladdin Records for another of her charges, pianist Amos Milburn, and Cullum saw the same sort of opportunity within Hopkins' dusty country blues. Alexander wasn't part of the deal; instead, Cullum paired Hopkins with pianist Wilson "Thunder" Smith, sensibly rechristened the guitarist Lightnin', and presto! Hopkins was very soon an Aladdin recording artist. "Katie May," cut on November 9, 1946, in L.A. with Smith lending a hand on the 88s, was Lightnin' Hopkins' first regional

seller of note. He recorded prolifically for Aladdin in both L.A. and Houston into 1948, scoring a national R&B hit with his "Shotgun Blues." "Short Haired Woman," "Abilene," and "Big Mama Jump," among many Aladdin gems, were evocative Texas blues rooted in an earlier era.

A load of other labels recorded the wily Hopkins after that, both in a solo context and with a small rhythm section—Modern/RPM (his uncompromising "Tim Moore's Farm" was an R&B hit in 1949), Gold Star (where he hit with "T-Model Blues" that same year), Sittin' in With ("Give Me Central 209" and "Coffee Blues" were national chart entries in 1952) and its Jax subsidiary, the major labels Mercury and Decca, and in 1954, a remarkable batch of sides for Herald where Hopkins played blistering electric guitar on a series of blasting rockers ("Lightnin's Boogie," "Lightnin's Special," the amazing "Hopkins' Sky Hop") in front of drummer Ben Turner and bassist Donald Cooks (who must have had bleeding fingers, so torrid were some of the tempos).

But Hopkins' style was apparently too rustic and old-fashioned for the new generation of rock 'n' roll enthusiasts (they should have checked out "Hopkins' Sky Hop"). He was back on the Houston scene by 1959, largely forgotten. Fortunately, folklorist Mack McCormick rediscovered the guitarist, who was dusted off and presented as a folk-blues artist—a role that Hopkins was born to play. Pioneering musicologist Sam Charters produced Hopkins in a solo context for Folkways Records that same year, cutting an entire LP in Hopkins' tiny apartment (on a borrowed guitar). The results helped introduced his music to an entirely new audience.

Lightnin' Hopkins went from gigging at back-alley gin joints to starring at collegiate coffeehouses, appearing on TV programs and touring Europe to boot. His once-flagging recording career went right through the roof, with albums for World Pacific, Vee-Jay, Bluesville, Bobby Robinson's Fire label (where he cut his classic "Mojo Hand" in 1960), Candid, Arhoolie, Prestige, Verve, and in 1965, the first of several LPs for Stan Lewis' Shreveport-based Jewel logo.

Hopkins generally demanded full payment before he'd deign to sit down and record, and seldom indulged a producer's desire for more than one take of any song. His singular sense of country time befuddled more than a few unseasoned musicians; from the 1960s on, his solo work is usually preferable to band-backed material.

Filmmaker Les Blank captured the Texas troubadour's informal lifestyle most vividly in his acclaimed 1967 documentary, *The Blues Accordin' to Lightnin' Hopkins*. As one of the last great country bluesmen, Hopkins was a fascinating figure who bridged the gap between rural and urban styles. —*Bill Dahl*

Blues Train / 1951 / Mainstream ✦✦✦✦
Classic sides from Hopkins' 1950-1951 stint with Bobby Shad's Sittin' In With logo. The disc's 15 selections include two of his biggest hits, "Hello Central" and "Coffee Blues." —*Bill Dahl*

Lightnin' Hopkins / 1959 / Smithsonian/Folkways ✦✦✦✦
Lightnin' Hopkins was a master storyteller, underrated guitarist, and marvelous performer whose albums could be irritating, inspirational, or uneven, but were seldom predictable or tepid. This 1959 session, reissued without bonus cuts or alternate takes, has mostly short, crisply narrated anecdotes or songs with ironic resolutions sung in Hopkins' usual declarative, wry tone. His "Reminiscences of Blind Lemon" spins one of his wonderful yarns, while "See That My Grave Is Clean" and "Bad Luck and Trouble" pivot around his sparse guitar and emphatic, dry vocals. —*Ron Wynn*

How Many More Years I Got / 1962 / Fantasy ✦✦✦
Repackaging of three albums, *Walkin' This Road by Myself*, *Lightnin' & Co.* and *Smokes like Lightnin'*. Lightnin' plays electric with small band support on these, which probably come the closest to what he sounded like in the juke joints around Houston in the early '60s. —*Cub Koda*

Blue Lightnin' / 1965 / Jewel ✦✦✦

The Herald Material 1954 / 1988 / Collectables ✦✦✦✦
Lightnin' Hopkins in a heavily amplified mode (especially for 1954!) and tearing it up with some of the wildest licks of his long and storied career! It's hard to fathom a more torrid tempo than the one he employs for "Hopkins' Sky Hop," and "Flash Lightnin'," "Lightnin's Boogie," and "Lightnin' Stomp" aren't far behind. Alas, Hopkins' Herald waxings didn't sell particularly well—though they're downright astonishing in retrospect. —*Bill Dahl*

The Herald Recordings, Vol. 2 / 1989 / Collectables ✦✦✦✦
Hopkins left a ton of tapes behind at New York-based Herald Records—enough to support this second volume of 1954 gems. —*Bill Dahl*

Gold Star Sessions, Vol. 1 / 1991 / Arhoolie ✦✦✦✦
The first of two discs devoted to Hopkins' extensive recording activities during the late '40s for Bill Quinn's Gold Star logo. —*Bill Dahl*

Gold Star Sessions, Vol. 2 / 1991 / Arhoolie ✦✦✦✦
More wonderfully sparse ruminations by the Texas blues troubadour for Quinn's Gold Star label. Hopkins was amazingly prolific during his first

few years of recording, and nearly everything he did back then has great artistic merit. —*Bill Dahl*

☆ **The Complete Aladdin Recordings** / 1991 / Aladdin/EMI ✦✦✦✦✦
This is where it all began for the Houston troubadour: 43 solo sides, as evocative and stark as any he ever did, from 1946-1948. The first 13 sides find the guitarist in tandem with pianist Wilson "Thunder" Smith (who handles the vocals on a few tracks), but after that, old Lightnin' Hopkins went the solo route. "Katie May," "Short Haired Woman," "Abilene," "Shotgun"—all these and more rate with his seminal performances. —*Bill Dahl*

☆ **Complete Prestige/Bluesville Recordings** / 1991 / Bluesville ✦✦✦✦✦
This seven-disc boxed set of Hopkins' complete Prestige/Bluesville recordings includes Sam Charters' brilliant liner notes. —*Jas Obrecht*

Sittin' In With / 1992 / Mainstream ✦✦✦✦
The second installment of Sittin' in With masters, some with bassist Donald Cooks and drummer Connie Kroll providing rock-solid support (L.C. Williams takes over as vocalist for two cuts). Supple boogies and dusty rural blues, all woven expertly by the Texas guitarist. —*Bill Dahl*

Houston Bound / 1993 / Relic ✦✦✦✦
Thirteen of the last sides he cut for his former R&B audience. Under Bobby Robinson's tutelage, Hopkins' 1960 Fire sides rank with his finest—especially his boogie-based "Mojo Hand," a title he subsequently remade early and often. —*Bill Dahl*

★ **Mojo Hand: The Anthology** / May 18, 1993 / Rhino ✦✦✦✦✦
As with its John Lee Hooker two-disc set, Rhino offers a very pleasant way to begin serious appreciation of Hopkins' humongous recorded legacy with this 41-track anthology. His Aladdin, Gold Star, RPM, Sittin' in With, and Mercury output are all liberally sampled on disc one, and there are a half dozen of those electrifying 1954 Herald sides that verged on rock 'n' roll. Disc two is a less exciting affair, those 1960s folk-blues and later efforts usually paling in comparison to seminal early work. Still, for a cogent overview of the guitarist's daunting discography, this is the place to start. —*Bill Dahl*

Big Walter "Shakey" Horton

b. Apr. 6, 1917, Horn Lake, MS, **d.** Dec. 8, 1981, Chicago, IL
Harmonica, Vocals / Electric Chicago Blues, Electric Blues
Big Walter "Shakey" Horton is one of the all-time great blues harp (harmonica) players. Along with Little Walter, Horton defined modern amplified Chicago-style harmonica. There is no harp player (and that includes Little Walter) with Horton's big tone and spacious sense of time. Horton (who is said to have been somewhat shy) was not a natural group leader and therefore has produced few solo albums. His best work is as a sideman; his backup harmonica and virtuoso harp solos have graced many great Chicago blues recordings—turning an otherwise good cut into a dynamite jam.

Walter is the master of the single note and his characteristic walking bass line (usually with a deep tone and selection of notes that is unsurpassed) is instantly recognizable. As an accompanist, he has few equals. His backup harp is always unobtrusive yet bright and fresh—enhancing whatever else is going on. Give Big Walter a chance to solo and you are in for some of the most tasteful lines Chicago-style harp has ever produced. He made a specialty of playing entire tunes (often in blues style) on the harmonica ("La Cucaracha," "Careless Love," "I Almost Lost My Mind," etc.). This might sound trite, but give them a listen. You'll see.

As for harmonicas, he used Hohner's Marine Band. He was just as comfortable playing first position (A harp in the key of A) as with the more standard cross harp (D harp in the key of A). He did not do much with chromatic harmonica. Although Big Walter could play in the style of other harp players (and was often asked to do so), he has no credible imitators. He is one of a kind.

Walter Horton was born in Horn Lake, MS, on April 6, 1917, but his mother soon moved to Memphis, where Walter taught himself how to play the harmonica at five years of age. He later learned more about his instrument by working with harp players Will Shade and Hammie Nixon.

In the late '20s, he performed and recorded with the Memphis Jug Band (1927) and generally worked the Southern dance and juke-joint circuit as well as Memphis street corners. Horton moved to Chicago in the late '40s, but was often to be found back in Memphis for recording dates with Sun and Modern/RPM. He claimed to be blowing amplified harp as early as 1940, which would make him the first. Johnny Shines recalls that Sonny Boy Williamson (Rice Miller) used to come to Walter for lessons. He also says that he used the name "Little Walter" before Little Walter Jacobs did, but gave it up to Jacobs. Jacobs acknowledges that he "ran" with Big Walter in Memphis during the 1940s. Horton later called himself "Big Walter" to distinguish himself. The term "Shakey" came from the way he moved his head while playing.

He recorded four sides in 1951 for the Modern/RPM label under the name "Mumbles," but was not fond of that moniker. It was not until

1953 that he really left Memphis and relocated to Chicago to work as a sideman with his friend Eddie Taylor. He soon joined the Muddy Waters band (replacing Junior Wells, who had been drafted into the military) and played with Muddy for about a year.

Over the next few years, Horton worked with Chicago blues artists such as Johnny Shines, Jimmy Rogers, and Otis Rush—both in the Chicago blues clubs and at record studios. He recorded with Chess, Cobra, and States throughout the 1950s. During the 1960s, Horton continued to work with Jimmy Rogers, Shines, Tampa Red, Big Mama Thornton, Robert Nighthawk, Johnny Young, and Howlin' Wolf. In the 1970s, Walter was active in the blues clubs, in recording studios, and also began to appear at blues and folk festivals—primarily with Willie Dixon's Blues All-Stars. He died in Chicago on Dec. 8, 1981, and was inducted into the Blues Foundation's Hall of Fame in 1982.

While his early acoustic recordings in Memphis (1951-1954) are excellent, it is the recordings from the late '50s and mid-'60s that are unrivaled. When Horton's music is discussed in print, often the reference is to his later albums on Blind Pig (*Can't Keep Lovin' You* and *Fine Cuts*) and Alligator (*Big Walter Horton with Carey Bell*). I don't want to take anything away from these albums, but this is not what has made Walter a legend. Here is what has:

The recording of "Easy" with guitarist Jimmy DeBerry (recorded by Sam Phillips of Sun Records in the early '50s) is a sheer instrumental that remains unrivaled for sheer power. For a superb example of Big Walter playing behind Muddy Waters (and soloing), try the cut "Mad Love (I Want You to Love Me)" that was recorded in 1953. Walter also plays on the classic Jimmy Rogers tune "Walking by Myself," on the Otis Rush tune "I Can't Quit You Baby," and many others. Also hear great Walter on the Flyright album, *Johnny Shines & Robert Lockwood, Joe Hill Louis: The Be-bop Boy* on Bear Family, *Memphis Harmonica 1951-1954* on Sun, and *The Blues Came Down from Memphis* on Charly. This last album contains the incredible instrumental, "Easy."

Walter's singing is seldom mentioned except in an apologetic way. This is something I have never understood. I love to hear Walter sing and his singing style has all the elements of his harp playing, in particular, sincerity and (above all) humor. Make a point to listen to some Big Walter songs like "Need My Baby," "Everybody's Fishin'," and "Have a Good Time." They are priceless. His original recording of "Hard Hearted Woman" on the album *Chicago Blues*—the Early Fifties (Blues Classics) never fails to raise the hair on the back of my neck. His hard-to-find first album for Chess, *The Soul of Blues Harmonica*, is also worth a listen, although not definitive.

But if you want to hear Walter at his best, pick up the Vanguard CD *Chicago/The Blues/Today!, Volume 3* and listen to the music Walter lays down. Both as backup harp and in solos, this is not only classic Big Walter, but Chicago blues at its finest—not to be missed. The music on this album is incredible—Horton's contrapuntal backup harp seems to float in the background, loping along, always stretching and opening up the time. And Horton's taste in notes and depth of tone is unparalleled in the history of amplified Chicago-style harmonica. As Willie Dixon says, "Big Walter is the best harmonica player I ever heard." I agree. He was the man. —*Michael Erlewine*

The Soul of Blues Harmonica / Jan. 13, 1964 / MCA/Chess ✦✦✦
Big Walter's first album and with an all-star cast—Buddy Guy (guitar), Jack Myers (bass), Willie Dixon (vocals), and Willie Smith (drums). Although not definitive, this album is worth seeking out for Horton fans. It features him in a variety of musical styles, including a good rendition of "Hard Hearted Woman" and a wild version of "La Cucarach." —*Michael Erlewine*

★ **Chicago/The Blues/Today!, Vol. 3** / 1967 / Vanguard ✦✦✦✦✦
One of the all-time great blues albums. Period. It features Big Walter with the Johnny Shines Blues Band, the Johnny Young South Side Blues Band, and Big Walter Horton's Blues Harp Band (with Charlie Musselwhite). The timing and sense of musical spaciousness are incredible. Walter's backup harp and harmonica solos mark a high point in his career. A must-hear. —*Michael Erlewine*

Offer You Can't Refuse [1 Side] / 1972 / Red Lightnin' ✦✦✦
An album released on the Red Lightnin' label in 1972 consisting of one side of Big Walter Horton and the other side with very early Paul Butterfield (1963) (See: Paul Butterfield). The Horton side consists of eight tracks of Horton with guitarist Robert Nighthawk (no bass or drums). Nighthawk is playing pure backup here, very little else. It is not clear when these were recorded. Perhaps not classic Walter, but any Big Walter is worth a listen. There are three instrumentals that make for good listening, including a version of "Easy" (not up to the original Walter recording). The instrumental "West Side Blues" has some interesting Walter harp licks that I have not heard elsewhere. The other five cuts are Walter singing. Of these, there is a great version of "Louise" and Walter singing of "Tin Pan Alley" which never fails to raise the hair on the back of my neck. If you can find this album, it is good to have. —*Michael Erlewine*

Live at the El Mocambo / 1973 / Red Lightnin' ✦
Recorded at the El Mocambo Club in Toronto on July 25, 1973, this is not vintage Horton. —*Michael Erlewine*

Big Walter Horton with Carey Bell / Jan. 1973 / Alligator ✦✦✦✦
The teacher/pupil angle might be a bit unwieldy here—Bell was already a formidable harpist in his own right by 1972, when Horton made this album—but there's no denying that a stylistic bond existed between the two. A showcase for the often recalcitrant harp master, and only his second domestic set as a leader. —*Bill Dahl*

Fine Cuts / Apr. 1979 / Blind Pig ✦✦✦✦
This is perhaps the best of the later Horton material from the late '70s when he was working with John Nicholas. Horton reworks many of his earlier classics including "Everybody's Fishin'," "Need My Baby," and "La Cucaracha." Not as riveting as the originals, but any Big Walter is worth a listen. —*Michael Erlewine*

Little Boy Blue / 1980 / JSP ✦✦✦
A 1980 live recording in Boston. Working with a pickup band consisting of Ronnie Earl on guitar, Mudcat Ward on bass, and Ola Dixon on drums, Horton catches fire and quite simply blows his heart out. The album features some of Horton's best late-period playing. —*Cub Koda*

Harmonica Blues Kings / May 1987 / Pearl Flapper ✦✦✦✦
Six cuts (one side) of an album shared with Alfred Harris. This is very early amplified Walter, recorded in the fall of 1954 for the Black-owned United/States labels. On four of the cuts, Big Walter is playing backup harp and solos for singer Tommy Brown; the other two cuts represent Big Walter's first Chicago record under his own name. Includes the definitive recording of the classic Walter tune "Hard Hearted Woman." —*Michael Erlewine*

Mouth Harp Maestro / 1988 / Ace ✦✦✦✦
These 16 cuts are from the Sam Phillips recordings from the early '50s. Features Walter on acoustic harp. Contains many of the same cuts on the Kent/Crown album, but lacks the amplified songs given there. —*Michael Erlewine*

Can't Keep Lovin' You / 1989 / Blind Pig ✦✦✦
Probably from the mid-'70s, this is later Horton, with John Nicholas on guitar and Ron Levy on piano. The album features a variety of material, including a good version of "Hard Hearted Woman." Not vintage, but worth a listen. —*Michael Erlewine*

Memphis Recordings 1951 / 1991 / Kent ✦✦✦✦
These are the Modern/Cobra masters—17 cuts from the sessions Walter did with Sam Phillips in 1951, including several alternate takes. This is mostly great acoustic harp, but it does contain the songs "Have a Good Time," and "Need My Baby" with Walter playing amplified harp—and great songs and solos these are! Worth finding. —*Michael Erlewine*

Eddie James "Son" House, Jr,

b. Mar. 21, 1902, Riverton, MS, d. Mar. 21, 1988, Detroit, MI
Guitar, Vocals / Acoustic Delta Blues
Son House's place, not only in the history of Delta blues but in the overall history of the music, is a very high one indeed. He was a major innovator of the Delta style, along with his playing partners Charlie Patton and Willie Brown. Few listening experiences in the blues are as intense as hearing one of Son House's original 1930s recordings for the Paramount label. Although it is entombed in a hailstorm of surface noise and scratches, one can still be awe-struck at the emotional fervor House puts into his singing and slide playing. Little wonder, then, that the man became more than just an influence on some White English kid with a big amp; he was the main source of inspiration to both Muddy Waters and Robert Johnson, and it doesn't get much more pivotal than that. Even after his rediscovery in the mid-'60s, House was such a potent musical force that what would have been a normally genteel performance by any other bluesmen in a 'folk' setting, turned into a night in the nastiest juke joint you could imagine, scaring the daylights out of young White enthusiasts expecting something far more prosaic and comfortable. When the man hit the downbeat on his National steel-bodied guitar and you saw his eyes disappear into the back of his head, you knew you were going to hear some blues. And when he wasn't shouting the blues, he was singing spirituals, a cappella. Right up to the end, no bluesman was torn between the sacred and the profane more than Son House.

He was born Eddie James House, Jr., on March 21, 1902, in Riverton, MS. By the age of 15 he was preaching the gospel in various Baptist churches as the family seemingly wandered from one plantation to the next. He didn't even bother picking up a guitar until he turned 25; to quote House, "I didn't like no guitar when I first heard it; oh gee, I couldn't stand a guy playin' a guitar. I didn't like none of it." But Son hated plantation labor even more and had developed a taste for corn whiskey. After drunkenly launching into a blues at a house frolic in Lyon, MS, one night and picking up some coin for doing it, the die

seemed to be cast; Son House may have been a preacher, but he was part of the blues world now.

The blues life is said to be a life full of trouble. House found a barrel of it one night at another house frolic in Lyon. He shot a man dead that night and was sentenced to imprisonment at Parchman Farm. He ended up serving only two years of his sentence, with his parents both lobbying hard for his release, claiming self defense. Upon his release—after a Clarksdale judge told him never to set foot in town again—he started a new life in the Delta as a full-time man of the blues.

After hitchhiking and hoboing the rails, he made it to Lula, MS, and ran into the most legendary character the blues had to offer at that point, the one and only Charlie Patton. He followed Patton to Grafton, WI, and recorded a handful of sides for the Paramount label. The absolutely demonic performances House laid down on these three two-part 78s ("My Black Mama," "Preachin' the Blues," and "Dry Spell Blues," with an unreleased test acetate of "Walkin' Blues" showing up decades later) cut through the hisses and pops like a brick through a stained glass window.

It was those recordings that led Alan Lomax to his door in 1941 to record him for the Library of Congress. Lomax was cutting acetates on a "portable" recording machine weighing over 300 pounds. House was still playing (actually at the peak of his powers, some would say), but had backed off a bit since Charlie Patton died in 1934. House did some tunes solo, as Lomax asked him to do, but also cut a session backed by a rocking little string band. As the band laid down long and loose (some tracks went on for over six minutes) versions of their favorite numbers, all that was missing was the guitars being plugged in and a drummer's back beat and you were getting a glimpse of the future of the music.

But just as House had gone a full decade without recording, this time after the Lomax recordings, he just as quickly disappeared, moving to Rochester, NY. When folk blues researchers finally found him in 1964, he cheerfully exclaimed that he hadn't touched a guitar in years. One of the researchers, a young guitarist named Alan Wilson (later of the blues-rock group Canned Heat), literally sat down and retaught Son House how to play like Son House. Once the old master was up to speed, the festival and coffeehouse circuit became his oyster. He recorded again, the recordings becoming an important introduction to his music and, for some, a lot easier to take than those old Paramount 78s from a strict audio standpoint. In 1965 he played Carnegie Hall and four years later found himself the subject of an eponymously titled film documentary. Everywhere he played he was besieged by young fans asking him about Robert Johnson, Charlie Patton, and others. For young White blues fans, these were merely exotic names from the past, heard only on old, highly prized recordings; for Son House they were flesh and blood contemporaries.

He fell into ill health by the early '70s; what was later diagnosed as both Alzheimer's and Parkinson's disease first affected his memory and his ability to recall songs onstage and, later, his hands, which shook so badly he finally had to give up the guitar and live performing by 1976. He lived quietly in Detroit, MI, for another 12 years, passing away on October 19, 1988. —*Cub Koda*

★ **Delta Blues** / 1991 / Biograph ✦✦✦✦✦
In 1941 and 1942 folklorist Alan Lomax recorded these sides on House on a pair of field trips with a bulky, 300-pound acetate cutting machine for the Library of Congress. House was in peak form and the sides Lomax recorded are absolutely revelatory. The 1941 session finds him in the company of a driving little string band combo with the legendary Willie Brown (the man mentioned in Robert Johnson's "Crossroads") on second guitar. The effect of hearing Son House in this context is fairly astounding. The 1942 batch are solo recordings and equally as riveting. While there are other versions of these sides available in import form, this Biograph features the best sound restoration. —*Cub Koda*

● **Father of the Delta Blues: The Complete 1965 Sessions** / 1992 / CBS ✦✦✦✦
After being rediscovered by the folk-blues community in the early '60s, Son House rose to the occasion and recorded this magnificent set of performances. Allowed to stretch out past the shorter running time of the original 78s, House turns in wonderful, steaming performances of some of his best-known material. On some tracks, House is supplemented by folk-blues researcher/musician Alan Wilson, who would later become a member of the blues-rock group Canned Heat and here plays some nice second guitar and harmonica on several cuts. This two-disc set features alternate takes, some unissued material and some studio chatter from producer John Hammond, Sr. that occasionally hints at the chaotic nature inherent to some of these '60s "rediscovery" sessions. While not as overpowering as his earlier work (what could be?), all of these sides are so power-packed with sheer emotional involvement from House, they're an indispensable part of his canonade. —*Cub Koda*

☆ **Masters of the Delta Blues: The Friends of Charlie Patton** / 1994 / Yazoo ✦✦✦✦✦
If you've only heard Son House's 1965 rediscovery recordings for Colum-

bia (or his excellent 1941-1942 Library of Congress sessions), boy, are you in for a shock. This various artists compilation collects up House's original 1930 recordings for the Paramount label, some of the rarest and hardest to find 78s in blues history. Recorded in Grafton, WI, House sounds positively demonic on the six issued titles (all of them two-part numbers, each being a separate take, rather than a single performance spread over both sides of a single) and with the inclusion of a previously unissued test acetate of "Walking Blues," this is the most complete document of his first recordings that has survived on this important Delta bluesman. The original Paramount 78s were always considered of inferior pressing quality even back in the days when turntables were called victrolas and the hailstorm of surface noise on these sides seems by and large resistant to all forms of modern noise reduction devices employed here. But House's performances here cut through the crackles, pops and hisses like slicing up a cold stick of butter with a soldering iron. Absolutely indispensable. — *Cub Koda*

Howlin' Wolf (Chester Arthur Burnett)

b. Jun. 10, 1910, West Point, MS, **d.** Jan. 10, 1978, Hines, IL
Guitar, Harmonica, Vocals / R&B, Electric Chicago Blues
In the history of the blues, there has never been anyone quite like the Howlin' Wolf. Six foot three and close to 300 pounds in his salad days, the Wolf was the primal force of the music spun out to its ultimate conclusion. A Robert Johnson may have possessed more lyrical insight, a Muddy Waters more dignity, and a B.B. King certainly more technical expertise, but no one could match him for the singular ability to rock the house down to the foundation while simultaneously scaring its patrons out of their wits.

He was born in West Point, MS, and named after the 21st president of the United States. His father was a farmer and Wolf took to it as well until his 18th birthday, when a chance meeting with Delta blues legend Charlie Patton changed his life forever. Though he never came close to learning the subtleties of Patton's complex guitar technique, two of the major components of Wolf's style (Patton's inimitable growl of a voice and his propensity for entertaining) were learned first-hand from the Delta blues master. Wolf's hard-driving, rhythmic style on harmonica developed when Aleck "Rice" Miller (Sonny Boy Williamson) married his half-sister Mary and taught him the rudiments of the instrument. He started playing in the early '30s as a strict Patton imitator, while others recall him at decades' end rocking the juke joints with a neck-rack harmonica and one of the first electric guitars anyone had ever seen. After a four-year stretch in the Army, he settled down as a farmer and weekend player in West Memphis, AR, and it was here that Wolf's career in music began in earnest.

By 1948 he had established himself within the community as a radio personality. As a means of advertising his own local appearances, Wolf had a 15-minute radio show on KWEM in West Memphis, interspersing his down-home blues with farm reports and like-minded advertising that he sold himself. But a change in Wolf's sound that would alter everything that came after was soon in coming because when listeners tuned in for Wolf's show, the sound was up-to-the-minute electric. Wolf had put his first band together, featuring the explosive guitar work of Willie Johnson, whose aggressive style not only perfectly suited Wolf's sound, but aurally extended and amplified the violence and nastiness of it as well. In any discussion of Wolf's early success—live, over the airwaves, and on record—the importance of Willie Johnson cannot be overestimated.

Wolf finally started recording in 1951, when he caught the ear of Sam Phillips, who first heard him on his morning radio show. The music Wolf made in the Memphis Recording Service studio was full of passion and zest, and Phillips simultaneously leased the results to the Bihari brothers in Los Angeles and Leonard Chess in Chicago. Suddenly Howlin' Wolf had two hits at the same time on the R&B charts, with two record companies claiming to have him exclusively under contract. Chess finally won him over and, as Wolf would proudly relate years later, "I had a four-thousand-dollar car and $3,900 in my pocket. I'm the onliest one drove out of the South like a gentleman." It was the winter of 1953, and Chicago would be his new home.

When Wolf entered the Chess studios the next year, the violent aggression of the Memphis sides wa being replaced with a Chicago backbeat and, with very little fanfare, a new member in the band. Hubert Sumlin proved himself to be the Wolf's longest-running musical associate. He first appears as a rhythm guitarist on a 1954 session, and within a few years' time his style had fully matured to take over the role of lead guitarist in the band by early 1958. In what can only be described as an "angular attack," Sumlin played almost no chords behind Wolf, sometimes soloing right through his vocals, featuring wild skitterings up and down the fingerboard and biting single notes. If Willie Johnson was Wolf's second voice in his early recording career, then Hubert Sumlin would pick up the gauntlet and run with it right to the end of the howler's life. By 1956, Wolf was in the R&B charts again, racking up hits with "Evil" and "Smokestack Lightnin." He remained a

top attraction both on the Chicago circuit and on the road. His records, while seldom showing up on the national charts, were still selling in decent numbers down South. But by 1960, Wolf was teamed up with Chess staff writer Willie Dixon and for the next five years, he would record almost nothing but songs written by Dixon. The magic combination of Wolf's voice, Sumlin's guitar and Dixon's tunes sold a lot of records and brought the 50-year-old bluesman roaring into the next decade with a considerable flourish. The mid-'60s saw him touring Europe regularly with "Smokestack Lightnin'" becoming a hit in England some eight years after its American release. Certainly any list of Wolf's greatest sides would have to include "I Ain't Superstitious," "Little Red Rooster," "Shake for Me," "Back Door Man," "Spoonful," and "Wang Dang Doodle," Dixon compositions all. While almost all of them would eventually become Chicago blues standards, their greatest cache occurred when rock bands the world over started mining the Chess catalog for all it was worth. One of these bands was the Rolling Stones, whose cover of "The Red Rooster" became a No. 1 record in England. At the height of the British Invasion, the Stones came to America in 1965 for an appearance on ABC-TV's rock music show, *Shindig*. Their main stipulation for appearing on the program was that Howlin' Wolf would be their special guest. With the Stones sitting worshipfully at his feet, the Wolf performed a storming version of "How Many More Years," being seen on his network-TV debut by an audience of a few million. Wolf never forgot the respect the Stones paid him, and he spoke of them highly right up to his final days.

Dixon and Wolf parted company by 1964 and Wolf was back in the studio doing his own songs. One of the classics to emerge from this period was "Killing Floor," featuring a modern backbeat and an incredibly catchy guitar riff from Sumlin. Catchy enough for Led Zeppelin to appropriate it for one of their early albums, cheerfully crediting it to themselves in much the same manner as they had done with numerous other blues standards. By the end of the decade, Wolf's material was being recorded by artists including the Doors, the Electric Flag, the Blues Project, Cream, and Jeff Beck. The result of all these covers brought Wolf the belated acclaim of a young, White audience. Chess' response to this was to bring him into the studio for a "psychedelic" album, truly the most dreadful of his career. His last big payday came when Chess sent him over to England in 1970 to capitalize on the then-current trend of *London Session* albums, recording with Eric Clapton on lead guitar and other British superstars. Wolf's health was not the best, but the session was miles above the earlier, ill-advised attempt to update Wolf's sound for a younger audience.

As the '70s moved on, the end of the trail started coming closer. By now Wolf was a very sick man; he had survived numerous heart attacks and was suffering kidney damage from an automobile accident that sent him flying through the car's windshield. His bandleader Eddie Shaw firmly rationed Wolf to a meager half-dozen songs per set. Occasionally some of the old fire would come blazing forth from some untapped wellspring and his final live and studio recordings show that he could still tear the house apart when the spirit moved him. He entered the Veterans Administration Hospital in 1976 and passed away on January 10.

His passing did not go unrecognized. A life-size statue of him was erected shortly after in a Chicago park. Eddie Shaw kept his memory and music alive by keeping his band, the Wolf Gang, together for several years afterward. A child-education center in Chicago was named in his honor, and in 1980 he was inducted into the Blues Foundation Hall of Fame. In 1991 he was inducted into the Rock & Roll Hall of Fame. A couple of years later, his face was on a United States postage stamp. Live performance footage of him exists in the CD-ROM computer format. — *Cub Koda*

The Real Folk Blues / 1963 / MCA/Chess ✦✦✦✦

This was originally released by Chess in 1966 to capitalize on the then-current folk music boom. The music, however—a collection of Wolf singles from 1956 to 1965—is full-blown electric featuring a nice sampling of Wolf originals with a smattering of Willie Dixon tunes. Some of the man's best middle-period work is aboard here; "Killing Floor," "Louise," the hair-raisingly somber "Natchez Burning," and Wolf's version of the old standard "Sitting on Top of the World," which would become his set closer in later years. The Mobile Fidelity version sounds as sonically sharp as anything you've ever heard on this artist and its heftier price tag is somewhat justified by the inclusion of two bonus cuts. But those on a budget who just want the music minus the high-minded audiophile concerns will be happy to note that this is also available as a Chess budget reissue. — *Cub Koda*

More Real Folk Blues / 1967 / MCA/Chess ✦✦✦✦

This companion volume to the *Real Folk Blues* album was issued in 1967 (after the Wolf had appeared on network television with the Rolling Stones, alluded to in the original liner notes) and couldn't be more dissimilar in content to the first one if you had planned it that way. Whereas the previous volume highlighted middle period Wolf, this one goes all the way back to his earliest Chess sessions, many of which sound like leftover Memphis sides. The chaotic opener, "Just My Kind," sets a familiar Wolf theme to a "Rollin' and Tumblin'" format played at breakneck speed and what the track lacks in fidelity is more than made up in sheer energy. For a classic example of Wolf's ensemble Chicago sound, it's pretty tough to beat "I Have a Little Gir," where the various members of his band all seem to be soloing simultaneously—not unlike a Dixieland band—right through Wolf's vocals. For downright scary, the demonic-sounding "I'll Be Around" is an absolute must-hear. Wolf's harp solo on this slow blues is one of his best, and the vocal that frames it sounds as if the microphone is going to explode at any second. As soul singer Christine Ohlman commented upon hearing this track for the first time, "Boy, I'd sure hate to be the woman he's singing that one to." —*Cub Koda*

Memphis Days . . . / 1989 / Bear Family ✦✦✦✦
These are Wolf's earliest and rarest sides recorded at the Sun studios, as raw and explosive as blues records come. Much of this was issued on various European albums during the '70s, always transferred off of muffled-sounding copy tapes. These 21 tracks (all but two of them off the master tapes) featuring the amp-on-11 guitar work of Willie Johnson and the cave man drumming of Willie Steele, are loose and somewhat chaotic, with Wolf sounding utterly demonic. The real bonus on this volume is the first-time inclusion of both sides of the only known acetate of Wolf's first session at Sam Phillip's 706 Union Avenue studio from 1951. With only Johnson and Steele in support (no bass, no piano), these early versions of "How Many More Years" and "Baby Ride with Me (Riding in the Moonlight)" are Wolf at his most primitive. —*Cub Koda*

Memphis Days: Definitive Edition, Vol. 2 / 1989 / Bear Family ✦✦✦✦
The second volume in this series collects all the known Memphis recordings that were either issued by or originally offered to Chess. As such, it stands as a marvelous collection of Wolf's early 78s for that label. But what truly puts it over is the added bonus of a newly discovered acetate featuring several unissued versions of "How Many More Years" and "Baby Ride with Me (Riding in the Moonlight)." Much of this volume is pulled from discs, but the overall sound is good and the performances make it yet another must-have. —*Cub Koda*

☆ **The Chess Box** / 1991 / MCA/Chess ✦✦✦✦✦
This three-CD box set currently rates as the best—and most digestible—overview of Wolf's career. Disc one starts with the Memphis sides that eventually brought him to the label, including hits like "How Many More Years," but also compiling unissued sides that had previously only been available on vinyl bootlegs of dubious origin and fidelity. The disc finishes with an excellent cross section of early Chicago sessions including classic Wolf tracks like "Evil," "Forty Four," "I'll Be Around," and "Who Will Be Next." Disc two picks it up from there, guiding us from mid- to late-'50s barnburners like "The Natchez Burnin'" and "I Better Go Now" to the bulk of the Willie Dixon classics. The final disc runs out the last of the Dixon sessions into mid-'60s classics like "Killing Floor," taking us to a nice selection of his final recordings. A really nice bonus on this box set is the inclusion on the first two discs of snippets from a 1968 Howlin' Wolf interview and two performances of Wolf playing solo acoustic. Definitely not the place to start (unless you have money to burn), but maybe just the perfect place to end up. —*Cub Koda*

☆ **Howlin' Wolf Rides Again** / 1993 / Flair/Virgin ✦✦✦✦✦
While both Bear Family sets deal with a largely unissued wealth of material, this collection is devoted in the main to all the Memphis recordings from 1951 and 1952 that saw the light of day on a number of Los Angeles-based labels owned by the Bihari brothers, being issued and reissued and reissued again on a plethora of $1.98 budget albums. Featuring recordings done in Sam Phillips' Memphis Recording Service and surreptitious sessions recorded by a young Ike Turner in makeshift studios, these 18 sides are the missing piece of the puzzle in absorbing Wolf's early pre-Chess period. It also helps that this just happens to be some of the nastiest-sounding blues ever recorded. With no tracks being duplicated from the two Bear Family *Memphis Days* volumes, and sonics far surpassing all previous issues of this material (every last one of them horribly marred by an annoying 60 cycle hum), this is an essential part of any Wolf collection. Alternate take freaks will revel in the inclusion of two extra takes of "Riding in the Moonlight" from an earlier and different session than the issued version also included. While not quite as essential as his first two Chess albums (and if we were making a judgment call on just passionate performances alone, even that would be debatable), this is definitely the next stop along the way in absorbing the raw genius of Howlin' Wolf. —*Cub Koda*

Ain't Gonna Be Your Dog / 1994 / MCA/Chess ✦✦✦✦
This double-disc set features 42 rare and unissued performances, effectively cleaning out the Chess vaults of all but alternate takes of alternate takes. But these are no bottom-of-the-barrel scrapings here; quite the opposite. The first 14 tunes collect the remainder of his Memphis recordings for Sam Phillips while the rest does the bootleggers one better, compiling masters that were previously available only on bad-sounding '70s vinyl albums. There's another snippet from his 1968 interview, along with four more acoustic numbers from that same session (done, it turns

out, as a promotional piece of sorts to preview his "soon to be released psychedelic album," which Wolf always dismissed as "birds"t"), sadly the only time Chess ever tried to record him as a solo artist. A wonderful companion piece to any other Wolf collection you might own. —*Cub Koda*

★ **Howlin' Wolf/Moanin' in the Moonlight** / MCA/Chess ✦✦✦✦✦
Wolf's first and second Chess albums, released in 1959 and 1962 respectively, are essential listening of the highest order. Compiled—as were all early blues albums—from various single sessions (not necessarily a bad thing, either), blues fans will probably debate endlessly about which of these two albums is the perfect introduction to his music. But the MCA-Chess CD issue renders all arguments moot as both albums appear on one disc, making this one of the true best buys around today. Wolf's debut opus—curiously tacked on here after his second album—features all of his early hits ("How Many More Years," "Moanin' at Midnight," "Smokestack Lightning," "Forty Four," "Evil," and "I Asked for Water [She Gave Me Gasoline]") and is a pretty potent collection in its own right. But it is the follow-up (always referred to as 'the rocking chair album' because of Don Bronstein's distinctive cover art) where the equally potent teaming of Willie Dixon and Wolf produced one Chicago Blues classic ("Spoonful," "Little Red Rooster," "Back Door Man," and "Wang Dang Doodle") after another. It's also with this marvelous batch of sides that one can clearly hear lead guitarist Hubert Sumlin coming into his own as a blues picking legend. The number of blues acolytes, both Black and White, who wore the grooves down to mush learning the songs and guitar licks off these two albums would fill a book all by itself. If you have to narrow it down to just one Howlin' Wolf purchase for the collection, this would be the one to have and undoubtedly the place to start. This and *The Best of Muddy Waters* are the essential building blocks of any Chicago Blues collection. And seldom does the music come with this much personality and brute force. —*Cub Koda*

Ivory Joe Hunter

b. Oct. 10, 1914, Kirbyville, TX, d. Nov. 8, 1974, Memphis, TN
Piano, Vocals / R&B
Bespectacled and velvet-smooth in the vocal department, pianist Ivory Joe Hunter appeared much too mild-mannered to be a rock 'n' roller. But when the rebellious music first crashed the American consciousness in the mid-'50s, there was Ivory Joe, deftly delivering his blues ballad "Since I Met You Baby" right alongside the wildest pioneers of the era.

Hunter was already a grizzled R&B vet by that time who had first heard his voice on a 1933 Library of Congress cylinder recording made in Texas (where he grew up). In later years he did sessions as both a soul singer and a country and western artist. As a songwriter, Hunter claimed over 7,000 compositions. —*Bill Dahl*

● **Since I Met You Baby: The Best of Ivory Joe Hunter** / 1994 / Razor & Tie ✦✦✦✦
Bespectacled pianist Ivory Joe Hunter's crooning blues balladry made him a hot commodity from the late '40s through the late '50s, but he could rock reasonably hard, too. He does both on this wonderful survey of his 1949-1958 MGM and Atlantic sides—"I Need You So," "I Almost Lost My Mind," and the title item are sophisticated and mellow, while "Rockin' Chair Boogie," "Love Is a Hurting Game," and "Shooty Booty" find the pianist in decidedly unsentimental moods. —*Bill Dahl*

Mississippi John Hurt

b. Jul. 1, 1893, Teoc, MS, d. Nov. 2, 1966, Grenada, MS
Guitar, Harmonica, Vocals / Blues, Acoustic Blues
The history of Mississippi John Hurt reads like a real Cinderella story. Born John Smith Hurt on July 3, 1893, in Teoc (Carroll Co.), MS, he moved with his family to Avalon, MS (where he grew up), when he was two. One of ten children (who all played music of one sort or another), Hurt was the most into it and taught himself how to play. Years later, when his White landlord asked how he came up with his melodies, he replied, "Well sir, I just make it sound like I think it should."

Although he learned to read and write, he did not attend school past the fourth grade. As a young adult, he became a sharecropper or tenant farmer for many years, but finally gave that up and switched to day labor. For fun and extra cash, Hurt joined other local guitarists and fiddlers for church suppers and town dances in surrounding towns. Hurt soon became a popular favorite at these local functions.

In the late '20s, a well-known fiddler named Willie Narmour, with whom Hurt often played, was spotted by a talent scout for Okeh Phonograph, a division of Columbia Records. When asked about other talented local musicians, Narmour gave the name of John Hurt and directions on how to find him. Okeh found and interviewed Hurt, had him play a few songs, and decided to record him, provided he was willing to travel to Memphis and New York.

Hurt recorded two songs in February of 1928 while in Memphis, "Frankie" and "Nobody's Dirty Business," and these were released by Okeh. That December Hurt traveled to New York City to record five more sides. During that visit he met Lonnie Johnson, but made a point of declaring that he cribbed nothing from that great guitarist. Hurt's records did not sell in great numbers, perhaps in the hundreds. After his short musical excursion, Hurt returned to Avalon and went back to sharecropping and playing music just about every Saturday night in the towns surrounding his home.

That could have been the end of Hurt's national career had not two young blues musicians from Washington, D.C., Tom Hoskins and Mike Stewart, come across the original Okeh recording of "Avalon Blues." This was in 1963. Intrigued by John's intricate finger-picking style, they came up with the idea of trying to locate some of the original artists, should they still be alive. They checked the Mississippi maps, but no town named Avalon could be found. However, after locating an 1878 atlas, sure enough, there was an Avalon marked on a rural road running between Greenwood and Grenada. On hope and a whim, the two blues archivists headed south armed with a tape recorder. With the help of the old map, they found Avalon with its single gas station/store and inquired about John Hurt.

They were floored to see the attendant point down the road and say that Hurt's house was "About a mile down that road, third mailbox up the hill. Can't miss it." Hurt, 71 years of age, was still able to sing and play about as well as he had before. They recorded him and returned to Washington with the precious taped results.

From the Spring of 1963, when he was brought to Washington, D.C., to perform, until his death in 1966, Hurt played all over the Northeast at clubs and folk festivals, including twice at the Newport Folk Festival. Much admired by his new-found audience, Hurt loved his late success and gave as much as he got. He was befriended by fellow performers like Doc Watson, Fred McDowell, and Elizabeth Cotten. In the end, he retired to a small home in Granada, MS, not far from his home town of Avalon.

Mississippi John Hurt is an exquisite country-blues singer/guitarist with a subtle voice and refined finger-picking guitar style. As mentioned, he recorded in the '20s and again in the '60s, and both periods are well worth hearing. Here is acoustic country-blues with real technical clarity that is also comforting and easy to listen to. There is a gospel flavor in Hurt's blues. Mississippi John Hurt projects a sense of dignity and kindness through all of his recordings. If you have trouble with the occasional heaviness of many blues players, you may find Hurt refreshing. —Michael Erlewine

Worried Blues / Apr. 1963 / Rounder ✦✦✦✦
This is some of the Vanguard material recorded in April of 1963, not long after Hurt's rediscovery. It contains ten tracks with "Worried Blues" and "Oh Mary Don't You Weep." —Michael Erlewine

Memorial Anthology / Dec. 1964 / Adelphi ✦✦✦✦
Mississippi John Hurt's mid-'60s performances were usually distinctive and sometimes staggering. His guitar work was crisp, attractive and frequently brilliant, although his vocals were the real hook. Hurt's narratives, storytelling ability and general communicative powers were at their peak on this two-CD set, which has languished in a vault for nearly 30 years. Hurt covers such traditional numbers as "C.C. Rider" and "Staggerlee" with vigor, plays several originals, sometimes shifts to gospel, and does everything in an unassuming way that nevertheless grabs your attention. The set's treasure is a 31-minute interview with Pete Seeger in which Hurt lays bare his life, times and personality, doing so in the same steady, casual, gripping fashion that underscored his singing and playing. —Ron Wynn

Avalon Blues / 1965 / Rounder ✦✦✦✦
Recorded in April of 1963, these are part of the legacy of Hurt after his rediscovery. Contains "Avalon Blues," "Candyman Blues"—11 cuts in all. Great. —Michael Erlewine

Today / 1966 / Vanguard ✦✦✦✦
These is material recorded after his rediscovery in 1963. Includes classic Hurt tunes like "Candy Man" and "Coffee Blues." Wonderful listening. —Michael Erlewine

The Immortal / 1967 / Vanguard ✦✦✦✦
This is the best of Hurt's '60s "rediscovery-era" recordings. —Mark A. Humphrey

The Mississippi John Hurt / 1968 / Vanguard ✦✦✦
A great double-album collection of '60s Hurt. —Michael Erlewine

The Best of Mississippi John Hurt / 1968 / Vanguard ✦✦✦✦
Contrary to what this title would make one believe, this record is not a collection of previously available recordings by Mississippi John Hurt—rather, it is a complete concert from Oberlin College on April 15, 1965. Regardless, the title is justified, as the concert features Hurt in excellent form doing most of his best known classic songs from the 1920s as well as newer compositions. —Bruce Eder

Last Sessions / 1970 / Vanguard ✦✦✦✦
Recorded in New York during February and July of 1966, the 17 songs on this collection represent Mississippi John Hurt's final studio efforts. It is

astonishing that this man, in the final months of his life, could do 17 songs that were the equal of anything he had done at his first sessions 45 years earlier, his playing (supported on some tracks with producer Patrick Sky on second guitar) as alluringly complex as ever and his voice still in top form. Hurt is brilliant throughout, his voice overpowering in its mixture of warmth, gentleness, and power, and in addition to the expected crop of standards and originals, he covers songs by Bukka White ("Poor Boy, Long Ways from Home") and Leadbelly ("Goodnight Irene")—all of it is worthwhile, with some tracks, such as "Let the Mermaids Flirt with Me" especially haunting. —Bruce Eder

★ **1928 Sessions** / 1988 / Yazoo ✦✦✦✦✦
The 13 original 1928 recordings of Hurt. Justifiably legendary, with gentle grace and power on these understated vocal and fingerpicking masterpieces. These are the ones to hear, although all Hurt is worth listening to. —Michael Erlewine

The Greatest Songsters: Complete Works (1927-1929) / 1990 / Document ✦✦✦✦
You can get a lot of arguments started about which Mississippi blues musician is the best, so let's just say that this is first-rate Mississippi John Hurt material and leave it at that. —Ron Wynn

J. B. Hutto (Joseph Benjamin Hutto)

b. Apr. 26, 1926, Blackville, SC, **d.** Jun. 12, 1983, Harvey, IL
Guitar, Vocals / Electric Chicago Blues

J.B. Hutto—along with Hound Dog Taylor—was one of the last great slide guitar disciples of Elmore James to make it into the modern age. Hutto's huge voice, largely incomprehensible diction and slash and burn playing was Chicago blues with a fierce, raw edge all its own. He entered the world of music back home in Augusta, GA, singing in the family-oriented group the Golden Crowns Gospel Singers. He came north to Chicago in the mid-'40s, teaching himself guitar and eventually landing his first paying job as a member of Johnny Ferguson and His Twisters. His recording career started in 1954 with two sessions for the Chance label supported by his original combo the Hawks (featuring George Mayweather on harmonica, Porkchop Hines on washboard traps and Joe Custom on rhythm guitar), resulting in six of the nine songs recorded being issued as singles to scant acclaim. After breaking up the original band, Hutto worked outside of music for a good decade. He resurfaced around 1964 with a stripped-down, two guitars-drums-no bass trio version of the Hawks, working regularly at Turner's Blue Lounge and recording blistering new sides for the first time in as many years. From there, he never looked back and once again became a full-time bluesman. For the next 12 years Hutto gigged and recorded with various groups of musicians—always billed as the Hawks—working with electric bass players for the first time and recording for small labels, both here and overseas. After fellow slide man Hound Dog Taylor's death in 1976, J.B. "inherited" his backup band, the Houserockers. Although never formally recorded in a studio, this short-lived collaboration of Hutto with guitarist Brewer Phillips and drummer Ted Harvey produced live shows that would musically careen in a single performance from smoldering intense to utter chaos. Within a year, Hutto would be lured to Boston where he put together a mixed group of "New Hawks," recording and touring America and Europe right up until his death in the mid-'80s. Hutto was an incredibly dynamic live performer, dressed in hot pink suits with headgear ranging from a shriner's fez to high-plains-drifters' hats, snaking through the crowd and dancing on tabletops. And this good-time approach to the music held sway on his recordings as well, giving a loose, barroom feel to almost all of them, regardless of who was backing him. —Cub Koda

Masters of Modern Blues / 1966 / Testament ✦✦✦✦
1966 was a banner year for Hutto and his Hawks—in addition to laying down the lion's share of his killer Delmark album, the slide master also waxed a similarly incendiary set for Pete Welding's Testament logo. Vicious versions of "Pet Cream Man," "Lulubelle's Here," and "Bluebird" are but a few of its charms, with Big Walter Horton's unmistakable harp winding through the proceedings. —Bill Dahl

☆ **Chicago/The Blues/Today!, Vol. 1** / 1967 / Vanguard ✦✦✦✦✦
Hutto only has five tracks on this album, sharing it with great solo turns by Junior Wells and Otis Spann, but it's truly the place to start, because it doesn't get much better than this: "Too Much Alcohol," "Please Help," "Going Ahead," and "That's The Truth" are all classics; and Hutto is in perfect form throughou,t with swinging support from the Turner's Blue Lounge version of the Hawks, bass-rhythm guitarist Herman Hassell, and former Bo Diddley drummer Frank Kirkland. Sound is crystal clear. —Cub Koda

● **Hawk Squat!** / 1968 / Delmark ✦✦✦✦
The raw-as-an-open-wound Chicago slide guitarist outdid himself throughout an outrageously raucous album (most of it waxed in mono 1966) anchored by an impossible-to-ignore "Hip-Shakin'," the blaring title cut, and savage renditions of "20% Alcohol" and "Notoriety Woman." Sunny-

land Slim augments Hutto's Hawks on organ, rather than his customary piano. —*Bill Dahl*

Slideslinger / Apr. 1, 1982 / Evidence ✦✦✦

And the Houserockers Live 1977 / 1991 / Wolf ✦✦✦
Culled from a couple of nights in a Boston jazz club and recorded on a cassette deck with two microphones, this stunning document of Hutto with Hound Dog Taylor's band in support gives new meaning to the phrase raw 'n' steamy. Although the trio is fleshed out at this point by the addition of a fairly obtrusive bass player (Mark Harris) and a guest piano man on a couple of tracks, the sheet metal tone of Phillips' and Hutto's twin Telecaster attack cuts through the murkiest of mixes and Ted Harvey swings mightily. —*Cub Koda*

Papa Charlie Jackson (Charlie Carter)

b. 1885, New Orleans, LA, d. 1938, Chicago, IL
Banjo, Guitar, Ukulele, Vocals / Acoustic Country Blues
Papa Charlie Jackson was the first bluesman to record, beginning in 1924 with the Paramount label, playing a hybrid banjo-guitar (six strings tuned like a guitar but with a banjo body that gave it a lighter resonance) and ukelele. And apart from his records and their recording dates, little else is known for sure about this pioneering blues performer, other than his probable city of birth, New Orleans—even his death in Chicago during 1938 is more probability than established fact.

Jackson spent his teen years as a singer/performer in minstrel and medicine shows and is known to have busked around Chicago in the early '20s. In August of 1924, Jackson made his first record, "Papa's Lawdy Lawdy Blues" and "Airy Man Blues," for a Paramount label. He followed this up a month later with "Salt Lake City Blues" and "Salty Dog Blues," which became one of his signature tunes. Jackson made his first duet recording in 1925 ("Mister Man, Parts 1 and 2," with singer Ida Cox, again for Paramount, and later cut duets with Ma Rainey and future Oscar-winning actress Hattie McDaniel.

He was already regarded as one of the Paramount label's more successful recording artists, and all but a handful of his recordings were done for Paramount over the next decade. Jackson switched to guitar on some of his late '20s recordings, and occasionally played the ukelele as well, although he was back to using the five-string hybrid in 1934, when he cut his final sessions. For reasons that nobody has ever established, he parted company with Paramount after 1930, and never recorded for the label again, even though Paramount lasted another two years before going under amid the hardships of the Great Depression. His last sides for the label, "You Got That Wrong" and "Self Experience," were highly personal songs dealing with romance and an apparent brush with the law, after which he disappeared from recording for four years. Jackson continued performing, however, and he returned to the recording studio again in November of 1934 for sessions on the Okeh label, including three songs cut with his friend Big Bill Broonzy, which were never issued. Jackson was an important influence on Broonzy, who outlived his mentor by 20 years.

Papa Charlie Jackson remains a shadowy figure; he is considered a highly influential figure in the blues, though not quite a major blues figure, apart from the fact that he was the first male singer/guitarist who played the blues to get to record. His recordings are all eminently listenable, although most are not blues, but fall into such related areas as ragtime and hokum. At this writing, the only extant collections consist of three Austrian-produced CDs. —*Bruce Eder*

● **Fat Mouth** / 1970 / Yazoo ✦✦✦✦
The best single-disc retrospective of this early country blues artist. —*Cub Koda*

Elmore James

b. Jan. 27, 1918, Richland, MS, d. May 24, 1963, Chicago, IL
Guitar, Vocals / Electric Chicago Blues
No two ways about it, the most influential slide guitarist of the postwar period was Elmore James, hands down. Although his early demise from heart failure kept him from enjoying the fruits of the '60s blues revival as his contemporaries Muddy Waters and Howlin' Wolf did, James was influential. And that influence continues to the present—in approach, attitude, and tone—in just about every guitar player who puts a slide on his finger and wails the blues. As a guitarist, James wrote the book, his slide style influencing the likes of Hound Dog Taylor, Joe Carter, his cousin Homesick James, and J.B. Hutto, while his seldom-heard single-string work had an equally profound effect on B.B. King and Chuck Berry. His signature lick—an electric updating of Robert Johnson's "I Believe I'll Dust My Broom" and one that Elmore recorded in infinite variations from day one to his last session—is so much a part of the essential blues fabric of guitar licks that no one attempting to play slide guitar can do it without being compared to Elmore James. Others may have had more technique—Robert Nighthawk and Earl Hooker immediately come to mind—but James had the sound and all the feeling. A

radio repairman by trade, James reworked his guitar amplifiers in his spare time, getting them to produce raw, distorted sounds that wouldn't resurface until the advent of heavy rock amplification in the late '60s. This amp on 11 approach was hot-wired to one of the strongest emotional approaches to the blues ever recorded. There is never a time when you're listening to one of his records that you feel—no matter how familiar the structure—that he's phoning it in just to grab a quick session check. Elmore James always gave it everything he had, everything he could emotionally invest in a number. This commitment of spirit is something that shows up time and again when listening to multiple takes from his session masters. The sheer repetitiveness of the recording process would dim almost anyone's creative fires, but James always seemed to give it 100% every time the red light went on. Few blues singers had a voice that could compete with James'; it was loud, forceful, prone to "catch" or break up in the high registers, almost sounding on the verge of hysteria at certain moments. Evidently the times back in the mid-'30s when James had Robert Johnson as a playing companion had deep influence on him, not only in his choice of material, but in his presentation.

Backing the twin torrents of James' guitar and voice was one of the greatest—and earliest—Chicago blues bands. Named after James' big hit, the Broomdusters featured Little Johnny Jones on piano, J.T. Brown on tenor sax, and Elmore's cousin, Homesick James, on rhythm guitar. This talented nucleus was often augmented by a second saxophone, and the drummer changed frequently. But this was the band that could go toe to toe in a battle of the blues against the bands of Muddy Waters or Howlin' Wolf and always hold their own, if not walk with the show. Using a stomping beat, James' slashing guitar, Jones' two-fisted piano delivery, Homesick's rudimentary boogie bass rhythm, and Brown's braying nanny-goat sax leads, the Broomdusters were as loud, powerful, and popular as any blues band the Windy City had to offer.

But as urban as their sound was, it had roots in James' hometown of Canton, MS. He was born there on January 27, 1918, the illegitimate son of Leola Brooks and later given the surname of his stepfather, Joe Willie James. He adapted to music at an early age, learning to play bottleneck on a homemade instrument fashioned out of a broom handle and a lard can. By the age of 14, he was a weekend musician, working the various country suppers and juke joints in the area under the names "Cleanhead" or Joe Willie James. Although he confined himself the area around Belzoni, he would work with traveling players coming through like Robert Johnson, Howlin' Wolf, and Sonny Boy Williamson. By the late '30s he had formed his first band and was working the Southern state area with Sonny Boy until World War II broke out. He spent three years with the Navy in Guam. When he was discharged, he picked up where he left off, moving for a while to Memphis, working in clubs with Eddie Taylor and his cousin Homesick James. Elmore was also one of the first "guest stars" on the popular "King Biscuit Time" radio show on KFFA in Helena, AR, also doing stints on the "Talaho Syrup" show on Yazoo City's WAZF and the "Hadacol" show on KWEM in West Memphis. Nervous and unsure of his abilities as a recording artist, James was surreptitiously recorded by Lillian McMurray of Trumpet Records at the tail end of a Sonny Boy session doing his now signature tune, "Dust My Broom." The legend has it that James didn't even stay around long enough to hear the playback, much less record a second side. Mrs. McMurray stuck a local singer (Bo Bo Thomas) on the flip side, and the record became the surprise R&B hit of 1951, making the Top Ten and making a recording star out of James. With a few months left on his Trumpet contract, James was recorded by the Bihari brothers for their Modern label subsidiaries, Flair and Meteor, but the results were left in the can until James' contract ran out. In the meantime, James had moved to Chicago and cut a quick session for Chess, which resulted in one single being issued and just as quickly yanked off the market as the Biharis swooped in to protect their investment. This period of activity found James assembling the nucleus of the Broomdusters, and several fine recordings were issued over the next few years on a plethora of Bihari-owned labels, with several of them charting and most all of them becoming certified blues classics.

By this time James had established a beach-head in the clubs of Chicago as one of the most popular live acts and regularly broadcast over WPOA under the aegis of disc-jockey Big Bill Hill. In 1957, with his contract with the Biharis at an end, he recorded several successful sides for Mel London's Chief label, all of them later being issued on the larger Vee-Jay label. His health—always fragile due to a recurring heart condition—sent him back home to Jackson, MS, where he temporarily sat aside his playing for work as a disc jockey or radio repair man. He came back to Chicago to record a session for Chess, then just as quickly broke contract to sign with Bobby Robinson's Fire label, producing the classic "The Sky Is Crying" and numerous others. Running afoul of the Chicago musician's union, he returned to Mississippi, doing sessions in New York and New Orleans while waiting for Big Bill Hill to sort things out. In August 1963 James returned to Chicago, ready to resume his on-again, off-again playing career—his records were still being regularly issued and reissued on a variety of labels—when he suffered his final heart attack. —*Cub Koda*

Whose Muddy Shoes / 1969 / MCA/Chess ✦✦✦✦
James had recorded a session for Chess in 1953 before settling down with the Bihari brothers and again in 1960, shortly before starting his final recordings for Bobby Robinson's Fire, Fury, and Enjoy labels. This collects all of them on CD with the bonus addition of an alternate take of "The Sun Is Shining," which can be interpreted as a precursor to his later hit "The Sky Is Crying." The earlier sides from 1953 lack his inimitable slide, but the 1960 session produced classics like "Talk to Me Baby," "Madison Blues," and a powerful reading of T-Bone Walker's "Stormy Monday." These tracks of James working with the Chess production team are delightfully fleshed out with a half dozen gems by the highly underrated John Brim, some of which include stellar harp work by Little Walter ("Rattlesnake," "Be Careful"—on which Walter stops playing in several spots to become an ad-lib backup vocalist—and "You Got Me") as well as the original version of "Ice Cream Man," better known to rock fans from Van Halen's cover version of it from their debut album. —*Cub Koda*

☆ **The Original Meteor and Flair Sides** / 1984 / Ace ✦✦✦✦✦
The best of James' early-'50s sides with stunning slide and driving band support. At the top of his form, this is a perfect introduction to his music. —*Cub Koda*

Rollin' & Tumblin': The Best of Elmore James / 1992 / Relic ✦✦✦✦
Although the Capricorn box set does a great job of rounding up at least one take of everything James cut for Bobby Robinson's Fire and Enjoy labels, if you want (or need) to sweat it down to bare essentials, this is the one to grab out of the blues bin and take home. The remastering by Little Walter Devenne on this single disc is exemplar,y and for late period Elmore, this truly is the best of the best. —*Cub Koda*

☆ **King of the Slide Guitar** / 1992 / Warner Brothers ✦✦✦✦✦
James' last great recordings occurred in the 1960s when he was signed by New York producer/label owner Bobby Robinson. Unlike many of his contemporaries, James seemingly got better as the years went by; and while none of the sides features a slide guitar anywhere near as nasty as his early Modern and Flair recordings, he's still obviously giving it all on each and every side. These recordings are the ones most commonly issued on James and have surfaced on so many different compilations—all with varying levels of sound quality—that it would be futile to list them all here. Fortunately, to make things easier we have this two-disc 50-song box set rounding up at least one extant take of everything James recorded with Robinson at the helm. Some are recuts of his best known tunes; "Dust My Broom" resurfaces here in two versions from two different sessions, and the version of "It Hurts Me, Too" included here—it was originally cut for Chief in the late '50s—became a posthumous hit for him. But the majority breaks new ground and stands as some of James' most emotion-laden work. Nice essays in the booklet make up for the disgusting art work that adorns the box. —*Cub Koda*

★ **The Sky Is Crying: The History of Elmore James** / 1993 / Rhino ✦✦✦✦✦
With the confusing plethora of Elmore James discs out on the market, this is truly the place to start, featuring the best of his work culled from several labels. Highlights include James' original recording of "Dust My Broom," "It Hurts Me, Too," "T.V. Mama" (with James backing Big Joe Turner) and the title track, one of the best slow blues ever created. Slide guitar doesn't get much better than this, making this particular compilation not only a perfect introduction to James' music, but an essential piece for any blues collection. —*Cub Koda*

☆ **The Classic Recordings** / 1993 / Flair/Virgin ✦✦✦✦✦
After James hit the national charts with his Trumpet recording of "Dust My Broom," he came to record for the Bihari brothers, first for their Meteor subsidiary, then for their Flair and Modern labels. This multi-disc retrospective rounds up every existing master James recorded for the Biharis, plus his backup work behind band members Johnny Jones and J.T. Brown. James' guitar tone is distorted and overamped to the extreme; this is the sound that changed the face of slide guitar forever, influencing everyone from Hound Dog Taylor to J.B. Hutto to George Thorogood and everybody in between. The intensity of James' vocals is nothing short of riveting, and the material collected here (along with breakdowns, studio chat, etc.) is simply the best of James' early-'50s sides and a box set well worth saving for.—*Cub Koda*

Best of Elmore James: Early Years / 1995 / Ace ✦✦✦
This breaks down James' Modern recordings into a single disc retrospective, and a fine one it is, too. This compiles the A and B sides of every single recorded for the Bihari brothers, with the original Trumpet recording of "Dust My Broom" standing in the place of "1839 Blues." If you really want to hear James at his wildest and most unfettered and don't want to wade through a pile of alternate takes to get to it, we heartily suggest adding this one to the collection. Import. —*Cub Koda*

Dust My Broom: The Best of Elmore James, Vol. 2 / Relic ✦✦✦✦
A second Relic volume of classics from the Fire/Fury/Enjoy vaults that picks up where the company's first one left off. Even if you already own Capricorn's definitive two-disc collection of his Bobby Robinson-produced sides, you're missing one gem here: "Poor Little Angel Child," which features the robust vocal talent of harpist Sam Myers. Great sound quality throughout, with many stereo items. —*Bill Dahl*

Etta James (Etta James Hawkins)

b. Jan. 25, 1938, Los Angeles, CA
Vocals / Soul, R&B, Soul Blues

Few R&B singers have endured tragic travails on the monumental level that Etta James has and remain on earth to talk about it. The lady's no shrinking violet; her recent autobiography, *Rage to Survive*, describes her past (including numerous drug addictions) in sordid detail.

But her personal problems have seldom affected her singing. James has hung in there from the age of R&B and doo wop in the mid-'50s through soul's late-'60s heyday and right up to today (when her 1994 disc *Mystery Lady* paid loving jazz-based tribute to one of her idols, Billie Holiday). Etta James' voice has deepened over the years and coarsened more than a little, but still conveys remarkable passion and pain.

Jamesetta Hawkins was a child gospel prodigy, singing in her Los Angeles Baptist church choir (and over the radio) when she was only five years old under the tutelage of Professor James Earle Hines. She moved to San Francisco in 1950, soon teaming with two other girls to form a singing group. When she was 14, bandleader Johnny Otis gave the trio an audition. He particularly dug their answer song to Hank Ballard & the Midnighters' "Work with Me Annie."

Against her mother's wishes, the young singer embarked for L.A. to record "Roll with Me Henry" with the Otis band and vocalist Richard Berry in 1954 for Modern Records. Otis inverted her first name to devise her stage handle and dubbed her vocal group the Peaches (also Etta's nickname). "Roll with Me Henry," renamed "The Wallflower" when some radio programmers objected to the original title's connotations, topped the R&B charts in 1955.

The Peaches dropped from the tree shortly thereafter, but Etta James kept on singing for Modern throughout much of the decade. "Good Rockin' Daddy" also did quite well for her later in 1955, but deserving follow-ups such as "W-O-M-A-N" and "Tough Lover" (the latter a torrid rocker cut in New Orleans with Lee Allen on sax) failed to catch on.

James landed at Chicago's Chess Records in 1960, signing with their Argo subsidiary. Immediately, her recording career kicked into high gear; not only did a pair of duets with her then-boyfriend (Moonglows lead singer Harvey Fuqua) chart, her own sides chased each other up the R&B lists as well. Leonard Chess viewed James as a classy ballad singer with pop crossover potential, backing her with lush violin orchestrations for 1961's luscious "At Last" and "Trust in Me." But James' rougher side wasn't forsaken—the gospel-charged "Something's Got a Hold On Me" in 1962, a kinetic 1963 live LP (*Etta James Rocks the House*), and a blues-soaked 1966 duet with childhood pal Sugar Pie DeSanto, "In the Basement," ensured that.

Although Chess hosted its own killer house band, James traveled to Rick Hall's Fame studios in Muscle Shoals in 1967 and emerged with one of her all-time classics. "Tell Mama" was a searing slice of upbeat Southern soul that contrasted markedly with another standout from the same sessions, the spine-chilling ballad "I'd Rather Go Blind." Despite the death of Leonard Chess, Etta James remained at the label into 1975, experimenting toward the end with a more rock-based approach.

There were some mighty lean years, both personally and professionally, for Miss Peaches. But she got back on track recording-wise in 1988 with a set for Island, *Seven Year Itch*, that reaffirmed her Southern soul mastery. Her last few albums have been a varied lot—1990's *Sticking to My Guns* was contemporary in the extreme; 1992's Jerry Wexler-produced *The Right Time* for Elektra was slickly soulful, and her most recent outings have explored jazz.

In concert, Etta James is a sassy, no-holds-barred performer whose suggestive stage antics sometimes border on the obscene. She's paid her dues many times over as an R&B and soul pioneer; long may she continue to shock the uninitiated. —*Bill Dahl*

★ **At Last** / 1961 / MCA/Chess ✦✦✦✦✦
Most of these are also on *Greatest Sides*. Those that are not are well worth hearing. —*George Bedard*

The Second Time Around / 1961 / MCA/Chess ✦✦✦✦
Etta James' second album isn't what you pull off the shelf when you want to hear her belt some soul. Like her debut, it found Chess presenting her as more or less a pop singer, using orchestration arranged and conducted by Riley Hampton, and tackling mostly popular standards of the '40s. If you're not a purist, this approach won't bother you in the least; James sings with gusto, proving that she could more than hold her own in this idiom as well. R&B isn't entirely neglected either, with the rousing "Seven Day Fool" (co-written by Berry Gordy, Jr.) a standout; "Don't Cry

Baby" and "Fool That I Am" were R&B hits that made a mild impression on the pop charts as well. —Richie Unterberger

☆ **Rocks the House** / 1964 / MCA/Chess ✦✦✦✦✦
Simply one of the greatest live blues albums ever captured on tape. Cut in 1963 at the New Era Club in Nashville, the set finds Etta James in stellar shape as she forcefully delivers her own "Something's Got a Hold on Me" and "Seven Day Fool" interspersed with a diet of sizzling covers ("What'd I Say," "Sweet Little Angel," "Money," "Ooh Poo Pah Doo"). The CD incarnation adds three more great titles, including an impassioned reprise of her "All I Could Do Is Cry." Guitarist David T. Walker is outstanding whenever he solos. —Bill Dahl

Call My Name / 1967 / Cadet ✦✦✦✦
Still unavailable digitally, James' 1966 LP is dynamite Chicago soul, with the vaunted Chess house band in uplifting support. Among the many standouts are "I'm So Glad (I Found Love in You)," "It Must Be Your Love," and "Don't Pick Me for Your Fool." —Bill Dahl

Tell Mama / 1968 / MCA/Chess ✦✦✦✦
Leonard Chess dispatched Etta James to Muscle Shoals in 1967, and the move paid off with one of her best and most soul-searing Cadet albums. Produced by Rick Hall, the resultant album boasted a relentlessly driving title cut, the moving soul ballad "I'd Rather Go Blind," sizzling covers of Otis Redding's "Security" and Jimmy Hughes' "Don't Lose Your Good Thing," and a pair of fine Don Covay copyrights. The skin-tight session aces at Fame Studios really did themselves proud behind Miss Peaches. —Bill Dahl

R&B Dynamite / 1987 / Virgin ✦✦✦✦
The singer in her precocious formative years, headed by her 1955 R&B smash "Roll with Me Henry" (aka "The Wallflower"). James' follow-ups included the driving "Good Rockin' Daddy," a bluesy "W-O-M-A-N," and the New Orleans raveup "Tough Lover," which found her backed by the gang at Cosimo's (notably saxman Lee Allen). Even though her tenure at Modern Records produced only a handful of hits, these 22 cuts are delightful artifacts of the belter's earliest days. —Bill Dahl

How Strong Is a Woman: The Island Sessions / 1993 / 4th & Broadway ✦✦✦
How Strong Is a Woman collects the highlights from Etta James' late '80s and early '90s stint at Island Records. Although she didn't record any new classics while she was at the label, she demonstrated time and time again that she hadn't lost much of her vocal power and that she remained vital 40 years after she began recording. How Strong Is a Woman offers positive proof of that and is a good sampling of her work for Island. —Thom Owens

★ **The Essential Etta James** / Jun. 8, 1993 / MCA/Chess ✦✦✦✦✦
Forty-four tracks summarizing the long and brilliant Chess tenure of Miss Peaches, opening with her 1960 smash "All I Could Do Was Cry"; encompassing such sterling, fully orchestrated ballads as "At Last," "My Dearest Darling," and "Trust in Me"; and continuing through her 1961 gospel rocker "Something's Got a Hold on Me"; the Chicago soul standouts "I Prefer You" and "842-3089"; and her 1967 Muscle Shoals-cut smash "Tell Mama." A few of the '70s sides that conclude the two-disc set seem makeweight when compared to what preceded them, but most of the essentials are aboard. —Bill Dahl

These Foolish Things / 1995 / MCA/Chess ✦✦✦✦
James has long been a masterful blues balladeer—a talent spotlighted throughout the course of this 14-song collection. Some tracks are cushioned by string-enriched arrangements, others—notably 1965's passionate "Only Time Will Tell"—are melodic Chicago soul. Four tracks are previously unreleased, including her reading of Billie Holiday's "Lover Man." —Bill Dahl

Skip James (Nehemiah Curtis James)

b. 1902, d. 1969
Organ, Guitar, Piano, Kazoo, Vocals / Acoustic Delta Blues, Acoustic Mississippi Blues
Among the earliest and most influential Delta bluesmen to record, Skip James was the best known proponent of the so-called Bentonia school of blues players, a genre strain invested with as much fanciful scholarly "research" as any. Coupling an oddball guitar tuning set against eerie, falsetto vocals, James' early recordings could make the hair stand up on the back of your neck. Even more surprising was when blues scholars rediscovered him in the '60s and found his singing and playing skills intact. Influencing everyone from a young Robert Johnson ("Devil Got My Woman" became the basis of Johnson's "Hellhound on My Trail") to Eric Clapton (who recorded James' "I'm So Glad" on the first Cream album), Skip James' music, while from a commonly shared regional tradition, remains infused with his own unique personal spirit. —Cub Koda

☆ **Skip James Today!** / 1965 / Vanguard ✦✦✦✦✦
As quiet as it was kept then, Skip James might have made the best music of anyone who resurfaced during the mid-'60s "rediscovery" era for Mis-

sissippi country blues types. Certainly, there weren't many albums made during that time as good as this one; wonderful vocals, superb guitar and a couple of tunes with tasty piano make this essential. —Ron Wynn

★ **Complete Early Recordings** / 1994 / Yazoo ✦✦✦✦✦
Complete Early Recordings collects 18 tracks Skip James recorded in the early '30s. The single-disc compilation features all of his classic songs in their original versions, including "I'm So Glad." It's a concise and thorough collection and it's essential to any blues library. —Thom Owens

Blind Lemon Jefferson

b. Jul. 11, 1897, Couchman, TX, d. Dec. 1929
Guitar, Vocals / Blues, Texas Acoustic Blues
One of the first blues-guitar stars, Blind Lemon Jefferson became the most famous bluesman of the Roaring Twenties. His 78s shattered racial barriers, becoming popular from coast to coast and influencing a generation of musicians. His best songs forged original, imagistic themes with inventive arrangements and brilliantly improvised solos. He was a serious showman, balancing a driving, unpredictable guitar style with a booming, two-octave voice. His guitar became a second voice that complemented rather than repeated his lyrics. He often halted rhythm at the end of vocal lines to launch into elaborate solo flourishes, and he could play in unusual meters with a great deal of drive and flash. A man well acquainted with booze, gambling, and heavy-hipped mamas, Blind Lemon lived the rough-and-tumble themes that dominate his songs. Portraits of Afro-American life during the early 1900s, his lyrics create a unique body of poetry—humorous and harrowing, jivey and risqué, a stunning view of society from the perspective of someone at the bottom. To this day, he ranks among the most gifted and individualistic artists in blues history. —Jas Obrecht

★ **King of the Country Blues** / 1985 / Yazoo ✦✦✦✦✦
King of the Country Blues compiles 28 of Blind Lemon Jefferson's finest songs, all presented in the original '20s versions. It is the finest introduction to the guitarist—as well as the most effective, concise retrospective—ever assembled. —Thom Owens

Complete Recorded Works, Vol. 1-4 / Document ✦✦✦
Over the course of four separate CDs, Document compiled everything Blind Lemon Jefferson recorded in the '20s. Although there is an immense amount of brilliant music here—he was one of the great bluesmen of the '20s, after all—the sequencing and presentation make the series useful only to completists and historians. Other listeners will be better served by more concise collections. —Thom Owens

Blind Willie Johnson

b. 1890, d. 1947
Guitar, Vocals / Blues Gospel
A guitar-playing evangelist with a scary, emotion-charged voice, Blind Willie Johnson played the most exquisite slide ever heard. Void of frivolity and uncertainty, his 78s were clearly the work of a pained believer seeking street-corner redemption with a guitar and a tin cup. He was gifted with an incomparable sense of timing and tone, using his pocket-knife slide to duplicate his vocal inflections or to produce an unforgettable phrase from a single strike of a string. With its wide, rough vibrato, his voice was as fierce as Charles Patton's or Son House's, but much easier to understand.

In 1927 Johnson became one of the first gospel guitarists on 78. Among his 30 recorded songs is the landmark instrumental "Dark Was the Night, Cold Was the Ground," described by Ry Cooder as "the most transcendent piece in all American music." Johnson spent most of his life singing for the Baptist Church or playing for tips on the streets of Beaumont, TX. He died of pneumonia in the late '40s after his wife made him sleep on wet bedding after a house fire. Decades later, his music echoed in the styles of Mississippi Fred McDowell and Mance Lipscomb. He remains a slide guitarist without parallel, a player so perfect he's impossible to adequately imitate. —Jas Obrecht and Sandra Brennan

☆ **Praise God I'm Satisfied** / 1989 / Yazoo ✦✦✦✦✦
Pre-war gospel blues at its most harrowing and transcendental, this is unsurpassed slide guitar. —Jas Obrecht

Sweeter As the Years Go By / 1990 / Yazoo ✦✦✦✦
Blind Willie Johnson was perhaps the finest singing evangelist of all time. While the 16 tracks on this CD aren't as striking as those on the seminal Praise God I'm Satisfied, they're still invigorating and a vital part of his legacy. Johnson played acoustic rather than slide on several cuts, and didn't take flamboyant solos or add slashing counterpoint. But he demonstrated a skillful use of repetition and outstanding rhythmic and melodic skills. Johnson teamed with Willie B. Harris on several songs, and her rough, cutting voice proved an ideal match for his equally ragged sound. —Ron Wynn

★ **Complete Recordings of Blind Willie Johnson** / Apr. 27, 1993 / Columbia ✦✦✦✦✦

If you've never heard Blind Willie Johnson, you are in for one of the great, bone-chilling treats in music. Johnson played slide guitar and sang in a rasping, false bass that could freeze the blood. But no bluesman was he; this was gospel music of the highest order, full of emotion and heartfelt commitment. Of all the guitar-playing evangelists, Blind Willie Johnson may have been the very best. Though not related by bloodlines to Robert Johnson, comparisons in emotional commitment from both men cannot be helped. This two-CD anthology collects everything known to exist, and that's a lot of stark, harrowing emotional commitment no matter how you slice it. Not for the faint of heart, but hey, the good stuff never is. —*Cub Koda*

Johnnie Johnson

b. Jul. 8, 1924
Piano / R&B, Rock 'n' Roll, Blues Piano
A great boogie-woogie pianist, Johnnie Johnson's a self-taught player who's integrated the influence of Meade "Lux" Lewis, Earl Hines, and Clarence "Pinetop" Smith in his own delightful style. Johnson's professional career began after he ended a stint in the Army in 1946. His association with Chuck Berry began in 1952, when he hired Berry as the guitarist for his Sir John Trio. Berry shortly graduated to head songwriter and then group leader. Berry was signed to a Chess solo deal after Muddy Waters suggested the group audition. Berry recruited Johnson for the sessions, and his flaming piano riffs and licks were a vital ingredient on all Berry's fabulous singles. Berry's been quoted as saying "Johnny B. Goode" was written for Johnson. After leaving Berry in the '60s, Johnson played for a time with Albert King. He began heading his own band in the '70s. Johnson was featured in the Berry concert/retrospective film *Hail! Hail! Rock and Roll* and played on Keith Richards' debut solo release. He's recorded as a leader for Pulsar and Elektra, and also recorded with the Kentucky Headhunters. —*Ron Wynn*

● **Blue Hand Johnnie** / 1988 / Evidence ✦✦✦✦
Johnnie Johnson's rolling, barrelling licks are as enticing as ever on this reissue, but there are some other things that are not so grand. These include barely tolerable vocalists Barbara Carr and Stacy Johnson, whose enthusiasm is commendable, but whose vocals often get in the way. Johnson's covers of Fats Washington's "O.J. Blues" and "Black Nights" are great, as are his versions of "Honky Tonk" and "See See Rider." But he falters on "Baby, What You Want Me To," in part because he does not convey either the original's loping stride or laconic quality, and because it is not the kind of peppy arrangement and backbeat suited to his style. A decent effort that might have been superior with a couple of added touches. —*Ron Wynn*

Johnnie B. Bad / 1991 / Elektra/Nonesuch ✦✦✦✦
Keith Richards, Eric Clapton, and various NRBQ members guest on this pianist's inconsistent major-label debut. —*Bill Dahl*

Lonnie Johnson (Alonzo Johnson)

b. Feb. 8, 1889, New Orleans, LA, d. Jun. 16, 1970, Toronto, Canada
Guitar, Vocals / Blues, Acoustic Blues, Classic Jazz, Jazz Blues
Blues guitar simply would not have developed in the manner that it did if not for the prolific brilliance of Lonnie Johnson. He was there to help define the instrument's future within the genre and the genre's future itself at the very beginning, his melodic conception so far advanced from most of his pre-war peers as to inhabit a plane all his own. For more than 40 years, Johnson played blues, jazz, and ballads his way; he was a true blues originator whose influence hung heavy on a host of subsequent blues immortals.

Johnson's extreme versatility doubtless stemmed in great part from growing up in the musically diverse Crescent City. Violin caught his ear initially, but he eventually made the guitar his passion, developing a style so fluid and inexorably melodic that instrumental backing seemed superfluous. He signed up with OKeh Records in 1925 and commenced to recording at an astonishing pace—between 1925 and 1932, he cut an estimated 130 waxings. The red-hot duets he recorded with White jazz guitarist Eddie Lang (masquerading as Blind Willie Dunn) in 1928-29 were utterly groundbreaking in their ceaseless invention. Johnson also recorded pioneering jazz efforts in 1927 with no less than Louis Armstrong's Hot Five and Duke Ellington's orchestra.

After enduring the Depression and moving to Chicago, Johnson came back to recording life with Bluebird for a five-year stint beginning in 1939. Under the ubiquitous Lester Melrose's supervision, Johnson picked up right where he left off, selling quite a few copies of "He's a Jelly Roll Baker" for old Nipper. Johnson went with Cincinnati-based King Records in 1947 and promptly enjoyed one of the biggest hits of his uncommonly long career with the mellow ballad "Tomorrow Night," which topped the R&B charts for seven weeks in 1948. More hits followed posthaste: "Pleasing You (As Long as I Live)," "So Tired," and "Confused."

Time seemed to have passed Johnson by during the late '50s. He was toiling as a hotel janitor in Philadelphia when banjo player Elmer Snowden alerted Chris Albertson to his whereabouts. That rekindled a major comeback, Johnson cutting a series of albums for Prestige's Bluesville subsidary during the early '60s and venturing to Europe under the auspices of Horst Lippmann and Fritz Rau's American Folk Blues Festival banner in 1963. Finally, in 1969, Johnson was hit by a car in Toronto and died a year later from the effects of the accident.

Johnson's influence was massive, touching everyone from Robert Johnson, whose seminal approach bore strong resemblance to that of his older namesake, to Elvis Presley and Jerry Lee Lewis, who each paid heartfelt tribute with versions of "Tomorrow Night" while at Sun. —*Bill Dahl*

Losing Game / 1960 / Bluesville ✦✦✦✦
Johnson recorded prolifically for Prestige's Bluesville during his early-'60s comeback; this 1960 set is a typically gorgeous solo outing that ranges from torchy standards of the Tin Pan Alley species ("What a Difference a Day Makes," "Summertime") to bluesier pursuits of his own creation. —*Bill Dahl*

★ **Blues and Ballads** / Apr. 1960 / Bluesville ✦✦✦✦✦
Later Johnson, doing blues and ballads with jazz guitarist Elmer Snowden. Johnson's vocals are refined and sensitive. It is hard to hear him sing his own composition "I Found a Dream" and remain unmoved. Such a lovely album. —*Michael Erlewine*

Blues, Ballads and Jumpin' Jazz / Apr. 1960 / Bluesville ✦✦✦✦
This is an unusual CD. In 1960 guitarists Lonnie Johnson and Elmer Snowden (along with bassist Wendell Marshall) teamed up for *Blues and Ballads*, which was primarily a showcase for Johnson's blues vocals. This previously unreleased set from the same session has six instrumentals and just four vocals with Snowden generally in the lead. The two guitarists are heard good-naturedly suggesting songs before launching into spontaneous improvisations, and the results sound like an intimate concert. Highlights of this fun outing include "Lester Leaps In," "C-Jam Blues," and "Careless Love." —*Scott Yanow*

Idle Hours / Jul. 1961 / Bluesville ✦✦✦

The Complete Folkways Recordings / 1967 / Smithsonian/Folkways ✦✦✦✦
An even two dozen solo performances from late in the legendary guitarist's amazing career (1967), but chock full of stellar moments all the same. Artists of Johnson's versatility were rare even then—he brings a multitude of shadings to "My Mother's Eyes" and "How Deep Is the Ocean," then delivers a saucy "Juice Headed Baby" with the same stunning complexity. —*Bill Dahl*

Another Night to Cry / 1978 / Bluesville ✦✦✦

The Originator of Modern Guitar Blues / 1980 / Blues Boy ✦✦✦✦
Later Lonnie Johnson, demonstrating his proficiency on everything from pop to blues and R&B. It's excellently remastered, sequenced and presented, covering 1940s and '50s cuts. —*Ron Wynn*

★ **Steppin' on the Blues** / 1991 / Columbia/Legacy ✦✦✦✦✦
Groundbreaking guitar work of dazzling complexity that never fails to amaze—and this stuff was cut in the 1920s!! Johnson's astonishingly fluid guitar work was massively influential (Robert Johnson, for one, was greatly swayed by his waxings), and his no-nonsense vocals (frequently laced with threats of violence—"Got the Blues for Murder Only" and "She's Making Whoopee in Hell Tonight" are prime examples on this 19-cut collection) are scarcely less impressive. Johnson's torrid guitar duets with jazzman Eddie Lang retain their sense of legend nearly seven decades after they were cut. —*Bill Dahl*

He's a Jelly Roll Baker / Sep. 1992 / Bluebird ✦✦✦✦
This 20-song collection covers 1930s and '40s material in which Johnson primarily performs blues tunes, doing salty, sassy, mournful, and suggestive numbers in a distinctive, memorable fashion. His vocals on "Rambler's Blues," "In Love Again," the title cut, and several others are framed by brilliant, creative playing and excellent support from such pianists as Blind John Davis, Lil Hardin Armstrong, and Joshua Altheimer. This is tight, intuitive music in which Johnson sets the tone and dominates the songs. If you're unaware of Lonnie Johnson's brilliant blues material, here's an excellent introduction. —*Ron Wynn*

Stompin' at the Penny / 1995 / Columbia/Legacy ✦✦

Me and My Crazy Self / Charly ✦✦✦✦
With a firm emphasis on the less schmaltzy side of Johnson's 1947-1952 stint at Cincinnati's King Records, this 20-tracker finds the blues pioneer coming into the age of electric blues and R&B quite adroitly. His dignified vocal style similarly weathered the ensuing decades nicely—"You Can't Buy Love," "Friendless Blues," and the title track are bittersweet outings sporting multiple levels of subtlety. —*Bill Dahl*

Luther Johnson

b. Aug. 30, 1934, Davisboro, GA, **d.** Mar. 18, 1976
Guitar / Chicago Blues

The confusing plethora of artists working under the name of Luther (nickname here) Johnson can leave even those with a decent knowledge of blues in a major state of confusion. But in this biographical entry, we concern ourselves with the life and times of Luther "Georgia Boy/Snake Boy" Johnson who, to make matters even more confusing, also worked and recorded under the names Little Luther and Luther King.

He was born in 1934 in Davisboro, GA, which explains at least one of his nicknames, but it turns out his real name wasn't even Luther, but Lucius. One of ten children, he started playing guitar at the age of seven. He soon ran away from home and was in a reform school by 1947. A three-year stint in the Army followed. Upon his discharge, he played guitar as a member of the Milwaukee Supreme Angels gospel group, working the local church circuit. But the blues bug hit, and he soon had his own blues trio together, settling in Chicago by the early '60s. He played for a while with Elmore James and was a regular fixture in the Muddy Waters band by the mid-'60s. He recorded as Little Luther for Chess in the mid-'60s ("The Twirl," available on the Ace anthology, *Houserockin' Blues*, listed in the compilation section) and by 1970 was relocated to Boston, MA, working as a solo artist. The next five years found him working steadily on the college and blues festival circuit. Cancer overtook him on March 18, 1976. *— Cub Koda*

● **Lonesome in My Bedroom** / Dec. 18, 1975 / Evidence ✦✦✦✦
This was Johnson's final album before his death in 1976, and it was originally cut for Black and Blue (now reissued with three bonus tracks). While various tracks reflect the influence of Muddy Waters, Jimmy Reed, and John Lee Hooker, Johnson's own inimitable vocals, raspy lines and tart guitar eventually create his own aura. He is nicely backed by drummer Fred Below, bassist Dave Myers, guitar burner Lonnie Brooks and the solid rhythm work of Hubert Sumlin. This was a fine session for a good, occasionally outstanding blues artist. *—Ron Wynn*

Get Down to the Nitty Gritty / 1976 / New Rose ✦✦✦

Luther "Guitar Jr." Johnson

b. Aug. 30, 1934, Itta Bena, MS, **d.** Mar. 18, 1976
Guitar, Vocals / Modern Electric Blues, Blues, Electric Blues

Of the three blues guitarists answering to the name of Luther Johnson, this West Side-styled veteran is probably the best-known. Adding to the general confusion surrounding the triumvirate: like Luther "Georgia Boy" Johnson, "Guitar Junior" spent a lengthy stint in the top-seeded band of Muddy Waters (1972-1979).

Gospel and blues intersected in young Luther Johnson's life while he was still in Mississippi. But after he moved to Chicago in the mid-'50s, blues was his main passion. he worked with Ray Scott and Tall Milton Shelton before taking over the latter's combo in 1962. Magic Sam was a major stylistic inspiration to Johnson during the mid-'60s (Johnson spent a couple of years in Sam's band). The West Side approach remains integral to Johnson's sound today, even though he moved to the Boston area during the early '80s.

Johnson's 1976 debut album, *Luther's Blues*, was cut during a European tour with Muddy Waters. By 1980, he was on his own, recording with the Nighthawks as well as four tracks on Alligator's second series of *Living Chicago Blues* anthologies. With his own band, the Magic Rockers, and the Roomful of Blues horn section, Johnson released *Doin' the Sugar Too* on Rooster Blues in 1984. Since 1990, Johnson has been signed to Ron Levy's Bullseye Blues logo; his three albums for the label have been sizzling, soul-tinged blues (with a strong West Side flavor often slicing through). *— Bill Dahl*

Luther's Blues / Nov. 1, 1976 / Evidence ✦✦✦

Doin' the Sugar Too / 1984 / Rooster Blues ✦✦✦

I Want to Groove with You / 1990 / Bullseye Blues ✦✦✦✦
Now this is more like it. Johnson and his New England-based Magic Rockers sizzle the hide off the genre with tough West Side-styled grooves redolent of Johnson's Chicago upbringing but up-to-the-minute in their execution. With this set, Johnson fully came into his own as a recording artist. *—Bill Dahl*

Country Sugar Papa / Mar. 30, 1994 / Bullseye Blues ✦✦✦✦
Johnson's third and final album for producer Ron Levy's Bullseye Blues diskery is every bit as spellbinding as the prior pair. Whether fronting his latest batch of Magic Rockers or going it alone, Johnson is totally convincing. *—Bill Dahl*

● **Slammin' on the West Side** / 1996 / Telarc ✦✦✦✦
Lousy album title, great album. Johnson hasn't been based out of Chicago in years, but that sound remains at the heart of his approach—even when he's recording in Louisiana with a funky New Orleans rhythm section (bassist George Porter, Jr., and drummer Herman Ernest). Jump blues in the form of Buddy Johnson's "A Pretty Girl (A Cadillac and Some

Money)," the Magic Sam tribute "Hard Times (Have Surely Come)," the solo acoustic "Get Up and Go," a soul-slanted "Every Woman Needs to Be Loved"—Johnson smokes 'em all. *—Bill Dahl*

Luther "Houserocker" Johnson

Guitar, Vocals / Modern Electric Blues

The latest Luther Johnson to add his name to the blues directory is an adept singer/guitarist who is a current favorite on the Atlanta blues scene. Proficient in various shadings of the electric blues idiom, Johnson has recently extended his repertoire from covers of blues standards to his own material, performed with the same '50s/'60s flavor.

Johnson taught himself how to play guitar when he was a teenager in Atlanta by listening to records. Soon he began playing guitar in pickup bands, which gave him the opportunity to support such touring musicians as Johnny Winter. After several years playing in bar bands, Johnson formed his own group, the Houserockers.

The Houserockers played bars and clubs around Georgia for several years, eventually landing a record contract with Ichiban in 1989. That same year, Johnson released his debut album, *Takin' a Bite Outta the Blues*. Two years later, his second record, *Houserockin' Daddy*, appeared. Luther "Houserocker" Johnson continued to tour the US. throughout the '90s. *—Jim O'Neal and Stephen Thomas Erlewine*

Takin' a Bite Outta the Blues / 1989 / Ichiban ✦✦✦

● **Houserockin' Daddy** / 1991 / Ichiban ✦✦✦✦
Johnson is a traditional electric bluesman (now living and working in the Atlanta area) who was heavily influenced by Jimmy Reed. The album includes covers of Jimmy Reed, Lightnin' Slim, Howlin' Wolf, and Guitar Slim tunes. It's simple, driving, to the point, streamlined, no-frills blues. *—Niles J. Frantz*

Robert Johnson

b. May 8, 1911, Hazlehurst, MS, **d.** Aug. 16, 1938, Greenwood, MS
Guitar, Vocals / Acoustic Delta Blues

If the blues has a truly mythic figure, one whose story hangs over the music the way a Charlie Parker does over jazz or a Hank Williams does over country, it's Robert Johnson, certainly the most celebrated figure in the history of the blues. Of course his legend is immensely fortified by the fact that Johnson left behind a small legacy of recordings that are considered the emotional apex of the music itself. These recordings have entered not only the realm of blues standards ("Love in Vain," "Crossroads," "Sweet Home Chicago," "Stop Breaking Down"), but have been adapted by rock 'n' roll artists as diverse as the Rolling Stones, Steve Miller, Led Zeppelin, and Eric Clapton. While there are historical naysayers who would be more comfortable downplaying his skills and achievements (most of whom have never made a convincing case as to the source of his apocalyptic visions), Robert Johnson remains a potent force. As a singer, composer, and guitarist of considerable skill, he produced some of the genre's best music and is the ultimate blues legend. Doomed, haunted, driven by demons, a tormented genius dead at an early age, all of these make him a character of mythology.

The legend of his life goes something like this: Robert Johnson was a young Black man living on a plantation in rural Mississippi. Branded with a burning desire to become great blues musician, he was instructed to take his guitar to a crossroad near Dockery's plantation at midnight. There he was met by a large Black man (the Devil) who took the guitar from Johnson, tuned it, and handed it back. Within less than a year, in exchange for his everlasting soul, Robert Johnson became the king of the Delta blues singers, able to play, sing, and create the greatest blues anyone had ever heard.

As success came with live performances and phonograph recordings, Johnson remained tormented, constantly haunted by nightmares of hellhounds on his trail, his pain and mental anguish finding release only in the writing and performing of his music. Just as he was to be brought to Carnegie Hall to perform in John Hammond's first Spirituals to Swing concert, the news came from Mississippi; Robert Johnson was dead, poisoned by a jealous husband while playing a jook joint. Those who were there swear he was last seen alive foaming at the mouth, crawling around on all fours, hissing and snapping at onlookers like a mad dog. His dying words (either spoken or written on a piece of scrap paper) were, "I pray that my Redeemer will come and take me from my grave." He was buried in a pine box in an unmarked grave, his deal with the Devil at an end.

Of course, Johnson's influences in the real world were far more disparate than the legend suggests. As a teenage plantation worker, Johnson fooled with a harmonica a little bit, but seemingly had no major musical skills to speak of. Every attempt to sit in with local titans of the stature of Son House, Charlie Patton, Willie Brown, and others brought howls of derision from the older bluesmen. Son House: "We'd all play for the Saturday night balls, and there'd be this little boy hanging around. That was Robert Johnson. He blew a harmonica then, and he was pretty good at that, but he wanted to play a guitar. He'd sit at our feet and play during the breaks and such another racket you'd never heard." Johnson married young and left Robinsonville, wandering the Delta and using Hazelhurst as base, determined to become a full-time professional musician after his wife died during childbirth. Johnson returned to Robinsonville a few years later, and when he encountered House and Willie Brown at a juke joint in Banks, MS, according to House, "When he finished all our mouths were standing open. I said, 'Well, ain't that fast! He's gone now!'" To a man, there was only one explanation as how Johnson had gotten *that* good *that* fast; he had sold his soul to the Devil.

But Johnson's skills were acquired in a far more conventional manner, born more of a concentrated Christian work ethic than a Faustian bargain with old Scratch. He idolized the Delta recording star Lonnie Johnson—sometimes introducing himself to newcomers as "Robert Lonnie, one of the Johnson brothers"—and he drew his style from the music of Scrapper Blackwell, Skip James, and Kokomo Arnold. His slide style certainly came from hours of watching local stars like Charlie Patton and Son House, among others. Perhaps the biggest influence, however, came from an unrecorded bluesman named Ike Zinneman. We'll never really know what Zinneman's music sounded like (we do know from various reports that he liked to practice late at night in the local graveyard, sitting on tombstones while he strummed away) or how much of his personal muse he imparted to Johnson, if any. What *is* known is that after a year or so under Zinneman's tutelage, Johnson returned with an encyclopedic knowledge of his instrument, an ability to sing and play in a multiplicity of styles, and a very carefully worked out approach to song construction, keeping his original lyrics with him in a personal digest. As an itinerant musician, playing at country suppers as well as on the street, he could play and sing everything from blues pieces to the pop and hillbilly tunes of the day. His most enduring contribution, the boogie bass line played on the bottom strings of the guitar (adapted from piano players), has become part and parcel of the sound most people associate with down-home blues. It is a sound so very much a part of the music's fabric that the listener cannot imagine the styles of Jimmy Reed, Elmore James, Eddie Taylor, Lightnin' Slim, Hound Dog Taylor, or a hundred lesser lights without that essential component. As his playing partner Johnny Shines put it, "Some of the things that Robert did with the guitar affected the way everybody played. He'd do rundowns and turnbacks. He'd do repeats. None of this was being done. In the early '30s, boogie on the guitar was rare, something to be heard. Because of Robert, people learned to complement theirselves, carrying their own bass as their own lead with this one instrument."

Although Robert Johnson never recorded as much as Lonnie Johnson, Charlie Patton, or Blind Lemon Jefferson, he certainly traveled more than all of them put together. After his first recordings came out and "Terraplane Blues" became his signature tune (a so-called "race" record selling over three or four thousand copies in the early to mid-'30s was considered a hit), Johnson hit the road, playing anywhere and everywhere. Instilled with a seemingly unquenchable desire to experience new places and things, his wandering nature took him up and down the Delta and as far afield as St. Louis, Chicago, Detroit (where he performed over the radio on the "Elder Moten Hour"), and New York City, places Son House and Charlie Patton had seen only in the movies, if that. But the end came at a Saturday-night dance at a juke joint in Three Forks, MS, in August 1938. Playing with Honeyboy Edwards and Sonny Boy Williamson (Rice Miller), Johnson was given a jug of moonshine whiskey laced with either poison or lye, presumably by the husband of a woman the singer had made advances toward. He continued playing into the night until he was too sick to go on, and was brought back to a boarding house in Greenwood. He lay sick for several days, successfully sweating the poison out of his system, but caught pneumonia and died on August 16. The legend was just beginning.

In the mid-'60s, Columbia Records released *King of the Delta Blues Singers,* the first compilation of Johnson's music and one of the earliest collections of pure country blues. Rife with liner notes full of romantic speculation, little in the way of hard information, and a painting instead of a picture, this for years was the world's sole introduction to the music and the legend, doing much to promote both. A second volume—collecting the other master takes and issuing a few of the alternates—was released in the '70s, giving fans a first-hand listen to music that had been circulated only through bootleg tapes and albums or cover versions by English rock stars. Finally in 1991—after years of litigation—a complete two-CD box set was released with every scrap of Johnson material known to exist plus the holy grail of the blues; the publishing of the only two known photographs of the man himself. Columbia's parent company, Sony, was hoping that sales might hit 20,000. The box set sold more than a million units, the first blues recordings ever to do so.—*Cub Koda*

☆ **King of the Delta Blues Singers** / 1961 / Columbia ✦✦✦✦✦
Reading about the power inherent in Robert Johnson's music is one thing, but actually experiencing it is another matter entirely. Here's where you go to find it. The gold-disc edition of this album is certainly worth the extra money, as it was mastered off newly discovered safety tapes of quality far superior to even that of the 1991 box set. If there is such a thing as a "greatest hits" package available on Johnson, this landmark album would come very close indeed. The majority of Johnson's best-known tunes are aboard; "Crossroads," "Terraplane Blues," "Me and the Devil Blues," "Come On in My Kitchen," and the apocalyptic visions contained in "Hellhound on My Trail" are the blues at its finest, the lyrics sheer poetry. If you are starting your blues collection, be sure to make this your first purchase. —*Cub Koda*

☆ **King of the Delta Blues Singers, Vol. 2** / 1970 / Columbia ✦✦✦✦✦
This second volume—although made somewhat superfluous by the arrival two decades later of the box set—contains the rest of the issued takes and some, but not all, of the alternate takes. The music is excellent, featuring the first album appearance of "Love in Vain." —*Cub Koda*

★ **The Complete Recordings** / 1990 / Columbia/Legacy ✦✦✦✦✦
A double-disc box set containing everything Robert Johnson ever recorded, *The Complete Recordings* is essential listening, but it is also slightly problematic. The problems aren't in the music itself, of course, which is stunning, and the fidelity of the recordings is the best it ever has been or ever will be. Instead, it's in the track sequencing. As the title implies, *The Complete Recordings* contains all of Johnson's recorded material, including a generous selection of alternate takes. All of the alternates are sequenced directly after the master, which can make listening to the album a little intimidating and tedious for novices. Certainly, the alternates can be programmed out with a CD player, but the set would have been more palatable if the alternate takes were presented on a separate disc. Nevertheless, this is a minor complaint—Robert Johnson's music retains its power no matter what context it is presented in. He, without question, deserves this kind of deluxe box-set treatment. —*Stephen Thomas Erlewine*

Tommy Johnson

b. 1896, Terry, MS, **d.** Nov. 1, 1956, Crystal Springs, MS
Guitar, Kazoo, Vocals / Acoustic Delta Blues, Acoustic Mississippi Blues
Next to Son House and Charlie Patton, no one was more important to the development of pre-Robert Johnson Delta blues than Tommy Johnson. Armed with a powerful voice that could go from a growl to an eerie falsetto range and a guitar style that had all of the early figures and licks of the Delta style clearly delineated, Johnson only recorded for two years—from 1928 to 1930—but left behind a body of work that's hard to ignore.

The legend of Tommy Johnson is even harder to ignore. The stories about his live performances—where he would play the guitar behind his neck in emulation of Charlie Patton's showboating while hollering the blues at full-throated level for hours without a break—are part of it. So is his uncontrolled womanizing and alcoholism, both of which constantly got him in trouble. Johnson's addiction to spirits was so pronounced that he was often seen drinking Sterno-denatured alcohol used for artificial heat—or shoe polish strained through bread for the kick each could offer when whiskey wasn't affordable or available in dry counties throughout the South. Then there's the crossroads story. Yes, years before the deal with the Devil at a deserted Delta crossroad was being used as an explanation of the other-worldly abilities of young Robert Johnson, the story was being told repeatedly about Tommy, often by the man himself to reinforce his abilities to doubting audiences.

Then there's the music. His "Cool Water Blues" got amped up in the '50s by one of his early admirers, Howlin' Wolf, and became "I Asked for Water (She Brought Me Gasoline)." Another signature piece, his "Maggie Campbell," came with a chord progression that was used for infinite variations by blues players dating all the way back to his contemporary Charlie Patton through Robert Nighthawk. His best-known numbers have survived to modern times; "Big Road Blues" is probably best known to contemporary blues fans from adaptations by Floyd Jones and others, while his "Canned Heat Blues"—a bone-chilling account of his complete addiction to alcohol and his slavish attempts to score it by whatever means necessary—was the tune that gave a California blues-rock band their name. After awhile, all of the above starts adding up, no matter how you slice it. Tommy Johnson was one tough hombre, and a real piece of work.—*Cub Koda*

★ **Complete Recorded Works** / Document ✦✦✦✦✦
The complete Victor and Paramount sides from 1928-1929 are sequenced in chronological order. —*Jas Obrecht*

Curtis Jones

b. Aug. 18, 1906, Naples, TX, **d.** Sep. 11, 1971, Munich, Germany
Piano, Vocals / Electric Chicago Blues, Piano Blues
The origins of the blues standard "Tin Pan Alley" can be traced directly back to pianist Curtis Jones, who also enjoyed considerable success in

1937 with his "Lonesome Bedroom Blues" for Vocalion (a song inspired by a breakup with his wife).

Jones started out on guitar but switched to the 88s after moving to Dallas. He arrived in Chicago in 1936 and recorded for Vocalion, Bluebird, and Okeh from 1937 to 1941. But the war ended his recording career until 1953, when powerful deejay Al Benson issued a one-off single by Jones, "Wrong Blues"/"Cool Playing Blues," on his Parrot label with L.C. McKinley on guitar. In 1960, Jones waxed his debut album, *Trouble Blues*, for Prestige's Bluesville subsidiary with a classy crew of New York session aces and Chicagoan Johnny "Big Moose" Walker on guitar. By then, his audience was shifting drastically, as he became a fixture on the Chicago folk circuit. His next LP, *Lonesome Bedroom Blues*, was a 1962 solo affair for Delmark offering definitive renditions of the title cut and "Tin Pan Alley." Jones left Chicago permanently in January of 1962, settling in Europe and extensively touring the continent until his death in 1971. — *Bill Dahl*

● **Trouble Blues** / 1983 / Original Blues Classics ◆◆◆◆
The taciturn pianist in the company of a fine New York rhythm section and Johnny "Big Moose" Walker (but on guitar, not piano) made for a winning combination on this 1960 album. Jones delivers his downbeat "Suicide Blues," "Low Down Worried Blues," "Lonesome Bedroom Blues" . . . well, you get the picture. Jones wasn't exactly an upbeat kind of guy. The compilers did unearth a bonus for the CD version: Jones' treatment of "Pinetop Boogie." — *Bill Dahl*

Little Johnny Jones

b. Nov. 1, 1924, Jackson, MS, **d.** Nov. 19, 1964, Chicago, IL
Harmonica, Piano, Vocals / Piano Blues
One of the great blues piano men of all time, Johnny Jones is well known for his striking work on a number of seminal sides by slide guitar legend Elmore James. He recorded very little as a solo artist, but what few recordings exist are all classics of the Chicago style.

Born and raised in Mississippi, Jones learned to play piano when he was a child. In the mid-'40s, he and his faimly moved to Chicago and within a few years, he was playing concerts with Tampa Red. In 1949, he cut his first recording session, appearing on several sides with Tampa Red; between 1949 and 1951, he recorded several songs with Tampa Red. The year after his recording debut, Jones recorded two songs for Aristocrat. On these songs, he was supported by Muddy Waters, whom Jones had supported earlier in that same session.

In 1951, Johnny Jones began a working relationship with Elmore James that would prove to be his most productive and creative. Throughout the '50s, he performed and recorded with James, appearing on most of the slide guitarist's classic singles. In the late '50s, Jones left James and began performing with Magic Sam. During the early '60s, Jones worked as a session pianist, appearing on many classic Chicago blues sides, including numbers by Howlin' Wolf and Jimmy Reed. Johnny Jones continued working until he developed lung cancer in 1963. He died the following year. — *Cub Koda and Stephen Thomas Erlewine*

● **Johnny Jones with Billy Boy Arnold** / 1979 / Alligator ◆◆◆◆
Thank heaven Norman Dayron had the presence of mind to capture these sides by Chicago pianist Johnny Jones when he played at the Fickle Pickle in 1963—as little as remains on tape of his talents as a singer, we're eternally indebted to Dayron. Jones' insinuating vocals and bedrock 88s are abetted by harpist Billy Boy Arnold on these performances, and that's it—he had no rhythm section to fall back on. — *Bill Dahl*

Keb' Mo'

Guitar, Vocals / Modern Blues
Keb' Mo' draws heavily on the old-fashioned country blues style of Robert Johnson, but keeps his sound contemporary with touches of soul and folksy storytelling. He writes much of his own material and has applied his acoustic, electric, and slide guitar skills to jazz and rock-oriented bands in the past as well. Born Kevin Moore in Los Angeles to parents of Southern descent, he was exposed to gospel music at a young age. At 21, Moore joined an R&B band later hired for a tour by Papa John Creach and played on three of Creach's albums. Opening for jazz and rock artists such as the Mahavishnu Orchestra, Jefferson Starship, and Loggins & Messina helped broaden Moore's horizons and musical abilities. Moore cut an R&B-based solo album, *Rainmaker*, in 1980 for Casablanca, which promptly folded. In 1983, he joined Monk Higgins' band as a guitarist and met a number of blues musicians who collectively increased his understanding of the music. He subsequently joined a vocal group called the Rose Brothers and gigged around L.A. 1990 found Moore portraying a Delta bluesman in a local play called *Rabbit Foot* and he later played Robert Johnson in a docudrama called *Can't You Hear the Wind Howl?* He released his self-titled debut album as Keb' Mo' in 1994, featuring two Robert Johnson covers, 11 songs written or co-written by Moore, and his guitar and banjo work. Keb' Mo' per-

formed a well-received set at the 1995 Newport Folk Festival. — *Steve Huey*

● **Keb' Mo'** / 1995 / OKeh/550/Epic ◆◆◆◆
Keb' Mo's self-titled debut is an edgy, ambitious collection of gritty country blues. Keb' Mo' pushes into new directions, trying to incorporate some of the sensibilities of the slacker revolution without losing touch of the tradition that makes the blues the breathing, vital art form it is. His attempts aren't always successful, but his gutsy guitar playing and impassioned vocals, as well as his surprisingly accomplished songwriting, make *Ke'b Mo'* a debut to treasure. — *Thom Owens*

Albert King

b. Apr. 25, 1923, Indianola, MS, **d.** Dec. 21, 1992
Guitar, Vocals / Soul, R&B, Modern Electric Blues
Albert King is truly a "King of the Blues," although he doesn't hold that title (B.B. does). Along with B.B. and Freddie King, Albert King is one of the major influences on blues and rock guitar players. Without him, modern guitar music would not sound as it does—his style has influenced both Black and White blues players from Otis Rush and Robert Cray to Eric Clapton and Stevie Ray Vaughan. It's important to note that while almost all modern blues guitarists seldom play for long without falling into a B.B. King guitar cliché, Albert King never does—he's had his own style and unique tone from the beginning.

Albert King plays guitar left-handed, without re-stringing the guitar from the right-handed setup; this "upside-down" playing accounts for his difference in tone, since he pulls down on the same strings that most players push up on when bending the blues notes. King's massive tone and totally unique way of squeezing bends out of a guitar string has had a major impact. Many young White guitarists—especially rock 'n' rollers—have been influenced by King's playing, and many players who emulate his style may never have heard of Albert King, let alone heard his music. His style is immediately distinguishable from all other blues guitarists, and he's one of the most important blues guitarists to ever pick up the electric guitar.

Born in Indianola, MS, but raised in Forrest City, AR, Albert King (born Albert Nelson) taught himself how to play guitar when he was a child, building his own instrument out of a cigar box. At first, he played with gospel groups—most notably the Harmony Kings—but after hearing Blind Lemon Jefferson, Lonnie Johnson, and several other blues musicians, he solely played the blues. In 1950, he met MC Reeder, who owned the T-99 nightclub in Osceola, AR. King moved to Osceloa shortly afterward, joining the T-99's house band, the In the Groove Boys. The band played several local Arkansas gigs besides the T-99, including several shows for a local radio station.

After enjoying success in the Arkansas area, King moved to Gary, IN, in 1953, where he joined a band that also featured Jimmy Reed and John Brim. Both Reed and Brim were guitarists, which forced King to play drums in the group. At this time, he adopted the name Albert King, which he assumed after B.B. King's "Three O'Clock Blues" became a huge hit. King met Willie Dixon shortly after moving to Gary, and the bassist/songwriter helped the guitarist set up an audition at Parrot Records. King passed the audition and cut his first session late in 1953. Five songs were recorded during the session and only one single, "Be on Your Merry Way" / "Bad Luck Blues," was released; the other tracks appeared on various compilations over the next four decades. Although it sold respectably, the single didn't gather enough attention to earn him another session with Parrot. In early 1954, King returned to Osceola and re-joined the In the Groove Boys; he stayed in Arkansas for the next two years.

In 1956, King moved to St. Louis, where he initially sat in with local bands. By the fall of 1956, King was headlining several clubs in the area. King continued to play the St. Louis circuit, honing his style. During these years, he began playing his signature Gibson Flying V, which he named Lucy. By 1958, King was quite popular in St. Louis, which led to a contract with the fledgling Bobbin Records in the summer of 1959. On his first Bobbin recordings, King recorded with a pianist and a small horn section, which made the music sound closer to jump blues than Delta or Chicago blues. Nevertheless, his guitar was taking a center stage and it was clear that he had developed a unique, forceful sound. King's records for Bobbin sold well in the St. Louis area, enough so that King Records leased the "Don't Throw Your Love on Me So Strong" single from the smaller label. When the single was released nationally late in 1961, it became a hit, reaching No. 14 on the R&B charts. King Records continued to lease more material from Bobbin—including a full album, *The Big Blues*, which was released in 1963—but nothing else approached the initial success of "Don't Throw Your Love on Me So Strong." Bobbin also leased material to Chess, which appeared in the late '60s.

Albert King left Bobbin in late 1962 and recorded one session for King Records in the spring of 1963, which was much more pop-oriented than his previous work; the singles issued from the session failed to sell.

Within a year, he cut four songs for the local St. Louis independent label Coun-Tree, which was run by a jazz singer named Leo Gooden. Though these singles didn't appear in many cities—St. Louis, Chicago, and Kansas City were the only three to register sales—they foreshadowed his coming work with Stax Records. Furthermore, they were very popular within St. Louis, so much so that Gooden resented King's success and pushed him off the label.

After his stint at Coun-Tree, Albert King signed with Stax Records in 1966. His records for Stax would bring him stardom, both within blues and rock circles. All of his '60s Stax sides were recorded with the label's house band, Booker T. & the MGs, which gave his blues a sleek, soulful sound. That soul underpinning gave King crossover appeal, as evidenced by his R&B chart hits—"Laundromat Blues" (1966) and "Cross Cut Saw" (1967) both went Top 40, while "Born Under a Bad Sign" (1967) charted in the Top 50. Furthermore, King's style was appropriated by several rock 'n' roll players, most notably Jimi Hendrix and Eric Clapton, who copied Albert's "Personal Manager" guitar solo on the Cream song, "Strange Brew." Albert King's first album for Stax, 1967's *Born Under a Bad Sign*, was a collection of his singles for the label and became one of the most popular and influential blues albums of the late '60s. Beginning in 1968, Albert King was playing not only to blues audiences, but also to crowds of young rock 'n' rollers. He frequently played at the Fillmore West in San Francisco and he even recorded an album, *Live Wire / Blues Power*, at the hall in the summer of 1968.

Early in 1969, King recorded *Years Gone By*, his first true studio album. Later that year, he recorded a tribute album to Elvis Presley (*King Does the King's Things*) and a jam session with Steve Cropper and Pops Staples (*Jammed Together*), in addition to performing a concert with the St. Louis Symphony Orchestra. For the next few years, Albert toured America and Europe, returning to the studio in 1971, to record the *Lovejoy* album. In 1972, he recorded *I'll Play the Blues for You*, which featured accompaniment from the Bar-Kays, the Memphis Horns, and the Movement. The album was rooted in the blues, but featured distinctively modern soul and funk overtones.

By the mid-'70s, Stax was suffering major financial problems, so King left the label for Utopia, a small subsidiary of RCA Records. Albert released two albums on Utopia, which featured some concessions to the constraints of commercial soul productions. Although he had a few hits at Utopia, his time there was essentially a transitional period, where he discovered that it was better to follow a straight blues direction and abandon contemporary soul crossovers. King's subtle shift in style was evident on his first albums for Tomato Records, the label he signed with in 1978. Albert stayed at Tomato for several years, switching to Fantasy in 1983, releasing two albums for the label.

In the mid-'80s, Albert King announced his retirement, but it was short-lived—he continued to regularly play concerts and festivals throughout America and Europe for the rest of the decade. King continued to perform until his sudden death in 1992, when he suffered a fatal heart attack on December 21. The loss to the blues was a major one—although many guitarists have tried, no one can replace King's distinctive, trailblazing style. Albert King is a tough act to follow. —*Daniel Erlewine and Stephen Thomas Erlewine*

★ **Born under a Bad Sign** / 1967 / Stax ✦✦✦✦✦
One day this southpaw was playing little clubs in Osceola, AR, the next he was headlining rock ballrooms like the Fillmore. This is the album that changed everything—including seemingly 90% of the blues and rock guitarists on the landscape. Backed by Booker T. & the MGs and the Memphis Horns, King proved he was every bit as hip as they, not to mention flexible. In fact, as throughout his career, he used a relatively small vocabulary of licks, but gave them slightly different timing and English, depending on the groove and the surroundings. The result was a whole new language. This LP is one big classic from top to bottom. "Crosscut Saw," "Oh, Pretty Woman," "The Hunter," "As the Years Go Passing By," "Personal Manager," the title tune—every track is a must-have. —*Dan Forte*

Live Wire/Blues Power / 1968 / Stax ✦✦✦✦
Live Wire/Blues Power is one of Albert King's definitive albums. Recorded live at the Fillmore Auditorium in 1968, the guitarist is at the top of his form throughout the record—his solos are intense and piercing. The band is fine, but ultimately it's King's show—he makes Herbie Hancock's "Watermelon Man" dirty and funky and wrings out all the emotion from "Blues at Sunrise." —*Thom Owens*

Albert King: King of the Blues Guitar / 1969 / Atlantic ✦✦✦✦
No blues guitarist who emerged during the '60s wielded more influence. This incendiary collection contains his best '60s workouts for Stax. —*Bill Dahl*

★ **King of the Blues Guitar** / 1969 / Atlantic ✦✦✦✦✦
Atlantic's original vinyl edition of this was comprised of Albert's Stax singles—a few from *Born under a Bad Sign*, along with "Cold Feet," "I Love Lucy" (two of King's patented monologues), and the beautiful "You're Gonna Need Me." Great stuff. Even greater, though, is the CD reissue,

which includes those singles (which didn't appear on any other LPs) and all of *Born under a Bad Sign*. Need I say more? —*Dan Forte*

Lovejoy / 1971 / Stax ✦✦✦

I'll Play the Blues for You / 1972 / Stax ✦✦✦✦
A moody, R&B-influenced set with plenty of intensity. —*Bill Dahl*

The Pinch / 1976 / Stax ✦✦✦

The Blues Don't Change / 1977 / Stax ✦✦✦
Previously titled *The Pinch* when it was issued on LP in 1977, this material was actually recorded in 1973 and 1974. These are some of King's most soul-oriented sessions, with contributions from the Memphis Horns and a couple of the MGs. Blues-oriented fans may find this one of his lesser efforts, putting less emphasis on King's guitar work than usual, and more on the vocals and arrangements. This approach has its merits, though, as it's one of the more relaxed items in the King catalog, with none of the occasional excess that crept into his blues guitar solos. —*Richie Unterberger*

Chronicle (With Little Milton) / 1979 / Stax ✦✦✦
This compilation has a leftover feel; the liner notes provide no sources and dates, admitting only that these are "Stax recordings, some never before available on LP." If you're a big fan of one or both of the artists involved, though, it's not bad, with a quality that's generally consistent with their fully baked Stax-era albums, though the King half of the program is somewhat superior to the Milton tracks. —*Richie Unterberger*

Albert King Live / 1979 / Tomato ✦✦✦

Tomato Years / 197_ / Rhino/Tomato ✦✦✦

In San Francisco-Crosscut Saw / Mar. 1983 / Stax ✦✦✦
A reissue of King's 1983 LP *San Francisco '83* (a studio album, not a live one), with the addition of two previously unreleased cuts. His first new release in five years, it wasn't one of King's better records. But it did represent a return to a basic five-piece sound, an improvement upon his over-produced outings of the late '70s. —*Richie Unterberger*

Blues at Sunrise: Live at Montreux / 1988 / Stax ✦✦✦

Let's Have a Natural Ball / 1989 / Modern Blues ✦✦✦✦
Great compilation of King's Bobbin sides of the late '50s and early '60s. —*Bill Dahl*

Wednesday Night in San Francisco: Recorded Live at the Fillmore Auditorium / 1990 / Stax ✦✦✦

Thursday Night in San Francisco: Recorded Live at the Fillmore Auditorium / 1990 / Stax ✦✦✦

The Best of Albert King, Vol. 1 / 1991 / Stax ✦✦✦✦
"The best of Albert King"? More like the best material that he happened to record for Stax between 1968 and 1973. Even that's debatable, the 13 tracks including covers such as "Honky Tonk Woman," "Sky Is Crying," and "Hound Dog." It does present a reasonable cross-section of his soul-inflected work of the period, drawing from over a half-dozen LPs and a couple of singles, though you might be as well or better off with his more focused individual titles. And for the true "best of Albert King," Rhino's *Ultimate Collection* remains the hands-down winner. —*Richie Unterberger*

★ **Ultimate Collection** / 1993 / Rhino ✦✦✦✦✦
This two-disc set covers a few early songs, but concentrates on the inspired blend of soul, blues, and rock that King made famous in the 1960s and '70s. Many songs, such as "Laundromat Blues," "Crosscut Saw," "I'll Play the Blues for You" and of course "Born Under a Bad Sign," featured simple riffs, catchy lyrics, and solid grooves parlayed into memorable performances through King's confident vocals and soaring solos. To be sure, there were formulaic numbers, and after a time King's solos and note choices were as much show biz effect as they were exciting, but the anthology's live cuts show that King was always capable of surprise and invention on the bandstand. The later numbers aren't quite as powerful, but King's rendition of "Phone Booth" shows his successors and imitators what legitimate blues playing is all about. —*Ron Wynn*

Hard Bargain / Feb. 1996 / Stax ✦✦✦

B.B. King (Riley B. King)

b. Sep. 16, 1925, Indianola, MS
Guitar, Vocals / R&B, Modern Electric Blues
Universally hailed as the reigning king of the blues, the legendary B.B. King is without a doubt the single most important electric guitarist of the last half century. A contemporary blues guitar solo without at least a couple of recognizable King-inspired bent notes is all but unimaginable, and he remains a supremely confident singer capable of wringing every nuance from any lyric (and he's tried his hand at many an unlikely song—anybody recall his version of "Love Me Tender"?).

Yet B.B. King remains an intrinsically humble superstar, an utterly accessible icon who welcomes visitors into his dressing room with self-effacing graciousness. Between 1951 and 1985, King notched an amazing 74 entries on *Billboard*'s R&B charts, and he was one of the few full-fledged blues artists to score a major pop hit when his 1970 smash "The Thrill Is Gone" crossed over to mainstream success (engendering memorable appearances on *The Ed Sullivan Show* and *American Bandstand!*).

The seeds of King's enduring talent were sown deep in the blues-rich Mississippi Delta. That's where Riley B. King was sired—in Itta Bena, to be exact. By no means was his childhood easy. Young Riley was shuttled between his mother's home and his grandmother's residence. The youth put in long days working as a sharecropper and devoutly sang the Lord's praises at church before moving to Indianola—another town located in the very heart of the Delta—in 1943.

Country and gospel music left an indelible impression on King's musical mindset as he matured, along with the styles of blues greats T-Bone Walker and Lonnie Johnson and jazz geniuses Charlie Christian and Django Reinhardt. In 1946, B.B. King set off for Memphis to look up his cousin, rough-edged country blues guitarist Bukka White. For ten invaluable months, White taught his eager young relative the finer points of playing blues guitar. After returning briefly to Indianola and the sharecropper's eternal struggle with his wife Martha, King arrived in Memphis once again in late 1948. This time, he stuck around for a while.

King was soon broadcasting his music live via Memphis radio station WDIA, a frequency that had only recently switched to a pioneering all-Black format. Local club owners preferred that their attractions also held down radio gigs so they could plug their nightly appearances on the air. When WDIA deejay Maurice "Hot Rod" Hulbert exited his air-shift, King took over his record-spinning duties. At first tagged "The Pep-tikon Boy" (an alcohol-loaded elixir that rivaled Hadacol) when WDIA put him on the air, King's on-air handle became the "Beale Street Blues Boy," later shortened to Blues Boy and then a far snappier B.B.

1949 was a four-star breakthrough year for King. He cut his first four tracks for Jim Bulleit's Bullet Records (including a number entitled "Miss Martha King" after his wife), then signed a contract with the Bihari brothers' Los Angeles-based RPM Records. King cut a plethora of sides in Memphis over the next couple of years for RPM, many of them produced by a relative newcomer named Sam Phillips (whose Sun Records was still a distant dream at that point in time). Phillips was independently producing sides for both the Biharis and Chess; his stable also included Howlin' Wolf, Rosco Gordon, and fellow WDIA personality Rufus Thomas.

The Biharis also recorded some of King's early output themselves, erecting portable recording equipment wherever they could locate a suitable facility. King's first national R&B chart-topper in 1951, "Three O'Clock Blues" (previously waxed by Lowell Fulson), was cut at a Memphis YMCA. King's Memphis running partners included vocalist Bobby Bland, drummer Earl Forest, and ballad-singing pianist Johnny Ace. When King hit the road to promote "Three O'Clock Blues," he handed the group, known as the Beale Streeters, over to Ace.

It was during this era that King first named his beloved guitar "Lucille." Seems that while he was playing a joint in a little Arkansas town called Twist, fisticuffs broke out between two jealous suitors over a lady. The brawlers knocked over a kerosene-filled garbage pail that was heating the place, setting the room ablaze. In the frantic scramble to escape the flames, King left his guitar inside. He foolishly ran back in to retrieve it, dodging the flames and almost losing his life. When the smoke had cleared, King learned that the lady who had inspired such violent passion was named Lucille. Plenty of Lucilles have passed through his hands since; Gibson has even marketed a B.B.-approved guitar model under the name.

The 1950s saw King establish himself as a perennially formidable hitmaking force in the R&B field. Recording mostly in L.A. (the WDIA airshift became impossible to maintain by 1953 due to King's endless touring) for RPM and its successor Kent, King scored 20 chart items during that musically tumultuous decade, including such memorable efforts as "You Know I Love You" (1952); "Woke Up This Morning" and "Please Love Me" (1953); "When My Heart Beats like a Hammer," "Whole Lotta' Love," and "You Upset Me Baby" (1954); "Every Day I Have the Blues" (another Fulson remake), the dreamy blues ballad "Sneakin' Around," and "Ten Long Years" (1955); "Bad Luck," "Sweet Little Angel," and a Platters-like "On My Word of Honor" (1956); and "Please Accept My Love" (first cut by Jimmy Wilson) in 1958. King's guitar attack grew more aggressive and pointed as the decade progressed, influencing a legion of up-and-coming axemen across the nation.

In 1960, King's impassioned two-sided revival of Joe Turner's "Sweet Sixteen" became another mammoth seller, and his "Got a Right to Love My Baby" and "Partin' Time" weren't far behind. But Kent couldn't hang onto a star like King forever (and he may have been tired of watching his new LPs consigned directly into the 99-cent bins on the Biharis' cheapo Crown logo). King moved over to ABC-Paramount Records in 1962, following the lead of Lloyd Price, Ray Charles, and before long, Fats Domino. In November of 1964, the guitarist cut his seminal *Live at the Regal* album at the fabled Chicago theater, and excitement virtually

leapt out of the grooves. That same year, he enjoyed a minor hit with "How Blue Can You Get," one of his many signature tunes. 1966's "Don't Answer the Door" and "Paying the Cost to Be the Boss" two years later were Top Ten R&B entries, and the socially charged and funk-tinged "Why I Sing the Blues" just missed achieving the same status in 1969.

Across-the-board stardom finally arrived in 1969 for the deserving guitarist, when he crashed the mainstream consciousness in a big way with a stately, violin-drenched minor-key treatment of Roy Hawkins' "The Thrill Is Gone" that was quite a departure from the concise horn-powered backing King had customarily employed. At last, pop audiences were convinced that they should get to know King better: not only was the track a No. 3 R&B smash, it vaulted to the upper reaches of the pop lists as well.

King was one of a precious few bluesmen to score hits consistently during the 1970s, and for good reason: he wasn't afraid to experiment with the idiom. In 1973, he ventured to Philadelphia to record a pair of huge sellers, "To Know You Is to Love You" and "I Like to Live the Love," with the same silky rhythm section that powered the hits of the Spinners and the O'Jays. In 1976, he teamed up with his old cohort Bland to wax some well-received duets. And in 1978, he joined forces with the jazzy Crusaders to make the gloriously funky "Never Make Your Move Too Soon" and an inspiring "When It All Comes Down." Occasionally, the daring deviations veered off-course—*Love Me Tender,* an album that attempted to harness the Nashville country sound, was an artistic disaster.

Although his concerts have long been as consistently satisfying as anyone's now working in the field (and he remains a road warrior of remarkable resiliency who used to gig an average of 300 nights a year), King has tempered his studio activities somewhat. Still, his 1993 MCA disc *Blues Summit* was a return to form, as King duetted with his peers (John Lee Hooker, Etta James, Lowell Fulson, Koko Taylor) on a program of standards.

King's immediately recognizable guitar style, utilizing a trademark trill that approximates the bottleneck sound shown him by cousin Bukka White all those decades ago, has long set him apart from his contemporaries. Add his patented pleading vocal style and you have the most influential and innovative bluesman of the post-war period. There can be little doubt that B.B. King will reign as the genre's undisputed king (and goodwill ambassador) for as long as he lives. —*Bill Dahl*

My Kind of Blues / 1961 / Crown ✦✦✦

★ **King of the Blues** / Jul. 1961 / MCA ✦✦✦✦✦
No way can a mere four discs cover every facet of the blues king's amazing recording career, but MCA makes a valiant stab at it. The first two discs, as expected, are immaculate: opening with his Bullet Records debut ("Miss Martha King"), the box continues with a handful of pivotal RPM/Kent masters before digging into his 1960s ABC-Paramount material ("I'm Gonna Sit in 'Til You Give In" and "My Baby's Comin' Home" are little-recalled gems). The hits—"The Thrill Is Gone," "Why I Sing the Blues," "To Know You Is to Love You"—are all here, and if much of the fourth disc is pretty disposable, it only mirrors King's own winding down in the studio. —*Bill Dahl*

★ **Live at the Regal** / 1965 / ABC/MCA ✦✦✦✦✦
This is one of the all-time classic live albums. Recorded in 1964, it captures King in his prime playing to a *very* enthusiastic Black audience. He stretches out on guitar in a way he doesn't on his studio recordings—his guitar sound (it's a joy to hear him switching around and playing with different settings and guitar tones) has a vibrancy and, sometimes, a wild edge that doesn't get captured in the studio. This is a must for B.B. King fans. —*George Bedard*

Lucille / 1968 / MCA ✦✦✦✦
A decent but short (nine songs) late '60s set, with somewhat sparser production than he'd employ with the beefier arrangements of the "Thrill Is Gone" era. Brass and stinging guitar plays a part on all of the songs, leading off with the eight-minute title track, a spoken narrative about his famous guitar. —*Richie Unterberger*

Live and Well / 1969 / MCA ✦✦✦

Completely Well / 1969 / MCA ✦✦✦✦
Containing "The Thrill Is Gone," the violin-soaked minor-key blues that broke him permanently onto the pop circuit, this album is solid but hardly earthshattering, with a revival of Jay McShann's "Confessin' the Blues" and the heated "So Excited" to its credit. —*Bill Dahl*

Live at Cook County Jail / 1971 / MCA ✦✦✦✦
Some veteran King aficionados have been known to tout this album as superior to the massively acclaimed *Live at the Regal.* Either way, it's a crisply paced concert recording for a very appreciative audience. —*Bill Dahl*

To Know You Is to Love You / 1973 / MCA ✦✦✦
The combination of King and the Philly rhythm section that powered hits by the O'Jays, Spinners, and Stylistics proved a surprisingly adroit one. Two huge hits came from this album, the Stevie Wonder/Syreeta Wright-

penend title track and "I Like to Live the Love," both of them intriguing updates of King's tried-and-true style. —*Bill Dahl*

Great Moments with B.B. King / 1981 / MCA ✦✦✦✦
Very solid 23-track package culled from some of King's best mid-to-late-'60s ABC-Paramount and BluesWay LPs. Some of the best cuts stem from a sizzling live album; "Gambler's Blues," "Waitin' on You," and a stunning "Night Life" find his reverb level rising to the boiling point. A brassy "That's Wrong Little Mama," "Dance with Me," and "Heartbreaker" connect like consecutive right hooks, and his rousing smash "Paying the Cost to Be the Boss" is also on board. —*Bill Dahl*

Do the Boogie! B.B. King's Early '50s Classics / 1988 / Flair ✦✦✦✦
20 killer tracks from B.B. King's 1950s heyday, including quite a few alternate takes and a few tough-to-locate items ("Bye Bye Baby," "Dark Is the Night," "Jump with You Baby"). Many of the titles are familiar ones—"Woke Up This Morning," "Every Day," "Please Love Me," "Whole Lotta Love"—but often as not, compiler Ray Topping unearthed contrasting versions from the same sessions that shed new, fascinating light on King's studio techniques. —*Bill Dahl*

The Best of B.B. King, Vol. 1 / 1991 / Flair ✦✦✦
A 20-track this compilation that should have been a great deal better than it is. The disc embarrassingly uses an inferior remake of King's classic "Whole Lotta Love" instead of the original, while drums and electric bass have been clumsily overdubbed on the original takes of "You Upset Me Baby," "Every Day," and "Please Love Me," absolutely ruining them. What a shame, since two-thirds of the collection is just fine. —*Bill Dahl*

Spotlight on Lucille / 1991 / Flair ✦✦✦✦
From the contemporary-looking cover, this would appear to be recently recorded material. But wait—these are all 1950s/early-'60s instrumentals from the Modern/Kent vaults, spotlighting B.B. King's pristine lead guitar in an often jazzier mode than he usually adopted in the studio. His workout on Louis Jordan's "Just like a Woman" is a tour de force that's been reissued often, but much of the compilation is rare stuff that gives Lucille her full due. —*Bill Dahl*

The Fabulous B.B. King / 1991 / Flair ✦✦

☆ **Singin' the Blues/The Blues** / 1992 / Flair ✦✦✦✦✦
Two great original Crown albums from the '50s appear on one import CD, including most of King's Top Ten R&B hits from the period: "3 O'Clock Blues," "Please Love Me," "You Upset Me Baby," "You Know I Love You," "Woke Up This Morning," and "Sweet Little Angel," plus one of his best, "Crying Won't Help You." This is the stuff that was so hugely influential to other blues guitarists and singers in its original recorded version. Here is lots of the real early, gritty stuff: "That Ain't the Way to Do It," "When My Heart Beats like a Hammer," and "Don't You Want a Man like Me?" The guitar intro to "Early in the Morning" is one of the finest examples of King in a jazzy mode. Great guitar! —*George Bedard*

Heart and Soul / 1992 / Pointblank ✦✦✦

Blues Summit / 1993 / MCA ✦✦✦

My Sweet Little Angel / Oct. 5, 1993 / Flair ✦✦✦✦
Another 21-track anthology chock full of alternate takes and previously unreleased masters from B.B. King's 1950s stint at RPM/Kent. A wild cross-section of material—signature items like "Sweet Little Angel" and "Please Accept My Love," an off-the-wall reading of Tony Bennett's "In the Middle of an Island," and best of all, a torrid, jazzy instrumental called "String Bean" that finds King pulling some astounding guitar tricks out of a seemingly bottomless bag. —*Bill Dahl*

Earl King

b. Feb. 2, 1934, New Orleans, LA
Guitar, Vocals / Soul, R&B, Electric New Orleans Blues
Unilaterally respected around his Crescent City homebase as both a performer and a songwriter, guitarist Earl King has been a prime New Orleans R&B force for more than four decades—and he shows no signs of slowing down.

Born Earl Johnson, the youngster considered the platters of Texas guitarists T-Bone Walker and Gatemouth Brown almost as fascinating as the live performances of local luminaries Smiley Lewis and Tuts Washington. King met his major influence and mentor, Guitar Slim, at the Club Tijuana, one of King's favorite haunts (along with the Dew Drop, of course), the two becoming fast friends. Still billed as Earl Johnson, the guitarist debuted on wax in 1953 on Savoy with "Have You Gone Crazy" (with pal Huey "Piano" Smith making the first of many memorable supporting appearances on his platters).

Johnson became Earl King upon signing with Specialty the next year (label head Art Rupe intended to name him King Earl, but the typesetter reversed the names!). "A Mother's Love," King's first Specialty offering, was an especially accurate Guitar Slim homage produced by Johnny Vincent, who would soon launch his own label, Ace Records, with King one of his principal artists. King's first Ace single, the seminal two-chord south Louisiana blues "Those Lonely, Lonely Nights," proved a national

R&B hit (despite a soundalike cover by Johnny "Guitar" Watson). Smith's rolling piano undoubtedly helped make the track a hit.

King remained with Ace through the rest of the decade, waxing an unbroken string of great New Orleans R&B sides with the unparalleled house band at Cosimo's studio. But he moved over to Imperial to work with producer Dave Bartholomew in 1960, cutting the classic "Come On" (also known as "Let the Good Times Roll") and 1961's humorous "Trick Bag" and managing a second chart item in 1962 with "Always a First Time." King wrote standout tunes for Fats Domino, Professor Longhair, and Lee Dorsey during the '60s.

Although a potential 1963 pact with Motown was scuttled at the last instant, King admirably rode out the rough spots during the late '60s and '70s. Since signing with Black Top, his performing career has been rejuvenated; 1990's *Sexual Telepathy* and *Hard River to Cross* three years later were both superlative albums. —*Bill Dahl*

Street Parade / 1981 / Charly ✦✦✦
Funky 1972 tracks that should have fueled a comeback for the Crescent City mainstay but didn't (a lease deal with Atlantic fell through). Allen Toussaint was apparently in charge of the sessions, which produced updates of "Mama and Papa" and "A Mother's Love" as well as a bevy of fresh nuggets (notably the fanciful "Medieval Days," later revived by King on Black Top), and the two-part title item. —*Bill Dahl*

Sexual Telepathy / 1990 / Black Top ✦✦✦✦
Reunited with a more sympathetic New Orleans rhythm section (bassist George Porter, Jr., and drummer Kenny Blevins) and a funkier horn section, King excelled handsomely on this uncommonly strong outing. As we've come to expect from him, he brought a sheaf of new originals to the sessions, from a saucy "Sexual Telepathy" to a heartwarming "Happy Little Nobody's Waggy Tail Dog." Remakes of his "Always a First Time" and "A Weary Silent Night" were welcome inclusions (especially since we can't easily lay our hands on the originals!). —*Bill Dahl*

Hard River to Cross / 1993 / Black Top ✦✦✦✦
The quirky guitarist with the endlessly wavy hair made it two winners in a row with this one. Snooks Eaglin guests on guitar for three tracks, including the hilarious "Big Foot" and a joyous "No City like New Orleans," while Porter and drummer Herman Ernest III lay down scintillating grooves behind King's ringing axe and wise vocals. —*Bill Dahl*

● **Those Lonely, Lonely Nights** / 1993 / P-Vine ✦✦✦✦
Why must New Orleans guitarist Earl King's 1950s material be so difficult to locate on CD? This expensive Japanese import does the job handily, if you can find it—all eight of King's Guitar Slim-influenced Specialty sides (including "A Mother's Love" and its rocking flip, "I'm Your Best Bet Baby") and 17 of his terrific efforts for Ace, including the hit title track, the equally moving "My Love Is Strong," and the jumping "Everybody's Carried Away," "Little Girl," and "I'll Take You Back Home." —*Bill Dahl*

Freddie King (Freddy King)

b. Sep. 3, 1934, Gilmer, TX, **d.** Dec. 28, 1976, Dallas, TX
Guitar, Vocals / Modern Electric Blues
Guitarist Freddie King rode to fame in the early '60s with catchy instrumentals that became instant bandstand fodder for fellow bluesmen and White rock bands alike. Employing a more down-home (thumb and finger picks) approach to the B.B. King single-string style of playing, King enjoyed success on a variety of different record labels. Furthermore, he was one of the first bluesmen to employ a racially integrated group onstage behind him. Influenced by Eddie Taylor, Jimmy Rogers, and Robert Jr. Lockwood, King went on to influence Eric Clapton, Mick Taylor, Stevie Ray Vaughan, and Lonnie Mack, among many others.

Freddie King (who was originally billed as "Freddy" early in his career) was born and raised in Gilmer, TX, where he learned how to play guitar as a child. By the time he was a teenager, he had grown to love the rough, electrified sounds of Chicago blues. In 1950, when he was 16 years old, his family moved to Chicago, where he began frequenting local blues clubs, listening to musicians like Muddy Waters, Jimmy Rogers, Robert Jr. Lockwood, Little Walter, and Eddie Taylor.. In the mid-'50s, King began playing on sessions for Parrot and Chess Records, as well as playing with Earlee Payton's Blues Cats and the Little Sonny Cooper Band. Freddie King didn't cut his own record until 1957, when he recorded "Country Boy" for the small independent label El-Bee. The single failed to gain much attention.

Three years later, King signed with Federal Records, a subsidiary of King Records, and recorded his first single for the label, "You've Got to Love Her with a Feeling," in August of 1960. The single appeared the following month and became a minor hit. "You've Got to Love Her with Feeling" was followed by "Hide Away," the song that would become Freddie King's signature tune and most influential recording. "Hide Away" was adapted by King and Magic Sam from a Hound Dog Taylor instrumental and named after one of the most popular bars in Chicago. The single was released as the B-side of "I Love the Woman" (his singles featured a vocal A-side and an instrumental B-side) in the fall of 1961, and it became a major hit, reachingNo. 5 on the R&B charts and No. 29

on the pop charts. King's first album, *Freddy King Sings,* appeared in 1961 and it was followed later that year by *Let's Hide Away and Dance Away with Freddy King: Strictly Instrumental.* Throughout 1961, he turned out a series of instrumentals—including "San-Ho-Zay," "The Stumble," and "I'm Tore Down"—which became blues classics. "Lonesome Whistle Blues," "San-Ho-Zay," and "I'm Tore Down" all became Top Ten R&B hits that year.

Freddy King continued to record for King Records until 1968, with a second instrumental album (*Freddy King Gives You a Bonanza of Instrumentals*) appearing in 1965, although none of his singles became hits. Nevertheless, his influence was heard in blues and rock guitarists throughout the '60s—Eric Clapton made "Hide Away" his showcase number in 1965. King signed with Atlantic/Cotillion in late 1968, releasing two albums the following year; both collections were produced by King Curtis. After their release, King and Atlantic/Cotillion parted ways.

King landed a new record contract with Leon Russell's Shelter Records in the fall of 1970. He recorded three albums for Shelter in the early '70s, all of which sold well. In addition to respectable sales, his concerts were also quite popular with both blues and rock audiences. In 1974, he signed a contract with RSO Records and he released *Burglar,* which was produced and recorded with Clapton. Following the release of *Burglar,* King toured America, Europe, and Australia. In 1975, he released his second RSO album, *Larger than Life.*

Throughout 1976 Freddie King toured America, even though his health was declining. On December 28, 1976, King died of heart failure. Although his passing was premature—he was only 42 years old—Freddie King's influence could still be heard in blues and rock guitarists 20 years after his death. *—Stephen Thomas Erlewine & Cub Koda*

Getting Ready / 1971 / DCC ✦✦✦
The first of King's three albums for Leon Russell's Shelter label set the tone for his work for the company: competent electric blues with a prominent rock/soul influence. King sings and plays well, but neither the sidemen nor the material challenge him to scale significant heights. Part of the problem is that Freddie himself wrote none of the songs, which are divided between Chicago blues standards and material supplied by Leon Russell and Don Nix. The entire album is included on the compilation *King of the Blues. —Richie Unterberger*

Just Pickin' / 1986 / Modern Blues ✦✦✦✦
Both of Freddy's all-instrumental albums for the King label (*Let's Hide Away and Dance Away with Freddy King* and *Freddy King Gives You a Bonanza of Instrumentals*) on one compact disc. "Hide Away", "The Stumble," and "San-Ho-Zay" are the numbers that made King's rep and influenced guitarists on both sides of the Atlantic. *—Cub Koda*

★ **Hide Away: The Best of Freddie King** / 1993 / Rhino ✦✦✦✦✦
Although not always placed in the upper echelon of blues performers alongside the other Kings (B.B. and Albert), Freddie King was a dynamo. He was a powerhouse, imaginative guitarist and a glorious, soulful vocalist who could belt out come-ons, shout with gusto, or wail in anguish. His instrumentals were also catchy, usually simply structured but vigorous and vividly articulated. This tremendous 20-cut sampler includes familiar hits like "Going Down" and the title cut, plus the shattering "Have You Ever Loved a Woman" and the poignant "Lonesome Whistle Blues." The tracks are exquisitely remastered and intelligently sequenced, and the notes are informative and thorough without being academic or fawning. *—Ron Wynn*

Kinsey Report

Group / Modern Electric Blues, Chicago Blues
This family band consists of Donald Kinsey (b. May 12, 1953, Gary, IN), (vocal, guitar); Ralph "Woody" Kinsey, (drums); Kenneth Kinsey, (bass); and Ronald Prince, (guitar). Solidly based in the blues as a result of lifelong training in the Big Daddy Kinsey household, the Kinsey scions are also versed in a broad range of music. The older brothers Donald and Ralph had an early blues-rock trio (White Lightnin') in the mid-'70s, long before they regrouped as the Kinsey Report in 1984 and began to launch new excursions into rock. Donald also recorded and toured with Albert King and with Bob Marley, and the influence of those giants (as well as that of Big Daddy Kinsey, naturally) show through in the music of The Kinsey Report. The band expertly covers all the bases from Chicago blues through reggae, rock, funk, and soul, and their recordings are also distinguished by the songwriting talents and self-contained production approach of the Kinseys. *—Jim O'Neal*

● **Edge of the City** / 1987 / Alligator ✦✦✦✦
An engaging, original blues-rock album comes from this family band. *—Niles J. Frantz*

Big Daddy Kinsey

b. Mar. 18, 1927, Pleasant Grove, MS
Guitar, Harmonica, Vocals / Modern Electric Blues, Chicago Blues
Long before Lester "Big Daddy" Kinsey and his clan hit the interna-

tional blues circuit, he established himself as the blues patriarch of Gary, IN, and as the Steeltown's answer to Muddy Waters. A slide guitarist and harp blower with roots in both the Mississippi Delta and postwar Chicago styles, Kinsey worked with local bands only long enough for his sons to mature into top-flight musicians, and since 1984 (when Big Daddy recorded his debut album, *Bad Situation*) the family act has become one of the hottest attractions in blues. Big Daddy's material ranges from deep blues in the Muddy Waters vein to hard-rocking blues with touches of funk and even reggae, courtesy of sons Donald and Ralph (who venture even further afield in their own outings as the Kinsey Report). *—Jim O'Neal*

Bad Situation (with the Kinsey Report) / 1985 / Rooster Blues ✦✦✦
Crisp, funky, and modern, *Bad Situation* shows Big Daddy and the band in fine form. *—Bill Dahl*

Midnight Drive / 1989 / Alligator ✦✦✦
With *Midnight Drive,* Big Daddy Kinsey attempts to expand the sonic palette of blues by adding elements of funk and hard rock. Although there are some interesting moments—primarily in the skillful solos—the music often falls flat and the songwriting isn't distinctive. Kinsey's attempts at diversity are admirable, but ultimately unsuccessful. *—Thom Owens*

● **Can't Let Go** / 1990 / Blind Pig ✦✦✦✦
Fine patriarchal blues from this little-known Chicago artist, backed by his sons (Kinsey Report). *—Cub Koda*

Powerhouse / 1991 / Pointblank ✦✦✦
This hard-rock album is spiced (lightly) with blues. *—Niles J. Frantz*

Eddie Kirkland

b. Aug. 16, 1928, Jamaica
Guitar, Harmonica, Vocals / Modern Electric Blues
How many Jamaican-born bluesmen have recorded with John Lee Hooker and toured with Otis Redding? It's a safe bet there's only one: Eddie Kirkland, who's engaged in some astonishing onstage acrobatics over the decades (like standing on his head while playing guitar on TV's "Don Kirshner's Rock Concert").

But you won't find any ersatz reggae grooves cluttering Kirkland's work. He was brought up around Dothan, AL, before heading north to Detroit in 1943. There he hooked up with Hooker five years later, recording with him for several labels as well as under his own name for RPM in 1952, King in 1953, and Fortune in 1959. Tru-Sound Records, a Prestige subsidiary, invited Kirkland to Englewood Cliffs, NJ, in 1961-62 to wax his first album, *It's the Blues Man!* The polished R&B band of saxist King Curtis crashed into Kirkland's intense vocals, raucous guitar, and harmonica throughout the exciting set.

Exiting the Motor City for Macon, GA, in 1962, Kirkland signed on with Otis Redding as a sideman and show opener not long thereafter. Redding introduced Kirkland to Stax/Volt co-owner Jim Stewart, who flipped over Eddie's primal dance workout "The Hawg." It was issued on Volt in 1963, billed to Eddie Kirk. By the dawn of the 1970s, Kirkland was recording for Pete Lowry's Trix label. More recently, he's waxed three CDs for Deluge (his latest, an unpredictable *Where You Get Your Sugar?,* emerged in 1995). *—Bill Dahl*

It's the Blues Man! / 1961 / Original Blues Classics ✦✦✦✦
Wildman guitarist/harpist Kirkland brought his notoriously rough-hewn attack to this vicious 1962 album for Tru-Sound, joined by a very accomplished combo led by saxman extraordinaire King Curtis and including guitarist Bill Doggett. As the crew honed in on common stylistic ground, the energy levels soared sky-high, Kirkland roaring "Man of Stone," "Train Done Gone," and "I Tried" with ferocious fervor. *—Bill Dahl*

● **Three Shades of the Blues** / 198 / Original Blues Classics ✦✦✦✦
Kirkland's eight sides on this compilation are as hard-driving and intense as you could possibly ask for. It includes four sides each from B.B. King disciple Mr. Bo and the Ohio Untouchables, with dazzling guitar work from Robert Ward on the latter. *—Cub Koda*

Some Like It Raw / Sep. 1993 / Deluge ✦✦✦

Koerner, Ray & Glover

Group / Acoustic Blues
In today's climate of a blues band seemingly on every corner with "the next Stevie Ray Vaughan" being touted every other minute, it's hard to imagine a time when being a White blues singer was considered kind of a novelty. But in those heady times of the early '60s and the folk and blues revival, that's exactly how it was. Into this milieu came three young men who knew it, understood it, and could play and sing it; their names were Koerner, Ray, and Glover. They were folkies, to be sure, but the three of them did a lot—together and separately—to bring the blues to a White audience; in many ways they set things in place that have become standards of the Caucasian presentation of the music over the years. They were attending the University of Minnesota, drawn together

by their interest in the music. They chose colorful nicknames: "Spider" John Koerner, the Jesse Fuller and Big Joe Williams of the group; Dave "Snaker" Ray, a 12-string-playing Leadbelly aficionado; and Tony "Little Sun" Glover on harmonica, holding up the Sonny Terry end of things.

They worked in various configurations within the trio, often doing solo turns and duets, but seldom all three of them together. Their break-through album was *Blues, Rags and Hollers*, released in 1963. While recording two excellent follow-ups for Elektra, both Koerner and Ray released fine solo albums. Tony Glover put together one of the very first books on how to play blues harmonica (*Blues Harp*) around this time, and its excellence and conciseness still make it the how-to book of choice for all aspiring harmonica players. Both Koerner and Ray still maintain an active performing schedule, and every so often the three of them get back together for a concert. *—Cub Koda*

● **Lots More Blues Rags and Hollers** / 1964 / Elektra ◆◆◆◆

Alexis Korner (Alexis Koerner)

b. Apr. 19, 1928, Paris, France, **d.** Jan. 1, 1984, London, England
Guitar, Vocals / R&B, Electric British Blues, British Blues
The cofounder of British blues (with Cyril Davies), guitarist Alexis Kor-ner never achieved anything like the fame of the younger players who learned from him (among them Charlie Watts, who played in Blues Incorporated). Gifted though he was, Korner lacked the vocal skills or the commercial edge needed for mass success. After splitting up the last of his various incarnations of Blues Incorporated, he began populariz-ing the blues as the host of a children's TV show. He toured with the Rolling Stones in the mid-'70s, then formed his last (and best) band, Rocket 88, late in the decade, prior to his sudden death in the early '80s. *—Bruce Eder*

R&B from the Marquee / 1962 / Ace of Clubs ◆◆◆◆
Britain's first home-grown blues album to make the UK charts is a land-mark with good playing, even if none of the flash associated with Korner alumni like the Rolling Stones or Yardbirds is present. *—Bruce Eder*

New Generation of Blues / 1968 / Beat Goes On ◆◆◆
A basically competent, though hardly enthralling, effort from the British bluesman that alternates between minimally produced, acoustic-fla-vored production and fuller arrangements with jazzy touches of flute and upright bass. Korner wrote about half of the material, leaving the rest of the space open for R&B/blues covers and adaptations of tradi-tional standards. "The Same for You" has a strange, ever-so-slight psyche-delic influence, with its swirling flute, fake fadeout, and odd anti-estab-lishment lyrics. Korner's voice is (and always would be) a tuneless bark, but it sounds better here than it did on the first album to prominently feature his vocals (*I Wonder Who*, 1967). As such, this album is one of the best representations of Korner as a frontman. *—Richie Unterberger*

Bootleg Him! / 1972 / Warner Brothers ◆◆◆◆
The best of all the Korner anthologies, boasting unreleased tapes and a lot of interesting one-off recordings from the various nooks and crannies of his career. *—Bruce Eder*

Rocket 88 / 1981 / Atlantic ◆◆◆◆
Arguably the best record ever for an offshoot of the Rolling Stones, with Korner on guitar, Ian Stewart on piano, Charlie Watts on drums, and Jack Bruce on upright bass. This has tight, rippling, rollicking interpretations of blues and jazz standards and is a seminal part of any collection. *—Bruce Eder*

● **The Alexis Korner Collection** / 1988 / Castle ◆◆◆◆
A strong import anthology featuring Korner's various bands over the years. Probably the best extant collection. *—Bruce Eder*

The Smokin' Joe Kubek Band

Guitar, Vocals / Modern Electric Texas Blues
Another young Texas axeman from the old school, Smokin' Joe Kubek issued his band's debut disc in 1991 on Bullseye Blues, *Steppin' Out Texas Style*. Kubek was already playing his smokin' guitar on the Lone State chitlin circuit at age 14, supporting such musicians as Freddie King. Soon, he formed his own band and began playing a number of bars across Dallas. In the '80s, he met guitarist/vocalist B'nois King, a native of Monroe, LA, and the duo formed the first edition of the Smokin' Joe Kubek Band.

The Smokin' Joe Kubek Band began playing the rest of the South-west in the late '80s. In 1991, they signed to Bullseye Blues, releasing their debut *Steppin' Out Texas Style* the same year. After its release, the band launched their first national tour. *—Bill Dahl and Stephen Tho-mas Erlewine*

● **Steppin' out Texas Style** / 1991 / Bullseye Blues ◆◆◆◆
Smokin' Joe Kubek's debut album is a delight. Kubek leads his band through a set of smoking hot Texas and Memphis blues, delivered with passion—they can play this music with precision, but they choose to be looser and more fun than most traditionalists. Kubek's skillful guitarist

and B'nois King, his vocalist and rhythm guitarist, can play nearly as well; their duels are the high watermark of an already wonderful album. *—Thom Owens*

Chain Smokin' Texas Style / 1992 / Bullseye Blues ◆◆◆
Texas Cadillac / 1993 / Bullseye Blues ◆◆◆◆
Smokin' Joe Kubek's third Rounder album juggles blues-rock originals with faithful, exuberant covers of Jimmy Reed, Willie Dixon, Muddy Waters, and Little Walter Jacobs, among others. Kubek is a good, some-times captivating, guitarist and entertaining singer, if not the greatest pure vocalist, and the band rips through the 11 cuts in a relaxed, yet pas-sionate fashion. But it's hard for any longtime blues fan to get excited over hearing another version of "Little Red Rooster" or "Mean Old World"; it's impossible to reinvent Delta, urban, Texas, or West Coast blues. The solution is probably to make the best music you can and hope you hook those willing to listen to contemporary blues rather than spurn it for the originals. *—Ron Wynn*

Sammy Lawhorn

b. Jul. 12, 1935, **d.** Apr. 29, 1990
Guitar
Guitarist Sammy Lawhorn was born Samuel David Lawhorn on July 12, 1935, in Little Rock, AR. He was raised in the South by his grandpar-ents after his mother and stepfather moved to Chicago. He first heard live guitar from blind guitar players on the street and soon was learning the instrument. Starting with a ukulele, graduating to an acoustic (Stella), and finally getting an electric (Supro), Lawhorn learned to play the guitar in about two years.

As a teenager he worked as a King Biscuit Boy for Sonny Boy Will-iamson II and learned slide guitar from Houston Stackhouse. After a stint in the service, Lawhorn returned to Arkansas and played and/or recorded with Willie C. Cobbs, the Five Royals, Eddie Boyd, and Roy Brown.

He moved to Chicago in the early '60s and became part of the house band at Theresa's, one of Chicago's main blues clubs. He worked on and off with Muddy Waters for about ten years and toured with that band. Lawhorn became best known as the resident guitarist at Theresa's club, where he played behind just about any great blues artist you could name. His influences were T-Bone Walker, Lightnin' Hopkins, Pee Wee Crayton, Lowell Fulson, and Muddy Waters. He was especially drawn to slide and Hawaiian-style guitar, and became well known for his use of the tremolo bar. He is considered one of finest examples of postwar-style Chicago blues guitar. He can be heard on recordings of Muddy Waters, Big Mama Thornton, Otis Spann, Junior Wells, John Lee Hooker, Eddie Boyd, and many others. Lawhorn died April 29, 1990, in Chicago. *—Michael Erlewine*

Sam Lay

b. Mar. 20, 1935, Birmingham, AL
Drums, Vocals / Chicago Blues
Sam Lay was born March 20, 1935, in Birmingham, AL, and began his career as a drummer in Cleveland in 1954, working with the Moon Dog Combo. In 1957 he joined the Original Thunderbirds and stayed with that group until 1959, when he left for Chicago to work with the legend-ary Little Walter.

Lay began to work with Howlin' Wolf in 1960 and spent the next six years with that group. He and bassist Jerome Arnold were hired away from Wolf's band by Paul Butterfield in 1966 and became part of the Paul Butterfield Blues Band, recording that classic first album. Lay toured with Butterfield until late year when he accidentally shot him-self.

Sam Lay backed Bob Dylan at the historic 1965 Newport Folk Festi-val, when Dylan first introduced electric-rock to the folk crowd. He went on to record with Dylan on *Highway 61 Revisited*. He can be heard on more than 40 classic Chess blues recordings, and his famous double-shuffle is the envy of every would-be blues drummer. In 1969, Lay played drums for the Muddy Waters *Fathers and Sons* album, now a classic. He also was the original drummer for the James Cotton Blues Band.

Later in 1969, he also worked with the Siegel-Schwall Band. He went on to form the Sam Lay Blues Revival Band, which has involved many players over the years including Jimmy Rogers, George "Wild Child" Butler, Eddie Taylor, and others.

Sam Lay was inducted into the Blues Hall of Fame in 1992 and received a nomination for a W.C. Handy award. He formed the Sam Lay Blues Band and has had recent recordings on Appaloosa Records (*Shuf-fle Master, Sam Lay Live*) and on Alligator with the Siegel-Schwall Band, with whom he often plays. A 1996 release on Evidence is in the can. *—Michael Erlewine*

● **Shuffle Master** / 1992 / Appaloosa ◆◆◆◆

Lazy Lester

b. Jun. 20, 1933, Torras, LA
Guitar, Harmonica, Percussion, Vocals, Washboard / Electric Louisiana Blues

His colorful sobriquet (supplied by prolific south Louisiana producer J.D. Miller) to the contrary, harpist Lazy Lester swears he never was all that lethargic. But he seldom was in much of a hurry either, although the relentless pace of his Excello Records swamp blues classics "I'm a Lover Not a Fighter" and "I Hear You Knockin'" might contradict that statement too.

While growing up outside of Baton Rouge, Leslie Johnson was influenced by Jimmy Reed and Little Walter. But his entree into playing professionally arrived quite by accident: while riding on a bus sometime in the mid-'50s, he met guitarist Lightnin' Slim, who was searching fruitlessly for an AWOL harpist. The two's styles meshed seamlessly, and Lester became Slim's harpist of choice.

In 1956, Lester stepped out front at Miller's Crowley, LA, studios for the first time. During an extended stint at Excello that stretched into 1965, he waxed such gems as "Sugar Coated Love," "If You Think I've Lost You," and "The Same Thing Could Happen to You." Lester proved invaluable as an imaginative sideman for Miller, utilizing everything from cardboard boxes and claves to whacking on newspapers in order to locate the correct percussive sound for the producer's output.

Lester gave up playing for almost two decades (and didn't particularly miss it, either), settling in Pontiac, MI, in 1975. But Fred Reif (Lester's manager, booking agent, and rubboard player) convinced the harpist that a return to action was in order, inaugurating a comeback that included a nice 1988 album for Alligator, *Harp & Soul*. His swamp blues sound remains as atmospheric (and dare we say it, energetic) as ever. *—Bill Dahl*

☆ **True Blues** / 196X / Excello ◆◆◆◆◆
His original album collects the best of the early Excello sides. Includes "Sugar Coated Love," "I Hear You Knockin'," and "I'm a Lover, Not a Fighter." *—Cub Koda*

Harp and Soul / 1988 / Alligator ◆◆◆◆
After a lengthy hiatus from the music business, Lester was in the midst of his comeback when he waxed this album for Alligator. The overall sound is redolent of those Louisiana swamp blues classics, but with a cannily updated contemporary edge ?that works well. *—Bill Dahl*

Rides Again / 1988 / Sunjay ◆◆◆◆
His original rediscovery album pairs him with English blues musicians, with surprisingly great results. *—Cub Koda*

Lazy Lester / 1989 / Flyright ◆◆◆◆
Alternate takes and unissued titles from the cache of producer J.D. Miller, whose tiny Crowley, LA, studio was the prime site for recording swamp blues during the '50s and '60s. A fine companion to AVI's essential Lester compilation. *—Bill Dahl*

★ **I Hear You Knockin'!!!** / 1995 / Excello/AVI ◆◆◆◆◆
Southern Louisiana swamp blues doesn't get more infectious or atmospheric than in the hands of Lazy Lester, whose late-'50s/early-'60s catalog for Excello Records (produced by the legendary J.D. Miller) is splendidly summarized with the 30 sides here. Lester's insistent harp and laconic vocals shine brightly on the rollicking "I'm a Lover, Not a Fighter," "Sugar Coated Love," "I Hear You Knockin'," and "If You Think I've Lost You," serving to help define the genre's timeless appeal. *—Bill Dahl*

Legendary Blues Band

Group / Electric Chicago Blues
The Legendary Blues Band includes Calvin Jones (b. 1926, Greenwood, MS; bass, violin); Willie Smith (b. 1935, Helena, AR; drum); and various others on vocals, guitar, harmonica, and piano. When the Muddy Waters band quit the master en masse in 1980, most of the sidemen stuck together and formed their own group. The Legendary Blues Band, as they were named, included Pinetop Perkins, Jerry Portnoy, Willie Smith, and Calvin Jones throughout its early years. Short-term member Louis Myers, another Muddy Waters alumnus, appeared as guitarist on the band's first album (Rounder, 1981). The band has since changed personnel with some regularity, and while its lineup has become progressively less "legendary" in name or historic associations, its music has remained solid and true to the mainstream Chicago style. In a later configuration, they even made the *Billboard* Black Music charts. Recent albums have featured guitarist Billy Flynn and harmonicist Madison Slim. The rhythm section of Jones and Smith has anchored the unit throughout the changes, never failing to deliver the Chicago blues with aplomb. *—Jim O'Neal*

● **Red Hot 'n' Blue** / 1983 / Rounder ◆◆◆◆
Very solid vocals by Pinetop Perkins and Calvin Jones. Above-average LBB set. *—Bill Dahl*

Keepin' the Blues Alive / 1990 / Ichiban ◆◆◆◆
Only bassist Calvin Jones and drummer Willie Smith remain from Muddy Waters' old crew, but guitarist John Julch helps keep the traditional Chicago sound in place. *—Bill Dahl*

Money Talks / 1993 / Wild Dog ◆◆◆
All of a sudden, on their 1993's *Money Talks*, drummer Willie Smith has become a very credible singer. *—Bill Dahl*

J.B. Lenoir

b. May 5, 1929, Monticello, MS, **d.** Apr. 29, 1967, Urbana, IL
Guitar, Vocals / Electric Chicago Blues
Newcomers to his considerable legacy could be forgiven for questioning J.B. Lenoir's gender upon first hearing his rocking waxings. Lenoir's exceptionally high-pitched vocal range is a fooler, but it only adds to the singular appeal of his music. His politically charged "Eisenhower Blues" allegedly caused all sorts of nasty repercussions upon its 1954 emergence on Al Benson's Parrot logo (it was quickly pulled off the shelves and replaced with Lenoir's less controversially titled "Tax Paying Blues"). J.B. (that was his entire legal handle) fell under the spell of Blind Lemon Jefferson as a wee lad, thanks to his guitar-wielding dad. Lightnin' Hopkins and Arthur Crudup were also cited as early influences. Lenoir spent time in New Orleans before arriving in Chicago in the late '40s. Boogie grooves were integral to Lenoir's infectious routine from the get-go, although his first single for Chess in 1951, "Korea Blues," was another slice of topical commentary. From late 1951 to 1953, he waxed several dates for Joe Brown's JOB logo in the company of pianist Sunnyland Slim, drummer Alfred Wallace, and on the romping "The Mojo," saxist J.T. Brown.

Lenoir waxed his most enduring piece, the infectious (and often-covered) "Mama Talk to Your Daughter," in 1954 for Al Benson's Parrot label. Lenoir's 1954-55 Parrot output and 1955-58 Checker catalog contained a raft of terrific performances, including a humorously defiant "Don't Touch My Head" (detailing his brand-new process hairdo) and "Natural Man." Lenoir's sound was unique: saxes (usually Alex Atkins and Ernest Cotton) wailed in unison behind Lenoir's boogie-driven rhythm guitar as drummer Al Galvin pounded out a rudimentary backbeat everywhere but where it customarily lays. Somehow, it all fit together.

Scattered singles for Shad in 1958 and Vee-Jay two years later kept Lenoir's name in the public eye. His music was growing substantially by the time he hooked up with USA Records in 1963 (witness the 45's billing: J.B. Lenoir & his African Hunch Rhythm). Even more unusual were the two acoustic albums he cut for German blues promoter Horst Lippmann in 1965 and 1966. *Alabama Blues* and *Down in Mississippi* were done in Chicago under Willie Dixon's supervision, Lenoir now free to elaborate on whatever troubled his mind ("Alabama March," "Vietnam Blues," "Shot on James Meredith").

Little did Lenoir know his time was quickly running out. By the time of his 1967 death, the guitarist had moved to downstate Champaign—and that's where he died, probably as a delayed result of an auto accident he was involved in three weeks prior to his actual death. *—Bill Dahl*

Down in Mississippi / 1966 / L&R
Recorded in September 1966, shortly before his death the following spring, this session was Lenoir's most effective fusion of acoustic blues, African percussion, and contemporary, topical songwriting. "Round And Round," "Voodoo Music," and "Feelin' Good" bring the African influence to the fore, while J.B. addresses tough issues like Vietnam and discrimination more directly than any other bluesman of the time on cuts like "Down In Mississippi," "Shot On Meredith," and "Vietnam Blues." Supervised by Willie Dixon, this recording also featured top Chicago blues drummer Fred Below. *—Richie Unterberger*

Natural Man / 1968 / MCA/Chess ◆◆◆◆
This collection of J.B.'s mid-'50s tenure at the label—originally issued in the '70s—duplicates two songs from the Parrot collection (a label which Chess later acquired), but the rest of it is more than worth the effort to seek out. The rocking "Don't Touch My Head," the topical "Eisenhower Blues," and the sexually ambiguous, chaotic, and cool title track are but a few of the magical highlights aboard. Either this or the Parrot sides will do in a pinch, but I can't imagine being without either one. *—Cub Koda*

★ **The Parrot Sessions, 1954-55: Vintage Chicago Blues** / 1989 / Relic ◆◆◆◆◆
Lenoir's sound really got locked in during this period, using twin saxes, himself on boogie rhythm guitar (with an occasional minimal solo), revolving piano and bass stools and Al Gavin—certainly the strangest of all Chicago drummers—constantly turning the beat around. This is J.B. at his creative and performing best, including his best known songs, "Mama Talk to Your Daughter" (with the famous "one note for 12 bars" guitar solo), "Eisenhower Blues" and "Give Me One More Shot," where Gavin starts out the tune on the wrong beat, gets on the right beat by mistake, then "corrects" himself! Lyrics as metaphorically powerful as

any in the blues against grooves alternating between low-down slow ones and Lenoir's patented boogie. —*Cub Koda*

His J.O.B. Recordings 1951-54 / 1991 / Paula/Flyright ✦✦✦✦
These are Lenoir's earliest sides in a very stripped-down setting compared to the Parrot and Chess sides. Over half of the 14 sides feature Lenoir on guitar with only Sunnyland Slim on piano and Alfred Wallace on drums in support, with J.T. Brown on tenor sax aboard for the next session. They all suffer from a curiously muffled sound, but early delights like "The Mojo (Boogie)" and "Let's Roll" make all audio points mute. This CD also includes seven tracks fronted by Sunnyland Slim recorded the same day with Lenoir in a supporting role. —*Cub Koda*

Vietnam Blues: The Complete L&R Recordings / 1995 / Evidence ✦✦✦✦

Ron Levy's Wild Kingdom

Organ, Piano / Modern Electric Blues, Groove
Ron Levy (born Reuvin Zev ben Yehoshua Ha Levi) was born on May 29, 1951, in Cambridge, MA. Although Levy grew up playing clarinet, he switched to piano at age 13 after attending a Ray Charles concert. Then, influenced by Jimmy Smith, Booker T., and Billy Preston, he picked up on the Hammond organ. Within a few years he was working in the Boston area backing up blues acts. Albert King discovered and hired him in 1971, while Levy was still in high school. They worked together for 18 months. He then went on to B.B. King's band and worked with King for almost seven years. From 1976 until 1980, Levy worked with the Rhythm Rockers and it was here that he met guitarist Ronnie Earl. Levy joined the Roomful of Blues from 1983 to 1987. Levy's own band, Ron Levy's Wild Kingdom, has recorded a number of fine albums for Black Top, Rounder, and Bullseye. —*Michael Erlewine*

Ron Levy's Wild Kingdom / May 1987 / Black Top ✦✦✦
Ten tunes with an all-star cast including Ronnie Earl (guitar), Kim Wilson (harmonica), Greg Piccolo (sax), Wayne Bennett (guitar), and other excellent players. Plenty of fine guitar, keyboards, harmonica, and uptempo blues music. —*Michael Erlewine*

Safari to New Orleans / 1988 / Black Top ✦✦✦
Ron Levy's piano playing shines throughout *Safari to New Orleans*, but he fails to come up with enough strong songs to make the album memorable. —*Thom Owens*

★ **B-3 Blues and Grooves** / Apr. 1, 1993 / Bullseye Blues ✦✦✦✦
Ron Levy is one of the finest young masters of the Hammond B-3. Here are 11 soul-satisfying cuts that feature Levy's funky keyboard playing—many written by Levy himself. Those who look for B-3 jams in the soul-jazz vein that are as funky as can be will not be disappointed. This is a great CD to own. —*Michael Erlewine*

Furry Lewis (Walter Lewis)

b. Mar. 6, 1893, Greenwood, MS, d. Sep. 14, 1981, Memphis, TN
Guitar, Harmonica, Vocals / Acoustic Memphis Blues
Furry Lewis was the only blues singer of the 1920s to achieve major media attention in the 1960s and 1970s. One of the most recorded of Memphis-based guitarists of the late '20s, Lewis' subsequent fame 40 years later was based largely on the strength of those early sides. One of the very best blues storytellers, and an extremely nimble-fingered guitarist right into his seventies, he was equally adept at blues and ragtime, and made the most out of an understated, rather than an overtly flamboyant, style.

Lewis' real musical start took place on Beale Street in the late teens, where he began his career. He picked up bottleneck playing early on and tried to learn the harmonica, but never quite got the hang of it. Lewis started playing traveling medicine shows, and it was in this setting that he began showing off an uncommonly flashy visual style, including playing the guitar behind his head.

Lewis' recording career began in April 1927, with a trip to Chicago with fellow guitarist Landers Walton to record for the Vocalion label, which resulted in five songs, also featuring mandolin player Charles Jackson on three of the numbers. The songs proved that Lewis was a natural in the recording studio, playing to the microphone as easily as he did to audiences in person, but they were not, strictly speaking, representative of Lewis' usual sound, because they featured two backup musicians. In October 1927 Lewis was back in Chicago to cut six more songs, this time with nothing but his voice and his own guitar. Lewis seldom played with anyone else, partly because of his loose bar structures, which made it very difficult for anyone to follow him. The interplay of his voice and guitar, on record and in person, made him a very effective showman in both venues. Lewis' records, however, did not sell well, and he never developed more than a cult following in and around Memphis. A few of his records, however, lingered in the memory far beyond their relatively modest sales, most notably "John Henry" and "Kassie Jones—Parts 1 and 2," arguably one of the great blues recordings of the 1920s. Lewis gave up music as a profession during the mid-1930s, when

the Depression reduced the market for country blues. At the end of the 1950s, however, folksong/blues scholar Sam Charters discovered Lewis and persuaded him to resume his music career. In the interim, all of the blues stars who'd made their careers in Memphis during the 1930s had passed on or retired, and Lewis was a living repository of styles and songs that, otherwise, were scarcely within living memory of most Americans.

Lewis returned to the studio under Charters' direction and cut two albums for the Prestige/Bluesville labels in 1961. These showed Lewis in excellent form, his voice as good as ever and his technique on the guitar still dazzling. Audiences—initially hardcore blues and folk enthusiasts, and later more casual listeners—were delighted, fascinated, charmed, and deeply moved by what they heard. Gradually, as the 1960s and the ensuing blues boom wore on, Lewis emerged as one of the favorite rediscovered stars of the 1930s, playing festivals, appearing on talk shows, and being interviewed. He proved to be a skilled public figure, regaling audiences with stories of his life that were both funny and poignantly revealing, claiming certain achievements (such as being the inventor of bottleneck guitar) in dubious manner, and delighting the public. After his retirement from working for the city of Memphis, he also taught in an antipoverty program in the city.

Furry Lewis became a blues celebrity during the 1970s, after a profile in *Playboy* magazine and appearances on "The Tonight Show," and managed a few film and television appearances, including one as himself in the Burt Reynolds action/comedy *W.W. and the Dixie Dance Kings*. By this time he had several new recordings to his credit, and if the material wasn't as vital as the sides he'd cut at the end of the '20s, it was still valid and exceptionally fine blues, and paid him some money for his efforts. Lewis died in 1981 a beloved figure and a recognized giant in the world of blues. His music continues to sell well, and attract new listeners more than 15 years later. —*Bruce Eder*

Back on My Feet Again / 1961 / Bluesway ✦✦✦
An April 1961 session of traditional material such as "Shake 'Em on Down," "John Henry," "Roberta," and "St. Louis Blues." The album has been combined with another 1961 LP, *Done Changed My Mind*, for the CD compilation *Shake 'Em on Down*. —*Richie Unterberger*

Done Changed My Mind / 1962 / Bluesville ✦✦✦
A May 1961 session of traditional material along the lines of "Casey Jones" and "Frankie and Johnnie." It's been combined with a similar 1961 LP, *Back on My Feet Again*, onto one disc for the CD reissue compilation *Shake 'Em on Down*. —*Richie Unterberger*

☆ **Shake 'Em on Down** / 1972 / Fantasy ✦✦✦✦✦
A 20-song single CD reissue of Lewis' first modern commercial recordings, done for two Prestige/Bluesville albums (*Back On My Feet Again*, *Done Changed My Mind*) in April and May of 1961 at Sun Studios in Memphis. Lewis is in brilliant form throughout, his fingers nearly as fast and his voice as rich as they were 30-odd years earlier. The disc includes the definitive version of "John Henry" (not just Lewis' definitive version)—one of the greatest vocal performances ever put on record, and a guitar workout so dazzling that you'd swear there was more than one guy playing. What's more, with the extended running time available on tape (Lewis' sessions in the 1920s having been captured on 78 rpm discs with limited running times), he really stretches out here and obviously loves doing it. The slight reverb in the studio also gives Lewis a larger-than-life stature on this recording. —*Bruce Eder*

Fourth and Beale / 1975 / Lucky Seven ✦✦✦
Recorded in Memphis on March 5, 1969, with Lewis in bed—essentially an impromptu concert for the microphone and whoever happened to be there—these nine tracks show Lewis to fairly good advantage. They're more laidback than his work at the other end of the decade for Prestige/Bluesville, with Lewis playing more slowly and singing more roughly than those earlier sessions. His slide work is still stingingly effective, however, and his voice still highly expressive, and he knows how to put over a song even at this late date, playing with an almost hypnotic intensity—the songs include new renditions of "John Henry" and "Casey Jones," as well as "When the Saints Go Marching In" and W.C. Handy's "St. Louis Blues." —*Bruce Eder*

★ **In His Prime (1927-1928)** / 1988 / Yazoo ✦✦✦✦✦
The best overview of Lewis' classic late-'20s sides, containing 14 songs from the period (though not "John Henry"), all of which are crisply remastered, showing off both his superb guitar playing and his brilliantly expressive singing (the vocal performance on "Falling Down Blues" alone is worth the price of the disc) to excellent advantage. A seminal part of any blues collection, as well as any collection of Lewis' material. —*Bruce Eder*

☆ **Furry Lewis: Complete Works (1927-1929)** / 1990 / Document ✦✦✦✦✦
This Austrian import would be the finest single collection of Furry Lewis' work, covering his Vocalion and Victor sides, if it only included "Kassie Jones-Part 2," which it does not. But otherwise it is as comprehensive a collection as has been put together on Lewis' work. "John Henry" is

included, as is the laidback "Mr. Furry's Blues," the latter featuring Charles Jackson (or Johnson) on mandolin. Some of the tracks have more noise than we might like, but overall this is a good representation of Lewis' work. —*Bruce Eder*

Jimmy Liggins

b. Oct. 14, 1922, Newby, OK, **d.** Jul. 18, 1983, Durham, NC
Guitar / R&B, Jump Blues
Another of the jump blues specialists whose romping output can be pinpointed as a direct precursor of rock 'n' roll, guitarist Jimmy Liggins was a far more aggressive bandleader than his older brother Joe, right down to the names of their respective combos (Joe led the polished Honeydrippers; Jimmy proudly fronted the Drops of Joy).

Inspired by the success of his brother (Jimmy toiled as Joe's chauffeur for a year), the ex-pugilist jumped into the recording field in 1947 on Art Rupe's Specialty logo. His "Tear Drop Blues" pierced the R&B Top Ten the next year, while "Careful Love" and "Don't Put Me Down" hit for him in 1949. But it's Liggins' rough-and-ready rockers—"Cadillac Boogie," "Saturday Night Boogie Woogie Man," and the loopy one-chord workout "Drunk" (his last smash in 1953)—that mark Liggins as one of rock's forefathers. His roaring sax section at Specialty was populated by first-rate redmen such as Harold Land, Charlie "Little Jazz" Ferguson, and the omnipresent Maxwell Davis.

Liggins left Specialty in 1954, stopping off at Aladdin long enough to wax the classic-to-be "I Ain't Drunk" (much later covered by Albert Collins) before fading from the scene. —*Bill Dahl*

● **And His Drops of Joy** / 1989 / Specialty ◆◆◆◆
Guitarist Jimmy Liggins swung considerably harder than his brother Joe during his 1947-1953 Specialty stint, presaging rock's rise with his torrid jump blues "Cadillac Boogie," "Saturday Night Boogie Woogie Man," and the marvelously loopy "Drunk." Twenty-five of his best are right here. —*Bill Dahl*

Rough Weather Blues, Vol. 2 / 1992 / Specialty ◆◆◆◆
Twenty-five more Specialty cookers, including an undubbed version of "Drunk," plenty of horn-leavened jump blues outings, and several unissued artifacts (including a rare example of the Drops of Joy getting jazzy on "Now's the Time"). —*Bill Dahl*

Joe Liggins

b. 1915, Guthrie, OK, **d.** Aug. 1, 1987
Piano / R&B, Electric Jump Blues, Jump Blues
Pianist Joe Liggins and his band, the Honeydrippers, tore up the R&B charts during the late '40s and early '50s with their polished brand of polite R&B. Liggins scored massive hits with "The Honeydripper" in 1945 and "Pink Champagne" five years later, posting a great many more solid sellers in between.

Born in Oklahoma, Liggins moved to San Diego in 1932. He moved to Los Angeles in 1939 and played with various outfits, including Sammy Franklin's California Rhythm Rascals. When Franklin took an unwise pass on recording Liggins' infectious "The Honeydripper," the bespectacled pianist assembled his own band and waxed the tune for Leon Rene's Exclusive logo. The upshot: an R&B chart-topper. Nine more hits followed on Exclusive over the next three years, including the schmaltzy "Got a Right to Cry," the often-covered "Tanya" (Chicago guitarist Earl Hooker waxed a delicious version) and "Roll 'Em."

In 1950, Joe joined his brother Jimmy at Specialty Records. More hits immediately followed: "Rag Mop," the number one R&B smash "Pink Champagne," "Little Joe's Boogie," and "Frankie Lee." During this period, the Honeydrippers prominently featured saxists Willie Jackson and James Jackson, Jr. Liggins stuck around Specialty into 1954, later turning up with solitary singles on Mercury and Aladdin. But time had passed Liggins by, at least right then; later, his sophisticated approach later came back into fashion, and he led a little big band until his death. —*Bill Dahl*

★ **Joe Liggins and the Honeydrippers** / 1990 / Specialty ◆◆◆◆◆
Pianist Joe Liggins presented a fairly sophisticated brand of swinging jump blues to jitterbuggers during the early '50s, when his irresistible "Pink Champagne" scaled the R&B charts. Twenty-five of his very best 1950-1954 Specialty sides grace this collection, including a tasty remake of "The Honeydripper" "Rhythm in the Barnyard," and the syncopated "Going Back to New Orleans" (recently revived by Dr. John). —*Bill Dahl*

Dripper's Boogie, Vol. 2 / 1992 / Specialty ◆◆◆◆
An encore helping of 20 rarities by Joe Liggins from Specialty, dotted with unissued discoveries (including two versions of "Little Joe's Boogie" and "Hey, Betty Martin") from 1950-1954. —*Bill Dahl*

Lightnin' Slim

b. Mar. 13, 1913, St. Louis, MO, **d.** Jul. 24, 1974, Detroit, MI
Guitar, Vocals / Electric Louisiana Blues
The acknowledged kingpin of the Louisiana school of blues, Lightnin'

Slim's style was built on his grainy but expressive vocals and rudimentary guitar work, with usually nothing more than a harmonica and a drummer in support. It was down-home country blues edged two steps further into the mainstream; first by virtue of Lightnin's electric guitar, and secondly by the sound of the local Crowley musicians who backed him being bathed in simmering, pulsating tape echo. As the first great star of producer J.D. Miller's blues talent stable, the formula was a successful one, scoring him regional hits that were issued on the Nashville-based Excello label for over a decade, one of them, "Rooster Blues," making the national R&B charts in 1959. Combining the country ambience of a Lightnin' Hopkins with the plodding insistency of a Muddy Waters, Slim's music remained uniquely his own, the perfect blues raconteur, even when reshaping other's material to his dark, somber style. He also possessed one of the truly great voices of the blues; unadorned and unaffected, making the world-weariness of a Sonny Boy Williamson sound like the second coming of Good Time Charlie by comparison. His exhortation to "blow your harmonica, son" has become one of the great, mournful catchphrases of the blues, and even on his most rockin' numbers, there's a sense that you are listening less to an uptempo offering than a slow blues just being played faster. Lightnin' always sounded as if bad luck just moved into his home approximately an hour after his mother-in-law did.

He was born Otis Hicks in St. Louis, MO, on March 15, 1913. After 13 years of living on a farm outside of the city, the Hicks family moved to Louisiana, first settling in St. Francisville. Young Otis took to the guitar early, first shown the rudiments by his father, then later by his older brother, Layfield. Given his output, it's highly doubtful that either his father or brother knew how to play in any key other than E natural, as Lightnin' used the same patterns over and over on his recordings, only changing keys when he used a capo or had his guitar de-tuned a full step.

But the rudiments were all he needed, and by the late '30s/early '40s he was a mainstay of the local picnic/country supper circuit around St. Francisville. In 1946, he moved to Baton Rouge and started to make a name for himself on the local circuit, first working as a member of Big Poppa's band, then on his own.

The '50s dawned with harmonica player Schoolboy Cleve in tow, working club dates and broadcasting over the radio together. It was local disc jockey Ray "Diggy Do" Meaders who then persuaded Miller to record him. He recorded for 12 years as an Excello artist, starting out originally on Miller's Feature label. As the late '60s found Lightnin' Slim working and living in Detroit, a second career blossomed as European blues audiences brought him over to tour. During the early '70s, Lightnin' recording sporadically, while performing as part of the American Blues Legends tour until his death in 1974. Lazy, rolling and insistent, Lightnin' Slim is Louisiana blues at its finest. —*Cub Koda*

Bell Ringer / 1987 / Excello ◆◆◆◆
Superb early Slim Excello material. He never sang with more clarity or conviction, nor did his harmonica or guitar playing ever sound more electrifying than on these songs, many of which were popular singles. Other than Rice Miller's (Sonny Boy Williamson II) definitive anthem, Slim's rendition of "Don't Start Me to Talking" is the finest. —*Ron Wynn*

★ **Rooster Blues** / 1987 / Excello ◆◆◆◆◆
Stark, sparse, swamp blues with the deepest tone in the South Louisiana genre's history. Lightnin' Slim was an Excello mainstay from the mid-'50s to the mid-'60s; 18 of his best J.D. Miller-produced sides reside here. The title track, "Hoo-Doo Blues," "GI Slim," "Tom Cat Blues," and the ribald "It's Mighty Crazy" rate with the guitarist's seminal efforts. —*Bill Dahl*

I'm Evil / 1995 / Excello/AVI ◆◆◆◆
A goldmine of 27 1950s/1960s obscurities from one of the lonesomest bayou blues greats ever. Filled with alternate takes and outright unissued efforts, *I'm Evil* reverberates with lowdown treatises that cut to the heart and soul of the swamp. "Bad Luck," "Mean Ol' Lonesome Train," and "Rock Me Mama" are pure, unadulterated Louisiana blues of the highest order. —*Bill Dahl*

Lil' Ed and the Blues Imperials (Lil' Ed Williams)

Guitar, Vocals / Modern Electric Blues
Lil' Ed and the Blues Imperials include Lil' Ed Williams (vocal, guitar); "Pookie" Young (bass); and various others on guitar and drums. Lil' Ed Williams learned his trade as a teenager from his uncle, Chicago slide-guitarist J.B. Hutto, and the resemblance to Hutto, vocally and instrumentally, continues to be no less amazing some 20 years later. If Ed, half-brother Pookie Young, and the latest members of the revamped Blues Imperials never do much to modernize their blues or develop a new sound, that will be just fine with the band's growing legion of followers ("Ed Heads," no less), to whom the raucous, rocking slide guitar heritage of Hutto, Hound Dog Taylor, and Elmore James is blues nirvana. —*Jim O'Neal*

Roughhousin' / 1986 / Alligator ✦✦✦
Wild & greasy blues at its best, a two-song session for an anthology turned into an all-night, live-in-the-studio jam. Sounds like it was great fun. —*Niles J. Frantz*

● **Chicken Gravy & Biscuits** / 1989 / Alligator ✦✦✦✦
Wild, raw, rough-edged Chicago slide guitar blues, this is jumpin', partyin' music in the tradition of Hound Dog Taylor and J.B. Hutto (Lil' Ed's uncle). Recorded live in the studio with no overdubs, it includes nine original compositions plus covers of Hutto and Albert Collins tunes. —*Niles J. Frantz*

What You See Is What You Get / 1992 / Alligator ✦✦✦
There's enough greasy slide guitar blues on *What You See Is What You Get* to satisfy fans of Lil' Ed Williams, but it doesn't rank as one of his best albums. Though there are a couple of ripping tracks—particularly the off-beat "Life Is like Gambling"—Williams sounds a little tired, and, ultimately, that flagging energy is what sinks the album. —*Thom Owens*

Little Charlie and the Nightcats

Group / Modern Electric Blues
Little Charlie and The Nightcats have been bringing West Coast clubgoers to their feet with their eclectic blues-infused repertoire since the mid-'70s. Drawing from styles ranging from Chicago and jazzy West Coast blues to Texas Swing to rockabilly to surf music and R&B, the Nightcats sing mostly original songs and are noted for their wry, satirical lyrics. They also perform adaptations of obscure older tunes. Though they primarily perform in California and Oregon, the Nightcats frequently tour across the continent, and have even toured Europe. They feature a talented lineup that centers upon extraordinary harp player/songwriter/singer Rick Estrin and versatile guitarist Little Charlie Baty. Dobie Strange on drums and bass player Ronnie James Weber, who joined the Nightcats in the mid-'90s, round out the lineup. —*Sandra Brennan*

● **Disturbing the Peace** / 1988 / Alligator ✦✦✦✦
These are jumpin' blues with wild antics, a good sense of humor, tons of fun, often outrageous. Very, very good guitar comes from Charlie Baty and interesting harp from lead vocalist Rick Estrin. —*Niles J. Frantz*

Captured Live / 1991 / Alligator ✦✦✦
This enjoyable live set captures the group's manic energy. —*Niles J. Frantz*

Night Vision / 1993 / Alligator ✦✦✦

Little Milton (Milton Campbell)

b. Sep. 7, 1934, Inverness, MS
Guitar, Vocals / Soul, R&B, Soul Blues, Boogie-Woogie
One of the great blues guitarists, singers, and composers of all time, Milton began his recording career in Memphis with Sun Records in 1953. Small-label singles followed for Meteor and Bobbin before he landed at Chess records in Chicago in 1961. He became one of the best-selling blues artists of the '60s, with many hit singles, including a No. 1 R&B hit "We're Gonna Make It" and items such as "Feel So Bad," "If Walls Could Talk," and "Baby I Love You." There may be soap-opera elements in much of Milton's work, but it is always done with flair and good humor. While the mold was pretty much established during his Checker period, it also worked with his later affiliations at Stax and Glades. His Malaco recordings (dating from 1984) bring the formula of strings, horns, and background vocals up to date, but the blues artistry of Milton still shines through. —*Bob Porter*

If Walls Could Talk / 1970 / MCA/Chess ✦✦✦✦
On *If Walls Could Talk* Little Milton continues to fuse blues with soul—if anything, the album leans toward soul more than blues. Supported by a band with a thick, wailing horn section, Little Milton sings and plays with power. Though there are a couple of wonderful solos, the focus of the record is on the songs, which all sound terrific, thanks to Milton's compassionate vocals. —*Thom Owens*

Grits Ain't Groceries / Jan. 1970 / Checker ✦✦✦
Grits Ain't Groceries is another set of soul and R&B songs from the blues guitarist Little Milton, highlighted by the scorching title track. —*Thom Owens*

Greatest Hits / 1972 / MCA/Chess ✦✦✦
Greatest Hits offers a good sampling of Little Milton's singles for Chess Records in the '60s, including the hits "We're Gonna Make It" and "If Walls Could Talk." It may be a little brief, but there are no bad songs on the record at all and it's an excellent introduction to the guitarist's talents. —*Thom Owens*

Waiting for Little Milton / 1973 / Stax ✦✦✦
Although Little Milton's Stax recordings aren't as blues-oriented as his classic Chess and Checker recordings, there are still plenty of things to recommend about them. Primarily, they're of interest because they focus on his soulful vocals and those vocals shine on *Waiting for Little Milton*.

On the whole, the album is a little uneven—the songs aren't always first-rate and the production is a little too smooth—but the performances make it worthwhile for most dedicated fans. —*Thom Owens*

Chronicle / 1979 / Stax ✦✦✦✦
This compilation has a leftover feel; the liner notes provide no sources and dates, admitting only that these are "Stax recordings, some never before available on LP." If you're a big fan of one or both of the artists involved, though, it's not bad, with a quality that's generally consistent with their fully-baked Stax-era albums. The Milton half of the program is somewhat inferior to the King tracks, the singer taking a misstep with his version of Charlie Rich's country smash "Behind Closed Doors." —*Richie Unterberger*

Age Ain't Nothin' But a Number / 1983 / Mobile Fidelity ✦✦✦

Greatest Sides / 1984 / MCA/Chess ✦✦✦✦
Greatest Sides contains a few of Little Milton's best cuts—including "We're Gonna Make It"—but the packaging isn't very good and the songs are presented haphazardly. There might be some good music on *Greatest Sides*, but there are far better compilations to purchase. —*Thom Owens*

★ **Sun Masters** / 1990 / Rounder ✦✦✦✦✦
While he was at Sun, Little Milton tried a variety of different sounds and styles—sounding like everybody from Elmore James and B.B. King to Fats Domino—which was all tied together by his raw, manic lead guitar. *The Sun Masters* collects many of Milton's absolute finest moments—he never again sounded quite as wild or reckless, either vocally or instrumentally, as he does here. —*Thom Owens*

Greatest Hits / Sep. 5, 1995 / Malaco ✦✦✦
For fans of Little Milton's Chess, Checker, and Sun sides, his '80s records for Malaco aren't particularly attractive, since they are slicker and more polished. Nevertheless, he cut several first-rate songs for the label, songs that showcase his considerable guitar and vocal talents, and the majority of those songs are collected on *Greatest Hits*. It's a solid introduction to the latter part of Milton's career. —*Thom Owens*

We're Gonna Make It/Little Milton Sings Big Blues / 199_ / MCA/Chess ✦✦✦✦
Two of Milton's classic mid-'60s Chess albums on one CD makes for a great value. —*Bill Dahl*

Little Walter (Marion Walter Jacobs)

b. May 1, 1930, Marksville, LA, **d.** Feb. 15, 1968, Chicago, IL
Guitar, Harmonica, Vocals / R&B, Electric Chicago Blues
Who's the king of all postwar blues harpists, Chicago division or otherwise? Why, the virtuosic Little Walter, without a solitary doubt. The fiery harmonica wizard took the humble mouth organ in dazzling amplified directions that were unimaginable prior to his ascendancy. His daring instrumental innovations were so fresh, startling, and ahead of their time that they sometimes sported a jazz sensibility, soaring and swooping in front of snarling guitars and swinging rhythms perfectly suited to Walter's pioneering flights of fancy.

Marion Walter Jacobs was by most accounts an unruly but vastly talented youth who abandoned his rural Louisiana home for the bright lights of New Orleans at age 12. Walter gradually journeyed north from there, pausing in Helena (where he hung out with the wizened Sonny Boy Williamson), Memphis, and St. Louis before arriving in Chicago in 1946.

The thriving Maxwell Street strip offered a spot for the still-teenaged phenom to hawk his wares. He fell in with local royalty—Tampa Red and Big Bill Broonzy—and debuted on wax that same year for the tiny Ora-Nelle logo ("I Just Keep Loving Her") in the company of Jimmy Rogers and guitarist Othum Brown. Walter joined forces with Muddy Waters in 1948; the resulting stylistic tremors are still being felt today. Along with Rogers and Baby Face Leroy Foster, this super-confident young aggregation became informally known as the Headhunters. They would saunter into South Side clubs, mount the stage, and proceed to calmly "cut the heads" of whomever was booked there that evening.

By 1950 Walter was firmly entrenched as Muddy Waters' studio harpist at Chess as well (long after Walter had split the Muddy Waters band, Leonard Chess insisted on his participation on waxings—why split up an unbeatable combination?). That's how Walter came to record his breakthrough 1952 R&B chart-topper "Juke"—the romping instrumental was laid down at the tail end of a Waters session. Suddenly Walter was a star on his own, combining his stunning talents with those of the Aces (guitarists Louis and David Myers and drummer Fred Below) and advancing the conception of blues harmonica another few light years with every session he made for Checker Records.

From 1952 to 1958, Walter notched 14 Top Ten R&B hits, including "Sad Hours," "Mean Old World," "Tell Me Mama," "Off the Wall," "Blues with a Feeling," "You're So Fine," a threatening "You Better Watch Yourself," the mournful "Last Night," and a rocking "My Babe" that was Willie Dixon's secularized treatment of the traditional gospel lament

"This Train." Throughout his Checker tenure, Walter alternated spine-chilling instrumentals with gritty vocals (he's always been underrated in that department; he wasn't Muddy Waters or the Wolf, but who was?).

Walter used the chromatic harp in ways never before envisioned (check out his 1956 free-form instrumental "Teenage Beat," with Robert Jr. Lockwood and Luther Tucker manning the guitars, for proof positive). 1959's determined "Everything Gonna Be Alright" was Walter's last trip to the hit lists; Chicago blues had faded to a commercial nonentity by then unless your name was Jimmy Reed.

Tragically, the '60s saw the harp genius slide steadily into an alcohol-hastened state of unreliability, his once-handsome face becoming a roadmap of scars. Walter's eternally vicious temper led to his violent undoing in 1968. He was involved in a street fight (apparently on the losing end, judging from the outcome) and died from the incident's after-effects at age 37. His influence remains inescapable to this day—it's unlikely that a blues harpist exists on the face of this earth who doesn't worship Little Walter. —*Bill Dahl*

★ **Best** / 1958 / MCA/Chess ✦✦✦✦✦
If there's a blues harmonica player alive today who doesn't have a copy of this landmark album in their collection, they're either lying or had their copy of it stolen by another harmonica player. This 12-song collection is the one that every harmonica player across the board cut their teeth on. All the hits are here: "My Babe," "Blues with a Feeling," "You Better Watch Yourself," "Off the Wall," "Mean Old World," and the instrumental that catapulted him from the sideman chair in Muddy Waters' band to the top of the R&B charts in 1952, "Juke." Walter's influence to this very day is so pervasive over the landscape of the instrument that this collection of singles is truly: 1) one of the all-time greatest blues harmonica albums, 2) one of the all-time greatest Chicago blues albums, and 3) one of the first ten albums you should purchase if you're you're building your blues collection from the ground floor up. —*Cub Koda*

Hate to See You Go / 1969 / MCA/Chess ✦✦✦✦
Another solid collection of tracks recorded between 1952 and 1960 that originally appeared in 1969 as part of the short-lived Chess Vintage Blues Masters series. Three of the tracks overlap with the budget compilation *The Best of Little Walter, Volume 2*, but the other 12 are just too good to pass by because of a minor programming gaffe. Standout cuts abound just about anywhere the laser beam falls, but the set closer, the minor-key masterpiece "Blue and Lonesome," just may be the most emotionally terrifying masterpiece of Walter's illustrious career. —*Cub Koda*

The Blues World of Little Walter / 1988 / Delmark ✦✦✦
If you really want to hear what Little Walter sounded like in his pre-amplified days and early stages of development with the Muddy Waters band, this is the one to get. The title is a bit of a misnomer as Walter is featured more as a sideman to Baby Face Leroy, Muddy Waters, and others on early Parkway, Regal, and Savoy sides, but it's clear that Walter at this stage of the game should have been paying royalties to both Sonny Boys and Walter Horton in particular. One of the high points features explosive slide work from Waters on a pre-Chess version of "Rollin' and Tumblin'," as crude a version as you'll ever hear and certainly not to be missed. Although many of these sides have appeared on other compilations (usually taped up off of old scratchy 78s), this one features superior sound taken from the original lacquer masters. —*Cub Koda*

☆ **The Best of Little Walter, Vol. 2** / 1989 / MCA/Chess ✦✦✦✦✦
This ten-song budget compilation continues the overview of Walter's enormous output for the Chess label. For rock fans, the most familiar track on here is the original version of "Boom Boom (Out Go the Lights)." But there's more where that came from, including the smoking uptempo "It Ain't Right," the blistering instrumental "Boogie," and the soulful stroll of "I Don't Play." Another bonus is the inclusion of an early Muddy Waters instrumental featuring Walter on acoustic harp, "Evans' Shuffle." A great, cost-effective way to add some more Walter to the collection. —*Cub Koda*

☆ **The Chess Years 1952-1963** / 1992 / Charly ✦✦✦✦✦
Damn near everything (*Blues with a Feeling* popped any semblance of absolute completion) that the Chicago harp genius ever waxed for Chess (95 sides in all), spread over four generously programmed discs. Particularly revealing are the lengthy snippets of studio chatter on the final rarities disc—Sonny Boy had nothing on Walter when it came to verbally sparring in the studio with Leonard Chess! —*Bill Dahl*

★ **The Essential** / Jun. 8, 1993 / MCA/Chess ✦✦✦✦✦
In many ways, this supplants the original single disc, *Best of Little Walter*, and appends it with 35 more classics of Chicago blues harp genius, although one track from the original 12-song lineup is (perhaps purposely) left off. If you want to start your Walter collection with a nice generous helping of his best, this one runs the entire gamut of his solo career, from the classic 1952 instrumental "Juke" up to the Willie Dixon-penned "Dead Presidents." 46 tracks, one dynamite booklet, nice remastering, a great value for the cash outlay involved and best of all, an album title that truly delivers the goods. —*Cub Koda*

Blues with a Feeling / Oct. 24, 1995 / MCA/Chess ✦✦✦✦
Blues with a Feeling is a two-CD, 40-track compilation that makes the perfect audio bookend to *The Essential Little Walter* (or the single disc *The Best of Little Walter* for those on a budget) by systematically combing the Chess vaults and rounding up the best stuff. The rarities (including the low-down "Tonight with a Fool," possibly the rarest Walter Checker single of all and one whose title never shows up in the lyrics) are all noteworthy by their inclusion. But the alternate takes are the real motherlode here; everyone of 'em has got some kind of major screwup while showing Walter's penchant for putting a new spin on a tune every time the engineer hit the "record" button. Little Walter was a blues genius, and once you've absorbed the influential hits, here's exactly where you go next to get the rest of the story. —*Cub Koda*

Johnny Littlejohn (John Funchess)

b. Apr. 16, 1931, Lake, MS, **d.** Feb. 1, 1994, Chicago, IL
Guitar, Vocals / Electric Chicago Blues
Johnny Littlejohn's stunning mastery of the slide guitar somehow never launched him into the major leagues of bluesdom. Only on a handful of occasions was the Chicago veteran's vicious bottleneck attack captured effectively on wax, but anyone who experienced one of his late-night sessions as a special musical guest on the Windy City circuit will never forget the crashing passion in his delivery. —*Bill Dahl*

● **Chicago Blues Stars** / 1991 / Arhoolie ✦✦✦✦
Slide guitar master Littlejohn was already overdue for the full-length album treatment when he waxed this stellar set for Arhoolie in 1969 (enhanced by three bonus cuts on the CD version). A sizzling Chicago combo provides sterling backing as Littlejohn sears the strings on "Dream," "Shake Your Moneymaker," and a rough-edged adaptation of Brook Benton's "Kiddeo," his powerhouse vocals consistently stunning. —*Bill Dahl*

Robert Jr. Lockwood

b. Mar. 27, 1915, Marvell, AR
Guitar, Harmonica, Vocals / Chicago Blues, Electric Delta Blues, Acoustic Delta Blues
Robert Jr. Lockwood learned his blues first-hand from an unimpeachable source: the immortal Robert Johnson. Lockwood can still conjure up the bone-chilling Johnson sound whenever he so desires, but he's never been one to linger in the past for long—which accounts for the jazzy swing he often brings to the licks he plays on his 12-string electric guitar.

Now past the age of 80, Lockwood is one of the last living links to the glorious Johnson legacy. When Lockwood's mother became romantically involved with the charismatic rambler in Helena, AR, the quiet teenager suddenly gained a role model and a close friend—so close that Lockwood considered himself Johnson's stepson. Robert Jr. learned how to play guitar very quickly with Johnson's expert help, assimilating Johnson's technique inside and out.

Following Johnson's tragic murder in 1938, Lockwood embarked on his own intriguing musical journey. He was among the first bluesmen to score an electric guitar in 1938 and eventually made his way to Chicago, where he cut four seminal tracks for Bluebird. Jazz elements steadily crept into Lockwood's dazzling fretwork, although his role as Sonny Boy Williamson's musical partner on the fabled KFFA *King Biscuit Time* radio broadcasts during the early '40s out of Helena, AR, probably didn't emphasize that side of his dexterity all that much.

Settling in Chicago in 1950, Lockwood swiftly gained a reputation as a versatile in-demand studio sideman, recording behind harp genius Little Walter, piano masters Sunnyland Slim and Eddie Boyd, and plenty more. Solo recording opportunities were scarce, though Lockwood did cut fine singles for Mercury in 1951 ("I'm Gonna Dig Myself a Hole" and a very early "Dust My Broom") and JOB in 1955 ("Sweet Woman from Maine"/"Aw Aw Baby").

Lockwood's best modern work as a leader was done for Pete Lowry's Trix label, including some startling workouts on the 12-string axe that he daringly added to his arsenal in 1965. He later joined forces with fellow Johnson disciple Johnny Shines for two eclectic early-'80s Rounder albums. Intent on satisfying his own instincts first and foremost, the sometimes taciturn Lockwood is a priceless connection between past and present. —*Bill Dahl*

Contrasts / 1974 / Trix ✦✦✦✦
Robert Jr. Lockwood has never been a conventional musician or blues artist. This was one of a pair of spectacular albums done for Trix in the 1970s. Johnson's version of "Driving Wheel" maintains the spirit of Roosevelt Sykes' familiar rendition, but has his own compelling twists. Otherwise, the session featured Lockwood songs, and he demonstrated the probing, animated qualities that made him a legend and a survivor. —*Ron Wynn*

Hangin' On / 1979 / Rounder ✦✦✦
Two of the principal keepers of the Robert Johnson flame joined forces for a Rounder LP that's stunning in its non-conformity to what purists might like to hear from the two veterans. Jazz and swing influences invest much of the LP, the pair sharing vocal and guitar duties. —*Bill Dahl*

● **Plays Robert and Robert** / Nov. 28, 1982 / Black & Blue ✦✦✦✦
Lockwood in a beautifully recorded solo context (cut in France in 1982 for Black & Blue), doing what he does best—his own songs and those of his legendary mentor, Robert Johnson. Purists may quiver at Lockwood's use of the 12-string guitar as his primary axe, but he long ago made the instrument his own blues tool of choice, and he handles its nuances expertly. —*Bill Dahl*

Robert Lockwood / 1991 / Paula ✦✦✦✦
All 20 of these tracks were recorded for JOB in the early '50s, but only half feature Lockwood; the others are Johnny Shines solo sides. The title is a bit misleading; the Lockwood tracks, recorded in 1951 and 1955, mix genuine Lockwood solo performances with sides on which he supported Sunnyland Slim and Alfred Wallace. It's decent, sparse, early Chicago blues, though not as good as the preceding Shines tracks on the disc. —*Richie Unterberger*

Cripple Clarence Lofton (Albert Clemens)

b. Mar. 28, 1887, Kingsport, TN, d. Jan. 9, 1957, Chicago, IL
Piano, Vocals / Piano Blues
Cripple Clarence Lofton is one of those colorful names that adorned many an album collection of early boogie-woogie piano 78s in the early days of the '60s folk-blues revival. Lofton's technique—or lack of it—stemmed more from a tent show background, and those listening to his earliest and most energetic recordings will quickly attest that hitting every note or making every chord change precisely were not exactly high priorities with him. But this wild, high energy act got the young showman noticed quickly and by the early '30s, he was so much a fixture of the Chicago night life firmament that he had his own Windy City nightclub, the oddly named Big Apple. Lofton remained on the scene, cutting sides for the Gennett, Vocalion, Solo Art, Riverside, Session, and Pax labels into the '40s. When the boogie-woogie craze cooled off and eventually died down in the late '40s, Lofton went into early retirement, staying around Chicago until his death in 1957 from a blood clot in the brain. —*Cub Koda*

Cripple Lofton and Walter Davis / Yazoo ✦✦✦✦
Marvelous blues piano and singing from Cripple Clarence Lofton, and nearly as fine an effort from Walter Davis. —*Ron Wynn*

● **Cripple Clarence Lofton, Vol. 1** / RST ✦✦✦✦
Some of Lofton's best, with the selections "Strut That Thing," "Monkey Man Blues," and "Pitchin' Boogie" being particular standouts. (Import) —*Cub Koda*

Willie Love

b. Nov. 4, 1906, Duncan, MS, d. Aug. 19, 1953, Jackson, MS
Piano, Vocals / Acoustic Delta Blues, Electric Delta Piano Blues
Harpist Rice Miller, known to his legion of fans across the Delta as Sonny Boy Williamson, first encountered pianist Willie Love in Greenville, MS, in 1942. The talented pair played regularly on Nelson Street, the main drag of the Black section of Greenville, musically intertwining with remarkable empathy. And it was Williamson who brought Love into the fold at Trumpet Records (the label responsible for Love's entire recorded legacy as a leader).

Love was deeply influenced by Leroy Carr and equally conversant with boogies and down-in-the-alley blues. He played piano on several of Sonny Boy Williamson's Trumpet sessions, but Love didn't utilize his pal on any of his own 1951-1953 dates for the Jackson, MS, label. Love's debut, "Take It Easy, Baby," was a rollicking boogie outing, and he followed it up with the equally sturdy "Everybody's Fishing," "Vanity Dresser Boogie," and "Nelson Street Blues." Love's last session in April of 1953 found him backed by a White bassist and drummer—certainly a rarity for the era. Four months later, Love, who had long suffered from alcoholism, was dead. —*Bill Dahl*

● **Clownin' with the World** / 1993 / Alligator ✦✦✦✦
Instead of assembling a single disc highlighting this Delta piano great, Alligator has spread pianist Willie Love's Trumpet catalog over three marvelous anthologies drawn from the early-'50s archives of Lillian McMurry's Trumpet Records. After eight terrific sides by Sonny Boy, Love pounds out "Take It Easy, Baby," "Little Car Blues," "Feed My Body to the Fishes," and five more, conjuring up a steamy Delta juke joint ambience. —*Bill Dahl*

Delta Blues: 1951 / 1993 / Alligator ✦✦✦
Six more classic 1951 performances by Love from Trumpet's vaults, including the romping "Everybody's Fishing," "My Own Boogie," and "Vanity Dresser Boogie." The pianist shares this disc with country blues-

men Luther Huff and the omnipresent Big Joe Williams; both turned in some inspired work for Lillian McMurry's logo. —*Bill Dahl*

Shout Brother Shout / Oldie Blues ✦✦✦✦
A more varied mix of musical styles than on the first two anthologies (everything from Wally Mercer's rocking R&B to Beverly White's schmaltzy lounge sounds). Love leads three more solid sides from 1953: the title item, "Way Back," and "Willie Mae." —*Bill Dahl*

Willie Mabon

b. Oct. 24, 1925, Hollywood, TN, d. Apr. 19, 1985, Paris, France
Piano, Vocals / R&B, Blues, Piano Blues
The sly, insinuating vocals and chunky piano style of Willie Mabon won the heart of many an R&B fan during the early '50s. His salty Chess waxings "I Don't Know," "I'm Mad," and "Poison Ivy" established the pianist as a genuine Chicago blues force, but he faded as an R&B hitmaker at the dawn of rock 'n' roll.

Mabon was already well-grounded in blues tradition from his Memphis upbringing when he hit Chicago in 1942. Schooled in jazz as well as blues, Mabon found the latter his ticket to stardom. His first sides were a 1949 78 for Apollo as Big Willie and some 1950 outings for Aristocrat and Chess with guitarist Earl Dranes as the Blues-rockers.

But Mabon's asking price for a night's work rose dramatically when his 1952 debut release on Parrot, "I Don't Know," topped the R&B charts for eight weeks after being sold to Chess. From then on, Mabon was a Chess artist, returning to the top R&B slot the next year with the ominous "I'm Mad" and cracking the Top Ten anew with "Poison Ivy" in 1954. Mabon's original version of Willie Dixon's hoodoo-driven "The Seventh Son" bombed in 1955, as did the remainder of his fine Chess catalog.

Mabon never regained his momentum after leaving Chess. He stopped at Federal in 1957, Mad in 1960, Formal in 1962, and USA in 1963-64. Mabon sat out much of the late '60s but came back strong after moving to Paris in 1972, recording and touring Europe prolifically until his death. —*Bill Dahl*

● **Seventh Son** / 1993 / Charly ✦✦✦✦
Since MCA hasn't gotten around to this insinuating character's splendid Chess catalog as yet, we'll have to opt for a 16-song import that encompasses his three major hits "I Don't Know," "I'm Mad" (here in alternate take form, for whatever reason), and the Mel London-penned "Poison Ivy." Mabon's urban R&B approach was something of a departure for the Delta-rooted blues prevalent at Chess at the time, but his laconic vocals on "The Seventh Son," "Knock on Wood," and "Got to Have It" made him a star (albeit briefly). —*Bill Dahl*

Lonnie Mack

b. Jul. 18, 1941, Harrison, IN
Guitar, Vocals / R&B, Rock 'n' Roll, Modern Electric Blues, Instrumental Rock
When Lonnie Mack sings the blues, country strains are sure to infiltrate. Conversely, if he digs into a humping rockabilly groove, strong signs of deep-down blues influence are bound to invade. Par for the course for any musician who cites both Bobby Bland and George Jones as pervasive influences.

Fact is, Lonnie Mack's lightning-fast, vibrato-enriched, whammy bar-hammered guitar style has influenced many a picker too—including Stevie Ray Vaughan, who idolized Mack's early singles for Fraternity and later co-produced and played on Mack's 1985 comeback LP for Alligator, *Strike Like Lightning*.

Growing up in rural Indiana not far from Cincinnati, Lonnie McIntosh was exposed to a heady combination of R&B and hillbilly. In 1958, he bought the seventh Gibson Flying V guitar ever manufactured and played the roadhouse circuit around Indiana, Ohio, and Kentucky. Mack has steadfastly cited another local legend, guitarist Robert Ward, as the man whose watery-sounding Magnatone amplifier inspired his own use of the same brand.

Session work ensued during the early '60s behind Hank Ballard, Freddy King, and James Brown for Cincy's principal label, Syd Nathan's King Records. At the tail end of a 1963 date for another local diskery, Fraternity Records, Mack stepped out front to cut a searing instrumental treatment of Chuck Berry's "Memphis." Fraternity put the number out, and it leapt all the way up to the Top Five on *Billboard's* pop charts!

Its hit follow-up, the frantic "Wham!," was even more amazing from a guitaristic perspective, with Mack's lickety-split whammy-bar-fired playing driven like a locomotive by a hard-charging horn section. Mack's vocal skills were equally potent; R&B stations began to play his soul ballad "Where There's a Will" until they discovered Mack was of the Caucasian persuasion, then dropped it like a hot potato (its flip, a sizzling vocal remake of Jimmy Reed's "Baby, What's Wrong," was a minor pop hit in late 1963).

Mack waxed a load of killer material for Fraternity during the mid-'60s, much of it not seeing the light of day until later on. A deal with Ele-

Blues History

Music Map

African Roots

| Work Songs, Field Hollers | Church & Gospel Music
Standard Quartette (rec. 1894)
Dinwiddie Colored Quartet (rec. 1902)
Apollo Male Quartette (rec. 1912) | Black Entertainment
Minstrel, Ragtime, String Bands | Medicine Shows
Papa Charlie Jackson — Pink Anderson
Daddy Stovepipe |

| Early Blues Recorders (ca. 1920)
W. C. Handy (1873-1958) — Perry Bradford (1893-1970)
Clarence Williams (1898-1965) | Songsters
Henry Thomas (1874-1950) — Frank Stokes (1888-1955)
Peg Leg Howell (1888-1966) — Leadbelly (1889-1949)
Mance Lipscomb (1895-1976) — Mississippi John Hurt (1893-1966) |

Classic Female Blues Singers
Mamie Smith (1883-1946) — Ma Rainey (1886-1939)
Bessie Smith (1894-1937) — Lucille Bogan (1897-1948)
Sara Martin (1884-1955) — Clara Smith (1894-1935)
Ida Cox (1896-1967) — Sippie Wallace (1898-1986)
Victoria Spivey (1906-1976) — Chippie Hill (1905-1950)

Postwar Female Blues
Big Maybelle (1924-1972) — Big Mama Thornton (1926-1984)
Little Esther Phillips (1935)

Religious Music That Influenced Blues
Blind Willie Johnson (1900-1947)

Piano Blues

Origins — 1890s — Barrelhouses, Railroad & Lumber Camps

Clarence "Pine Top" Smith (1904-1929)
Cow Cow Davenport (1894-1955) — George Thomas
Henry Townsend (1929-1971) — Roosevelt Sykes (1906-1983)
Albert Ammons (1907-1949) — Meade "Lux" Lewis (1905-1964)
Big Maceo (1905-1953) — Sunnyland Slim (1907)
Peetie Wheatstraw (1902-1941) — Leroy Carr (1905-1935)
Johnnie Jones (1949-1964) — Otis Spann (1930-1970)
Pinetop Perkins (1913)

Major Influences
Lonnie Johnson (1889-1970)
Blind Lemon Jefferson (1897-1929)

Mississippi Blues

Delta-Style Blues
Charley Patton (1887-1934) — Willie Brown (1900-1952)
Son House (1902-1971) — Robert Johnson (1911-1938)
Fred McDowell (1904-1972) — Bukka White (1906-1977)
Big Joe Williams (1903-1982) — Arthur Crudup (1905-1974)
Tommy McClennan (1908-ca. 1962)
John Lee Hooker (1917)

Jackson-Style Blues
Rubin Lacy (1901-1972) — Ishmon Bracey (1901-1970)
Charles McCoy (1909-1950) — Tommy Johnson (1896-1956)

Bentonia-Blues
Henry Stuckey (1897-1966) —Skip James (1902-1969)
Jack Owens (1904)

Regional Down-Home Blues

Atlanta
Barbecue Bob (Robert Hicks) (1902-1931)
Blind Willie McTell (1901-1959) — Curley Weaver (1906-1962)
Buddy Moss (1906)

Piedmont School
Blind Blake (1890-1933) — Blind Boy Fuller (1908-1941)
Sonny Terry (1911-1984) —Brownie McGhee (1915)
Rev. Gary Davis (1896-1972)

Tennessee

Memphis Jug Bands
Gus Cannon's (1885-1979) Jug Stompers — Memphis Jug Band
Will Shade (1898-1966) — Noah Lewis (1895-1961)

Memphis
Furry Lewis (1893-1981) — Frank Stokes (1888-1955)
Robert Wilkins (1896-1987) — Memphis Minnie (1897-1973)

Brownsville, Tennessee
Sleepy John Estes (1899-1977)
Yank Rachell (1910) — Sonny Boy Williamson (1914-1948)

The End of World War II — The Rise of Live Blues Radio — "King Biscuit Time" — KFFA — Helena, Arkansas 1941

Sonny Boy Williamson II (Rice Miller) (1899-1965) — Robert Lockwood Jr (1915) — Willie Love (1906-1953)
Joe Willie Wilkins (1923-1979) — Houston Stackhouse (1910-1981) — Peck Curtis (1912-1970)
Doctor Isaiah Ross (1925) — Elmore James (1918-1963) — Hound Dog Taylor (1917-1975)

Blues History

Music Map

Chicago
The Bluebird Sound (mid '30s - late '40s)
Producer: Lester Melrose
Recorded:
Big Bill Broonzy — Washboard Sam (1935-1964) — Jazz Gillum
Tampa Red — Memphis Minnie — Walter Davis
Sonny Boy Williamson — Big Joe Williams — Arthur Crudup
Tommy McClennan — Henry Townsend (1909)

Chicago — Early Artists
Big Bill Broonzy (1893-1958) — Tampa Red (1900-1981)
Jazz Gillum (1904-1966) — Leroy Carr (1905-1935)
Big Maceo (1905-1953) — Robert Nighthawk (1909-1967)
Scrapper Blackwell (1903-1962) — Kokomo Arnold (1901-1968)
Sonny Boy Williamson (1914-1948)

Chess Records
Producer: Leonard Chess
Recorded
Muddy Waters — Little Walter — Elmore James
Howlin' Wolf — Buddy Guy — Sonny Boy Williamson II
Jimmy Rogers

The Muddy Waters Band
Muddy Waters (1915-1983) — Little Walter (1930-1968)
Jimmy Rogers (1924) — Otis Spann (1930-1970)

The Howlin' Wolf Band
Memphis ca. 1952
Howlin' Wolf — Willie Johnson — Willie Steele

Chicago ca. 1954-1975
Hubert Sumlin — Henry Gray — Eddie Shaw
Sam Lay — Detroit Jr. — Jody Williams

2nd Generation Chicago Bands
Buddy Guy (1936) — Otis Rush (1934) — Junior Wells (1934)
James Cotton (1935) — Magic Sam (1937-1969)
Hound Dog Taylor (1917-1975) & the Houserockers

Postwar Chicago Harmonica
Little Walter — Big Walter Horton — Snooky Pryor
Jimmy Reed — James Cotton — Billy Boy Arnold
Junior Wells — George "Harmonica" Smith
Sonny Boy Williamson II

Jimmy Reed — Eddie Taylor

Modern Postwar Blues Guitar
T-Bone Walker (1910-1975)
B. B. King — Albert King — Freddy King

Texas Guitar
Clarence Gatemouth Brown (1924) — Lowell Fulson (1921)
Albert Collins (1932) — Johnny Copeland (1937)

Chicago Guitar
Mississippi - influenced:
Elmore James — Eddie Taylor — Johnny Young
Johnny Shines — Homesick James — Hound Dog Taylor
Earl Hooker — Joe Carter — J. B. Hutto — Louis Myers
B. B. King - influenced (West Side School):
Otis Rush — Magic Sam — Buddy Guy — Hubert Sumlin
Magic Slim (1937) — Son Seals (1942) — Lonnie Brooks (1933)

Jump Blues
Big Joe Turner (1911-1985) — Amos Milburn (1927-1980)
Roy Brown (1920-1981) — Wynonie Harris (1915-1969)

Texas Bluesmen
Smokey Hogg (1908) — Lightnin' Hopkins (1912-1982)
Lil Son Jackson (1915-1976) — Frankie Lee Sims (1917-1970)

West Coast
Jimmy McCracklin (1921) — Lowell Fulson (1921)
Percy Mayfield (1920-1984) — Jesse Fuller (1896-1976)
K. C. Douglas (1913-1975) — Floyd Dixon (1929)
Charles Brown (1920) — Johnny Otis (1921)
Jimmy Witherspoon (1923) — Pee Wee Crayton (1914)

Detroit
John Lee Hooker (1917) — Baby Boy Warren (1919-1977)
Bobo Jenkins (1916) — Eddie Burns (1928)
Eddie Kirkland (1928)

The Memphis Sound
Producer: Sam Phillips/Sun Records
Originally Recorded:
B. B. King — Howlin' Wolf — Bobby Bland — Junior Parker
Big Walter Horton — Joe Hill Louis — Willie Nix — Dr. Ross
Ike Turner — Roscoe Gordon

New Orleans
Professor Longhair (1918-1980) — Guitar Slim (1907-1975)

Zydeco
Clifton Chenier (1925-1987) — Boozoo Chavis
Rockin' Dopsie — Fernest Arceneaux

Louisiana (Excello Records)
Lightnin' Slim (1913-1974) — Slim Harpo (1924-1970)
Lonesome Sundown (1928) — Lazy Lester (1933)
Silas Hogan (1911)

Robert Pete Williams (1914-1980)

More Modern Blues - Mid '60s to present:
Country Blues (White Interpreters)
John Hammond (1942) — Dave Van Ronk (1936)
John Koerner (1938) — Rory Block
Some Electric Blues
Paul Butterfield (1942-1987) — Michael Bloomfield (1944-1981)
Taj Mahal (1940) — Johnny Winter (1944)
Elvin Bishop (1942) — Roy Buchanan (1939-1988)
Lil' Ed and the Blues Imperials – Roomful of Blues
Fabulous Thunderbirds – Stevie Ray Vaughan (1956-1990)
Robert Cray (1953) — William Clarke

Soul Blues
Junior Parker — Bobby Blue Bland (1930)
Little Milton (1934) — Little Johnny Taylor (1943) — Otis Clay
Z.Z. Hill (1940-1984)

ktra Records inspired by a 1968 *Rolling Stone* article profiling Mack should have led to major stardom, but his three Elektra albums were less consistent than the Fraternity material. (Elektra also reissued his only Fraternity LP, the seminal *The Wham of That Memphis Man*.)

Disgusted with the record business, Lonnie Mack retreated back to Indiana for a while, eventually signing with Capitol and waxing a couple of obscure country-based LPs. Finally, at Vaughan's behest, Mack abandoned his Indiana comfort zone for hipper Austin, TX, and began to reassert himself nationally. Vaughan masterminded the stunning *Strike like Lightning* in 1985; later that year, Mack co-starred with Alligator labelmates Albert Collins and Roy Buchanan at Carnegie Hall (a concert marketed on home video as *Further on Down the Road*).

Mack's most recent album from 1990, *Live! Attack of the Killer V*, was captured on tape at a suburban Chicago venue called FitzGerald's and once again showed why Lonnie Mack is venerated by anyone who's even remotely into savage guitar playing. —*Bill Dahl*

★ **The Wham of that Memphis Man** / 1963 / Alligator ✦✦✦✦✦
This is a vinyl reissue of Lonnie's first album for the Fraternity in 1964, the one thousands of guitarists cut their teeth on. Muddy Waters once sang, "the blues had a baby and they named the baby rock'n'roll." This is the album that proves it. Instrumental versions of R&B hits ("Memphis," "Susie Q," "The Bounce") rebound against heartfelt soul numbers ("Farther Down the Road," "Why?") right next to dazzling fretboard blues romps both slow and fast ("Wham!," "Down and Out"). Lonnie sings his rear end off, the band—with saxes and Hammond organ and pumping soul bass—is right in there, and Mack's vibrato- drenched guitar stings, wounds, and amazes. It remains his defining moment. —*Cub Koda*

Glad I'm in the Band / 1969 / Elektra ✦✦✦
With the exception of his comeback album for Alligator, *Strike like Lightning*, nothing Mack has done since leaving Fraternity Records has come close to the wham-fisted brilliance of those seminal sides. This LP isn't bad at all, though—besides passable remakes of "Memphis" and "Why," Mack attacks Frankie Ford's "Roberta," Ted Taylor's "Stay Away from My Baby," and Little Willie John's "Let Them Talk" with a slightly rockier edge than his previous stuff. R&B vet Maxwell Davis did the horn charts. —*Bill Dahl*

Whatever's Right / 1969 / Elektra ✦✦✦

Strike like Lightning / 1985 / Alligator ✦✦✦
Co-produced by Stevie Ray Vaughan, this was Lonnie's ticket back to the show after a few years on the sidelines. To say it was an inspired date would be putting it mildly. With his batteries recharged, Mack was in peak form, playing and singing better than ever. A highlight is an inspired duet between Stevie and Lonnie on "Wham (Double Whammy)," going toe to toe for several choruses. —*Cub Koda*

Second Sight / 1987 / Alligator ✦✦✦

Live: Attack of the Killer V / 1990 / Alligator ✦✦✦
Cut in front of an appreciative throng at FitzGerald's in suburban Chicago, Mack cuts loose the way he so often does in concert, sticking almost exclusively to his Alligator-era tunes ("Satisfy Suzie," "Cincinnati Jail," the tortured soul ballad "Stop") and never looking too far backwards. —*Bill Dahl*

Lonnie on the Move / Ace ✦✦✦✦
Criminally, Mack's LP *The Wham of That Memphis Man* remains unavailable on CD. But that doesn't mean Mack's Fraternity work is totally unrepresented in the digital racks. These 19 Flying V-soaked sides pack the same punch and hail from the same mid-'60s timeframe. He unleashes his vibrato-drenched axe on the torrid "Soul Express," "Lonnie on the Move," "Florence of Arabia," and an astonishing instrumental version of "Stand by Me" that'll send aspiring guitarists' jaws crashing to the floor. For a change of pace, "Men at Play" mines a jazzy walking groove to satisfying ends. —*Bill Dahl*

Magic Sam (Samuel Maghett)

b. Feb. 14, 1937, Grenada, MS, **d.** Dec. 1, 1969, Chicago, IL
Guitar, Vocals / R&B, Modern Electric Blues, Electric Chicago Blues
No blues guitarist better represented the adventurous modern sound of Chicago's West Side more proudly than Sam Maghett. He died tragically young (at age 32 of a heart attack), right when he was on the brink of climbing the ladder to legitimate stardom—but Magic Sam left behind a thick legacy of bone-cutting blues that remains eminently influential around his old stomping grounds to this day.

Sam's tremolo-rich staccato finger-picking was an entirely fresh phenomenon when he premiered it on Eli Toscano's Cobra label in 1957. His Cobra debut single, "All Your Love," was an immediate local sensation; its unusual structure would be recycled time and again by Sam throughout his tragically truncated career. Sam's Cobra encores "Everything Gonna Be Alright" and "Easy Baby" borrowed much the same melody but were no less powerful; the emerging West Side sound was now officially committed to vinyl. Not everything Sam cut utilized the tune; "21 Days in Jail" was a pseudo-rockabilly smoker with hellacious lead gui-

tar from Sam and thundering slap bass from the ubiquitous Willie Dixon. Sam also backed Shakey Jake Harris on his lone 45 for Cobra's Artistic subsidiary, "Call Me If You Need Me."

After Cobra folded, Sam didn't follow labelmates Otis Rush and Magic Slim over to Chess. Instead, after enduring an unpleasant Army experience that apparently landed him in jail for desertion, Sam opted to go with Mel London's Chief logo in 1960. His raw-boned West Side adaptation of Fats Domino's mournful "Every Night About This Time" was the unalloyed highlight of his stay at Chief; some other Chief offerings were less compelling.

Gigs on the West Side remained plentiful for the charismatic guitarist, but recording opportunities proved sparse until 1966, when Sam made a 45 for Crash Records. "Out of Bad Luck" brought back that trademark melody again, but it remained as shattering as ever. Another notable 1966 side, the plaintive "That's Why I'm Crying," wound up on Delmark's *Sweet Home Chicago* anthology, along with Sam's stunning clippity-clop boogie instrumental "Riding High" (aided by the muscular tenor sax of Eddie Shaw).

Delmark Records was the conduit for Magic Sam's two seminal albums, 1967's *West Side Soul* and the following year's *Black Magic*. Both LPs showcased the entire breadth of Sam's West Side attack: the first ranged from the soul-laced "That's All I Need" and a searing "I Feel So Good" to the blistering instrumental "Lookin' Good" and definitive remakes of "Mama Talk to Your Daughter" and "Sweet Home Chicago," while *Black Magic* benefitted from Shaw's jabbing, raspy sax as Sam blasted through the funky "You Belong to Me," an impassioned "What Have I Done Wrong," and a personalized treatment of Freddy King's "San-Ho-Zay."

Sam's reputation was growing exponentially. He wowed an overflow throng at the 1969 Ann Arbor Blues Festival, and Stax was reportedly primed to sign him when his Delmark commitment was over. However, heart problems were fast taking their toll on Sam's health. On the first morning of December of 1969, he complained of heartburn, collapsed, and died.

Even now, more than a quarter century after his passing, Magic Sam remains the king of West Side blues. That's unlikely to change as long as the sub-genre is alive and kicking. —*Bill Dahl*

Magic Touch / 1966 / Black Top ✦✦✦✦
Another rare glimpse at Magic Sam hard at work, this time at another fabled West Side haunt, Sylvio's, in 1966. No saxes this time, but uncle Shakey Jake was around for a few guest shots, while bassist Mac Thompson and drummer Odie Payne provide supple backing as Sam launches into another terrific set of numbers that for the most part he never recorded in the studio—songs by Freddy King, Albert Collins, James Robins, Junior Parker, and Jimmy McCracklin that brilliantly suited his soaring pipes and singular guitar style. —*Bill Dahl*

★ **West Side Soul** / 1968 / Delmark ✦✦✦✦✦
One of the truly essential Chicago blues albums of the 1960s. There's not a weak piece of filler on it—Sam exudes West Side sizzle as he busts loose on "I Don't Want No Woman," "I Need You So Bad," definitive covers of "Sweet Home Chicago" and "Mama Talk to Your Daughter," the clippity-clop finger-twisting instrumental "Lookin' Good," and a soul-slanted "That's All I Need." —*Bill Dahl*

Black Magic / 1969 / Delmark ✦✦✦✦
With the key addition of raspy saxist Eddie Shaw to urge him on, Sam's Delmark encore was another instant classic, containing his R&B-slanted "You Belong to Me" and "What Have I Done Wrong," the bandstand favorites "Just a Little Bit" and "Same Old Blues," and a personalized treatment of Freddy King's "San-Ho-Zay." The album also proved his swan song; he was dead a year later. —*Bill Dahl*

Live at Ann Arbor and in Chicago / Jul. 1982 / Delmark ✦✦✦
Don't let the homemade recording quality put you off for a second, because this is Magic Sam at his whiplash best. —*Cub Koda*

Late Great Magic Sam / 1984 / Evidence ✦✦✦
The ten 1963-1964 sides that make up the majority of this set have sort of fallen through the historical cracks over the years. They didn't deserve such shoddy treatment—Sam didn't record "Back Door Friend" or "Hi-Heel Sneakers" anywhere else, and he's in top shape throughout. Two live tracks at the set's close from 1969 don't add much to the overall package. —*Bill Dahl*

Magic Sam Legacy / 1989 / Delmark ✦✦✦✦
Alternate takes and unissued surprises from the *West Side Soul* and *Black Magic* sessions, along with a couple of welcome 1966 sides ("I Feel So Good" and "Lookin' Good") that didn't see the light of day when they were recorded. Sam's versions of Jimmy Rogers' "Walkin' by Myself" and "That Ain't It" are important additions to his immortal legacy. —*Bill Dahl*

Live at the Alex Club / 1990 / Delmark ✦✦✦✦
For the first half of this frequently amazing disc, Magic Sam plays for his West Side homefolks at the Alex Club. The time is 1963-64, he's backed

by saxists A.C. Reed and Eddie Shaw and his longtime bassist, Mac Thompson, and he's blasting the hits of the day with a joyous abandon. A little over six years later, Sam wowed the Ann Arbor Blues Festival with a sensational trio set just as inordinately powerful in its own way. Sound quality is rough on both artifacts, but no matter. —*Bill Dahl*

★ **1957-1966** / 1991 / Paula ✦✦✦✦✦
Never mind Otis Rush and Buddy Guy—this is the bedrock document of Chicago's West Side blues guitar movement. Ten seminal numbers that constitute Sam's complete Cobra stash (notably "All Your Love," "Easy Baby," and the rockabilly-tinged "21 Days in Jail"), another pair by his harp-blowing uncle Shakey Jake, five numbers from 1960 that first appeared on Mel London's Chief logo (a tortured cover of Fats Domino's "Every Night About This Time" is the killer), and a couple of solid 1966 outings that reinforce Sam's standing as the king of the West Side before his untimely demise. —*Bill Dahl*

Taj Mahal (Henry Saint Clair Fredericks)

b. May 17, 1942, New York City, NY
Banjo, Bass, Guitar, Piano, Vocals / Modern Acoustic Blues
Since the mid-'60s, Taj Mahal has played a vital role in the preservation of traditional blues and African-American roots music. He is a singer, songwriter, composer, and a noted musicologist who through intensive research creates authentic, rootsy compositions that, while remaining true to tradition, are still relevant to modern audiences and always bear his own unique stamp. Though he frequently ventures into different genres, Mahal's heart and soul belongs to the old-time country blues.

Mahal made his own recording debut for Columbia in 1968 with a self-titled album. He recorded several more albums for the label through the early '70s and at the same time established himself as a popular, charismatic yet laidback performer, known for his adventurousness, gentle wit, and intelligence. As the years have passed, Mahal has become known as a musical chameleon, changing and mixing up genres to suit his current interests. He has even recorded children's albums that are anything but childish in their content. Many albums, such as *Like Never Before* (1991) contain an eclectic assortment of styles covering both old songs and his new compositions. —*Sandra Brennan*

Taj Mahal / 1968 / Columbia ✦✦✦✦
His self-titled debut, with Ry Cooder and Jesse Ed Davis, is first and foremost. —*Mark A. Humphrey*

Natch'l Blues / 1968 / Columbia ✦✦✦✦
For some reason, Taj Mahal gets the back of the hand treatment from a lot of blues purists. Sure, his records can get very self-indulgent, but when he turns to blues, you can hear a lot worse than Mahal. This was among his best LPs, with both strong originals and good remakes. —*Ron Wynn*

Giant Step / 1969 / Columbia ✦✦✦
Giant Step/De Old Folks at Home is a two-record set that features one album of Delta blues that was recorded with a full electric band and one album of solo acoustic blues. The electric record is the better collection, but only by a small margin—the acoustic record suffers from poor production that prevents a listener from completely connecting with Taj Mahal's blues. Nevertheless, there are terrific moments on both records and, on the whole, it is one of his finest albums. —*Thom Owens*

Happy Just to Be like I Am / 1971 / Mobile Fidelity ✦✦✦✦
With *Happy Just to Be Like I Am*, Taj Mahal offers another (possibly his most effective) course in roots music, this time dabbling in Caribbean rhythms in addition to his more-or-less standard take on acoustic country blues. While his good intentions and craftsmanlike execution can't be denied, one hopes the listener will eventually decide to seek out the inspirations for these recordings. —*AMG*

Recycling the Blues and Other Related Stuff / 1972 / Mobile Fidelity ✦✦✦
The title *Recycling the Blues and Other Related Stuff* certainly sums up the album quite well—that's exactly what Taj Mahal had been doing for several years by this point. The first side features laidback in-the-studio work with some nice gospel-inflected backup from the Pointer Sisters. The second (and preferable) side offers a good look at Mahal's stage show. —*AMG*

Ooh So Good 'n' Blues / 1973 / Columbia ✦✦✦
Ooh So Good 'n' Blues takes a more straight-ahead approach that, with the exception of the the jazzy misstep titled "Teacup's Jazzy Blues Tune," keeps the experimentation down to a minimum. As a result, this is one of his most consistently enjoyable and even albums. —*AMG*

● **Anthology, Vol. 1** / 1976 / Columbia ✦✦✦✦
Taj Mahal's often-indulgent experimentations have flawed most of his albums to different degrees; *The Taj Mahal Anthology, Vol. 1* rights these self-inflicted wrongs by compiling a coherent look at his early career (1966-1971). Though this collection is currently out of print, it provides the best introduction to his easy-going take on the blues. —*AMG*

● **The Best of Taj Mahal, Vol. 1** / 1981 / Columbia ✦✦✦✦
Best of Taj Mahal provides a concise career overview with a broader scope than *Anthology, Vol. 1*. —*AMG*

Shake Sugaree / Sep. 1988 / Music for Little People ✦✦✦

Taj's Blues / Jun. 16, 1992 / Columbia/Legacy ✦✦✦✦
Taj's Blues is an entertainingly diverse record, featuring a variety of blues and roots-music styles, all fused together into a distinctive sound of its own. Half of the album is played on acoustic, the other with an electric band (which includes guitarists Ry Cooder and Jesse Davis on a handful of tracks), which gives a pretty good impression of the range of Mahal's talents. It's a good collection, featuring many of his best performances for Columbia, including "Statesboro Blues" and "Leaving Trunk," as well as the unreleased "East Bay Woman." —*Thom Owens*

Dancing the Blues / 1993 / Private Music ✦✦✦

Percy Mayfield

b. Aug. 12, 1920, Minden, LA, d. Aug. 11, 1984, Los Angeles, CA
Piano, Vocals / Soul, R&B, West Coast Blues
A masterful songwriter whose touching blues ballad "Please Send Me Someone to Love," a multi-layered universal lament, was a No. 1 R&B hit in 1950, Percy Mayfield had the world by the tail until a horrific 1952 auto wreck left him facially disfigured. That didn't stop the poet laureate of the blues from writing in prolific fashion, though. As Ray Charles' favorite scribe during the '60s, he handed the Genius such gems as "Hit the Road, Jack" and "At the Club."

Like so many of his postwar L.A. contemporaries, Mayfield got his musical start in Texas but moved to the coast during the war. Surmising that Jimmy Witherspoon might like to perform a tune he'd penned called "Two Years of Torture," Mayfield targeted Supreme Records as a possible buyer for his song. But the bosses at Supreme liked his own gentle reading so much that they insisted he wax it himself in 1947 with an all-star band that included saxist Maxwell Davis, guitarist Chuck Norris, and pianist Willard McDaniel.

Art Rupe's Specialty logo signed Mayfield in 1950 and scored a solid string of R&B smashes over the next couple of years. "Please Send Me Someone to Love" and its equally potent flip "Strange Things Happening" were followed in the charts by "Lost Love," "What a Fool I Was," "Prayin' for Your Return," "Cry Baby," and "Big Question," cementing Mayfield's reputation as a blues balladeer of the highest order. Davis handled sax duties on most of Mayfield's Specialty sides as well. Mayfield's lyrics were usually as insightfully downbeat as his tempos; he was a true master at expressing his innermost feelings, laced with vulnerability and pathos (his "Life Is Suicide" and "The River's Invitation" are two prime examples).

Even though his touring was drastically curtailed after the accident, Mayfield hung in there as a Specialty artist through 1954, switching to Chess in 1955-56 and Imperial in 1959. Charles proved thankful enough for Mayfield's genius to sign him to his Tangerine logo in 1962; over the next five years, the singer waxed a series of inexorably classy outings, many with Brother Ray's band (notably "My Jug and I" in 1964 and "Give Me Time to Explain" the next year). It's a rare veteran blues artist indeed who hasn't taken a whack at one or more Mayfield copyrights. Mayfield himself persisted into the '70s, scoring minor chart items for RCA and Atlantic while performing on a limited basis until his death in 1984. —*Bill Dahl*

My Jug and I / 1962 / Tangerine ✦✦✦✦
Mayfield's gentle vocal delivery and the big, brassy sound of Ray Charles' orchestra were a match made in heaven. Mayfield brought some first-class material to this party (which begs for CD reissue): "My Jug and I," "Stranger in My Own Home Town" (later covered by Elvis Presley), the untypically jumping "Give Me Time to Explain," and a handful of Specialty remakes. —*Bill Dahl*

Bought Blues / 1969 / Tangerine ✦✦✦✦
Another elegant, beautifully arranged collection fraught with brilliant, sometimes heartbreaking material: "Ha Ha in the Daytime," "We Both Must Cry," "My Bottle Is My Companion." —*Bill Dahl*

★ **Poet of the Blues** / 1990 / Specialty ✦✦✦✦✦
The insightful songwriting skills of this West Coaster were matched by his wry, plaintive vocal delivery (Mayfield was usually his own best interpreter). The 25 sides here date from his hit-laden 1950-1954 stay at Art Rupe's Specialty logo and include his universal lament "Please Send Me Someone to Love," the resolutely downbeat "Strange Things Happening" and "Lost Love," and an ironic "The River's Invitation." Saxman Maxwell Davis led the horn-powered combos, providing support behind Mayfield. —*Bill Dahl*

Memory Pain / Specialty ✦✦✦✦
Twenty-five more nuggets from the voluminous Specialty vaults, including alternate takes of some of his biggest smashes, a plethora of unissued stuff, both sides of his 1957 single for the label that showed him

coping subtly with the rocking changes sweeping the R&B world, and ending with a 1960 demo of his classic "Hit the Road, Jack." —*Bill Dahl*

For Collectors Only / Specialty ✦✦✦
This gives a deeper look at Mayfield's early career. Alternate takes and unissued material are included. —*Hank Davis*

Jerry McCain

b. Jun. 18, 1930, Gadsden, AL
Guitar, Harmonica, Trumpet, Drums, Vocals / R&B, Modern Electric Blues

Not only is Alabama-born Jerry McCain a terrific amplified harpist, he's also one of the funniest songwriters working the genre. He has been for more than four decades, as anyone who's dug his out-of-control 1950s Excello rockers "My Next Door Neighbor" and "Trying to Please" will gladly testify.

Little Walter was McCain's main man on harp, an instrument McCain began playing at age five. Walter passed through Gadsden one fateful night in 1953 with his Aces, offering encouragement and a chance to jam at a local nightpot. That same year, "Boogie" McCain made his vinyl debut for Lillian McMurry's Trumpet label in Jackson, MS, with "East of the Sun"/"Wine-O-Wine." His brother Walter played drums on the sides. McCain's 1954 Trumpet encore, "Stay out of Automobiles"/"Love to Make Up," was solid Southern blues but barely hinted at the galvanic energy of his subsequent output.

Jerry McCain signed with Ernie Young's Nashville-based Excello logo in 1955, cutting "That's What They Want" with his usual sidekick, Christopher Collins, on guitar. "Run, Uncle John! Run," "Trying to Please," the torrid "My Next Door Neighbor" (a prior homemade demo version of the track that surfaced much later was even crazier!)," and "The Jig's Up" ranked with McCain's best 1955-57 Excello efforts.

The harpist is probably best-known for his two-sided 1960 gem for Rex Records, "She's Tough"/"Steady." The Fabulous Thunderbirds later appropriated the insinuating mid-tempo A-side, while McCain's harp chops were strikingly showcased on the flip. McCain waxed three 45s for Okeh in Nashville in 1962, utilizing Music Row mainstays Floyd Cramer, Grady Martin, and Boots Randolph as his backup for "Red Top" and "Jet Stream." A series of 1965-68 sides for Stan Lewis' Shreveport-based Jewel Records included a tailor-made tribute to the company, "728 Texas (Where the Action Is)" (Jewel's address).

After too many years spent in relative obscurity, McCain rejuvenated his fortunes in 1989 by signing with Ichiban Records and waxing a series of outings that displayed both his irreverent wit and a social conscience rare on the contemporary circuit. —*Bill Dahl*

Choo Choo Rock / 1981 / White Label ✦✦✦✦
These demo recordings for Excello (ca. 1956) are wild and raucous, featuring overamplified guitars, crashing drums, and bizarre lyrics. What a rock 'n' roll album by Little Walter might have sounded like. —*Cub Koda*

Strange Kind of Feelin' / 1990 / Acoustic Archives ✦✦✦

● **That's What They Want: The Best of Jerry McCain** / 1995 / AVI-Excello ✦✦✦✦
McCain has always marched to the beat of a different drummer and the proof of it is right here, 23 recordings that define the place where the blues and rock 'n' roll meet at the end of a dark alley. The first 12 tracks are McCain's complete singles output for Excello Records, the sides upon which most of his reputation rests. From the bravado of the title track to the rocking insanity of "Trying to Please," this music is as special as it comes. The following 11 tracks come from homemade demo tapes circa 1955 that were cut in Jerry's living room with a single-mike, one-track home tape recorder. Featuring grinding, massively distorted guitars, crashing drum,s and lyrical texts concerning themselves with going crazy to rock 'n' roll, rock 'n' roll as salvation ("Rock and Roll Ball," "Geronimo's Rock"), or going crazy from outside, worldly pressures ("Bell in My Heart," "My Next Door Neighbors"), these masterpieces answer the question: what would a rock 'n' roll album by Little Walter have sounded like? —*AMG*

Delbert McClinton

b. Nov. 4, 1940
Harmonica, Vocals / R&B, Modern Electric Blues, Blues-Rock, Country-Rock

A Texas music institution, McClinton honed his musical chops to razor sharpness as a teenage harmonica man learning firsthand from blues legends traveling thru the area. His harp work on Bruce Channel's hit, "Hey Baby", got him on the big time circuit, making it over to tour England and eventually giving harmonica lessons to a young John Lennon. Much behind the scenes work throughout the '60s ensued with McClinton fronting the Rondells, who hit the Hot 100 with "If You Really Want Me To, I'll Go." He hit the charts again in the '70s with Glen Clark as Delbert and Glen. Around this period, McClinton's songs started getting covered by country acts, Waylon Jennings and Emmylou Harris

both having hits with his material. The Blues Brothers used his "B-Movie Box Car Blues" on their first album and their hit movie. He has continued to release idiosyncratic solo efforts and guest on albums with everyone from Roy Buchanan to Bonnie Raitt. —*Cub Koda*

● **The Best of Delbert McClinton** / 1989 / Curb ✦✦✦✦
This adequate overview contains mostly familiar material but lacks the cohesiveness of his best early albums. —*Rick Clark*

Live from Austin / 1989 / Alligator ✦✦✦
This rock-solid, gritty roadhouse R&B is performed with a no-nonsense spirit. —*Rick Clark*

Never Been Rocked Enough / 1992 / Curb ✦✦✦

Jimmy McCracklin

b. Aug. 13, 1921, St. Louis, MO
Piano, Vocals / R&B, Electric West Coast Blues, Acoustic West Coast Blues, West Coast Blues

A full half-century from when he started out in the blues business, Jimmy McCracklin is still touring, recording, and acting like a much younger man. In fact, he vehemently disputes this commonly accepted birthdate—but since he began recording back in 1945, it seems reasonable.

McCracklin recorded for a daunting array of tiny labels in Los Angeles and Oakland prior to touching down with Modern in 1949-50, Swing Time the next year, and Peacock in 1952-54. Early in his recording career, McCracklin had Robert Kelton on guitar, but by 1951, Lafayette "Thing" Thomas was installed as the searing guitarist with McCracklin's Blues Blasters and remained invaluable to the pianist into the early '60s.

By 1954 the pianist was back with the Bihari brothers' Modern logo and really coming into his own with a sax-driven sound. "Couldn't Be a Dream" was hilariously surreal, McCracklin detailing his night out with a woman sent straight from hell, while a 1955 session found him doubling credibly on harp.

A series of sessions for Bay Area producer Bob Geddins' Irma label in 1956 (many of which later turned up on Imperial) preceded McCracklin's long-awaited first major hit. Seldom had he written a simpler song than "The Walk," a rudimentary dance number with a good groove that Checker Records put on the market in 1958. It went Top Ten on both the R&B and pop charts, and McCracklin was suddenly rubbing elbows with Dick Clark on network TV.

The nomadic pianist left Chess after a few more 45s, pausing at Mercury (where he cut a torrid "Georgia Slop" in 1959, later revived by Big Al Dowling) before returning to the hit parade with the tough R&B workout "Just Got to Know" in 1961 for Art-Tone Records. A similar follow-up, "Shame, Shame, Shame," also did well for the next year. Those sides eventually resurfaced on Imperial, where he hit twice in 1965 with " Everyt Night, Every Day" (later covered by Magic Sam) and the uncompromising "Think" and "My Answer" in 1966.

McCracklin's songwriting skills shouldn't be overlooked as an integral factor in his enduring success. He penned the funky "Tramp" for guitarist Lowell Fulson and watched his old pal take it to the rarified end of the R&B lists in 1967, only to be eclipsed by a sassy duet cover by Stax stalwarts Otis Redding and Carla Thomas a scant few months later.

Two recent discs for Bullseye Blues prove that McCracklin still packs a knockout punch from behind his piano—no matter what his birth certificate says. —*Bill Dahl*

I Just Gotta Know / 1961 / Imperial ✦✦✦✦
It's always a "Shame, Shame, Shame" (to quote one of this LP's best numbers) when a 35-year-old slab of vinyl must be cited as what may be an artist's finest collection—but since no one has yet touched McCracklin's massive '60s Imperial catalog for CD reissue, here you go! Contains his definitive soul-tinged ballad "Just Got to Know," the Amos Milburn-derived jump blues "Club Savoy," and several more late-'50s rockers that Imperial acquired from various small concerns after he began to hit with regularity. —*Bill Dahl*

● **My Answer** / 1966 / Imperial ✦✦✦✦
Conveniently enough, Imperial slapped together what amounts to a greatest-hits set here, and it serves as the best available introduction to the pianist's '60s catalog. Contains "Just Got to Know," "Every Night, Every Day," "Think," "Steppin' Up in Class," and the title item—every one of them occupying an intriguing island midway between blues and soul. —*Bill Dahl*

High on the Blues / 1971 / Stax ✦✦✦
Given that this was co-produced by Al Jackson (of Booker T. & the MGs) and Willie Mitchell (of Hi Records), and adds embellishment by the Memphis Horns, it's unsurprising that this is very much a soul-blues record. It's a workmanlike effort with an early-'70s Stax period feel, including remakes of two of his past R&B singles, "Think" and "Just Got to Know." The CD reissue adds a couple of previously unreleased bonus tracks. —*Richie Unterberger*

Jimmy McCracklin: The Mercury Recordings / 1992 / Bear Family
✦✦✦✦

McCracklin's liaison with Mercury was relatively brief, from late 1958 to the fall of 1960, and Bear Family has only managed to locate 13 songs for this CD. But it's a rewarding chapter in the pianist's endlessly nomadic recording career, featuring his original dance tunes "Georgia Slop" and "Let's Do It (The Chicken Scratch)," a New Orleans-cut cover of Johnny Cash's "Folsom Prison Blues," and some smoothly arranged (by Clyde Otis, Brook Benton's collaborator) pop/R&B outings that suggest Mercury had big plans for McCracklin that never quite panned out. —*Bill Dahl*

Roots of Rhythm & Blues / Roots ✦✦✦✦

The country of origin of this disc remains murky, but its 18 McCracklin tracks, from his 1957-58 layover at Chess (there was a belated 1962 date as well), are in dire need of domestic reissue—so until that happens, this one (shared with Paul Gayten) will just have to do. McCracklin's smash dance tune "The Walk" is here, along with the amusing playlet "He Knows the Rules" (immaculate axe by Lafayette Thomas), a jumping "Everybody Rock," and another workout that didn't fare as well, "The Wobble." —*Bill Dahl*

Blast 'em Dead! / Ace ✦✦✦✦

McCracklin's vast catalog is perhaps more fully appreciated overseas than in his home. British Ace assembled 18 of the piano-pounder's Duke waxings for this searing LP, which features frequent interjections from guitarist Lafayette Thomas. Jumping stuff! —*Bill Dahl*

Mississippi Fred McDowell

b. Jan. 12, 1904, Rossville, TN, **d.** Jul. 3, 1972, Memphis, TN
Guitar, Vocals / Blues, Acoustic Delta Blues

When Mississippi Fred McDowell proclaimed on one of his last albums, "I do not play no rock 'n' roll," it was less a boast by an aging musician swept aside by the big beat than a mere statement of fact. As a stylist and purveyor of the original Delta blues, he was superb; equal parts Charlie Patton and Son House coming to the fore through his roughed up vocals and slashing bottleneck style of guitar playing. McDowell *knew* he was the real deal and while others were diluting and updating their sound to keep pace with the changing times and audiences, Mississippi Fred stood out from the rest of the pack simply by not changing his style one iota. Though he scorned the amplified rock sound with a passion matched by few country bluesmen, he certainly had no qualms about passing any of his musical secrets along to his young, White acolytes, prompting several of them—including a young Bonnie Raitt—to develop slide guitar techniques of their own. Although generally lumped in with other blues "rediscoveries" from the '60s, the most amazing thing about him was that this rich repository of Delta blues had never recorded in the '20s or early '30s, didn't get "discovered" until 1959, and didn't become a full-time professional musician until the mid-'60s.

He was born in 1904 in Rossville, TN, and was playing the guitar by the age of 14 with a slide hollowed out of a steer bone. His parents died when Fred was a youngster and the wandering life of a traveling musician soon took hold. The 1920s saw him playing for tips on the street around Memphis, TN, the hoboing life eventually setting him down in Como, MS, where he lived the rest of his life. There McDowell split his time between farming and keeping up with his music by playing weekends for various fish fries, picnics, and house parties in the immediate area. This pattern stayed largely unchanged for the next 30 years until he was discovered in 1959 by folklorist Alan Lomax. Lomax was the first to record this semi-professional bluesman, the results of which were released as part of an American folk music series on the Atlantic label. McDowell, for his part, was happy to have some sounds on records, but continued with his farming and playing for tips outside of Stuckey's candy store in Como for spare change. It wasn't until Chris Strachwitz—folk blues enthusiast and owner of the fledgling Arhoolie label—came searching for McDowell to record him that the bluesman's fortunes began to change dramatically.

Two albums, *Fred McDowell, Volume 1 and Volume 2*, were released on Arhoolie in the mid-'60s, and the shock waves were felt throughout the folk-blues community. Here was a bluesman with a repertoire of uncommon depth, putting it over with great emotional force and to top it all off, had seemingly slipped through the cracks of late-'20s/early-'30s field recordings. No scratchy, highly prized 78s on Paramount or Vocalion to use as a yardstick to measure his current worth, no romantic stories about him disappearing into the Delta for decades at a time to become a professional gambler or a preacher. No, Mississippi Fred McDowell had been in his adopted home state, farming and playing all along, and the world coming to his doorstep seemed to ruffle him no more than the little boy down the street delivering the local newspaper.

The success of the Arhoolie recordings suddenly found McDowell very much in demand on the folk and festival circuit, where his quiet, good-natured performances left many a fan utterly spellbound. Working everything from the Newport Folk Festival to coffeehouse dates to becoming a member of the American Folk Blues Festival in Europe, McDowell suddenly had more listings in his resume in a couple of years than he had in the previous three decades combined. He was also well documented on film, with appearances in *The Blues Maker* (1968), his own documentary *Fred McDowell* (1969) and *Roots of American Music: Country and Urban Music* (1970) among them. By the end of the decade, he was signed to do a one-off album for Capitol Records (the aforementioned *I Do Not Play No Rock 'n' Roll*) and his tunes were being mainstreamed into the blues-rock firmament by artists like Bonnie Raitt (who recorded several of his tunes, including notable versions of "Write Me a Few Lines" and "Kokomo") and the Rolling Stones, who included a very authentic version of his classic "You Got to Move" on their *Sticky Fingers* album. Unfortunately, this career largess didn't last much longer, as McDowell was diagnosed with cancer while performing dates into 1971. His playing days suddenly behind him, he lingered for a few months into July of 1972, finally succumbing to the disease at age 68. And right to the end, the man remained true to his word; he didn't play any rock 'n' roll, just the straight, natural blues. —*Cub Koda*

★ **Mississippi Delta Blues** / Aug. 1964 / Arhoolie ✦✦✦✦✦

With 19 great tracks (1964-1965) of bottleneck slide guitar, the release also features excellent liner notes. —*Jas Obrecht*

My Home Is in the Delta / Sep. 1964 / Testament ✦✦✦✦

Mississippi Fred McDowell's home may have been in the Delta, but his music belonged to the world. This is heartfelt, raw, glorious country blues, delivered without an ounce of pretension or nostalgia. —*Ron Wynn*

Mississippi Blues / Dec. 1965 / Black Lion ✦✦✦

"Mississippi" Fred McDowell played simple, haunting blues with vivid, demonstrative passion and power. He wasn't a great guitarist, but his voicings and backings were always memorable, while his singing never lacked intensity or conviction or failed to hold interest. This 1965 set contains mostly McDowell compositions, with the exception of the set's final number, a nearly seven-minute exposition of Big Bill Broonzy's "Louise." Assisted only at times by his wife Annie, Fred McDowell makes every song entertaining, whether it's humorous, poignant, reflective, or bemused. —*Ron Wynn*

Long Way from Home / 1966 / Original Blues Classics ✦✦✦

Good no-frills set of acoustic solo blues on bottleneck guitar. The accent is on traditional material, including "Milk Cow Blues," "John Henry," "Big Fat Mama," and the title track. —*Richie Unterberger*

Amazing Grace / 1966 / Testament ✦✦✦✦

The connection between rural blues and spiritual music is sometimes overlooked. This 1966 recording, featuring McDowell, his guitar, and the Hunter's Chapel Singers of Como, MS (including his wife Annie Mae), is one of the best illustrations of how closely the styles can be linked. McDowell and company perform what the record subtitle calls "Mississippi Delta spirituals" on this stark and moving set, which includes a version of one of his signature tunes, "You Got to Move." The CD reissue adds three previously unreleased tracks. —*Richie Unterberger*

I Do Not Play No Rock 'n' Roll / 1969 / Capitol ✦✦✦✦

Blues purists were disappointed to hear McDowell pick up an electric guitar for the first time on this LP, as well as work with a young, White rhythm section. To the rest of us, this session sounds pretty good, Fred's vocals, guitar playing, and integrity coming through just as strongly as they had on his acoustic work. The title track, and the rap that opens it up, is a mini-classic in its own right—if McDowell does not play no rock 'n' roll, as he claims, he certainly keeps a beat pretty well. The album, as well as a second one cut at the same sessions (released on the Just Sunshine label) and some previously unreleased tracks, was released as an expanded double CD by Capitol in 1995. —*Richie Unterberger*

I Do Not Play No Rock 'n' Roll: Complete Sessions / Oct. 24, 1995 / Capitol ✦✦✦✦

A reissue of his popular 1969 electric album, expanded into a double CD with the addition of other material recorded at the same sessions (most of which was issued on an LP on the Just Sunshine label). It makes more sense to pick this up rather than the original vinyl album, as it rounds up all the material recorded at the *I Do Not Play No Rock 'N' Roll* sessions in November 1969, and adds lengthy liner notes. —*Richie Unterberger*

Brownie McGhee (Walter McGhee)

b. Nov. 30, 1915, Knoxville, TN, **d.** Feb. 23, 1996, Oakland, CA
Guitar, Piano, Kazoo, Vocals / Acoustic Country Blues, Piedmont Blues

Brownie McGhee's death represents an enormous and irreplaceable loss to the blues field. Although he had been semi-retired and suffering from stomach cancer, the guitarist was still the leading Piedmont-style bluesman on the planet, venerated worldwide for his prolific activities both on his own and with his longtime partner, the blind harpist Sonny Terry. Together, McGhee and Terry worked for decades in an acoustic folk-blues bag, singing ancient ditties like "John Henry" and "Pick a

Bale of Cotton" for appreciative audiences worldwide. But McGhee was capable of a great deal more. Throughout the immediate postwar era, he cut electric blues and R&B on the New York scene, even enjoying a huge R&B hit in 1948 with "My Fault" for Savoy (Hal "Cornbread" Singer handled tenor sax duties on the 78).

Walter Brown McGhee grew up in Kingsport, TN. He contracted polio at the age of four, which left him with a serious limp and plenty of time away from school to practice the guitar chords that he'd learned from his father, Duff McGhee. Brownie's younger brother, Granville McGhee, was also a talented guitarist who later hit big with the romping "Drinkin' Wine Spo-Dee-O-Dee"; he earned his nickname, "Stick," by pushing his crippled sibling around in a small cart propelled by a stick.

A 1937 operation sponsored by the March of Dimes restored most of McGhee's mobility. Off he went as soon as he recovered, traveling and playing throughout the Southeast. His jaunts brought him into contact with washboard player George "Oh Red" (or "Bull City Red") Washington in 1940, who in turn introduced McGhee to talent scout J. B. Long. Long got him a recording contract with Okeh/Columbia in 1940; his debut session in Chicago produced a dozen tracks over two days.

After the end of World War II, McGhee began to record most prolifically, both with and without Terry, for a myriad of R&B labels: Savoy (where he cut "Robbie Doby Boogie" in 1948 and "New Baseball Boogie" the next year), Alert, London, Derby, Sittin' in With and its Jax subsidiary in 1952, Jackson, Bobby Robinson's Red Robin logo (1953), Dot, and Harlem, before crossing over to the folk audience during the late '50s with Terry at his side. One of McGhee's last dates for Savoy in 1958 produced the remarkably contemporary "Living with the Blues," with Roy Gaines and Carl Lynch blasting away on lead guitars and a sound light years removed from the staid folk world.

McGhee and Terry were among the first blues artists to tour Europe during the 1950s, and they ventured overseas often after that. Their plethora of late-'50s/early-'60s albums for Folkways, Choice, World Pacific, Bluesville, and Fantasy presented the duo in acoustic folk trappings only, their Piedmont-style musical interplay a constant (if gradually more predictable) delight.

The wheels finally came off the partnership of McGhee and Terry during the mid-'70s. Toward the end, they preferred not to share a stage with one another (Terry would play with another guitarist, then McGhee would do a solo), let alone communicate. One of McGhee's final concert appearances came at the 1995 Chicago Blues Festival; his voice was a tad less robust than usual, but no less moving, and his rich, full-bodied acoustic guitar work cut through the cool evening air with alacrity. His like won't pass this way again. —Bill Dahl

Brownie McGhee and Sonny Terry Sing / 1958 / Smithsonian/Folkways ✦✦✦✦
One of the duo's best acoustic folk-blues collaborations, originally issued in 1958. They convincingly run through a very enjoyable series of collaborations marked by affectionate interplay, with drummer Gene Moore adding rhythmic power. —Bill Dahl

Back Country Blues / Nov. 1958 / Savoy ✦✦✦✦
Brownie McGhee's solo material had a certain charm and compelling quality missing from his collaborations with Terry. For whatever reason, he tended to try more things alone and vary his approach, sound, and delivery. This is first-rate country and topical material, delivered without the forced humor that eventually made his dates with Terry more camp than substance. —Ron Wynn

At the 2nd Fret / Mar. 1963 / Bluesville ✦✦✦✦
Brownie McGhee and Sonny Terry were the ultimate blues duo; McGhee's stylized singing and light, flickering guitar was wonderfully contrasted by Terry's sweeping, whirling harmonica solos and intense, country-tinged singing. They were in great form during the ten tunes featured on this live date, recently reissued on CD. Sometimes, as on "Custard Pie" or "Barking Bull Dog," they're funny; at other times, they were prophetic, chilling, or moving. This is Piedmont blues at its best, and this disc's tremendous remastering provides a strong sonic framework. —Ron Wynn

Hometown Blues / 1990 / Mainstream ✦✦✦✦
Plenty of delightful interplay between McGhee and Terry recommends these 18 1948-1951 sides for producer Bobby Shad for his Sittin' in With label, but they predate the duo's later folk period by a longshot. Back then, they were still aiming their output solely at the R&B crowd—meaning "Man Ain't Nothin' But a Fool," "Bad Blood," "The Woman Is Killing Me," and "Dissatisfied Woman" are straightahead, uncompromising New York-style blues. —Bill Dahl

● **Folkways Years, 1945-1959** / 1991 / Smithsonian/Folkways ✦✦✦✦
Brownie McGhee was among the last generation of blues musicians with deep country and traditional ties who maintained some level of popularity into the '50s. The onslaught of electrified urban blues would change the music's direction and result in many Delta and country artists losing stature among the genre's core constituency. But McGhee managed to continue working, both with longtime musical companion Sonny Terry

and as a solo act. The 17 cuts presented on this reissued CD were taken from six McGhee albums and include ballads, folk tunes, originals, and comedic numbers depicting the versatility and idiomatic range that was commonplace in McGhee's music. —Ron Wynn

★ **Complete Brownie McGhee** / 1994 / Columbia/Legacy ✦✦✦✦✦
Well, complete as far as his pre-war country blues waxings for Okeh sans Sonny Terry (except for one or two where the whooping harpist provided accompaniment). McGhee was working firmly in the Piedmont tradition by 1940, when he signed with Okeh and began cutting the 47 enlightening sides here, which represent some of the purest country blues he ever committed to posterity. —Bill Dahl

"Blind" Willie McTell (William Samuel McTell)

b. May 5, 1901, Thomson, GA, d. Aug. 19, 1959, Milledgeville, GA
Guitar, Harmonica, Accordion, Vocals / Acoustic Country Blues
Willie Samuel McTell was one of the blues' greatest guitarists, and also one of the finest singers ever to work in blues. A major figure with a local following in Atlanta from the 1920s onward, he recorded dozens of sides throughout the 1930s under a multitude of names—all the better to juggle "exclusive" relationships with many different record labels at once—including Blind Willie, Blind Sammie, Hot Shot Willie, and Georgia Bill, as a back-up musician to Ruth Mary Willis.

McTell was born in Thomson, Georgia, near Augusta, and raised near Statesboro. He was probably born blind, although early in his life he could perceive light in one eye. His blindness never became a major impediment, however, and it was said that his sense of hearing and touch were extraordinary. His first instruments were the harmonica and the accordion, but as soon as he was big enough he took up the guitar and showed immediate aptitude on the new instrument. He played a standard six-string acoustic until the mid-'20s, and never entirely abandoned the instrument, but from the beginning of his recording career, he used a 12-string acoustic in the studio almost exclusively. McTell's technique on the 12-string instrument was unique. Unlike virtually every other bluesman who used one, he relied not on its resonances as a rhythm instrument, but, instead, displayed a nimble, elegant slide and finger-picking style that made it sound like more than one guitar at any given moment.

McTell's recording career began in late 1927 with two sessions for Victor records, eight sides including "Statesboro Blues." McTell's earliest sides were superb examples of storytelling in music, coupled with dazzling guitar work. All of McTell's music showed extraordinary power, some of it delightfully raucous ragtime, other examples evoking darker, lonelier sides of the blues, all of it displaying astonishingly rich guitar work.

Like many bluesmen, he recorded under different names simultaneously, and was even signed to Columbia and Okeh Records, two companies that ended up merged at the end of the 1930s, at the same time under two names. His recording career never gave McTell quite as much success as he had hoped, partly due to the fact that some of his best work appeared during the depths of the Depression.

McTell was well known enough that Library of Congress archivist John Lomax felt compelled to record him in 1940, although during the war, like many other acoustic country bluesmen, his recording career came to a halt. Luckily for McTell and generations of listeners after him, however, there was a brief revival of interest in acoustic country blues after World War II that brought him back into the studio. Amazingly enough, the newly founded Atlantic Records—which was more noted for its recordings of jazz and R&B—took an interest in McTell and cut 15 songs with him in Atlanta during 1949. The one single released from these sessions, however, didn't sell, and most of those recordings remained unheard for more than 20 years after they were made. He was rediscovered in 1956, just in time to get one more historic session down on tape. He left music soon after, to become a pastor of a local church, and he died of a brain hemorrhage in 1959, his passing so unnoticed at the time that certain reissues in the 1970s referred to McTell as still being alive in the 1960s.

Blind Willie McTell was one of the giants of the blues, as a guitarist and as a singer and recording artist. Hardly any of his work as passed down to us on record is less than first rate, and this makes most any collection of his music worthwhile. A studious and highly skilled musician whose skills transcended the blues, he was equally adept at ragtime, spirituals, story-songs, hillbilly numbers, and popular tunes, excelling in all of these genres. He could read and write music in braille, which gave him an edge on many of his sighted contemporaries, and was also a brilliant improvisor on the guitar, as is evident from his records. McTell always gave an excellent account of himself, even in his final years of performing and recording. —Bruce Eder

☆ **Atlanta Twelve String** / 1949 / Atlantic ✦✦✦✦✦
In 1949, a brief flurry of interest in old-time country blues resulted in this 15-song session by McTell for the newly formed Atlantic Records during 1949. Only two songs, "Kill It Kid" and "Broke Down Engine

Blues," were ever issued on a failed single, and the session was forgotten until almost 20 years later. McTell is mostly solo here, vividly captured on acoustic 12-string (his sometime partner Curley Weaver may have been present on some tracks), and in excellent form. The playing and the repertory are representative of McTell as he was at this point in his career, a blues veteran rolling through his paces without skipping a beat and quietly electrifying the listener. Songs include "Dying Crapshooter's Blues," "The Razor Ball," and "Ain't I Grand to Live a Christian." *—Bruce Eder*

☆ **Pig 'n' Whistle Red** / 1950 / Biograph ✦✦✦✦✦
This collection of 20 songs, cut by McTell with Curley Weaver on second guitar and sharing the vocals, was left out of many McTell biographical accounts until it resurfaced in 1993. Cut for Regal Records in 1950, it's a remarkable document, capturing McTell and Weaver in vivid modern sound, and includes remakes of McTell's 1933 "Talkin' to You Mama" and "Good Little Thing" as well as more recent material that the two had been doing, and even outtakes, showing very different interpretations of the 1920s pop standard "Pal of Mine" and the gospel number "Sending Up My Timber." The sheer diversity of material makes this an indispensable (as well as a delightful) recording, and except for some minor tape damage on "A to Z Blues" and one other cut, there are few technical flaws here. The playing is so sharp and crisp, and the vocals so delicate in their textures, that this has to be considered essential to any serious blues collection. McTell and Weaver were a legendary duo in Atlanta from before World War II, and it is nothing less than a gift to have them still together and in excellent form on this postwar recording. *—Bruce Eder*

Last Session / 1956 / Bluesville ✦✦✦✦
This recording has a less-than-stellar reputation, principally because it was done so late in McTell's career, and it is true that he lacks some of the edge, especially in his singing, that he showed on his other postwar recordings. On the other hand, his 12-string playing is about as nimble as ever and a real treat. McTell cut these sides for record store owner Ed Rhodes, who had begun taping local bluesmen at his shop in Atlanta in the hope of releasing some of it—McTell took to the idea of recording only slowly, then turned up one night and played for the microphone and anyone who happened to be listening, finishing a pint of bourbon in the process—the result was a pricelessly intimate document, some of the words slurred here and there, but brilliantly expressive and stunningly played. No apologies are needed for "The Dyin' Crapshooter's Blues," "Don't Forget It," or "Salty Dog," however. McTell lived a few more years but never recorded again, which is a pity because based on this tape he still had a lot to show people. Rhodes never did anything with the tapes, and might've junked them if he hadn't remembered how important the McTell material was—they turned out to be the only tapes he saved, out of all he'd recorded. *—Bruce Eder*

☆ **Complete Recorded Works, Vol. 1 (1927-1931)** / 1990 / Document ✦✦✦✦✦
Of all the compilations of McTell's early work, this is probably the most rewarding, because it includes both his Victor songs (including "Statesboro Blues") and his Columbia sides (which have been issued separately by Columbia-Legacy), and RCA-BMG seems to be in no hurry to put any of the Victor material out as a comprehensive collection. The songs all have some noise—there are no "masters" to speak of on acoustic blues of this vintage—but none of it is overly obtrusive, and the orderly chronology is very illuminating. Subsequent volumes from Document are also worthwhile, but Sony-Legacy does have superior workmanship in dealing with much of the same material. *—Bruce Eder*

★ **Blind Willey McTell: The Early Years 1927-33** / 1990 / Yazoo ✦✦✦✦✦
A good sampler, it emphasizes 12-string guitar. *—Jas Obrecht*

☆ **The Definitive Blind Willie McTell** / 1994 / Columbia/Legacy ✦✦✦✦✦
This double-CD set is a little misleading. It is definitive, but only in terms of McTell's Columbia and Okeh sides—you won't find "Statesboro Blues" or his other essential sides here, because they were done for Victor. But the material that is here is all worthwhile, and this is the best single source for McTell's work for those labels (done under a variety of names) from the mid-'30s, very nicely remastered and thoroughly annotated, although producer Lawrence Cohn concedes that even Sony-Legacy was unable to locate sources on a handful of songs that McTell is known to have recorded. *—Bruce Eder*

Memphis Jug Band

Group / Acoustic Memphis Blues
One of the definitive jug bands of the '20s and early '30s, this seminal group was comprised of Will Shade, Will Weldon, Hattie Hart, Charlie Polk, Walter Horton, and others, in various configurations.

Guitarist/harpist Will Shade formed the Memphis Jug Band in the Beale Street section of Memphis in the mid-'20s. A few years after their formation, Shade signed a contract with Victor Records in 1927. Over the next seven years, Shade and the Memphis Jug Band recorded nearly 60 songs for the record label. During this time, a number of musicians

passed through the group, including Big Walter Horton, Furry Lewis, and Casey Bill Weldon. Throughout all of the various lineup incarnations, Shade provided direction for the group. The Memphis Jug Band played a freewheeling mixture of blues, ragtime, vaudeville, folk, and jazz, which was all delivered with good-time humor. That loose spirit kept the group and its records popular throughout the early '30s.

Although the group's popularity dipped sharply in the mid-'30s, Will Shade continued to lead the group in various incarnations until his death in 1966. *—Cub Koda & Stephen Thomas Erlewine*

★ **Memphis Jug Band** / Yazoo ✦✦✦✦✦
This definitive 28-song collection by the city's finest jug band spans their output from 1927 to 1934. *—John Floyd*

Memphis Minnie (Lizzie Douglas)

b. Jun. 3, 1897, Algiers, LA, **d.** Aug. 6, 1973, Memphis, TN
Banjo, Guitar, Vocals / Acoustic Memphis Blues
Tracking down the ultimate woman blues guitar hero is problematic because woman blues singers seldom recorded as guitar players and woman guitar players (such as Rosetta Tharpe and Sister O. M. Terrell) were seldom recorded playing blues. Excluding contemporary artists, the most notable exception to this pattern was Memphis Minnie. The most popular and prolific blueswoman outside the vaudeville tradition, she earned the respect of critics, the support of record-buying fans, and the unqualified praise of the blues artists she worked with throughout her long career. Despite her Southern roots and popularity, she was as much a Chicago blues artist as anyone in her day. Big Bill Broonzy recalls her beating both him and Tampa Red in a guitar contest and claims she was the best woman guitarist he had ever heard. Tough enough to endure in a hard business, she earned the respect of her peers with her solid musicianship and recorded good blues over four decades for Columbia, Vocalion, Bluebird, Okeh, Regal, Checker, and JOB. She also proved to have as good taste in musical husbands as music and sustained working marriages with guitarists Casey Bill Weldon, Joe McCoy, and Ernest Lawlers. Their guitar duets span the spectrum of African-American folk and popular music, including spirituals, comic dialogs, and old-time dance pieces, but Memphis Minnie's best work consisted of deep blues like "Moaning the Blues." More than a good woman blues guitarist and singer, Memphis Minnie holds her own against the best blues artists of her time, and her work has special resonance for today's aspiring guitarists. *—Barry Lee Pearson*

★ **Hoodoo Lady (1933-1937)** / 1933-1937 / Columbia ✦✦✦✦✦
Great early stuff. *—Mark A. Humphrey*

I Ain't No Bad Gal / 1988 / Portrait ✦✦✦
Minnie was the toughest guitar-picking femme of bluesdom, with plugged-in 1941 performances that included "Me and My Chauffeur Blues." *—Mark A. Humphrey*

☆ **And Kansas Joe: 1929-1934** / 1991 / Document ✦✦✦✦✦
Minnie's earliest recordings with first husband Kansas Joe McCoy. Includes "I Want That," "Bumble Bee," "Squat It," "I Don't Want That Junk Outta You," and the original version of "When the Levee Breaks," later covered by (and re-credited to) Led Zeppelin. *—Cub Koda*

Traveling Blues / Aldabra ✦✦✦✦
Traveling Blues collects a number of sessions recorded with Kansas Joe McCoy, Memphis Minnie's second husband. Make no mistake about it—with her impassioned vocals, Memphis Minnie controls these recordings. Although most of these cuts are available on better collections, this album sounds fine and contains a wealth of terrific music. *—Thom Owens*

Memphis Slim (Peter Chatman)

b. Sep. 3, 1915, Memphis, TN, **d.** Feb. 24, 1988, Paris, France
Piano, Vocals / R&B, Piano Blues
An amazingly prolific artist who brought a brisk air of urban sophistication to his frequently stunning presentation, Memphis Slim assuredly ranks with the greatest blues pianists of all time. He was smart enough to take Big Bill Broonzy's early advice about developing a style to call his own to heart, instead of imitating the man's idol, Roosevelt Sykes. Soon enough, other 88s pounders were copying Slim rather than the other way around—his thundering ivories attack set him apart from most of his contemporaries, while his deeply burnished voice possessed a commanding authority.

As befits his stage name, John Chatman was born and raised in Memphis—a great place to commit to a career as a bluesman. Sometime in the late '30s, he resettled in Chicago and began recording as a leader in 1939 for Okeh, then switched over to Bluebird the next year. Around the same time, Slim joined forces with Broonzy, then the dominant force on the local blues scene. After serving as Broonzy's invaluable accompanist for a few years, Slim emerged as his own man in 1944.

After the close of World War II, Slim joined Hy-Tone Records, cutting eight tracks that were later picked up by King. Lee Egalnick's Miracle label reeled in the pianist in 1947; backed by his jumping band, the House Rockers (its members usually included saxists Alex Atkins and Ernest Cotton), Slim recorded his classic "Lend Me Your Love" and "Rockin' the House."

The pianist kept on label-hopping, moving from Miracle to Peacock to Premium (where he waxed the first version of his uncommonly wise down-tempo blues "Mother Earth") to Chess to Mercury before staying put at Chicago's United Records from 1952 to 1954. Before the decade was through, the pianist landed at Vee-Jay Records, where he cut definitive versions of his best-known songs with Matt Murphy and a stellar combo in gorgeously sympathetic support (Murphy was nothing short of spectacular throughout).

Slim exhibited his perpetually independent mindset by leaving the country for good in 1962. A tour of Europe in partnership with bassist Willie Dixon a couple of years earlier had so intrigued the pianist that he permanently moved to Paris, where recording and touring possibilities seemed limitless and the veteran pianist was treated with the respect too often denied even African-American blues stars at home back then. He remained there until his 1988 death, enjoying his stature as expatriate blues royalty. *—Bill Dahl*

At the Gate of Horn / 1959 / Vee-Jay ✦✦✦✦
Only this disc's short length (34 minutes) qualifies as something worthy of complaint; otherwise this is seminal blues piano, performed by a great player and singer, Memphis Slim. This 1959 session had everything: super piano solos, a strong lineup of horn players, clever, well-written and sung lyrics, and a seamless pace that kept things moving briskly from beginning to end. Other than Slim, instrumental honors go to guitarist Matt Murphy, a marvelous accompanist who was able to blend sophistication, technique, and earthiness into one dynamic package. Even at its bargain-basement length, *At the Gate of Horn* belongs in any blues fan's library. *—Ron Wynn*

Memphis Slim / 1961 / MCA/Chess ✦✦✦✦
A straight CD reissue of a vintage Chess LP, its contents dating back to the early '50s and most tracks originally issued on the Premium logo. Includes an early and very nice reading of "Mother Earth"; also sharp as a tack is "Rockin' the Pad." In an unusual move, Slim is joined by a smooth vocal group, the Vagabonds, for "Really Got the Blues." *—Bill Dahl*

The Real Folk Blues / 1966 / MCA/Chess ✦✦✦✦
Lots of duplication with the other Chess reissue CD here, so take your pick. Or pick 'em both up—you can't go wrong with either one of these early-'50s collections. *—Bill Dahl*

Mother Earth / 1969 / Buddah ✦✦✦
Excellent singing and rousing, sparkling barrelhouse, boogie-woogie and straight blues piano playing from a certified legend. Memphis Slim wasn't shy about making records, and they were seldom not worth hearing. This one didn't break the string of quality efforts. *—Ron Wynn*

★ **Rockin' the Blues** / 1981 / Charly ✦✦✦✦✦
The most complete gathering of Slim's 1958-1959 Vee-Jay output available on disc (16 songs to the even dozen on the *Gate of Horn* domestic disc) and the best-sounding too. This is the crowning achievement in Memphis Slim's massive legacy—he delivers his classics one right after another, backed by his unparalleled combo that was anchored by Matt "Guitar" Murphy's startlingly fresh solos. Along with the standbys—"Messin' Around," "Mother Earth," "Wish Me Well"—there's the catchy instrumental "Steppin' Out," later covered by Eric Clapton; the romping "What's the Matter," and a blistering "Rockin' the House" where the band nearly sails right out of the studio! *—Bill Dahl*

I Just Keep on Singing the Blues / 1981 / Muse ✦✦✦
He kept singing and playing the blues with gusto and distinction his entire career. This came a bit later in the Memphis Slim legacy, when he was more of an established artist than a maverick performer, but it's still almost as essential as his landmark recordings from the 1950s. *—Ron Wynn*

Lonesome / 1994 / Drive Archive ✦✦✦✦
Sound quality isn't exactly superb here on this 1961 album first out on Strand, but the contents are. Another House Rockers album featuring Murphy, saxists John Calvin and Johnny Board, bassist Sam Chatman, and drummer Billie Stepney flying high on "Let the Good Times Roll Creole" (likely the only time Slim and Bill Haley battled it out for bragging rights on a tune), the crackling title track, and a very oddly titled "What Is the Mare-Rack." Slim wouldn't make any more albums with this band (after all, they didn't relocate to Paris with him), making it all the more precious. *—Bill Dahl*

Life Is Like That / Charly ✦✦✦✦
Some of Slim's earliest postwar sides for Miracle and King (1946-1949), and some of his best. He'd already assembled his little combo with saxists Alex Atkins and Ernest Cotton by that time (interchangeable bassists included Willie Dixon and Big Crawford; no drums necessary) and the classics were flowing: "Lend Me Your Love," "Nobody Loves Me"

(adapted by Lowell Fulson as "Every Day I Have the Blues"), and the luxurious "Messin' Around with the Blues." *—Bill Dahl*

Big Maceo Merriweather (Major Merriweather)

b. Mar. 31, 1905, Atlanta, GA, **d.** Feb. 26, 1953, Chicago, IL
Piano, Vocals / Chicago Blues, Piano Blues
The thundering 88s of Big Maceo Merriweather helped pave the way for the great Chicago blues pianists of the 1950s—men like Johnny Jones, Otis Spann, and Henry Gray. Unfortunately, Merriweather wouldn't be around to enjoy their innovations—he died a few years after suffering a debilitating stroke in 1946.

Major Merriweather was already a seasoned pianist when he arrived in Detroit in 1924. After working around the Motor City scene, he ventured to Chicago in 1941 to make his recording debut for producer Lester Melrose and RCA Victor's Bluebird subsidiary. His first day in the studio produced 14 tracks—six of his own and eight more as accompanist to renowned Chicago guitarist Tampa Red. One of his initial efforts, "Worried Life Blues," has passed into blues standard status (Chuck Berry was hip to it, covering it for Chess).

Merriweather remained Tampa Red's favorite pianistic accompanist after that, gigging extensively with him and Big Bill Broonzy on Chicago's South Side. The pianist cut a series of terrific sessions as a leader for Bluebird in 1941-42 and 1945 (the latter including his tour de force, "Chicago Breakdown") before the stroke paralyzed his right side. He tried to overcome it, cutting for Victor in 1947 with Eddie Boyd assuming piano duties and again for Specialty in 1949 with Johnny Jones, this time at the stool. His health fading steadily after that, Merriweather died in 1953. *—Bill Dahl*

★ **King of Chicago Blues Piano, Vols. 1 & 2** / Arhoolie ✦✦✦✦✦
A slightly truncated CD version of the RCA two-record set that first anthologized the thundering 1940s RCA Bluebird sides of pianist Big Maceo (25 cuts on the CD, 32 on the vinyl). The CD opens with Maceo's immortal blues "Worried Life Blues," closes with his instrumental tour de force "Chicago Breakdown," and boasts a great deal of blues piano magic in between. *—Bill Dahl*

Amos Milburn

b. Apr. 1, 1927, Houston, TX, **d.** Jan. 3, 1980, Houston, TX
Piano, Vocals / R&B, Piano Blues, Electric Jump Blues
Boogie piano master Amos Milburn was born in Houston, and he died there a short 52 years later. In between, he pounded out some of the most hellacious boogies of the postwar era, usually recording in Los Angeles for Aladdin Records and specializing in good-natured upbeat romps about booze and its effects (both positive and negative) that proved massive hits during the immediate pre-rock era.

The first of Milburn's 19 Top Ten R&B smashes came in 1948 with his party classic "Chicken Shack Boogie," which paced the charts and anointed his band with a worthy name (the Aladdin Chickenshackers, natch). A velvet-smooth "Bewildered" displayed the cool after-hours side of Milburn's persona as it streaked up the charts later that year, but it was rollicking horn-driven material such as "Roomin' House Boogie" and "Sax Shack Boogie" that Milburn was renowned for. Milburn's rumbling 88s influenced a variety of famous artists, notably Fats Domino.

With the ascent of "Bad, Bad Whiskey" to the peak of the charts in 1950, Milburn embarked on a string of similarly boozy smashes: "Thinking and Drinking," "Let Me Go Home Whiskey," "One Bourbon, One Scotch, One Beer," and "Good Good Whiskey" (his last hit in 1954). Berry Gordy gave Milburn a comeback forum in 1962, issuing an album on Motown predominated by remakes of his old hits that doesn't deserve its extreme rarity today (even Little Stevie Wonder pitched in on harp for the sessions). Nothing could jump-start the pianist's fading career by then, though. His health deteriorated to the point where a string of strokes limited his mobility and his left leg was eventually amputated. Not too long after, one of the greatest pioneers in the history of R&B was dead. *—Bill Dahl*

☆ **The Complete Aladdin Recordings of Amos Milburn** / 1994 / Mosaic ✦✦✦✦✦
Seven discs tracing the entire 1946-1957 Aladdin Records legacy of jump blues pioneer Amos Milburn, whose rippling boogie-based piano talent and predilection for songs about booze made him a postwar R&B superstar. One hundred forty tracks in all (including plenty of unissued goodies) tab this as the ultimate collection for Milburn fans. He boogied like a champ at his first L.A. date for Aladdin, with a thundering "Down the Road Apiece" and rocked equally hard a decade later down in New Orleans when he was recutting "Chicken Shack Boogie" with the crew at Cosimo's. Mosaic does their usual elegant presentational job on this R&B legend, not skimping on a thing. Fabulous boxed set. *—Bill Dahl*

★ **Down the Road Apiece: The Best of Amos Milburn** / Jan. 11, 1994 / EMI America ✦✦✦✦✦
Pianist Amos Milburn mixed boogie-woogie with vocal energy and

intensity to forge a style that was among early R&B's most exciting and appealing. Milburn's 1940s and '50s singles were sometimes fiery and sometimes silly, ranging from drinking songs and celebratory uptempo numbers to stomping instrumentals and an occasional blues or love tune. This excellent 26-track anthology contains such classic Milburn anthems as "Chicken Shack Boogie," "One Bourbon, One Scotch, One Beer," "Let's Have a Party," and "Bad, Bad Whiskey," as well as lesser-known but just as spirited romps. The mastering bolsters the sound, but doesn't deaden it, while Joseph Laredo's liner notes clearly and completely outline Milburn's musical and cultural/historical significance. *—Ron Wynn*

Blues, Barrelhouse and Boogie Woogie: The Best of Amos Milburn, 1946-1955 / 1996 / Capitol ✦✦✦✦

Here's a very reasonable compromise between the pricey Mosaic box and EMI's incomplete single-disc treatment of Milburn's Aladdin legacy: a three-disc, 66-song package that's heavy on boogies and blues and slightly deficient in the ballad department (to that end, his smash "Bewildered" was left off). Everything that is aboard is top-drawer, though—the booze odes, many a party rocker, and a plethora of the double-entendre blues that Milburn reveled in during his early years. The absent 1956 remake of "Chicken Shack Boogie" is a humongous omission, though. *—Bill Dahl*

The Motown Sessions, 1962-1964 / Feb. 1996 / Motown ✦✦✦✦

Signed to Motown years after his peak as an R&B star, Milburn's association with the label turned out to be something of a non-event, producing only an obscure album and flop single. A commercial non-event, that is; Milburn's skills were still intact, resulting in some fine if somewhat uncharacteristic performances. This compilation reissues that album (*Return of the Blues Boss*) and adds seven unreleased tracks. Milburn may still have been singing blues/R&B, but he was with Motown, which meant that a fair amount of soul-pop flavor inevitably seeped through. You can hear it in the occasional female backup vocals, swinging brass arrangements, and even a brief harmonica solo by Stevie Wonder on "Chicken Shack Boogie"; the arrangement on "I'll Make It Up to You Somehow" wouldn't have been out of place on an early Mary Wells single. The results are pleasantly surprising, updating Milburn's sound (which would have been quite anachronistic in the early 1960s) into the early soul era. The material is pretty strong, including both bluesy ballads and more uptempo numbers that don't totally smother his boogie-woogie roots. *—Richie Unterberger*

Roy Milton

b. Jul. 31, 1907, Wynnewood, OK, d. Sep. 18, 1983, Los Angeles, CA
Drums, Vocals / R&B, Electric Jump Blues, Blues Jazz
As in-the-pocket drummer of his own jump blues combo, the Solid Senders, Roy Milton was in a perfect position to drive his outfit just as hard or soft as he so desired. With his stellar sense of swing, Milton did just that; his steady backbeat on his 1946 single for Art Rupe's fledgling Juke Box imprint, "R.M. Blues," helped steer it to the uppermost reaches of the R&B charts (that assured vocal didn't hurt either).

"R.M. Blues" was such a huge seller that it established Juke Box (soon to be renamed Specialty) as a viable concern for the long haul. Rupe knew a good thing when he saw it, recording Milton early and often through 1953. He was rewarded with 19 Top Ten R&B hits by the Solid Senders. Sadly, even though he helped pioneer the postwar R&B medium, rock 'n' roll had rendered Roy Milton an anachronism.

The drummer remained active nonetheless, thrilling the throng at the 1970 Monterey Jazz Festival as part of Johnny Otis' all-star troupe. It's a safe bet he was swinging until the very end. *—Bill Dahl*

★ **Roy Milton and His Solid Senders** / 1990 / Specialty ✦✦✦✦✦

Certainly this is the place to go for Milton's most popular and influential material—a whopping 18 of the 25 cuts made the R&B Top Ten in the late '40s and early '50s. These include such classics as "R.M. Blues," "The Hucklebuck," and "Hop, Skip & Jump" (given a great rockabilly treatment in the 1950s by the Collins Kids). All of the tracks are prime jump blues, Milton occasionally slowing down the boogies into ballads; one number ("Thrill Me") features fellow jump blues star Camille Howard on vocals. *—Richie Unterberger*

Groovy Blues, Vol. 2 / 1992 / Specialty ✦✦✦✦

The rarities and unissued material begin to pop up on *Vol. 2*, making it even more of a feast for collectors. Milton's Solid Senders, featuring pianist/singer Camille Howard, guitarist Johnny Rogers, and a crew of roaring saxmen, were one of the tightest and most respected on the Coast. *—Bill Dahl*

Blowin' with Roy / 1994 / Specialty ✦✦✦✦

The third and presumably final entry in Specialty's exhaustive Milton reissue series is by no means a make-weight affair. Even when the Solid Senders tackled Tin Pan Alley fare like "Along the Navajo Trail," "Coquette," and "When I Grow Too Old to Dream," they swung 'em. More late-'40s/early-'50s rarities and unissued items galore. *—Bill Dahl*

Mississippi Sheiks

Group / Acoustic Country Blues
One of the classic string bands of the late '20s and early '30s, this group featured the talents of Walter Vinson, Bo Carter, and Lonnie Chatmon in various configurations.

Based in Jackson, MS, the group took their name from the Rudolph Valentino movie *The Sheik*. Several years after they began performing, the group recorded their first session in 1930. Over the next five years, they cut nearly 70 songs, which ranged from old-timey string songs to racy blues. During this time, the core of the group consisted of fiddler Lonnie Chatmon and guitarist Walter Vinson, with guitarists Bo Carter and Sam Chatmon joining the group frequently; both Carter and Sam also had successful solo careers, which occasionally prevented them from performing with the group.

The Mississippi Sheiks retained their popularity until the end of the '30s, when they slowly faded away from view. *—Cub Koda and Stephen Thomas Erlewine*

★ **Stop and Listen** / Yazoo ✦✦✦✦✦

Stop and Listen collects 20 tracks the Mississippi Sheiks recorded in the early '30s, gathering together most of their best-known material (including "Sitting on Top of the World"), plus the previously unreleased "Livin' in a Strain." These records are of significant historical importance and this is the definitive compilation of this groundbreaking—and popular—string band. *—Thom Owens*

Little Brother Montgomery

b. Apr. 18, 1906, Kentwood, LA, d. Sep. 6, 1985, Champaign, IL
Piano, Vocals / Piano Blues
A notable influence to the likes of Sunnyland Slim and Otis Spann, pianist "Little Brother" Montgomery's lengthy career spanned both the earliest years of blues history and the electrified Chicago scene of the 1950s.

By age 11, Montgomery had given up on attending school to instead play in Louisiana juke joints. He came to Chicago as early as 1926 and made his first 78s in 1930 for Paramount (the booty that day in Grafton, WI, included two of Montgomery's enduring signature items, "Vicksburg Blues" and "No Special Rider"). Bluebird recorded Montgomery more prolifically in 1935-36 in New Orleans.

In 1942, Little Brother Montgomery settled down to a life of steady club gigs in Chicago, his repertoire alternating between blues and traditional jazz (he played Carnegie Hall with Kid Ory's Dixieland band in 1949). Otis Rush benefitted from his sensitive accompaniment on several of his 1957-58 Cobra dates, while Buddy Guy recruited him for similar duties when he nailed Montgomery's "First Time I Met the Blues" in a supercharged revival for Chess in 1960. That same year, Montgomery cut a fine album for Bluesville with guitarist Lafayette "Thing" Thomas that remains one of his most satisfying sets. *—Bill Dahl*

● **Tasty Blues** / 1960 / Original Blues Classics ✦✦✦✦

Unfortunately not available on CD, here's a very attractive example of a pianist with roots dug deep in pre-war tradition updating his style just enough to sound contemporary for 1960. With a little help from bassist Julian Euell and Lafayette Thomas (better known as Jimmy McCracklin's guitarist), Montgomery swoops through his seminal "Vicksburg Blues" and "No Special Rider" with enthusiasm and élan. *—Bill Dahl*

Goodbye Mister Blues / 1973-1976 / Delmark ✦✦✦

While Eurreal "Little Brother" Montgomery was among blues' greatest barrelhouse and boogie pianists, he was also well versed in traditional jazz. This disc's 13 cuts feature him working with The State Street Swingers, an early jazz unit, doing faithful recreations of such chestnuts as "South Rampart St. Parade," "Riverside Blues" and "Panama Rag." Montgomery's vocals were stately, yet exuberant, while his piano solos were loose and firmly in the spirit, showing the link between early jazz and blues. While the emphasis is more on interaction and ensemble playing than individual voices, players expertly maximized their solo time. This is a fine example of a vintage style. *—Ron Wynn*

Charlie Musselwhite

b. Jan. 31, 1944, Kosciusko, MS
Guitar, Harmonica, Vocals / Electric Chicago Blues
Harmonica wizard Norton Buffalo can recollect a time when his record collection had been whittled down to only the bare essentials: *The Paul Butterfield Blues Band* and *Stand Back! Here Comes Charley Musselwhite's South Side Band*. Butterfield and Musselwhite will probably be forever linked as the two most interesting, arguably most important, products of the "White blues movement" of the mid- to late- '60s—not only because they were near the forefront chronologically, but because each stands out as being especially faithful to the style. Each certainly earned the respect of his legendary mentors. No less than the late Big Joe Williams said, "Charlie Musselwhite is one of the greatest living

harp players of country blues. He is right up there with Sonny Boy Williams, and he's been my harp player ever since Sonny Boy got killed."

It's interesting that Big Joe specifies "country" blues, because, even though he made his mark leading electric bands in Chicago and San Francisco, Musselwhite began playing blues with people he'd read about in Sam Charters' *Country Blues*—Memphis greats like Furry Lewis, Will Shade, and Gus Cannon. It was these rural roots that set him apart from Butterfield, and decades later Musselwhite began incorporating his first instrument, guitar.

When his aforementioned debut LP became a standard on San Francisco's underground radio, Musselwhite played the Fillmore Auditorium and never returned to the Windy City. Leading bands that featured greats like guitarists Harvey Mandel, Freddie Roulette, Luther Tucker, Louis Myers, Robben Ford, Fenton Robinson, and Junior Watson, Musselwhite played steadily around Bay Area bars and mounted somewhat low-profile national tours. It wasn't until the late '80s, when he conquered a career-long drinking problem, that Musselwhite began touring worldwide to rave notices. Today he is busier than ever. —*Dan Forte*

★ **Stand Back! Here Comes Charley Musselwhite's Southside Band** / 1967 / Vanguard ♦♦♦♦♦
Vanguard may have spelled his name wrong (he prefers Charlie or Charles), but the word was out as soon as this solo debut was released: Here was a harpist every bit as authentic, as emotional, in some ways as adventuresome, as Paul Butterfield. Similarly leading a Chicago band with a veteran Black rhythm section (Fred Below on drums, Bob Anderson on bass) and rock-influenced soloists (keyboardist Barry Goldberg, guitarist Harvey Mandel), Musselwhite played with a depth that belied his age—only 22 when this was cut! His gruff vocals were considerably more affected than they would become later (clearer, more relaxed), but his renditions of "Help Me," "Early in the Morning," and his own "Strange Land" stand the test of time. He let his harmonica speak even more authoritatively on instrumentals like "39th and Indiana" (essentially "It Hurts Me Too" sans lyrics) and "Cha Cha the Blues," and his version of jazz arranger Duke Pearson's gospel-tinged "Cristo Redentor" has become his signature song—associated with Musselwhite probably more so than with trumpeter Donald Byrd, who originally recorded the song for Blue Note. Goldberg is in fine form (particularly on organ), but Mandel's snakey, stuttering style really stands out—notably on "Help Me," his quirky original "4 P.M.," and "Chicken Shack," where he truly makes you think your record is skipping. —*Dan Forte*

Louisiana Fog / 1968 / Cherry Red ♦♦♦

★ **Tennessee Woman** / 1969 / Vanguard ♦♦♦♦♦
The addition of jazz pianist Skip Rose gave a new dimension to the ensemble sound, and provided a perfect foil to Charlie's own soloing—especially on the re-take of "Cristo Redentor," extended to 11 minutes, shifting to double-time in spots. Rose's instrumental, "A Nice Day for Something," is a welcome change of pace, and Musselwhite's "Blue Feeling Today" compares favorably to fine covers of Little Walter and Fenton Robinson tunes. —*Dan Forte*

Takin' My Time / 1974 / Arhoolie ♦♦♦♦
Another talented and original ensemble—Rose still on piano, with the Ford brothers (Pat and Robben) on drums and guitar, respectively. Again, Rose contributes an original departure, the solo piano ballad "Two Little Girls"—and, as usual, it is to Musselwhite's credit that he welcomed such far-from-blues mood swings. Otherwise, the band's (especially Robben's) jazzier leanings were checked at the studio door, and Robben's guitar is mixed too low throughout. At this stage, Musselwhite was changing personnel too quickly to give any unit a second chance in the studio, which would have been especially interesting with this outfit. —*Dan Forte*

Harmonica According to Charlie / 1979 / Kicking Mule ♦♦♦
Ostensibly an instructional blues harp album (with an exhaustive accompanying book penned by Musselwhite), this is emotional and listenable rather than academic. Mullelwhite covers a wide range of blues styles (and harp positions), and ventures to the outer fringes of the genre for the instrumentals "Hard Times" (from Ray Charles' sax man David "Fathead" Newman) and his Latin original "Azul Para Amparo" (backed only by guitarist Sam Mitchell). The English studio band is sympathetic, especially pianist Bob Hall. —*Dan Forte*

Memphis Tennessee / 1984 / Mobile Fidelity ♦♦♦♦
Though steel guitarist Freddie Roulette was pictured on *Tennessee Woman*, he did not play on the album; luckily he is given ample space here, and the combination of his eerie vocal-like sound, Jack Myers' solid but adventurous bass playing, and Skip Rose' jazz piano voicings made this edition of the Musselwhite band one of the most original blues outfits ever. Musselwhite is in fine form as well, on a rock solid cover of Muddy's "Trouble No More," a lyrical reading of "Willow Weep for Me," and his harp tour de force "Arkansas Boogie." —*Dan Forte*

Tell Me Where Have All the Good Times Gone / 1984 / Blue Rock ♦♦♦♦
Drummer/label head Pat Ford reunited with Musselwhite and brought

along brother Robben on guitar, producing this return to form. Musselwhite is up to the task in all departments—singing, playing (great tone), and especially songwriting (the title tune and "Seemed like the Whole World Was Crying," inspired by Muddy Waters' death)—but it had been a while since Robben had played lowdown blues (touring with Joni Mitchell, putting in countless hours in L.A. studios). Pianist Clay Cotten is in fine form, and it may have been wiser to give the guitar chair to Tim Kaihatsu, who by this time had seniority (in terms of hours on the bandstand with Musselwhite) over any of Musselwhite's alumni. The to-be-expected-by-now deviations this time out: Don and Dewey's "Stretchin' Out," an impressive chromatic harp rendering of "Exodus," and Musselwhite's solo guitar outting, "Baby-O." Easily Musselwhite's best-engineered album (nice job, Greg Goodwin). —*Dan Forte*

In My Time / 1993 / Alligator ♦♦♦♦
Charlie Musselwhite takes four different approaches on this Alligator release. On two tracks, he turns to guitar, proving a competent instrumentalist and convincing singer in a vintage Delta style. He also does two gospel numbers backed by the legendary Blind Boys of Alabama, which are heartfelt, but not exactly triumphs. Musselwhite reveals his jazz influence on three tracks, making them entertaining harmonica workouts. But for blues fans, Musselwhite's biting licks and spiraling riffs are best featured on such numbers as "If I Should Have Bad Luck" and "Leaving Blues." Despite the diverse strains, Musselwhite retains credibility throughout while displaying the wide range of sources from which he's forged his distinctive style. —*Ron Wynn*

Blues Never Die / Vanguard ♦♦♦♦
This may be an overview of Musselwhite's career (from the late '60s to the present—with some previously unreleased tracks, including the title cut), but it is not the best introduction to the artist. For that, his Vanguard '60s output is still recommended, along with the 1984 session on Blue Rock'it and Alligator's *In My Time*. —*Dan Forte*

Mark Naftalin

b. 1944, Minneapolis, MN
Organ, Guitar, Piano, Accordion, Keyboards, Vibes
Blues musician, composer, and producer Mark Naftalin played keyboards with the original Paul Butterfield Blues Band from 1965 to 1968. Since then he has recorded with top blues players like John Lee Hooker, Otis Rush, Percy Mayfield, James Cotton, Michael Bloomfield, Lowell Fulson, Big Joe Turner, and dozens of others—a sideman on more than 100 albums.

Naftalin is sought after for his elegant, understated keyboard accompaniment and tasty solos. Although first known as an organist, he has also recorded on piano, guitar, accordion, vibes, and various electric keyboards. In his solo concerts he plays mostly acoustic piano. Born in Minneapolis, MN, in 1944, Naftalin moved to Chicago in 1961 and enrolled at the University of Chicago, where he jammed on piano at many of the campus "twist parties," the rage at the time. It was at these parties that Naftalin had his first opportunity to play with harmonica player Paul Butterfield and guitarist Elvin Bishop, the nucleus of what was to become the Paul Butterfield Blues Band.

In 1964 Naftalin moved to New York City, where he spent a year at the Mannes College of Music, and it was there that he sat in with the Butterfield band during a recording session warmup song, playing the Hammond organ (for the first time!). Michael Bloomfield had recently joined the band. The group liked the organ sound (and his playing), and Naftalin went on to record eight of the 11 songs on the first Butterfield album that very day. Butterfield asked Naftalin to join the group during that first session.

In the late '60s, after the first four Butterfield albums, Naftalin went out on his own, settling in the San Francisco Bay area. There he put together the Mark Naftalin Rhythm and Blues Revue and has been active in blues and rock recording sessions, solo gigs, and revue shows, and as a producer of concerts, festivals, and radio shows. He also played with Michael Bloomfield as a duo and in a band.

Currently Naftalin performs, both solo and ensemble, in the Bay Area and elsewhere, often with slide guitar virtuoso Ron Thompson, a longtime associate. —*Michael Erlewine*

Kenny Neal

b. Oct. 14, 1957, Los Angeles, CA
Bass, Guitar, Harmonica, Piano, Vocals / Modern Electric Blues
The future of Baton Rouge swamp blues lies squarely in multi-instrumentalist Kenny Neal's capable hands. Along with a select few others (Larry Garner, for one), the second-generation southern Louisiana bluesman is entirely cognizant of the region's venerable blues tradition and imaginative enough to steer it in fresh directions—as his five albums for Alligator confirm. In 1987, Kenny Neal cut his debut LP for Florida producer Bob Greenlee—a stunningly updated swamp feast initially marketed on King Snake Records as *Bio on the Bayou*. Alligator

picked it up the following year, retitled it *Big News from Baton Rouge!!*, and young Neal was on his way.

Neal's sizzling guitar work, sturdy harp, and gravelly, aged-beyond-his-years vocals have served him well ever since. An acclaimed 1991 stint on Broadway in a production of *Mule Bone* found him performing acoustic versions of Langston Hughes' poetry set to music by Taj Mahal. His last Alligator set, 1994's *Hoodoo Moon*, rates as one of his most satisfying outings to date. —*Bill Dahl*

Big News from Baton Rouge!! / 1987 / Alligator ✦✦✦✦
The debut release for the second-generation bayou blues guitarist/harpist, whose gruff-before-their-time vocals retain their swamp sensibility while assuming a bright contemporary feel that tabs him as a leading contender for future blues stardom. —*Bill Dahl*

Devil Child / 1988 / Alligator ✦✦✦✦
Backed by a punchy horn section and sizzling rhythms, Neal didn't suffer from any sophomore jinx. Between Neal, his bass-playing co-producer Bob Greenlee, and drummer Jim Payne, there's some very crafty songwriting going on here—"Any Fool Will Do," "Bad Check," and "Can't Have Your Cake (And Eat It Too)" are among the standouts. —*Bill Dahl*

Walking on Fire / 1991 / Alligator ✦✦✦✦
Another in the remarkably consistent Alligator catalog of Kenny Neal that strikingly captures his contemporary Baton Rouge blues sound. He gets a little hot help from the Horny Horns—alto saxist Maceo Parker and trombonist Fred Wesley—who once filled a smiliar role behind the Godfather of Soul himself, James Brown. Two songs find Neal going the unplugged route, just as he had performed them in the Broadway musical *Mule Bone*. —*Bill Dahl*

● **Bayou Blood** / 1992 / Alligator ✦✦✦✦
You really can't go wrong with any of the guitarist's fine Alligator albums, but this one sparkles as brightly as any, with memorable outings like "Right Train, Wrong Track," "That Knife Don't Cut No More," and the steamy title track. Neal's albums are invariably dominated by well-chosen originals—no small feat these days. —*Bill Dahl*

Hoodoo Moon / 1994 / Alligator ✦✦✦✦
Neal is one of the most impressive young blues artists on the scene today—a fact borne out by the contents of this collection. Ably backed by a band that includes his brother Noel on bass and keyboardist Lucky Peterson, Neal indulges in a couple of covers this time, but the majority of the disc is original and incendiary. —*Bill Dahl*

Robert Nighthawk (Robert McCollum)

b. Nov. 30, 1909, Helena, AR, **d.** Nov. 5, 1967, Helena, AR
Guitar, Harmonica, Vocals / Electric Chicago Blues, Acoustic Chicago Blues
Of all the pivotal figures in blues history, certainly one of the most important was Robert Nighthawk. He bridged the gap between Delta and Chicago blues effortlessly, taking his slide cues from Tampa Red and stamping them with a Mississippi edge learned firsthand from his cousin, Houston Stackhouse. Though he recorded from the '30s into the early '40s under a variety of names—Robert Lee McCoy, Rambling Bob, Peetie's Boy—he finally took his lasting sobriquet of Robert Nighthawk from the title of his first record, "Prowling Night Hawk." It should be noted that the huge lapses in the man's discography are direct results of his rambling nature, taciturnity, and seeming disinterest in making records. Once you got him into a studio, the results were almost always of a uniform excellence. But it might be two years or more between sessions!

Robert Nighthawk is not a name that regularly gets bandied about in discussions of the all-time greats of the blues. But well it should, because his legacy was all-pervasive; his resonant voice and creamy smooth slide guitar playing (in standard tuning, unusual for a bluesman) would influence players for generations to come, and many of his songs would later become blues standards. —*Cub Koda*

Bricks in My Pillow / 1977 / Pearl Flapper ✦✦✦
Complete Recorded Works (1937-1940) / 1985 / Wolf ✦✦✦✦
For a glimpse into Nighthawk's earliest sides for the Victor label, this is the place to go. The sound—all of it taken off old 78s with little regard for modern noise reduction—is less than stellar, but the performances are nothing but. This includes the tune that gave him his permanent nom de plume, "Prowling Night Hawk." —*Cub Koda*

★ **Live on Maxwell Street** / 1988 / Rounder ✦✦✦✦✦
Recorded by Norman Dayron live on the street (one can actually hear cars driving by!) in 1964 with just Robert Whitehead on drums and John Lee Granderson on rhythm guitar in support, Nighthawk's slide playing (and single string soloing, for that matter) is nothing short of elegant and explosive. Highlights include "The Maxwell Street Medley," which combines his two big hits "Anna Lee" and "Sweet Black Angel," a mind-altering 12-bar solo on "The Time Have Come," which proves that Nighthawk's lead playing was just as well developed as his slide work, and a couple of wild instrumentals with Carey Bell sitting in on harmonica.

Nighthawk sounds cool as a cucumber, presiding over everything with an almost genial charm while laying the toughest sounds imaginable. One of the top three greatest live blues albums of all time. —*Cub Koda*

Jimmy Oden (James Burke Oden)

b. Jun. 26, 1903, Nashville, TN, **d.** Dec. 30, 1977, Chicago, IL
Piano, Vocals / Electric Chicago Blues, Piano Blues
Few blues songs have stood the test of Father Time as enduringly as "Goin' Down Slow." Its composer, St. Louis Jimmy Oden, pondered rather impressively himself—he recorded during the early '30s and was still at it more than three decades later.

If not for a move to St. Louis circa 1917, James Oden might have been known as Nashville Jimmy. He fell in with pianist Roosevelt Sykes on the 1920s Gateway City blues circuit (the two remained frequent musical partners through the ensuing decades). Oden enjoyed a prolific recording career during the 1930s and '40s, appearing on Champion, Bluebird (where he hit with "Goin' Down Slow" in 1941), Columbia, Bullet in 1947, Miracle, Aristocrat (where he cut "Florida Hurricane" in 1948 accompanied by pianist Sunnyland Slim and a young guitarist named Muddy Waters), Mercury, Savoy, and Apollo. Singles for Duke (with Sykes on piano) and Parrot (a 1955 remake of "Goin' Down Slow") set the stage for Oden's 1960 album for Prestige's Bluesville subsidiary (naturally, it included yet another reprise of "Goin' Down Slow"). Oden was backed by guitarist Jimmie Lee Robinson and a swinging New York rhythm section. As much a composer as a performer, Oden wrote "Soon Forgotten" and "Take the Bitter with the Sweet" for Muddy Waters. —*Bill Dahl*

● **1932-1948** / Story of Blues ✦✦✦✦
A solid sixteen-track import collection of Oden's earliest and best sides. —*Cub Koda*

Johnny Otis

b. Dec. 28, 1921, Vallejo, CA
Piano, Drums, Vocals, Vibes / R&B, Electric West Coast Blues, West Coast Blues
Johnny Otis has modeled an amazing number of contrasting musical hats over a career spanning more than half a century. Bandleader, record producer, talent scout, label owner, nightclub impresario, disc jockey, TV variety show host, author, R&B pioneer, rock 'n' roll star—Otis has answered to all those descriptions and quite a few more. Not bad for a Greek-American who loved jazz and R&B so fervently that he adopted the African-American culture as his own.

California-born John Veliotes changed his name to the Blacker-sounding "Otis" when he was in his teens. Drums were his first passion—he spent time behind the traps with the Oakland-based orchestra of Count Otis Matthews and kept time for various Midwestern swing outfits before settling in Los Angeles during the mid-'40s. Later, R&B replaced jazz in Otis' heart; he pared the big band down and discovered young talent such as the Robins, vocalists Mel Walker and Little Esther Phillips, and guitarist Pete Lewis that would serve him well in years to come.

Otis signed with Newark, NJ-based Savoy Records in 1949, and the R&B hits came in droves: "Double Crossing Blues," "Mistrustin' Blues," and "Cupid's Boogie" all hit No. 1 that year. Otis was a masterful talent scout; among his platinum-edged discoveries were Jackie Wilson, Little Willie John, Hank Ballard, and Etta James (he produced her debut smash "Roll with Me Henry").

In 1955 Otis took studio matters into his own hands, starting up his own label, Dig Records, to showcase his own work as well as his latest discoveries (including Arthur Lee Maye & the Crowns, Tony Allen, and Mel Williams). Rock 'n' roll was at its zenith in 1957, when the multi-instrumentalist signed on with Capitol Records; billed as the Johnny Otis Show, he set the R&B and pop charts ablaze in 1958 with his shave-and-a-haircut beat, "Willie and the Hand Jive," taking the vocal himself (other singers then with the Otis Show included Mel Williams and the gargantuan Marie Adams and The Three Tons of Joy). During the late '50s, Otis hosted his own variety program on L.A. television, starring his entire troupe.

In recent years, the multi-talented Otis added operating a California health-food emporium to his endless list of wide-ranging accomplishments. If blues boasts a renaissance man amongst its ranks, Johnny Otis surely fills that bill. —*Bill Dahl*

The Johnny Otis Show / 1958 / Savoy ✦✦✦✦
Some of the R&B bandleader's earliest and best work (1945-51) for Savoy. The cast includes singers Little Esther and Mel Walker, the Robins, and guitarist Pete Lewis. —*Bill Dahl*

The Capitol Years / 1988 / Capitol ✦✦✦✦
Unfortunately now out of print, this set anthologizes Otis' late-'50s rise to rock 'n' roll fame, thanks to his shave-and-a-haircut special "Willie and the Hand Jive." Like every other style of R&B Otis drifted into, he excelled

at it—"Castin' My Spell," "Crazy Country Hop," "Willie Did the Cha Cha," and "Three Girls Named Molly" are catchy rockers. Otis had a terrific band—guitarist Jimmy Nolen (later James Brown's main axeman), pianist Ernie Freeman, drummer Earl Palmer, and a tight horn section (along with singers Marie Adams and Mel Williams) gave him all the help he could possibly need. —*Bill Dahl*

Be Bop Baby Blues / 1989 / Night Train ✦✦✦
A bit skimpy at 14 songs, this disc casts Otis mostly in a bandleader role on late-'40s sides culled from the Excelsior, Supreme, and Swing Time labels. Vocalists fronting the Otis outfit include the extremely obscure Joe Swift, Earl Jackson, Clifford "Fat Man" Blivens, and Johnny Crawford. Swinging, horn-leavened jump blues all the way. —*Bill Dahl*

Creepin' with the Cats: The Legendary Dig Masters / 1991 / Ace ✦✦✦
Twenty-two tracks, almost half previously unreleased, from circa 1956-57 that Otis recorded for his own short-lived Dig label. Not as vivacious as the sides he recorded for Capitol in the late '50s, this is spirited but generic jump blues/R&B, divided evenly between vocals and instrumentals. Occasional cuts like the silly novelty instrumental "Ali Baba's Boogie" stand out from the pack. The one commanding greatest interest is "Hey! Hey! Hey!," which served as the model for Little Richard's version, which in turned was covered by the Beatles in the mid-'60s (as "Kansas City"). —*Richie Unterberger*

★ **The Original Johnny Otis Show** / 1994 / Savoy Jazz ✦✦✦✦✦
Twenty-seven of the Otis aggregation's best early sides for Savoy and Excelsior, including a slew of the group's early-'50s Little Esther and/or Mel Walker-fronted R&B smashes ("Mistrustin' Blues," "Cry Baby," "Sunset to Dawn"). Jimmy Rushing and the Robins also share vocal duties, as does Otis himself on a jumping "All Nite Long." This is one time when the bonus cuts are on the vinyl version—it contained 32 cuts appearing on a *Complete Disc* that Savoy Jazz reissued at the same time as this CD. The original artwork and liner notes have been reduced so much for the CD that they're unreadable (Pete Welding's essay deserves more respect). —*Bill Dahl*

Too Late to Holler / 1995 / Night Train ✦✦✦✦
A more generous selection of late-'40s Swing Time and Excelsior sides, again featuring Swift (who dominates the compilation), Jackson, and Blivens in front of the powerful Otis orchestra. Very little duplication exists between the two discs. —*Bill Dahl*

Let's Live It Up / Charly ✦✦✦
Otis stopped off at King Records for a while during the early '60s, making clever 45s that no one paid much attention to. Twenty-two of them are here, including five by the late Johnny "Guitar" Watson (whose "In the Evenin'" is chillingly direct). It's a mixed bag—vocal group stuff, twist workouts, and the inevitable sequel "Hand Jive One More Time" (alas, nobody did). —*Bill Dahl*

Junior Parker (Herman Parker)

b. May 27, 1932, Clarksdale, MS, **d.** Nov. 18, 1971, Chicago, IL
Harmonica, Vocals / Soul, R&B, Soul Blues, Electric Memphis Blues
His velvet-smooth vocal delivery to the contrary, Junior Parker was a product of the fertile postwar Memphis blues circuit whose wonderfully understated harp style was personally mentored by none other than regional icon Sonny Boy Williamson.

Parker and his band, the Blue Flames (including Floyd Murphy, Matt's brother, on guitar), landed at Sun Records in 1953 and promptly scored a hit with their rollicking "Feelin' Good." Later that year, Little Junior cut a fiery "Love My Baby" and a laidback "Mystery Train" for Sun.

Before 1953 was through, the polished Junior Parker had moved on to Don Robey's Duke imprint in Houston. It took a while for the harpist to regain his hitmaking momentum, but he scored big in 1957 with the smooth "Next Time You See Me."

Criss-crossing the country as headliner with the Blues Consolidated package (his support act was labelmate Bobby Bland), Parker developed a breathtaking brass-powered sound (usually the work of trumpeter/Duke-house-bandleader Joe Scott) that pushed his honeyed vocals and intermittent harp solos with exceptional power. Parker's updated remake of Roosevelt Sykes' "Driving Wheel" was a huge R&B hit in 1961, as was the surging "In the Dark" (the R&B dance workout "Annie Get Your Yo-Yo" followed suit the next year).

Parker was exceptionally versatile—whether delivering "Mother-in-Law Blues" and "Sweet Home Chicago" in faithful down-home fashion, courting the teenage market with "Barefoot Rock," or tastefully howling Harold Burrage's "Crying for My Baby" (another hit for him in 1965) in front of a punchy horn section, Parker was the consummate modern blues artist, with one foot planted in Southern blues and the other in uptown R&B. A brain tumor tragically silenced Junior Parker's magic-carpet voice in late 1971 before he reached his 40th birthday. —*Bill Dahl*

The ABC Collection / 1976 / ABC ✦✦✦✦
Housed in something that looks vaguely like a square gray envelope that's guaranteed to wear out if you're not careful, this album is still one of the only places to locate many of Parker's best 1958-1966 Duke sides (unless you've got the 45s salted away somewhere). "Man or Mouse," "Dangerous Woman," the two-part "These Kind of Blues," and "I'll Forget About You" are prime vehicles for Parker's uncommonly smooth vocals and occasional harp blasts. —*Bill Dahl*

Mystery Train / 1990 / Rounder ✦✦✦✦
This excellent little compilation features at least one extant take of everything Junior and his original band, the Blue Flames, recorded at Sun Records between 1952 to 1954. His debut single for the label and his first hit, the classic "Feelin' Good," is aboard as well as the equally fine (but originally unissued) "Feelin' Bad." His leanings toward smoother Roy Brown stylings are evident with tracks like "Fussing and Fighting Blues" and "Sitting and Thinking," but the follow-up to his first Sun single, the original version of "Mystery Train" and two takes of the flip side, "Love My Baby," are the must-hears on this collection. Fleshing out Parker's meager output for Sun are essential early tracks from James Cotton. Cotton doesn't blow harp on any of these, but the sax-dominated "My Baby," and especially "Cotton Crop Blues" and "Hold Me in Your Arms" with Pat Hare on super-distorted blistering guitar are Memphis-'50s blues at its apex. Hare himself also rounds out the compilation with two tracks, the prophetic "I'm Gonna Murder My Baby" (Hare did exactly that and spent the rest of his life behind bars as a result) and the previously unissued "Bonus Pay." Don't let the short running time of this CD stop you from picking this one up; the music is beyond excellent. —*Cub Koda*

★ **Junior's Blues/The Duke Recordings, Vol. 1** / 1992 / MCA ✦✦✦✦✦
After the non-success of "Mystery Train" on the R&B charts, Parker jumped contract and signed with Don Robey's Houston-based Duke Records. With his smooth vocal approach, Parker clearly envisioned himself as the next Roy or Charles Brown. But from the evidence of these early sides, it's clear that Robey wanted to piggyback off the success of the Sun sound. Tracks like "I Wanna Ramble" were virtual carbon copies of the "Feelin' Good" riff and Parker's recasting of old favorites like Robert Johnson's "Sweet Home Chicago," Roosevelt Sykes' "Driving Wheel," "Yonder's Wall" and "Mother-in-Law Blues," were all clearly in the downhome vein that Parker felt was too "old timey" for an up-to-date musician/vocalist of his caliber. His first big hit for the label, the horn-driven "Next Time You See Me" is here with others in the same vein, but this otherwise excellent collection is curiously missing "Pretty Baby," Parker's version of Howlin' Wolf's "Riding in the Moonlight," certainly one of his best. —*Cub Koda*

Charley Patton

b. 1887, **d.** 1934
Guitar, Vocals / Acoustic Delta Blues
If the Delta country blues has a convenient source point, it would probably be Charley Patton, its first great star. His hoarse, impassioned singing style, fluid guitar playing and unrelenting beat made him the original king of the Delta blues. Much more than your average itinerant musician, Patton was an acknowledged celebrity and a seminal influence on musicians throughout the Delta. Rather than bumming his way from town to town, Patton would be called up to play at plantation dances, juke joints and the like. He'd pack them in like sardines everywhere he went, and the emotional sway he held over his audiences caused him to be tossed off of more than one plantation by the ownership, simply because workers would leave crops unattended to listen to him play any time he picked up a guitar. He epitomized the image of a '20s "sport" blues singer; rakish, raffish, easy to provoke, capable of downing massive quantities of food and liquor, a woman on each arm with a flashy, expensive looking guitar fitted with a strap and kept in a traveling case by his side, only to be opened up when there was money or good times involved. His records—especially his first and biggest hit, "Pony Blues"—could be heard on phonographs throughout the South. Although he was certainly not the first Delta bluesman to record, he quickly became one of the genre's most popular. By late-'20s Mississippi plantation standards, Charley Patton was a star, a genuine celebrity.

Although Patton was roughly five foot, five inches tall and only weighed a spartan 135 pounds, his gravelly, high-energy singing style (even on ballads and gospel tunes it sounded this way) made him sound like a man twice his weight and half again his size. Sleepy John Estes claimed he was the loudest blues singer he ever heard and it was rumored that his voice was loud enough to carry outdoors at a dance up to 500 yards away without amplification. His vaudeville-style vocal asides—which on record give the effect of two people talking to each other—along with the sound of his whiskey- and cigarette-scarred voice, would become major elements of the vocal style of one of his students, a young Howlin' Wolf. His guitar playing was no less impressive, fueled with a propulsive beat and a keen rhythmic sense that would later plant seeds in the boogie style of John Lee Hooker. Patton is generally regarded as one of the original architects of putting blues into a strong, syncopated rhythm and the strident tone he achieves on record was achieved by tuning his guitar a step to a step and a half above standard pitch instead of using a capo. His compositional skills on the instrument are illustrated by his penchant for finding and utilizing several different themes as background accompaniment in a single song. His slide work—either played in his lap like a Hawaiian guitar and fretted with a pocket knife or in the more conventional manner with a brass pipe for a bottleneck—was no less inspiring, finishing vocal phrases for him and influencing contemporaries like Son House and up and coming youngsters like Robert Johnson. He also popped his bass strings (a technique he developed some 40 years before funk bass players started doing the same thing), beat his guitar like a drum and stomped his feet to reinforce certain beats or to create counter rhythms, all of which can be heard on various recordings. Rhythm and excitement were the bywords of his style.

The second, and equally important, part of Patton's legacy handed down to succeeding blues generations was his propensity for entertaining. One of the reasons for Charlie Patton's enormous popularity in the South stems from him being a consummate barrelhouse entertainer. Most of the now-common guitar gymnastics modern audiences have come to associate with the likes of a Jimi Hendrix, in fact originated with Patton. His ability to "entertain the peoples" and rock the house with a hell-raising ferociousness left an indelible impression on audiences and fellow bluesmen alike. His music embraced everything from blues, ballads, and ragtime to gospel. And so keen were Patton's abilities in setting mood and ambience, that he could bring a barrelhouse frolic to a complete stop by launching into an impromptu performance of nothing but religious-themed selections and still manage to hold his audience spellbound. Because he possessed the heart of a bluesman with the mindset of a vaudeville performer, hearing Patton for the first time can be a bit overwhelming; it's a lot to take in as the music and performances can careen from emotionally intense to buffoonishly comic, sometimes within a single selection. It is all strongly rooted in '20s Black dance music and even on the religious tunes in his repertoire, Patton fuels it all with a strong rhythmic pulse.

He first recorded in 1929 for the Paramount label and within a year's time, he was not only the largest-selling blues artist but—in a whirlwind of recording activity—also the music's most prolific. Patton was also responsible for hooking up fellow players Willie Brown and Son House with their first chances to record. It is probably best to issue a blanket audio disclaimer of some kind when listening to Patton's total recorded legacy, some 60 odd tracks total, his final session done only a couple of months before his death in 1934. We will never know what Patton's Paramount masters really sounded like. When the company went out of business, the metal masters were sold off as scrap, some of it used to line chicken coops! All that's left are the original 78s—rumored to have been made out of inferior pressing material commonly used to make bowling balls (!)—and all of them are scratched and heavily played, making all attempts at sound retrieval by current noise-reduction processing a tall order indeed. That said, it is still music well worth seeking out and not just for its place in history. Patton's music gives us the first flowering of the Delta blues form, before it became homogenized with turnarounds and 12-bar restrictions, and few humans went at it so aggressively. —*Cub Koda*

★ **Founder of the Delta Blues** / 1969 / Yazoo ✦✦✦✦✦
A cornerstone of any blues collection, this is where you start. As compilations go, this originally started life as a double record set featuring all of Patton's best known titles and sound wise was miles above all previous versions. Its compact disc incarnation here trims the tune list to 24 tracks, but all the seminal tracks are here: "Pony Blues," "High Water Everywhere," "Screamin' and Hollerin' the Blues," "A Spoonful of Blues," "Shake It and Break It" and the wistful "Poor Me," recorded at his final session in 1934, a scant two months before he died. —*Cub Koda*

☆ **King of the Delta Blues** / 1991 / Yazoo ✦✦✦✦✦
This excellent companion volume to the above pulls together 23 more Patton tracks (including some alternate takes that were for years thought to be lost) to give a much more complete look at this amazing artist. It's interesting here to compare the tracks from his final session to his halcyon output from 1929. Highlights include "Mean Black Cat Blues," Patton's adaptation of "Sitting on top of the World" ("Some Summer Day") and both parts of "Prayer of Death," originally issued under the nom de plume of "Elder J.J. Hadley." The sound on this collection is vastly superior from a noise reduction standpoint to its companion volume. —*Cub Koda*

Complete Recorded Works, Vols. 1-3 / Document ✦✦✦

Odie Payne

b. Aug. 27, 1926, **d.** Mar. 1, 1989, Chicago, IL
Drums
Drummer Odie Payne was born in Chicago on August 27, 1926. After

release from the military, Payne studied drums and graduated with high honors from the Roy C. Knapp School of Percussion. While playing with pianist Johnny Jones in 1949, Payne met Tampa Red and soon joined Red's band. In 1952 Payne and pianist Johnny Jones became part of Elmore James' dance band the Broomdusters. Payne stayed with the band for three years, but recorded with James until 1959—recording some 31 singles. He became a highly sought after studio musician and, in the later 1950s, played on many essential recordings for the Cobra label, for artists like Otis Rush, Magic Sam, and Buddy Guy. Odie Payne developed the famous double-shuffle, later used by Fred Below and Sam Lay to great effect. Payne recorded for Chess including a number of classic Chuck Berry tunes like "Nadine" and "No Particular Place to Go." He recorded with most of the great Chicago blues artists: Otis Rush, Sonny Boy Williamson II, Muddy Waters, Jimmy Rogers, Eddie Taylor, Magic Sam, Yank Rachell, Sleepy John Estes, Little Brother Montgomery, Memphis Minnie, and many others.
—*Michael Erlewine*

Peg Leg Sam

b. Dec. 18, 1911, Jonesville, SC, **d.** Nov. 27, 1977, Jonesville, SC
Harmonica, Vocals / Acoustic Country Blues
Peg Leg Sam was a performer to be treasured, a member of what may have been the last authentic traveling medicine show, a harmonica virtuoso, and an extraordinary entertainer. Born Arthur Jackson, he acquired his nickname after a hoboing accident in 1930. His medicine show career began in 1938, and his repertoire—finally recorded only in the early '70s—reflected the rustic nature of the traveling show. "Peg" delivered comedy routines, bawdy toasts, and monologs; performed tricks with his harps (often playing two at once); and served up some juicy Piedmont blues (sometimes with a guitar accompanist, but most often by himself). Peg Leg Sam gave his last medicine-show performance in 1972 in North Carolina and was still in fine fettle when he started making the rounds of folk and blues festivals in his last years.
—*Jim O'Neal*

● **Joshua** / Sep. 1990 / Tomato ✦✦✦✦
These are rootsy '70s performances by this Southeastern country-blues harmonica player and singer. —*Mark A. Humphrey*

Pinetop Perkins

b. Jul. 13, 1913, Belzoni, MS
Guitar, Piano, Vocals / Piano Blues
He admittedly wasn't the originator of the seminal piano piece "Pinetop's Boogie Woogie," but it's a safe bet that more people associate it nowadays with Pinetop Perkins than with the man who devised it in the first place, Clarence "Pinetop" Smith.

Although it seems as though he's been around Chicago forever, the Mississippi native actually got a relatively late start on his path to Windy City immortality. It was only when Muddy Waters took him on to replace Otis Spann in 1969 that Perkins' rolling mastery of the ivories began to assume outsized proportions.

Perkins had traveled to Helena with Robert Nighthawk in 1943, playing with the elegant slide guitarist on Nighthawk's KFFA radio program. Perkins soon switched over to rival Sonny Boy Williamson's beloved *King Biscuit Time* radio show in Helena, where he remained for an extended period. Perkins accompanied Nighthawk on a 1950 session for the Chess brothers that produced "Jackson Town Gal," but Chicago couldn't hold him at the time.

Nighthawk disciple Earl Hooker recruited Perkins during the early '50s. They hit the road, pausing at Sam Phillips' studios in Memphis long enough for Perkins to wax his first version of "Pinetop's Boogie Woogie" in 1953. He settled in downstate Illinois for a spell, then relocated to Chicago. Music gradually was relegated to the back burner until Hooker coaxed him into working on an LP for Arhoolie in 1968. When Spann split from Muddy Waters, the stage was set for Pinetop Perkins' reemergence.

After more than a decade with the Man, Perkins and his bandmates left en masse to form the Legendary Blues Band. Their early Rounder albums (*Life of Ease, Red Hot 'n' Blue*) prominently spotlighted Perkins' rippling 88s and rich vocals. —*Bill Dahl*

Boogie Woogie King / Nov. 1, 1976 / Evidence ✦✦✦

● **After Hours** / 1986 / Blind Pig ✦✦✦✦
Easy-grooving blues and boogie backed by the competent New York City-based blues band Little Mike and the Tornadoes. Though Perkins followed Otis Spann as the piano player in the Muddy Waters band, these are their first domestically available recordings under his own name. —*Niles J. Frantz*

Pinetop's Boogie Woogie / 1992 / Antone's ✦✦✦✦
The maze of new and recent discs by this veteran Chicago piano man can be daunting, but rest assured that this is one of his best to date. Many of the songs are Perkins standbys—"Kidney Stew," "Caledonia," and, of

course, "Pinetop's Boogie Woogie"—but the backing here is so stellar (sidemen include harpists James Cotton and Kim Wilson; guitarists Matt Murphy, Jimmy Rogers, Hubert Sumlin, and Duke Robillard; and several driving rhythm sections) that the project rises above most of Perkins' output. —*Bill Dahl*

Portrait of a Delta Bluesman / 1993 / Vanguard ✦✦✦✦
Considerably more ambitious than just another Perkins set, this solo disc intersperses key songs from his storied history with interview segments that reveal much about the man himself, from his Delta beginnings to when he replaced Otis Spann in Muddy Waters' vaunted band. —*Bill Dahl*

Lucky Peterson

b. Dec. 13, 1964, Buffalo, NY
Organ, Bass, Guitar, Piano, Drums, Vocals / Modern Electric Blues
Child-prodigy status is sometimes difficult to overcome upon reaching maturity. Not so for Lucky Peterson—he's far bigger (in more ways than one) on the contemporary blues circuit than he was at the precocious age of six, when he scored a national R&B hit with the Willie Dixon-produced "1-2-3-4."

Little Lucky Peterson was lucky to be born into a musical family. His dad, James Peterson, owned the Governor's Inn, a popular Buffalo, NY, blues nightclub that booked the biggies: Jimmy Reed, Muddy Waters, Bill Doggett. The latter's mighty Hammond B-3 organ fascinated the four-and-a-half-year-old lad, and soon Peterson was on his way under Dixon's tutelage. "1-2-3-4" got Peterson on *The Tonight Show* and *The Ed Sullivan Show*, but he didn't rest on his laurels—he was doubling on guitar at age eight, and at 17, he signed on as Little Milton's keyboardist for three years.

A three-year stint with Bobby Bland preceded Peterson's solo career launch, which took off when he struck up a musical relationship with Florida-based producer Bob Greenlee. Two Greenlee-produced albums for Alligator, 1989's *Lucky Strikes!* and the following year's *Triple Play*, remain his finest recorded offerings. —*Bill Dahl*

Ridin' / Mar. 1984 / Evidence ✦✦✦✦
As a child prodigy, keyboardist and organist Lucky Peterson's exploits were legendary. The stories grew even more widespread as he became a teen and stints with Little Milton and Bobby "Blue" Bland only added to his fame. But Peterson's records have not always justified or reaffirmed his reputation. That is not the case with the cuts on this 1984 set, recently reissued by Evidence. The spiraling solos, excellent bridges, turnbacks, pedal maneuvers, and soulful accompaniment are executed with a relaxed edge and confident precision. If you have wondered whether Lucky Peterson deserves the hype and major label bonanza, these songs are the real deal. —*Ron Wynn*

Lucky Strikes / 1989 / Alligator ✦✦✦✦
Peterson's real coming-out party as a mature blues triple threat: his guitar and keyboard skills are prodigious (though he's no longer a child prodigy), and his vocals on "Pounding of My Heart," "Can't Get No Loving on the Telephone," and "Heart Attack" (all written by producer/bassist Bob Greenlee) served notice that more than luck was involved in Peterson's adult rise to fame. —*Bill Dahl*

● **Triple Play** / 1990 / Alligator ✦✦✦✦
Even more impressive than his previous Alligator set, thanks to top-flight material like "Don't Cloud Up on Me," "Let the Chips Fall Where They May," and "Locked Out of Love," the fine house band at Greenlee's King Snake studios, and Peterson's own rapidly developing attack on two instruments. —*Bill Dahl*

I'm Ready / Aug. 1992 / Verve ✦✦✦

Piano Red (William Lee Perryman)

b. Oct. 19, 1911, Hampton, GA, **d.** Jul. 25, 1985, Decatur, GA
Piano, Vocals / Piano Blues
Willie Perryman went by two nicknames during his lengthy career, both of them thoroughly apt. He was known as Piano Red because of his albino skin pigmentation for most of his performing life. But they called him Doctor Feelgood during the '60s, and that's precisely what his raucous, barrelhouse-styled vocals and piano were guaranteed to do: cure anyone's ills and make them feel good. In 1950, Red's big break arrived when he signed with RCA Victor. His debut Victor offering, the typically rowdy "Rockin' with Red," was a huge R&B hit, peaking at No. 5 on *Billboard*'s charts. "Red's Boogie," another pounding rocker from the pianist's first RCA date, also proved a huge smash, as did the rag-tinged "The Wrong Yo Yo," "Just Right Bounce," and "Laying the Boogie" in 1951. Red became an Atlanta mainstay in the clubs and over the radio, recording prolifically for RCA through 1958 both there and in New York.

A 1959 single for Checker called "Get Up Mare" and eight tracks for the tiny Jax label preceded the rise of Red's new guise, Dr. Feelgood & the Interns, who debuted on Columbia's Okeh subsidiary in 1961 with a

self-named rocker, "Doctor Feel-Good," that propelled the aging piano pounder into the pop charts for the first time. Its flipside, "Mister Moonlight" (penned and ostensibly sung by bandmember Roy Lee Johnson), found its way into the repertoire of the Beatles. Red remained ensconced at Muhlenbrink's Saloon in Atlanta from 1969 through 1979, sandwiching in extensive European tours along the way. He was diagnosed with cancer in 1984 and died the following year. —*Bill Dahl*

Jump Man, Jump / 1956 / Groove ✦✦✦✦
Raucous barrelhouse blues and boogies with a hot R&B combo on these swinging sides. —*Bill Dahl*

Atlanta Bounce / 1992 / Arhoolie ✦✦✦
The Doctor's In! / 1993 / Bear Family ✦✦✦✦
As usual, Bear Family does Piano Red up right: four discs packed to the brim with everything you'd ever want or need—the entirety of his 1950-1958 stint at RCA and Groove (including his smashes "Rockin' with Red" and "Right String but the Wrong Yo Yo"); subsequent dates for Checker (six of eight tracks from this 1958 date were previously unreleased), Jax, and Okeh, where he was musically reborn as Dr. Feelgood and the Interns in 1961 and rocked unrepentantly on his signature "Doctor Feel-Good," "What's Up Doc," and "Bald-Headed Lena." A nonstop good time—no easy task over four jam-packed discs! —*Bill Dahl*

● **Wildfire** / Matchbox ✦✦✦✦
A dozen tracks of Red at his poundin' best. —*Cub Koda*

Professor Longhair (Henry Roeland Byrd)

b. Dec. 19, 1918, Bogalusa, LA, **d.** Jan. 30, 1980, New Orleans, LA
Piano, Vocals / Rock & Roll, New Orleans R&B
Justly worshipped a decade-and-a-half after his death as a founding father of New Orleans R&B, Roy "Professor Longhair" Byrd was nevertheless so down-and-out at one point in his long career that he was reduced to sweeping the floors in a record shop that once could have moved his platters by the boxful.

That Fess made such a marvelous comeback testifies to the resiliency of this late legend, whose Latin-tinged rhumba-rocking piano style and croaking, yodeling vocals were as singular and spicy as the second-line beats that power his hometown's musical heartbeat. Byrd brought an irresistible Caribbean feel to his playing, full of rolling flourishes that every Crescent City ivories man had to learn inside out (Fats Domino, Huey Smith, and Allen Toussaint all paid homage early and often).

The pianist made great records for Atlantic in 1949, Federal in 1951, Wasco in 1952, and Atlantic again in 1953 (producing the immortal "Tipitina," a romping "In the Night," and the lyrically impenetrable boogie "Ball the Wall"). After recuperating from a minor stroke, Longhair came back on Lee Rupe's Ebb logo in 1957 with a storming "No Buts—No Maybes." He revived his "Go to the Mardi Gras" for Joe Ruffino's Ron imprint in 1959; this is the version that surfaces every year at Mardi Gras in New Orleans.

Other than the ambitiously arranged "Big Chief" in 1964 for Watch Records, the '60s held little charm for Longhair. He hit the skids, abandoning his piano playing until a booking at the fledgling 1971 Jazz & Heritage Festival put him on the comeback trail. He made a slew of albums in the last decade of his life, topped off by a terrific set for Alligator, *Crawfish Fiesta*.

Longhair triumphantly appeared on the PBS-TV concert series *Soundstage* (with Dr. John, Earl King, and the Meters), co-starred in the documentary *Piano Players Rarely Ever Play Together* (which became a memorial tribute when Longhair died in the middle of its filming; funeral footage was included), and saw a group of his admirers buy a local watering hole in 1977 and rechristen it Tipitina's after his famous song. He played there regularly when he wasn't on the road; it remains a thriving operation.

Longhair went to bed on January 30, 1980, and never woke up. A heart attack in the night stilled one of New Orleans' seminal R&B stars, but his music is played in his hometown so often and so reverently, you'd swear he was still around. —*Bill Dahl*

Rock 'n' Roll Gumbo / 1977 / Dancing Cat ✦✦✦✦
It features great renditions of New Orleans standards such as "Junco Partner" and "Rockin' Pneumonia" with an all-star band that features Clarence "Gatemouth" Brown on guitar and violin. —*Bruce Boyd Raeburn*

Crawfish Fiesta / 1980 / Alligator ✦✦✦✦
Probably the best of all the many albums Longhair waxed during his comeback. A tremendously tight combo featuring three horns and Dr. John on guitar delightfully back the Professor every step of the way as he recasts Solomon Burke's "Cry to Me" and Fats Domino's "Whole Lotta Loving" in his own indelible image and roars, yodels, and whistles out wonderful remakes of his own oldies "Big Chief" and "Bald Head." —*Bill Dahl*

New Orleans Piano / 1989 / Atlantic ✦✦✦✦
All 16 of the Atlantic sides from 1949 and 1953 (including a handful of alternate takes) on one glorious disc. Longhair's work for the label was

notoriously marvelous—this version of "Mardi Gras in New Orleans" reeks of revelry in the streets of the French Quarter; "She Walks Right In" and "Walk Your Blues Away" ride a bedrock boogie, and "In the Night" bounces atop a parade-beat shuffle groove and hard-charging saxes. —*Bill Dahl*

Mardi Gras in Baton Rouge / 1991 / Rhino ✦✦✦✦
Some of the earliest sides from Longhair's rediscovery period (1971-72), featuring a lot of tunes inexorably associated with him through previous versions and a few ("Jambalaya," "Sick and Tired") that weren't. An added bonus is the magical presence of guitarist Snooks Eaglin, whose approach is every bit as singular as the Professor's was. —*Bill Dahl*

★ **Fess: Professor Longhair Anthology** / 1993 / Rhino ✦✦✦✦✦
The rhumba-rocking rhythms of Roy "Professor Longhair" Byrd live on throughout Rhino's 40-track retrospective of the New Orleans icon's amazing legacy. Most of the seminal stuff arrives early on: "Bald Head," the rollicking ode Byrd cut for Mercury in 1950, is followed by a raft of classics from his 1949 and 1953 Atlantic dates ("Tipitina," "Ball the Wall," "Who's Been Fooling You"), the storming 1957 "No Buts—No Maybes" and "Baby Let Me Hold Your Hand" for Ebb, and his beloved "Go to the Mardi Gras" as waxed for Ron in 1959. The second disc is a hodge-podge of material from his 1970s comeback, all of it wonderful in its own way but not as essential as the early work. —*Bill Dahl*

Houseparty New Orleans Style / 1994 / Rounder ✦✦✦✦
Boiling blues and trademark Afro-Latin and boogie-woogie riffs were the menu when Professor Longhair brought his Crescent City music show to Baton Rouge and Memphis in 1971 and 1972, respectively. The 15 numbers on this set matched the great pianist with an esteemed array of musicians that included outstanding guitarist Snooks Eaglin on both sessions, and fine rhythm sections as well. Eaglin's flashy, inventive solos were excellent contrasts to Longhair's rippling keyboard flurries and distinctive mix of yodels, yells, cries and shouts. —*Ron Wynn*

Snooky Pryor (James Edward Pryor)

b. Sep. 15, 1921, Lambert, MS
Harmonica, Drums, Vocals / Electric Chicago Blues
Only in the last few years has Snooky Pryor finally begun to receive full credit for the mammoth role he played in shaping the amplified Chicago blues harp sound during the postwar era. He's long claimed he was the first harpist to run his sound through a public-address system around the Windy City—and since nobody's around to refute the claim at this point, we'll have to accept it! He's still quite active musically, having cut two potent discs for Austin, TX-based Antone's Records in recent years.

He hit Chicago for the first time in 1940, later serving in the Army at nearby Fort Sheridan. Playing his harp through powerful PA systems gave Pryor the idea to acquire his own portable rig once he left the service. Armed with a primitive amp, he dazzled the folks on Maxwell Street in late 1945 with his massively amplified harp.

Pryor made some groundbreaking 78s during the immediate postwar Chicago blues era. Teaming with guitarist Moody Jones, he waxed "Telephone Blues" and "Boogie" for Planet Records in 1948, encoring the next year with "Boogy Fool"/"Raisin' Sand" for JOB with Jones on bass and guitarist Baby Face Leroy Foster in support. Pryor made more more classic sides for JOB (1952-53), Parrot (1953), and Vee-Jay ("Someone to Love Me"/"Judgment Day") in 1956, but commercial success never materialized. He wound down his blues-playing in the early '60s, finally chucking it all and moving to downstate Ullin, IL, in 1967.

For a long while, Pryor's whereabouts were unknown. But the 1987 Blind Pig album, *Snooky,* produced by guitarist Steve Freund, announced to the world that the veteran harpist was alive and well, his chops still honed. —*Bill Dahl*

★ **Snooky Pryor** / 1969 / Paula/Flyright ✦✦✦✦✦
If anyone doubts the longevity and journeyman greatness of Snooky Pryor, this collection of sides should do much to quiet them. Starting with the 1947 Floyd Jones (the classic "Stockyard Blues") and Johnny Young sessions for Old Swingmaster with Snooky in support and running right from the early '50s into the early '60s sides for the JOB label with "Boogie Twist" (his Vee-Jay and Parrot sides are not here), this is ground-floor Chicago blues one step removed from Maxwell Street. Lots of unissued sides—all of them great—plus the inclusion of the instrumental "Boogie," which became the blueprint for Little Walter's hit "Juke." Pryor's finest moments on wax. —*Cub Koda*

In This Mess up to My Chest / 1994 / Antone's ✦✦✦✦
Pryor reaffirms his mastery of postwar blues harp over the course of this sturdy set, again done with the help of some fine Texas and Chicago players. Pryor's downhome vocals shine on the distinctive "Bury You in a Paper Sack" and "Stick Way Out Behind." —*Bill Dahl*

Snooky / Blind Pig ✦✦✦✦
An outstanding comeback effort by Chicago harp pioneer Snooky Pryor, whose timeless sound meshed well with a Windy City trio led by pro-

ducer/guitarist Steve Freund for this set. Mostly Pryor's own stuff—"Why You Want to Do Me like That," "That's the Way to Do It," "Cheatin' and Lyin'"—with his fat-toned harp weathering the decades quite nicely. —*Bill Dahl*

Hand Me Down Blues / Relic ✦✦✦✦
A nice 16-track compilation of rare blues material from the Parrot label, this features both sides of Snooky's lone single for the label, "Crosstown Blues" and "I Want You for Yourself." Also features obscure and unissued tracks by Little Willie Foster ("Four Day Jump"), Dusty Brown ("Yes She's Gone"), John Brim ("Gary Stomp"), Sunnyland Slim ("Devil Is a Busy Man"), early Albert King ("Little Boy Blue" and the title track), plus Henry Gray with four previously unissued sides, all of them sloppy and great. —*Cub Koda*

Ma Rainey (Gertrude Rainey)

b. Apr. 26, 1886, Columbus, GA, **d.** Dec. 22, 1939, Columbus, GA
Vocals / Classic Female Blues
Ma Rainey wasn't the first blues singer to make records, but by all rights she probably should have been. In an era when women were the marquee names in blues, Ma Rainey was once the most celebrated of all—the "Mother of the Blues" had been singing the music for more than 20 years before she made her recording debut (Paramount, 1923). With the advent of blues records, she became even more influential, immortalizing such songs as "See See Rider," "Bo-Weevil Blues," and "Ma Rainey's Black Bottom." Like the other classic blues divas, she had a repertoire of pop and minstrel songs as well as blues, but she maintained a heavier, tougher vocal delivery than the cabaret blues singers who followed. Ma Rainey's records featured her with jug bands, guitar duos, and bluesmen such as Tampa Red and Blind Blake, in addition to the more customary horns-and-piano jazz-band accompaniment (occasionally including such luminaries as Louis Armstrong, Kid Ory, and Fletcher Henderson).

In 1923, Ma Rainey signed a contract with Paramount Records. Although her recording career lasted a mere six years—her final sessions were in 1928—she recorded more than 100 songs and many of them, including "C.C. Rider" and "Bo Weevil Blues," became genuine blues classics. During these sessions, she was supported by some of the most talented blues and jazz musicians of her era, including Louis Armstrong, Fletcher Henderson, Coleman Hawkins, Buster Bailey, and Lovie Austin.

Rainey's recordings and performances were extremely popular among Black audiences, particularly in the South. After reaching the height of her popularity in the late '20s, Rainey's career faded away in the early '30s as female blues singing became less popular with the blues audience. She retired from performing in 1933, settling down in her hometown of Columbus. In 1939, Ma Rainey died of a heart attack. She left behind an immense recorded legacy, which continued to move and influence successive generations of blues, country, and rock 'n' roll musicians. In 1983, Rainey was inducted into the Blues Foundation's Hall of Fame; seven years later, she was inducted into the Rock & Roll Hall of Fame. —*Jim O'Neal and Stephen Thomas Erlewine*

★ **Ma Rainey's Black Bottom** / Jun. 1975 / Milestone ✦✦✦✦✦
The archetypical "classic" blues femme belter on 1924-1928 recordings, with Fletcher Henderson on piano and Coleman Hawkins bass sax on two tracks. —*Mark A. Humphrey*

A. C. Reed

b. May 9, 1926, Wardell, MO, **d.** 1976
Saxophone, Vocals / Electric Chicago Blues
One of a handful of sax players to ever assume a featured role as singer/bandleader in Chicago blues, Aaron Corthen once based his act on a reputed relationship with Jimmy Reed, going so far as to assume the last name in addition to the musical posture. After years of sideman duty with Buddy Guy, Albert Collins, and others, recording occasional singles along the way, A. C. hit his songwriting wit to the fore and came up with a successful new persona—that of the anti-blues bluesman. Coproducing his own albums with sidekick Casey Jones, Reed has become noted for titles such as "Take These Blues and Shove 'Em," "I Am Fed Up with This Music," and "I'm in the Wrong Business." Despite the comic-yet-sincere sentiments expressed, Reed has remained a bluesman through and through. —*Jim O'Neal*

Take These Blues and Shove 'Em / 1982 / Rooster Blues ✦✦✦
The first of the saxist's humorous diatribes detailing his tongue-in-cheek hatred of his life's calling. His argument doesn't hold water, though, since the LP is so refreshingly funky ("I Am Fed Up with This Music" remains a bandstand staple for him) and enjoyable. Drummer Casey Jones, Reed's longtime bandmate behind Albert Collins, co-produced with the sardonic horn man. —*Bill Dahl*

● **I'm in the Wrong Business** / 1987 / Alligator ✦✦✦✦
Solid, soulful blues, often with humorous, self-deprecating lyrics, comes

from the well-respected vocalist, tenor player, composer, and veteran of the bands of Albert Collins, Buddy Guy, Magic Sam, and Son Seals. Reed has been called "the definitive Chicago blues sax player." This album features Reed's band, with guests Bonnie Raitt and Stevie Ray Vaughan. —*Niles J. Frantz*

Jimmy Reed (Mathis James Reed)

b. Sep. 6, 1925, Dunleith, MS, **d.** Aug. 29, 1976, Oakland, CA
Guitar, Harmonica, Vocals / R&B, Electric Chicago Blues
There's simply no sound in the blues as easily digestible, accessible, instantly recognizable and as easy to play and sing as the music of Jimmy Reed. His best-known songs—"Baby, What You Want Me to Do," "Bright Lights, Big City," "Honest I Do," "You Don't Have to Go," "Going to New York," "Ain't That Lovin' You Baby," and "Big Boss Man"—have become such an integral part of the standard blues repertoire, it's almost as if they have existed forever. Because his style was simple and easily imitated, his songs were accessible to just about everyone from high school garage bands having a go at it to Elvis Presley, Charlie Rich, Lou Rawls, Hank Williams, Jr., and the Rolling Stones, making him—in the long run—perhaps the most influential bluesman of all. His bottom string boogie rhythm guitar patterns (all furnished by boyhood friend and longtime musical partner Eddie Taylor), simple two-string turnarounds, countryish harmonica solos (all played in a neck rack attachment hung around his neck) and mush-mouthed vocals were probably the first exposure most White folks had to the blues. And his music—lazy, loping, and insistent and constantly built and reconstructed single after single on the same sturdy frame—was a formula that proved to be enormously successful and influential, both with middle-aged Blacks and young White audiences for a good dozen years. Jimmy Reed records hit the R&B charts with amazing frequency and crossed over onto the pop charts on many occasions, a rare feat for an unreconstructed bluesman. This is all the more amazing simply because Reed's music was nothing special on the surface; he possessed absolutely no technical expertise on either of his chosen instruments and his vocals certainly lacked the fierce declamatory intensity of Howlin' Wolf or Muddy Waters. But it was exactly that lack of in-your-face musical confrontation that made Jimmy Reed a welcome addition to everybody's record collection back in the '50s and '60s.

Reed was born on September 6, 1925, on a plantation in or around the small burg of Dunleith, MS. He stayed around the area until he was 15, learning the rudiments of harmonica and guitar from his buddy Eddie Taylor, who was then making a name for himself as a semi-pro musician. Reed moved to Chicago in 1943 but was quickly drafted into the Navy, where he served for two years. After a quick trip back to Mississippi and marriage to his beloved Mary (known to blues fans as "Mama Reed"), he relocated to Gary, IN, and found work at an Armour Foods meat packing plant while simultaneously breaking into the burgeoning blues scene around Gary and neighboring Chicago. The early '50s found him working as a sideman with John Brim's Gary Kings and playing on the street for tips with Willie Joe Duncan, a shadowy figure who played an amplified, homemade one-string instrument called a unitar. After failing an audition with Chess Records (his later chart success would be a constant thorn in the side of the firm), Brim's drummer at the time—improbably enough, future blues guitar legend Albert King—brought him to the newly formed Vee-Jay Records, where his first recordings were made. It was during this time that he started playing again with Eddie Taylor, a musical partnership that would last off and on until Reed's death. Success was slow in coming, but when his third single, "You Don't Have to Go" backed with "Boogie in the Dark," made the No. 5 slot on *Billboard*'s R&B charts, the hits pretty much kept on coming for the next decade.

While revisionist blues historians like to make a big deal about either the lack of variety of his work or how later recordings turned him into a mere parody of himself, the public just couldn't get enough of it. Jimmy Reed placed 11 songs on the *Billboard* Hot 100 pop charts and 14 on the R&B charts, a figure that even a much more sophisticated artist like B.B. King couldn't top. To paraphrase the old saying, nobody liked Jimmy Reed but the people.

Reed's slow descent into the ravages of alcoholism and epilepsy roughly paralleled the decline of Vee-Jay Records, which went out of business at approximately the same time that his final 45 was released, "Don't Think I'm Through." His manager, Al Smith, quickly arranged a contract with the newly formed ABC-Bluesway label, and a handful of albums were released into the '70s, all of them sounding as if they had been cut on a musical assembly line. Jimmy did one last album, a horrible attempt to update his sound with funk beats and wah-wah pedals, before becoming a virtual recluse in his final years. He finally received proper medical attention for his epilepsy and quit drinking, but it was too late and he died trying to make a comeback on the blues festival circuit on August 29, 1976.

All of this is sad beyond belief, simply because there's so much joy in Jimmy Reed's music. And it's that joy that becomes evident every time

you give one of his classic sides a spin. Although his bare-bones style influenced everyone from British Invasion combos to the entire school of Louisiana swamp blues artists (Slim Harpo and Jimmy Anderson in particular), the simple indisputable fact remains that—like so many of the other originators in the genre—there was only one Jimmy Reed. —*Cub Koda*

★ **Live at Carnegie Hall/Best of Jimmy Reed** / 1961 / Mobile Fidelity ✦✦✦✦✦
Not a live album at all, this is actually two LPs of Reed's finest studio efforts for Vee-Jay. —*Bill Dahl*

Jimmy Reed / 1965 / Paula/Flyright ✦✦✦

Classic Recordings / 1995 / Tomato ✦✦✦✦
This three-CD, 55-song box is the most comprehensive domestic retrospective of Reed's career (a six-CD box is available on import). The material is fine and consistent, but this isn't the best deal for either the average fan or the completist. Reed is one of the most homogenous blues greats, and unless your interest is deep, three CDs at once will become monotonous; you're better off with one of the several fine single-disc compilations available. Also, this has no information whatsoever on release dates or sessions, and inexplicably omits one of his two Top 40 hits, "Honest I Do" (covered by the Rolling Stones on their first album). —*Richie Unterberger*

★ **Speak the Lyrics to Me, Mama Reed** / Vee-Jay ✦✦✦✦✦
Although many *Best of Jimmy Reed* compilations exist on the market (most with variable sound quality and maddening duplication), this 25-tracker is currently the one to beat. Including all the influential hits and a few of the best rare ones ("You Upset My Mind" and the single version of "Little Rain," different than the take on his debut album), this features impeccable sound (except on the disc transfer of Reed's first single, "High and Lonesome") and is the perfect place to start. —*Cub Koda*

Sonny Rhodes

b. Nov. 3, 1940, Smithville, TX
Bass, Guitar, Steel Guitar, Vocals / Modern Electric Blues
Blues guitarist, singe,r and songwriter Sonny Rhodes is such a talented songwriter, so full of musical ideas, that he's destined to inherit the seats left open by the untimely passing of blues greats like Albert King and Albert Collins.

Rhodes recorded a single for Domino Records in Austin, "I'll Never Let You Go When Something Is Wrong," in 1958, while he was serving in the Navy. Rhodes returned to California while in his mid-20s, and lived in Fresno for a few years before hooking up a deal with Galaxy Records in Oakland. In 1966, he recorded a single, "I Don't Love You No More." He recorded another single for Galaxy in 1967 and then in 1978, out of total frustration with the San Francisco Bay Area record companies, he recorded "Cigarette Blues" on his own Rhodesway label. Rhodes toured Europe in 1976, and that opened a whole new European market to him. In desperation again, Rhodes went into the studio again to record an album in 1985, *Just Blues*, on his own Rhodesway label.

Fortunately, things have been on track for Rhodes since the late '80s, when he began recording first for the Ichiban label and later for Kingsnake. —*Richard Skelly*

Disciple of the Blues / 1991 / Ichiban ✦✦✦✦
This be-turbaned bluesman plays lap steel guitar. This is a good one, but he's got an even better one in him. —*Niles J. Frantz*

● **Livin' Too Close to the Edge** / 1992 / Ichiban ✦✦✦✦
Livin' Too Close to the Edge is an exciting, blistering set of contemporary blues, drivin by Sonny Rhodes' innovative lap steel playing. —*Thom Owens*

Tommy Ridgley

b. Oct. 30, 1925, New Orleans, LA
Piano, Vocals / R&B, Electric New Orleans Blues, Dixieland
Tommy Ridgley has been right with the New Orleans rhythm and blues movement ever since the early Imperial recording era, achieving his share of local renown and regional success despite a lack of national hits. Influenced in his younger days by the blues-shouting style of Roy Brown and Big Joe Turner, Ridgley eventually became known for his ballad singing; a similarity to Chuck Willis also earned him the title "The New King of the Stroll." After recording for Imperial, Atlantic, and Herald, Ridgley turned to local New Orleans labels in the '60s. After an ensuing lull, he has been recording again in recent years and is still a talent to be reckoned with. —*Jim O'Neal*

● **The New Orleans King of the Stroll** / 1988 / Rounder ✦✦✦✦
Tommy Ridgley was a solid R&B vocalist who was quite successful with novelty tunes and silly songs, but was also a good romantic balladeer. This 15-track collection mostly covers Ridgley material from 1960 to 1964 for the Ric label, and ranges from laments like "Please Hurry Home" and "I Love You Yes I Do" to such comic material and dance-

based numbers as "Double Eyed Whammy" and "The Girl from Kooka Monga." Ridgley wasn't as booming or dynamic as some other Crescent City vocalists, but he made several nice period pieces and soul tunes, several of which are on this set. —*Ron Wynn*

Since the Blues Began / 1995 / Black Top ◆◆◆◆
The veteran New Orleans singer remains a contemporary force to be reckoned with. Guitarist Snooks Eaglin, bassist George Porter, Jr., and saxist Kaz Kazanoff help Ridgley out on what's easily his finest contemporary release. There are a handful of remakes of his earlier triumphs, but for the most part, he is commendably living in the present, incorporating funk-tinged rhythms into his delectable musical gumbo. —*Bill Dahl*

The Herald Recordings / Collectables ◆◆◆◆
There's some very nice late-'50s New Orleans R&B recommending this 17-track collection, along with a few superfluous instrumental backing tracks that could have safely been jettisoned altogether. Ridgley's stint at Herald included the sizzling "When I Meet My Girl," "Baby Do Little," and several more impressive rocking efforts, backed by the esteemed crew at Cosimo's Crescent City studio—saxist Lee Allen, etc. —*Bill Dahl*

Fenton Robinson

b. Sep. 23, 1935, Minter City, MS
Guitar, Vocals / Modern Electric Blues, Chicago Blues
"The Mellow Blues Genius," as his Japanese fans have dubbed him, is a widely praised and honored artist, yet Robinson has had to struggle financially throughout a career that has most often found him an undeniably distinctive and original stylist in search of a market. After recording in a Memphis-based blues style early in his career (Meteor, 1957, and Duke, 1959), Robinson moved from Arkansas to Chicago in 1961 and began staking out his own stylistic territory, one that made use of his extensive and growing knowledge of musical structures and progressions. His well-known "Somebody Loan Me a Dime" (Palos, 1967, later re-recorded for Alligator) was an early culmination of his blues vision. A thinking man of the blues, Robinson seems forever ready to explore something new, continually experimenting with his fluid, jazz-flavored blues, perhaps just too far ahead or too far removed for the rest of the blues world to catch up. —*Jim O'Neal*

★ **Somebody Loan Me a Dime** / 1974 / Alligator ◆◆◆◆◆
One of the most subtly satisfying electric blues albums of the 1970s. Robinson never did quite fit the "Genuine Houserocking Music" image of Alligator Records—his deep, rich baritone sounds more like a magic carpet than a piece of barbed wire, and he speaks in jazz-inflected tongues, full of complex surprises. The title track hits with amazing power, as do the chugging "The Getaway," a hard-swinging "You Say You're Leaving," and the minor-key "You Don't Know What Love Is." In every case, Robinson had recorded them before, but thanks to Bruce Iglauer's superb production, a terrific band, and Robinson's musicianship, these versions reign supreme. —*Bill Dahl*

I Hear Some Blues Downstairs / 1977 / Alligator ◆◆◆
A disappointment in its inconsistency following such a mammoth triumph as his previous set, yet not without its mellow delights. The title track is atypically playful; Robinson's revisiting of the mournful "As the Years Go Passing By" is a moving journey, and his T-Bone Walker tribute "Tell Me What's the Reason" swings deftly. On the other hand, a superfluous remake of Rosco Gordon's "Just a Little Bit" goes nowhere, and nobody really needed another "Killing Floor." —*Bill Dahl*

Nightflight / 1984 / Alligator ◆◆◆
For the most part, another easygoing trip to the mellower side of contemporary blues, Robinson's jazzy tone and buttery vocals applied to a couple of his '50s-era numbers ("Crazy Crazy Lovin'" and "Schoolboy") along with some intriguing new items and Lowell Fulson's mournful "Sinner's Prayer." Tasty backing helps, too. —*Bill Dahl*

Special Road / Apr. 1989 / Evidence ◆◆◆

Jimmy Rogers (James A. Lane)

b. Jun. 3, 1924, Ruleville, MS
Guitar, Harmonica, Piano, Vocals / R&B, Electric Chicago Blues
Guitarist Jimmy Rogers is the last living connection to the groundbreaking first Chicago band of Muddy Waters (informally dubbed the Headhunters for their penchant of dropping by other musicians' gigs and "cutting their heads" with a superior onstage performance). Instead of basking in worldwide veneration, he's merely a well-respected Chicago elder boasting a seminal 1950s Chess Records catalog, both behind Waters and on his own. Rogers made his recorded debut as a leader in 1947 for the tiny Ora-Nelle logo, then saw his efforts for Regal and Apollo lie unissued.

Those labels' monumental errors in judgment were the gain of Leonard Chess, who recognized the comparatively smooth-voiced Rogers' potential as a blues star in his own right. (He first played with Muddy Waters on an Aristocrat 78 in 1949 and remained his indispens-

able rhythm guitarist on wax into 1955.) With Walter and bassist Big Crawford laying down support, Rogers' debut Chess single in 1950, "That's All Right," has earned standard status after countless covers, but his version still reigns supreme.

In 1955, Rogers left Muddy Waters to venture out as a bandleader, cutting another gem, "You're the One," for Chess. He made his only appearance on *Billboard*'s R&B charts in early 1957 with the driving "Walking by Myself," which boasted a stunning harp solo from Big Walter Horton (a last-second stand-in for no-show Good Rockin' Charles). The tune itself was an adaptation of a T-Bone Walker tune, "Why Not," that Rogers had played rhythm guitar on when Walker cut it for Atlantic. By 1957, blues was losing favor at Chess, the label reaping the rewards of rock via Chuck Berry and Bo Diddley. Rogers' platters slowed to a trickle, though his 1959 Chess farewell, "Rock This House," ranked with his most exciting outings (Reggie Boyd's light-fingered guitar wasn't the least of its charms).

Rogers virtually retired from music for a time during the 1960s, operating a West Side clothing shop that burned down in the aftermath of Dr. Martin Luther King's tragic assassination. He returned to the studio in 1972 for Leon Russell's Shelter logo, cutting his first LP, *Gold-Tailed Bird* (with help from the Aces and Freddie King). There have been a few more fine albums since then, notably *Ludella*, a 1990 set for Antone's. —*Bill Dahl*

Sloppy Drunk / Dec. 8, 1973-Dec. 15, 1973 / Black & Blue ◆◆◆

★ **Chicago Bound** / 1976 / MCA/Chess ◆◆◆◆◆
The logical place to inaugurate any Rogers collection is this perennially acclaimed 14-song retrospective of the guitarist's 1950s Chess years. Most of the big ones are here for your perusal: "That's All Right," "Sloppy Drunk," "You're the One," "Walking by Myself," and the thundering title track. Peerless band support from the likes of Muddy Waters, Little Walter, Otis Spann, and Walter Horton. This is a cornerstone of Chicago blues history. —*Bill Dahl*

☆ **That's All Right** / 1989 / Charly ◆◆◆◆◆
Quite a few important items from Rogers' classic Chess catalog that aren't on *Chicago Bound* turn up on this 24-track British import (along with the prerequisite hits, natch), notably a torrid "Rock This House" (Reggie Boyd's mercurial guitar solos are stunning), the downcast "The World's in a Tangle," a rhumba-beat "My Baby Don't Love Me No More" with a tremendous Walter Horton harp solo, and the bizarre "My Last Meal." —*Bill Dahl*

Ludella / 1990 / Antone's ◆◆◆◆
One of the most enriching contemporary items in Rogers' growing album catalog. Combining studio tracks with live performances, the set treads heavily on the past, with loving renditions of "Rock This House," "Ludella," "Sloppy Drunk," and "Chicago Bound." Kim Wilson proves a worthy harp disciple of Little Walter, while bassist Bob Stroger and drummer Ted Harveylay down supple grooves behind the blues great. —*Bill Dahl*

Chicago Blues Masters, Vol. 2 / 1995 / Capitol ◆◆◆◆
Rogers reemerged after a long layoff with a 1972 album for Leon Russell's Shelter label called *Gold Tailed Bird*. It wasn't the equivalent of his immortal Chess stuff, but the Shelter sides, here in their entirety, are pretty decent themselves (and no wonder, with the Aces, Freddy King, and reliable Chicago pianist Bob Riedy all involved). A few extra numbers not on the original Shelter LP make this 18-song set even more solid. —*Bill Dahl*

Otis Rush

b. Apr. 29, 1934, Philadelphia, MS
Guitar, Vocals / Soul, R&B, Electric Chicago Blues
Breaking into the R&B Top Ten his very first time out in 1956 with the startlingly intense slow blues "I Can't Quit You Baby," southpaw guitarist Otis Rush subsequently established himself as one of the premier bluesmen on the Chicago circuit. He remains so today.

Rush is often credited with being one of the architects of the West side guitar style, along with Magic Sam and Buddy Guy. It's a nebulous honor, since Otis Rush played clubs on Chicago's South Side just as frequently during the sound's late-'50s incubation period. Nevertheless, his status as a prime Chicago innovator is eternally assured by the ringing, vibrato-enhanced guitar work that remains his stock-in-trade and a tortured, super-intense vocal delivery that can force the hairs on the back of your neck upwards in silent salute.

Rush came to Chicago in 1948, met Muddy Waters, and knew instantly what he wanted to do with the rest of his life. The omnipresent Willie Dixon caught Rush's act and signed him to Eli Toscano's Cobra Records in 1956. The frighteningly intense "I Can't Quit You Baby" was the maiden effort for both artist and label, streaking to No. 6 on *Billboard*'s R&B chart.

His 1956-58 Cobra legacy is a magnificent one, distinguished by the Dixon-produced minor-key masterpieces "Double Trouble" and "My

Love Will Never Die," the nails-tough "Three Times a Fool" and "Keep on Loving Me Baby," and the rhumba-rocking classic "All Your Love (I Miss Loving)." Rush apparently dashed off the latter tune in the car en route to Cobra's West Roosevelt Road studios, where he would cut it with the nucleus of Ike Turner's combo.

After Cobra closed up shop, Rush's recording fortunes mostly floundered. Finally, in 1994, the career of this Chicago blues legend began traveling in the right direction. *Ain't Enough Comin' In,* his first studio album in 16 years, was released on Mercury and ended up topping many blues critics' year-end lists. Produced spotlessly by John Porter with a skin-tight band, Rush roared a set of nothing but covers—but did them all his way, his blistering guitar consistently to the fore.

Once again, a series of personal problems threatened to end Rush's long-overdue return to national prominence before it got off the ground. But he's been in top-notch form the last year-and-a-half, fronting a tight band that's entirely sympathetic to the guitarist's sizzling approach. Rush recently signed with the House of Blues' fledgling record label, instantly granting that company a large dose of credibility and setting himself up for another large-scale career push when the album is completed.

It still may not be too late for Otis Rush to assume his rightful throne as Chicago's blues king. —*Bill Dahl*

Mourning in the Morning / Aug. 1969 / Atlantic ✦✦✦
Panned by many a critic upon its 1969 release, Otis Rush's trip to Muscle Shoals sounds pretty fine now. The house band (including Duane Allman and drummer Roger Hawkins) picks up on Rush's harrowing vibe and runs with it on the stunning "Gambler's Blues," a chomping "Feel So Bad," and a shimmering instrumental treatment of Aretha Franklin's "Baby I Love You." —*Bill Dahl*

Door to Door (With Albert King) / Jun. 1970 / MCA/Chess ✦✦✦✦
Although Albert King is pictured on the front cover and has the lion's share of tracks on this excellent compilation, six of the 14 tracks come from Rush's shortlived tenure with the label and are some of his very best. Chronologically, these are his next recordings after the Cobra sides; and they carry a lot of the emotional wallop of those tracks, albeit with much loftier production values, with much of it recorded in early stereo. Oddly enough, some of the material ("All Your Love," "I'm Satisfied [Keep on Loving Me Baby]") were remakes—albeit great ones—of tunes that Cobra had already released as singles! But Rush's performance of "So Many Roads" (featuring one of the greatest slow blues guitar solos of all time) should not be missed at any cost. —*Cub Koda*

Screamin' and Cryin' / Nov. 26, 1974 / Evidence ✦✦✦

Cold Day in Hell / 1976 / Delmark ✦✦✦
Inconsistent but sometimes riveting 1975 studio set that hits some high highs (a crunchy "Cut You a Loose," the lickety-split jazzy instrumental "Motoring Along") right alongside some incredibly indulgent moments. But that's Otis—the transcendent instants are worth the hassle. —*Bill Dahl*

Right Place, Wrong Time / Feb. 1976 / Hightone ✦✦✦✦
Among the undisputed high points in Rush' checkered career is this 1971 studio set, originally done for Capitol (who astonishingly took a pass on the finished product). Rush has seldom sounded more convincing vocally than on the title track, and his surging reading of Ike Turner's "I'm Tore Up" rates with his best uptempo vehicles. —*Bill Dahl*

Live in Europe / Oct. 1977 / Evidence ✦✦✦✦
Recorded in France, this ten song-set finds Otis backed by strong trio support throughout in a delightfully engaged performance. Though several live albums exist, seldomhave his declamatory vocals and stinging left-handed upside down guitar style been so well documented. Rush puts forth solo after solo, each with its own unique set of twists and turns, making this a veritable textbook of what he does best. Inspired listening and highly recommended. —*Cub Koda*

★ **Cobra Recordings, 1956-1958** / 1989 / Paula/Flyright ✦✦✦✦✦
Otis Rush's debut recordings for the Cobra label are defining moments of Chicago blues. Seldom had a young Windy City artist recorded with this much harrowing emotion in both his singing and playing, simultaneously connecting with the best that Delta blues had to offer while plunging headlong into the electric future. These are the songs that continue to be the building blocks of his legend; "All Your Love," "Double Trouble," "I Can't Quit You, Baby," "Groaning The Blues," "It Takes Time," and "Checking On My Baby" are all masterpieces. This single-disc collection features all 16 Cobra sides issued as singles plus the bonus of four alternate takes, all presented here with the best sound to date. These are milestone recordings in the history of the blues and an essential part of anyone's collection. —*Cub Koda*

Ain't Enough Comin' In / 1994 / This Way Up ✦✦✦✦
With sympathetic production from John Porter, a great lineup of players who follow him every bluesy turn of the way, and a dozen well-chosen pieces of material, Rush wipes the "uninspired album" slate clean with this one. Everything that makes Otis a unique master of his form is here

to savor, from his passionate vocals to the shimmering finger vibrato he applies to the liquid tones of his Fender Stratocaster. While Rush has tackled some of this material on other outings, never has it been served up as passionately as it is here. Even the re-cut of his famous Duke 45 "Homework" burns with a new intensity that makes you believe that this is one opportunity that Rush—at least this time—refused to let go by the boards. —*Cub Koda*

So Many Roads: Live / Aug. 1, 1995 / Delmark ✦✦✦✦
There's a pile of Otis Rush live albums in the bins now, but this was the one that made everybody sit up and take notice and it's still his best. Recorded live outdoors in a Tokyo park in the summer of 1975 with thousands of fans hanging on every note and word, Otis digs deep and delivers some of the most inspired singing and playing he's ever committed to magnetic tape. All the performances are of a nice, comfortable length, with none of the interminable soloing that mars other Rush live sets. This is the one to have. —*Cub Koda*

Saffire

Group / Modern Acoustic Blues
The women from Saffire at one point in the early '90s just considered themselves blues historians, but since their performing career has gotten launched on the festival circuit, they've become much more than that. All three have developed into talented songwriters. Since blues fans are always looking for fresh themes or new twists on old themes, this trio is a sought-after club and festival act. The core members of this Virginia-based group include pianist Ann Rabson (b. April 12, 1945) and Gaye Adegbalola (b. March 21, 1944), and while the trio was accompanied for a while by bassist Earlene Lewis, she has since left the group. Lewis was replaced by mandolinist Andra Faye McIntosh, also from the Washington, D.C./Virginia area. The group's fundamental appeal—to growing numbers of music fans who don't know much about blues—is their original songs and their ability to dig up and reinterpret old blues gems from the 1920s and '30s. They specialize in songs made by the sassy original blues divas including Bessie Smith, Ma Rainey, Memphis Minnie, and Ida Cox. —*Richard Skelly*

The Middle Aged Blues / 1989 / Saffire ✦✦✦

The Uppity Blues Women / 1990 / Alligator ✦✦✦
Saffire's debut album, *The Uppity Blues Women,* takes the best moments from their independently released tape and adds a number of songs that weren't on the cassette. The result is a stronger, funnier, and heartfelt record. It doesn't hurt that Alligator could give the group a clean production, where their voices simply leap out from the speakers. The result is an album that provides a boisterous and thought-provoking listen. —*Thom Owens*

● **Hot Flash** / 1991 / Alligator ✦✦✦✦
In many ways, *Hot Flash* is the definitive Saffire album. Racy and sassy—and to some tastes cutesy—the album is a fun, free-thinking update of classic female blues, performed with gusto and verve. The instrumentation is sparse—a piano, guitar, bass, harmonica, and kazoo provide the foundation of the music—but the focus of these songs is solely on the vocals, which are vigorous and humorous and if you share Saffire's sense of humor, it's a rollicking good time. —*Thom Owens*

Satan and Adam

Group / Modern Acoustic Blues
The blues duo of guitarist, singer and songwriter Sterling Magee and harmonica player Adam Gussow have paid their dues. They began their career on the street. On the corner of Seventh Avenue and 125th Street, to be exact, and within a matter of weeks, they were drawing crowds to their corner, people pausing on their way home from work to stop and listen. For five years, nearly every afternoon that weather permitted, the pair would meet on the corner and Magee would set up his simple stool, drum kit, guita,r and amplifier. Using a combination of foot stomps, tambourines, hi-hat cymbals and his guitar, Magee gives the duo a full sound.

Magee and Gussow specialize in funky, gritty, electric urban blues, and there are few groups or artists anywhere who sound anything remotely like them. Gussow's exquisite harmonica solos complement the driving, open-toned guitar playing of Magee, who prefers to be called Mr. Satan, and who frequently refers to Gussow in live performances as Mr. Gussow.

The pair have such a unique sound, it seems they're destined for a major label, given their knowledge and experience with blues. Magee, born May 20, 1936, in Mississippi and raised in Florida, began his career playing piano in churches in both states. Since the early '80s, he's played on Harlem streets, but in the 1960s he was a key session guitarist, playing on recordings by James Brown, King Curtis, George Benson and others. Adam Gussow, born April 3, 1958 and raised in Rockland County, NY, was a Princeton-educated harmonica player who had a little uptown apartment, and in passing Magee one day on the street in

1985, he asked if he could sit in on harmonica. That was the start of a musical and social relationship between the two that continues to this day.

Satan and Adam have redefined and shaped the sound of modern blues so much that "I Want You" from their *Harlem Blues* debut was included on a Rhino Records release, *Modern Blues of the 1990s*. —*Richard Skelly*

● **Harlem Blues** / 1991 / Flying Fish ✦✦✦✦
Harlem Blues sounds exactly like how Satan & Adam would sound playing on a street corner—it's raw and tough, with a surprisingly adventurous streak. Satan & Adam stick to a basic acoustic blues duo, but their rhythms and techniques occasionally stray into funkier, jazzier territory. And that sense of careening unpredictability is what makes *Harlem Blues* so entertaining—they might be playing blues in a traditional style, but the end result is anything but traditional. —*Thom Owens*

Mother Mojo / Jan. 1993 / Flying Fish ✦✦✦
Mother Mojo was an excellent follow-up to Satan & Adam's first-rate debut, *Harlem Blues*. The duo hasn't abandoned their minimalist guitar and harp blues, but there is a loose energy that keeps the music fresh and consistently engaging. —*Thom Owens*

Son Seals

b. Aug. 13, 1942, Osceola, AR
Guitar, Drums, Vocals / Electric Chicago Blues
It all started with a phone call from Wesley Race, who was at the Flamingo Club on Chicago's South Side, to Alligator Records owner Bruce Iglauer. Race was raving about a new find, a young guitarist named Son Seals. He held the phone in the direction of the bandstand, so Iglauer could get an on-site report. It didn't take long for Iglauer to scramble into action. Alligator issued Seals' 1973 eponymous debut album, which was followed by six more.

Seals' jagged, uncompromising guitar riffs and gruff vocals were showcased very effectively on that 1973 debut set, which contained his "Your Love Is like a Cancer" and a raging instrumental called "Hot Sauce." *Midnight Son*, his 1976 encore, was by comparison a much slicker affair, with tight horns, funkier grooves, and a set list that included "Telephone Angel" and "On My Knees." Seals cut a live LP in 1978 at Wise Fools Pub; another studio concoction, *Chicago Fire*, in 1980; and a solid set in 1984, *Bad Axe*, before having a disagreement with Iglauer that was patched up in 1991 with the release of his sixth Alligator set, *Living in the Danger Zone. Nothing but the Truth* followed in 1994.. —*Bill Dahl*

The Son Seals Blues Band / 1973 / Alligator ✦✦✦✦
The Chicago mainstay's debut album was a rough, gruff, no-nonsense affair typified by the decidedly unsentimental track "Your Love Is like a Cancer." Seals wasn't all that far removed from his Southern roots at this point, and his slashing guitar work sports a strikingly raw feel on his originals "Look Now, Baby," "Cotton Picking Blues," and "Hot Sauce" (the latter a blistering instrumental that sounds a bit like the theme from *Batman* played sideways). —*Bill Dahl*

● **Midnight Son** / Jun. 1977 / Alligator ✦✦✦✦
A much more polished set than its predecessor, *Midnight Son* is a particularly effective effort with several numbers that remain in Seals' onstage repertoire to this day—"Telephone Angel," "On My Knees," the jumping "Four Full Seasons of Love." The addition of a brisk horn section enhanced his staccato guitar attack and uncompromising vocals, rendering this his best set to date. —*Bill Dahl*

Live and Burning / 1978 / Alligator ✦✦✦✦
This album lives up to its billing. Seals' smoking set, caught live at Chicago's long-gone (and definitely lamented) Wise Fools Pub, finds him attacking a sharp cross-section of material—Detroit Junior's deliberate "Call My Job," Elmore James' "I Can't Hold Out," his own "Help Me, Somebody"—with an outstanding band in tow: saxist A.C. Reed, guitarist Lacy Gibson, pianist Alberto Gianquinto, bassist Snapper Mitchum, and drummer Tony Gooden. —*Bill Dahl*

Bad Axe / 1984 / Alligator ✦✦✦✦
One of Son Seals' finest collections, studded with vicious performances ranging from covers of Eddie Vinson's "Person to Person" and Little Sonny's "Going Home (Where Women Got Meat on Their Bones)" to his own "Can't Stand to See Her Cry," and the swaggering "Cold Blood." Top-drawer Windy City studio musicians lay down skin-tight grooves throughout. —*Bill Dahl*

Nothing But the Truth / 1994 / Alligator ✦✦✦✦
The grotesque cover illustration is an abomination, but the contents are right in the growling grizzly bear style that we've come to expect. Only four Seals-penned originals, but the R&B-laced "Life Is Hard" and "I'm Gonna Take It All Back" are quality efforts. So is his heartfelt tribute to Hound Dog Taylor, "Sadie." —*Bill Dahl*

Eddie Shaw

b. Mar. 20, 1937, Stringtown, MS
Saxophone / Electric Chicago Blues
When it comes to blues, Chicago's strictly a guitar and harmonica town. Saxophonists who make a living leading a blues band in the Windy City are scarce as hen's teeth. But Eddie Shaw has done precisely that ever since his longtime boss, Howlin' Wolf, died in 1976.

The powerfully constructed tenor saxist has rubbed elbows with an amazing array of luminaries over his 40-plus years in the business. Shaw's own recording career finally took off during the late '70s, with a standout appearance on Alligator's *Living Chicago Blues* anthologies in 1978, his own LPs for Simmons and Rooster Blues, and fine recent discs for Rooster Blues (*In the Land of the Crossroads*) and Austrian Wolf (*Home Alone*). —*Bill Dahl*

Movin' and Groovin' Man / May 14, 1982 / Evidence ✦✦✦
King of the Road / Sep. 1986 / Rooster Blues ✦✦✦✦
A revealing compilation of the ballsy Chicago saxist's earlier work (1966-1984) that certainly deserves to be on CD but isn't yet. "Blues for the West Side" and "Lookin' Good," both with Magic Sam on guitar, are highlights of Shaw's entire career, while his vocal talents are well-served on "It's All Right," an amusing "I Don't Trust Nobody," and his touching tribute "Blues Men of Yesterday." —*Bill Dahl*

● **In the Land of the Crossroads** / 1992 / Rooster Blues ✦✦✦✦
The best contemporary Shaw offering, cut in his old Mississippi stomping grounds with his trusty combo, the Wolf Gang. Lots of lyrically unusual originals—"Dunkin' Donut Woman," "Wine Head Hole," and "She Didn't Tell Me Everything," for starters—and Shaw's usual diamond-hard horn lines and commanding vocals make this a standout selection. —*Bill Dahl*

Kenny Wayne Shepherd

b. Jun. 12, 1977, Shreveport, LA
Guitar, Vocals / Modern Electric Blues
Kenny Wayne Shepherd and his group have exploded onto the scene in the mid-'90s and garnered huge amounts of airplay on commercial radio, which historically has not been a solid home for blues and blues-rock music, with the exception of Stevie Ray Vaughan in the mid-'80s. *Ledbetter Heights*, his first album was an immediate hit, selling more than 500,000 copies by early 1996. Most blues records never achieve that level of commercial success, much less ones released by artists that are still in their teens.

Although Shepherd—who has been influenced by (and has played with) guitarists Stevie Ray Vaughan, Albert King, Slash, Robert Cray, and Duane Allman—is definitely a performer who thrives in front of an audience, *Ledbetter Heights* is impressive for its range of styles: acoustic blues, rockin' blues, Texas blues, Louisiana blues. The only style that he doesn't tackle is Chicago blues, owing to Shepherd's home base smack dab in the middle of the Texas triangle. —*Steve Huey & Richard Skelly*

● **Ledbetter Heights** / Oct. 1995 / Giant ✦✦✦✦
You would never guess from Kenny Wayne Shepherd's fiery playing that the guitarist is still only in his teens. On his debut, *Ledbetter Heights*, Shepherd burns through a set of rather generic blues-rock ravers that are made special by his exceptional technique. It may still be a while before he says something original, but he plays with style, energy, and dedication, which is more than enough for a debut album. —*Thom Owens*

Johnny Shines (John Ned Shines)

b. Apr. 26, 1915, Frayser, TN, d. Apr. 20, 1992, Chicago, IL
Guitar, Vocals / Electric Delta Blues, Acoustic Delta Blues
Johnny Shines' best material crackles with energy. In his prime, his slashing slide guitar carried more of the spirit of his onetime running mate Robert Johnson than any other traditional blues artist. Shines, however, was never a Johnson imitator. He had his own sound, his own guitar style, and a voice that could take you on a roller coaster ride. (However, he did learn from Johnson and his classic recordings. "Ramblin'" and "Dynaflow Blues" feel like Johnson's best work.) Shines had too much personal magnetism to be confused with anyone else. Like many artists of his generation, he was also master of the spoken word, a gifted storyteller, a social critic, and a historian dedicated to telling the truth. On stage or off, he pulled no punches, and his independent spirit and readiness to fight for what he perceived to be fair no doubt ruffled the feathers of the movers and shakers in Chicago's blues business.

Shine's distinctive style and songwriting skills should have brought him fame and fortune in music, but such was not the case. During the '40s and '50s, when he was at his peak, he only issued a handful of records. Although critically acclaimed today, these were not sufficient to keep him in the business at the time. Working outside of music in the '50s and over much of his career, he returned to the studio with Pete Welding in the '60s. These Chicago sessions showed his musical power had not diminished. Subsequent recordings, including his collaboration with Robert Jr. Lockwood, have maintained a high quality. His later guitar work was hampered by a stroke, but he remained a powerful artist sustained by one of the all-time great blues voices, until his death in 1992. —*Barry Lee Pearson*

Last Night Dream / 1968 / Warner Brothers ✦✦✦✦
It's no wonder that this album, cut in 1968 with British blues maven Mike Vernon at the helm, works so well. When you team a rejuvenated Shines with his longtime compadres Horton, Spann, bassist Willie Dixon, and drummer Clifton James, a little blues history was bound to be made. —*Bill Dahl*

Johnny Shines with Big Walter Horton / Nov. 1969 / Testament ✦✦✦✦
Outstanding late-'60s Shines material matching him with a sterling lineup. Big Walter Horton is awesome on harmonica, a young Luther Allison doesn't dissipate his brilliance on haphazard soul and funk, and pianist Otis Spann and drummer Fred Below are super on their cuts. The date combines 1966 and 1969 sessions; there's another LP with a full collection culled from 1966. —*Ron Wynn*

Hey Ba-Ba-Re-Bop / 1978 / Rounder ✦✦✦✦
Delta blues vocalist, guitarist, and composer Johnny Shines hadn't yet encountered the physical difficulties that made his final years so troubling when he recorded the 13 selections on this CD. He could still sing and moan with intensity and passion, hold a crowd hypnotized with his remembrances and asides, and play with a mix of fury and charm. While the menu includes oft-performed chestnuts "Sweet Home Chicago," "Terraplane Blues," and "Milk Cow Blues," there wasn't anything staid or predictable about the way Shines ripped through the lyrics and presented the music. If you missed it the first time around, grab this one immediately. —*Ron Wynn*

★ **Johnny Shines and Robert Lockwood** / 1979 / Paula/Flyright ✦✦✦✦✦
Shines has half of this 20-track disc, the remainder being devoted to sides from the same era featuring Robert Lockwood. Recorded in 1952 and 1953 for the JOB label, this is Shines at his most primal, working with a drumless trio; Big Walter Horton plays harmonica on the 1953 sides. These tracks decidedly outshine the Lockwood efforts (also recorded for JOB in the early '50s), some of which only feature Robert as a sideman. —*Richie Unterberger*

Masters of Modern Blues / 1994 / Testament ✦✦✦✦
After stepping away from the music business altogether for a while, Shines came back strong during the mid-'60s, recording far more prolifically than his first time around. This 1966 date is one of his best, spotlighting his booming pipes and sturdy guitar in front of an all-star Chicago crew: Walter Horton on harp, pianist Otis Spann, and drummer Fred Below. —*Bill Dahl*

Siegel-Schwall Band

Group / Modern Electric Blues, Electric Chicago Blues
Paul Butterfield and Elvin Bishop were not the only White dudes that formed a blues band in Chicago in the early '60s. Siegel and Jim Schwall formed the Siegel-Schwall Band in the mid-'60s in Chicago and worked as a duo playing blues clubs like Pepper's Lounge, where they were the house band. All of the great blues players would sit in—all the time. Corky Siegel played harp and electric Wurlitzer piano, with an abbreviated drum set stashed under the piano; Jim Schwall played guitar and mandolin. Both sang.

The Siegel-Schwall Band approach to music (and blues) was lighter than groups like Butterfield or Musselwhite, representing more of a fusion of blues and more country-oriented material. They seldom played at high volume, stressed group cooperation, and shared the solo spotlight.

When the Butterfield band left their in gig at Big John's on Chicago's North Side, it was the Siegel-Schwall Band that took their place. Signed by Vanguard scout Sam Charters in 1965, they released their first album in 1966, the first of five they would do with that label. Bass player Jack Dawson, formerly of the Prime Movers Blues Band, joined the band in 1967.

In 1969 the band toured, playing the Fillmore West, blues/folk festivals, and many club dates—one of several White blues bands that introduced the blues genre to millions of Americans during that era. They were, however, the first blues band to record with a full orchestra, performing *Three Pieces for Blues Band and Symphony Orchestra* in 1971 with the San Francisco Orchestra. Later that year, the band signed with RCA (Wooden Nickel) and produced five albums in the next four years. The band broke up in 1974.

In 1987 the band reformed and produced a live album on Alligator, *The Siegel-Schwall Reunion Concert.* Jim Schwall is a university professor of music in Kalamazoo, MI. Corky Siegel has been involved in many projects over the years that fuse classical music with blues, including his current group Chamber Blues —a string quartet, with a percussionist

(tabla), and Siegel on piano and harmonica. And on rare occasions, the old band still gets together and performs. —*Michael Erlewine*

Siegel-Schwall Band / 1966 / Vanguard ✦✦✦
Say Siegel-Schwall / 1967 / Vanguard ✦✦✦✦
This was the group's breakthrough album. Corky Siegel's emotional harp work and foxy, sly (almost cutesy) vocals, coupled with a hot rhythm section and Jim Schwall's cardboard-sounding acoustic-with-a-pickup guitar work, made this the one that connected big with White audiences. Some of it rocks, some of it boogies, some of it's downright creepy and eerie. Worth seeking out. —*Cub Koda*

Shake / 1968 / Vanguard ✦✦✦
Shake! was probably the group's second best album and the one that came the closest to representing their live act. The highlight is their take on Howlin' Wolf's "Shake for Me." Lots of fun and fireworks on this one, the sound of a band at the top of their game. —*Cub Koda*

The Best of Siegel-Schwall / Dec. 1974 / Vanguard ✦✦✦✦
Vinyl best-of compilation that hits a few (but not all) of the high notes of their tenure with Vanguard Records. —*Cub Koda*

● **Where We Walked (1966-1970)** / 1991 / Vanguard ✦✦✦✦
A very nice, fairly thorough, compilation that supersedes the old vinyl collection on several levels; nice mastering, better notes, and nicer selection. For a basic introduction to their sound, this one's hard to beat. —*Cub Koda*

Frankie Lee Sims

b. Apr. 30, 1917, New Orleans, LA, d. May 10, 1970, Dallas, TX
Guitar, Vocals / Electric Texas Blues
A cousin of Lightnin' Hopkins (and supposedly a nephew of Texas Alexander), Sims recorded in the late '40s for Texas labels like Bluebonnet before scoring a sizeable blues hit for Specialty in the early '50s with his signature number, "Lucy Mae Blues." Sims worked in a style similar to Hopkins, only much more percussive and electric, and with a better ability to work with full bands than his more celebrated cousin. His lyrics borrow from traditional sources with inventive twists of their own, while the music at times sounds like a strong precursor to rock 'n' roll. —*Cub Koda*

● **Lucy Mae Blues** / 1970 / Specialty ✦✦✦✦
This collection of Sims' Specialty sides, primarily in a drums and electric guitar format, is pretty hard to beat. It combines all of the original singles, the extra tracks from his lone album, plus unissued material, and—until further alternate takes come to light—the best overview of his tenure with the label. Some tracks are augmented with harmonica and/or string bass, but it's Frankie Lee's guitar and sly vocals that drive things along. Until his early Bluebonnet and later Ace material is cobbled together to complete the picture, this compilation is all you'll need. —*Cub Koda*

Bessie Smith

b. Apr. 15, 1894, Chattanooga, TN, d. Sep. 26, 1937, Clarksdale, MS
Vocals / Blues, Classic Female Blues, Classic Jazz
The first major blues and jazz singer on record and one of the most powerful of all time, Bessie Smith earned the title of "The Empress of the Blues." Even on her first records in 1923, her passionate voice overcame the primitive recording quality of the day and still communicates easily to today's listeners (which is not true of any other singer from that early period). At a time when the blues were in and most vocalists (particularly vaudevillians) were being dubbed "blues singers," Bessie Smith simply had no competition.

Back in 1912, Bessie Smith sang in the same show as Ma Rainey, who took her under her wing and coached her. Although Rainey would achieve a measure of fame throughout her career, she was soon surpassed by her protégé. In 1920 Smith had her own show in Atlantic City, and in 1923 she moved to New York. She was soon signed by Columbia, and her first recording (Alberta Hunter's "Downhearted Blues") made her famous. Bessie worked and recorded steadily throughout the decade, using many top musicians as sidemen on sessions, including Louis Armstrong, Joe Smith (her favorite cornetist), James P. Johnson, and Charlie Green. Her summer tent show, "Harlem Frolics," was a big success during 1925-27, and "Mississippi Days" in 1928 kept the momentum going. However, by 1929 the blues were out-of-fashion and Bessie Smith's career was declining, despite being at the peak of her powers (and still only 35!). She appeared in *St. Louis Blues* that year (a low-budget movie short that contains the only footage of her), but her hit recording of "Nobody Knows You When You're Down and Out" predicted her leaner Depression years. Although she was dropped by Columbia in 1931 and made her final recordings on a four-song session in 1933, Bessie Smith kept on working. She played the Apollo in 1935 and substituted for Billie Holiday in the show *Stars over Broadway.* The chances are very good that she would have made a comeback, starting with a Carnegie Hall appearance at John Hammond's upcoming "From

Spirituals to Swing" concert, but she was killed in a car crash in Missouri. —*Scott Yanow*

☆ **The Complete Recordings, Vol. 1** / Feb. 16, 1923-Apr. 8, 1924 / Columbia/Legacy ✦✦✦✦✦
In the 1970s Bessie Smith's recordings were reissued on five double LPs. Her CD reissue series also has five volumes (the first four are double-CD sets), with the main difference being that the final volume includes all of her rare alternate takes (which were bypassed on LP). The first set (which, as with all of the CD volumes, is housed in an oversize box that includes an informative booklet) contains her first 38 recordings. During this early era, Bessie Smith had no competitors on record, and she was one of the few vocalists who could overcome the primitive recording techniques; her power really comes through. Her very first recording (Alberta Hunter's "Down-Hearted Blues") was a big hit and is one of the highlights of this set, along with "'Tain't Nobody's Bizness If I Do" (two decades before Billie Holiday), "Jail-House Blues," and "Ticket Agent, Ease Your Window Down." Smith's accompaniment is nothing that special (usually just a piano and maybe a weak horn or two) but she dominates the music anyway, even on two vocal duets with her rival Clara Smith. All of these volumes reward close listenings and are full of timeless recordings. —*Scott Yanow*

☆ **The Complete Recordings, Vol. 2 (1924-1925)** / Apr. 8, 1924-Nov. 18, 1925 / Columbia/Legacy ✦✦✦✦✦
Bessie Smith, even on the evidence of her earliest recordings, well deserved the title "Empress of the Blues," for in the 1920s there was no one in her league for emotional intensity, honest blues feeling, and power. The second of five volumes finds her accompaniment improving rapidly with such sympathetic sidemen as trombonist Charlie Green, cornetist Joe Smith, and clarinetist Buster Bailey often helping her out. However, they are overshadowed by Louis Armstrong, whose two sessions with Smith (nine songs in all) fall into the time period of this second set; particularly classic are their versions of "St. Louis Blues," "Careless Love Blues," and "I Ain't Gonna Play No Second Fiddle." Other gems on this essential set include "Cake Walkin' Babies from Home," "The Yellow Dog Blues," and "At the Christmas Ball." —*Scott Yanow*

The Complete Recordings, Vol. 3 / Nov. 20, 1925-Feb. 16, 1928 / Columbia/Legacy ✦✦✦✦
On the third of five volumes, the great Bessie Smith is greatly assisted on some of the 39 selections by a few of her favorite sidemen: cornetist Joe Smith, trombonist Charlie Green, and clarinetist Buster Bailey. But the most important of her musicians was pianist James P. Johnson, who makes his first appearance in 1927 and can be heard on four duets with Bessie, including the monumental "Back Water Blues." —*Scott Yanow*

The Complete Recordings, Vol. 4 / Feb. 21, 1928-Jun. 11, 1931 / Columbia/Legacy ✦✦✦✦
The fourth of five volumes traces her career from a period when her popularity was at its height down to just six songs away from the halt of her recording career. But although her commercial fortunes might have slipped, Bessie Smith never declined, and these later recordings are consistently powerful. —*Scott Yanow*

The Complete Recordings, Vol. 5: The Final Chapter / May 6, 1925-Nov. 24, 1933 / Sony/Legacy ✦✦✦✦
Bessie Smith cut 160 sides for the Columbia and Okeh labels between 1923 and 1933, and the four previous two-CD/cassette boxed sets of her complete recordings released in the 1990s covered 156 of them, which introduces the question, what can a fifth two-CD/cassette boxed set contain in addition to the remaining six cuts? First, there are five previously unreleased alternate takes; second, there is the 15-minute low-fi soundtrack to the two-reel *St. Louis Blues*, which constitutes the only film of Smith; and third, taking up all of the second CD/cassette, there are 72 minutes of interview tapes of Ruby Smith, Bessie Smith's niece, who traveled as part of her show. The box contains a "Parental Advisory—Explicit Lyrics" warning because of the nature of Ruby Smith's reminiscences. You won't learn much about Bessie Smith's music from her niece's remarks, but you will learn a lot about her sexual preferences. —*William Ruhlmann*

★ **The Bessie Smith Collection [Columbia Jazz Masterpieces]** / Dec. 1989 / Columbia ✦✦✦✦✦
While there's no denying the importance and quality of Columbia/Legacy's *Complete Recordings* series, nine discs may seem a bit intimidating to the newcomer. *Collection*, a mid-priced, 16-track collection that spans most of Smith's career, ultimately does a better service to the casual listener with a limited budget. This is probably the best introduction—undoubtedly many will seek out the more comprehensive packages afterwards. —*Chris Woodstra*

George Harmonica Smith

b. Apr. 22, 1924, Helena, AR, d. Oct. 2, 1983, Los Angeles, CA
Harmonica, Vocals / Electric Harmonica Blues
George Smith was born April 22, 1924, in Helena, AR, but was raised in

Cairo, IL. At age four, Smith was already taking harp lessons from his mother, a guitar player and a somewhat stern taskmaster—it was a case of get-it-right-or-else. In his early teens, he started hoboing around the towns in the South and later joined Early Woods, a country band with Early Woods on fiddle and Curtis Gould on spoons. He also worked with a gospel group in Mississippi called the Jackson Jubilee Singers.

Smith moved to Rock Island, IL, in 1941 and played with a group that included Francis Clay on drums. There is evidence that he was one of the first to amplify his harp. While working at the Dixie Theater, he took an old 16mm cinema projector, extracted the amplifier/speaker, and began using this on the streets.

His influences include Larry Adler and later Little Walter. Smith would sometimes bill himself as Little Walter Jr. or Big Walter. He played in a number of bands, including one with a young guitarist named Otis Rush, and later went on the roal with the Muddy Waters Band, after replacing Henry Strong.

In 1954 he was offered a permanent job at the Orchid Room in Kansas City where, early in 1955, Joe Bihari of Modern Records (on a scouting trip) heard Smith, and signed him to Modern. These recording sessions were released under the name Little George Smith, and included "Telephone Blues" and "Blues in the Dark." The records were a success.

Smith traveled with Little Willie John and Champion Jack Dupree on one of the Universal Attractions tours. While on the tour, he recorded with Champion Jack Dupree in November of 1955 in Cincinnati, producing "Sharp Harp" and "Overhead Blues." The tour ended in Los Angeles and Smith settled down—spending the rest of his life in that city.

In the late '50s he recorded for J&M, Lapel, Melker, and Caddy under the names Harmonica King or Little Walter Junior. He also worked with Big Mama Thornton on many shows.

In 1960 Smith met producer Nat McCoy, who owned the Soloplay and Carolyn labels, with whom he recorded ten singles under the name of George Allen. In 1966, while Muddy Waters was on the West Coast, he asked Smith to join him, and they worked together for a while, recording for Spivey Records.

Smith's first album on World Pacific, *A Tribute to Little Walter*, was released in 1968. In 1969 Bob Thiele produced an excellent solo album of Smith on Bluesway, and later made use of Smith as a sideman for his Blues Times label, including sets with T-Bone Walker, and Harmonica Slim. Smith met Rod Piazza, a young White harp player, and they formed the Southside Blues Band, later known as Bacon Fat.

In 1969, Smith signed with UK producer Mike Vernon and did the *No Time for Jive* album. Smith was less active in the 1970s, appearing with Eddie Taylor and Big Mama Thornton. Around 1977, Smith became friends with William Clarke and they began working together. Their working relationship and friendship continued until Smith died on October 1, 1983.

William Clarke, Smith's protégé, writes, "He had a technique on the chromatic harp where he would play two notes at once, but one octave apart. He would get an organ-type sound by doing this. George really knew how to make his notes count by not playing too much and taking his time by letting the music unfold easily. He could also swing like crazy and was a first-class entertainer. I have heard from a friend that they had seen George Smith in the 1950s playing a club in Chicago, tap dancing around everybody's drinks on top of the bar while playing his harp.

"I have been with him in church and seen him play amplified harmonica by himself. This was very soulful. I have never heard George play a song the same way twice. He was very creative and played directly from his heart. He admired all great musicians but had his own sound and style. He was a true original. Mr. Smith would always give 100% on stage whether or not there were 1 or 1,000 people listening. This was his performing style, always.

"George Smith greatly admired harmonica player Larry Adler, and although Adler used the octave technique on the harp also, George really was the one that developed this to its full potential. Before Mr. Smith, nobody in blues had used this octave technique. An extremely kind and gentle man, George always went all out to help other harmonica players. Everybody liked George Smith. He played a huge role in advancing blues harmonica and should never be forgotten. You can hear the influence of George Smith in most everyone playing blues harmonica today, whether directly or indirectly. He also was a great blues singer. He had a huge baritone voice that conveyed great emotion and soulfulness."
—*Michael Erlewine*

● **Tribute to Little Walter** / 1968 / World Pacific ✦✦✦✦
The L.A. harp ace pays tribute to one of his peers and influences with a well-conceived set of Little Walter covers. —*Bill Dahl*

No Time to Jive / 1970 / Blue Horizon ✦✦✦
Laidback L.A. session from 1969 produced by Mike Vernon for his Blue Horizon label that's dominated by a mellow feel. There are a few upbeat items—"Before You Do Your Thing (You'd Better Think)" and "Soul

Feet"—but mostly George sits back and blows with a relaxed ease. His sidemen include guitarists Pee Wee Crayton and Marshall Hooks, pianist J.D. Nicholson, and drummer Richard Innes. —*Bill Dahl*

● **Harmonica Ace** / 1993 / Capitol ✦✦✦✦
Smith's fat-toned amplified harmonica marks him as one of the humble instrument's leading innovators of the mid-'50s—especially the hautning "Blues in the Dark," "Telephone Blues," and the roaring "Down in New Orleans." Smith's vocals are equally commanding. —*Bill Dahl*

Otis Spann

b. Mar. 21, 1930, Jackson, MS, d. Apr. 24, 1970, Chicago, IL
Piano, Vocals / R&B, Electric Chicago Blues, Piano Blues
An integral member of the Muddy Waters band of the 1950s and 1960s, pianist Otis Spann took his sweet time in launching a full-fledged solo career. But his own discography is a satisfying one nonetheless, offering ample proof as to why so many aficionados considered him then and now as Chicago's leading postwar blues pianist.

Spann played on most of Waters' classic Chess waxings between 1953 and 1969, his rippling 88s providing the drive on Waters' seminal 1960 live version of "Got My Mojo Working."

Spann gigged on his own and with guitarist Morris Pejoe before hooking up with Waters in 1952. His first Chess date behind the Chicago icon the next year produced "Blow Wind Blow." Subsequent Waters classics sporting Spann's ivories include "Hoochie Coochie Man," "I'm Ready," and "Just Make Love to Me."

Strangely, Chess somehow failed to recognize Spann's vocal abilities. His own Chess output was limited to a 1954 single, "It Must Have Been the Devil," that featured B.B. King on guitar, and sessions in 1956 and 1963 that remained in the can for decades. So Spann looked elsewhere, waxing a stunning album for Candid with guitarist Robert Jr. Lockwood in 1960, a largely solo outing in 1963 that was cut in Copenhagen, a set for British Decca the following year that found him in the company of Waters and Eric Clapton, and a 1964 LP for Prestige where Spann shared vocal duties with bandmate James Cotton. Testament and Vanguard both recorded Spann as a leader in 1965.

Spann's last few years with Muddy Waters were memorable for their collaboration on the Chess set *Fathers and Sons*, but the pianist was clearly ready to launch a solo career, recording a set for Blue Horizon with British blues-rockers Fleetwood Mac that produced Spann's laid-back "Hungry Country Girl." He finally turned the piano chair in the Waters band over to Pinetop Perkins in 1969, but fate didn't grant Spann long to achieve solo stardom. He was stricken with cancer and died in April of 1970. —*Bill Dahl*

Otis Spann Is the Blues / Aug. 1960 / Candid ✦✦✦✦
He may not have been *the* blues, but he was sure close to being *the blues pianist.* Spann provided wonderful, imaginative, tasty piano solos and better-than-average vocals, and was arguably the best player whose style was more restrained than animated. Not that he couldn't rock the house, but Spann's forte was making you think as well as making you dance. —*Ron Wynn*

● **Complete Candid Recordings**—Otis Spann/Lightnin' Hopkins Sessions / Aug. 23, 1960 / Mosaic ✦✦✦✦
With Robert Lockwood, Jr. Two classic Spann albums: *Otis Spann Is the Blues* and *Walkin' the Blues*. Early, potent Spann with flawless liner notes and a complete discography. Also included are the Candid sessions of Lightnin' Hopkins. —*Michael Erlewine*

Blues of Otis Spann . . . Plus / 1993 / See for Miles ✦✦✦
A Mike Vernon-produced British album from 1964 that was one of Spann's first full-length dates as a leader. Nice band, too: Muddy Waters on guitar, bassist Ransom Knowling, and drummer Willie "Big Eyes" Smith, along with a young Eric Clapton playing on a couple of cuts. Spann plays a harpsichord on a few items; needless to say, they aren't the album's shining moments! —*Bill Dahl*

Down to Earth / 1995 / MCA ✦✦✦✦
Both of the great Chicago pianist's albums for ABC-Bluesway, characterized by rippling piano and ruminative vocals. Backed in style by his mates in the Muddy Waters band (including the man himself), Spann responds to a studio full of people on "Popcorn Man," "Steel Mill Blues," and "Nobody Knows Chicago like I Do." Spann's 1967 encore LP united him in the studio with wife Lucille for several vocals. —*Bill Dahl*

Hubert Sumlin

b. Nov. 16, 1931, Greenwood, MS
Guitar, Vocals / Electric Chicago Blues
Quiet and extremely unassuming off the bandstand, Hubert Sumlin played a style of guitar incendiary enough to stand tall beside the immortal Howlin' Wolf. The Wolf was Sumlin's imposing mentor for more than two decades, and it proved a mutually beneficial relationship; Sumlin's twisting, darting, unpredictable lead guitar constantly energized the Wolf's 1960s Chess sides, even when the songs them-

selves (check out "Do the Do" or "Mama's Baby" for conclusive proof) were less than stellar.

Sumlin learned his craft nightly on the bandstand behind Wolf, his confidence growing as he graduated from rhythm guitar duties to lead. By the dawn of the '60s, Sumlin's slashing axe was a prominent component on the great majority of Wolf's waxings. Only in the last few years has Sumlin allowed his vocal talents to shine. He's recorded solo sets for Black Top and Blind Pig that show him to be an understated but effective singer—and his guitar continues to communicate most forcefully. —*Bill Dahl*

Blues Anytime! / 1994 / Evidence ✦✦✦✦
A remarkable 1964 session produced by Horst Lippmann behind the Iron Curtain in East Germany that found Sumlin trying for the first time on record to sing. He played both electric and acoustic axe on the historic date, sharing the singing with more experienced hands Willie Dixon and Sunnyland Slim (Clifton James is on drums). All three Chicago legends acquit themselves well. —*Bill Dahl*

Healing Feeling / Black Top ✦✦✦
An improvement over his previous Black Top disc, especially on Sumlin's two vocal showcases, "Come Back Little Girl" and "Honey Dumplins." James "Thunderbird" Davis is also on board in a guest role, though he has to share his mike time with the considerably less remarkable Darrell Nulisch, who dominates the vocals. —*Bill Dahl*

● **Heart and Soul** / Blind Pig ✦✦✦✦
The veteran guitarist sounds more confident and expressive vocally here than on any other of his contemporary recordings. Backing by harpist James Cotton, along with Little Mike and the Tornadoes, is nicely understated, affording Sumlin just enough drive without drowning his easygoing vocals (no small feat). —*Bill Dahl*

Sunnyland Slim (Albert Luandrew)

b. Sep. 5, 1907, Vance, MS, d. Mar. 17, 1995, Chicago, IL
Piano, Vocals / Piano Blues
Exhibiting truly amazing longevity that was commensurate with his powerful, imposing physical build, Sunnyland Slim's status as a beloved Chicago piano patriarch endured long after most of his peers had perished. For more than 50 years, the towering Sunnyland had rumbled the ivories around the Windy City, playing with virtually every local luminary imaginable and backing the great majority in the studio at one time or another.

Slim moved to Chicago in 1939 and set up shop as an in-demand piano man, playing for a spell with John Lee "Sonny Boy" Williamson before waxing eight sides for RCA Victor in 1947 under the somewhat misleading handle of "Doctor Clayton's Buddy." If it hadn't been for the helpful Sunnyland, Muddy Waters may not have found his way onto Chess; it was at the pianist's 1947 session for Aristocrat that the Chess brothers made Waters' acquaintance.

Aristocrat (which issued his harrowing "Johnson Machine Gun") was but one of a myriad of labels that Sunnyland recorded for between 1948 and 1956: HighTone, Opera, Chance, Tempo-Tone, Mercury, Apollo, JOB, Regal, Vee-Jay (unissued), Blue Lake, Club 51, and Cobra all cut dates on Slim, whose vocals thundered with the same resonant authority as his 88s. In addition, his distinctive playing enlivened hundreds of sessions by other artists during the same time frame.

Like a deep-rooted tree, Sunnyland Slim persevered despite the passing decades. For a time, he helmed his own label, Airway Records. As late as 1985, he made a fine set for the Red Beans logo, *Chicago Jump*, backed by the same crack combo that shared the stage with him every Sunday evening at a popular North side club called B.L.U.E.S. for some 12 years.

There were times when the pianist fell seriously ill, but he always defied the odds and returned to action, warbling his trademark Woody Woodpecker chortle and kicking off one more exultant slow blues as he had done for the previous half century. Finally, after a calamitous fall on the ice coming home from a gig led to numerous complications, Sunnyland Slim finally died of kidney failure in 1995. He's sorely missed. —*Bill Dahl*

House Rent Party / 1949 / Delmark ✦✦✦✦
From deep in the vaults of Apollo Records comes this sensational collection of 1949 artifacts by the veteran pianist, along with sides by singer St. Louis Jimmy, young pianist Willie Mabon, and two unissued sides by guitarist Jimmy Rogers (including a pre-Chess rendition of his seminal "That's All Right"). Slim's mighty roar shines on "Brown Skin Woman," "I'm Just a Lonesome Man," and "Bad Times (Cost of Living)," all from the emerging heyday of the genre. —*Bill Dahl*

● **Slim's Shout** / 1969 / Prestige ✦✦✦✦
You wouldn't think that transporting one of Chicago's reigning piano patriarchs to Englewood Cliffs, NJ, would produce such a fine album, but this 1960 set cooks from beginning to end. His swinging New York rhythm section has no trouble following Slim's bedrock piano, and the

estimable King Curtis peels off diamond-hard tenor sax solos in the great
Texas tradition that also mesh seamlessly. Slim runs through his standards—"The Devil Is a Busy Man," "Shake It," "It's You Baby"—in gorgeous stereo, and two unissued bonus cuts (including another of his best-
known tunes, "Everytime I Get to Drinking") make the CD reissue even
more appealing. —*Bill Dahl*

Chicago Jump / Apr. 1986 / Evidence ✦✦✦✦
The last of Slim's great band-backed albums, cut with yeoman help from
his longtime combo (guitarist Steve Freund and drummer Robert Covington share the vocals). At the heart of the matter are Slim's rolling 88s
and still-commanding vocals, invested with experience beyond all com-
prehension. —*Bill Dahl*

Be Careful How You Vote / 1989 / Earwig ✦✦✦

Live at the D.C. Blues Society / Mapleshade ✦✦✦

Roosevelt Sykes

b. Jan. 31, 1906, Elmar, AR, d. Jul. 17, 1983, New Orleans, LA
Piano, Vocals / Piano Blues
Next time someone voices the goofball opinion that blues is simply too
depressing to embrace, sit 'em down and expose 'em to a heady dose of
Roosevelt Sykes. If he doesn't change their minds, nothing will. There
was nothing downbeat about his roly-poly, effervescent pianist (nicknamed "Honeydripper" for his youthful prowess around the girls),
whose lengthy career spanned the pre-war and postwar eras with no
interruption whatsoever. Sykes' romping boogies and hilariously risqué
lyrics (his double-entendre gems included "Dirty Mother for You," "Ice
Cream Freezer," and "Peeping Tom") characterize his monumental contributions to the blues idiom—he was a pioneering piano-pounder
responsible for the seminal pieces "44 Blues," "Driving Wheel," and
"Night Time Is the Right Time."
    Precious few pianists could boast the thundering boogie prowess of
Roosevelt Sykes—and even fewer could chase away the blues with his
blues as the rotund cigar-chomping 88s ace did. —*Bill Dahl*

The Return of Roosevelt Sykes / 1960 / Bluesville ✦✦✦✦
Sykes' lyrical images are as vivid and amusing as ever on this 1960 set,
with titles like "Set the Meat Outdoors" and "Hangover" among its standouts. Other than drummer Jump Jackson, the quartet behind the pianist
is pretty obscure, but they rock his boogies with a vengeance. Contains a
nice remake of his classic "Drivin' Wheel." —*Bill Dahl*

The Honeydripper / 1961 / Prestige ✦✦✦✦
Roosevelt Sykes expertly fit his classic down-ome piano riffs and style
into a fabric that also contained elements of soul, funk ,and R&B. The
nine-cut date, reissued by Original Blues Classics, included such laments
as "I Hate to Be Alone," "Lonely Day" and "She Ain't for Nobody," as well
as the poignant "Yes Lawd" and less weighty "Satellite Baby" and "Jailbait." Besides Sykes' alternately bemused, ironic, and inviting vocals,
there's superb tenor sax support from King Curtis, Robert Banks' tasty
organ, and steady, nimble bass and drum assistance by Leonard Gaskins
and drummer Belton Evans. —*Ron Wynn*

Gold Mine: Live in Europe / 1991 / Delmark ✦✦✦
Solid 1966 solo set, cut during one of the effervescent piano pounder's
frequent overseas jaunts and originally issued on Delmark as *In Europe*.
A winning combination of material ancient even back then ("44 Blues,"
the jaunty boogie "Boot That Thing") and fresh numbers. —*Bill Dahl*

Blues by Roosevelt "The Honeydripper" Sykes / 1995 / Smithsonian/
Folkaways ✦✦✦✦
Other than a cameo piano appearance by his producer (and peer) Memphis Slim on the appropriately titled "Memphis Slim Rock," this is a stellar solo outing by the prolific pianist. He belts out a booming "Sweet Old
Chicago," takes a trip to Chicago's South Side on "47th Street Jive," and
indulges in a little ribald imagery for "The Sweet Root Man." —*Bill Dahl*

● **Boogie Honky Tonk** / Oldie Blues ✦✦✦✦
Vinyl compilation of the pianist's 1944-1947 output for RCA with his
jumping little combo, the Honeydrippers, all of it cut in Chicago. Backed
by a myriad of swinging Windy City sidemen (saxists Leon Washington,
J.T. Brown, and Bill Casimir; bassist Ransom Knowling, and drummers
Jump Jackson and Judge Riley), Sykes rips through "Peeping Tom," the
wonderfully titled "Flames of Jive," and his often-covered "Sunny Road"
with ebullient charm. —*Bill Dahl*

Tampa Red (Hudson Whittaker)

b. Jan. 8, 1904, Smithville, GA, d. Mar. 19, 1981, Chicago, IL
*Guitar, Piano, Kazoo, Vocals / Electric Chicago Blues, Blues, Acoustic
Chicago Blues*
Out of the dozens of fine slide guitarists who recorded blues, only a
handful—Elmore James, Muddy Waters, and Robert Johnson, for example—left a clear imprint on tradition by creating a recognizable and
widely imitated instrumental style. Tampa Red was another influential
musical model. During his heyday in the '20s and '30s, he was billed as

"The Guitar Wizard," and his stunning slide work on steel National or
electric guitar shows why he earned the title. His 30-year recording
career produced hundreds of sides: hokum, pop, and jive, but mostly
blues (including classic compositions "Anna Lou Blues," "Black Angel
Blues," "Crying Won't Help You," "It Hurts Me Too," and "Love Her with
a Feeling"). Early in Red's career, he teamed up with pianist, songwriter,
and latter-day gospel composer Georgia Tom Dorsey, collaborating on
double entendre classics like "Tight like That."
    Today's listener will enjoy Tampa Red's expressive vocals and per-
haps be taken aback by his kazoo solos. His songwriting has stood the
test of time, and any serious slide guitar student had better be familiar
with Red's guitar wizardry. —*Barry Lee Pearson*

★ **Bottleneck Guitar (1928-1937)** / 1974 / Yazoo ✦✦✦✦
Prime cuts from one of the greatest guitarists ever to strap on a slide.
—*Cub Koda*

☆ **Tampa Red: Guitar Wizard** / Oct. 1975 / RCA ✦✦✦✦✦
Thirty-two of Red's premier tracks from his RCA Bluebird days dating
from 1934-1953 (talk about longevity!) on two slabs of vinyl (with
exhaustive liner notes by Jim O'Neal). Red's rousing kazoo blasts power
many of these essential sides, which feature legends like pianists Black
Bob, Blind John Davis, and Johnny Jones in support roles. Red's last few
Victor sides were right in the stylistic heart of the later Chicago sound;
the remarkable Latin-tinged "Rambler's Blues" boasts a spine-tingling
amplified harp solo from Big Walter Horton. —*Bill Dahl*

Don't Tampa with the Blues / 1982 / Bluesville ✦✦✦
The kazoo-toting bluesman wasn't as powerful a presence when he came
back in 1960 to record this set in a solo setting as he was in his Bluebird
heyday, but it's hard to resist these agreeable versions of "Let Me Play
with Your Poodle," "Love Her with a Feeling," and "It's Tight like That"
nonetheless. —*Bill Dahl*

The Guitar Wizard [CD] / 1994 / Columbia/Legacy ✦✦✦✦
Some of the earliest work (1928-1934) by the slide guitar great, ranging
from the irresistible hokum he served up with piano-playing partner
"Georgia Tom" Dorsey ("Dead Cats on the Line," "No Matter How She
Done It") to the gorgeous "Black Angel Blues" (eventually known as
"Sweet Little Angel") and the solo guitar masterpieces "Things 'bout
Comin' My Way" and "Denver Blues." —*Bill Dahl*

★ **It Hurts Me Too: The Essential Recordings** / 1995 / Indigo ✦✦✦✦✦
A magnificent primer on the catalog of this prolific guitar/kazoo ace that
spans 1928-1942. Opening with his immortal hokum duet with "Georgia
Tom" Dorsey, the bawdy "It's Tight like That," the disc makes clear just
how seminal Red's Chicago-cut output was—here are the original versions of "It Hurts Me Too," "Love with a Feeling," "Don't You Lie to Me,"
and the double-entendre hoots "She Wants to Sell My Monkey" and "Let
Me Play with Your Poodle." —*Bill Dahl*

Eddie Taylor

b. Jan. 29, 1923, Benoit, MS, d. Dec. 25, 1985, Chicago, IL
Guitar, Vocals / R&B, Electric Chicago Blues
When you're talking about the patented Jimmy Reed laconic shuffle
sound, you're talking about Eddie Taylor just as much as Reed himself.
Taylor was the glue that kept Reed's lowdown grooves from falling into
serious disrepair. His rock-steady rhythm guitar powered the great
majority of Reed's Vee-Jay sides during the 1950s and early '60s, and he
even found time to wax a few classic sides of his own for Vee-Jay during
the mid-'50s.
    Eddie Taylor was as versatile a blues guitarist as anyone could ever
hope to encounter. His style was deeply rooted in Delta tradition, but he
could snap off a modern funk-tinged groove just as convincingly as a
straight shuffle. —*Bill Dahl*

I Feel So Bad / 1972 / HighTone ✦✦✦✦
One of the Chicago guitarist's most satisfying contemporary albums, this
1972 set (first issued on Advent) was cut not in the Windy City, but in L.A.
in 1972 with a combo featuring Phillip Walker on second guitar and
George Smith on harp. Taylor was no strict traditionalist; he was as conversant with funk-tinged modern rhythms as with Delta-based
styles—and he exhibits both sides of his musical personality on this one.
—*Bill Dahl*

★ **Bad Boy** / 1993 / Charly ✦✦✦✦✦
The Delta-rooted mid-'50s Vee-Jay label classics by perennially underrated Chicago guitarist Eddie Taylor, who stepped out of Jimmy Reed's
shadow long enough to leave behind "Bad Boy," "Big Town Playboy,"
"Ride 'em on Down," the bouncy "I'm Gonna Love You," and several
more brilliant sides. Fifteen songs in all, including five from 1964 that
are scarcely less impressive than his previous stuff. —*Bill Dahl*

My Heart Is Bleeding / 1994 / Evidence ✦✦✦

★ **Ride 'em on Down** / Charly ✦✦✦✦✦
An absolutely essential 24-track collection that alternates 12 of Eddie's
classic Vee-Jay sides (including "Bad Boy," "Big Town Playboy," "Find My

Baby," "Looking for Trouble" and the title track) with a dozen more early Jimmy Reed sides with Taylor in support. As a collection of Taylor's best solo sides, it's as complete as any on the market. As a sample of Taylor's impeccable backup work behind Reed—while containing no hits—it stands by itself as a very nice collection of rarities that shows both artists off to good advantage. As a document of early '50s Chicago blues, it's a major brick in the wall. As seamless blues groove listening, consider it a must-have. —*Cub Koda*

Hound Dog Taylor (Theodore Roosevelt Taylor)

b. Apr. 12, 1915, Natchez, MS, **d.** Dec. 17, 1975, Chicago, IL
Guitar, Vocals / Electric Chicago Blues
Alligator Records, Chicago's leading contemporary blues label, might never have been launched at all if not for the crashing, slashing slide guitar antics of Hound Dog Taylor. Bruce Iglauer, then an employee of Delmark Records, couldn't convince his boss, Bob Koester, of Taylor's potential, so Iglauer took matters into his own hands. In 1971, Alligator was born for the express purpose of releasing Hound Dog's debut album. We all know what transpired after that.

Taylor's relentlessly raucous band, the HouseRockers, consisted of only two men, though their combined racket sounded like quite a few more. Second guitarist Brewer Phillips, who often supplied buzzing pseudo-bass lines on his guitar, had developed such an empathy with Taylor that their guitars intertwined with ESP-like force, while drummer Ted Harvey kept everything moving along at a brisk pace.

Their eponymous 1971 debut LP contained the typically rowdy "Give Me Back My Wig," while Taylor's first Alligator encore in 1973, *Natural Boogie*, boasted the hypnotic "Sadie" and a stomping "Roll Your Moneymaker." *Beware of the Dog*, a live set, vividly captured the good-time vibe that the perpetually beaming guitarist emanated, but Taylor didn't live to see its release—he died of cancer shortly before it hit the shelves.

Hound Dog Taylor was the obvious inspiration for Alligator's "Genuine Houserocking Music" motto, a credo Iglauer's firm still tries to live up to today. He wasn't the most accomplished of slide guitarists, but Hound Dog Taylor could definitely rock any house he played at. —*Bill Dahl*

★ **Hound Dog Taylor and The Houserockers** / 1971 / Alligator ✦✦✦✦✦
The first album and the perfect place to start. Wild, raucous, crazy music straight out of the South Side clubs. The incessant drive of Hound Dog's playing is best heard on "Give Me Back My Wig," "55th Street Boogie," and "Taylor's Rock," while the sound of Brewer Phillips' Telecaster on "Phillips' Theme" gives new meaning to the phrase "sheet metal tone." One of the greatest slide guitar albums of all time. —*Cub Koda*

Natural Boogie / 1973 / Alligator ✦✦✦✦
Hound Dog's second album was every bit as wild as the first, bringing with it a fatter sound and a wider range of emotions and music. A recut here of Hound Dog's first single, "Take Five," totally burns the original, while the smoldering intensity of "See Me in the Evening" and "Sadie" take this album to places the first one never reached. —*Cub Koda*

Beware of the Dog / 1975 / Alligator ✦✦✦✦
This was Hound Dog's posthumous live album containing performances that are even steamier than the first two studio albums, if such a notion is possible. For lowdown slow blues, it's hard to beat the heartfelt closer "Freddie's Blues," and for surreal moments on wax, it's equally hard to beat the funkhouse-turned-looney-bin dementia of "Let's Get Funky" or the hopped up hillbilly fever rendition of "Comin' Around the Mountain." —*Cub Koda*

Genuine Houserocking Music / 1982 / Alligator ✦✦✦
With Alligator label president Bruce Iglauer recording some 20 or 30 tracks over two nights everytime the band went into the studio, there were bound to be some really great tracks lurking in the vaults, and here they are. Noteworthy for the great performance of Robert Johnson's "Crossroads," (previously available only as a Japanese 45) but also for the "rock 'n' roll" inclusion of "What'd I Say" and Brewer Phillips' take on "Kansas City." No bottom of the barrel scrapings here. —*Cub Koda*

Live at Joe's Place / 1992 / New Rose ✦✦✦✦
1972 live recordings in Boston. They're drunk, they're out of tune, but the crowd goes nuts and the vibe cancels out any musical inconsistencies. Doesn't really add anything to the Alligator legacy, as it's extremely loose and chaotic, but it's great fun anyway. —*Cub Koda*

Have Some Fun / 1992 / Wolf ✦✦✦
More 1972 live recordings from Joe's Place. Different song selection, somewhat better fidelity. Confusingly for people who'll want to order this as an import, it's issued under the name "The Houserockers," with only Hound Dog's photo on the front! —*Cub Koda*

Freddie's Blues / 1993 / Wolf ✦✦✦
This is the third volume of live recordings from Joe's Place in Cambridge, MS, in 1972. Six of the 11 tunes here are instrumentals (four of them featuring the lead guitar of Brewer Phillips), and while Taylor and the Houserockers are generally in rare form here, some chaotic moments ("Let's

Get Funky") do abound, but that's half the fun and charm of it all. —*Cub Koda*

Koko Taylor

b. Sep. 28, 1935, Memphis, TN
Vocals / R&B, Electric Chicago Blues
She's the undisputed queen of Chicago blues. Has been for decades. And truthfully, no one has even mounted a serious challenge to Koko Taylor's reign in recent memory. In 1962 Willie Dixon caught Taylor's act and took over as her mentor. He produced her 1963 debut 45 for USA, "Honky Tonky," then got her signed to Chess. There she enjoyed one of the last legitimate Chicago blues hits with her rousing rendition of the Dixon-penned party classic "Wang Dang Doodle." It went all the way to No. 4 on *Billboard*'s R&B charts in 1966. Dixon's role as writer/producer was a prominent one on Taylor's eponymous Chess debut LP, but none of her encores enjoyed the same success level as "Wang Dang Doodle" (still her enduring signature song).

After a dry spell, Taylor joined Bruce Iglauer's Alligator Records in 1975 (she was the fledgling label's first female artist). Her Grammy-nominated Alligator album debut, *I Got What It Takes*, catapulted Koko Taylor back into the blues limelight, and six more sets for the label have kept her there. —*Bill Dahl*

Koko Taylor / 1968 / MCA/Chess ✦✦✦✦
Straight digital reissue of Taylor's debut Chess album. Produced by Willie Dixon(who can intermittently be heard as a duet partner), the set is one of the strongest representations of the belter's Chess days available, with her immortal smash "Wang Dang Doodle," the chunky "Twenty-nine Ways," "I'm a Little Mixed Up," and "Don't Mess with the Messer." Top-flight session musicians on Taylor's 1965-1969 output included guitarists Buddy Guy, Matt Murphy, and Johnny Shines and saxman Gene "Daddy G" Barge. —*Bill Dahl*

South Side Lady / Dec. 1, 1973 / Evidence ✦✦✦

I Got What It Takes / 1975 / Alligator ✦✦✦✦
The queen's first album for Alligator, and still one of her very best to date. A tasty combo sparked by guitarists Mighty Joe Young and Sammy Lawhorn and saxist Abb Locke provide sharp support as the clear-voiced Taylor belts Bobby Saxton's "Trying to Make a Living," Magic Sam's "That's Why I'm Crying," her own "Honkey Tonkey" and "Voodoo Woman," and Ruth Brown's swinging "Mama, He Treats Your Daughter Mean." —*Bill Dahl*

Queen of the Blues / 1975 / Alligator ✦✦✦✦
Co-producer Bruce Iglauer anticipated a future trend by making this a set filled with cameos—but the presence of Lonnie Brooks, James Cotton, Albert Collins, and Son Seals is entirely warranted, and the contributions of each work quite well in the context of the whole. Taylor's gritty "I Cried like a Baby" and a snazzy remake of Ann Peebles' "Come to Mama" are among the many highlights. —*Bill Dahl*

★ **What It Takes: The Chess Years** / 1977 / MCA/Chess ✦✦✦✦✦
With 18 tracks spanning 1964-1971, this compilation receives the nod over the shorter *Koko Taylor* (eight cuts double off anyway). Opening with her nails-tough "I Got What It Takes," the disc boasts "Wang Dang Doodle," several sides never before on album, and the strange previously unissued "Blue Prelude." Four 1971 tracks from Taylor's tough-to-find second Chess album, *Basic Soul*, are aboard (including "Bills, Bills and More Bills" and her queenly version of "Let Me Love You Baby"). Producer Willie Dixon's guiding hand is apparent everywhere. —*Bill Dahl*

The Earthshaker / 1978 / Alligator ✦✦✦✦
Koko Taylor's Alligator encore harbored tunes that pepper her set list to this day—the grinding "I'm a Woman" and the party-down specials "Let the Good Times Roll" and "Hey Bartender." Her uncompromising slow blues "Please Don't Dog Me" and a sassy remake of Irma Thomas' "You Can Have My Husband" also stand out, as does the fine backing by guitarists Sammy Lawhorn and Johnny B. Moore, pianist Pinetop Perkins, and saxman Abb Locke. —*Bill Dahl*

Force of Nature / 1993 / Alligator ✦✦✦✦
A solid contemporary blues album that ranges from Taylor's own "Spellbound" and "Put the Pot On" to a rendition of Toussaint McCall's tender soul lament "Nothing Takes the Place of You," and a saucy revival of the old Ike and Tina Turner R&B gem "If I Can't Be First." Gene Barge once again penned the horn charts, Carey Bell contributes his usual harp mastery to Taylor's remake of Little Milton's "Mother Nature," and only Buddy Guy's over-the-top guitar histrionics on "Born under a Bad Sign" grate. Long may the queen reign! —*Bill Dahl*

Little Johnny Taylor (Johnny Lamar Taylor)

b. Feb. 11, 1943, Memphis, TN
Vocals / Soul, R&B, Soul Blues
A former member of the Mighty Clouds of Joy best known for his mod-

ern-day blues classic "Part Time Love" (Galaxy, 1963), Taylor has long been one of America's top gospel-based blues vocalists, though not always one of the most visible. As the story goes, his failure to tour behind "Part Time Love" allowed a like-named rival, Johnnie Taylor, to step in and reap the benefits; Johnnie later recorded the song himself for Stax. LJT has been a chitlin-circuit favorite but has remained within that sphere, recording consistently enough to keep his name going. His early-'70s work for Ronn (including "Everybody Knows About My Good Thing," "It's My Fault Darling," and "Open House at My House") clearly presaged the popular Malaco soul-blues sound of the '80s and '90s. The confusing Taylor rivalry has continued: with Johnnie now at Malaco, Little Johnny signed with the label's main competitor, Ichiban, in 1988. —Jim O'Neal

● **Greatest Hits** / Fantasy ✦✦✦✦
The gospel-tinged and decidedly soul-inflected 1963-1968 blues sides of Little Johnny Taylor on Galaxy Records benefitted from marvelous horn-powered arrangements by Ray Shanklin that brilliantly pushed Taylor's melismatic vocals. Naturally, the impassioned "Part Time Love" is included, along with the Bobby Bland-tinged mid-tempo groover "You'll Need Another Favor," a delicious "Since I Found a New Love," and the blistering "You Win, I Lose." Seventeen tracks in all, many of them bolstered by Arthur Wright's stinging guitar. —Bill Dahl

Super Taylors / 1974 / Ronn ✦✦✦
Now here's a relic from Taylor's prolific early '70s Ronn tenure that is available on CD. Although they weren't related (except by label), the "Super Taylors" shared this album like long-lost brothers. Four duets find the two complementing one another most soulfully; otherwise, the album is comprised of solo sides by both (including Little Johnny's "Everybody Knows About My Good Thing"). —Bill Dahl

Johnnie "Geechie" Temple

b. Oct. 18, 1906, Canton, MS, **d.** Nov. 22, 1968, Jackson, MS
Guitar, Vocals / Urban Blues, Delta Blues
Johnnie Temple is one of the great unsung heroes of the blues. A contemporary of Skip James, Son House, and other Delta legends, Temple was one of the very first to develop the now-standard bottom-string boogie bass figure, generally credited to Robert Johnson.
Born and raised in Mississippi, Temple learned to play guitar and mandolin as a child. By the time he was a teenager, he was playing house parties and various other local events. Temple moved to Chicago in the early '30s, where he quickly became part of the town's blues scene. Often, he performed with Charlie and Joe McCoy. In 1935, Temple began recording, releasing "Louise Louise Blues" the following year on Decca Records.
Although he never achieved stardom, Temple's records—which were released on a variety of record labels—sold consistently throughout the late '30s and '40s. In the '50s, his recording career stopped, but he continued to perform, frequently with Big Walter Horton and Billy Boy Arnold. Once electrified post-war blues overtook acoustic blues in the mid-'50s, Temple left Chicago and moved to Mississippi. After he returned to his home state, he played clubs and juke joints around the Jackson area for a few years before he disappeared from the scene. Johnny Temple died in 1968. —Cub Koda & Stephen Thomas Erlewine

1935-39 / Document ✦✦✦✦
A solid collection of Temple's earliest sides, including the killer "Lead Pencil Blues." —Cub Koda

Sonny Terry

b. Oct. 24, 1911, Greensboro, GA, **d.** Mar. 11, 1986, Mineola, NY
Harmonica, Vocals / Blues, Acoustic Blues, Acoustic Country Blues, Electric Blues, Piedmont Blues, Folk-Blues
The joyous whoop that Sonny Terry naturally emitted between raucous harp blasts was as distinctive a signature sound as can possibly be imagined. Only a handful of blues harmonicists wielded as much of a lasting influence on the genre as did the sightless Terry (Buster Brown, for one, copied the whoop and all), who recorded some fine urban blues as a bandleader in addition to serving as guitarist Brownie McGhee's longtime duet partner.
Terry had met McGhee in 1939, and they joined forces, playing together on a 1941 McGhee date for Okeh and settling in New York as a duo in 1942. There they broke into the folk scene, working alongside Leadbelly, Josh White, and Woody Guthrie.
While Brownie McGhee was incredibly prolific in the studio during the mid-'40s, Terry was somewhat less so as a leader. Terry made some nice sides in an R&B mode for Jax, Jackson, Red Robin, RCA Victor, Groove, Harlem, Old Town, and Ember during the '50s, usually with Brownie close by on guitar. But it was the folk boom of the late '50s and early '60s that made Brownie and Sonny household names (at least among folk aficionados). They toured long and hard as a duo, cutting a horde of endearing acoustic duet LPs along the way, before scuttling

their decades-long partnership amidst a fair amount of reported acrimony during the mid-'70s. —Bill Dahl

★ **The Folkways Years, 1944-1963** / 1944-1963 / Smithsonian/Folkways ✦✦✦✦✦
While he's best known as guitarist Brownie McGhee's longtime partner, harmonica ace and vocalist Sonny Terry made many excellent recordings as a solo act, and recorded with Blind Boy Fuller and others. The 17 songs on this anthology include Terry playing with McGhee's brother Stick, Pete Seeger, and others, as well as several featuring Terry's biting harmonica and wry leads relating stories of failure, triumph, and resiliency, backed by McGhee's flickering but always audible guitar. The title is a bit misleading, since the earliest date for any session is 1946 (one number), and most are done between 1955 and 1959. —Ron Wynn

Whoopin' / 1984 / Alligator ✦✦✦✦
The textbook charge usually levelled against Alligator sessions are that they're sanitized. You couldn't lodge that one against this set with a straight face; if anything, somebody turned Sonny Terry loose. It didn't hurt that Johnny Winter was around on guitar and piano, playing gritty blues with a passion. It didn't help that Terry didn't put any amplified muscle behind his harmonica, however. Otherwise, this is a strong session. —Ron Wynn

Sonny Terry / 1987 / Collectables ✦✦✦✦
Harmonica player and vocalist Sonny Terry cut some stunning material for Gotham in the early '50s. Some of it was issued, and much of it wasn't. This is a healthy chunk of things that were and weren't released, with good remastering embellishing Terry's cutting vocals and splintering harmonica. —Ron Wynn

Sonny Terry / 1995 / Capitol ✦✦✦✦
Some of the whooping harmonicist's finest stuff as a bandleader, dating from his 1947-1950 Capitol Records tenure. Brownie McGhee handles the guitar on two sessions, his brother Stick on the other two, but Terry is front and center on all. Contains all 16 numbers Terry did for the major label, notably "Whoopin' the Blues," "Custard Pie Blues," and "Beer Garden Blues." —Bill Dahl

Henry Thomas

b. 1874
Vocals / Acoustic Country Blues
Texas songster Henry Thomas remains a relative stranger who made some great recordings, then returned to obscurity. Evidence suggests he was an itinerant street musician, a musical hobo who rode the rails across Texas and possibly to the World Fairs in St. Louis and Chicago just before and after the turn of the century. Most agree he was the oldest African-American folk artist to produce a significant body of recordings. His projected 1874 birthdate would predate Charley Patton by a good 17 years. Like Patton and a handful of other musicians generally termed songsters (including John Hurt, Jim Jackson, Mance Lipscomb, Furry Lewis, and Leadbelly), Thomas' repertoire bridged the 19th and 20th centuries, providing a compelling glimpse into a wide range of African-American musical genres. The 23 songs he cut for Vocalion between 1927 and 1929 include a spiritual, ballads, reels, dance songs, and eight selections titled blues. Obviously dance music, his songs are geared to older dance styles shared by Black and White audiences. Thomas' sound, like his repertoire, is unique. He capoed his guitar high up the neck and strummed it in the manner of a banjo, favoring dance rhythm over complex fingerwork. On many of his pieces, he simultaneously played the quills or panpipes, a common but seldom-recorded African-American folk instrument indigenous to Mississippi, Louisiana, and Texas. Combining the quills, a limited-range melody instrument, with his banjo-like strummed guitar produced one of the most memorable sounds in American folk music. For example, his lead-in on "Bull Doze Blues" still worked as a hook when recycled 40 years later by blues/rockers Canned Heat in their version of "Going Up the Country." "Ragtime Texas," as Thomas was known, provides a welcome inroad to 19th-century dance music, but his music is neither obscure nor merely educational: it has a timeless quality—and while it may be an acquired taste, once you catch on to it, you're hooked. —Barry Lee Pearson

★ **Texas Worried Blues** / Yazoo ✦✦✦✦✦
Songster Thomas plays a cross-section of blues and pre-blues with a unique guitar-and-panpipes instrumentation. Although it may sound archaic to the beginner, given time it will get your toes tapping and quickly become a favorite. —Barry Lee Pearson

"Big Mama" Thornton (Willie Mae Thornton)

b. Dec. 11, 1926, Montgomery, AL, **d.** Jul. 25, 1984, Los Angeles, CA
Harmonica, Drums, Vocals / Electric West Coast Blues
Willie Mae "Big Mama" Thornton only notched one national hit in her lifetime, but it was a true monster. "Hound Dog" held down the top slot on *Billboard's* R&B charts for seven long weeks in 1953. Alas, Elvis Pres-

ley's rocking 1956 cover was even bigger, effectively obscuring Thornton's chief claim to immortality.

That's a damned shame, because Thornton's menacing growl was indeed something special. The hefty belter first opened her pipes in church but soon embraced the blues. She toured with Sammy Green's Hot Harlem Revue during the 1940s. Thornton was ensconced on the Houston circuit when Peacock Records boss Don Robey signed her in 1951. She debuted on Peacock with "Partnership Blues" that year, backed by trumpeter Joe Scott's band.

But it was her third Peacock date with Johnny Otis' band that proved the winner. With Pete Lewis laying down some truly nasty guitar behind her, Big Mama shouted "Hound Dog," a tune whose authorship remains a bone of contention to this day (both Otis and the team of Jerry Leiber and Mike Stoller claim responsibility), and soon hit the road a star.

Thornton was a tough cookie. She dressed like a man and took no guff from anyone, even as the pounds fell off her once-ample frame and she became downright scrawny during the last years of her life. Medical personnel found her lifeless body in an L.A. rooming house in 1984. —*Bill Dahl*

● **Hound Dog: The Peacock Recordings** / 1992 / MCA ◆◆◆◆
Let's face it, Big Mama Thornton will always be chiefly recalled for her growling 1952 reading of the Jerry Leiber-Mike Stoller classic "Hound Dog." But the other 17 sides on this collection of her 1952-1957 output for Don Robey's Peacock Records aren't exactly makeweight. Thornton's mighty roar was backed by the jumping combos of Johnny Otis and saxist Bill Harvey, producing additional gems in "My Man Called Me," "They Call Me Big Mama," "The Fish," and a duet with the ill-fated Johnny Ace, "Yes Baby." —*Bill Dahl*

Luther Tucker

b. Jan. 20, 1936, Memphis, TN, **d.** Jun. 18, 1993, Greenbrae, CA
Guitar / Chicago Blues
Guitarist Luther Tucker worked with Little Walter Jacobs for seven years and played on many of Walter's classic sides. He also recorded with Otis Rush, Robben Ford, Sonny Boy Williamson II, Jimmy Rogers, Snooky Pryor, Muddy Waters, John Lee Hooker, Elvin Bishop, and James Cotton.

In the mid-'60s, Tucker was featured in the James Cotton Blues Band and traveled with that band extensively. He relocated to Marin County, CA, in 1973 and formed the Luther Tucker Band. He played in clubs in the San Francisco Bay Area until his death on June 18, 1993, in Greenbrae, CA. Luther Tucker, who was soft-spoken and even shy, was one of a handful of backup artists (the Four Aces/Jukes were others) who helped to create and shape the small combo sound of Chicago blues. Unfortunately, they seldom get much credit. Yet, as the history of Chicago blues gets written, there will be more and more time to discover the wonderful understated rhythmic guitar mastery of Luther Tucker. —*Michael Erlewine*

Sad Hours / Antone's ◆◆◆◆
Sadly, this disc was issued posthumously. —*Bill Dahl*

Big Joe Turner

b. May 18, 1911, Kansas City, MO, **d.** Nov. 24, 1985, Inglewood, CA
Vocals / R&B, Rock 'n' Roll, Blues, Jazz, Swing, Jump Blues
The premier blues shouter of the postwar era, Big Joe Turner's roar could rattle the very foundation of any gin joint he sang within—and that's without a microphone. Turner was a resilient figure in the history of blues—he effortlessly spanned boogie-woogie, jump blues, even the first wave of rock 'n' roll, enjoying great success in each genre.

Turner, whose powerful physique certainly matched his vocal might, was a product of the swinging, wide-open Kansas City scene. Even in his teens, the big-boned Turner looked entirely mature enough to gain entry to various K.C. niteries. He ended up simultaneously tending bar and singing the blues before hooking up with boogie piano master Pete Johnson during the early '30s. Theirs was a partnership that would endure for 13 years.

The pair initially traveled to New York at John Hammond's behest in 1936. On December 23, 1938, they appeared on the fabled Spirituals to Swing concert at Carnegie Hall on a bill with Big Bill Broonzy, Sonny Terry, the Golden Gate Quartet, and Count Basie. Big Joe and Johnson performed "Low Down Dog" and "It's All Right, Baby" on the historic show, kicking off a boogie-woogie craze that landed them a long-running slot at the Cafe Society (along with piano giants Meade Lux Lewis and Albert Ammons).

As 1938 came to a close, Turner and Johnson waxed the thundering "Roll 'em Pete" for Vocalion. It was a thrilling up-tempo number anchored by Johnson's crashing 88s, and Turner would re-record it many times over the decades. In 1940, the massive shouter moved over to Decca and cut "Piney Brown Blues" with Johnson rippling the ivories.

Turner ventured out to the West Coast during the war years, building quite a following while ensconced on the L.A. circuit. In 1945, he signed

on with National Records and cut some fine small combo platters under Herb Abramson's supervision. Turner remained with National through 1947, belting an exuberant "My Gal's a Jockey" that became his first national R&B smash.

Few West Coast indie labels of the late '40s didn't boast at least one or two Turner titles in their catalogs. The shouter bounced from RPM to Down Beat/Swing Time to MGM (all those dates were anchored by Johnson's piano) to Texas-based Freedom (which moved some of their masters to Specialty) in 1950 (his New Orleans backing crew there included a young Fats Domino on piano). But apart from the 1950 Freedom 78, "Still in the Dark," none of Big Joe's records were selling particularly well. When Atlantic Records bosses Abramson and Ahmet Ertegun fortuitously dropped by the Apollo Theater to check out Count Basie's band one day, they discovered that Turner had temporarily replaced Jimmy Rushing as the Basie band's front man, and he was having a tough go of it. Atlantic picked up his spirits by picking up his recording contract, and Big Joe Turner's heyday was about to commence. At Turner's first Atlantic date in April of 1951, he imparted a gorgeously world-weary reading to the moving blues ballad "Chains of Love" (co-penned by Ertegun and pianist Harry Van Walls) that restored him to the uppermost reaches of the R&B charts. From there, the hits came in droves: "Chill Is On," "Sweet Sixteen," and "Don't You Cry" were all done in New York, and all hit big.

Big Joe Turner had no problem whatsoever adapting his prodigious pipes to whatever regional setting he was in. In 1953, he cut his first R&B chart-topper, the storming rocker "Honey Hush," in New Orleans, with trombonist Pluma Davis and tenor saxman Lee Allen in rip-roaring support. Before the year was through, he stopped off in Chicago to record with slide guitarist Elmore James' considerably rougher-edged combo and hit again with the salacious "T.V. Mama."

Prolific Atlantic house writer Jesse Stone was the source of Turner's biggest smash of all, "Shake, Rattle and Roll," which proved his second chart-topper in 1954. With the Atlantic braintrust reportedly chiming in on the chorus behind Turner's rumbling lead, the song sported enough pop possibilities to merit a considerably cleaned-up cover by Bill Haley & the Comets. Suddenly, at the age of 43, Big Joe Turner was a rock star. His jumping follow-ups—"Well All Right," "Flip Flop and Fly," "Hide and Seek," "Morning, Noon and Night," "The Chicken and the Hawk"—all mined the same goodtime groove as "Shake, Rattle and Roll," with crisp backing from New York's top session aces and typically superb production by Ertegun and Jerry Wexler. Turner stayed on at Atlantic into 1959, but nobody bought his violin-enriched remake of "Chains of Love." The '60s didn't produce too much of lasting substance for the shouter—he actually cut an album with longtime admirer Haley and his latest batch of Comets in Mexico City in 1966!

But by the tail end of the decade, Big Joe Turner's essential contributions to blues history were beginning to receive proper recognition; he cut LPs for Bluesway and Blues Time. During the '70s and '80s, Turner recorded prolifically for Norman Granz's jazz-oriented Pablo label. These were super-relaxed impromptu sessions that often paired the allegedly illiterate shouter with various jazz luminaries in what amounted to loosely-run jam sessions. Turner contentedly roared the familiar lyrics of one or another of his hits, then sat back while somebody took a lengthy solo. Other notable album projects included a 1983 collaboration with Roomful of Blues, *Blues Train*, for Muse. Health problems and the size of his humongous frame forced him to sit down during his latter-day performances, Turner continued to tour until shortly before his death in 1985. They called him the Boss of the Blues, and the appellation was truly a fitting one: when Big Joe Turner shouted a lyric, you were definitely at his beck and call. —*Bill Dahl*

★ **Big, Bad and Blue: The Big Joe Turner Anthology** / Dec. 30, 1938-Jan. 26, 1983 / Rhino ◆◆◆◆◆
Rhino has done a stellar job of cross-licensing to present an exhaustive three-disc, 62-track compilation that traces the booming jump blues belter's recording career from its Kansas City-bred beginnings with pianist Pete Johnson in 1938 through the postwar years with the National, Aladdin, Down Beat, and Freedom labels and on into his R&B heyday on Atlantic from 1951 to 1959. Of course, all the great prototypical rockers are aboard—"Honey Hush," "Shake, Rattle and Roll," "Flip Flop and Fly," "Corrine Corrina"—and the set closes with three far more recent entries that are the weakest tracks on the entire anthology. The sheer power of Big Joe's pipes is overwhelming, his combos cooked mercilessly, and this set is one to get. —*Bill Dahl*

☆ **Complete 1940-1944** / Nov. 11, 1940-Nov. 13, 1944 / Official ◆◆◆◆◆
Big Joe Turner's 25 Decca recordings are all included on this excellent set. The music is consistently exciting and finds the blues singer in prime form. His accompaniment is quite varied and always colorful with such pianists as Art Tatum, Pete Johnson, Willie "The Lion" Smith (a perfect match), Sam Price and the surprisingly effective Freddie Slack all getting their spots. Turner had a remarkably long and commercially successful career considering that he never changed his basic approach; he just never went out of style. —*Scott Yanow*

Every Day in the Week / 1941 04 1 / Decca ✦✦✦
Most of the material on this grab bag dates from early- and mid-'40s sessions for Decca. Rather muted and jazzy in feel, they're made more interesting or tedious, depending on your perspective, by the inclusion of many alternate takes (some previously unissued). As these are grouped together one after another, it can make tough listening for the general fan, although Turner completists will appreciate the attention to detail. Rounding out the collection are four 1963-64 tracks that awkwardly update Turner's R&B with modern soul and pop touches, and a track from a 1967 Bluesway LP. —*Richie Unterberger*

Tell Me Pretty Baby / Nov. 1947-1949 / Arhoolie ✦✦✦✦
Lusty, romping jump blues and boogies from 1947-1949 that teams Big Joe Turner with his longtime piano partner Pete Johnson and a coterie of solid L.A. sessioneers. The two dozen entries include party rockers like "Wine-O-Baby Boogie," "Christmas Date Boogie," "I Don't Dig It," and an incredibly raunchy two-part "Around the Clock Blues" (where Turner spends his time in a by-the-hour sexual tryst). —*Bill Dahl*

★ **Greatest Hits** / Apr. 19, 1951-Jan. 22, 1958 / Atlantic ✦✦✦✦✦
The best single-disc collection available of Turner's seminal 1950s Atlantic sides (21 sides in all). Most of the essential stuff is here—the world-weary blues ballads "Chains of Love" and "Sweet Sixteen," the rockers "Shake, Rattle and Roll," "Flip Flop and Fly," and "Boogie Woogie Country Girl," and a lusty "Well All Right" that rates with Turner's best jump blues outings ever. —*Bill Dahl*

Things That I Used to Do / Feb. 8, 1977 / Original Jazz Classics ✦✦✦✦
This is one of Big Joe Turner's best albums of his last period. Turner is in fine form and joined by some superb blues and jazz musicians. Altoist Eddie "Cleanhead" Vinson (pity that he didn't have a vocal duet with Turner) and trumpeter Blue Mitchell get solo space as does the veteran R&B tenor Wild Bill Moore, pianist Lloyd Glenn and guitarist Gary Bell. Mitchell can be heard on many of the tunes, setting hot ensemble riffs. There are some loose spots but the spirit is definitely there and Turner's voice can be heard still in its prime on such tunes as "Jelly Jelly Blues," "Shake It and Break It" and "St. Louis Blues." Fun music. —*Scott Yanow*

Rhythm and Blues Years / 1986 / Atlantic ✦✦✦✦
Picks up the rest of the 1950s Atlantic Records motherlode. The Chicago-cut double-entendre gem "TV Mama" (with Elmore James on guitar), the lighthearted rockers "Rock a While," "Morning Noon and Night," and "Lipstick, Powder and Paint," and a rip-snorting remake of Turner's classic "Roll 'em Pete," here titled "(We're Gonna) Jump for Joy," that in its own way rivals the original (King Curtis' blistering sax solo doesn't hurt), are among the many highlights on the 28-song collection. —*Bill Dahl*

I've Been to Kansas City, Vol. 1 / 1990 / Decca/MCA ✦✦✦✦
Sixteen of Big Joe's earliest sides (1940-1941) for Decca, many but not all with the immortal pianist Pete Johnson rolling the ivories behind the Kansas City shouter (other sidemen include pianists Art Tatum, Sammy Price, and Willie "The Lion" Smith, guitarist Oscar Moore, and trumpet ace Hot Lips Page). Big Joe sounds young and virile on "Piney Brown Blues," "Wee Baby Blues," and "Nobody in Mind," and there's an early reading of "Corrine, Corrina" that's considerably different from his subsequent rock 'n' roll hit version. —*Bill Dahl*

Have No Fear, Big Joe Turner Is Here / 1994 / Savoy Jazz ✦✦✦✦
Producer Herb Abramson's first encounters with Big Joe Turner weren't at Atlantic, but for the National logo, where Turner paused from 1945 to 1947 and cut the 26 swinging numbers on this collection. For once, the CD format limits the amount of selections rather than enlarges it; the original two-LP version of this package boasted a few more cuts. Pete Johnson returns to run the 88s on the first seven numbers (including a two-part cover of Saunders King's "S.K. Blues"), and familiar names like saxman Wild Bill Moore and drummer Red Saunders also turn up. "Sally Zu-Zazz," "I Got Love for Sale," and "My Gal's a Jockey" capture the peerless shouter at his ribald best. —*Bill Dahl*

Jumpin' with Joe: The Complete Aladdin and Imperial Recordings / Jan. 11, 1994 / EMI America ✦✦✦✦
Big Joe Turner's remarkable recordings for Atlantic and Decca have been frequently reissued and evaluated. But his singles for other labels haven't gotten similar treatment, which makes this 18-cut single-disc anthology of Aladdin and Imperial material so welcome. These were recorded in the late '40s and early '50s and were closer to the Kansas City swing Turner had done earlier in his career; there was more emphasis on lyric interpretation, swing, and timing than sheer volume and volcanic, non-stop hollering. Although these songs aren't remembered as fondly as the landmark Atlantic numbers, they're just as important a part of Turner's legacy. —*Ron Wynn*

Joe Louis Walker

b. Dec. 25, 1949, San Francisco, CA
Guitar, Vocals / R&B, Modern Electric Blues
Without a doubt one of the most exciting and innovative artists gracing contemporary blues, guitarist Joe Louis Walker has glowed like a shin-ing blue beacon over the last decade. His 1986 debut album for HighTone, *Cold Is the Night*, announced his arrival in stunning fashion; his subsequent output on HighTone and Verve has only served to further establish Walker as one of the leading younger bluesmen on the scene.

Walker traveled a circuitous route to get to where he is today. At age 14, he took up the guitar, playing blues (with an occasional foray into psychedelic rock) on the mushrooming San Francisco circuit.

But by 1975, Walker was burned out on blues and turned to God, singing for the next decade with a gospel group, the Spiritual Corinthians. When the Corinthians played the 1985 New Orleans Jazz & Heritage Festival, Walker was inspired to embrace his blues roots again. He assembled a band, the Boss Talkers, and wrote some stunning originals that ended up on *Cold Is the Night* (co-produced by Bruce Bromberg and Dennis Walker).

Joe Louis Walker is quite the total package, as tremendously assured on a down-in-the-alley acoustic solo outing as he is performing a thoroughly modern R&B-laced number with his latest crew of Boss Talkers. Expect more great things from him in years to come. —*Bill Dahl*

Cold Is the Night / 1986 / HighTone ✦✦✦✦
The Bay Area blues guitarist's debut album sounds underproduced compared to what would soon follow—and that's no knock. Walker's gritty, expressive vocals and ringing, concise guitar work shine through loud and clear in front of his band, the Boss Talkers. Walker and his producers Dennis Walker and Bruce Bromberg wrote virtually the entire set, including the slashing "Cold Is the Night," "Don't Play Games," and "One Woman." —*Bill Dahl*

● **The Gift** / 1988 / HighTone ✦✦✦✦
Although it didn't enjoy the major label hype that his current output does, Walker's HighTone encore just may be his finest album of all, filled with soulful vocal performances, bone-cutting guitar work, and tight backing from the Boss Talkers and the Memphis Horns. Honestly, you can't go wrong with any of Walker's remarkably consistent HighTone discs—but give this one the slightest of edges over the rest. —*Bill Dahl*

Blue Soul / 1989 / Hightone ✦✦✦✦
Another winner sporting memorable songs ("T.L.C.," "Personal Baby," "City of Angels," "Prove Your Love"), sinuous grooves, and a whole lot of vicious guitar from one of the hottest relatively young bluesmen on the circuit. He goes it alone on the finale, "I'll Get to Heaven on My Own," sounding as conversant with the country blues tradition as he does with the contemporary stuff. —*Bill Dahl*

Blues Survivor / Oct. 19, 1993 / Verve ✦✦✦

T-Bone Walker (Aaron Thibeaux Walker)

b. May 28, 1910, Linden, TX, **d.** Mar. 16, 1975, Los Angeles, CA
Guitar, Vocals / Electric Texas Blues
Modern electric blues guitar can be traced directly back to this Texas-born pioneer, who began amplifying his sumptuous lead lines for public consumption circa 1940 and thus initiated a revolution so total that its tremors are still being felt today.

Few major postwar blues guitarists come to mind that don't owe T-Bone Walker an unpayable debt of gratitude. B.B. King has long cited him as a primary influence, marveling at Walker's penchant for holding the body of his guitar outward while he played it. Gatemouth Brown, Pee Wee Crayton, Goree Carter, Pete Mayes, and a wealth of other prominent Texas-bred axemen came stylistically right out of Walker during the late '40s and early '50s.

In 1929, Walker made his recording debut with a single 78 for Columbia, "Wichita Falls Blues"/"Trinity River Blues," billed as Oak Cliff T-Bone. Pianist Douglas Fernell was his musical partner for the disc. Walker was exposed to some pretty outstanding guitar talent during his formative years; besides Jefferson, Charlie Christian—who would totally transform the role of the guitar in jazz with his electrified riffs much as Walker would with blues—was one of his playing partners circa 1933.

T-Bone Walker split the Southwest for Los Angeles during the mid-'30s, earning his keep with saxist Big Jim Wynn's band with his feet rather than his hands as a dancer. Popular bandleader Les Hite hired Walker as his vocalist in 1939. Walker sang "T-Bone Blues" with the Hite aggregation for Varsity Records in 1940, but didn't play guitar on the outing. It was about then, though, that his fascination with electrifying his axe bore fruit; he played L.A. clubs with his daring new toy after assembling his own combo, engaging in acrobatic stage moves—splits, playing behind his back—to further enliven his show.

Capitol Records as a fledgling Hollywood concern in 1942, when Walker signed on and cut "Mean Old World" and "I Got a Break Baby" with boogie master Freddie Slack hammering the 88s. This was the first sign of the T-Bone Walker that blues guitar aficionados know and love, his fluid, elegant riffs and mellow, burnished vocals setting a standard that all future blues guitarists would measure themselves by.

Chicago's Rhumboogie Club served as Walker's home away from home during a good portion of the war years. He even cut a few sides for the joint's house label in 1945 under the direction of pianist Marl Young. But after a solitary session that same year for Old Swingmaster that soon made its way onto another newly established logo, Mercury, Walker signed with L.A.-based Black & White Records in 1946 and proceeded to amass a stunning legacy.

The immortal "Call It Stormy Monday (But Tuesday Is Just as Bad)" was the product of a 1947 Black & White date with Teddy Buckner on trumpet and invaluable pianist Lloyd Glenn in the backing quintet. Many of Walker's best sides were smoky after-hours blues, though an occasional uptempo entry—"T-Bone Jumps Again," a storming instrumental from the same date, for example—illustrated his nimble dexterity at faster speeds.

Walker recorded prolifically for Black & White until the close of 1947, waxing classics like the often-covered "T-Bone Shuffle" and "West Side Baby," though many of the sides came out on Capitol after the demise of Black & White. In 1950, Walker turned up on Imperial. His first date for the L.A. indie elicited the after-hours gem "Glamour Girl" and perhaps the penultimate jumping instrumental in his repertoire, "Strollin' with Bones" (Snake Sims' drum kit cracks like a whip behind Walker's impeccable licks).

Walker's 1950-54 Imperial stint was studded with more classics: "The Hustle Is On," "Cold Cold Feeling," "Blue Mood," "Vida Lee" (named for his wife), "Party Girl," and, from a 1952 New Orleans jaunt, "Railroad Station Blues," which was produced by Dave Bartholomew. Atlantic was T-Bone Walker's next stop in 1955; his first date for them was an unlikely but successful collaboration with a crew of Chicago mainstays (harpist Junior Wells, guitarist Jimmy Rogers, and bassist Ransom Knowling among them). Rogers found the experience especially useful; he later adapted Walker's "Why Not" as his own Chess hit "Walking by Myself."

With a slightly more sympathetic L.A. band in staunch support, Walker cut two follow-up sessions for Atlantic in 1956-57. The latter date produced some amazing instrumentals ("Two Bones and a Pick," "Bluesrock," "Shufflin' the Blues") that saw him duelling it out with his nephew and jazzman Barney Kessel (Walker emerged victorious in every case).

Unfortunately, the remainder of Walker's discography isn't of the same sterling quality for the most part. As it had with so many of his peers from the postwar R&B era, rock's rise had made Walker's classy style an anachronism (at least during much of the 1960s).

No amount of written accolades can fully convey the monumental importance of what T-Bone Walker gave to the blues. He was the idiom's first true lead guitarist, and undeniably one of its very best. —*Bill Dahl*

☆ **T Bone Blues** / 1959 / Atlantic ✦✦✦✦✦
Walker's finest mid-period album. Classics abound any place you look, and T-Bone's guitar work is nothing short of extraordinary. —*Cub Koda*

Inventor of the Electric Guitar Blues / 1983 / Blues Boy ✦✦✦✦
Some formative and masterful recordings by Aaron T-Bone Walker, among the greatest pure vocalists in modern blues history. The find is a side with Walker playing 1929 country blues and sounding just as comfortable and exciting as he does on the 16 other 1940s and '50s numbers. —*Ron Wynn*

☆ **The Complete Recordings of T-Bone Walker 1940-1954** / Oct. 1990 / Mosaic ✦✦✦✦✦
A six-CD boxed set—an education in the lineage of urban blues. It appears that T-Bone Walker had a greater influence on urban blues players than any other single talent. His guitar, vocals, song selection, and sheer style live on in nearly every blues performer. He is the master. —*Michael Erlewine*

★ **The Complete Imperial Recordings** / 1991 / EMI America ✦✦✦✦✦
Another essential T-Bone Walker stake, this time a two-disc dish with 52 sensational tracks from his stint at Lew Chudd's Imperial Records. Whether waxing with his own jump blues unit in L.A. or Dave Bartholomew's hard-drivers in New Orleans, Walker always stayed true to his vision, and the proof was in the grooves: "Glamour Girl," "The Hustle Is On," "Tell Me What's the Reason," "High Society," "Cold, Cold Feeling," and the immaculate jumping instrumental "Strollin' with Bones" all date from this historic period of Walker's legacy. —*Bill Dahl*

☆ **Complete Capitol/Black and White Recordings** / 1995 / Capitol ✦✦✦✦✦
Three-CD, 75-track box of T-Bone Walker's recordings for the Capitol and Black and White labels in the 1940s. From a historical perspective, this is perhaps the most important phase of Walker's evolution. It was here that he perfected his electric guitar style, becoming an important influence on everyone from B.B. King down. It was also here that he acted as one of the key players in small combo West Coast bands' transition from jazz to a more jump blues/R&B-oriented sound (though most of these sides retain a pretty strong jazz flavor). These sessions, which include the original version of his most famous tune ("Call It Stormy Monday"), have previously been chopped up into small morsels for reissue, or incorporated into the mammoth limited-edition Mosaic box set; this isolates

them more conveniently. At the same time, it may be too extensive for some listeners, especially with the abundance of alternate takes (which are placed right after the official versions). Excellent liner notes, although the discographical information is surprisingly inconsistent. —*Richie Unterberger*

T-Bones Blues / Atlantic ✦✦✦✦
The last truly indispensable disc of the great guitar hero's career, and perhaps the most innately satisfying of all—these mid-'50s recordings boast magnificent presence, with Walker's axe so crisp and clear it seems as though he's sitting right next to you as he delivers a luxurious remake of "Call It Stormy Monday." Atlantic took some chances with Bone, dispatching him to Chicago for a 1955 date with Junior Wells and Jimmy Rogers that produced "Why Not" and "Papa Ain't Salty." Even better were the 1956-57 L.A. dates that produced the scalding instrumentals "Two Bones and a Pick" (the latter finding Walker duelling it out with nephew R.S. Rankin and jazzman Barney Kessel). —*Bill Dahl*

Sippie Wallace (Beulah Wallace)

b. Nov. 1, 1898, Houston, TX, **d.** Nov. 1, 1986, Detroit, MI
Vocals / Classic Female Blues, Blues
A classic female blues singer from the '20s, Wallace kept performing and recording until her death. She was a major influence on a young Bonnie Raitt, who recorded several of Wallace's songs and performed live with her.

In 1923, Sippie, Hersal, and their older brother George moved to Chicago, where Sippie became part of the city's jazz scene. By the end of the year, she had earned a contract with Okeh Records. Her first two songs for the label, "Shorty George" and "Up the Country Blues," were hits and Sippie soon became a star. Throughout the '20s, she produced a series of singles that were nearly all hits. Wallace's Okeh recordings featured a number of celebrated jazz musicians, including Louis Armstrong, Eddie Heywood, King Oliver, and Clarence Williams; both Hersal and George Thomas performed on Sippie's records as well, in addition to supporting her at concerts. Between 1923 and 1927, she recorded over 40 songs for the OKeh. Many of the songs that were Wallace originals or co-written by Sippie and her brothers.

In 1926, Hersal Thomas died of food poisoning, but Sippie Wallace continued to perform and record. Within a few years, however, she stopped performing regularly. After her contract with OKeh was finished in the late '20s, she moved to Detroit in 1929. In the early '30s, Wallace stopped recording, only performing the occasional gig. In 1936, both George Thomas and her husband Matt died. Following their deaths, Sippie joined the Leland Baptist Church in Detroit, where she was an organist and vocalist; she stayed with the church for the next 40 years.

Between 1936 and 1966, Sippie Wallace was inactive on the blues scene—she only performed a handful of concerts and cut a few records. In 1966, she was lured out of retirement by her friend Victoria Spivey, who convinced Sippie to join the thriving blues and folk festival circuit. Wallace not only joined the circuit, she began recording again.

In 1970, Sippie Wallace suffered a stroke, but she was able to continue recording and performing, although not as frequently as she had before. In 1982, Bonnie Raitt—who had longe claimed Sippie as a major influence—helped Wallace land a contract with Atlantic Records. Raitt produced the resulting album, *Sippie*, which was released in 1983. *Sippie* won the W.C. Handy Award for best blues album of the year and was nominated for a Grammy. The album turned out to be Sippie Wallace's last recording—she died in 1986, when she was 88 years old. —*Stephen Thomas Erlewine & Cub Koda*

Women Be Wise / 1992 / Alligator ✦✦✦

● **1923-1929** / Document ✦✦✦✦
Sippie's earliest and best sides, including "I'm a Mighty Tight Woman." —*Cub Koda*

Robert Ward

b. Oct. 15, 1938
Guitar, Vocals / R&B, Soul Blues
Comeback tales don't come any more heartwarming (or unlikely) than Robert Ward's. Totally off the scene and thought by many aficionados to be dead, Ward's chance encounter with guitar-shop owner Dave Hussong in Dayton, OH, set off a rapid chain of events that culminated in Ward's 1990 debut album for Black Top, *Fear No Evil*, and a second chance at the brass ring.

Ward's first taste of stardom came as leader of the Ohio Untouchables (who later mutated into the Ohio Players long after Ward's departure) during the early '60s. Inspired by hard-bitten FBI man Eliott Ness on TV's *The Untouchables*, Ward recruited bassist Levoy Fredrick and drummer Cornelius Johnson to form the first edition of the Ohio Untouchables. Ward's trademark vibrato-soaked guitar sound was the direct result of acquiring a Magnatone amplifier at a Dayton music store. Lonnie Mack was so entranced by the watery sound of Ward's amp that he bought a Magnatone as well; both still utilize the same trademark sound to this day.

Detroit producer Robert West signed the Untouchables to his LuPine logo in 1962. Ward's quirky touch was beautifully exhibited on the hard-bitten "I'm Tired," a chilling doo wop-tinged "Forgive Me Darling," and the exotic "Your Love Is Amazing" for LuPine. In addition, the Untouchables backed Wilson Pickett and the Falcons on their gospel-charged 1962 smash "I Found a Love."

Ward and his band also briefly recorded for Detroit's Thelma Records, waxing the driving blues "Your Love Is Real" and a soul-sending "I'm Gonna Cry a River." Ward left the Untouchables in 1965.

During the early '70s, Ward worked as a session guitarist at Motown, playing behind the Temptations and the Undisputed Truth. But when his wife died in 1977, Ward hit the skids. He moved back to Georgia, and served a year in jail at one point. In 1990, that auspicious encounter with Hussong started the ball rolling for Ward's return to action. Black Top boss Hammond Scott signed the guitarist and produced the amazing *Fear No Evil* and a credible 1993 follow-up, *Rhythm of the People.* The label recently issued a third set, *Black Bottom*, that once again captured Ward's curiously mystical appeal. Today, Ward lives in tiny Dry Branch, GA, with his second wife Roberta, who contributed background vocals to his encore album. *—Bill Dahl*

★ **Fear No Evil** / 1991 / Black Top ✦✦✦✦✦
One of the most amazing comeback stories of the modern blues era was ignited by this astonishing album. Robert Ward hadn't recorded as a leader in close to a quarter century, but his melismatic, almost mystical vocal quality and quirky, vibrato-enriched guitar sound utterly vital and electrifying as he revives some of his own obscure oldies ("Your Love Is Amazing," "Forgive Me Darling," "Strictly Reserved for You") and debuts a few new compositions for good measure. One of the classic blues/soul albums of the '90s. *—Bill Dahl*

Hot Stuff / 1995 / Relic ✦✦✦✦
These are the first magnificent 1960s waxings of guitarist Robert Ward & the Ohio Untouchables for the tiny LuPine, Thelma, and Groove City logos; full of fiery soul, watery, vibrato-enhanced axe, and sinuous rhythms. Ward's piercing vocals on "I'm Tired," "Your Love Is Amazing," and "Fear No Evil" are mesmerizing. Also aboard are four classic cuts by the Wilson Pickett-led Falcons from 1962 with the Untouchables in support (the gospel-soaked "I Found a Love" was a legit smash, while Ward sears the strings on their "Let's Kiss and Make Up"). *—Bill Dahl*

Black Bottom / Oct. 17, 1995 / Black Top ✦✦✦✦
Now this is more like it. Ward is back in top form for his third Black Top outing, with better songs (most of them originals), skin-tight support from the Black Top house band, and plenty of that singularly gurgly guitar that inspired Lonnie Mack to follow Ward's lead and buy a Magnatone amp when he was starting out. *—Bill Dahl*

Muddy Waters (McKinley Morganfield)

b. Apr. 4, 1915, Rolling Fort, MS, **d.** Apr. 30, 1983, Westmont, IL
Guitar, Vocals / R&B, Electric Chicago Blues
A postwar Chicago blues scene without the magnificent contributions of Muddy Waters is absolutely unimaginable. From the late '40s on, he eloquently defined the city's aggressive, swaggering, Delta-rooted sound with his declamatory vocals and piercing slide guitar attack. When he passed away in 1983, the Windy City would never quite recover.

Like many of his contemporaries on the Chicago circuit, Waters was a product of the fertile Mississippi Delta. Born McKinley Morganfield in Rolling Fort, he grew up in nearby Clarksdale on Stovall's Plantation. His idol was the powerful Son House, a Delta patriarch whose flailing slide work and intimidating intensity Waters would emulate in his own fashion. Musicologist Alan Lomax traveled through Stovall's in August of 1941 under the auspices of the Library of Congress, in search of new talent for purposes of field recording. With the discovery of Morganfield, Lomax must have immediately known he'd stumbled across someone very special.

Setting up his portable recording rig in the Delta bluesman's house, Lomax captured for Library of Congress posterity Waters' mesmerizing rendition of "I Be's Troubled," which became his first big seller when he recut it a few years later for the Chess brothers' Aristocrat logo as "I Can't Be Satisfied." Lomax returned the next summer to record his bottleneck-wielding find more extensively, also cutting sides by the Son Simms Four (a string band that Waters belonged to).

Waters was renowned for his blues-playing prowess across the Delta, but that was about it until 1943, when he left for the bright lights of Chicago. By the mid-'40s, Waters' slide skills were becoming a recognized entity on Chicago's South Side, where he shared a stage or two with pianists Sunnyland Slim and Eddie Boyd and guitarist Blue Smitty. Producer Lester Melrose, who still had the local recording scene pretty much sewn up in 1946, accompanied Waters into the studio to wax a

date for Columbia, but the urban nature of the sides didn't electrify anyone in the label's hierarchy and remained unissued for decades.

Sunnyland Slim played a large role in launching the career of Muddy Waters. The pianist invited him to provide accompaniment for his 1947 Aristocrat session that would produce "Johnson Machine Gun." When Sunnyland was finished that auspicious day, Waters sang a pair of numbers, "Little Anna Mae" and "Gypsy Woman," that would become his own Aristocrat debut 78. They were rawer than the Columbia stuff, but not as inexorably down-home as "I Can't Be Satisfied" and its flip, "I Feel like Going Home" (the latter was his first national R&B hit in 1948). With Big Crawford slapping the bass behind Waters' gruff growl and slashing slide, "I Can't Be Satisfied" was such a local sensation that even Muddy Waters himself had a hard time buying a copy down on Maxwell Street.

He assembled a band that was so tight and vicious on stage that they were informally known as the Headhunters; they'd come into a bar where a band was playing, ask to sit in, and then "cut the heads" of their competitors with their superior musicianship. Little Walter, of course, would single-handedly revolutionize the role of the harmonica within the Chicago blues hierarchy; Jimmy Rogers was an utterly dependable second guitarist, and Baby Face Leroy Foster could play both drums and guitar. On top of their instrumental skills, all four men could sing powerfully.

In 1951 Waters climbed the R&B charts no less than four times, beginning with "Louisiana Blues," and continuing through "Long Distance Call," "Honey Bee," and "Still a Fool."

"Mad Love," his only chart bow in 1953, is noteworthy as the first hit to feature the rolling piano of Otis Spann, who would anchor the Waters aggregation for the next 16 years. By this time, Foster was long gone from the band, but Rogers remained, and Chess insisted that Walter—by then a popular act in his own right—make nearly every Waters session into 1958 (why break up a winning combination?). There was one downside to having such a peerless band; as the ensemble work got tighter and more urbanized, Waters' trademark slide guitar was largely absent on many of his Chess waxings.

Willie Dixon was playing an increasingly important role in Muddy Waters' success. In addition to slapping his upright bass on Waters' platters, the burly Dixon was writing one future bedrock standard after another for him: "I'm Your Hoochie Coochie Man," "Just Make Love to Me," and "I'm Ready."

When labelmate Bo Diddley borrowed Waters' swaggering beat for his strutting "I'm a Man" in 1955, Muddy turned around and did him tit for tat by reworking the tune ever so slightly as "Mannish Boy" and enjoying his own hit. "Sugar Sweet," a piledriving rocker with Spann's 88s anchoring the proceedings, also did well that year. 1956 brought three more R&B smashes: "Trouble No More," "Forty Days & Forty Nights," and "Don't Go No Farther."

After that, there was only one more chart item, 1958's typically uncompromising (and metaphorically loaded) "Close to You." But Waters' Chess output was still of uniformly stellar quality, boasting gems like "Walking Thru the Park" and "She's Nineteen Years Old," among the first sides to feature James Cotton's harp instead of Walter's, in 1958.

Cotton was apparently the bandmember that first turned Muddy on to "Got My Mojo Working," originally cut by Ann Cole in New York. Waters' 1956 cover was pleasing enough but went nowhere on the charts. But when the band launched into a supercharged version of the same tune at the 1960 Newport Jazz Festival, Cotton and Spann put an entirely new groove to it, making it an instant classic (fortuitously, Chess was on hand to capture the festivities on tape).

The personnel of the Waters band was much more fluid during the 1960s, but he always whipped them into first-rate shape. Guitarists Pee Wee Madison and Luther "Snake Boy" Johnson, and Sammy Lawhorn, harpists Mojo Buford and George Smith, bassists Jimmy Lee Morris and Calvin "Fuzz" Jones, and drummers Francis Clay and Willie "Big Eyes" Smith (along with Spann, of course) all passed through the ranks.

In 1964, Waters cut a two-sided gem for Chess, "The Same Thing"/ "You Can't Lose What You Never Had," that boasted a distinct 1950s feel in its sparse, reflexive approach. Most of his subsequent Chess catalog, though, is fairly forgettable.After a period of steady touring worldwide but little standout recording activity, Waters' studio fortunes were resuscitated by another of his legion of disciples, guitarist Johnny Winter. Signed to Blue Sky, a Columbia subsidiary, Waters found himself during the making of the LP *Hard Again*—backed by pianist Pinetop Perkins, drummer Willie Smith, and guitarist Bob Margolin from his touring band, Cotton on harp, and Winter' slam-bang guitar. Waters roared like a lion who had just awoken from a long nap.

Three subsequent Blue Sky albums continued the heartwarming back-to-the-basics campaign. In 1980, his entire combo split to form the Legendary Blues Band; needless to note, he didn't have much trouble assembling another one (new members included pianist Lovie Lee, guitarist John Primer, and the harpist Mojo Buford).

By the time of his death in 1983, Muddy Waters' exalted place in the history of blues (and 20th-century popular music, for that matter) was eternally assured. The Chicago blues genre that he turned upside down during the years following World War II would never recover—and that's a debt we'll never be able to repay. —*Bill Dahl*

☆ **Muddy Waters at Newport** / 1960 / MCA/Chess ✦✦✦✦✦
For many back in the early '60s, this was their first exposure to live recorded blues, and it's still pretty impressive. Muddy, with a band featuring Otis Spann, James Cotton, and guitarist Pat Hare, lays it down tough and cool with a set that literally had 'em dancing in the aisles by the set closer, a ripping version of "Got My Mojo Working," reprised in a shorter, encore version. Kicking off with a version of "I've Got My Brand on You" that positively burns the relatively tame (by comparison) studio take, Waters heads full bore through impressive versions of "Hoochie Coochie Man," Big Bill Broonzy's "Feel So Good" and "Tiger in Your Tank." A great breakthrough moment in blues history, preserved for posterity. —*Cub Koda*

Muddy Waters Sings Big Bill Broonzy / 1964 / MCA/Chess ✦✦✦✦
Waters' tribute album to the man who gave him his start on the Chicago circuit, this stuff doesn't sound much like Broonzy so much as a virtual recasting of his songs into Muddy's electric Chicago style. Evidently the first time Waters and his band were recorded in stereo, the highlights include high voltage takes on "When I Get to Drinkin'" and "The Mopper's Blues," with some really great harp from James Cotton as a bonus. —*Cub Koda*

The Real Folk Blues / 1965 / MCA/Chess ✦✦✦✦
Once Chess discovered a White folk-blues audience ripe and ready to hear the real thing, they released a series of albums under the *Real Folk Blues* banner. This is one of the best entries in the series, a mixed bag of early Chess sides from 1949-1954. Some of it hearkens back to Muddy's first recordings for Aristocrat with only Big Crawford on string in support, with some wonderful full band sides rounding out the package to give everyone the big picture. A couple of highlights are the cha cha/shuffle strut of the band charging through "Walkin' Through the Park" and the "I'm a Man"-derived nastiness of "Mannish Boy." —*Cub Koda*

Blues from Big Bill's Copacabana / 1967 / MCA/Chess ✦✦✦✦
Originally released as *Folk Festival of the Blues* on Chess' Argo subsidiary, the reissue gets the title right the second time around, a live document of a steamy night in a Chicago blues club. Chicago blues disc jockey Big Bill Hill intros the band and the assembled stars (one of whom, Little Walter, is nowhere to be found on this disc), then Buddy Guy's band rips into "Wee Wee Baby," sung in three-part harmony by Buddy, Muddy Waters and Willie Dixon. Some of the tracks here are ringers; Sonny Boy Williamson's "Bring It On Home" and a stray Buddy Guy track are actually studio takes with fake applause dubbed on. But the two from Howlin' Wolf and *everything* here from Muddy are as real as it gets; funky, out of tune in spots, with the crowd literally sweating all over the tape. Muddy's versions (with Otis Spann sitting in with the band) of "Clouds In My Heart" and "She's 19 Years Old" are nothing short of brilliant and the only thing better than this aural document would be to have actually been there right down front. Simply raw and amazing. —*Cub Koda*

More Real Folk Blues / 1967 / MCA/Chess ✦✦✦✦
The companion volume to the first Waters entry in the series is even more down home than the first. Featuring another brace of early Chess sides from 1948-1952, this release includes some essential tracks not found on *The Chess Box*. With the bludgeoning stomp of "She's Alright" featuring Elgin Evans' kickass drumming and the moody introspection of "My Life Is Ruined" among the numerous highlights, this is a fine budget package that Muddy fans (and lovers of early Chicago blues) shouldn't overlook. —*Cub Koda*

They Call Me Muddy Waters / 1970 / MCA/Chess ✦✦✦
Upon its original 1970 release, this was a Grammy winner for Best Ethnic/Traditional Recording. A quarter of a century later, it seems like an interesting, but diffuse, collection of Muddy Waters tracks, running chronologically from 1951 up to 1967. Excepting the title track and a couple others, there's nothing really indispensable here. A good one to add to the collection after you've picked up a half dozen others. —*Cub Koda*

Live at Mister Kelly's / Jun. 1971 / MCA/Chess ✦✦✦

Hard Again / May 1977 / Blue Sky ✦✦✦

Rare and Unissued / 1984 / MCA/Chess ✦✦✦✦
Compiler Dick Shurman rummaged around in the voluminous Chess vaults long enough to emerge with this sterling 14-song collection of unissued and rare sides, most of them dating from Waters' 1947-1954 heyday. "Little Anna Mae," "Feel like Going Home," and "You're Gonna Miss Me" spotlight his stark Delta roots; "Stuff You Gotta Watch," "Smokestack Lightnin'," and "Born Lover" boast fuller Waters bands of immense power and drive. —*Bill Dahl*

Fathers and Sons / 1987 / Vogue ✦✦✦

★ **The Best of Muddy Waters** / 1987 / MCA/Chess ✦✦✦✦✦
If you're building your Muddy Waters collection from the ground up, you can do no better than this compact disc reissue of his first album featuring 12 tightly compacted gems of seminal Chicago blues. This release features the original versions of "I'm Your Hoochie-Coochie Man," "Long Distance Call," "I'm Ready," "Honey Bee," "I Just Wanna Make Love to You," "Still a Fool," and a song called "Rollin' Stone," which provided the name inspiration for a hippie rock magazine and a group of British musicians.More than 30 years after its original release, it still stands as the perfect introduction to his music and one of the top five greatest Chicago blues albums of all time. —*Cub Koda*

Trouble No More/Singles (1955-1959) / 1989 / MCA/Chess ✦✦✦✦
This is an excellent compilation of some of Muddy Waters' lesser-anthologized singles, all of them dating from the late '50s. Some were surprisingly hard to acquire in any form until this appeared; the original version of "Got My Mojo Working," for instance, as well as some of his higher-profile tracks, like "Rock Me," "Trouble No More," "Close to You," and "Don't Go No Further." All of these tracks appear on the *Chess Box*, so if you have that one, you don't need this one. But if you don't, you do. —*Richie Unterberger and Cub Koda*

★ **The Chess Box** / Mar. 1990 / MCA/Chess ✦✦✦✦✦
Multi-disc box sets are a nettlesome proposition for the casual blues fan and even some hardliners. Most folks just don't have the time or the attention span to stay with one artist over the course of three to four hours of material, and because the very best sides are usually spread out over the various discs, just popping one in might not give you the artistic quick fix you're seeking. But if you've decided that Waters is your main man and you want to build a Chicago blues collection that's comprehensive and expansive, this three-disc box just might be your first stop. While there's a European box that's far more exhaustive (and expensive, sporting both dodgy sound quality and dubious legality), this one is far easier to digest. If you want to go for the big one, this is it. —*Cub Koda*

Blues Sky / Jun. 16, 1992 / Columbia/Legacy ✦✦✦✦
This is a nice collection, pairing down the best of the material Waters recorded for the Blue Sky label between 1976 to 1980. With Johnny Winter in the producer's chair, the backings are sympathetic, and the songs are great (some of them remakes of earlier Chess material). These are the tracks that garnered three consecutive Grammy Awards (for Best Ethnic or Traditional Recording) for Waters. Not the place to start by any means, but definitely worth a listen or two. —*Cub Koda*

☆ **The Complete Plantation Recordings** / Jun. 8, 1993 / MCA ✦✦✦✦✦
At long last, Muddy's historic 1941-1942 Library of Congress field recordings are collected in one place, with the best fidelity that's been heard thus far. Waters performs solo pieces (you can hear his slide rattling against the fretboard in spots) and band pieces with the Son Sims Four, "Rosalie" being a blueprint for his later Chicago style. Of particular note are the inclusion of several interview segments with Muddy from that embryonic period and a photo of Muddy playing on the porch of his cabin, dressed up and looking sharper than any Mississippi sharecropper on Stovall's plantation you could possibly imagine. This is much more than just an important historical document; this is some really fine music imbued with a sense of place and time and loads of ambience. Beyond essential. —*Cub Koda*

One More Mile / 1994 / MCA/Chess ✦✦✦✦
A double CD of 41 tracks, none of which is found on the box set. With only three exceptions, none of them has ever been available on an American album before, and quite a few were never previously released anywhere. During most of his stay at Chess, Waters' output was remarkably prolific and consistent. If you are interested enough in him to own more than one of his albums, you'll like what you hear on this collection, which matches or nearly matches the standards of his best work. Lots of rarities spanning the late '40s to the early '70s, with some special points of interest: the original 1955 version of "I Want to Be Loved," covered by the Rolling Stones on the B-side of their very first single, finally makes its first appearance on an American LP, and the final 11 songs are from a previously unreleased 1972 Swiss radio broadcast, showcasing Waters in a drummerless trio. —*Richie Unterberger*

Johnny Guitar Watson

b. Feb. 3, 1935, Houston, TX, **d.** May 17, 1996
Guitar, Vocals / Soul, R&B, Blues, Urban, Club/Dance
"Reinvention" could just as easily have been Johnny "Guitar" Watson's middle name. The multi-talented performer parlayed his stunning guitar skills into a vaunted reputation as one of the hottest blues axemen on the West Coast during the 1950s. But that admirable trait wasn't paying the bills as the 1970s rolled in. So he totally changed his image to that of a pimp-styled funkster, enjoying more popularity than ever

before for his down-and-dirty R&B smashes "A Real Mother for Ya" and "Superman Lover."

Watson's roots resided within the fertile blues scene of Houston. As a teen, he played with fellow Texas future greats Albert Collins and Johnny Copeland. But he left Houston for Los Angeles when he was only 15 years old. Back then, Watson's main instrument was piano; that's what he played with Chuck Higgins' band when the saxist cut "Motorhead Baby" for Combo in 1952 (Watson also handled vocal duties).

He was listed as Young John Watson when he signed with Federal in 1953. His first sides for the King subsidiary found him still tinkling the ivories, but by 1954, when he dreamed up the absolutely astonishing instrumental "Space Guitar," the youth (he was two days short of his 17th birthday!) had switched over to guitar. "Space Guitar" ranks with the greatest achievements of its era—Watson's blistering rapid-fire attack, done without the aid of a pick, presages futuristic effects that rock guitarists still hadn't mastered another 15 years down the line.

Watson moved over to the Bihari brothers' RPM label in 1955 and waxed some of the toughest upbeat blues of their timeframe (usually under saxist Maxwell Davis' supervision). "Hot Little Mama," "Too Tired," and "Oh Baby" scorched the strings with their blazing attack; "Someone Cares for Me" was a churchy Ray Charles-styled slow-dragger, and "Three Hours Past Midnight" cut bone-deep with its outrageous guitar work and laidback vocal (Watson's cool phrasing as a singer was scarcely less distinctive than his playing). He scored his first hit in 1955 for RPM with a note-perfect cover of New Orleanian Earl King's two-chord swamp ballad "Those Lonely, Lonely Nights."

Though he cut a demo version of the tune while at RPM, Watson's first released version of "Gangster of Love" emerged in 1957 on Keen. Singles for Class ("One Kiss"), Goth, Arvee, and Escort preceded a hookup with Johnny Otis at King during the early '60s. He recut "Gangster" for King, and dented the R&B charts again in 1962 with his impassioned, violin-enriched blues ballad "Cuttin' In."

Never content to remain in one stylistic bag for long, Watson landed at Chess just long enough to cut a jazz album in 1964 that placed him back behind the 88s. Along with longtime pal Larry Williams, Watson rocked England in 1965 (their dynamic repartee was captured for posterity by British Decca). Their partnership lasted stateside through several singles and an LP for Okeh; among their achievements as a duo was the first vocal hit on "Mercy, Mercy, Mercy" in 1967.

Little had been heard of this musical chameleon before he returned decked out in funk threads during the mid-'70s. He hit with "I Don't Want to Be a Lone Ranger" for Fantasy before putting together an incredible run at DJM Records paced by "A Real Mother for Ya" in 1977 and an updated "Gangster of Love" the next year.

After a typically clever "Strike on Computers" nicked the R&B lists in 1984, Watson again seemed to fall off the planet. But counting this remarkable performer out was always a mistake. Bow Wow, his 1994 album for Al Bell's Bellmark logo, returned him to prominence and earned a Grammy nomination for best contemporary blues album, even though its contents were pure old school funk. Sadly, in the midst of a truly heartwarming comeback campaign, Watson passed away while touring Japan in 1996. —Bill Dahl

★ **Gangster of Love** / Charly ◆◆◆◆◆
The innovative guitar wizard when he was young and wearing his Texas blues roots prominently on his sleeve. Watson spent two stints at King/Federal, both of them sampled here: his 1953-54 output includes the incomparable "Space Guitar," a sizzling "Half Pint of Whiskey," and a woozy "Gettin' Drunk." The 1961-63 King stuff is headed by the definitive version of "Gangster of Love," the searing soul-tinged "Cuttin' In," and a chunky "Broke and Lonely." —Bill Dahl

Blues Soul / 1965 / MCA/Chess ◆◆◆

Ain't That a Bitch / 1976 / Collectables ◆◆◆◆
The first of Watson's monstrously popular funk-based albums for DJM, and in all likelihood, the best of the lot. The title cut of the 1976 album is a sardonic gem, Watson's sinuous guitar licks a far cry from his brash '50s sound. The intimate "I Want to Ta-Ta You Baby," "Superman Lover," and "I Need It" also rate with Watson's most alluring old school R&B output. —Bill Dahl

Real Mother / 1977 / Collectables ◆◆◆
Obviously, the storming funk workout that gives this 1977 gold album its title is the album's principal draw (it's been covered countless times, but never duplicated). As was his wont by this time, the multitalented Watson plays everything except drums and horns. —Bill Dahl

I Heard That / 1985 / Charly ◆◆◆◆
King-Federal sides from the 1950s and '60s includes the amazing "Space Guitar." —Bill Dahl

Three Hours Past Midnight / 1991 / Flair ◆◆◆◆
Watson's mid-'50s catalog for the Bihari brothers' Flair logo is unassailable, with searing rockers like "Oh Baby," "Hot Little Mama," and "Ruben," and the blistering slow blues title cut. Unfortunately, this 16-song collection utilizes inferior alternate takes on several of the most important titles.But it contains both sides of his rare 1959 single for Class, "One Kiss"/"The Bear." —Bill Dahl

● **Gonna Hit That Highway: The Complete RPM Recordings** / 1992 / P-Vine ◆◆◆◆
No such omissions with this two-disc Japanese set—not only are the official versions of all of Watson's vicious RPM sides here, so are a plethora of alternate takes and extreme rarities (including a demo version of "Gangster of Love" as "Love Bandit"). Could be tough to locate, but for anyone seriously into this brilliant guitarist's early blues output, absolutely essential! —Bill Dahl

Listen/I Don't Want to Be Alone, Stranger / 1992 / Ace ◆◆◆◆
Watson's first two funk-slanted albums, combined conveniently on one disc. Listen dates from 1973, I Don't Want to Be Alone from two years later, and both are very together funk outings with a heady dose of modern blues at their core. —Bill Dahl

Curley Weaver

b. Mar. 26, 1906, Covington, GA, d. Sep. 20, 1962, Almon, GA
Guitar, Vocals / Acoustic Country Blues

Curley Weaver, who was known for much of his life as "the Georgia Guitar Wizard," is only just beginning to be appreciated as one of the best players ever to pick up a six-string instrument. Although he recorded a fair number of sides on his own during the 1920s and 1930s, Weaver was most commonly heard in performances and recordings in association with his better known colleagues Blind Willie McTell (with whom he worked from the 1930s until the early 1950s), Barbecue Bob, and Buddy Moss.

At age 19, Weaver teamed up with harmonica player Eddie Mapp, and moved to Atlanta. There he hooked up with Barbecue Bob and Charlie Lincoln, who quickly showed their younger friend the ins-and-outs of busking on Decatur Street, the heart of Atlanta's Black entertainment district, with its bars, restaurants, clubs, and theaters.

The association between the three guitarists was to prove providential. Barbecue Bob emerged as a local star first and, as a consequence, was also the first to go into the recording studio for the Columbia Records label in 1927—his first releases sold well, and he, in turn, arranged for his brother and Curley Weaver to make their debuts in the studio the following year. Weaver paid his first visit to the recording studio in Atlanta on October 26, 1928, laying down two tracks, "Sweet Petunia" and "No No Blues."

Although many of Weaver's recording sessions in the 1930s were in New York, he kept his home base in Atlanta for his entire life, and it was while playing at clubs, parties, dances, picnics, and even on streetcorners in the early part of the decade that he struck up the most important professional relationship of his life, with Blind Willie McTell. A renowned 12-string guitarist, McTell had begun his recording career in 1927, and was a local legend around Atlanta. The two played and recorded together for 20 years or more, and comprised one of the most important and celebrated East Coast blues teams in history. Weaver's most renowned recordings were done in association either with McTell or Moss, the latter under the guise of the Georgia Browns, during the mid-'30s. His playing, either on its own or in association with either McTell or Moss, was nothing less than dazzling.

Curley Weaver was, by virtue of his virtuosity and the associations that he kept throughout his life and career, a guitarist's guitarist, a virtuoso among a small coterie of Atlanta-based guitar wizards. He never had the renown of Blind Willie McTell, but he was Willie's equal and match in just about every conceivable respect as a player and singer, his six-string being perfectly mated to Willie's 12-string. When he was playing or recording with McTell, Buddy Moss, or Barbecue Bob, the results were the blues equivalent of what rock people later would've called a "super-session" except that, as a listen to the surviving records reveals, the results were more natural and overpowering—these guys genuinely liked each other, and loved playing together, and it shows beyond the virtuosity of the music, in the warmth and elegance of the playing and the sound. —Bruce Eder

★ **Georgia Guitar Wizard (1928-1935)** / 1987 / Story of Blues ◆◆◆◆◆
These are 16 of the greatest blues sides ever to come out of Atlanta, and a match for the best work of Blind Willie McTell, Barbecue Bob, and Buddy Moss (whose harmonica playing on the Georgia Browns' "Decatur Street 81" reveals him to be an equally formidable talent on that instrument), who are all over these sides as well. The sound is a little rough at times, and even more than a little, and there are some major gaps between 1929 and 1933—including his renowned "Guitar Rag"—but none of the flaws does violence to the music, and all that is here is worth the price of admission. One important bonus—the presence of "Oh Lawdy Mama," the song that later, in Willie Dixon's hands, evolved into the blues standard "Down in the Bottom" (an unreleased version was even cut by the Rolling Stones, in what might be their best early blues side); it had been cut by Buddy Moss a year earlier as a solo number. —Bruce Eder

☆ **Complete Studio Recordings** / 1990 / Document ✦✦✦✦✦
Weaver's complete recordings, taking into account all of the sessions for
Moss, McTell, et al., where he played guitar, would comprise a lot more
than the 19 tracks here, but that's no reason not to spring for this slightly
more expensive collection, which doesn't entirely overlap with the *Story
of Blues* disc. —*Bruce Eder*

Katie Webster

b. Jan. 9, 1939, Houston, TX, **d.** , Houston, TX
Organ, Harmonica, Piano, Vocals / R&B, Electric New Orleans Blues
A piano-pounding institution on the southern Louisiana swamp blues
scene during the late '50s and early '60s, Katie Webster later grabbed a
long-deserved share of national recognition with three recent Alligator
albums before a 1993 stroke temporarily shelved her. Local guitarist
Ashton Savoy took her under his wing, sharing her 1958 debut 45 for
the Kry logo ("Baby Baby"). Webster rapidly became an invaluable studio sessioneer for Louisiana producers J.D. Miller in Crowley and Eddie
Shuler in Lake Charles. The young pianist also waxed some terrific
sides of her own for Miller from 1959 to 1961 for his Rocko, Action, and
Spot labels (where she introduced a dance called "The Katie Lee"). Webster led her own band, the Uptighters, at the same time she was spending her days in the studio. In 1964, she guested with Otis Redding's band
at the Bamboo Club in Lake Charles and so impressed the charismatic
Redding that he absconded with her. For the next three years, Webster
served as his opening act! The 1970s were pretty much a lost decade for
Katie Webster as she took care of her ailing parents in Oakland, CA. But
in 1982 a European tour beckoned, and she journeyed overseas for the
first of many such jaunts. The Alligator connection commenced in 1988
with some high-profile help: Bonnie Raitt, Robert Cray, and Kim Wilson
all made guest appearances on *The Swamp Boogie Queen*. The lovably
extroverted boogie pianist encored with *Two-Fisted Mama!* and *No Foolin'* before suffering a stroke. —*Bill Dahl*

Swamp Boogie Queen / 1988 / Alligator ✦✦✦✦
Lovable Katie Webster had some high-profile help for this impressive
comeback album—Bonnie Raitt shares the vocal on "Somebody's on
Your Case" and plays guitar on "On the Run"; Kim Wilson duets with
Webster for a cover of Johnnie Taylor's "Who's Making Love" (a track that
Robert Cray contributes crisp guitar to). Throughout, Webster's vocals are
throatier than they used to be (she soulfully covers one-time mentor Otis
Redding's "Fa-Fa-Fa-Fa-Fa [Sad Song]" and "Try a Little Tenderness"),
while her driving left hand still lays down some powerhouse boogie
rhythms. —*Bill Dahl*

Two-Fisted Mama! / 1990 / Alligator ✦✦✦✦
Another impressive showcase for Katie Webster's rollicking 88s and
earthy vocals. Other than the Memphis Horns, no special guests this
time—just Webster and her tight trio (anchored by guitarist Vasti Jackson). —*Bill Dahl*

● **Katie Webster** / 1991 / Paula ✦✦✦✦
Webster is at her full bayou-bred boogie-blues best here, when she was
the queen of south Louisiana's swamp sessioneers. Webster's own late-
'50s/early-'60s output for producer J.D. Miller was no less captivating;
her self-named dance number "The Katie Lee" and "Mama Don't Allow,"
which uproots the Gary US Bonds party vibe to New Orleans, are two of
the best items on the 20-track disc. There's also her blues-drenched "No
Bread, No Meat" and a nice version of "Sea of Love." (Webster added the
gently rolling piano to Phil Phillips' original hit.) —*Bill Dahl*

Junior Wells (Amos Blackmore)

b. Dec. 9, 1934, Memphis, TN
Harmonica, Vocals / R&B, Electric Chicago Blues
Wells started on the streets of Chicago, playing for tips as a teenager, and
graduated to house parties with the Aces, who became Little Walter's
Jukes when Wells replaced him in Muddy Waters's band. Wells recorded
on his own throughout the '50s and into the early '60s for a spate of
smaller, Chicago-based labels, then came to national attention by teaming up with guitarist Buddy Guy in the mid-'60s and recording a brilliant set of landmark recordings for collector-oriented labels like Delmark and Vanguard. Generally acknowledged as the last of the great
Chicago harmonica players, Wells continues to record and perform to
the present day, his skills honed to a fine edge, a perfect ambassador for
the music he's represented for so long. —*Cub Koda*

★ **Hoodoo Man Blues** / 1965 / Delmark ✦✦✦✦✦
One of the truly classic blues albums of the 1960s, and one of the first to
fully document the smoky ambience of a night at a West Side nightspot
in the superior acoustics of a recording studio. Wells just set up with his
usual cohorts—guitarist Buddy Guy (billed as "Friendly Chap" on first
vinyl pressings), bassist Jack Myers, and drummer Billy Warren—and
proceeded to blow up a storm, bringing an immediacy to "Snatch It Back
and Hold It," "You Don't Love Me," "Chitlin Con Carne," and the rest that
is absolutely mesmerizing. —*Bill Dahl*

On Tap / 1966 / Delmark ✦✦✦
Underrated collection boasting a contemporary, funky edge driven by
guitarists Phil Guy and Sammy Lawhorn, keyboardist Big Moose
Walker, and saxman A.C. Reed. Especially potent is the crackling "The
Train I Ride," a kissin' cousin to Little Junior Parker's "Mystery Train."
—*Bill Dahl*

South Side Blues Jam / 1967 / Delmark ✦✦✦
Enjoyable but less electrifying follow-up to *Hoodoo Man Blues*. It's
looser, with longer songs that afford more room to stretch out instrumentally but don't quite equal the stunning precision of what came before.
Buddy Guy returns on guitar; Otis Spann is the pianist, and Fred Below
keeps superb time. —*Bill Dahl*

You're Tuff Enough / 1968 / Blue Rock ✦✦✦✦
Another period of the veteran Chicago harp man's career that awaits CD
documentation—and one of the most exciting. Wells' late-'60s output for
Bright Star and Mercury's Blue Rock subsidiary frequently found him
mining funky James Brown grooves (with a bluesy base, of course) to
great effect—"Up in Heah" and his national smash "You're Tuff Enough"
are marvelous examples of his refusal to bend to purists' wishes (though
there's a glorious version of Bobby Bland's blues-soaked "You're the One"
that benefits handily from Sammy Lawhorn's delicate guitar work).
—*Bill Dahl*

Comin' at You / 1968 / Vanguard ✦✦✦
Another eminently solid outing by the legendary harpist that captures
his trademark barroom bravado in a studio setting. The band is quite
tight—Buddy Guy and Lefty Dizz are the guitarists, Douglas Fagan plays
sax, and Clark Terry, believe it or not, occupies a third of the trumpet section—and the set list is dominated by oldies from both Sonny Boys,
Willie Dixon, and John D. Loudermilk (Junior invests his "Tobacco Road"
with a lights-out toughness that the Nashville Teens could never even
imagine). —*Bill Dahl*

Live at the Golden Bear / Dec. 1969 / Blue Rock ✦✦✦
The swaggering harpman took his act on the road to Huntington Beach,
CA, to do this live set with his touring quartet of the moment. Virtually
nothing but blues and soul standards that show his wide stylistic
range—alongside tunes by Muddy Waters, both Sonny Boys, and the
Wolf resides an impassioned reading of James Brown's "Please, Please,
Please." —*Bill Dahl*

In My Younger Days / 1971 / Red Lightnin' ✦✦
Good collection of 16 early sides from 1953-62. The earliest tracks are
straight blues, and Wells at his most conventional. Starting with the late-
'50s performances, he began to broaden his influences into his trademark blend of blues, R&B, rock, and even some Latin music. Earl Hooker
lends his guitar to the early-'60s tracks, which are highlighted by the
original version of his signature tune, "Messin' with the Kid." —*Richie
Unterberger*

Play the Blues / 1972 / Atlantic ✦✦✦

Blues Hit Big Town / 1977 / Delmark ✦✦✦✦
Why isn't this seminal collection of the harpist's earliest 1953-1954 sides
for States Records available on CD? Its Chicago blues treasures include
Wells' first waxing of "Hoodoo Man," a jumping "Cut That Out" and
"Tomorrow Night," and slashing showcases for the young bluesman's
amplified harp: "Eagle Rock" and "Junior's Wail." Junior's sidemen are the
absolute cream of the crop—Muddy Waters, the Aces, Elmore James, and
pianists Otis Spann and Johnny Jones—making these 12 sides all the
more indispensable. —*Bill Dahl*

Pleading the Blues / Oct. 31, 1979 / Isabel ✦✦✦

Harp Attack! / 1990 / Alligator ✦✦✦✦
Along with his Windy City peers James Cotton, Carey Bell, and Billy
Branch, Wells trades harp solos and vocals on this raucous meeting of
the minds. Junior's front and center on a fine rendition of Sonny Boy II's
"Keep Your Hands Out of My Pockets" and the tailor-made "Somebody
Changed the Lock" and "Broke and Hungry," relishing the camaraderie
between himself and his fellow harmonica giants. —*Bill Dahl*

● **1957-1966** / 1991 / Paula ✦✦✦✦
The indispensable sides for Mel London's Profile, Chief, and Age labels
(and a few for USA Records that directly followed). Backed by a modern-
sounding crew that included immaculate guitarist Earl Hooker, saxist
A.C. Reed, and keyboardist Johnny "Big Moose" Walker, Wells enjoyed a
considerable R&B hit with the grinding "Little by Little," glides atop a
churning rhythm groove on the original "Messin' with the Kid," rocks
"Lovey Dovey Lovely One" and the hokey-but-fun "I Need Me a Car," and
blows some husky amplified harmonica on "Cha Cha Cha in Blue" and
"Calling All Blues." —*Bill Dahl*

Artie White

b. Apr. 16, 1937, Vicksburg, MS
Vocals / Soul, R&B, Soul Blues
Very few Chicago blues artists were able to pierce the R&B charts dur-

ing the 1970s, when interest in the genre was at rock-bottom. But smooth-voiced Artie "Blues Boy" White managed the rare feat with his 1977 single for Altee, "Leanin' Tree." White signed with Ichiban in 1987 and waxed six fine sets in the soul-blues vein (enough to merit a *Best Of* CD in 1991, which made seven), utilizing Chicago songwriter Bob Jones (the composer of "Leanin' Tree") and labelmate Travis Haddix as chief sources of material. On 1989's *Thangs Got to Change*, White enjoyed the presence of Little Milton Campbell, one of his prime influences, on lead guitar. *—Bill Dahl*

Blues Boy / 1985 / Ronn ✦✦✦✦
Blues Boy's first album, dating back to the mid-'80s, also ranks as one of his most soulfully satisfying, thanks to the contemporary grooves of a Chicago outfit called Amuzement Park and White's smoky, Little Milton-influenced vocal delivery. He delivers a fine remake of his own modern blues "Leanin' Tree" and Little Beaver's "Jimmie" and adapts Aretha Franklin's "Chain of Fools" to his own rich vocal range. *—Bill Dahl*

Nothing Takes the Place of You / 1987 / Ichiban ✦✦✦
Artie White's Ichiban debut is typically confident and soulful. Along with standards by Toussaint McCall and Willie Nelson, White does a solid job on a sheaf of original material and Z.Z. Hill's anguished "I Need Someone." *—Bill Dahl*

Hit and Run / 1992 / Ichiban ✦✦✦✦
Without a great deal of fanfare, Artie White released a steady stream of quality contemporary releases on Ichiban, each straddling the sometimes imperceptible fence between blues and deep soul. This one's no exception—backed by a Chicago combo called Masheen Co., White delivers originals penned by Travis Haddix, Bob Jones (the title cut), and himself in assured, smooth style. *—Bill Dahl*

● **The Best of Artie White** / Ichiban ✦✦✦✦
A well-selected 12-song overview of White's prolific tenure at Ichiban. His delivery, pitched somewhere between blues and soul, is equally effective on the contemporary blues-based items "Hattie Mae" and "Jodie," the soul-slanted "Dark End of the Street" (though he can't give James Carr a run for his money in the intensity department,) and Toussaint McCall's tender "Nothing Takes the Place of You." *—Bill Dahl*

Bukka White (Booket T. Washington White)

b. Nov. 12, 1909, Houston, TX, **d.** Feb. 26, 1977, Memphis, TN
Guitar, Harmonica, Piano, Vocals / Acoustic Delta Blues
Achieving a distinctive musical voice is a highly prized blues value, yet few artists develop an easily recognizable vocal and instrumental style that is uniquely theirs. Bukka White was one of those remarkable artists with an overall approach and composition style that were unusual, yet he was a popular house party musician and a successful recording artist. Although he had a second career during the blues revival and remained a powerful performer, his best work was on his 1937 and 1940 Vocalion sides, reissued by Columbia. They feature down-home country-blues at its best: personal, moving, and instrumentally compelling. White's percussive approach to his open G-tuned steel National can be imitated but not duplicated. Like other Delta artists, White's sound was melodically simple but rhythmically complex. Sporting an attack vaguely reminiscent of Big Joe Williams, White worked his guitar like a drum, adding rhythmic nuances with his chording hand on the guitar neck. On his '40s session, he added further percussive rhythm. Many of White's pieces employ spoken or chanted passages, especially his train songs, which combined talking blues and train effects. His compositions generally either fall outside mainstream blues or bridge sacred and secular traditions, as in his classic "Fixing to Die." Moody and introspective, his songs let you into his life, detailing his experiences as a prisoner at Mississippi's notorious Parchman Farm or as a hobo riding the rails. His dance songs, such as "Bukka's Jitterbug Swing," aptly demonstrate his skills as a houseparty performer and bear out his reputation as a breakdown artist, which means people danced so hard to his beat that they literally broke the floors down at the jukes and plantation balls over which he reigned. *—Barry Lee Pearson*

Three Shades of Blues / 1989 / Biograph ✦✦✦
★ **The Complete Bukka White** / 1994 / Columbia ✦✦✦✦✦
All of Bukka White's landmark recordings for Vocalion and Okeh Records are collected on this brilliant single disc. *—AMG*

Robert Wilkins (Rev. Robert Timothy Wilkins)

b. Jan. 16, 1896, Hernando, MS, **d.** May 26, 1987, Memphis, TN
Guitar, Vocals / Acoustic Country Blues, Acoustic Memphis Blues
A superior guitarist, Robert Wilkins projected a relaxed ease on his exquisite country-blues 78s. He was working as a Pullman porter in Memphis when he was hired by Victor to record in 1928. He was soon back in the studio for Brunswick and Vocalion. The 1929 "That's No Way to Get Along," the most famous of his pre-war 78s, was covered by the Rolling Stones as "Prodigal Son." Wilkins' great Mississippi vibrato was similar to that of Frank Stokes and Joe Callicott, and his records show

considerable finesse with rag and blues guitar. Ungoverned by standard 12-bar conventions, Wilkins created his own structures and was especially strong in open E, as heard in "That's No Way to Get Along" and the spooky one-chord "Rollin' Stone." He crafted lyrics into coherent narratives, carefully avoiding any hint of the risqué. He showed up at the Chicago World's Fair but did most of his playing in Memphis and Hernando. Unnerving violence at a houseparty prompted him to quit the blues in 1936 and find Jesus. In 1964 a rediscovered Rev. Robert Wilkins, spiritual singer and minister of the Church of God in Christ, hit the folk circuit and made some deeply moving records. He refused to play blues but did recycle some old riffs. Near the end of his life, Rev. Wilkins was seen working as a root doctor on a Memphis side street. He lived to be 91. *—Jas Obrecht*

● **The Original Rolling Stone** / 1980 / Yazoo ✦✦✦✦
These 14 pre-war tracks include adequate liner notes. *—Jas Obrecht*

Big Joe Williams

b. Oct. 16, 1903, Crawford, MS, **d.** Dec. 17, 1982, Macon, MS
Guitar, Vocals / Electric Delta Blues, Acoustic Delta Blues
Big Joe Williams may have been the most cantankerous human being who ever walked the earth with guitar in hand. At the same time, he was an incredible blues musician: a gifted songwriter, a powerhouse vocalist, and an exceptional idiosyncratic guitarist. Despite his deserved reputation as a fighter (documented in Michael Bloomfield's bizarre booklet *Me and Big Joe*), artists who knew him well treated him as a respected elder statesman. Even so, they may not have chosen to play with him, because—as with other older Delta artists—if you played with him you played by his rules.

As protégé David "Honeyboy" Edwards described him, Williams in his early Delta days was a walking musician who played work camps, jukes, store porches, streets, and alleys from New Orleans to Chicago. He recorded through five decades for Vocalion, Okeh, Paramount, Bluebird, Prestige, Delmark, and many others. As a youngster, I met him in Delmark owner Bob Koester's store, the Jazz Record Mart. At the time, Big Joe was living there when not on his constant travels. According to Charlie Musselwhite, he and Big Joe kicked off the blues revival in Chicago in the '60s.

When I saw him playing at Mike Bloomfield's "blues night" at the Fickle Pickle, Williams was playing an electric nine-string guitar through a small ramshackle amp with a pie plate nailed to it and a beer can dangling against that. When he played, everything rattled but Big Joe himself. The total effect of this incredible apparatus produced the most buzzing, sizzling, African-sounding music I have ever heard. *—Barry Lee Pearson*

Nine String Guitar Blues / 1961 / Delmark ✦✦✦✦
The title says it all—Big Joe Williams plays a custom-made nine-string guitar, which sounds like no other instrument in existence. That alone would give his stripped-down acoustic Delta blues a new spin, but he brings so much grit and passion to his performances, they would have sounded fresh and vital anyway. *—Thom Owens*

Blues on Highway 49 / 1961 / Delmark ✦✦✦
One of Big Joe Williams' better releases, *Blues on Highway 49* is a tense, gritty set of roadhouse blues. Williams' stinging playing and singing bring out the best in such songs as "Tijuana Blues" and "45 Blues"—he shows exactly how Delta blues could be updated. *—Thom Owens*

Back to the Country / 1964 / Testament ✦✦✦✦
Fellow Mississippians Jimmy Brown on fiddle and Willie Lee Harris on harmonica augment Big Joe's down-home Delta blues from the blues revival of the '70s. *—Barry Lee Pearson*

● **Early Recordings 1935-41** / 1965 / Mamlish ✦✦✦✦
This blues legend and guitar wizard's best initial Bluebird recordings, including the best versions of "49 Highway" and "Baby Please Don't Go" from 1935. *—Barry Lee Pearson*

Stavin' Chain Blues / 1966 / Delmark ✦✦✦✦
A CD reissue of 1958 recordings, it includes four previously unreleased tracks. This is raw but beautiful country-blues, featuring the otherworldly sound of Big Joe's nine-string guitar. *—Niles J. Frantz*

● **Shake Your Boogie** / 1990 / Arhoolie ✦✦✦✦
Arhoolie reissued two of Big Joe Williams' seminal rediscovery albums on one disc in 1990. The first, 1960's *Tough Times*, ranks among his best; the second, 1969's *Thinking of What They Did*, isn't as strong, but the two albums provide an excellent introduction to this Delta bluesman. *—Stephen Thomas Erlewine*

Delta Blues: 1951 / 1991 / Trumpet ✦✦✦✦
Although the early '50s were not a great time for delta blues musicians, there remained some proficient players performing in this vein throughout the South. The three presented on this new collecion of classic Trumpet recordings include Big Joe Williams, known for his nine-string guitar and robust singing, Luther Huff, a good, if derivative vocalist/guitarist, and the spry pianist and vocalist Willie Love, an exuberant performer

whose Three Aces band at various times contained Elmore James and Little Milton. This anthology includes 18 selections that show the link between older, traditional blues and the urban, electric sounds that emerged as the idiom's dominant form later in the decade. —*Ron Wynn*

Robert Pete Williams

b. Mar. 14, 1914, Zachary, LA, d. Dec. 31, 1980, Rosedale, LA
Guitar, Vocals / Acoustic Louisiana Blues
Discovered in the Louisiana State Penitentiary, Robert Pete Williams became one of the great blues discoveries during the folk boom of the early '60s. His disregard for conventional patterns, tunings, and structures kept him from a wider audience, but his music remains one of the great, intense treats of the blues. —*Cub Koda*

★ **Angola Prisoner's Blues** / Mar. 1961 / Arhoolie ✦✦✦✦✦
Not enough great things to say about this one, one of the finest field recordings ever done anywhere. If Robert Pete's "Prisoner's Talking Blues" doesn't move you, check your heart into your refrigerator's freezer section. —*Cub Koda*

Rural Blues (With Snooks Eaglin) / 197X / Storyville ✦✦✦✦
Not only does Snooks Eaglin prove a fine partner for Robert Pete Williams, but his vocals and playing have seldom been more disciplined and exciting. —*Ron Wynn*

Robert Pete Williams, Vol. 1 / 1994 / Arhoolie ✦✦✦

Robert Pete Williams, Vol. 2 / 1994 / Arhoolie ✦✦✦

When a Man Takes the Blues / 1994 / Arhoolie ✦✦✦✦
Important collection of Williams' best early work. —*Bill Dahl*

Sonny Boy Williamson I (John Lee Williamson)

b. Mar. 30, 1914, Jackson, TN, d. Jun. 1, 1948, Chicago, IL
Harmonica, Vocals / Chicago Blues, Blues, Acoustic Chicago Blues
Easily the most important harmonica player of the pre-war era, John Lee Williamson almost single-handedly made the humble mouth organ a worthy lead instrument for blues bands—leading the way for the amazing innovations of Little Walter and a platoon of others to follow. If not for his tragic murder in 1948 while on his way home from a Chicago gin mill, Williamson would doubtless have been right there alongside them, exploring new and exciting directions.

It can safely be noted that Williamson made the most of his limited time on the planet. Already a harp virtuoso in his teens, the first Sonny Boy (Rice Miller) would adopt the same moniker down in the Delta) learned from Hammie Nixon and Noah Lewis and rambled with Sleepy John Estes and Yank Rachell before settling in Chicago in 1934.

Williamson's extreme versatility and consistent ingenuity won him a Bluebird recording contract in 1937. Under the direction of the ubiquitous Lester Melrose, Sonny Boy Williamson recorded prolifically for Victor both as a leader and behind others in the vast Melrose stable (including Robert Lee McCoy and Big Joe Williams, who in turn played on some of Williamson's sides).

Williamson commenced his sensational recording career with a resounding bang. His first vocal offering on Bluebird was "Good Morning School Girl," covered countless times across the decades. Sonny Boy cut more than 120 sides in all for RCA from 1937 to 1947, many of them turning up in the postwar repertoires of various Chicago blues giants. His call-and-response style of alternating vocal passages with pungent harmonica blasts was a development of mammoth proportions that would be adopted across-the-board by virtually every blues harpist to follow in his wake.

But Sonny Boy Williamson wouldn't live to reap any appreciable rewards from his inventions. He died at the age of 34, while at the zenith of his popularity (his romping "Shake That Boogie" was a national R&B hit in 1947 on Victor), from a violent bludgeoning about the head that occurred during a strong-arm robbery on the South Side. "Better Cut That Out," another storming rocker later appropriated by Junior Wells, became a posthumous hit for Williamson in late 1948. It was the very last song he had committed to posterity. Wells was only a one young harpist to display his enduring allegiance; a teenaged Billy Boy Arnold had recently summoned up the nerve to knock on his idol's door to ask for lessons. The accommodating Sonny Boy Williamson was only too happy to oblige, a kindness Arnold has never forgotten (nor does he fail to pay tribute to his eternal main man every chance he gets). Such is the lasting legacy of the blues' first great harmonicist. —*Bill Dahl*

Throw a Boogie Woogie (With Big Joe Williams) / Apr. 1990 / RCA ✦✦✦✦
Eight indispensable Bluebird sides dating from 1937-38—right at the very beginning of his reign as king of blues harpists—that display precisely why Williamson was such a revered innovator (and continues to be even now). Highlights include his classic "Good Morning School Girl" and "Sugar Mama Blues." He shares the disc with itinerant rambler Big Joe Williams, whose eight 1937-41 selections include six featuring Sonny Boy playing harp behind the nine-string guitarist. —*Bill Dahl*

★ **Sugar Mama** / 1995 / Indigo ✦✦✦✦✦
A well-researched 24-track compendium of the first Sonny Boy Williamson's massively influential Bluebird catalog that spans 1937-1942. Besides being such an innovator on the mouth organ, Williamson's songs themselves have stood the test of time strikingly—"Good Morning School Girl," "Blue Bird Blues," "Decoration Blues," "Sloppy Drunk Blues," and many more on the collection are recognized classics. —*Bill Dahl*

Complete Recorded Works, Vols. 1-5 / Document ✦✦✦✦
His complete works 1937-1947 in chronological order. Sonny Boy was a major influence (both harmonica and vocals) on many of the younger Chicago bluesmen, Junior Wells in particular. —*Michael Erlewine*

Sonny Boy Williamson, Vol. 1; 1937-39 / Qualiton ✦✦✦✦
This artist was perhaps the most significant pioneer of the city-styled, horn-oriented blues harp—a style brought to perfection by Little Walter. Williamson adapted the country-styled, chordal-rhythmic technique that he learned from Noah Lewis and Hammie Nixon to suit the demands of the evolving urban blues styles. These 24 tracks include Sonny Boy's first six records cut in 1937 and sport an imposing list of sidemen: Robert Nighthawk, Big Joe Williams, Henry Townsend, Walter Davis, Yank Rachel, Big Bill Broonzy, and Speckled Red. This is a definitive collection. —*Larry Hoffman*

Sonny Boy Williamson II (Aleck Ford "Rice" Miller)

b. Dec. 5, 1899, Glendora, MS, d. May 25, 1965, Helena, AR
Harmonica, Vocals / R&B, Electric Chicago Blues, Blues, Electric Delta Blues
Sonny Boy Williamson was, in many ways, the ultimate blues legend. By the time of his death in 1965, he had been around long enough to have played with Robert Johnson at the start of his career and Eric Clapton, Jimmy Page, and Robbie Robertson at the end of it. In between, he drank a lot of whiskey, had a successful radio show for 15 years, and sang some of the greatest blues ever etched into black phonograph records. His delivery was sly, evil, and world-weary, while his harp playing was full of short, rhythmic bursts one minute and powerful, impassioned blowing the next. His songs were chock full of mordant wit, largely autobiographical lyrics that hold up to the scrutiny of the printed page. Though he took his name from another well-known harmonica player, no one really sounded like him.

A moody, bitter, and suspicious man, no one wove such a confusing web of misinformation as Sonny Boy Williamson II. Even his birth date (either 1897 or 1909) and real name (Aleck or Alex or Willie "Rice"—which may or may not be a nickname—Miller or Ford) cannot be verified with absolute certainty. Of his childhood days in Mississippi, absolutely nothing is known. What is known is that by the mid-'30s, he was traveling the Delta, working under the alias of Little Boy Blue. With blues legends like Robert Johnson, Robert Nighthawk, Robert Jr. Lockwood, and Elmore James as interchangeable playing partners, he worked the juke joints and country suppers of the era. By the early '40s he was the star of KFFA's "King Biscuit Time," the first live blues radio show to hit the American airwaves. As one of the major ruses in blues history, his sponsor—the Interstate Grocery Company—felt they could push more sacks of their King Biscuit Flour with Miller posing as Chicago harmonica star John Lee "Sonny Boy" Williamson. In today's everybody-knows-everything video age, it's hard to think that such an idea would work, much less prosper. After all, the real Sonny Boy was a national recording star, and Miller's vocal and harmonica style was in no way derivative of him. But Williamson had no desire to tour in the South, so prosper it did, and when John Lee was murdered in Chicago, Miller became—in his own words—"the original Sonny Boy." Among his fellow musicians, he was usually still referred to as Rice Miller, but to the rest of the world he did, indeed, become the Sonny Boy Williamson.

The show was an immediate hit, prompting IGC to introduce Sonny Boy Corn Meal, complete with a likeness of Williamson on the front of the package. With all this local success, however, Sonny Boy was not particularly anxious to record. Though he often claimed in his twilight years that he had recorded in the '30s, no evidence appears. Lillian McMurray, the owner of Trumpet Records in Jackson, MS, had tracked him down at a boarding house in nearby Belzoni and enticed him to record for her. The music Sonny Boy made for her between 1951 and 1954 shows him in peak form. Williamson struck paydirt on his first Trumpet release, "Eyesight to the Blind," and though the later production on his Chess records would make the Trumpet sides seem woefully under-recorded by comparison; they nonetheless stand today as classic performances, capturing juke-joint music in one of its finest hours.

Another major contribution to the history of the blues occurred when Sonny Boy brought "King Biscuit Time" guest star Elmore James into the studio for a session. With Williamson blowing harp, a drummer keeping time, and the tape machine running surreptitiously, James recorded the first version of what would become his signature tune, Robert Johnson's "Dust My Broom." By this time Sonny Boy married his second wife, Mattie Gordon. This would prove to be the longest and most enduring relationship of his life, outside of music, with Mattie putting up with the man's rambling ways. On two different occasions Sonny Boy moved to Detroit, taking up residence in the Baby Boy Warren band for brief periods, and contributing earth-shattering solos on Warren sides for Blue Lake and Excello in 1954.

By early 1955, after leasing a single to Ace, McMurray had sold Williamson's contract to Buster Williams in Memphis, who in turn sold it to Leonard Chess in Chicago. All the pieces were finally tumbling into place, and Sonny Boy finally had a reason to take up permanent residence north of the Mason-Dixon line; he now was officially a Chess recording artist. His first session for Chess took place on August 12, 1955, and the single pulled from it, "Don't Start Me to Talkin'," started doing brisk business on the R&B charts. By his second session for the label, he was reunited with longtime musical partner Robert Jr. Lockwood. Lockwood—who had been one of the original King Biscuit Boys—had become de facto house guitarist for Chess, as well as moonlighting for other Chicago labels. With Lockwood's combination of Robert Johnson rhythms and jazz chord embellishments, Williamson's harp and parched vocals sounded fresher than ever, and Lockwood's contributions to the success of Sonny Boy's Chess recordings cannot be overestimated. Williamson had a remarkable penchant for pulling a disappearing act for months at a time. Sometimes, when Chicago bookings got too lean, he would head back to Arkansas, fronting the "King Biscuit" radio show for brief periods. In 1963 he was headed to Europe for the first time, as part of the American Folk Blues Festival. The folk music boom was in full swing, and Europeans were bringing over blues artists, to face wildly appreciative White audiences for the first time. Sonny Boy unleashed his bag of tricks and stole the show every night.

He loved Europe and stayed behind in Britain when the tour headed home. He started working the teenage beat club circuit, touring and recording with the Yardbirds and the Animals. On the beat blues tours, Sonny Boy was dignified and laidback. But in the beat club setting, with young, White bands playing behind him, he'd pull out every juke-joint trick he'd used with the King Biscuit Entertainers and drive the kids nuts. "Help Me" became a surprise hit in Britain and across Europe. Now in his mid-60s, Williamson was truly appreciative of all the attention, and contemplated moving to Europe permanently. But after getting a harlequin, two-tone, city gentleman's suit made up for himself, he headed back to the States—and the Chess studios—for some final sessions. When he returned to England in 1964, it was as a conquering hero. One of his final recordings, with Jimmy Page on guitar, was entitled "I'm Trying to Make London My Home."

In 1965 he headed back to Mississippi one last time and took over the "King Biscuit" show again. After hoboing his way around the United States for 30-odd years, and playing to appreciative audiences throughout Europe, Sonny Boy had a good reason for returning to the Delta; he had come home to die. He would enlist the help of old friends like Houston Stackhouse and Peck Curtis to take him around to all the back-road spots he had seen as a boy, sometimes paying his respects to old friends, other days just whiling away an afternoon on the banks of a river fishing. On May 25, 1965, Curtis found Williamson lying in bed, dead of an apparent heart attack. He was buried in the Whitfield Cemetery in Tutwiler, MS, and his funeral was well-attended. As Houston Stackhouse said, "He was well thought of through that country." —*Cub Koda*

Down and out Blues / 1959 / MCA/Chess ✦✦✦✦
Retaining photographer Don Bronstein's cover shot of a disheveled bum lying on the sidewalk (some former Chess artist, perhaps?) Sonny Boy Williamson's original 1959 album made it to digital reissue but has now been supplanted by MCA's exhaustive *The Essential Sonny Boy Williamson.* Still, for a budget price, there's a dozen unforgettable tracks: "Don't Start Me to Talkin'," his Checker debut; "All My Love in Vain," "Wake Up Baby," "99," "Cross My Heart," "Let Me Explain," and "The Key (To Your Door)." —*Bill Dahl*

The Real Folk Blues / 1965 / MCA/Chess ✦✦✦✦
Except for "Dissatisfied," cut in 1957, everything on this dozen-track comp dates from 1960-63 and holds "One Way Out," "Checkin' Up on My Baby," "Trust My Baby," and the catchy, country-tinged "Peach Tree," which drives along with a pronounced bounce. —*Bill Dahl*

More Real Folk Blues / Sep. 1967 / MCA/Chess ✦✦✦✦
More good early-'60s Chess recordings from Sonny Boy Williamson. "Help Me," "Bye Bye Bird," and "Nine Below Zero" have been covered by numerous blues and rock acts. Most of the songs, however, show up on the *Essential* best-of collection. —*Richie Unterberger*

One Way Out / 1968 / MCA/Chess ✦✦✦✦
Sly son-of-a-gun that he was, Sonny Boy Williamson found a way to weld the twist to the blues with his rousing 1961 title track, with guitarists Robert Jr. Lockwood and Luther Tucker positively blazing in supple support. Fourteen more gems make this one a must: 1955's "Good Evening Everybody," "Work with Me" and "You Killing Me," all with Muddy Waters and Jimmy Rogers in support; the sturdy "Keep It to Yourself"

from the next year, and a forceful "This Is My Apartment." —*Bill Dahl*

Bummer Road / 1969 / MCA/Chess ✦✦✦✦
Yes, this is the album where Williamson and Leonard Chess get down to some serious cussing during their hilariously heated exchange while recording "Little Village." But there are plenty more reasons to pick up this CD: his lascivious Yuletide ditty "Santa Claus," the stirring "Unseen Eye" and "Keep Your Hand Out of My Pocket," the leering "She Got Next to Me." Everything here was done between 1957 and 1960—prime years for the wily harpist at Chess. —*Bill Dahl*

★ **King Biscuit Time** / 1989 / Arhoolie ✦✦✦✦✦
Sonny Boy's early Trumpet sides, 1951. The original "Eyesight to the Blind," "Nine Below Zero" and "Mighty Long Time" are Sonny Boy at his very best. Added bonuses include Williamson backing Elmore James on his original recording of "Dust My Broom" and a live KFFA broadcast from 1965. —*Cub Koda*

Clownin' with the World / 1989 / Trumpet ✦✦✦✦
This batch of mostly unreleased Trumpet blues cuts from the early '50s offers some sizzling, if sometimes uneven, material by Sonny Boy Williamson II (Rice Miller) and Willie Love. Each gets eight numbers, with Williamson's being recorded both in Houston and Jackson, MS, while Love did all of his in Jackson. Williamson's ripping, searing harmonica and craggy vocals were then becoming popular, while Love's equally decisive singing and wild, carefree tunes were also attracting big audiences. This is undiluted, frequently chaotic, and always enjoyable music. —*Ron Wynn*

Keep It to Ourselves / 1992 / Alligator ✦✦✦✦
An intimate 1963 collection of Sonny Boy Williamson in solo and duet (with guitarist Matt Murphy) formats; on three tracks, pianist Memphis Slim hops aboard. This delightful addendum to Williamson's electric output of the same era was cut in Denmark and first issued on Storyville. —*Bill Dahl*

★ **The Essential Sonny Boy Williamson** / Jun. 8, 1993 / MCA/Chess ✦✦✦✦✦
Two-disc compilation offering 45 of the wizened harmonica genius' best efforts for the Chess brothers, this is the best domestic Williamson package you'll find. Not everything you might want, but pretty close to it: "Don't Start Me to Talkin'," "Let Me Explain," "The Key (To Your Door)" (an alternate take), "Bring It on Home," "Help Me," "One Way Out," "Your Funeral and My Trial," and plenty more. With Robert Jr. Lockwood and Luther Tucker peeling off sizzling guitar riffs behind him, Williamson always had a trick or two up his sleeve until the end. —*Bill Dahl*

Goin' in Your Direction / 1994 / Trumpet ✦✦✦✦
Alligator continues its Trumpet reissue series with an excellent 15-cut anthology covering early Rice Miller (Sonny Boy Williamson II) material, some of it also including guitarist Arthur "Big Boy" Crudup and guitarist Bobo "Slim" Thomas. Miller was honing the uncanny technique that made him a harmonica legend, playing long overtones, spitting lines, droning and angular phrases that are now part of blues lore. His voice was gaining strength and stature, and he repeatedly demonstrated the kind of vocal character and instrumental acumen later immortalized on his Chess sessions. Alligator has found a genuine treasure chest with this series. —*Ron Wynn*

Trumpet Masters, Vol. 5: From the Bottom / Collectables ✦✦✦✦
As you would expect, Sonny Boy Williamson II's Trumpet sides were rough, raspy and combative, punctuated by biting harmonica and accented by his piercing vocals. This CD cleans up the sound a bit, but not enough to rob it of its energy or grit. —*Ron Wynn*

Jimmy Witherspoon (James Witherspoon)

b. Aug. 8, 1923, Gurdon, AK
Vocals / Blues, Swing, Jazz Blues

One of the great blues singers of the post-World War II period, Witherspoon began recording with Jay McShann for Philo and Mercury in 1945 and 1946. His own first recordings, using McShann's band, resulted in a No. 1 R&B hit in 1949 with "Ain't Nobody's Business Parts 1 & 2" on Supreme Records. Live performances of "No Rollin' Blues" and "Big Fine Girl" provided Spoon with two more hits in 1950. Later singles were tried for Federal, Chess, Atco, Vee-Jay, and others with little success. His album *Live at the Monterey Jazz Festival* (HiFi Jazz) from 1959 lifted him back into the limelight. Partnerships with Ben Webster (tenor sax) or Groove Holmes (organ) were recorded, and some memorable music resulted, but Jimmy's best '60s album is *Evenin' Blues* (Prestige), which features T-Bone Walker on guitar and Clifford Scott on saxophone. Inactive for a time in the '70s due to throat cancer, Witherspoon has made a complete recovery and made one of his most memorable albums for Muse Records (*Midnight Lady Called the Blues*). Muse also released an album recorded in France, featuring Witherspoon with The Savoy Sultans. His newer records lack the spark of some of his earlier work, but given the proper circumstances Jimmy Witherspoon always delivers. —*Bob Porter*

Baby Baby Baby / 1963 / Original Blues Classics ✦✦✦

Blues Around the Clock / Nov. 5, 1963 / Original Blues Classics ✦✦✦

Evenin' Blues / 1964 / Original Blues Classics ✦✦✦✦

A good relaxed (but not laidback) session, and one of his bluesier ones, with organ, Clifford Scott (who played on Bill Doggett's "Honky Tonk") on sax, and T-Bone Walker on guitar. Nothing too adventurous about the song selection, including well-traveled items like "Good Rockin' Tonight" and "Kansas City," but Witherspoon sings them with ingratiating soul, reaching his peaks on his cover of "Don't Let Go" (perhaps better than the hit version by Roy Hamilton) and the late-night ambience of the title track. The CD reissue adds previously unissued alternate takes of four of the songs. —*Richie Unterberger*

● **Hey Mr. Landlord** / 1965 / Route 66 ✦✦✦✦

This is a thorough import survey of Witherspoon's earlier (1945-56) blues-shoutin' days. —*Hank Davis*

Spoon So Easy: The Chess Years / 1990 / MCA/Chess ✦✦✦✦

Spoon So Easy: The Chess Years is an excellent retrospective of Jimmy Witherspoon's stint at Chess Records. During this time he was moving closer to jump blues and R&B than jazz, but his music wasn't suffering at all—he sounds vigorous throughout these sessions. It's a brief sampler—only 12 songs on the disc—but it collects the cream of a somewhat checkered era for Witherspoon. —*Thom Owens*

★ **Blowin' in from Kansas City** / 1993 / Capitol ✦✦✦✦✦

These 20 tunes pair the great Mr. Witherspoon with the finest jazz, jump, and blues talent around. Jay McShann, Maxwell Davis, Tiny Webb, and Chuck Norris are only a few of the first-rate session-men and arrangers who grace the tracks of this essential CD. A special mention must be made of tenor sax legend Ben Webster, whose solo on "I'm Going Around in Circles" is simply magnificent. This is quintessential Kansas City blues. Of all the shouters, Witherspoon is perhaps the greatest singer. —*Larry Hoffman*

Jay's Blues / Charly ✦✦✦✦

Jay's Blues is a fine collection of early-'50s jump blues sides that Jimmy Witherspoon cut for Federal Records. This 23-track collection offers a good retrospective of one of Witherspoon's most neglected—and admittedly uneven—periods. —*Thom Owens*

Billy Wright

b. May 21, 1932, Atlanta, GA, **d.** Oct. 27, 1991, Atlanta, GA

Vocals / R&B

A prime influence on Little Richard during his formative years, "Prince of the Blues" Billy Wright's hearty shouting delivery was an Atlanta staple during the postwar years.

Wright's 1949 Savoy debut, "Blues for My Baby," shot up to No. 3 on *Billboard's* R&B charts, and its flip, "You Satisfy," did almost as well. Two more of Wright's Savoy 78s, "Stacked Deck" and "Hey Little Girl," were also Top Ten R&B entries in 1951. The flamboyant Wright set his pal Little Richard up with powerful WGST deejay Zenas Sears, who scored the newcomer his first contract with RCA in 1951. It's no knock on Richard to note that his early sides sound very much like Billy Wright. Wright later emceed shows in Atlanta, remaining active until a stroke in the mid-'70s slowed him down. —*Bill Dahl*

Goin' Down Slow (Blues, Soul & Early R 'n' R, Vol. 1) / 1984 / Savoy ✦✦✦✦

Crying and pleading the blues, Wright's early-'50s Savoy output was very influential. —*Bill Dahl*

● **Billy Wright** / 1994 / Savoy Jazz ✦✦✦✦

Fifteen of the Atlanta jump blues shouter's very best outings for Savoy, spanning 1949-1954. Wright's pleading style, a large influence indeed on a developing Little Richard, is irresistibly spotlighted on "After Awhile," "I Remember," and the romping "Billy's Boogie Blues." —*Bill Dahl*

Jimmy Yancey

b. 1894, Chicago, IL, **d.** Sep. 17, 1951, Chicago, IL

Piano / Blues, Boogie-Woogie

One of the pioneers of boogie-woogie piano, Jimmy Yancey was generally more subtle than the more famous Albert Ammons, Pete Johnson, and Meade Lux Lewis, falling as much into the blues genre as jazz. Yancey, who could romp as well as anyone, made many of his most memorable recordings at slower tempos. No matter what key he played in, Yancey ended every song in E flat, leading to hilarious conclusions to some recordings. He worked in vaudeville as a singer and tap dancer, starting at age six, and in 1915 settled in Chicago as a pianist. But Yancey spent his last 26 years (from 1925 on) earning his living as a groundskeeper at Comiskey Park for the Chicago White Sox. He played part-time in local clubs and began recording in 1939, on a few occasions backing his wife, singer Mama Yancey. Jimmy Yancey never achieved the fame of his contemporaries but he remained a major influence on all practitioners in the genre. —*Scott Yanow*

★ **Complete Recorded Works, Vol. 1** / May 4, 1939+Sep. 6, 1940 / Document ✦✦✦✦✦

Yancey's earliest and best sides for the Solo Art label. Beautiful and sensitive performances. —*Cub Koda*

● **Complete Recorded Works, Vol. 2 (1939-1950)** / Feb. 23, 1940-Dec. 1943 / Document ✦✦✦✦

On the second of three CDs that trace virtually his entire recording career, pianist Jimmy Yancey is showcased on a variety of solo tracks. Two numbers from February 1940 are highlighted by the classic "Bear Trap Blues." There are a couple of numbers made for the tiny Art Center Jazz Gems label, a four-song (plus two alternate takes) definitive set cut for Bluebird (which includes "Death Letter Blues" and "Yancey's Bugle Call"), and nine songs (five previously unissued) from 1943; on one version of "How Long Blues," Mama Yancey sings, while Jimmy switches to the spooky-sounding harmonium. This set also has Jimmy Yancey's only four recorded vocals, which are quite effective even though his voice is limited. All three volumes in this series are highly recommended . —*Scott Yanow*

Vol. 3 (1943-1950) / Dec. 1943-Dec. 23, 1950 / Document ✦✦✦✦

The third of three CDs tracing the recording career of the unique boogie-woogie pianist Jimmy Yancey, whose subtlety could often result in some dramatic music, completes his December 1943 session and also has his December 23, 1950 solo set; his final recordings from July 1951 are available on an Atlantic release. The 1943 titles, three of which were previously unreleased, include two with Mama Yancey vocals (on one Jimmy switches to harmonium) and is highlighted by "White Sox Stomp," "Yancey Special" and two versions of "Pallet on the Floor." After the six fine titles from 1950, this CD finishes off with the only four numbers that Jimmy's older brother, the more ragtime-oriented Alonzo Yancey, ever recorded. Although his style was different, on "Ecstatic Rag" Alonzo does sound a bit like Jimmy. All three of these Document CDs, plus the Atlantic set, are highly recommended and preferable to the piecemeal domestic Bluebird reissues. —*Scott Yanow*

★ **Chicago Piano, Vol. 1** / Jul. 18, 1951 / Atlantic ✦✦✦✦✦

Jimmy Yancey was a pioneer boogie-woogie pianist but, unlike many of the other pacesetters, he had a gentle and thoughtful style that also crossed over into the blues. This Atlantic CD, a straight reissue of the 1972 LP, contains Yancey's final recordings, cut just eight weeks before his death from diabetes. The pianist is in fine form on these introspective and often emotional performances which, with the exception of Meade Lux Lewis' "Yancey Special" and the traditional "Make Me a Pallet on the Floor," are composed entirely of Yancey's originals. His wife Mama Yancey does five vocals on this memorable set of classic blues. —*Scott Yanow*

Mighty Joe Young

b. Sep. 23, 1927, Shreveport, LA

Guitar, Vocals / Electric Chicago Blues

Although physical problems have curtailed his guitar playing in recent years, there was a time during the late '70s and early '80s when Mighty Joe Young was one of the leading blues guitarists on Chicago's budding North Side blues circuit. Young hit his stride in 1961 with the sizzling "Why Baby"/"Empty Arms" for Bobby Robinson's Fire label. Young gigged as Otis Rush's rhythm guitarist from 1960 to 1963 and cut a series of excellent Chicago blues 45s for a variety of labels.

Delmark issued Young's solo album debut, *Blues with a Touch of Soul*, in 1970, but a pair of mid-'70s LPs for Ovation (1974's *Chicken Heads* and an eponymous set in 1976) showcased the guitarist's blues-soul synthesis far more effectively. Young's main local haunt during the '70s and early '80s was Wise Fools Pub, where he packed 'em in nightly (with Freddy King's brother, Benny Turner, on bass). —*Bill Dahl*

Chicken Heads / 1974 / Ovation ✦✦✦✦

One of Mighty Joe Young's best efforts (and one that's not out on CD), an up-to-the-minute effort that combines soul and blues most effectively. Predominantly original material that suits his booming vocals and stinging guitar well. Nice band, too: bassist Louis Satterfield, drummer Ira Gates, and keyboardist Floyd Morris were all veterans of the '60s soul session scene. —*Bill Dahl*

● **Mighty Joe Young** / 1976 / Ovation ✦✦✦✦

Another out-of-print collection that's the crown jewel in Young's album discography. Many of Young's finest originals—"Need a Friend," "Takes Money," "Take My Advice (She Likes the Blues and Barbecue)"—reside in their most memorable recorded forms on this worthwhile LP. —*Bill Dahl*

Various Artists

Alligator Records—25th Anniversary Collection / Mar. 1996 / Alligator ✦✦✦✦✦

It's hard to believe that Alligator Records has been around for 25 years, but indeed it's true. Yet, it's a bit hard to remember a time in the blues bizz when Alligator *wasn't* on the scene. It's also pretty amazing to realize the state of the indie blues label way back then and how much label prexy Bruce Iglauer has changed the whole ballgame in the intervening years. They couldn't have pulled it off if the music wasn't great to begin with, and here's where you go to get a real nice sampling of it. This is a specially priced, two CDs for the price of one photocube set, loaded with great stuff from Charlie Musselwhite, Koko Taylor, Lonnie Brooks, Johnny Winter, Billy Boy Arnold, Lonnie Mack, and a host of others who've trotted their wares on the label over the years. Besides giving the novice one great introduction to the label (as the music runs from traditional to modern), the big bonus here is a treasure trove of previously unissued tracks from Roy Buchanan (a chaotic version of Link Wray's "Jack the Ripper"), Floyd Dixon (a recut of his Blues Brothers' approved hit "Hey Bartender"), Albert Collins and Johnny Copeland in a marvelous outtake from the *Showdown!* album ("Something to Remember You By") and the band that started it all, Hound Dog Taylor & the HouseRockers, with a crazed version of Elmore James' "Look on Yonder's Wall," as sloppy as it is cool. While some naysayers in the blues community tend to diss Alligator for being too slick, this double set shows that Mssrs. Iglauer and company have done more than any other in promoting and fostering the music while simultaneously moving it away from the mummified scholarly leanings of other labels. Very good stuff and at these prices, a bargain and then some. —*Cub Koda*

Ann Arbor Blues and Jazz Festival, Vol. 3 / Mar. 19, 1996 / Schoolkids ✦✦✦
Like the previous two installments in Schoolkids Records' *Ann Arbor Blues & Jazz Festival* series, the sound on *Vol. 3: Grind It! Roosevelt Sykes & Victoria Spivey* is pretty poor. There are plenty of poor fades and mixes, not to mention dropouts. When you're dealing with historical recordings such as this, you can handle poor fidelity if you're getting good music, which is the case here. Both Roosevelt Sykes and Victoria Spivey are captured at the top of the form, playing with vigor and style, even though they were nearing the end of their careers. And that's what makes this music special—these are among the last recordings of Sykes or Spivey, and they prove that the musicians remained vital until the very end. That revelation alone makes the poor sound quality tolerable. —*Thom Owens*

Ann Arbor Blues and Jazz Festival, Vol. 4 / Mar. 19, 1996 / Schoolkids ✦✦✦
Once again in this series, the sound is often poor, but if low-down gutbucket juke-joint blues floats your boat, then the nine selections (two of them, "Me and the Devil Blues" and "Down So Long," are both only accessible on this disc as track three, even though they're not a medley, hmmmmm) by the King Biscuit Boys is just the thing you've been waiting to hear. They were fronted by Houston Stackhouse and Joe Willie Wilkins on guitars and Sonny Blake on harmonica.
The Walter Horton set brings back a flood of positive memories for this writer. Volume and fader fluctuations aside, Horton was having the time of his life and the backing band of Johnny Nicholas on guitar, Fran Christina on drums, and Sarah Brown on bass from Nicholas' band, the Boogie Brothers, were following Big Walter's every crazy musical move without ever letting go of the groove, no small feat, believe me. —*Cub Koda*

The Atlantic Blues Box / 1986 / Atlantic ✦✦✦✦✦
The Atlantic Blues Box includes four discs, with each focusing on a different style—vocalists, Chicago, guitar, and piano (each available separately as well). If you've got the money, this is a worthwhile addition to any blues collection. —*Bill Dahl*

Baby, Let's Burn / 1992 / Flyright ✦✦✦
A thoroughly delicious slice of down-home Louisiana blues (21 tracks in all) by some of the lesser known artists who recorded for the Excello label. The seven tracks by Jimmy Reed sound-alike Jimmy Anderson are choice listening, while "I Don't Know Why" by the mysterious Boogie Jake is as low-down as it gets. —*Cub Koda*

Bad, Bad Whiskey (The Galaxy Masters) / 1994 / Specialty ✦✦✦✦✦
A subsidiary of Fantasy, the Galaxy label recorded a diverse assortment of soul and R&B in the 1960s and early '70s. This is a 26-track compilation of highlights from the company's output, covering 1962 to 1972. Landing the occasional minor R&B chart hit, Galaxy couldn't be said to have an especially distinctive label sound, though their efforts were on the whole bluesier than much soul of the era. But this is still a decent grab bag of odds and ends from soul's vintage period, with obscure sides by well-known performers like Betty Everett, Little Johnny Taylor, Lenny Williams, Charles Brown, Johnny "Guitar" Watson, Merl Saunders, and a host of unknowns. Especially good are the three sides by Rodger Collins, whose 1966 single "She's Looking Good" (which leads off the CD) was one of the better regional soul hits of the '60s and was covered by Wilson Pickett for a Top 20 smash a couple of years later. —*Richie Unterberger*

The Beauty of the Blues / 1991 / Columbia/Legacy ✦✦✦✦
This is a beautiful 18-track collection from a sampling of Columbia/Legacy's *Roots 'n' Blues* series. The recordings, from 1929-1947, include a wide variety of traditional blues and blues-related styles. Excellent

sound, with music from Robert Johnson, Big Bill Broonzy, and others. —*Niles J. Frantz*

Before the Blues, Vol. 1 / 1996 / Yazoo ✦✦✦

The Best of Duke-Peacock Blues / 1992 / MCA ✦✦✦
Interesting collection of sides from this seminal Texas label. Highlights includes tracks by Bobby Bland ("Stormy Monday," "Turn On Your Lovelight"), Otis Rush ("Homework"), Junior Parker ("Driving Wheel"), and Larry Davis' original version of "Texas Flood," made popular to a new audience by Stevie Ray Vaughn. —*Cub Koda*

☆ **Blue Flames: Sun Blues Collection** / 1990 / Rhino ✦✦✦✦✦
A skimpy (18 songs) but tremendous set of Sam Phillips' gutbucket blues recordings, all are of early-'50s vintage and exquisitely remastered. Most of the big names are here. —*John Floyd*

The Blues Came Down from Memphis / Charly ✦✦✦✦✦
Nice overview of Sun Records' early '50s blues recordings on a single CD, primarily sticking to an issued singles format. Perfect place to start. —*Cub Koda*

Blues Hangover / 1995 / AVI-Excello ✦✦✦✦
This two-disc, 43-track collection contains a treasure trove of rare and unissued performances from the vaults of Excello Records. All but one of the 17 tracks collected on the first disc were produced by Jay Miller in his Crowley, LA studio, home of Excello's unmistakable "swamp blues" sound. The first ten tracks are by Jimmy Anderson, who impersonates the vocal and harmonica style of Jimmy Reed so pervasively, it's downright eerie. Three tracks from Whispering Smith, a stray Lightnin' Slim cut, and both sides of the mysterious Blue Charlie single are aboard, as well as rare singles from the equally mysterious Ole Sonny Boy, Little Al (Gunter) and Little Sonny. But the true find here is the first time release of 15 tracks from a 1966 audition tape by one Early Drane. For all intents and purposes, this appears to be the same "Earl Draines" that recorded for the label as part of the Blues-rockers ("Calling All Cows") in the mid-'50s. But these remarkable tapes are the man alone in his living room, singing and playing a quirky collection of original material, blues and gospel covers that careen from brilliant to downright loony. Add to this lineup four tracks by Detroit bluesman Baby Boy Warren (featuring Sonny Boy Williamson on harmonica) and two early-'60s stereo swingers by the little known James Stewart and you've got an Excello rarities package that's pretty hard to beat. —*AMG*

Blues Is Killin' Me / 1991 / Paula/Flyright ✦✦✦✦✦
20-track, rock-solid collection of classic blues sides from Chicago's JOB label, primarily focusing on both sides of original-issue 78s by Floyd Jones, Memphis Minnie, Baby Face Leroy, and Little Hudson's Red Devil Trio with a few unissued surprises rounding out the already excellent package. —*Cub Koda*

Blues Masters, Vol. 10: Blues Roots / 1993 / Rhino ✦✦✦
Expertly compiled, annotated, and in most cases recorded by pioneering blues researcher Samuel Charters, this volume explores all areas of the blues' origins. Featuring devastating recordings of prison work hands, native African music to Texas prison songs, this is as hardcore a collection as you're likely to find, yet still very accessible to the average fan. —*Cub Koda*

☆ **Blues Masters, Vol. 11: Classic Blues Women** / 1993 / Rhino ✦✦✦✦✦
Although it is now a male-dominated field, the earliest to record and have success in the blues field were women. This volume not only collects many of the great recordings by these women (Mamie, Trixie and Bessie Smith, Billie Holiday, Sippie Wallace, Ma Rainey), but also holds the distinction in the series of being one of the few that offers multiple selections by some of these artists. Highly recommended. —*Cub Koda*

☆ **Blues Masters, Vol. 12: Memphis Blues** / 1993 / Rhino ✦✦✦✦
Running the blues history of America's craziest city from early offerings by Cannon's Jug Stompers and the Memphis Jug Band to early Sun recordings from the '50s by Junior Parker, Rufus Thomas, and Joe Hill Louis, this is undoubtedly one of the best compiled volumes in the series. —*Cub Koda*

Blues Masters, Vol. 13: New York City Blues / 1993 / Rhino ✦✦✦✦✦
While other volumes in the series showcase the down-home aspects of the music, this one highlights the big-band sound. Great sides by Lionel Hampton ("Hamp's Boogie Woogie"), Duke Ellington, Buddy Johnson, Count Basie, Sam "The Man" Taylor ("Oo-Wee"), and Lucky Millinder showcase a side to the music that is seldom heard. —*Cub Koda*

★ **Blues Masters, Vol. 14: More Jump Blues** / 1993 / Rhino ✦✦✦✦✦
Just as essential as the previous Rhino jump blues collection (vol. 5 of the *Blues Masters* series), this has classics by Floyd Dixon ("Hey Bartender"), Joe Liggins ("Pink Champagne"), Joe Turner, Wynonie Harris, Ruth Brown, Big Maybelle, and Louis Jordan. It also takes some chances by presenting cuts by performers not strictly identified with the style, like Louis Prima, Bobby Charles (the original version of Bill Haley's "See You Later Alligator"), Little Richard, and Faye Adams, whose rousing "I'll Be True" is a touchstone of early R&B. —*Richie Unterberger*

Blues Masters, Vol. 15: Slide Guitar Classics / 1993 / Rhino ✦✦✦✦✦
The final volume in the series (at least for now) features seminal and classic tracks from Elmore James ("Dust My Broom"), Muddy Waters ("Honey Bee"), and Hound Dog Taylor to modern-day disciples like Johnny Winter and Ry Cooder. Blind Willie Johnson's "Dark Was the Night, Cold Was the Ground" is worth the price of admission alone. — *Cub Koda*

☆ **Blues Masters, Vol. 1: Urban Blues** / 1992 / Rhino ✦✦✦✦✦
While more horn driven and less guitar-reliant than other forms of blues, the urban style nonetheless provides its own spectacular highlights, some of the best of which are right here. The first volume in this 15-volume series features classic performances by Eddie "Cleanhead" Vinson, Dinah Washington, T-Bone Walker, Charles Brown, Joe Turner, and Jimmy Witherspoon. Where the blues meets the jazz and heads uptown for a party. — *Cub Koda*

☆ **Blues Masters, Vol. 2: Post-War Chicago Blues** / 1992 / Rhino ✦✦✦✦✦
Excellent 18-track compendium of all the major movers and shakers who helped shape the Chicago blues scene in the '50s. Everyone is well represented here, and major stars like Muddy Waters and Howlin' Wolf stand next to behind-the-scenes geniuses like Earl Hooker and Jody Williams for an interesting, accurate, blend. — *Cub Koda*

☆ **Blues Masters, Vol. 3: Texas Blues** / 1992 / Rhino ✦✦✦✦✦
The best that the Lone Star State has had to offer over a 60-year period is right here, from Blind Lemon Jefferson's "Match Box Blues" (1927) to Stevie Ray Vaughn's live version of "Flood Down in Texas (Texas Flood)" from 1986. This compilation also features great sides by the Fabulous Thunderbirds, Lightnin' Hopkins, T-Bone Walker, and Albert Collins. As an introduction to the Texas blues style, this is a pretty darn good one. — *Cub Koda*

★ **Blues Masters, Vol. 4: Harmonica Classics** / 1992 / Rhino ✦✦✦✦✦
If both sides of McCain's lone 1961 single for the Mississippi Rex label weren't so great, we probably would only be listing this excellent compilation in the back of the book. But if massive amplified harp tone is what you're looking for, then step up to the volume control and crank it for McCain's instrumental "Steady." Ironically, Jerry's biggest hit and most well known track, "She's Tough"–the flipside–has so far eluded compilation onto compact disc. This excellent collection also includes seminal tracks from Little Walter, Big Walter Horton, Paul Butterfield, Jimmy Reed, Lazy Lester, Slim Harpo, Junior Wells, and Charlie Musselwhite. — *AMG*

☆ **Blues Masters, Vol. 5: Jump Blues Classics** / 1992 / Rhino ✦✦✦✦✦
Jump blues, of course, was crucial to the birth of R&B and rock 'n' roll. More important, the infectious swing, grit, and humor were great in themselves. *Jump Blues Classics* collects 18 tracks from the golden days of the genre in the late '40s and 1950s. Most of the pioneers of the style are here—Joe Turner, Wynonie Harris, Roy Brown, Ruth Brown, Roy Milton, Big Jay McNeely, and others, even Louis Prima. The collection includes several cuts that were revived to become rock 'n' roll classics, including "The Train Kept A-Rollin' " (Tiny Bradshaw), "Shake, Rattle, and Roll" (Joe Turner), "Good Rockin' Tonight" (Wynonie Harris), "Hound Dog" (Big Mama Thornton), and the little-known original, pre-Muddy Waters version of "Got My Mojo Working" (Ann Cole). This is, of course, just the surface of a genre that was hugely successful in its time, producing hundreds of memorable recordings. This well-annotated anthology is a good starting point and a good representative sampling for those who only want the cream of the crop in their collection. — *Richie Unterberger*

★ **Blues Masters, Vol. 6: Blues Originals** / 1993 / Rhino ✦✦✦✦✦
It's unfortunate, but it's true: the original versions of many blues classics aren't nearly as well known as their hit covers by (usually White) rock groups. That's not to say that some of these covers aren't great as well, but it's both educational and enjoyable to hear them from the source's mouth. *Blues Originals* contains 18 original versions of classics that went on to reach a wide audience via covers by the Stones, Yardbirds, Elvis, Led Zeppelin, the Doors, and others. The Chess stable of Howlin' Wolf, Muddy Waters, Bo Diddley, Little Walter, and Sonny Boy Williamson is represented here, of course, along with standards by Elmore James, Otis Rush, Robert Johnson, Slim Harpo, and Jimmy Reed. Mixed in with great and fairly available performances like Bo Diddley's "I'm a Man" and Howlin' Wolf's "Back Door Man" are some quite obscure and collectable delights. Arthur Crudup's original version of "That's All Right," covered by Elvis Presley for his first single, has been surprisingly hard to find over the years; ditto for Muddy Waters' "You Need Love," which formed the blueprint for Led Zeppelin's "Whole Lotta Love." Even most Yardbirds fanatics are unaware that the prototype for "Lost Woman" was taken from (and retitled from) an obscure Snooky Pryor single, "Someone to Love Me." And even many Chicago blues fanatics will be surprised to find the original version of "Got My Mojo Working," which was not recorded by Muddy Waters, but little-known jump blues singer Ann Cole. A fine collection, mixing together famous standards and obscure gems with thorough liner notes. — *Richie Unterberger*

Blues Masters, Vol. 7: Blues Revival / 1993 / Rhino ✦✦✦✦✦
It's hard to believe from the vantage point of a period when blues songs are used for network television commercials, but it wasn't so long ago that the blues was, though hardly in danger of extinction, certainly limited to a pretty specialized audience. The blues revival of the early '60s brought the music back into the spotlight through its prominence at major folk festivals and college concerts, the rediscovery of lost legends like Skip James and Mississippi John Hurt, and the efforts of several musicians and record labels to popularize the work of the form's originators. *Blues Revival* covers a lot of these bases. This 17-track collection includes some of the biggest hit blues singles of the '60s (by Jimmy Reed, John Lee Hooker, Slim Harpo, and B.B. King), '60s recordings by acoustic Delta blues giants like Mississippi Fred McDowell and Son House, hot electric Chicago blues by Junior Wells and Muddy Waters, and White, rock-oriented revivalists like Paul Butterfield, John Mayall, and Canned Heat. Seasoned collectors won't find anything too obscure here, but it's a handy primer to some of the best blues recorded during an era in which the idiom reestablished itself as a vital and living form. — *Richie Unterberger*

Blues Masters, Vol. 8: Mississippi Delta Blues / 1993 / Rhino ✦✦✦
The title for this volume is a bit of a misnomer. While there is easily half a compilation's worth of authentic acoustic material here (including classics by Tommy Johnson, Charlie Patton, Willie Brown, and Robert Johnson), the inclusion of tracks by B.B. and Albert King and recorded-in-Chicago sides by Howlin' Wolf, Elmore James, and Robert Nighthawk do much to blur the distinctiveness of this package. — *Cub Koda*

Blues Masters, Vol. 9: Postmodern Blues / 1993 / Rhino ✦✦✦✦✦
A wonderful compendium of artists and styles illustrating the coming of blues into the mainstream. This volume features representative tracks by B.B. King, Albert Collins, Albert King, George Thorogood, Stevie Ray Vaughn, Johnny Winter, and the Fabulous Thunderbirds. The modern sound at its best, and most diverse. — *Cub Koda*

Blues at the Newport Folk Festival / 1959 / Vanguard ✦✦✦
Blues at Newport—Newport Folk Festival 1959-64 offers fine performances by John Hurt, Skip James, Rev. Gary Davis, Robert Wilkins, and others. — *Mark A. Humphrey*

Blues in the Mississippi Night / Jul. 13, 1991 / Rykodisc ✦✦✦✦✦
This pioneering, documentary-style recording was produced by Alan Lomax and laid unissued for decades after its 1946 recording due to its frank discussion of racism by Big Bill Broonzy, Sonny Boy Williamson, and Memphis Slim. — *Bill Dahl*

The Bluesville Years, Vol. 1: Big Blues, Honks and Wails / 1995 / Prestige ✦✦✦
For almost a decade Bluesville operated as a subsidiary label to the indie jazz pioneer Prestige Records. With a chaotic catalog, they issued everything from barrelhouse piano players working with hipster jazz combos to semipro street singers to tons of Lightnin' Hopkins albums. What we have here are the beginnings of the modern blues album as we know it. The first entry in the series, *Big Blues, Honks and Wails*, features tracks by piano giants Sunnyland Slim and Roosevelt Sykes and uptown blues belters Mildred Anderson, Jimmy Witherspoon, and Al Smith paired with small, jazz-oriented combos with sax legends Kurtis Kurtis, Eddie "Lockjaw" Davis, and Clifford Scott honkin' away. — *Cub Koda*

The Bluesville Years, Vol. 2: Feelin' Down on the South Side / 1995 / Prestige ✦✦✦
Feelin' Down on the South Side culls the best of the albums that were cut in Chicago, with topflight selections by Billy Boy Arnold, Homesick James, Otis Spann and James Cotton. Cotton's "One More Mile to Go", with its voodoo backup chorus from the Muddy Waters band, is downright bone-chilling and eerie. — *Cub Koda*

The Bluesville Years, Vol. 3: Beale Street Get-Down / 1995 / Prestige ✦✦✦
Beale Street Get-Down is the folksiest of the bunch, most of it recorded at the Sun studios in Memphis, with country-blues guitarists Furry Lewis and Memphis Willie B. (Borum) and pianist Memphis Slim all contributing to the fray. — *Cub Koda*

The Bluesville Years, Vol. 4: In the Key of Blues / 1995 / Prestige ✦✦✦
The final volume, *In the Key of Blues*, features an all-piano fest with boogies and blues from Mercy Dee Walton, Little Brother Montgomery, Curtis Jones, and still more from Sykes and Memphis Slim. — *Cub Koda*

Boogie Woogie Blues / Sep. 1922-Apr. 1927 / Biograph ✦✦✦
Biograph has come out with many releases of piano rolls through the years. This CD has some by Cow Cow Davenport, James P. Johnson, Clarence Williams, Jimmy Blythe, Hersal Thomas, Lemuel Fowler, and two totally forgotten names: Everett Robbins and Clarence Johnson. As is usual with piano rolls, the rhythms are inflexible and the touch a bit unnatural, so it may take listeners a while to get used to these performances. The emphasis is more on blues than on boogie-woogie, but in general the music is fine for this idiom although not as lively as real piano solos. — *Scott Yanow*

☆ **Chess Blues** / 1992 / MCA ♦♦♦♦♦
Superlative four CD box set, featuring important tracks by all the main stars of the label (Muddy Waters, Howlin' Wolf, Little Walter, Sonny Boy Williamson), as well as much previously unreleased material. A well-done retrospective of Chicago blues in its heyday, as recorded by America's greatest blues label, Chess. —*Cub Koda*

Chicago Blues Anthology / 1984 / Chess ♦♦♦♦♦
A wonderful 24-cut set of raw, early Chicago blues from the Chess label, Delta blues influences are evident in the work of Johnny Shines, Robert Nighthawk, and Floyd Jones. A more modern, urban style is shown by Buddy Guy and Otis Rush on this worthwhile collection. —*Niles J. Frantz*

Chicago Blues Harmonicas / 1990 / Paula/Flyright ♦♦♦♦♦
The four remaining JOB sides by Pryor ("Boogy Fool," "Raisin' Sand," "Cryin' Shame," and "Eighty Nine Ten") are to be found here on this compilation, with Snooky also found in support on two tracks from a 1949 Baby Face Leroy session. With the other 13 tracks including John Lee Henley's "Rhythm Rockin' Boogie," Walter Horton's "Have a Good Time," and rare but notable sides by Sonny Boy Williamson, Little Willie Foster, and Louis Myers and the Aces, this is a harmonica rarities package that's pretty tough to beat. —*Cub Koda*

Chicago Boogie: 1947 / 1983 / St. George ♦♦♦♦♦
All the earliest Maxwell Street acetate recordings from the short-lived Ora Nelle label, featuring the earliest sides of Little Walter, Jimmy Rogers, Johnny Young and Othum Brown. Delta bluesman Johnny Temple's "Olds 98 Blues," done Robert Johnson style with an electric guitar, is a particular standout. —*Cub Koda*

☆ **Chicago: The Blues Today!, Vol. 1** / Oct. 1966 / Vanguard ♦♦♦♦♦
Junior Wells, J.B. Hutto, and Otis Spann are all superlative on this groundbreaking 1966 anthology. —*Bill Dahl*

☆ **Chicago: The Blues Today!, Vol. 2** / 1966 / Vanguard ♦♦♦♦♦
This series (three volumes) is one of the enduring gems from producer Sam Charters' tenure with Vanguard Records in the '60s. James Cotton's vocals and harp playing are both in top form on his five tracks; among them Ike Turner's "Rocket 88" and a makeover of Charles Brown's "Black Night." Slide guitarist Homesick James and his Dusters are fierce in Elmore's "Dust My Broom" and "Set a Date," and Otis Rush is simply magnificent on his five tracks, which include "It's a Mean Old World" and "I Can't Quit You, Baby." This disc is certain to climb to the Top Ten of any blues fan's collection. —*Larry Hoffman*

☆ **Chicago: The Blues Today!, Vol. 3** / 1966 / Vanguard ♦♦♦♦
This is one of the all-time great blues series ever recorded. Aside from the classic Chess albums (Muddy Waters, Little Walter, Howlin' Wolf, etc.), there is no better introduction to Chicago-style blues than this three-volume set. Each one is incredible. This third album contains the Johnny Shines Blues Band, Johnny Young's South Side Blues Band, and Big Walter Horton's Blues Harp Band with Memphis Charlie Musselwhite. Here are the original Chicago artists who have grown up and played together for most of their lives, so the musical time is spacious—wide open. This is South Side Chicago blues with a trace of country at its best. Big Walter Horton plays some of the best harmonica of his career on this album. Listening to Horton on backup and solo harp is an education. This album is definitive. —*Michael Erlewine*

The Cobra Records Story / 1993 / Capricorn ♦♦♦♦♦
This two-disc examination of Chicago's mid-to-late-'50s label features West Side blues classics by Otis Rush, Buddy Guy, and Magic Sam. —*Bill Dahl*

The Copulatin' Blues Compact Disc / Apr. 29, 1929-Feb. 5, 1940 / Stash ♦♦♦
The Stash label began in 1976 with a dozen or so LPs that featured subject matter from the 1930s than was considered risque for the period. In the case of this album, the 16 selections all have to do with sex; several cuts were previously unreleased and few had very wide circulation. Such top jazz and blues artists as Sidney Bechet, Lil Johnson, Bessie Smith ("Do Your Duty" and "I Need a Little Sugar in My Bowl"), the Harlem Hamfats, Merline Johnson, Tampa Red, Grant & Wilson, Jelly Roll Morton ("Winin' Boy"), and Lucille Bogan (an absolutely filthy "Shave 'Em Dry") are heard from. Some of this music has been reissued by Stash through its subsidiary Jass on CD but not in the same format. —*Scott Yanow*

The Copulatin' Blues, Vol. 2 / Jan. 26, 1929-1955 / Stash ♦♦♦
This collection contains a truthful warning and description: "A Party Record for Adults—Screen Before Airplay." It is doubtful if more than a couple of these 15 selections could be played on the radio, even now. Mostly dating from the 1930s, the risque performances include several (including a very profane "parody" by the Clovers in the 1950s) that were previously unissued. Best is "The Duck's Yas Yas" by Eddie Johnson and his Crackerjacks, "It Feels So Good" by the Hokum Boys, and the classic "Pussy" by Harry Roy's Bat Club Boys. —*Scott Yanow*

☆ **Country Blues Bottleneck Guitar Classics** / 1972 / Yazoo ♦♦♦♦♦
The first and possibly best anthology of pre-war bottleneck guitar (1926-1937), this includes the singing slides of Robert Johnson, Bukka White, Memphis Minnie, and—although scarcely country blues—a stunning "St. Louis Blues" by Jim and Bob, the Genial Hawaiians! —*Mark A. Humphrey*

Deep Blue: 25 Years of Blues on Rounder Records / Sep. 12, 1995 / Rounder ♦♦♦
Over the course of two CDs, *Deep Blue*—25 Years of Blues on Rounder Records rounds up the highlights of Rounder's blues catalog, including tracks from Professor Longhair, Clarence "Gatemouth" Brown, Lowell Fulson, Robert Nighthawk, Champion Jack Dupree, Luther "Guitar Junior" Johnson, Ronnie Earl, and Smokin' Joe Kubek, among many others. It's a fairly consistent collection, giving a good representation of the record label's catalog. —*Stephen Thomas Erlewine*

Delta Blues: 1951 / 1990 / Acoustic Archives ♦♦♦♦♦
Great compilation from Jackson, Mississippi's Trumpet Records. Features early-50s sides by Big Joe Williams, wonderful acoustic duets by the Huff Brothers, and the last recordings of original King Biscuit Boy Willie Love. A wonderful document. —*AMG*

Don't Leave Me Here / Yazoo ♦♦♦♦♦
Don't Leave Me Here—Blues of Texas, Arkansas & Louisiana is a 14-track country-blues collection of recordings from 1927-1932. This contains a variety of traditional acoustic blues styles from the Gulf Coast area. Highlights include King Solomon Hill and Little Hat Jones. —*Niles J. Frantz*

Drop Down Mama / 1970 / Chess ♦♦♦♦♦
Nighthawk's early sides for Chess back when they were still called Aristocrat. Includes the original "Sweet Black Angel," which later became a hit for B.B. King as "Sweet Little Angel," and "Anna Lee," two of his very best. Even with minimal band support on these sides, Nighthawk's voice and slide guitar resonates like an orchestra. This wonderful compilation also features seminal tracks by Johnny Shines ("So Glad I Found You"), Floyd Jones ("Dark Road"), Big Boy Spires ("One of These Days"), and Honeyboy Edwards doing the title track with a full band. Truly a compilation that should be residing in everyone's collection. —*Cub Koda*

☆ **Duke-Peacock's Greatest Hits** / 1992 / MCA ♦♦♦♦♦
Don Robey, something of an infamous figure even in the rough-and-tumble world of 1950s R&B labels, owned one of the first successful black-owned labels in the country, and his output was rich and varied. *Duke-Peacock's Greatest Hits* offers a revealing overview of his operation, beginning with major hits by two of the company's humongous female belters—Big Mama Thornton's "Hound Dog" and Marie Adams' "I'm Gonna Play the Honky Tonks." Johnny Ace, Bobby Bland, and Junior Parker are represented by a few of their biggest hits, but it's the relatively unknown "Pack Fair and Square" by San Antonio pianist Big Walter Price that wields a knockout punch. Vocal groups aren't forgotten, with sides by Norman Fox and the Rob Roys and the El Torros, and a foray into "rockabilly" is recalled by the Original Casuals' "So Tough." —*Bill Dahl*

☆ **The Earliest Negro Vocal Quartets (1894-1928)** / Document ♦♦♦♦♦
A strong collection of mostly religious sides by some pioneering a cappella groups, beginning with an 1894 cylinder by the Standard Quartet. —*Kip Lornell*

Early American Blues Classics / 1994 / Yazoo ♦♦♦♦
Blues compilations come and go, but seldom has one struck the mother lode of obscure country blues as well as this one. Pulled from various private collections, these are discs so rare that in some cases the listener is experiencing a selection taped from the only copy known to exist. Using the NoNoise digital restoration system for transfer to compact disc, the sound is still extremely noisy by modern-day standards. But the power and drive contained on these selections (including classics by Garfield Akers, Joe Callicott, Geeshie Wiley, and King Solomon Hill) is only rivaled by the best of Robert Johnson or Son House, making all audiophile concerns mute. —*Cub Koda*

East Coast Blues: 1926-1935 / Yazoo ♦♦♦♦♦
A fine assortment from Carl Martin, Willie Walker, William Moore, Blind Blake, Bayless Rose, and other East Coast guitarists. There are several very traditional blues like "Black Dog Blues" and "Crow Jane," plus lots of good ragtime guitar. For serious guitar players and Piedmont blues fans. —*Barry Lee Pearson*

Excello Harmonica Blues Variety / 1994 / ♦♦♦♦
This is a 39-track, double-CD package collecting various stray cuts in the Excello vaults by artists who didn't leave enough tracks behind to justify having compilations under their own names. The highlights include nine tracks by Jimmy Reed sound alike Jimmy Anderson, Lightnin' Slim sideman Lazy Lester, and ten tracks by Jerry McCain and His Upstarts. Add to this stray singles by Baby Boy Warren (with Sonny Boy Williamson), Little Sonny, Whispering Smith, and the obscure Ole Sonny Boy and you have a package that fills up the holes in your Excello collection quite

nicely. Over half of the tracks are dubbed from disc, but the music's fine just the same. —*Cub Koda*

The Fifties: Juke Joint Blues / Capitol ✦✦✦✦✦
This is a valuable look at some of the toughest Delta and West Coast blues sides issued by Modern Records in the 1950s. —*Bill Dahl*

Genuine Houserockin' Music, Vol. 1 / 1986 / Alligator ✦✦✦✦✦
These virtually interchangeable samplers of good-time, high-energy, modern R&B were produced by Chicago's Alligator label. Lonnie Brooks, Lonnie Mack, Koko Taylor, Fenton Robinson, Albert Collins, and others are included. Slick and well produced. —*Hank Davis*

Gonna Head for Home / Flyright ✦✦✦✦✦
Nice compendium of rare and unissued Excello sides by lesser-known names (Boogie Jake, Mr. Calhoun, Silas Hogan, and Jimmy Anderson) who recorded for the label. Excellent Louisiana swamp blues, crude and low-down. —*AMG*

Got My Mojo Working / 1991 / Flyright ✦✦✦✦
Collection of blues sides recorded for New York's Baton label in the mid-to late-'50s, featuring Chris Kenner's first recording and Ann Cole's original, pre-Muddy Waters version performance of the title track. —*Cub Koda*

Great Blues Guitarists: String Dazzlers / Aug. 1991 / Columbia/Legacy ✦✦✦
A high-quality survey of some of the finest blues guitar players, these were recorded from 1924-1940. It includes, among others, Tampa Red, Blind Willie Johnson, and Big Bill Broonzy. Highlights include three instrumental duets featuring Lonnie Johnson and Eddie Lang. They take your breath away. —*Niles J. Frantz*

☆ **The Great Bluesman at Newport** / 1976 / Vanguard ✦✦✦✦✦
These performances come from 1959-1965 by rediscovery legends Son House, Mississippi John Hurt, Skip James, Sleepy John Estes, and other compelling singers and guitarists such as Robert Pete Williams, John Lee Hooker, and Mississippi Fred McDowell. —*Mark A. Humphrey*

● **The Greatest in Country Blues (1929-1956), Vol. 1** / Story of Blues ✦✦✦✦✦
Story of the Blues has provided one of the best introductions to acoustic country blues with its three-volume *Greatest in Country Blues* series. While it collects most of the major figures as well as the obscure and their finest performances, there are a certain number of odd omissions such as Reverend Gary Davis and Robert Nighthawk that prevent it from being the definitive country blues set. Nevertheless, each of the three volumes is an invaluable reference as well as an interesting listen for both the specialist and the novice. —*Chris Woodstra*

● **The Greatest in Country Blues (1929-1956), Vol. 2** / Story Of Blues ✦✦✦✦✦
Anyone interested in a survey of early blues will be thrilled with having any of these three historical volumes, suited to both novice and connoisseur alike. Each provides a dazzling, panoramic survey of artists both famous and obscure and covers every region known to have nurtured the music. *Vol. 2* features Skip James' "Devil Got My Woman," Robert Johnson's "Preaching' Blues," and Kokomo Arnold's "Paddlin' Madeline Blues." From Texas Alexander there is a version of "Levee Camp Moan Blues" which is made timeless by the incomparable guitar of Lonnie Johnson. Great instrumentals like Palmer McAbee's "Railroad Piece" and the Dallas String Band's "Dallas Rag" add spice, and there are also first-rate entries by more obscure giants like King Solomon Hill, George "Bullet" Williams, "Hi" Henry Brown, and Blind Joe Taggart. —*Larry Hoffman*

Hand Me Down Blues Chicago Style / 1990 / Relic ✦✦✦✦✦
One of the finest 1950s Chicago blues compilations in existence, taken from the vaults of Parrot-Blue Lake Records. Unissued sides and rare singles create an incredible ambience here. Essential listening. —*Cub Koda*

Harmonica Blues Kings / 1986 / Delmark ✦✦✦✦✦
Featuring a side each of Big Walter Horton and Alfred "Blues King" Harris in primarily supporting roles behind various vocalists from the vaults of United/States Records, 1954. Raw, lively harmonica and another missing piece of the early Chicago blues puzzle. —*AMG*

Harp Attack! / 1990 / Alligator ✦✦✦✦
Along with his Windy City peers James Cotton, Carey Bell, and Billy Branch, Wells trades harp solos and vocals on this raucous meeting of the minds. Junior's front and center on a fine rendition of Sonny Boy, II's "Keep Your Hands Out of My Pockets" and the tailor-made "Somebody Changed the Lock" and "Broke and Hungry," obviously relishing the camaraderie between himself and his fellow harmonica giants. —*Bill Dahl*

House Rockin' Blues / 1995 / Ace ✦✦✦✦
Compilations of vintage Chess material seem to be plentiful these days, but this excellent collection of strictly uptempo material should not be passed by at any cost. With a healthy 27 tracks aboard, the highlights are numerous, with the label's stars and second- stringers like Howlin' Wolf, J.B. Lenoir, John Brim, Billy Boy Arnold, Bo Diddley, Willie Mabon,

Elmore James, and Otis Rush all present and accounted for. But rather than opt for the same tracks that have been around the block time and again, true obscurities like the anonymous Little Luther's "The Twirl," G.L. Crockett's "Look Out Mabel," the previously unissued Robert Nighthawk with Buddy Guy shuffle, "Someday," "Tired of Crying over You" by Morris Pejoe, and "He Knows the Rules" by Jimmy McCracklin pepper the mix to keep the collectors happy as well. If the boogie side of the Chess cannonade is your particular cup of coffee, this collection is the one you'll keep going back to time and again. Great! —*Cub Koda*

If It Ain't a Hit . . . / Zu-Zazz ✦✦✦✦✦
X-rated blues is the theme here, with selections ranging from totally raunchy to mildly titillating with great listening and a full dollop of humor throughout. Features under-the-counter performances by Jackie Wilson, LaVern Baker, Chick Willis, the Clovers, and the Fred Wolff Combo. Blues with a nudge and a wink to it. —*Cub Koda*

Independent Women's Blues, Vol. 1: Mean Mothers / Rosetta ✦✦✦
Independent Women's Blues is an excellent, four-disc series of early blues and jazz recordings by women—all come highly recommended for not only the abundance of rarities but also for the quality of the music. *Vol. 1*, subtitled *Mean Mothers*, includes selections from Billie Holiday, Ida Cox, and Bessie Brown. —*Chris Woodstra*

Jackson Blues: 1928-1938 / Yazoo ✦✦✦✦✦
Featured are Tommy Johnson and the school of Delta blues he inspired in Jackson, MS. —*Mark A. Humphrey*

Jewel/Paula Records . . . / 1993 / Capricorn ✦✦✦
Jewel and Paula were started by Stan Lewis, a record store owner and mail-order operator specializing in the kind of R&B, blues, soul, and gospel tunes that many people enjoyed, but were undervalued by most major record labels. Lewis moved into the record business during the mid-'60s, signing raw artists who made music light-years away from slick pop fare. This two-disc anthology features prime Jewel and Paula acts from the 1960s, '70s, and '80s. The first disc includes urgent soul tunes from Toussaint McCall and Ted Taylor, Delta blues from Frank Foster, classic shouting R&B from Joe Turner, the smoother R&B sound of Charles Brown, Lightnin' Hopkins, John Lee Hooker, and others. The second disc is just as distinguished, featuring Little Johnny Taylor, Fontella Bass, Ike and Tina Turner, Buster Benton and Ted Taylor, then-budding stars Bobby Rush and Artie "Blues Boy" White, plus other regional attractions. —*Ron Wynn*

Legends of Guitar: Electric Blues, Vol. 1 / Rhino ✦✦✦✦✦
This very consistent post-war blues-guitar collection includes Muddy Waters, T-Bone Walker, B.B. King, Guitar Slim, Earl Hooker, and Otis Rush contributing their vintage classics. —*Bill Dahl*

Legends of Guitar: Electric Blues, Vol. 2 / 1991 / Rhino ✦✦✦
Slightly less consistent than its predecessor, it's still loaded with gems—18 tracks including Clarence Gatemouth Brown, Albert Collins, Lowell Fulson, Magic Sam, etc. —*Bill Dahl*

Legends of the Blues, Vol. 2 / CBS ✦✦✦✦✦
Vol. 2 is just as diverse and entertaining as *Vol. 1*, though the artists included are, in general, somewhat less well known. This collection (featuring recordings from 1929 to 1941, presented in chronological order) includes piano blues from Roosevelt Sykes, Charlie Spand, and Champion Jack Dupree; guitar greats Tampa Red, Buddy Boss, and Casey Bill Weldon; and "classic" blues from Lil' Johnson, Victoria Spivey, and Bessie Jackson. Also here is one of T-Bone Walker's first-ever recordings (as "Oak Cliff T-Bone" from 1929) as well as 13 sides that are previously unissued by Columbia or that alternate takes of issued recordings. —*Niles J. Frantz*

Living Chicago Blues, Vol. 1 / 1978 / Alligator ✦✦✦✦✦
Arguably the best entry in this pioneering anthology series, this features excellent sides by guitarist Jimmy Johnson and saxophonist Eddie Shaw. —*Bill Dahl*

Living Chicago Blues, Vol. 3 / 1980 / Alligator ✦✦✦
Laconic saxman A.C. Reed and crisp guitarist Lacy Gibson are standouts. —*Bill Dahl*

Living Chicago Blues, Vol. 4 / 1980 / Alligator ✦✦✦
Not quite as strong, although witty pianist Detroit Jr. and guitarist Andrew Brown contribute strong tracks. —*Bill Dahl*

Lonesome Road Blues: 15 Years in the Mississippi Delta, 1926-1941 / Yazoo ✦✦✦✦✦
Tommy Johnson's influence is again here on *Lonesome Road Blues—15 Years in the Mississippi Delta*, which includes other fine pre-war Delta blues. —*Mark A. Humphrey*

Low Blows: An Anthology of Chicago Harmonica Blues / 1994 / Rooster ✦✦✦
Scattershot compilation of great, early-'70s recordings by Chicago's better-known (Walter Horton, Carey Bell) and lesser-known (Big John Wrencher, Good Rockin' Charles Edwards) harmonica men. Another missing chapter in blues history. —*Cub Koda*

☆ **Mama Let Me Lay It on You (1926-1936)** / Yazoo ✦✦✦✦✦
A fine collection of East Coast blues, including vintage Josh White, Pink Anderson, and guitarists Blind Blake and Willie Walker. —*Barry Lee Pearson*

☆ **Masters of the Delta Blues: The Friends of Charlie Patton** / 1991 / Yazoo ✦✦✦✦✦
Subtitled "The Friends of Charlie Patton", this CD perfectly anthologizes some of the best and rarest tracks by early Delta blues legends like Son House, Tommy Johnson, and Bukka White. Rough sounds in spots, but indispensable nonetheless. —*Cub Koda*

☆ **Mean Old World: The Blues from 1940 to 1994 Smithsonian Blues Box** / 1996 / Smithsonian Institution Press ✦✦✦✦✦
This four-disc set is just what you might expect from Smithsonian—comprehensive and well conceived. It contains representative major blues figures for each time period for the years 1940 through 1994—everyone from Ma Rainey to Taj Mahal. For most periods, the selection is excellent. The only downside to this approach is that for time periods with great blues activity, some major artists have been dropped from the collection, while for other time periods with low blues activity, minor artists are included. This approach results in biographies and selections for artists like Earl Hooker, Big Walter Horton, and J.B. Hutto missing from the collection. Aside from the above complaint, this is the best collection for its size (four discs) that has been produced to date. The artists selected and the selections for each of the artists are in most cases excellent—the best of the best, so to speak. This is a veritable tour of the best in recorded blues.
The 90-page liner notes by Larry Hoffman contain copious notes on the various selections, including artist biographies (and photos!), comments on the takes, etc.—perhaps the most thorough liner notes of its kind. The introductory essay focuses more on race relations than on the blues music. —*Michael Erlewine*

Memphis Masters: Early American Blues Classics / 1994 / ✦✦✦✦
A companion to Yazoo's excellent *Mississippi Masters* collection, this time focusing on Memphis artists recorded between 1927 to 1934. The tracks collected here offer up a musical ambience that accurately depicts time and place with classic selections from acknowledged area kingpins Frank Stokes, Furry Lewis, Gus Cannon's Jug Stompers, Memphis Minnie, Joe McCoy, and Jack Kelly. Like its companion volume, this 20-track compilation is mastered direct from extremely rare old 78s—in some cases, the only copies known to exist—and the sound varies wildly from track to track. But the music is so great and of such major historical significance, the 78 surface noise that remains only seems to add to the charm and romance of it all. —*Cub Koda*

Mississippi Delta Blues in the 1960's, Vol. 2 / 1994 / Arhoolie ✦✦✦
The second of a two-disc Arhoolie collection featuring late-'60s Delta blues again mixes tracks from familiar names and underrecorded performers. There are 11 cuts from Joe Callicot, among them the superb "Traveling Mama Blues" and "Fare Thee Well Blues," both of which Callicot originally performed in 1930, when he was at his vocal and playing peak. R.L. Burnside is revered inside the Mississippi Delta but has a very low profile beyond it. He's featured on nine late-'60s tunes, four previously unissued. Burnside's ragged guitar riffs and dynamic voice rip through a variety of material, from the novelty cut "Skinny Woman" to the double-entendre "See My Jumper Hangin' Out on the Line" and masterful "Walking Blues." Houston Stackhouse concludes the session with four interesting tunes, three previously unissued on Arhoolie. —*Ron Wynn*

Mississippi Delta Blues, Vol. 1: Blow My Blues Away / 1994 / Arhoolie ✦✦✦
George Mitchell still recorded several vibrant, distinctive Delta blues performances here. The artists he chronicled ranged from such legendary greats as Robert Nighthawk, Johnny Woods, and Fred McDowell to obscure but exciting performers such as Napoleon Strickland, Peck Curtis, and Do-Boy Diamond. Their songs were quite simple; many were reworked tunes they had heard and/or played all their lives. They performed with no fanfare, sophisticated support to cover flaws, or pretension. The songs were about heartbreak, anguish, disappointment, and indignation, and sometimes about getting drunk, sexual potency, or whatever else came to mind. There are 12 unreleased cuts among these 23 numbers, and the mastering and notes provide an added bonus to this nice set. —*Ron Wynn*

☆ **Mississippi Girls** / Sep. 1991 / Story Of Blues ✦✦✦✦✦
This is an important collection because it helps fill the gap in the recorded history of blueswomen who played and sang outside of the well-known sphere of the "classic singers" such as Ma Rainey and Bessie Smith. The highlights here are the two recordings of Mattie Delaney, a wonderful singer/guitarist about whom almost nothing is known. Fine also are the more rough-hewn offerings of Rosie Mae Moore,who is accompanied by talented veterans Charlie McCoy and Ishmon Bracey. Although the Geechie Wiley/Elvie Thomas duets are marred by a scratchy background, they also are well worth hearing. —*Larry Hoffman*

Modern Chicago Blues / Aug. 1965 / Testament ✦✦✦✦
Big John Wrencher never recorded much,and so *any* documentation on this elusive artist is most welcome. On this compilation, he only appears on two tracks; the first, "Blues Before Sunrise," is a leftover from the October 1964 trio session with Robert Nighthawk and Johnny Young. The other, "I'm Going to Detroit," is another trio effort, but this time featuring Young on mandolin and John Lee Granderson on guitar, and sounds like it could have been taken from a late-'40s Maxwell Street recording session. Comparing this track to Wrencher's solo album shows that the intervening time had done much to coarsen up his approach, especially in the vocal department. Nice photo on the inside booklet of Big John playing on the street with Johnny Young too. —*Cub Koda*

Mojo Working: The Best of Ace Blues / 1995 / Ace ✦✦✦✦
This 20-track collection puts together essential tracks by some of the biggest names in the genre. Elmore James, John Lee Hooker, Smokey Hogg, B.B. King, Slim Harpo, Albert King, Lowell Fulson, Lonesome Sundown, Howlin' Wolf, Johnny "Guitar" Watson, Arthur Gunter, Lazy Lester, Pee Wee Crayton, Ike Turner,and Lazy Lester are all represented by at least one track apiece and, in most cases, some of their representative work. A pretty great primer that not only serves as something of a greatest-hits package for the novice, but just plain great listening for the hardliners as well. —*Cub Koda*

News & Blues: Telling It Like It Is / Feb. 1991 / Columbia ✦✦✦✦✦
Like any form of popular music, the blues has reflected the social conditions of the times, sometimes quite explicitly. *News & the Blues* offers 20 songs from the Columbia vaults from between 1927 and 1947. The Depression is reflected often, as expected, but there are also songs about natural disasters, public figures like Joe Louis, World War II, and even the atomic bomb. Memphis Minnie and Bill Gaither even take the step of recording specific tributes to other blues singers (Ma Rainey and Leroy Carr, respectively). Many of the performers are well known—Bessie Smith, Mississippi John Hurt, Big Bill Broonzy, Charlie Patton, Memphis Minnie, Bukka White—and several others are unknown to any but blues scholars (Jack Kelly, Homer Harris, Alfred Fields). Like several of Columbia's anthologies that are loosely grouped under a theme, you don't necessarily have to have a keen interest in the album concept to appreciate the music, which is an above-average gathering of early blues tracks of various styles. —*Richie Unterberger*

Old Town Blues, Vol. 1: Downtown Sides / 1993 / Ace ✦✦✦
Twenty-two blues tracks recorded in the 1950s for New York's Old Town label, most of which were unissued at the time. The heart of this anthology is the 11 songs by Sonny Terry & Brownie McGhee, who do electrified city blues with an audible influence from Chicago performers like Bo Diddley and Jimmy Reed. It's not the style they're most renowned for, perhaps, but the results are pretty good. The rest of the CD is a hodgepodge of miscellany, including decent raw electric blues from James Wayne, fairly anonymous sides by Little Willie and Bob Gaddy, and a couple of rare Willie Dixon items from an unissued acetate of demos. —*Richie Unterberger*

Orig. American Folk Blues Festival / 1962 / PolyGram ✦✦✦✦✦
Recorded live in a studio in Hamburg, Germany, in October 1962. Includes artists involved with that year's American Folk Blues Festival tour. With generally relaxed and reflective performances. The artists include T-Bone Walker, Sonny Terry, and John Lee Hooker. —*Cub Koda*

Out of the Blue [Rykodisc] / 1985 / Rykodisc ✦✦✦✦✦
A 17-cut sampler of some of Rounder's blues and blues-related releases of the period, it features "straight" blues from J.B. Hutto, Phillip Walker, and Johnny Copeland; blues-rock from the Nighthawks and George Thorogood; soulful blues from Johnny Adams and Ted Hawkins; plus cuts from Buckwheat Zydeco, piano great James Booker, John Hammond, Solomon Burke, and several more. The Adams, Walker, and Copeland cuts are particularly nice, as is one entry from Marcia Ball and the Legendary Blues Band. —*Niles J. Frantz*

☆ **Play My Juke Box: East Coast Blues (1943-1954)** / Flyright ✦✦✦✦✦
Bruce Bastin's English Flyright label—only one of the magnificent tributaries of his Interstate Music Company—has consistently demonstrated a union of fine scholarship and great music. This collection of mostly little-known East Coast blues artists is no exception. There are seven tracks of singer/guitarists, four harp/guitar duets, four piano/guitar pairings, two guitar duos, and one arresting cut featuring three harps plus vocal. Artists such as Skoodle-Dum-Doo & Sheffield, Boy Green, Robert Lee Westmoreland, Marilyn Scott, and Sonny Jones serve up a startling reminder of all the amazing talent that has gone unrecognized over the years. —*Larry Hoffman*

Raunchy Business: Hot Nuts & Lollypops / Aug. 1991 / Columbia ✦✦✦✦✦
This is a sampler of risque blues. —*Mark A. Humphrey*

Reefer Songs: Original Jazz & Blues Vocals / Jun. 17, 1932-Nov. 2, 1945 / Stash ✦✦✦✦✦
This LP was the very first release by the Stash label, and as with its first

dozen or so collections, it features vintage material that deals with illicit subject matter. Many of the best marijuana and drug-based recordings are on this set, including Stuff Smith's "Here Comes the Man with the Jive" (which features some hot Jonah Jones trumpet), Trixie Smith's "Jack I'm Mellow," Barney Bigard's "Sweet Marijuana Brown" (which has Art Tatum on piano), Andy Kirk's "All the Jive Is Gone," and Harry "The Hipster" Gibson's classic "Who Put the Benzedrine in Mrs. Murphy's Ovaltine?" Other performers include Cab Calloway, Benny Goodman, Buster Bailey, Sidney Bechet, the Harlem Hamfats, Chick Webb, and Clarence Williams. Some of this material has since been reissued on CD, but the original set is still the best. —*Scott Yanow*

Roots 'n' Blues: The Retrospective 1925-1950 / Jun. 30, 1992 / CBS ✦✦✦✦✦

Roots 'n' Blues: The Retrospective presents five hours of music over four discs, covering the traditional recordings made by Columbia Records and its associated labels from 1925 to 1950. As an all-inclusive survey of American roots music, this set is an invaluable library piece and a good reference, but where this collection really stands out is in its presentation. The collection does a better service than the more academic studies by including a variety of styles—including early string-band recordings, spirituals, jugbands, blues, cajun, and country music, mixing the better-known artists with the more obscure—in the end, the diversity makes for good listening as well as a good learning experience. —*Chris Woodstra*

Roots of Rhythm & Blues: A Tribute to the Robert Johnson Era / Sep. 1, 1992 / CBS ✦✦✦✦✦

This live program featured some of the late legend's old partners—Honeyboy Edwards, Johnny Shines, Robert Jr. Lockwood—and some of his contemporary successors, such as Lionel Pitchford, Cephas and Wiggins paying heartfelt tribute. —*Bill Dahl*

☆ **Roots of Robert Johnson** / 1990 / Yazoo ✦✦✦✦✦

Robert Johnson's small body of recordings have become almost larger than life. Many novice listeners probably think the Delta blues began and ended with him. This 14-song collection traces the origins of Johnson's music, uncovering the roots of his tormented, anguished lyrics, and the origins of his wildly influential guitar style. Some of the finest songs by luminaries like Skip James, Charlie Patton, Son House, Kokomo Arnold, and Lonnie Johnson are included. It's not only of use for Johnson archivists but for anyone interested in the greatest pre-war Delta blues. —*Bruce Boyd Raeburn*

Sissy Man Blues: Str't & Gay Blues / Vintage Jazz ✦✦✦

Twenty-five straight and gay blues from 1924-1941 are featured, by various artists. —*Jas Obrecht*

☆ **The Slide Guitar: Bottles, Knives, & Steel** / Feb. 1991 / Columbia/Legacy ✦✦✦✦✦

A super collection of slide guitar pieces in such styles as blues, hokum, gospel, and dance songs from Blind Willie Johnson, Tampa Red, Bukka White, and other bottleneck masters. The Leadbelly cut, "Packing Trunk Blues," shows off his masterful slide style. For every blues guitarist. —*Barry Lee Pearson*

● **The Sound of the Delta** / Jun. 1966 / Testament ✦✦✦✦✦

Blues scholar Pete Welding assembled these 19 recordings—most solo, all acoustic, most featuring guitar and vocal—between 1963 and 1965, just as the blues revival was gathering steam. This isn't the best Delta blues compilation, as an introduction or a general sampler. If you can't get enough of the stuff, though, it certainly stands up well. Big Joe Williams and Fred McDowell are the only well-known performers, but the others—obscure names like Arthur Weston and the delightfully raw-voiced Ruby McCoy—are generally in the same league. It's well recorded, and contains a reasonable variety of styles. The CD reissue adds bonus tracks by Williams and Avery Brady that were not included on the original version. —*Richie Unterberger*

Southern Rhythm & Rock / Rhino ✦✦✦

Southern Rhythm & Rock (The Best of Excello Records—Vol. 2) is the second volume of the Excello Records collection, with its companion *Sound of the Swamp.* This volume rounds up some wild and woolly R&B obscurities. —*John Floyd*

Stone Rock Blues / 1994 / Chess ✦✦✦

"The original recordings of songs covered by the Rolling Stones" is heavy on the blues, R&B, and early rock 'n' roll chestnuts they gleaned from Chess Records. Chuck Berry and Muddy Waters are, unsurprisingly, the most heavily represented artists here; seven Chuck tunes, five by Muddy (one of which, "Rollin' Stone," wasn't recorded by the Stones, but is included because it inspired their name). The 18-song collection is filled out by a couple of Bo Diddley tracks, Howlin' Wolf's "Little Red Rooster," and three songs outside of Chess' black music axis. —*Richie Unterberger*

Sun Records Harmonica Classics / 1990 / Rounder ✦✦✦✦✦

Brilliant compilation of blues sides cut at the Sun studios in the early '50s, featuring indispensable tracks by Walter Horton ("Easy" being one of the greatest harmonica instrumentals of all time), Joe Hill Louis, and Doctor Ross. —*Cub Koda*

Sun Records: The Blues Years / Charly ✦✦✦✦✦

Gigantic nine-record box with a 44-page booklet, this comes the closest to documenting the wide breadth of blues recordings done by Sam Phillips at the Sun studios in Memphis during the early '50s. A landmark achievement. —*Cub Koda*

Superblues, Vol. 1: All-Time Classic Blues Hits / 1990 / Stax ✦✦✦✦✦

The three-volume *Superblues* series may not have enough rare/unusual items for the collector, or enough of a solid connecting thread for the more general listener. For those who just want a varied assortment of top-notch blues (mostly from the '50s and '60s) in their collection, though, they're good deals. They cover a pretty wide territory of both top blues stars and lesser-known singers, drawn more from urbane R&B- and jump blues-influenced cuts than most similar compilations. They also have generous playing times, and offer enough liner notes to provide a context for nonexperts. Vol. 1 has classics by B.B. King, Ike & Tina Turner, Jimmy Reed, Koko Taylor, Bobby "Blue" Bland, Albert King, Little Milton, Howlin' Wolf, and others. —*Richie Unterberger*

Superblues: All-Time Classic Blues Hits / 1991 / Stax ✦✦✦✦✦

More soul and R&B influences are heard on this volume than the first, though it's not a detriment. The 18 tracks include prize items by Guitar Slim, Lloyd Price, Lowell Fulson, Elmore James, and Sonny Boy Williamson, with some bluesy Southern soul by O.V. Wright and Johnnie Taylor. Also has some little-anthologized gems, most notably Gene Allison's "You Can Make It If You Try" (covered by the Rolling Stones on their first album) and Jimmy Hughes's magnificent bluesy soul ballad, "Steal Away." —*Richie Unterberger*

Superblues: All-Time Classic Blues Hits, Vol. 3 / 1995 / Stax ✦✦✦✦✦

Another solid outing in the *Superblues* series. The 19 cuts include classics by Little Walter, Elmore James, Jimmy Reed, and Billy Boy Arnold ("I Wish You Would"); vintage jump blues by Jimmy Liggins, Joe Liggins, and Camille Howard; and soul blues by Little Johnny Taylor and Little Milton. This has a significantly higher percentage of obscure names than the previous two volumes, with worthy items (some of which were one-shot R&B hits) by Mercy Dee Walton, Larry Dale, Eddie Taylor, Larry Birdsong, Larry Davis, Ted Taylor, Frankie Lee Sims, and others. —*Richie Unterberger*

Taste of Blues, Vol. 1 / 1993 / Vee-Jay ✦✦✦✦

At 25 tracks, 69 minutes of running time, and musician/historian Billy Vera doing the compilation, there's little to quibble about here, as all the selections are first rate. Kicking off with the one-two punch of Jimmy Reed's "Boogie in the Dark" and Eddie Taylor's "Bad Boy," other highlights include J.B. Lenoir's thinly veiled rewrite of Ray Charles' classic ("Do What I Say"), the hopelessly obscure Morris Pejoe's "Hurt My Feelings," while Billy "The Kid" Emerson's "Every Woman I Know (Is Crazy About an Automobile)" just may be one of the finest car songs of all time. Add to the mix Snooky Pryor's "Judgement Day," a pair of Elmore James classics (the original versions of "It Hurts Me Too" and "The 12 Year Old Boy"), Billy Boy Arnold's "Rockinitis," John Lee Hooker's live at Newport performance of "Tupelo," and Pee Wee Crayton's scorching guitar solo on "The Telephone Is Ringing," and you have a compilation that's mighty hard to beat. Sound quality on all this is first rate, thanks to the digital remastering work of Bob Fisher. —*Cub Koda*

A Taste of the Blues, Vol. 2 / Oct. 1993 / Vee-Jay ✦✦✦

A 26-track comp of more obscure and rare Vee-Jay sides, this time featuring a previously unissued Snooky Pryor track, "You Tried to Ruin Me." Also includes tracks from Elmore James, Eddie Taylor, and Pee Wee Crayton, plus the added bonus of the first-time CD issue of Jimmy Reed's "I'm Gonna Ruin You." —*Cub Koda*

Texas Blues / 1992 / Arhoolie ✦✦✦✦✦

This excellent collection features eight little-known blues artists who recorded for Bill Quinn's Gold Star label in Houston. There are 27 tracks in all—split unequally between acoustic guitar/vocal (16) and piano/vocal (11). Lil' Son Jackson is perhaps the best known, and his ten tracks are all good, rocking acoustic blues. There are also tunes by L.C. Williams, a polished and imaginative guitarist, and one magnificent track by the obscure Buddy Chiles. —*Larry Hoffman*

Texas Country Blues 1948-1951 / 1994 / Flyright ✦✦✦

Another entry in Flyright's ongoing quest to present the rare and the wonderful, this collects some impossibly hard-to-find Texas 78s originally released on short-lived, dime-sized labels like Talent, Freedom, Nucraft, ARC, Bluebonnet, and the colorfully named Oklahoma Tornado! Honeyboy Edwards and Frankie Lee Sims are the only "big names" aboard, but the remainder of the tracks featuring Rattlesnake Cooper, James Tisdom, Andrew Thomas, Willie Lane, Monister Parker, Leroy "Country" Johnson, and others clearly illustrate how big the looming presence (both commercially and artistically) of Lightnin' Hopkins already was at this early stage of the game. —*Cub Koda*

Texas Guitar Greats / 1991 / Collectables ✦✦✦

Texas blues, boogie, and blues-rock recorded from 1962-1988, it includes several previously unreleased cuts, with Johnny Winter, Freddie King,

Gatemouth Brown, and Johnny Copeland, among others. —*Niles J. Frantz*

☆ **Texas Music: Postwar Blues Combos** / 1994 / Rhino ✦✦✦✦
Texas blues is harder to define and pigeonhole than, say, Chicago electric blues, or Mississippi Delta country blues. In general terms, the Texas blues of the immediate post-war era featured hard-driving, jazzy guitar lines, a jump blues influence, occasional brass, and a generally lighter, sunnier attitude than its more famous Chicago cousin. This is a fine 18-song survey of Texas blues from the late '40s to the early '70s, including both giants (T-Bone Walker, Bobby Bland, Freddie King, Albert Collins) and names that are known only to blues collectors (Frankie Lee Sims, Goree Carter, Zuzu Bollin). Some of the selections, even by some of the more well-known names, are rare; there are mighty hard-to-find '50s singles by Collins, Gatemouth Brown, and Johnny Copeland (as well as one very well-known single, Ivory Joe Hunter's "Since I Met You Baby"). There are a good variety of styles here, encompassing both bluesy ballads and boogies; the thrilling instrumental string-benders by Clarence Green, Albert Collins, and T-Bone Walker may be the highlights. Whatever your preference, it's a fine survey/introduction to vintage Texas electric blues, and it's a good bet that even listeners with big blues collections won't have a lot of the rarities here. —*Richie Unterberger*

★ **Texas Piano Blues 1929-48** / Story of Blues ✦✦✦✦✦
This is a good collection of piano-accompanied vocals sporting bluesmen who worked the lumber camps and oil fields of rural Texas, as well as the red-light districts of cities like Galveston and Houston. Big Boy Knox shows a strong city influence in his decorative right-hand work, as does Robert Cooper, whose playing points to the influence of Fats Waller. Joe Pullem is on board with his hit, "Black Gal," which is perhaps overstated by three takes and a variation. The vocals are good, however, and the piano playing is uniformly excellent. Stylistically, this music falls somewhere between ragtime, blues, and vaudeville. —*Larry Hoffman*

■ **The Real Blues Brothers** / 1987 / DCC ✦✦✦✦
This is a nice Vee-Jay collection with representative cuts from Pee Wee Crayton, John Lee Hooker, Jimmy Reed, Lightnin' Hopkins, Billy Boy Arnold, Memphis Slim, and a stray track from Brownie McGhee and Sonny Terry. The big ticket for collectors on this one, however, is the inexplicable bonus of a previously unissued Eddie Taylor number, "Leave This Neighborhood," reason enough for hard-core fans to want to add this one to the collection. —*Cub Koda*

Them Dirty Blues / Jass ✦✦✦✦
The thin line between provocative and obscene, suggestive and disgust-

ing, gets examined and stretched throughout the 50 tracks presented on the 1989 two-disc set *Them Dirty Blues*. Many of these songs could be deemed sexist using a '90s measuring stick; on the other hand, many are also quite funny, language notwithstanding. They reflect a time when audiences were willing to accept songs with either overt carnal themes or with an implicit, yet rather pronounced sexuality. —*Ron Wynn*

Tomato Delta Blues Package / 1994 / Tomato/Rhino ✦✦✦
While there's no denying the greatness of the performers spotlighted on this 16-track anthology, Tomato/Rhino played a bit loose with its definition of "Delta blues." Leadbelly, for example, was more of a classic folk singer with blues ties, while Sonny Terry and Brownie McGhee were Piedmont blues performers, and the songs by Howlin' (not Howling) Wolf and the Little Walter/Otis Rush duo aren't Delta blues either. Licensing problems probably reared their heads here; witness the absence of Charlie Patton, Robert Johnson, Son House, Tommy Johnson, or Sonny Boy Williamson (John Lee). There's still some good material, notably Arthur "Big Boy" Crudup, Mississippi Fred McDowell, Johnny Shines, Mississippi John Hurt, and decent (though hardly sensational) Lightnin' Hopkins and John Lee Hooker. —*Ron Wynn*

Voice of the Blues . . . / Dec. 1976 / Yazoo ✦✦✦✦
Voice of the Blues—Bottleneck Guitar Masterpieces contains an eclectic hodgepodge of pre-war slide-guitar styles, encompassing everything from blues and Hawaiian to ragtime and country. —*John Floyd*

White Country Blues, 1926-1938 . . . / Apr. 27, 1993 / CBS ✦✦✦✦
Country artists sing pre-war blues-influenced songs. —*Bill Dahl*

Wizards from the Southside / Chess ✦✦✦✦✦
This is a great sampler of the finest in classic Chicago blues—perfect for those listeners who are looking for a taste of the best of the genre. Included are "Evil" by Howlin' Wolf (two wolf-tracks in all); "Rollin' and Tumblin" by Muddy Waters (five); "Walkin' the Boogie" by John Lee Hooker (one); "Bring It on Home" by Sonny Boy Williamson (one), "I'm a Man" by Bo Diddley (two); and "Mellow Down Easy" by Little Walter (two). All of these fabulous sides were cut between 1950 and 1961—the golden era of South Side Chicago blues. —*Larry Hoffman*

Wrapped in My Baby / 1989 / Pearl Flapper ✦✦✦✦✦
Basement rehearsal recordings from the early '50s for the United/States labels, featuring Morris Pejoe's raw 'n' rockin' "Let's Get High" from a full unissued session, plus four amazing sides from Arthur "Big Boy" Spires. Another missing chapter of Chicago blues history brought to light, simply incredible. —*Cub Koda*

GOSPEL

Religion has existed for thousands of years, but gospel music is just a few decades old. The term was coined by blues pianist Thomas A. Dorsey in 1920 soon after he wrote "If You See My Savior," his first religious song. After Dorsey established a firm that published his "gospel" songs and those of others (the first such company), the name stuck.

Gospel music was born out of the blood, sweat, and tears of African slaves working on Southern plantations and in cotton fields. They attended segregated Protestant churches, where White ministers led them in worship. Over time, Blacks combined the Southern folk music, Protestant hymns, and European elements of the worship service with their African traditions and Negro spirituals (which were not religious songs but songs of vexation, e.g., "Nobody Knows the Trouble I've Seen"), and the distinct Black gospel sound was born In those early years, gospel was segregated along racial lines: Southern gospel became a catchword for White gospel when Black gospel was equally Southern in its styling. Mahalia Jackson was the primary influence of her era, although the Swan Silvertones, the Clara Ward Singers, the Five Blind Boys, and others made significant contributions to early gospel. In Southern gospel, the Speers reigned "king of the charts," winning contracts on major labels such as Columbia and RCA, where they recorded such standards as "I'm Building a Bridge" and "I'll Meet You in the Morning."

As the '50s approached, there was a greater amalgamation of gospel, folk, and blues styles, which together were the foundation of rock 'n' roll. Elvis Presley, Jerry Lee Lewis, and Little Richard were just a few of the singers with strong gospel backgrounds to make the leap into the secular arena. Groups like the Soul Stirrers and the Pilgrim Travelers supplied secular music with Sam Cooke, Johnnie Taylor, Lou Rawls, and others.

In the '70s, social movements began to influence what the White gospel young adults were recording. Artists such as Larry Norman pioneered "Jesus Rock." When a contemporary Christian music (CCM) magazine writer asked him if his 1969 Upon This Rock album was the first Christian rock album, Norman was cautious. "I can't really tell you if it was the first Christian rock album or not," he said. "I had never heard any. I was a Baptist, and the only Christian

songs I had ever heard were the hymns and Negro spirituals . . . . So when Elvis Presley came along in 1956, and all those other boys, I thought, 'That's nothing new.' They were just stealing Black church music . . . so I decided to steal it back."

A similar revolution was taking place among young Black musicians who had tired of the same old "church" beat. Edwin Hawkins has taken a lot of credit for sparking the contemporary Black gospel movement. Actually, Rance Allen was doing it better, and long before Hawkins. Toward the very late '70s, Andrae Crouch did the unthinkable: he began making music that not only pleased his Black constituency and a progressive White audience but also touched mainstream pop. Amy Grant would pick up on Crouch's theme and run with it.

During the '80s, gospel had its most lucrative decade to date. Many of the biggest hits were by women. Shirley Caesar and Tramaine Hawkins crisscrossed the traditional and contemporary Black audiences. Sandi Patti held down the inspirational arena while Amy Grant held the pop-rock youth market. Grant's success and subsequent influence in pop led to a lot of copycatting An area women did not get into was heavy metal, or heaven's metal, as it's called in CCM. Bands that grew up on Aerosmith, Led Zeppelin, Black Sabbath, and other premier hard rock outfits began to merge Christian lyrics with this type of music. Petra and Stryper are examples.

During the '90s, gospel and CCM began crossing over into the mainstream in a variety of ways. Not only did Amy Grant establish herself as a popular secular vocalist, but Christian acts were able to crossover into the pop charts without abandoning their inspirational roots. Partially, this is because Billboard began including Gospel albums on their album charts, which resulted in Michael W. Smith having a Top 20 hit. But it is also because the music opened itself up to contemporary production techniques—by the mid-'90s, CCM bands like the folk-rock Jars of Clay and the hip-hop DC Talk were getting secular play with their inspirational material, and Kirk Franklin & the Family consistently charted in the Top 20 on the R&B charts. The diversity of these successful CCM artists signals the depth and variety within contemporary gospel, as well as proving that gospel music is undergoing a renaissance during the '90s. —Bil Carpenter

Jimmy A.

Guitar, Vocals
The cofounder of '80s alternative pop band Vector, Jimmy Abegg has also worked extensively with Charlie Peacock. He strikes out on his own with creative solo efforts that feature his exceptional guitar work and low-key vocal approach. —Thom Granger

● **Entertaining Angels** / 1991 / Sparrow ♦♦♦♦
Appealing guitar-pop record in the Charlie Peacock tradition. Peacock appears here, as does vocalist Vince Ebo, most notably on "Thin but Strong Cord," where the two share lead vocals with Abegg. But it's Abegg's show down the line, as he writes and produces the bulk of the material, showing real promise. —Brian Mansfield

Secrets / 1994 / Small World ♦♦♦

Abyssinian Baptist Gospel Choir

Gospel
Prof. Alex Bradford directed this choir, some of whose members recorded with the famous Back Home Choir of Newark. —Opal Louis Nations

● **Shakin' the Rafters** / 1960 / Columbia/Legacy ♦♦♦♦
An energetic choral release spotlighting one of the most popular, large (100-plus) vocal aggregations of the '60s. —Ron Wynn

Acappella

Inspirational
Founded by Keith Lancaster, whose Church of Christ background did not permit instrumental music in worship, this male vocal ensemble established itself making clever recordings using a variety of sounds created by the human voice. —Thom Granger

● **Better than Life** / 1987 / Word ♦♦♦♦
Soft, synchronized a cappella on original songs. —Bil Carpenter

Hymns for all the World / Dec. 6, 1994 / Word/Epic ♦♦♦
Hymns for All the World is a gentle, reassuring collection of some of the world's greatest hymns performed with grace. —Sara Sytsma

Adam Again

CCM, Alternative Pop-Rock
Adam Again, an alternative rock act from Southern California, anticipated the synthesis of rock and funk to be later expressed by groups such as the Red Hot Chili Peppers and Spin Doctors. The band consists of Gene Eugene (lead vocals, guitar, keyboards), Riki Michele (backing vocals), Paul Valadez (bass), and John Knox (drums). Saxophonist Dan Michaels was a full-time member for the first album but has appeared only sporadically as a guest since then. Group leader Gene Eugene is also a talented producer in Christian alternative music. —Thom Granger

In a New World of Time / 1987 / Blue Collar ♦♦♦
The original Howard Finster cover let hipsters know something was worth checking out on this first effort. —*Thom Granger*

Ten Songs / 1988 / Broken ♦♦♦
The band's style begins to solidify here. Included is a killer cover of "Ain't No Sunshine." —*Thom Granger*

● **Homeboys** / 1990 / Broken ♦♦♦♦
Urban rock music meets urban concerns on this excellent collection, including a cover of Marvin Gaye's "Inner City Blues." —*Thom Granger*

Dig / Brainstorm ♦♦♦
This emotionally powerful set is less than easy to listen to, due to clues that leader Eugene's marriage to vocalist Riki Michele was coming apart at the seams. —*Thom Granger*

Rance Allen Group

Urban, Black Gospel
This Detroit-based, traditionally trained Black gospel group formed in the '60s and was the first traditional gospel group to incorporate rock, jazz, and soul in their music. They were harbingers of the contemporary Christian music movement popularized in the late '70s by Andrae Crouch, Amy Grant, and the Winans.
Rance Allen scored a Top 30 R&B hit in 1979 with "I Belong to You," one of two Stax singles that year to make the charts. His recordings for Gospel Truth, Capitol, and Stax proved quite popular among gospel audiences and had some success attracting soul fans as well. —*Bil Carpenter and Ron Wynn*

Ain't no Need of Crying / 1958 / Stax ♦♦♦♦
Rance Allen's brand of soul-tinged gospel is at its best on this release. The title track cracked the R&B charts, and Allen's soaring voice, coupled with the fine harmonies provided by his brothers Tom, Steve, and Esau, as well as assistance from cousins Judy, Linda, and Annie Mendez, results in some arresting songs. —*Ron Wynn*

Straight from the Heart / 1972 / Stax ♦♦♦
Gospel singer Rance Allen enjoyed some crossover soul success in the early '70s, recording on Stax' Gospel Truth label. His explosive, soaring voice is especially effective on upper-register notes and inspirational ballads. This is one of his biggest albums, especially the single "I Belong To You." —*Ron Wynn*

★ **Soulful Experience** / 1975 / Truth ♦♦♦♦♦
Another in a string of well-produced gospel albums incorporating soul influences and relying on Rance Allen's booming, yet also anguished and soulful delivery. This LP contains examples of Allen's ability to explode in the upper register and generate a high-pitched cry that is dazzling and effective. —*Ron Wynn*

I Feel Like Goin' On / 1980 / Stax ♦♦♦
Although not as smartly produced or containing compositions as memorable as some earlier releases, Rance Allen still generated mild R&B attention with this LP, as well as the usual good response in gospel circles. But the Allen style was becoming more predictable, and would soon lose favor as huge choirs and slick, urban contemporary-style groups and artists began to dominate the modern gospel scene. —*Ron Wynn*

Best of the Rance Allen Group / 1988 / Stax ♦♦♦♦
Creative, influential hits with a Memphis flavor. —*Bil Carpenter*

Phenomenon / 1991 / Bellmark ♦♦♦
This set is consistent with earlier recordings. —*Bil Carpenter*

Margaret Allison

Piano, Vocals / Black Gospel
Margaret Allison and the Angelic Gospel Singers formed in 1944. Their "Touch Me Lord Jesus" (Gotham) was a No. 13 single on R&B charts in August 1949. Known for a traditional-style quartet music, their current lineup includes Allison, Darryl, and John Richmond; Frances Leggett; and Theresa McDowell. —*Bil Carpenter*

● **Out of the Depths** / 1987 / Malaco ♦♦♦♦
An album of traditional cuts featuring "It Could've Been the Other Way" and "Up Above My Head." —*Bil Carpenter*

He's my Ever Present Help / 1992 / Malaco ♦♦♦
An album of new traditional favorites, it features the title song and "I'll Go." —*Bil Carpenter*

My Sweet Home / Nashboro ♦♦♦
"Jesus Is All the World to Me" and "Goin' over Yonder" are outstanding. —*Bil Carpenter*

Inez Andrews

b. Oct. 19, 1935
Vocals / Soul, Black Gospel
Inez Andrews' powerful contralto voice has been among gospel's great-

---

Gospel Terms

BLACK GOSPEL — An art form that is essentially Black in tone. The term was coined around the popularity of Thomas Dorsey's "Precious Lord." Black gospel is usually traditional music, often choir-oriented. Mahalia Jackson, Clara Ward Singers, James Cleveland, etc.

CONTEMPORARY CHRISTIAN MUSIC — This style of gospel picked up where Jesus rock left off, incorporating more funky and harder music elements, often soft-rock. Amy Grant, Michael W. Smith, and BeBe & CeCe Winans are such performers.

HEAVEN'S METAL — "Heavy metal meets gospel lyrics" is how this style is best defined. Strong bass lines, electric/amplified guitar riffs, and steel drumming. Stryper, Bloodgood, and the latter-day Petra coterie exemplify this form.

INSPIRATIONAL — Not unlike middle-of-the-road (MOR) music in the pop sphere, easy-listening, or adult contemporary. Heavy on strings and grandiose orchestrations. Sandi Patti, Dallas Holm, and Dino fall into this category.

JESUS ROCK — A contemporary "White" music style popularized in the late '60s and early '70s, coinciding with the Jesus movement. Pioneers of the form brought rhythm & blues, rock 'n' roll, and folk elements into standard praise tunes. Larry Norman and Randy Stonehill were among the purveyors of the form.

QUARTET SINGING — Based on the old barbershop quartet styles, with gospel lyrics. Usually four-part harmony performed by traditional Black gospel or Southern gospel musicians. Usually performed by males.

SOUTHERN GOSPEL — A country music gospel art form with emphasis on steel and rhythm guitars as its foundation. Draws on bluegrass, blues, and hillbilly elements. Southern gospel groups tend to use four-part harmony with a high tenor and baritone. The Happy Goodmans, the Speers, and Gold City are examples.

SPIRITUAL — A Black gospel art form rising from the Negro spirituals and blues tradition. Characterized by wailing and guttural sounds. Inez Andrews and Shirley Caesar are examples.

STREET POETRY — Whether the term developed in Christian circles is uncertain; however, Christian rap musicians prefer this term to "rap." An urban, funk style of rap with, in this case, Christian lyrics. —*Bil Carpenter*

---

est since her days with The Caravans in the late '50s. Andrews' nickname, "Songbird," was taken by Don Robey when he formed a gospel subsidiary label of his Backbeat/Peacock operation. Andrews was among the first gospel artists he signed. She later recorded for Savoy and Spirit Feel. —*Ron Wynn*

● **Lord Don't Move the Mountain** / 1972 / MCA ♦♦♦♦
This crossover pop album has a traditional mood. —*Bil Carpenter*

If Jesus Came to Your Town Today / 1988 / Miracle ♦♦♦
This album features Inez Andrews' famous parched, weary leads and earnest, at times serene, tone. She includes one pop tune, Curtis Mayfield's "People Get Ready," restoring the spiritual/church element often missing from other renditions. "Praise the Lord" and "We've Got Work to Do" are the tribute pieces, while "If Jesus Came to Your Town Today" mixes a sociopolitical undercurrent with a plea for believers to get their act together. Andrews can still wail and shout, and it's great that she's getting the opportunity to do so without having to compete with a funk backbeat or multi-tracked synthesizers and cloying background vocalists. —*Ron Wynn, Rejoice*

Raise up a Nation / 1991 / Word ♦♦♦
These traditional Black arrangements are backed with a choir. —*Bil Carpenter*

Vanessa Bell Armstrong

b. Oct. 2, 1953, Detroit, MI
Vocals / Soul, Gospel
With a style reminiscent of Aretha Franklin, soulful Vanessa Bell Armstrong has been belting out R&B-flavored contemporary gospel since the '80s. A native of Detroit and mother of five, she got her start working with Dr. Mattie Moss Clark. She has gone on to work in both gospel and secular music. She did the theme song for the television series *Amen*, where her links to Rev. Al Green (and to Rev. Claude Jeter) were evident.

She's recorded urban contemporary ballads and lyrically neutral material for Jive, and done gospel for Muscle Shoals, Sound Gospel, and Onyx, subsidiaries of Malaco. —*Bil Carpenter and Ron Wynn*

Peace Be Still / 1984 / Benson ✦✦✦✦
Traditional hymns that are given "Holiness" treatment. —*Bil Carpenter*

Vanessa Bell Armstrong / 1987 / Jive/Novus ✦✦✦
This contemporary urban gospel has a traditional shouting style and vague lyrics for its gospel content. —*Bil Carpenter*

Wonderful One / 1990 / Jive/Novus ✦✦✦
While the songs range from spectacular to disapponting, Vanessa Bell Armstrong's singing is uniformly excellent on this '90 collection of crossover gospel and light, urban contemporary pop and R&B. Armstrong's declarative, assertive delivery and triumphant manner make the good songs great and the one or two great ones unforgettable. —*Ron Wynn*

● **Greatest Hits** / 1990 / Malaco ✦✦✦✦

Secret Is Out / 1995 / Verity ✦✦✦
On *The Secret Is Out*, Vanessa Bell Armstrong turns in one of her most straightforward gospel recordings, with all of the material being written and produced by John P. Kee, whose choir provides musical support. —*Stephen Thomas Erlewine*

Susan Ashton

Vocals / CCM
Texas-born Ashton sang backup for Wayne Watson and Dallas Holm before going solo. *Wakened by the Wind* became one of CCM's most successful debut albums, garnering Ashton five hit singles and a Dove Award nomination for best new artist. Having Brown Bannister and Wayne Kirkpatrick, two people essential in Amy Grant's success, didn't hurt her, either. Her 1992 follow-up *Angels of Mercy* expanded both her musical and her emotional vocabularies. —*Brian Mansfield*

Wakened by the Wind / 1991 / Sparrow ✦✦✦
This debut is in the contemporary-folk vein, a la Shawn Colvin (whose voice Ashton's closely resembles). Ashton gets most of her material from producer Wayne Kirkpatrick, also one of CCM's top songwriters; she contributes to three, including the countryish "Ball and Chain." —*Brian Mansfield*

Angels of Mercy / 1992 / Sparrow ✦✦✦✦
No sophomore slump here, as Ashton reaches for more and gets it. The topics are more complex—the devastating rumor mongering of "Started as a Whisper," the mysteries of salvation and fallibility in "Alice in Wonderland"—and the music is more dramatic. —*Brian Mansfield*

● **So Far, the Best of Susan Ashton, Vol. 1** / Aug. 29, 1995 / Sparrow ✦✦✦✦
So Far, the Best of Susan Ashton, Vol. 1 conveniently collects highlights from the inspirational adult contemporary singer. —*Stephen Thomas Erlewine*

John Austin

b. 1969
Guitar, Harmonica, Vocals / CCM
Born in Chicago, Austin began his career just after high school. He plays acoustic guitar and harmonica and writes most of his own material. Based on his first effort alone, he's made a contribution to linking authentic gospel messages with uncommercial light-rock/folk styles. His firm but mellow vocal style is reminiscent of '60s folk heroes such as the Byrds. —*Bil Carpenter*

● **The Embarrassing Young** / 1992 / Glasshouse ✦✦✦✦
Austin's debut album contains 12 songs discussing relationships and Christianity in a nonproselytizing manner. Heavy guitar emphasis on mostly light-rock and alternative-style cuts. Musical support comes from Buddy Miller, Mark Heard, and a choir. Harmony vocals are supplied by Austin's singing partner, Erin Echo. —*Bil Carpenter*

Dr. Morgan Babb

Vocals
Dr. Morgan Babb first made gospel history as the remarkable lead vocalist of the Radio Four. He later made a series of stirring recordings for Nashboro as a solo vocalist. —*Ron Wynn*

● **I Will not Bow** / 1995 / Nashboro ✦✦✦✦
This collection, first issued by Nashboro in 1975, is a grab bag of songs and sermonettes recorded at Baptist churches in Cleveland, St. Louis, Atlanta, and Babb's own ministry in Nashville for his weekly radio broadcasts. Not only a soul-stirring preacher, Babb is a fine singer who adds both power and compassion to songs like "No Friend like Jesus" and the rousing "Invitation." It includes a hilarious interview with Renate Johnstone, staff writer for London's BBC (*Radio Times*). —*Opal Louis Nations, Roots and Rhythm Newsletter*

Philip Bailey

b. May 8, 1951, Denver, CO
Conga, Vocals / Soul, Urban
The falsetto-singing co-lead vocalist in Earth, Wind & Fire, Philip Bailey, launched a solo career during the band's hiatus, resulting in his hit duet with Phil Collins, "Easy Lover," in 1985. He also makes gospel records.

Bailey has continued the juggling act between urban contemporary material and gospel through the '80s and '90s. —*William Ruhlmann and Ron Wynn*

Continuation / 1983 / CBS ✦✦
Philip Bailey's debut solo album. —*William Ruhlmann*

The Wonders of His Love / 1985 / Word ✦✦
Philip Bailey's debut gospel album. —*William Ruhlmann*

● **Chinese Wall** / 1985 / Columbia ✦✦✦✦
At the time Philip Bailey persuaded Phil Collins to produce his second solo album, *Chinese Wall*, Collins was among the hottest pop stars in the world. The advantage to that, of course, is the exposure it affords, and after the merely modest success of his debut solo album, *Continuation*, Bailey needed the reflected glory. On the other hand, it's hard to shine in such a glare, and although Bailey's name was on the gold-selling hit single "Easy Lover," a duet with Collins that helped the album take off, it's Collins' singing and drumming that one remembers. Elsewhere, tunes like "Photogenic Memory" and "Walking On The Chinese Wall" better represent Bailey's ability to handle a variety of material from ballads to techno dance tracks with his elastic falsetto. Still, *Chinese Wall* was a gold-selling standoff that made Bailey a solo hitmaker without really establishing him on his own. —*William Ruhlmann*

Triumph / 1986 / Word ✦✦

Family Affair / 1989 / Word ✦✦

Inside Out / 1990 / CBS ✦✦
Philip Bailey turned to Nile Rodgers to produce *Inside Out*, his followup to *Chinese Wall*, and though Rodgers didn't turn it into a dance record on the order of his old band Chic (the sort of thing he did do to other clients), the result is no more than pedestrian Black pop, which is why Bailey's secular solo career ran out of gas at this point and he willingly re-upped with the new edition of Earth, Wind & Fire. He didn't make another secular solo album for eight years. —*William Ruhlmann*

● **The Best of Philip Bailey: A Gospel Collection** / Word ✦✦✦✦
This is a compilation album culled from Philip Bailey's three gospel albums, *The Wonders Of His Love*, *Triumph*, and *Family Affair*. Bailey brings the same creamy pop production and warm falsetto singing to his inspirational work that he does to his solo albums and to Earth, Wind & Fire, although he is far gentler here (except when he's being religiously righteous on "Call to War"). Note that this is listed as the pick among his gospel albums, not his entire solo catalog. —*William Ruhlmann*

Bishop Jeff Banks

Vocals / Black Gospel
The Banks Brothers were pupils of Mary Johnson Davis. They enjoyed some success teaming with the Greater Harvest Choir in the '60s for Savoy. —*Ron Wynn*

● **Caught up in the Rapture** / 1987 / Savoy ✦✦✦✦
A traditional spiritual choir sound, also featuring vocalist Donald Malloy. —*Bil Carpenter*

Love Lifted Me / Savoy ✦✦✦
Traditional Black gospel. —*Bil Carpenter*

Barnes and Brown

Black Gospel
Rev. F.C. Barnes and Janice Brown of North Carolina, where they are pastors at Red Budd Holy Church in Rocky Mountain, came together to record many traditional albums in the '80s. —*Bil Carpenter*

Rough Side of the Mountain / 1980 / Atlanta International ✦✦✦✦
Mellow, bluesy, traditional Black gospel. —*Bil Carpenter*

The Barrett Sisters

Vocals / Black Gospel
Delois, Billie, and Rodessa Barrett began singing in the Chicago-based Morning Star Baptist Church as children in the '40s. Under the direction of their aunt, Mattie Dacus, they were originally known as the Barrett and Hudson Singers before becoming the Barrett Sisters. Delois was recruited for the Roberta Martin Singers while a senior at Englewood High. After graduation, she joined Martin's group full time and remained a member for 18 years. Rodessa Barrett became a choral director of Galileo Baptist church, and Billie Barrett became a church soloist after taking voice lessons at the American Music Conservatory. They formed the Barrett Sisters in 1962 and have remained together

ever since. Their first LP was recorded for Savoy in 1963. They currently record for I Am Records in Chicago. —*Ron Wynn*

Nobody Does It Better / Word ✦✦✦✦
One of the hottest gospel albums ever from this great trio. Their shimmering voices and precise, yet spontaneous-sounding, interaction on every tune expertly convey gospel's hypnotic charm. They're particularly inspiring on "Christ Is All," "Rapture," "All My Help," and "Nobody But Jesus." They haven't de-emphasized the overt religious base of the songs or tried to hedge the themes and lyrics. Anyone who doubted whether a trio could sustain the same clout and drive as a quartet or large group should hear "Walk and Talk" or "Fly Away"; The Barretts can sing up a storm. —*Ron Wynn*

What a Wonderful World / I Am ✦✦✦
A more contemporary production, geared toward fans of a modern approach. —*Ron Wynn*

● **What Will You Do with Your Life** / Savoy ✦✦✦✦
Classic "golden age" gospel, shouting vocals, and tight harmonies. —*Ron Wynn*

Sweet Emma Barrett

b. Mar. 25, 1897, New Orleans, LA, **d.** Jan. 28, 1983, New Orleans, LA
Piano, Vocals / Blues, Gospel, New Orleans Jazz
Sweet Emma was a stalwart performer, a powerhouse singer and a bluesy, driving pianist. Barrett's career began in the early '20s, and she became known as the "bell gal" for her habit of wearing red garters with bells that jingled while she sang and played. Barrett was part of the Original Tuxedo Orchestra in the '20s and '30s. The group was initially co-led by Papa Celestin and William Ridgley. Ridgley took over from 1925-1936. Barrett also sang and played with Sidney Desvigne, John Robichaux, and A. J. Piron. She appeared at Happy Landing in the '50s, and became a Preservation Hall regular after 1961. She overcame a 1967 stroke that caused paralysis on her left side and kept performing playing, with only her right hand until her death. —*Ron Wynn*

● **Sweet Emma**—New Orleans: The Living Legends / Jan. 1961 / Original Jazz Classics ✦✦✦✦
This CD reissue of the future members of the Preservation Hall Jazz Band is at such a high level it makes one wonder why this group had so many erratic recordings. Pianist Emma Barrett (who also takes four vocals) is in fine form, and trombonist Jim Robinson was always a major asset to any New Orleans jazz band; but it is the performances of trumpeter Percy Humphrey (who never sounded better on record) and his brother, clarinetist Willie, that really makes this music special. Together the septet plays such songs as "Bill Bailey," "Just a Little While to Stay Here," and "The Saints" with drive, enthusiasm, and surprising musicianship. It's essential music for all New Orleans jazz fans. —*Scott Yanow*

Sweet Emma Barrett and Her New Orleans Music / Sep. 1963 / Southland ✦✦✦
This is both classic blues, done in the requisite sassy, double-entendre fashion, and traditional jazz that also touches on gospel, brass band, and other pop styles. Although not the finest pure singer, Sweet Emma could belt out numbers and make suggestive remarks with abandon. —*Ron Wynn*

Sweet Emma and Her Preservation Hall Jazz Band / Oct. 18, 1964 / Preservation Hall ✦✦✦

New Orleans Traditional Jazz / 1992 / Mardi Gras ✦✦✦
A '92 reissue featuring noted classic blues and traditional New Orleans jazz vocalist Sweet Emma Barrett. She lived up to her reputation, belting out the one-liners, double entendres, and innuendo with gusto, then turning poignant or bemused when necessary. Her fine vocals were backed by fairly routine support, but hearing Sweet Emma Barrett made everything worthwhile. —*Ron Wynn*

Martha and Fontella Bass

b. Jul. 3, 1940, St. Louis, MO
Vocals / R&B, Gospel
They are progressive gospel singers, although Fontella is better known for her R&B hit "Rescue Me." —*Michael G. Nastos*

From the Root to the Source / 1980 / Soul Note ✦✦✦✦
Traditional and gospel music updated. Quintessential music, with Amina Myers on piano. —*Michael G. Nastos*

● **Martha Sings Mahalia** / Chess ✦✦✦✦
Martha Bass paid homage to the great Mahalia Jackson with poignant, exuberantly performed versions of her best songs. Although neither as gifted as Jackson and not from her more formalized gospel tradition, Bass nonetheless offered credible tributes to gospel's all-time queen, while demonstrating her own considerable powers. —*Ron Wynn*

Margaret Becker

Guitar, Vocals / CCM
The hardest female rocker/guitarist in CCM, she was influenced by a variety of styles that she incorporates into a unique sound, most built on guitar arrangements. Her hardy vocals cut through any style. —*Bil Carpenter*

Never for Nothing / 1987 / Sparrow ✦✦✦
A debut with strident proselytizing. —*Bil Carpenter*

The Reckoning / 1988 / Sparrow ✦✦✦
Spiritual renewal and thickly textured rock music. —*Bil Carpenter*

Immigrant's Daughter / 1990 / Sparrow ✦✦✦✦
She sings about degrees of holiness, with a minimalist-rock background. —*Bil Carpenter*

Simple House / 1991 / Sparrow ✦✦✦
British influences on the usual power rock. —*Bil Carpenter*

★ **Steps of Faith 1985-1992** / 1992 / Sparrow ✦✦✦✦✦
Becker's best, with a heavy emphasis on *Immigrant's Daughter* and *Simple House*, shows just what a talented pop stylist she is. The one new cut, "This Love," is essential Becker. —*Brian Mansfield*

Soul / May 18, 1993 / Sparrow ✦✦✦
Shows movement toward European pop/R&B, influenced by artist Annie Lennox and producer Charlie Peacock. —*Thom Granger*

Scott Blackwell

Keyboards
A former secular club DJ/mixmaster, Blackwell brought his skills to the church, causing youth group leaders worldwide to ponder whether dancing is a sin. —*Thom Granger*

Walk on the Wild Side / 1992 / Myx ✦✦✦
Producer Blackwell introduces original tunes, and his stable of vocalist proteges intend to move feet. —*Thom Granger*

● **A Myx'd Trip to a Gospel House** / 1992 / Myx ✦✦✦✦
Several classic contemporary gospel tunes are fairly radically remixed with a house attack, with fun results. —*Thom Granger*

Robert Blair and the Fantastic Violinaires

Black Gospel
Blair began his contemporary quartet in the '60s and became known for his Julius Cheeks-like falsetto shouting and raving. While their recent AIR Records albums have been good, their best music was recorded in the '60s on the Chess and Checker labels. —*Bil Carpenter*

The Pink Tornado / 1988 / Atlanta International ✦✦✦✦
Smooth, old-style traditional gospel, with Blair's renowned panting on the title track. A younger member does falsetto on "People Get Ready." —*Bil Carpenter*

Sing with the Angels / Malaco ✦✦✦
This strong material has passionate vocals. —*Hank Davis*

Today Is the Day / Malaco ✦✦✦✦
Excellent modern gospel from an eight-man "quintet." —*Hank Davis*

● **Their Greatest Sides, Vol. 1** / MCA ✦✦✦✦
A collection of some of their best Chess album sides from the '50s and '60s, featuring Robert Blair. Includes "Mother Used to Hold Me," a song known to reduce entire audiences to tears. —*Billy C. Wirtz*

Debby Boone

b. Sep. 22, 1956, Hackensack, NJ
Vocals / Gospel, Inspirational
This light-voiced singer was born in Hackensack, NJ, and is especially known for the No. 1 pop hit "You Light up My Life" (1979). She has done easy-listening albums and a string of CCM and inspirational albums. —*Bil Carpenter*

The Best of Debby Boone / 1986 / Capitol ✦✦✦
Pop hits from the late '70s. —*Bil Carpenter*

Friends for Life / 1987 / Benson ✦✦✦✦
This is an inspirational/pop offering, featuring "Every Generation." —*Bil Carpenter*

● **Reflections** / 1988 / Benson ✦✦✦✦
Includes her biggest gospel hits. —*Bil Carpenter*

Professor Alex Bradford

b. 1926, Bessemer, AL, **d.** Feb. 15, 1978, Newark, NJ
Piano, Vocals / Black Gospel
In a genre filled with slightly eccentric and certainly colorful performers, the flamboyant, complex, and innovative Alex Bradford (aka the Professor) was a character among characters. A talented singer, key-

boardist, songwriter, and choir director as well as a charismatic, theatrical showman, he was firmly grounded in gospel traditions, yet always kept an ear tuned to the rhythms and innovations of jazz and pop music, both of which he integrated into a style that has had considerable influence on both gospel and pop performers. He was a versatile performer and singer with a range that moved from a tremendous, at times raspy, baritone to a high soprano whoop that in his prime easily made it to the rarified realm of high A. His piano playing, blues-infused phrasing, and soulful tone had great impact on Ray Charles; and his singing style had great effect on young gospel singer James Cleveland, who went on to become one of the all-time greats. As a songwriter, Bradford penned numerous modern gospel standards, including "I'm Too Close to Heaven and I Can't Turn Around" and "Let God Abide." He also wrote for such secular singers as Charles and La Vern Baker and may in that regard may be one of the grandfathers of the '60s soul music.

He was born in Bessemer, AL. Though raised in poverty during the Depression, Bradford got dance and music lessons from jazz pianist Martha Belle Hall. After making his vaudeville debut, six-year-old Bradford became captivated by the music of the sanctified church. Other influences included quartets such as the Blue Jays, the Kings of Harmony, and especially the Swan Silvertones. Wild pianist Prophet Jones, who would play the piano with his feet, was also a great influence. Cab Calloway inspired his pantomime antics and dance steps, and Georgia Lee Stafford, the "Songbird of the South," inspired his amazing soprano falsetto. Queen C. Anderson, a singer for Reverend Brewster, also profoundly affected Bradford.

He formed the Bradfordettes, where he gained notoriety for elaborate, rather secular choreography. His mother sent him to New York, where Bradford formed the Bronx Gospelaires. Eventually he returned to Bessmer to attend private school. Later he became a school teacher and earned the moniker "Professor." While serving in the military, he frequently performed at camp shows. As an ordained minister he also preached in Mother Hargrove Bishop Universal Spiritual Church of Birmingham. After his discharge, Bradford took several laborer jobs in Chicago to support his first wife. He also moonlighted in piano bars until he began making inroads with ruling gospel divas Mahalia Jackson, Roberta Martin, and Sallie Martin.

In the early '50s Bradford began touring and performing in several groups and writing songs for Jackson and both Martins until founding the eight-member Bradford Specials in 1954. Before that, only women, such as the Ward Sisters, sang in such groups, with the men preferring quintets or quartets. With their full-length black robes trimmed with pastel-colored stoles, and with their falsetto harmonies, the Bradford Specials caused a not entirely positive stir on their first Southern tour. Upon returning to Chicago, they recorded Bradford's "Too Close to Heaven" and found themselves with a million-seller. Suddenly Bradford was hailed as the "Singing Rage of the Gospel Age," and his carefully choreographed performances were in great demand. He and the group remained hot through the '50s. In the early '60s Bradford's career began to wane, but it was revitalized after he was cast in the gospel musical *Black Nativity* opposite Marion Williams. The show was somewhat successful in the States, but in Europe it was a smash hit. Later in the decade Bradford took a company to Australia and then returned to Europe, where he found many devoted fans. In the early '70s he returned to found, direct, and occasionally perform with the Greater Abyssinian Baptist Choir of Newark, NJ. He also returned to the stage in a City Centerproduction of *Black Alice* and in a college production (with a new incarnation of the Bradford Singers) of *Dark of the Moon.* While haggling over details of his gospel musical, *Your Arms Too Short to Box with God,* Bradford suffered a stroke. He died a few weeks later, in early 1978. *—Sandra Brennan*

Too Close / 1953-1958 / Specialty ✦✦✦✦
Rev. Alex Bradford was an amazing singer, prolific composer, and outstanding pianist whose work in the '50s was extremely influential. His flamboyant, exuberant manner and slashing style were imitated by many secular singers and served as a blueprint for the emergence of a sound that would eventually be labeled "soul." This 29-song package includes his biggest hits, particularly the incredible "Too Close To Heaven," a remarkable three-minute piece that merges theatrics, lyrical metaphors, and fire-breathing vocals into a transcendent tour-de-force. There are also seven newly released numbers, including "Move Upstairs," a 1958 duet between Bradford and Bessie Griffin. *—Ron Wynn*

● **The Best of Alex Bradford** / Specialty ✦✦✦✦
A comprehensive selection of his fiery, stomping cuts with the Bradford Specials all-male quintet. *—Ron Wynn*

He Lifted Me / Specialty ✦✦✦
A good "hard gospel" outing, spiced with animated leads from Bradford. *—Ron Wynn*

Rainbow in the Sky / Specialty ✦✦✦✦
A broad range of formats and self-penned songs by one of gospel's great-

est writers, producers, and soloists. Some are issued for the first time here (ca. 1954-58). *—Opal Louis Nations*

Walking with the King / Savgos ✦✦✦
Prof. Alex Bradford delivers a series of smashing, aggressive, animated hard gospel anthems here, singing with the fire and fury normally associated with Golden Age material, yet also incorporating some elements of modern production. While not quite as majestic as Brother Joe May, Bradford could moan, shout, and holler with almost any singing evangelist, and he demonstrates that on these numbers. *—Ron Wynn*

Willmer Broadnax

b. 1916
Vocals / Black Gospel
This bespectacled, dynamic lead tenor worked with various groups in Southern California before gaining a wider audience when he joined the Spirit of Memphis in 1950. Listed variously during his career as Willmer, Wilmer, Wilbur, and Willie "Little Ax" Broadnax, the "ringing tenor" led the Southern Gospel Singers, the Golden Echoes, and later the Spirit of Memphis Quartet during the '50s. *—Bil Carpenter and Kip Lornell*

● **So Many Years** / Gospel Jubilee ✦✦✦✦
Broadnax' unique and influential voice in a variety of settings. *—Kip Lornell*

Brooklyn All-Stars

Gospel
The Brooklyn All-Stars are an internationally recognized male group who have been performing since 1950. They have won numerous awards and racked up two gold albums. Original members include the group's founder, Thomas J. Spann, Hardie Clifton, and Sam Thomas. They recorded several cuts for Peacock in 1959, including "Rest Awhile" and "Meet Me in Galilee." Their early years were difficult. They often traveled to engagements stuffed into a single car, relying on parishioners' hospitality for food and lodging because they were not permitted into restaurants and motels. Things improved over the '60s, and they established themselves as a fine traditional gospel act. Between 1971 and 1978 they were annually voted the No. 1 gospel group in the US. Their biggest selling hits are "When I Stood on the Banks of Jordan" and "He Touched Me and Made Me Whole" on Jewel, the label they have been with since 1971. During the '80s, the All-Stars embarked upon a series of world tours. *—Sandra Brennan*

● **Our Greatest Hits** / Nashboro ✦✦✦✦
Powerful material drawn from a variety of '60s and '70s Nashboro albums, it's led principally by the soaring tenor of the underrated Hardie Clifton. *—Opal Louis Nations*

Archie Brownlee and the Five Blind Boys of Mississippi

Vocals
Archie Brownlee's amazing vocal flights and theatrics helped make the Original Five Blind Boys of Mississippi one of the greatest quartets of all time. They were originally recorded by the Library of Congress in 1937, doing comic and game tunes. Brownlee became a star in the '40s and early '50s. He died of a heart attack in the late '50s. *—Ron Wynn*

● **You Done What the Doctor Couldn't Do** / Gospel Jubilee ✦✦✦✦
Eighteen stunning hard gospel performances (recorded between 1948-59) by arguably the greatest practitioners of the art. Brownlee was master of controlled vocal pandemonium, his deft leaps from the decorous to the delirious prompting the faithful to "fall out" in ecstatic fits. His "Amazing Grace" becomes an extraordinary plea for deliverance, while the Blind Boys' vamp on the Lord's Prayer ("World Prayer") is a beautifully tiered tour de force of prayer and song. Anyone wanting to experience the fervor of hard gospel at its intense, yet artful, best should hear this profoundly heartfelt and masterfully performed music. *—Mark Humphrey, Roundup Newsletter*

Rev. Milton Brunson

Vocals / Black Gospel
Brunson founded the Chicago-based Thompson Community Singers in 1948 and is pastor of Christ Tabernacle Baptist Church in that city. *—Bil Carpenter*

Available to You / 1988 / Word ✦✦✦✦
Traditional, Black-choir mass music. *—Bil Carpenter*

Open Our Eyes / 1990 / Word ✦✦✦
More of the same. *—Bil Carpenter*

● **Greatest Hits** / Jul. 1996 / Sony ✦✦✦✦
Milton Brunson's *Greatest Hits* collects all of his gospel choir's biggest hits and most popular songs—including "He Cares for You," "I'm Free,"

"Lord I Believe," and "Jesus Rose"—on one disc, making it a perfect introduction to one of the most successful and acclaimed gospel choirs of the '90s. —*Leo Stanley*

Shirley Caesar

b. Oct. 13, 1938, Durham, NC
Vocals / Black Gospel
Born in Durham, NC, Caesar sang with the Caravans in the early '60s, before going solo in 1966. She is a strict traditionalist known for her shouting style and evangelizing messages. —*Bil Carpenter*

First Lady / 1977 / Hob ✦✦✦
Secular songs and Christian themes are mixed here. —*Bil Carpenter*

Live in Chicago with Rev. Milton Brunson and the Thompson Community Singers / 1988 / Word ✦✦✦
Including traditional Black gospel testifying, singing, and storytelling, this album was recorded with the Thompson Community Singers and Albertina Walker. —*Bil Carpenter*

Celebration / 1990 / Myrrh ✦✦✦
As this fine pop-gospel hit album confirms, Caesar has always managed to steer a course between conservatism and selling out, in the enduring gospel tradition of drawing on the secular music of its time. —*John Storm Roberts, Original Music*

● **Her Very Best** / 1991 / Word ✦✦✦✦
This collection is taken from four of her '80s Word albums, plus two unreleased cuts (20 in all). Moments of glory include the choir-backed "Jesus, I Love Calling Your Name," and "Sailing on the Sea of Your Love," with Al Green sharing lead vocals. The set also features an extremely interesting rendition, in good Nashville style, of the country-gospel classic "No Charge." —*Opal Louis Nations, Roots & Rhythm Newsletter*

● **I Remember Mama** / Feb. 25, 1992 / Word ✦✦✦✦
Shirley Caesar's poignant rembrances of her mother set the stage for this album that mixed sentimental fare with rocking evangelism and surging performances. No Golden Age gospel artists have been more successful at retaining their zeal while adapting to contemporary production and arranging tendencies than Caesar. She doesn't compromise her lyrical message but will hold still for electronics, strings, and even an occasional funk backbeat. —*Ron Wynn*

Jesus, I Love Calling Your Name / Apr. 28, 1992 / Word ✦✦✦
More fervent lyrical material from Shirley Caesar, backed by both choral and contemporary production and arrangements. The results aren't always successful, but when they click, they are masterful. The title track was a sizable hit on gospel radio. —*Ron Wynn*

Sailin' / Apr. 28, 1992 / Word ✦✦✦✦
Shirley Caesar and Rev. Al Green make a magnificent team on the title track, which helped win each a Grammy. Caesar's evocative leads and Green's shimmering harmonies and equally spectacular leads are a session highlight, although there are some other fine numbers spotlighting Caesar as well. —*Ron Wynn*

Just a Word / Jul. 1996 / Sony ✦✦✦✦
Not strictly a Shirley Caesar album, *Just a Word* nevertheless is a good showcase of mid-'90s contemporary gospel music. Recorded on the final day of the Outreach Convention, *Just A Word* features four songs with Caesar's lead vocals and a host of other gospel vocalists and musicians, singing both standards and new gospel songs. The performances are energetic and invigorating, demonstrating that traditional gospel is nearly always best heard in a live setting. —*Leo Stanley*

Rejoice / Myrrh ✦✦✦✦
The title track features Shirley Caesar in peak form, soaring, shouting, and declaring her love for God. The LP overall isn't quite as strong as some other Caesar releases, lacking consistent material or top performances. Still, Caesar often manages to salvage things solely with her vocal power and personality. —*Ron Wynn*

The Best of Shirley Caesar with the Caravans / Savoy ✦✦✦✦
This anthology covers Caesar's Savoy material during the initial period after she left the Caravans. It's mostly traditional gospel, often superbly performed, though not as well produced or engineered as her later releases for Word. —*Ron Wynn*

Caravans

Arguably the greatest women's gospel group ever, the Caravans at one time included contralto Albertina Walker, contralto (and former contender for Mahalia Jackson's throne) Bessie Griffin, first soprano Inez Andrews, wailing soprano "Little" Shirley Caesar, coloratura Dolores Washington, Dorothy Norwood, Cassietta George, and the Reverend James Cleveland on piano. At the height of their unequaled popularity between the late '50s and mid-'60s, they were known for unusual rapport that made it seem as if the singers were telepathically linked during their improvisation-filled performances. The group's founder, Albertina Walker, originally sang with top Chicago soloist Tom Anderson's

group and in 1952 took a few other former group members to form the Caravans. The group became a training ground for female gospel stars, and many of its members have gone on to become important figures in gospel. In the mid-'50s, Cleveland joined the group. Already a noted preacher and musical arranger, he functioned as the pianist and monologist, telling stories that the singers would punctuate and illustrate with music. Cleveland also helped to hone the group's skill. Singer-songwriter Cassietta George joined the Caravans in 1954. During the '50s, the group recorded primarily for Savoy; they switched to Vee-Jay in 1962 and remained with them through 1965. Cleveland was replaced by James Herndon in 1962. The group disbanded in 1966 after the departure of their main star, the fiery Shirley Caesar. Since then, Walker has occasionally hosted reunion performances. —*Sandra Brennan*

★ **'Til I Meet The Lord** / ✦✦✦✦✦
The collection here is taken from the two Vee-Jay albums recorded in the early '60s. Featured singers include founder, manager, and lead Albertina ("Tina") Walker, ably supported by Cassietta George, the great Shirley Caesar, and Josephine Howard, supported by James Herndon and Kenneth Woods on organ and piano. There's some fine high-spirited moments with Walker's raspy wails and Caesar's amazing glissandos. —*Opal Louis Nations, Roots & Rhythm Newsletter*

The Best of the Caravans / Savoy ✦✦✦✦
This doesn't necessarily contain their best material, only those songs that garnered either chart success or radio airplay during the 1950s and early '60s. Walker, Andrews, and Caesar are the artists featured most prominently. —*Ron Wynn*

Michael Card

b. Apr. 11, 1957
Dulcimer, Banjo, Guitar, Piano, Violin / Inspirational
Called the "Christian Dan Fogelberg" for his folk guitar style and Bible-based songs, Card learned the banjo from country legend Earl Scruggs and later picked up piano, dulcimer, guitar, and violin. He dropped out of a Ph.D. program to go into the music business. —*Bil Carpenter*

The Final Word / 1987 / Sparrow ✦✦✦✦
Pensive, acoustic, and spiritually correct. —*Bil Carpenter*

The Way of Wisdom / 1991 / Sparrow ✦✦✦
This superb effort has mellow instrumentation and potent lyrics. —*Bil Carpenter*

● **Joy in the Journey** / 1994 / Sparrow ✦✦✦✦
Card's best known songs are collected here, with the earliest ones newly re-recorded for this album. —*Thom Granger*

Brother to Brother / Jun. 25, 1996 / Sony ✦✦✦
Brother to Brother is a beautiful duet album, featuring Michael Card's trademark pop sound spike with worldbeat flourishes. The results may be a little uneven, but it's always engaging and frequently lovely. —*Rodney Batdorf*

Carman

b. Jan. 19, 1956
Vocals / CCM
Born Dominic Licciardello, he was "saved" at an Andrae Crouch concert. After he was discovered by Bill Gaither, he started his own ministry with a recording arm. He sings in CCM and R&B formats, with a heavy evangelistic message. —*Bil Carpenter*

Live . . . Radically Saved / 1988 / Benson ✦✦✦✦
A breakthrough album with Christian rap, R&B, and a little rock. —*Bil Carpenter*

Shakin' the House / 1991 / Benson ✦✦✦
A live Black gospel revival set with Commissioned and the Christ Church Choir. —*Bil Carpenter*

● **The Absolute Best** / 1993 / Sparrow ✦✦✦✦
A collection of what this unconventional artist does best, it spotlights his story-songs and hits and features one new song produced by David Foster. —*Thom Granger*

The Standard / Sep. 27, 1993 / Sparrow ✦✦✦
Carman tries his hand at some new musical directions, with less extended stories and more song-oriented material, alienating some old fans but winning some new ones in the process. —*Thom Granger*

Sister Wynona Carr

b. Aug. 23, 1924, Cleveland, OH, **d.** 1976
Vocals / R&B, Gospel
One of the top gospel artists on the Specialty label during the early '50s, Carr later made some fine R&B. Born in Cleveland, Carr moved to Detroit and joined Rev. C.L. Franklin's New Bethel Baptist Church Choir. She began cutting gospel as Sister Wynona Carr for Los Angeles-based Specialty in 1949, enjoying success with "The Ball Game." Carr went

secular in 1955, rocking out on "Boppity Bop (Boogity Bop)" and "Nursery Rhyme Rock." Her lone R&B chart item in 1957, the bluesy "Should I Ever Love Again," was covered by rockabilly great Gene Vincent.

Wynona Carr's secular and gospel material has been reissued by Fantasy, holder of the Specialty catalog. —*Bill Dahl*

Jump Jack Jump! / 1985 / Specialty ✦✦✦✦
This 24-track set covers Carr's R&B tunes, with many unissued but fine tunes such as "If These Walls Could Speak," "Finders Keepers," and "Weather Man" finally getting out of the vault. The CD also includes her trademark upbeat, sassy songs, "Jump Jack Jump," "Boppity Bop (Boogity Boop)," "Ding Dong Daddy" and "Nursery Rhyme Rock." Thematic variety wasn't her label's strong suit when it came to material, and they might have done better with more numbers like "Please Mr. Jailer" and "It's Raining Outside" and a few less boogies and jump pieces. —*Ron Wynn*

★ **Dragnet for Jesus** / 1992 / Specialty ✦✦✦✦✦
Carr is a long-overlooked gospel writer, producer, and soloist—the Billie Holiday of gospel. The priceless material on this album is circa 1949-1954. —*Opal Louis Nations*

The Cathedrals

Southern Gospel
Formed in 1965, this traditional Southern gospel group (also known as the Cathedral Quartet) appeared regularly on Rex Humbard's "Cathedral of Tomorrow" broadcast in the '60s. The Cathedrals are led by bass George Younce and alto Glen Payne, who are known for their humorous onstage exchanges. Originally Humbard formed them as a trio, but soon they became a quartet comprising Payne, Younce, Danny Koker, and Bobby Clark. Both Payne and Younce have remained with the group; the other two spots have been filled by a number of singers. As of 1994, the tenor and baritone vocals are provided by Ernie Haase and Scott Fowler, with piano accompaniment by Roger Bennett. The Cathedral Quartet remained with Humbard until 1969 and then set out on their own, traveling from gig to gig in a converted egg truck until they could afford tour buses. Over the next decade the group became one of the most popular Southern gospel groups. In 1977 they won their first Grammy for best gospel performance, going on to win in 1978, 1979, and 1982 as well. In 1977 they also won Dove Awards for male group of the year and best Southern gospel album (for *Then . . . and Now*) by the Gospel Music Association. In 1979 Koker and Clark left the group, beginning a long stream of replacements; pianist Roger Bennett joined up. During the '70s and '80s the Cathedrals had a long stream of No. 1 gospel hits, including "Step into the Water," "Can He, Could He, Would He," and "I've Just Started Living." From 1986 through 1990 the Cathedrals were featured at Bill Gaither's Praise Gathering for Believers. In 1988 they became the first Southern gospel group to record in England with the London Philharmonic Orchestra, for the album *Symphony of Praise*. During the mid- to late '80s the Cathedrals garnered numerous awards from the GMA. In 1989, the group's 25th anniversary, *Gospel Music Voice* named them group of the year, and *Cash Box* named their *Goin' in Style* Southern gospel album of the year. —*Sandra Brennan*

● **Cathedrals Collection, Vol. 1** / 1988 / Benson ✦✦✦✦
A fine collection of recent hits, styled in the manner of their old hits. —*Bil Carpenter*

Gary Chapman

Guitar, Vocals
Texas-born songwriter Chapman came to early fame with "My Father's Eyes," made popular by Amy Grant, whom he later married. He has also had songs recorded by T.G. Sheppard, Kenny Rogers, and other country artists. —*Thom Granger*

Light Inside / 1994 / Reunion ✦✦✦
Grammy-winning producer Michael Omartian teams with Chapman for a comfortably satisfying album, including remakes of two songs from his earlier (and out of print) Lamb and Lion albums. —*Thom Granger*

● **Everyday Man** / RCA ✦✦✦✦
Chapman's album marries pop and country having the unfortunate effect of missing the moment with both audiences. —*Thom Granger*

Steven Curtis Chapman

Guitar, Vocals / CCM
Singer-songwriter Steven Curtis Chapman, whose music is a cross between '70s-style light rock and orchestrated pop, has been one of the most prominent performers of contemporary Christian music during the '80s and '90s. Born and raised in Paducah, KY, Chapman learned to play several instruments while hanging out in his father's music store, excelling at guitar and piano. Chapman enrolled as a pre-med student at Anderson College in Indiana. He soon decided to pursue a music career and dropped out to go to Nashville, where he began working in a music

show at Opryland USA. When not performing, he was busy writing songs, a skill he learned from his father. One of his tunes was recorded by the Imperials, a prominent gospel group. Although several different labels and music publishers were interested in Chapman, he decided to sign with Sparrow, the major Christian music company, in 1987. That year he cut his first album, First Hand. The first single released from the album, "Weak Days," made it to No. 2 on the contemporary Christian chart. His second album, 1988's *Real Life Conversations*, earned him four more hits, including the No. 1 song "His Eyes." Co-written with James Isaac Elliott, it earned the Contemporary Recorded Song of the Year award from the Gospel Music Association in 1989. That year he also won a GMA award for best songwriter of the year. Released later that year, his third album, *More to This Life*, contained four No. 1 hits and in 1990 earned him an unprecedented ten nominations at the GMA Awards (he actually won five of those ten). His next album, *For the Sake of the Call*, which contained five No. 1 singles and earned him another slew of GMA awards and his first Grammy in the best pop gospel album category, only strengthened his position as the king of Christian music. In 1992 Chapman made a successful bid to attract a more mainstream audience with *The Great Adventure*, which also won a Grammy, and its accompanying title track video. When Sparrow Records was purchased by EMI/Liberty, they began marketing the album in discount stores, and in 1993 it went gold. He began performing material from the album on the road, which spawned a live album and video called *The Live Adventure*. In 1993 the live album won more GMA awards and earned Chapman a new award from *American Songwriter* magazine, songwriter and artist of the year. Many of country's brightest stars, including Sandi Patti, Billy Dean, Glen Campbell, and Roger Whitaker, have recorded Chapman's songs. He released his seventh album, *Heaven in the Real World*, in 1994 and embarked on a major tour. —*Sandra Brennan*

First Hand / 1987 / Sparrow ✦✦✦
Chapman's freshman debut is infused with country, soft rock, and pop. —*Bil Carpenter*

Real Life Conversations / 1988 / Sparrow ✦✦✦✦
Harder-edged, elaborate, guitar-focused light rock. —*Bil Carpenter*

★ **For the Sake of the Call** / 1990 / Sparrow ✦✦✦✦✦
Chapman's songwriting voice continues to mature, and the stirring title anthem helped make this his most successful album. —*Brian Mansfield*

The Great Adventure / 1992 / Sparrow ✦✦✦
Chapman flirts with country, rap, and Springsteenian rock on his most ambitious project, both musically and lyrically. Includes guest appearances from Ricky Skaggs, DC Talk, and BeBe Winans. —*Brian Mansfield*

Heaven in the Real World / 1994 / Sparrow ✦✦✦
Chapman moves into rockier, more electrified territory with his down-home story songs and values. —*Thom Granger*

The Choir

CCM
Atmospheric alternative rock bands like Cocteau Twins and My Bloody Valentine influenced this alternative-Christian rock group. More melodic than most, the Choir has strong enough songs to cross into pop. —*Thom Granger*

Wide-Eyed Wonder / 1990 / Word ✦✦✦
More accessible than *Kangaroo*, this album helped the band build a larger following through Christian rock radio. —*Thom Granger*

● **Circle Slide** / 1991 / Word ✦✦✦✦
Its best set to date, marked by the band's usual high standards of songwriting, extended soloing and better production. —*Thom Granger*

Speckled Bird / 1994 / REX ✦✦✦
The national release of songs from its indie album *Kissers and Killers*, along with the few new tunes, showed increasing love for the noise pop genre. —*Thom Granger*

Chase the Kangaroo / Word ✦✦✦
First movement into Euro alternative guitar pop, sets direction for later albums. —*Thom Granger*

Diamonds and Rain / Word ✦✦

Chosen Gospel Singers

Gospel
Among the original members were Lou Rawls, Joe Hinton, and Joe Medwick, all of whom went on to successful secular careers. Largely an a cappella group, they later became the Gospel Keynotes with the searing lead vocals of Paul Beasley. —*Bil Carpenter*

● **The Lifeboat** / 1954 / Specialty ✦✦✦✦
Featured are previously unreleased tracks, alternate takes, and long-out-of-print gems by this major gospel quartet, led at times by Lou Rawls. —*Opal Louis Nations*

Meet the Selah Jubilees / ✦✦✦
The Chosen Gospel Singers were a spiritual group in the sanctified style, fronting such vocalists as the sing-and-preach Bob Crutcher, Joe Johnson from the Trumpeteers, jazz-soul singer Lou Rawls, and the hard-working Tommy Ellison, who went on to form the Five Singing Stars. These are exciting selections from various labels, recorded between 1952 and 1963. Side B features the great Thermon Ruth and the Selah Singers, who sang both R&B and gospel under various aliases during the '40s and '50s. The material here from their postwar Arista, Continental, Gotham, and Mercury period is entirely gospel—close jubilee harmonies with sparse accompaniment. The songs are taken from rare 45s and 78s. Good overall sound quality (cassette only). *—Opal Louis Nations, Roots and Rhythm Newsletter*

Chuck Wagon Gang

Gospel, Southern Gospel
The Chuck Wagon Gang has been around since 1936, and though it has undergone many personnel changes over the years, its sound and devotion to old-fashioned gospel have remained much the same. The band provides an important link between country music and traditional sacred songs of the South.

The original incarnation of the Chuck Wagon Gang wasDavid Parker Carter, his son Jim (born Ernest), daughter Rose (born Rosa Lola), and daughter Effie. Dad Carter was born in Kentucky, but was raised in Clay County, TX. He was enrolled in a singing school there when he met Carrie Brooks, whom he married in 1909. They bore eight children, and to support them Carter worked for the Rock Island Railroad. At times he and the family also picked cotton. The band formed around 1935 when the illness of one of the children left the family destitute. For additional income, Dad Carter talked the management at station KFYO Lubbock to hiring him to host a daily radio program for $12.50 a week. The original group was called the Carter Quartet; and in it Dad sang tenor, Jim sang bass and played guitar, while Rose and Effie sang soprano and alto. They were popular and soon began earning $15 per week. The following year the Carters moved to WBAP and billed themselves as the Chuck Wagon Gang; they sang a variety of secular and sometimes sacred songs. Their earliest recording session for ARC produced country singles rather than gospel. They gradually became more gospel-oriented and by the late '40s had switched over completely. In 1942 they spent a few months at a Tulsa radio station.

The Chucks broke up for the duration of World War II. Afterward they reunited and returned to WBAP, remaining primarily a radio band. They began recording again in 1948 for Columbia. Two years later Wally Fowler had them perform at one of his all-night singing conventions in Augusta, GA. They became a full-time touring band after that. During the early '50s the band underwent the first of many membership changes. Jim left in 1953 and was replaced by Howard Gordon; he remained with the Chucks until he died in 1967. Another brother, Roy, joined and sang bass in Jim's stead. Dad Carter retired in 1955 and was at first replaced by Eddie Carter. In the late '50s non-family members such as Alynn Billodeau, Patrick McKeehan, Ronnie Page, and Ronnie Crittenden spent time with the Chuck Wagon Gang. The band kept touring part-time and making records. By 1975, the Chucks had made 408 masters. They stopped recording for a time and underwent more personnel changes. They resumed recording around 1978, mostly on the Copperfield label. In 1987 they once again became a full-time band, with new members joining the last of the Carters, Roy and his sister Ruth Ellen Yates. In 1984 Dad Carter, who had died in 1963, was inducted into the Gospel Music Hall of Fame. In the late '80s the Chuck Wagon Gang was named gospel artist or group of the year by *Music City News* for five years in a row. In 1990 Bob Terrell published an authorized history of the group, *The Chuck Wagon Gang: A Legend Lives On. —Sandra Brennan*

● **Greatest Hits** / 1920 / Arrival ✦✦✦✦
Featuring 16 tracks, *Greatest Hits* is a solid compilation of some of the Chuck Wagon Gang's best tracks and offers a good introduction to this contemporary country-gospel vocal group. *—Stephen Thomas Erlewine*

Old Time Hymns, Vol. 2 / 1921 / Arrival ✦✦✦
The Chuck Wagon Gang's heartfelt renditions of some well known traditional hymns are somewhat hampered by the sterile production, but their strong performances carry the disc. *—Stephen Thomas Erlewine*

Family Tradition / 1973 / K-Tel ✦✦✦
It contains "Standing on the Promises" and other performances that show that throughout the many lineup changes this group has experienced, their sound remains a constant. *—AMG*

Looking Away to Heaven / 1976 / CBS ✦✦✦
This is one of the best of the Columbia sets. *—Charles S. Wolfe*

☆ **Columbia Historic Edition** / 1990 / CBS ✦✦✦✦✦
The best set of the group's vintage '30s and '40s sides is well mastered, with excellent annotations. *—Charles S. Wolfe*

In Harmony / Copperfield ✦✦✦
Features "We Are Climbing" and other gospel favorites. *—AMG*

● **Historic Edition** / CBS ✦✦✦✦

Rev. James Cleveland

b. Dec. 5, 1932, Chicago, IL, **d.** Feb. 9, 1991
Piano, Vocals / Black Gospel
Born in Chicago, Cleveland was one of the pioneers of the trend toward mass choirs that developed in the '50s. He led the movement in Southern California but maintained his national reputation as a teacher, performer, and recording artist until his death in 1991. He played the piano behind the Roberta Martin Singers in the '50s and moonlighted with the Caravans during the same period. By the early '60s he had branched out on his own and gained a Savoy Records contract. He started the "traditional Black choir sound" with the 1962 *Peace Be Still* and continued to promote the sound through the founding of the Gospel Music Workshop of America in 1968 to train mass choirs in the Cleveland sound. *—Bil Carpenter*

★ **Peace Be Still** / 1962 / Savoy ✦✦✦✦✦
A set of original Cleveland tunes and traditional hymns done in the choir format he pioneered with The Angelic Choir of New Jersey. This live recording, done with crude technology, is helped somewhat by the high-fidelity pressing. It includes "I Had a Talk with God" and "I'll Wear a Crown." Cleveland's gruff vocals appear on most cuts. *—Bil Carpenter*

● **Having Church** / 1991 / Savoy Gospel ✦✦✦✦
There are those who claim Cleveland's later recordings with The Southern California Community Choir don't quite match those with the group from Nutley, NJ. Perhaps—even probably. He's also lost some power as he's gotten older. But whether led by Cleveland or by other singers (notably the magisterial Lavora Wilson) the material on this CD is powerful and joyous enough to make that kind of distinction irrelevant. *—John Storm Roberts, Original Music*

Victory Shall Be Mine / 1991 / Savoy ✦✦✦
This is among Cleveland's best later works. *—Kip Lornell*

Gospel Music Workshop of America / Savoy Gospel ✦✦✦✦
A typically strong Cleveland performance with an all-star choir. *—Kip Lornell*

Live at Carnegie Hall / Savoy ✦✦✦✦
A Grammy winner. *—Ron Wynn*

Rev. James Cleveland / Nashboro ✦✦✦
James Cleveland is, of course, one of the great names of contemporary gospel music, a master preacher and soloist, and one of those who developed the choir style until it has almost obliterated quartet singing. But his present fame, of course, was built on youthful brilliance, and this fine (deleted) set testifies to that. This is the young Cleveland, sparkling new and with the freshness of a revelation in process. *—John Storm Roberts, Original Music*

Dorothy Love Coates

b. 1930, Birmingham, AL
Vocals / Black Gospel
Born in Birmingham, AL, Coates started singing in the '40s with The Original Gospel Harmonettes, who had the hits "I'm Sealed" and "Get Away." *—Bil Carpenter*

☆ **Get on Board** / 1956 / Specialty ✦✦✦✦✦
With The Original Gospel Harmonettes, here are 24 exciting songs (circa 1951-56) supported by Herbert "Pee Wee" Pickard, gospel's organist supreme. *—Opal Louis Nations*

★ **The Best of Dorothy Love Coates, Vols. 1 & 2** / 1957 / Specialty ✦✦✦✦✦
A great overview that spotlights the ragged Coates voice and collects many of her best compositions. *—Ron Wynn*

The Best of Dorothy Love Coates/Orig. Gospel Harmonettes, Vol. 2 / 1991 / Specialty ✦✦✦
...The group sang hard and sanctified to the point of almost total exhaustion. They're one of the truly great post-war female gospel quintets. This has great improved sound. *—Opal Louis Nations, Roots & Rhythm Newsletter*

The Original Gospel, Vols. 1 & 2 / Specialty ✦✦✦
Dynamic lead vocals from Coates, plus superb harmonizing and rollicking instrumental accompaniment. *—Ron Wynn*

Daryl Coley

b. 1955, San Francisco, CA
Clarinet, Piano, Keyboards / Urban, Jazz, Black Gospel
Born in San Francisco, Coley grew up on jazz music and learned to play clarinet and piano. He played keyboards for The Hawkins Family from 1977 until he left to collaborate with James Cleveland in 1983. Later he

worked with jazz artists Nancy Wilson and Rodney Franklin and pop singer Philip Bailey. —*Bil Carpenter*

I'll Be with You / 1988 / Light ✦✦✦
Coley shows his jazz technique on the heavily improvisational title cut, with breaks and gaps throughout. Further, the vocal arrangements are not in standard choir style. Otherwise, this is mostly upbeat Black gospel. —*Bil Carpenter*

Live . . . He's Right on Time / 1990 / Sparrow ✦✦✦✦
This live fusion of jazz, classical, and traditional gospel is wrapped up in Coley's zestful, upbeat arrangements. —*Bil Carpenter*

● **Collection** / 1995 / Sparrow ✦✦✦✦

Beyond the Veil: Live at Bobby Jones Gospel XIII / Jun. 25, 1996 / Forefront ✦✦✦
Beyond The Veil: Live At Bobby Jones Gospel XIII captures the invigorating energy of Daryl Coley's live shows, conveying the rootsy joy of traditional gospel music. —*Rodney Batdorf*

Commissioned

CCM
An urban Black gospel band with crossover appeal. In concert they are an extremely evangelistic group who put on such a dramatic show that the altars are routinely packed with repenters after their performances. Members Fred Hammond and Keith Staten have done solo projects. —*Bil Carpenter*

Will You Be Ready? / 1989 / Light ✦✦✦
A mix of contemporary and traditional spirituals. —*Bil Carpenter*

● **State of Mind** / 1991 / Benson ✦✦✦✦
This R&B/urban CCM spectacle has tight harmonies. —*Bil Carpenter*

Andrae Crouch

b. Jun. 1, 1950, San Francisco, CA
Piano / CCM, Christian Rock
A pioneer in contemporary gospel music, Crouch combined the classic motif of call-and-response and solo with choir approach with pop songwriting techniques and production, resulting in albums accepted by both Black and White audiences. Many of Crouch's early songs are now considered "Jesus Music" standards. After a ten-year hiatus from recording, during which he dabbled in music for film and TV scores, Crouch signed with Quincy Jones' Qwest label for a triumphant return to form with *Mercy*. —*Thom Granger*

☆ **Andrae Crouch and The Disciples** / 1978 / Light ✦✦✦✦✦
*Andrae Crouch and the Disciples—*Live in London has all the groundbreaking rock riffs, motifs, and crossover elements that had him labeled a "devil" by conservatives. —*Bil Carpenter*

Let's Worship Him / May 1993 / Arrival ✦✦✦
Featuring driving beats and funky guitars as well as more contemplative slower numbers, *Let's Worship Him* is a good compilation of Crouch's late-'70s and early-'80s work. —*Stephen Thomas Erlewine*

Mercy / 1994 / Qwest ✦✦✦
A potpourri of musical styles from Caribbean to African, laid down with impeccable taste in arrangment and production, exceeded the expectations that come from ten years away from the studio. —*Thom Granger*

● **His Best** / Arrival ✦✦✦✦
As the title suggests, *His Best* features some of Crouch's finest moments from the early '70s, including "Jesus Is the Answer" and "My Tribute." A good introduction to this popular gospel singer. —*Stephen Thomas Erlewine*

Daniel Amos (Da)

CCM
Daniel Amos started out as a Gram Parsons-influenced country band. By the late '70s, the group had become a rock band, but the collapse of its record label delayed the release of the landmark *Horrendous Disc*. During that time, frontman Terry Taylor discovered Elvis Costello and the Talking Heads. The few fans who stuck around during the band's three-year recording absence were shocked to hear the new wave *Alarma!* released hot on the heels of the mainstream *Horrendous Disc*. The band, also known as Da, now follows its own music with little concern for audiences and marketing. Taylor has become one of the most influential figures in Christian rock, as both a performer and a producer (Randy Stonehill, Jacob's Trouble, Scattered Few). —*Brian Mansfield*

Daniel Amos / 1976 / Maranatha Music ✦✦✦✦
Christian country-rock, along the lines of the Flying Burrito Brothers, but hardly *Gilded Palace of Sin*. However, Gram Parsons sideman Al Perkins does contribute pedal steel. —*Brian Mansfield*

Shotgun Angel / 1977 / Maranatha Music ✦✦✦✦
This country-rock album, tighter than *Daniel Amos* with added pop har-

monies, is Christian music's answer to the Eagles. One of the most popular albums of its time. —*Brian Mansfield*

Doppelganger / 1982 / Stunt ✦✦✦✦
After making (but before releasing) *Horrendous Disc*, Terry Taylor discovered new wave, and Daniel Amos was never the same. *Alarma!!* stripped the band to bare bones, but *Doppelganger* returned the production values that typified Daniel Amos records. *Doppelganger* is the second of the four-part *Alarma!!* saga, but it works just fine on its own. Stunt's 1992 reissue of the album includes three live bonus tracks. —*Brian Mansfield*

★ **Kalhoun** / 1991 / Brainstorm ✦✦✦✦✦
"It's the magic word they claim came down from ancient Babylon," Taylor sings, by way of explaining the title word. "Don't know exactly what it means, it's just a sacred kind of thing." Satirical, often scathing, this rock brooks no compromise. —*Brian Mansfield*

Horrendous Disc / Feb. 1992 / Solid Rock ✦✦✦✦
The country influences of *Daniel Amos* and *Shotgun Angel* almost gone, *Horrendous Disc* established Daniel Amos as a rock band with huge melodies and huge guitars, sweetened by Beatles-influenced harmonies. —*Brian Mansfield*

● **Motor Cycle** / 1993 / Brainstorm ✦✦✦✦
A swirling, sonic song cycle, more accessible than most of DA's catalog, has great production and tons of Beatlesque fun. —*Thom Granger*

Bibleland / 1994 / Word ✦✦✦
A return to a harder-edged alternative rock sound, it's less melodic but very much alive. —*Thom Granger*

Vox Humana / ✦✦✦

Darn Floor Big Bite / Frontline ✦✦

Fearful Symmetry / Frontline ✦✦

Davis Sisters

Black Gospel
The group was founded by Ruth "Baby Sis" Davis in Philadelphia. Other members included Alfreda, Audrey, and Thelma Davis; Imogene Greene; Curtis Dublin on piano; and Jackie Verdell, lead vocalist. They recorded for Savoy until 1962. Verdell recorded secular sides for Peacock 1961-1964. Though a quintet, they sounded like a small choir with their full sound. —*Bil Carpenter*

Get Right with God / 1993 / Hob ✦✦✦

★ **The Best of the Davis Sisters** / Savoy ✦✦✦✦✦
A remarkable family gospel unit, plagued by personal tragedies. A nice anthology of their Savoy songs. —*Ron Wynn*

DC Talk

Christian Rap
Interracial trio DC Talk's blend of pop, hip-hop, and rap has brought them gold-record status over the course of three albums distributed primarily in the Christian market. —*Thom Granger*

DC Talk / 1988 / ForeFront ✦✦

Nu Thang / 1991 / Heartwarming ✦✦✦
Crossover, pop-style Christian rap. —*Bil Carpenter*

★ **Free at Last** / 1992 / ForeFront ✦✦✦✦✦
Its breakthrough album expands the group's musical boundaries and appeal, with impressive covers of "Jesus Is Just Alright" and "Lean on Me," and the trio's best original compositions to date. —*Thom Granger*

Jesus Freak / 1995 / Chordant ✦✦✦
After building a dedicated following with three albums of Christian hip-hop, DC Talk makes a play for crossover success with *Jesus Freak*. As the title indicates, the group hasn't abandoned its religious base. Keeping a solid hip-hop foundation, the trio adds elements of soul, psychedelic rock, and pop, making *Jesus Freak* their most ambitious album to date. It also happens to be their best. DC Talk fuses their diverse influences with style and grace, making the music sound seamless. The lyrics avoid cliches, managing to celebrate Christianity without sounding preachy. With its musical diversity and well-crafted lyrics, *Jesus Freak* is the album that will convince secular listeners that DC Talk is worth a listen. —*Stephen Thomas Erlewine*

De Garmo & Key

CCM
Eddie De Garmo and Dana Key are Memphis-reared guitar rockers who started with the Globe band in early 1972 and later created the Christian rock group called the Christian Band, changing the name to De Garmo and Key later in the decade. They were influenced by ZZ Top, Jimi Hendrix, and ELP. . —*Bil Carpenter*

Straight On / 1979 / Lion and Lamb ✦✦✦
Bluesy Southern rock that was ahead of its time. —*Bil Carpenter*

● **Destined to Win** / 1992 / Benson ✦✦✦✦
A greatest-hits collection, it features most of the radio favorites and an acoustic medley of earlier material. — *Thom Granger*

Heat It Up / 1993 / Benson ✦✦✦
The duo celebrates its 15th year by producing a well rounded example of everything it does: pop songs, rockers, and ballads. — *Thom Granger*

To Extremes / 1994 / Benson ✦✦✦✦
Mid-age crises cause D and K to churn out its hardest rocking effort in years, highlighted by some stellar guitar soloing by Key. — *Thom Granger*

No Turning Back/Live / Lion & Lamb ✦✦✦✦
A good sampler of the band's early sound, typified by Kansas/Emerson, Lake and Palmer-type guitar/keyboard interplay, before the band ventured into poppier waters. — *Thom Granger*

Feels Good to Be Forgiven / Heartwarming ✦✦✦
A solo effort by Eddie De Garmo. Bluesy Southern rock. — *Bil Carpenter*

Go to the Top / Benson ✦✦✦
A good example of D&K's pop side, it has compact, catchy (if somewhat cliched) tunes with enough hooks to land the band a larger following. — *Thom Granger*

The Journey / Heartwarming ✦✦✦
A light, soft-rock solo effort by Dana Key. — *Bil Carpenter*

The Pledge / Power Discs ✦✦

The Dixie Hummingbirds

Black Gospel
The Dixie Hummingbirds are among the granddaddies of Black gospel music and have provided that genre—plus pop and soul music—with numerous innovative traditions. The quartet was founded in Greensville, SC, by baritone James Davis. Under his strict leadership, the quartet sang and recorded (for Decca) slick jubilee-style songs such as "Joshua Journeyed to Jericho." Lead singer Ira Tucker, one of gospel music's all-time greats, joined the group soon after their formation, as did bass singer William Bobo, who got his start singing for the Heavenly Gospel Singers, with whom he recorded about 12 singles for Bluebird. At that time the Hummingbirds were struggling and could barely afford to travel to performances. Still, they persisted with their Southern tours and soon developed a large, devoted fan base and earned a reputation for being one of the finest gospel quartets around. Over the next five years the Hummingbirds' sound evolved in distinct phases. At first they sang in a blues-inflected folk style; then they moved on to jubilee singing with its close and more sophisticated harmonizing. Their third phase was closer to pure gospel, and they frequently sang rousing, hard adaptations of old Baptist hymns.

Around 1942, after the four had moved to Philadelphia, Tucker broke free from the tradition of standing still while singing and, in emulation of fiery rural preachers, began tearing up and down the aisles and acting out his songs. He then began hip-slapping and, in 1944, started leaping off stages. The Hummingbirds' notoriety grew when Paul Owens joined the group. In performance, he and Tucker began an elaborate vocal interplay in which one would begin a line and the other would finish it, matching the other note for note. They were so tight that one would join in, perfectly on key, before the other even finished.

In 1942 they began to sing on a Philadelphia radio station using the names the Jericho Boys and the Swanee Quintet. As the former they were picked up by producer John Hammond, who booked them at the most popular showcase for African-American talent in Greenwich Village, the Cafe Society. By the mid-'40s, they were living quite well but had yet to attain the success of such groups as the Golden Gate Quartet. In 1945 they began recording on Apollo and Gotham. In 1952 they signed with Peacock, where they have remained. Classic tracks from the early '50s include "Trouble in My Way." During this period Tucker began perfecting his improvisational style, while the other Hummingbirds began advancing into even more complex, daring harmonies. Paul Owens left the group and was replaced by baritone James Walker. The Hummingbirds added guitarist Howard Carroll, whose style has been compared to that of B.B. King.

The Dixie Hummingbirds retired for a while but by the late '60s returned, creating a fresh take on gospel by adding stronger elements of rock, jazz, and blues. In 1973 they regained national exposure by singing backup on Paul Simon's hit "Loves Me Like a Rock," a tune they recorded on an album of the same name later that year.

Bass Willie Bobo died in 1976, and James Davis retired in 1984. Ira Tucker and James Walker continue to perform in the '90s.. — *Sandra Brennan*

Christian Testimonial / 1959 / MCA ✦✦✦
Includes "The Devil Can't Harm a Praying Man." — *Bil Carpenter*

The Best of the Dixie Hummingbirds / 1973 / MCA ✦✦✦✦
A short (12 cuts) selection that is hardly their best, but still a worthwhile collection of sides from the early '60s. — *Kip Lornell*

★ **Live** / 1976 / Mobile Fidelity ✦✦✦✦✦
With 75 minutes of fine performances, good sound quality, and a varied repertoire this is the one to buy. — *Kip Lornell*

In the Storm Too Long / Gospel Jubilee ✦✦✦✦
Their classic early recordings from 1939-1949. This is their pre-Peacock Records material, from before lead singer James Walker joined the quartet. — *Kip Lornell*

Thomas A. Dorsey

b. 1899, d. Jan. 23, 1993
Guitar, Piano, Vocals / Gospel, Acoustic Chicago Blues
One of the key figures in the development of modern gospel music, composer Thomas Andrew Dorsey helped bring the blues to contemporary gospel music. It was he who coined the term "gospel songs" in the 1920s; prior to that they were called evangelistic songs. Dorsey was a versatile composer whose songs ranged from sentimental syrup to rol-licking hard-gospel. Though he composed many gospel standards, his biggest mainstream song is "Precious Lord," which has been recorded by artists ranging from the Heavenly Gospel Singers to Red Foley to Elvis Presley. Other well known Dorsey works include his adaptations of "We Shall Walk Through the Valley in Peace," "I'm Gonna Live the Life I Sing About in My Song," and "Singing in My Soul."

A native of Atlanta, GA, Thomas Dorsey was the son of a Southern Baptist preacher. Though greatly influenced by Dr. Watts hymns, Dorsey also listened to early jazz and blues. A child prodigy, Dorsey taught himself to play a number of instruments. He got his start playing blues and ragtime piano. As a young man, Dorsey billed himself as "Georgia Tom," and began writing notorious, witty, and double entrendre-filled blues and accompanying blues legend Ma Rainey in Chicago. Though performing secular music, Dorsey was interested in religious music and particularly the blues-tinged songs of composer C.A. Tindley, another father of modern gospel.

In 1926, during Dorsey's recovery from a lingering illness, his son suddenly died of acute appendicitis. Dorsey claims to have been visited by a heavenly messenger, who directed the composer to write "If You See My Savior, Tell Him That You Saw Me." He sent out 500 copies of the song to various churches; but it did not become a hit until 1930, when it was sung at the Jubilee Session of National Baptist Convention in Chicago. Impressed by the song, the convention directors Lucie Campbell and E.W. Isacc suggested he sell his music.

Dorsey wrote most prolifically during the Depression and created a new sub-genre, "gospel blues." Dorsey also created and led gospel choirs. A mutual friend introduced him to young shouter Sallie Martin, and he invited her to join his group at the Ebenezer Baptist Church. She eventually became his main soloist and business partner. She helped him understand the huge untapped market for gospel sheet music, and between 1932 and 1940 they toured across the country setting up choirs to demonstrate his music during his "Evening with Dorsey" performances. Together Dorsey and Martin founded the first Gospel Singers Convention. Martin ended their partnership in 1940, but he continued hosting those performances through 1944. From 1939 through 1944 he toured with Mahalia Jackson. Dorsey retired from traveling and composing in the 1960s but remained the director of the Convention for many years. He died at the age of 93. — *Sandra Brennan*

★ **Precious Lord** / 1994 / Columbia/Legacy ✦✦✦✦✦
Precious Lord collects 18 of Dorsey's greatest songs, offering a terrific introduction to one of the greatest gospel country blues singers of the '30s. — *Thom Owens*

Come On Mama, Do That Dance 1931-1940 / Yazoo ✦✦✦✦
Hard to believe that America's greatest writer of gospel songs could come up with this solid a collection of risqué blues tunes in his earlier, "sinful" days. Believe it. — *Cub Koda*

Complete Recorded Works, Vols. 1-2 / Document ✦✦✦
The two-volume *Complete Recorded Works* contains everything Dorsey recorded between 1928 and 1934, including all of his inspirational and secular material. Most listeners will be better served with the compilations *Precious Lord* and *Come On Mama, Do That Dance*, which separate his gospel recordings from his racy blues records. Historians and completists, however, will find this series necessary. — *Thom Owens*

O'landa Draper and the Associates

Black Gospel
Draper attended Memphis State University, where he formed a mass choir (the Associates) that later performed with Shirley Caesar (on "Hold My Mule"), the Winans, Timothy Wright, and Myrna Summers. — *Bil Carpenter*

● **Above and Beyond** / 1990 / Word ✦✦✦✦
Contemporary Memphis-based choir; good singing, heavily arranged. — *Ron Wynn*

Do It Again / 1990 / Word ✦✦✦

Bryan Duncan

Vocals / Gospel, CCM, Reggae, Christian Rap
The former lead singer for Sweet Comfort Band has cut a bushel of albums as a solo artist but honed both his singing craft and lyrical perspective in the early '90s. — *Thom Granger*

Strong Medicine / 1989 / Word ✦✦✦
Reggae, rap, and the strong title-track ballad. — *Bil Carpenter*

Now and Then / 1989 / Light ✦✦✦
A collection of biggest hits from Duncan's early solo albums. — *Thom Granger*

Anonymous Confessions of a Lunatic Friend / 1991 / Word ✦✦✦
Duncan's extroverted comic side is balanced with a few tunes featuring a new, more confessional tone. — *Thom Granger*

● **Mercy** / Jan. 19, 1993 / Word ✦✦✦✦
Arguably his best album. Duncan digs deep to deal with the things he's been avoiding and turns in the best songs and vocal performances of his career. — *Thom Granger*

Slow Revival / 1994 / Myrrh ✦✦✦
Continuing with the themes spotlighted on *Mercy*, this album delivers even better lyrical expressions of the ideas. Ballad-heavy and lacking the variety of earlier work. — *Thom Granger*

My Utmost for His Highest: Quiet Prayers / Jul. 1996 / Sony ✦✦✦✦
Quiet Prayers is Bryan Duncan's installment in the *My Utmost for His Highest* series, and it ranks as one of the best, not only in the series, but in his catalog. Most of the album consists of covers of contemporary Christian songs, but there are also a couple of originals, like "When I Turn to You." No matter who wrote the song, Duncan delivers it convincingly, and his smooth, country-tinged mainstream pop style is appealingly melodic on every cut on the record. — *Rodney Batdorf*

Michael English

Vocals / Gospel, CCM
Michael English's roots are in Southern Gospel. He performed with the Singing Americans, the Goodmans, the Gaither Trio and the Gaither Vocal Band before going solo in 1991. English began drawing attention when he recorded "I Bowed on My Knees and Cried Holy," first with the Singing Americans, then with the Brooklyn Tabernacle Choir. English has won Dove Awards for best new artist and best male vocalist. — *Brian Mansfield*

● **Michael English** / 1991 / Warner Alliance ✦✦✦✦
This wildly successful debut rides the line between adult contemporary and dance-pop. But the real draw is English's eloquent voice, showcased to great effect on "Heaven" and "Solid As the Rock." — *Brian Mansfield*

Hope / 1993 / Warner Alliance ✦✦✦
English traded the sophomore slump for a scandal, as his second solo album made him even more popular, taking home the Dove Award for artist of the year in '94, only to leave gospel music a week later as a result of an extramarital affair, after which his label dropped him from its roster. — *Thom Granger*

Healing / 1995 / Curb ✦✦✦

Freedom / Jul. 1996 / Curb ✦✦✦✦
Freedom is Michael English's first purely secular effort. With its slick production and layers of synthesizers and lush guitars, the album is clearly intended to cross over to adult contemporary and easy hits radio stations. On the surface it would appear that English's stab at pop acceptance is successful. He has a pleasant voice and a winning personality, not to mention good looks. What he doesn't have on *Freedom* is a set of songs that match the standards of pop radio. Every now and then there are strong hooks—such as "Your Love Amazes Me" and "Love Has a Mind of Its Own"—but, more often, the music is bland and undistinguished, simply coasting along on its own stylish production. *Freedom* works well as pleasant background music, but there is nothing to remember once the songs are over. — *Rodney Batdorf*

Evie (Tornquist)

Vocals / Inspirational
This Norwegian singer made emphatic pop/inspirational albums in the '70s and '80s. She was the most popular woman in contemporary White gospel before the advent of Amy Grant and Sandi Patti. — *Bil Carpenter*

● **When All Is Said and Done** / 1986 / Word ✦✦✦✦
Tornquist's light voice really rocks on these mid-tempo songs of joy. — *Bil Carpenter*

Mirror / Word ✦✦✦✦

The Fairfield Four

Gospel
During the 1940s the Fairfield Four were among the top ranked gospel quartets, along with the Dixie Hummingbirds, Five Blind Boys, and the Soul Stirrers. Originally a gospel duet created in the early '20s by the pastor of Fairfield Baptist Church in Nashville to occupy his sons, Harry and Rufus Carrethers, they became a gospel trio with the addition of John Battle. The group was transformed into a jubilee quartet by the '30s and began the first of numerous personnel changes. They recorded for RCA Victor and Columbia and were known for their re-interpretation of standard hymns, featuring bright, close baritone and tenor harmonies. They moved easily from deep, rolling basslines to the staccato upper peaks of the tenor range, with precise, intricate harmonies and ever-shifting leads. They reached their broadest audience when the Sunway Vitamin Company sponsored a nationally broadcast daily radio show on WLAC, Nashville. They continued touring. It was a grueling schedule, and often the group would be missing a member or two on the show. In 1942 the quartet recorded for the Library of Congress; but by 1950 it all became too much, and coupled with some financial trouble and a dwindling radio audience, the Fairfield Four broke up, though one member, Reverend Sam McCary, used the group name to perform with other quartets. In 1980 the Fairfield Four from the '40s was reunited for a concert in Birmingham, AL, by Black gospel specialist Doug Seroff. In 1989 they were designated National Heritage Fellows by the National Endowment for the Arts. — *Sandra Brennan & Bil Carpenter*

★ **Angels Watching over Me** / 1991 / P-Vine ✦✦✦✦✦

Standing in the Safety Zone / 1992 / Warner Brothers ✦✦✦✦
The Fairfield Four were once among the finest hard gospel ensembles around. This wonderful release features awesome harmonies, a guest appearance from the Nashville Bluegrass Band on "Roll, Jordan Roll," and soaring, magnificent lead vocals from Walter Settles, Isaac Freeman, and W.L. Richardson. Old-time gospel at its best, vividly presented via contemporary technology. — *Ron Wynn*

Fairfield Four / ✦✦✦✦
Here are 33 cuts by the exciting jubilee quartet, still performing (after more than 68 years) a cappella. Contains long-out-of-print material, plus two by Joe Henderson, the group's basso in 1960. It's close harmony '50s singing at its best with the legendary Sam McCrary on "hard tenor" lead and the unbeatable Isaac "Dickie" Freeman on occasional bass lead. One of today's best traditional quartets. Very good sound quality (cassette only). — *Opal Louis Nations, Roots & Rhythm Newsletter*

One Religion / ✦✦✦
This is a prize collection of some of Fairfield Four's Dot recordings spanning the years 1951 through 1953. The group on these sides is composed of Reverend Sam McCrary—lead, Willie Love—second tenor, James Hill—baritone, and Willie Frank Lewis—bass. Some of these cuts are thought to be alternate takes of earlier Bullet recordings made during the late '40s. Classic a cappella singing reminiscent of early Spirit of Memphis material. Excellent notes by gospel researcher Tony Heilbut. — *Opal Louis Nations, Roots and Rhythm Newsletter*

Fernando

b. Ecuador
Vocals / CCM
Born in Ecuador, raised in California, Fernando began his career in the late '80s. With a rather smooth singing voice, he tends to record pop-ish urban dance music and an occasional message rap tune. He's one of the first Hispanics to make a strong presence in gospel music; however, because of his outspoken pride in his Latin heritage, he's also become a visible role model to young Hispanics (mostly of a non-traditional Protestant bent) who are increasingly beginning to listen to gospel music. — *Bil Carpenter*

● **True Love** / 1990 / Movin' Up ✦✦✦✦
This is all-English, Top 40 pop-style gospel with catchy hooks, heavy use of background vocals, and sequenced instrumentation. — *Bil Carpenter*

Latin Perspective / 1992 / Movin' Up ✦✦✦
His second album has a definite mix of urban Black music and traditional South American music styles, with a few English/Spanish cuts. — *Bil Carpenter*

The Five Blind Boys of Alabama

Black Gospel
Evolving from the Happyland Jubilee Singers, this traditional Black gospel quartet was formed in 1937 at the Talladega Institute for the Deaf and Blind in Alabama. By the '40s they had become "the Blind Boys" and recorded for Specialty, Vee-Jay, Savoy, and Elektra. Their first hit was "I Can See Everybody's Mother but Mine" in 1949. Current lineup: Joe Watson, Jimmy Carter, Sam and Bobby Butler, Curtis Foster, Johnny Fields, and Clarence Fountain. They appeared on Broadway in *Gospel at Colonus*. — *Bil Carpenter*

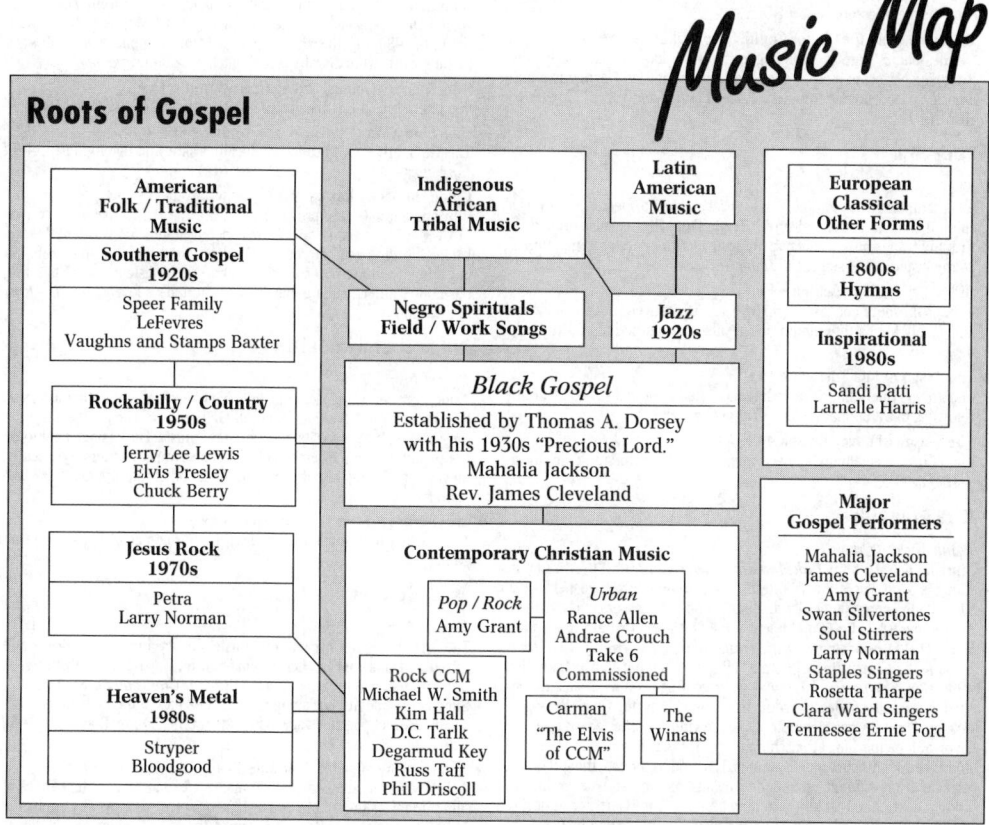

Music Map

Roots of Gospel

| American Folk / Traditional Music | Indigenous African Tribal Music | Latin American Music | European Classical Other Forms |

Southern Gospel 1920s

Speer Family
LeFevres
Vaughns and Stamps Baxter

Negro Spirituals Field / Work Songs

Jazz 1920s

1800s Hymns

Inspirational 1980s

Sandi Patti
Larnelle Harris

Rockabilly / Country 1950s

Jerry Lee Lewis
Elvis Presley
Chuck Berry

Black Gospel

Established by Thomas A. Dorsey with his 1930s "Precious Lord." Mahalia Jackson Rev. James Cleveland

Major Gospel Performers

Mahalia Jackson
James Cleveland
Amy Grant
Swan Silvertones
Soul Stirrers
Larry Norman
Staples Singers
Rosetta Tharpe
Clara Ward Singers
Tennessee Ernie Ford

Jesus Rock 1970s

Petra
Larry Norman

Contemporary Christian Music

| Pop / Rock Amy Grant | Urban Rance Allen Andrae Crouch Take 6 Commissioned |

Rock CCM
Michael W. Smith
Kim Hall
D.C. Tarlk
Degarmud Key
Russ Taff
Phil Driscoll

Carman "The Elvis of CCM"

The Winans

Heaven's Metal 1980s

Stryper
Bloodgood

★ **The Sermon** / 1953-1956 / Specialty/Fantasy ♦♦♦♦♦
The Five Blind Boys of Alabama were among the most dynamic, energetic gospel quartets to emerge during the '50s "Golden Age." Led by the exuberant Clarence Fountain, they were more open to musical experimentation than most of their contemporaries, something quite evident on this 27-track compilation featuring cuts done during the mid-'50s for Specialty. Besides Fountain's smashing voice, the set is distinguished by the contributions of four singing preachers (Paul Exkano, Samuel K. Lewis, George W. Warren, and Percell Perkins) and the insertion of jazz, Latin, and comedic elements into the musical mix. —*Ron Wynn*

The Five Blind Boys of Alabama / Gospel Heritage ♦♦♦♦
An excellent 16-track anthology, it predates their Specialty recordings by four years, with leads shared by Clarence Fountain and the legendary Paul Excano. With scholarly notes and photos, it's a must for collectors. —*Hank Davis*

● **Oh Lord Stand by Me/Marching up to Zion** / Specialty ♦♦♦♦
These superb '50s Specialty sides have hair-raising leads from Clarence Fountain, Rev. Samuel K. Lewis, and Rev. Percell Perkins. —*Hank Davis*

The Five Blind Boys of Mississippi

Black Gospel
The Five Blind Boys Of Mississippi are among the greatest singing groups in popular music history. Their smashing harmonies and the leads of Archie Brownlee influenced not only numerous gospel ensembles but such secular artists as Ray Charles. Their origins date from the '30s, when Archie Brownlee (Brownley in some accounts), Joseph Ford, Lawrence Abrams, and Lloyd Woodard formed a quartet. They were students at the Piney Woods School near Jackson, MS. They began as the Cotton Blossom Singers and did both spiritual and secular material. The quartet sang on the school grounds in 1936 and were recorded in 1937 by Alan Lomax for the Library of Congress. After graduation they decided to become professional singers and for a time performed under dual identities; they were the Cotton Blossom Singers for popular songs and the Jackson Harmoneers for gospel. They became a quintet when

Melvin Henderson joined. When Percell Perkins replaced Henderson in the mid-'40s, they became the Five Blind Boys, although Perkins, who doubled as their manager, was not blind. They made their recording debut for Excelsior in 1946, after meeting label owner Leon Rene in Cleveland. They recorded for Coleman in 1948, the same year Joseph Ford was replaced by J.T. Clinkscales. But when they joined Don Robey's Peacock label in 1950, the Five Blind Boys became superstars. The single "Our Father" was a Top Ten R&B hit, and they recorded 27 singles and five albums for Peacock through the '60s. Brownlee died in New Orleans in 1960. His riveting, chilling screams and yells were among gospel's most amazing. Perkins left the group soon after becoming a minister. The list of replacements included Revs. Samy Lewis and George Warren, as well as Tiny Powell. Roscoe Robinson took over for Brownlee, and was assisted by second lead Willmer Broadnax, who was also a masterful singer. The Five Blind Boys continued into the '90s. Woodard died in the mid-'70s, and Lawrence Abrams in 1982. But the group was still going as of 1993. *Counting on Jesus*, their most recent release, was issued on Soul-Potion Records. —*Ron Wynn*

★ **Best of the Five Blind Boys of Mississippi, Vol. 1** / 1973 / MCA ♦♦♦♦♦
These Specialty recordings represent some of the best by the greatest "quartet" ever. Featuring the wondrous Archie Brownlee. —*Kip Lornell and Ron Wynn*

My Desire/There's a God Somewhere / 1974 / Mobile Fidelity ♦♦♦
My Desire/There's a God Somewhere combines two fine albums from the Peacock vaults. The group was also known as the Original Five Blind Boys and the Jackson Harmoneers. Lead vocals by Brownlee have been known to reduce grown men to tears. Powerful material! —*Hank Davis*

Best of Five Blind Boys / Chameleon ♦♦♦♦
Here are 11 great sides recorded for Vee-Jay in the late '50s featuring the soaring lead vocals of the magnificent Archie Brownlee. —*Roots and Rhythm Newsletter*

Best of the Five Blind Boys of Mississippi, Vol. 2 / MCA ♦♦♦
More gems from this seminal ensemble. —*Ron Wynn*

Soon I'll Be Done / Chess ✦✦✦
The Chess edition, with the first sighted member, Roscoe Robinson, who shares lead work with Wilmer "Little Ax" Broadnax. It doesn't quite equal its predecessors. —*Ron Wynn*

You Done What the Doctor Couldn't Do / Jubilee ✦✦✦✦
Quintessential "hard" gospel singing from the late '40s and early '50s. Brownlee performs most of the lead chores, with vital dynamism and occasional lead singing from Rev. Percell Perkins and Vance "Tiny" Powell. —*Kip Lornell*

Four Him

CCM
A contemporary inspirational male vocal quartet formed originally as a spin-off from larger choral group Truth, Four Him is spearheaded by Kirk Sullivan, whose distinctive phrasing has influenced a generation of young inspirational singers. —*Thom Granger*

Ride / Oct. 4, 1994 / Benson ✦✦✦
Though the foursome teamed up with super-producer Michael Omartian and others for its fifth album, the results showed nothing particularly new. —*Thom Granger*

● **The Basics of Life** / Benson ✦✦✦✦
The group's breakthough recording has a title song that says it all about returning to traditional values. —*Thom Granger*

The Season of Love / Benson ✦✦✦
This Christmas album showed more musical diversity than most. —*Thom Granger*

Kirk Franklin

Piano, Vocals / Urban
Since his debut album, *Kirk Franklin and the Family* in 1993, Kirk Franklin has been one of the brightest stars in contemporary gospel music. The album spent 100 weeks topping *Billboard*'s gospel charts, crossed over to the R&B charts, and became the first gospel album to go platinum. His second album, *Kirk Franklin and the Family Christmas* became the genre's first Christmas album to make it to No. 1, and his 1996 album, *Whatcha Lookin' 4*, went gold as soon as it was distributed. It is small wonder that some have hailed him "the Garth Brooks of gospel." Franklin remains humble, eschewing the title "entertainer" in favor of labeling himself a "church boy." He is a devout Christian and does not take his success for granted. His road to the top, though quick, was far from smooth. Abandoned by his mother and never having known his father, Franklin was reared by his Aunt Gertrude, a deeply religious woman who raised him as a strict Baptist. When he was four, she paid for his piano lessons by collecting aluminum cans. Franklin is a natural musician who could sight-read and play by ear with equal facility. At age 11 he was leading the Mt. Rose Baptist Church adult choir near Dallas. Franklin began rebelling in his teens and getting into trouble until one of his friends was accidentally shot and killed at age 15. Realizing that he had chosen a bad road, Franklin returned to the fold and began composing songs, recording, and conducting. Since 1991 he has been backed up by his 17-member choir the Family, a group comprising friends and associates from his younger days. —*Sandra Brennan*

● **Kirk Franklin and the Family** / Jun. 29, 1993 / Sparrow ✦✦✦✦
Whatcha Lookin' 4 / 1995 / Gospo Centric ✦✦✦

Rev. C. L. Franklin

Vocals / Black Gospel
The pastor of Detroit's Bethel Baptist Church, a confidant of Martin Luther King Jr., and father of Aretha Franklin, this charismatic preacher is known for "hair-raising" sermons. —*Bil Carpenter*

23rd Psalm / 1976 / Jewel ✦✦✦✦
Both a performance and a lesson, this improvised and yet tightly structured sermon weaves its message around and between the words of possibly the best-known passage in the Bible. Tremendously moving—if you're into qawwali or kriti, you ought to listen to this, even if you don't care that it's an example of the US' leading form of oral literature. —*Carl Hoyt, Original Music*

● **Give Me This Mountain** / ✦✦✦✦
The African-American sermon has been little written about, and then usually ponderously. Jeff Todd Titon breaks the mold with a collection of annotated sermons and biographical notes about one of the greatest of preachers. Note: most of Franklin's recorded sermons are out of print, and all are very rare. —*John Storm Roberts, Original Music*

The Eagle Stirreth in Her Nest / Jewel ✦✦✦✦
This wrenching, sweaty, hellfire sermon was recorded for Joe Von Battle in the mid-'50s. —*Bil Carpenter*

Billy and Sarah Gaines

CCM
A husband/wife duo who met while students on the Virginia Commonwealth University campus, they sang with the CCM group Living Sacrifice until 1980. Together they sing in CCM/inspirational style. Billy's is a mellow voice, while Sarah's is high-pitched. —*Bil Carpenter*

Billy & Sarah Gaines / 1986 / Heartwarming ✦✦✦
Pop praise music, this also features stirring ballads. —*Bil Carpenter*

● **He'll Find a Way** / 1988 / Heartwarming ✦✦✦✦
This R&B, urban CCM collection includes slow and uptempo cuts. —*Bil Carpenter*

Come On Back / Jun. 25, 1996 / Warner Brothers ✦✦✦✦
Billy and Sarah Gaines prove why they are one of the most popular duos in CCM with *Come On Back*, their debut album for Warner Alliance. Under the direction of producer Michael Omartian, the duo crafts an engaging, soothing pop sound that charms the listener with its lilting harmonies and cascading melodies. In short, it's a lovely album. —*Rodney Batdorf*

Bill and Gloria Gaither

Gospel, Inspirational
Aside from recording as a duo, they have recorded with other artists as the Gaither Vocal Band and the Bill Gaither Trio. The Gaithers are the most successful songwriters in Christian music. Their songs tend to be praise- and worship-oriented but often cross music barriers stylistically; however, their most significant material is contemporary pop. —*Bil Carpenter*

● **Live Across America** / 1980 / Word ✦✦✦✦
This fine live double album includes their '70s pop-gospel hits. —*Bil Carpenter*

M. C. Ge Gee

Vocals / Christian Rap
The first female in Christian rap music, she was born in the Bronx and raised in Dallas, where her parents run an inner-city youth outreach program that was the subject of the film *The Cross and the Switchblade*. She's neither a hard nor a pop rapper. She's picked up the serious issue-oriented street-poetry legacy of her late brother, D-Boy Rodriguez. —*Bil Carpenter*

● **And Now the Mission Continues** / 1991 / Frontline ✦✦✦✦
A Tim Miner production of midrange rap. Urban funk with spare sampling. Most of the album is message-oriented, such as "I Caught the Mike," a pickup of D-Boy's "I Dropped the Mike," which speaks to the continuance of his ministry to youth. —*Bil Carpenter*

Jon Gibson

b. Apr. 27, 1940
Vocals
Blue-eyed soulster Jon Gibson's instincts and songwriting made his too-close-for-comfort Stevie Wonder-like vocals worth tolerating. His later albums are the better, as Gibson evolved into a vocal style more his own. The songs and production are improved as well. —*Thom Granger*

Body and Soul / 1989 / Frontline ✦✦✦
Included is a remake of mentor Wonder's "Have a Talk with God," featuring Stevie's own harmonica on the solo. —*Thom Granger*

Jesus Loves Ya / 1990 / Frontline ✦✦✦
A solid outing, it features hits like "Love Come Down" and the title cut. —*Thom Granger*

● **Hits** / 1991 / Frontline ✦✦✦✦
A good place to start with Gibson, it features most of his hits, a Scott Blackwell remix of "Jesus Loves Ya," and a new Christmas song. —*Thom Granger*

Forever Friends / 1992 / Frontline ✦✦✦
More slammin' blue-eyed soul comes from the still less-than-well-known stylist. —*Thom Granger*

Change of Heart / Frontline ✦✦✦
Featured is a remake of James Ingram's "Yah Mo B There" and a duet with MC Hammer on "The Wall." —*Thom Granger*

Golden Eagle Gospel Singers

Black Gospel
An Alabamian a cappella outfit that later developed roots in Chicago, the Golden Eagles were formed in the '30s by Thelma Byrd. On a level with the Golden Gate Quartet, their popularity was strongest in the Midwest. Unlike other groups of the time, who were usually male and Baptist, this one was coed and Sanctified. Much of their music had a fast-paced blues feel, most notably on 1937's "Tone the Bell" and 1940's

"He's My Rock," which showcased Hammie Nixon on blues harmonica. They recorded for Decca. —*Bil Carpenter*

● **Complete Recordings 1937-1940** / ✦✦✦✦
The Golden Eagle Gospel Singers / Eden ✦✦✦✦
These are gems from the three Chicago sessions (ca. 1937-1940) of this important mixed ten-member aggregation led by Thelma Byrd and supported at times by Hammie Nixon. —*Opal Louis Nations*

Golden Gate Quartet

Black Gospel
Pioneer Virginia gospel/pop quartet of the '30s and '40s. Calling their innovative approach to sacred hymns "jubilee" singing, the Golden Gate Quartet, propelled by Willie Johnson and William Langford, enjoyed massive acceptance outside the church. Their smooth Mills Brothers-influenced harmonies made the Gates naturals for pop crossover success, and they began recording for Victor in 1937. National radio broadcasts and an appearance on John Hammond's 1938 "Spirituals to Swing" concert at Carnegie Hall made them coast-to-coast favorites. By 1941 the Gates were recording for Columbia minus Langford, and movie appearances were frequent:, including *Star Spangled Rhythm*, *Hollywood Canteen*, and *Hit Parade of 1943*. Experiments during the late '40s with R&B didn't pan out, and Johnson defected to the Jubilaires in 1948. The group emigrated to France in 1959; led by veteran bass singer Orlando Wilson, the Golden Gate Quartet's vocal blend is as powerful as ever. —*Bill Dahl*

Travelin' Shoes / Sep. 1992 / Bluebird ✦✦✦✦

★ **35 Historic Recordings** / RCA ✦✦✦✦✦
These breathtaking sides from 1937-1939 are largely a cappella, with both gospel and pop music. The album includes a landmark version of "Stormy Weather" that is at the root of doo wop. —*Hank Davis*

Nobody Knows / Ibach ✦✦✦✦
Another adequate recording by this once-mighty group. —*Kip Lornell*

Spirituals to Swing / Jazz Time ✦✦✦✦
An inspired effort, recorded between 1955 and 1969. —*Kip Lornell*

☆ **Swing Down, Chariot** / Columbia/Legacy ✦✦✦✦✦
The most influential jubilee quartet of the late '30s and '40s, in inspired and deftly syncopated performances. —*Mark A. Humphrey*

The Golden Gate Quartet / Carrere ✦✦✦
Recent recordings of familiar spirituals ("Shadrack," "Joshua Fit the Battle of Jericho," "Amen," "Glory Glory Hallelujah") are mixed in with a predominantly pop repertoire ("Blue Suede Shoes," "The Great Pretender," "Only You," "Frankie and Johnny"). Eighteen tunes from this latter-day incarnation of the influential gospel group. —*Roots & Rhythm Newsletter*

The Happy Goodman Family

Southern Gospel
For nearly four decades the Happy Goodman Family brightened the world with their gospel songs. They were founded in Alabama in the 1940s by Howard and Gussie Goodman. Over the years they expanded and changed membership until finally becoming a quartet composed of Ruth, Sam, Rusty, and Bob Goodman. They were joined by Vestal Goodman and the only non-Goodman, tenor Johnny Cook. The family was most successful during the '60s and '70s. In 1968 their album *The Happy Gospel of the Happy Goodmans* won a Grammy for best gospel album. The next year Vestal received a Dove Award for female vocalist of the year. The Happy Goodmans were some of the first members of the TV show "The Gospel Singing Jubilee," which won numerous Dove awards. —*Sandra Brennan*

● **Greatest Hits** / 1985 / Canaan ✦✦✦✦
A live recording of the Goodman Family's country gospel. —*Bil Carpenter*

The Gospel Harmonettes

Black Gospel
A recently formed female a cappella harmony group from central Alabama, the Gospel Harmonettes have strong roots in the Baptist Church and Jefferson County singing tradition. —*Kip Lornell*

● **Camp Meeting** / 1993 / Vee-Jay ✦✦✦✦
The link between gospel music and the civil rights era has never been clearer than on the two albums that comprise this CD reissue. Both issued in the mid-'60s, the rough-hewn, earthy, bluesy voice of Dorothy "Love" Coates and her inspirational songs were tailor-made to elevate the spirits of those fighting for social justice. Numbers like "Camp Meeting," "I Won't Let Go," "The Righteous On The March," and "Step By Step" don't have overt political lyrics but certainly speak to the victories anticipated by civil rights workers. There's also plenty of more traditional spiritual material, sung with passionate belief. —*Ron Wynn*

Gospel Hummingbirds

The Gospel Hummingbirds play a combination of traditional (in a style similar to the Swan Silvertones, one of the Hummer's chief inspirations) and modern electrified blues and soul-injected gospel and for the past couple of decades have performed at religious gatherings, nightclubs, rock concerts, and blues festivals. Regardless of where they perform, their joyful praises to God remain the same. The Oakland-based group has been together since the 1970s and was founded by the father of lead vocalist and bass guitar player Joe A. Thomas, who began playing bass with the Hummingbirds when he was only eight. As of 1995, the rest of the lineup included Roy Tyler, Clarence Nichols, James Gibson, Jr., and Mark Smith, Sr. —*Sandra Brennan*

● **Steppin' Out** / 1992 / Blind Pig ✦✦✦✦
Taking Flight / Nov. 1995 / Blind Pig ✦✦✦

Amy Grant

b. Nov. 25, 1960, Augusta, GA
Vocals / CCM, Adult Contemporary, Pop
Amy Grant is not only one of the most influential singers in contemporary Christian music, but also a successful pop star. She was born in Nashville, the youngest of four children. She released her self-titled debut album at age 15 after signing with Myrrh/Word Records in 1979. In 1982 she married singer-songwriter Gary Chapman, who was to become her co-writer by the late 1980s. Grant became a bona fide gospel star in 1982 after the release of *Age to Age*, which won her a Grammy for best female gospel performance and three Dove Awards, including artist of the year. In 1984 she released a Christmas album and *Straight Ahead*, which won Grant another Dove award. One cut from the album, "Angels," which she co-wrote, won her another Grammy. In 1985, *Age to Age* was certified platinum, and her other two albums went gold. Her 1985 album, *Unguarded*, soon followed suit and won her a Grammy. Grant caused an uproar amongst her loyal gospel audience with this album, which sported two successful pop crossover singles, "Find a Way" and "Wise Up." A year later she made it to No. 1 on the pop charts with "The Next Time I Fall," a duet with Peter Cetera. Throughout the '80s Grant's albums went gold and platinum and won awards. She signed with A&M in 1990 and began focusing less on her squeaky clean gospel singer persona, trying to project a more contemporary, sexy (albeit in a wholesome way) pop image. In 1991 she had three big hit singles on the pop charts: the number one "Baby Baby," "Every Heartbeat," and "That's What Love Is For." By the end of the year the album had gone double platinum and continued to be a big seller. Grant frequently donates her time to humanitarian efforts and has received honors from the American Cancer Society, the State of Tennessee, the Nashville Chamber of Commerce, and St. John's University, which gave her its Pax Christi Award. —*Sandra Brennan*

Unguarded / 1985 / Reunion ✦✦✦
The artist's first foray into crossover featured dance-pop music, and yielded a Top 20 hit, "Find a Way." —*Thom Granger*

The Collection / 1986 / Reunion ✦✦✦✦
This early gospel hits package includes "El Shaddai." —*Bil Carpenter*

Lead Me On / 1989 / A&M ✦✦✦✦
Grant's best album, all things considered, is a mature statement of faith that digs deeper than most of the genre, with songs that remain relevant. —*Thom Granger*

● **Heart in Motion** / 1991 / A&M ✦✦✦✦
Her mainstream multi-platinum breakthrough, a pure pop treat that yielded a handful of hits and established her as a pop star in the general market. Not a gospel album, but the album's closer, "Hope Set High," left the cards face up on the table. —*Thom Granger*

House of Love / 1994 / A&M ✦✦✦
After a duo of detours (a youth worship record and a second Christmas offering), Grant returns with an album that doesn't even pretend to be gospel, but still reflects her ideologies. Mellower than *Heart in Motion*, the album sounds more like *Lead Me On*, but doesn't plumb its depths. —*Thom Granger*

Keith Green

d. Jun. 1982
Piano, Vocals / Inspirational
Green founded Last Days Ministries with his wife, Melody, in the late '70s. A reformer trying to purge the church of unbiblical habits, his music was lyrically a mix of Jesus Movement protest and 19th-century evangelistic writings. He died in a plane crash in 1982. —*Bil Carpenter*

● **The Ministry Years, Vol. 1** / 1987 / Sparrow ✦✦✦✦
Green makes the piano keys sing. —*Bil Carpenter*

The Ministry Years, Vol. 2 / 1988 / Sparrow ✦✦✦
Theological questioning and stirring MOR. —*Bil Carpenter*

No Compromise / 1990 / Sparrow ◆◆◆◆
Green tackles controversial doctrinal issues and still makes you want to listen. — *Thom Grainger*

For Him Who Has Ears to Hear / 1991 / Sparrow ◆◆◆◆
The debut of a major songwriter in Christian music. — *Thom Grainger*

The Harmonizing Four

Black Gospel
The Richmond, VA-based Harmonizing Four were an offbeat but innovative gospel quartet who were most popular during the '40s and '50s but performed through the 1970s. Between 1929 and 1957 the Four were best known for their singing jubilee style; but after signing with Vee-Jay records in 1957, they began to establish a reputation for extraordinarily close harmonies and a smooth mellow sound. Whereas most male-gospel quartets were led by tenors or baritones, the Harmonizing Four often spotlighted basso profundo Jimmy Jones, who possessed one of the deepest voices ever heard in gospel. (Jones' rendition of "Motherless Child" with the haunting, crooning three in the background is guaranteed to raise goosebumps.) Though the Harmonizing Four recorded prolifically, little is known about the group's formation and early history, because the group's leader and manager, Joseph "Gospel Joe" Williams, forbade any of the group members to discuss the group unless they were paid in advance. It is known that they made their debut at a grammar school in South Richmond on October 27, 1927. Charter members included Levi Handly and Thomas "Goat' Johnson. Williams joined in 1933, and in 1941 guitarist/vocalist Lonnie Smith rounded out the group. They began recording for Decca in 1943, and it is believed that Sister Rosetta Tharpe connected them with the label. The Harmonizing Four subsequently appeared on some of Tharpe's albums and sang at her enormous gospel wedding in the early '50s. In the late '50s, the Four recorded for the Newark-based Coleman label. They then did a stint with Philly-located Gotham until 1952. After their time with Vee-Jay in the late '50s, the Harmonizing Four recorded for Nashboro. — *Sandra Brennan*

The Best of the Harmonizing Four / Capitol ◆◆◆
Featured is the bass voice of Ellis Johnson or the legendary Jimmy Jones. — *Opal Louis Nations*

★ **Gospel in My Soul** / Chameleon ◆◆◆◆◆
This truly fine collection of 11 close-quartet gospel songs is from Vee-Jay sessions conducted during the late '50s and issued on a Vee-Jay LP in the early '60s. This is one of the few worthwhile Vee-Jay quartet albums that has never been reissued over the ensuing years. The Richmond group is led here by Thomas Johnson (first tenor) and his son Ellis Johnson (bass). Other members of long standing include Lonnie Smith and Joe Williams. An excellent collection. — *Opal Louis Nations, Roots and Rhythm Newsletter*

Child of a King / Peacock ◆◆◆
Includes "Nobody Knows" and the original gospel cut of "Stand by Me," later popularized by Ben E. King. — *Bil Carpenter*

Larnelle Harris

Percussion, Saxophone, Vocals / Inspirational
This singer, saxophonist, and percussionist was at one time a member of the Spurrlows, First Gear, and the Gaither Vocal Band gospel groups. — *Bil Carpenter*

From a Servant's Heart / 1987 / Heartwarming ◆◆◆
Inspirational best. — *Bil Carpenter*

The Father Hath Provided / 1988 / Heartwarming ◆◆◆◆
Signs of pop progression with a little soul. — *Bil Carpenter*

● **The Best of 10 Years, Vol. 1** / 1991 / Benson ◆◆◆◆
Few performers have powerful enough voices to overwhelm the pseudo-orchestral arrangements of modern inspirational music; Harris does. With *Volume 2*, this provides an excellent overview of the singer's work. — *Brian Mansfield*

The Best of 10 Years, Vol. 2 / 1991 / Benson ◆◆◆◆
This gets the edge over *Volume One* because it has the soulful "Friends in High Places" and "I Can Begin Again" from 1989's *I Can Begin Again* album. — *Brian Mansfield*

Unbelievable Love / Oct. 1995 / Benson ◆◆◆
Unbelievable Love is another typically solid album from Larnelle Harris. The record ranges from slow groove R&B and Motown to ska and sweeping ballads. Throughout the album, Harris turns in a fine performance, proving why he has sustained his popularity over the course of two decades. — *Sara Sytsma*

The Edwin Hawkins Singers

Gospel
Through his mass choir worship seminars, Edwin Hawkins has kept tra-

ditional Black gospel styles in vogue, particularly among youth. — *Bil Carpenter*

Oh Happy Day / 1969 / Pair ◆◆◆◆
A classic traditional Black gospel recording from 1969. — *Bil Carpenter*

● **The Best of the Edwin Hawkins Singers** / 1985 / Savoy ◆◆◆◆
After becoming the Edwin Hawkins Singers, the group became crossover sensations when their single "Oh Happy Day" cracked the Top Ten on both the pop and R&B charts in 1969, peaking at No. 2 R&B (No. 4 pop). It was their biggest hit and one of the seminal tunes in contemporary gospel history. This collection features other successful Hawkins family numbers. Dorothy Morrison later went on to a solo career. — *Ron Wynn*

Face to Face / 1989 / Lection ◆◆◆
Contemporary, with a spiritual mass choir sound. — *Bil Carpenter*

Tramaine Hawkins

Vocals / Soul, Urban, Black Gospel
Born Tramaine Davis in San Francisco and raised in Berkeley, Tramaine Hawkins is the granddaughter of Bishop E. E. Cleveland, one of the founders of the Church of God in Christ Church, the largest Black Pentecostal organization in the US. She got her start as a teenager, performing in 1968 with the Edwin Hawkins Singers during the homemade recording session that produced the crossover smash "Oh Happy Day," the biggest selling gospel single to date. In the early '70s she married Walter Hawkins, Edwin's brother. He went on to lead the Berkeley Love Center Church of God in Christ Church. There she sang lead soprano with her husband's Love Center Choir and appeared on the *Love Alive* album, a recorded Sunday session featuring her husband's sermon, Edwin on piano, and Hawkins on lead vocals. It and the followup, *Love Alive II*, were both best-sellers.

Hawkins began her solo recording career in the mid-'80s. She draws from a variety of genres, and her albums demonstrate that she is as much at home shouting traditional tunes as she is belting out the blues, crooning silky-smooth soul numbers, or even delivering hard-driving urban funk. Her tendency to use popular music has caused controversy amongst conservative saints and even caused some to question her faith, but a close listen to her music demonstrates that even though her music has "crossed-over," her faith and good intentions are rock-solid. — *Sandra Brennan*

● **The Joy That Floods My Soul** / 1988 / Sparrow ◆◆◆◆
Tramaine Hawkins has sometimes drawn fire from conservative types for being too risky and experimental in her work . . . There shouldn't be any such worries with *The Joy That Floods My Soul*. The mood is more restrained, the arrangements less linked to prominent, driving backbeats, and Hawkins' rising, glorious soprano is assisted by swirling voices and a soulful choir rather than a barrage of synthesizers and blaring guitars. — *Ron Wynn*

The Search Is Over / 1989 / Word ◆◆◆
Urban-funk/R&B, crossover gospel. — *Bil Carpenter*

Tramaine Hawkins Live / 1990 / Sparrow ◆◆◆◆
Traditional Black gospel belting. — *Bil Carpenter*

Mark Heard

Guitar, Vocals / Folk
Mark Heard was a brilliant, poetic singer-songwriter whose work displayed a deep spirituality and honesty uncommon in CCM. Heard died in 1992 of heart failure; *High Noon* recaps the best material of his last three albums. — *Thom Granger*

Stop the Dominoes / 1981 / Home Sweet Home ◆◆◆
More straight rock 'n' roll than his later efforts, it also has more obviously Christian-oriented songs. — *Richard Meyer*

Dry Bones Dance / 1990 / Fingerprint ◆◆◆◆
Includes the great "House of Broken Dreams," the rockin' "Rise from the Ruins," and "Lonely Road." This great acoustic album is very forceful but never forced. Each song has drive and committed vocals. — *Richard Meyer*

Second Hand / 1991 / Fingerprint ◆◆◆◆
On this album Heard has adopted a more contemporary electric sound. His songs keep getting stronger. Key tracks are "Nod over Coffee," "Love Is not the Only Thing," and "Look over Your Shoulder." Highly recommended. — *Richard Meyer*

Satellite Sky / 1992 / Fingerprint ◆◆◆
Mark Heard has gone into overdrive on this, his third Fingerprint CD. Most songs are arranged around his electrified metal-bodied mandolin. The personal spiritual message is still here in full force, but the songs stand up well. "Tip of My Tongue," "Love Is So Blind," and "Satellite Sky" are key tracks. — *Richard Meyer*

● **High Noon** / 1993 / Myrrh ✦✦✦✦
Excellent collection of tracks selected from Heard's last three recordings, all of which were exemplary. —*Thom Granger*

Reflections of a Former Life / 1994 / Home Sweet Home ✦✦✦
The only way to get even a smattering of Heard's early recordings for Home Sweet Home is this CD collection, unmercifully brief and hardly a substitute for the real things. —*Thom Granger*

Highway QCs

Black Gospel
This quartet was started in the '40s. Over the years, the lead singers have included Sam Cooke, Johnnie Taylor, Willie Rogers, and Spencer Taylor. —*Bil Carpenter*

● **Jesus Is Waiting** / Vee-Jay ✦✦✦✦
The Highway QCs were considered gospel's greatest farm team, the place where aspiring quartet lead singers would hone their skills before joining an "A-list" group. But that doesn't mean the group made inferior music; the songs on *Jesus Is Waiting*, a single-disc collection combining two albums they cut in the mid-'50s and early '60s, can stand with any issued by the better name ensembles. A youthful Johnnie Taylor soars, whoops, and moans through songs done from 1955-1957, while Spencer Taylor comes on with equal might and ferocity on the later material. They may not have had the reputations or kept their members as long, but at times the Highway QCs made music that resounded with as much fury as anyone on the gospel trail. —*Ron Wynn*

The Best of the Highway [QCS] / Chameleon ✦✦✦✦
A respectable collection for the group that acted as a feeder for the Soul Stirrers and other first-echelon groups. Prior editions included Johnnie Taylor and the unrecorded Sam Cooke and O. V. Wright. —*Ron Wynn*

The Lord Is Sweet / Peacock ✦✦✦
Includes "Changes at the End" and "Rock Me." —*Bil Carpenter*

Kim Hill

Guitar, Vocals / CCM, Folk-Rock
This Mississippi guitarist with a folk-rock style akin to James Taylor and Suzanne Vega has a sturdy, low-alto vocal style. —*Bil Carpenter*

Kim Hill / 1982 / Reunion ✦✦✦✦
Semi-philosophical mid-tempo worship songs. —*Bil Carpenter*

Brave Heart / 1991 / Reunion ✦✦✦

Talk About Life / Jun. 1993 / Reunion ✦✦✦
Honest looks at life crises in an acoustic setting. —*Bil Carpenter*

● **So Far So Good** / May 24, 1994 / BNA ✦✦✦✦
Hill's first foray into country is of the more current pop/folk- flavored approach, featuring many contemporary Christian musicans on the project. —*Thom Granger*

Testimony / 1995 / Reunion/BMG ✦✦✦

Dallas Holm

Vocals / Inspirational
Holm is a singer and songwriter. In spite of a restrained, undistinctive, flat vocal style, Holm convincingly brings life to ballads such as his signature song, "Rise Again." —*Bil Carpenter*

Beyond the Curtain / 1988 / Dayspring ✦✦✦✦
Inspirational reworking of "Rise Again." —*Bil Carpenter*

● **The Early Works: Best of Dallas Holm** / Benson ✦✦✦✦
Adult contemporary pop. This album collects the finer moments of Holmes' first period. —*Bil Carpenter*

The Imperials

Inspirational
The Imperials have been making music since 1964 and have in that time undergone many personnel and stylistic changes before returning to the close harmonies and straight Southern gospel songs that originally made them popular. As of the mid-'90s, Armond Morales is the only remaining charter member of the Imperials. It was he and Jake Hess who founded the quintet. Over the years 18 different singers have come and gone, including such legendary singers as Russ Taff, Paul Smith, and Gary McSpadden. Other CCM pop performers such as Jonathan Pierce also got their start with the Imperials.
The Imperials have released more than 40 albums and had 14 No.1 songs. They have also won four Grammy awards and 13 Dove awards, making the Imperials, despite (or because of) their many style changes, one of the most popular Christian bands ever. But in 1987 they stirred up controversy and lost many of their oldest fans when they adopted a harder rock/techno pop sound on *This Year's Model*. *Stir It Up* and *Love's Still Changing Hearts* continued in the same vein. Morales considers those albums part of an identity crisis for the band. They lost

touch with their original direction and purpose, which was to sing joyful music and minister to the church. The Imperials reverted to that mission when Morales brought two ordained ministers, Steve Ferguson and Jeff Walker, on board. Neither had experience in mainstream Christian music, and they were more interested in spreading the word than selling albums.
The Imperials have scaled down their act, opting for simple accompaniment and church performances in lieu of stadium and large concert gigs. Albums such as *Til' He Comes* have lost the hard edge of earlier albums, and slowly their old fans are starting to return. —*Sandra Brennan*

Big God / 1991 / Star Song ✦✦✦
Synthesizers and electric guitars—their hippest date yet. —*Bil Carpenter*

● **The Very Best of the Imperials** / Word ✦✦✦✦
Contemporary pop from the '70s and '80s. —*Bil Carpenter*

Mahalia Jackson

b. Oct. 1911, New Orleans, LA, **d.** Jan. 27, 1972, Chicago, IL
Vocals / Blues, Black Gospel
With her inimitable, expressive contralto, Mahalia Jackson was the Queen Mother of gospel music. Over her 40-year career, she was responsible not only for influencing countless gospel singers but for introducing White audiences to the beauty, joy, and power of Black gospel music.
Jackson was born in a moderately poor area of New Orleans, the daughter of Johnny Jackson, Jr. and Charity Clark. Though she remained a devout Baptist all her life, Jackson was heavily influenced by the rhythmic, joyful music emanating from the sanctified church near their home. She made her debut at age four singing "Jesus Loves Me" in front of a congregation at the Plymouth Rock Baptist Church. Even then she showed rare talent and control. When she got a little older, Jackson joined a junior choir. Though she sang Baptist hymns, she began to infuse them with a little of the sanctified shouting she'd heard so often at home; and it was from the Holy Rollers that she got her idiosyncratic sense of timing. Her other major influences were Bessie Smith and the great Ma Rainey, who inspired the distinctive blue notes found in many of Mahalia Jackson's songs. In 1927, when she was 16 years old, Jackson dropped out of the eighth grade and moved to Chicago.
The Sunday after she arrived, Jackson attended the Greater Salem Baptist Church. Finding the service moving, she spontaneously rose up to sing her favorite hymn, "Hand Me Down My Silver Trumpet, Gabriel." She was asked to join the choir, and a few months later she became a lead singer. When not in church, she worked as a domestic and as a laundress until she became a charter member of the Johnson Gospel Singers, a group founded by the pastor's son, Robert Johnson. After a rocky debut—Pastor Johnson was outraged by the provocative movements Jackson unconsciously employed while cutting loose on her solos—the group became popular and then branched out, performing throughout the city. The Johnson Singers are said to be the first organized gospel group to work professionally. Robert Johnson even wrote and staged plays starring himself and Jackson. The Johnsons remained together through the early '30s; after their breakup Jackson began her solo career singing in church and at political rallies and began to build a strong following throughout the Midwest.
Thanks to Dr. Frank J. Hawkins, a prominent deacon in her church, Jackson met Ink Williams, an important record producer and repertoire director of the Race Division at Decca Records. In 1937 she and her accompanist, Esthete Allen, recorded four singles for Decca and Jackson became the first gospel singer to record on that label. Her first release was "God's Gonna Separate the Wheat from the Tare," a lively adaptation of an old Southern wake song. On two of those singles, "God Shall Wipe All Tears Away" and "Keep Me Every Day," Jackson had Allen play an organ, thus making her the first gospel artist to use one on a recording. Unfortunately, none of her early recordings were more than perfunctorily promoted. Earlier that year Jackson had also agreed to become a demo singer for composer Thomas A. Dorsey. Jackson began touring the Midwest. To augment her income, she borrowed a few recipes for cosmetics from her former mother-in-law, a beautician, and began making and selling her own. She then attended the Scott Institute of Beauty Culture and opened the tiny Mahalia's Beauty Shop.
In 1946 she warily took a crack at recording for Apollo. Once again, her first four singles did not make much of an impression, and the label owner, Bess Berman, considered dropping Jackson until producer Art Freeman convinced her to give Jackson one final try. Freeman had Jackson record "Move On Up a Little Longer," a song he had overheard her singing during a warm-up session. Released in 1948, the tune sold over a million copies and was the biggest gospel record of its time. That year she was further honored by being designated the first "official" soloist of the National Baptist Convention. She began appearing on Chicago journalist Studs Terkel's local television show in 1951; and in 1952, after the success of her Apollo record "I Can Put My Trust in Jesus" that won her a prize at the French Academy, she embarked upon a European concert

tour. The Europeans adored her and hailed her as one of the greatest singers in North America.

In 1954 CBS radio contracted Jackson to host and perform on a nationally broadcast Sunday night program. With Mildred Falls on piano, organist Ralph Jones, and the lily white Jack Halloran Quartet for backup, Jackson became the first African-American gospel artist to gain a major following with White audiences. Both that program and a subsequent television show were very successful, but she ended up getting cancelled when sponsors became leery of backing the show after Jackson, during a particularly powerful performance, jubilantly exclaimed "Glory!" Later that year she signed to Columbia Records. Now under control by a major label, Jackson was no longer allowed to sing the brilliant improvisations, intricate variations, and delicate interplay between her and her accompanist that made her a star. Instead she was saddled with strict time constraints and asked to sing mainstream, pop-flavored variations on standard hymns and spirituals, often backed by a full band or choir, in addition to her simpler, freer hard-gospel numbers, which are still considered among her finest. Still, while purists derided her for crossing over, Jackson sang beautifully; and her popularity soared with such chestnuts as "Rusty Old Halo" and "The Lord Is a Busy Man." She debuted on the "Ed Sullivan Show" in 1956 and received a standing ovation. In 1958 she made a huge splash at the Newport Jazz Festival. She went on to record with such artists as Percy Faith, Duke Ellington, and even Harpo Marx. Meanwhile rival performers and old-time fans continued to shake their heads, believing that commercialization had quenched the fire that had been Mahalia. Fortunately, she occasionally performed with other gospel singers and proved them dead wrong.

In 1960 Jackson sang at President Kennedy's inauguration. A little later she became close friends with Dr. Martin Luther King. It was she who brought him to Chicago and she who sang the opening hymn, "I've Been Buked and I've Been Scorned" before his history-making speech on the day of the 1963 March on Washington. During these years, Jackson was active in community politics, a spokesperson for African-American rights, and was known for generously helping up-and-coming gospel singers and funding the educations of under-privileged Blacks. The assassination of Martin Luther King devastated her, and she backed out of politics.

She married again in 1965 and, subsequently, an ugly divorce caused a major scandal that damaged her image. She then suffered several minor heart attacks and rapidly lost 100 pounds. In the late '60s she remarried her second ex-husband, and continued touring; she gave her farewell concert in Germany in 1971. When she died in 1972, there were two funerals: an enormous, nationally publicized one in Chicago attended by most of gospel's legends and featuring farewell songs by J. Robert Bradley, Robert Anderson, and Aretha Franklin; and one in New Orleans, where she was buried. —*Sandra Brennan*

In the Upper Room / 1965 / Vogue ✦✦✦✦

Sings America's Favorite Hymns / 1977 / Columbia ✦✦✦
Another cross-section of Jackson's '50s and '60s work. —*Kip Lornell*

★ **Gospels, Spirituals and Hymns** / 1991 / Columbia/Legacy ✦✦✦✦✦
With a wonderful booklet, this is the best sampling of '50s and '60s work. —*Kip Lornell*

☆ **Mahalia Jackson, Vol. 2** / Jul. 28, 1992 / Columbia/Legacy ✦✦✦✦✦
With its excellent sound and liner notes, the second box set of Mahalia Jackson's Columbia recordings is just as essential as the first. —*AMG*

Go Tell It on the Mountain / 1993 / Arrival ✦✦✦
This disc features ten of the original Apollo tracks by the great Mahalia Jackson. In addition to the title track, the disc includes "Nobody Knows," "Just As I Am," and "Amazing Grace." If you like gospel music, this is the real thing! —*Jim Worbois*

☆ **Live at Newport** / 1994 / Sony ✦✦✦✦✦

Amazing Grace / Sony ✦✦✦✦
A nice sampling of Jackson's later recordings. —*Kip Lornell*

Live in Antibes / French Concerts ✦✦✦
A nice concert performance from late in her career. —*Kip Lornell*

Les Plus Grands Themes / ✦✦✦
It's a joy to hear Mahalia Jackson's early-'50s Apollo sides in good, clean digitalized stereo. The quality here is better than all previous reissue material. Soaring and sometimes graceful vocal dynamics by this great diva of gospel and spirituals, but there's a shameful lack of pictures and book notes. This is 18 of the best. —*Opal Louis Nations, Roots and Rhythm Newsletter*

Jacob's Trouble

CCM, Pop-Rock
A Georgia-based band, they're influenced by '60s pop (Beatles, Byrds, Monkees) and Christian alternative mentor Terry Taylor, who also produced the band's first two records. —*Thom Granger*

● **Let the Truth Run Wild** / 1992 / Alarma ✦✦✦✦
Produced by the late Mark Heard. —*Thom Granger*

Jacob's Trouble / 1993 / Alarma ✦✦✦
Its first self-produced effort was an attempt to forge a more original style. —*Thom Granger*

Diggin' Up Bones / 1994 / Alarma ✦✦✦
A collection of outtakes, demos, and covers. —*Thom Granger*

Brother Vernard Johnson

Saxophone / Gospel, Jazz, Inspirational
This saxophonist earned a doctorate in musicology from Southwestern Baptist Theological Seminary in 1982. Influenced by R&B sax man King Curtis, he played in a Kansas City jazz group. Now he plays only gospel-oriented music, touring with a 13-member combo. —*Bil Carpenter*

I'm Alive! / 1991 / Nonesuch ✦✦✦
Contains some good sax solos, derivative arrangements, timid percussion. —*Ron Wynn*

● **I'm Alive** / American Explorer ✦✦✦✦
One big collective kudo to Nonesuch's classy *American Explorer* series for managing to bring out the absolute best in five wonderful musicians. In the cases of Chuck Berry pianist/mentor Johnnie Johnson, rockabilly Charlie Feathers, and gospel saxophonist Vernard Johnson, you also find yourself grateful that a label would slip the elastic off its bankroll long enough to record these guys this way—anyone who's ever heard them knows it was overdue. Boozoo Chavis' album is a surprise because it's so much stronger than both his early novelties and the boozy monotony that overwhelms some of his live gigs. And Texan songwriter Jimmie Dale Gilmore's *After Awhile* is his best work ever. Any one and perhaps all of these fine records deserve to be on a best-of-1991 list. —*Roundup Newsletter*

Phil Keaggy

Guitar / Folk, Pop-Rock
Phil Keaggy is an all-around excellent guitarist who has been a part of the CCM scene formore than two decades. Born and raised in Ohio into a Catholic family of ten, Keaggy loved music and spent hours listening to such singers as Johnny Ray and Elvis Presley. He began imitating the latter as young as age four. Keaggy was also exposed to other kinds of music and became well-versed in classical. His first guitar was a late '50s Gretsch Anniversary model. His father bought him a Sears Silvertone when Phil was ten, and by the end of fifth grade he was playing in front of his entire school. Three years later Keaggy was playing professionally with the Squires. He and a longtime friend, drummer John Sferra, founded Glass Harp in the late '60s, when he was in the eleventh grade. They soon became known as one of the most innovative power trios around; even though they weren't together long enough to break through commercially. They had a contract with Decca, toured the country several times, and had a growing base of devoted fans, many of whom were knocked out by Keaggy's lightning-fast guitar riffs and experimental sounds. At its pinnacle, Glass Harp was opening for such major acts as Iron Butterfly, Yes, Traffic, and Chicago.

Keaggy was exposed to, and partook of, his share of drugs. His life changed dramatically on February 14, 1970. While he was lying in a hotel room suffering a bad LSD trip, his parents were involved in a head-on crash. His mother died, spawning a crisis for Keaggy that led to his becoming a born-again Christian. In the early '70s Keaggy took to testifying before bewildered Glass Harp listeners after concerts.

He left Glass Harp in 1972 and the following year recorded his first solo album, *What a Day*. He then spent many years working with a Christian fellowship. Keaggy has released more than a dozen albums, earning critical acclaim for both his virtuosity on guitar and his songwriting, which ranges from the Beatle-esque pop of *Sunday's Child* to more subtle intrumentals. He occasionally joins Glass Harp for reunion concerts. —*Sandra Brennan*

The Wind and the Wheat / 1987 / A&M ✦✦✦
Several pieces of brilliant solo acoustic guitar and others with a small group ensemble. —*Paul Kohler*

★ **Phil Keaggy and Sunday's Child** / 1988 / Word ✦✦✦✦✦
Fans of Anglo-pop-rock should love this outing, which has all the tuneful appeal of Crowded House or Jellyfish. Produced by Lynn Nichols (who later helped form Chagall Guevara), *Phil Keaggy and Sunday's Child* sparkles with a fine mix of chiming Rickenbacker guitars and soaring harmonies. Occasionally the Brit-pop focus gives way to a sturdy hard rock sound, but it's still very well executed. Among the many highlights included are "Sunday's Child," "Tell Me How You Feel," and "I'm Gonna Get You Now." —*Rick Clark*

Love Broke Thru / 1990 / Myrrh ✦✦✦
These are extended, McCartneyesque guitar solos. Stirring pop-rock. —*Bil Carpenter*

Town to Town/Ph'lip Side/Play Thru Me / 1990 / Myrrh ✦✦✦

Keaggy's early music is rather dated, so while there's some impressive guitar work and some good songs on the two-CD reissue (material 1980-1982), there's a lot to wade through. —*Brian Mansfield*

What a Day/Love Broke Thru / 1990 / Myrrh ✦✦✦✦

Keaggy's solo albums from 1973 and 1976, reissued here on one CD, remain among his best. Keaggy was one of the first contemporary Christian musicians to bring an original melodic sense to his songs (indebted as he was to Paul McCartney), and his lyrical naivete comes across as refreshing rather than insipid. —*Brian Mansfield*

Find Me in These Fields / 1990 / Word ✦✦✦✦

His hooks are still firmly rooted in the '60s, but they're big ol' hooks, and a crack backing band makes this a power-pop classic interspersed with guitar instrumentals. —*Brian Mansfield*

Beyond Nature / 1991 / Word ✦✦✦

This album of solo acoustic guitar and small-group music is an excellent recording. —*Paul Kohler*

★ **Crimson and Blue** / 1994 / Word ✦✦✦✦✦

A tour-de-force of '60s and '70s power trios and extended jams, it has songwriting a few cuts above most of the material that inspired it. Features cover of Badfinger's "Baby Blue" and the Van Morrison tune "When Will I Learn (To Live in God)." —*Thom Granger*

220 / Sep. 3, 1996 / Chordant ✦✦✦

Cristy Lane (Eleanor Johnston)

b. Jan. 8, 1940, Peoria, IL
Vocals / Inspirational

Cristy Lane is best remembered for her 1979 hit, "One Day at a Time," one of the biggest-selling gospel songs of all time. She was born Eleanor Johnston to a family of 12 in Peoria, IL. She married Lee Stoller at age 17, and her husband began promoting her talents with a demo tape, which he carried everywhere. He eventually convinced nightclub singer Bobby Mac, who sang in Waynes Club in Peoria, to let him bring his wife to the club to sing. He made another demo tape and began sending it to radio stations and established performers. *National Barn Dance* eventually hired her for $87. She took a stage name from a local deejay, "Chris Lane."

In 1966 Stoller directed his wife toward Nashville. He had her dye her naturally dark hair blond, and once in Music City, paid to have her record two songs she had written, "Stop Fooling with Me" and "Heart in the Sand." Stoller then began taking the demo directly to record companies, but he had no luck until he decided to market her himself through K-Ark record distributors. They manufactured 800 records for the Stollers, who sent 300 of them to national radio stations. Again, nothing happened, and Lane went back to performing at the club they owned together. In 1969 Stoller took her on an ill-advised tour of Vietnam, on which she performed 120 shows for the troops and was involved in a helicopter crash that left her stranded in the midst of a battle.

Upon her return to the States, Lane returned to the club circuits and military bases. In 1972 the Stoller family moved to a Nashville suburb and continued its attempts to get Lane's career off the ground. Stoller formed LS Records in the mid-'70s and finally found success with Cristy's debut single, "Tryin' to Forget About You," and its follow-up, "Sweet Deceiver," appeared on the charts in 1977. That year she also made it to the Top Ten and the Top 20 with "Let Me Down Easy" and "Shake Me I Rattle," respectively. Lane scored three more hits the next year and in 1979 was named the ACM's new vocalist of the year. During the ceremony, Lane sang "I Just Can't Stay Married to You," which later became a Top Five hit. In late 1979 Lane signed to United Artists Records and had three more hits before persuading the label to release "One Day at a Time." After that song's tremendous success, she released "Sweet Sexy Eyes" in 1980; it was her final Top Ten hit. Lane marketed her 1986 album *One Day at a Time* on television, which helped it become one of the top-selling albums in the world. During the '90s Lane has spent most of her time performing at her theater in Branson, MO. —*Sandra Brennan*

One Day at a Time / 1978 / Arrival ✦✦✦✦

Soft-pop gospel. —*Bil Carpenter*

● **Footprints in the Sand** / 1983 / Liberty ✦✦✦✦

Because of the strong selection of songs and consistent performances, this compilation is the one to get. —*Stephen Thomas Erlewine*

Amazing Grace, Vol. 2 / 1986 / Arrival ✦✦✦

A solid, if unspectacular, set of popular gospel tunes that are nicely performed by Lane, even if she is occasionally dominated by an intrusive synthesizer. —*Stephen Thomas Erlewine*

All in His Hands / 1989 / Heartwarming ✦✦✦

Lane's pristine sounds come through best on the '50s-style "He Loves Me Still." —*Bil Carpenter*

My Best to You / 1992 / Arrival ✦✦✦

A good compilation of some of Lane's most popular gospel material, which is somewhat undermined by the number of tracks duplicated from *Footprints in the Sand.* —*Stephen Thomas Erlewine*

Joe Ligon

Vocals

Alabama-born vocalist Joe Ligon was the original lead vocalist of the Mighty Clouds of Joy. His sound and approach reflected the influence of both the Rev. Julius Cheeks and Curtis Mayfield. He has remained their lead singer since the '60s, when they signed with Peacock Records. —*Ron Wynn*

● **Old Revival Back Home** / Word ✦✦✦✦

Sallie Martin Singers

Black Gospel

With a raspy, unmodulated voice of limited range, noted for its extraordinary energy and volume, Sallie Martin was not the sweetest of gospel singers, but despite her shortcomings as a singer, she is considered the "Mother of Gospel," and is credited for introducing mainstream audiences to the genre. Though she performed for many years, and wrote a few important songs, Martin is best remembered as a promoter who arranged many cross-country tours for new performers and as the groundbreaking cofounder of the Martin and Morris Publishing Company, which became the largest publisher of gospel music in the US

She was born in tiny Pittfield, GA. Her father died when she was young, and she was raised by her mother and grandparents on their little farm. As the local church also functioned as the village school, her religion was always with her and colored every aspect of her young life. Her love of singing came from her mother. It was a strict Baptist household, and Martin credits most of her own exceptional self-discipline to her folks. Martin was educated through the eighth grade and after that worked menial jobs in Atlanta for a while. Joining a Holiness church, she soon discovered an abiding love for the energetic sanctified music she heard there. By the '20s she was married and the mother of a son. She divorced in 1929. While struggling to support her child she became increasingly interested in gospel and the music of Thomas A. Dorsey. A mutual friend arranged an audition with him for Martin and led to her joining his group at the Ebenezer Baptist Church in February 1932. Not long afterward she became their soloist.

As Dorsey's reputation as a songwriter grew, Martin began realizing that there was a vast untapped market for gospel sheet music and began helping Dorsey make his more readily available by demonstrating his music with specially organized choirs. Dorsey and Martin began travelling the Midwest creating choruses and sponsoring such young talents as Roberta Martin and Mahalia Jackson. She and Dorsey also organized the first annual festival for such gospel choirs, the Gospel Singers Convention. Afterward, she became the first major gospel singer to make an impact on the West Coast. In 1940 she split up with Dorsey and began working on a solo career. Her music publishing company came about after Reverend Clarence Cobbs suggested she team up with young songwriter Kenneth Morris. She eventually hooked up with pianist Roberta Martin to form the Martin and Martin Gospel Singers, an all-male group. She then went on to create the first all-female gospel group, the Sallie Martin Singers, advertising their songs via Martin's choir. The music and the messengers travelled across the country and developed a fan base that transcended racial boundaries.

In 1942 Martin's adopted daughter Cora, after gaining experience with other choirs, joined her mother's group as a soloist. In 1946 Sallie Martin opened a Martin and Morris Studio and added male vocalists to her singers. In 1950, her publishing house hooked up with Specialty Records to distribute music printed by Venice Music, Inc. Specialty Records was the home of some of gospel's greatest acts, including the Soul Stirrers, the Swan Silvertones, Wynona Carr, Alex Bradford, Bessie Griffin, and Dorothy Love Coates. Together Venice and Martin and Morris became the powerhouse institution of gospel music; later that year Martin's own singers began recording on Specialty. Before that the Sallie Martin Singers had recorded on Bronze, Aladdin, Exclusive, and Capitol. As recording artists, they had several successful 78s. In 1952 her daughter Cora, tired from constantly touring, left the Sallie Martin Singers. Shortly thereafter Sallie Martin disbanded the group. She continued her longtime work with the St. Paul Baptist Church in Los Angeles. Martin also placed greater focus on her business and real estate ventures (she was an astute business woman and became relatively wealthy), as well as working tirelessly for various charities until around 1960, when she returned to Chicago to create a new version of the Sallie Martin Singers. When not working with the group, Martin hosted performances in Chicago churches and occasionally performed herself. —*Sandra Brennan*

Throw Out the Lifeline / 1950-1952 / Specialty ✦✦✦✦
Sallie Martin was a gospel institution, a mentor, performer, composer, and publisher who helped nurture careers and provided exposure for many performers throughout her lifetime. The Sallie Martin Singers have had almost none of their output made available until now. The 28 selections (plus a 29th that spotlights her adopted daughter Cora) aren't quite as freewheeling and rampaging as the quartets, but are no less powerful and expressive, whether it's Sallie Martin, Cora Martin, or Cora Weston on leads, or the group teaming with special guest Brother Joe May. This is vintage, joyous material from a group that's been sorely overlooked. — *Ron Wynn*

Precious Lord / 1993 / Vee-Jay ✦✦✦✦
Sallie Martin disbanded her famous singing group in the '50s when her daughter told her she didn't want to do any more tours. She briefly resurrected two new editions in the early '60s and cut two albums for Vee-Jay before disbanding them again. Although the 23 songs on this single disc reissue aren't as glorious or memorable as the group's Specialty recordings, they are still valuable, both to hear Martin's rough but effective leads and harmonizing with new vocalists, and also because the resignation and mournful quality in Martin's singing during the 1963 sessions were an indication that she'd had enough of the performance/recording/touring grind. — *Ron Wynn*

★ **Throw Out The Lifeline** / 1993 / ✦✦✦✦✦
The most instrumentation these tracks ever had was an organ, a piano, and an occasional drum. These 29 tracks are Black congregational-styled numbers, 23 of them previously unissued. The sides include six selections where Sallie and Cora joined the singers. Most of the rest find Sallie and Cora trading leads. A fine example of Sallie's powers shows up on "Ain't That Good News." — *Bil Carpenter*

The Roberta Martin Singers

Black Gospel
Talented pianist Roberta Martin started a quartet with Theodore Frye in the '30s. This aggregation evolved into the Roberta Martin Singers by the '50s. It is now known that she copied the piano style of blind pianist Arizona Dranes, who also influenced the Ward Singers. Martin's singers sang loudly and dramatically. She wasn't concerned about a harmonious sound; when one member of the group was leading a song, whether male or female, you could easily identify the backing voices. This lack of synchronicity made the group's urgent sound a unique and welcome change amid the repetitive quartets of the time. Robert Anderson was one of Martin's principal singers. She herself was referred to as the Helen Hayes of the Gospel World. She died in 1969. — *Bil Carpenter*

● **The Roberta Martin Singers** / Savoy ✦✦✦✦
Most of Martin's best early work from the late '40s through the '50s is out of print, but this is a nice introduction. — *Kip Lornell*

Brother Joe May

d. 1972
Vocals / Black Gospel
In a voice as big as thunder, Brother Joe May sang a stirring mix of sanctified soul and sweet-hot blues that brought the saints to their knees. At the height of his distinguished career, May, dubbed the "Thunderbolt of the Midwest" by his mentor, Willie Mae Smith, was considered the king of gospel performers. In the rural South, where he was most popular, days, scholarships, and dinners were named in his honor.

He was born in Macon, MS, and moved to St. Louis as a teen. He married young and produced a pack of children whom he supported by working at a chemical plant. When not working and child-rearing, May would sing with area quartets such as the Smith Jubilee Singers. But May had an individualistic style that made him ill-suited to group singing, so he began learning more about solo singing. At that time he idolized Willie Mae Ford Smith. Mother Smith took him in as her student and chief supporter. From her, May learned phrasing and how to use his tenor voice to blow listeners away one minute and sweetly lull them back to the fold the next. Most of his physical mannerisms he also learned from her. Eventually the two teamed up and toured together.

In 1949 he made a huge impression performing at Thomas A. Dorsey's Singers Convention, and this led to a recording contract with Specialty. His first recordings closely resembled those of Smith's "Old Ship of Zion" and "Search Me Lord," which became Brother May's biggest hit. The success with Specialty enabled May to settle down and send his children to college. He left the label in the late '50s to sign with Nashboro. May frequently appeared in package tours and was at home singing with such legendary performers as Mahalia Jackson, from whom he derived much of his bluesiness. When Jackson's career was just igniting, it was May and Mother Smith who handed Jackson her first $1,000 check. It was while with Nashboro that he began firmly establishing himself in the South. May joined the cast of *Black Nativity*, a Broadway musical featuring Marion Williams, in the 1960s and

toured North America and Europe. Afterward, he went back to the South. In the early '70s he had a stroke that weakened but did not destroy him; as soon as he had recovered, he resumed touring. He had a minor hit with "Don't Let the Devil Ride. May died on the road a few months after Mahalia Jackson passed on. — *Sandra Brennan*

☆ **Thank You Lord for One More Day** / 1967 / Specialty ✦✦✦✦✦
Excellent hard gospel, with occasional support from Sister Wynona Carr and the Pilgrim Travelers. — *Ron Wynn*

★ **In Loving Memory . . .** / 1974 / Specialty ✦✦✦✦✦
A collection of May's finest shouts and duets, supported on some cuts by the Pilgrim Travelers, the Sallie Martin Singers, or a live audience. — *Ron Wynn*

Search Me, Lord / 1974 / Specialty ✦✦✦✦
Authoritative gospel and energized vocals with support from the Pilgrim Travelers and the Sallie Martin Singers. — *Ron Wynn*

Thunderbolt of the Middle West / 1974 / Specialty ✦✦✦
Brother Joe May, the baritone belter from Macon, MS, could, without much effort, move a church through the power of his voice. On these recordings culled from 1952-1955 sessions, May is ably supported by the vocalizing of the Sallie Martin Singers, Sister Wynona Carr, Annette May, and the Pilgrim Travelers. There are 17 lung-splitting solo outings, ten previously unissued. It includes such hits as "Search Me Lord" and "I'm Gonna Live the Life I Sing About in My Song." He was the Caruso of postwar gospel. — *Opal Louis Nations, Roots and Rhythm Newsletter*

Brother Joe May Live, 1952-1955 / 1994 / Specialty ✦✦✦✦
Brother Joe May earned his "Thunderbolt of the Midwest" nickname with incandescent, riveting vocals that could blow a roof off or reduce listeners to tears, often at the same time. The 16 tracks on this CD were done live, usually at services or during church performances, and they frequently paired him with The Sallie Martin Singers. While they and Prof. Earle Hines are fine, May is in another dimension. His flamboyant, dynamic voice shudders, roars, rises, moans, and flails, and he fortifies the songs with commentary that's nearly as inspiring. Even devout atheists will be impressed by the power of Brother Joe May. — *Ron Wynn*

Brother Joe May Story / ✦✦✦
Here's a 1972 two-record set of 24 gospel songs made popular by Brother Joe May between 1958, when he joined Nashboro after nine years on Specialty, and his demise. Macon-born May was a Pentecostal practioner of the Willie Mae Ford Smith school of gospel singing. May's powerful tenor impressed and inspired many. This set includes some live church recordings and sides made with the Joe May Singers. A notable cut is the rousing "I've Been Dipped in the Water." This is a fine collection. — *Opal Louis Nations, Roots and Rhythm Newsletter*

David Meece

b. 1952
Piano, Vocals / CCM
Light pop singer-songwriter David Meece's chameleon-like tendencies have made for an uneven catalog; nevertheless, many of his songs have been smash hits on Christian radio. — *Thom Granger*

● **Chronology** / 1940 / Word ✦✦✦✦
The best songs from his years with the Myrrh label, making for a good introduction to the artist. — *Thom Granger*

Front Row / 1982 / Myrrh ✦✦
Candle in the Rain / 1987 / Myrrh ✦✦✦
Meece teamed with Gino and Joe Vanelli for this set, resulting in a different musical approach, with good results. — *Thom Granger*

Learning to Trust / 1989 / Two-One-Four ✦✦✦
A pivotal recording for Meece. The artist deals with his troubled family history, and crafts some of his best songs in the process. — *Thom Granger*

Once in a Lifetime / 1993 / Star Song ✦✦

The Mighty Clouds of Joy

Soul, R&B, Black Gospel
Formed in Los Angeles ca. 1959, the original members were Ermant and Elmer Franklin, Joe Ligon, Johnny Martin, Leon Polk, and Richard Wallace. They had some R&B hits in the 1974-1977 period with "Mighty High" and "Time." They have consistently adjusted their repertoire according to current trends, having played everything from traditional Black gospel to light rock. — *Bil Carpenter*

A Bright Side / 1960 / MCA ✦✦✦
Includes the title sermonette and other quartet-style cuts. — *Bil Carpenter*

The Best of the Mighty Clouds of Joy, Vol. 2 / 1973 / MCA ✦✦
The Best of the Mighty Clouds of Joy / 1973 / MCA ✦✦✦✦
The title is a bit misleading, but it's still a fair sample of the group's most popular performances. — *Kip Lornell*

The Best of the Mighty Clouds of Joy, Vol. 2 / 1973 / MCA ✦✦✦
A hodgepodge of lesser material from their Peacock albums and singles. Vol. 2 includes some nice sides, but it's weaker than the first volume. —*Kip Lornell*

● **Live and Direct** / 1977 / ABC ✦✦✦✦

Geoff Moore

Vocals / CCM
Second-generation CCM artist Moore was influenced by Russ Taff and others; he creates dependable, heartland pop-rock. —*Thom Granger*

All the Good Music / 1987 / Benson ✦✦✦
This anthology of early music was created for the Benson label. —*Thom Granger*

Home Run / 1995 / ✦✦✦✦
Geoff Moore followed up his 1992 Dove award-winning song "The Great Adventure" with *Home Run*, which continued his collaboration with Steven Curtis Chapman on two songs. Moore turns in rootsy, driving, inspirational pop-rock. —*Stephen Thomas Erlewine*

● **Pure and Simple** / Fore Front Comm. Group ✦✦✦✦
This set represents a band at its peak as a rock act; later albums would feature more pop-oriented material. —*Thom Granger*

Rich Mullins

b. 1955
Dulcimer, Piano, Vocals / CCM
A songwriter whose distinctive point of view makes for some of the more thoughtful lyrics in the genre, Mullins also allows his Celtic/American heritage to influence the instrumental side of his music; the combination has produced some essential albums in contemporary Christian music. —*Thom Granger*

Winds of Heaven, Stuff of Earth / May 1989 / Reunion ✦✦✦
Mullins' vision begins to take shape, with help from producer Reed Arvin, on the album that features the now-classic,"Awesome God." —*Thom Granger*

The World As Best As I Remember It / 1991 / Reunion ✦✦

☆ **The World As Best As I Remember It, Vol. 2** / 1992 / Reunion ✦✦✦✦✦
A near-perfect song cycle, it featured moments worthy of the best in pop music history. —*Thom Granger*

A Liturgy, a Legacy and a Ragamuffin Band / Oct. 26, 1993 / Reunion ✦✦✦✦
Mullins' originals reflecting on the concept of legacy are used as liturgical motifs, making for a thoroughly contemporary and powerful worship experience and artistic statement. —*Thom Granger*

★ **Songs** / Jul. 1996 / Reunion ✦✦✦✦✦
Songs collects 16 of Rich Mullins' best and most popular songs, offering a perfect introduction to one of the most delightful and provocative singer-songwriters in CCM. —*Rodney Batdorf*

★ **Collection of Songs** / Jul. 1996 / Reunion ✦✦✦✦✦
During the late '80s and early '90s, Rich Mullins was one of the most popular contemporary Christian artists in America, having ten No. 1 CCM hits over the course of a decade. All of his biggest hits for Reunion records—including "Awesome God" and his original version of Amy Grant's "Sing Your Praise to the Lord"—are compiled on *Collection of Songs*, making this the perfect introduction to the Christian singer-songwriter. —*Rodney Batdorf*

Larry Norman

Guitar, Vocals / Christian Rock
One of the founding fathers of 'Jesus Music' in the late '60s, Norman left L.A. band People! to record *Upon This Rock* in late 1969, which, along with Mylon LeFevre's solo debut, marked the beginnings of the genre. His *Only Visiting This Planet* was, and still is for many, a high-water mark for Christian rock. Recent years have found him recording and touring less and less, paritally due to health problems. —*Thom Granger*

● **Upon This Rock** / 1969 / Kingsway ✦✦✦✦
Counterculture, psychedelic pop. —*Bil Carpenter*

Only Visiting This Planet / 1972 / Street Level ✦✦✦✦
Contains sociopolitical statements with hard-edged, Jesus-rock zeal. —*Bil Carpenter*

Dorothy Norwood

Vocals / Black Gospel
A former member of the Chimes and the Caravans, Dorothy Norwood is a shouter best known for her strong, raspy voice and her tendency to sing songs about children who stray from their all-suffering mothers. She left the Caravans in the 1960s and became a solo act. Much later

Norwood became a producer and has worked to introduce new gospel performers. —*Sandra Brennan*

Mother's Son / 1972 / Word ✦✦✦
The eight songs on Dorothy Norwood's *A Mother's Son* are ideal showcases for her skill as a master of the song sermon. She uses the war symbolism to marvelous effect on "Battle Field," sounds purposely animated on "Mt. Zion," and turns "I See God Making A Way For You" and "Leave It in the Hand of the Lord" into stirring testaments of belief. Her voice, emphatic pace, and dramatic embellishments are the LP's core; there's sparse background and almost no defined instrumental sound. But Norwood is certainly up to the task; her glorious voice and triumphant spirit make *A Mother's Son* another outstanding classic. —*Ron Wynn, Rejoice*

Live / 1992 / Malaco ✦✦✦
An enthusiastic performance, but the energy level dips whenever Norwood stops singing. —*Ron Wynn*

● **Best of Dorothy Norwood** / Jul. 1996 / Intersound ✦✦✦✦
All of Dorothy Norwood's biggest hits and most popular songs are collected on *The Best of Dorothy Norwood*, making it a perfect introduction to her career. —*Rodney Batdorf*

● **Denied Mother** / Savoy ✦✦✦✦
Norwood's spectacular vocals are supported by the Combined Choir of Atlanta, GA. One of Norwood's greatest song sermons is the title track. —*Ron Wynn*

Faithful Daughter / Savoy ✦✦✦
This has another classic single in the title track. —*Ron Wynn*

Look What They've Done to My Child / Savoy ✦✦✦
Wonderful anthemic vocals and a textbook selection that's a blueprint of gospel storytelling and lyric imagery. —*Ron Wynn*

A Wonderful Day: Live / I Am ✦✦✦
Fine singing, but an overabundance of pop/contemporary devices and instrumentation. —*Ron Wynn*

Michael Omartian

Keyboards, Vocals / CCM
Michael Omartian has enjoyed considerable success in the CCM and secular music fields as a session sideman, songwriter, solo artist, and producer. During the '70s, Omartian's distinctive keyboard work graced projects by Loggins and Messina and Steely Dan. As a producer, Omartian worked with Christopher Cross (cleaning up at the 1981 Grammys with Cross' self-titled debut), as well as Donna Summer and Amy Grant (notably her platinum *Heart in Motion* album). During the mid-'70s Omartian's solo work helped set the standard for high-caliber pop statements that rivaled the best the secular world had to offer. Omartian continues to release solo efforts. —*Rick Clark*

The Race / 1991 / Epic ✦✦✦
On *The Race*, Omartian collaborates with singer-songwriter Michael Anderson and Bruce Sudano (formerly with Brooklyn Dreams). The style is contemporary keyboard-heavy pop, with several songs sporting strong melodic hooks (particularly "Faithful Forever" and "Heartbreak City"). —*Rick Clark*

★ **White Horse/Adam Again** / 1991 / Myrrh ✦✦✦✦✦
This CD combines Omartian's first two solo albums, *White Horse* (1974) and *Adam Again* (1975), both very important to CCM because they heralded the advent of advanced production techniques and sophisticated, multilayered lyrical imagery that went beyond standard gospel metaphors. Musically, these two albums are probably Omartian's most adventurous statements. Highlights include the reflective "Right from the Start" and "The Orphan," as well as the celebratory "Ain't You Glad" and the sweeping ballad "Annie the Poet." "White Horse," "Take Me Down," and "Silver Fish" showcase Omartian's fine arranging and keyboard chops. Nevertheless, certain tracks haven't aged very gracefully, particularly "Alive and Well," which instrumentally sounds like a cliched '70s "Rockford Files"-style TV soundtrack. Both albums use the cream of Los Angeles' "A-list" session sidemen, including Lee Ritenour, Leland Sklar, David Hungate, Larry Carlton, and Victor Feldman. —*Rick Clark*

One Bad Pig

Christian Rock
This punk quartet started as a lark for a youth rally in the band's Austin, TX, hometown. The positive reception led to a relatively long career, but the members of the band seemed to understand neither punk's culture nor its philosophy and ended up, depending on where you stood in the audience, as either a generic thrash band or a punk parody. —*Brian Mansfield*

● **I Scream Sunday** / Sep. 17, 1991 / Word ✦✦✦✦
These uninspired punk thrashings, produced by White Heart's Billy Smiley, quickly get tedious. But "Man in Black," a duet with (believe it or not) Johnny Cash, shows the exact spot where punk and Christianity inter-

sect. And Cash comes off as a more committed punk than anybody in the band. —*Brian Mansfield*

Shun Pace-Rhodes

Vocals / Black Gospel

Pace-Rhodes hails from a family of singers active in the Church of God in Christ (COGIC) music movement. She and her siblings formed the Anointed Pace Sisters of Atlanta in the mid-'70s and were known for their contemporary R&B gospel sound. She sang "That Name" on one of Edwin Hawkins' seminal Music and Arts albums in 1987. It was he who personally went to the head of Savoy-Malaco Records and suggested they sign the belting singer as a solo artist, and they did. Rather than cutting her chops on modern styles, Pace-Rhodes sang music that recalls the days of Mahalia Jackson and the Ward Singers. —*Bil Carpenter*

● **He Lives** / 1992 / Savoy Gospel ✦✦✦✦
From the most astonishing traditional female gospel soloist in the church today. Her powerhouse pipes are supported by the Showers of Blessing Choir and the Voices of Power from Atlanta, GA. —*Opal Louis Nations*

Twila Paris

b. 1958

Vocals / Easy Listening, Inspirational

One of modern inspirational music's most prolific singer-songwriters, Paris has already made a formidable contribution to the church worldwide, as a number of her songs have been incorporated into hymnals. —*Thom Granger*

Cry for the Desert / 1991 / JCI ✦✦✦
Intimate, light praise/pop music, with Brown Bannister producing. —*Bil Carpenter*

Sanctuary / 1991 / Star Song ✦✦✦
Produced by contemporary instrumentalist Richard Souther, this album set new musical standards in the inspirational field for arrangement and production ideas. —*Thom Granger*

● **Heart That Knows You** / 1993 / Star Song ✦✦✦✦
This best-of collection (radio hits and re-recordings) of early classics serves to introduce the uninitiated. —*Thom Granger*

Beyond a Dream / 1994 / Star Song ✦✦✦
Paris spun a few heads with this one, featuring her most contemporary material to date, and a bit of a new and more confident vocal approach to match it. —*Thom Granger*

Where I Stand / 1996 / Sparrow ✦✦✦✦
Twila Paris continues to become more pop-oriented with each of her releases, but that's not necessarily a bad thing. Although *Where I Stand* could be mistaken for any number of records cluttering the adult contemporary radio stations, Paris performs with style and grace, which is what saves the album from being either a sell-out or a wash-out. Some stronger songwriting would have made the album even more enticing, but as it stands, *Where I Stand* is simply another pleasurable record in her deep catalog. —*Rodney Batdorf*

The Early Works / Benson ✦✦✦✦
A good anthology of Paris' first few albums, it features songs like "The Warrior Is a Child" and "We Will Glorify." —*Thom Granger*

Squire Parsons

b. Newton, WV

Vocals / Southern Gospel

Born in Newton, WV, Parsons began his gospel career singing with the Calvary Men. In 1975 he joined the Kingsmen as a baritone, but he left in 1979 to pursue a solo career and has since recorded 25 Southern-gospel/MOR albums. Parsons won six *Singing News Magazine* awards, including the prestigious Marvin Norcross Award in 1990. "Sweet Beulah Land" was a No. 1 song on Southern gospel charts in 1981. —*Bil Carpenter*

● **His Very Best** / Heartwarming ✦✦✦✦
Includes "Hello Mama," "Jesus Is the Door," and "Sweet Beulah Land." —*Bil Carpenter*

Sandi Patti

b. Jul. 14, 1957, Oklahoma City, OK

Piano, Vocals / Inspirational

Known as "The Voice," Sandi Patti is one of the biggest stars in CCM and over a 15-year period (from the early '80s) has earned three platinum albums, five gold albums, 33 Dove Awards, and five Grammys. Her debut album sold 11 million copies. Known for her versatility, Patti draws from pop to ballads to modernized gospel standards.

Born Sandi Patty in Oklahoma City, she made her performing debut singing "Jesus Loves Me" at church when she was only two. A few years later, she and her two young brothers billed themselves as the Ron Patty Family and began singing gospel at small churches across the country. She later studied voice at San Diego State University and then majored in music at Anderson College, Indiana. She earned extra cash at the latter singing commercial jingles. Before graduating from Anderson, Patti married John Helvering, who has had a major influence on her career. He was her biggest fan and helped her record her self-produced debut album *For My Friends*. A printer's mistake changed her last name from Patty to Patti, and the name stuck.

In 1979 she signed to an independent label and that year released *Sandi's Song*. She then began a series of musical ministry tours and realized she'd found her calling. She won her first two Dove Awards in 1982 for *Lift up the Lord*. For Patti, it was straight up from there. She launched her first major US tour in 1984 to promote *Songs from the Heart*. As a singer she is noted for her powerful, flexible voice and her ability to climb effortlessly to a high C. Patti has appeared on numerous television shows and has sung for presidents, on awards shows, and, in 1988, for a CBS special, "We the People," at that year's Republican National Convention. She also managed to find time to bear four children.

At the height of her career, Patti was an inspiration and role model of a good Christian wife for millions. But in 1992 she filed for divorce. By 1995 she admitted to having had two affairs while married to Helvering, one briefly at the beginning of her marriage, and a more serious one later on. Her problems generated much controversy in the CCM business. Many radio stations pulled her material. World Records temporarily postponed the release of her 1995 Christmas album, and many fans were left shocked and disillusioned. Word Records still offers her back catalogue and publicly supports her, but her career has been in limbo ever since. —*Sandra Brennan*

Another Time, Another Place / 1973 / Word ✦✦✦
A pop crossover setting. —*Bil Carpenter*

A Morning like This / 1986 / Word ✦✦✦✦
An inspirational tour de force, this features sweet string arrangements. —*Bil Carpenter*

● **Finest Moments** / 1990 / Word ✦✦✦✦
Her greatest hits. —*Bil Carpenter*

Le Voyage / May 25, 1993 / Epic ✦✦✦
Patti stretches out a bit, musically and lyrically, with a sort of *Pilgrim's Progress* set to adult contemporary music and more use of lyrical metaphors than before. —*Thom Granger*

Hymns Just for You / Word ✦✦✦
These traditional hymns are given Patti's heartfelt imprint. —*Bil Carpenter*

Songs from the Heart / Word ✦✦✦
A mix of light CCM and pop-gospel. —*Bil Carpenter*

Charlie Peacock

Keyboards, Vocals / Christian Rock

This White soul singer's combination of Smokey Robinson-influenced falsetto vocals and cerebral lyrics has helped him develop one of CCM's most individual sounds. He co-wrote Amy Grant's 1991 hit "Every Heartbeat." A sought-after producer, he has worked with Margaret Becker, the Choir, the 77's, and Jimmy A. —*Brian Mansfield*

The Secret of Time / 1990 / Sparrow ✦✦✦
Because of their low-budget production, early Peacock projects classified him as "alternative." "Put the Love Back into Love," "Almost Threw It Away," and "Heaven Is a Real Place" suggested that he had more of an affinity for soul, but "Experience" showed that he still needed to learn that the best grooves are created by instinct, not academia. —*Brian Mansfield*

★ **Love Life** / 1991 / Sparrow ✦✦✦✦✦
Peacock's concept album about the correlation between a man's spiritual relationship with God and his physical relationship with his wife is the masterpiece that *The Secret of Time* pointed to. "After Loving You" made no bones about the object of its affections; it was an unabashed love song for Peacock's wife. But what really shook up the Christian audiences was the sensuous funk of "Kiss Me Like a Woman," nothing less than the first Christian song about foreplay (and a scathing indictment of pop radio). —*Brian Mansfield*

West Coast Diaries, Vols. 1-3 / 1991 / Sparrow ✦✦✦✦
Peacock released these demos and live recordings as individual albums between 1986 and 1988. Although these recordings show his tendency to over-intellectualize his music, they're still worth having (especially *Volume Two*, which captures an acoustic concert with guitarist Jimmy A and vocalist Vince Ebo). —*Brian Mansfield*

Coram Deo: In the Presence of God / 1992 / Sparrow ✦✦✦
This worship-oriented project featuring Michael Card, Michael English, and Susan Ashton reflects writer/producer Charlie Peacock's ongoing

preoccupation with Christian life and the omnipresence of God. —*Brian Mansfield*

Strange Language / Jun. 25, 1996 / Forefront ✦✦✦✦
Charlie Peacock again demonstrates why he is one of the top songwriters of contemporary christian music in the '90s. He likes to push the boundaries of CCM, adding elements of modern, alternative rock, dance music, and jazz to his bedrock pop sound. It's an invigorating listen. *Strange Language* is one of the most ambitious CCM albums of the mid-'90s, as well as one of most rewarding. —*Rodney Batdorf*

Maggie Staton Peebles

Vocals / Gospel, Black Gospel
Peebles first sang with the Jewell Gospel Trio in the '50s and had nine gold records on Nashboro. Then she became a schoolteacher, returning to gospel in 1988. She has a melodious and sweetly powerful voice. —*Bil Carpenter*

Born Again / Winston-Derek ✦✦✦
Black gospel standards of the '50s redone in the '90s. —*Bil Carpenter*

● **First Fruits** / Winston-Derek ✦✦✦✦
Recorded with a simple rhythm section and traditional arrangements. —*Bil Carpenter*

This Soul of Mine / Winston-Derek ✦✦✦
Piano-activated Black gospel. —*Bil Carpenter*

Petra

Gospel, Christian Rock
Founded by guitarist Bob Hartman, Petra is Christian rock's biggest and longest-running band. Their first album was released in 1974, and the group is still pleasing arena-rock fans with catchy anthems and ballads. —*Thom Granger*

Petra / 1974 / Word ✦✦✦
A musician's album in a blues/country-rock guitar style. —*Bil Carpenter*

● **This Means War** / 1987 / Star Song ✦✦✦✦
Unseen Power / 1992 / Word ✦✦✦✦
This is a warm, crisp production, aside from its metal and bluesy-pop. —*Bil Carpenter*

No Doubt / 1995 / Word/Epic ✦✦✦✦
The addition of keyboardist Jim Cooper and guitarist David Lichens has not changed Petra's sound. The band's songwriting is strong throughout the record, alternating between their patented fist-pumping anthems and inspirational ballads, all devoted to the Lord. —*David Jehnzen*

PFR

Originally called Inside Out, PFR was formed in Minnesota by Mark Nash, Joel Hanson, and Patrick Andrew. For their 1992 album debut on Sparrow, the trio changed their name to Pray for Rain; they changed it to PFR for *Goldie's Last Days*. —*John Bush*

Pray for Rain / Jul. 27, 1992 / Vireo ✦✦✦
● **Goldie's Last Day** / 1993 / Sparrow ✦✦✦✦
Renamed PFR, the band displays a wider range of material and arrangements on its second outing. —*Thom Granger*

Great Lengths / 1994 / Sparrow ✦✦✦
Them / 1996 / Vireo ✦✦✦

Leslie Phillips

Synthesizer, Vocals / CCM
Gospel music's she-rebel, Phillips left the gospel industry in the late '80s because of its confining nature. She now records secular material on Virgin Records with producer and husband T-Bone Burnett, under the name of Sam Phillips. —*Bil Carpenter*

● **Recollection** / 1987 / Myrrh ✦✦✦✦
A greatest-hits package. —*Bil Carpenter*

The Turning / Word ✦✦✦
Emotionally truthful CCM with eccentric instrumentation. —*Bil Carpenter*

Pilgrim Jubilees

Black Gospel
Since the early '50s the Pilgrim Jubilee Singers have used their rockin' hard gospel music as a powerful means of testifying their faith, love, and charitable hope that humanity will find a way to bring itself closer to the Kingdom of Heaven. Over its long history, the group has undergone numerous personnel changes. The first incarnation originated on the Mississippi Delta in the 1940s with Elgie and Theophlis Graham, but the most famous version of the Pilgrim Jubilees began in Chicago in 1952, when younger brothers Clay and Cleve Graham resurrected the

Southern White Gospel

Gospel songs from the beginning made up a large part of the country music repertoire. Two subgroups quickly formed. First came the traditional British ecclesiastical songs, reflecting a fundamental Protestant view of life as a vale of tears and suffering. But another form of gospel songs, one that tolerated joy in both worlds, became increasingly popular because of the upbeat, optimistic message of its lyrics and its fast-tempo melody. Whatever the mood of the musicians and audience, there was an appropriate gospel song: If you are feeling unreasonably good, "This World Is Not My Home" will bring you crashing back to earth; but if your daily life has so much real woe and suffering that a gospel dirge woud be the last nail in your coffin, then request the band to play "I'll Fly Away" or "God Put a Rainbow in the Cloud." Southerners, Black and White alike, found gospel music a contrast to country music's standard fare of songs about family and home, good love and broken love, working men and failures, rambling and jail.

Most of country's great performers learned gospel music first, and a large number returned to it after the pressures of the business drove them to self-destruction—in the old days with alcohol, but more recently with drugs. Thus, gospel songs often have saved not only the audience but the performers, who in the very act of singing "Amazing Grace" have found what the lyrics promise.

Because the church often offered the only opportunity for singing and musicmaking (fiddle and banjo music especially were thought to be the devil's music in the old days), country performers since the '50s have made it standard fare to record a gospel album after "making it" with mass-audience material. The Carter Family, Uncle Dave Macon, Roy Acuff, Bill Monroe, Hank Williams, Red Foley, Tennessee Ernie Ford, Elvis Presley, George Jones, Ricky Skaggs—these are only a few of the legions of country stars who have showcased gospel music in their careers. Bluegrass music, with its base of tradition, emphasizes gospel songs, often sung a cappella. The Lewis Family is the best example of a bluegrass/country group that has established a good reputation over the years by performing gospel and pretty much only gospel. Meanwhile, the Oak Ridge Boys, the epitome of country/rock in the '80s, began as a gospel group. So did the Statler Brothers, who toured as the Kingsmen with Johnny Cash in 1963. Southern gospel is now a subgenre of country music, with its own charts and awards and many groups who perform nothing but gospel. From the earliest country recordings through the most recent, gospel has permeated country music. —*David Vinopal*

group. They have remained the group's spiritual and musical core. While growing up in Mississippi, all four Graham brothers were trained to sing. Theophlis left the first group to live in Chicago. The rest of his brothers followed in 1951, and briefly all four sang in the group. The Pilgrims Jubilees toured quite a bit when not working their day-jobs, which for the Graham brothers was barbering in their separate shops, and this proved too much for the older brothers, who gradually dropped out. Shortly thereafter Clay and Cleve invited baritone Major Roberson and lead singer Percy Clark to join. They also took on guitarist Richard Crume and bassist Roosevelt English. They began recording and through the 1950s released sides and albums for assorted labels, including Peacock, Chance, and Nashboro. Soon after signing with Peacock in 1960, the band gained national exposure with their label debut, "Stretch Out." Its success allowed the Pilgrim Jubilees to finally go professional. Crume eventually left the group to join the Soul Stirrers. The other three have remained together and have carried on into the '90s. —*Sandra Brennan*

★ **Walk On/The Old Ship of Zion** / 1964 / Mobile Fidelity ✦✦✦✦✦
Back to Basics / 1990 / Malaco ✦✦✦
Another solid effort recorded by this label, which helped to bring good Southern gospel music into the '90s. —*Kip Lornell*

Gospel Roots / 1990 / Malaco ✦✦✦✦
This dynamic album shows why the Pilgrim Jubilees have remained one of the most respected "hard" gospel groups for many years. —*Kip Lornell*

The Old Ship of Zion / Peacock ✦✦✦
This one includes "Pearly Gates" and "If You Don't Mind." —*Bil Carpenter*

Pilgrim Travelers

Black Gospel
From the early to mid-'50s the Pilgrim Travelers were among the most popular gospel quartets on the circuit, appearing everywhere from churches to huge filled-to-capacity stadiums across the country. They are known for their mixture of hard and soft gospel. In the early '50s they were among the first acts to sign to Art Rupe's Specialty label. They became the label's most prolific recording artists. The group's origins go back to the early '30s and the Pleasant Grove Baptist Church in Houston, TX. They started performing locally and in 1942 traveled to California. Their first big break came in 1944, when they won a national gig touring with the Soul Stirrers, one of gospel's most popular groups. They recorded for Bob Geddin's Big Town label in Oakland and for the Greenwood label for L.A. record shop owner Mrs. Greenwood. It was she who hooked the Pilgrim Travelers up with Rupe. Between 1947 and late 1953 the group's line-up included lead vocalists Kylo Turner and Keith Barber, tenor J.W. Alexander, baritone Jesse Whitaker, and bass Raphael Taylor. In 1953 they were joined briefly by a third lead singer, Walter Budgett, who left in 1954. Later that year bass George McCurn replaced Raphael Taylor. Occasionally the Pilgrim Travelers stirred up controversy, first with their unique "walking rhythm" and then in 1955 when they released two singles containing saxophone music. The latter offended many gospel purists, who associated horns with the more worldly jazz. Their last recording session for Specialty was in 1956. A few years later, after a major car accident, the second since 1950, they went their separate ways. At that time singer Lou Rawls was leading the group. In 1962 Rawls used the name Pilgrim Travelers on a gospel album produced by Alexander for Capitol. Later James Wafer and Jesse Whitaker traveled a few years as the New Pilgrim Travelers and recorded on Proverb, but they could never recapture the glory of their earlier years. — *Sandra Brennan*

Shake My Mother's Hand / 1977 / Specialty ✦✦✦

● **The Best of . . . , Vols. 1 & 2** / 1990 / Specialty ✦✦✦✦
An aptly named sampler of early sides from the huge Specialty vaults, with the legendary Kylo Turner and Keith Barber on leads. — *Kip Lornell*

Walking Rhythm / 1992 / Specialty ✦✦✦✦
This is the first of two CD collections of prime a cappella close harmony gospel in walking rhythm by the Pilgrim Travelers. Contained are unissued, alternate, and previously issued-on-wax sides from Kylo Turner and Keith Barber, who fronted L.A.'s Travelers during the 1947-1956 Specialty sojourn. The quintet cut over 100 sides during this time. The selection here is drawn from 1947 through 1951. They're taken from original 16-inch metal masters and filtered through a non-noise system to produce fine presence and sound clarity. — *Opal Louis Nations, Roots & Rhythm Newsletter*

Better Than That / Specialty ✦✦✦
The Pilgrim Travelers were Specialty's most prolific group. They were versatile enough to be sensational as an a cappella unit, and almost as magnificent with instrumental accompaniment. The 28 cuts from this most recent anthology show them adjusting to instrumental support, as lead vocalists Kylo Turner and Keith Barber effectively duel and contrast with organs, keyboards, bass, and drums. The collection also contains 13 previously unissued songs, most of them incredible unaccompanied performances. — *Ron Wynn*

Everytime I Feel the Spirit / Chameleon ✦✦✦
This is a tepid collection of traditional gospel sung in the Pilgrims' inimitable style without the bite of earlier work for Specialty, Andex, and Capitol. The album, first issued on Kent in 1971, contains the voices of lead singer Kylo Turner, who joined the group in 1945, and J.W. Alexander, also a member of long standing who managed the group and produced many of the outfit's later post-Specialty recordings. The songs cut at these sessions should have proven more exciting, as Harold Battiste handled the musical arrangements, but somehow the group lacked enthusiasm. — *Opal Louis Nations, Roots and Rhythm Newsletter*

Dottie Rambo

b. Mar. 2, 1934, Madison, KY
Guitar, Vocals / Southern Gospel
Dottie was born in Madison, KY. (She is the wife of Buck Rambo, mother to Reba Rambo, and mother-in-law to Dony McGuire.) She is more influential for the 700 or more worshipful songs she's written over the years, which have inspired facsimiles and numerous covers, than for her own career as a Southern gospel singer or as one of the first female lead guitarists in gospel. — *Bil Carpenter*

● **The Best of the Rambos, Vols. 1 & 2** / NK ✦✦✦✦
Dottie and Buck's country gospel. — *Bil Carpenter*

Soul of Me / Heartwarming ✦✦✦
Late-'60s soulful Southern gospel. — *Bil Carpenter*

Sunshine Shine on Me / Heartwarming ✦✦✦
Mainstream Southern gospel from the '60s. — *Bil Carpenter*

This Is My Valley / Heartwarming ✦✦✦
Rambo's warm voice on moody Southern gospel ballads. — *Bil Carpenter*

Reverend. D.C. Rice

b. 1888, d. Mar. 1973
Vocals / Black Gospel
The sound of Reverend D.C. Rice is one part fiery preachin' and two parts scratchy-but-sanctified singin'. It is also heavily influenced by the 78s of Reverend J.M. Gates and Reverend F.W. McGee. Born and raised a Baptist's son in Barbour County, AL, Rice left his rural home and moved to Chicago. He joined Bishop Hill's Pentecostal congregation at the Church of the Living God. In 1917 Rice claims he found salvation. Around 1920, after the death of Bishop Hill, Rice became the leader of a tiny Church of the Living God congregation. He was a strong preacher and soon found himself attracting a following. After hearing the recordings of the aforementioned preachers, he was inspired to make his own records and went to Vocalion to meet Jack Knapp. Knapp sent some folks to Rice's next Sunday gathering but was unimpressed. A few days later Knapp had a sudden, inexplicable change of heart and called Rice in to record in exchange for $75 a side, but no royalties. On these sungsermons, Rice was accompanied by percussion, a trombone, piano, and bass. The ensuing discs, of which *I'm on the Battlefield of the Lord* (1929) is his best known, were distributed liberally throughout Chicago; and by August 1928 he had ten singles out and was giving Sunday services on the radio. He continued recording for Vocalion through 1930. He twice tried to sign to Paramount but got no contract and moved to lead a church in Jackson, AL, for two years. He then began preaching at the Oak Street Holiness Church in Montgomery. In 1941 Rice was appointed Bishop of the Apostolistic (sic) Overcoming Holy Church of God, for Alabama, Florida, and Georgia. Though he made other recordings after Vocalion, they have been lost. — *Sandra Brennan*

Rev. D. C. Rice / Document ✦✦✦✦
More than 20 exemplary performances of jazz-accompanied, sanctified singing and preaching. — *Kip Lornell*

★ **Complete Recorded Works (1928-1930)** / Document ✦✦✦✦✦

Seawind

CCM
This influential late '70s pop-jazz outfit boasted in-the-pocket grooves, clever horn charts, and Pauline Wilson's signature vocals set to lyrics that (more often than not) clearly communicated a Christian worldview. Seawind's career produced only three albums, but Pauline and husband/drummer Bob released an album in the early '80s, and various other members have made their mark in the L.A. studios, playing on a myriad of projects. — *Thom Granger*

Seawind / 1976 / CTI ✦✦✦
Their first outing featured more instrumental than vocal music, but the band still made its point with songs like "He Loves You" and "Devil Is a Liar." — *Thom Granger*

● **Window of a Child** / 1977 / CTI ✦✦✦✦
Though Seawind's second recording came only a year after its debut, this album represents its finest artistic statement, with lyrics that spoke plainly, yet poetically, and funky jazz-pop music. — *Thom Granger*

Light the Light / 1979 / Horizon ✦✦✦
Their third album with the A&M-owned Horizon label exposed the band to new audiences, but some Christians felt the message was watered down in the process. — *Thom Granger*

2nd Chapter of Acts

Church, CCM
This major Christian-rock act, which began in the early '70s, was defined by the sibling harmonies of Annie Herring, Matthew Ward, and Nelly Greisen. Their music brought complex song structures to inspirational music. Their best-known song was 1974's "Easter Song," which achieved mainstream radio airplay (and featured Michael Been, later founder of the Call, on bass). The group's self-deprecating attitudes may have kept them from achieving the renown of some contemporaries. Herring and Ward continued to record after the group disbanded in 1988. — *Brian Mansfield*

● **20** / 1992 / Sparrow ✦✦✦✦
Twentieth-anniversary retrospective is a 41-track overview of the music of this influential group. Includes three early singles for MGM and two previously unreleased cuts. — *Brian Mansfield*

Sensational Nightingales

Black Gospel
The Sensational Nightingales were assembled in the '40s. In 1957 they

appeared on the Gospel Train tour with the Clara Ward Singers and five other big-name gospel acts. Members included Julius Cheeks (lead), Carl Coates (bass), JoJo Wallace (tenor), Howard Carroll (baritone), and Paul Gwens (tenor). Their hit was "See How They Done My Lord." One of the earliest gospel quintets, they still record and tour. Many of their '50s and '60s sides (found on MCA reissues) feature the stunning vocals of Reverend Julius Cheeks. As with Archie Brownlee, Cheeks reaches an intensity that distorts the recordings, and his style has been heavily "borrowed" by Bobby Bland, Wilson Pickett, and others. The later recordings by Charles Johnson are smoother and slicker, but still top-notch. —*Bil Carpenter and Billy C. Wirtz*

The Best of the Sensational Nightingales / 1978 / MCA ✦✦✦✦
Twelve selections featuring Cheeks, Johnson, and Herbert Robertson. This album is first-rate, five-star, indespensable, and available as a budget reissue! —*Billy C. Wirtz*

Victory Is Mine / 1980 / Malaco ✦✦✦
This release has soaring unison vocals on such songs as "He'll Answer Prayer," "He May Not Knock No More," and "Occupy Till He Comes." They also put a nice contemporary touch on "Power in the Blood," and "Open Up My Eyes" has a moving, personalized approach. This isn't earthshaking material, but it's well done and faithful to the genre in mood and approach. —*Ron Wynn, Rejoice*

● **Heart and Soul/You Know Not...** / Mobile Fidelity ✦✦✦✦
The CD remastering of these two early-'70s albums by this fine harmony quintet is well worth owning. *Heart and Soul* is taken from the better pre-Paramount days (1970-1971), and *You Know Not the Hour* presents the group in a later, more hymnal, more hymnal song setting, both with Charles Johnson on lead. —*Kip Lornell*

The 77s

Christian Rock
This quintessential Christian rock band was fronted by vocalist and guitarist Mike Roe. The band's albums make few concessions for CCM compatibility. (Their live album, *88*, for instance, includes a rave-up of the Yardbirds' "Over Under Sideways Down.") Drummer Aaron Smith played with Ray Charles and the Temptations. New band members—bassist Mark Harmon and keyboardist David Leonhardt—made their full-album debut with the band in late 1992 and promise a new direction for the group. —*Brian Mansfield*

The 77s / 1987 / Exit ✦✦✦✦
This promising debut shows a band equally influenced by Bob Dylan and blues-rock. Includes their concert favorite, "The Lust, the Flesh, the Eyes and the Pride of Life," and a killer anthem, "Do It for Love." —*Brian Mansfield*

★ **Sticks and Stones** / 1990 / Brainstorm ✦✦✦✦✦
After the departure of keyboardist Mark Tootle, Mike Roe emerged as the dominant figure in the 77s. *Sticks and Stones* points the way to the 77s of the future: biting, guitar-dominated rock with provocative lyrics epitomized by "Perfect Blues." Included are new recordings of the four best songs from *The 77s*. —*Brian Mansfield*

Seventy Sevens / 1992 / Brainstorm ✦✦✦
A mostly pop collection, with the exception of the Zeppelin-like "Woody" and the unlisted 'title' cut, an eight-minute Middle Eastern rave-up. —*Thom Granger*

Drowning with Land in Sight / 1994 / Myrrh ✦✦✦
Again, an uneven but important album, beginning with a dead-on cover of the Led Zep arrangement on "Nobody's Fault but Mine," and evolving into a hard look at some of life's most challenging realities such as a relationship's dissolution and its effects on the human spirit. —*Thom Granger*

George Beverly Shea

Vocals
Gospel singer-songwriter George Beverly Shea has spent most of his more than 45-year career closely associated with evangelist Billy Graham; his best-known song is "How Great Thou Art," written by Reverend Stuart K. Hine in the 1920s. Shea is also a writer of popular hymns such as "The Wonder of It All." He was born in Winchester, Ontario, the son of a Wesleyan Methodist minister. He was raised in New York and New Jersey parsonages and spent much time as a youth singing in various church choirs. He briefly attended Houghton College in New York, but his family's financial difficulties forced him to drop out. Shea began working as a clerk but continued to receive voice lessons and sing in churches and on local religious radio stations. The latter led to an audition for the Lynn Murray Singers; because they sang secular music, he declined an invitation to join them. He married his high school sweetheart in 1934 and moved to Chicago. In 1944 Shea got national exposure when he was hired to appear on "Club Time," a show he sang with for the next eight years. Shea also became prominent in the Youth for

Christ movement of the '40s and '50s. He hooked up with Graham in 1947 and signed to RCA Victor in 1951. In 1965 *Southland Favorites* received a Grammy for best gospel or other religious recording (musical). Shea was inducted into the Gospel Music Association Hall of Fame in 1978. —*Sandra Brennan*

● **My Favorite Songs (Best of George Beverly Shea)** / Word ✦✦✦✦

Michael W. Smith

b. Kenova, VA
Keyboards, Vocals / CCM, Adult Contemporary
Michael Whitaker Smith has become one of the most enduringly popular artists on the christian contemporary music front and is finding considerable success as a mainstream artist.

He was born in Kenova, WV, the son of an oil refinery worker and a caterer. He became a devout Christian at age ten and spent his teens hanging around with fellow believers who frequently gathered to play and make music. After high school that group split up and Smith turned to alcohol, drugs, and wild times. He scraped through a couple of semesters of college and began honing his songwriting skills. In 1978 a songwriting company expressed interest; and he moved to Nashville, where he played with local bands, including Rose. He was still heavily into drugs and continued using until October 1979, when he suffered a sort of breakdown that culminated in recommitting to Christ. He joined a new CCM group, Higher Ground, as keyboardist, and while touring with them, Smith cleaned up his act.

In 1981 he signed with Meadowgreen Music as a staff writer; over the next few years he provided gospel hits for such artists as Sandi Patti, Kathy Troccoli, Bill Gaither, and Amy Grant. He began touring as a keyboardist with Grant in 1982 and the next year, after releasing his first album, *The Michael W. Smith Project*, became her opening act. His debut album garnered a Grammy nomination for best gospel performance. Smith became a headliner after the release of *Michael W. Smith 2*. Afterward he changed musical directions and began recording more rock-oriented music to reach a younger audience. As a result, some of his songs became more secular and began breaking through to mainstream audiences. His first real shot at mainstream music came in 1991 when his label, Reunion Records, allowed Geffen Records to distribute his albums. They chose a two-pronged promo campaign, with ads designed to appeal to both CCM and mainstream pop audiences. This has caused some controversy among his more religious fans, who feared that Smith was selling out to the more lucrative secular market. Smith has won both Dove and Grammy Awards, has topped *Billboard* charts, and has been hailed by *Keyboard* magazine as one of the top keyboardists in rock. —*Sandra Brennan*

The Big Picture / Feb. 1986 / Reunion ✦✦✦✦
 Smith's most rock-oriented project garnered him more critical acclaim and less airplay and sales. —*Thom Granger*

The Live Set / Mar. 1987 / Reunion ✦✦✦
A jammin' rock-concert aura. —*Bil Carpenter*

The Michael W. Smith Project / Dec. 1987 / Reunion ✦✦✦
Worshipful, inspirational pop. —*Bil Carpenter*

I 2 Eye / 1989 / Reunion ✦✦✦
A mix of mature pop and soft rock. —*Bil Carpenter*

Michael W. Smith 2 / 1989 / Reunion ✦✦

Go West Young Man / 1990 / Reunion ✦✦✦
The artist's first foray into crossover territory includes "Place in This World," which landed on the pop charts and raised the stakes for a new level of acceptance. —*Thom Granger*

Change Your World / 1992 / Reunion ✦✦✦✦
Smith's biggest pop production changed his own world, bringing a bevy of hits in both gospel and pop markets, as well as a new level of touring activity. —*Thom Granger*

★ **Wonder Years** / 1993 / Reunion ✦✦✦✦✦
This deluxe two-disc boxed set of Smith's best 35 songs includes elaborate packaging and commentary from the artist. —*Thom Granger*

☆ **The First Decade: 1983-1993** / Oct. 12, 1993 / Reunion ✦✦✦✦✦
A one-disc greatest hits collection, it features two new songs with a decidedly more mainstream approach. —*Thom Granger*

I'll Lead You Home / Oct. 1995 / Reunion ✦✦✦✦
I'll Lead You Home became the highest-debuting Christian album in chart history and it's easy to see why. Produced by Patrick Leonard, the album consolidates Michael W. Smith's inspirational and pop success, combining gospel songs with glistening, immaculate pop production. Smith had earned pop fans with *Change Your World; I'll Lead You Home* shows that his inspirational records are as good as his pop records. They share the same kind of mainstream pop production; the layered synths and guitars speak to listeners nearly as much as Smith's voice itself. —*Stephen Thomas Erlewine*

Reverend Dan Smith

b. 1911, Alabama
Harmonica, Vocals / Blues Gospel
Smith sang in church and played harmonica as a child. He didn't begin his professional career until the early '60s, when he played behind folk legends Rev. Gary Davis and Pete Seeger. His musical style is overwhelmingly oriented to Chicago blues. —*Bil Carpenter*

● **Just Keep Goin' On** / 1992 / Glasshouse ✦✦✦✦
All original gospel material set to a 12-bar blues backbeat. Harmonica is the instrumental focus, and the songs are separated by short testimonies by Smith in his folksy gravel of a voice. —*Bil Carpenter*

Mother Smith

b. 1906, Rolling Fort, MS
Vocals / Black Gospel
Mother Smith was involved with Thomas Dorsey's National Convention of Gospel Choirs and Choruses and had a 1937 hit with "If You Just Keep Still." Smith had a blues-like contralto and was known for her dramatic vocal fits and improvisational skills on cuts like "Take Your Burdens to the Lord." She performed and recorded sparingly but was influential by starting a tradition of opening a song with a sermonette. She was one of the most important gospel singers to emerge in the '30s. —*Bil Carpenter and Kip Lornell*

● **Mother Willie Mae Ford Smith** / Spirit Feel ✦✦✦✦
Mother Willie Mae Ford Smith and Her Children is a compilation that highlights some of the best performances by Ms. Smith and her musical progeny. —*Kip Lornell*

Willie Mae Ford Smith / Savoy ✦✦✦✦
Includes "I Must Tell Jesus" and "He Never Left Me Alone." —*Bil Carpenter*

Going on with the Spirit / Nashboro ✦✦✦
Of special note: "Give Me Wings" and "I've Got a Secret." —*Bil Carpenter*

Steven Soles

Guitar, Vocals
Former Dylan sideman (on the Rolling Thunder Revue) and Alpha Band member (with T-Bone Burnett), Soles made two CCM albums in the early '80s that were critically acclaimed, if little heard. —*Thom Granger*

Promise / 1980 / Maranatha Music ✦✦✦
A statement of faith by Soles, it includes third Alpha Band-member David Mansfield. —*Thom Granger*

● **Walk by Love** / 1982 / Good News ✦✦✦✦
More commercial than *The Promise*, this second solo album features catchier songs and fuller pop arrangements. —*Thom Granger*

The Soul Stirrers

Soul, Black Gospel
A legendary gospel group known best for introducing Sam Cooke's mellifluous voice to the world, the Soul Stirrers were tremendously influential on the Black gospel scene from the mid-'30s on. They are considered the fathers of the contemporary all-male quartet sound, and their influence can be heard in both gospel and soul music. Formed in Trinity, TX, in 1927, the group soon moved their base of operations to Chicago and recorded for the Library of Congress in 1936. At that time they veered away from the traditional quartet repertoire of jubilees and old spirituals, preferring to focus on new gospel music. This led to criticism, as many believed quartets had no business singing church music. The Soul Stirrers often wrote their own songs or adapted older ones to their styles. They also became the first quartet to add a second lead, thereby freeing up their first lead to do extensive solos with a full quartet behind him, an innovation that was controversial then but has since become a standard practice. In 1936 the Soul Stirrers added lead tenor R.H. Harris. Harris was a great innovator whose advanced concept of modern gospel harmony included alternating leads between two singers, ad-libbing, and the chanting of key words behind the lead while the lead sang at a pace just different enough to create a complex, syncopated sound. These ideas helped make the Soul Stirrers one of the nation's top gospel acts from the '40s on. Harris was replaced by Cooke in 1950, and the charismatic young singer led the group to new heights on Specialty Records through 1956. When Cooke left to go pop, he was succeeded by Jonnie Taylor, who was later to experience soul hitdom himself. Jimmy Outler and James Phelps also handled front work for a time, and by the mid-'60s, when they were signed to Chess, Willie Rogers and Martin Jacox traded leads. A quarter-century later, Rogers and Jacox still lead the active group. —*Bill Dahl and Sandra Brennan*

Heaven Is My Home / 1953-1959 / Specialty/Original ✦✦✦✦
The Soul Stirrers have been gospel's most honored and recognized vocal group since the '40s, when R.H. Harris made musical history by shifting the genre's focus from unison singing to improvisational theatrics and inter-group dynamics. The selections on their most recent reissue cover a significant and too often ignored aspect of the ensemble's history, the music of its other premier lead singers besides Harris and Sam Cooke. Paul Foster and Johnnie Taylor, the set's featured vocalists, weren't virtuosos like Harris or Cooke; they relied on timing, delivery, and fervor. —*Ron Wynn*

The Original Soul Stirrers Featuring Sam Cooke / 1964 / Specialty ✦✦✦✦

In the Beginning / 1991 / Ace ✦✦✦✦
Here's a great collection of Specialty recordings done by Sam Cooke, solo and with the Soul Stirrers in the early/mid-'50s. There's fine gospel singing on "He's My Friend," "'Til the End," "Jesus, I'll Never Forget," "I Don't Want to Cry," "Lovable," and "Forever." The CD issue has several extra tracks. —*Roots and Rhythm Newsletter*

Sam Cooke with the Soul Stirrers / 1992 / Specialty ✦✦✦
This 1992 reissue features previously unreleased material. Sam Cooke incorporated the styles of Archie Brownlee, R. H. Harris, and Julius Cheeks (along with his own natural abilities) to become the best all-around gospel and R&B singer ever. This recording gives 25 reasons why people might say that. —*Billy C. Wirtz*

Jesus Gave Me Water / 1992 / Specialty ✦✦✦✦
Sam Cooke was one of the most original and influential vocal stylists of all time. You can hear him in all his glory (1951-1955) without edits or overdubs; his peerless, soaring melismas are a joy. Catch also the anguished spiritual tones of the great Paul Foste, Sr., as he alternates sparingly with Cooke. The first eight cuts are a cappella. The album includes the "long" version (one of three unissued renderings) of "All Right Now," sung blazingly by gospel's hardest lead, Reverend "June" Julius Cheeks. —*Opal Louis Nations, Roots and Rhythm Newsletter*

★ **The Soul Stirrers** / Specialty ✦✦✦✦✦
Here's a compilation of the group that is synonymous with intense, inspirational, highly-perfected gospel singing. The material—which includes "Wonderful" and "Touch the Hem of His Garment"—spans a decade and features the lead voices of Johnnie Taylor, R.H. Harris, and Paul Foster in addition to Sam Cooke. —*Roundup Newsletter*

● **The Gospel Soul of Sam Cooke, Vol. 2** / Specialty ✦✦✦✦
This work is being promoted under Sam Cooke's name, but it's really the Stirrers' show, with first-class titles like "Farther Along" and "I'm So Glad." Some of Cooke's greatest moments, ca. 1951-1955, with great second-lead support from Paul Foster Sr. Includes three previously unreleased cuts. —*Kip Lornell*

Shine on Me / Specialty ✦✦✦✦
This contains 26 previously released tracks, alternate takes, and unissued tracks (ca. 1950) by the legendary quintet and features postwar gospel's finest and most influential soloist, R.H. Harris. —*Opal Louis Nations*

The Last Mile of the Way / Specialty ✦✦✦
While the Soul Stirrers' catalog has been thoroughly documented on past Specialty reissues, the 28 tracks presented on this set show that even their secondary and/or alternate cuts were outstanding. They pioneered the use of a double lead, with Sam Cooke's wondrous tenor contrasted by several other superb vocalists from Paul Foster to Julius Cheeks. There's even one cut where guitarist Bob King takes a turn at the microphone and doesn't disgrace himself. Although many of these songs have been previously released, it's instructive to hear the discussions and fragments that show the Soul Stirrers experimenting and perfecting the formula that made gospel history. —*Ron Wynn*

Sounds of Blackness

Urban, CCM, Reggae
This 30-piece choir and orchestra, formed in 1971 by Gary Hines at Macalester College in Minnesota, combine traditional African elements with contemporary R&B. —*Bil Carpenter*

● **The Evolution of Gospel** / 1991 / Perspective ✦✦✦✦
Primitive, funky, secularized gospel. —*Bil Carpenter*

The Speer Family

Southern Gospel
The Speer Family emerged when there were countless Southern gospel quartets and are noteworthy because of their longevity. Though personnel has changed over the years, their music in the '90s is true to the music they were making when the group was formed by patriarch G.T. in 1921. This group is an important reference point in appreciation of traditional Southern gospel quartet singing.

G.T. Speer was born in a rural community near Fayetteville, GA, and worked as a teacher at the Stamps-Baxter School of Music in Dallas. He also taught at the Vaughan School of Music, Lawrenceburg, TN. The first incarnation of the Speers was formed with his wife, Lena, and his sister and her husband in 1921. It was innovative because until then, gospel groups were almost always completely male. Despite the trepidation of the naysayers, G.T. persisted with his original lineup, and much to the surprise of gospel "purists," became popular. He also strayed from the norm by having the Speers sing only gospel music. Soon other groups followed suit.

In 1925 his sister and brother-in-law left, and G.T. and Lena added their children, Rosa Nell and Mary Tom, to the line-up. They eventually left to raise their own children, but returned to become permanent members a few years later. Over the years, the Speers Family often contained other musicians, most notably Harold Lane, who spent two decades with them.

Through the '50s and '60s the Speers were frequent guests on radio station WLAC Nashville. In 1966 G.T. suddenly died and became the first person inducted into the "deceased" category of the Gospel Music Hall of Fame. Lena died the next year, and became the second to be inducted in the same institution in 1972. During their long career the group has won numerous awards and honors, but one of the highest came in 1981 on the group's 60th anniversary, when they were entered into the Congressional Record and received a plaque that contained their first commercial record. To celebrate these events the Benson Company distributed a commemorative anniversary album and packaged a multimedia presentation chronicling the family's history. The Speer Family continues to record and perform. In 1993 they released *A Beautiful Day. —Sandra Brennan and Bil Carpenter*

Hallelujah Time / 1990 / HB ◆◆◆

● **He's Still in the Fire** / 1990 / HB ◆◆◆◆

All Night Singing / 1991 / Starday ◆◆◆

Hallelujah / 1991 / Heartwarming ◆◆◆

The Speer Family / Powerpak ◆◆◆

The Staple Singers

Soul, Gospel

The Staples' story goes all the way back to Winona, MS, in 1915. It was then and there that patriarch Roebuck Staples entered the world. A contemporary and familiar of Charley Patton, Roebuck quickly became adept as a solo blues guitarist, entertaining at local dances and picnics. Gradually drawn to the church, by 1937 he was singing and playing guitar with a spiritual group, the Golden Trumpets, based in Drew, MS. Moving to Chicago four years later, he continued playing gospel music with the Windy City's Trumpet Jubilees. A decade later Pops Staples (as he had become known) presented two of his daughters, Cleotha and Mavis, and his son Pervis in front of a church audience, and the Staple Singers were born.

The Staples recorded in an older, slightly archaic, deeply Southern spiritual style, first for United and then for Vee-Jay. Pops and Mavis Staples shared lead vocal chores, with most records underpinned by Pops' heavily reverbed Mississippi cottonpatch guitar. In 1960 the Staples signed with Riverside, a label that specialized in jazz and folk. With Riverside and later Epic, the Staples attempted to move into the then-burgeoning White folk boom. Two Epic releases, "Why (Am I Treated So Bad)" and a cover of Stephen Stills' "For What It's Worth," briefly graced the pop charts in 1967.

In 1968 the Staples signed with Memphis-based Stax. The first two albums, *Soul Folk in Action* and *We'll Get Over*, were produced by Steve Cropper and backed by Booker T & The MG's. The Staples were now singing entirely contemporary "message" songs such as "Long Walk to D.C." and "When Will We Be Paid." In 1970 Pervis Staples left and was replaced by sister Yvonne Staples. Even more significantly, Al Bell took over production chores. Bell took them to Muscle Shoals, and things got decidedly funky.

Starting with "Heavy Makes You Happy (Sha-Na-Boom Boom)" and "I'll Take You There," the Staples counted 12 chart hits at Stax. When Stax encountered financial problems, Curtis Mayfield signed the Staples to his Curtom label and produced a number one hit in "Let's Do It Again." The Staples went on to continued chart success, albeit less spectacularly, with Warner through 1979. One more album followed on 20th Century-Fox in 1981. After a three-year hiatus, they signed a two-album deal with Private I and hit the R&B charts five more times, once with an unlikely cover of Talking Heads' "Slippery People."

The Staple Singers found a new audience in 1994 when they teamed with Marty Stuart to perform "The Weight" on the *Rhythm, Country and Blues* LP for MCA. *—Rob Bowman*

Uncloudy Day/Will the Circle Be Unbroken / 1955-1960 / Vee-Jay ◆◆◆◆

The Staple Singers brilliantly fused gospel, folk, blues, and soul in a cohesive, commercially potent sound in the '50s and '60s. They perfected this approach during their tenure at Vee-Jay, the first label that allowed the twangy, expert guitar licks of Roebuck "Pop" Staples to be heard in the group's mix and fully presented their harmonies. This single disc contains two pivotal Staples albums: *Uncloudy Day* includes such gospel

favorites as "I Know I Got Religion" and "Let Me Ride," while *Will the Circle Be Unbroken* offers the splendid title track, plus masterpieces like "Pray On" and "Come Up in Glory." *—Ron Wynn*

Great Day / 1963 / Milestone ◆◆◆

This two-album Fantasy reissue is an anthology of the material the Staples recorded for Riverside between 1960 and 1963. For Riverside, the Staples recorded mostly gospel, but the shouting was toned down a bit. A few modern-day "message" songs make their way into their repertoire, including Bob Dylan's "Masters of War." Not quite as cataclysmic as their Vee-Jay material, but still essential. *—Rob Bowman*

Make You Happy / 1971 / Epic ◆◆◆

From Riverside, the Staples moved on to Columbia subsidiary Epic in 1964. With Epic they delved further into the secular realm, hitting the pop charts twice with Pops Staples' plaintive "Why Am (I Treated So Bad)?" and a cover of Stephen Stills' "For What It's Worth." Both are included on this two-disc anthology, as is a stunning side of live performance. *—Rob Bowman*

Freedom Highway / 1965 / CBS ◆◆◆

A reissue of their first great Riverside collection, with "Daddy" Roebuck and the legendary Mavis Staples as leads. The Staples once again mix a positive political message with a dash of religion. *—Kip Lornell*

Soul Folk in Action / 1968 / Stax ◆◆◆

The Staples' debut Stax release includes covers of Otis Redding's "(Sittin' On) The Dock of the Bay" and the Band's "The Weight." Steve Cropper produced and the Stax songwriting staff concocted a number of socially concious lyrics, the most notable being "Long Walk to D.C." *—Rob Bowman*

Pray On / 1968 / Hob ◆◆◆◆

The Staple Singers recorded ten 78s over a four-year period for Chicago's Vee-Jay. These have been reissued countless times in various forms. The Charly CD is simply the most recent. For Vee-Jay The Staples recorded a number of Pops Staples originals as well as radical rearrangements of standards. Pops Staples and Mavis Staples shared the lead singing chores, with Pervis and Cleotha Staples moaning in the background. Superb gospel shouting. *—Rob Bowman*

We'll Get Over / 1970 / Stax ◆◆◆

Their second Stax release was similar to *Soul Folk in Action*. The album's highlight is Randall Stewart's "When Will We Be Paid?" *—Rob Bowman*

The Staple Swingers / 1971 / Stax ◆◆◆

The Staples' first album produced by Al Bell and recorded in Muscle Shoals hit the winning formula. Other changes saw Pervis Staples departing just before the album was recorded and being replaced by sister Yvonne Staples. Everything was now in place for the Staples' golden years. Three songs, "Heavy Makes You Happy," "Love Is Plentiful," and "You've Got to Earn It," all charted. *—Rob Bowman*

Be Attitude: Respect Yourself / 1972 / Stax ◆◆◆

The Staples' finest single album, containing three Top Ten R&B hits: "Respect Yourself," "I'll Take You There," and "This World." The first two also were pop Top 20s, "I'll Take You There" going all the way to No. 1. *—Rob Bowman*

Be What You Are / 1973 / Stax ◆◆◆

Continuing in the same vein, *Be What You Are* contained three chart hits: the title song, "If You're Ready (Come Go with Me)," and "Touch a Hand, Make a Friend." The Stax songwriters, combined with Mavis Staples' unbelievably seductive vocals, were on a roll. *—Rob Bowman*

City in the Sky / 1974 / Stax ◆◆◆

Stax was teetering on its last legs, but the label still managed to squeeze two final chart hits out of the Staple Singers in the title cut and "My Main Man." A cut below the previous three albums. *—Rob Bowman*

Best of the Staple Singers [Stax] / 1975 / Buddah ◆◆◆

Exactly what the title implies—seven monster soul hits plus three judiciously chosen album cuts. One chart hit, "Oh La De Dah," makes its only album appearance here. This disc is nearly too rich for one sitting. Early-'70s soul simply does not get better. *—Rob Bowman*

Let's Do It Again / 1975 / Curtom ◆◆◆

As Stax neared bankruptcy, the Staples signed with Curtis Mayfield's Curtom label for this soundtrack album. The title track was a No. 1 hit, and "New Orleans" reached No. 70, returning the Staples to the upper echelons of the charts for the last time. *—Rob Bowman*

● **Chronicle** / 1979 / Stax ◆◆◆◆

This 1979 greatest-hits collection by Roebuck Staples and daughters Mavis, Yvonne, and Cleo shines a light on their moving harmonies and earthy, funky gospel sound. It includes "Heavy Makes You Happy (Sha-Na-Boom-Boom)," "Respect Yourself," and "Be What You Are." *—Roundup Newsletter*

★ **Best Of** / Stax ✦✦✦✦✦
This is a double Vee-Jay set of prime Staples sides, 27 songs picked from the 33 cuts on three Vee-Jay albums that constitute the group's best gospel period (1955-1961). The group's close country (Mississippi) harmony, sharpened by the riveting Delta blues guitar stylings of Pops Staples, is topped off by the impassioned virtuosity of lead singer Mavis Staples, who could reach low into bass notes, then scream and moan her heart out. It includes "Uncloudy Day," "Swing Low," "Pray On," "Stand by Me," "If I Could Hear My Mother Pray Again," "I Know I Got Religion," and "Sit Down Servant." About a dozen tracks are duplicated on a New Cross LP. — *Opal Louis Nations, Roots and Rhythm Newsletter*

Candi Staton (Candi Staton-Sussewell)

b. Mar. 13, 1940, Hanceville, AL
Vocals / Gospel, Urban
A sensitive Southern soul singer, Candi Staton got her start recording with famed producer Rick Hall in his Muscle Shoals studio in the early '70s. The association was productive enough to net her a modest pop hit in 1970 with a soulful reworking of Tammy Wynnette's "Stand By Your Man." Later she signed with Warner Bros. Records, where she recorded her biggest hit, the Top 20 disco ballad "Young Hearts Run Free." Unfortunately, Staton suffered from benign neglect at the label, as Warner Bros. wasn't giving her adequate material and production, though she dented the charts again in 1979 with the dance track "Victim." Today Staton has eschewed secular music in favor of gospel, and in doing so she makes frequent appearances on Paul Crouch's Trinity Broadcasting Network, as well as Pat Robertson's "700 Club." — *John Lowe*

I'm Just a Prisoner / 1969 / ✦✦✦✦
Rick Hall's horns, creeping piano, and Staton's grit. — *Bil Carpenter*

Young Hearts Run Free / 1976 / Warner Brothers ✦✦✦
Soul meets disco on this classy dance record with tender downbeats. — *Bil Carpenter*

Love Lifted Me / 1988 / Beracah ✦✦✦✦
Traditional gospel reflecting her deep-South roots. — *Bil Carpenter*

Stand Up and Be a Witness / 1990 / Beracah ✦✦✦
Urban, upbeat psalms and exhortations. — *Bil Carpenter*

★ **The Best of Candi Staton** / Nov. 1995 / Warner Archives ✦✦✦✦✦
Candi Staton deserved better. Like many of her counterparts during the disco era, Staton suffered from artistic disintegration at the hands of producers who were not sympathetic to her talents. All the essential tracks are here, including a beautiful rendition of "Precious Lord, Take My Hand." — *John Lowe*

Standing on the Promises / Beracah ✦✦

Randy Stonehill

Guitar, Vocals / CCM
Veteran singer-songwriter Randy Stonehill works primarily in acoustic-based settings but also loves to rock, and displays the occasional penchant for satire. — *Thom Granger*

Welcome to Paradise / 1976 / Solid Rock ✦✦✦✦
Stonehill's first album to receive widespread distribution, this early 'Jesus Rock' masterpiece still stands the test of time, mostly due to top-notch songwriting. Unfortunately, it's out of print. — *Thom Granger*

Between the Glory and the Flame / 1981 / Myrhh ✦✦✦
The first pairing with Daniel Amos' leader Terry Taylor producing, this stripped down pop-rocker reflects the new wave trends of the time. — *Thom Granger*

Equator / 1982 / Myrrh ✦✦✦
The artist's most successful record veers from radio-ready ballads to quirky pop peculiarities. — *Thom Granger*

Wild Frontier / 1986 / Word ✦✦✦
After two unsatisfying forays into the more commercial trappings of pop, Stonehill formed a new association with producer/player Dave Perkins with larger-than-life rock arrangements and vocals. — *Thom Granger*

★ **Return to Paradise** / 1989 / Word ✦✦✦✦✦
Stonehill's work on this essential collection with Mark Heard (who produced) resulted in the most consistent group of thoughtful, introspective songs in years. — *Thom Granger*

Wonderama / 1991 / Myrhh ✦✦✦
Randy reunited with Terry Taylor for a psychedelic, Beatlesque song cycle that may have set the stage for Taylor's own version of the same with Daniel Amos, *Motor Cycle*. — *Thom Granger*

Stories / 1993 / Myrrh ✦✦✦
A collection of Stonehill's story-songs, mostly ballads, is culled from his Myrrh releases. — *Thom Granger*

Stryper

Heaven's Metal, Hard Rock
A hard rock/heavy metal CCM quartet founded in Orange County, CA, in 1983. At the time they signed to Enigma Records in 1984, the group consisted of lead singer Michael Sweet, guitarist Oz Fox, bassist Timothy Gaines, and drummer Robert Sweet. Their first recording was the mini-album *The Yellow and Black Attack*, followed by 1985's full-length album *Soldiers Under Command*, which reached No. 84 on the charts. Enigma remixed *The Yellow and Black Attack* and added two songs in 1986, and the new version hit No. 103. *To Hell with the Devil* (1986) went gold and earned the band a Grammy nomination. *In God We Trust* (1988) repeated this success. *Against the Law* (1990) was somewhat less of a hit. — *William Ruhlmann*

In God We Trust / 1988 / Hollywood ✦✦✦
Balanced soft-rock/metal guitar licks. — *Bil Carpenter*

★ **Can't Stop the Rock** / 1991 / Hollywood ✦✦✦✦✦
Can't Stop the Rock: The Stryper Collection 1984-1991 features thundering drums, wailing guitars, keening choruses, pseudo-castrati singing—all the accoutrements of metal, and here in the service of the Lord. This best-of selects from the group's five previous recordings. — *William Ruhlmann*

Swan Silvertones (Four Harmony Kings)

Black Gospel
The Swan Silvertones are a premiere gospel group. The a cappella quartet Four Harmony Kings was created by tenor Claude Jeter in 1938 in Coalwood, WV, but the name was changed to the Swan Silvertones when they began a 15-minute radio show sponsored by the Swan Bakery Company in Knoxville in 1942. They developed a national reputation during their contract with King Records from 1946 to 1951, recording some 21 recordings (mostly in the jubilee gospel style) including "I Cried Holy" and "Go Ahead." They joined Specialty Records from 1951 to 1953, but issued only four singles (in a more contemporary, harder style) before they were dropped by that label. The early group had lead singers Jeter and Solomon Womack, tenors Robert Crenshaw and John Manson, baritone John H. Myles, and bass Henry K. Bossard.
They really came into their own when they recorded with Vee-Jay through 1964. The smoother Vee-Jay sound was probably due to arranger Paul Owens, who joined the group in 1952. Influenced by jazz-vocal groups like the Four Freshmen and the Hi-Los, Owens smoothed out the sound and made it more contemporary, even progressive. Starting in 1956 the group began adding instruments to what had been up until then a purely vocal sound. The excellent guitarist Linwood Hargrove added greatly to the emerging Vee-Jay sound, and the additions (on recordings) of jazz sidemen Bob Cranshaw on bass and Walter Perkins —founding members of MJT (3)—on drums completed the sound.
Perhaps their greatest hit was "Oh Mary Don't You Weep," released in 1959—an incredible listening experience. It is in this song that Claude Jeter intones the phrase "I'll be a bridge over deep water, if you trust in my name" that inspired Paul Simon to compose "Bridge Over Troubled Water" some years later. The Swan Silvertones had a great effect on many rock (Al Kooper) and country (Gary Stewart) artists. During their nine years at Vee-Jay, the main members of the group were tenor (and falsetto) Claude Jeter, baritone John H. Myles, tenor Paul Owens, and bass William Conner. Other singers in the group during that time were tenors Dewey Young, Robert Crutcher, and Louis Johnson. When Vee-Jay closed in 1965, the group moved to Hob records, where they did one last album before Claude Jeter left to record on his own and focus on his ministry. — *Michael Erlewine*

Heavenly Light / 1952 / Specialty ✦✦✦✦
The Swan Silvertones recorded for Specialty Records from 1952 until 1955, and it's generally not considered a prime period. But this set of newly released performances from the early '50s shows that they did turn in some top-flight outings during that period. Ten of the tracks were done live before hollering, celebrating audiences that weren't attending a concert, but participating in a spiritual renewal. The other eight are studio numbers, but they contain the same intensity and spark. — *Ron Wynn*

Pray for Me / 1956-1961 / Vee-Jay ✦✦✦
This is early Swan Silvertones on Vee-Jay, recorded in sessions in 1956, 1957, and 1961 but not compiled and released as an album until 1974. It is available on the Vee-Jay two-fer *The Swan Silvertones* along with another great album, *Let's Go to Church Together*. — *Michael Erlewine*

☆ **Let's Go to Church Together** / 1964 / Vee-Jay ✦✦✦✦✦
This is quintessential Swan Silvertones at their peak. Songs like "Love Lifted Me" and "I'll Be Satisfied" capture some of the finest work of this legendary group. — *Michael Erlewine*

Day by Day / 1972 / Savoy ✦✦

Get Right with the Swan Silvertones / 1982 / Rhino ✦✦✦✦
A reissue of various '50s and '60s singles and album sides plus two unis-sued cuts. Lead vocal dynamics from Reverend Claude Jeter, Paul Owens, and Louis Johnson. This well rounded and amply annotated cross-section deserves serious consideration. —*Kip Lornell*

★ **Swan Silverstones** / 1993 / Specialty ✦✦✦✦✦
Here is perhaps the best of the Vee-Jay albums (12 tracks) of vintage Swan Silverstones. These tracks came from six sessions for Vee-Jay when the group was at its creative peak—perhaps the single best album they ever put out. It contains their hit "Oh Mary Don't You Weep," "How I Got Over," "My Rock," "The Lord's Prayer," "When Jesus Comes," and "Great Day in December"—all incredible music experiences. —*Michael Erlewine*

★ **Swan Silvertones/Singin' in My Soul** / Oct. 1993 / Vee-Jay ✦✦✦✦✦
Here is one CD with two classic Vee-Jay albums (24 tracks) of vintage Swan Silvertones. Both albums came from six sessions for Vee-Jay when the group was at its creative peak. The album *Swan Silvertones* is per-haps the single best album they ever put out. *Singin' in My Soul* has 12 more prime Vee-Jay cuts. —*Michael Erlewine*

☆ **Best of Swan Silvertones** / Chameleon ✦✦✦✦✦
This is a reissue of a Vee-Jay LP drawn principally from other Vee-Jay albums issued in 1960 and 1963. Reverend Claude Jeter's swooping fal-setto is heard in all its magnificence. So is the preaching style of Louis Johnson and the soft, soulful tones of the great Paul Owens. It contains definitive quintet versions of "The Lord's Prayer," "Blessed Quietness," "Jesus Remembers," and "Great Day in December." These cuts are post-war gospel milestones and memories of how dramatic and spiritually uplifting gospel music had become. It's a must for all serious collectors of postwar gospel music if you don't already have the reissue of these tracks on Rhino or New Cross. —*Opal Louis Nations, Roots and Rhythm News-letter*

☆ **Pray For Me/Let's Go to Church Together** / Vee-Jay ✦✦✦✦✦
The Swan Silvertones perfected their shimmering, explosive vocals while on Vee-Jay Records from 1956-1964. The elastic, dazzling falsetto of Claude Jeter, which was later adapted and reworked by Al Green, was contrasted by any number of powerful second lead singers within the group: Paul Owens, Louis Johnson, or Azell Monk. The songs on this disc, with one exception, cover the Silvertones' last great period and offer resounding harmonies, soaring leads, and remarkable music. The lead selection, "Sinners Crossroad," is actually the Silver Quintette, an Indiana group probably most famous for having on its roster two future soul stars, Roscoe Robinson and Joe Henderson. —*Ron Wynn*

☆ **My Rock/Love Lifted Me** / Specialty ✦✦✦✦✦
Some of the best hard-gospel harmonizing from the mid-'50s, most nota-bly "How I Got Over" and "My Rock." The group's toughest sides, with firm conviction from lead soloists Solomon Womack, Rev. Bob Cren-shaw, Dewey Young, and Paul Owens.—*Kip Lornell*

Singing' in My Soul / Vee-Jay ✦✦✦✦
Here is one of the classic Vee-Jay albums (12 tracks) of vintage Swan Sil-vertones. These tracks came from six sessions for Vee-Jay when the group was at its creative peak. The album includes "End of My Journey," "Jesus is Alright with Me," and their version of "Rock My Soul." —*Michael Erlewine*

Swirling Eddies

CCM, Alternative Pop-Rock
Another Terry Taylor spin-off (consisting of Adam Again's Gene Eugene and various members of Daniel Amos and related bands listed under pseudonyms), Swirling Eddies mix rock and satire with humorous (and occasionally profound) results. —*Thom Granger*

● **Let's Spin** / 1988 / Alarma ✦✦✦✦
Outdoor Elvis / 1989 / Alarma ✦✦✦
Zoom Daddy / 1994 / Alarma ✦✦✦

Russ Taff

b. 1953
Vocals / CCM
Taff first gained recognition as lead vocalist for the Imperials (1977-1981), but quickly gained a reputation as one of Christian music's most powerful and versatile artists, one whose music could hold its own against the best mainstream acts. His dynamic vocals reflect both the joys and the struggles of the Christian faith. —*Brian Mansfield*

Medals / 1985 / Horizon ✦✦✦
The second solo set showcases '80s pop styles and hooky songs, resulting in a CCM classic. —*Thom Granger*

Russ Taff / 1987 / Word ✦✦✦
This self-titled effort finds Taff trying to find himself. A cathartic album, it's less accessible but deeply felt. —*Thom Granger*

★ **The Way Home** / 1990 / Word ✦✦✦✦✦
Taff serves up his best effort here, a blend of well-crafted acoustic pop and roots-rock that deserved to be heard beyond the walls of CCM. —*Thom Granger*

★ **Under Their Influence, Vol. 1** / 1991 / Word ✦✦✦✦✦
The musical roots of most CCM artists lie pretty close to the surface, but that's not the case with Taff, the son of a Pentecostal evangelist who preached in California migrant territory. Here Taff pays tribute to Blind Willie Johnson, Brother Joe May, and Mahalia Jackson, among others, with an album that provides the link between gut-level gospel and Southern rock. —*Brian Mansfield*

Take 6

Gospel, Jazz, Bop, Free Funk
An innovative vocal sextet, Take 6 has an uncanny sense of history and taste. They combine classic gospel quartet singing with the jazzier approach of groups like Gene Puerling's Hi-Lo's and Singers Unlimited for unparalled arrangements and musicianship. —*Thom Granger*

● **Take 6** / 1988 / Reprise ✦✦✦✦
The collective exchanges and massed harmonies of six Nashville gospel vocalists make this an unusual, often spectacular release. The approach more closely echoes classic jubilee than the more common quartet gos-pel. — *Ron Wynn*

So Much 2 Say / 1990 / Warner Alliance ✦✦✦
Slightly more contemporary than their debut. —*Bil Carpenter*

Join the Band / 1994 / Warner Brothers ✦✦✦
The group branches out with instrumental backing throughout for the first time, with appearances by Ray Charles, Stevie Wonder, Queen Lati-fah, and a host of stellar sidemen. —*Thom Granger*

Steve Taylor

Guitar, Vocals / CCM
Sometimes referred to as the "clown prince of Christian music," Steve Taylor brought sarcasm and satire to Christian music. His acerbic lyrics engendered enough controversy to place him among the most visible Christian rockers of the mid-'80s. Ultimately he felt stifled by the indus-try and quit recording for the Christian market, but resurfaced as the lead singer of Chagall Guevara in 1991. He resumed his solo career in 1994. —*Brian Mansfield*

I Predict 1990 / 1987 / Myrrh ✦✦✦✦
It's small surprise the Christian community all but disowned Taylor after songs like "I Blew Up the Clinic Real Good" and "Since I Gave Up Hope I Feel a Lot Better." The songs on *I Predict 1990* don't look for easy answers—they rarely look for answers at all—and they're often unset-tling. But half of Taylor's point is that life rarely gives easy answers. The other half is in the final song: "Harder to Believe than Not To." —*Brian Mansfield*

★ **The Best We Could Find** / 1988 / Sparrow ✦✦✦✦✦
This compilation makes an excellent introduction to Taylor's iconoclastic songwriting, with music that frequently sounds like a new-wave Chris-tian sideshow. Taylor gets his licks in on modern culture with "Meltdown (At Madame Tussaud's)," but he more often turns his gaze on the church with songs like "I Want to Be a Clone" and "This Disco (Used to Be a Cute Cathedral)." —*Brian Mansfield*

Squint / 1993 / Warner Alliance ✦✦✦
Taylor returns as a solo act with a renewed sense of satiric mission and great music to surround his incisive lyrics. —*Thom Granger*

Pat Terry

Harp, Vocals
A Georgia-based artist, Terry was one of the few in early Jesus music worth his salt as a songwriter. The Pat Terry Group produced a handful of interesting pop CCM albums in the mid-to-late '70s, but couldn't pre-pare fans for the trio of artful, introspective solo records made in the early '80s with Mark Heard that were to be his last in the gospel market. Terry still writes, now for the country market. —*Thom Granger*

Songs of the South / 1976 / Myrrh ✦✦✦
Simple acoustic pop, it features "Home Where I Belong" and "Happy Man," later to be hits for B.J. Thomas. —*Thom Granger*

Humanity Gangsters / 1982 / Myrrh ✦✦✦
His first solo album finds Terry restless, coming up with more questions than answers, and arguably making better music (with the help of pro-ducer Mark Heard, who also contributes guitars) than any of his albums with the Group. —*Thom Granger*

★ **Film at Eleven** / 1983 / Myrrh ✦✦✦✦✦
The second of three albums produced with Heard finds the artist speak-ing eloquently to the issues of life from a distinctly Christian, though less

dogmatic, point of view than his earlier songs, making for an album that, like many of Heard's, stands the test of time. — *Thom Granger*

Silence / 1984 / Myrrh ◆◆◆

Terry completed his trilogy with another strong collection that features Leslie (now Sam) Phillips on "Man of Sorrows." — *Thom Granger*

Sister Rosetta Tharpe

b. Mar. 20, 1921, Cotton Plant, AR, d. Oct. 9, 1973, Philadelphia, PA
Guitar, Vocals / Blues, Black Gospel, United States

Sister Rosetta Tharpe was one of the most popular gospel singers of the '30s, '40s, and early '50s. She was also a pioneer in that her success helped ease the way for other female gospel singers such as Marion Williams and, most notably, Sister O.M. Terrell. With her natural flamboyance, secular affectations, and tendency to perform blues and swing-influenced gospel in both clubs and in church, Tharpe also generated controversy among the sanctified saints who comprised her biggest audience.

Rosetta Tharpe was born in Cotton Plant, AR, the daughter of Katie Bell Nubin (better known as Mother Bell), a shouter and devoted saint. Her mother frequently attended Holiness conventions throughout the South and Midwest. She and Tharpe eventually settled in Chicago, where the six-year-old Tharpe made her performing debut singing and playing guitar before 1,000 parishioners. This led to the girl's touring with P.W. McGhee's tent revivals, where she would wow audiences with such tunes as "The Day Is Past and Gone" and "I Looked Down the Line." Not only was Tharpe an excellent singer, with a powerful but lightly toned voice, she was also an accomplished guitarist with a style close to that of bluesman Big Bill Broonzy. Her own playing style is said to have influenced a number of other blues guitarists such as Brother Willie Eason and Utah Smith.

Signing with Decca in 1938, she recorded such major hits as "Rock Me," "That's All," and her best-known song, "This Train," all of which have since become gospel standards. The success of her records led the charismatic Sister Tharpe to begin performing with such big bands as Lucky Millinder and Benny Goodman. Tharpe had an excellent ability to judge an audience and always tailored her recordings and performances to fit a particular crowd. She soon began performing at churches, in stadiums, and in New York's Cotton Club and Cafe Society Downtown in New York; in 1939, Tharpe was profiled in *Life* magazine. During WW II she and the Golden Gate Quartet were the only Black gospel singers to record on V-Discs. During the war she toured with a variety of quartets, including her favorites, the Dixie Hummingbirds. By this time she had become a major star and her songs frequently made it to the Top Ten on the race-record charts. In 1945 she and Roy Acuff performed on an educational radio show about venereal disease. Tharpe teamed up with Marie Knight in 1946 to record a number of exceptional singles, beginning with "Up Above My Head." The duo then began touring with various quartets. Tharpe also recorded and toured with Mother Bell and different choirs.

In 1951 she married Russell Morrison, the former manager for the Ink Spots. She and Madame Knight caused considerable outrage amongst their devoted fans in the early '50s when they began making blues records. Tharpe didn't like the change, and she attempted to return to the fold. Unfortunately, her former fans felt she'd betrayed them by "selling out," and many turned their backs upon her. By the mid-'50s she had gone from filling stadiums and ballrooms and having hit records to barely being able to fill clubs. She went to Europe to sing in clubs, and a year later she returned to sing in churches around the South. To augment her meager income, Tharpe would also hawk perfume, nylons, and recordings after each performance.

By 1960, she had regained her high profile when she impressed audiences with an emotionally charged two-night stay at the Apollo. By this time her voice had deepened an octave and had lost its girlish tone, but this only served to improve her singing. Later in the decade, she and Muddy Waters embarked upon a European tour and by the mid-'60s had become popular again, but on a much smaller scale. Instead of playing major concert halls, she found herself playing small churches in backwater towns, but Tharpe was happy with the change, finding herself back in touch with genuine country/folk and making enough to live comfortably. In 1967 she appeared at the Newport Folk Festival. She then went on to record again for Savoy.

While on a European tour in 1970, Sister Tharpe suffered a stroke and ended up losing a leg. Her speech was impaired but not her singing. Despite the setbacks, she continued singing and began touring with the Nightingales in 1972. In 1973, she was scheduled for a recording session with Savoy, but on the appointed day suffered a massive stroke and died the next morning. Despite her popularity and importance, Sister Rosetta Tharpe was buried with little of the fanfare and hoopla that characterized the funerals of the two other female gospel greats, Clara Ward and Mahalia Jackson. — *Sandra Brennan*

Gospel Train, Vol. 2 / 1960 / Lection ◆◆◆

This was recorded later than the material on *Volume 1*, some of Sister Rosetta's worst, most-overproduced recordings. — *Opal Louis Nations*

Live in Paris: 1964 / 1964 / French Concerts ◆◆◆

A nice, rather folk-like concert performance in front of an enthusiastic audience. — *Kip Lornell*

Live at the Hot Club de France / 1966 / Milan ◆◆◆

This recording, done in front of French audiences in 1966, starts out as a polite, folky affair. Sister Rosetta Tharpe, perhaps a bit shy in the overseas concert setting, plays it safe with "This Train," "Jesus Met the Woman at the Well," and "He's Got the Whole World in His Hands." Then comes the rip-roaring intro to "Walk All over God's Heaven," and Tharpe hits her testifyin' stride, and that husky voice can do no wrong (except overloading the mike once in awhile). Her electric guitar is way down in the mix, but thankfully the engineer was paying attention to her show-stopping solo on "Joshua Fit the Battle." Of the 12 selections, most are standard spirituals. — *Myles Boisen, Roots and Rhythm Newsletter*

Gospel 1938-1943 / Frémeaux & Associés ◆◆◆◆

Ironically, singer/guitarist Sister Rosetta Tharpe's twin gospel and blues careers stunted both, and the fact that she was a woman singing solo in an era of male quartets didn't help. But she was one of the finest of all solo gospel singers and a highly individual one. These stunning, mostly acoustic, performances are pinnacles of the African-American religious tradition. — *John Storm Roberts, Original Music*

● **Sacred and Secular** / Rosetta ◆◆◆◆

A beautiful collection of 16 recordings covering 1941 through 1969. Sister Rosetta Tharpe recorded religious songs, jazz and blues, though the majority of her recordings were religious, and this emphasis is followed on this reissue. The recordings here feature her with various groups, including Lucky Millinder's band (with whom she worked for many years), Leroy Kirkland's Orchestra, and smaller groups featuring Sam Price and others. Excellent sound, full discographical details, and extensive notes in a beautiful fold-out jacket with great photos. — *Roots & Rhythm Newsletter*

Kathy Troccoli

Vocals / CCM, Adult Contemporary

Next to Amy Grant and Sandi Patti, New Yorker Kathy Troccoli was probably CCM's most popular female singer before leaving the business in 1986 when her record label, Reunion, couldn't produce the mainstream stardom she sought. Troccoli returned to Reunion when the label had mainstream possibilities (after signing a distribution pact with Geffen) to release hit *Pure Attraction* in 1991. — *Brian Mansfield*

Pure Attraction / 1991 / Reunion ◆◆◆◆

Troccoli's first recording after a five-year absence was her most commercial, with the Diane Warren-penned "Everything Changes" hitting Top Five on CHR radio. Troccoli had developed her songwriting during her time away; she wrote seven of *Pure Attraction*'s cuts, emphasizing the torch-song style she loves. — *Brian Mansfield*

● **Kathy Troccoli** / 1994 / RCA ◆◆◆◆

Sounds of Heaven / Sep. 26, 1995 / Reunion ◆◆◆

The Trumpeters

Black Gospel

Influenced by the Golden Gate Quartet and led by the spectacular singing of Joe Johnson, this quartet hit the public's consciousness in the late '40s with "Milky White Way," recorded for Score Records. Other members included Raleigh Turnage (tenor), Joseph Armstrong (baritone), and James Keels (bass). There were numerous personnel changes, and they disbanded upon Johnson's death in 1948. — *Bil Carpenter and Kip Lornell*

★ **Milky White Way** / 1956 / Score ◆◆◆◆◆

A wonderful sampling of the recordings made by this first-rate a cappella vocal group during the late '40s and early '50s. The title cut became one of this postwar quartet's heaviest-selling gospel 78s. Fine, smooth lead choruses from Joseph Johnson. — *Kip Lornell*

The Twelfth Tribe

Christian Rap

The California duo of Dave Portillo and Eddie Sierra began rapping in 1985 under the name of Deity. Influenced by soul and heavy metal, they like the rap of Kool Moe Dee, Houdini, and the Fat Boys. They take their name from the twelfth tribe of Israel, the Benjamites, mighty warriors. They portray a tougher image than most Christian rap artists and have a hard, street rap sound. — *Bil Carpenter*

● **Knowledge Is the Tribe of Life** / 1991 / Frontline ◆◆◆◆

Produced, engineered, and mixed by master urban dance musician Scott Blackwell, who easily moves into the hard, funky side of Christian rap here. There are 15 rhymes on war, peace, and knowing God. The sound is very Black, very hard, with a few metal elements; a good set, though not overly original outside of the gospel music industry. —*Bil Carpenter*

Albertina Walker

b. Aug. 1930, Chicago, IL
Vocals / Black Gospel
Born in Chicago, Walker sang with the Pete Williams Singers and the Robert Anderson Singers before forming the Caravans in 1951. Among the Caravans' classics were "Mary Don't You Weep," "Soldiers in the Army," "The Solid Rock," and "The Blood Will Never Lose Its Power." Since 1960 Walker has been a solo singer, maintaining her ties to traditional gospel. —*Bil Carpenter*

Tell the Angels / 1960 / Savoy ✦✦✦
Her 1960 debut, after the Caravans. —*Bil Carpenter*

● God Is Love / 1975 / Lection ✦✦✦✦
A fine collection by this influential performer. —*Kip Lornell*

You Believed in Me / 1991 / Benson ✦✦✦
This recent album includes "Working on a Building." —*Bil Carpenter*

The Best Is Yet to Come / Savoy ✦✦

My Time Is Not Over / Word ✦✦

Clara Ward and the Ward Singers

Gospel, Black Gospel
Clara Ward, along with Sister Rosetta Tharpe and Mahalia Jackson, is among the holy trinity of legendary female singers who have had untold influence on the development and direction of Black gospel music. She was also one of the most controversial figures, causing great scandal by deciding to commercialize her flamboyant Clara Ward Singers and have them perform in such iniquitous dens as Vegas, nightclubs, and even Disneyland. Sporting dazzlingly colorful gowns, gobs of jewelry, and enormous wigs, they sang only mainstream gospel hits but engaged in such unabashed clowning that critics felt the Wards brought ridicule to all gospel singers. But despite these failings, no one would deny that the Wards, who have launched the careers of such gospel legends as Marion Williams, were one of the greatest gospel groups ever. And though Clara herself was an exquisite soloist (many quarters consider her better than Mahalia), she preferred to let Williams lead, while she accompanied the group on piano.

The driving force behind Ward's illustrious career was her mother, Gertrude Mae Murphy Ward, who functioned not only as her promoter, guide, and prime cheerleader, but also as Clara's spiritual rock, keeping her daughter close to the church. In classic stage-mother fashion, Gertrude insisted that Clara remain in show business, even when the young woman's devotion to it faltered. A native of South Carolina, Gertrude, herself a talented singer, had grown up in terrible poverty, finding comfort and devotion in her church. She and her husband moved to Philadelphia in the 1920s and bore Willa and Clara. The little family remained impoverished through the Depression, but in 1931 things changed after Gertrude had a vision telling her to sing. Thus inspired, she founded a family group starring young Clara on lead vocals and the piano. Even then, the Wards were influential and helped Professor Thomas A. Dorsey and Sallie Martin establish themselves in Philadelphia. Mother Ward proved herself to be an exceptional promoter, and by the mid-'40s, following a tremendous performance at the 1943 National Baptist Convention, found herself helming a major attraction. At this time, the group took on two new members Henrietta Waddy and versatile teenage sensation Marion Williams, whom the Wards discovered in Miami to augment Clara's gorgeous alto. Deep-voiced Frances Steadman and soprano shouter Kitty Parham rounded out the group. In addition to being a singer and gifted pianist, Clara was also an excellent arranger, noted for her innovations such as setting the gospel standard "Surely" (their biggest hit) to a waltz beat. Another innovation was leader Clara's tendency to have group members switch leads in the midst of a song. Though she allowed Williams to do most of the solo shouting, she would frequently solo. In addition to performing, Mother Ward and Clara also published the music of Reverend Brewster.

The Ward Singers hooked up with the charismatic singing Detroit preacher Reverend C. L. Franklin in the early '50s. After he became a major star, he and Clara continued touring and even performed in the Middle East. Much later, Clara would have great influence on the Reverend's superstar daughter Aretha Franklin, Ward's protégé. The group exchanged their traditional choir robes for elaborate (some might even say bizarre) costumes in the mid-'50s and continued touring extensively until 1958, when the rigorous road life, coupled with the fact that Williams and the others saw little of the group's profits while the Wards made out like bandits, caused the others to leave. Mother Ward hired new singers such as Thelma Jackson and Carrie Williams, but even though they, were excellent, the public preferred the originals and their popularity waned until 1962 when they began performing in Vegas.

Next Clara starred in a Broadway production by Langston Hughes, who was trying to recapture the success of *Black Nativity*, an internationally popular production that starred Alex Bradford and Marion Williams. The play bombed, and Ward again played clubs and then Disneyland. Eventually the Wards began performing in Europe and Asia to great success. As the '60s progressed, Clara began slowly moving towards music bordering gospel and secular pop. But though she frequently waded into the mainstream, Ward's heart always belonged to gospel, and that is where she always did best. Her biggest hit was "How I Got Over."

Clara Ward continued performing through the '60s, even after suffering a debilitating stroke. She died in 1973 and her mother, to mourn the occasion, staged two elaborate, star-studded funerals, one in Philadelphia and the other in Los Angeles. Later Gertrude Ward made a new version of the Ward Singers to keep her daughter's memory alive, until she joined Clara in eternal peace about a decade later. —*Sandra Brennan*

The Clara Ward Singers / Roulette ✦✦✦
Includes pleasant but not essential selections by this popular group. —*Kip Lornell*

Surely God Is Able / Savgos ✦✦✦
The Pilgrim Jubilees were among the greatest of Mississippi quartets: subtle swing, fine guitar, and a terrific time-sense. The Ward Singers brought quartet singing to a pinnacle in the 1950s, and this album has some of their most moving songs, among them "Surely God Is Able" and "He Knows How Much I Can Bear." (The cover's claim of mid-price status became history when the label changed hands.) —*John Storm Roberts, Original Music*

The Best Of / Savoy ✦✦✦
The Clara Ward Singers have been called the greatest group, together with the Roberta Martin Singers, produced by gospel. Stylistically the Ward Singers represented an early stage in the move to a deliberate and dramatic use of a fervor that had once been purely religious. —*John Storm Roberts, Original Music*

Gospel Soul of Clara Ward / ✦✦✦✦
A surprising set of joyful-sounding gospel songs recorded some time in the early '70s that gives an idea of how magnificent the Ward Singers sounded in their heyday. All the songs are carefully arranged to evoke the feel of a live church performance, with high-spirited renditions of "What Jesus Is to Me" and "It May Be the Best for Me." There's lots of jubilant singing and tambourine banging. —*Opal Louis Nations, Roots and Rhythm Newsletter*

★ Clara Ward Singers / ✦✦✦✦✦
These 22 sides recorded for the Roulette label in 1963 are solid gospel winners featuring the unbeatable voice of Clara Ward. An added feature in these jubilant surroundings is a fantastic unnamed slide guitarist, who really goes to town on a few numbers. This is excellent. —*Myles Boisen, Roots and Rhythm Newsletter*

Ernestine Washington

Vocals / Black Gospel
Born in Arkansas, Madame Ernestine B. Washington grew up on the sanctified gospel of the '20s, singing primarily for her husband's church and denomination, Washington Temple C.O.G.I.C. Though inspired by the controlled Baptist style of the Roberta Martin Singers, she had a strident voice and was known to be a singing shouter in the mode of Mahalia Jackson. Her rare and most important recordings were executed from the late '40s through the '50s. —*Bil Carpenter*

● In Washington Temple / Collectors Issue ✦✦✦✦
Sensational solos are supported rousingly by Brooklyn's Congregation of the Washington Temple C.O.G.I.C. A re-issue of material recorded in 1958. —*Opal Louis Nations*

White Heart

Christian Rock
A band of "musician's musicians" with a revolving-door membership, their sound borders on hard-rock/prog-rock. Original vocalist Steve Green became a major inspirational act as a solo artist. Founder and guitarist Dann Huff became Los Angeles' premier studio guitarist in the late '80s before forming the arena rock group Giant; bassist Tommy Sims joined Bruce Springsteen's road band in 1992. —*Brian Mansfield*

Freedom / 1989 / Sparrow ✦✦✦
White Heart took the album's name to heart, allowing themselves more creative leeway on this than on any previous album. Most Christian arena rock sounds derivative of its secular counterparts—not *Freedom*; even its weak spots are undeniably original. —*Brian Mansfield*

Souvenirs / 1990 / Sparrow ✦✦✦✦
White Heart found its voice in 1986 with *Don't Wait for the Movie*, the first album with lead singer Rick Florian. *Souvenirs* collects the produc-

tive years that followed, including five tracks from *Freedom* and an unusual hard-rock "The Little Drummer Boy." —*Brian Mansfield*

Powerhouse / 1991 / 214 ♦♦

Tales of Wonder / 1992 / Star Song ♦♦♦
The band turns in its most popular album in years, showing continued growth and depth in its songwriting, better than the simplistic anthems that typify the arena rock genre. —*Thom Granger*

● **Highlands** / 1994 / Star Song ♦♦♦♦
Another artistic high-water mark for the band, which now includes Adam Again member Jon Knox on drums. The influence of '70s prog-rockers like Yes and Kansas is interwoven with Celtic themes for a Christian rock classic. —*Thom Granger*

The Williams Brothers

Black Gospel
The group was organized in 1960 by Leon "Pop" Williams, who is the founder and father of the Williams Brothers. They were known as the Little Williams Brothers, but as the group grew in talent, experience, and performance, the name changed to the Sensational Williams Brothers. Today the group is called the Williams Brothers. All of the group members were born and reared in Mississippi in a little community called "Smithdale," about 100 miles south of Jackson, where a road has been named in their honor. They have been writing and arranging most of their music since 1970 and producing since 1979. The group recorded its first album in 1973 on the Songbird label, which included the instant hit "Jesus Will Fix It." Since then they have recorded 16 albums listed as Top Ten in *Billboard* and *Cashbox* magazines, out of which came three No. 1 records and a Grammy nomination. Their repertoire of hits includes songs such as "Jesus Will Never Say No," "I Won't Let Go My Faith," "He'll Understand," "Sweep Around Your Own Front Door," and "A Ship Like Mine." They also performed on the Winans' grammy-winning song, "Ain't No Need to Worry," featuring Anita Baker. In April 1991 the group formed their own record label, Blackberry Records, the first Black-owned and-operated label in the state of Mississippi that has major distribution. Their first release on the label, "This Is Your Night," reached No. 4 on the *Billboard* gospel chart. —*Billy C. Wirtz*

● **Ain't Love Wonderful** / Malaco ♦♦♦♦
Strong material and solid production. —*Hank Davis*

Blessed / Malaco ♦♦♦♦
Slick, well-crafted modern gospel, complete with synthesizer, strings, and percussion overdubs. —*Hank Davis*

Hand in Hand / Malaco ♦♦♦
For proof that change is not decay, look no further. The sermonette "The Goat" might have come off an early Clouds single, and time and again the accompaniment returns to the great, simple, classic piano/organ combination. But the four Williams Brothers are up for 'most anything, including Walter Hawkins on one track and rappers on another. —*John Storm Roberts, Original Music*

Dewey Williams

Vocals / Black Gospel
Born at the turn of the century, Williams has been the leader of the African-American shape-note movement in Southern Alabama for over 50 years. In the late '80s, he was honored with a Heritage Award from the National Endowment for the Arts/Folk Arts. —*Kip Lornell*

★ **Wiregrass Notes: Black Sacred Harp Singing from the South** / Wiregrass Music ♦♦♦♦♦
This is a self-produced cassette of a rare Black religious tradition that is downhome and unique. —*Kip Lornell*

Marion Williams

b. Aug. 29, 1927, Miami, FL, d. Jul. 2, 1994
Vocals / Black Gospel
With an amazing grace, a powerful, yet lyrical voice, and unmatched improvisation skills, Marion Williams punctuated her sanctified "shouting" with gut-wrenching growls, low moans, joyful whoops, and soaring, angelic falsettos that made her one of the most influential singers in gospel music. In her heyday she was hailed by some critics as one of the greatest singers in the US.
Williams was born in a Miami ghetto, the daughter of a West Indian butcher and a South Carolina laundry woman. When not working, her father would give music lessons; her devout mother introduced her to religion. Williams' own love of gospel music began in childhood, and she would sing it and listen to it at every opportunity. One of her older brothers frequently played blues and jazz on the family jukebox. Though gospel was Williams' main musical interest, her music is infused with elements of those jukebox tunes as well as the calypso music played throughout her neighborhood. When she was nine, her father died. At age 14 Williams quit school to work all day in the laun-

dry beside her mother. Later the responsibility for supporting the family fell totally on Williams' shoulders when her mother lost both legs due to diabetes. Still her interest in sanctified gospel continued, and on weekends she sang in church programs and street corners. She was particularly inspired by the Smith Jubilee Singers (her favorites) and the Kings of Harmony. Influential soloists included such women as Mary Johnson Davis and particularly Sister Rosetta Tharpe. Williams' extraordinary singing attracted considerable attention, but though attempts were made to steer her into everything from opera to the blues, she was determined to spread the gospel and by 1946 was known as the best gospel soloist in Miami.
While at a Clara Ward and the Ward Singers program, Williams was called up to sing. Impressed, Clara and Gertrude Ward invited the young singer to join their nationally known group. The following year, she joined the Wards and remained with them for the next 11 years as their star attraction. Her natural sparkle and enthusiasm in performance earned her the nickname "Miss Personality." She made her recording debut singing "How Far Am I from Canaan" with the Ward Singers in 1948 for Savoy. It was the Rev. W. Herbert Brewster-penned "Surely God Is Able" that made Williams and the Ward Singers stars. During their dynamic performances, it was not uncommon for audience members to fall out in frenzied ecstasy, something Williams encouraged by getting right down into the audience, sashaying about, shouting at the top of her lungs, occasionally sitting upon listeners' laps, and even literally trying to pack up the earthly goods of audience members during her renditions of her second big hit, "Packin' Up." She put so much into her performances with the Ward Singers that in time she began suffering "nervous spells" in which she would yell just to express the remaining energy generated by singing those high notes. Williams and a few others from the group left in 1958 to form Stars of Faith.
The Stars of Faith got off to a rocky start, as they lacked many of the things that made the Wards great, including Gertrude's ability to manage, Clara's driving vision, and Brewster's exquisite songs. It did not help that Williams was not putting the energy into singing that she did with the Wards. She frequently allowed other group members to do the shouting and avoided the vocal extremes that characterized her earlier work. The lull continued until 1961, when she again found Jesus and approached music with renewed vigor. She and the Stars got major exposure when they appeared in the off-Broadway production *Black Nativity* and began touring North America and Europe. Williams left the group in 1965 to launch a solo career. Returning to Europe, she appeared in an unsuccessful show until her mother's death caused her to go back to Miami. It was at her mother's funeral that she became committed, bringing back her old fire to her new career. Starting at Yale, Williams began a long series of college campus tours that gave her the opportunity to thrill audiences in North America, Europe (where she also appeared at jazz festivals), Africa, and the Caribbean with stirring renditions of such great songs as "Jesus Is All" and her biggest solo hit, the reflective "Standing Here Wondering Which Way to Go."
hough she died in 1994, Marion Williams' influence upon contemporary music continues to be felt. Back in the '50s, her unique singing style, that inimitable hollering and whooping, inspired artists such as Little Richard and the Isley Brothers. —*Sandra Brennan*

O Holy Night / 1959 / Savoy ♦♦♦
A Christmas album with the Stars of Faith. —*Bil Carpenter*

Surely God Is Able / 1989 / Spirit Feel ♦♦♦♦
A very strong soloist who reworked classic gospel material from the '30s and '40s into a wonderful album. —*Kip Lornell*

★ **Strong Again** / 1991 / Spirit Feel ♦♦♦♦♦
Eclectic though satisfying 20-cut album by this major singer, her most impressive solo set in recent years. Sparse accompaniment; mainly traditional material. Excellent. —*Kip Lornell*

Can't Keep It to Myself / 1993 / Shanachie ♦♦♦♦
Marion Williams has majesty in her voice, power in her delivery, and a compelling, dynamic quality that underscores her vocals. This new disc features 22 awesome performances recorded with minimal, sympathetic accompaniment and little production support; just mostly Williams' smashing, note-bending, soaring vocals. She flies on slow, bluesy numbers, testifies and shouts on originals like "Ride in the Clouds" and "I'll Never Return No More" and turns standards such as Roberta Martin's "God's Amazing Grace" and Reverend Thomas A. Dorsey's "Live the Life I Sing About in My Song" into gripping, fresh reaffirmations of her own faith. —*Ron Wynn*

Somebody Bigger Than You and I / Relic ♦♦♦
Her first album after leaving the Ward Singers. Recorded in 1958, it includes "I Can't Forget." —*Bil Carpenter*

The Winans

Urban, CCM, Black Gospel
These four brothers hail from Detroit, MI. Their contemporary Black

gospel style reflects traditional Black gospel roots. They sang gospel all their lives and began their professional careers in the '80s. Marvin, Carvin, Ronald, and Michael have performed several times with the likes of Michael McDonald, Anita Baker, and Vanessa Bell Armstrong. — *Bil Carpenter*

Let My People Go / 1985 / Qwest ✦✦✦
Their distinctive, muddy, percussive, and jazzy sound. — *Bil Carpenter*

Return / 1990 / Qwest ✦✦✦
New jack swing and urban soul. — *Bil Carpenter*

● **Tomorrow** / Light ✦✦✦✦
The title track was the hymn of the '80s. — *Bil Carpenter*

Live at Carnegie Hall / Qwest ✦✦✦
A dynamic concert, with all the hits drawn out, on this double album. — *Bil Carpenter*

BeBe and CeCe Winans

Soul, Gospel, Urban
Detroit-born brother and sister BeBe (Benjamin) and CeCe (Priscilla) Winans are part of the gospel-singing Winans family that includes their four brothers. As a duo, BeBe and CeCe maintain the gospel message, although their records have the production values and style of contemporary R&B. They released their debut album, *BeBe & CeCe Winans,* in 1987 and scored a moderate hit (No. 49) in the R&B charts with the single "I.O.U. Me" on the R&B and adult-contemporary charts. This earned them three Grammy nominations and one award (gospel). Their second album, *Heaven,* came in 1988 and found them scoring three R&B hits with the title track, "Lost Without You," and "Celebrate Life." The album reached the R&B Top Ten (No. 95 in the pop chart) and went gold. The platinum-selling *Different Lifestyles* was their biggest hit yet, topping the R&B album chart and featuring "Addictive Love" and "I'll Take You There." — *William Ruhlmann*

Lord Lift Us Up / 1985 / PTL ✦✦✦✦
Pop-oriented praise tunes. — *Bil Carpenter*

Bebe and Cece Winans / 1987 / Capitol ✦✦✦
R&B, urban-crossover CCM ballads. — *Bil Carpenter*

● **Heaven** / Sep. 1988 / Capitol ✦✦✦✦
If you listen carefully, the songs *are* about Jesus rather than love sweet love, but even a casual hearing lets you know this is one of the most soulful duos to come along since Marvin Gaye and Tammi Terrell. Keith Thomas gives the production a contemporary R&B sheen. — *William Ruhlmann*

Relationships / 1994 / Capitol ✦✦✦
The duo's first outing without the involvement of producer Keith Thomas finds them heading toward more downtempo, ballad-heavy R&B. — *Thom Granger*

Various Artists

☆ **Ain't That Good News** / Specialty ✦✦✦✦✦
Super '50s gospel from the Specialty vaults, compiled by Barrett Hansen (aka Dr. Demento). Each cut is a true gem. Of special interest to audiophiles: the tracks carefully segue into each other, with no space between (which could be annoying to some). A spellbinding effect and a great album. — *Barry Lee Pearson*

At the Foot of the Cross / 1991 / Glasshouse ✦✦✦
A unique worship-oriented album, it's spearheaded by alternative rock artists Steve Hindalong and Derri Daugherty (from the Choir), and a variety of guests. The album mixes traditional church liturgical ideas, some with Latin texts, with less than traditional church music for another part of the congregation. — *Thom Granger*

Bless My Bones / Rounder ✦✦✦✦✦
Bless My Bones: Memphis Gospel Radio—1950s highlights eight stellar ensembles in a stunning set of radio transcriptions from Memphis' WDIA. Includes "99 & 1/2 Won't Do" by the Song Birds of the South and "Milky White Way" by the Spirit of Memphis, as well as tracks by the Dixie Nightingales, Southern Wonders, and Sunset Travelers. — *John Floyd*

Gospel Stars in Concert / 197_ / Specialty ✦✦✦✦✦
These historically and spiritually important early-'50s live performances were recorded by the Gospel Harmonettes with Dorothy Love Coates, Brother Joe May, and the Pilgrim Travelers. Side two features three riveting cuts by Sam Cooke and the Soul Stirrers. — *John Floyd*

The Gospel Tradition: Roots & Branches, Vol. 1 / 1991 / Columbia/Legacy ✦✦✦✦✦
One of the few gospel collections that ignores the barriers between White and Black gospel music, *The Gospel Tradition: The Roots and the Branches*—Vol. 1 contrasts the blues of Bessie Smith and the western swing of Bob Wills, the rough edge of Mitchell's Christian Singers and

the smooth polish of the Sons of the Pioneers. Lots of obscure sides dating back to 1927, and a wide range of styles from sanctified women to choral spirituals. — *Brian Mansfield*

☆ **Great Golden Gospel Hits, Vol. 4** / Savoy ✦✦✦✦✦
This is a tremendous and far-reaching assortment of vintage gospel by such masters as the Ward Singers, the Davis Sisters, the Staples Singers, and the Gospel Harmonettes. — *John Floyd*

Greatest Gospel Gems / 1991 / Specialty ✦✦✦✦✦
An excellent 24-song sampling of '50s and '60s sacred testifying from the vaults of Specialty Records, it includes essential cuts from Dorothy Love Coates, the Swan Silvertones, and Sam Cooke and the Soul Stirrers. — *John Floyd*

I Hear Music in the Air: A Treasury of Gospel Music / 1990 / RCA ✦✦✦✦✦
I Hear the Music in the Air: A Treasury of Gospel Music offers great quartet-style singing (and three mini-sermons too!) for RCA Victor between 1926 and 1942. It features the likes of the Golden Gate Jubilee Quartet, the Morris Brown Quartet, and the Southern Sons. It also includes the first recording of Thomas Dorsey's "Precious Lord, Take My Hand," performed in 1937 by the Heavenly Gospel Singers. — *Brian Mansfield*

★ **Jubilation, Vol. 1 (Black Gospel)** / Jan. 1992 / Rhino ✦✦✦✦✦
Jubilation: Great Gospel Performances, Vol. 1 offers a first-rate introduction and overview of the key players in Black gospel, including stellar performances by Mahalia Jackson, the Soul Stirrers, the Swan Silvertones, Shirley Caesar, Aretha Franklin and James Cleveland, and many other wonderful artists. — *Thom Owens*

☆ **Jubilation, Vol. 2 (More Black Gospel)** / Feb. 1992 / Rhino ✦✦✦✦✦
Like the title says, there's more of the same as the first volume, including the Staples Singers, the Original Gospel Harmonettes, Prof. Alex Bradford, the Harmonizing Four, Sam Cooke with the Soul Stirrers, and more. — *AMG*

☆ **Jubilation, Vol. 3 (Country Gospel)** / Mar. 1992 / Rhino ✦✦✦✦
Although slightly weaker than the first two, this features tracks by Hank Williams, Kitty Wells, Patsy Cline, the Carter Family, the Louvin Brothers, Webb Pierce, Doyle Lawson & Quicksilver, Bill Monroe, and others. — *AMG*

No Compromise: Remembering the Music of Keith Green / 1992 / Sparrow ✦✦✦✦✦
Petra, Steven Curtis Chapman, Russ Taff, and others cover songs by the late Keith Green, probably CCM's most influential early songwriter and performer. Most of the chosen material has worn fairly well over the years. — *Brian Mansfield*

Preachin' the Gospel: Holy Blues / Apr. 9, 1991 / Columbia ✦✦✦✦✦
Serious inspiration from Blind Willie Johnson, Arizona Dranes, Josh White, Washington Phillips, and others comes from this digitally cleaned-up recording. — *Jas Obrecht*

Raisin' the Roof: The Peacock Recordings Of… / Mobile Fidelity ✦✦✦✦✦
This indispensable early-'60s Sunsets material includes O.V. Wright, Rev. Julius Cheeks and the 4 Knights, plus great Swan Silvertones material led by Claude Jeter and Louis Johnson, from '60s Vee-Jay sources. — *Opal Louis Nations*

Something Got a Hold on Me: A Treasury of Sacred / RCA ✦✦✦✦✦
Gospel and spiritually oriented vintage country sides from 1927-41. Includes cuts by some giants of early country—Carter Family, the Monroe Brothers, the Blue Sky Boys, and Uncle Dave Macon—as well as lesser-known but influential figures like the Dixon Brothers and Wade Mainer. Most of these singers hail from brother or family acts, and the great harmony vocals that result are the highlights of this set. — *Richie Unterberger*

The Soul of Chicago / 1993 / Shanachie ✦✦✦
Distinguished gospel music critic, author, producer, and label executive Anthony Heilbut has provided many wonderful anthologies. For this one, he has taken 11 surviving artists from the golden age and recorded them in a traditional setting with their familiar spare backings (mostly piano, guitar, and organ). The results are both impressive and memorable; Robert Anderson, Delois Barrett Campbell, Rev. Samuel Patterson, Gladys Beamon Gregory and the Gay Family, among others, don't just sound good, but almost as fabulous as they did in their heyday. They have the spirit just as if they were performing and recording all the time, yet many of them have not sung regularly in decades. The quality of this masterful session blows most contemporary gospel out of the water. — *Ron Wynn*

Stained Glass Hour / 1992 / Rounder ✦✦✦✦✦
Ricky Skaggs dominates this collection, both as a bandleader and as a member of Boone Creek and J. D. Crowe and the New South. Beyond that, *Stained Glass Hour: Bluegrass and Old-Timey Gospel Music* is an excellent sampler of religious-based bluegrass, past (the Blue Sky Boys,

the Johnson Mountain Boys) and present (the Nashville Bluegrass Band, Dry Branch Fire Squad). —*Brian Mansfield*

Strong Hand of Love / 1994 / Word/Epic ◆◆◆
This is a tribute to the late Mark Heard, songwriter, instrumentalist, and producer. A devoted Christian, Heard was able to infuse his sense of faith in his songs without their being limited solely to that audience. His intricate lyrics show a high poetic intelligence combined with a frenzy of rock 'n' roll and textured acoustic music. It is from Heard's own final three albums that most of these songs are drawn. Some of the heartfelt performances are "Nod over Coffee" sung by Pierce Pettis (who had been produced by Heard), Victoria Williams' "What Kind of Friend," and Bruce Cockburn's mature interpretation of "Strong Hand of Love." As with the best tributes, this collection stands on its own, but sends you back to Mark Heard's own great performances. —*Richard Meyer*

Ten Years of Black Country Religion / Yazoo ◆◆◆◆◆
A first-class overview of Southern rural religious music, including striking performances by Jaybird Coleman and Crumpton & Summers. —*Kip Lornell*

☆ **The Great Gospel Men** / Shanachie ◆◆◆◆◆
A wide range of magnificent vocals are displayed on *The Great Gospel Men*, a 27-song anthology. Some names such as Brother Joe May, Rev. James Cleveland, and Professor Alex Bradford are familiar even to non-gospel fans; others, like the intense Robert Anderson, Professor J. Earle Hines, Norsalus McKissick, Robert Bradley, and R.L. Knowles are known only to the hard core, and even they probably haven't heard many songs by any one artist. This collection alternates between slow and fast pieces, giving each artist a chance to demonstrate their skills. —*Ron Wynn*

☆ **The Great Gospel Women** / Shanachie ◆◆◆◆◆
Like its male counterpart, this anthology spotlights contributions from both famous stars (Mahalia Jackson, Marion Williams, Dorothy Love Coates, Sister Rosetta Tharpe) and obscure figures (Mary Johnson Davis, Jessie Mae Renfro, Lucy Smith, and Goldia Haynes, among others), presenting a hefty 31 selections. While some might quibble that celebrated stars Jackson and Williams get six tracks apiece, it's hard to argue with the greatness of what's presented by them. Others who give head-turning performances include Frances Steadman, Roberta Martin, and Clara Ward. —*Ron Wynn*

White Spirituals from the Sacred Harp / New World ◆◆◆◆◆
The polyphonic shape-note tradition provides what is surely some of the world's most beautiful folk choral singing. This continuously stunning collection, recorded by Alan Lomax at the Alabama Sacred Harp Convention in 1959, is enriched by his historical and musical notes. —*John Storm Roberts*

Women of Gospel's Golden Age, Vol. 1 / 1994 / Specialty ◆◆◆◆
Although women have been at the forefront of gospel innovation since the beginning, the domination of male quartets may have fooled some into thinking they weren't that important. Anyone holding that mistaken impression will surely know better after hearing the 28 remarkable cuts on this valuable anthology. New Orleans' wondrous Bessie Griffin, whose vibrant, dazzling voice was overlooked due to Mahalia Jackson, gets the spotlight with six amazing numbers. She's not alone there, however; everyone from the famous Clara Ward Singers and Dorothy Love Coates to the lesser-known Sallie Martin Singers sounds fantastic. —*Ron Wynn*

COUNTRY

Country music is facts-of-life music. It's the music of experience. More than with other music genres (with the possible exception of the blues), country music echoes and reflects the heights and depths of the collective lives of its audience, who up until the '70s were predominantly working class, White, and rural. Willie Nelson, Waylon Jennings, Dolly Parton, Kenny Rogers, Roy Clark, and other superstars in the '70s brought country music to a new and huge audience—the middle class, the educated, and the urban listeners—in the process changing the direction of the music. Yet this was only another step in what has been a continuous evolution in country music.

In this American music form, the older styles are revered and retained rather than discarded, so that they remain dear to their listeners, while at the same time contemporary country heads off into new territory, thus attracting a new group of listeners. It's always been this way, since the day country music went commercial with its first record in the mid-'20s. Though to a degree change-resistant because of its adherence to tradition, country in fact changes as the lives of its listeners change. And this is the common bond of all these styles from the '20s to the present: it's all facts-of-life music, from the hillbilly string-bands of the '20s through the cowboys and honky tonkers and outlaws and even up to the creamy country-pop sounds of Randy Travis, Dolly Parton, the Judds, and Ricky Skaggs. Country music's singers and musicians perform music they have lived. And now, because country music has become a major force in the record industry — in fact, the major force, with Garth Brooks and number of records sold — it has been given the respect and attention long lav-

ished upon jazz, blues, and rock When the lines of distinction between country and other genres of music begin to blur, traditional country reasserts itself, thus preventing the country sound from evolving to the point of equivalence with pop. Judge George Hay, founder of the Grand Ole Opry, said it best in the mid '20s when he admonished performers with "Keep it close to the ground, boys," if they strayed from the country style that prevailed at the time. The essence of country music has remained pretty much intact ever since. Its repertory derives from folk, minstrel, medicine show, vaudeville, and gospel music.

Country's subject matter falls into some general categories: home and family, working-man blues, death and sorrow, cheatin', good love gone bad, prison, trains and trucks and travelling, disasters, booze and sorrow-drowning, and gospel songs (which can uplift with promised redemption or depress with likely damnation). Sobering material, but true-to-life: to paraphrase Hank Williams, none of us will ever get out of this world alive. And enough country music tells us of the good love and fun possible on this earth before we pass over to Canaan's land, that we keep on the sunny side of life, at least occasionally.

Kris Kristofferson says that if a song sounds country, it is. Add to this generalizations about instrumentation (fiddle, banjo, dobro, steel guitar, guitar, harmonica, mandolin), about vocals (pure, often stark and rough-edged, highly emotional), and about country performers (revered by and loving of their fans), and we probably know enough to stop reading and start listening to the music. — *David Vinopal*

Roy Acuff (Roy Claxton Acuff)

b. Sep. 15, 1903, Maynardsville, TN, **d.** Nov. 23, 1992
Harmonica, Violin, Vocals / Traditional Country
Roy Acuff was called the King of Country Music, and for more than 60 years, he lived up to that title. If any performer embodied country music, it was Roy Acuff. Throughout his career, Acuff was a champion for traditional country values, enforcing his beliefs as a performer, a music publisher, and as the Grand Master of the Grand Ole Opry. Acuff was the first country music superstar after the death of Jimmie Rodgers, pioneering an influential vocal style that complemented the spare, simple songs he was performing. Generations of artists, from Hank Williams to George Jones have been influenced by Acuff, and countless others have paid respect to him. At the time of his death in 1992, he was still actively involved in the Grand Ole Opry, and was as popular as ever.

Originally, Acuff didn't plan to be a singer. Acuff sang in the church choir as a schoolboy, but he was more interested in sports, particularly baseball. Not only was he attracted to the sport, he had a wild streak—after his family moved to Knoxville, he was frequently arrested for fighting. Acuff continued to concentrate on playing ball, eventually becoming strong enough to earn a tryout at for the Major Leagues. However, that tryout never took place. Before he had a chance to play, he was overcome by a severe sunstroke while he was on a fishing trip; after the sunstroke, Acuff suffered a nervous breakdown. While he was recovering, he decided that a career in baseball was no longer possible, so he decided to become an entertainer. He began to learn the fiddle and became an apprentice of Doc Hauer, a local medicine show man.

While traveling with the medicine show, Acuff learned how to be a performer—he learned how to sing, how to imitate, how to entertain, how to put on a show. Soon, Acuff joined the Tennessee Crackerjacks, who had a regular slot on the Knoxville radio station, WROL. Although he was performing frequently, he wasn't making any significant headway, failing to become a star in Tennessee. One song changed that situation—"The Great Speckled Bird," an old gospel tune that had become

popular with the Church of God sect. After another radio entertainer wrote the words out to the song, Acuff began performing it in his shows. Quickly, he became popular throughout the eastern part of Tennessee and was asked to record the song by ARC, a record label with national distribution. Acuff headed north to Chicago for a recording session, which resulted in 20 different songs. In addition to "The Great Speckled Bird," he recorded "Steamboat Whistle Blues" and "The Wabash Cannonball," another Tennessee standard which featured the singer imitating the sound of a train whistle; he also made a handful of risque numbers during these sessions, which were released under the name the Bang Boys.

In 1938, the Grand Ole Opry invited Roy Acuff to audition for the show. During the show, he sang "The Great Speckled Bird," and became an instant hit, prompting the Opry to hire him full-time. Before he was given his regular slot, the Opry insisted that he change the name of his band to the Smoky Mountain Boys. The following year, Acuff reassembled his band, with the most notable addition being Bashful Brother Oswald (Pete Kirby), a dobro player that sang high harmonies.

Roy Acuff became a national superstar during the '40s, scoring a long string of hit records, which included the classics "The Wreck on the Highway," "The Precious Jewel," and "Beneath That Lonely Mound of Clay," among many others. During this time, he discovered that there was a potential gold mine in music publishing. Acuff had printed his own songbook, which sold a staggering 100,000 copies. Publishers in New York tried to acquire the rights to his songs, but the success of the songbook convinced Acuff to hold on to the songs and seek out the help of Fred Rose, a professional songwriter and pianist working in Chicago. The pair founded Acuff-Rose Publications in October, 1942, using Acuff's songs as its base; Rose also added his songs, including "Faded Love," "Deep Water," and "Blue Eyes Crying in the Rain." Acuff-Rose was an immediate success and over the next two decades, many of the most popular songs and songwriters were the property of the company, including the songs of Hank Williams, the Louvin Brothers, Don Gibson, Roy Orbison, the

Everly Brothers, John D. Loudermilk, Boudleaux and Felice Bryant, and Redd Stewart and Pee Wee King's "Tennessee Waltz."

In the late '40s, Acuff continued to rule the country charts, as well as scoring a number of pop crossovers ("The Prodigal Son," "I'll Forgive You, But I Can't Forget"). For most of the '50s, he concentrated on touring—he didn't have a single charting record between 1947 and 1958, returning with the Top Ten hit "Once More," as well as two other Top 20 singles, "So Many Times" and "Come and Knock." The '60s yielded some hits, yet he continued to concentrate on touring; by the end of the decade, he decided to leave the road, staying at the Grand Ole Opry.

The beginning of the '80s was a difficult period for Acuff, as he experienced the death of his wife and several longtime band members, including pianist Jimmie Riddle and fiddler Howdy Forrester. In 1987, he released his final charting record, an inspirational duet with Charlie Louvin called "The Precious Jewel." As his health began to decline in the late '80s, Acuff built a house near the Opry so he could greet friends and fans. In 1992, he became the first living performer to be inducted to the Country Music Hall of Fame. Several months later, he passed away, leaving behind a legacy that isn't limited to his music. Through his records, his performances and Acuff-Rose, Roy Acuff has had an enormous effect on shaping the role of country music in the 20th century; it is hard to imagine the music without him. —*Stephen Thomas Erlewine*

Fly Birdie Fly '39-41 / Rounder ✦✦✦✦
The songs on *Fly Birdie Fly* were recorded in 1939-1941, as he was flying high as a new star of the Opry. Although these tracks are not his best-known, these blues and gospel songs are rowdier than his reputation and as good as his classics. —*Michael McCall*

The Best of Roy Acuff / 1970 / Curb ✦✦✦
These selections were taken from his '60s work for Hickory Records. Not as important as his earlier work, it's powerful nonetheless. The instrumentation is slicker; the voice remains as chilling as ever. —*Michael McCall*

Greatest Hits [Columbia] / 1970 / Columbia ✦✦✦✦
Contains the original versions of Acuff's classic, groundbreaking work—"The Great Speckled Bird," "Wabash Cannonball," "Night Train to Memphis," "Were You There When They Crucified My Lord," and "Fire Ball Mail." —*Stephen Thomas Erlewine*

☆ **Columbia Historic Edition** / 1985 / Columbia ✦✦✦✦✦
It has many of his early landmark recordings, including his first recording of "Wabash Cannonball," on which he blows the train whistle and bows the fiddle, but the vocals are by Dynamite Hatcher, a bandmember. Other songs do feature some of Acuff's earliest singing. It's a good representation of his initial string-band sound. —*Michael McCall*

☆ **Steamboat Whistle Blues** / 1985 / Rounder ✦✦✦✦✦
Steamboat Whistle Blues is a collection of fine early Roy Acuff band versions of blues, pop, and old-time country, recorded between 1936-1939. —*Barry Lee Pearson*

Best of Roy Acuff [Curb] / 1991 / Curb ✦✦✦
The Best of Roy Acuff is a collection of '60s hits and a number of re-recordings Acuff made in the '60s while signed to Hickory Records, a label he began with his publishing partner Fred Rose. By this point, Acuff's recording career was no longer successful; he concentrated on the Grand Ole Opry. Nevertheless, these re-recordings are entertaining, although they are considerably slicker and less affecting than his early, groundbreaking tracks. As a sampler of Acuff's '60s sound, *The Best of* is effective. Bear in mind, the disc only has ten tracks, so while it may be bargain-priced, it's not necessarily a bargain. —*Stephen Thomas Erlewine*

★ **The Essential Roy Acuff (1936-1949)** / 1992 / Columbia/Legacy ✦✦✦✦✦
The Essential Roy Acuff (1936-1949) contains the original versions of "The Great Speckled Bird," "Night Train to Memphis," "The Precious Jewel," and "Wabash Cannon Ball," and 16 other tracks that were cut at the peak of his recording career. —*Stephen Thomas Erlewine*

Alabama

Country-Rock
Before Alabama, bands were usually relegated to a supporting role in country music. In the first part of the century, bands were popular with audiences across the country, but as recordings became available, nearly every popular recording artist was a vocalist, not a group. Alabama was the group that made country bands popular again. Emerging in the late '70s, the band had roots in both country and rock; in fact, many of their musical concepts, particularly the idea of a performing band, owed more to rock and pop than hardcore country. However, there is no denying that Alabama is a country band—their pop instincts may come from rock, but their harmonies, songwriting and approach are indebted to country, particularly the Bakersfield sound of Merle Haggard, bluegrass, and the sound of Nashville pop. Their sleek, country-rock sound made the group the most popular country group in history, selling more records than any

other artist of the '80s and earning stacks of awards. First cousins Randy Owen (b. Dec. 14, 1949; lead vocal, rhythm guitar) and Teddy Gentry (b. Jan. 22, 1952; vocals, bass) form the core of Alabama. Owen and Gentry grew up on separate cotton farms on Lookout Mountain in Alabama, but the pair learned how to play guitar together; the duo also had sung in church before they were six years old. On their own, Gentry and Owen played in a number of different bands during the '60s, playing country, bluegrass, and pop on different occasions. During high school, the duo teamed with another cousin, Jeff Cook (b. Aug. 27, 1949; lead guitar, vocals, keyboards, fiddle), to form Young Country in 1969. Before joining his cousins, Cook had played in a number of bands and was a rock 'n' roll DJ. Young Country's first gig was at a high school talent contest, where they performed a Merle Haggard song; the band won first prize at the contest, a trip to the Grand Ole Opry. However, the group was fairly inactive as Owen and Cook went to college.

After Randy Owen and Jeff Cook graduated from college, they moved with Teddy Gentry to Anniston, Alabama, with the intention of keeping the band together. Sharing an apartment, the band practiced at night and performed manual labor during the day. They changed their name to Wildcountry in 1972, adding drummer Bennet Vartanian to the lineup. The following year, the band made the decision to become professional musicians, quitting their jobs and playing a number of bars in the Southeast. During this time, Wildcountry began writing their own songs, including "My Home's In Alabama." Vartanian left the band soon after they turned professional; after losing four more drummers, they added Rick Scott to the lineup in 1974.

Wildcountry changed their name to Alabama in 1977, the same year they signed a one-record contract with GRT. The resulting single, "I Wanna Be With You Tonight," was a minor success, peaking in the Top 80. Nevertheless, the single's performance was an indication that Alabama was one of the most popular bands in the Southeast; at the end of the decade, the group was playing over 300 shows a year. After "I Wanna Be With You Tonight," the group borrowed $4,000 from a Fort Payne bank, using the money to record and release their own records, which they sold at their shows. When GRT declared bankruptcy a year after the release of "I Wanna Be With You Tonight," Alabama discovered that they were forbidden from recording with another label because of a hidden clause in their contract. For two years, the band raised money to buy out their contract. In 1979, they were finally able to begin recording again. That same year, Scott left the band. Scott was replaced by Mark Herndon, a former rock drummer who helped give Alabama its signature sound.

Later in 1979, Alabama self-recorded and released an album, hiring an independent record promoter to help them get radio play for the single, "I Wanna Come Over." The band also sent hundreds of hand-written letters to program directors and DJs across the country. "I Wanna Come Over" gained the attention of MDJ Records, a small label based in Dallas. MDJ released the single, and it reached No. 33 on the charts. In 1980, MDJ released the group's "My Home's In Alabama," which made it into the Top 20. Based on the single's success, Alabama performed at the Country Music New Faces show, where they were spotted by an RCA Records talent scout, who signed them after the show.

Alabama released its first RCA single, "Tennessee River," late in 1980. Produced by Harold Shedd, the song began a remarkable streak of 21 No. 1 hits (interrupted by the 1982 holiday single, "Christmas in Dixie"), which ran until 1987; after one No.7 hit, the streak resumed for another six singles, resulting in a total of 27 No. 1 singles during the decade. Taken alone, the amount of chart-topping singles is proof of Alabama's popularity, but they also won numerous awards, had seven multi-platinum albums, and crossed over to the pop charts nine times in the '80s.

In the '90s, their popularity declined somewhat, yet they were still having hit singles and gold and platinum albums with regularity. It's unlikely that any other country group will be able to surpass the success of Alabama. —*Stephen Thomas Erlewine*

My Home's in Alabama / 1980 / RCA ✦✦✦✦
This is the album that started it all for Alabama. Their Southern-rock influences are obvious but encased in a country context. The title track's sentiment is overwhelming, whether you're from Alabama or Iowa. —*Tom Roland*

Feels So Right / 1981 / RCA ✦✦✦✦
On their second album, Alabama's apparently more comfortable with the studio. The harmonies are tighter than in the debut, but the material selection—heavy on uptempo tunes—shows that the club mentality developed at the Bowery is still very much intact. Three hits—the title track, "Love in the First Degree," "Old Flame"—but nearly all the extra cuts are strong as well. —*Tom Roland*

Mountain Music / 1982 / RCA ✦✦✦✦
This is their best effort. The group hadn't quite fallen into any formulas, and as a result, they cover the stylistic gamut pretty well. The title track practically defined what country groups have strived to accomplish, and the group slides easily from sentiment, to social relevance, to out-and-out partying. —*Tom Roland*

Country Styles

BAKERSFIELD SOUND— Bakersfield was the first genre of country music to rely heavily on electric instrumentation, as well as a defined backbeat—in other words, it was the first to be significantly influenced by rock 'n' roll. Named after the town of Bakersfield, CA, where a great majority of the artists performed, the sound was pioneered by Wynn Stewart and popularized by Buck Owens and Merle Haggard. Using telecaster guitars, the singers developed a clean, ringing sound that stood in direct opposition to the produced, string-laden Nashville sound. The Bakersfield sound became one of the most popular—and arguably the most influential—country genres of the '60s, setting the stage for country-rock and outlaw, as well as reviving the spirit of honky tonk.

CONTEMPORARY COUNTRY— Contemporary country followed the Urban Cowboy movement and preceded the rise of Garth Brooks. It incorporated subtle pop-production techniques, occasionally using synthesizers but always sounding slick and polished. At times, the country roots of contemporary country were fairly well-hidden beneath pop trappings, but new traditionalists like George Strait and Randy Travis also fit into the genre.

COUNTRY-FOLK— Country-folk is a hybrid of country music and folk. Generally, the music is based on acoustic guitars and is gentler than most country music. Also, country-folk is dominated by singer-songwriters who write and record their own material in the manner of most folk singer-songwriters.

COUNTRY-POP— Country-pop uses country instrumentation and song structures but adds a greater inclination toward pop melody on a lusher, more orchestrated production.

COWBOY— Cowboy songs include both traditional western songs and songs from western movies. Most of the songs are performed on acoustic guitars (though movie songs have much more elaborate instrumentation, frequently featuring orchestras) and are about Western themes.

HONKY TONK— Honky tonk is the most recognizable genre of country music. It's spare and direct, with acoustic guitars, steel guitars, fiddles, and a high, lonesome vocal. Ernest Tubb was the first honky tonk musician to popularize the genre, but Hank Williams, George Jones, and Lefty Frizzell became the definitive artists in the '50s.

NASHVILLE SOUND/COUNTRYPOLITAN— Countrypolitan, an outgrowth of the Nashville sound of the '50s, is among the most commercially-oriented genres of country music. The Nashville sound emerged in the '50s as a way to bring country music to a broad pop audience. The movement was led by Chet Atkins, who was the head of RCA Records country division. Atkins designed a smooth, commercial sound that relied on country song structures but abandoned all of the hillbilly and honky tonk instrumentation. He hired session musicians and coordinated pop-oriented, jazz-tinged productions. Similarly, Owen Bradley created productions—most notably with Patsy Cline—that featured sophisticated productions and smooth, textured instrumentation. Eventually, most records from Nashville featured this style of production and the Nashville sound began to incorporate strings and vocal choirs.

In the late '60s, the Nashville Sound evolved into countrypolitan, which emphasized these kinds of pop production flourishes. Featuring layers of keyboards, guitars, strings, and vocals, countrypolitan records were designed to crossover to pop radio and they frequently did. The sound dominated the country charts in the '70s and stayed popular until the early '80s.

NEW TRADITIONALIST— New traditionalists refers to the legions of young country singers that emerged in the late '80s. These artists reworked and updated the classic sounds of honky tonk and traditional country, adding contemporary production touches to make it more commercially viable—even with the flourishes, the music was essentially hardcore country. After the first wave of new traditionalists (George Strait, Randy Travis, Dwight Yoakum), the genre became a bit slicker and demonstrated more overt rock influences, but the new traditionalists continued to dominate the country charts in one form or another until the mid-'90s.

OUTLAW COUNTRY— Outlaw country was one of the more significant trends in country music in the '70s. During that decade, many of the most popular hardcore country singers of the '60s— from George Jones to Merle Haggard—softened their sound slightly, moving away from their honky tonk roots. While the outlaws weren't strictly honky tonk—they were as much storytellers in the tradition of folk songwriters as they were honky tonk vocalists—they kept that spirit alive. Outlaws didn't play by Nashville's rules. They didn't change their music to fit the heavily-produced, pop-oriented Nashville sound, nor did they go out of their way to fit into the accepted conventions of country music. Instead, they created an edgy form of hardcore country that was influenced by rock 'n' roll, folk, and blues. Ironically, two of the leading figures of the movement—Waylon Jennings and Willie Nelson—had their roots in the music industry, but by the time they came into their own as recording artists in the mid-'70s, they had developed a unique, defiant way of performing. Several other musicians—including David Allan Coe, Billy Joe Shaver, and Tompall Glaser—followed in their footsteps, and the outlaws were quite popular for a period of three to four years. At the end of the '70s, the urban cowboy movement easily eclipsed the outlaw movement in terms of commercial appeal, but the outlaws had a lasting influence. During the '80s, certain neo-traditionalists owed a bit of their sound to the outlaws, while a whole breed of songwriters, led by Steve Earle, demonstrated a massive debt to the outlaws and their fusion of country, folk, and rock.

WESTERN SWING— Western swing was the most eclectic form of country music and in its free-wheeling diversity, it set the stage for rock 'n' roll. Based in traditional string band music, Western swing also incorporated traditional pop melodies, jazz improvisation, blues and folk, creating a wildly entertaining and eclectic form of American music. Bob Wills and Milton Brown popularized the genre in the '30s and Wills became known as the father of the genre, since he remained popular for several decades, and had a remarkable string of hit singles. Although it sometimes faded from view, Western swing remained popular throughout the 20th century, occasionally experiencing upswings in popularity, such as the early '70s and the early '90s.

The Closer You Get / 1983 / RCA ✦✦✦✦
On their fourth album, Alabama shows signs that their hit-making approach was becoming a slick, well-produced formula, but when the formula produces hits like the title track and "Dixieland Delight," it's useless to complain. — *Stephen Thomas Erlewine*

40 Hour Week / 1985 / RCA ✦✦✦✦
Opening with the driving title track, *40 Hour Week* encapsulates why Alabama was the top country group of the '80s. Alternating between restrained rockers and well-crafted ballads, it captures the band at its peak. Nevertheless, it isn't quite as strong as their first albums—the performances and production are a bit too mannered—but its professionalism is appealing. And that professionalism made *40 Hour Week* the group's most popular album, as it crossed over into the pop Top Ten. — *Stephen Thomas Erlewine*

★ **Greatest Hits** / 1986 / RCA ✦✦✦✦✦
This batch of hits made them the most successful country act of the 80s. More than the best available sampler of their much-imitated group sound, it also reflects state-of-the-art Nashville Sound the moment before Randy Travis hit. — *Dan Cooper*

Southern Star / 1989 / RCA ✦✦✦✦
After eight very successful years with record producer Harold Shedd,

Alabama wisely opts for change. Half the album is recorded with Josh Leo and Larry Lee, the other half with Barry Beckett, and the guys from Fort Payne attack the project with a little more energy than in some of their prior efforts. Get it on CD—three of the four "bonus" tracks are substantial. — *Tom Roland*

Greatest Hits, Vol. 2 / 1991 / RCA ✦✦✦✦
Companion piece to the above with more emphasis on ballad material. —*Cub Koda*

American Pride / 1992 / RCA ✦✦✦

Cheap Seats / 1993 / RCA ✦✦✦

Greatest Hits, Vol. 3 / 1994 / RCA ✦✦✦✦
Like most country artists, Alabama made better singles than albums, rarely releasing a bad song for a single. Their third greatest hits compilation collects their biggest and best hits of the late '80s and early '90s, making it a worthwhile addition to a contemporary country library. —*Stephen Thomas Erlewine*

Deborah Allen

b. Sep. 30, 1953, Memphis, TN
Vocals
An adventurous singer who claims to have been heavily influenced by

Patsy Cline, Deborah Allen's best work blends the punched-up swamp blues of her native Memphis with aggressive pop-country. She scored her first hits in 1979 when Mary Reeves selected her to dub her voice on three tracks by the late Jim Reeves. Allen had wanted to be a country music singer since she was four. At age 17, she went to Nashville, where she worked as a waitress in a pancake house. Legend has it that one of her customers was Roy Orbison, who hired her on the spot as a backup singer for his next session after she convinced him of her singing ability. Allen then worked at Opryland on the General Jackson showboat and then went on an international tour as a singer and dancer with Tennessee Ernie Ford's show. Jim Stafford then hired her to appear on his summer TV show in California and as an opening act for his concerts. In 1980, she recorded her debut album, *Trouble in Paradise*, for Capitol; the album contained one Top 20 single, "You (Make Me Wonder Why)." In 1983, she released the mini-album *Cheat the Night*, which contained three major singles; she wrote all three, including "Baby I Lied." The success of this short album led to the full album *Let Me Be the First* in 1984. Afterwards, Allen stopped performing and became a songwriter, frequently collaborating with then-husband Rafe Van Hoy. Among the hits she has written are Janie Fricke's "Don't Worry 'Bout Me Baby" and Tanya Tucker's "Can I See You Tonight."

She came back to country singing with a sassy vengeance in 1993 with the album *Delta Dreamland*. Her first single, "Rock Me," was released with a rather raw concept video. While her career started out with modest promise, the gutsy Deborah Allen has grown into one of the major country music talents of the 1990s. —*Sandra Brennan*

Let Me Be the First / 1984 / RCA ✦✦✦
Working again with husband/producer/co-writer Rafe Van Hoy, Allen attempts an artful, electronic style of country-pop that proved too progressive for the country mainstream. —*Michael McCall*

● **Delta Dreamland** / 1993 / Warner Bros. ✦✦✦✦
Allen comes roaring back with another Van Hoy collaboration, this one produced before signing a record contract. Bluesy, sexy and intimately powerful, it rocks stronger than anything she previously offered. —*Michael McCall*

All That I Am / 1994 / Giant ✦✦✦✦
Allen pushes her steamy sensuality even more to the forefront here in another strong collection. —*Michael McCall*

Cheat the Night / RCA ✦✦✦✦
An EP features her two best-known hits of the 1980s, "Baby I Lied" and "I've Been Wrong Before." It's sweeter and softer-edged than her '90s work. —*Michael McCall*

Rex Allen

b. Dec. 31, 1922, Willcox, AZ
Guitar, Vocals
Better-known as the Arizona Cowboy, Rex Allen was the last of Hollywood's singing cowboys. Between 1950 and 1954, Allen starred in 19 movies for Republic studios. The films launched a popular recording career for Allen, as he had several hit singles and albums in the early '50s, before the singing cowboys slowly disappeared from the charts.

The son of a fiddle-player, Rex Allen was given his first guitar when he was 11 years old; his father intended Rex to support him at dances. Shortly afterwards, Rex began singing. After he finished high school, Allen was hired as a performer by a Phoenix radio stations, but he only stayed there for a brief time. Instead, he hit the rodeo circuit. His career as a rodeo rider was short-lived, as he suffered an injury from a bull. The injury led Allen back to singing, and he was hired by WTTM in Trenton, New Jersey in 1943.

After he left WTTM, Rex Allen joined the Sleepy Hollow Ranch gang in Pennsylvania. During the summer of 1946, Allen was spotted by Lulubelle and Scotty; impressed, the duo recommended that he try out for the National Born Dance and WLS in Chicago. Allen became a popular performer in the windy city, which led him to become one of the first country-western artists signed by Mercury Records. Mercury released several of Allen's singles before he had a hit with "Afraid" in 1949. That same year, Allen went to Hollywood.

Bringing along a CBS Network radio program, Rex Allen approached Republic Pictures. The studio signed the singer to a star in a film, *The Arizona Cowboy*, which was released in 1950. The movie was a success, beginning a string of 19 pictures that ran until February 1954. All of the movies were musical westerns, starring Allen with a rotating cast of sidekicks. Frequently, he would star with Slim Pickens, but Buddy Ebsen and Fuzzy Knight also made their appearances in Allen's films.

Allen's film successes led to a hit record in 1951, "Sparrow in the Tree Top." Released on Mercury Records, the single climbed into the country Top Ten and made it into the pop Top 30. Soon after its release, Allen signed with Decca Records, who released his biggest hit, 1953's "Crying in the Chapel"; the song peaked in the Top Five and reached the Top Ten pop charts. In the latter half of the decade, he made a number of albums

composed of Western songs. During this time, he acted in 39 episodes of the television program, *Frontier Doctor*.

By the '60s, Rex Allen had re-signed with Mercury Records, which led to several minor hits and one major success—1962's "Don't Go Near the Indians," which returned the singer to the country Top Ten and the pop Top 20. On his '60s stint at Mercury, Allen had two other significant hits—1961's "Marines Let's Go" and "Tear After Tear" in 1964. In the late '60s, the singer went back to Decca Records, which resulted in one minor hit in 1968, "Tiny Bubbles." During this time and the early '70s, he recorded albums for Disneyland, Buena Vista, and JMI. However, he was more prominent in this era as a narrator for many Walt Disney films and television programs, as well as a voice in several Disney cartoons.

In the '80s, Allen's oldest son, Rex Allen Jr., became a star in his own right. A museum in his hometown Willcox was dedicated to Rex Allen, and the Governor of Arizona honored him. Allen occasionally appeared at Western film fairs, where he remained as popular as ever. —*Stephen Thomas Erlewine*

● **Voice of the West** / Aug. 1986 / Bear Family ✦✦✦✦
Voice of the West collects songs Rex Allen recorded in the early '70s with producer Jack Clement, who cut away the cinematic strings that dominated Allen's previous recordings. Instead, he leaves the singing cowboy with simple, straightforward production that accentuates the western roots of his music. Not only does he play traditional cowboy classics, he does a handful of contemporary country numbers. It might not have his classic hits, but *Voice of the West* gives a good sense of the scope of Allen's talents. —*Stephen Thomas Erlewine*

Terry Allen

b. May 7, 1943, Wichita, KS
Keyboards, Vocals / Country-Rock
There may be no greater maverick than Terry Allen in all of late-20th century country music. Along with Jimmie Dale Gilmore, Joe Ely, and Butch Hancock—all of whom he's known and collaborated with—Allen is a standardbearer of the Lubbock, TX, country scene. Though not widely heralded, this is perhaps the most progressive movement in all of contemporary country, digging into modern-day concerns with a gutsy, liberal perspective, while maintaining a firm musical grounding in regional country and folk traditions. Allen is perhaps the most ambitious of them all, writing complex song cycles that are performed with the help of fellow eclectics ranging from Lowell George to David Byrne.

Allen's audience, like those of the other Lubbock pioneers, is not the country mainstream. Indeed, his principal appeal may not lie with the country audience at all (though his music definitely *is* country), but with open-minded alternative folk and rock listeners. Unlike most current country artists, his words aim to question and confront hard day-to-day realities, rather than offer conservative clichés or maudlin comforts to shield listeners from those realities. He does so with a humor and irreverence that will also find little sympathy in Nashville or Middle America.

Country music is just one of Allen's artistic pursuits, perhaps accounting to some degree for his wide perspective. The renaissance man is also an internationally recognized artist with three NEA grants and a Guggenheim Fellowship to his credit. He's also a true multimedia performer, having done work in the mediums of painting, sculpture, film, video, installation, theater, and poetry. Just a few of his more interesting projects, for instance, were writing the music for *Amerasia*, a film about American servicemen living in Thailand after the Vietnam War; writing a new national anthem (with Ely, Hancock, and Gilmore) in conjunction with a book about Vietnam; and collaborating with his wife Jo Harvey Allen, Ely, and Hancock on the production of the acclaimed stage play *Chippy*.

But Allen is not a country music dilettante, having written songs for Bobby Bare and Robert Earl Keen. Outside of the strict country sphere, he wrote "New Delhi Freight Train" for Little Feat, and contributed a few songs to the soundtrack of David Byrne's *True Stories* film. The cinema has always been an inspiration or influence upon Allen's work. His first album, *Juarez* (from the mid-'70s), was a conceptual work that originated as a soundtrack to an imaginary film, evolving in performance to a set of songs inspired by Mexican imagery.

1979's *Lubbock (On Everything)* is considered his most significant album. Inspired by his experiences growing up in the Texan town, it won praise for observing the details of regional life and characters with a sensitivity and wit more akin to rock and folk singer-songwriters than country ones. Allen's music (if not his lyrics), however, remain very much in the Texan country tradition.

With many artistic projects always in the works, Allen has never had the need to record frequently. 1996's *Human Remains*, though, found his singing and songwriting prowess undimmed. He also expanded his musical horizons significantly with support from such noted stars and cult figures as David Byrne, Lucinda Williams, Ponty Bone, Lloyd Maines, and Joe Ely. —*Richie Unterberger*

● **Lubbock on Everything** / 1979 / Sugar Hill ✦✦✦✦
In the view of most critics this is Allen's definitive statement, examining mundane and eccentric small town lives with a sympathetic but penetrating wit that is rare in country music. The musical arrangements are much plainer than the ones Allen would craft in his much more recent *Human Remains*. Still, you won't find songs about a Wolfman of Del Rio, a football star who ends up in the pen after a series of post-high school failures, or middle aged women fighting for beauty on many other country albums. —*Richie Unterberger*

Human Remains / Jan. 23, 1996 / Sugar Hill ✦✦✦✦
The conceptual scope of *Human Remains* is not nearly as ambitious as *Lubbock*. But the gutsier and more varied musical arrangements—crafted with help from Lloyd Maines, David Byrne, Joe Ely, Lucinda Williams, and many others—may make this a better introduction into Allen's world. —*Richie Unterberger*

John Anderson

b. Dec. 12, 1955, Apopka, FL
Guitar, Vocals / Country
Growing up in Apopka, FL, John Anderson was enamored with the Beatles and the Rolling Stones, like most of his peers. But, when he heard a Merle Haggard album at age 15, he found his true calling. Anderson headed for Nashville, where he showed up unannounced on his sister's doorstep. He took low-paying club jobs in Music City's Printer's Alley for experience, and worked a variety of places for money in the early '70s. In one of those jobs, he actually helped do roofing on the Grand Ole Opry House, before its opening in 1974. Signed to Warner Brothers in the late '70s, Anderson's first album hit the streets in 1980, bringing with it critical acclaim for his attention to country tradition. Adding a vocal strain to the phrasing he picked up from Haggard and Lefty Frizzell, Anderson captured the Country Music Association's Horizon award for 1983, given to an artist who makes the most career progress. "Swingin'," which, at 1.3 million in sales, is the best-selling single in Warner history, also reeled in the CMA's Single of the Year trophy. Unfortunately Anderson fell out of favor with country radio within two years and future albums failed to capitalize on his earlier momentum. With the help of producer James Stroud, Anderson's career was revitalized in 1992 with the release of his first BNA Records release, *Seminole Wind*, and the single "Straight Tequila Night." He followed with *Solid 'til I Die* in 1993, *Country 'til I Die* in 1994 and *Paradise* in 1996. —*Tom Roland*

John Anderson 2 / 1981 / Warner Bros. ✦✦✦✦
His second album (obviously), this traditionally minded package contrasted with the bulk of the material released in the same *Urban Cowboy*—influenced time period. His cover of Lefty Frizzell's "I Love You a Thousand Ways" shows his roots nicely, and "I'm Just an Old Chunk of Coal (But I'm Gonna Be a Diamond Someday)" is simply classic. —*Tom Roland*

Wild & Blue / 1982 / Warner Bros. ✦✦✦

★ **Greatest Hits** / 1984 / Warner Bros. ✦✦✦✦✦
Greatest Hits covers John Anderson's biggest hits from the early '80s, including the Top Ten singles "I Just Came Home to Count the Memories," "She Sure Got Away With My Heart," "Chicken Truck," "1959," "Would You Catch a Falling Star," "I'm Just An Old Chunk of Coal (But I'm Gonna Be A Diamond Someday)," and the No. 1 hits "Wild and Blue," "Swingin'," and "Black Sheep." —*Thom Owens*

Greatest Hits, Vol. 2 / 1990 / Warner Bros. ✦✦✦✦
Anderson keeps up the momentum. —*Dan Heilman*

Seminole Wind / 1992 / RCA ✦✦✦✦
A solid comeback album, it re-established Anderson as one of the most emotionally moving stylists of his generation. The title song features pointed social commentary about the ecological destruction of his native Florida. —*Michael McCall*

Solid Ground / Jun. 1993 / BNA ✦✦✦

Paradise / Jan. 30, 1996 / BNA ✦✦✦
Featuring guest appearances by Levon Helm and Mark Knopfler, John Anderson's *Paradise* is a typically consistent effort from the singer, featuring a handful of great songs that cancel out the fair amount of filler on the record. —*Sara Sytsma*

Lynn Anderson (Lynn Rene Anderson)

b. Sep. 26, 1947, Grand Forks, ND
Vocals / Country-Pop
Vocalist, songwriter, and guitarist Lynn Anderson is best remembered for her gigantic 1971 crossover hit "Rose Garden." The daughter of songwriters Casey and Liz Anderson, she was born in North Dakota and raised in northern California. By the time she was a teen, Anderson was singing, dancing and playing the guitar. She was studying at American River College in 1965 when she joined *Country Corners* in Sacramento, where she stayed until 1966. When her mother Liz went to Nashville to collect a BMI Award for writing Merle Haggard's first hit song "Strang-

ers," Anderson accompanied her. She and her mother sang at a party during the Disc Jockey Convention and she was noticed by Slim Williamson of Chart Records, who signed her to his struggling label hoping she could help make it into a major independent record company. She recorded her first single at the end of 1965 with Jerry Lane. She released her first solo single, "In Person," in 1966, and a year later, Lawrence Welk invited her to become a regular on his show. She was named Most Promising Female Vocalist in a *Cash Box* DJ poll, which led to her debuting at the Grand Ole Opry and releasing her first album, *Ride, Ride, Ride*. In addition to her budding singing career, Anderson was also becoming well-known as an expert rider on the equestrian circuit.

In 1968 Anderson married songwriter/producer Glenn Sutton. That year she was also named Best Female Vocalist by ACM and left the Welk show to record for Chart until 1970, by which time she had recorded over 100 songs; some of them, such as "Big Girls Don't Cry" (1968) and "That's a No-No," made it to the Top Ten.

After she left Chart for Columbia, she released three singles before "Rose Garden" from an album of the same name. The single was internationally popular and topped both the country and pop charts. Among the awards Anderson garnered for the tune were a 1970 Grammy for Best Female Country Vocal Performance and CMA's Best Female Vocalist. Anderson continued her affiliation with Columbia until 1981 and had numerous Top Ten hits; some of her tunes, such as "Even Cowboys Get the Blues" (1980), have become country music standards. Anderson recorded *Back* for Permian in 1983, which produced two hits. One year later, Anderson released a single for MCA and then stopped recording for the next two years. In 1986, she signed with Mercury and staged a comeback with her album *What She Does Best*, which contained several hits. She then was honored with *Record World's* Country Artist of the Decade award. —*Sandra Brennan*

● **Greatest Hits** / 1972 / RCA ✦✦✦✦
With big pipes, big production, and big hits from the mid-to-late '60s, including "Rose Garden." —*Mark A. Humphrey*

Eddy Arnold

b. May 15, 1918, Madisonville, TN
Guitar, Vocals / Traditional Country
Eddy Arnold moved hillbilly music to the city, creating a sleek sound that relied on his smooth voice and occasionally lush orchestrations. In the process, he became the most popular country performer of the century, spending more weeks at the top of the charts than any other artist. Arnold not only had 28 No. 1 singles, he has more charting singles than any other artist. More than any other country performer of the post-war era, he was responsible for bringing the music to the masses, to people that wouldn't normally listen to country music. Arnold was initially influenced by cowboy singers like Gene Autry, but as his career progressed, he shaped his phrasing in the style of Pete Cassell. Nevertheless, he was more of a crooner than a hillbilly singer, which is a large reason why he was embraced by the entertainment industry at large, and frequently crossed over to the pop charts. Arnold's career ran strong into the '90s. Although his records didn't dominate the charts like they did during the '40s and '50s, he continued to fill concert halls and reissues of his older recordings sold well.

Raised on a farm in Tennessee, Arnold was given a guitar at the age of ten by his mother. His father, who had played fiddle and bass, died the following year. Arnold left school so he could help out on the farm. However, he began playing dances whenever he had the chance. Several years later, he made his first radio appearance on a station in Jackson. Arnold then moved to St. Louis, where he played in night clubs with fiddler Speedy McNatt. In St. Louis, Arnold landed a regular spot on WMPS Memphis, spending six years at the radio station. Through the show, the singer earned a dedicated following of fans.

During World War II, Eddy Arnold became part of the R.J. Reynolds' Camel Caravan, which featured Redd Stewart, Pee Wee King's Golden West Cowboys, Minnie Pearl, and San Antonio Rose. The troupe performed for US troops throughout America, as well some selected dates in Panama. After the Camel Caravan, Arnold became the featured singer in the Golden West Cowboys while they performed on the Grand Ole Opry. At first, he appeared under the name "The Tennessee Plowboy," a nickname that followed him throughout his career.

Arnold recorded his first single, "Mommy Please Stay Home With Me," in 1944 for RCA Victor. At RCA, the singer received the guidance of the label's A&R head, Steve Sholes, which proved to be invaluable help for his career.

Eddy Arnold pursued a solo career in 1945, the same year he got married to Sally Gayhart. "Each Minute Seems A Million Years," released on RCA's Bluebird division that same year, became his first charting record, peaking in the Top Five. Arnold's career really took off the following year, when "That's How Much I Love You" peaked in the Top Three, staying there for 16 weeks and selling over 650,000 copies; its flip-side, "Chained to a Memory," also climbed into the Top Three. Arnold followed the single's success with two No. 1 hits in 1947, "What Is Life Without Love" and

"It's A Sin." However, that didn't compare to the success of his next record, "I'll Hold You In My Heart (Till I Can Hold You In My Arms)." The single spent 46 weeks on the charts, with 21 of those weeks spent at the top; it also crossed over to the pop charts, reaching the Top 30. In the process, it became the No. 1 single of the decade. "I'll Hold You In My Heart" confirmed that Arnold had become a country superstar, as did the performance of his 1948 singles. All of his nine singles went into the Top Five, and five of them went to No. 1, including "Anytime," "What A Fool I Was," "Texarkana Baby," "Just A Little Lovin' (Will Go a Long, Long Way)," "My Daddy Is Only A Picture," and "Bouquet of Roses," which stayed at the top for 19 weeks. In total, Arnold racked up over 40 weeks on top of the charts during 1948, becoming the No. 1 country star in America. He headlined all the radio shows and concerts he appeared on, and he was in demand throughout the nation. By the end of the year, Colonel Tom Parker had become his manager; Parker would later become Elvis Presley's manager. Throughout 1949, he continued to dominate the charts, releasing a succession of Top Ten singles, including the No. 1 "Don't Rob Another Man's Castle," "One Kiss Too Many," "I'm Throwing Rice (At the Girl I Love)," and "Take Me In Your Arms and Hold Me."

Eddy Arnold became a familiar face not only to country fans, but to the general public in the early '50s. He toured all of the US, as well as several foreign countries. All of the major television shows of the era, including *The Perry Como Show* and *Arthur Godfrey's Talent Scouts*, featured the singer. Indeed, he became so popular that he was the first country star to have his own television show, *Eddy Arnold Time*. The show originally aired on NBC, but it later moved to ABC. Through all of this, his string of Top Ten hits remained unbroken, even though he didn't have another crossover pop hit until 1954. Nevertheless, the sheer amount of country hits was overwhelming: in 1950 he had seven, 13 in 1951 (including the No. 1 hits "There's Been A Change In Me," "Kentucky Waltz," "I Wanna Play House With You," "Easy on the Eyes," and "A Full Time Job"). The hits, including "Eddy's Song" (composed of the titles of previous hits), "How's the World Treating You?," "I Really Don't Want To Know," "My Everything," "The Cattle Call," "That Do Make It Nice," "Just Call Me Lonesome," and "The Richest Man (In the World)," continued to come in force until 1956.

Between 1956 and 1964, Arnold continued to chart, but he wasn't reaching the Top Ten at the same frequency of the previous decade. During this time, his style was beginning to change, as he was shedding his rootsy style for a slicker, polished sound that was more appropriate for urban settings than rural territories. Arnold became a crooner, complete with subdued instrumental backings, highlighted by gentle steel guitars and the occasional orchestra. The change in musical direction was a major commercial success, sparking a new era of chart dominance that began in 1965 with "What's He Doing In My World." Not only did he return to the top of the country charts, he once again crossed over to the pop charts. Arnold's second streak of major hits ran until 1969. During this time, he earned several No. 1 and Top Ten singles, all of which were pop hits as well, including "Make the World Go Away," "I Want To Go With You," "The Last Word in Lonesome," "Somebody Like Me," "Lonely Again," "Turn the World Around," "Then You Can Tell Me Goodbye," "They Don't Make Love Like They Used To," and "Please Don't Go."

In the early '70s, Arnold continued to appear on the country charts, although his pop hits dried up. The singer signed with MGM in 1972, ending 27 straight years at RCA. Arnold spent only four years at MGM, landing only one major hit, 1974's "I Wish That I Had Loved You Better." Returning to RCA in 1976, he closed out the decade with two hits—"Cowboy" (1976) and "If Everyone Had Someone Like You" (1978). Arnold managed to put two songs into the Top Ten in 1980 ("Let's Get It While The Gettin's Good," "That's What I Get For Loving You"), making him one of the few artists that charted in five different decades. He continued to record in the '90s, although he has yet to chart a hit single. Nevertheless, his concert and television appearances remained popular.

Beginning in the '60s, Eddy Arnold was bestowed with numerous awards. In 1966, he was inducted into the Country Music Hall of Fame. The following year, he was the first "Entertainer of the Year" named by the CMA. The ACM gave him the "Pioneer Award' in 1984; three years later, the Songwriters Guild gave him "The President's Award." Perhaps the truest gauge of his success is his record sales. Over the course of his career, he has sold over 85 million records, making him one of the most successful artists of the century. —*Stephen Thomas Erlewine*

Anytime/Eddy Arnold and His Guitar / 1952 / RCA ✦✦✦✦
The fine, early country material ("Bouquet of Roses," "Molly Darling") features Little Roy Wiggins on steel guitar. —*Richard Lieberson*

Cattle Call/Thereby Hangs a Tale / 1963 / Bear Family ✦✦✦✦
Two of Eddy Arnold's early RCA/Victor albums, *Cattle Call* and *Thereby Hangs a Tale*, were combined on this single-disc from Bear Family. Though fans of Arnold's earliest records will find plenty of interest, the disc is primarily of historical interest—there are better places to listen to his early material. —*Stephen Thomas Erlewine*

★ **The Best of Eddy Arnold [RCA]** / 1967 / RCA ✦✦✦✦✦
His smooth, lushly produced crossover hits upset the traditional crowd, but they represent some of the most romantic country recordings of the era. Featured is "Make the World Go Away," "Anytime," "Bouquet of Roses," "The Last Word in Lonesome Is Me," and a re-recording of his classic "Cattle Call." —*Michael McCall*

Last of the Love Song Singers: Then & Now / 1993 / RCA ✦✦✦✦
The double-disc box set *Last of the Love Song Singers: Then and Now* is a wasted opportunity. The first disc, called *Then*, is a quick overview of some of Arnold's biggest hits that doesn't offer enough songs. The second disc, titled *Now*, is a collection of new recordings. Though they aren't bad, the new recordings devalue the set's worth as a retrospective and as an introduction. —*Stephen Thomas Erlewine*

Essential Eddy Arnold / Jun. 18, 1996 / RCA ✦✦✦✦
The Essential Eddy Arnold contains the majority of Eddy Arnold's biggest hits, including "Make the World Go Away" and "Cattle Call." It's the only single-disc retrospective that offers a reasonably thorough overview of his hit singles, making it an ideal introduction and—considering that the two-disc box set *Last of the Love Song Singers* contained an entire disc of newly recorded material—the only currently available retrospective that could be considered definitive. —*Thom Owens*

Asleep at the Wheel

Western Swing
The enduring Western swing revivalist band Asleep at the Wheel helped popularize the genre in the '70s and went on to a popular career as performing and recording artists. Their eclectic, freewheeling music earned the group a dedicated following of both fans and critics since the start of their career in the '70s. Over the course of their career, a number of musicians have passed through the group—more than 80, to be precise—but throughout the years, the vision of guitarist Ray Benson has kept the band together.

Asleep At The Wheel was founded by Ray Benson (vocals, lead guitar) and Leroy Preston (drums, guitar, vocals) in 1970. The pair met through Benson's sister, who was attending Northeastern College in Boston with Preston while Benson was living on a rent-free 1,500 acre farm in West Virginia. Benson, Preston, and Benson's longtime friend Reuben "Lucky Oceans" Gosfield (steel guitar, drums) formed a straightforward country band and began playing at local bars and lodges in Virginia. They were soon joined by guitarist/singer Chris O'Connell, who had just graduated from high school. In 1971, Commander Cody saw the group performing in Washington, DC, and was impressed enough to send his manager Joe Kerr to meet with the band. They signed with Kerr, who convinced the band to move to San Francisco late in that year. Keyboardist Floyd Domino (b. Jim Haber) joined the band following an inaugural 30-day tour with Stoney Edwards.

After Domino joined the group, Asleep At The Wheel landed a permanent gig at the Longbranch Saloon in Berkeley. They soon cultivated a solid fan base and signed with United Artists Records. Their first album, *Comin' Right At Ya*, was released in 1973. In 1974, they moved to Austin, TX, which eventually became their home base. That year, they released an eponymous album on Epic Records and had their first minor hit, a remake of Louis Jordan's "Choo Choo Ch'Boogie."

Asleep At The Wheel added two members, fiddler Lisa Silver and trumpeter Bobby Womack, and moved to Capitol Records in 1975. Their first album for the label, *Texas Gold*, was their most popular breakthrough, reaching the pop charts and spawning the hit single "The Letter That Johnny Walker Red." The album generated four more hits, and later that year they released *Wheelin' and Dealin'*. By that time four more members, including accordion player Jo-El Sonnier, had joined the lineup. For the rest of the decade, Asleep At The Wheel was one of the most popular country artists in America. In 1977, they were voted Best Touring Band by the ACM, and won a Grammy for Best Country Instrumental Performance for the single "One O'Clock Jump" in 1978.

1980 was a year of setbacks for Asleep At The Wheel; Lucky Oceans left the band, and the remaining members soon found that they were over $200,000 in debt. To keep afloat, the group performed TV commercials for Budweiser and worked on movie soundtracks. Shortly afterwards, the group lost Chris O'Connell, who quit the band to have a baby. In addition to their internal difficulties in the early '80s, Asleep At The Wheel had trouble selling records. The group had a hit album with *Framed* in 1980, but that was their last release for over half a decade. After their self-titled album for MCA-Dot flopped in 1985, Benson tried his hand at producing, working with such artists as Aaron Neville, Rob Wasserman, Willie Nelson, and Bruce Hornsby.

Things began turning around for Asleep At The Wheel in 1986 when they were named Country Band of the Year by the National Association of Campus Activities. By the time they signed with Epic Records in 1987, the group had gone through a number of personnel changes. The band now consisted of Benson, Chris O'Connell (who had returned from her leave of absence), fiddler Larry Franklin, fiddler Johnny Gimble, bassist

Jon Mitchell, pianist/accordionist Tim Alexander, steel guitarist John Ely, saxophonist Mike Francis, and David Sanger. *Asleep at the Wheel 10,* the group's first album for Epic, was released in 1987 and became the hit they needed. The album launched several hit singles, including "House of Blue Lights," "Way Down Texas Way," and the Grammy-winning instrumental album track, "String of Pars." Their next Epic album, *Western Standard Time,* came out in 1988 and led to another Grammy for the instrumental "Sugarfoot Rag."

In 1990, Asleep At the Wheel signed with Arista and recorded *Keepin' Me Up Nights.* Two years later, they released *Greatest Hits Live and Kickin',* after which most of the band members left the group. In 1993, a re-formed lineup featuring Benson, fiddler Rickey Turpin, bassist David Earl Miller, drummer Tommy Beavers, and steel guitarist Cindy Cash-Dollar released *Tribute to the Music of Bob Wills and the Texas Playboys* on Liberty. Featuring a number of guest artists, including several original Texas Playboys, Merle Haggard, Willie Nelson, Lyle Lovett, Vince Gill, Chet Atkins, Suzy Bogguss, Brooks & Dunn, George Strait, Dolly Parton, and Garth Brooks, the album received the best reviews of any of the group's records and became a big hit. —*Sandra Brennan*

Asleep at the Wheel [Epic] / 1974 / Epic ✦✦✦

Asleep at the Wheel [Dot] / 1985 / Dot ✦✦✦✦
Benson by now is revealing a romantic baritone as well as his usual sublime swing. Guest appearances come from Bonnie Raitt and Willie Nelson. —*Michael McCall*

● **Live & Kickin': Greatest Hits** / Aug. 1991 / Arista ✦✦✦✦
Recorded at an Austin roadhouse, *Live and Kickin': Greatest Hits* showcases Asleep at the Wheel running through their best-known material in a kinetic live setting. It's a great introduction to the band—they are never better than they are in concert, and the selection brings out the best in the musicians. —*Stephen Thomas Erlewine*

Best of / 1992 / CEMA ✦✦✦✦
Features "Route 66," "Bump Bounce Boogie," "Texas, Me & You," and others. —*AMG*

Tribute to the Music of Bob Wills & The Texas Playboys / Oct. 25, 1993 / Liberty ✦✦✦✦
Benson and The Wheel invite a bus full of guests to pay homage to the King of Western swing and do so with joyful, rollicking fun. Garth Brooks, Vince Gill, George Strait, Dolly Parton, Marty Stuart, and Suzy Bogguss are among those enjoying themselves on this exemplary album. —*Michael McCall*

Chet Atkins (Chester Burton Atkins)

b. Jun. 20, 1924, Luttrell, TN
Fiddle, Guitar / Nashville Sound/Countripolitan
Without Chet Atkins, country music may never have crossed over into the pop charts in the '50s and '60s. Although he has recorded hundreds of solo records, Chet Atkins' largest influence came as a session musician and a record producer. During the '50s and '60s, he helped create the Nashville sound, a style of country music that owed nearly as much to pop as it did to honky tonks.

And as a guitarist, he is without parallel. Atkins' style grew out of his admiration for Merle Travis, expanding Travis' signature syncopated thumb and fingers roll into new territory.

Interestingly, Chet Atkins didn't begin his musical career by playing guitar. On the recommendation of his older brother, Lowell, he began playing the fiddle as a child. However, Chet was still attracted to the guitar and at the age of nine, he traded a pistol for a guitar. Atkins learned his instrument rapidly, becoming an accomplished player by the time he left high school in 1941. Using a variety of contacts, he wound up performing on the *Bill Carlisle Show* on WNOX in Knoxville, TN, as well as becoming part of the Dixie Swingers. Atkins worked with Homer and Jethro while he was at the radio station. After three years, he moved to a radio station in Cincinnati.

Supporting Red Foley, Atkins made his first appearance at the Grand Ole Opry in 1946. That same year, he made his first records, recording for Bullet. Atkins also began making regular performances on the WRVA radio station in Richmond, VA, but he was repeatedly fired because the musical arrangements differed from the expectations of the station's executives. He eventually moved to Springfield, MO, working for the KWTO station. A tape of one of Atkins' performances was sent to RCA Victor's office in Chicago. Eventually, it worked its way to Steve Sholes, the head of country music at RCA. Sholes had heard Atkins previously and had been trying to find him for several years. By this time, Atkins had moved to Denver, CO, and was playing with Shorty Thompson and His Rangers. Upon receiving the call from RCA, he moved to Nashville to record.

Once he arrived in Nashville, Chet recorded eight tracks for the label, five of which featured the guitarist singing. Impressed by his playing, Sholes made Atkins the studio guitarist for all of RCA studio's Nashville sessions in 1949. The following year, Mother Maybelle and the Carter Sisters hired him as a regular on the Grand Ole Opry, making his place

in Nashville's musical community secure. While he worked for RCA, he played on many hit records and helped fashion the Nashville sound. RCA appreciated his work and made him a consultant to the company's Nashville division in 1953. That year, the label began to issue a number of instrumental albums that showcased Atkins' considerable talents. Two years later, he scored his first hit with a version of "Mr. Sandman"; it was followed by "Silver Bell," a duet with Hank Snow. By the late '50s, Chet Atkins was known throughout the music industry as a first-rate player. Not only did his records sell well, he designed guitars for Gibson and Gretsch; models of these instruments continued to sell in the '90s.

Steve Sholes left for New York in 1957 to act as head of pop A&R, leaving Atkins as the manager of RCA's Nashville division. However, the guitarist didn't abandon performing, and throughout the early '60s his star continued to rise. He played the Newport Jazz Festival in 1960; in 1961, he performed at the White House. Atkins had his first Top Five hit in 1965 with a reworking of Boots Randolph's "Yakety Sax", retitled "Yakety Axe"; in addition to being a sizable country hit, the song crossed over to the pop charts. Atkins' role behind the scene was thriving as well. He produced hits for the majority of RCA's Nashville acts, including Elvis Presley and Eddy Arnold, and discovered a wealth of talent, including Don Gibson, Waylon Jennings, Floyd Cramer, Charley Pride, Bobby Bare, and Connie Smith. Because of his consistent track record, Atkins was promoted to vice- president of RCA's country division when Steve Sholes died in 1968.

The following year, Atkins had his last major hit single, "Country Gentleman." In the late '60s and early '70s, several minor hits followed, but only one song, "Prissy" (1968), made it into the Top 40. Instead, the guitarist's major musical contribution in the early part of the '70s was with Homer and Jethro. Under the name the Nashville String Band, the trio released five albums between 1970 and 1972. Following Homer's death, Atkins continued to work with Jethro.

Atkins continued to record for RCA throughout the '70s, although he was creatively stifled by the label by the end of the decade. The guitarist wanted to record a jazz album, but he was met with resistance by the label. In 1982, he left RCA and signed with Columbia, releasing his first album for the label, *Work It Out With Chet Atkins,* in 1983. During his time at Columbia, Atkins departed from his traditional country roots, demonstrating that he was a bold and tasteful jazz guitarist as well. He did return to country on occasion, particularly on duet albums with Mark Knopfler and Jerry Reed, but by and large, Atkins' Columbia records demonstrated a more adventurous guitarist than was previously captured on his RCA albums.

Throughout his career, Chet Atkins earned numerous awards, including 11 Grammy awards and nine CMA "Instrumentalist of the Year" honors, as well as a "Lifetime Achievement Award" from NARAS. Although his award list is impressive, they only begin to convey his contribution to country music. —*Stephen Thomas Erlewine*

Chet Atkins Picks on the Beatles / 1965 / RCA ✦✦

Stay Tuned / 1985 / CBS ✦✦✦✦
This first-rate session teams Atkins with George Benson, Earl Klugh, Larry Carlton, and Mark Knopfler. —*Ron Wynn*

C.G.P. / 1988 / CBS ✦✦✦✦
Great picking and guitar technique. —*Ron Wynn*

Neck & Neck / Feb. 1991 / Columbia ✦✦✦✦
Working with Dire Straits guitarist Mark Knopfler had a rejuvenating influence on Chet Atkins. Knopfler has Atkins moving toward his country roots, but both guitarists still play with a tasteful, jazzy sensibility—however, Atkins has abandoned the overt jazz-fusion pretensions that sank most of his '80s records. With its direct, understated approach, *Neck and Neck* is the most focused and arguably the most rewarding record Atkins has released. —*Stephen Thomas Erlewine*

★ **The RCA Years** / Oct. 1992 / RCA ✦✦✦✦✦
The RCA Years—1947-1981 isn't quite a definitive compilation, but it is the closest attempt at a comprehensive retrospective to date. Chet Atkins compiled the set himself, which means it's filled with idiosyncratic selections that don't necessarily represent him at his most representative. Nevertheless, *The RCA Years* does give a sense of Atkins' accomplishments and the breadth of his talents. —*Stephen Thomas Erlewine*

Galloping Guitar / 1993 / Bear Family ✦✦✦✦
A wonderful multi-disc boxed set retrospective of Atkins' earliest recordings. Casual fans will be surprised to hear that Chet was originally marketed as a vocalist/guitarist, much the same as then-popular-Merle Travis was on Capitol. His eventual move to strict instrumentals doesn't come until the end of this box set, with guest vocalists flitting in and out of the picture, but Atkins' guitar is solid throughout. —*Cub Koda*

Almost Alone / Mar. 12, 1996 / Columbia ✦✦✦
On this album of nearly solo guitar instrumentals, Chet Atkins plays with his usual ease and dexterity, beginning with some tasty originals and gradually moving into such standards as "Mr. Bojangles" and "Cheek to Cheek." The most unusual track is the in-concert vocal performance "I Still Write Your Name in the Snow," which is a bit more risque

than you might expect, but makes a welcome change of pace. — *William Ruhlmann*

Essential Chet Atkins / Jun. 18, 1996 / RCA ✦✦✦✦
Since *The Essential Chet Atkins* concentrates on his instrumental tracks—including hits like "Mr. Sandman" and "Yakety Axe"—it functions as the best single-disc retrospective of the guitarist. It is also one of the only collections that concisely demonstrates his subtly dazzling virtuosity. — *Thom Owens*

Gene Autry (Orvin Gene Autry)

b. Sep. 29, 1907, Tioga, TX
Guitar, Vocals / Cowboy
In 1934, Gene Autry rode into Hollywood and became the prototypical singing cowboy—a handsome, gun-toting yodeler who came to town and set things right. He defeated the black-clad forces of evil, treated his clever horse kindly, married the prettiest girl, and found time to sing about it all. A country that was little interested in singing hillbillies flocked to the theaters to see the guitar-strumming embodiment of truth, justice, and the American way (the *western* American way) prevail over the baddies in the black hats. This romantic and fanciful image of the Golden West did much to help Americans forget the Depression and look beyond into the sunset. This national fascination with that-which-never-was dominated country music in the '40s and has reappeared, from Marty "El Paso" Robbins through Michael Martin Murphey and Riders in the Sky.

The cowboy song trail had been blazed before, by real or pretend cowboys such as Carl T. Sprague, Jules Verne Allen, Goebel Reeves, and even Jimmie Rodgers, but it was Gene Autry who caused the "country-western" term that for nearly fifty years has been commonly used (though inaccurately) to refer to country music in general. Hollywood studios discovered the gold mine personified by Ray Whitley, Eddie Dean, Jimmy Wakely, Rex Allen, Johnny Bond, Tex Ritter, and Roy Rogers (the latter being Autry's chief rival for the affection of every red-blooded American youth through the '40s).

Autry's bit-singing role in Ken Maynard's *In Old Santa Fe* led to the gun-and-guitar hero who lives on in country music, though ebbing and flowing with the times. The horse opera is out of style but the boots are in; yodeling is corny but sequined suits are hip (thanks perhaps to Porter Wagoner alone). Six-shooters frighten many people but not clichéd cowboy hats, which are now appendages to Garth Brooks, George Strait, Clint Black, and many contemporaries who hope the Look will lead them to that perfect happiness with which each cowboy movie ended. The Outlaw fad and *Urban Cowboy* fallout show that at least part of the country doesn't want to let go of what Gene Autry started. To sum up Autry's philosophy in one sentence, "After I get back in the saddle again, I'll be riding down the canyon to see that silver-haired daddy of mine who lives south of the border, near Mexicali Rose." America and Americana were never the same after Gene Autry. — *David Vinopal*

★ **The Essential Gene Autry** / Aug. 18, 1992 / Columbia/Legacy ✦✦✦✦✦
The Essential Gene Autry contains 18 of his biggest hits, recorded between 1933 and 1946. Although it doesn't have any of his early RCA tracks, the disc remains a definitive retrospective, featuring all of his best-known material. — *Stephen Thomas Erlewine*

Columbia Historic Edition / Columbia ✦✦✦✦
Columbia Historic Edition is a brief but effective introduction to Gene Autry, featuring ten of his big hits from the '40s. Although it is a good collection, it isn't as generous with its selection as *The Essential Gene Autry*, which has 18 tracks (including four that are on *Historic Edition*) and is a preferable collection. — *Stephen Thomas Erlewine*

Hoyt Axton

b. Mar. 25, 1938, Duncan, OK
Guitar, Vocals / Traditional Country
Hoyt Axton has enjoyed an amazingly diverse career as a songwriter, recording artist, and movie actor. While Axton is rooted equally in the folk and country traditions, his pop smarts have enabled him to land substantial hits with numerous artists. Among the artists who have recorded Axton's songs are Three Dog Night ("Joy to the World," "Never Been to Spain"), The Kingston Trio ("Greenback Dollar"), Steppenwolf ("The Pusher," "Snowblind Friend"), and Ringo Starr ("No No Song"), as well as Waylon Jennings, Glen Campbell, Tanya Tucker, John Denver, and Commander Cody. As an artist, Axton has released a string of remarkably consistent albums that feature his warm baritone and wry earthy lyrical style.

Axton is the son of Mae Boren Axton, a former English and drama teacher in Duncan, OK. He was inspired to become a songwriter and performer by his own mother, who had abandoned her teaching career to become a distinguished songwriter whose best work, "Heartbreak Hotel," was immortalized by Elvis Presley in 1956. Axton's mother taught him much about traditional music. She also made him take classical piano lessons until he made clear his preference for boogie-woogie music. He learned to play guitar while a teenager. A beefy, athletically inclined youth, Axton went to Oklahoma State University on a football scholarship, where he played music informally for his buddies. By the late '50s, Axton had just served a stint in the Navy and began an interest in folk music that led him to perform on the California coffeehouse circuit. He had his first real songwriting success in 1962 with "Greenback Dollar," a song he had co-written with Ken Ramsey. Though it didn't make much money for him, it did lead to his signing with Horizon Records. His debut album was *The Balladeer*. After recording another album for Horizon, Axton switched to Vee-Jay Records where he made four albums, including *Saturday's Child*. More albums for different labels followed, but Axton didn't really hit it big until he began opening for the pop group Three Dog Night in 1969. When they recorded his song "Joy to the World," he found himself with a gigantic international crossover hit. Between 1969 and 1971, Axton recorded three albums, one, *My Griffin is Gone* for Columbia, and the others, including *Joy to the World*, for Capitol. As a singer, Axton (who had by then signed to A&M Records) first hit the charts in 1974 with two Top Ten tunes: "When the Morning Comes" and "Boney Fingers." As a recording artist, Axton's albums have included guest performances from many distinguished artists including Linda Rondstadt, John Hartford, Nicolette Larson, the Ozark Mountain Daredevils, and the Miracles, a noted soul group. Axton moved to MCA in 1977, where he produced one of his best albums, *Snowblind Friend*. He left the label to found his own Jeremiah Records in 1978. The following year, his *Rusty Old Halo* album produced two major hits, "Della and the Dealer" and the title track. He has continued to record steadily.

Axton made his acting debut in 1966, and has since appeared in many feature films and television shows, including 1979's *Black Stallion*. For someone who claims not to have any acting talent, he certainly gave a sensitive, believable performance as a doomed gambler and caring father. Other films include 1994's *Season of Change*. — *Sandra Brennan and Rick Clark*

My Griffin Is Gone / 1969 / Columbia ✦✦✦

Joy to the World / 1971 / Capitol ✦✦✦

Life Machine / 1974 / A&M ✦✦✦✦
Among Axton's many albums, *Life Machine* features some of his best writing. "When the Morning Comes" and "Boney Fingers" are highlights. — *Rick Clark*

Southbound / 1975 / A&M ✦✦✦✦
Another solid effort, it includes "Pride of Man" and "Lion in the Winter." — *Rick Clark*

Snowblind Friend / 1977 / MCA ✦✦✦

● **Road Songs** / 1977 / A&M ✦✦✦✦
Featuring instrumental support from James Burton and backing vocals from Linda Ronstadt, *Road Songs* has a good cross-section of Axton's best-known songs, including "Boney Fingers" and "The No- No Song," making it a good introduction to the songwriter. — *Stephen Thomas Erlewine*

David Ball

b. May 3, 1959, Rock Hill, SC
Guitar, Vocals / Contemporary Country
Distinguished singer-songwriter David Ball has been playfully dubbed the "human jukebox" by producer Blake Chancey for his inability to pass a guitar without picking it up and playing upbeat Bob Willis-influenced music. A talented performer with a friendly, laidback attitude, Ball earned a CMA Song of the Year award and was nominated for their Horizon award in 1996.

Born in Rock Hill, SC, the son of a Baptist minister, Ball was influenced by a Fred Kirby concert in Charlotte, NC, that his parents took him to see when he was only five. He got his own start a few years later when he received a ukulele for Christmas and a Stella guitar for his birthday. He began jamming frequently with other musicians. Ball made his formal debut singing a song he'd penned with his group The Strangers during a 7th grade talent show. After mastering the bass, the teenaged Ball began appearing on the folk festival circuit. Just after graduation, he founded the trio Uncle Walt's Band and moved to Austin, TX, where he discovered the music of Willis. He remained in Texas, playing "dance-hall music" through the late '80s when he landed a contract with Nashville producer Blake Chancey. In between he and Uncle Walt's Band recorded two albums in the early '80s including *Girl on the Sunny Shore* (1980). A little while later, the A&R director at Warner Brothers requested that Ball audition for him. He was impressed, and Ball released his debut album for the label *Thinkin' Problem*. The album went gold, and the video made it to No. 1. He followed with *Starlite Lounge* in June of 1996. — *Sandra Brennan*

● **Thinkin' Problem** / 1994 / Warner Bros. ✦✦✦✦
This hard-country album has a cerebral twist, as the title song suggests. Ball, 41 when this album came out, had a craggy Texas face and a voice

to match. When he has material to match, such as "Thinkin' Problem" or the ballad "When the Thought of You Catches up with Me," he's the kind of singer neo-traditional country fans dream about. —*Brian Mansfield*

Starlite Lounge / Jun. 25, 1996 / Warner Bros. ✦✦✦✦
Starlite Lounge is another set of gritty, contemporary honky tonk from David Ball, highlighted by his gutsy vocals and no-holds-barred approach. Ball doesn't treat honky tonk as a museum piece, but he has respect for its roots—he tears through the songs with energy and conviction, making *Starlite Lounge* an invigorating listen. —*Thom Owens*

Moe Bandy

b. Feb. 12, 1944, Meridan, MS
Guitar, Vocals / Honky Tonk

Moe Bandy was one of the most popular country singers of the '70s, turning out a series of hits in the latter half of the decade that made many fans and critics believe he was one of the great honky tonk singers. Bandy's songs never strayed far from the traditional bar-room fare—delivered with a knowing sense of humor, loving, cheating, drinking, and patriotic songs form the core of his repertoire. Throughout the late '70s and early '80s, the singer racked up hits. A decade after his career took off, his audience declined somewhat, yet through his theater in Branson, MO, he remained popular in the '90s.

Bandy was born in Meridian, MS, the birthplace of Jimmie Rodgers. In fact, Bandy's grandfather worked with Rodgers on the railroad, so it's no surprise that the singer first fell in love with country music through the Jimmie Rodgers and Hank Williams records that were in his house. Bandy's family moved to San Antonio, Texas when he was six. During high school, he was a rodeo rider, but his career came to a halt after he suffered too many injuries. Once he left school, Bandy was a sheet metal worker, singing in country nightclubs. He landed a one-record deal with Satin Records in 1964. The label released Bandy's original song "Lonely Lady," but the record made no impact. Nevertheless, he continued to perform in various Texan honky tonks.

In 1972, Bandy met record producer Ray Baker on a hunting trip and convinced him to listen to some demo tapes he had made. Provided that the singer could pay for the sessions, Baker agreed to produce the record. Excited by his new prospect, Bandy pawned his furniture and financed a session. Once they were released, the records went nowhere. The following year, the singer took out a loan to pay for another recording session resulting in "I Just Started Hatin' Cheatin' Songs Today" which Baker released for Footprint Records, manufacturing only 500 copies. Unlike Bandy's previous records, the single began to sell. GRC acquired the rights to the record and released it nationally. Although it eventually became a Top 20 hit, Bandy kept his job as a sheet metal worker.

Moe Bandy followed "I Just Started Hatin' Cheatin' Songs Today" with several singles on GRC, including the Top Ten hits "It Was So Easy to Find an Unhappy Woman" (1974) and "Bandy the Rodeo Clown" (1975), which was written by Lefty Frizzell and Whitey Shafer. Bandy signed with Columbia Records in 1975, keeping Baker as a producer. "Hank Williams You Changed My Life," his first single for the label, was an instant No. 3 hit, leading to his "Most Promising Male Vocalist" award from the Academy of Country Music. Bandy's string of hit singles in 1976—including "Here I Am Drunk Again" and "She Took More Than Her Share"—confirmed that he was one of the most popular singers of the latter half of the decade. The following two years were equally successful for the singer, with "I'm Sorry for You My Friend," "Cowboys Aren't Supposed to Cry," "She Just Loved the Cheatin' Out of Me," "That's What Makes the Jukebox Play," and "Two Lonely People."

Bandy's career reached a peak in 1979 when he teamed up with Janie Fricke for "It's a Cheatin' Situation." The song became a No. 3 hit and won the "Song of the Year" award from ACM. Bandy had another successful duet that year with Joe Stampley in *Just Good Ole Boys*, which became one of the most popular albums of the year, spawning the No. 1 title track and the Top Ten "Holding the Bag." Pairing with Stampley was an award-winning combination, as the duo won the Country Music Association's "Duet of the Year" and the ACM's "Duo of the Year" in 1980. Moe also had a pair of major solo hits, with the No. 1 "I Cheated Me Right Out of Her" and the Top Ten "Barstool Mountain."

During 1980, Moe Bandy's winning streak continued with the Top Ten hits "Yesterday Once More" and "Following the Feeling," a duet with Judy Bailey. Bandy teamed up with Stampley again in 1981, which proved as successful as their first outing. They again reached the Top Ten with "Hey Moe Hey Joe," and charted again with "Honky Tonk Queen." With "My Woman Loves the Devil Out of Me" and "Rodeo Romeo," Bandy had a pair of solo hits the same year. For the next two years, he regularly charted in the Top 20, both as a solo act and with various duet partners, including Becky Hobbs on the Top Ten 1983 hit "Let's Get Over Them Together." However, none of his songs caused the sensation of "Where's the Dress," a parody of Culture Club's Boy George recorded with Joe Stampley. Although Boy George sued the duo, the song was a major hit,

winning an award for Best Country Video from the America Video Awards and the New York Film Festival.

Bandy switched record labels in 1986, signing with MCA/Curb. Not only did he change labels, he changed producers, abandoning his old collaborator Ray Baker for Jerry Kennedy. Appropriately, the sound of the singer's records changed as well. No longer were they the modern-day honky tonk, they were slicker and more pop-oriented. Ironically, the change in sound didn't bring about more commercial success. For a brief time, Bandy continued to have Top Ten hits, including "Till I'm Too Old to Die Young" (1987) and "Americana" (1988), which became presidential candidate George Bush's campaign theme song; Bandy played Bush's Presidential Inauguration, as well as playing the White House twice in 1989. However, he wasn't faring as well on the country charts. His albums became increasingly safer and smoother, yet they failed to reach the peaks of his rowdier early material.

Moe Bandy opened the Moe Bandy Americana Theatre in 1991, becoming one of many country performers to establish themselves in Branson, MO. Bandy frequently performs in the 900-seat venue with his Americana Band. In the '90s, his theater was more popular than his records, but for a time in the late '70s and early '80s he was one of the most popular and exciting singers recording. —*Stephen Thomas Erlewine*

The Best of Moe Bandy, Vol. 1 / 1977 / Columbia ✦✦✦✦
Best of Moe Bandy, Vol. 1 covers the honky tonk singer's first big hits, including "It Was Always So Easy (To Find an Unhappy Woman)" and "Hank Williams, You Wrote My Life." Although it has a good song selection, it has since been replaced by the more comprehensive collection *Honky Tonk Amnesia*. —*Stephen Thomas Erlewine*

Greatest Hits [Curb] / 1982 / Curb ✦✦✦✦
Moe Bandy's late-'80s hits for Curb records are collected on this brief album. By this time, he had tamed a lot of the rowdier aspects of his music, settling into a smoother rhythm. There are some genuine overlooked gems here, but fans of his gut-level honky tonk might be disappointed. Nevertheless, it's a first-rate retrospective of a generally overlooked era. —*Stephen Thomas Erlewine*

Greatest Hits [Moe Bandy & Joe Stampley] / 1982 / Columbia ✦✦✦✦
Carousing, drinking, and dodging wives are the order of the day here. "Holding the Bag" and "Tell Ole I Ain't Here, He Better Get on Home" are particularly amusing, but the biggest laughs come with the transvestite storyline of "Honky Tonk Queen." —*Tom Roland*

You Haven't Heard the Last of Me / 1987 / MCA ✦✦✦

Many Mansions / 1989 / Curb ✦✦✦
A fine title song about homelessness, among others. —*Mark A. Humphrey*

★ **Honky Tonk Amnesia: The Best of Moe Bandy** / Feb. 20, 1996 / Razor & Tie ✦✦✦✦✦
Honky Tonk Amnesia is the first comprehensive collection of Moe Bandy's career, featuring all of his biggest hits on Columbia, plus a couple of his duets with Joe Stampley. Bandy's strength is his conviction—at his best, he was a straightahead, no-frills honky tonker and there is nothing but his best on this disc. It's the essential Bandy album. —*Stephen Thomas Erlewine*

Bobby Bare

b. Apr. 7, 1935, Ironton, OH
Guitar, Vocals / Traditional Country

Bobby Bare's story is nearly as fascinating as his music. Bare's mother died when he was five. His father couldn't earn enough money to feed his children, forcing the family to split up. Bobby was working on a farm by the time he was fifteen years old, later working in factories and selling ice cream to support himself. Building his first guitar, he began playing music in his late teens, performing with a local Ohio band in Springfield.

In the late '50s, he moved out to Los Angeles. Bare's first appearance on record was in 1958; he recorded a talking blues version of "The All American Boy" while sitting in for Bill Parsons, to whom the single was erroneously credited. A number of labels refused the record before the Ohio-based Fraternity Records bought it for $50; the fee also included the publishing rights. "The All American Boy" was released in 1958 and it surprisingly became the second-biggest single in the US that December, crossing over to the pop charts and peaking at No. 3. The single was also a big hit in the UK, reaching No. 22.

Before Bobby Bare could capitalize on his success, he was drafted into the armed forces. While he was on duty, Fraternity hired another singer to become Bill Parsons and sent him out on tour. After Bare left the army, he became roommates with Willie Nelson. During this time, he decided to become a pop singer. Soon, he was touring with rock-pop stars like Roy Orbison and Bobby Darin, recording records for a number of California labels. Meanwhile, his songs were being recorded by a number of artists; three of his tunes were featured in the Chubby Checker movie, *Teenage Millionaire.*

Even though he was having some modest success, Bare decided he wasn't fulfilled playing pop music. Instead, he turned back to country, developing a distinctive blend of country, folk, and pop. In 1962, Chet Atkins signed him to RCA Records. By the end of the year, he had a hit with "Shame On You," which was notable for being one of the first records out of Nashville to make concessions to the pop charts by featuring horns. The production worked, as the single broke into the pop charts. The following year, he recorded Mel Tillis and Danny Dill's "Detroit City," which became his second straight single to make both the country and pop charts. Bare followed up the single with a traditional folk song, "500 Miles From Home." It was another big hit for the singer, peaking in the Top Ten on both the country and pop charts. Bare continued to rack up hits in 1964 and 1965, as well as appearing in the western movie, *A Distant Trumpet.*

As the '60s progressed, Bobby Bare continued to blur the lines between country and folk, as he was influenced by songwriters like Bob Dylan, recording material by Dylan and several of his contemporaries. Not only did he explore American folk, but Bare traveled to England, where he was popular. In 1968, he recorded an album, *The English Country Side,* with a Liverpool country band called the Hillsiders, which signaled his artistic drive.

Bare switched record labels in 1970, signing with Mercury Records. He stayed at the label for two years, producing a string of Top Ten hits, including "How I Got To Memphis," "Please Don't Tell Me How the Story Ends," and "Come Sundown." Upon leaving Mercury, he recorded an album for United Artists called *This is Bare Country,* which remained unreleased until 1976; instead, the label released a collection, *The Very Best of Bobby Bare.* After leaving UA, he re-signed with RCA in 1973.

Later in 1973, Bare released a double album of Shel Silverstein songs, *Bobby Bare Sings Lullabys, Legends and Lies.* Not only did the album represent the beginning of a collaboration with Silverstein, it was arguably the first country concept album, adding fire to the outlaw movement of the '70s in the process. The record was a hit with country audiences as well as rock fans, gaining airplay on FM radio stations. The following year, he had his first No. 1 single with "Marie Laveau." Bare released another record of Silverstein songs, *Bobby Bare and the Family Singin' in the Kitchen,* in 1975. Unfortunately, the singer's oldest daughter died shortly after recording the album; she was only 15.

In 1977, Bare received a major publicity push from Bill Graham, the legendary rock concert promoter. Graham signed the singer to his management company, proclaiming that Bare was the "Springsteen of country music." Soon, the singer found new audiences at college campuses and Canada. He switched record labels the same year, recording the self-produced *Bare* for Columbia. Two years later, he released *Sleeper Whenever I Fall,* which featured contributions from Rodney Crowell and rearranged rock 'n' roll songs like the Rolling Stones' "The Last Time" and the Byrds' "Feel A Whole Lot Better." Bare resumed his collaboration with Silverstein in 1980, releasing the live collection *Down and Dirty,* which spawned two humorous hits, "Numbers" and "Tequila Sheila." The following year, he released *As Is,* which showed that he was continuing to record a diverse selection of songwriters, including Townes Van Zandt, J.J. Cale, and Guy Clark.

Despite the fact that his work was consistently critically acclaimed, Bare's record sales began to slip in the early '80s, as the 1982 Silverstein collaboration *Drinkin' From the Bottle, Singin' From the Heart* and his 1985 record for EMI failed to launch any major hit singles. Nevertheless, Bobby Bare retained a devoted following in the US and the UK into the '90s, and his influence on contemporary country music is evident. *— Stephen Thomas Erlewine*

Lullabys, Legends and Lies / 1973 / Bear Family ✦✦✦

☆ **This Is Bobby Bare** / 1973 / RCA ✦✦✦✦✦
The best assortment of his '60s work includes such classic hits as "Detroit City," "500 Miles from Home," and "Streets of Baltimore" as well as country-folk versions of "Four Strong Winds," "Miller's Cave," and "Long Black Veil." *—Michael McCall*

Cowboys & Daddys / 1975 / RCA ✦✦✦✦
Instead of singing about outlaws and rhinestone cowboys, Bare's songs speak of the struggles and joys of those who truly make their home on the range. *—Michael McCall*

Sleeper Wherever I Fall / 1978 / Columbia ✦✦✦

As Is / 1981 / Columbia ✦✦✦✦
Produced by Rodney Crowell, it's a solid collection of good songs in which Bare's sly, low-key charms shine. *—Michael McCall*

★ **Best of Bobby Bare** / 1994 / Razor & Tie ✦✦✦✦✦
The single-disc collection *The Best of Bobby Bare* offers the first comprehensive overview of his big '60s and early-'70s hits, including "Detroit City," "The Long Black Veil," and "500 Miles from Home," making it the place to start. *— Stephen Thomas Erlewine*

Mercury Years / Bear Family ✦✦✦✦
Bear Family has issued Bobby Bare's entire recordings for Mercury on a three-disc box set. Bare was only at Mercury for two years, but that time did produce a handful of his finest singles, including "How I Got to Memphis," "Please Don't Tell Me How the Story Ends," and "Come Sundown," a duet with Kris Kristofferson. Though the music is quite good, the set remains of interest only to completists, since there is simply too much music for casual listeners. Nevertheless, it's a necessary purchase for devoted Bare fans. *— Stephen Thomas Erlewine*

Greatest Hits / RCA ✦✦✦

Detroit City / 500 Miles Away From Home / RCA ✦✦✦✦
Bobby Bare's first two albums, *Detroit City* and *500 Miles Away From Home,* are combined on this single disc. Though there are some weak tracks, this is one of the strongest and most exciting collections of Bare's music, showcasing the songwriter in his earliest stages. He might not have perfected his sound, but it is thrilling to hear him sort it out. *—Stephen Thomas Erlewine*

The Bellamy Brothers

Country-Rock, Country-Pop
Howard (b. Feb. 2, 1946) and David (b. Sept. 16, 1950) Bellamy. Growing up on a Florida farm that's been in the family since the Civil War, the Bellamys have an understandable interest in their roots—geographical, genealogical, and musical. The latter area is a mixed bag, evidenced in a line from "Kids of the Baby Boom": "We had sympathy for the devil and the Rolling Stones/Then we got a little older, we found Haggard & Jones." Entranced by the Beatles and Crosby, Stills, Nash & Young, the Bellamys also heard island rhythms and melodies from the migrant workers who labored in Florida. They performed as an opening act with a local R&B band that worked the same stage as Little Anthony & the Imperials and Percy Sledge, and signed up in the late '60s with Jericho, a Southern-rock band. Ultimately, David's song "Spiders and Snakes" was recorded by Jim Stafford, and the Brothers ended up in Los Angeles. Through happenstance, a producer heard Howard singing while working as a roadie for Neil Diamond, and in short order, they recorded "Let Your Love Flow," which hit No. 1 on the pop charts during 1976. Within a year they were certified has-beens in the US, though they continued to find success in Europe. Finally, they found their niche in the US on the country chart in 1979 with "If I Said You Have a Beautiful Body Would You Hold It Against Me," nominated for a Grammy. It began a series of double-entendre songs that kept them from favor with the critics, but they quietly evolved through experimentation into one of country's most daring acts. With "You're My Favorite Star" and "Get into Reggae Cowboy," they melded country with Jamaican reggae, and they matched up country and another surprising genre with the self-explanatory title "Country Rap." The Bellamys also made great strides lyrically, particularly in their thirtysomething trilogy: "Old Hippie," "Kids of the Baby Boom," and "Rebels without a Clue." The Bellamy Brothers have racked up more Top Ten country singles than any other duo in history, yet remain one of the format's most underrated acts. *— Tom Roland*

Two & Only / 1979 / Warner Bros. ✦✦✦

You Can Get Crazy / 1980 / Warner Bros. ✦✦✦

● **Greatest Hits** / 1982 / MCA ✦✦✦✦
This contains such hits as "Dancin' Cowboys," "Redneck Girl," "Let Your Love Flow," "Lovers Live Longer," and others. *—AMG*

When We Were Boys / 1982 / Elektra ✦✦✦✦
Michael Lloyd, probably best-known as the producer on Shaun Cassidy's "Da Doo Ron Ron," oversaw the brothers' cute, early country years. In this album, they were given the reins for the first time, leading to a more serious, reflective and simple approach. Also for the first time, they recorded the album at their own home studio, located on their farm in Darby, FL. *— Tom Roland*

Greatest Hits, Vol. 2 / 1986 / MCA ✦✦✦✦
The second volume contains "Strong Weakness," "Feelin' the Feelin'," "Too Much Is Not Enough," and others. *—AMG*

Country Rap / 1987 / MCA ✦✦✦

Rebels Without a Clue / Sep. 19, 1988 / MCA ✦✦✦

Greatest Hits, Vol. 3 / 1989 / MCA ✦✦✦✦
This member of the series contains "The Center of My Universe," "Big Love," "Hillbilly Hell," "Santa Fe," and other hits. *—AMG*

Rip off the Knob / Aug. 1, 1993 / Bellamy Brothers ✦✦✦

Matraca Berg

b. 1964
Vocals / Contemporary Country
The daughter of country songwriter and session singer Icee Berg, Matraca Berg has written songs for most of Nashville's leading ladies, including Reba McEntire ("The Last One to Know"), Suzy Bogguss ("Hey Cinderella"), Trisha Yearwood ("Wrong Side of Memphis"), and Pam Tillis

("Calico Plains"). Matraca got her start while still a teen when her mother took her to several music publishing houses. At Tree Publishing, Berg met and teamed up with Bobby Braddock. Their first song, "Faking Love," became a No. 1 hit in 1983 for T.G. Sheppard and Karen Brooks. She then became a keyboardist for the rock-oriented Kevin Stewart Band. Two years later, Berg returned to Nashville and continued to write songs, but never considered singing them herself until 1990, when she released her first album, *Lying to the Moon*, which spawned the Top 40 single "Baby, Walk On." The following year, four more singles from *Lying to the Moon* made respectable showings on the chart. RCA Nashville refused a second album from Berg, so the songwriter moved to the label's pop music division, releasing her second album, *The Speed of Grace*, in 1993. —*Sandra Brennan*

● **Lying to the Moon** / 1990 / RCA ✦✦✦✦
An enchanting album from one of Nashville's best female songwriting voices, this album included two minor hits, "Baby, Walk On" and "The Things You Left Undone." The title track eventually became something of a Nashville standard, being recorded by Trisha Yearwood, Robin & Linda Williams and by Berg on *The Speed of Grace*. —*Brian Mansfield*

The Speed of Grace / Nov. 1993 / RCA ✦✦✦
After RCA Nashville refused a second album, Berg moved to the label's pop division, recording an album primarily with such L.A. studio musicians as guitarist Michael Landau and drummer Jim Keltner. The results highlighted Berg's bluesy side, but, aside from a cover of Dolly Parton's "Jolene" recorded with her Nashville buddies, lacked the acoustic Southern mysticism of *Lying to the Moon*. —*Brian Mansfield*

John Berry

Vocals / Contemporary Country
John Berry is a hot young country artist who in 1996 was nominated for both the "Male Vocalist of the Year" award and the Horizon Award by the Country Music Association. In the early '90s, he released his 1993 eponymous debut album for Liberty that featured the Top 30 song "Kiss Me in the Car." Berry was born in South Carolina but raised in Atlanta, GA, before signing to Liberty, he released a few solo albums. In 1994, a hectic tour schedule was interrupted when Berry underwent brain surgery to remove a cyst. On the same day of the surgery, he had his single "Your Love Amazes Me" hit No. 1 on the country charts. Berry's next album *Standing on the Edge*, with its popular title cut, earned him recognition by the CMA. —*Sandra Brennan*

John Berry / Jun. 7, 1993 / Liberty ✦✦✦✦

Saddle The Wind / Nov. 15, 1994 / Patriot ✦✦✦

Things Are Not The Same / Nov. 15, 1994 / Liberty ✦✦✦

● **Standing on the Edge** / 1995 / Patriot/Liberty ✦✦✦✦

Clint Black

b. 1962, Long Branch, NJ
Guitar, Vocals / Contemporary Country, New Traditionalist
A country music traditionalist from Texas, Clint Black was one of the first artists to kick-start the mass-market popularity of country in the '90s. Black also is one of the first artists of a generation that was equally inspired by rock-oriented pop—like '70s singer-songwriters and '60s rock 'n' roll—as well as country artists like Merle Haggard, Bob Wills, and George Jones. He offered a shiny, marketable version of traditional country and in the process, paved the way for a new generation of country artists, particularly Garth Brooks. After Brooks broke through into the pop mainstream, Black's career began to fade somewhat, but he remained one of the most popular and acclaimed vocalists of the '90s.

Clint Black was born in New Jersey, but raised in Katy, TX, a suburb of Houston. As a child, he listened to both country and rock 'n' roll, but he didn't begin playing guitar until the age of 13, when he started playing harmonica. Two years later, he began writing songs, as well as performing in his brother Kevin's band, where he played bass and sang. In the early '80s, he began busking on the streets of Katy, eventually working his way into coffeehouses, bars, and nightclubs.

In 1987, Clint met Hayden Nicholas, a guitarist and songwriter that had a home studio. Nicholas and Black began collaborating together, writing songs and recording demos; Hayden would become the bandleader for Clint, playing lead guitar and co-writing a large majority of his hit singles. A tape of their songs made its way to Bill Ham, the manager of ZZ Top. Impressed with the tape, Ham became Black's manager; the singer had a contract with RCA Nashville by the end of 1988.

"A Better Man," Black's first single, was released early in 1989 and it went to No. 1—he was the first new male country artist to have a No. 1 hit with his debut single in 15 years. Clint was an immediate sensation throughout country music and he played the Grand Ole Opry in April, one month before his debut album, *Killin' Time*, was released. *Killin' Time* was an immediate hit, going gold within six months and spawning four other hit singles, including the No. 1 hits "Killin' Time," "Nobody's Home," and "Walkin' Away." At the end of 1989, he won the Country

Music Association's Horizon Award, as well that organization's Best Male Vocalist award. He also won Best Album, Single, Best Male Vocalist, and Best New Male Vocalist awards from the Academy of Country Music and the NSAI Songwriter/Artists of the Year Award. By the end 1990, *Killin' Time* sold over two million copies in America.

Black released his second album, *Put Yourself in My Shoes*, in 1990. Like the debut, *Put Yourself in My Shoes* was a major success, spawning four Top Ten hits—"Put Yourself in My Shoes," "One More Payment," and the No. 1s "Loving Blind" and "Where Are You Now"—selling over two million copies and peaking at No. 18 on the pop charts. Even though it sold well, it didn't receive the same critical acclaim as the debut. Nevertheless, Black was named Best Male Vocalist that same year.

Throughout 1990, Black was on tour with Alabama and appearing on television shows across the country. In 1991, several singles from *Put Yourself in My Shoes* charted and he was inducted into the Grand Ole Opry. On New Year's Eve of 1991, he married the television actress Lisa Hartman. Clint Black began 1992 in a lawsuit with his manager Bill Ham. Black claimed that his original contract gave Ham too large of a percentage of the singer's royalties and publishing rights. For seven months he was embroiled in the lawsuit, during which he was recording his third album. By the summer, the suit was settled and his new album, *The Hard Way*, finally was released. *The Hard Way* received positive reviews and became an immediate hit, peaking at No. 2 on the country charts and crossing over into the pop Top Ten. The first single from the album, "We Tell Ourselves," reached No. 1 that summer. Black began a lengthy world tour in June of 1992 to support *The Hard Way*.

Although it was a success, *The Hard Way* wasn't as popular as Black's first two records, selling no more than a million copies. *No Time to Kill*, his fourth album (released in 1993), continued the stagnation in his record sales, even though its sales were more than respectable—the album went platinum and spawned the hit single, "When My Ship Comes In." During the fall of 1994, Clint Black released his fifth album, *One Emotion*. —*Stephen Thomas Erlewine*

★ **Killin' Time** / 1989 / RCA ✦✦✦✦✦
Black's accessible brand of Texas country burned up the charts upon its release, selling two million copies and yielding the hit singles "Better Man," "Killin' Time," "Nobody's Home," Walkin' Away," and "Nothing's News." —*Brian Mansfield*

Put Yourself in My Shoes / 1990 / RCA ✦✦✦

The Hard Way / 1992 / RCA ✦✦✦✦
Back to form, Black put some of his most exciting singles on his third album. "We Tell Ourselves" rocked without resorting to Southern boogie, and "When My Ship Comes In" contained a masterful chorus. The album also included the hit "Burn One Down." —*Brian Mansfield*

No Time to Kill / Jul. 1993 / RCA ✦✦✦

One Emotion / 1994 / RCA ✦✦✦

The Blue Sky Boys

Old-Time
In the '30s brother duets were common in country music: Among the better known were the Monroes, the Delmores, the Dixons, and the Carlisles. Bill And Earl Bolick, who in 1936 were ready to make their first recording, followed their producer's suggestion that they should be "different" by avoiding the word *brother*. From "Blue Ridge Mountains, Land of the Sky" they took two words and named their act. But The Bolicks would have been different without the new name. Their intricate, simple harmonies, their perfectly matching voices, and their unadorned mandolin and guitar instrumental backing set them off from the competition, so much so that two generations of subsequent duet singers echo them, some without realizing it. The Everly Brothers and the Louvin Brothers, themselves recognized as exceptional vocal duets, acknowledge the influence of the Blue Sky Boys.

In the '50s, when tastes in country music changed drastically, the Blue Sky Boys retired from music rather than forsake their love of old mountain ballads for the uptempo popularity of electric instruments, drums, and honky tonk. In the '60s they were coaxed to come out of retirement, playing an occasional college date during the hootenanny phenomenon and recording albums in 1963, 1965, and 1976.

No one in country music has done vocal duets better than the Blue Sky Boys. If your taste runs more to Conway & Loretta, George & Tammy, or Wynonna & Naomi, listen to the effortless, exquisite singing of Bill and Earl Bolick. See where it all started. —*David Vinopal*

★ **There'll Come a Time / Can't You Hear That Nightbird** / 1936 / Blue Tone ✦✦✦✦✦
Sacred songs, weepers, and hillbilly heart-singing at its best. —*Mark A. Humphrey*

☆ **Within the Circle / Who Wouldn't Be Lonely** / 1937 / Blue Tone ✦✦✦✦✦
This genuine classic contains old-time recordings from 1937-1938. —*AMG*

The In Concert '64 / Rounder ◆◆◆◆
This is an excellent "rediscovery" concert of this legendary '30s brother duo. —*Mark A. Humphrey*

Suzy Bogguss

b. Dec. 30, 1956, Aledo, IL
Vocals / Country-Pop, Contemporary Country
Free-spirited Suzy Bogguss successfully straddled the line between traditional and mainstream country, and in the process, she became one of the most popular and critically acclaimed female country singers of the late '80s and early '90s. Born in Aledo, IL, Bogguss is the youngest of four children and sang in the Aledo Presbyterian Church Angel Choir at age five. As a young adult, Bogguss planned to be a metalsmith and graduated from Illinois State University with a B.A. in art, but instead became interested in the guitar and began singing. Living in a trailer with her dog Duchess, she played whenever and wherever she could find an audience; soon Bogguss had developed a sizable following throughout the Midwest, Northeast, and Canada. She appeared on a television special on a Peoria public television station, and after a positive viewer response, she came back to host and star in two more shows. Not long afterward, Bogguss was hired as an opener for such acts as Dan Seals and Asleep at the Wheel, and toured the West and Mexico.

In 1985, she headed to Nashville and got a job singing in a rib joint and doing studio session work. She recorded an album at Wendy Waldman's studio and began giving copies to local radio stations and magazines, receiving glowing reviews. She got a gig singing at Dolly Parton's Dollywood theme park in Pigeon Forge, TN, and this led to a contract with Capitol Nashville and an appearance on TNN's "Nashville Now," where Chet Atkins invited her to open his concert at the Ordway Theater in St. Paul, MN. Bogguss' first two Capitol singles, "I Don't Want to Set the World on Fire" and "Love Will Never Slip Away," were released in 1987 and became minor hits. In 1988, she demonstrated her prowess as a yodeler in "I Want to Be a Cowboy's Sweetheart," a song which also had modest success on the charts. She and producer Wendy Waldman cut her first major label album, *Somewhere Between*, in 1989. Several tracks from the record became hits and Bogguss was named the ACM's Best Female Artist of 1989. Her next album, 1990's *Moment of Truth*, did fairly well, but her third, *Aces*, went gold in 1992, a year after it was released. *Voices in the Wind*, Bogguss' fourth album, was released that year; it went gold and spawned a string of Top Ten hits, including a the No. 2 hit "Drive South," which was written by John Hiatt and won her the CMA Horizon Award. In 1994, she released her fifth album, *Simpatico*, as well as a greatest hits collection, and 1996 she released *Give Me Some Wheels*. —*Sandra Brennan*

★ **Somewhere Between** / 1988 / Capitol ◆◆◆◆◆
A fabulous, truly surprising debut, this album firmly plants one foot in the past and the other in the Nashville mainstream. The best songs here come from country legends. Merle Haggard penned the powerhouse title cut, "My Sweet Love Ain't Around" came from Hank Williams, and "I Want To Be a Cowboy's Sweetheart" was an old Patsy Montana tune. The new stuff was pretty danged good, too: "Cross My Heart," written by Verlon Thompson and Kye Fleming, was the album's highest-charting single. —*Brian Mansfield*

Moment of Truth / 1990 / Capitol Nashville ◆◆◆

Aces / 1991 / Capitol Nashville ◆◆◆◆
The new strategy paid off here: Bogguss took Cheryl Wheeler's "Aces" and Nanci Griffith's "Outbound Plane" into the Top Ten. She also hit with "Someday Soon" and "Letting Go." This is the album that won her the CMA's Horizon Award, five years after her first single. —*Brian Mansfield*

Voices in the Wind / 1992 / Liberty ◆◆◆

Somethin' up My Sleeve / Sep. 13, 1993 / Liberty ◆◆◆
Includes "Hey Cinderella," which Bogguss wrote with Matraca Berg; "Just Like the Weather," which she wrote with husband Doug Crider; and "Souvenirs," a remarkably understated indictment of materialism by Gretchen Peters. The title track is a duet with Billy Dean. —*Brian Mansfield*

Greatest Hits / Mar. 8, 1994 / Liberty ◆◆◆◆
Ten of Bogguss' best are included, from "I Want to Be a Cowboy's Sweetheart" to 1993's "Heartache." The album doesn't contain anything from *Something up My Sleeve*, but it does have "Hopelessly Yours," a duet with Lee Greenwood, that hadn't appeared on any of Bogguss' other albums. —*Brian Mansfield*

Simpatico / Oct. 1994 / Liberty ◆◆◆
Simpatico is a laidback, charming duet album with Chet Atkins. The duo covers a lot of ground, beginning with Jimmie Rogers' "In the Jailhouse Now," running through Elton John's "Sorry Seems to Be the Hardest Word," and playing a couple of nice, understated originals. Although it isn't a strict country record—there are quite a bit of pop flourishes scattered throughout the record—it's a charmingly low-key listen. —*Stephen Thomas Erlewine*

Give Me Some Wheels / 1996 / Capitol ◆◆◆

Boxcar Willie (Lecil Travis Martin)

b. Sep. 1, 1931, Sterret, TX
Guitar, Vocals
Boxcar Willie is perhaps the most successful invented character in the history of country music. With his kitschy persona and stage act—highlighted by his amazingly accurate impersonation of a train whistle—Willie played into the stereotype of the lovable, good-natured hobo that spent his life riding the rails and singing songs. Since his popularity had more to do with his image than his music, it makes sense that he was massively successful in England, where he personified Americana. Willie's English success carried him over to American success in the early '80s, where he ironically was perceived as carrying the torch for traditional country, because he kept the stereotypes alive.

Born Lecil Travis Martin, Boxcar Willie never worked on the railroads—his father did. However, Willie loved the railroads and kept running away to ride the trains when he was a child. He also loved country music, particularly the songs of Jimmie Rodgers, Roy Acuff, and Ernest Tubb; as a young man, he would also develop an affection for Hank Williams. As a teenager, Boxcar Willie would perform under his given name, eventually becoming a regular on the Big D Jamboree in Dallas, TX. In his early twenties, he served in the Air Force. After he left the service, he continued to sing in clubs and radio shows.

In the late '50s, he began performing as Marty Martin, while working blue collar jobs during the day. Marty Martin actually released an album, *Marty Martin Sings Country Music and Stuff Like That*, around 1958, but it was ignored. In the mid-'60s, Martin wrote a song called "Boxcar Willie," based on a hobo he saw on a train that looked like Willie Nelson. Martin continued to struggle in his musical career until the mid-'70s. By that time, he had become a DJ in Corpus Christi, TX. In 1975, he decided to risk everything he had on one final chance at stardom. He moved to Nashville and developed the Boxcar Willie character, using his song as the foundation.

Initially, Boxcar Willie wasn't very successful, but he had a lucky break in 1976 when he was called in to replace a sick George Jones at a Nashville club. During that performance, he was spotted by Drew Taylor, a Scottish booking agent. Taylor brought Boxcar Willie over to England for a tour, where he was enthusiastically received. Later that year, he released his first album which was a moderate success in the UK. Through the rest of the '70s, Willie toured Britain and every tour was more successful, culminating in a performance at the International Country Music Festival at Wembley in 1979. After his Wembley show was finished, he received a standing ovation—the performance established Boxcar Willie as a star. His next album, *King of the Road*, became a humongous success in England, reaching No. 5 on the album charts; the record was helped immeasurably by its accompanying television advertisements, which sold the record through the mail.

By the end of 1980, Willie had become the most successful country artist in England and his American success had just begun. *King of the Road* was available through an American television advertisement, "Train Medley" was a minor hit on the country charts, and he was becoming a popular attraction on US concert circuits. In 1981, he received a spot on the Country Music Hall of Fame's Walkway of the Stars and became a member of the Grand Ole Opry.

Boxcar Willie enjoyed his time in the spotlight, becoming a regular on the television show *Hee Haw* in 1982 and turning out albums as fast as he could make them. "Bad News" became his only American country Top 40 hit in 1982. In 1985, he played a hobo in *Sweet Dreams*, a film about Patsy Cline. By the mid-'80s, his star had faded, but he remained a popular concert attraction, particularly in England, into the '90s. —*Stephen Thomas Erlewine*

Boxcar Willie / 1976 / MCA ◆◆◆◆
Never issued on compact disc, *Boxcar Willie* remains one of the hobo's best albums, highlighted by a guest appearance by Willie Nelson. —*Stephen Thomas Erlewine*

● **The Collection** / 1987 / Castle ◆◆◆◆
Castle's *The Collection* is the best Boxcar Willie compilation ever assembled, featuring his signature hit, "Train Medley," as well as several other songs in a similar vein. Appropriately, *The Collection* was only released in England, the country that made Boxcar Willie famous. —*Stephen Thomas Erlewine*

Best Loved Favorites / 1989 / Vanguard ◆◆◆◆
Best Loved Favorites is not a greatest hits collection from Boxcar Willie, but rather, a selection of some of the most popular and enduring country standards, performed by the singing hobo. Willie is in good voice throughout and with songs like "In the Jailhouse Now" and "Blue Moon of Kentucky," it's an entertaining listen. —*Stephen Thomas Erlewine*

Rocky Box: Rockabilly / 1993 / K-Tel ◆◆◆
Country music's favorite fake hobo teams up with the Midwest's top roots-music combo for a spirited, if at times surreal, outing. The Skele-

tons, featuring D. Clinton Thompson's excellent fretboard work, provides perfect retro backing on everything, while Boxcar is quite at home on traditional '50s boppers like "Mystery Train" and "Rockin' Bones." But the true candidate for the twilight zone is his version here of "Achy Breaky Heart," complete with his patented train whistle. It doesn't get much weirder than this in any style of music. —Cub Koda

King of the Road / Mainstreet ✦✦✦✦
King of the Road is the album that made Boxcar Willie famous. Advertised on English television, the record wound up climbing to No. 5 on the UK charts, setting the stage for his breakthrough success in the US and Canada. *King of the Road* consists of a number of traditional country songs, including "Wabash Cannonball," "San Antonio Rose," "You Are My Sunshine," "Mule Train," "Rolling in My Sweet Baby's Arms," and three Hank Williams songs, with a couple of cute originals thrown in for good measure. Although it doesn't have his signature song, "Train Medley," it remains his best album. —Stephen Thomas Erlewine

Bill Boyd

b. Sep. 29, 1910, Fannin County, TX
Guitar, Vocals / Western Swing
For true fans of Western swing music, Bill Boyd rates right up there with his contemporary, Bob Wills, even though the two utilize very different styles. Whereas Wills and his Playboys often used horns and recorded songs from a variety of genres, Boyd has remained true to his western roots, using only a string-band, the Cowboy Ramblers. Boyd was popular in the Southwest for over 20 years and was behind a number of enduring hit songs.

Born on a ranch and cotton farm near Ladonia, Texas, Boyd grew up as a working cowboy, learning the traditional songs from the impromptu campfire jam sessions of the ranch hands. Both Boyd and his younger brother frequently sang with the cowboys as did their parents. The boys got to be pretty good and in 1926, made their debut on KFPM in Greenville. The Boyd family moved to Dallas in 1929, and when not studying at the Dallas Technical High School, Boyd played in a band that included fiddler Art Davis. By this time, Boyd knew he wanted a career in music. At this time, there was a large active radio scene in Dallas then and Boyd jumped right in, first with a band on WFAA and then with the first incarnation of the Cowboy Ramblers in 1932 on WRR. Included in Boyd's new band was his brother Jim on bass, fiddler Art Davis, and Walter Kirkes on tenor banjo. When not actually performing, Boyd was out recruiting new sponsors and in this way managed to survive the Depression.

In 1934, he and the band moved to San Antonio to record a few singles for Bluebird ranging from traditional cowboy tunes such as "The Strawberry Roan" to instrumentals such as "The Lost Wagon." Hits included the standard "Under the Double Eagle" and "Going Back to My Texas Home." They then began recording regularly with RCA and in the late '30s, increased their membership to ten. Among their better known members was fiddler Carroll Hubbard, piano player Knocky Parker, and steel guitar player Wilson "Lefty" Perkins. During their long association with RCA, Boyd and the Ramblers recorded over 229 singles. In the early '40s, they appeared in six Hollywood films including *Raiders of the West* and *Prairie Pals*. The popularity of live radio in Dallas began fading in the '50s, causing Boyd to become a DJ. —Sandra Brennan

● **Bill Boyd's Cowboy Ramblers** / RCA Bluebird ✦✦✦✦
The double album *Bill Boyd's Cowboy Ramblers* contains most the Western swing band's greatest hits, making it a definitive retrospective. Unfortunately, it's scarce and out of print, but it remains the one collection to own. —Stephen Thomas Erlewine

With His Cowboy Ramblers 1934-1947 / ✦✦✦✦
This features "On the Texas Plains," "You're Just About Right," "Boyd's Blues," and more. —AMG

Brooks & Dunn

Contemporary Country
Kix Brooks and Ronnie Dunn were the most popular country duo since the Judds and, in the process, became one of the biggest country artists of the '90s. Brooks & Dunn's music runs from hard-edged honky tonk to radio-ready contemporary ballads.

Both Kix Brooks (born and raised in Shreveport, LA) and Ronnie Dunn (born and raised in Coleman, TX) were sons of pipefitters. As a youth, Brooks was influenced by a variety of regional musical styles ranging from Cajun to blues to jazz to country. He was first inspired towards a musical career by his neighbor Johnny Horton. A friend of Horton's daughter, he would frequently visit their home and become dazzled by all the gold records on Horton's wall. Brooks made his performing debut at the age of 12, singing with Horton's daughter.

Brooks he continued performing in clubs and at other venues through high school; he also began writing songs frequently. After spending one year in college, he dropped out to work on the Alaskan pipeline. After a while, he moved to Maine, where he performed at ski resorts. Eventually he landed in Nashville where he worked odd jobs while looking for a

break. Eventually, he joined Don Gant's newly established Tree Publishing company. Shortly afterwards artists like the Nitty Gritty Dirt Band, John Conlee, and Highway 101 began finding success with Kix Brooks tunes. In 1983, he launched his own recording career with "Baby, When Your Heart Breaks Down" for Avion. He didn't record again until 1989, when he released his eponymous solo debut.

Ronnie Dunn's journey to Music City was quite different. His father had been a guitarist and sang in a traditional mountain string band as a hobby. While still in high school Dunn learned to play bass. He eventually he began studying psychiatry and religion at Abilene Christian College. It was his intention to become a Baptist preacher, but he became increasingly infatuated with music, and he spent many evenings performing in honky tonk bars. After several months, he was caught performing by the administrators of the school and he was forced to choose between the clergy or his music. He chose music. Afterwards, Dunn and his family moved to Tulsa where he began leading the house band at Duke's Country. This led to a record contract with the independent Churchill label. At Churchill, he had two moderate hits in 1983 and 1984. Dunn moved to Nashville via a Marlboro talent contest. At first, he didn't know he had entered the contest—his friend Jimmy Oldecker, who was drumming for Eric Clapton at the time, submitted one of Dunn's tapes unbeknownst to the songwriter. Dunn won the regionals in Tulsa with a hastily assembled band. After the regionals, he went to Nashville's Bullpen Lounge for the finals where he won $30,000 and a recording session with one of Music City's biggest producers, Scott Hendricks. The two hit it off and for a while, Dunn would send Hendricks his newest material. Hendricks saw that some of it got to Tim DuBois, the head of Arista. Eventually Dunn decided to relocate to Nashville.

Upon his arrival in Nashville, Dunn joined Tree Publishing and met Brooks. The two hit it off and soon began not only writing together, but also performing. DuBois was pleased by the new duo and offered them a recording contract. The two started out with a bang in 1990 when their debut single "Brand New Man" shot up to No. 1, as did their follow-up "My Next Broken Heart." The following year their debut album Brand New Man was released and became an immediate success. Later in 1992, they had yet another No. 1 hit with "Neon Moon," but it was the single's flip-side "Boot Scootin' Boogie" that provided them with their biggest hit to date. At the end of the year, Brooks & Dunn were named the Country Music Association's "Vocal Duo of the Year," an honor they won the following year as well. By 1993, their first album had gone triple platinum and rather than performing as an opening act for such performers as Reba McEntire and Alabama, they became the headliners. That year, they also released their second album *Hard Workin' Man*, and their string of hits continued. In 1996, they released their fourth album, *Borderline*, and had a major hit with their cover of B.W. Stevenson's old pop hit "My Maria" (one of the few hits they did not write). —Sandra Brennan

● **Brand New Man** / 1991 / Arista ✦✦✦✦
The title tale of love and redemption was a classic single for all the same reasons that made this would-be modern cowboy duo such a winner: tightly constructed choruses; a perfect balance between romance, macho swagger, and Wild-West imagery; and bracing harmonies that'll clear the trail dust out of your throat quicker than a shot of good whiskey. Four singles from *Brand New Man* topped the country charts: the title tune, "My Next Broken Heart," "Neon Moon," and "Boot Scootin' Boogie." —Brian Mansfield

Hard Workin' Man / 1993 / Arista ✦✦✦
As with most second albums, the successful traits started to isolate themselves on *Hard Workin' Man:* Macho stuff like "Hard Workin' Man" and "Rock My World (Little Country Girl)" rocked harder than anything on *Brand New Man*, though B&D made sure their women came off as good as they did (catch the "and women too" tag on "Hard Workin' Man"). The slower songs ("That Ain't No Way to Go," "She Used to Be Mine") tended towards the sort of evocative images that ran all through the debut. The pair never put all the elements together they way they did the first time, but they came close enough that few people noticed. —Brian Mansfield

Waitin' On Sundown / Sep. 27, 1994 / Arista ✦✦✦
Waitin' On Sundown didn't depart from Brooks & Dunn's formula much, but the fans didn't mind—it sold over three million albums, anyway. By this point, the duo's albums have become a handful of solid singles—this time out, they were "Little Miss Honky Tonk," "She's Not the Cheatin' Kind," and "You're Gonna Miss Me When I'm Gone"—surrounded by filler, but the hits will make the fans forgive the filler. —Thom Owens

Borderline / Apr. 1996 / Arista ✦✦

Garth Brooks

b. Feb. 7, 1962, Tulsa, OK
Guitar, Vocals / Contemporary Country
Garth Brooks is a pivotal figure in the history of country music, no matter how much some country purists would like to deny it. With his com-

mercially savvy fusion of post-Merle Haggard country, honky tonk, post-folk-rock sensitive singer-songwriter sensibilities, and '70s arena-rock dramatics, Brooks brought country music to a new audience in the '90s—namely, a mass audience. Before Brooks, it was inconceivable for a country artist to sell a million copies. He shattered that barrier in 1991, when his second album, *No Fences*, began its chart domination and its follow-up, *Ropin' the Wind*, became the first country album to debut at the top of the pop charts. *No Fences* would eventually sell a record-shattering 13 million copies. After Garth, country music had successfully carved a permanent place for itself on the pop charts. In the process, it lost a lot of the traditionalism that had always been its hallmark, and that is precisely why Brooks is important.

Garth Brooks is the son of Troyal and Colleen Carroll Brooks. Colleen was a country singer herself, recording a handful of records for Capitol in the mid-'50s that never experienced any chart success. As a child, Garth was interested in music and frequently sang at family gatherings, but he concentrated on athletics. He received a partial athletic scholarship at Oklahoma State University as a javelin tosser, but he wound up dropping the sport during his collegiate career. While he was at college, Brooks began singing in local Oklahoma clubs, often with lead guitarist Ty England.

After he graduated with an advertising degree in December of 1984, Garth Brooks decided to try to forge out a career as a country singer. In 1985 he moved to Nashville with hopes of being discovered by a record label. Twenty-three hours after moving to Nashville, he returned to Oklahoma, frustrated with the industry, his prospects, and his naive dreams. Brooks continued to perform in Oklahoma clubs, and in 1986, he married his college girlfriend, Sandy Mahl.

The couple moved to Nashville in 1987, this time with a better idea of how the music industry operated. Brooks began making connections with various songwriters and producers, and he sang on a lot of songwriters' demo tapes. Although he had made several connections within the industry and he had a powerful management team, every label in town was refusing to sign him. In 1988, six weeks after Capitol Records passed on his demo, one of the label's executives saw Brooks sing at a local club. Impressed with the performance, the executive convinced the label to sign Garth.

Brooks recorded his first album with producer Allen Reynolds at the end of 1988; the self-titled debut appeared early in 1989. The album was an instant success, with its first single, "Much Too Young (To Feel This Damn Old)," climbing into the country Top Ten. Garth's debut was a success, crossing over into the pop album charts, but it was overshadowed by the blockbuster appeal of Clint Black, as well other similar new male vocalists like Travis Tritt and Alan Jackson. Within a year, Brooks would tower above them all with his surprise, widespread success.

Garth Brooks had three other hit singles—the No. 1 "If Tomorrow Never Comes," the No. 2 "Not Counting You," and the No. 1 "The Dance"—but it was his second album, *No Fences*, that established him as a superstar. *No Fences* was released in the fall of 1990, preceded by the massive hit single "Friends in Low Places." *No Fences* spent 23 weeks at the top of the country charts and sold 700,000 copies within the first ten days of its release. Throughout 1990 and 1991, Brooks had a string of No. 1 country hits from the album, including "Unanswered Prayers," "Two of a Kind, Workin' on a Full House," and "The Thunder Rolls." By 1993, *No Fences* would sell over ten million copies.

Not only did his record sales break all the accepted country conventions, but so did Garth Brooks' concerts. By the end of 1990, he was selling out stadiums within minutes and was putting on stadium-sized shows, patterned after '70s rock extravaganzas. Brooks used a cordless, headset microphone so he could run around his large stage. He had an elaborate light show, explosions, and even a harness so he could swing out above the crowd and sing to them. It was the first time any country artist incorporated such rock 'n' roll techniques into their stageshows.

Ropin' the Wind, Garth's third album, was released in September of 1991 and became the first country record to debut at the top of the pop charts. *Ropin' the Wind* matched the success of *No Fences*, selling over ten million copies within its first two years of release and spawning the No. 1 hit singles "Shameless," "What She's Doing Now," and "The River."

By the end of 1991, Brooks had become a genuine popular music phenomenon—even his 1992 Christmas album, *Beyond the Season*, went multi-platinum—and there were no signs of his momentum slowing down. Naturally, a backlash began to develop in the fall of 1992, beginning with the release of "We Shall Be Free," the first single from his fourth album. Featuring a strong gospel underpinning, the single stalled at No. 12 and many radio stations refused to play it. It was indicative of the eclectic nature of his forthcoming album, *The Chase*, which pushed the boundaries of contemporary country. *The Chase* debuted at No. 1 upon its October 1992 release and by the end of the year, it sold over five million copies. Nevertheless, that number was half the size of the figures

for his two previous albums and there was speculation in the media that Brooks' career had already peaked.

Sensing that he was in danger of losing his core audience, Brooks returned to straight country with 1993's *In Pieces*. The album was critically-acclaimed and sold several million copies, though it was clear that Garth would not reach the stratospheric commercial heights of *No Fences* and *Ropin' the Wind* again. Even so, he remained one of the most successful artists in popular music, one of the few that was guaranteed to sell millions of records with each new album, as well as sell out concerts around the world.

The Hits, which was only available for a year, was released in the fall of 1994 and would eventually sell over eight million albums. Garth Brooks released *Fresh Horses*, his first album of new material in two years, in November of 1995; within six months of its release, it had sold over three million copies. —*Stephen Thomas Erlewine*

Garth Brooks / Apr. 12, 1989 / Capitol ✦✦✦

☆ **No Fences** / Aug. 27, 1990 / Capitol ✦✦✦✦✦
Essentially, Garth Brooks' second album *No Fences* follows the same pattern as his debut album, but it is a more assured and risky record. Brooks still performs neo-traditional country, such as the honky tonk hit "Friends in Low Places," but now he twists it around with clever pop hooks. Those pop-rock influences are most apparent on the ballads, which alternate between sensitive folk-rock and power-ballad bombast. But what made *No Fences* such a success is how seamlessly he blends the two seemingly opposing genres, and how he chose a set of material that makes his genre-bending sound subtle and natural. Of course, it doesn't hurt that the songs are consistently entertaining, either. —*Stephen Thomas Erlewine*

Ropin' the Wind / Sep. 1991 / Liberty ✦✦✦✦
With *Ropin' the Wind*, Garth Brooks began to make his '70s rock influences more explicit. Naturally, that was most notable in his reworking of Billy Joel's "Shameless," which he transformed from a rock power ballad into contemporary country. But that influence is also evident on ambitious epics like "The River" and even the honky tonk ravers of "Papa Loved Mama" and "Rodeo." Some might say that those rock influences are what made Brooks a crossover success, but he wouldn't have been nearly as successful if he didn't have a tangible country foundation to his music—even when he comes close to standard arena rock bombast, there a gritty steel guitars or vocal inflections that prove he is trying to expand country's vocabulary, not trying to exploit it. —*Stephen Thomas Erlewine*

The Chase / Oct. 1992 / Liberty ✦✦✦

In Pieces / Aug. 23, 1993 / Liberty ✦✦✦✦
After the relative commercial disappointment of *The Chase*, Garth Brooks toned down his experimental eclecticism on *In Pieces*. Alternating between heavily rock-influenced numbers, dramatic ballads, and revamped honky tonk, *In Pieces* appeals to the audience that found *The Chase* too pretentious and overly serious. That doesn't mean Brooks abandoned his desire to bend the rules—he's just masked his more ambitious material with crowd-pleasing uptempo numbers like "American Honky-Tonk Bar Association" and "Ain't Going Down (Til the Sun Comes Up)." *In Pieces* is an album that was made for the fans and it shows—it is one of Brooks' most energetic and exciting collections. —*Stephen Thomas Erlewine*

★ **The Hits** / 1994 / Liberty ✦✦✦✦✦
The Hits is exactly what it says it is—18 of Garth Brooks' biggest hits, including his first 14 No. 1 singles. Although he has good album tracks on each of his records, this is the essential Garth Brooks album—it gives a good sense of the singer's talents, especially his underappreciated eclecticism. *The Hits* was only in print for a year, but it sold in excess of eight million copies, so it could hardly be called a limited edition. —*Stephen Thomas Erlewine*

Fresh Horses / Nov. 21, 1995 / Capitol Nashville ✦✦✦

Brother Phelps

Contemporary Country
The duo of Brother Phelps consists of singer-songwriter/bassist Doug and singer-songwriter/guitarist Ricky Lee Phelps, who left the Kentucky Headhunters in 1992 following *Electric Barnyard* due to objections that the group was leaving its country roots for straightahead rock 'n' roll. The name Brother Phelps, which came about after they held a nationwide contest on TNN's *Crook & Chase*, is a tribute to their father, an Assembly of God preacher nicknamed Brother Phelps by his congregation. The Phelps brothers began playing together as teens and have developed a style of close harmony singing reminiscent of the Everly Brothers. In 1992, they were signed to the newly formed Asylum Records in Nashville; their debut album, *Let Go*, was in a much more traditional country vein than their work with the Kentucky Headhunters. In mid-1993, the title track hit the Top Ten and stayed there for five months; it was fol-

lowed up with "Were You Really Livin'." Brother Phelps released its second album early in 1995. — *Sandra Brennan*

Let Go / Aug. 3, 1993 / Asylum ✦✦✦
Much more low-key than most people expected, *Let Go* proves that the Brother Phelps were the smarts behind the Kentucky Headhunters. The title cut was a breezy single that recalled Buddy Holly, and elsewhere on the album the Brother Phelps made judicious use of Southern boogie ("Were You Really Livin'") and strings ("What Goes Around"). Not a perfect album, and not as good as the Headhunters at their peak, but *Let Go* still contains some mighty nice listening. — *Brian Mansfield*

● **Any Way the Wind Blows** / Mar. 7, 1995 / Asylum ✦✦✦✦
Any Way the Wind Blows doesn't stray from the laidback, rootsy vibe of the Brother Phelps' debut, but it boasts a more assured performance and a stronger set of songs, making it a more engaging listen. — *Stephen Thomas Erlewine*

Jim Ed Brown (James Edward Brown)

b. Mar. 1, 1934, Sparkman, AK
Vocals / Honky Tonk
Jim Ed Brown came to fame as a member of the '50s vocal group the Browns, where he was the band's lead male vocalist. In 1965, when the group was still together, he embarked on a solo career that would eventually eclipse the success of the Browns.

Brown and his older sister, Maxine, began performing while he was still in high school. In 1954, the duo signed a contract with the Fabor label, where they released five singles. Later that year, their sister Bonnie joined the duo and they became the Browns. From 1956 until 1967, the Browns were signed to RCA records, where they had a number of moderately successful hit singles, highlighted by the 1959 No. 1 "The Three Bells."

Brown began his solo career in 1965, two years before the Browns disbanded. Initially, he didn't have much success and just scraped the bottom of the country Top 40. Once the Browns disbanded, Brown began to have more substantial hits, beginning with the No. 18 single "You Can Have Her," which was a cover of the Roy Hamilton hit. That was followed by the beer-drinking anthem "Pop A Top," which climbed to No. 3. Although his next single, "Bottle, Bottle," reached No. 13, Brown didn't have any major hits for the rest of the '60s.

As his chart performance stagnated in 1968, he formed a backing group called the Gems and began a residency at the Sahara Tahoe's Juniper Lounge. In 1969, he hosted the syndicated television show, *The Country Place,* which ran until 1970.

As *The Country Place* was ending its run, Brown had his first major hit since "Pop A Top," with the No. 4 single "Morning." Again, he wasn't able to immediately follow "Morning" with another Top Ten hit, but he began charting more frequently. In 1973, he had two Top Ten hits, "Southern Loving and "Sometime Sunshine," which were followed by the Top Ten "It's That Time of Night" in early 1974.

Jim Ed Brown had his greatest success in the late '70s, when he regularly dueted with Helen Cornelius. The duo had six Top Ten hits between 1976 and 1980, including their debut single, "I Don't Want To Have To Marry You," which went to No. 1 in 1976. During this time, he had some solo hits, but only two of them broke the Top 40. Brown and Cornelius ended their partnership in 1971, following the No. 13 hit "Don't Bother to Knock."

After the breakup of his duo with Helen Cornelius, Jim Ed Brown pretty much retired from recording. He made the occasional appearance on the Grand Ole Opry and he sometimes reunited with Cornelius. Brown also hosted TV game shows and talent contests throughout the '80s. Toward the end of the decade, he opened the Jim Ed Brown Theater near Opryland in Nashville, Tennessee, where he performed regularly well into the '90s. — *Stephen Thomas Erlewine*

Greatest Hits / Feb. 1992 / RCA ✦✦✦✦
Greatest Hits collects the biggest hits from Jim Ed Brown's duets with Helen Cornelius, including the Top Ten hits "I Don't Want To Have To Marry You," "Saying Hello, Saying I Love You, Saying Goodbye," "Lying In Love With You," "If the World Ran Out of Love Tonight," and "Fools," among several others. — *Stephen Thomas Erlewine*

● **Essential Series** / Jan. 30, 1996 / RCA ✦✦✦✦
Essential Series collects all of Jim Ed Brown's solo hits, as well as a selection of his duets with the Browns, making it the definitive compilation of his inconsistent, but enjoyable, career. — *Stephen Thomas Erlewine*

Junior Brown

Guitar, Vocals / Honky Tonk, New Traditionalist
Nothing inspires a yawn quite so fast as hearing a new hot country artist's obligatory talk about his Jones and Haggard influences. But when a singer/picker starts talking about Ernest Tubb, Jimi Hendrix, and the Ventures—and backs it up on record—better close your mouth and listen. Actually, Junior Brown (who hit the bigtime in 1993 after twenty-plus

years on the Southwest roadhouse circuit) doesn't like to talk about his influences—probably because they have nothing, and everything, to do with his style. A monster picker, he plays the "guit-steel," a double-neck, combined electric and steel guitar of his own invention. His vocals, though sometimes shaded towards Tubb for comic effect, are always instantly recognizable as his own. His brilliant, idiosyncratic songwriting, more so. None of which really explains the complete package that is Junior Brown, a honky tonk man out of time. So-called hot country ain't nothing but a plate-warmer compared to the heat this guy turns up. — *Dan Cooper*

12 Shades of Brown / 1989 / Curb ✦✦✦✦
Brown's debut deck shines like gold with standout original material like "They Don't Choose to Live That Way," "My Hillbilly Hula Gal," and "My Baby Don't Dance to Nothing but Ernest Tubb" being particular noteworthy. Possessing a voice that will curl the hair on the back of your neck while both single-string and slide stylings on his twin neck "guit-steel," this is a mighty-talented fella, neo-traditionalist or not. — *Cub Koda*

● **Guit with It** / Aug. 24, 1993 / Capitol/Curb ✦✦✦✦
Junior Brown's rumbling, strikingly deep voice, tasty electric and steel guitar playing, and splendid honky tonk and Western swing songs have made him a sensation in country circles. There's nothing phony or cliched about Brown's music; this is the genuine, untutored, undiluted article. Brown can sing tunes requiring sincerity, ache, or irony with equal flair. The CD's 12 cuts include the nearly 12-minute "Guit-Steel Blues," a sharp cover of Hank Garland's "Sugarfoot Stomp," and the bittersweet "Doin' What Comes Easy To A Fool" and "Holding Pattern." Brown is as vital and refreshing as early John Anderson or Randy Travis. — *Ron Wynn*

Junior High / Jul. 18, 1995 / Curb ✦✦✦
Junior High is an EP that features re-recorded versions of "Highway Patrol," "Sugarfoot Rag," and "My Wife Thinks You're Dead," plus two new songs, "That's Easy for You to Say" and "Lovely Hula Hands." It's a minor entry in Brown's catalog, but it is an enjoyable one, even if it is only necessary for diehard fans. — *Stephen Thomas Erlewine*

Semi-Crazy / May 1996 / Curb ✦✦✦✦
On *Semi-Crazy,* Junior Brown's third full-length album, the suit-and-tied Texas singer's clever lyrics, Ernest Tubb-like voice, and virtuoso guitar playing (on his custom-made, double-necked "guit-steel," that allows him to switch quickly between picking and steel playing) are once again intact and on the mark. *Semi-Crazy* may not bowl Brown fans over immediately—he offers no new twists as either a writer or player. On the other hand, because Brown is one of country music's most stunning guitarists (imagine Ornette Coleman crossed with Speedy West)—not to mention possessing a truly original sound—it's hard not to fall for the classic Brown sound of "I Hung It Up" (a standout for the guitar work), "Gotta Get Up Every Morning," and the fun-loving title track (his duet partner, Red Simpson, penned Brown's earlier song "Highway Patrol"). — *Kurt Wolff*

Marty Brown

b. 1965
Guitar, Vocals / Traditional Country
Marty Brown, a native of the tobacco-farming community of Maceo, KY, is the kind of guy myths spring up around. He hitchhiked into Nashville with little more than his guitar, a cheap demo tape, and a knowledge of the music industry he'd picked up from TNN. (He's said to have accosted producer Barry Beckett at a music-biz function and said, "I know you! I saw you in a video.") It turned out that was enough. A featured segment on the network news show *48 Hours* and an unannounced visit to performing rights organization BMI led to a scramble to sign Brown to a recording deal.

Brown's pinched voice is a throwback to an earlier time, sort of a Kentucky hill version of Jimmie Rodgers. He recorded three albums for MCA and won a small but strong fan base through a national tour with Jimmie Dale Gilmore and, later, a couple of solo tours playing at Wal-Marts across the country. But while his albums and concerts were critically acclaimed, Brown never had a radio hit, and MCA eventually dropped him. In 1996, however, he was snatched up by the Oakland, CA, indie label HighTone (onetime home to Jimmie Dale Gilmore, Joe Ely, and Robert Cray). He was due to release his debut for the label later that same year. — *Brian Mansfield & Kurt Wolff*

High & Dry / 1991 / MCA ✦✦✦
If everything here were as pure a hillbilly distillation as the title track or the loopy "Old King Kong," Brown might come off like a simple hick with limited nostalgia appeal. But his range is surprisingly wide. Brown's ballads—"I'll Climb Any Mountain" and "Wildest Dreams"—though simple, build to stunning, emotional climaxes. "Every Now and Then" is the equal of many of the Everly Brothers' best. And "Nobody Knows" is surely one of the most lonesome wails in a long, long time. — *Brian Mansfield*

● **Wild Kentucky Skies** / 1993 / MCA ✦✦✦✦
One of the best things about Marty Brown's music is that it possesses the qualities that people both love and hate about country music. Brown takes a sure-fire hit song, "I Don't Wanna See You," then sings it in a voice that won't let folks forget just how backwoods country music can be. Songs like "It Must Be the Rain" and "Let's Begin Again" have soaring choruses that recall the Everlys at their best. On the other hand, "No Honky Tonkin' Tonight" and "I'd Rather Fish Than Fight" put to shame the lip service some singers pay to Hank Williams, Sr., and Jimmie Rodgers. With the eerie "She's Gone," Brown takes the country death ballad into territory it's never seen before, and he follows it with the sentimental "Kentucky Skies." Brown is pure country without being purist. Flatly put, he's a hillbilly and proud of it. — *Brian Mansfield*

Cryin', Lovin', Leavin' / 1994 / MCA ✦✦✦✦
By his third album, Brown and producer Richard Bennett could be pretty confident they weren't going to get any radio play, so they just cut loose and made as pure an album as Brown had in him. "You Must Be Mistakin' Me" and "Too Blue to Crow" possess a country sound so hard, they make most New Traditionalists sound like Muzak. Brown cuts Moon Mullican's "Cherokee Boogie," sings "Shameless Lies" with Melba Montgomery, shamelessly cops from Buddy Holly's "Crying, Waiting, Hoping" with the title cut, and finishes with a gorgeous duet with Joy Lynn White on "I Love Only You." — *Brian Mansfield*

Milton Brown

b. Sep. 8, 1903, Stephenville, TX, d. Apr. 13, 1936
Vocals
In April, 1936, when Milton Brown was killed in a wreck on a Texas highway (his car's speedometer was found frozen at 93 mph), he was fronting a take-no-prisoners swing band every bit as popular in the Lone Star State as Bob Wills' band. In fact, Brown and Wills had been bandmates in the Wills Fiddle Band, the Alladin Laddies, and the original Light Crust Doughboys, before Brown split off to form the Musical Brownies in 1932. The latter dancehall outfit recorded for Bluebird in 1934, and for Decca in 1935-36. Whether Brown, had he lived, would have attained the iconographic stature of his friendly rival Wills is anybody's guess. Certainly the music he left behind deserves wider recognition. — *Dan Cooper*

Taking Off! / 1977 / String ✦✦✦✦
More Decca material, it includes a couple of 1937 cuts recorded without Brown after he died. — *Dan Cooper*

☆ **Complete Recordings of the Father of Western Swing 1932-1937** / 1996 / Texas Rose ✦✦✦✦✦
The Complete Recordings of the Father of Western Swing 1932-1937 is exactly what its title suggests—everything Milton Brown and His Musical Brownies recorded for both Victor and Decca Records, spread out over five compact discs. The very comprehensiveness of the box makes it appealing only to serious country music historians and dedicated fans, but within these five discs is some of the most groundbreaking, influential—and just plain enjoyable—popular music of the early 20th century. For those willing to make the investment, it is well worth the money. — *Stephen Thomas Erlewine*

☆ **With His Musical Brownies 1934** / Texas Rose ✦✦✦✦✦
Containing the complete Bluebird recordings of 1934, it showcases fiddler Cecil Brower and pianist Fred "Papa" Calhoun on a typically wild assortment of blues, pop, jazz, and fiddle tunes. — *Dan Cooper*

★ **Pioneer Western Swing Band (1935-1936)** / MCA ✦✦✦✦✦
On this twelve-cut collection from Brown's brilliant Decca sessions, the same core band appears as on the Bluebird sides. There's the additional firepower of a second fiddle hero, Cliff Bruner, and Bob Dunn, one of the first real geniuses of the steel guitar. — *Dan Cooper*

T. Graham Brown

b. Oct. 30, 1954, Arabi, GA
Vocals / Country
Asked to describe his own music, "His T-Ness" calls it "Otis Redding meets George Jones." With the smoky timbre of rocker Chris Rea and the passionate energy of Joe Cocker, Brown possesses as much "blue-eyed soul" as Boz Scaggs or Hall & Oates. A former All-State baseball player in Georgia, Brown gave up the sport when he rode the bench on his college team. He put together a band for the Holiday Inn lounge, and in 1982 his wife Sheila convinced him it was time to head to Nashville. There, he became immersed in the world of jingles, working for McDonald's, Kraft, Coca Cola, and Taco Bell. He also sang the demo of "1982" that Randy Travis eventually recorded. His sound is a bit unusual for country music, and that's appropriate for Brown, who does nothing the same way as anyone else. Cases in point: he named his band the Rack of Spam, and named his first child Acme. — *Tom Roland*

I Tell It Like It Used to Be / 1986 / Capitol ✦✦✦✦
With the sessions split between Nashville's Woodland Studio and Muscle Shoals, T. Graham Brown's debut often sounds affectionately like the raw, impassioned work of a garage band. — *Tom Roland*

Brilliant Conversationalist / 1987 / Capitol ✦✦✦
With blaring horns and bluesy growled vocals, this record has more to do with Southside Johnny than any country band one could name. That aside, there are some nice songs on here. Not a great record but if this is your type of thing, you could do worse. — *Jim Worbois*

● **The Best of T. Graham Brown** / 1992 / Liberty ✦✦✦✦
It contains "With This Ring," "Never Say Never," and "Moonshadow Road," among other hits. — *AMG*

The Browns

Maxine Brown (b. Apr. 27, 1931) and Jim Ed Brown (b. Apr. 1, 1934) of Sparkman, AR had been singing together for several years when, in 1954, their sister Bonnie (b. Jul. 31, 1937) joined them. Calling themselves the Browns, the sibling harmony trio struck gold in 1959 with "The Three Bells," a crossover smash that spent four weeks atop the Billboard pop chart and ten weeks at No. 1 country. They broke up in 1967, though Jim Ed scored solo hits into the '80s. — *Dan Cooper*

● **20 of the Best** / 1985 / RCA ✦✦✦✦
20 of the Best collects the great majority of the Browns' biggest hits. Even though it bypasses early hits like "Looking Back to See," "Here Today and Gone Tomorrow," "I Take the Chance," and "I Heard the Bluebirds Sing"—which were all recorded under the name Jim Edward, Maxine & Bonnie Brown (with the exception of "Looking Back to See," which was recorded without Bonnie)—the compilation is the only recent set to attempt a concise retrospective of the vocal group. — *Stephen Thomas Erlewine*

Looking Back To See / Sep. 1986 / Bear Family ✦✦✦

Three Bells / 1993 / Bear Family ✦✦✦✦
It is a lesson in reissue absurdity that The Browns, whose popularity has warranted this attractive, but expensive, eight-CD box set, have no single-disc compilation available as of mid-1994. But if you know you're a fan, you can do no better than this collection of their complete RCA recordings. — *Dan Cooper*

Ed Bruce

b. Dec. 29, 1939
Vocals / Country, Rock 'n' Roll
Born in Arkansas, raised in Memphis, Ed Bruce signed first with the rockabilly-heavy Sun Records, and later with the soul-oriented Septre label. But Bruce's deep resonance and laidback approach to life were more suited to country. He was able to move to Nashville with the help of Tommy Roe's pop hit "Sheila"; Bruce wrote the B-side, and collected enough royalties when it sold a million copies to swing a new home base. A jack-of-all-trades in the business, he's done some acting (the "Bret Maverick" series); some radio work (on Nashville's WSM); some jingle-singing (United Airlines, Burger King, Tennessee Tourism, among many others); and some songwriting ("Mammas, Don't Let Your Babies Grow up to Be Cowboys," "Texas When I Die," and "See the Big Man Cry"). A journeyman recording artist, Bruce found brief success in the early '80s with a string of singles for MCA Records. — *Tom Roland*

Greatest Hits / 1986 / MCA ✦✦✦✦
This album documents the most rewarding period of Ed Bruce's recording career. Easygoing, mid-tempo love songs dominate, particularly with "You're the Best Break This Old Heart Ever Had," "Ever, Never Lovin' You," and "You're Leavin' Here Tonight." The reflective "After All" is permanently haunting. — *Tom Roland*

● **The Best Of Ed Bruce** / 1995 / Varese Sarabande ✦✦✦✦
18 songs from 1975 to 1986, all but two of which were country hits, a half dozen making the Top Ten. Includes the original 1975 version of "Mammas Don't Let Your Babies Grow Up To Be Cowboys," a No. 1 duet for Waylon Jennings and Willie Nelson a few years later; "The Last Cowboy Song," which features a guest vocal by Nelson; and the "Theme From Bret Maverick." — *Richie Unterberger*

Cliff Bruner

Fiddle / Honky Tonk
Like his former boss, Milton Brown, ace Texas fiddler Cliff Bruner led a prewar Western swing band as steeped in jazz and blues as traditional hoedown music. Based in the Houston-Beaumont region (as opposed to Dallas-Fort Worth) his Texas Wanderers featured several former members of Milton Brown's Musical Brownies, including the immortal steel guitar man Bob Dunn. honky tonk singer/pianist Moon Mullican also came to prominence as a member of Bruner's band. — *Dan Cooper*

★ **Cliff Bruner's Texas Wanderers** / 1983 / Texas Rose ✦✦✦✦✦
This is a fine compilation covering the years 1937-44. Beaucoups chops from the aforementioned Bruner, Dunn and Mullican, as well as Leo Raley, the first Western swinger to "plug in" a mandolin. —*Dan Cooper*

Jimmy Bryant

Guitar / Country
With steel guitar wizard Speedy West, guitarist Jimmy Bryant formed half of the hottest country guitar duo of the '50s. With lightning speed and jazz-fueled taste for improvisation and adventure, Bryant's boogies, polkas, and country swing—recorded with West and as a solo artist—remain among the most exciting instrumental country recordings of all time. Bryant also waxed major contributions to the early recordings of singers like Tennessee Ernie Ford, Merrill E. Moore, Kay Starr, Billy May, and Ella Mae Morse, and has influenced country guitarists like Buck Owens, James Burton, and Albert Lee. While he enjoyed a career that spanned several decades, it was his sessions with Capitol Records in the early '50s that allowed him his fullest freedom to strut his stuff. —*Richie Unterberger*

Country Cabin Jazz / 196_ / Longhorn ✦✦✦✦
Featuring Speedy West on steel guitar and Billy Strange on rhythm, Bryant runs through a dozen swinging instrumentals with panache on this "country jam session." —*Richie Unterberger*

● **Guitar Take-Off** / 1989 / See For Miles ✦✦✦✦
Indisputably the best Bryant compilation. 20 tracks from 1951 to 1955, many taken from rare singles, and many also featuring Speedy West. Also includes cuts by Ella Mae Morse, Tennessee Ernie Ford, Merrill E. Moore, and Billy May that feature Jimmy as a sessionman. "Stratosphere Boogie" and "Catfish Boogie" are breathtaking Bryant/West duels. —*Richie Unterberger*

Bryant's Back in Town / Longhorn ✦✦✦

Jethro Burns (Homer and Jethro)

b. 1920, **d.** Feb. 4, 1989
Instrumental, Mandolin
Behind the country hayseed garb, the hick patter, and the outrageous parodies of popular songs lay mandolin player Kenneth "Jethro" Burns and guitarist Henry "Homer" Haynes, expert jazz musicians who for nearly four decades were country comedy's most visible duo. Their exaggerated hillbilly appearance and zany send-ups of songs belie the cleverness of their comedy and the extraordinarily high quality of their music.
Both from Knoxville, TN, they billed themselves first as the String Dusters but moved to comedy in 1936 when they created the Homer and Jethro characters that were intact until Haynes' death in 1971. And they made a good living from these rubes, winning a Grammy in 1959, starring in Las Vegas, and appearing regularly on TV, including "The Tonight Show." Although they canned the country corn occasionally (as in *Playing It Straight*, a 1962 album), their onstage wit and parodies of well-known songs ranging from the opera to the Opry made them famous. Regarding his "Jambalaya" being turned into "Jam Bowl Liar," Hank Williams said you know a song's good when it's been given the Homer and Jethro treatment. Other zingers include "She Was Bitten on the Udder by an Adder," "Mama, Get the Hammer (There's a Fly on Papa's Head)," and "I've Got Tears in My Ears from Lying on My Back in Bed While I Cry over You." What other act could put out a hit album titled *The Worst of Homer and Jethro?* Only they could be so creatively, zanily bad that they were excellent. Shortly after Haynes' death, in a series of swing jazz albums, Burns has shown why he's been considered the best mandolin player of a generation and, in the opinion of many, the best who has ever lived. —*David Vinopal*

Jethro Live / 1990 / Flying Fish ✦✦✦
Some laughs are included, and much "mando-marvelosity." —*Mark A. Humphrey*

● **Tea for One** / Kaleidoscope ✦✦✦✦
Known for cornball comedy as half of Homer & Jethro, Burns was also a deft swing-style mandolinist. This album features Jethro Burns and his mandolin and no one else. —*Mark A. Humphrey*

☆ **Back to Back** / Kaleidoscope ✦✦✦✦✦
The two modern giants of mandolin, Jethro Burns and Tiny Moore, are backed by guitar-great Eldon Shamblin of Bob Wills' Texas Playboys. —*David Vinopal*

Tracy Byrd

b. Beaumont, TX
Guitar, Vocals / Contemporary Country
Singer-songwriter/guitarist Tracy Byrd is part of a movement of contemporary country performers trying to move away from the trend toward pop-country and back towards the more traditional sounds of the genre; his rising popularity seems to show that many fans have similar feelings. He began his career while studying business at Lamar University in

Beaumont, TX, in a rather odd way—he sang "Your Cheatin' Heart" in a shopping mall "recording studio," and the saleswoman was impressed enough to invite him to perform in a monthly amateur talent show. His success there inspired him to pursue music, working his solo act at night and doing odd jobs during the day. He got a job playing with Mark Chesnutt at the Cutters nightclub in Beaumont. After Chesnutt became a success and hit the road, Byrd formed a new group, Only Way to Fly, which became the club's house band. He went to Nashville nearly a year later, but the trip wasn't successful. On his return trip, he was showcased, and did a successful solo audition for MCA executives Bruce Hinton and Tony Brown. His first MCA album was produced by Keith Steagall. The first single from his self-titled debut, "That's the Thing About a Memory," made it to the charts as a minor hit in 1992. The next single, "Someone to Give My Love To," made the Top 50, but the third single, "Holdin' Heaven," climbed all the way to No. 1 in 1993. Byrd released his Jerry Crutchfield-produced second album, *No Ordinary Man*, in 1994, which featured the two collaborating on the title track and "Redneck Roses." The single "Lifestyles of the Not So Rich and Famous" made the Top 20. *Love Lessons*, Byrd's third album, was released in 1995. —*Sandra Brennan*

Tracy Byrd / 1993 / MCA ✦✦✦
Tracy Byrd's self-titled debut is an uneven but appealing set of new traditionalist country, highlighted by the No. 1 hit, "Holdin' Heaven." On about half of the album's tracks, Byrd sounds confident and skillful, but on the other half, he sounds unsure and timid. Which just means that *Tracy Byrd* is a promising debut album, not a great one. —*Thom Owens*

● **No Ordinary Man** / 1994 / MCA ✦✦✦✦
No Ordinary Man, Tracy Byrd's second album, was his breakthrough record and its easy to see why. While he was still sorting out the ins and outs of recording on his debut album, Byrd sounds raw, vibrant, and confident throughout *No Ordinary Man*, which is clear from the record's first single, "Lifestyles of the Not So Rich and Famous," and the first-rate weeper "The Keeper of the Stars." Byrd plays ballads and uptempo dance numbers equally well and his set of material on the album is fairly consistent, making the album his best to date. —*Thom Owens*

Love Lessons / 1995 / MCA ✦✦✦
On his third album *Love Lessons*, Tracy Byrd doesn't come up with quite as winning a collection as he did on *No Ordinary Man*, but he comes close enough to make the record a worthwhile purchase for fans. —*Thom Owens*

Glen Campbell (Glen Travis Campbell)

b. Apr. 22, 1936, Delight, AR
Banjo, Guitar, Vocals / Country-Pop
Playing guitar on the Los Angeles session circuit, Glen Campbell got involved in such memorable releases as "Strangers in the Night," by Frank Sinatra; "I'm a Believer," by the Monkees; "Viva Las Vegas," by Elvis Presley; and "The Legend of Bonnie & Clyde," by Merle Haggard. Campbell also toured as Brian Wilson's stand-in with the Beach Boys. But his own recording career was hardly rewarding at the start. After several albums, he was about to give it up when a song called "Gentle on my Mind" emerged with a smattering of success. Encouraged, he continued recording, and exploded with the release of "By the Time I Get to Phoenix." A string of hits followed—not to mention the network TV show "The Glen Campbell Goodtime Hour"—and within short order, he was selling more records than his labelmates, the Beatles. But his successes didn't sustain. He tailed off in the early '70s, re-emerged with the release of "Rhinestone Cowboy" in 1975, and continued through several more up-and-down periods. Campbell's vocal range, good looks, and sense of humor all combined to make him one of country music's best-recognized personalities, even when the music didn't work commercially. —*Tom Roland*

☆ **Glen Campbell's Greatest Hits** / 1971 / Capitol ✦✦✦✦✦
It covers the most productive period of his recording career, the years in which Al De Lory's soaring string arrangements, Jimmy Webb's snapshot songs, and the identifiable low-tuned guitars vaulted Campbell to the upper strata of both the country and pop charts. You simply weren't alive if you didn't hear "Wichita Lineman," "Galveston," or "Try a Little Kindness." —*Tom Roland*

★ **The Very Best of Glen Campbell** / Mar. 20, 1987 / Liberty ✦✦✦✦✦
The Very Best of Glen Campbell features 15 of his biggest hits, from "Gentle on My Mind" and "Wichita Lineman" to "Rhinestone Cowboy," making it the place to get acquainted with Campbell's career. —*Stephen Thomas Erlewine*

Greatest Country Hits / 1990 / Curb ✦✦✦
A hodgepodge of material from the mid-'70s through 1989, this displays a variety of Glen Campbell approaches to country. "She's Gone, Gone, Gone" is twangy enough to do originator Lefty Frizzell justice. "Still Within the Sound of My Voice" catches Campbell at his most sensitive, and "Southern Nights" is just plain fun. —*Tom Roland*

Essential, Vol. 2 / 1995 / Capitol ✦✦✦✦
The second installment of *The Essential* series features some of Glen Campbell's biggest hits, including "Rhinestone Cowboy" and "Gentle on My Mind," as well as several live tracks, album cuts, instrumentals, and a couple of previously unreleased songs. All of the material was recorded between 1962 and 1978. —*Stephen Thomas Erlewine*

Essential, Vol. 3 / Oct. 10, 1995 / Capitol ✦✦✦✦
The third installment of Glen Campbell's *Essential* series features his No. 1 hit "Wichita Lineman" among a handful of other hit singles and selected rarities. —*Thom Owens*

Essential, Vol. 1 / Capitol ✦✦✦✦
The first volume of *The Essential Glen Campbell* establishes the pattern of familiar hits and fascinating rarities that make the series a worthwhile purchase for both devoted and casual fans. Although it doesn't follow a strict chronological running order, it offers a good cross-section of his late-'60s and-'70s hits. —*Thom Owens*

Mary-Chapin Carpenter

b. Feb. 21, 1958, Princeton, NJ
Guitar, Vocals / Contemporary Country
Mary-Chapin Carpenter was part of a small movement of folk-influenced, country singer-songwriters of the late '80s. Although many of these performers never achieved commercial success, Carpenter was able to channel her anti-Nashville approach into chart success and industry awards by the early '90s.

Carpenter was born and raised in Princeton, NJ, the daughter of a *Life* magazine executive; she spent two years of her childhood in Japan, when her father was launching the Asian edition of *Life.* During the folk explosion of the early '60s, her mother had begun to play guitar. When Mary-Chapin became interested in music as a child, her mother gave her her guitar. Carpenter played music during her high school years, but she didn't actively pursue it as a career. In 1974, her family moved to Washington DC, where she became involved in the city's folk music scene. After graduating from high school in the mid-'70s, she spent a year travelling Europe; when she was finished, she enrolled at Brown University, where she was an American Civilization major.

Following her college graduation, she became deeply involved in the Washington-area folk scene, performing a mixture of originals, contemporary singer-songwriter material, and pop covers. Carpenter met guitarist John Jennings during the early '80s and the pair began performing together. Eventually, the duo made a demo tape of their songs, which they sold at their concerts. The tape wound up at Columbia Records, who offered Carpenter an audition. By early 1987, the label had signed her as a recording artist. Her first album, *Hometown Girl,* was released that year.

Hometown Girl and its follow-up, *State of the Heart* (1989), earned her a dedicated cult following, as well as two Top Ten singles, "Never Had It So Good" and "Quittin' Time." Country radio was hesitant to play her soft, folkie, feminist material, but she received good reviews and airplay on more progressive country stations, as well as college radio. *Shooting Straight in the Dark,* released in 1990, managed to break down a lot of the barriers that stood in her way. "Down At the Twist and Shout" became a No. 2 single and the album sold well, setting the stage for her breakthrough album, 1992's *Come On Come On.*

Come On Come On signalled a slight change in direction for Carpenter—although there were still folk songs, she felt freer to loosen up on honky tonk and country-rock songs, which resulted in several hit singles. Two of the singles from the album, "I Feel Lucky" and "Passionate Kisses" hit No. 4, and "He Thinks He'll Keep Her" became her first No. 1. *Come On Come On* would eventually sell over two million copies. *Stones in the Road,* her fifth album, released in 1994, concentrated on the folkier material, but it was still a major success, selling over a million copies within the first six months of release. —*Stephen Thomas Erlewine*

Hometown Girl / Feb. 1987 / Columbia ✦✦✦

State of the Heart / 1989 / Columbia ✦✦✦✦
Carpenter, a folkie, eventually turned to the country market, especially on her third album, *Shooting Straight in the Dark.* On this, her second, she's still in transition, which makes her more thoughtful than the average country singer and catchier than the average folkie, especially on her breakthrough country hit, "Never Had It So Good." Also includes "Quittin' Time," "Something of a Dreamer," and "How Do." —*William Ruhlmann*

Shooting Straight in the Dark / 1990 / Columbia ✦✦✦✦
Carpenter's third album expanded on the promise of her breakthrough, with the Searchers-style pop of "Going out Tonight" and a guest spot from Beausoleil on the Cajun-rooted "Down at the Twist and Shout." It also held some of her most penetrating, introspective songs, with payoff lines that would impress Elvis Costello. The album contains the singles "You Win Again" and "Right Now." —*Brian Mansfield*

● **Come on Come on** / 1992 / Columbia ✦✦✦✦
The ultra-serious *Shooting Straight in the Dark* left Carpenter in need of a breather, which she took by covering Dire Straits' "The Bug" and Lucinda Williams' "Passionate Kisses." On "I Feel Lucky," she won the lottery and flirted with Dwight Yoakam and Lyle Lovett in a bar. It's tough to say which she enjoyed more. The line about winning the lottery might have been prescience on Carpenter's part—*Come on Come on* sold more than two million copies and generated six hit singles, including "Not Too Much to Ask" with Joe Diffie, "The Hard Way," and the Geritol-inspired "He Thinks He'll Keep Her," her first No. 1 according to *Billboard.* —*Brian Mansfield*

Stones in the Road / 1994 / Columbia ✦✦✦✦
With *Stones in the Road,* Mary Chapin Carpenter stripped her sound down and returned to the core of her music—namely, her singer-songwriter roots. Although the lyrics are among her best, Carpenter unfortunately cut back the number of hooks and melodies in her songs. Previously, she found a nice balance between the two, but here, she concentrates on the lyrics to the detriment of the actual songs. The sound of *Stones in the Road* is pleasant, but there aren't any songs that stick in your head after the record is finished. —*Thom Owens*

The Carter Family

Fiddle, Guitar, Autoharp, Vocals / Traditional Country, Appalachia
The most influential group in country music history, the Carter Family switched the emphasis from hillbilly instrumentals to vocals, made scores of their songs part of the standard country music canon, and made a style of guitar-playing, "Carter-picking," the dominant technique for decades. For nearly 70 years the Carters' "Wildwood Flower" was first choice of most young country people learning to play the guitar. In 1970 the original Carter Family became the first group elected to the Country Music Hall of Fame.

In a remarkable coincidence, on Aug 1-4, 1927, the first two stars ("superstars" in today's inflation) were recorded in Bristol, TN, by an RCA scout looking for rural talent. One was the great Mississippi Blue Yodeler, Jimmie Rodgers; the other was a family group consisting of Alvin P. Carter, his wife Sara, and their sister-in-law, Maybelle. These three—a gaunt, shy gospel quartet member and two reserved country girls—sang a pure, simple harmony that influenced not only the numerous other family groups of the '30s and the '40s, but Woody Guthrie, Bill Monroe, the Kingston Trio, Doc Watson, Bob Dylan, and Emmylou Harris, to mention just a few. It's unlikely that bluegrass music would have existed without the Carter Family.

A.P., the family patriarch, collected hundreds of British/Appalachian folk songs and, in arranging these for recording, both enhanced the pure beauty of these "facts-of-life tunes" and at the same time saved them for future generations. Those hundreds of songs the trio found around their Virginia and Tennessee homes, after being sung by A.P., Sara, and Maybelle, became *Carter* songs, even though they were folksongs and in the public domain. Among the more than 300 sides they recorded are "Worried Man Blues," "Wabash Cannonball," "Will the Circle Be Unbroken," "Wildwood Flower," and "Keep on the Sunny Side," their radio theme.

The Carter Family's instrumental backup, like their vocals, was unique. On her Gibson L-5 guitar, Maybelle played a bass-strings lead (the guitar being tuned down from the standard pitch) that is the mainstay of bluegrass guitarists to the present. Sara accompanied her on the autoharp or on a second guitar, while A.P. devoted his talent to singing a haunting though idiosyncratic bass or baritone. Although the original Carter Family disbanded in 1943, enough of their recordings remained in the vaults to keep the group current through the '40s. Maybelle, through a Flatt and Scruggs album of Carter material, found a new and younger audience in the '60s; her work on the famous three-record album *Will the Circle Be Unbroken* (under the aegis of the Nitty Gritty Dirt Band), blended the old-guard country with the new, restoring to her the fame of 40 years earlier. This time, though, the audience was predominantly urban and educated. —*David Vinopal*

☆ **'mid the Green Fields of Virginia** / 1963 / RCA ✦✦✦✦✦
The Carter Family was the most important group in early country music, and this 16-track album selects some of their most notable initial recordings from the late '20s and early '30s, among them "My Clinch Mountain Home" and their theme song "Keep on the Sunny Side." —*William Ruhlmann*

Diamonds in the Rough / 1990 / Copper Creek ✦✦✦

★ **Country Music Hall of Fame** / 1991 / MCA ✦✦✦✦✦
After ending an eight-year association with Victor Records, the Carter Family recorded 60 sides for Decca between 1936 and 1938; 15 of those recordings are collected here. Decca wanted to emphasize new material; this posed no problem for A.P. Carter, who was long accustomed to taking copyright credit for minor rewrites of other people's songs. The Decca songs are less familiar than the recordings for Victor or, later, OKeh, but they're worth hearing. —*Brian Mansfield*

☆ **My Clinch Mountain Home–Their Complete Victor Recordings**,
1928-1929 / 1993 / Rounder ✦✦✦✦✦
A.P. Carter, his wife Sara, and her cousin Maybelle were now established RCA Victor recording artists by the time these 1928-1929 recordings were made. But the music is no less real, raw and compelling. Highlights include the title track, "I'm Thinking Tonight of My Blue Eyes," and "Forsaken Love." —*Cub Koda*

★ **Anchored in Love: Their Complete Victor Recordings, Vol. 1:**
1927-1928 / 1993 / Rounder ✦✦✦✦✦
The first volume in Rounder's chronicling of The Carter Family's complete Victor recordings starts at the beginning with the debut album from Bristol, Tennessee in 1927 that changed country music forever. Including the original versions of "Keep on the Sunny Side," "Wildwood Flower," and "Little Darling Pal of Mine," this is country music on the ground floor. —*Cub Koda*

☆ **My Clinch Mountain Home: Their Complete Victor Recordings,**
Vol. 2: 1928-1929 / Oct. 1, 1993 / Rounder ✦✦✦✦✦
A.P. Carter, his wife Sara, and her cousin Maybelle were now established RCA Victor recording artists by the time these 1928-1929 recordings were made. But the music is no less real, raw and compelling. Highlights include the title track, "I'm Thinking Tonight of My Blue Eyes," and "Forsaken Love." —*Cub Koda*

☆ **When the Roses Bloom in Dixieland: Their Complete Recordings,**
Vol. 3: 1929-1930 / Oct. 31, 1995 / Rounder ✦✦✦✦✦
The third volume in Rounder's projected eight-disc series of the Carter Family's 1927-1941 recordings for RCA Victor picks up in Atlanta, GA, in November 1929, where the family records ten tracks—including "Motherless Children," "Wabash Cannonball," and "Jimmy Brown the Newsboy," among other country classics—then travels to Memphis for six tracks from the Carters' fifth recording session in May 1930. — *William Ruhlmann*

☆ **Worried Man Blues: Their Complete Recordings, Vol. 4: 1930 /**
Oct. 31, 1995 / Rounder ✦✦✦✦✦
The fourth volume in Rounder's projected eight-disc series of the Carter Family's 1927-1941 recordings for RCA Victor picks up in Memphis, TN, in May 1930 and continues in the same city in November for 16 sides, including the title track and "Lonesome Valley." There are an unusually large number of three-part harmony vocals in this set, much of which is given over to gospel songs. The only complaints about this brilliant chronological series are that it could be accomplished faster: This disc runs less than 48 minutes, and Rounder seems to be doling out the albums at a rate of two every two years, which means that it could take until the end of 1999 to hear them all. (The fifth volume, *Sunshine in the Shadows–Their Complete Victor Recordings 1931-1932* was scheduled for release June 18, 1996, speeding up the schedule somewhat.) — *William Ruhlmann*

Sunshine in the Shadows: Their Complete Victor Recordings, Vol.
5: 1931-1932 / 1996 / Rounder ✦✦✦✦
Sixteen tracks from 1931 and 1932, originally recorded for Victor, most penned by A.P. Carter. It displays the Carters' usual unadorned consistency, moving harmonies, and accomplished picking; "Picture on the Wall," "Where We'll Never Grow Old," and "Lonesome for You" are just some of the more striking examples of their skill with material that is both humble and mournfully evocative. Of special interest are a few songs (and a couple corny sketches) on which the clan is joined by Jimmie Rodgers, the most influential country act of the day barring the Carters themselves. —*Richie Unterberger*

Clinch Mountain Treasures /1993 / County ✦✦✦✦
As the title suggests, the songs are treasures, but they're not among the seminal group's best-known songs. Recorded for OKeh Records in Chicago in 1940, it captures the group's instrumentation and vocals at their most incisive. —*Michael McCall*

Carlene Carter

b. Sep. 26, 1955, Nashville, TN
Guitar, Vocals / Roots-Rock, New Traditionalist
Carlene Carter has always straddled the line between country and rock. Beginning her career as a rock singer in the mid-'70s, she became immersed in the new wave in the late '70s, before emerging as a new country singer in the late '80s, Throughout it all, her music has always infused roots music—whether it's country or rock 'n' roll—with a nervy, edgy energy.
Carlene is the daughter of June Carter and Carl Smith, who divorced when their daughter was just two. June would frequently take her daughter on the Carter Family tours, which meant that Carlene developed a musical interest at an early age. When she was 12, her mother married Johnny Cash. Following the marriage, Carlene and her stepsister Rosanne Cash became backup singers in the Carter/Cash touring show.
At the age of 15 she married Joe Simpkins and had a child; they were divorced within a few years. Carter enrolled in college as a piano major

in her late teens, but she never graduated. At 19, she married Jack Routh; they were divorced within two years.
In 1978, she decided to pursue a musical career, heading to Los Angeles where she received a record contract with Warner Brothers. Her debut album, *Carlene Carter*, was a rock 'n' roll record recorded in London with Graham Parker's backing band, the Rumour. The following year, she released her second album, *Two Sides to Every Woman*, which featured support from the Doobie Brothers. That same year she married singer-songwriter/producer Nick Lowe, who was currently the co-leader of the new wave rock 'n' roll revival band, Rockpile. Lowe helped Carter shape her musical direction in the early '80s and her third album—the new wave-inflected country-rock record *Musical Shapes* (1980)—showed the influence of Lowe, Rockpile, and Dave Edmunds. Although the album was critically acclaimed, it was a commercial failure. She followed *Musical Shapes* in 1981 with *Blue Nun*, which continued to pursue a new-wave country direction; like its predecessor, it was ignored.
During the early '80s, Carter was shut off from the country community because she was living in England with Lowe. After *Blue Nun*, she stopped recording, choosing to perform solo shows instead; she also had a starring role in the theatrical production *Pump Boys and Dinettes*. Carter and Lowe's marriage collapsed in the mid-'80s and she returned to the states, where she became part of the touring Carter Family.
In 1989, she began work on a comeback record with Howie Epstein, the bassist for Tom Petty & the Heartbreakers. That same year, she dueted with Southern Comfort on the Top 40 hit, "Time's Up." Reprise signed Carter in 1990 and she released her overdue fifth album, *I Fell in Love*, later that year. *I Fell In Love* still had rock influences, but it was a more straightforward country record than her previous albums, and country radio paid attention. The album became a hit and two singles, "I Fell In Love" and "Come On Back," climbed all the way to No.3. *Little Love Letters*, her 1993 follow-up (which was released on Giant Records), was equally successful; its first single, "Every Little Thing," was another No. 3 hit. *Little Acts of Treason*, her 1995 album, wasn't as big a hit as its two predecessors, but it still enjoyed moderate success on the country charts. —*Stephen Thomas Erlewine*

Carlene Carter / 1978 / Warner Bros. ✦✦✦

Two Sides to Every Woman / 1979 / Warner Bros. ✦✦✦

Musical Shapes / 1980 / F Beat ✦✦✦✦
This is Carter's masterpiece to date. Great songs and production that could easily fit into today's climate of country radio. —*Cub Koda*

Blue Nun / 1981 / F Beat ✦✦✦
Carter's American label passed on this one, and it's too bad. While it's not one of her best albums, when she's on, she's dead on. It's interesting from a historical point because it somewhat chronicles her musical associations with former-husband Nick Lowe and Paul Carrack (ex-Ace, Squeeze, Mike and the Mechanics). —*Jim Worbois*

C'est C Bon / 1983 / Razor & Tie ✦✦

● **I Fell in Love** / 1990 / Reprise ✦✦✦✦
This comeback album has a perfect mix of old (A.P. Carter's "My Dixie Darlin'") and new (guest spots from Dave Edmunds, David Lindley, and Albert Lee). If Carter hasn't come to terms with her love for rock and her duty to heritage, she's at least learned to balance them. —*Brian Mansfield*

Musical Shapes/Blue Nun / 1992 / Demon ✦✦✦✦
Demon Records reissued Carlene Carter's *Musical Shapes* and *Blue Nun* on one disc in 1992. Neither album is straight country—with their propulsive rhythms and jangling guitars, they exhibit the influence of her then-current husband Nick Lowe—but *Musical Shapes* is one of her best records, and worth getting in any form. —*Stephen Thomas Erlewine*

Little Love Letters / 1993 / Giant ✦✦✦✦
This is the album fans always dreamed she would make. While it shows off her love of, and ability to handle, various styles of music, she never loses her direction. —*Jim Worbois*

Little Acts of Treason / Oct. 1995 / Giant ✦✦✦
Carlene Carter's *Little Acts of Treason* doesn't break much new ground for the singer, but that's not necessarily a bad thing. While she continues in the same vein as *Little Love Letters*, the music is done well, even if the album isn't as infectious and catchy as her previous album. —*Stephen Thomas Erlewine*

Johnny Cash (John R. Cash)

b. Feb. 26, 1932, Kingsland, AR
Guitar, Vocals / Traditional Country
Johnny Cash was one of the most imposing and influential figures in post-World War II country music. With his deep, resonant baritone and spare, percussive guitar, he had a basic, distinctive sound. Cash didn't sound like Nashville, nor did he sound like honky tonk or rock 'n' roll. He created his own subgenre, falling halfway between the blunt emotional honesty of folk, the rebelliousness of rock 'n' roll, and the world-weariness of country. Cash's career coincided with the birth of rock 'n' roll, and

his rebellious attitude and simple, direct musical attack shared a lot of similarities with rock. However, there was a deep sense of history—as he would later illustrate with his series of historical albums—that kept him forever tied with country. And he was one of country music's biggest stars of the '50s and '60s, scoring well over 100 hit singles.

Johnny Cash was born and raised in Arkansas, moving to Dyess when he was three. By the time he was 12 years old, Cash had begun writing his own songs. Johnny was inspired by the country songs he had heard on the radio. While he was in high school, he sang on the Arkansas radio station KLCN. Johnny Cash graduated from college in 1950, moving to Detroit to work in an auto factory for a brief while. With the outbreak of the Korean War, he enlisted in the Air Force. While he was in the Air Force, Cash bought his first guitar and taught himself to play. He began writing songs in earnest, including "Folsom Prison Blues." Cash left the Air Force in 1954, married a Texas woman named Vivian Leberto, and moved to Memphis, where he took a radio announcing course at a broadcasting school on the GI Bill. During the evenings, he played country music in a trio that also consisted of guitarist Luther Perkins and bassist Marshall Grant. The trio occasionally played for free on a local radio station, KWEM, and tried to secure gigs and an audition at Sun Records.

Cash finally landed an audition with Sun Records and its founder, Sam Phillips, in 1955. Initially, Cash presented himself as a gospel singer, but Phillips turned him down. Phillips asked him to come back with something more commercial. Cash returned with "Hey Porter," which immediately caught Phillips' ear. Soon, Cash released "Cry Cry Cry" / "Hey Porter" as his debut single for Sun. On the single, Phillips billed Cash as "Johnny" which upset the singer, because he felt it sounded too young; the record producer also dubbed Perkins and Grant the Tennessee Two. "Cry Cry Cry" became a success upon its release in 1955, entering the country charts at No. 14 and leading to a spot on the "Louisiana Hayride," where he stayed for nearly a year. A second single, "Folsom Prison Blues," reached the country Top Five in early 1956 and its follow-up, "I Walk the Line," was No. 1 for six weeks and crossed over into the pop Top 20.

Johnny Cash had an equally successful year in 1957, scoring several Top Ten country hits including the Top 15 "Give My Love to Rose." Cash also made his Grand Ole Opry debut that year, appearing all in black where the other performers were decked out in flamboyant, rhinestone-studded outfits. Eventually, he earned the nickname of "The Man in Black." Cash became the first Sun artist to release a long-playing album in November of 1957, when *Johnny Cash with His Hot and Blue Guitar* hit the stores. Cash's success continued to roll throughout 1958, as he earned his biggest hit, "Ballad of a Teenage Queen" (No. 1 for ten weeks), as well another No. 1 single, "Guess Things Happen That Way." For most of 1958, Cash attempted to record a gospel album, but Sun refused to allow him to record one. Sun also was unwilling to increase Cash's record royalties. Both of these were deciding factors in the vocalist's decision to sign with Columbia Records in 1958. By the end of the year, he had released his first single for the label, "All Over Again," which became another Top Five success. Sun continued to release singles and albums of unissued Cash material into the '60s.

"Don't Take Your Guns to Town," Cash's second single for Columbia, was one of his biggest hits, reaching the top of the country charts and crossing over into the pop charts in the beginning of 1959. Throughout that year, Columbia and Sun singles vied for the top of the charts. Generally, the Columbia releases—"Frankie's Man Johnny," "I Got Stripes," and "Five Feet High and Rising"—fared better than the Sun singles, but "Luther Played the Boogie" did climb into the Top Ten. That same year, Cash had the chance to make his gospel record—*Hymns by Johnny Cash*—which kicked off a series of thematic albums that ran into the '70s.

The Tennessee Two became the Tennessee Three in 1960 with the addition of drummer W.S. Holland. Though he was continuing to have hits, the relentless pace of his career was beginning to take its toll on Cash. In 1959, he had begun taking amphetamines to help him get through his schedule of nearly 300 shows a year. By 1961, his drug intake had increased dramatically and his work was affected, which is reflected by a declining number of hit singles and albums. By 1963, he had moved to New York, leaving his family behind. He was running into trouble with the law, most notably for starting a forest fire out West.

June Carter—who was the wife of one of Cash's drinking buddies, Carl Smith—would provide Cash with his return to the top of the charts with "Ring of Fire," which she co-wrote with Merle Kilgore. "Ring of Fire" spent seven weeks on the top of the charts and was a Top 20 pop hit. Cash continued his success in 1964, as "Understand Your Man" became a No. 1 hit. However, Cash's comeback was short-lived, as he sank further into addiction and his hit singles arrived sporadically. Cash was arrested in El Paso for attempting to smuggle amphetamines into the country through his guitar case in 1965. That same year, the Grand Ole Opry refused to have him perform and he wrecked the establishment's footlights. In 1966, his wife Vivian filed for divorce. After the divorce, Cash

moved to Nashville. At first, he was as destructive as he ever had been, but he became close friends with June Carter, who had divorced Carl Smith. With Carter's help, he was able to shake his addictions; she also converted Cash to fundamentalist Christianity. His career began to bounce back as "Jackson" and "Rosanna's Going Wild" became Top Three hits. Early in 1968, Cash proposed marriage to Carter during a concert; the pair were married in the spring of 1968.

In 1968, Johnny Cash recorded and released his most popular album, *Johnny Cash at Folsom Prison*. Recorded during a prison concert, the album spawned the No. 1 country hit "Folsom Prison Blues," which also crossed over into the pop charts. By the end of the year, the record had gone gold. The following year, he released a sequel, *Johnny Cash at San Quentin*, which had his only Top Ten pop single, "A Boy Named Sue," which peaked at No. 3; it also hit No. 1 on the country charts. Johnny Cash guested on Bob Dylan's 1969 country-rock album, *Nashville Skyline*. Dylan returned the favor by appearing on the first episode of *The Johnny Cash Show*, the singer's television program for ABC. *The Johnny Cash Show* ran for two years, between 1969 and 1971. Johnny Cash was reaching a second peak of popularity in 1970. In addition to his television show, he performed for President Richard Nixon at the White House, acted with Kirk Douglas in *The Gunfight*, sang with John Williams and the Boston Pops Orchestra, and he was the subject of a documentary film. His record sales were equally healthy, as "Sunday Morning Coming Down" and "Flesh and Blood" were No. 1 hits. Throughout 1971, Cash continued to have hits, including the Top Three "Man in Black." Both Cash and Carter became more socially active in the early '70s, campaigning for the civil rights of Native Americans and prisoners, as well as frequently working with Billy Graham.

In the mid-'70s, Cash's presence on the country charts began to decline, but he continued to have a series of minor hits and the occasional chart topper like 1976's "One Piece at a Time," or Top Ten hits like the Waylon Jennings duet "There Ain't No Good Chain Gang" and "(Ghost) Riders in the Sky." *Man in Black*, Johnny Cash's autobiography, was published in 1975. In 1980, Johnny Cash became the youngest inductee to the Country Music Hall of Fame. However, the '80s were a rough time for Cash, as his record sales continued to decline and he ran into trouble with Columbia. Cash, Carl Perkins, and Jerry Lee Lewis teamed up to record *The Survivors* in 1982, which was a mild success. The Highwaymen—a band featuring Cash, Waylon Jennings, Willie Nelson, and Kris Kristofferson—released their first album in 1985, which was also moderately successful. The following year, Cash and Columbia Records ended their relationship and he signed with Mercury Nashville. The new label didn't prove to be a success, as the company and the singer fought over stylistic direction. Furthermore, country radio had begun to favor more contemporary artists, and Cash soon found himself shut out of the charts. Nevertheless, he continued to be a popular concert performer.

The Highwaymen recorded a second album in 1992 and it was more commercially successful than any of Cash's Mercury records. Around that time, his contract with Mercury ended. In 1993, he signed a contract with American Records. His first album for the label, *American Recordings*, was produced by the label's founder, Rick Rubin, and was a stark, acoustic collection of songs. *American Recordings*, while not a blockbuster success, revived his career critically and brought him in touch with a younger, rock-oriented audience. In 1995, the Highwaymen released their third album, *The Road Goes on Forever*. The following year, Johnny Cash released his second album for American Records. —*Stephen Thomas Erlewine*

Now, There Was a Song! / 1960 / Columbia ✦✦✦✦
This is an outstanding album of covers of old country songs, from the familiar (Ernest Tubb, Hank Williams, George Jones) to lesser-known gems. —*Michael McCall*

Blood Sweat & Tears / 1963 / Columbia ✦✦✦
Continuing his early-'60s focus on concept albums, this one pays tribute to the working man. It includes the hit "Busted." —*Michael McCall*

Bitter Tears / 1964 / Columbia ✦✦✦✦
Another concept album, this one is devoted to the trials of the American Indian—a bold move for a country singer in 1964. —*Michael McCall*

★ **At Folsom Prison & San Quentin** / 196_ / Columbia ✦✦✦✦✦
Originally released in two different double-album sets, these albums have been packaged together on CD. There's a certain tension inherent in the concept of playing live to a bunch of convicts, and the tension—as well as Cash's ability to cope with it—is very present. —*Tom Roland*

☆ **Columbia Records 1958-1986** / 1987 / Columbia ✦✦✦✦✦
Columbia Records 1958-1986 is a terrific single-disc sampler of Cash's lengthy career at Columbia Records, featuring a total of 20 songs, including the classic hits "Ring of Fire," "I Still Miss Someone," "Don't Take Your Guns to Town," "Five Feet High and Rising," "Sunday Mornin' Coming Down," and "A Boy Name Sue." If you just need his latter-day hits, it's the perfect compilation. —*Stephen Thomas Erlewine*

★ **The Sun Years** / 1990 / Rhino ✦✦✦✦✦
Rhino's single-disc compilation *The Sun Years* contains 18 highlights from Johnny Cash's early years, including nearly every one of his hits for the label. During his time at Sun, Cash established his sound and these songs—"Cry! Cry! Cry!," "Folsom Prison Blues," "I Walk the Line"—remained the core of his repertoire throughout his entire career. Hit singles like "There You Go," "Guess Things Happen That Way," and "Luther Played the Boogie" round out *The Sun Years* in an exemplary fashion. There might be more comprehensive collections of Cash's Sun recordings than *The Sun Years*, but this disc contains everything you need to know. —*Stephen Thomas Erlewine*

Man In Black: 1954-1958 / Sep. 1990 / Bear Family ✦✦✦✦
The Man In Black: 1954-1958 is a five-disc box set that includes everything Johnny Cash recorded for Sun Records, plus the fruits of his first year with Columbia Records. In addition to all of the classic singles—from "Hey Porter" to "Don't Take Your Guns To Town," they're all here—there is a wealth of unreleased material and alternate takes, including a disc that captures an entire recording session from his early days with Columbia. The problem with the set is its very comprehensiveness—only dedicated fans or historians can listen to this much music, especially with all of the alternate takes mixed in with the official versions. And the disc with the recording session isn't interesting—it's a curiosity that makes for tedious listening. Certainly anyone that is willing to invest in this expensive box will find it rewarding, but only serious listeners should consider purchasing the set. —*Stephen Thomas Erlewine*

Come Along and Ride This Train / 1991 / Bear Family ✦✦✦✦
The four CDs in this set contain 87 tracks originally released on 7 albums from 1960-1977, all about life in the USA. Selections include "The Gettysburg Address," "Casey Jones," "From Sea to Shining Sea," "Busted," and many more. —*AMG*

☆ **The Essential Johnny Cash 1955-1983** / 1992 / Columbia/Legacy ✦✦✦✦✦
A three-CD set, this one traces his career from his Sun beginnings with "Hey Porter" and "Cry! Cry! Cry!" through the close of his Columbia association. It includes the obvious high points along the way ("Folsom Prison Blues," "Ring of Fire," etc.), but also packs in more obscure hits (like "Blistered" and "Singin' in Vietnam Talkin' Blues"), plus material from some of his later albums, and several appropriate gospel tracks. —*Tom Roland*

American Recordings / 1994 / American ✦✦✦✦
A stark, masterful album featuring Cash and his guitar, it captures the essence of his distinctive talent while confirming his stature as one of the most affecting artists of his time. —*Michael McCall*

The Man In Black: 1963-1969 / Feb. 1996 / Bear Family ✦✦✦✦
The Man in Black: 1963-1969 is Bear Family's fourth box set of Johnny Cash recordings and the third in *The Man In Black* series. *1963-1969* picks up where the previous *Man In Black* box left off—in the beginning of the '60s, after Cash established himself as a hitmaker for Columbia. It collects all of the music Cash made for Columbia Records between 1963 and 1969, including outtakes and alternate versions but not the albums that were issued on the *Come Along and Ride This Train* set. Again, this collection is more for collectors and scholars than fans. There is terrific music here, but the strict chronological order—sequenced by the session date, not release date—makes listening to each disc somewhat tiring. —*Stephen Thomas Erlewine*

The Man In Black: 1959-1962 / 1990 / Bear Family ✦✦✦✦
Picking up where the previous set left off, this collection has all of the recordings Johnny Cash made for Columbia between '59 and '62; the only music that was left off are his historical albums, which Bear Family had already released on *Come Along on Ride Train*. Like the other set, it has an abundance of alternate takes and outtakes, plus a disc that captures an actual recording session. Again, it is primarily of interest for historians and dedicated fans willing to take the time to delve deeply into this music—since the songs are presented in chronological order according to their session date, it doesn't make for casual listening. —*Stephen Thomas Erlewine*

Rosanne Cash

b. May 24, 1955, Memphis, TN
Guitar, Vocals / Contemporary Country
Reba McEntire sells more records, but Rosanne Cash, the daughter of Johnny Cash, may be the greatest woman currently working in country. Her brand of art, however, has never been confined to the cut-and-dried traditions of C&W, nor can she be pigeonholed as an "outlaw" upstart. Cash works within the context of country much as Bob Wills did: By bringing her unique perspectives to the genre, she has somehow eclipsed it, changing its patterns to suit her creative needs and tailoring it to encompass the complexities of her vision.
Her first hit, the self-penned "Seven Year Ache," was a crossover smash for several reasons; the sentiments of the song contradicted the

roles enforced on female country artists, and the backbeat had more in common with Bonnie Raitt than Kitty Wells. Although many of her best personality-defining songs have come from outside writers, over the last few years Cash has blossomed into a clever and soul-searching songwriter. 1990's *Interiors*, produced and written entirely by Cash, uncompromisingly picked apart the disintegration of her marriage to Rodney Crowell. It remains a moody, unsettling masterpiece.
Cash followed with *The Wheel* in 1993 and while sales were disappointing, the album received considerable critical acclaim. In 1996, she released *10 Song Demo*.
At her best, Cash sounds like a meeting of Patsy Cline, Joni Mitchell, and Chrissie Hynde: she has a full-bodied vocal style reminiscent of Cline's, she manifests her emotions with the persistence of Mitchell, and she has the confidence and attitude of Hynde. —*John Floyd*

Right or Wrong / 1979 / Columbia ✦✦✦
Cash's impressive debut featured a solid collection of Nashville-meets-California singer-songwriter country-rock, with occasional stylistic nods to folk and light R&B. "No Memories Hangin' 'Round" was a hit duet with Bobby Bare, and "Couldn't Do Nothin' Right" and "Take Me Take Me" also charted. Other highlights include "Man Smart Woman Smarter," "Better Start Turnin' 'Em Down," and the aching ballad "Anybody's Darlin' (Anything but Mine)," one of the finest performances of her career. —*Rick Clark*

★ **Seven Year Ache** / 1981 / Columbia ✦✦✦✦✦
Cash was arguably the most important artist to emerge in country music in the early '80s, and this was her breakthrough album, which introduced a new, assertive, passionate stance to women in country and also helped foster the crossover between folk, rock, and country. Cash's songwriting (the title track and "Blue Moon with a Heartache") was first-rate, and her choices from others, notably Leroy Preston's "My Baby Thinks He's a Train," were equally strong. —*William Ruhlmann*

Somewhere in the Stars / 1982 / Columbia ✦✦✦
A terrific collection, including Rodney Crowell's "Ain't No Money," and Tom T. Hall's "That's How I Got to Memphis." —*William Ruhlmann*

Rhythm & Romance / 1985 / Columbia ✦✦✦
Cash expected criticism for this album, and got it but didn't deserve it. The orange hair and pink fingernails on the cover visually illustrate the musical risks she took in working with Eddie Rabbitt's former producer, David Malloy, and the result is a scorcher. Best cuts: Grammy-winner "I Don't Know Why You Don't Want Me" and "Halfway House." —*Tom Roland*

King's Record Shop / 1988 / Columbia ✦✦✦
After writing most of 1985's *Rhythm & Romance*, Cash returned to largely interpretive work on this powerful collection highlighted by Eliza Gilkyson's feminist anthem "Rosie Strike Back" and her father Johnny Cash's "Tennessee Flat Top Box." —*William Ruhlmann*

Hits 1979-1989 / 1989 / Columbia ✦✦✦
Ten years' worth of hits includes "I Don't Want to Spoil the Party," "Seven Year Ache," "Black and White," and others. —*AMG*

☆ **Interiors** / 1990 / Columbia ✦✦✦✦✦
What makes *Interiors* brilliant isn't that Cash produced herself for the first time nor that she wrote all the songs. It's that *Interiors*—the last album Cash made for Columbia's Nashville division—meticulously chronicles the unraveling of a terribly dysfunctional relationship, namely Cash's marriage to Rodney Crowell. Cash gets at the psychology behind country's cheating and drinking themes—the emotional anesthetic of addictions, the desperate grasping for love in affairs. The arrangements are stripped as bare as Cash's soul, but *Interiors* is country at its core. —*Brian Mansfield*

The Wheel / Jan. 19, 1993 / Columbia ✦✦✦✦
Like the dark, cathartic *Interiors, The Wheel* is an introspective, soul-searching set of confessional songs revolving around love and relationships. While many of the themes and emotions of *Interiors* are repeated on *The Wheel*, Roseanne Cash hasn't repeated herself, either lyrically or musically. Working from the same combination of folk and country that has fueled her songwriting throughout her career, she has created an album of subtle, melodic grace that helps convey the deep feelings of her lyrics. It's an immaculately produced album, but that never detracts from the emotional core of Cash's music. —*Stephen Thomas Erlewine*

Retrospective / Nov. 7, 1995 / Columbia ✦✦✦

10 Song Demo / Apr. 2, 1996 / Capitol ✦✦✦
Despite its title, *10 Song Demo* isn't really a demo tape, but it is what the title suggests—a stripped-down, direct collection of songs (for the record, there are 11 songs, not ten). Conceptually, it is a brilliant way to signal that Rosanne Cash has severed ties with Nashville, as well as beginning her contract with Capitol Records. However, the album doesn't completely work. Essentially, *10 Song Demo* is a statement from Cash that she is no longer strictly a country singer, but an all-around singer-songwriter. Of course, she has always bent the rules of country music, so this isn't a big departure, as far as songwriting goes. Musically, however, the

spare, simple arrangements lack all of the country and pop production flourishes that marked her last two albums. Though it initially sounds fine, there isn't much variation to the music, and her melodies are frequently uncompelling. That can't be said of her lyrics—they are as cutting, emotional, and affecting as they have been, and they are the main reason for listening to *10 Song Demo.* —*Stephen Thomas Erlewine*

Beth Nielsen Chapman

Vocals / Contemporary Country, Singer-Songwriter
A Nashville-based singer-songwriter who has written several No. 1 country hits, her own work leans more toward contemporary adult pop. Her songs are melodic, her themes mostly romantic and obsessed with inner journeys. Comparable to Carole King or the earnest side of Elton John, her range covers insistent pop-rock, intimate ballads, sensual soul, and solemn spirituals, all done with an undercurrent of revelation and intelligence. —*Michael McCall*

Hearing It First / 1980 / Capitol ◆◆◆
● **Beth Nielsen Chapman** / Sep. 25, 1990 / Reprise ◆◆◆◆
Chapman moved to Nashville in 1985, and the influence of the city's focus on songcraft helped her hone her poetic sensibilities into powerful, personal pop tunes. It includes a strong version of "Down on My Knees," a song covered by country singer Trisha Yearwood. —*Michael McCall*

You Hold the Key / 1993 / Reprise ◆◆◆◆
The arrangements are peppier, but the subject matter as intensely internal as on her previous album. —*Michael McCall*

Mark Chesnutt

Vocals / Contemporary Country, New Traditionalist
The son of a country singer, Mark Chesnutt grew up in his father's footsteps. He started singing at Gilley's (the club Urban Cowboy made famous) at 17, and cut independent singles before signing to MCA. His debut album, 1990's *Too Cold at Home*, made him a dark-horse hat act, as he was initially overshadowed by the success of Garth Brooks and Clint Black. On his second album, the humor and personality in his delivery showed through, and Chesnutt made a name for himself with the likes of "Old Flames Have New Names" and "I'll Think of Something." —*Brian Mansfield*

Too Cold at Home / 1990 / MCA ◆◆◆◆
An impressive traditional country debut that often drew on George Jones and Texas swing, *Too Cold at Home* started Chesnutt off strong with the hits "Too Cold at Home," "Brother Jukebox," "Blame It on Texas," and "Your Love Is a Miracle." It also included a version of "Friends in Low Places" that came out at almost exactly the same time Garth Brooks' did. —*Brian Mansfield*

● **Longnecks & Short Stories** / 1992 / MCA ◆◆◆◆
Longnecks heralded the emergence of a Texas voice that contained both the knack for humor ("Old Flames Have New Names," "Bubba Shot the Jukebox"), and the depth for heartache ("I'll Think of Something"). —*Brian Mansfield*

Almost Goodbye / Jun. 22, 1993 / MCA ◆◆◆
Weak material weighs down Chesnutt's third release, though he still sings them like the most romantic Western swinger since George Strait. "Almost Goodbye" is backed by a string arrangement as powerful as the one on "I'll Think of Something," but songs like "Texas Is Bigger" and "My Heart's Too Broke" aren't the attention-grabbers "Old Flames Have New Names" and "Bubba Shot the Jukebox" are. One of Chesnutt's biggest strengths is his casual delivery, but *Almost Goodbye* sounds too easy. "Almost Goodbye" and "It Sure Is Monday" both topped the singles charts. —*Brian Mansfield*

What A Way To Live / 1994 / MCA ◆◆◆
Like its predecessor *Almost Goodbye*, this album is dogged by inconsistent material, but Chesnutt's fine singing manages to save most of the weaker material from being a bore. —*Stephen Thomas Erlewine*

Wings / Oct. 3, 1995 / Decca ◆◆◆◆
Wings is one of Mark Chesnutt's most impressive efforts, showing the singer expanding his sonic template by stepping away from the commercial leanings of his recent material, and leaving a slight pop and rock influence to his straightforward traditional country. What really makes the album rank among his best is the consistent quality of songwriting. Featuring songwriters like Jim Lauderdale and Todd Snider, *Wings* is filled with first-rate material that pushes at the borders of contemporary country while preserving its heritage. Ranging from romantic ballads to Bakersfield-type raveups, the record showcases Chesnutt at his finest. —*Stephen Thomas Erlewine*

Guy Clark

b. Nov. 6, 1941, Rockport, TX
Guitar, Vocals / Singer-Songwriter
Guy Clark doesn't just write songs, he crafts them with the kind of

hands-on care and respect that a master carpenter (a favorite image of his) would have when faced with a stack of rare hardwood. Clark works slowly and with strict attention to detail—he's only recorded eight albums since he was first signed to RCA in the early '70s—but he has produced an impressive collection of timeless gems, leaving very little waste behind. His albums have never met with much commercial success, but the emotional level of his work consistently transcends sales figures and musical genres. He remains the kind of songwriter whom young artists study and seasoned writers (and listeners) admire.

Clark was born in the West Texas town of Monahans, where he was raised mostly by his grandmother (his mother worked and his father was in the Army) who ran the town hotel. One of her residents was an oil-well driller who would later end up the subject of one of Clark's most moving and stunningly beautiful songs, "Desperados Waiting for a Train." Many of Clark's songs, in fact, have centered around his days growing up in West Texas, including "Texas 1947" (from his debut album) and the 1992 song "Boats to Build," which hearkened back to a summer job he once had as a teenager on the Gulf Coast.

The first songs Clark learned were mostly in Spanish. Later, when he moved to Houston and began working the folk-music circuit, he met fellow songwriter Townes Van Zandt (the two still often tour together) and blues singers Lightnin' Hopkins and Mance Lipscomb. It was here that Clark began playing and writing his sturdy brand of folk- and blues-influenced country music. In the late '60s, Clark moved to California, living first in San Francisco (where he met and married his wife Susanna, a painter and songwriter) and then in Los Angeles, where he worked in the Dopera Brothers' dobro factory. Tiring quickly of Southern California (sentiments he expressed in another of his classics, "L.A. Freeway"), he and Susanna packed up and headed for Nashville in 1971, where he picked up work as a writer with publishing companies and, eventually, a recording contract with RCA. Clark's first album, *Old No. 1*, came out in 1975, a few years after Jerry Jeff Walker had turned "L.A. Freeway" into a minor hit. By this time Clark was considered one of the most promising young writers in country music, and while he didn't live in Texas anymore, the state's influence still ran thick in his blood.

Clark recorded one more album for RCA, *Texas Cookin',* in 1976 before switching to Warner Bros. for his next three albums, released between 1978 and 1983. Three of his songs from these albums cracked the Top 100. By the mid-'80s, however, a number of his songs had been made into hits by country stars such as Johnny Cash, David Allen Coe, Ricky Skaggs (who took "Heartbroke" to No. 1), George Strait, Vince Gill, and the Highwaymen. Clark continued to work as a writer but didn't record again until 1988's *Old Friends*, released by Sugar Hill. He then switched labels once more, this time to Asylum, who released his 1992 album *Boats to Build* as part of their acclaimed American Explorer series. His eighth album, *Dublin Blues*, came out in 1995, and among its finely crafted moments is a re-reading of one of his most enduring songs, "Randall Knife," about the death of his father. —*Kurt Wolff*

● **Old #1** / 1975 / Sugar Hill ◆◆◆◆
Every song is a classic. Clark is backed by Chip Young, Steve Gibson, Johnny Gimble, Rodney Crowell, Emmylou Harris, Steve Earle, and others. Start your collection here. —*Chip Renner*

Texas Cookin' / 1976 / Sugar Hill ◆◆◆
The songs here are more Nashville, hitting many emotions. "Texas Cookin'," "Virginia's Reel," and "Broken Hearted" are all great songs. What a way to finish the album, as Clark and Johnny Cash sing "The Last Gunfighter Ballad." —*Chip Renner*

Fool on the Roof / 1978 / Warner Bros. ◆◆◆◆
This very-overlooked album is more country than his first two RCA albums. Just listen to the vocals (with the Whites, Rodney Crowell, Don Everly, Gordon Payne) and the words. You'll find this album grows on you. —*Chip Renner*

The South Coast of Texas / 1981 / Warner Bros. ◆◆◆

Better Days / 1983 / Warner Bros. ◆◆◆

Old Friends / 1988 / Sugar Hill ◆◆◆◆
Clark's finest moment. The production allows Clark to present his songs without any distractions. Sam Bush, Verlon Thompson, Michael Henderson, and Vince Gill blend with Clark perfectly, as do Rosanne Cash and Emmylou Harris. —*Chip Renner*

Boats to Build / 1992 / Elektra/Nonesuch ◆◆◆◆
As unadorned and uncontrived as ever, Clark's masterful songs get to the heart of the matter and stay there. —*Michael McCall*

Craftsmen / 1995 / Philo ◆◆◆

Dublin Blues / Apr. 4, 1995 / Elektra ◆◆◆

Roy Clark (Roy Linwood Clark)

b. Apr. 15, 1933, Meherrin, VA
Banjo, Fiddle, Guitar, Vocals / Traditional Country, Country-Pop
In the '70s Roy Clark symbolized country music in the US and abroad. Between guest-hosting for Johnny Carson on "The Tonight Show" and

performing to packed houses in the Soviet Union on a tour that sold out all 18 concerts, he used his musical talent and his entertaining personality to bring country music into homes across the world. As one of the hosts of TV's "Hee Haw" (Buck Owens was the other), for more than 20 years Clark picked and sang and offered kountry korn to 30 million people weekly. He is first and foremost an entertainer, drawing crowds at venues as different as Las Vegas, Atlantic City, and the Opry. His middle-of-the-road approach has filled a national void, with Clark offering music more country than Kenny Rogers but less country than Waylon Jennings. Among his numerous vocal hits are "Yesterday When I Was Young" and "Thank God and Greyhound." Instrumentally he has won awards, for both guitar and banjo. Multi-talented Clark co-starred on the silver screen with Mel Tillis, in the comedy *Uphill All the Way*. Roy Clark's popularity will continue as long as he wants to stay in the business. Bob Hope refers to Clark as "the consummate entertainer." —*David Vinopal*

● **Greatest Hits** / Sep. 12, 1995 / Varese ✦✦✦✦
By concentrating on his biggest straight country hits and sidestepping many of the novelty numbers that were associated with *Hee-Haw*, the 14-song *Greatest Hits* makes a case for Roy Clark's talents as songwriter and performer, providing a good introduction to his career. —*Stephen Thomas Erlewine*

Patsy Cline (Virginia Patterson Hensley)

b. Sep. 8, 1932, Gore, VA, **d.** Mar. 5, 1963, Camden, TN
Piano, Vocals / Traditional Country, Rockabilly, Nashville Sound/ Countrypolitan
One of the greatest singers in the history of country music, Patsy Cline also helped blaze a trail for female singers to assert themselves as an integral part of the Nashville-dominated country music industry. She was not alone in this regard; Kitty Wells had become a star several years before Cline's big hits in the early '60s. Brenda Lee, who shared Cline's producer, did just as much to create a country-pop crossover during the same era; Skeeter Davis briefly enjoyed similar success. Cline has the most legendary aura of any female country singer, however, perhaps due to an early death that cut her off just after she had entered her prime.

Cline began recording in the mid-'50s, and although she recorded quite a bit of material between 1955 and 1960 (17 singles in all), only one of them was a hit. That song, "Walkin' After Midnight," was both a classic and a Top 20 pop smash. Those who are accustomed to Cline's famous early-'60s hits are in for a bit of a shock when surveying her 1950s sessions (which have been reissued on several Rhino compilations). At times she sang flat-out rockabilly; she also tried some churchy tear-weepers. She couldn't follow up "Walkin' After Midnight," however, in part because of an exploitive deal that limited her to songs from one publishing company.

Circumstances were not wholly to blame for Cline's commercial failures. She would have never made it as a rockabilly singer, lacking the conviction of Wanda Jackson or the spunk of Brenda Lee. In fact, in comparison with her best work, she sounds rather stiff and ill-at-ease on most of her early singles. Things took a radical turn for the better on all fronts in 1960, when her initial contract expired. With the help of producer Owen Bradley (who had worked on her sessions all along), Cline began selecting material that was both more suitable and of a higher quality than her previous outings.

"I Fall to Pieces," cut at the very first session where Cline was at liberty to record what she wanted, was the turning point in her career. Reaching No. 1 in the country charts and No. 12 pop, it was the first of several country-pop crossovers she was to enjoy over the next couple of years. More important, it set a prototype for commercial Nashville country at its best. Owen Bradley crafted lush orchestral arrangements, with weeping strings and backup vocals by the Jordanaires, that owed more to pop (in the best sense) than country.

The country elements were provided by the cream of Nashville's session musicians, including guitarist Hank Garland, pianist Floyd Cramer, and drummer Buddy Harman. Patsy's voice sounded richer, more confident, and more mature, with ageless wise and vulnerable qualities that have enabled her records to maintain their appeal with subsequent generations. When k.d. lang recorded her 1988 album *Shadowland* with Owen Bradley, it was this phase of Cline's career that she was specifically attempting to emulate.

It's arguable that too much has been made of Cline's crossover appeal to the pop market. Brenda Lee, whose records were graced with similar Bradley productions, was actually more successful in this area (although her records were likely targeted towards a younger audience). Cline's appeal was undeniably more adult, but she was always more successful with country listeners. Her final four Top Ten country singles, in fact, didn't make the pop Top 40.

Despite a severe auto accident in 1961, Cline remained hot through 1961 and 1962, with "Crazy" and "She's Got You" both becoming big country and pop hits. Much of her achingly romantic material was supplied by fresh talent like Hank Cochran, Harlan Howard, and Willie Nelson (who penned "Crazy"). Although her commercial momentum had

faded slightly, she was still at the top of her game when she died in a plane crash in March of 1963, at the age of 30. She was only a big star for a couple of years, but her influence was and remains huge. While the standards of professionalism on her recordings have been emulated ever since, they've rarely been complemented by as much palpable, at times heartbreaking emotion in the performances. For those who could do without some of the more elaborate arrangements of her later years, many of her relatively unadorned appearances on radio broadcasts have been thankfully preserved and issued. —*Richie Unterberger*

★ **Patsy Cline's Greatest Hits** / 1967 / Decca ✦✦✦✦✦
This is the standard collection of Patsy Cline's most successful singles, containing among its 12 tracks seven of her eight Top Ten country hits, 1957-1963. Since its release, the album has sold four million copies, and at this writing, it is enjoying its 66th consecutive week at No. 1 in *Billboard* magazine's Top Country Catalog Albums chart, a chart that has been in existence for 66 weeks. —*William Ruhlmann*

Live at the Opry / 1988 / MCA ✦✦✦
As everyone who listened to the Ryman opry knows, even a good singer can sound pretty bad live over the radio. Cline sounds simply great, with no studio effects and a sometimes pedestrian backup. —*George Bedard*

Live, Vol. 2 / 1989 / MCA ✦✦✦✦
A sequel to *Live at the Opry*, it's not called *Live at the Opry Vol. 2* because it wasn't taken from Opry broadcasts, but from radio shows produced for the US Navy and Armed Forces. The twelve performances date from 1956 to 1962, and are of special interest in that they include five songs that she never recorded in the studio for commercial release, including numbers by Roger Miller, Webb Pierce, and Sonny James. Cline's in good form throughout, the fidelity is very good, and the arrangements are on the whole considerably sparer than her studio recordings were wont to employ. The straightahead reading of "Strange," a top-notch 1962 Mel Tillis composition that went on the B-side of "She's Got You," is a particular highlight. A good album that will appeal to most country fans, not just Cline collectors. —*Richie Unterberger*

☆ **The Patsy Cline Collection** / 1991 / MCA ✦✦✦✦✦
With four hours and 25 minutes of music (104 cuts), this is pretty much the definitive Cline collection. It's got all the hits, 16 previously unreleased tracks (including some live radio transcriptions), even some silliness, like "Tra Le La La Triangle." But in only ten years of recording, Cline became the most influential female vocalist in country music, so she's worth it. —*Brian Mansfield*

David Allan Coe

b. Sep. 6, 1939, Akron, OH
Guitar, Vocals / Traditional Country, Outlaw Country
A lifelong renegade, singer-songwriter David Allan Coe is truly one of the most colorful and unpredictable characters in country music history. He was one of the pioneering artists of the outlaw country movement of the '70s. Although he didn't have many big hits—only three of his singles hit the Top Ten over the course of his career—he was one of the biggest cult figures in country music in the late '70s and early '80s.

Born in Akron, OH, Coe first got into trouble with the law at age nine. As a result, he was sent to reform school. For the next 20 years, Coe never spent more than a handful of months outside of a correctional facility—he spent much of his twenties in the Ohio State Penitentiary. Released from prison in 1967, the wild-haired, earring-wearing, heavily tattooed Coe went straight for Nashville where, at first, he lived in a hearse that he parked in front of the old Ryman Auditorium, the home of the Grand Ole Opry. Although he didn't conform to Nashville's professional standards, he soon gained the attention of the independent label, Plantation Records. Plantation released Coe's debut album *Penitentiary Blues* in 1968 and it was followed by volume two within a year of its release. All of the songs on the albums were based on his prison experiences.

Following the release of the *Penitentiary Blues* albums, Coe toured with Grand Funk Railroad, and continued to draw as much from rock's traditions as he did from country. Soon, he began performing in a rhinestone suit given to him by Mel Tillis, as well as a Lone Ranger mask. Because of his outlandish appearance, he began calling himself the "Masked Rhinestone Cowboy." Coe's concerts became notorious for their unpredictability—frequently he would roar up on stage astride his enormous Harley, and swearing at the audience. He cultivated a large cult following with this act, but he couldn't break into the mainstream. However, other artists could with Coe's songs—in 1972, Billie Jo Spears had a minor hit with his "Souvenirs & California Mem'rys." In 1973, Tanya Tucker had a No. 1 hit with Coe's "Would You Lay with Me (in a Field of Stone)," and the song would win a BMI award later that year. After Tucker's hit, David Allan Coe suddenly became one of Nashville's hottest songwriters and some of the biggest country artists—including Willie Nelson, George Jones, and Tammy Wynette—recorded his tunes. All of the attention on Coe's songs led to his own record contract with Columbia Records.

Coe's first two singles for Columbia didn't come close to the country Top 40 but his 1975 cover of Steve Goodman's "You Never Even Called Me by My Name" cracked the Top Ten. Although he had a string of moderate hits after "You Never Even Called Me By My Name," he rarely cracked the country Top 40. During his 13-year association with Columbia, he released 26 albums including the double-album set *For the Record... The First Ten Years* (1984), *Son of the South* (1986) featuring Willie, Waylon, Jessi Colter and other "outlaws," and his highly regarded *Matter of Life... .and Death* (1987). In 1977, Johnny Paycheck took Coe's "Take This Job and Shove It" to No. 1 on the charts and the song became the songwriter's best-known work.

Although Coe had a successful career, it was one plagued with many setbacks. The conservative Nashville music industry frequently snubbed him and he had tax problems with the IRS. At one time, they seized his Key West home, and he went to live in a Tennessee cave until he got back on his feet.

Towards the end of the '80s, Coe remarried and began to settle down. Throughout the '90s, he was a popular concert attraction in America and Europe. In addition to his musical career, Coe also acted in a few movies including *The Last Days of Frank and Jesse James*. He has also published a novel, *Psychopath*, and an autobiography. Though presenting a slightly less radical image, the original outlaw is alive and well inside Coe, who continues to record and perform songs such as "Lead Me Not into Temptation (I Can Get There by Myself)." —*Sandra Brennan*

Once upon a Rhyme / 1974 / Columbia ✦✦✦
Whether doing one of his own songs or breathing new life into a tune like "Fraulein," few can touch Coe. This album is full of good songs and strong performances and is well worth looking for. —*Jim Worbois*

Longhaired Redneck / 1976 / Columbia ✦✦✦
This is '70s outlaw country at its most virulent. The tattoos and biker bravado thinly conceal Coe's sentimentality. —*Mark A. Humphrey*

Greatest Hits / 1978 / Columbia ✦✦✦✦
This is all you need to know about this ex-con turned country con-man/songwriter. He was one of country's more intriguing egos from the '70s. —*Mark A. Humphrey*

● **For the Record: The First 10 Years** / 1985 / Columbia ✦✦✦✦
This is an overview of Coe's Columbia sides. —*Mark A. Humphrey*

Super Hits, Vol. 2 / Mar. 19, 1996 / Columbia ✦✦✦

Mark Collie

Guitar, Vocals / New Traditionalist
The music of singer-songwriter Mark Collie is a lively blend of straightahead rock 'n' roll and traditional country. He was born in Waynesboro, TN, one of six children, and grew up listening to country music. He was most influenced by the fiery piano playing of Jerry Lee Lewis, the guitar playing of Carl Perkins, and the songwriting skills of Willie Nelson and Kris Kristofferson. While young, Collie learned to play guitar and piano and joined a band when he was 12. In high school, he worked as a parttime DJ at the local radio station. Following his high school graduation, he joined several bands and toured the Southwest. He later stayed with his brother in Hawaii, playing in different bands for over a year and a half. In 1982, Collie, encouraged by his wife, moved to Nashville to become a full-time songwriter at a publishing house. When no one hired him, he began singing his own songs to live audiences and picked up a following when he began doing monthly performances at the Douglas Corner Cafe. This led to a showcase in 1989, which in turn led MCA/Nashville Executive Vice President Tony Brown to sign him. Collie's first MCA single, "Something with a Ring to It," came out and made it to the Top 60 in 1990. His next single, "Looks Aren't Everything," made it to the Top 40; both songs appeared on his first album, *Harden County Line* (1990), which was produced by Brown and Doug Johnson. Collie wrote or co-wrote every song on the album. Collie then hit the road and played with Reba McEntire, Conway Twitty, and Charlie Daniels. He made it to the Top 20 for the first time in 1991 and then released his second album *Born and Raised in Black & White*, which produced two Top 40 hits, including "She's Never Coming Back." The following year, the album produced one additional minor hit and the Top Five single "Even the Man in the Moon Is Crying." His third album, *Mark Collie*, was released in 1993 and continued to fare well with such popular tunes as "Born to Love You" and "Shame, Shame, Shame, Shame." *Unleashed*, Collie's fourth album, appeared in 1994. After its release, he signed with Warner Records, who released *Tennessee Plates* in 1995. —*Sandra Brennan*

Born & Raised in Black & White / 1985 / MCA ✦✦✦
The first half of Collie's second album contained some smartly written songs, including "She's Never Coming Back" and "Calloused Hands," but some of the first album's edge had been smoothed off. —*Brian Mansfield*

Hardin County Line / 1990 / MCA ✦✦✦✦
This honky tonk rebel's debut evokes the heart of '50s country, with

detailed and compassionate songwriting, wildcat vocals, and guitar by James Burton. One song, "Looks Aren't Everything," hit the Top 40, while two others, "Hardin County Line" and "Something with a Ring to It," didn't fare quite so well. —*John Floyd & Brian Mansfield*

● **Mark Collie** / 1993 / MCA ✦✦✦✦
At once a move to the mainstream and a return to Collie's West Tennessee rockabilly roots, the album worked fairly well. "Even the Man in the Moon Is Crying" and "Born To Love You" were Collie's first Top Ten hits, and "Shame Shame Shame Shame" rocked as hard as anything he'd done. —*Brian Mansfield*

Unleashed / 1994 / MCA ✦✦✦
In the same vein as *Mark Collie*, this album is more aggressive. "It Is No Secret" followed in Collie's tradition of mid-tempo romantic singles, while he rocks it up elsewhere. —*Brian Mansfield*

Tennessee Plates / Jul. 18, 1995 / Warner Bros. ✦✦✦
Tennessee Plates delivers the edgy rockabilly punch that fans have come to expect from Mark Collie, but not in quite as a consistent fashion as some of his earlier records. Although it has its share of love songs, the album does continue the stripped-down, direct approach of *Unleashed*—it just doesn't have the same amount of high-quality songs. That said, the best songs on the record are very good indeed, and make the album a fun, entertaining listen. —*Thom Owens*

Jessi Colter (Miriam Johnson Eddy)

b. May 25, 1947, Phoenix, AZ
Piano, Vocals / Outlaw Country
Born Mariam Johnson, this talented singer-songwriter was a church pianist by age 11. At 16 she married guitarist Duane Eddy; an alliance that led to her making some of her first recordings. During this period she also began to make a name for herself as a songwriter (as Miriam Eddy) as her compositions began being covered by such artists as Don Gibson, Eddy Arnold, and Anita Carter. Her stage name, Jessi Colter, was inspired by a great, great uncle who'd ridden with the James Gang. In 1969, she and Waylon Jennings were married and within a year, they began recording duets together. In 1974 she landed a contract with Capitol which resulted in several hits including "I'm Not Lisa." —*Jim Worbois*

● **Jessi** / 1976 / Capitol ✦✦✦✦
After the success of "I'm Not Lisa" it's surprising that this record wasn't more popular than it was. Many of these songs are better than her big hit. —*Jim Worbois*

Diamond in the Rough / 1976 / Capitol ✦✦✦✦

Leather and Lace / 1981 / RCA ✦✦

Confederate Railroad

Contemporary Country
Georgia-based Confederate Railroad is the contemporary cousin to such outlaw Southern-rockers as the Allman Brothers, Lynyrd Skynard, and Hank Williams, Jr. These rockers with their scruffy biker clothes and hard-edged good-time music got their start as a club band in the late '80s. They were founded by lead vocalist/guitarist Danny Shirley, who had been playing the club circuit with his Danny Shirley band since the early '80s. Shirley signed to an independent label in 1984 and made it to the lower reaches of the charts over the next two years with his best-known song being "Love and Let Love." Early in their career, Confederate Railroad, comprised of drummer Mark Dufresne, bassist Wayne Secrest, keyboardist Chris McDaniel, lead guitarist Michael Lamb and steel guitarist Gates Nichols, frequently played at Miss Kitty's in Marietta, GA. In 1991, they signed to the Nashville Division of Atlantic Records and released a self-titled album the following year. It produced several hits including "Jesus and Mama" (Top Five) and "Queen Memphis" (Top Three), but it was with the B-side of their "When You Leave That Way You Can Never Go Back," that they really gained notoriety. Both the song and the resulting video for "Trashy Women" got considerable media exposure and it made it to the Top Ten on the country charts. In 1994, they released *Notorious* and within less than two months, it went gold. —*Sandra Brennan*

Confederate Railroad / 1992 / Atlantic ✦✦✦
Featured are "Queen of Memphis," "Time Off for Bad Behavior," and "She Took It like a Man," among other hits. —*AMG*

● **Notorious** / 1994 / Atlantic ✦✦✦✦
Despite its unkempt, biker image, Confederate Railroad is a country band in the tradition of Alabama. Rooted in traditional country sounds and values, both bands also have the breadth to appeal to those outside the genre (in CR's case, Southern-rockers). The group rocks hardest on the funny stuff ("Elvis & Andy," "Move over Madonna") but gets serious with some impressive ballads ("Daddy Never Was the Cadillac Kind," "Summer in Dixie," "Three Verses"). —*Brian Mansfield*

When and Where / 1995 / Atlantic ✦✦✦✦
By their third album, Confederate Railroad had established their fusion of Lynyrd Skynyrd and Alabama and knew what worked and what

didn't. In other words, *When and Where* offers nothing new from the band, but it is far from a bad record. The group has gotten predictable, but they continue to shine, whether it's on the rowdy rockers or the surprisingly smooth, radio-ready ballads. They do have a problem coming up with a batch of consistent material, but the album is as enjoyable as its predecessor and nearly as solid. —*Thom Owens*

● **Greatest Hits** / Jun. 18, 1996 / Atlantic ✦✦✦✦
Greatest Hits compiles Confederate Railroad's biggest hits, including all of their Top Ten singles, as well as several singles that never made it quite as far up the charts. As an added bonus, the group has added two new songs—which aren't particularly noteworthy—to lure fans that already own all the band's albums to the new collection. Even with the addition of the new songs, *Greatest Hits* remains the province of casual fans—it serves up all the hits in an engaging, concise manner. —*Stephen Thomas Erlewine*

John Conlee

b. Aug. 11, 1946, Versailles, KY
Guitar, Vocals / Country
Born and raised on a 200-acre farm in Versailles, KY, Conlee has continued to till the soil on his own farm in suburban Nashville, even since "hitting it big." Music was—and still is—a hobby as much as a career to him; he didn't even sign his first recording contract until age 30. Instead, he pursued work as a mortician (he still maintains his license in Kentucky) and worked as a disc jockey at a number of radio stations, including Nashville's WLAC, where he made numerous contacts on Music Row. One of his tapes attracted ABC Records, but Conlee's gruff, down-to-earth delivery wasn't an immediate success. It took a couple of years before "Rose Colored Glasses"—one of the few songs he's written himself—exploded in 1978. A self-avowed homebody, Conlee was never particularly enamored with touring, and devoted most of his career time to the recording process instead, particularly his song selection. Noted for an astute sense of quality material (he was ably assisted through the bulk of his career by record producer and former Jim Reeves sideman Bud Logan), he made albums that rarely, if ever, contained "fluff." Even when they're not commercial, Conlee's songs are always interesting. —*Tom Roland*

With Love / 1981 / MCA ✦✦✦✦
Nine of the ten cuts in this package came from Tree Publishing, meaning that Conlee and producer Bud Logan limited themselves unnecessarily. But Conlee is extremely convincing on "Only Oklahoma Away" and "What's Forever For," not to mention the mysterious "Miss Emily's Picture." —*Tom Roland*

John Conlee's Greatest Hits / 1983 / MCA ✦✦✦✦
With virtually every detail of the real world, the songs cover (in)fidelity ("She Can't Say That Anymore," "Baby, You're Something"), relationship issues ("Friday Night Blues"), and personal finance ("Busted," "Common Man"). The asylum piece, "I Don't Remember Loving You," is eternally vivid. —*Tom Roland*

● **20 Greatest Hits** / 1987 / MCA ✦✦✦✦
20 Greatest Hits combines material from Conlee's *Greatest Hits* and *Greatest Hits, Vol. 2*, leaving off one track from each record ("Baby, You're Something" and "Lifetime Guarantee," respectively). As such, it offers a perfect retrospective of his career. —*Stephen Thomas Erlewine*

Earl Thomas Conley

b. Oct. 17, 1941, Portsmouth, OH
Vocals / Country
Early in his career, Earl Thomas Conley's music picked up the label "thinking man's country." An accurate description—Conley looks into the heart and soul of his characters, finding the motivations for their actions and beliefs. In the process, the astute listener can find fragments of him/ herself in nearly any Conley creation. Born into poverty in Portsmouth, OH, Conley struggled with the limits of his social class. He aspired to be a painter or actor but found that his aspirations for music lingered after the other interests died down. Influenced by everything from Hank Williams to The Eagles, Conley delved into the details of writing, trying to learn the craft by following the rules and regulations of the Music Row songwriting community. Eventually, torn by the limits of the "law," he found his own niche by breaking many of those same rules. His public self-analysis—in both his songs and his interviews—has proven inspirational to some, bothersome to others, but Conley has evolved stylistically, even though the thinking man label continues to follow him. He's admittedly chased a more commercial sound, with a certain degree of success, but the run for the dollars also put him into a financial bind. He spent part of the late '80s and early '90s overworking himself to pay off his debts. Although he has been a hitmaker for more than a decade, his contributions to country have often gone almost unnoticed. —*Tom Roland*

Blue Pearl / 1980 / Sunbird ✦✦✦
This is the album that earned Conley the thinking-man label. "Middle-

Age Madness" and "Blue and Green" stand out as classically written profiles of people in pain. "Silent Treatment," "Fire and Smoke," and "You Don't Have to Go Too Far" possess a captivating, slick sheen that belies their raw approach. —*Tom Roland*

Don't Make It Easy for Me / 1983 / RCA ✦✦✦✦
Conley speaks of "programming" himself to write, and in setting the tone for this album—as well as the follow-up, *Treadin' Water*—he programmed "radio records" into his consciousness. The result: a driving, rock-inflected package that yielded four No. 1 singles—the first time an album did that in any format. The title track and "Your Love's on the Line" are particularly listenable, but there's not a bad cut on it. —*Tom Roland*

● **The Best of Earl Thomas Conley, Vol. 1** / 1988 / RCA ✦✦✦✦
As much as any of his '80s peers, Conley might have benefited from moving his sound towards harder country. The hits he did score ("Fire & Smoke," and "Somewhere Between Right and Wrong," are among the ones on this album) projected a voice ideally suited to a more Whitley-esque setting. —*Dan Cooper*

Greatest Hits, Vol. 2 / 1990 / RCA ✦✦✦✦
Conley is one of the hottest recording artists of the '80s. While this album isn't quite as strong as the first hits package, it shouldn't be ignored. Also features two new tracks. —*Jim Worbois*

● **Essential** / Apr. 1996 / RCA ✦✦✦✦
Featuring the great majority of hits plus an intriguing batch of rarities, *Essential* offers the best retrospective of Conley's career. —*Stephen Thomas Erlewine*

Spade Cooley (Donell C. Cooley)

b. Feb. 22, 1910, Grand, OK , **d.** 1969
Fiddle, Cello
A one-time king of Western swing, Spade turned professional at age 8 as a fiddle player at square dances. By the '30s he had moved to Hollywood where he picked up "extra" work (which eventually led to actual roles) at several different studios. Through out the '40s he led a very successful band (sometimes with more than 20 members) which resulted in his leasing the Santa Monica Ballroom as a homebase for the band. His career was cut short when he was jailed for killing his wife. Shortly after his release from prison, he suffered a heart attack and died. —*Jim Worbois*

● **Spadella: The Essential** / 1994 / Columbia/Legacy ✦✦✦✦
Spadella: The Essential Spade Cooley collects 20 highlights from Cooley's stint as one of the most popular Western swing bandleaders in America. All of the selections on the album were recorded between 1945 and 1946, when Cooley and his group scored six straight Top Ten singles, all of which are included here ("You Can't Break My Heart" is in an alternate version). This is when the group was at its peak and vocalist Tex Williams was always in stellar form. Though it doesn't cover his entire career, *Spadella* remains the one essential Cooley compilation. —*Stephen Thomas Erlewine*

Stoney Cooper & Wilma Lee

Traditional Country
Stoney (b. 1918) and Wilma Lee Cooper (b. 1921), a husband-and-wife Opry act, were famed for their powerful stage presence and their authentic material that fell between mountain folk music and bluegrass. Since fiddler Stoney's death, Wilma has continued on the Opry. When she sings a song, it stays sung. —*David Vinopal*

● **Classic Early Recordings** / County ✦✦✦✦
Originally recorded between 1949 and 1953, the wife-and-husband duo let it fly with passionate zeal on these old-time mountain and gospel songs. Wilma Lee could shake the coal out of the hills with her raw and full-throated voice, and she didn't bother with nuance. —*Michael McCall*

Billy "Crash" Craddock (Mr. Country Rock)

b. Jun. 16, 1939, Greensboro, NC
Guitar, Vocals / Country
People often associate the "Crash" nickname with auto racing, but Craddock actually got it as a halfback in high school, crashing into linemen who were twice his size. Growing up in Greensboro, NC, he pantomimed Grand Ole Opry shows in the family's barn with a broomstick as a microphone, alternately pretending he was Hank Williams, Faron Young, or Carl Smith. But when he signed a recording contract in the late '50s, Columbia tried to mold him as a teen idol, much like Elvis Presley or Fabian. It didn't work in the US, but "Crash" did pick up a trio of hits in Australia. Fifteen years later, he finally got his chance in country music when record producer Ron Chancey signed him to his Cartwheel label. With a knack for doing re-makes of pop hits like "Knock Three Times" and "Ruby Baby"—and for adding a certain energy to the country idiom—Craddock picked up the nickname "Mr. Country-rock." —*Tom Roland*

● **Crash's Smashes** / Feb. 20, 1996 / Razor & Tie ✦✦✦✦
Crash's Smashes offers the best retrospective of Billy "Crash" Croad-dock's career, featuring a good cross-section of his '50s rockabilly material and his '70s country-rock hits. —*Stephen Thomas Erlewine*

Floyd Cramer

b. Oct. 27, 1933, Shreveport, LA
Piano / Instrumental Pop, Nashville Sound/Countrypolitan
Floyd Cramer is the best known piano player in country music. Chet Atkins suggested that Floyd become a session player, which he did in 1955; for the next ten years he must have recorded on one-quarter of all releases during the peak of the "Nashville Sound" (middle-of-the-road country-flavored music). Floyd's highly distinctive piano playing results from his "slip-note" style (one note forward, one note back) that made an immediate hit with the fans. He wrote his famous "Last Date," an instrumental hit, in 1960. —*David Vinopal*

★ **The Best of Floyd Cramer** / 1970 / RCA ✦✦✦✦✦
The Best of Floyd Cramer is a cheap collection and its 12 tracks don't provide a definitive retrospective, but it has enough hits—including "Last Date" and "San Antonio Rose"— to satisfy many fans. —*Stephen Thomas Erlewine*

Collector's Series / May 23, 1995 / RCA ✦✦✦✦
Collector's Seres is a reasonably thorough overview of Floyd Cramer's career, offering nearly every one of his hits in its original version. —*Stephen Thomas Erlewine*

Rodney Crowell

b. Aug. 7, 1950, Houston, TX
Guitar, Vocals / Country-Rock, Contemporary Country
The consummate singer-songwriter, Crowell "grew up in Houston off of Wayside Drive" (as he says in the lyrics of Waylon Jennings' "I Ain't Living Long Like This"), latching onto everything from Hank Williams to Chuck Berry and Elvis Presley. He played as a kid in his dad's local band, and packed up with friend Donovan Cowart (now a successful engineer) to move to Nashville, lured by a "promoter's" promise of an opening slot on a major concert tour with a name entertainer. Once he got there, he realized he'd been "taken," but Crowell decided to stay, and worked his way up from lounge singer to membership in Emmylou Harris's Hot Band. From there, he earned a reputation for his evaluation of material and for his arranging "smarts," and picked up plenty of action as a songwriter and producer. His production credits include projects with now-ex-wife Rosanne Cash, Guy Clark, Bobby Bare, and Sissy Spacek, while his songwriting includes: "Leaving Louisiana in the Broad Daylight," "Somewhere Tonight," "Til I Gain Control Again," and "Shame on the Moon." Despite critical acclaim for his recording efforts, Crowell was unable to harness commercial success for a decade, but that problem ended with 1988's *Diamonds & Dirt* album. —*Tom Roland*

Ain't Living Long Like This / 1978 / Warner Bros. ✦✦✦
Before Rodney Crowell began to have hits of his own, his albums were often raided by other artists for hits. This album features Crowell compositions that became hits for the Oak Ridge Boys, the Nitty Gritty Dirt Band, and Waylon Jennings. It's worth checking out to hear how they were originally done. —*Jim Worbois*

But What Will the Neighbors Think / 1980 / Warner Bros. ✦✦

Rodney Crowell / 1981 / Warner Bros. ✦✦✦
Crowell plays down his performance on this album. Yes, he's a bit cool toward the material vocally on occasion, but the overall effect is raw, energetic, and natural, in the best garage-band tradition. A good mix of club rock 'n' roll and country-rock, with, incidentally, his own renditions of "Till I Gain Control Again" and "Shame on the Moon." —*Tom Roland*

Street Language / 1986 / Columbia ✦✦

Diamonds & Dirt / 1988 / Columbia ✦✦✦✦
Record-producer Tony Brown convinced Crowell to do this one quickly and not second-guess himself; the advice paid off. Leaning hard on the country shuffle, Crowell broke through with this package—live, honest, and unassuming. It yielded five hits, including the Grammy-winning "After All This Time," but the best cut might be the tantalizing "I Know You're Married." —*Tom Roland*

Keys to the Highway / 1989 / Columbia ✦✦✦✦
This wide-ranging set combines soul, blues, rock, and the country shuffle. Recorded shortly after the May 1989 death of Crowell's father, it's surprisingly upbeat and hopeful in its approach. Still, the two brooding songs most closely linked to James Crowell's passing, "Many a Long and Lonesome Highway" and "Things I Wish I'd Said", stand out most. —*Tom Roland*

● **The Rodney Crowell Collection** / 1989 / Warner Bros. ✦✦✦✦
The best of Crowell's uneven but occasionally brilliant early recordings is condensed into one neat little package. It includes "Shame on the

Moon," which Bob Seger rightly turned into a pop hit. This isn't *Diamonds & Dirt*, but it's a good start. —*Brian Mansfield*

Life Is Messy / May 12, 1992 / Columbia ✦✦✦
Featured are "It's Not for Me to Judge," "I Hardly Know How to Be Myself," "Lovin' All Night," and more. —*AMG*

● **Greatest Hits** / 1993 / Columbia ✦✦✦✦
The music on *Greatest Hits* is taken from an era when Rodney Crowell actually had hits, including the No. 1s "I Couldn't Leave You If I Tried," "She's Crazy for Leavin'," and "After All This Time." Those songs and several more are collected on *Greatest Hits*, making it a fine introduction to the singer-songwriter. —*Stephen Thomas Erlewine*

Let the Picture Paint Itself / 1994 / MCA ✦✦✦
So much of Crowell's best work has been co-produced by MCA executive Tony Brown, it seemed inevitable he would wind up at MCA himself. This, his first release for his new label, emphasizes Crowell, the thoughtful songwriter, over Crowell the neo-honky tonk bandleader. It's a fair trade, but requires repeat listening to fully appreciate. —*Dan Cooper*

Jewel of The South / 1995 / MCA ✦✦✦
Crowell tries to stretch out a bit too much on *Jewel of the South*, but it remains a fine album, nonetheless. Featuring guest performances by the Mavericks' Raul Malo, Bela Fleck, Vince Gill, Kim Richey, and Billy Joe Walker Jr. among others, the album tries to do too many things, but it does enough of them well enough to make it an entertaining listen. —*Thom Owens*

Billy Ray Cyrus

b. Aug. 25, 1961, Flatwoods, KY
Guitar, Vocals / Contemporary Country
Enamored of baseball, Billy Ray Cyrus intended to become another Johnny Bench as he grew up in Flatlands, KY. While attending Georgetown College on a baseball scholarship, he bought a guitar, and decided immediately that athletics wasn't the proper direction for his life. Instead, he formed a band called Sly Dog with his brother and gave himself a ten-month deadline for finding a place to play. One week prior to that cut-off date, the group went to work as the house band for a club in Ironton, OH, where they remained for two years. When a 1984 fire destroyed the bar— and Cyrus' equipment—he moved to Los Angeles to pursue his career. Eventually, he decided to return to Kentucky and he commuted regularly from there to Nashville in search of a record deal. Grand Ole Opry star Del Reeves got Mercury Records to take a look, and division head Harold Shedd signed him in the summer of 1990. When his first album came out in mid-1992, Cyrus—with his good looks, sculpted body and the infectious "Achy, Breaky Heart"—became an instant groundbreaking sensation. "Achy, Breaky Heart" made his debut album, *Some Gave All*, a blockbuster success; it sold over six million albums by the end of 1993.
    Cyrus wasn't able to match the sales of his debut, but 1993's *It Won't Be the Last* sold over two million and his 1994 record, *Storm in the Heartland*, went platinum. *Trail of Tears*, Cyrus' fourth album, was released in the summer of 1996. —*Tom Roland*

● **Some Gave All** / 1992 / Mercury ✦✦✦✦
Some Gave All became the first debut album by a country artist to enter the pop charts at No. 1 (it hit No. 1 on the country charts as well). The album's sales were fueled by the breakout single "Achy, Breaky Heart," which offered Southern-fried Rolling Stones rhythms and a goofy chorus with a hook so big it demanded a reaction. Not one to eschew the obvious, Cyrus pumped his songs full of as much rock 'n' roll as the market would bear, so songs like "Could've Been Me" and "Never Thought I'd Fall in Love with You" appealed to young fans who had just discovered the possibilities (both musical and sexual) of country music. —*Brian Mansfield*

It Won't Be the Last / Jun. 22, 1993 / Mercury ✦✦

Storm in the Heartland / 1994 / Mercury ✦✦✦
Although it didn't win him any new fans, *Storm in the Heartland* delivered what Billy Ray Cyrus' fans wanted to hear—good-humored rockers and powerful ballads. In fact, it was a stronger, more assured effort than *It Won't Be the Last*, offering a catchier batch of songs, even though it doesn't have the goofy charm of *Some Gave All*. —*Stephen Thomas Erlewine*

Trail Of Tears / 1996 / Mercury ✦✦✦
Trail of Tears is the most personal and most successful album Billy Ray Cyrus has recorded to date. Cyrus' elaborates his pop-oriented country with some rootsy production flourishes—the album sounds edgier and grittier than any of his previous records. Furthermore, Cyrus delivers both his originals and the covers with conviction, far more conviction than could have been believed possible from his first two albums. In fact, *Trail of Tears* suggests that he may be able to carve out a successful career for himself, after all. —*Thom Owens*

Charlie Daniels Band

Fiddle, Guitar, Violin, Vocals / Traditional Country, Country-Rock
A talented and showy fiddler, Charlie Daniels and his band fuse hardcore country with a hard-edged Southern-rock boogie and blues. The group—which has had a rotating cast of musicians over the years—has always been known for their instrumental dexterity, but they were also notorious for their down-home, good-old boy attitude; in the early '80s they became a virtual symbol of conservative country values. Daniels and his band experienced the height of their popularity at the end of the '70s and early '80s, but they remained a popular concert attraction well into the '90s.

Charlie Daniels was born and raised in North Carolina, playing fiddle and guitar in several bands during his teenage years. At the age of 21, he decided become a professional musician, assembling an instrumental rock 'n' roll combo called the Jaguars. The group landed a recording session for Epic Records in 1959 with Bob Johnson, who would later become Columbia Records' leading folk and country producer. The record didn't receive much attention, but the band continued to play and Daniels continued to write songs. One of his originals, "It Hurts Me," was recorded by Elvis Presley in 1963. By the late '60s, it had become clear that the Jaguars weren't going to hit the big time, so Johnston recommended to Daniels that he move to Nashville to become a session musician. Daniels followed the advice and he became one of the most popular fiddlers in Nashville. He played on several Bob Dylan albums—*Nashville Skyline, Self Portrait, New Morning,* and *Dylan* as well as Ringo Starr's 1970 record *Beaucoups of Blues.* He also became part of Leonard Cohen's touring band in the late '60s and produced the Youngbloods' *Elephant Memory* album around the same time.

Daniels cut an album for Capitol Records in the early '70s which was ignored. In 1972, he formed the Charlie Daniels Band, using the Southern-rock of the Allman Brothers as a blueprint. The band comprised Daniels (lead guitar, vocals, fiddle), lead guitarist Don Murray, bassist Charlie Hayward, drummer Don Murray, and keyboardist Joe DiGregorio. The formula worked and in 1973 they had a minor hit with "Uneasy Rider," which was released on Kama Sutra Records. In 1974, they released *Fire on the Mountain,* which became a gold record within months of its release, thanks to the Top 40 country hit "Texas"; the album would eventually go platinum. *Saddle Tramp,* released in 1976, was nearly as successful, going gold.

Throughout the mid-'70s, the Charlie Daniels Band pursued a Southern-rock direction. They were moderately successful, but they never had a breakthrough hit either on the pop or country charts. By the late '70s, Daniels sensed that the audience for Southern-rock was evaporating, so he refashioned the band as a more straightforward country band. The change paid off in 1979 when the single "The Devil Went Down to Georgia" became a No. 1 hit, crossing over into the pop charts, where it hit No. 3. The song was named the Country Music Association's Single of the Year and helped its accompanying album, *Million Mile Reflections,* become a multi-platinum success. Daniels wasn't able to follow "The Devil Went Down to Georgia" with another blockbuster single on the country charts, ironically, but he had several rock crossover successes in the years following the success of *Million Mile Reflections—Full Moon* (1980) which went platinum and 1982's *Windows* went gold.

Although he continued to sell respectably throughout the '80s, he didn't have a big hit until 1989's *Simple Man,* which went gold. In the '90s, his records failed to chart well, although he remained a popular concert draw. —*Stephen Thomas Erlewine*

☆ **Fire on the Mountain** / 1975 / Epic ♦♦♦♦♦
Fire on the Mountain is the Charlie Daniels Band's finest moment. Daniels finds the perfect middle ground between Southern-rock boogie and hillbilly honky tonk, creating a sound that rocked hard but still had down-home roots. Although he would delve deeper into country, he would never make a stronger, more enjoyable album. —*Thom Owens*

Saddle Tramp / 1976 / Epic ♦♦♦

High Lonesome / 1976 / Epic ♦♦♦

Million Mile Reflections / 1979 / Epic ♦♦♦
Despite the inclusion of the hit "Devil Went Down to Georgia," this is, at best, a mediocre record. Certainly not for everyone, Daniels' fans will still enjoy it. —*Jim Worbois*

● **A Decade of Hits** / 1983 / Epic ♦♦♦♦
An all-too-brief summing-up. —*Dan Heilman*

Renegade / 1991 / Epic ♦♦♦♦
This strong collection of Daniels songs rocks harder than usual, despite showing his soft side on "Little Folks" and "Fathers and Sons." Daniels practically gives a cultural history of the violin on "Talk to Me Fiddle," the album's most unusual song, and continues to extol the virtues of country living ("The Twang Factor") and patriotism ("Let Freedom Ring"). —*Brian Mansfield*

● **All-Time Greatest Hits** / 1993 / Epic ♦♦♦♦
This traces his career from early highpoints—"Long Haired Country Boy," "The South's Gonna Do It," "The Devil Went Down to Georgia"—to the desperate attempts to revive his late career with self-referential updates ("Uneasy Rider '88") and jingoistic, red-baiting blather ("Simple Man") that was out of date before he released it. —*Michael McCall*

Jimmie Davis (James Houston Davis)

b. Sep. 11, 1902, Quitman, LA
Guitar, Vocals / Traditional Country
The Jimmie Davis story, in which a White man from Louisiana cuts some of the raunchiest, double-entendre blues of the prewar country era; then, armed with a Masters degree and royalties from the original 1940 version of "You Are My Sunshine," enjoys a second career as the pious, segregationist, twice-elected governor of his home state. Along the way, he also enjoys massive (and well-deserved) hits with "Nobody's Darling But Mine" (1934), and Floyd Tillman's brilliant "It Makes No Difference Now" (1938). —*Dan Cooper*

Barnyard Stomp / 1988 / Bear Family ♦♦♦

● **Country Music Hall of Fame** / 1991 / MCA ♦♦♦♦
1934-53 sides by this hillbilly crooner with a penchant for blues include "You Are My Sunshine." —*Mark A. Humphrey*

Link Davis

Saxophone, Vocals
Multi-instrumentalist Link Davis recorded Western swing, Cajun, and rockabilly over the course of his career. His most notable singles, cut for the OKeh label in the early fifties, were aimed at both the hillbilly and Cajun markets. Few, if any, artists bisected those genres as neatly as Davis. The Cajun influence is most audible in Link's vocals, which have an easygoing slur that often seems on the verge of bursting into chuckles. He recorded sides for the Starday label later in the fifties that were more rock 'n' roll-influenced, and earned a couple footnotes in rock 'n' roll history by playing saxophone on The Big Bopper's "Chantilly Lace" and Johnny Preston's "Running Bear." —*Richie Unterberger*

Big Mamou / 1989 / Edsel ♦♦♦
16 tracks recorded for OKeh from 1952-54. A standout among these waltzing numbers is "Falling For You," a riveting call-and-response boogie with a great steel guitar solo. —*Richie Unterberger*

Skeeter Davis (Mary Frances Penick)

b. Dec. 30, 1931, Dry Ridge, KY
Vocals / Traditional Country, Country-Rock
Skeeter Davis has never gotten a lot of critical attention, but in the '50s and '60s, she recorded some of the most accessible crossover country music, occasionally skirting rock 'n' roll. Born Mary Penick, Davis took her last name after forming a duo with Betty Jack Davis, the Davis Sisters. Their 1953 single "I Forgot More than You'll Ever Know" was a big country hit; its B-side, the remarkable "Rock-A-Bye Boogie," foreshadowed rockabilly. That same year, however, the duo's career was cut short by a tragic car accident in which Betty Jack Davis was killed, and Skeeter was severely injured. Skeeter did attempt to revive the Davis Sisters with Betty Jack's sister, but was soon working as a solo artist.

In the early '60s, Davis followed the heels of Brenda Lee and Patsy Cline to become one of the first big-selling female country crossover acts, although her pop success was pretty short-lived. The weepy ballad "The End of the World," was a massive hit, reaching No. 2 in 1963. "I Can't Stay Mad at You," a Top Ten hit the same year, was downright rock 'n' roll; penned by Goffin and King, it sounded like (and was) an authentic Brill Building girl group-styled classic. Goffin and King also wrote another successful girl group knockoff for her, "Let Me Get Close to You," although such efforts were the exception rather than the rule. Usually she sang sentimental, country-oriented tunes with enough pop hooks to catch the ears of a wider audience, such as "I Will."

Davis concentrated on the country market after the early '60s, although she never seemed too comfortable limiting herself to the Nashville crowd. She recorded a Buddy Holly tribute album in 1967, when Holly wasn't a hot ticket with either the country or the rock audience. But she certainly didn't reject country conventions either: she performed on the Grand Ole Opry, and recorded duets with Bobby Bare, Porter Wagoner, and George Hamilton IV. In the '80s, she had a mild comeback with the rock crowd after recording an album with NRBQ; she also married NRBQ's bass player, Joey Spampinato. —*Richie Unterberger*

The End of the World / 1963 / RCA ♦♦♦
Recorded at the peak of Davis' brief stardom, this emphasizes the weepy country-pop that gave her a No. 2 pop hit with the title track. Nothing here measures up to that wonderful smash, but it's tasteful enough period Nashville country. Producers Anita Kerr and Chet Atkins ensure that the LP measures up to state-of-the-art country-pop production by double-tracking Skeeter's vocals against a background of strings and

lazy barroom piano runs. They let her loose on Little Eva's "Keep Your Hands Off My Baby," which is replete with primitive fuzzy guitar. Though it may sound enticing, the result is actually kind of lousy and ill-fitting. —*Richie Unterberger*

The Best of Skeeter Davis / 1965 / RCA ✦✦✦✦
Skeeter fused country, pop, and even occasional girl-group sounds during her commercial peak in the early '60s, which found her at her most fetching and tuneful. This has twelve of her most successful recordings of the era, including the huge ballad "The End Of The World," which hit No. 2 on the pop charts in 1963, and Goffin/King's irresistible girl-group composition "I Can't Stay Mad At You," which reached the Top Ten the same year. —*Richie Unterberger*

My Heart's in the Country / 1966 / RCA ✦✦✦
The cover art, with Skeeter fondling farm animals in front of the barn and extolling the rural life in the liner notes, makes a pretty determined effort at presenting Davis in as much of a pure country light as possible. The actual music, by and large, follows suit. Produced by Felton Jarvis in Nashville, it's plainer and more traditional in mood than her work with Chet Atkins and Anita Kerr. The strings are banished and the guitar picking and fiddles are at the forefront, although the vocals are still double-tracked. It's kind of an average effort, without any particular flaws or standout material. Includes compositions by Dolly Parton and Loretta Lynn, as well as Skeeter's rendition of the traditional "Goin' Down the Road (Feelin' Bad)." —*Richie Unterberger*

Skeeter Davis Sings Buddy Holly / 1967 / RCA Victor ✦✦✦
Twelve Holly covers, produced by Felton Jarvis in Nashville and featuring Waylon Jennings on guitar, at a time when neither Davis nor Holly were exactly in the forefront of pop's collective consciousness. A modest accomplishment, this LP is nevertheless fairly worthwhile, with a much more upbeat sound than Davis' early-'60s recordings. The arrangements are pretty straightforward and close to the originals, with solid country-rock backing and occasional light, tasteful strings. —*Richie Unterberger*

Best Of Skeeter Davis Vol. 2 / 1973 / RCA ✦✦✦
A ridiculously uneven collection, veering between solid country uptempo numbers to pathetic weepers (which could be either effective or embarrassing), a fine girl-group pastiche, a stupid courtroom divorce song, and a couple lousy covers of early-'70s pop hits ("One Tin Soldier"?!). By far the best cut is her girl-group take on Goffin-King's "Let Me Get Close To You," which is in the same class as her similar 1963 Top Ten pop hit "I Can't Stay Mad At You" (also written by Goffin-King). "Sunglasses" is an out-of-character pop number by John Loudermilk, and a couple of the straight country tunes are decent, but this is a very scattershot compilation; surely Skeeter recorded enough decent material to warrant a better selection. —*Richie Unterberger*

She Sings, They Play / 1985 / Rounder ✦✦✦
Skeeter Davis, a prolific country singer since the '50s, teamed up with the versatile NRBQ for this delightful collaboration. Nashville with a kick. —*Jeff Tamarkin*

● **Essential Skeeter Davis** / 1996 / RCA ✦✦✦✦
Featuring 20 tracks, *The Essential Skeeter Davis* collects all of her big hits from both the country and pop charts, making it the one definitive compilation. —*Stephen Thomas Erlewine*

Billy Dean

b. Apr. 1, 1962
Guitar, Vocals / Contemporary Country
Billy Dean received a basketball scholarship to attend East Central Junior College in Decatur, MS, where he majored in physical education, but instead of wearing a whistle around his neck, he opted for a guitar strap. Inspired by Merle Haggard, Marty Robbins, and Dean Martin, he played the club circuit along the Gulf Coast in Florida and used national talent contests as a vehicle for his music. He made the finals of the Wrangler Country *Star Search* in 1982, then won as a Male Vocalist champ on Ed McMahon's *Star Search* program in 1988. Even before the release of his debut album, *Young Man*, he'd already gone on tour as an opening act for Mel Tillis, Gary Morris, and Ronnie Milsap. He's contributed to commercials for Valvoline, McDonald's, and Chevrolet, and had an acting role in the brief Elvis series on ABC-TV in 1990.

His good looks are undeniable, but Dean has the talent to match, as proven when he won the Academy of Country Music's Song of the Year award for the enormously sensitive "Somewhere in My Broken Heart," co-written with Richard Leigh ("Don't It Make My Brown Eyes Blue," "Come from the Heart"). —*Tom Roland*

Young Man / 1990 / Liberty ✦✦✦✦
Nashville launched so many new acts from 1989-1992 that many who deserved a shot went overlooked. Thanks in part to his own songwriting skills, and to signing with SBK Records, which had just one country act to push, he got a good listen and was able to capitalize with a strong debut. His vocals aren't unique, but he sings with strength and convic-

tion, regardless of the style. You can't go wrong with "Somewhere in My Broken Heart." —*Tom Roland*

Billy Dean / 1991 / Liberty ✦✦✦✦
Billy Dean's second album follows the same pattern that made his first so popular: a strong emphasis on the ballads on which his supple baritone thrives. The rollicking "Hammer Down" flies in the face of everything else, but even there the message remains the same: obvious but effective. —*Brian Mansfield*

Fire in the Dark / 1993 / Liberty ✦✦✦
Like *Billy Dean* before it, *Fire in the Dark* doesn't stray from the pattern Dean established on *Young Man*, which might not necessarily be a bad thing. However, there is the problem of diminishing returns—each time he goes back to the well, he's coming back with a lesser number of first-rate songs. There are highlights on *Fire in the Dark*, but nothing on the album represents a progress from his first two albums. —*Thom Owens*

Men'll be Boys / 1994 / Capitol ✦✦

● **Greatest Hits** / Mar. 8, 1994 / Liberty ✦✦✦✦
As the title implies, *Greatest Hits* collects Billy Dean's biggest hit singles, which usually happen to be the best parts of his albums. Consequently, *Greatest Hits* is Dean's most consistent and enjoyable album. —*Thom Owens*

It's What I Do / Apr. 1996 / Capitol ✦✦

Jimmy Dean

b. Aug. 10, 1928, Plainview, TX
Guitar, Piano, Accordion, Vocals / Traditional Country, Country-Pop
To the general public, singer-songwriter Jimmy Dean is best-known for his sausages and processed meats. However, he had a string of country hits in the early '60s. Most of his material consisted of narrative songs that were half-spoken half-sung as can be heard in his most famous number "Big Bad John," his story of a courageous ex-con turned miner.

Born in Seth Ward, TX, Dean spent his early years in dire poverty as his mother was barely able to make a living at the barbershop she ran. He joined the Merchant Marines in his late teens and two years later entered the Air Force. Dean founded his first band, the Tennessee Haymakers, while stationed at Bolling Air Force Base located near Washington, DC. He and the Haymakers played on base and in local clubs. Following his discharge, Dean remained in the area and founded the Texas Wildcats. Dean didn't get his first real break until 1952 when he became managed by promoter Connie B. Gay, who arranged for him to tour US military bases in the Caribbean. Later that year, he made his debut single, "Bumming Around," for 4 Star Records. It took a year for the song to peak at No. 5 on the country charts. Later Gay got Dean national exposure by putting him on the nationally syndicated Washington-based *Town and Country Jamboree*.

Dean became popular and eventually CBS gave him his own *Jimmy Dean Show*. Unfortunately, it was on at 7:00 AM and fizzled. Dean signed to Columbia Records in 1957 and though he released ten singles, he didn't have a hit until 1961 when he released "Big Bad John," the first song he'd ever written. The song topped the country charts, then the pop charts and even made it to No. 2 in Great Britain. His follow-up, "Dear Ivan," came out in 1962 and it was a more moderate crossover success. Like the first it was a narrative, as was his next single, which also made it to the charts. Later that year, yet another story-song, "PT109," the story of JFK's famous boat, provided a timely hit. In 1963, Dean launched a new incarnation of his short-lived TV show on ABC. It aired during the days through 1966 and was very successful. In 1964, he tried a nighttime version as well, but it wasn't as popular. Both shows folded in 1966. In the meantime, he had three more hits, including a cover of Hank Williams' "Mind Your Own Business."

Dean continued having hits of varying levels through the early '70s. Things stalled out for a while, but then in 1976, he suddenly had a gold record when his narrative song "I.O.U." became a Top Ten country hit. Beginning in the late '70s, Dean turned his concentration to his meat business, eventually making the company a multi-million dollar empire. —*Sandra Brennan*

● **American Originals** / 1989 / Columbia ✦✦✦✦
American Originals collects ten of Jimmy Dean's biggest hits from Columbia Records, featuring everything from "Big Bad John" to "The First Thing Ev'ry Morning (And the Last Thing Ev'ry Night)." It only covers five years—between 1961 and 1965—but it offers the best introduction to his sound. —*Stephen Thomas Erlewine*

The Delmore Brothers

Old-Time, Traditional Country, Honky Tonk
The Delmore Brothers are not nearly as well-known as such early country giants as the Carter Family, Jimmie Rodgers, Bob Wills, and Hank Williams. The reasons for this, upon close inspection of their work, are not readily apparent. They were one of the greatest early country harmonizers, drawing from both gospel and Appalachian folk. They were

skilled songwriters, penning literally hundreds of songs, many of which have proven to be durable. Most importantly, they were among the few early traditional country acts to change with the times, and pioneer some of those changes. Their recordings from the latter half of the '40s married traditional country to boogie beats and bluesy riffs. In this respect they laid a foundation for rockabilly and early rock 'n' roll, and rate among the most important White progenitors of those forms.

The Delmores were born into poverty in Elkmont, AL, as the sons of tenant farmers. Alton (b. Dec. 25, 1908) would write most of the duo's original material, although his younger brother Rabon (b. Dec. 3, 1916) was also a competent writer. Performing on guitar and vocals from early ages, they were playing as a pair by the time Rabon was ten years old. In the early '30s, they were confident enough to enter professional music, auditioning for Columbia in 1931 and successfully auditioning for Nashville radio station WSM the following year.

Throughout the '30s, the Delmore Brothers recorded often, as well as performing on several radio stations. They probably gained their earliest fame, however, from their long-running stint with the Grand Ole Opry between 1932 and 1938. The music emphasized their beautiful soft harmonies, accomplished guitar picking, and strong original compositions. Unusual for that time (or any other), the Delmores would switch high and low harmony parts from song to song (or even within the same song), although Alton would usually sing lead. Whether performing their own songs, traditional ones, or gospel, they brought a strong bluesy feeling to both their music and their vocals. It's that element, perhaps, that enables the Delmores, more than many other acts of the time, to speak to listeners of subsequent generations. Not to be underestimated either are their down-to-earth lyrical concerns, which address commonplace struggles and lost love with grace and redeeming, good-natured humor, rarely resorting to cornball tears.

In 1944, the Delmores signed with King, inaugurating an era which found them delving into and innovating more modern forms of country. Although their first sides for the label stuck to a traditional mold, in 1946 they expanded from their acoustic two-piece arrangements into full-band backup, with bass, mandolin, steel guitar, fiddle, harmonica, and additional guitars. Some of those additional guitars were supplied by Merle Travis, who credited Alton Delmore as a key influence.

In retrospect, however, the most important backup musician on these sides was Wayne Raney, who played a "choke" style of harmonica that was heavily influenced by the blues. The Delmores were also leaning increasingly towards uptempo material that reflected the upsurge in Western swing and boogie-woogie. By the end of 1947, they were also using electric guitar and drums. Raney (who also sang) in effect acted as a third member of the Delmores in the late '40s and early '50s, when they plunged full-tilt into hillbilly boogie.

These are the most widely available and, in some ways, best Delmore Brothers sides. They were also the most successful, and in the late '40s the brothers reached their commercial peak, releasing a series of hard-driving boogies with thumping backbeats and bluesy structures. Arguably they milked the cow dry, recording "Hillbilly Boogie," "Steamboat Bill Boogie," "Barnyard Boogie," "Mobile Boogie," "Freight Train Boogie," and even "Pan American Boogie."

These were usually exciting performances, though, featuring extended guitar solos that clearly looked forward to the rock era. Listen, for instance, to the lengthy guitar breaks of "Beale Street Boogies" (unreleased at the time)—very few, if any, White or Black artists were riffing so extensively in 1947. And of course "Beale Street" itself was a tribute to the most famous musical street in Memphis, the city that did so much to cross-fertilize Black and White roots music into what became rock 'n' roll.

The Delmores didn't stick entirely to boogies during the King era, also releasing some slower bluesy material. One of these, the original "Blues Stay Away from Me," became their biggest hit, and indeed the most famous Delmore Brothers song of all, often covered by subsequent country and pop artists. Interestingly, the Delmores continued to record gospel on the side, as part of the Brown's Ferry Four, a quartet which also included (at various points) Grandpa Jones, Merle Travis, and Red Foley.

As influential as the Delmores' King sides may have been on the future of American pop, the Delmores themselves would not be able to capitalize on that future. By the early '50s, their commercial success was fading. After the death of his young daughter, Alton drank heavily; worse, Rabon died of lung cancer on December 4, 1952. Alton (like longtime accompanist Wayne Raney) did record some material as a solo act, in both the gospel and rockabilly fields. Alton was way too old to begin a new career as a rockabilly singer, though, and he didn't record much for the last decade of his life. He wrote the hard-to-find autobiography *Truth Is Stranger than Fiction* (published posthumously in 1977 by CMF) before dying on June 9, 1964. By that time the Delmore Brothers' work had already proven extremely influential, particularly on the harmonies of fellow sibling acts like the Louvin Brothers and the Everly Brothers. They left behind an extraordinary lengthy and consistent body of recorded work—virtually none of their sides are lousy, at least the ones which

have been reissued. Much of the Delmores' early material, unfortunately, can be hard to locate, although many of the King sides have recently been reissued on CD. —*Richie Unterberger*

Weary Lonesome Blues / 1983 / Old Homestead ✦✦✦✦
Unfortunately, there's no documentation on this 18-song set, but it's a safe guess that the tracks date from the 1930s and early 1940s. It's another strong and varied set of blues, ballads, and spirituals, duplicating virtually nothing from the other Delmore Brothers reissues that have been compiled. —*Richie Unterberger*

Singing My Troubles Away / 1984 / Old Homestead ✦✦✦
The Delmores recorded over two hundred sides, many of which have been reissued by Old Homestead. The quality is so consistently high and the material so similar in focus, that there's really little to differentiate them; if you like their sound, you'll like any given album. This one focuses mostly on their early days in the '30s, reaching back as far as 1933 (a couple of previously unissued cuts in a much more boogie-oriented style from 1946 and 1947 are also included). Perhaps more traditional in focus than some of their other compilations, it includes a fair number of blues-derived tunes. The harmonies and guitar playing are consistently fine. —*Richie Unterberger*

When They Let the Hammer Fall / 1984 / Bear Family ✦✦✦✦
Contains 18 of the "boogie" sides this great country duo cut (with harmonica player Wayne Raney) between 1945 and 1952, though it inexplicably fails to include their biggest hit from this time, "Blues Stay Away From Me" (later recorded by Johnny Burnette and Gene Vincent). This is the bluesiest and most raucous material cut by the harmonizing siblings. These tunes sound about as close to rock 'n' roll as any other music recorded by white musicians prior to the '50s, and still makes fine party music today, with its thumping shuffle beats, bluesy solos, and loose abandon. The great "Beale Street Boogie," cut in 1947 (and unissued at the time), is one of the dozens of songs which could make a strong case for being the first rock 'n' roll record. There's a classic opening bluesy call-and-response riff, a long electric guitar solo duel, and appropriate homage to Memphis' famed Beale Street, certainly one of the locales most responsible for brewing together the basic ingredients of rock 'n' roll—"the Beale Street Boogie is eight beats to the bar," they sing in unison, just in case you don't get the point. Compared to their early recordings, the Delmores seem less pious and devout on these sessions and more concerned with celebration than lamentation. —*Richie Unterberger*

Lonesome Yodel Blues / 1985 / Old Homestead ✦✦✦✦
Eighteen of their early sides, recorded between 1933 and 1940, focusing on the more traditional elements of their repertoire. As the title implies, the brothers do often actually yodel throughout the proceedings, although in a more restrained fashioned than many of their peers. Remastered nicely from original copies of these rare singles, though some unavoidable surface noise is evident. —*Richie Unterberger*

Early Sacred Songs / 1985 / Old Homestead ✦✦✦✦
Fourteen of their more spiritually-inclined tracks, mostly cut between 1935 and 1940. Those who favor secular material over gospel or traditional spirituals shouldn't be wary of this release because of its lyrical content. If you enjoy early country harmonizing, or any of the other material the Delmores cut in their early days, you'll like this as well. Aside from the nominally different lyrical concerns (presented here with humility and without preaching), the basic strengths of the pair remain intact: peerless close harmonizing, fine acoustic guitar playing, and strong songs that can be enjoyed regardless of what your faith (or lack thereof) may be. —*Richie Unterberger*

Sand Mountain Blues / 1986 / County ✦✦✦
The Delmores' recordings for King in the mid-'40s found them shifting away from traditional sounds into more energetic boogies that foreshadowed—however faintly—the blend of R&B and country that would give birth to rock 'n' roll. This has 14 sides from 1944-49, some of which feature such stellar sidemen as guitarist Merle Travis, mandolinist Jethro Burns, and harmonica player Wayne Raney. —*Richie Unterberger*

★ **Freight Train Boogie** / 1993 / Ace ✦✦✦✦✦
It's kind of a toss-up as to whether this or the German *When They Let the Hammer Down* is the best compilation of the Delmores' finest work from the late '40s and early '50s. *When They Let the Hammer Down* is more raucous and uptempo; the 20-track *Freight Train Boogie*, though, has more variety. *Freight Train Boogie* is much easier to locate in the US than *When They Let the Hammer Down*. In addition, there's a fair amount of duplication between the anthologies, though each includes several noteworthy songs not on the other. In any case, you won't be disappointed by *Freight Train Boogie*, whether it's your first exposure to the Delmores or not. Featuring King material from 1946-1951, it has plenty of high-spirited country boogies, balanced by more traditionally folk-oriented material ("Sand Mountain Blues," "Weary Day") and bluesy, slower numbers, including their biggest hit (and one of their best), "Blues Stay Away From Me." These sides were not only some of the finest country

music of the era, but important building blocks of rockabilly and early rock 'n' roll. —*Richie Unterberger*

Brown's Ferry Blues / County ◆◆◆
The Delmores recorded a great wealth of material in the '30s and early '40s, encompassing both country and sacred songs; many of these sides have been reissued on the County label. All of them are good. *Brown's Ferry Blues* may be recommended as an introductory volume because of its range of material (ranging from 1933 to 1941), much of which is bluesy in nature. —*Richie Unterberger*

Desert Rose Band

Country-Rock
The Desert Rose Band came to be in 1985. One of the founders is Chris Hillman, a former member of the Byrds and the Flying Burrito Brothers. Hillman sang lead vocals, played guitar and mandolin and functioned as the group's primary songwriter. The original line-up included banjoist/ guitarist Herb Pedersen, guitarist John Jorgenson, pedal steel guitarist Jay Dee Maness, bassist Bill Bryson, and drummer Steve Duncan. Nearly all of the members were professional studio musicians before joining the Desert Rose Band. In 1986, the Desert Rose Band signed to MCA/Curb and released a cover of Johnny and Jack's hit "Ashes of Love." The song hit the Top 30 the following year, as did their self-titled debut album. *The Desert Rose Band* produced three Top Ten singles, including the No. 1 "He's Back and I'm Blue," and was nominated for a Grammy. In 1988, the group released their second album, *Running*, and by the end of the year were named "Touring Band of the Year" by the ACM. They received this honor three more times. Among their subsequent hits were the No. 2 hit "Summer Wind" and the chart topper "I Still Believe in You." The band's 1989 album *Pages of Life* spawned three more major hits including the Top Ten "Story of Love," which would prove to be their last major hit.

In the early '90s, the Desert Rose Band had a string of minor hits. In 1992, the group's lineup underwent a few changes in 1992 when Duncan was replaced by Tim Grogan, Maness was replaced by Tom Brumley, and Jeff Ross replaced Jorgenson. The new lineup of the Desert Rose Band recorded three more albums, *True Love* (1992), *Traditional* and *Life Goes On* (both 1993). The Desert Rose Band broke up in 1994. —*Sandra Brennan*

The Desert Rose Band [Curb] / 1987 / Curb ◆◆◆
For those concerned that California country might have disappeared, the mid-'80s emergence of the Desert Rose Band, Southern Pacific, and Dwight Yoakam put those fears to rest. While S-Pac leaned toward country-rock, and Yoakam hits hard on the honky tonk sound, TDRB offers just a tinge of bluegrass, lots of energy, and intriguing harmonies. —*Tom Roland*

Running / 1988 / Curb ◆◆◆

● **A Dozen Roses: Greatest Hits** / 1991 / Capitol ◆◆◆◆
A showcase for Hillman's pop-country vocals and the considerable chops of bandmembers such as Herb Pedersen. Together they made some of the best country singles of the late '80s, all collected here. —*William Ruhlmann*

Diamond Rio

Progressive Bluegrass, Contemporary Country
A group that began playing bluegrass at Opryland USA as the Tennessee River Boys, Diamond Rio became one of the most sudden success stories of modern country music. Diamond Rio's initial release, "Meet in the Middle," topped the charts (the first debut single by a group to do so) in 1991; the band followed with more hits and an Academy of Country Music Group of the Year award. The band's bluegrass pedigree (bassist Dana Williams is a nephew of the Osborne Brothers; other members have played for Vassar Clements and J.D. Crowe) helped establish the image of a new country band with traditional ties. The picking's hot, thanks especially to guitarist Jimmy Olander, and the sextet's tight harmonies complement Marty Roe's smooth tenor lead. —*Brian Mansfield*

● **Diamond Rio** / 1991 / Arista ◆◆◆◆
One of the most successful debut albums in country music, *Diamond Rio* sparked plenty of hits—"Meet in the Middle," "Mama Don't Forget to Pray for Me," "Nowhere Bound," "Norma Jean Riley"—by combining bluegrass harmonies, old-fashioned country virtues, and just enough rock to keep things moving. —*Brian Mansfield*

Close to the Edge / 1992 / Arista ◆◆◆
On *Close to the Edge*, Diamond Rio took the cue from their debut's best songs and created an entire album cut from the same cloth. Diamond Rio's strongest material emphasizes the virtues of God, family, and honest living—traditional stuff, no doubt influenced by the members' bluegrass background. But while most folks who'd claim divine intervention in their relationship sound sappy at best, Marty Roe comes off earnest and convincing. Unfortunately, amid hits like "In a Week or Two" and "Oh Me, Oh My, Sweet Baby," *Close to the Edge* reveals such weaknesses

as a penchant for bad puns ("This Romeo ain't got Julie Yet"—ouch!). —*Brian Mansfield*

Love a Little Stronger / 1994 / Arista ◆◆◆
Spurred by the relatively lackluster performance of *Close to the Edge* (it barely went gold compared to the debut's platinum), Diamond Rio explored the musical possibilities of its talents rather than digging for easy commercial success. The instrumentalists, particularly Jimmy Olander and mandolinist Gene Johnson, assume larger roles on songs like "Love a Little Stronger" and the instrumental "Appalachian Dream," but they rarely show off. The band members even tap into an acoustic jazz-rock mode for "Kentucky Mine," one of the best songs they've ever recorded. —*Brian Mansfield*

IV / Feb. 27, 1996 / Arista ◆◆◆◆

Little Jimmy Dickens

b. Dec. 19, 1925, Bold, WV
Guitar, Vocals / Traditional Country
Little Jimmy Dickens is the master of the country novelty song, as well as a renowned ballad singer. He also known for his diminutive stature—he's less than five feet tall—and his affection for flamboyant, rhinestone-studded outfits and country humor. Although he never had a consistent presence on the charts, he managed to have hits in every decade between the '40s and the '70s, and he became one of the Grand Ole Opry's most popular performers.

Dickens was the 13th child of a West Virginian farmer. During his childhood, he fell in love with music and had a dream of performing on the Grand Ole Opry. He began performing professionally while he was a student at the University of West Virginia in the late '30s, singing on a local radio station. Dickens left school shortly after he received his regular radio job. He began travelling around the country, singing on radio shows in Indiana, Ohio, and Michigan under the name Jimmy the Kid. Roy Acuff heard Dickens sing on a radio show in Saginaw, MI, and invited him to sing on the Grand Ole Opry.

In 1949, Dickens—who was now using the name Little Jimmy Dickens—became a permanent member of the Grand Ole Opry. That year, he also signed a record contract with Columbia Records, releasing his first single, "Take An Old Cold Tater and Wait," in the spring of 1949. The song became a Top Ten hit and launched a string of hit novelty, ballad, and honky tonk singles that lasted for a year, which included "Country Boy," "A-Sleeping At the Foot of the Bed," "Hillbilly Fever," and "My Heart's Bouquet." Early in the '50s, he formed a band called the Country Boys, which featured a steel guitar, two lead guitars and drums. With their spirited, traditional country approach and vague rockabilly inflections, the band didn't sound like their Nashville contemporaries. Perhaps that's why Dickens only had one hit between 1950 and 1962—1954's "Out Behind the Barn."

Dickens bounced back to the Top Ten with the ballad "The Violet and the Rose" in 1962. Three years later, he had his biggest hit, "May the Bird of Paradise Fly Up Your Nose." The single topped the country charts and crossed over to No. 15 on the pop charts. Although his next single, "When the Ship Hit the Sand," was moderately successful, Dickens wasn't able to replicate his earlier success. In 1968, he stopped recording for Columbia, signing with Decca Records, where he had three minor hits in the late '60s and early '70s. In 1971, he moved to United Artists, which resulted in two more small hits, but by that time he had begun to concentrate on performing as his main creative outlet. Dickens continued to tour and perform at the Grand Ole Opry into the '90s, becoming one of the most beloved characters in country music. —*Stephen Thomas Erlewine*

● **I'm Little But I'm Loud: The Little Jimmy Dickens Collection** / May 1996 / Razor & Tie ◆◆◆◆
This is a thorough retrospective of Dickens' prime years, running from the 1949 Top Ten hit "Take and Old Cold 'Tater (And Wait)" to the 1967 Top 40 hit "Country Music Lover." In between those two songs are no less than 20 tracks, including all of his Top Ten hits—"Country Boy," "My Heart's Bouquet," "A-Sleeping At the Foot of the Bed," "Hillbilly Fever," "Out Behind the Barn," "The Violet and A Rose," and the No. 1 "May the Bird of Paradise Fly Up Your Nose." —*Stephen Thomas Erlewine*

Joe Diffie

b. 1958
Vocals / Progressive Country, Contemporary Country, New Traditionalist
Joe Diffie is among the new generation of artists who blend traditional country sounds with '90s sensibilities. Born to a musical family in Tulsa, OK, Diffie was a member of his high school gospel group, Genesis II, and a member of the local rock group Blitz. While young, he also belonged to the gospel group Higher Purpose and the bluegrass band the Special Edition. After college, Diffie worked in the Texas oil fields and in a foundry, as the Special Edition began to gain an audience and appeared in several festivals. He then began playing country music with his aunt Dawn

Anita and his sister Monica. Soon, one of Diffie's early songs, "Love on the Rocks," was recorded by Hank Thompson. With the help of pal Cecil Petty, Diffie moved to Nashville and began working for Gibson Guitars while continuing to write songs. Holly Dunn recorded one of his collaborations, "There Goes My Heart Again," in 1989. Bob Montgomery, who had been wanting to sign Diffie to Epic for some time, finally did so a year later.

Diffie's debut single, "Home," climbed to No. 1 in 1990; that year he also debuted at the Grand Ole Opry. This was followed by three Top Five hits, all of which he co-wrote. His 1990 debut album *A Thousand Winding Roads* was produced by Bob Montgomery and Johnny Slate. Diffie's second album, *Regular Joe*, contained several hits, including the No. 5 "Is It Cold in Here." In 1993, he released his third album, *Honky Tonk Attitude*. *Third Rock from the Sun* appeared in 1994 and *Life's So Funny* was released the following year. — *Sandra Brennan*

A Thousand Winding Roads / 1990 / Epic ♦♦♦♦
This likeable new country voice from Oklahoma praises home and hearth. — *Mark A. Humphrey*

● **Regular Joe** / 1992 / Epic ♦♦♦♦
Diffie's second album has all the clichés of country music, and all the good stuff too. If "Ain't That Bad Enough" is a run-of-the-mill song, Diffie rescues it by tearing the melody loose from its mooring. He's also willing to push the line: of all Diffie's country heroes—and you'll be able to name them after one listen—maybe only Merle Haggard would rock out as hard as Diffie does on the title track. — *Brian Mansfield*

Honky Tonk Attitude / Apr. 20, 1993 / Epic ♦♦♦
Taking a cue from some of his peers, balladeer Diffie makes a point to get rowdy on this, his most commercially successful album to date. Besides the title track, it includes the hits "Prop Me up Beside the Jukebox (If I Die)" and "John Deere Green." — *Dan Cooper*

Third Rock from the Sun / 1994 / Epic ♦♦♦♦
Third Rock from the Sun represents a bit of a musical departure for Joe Diffie. Though he keeps his basic honky tonk roots, he experiments more, adding more rock flourishes to his sound. Not all of his attempts are successful, but his ballads are frequently compelling. Nevertheless, it's a little distressing that he has only written one song on the album—there's no reason for his well to dry up by only his fourth record. — *Thom Owens*

Life's So Funny / 1995 / Epic ♦♦♦
Led by the tongue-in-cheek single "Bigger Than the Beatles," Joe Diffie's fifth album *Life's So Funny* delivers the relaxed, funny contemporary country that fans have come to expect from the singer. *Life's So Funny* isn't as consistently engaging as his previous *Third Rock From the Sun*, yet its warm sense of humor and varied collection of ballads and mid-tempo rockers makes it a worthy follow-up to the most popular record Diffie ever released. — *Thom Owens*

Dave Dudley (Dave Darwin Pedruska)

b. May 3, 1928, Spencer, WI
Guitar, Vocals / Traditional Country
Dudley was one of country music's biggest troubadours of trucker songs. "Six Days on the Road," a No. 2 country hit in 1963, was the first of a string of classic songs in the idiom. Between 1961 and 1980, Dudley scored 41 hits. Currently there isn't an adequate domestically available collection on compact disc. — *Rick Clark*

● **20 Great Truck Hits: Dave Dudley** / 1983 / EMI ♦♦♦♦
This Swedish import collection includes a smattering of Dudley's hits like "Six Days on the Road," "Counterfeit Cowboy," and "Me and Ole C.B." — *Rick Clark*

Holly Dunn

Vocals / Contemporary Country
Singer-songwriter Holly Dunn, the sister of talented Nashville songwriter Chris Waters, had barely graduated from college when she found herself soaring to success. Dunn had her first group in high school—she was the lead singer of the Freedom Folk, which was selected to represent Texas at the bicentennial celebrations at the White House. The band went on to tour the South and appear on television. Dunn later became a member of the Abilene Christian University USO touring choir, the Hilltop Singers. In 1978, a song she had co-written with her brother, "Out of Sight, Not Out of Mind," was recorded by Christy Lane. She moved to Nashville to join her brother after obtaining her degree. At first she worked odd jobs and sang demos for music publishers before signing with CBS Songs, where her brother also worked. In 1984, Dunn was hired as a songwriter for MTM by producer Tommy West, and several top female singers recorded her songs, including Louise Mandrell, who took "I'm Not Through Loving You Yet" to the country Top Ten.

In 1985, Dunn signed with MTM records and released three singles which became minor hits. Dunn's eponymous debut appeared in 1986, around the same time "Daddy's Hands" was released. "Daddy's Hands"

became her breakthrough hit, reaching the country Top Ten. She was named Top New Female Vocalist by the Academy of Country Music and the album received two Grammy nominations. Her next album, 1987's *Cornerstone*, contained two Top Five hits and won Dunn the Country Music Association's Horizon Award. She made her debut as a producer with her next album, 1988's *Across the Rio Grande*. MTM went out of business in 1988 and Dunn signed with Warner. Her first Warner album, *The Blue Rose of Texas*, produced her first No. 1 hit, "Are You Gonna Love Me." In 1991, following a chart slump, her label released *Milestones: Greatest Hits*. A small controversy erupted over one of the songs, "Maybe I Mean Yes," because some listeners felt it encouraged women to blame themselves for date rape, and Dunn had the song pulled from the album. During the '90s, her popularity declined, resulting in Dunn's departure from Warner in 1993. In 1995, she released *Life And Love And All The Stages* on River North Nashville. — *Sandra Brennan*

The Blue Rose of Texas / 1989 / Warner Bros. ♦♦♦
This "nu-country/pop" belter has an occasional rock punch and a Western swing and sway. — *Mark A. Humphrey*

Heart Full of Love / 1990 / Warner Bros. ♦♦♦
Here are more of Dunn's radio-friendly songs. — *Mark A. Humphrey*

● **Milestones: Greatest Hits** / 1991 / Warner Bros. ♦♦♦♦
This best-of contains "Maybe I Mean Yes," "Daddy's Hands," and other favorites. — *AMG*

Getting It Dunn / 1992 / Warner Bros. ♦♦♦♦
It contains the hits "You Say You Will," "A Simple I Love You," "No Love Have," and others. — *AMG*

Steve Earle

Guitar, Vocals / Country-Rock, Singer-Songwriter, New Traditionalist
When Steve Earle released his 1986 debut *Guitar Town*, he had already developed quite a reputation as an exceptional singer-songwriter in the Nashville music community. Nevertheless, that album's tough-as-nails lyrical and musical delivery immediately made Earle an outsider for the generally polite country-radio format. With each subsequent album, Earle has integrated a harder rock sound, helping him gain entrance on FM rock playlists. — *Rick Clark*

● **Guitar Town** / 1986 / MCA ♦♦♦♦
Steve Earle rode a suspiciously rocking band into Nashville and up to the top of the country charts with this album, after which it was decided he was just a little too extreme for the country market, which means this record is "on the edge" in more ways than one. — *William Ruhlmann*

Early Tracks / 1987 / Epic ♦♦♦

Exit O / 1987 / MCA ♦♦♦

Copperhead Road / 1988 / MCA ♦♦♦
Earle finally got around to re-recording his classic "The Devil's Right Hand" on an album that is a potent combination of hillbilly attitude and rude rock 'n' roll. Irish punk-folksters the Pogues pitch in on some of the proceedings. The title track became Earle's first FM rock hit. — *William Ruhlmann & Rick Clark*

The Hard Way / 1990 / MCA ♦♦♦
Some of Earle's best songwriting is on this album. The anthemic "The Other Kind" is a classic. On "Country Girl," Earle and his band (The Dukes) do their best NRBQ grooves. "Billy Austin" is a compassionate character sketch of a Native American on death row. Former Lone Justice lead singer Maria McKee offers vocal support on this album. On the down side, the subtleties of these songs are occasionally buried under a sea of cinematic production. Earle sometimes sounds too tired to emote anything, and the heavily compressed mix doesn't help matters. Regardless, fans of rock which contains well-written lyrics might enjoy this. — *Rick Clark*

Shut up and Die Like an Aviator (Live) / 1991 / MCA ♦♦

● **Essential Steve Earle** / 1993 / MCA ♦♦♦♦
Steve Earle lives up to the title billing here. While some of Earle's recent work (and live shows) have inclined to excess, this disc collects lean, mean, and vital material from Earle's first three outings—the country-rock masterpiece *Guitar Town*, the inward-looking *Exit O*, and the angry lashing out of *Copperhead Road*. *Essential* is topped off by "Continental Trailways Blues," previously available only on a 1987 compilation. Thirteen tracks is a little skimpy; some rarities from the vaults would have been a nice touch. — *Roch Parisien*

Train A Comin' / 1995 / Winter Harvest ♦♦♦♦
Supported by Norman Blake, Roy Husky, and Peter Rowan, Steve has made a comeback record of sorts. Its a greasy, homey, soulful country-folk album that sounds great and keeps asking to be played again. This is an album full of stories of men with hard hearts and broken lives. He sings with a believable voice, which is all too rare these days. He turns in a breezy "I'm Looking Through You" to top it all off, reminiscent of the mid-'60s *Beatle Country* album by the Charles River Valley Boys. — *Richard Meyer*

I Feel Alright / Mar. 5, 1996 / Warner Bros. ✦✦✦✦
"Be careful what you wish for friends, I've been to hell and now I'm back again," Earle sings on the title track of *I Feel Alright*, immediately drawing us into one of the finest albums of his career. This is the Steve Earle we've been waiting for, as unadorned, unashamed, and plain-faced honest about his roots, dreams, and dirty past lives as any of country music's most heralded singers. From the drifting, hard-loving woman in "Now She's Gone" to withdrawn junkie in the ghostly "CCKMP" ("cocaine cannot kill my pain") to the teenage outlaw in "Billy and Bonnie," Earle's characters are a string of loners, often down and out but at the same time loyal, self-aware romantics right to the bitter end. Few artists can give us a picture of life's other side with such electrifying clarity. But despite its subject, "I Feel Alright" is imbued with true moments of hope. The closing duet with Lucinda Williams, "You're Still Standin' There," for example, is as strong a statement of faith as any Earle has written. —*Kurt Wolf*

Ain't Ever Satisfied / Jul. 1996 / HIPP ✦✦✦✦
Although his life was plagued with troubles during the late '80s, Steve Earle wrote a wealth of first-rate songs during that time and the majority of those tunes are collected on the double-disc set, *Ain't Ever Satisfied*. Spanning his career from 1985's *Guitar Town* to 1991's *The Hard Way*, *Ain't Ever Satisfied* hits nearly every high point from his studio albums and throws in a handful of rarities, including live covers of the Rolling Stones and Bruce Springsteen, for good measure. It's an excellent retrospective, illustrating exactly why Earle was one of the most acclaimed country singer-songwriters of the latter half of the '80s. —*Thom Owens*

Exile

Country-Rock, Country-Pop
Although the Kentucky-based group Exile's first hit "Kiss You All Over" was a major pop charter, they experienced their greatest success as a country band in the latter half of the '80s. Exile was co-founded by J.P. Pennington, the son of former Coon Creek Girl Lily May Ledford, in 1963. Originally known as the Exiles, they got their start touring with Dick Clark in 1965. In 1973, they changed their name to Exile and had their first minor chart success with "Try It On." They followed this up with "Kiss You All Over," which hit No. 1 on the US pop charts in 1978. After delivering several unsuccessful follow-ups to their hit single, Exile returned to Kentucky to retool their sound by working in local clubs.

Exile soon gained a popular following in Kentucky and several of their songs from this era were covered by major artists such as Janie Fricke ("It Ain't Easy Being Easy") and Alabama ("The Closer You Get"). By the time they finally re-emerged onto the country music scene in the '80s, the band had gone from mellow pop band to a high voltage five-piece band of Southern-rockers consisting of Pennington, Les Taylor, Sonny Lemaire, Marlon Hargis, and Steve Goetzman. The group signed to Epic Records in 1983 and their first country single, "High Cost of Leaving," reached No. 24. An eponymous album followed and produced two chart-toppers, "Woke Up in Love" and "I Don't Wanna Be a Memory."

In 1984, Exile's second country album *Kentucky Hearts*, provided three more No. 1 hits including "Crazy for Your Love." Released in 1985, *Hang on to Your Heart* was even more successful, producing four No. 1 singles, including the title track and "I Could Get Used to You." In 1986, Sonny Lemairre won BMI's award for Songwriter of the Year. During 1986, Exile took an extended break, returning with *Shelter from the Night* in 1987. Although it contained the No. 1 hit "I Can't Get Close Enough," the album wasn't as successful as its predecessors. The band then underwent personnel changes over the next two years. First Marlon Hargis was replaced by keyboardist Lee Carroll. Les Taylor left the group in 1989 with Mark Jones replacing him. Finally, after nearly three decades, J.P. Pennington left and guitar player Paul Martin took his place. Exile signed to Arista in 1990 and later released *Still Standing*. The album produced two Top Ten hits, "Nobody's Talking" and "Yet." The group released one more album for Arista, 1991's *Justice;* the album contained the hit "Even Now." Arista dropped the group in 1993. Left without a record label, Exile decided to disband. —*Sandra Brennan*

● **Greatest Hits** / 1986 / Epic ✦✦✦✦
Exile—Greatest Hits offers a good cross-section of the band's late '70s and early '80s country-rock hits, including "Kiss You All Over" and "Woke Up In Love." —*Stephen Thomas Erlewine*

The Complete Collection / 1991 / Curb ✦✦✦✦
The Complete Collection is a good summation of Exile's '80s career, concentrating on lesser-known tracks, not chart-toppers. For the big hits, stick with *Greatest Hits*, but if you want to dig a little deeper, start with *The Complete Collection.* —*Stephen Thomas Erlewine*

Donna Fargo   (Yvonne Vaughn)

b. Nov. 10, 1949
Guitar, Vocals / Country, Country-Pop
In the early '70s, Donna Fargo was an unusual country star for a couple of reasons. She was one of the few female country singers to write her own material, and one of the few country singers of any sort to cross over

to the pop charts in a big way, which she did in 1972 with "The Happiest Girl In The Whole USA." (No. 11) and "Funny Face" (No. 5). She never made the pop Top 40 again, but placed over a dozen more singles in the country Top Ten in the '70s, most written by herself. As an artist, she was squarely in the mainstream, her slightly lisping voice delivering upbeat, sweetly produced homilies to romance, home, and America. She faded after developing multiple sclerosis in 1979, although she continued writing and performing. —*Richie Unterberger*

● **The Best of Donna Fargo** / 1995 / Varese Sarabande ✦✦✦✦
Eighteen songs, all but one from dating from her 1972-75 prime, when she recorded for Dot. Contains ten Top Ten country hits, including of course "Funny Face" and "The Happiest Girl In The Whole USA." —*Richie Unterberger*

Freddy Fender   (Baldemar Huerta)

b. Jun. 4, 1937, San Benito, TX
Guitar, Vocals / Rock 'n' Roll, Traditional Country, Country-Pop, Tex-Mex
With Johnny Rodriguez in the '70s, Freddy Fender popularized Tex-Mex music and helped to create a national interest in the genre. Born Baldemar Huerta, the son of Texas migrant farmers, Fender started in R&B, moving to country songs in which he alternated lyrics in Spanish and English. In 1975 he had three monster No. 1 hits, "Before the Next Teardrop Falls" and "Wasted Days and Wasted Nights," followed by "Secret Love." Further success eluded him for fifteen years, until he became part of the Texas Tornados. —*David Vinopal*

Before the Next Teardrop Falls / 1975 / Collectibles ✦✦✦
Textbook blend of Tex-Mex and country, spiced by Fender's immortal hit. —*Ron Wynn*

The Best of Freddie Fender / 1977 / MCA ✦✦✦✦
The Best of Freddie Fender collects all of his biggest hits from the early '70s, making it an excellent introduction to the singer. —*Thom Owens*

Early Years: 1959-1963 / 1986 / Krazy Kat ✦✦✦
These 16 sides are taken from rare regional singles that were cut for tiny labels in the days when Fender was only known in Texas and Louisiana. While Fender's earliest recordings were in Spanish, he only sings in English on these cuts of decent, though not thrilling, early swamp-pop. Freddy takes his inspiration from rockabilly, doo wop, Tex-Mex, and smoldering R&B ballads on these singles, which include his first (and possibly best) version of "Wasted Days and Wasted Nights." One of the relatively few early rock performers to flavor his sound with Texas border music, these sides were most likely influential on Doug Sahm, although they were unheard by a national audience. —*Richie Unterberger*

● **Collection** / 1991 / Reprise ✦✦✦✦
Collection covers a bit more territory than *The Best of Freddie Fender*, but it doesn't have quite as many tracks. Nevertheless, it has the same essential singles as the previous compilation, as well as some songs that aren't on *The Best of*—consequently, it is just as good an introduction as *Collection.* —*Thom Owens*

Flatlanders

Country
The Flatlanders became legends long after they broke up because the band's three primary members—Jimmie Dale Gilmore, Joe Ely, and Butch Hancock—each attracted a large, loyal cult following as solo performers. In 1972, when their lone album was recorded, they were part-time musicians who hooked up after each returned to their native Texas after exploring some different region of the world. The record wasn't released, and they went their separate ways, each abandoning music briefly. Their careers continued to intertwine in the ensuing decades with great results. —*Michael McCall*

● **More a Legend Than A Band** / 1990 / Rounder ✦✦✦✦
The title refers to the status these "lost" tapes acquired as time passed and the reputations of Ely, Gilmore, and Hancock grew. The music itself is odd and effective, a blend of old-time acoustic music (including a musical saw) matched with lyrics that look at the world as only modern Texas mystics could. Gilmore takes most of the lead vocals. It features the first recorded versions of two of his classics, "Dallas" and "Tonight I'm Gonna Go Downtown." —*Michael McCall*

Rosie Flores

Guitar / Country, Rockabilly
Since the late '70s, guitarist, singer, and songwriter Rosie Flores has been a steady figure on the alternative country scene in both Austin, TX, and Los Angeles, CA. She's a hard-working, independently minded artist who's well-respected for her gritty, energetic vocals and fiery guitar solos.

Flores' first band was Rosie and the Screamers—based in Southern California during the punk-rock era of the late '70s—who played hard country and rockabilly material, much of it written by Flores. A few years later she began working as a solo acoustic artist, but eventually formed an all-female band, the Screaming Sirens, who recorded the album *Fiesta* in 1984. In 1987 Flores recorded her first solo album, *Rosie Flores*, produced by Pete Anderson (Dwight Yoakam's producer and guitarist) and released by Warner Bros. Flores eventually parted ways with Warner Bros. and signed to the indie label HighTone. In 1992 she released her second solo album, *After the Farm*, followed by *Once More with Feeling* a year later. Flores then spent the better part of 1994 playing lead guitar in Butch Hancock's band. In 1995 Flores recorded *Rockabilly Filly*, a spirited tribute to the music she grew up with. The album featured duets with her longtime idols Wanda Jackson and Janis Martin, both of whom Flores brought out of retirement for the project. The album led to a cross-country tour with Jackson, who hadn't played in nightclubs in over 20 years. —*Kurt Wolff*

● **Rosie Flores** / 1987 / Reprise ♦♦♦♦
Produced by Pete Anderson, Rosie Flores' debut made her out to be the female answer to Dwight Yoakam. Flores probably felt like that image straitjacketed her, but from a musical standpoint, it worked beautifully, incorporating Flores' San Antonio roots into Anderson's California country vision. Includes "Crying over You," "Somebody Loses, Somebody Wins," and "Blue Side of Town," which Patty Loveless wouldn't do nearly as well the following year. —*Brian Mansfield*

After the Farm / 1992 / Hightone ♦♦♦
From start to finish, there is something special about this CD. Flores is a great guitarist, backed by Greg Liesz, David Lindley, Duane "DJ" Jarvis, and Dusty Wakeman. They rock, with some great slide-guitar work. If you like your country hard, you'll love it. —*Chip Renner*

Once More with Feeling / 1993 / Hightone ♦♦♦
Closer to modern commercial country than *After the Farm*, *Once More with Feeling* doesn't have the sleekly professional touch of *Rosie Flores*, but it's not without its charms. It includes a duet with Joe Ely ("Love and Danger," which Flores wrote with Jason & The Scorchers' Jason Ringenberg). Other songs are contributed by Wendy Waldman ("Ruin This Romance") and Katy Moffatt ("Real Man"). —*Brian Mansfield*

Rockabilly Filly / Oct. 1995 / Hightone ♦♦♦
As the title indicates, *Rockabilly Filly* is Rosie Flores' first album that consists entirely of rockabilly tunes. Of course, she has always flirted with the genre, but it is refreshing to hear her take a full-fledged plunge. It's all the more impressive when you consider that it was recorded after she recovered from a wrist-shattering accident—she plays with the vitality of a wild, young rockabilly cat throughout the album. —*Sara Sytsma*

Red Foley (Clyde Julian Foley)

b. Jun. 17, 1910, Blue Lick, KY, **d.** Sep. 19, 1968, Fory Wayne, IN
Guitar, Vocals / Traditional Country, Honky Tonk, Country Gospel
Hall of Fame member Clyde Julian "Red" Foley was graced with a rich baritone voice and a personality that made him a natural star. In 1950 he scored with three No. 1s, "Chattanoogie Shoe Shine Boy," "Steal Away," and "Just a Closer Walk with Thee," the latter two directing him toward religious material for the rest of his career, including his signature song, "Peace in the Valley." In 1954 he hosted the "Ozark Jubilee," one of the earliest country TV shows. He continued making appearances right up to his death. —*David Vinopal*

Beyond the Sunset / 1956 / MCA ♦♦♦♦
Foley's gospel albums ranked with Tennessee Ernie Ford's as the most popular of the era among country fans. This is his best. —*Michael McCall*

Red and Ernie / 1956 / Decca ♦♦♦♦
Foley recorded four albums with his good friend Ernest Tubb, whose good humor always managed to bring out the best in his partner. —*Michael McCall*

★ **Country Music Hall of Fame** / 1991 / MCA ♦♦♦♦♦
Country Music Hall of Fame contains a good cross-section of Red Foley's heyday in the late '40s and early '50s. All of the selections of this 16-track, single-disc compilation were recorded for Decca Records. While not all of his hits are present—even some of his biggest singles, including "Smoke On Your Water," are missing—but most of the essential items ("Chattanoogie Shoe Shine Boy," "Tennessee Saturday Night," "Peace In the Valley") are here, making it an essential introduction to one of country's biggest stars. —*Stephen Thomas Erlewine*

Tennessee Ernie Ford

b. Feb. 13, 1919, Bristol, TN, **d.** Oct. 17, 1991, Los Angeles, CA
Vocals / Traditional Country, Country Gospel
This radio announcer quickly changed careers when "Smokey Mountain Boogie," "The Cry of the Wild Goose," "Mule Train," and his self-penned rockabilly song "Shotgun Boogie" made him a star in 1950. The best was yet to come. In 1955 he recorded Merle Travis' superb "Sixteen Tons," a grimly real song about life in the coal mines that sold more than 4 million copies over the next ten years. Ernie's TV show on NBC lasted until he

grew tired of it (six years), at which time he took his warm bass voice out of the business for a while; when he returned, it was mainly to gospel, on material that was beautifully suited to his exceptional voice. His *Hymns* album is considered the first country album to sell a million. This gentleman of country music died in 1991, shortly after a TV special tribute to him. —*David Vinopal*

★ **16 Tons of Boogie: the Best of . . .** / 1990 / Rhino ♦♦♦♦♦
In his later years, Ford's little pea-pickin' heart was closely associated with gospel and patriotic music, but in earlier years he knew how to—as the album title says—boogie. This includes all the essential material from that period: "Sixteen Tons," "The Shot Gun Boogie," "Mule Train," and "Blackberry Boogie," for starters. —*Tom Roland*

Country Gospel Classics, Vol. 1 & 2 / 1991 / Capitol ♦♦♦♦
The '60s follow-up to the previous decade's *All-Time Greatest Hymns* wasn't as overwhelmingly successful, but it holds up better. The interplay between Ford's baritone and the Jordanaires' harmony support is beautiful. —*Michael McCall*

Sings Songs of the Civil War / Feb. 4, 1991 / Capitol ♦♦♦
The 1991 release combines two evocative albums of Civil War-era songs Ford recorded for that conflict's centennial remembrance in 1961. His somber style perfectly fits the subject matter. —*Michael McCall*

Red, White & Blue / Jun. 24, 1991 / Capitol ♦♦♦
This gathers together his patriotic songs, including the complete *America the Beautiful* LP from 1970. —*Michael McCall*

Foster & Lloyd

Progressive Country
Radney Foster (from Del Rio, TX) and Bill Lloyd (from Bowling Green, KY) specialized in a smart synthesis of country, rock, and pop as the duo Foster & Lloyd. Between 1987 and 1990 they cut three albums for RCA, landing four Top Five singles in the process. Unlike many Nashville acts, Foster & Lloyd wrote and produced their own recordings. Their albums, all very enjoyable listens for their roots-rock immediacy, set them apart from their country contemporaries. —*Rick Clark*

Foster & Lloyd / 1987 / RCA ♦♦♦
This self-titled debut effort contains the duo's most recognizable radio tracks, particularly "Crazy over You," a Top Five hit. Other hits included here are "Sure Thing," "What Do You Want from Me This Time?," and "Texas in 1880." —*Rick Clark*

Faster & Llouder / 1989 / RCA ♦♦♦♦
Foster & Lloyd's sophomore effort presented a harder, edgier collection of songs, which were even stronger than the ones found on their first album. Highlights include "Happy for Awhile," the roots-rocker "Fat Lady Sings," and the title track. Power-pop artist Marshall Crenshaw guested on "She Knows What She Wants." —*Rick Clark*

Version of the Truth / 1990 / RCA ♦♦♦

● **Essential Foster & Lloyd** / Apr. 1996 / RCA ♦♦♦♦
The Essential Foster & Lloyd groups together 19 tracks by this influential duo who scored several hits in the '80s. The two merged Lloyd's melodic pop smarts with Foster's Texas literary soul, giving them catchiness and substance in the same package. They also could rock out, leaning toward a rockabilly energy that didn't carry a trace of the redneck swagger of Southern-rock. Instead, this was solid, clean-rocking fun with brains. The duo split in 1990 after three albums, but this collection is a good reminder that they anticipated the country youth movement that followed them. —*Michael McCall*

Radney Foster

Guitar, Vocals / Contemporary Country, New Traditionalist
Half of the popular duo Foster & Lloyd (Bill); 1993 saw Radney release his first solo album *Del Rio, TX 1953*, which yielded several hit singles.
Foster and Lloyd had first teamed up at MTM where each was employed. Together and singly they wrote hits for artists such as Holly Dunn and Sweethearts of the Rodeo. —*Jim Worbois*

● **Del Rio, Texas, 1959** / 1992 / Arista ♦♦♦♦
Radney Foster's first album since dissolving the much-missed Foster & Lloyd duo is a tribute to the songwriter's coming of age in small-town Texas and all the musical baggage that stowed aboard for the ride. On many of the tracks, Foster seems a little too conscious of wanting to deliver a pure country effort. The songs are solid, but there's a slight archival feel to the result. I admit that personal biases may be at work here, having been a Foster & Lloyd fan, but it's the more contemporary hybrids that strike me as the disc's best moments. The gutsy "A Fine Line," the infectious "Nobody Wins" (with Mary Chapin Carpenter on background vocals), and the gospelly country-rocker "Hammer and Nails" are worth the price of admission alone. —*Roch Parisien*

Labor Of Love / 1995 / Arista ♦♦

Janie Fricke

b. Dec. 19, 1952, South Whitney, IN
Guitar, Vocals / Country-Pop
This versatile Indiana native made a good living writing jingles and singing backup until Nashville realized her talent as a solo star. In 1982 she had her first No. 1 with "Don't Worry About Me Baby," leading to her being named Country Music Association Female Vocalist of the Year two years running. —*David Vinopal*

It Ain't Easy / 1982 / CBS ✦✦✦
The versatility that made Fricke a jingles success might have been a liability as a solo performer. She's so adaptable that her voice might not have been distinctive enough. Here she sounds like a strong woman who's very familiar with heartache, and producer Bob Montgomery gives her some rockin' material to shout on. —*Tom Roland*

● **17 Greatest Hits** / 1986 / CBS ✦✦✦✦
Just like the title says—17 of Fricke's biggest hits from the early '80s, including the No. 1 hits "He's A Heartache (Looking for a Place to Happen)," "It Ain't Easy Bein' Easy," "Don't Worry 'Bout Me Baby," and "Your Heart's Not In It." —*Thom Owens*

Lefty Frizzell (William Orville Frizzell)

b. Mar. 31, 1928, Corsicana, TX, **d.** Jul. 19, 1975, Nashville, TN
Guitar, Vocals / Traditional Country, Honky Tonk
Lefty Frizzell was the definitive honky tonk singer, the vocalist that set the style for generations of vocalists that followed him. Frizzell smoothed out the rough edges of honky tonk by singing longer, flowing phrases—essentially, he made honky tonk more acceptable for the mainstream without losing its gritty, bar-room roots. In the process, he changed the way country vocalists sang forever. From George Jones, Merle Haggard, and Willie Nelson to George Strait, John Anderson, Randy Travis, and Keith Whitley, hundreds of artists have emulated and expanded Lefty's innovations. Frizzell's singing became the foundation of how hard country should be sung.

Despite his influence, there was a time when Lefty Frizzell wasn't regarded as one of country's definitive artists. Unlike Hank Williams—the only contemporary of Lefty that had greater influence—he didn't die young, leaving behind a romantic legend. After his popularity peaked in the early and mid-'50s, Frizzell continued to record, without having much success. However, his recordings continued to reach new listeners and his reputation was restored by the new traditionalists of the '80s, nearly ten years after Lefty's death.

Lefty Frizzell (born William Orville Frizzell) was born in Corisicana, TX, in 1928, a son of an oiler; he was the first of eight children. During his childhood, his family moved to El Dorado, AR. As a child he was called Sonny, but his nickname changed to Lefty when he was 14, because he won a schoolyard fight; it was later suggested that he earned his nickname after winning a Golden Gloves boxing match, but that was eventually proven to be a hatched publicity stunt by his record company. Initially, Lefty was attracted to music through his parents' Jimmie Rodgers records. He began singing professionally before he was a teenager, landing a regular spot on KELD El Dorado.

Frizzell spent his teenage years playing throughout the region, singing on radio shows, in nightclubs, for dances, and in talent contests. He travelled throughout the south, playing in Arkansas, Texas, New Mexico, and even Las Vegas. During this time, he was refining his style, drawing from influences like Jimmie Rodgers, Ernest Tubb, and Ted Daffan. Lefty's career was going fine until he was arrested in the mid-'40s, serving a jail sentence for statutory rape.

Frizzell's run-in with the law led him away from music, as he temporarily worked in the oil fields with his father. However, his time as an oiler was brief and he was soon performing in clubs again. By 1950, he had landed a regular job at the Texas club Ace of Clubs, where he developed a dedicated following of fans. At one of his concerts at the Ace of Clubs he caught the attention of Jim Beck, the owner of a local recording studio. Beck recorded music for several major record labels, and he also had connections within the publishing industry. Impressed with Lefty's performance, he invited the singer to make some demos at the studio. In April of 1950, Frizzell cut several demos of his original songs, including a new song called "If You've Got the Money, I've Got the Time," which Beck took to Nashville. Beck intended to pitch the song to Little Jimmy Dickens, but Dickens disliked the song. However, Columbia record producer Don Law heard the tape and liked Frizzell's voice. After hearing Lefty live in concert, Law signed the singer to Columbia; within a few months, he had his first recording session.

"If You've Got the Money, I've Got the Time," Lefty's first single, climbed to No. 1 upon its release. It was a huge hit—its B-side, "I Love You a Thousand Ways," even hit No. 1—with other artists hurrying into the studio to cut their own versions; over 40 performers wound up recording the song. Within 17 days of the single's release, Columbia had Frizzell record another single. The result, "Look What Thoughts Will

Do"/"Shine, Shave, Shower (It's Saturday)," wasn't as big a hit, but it did reach the Top Ten.

By now, the Lefty Frizzell sound was being perfected by the vocalist and Don Law. Frizzell was working with a core group of Dallas-based studio musicians, highlighted by pianist Madge Sutee. In the beginning of 1951, he formed the Western Cherokees, which was led by Blackie Crawford. Soon, the Western Cherokees became his primary band for both live and recording situations. Lefty was in the studio frequently, recording singles. His third single, "I Want to Be with You Always," was No. 1 for 11 weeks and its follow-up, "Always Late (With Your Kisses)," spent 12 weeks. At one point in early 1951, he had a total of four songs in the country Top Ten, setting a record that was never broken. Frizzell was a popular concert attraction, playing shows with the "Louisiana Hayride" and the Grand Ole Opry. He had three more Top Ten hits in 1951—"Mom and Dad's Waltz," "Travelin' Blues," and the No. 1 "Give Me More, More, More (Of Your Kisses)."

The hits continued throughout 1952, as "How Long Will It Take (To Stop Loving You)," "Don't Stay Away (Till Love Grows Cold)," "Forever (And Always)," "I'm An Old, Old Man (Tryin' to Live While I Can)" all went to the Top Ten. Even though he was at the peak of his popularity, things began to unravel for Lefty behind the scenes. Frizzell fired both his manager and his band. He joined the Grand Ole Opry, but he decided he didn't like it and left almost immediately. Lefty was earning a lot of money but he was spending nearly all of it. He worked with Wayne Raney, but the sessions were a failure. In early 1953, he moved from Texas to Los Angeles, where he got a regular job on Town Hall Party. That year, he had only one hit—the Top Ten "(Honey, Baby, Hurry!) Bring Your Sweet Self Back to Me."

Early in 1954, he reached the Top Ten with "Run 'Em Off," but it would be his last Top Ten record for five years. During the mid-'50s, Frizzell felt burned out and he didn't have the energy to invest in his career. He had a total of two hits between 1954 and 1959—"I Love You Mostly" in 1955, "Cigarettes and Coffee Blues"—because he decided to stop recording. Lefty was frustrated that Columbia wasn't releasing what he believed to be his best material, so he simply stopped writing and recording songs. However, he did tour sporadically, occasionally with his brother, David Frizzell.

Deciding it was time for a change, he began working with Jim Denny's Nashville-based Cedarwood publishing company in 1959. Cedarwood gave him "The Long Black Veil," a song written by Danny Dill and Marijohn Wilkin that had overt folk music influences. Lefty recorded the song and it became a surprise Top Ten hit in the summer of 1959. Encouraged by its success, Frizzell moved to Nashville in 1961, after Town Hall Party closed in 1960. He began touring and recording at a more rapid rate, although it only resulted in a couple of minor hits. Lefty's last big hit arrived early in 1964, when "Saginaw, Michigan" climbed to No. 1 and spent four weeks on the top of the charts. After that, he came close to the Top Ten with 1965's "She's Gone Gone Gone," but he usually struggled to have any of his songs break the Top 20 for the next decade.

Frizzell didn't stop recording, but he did develop a debilitating alcohol problem that came to plague him throughout the late '60s and '70s. However, alcohol wasn't the only thing holding his career back—Columbia was only releasing handfuls of albums and singles, though Lefty was recording an abundance of material. Since his records weren't as successful, he drastically cut back the number of concerts he performed. In 1968, he cut some songs with June Stearns under the name Agnes and Orville, but none of the tracks became hits. The lack of success helped him sink deeper into alcoholism.

In 1972, Lefty left Columbia, signing with ABC Records. Though the change in labels helped revitalize him artistically, he didn't sell that many more records. However, he did have the enthusiasm to record albums, as well as play concerts and television shows. Frizzell's alcohol addiction worsened and he developed high blood pressure, but he wouldn't take the medication because he thought it would interfere with his drinking. As a result, he looked older than his 47 years when he died of a stroke in 1975.

Years of mediocre and mis-marketed records had diminished Lefty Frizzell's reputation, but after his death, a new generation of artists hailed him as an influence and an idol. Merle Haggard, Willie Nelson, and George Jones had all sung his praises before, but in the mid-'80s, the kind words of George Strait and Randy Travis were supported by a series of reissues, beginning with Bear Family's 14-LP set, *His Life*—His Music (later replaced by the 12-CD *Life's Like Poetry*). In 1982, he was inducted into the Country Music Hall of Fame, but the greatest testament to his music remains the fact that his voice can be heard in every hard country singer that followed. —*Stephen Thomas Erlewine*

☆ **Treasures Untold** / 1980 / Rounder ✦✦✦✦✦
A wonderful selection of early performances, it's rugged Texas honky tonk delivered in a mellifluous drawl that Merle Haggard and others emulated. An archetype. —*Mark A. Humphrey*

★ **The Best of Lefty Frizzell** / 1991 / Rhino ✦✦✦✦✦
These 18 tracks cover 15 years (1950-65) in the career of a singer whom Merle Haggard once called "the most unique thing that ever happened to country music." Included are such timeless Frizzell gems as "If You've Got the Money, I've Got the Time," "I Love You a Thousand Ways," "I Want to Be with You Always," "Always Late (With Your Kisses)," and "The Long Black Veil." This is a must-hear for anyone interested in the origins of a vocal style so influential it rules country radio to this very day. *—Dan Cooper*

American Originals / Columbia ✦✦✦✦
American Originals collects most of Frizzell's biggest hits, but all of those are available in a more cohesive fashion on Rhino's *The Best of Lefty Frizzell*. Nevertheless, there are some songs on *American Originals* that aren't on *The Best of Lefty Frizzell*, and it does offer a good 10-song sampling of some of his best work, even if the presentation is decidedly haphazard. *— Stephen Thomas Erlewine*

Life's Like Poetry / Bear Family ✦✦✦✦
Life's Like Poetry is a gigantic, 12-disc box set that includes all of Lefty Frizzell's recordings for Columbia and ABC, plus early demos, a session with Jay Miller, and several radio transcriptions—everything he recorded between 1950 and 1975. Certainly, the box is designed for collectors—no one but the most devoted fan could listen to all 330 tracks. Though all of his classic material is included, there is also a fair share of mediocre material, including some ill-advised attempts at country-pop. Nevertheless, there are gems sprinkled throughout the collection and it offers proof of his far-reaching talents and influence, as well as demonstrating that several of Lefty's later recordings were as worthwhile as his early singles. For any serious fan, it is an indispensable collection. *— Stephen Thomas Erlewine*

Gatlin Brothers

Traditional Country, Country-Pop
With his brothers Rudy and Steve, strong-voiced Larry Gatlin sang gospel songs in childhood. His first break came when he worked with the Imperials in Las Vegas, as part of Jimmy Dean's show. The late Dottie West gave him a hand by recording his compositions, and Johnny Cash used some of his songs in his *Gospel Road* movie. Gatlin's first album, *The Pilgrim*, came out in 1974, and his "Broken Lady" single was a hit in 1975, leading to a Grammy. In the latter part of the '70s he had numerous No. 1 hits, with "I Wish You Were Someone I Love" and "All the Gold in California." In the '80s, Gatlin and his brothers were as hot as any in the business. Due to medical problems with Larry's vocal chords, the three brothers announced that at the end of 1992 they would disband. *—David Vinopal*

Greatest Hits / 1978 / Columbia ✦✦✦✦
The first volume of the Gatlin Brothers' *Greatest Hits* concentrates on Larry Gatlin's solo hits. *—AMG*

Straight Ahead / 1979 / Columbia ✦✦✦✦
Occasionally overstated but predominantly satisfying, it's got a little jazz, a little gospel, a little pop, and a little country. Every country fan knows "All the Gold in California," but the best cuts are the controversial "Midnight Choir (Mogen David)," and a sweet little number: "Taking Somebody with Me When I Fall." *— Tom Roland*

Help Yourself / 1980 / Columbia ✦✦✦
Heavy on ballads that effectively show off the Gatlins' trademark genetic harmony. As always, all ten cuts are written by Larry; "Daytime Heroes," a nod to Prince Valium and the soaps, is most inspired. the Gatlin Brothers recorded "Songwriter's Trilogy" live—whether insightful or self-indulgent depends on the listener's viewpoint. *— Tom Roland*

Greatest Hits, Vol. 2 / 1983 / Columbia ✦✦✦✦
Greatest Hits, Vol. 2 features the best of The Gatlin Brothers' late '70s hits. *—AMG*

● **Best of the Gatlins: All the Gold in California** / 1996 / Columbia/ Legacy ✦✦✦✦
This 18-track compilation traces the work of Larry Gatlin, his brothers, family, and friends (as the various billings on the records had it) from 1975 to 1988. A greatest-hits collection, it slightly favors Gatlin's early work, including "Sweet Becky Walker" and "Delta Dirt," which were among his first chart singles, while skipping "Night Time Magic" and "Nothing But Your Love Hatters," which were bigger hits. Otherwise, it's all country Top Ten singles, including the No. 1 hits "I've Done Enough Dyin' Today," "All the Gold in California," and "Houston (Means I'm One Day Closer to You)." Gatlin, who wrote all the songs and sings all the lead vocals, has a traditionalist bent, though the productions are not as lush as the '60s Nashville sound, the romantic lyrics are more erotic (it was the '70s, after all), and the best songs, such as "All The Gold In California," are unique efforts thematically and musically. (The unnecessarily brief 55-minute CD running time probably is due to song publishing royalties: all the albums in Columbia/Legacy's Country Classics series have only 18 tracks.) *— William Ruhlmann*

Crystal Gayle (Brenda Gail Webb)

b. Jan. 9, 1951, Paintsville, KY
Vocals / Country-Pop
Younger sister of Loretta Lynn, Crystal Gayle began her career when her debut single "I Cried (the Blue Right out of My Eyes)" charted high in 1970. While Lynn became a superstar with traditional country material, Gayle reached the top of her profession with songs that are more pop-oriented, such as "Don't It Make My Brown Eyes Blue" (1977). She's scored many No. 1 hits and collected numerous awards. *—David Vinopal*

All-Time Greatest Hits / 1974 / Curb ✦✦✦
Besides covering many of the hits that appear on *Classic Crystal*, this one also has Gayle's debut single, "I've Cried (The Blue Right out of My Eyes)," which was written by her sister, Loretta Lynn. *—Dan Cooper*

● **Classic Crystal** / 1979 / EMI America ✦✦✦✦
Of Gayle's many overlapping hits collections, this one's the best. Given her crossover success ("Don't It Make My Brown Eyes Blue," included here, hit No. 2 pop) it's interesting to note that all of these tracks were produced by Allen Reynolds, known these days for his work with Garth Brooks. *—Dan Cooper*

True Love / 1982 / Elektra ✦✦✦✦
When Gayle delivered the album to then-Elektra-division-head Jimmy Bowen, he complained that it rocked too much. Producer Allen Reynolds refused to make changes, so Bowen produced three new tracks that seem out of place. Yeah, the Reynolds tracks do rock. So what? Gayle gives some of her best performances ever on "Our Love Is on the Faultline" and "Deeper in the Fire." *— Tom Roland*

Crystal Gayle's Greatest Hits / 1983 / CBS ✦✦✦✦
Always greatly influenced by pop sounds, Gayle embraced that aspect of her musical heritage more in the late '70s and early '80s than any other period. This set covers it well ("Half the Way" is classic), and provides a nice cover photo too. *— Tom Roland*

Bobbie Gentry (Roberta Streeter)

b. Jul. 27, 1944, Chickasaw County, MO
Guitar, Vocals / Country-Pop
Bobbie Gentry became an overnight star, moving from the Los Angeles School of Music to her smash single, "Ode to Billy Joe," a crossover hit in 1967 that led to three Grammy awards. Following this she did well on two duets with Glen Campbell, "Let It Be Me" and "All I Have to Do Is Dream." She hosted and starred on her own show for Britain's BBC in the late '60s and early '70s. *—David Vinopal*

● **Greatest Hits** / 1990 / Curb ✦✦✦✦
Featured are "Fancy," "Ode to Billie Joe," "Louisiana Man," and other hits. *—AMG*

Don Gibson

b. Apr. 3, 1928, Shelby, NC
Guitar, Vocals / Traditional Country, Country-Pop
Singer-songwriter Don Gibson was one of the most popular and influential forces in '50s and '60s country, scoring numerous hit singles as a performer and a songwriter. Gibson's music touched on both traditional country and highly-produced country-pop, which is part of the reason he had such a broad audience. For nearly a decade after his first hit single, "Sweet Dreams," in 1956, he was a reliable hitmaker and his songs have become country classics—they have been covered by a wide range of artists, including Patsy Cline, Ray Charles, Kitty Wells, Emmylou Harris, Neil Young, and Ronnie Milsap.

Gibson began playing guitar while he was a high school student in North Carolina, playing local radio stations and dances. In 1946, he became a regular with the Tennessee Barn Dance in Knoxville. Around the same time, he began recording western songs with the Sons of the Soil, both on Mercury and RCA Victor Records. In 1950, Gibson assumed control of the band, renaming them Don Gibson and his King Cotton Kinfolks and switching their musical direction to honky tonk. Although their sound was more focused, they remained unsuccessful. Gibson continued to perform on the radio, as well as Esslinger's Club in Tennessee. At the nightclub, Wesley Rose saw Gibson perform and offered him a writing contract. Don would only accept the deal if he was allowed to record. Rose managed to get Gibson a contract with Columbia, which proved unsuccessful. Again, Rose secured him another contract, this time with MGM. Gibson's first single for the label, "Sweet Dreams," became a Top Ten hit and was covered by Faron Young, who took it to No. 3.

Following the success of "Sweet Dreams," Gibson was signed to RCA in 1957 by Chet Atkins, who would become his producer for the next seven years. Released early in 1958, Don's first RCA single, "Oh Lonesome Me," was a blockbuster, spending eight weeks at the top of the country charts and crossing over into the pop Top Ten. Gibson and Atkins developed a pop-friendly style which featured rock 'n' roll flourishes that brought him to a larger audience. In the course of 1958-1961, Gibson had a total of 11 Top Ten singles, including "I Can't Stop Lovin'

You," "Blue Blue Day," "Who Cares," "Don't Tell Me Your Troubles," "Just One Time," "Sea of Heartbreak," and "Lonesome Number One."

Although his career wasn't as successful in the latter half of the '60s, he still had the occasional Top Ten single, including "(Yes) I'm Hurting" (1966), "Funny, Familiar, Forgotten, Feelings" (1966), "Rings of Gold" (1969), and "There's A Story (Goin' Round)" (1969). During the late '60s, he suffered from alcoholism and drug addiction, but he cleaned up in the early '70s, which led to a comeback in 1971. Switching record labels from RCA to Hickory, Gibson had a Top Ten hit with "Country Green" in 1972. The following summer, he had his last No. 1 single, "Woman (Sensuous Woman)." He also had a series of duets with Sue Thompson between 1971 and 1976, which were all moderately successful. After two Top Ten hits in 1974—"One Day at a Time" and "Bring Back Your Love to Me"—he settled into a string of minor hits that ran until 1980's "Love Fires." During the '80s and '90s, he continued to tour and perform at the Grand Ole Opry. *— Stephen Thomas Erlewine*

★ **A Legend in His Time** / 1988 / Bear Family ✦✦✦✦✦
A Legend in His Time contains 26 tracks from Don Gibson's peak years of 1957-1965, including all of his country Top Ten hits ("Oh Lonesome Me," "I Can't Stop Lovin' You," "Blue Blue Day," "Sweet Dreams," and several others), as well as a selection of lesser-known material that is all first-rate. It's the definitive retrospective. Although hardcore fans will want Bear Family's box sets and casual fans might want a collection that's a little more concise, *A Legend in His Time* has every essential item from the classic singer-songwriter. *— Stephen Thomas Erlewine*

★ **All-Time Greatest Hits** / 1990 / RCA ✦✦✦✦✦
All-Time Greatest Hits lives up to its title. The album contains 20 of Don Gibson's RCA singles, including all of his big hits—"Oh Lonesome Me," "Sweet Dreams," "I Can't Stop Loving You," and many more. It's a definitive compilation—it has all the necessary songs and illustrates Gibson's songwriting genius quite effectively. *— Stephen Thomas Erlewine*

18 Greatest Hits / 1991 / Curb ✦✦✦
Gibson's best-known hits were recorded in the late '50s and early '60s for RCA with Chet Atkins producing. These recordings are drawn from his work for Hickory Records in the early '70s. They include "Woman, Sensuous Woman," "Country Green" and several remakes of his earlier hits. *—Michael McCall*

The Singer, the Songwriter (1949-1960) / 1991 / Bear Family ✦✦✦✦
Although it contains way too much material for most listeners, completists and historians will find the multi-disc box *The Singer, The Songwriter (1949-1960)* invaluable. Containing every song that Gibson cut for MGM and RCA during that period—including several demos—the set offers plenty of brilliant music, but it's mixed in with mediocre material that is all too indicative of its era. The best of Gibson's songs transcends their time quite effortlessly, and all of those songs are here, but they're more effectively heard on other compilations. However, this set is fascinating for the diehard fan, even if the sheer extensiveness of the set is a little intimidating. *— Stephen Thomas Erlewine*

Vince Gill

b. Apr. 1, 1957, Norman, OK
Guitar, Vocals / Contemporary Country, New Traditionalist
Vince Gill was one of the most popular mainstream country performers of the early '90s. Gill grew up in Oklahoma playing banjo and guitar with local bluegrass musicians. At age 18 he joined The Bluegrass Alliance in Louisville, KY, and played alongside band members Sam Bush and Dan Crary. After one year, he went to Los Angeles to play with Byron Berline and his band Sundance. Two years later he accompanied a friend to an audition for Pure Prairie League. The band members remembered Gill because his high school band Mountain Smoke had opened for them years before, and immediately offered him a job. In 1979 he became the band's lead singer. During his three years with them, the band had a Top 40 pop hit with his song "I'm Almost Ready" (1980). He left Pure Prairie League soon after the single's success to spend time with his then-pregnant wife Janis Oliver, a well-known bluegrass singer on the West Coast. After the birth of their child, Gill contacted Rodney Crowell to see if his band Cherry Bomb needed guitarist. Gill joined Crowell's group and, shortly afterward, former Cherry Bomb keyboard player Tony Brown signed Gill to a solo contract at RCA.

In 1984, Gill moved his family to Nashville and cut his debut EP, *Turn Me Loose*. His second single, "Victim of Life's Circumstances," cracked the country Top 40, beginning a string of hit singles that ran well into the '90s. The Academy of Country Music named Gill the Top New Male Vocalist of the Year in 1984. In 1985, Gill had one Top 40 and two Top Ten hits including "If It Weren't for Him," which featured harmonies from Rosanne Cash. In addition to his 12 hit singles, Gill sang harmonies and played guitar on over 120 records, wrote and co-wrote songs with artists like Rosanne Cash, and toured with Emmylou Harris' band during the latter half of the '80s. In 1989, Gill's career fired up again after he signed with MCA. His first album with the label, *When I Call Your Name*,

produced the Top 25 hit "Never Alone," a song co-written with Cash. Following "Oklahoma Swing," a No. 13 hit duet with Reba McEntire in 1990, Gill released "Never Knew Lonely," a No. 3 hit in the fall of 1990 that began a string of Top Ten hits that ran for five straight years. By the end of 1990, *When I Call Your Name* had gone platinum and he received a Grammy for Best Male Country Performance for the album's title cut. Gill's 1991 album *Pocket Full of Gold* went platinum a year after its release, and more hits and accolades followed.

By the time he was asked to joined the *Grand Ole Opry* in 1992, Gill had become a bona fide superstar—his '92 album *I Still Believe in You* went platinum within two months of its release. He had three Top Three hits in 1993, including "One More Chance." In 1993, Gill's RCA best-of album went gold, as did his Christmas album *Let There Be Peace on Earth*. In 1994, he released *When Love Finds You*, which hit the Top Three on the country album charts and crossed over to land on the Top Ten pop album chart. That year he won the Country Music Academy's Entertainer of the Year award and Male Vocalist of the Year, making him the biggest CMA award winner of all time. In June of 1996, Gill released *High Lonesome Sound*. *— Sandra Brennan*

When I Call Your Name / 1989 / MCA ✦✦✦✦
"Oklahoma Swing," Gill's duet with Reba McEntire, announced his return to a rootsier sound after leaving RCA. But it was the title cut, with Patty Loveless providing the harmonies, that soared highest from car radios and announced the arrival of a major star. *—Dan Cooper*

Pocket Full of Gold / 1991 / MCA ✦✦✦✦
A hit album with high bluegrass vocals, traditional country arrangement, and contemporary production. *—Mark A. Humphrey*

I Still Believe in You / 1992 / MCA ✦✦✦✦
Lots of folks inject a shot of R&B clichés into their honky tonk and call it country soul. Vince Gill is country's real soul man, and not because of a familiarity with Black artists' catalogues (though "Nothin' Like a Woman" comes close to sounding what lovers imagine Percy Sledge's "When a Man Loves a Woman" to be). It's because Gill's voice captures pain and promise, love and loneliness—all in a distillation so smooth that you don't even notice it sneaking up to blindside you. With his high tenor harmonies on songs like "Tryin' to Get Over You" and "No Future in the Past," you might even call this bluegrass soul—and you know that's gotta be lonesome. *—Brian Mansfield*

Let There Be Peace on Earth / 1993 / MCA ✦✦✦✦
Christmas music releases have become a country music tradition, but the result is often generic mushy background instrumentation on the same moldy standards. Guilty of this is Vince Gill, whose *Let There Be Peace On Earth* is as cliché-ridden as they come. *—Roch Parisien*

When Love Finds You / 1994 / MCA ✦✦✦
That Vince Gill—he sure is a nice guy. But at this point, we sure would welcome some serious nastiness from him to keep us awake. *—Dan Cooper*

● **The Essential Vince Gill** / 1995 / RCA ✦✦✦✦
The Essential Vince Gill collects highlights from the singer's pop-inflected material for RCA in the early '80s. While Gill didn't have as many hits during this era, the best songs stand up well next to his better-known songs. *—Thom Owens*

● **Souvenirs** / Nov. 21, 1995 / MCA Nashville ✦✦✦✦
Souvenirs collects the greatest hits from Vince Gill's most popular period—his recordings for MCA in the late '80s and early '90s. As such, it contains a wealth of first-rate songs and hits—including the No. 1 hits "I Still Believe In You" and "Don't Let Our Love Start Slippin' Away"—and functions as a good introduction to his music. *—Thom Owens*

High Lonesome Sound / Jun. 1996 / MCA ✦✦✦

Mickey Gilley

b. Mar. 9, 1937, Ferriday, LA
Piano, Vocals / Traditional Country, Honky Tonk
For most of his career, pianist/vocalist Mickey Gilley lived in the shadow of his cousin, Jerry Lee Lewis, playing a similar fusion of country, rock, blues, and R&B. In the early '70s, he managed to break through into country stardom, but it wasn't until the late '70s, when he became associated with the Urban Cowboy movement, that he became a superstar.

Gilley, like Lewis, was raised in Ferriday, LA. It wasn't until Jerry Lee had a hit with his first Sun single, "Crazy Arms," that Mickey decided he wanted to pursue a musical career. Gilley began recording for a number of independent Texas labels without much success in the late '50s. In the early '60s, he became a local favorite by playing a never-ending series of bars and clubs. A few singles became Texas hits, but he didn't have a national hit until 1968 with the minor hit "Now I Can Live Again" on Paula Records.

In 1970, he opened Gilley's Club in Pasadena; the honky tonk had previously been known as Sherry's Club and its owner, Sherwood Cryer, asked Mickey to re-open the bar with him. In 1974, he had another local hit with "Room Full of Roses," which was released on Astro Records.

Playboy Records, which was distributed by Epic, heard the record and acquired national distribution for the single. It became a No. 1 country hit, crossing over to No. 50 on the pop charts. "Room Full of Roses" launched a string of updated, countrypolitan-inflected honky tonk hits for Gilly that ran for just over a decade. Gilley racked up 16 No. 1 hits besides "Room Full of Roses," including "I Overlooked an Orchid," "City Lights," She's Pulling Me Back Again," "True Love Ways," "Stand By Me," "That's All That Matters," and "A Headache Tomorrow (Or a Heartache Tonight)."

Gilley signed with Epic Records after Playboy folded in 1978. The following year, the film *Urban Cowboy*—which was based on Gilley's Club and featured a cameo by Mickey, as well as several of his songs—brought him to national attention, which resulted in a string of six straight No. 1 singles. He continued to have Top Ten hits until 1986, when his career began to slip. The late '80s were plagued with problems for Gilley. Not only had a new generation of country singers replaced him on the charts, he had financial problems which culminated in the closing of Gilley's Club. Mickey turned his career around in the early '90s, when he became one of the first country stars to open a permanent theater in Branson, MO. Although he recorded some albums in the '90s—which were primarily available through television advertisements—he focused his career on the theater. —*Stephen Thomas Erlewine*

Live at Gilley's / 1978 / Epic ◆◆◆

That's All That Matters to Me / 1980 / Epic ◆◆◆◆
This is the album that benefited most from Gilley's *Urban Cowboy* associations, and there's a perfunctory back-cover shot of some cowboy riding a mechanical bull at Gilley's nightclub. Though Gilley the Balladeer became pretty formulaic during the progression of the '80s, it was a new wrinkle with this album, and he delivers it convincingly. Gilley says the title track is his best performance ever. —*Tom Roland*

Biggest Hits / 1982 / Epic ◆◆◆◆
This is a concise sampling of his '70s and '80s honky tonk hits. —*Mark A. Humphrey*

● **Ten Years of Hits** / 1984 / Epic ◆◆◆◆
It's a shame people have such a hard time dissociating Mickey Gilley from Stepford bulls. At his best, Jerry Lee Lewis' cousin has proven himself a legitimately soulful country singer, as evidenced here on No. 1 hits like "That's All That Matters to Me" and "A Headache Tomorrow (Or a Heartache Tonight)." —*Dan Cooper*

Jimmie Dale Gilmore

Guitar, Vocals / Progressive Country, Contemporary Country, Singer-Songwriter, Country-Folk, Alternative Country-Rock
With his warm, warbling tenor voice and folksy, friendly approach to both his music and his audiences, Jimmie Dale Gilmore is an easy guy to like. His music is a rich blend of traditional country, folk, blues, and rock styles. His lyrics reflect both his philosophical interests and his inherent downhome nature. Since moving to Austin, Texas and reviving his career in the '80s, Gilmore has in many ways come to represent the current Austin music scene—its rootsy mix of country, rock, and folk music—the way Willie Nelson once reigned as king of the town's cosmic cowboys in the '70s.

Gilmore's roots go back to Tulia, a small West Texas town where his father played lead guitar in a country band. When Gilmore was in grade school the family moved to Lubbock, a Panhandle town known for being the starting point for a surprising number of musicians (including Buddy Holly, Waylon Jennings, Terry Allen, and Gilmore's onetime singing partners Butch Hancock and Joe Ely). Growing up in Lubbock, Gilmore met Butch Hancock when they were both 12, and they've remained friends and frequent musical collaborators ever since. Gilmore later met Terry Allen, who he says inspired him to write his own songs. One of the first songs Gilmore wrote, in fact—when he was around 20—was "Treat Me Like a Saturday Night," which is today one of his most enduring pieces. Later, another casual friend of Gilmore's, Joe Ely, turned him on to the music of Townes Van Zandt, which Gilmore says was a revelation for the way Van Zandt integrated the worlds of folk and country music.

Gilmore and Ely began playing music together around Lubbock as the T. Nickel House Band. Later, after a brief stint in Austin, Gilmore hooked up again back in Lubbock with Ely and Hancock and formed the Flatlanders, a now-legendary band that also included Steve Wesson, Tony Pearson, and several peripheral members. The group recorded an album in Nashville in 1972, but it was only ever released at the time on 8-track tape. (Long a collector's item, it was finally re-released by Rounder Records in 1990 under the title *More a Legend than a Band*.) A mix of acoustic folk, string-band country, and country blues, the album included another of Gilmore's best-known songs, "Dallas," which was actually released as a promo single at the time but generated little interest. By the end of the year the band had split up.

Gilmore moved to Denver, playing music only as a hobby. Ely, meanwhile, had won a record contract, and had recorded some of Gilmore's songs. In 1980, Gilmore moved back to Austin, where he began playing

regular gigs in local clubs. Finally, in 1988, Gilmore released his debut solo album, *Fair and Square*, on HighTone, Ely's label at the time. This and his 1989 follow-up, *Jimmie Dale Gilmore*, featured songs by Gilmore as well as Hancock and Ely played in a more straightforward honky tonk style than anything Gilmore has done previously or since. These two albums gained Gilmore newfound acclaim just as Austin itself was becoming a musical hot spot again. In 1990, the Flatlanders album was re-released and Virgin Australia put out *Two Roads*, a duet album with Hancock that was recorded live during the pair's Australian tour. Gilmore was soon signed to Elektra, which released *After Awhile* in 1991 as part of the label's American Explorer series. The album retained a country feeling, but was less honky tonk in nature, and it attracted Gilmore even more acclaim. Nashville showed little interest in Gilmore's brand of country music, but he earned the praise of many critics. His next album, *Spinning Around the Sun*, came out in 1993 and again featured a mix of contemporary and traditional country-flavored songs and a fuller instrumental sound fronted by Gilmore's rich, warm voice. In 1996 he released *Braver Newer World*, produced by T-Bone Burnett. —*Kurt Wolff*

Fair & Square / 1988 / Hightone ◆◆◆◆
If Willie Nelson were not so mellow and were still writing good songs, he would sound a lot like this soulful Texas singer-songwriter. —*Mark A. Humphrey*

Jimmie Dale Gilmore / 1989 / Hightone ◆◆◆
Featured are more good songs from Austin. —*Mark A. Humphrey*

● **After Awhile** / 1991 / Elektra/Nonesuch ◆◆◆◆
This is the pinnacle of a long and varied career for Gilmore and the most perfect New Country release since Rosanne Cash's *Interiors*. Great songs and dang-near-flawless performance are included. The present-day singer-songwriter refuses to die. —*Roundup Newsletter*

Spinning Around the Sun / 1993 / Elektra ◆◆◆◆
Recorded in Nashville with Emory Gordy Jr. (Patty Loveless' husband and producer), *Spinning Around the Sun* contains covers of Hank Williams' "I'm So Lonesome I Could Cry" and Elvis Presley's "I Was the One." If Gilmore's nasal voice weren't so uncommercial and his songs didn't still take flight with mystical tangents, some folks might start accusing him of going mainstream. —*Brian Mansfield*

Braver Newer World / Jun. 25, 1996 / Elektra ◆◆◆◆

Gosdin Brothers

Vern (1934) and Rex (1938) Gosdin seem to have always been on the fringe of what was happening musically and never quite seemed to get their due. A stint in the bluegrass band Golden State Boys in 1960 led to their joining future Byrd, Chris Hillman, in the Hillmen. Once Hillman had joined the Byrds, Vern found work as a session musician and continued to play bluegrass with Rex.

In 1966 they recorded with Gene Clark, who had recently left the Byrds, on the critically acclaimed *Gene Clark with the Gosdin Brothers*. Then, in 1967, they hit with the song "Hangin' On," but were not able to follow up. At this point, Vern dropped out of the business for several years.

Vern made a comeback in 1976 with a new version of "Hangin' On" and once again hit the road with Rex. While Vern, at last, found some success, charting more than 27 records over 12 years, Rex was not as lucky. Of the three chart records he had before his death in 1983, the biggest was a duet with Tommy Jennings (Waylon's brother). —*Jim Worbois*

Chiseled in Stone / 1988 / CBS ◆◆◆◆
The second coming of this veteran country balladeer during the late '80s. Righteous and wrenching. —*Mark A. Humphrey*

Alone / 1989 / CBS ◆◆◆
These are great performances. —*Mark A. Humphrey*

10 Years of Greatest Hits Newly Recorded / 1990 / CBS ◆◆◆◆
Gosdin has George Jones' keening desperation in his vocals and an ironic wit in his writing. A fine overview of a great artist. —*Mark A. Humphrey*

Out of My Heart / 1991 / CBS ◆◆◆◆
Bold bleating from "The Voice." —*Mark A. Humphrey*

● **Best of Vern Gosdin** / Warner Bros. ◆◆◆◆
The Best of Vern Gosdin contains ten of his late '70s hits. Although they bear all the hallmarks of the era—slick, string-laden productions—they remain pure, impressive country. Gosdin sounds especially good when Emmylou Harris or Janie Fricke provide harmonies. —*Thom Owens*

Vern Gosdin

b. Aug. 5, 1934
Guitar, Vocals / Traditional Country
Vern Gosdin is one of the best and most subtle of traditional vocalists in country music. Born in Woodland, AL, the sixth of nine children, Gosdin first learned to sing in church. His appreciation of country music came

from listening to his idols the Louvin Brothers on the Grand Ole Opry. It was an older brother who taught Gosdin to play guitar at age 13. When he was in his late teens, his family moved to Birmingham, AL, to host the *Gosdin Family Gospel Show* on a local radio station. Gosdin and his brother Rex moved to Long Beach, CA, in 1961. Both had day jobs, but at night played with the Golden State Boys, a bluegrass group that included Don Parmley. Later Chris Hillman joined the group and they changed their name to the Hillmen. In the mid-'60s, Hillman left to become the bassist for the Byrds and Vern and Rex teamed up to sing country music as the Gosdin Brothers. They then became the opening act for the Byrds. The Gosdins had their Top 40 country hit in 1967 with "Hangin On" for the independent Bakersfield International label.

By 1968, the Gosdins had broken up and Vern had moved to Atlanta to open a glass and mirror shop. Though he focused on raising his family and building his business, he occasionally performed at local clubs. Vern decided to re-attempt music as a career in 1976 and went to Nashville to re-record "Hangin On" for Elektra. The single reached the country Top 20. However, its B-side, "Yesterday's Gone"—which featured harmonies from Emmylou Harris—reached the Top Ten and suddenly Gosdin's career took off. The following year he had seven major hits including "Till the End," "Never My Love," and "Mother Country Music." His string of successes continued through 1978.

In 1980, Elektra shut down its country division and Gosdin signed to Ovation. The following year, he had Top Ten success with "Dream of Me" and in 1982 again made it to the Top Ten with "Today My World Slipped Away" for AMI. By this point, Gosdin had a number of hits beneath his belt and had been in the business a long time, but he wasn't quite a full-fledged country star. That changed in 1983, when he signed with Poly-gram's subsidiary, Compleat Records. In 1983, Gosdin had two Top Five hits—"If You're Gonna Do Me Wrong (Do It Right)" and "Way Down Deep." The following year was also a good one for the singer, as he had a No. 1 hit with "I Can Tell By the Way You Dance (You're Gonna Love Me Tonight)" and two additional Top Ten hits. His career hit another lull in the mid-'80s, but he bounced back into the Top Ten in 1987, when he signed with Columbia Records. That year, "Do You Believe Me Now" became a No. 4 hit and it was followed in 1988 by the No. 1 "Set 'Em Up Joe" and the Top Ten hit "Chiseled in Stone" which was named the Country Music Association's Song of the Year. In the early '90s, Gosdin's popularity declined—after 1990's "Is It Raining At Your House," he wasn't able to crack into the Top 40—but he continued recording and performing. —*Sandra Brennan*

There Is a Season / 1984 / Compleat ✦✦✦✦
Throughout the album, Emmylou Harris provides nice harmonies reminiscent of Rex Gosdin's style. Roger McGuinn adds vocals (background and accompanying) and the 12-string instrumental break to "Turn Turn Turn" (very different from the break on the Byrds' version). —*Jim Worbois*

If Jesus Comes Tomorrow / 1984 / Compleat ✦✦✦
If Jesus Comes Tomorrow (What Then) is part gospel standards, part complementary originals, all sung by a honky tonk voice hoping for heaven. —*Brian Mansfield*

The Best of Vern Gosdin / 1989 / Warner Bros. ✦✦✦✦
Some fine performances from the early and mid-'80s; they are a mite over-produced. Get his Columbia work first. —*Mark A. Humphrey*

10 Years of Hits—Newly Recorded / 1990 / Columbia ✦✦✦
As the title says, *10 Years of Hits*—Newly Recorded has seven of Gosdin's Compleat hits—like "I Can Tell By the Way You Dance (You're Gonna Love Me Tonight)—from the early '80s re-recorded for his new label, Columbia, as well as four new tracks. Although they aren't the originals, Gosdin is in good voice and the new versions nearly equal to the hit singles. —*Stephen Thomas Erlewine*

● **Super Hits** / 1994 / Columbia ✦✦✦✦
Super Hits collects all of the biggest hits Vern Gosdin had on Columbia Records in the late '80s, including all of his Top Ten hits and the No. 1 hits "I'm Still Crazy" and "Set 'Em Up Joe." —*Thom Owens*

Jack Greene

b. Jan. 7, 1930, Maryville, TN
Guitar, Drums, Vocals / Country
Hailing from Maryville, TN, Greene got his start in the record business as a vocalist in Ernest Tubb's band, but he hardly had the same almost-on-key "twang" as his boss. In fact, Greene's smooth, pleasant sound contrasted a great deal with Tubb's blue-collar intonation. Nicknamed "the Jolly Green Giant," Greene learned guitar and drums but mined his vocal chords for a solid string of hit records from 1966-1969, including one with Jeannie Seely, who joined his road show and recorded duets with him for several years.

A bit of trivia: In 1967, Greene became the first country artist ever to appear in the Macy's Thanksgiving Day Parade. —*Tom Roland*

● **Greatest Hits** / 1986 / Gusto ✦✦✦✦
This basically sums up his peak years and includes all the classics: "All the Time," "There Goes My Everything," and "Statue of a Fool." —*Tom Roland*

Nanci Griffith

b. Jul. 6, 1953, Seguin, TX
Guitar, Vocals / Folk, Progressive Country, Contemporary Country, Singer-Songwriter
Nanci Griffith emerged in the '80s as perhaps the most promising folk/country singer-songwriter of her day. Kathy Mattea had a 1986 hit with "Love at the Five and Dime," and Suzy Bogguss covered "Outbound Plane" in 1991; others, including Lynn Anderson, have recorded her songs as well. A former schoolteacher from near Austin, TX, Griffith first released *There's a Light Beyond These Woods* on her own B.F. Deal label in 1978, followed by three more albums for the folk label Philo that displayed an ear for detail and times past. 1987's *Lone Star State of Mind* was her first for the country division of MCA and included Julie Gold's soon-to-be standard "From a Distance." After three country albums, Griffith switched to MCA's Los Angeles division, where she has moved toward pop with 1989's *Storms* and 1991's *Late Night Grande Hotel*. —*Brian Mansfield & William Ruhlmann*

There's a Light Beyond These Woods / 1978 / Philo ✦✦
Poet in My Window / 1982 / Philo ✦✦
Once in a Very Blue Moon / 1984 / Philo ✦✦✦✦
After two promising albums, Nanci Griffith finally perfected her mixture of singer-songwriter folk and Texas-based country on this lovely collection, which features her own story-songs such as "Mary and Omie" and well-chosen covers such as the Pat Alger/Eugene Levine title tune. —*William Ruhlmann*

★ **The Last of the True Believers** / 1986 / Philo ✦✦✦✦✦
Griffith hit her peak as a songwriter with classics such as "Love at the Five and Dime" and "Banks of the Pontchartrain," while singing over an always-appropriate backup provided by the '80s new bluegrass specialists Bela Fleck, Mark O'Connor, and others. The album earned her a major-label contract with MCA and provided the basis of country singer Kathy Mattea's entire career, but it is also a pivotal '80s folk album. —*William Ruhlmann*

Lone Star State of Mind / 1987 / MCA ✦✦✦
Storms / 1987 / MCA ✦✦✦
One Fair Summer Evening / 1988 / MCA ✦✦✦
Recorded live in Houston in 1988, this album features Griffith in a stripped-down musical setting, with the emphasis on her sometimes delicate, sometimes hearty vocals. Included is "Once in a Very Blue Moon," "From a Distance," and "Love at the Five and Dime." —*Roundup Newsletter*

Little Love Affairs / 1988 / MCA ✦✦✦✦
All of Griffith's albums have songs to recommend them; of her country-folk albums, this one has the most written by her, as well as good tunes by Harlan Howard and fellow Texan Robert Earl Keen Jr. The first half's prime Griffith, and the second suggests that, if she'd stuck with country, she might have started outselling her press—Suzy Bogguss later turned "Outbound Plane" into a hit, and there's probably at least one more of those tucked away here. —*Brian Mansfield*

Late Night Grande Hotel / 1991 / MCA ✦✦✦
Two albums out of Nashville and Griffith doesn't even resemble the new-country/folkie role in which she was once cast. Britishers Rod Argent and Peter Van Hooke insulate Griffith with strings and moody atmospheres that complement her wallflower fantasies. She's perhaps partial to "Power Lines" and "Down 'n' Outer," both tales of folks who fall through society's cracks. Probably, come to think of it, because she identifies with them. —*Brian Mansfield*

Other Voices, Other Rooms / 1993 / Elektra ✦✦✦✦
Griffith pays homage to a wide cut of folk music heroes: Woody Guthrie, Townes Van Zandt, Bob Dylan, Kate Wolf, Malvina Reynolds, and John Prine, to name a few. She sounds looser and more spirited than usual, and her earnest adoration for the songs shines through in these compelling remakes. —*Michael McCall*

● **The MCA Years: a Retrospective** / 1993 / MCA ✦✦✦✦
Flyer / 1994 / Elektra ✦✦✦

Merle Haggard

b. Apr. 6, 1937, Bakersfield, CA
Fiddle, Guitar, Vocals / Traditional Country, Bakersfield Sound
As a performer and a songwriter, Merle Haggard was the most important country artist to emerge in the '60s. While his music remained hardcore country, he pushed the boundaries of the genre. Like his idol Bob Wills, his music was a melting pot that drew from all forms of traditional American music—country, jazz, blues, and folk—and in the process,

developed a distinctive style of his own. As a performer, singer, and musician, he was one of the best, influencing countless other artists. Not coincidentally, he was the best singer-songwriter in country music since Hank Williams, writing a body of songs that became classics. Throughout his career, Haggard has been a champion of the working man, largely due to his rough and tumble history.

It's impossible to separate Haggard's music from his life. Haggard's father died from a brain tumor when Merle was nine years old. After his father's death, Merle became rebellious. In an attempt to straighten her son out, his mother put him in several juvenile detention centers, but it had little effect on Merle's behavior. As a teenager, he fell in love with country music, particularly Bob Wills, Lefty Frizzell, and Hank Williams. When he was 12 years old, Haggard was given his first guitar by his older brother and taught himself how to play by listening to records. Throughout his adolescence, he was repeatedly sent to juvenile hall and repeatedly he escaped. In 1952, the courts decided he was incorrigible and sent him to the high-security Preston School of Industry. After getting out of PSI, Haggard went to see Lefty Frizzell in concert in Bakersfield. Before the show, he went backstage and he sang a couple songs for Frizzell. Lefty was so impressed, he refused to go onstage until Haggard was allowed to sing a song. Merle went out and sang a few songs to an enthusiastic response from the audience.

The reception persuaded Haggard to actively pursue a musical career. While he was working during the day in oilfields and farms, he performed in local Bakersfield clubs. In 1956, he married Leona Hobbs; the couple moved into his family's old converted boxcar. Throughout 1957, Haggard was plagued by financial problems, which made him turn to robbery. At the end of the year, he attempted to rob a restaurant. He was drunk at the time and thought it was three in the morning, but it was 10:30 in the evening and the establishment was still open. Haggard was arrested that day. Haggard was sentenced to a 15-year term and sent to San Quentin prison. Haggard served two years before he was released on parole in 1960. After his release, Merle moved back in with Leona and returned to manual labor. In the meantime, he sang at local clubs at night. After taking second place at a local talent contest, Haggard was asked to become a relief singer for a band led by Johnny Barnett. Soon, Merle was making enough money playing music that he could quit his ditch digging job. While he was singing with Barnett, he gained the attention of Fuzzy Owen, who owned the small record label Tally Records. Owen and his cousin Lewis Talley were instrumental in establishing Haggard's musical career. Owen made the first recording of Haggard, cutting a demo version of one of the singer's first songs, "Skid Row," and releasing a couple hundred copies of the tune. Shortly after the recording, Talley was able to land Haggard a job at Paul's Cocktail Lounge, which led to a slot on a local music television show.

During this time, Bakersfield country was beginning to become a national scene, largely due to the hit singles of Buck Owens. At a time when mainstream country was dominated by the lush, smooth countrypolitan sound of Nashville, Bakersfield country grew out of hardcore honky tonk, adding elements of Western swing. Bakersfield country also relied on electric instruments more than other subgenres of country, giving the music a driving, edgy flavor. During the late '50s, Tommy Collins and Wynn Stewart were two of the pioneering Bakersfield artists to have hits, and both were influential on Merle Haggard's career, musically as well as professionally.

For six months in 1962 and 1963, Merle played with Stewart's band in Las Vegas. During this time, Haggard heard Wynn's song "Sing a Sad Song" and asked the star if he could record it. Stewart gave him the song and Merle recorded it for Tally Records in 1963. Although Tally had minimal distribution, the record became a national hit, climbing to No. 19 on the country charts early in 1964. "Sam Hill," Haggard's second single, wasn't a success, and a duet with Bonnie Owens called "Just Between the Two of Us" broke into the Top 30. The next year, his version of Liz Anderson's "(My Friends Are Gonna Be) Strangers" broke him into the Top Ten and established him as a budding star. Capitol Records bought out his contract with Tally and Merle released "I'm Gonna Break Every Heart I Can," his first single for Capitol, in the fall of 1965. The single wasn't a success, scratching into the Top 50, but his next single, "Swinging Doors," was a smash hit, rocketing to No. 5 in the spring of 1966. Late in 1965, Haggard began recruiting a backing band and named them the Strangers.

Merle Haggard became a genuine country superstar in 1966, with three Top Ten hits, including "Swinging Doors," the No. 3 "The Bottle Let Me Down" and "The Fugitive" (later retitled "I'm a Lonesome Fugitive"). Haggard's songwriting was beginning to blossom and audiences embraced his music, sending his "I Threw Away the Rose" to No. 3 early in 1967. The single began a remarkable streak of 37 straight Top Ten hits, including 23 No. 1 singles. "I Threw Away the Rose" was followed by four straight No. 1 hits—"Branded Man," "Sing Me Back Home," "The Legend of Bonnie and Clyde," and "Mama Tried." With the exception of "Bonnie and Clyde," the songs represented a change in Haggard's songwriting, as he began to directly address his troubled history. While the songs were

personal, they also helped establish him as a voice for the working class. In 1968, he recorded his first conceptual album, *Same Train, Different Train: A Tribute to Jimmie Rodgers*. Released in early 1969, the record was not only an affectionate salute to one of Haggard's heroes, it reflected a fascination with American musical history and a desire to expand his music by adding stronger elements of Western swing, jazz, and blues.

Merle released three singles in 1969—"Hungry Eyes," "Workin' Man Blues," and "Okie from Muskogee"—and all three reached No. 1. In particular, "Okie from Muskogee" sparked a tremendous amount of attention. Written partially as a joke, the song was an attack on the liberal hippies that dominated American pop culture in the late '60s. The song struck a chord in audiences across the country, just missing the pop Top 40. Because of the song, Haggard was asked to endorse George Wallace, but he refused. Haggard released a sequel to "Okie" called "The Fightin' Side of Me" at the beginning of 1970, and it also shot to No. 1. That same year, he released *A Tribute to the Best Damn Fiddle Player in the World (Or My Salute to Bob Wills*, which helped spark a revival of Western swing in the '70s. Throughout 1971 and 1972, the hits kept coming, including "Soldier's Last Letter," "Someday We'll Look Back," "Daddy Frank (The Guitar Man)," "Carolyn," "Grandma Harp," "It's Not Love (But It's Not Bad)," and "I Wonder If They Ever Think of Me." In 1972, the governor of California, Ronald Reagan, granted Haggard a full pardon. The following year, his hit streak continued, and he scored his biggest hit, "If We Make It Through December," which peaked at No. 28 on the pop charts.

Haggard stayed with Capitol records until 1977, and never once did his grip on the American audience slip during his tenure there. In 1977, he switched labels, signing with MCA. During his time on MCA, he continued to have a number of hits, but his work was becoming slightly inconsistent. His first two singles for the record label, "If We're Not Back in Love by Monday" and "Ramblin' Fever," hit No. 2 and he continued to have hits with the label throughout the end of the decade and the first part of the '80s. "I'm Always on a Mountain When I Fall" and "It's Been a Great Afternoon" were No. 2 hits in 1978. In 1979, the only had two hits, while in 1980, two selections from the Clint Eastwood movie *Bronco Billy* reached the top three—"The Way I Am" and "Misery and Gin." The two hits paved the way for his two biggest singles with MCA, the No. 1 duet with Eastwood, "Bar Room Buddies," and the No. 1 "I Think I'll Just Stay Here and Drink." Early in 1981, Haggard had a Top Ten hit with "Leonard," a tribute to his old friend Tommy Collins.

Later that year, Haggard published his autobiography, *Sing Me Back Home*; he also left MCA and signed with Epic Records. Once he began recording for Epic, he began producing his own records, which gave the music a leaner sound. His first two singles for the label, "My Favorite Memory" and "Big City," were No. 1 hits. The following year, he released a duet album with George Jones, called *A Taste of Yesterday's Wine*, which featured the No. 1 single "Yesterday's Wine" and the Top Ten "C.C. Waterback." From 1983 until the beginning of 1985, Haggard continued to score No. 1 hits, including the duet with Willie Nelson, "Pancho and Lefty."

Merle's chart fortunes began to change in 1985, as a new breed of singers began to dominate the chart. Nearly every one of the artists, from George Strait to Randy Travis, was greatly influenced by Haggard, but their idol's new singles now had a tough time reaching the top of the charts. He had two Top Ten hits in 1986, and 1987's *Chill Factor* was a success, spawning the Top Ten title track and "Twinkle, Twinkle Lucky Star," which would prove to be his last No. 1 hit. In 1990, he signed with Curb Records, but he continued to have trouble reaching the charts; *1994* spawned his last Top 60 hit, "In My Next Life." In 1996, Haggard released *1996*, which received uniformly strong reviews but failed to make an impact on country charts.—*Stephen Thomas Erlewine*

Strangers / 1965 / Capitol ✦✦✦

☆ **Swinging Doors/The Bottle Let Me Down** / 1966 / Capitol ✦✦✦✦✦
Merle Haggard's third album, *Swinging Doors / The Bottle Let Me Down*, was assembled from a variety of singles and sessions like its two predecessors, but it contained a stronger overall selection of material than either album. In addition to the two masterpieces from which the album took its name, the record included a terrific version of Tommy Collins' "High On a Hilltop," plus excellent songs like "The Girl Turned Ripe," "If I Could Be Him," and "Someone Else You've Known." There are a few weak tracks, but Haggard and his band are in fine form, making the filler enjoyable. —*Stephen Thomas Erlewine*

Sing Me Back Home / 1968 / Capitol ✦✦✦✦

☆ **Same Train, Different Time** / 1969 / Bear Family ✦✦✦✦✦
Same Train, Different Time is Merle Haggard's affectionate tribute to Jimmy Rodgers. Haggard provides narration between the songs, offering tales of Rodgers' life and music. While the album is rooted in the past, the key to its success is how Haggard updates these traditional songs without losing sight of their roots. There are contemporary folk, country and blues influences scattered throughout the record, adding depth to the

music and proving that Rodgers' music is indeed timeless. —*Stephen Thomas Erlewine*

☆ **Tribute to the Best Damn Fiddle Player** / 1970 / Koch ✦✦✦✦✦
After releasing his tribute to Jimmie Rodgers, Merle Haggard immediately set about working on a tribute to his other major musical idol, Bob Wills. Haggard learned how to play fiddle and, within a month, he had recruited many of the original Playboys to augment the Strangers and begun recording the album that became *A Tribute to the Best Damn Fiddle Player: My Salute to Bob Wills*. Where *Same Train, Different Time* was a measured, heartfelt tribute, *Best Damn Fiddle Player* is a ragged, enthusiastic good time. Haggard, the Strangers and the Playboys play their hearts out, breathing in life to Wills warhorses like "Right or Wrong," "Stay A Little Longer," "Time Changes Everything," and "San Antonio Rose" while bringing attention to lesser-known songs like "Brain Cloudy Blues," "I Knew the Moment I Lost You" and "Old-Fashioned Love." The fact that Western swing re-established itself as a viable country genre after the release of *A Tribute to the Best Damn Fiddle Player* is a testament to the power and charm of this record. —*Stephen Thomas Erlewine*

I Love Dixie Blues . . . So I Recorded "live" in New Orleans / 1973 / Capitol ✦✦✦

His Greatest & His Best / 1985 / MCA ✦✦✦✦
Haggard's tenure on MCA was brief but productive. Highlights, all included here, were "If We're Not Back in Love by Monday," "Leonard" (a tribute to songwriter Tommy Collins), and "Misery and Gin." —*Dan Cooper*

Greatest Hits of the 80's / 1990 / Epic ✦✦✦

☆ **More of the Best** / 1990 / Rhino ✦✦✦✦✦
Rhino's *More of the Best* was designed to supplement *Capitol Collector's Series*, which explains why it is an odd, uneven collection. Since the very nature of the entire *Capitol Collector's Series* was to include the artist's biggest hits plus selected rarities and forgotten singles, the Capitol compilation was missing many of Merle Haggard's very best and most popular singles. *More of the Best* collects many of the most shocking omissions—"Sing A Sad Song," "Branded Man," "Mama Tried," "If We Make It Through December"—and adds album tracks like "Silver Wings" and "White Line Fever," as well as MCA hits like "I'm Always On A Mountain When I Fall," "It's Been a Great Afternoon," "Red Bandana," "Rainbow Stew," and "I Think I'll Just Stay Here and Drink." The result is an unven and slightly incoherent collection—it goes from 1963 to 1980 in under an hour—that is nevertheless enjoyable. However, *The Lonesome Fugitive* and *Down Every Road* anthologies have rendered *More of the Best* redundant, since both are more comprehensive and coherent. Still, *More of the Best* is a good sampler and it does contain a few tracks that are rarely included on other anthologies. —*Stephen Thomas Erlewine*

☆ **Capitol Collectors Series** / Jan. 29, 1990 / Capitol ✦✦✦✦
"The Bottle Let Me Down," "Workin' Man Blues," "Okie from Muskogee," and other songs come from the top country artist of the '60s and '70s, with picking from the likes of Glen D. Hardin, James Burton, Roy Nichols, and Ralph Mooney. —*AMG*

★ **Lonesome Fugitive: The Merle Haggard Anthology (1963-1977)** / 1995 / Razor & Tie ✦✦✦✦✦
This is an excellent double-disc retrospective of Hag's Capitol records. Over the course of the 40-track set, every hit country single Haggard had between 1963 and 1972 is included, as are the majority of his hits between 1973 and 1976. While not every great performance and song Merle recorded during this era is included—he was so prolific it would have been impossible to condense *everything* onto a double-disc set—*Lonesome Fugitive* remains a definitive collection. It has all of the hits, most of his greatest songs, and illustrates the depth of his music in the most concise manner possible. Furthermore, *Lonesome Fugitive* is the only place all of Haggard's classic hits are available on one collection, which means it is both the perfect introduction and a career-defining retrospective. —*Stephen Thomas Erlewine*

Untamed Hawk [box] / 1995 / Bear Family ✦✦✦✦

Vintage Collection Series / Jan. 23, 1996 / Capitol ✦✦✦✦
Vintage features a good cross-section of Merle Haggard's biggest hits, including "Mama Tried" and "Hungry Eyes," as well as a handful of rarities that should please both collectors and neophytes. Razor & Tie's *The Lonesome Fugitive* offers a more thorough overview and *Capitol Collector's Series* has more diversity, but *Vintage* offers a fine introduction to one of country's greatest singer-songwriters. —*Stephen Thomas Erlewine*

☆ **Down Every Road** / Apr. 1996 / Capitol ✦✦✦✦
Merle Haggard has been served by a countless number of compilations, but *Down Every Road* is the first multi-disc box set to attempt to give an overview of his career. Spanning from his first singles for Tally, through his glory days on Capitol to his scattershot later career, *Down Every Road* features every one of Haggard's necessary songs, as well as a couple of more obscure gems, including a handful of unreleased songs.

Though most casual fans will be better-served by *The Lonesome Fugitive*, a lean double-disc set that contains all of his essential songs, *Down Every Road* is ideal for listeners that want to dig a little deeper. It gives an excellent picture of the full scope of Haggard's talents as a songwriter and musician. —*Stephen Thomas Erlewine*

Tom T. Hall

b. May 25, 1936, Olive Hill, KY
Guitar, Vocals / Country-Pop
Tom T. Hall is known as a storyteller, a songwriter with a keen eye for detail and a knack for narrative. Many musicians have covered his songs—most notably Jeannie C. Riley's 1968 hit "Harper Valley P.T.A."—and he also has racked up a number of solo hits, including seven No. 1 singles.

Hall is the son of a brick-laying minister, who gave his child a guitar at the age of eight. He had already begun to write poetry, so it was a natural progression for him to begin writing songs. Hall began learning music and performing techniques from a local musician called Clayton Delaney. At the age of 11, his mother died. Four years later, his father was shot in a fishing accident, which prevented him from working. In order to support himself and his father, Hall quit school and took a job in a local garment factory. While he was working in the factory, he formed his first band, the Kentucky Travelers. The group played bluegrass and gigged at local schools, as well as a radio station in Morehead, KY. The station was sponsored by the Polar Bear Flour Company; Hall wrote a jingle for the company. After the Kentucky Travelers broke up, Hall became a DJ at the station.

In 1957, Hall enlisted in the Army and was stationed in Germany. While in Germany, he performed at local NCO clubs on the Armed Forces Radio Network, where he sang mostly original material, which usually had a comic bent to it. After four years of service, he was discharged in 1961. Once he returned to the states, he enrolled in Roanoke College as a journalism student; he supported himself by DJing at a radio station in Salem, VA.

One day a Nashville songwriter was visiting the Salem radio station and he heard Hall's songs. Impressed, the songwriter sent the songs to a publisher named Jimmy Key, who ran New Key Publishing. Key signed Hall as a songwriter, bringing the songs to a variety of recording artists. The first singer to have a hit with one of Tom's songs was Jimmy Newman, who brought "DJ for a Day" to No. 1 on the country charts in 1963. In early 1964, Dave Dudley took "Mad" to the Top Ten. The back-to-back success convinced Hall to move to Nashville, where he was to continue his career as a professional songwriter.

After Johnny Wright had a No. 1 hit with Hall's "Hello Vietnam," the music industry was pressuring Tom to become a performer. He decided to take the plunge in 1967, signing a contract with Mercury Records. His first single, "I Washed My Face in the Morning Dew," was released in the summer of 1967 and became a minor hit. Hall followed the single with two other singles in 1968 that failed to crack the Top 40. Then, in the late summer of 1968, Jeannie C. Riley had a major hit with Tom's "Harper Valley P.T.A.," which spent three weeks at the top of the charts and was voted the Single of the Year by the Country Music Association. Its success brought attention to Hall's own recording career, which was evident from the performance of "Ballad of Forty Dollars." The song became his first Top Ten hit, climbing all the way to No. 4.

Throughout 1969, he had a string of hit singles, culminated by the release of the No. 1 single "A Week In A Country Jail" at the end of the year. The following year was just as successful, as "Shoeshine Man" and "Salute to a Switchblade" both hit the Top Ten. In 1971, he had his second No. 1 single and his biggest hit, "The Year That Clayton Delaney Died," which was based on his childhood hero.

For most of the early '70s, Hall was a consistent hit-maker as well as a popular concert attraction. Between 1971 and 1976, he had five No. 1 hits besides "The Year That Clayton Delaney Died:" "Old Dogs, Children, and Watermelon Wine," "I Love, "Country Is," "I Care," and "Faster Horses (The Cowboy and the Poet)." Hall was appearing on television shows with regularity during this time, particularly *Hee Haw*. He also wrote a book on songwriting, which led to his authorship of a pair of books in the late '70s and early '80s—the semi-autobiography *The Storyteller's Nashville* (1979) and the novel *The Laughing Man of Woodmont* (1982).

Although he continued to have the occasional Top Ten hit in the late '70s—most notably the No. 4 "Your Man Loves You, Honey" (1977)—Hall didn't deliver hit singles as consistently as he did the first half of the decade. That pattern continued in the early '80s, when he began having trouble cracking the Top 40; only 1984's "P.S. I Love You," a cover of a 1934 Rudy Vallee hit, made it into the Top Ten. After 1986, Hall retired from recording, although artists continued to record his songs. In 1996, he delivered *Songs from Sopchoppy*, his first album in ten years. —*Stephen Thomas Erlewine*

☆ **In Search of a Song** / 1971 / Mercury ✦✦✦✦✦
Hall gathered his material while driving solo through rural America, and his songs are literal and compassionate—but not romantic or sentimen-

tal. Instead, he fills his heartland stories with extraordinary realism and humanity. —*Michael McCall*

Greatest Hits, Vol. 1 / 1972 / Mercury ✦✦✦✦
Greatest Hits contains the bulk of Tom T. Hall's biggest hits from the late '60s and early '70s, including all his Top Ten hits from that era—"Ballad of Forty Dollars," "Homecoming," "A Week In A Country Jail," "Shoeshine Man," "Salute to a Switchblade," "The Year that Clayton Delaney Died," and "Me and Jesus"—but the record only hints at the his talent as a songwriter. Many of his best songs are on *Greatest Hits* and the collection does avoid his tendency for cuteness (with only a couple of exceptions), making *Greatest Hits* a good introduction, even though it does bypass plenty of fine songs. —*Thom Owens*

Greatest Hits, Vol. 2 / 1975 / PolyGram ✦✦✦
Where *Greatest Hits* had the bulk of Tom T. Hall's greatest story songs, *Greatest Hits, Vol. 2* concentrates on his silly, cutesy songs, like "Sneaky Snake," "I Like Beer," "I Love," and "Old Dogs, Children and Watermelon Wine," among others. For fans of his detailed narratives, these songs can be quite grating, but for listeners that want all of these hits in one package, *Greatest Hits, Vol. 2* functions quite nicely. —*Thom Owens*

Greatest Hits, Vol. 3 / 1978 / Polydor ✦✦✦

★ **Essential Tom T. Hall** / 1988 / Mercury ✦✦✦✦✦
Tom T's songs are stories filled with interesting characters. Some of Hall's most interesting characters are gathered on this record which celebrates the first 20 years of his career as a performer. (Hall was a writer first with his most famous pre-performer song being "Harper Valley PTA.") Whether you're looking for a hits package (which this isn't, strictly speaking) or just want to learn more about Hall, this is a fine place to start. —*Jim Worbois*

Greatest Hits, Vols. 1 & 2 / 1993 / Mercury ✦✦✦✦
Greatest Hits, Vols. 1 & 2 combines Tom T. Hall's first two greatest hits albums on one CD. Although it is a good bargain, the two albums don't necessarily sit well together—the earlier story songs are considerably more heartfelt and substantial than the pseudo-novelties that comprise the latter songs. Nevertheless, the two-fer CD works as the best single-disc retrospective of Hall's career, although it still misses a couple of key tracks. —*Stephen Thomas Erlewine*

★ **Storyteller, Poet, Philosopher** / Nov. 14, 1995 / Mercury ✦✦✦✦✦
The double-disc box set *Storyteller, Poet, Philosopher* concentrates on Tom T. Hall's talents as a narrative songwriter, eschewing some of his better-known novelties for lesser-known, but better-written, serious songs. That doesn't mean the box is devoid of hits—all of the important ones are here. What that does mean is that *Storyteller, Poet, Philosopher* is the first Tom T. Hall compilation to accurately convey the scope of his talents, as well as his achievements. —*Thom Owens*

Songs From Sopchoppy / 1996 / Mercury ✦✦

Ballad of Forty Dollars/Homecoming / Bear Family ✦✦✦✦

I Witness Life/100 Children / Bear Family ✦✦✦✦
I Witness Life and *100 Children*, two of Tom T. Hall's excellent late '60s albums, are combined on this single compact disc. Although many of the best songs were featured on *Greatest Hits* and *Storyteller, Poet Philosopher*, these albums work well as individual records and they're well worth acquiring for any Hall fan. —*Thom Owens*

Emmylou Harris

b. Apr. 2, 1949, Birmingham, AL
Guitar, Vocals / Traditional Country, Progressive Country, Country-Rock, Contemporary Country, Folk-Rock
It's difficult to label Emmylou Harris, except to say everyone agrees that her voice is exceptionally, achingly beautiful. Her career, now heading toward the quarter-century mark, spans many types of music and at the moment rests in traditional country—sort of. In fact, Harris, who came to country with a hip, rock image, is now one of the most vocal proponents of pure country. In a decade that has begun with a mania for singers with oversized Stetsons, she has the taste and the credentials to suggest that maybe George Jones and Merle Haggard ought to be given a good listen too.

Her career began with folk music in the late '60s in NYC and around the Washington, DC, area, where she met Gram Parsons, formerly of the Byrds. It was Parsons who fine-tuned her appreciation for country music, particularly songs that featured heart-tugging harmony work, à la Louvin Brothers and Everly Brothers. For a brief spell Harris and Parsons worked together in his band the Fallen Angels. After his death in 1973, Harris went solo, pursuing a sound that melded strains of pure country with elements of singer-songwriter folk and acoustic-flavored rock into her sound.

It was with her second album, *Elite Hotel*, that Harris achieved some real success. *Elite Hotel* blended country standards and country-rock and yielded three No. 1 hits, including a remake of a Don Gibson song, "Sweet Dreams." Later on in her career, the traditional *Blue Kentucky Girl* brought Harris a Grammy. Another album, *Roses in the Snow*, rein-

forced her reputation as a superb interpreter of traditional country. In the '80s, she teamed up with Dolly Parton and Linda Ronstadt on *Trio*, a great commercial success and the only country album of that decade to reach the pop Top Ten. As a live performer, Harris has enjoyed a reputation for assembling stellar road bands, which have included British guitar ace Albert Lee and bluegrass journeyman Ricky Skaggs.

Given her versatility and broad musical taste, it's difficult to predict what albums we'll see from Emmylou Harris through the '90s; but whether it's country-rock or blues, ballads or bluegrass, you can be sure it will be done right—memorably right. —*David Vinopal*

Gliding Bird / 1970 / Amos ✦✦

☆ **Elite Hotel** / 1975 / Reprise ✦✦✦✦✦
Picking up the torch from her late partner, Gram Parsons, Emmylou Harris defined the country-rock hybrid of the '70s and '80s. Here she presents her own versions of Parsons' classics "Sin City" and "Wheels," gives a boost to up-and-comer Rodney Crowell, and even covers the Beatles, all in her heartbreaking voice and backed by a group of session stars soon aptly named "The Hot Band." —*William Ruhlmann*

Pieces of the Sky / 1975 / Reprise ✦✦✦✦
With a feathery voice that could knock people over, and a taste for vintage country music nurtured by Gram Parsons, Harris' career persona was already fully in place on this, her remarkable major-label debut. Included is "Boulder to Birmingham," one of her rare original tunes, and a performance that could give a dead man chicken skin. —*Dan Cooper*

Luxury Liner / 1977 / Warner Bros. ✦✦✦✦
While it's probably an impossibility for Harris to make a bad record, this would certainly be one of her more uninspired efforts. Many of the tracks, including those by her former mentor, Gram Parsons, feel lifeless. —*Jim Worbois*

★ **Profile (The Best of Emmylou Harris)** / 1978 / Warner Bros. ✦✦✦✦✦
Profile (The Best of Emmylou Harris) collects 12 of Harris' biggest hits from the mid-'70s, including the No. 1 hits "Together Again," "Sweet Dreams," "Two More Bottles of Wine," and the Top Ten hits "One of These Days," "If I Could Only Win Your Love," "You Never Can Tell," "Making Believe," and "To Daddy." —*Stephen Thomas Erlewine*

★ **A Quarter Moon in a Ten Cent Town** / 1978 / Warner Bros. ✦✦✦✦✦
Harris' albums of the period are uniformly strong, and the choices made here are predicated more than usual on personal taste. This album gets the nod largely for its definitive versions of the Crowell songs "Leaving Louisiana in the Broad Daylight" and "I Ain't Living Long like This." —*William Ruhlmann*

Blue Kentucky Girl / 1979 / Warner Bros. ✦✦✦
For the most part, this is a nice record filled with the kinds of songs and harmonies that no one does better than Harris. Unfortunately, one low point is her cover of "Hickory Wind" which she previously performed with Gram Parsons and which uses many of the same musicians Parsons used on his record. This version has none of the emotion of the former and, in fact, comes off rather lifeless. Still, don't let that sway you away from the rest of the record. —*Jim Worbois*

Roses in the Snow / 1980 / Warner Bros. ✦✦✦✦
The record label questioned Harris' decision to release an album featuring hybrid bluegrass—understandably, since it wasn't exactly in vogue. But Harris had Ricky Skaggs in her corner, and pulled it off with her usual flair. —*Tom Roland*

Evangeline / 1981 / Warner Bros. ✦✦✦
This rock-heavy package moves gracefully to bluegrass, folk, and jazz-inflected tracks as well. Thanks to contractual agreements, this is the only place you'll find the version of "Mister Sandman" that features Dolly Parton and Linda Ronstadt. —*Tom Roland*

Cimarron / Mar. 1981 / Warner Bros. ✦✦✦
One of Harris' best with everything in place to make it a real listening pleasure. In addition to many of her regular guests (Fayssoux Starling, two-thirds of the singing group the Whites, etc.), the album also features a duet with Don Williams, and the Amazing Rhythm Aces, with Barry Burton sitting in on guitar. —*Jim Worbois*

White Shoes / 1983 / Warner Bros. ✦✦✦
Harris tries on rock this time out and it fits as well as country. Her reading on "Diamonds Are a Girl's Best Friend" is nearly identical to T-Bone Burnett's own version from his *Trap Door* LP (not so strange since he arranged and sang on this version—Burnett's is a bit better, though.) —*Jim Worbois*

The Ballad of Sally Rose / 1985 / Warner Bros. ✦✦✦✦
Harris switched gears on this album, co-writing with Paul Kennerley a semi-autobiographical song cycle that makes you wonder why she had spent so much time interpreting the work of others. The album is unique in her catalog, but it's a successful attempt to try something different. —*William Ruhlmann*

At the Ryman / 1992 / Reprise ✦✦✦✦
This is the album debut of the Nashville Ramblers, her acoustic backing

band featuring Sam Bush and Roy Huskey, Jr., recorded over three nights in the former home of the Grand Ole Opry. Harris' choice of songs strikes a balance between hillbilly classics and folk-influenced rock, with Bill Monroe receiving the heaviest tribute but sharing space with Tex Owens, Bruce Springsteen, and John Fogerty. —*Brian Mansfield*

Cowgirl's Prayer / 1993 / Asylum ✦✦✦✦
This is a collection of reflective, wholly adult songs set to exquisitely austere arrangements. —*Michael McCall*

Wrecking Ball / Sep. 26, 1995 / Grapevine ✦✦✦

Hawkshaw Hawkins (Harold Hawkins)

b. Dec. 22, 1921, Huntington, WV, **d.** Mar. 5, 1963
Guitar, Vocals / Country
Born Harold F. Hawkins, Hawkshaw is a country singer, guitarist, songwriter, and entertainer. A large man (6 ft., 6 in.) with a deep singing voice, Hawkins was an immensely popular performer in country music for many years without the benefit of big record success. He started on radio, becoming a regular on WWVA's "Wheeling Jamboree" by 1946 and making his first records for the King label around that time. By 1953 he signed with RCA Victor and became a regular member of the Grand Ole Opry by 1955. Described as "the man with eleven and a half yards of personality," Hawkins was a warm and engaging performer both onstage and on records, able to pull off a wide variety of material from maudlin weepers to uptempo novelties. His label-jumping from Columbia in the late '50s and back to King by the early '60s moved his material closer to commercial mainstream country, but his time in the spotlight ran out when he perished in the same plane crash as Cowboy Copas and Patsy Cline. —*Cub Koda*

● **Hawkshaw Hawkins, Vol. 1** / 1988 / Deluxe ✦✦✦✦
Hawkshaw Hawkins, Vol. 1 has a cross-section of his King recordings, which were made between 1946 and 1953. Not all of his hits are included, but the collection does have "Sunny Side of the Mountain," "I Am Slowly Dying of a Broken Heart," and "Rattlesnakin' Daddy," which makes it an effective introduction. —*Stephen Thomas Erlewine*

Hawk 1953-61 / 1991 / Bear Family ✦✦✦✦
An excellent 3-CD boxed set. All the RCA-Victor and Columbia recordings, with superlative sound and liner notes. —*Cub Koda*

Jimmy Heap & the Melody Masters

Guitar, Vocals / Honky Tonk
Texas-born bandleader Heap put together the Melody Masters after World War II and quickly became an attraction on the roadhouse/dancehall circuit, mining similar turf to that of other Western swing bands of the area. Quite popular from the late '40s through early '50s, Heap & the Melody Masters are generally credited with one of the earliest versions of the country classic "Release Me," as well as several other hits, among them another country standard, "The Wild Side of Life." —*Cub Koda*

● **Release Me** / 1992 / Bear Family ✦✦✦✦
A great 30-track, single-disc compilation of Heap's earliest and best sides. Includes the title track, "Let's Do It Just Once," "It Takes a Heap of Lovin'," and "Ethyl in My Gas Tank (No Gal in My Arms)." This is great Western swing-style material in transition. —*Cub Koda*

Highway 101

Country-Rock, Country-Pop
The country-rock band Highway 101 formed in 1986 when Nitty Gritty Dirt Band manager Chuck Morris wanted a showcase for his newest discovery, Paulette Carlson, a talented singer and guitarist from Minnesota. Morris brought together guitarist/vocalist Jack Daniels, drummer/vocalist Cactus Moser, and bassist/guitarist/mandolin player Curtis Stone. All four original members were successful musicians before joining the band. Daniels and Stone had worked together in the late '70s, when they toured with Burton Cummings. After touring with Cummings, the duo formed the Lizards, who frequently played at the Palomino Club.
Carlson wrote Highway 101's debut single, "The Bed You Made for Me," which became a No. 4 hit in early 1987. The band's eponymous debut album, also released in 1987, produced two more hits—the No. 3 "Whiskey, If You Were a Woman" and "Somewhere Tonight," which became their first No. 1 hit.
Highway 101 went on to score numerous Top Ten singles, including three other No. 1 hits, in the latter half of the '80s. Between 1987-1989, the band was named Group of the Year by both the Academy of Country Music and the Country Music Association. In 1990, Carlson left the band to pursue a solo career, and the band brought in Nikki Nelson to replace her. Their first single with Nelson was the title cut from *Bing Bang Boom* (1991), which became a Top 15 single. However, the group wasn't as popular following the departure of Paulette Carlson—by the end of 1992, they could no longer crack the Top 40. Jack Daniels left the group in 1993, reducing it to a trio. The group signed with Liberty Records and released *The New Frontier*, which was a major commercial disappoint-

ment. In 1995, Carlson rejoined Highway 101 to celebrate their ten-year anniversary; the following year they released the aptly titled album *Reunion.* —*Sandra Brennan*

Highway 101 / 1987 / Warner Bros. ✦✦✦✦
The main thing that this country-rock quartet had going for it was lead singer Paulette Carlson, who approximated the throaty, torn vocal style of Stevie Nicks, but with a Southern accent. The group was best on its debut album, which included such characteristic hits as "Whiskey, If You Were a Woman" and "The Bed You Made for Me." —*William Ruhlmann*

Highway 101 2 / 1988 / Warner Bros. ✦✦✦
Highway 101's second album followed the same rocking country formula that made their debut a success, but its best songs—"Setting Me Up" and "Honky Tonk Heart"—are as good as anything on the first album. —*Thom Owens*

Paint the Town / 1989 / Warner Bros. ✦✦✦
Highway 101 was beginning to show signs of stagnation on *Paint the Town.* Although there were still some good songs on it—particularly the No. 1 single "Who's Lonely Now"—the quality of material wasn't as strong as their first two albums and the group was sounding tired, verging on the formulaic. —*Thom Owens*

● **Greatest Hits** / Sep. 11, 1990 / Warner Bros. ✦✦✦✦
Greatest Hits collects all of the hits from Highway 101's late '80s highwater mark, including the No. 1 hits "Somewhere Tonight" and "(Do You Love Me) Just Say Yes," plus the classic "Whiskey, If You Were A Woman." —*Thom Owens*

Bing Bang Boom / 1991 / Warner Bros. ✦✦

The New Frontier / Sep. 13, 1993 / Liberty ✦✦

Reunited / Feb. 27, 1996 / WillowTree Records ✦✦✦
Reunited was recorded around Highway 101's tenth anniversary. To celebrate, Paulette Carlson joined the band again and the difference is apparent. The band and Carlson need each other—they are more energetic together than they are apart. Unfortunately, Highway 101 didn't create an album of all-new material—out of the 12 tracks, four are re-recordings of their biggest hits. These are fine, but they don't have the spark of the originals, nor do they have the charm of the new songs. Though it isn't as good as their first two albums, it is better than either of their Liberty albums. —*Thom Owens*

Faith Hill

Vocals / Contemporary Country
Faith Hill was one of the most popular female singers of 1993 and 1994. Raised in Star, MS, by adoptive parents, Hill grew up idolizing Reba McEntire; as a youth would sing anywhere she could. When Faith was 19, she left Jackson and headed for Nashville, where she got a job selling T-shirts at Fan Fair. Eventually, she landed a job at Gary Morris' Nashville company. She worked there one year before a songwriter overheard her singing along with the radio. The songwriter asked her to sing demo tapes.
Hill made her professional debut singing with songwriter/musician Gary Burr, who went on to become her co-producer. After signing with Warner Brothers she released her debut single, "Wild One," in the fall of 1993. "Wild One" became a hit, spending four weeks at No. 1 on the country charts. Hill released her debut album, *Take Me as I Am,* in 1994. The record reached the Top Ten on the country charts and went gold within a year of its release. Also in 1994, her second single, "Piece of My Heart," also became a No. 1 hit. —*Sandra Brennan & Brian Mansfield*

Take Me As I Am / 1994 / Warner Bros. ✦✦✦✦
Whether she's singing songs associated with Janis Joplin ("Piece of My Heart") or Maura O'Connell ("I Would Be Stronger than That"), Faith Hill sounds every bit like the new-generation Reba McEntire heir her press makes her out to be. Hill sings with a natural tear in her voice that recalls McEntire without ever mimicking her. Hill sounds like a star on all ten cuts, whether she's fronting minimal acoustic accompaniment on "Just Around the Eyes" or rocking out on "Wild One." —*Brian Mansfield*

● **It Matters To Me** / 1995 / Warner Bros. ✦✦✦✦
On her second album, Faith Hill confirmed that *Take Me As I Am* was no fluke. Like her debut album, *It Matters to Me* is an ambitious, diverse set of contemporary country that proves Hill can tackle virtually every subgenre of country, singing rockers, ballads, socially-aware stories, and love songs with an equal amount of grace. The singles "Let's Go to Vegas" and "It Matters to Me" aren't the only strong songs here—the entire album is rich with first-rate songs, as well as superb singing from Hill, one of the most promising female vocalists of the mid-'90s. —*Stephen Thomas Erlewine*

Becky Hobbs

Piano
Becky Hobbs is a piano-pounding honky tonker who performs cheeky country boppers and hard-bitten ballads. An Oklahoma native, and

daughter of a violinist, she wanted to be a songwriter from the age of five. She began playing piano and making up tunes at age nine. When she was 14, Hobbs began writing Bob Dylan-influenced protest songs and was singing in a folk duo with her pal Beth Morrison. The following year she started the Four Faces of Eve, an all-girl band. While attending Tulsa University, she played in Sir Prize Package. In 1971 she was performing with Swampfox. Three years later she moved to Los Angeles, where she had some success as a songwriter providing songs for Helen Reddy and Jane Oliver before moving to Nashville.

In 1974, Hobbs released her self-titled debut album with MCA. The following year, she signed with Tatoo Records and released *From the Heartland*. Two years later, in 1978, Hobbs recorded "The More I Get the More I Want" for Mercury and had her first minor hit. Her next single, "I Can't Say Goodbye to You," made it to the Top 50. This led to three more minor hits. Meanwhile, she continued writing songs, which were usually recorded by other musicians. During the '80s, such performers as Lacy J. Dalton and the Tennessee Valley Boys had success with her songs.

In 1983, Hobbs scored a Top Ten hit for Columbia with "Let's Get Over Them Together," a duet with Moe Bandy. Over the next two years, she had four hits for Liberty/EMI-America, among them "Hottest 'Ex' in Texas." That year she had songs recorded by George Jones and Loretta Lynn ("We Sure Made Good Love"), Alabama ("I Want to Know You Before We Make Love," "Christmas Memories"), Moe Bandy and Joe Stampley ("Still on a Roll"), and Shelly West ("I'll Dance the Two Step," "How It All Went Wrong"). Hobb debuted on the *Grand Ole Opry* in 1985. Two years later she had hit songs recorded by Conway Twitty, Glen Campbell, and Emmylou Harris, who earned a Grammy nomination with Hobbs' "You Are."

Hobbs singed to MTM Records in 1988 and released the album *All Keyed Up*, which produced three successful singles including "Jones on the Jukebox." Over her career, Hobbs has won numerous awards, including first place in the American Song Festival for "I Can't Say Goodbye to You" and a BMI Performance Award for "I Want to Know You Before We Make Love." The British Academy of Country Music named her the Most Promising Act of 1989. In 1992 and her band the Heartthrobs toured Africa as part of the US Government agency Arts America. —*Sandra Brennan & Michael McCall*

● **All Keyed Up** / 1988 / RCA ✦✦✦✦
Originally released on MTM Records, her contract and album were picked up by RCA after MTM's demise. It was her sixth label in a decade, and getting a second chance with this worthy album didn't help much. She deserves better. —*Michael McCall*

Homer & Jethro

Comedy, Country, Country Humor
Henry "Homer" Haynes and Kenneth "Jethro" Burns remain country music's most famous comedy team, as well as one of its most enduring duos, more than 20 years after Homer's death ended their partnership. Their stock-in-trade was parodies of other songs, as well as cornball comic tunes, and their humor was supported by deft musicianship and great timing. Late in their career, they recorded several solid instrumental albums as the Nashville String Band. After Haynes' passing, Burns went on to record several albums highlighting his influential mandolin style. —*Michael McCall*

● **The Worst of Homer & Jethro** / 1957 / RCA ✦✦✦✦
Their best early parodies include the hilarious "How Much Is that Hound Dog in the Window?" and "Jam Bowl Liar," a recasting of Hank Williams' "Jambalaya." —*Michael McCall*

Playing It Straight / 1962 / RCA ✦✦✦✦
This shows off their instrumental talents. —*Michael McCall*

● **The Best of** / 1992 / RCA ✦✦✦✦
Their latter-day favorites include their version of the Beatles' "I Want to Hold Your Hand" and "The Battle of Kookamonga," based on Johnny Horton's "The Battle of New Orleans." —*Michael McCall*

Johnny Horton

b. Apr. 30, 1925, Tyler, TX
Vocals / Traditional Country, Honky Tonk
Although he is better-remembered for historical songs, Johnny Horton was one of the best and most popular honky tonk singers of the late '50s. Horton managed to infuse honky tonk with an urgent rockabilly underpinning. His career may have been cut short by a fatal car crash in 1960, but his music reverberated throughout the next three decades.

Horton was born in Los Angeles, CA in 1925, the son of sharecropping parents. During his childhood, his family continually moved between California and Texas, in an attempt to find work. His mother taught him how to play guitar at the age of 11. Horton graduated from high school in 1944 and attended a Methodist seminary with the intent of joining a ministry. After a short while, he left the seminary and began traveling

across the country, eventually moving to Alaska in 1949 to become a fisherman. While he was in Alaska, he began writing songs in earnest.

The following year, Johnny moved back to east Texas, where he entered a talent contest hosted by Jim Reeves, who was then an unknown vocalist. He won the contest, which encouraged him to pursue a career as a performer. Horton started out by playing talent contests throughout Texas, which is where he gained the attention of Fabor Robison, a music manager that was notorious for incompetence and scams. In early 1951, Robison became Horton's manager and managed to secure him a recording contract with Corman Records. However, shortly after his signing, the label folded. Robison then founded his own label, Abbott Records, with the specific intent of recording Johnny. None of these records had any chart success. During 1951, Johnny began performing on various Los Angeles TV shows and hosted a radio show in Pasadena, where he performed under the name "the Singing Fisherman." By early 1952, Robison had moved Horton to Mercury Records.

At the end of 1951, Horton relocated from California to Shreveport, LA, where he became a regular on the "Louisiana Hayride." However, Louisiana was filled with pitfalls—his first wife left him shortly after the move and Robison severed all ties with Johnny when he became Jim Reeves' manager. During 1952, Hank Williams rejoined the cast of the Hayride and became a kind of mentor for Horton. After Hank died on New Year's eve of 1952, Johnny became close with his widow, Billie Jean; the couple married in 1953.

Although he had a regular job on the Hayride, Horton's recording career was going nowhere—none of his Mercury records were selling and rock 'n' roll was beginning to overtake country's share of the market place. Johnny's fortunes changed in the latter half of 1955, when he hired Webb Pierce's manager Tillman Franks as his own manager and quit Mercury Records. Tillman had Pierce help him secure a contract for Horton with Columbia Records by the end of 1955. The change in record labels breathed life into Johnny's career. At his first Columbia session, he cut "Honky Tonk Man," his first single for the label which would eventually become a honky tonk classic. By the spring of 1956, the song had reached the country Top Ten and Horton was well on his way to becoming a star.

"Honky Tonk Man" was edgy enough to have Horton grouped in on the more country-oriented side of rockabilly. Wearing a large cowboy hat to hide his receding hairline, he became a popular concert attraction and racked up three more hit singles—"I'm A One-Woman Man" (No. 7), "I'm Coming Home" (No. 11), "The Woman I Need" (No. 9)—in the next year. However, the hits dried up just as quickly as they arrived; for the latter half of 1957 and 1958, he didn't hit the charts at all. Horton responded by cutting some rockabilly, which was beginning to fall out of favor by the time his singles were released.

In the fall of 1958, he bounced back with the Top Ten "All Grown Up," but it wasn't until the ballad "When It's Springtime in Alaska (It's Forty Below)" hit the charts in early 1959 that he achieved a comeback. The song fit neatly into the folk-based story songs that were becoming popular in the late '50s, and it climbed all the way to No. 1. Its success inspired his next single, "The Battle of New Orleans." Taken from a 1958 Jimmie Driftwood album, the song was a historical saga song like "When It's Springtime in Alaska," but it was far more humorous. It was also far more successful, topping the country charts for ten weeks and crossing over into the pop charts, where it was No. 1 for six weeks. After these back-to-back No. 1 successes, Horton concentrated solely on folky saga songs. "Johnny Reb" became a Top Ten hit in the fall of 1959 and "Sink the Bismarck" was a Top Ten hit in the spring of 1960, followed by the No. 1 hit "North to Alaska" in the fall of 1960.

Around the time of the November release of "North to Alaska," Horton claimed that he was getting premonitions of an early death. Sadly, his premonitions came true. On November 4, 1960, he suffered a car crash driving home to Shreveport after a concert in Austin, TX. Horton was still alive after the wreck, but he died on the way to the hospital; the other passengers in his car had severe injuries, but they survived.

Although he died early in his career, Johnny Horton left behind a recorded legacy that proved to be quite influential. Artists like George Jones and Dwight Yoakam have covered his songs, and echoes of Horton's music can still be heard in honky tonk and country-rock music well into the '90s. —*Stephen Thomas Erlewine*

Johnny Horton's Greatest Hits / 1961 / Columbia ✦✦✦
Johnny Horton's Greatest Hits concentrates on the singer's historical story songs, throwing in a handful of ballads and honky tonk numbers. It's not a bad listen—most of these songs were hits—but it doesn't accurately represent Horton's career, especially his hard country roots and his way with a ballad. —*Stephen Thomas Erlewine*

Rockin' Rollin' Johnny Horton / 1981 / Bear Family ✦✦✦✦
Although several of his hits are featured—including "Honky Tonk Man," "The Woman I Need," and "All Grown Up"—most of this album is comprised of obscurities, culled from his early career. The album veers between his rockabilly experiments and honky tonk. The entire CD is a highly enjoyable compilation for fans of his harder-edged music, even

though a handful of tracks haven't aged particularly well. — *Stephen Thomas Erlewine*

American Originals / 1989 / Columbia ✦✦✦✦
American Originals is a brief, 10-track collection that captures Horton's biggest hits. Though it gives a more balanced overview than *Greatest Hits*, it doesn't have the breadth of the double-disc set *Honky Tonk Man: The Essential Johnny Horton 1956-1960*, which is the definitive collection. — *Stephen Thomas Erlewine*

1956-1960 / 1991 / Bear Family ✦✦✦✦
Johnny Horton's complete recorded works for Columbia Records, as well as all of his demos, are collected on this four-disc box set. Although it certainly designed for collectors and die-hards, there is enough first-rate music on the set to make it a worthwhile investment for serious honky tonk fans. — *Stephen Thomas Erlewine*

★ **Honky Tonk Man: The Essential Johnny Horton 1956-1960** / 1996 / Columbia/Legacy ✦✦✦✦✦
The Bear Family box set is too exhaustive for most fans, and other Horton greatest hits collections have been on the skimpy side, making this two-CD, 36-track anthology the domestic compilation of choice. The early honky tonk sides, tinged with a bit of rockabilly, far outshine the historical sagas, though Horton found his greatest pop success with the latter. Both sides of the artist are featured here, for those who want both, or just one or the other. — *Richie Unterberger*

Ferlin Husky

b. Dec. 3, 1927, Flat River, MO
Guitar, Vocals / Traditional Country
Ferlin Husky had three separate careers. Out of the three, the best-known is his country-pop career, which brought him to the top of the charts in the late '50s, but he was also known as a honky tonk singer called Terry Preston and a country comic named Simon Crum. Of course, Preston and Crum are just footnotes to Husky's very popular career; Crum nearly became a household name as well. During the late '50s and early '60s, he had a string of Top 40 country hits, highlighted by two No. 1 hits—"Gone" and "Wings of a Dove"—which each spent ten weeks at the top. Husky wasn't able to sustain that momentum, but both of the songs became country classics. Born and raised outside on a Missouri farm, Ferlin Husky became infatuated with music and began to play guitar as a child. During World War II, he enlisted in the Merchant Marines, where he occasionally entertained the troops on board his ship. Following the war, he became a DJ in Missouri, then in Bakersfield, CA.

While he was in California, Ferlin began using the name Terry Preston, because he believed his given name sounded too rural. He also began singing in honky tonks, using the Preston name. At one of his gigs, Tennessee Ernie Ford's manager Cliffie Stone heard Husky and took him under his wing. Stone helped Husky secure a contract at Capitol Records in 1953. As soon as he signed with Capitol, he reverted to using Ferlin Husky as his performing name. Husky's first records were generally ignored. It wasn't until he sang on Jean Shepard's "A Dear John Letter," that he had a hit. "A Dear John Letter" became a No. 1 hit, but Husky wasn't able to follow it immediately with a solo hit, although the duo had a sequel, "Forgive Me John," later that year. Ferlin didn't have a solo hit until 1955, when "I Feel Better All Over (More Than Anywhere's Else)" and its flipside, "Little Tom," climbed into the country Top Ten. Around the same time, he developed his comic alter-ego, Simon Crum. Husky signed Crum to a separate record contract with Capitol and began releasing records under that name.

Ferlin racked up a consistent string of hits during the late '50s, reaching his peak in 1957, when "Gone" spent ten weeks at No. 1; the song crossed over into the pop charts, climbing to No. 4. That same year, he began an acting career, starting with a spot on the *Kraft TV Theatre* television program and the film *Mr. Rock & Roll*. In 1958, Simon Crum had a No. 2 hit with "Country Music Is Here To Stay." Though he had several hits in 1959, none of his songs broke the Top Ten. In 1960, he had his biggest hit, the gospel song "Wings of a Dove," which was No. 1 for a total of ten weeks and reached No. 12 on the pop charts. Despite the massive success of "Wings of a Dove," Husky wasn't able to sustain a presence on the country charts during the '60s. He remained a popular concert attraction, but he had no Top Ten hits between "Wings of a Dove" and "Once," which hit No. 4 in 1966. A year after "Once," Ferlin had his final Top Ten hit with "Just for You." In the late '60s, Husky managed to incorporate the slicker, heavily produced sounds of contemporary country-pop into his music, which resulted in his brief career revitalization.

Husky kept racking up minor hits until 1975. In 1977, he had heart surgery and briefly retired from performing. During the '80s and '90s, he performed regularly at the Grand Ole Opry, as well as Christy Lane's Theater in Branson, MO. — *Stephen Thomas Erlewine*

● **Capitol Collectors Series** / 1989 / Capitol ✦✦✦✦
Although *Capitol Collector's Series* is a fairly comprehensive overview of Ferlin Husky's hit-making peak, it's missing a couple of essential items, most notably his first hit, "A Dear John Letter." It concentrates on

his country-pop hits, picking up the great majority of his hits, including "Wings of a Dove," "Gone," "A Fallen Star," "Just for You," and 16 other songs. — *Stephen Thomas Erlewine*

Greatest Hits / 1990 / Curb ✦✦✦✦
Although it's brief and cheaply produced, *Greatest Hits* contains many of the essential Husky tracks, including "A Dear John Letter," which isn't on *Capitol Collector's Series*, "Gone," and "Wings Of a Dove." For the budget-conscious it isn't a bad purchase, although *Capitol Collector's Series* offers a greater selection for an equivalent price. — *Stephen Thomas Erlewine*

● **Vintage** / 1996 / Capitol ✦✦✦✦
Vintage contains nearly all of the essential items from Ferlin Husky's peak years at Capitol Records. Featuring almost 20 tracks, it's the closest thing to a definitive retrospective yet assembled. — *Thom Owens*

Alan Jackson

b. Oct. 17, 1958, Newnan, GA
Guitar, Vocals / Contemporary Country, New Traditionalist
Through the '80s and '90s, tall, laidback Alan Jackson quietly worked to become one of the most popular modern honky tonkers of his era. The youngest of four children, Jackson sang gospel music in church and with his family at home as a youth. As a teen, he sang at parties and choirs in a country duo. Jackson left school to sell cars and later work in construction. At the age of 20, he married his high school sweetheart. Jackson gradually got into performing music professionally, first by sitting in with other musicians, and then eventually starting his own band, Dixie Steel, with whom he played the local club circuit.

At this point, music was just a hobby for Jackson—he wrote a few songs in his spare time. His wife Denise, who was a flight attendant, played a major part in setting Jackson down the road to Nashville. Around 1985, she encountered Glen Campbell in an airport and asked the singer for some advice for her husband. Campbell gave her the address and phone number of his publishing company in Nashville. Jackson decided to sell his home and move to Nashville, bringing along a demo tape of some of his songs.

Campbell's company was impressed by Jackson's singing ability, but suggested he hone his songwriting a bit. To support himself and his family, Jackson took odd jobs, including working in the mailroom of the Nashville Network and doing some session and demo work. The following year, he went back and joined the staff of Glen Campbell Music. Jackson began writing songs—occasionally with a more experienced writer named Keith Stegall—that didn't always fit the typical Nashville formula and these he kept to himself. When not writing, he performed in local clubs. After a while, he hired Barry Coburn as his manager and he recorded a new demo tape with Stegall. The tape caught the attention of Arista Records, who were in the process of setting up a Nashville division and he became the first artist on the label. Jackson released his debut album, *Here in the Real World*, in 1990 and a year later it went platinum. It produced three consecutive Top Five hits and three chart toppers.

If 1990 was a good year for Jackson, 1991 was even better. His second album *Don't Rock the Jukebox* came out in the spring and went double-platinum within its first year of release. That same year, he became a member of the Grand Ole Opry. In the fall of 1992, he released *A Lot About Livin' (And a Little About Love)*, which became his most successful release, spawning no less than five Top Five singles, including the No. 1s "Love's Got a Hold On You," "She's Got the Rhythm (And I Got the Blues)," and "Chattahoochee." Jackson released a holiday album, *Honky Tonk Christmas*, in 1993. The following year, he delivered his follow-up *Who I Am*, which went double platinum within a year of its release and spawned the No. 1 hits "Summertime Blues," "Gone Country," "Livin' on Love," and "I Don't Even Know Your Name." In 1995, Jackson released *The Greatest Hits Collection*, which went triple platinum within a year of its release. — *Sandra Brennan*

Here in the Real World / 1990 / Arista ✦✦✦✦
"I'd Love You All Over Again" was Jackson's fifth single but his first No. 1. But any country fan of the time would also recognize the title track and "Chasin' That Neon Rainbow." — *Brian Mansfield*

Don't Rock the Jukebox / 1991 / Arista ✦✦✦
The album art is really ugly, but the music isn't—"Don't Rock the Jukebox," "Someday," "Love's Got a Hold on You," and "Dallas" all hit the top of the singles charts. And "Midnight in Montgomery," which details a ghostly encounter with Hank Williams' spirit, became a video classic. — *Brian Mansfield*

☆ **A Lot About Livin' (And a Little 'bout Love)** / 1992 / Arista ✦✦✦✦✦
By this third album—when many artists start to run out of ideas—Jackson sounds like he's just starting to hit his stride with songs like "Tonight I Climbed the Wall," "She's Got the Rhythm (And I Got the Blues)" (co-written with Randy Travis), and "Chattahoochee," one of country's great summer singles. He also continues a proud tradition of country artists covering blues tunes by singing "Mercury Blues" by a minor Bay Area bluesman named K.C. Douglas. — *Brian Mansfield*

Who I Am / 1994 / Arista ✦✦✦✦

The huge singles aren't as readily apparent here, but Jackson begins to reveal more of himself with his album. "Gone Country" is a subtly brilliant jab at people who discover country music only when there's money to be made. The joke is that Jackson leads the album with Eddie Cochran's teenage-angst anthem "Summertime Blues." Jackson pulls out chestnuts from the catalogues of Con Hunley and the Kendalls, and writes "Job Description" to explain to his daughter why daddy's never home. In a time when even artists had trouble telling all the young hat-acts apart, a personal statement like *Who I Am* was possibly the smartest move Jackson could have made. —*Brian Mansfield*

★ **Greatest Hits Collection** / Nov. 21, 1995 / Arista ✦✦✦✦✦

As the title indicates, all of Alan Jackson's greatest hits—including the No. 1 singles "Chattahoochee," "She's Got the Rhythm (And I Got the Blues)," "I'd Love You All Over Again," and "Don't Rock the Jukebox"—are collected on this single disc, making it the perfect introduction to the singer. —*Stephen Thomas Erlewine*

Stonewall Jackson

b. Nov. 6, 1932, Tabor City, NC
Guitar, Vocals / Traditional Country
The namesake and descendant of the famed Confederate general, Stonewall Jackson was one of the more popular country music stars of the early '60s, scoring a handful of Top Ten country hits and becoming a fixture at the Grand Ole Opry.

Jackson began singing professionally in the mid-'50s, moving to Nashville in 1956. Once in Nashville, he made a couple of demos for Acuff-Rose at their request. Wesley Rose heard the demo and set up an audition for Jackson at the Grand Ole Opry. Jackson became the first entertainer to join the Opry without a recording contract. Although he had signed a five-year contract with the Opry, Jackson was still desperately poor and his tattered clothing was all patched. After the audition, he was assigned to perform on the Friday Night Frolic before his official Opry debut. On the day of the performance, the audience thought he was a comic and began laughing at his raggedy clothing until Jackson began to sing. Backed by Ernest Tubb's Texas Troubadours, the audience demanded four encores. Afterward, Tubb bought the young singer some new clothing so he would look good for his subsequent Opry debut.

Eventually Jackson hit the road with Tubb. By the beginning of 1957, Stonewall signed a recording contract with Columbia Records. He cut his first record, "Don't Be Angry," in early 1957. The following year, Jackson's cover of George Jones' "Life to Go" became the singer's first major hit, peaking at No. 2 in early 1959. It was followed by "Waterloo," which became his first No. 1 hit, spending five weeks at the top of the country charts and hitting No. 4 on the pop charts. Following the success of "Waterloo," Jackson had a string of Top 40 hits that was highlighted by the Top Ten hits "Why I'm Walkin'" (No. 6, 1960), "A Wound Time Can't Erase" (No. 3, 1962), and "Loeona" (No. 9, 1962). Jackson's second No. 1 hit, "B.J. the D.J.," arrived in early 1964. During the latter half of the '60s, he reached the upper reaches of the Top 40 less frequently, scoring only one Top Ten hit—1967's "Stamp Out Loneliness"—during the last five years of the decade. By 1970, he wasn't even hitting the Top 40. He bounced back briefly in 1971, when he covered Lobo's "Me and You and a Dog Named Boo." Jackson left Columbia for MGM Records in 1973. Later that year, he had his last hit with "Herman Schwartz," which reached No. 41. After that, Jackson quietly entered a semi-retirement. He continued to record occasionally, releasing albums like the inspirational *Make Me Like a Child Again* for Myrhh. He also re-recorded versions of his old hits. Jackson continued to perform and occasionally record throughout the '80s and '90s. He privately published his autobiography, *From the Bottom Up*, in 1991. —*Sandra Brennan*

The Dynamite Stonewall Jackson / 1959 / Sony ✦✦✦✦

This collection of early hits—"Waterloo," "George Jones," "Life to Go," "Smoke Along the Track," "Why I'm Walking"—are almost all good songs, delivered in his powerful, homely but engaging voice. —*George Bedard*

● **American Originals** / 1989 / Columbia ✦✦✦✦

A re-packaging of many of Jackson's best-known songs includes the great "Don't Be Angry," "A Wound Time Can't Erase," and "Smoke Along the Tracks," the latter revived by Dwight Yoakam. For some unfathomable reason, "I Washed My Hands in Muddy Water" is missing. These kinds of omissions were standard place in this half-hearted oldies series. —*Michael McCall*

Wanda Jackson

b. Oct. 20, 1937, Maud, OK
Vocals / Rockabilly
Wanda Jackson was only halfway through high school when, in 1954, country singer Hank Thompson heard her on an Oklahoma City radio show and asked her to record with his band, the Brazos Valley Boys. By the end of the decade, Jackson had become one of America's first major

female country and rockabilly singers. Jackson was born in Oklahoma, but her father Tom—himself a country singer who quit because of the Depression—moved the family to California in 1941. He bought Wanda her first guitar two years later, gave her lessons, and encouraged her to play piano as well. In addition, he took her to see such acts as Tex Williams, Spade Cooley, and Bob Wills, which left a lasting impression on her young mind. Tom moved the family back to Oklahoma City when his daughter was 12 years old. In 1952, she won a local talent contest and was given a 15-minute daily show on KLPR. The program, soon upped to 30 minutes, lasted throughout Jackson's high school years. It's here that Thompson heard her sing. Jackson recorded several songs with the Brazos Valley Boys, including "You Can't Have My Love," a duet with Thompson's bandleader, Billy Gray. The song, on the Decca label, became a national hit, and Jackson's career was off and running. She had wanted to sign with Capitol, Thompson's label, but was turned down so she signed with Decca instead.

Jackson insisted on finishing high school before hitting the road. When she did, her father came with her. Her mother made and helped design Wanda's stage outfits. "I was the first one to put some glamour in the country music—fringe dresses, high heels, long earrings," Jackson says of these outfits. When Jackson first toured in 1955 and 1956, she was placed on a bill with none other than Elvis Presley. The two hit it off almost immediately. Jackson says it was Presley, along with her father, who encouraged her to sing rockabilly.

In 1956, Jackson finally signed with Capitol, a relationship that lasted until the early '70s. Her recording career bounced back and forth between country and rockabilly; she did this by often putting one song in each style on either side of a single. Jackson cut the rockabilly hit "Fujiyama Mama" in 1958, which became a major success in Japan. Her version of "Let's Have a Party," which Elvis had cut earlier, was a US Top 40 pop hit for her in 1960, after which she began calling her band the Party Timers. A year later, she was back in the country Top Ten with "Right or Wrong" and "In the Middle of a Heartache." In 1965, she topped the German charts with "Santa Domingo," sung in Dutch. In 1966, she hit the US Top 20 with "The Box It Came In" and "Tears Will Be the Chaser for the Wine." Jackson's popularity continued through the end of the decade.

Jackson toured regularly, was twice nominated for a Grammy, and was a big attraction in Las Vegas from the mid-'50s into the '70s. She married IBM programmer Wendell Goodman in 1961, and instead of quitting the business—as many women singers had done at the time—Goodman gave up his job in order to manage his wife's career. He also packaged Jackson's syndicated TV show, *Music Village*. In 1971, Jackson and her husband discovered Christianity, which she says saved their marriage. She released one gospel album on Capitol in 1972, *Praise the Lord*, before shifting to the Myrrh label for three more gospel albums. In 1977, she switched again, this time to Word Records, and released another two.

In the early '80s, Jackson was invited to Europe to play rockabilly and country festivals and to record. She's since been back numerous times. More recently, American country artists Pam Tillis, Jann Browne, and Rosie Flores have acknowledged Jackson as a major influence. In 1995, Flores released a rockabilly album, *Rockabilly Filly*, and invited Jackson, her longtime idol, to sing two duets on it with her. Jackson embarked on a major US tour with Flores later that year. It was her first secular tour in this country since the '70s, not to mention, her first time back in a nightclub atmosphere. —*Kurt Wolff*

There's a Party Goin' On / 1959 / Capitol ✦✦✦

While this doesn't have most of Wanda's best rockabilly sides, it's a pretty solid and energetic set. About half of it is taken up with retreads of the "Let's Have a Party" theme and covers of early rock hits like "Tweedlee Dee" and "Kansas City" which are, admittedly, well done. "Fallin'" and, especially, "Hard Headed Woman" are really fine cuts that rank among her best rock 'n' roll performances. The real surprise of this album is the lightning-speed rockabilly riffing by Roy Clark; his playing on "Hard Headed Woman" is downright savage, almost enough to redeem all those horrible "Hee Haw" programs. —*Richie Unterberger*

Rockin' with Wanda / 1960 / Capitol ✦✦✦✦

Absolutely the best collection of her rockabilly recordings, including her key 1956-60 singles—"Fujiyama Mama," "Mean Mean Man," "Hot Dog! That Made Him Mad," and others. A leading candidate for the best female rock 'n' roll album of the '50s. The British reissue adds four worthwhile bonus cuts, including the essential "Let's Have a Party." —*Richie Unterberger*

● **Rockin' in the Country: Best of Wanda Jackson** / 1990 / Rhino ✦✦✦✦

Perhaps the greatest of the rockabilly women, Wanda Jackson later turned to pure country. Rhino's compilation presents the best of both eras. —*Jeff Tamarkin*

Vintage Collection Series / Jan. 23, 1996 / Capitol ✦✦✦✦

This 20-track anthology of Jackson's early work is roughly equal to

Rhino's *Rockin' in the Country* in value. *Rockin' in the Country* offers a considerably wider range, chronologically speaking. *Vintage Collections*, on the other hand, focuses on 1956-61 recordings, affording greater depth for what is acknowledged as her most fertile period. Although it's issued on Capitol Nashville, it mixes rockabilly and straight country, including her biggest hits in each style ("Let's Have a Party," "Fujiyama Mama," "Right or Wrong") and some worthy obscurities. Those with an appetite for both rock 'n' roll and country will find this the best compilation of her work; those who want just the rock 'n' roll should look for the harder-to-find *Rockin' with Wanda* instead. *—Richie Unterberger*

Sonny James (Jimmy Loden)

b. May 1, 1929, Hackleburg, AL
Guitar, Vocals / Country-Pop, Nashville Sound/Countropolitan
Known as the Southern Gentleman, he had sixteen consecutive records between 1967 and 1971 that reached No. 1. His rich and mellow voice helped make him a crossover artist, starting with "Young Love," a pop hit in 1956. Even when his material was country, James presented it in a pop form acceptable to a large audience. Among his many hits are "Running Bear," "You're the Only World I Know," and "Take Good Care of Her." In the '60s he also appeared in the movies, including *Hillbilly in a Haunted House* with Lon Chaney, Jr. and *Las Vegas Hillbillies* with Jayne Mansfield. *—David Vinopal*

American Originals / 1989 / CBS ✦✦✦
American Originals is a cross-section of Sonny James' later hits from Columbia, beginning with the 1974 No. 1 "Is It Wrong (For Loving You)" and running through a selection of '70s hits. James was still popular during this period, even if he was showing signs of age. Although it is brief, *American Originals* provides a good summation of his later career. *—Stephen Thomas Erlewine*

● **Capitol Collector's Series** / 1990 / Capitol ✦✦✦✦
This album has 20 of Sonny James' chart-topping hits for Capitol Records, ranging from 1956's breakthrough "Young Love" to 1972's "When the Snow Is on the Roses." Although it's missing a handful of No. 1 hits, it remains a thorough, entertaining, and definitive compilation. *—Stephen Thomas Erlewine*

Waylon Jennings (Waylon Arnold Jennings)

b. Jun. 15, 1937, Littlefield, TX
Guitar, Vocals / Traditional Country, Progressive Country, Outlaw Country
The ultimate Outlaw, Waylon Jennings squeezed a lot of recording and a lot of living into the years between touring as Buddy Holly's bass player and recording the *Highwayman II* album in 1991. And all the time he fought against the lush but sterile Nashville Sound and against the Nashville establishment record labels that produced it. With fellow Texan and close friend Willie Nelson, Jennings changed the way things were done in Music City, including insisting on recording with their own bands, rather than with homogenized studio musicians of the Nashville feudal system.

In the early '60s, Jennings and his band the Waylors were doing well out of Phoenix. Chet Atkins learned about the talented singer and offered him a contract. Jennings' first singles did well enough ("Anita You're Dreaming," for example), but the husky, powerful voice, the faded-jeans image, and the raw and emotional material delivered with a rock beat scared some people in Nashville. He enjoyed moderate success through the '60s, recording and touring and building up an enthusiastic audience (*cult* would be accurate) for this unique sound.

In spite of all the talent, Jennings wasn't to become a major star until the '70s brought such influential albums as *Good Hearted Woman* (1972) and *Honky Tonk Heroes*, (1973). Then came the landmark album that sold millions, *Wanted: the Outlaws* (1976), that featured Jennings, Jessi Colter (his wife), Tompall Glaser, and Willie Nelson, performing eleven previously released songs. Jennings was a superstar and the Outlaws had won. As further proof, in 1978 the *Waylon & Willie* album was a runaway hit, remaining on the country and pop charts for over a year. His singles did as well as the albums, with such hits as "Luckenbach, Texas," "The Wurlitzer Prize," "I've Always Been Crazy," and "Amanda." Meanwhile, the Outlaw clones proliferated, leading (thanks to the mechanical bull movie) to the *Urban Cowboy* fad, and prompting Jennings to pen and record "Don't You Think This Outlaw Bit's Done Got out of Hand." But Jennings had racked up eight consecutive gold albums while keeping his musical integrity, and the direction of country music had been changed.

With his superstar status intact, Jennings recorded regularly in the '80s, but his popularity slipped a notch or two, having in fact nowhere to go but down. In 1985, Jennings, Willie Nelson, Johnny Cash, and Kris Kristofferson produced their *Highwayman* album, a best-seller that spawned a No. 1 single of the same title. Jennings, having done his music his way, has earned the right to rest on his laurels, should he choose to. *—David Vinopal*

☆ **Honky Tonk Heroes** / 1973 / Pair ✦✦✦✦
As he himself once noted, the "outlaw bit" got out of hand pretty fast. It's no accident that this, his defining outlaw-era album, hit the streets before the term ever did. Nine of the ten songs are from the pen of then-unknown Billy Joe Shaver, a gritty Texas songwriter from whom more would definitely be heard. *—Dan Cooper*

Early Years / 1979 / RCA ✦✦✦
This is pre-outlaw Jennings, though "Only Daddy That'll Walk the Line" is as tough as any of his '70s work. *—Dan Cooper*

★ **Greatest Hits** / 1979 / RCA ✦✦✦✦✦
Jennings' career dates back to his days as a Cricket in the '50s, but it wasn't until the '70s that he began to define a particular hard-edged subgenre of country music with his rock shuffles and his deep, sardonic voice on songs like "Lonesome, On'ry and Mean" and "Luckenbach, Texas," the best of which are included here. (A second volume, released in 1984, is also recommended.) *—William Ruhlmann*

Will the Wolf Survive / 1985 / MCA ✦✦✦
Moving to MCA after a long stay at RCA brought Jennings a new producer in Jimmy Bowen and a fresh approach, resulting in one of his better albums, typified by his version of The Los Lobos title track and a cover of Steve Earle's tailor-made "The Devil's Right Hand." *—William Ruhlmann*

Greatest Hits, Vol. 2 / 1985 / RCA ✦✦✦
This second volume contains Jennings' "Theme from the Dukes of Hazzard," "America," "I Ain't Living Long like This," and more. *—AMG*

Clean Shirt / Feb. 1991 / Epic ✦✦✦

★ **Only Daddy That'll Walk the Line: the RCA Years** / 1993 / Camden ✦✦✦✦
You wouldn't think that two CDs with 40 cuts could adequately summarize a career as important as Jennings', but quite the opposite is true. If anything, this box set highlights more than we might want to know of his creative rise, peak, and artistic decline. The first disc, covering the years 1965-74, will be a revelation to anyone unfamiliar with his luminous early work. On cuts like "Stop the World (And Let Me Off)" and "Just to Satisfy You" his struggle to free himself of the suffocating Nashville Sound is palpable. On "Lonesome, On'ry and Mean" and "I'm a Ramblin' Man," his success at doing the same is vicariously liberating. Disc two picks up in the midst of the revolution ("Are You Sure Hank Done It This Way?," "Bob Wills Is Still the King") and carries on through the Napoleonic expansion ("Luckenbach, Texas," a Top 40 pop hit). But the last quarter of the set is really quite depressing, as the performances become more and more self-consciously outlaw. Call "Theme from the Dukes of Hazard" Waterloo, if you will. The one gem from the 1980s, Jessi Colter's lovely "Storms Never Last," can be taken more than one way. *—Dan Cooper*

Right for the Time / May 21, 1996 / Justice ✦✦✦
Waylon Jennings' later albums have consistently been more interesting than those of most others from his generation. His new album, *Right for the Time*—his first for his new label, Justice Records—is one of his strongest of the '80s and '90s. His voice is rich and beautiful, his arrangements are spare and casual, and his songs explore life, love, and dreams with honesty and wisdom. He waxes nostalgic for small-town life on "Cactus Texas," and mixes bitter sentiments with a snap-crackle wit on "Kissing You Goodbye." Never shy about his feelings, Waylon again comments (as he has on recent albums) on the "new hats" in country music, doing so with good-natured sarcasm on the spoken-word acoustic song "Living Legends Pt. II." *—Kurt Wolff*

Essential Waylon Jennings / Jun. 18, 1996 / RCA ✦✦✦✦
The Essential Waylon Jennings may not contain every hit Jennings ever recorded or every fine album track he cut, but—as the title implies—it does have the bare-bones essentials ("Only Daddy That'll Walk the Line," "Are You Sure Hank Done It This Way," and several others), making it the best single-disc retrospective assembled on the groundbreaking country singer. *—Thom Owens*

Johnnie & Jack

Somewhat like the Delmore Brothers and Louvin Brothers, the brothers-in-law Johnnie & Jack (Johnnie Wright, b. May 13, 1914; and Jack Anglin, b. May 13, 1916, d. Mar. 8, 1963) connected the prewar Appalachian harmony era to the postwar commercial country era. To add an additional twist, their two most memorable hits, "Poison Love" and "Ashes of Love," were bluegrass-styled numbers propelled by a latin beat. In 1937, Johnnie married Muriel Deason, better known by her stage name, Kitty Wells. In 1963, Jack died in a car wreck, allegedly en route to Patsy Cline's funeral, though some say he was heading the opposite direction. *—Dan Cooper*

Johnnie & Jack and the Tennessee Mountain Boys / Bear Family ✦✦✦✦
Multi-disc box set of everything this country duo ever recorded. From their early bluegrass and gospel sides (some featuring Kitty Wells) to

their rhumba beat hits of the '50s, it's all here. With heartfelt singing and playing, great songwriting and much good humor in abundance, all box set retrospectives should be this much fun to listen to. Highly recommended. — *Cub Koda*

George Jones

b. Sep. 12, 1931, Saratoga, TX
Guitar, Vocals / Traditional Country, Honky Tonk, Nashville Sound/ Countrypolitan

By most accounts, George Jones is the finest vocalist in the recorded history of country music. Initially, he was a hardcore honky tonker in the tradition of Hank Williams, but over the course of his career he developed an affecting, nuanced ballad style. In the course of his career, he never left the top of the country charts, even as he suffered innumerable personal and professional difficulties. Only Eddy Arnold had more Top Ten hits than Jones, and George always stayed closer to the roots of hardcore country.

George Jones was born and raised in east Texas, near the city of Beaumont. At an early age, George displayed an affection for music. He enjoyed the gospel he heard in church and on the family's Carter Family records, but he truly became fascinated with country music, particularly Roy Acuff and Bill Monroe, when his family bought a radio when he was seven. When he was nine, his father bought him his first guitar. Soon, his father had George playing and singing on the streets on Beaumont, earning spare change. At 16, he ran away to Jasper, TX, where he sang at a local radio station. Jones married Dorothy, his first wife, in 1950 when he was 19 years old. The marriage collapsed within a year and he enlisted in the Marines at the end of 1951. Though the US was at war with Korea, Jones never served overseas—he was stationed at a military camp in California, where he kept singing in bars. After he was discharged, George immediately began performing again.

In 1953, Jones was discovered by record producer Pappy Daily, who was also the co-owner of Starday Records, a local Texas label. Impressed with Jones' potential, Daily signed the singer to Starday. "No Money in This Deal," Jones' first single, was released in early 1954, but it received no attention. Starday released three more singles that year, all of which were ignored. To pay the bills, Jones played Daily's radio show "Houston Jamboree" on KNUZ and became a DJ at KTRM in Beaumont. Jones released "Why, Baby, Why" late in the summer of 1955 and the single became his first hit. However, its momentum was halted by a cover version by Webb Pierce and Red Sovine that hit No. 1 on the country charts. Nevertheless, it became Starday's biggest hit, peaking at No.4.

George Jones was on the road to success and Pappy Daily secured the singer a spot on the "Louisiana Hayride," where he co-billed with Elvis Presley. Jones reached the Top Ten with regularity in 1956 with such singles as "What Am I Worth" and "Just One More." That same year, George recorded some rockabilly singles under the name Thumper Jones which were unsuccessful, both commercially and artistically. In August, he joined the cast of the Grand Ole Opry and his first album appeared by the end of the year. In 1957, Starday Records signed a distribution deal with Mercury Records and George Jones' records began appearing under the Mercury label. Pappy Daily began recording George in Nashville and Jones' first single for the new label, "Don't Stop the Music," was another Top Ten hit. Throughout 1958, he was landing near the top of the charts, culminating with "White Lightning," which spent five weeks at No. 1 in the spring of 1959. His next big hit arrived two years later, when the ballad "Tender Years" spent seven weeks at No. 1. "Tender Years" displayed a smoother production and larger arrangement than his previous hits, and it led the way toward Jones' later success as a balladeer.

In early 1962, Jones reached No. 5 with "Aching, Breaking Heart," which would turn out to be his last hit for Mercury Records. Pappy Daily became a staff producer for United Artists Records in 1962 and Jones followed him to the label. His first single for UA, "She Thinks I Still Care," was his third No. 1 hit and became a country standard. In 1963, Jones began performing and recording with Melba Montgomery. During the early '60s, mainstream country music was getting increasingly slick, but Jones and Montgomery's harmonies were raw and laden with bluegrass influences. Their first duet, "We Must Have Been Out of Our Minds," released in the spring of 1963, was their biggest hit, peaking at No. 3. The pair continued to record together throughout 1963 and 1964, although they never again had a Top Ten hit; they also reunited in 1966 and 1967, recording a couple of albums and singles for Musicor. Jones had a number of solo hits in 1963 and 1964 as well, peaking with the No. 3 "The Race Is On" in the fall of 1964.

Under the direction of Pappy Daily, George Jones moved to the new record label Musicor in 1965. Jones' first single for Musicor, "Things Have Gone to Pieces," was a Top Ten hit in the spring of 1965. Between 1965 and 1970, he had 17 Top Ten hits for Musicor. While at Musicor, Jones recorded almost 300 songs in five years. During that time, he cut a number of first-rate songs, including country classics like "Love Bug," "Walk Through This World with Me," and "A Good Year for the Roses." He also recorded a fair share of mediocre material and given the sheer

amount of songs he sang, that isn't surprising. Although Jones made a couple of records that were genuine tributes or experiments, he also tried to fit into contemporary country styles, such as the Bakersfield sound. Not all of the attempts resulted in hits, but he consistently charted the Top Ten his singles, if not with his albums. Musicor wound up flooding the market with George Jones records for the rest of the '60s. George's albums for Musicor tended to be arranged thematically and only two, his 1965 duet *George Jones & Gene Pitney* and 1969's *I'll Share My World with You*, charted. That meant that while Jones was one of the most popular and acclaimed singers in country music, there was still a surplus of material.

Like his discography, George Jones' personal life was spinning out of control. He was drinking heavily and began missing concerts. His wife Shirley filed for divorce in 1968, and George moved to Nashville, where he met Tammy Wynette, the most popular new female singer in country music. Soon, George and Tammy fell in love; Wynette soon left Chapel and she married Jones on February 16, 1969.

At the same time George married Tammy, tensions that had been building between Jones and his long-time producer Pappy Daily culminated. Jones was unhappy with the sound of his Musicor records, and he placed most of the blame on Daily. After his marriage, George wanted to record with Tammy, but Musicor wouldn't allow her to appear on her label, Epic, and Epic wouldn't let her sing on a Musicor album. Furthermore, Epic wanted to lure George away from Musicor. Jones was more than willing to leave, but he had to fulfill his contract before the company would let him go. While he continued recording material for Musicor, Epic entered contract negotiations with their rivals and halfway through 1971, Jones severed ties with Musicor and Pappy Daily. He signed away all the rights to his Musicor recordings in the process. The label continued to release Jones albums for a couple of years and they also licensed recordings to RCA, who released two singles and a series of budget-priced albums in the early '70s.

Jones signed with Epic Records in October of 1971. It was the culmination of a busy year for George, one that saw he and Tammy becoming the biggest stars in country music, racking up a number of Top Ten hits as solo artists, selling out concerts across the country as a duo, and appearing on television programs and publications throughout America. Jones had successfully remade his image from a short-haired, crazed honky tonker to more relaxed, sensitive balladeer. At the end of the year, he cut his first records for Epic.

George Jones' new record producer was Billy Sherrill, who had been responsible for Tammy Wynette's hit albums. Sherrill was known for his lush, string-laden productions and his precise, aggressive approach in the studio. Under his direction, musicians were there to obey his orders and that included the singers as well. Jones had been accustomed to the relaxed style of Pappy Daily, who was the polar opposite of Sherrill. As a result, the singer and producer were tense at first, but soon the pair developed a fruitful working relationship. With Sherrill, Jones became a full-fledged balladeer, sanding away the rough edges of his hardcore honky tonk roots.

"We Can Make It," his first solo single for Epic, was a celebration of Jones' marriage to Tammy written by Sherrill and Glenn Sutton. The song was a No. 2 hit early in 1972, kicking off a successful career at Epic. "The Ceremony," Jones and Wynette's second duet, followed "We Can Make It," and also became a Top Ten hit. Another marital-related song, "Loving You Could Never Be Better," followed its predecessors into the Top Ten at the end of 1972. By now, the couple's marriage was becoming a public soap opera, with their audience following each single as if they were news reports. Even though they were proclaiming their love through their music, the couple had begun to fight frequently. Jones was sinking deep into alcoholism and drug abuse, which escalated as the couple continued to tour together.

Though every single he released in 1973 went into the Top Ten, George Jones' personal life was getting increasingly difficult. Tammy Wynette filed for divorce in August, 1973. Shortly after she filed the papers, the couple decided to reconcile and her petition was withdrawn. Following her withdrawl, the duo had a No. 1 single with the appropriately titled "We're Gonna Hold On." In the summer of 1974, George had his first No. 1 hit since "Walk Through This World with Me" with "The Grand Tour," a song that drew a deft portrait of a broken marriage. He followed it with another No. 1 hit, "The Door." Not long after its release, he recorded "These Days (I Barely Get By)," which featured lyrics co-written by Tammy. Two days after he recorded the song, Wynette left Jones; they divorced within a year.

The late '70s were plagued with trouble for Jones. Between 1975 and the beginning of 1980, he had only two Top Ten solo hits—"These Days (I Barely Get By)" (1975) and "Her Name Is" (1976). Though they divorced, Jones and Wynette continued to record and tour together, and that is where he racked up the hits, beginning with the back-to-back 1976 No. 1 hits, "Golden Ring" and "Near You." The decrease in hits accurately reflects the downward spiral in Jones' health in the late '70s, when he became addicted not only to alcohol, but to cocaine as well. Jones became notorious for his drunken, intoxicated rampages, often involving both drugs and shotguns. George would disappear for days at a time. He began missing a substantial amount of concerts—in 1979 alone, he missed 54 shows—which earned him the nickname "No-Show Jones." Jones' career began to pick up in 1978, when he began flirting with rock 'n' roll, covering Chuck Berry's "Maybellene" with Johnny Paycheck and recording a duet with James Taylor called "Bartender's Blues." The success of the singles—both went Top Ten—led to an album of duets, *My Very Special Guests*, in 1979. Though it was poised to be a return to the top of the charts for George, he neglected to appear at the scheduled recording sessions and had to overdub his vocals after his partners recorded theirs. That same year, doctors told the singer he had to quit drinking, otherwise his life was in jeopardy. Jones checked into a rehab clinic, but left after a month, uncured. Due to his cocaine addiction, his weight had fallen from 150 pounds to a mere 100. Despite his declining health, Jones managed a comeback in 1980. It began with a Top Ten duet with Tammy Wynette, "Two Story House," early in the year, but the song that pushed him back to the top of the charts was the dramatic ballad "He Stopped Loving Her Today." The single hit No. 1 in the spring of the year, beginning a new series of Top Ten hits and No. 1 singles that ran through 1986. The string of hits was so successful, it rivaled the peak of his popularity in the '60s. "He Stopped Loving Her Today" was followed by the Top Ten "I'm Not Ready Yet" and an album, *I Am What I Am*, in the fall of the 1980. *I Am What I Am* became his most successful album, going platinum.

Throughout 1981 and 1983, he had eight Top Ten hits. Although he was having hits again, he hadn't kicked his addictions. Jones was still going on crazed, intoxicated rampages, which culminated with a televised police chase of George, who was driving drunk through the streets of Nashville. Following his arrest, Jones managed to shake his drug and alcohol addictions with the support of his fourth wife, Nancy Sepulvada. George and Nancy married in March of 1983. Soon after their marriage, he began to detoxicate and by the end of 1983, he had completed his rehabilitation.

George continued to have hits Top Ten hits regularly until 1987, when country radio became dominated by newer artists; ironically, the artists that kept him off the charts—singers like Randy Travis, Keith Whitley, and Dwight Yoakam—were heavily influenced by George himself. Jones and Sepulvada moved back to Nashville in 1987. In 1988, he recorded his final album with Billy Sherrill, *One Woman Man*. The title song, which was a hit for Johnny Horton in 1956, was George's final Top Ten hit. *One Woman Man* was his last record for Epic Records. After its release, he moved to MCA, releasing his first record for the label, *And Along Came Jones*, in the fall of 1991. In between its release and *One Woman Man* arrived a duet with Randy Travis, "A Few Ole Country Boys," that was a Top Ten hit in the fall of 1990. Jones' records for MCA didn't sell nearly as well as his Epic albums, but his albums usually were critically-acclaimed. In 1995, he reunited with Tammy Wynette to record *One*. In April of 1996, Jones published his autobiography, *I Lived To Tell It All*. —*Stephen Thomas Erlewine*

George Jones Salutes Hank Williams / 1960 / Mercury ✦✦✦✦
Country's greatest singer performs the songs of country's greatest writer. Liner notes by Elvis Costello. (The 1984 release is a 10-song abridged version of a longer, earlier set, Mercury SR 60257.) —*William Ruhlmann*

George Jones Sings Bob Wills / 1962 / Razor & Tie ✦✦✦
Rather than try to ape the Wills arrangements, producer Pappy Daily sets Jones up in front of a honky tonk combo and lets the Ol' Possum rip. The combo rips, too, on a couple of instrumentals. —*Dan Cooper*

The New Favorites of George Jones / 1962 / United Artists ✦✦✦
A good collection, it includes "Open Pit Mine," "Sometimes You Just Can't Win," "There's No Justice," and his big hit "She Thinks I Still Care." —*George Bedard*

George Jones Sings Like the Dickens! / 1964 / United Artists ✦✦✦
The Race Is on / 1965 / Razor & Tie ✦✦✦
The title track to *The Race Is on* is one of George Jones' biggest hits. With its galloping beat and clever, funny lyrics, the single gives the impression that the rest of the record is a return to honky tonk. Although there are several uptempo numbers, *The Race Is On* is dominated by ballads, like the majority of his UA albums. But *The Race Is On* boasts a stronger, more varied set of songs than most of his '60s albums, ranging from ballads ("They'll Never Take Her Love from Me"), to Western swing ("Time Changes Everything"), to honky tonk ("Don't Let the Stars Get in Your Eyes"). There are a couple of weak moments—ironically, one is "She's Mine," which was co-written by George—but the album remains one of his strongest from the mid-'60s. —*Stephen Thomas Erlewine*

☆ **George Jones with Love** / 1972 / Musicor ✦✦✦✦✦
It includes a couple of big production numbers—"A Good Year for the Roses" and "A Day in the Life of a Fool," and a nice rewrite of the gospel song "Never Grow Old," sung with Tammy Wynette and retitled "Never Grow Cold." —*George Bedard*

The Grand Tour / 1974 / Epic ✦✦✦
Included is the title-track tour de force, plus Johnny Paycheck's "Once You've Had the Best" and Mel Street's "Borrowed Angel." —*George Bedard*

★ **Anniversary: Ten Years of Hits** / 1982 / Epic ✦✦✦✦✦
This covers the first ten years of Jones' two-decade association with Epic Records, and more importantly, record-producer Billy Sherrill. Owing much to Sherrill's knack for locating quality material, the hits range from amusing ("Nothing Ever Hurt Me," "Her Name Is . . . "), to morbid ("He Stopped Loving Her Today"), to classic ("The Grand Tour," "A Picture of Me Without You"). Best cuts include "Bartender's Blues," "The Door," and "Still Doin' Time." —*Tom Roland*

Don't Stop the Music / 1987 / Ace ✦✦✦✦
The most extensive look at Jones' early Starday and Mercury recordings available, *Don't Stop the Music* is a perfect compliment to Rhino's collection. The disc's 22 tracks document the formative years (1954-61) where he grew from a Hank Williams soundalike to one of the most distinctive voices in country music. Essential listening worth seeking out. Import only. —*Chris Woodstra*

☆ **The Best of George Jones, Vol. 1: Hardcore Honky Tonk** / 1991 / Mercury ✦✦✦✦✦
This album contains the essential songs from George Jones' early career, including "Why Baby Why," "Just One More," "Color of the Blues," "The Window Up Above," "Aching Breaking Heart," and "Tall Tall Trees." There are a number of fine tracks that didn't make this 20-track single disc collection—the double-disc *Cup of Loneliness* is a more comprehensive set of these recordings for Starday and Mercury—but for most casual fans and listeners, *Hardcore Honky Tonk* is an ideal compilation. —*Stephen Thomas Erlewine*

★ **The Best of 1955-1967** / 1991 / Rhino ✦✦✦✦
This 18-track album is a good overview of George Jones' early career, containing most of the necessary hits from his first decade or so of hits. It's skewed toward his Mercury hits, featuring everything from "Why Baby Why" to "Aching Breaking Heart," picking up "Just One More," "The Window Up Above," and "Tender Years" along the way. Five wisely-chosen UA tracks are featured, as are four Musicor tracks. It doesn't have every hit from '55-'67, but *The Best of* does contain every truly necessary item Jones recorded during that time. —*Stephen Thomas Erlewine*

☆ **Cup of Loneliness: The Mercury Years** / 1994 / Mercury ✦✦✦✦✦
Jones was still developing his style on the earliest tracks on *Cup of Loneliness*, but this is the music that established him as one of the great vocalists of the 20th century, country or otherwise. *Cup of Loneliness* gathers together most of his Mercury recordings, as well as several highlights from his time at Starday. These recordings feature Jones at his purest—no strings, no backing vocals, only pure honky tonk. At the beginning of the double-disc set, traces of Hank Williams can be detected in Jones' vocals, but by the end of the first disc, Jones had become one of the most distinctive and popular country vocalists. His classic ballad style doesn't begin to develop until the end of the second disc. Mercury released two different versions of *Cup of Loneliness*—a standard two-disc set in a jewel box and a collector's edition that features extra songs; naturally, most fans will want the songs on the collector's edition, simply because they were recorded at a peak in Jones' career. —*Stephen Thomas Erlewine*

★ **The Spirit Of Country: The Essential George Jones** / 1994 / Epic/ Legacy ✦✦✦✦✦
As the only collection that draws from all the labels George Jones recorded for—only his later recordings for MCA are missing—this double-disc set is clearly a fine introduction to his prolific career. Since it was released on Epic/Legacy, it does favor the Billy Sherrill-produced '70s and '80s recordings. However, it does contain a majority of the truly essential from Starday, Mercury, UA, and Musicor. From "Why Baby Why" to "A Good Year for the Roses," most of his classic '50s and '60s songs are on the first disc, as are his first classic Epic recordings, "We Can Make It," "A Picture of Me (Without You)," and "The Grand Tour." The second disc is devoted to his '70s and '80s hits, adding greater detail to the ground *Anniversary* already covered. Although the set doesn't give his early, hardcore honky tonk recordings the proper showcase, *The Spirit of Country* is a necessary purchase—there is simply no better way to get acquainted with Jones' catalog and all of the twists and turns in his career. —*Stephen Thomas Erlewine*

All Time Greatest Hits [UA] / 1994 / Liberty ✦✦✦
Vintage Collection Series / Jan. 23, 1996 / Capitol ✦✦✦✦
Vintage collects nearly all of George Jones and Melba Montgomery's duets for United Artists. These songs, originally released on *What's In Our Hearts* and *Bluegrass Hootenanny*, illustrate how well-suited the pair was for each other—there may be a couple of weak songs, but there are no weak performances. In fact, *Vintage* makes a good argument that Montgomery was Jones' best duet partner. —*Stephen Thomas Erlewine*

Grandpa Jones (Louis Marshall Jones)

b. Oct. 20, 1913, Niagra, KY
Banjo, Guitar, Vocals / Old-Time, Country Humor
Louis Marshall "Grandpa" Jones is one person who has aged right into his makeup. His nickname reportedly was given to him by hillbilly crooner Bradley Kincaid when Jones was about 23 years old. His geezer image has thus been with him for over 55 years. In the early '40s, Jones, Merle Travis, and the Delmore Brothers formed the Brown's Ferry Four, an influential group. After the war, Jones joined the Opry, where he has appeared regularly ever since, often with his wife Ramona. Jones is among the last of the Uncle Dave Macon school of banjo picking and all-round entertaining. His years on "Hee Haw" made him even more famous; he was elected to the Country Music Hall of Fame in 1978.
—David Vinopal

● **Country Music Hall of Fame Series** / 1992 / MCA ✦✦✦✦
The banjo player's entire recorded output for Decca Records between 1956 and 1959, this includes a live performance and previously unreleased tracks. Jones sings about dogs and trains, rerecords some previous hits for King Records, and parodies Johnny Cash's "Don't Take Your Guns to Town." *—Brian Mansfield*

Wynonna Judd (Christina Ciminella Judd)

b. May 30, 1964, Ashland, KY
Guitar, Vocals / Contemporary Country
Wynonna Judd launched a solo career after the Judds disbanded in 1992. On her own, Wynonna has been more eclectic—drawing not only from country, but rock, pop, and folk—than she was as part of the duo that made her famous.

Wynonna was the first child of Michael and Diana Ciminella. When she was four years old, the family moved to Los Angeles. Shortly after the move, her parents divorced and she went to live with her mother. The pair changed their names to Naomi and Wynonna shortly after the divorce. The duo began performing together after they moved back to Kentucky in the early '80s. They went to Nashville, where they landed a recording contract in 1984. The Judds became the most popular duo in country music history during the '80s. In 1991, Naomi was forced to retire after she was diagnosed with a chronic liver disease.

Instead of retiring with her mother, Wynonna launched a solo career in 1992 with her eponymous solo album. *Wynonna* featured three consecutive No. 1 singles—"She Is His Only Need," "I Saw the Light," "No One Else On Earth"—and went triple platinum. The following year, she delivered her second album, *Tell Me Why*, which went platinum and spawned four Top Ten songs—"Tell Me Why," "A Bad Goodbye" (a duet with Clint Black), "Girls with Guitars," and "Rock Bottom." In early 1996, she released her third album, *Revelations*. It went platinum within four months of its release. *—Stephen Thomas Erlewine*

Wynonna / 1992 / Curb ✦✦✦
Daughter Judd stakes out her own territory. It's probably safe to say that she had more in her than most people guessed. From the tender "She Is His Only Need" to the Southern-rock 'n' soul of "No One Else on Earth," Wynonna sings with a smoldering sensuality that pulsed beneath the surface of the duo's best records—even "Live with Jesus" sounds sexy. After a few more albums like this, folks may not even remember the Judds. *—Brian Mansfield*

● **Tell Me Why** / May 11, 1993 / MCA ✦✦✦✦
Wynonna's second album, *Tell Me Why*, is a more confident and diverse collection than her debut. Drawing from sources as varied as gospel, folk, and blues-rock, Wynonna doesn't necessarily deliver a pure country album, but her blend of roots genres does qualify as a cleverly constructed contemporary country record. The selection of material is first-rate, but what makes *Tell Me Why* her best solo effort is how she ties all of the songs together with her assured—and surprisingly subtle—vocals. *—Thom Owens*

Revelations / 1996 / Curb ✦✦✦✦

The Judds

Contemporary Country
Naomi Judd and her daughter Wynonna were one of the most popular country music acts of the 1980s, eventually becoming the most successful duo in the genre's history. With Wynonna's strong bluesy style and Naomi's exquisite harmonies, the Judds presented an arresting image that was both homespun and city slick. During the eight years they performed together, they had many hits (14 No. 1 singles).

Born Dianna Ellen Judd in Ashland, Kentucky, Naomi was 18 when she gave birth to Wynonna. When Wynonna was four, Naomi—who had since given birth to Ashley and divorced the girls' father—decided to take her children to Los Angeles. Struggling to support her family over the next seven years, Naomi held a variety of jobs that ranged from modeling to working as the personal secretary for the Fifth Dimension. She was also in a relationship at that time, but when it turned abusive, she

decided to return to rural Kentucky in 1976, where they stayed until Wynonna was 12. They lived in an area with few modern conveniences and Naomi would not buy a television or a phone, so they entertained themselves by listening to local musicians and the Grand Ole Opry on the radio. A local singer named Songbird Yancy and her mother Minnie inspired the Judds to begin singing together. About a year later, when Wynonna was in her early teens, Naomi moved the family to northern California, where she intended to complete her nursing studies. By this time, she realized that her oldest daughter had real talent and decided to move them to Nashville to see if she and her daughter could build a music career.

The Judds arrived in Nashville in 1979 and while Naomi worked as a nurse, Wynonna finished high school. As they continued to hone their singing skills, they began performing occasionally on the early morning "Ralph Emery" show. Naomi also began making contacts in Nashville. Frequently, the Judds' idea of networking was to simply sit down and sing to whoever would listen. It was through such a live audition that the two came to be managed by Woody Bowles and Ken Stilts. Their managers brought a crudely recorded demo containing songs Naomi had written to noted producer Brent Maher. Impressed by the potential in Wynonna's still developing voice, and by the intelligence of Naomi's songs, Maher helped the duo get an audition with Dick Whitehouse at Curb Records. In turn, Whitehouse sent a demo to RCA, who requested a live demo with the group in Los Angeles. The Judds had no idea that the seven men they sang for represented the label's upper-level executives. With only Wynonna's guitar to accompany them, the women sang for 30 minutes and afterward were immediately offered a contract. In late 1983, they released their first single "Had a Dream (For the Heart)" and reached the country the Top 20. A mini-album, *The Judds: Wynonna and Naomi*, followed and a hastily assembled tour came after that.

With "Mama He's Crazy" in early 1984, the Judds began a streak of eight consecutive No. 1 hits. "Why Not Me," their second No. 1 hit, won the Country Music Association's Single of the Year award for 1984. That same year, the duo won their first Grammy, Best Country Performance by a Duo or Group with Vocal, and the Academy of Country Music's Top Vocal Duet award. For the remainder of their career, the Judds won a number of awards every year.

At the turn of the decade, Naomi had contracted chronic, acute hepatitis, an incurable, life-threatening disease. All the touring had seriously weakened her health and it began to show in 1990. For most of that year, she spent much of her time off stage bedridden and too weak to move. Eventually she went to the Mayo clinic for treatment. During one session they found a lump in her breast, but it turned out to be benign. Naomi's poor health led the duo to their disbandment in 1991. Before Naomi retired, the Judds embarked upon a 124-date farewell tour, called "Love Can Build a Bridge." It was grueling for Naomi and emotionally wrenching for Wynonna, who though encouraged by her mother and her managers to continue singing, was unsure about whether she wanted to go solo. By the end of 1991, she had decided to continue performing and signed a contract with MCA Records. Early in 1992, she released her eponymous debut album, which became a multi-platinum success and, in the process, launched a successful solo career for Wynonna. Naomi published her autobiography, *Love Can Build a Bridge*, in 1993. *—Sandra Brennan*

The Judds / 1983 / RCA ✦✦✦✦
This is the debut for the mother/daughter duo who became one of country's leading lights in the '80s. *—Mark A. Humphrey*

Why Not Me? / 1984 / RCA ✦✦✦✦
On their second album, Wynonna establishes herself as a fearsome and sultry belter. The production is built around an essentially acoustic base. *—Mark A. Humphrey*

Rockin' with the Rhythm / 1985 / RCA ✦✦✦
On the third album, "Have Mercy" and the title track (among others) kick with a funky glee that makes this the most plainly joyous Judds album. *—Mark A. Humphrey*

Heartland / 1987 / RCA ✦✦

★ **The Greatest Hits** / 1988 / RCA ✦✦✦✦✦
These singles document the rise of the Judds, who seemed, at times, to be singing for every bank teller, teacher, and struggling single mama in every small town in America. Songs like "Why Not Me," "Mama He's Crazy," and "Girl's Night Out" are more than country hits; they are like validation for every woman brave enough to believe in innocence even when she knows better. *—Dan Cooper*

River of Time / 1989 / RCA ✦✦✦

Love Can Build a Bridge / 1990 / RCA ✦✦✦
This was their final album together. *—Mark A. Humphrey*

Greatest Hits, Vol. 2 / 1991 / RCA ✦✦✦✦
While songs like "Young Love" and "Love Can Build a Bridge" continue to emphasize the Judds' warm and fuzzy middle-American sensibilities,

several other hits—"Let Me Tell You About Love," for instance, showcase the side of Wynonna influenced by Bonnie Raitt. —*Dan Cooper*

The Judds Collection 1983-1990 / 1992 / RCA ✦✦✦✦
The three-disc box set is an example of a wasted opportunity. Instead of providing a thorough, exhaustive overview of the duo's immensely popular career, the set simply combines their first two *Greatest Hits* albums with a disc of demos, which are only of interest to hardcore fans, who will already have all of the music on the first two discs. That leaves the set as being useful to no one—casual fans are better served by the individual collections, while dedicated fans are being ripped off by being forced to purchase two discs they already have if they want to get the rarities, which aren't that revelatory in the first place. —*Thom Owens*

★ **The Essential Judds** / Oct. 1995 / RCA ✦✦✦✦✦
The Essential Judds contains a great majority of the duo's biggest hits, as well as a wisely-chosen selection of rarities, making it a definitive compilation. —*Stephen Thomas Erlewine*

Toby Keith

Vocals / Contemporary Country
Toby Keith was one of many new traditionalist honky tonk singers that had a string of hit singles in the early '90s. Born in Oklahoma City, his interest in country music was sparked in childhood by the musicians who played at his grandmother's dinner club. Keith did not choose music as his career until losing his job as an operational manager in the oil industry. With nothing to do, he began playing in country-rock garage bands. Eventually he and some of the musicians he worked with teamed up to form Keith's Easy Money Band, which began playing at honky tonk dives in south Oklahoma City and neighboring Norman. Keith returned to the oil fields and later played football in the short-lived USFL while continuing to play music. By 1988, Keith was recording for independent labels and decided to try his luck in Nashville. He got his big break when former Alabama producer Harold Shedd, who worked for Mercury Records, heard Keith's demo and flew to Oklahoma to meet and listen to the band. He was impressed and offered Keith a record deal.

Toby Keith's eponymous debut album was released in 1993. The first single from the album, "Should've Been a Cowboy," became a No. 1 single and his next two singles—"He Ain't Worth Missing" and "A Little Less Talk and a Lot More Action"—made the Top Ten. In 1995, he released the seasonal album, *Christmas to Christmas*. In 1996, he delivered his second album, *Blue Moon*. —*Sandra Brennan*

Toby Keith / 1993 / PolyGram ✦✦
● **Blue Moon** / Apr. 1996 / A&M ✦✦✦✦

Kentucky Headhunters

Contemporary Country
The Kentucky Headhunters were a change of pace from the new traditionalists and country-pop that dominated the country charts at the end of the '80s. Instead of conforming to Nashville traditions, the Headhunters created a hybrid of honky tonk, blues and Southern-rock that appealed to both rock and country artists, as well as music critics. The group only stayed together for a few albums, but during their time together, they were one of the most popular fringe country acts of their era.

Consisting of members from two different southern families, the origins of the Kentucky Headhunters lie in 1968 when Fred and Richard Young began playing together with their cousins Greg Martin and Anthony Kenney at the Youngs' grandmother's home. Mark Orr also joined them a little later. The first incarnation of the band was called the Itchy Brothers and the group played together informally for over a decade. After about 13 years, the band members began launching separate careers. Richard Young went off to write songs for Acuff-Rose while Fred Young began touring with Sylvia. Martin became a member of Ronnie McDowell's band. Kenney just dropped out. While playing with McDowell, Martin met Doug Phelps. In 1985, Martin decided to reassemble the Itchy Brothers, but Kenney declined to join again, so they invited Phelps and later his brother Ricky Lee to join and the band became the Kentucky Headhunters.

The Kentucky Headhunters got their start playing twice monthly on the Chitlin' Show, a radio program on WLOC Munfordville, KY. From these 90-minute performances, the Headhunters built up a following. They sent an eight-song demo to Mercury and the label signed the group. The original demo tape was remixed and became the basis of their first album, 1989's *Pickin' On Nashville*. Upon its release, *Pickin' On Nashville* received overwhelmingly positive reviews and it quickly became a hit. "Dumas Walker" reached No. 15 in the spring of 1990, followed by the group's biggest hit, the No. 6 "Oh, Lonesome Me." After the album's tremendous success, the Headhunters were showered with awards from the Country Music Association, *Billboard*, and the Grammys. Afterward, they embarked on a long world tour. In 1991, the Kentucky Headhunters released their second album, *Electric Barnyard*. The album received

mixed reviews and weak sales, and none of its songs became hits. Nevertheless, the CMA named them Vocal Group of the Year.

In the summer of 1992, the Phelps brothers left the group to form Brothers Phelps, a more traditional country group. The remaining Headhunters brought former Itchy Brothers Anthony Kenney and Mark Orr to the group. The new lineup released *Rave On* in 1993. With *Rave On*, the Kentucky Headhunters began refashioning themselves as a bluesy Southern-rock act and they followed that direction on their subsequent album, *That'll Work*. —*Sandra Brennan*

Pickin' on Nashville / 1989 / Mercury ✦✦✦✦
As their album title suggests, The Headhunters aren't entirely comfortable with the country tag, which is appropriate when you hear their guitar-heavy, rambunctious music. The vocals have that twang, but these good old boys are often closer to Lynyrd Skynyrd than they are to Merle Haggard, and all the better for it. —*William Ruhlmann*

Electric Barnyard / 1991 / Mercury ✦✦✦
The Kentucky Headhunters aren't a remarkable country mutation, just a top-notch Southern-rock band with a sense of humor. "The Ballad of Davy Crockett" is the kind of clever novelty that won't work twice; "Big Mexican Dinner" is a novelty that doesn't even work the first time. Once again, the country and bluegrass covers—"Only Daddy That'll Walk the Line," "With Body and Soul"—are the highlights, and most of the originals (the Beatlesque shuffle "Always Makin' Love" aside) are offbeat, adequate filler. —*Brian Mansfield*

Rave On! / 1993 / Mercury ✦✦
● **Best Of The Kentucky Headhunters: Still Pickin'** / 1994 / Mercury ✦✦✦✦
The Best of the Kentucky Headhunters is a first-rate compilation of the highlights from the group's first three albums. Although their debut remains a worthwhile purchase, this collection salvages the good songs from the band's two uneven follow-ups to their exciting breakthrough first album. —*Thom Owens*

That'll Work / Elektra/Nonesuch ✦✦

Sammy Kershaw

Vocals / Contemporary Country, New Traditionalist
Sammy Kershaw's blend of honky tonk and Southern-rock made him a popular recording artist in the early '90s. The third cousin of legendary Cajun fiddler Doug Kershaw, Sammy was born in Kaplan, LA, the eldest of four children. He grew up listening to Hank Williams, Conway Twitty, Buck Owens, and Kershaw's idol, George Jones. When Kershaw was eleven, his grandfather gave him an electric guitar for Christmas; he debuted professionally at age 12 with J.B. Perry, a popular local musician for whom he had been working. With his mentor Perry, Kershaw toured the South, playing clubs and opening for several major acts; the repertoire included songs by Jones, Charlie Rich, Ray Charles and the Allman Brothers.

After overcoming financial difficulties which forced him to take day jobs, Kershaw joined Blackwater, which played the club circuit in the South and West. He also cut some independent solo singles, two of which were noticed in *Billboard*. By the late '80s, Kershaw was tired of the constant touring. To save his crumbling second marriage, he left music to work as a remodeling supervisor for Wal-Mart for two years. Eventually, songwriter Barry Jackson suggested that Kershaw send a demo and picture to Nashville. In 1991, Kershaw did a showcase there and was signed to Mercury Records.

Kershaw's first album, *Don't Go Near the Water*, contained the song "Cadillac Style," which peaked at No. 3 and spent five months on the charts. Kershaw's next two singles—"Don't Go Near the Water" and "Yard Sale"—reached the Top 20 and the fourth single, "Anywhere but Here," peaked at No. 10. *Haunted Heart*, his second album, was released in 1993. The first single, "She Don't Know She's Beautiful," became his first No. 1 hit and produced three more Top Ten singles—"Haunted Heart," "Queen of My Double Wide Trailer," and "I Can't Reach Her Anymore." In 1994, he released his third album, *Feelin' Good Train*, which went gold like its two predecessors; he also released the holiday album, *Christmas Time's A Comin'* in 1994. The retrospective *Hits: Chapter 1* was released in 1995. In 1996, Kershaw released his fourth studio album, *Politics, Religion and Her*. —*Sandra Brennan*

Don't Go Near the Water / 1991 / Mercury ✦✦✦
"Cadillac Style," Kershaw's first single, started him off strong. This album, which made his Jones influence explicit with a cover of "What Am I Worth," also produced the hits "Don't Go Near the Water," "Yard Sale" and "Anywhere but Here." —*Brian Mansfield*

Haunted Heart / 1993 / PolyGram ✦✦✦✦
The more you know about Sammy Kershaw, the more there is to like about his own albums. Though Kershaw doesn't write his own songs, he makes some of the most autobiographical albums to come from Music Row. If you know that Kershaw quit performing for a year and a half when it threatened his marriage, "Still Lovin' You" assumes greater sig-

nificance. Even a song as strange as "Queen of My Double Wide Trailer" makes more sense when you learn that Kershaw still owns a trailer in Louisiana, "in case things don't work out." Sure, he still sounded a lot like George Jones with a southern Louisiana accent. But *Haunted Heart* showed that Kershaw was coming into his own as a vocalist. Just as significant, he was choosing songs that set him apart from the pack. If some of those were as offbeat as "Double Wide Trailer" and "Neon Leon," well, that's just part of what made him distinctive. *—Brian Mansfield*

Feelin' Good Train / 1994 / Mercury ◆◆
"National Working Woman's Holiday" was a perfect example of Kershaw's strengths and weaknesses: few people, if any, had sung about the psychological toll the economic reality of the two-income family took on southern men whose mothers had probably stayed at home to raise them. Unfortunately, Kershaw addresses it with a song whose chorus sounds like it belongs on a T-shirt. He still sounds too much like Jones to be a great singer (just try to tell the two apart on the duet "Never Bit a Bullet Like This"—just try), but he gets in a couple of strong ballads with "If You Ever Come This Way Again" and "Southbound." It also contains a cover of the Amazing Rhythm Aces' 1975 hit "Third Rate Romance." *—Brian Mansfield*

● **Hits: Chapter 1** / Sep. 12, 1995 / Mercury Nashville ◆◆◆◆
Sammy Kershaw had only been recording for four years when he released *The Hits, Chapter 1,* but its appearance didn't seem premature. During that time, he had racked up a considerable number of Top Ten country hits, including the No. 1 hits "National Working Woman's Holiday" and "She Don't Know She's Beautiful." Both of those songs are included, as well as eight others that prove why he was one of the most popular country singers in the early '90s. *—Stephen Thomas Erlewine*

Politics, Religion and Her / 1996 / Mercury Nashville ◆◆
Sammy Kershaw knows the sights and smells of true honky tonks, but he keeps moving further away from the soulful slur and fun-loving style that made him sound so promising a few years ago. After too many novelty songs and misdirected pop-country moves, Kershaw tries to focus himself and get serious on *Politics, Religion and Her.* Unfortunately, his material fails him. A couple of powerful, soul-baring ballads only serve to show how superficial the rest of the song choices are. And his stiff version of Chuck Berry's "Memphis, Tennessee" would get the vote for worst cover of the year, except it gets topped by his pale take on Sammy Johns' ludicrous '70s hit, "Chevy Van." *—Michael McCall*

Clark Kessinger

Fiddle / Instrumental, Bluegrass
One of the greatest of old-time fiddlers, Kessinger and his nephew, Luches, were billed as the Kessinger Brothers and recorded for the Brunswick company in the late '20s, producing records that greatly influenced other fiddle players around the South. When Kessinger was "rediscovered" during the folk revival of 1960, he appeared on the Opry, giving two encores because of audience demand. He entered many of the better-known fiddle contests, winning first place and the title as World's Champion Fiddler at the 47th Annual Union Grove, when he was in his mid-80s. *—David Vinopal*

★ **Clark Kessinger: Fiddler** / 1966 / Smithsonian/Folkways ◆◆◆◆◆
These tunes are played with incredible drive. (Like all Folkways albums, it's now available on tape from Smithsonian/Folkways.) *—Charles S. Wolfe*

Clark Kessinger (Old-Time Music with Fiddle & Guitar) / 1984 / Rounder ◆◆◆◆
A West Virginian who began recording in 1928, Kessinger was rediscovered in the '60s and made several "comeback" albums, of which this is one of the best. *—Charles S. Wolfe*

Hal Ketchum

b. Apr. 9, 1953
Drums, Vocals / Country-Pop, Contemporary Country
Singer-songwriter/drummer Hal Ketchum was raised in the Adirondack Mountains in upstate New York near the Vermont border. Ketchum began drumming at age 15 and soon joined an R&B trio. At age 17, Ketchum moved to Florida and then to Texas, where he quickly got involved playing at a local dance hall and began to hone his songwriting skills. Ketchum went to Nashville in 1986 to write songs. Three years later he released his debut album, *Threadbare Alibis,* on Watermelon Records. The album was released in the US and Europe, and soon afterwards, Ketchum signed with Forerunner Music, which eventually led to a record contract with Curb.
Ketchum released his first Curb album, *Past the Point of Rescue,* in 1991. "Small Town Saturday Night," the first single from the album, reached No. 2 and the second single, "I Know Where Love Lives," reached No. 13; the latter song also won Ketchum a BMI award. On the strength of the two hit singles, the album went gold. In 1992, he scored two more hits and released his third album, *Sure, Love,* which produced three Top

20 hits, including the No. 2 "Hearts Are Gonna Roll." The following year, Ketchum joined the Grand Ole Opry. In 1994, he released his fourth album, *Every Little Word.* Although *Every Little Word* wasn't quite as successful as its predecessors, it still produced two Top 40 hits. In 1995, he released *Greatest Hits. —Sandra Brennan*

Threadbare Alibis / 1988 / Watermelon ◆◆◆
Recorded as Hal Michael Ketchum in Austin before he moved to Nashville, it's folkier and less musically focused than his country recordings. But the thoughtfulness that informs his best work is in place, as is the willingness to take chances with his songwriting. *—Michael McCall*

Past the Point of Rescue / 1991 / Curb ◆◆◆◆
Hal Ketchum writes simple, sometimes moving songs about relationships and/or life's dilemmas, and communicates them in an attractive, unadorned vocal package. But although many of these numbers espouse country themes, Ketchum's delivery, as well as the arrangements and sensibility, lean toward easy-listening pop and light folk. Certainly every country artist isn't a honky tonking, tough-talking, drinker whining about lost love, but Ketchum comes perilously close on "Past the Point Of Rescue" or his cover of the Vogues' "Five O'Clock World" to the super-smooth "Nashville Sound" of days past. *—Ron Wynn*

Sure Love / 1992 / Capitol ◆◆◆
Ketchum was surprised by the success of his major-label debut, and he followed up with a slicker, peppier album. The melodies are stout, and he's at his best on the working-class tributes "Mama Knows the Highway" and "Daddy's Oldsmobile." *—Michael McCall*

Every Little Word / 1994 / Curb ◆◆◆◆
Ketchum reconciles the thoughtfulness of his folkie heart with the verve of modern country, tapping into the directness and earthiness that ties them together. His most country album, it's his most consistent. *—Michael McCall*

● **Greatest Hits** / Mar. 26, 1996 / Curb ◆◆◆◆
Although it doesn't collect every worthwhile cut Ketchum recorded, *Greatest Hits* has the great majority of his big hits, making it a good introduction to the vocalist. *—Stephen Thomas Erlewine*

Claude King

b. Feb. 5, 1933, Shreveport, LA
Vocals / Traditional Country
Singer-songwriter and actor Claude King will best be remembered for his one big crossover hit "Wolverton Mountain." It was the song that gave him international attention and made him a bona fide country star.
King was a natural athlete as a child. When he was 12 years old, he learned how to play guitar. After he attended the University of Idaho, Moscow on a baseball scholarship he came back to his hometown to enroll in Meadows Draughan Business College. He then spent the '50s working as a construction engineer and performing music in local clubs and on TV and radio. King recorded his first singles for Gotham in 1952, but none of them were released.
In 1961, King signed to Columbia and released his first single, "Big River, Big Man." The song became a Top Ten country hit, as well as a minor pop hit. The follow-up "The Comancheros," also made it to the Top Ten in 1962. After "The Comancheros," King released "Wolverton Mountain," which spent nine weeks at the top of the country charts, and peaked at No. 6 on the pop charts. Two more hits—the Top Ten "The Burning of Atlanta" and the No. 11 "I've Got the World By the Tail"—followed that year, and he and his band, the Nashville Knights, became hot tickets. Through 1964, he continued his string of successes with singles like "Hey Lucille!," "Sam Hill," and "Building a Bridge," but his hits became more sporadic in the latter half of the '60s. King left Columbia in 1971 and began recording without success on independent labels. "Cotton Dan," which barely scraped the bottom of the charts, became his last hit in 1977. During his career, King also appeared in two feature films, *Swamp Girl* and *Year of the Wahoo.* He also appeared in the 1982 television mini-series *The Blue and the Gray. —Sandra Brennan*

● **American Originals** / 1990 / CBS ◆◆◆◆
Included are "Wolverton Mountain" and other '60s hits from Johnny Horton's pal. *—Mark A. Humphrey*

Kris Kristofferson

b. Jun. 22, 1936, Brownsville, TX
Guitar, Vocals / Traditional Country, Progressive Country, Singer-Songwriter
The '70s was a decade ripe and waiting for rebels. The Nashville establishment, though, which had sold a lot of records with the bland "Nashville Sound," wasn't quite ready for this songwriting former soldier who, with long beard and dressed in jeans, in 1970 walked on stage at the Country Music Association awards and got his award for "Sunday Morning Coming Down," a song that friend Johnny Cash had made a hit. When in the next year Janis Joplin sold a million with "Me and Bobby McGee", he was on his way, anti-establishment or not. Then Sammi

Smith's version of "Help Me Make It through the Night" was a hit on both the country and the pop charts, also in 1971; suddenly Kristofferson's creative lyrics and memorable music made the establishment forget about his image and created a cult following. In 1973, the year he and singer Rita Coolidge married, *The Silver Tongued Devil and I* went gold. Meanwhile, his duets with Coolidge sold well and produced two Grammys for them. It was at about this time that his record sales began to dip, so he stepped up a film acting career. Role followed role, among them *Cisco Pike, Pat Garrett and Billy the Kid, Alice Doesn't Live Here Anymore, Blume in Love, Rollover*, etc. Critics liked his work on the silver screen, writing that Kristofferson had real talent, that he wasn't only a singer who might sell tickets. He charted again, right into the '80s, but nothing like his phenomenal sales of the previous decade, though his collaboration with Johnny Cash, Willie Nelson, and Waylon Jennings on *Highwayman* (1985) produced another No. 1 album. This gifted songwriter, performer, and actor made success easier for subsequent musicians who, like him, don't fit into the mold. — *David Vinopal*

Kristofferson / 1970 / Monument ✦✦✦✦
This classic first album from Kristofferson showcases his versions of songs made famous by others. While he sometimes went to extremes to get these songs heard in the first place (landing a helicopter in Johnny Cash's yard in an effort to get the singer to hear his songs), this album should not be missed by anyone who's ever liked any of these songs. Once Monument realized what a talent they had, they reissued this record as *Me and Bobby McGee*. — *Jim Worbois*

The Silver Tongued Devil and I / 1971 / Monument ✦✦✦✦
This second album from Kristofferson continues where the first one left off: with more great songs that were readily snapped up and made into hits by other artists. In addition to original versions of songs that were hits by Bobby Bare and Ray Price, this album also features the first appearance of Rita Coolidge on one of Kristofferson's albums (billed as The Lady.) — *Jim Worbois*

☆ **Me & Bobby Mcgee** / 1971 / Monument ✦✦✦✦✦
In the late '60s and early '70s, Kris Kristofferson's adult, reality-based songs were the most shocking thing to hit Nashville in a long time, and what's more, they were hits. This album contains his own versions of some of the best, including the title song, "Help Me Make It through the Night," and "Sunday Mornin' Comin' Down." — *William Ruhlmann*

Border Lord / 1972 / One Way ✦✦✦✦
While the quality of the songwriting remains high on this album, the overall feel of the record is more "down." Monument seemed to be showing some faith in Kristofferson as an artist by releasing "Josie" as a single. Unfortunately, it wasn't a hit. Still, this album should not be missed. — *Jim Worbois*

Jesus Was a Capricorn / 1972 / Monument ✦✦✦
After a visit to the church of Jimmy Snow, Kristofferson was inspired to write the song that was his first hit as a performer: "Why Me." This is also the first time Kristofferson covered a song by another writer. Another strong album worth looking for. — *Jim Worbois*

★ **The Songs of Kristofferson** / 1977 / Monument ✦✦✦✦✦
This greatest-hits collection features most of the songs he wrote but that others turned into hits, including "Sunday Morning Coming Down," "The Pilgrim Number 33," "For the Good Times," "Help Me Make It Through the Night," and "Why Me." His idiosyncratic versions aren't pretty, but they're intimate and often powerful. — *Michael McCall*

Singer/Songwriter / 1991 / Monument ✦✦✦✦
An interesting concept: a two-disc set, one featuring Kristofferson's versions of 17 of his songs, the other featuring covers of the same songs by Ray Charles, Janis Joplin, Bob Dylan, Johnny Cash and others. — *Michael McCall*

Moment of Forever / 1995 / Justice ✦✦✦✦
With the help of producer Don Was and backing musicians like noted professional drummer Jim Keltner and the Heartbreakers' keyboardist, Benmont Tench, Kris Kristofferson turned in one of his best albums of the '80s and '90s with *A Moment of Forever*. Not all of the 14 songs are up to his classic '60s and '70s standards, but it's a consistently strong record, highlighted by the tough, well-constructed rootsy music. — *Stephen Thomas Erlewine*

k.d. lang

Vocals / Progressive Country, Singer-Songwriter, Alternative Pop-Rock
When k.d. lang released her first major label album in 1987, she caused considerable controversy within the traditional world of country music. With her vaguely campy approach, androgynous appearance, and rock-inflected music, very few observers knew what to make of her or her music, although no one questioned her considerable vocal talents. That confusion never quite dissipated over the course of her career, even when she abandoned country music for torchy adult contemporary pop in 1992, with her fourth album, *Ingenue*. Born in Alberta, Canada, lang was first drawn toward music while she was in college. In particular, she was

attracted to the music of Patsy Cline. She became acquainted with Cline's music while she was preparing to star in a collegiate theatrical production based on the vocalist's life. Soon, lang immersed herself in Cline's life and music and decided that she would pursue a career as a professional singer. With the help of guitarist/co-songwriter Ben Mink, she formed a band, named the re-clines in tribute to Patsy Cline, in 1983 and they recorded a debut album, *Friday Dance Promenade*, which received some positive notices in independent papers. A follow-up album, *A Truly Western Experience*, was released in 1984 and received even better reviews and led to national attention. In 1985, lang was named the Most Promising Female Vocalist by the Juno Awards.

All of the Canadian attention led to the interest of a number of American record labels. Sire signed lang in early 1986 and she recorded her first record for the label later that year. The result, *Angel with a Lariat*, was produced by Dave Edmunds and appeared in the fall of 1986. The mix of '50s-styled ballads, kitschy rockabilly and honky tonk numbers. The album garnered good reviews, especially from rock critics. The album had heavy support from college radio, as well as cutting-edge country stations. Though it was a mainstream hit in Canada and an underground smash in the US, Nashville resisted lang, especially her tongue-in-cheek concert appearances. As she was recording her second Nashville album in 1987, lang duetted with Roy Orbison on his old hit "Crying," which was recorded for the film *Hiding Out*. The single was released at the end of the year and it was hit, marking her first appearance on the country charts.

Shadowland, her second Sire album, made her debt to Patsy Cline explicit. Recorded with Cline's producer, Owen Bradley, the album lacked the campy humor of *Angel with a Lariat*, which helped it succeed in traditional country circles—"I'm Down to My Last Cigarette," the first single from the record, was her first to break the country Top 40. *Shadowland* became a sizable word-of-mouth hit, both in modern country and alternative music circles, which led to it going gold. The following year lang released the harder-edged *Absolute Torch and Twang*, which increased her mainstream American country audience, in addition to being a college radio and Canadian hit. lang won a Grammy—Best Country Vocal Performance, Female—for the album in 1989 and "Full Moon of Love" became a Top 25 hit in the summer of 1989. The attention made lang a minor celebrity, which meant that when she launched a protest against meat eating in 1990, it became a media sensation.

Before the release of her fourth album, lang declared that she was a lesbian in an interview in *The Advocate*, which could have been a risky proposition, since Nashville's industry was notorious for not accepting people that fell outside of the margins of the mainstream. However, the new album was not a country album. *Ingenue* was a set of adult contemporary pop that owed very little to country. Its first single, "Constant Craving," became an Top 40 American hit and won the Grammy Award for Best Pop Vocal Performance, Female, leading the album to platinum status in America, Britain, and Australia; it went double platinum in Canada.

Ingenue won lang a new audience, but she didn't immediately produce a follow-up to the album. Instead, her next recorded work was the largely instrumental soundtrack for Gus Van Zant's film adaptation of Tom Robbins' *Even Cowgirls Get the Blues* in 1993; the soundtrack was actually released several months before the film. It wasn't until 1995 that lang delivered *All You Can Eat*, her full-fledged follow-up to *Ingenue*. *All You Can Eat* continued the pop direction of its predecessor, showing no traces of country. The album didn't enjoy the mass commercial acceptance of *Ingenue*, but it was a moderate success, proving that she had a dedicated cult following. — *Stephen Thomas Erlewine*

A Truly Western Experience / 1984 / Bumstead ✦✦
k.d. lang's independent debut album is an uneven but exciting revamp of '50s country. She alternates between rocking honky tonk numbers and Patsy Cline-influenced weepers, sometimes assuming an ironic distance. It may be flawed, but *A Truly Western Experience* has an almost punky kick and illustrates why lang would soon be considered as the freshest female vocalist in country music in the late '80s. — *Stephen Thomas Erlewine*

Angel With a Lariat / 1987 / Sire ✦✦✦
On her debut album, big-voiced lang took a rockabilly approach, with Dave Edmunds as her perfect producer of choice. Edmunds brought out the sharp, rhythmic aspects of her band, the Reclines, and lang wailed over them. The record, which was underappreciated at the time of its release, was an amazingly confident first effort. — *William Ruhlmann*

● **Shadowland** / 1988 / Sire ✦✦✦✦
Rebuffed commercially, lang turned to veteran Nashville producer Owen Bradley for this genre exercise, which re-creates the kind of country diva style of Patsy Cline. It was an accomplished, if puzzling, effort that broke lang through to the country market, at least temporarily. — *William Ruhlmann*

Absolute Torch and Twang / 1989 / Sire ✦✦✦✦
As the title suggests, lang's third (and last country) album combines the best qualities of the first two—the affected-but-original country songwriting of *Angel with a Lariat* and the soaring, Patsy Cline-influenced vocals of *Shadowland*. —*Brian Mansfield*

Ingenue / 1992 / Sire ✦✦✦
Canada's angel with a lariat has chucked the spurs for this album in favor of a classic, Tin Pan Alley pop approach. lang's turnaround is a great success. *Ingenue* is an achingly beautiful work, all melancholy, longing, and heartbreak that strikes a perfect balance between the pain and pleasure of love. To stake out her own individual territory somewhere between Patsy Cline and Billie Holiday without relying on pop standards is a feat in itself. The ten original compositions allow full reign to lang's spectacularly expressive voice. One misses the sense of humor and playful spirit that has infused lang's music in the past, but that can wait until next time 'round when she's recovered from whatever major personal crisis served as inspiration for *Ingenue*. For now, listen and weep. —*Roch Parisien*

All You Can Eat / Oct. 10, 1995 / Sire ✦✦✦
k.d. lang followed through on the promise of her adult contemporary changeover *Ingenue* with *All You Can Eat*. A more experimental and realized record than its predecessor, there are more daring production touches on *All You Can Eat*—it's clear that she has been listening to contemporary pop, not just torch songs. It isn't immediately accessible—the production is low-key, the melodies are gentle and subtle (although her cutesy, tongue-in-cheek song titles suggest otherwise), and lang gives a nuanced, sophisticated performance. Though it lacks a standout song like the aching "Constant Craving," *All You Can Eat* has a more consistent set of songs and, given time, is a more rewarding listen. —*Stephen Thomas Erlewine*

Tracy Lawrence

Vocals / Contemporary Country
Tracy Lawrence was part of the new traditionalist honky tonk singers of the mid-'90s, producing a string of hit singles and critically-acclaimed albums. Born in Texas but raised in Foreman, AR, Lawrence played in his first band at age 16. In 1986, he enrolled at Southern Arkansas University, where he studied mass communications. He dropped out two years later to take a job singing with a Louisiana band. Following the band's breakup in 1990, Lawrence went to Nashville, where he worked as a telemarketer and ironworker. While looking for his big break, Lawrence began participating in talent contests and made enough from his winnings—he always took first or second place—to live on. One of those contests led to a spot on *Live at Libby's*, a local TV show. In 1991, Lawrence had a showcase at the Bluebird Cafe where he met Wayne Edwards, who would soon become his manager. Later that year, he signed with Atlantic Records and released his debut album, *Sticks and Stones*.

On May 31, 1991, Lawrence was celebrating the album's release with his longtime pal and former high-school girlfriend. As he walked her to the hotel door, three gun-toting youths robbed them and tried to force the two into the woman's room. Lawrence, fearing that his friend would be raped, resisted and was shot four times while his friend escaped. Two of the shots just nicked him, but a third had to be surgically removed from his knee and the fourth was deeply embedded in his pelvis, having landed dangerously close to a major artery. Fortunately, he recovered quickly and performed benefit shows to help him with his tremendous medical bills and ensuing physical therapy. His debut single, "Sticks and Stones," made it to No. 1 on the strength of the publicity surrounding the shooting. It began a streak on Top Ten singles that ran into 1996. In 1992, he was named *Billboard*'s Best New Male Artist and Top New Male Vocalist by the ACM. His second album, *Alibis*, went gold 17 days after its release and soon went platinum. The record spawned three straight No. 1 singles—"Alibis," "Can't Break It To My Heart," and "My Second Home." Lawrence's third album, *I See it Now*, was released in 1994; like its predecessors, it was a platinum success. *Live And Unplugged* was released in 1995 and it was followed by *Time Marches On* in 1996. —*Sandra Brennan*

Sticks and Stones / 1991 / Atlantic ✦✦✦
Among the hits to be found here are "Between Us," "Dancin' to Sweet 17," and "Paris." —*AMG*

Alibis / 1993 / Atlantic ✦✦✦✦

● **I See it Now** / Sep. 20, 1994 / Atlantic ✦✦✦✦

Live And Unplugged / Sep. 19, 1995 / Atlantic ✦✦✦

Time Marches On / Jan. 23, 1996 / Atlantic ✦✦✦
This album is another crowd-pleasing set of contemporary country. Like his previous albums, the song selection is a hit-or-miss affair, with about half of the songs failing to make much of an impression. The remainder, however, proves why Lawrence is one of the most popular singers in Nashville. —*Stephen Thomas Erlewine*

Chris LeDoux

Guitar, Vocals / Cowboy
Chris LeDoux is not only a successful country singer and songwriter, but also a champion rodeo rider. Born in Biloxi, MS, he and his family moved to Austin, TX, when he was 12. LeDoux won the Wyoming State Rodeo Championship, subsequently became Intercollegiate National Bareback Riding Champion, and reached the pinnacle of his rodeo career in 1976 when he became World Champion Bareback Rider. While riding and traveling, LeDoux began writing rodeo songs such as "Rodeo Life," "Bareback Jack," and "Bull Rider."

In 1980, he left the cowboy circuit to focus on a music career. He first recorded in a basement studio in Sheridan, and his father arranged a Nashville recording session with some of the city's best session players. His debut album was released on Lucky Man, a subsidiary of his family's music business American Cowboy Songs. For the next two decades, LeDoux recorded 22 albums on independent labels which contained a blend of originals and traditional cowboy songs. Many of those albums were sold on the rodeo circuit, and over the years he developed a loyal following. Between 1979 and 1980, LeDoux had three minor hits with "Lean, Mean and Hungry," "Ten Seconds in the Saddle," and "Caballo Diablo." By 1990, LeDoux had become popular enough to sign with Liberty Records. In addition to releasing new albums from LeDoux, the label arranged to reissue his earlier work. His first album for Liberty was *Western Underground*, which produced the minor hit, "This Cowboy Hat." The song made it to the Top 70, as did the follow-up "Working Man's Dollar."

In 1992 LeDoux teamed up with longtime friend Garth Brooks—who helped popularize LeDoux by mentioning his name in his 1989 hit "Much Too Young (To Feel This Damn Old)"—to sing the title track of *Watcha Gonna Do with a Cowboy*. The song became LeDoux's only Top Ten hit; following its success, LeDoux and Brooks toured together. In 1993, LeDoux had a Top 20 hit with "Cadillac Ranch," from *Under This Old Hat*, which also produced three more moderate hits. —*Sandra Brennan*

Rodeo Songs "Old & New" / 1973 / Liberty ✦✦✦✦
The title tells the tale. —*Mark A. Humphrey*

Western Underground / Jul. 22, 1991 / Liberty ✦✦✦
After nearly 20 years and as many self-produced albums, LeDoux found himself attracting attention as the rodeo singer mentioned in Garth Brooks' first hit, "Much Too Young (To Feel This Damn Old)." Brooks' company soon offered the cowboy his first major-label contract. Here, his producers try to turn him into a conventional Nashville hat act. —*Michael McCall*

Whatcha Gonna Do with a Cowboy / Jul. 20, 1992 / Liberty ✦✦✦✦
Brooks helps out his new friend again by joining him for a duet on the title cut, and LeDoux flashes more of his own personality and gritty charm. —*Michael McCall*

Under This Old Hat / Jul. 5, 1993 / Liberty ✦✦✦
LeDoux learns to rock, taking to the punched-up sound like he's been riding the horse all his life. Included is his wild 'n' woolly version of Joe Ely's "For Your Love." —*Michael McCall*

● **Best of Chris LeDoux** / Mar. 8, 1994 / Liberty ✦✦✦✦
12 tracks from the genuine rodeo cowboy and former bareback bronco-riding champion of country music. *The Best Of* collects the strongest tracks from *Western Underground*, *Whatcha Gonna Do With A Cowboy*, and *Under This Old Hat*, serving up an almost perfect blend of honesty and commercial tunefulness. —*Roch Parisien*

Brenda Lee (Brenda Mae Tarpley)

b. Dec. 11, 1944, Lithonia, GA
Vocals / Rock & Roll, Country-Pop, Pop-Rock
One of the biggest pop stars of the early '60s, Brenda Lee hasn't attracted as much critical respect as she deserves. She is sometimes inaccurately characterized as one of the few female teen idols. More crucially, the credit for achieving success with pop-country crossovers usually goes to Patsy Cline, although Lee's efforts in this era were arguably of equal importance. While she made few recordings of note after the mid-'60s, the best of her first decade is fine indeed, encompassing not just the pop ballads that were her biggest hits, but straight country and some surprisingly fierce rockabilly.

Lee was a child prodigy, appearing on national television by the age of ten, and making her first recordings for Decca the following year (1956). Her first few Decca singles, in fact, make a pretty fair bid for the best pre-teen rock 'n' roll performances this side of Michael Jackson. "BIGELOW 6-200," "Dynamite," and "Little Jonah" are all exceptionally powerful rockabilly performances, with robust vocals and white-hot backing from the cream of Nashville's session musicians (including Owen Bradley, Grady Martin, Hank Garland, and Floyd Cramer). Lee would not have her first big hits until 1960, when she tempered the rockabilly with teen idol pop on "Sweet Nothin's," which went to the Top Five.

The comparison between Lee and Cline is to be expected, given that both singers were produced by Owen Bradley in the early '60s. Naturally, many of the same session musicians and backup vocalists were employed. Brenda, however, had a bigger in with the pop audience, not just because she was still a teenager, but because her material was more pop than Cline's, and not as country. Between 1960 and 1962, she had a stunning series of huge hits—"I'm Sorry," "I Want to Be Wanted," "Emotions," "You Can Depend on Me," "Dum Dum," "Fool No. 1," "Break It to Me Gently," and "All Alone Am I" all made the Top Ten. Their crossover appeal is no mystery. While these were ballads, they were delivered with enough lovesick yearning to appeal to adolescents, and enough maturity for the adults. The first-class melodic songwriting and professional, orchestral production guaranteed that they would not be ghettoized in the country market.

Lee's last Top Ten pop hit was in 1963, with "Losing You." While she still had hits through the mid-'60s, these became smaller and less frequent with the rise of the British Invasion (although she remained very popular overseas). The best of her later hits, "Is It True?," was a surprisingly hard-rocking performance, recorded in 1964 in London with Jimmy Page on guitar. 1966's "Coming on Strong," however, would prove to be her last Top 20 entry.

In the early '70s, Lee reunited with Owen Bradley and, like so many early White rock 'n' roll stars, returned to country music. For a time she was fairly successful in this field, making the country Top Ten half a dozen times in 1973-74. Although she remained active as a recording and touring artist, for the last couple of decades she's been little more than a living legend, directing her intermittent artistic efforts to the country audience. —*Richie Unterberger*

Brenda Lee / 1960 / Decca ◆◆◆◆
Brenda Lee's nickname at 15 was "Miss Dynamite" and it's no lie. Some of her early hits are included—"Sweet Nothin's," "That's All You Gotta Do," plus "I'm Sorry," a great rocking reworking of "Weep No More My Lady," the bluesy "Be My Love Again," and "Just Let Me Dream." —*George Bedard*

The Brenda Lee Story (Her Greatest Hits) / 1974 / MCA ◆◆◆◆
This 22-song, two-LP set included the bulk of her biggest hits, although it misses some significant singles (like "Is It True?"). The two-volume *Anthology* CD, with nearly twice as much material, is a much better investment. —*Richie Unterberger*

★ **Anthology, Vols. 1 & 2 (1956-1980)** / 1991 / MCA ◆◆◆◆◆
A 40-song, two-CD collection, this proves Lee was the best White female rock singer of the pre-Beatles '60s. By the time she turned 18, Lee had hit the pop Top Ten 11 times. All of those cuts are here, from the innocently salacious "Sweet Nothin's" to the string-laden "I'm Sorry" and her remake of Earl "Fatha" Hines' "You Can Depend on Me." Her best country singles, "Johnny One Time" and "Big Four Poster Bed," are also included. The compilers wisely passed over some minor hits in favor of obscure sides like the odd rockabilly "Let's Jump the Broomstick," a cover of Edith Piaf's "If You Love Me (Really Love Me)," and "Is It True?" a middling hit from 1964, which features guitarist Jimmy Page (who is 11 months older than Lee). *Anthology* thoroughly traces Lee's development as a vocalist, from early-childish exuberance to mature, graceful phrasing. —*Brian Mansfield*

Johnny Lee (John Lee Harn)

b. Jul. 3, 1946, Texas City, TX
Guitar, Vocals / Adult Contemporary, Nashville Sound/Countrypolitan
Like many his age, Johnny Lee grew up on the music of Chuck Berry, Elvis Presley, and Jerry Lee Lewis. Raised on a dairy farm in Alta Loma, TX, he formed his first band, Johnny Lee & the Road Runners, during high school. He tricked his way into playing onstage with Mickey Gilley at a Houston club called the Nesadel, and that shot brought him a long-term run at Gilley's clubs. When *Urban Cowboy* was shot at Gilley's, record executive Irving Azoff offered Lee an opportunity to sing in the picture, and he ended up with a song that more than 20 artists had previously rejected. In his hands, that song—"Lookin' for Love"—became a million-seller and the musical centerpiece of the movie. Stardom occurred practically overnight for Lee, but it was a mixed bag. He and Gilley toured steadily; Lee got a substantial string of hits for about three years and ended up marrying "Dallas" starlet Charlene Tilton. But the marriage soured, he found his name constantly in the tabloids, and he was forced to record a large amount of same-sounding material. Nevertheless, Johnny Lee had an important role in a huge era for country music, and his easygoing vocal style still makes him very listenable. —*Tom Roland*

● **Greatest Hits** / 1983 / Full Moon ◆◆◆◆
Lots of mid-tempo love songs are here, much in the vein of "Lookin' for Love." Too bad Lee couldn't break out of that mold a little

sooner—"Sounds like Love" and "Hey Bartender" show some real teeth. —*Tom Roland*

Little Texas

Country-Rock, Contemporary Country
Drawing from country and rock 'n' roll, Little Texas was one of the more popular country bands of the early '90s. The origins of Little Texas lie in 1984, when vocalist Tim Rushlow teamed up with vocalist/acoustic guitarist Dwayne O'Brien in Arlington, TX. After two years of working together, Rushlow left for Nashville while O'Brien finished his chemistry degree at East Central State University, OK. The following year, he followed Rushlow to Music City. They were subsequently joined by lead guitarist Porter Howell and bass guitarist Duane Propes, both of whom were students at Belmont University, Nashville, and the group began touring. While performing in Massachusetts, they hooked up with keyboardist Brady Seals and drummer Del Gray. In 1988, future manager Christy DiNapoli convinced Doug Grau from Warner Brothers to come listen to one of the band's performances in Birmingham, and he signed them to the label.

Upon signing the contract, the group named themselves Little Texas after their old rehearsal spot on Little Texas Road and began touring the country in a beat-up van and a homemade trailer. By the end of 1990, they had enough material to record their debut album, *First Time for Everything*. The album was released in the summer of 1991, after the band's debut single, "Some Guys Have All the Love," became a Top Ten hit. The band really began to take off in 1994 with the release of their second album, *Big Time*. The album produced the No. 2 country hit "What Might Have Been," which also became a minor pop hit. This was followed by "God Blessed Texas," a line-dancing favorite which reached the Top Five. In early 1994, Little Texas scored its first No. 1 hit with "My Love," and *Big Time* went platinum. Later in 1994, the group released their third album, *Kick A Little*, which went platinum and produced the Top Ten singles "Kick A Little" and "Amy's Back in Austin." In 1995, Little Texas released *Greatest Hits*, which featured two new songs, including the No. 5 hit "Life Goes On." —*Sandra Brennan*

Little Texas / Mar. 3, 1992 / Warner Bros. ◆◆◆
Big Time / 1993 / Warner Bros. ◆◆◆
● **Greatest Hits** / Oct. 1995 / Warner Bros. ◆◆◆◆
Collecting all of Little Texas' best numbers, *Greatest Hits* is the perfect introduction to the country-pop band, as well as being their most consistent and enjoyable album. —*Stephen Thomas Erlewine*

Hank Locklin (Lawrence Hankins Locklin)

b. Feb. 15, 1918, McLellan, FL
Guitar, Vocals / Traditional Country, Honky Tonk
Hank Locklin, one of country music's great tenors, was born in the small town of McLellan located in the lumbering district of the Florida Panhandle. The youngest son of four children, he went to a one-room schoolhouse and was musical even as a young child. Hank was injured at the age of eight in an accident and the long recovery process was the time when he first begin to learn music. Although interested in the guitar early on, it was not until his mid-teens that he really began to master that instrument. Hank was active in music in high school (which he never finished), and at eighteen won first prize in a talent show. He went on to do spots on the local radio station as he became more and more interested in entertaining. By the mid-1940s he was playing on the radio and doing in-person performances in Florida and nearby states. For the next ten years or so, Locklin worked many jobs (musical and otherwise), played with a variety of groups, and, through a variety of trials, gradually worked his way up the country music ladder to recognition. (A good account of these years can be found in the Bear Family box liner notes, written by Otto Kissinger.)

His career did not really take off until he joined the RCA Victor label in the spring of 1955. Locklin's work with RCA has the added advantage that almost all of it was produced by Chet Atkins, often with Atkins himself on rhythm or lead guitar and with the added trills and fill-ins of Floyd Cramer on piano. The extreme simplicity of his early works makes this combination of his clear voice and these particular sidemen very effective. Everyone knows Hank's big hits—"Send Me the Pillow that You Dream On" (written by Locklin), "Geisha Girl," and "Please Help Me I'm Falling"—but real Locklin fans are in love with his very simple heartfelt tunes like "Who Am I to Cast the First Stone," "A Good Woman's Love," "Seven or Eleven," "I'm Tired of Bummin' Around," "Golden Wristwatch," "Sitting Alone at a Table for Two," and many others. These early songs are characterized by Locklin's crystal-clear tenor, the ultra-simplicity of the songs themselves, and their straight-to-the heart emotional plea. Kitty Wells has this same kind of gift. The result is a group of incredible songs that, first released as singles, later became available on Camden, RCA's budget label. Now, after many years of neglect, many of these songs are now available on the Bear family box *Hank Locklin, Please*

Help Me I'm Falling. Locklin stayed with the RCA label until the mid-1960s.

Locklin helped pioneer the idea of concept albums; his albums *Foreign Love* and *Irish Songs, Country Style* are examples. He also recorded an album tribute to Roy Acuff, *A Tribute to Roy Acuff, King of Country Music*. His Irish songs are pretty near definitive. As time goes by, the vocal chorus begins to creep into Locklin's albums a little more than purists might like, but his crystal-clear tenor never deserts him.

Hank hit the Top-Ten charts again in the 1968 with The Country Hall of Fame. In the 1970s he toured overseas often, was very popular in Ireland and Great Britain, and made at least one tour with Chet Atkins to the far East (Japan). After leaving RCA, he went on to record for a number of labels including MGM and Plantation. He is retired now and lives in Brewton, Alabama, only some 20 miles from his birthplace. —*Michael Erlewine*

☆ **Please Help Me I'm Falling [Box]** / Dec. 1995 / Bear Family ✦✦✦✦✦
This is a four-disc retrospective of Locklin's years with RCA Victor from 1955 through the mid-'60s. Of course Hank's big popular hits "Send Me the Pillow that You Dream On," "Geisha Girl," and "Please Help Me I'm Falling" are there. While a great many important early Locklin songs are missing from this collection ("I'm Tired of Bummin' Around," "Sitting Alone at a Table for Two," and "Golden Wristwatch"), many fine songs are included that have been unavailable for many years. Also included are a number of Locklin's concept albums: *Foreign Love* , *Irish Songs, Country Style*, plus his album tribute to Roy Acuff, *A Tribute to Roy Acuff, King of Country Music*.

Of course his early material on Four Star Records (pre-RCA) and his later material on MGM and Plantation are not here. Most of these songs in this box set are taken from albums that appeared on Camden and RCA. Unless RCA decides to release all the early Camden material, this fine box set from Bear Family is what we have for now. —*Michael Erlewine*

● **Hank Locklin** / Wrangler ✦✦✦✦
One of the most perfect early country albums ever recorded; heartwrenching songs sung in Locklin's perfect tenor—before the hits. It does not get any better than this. Hard-to-find album, but quintessential. —*Michael Erlewine*

The Louvin Brothers

Traditional Country
From the close-harmony brother acts of the '30s evolved Charlie (b. 1927) and Ira (Loudermilk) Louvin (1924-1965), ranking among the top duos in country music history. With Ira's incredibly high, pure tenor and Charlie's emotional and smooth melody tenor, they learned well from the Bolick brothers (the Blue Sky Boys), the Monroe Brothers, the Delmore Brothers, and other major family duos of the previous generation, preserving the old-time flavor, while bringing this genre into the '50s. When country music moved to a newer sound. Whatever type of songs they recorded—gospel, folk, hillbilly, or '50s pop—those songs became the Louvins. Add to the list the many Louvin compositions (for example, "If I Could Only Win Your Love," Emmylou Harris' first hit), and you have an act that is outstanding in country music history. Their career took a while to get going, partly because of interruptions from WW II and the Korean War. In the early '50s, after making a reputation for unexcelled gospel singing, the Louvins broadened their repertoire, recording "The Get Acquainted Waltz" (with Chet Atkins adding another guitar to Charlie's and to Ira's mandolin), a fair hit that showed success was reachable with non-religious music. The electric guitar, with the duo's unique harmony and Ira's exceptional tenor, created a sound that fans asked for in increasing numbers. In 1955, after ten unsuccessful auditions, they finally joined the Opry, where they performed to great acclaim until 1963, when they broke up. They had a number of hits, including the much-covered "When I Stop Dreaming." Ira continued on with a solo career. Charlie has remained with the Opry to this day, where his excellent voice has only improved with the years, scoring a major hit with "See the Big Man Cry, Mama." Driving home from a performance one night in 1965, Ira's car was struck in a head-on collision, killing probably the most exceptional high tenor country music has ever known. —*David Vinopal*

My Baby's Gone / 1960 / Stetson ✦✦✦✦
The Louvins' Capitol output was extremely consistent, and this 1960 LP (reissued on LP in England by Stetson) is no exception. Working under producer Ken Nelson, the traditional core of their harmonies and guitar remained intact, updated only very slightly with some fuller arrangements and mild pop touches. Most of the material is love laments, with "I Wish It Had Been a Dream" and "She Didn't Even Know I Was Gone" (mournfully heartbreaking even by country standards) being standouts. —*Richie Unterberger*

Songs That Tell a Story / 1981 / Rounder ✦✦✦✦
Arguably the greatest duet and brother act in country history, Ira and Charlie Louvin made remarkably moving, simply performed songs about their faith and lives, with only guitar and mandolin backing, and

reflecting the values of country with more sincerity and genuine feeling than hundreds of elaborately produced and packaged albums have since. Rounder issued these numbers on album in the late '70s, and reissued them on CD in 1991. The digital backdrop doesn't drain the authority from their voices; instead, it simply reaffirms the glory and splendor of the Louvins on 15 short, but brilliant gospel numbers. —*Ron Wynn*

Radio Favorites 1951-57 / 1987 / Country Music Foundation ✦✦✦✦
Here are 14 live performances of gospel and secular music, released here for the first time. The album includes "I Wish You Knew," "They've Got the Church Outnumbered," and more. —*AMG*

☆ **Close Harmony** / 1992 / Bear Family ✦✦✦✦✦
A gargantuan eight-disc box set, *Close Harmony* is essential for serious country fans and scholars. Collecting everything the Louvin Brothers recorded for Capitol, Apollo, Decca, and MGM, the set may have too much music for casual fans, but those willing to delve deeply into these 219 tracks will learn much—not only about the duo, but about the evolution of country music in the '50s. Many of the roots of contemporary country and rock 'n' roll are apparent throughout the set. —*Stephen Thomas Erlewine*

★ **When I Stop Dreaming: The Best of the Louvin Brothers** / 1995 / Razor & Tie ✦✦✦✦
Razor & Tie's single-disc collection *When I Stop Dreaming: The Best of the Louvin Brothers* contains all of the absolute essentials from the groundbreaking duo, including all of their biggest hits from the '50s. For most casual fans, it's not only the perfect introduction, it's the definitive compilation. —*Stephen Thomas Erlewine*

Patty Loveless (Patricia Ramey)

Vocals / Country-Rock, Contemporary Country
Patty Loveless born in Pikeville, KY, was one of the most popular female country vocalists of the late '80s and early '90s. Loveless drew from country's honky tonk tradition, adding a slight edge of rock 'n' roll.

Loveless began writing and singing songs with her older brother Roger before she was 12 years old. By the time she was 14, Loveless had an impressive repertoire of self-penned songs, and her brother took her to Nashville. There she met Porter Wagoner, who would become her close friend and mentor. Loveless got her first break upon meeting Doyle and Teddy Wilburn, who were searching for a singer to replace Loretta Lynn in the Wilburn Brothers. She became their featured singer for three years and signed to their publishing company, Surefire Music, as a songwriter after she graduated from high school. She also married ex-Wilburn drummer Terry Loveless. The newlyweds moved to his home at Kings Mountain near Charlotte, where they played in several local bands.

In 1985, Loveless went back to Nashville and recorded a demo tape, which attracted the attention of several record companies; two months later she signed with MCA and divorced her husband. Between 1985 and 1987, Loveless appeared on the Top 50 charts four times with songs such as "Wicked Ways" and "After All." Later in 1987, Loveless broke into the Top Ten and Top Five respectively with "If My Heart Had Windows" and "A Little Bit of Love." In 1988, Loveless' career rose meteorically when she released the album *Honky Tonk Angels*, which produced five tremendously successful singles, including the No. 1 hits "Timber I'm Falling in Love" and "Chains." Her 1990 album *On Down the Line* was also successful, as was 1991's *Up Against My Heart*, her final album for MCA. In 1993, the label released Loveless' *Greatest Hits* album. Later that year, she released *Only What I Feel*, her first album for Epic Records. Within a year, she album went gold, producing several hits, including the No. 1 "Blame It On Your Heart." In 1994, she released *When Fallen Angels Fly*, which also went gold and yielded several Top Ten hits. *Trouble With The Truth*, Loveless' eighth album, was released in 1996. —*Sandra Brennan*

If My Heart Had Windows / 1988 / MCA ✦✦✦
Included are fine songs by Steve Earle, Dallas Frazier, and others. —*Dan Heilman*

Honky Tonk Angel / 1988 / MCA ✦✦✦
The song subjects hardly classify Loveless as a honky tonk angel, at least by Hank Thompson's definition. But this was the album that established Loveless as a major presence, and it includes two of her biggest singles—"Chains," "Timber I'm Falling in Love"—and two of her best—"Blue Side of Town" and "Don't Toss Us Away," a duet with Rodney Crowell. —*Brian Mansfield*

On Down the Line / May 15, 1990 / MCA ✦✦✦
Featured are the hits "The Night's Too Long," "I've Got to Stop Loving You (And Start Living Again)," and "Blue Memories," among others. —*AMG*

Up Against My Heart / 1991 / MCA ✦✦✦
Loveless gets a little more adventurous with each album, though she never forgets to include sure-fire hits like "Hurt Me Bad (In a Real Good Way)" and "Jealous Bone." This time she invites comparisons to Patsy Cline with "Can't Stop Myself from Loving You" and implies that God is

female by switching the pronouns in Lyle Lovett's "God Will." —*Brian Mansfield*

Only What I Feel / Apr. 20, 1993 / Epic ✦✦✦✦
Loveless underwent throat surgery and switched labels before creating this album, and both helped. She sounds stronger and more impassioned than she had in years, and her artistic drive seemed more confident and determined. "Nothin' but the Wheel" ranks with her best ballads. —*Michael McCall*

● **Greatest Hits** / May 11, 1993 / MCA ✦✦✦✦
The inevitable hits compilation chronicling Patty Loveless' five years and five albums at MCA is, in the Nashville tradition, not exactly generous: It contains only ten tracks and runs 31.5 minutes. In that space, though, you get most of Loveless' big hits between 1988 and 1992, from "If My Heart Had Windows" to "Jealous Bone," and including the chart toppers "Timber I'm Falling In Love" and "Chains." Oddly, "A Little Bit In Love," which just missed hitting No. 1, is not included. The set traces Loveless' rise as part of the neo-traditionalism movement of the 1980s, a movement that had faded, and that Loveless was ready to move beyond, by the time she ended her tenure at MCA. The music included here is fine, bedrock country, but a little faceless for all its authenticity. This is one artist whose second hits collection is likely to be more interesting than her first. —*William Ruhlmann*

When Fallen Angels Fly / 1994 / Epic ✦✦✦✦
Patty Loveless expanded on the success of her comeback album, *Only What I Feel*, on its successor, *When Fallen Angels Fly*, which made the country Top Ten, went gold, spawned four Top Ten singles, and was named the Country Music Association's Album of the Year. Songs like the feisty hit "Halfway Down" had a bouncy rockabilly feel, and Loveless rode the rhythms well, while on the ballad "Here I Am," another hit, she sounded like a country Stevie Nicks. And then there was "I Try To Think About Elvis," a comic rocker that was one of the best pieces of material to turn up in Nashville that year, and that Loveless performed with just enough tongue in her cheek. Of course, there were a couple of those hopelessly hokey Gretchen Peters ballads, but even one of those, "You Don't Even Know Who I Am," was a hit. —*William Ruhlmann*

Trouble With The Truth / Jan. 23, 1996 / Epic ✦✦✦✦
On stage, Patty Loveless may be the antithesis of modern music stars. She can come across as shy, awkward, unsure of herself. On record, however, those traits help define the complexities she's capable of instilling in a good lyric. On *Trouble With the Truth*, she again crystallizes emotions to their core. When playing the part of a spurned lover, she can sound tough and direct without losing her vulnerability. When facing her own faults, as she does on the outstanding title song, she can sound contemplative and regretful without drowning in self-pity. When looking for a good time, she can sound rowdy and spirited without relying on silly novelty themes that overrun country radio. Loveless long ago established that she can be relied upon to dig up good material and elevate it with sensitivity and style. But, in recent years, one of country music's most consistently solid singers seems to keep raising her own stakes. *Trouble with the Truth* continues her streak of excellence. —*Michael McCall*

Loretta Lynn (Loretta Webb)

b. Apr. 14, 1935, Butcher's Hollow, KY
Guitar, Vocals / Traditional Country, Nashville Sound/Countrypolitan

Loretta Lynn is one of the classic country singers. During the '60s and '70s, she ruled the charts, racking up over 70 hits as a solo artist and a duet partner. Lynn helped forge the way for strong, independent women in country music.

As her song (and movie and book) says, Loretta Lynn is a coal miner's daughter, born in Butcher Hollow, KY, in 1934. As a child, she sang in church and a variety of local concerts. In January 1948, she married Oliver "Mooney" Lynn. She was 13 years old at the time. Following their marriage, the couple moved to Custer, WA, where they raised four children.

After a decade of motherhood, Lynn began performing her own songs in local clubs, backed by a band led by her brother, Jay Lee Webb. It took her a decade of gigging before she was noticed by a record label. In 1959, she signed a contract with Zero Records, which released her debut single, "I'm a Honky Tonk Girl," in 1960. The honky tonk ballad became a hit thanks to the insistent, independent promotion of Lynn and her husband. The pair would drive from one radio station to the next, getting the DJs to play her single, and sent out thousands of copies to stations. All of the effort paid off—the single reached No. 14 on the charts and attracted the attention of the Wilburn Brothers. The Wilburns hired Lynn to tour with them in 1960 and advised her to relocate to Nashville. She followed their advice and moved to the city in late 1960. After she arrived in Nashville, she signed with Decca Records. At Decca, she would work with Owen Bradley, who had produced Patsy Cline. Lynn released her first Decca single, "Success," in 1962 and it went straight to No. 6, beginning a string

of Top Ten singles that would run through the rest of the decade and throughout the next. She was a hard honky tonk singer for the first half of the '60s and rarely strayed from the genre. Although she still worked within the confines of honky tonk in the latter half of the decade, her sound became more personal, varied and ambitious, particularly lyrically. Beginning with 1966's No. 2 hit "You Ain't Woman Enough," Lynn began writing songs that had a feminist viewpoint, which was unheard of in country music. Her lyrical stance became more autobiographical and realistic as time wore on, highlighted by such hits as "Don't Come Home A'Drinkin' (With Lovin' on Your Mind)" (1966), "Your Squaw Is on the Warpath" (1968), "Woman of the World (Leave My World Alone)" (1969), and a tune about birth control called "The Pill" (1974).

Between 1966 and 1970, Loretta Lynn racked up 13 Top Ten hits, including four No. 1 hits—"Don't Come Home A'Drinkin'," "Fist City" (1968), "Woman of the World," and the autobiographical "Coal Miner's Daughter." In 1971, she began a professional partnership with Conway Twitty. As a duo, Lynn and Twitty had five consecutive No. 1 hits between 1971 and 1975—"After the Fire Is Gone" (1971), "Lead Me On" (1971), "Louisiana Woman, Mississippi Man" (1973), "As Soon As I Hang Up the Phone" (1974), and "Feelins'" (1974). The hit-streak kick-started what would become one of the most successful duos of country. For four consecutive years (1972-1975), Lynn and Twitty were named the Vocal Duo of the Year by the Country Music Association. In addition to their five No. 1 singles, they had seven other Top Ten hits between 1976 and 1981.

Loretta Lynn published her autobiography, *Coal Miner's Daughter*, in the mid-'70s. In 1980, the book was adapted for the screen, with Sissy Spacek as Lynn. The film was one of the most critically acclaimed and successful films of the year and Spacek would win the Academy Award for her performance. All of the attention surrounding the movie made Loretta Lynn a household name with the American mainstream. Although she continued to be a popular concert attraction throughout the '80s, she wasn't able to continue her domination of the country charts. "I Lie," her last Top Ten single, arrived in early 1982, while her last Top 40 single, "Heart Don't Do This to Me," was in 1985. In light of her declining record sales, Lynn backed away from recording frequently during the late '80s and '90s, concentrating on performing instead. In 1993, she recorded the *Honky Tonk Angels* album with Tammy Wynette and Dolly Parton. —*Stephen Thomas Erlewine*

☆ **Greatest Hits** / 1968 / MCA ✦✦✦✦✦
She had a big hand in raising Nashville's perception of women as capable and competent (although the city still has a way to go). "Don't Come Home A'Drinkin'" and "You Ain't Woman Enough" are particularly representative: sassy, honest, and aggressive. —*Tom Roland*

Greatest Hits, Vol. 2 / 1974 / MCA ✦✦✦✦
In the liner notes, Pete Axthelm cites "the range of her personality," and that range is evidenced here: reflective ("Coal Miner's Daughter"), feisty ("Fist City"), humorous ("One's on the Way"), and sentimental ("Love Is the Foundation"). —*Tom Roland*

★ **Country Music Hall of Fame** / 1991 / MCA ✦✦✦✦✦
Few greatest-hits packages pack the wallop of these 16 performances (1961-1976). This album includes duets with Ernest Tubb and Conway Twitty, men who knew to stand clear when Lynn wailed "Your Squaw Is on the Warpath" or "Fist City." —*Mark A. Humphrey*

☆ **Honky Tonk Girl: Collection** / 1994 / MCA ✦✦✦✦✦
Loretta Lynn's three-disc box set *Honky Tonk Girl* has the requisite rarities, but the real strength of the collection is how it offers all of her essential tracks—from 1960's "I'm A Honky Tonk Girl" to 1988's "Who Was That Stranger"—in one place. Not only are her classic hits like "Fist City" and "Coal Miner's Daughter" included, but so are most of her hit duets with Conway Twitty, such as "After the Fire Is Gone" and "As Soon As I Hang Up the Phone." A few hits are missing—notably "Louisiana Woman, Mississippi Man"—but *Honky Tonk Girl* remains the one comprehensive and essential Loretta Lynn collection. —*Stephen Thomas Erlewine*

Uncle Dave Macon (David Harrison)

b. Smartt Station, KY, **d.** 1952
Old-Time

David Harrison Macon didn't perform professionally until he was past 50, but he became one of the first superstars of country music. A talented banjoist and comic (and sometimes preacher and farmer), Uncle Dave Macon was the Grand Ole Opry's first major star and an audience favorite from 1925 until his death in 1952. He derived much of his repertoire and stage patter from vaudeville and minstrel shows, but his songs reflected on a wide variety of subjects from political corruption to current events like the advent of the automobile. His presence affected country music like none before it; even today a three-day festival, Uncle Dave Macon Days, is held in Murfreesboro, TN, the site of the National Old-Time Banjo Championship. —*Brian Mansfield*

● **Country Music Hall of Fame Series** / 1992 / MCA ✦✦✦✦
"Shout if you are happy!" Uncle Dave Macon exclaims during "Tom and Jerry" as Mazy Todd saws away at her fiddle. "Kill yo'self!" That's the kind of enthusiasm Macon brings to these 16 fine examples of string-band music, recorded between 1926 and 1934 for the Vocalion, Brunswick, and Champion labels. Macon frequently starts the songs with a spoken anecdote (including a plug for his Macon Midway Mule and Wagon Transportation Company). This collection is essentially an expanded version of *Uncle Dave Macon: First Featured Star of the Grand Ole Opry,* a retrospective issued in 1966 after his posthumous election to the Country Music Hall of Fame. —*Brian Mansfield*

Travelin' Down the Road / 1995 / Country/BMG ✦✦✦✦
This CD is a reissue containing many of Uncle Dave Macon's best sides. All these tunes were transfers from original 78s recorded in 1935. The sound is still quite clear and enjoyable. There is a good selection of religious and secular tunes, all performed with vitality. You can really hear what draws people to old-timey music after listening to these records. —*Richard Meyer*

The Maddox Brothers & Rose Maddox

Traditional Country
The Maddox Brothers (Cliff, Cal, Fred, Don, and "friendly Henry, the working girl's friend") and their sister Rose called themselves "America's Most Colorful Hillbilly Band." They weren't kidding. It wasn't just a matter of hillbilly couture—though with their matching Turk suits and spangles the family had style in spades. But colorful described their sound, as well. Throughout the '40s and '50s, they tore down the honky tonks from the Pacific Northwest to the Gulf Coast with slap-bass boogie and an iconoclastic attitude towards the stiffer mores of conventional country. In other words, they rocked the house. It all started in 1933, when the Maddox family—Charlie and Lula, and five of their seven children—hitchhiked and rode the rails from Boaz, AL, to California, where they worked in the migrant labor camps of the San Joaquin Valley. Fred Maddox quickly tired of picking fruit and wrangled a radio spot for his intensely musical family (which featured 11-year old Rose on decidedly raw lead vocals). On the air in Modesto by 1937, the group made their first records, for the 4-Star label, in 1946. From 1951 till 1956, they recorded for Columbia. At that point, the family act broke up, though Rose maintained a successful solo career for many years after. She still performs occasionally. —*Dan Cooper*

Rose Maddox Sing Bluegrass / 1962 / Capitol ✦✦✦✦
Of the many fine (and now rare) LPs she cut for Capitol, this humdinger is the best one to break your neck trying to find. On this bluegrass sung with honky tonk fire, sparks do fly. —*Dan Cooper*

Rockin' & Rollin' / Bear Family ✦✦✦✦
This German import contains a fair cross-section of their bizarre bluegrass/honky tonk/rockabilly madness. It includes "Ugly and Sloughy (That's the Way I Like 'Em)" and "The Death of Rock & Roll." —*George Bedard*

Columbia Historic Edition / CBS ✦✦✦✦
A too-short-lived (and too brief) LP, this sampler from their Columbia years showcases their relentless chops and outrageous sense of humor. Though the Bear Family LPs draw from the same source, a full CD collection of the Maddoxes' Columbia work is desperately needed. —*Dan Cooper*

Maddox Brothers & Rose on the Air, Vol. 1 & 2 / Arhoolie ✦✦✦✦
A fascinating document, this double-length cassette includes radio broadcasts from as early as 1940 (six years before the Maddoxes cut their first record) and on into the early '50s. It's not the place to find out if you're a Maddox family fan, but if you are one already, this collection (which includes their only appearance on the Grand Ole Opry) will give you a sense of what it must have been like to hear Rose wreak havoc with '50s gender roles by taking the lead on a cover of Hank Snow's "The Gold Rush Is Over." —*Dan Cooper*

★ **Maddox Brothers & Rose, 1946-1951, Vol. 1** / Arhoolie ✦✦✦✦✦
Consisting of 27 cuts from the years 1946-51, this disc is indispensable to anyone seeking a dose of vintage country music at its most hedonistically raucous. Though the archaic sound quality may make an audiophile cringe, the musical vitality of these boogie, blues, and ballad recordings is absolutely astonishing. So is the degree of nerve they show with their winking versions of "Whoa Sailor" and "Sally Let Your Bangs Hang Down." —*Dan Cooper*

☆ **Maddox Brothers & Rose: Their Original Hits** / Arhoolie ✦✦✦✦✦
Featured is the same material as above, except more of it. Only available on cassette, it combines the out-of-print Arhoolie LPs 5016 and 5017. —*Dan Cooper*

Barbara Mandrell

b. Dec. 25, 1948, Houston, TX
Guitar (Steel), Vocals / Country-Pop
A show-biz veteran of over thirty years, this country-pop superstar is the first artist to win the Country Music Association Entertainer of the Year award two consecutive years. She started early, touring with Johnny Cash when she was thirteen. Her first hit was with Otis Redding's "I've Been Loving You Too Long" in 1969. Among her many No. 1 records are "Sleepin' Single in a Double Bed," "I Was Country When Country Wasn't Cool," "Years," and "One of a Kind Pair of Fools." She and her sisters Louise and Irlene have received much TV play through their national show, on which each shows her versatility on many instruments. Her biography, *Get to the Heart: My Story,* recounts how her near-fatal auto accident of 1984 changed her life. —*David Vinopal*

The Best of Barbara Mandrell / 1979 / MCA ✦✦✦✦
The Best of Barbara Mandrell collects her biggest hits from the late '70s, including "After the Lovin'," "Married But Not to Each Other," "Tonight," "Woman to Woman," and "Sleeping Single in a Double Bed." —*Stephen Thomas Erlewine*

● **Greatest Hits** / 1985 / MCA ✦✦✦✦
Hank Williams definitely didn't do it this way. Nevertheless, "I Was Country When Country Wasn't Cool" summed up a lot of folks' feelings as the Travolta crowd tried to claim him as their own. Also included are the No. 1s "Sleeping Single in a Double Bed," "(If Loving You Is Wrong) I Don't Want to Be Right," and "Years." —*Dan Cooper*

Kathy Mattea

b. 1959
Guitar, Vocals / Country-Pop, Contemporary Country
Singer-songwriter Kathy Mattea primarily works in a country tradition, but her songs are tinged with the confessional folk of songwriters like Joni Mitchell, Buffy Sainte-Marie, and James Taylor. Mattea began playing guitar in junior high school; she also received operatic voice training during this time. Mattea became interested in bluegrass music while attending West Virginia University in the mid-'70s. In 1976, she joined the bluegrass group Pennsboro, and two years later, she dropped out of school to try her luck in Nashville. She spent a few years working as a waitress and tour guide before landing a job as a demo and jingle singer.

In 1983, Mattea signed to Mercury Records. The following year she released her eponymous debut album. Her first two singles, "Street Talk" and "Someone is Falling in Love," both reached the Top 30. "You've Got a Soft Place to Fall" and "That's Easy for You to Say" both went on to make the Top 50, and she was named Top New Country Artist of the Year by *Billboard* magazine. Following the release of her 1985 album *From My Heart,* Mattea was nominated for the CMA Horizon Award. The album produced three hits, with "He Won't Give In" making it to the Top 25. Her third album, 1986's *Walk the Way the Wind Blows,* provided her with her first Top Ten country hits, "Love At the Five and Dime," "Walk the Way the Wind Blows," "You're the Power," and "Train of Memories."

Untasted Honey, released in 1987, elevated Mattea to the status of a genuine star, as it produced the back-to-back No. 1 hits, "Goin' Gone" and "Eighteen Wheels and A Dozen Roses," which was named Single of the Year by the Country Music Association and the Academy of Country Music. In total, Mattea scored six major hits in 1987 and was named Top Female Vocalist by both academies. She married songwriter Jon Vezner in 1988 and subsequently released *Willow in the Wind,* which continued her successful streak. Mattea continued to have Top Ten hits into the early '90s, highlighted by 1989's "Where've You Been," which became a crossover hit on the adult contemporary charts and was named Song of the Year by both the CMA and ACM. The song also earned Mattea her first Grammy award for Best Female Country Vocal Performance. During the early '90s, Mattea's commercial standing declined somewhat. She was no longer able to reach the Top Ten with regularity, but she continued to have Top 40 hits throughout the decade. —*Sandra Brennan*

Walk the Way the Wind Blows / 1986 / Mercury ✦✦✦✦
An injection of brash, bluegrass-style energy gave her music a needed lift. This is her strongest collection, matching her folkie sensitivity with an innocent verve that is truly catchy. It includes her hit version of Nanci Griffith's "Love at the Five and Dime." —*Michael McCall*

Untasted Honey / Sep. 28, 1987 / Mercury ✦✦✦
Featured is one of her best uptempo tunes, "Untold Stories," and one of her most wistful ballads, "Life as We Knew It." —*Michael McCall*

● **A Collection of Hits** / 1990 / Mercury ✦✦✦✦
Kathy Mattea has risen to near the top of the Nashville ranks because of her haunting, soulful voice, well-produced recordings that have a simple, folkie directness, and, most especially, an amazing talent for picking the best songs being written for the country market, among them "Eighteen Wheels and a Dozen Roses," "Goin' Gone," and the heartbreaking "Where've You Been." —*William Ruhlmann*

Time Passes By / 1991 / Mercury ✦✦✦
On her most ambitious album, Mattea gets impeccably chosen songs (as usual) and strong supporting performances (from Emmylou Harris, Dougie MacLean, and the Roches). She doesn't write her own stuff, so she may not be the romantic dreamer of "Asking Us to Dance," but she sure sounds like it. Songs like "Time Passes By," co-written by husband Jon Vezner, suggest there's more honesty here than image. She can even make the half-baked "From a Distance" convincing. —*Brian Mansfield*

Lonesome Standard Time / 1992 / Mercury ✦✦✦✦
Mattea had vocal-cord surgery that threatened to end her career before she made *Lonesome Standard Time*, but you couldn't prove it by listening: her voice hasn't lost a bit of its deep alto warmth. *Lonesome Standard Time* isn't as ambitious as *Time Passes By*, but it's filled with lovely performances from Mattea's favorite sources: bluegrass ("Lonesome Standard Time"), gospel-influenced country ("Standing Knee Deep in a River [Dying of Thirst]"), and Nanci Griffith's ("Listen to the Radio"). —*Brian Mansfield*

Good News / 1993 / Mercury ✦✦✦
Mattea's outing is delightfully true to her folk-country style: ten moving, original pieces scoring a big zero on the saccharine and hackneyed front. A gorgeous voice, pristine production, and a true highlight of the season. —*Roch Parisien*

Walking Away a Winner / Oct. 1993 / Mercury ✦✦✦✦
Tired of having critics rave while radio programmers yawned, Mattea enlisted contempo-country producer Josh Leo to help brighten her sound for commercial consumption. It worked. The title cut was a hit right out of the box. —*Dan Cooper*

The Mavericks

Country-Rock, New Traditionalist
Fusing traditional country with traditional rock 'n' roll, the Mavericks became one of the most critically acclaimed and commercially successful groups of the early '90s. Led by singer-songwriter Raul Malo (b. August 7, 1965, Miami, FL), the band was formed in Florida in the late '80s. Malo had previously played in several different bands while he was in high school, as did bassist Robert Reynolds (born Robert Earl Reynolds, April 30, 1962, Kansas City, MO). The pair met at school and discovered they had similar musical tastes—they both enjoyed the music of Roy Orbison, Patsy Cline, Elvis Presley, Hank Williams, and Johnny Cash—and decided to form a band. Reynolds persuaded his best friend, Paul Deakin (born Paul Wylie Deakin, September 2, 1959, Miami, FL)—who had been a drummer in progressive rock bands before and had done some session work—to join the fledgling country band.

Taking the name the Mavericks, the band began playing rock clubs around the Miami area and built up a solid local following. The group chose to play rock clubs because the country bars only wanted to book bands that played covers and the Mavericks preferred to concentrate on original material. In the fall of 1990, the band released an eponymous independent album. The record worked its way onto playlists across Florida and made its way to Nashville, where it gained the attention of nearly every major record label.

In May of 1991, the group went to Nashville to play a showcase gig. Scouts from all of the town's major labels were in attendance, but the band decided to sign with MCA Records. Later that year, the Mavericks set about recording their first major label album; before the sessions began, they added lead guitarist David Lee Holt, who had previously played with Joe Ely, Rosie Flores, and Carlene Carter. Titled *From Hell to Paradise*, the record primarily consisted of Malo's original songs and was released in 1992. Although it was critically acclaimed, the album wasn't a commercial success; only a cover of Hank Williams' standard "Hey Good Lookin'" made the charts and that peaked at No. 74.

The Mavericks' commercial fortunes turned around with their second major label album, *What a Crying Shame*. Produced by Don Cook (Brooks & Dunn, Mark Collie), the album was more streamlined and focused. It became a hit upon its release early in 1994, with the title track becoming a Top 40 hit. Shortly after the release of *What a Crying Shame*, the group replaced Holt with Nick Kane (born Nicholas James Kane, August 21, 1954, Jerusalem, GA).

Throughout 1994, the band racked up Top 40 hit singles. "O What a Thrill" went to No. 18 in the summer, with "There Goes My Heart" reaching No. 20 in the fall. By the spring of 1995, *What a Crying Shame* had gone platinum. During the first half of 1995, the Mavericks recorded their fourth album, *Music for All Occasions*, which appeared in the fall of the year. Like its predecessor, it was critically acclaimed and a commercial success. By the spring of 1996, the album had gone gold. —*Stephen Thomas Erlewine*

Mavericks / 1990 / Y&T ✦✦✦
The group's first indie release, this album includes early versions of four songs recut for *From Hell to Paradise:* "The End of the Line," "This Broken Heart," and "A Better Way." —*Brian Mansfield*

From Hell to Paradise / 1992 / MCA ✦✦✦✦
In spite of Malo's Cuban heritage and the band's Miami roots—*because* of them, in fact—the Mavericks understand outsiders like Buck Owens and Hank Williams (both of whom the group cover) better than most of country's recent comers. And originals like "I Got You," "This Broken Heart," and the scathing title track, about Malo's aunt's escape from Cuban oppression, are so good the covers don't really matter. —*Brian Mansfield*

● **What a Crying Shame** / 1994 / MCA ✦✦✦✦
Superb, highly accessible follow-up to *From Hell to Paradise* included songs that made overt comparisons between Raul Malo and Roy Orbison ("I Should Have Been True," Jesse Winchester's "O What a Thrill"). Those who didn't realize the power of Malo's voice knew after those, when he didn't come off looking like a fool. Plenty of hot rockabilly shuffles are included, and the title track, with its Byrdsian guitar hook and bittersweet melody, became the first single by an "alternative" country act since Dwight Yoakam to break radio's Top 30. —*Brian Mansfield*

Music for All Occasions / Oct. 1995 / MCA ✦✦✦
With their third album, The Mavericks added slick country-pop to their arsenal of retro-country styles. The result straddles the line between affection and camp, since the band never goes completely overboard by drenching their songs with strings, and Raul Malo retains his aching Orbisonesque voice. However, that doesn't mean their songwriting has slipped, as all 11 originals are first-rate updated honky tonk ravers or countrypolitan numbers. And the closing cover of "Somethin' Stupid," recorded with Trisha Yearwood, is a fun, kitschy delight. —*Stephen Thomas Erlewine*

Martina McBride (Martina Maria Schiff)

b. Jul. 29, 1966, Sharon, KS
Vocals / Contemporary Country
A Kansas native who can sing with power and tenderness, Martina McBride started out in a more traditional country vein in the early '90s, then kicked up the beat and the tempo by her second album. McBride grew up in Texas, where she became infatuated with traditional country music. She began singing and playing keyboards at local clubs and barn dances with her father's band, the Schifters. After graduating from high-school, she began touring Kansas with a variety of country bands. Martina later married soundman John McBride and in 1990 moved with him to Nashville, where he worked for such stars as Charlie Daniels and Ricky Van Shelton while she waited tables and sang demos. John then produced a demo tape of her work and they tried sell it to several record labels. This led to a contract with RCA at the end of 1991. Around the same time, John became Garth Brooks' production manager, and Martina became his opening act.

McBride released her debut album, *The Time Has Come*, in 1992. It spent six months in the country album Top 50. The title track was released as her first single and it stayed on the charts for five months, while her next two, "That's Me" and "Cheap Whiskey," nearly cracked the Top 40. *The Way That I Am*, McBride's second album, was released in 1993 and it became her breakthrough. The record's first single, "My Baby Loves Me," reached No. 2 and "Life #9" also became a Top Ten hit. Her third album, *Wild Angels*, was released in the fall of 1995. It spawned the Top Ten single "Safe in the Arms of Love" and her first No. 1 hit, "Wild Angels." —*Sandra Brennan*

The Time Has Come / 1992 / RCA ✦✦✦
Her bold debut blends traditional country ("Cheap Whiskey," "That's Me") with acoustic rave-ups, as in the title song. —*Michael McCall*

● **The Way That I Am** / 1993 / RCA ✦✦✦✦
McBride revamps her image, flashing a new haircut and a more forceful, uptempo style. She matches the music with a feisty, daring collection of distinguished songs, including the hit "My Baby Loves Me" and the remarkable "Independence Day," about an abused wife who takes justice into her own hands. —*Michael McCall*

Wild Angels / Sep. 26, 1995 / RCA ✦✦✦
On *Wild Angels*, country singer Martina McBride continued to improve her skills, offering another selection of songs that showcased her incisive, emotional voice. —*David Jehnzen*

Neal McCoy

Vocals / Contemporary Country
Neal McCoy had a string of hit singles in the early '90s with his revivalist honky tonk. McCoy was born and raised in Jacksonville, TX, to Irish-Filipino parents who enjoyed a wide assortment of music. After graduating from high school, McCoy began playing the Texas honky tonk circuit and won a nightclub talent contest; during the contest, his performance was seen by Janie Fricke, who later helped him launch his career. Fricke arranged for McCoy to replace her as Charlie Pride's opening act when she left to pursue a full-fledged solo career in the early '80s. McCoy

remained with Pride for seven years, touring America, England, Australia, and New Zealand.

In 1988, McCoy released his first single, "That's How Much I Love You," as Neal McGoy; the record was a minor hit. In 1991, he signed to Atlantic, releasing his debut album, *At This Moment*, that same year. *At This Moment* produced two Top 50 singles—"If I Built a Fire" and "This Time I Hurt Her More (Than She Loves Me)." McCoy released his second album, *Where Forever Begins*, in 1992 but he didn't have a genuine hit until 1994's *No Doubt About It*, which produced the No. 1 singles "No Doubt About It" and "Wink." His success continued with 1995's *You Gotta Love That!*, which went platinum, and 1996's eponymous album. *—Sandra Brennan*

At This Moment / 1990 / Atlantic ✦✦✦
This debut's most notable song is its title track, a country version of the Billy Vera prom-night pop hit. *—Brian Mansfield*

Where Forever Begins / 1992 / Atlantic ✦✦✦
It includes the singles "Where Forever Begins," "There Ain't Nothin' I Don't Like About You," and "Now I Pray for Rain." *—Brian Mansfield*

● **No Doubt About It** / 1994 / Atlantic ✦✦✦✦
This Barry Beckett-produced disc was the first to capture the rock-influenced sound of McCoy's stage show (which usually included a rap version of the "Beverly Hillbillies" theme). Though McCoy had never had a single chart above No. 21, the album gave the singer his first two No. 1 hits. *—Brian Mansfield*

You Gotta Love That / 1995 / Atlantic ✦✦✦✦

Neal McCoy / Jun. 1996 / Atlantic ✦✦✦
Neal McCoy's eponymous album is another set of immaculately crafted contemporary country music. From McCoy's polished but heartfelt performance to the slick, seamless selection of songs, there isn't an obvious flaw on the album. Some may complain that McCoy's approach is getting a bit too predictable, but the highlights—including the favorite "Hillbilly Rap," which features segments of "Day-O," "The Ballad of Jed Clampett," and "Rapper's Delight"—are well worth the time of any fan. *—Thom Owens*

Ronnie McDowell

b. Mar. 26, 1950
Guitar, Vocals / Country
Raised in rural Portland, TN, north of Nashville, McDowell didn't take performing seriously until he was stationed in the Philippines with the navy. Appropriately, the first song he performed in public was "It's Now or Never," as Elvis Presley has had a huge impact on his career. McDowell wrote his first hit, "The King Is Gone," the day that Elvis died. Enough people shared his grief that a reported three million copies were sold. McDowell did all the Elvis vocal imitations for a 1979 Elvis TV movie, starring Kurt Russell, and he began to take on the image of an Elvis imitator. McDowell consciously distanced himself from those comparisons, which became easier when record producer Buddy Killen took over the reins of his career, bringing in solid uptempo material that consistently showcased McDowell's strong (though a bit nondescript) vocal talents. Now comfortable with his reputation, he's returned on occasion to more "Elvis" work, providing the vocal parts for the short-lived ABC series *Elvis* in 1990. *—Tom Roland*

● **Older Women and Other Greatest Hits** / 1987 / Epic ✦✦✦✦
McDowell fell into this "clone" thing for a couple of years where he remade his own hits; and all three soundalikes ("Older Women," "Wandering Eyes," "Watchin' Girls Go By") are curiously placed back-to-back. His later material is the most emotive, especially "I Dream of Women like You," "In a New York Minute," and "Love Talks," recorded with Exile. *—Tom Roland*

Reba McEntire (Reba Nell McEntire)

b. Mar. 28, 1954, Chockie, OK
Guitar, Vocals / Traditional Country, Contemporary Country
Reba McEntire was one of the most successful new country vocalists to emerge in the early '80s. The only problem was, she began her recording career in the mid-'70s. It may have taken her several years to reach the top of the country charts, but once she got there she stayed there—McEntire was the single most successful female country vocalist of the '80s and '90s, scoring a consistent stream of Top Ten singles and a grand total of 18 No. 1 singles.

McEntire is the daughter of Clark McEntire, a professional rodeo rider. As a child, Reba was a rodeo rider, as were her sisters Alice and Susie, and her brother Pake. While their father taught them how to ride, their mother Jackie taught them music. As young adults, the four siblings formed a vocal group that landed a local hit in 1971 with "The Ballad of John McEntire," a song dedicated to their grandfather.

The McEntire children intended to become a professional singing group, but those plans were thrown for a loop when Reba sang the national anthem at the National Rodeo Finals in Oklahoma City in 1974.

Red Steagall had heard her sing the anthem and immediately suggested that she go to Nashville and record a demo. McEntire was initially hesitant to pursue a solo career but the family eventually decided it was better for her to take the chance while it was there.

With some help from Steagall, Reba signed with Mercury Records in 1975, releasing her first record that same year. Initially, she was a traditional hard country singer at a time when the radio wasn't receptive to that sound—her first singles didn't come close to cracking the Top 40. Around the time of the release of her first album, she married Charlie Battles, a professional steer wrestler and bulldogger, and completed her teaching degree, in case her musical career floundered.

In 1978, Reba began to make some headway on the charts, as the double A-sided "Three Sheets in the Wind" / "I'd Really Love to See You Tonight" reached No. 20. However, she didn't have any significant hits until the summer of 1980, when "(You Lift Me) Up to Heaven" made it to No. 8. By this time, she had begun to cut more ballad-oriented material and the slight shift in musical direction paid off. McEntire stayed with Mercury Records for three more years. In that time, her audience dramatically expanded—at the end of 1982, she had her first No. 1 single, "Can't Even Get the Blues."

Reba McEntire switched labels in 1984, abandoning Mercury for MCA Records. At MCA, she established herself as one of the decade's most popular artists, selling over 20 million albums and winning four Female Vocalist of the Year awards from the Country Music Association. Between 1985 and 1992, she had 24 straight Top Ten hits, including 14 No. 1 singles. McEntire began toying with rock and pop influences, both in her music and in her image. Reba divorced Charlie Battles in 1987. Two years after the divorce, she married Narvel Blackstock, her road manager and steel guitarist; the pair assumed complete control of all aspects of her career, from recording to merchandising and marketing. In the '90s, Reba stayed as popular as she was in the previous decade, as both her albums and her singles consistently charted in the Top Ten, frequently at No. 1. McEntire also begun an acting career in the early '90s, appearing in TV movies and feature films, most notably the cult horror film, *Tremors. —Stephen Thomas Erlewine*

The Best of Reba McEntire / 1985 / Mercury ✦✦✦✦
This compilation of her late '70s and early '80s Polygram hits reflects future triumphs on MCA. *—Mark A. Humphrey*

My Kind of Country / 1986 / MCA ✦✦✦✦
McEntire's celebration of the back-to-basics movement in country has many country shuffles. These are her purest country performances and most straightforward productions. *—Mark A. Humphrey*

Whoever's in New England / 1986 / MCA ✦✦✦✦
This is the album that elevated McEntire from pretty good country singer to megastar. A number of the melodies have pop sensibilities, but the production is decidedly country. *—Tom Roland*

The Last One to Know / 1987 / MCA ✦✦✦
Recorded as McEntire went through the process of divorce from first husband Charlie Battles, it's understandably heavy on songs about breakups and the uncertainty of the future, "The Stairs"—about domestic violence—is particularly moving. Despite her personal pain, she still holds out hope in "Love Will Find Its Way to You." *—Tom Roland*

★ **Greatest Hits** / 1987 / MCA ✦✦✦✦✦
Reba McEntire's first collection of hits on MCA Records draws entirely from the beginning of her string of Top Ten hits in the mid-'80s. *Greatest Hits* cover her singles from 1984, 1985, and 1986 and features nearly every Top Ten hit she had, including the No. 1 hits "How Blue," "Somebody Should Leave," "Whoever's In New England," "Little Rock," "What Am I Gonna Do About You," and "One Promise Too Late." *—Stephen Thomas Erlewine*

☆ **For My Broken Heart** / 1991 / MCA ✦✦✦✦✦
Only the quietly moving "If I Had Only Known" might be considered a tribute to the members of McEntire's band who died in a 1990 plane crash, but the tragedy creeps into McEntire's voice and her song selection. Throughout the album, McEntire dwells on regrets, unvoiced feelings, and missed chances. The best songs aren't the hits "For My Broken Heart" and "Is There Life out There" but a group of evocative story-songs which unfold slowly, leaving loose threads and developing complex emotional undercurrents. *For My Broken Heart* may be the strongest album of McEntire's career; it's certainly her most heartbreaking. *—Brian Mansfield*

It's Your Call / 1992 / MCA ✦✦✦
McEntire possesses one of the most undeniably emotional voices in country music—one well-phrased word in her Oklahoma accent can start hearts breaking. The overwhelming number of ballads on *It's Your Call* take maximum advantage of that talent, especially on "Straight from You" and "The Heart Won't Lie," a duet with labelmate Vince Gill. While *It's Your Call* may have the same intensity of emotion as the double-platinum *For My Broken Heart*, it lacks similar depth—taken as a whole, these songs make McEntire sound like a victim, a role she no longer plays well. The ballads leave few places for McEntire's strength of

character, and the bluesy "Take It Back" and "Go Down Easy" only serve as breaks in the despair. McEntire showed her best on *For My Broken Heart;* while she's not holding back here, only casual or partial listeners will be moved as much. — *Brian Mansfield*

☆ **Greatest Hits, Vol. 2** / Oct. 1993 / MCA ✦✦✦✦✦
A collecting of Reba McEntire's biggest hits of the late '80s, including the No. 1 singles "You Lie," "For My Broken Heart," and her biggest hit, "Is There Life Out There." — *Stephen Thomas Erlewine*

Starting Over / Oct. 3, 1995 / MCA ✦✦✦
Starting Over isn't quite a rebirth for Reba McEntire; rather, it's a tribute to her formative influences. Consisting of nothing but covers of a selection of her favorite songs from the '50s, '60s, and '70s, the album is an engaging listen. Some of the tracks demonstrate her roots, while others are nothing more than entertainment. McEntire doesn't re-imagine these songs, but she delivers strong, confident performances that make them sound fresh. — *Stephen Thomas Erlewine*

Tim McGraw

Vocals / Contemporary Country
Tim McGraw is best-known for his hit single, "Indian Outlaw," a controversial single that made him a star in the mid-'90s.
McGraw is the son of the baseball player Tug McGraw. As a boy in Start, LA, Tim listened to country, Motown, rock 'n' roll, and R&B. Like his father, Tim was a natural athlete and attended Northeast Louisiana University on sports scholarships. McGraw didn't become interested in performing music until he bought a pawn shop guitar while attending college. He moved to Nashville in 1989 and later played gigs in the Deep South. He signed to Curb Records in 1990 and released his first single, "Welcome to the Club," two years later; the single reached the country Top 50. In 1993, he released his eponymous debut, which produced two more minor hits.
In 1994, McGraw released his second album, *Not A Moment Too Soon,* which contained "Indian Outlaw," his breakthrough single. The song reached No. 8 on the country charts and No. 15 on the pop charts amidst controversy about the Native American stereotypes presented in the lyrics. Nevertheless, the single made *Not A Moment Too Soon* a crossover hit—the album hit No. 2 on the pop charts and went triple-platinum within months of its release. "Don't Take the Girl," the follow-up single to "Indian Outlaw," was another crossover success, reaching No. 17 on the pop charts and No. 1 on the country charts. In 1995, McGraw released his third album, *All I Want,* which became another multi-platinum hit. — *Sandra Brennan*

Tim McGraw / 1993 / Capitol ✦✦✦
Three songs—"Welcome to the Club," "Memory Lane," and "Two Steppin' Mind"—appeared on the bottom half of the *Billboard* singles chart, which suggested McGraw had some talent but wasn't anything special. During a year that introduced Clay Walker and Doug Supernaw, hardly anybody noticed this young hat act. — *Brian Mansfield*

● **Not a Moment Too Soon** / Mar. 22, 1994 / Curb ✦✦✦✦
"Indian Outlaw," with its controversy and its resemblance to the Raiders' "Indian Reservation," made McGraw a star, and the ballad "Don't Take the Girl" reinforced the image. *Not a Moment Too Soon* contained better hooks than its predecessor, but it also belabored the obvious with songs like "It Don't Get Any Countrier Than This" and "Give It to Me Strait." — *Brian Mansfield*

All I Want / Sep. 19, 1995 / Curb ✦✦✦
Tim McGraw's albums always suffer from uneven material, but *All I Want* is a surprisingly consistent record that consolidates his strengths while expanding him into new territory. He hasn't abandoned the honky tonk and jokey country-rock that made his famous, but he's made it harder and more believable. Similarly, his ballads are heartfelt, delivered with convincing sincerity. In other words, he has grown musically and developed into a thoroughly entertaining vocalist. And that growth is what makes *All I Want* his best record. It is still fairly uneven, with several weak songs, but McGraw now knows how to disguise the flaws in the material with his singing. — *Stephen Thomas Erlewine*

Emmett Miller

Vocals
Although his vocal delivery was influential on several major country singers, Emmett Miller was basically a vaudeville singer, with far stronger aural links to Al Jolson than Merle Haggard. A White man performing in blackface, Miller was an exponent of the minstrel school of performance, touring widely with minstrel shows for several decades. The most influential aspect of his recordings was his yodeling trill, and there can be no doubt that it heavily influenced country singers such as Jimmie Rodgers, Lefty Frizzell, and Hank Williams (who learned "Lovesick Blues" from a Miller record). Bob Wills asked his early lead singer to

copy Miller's style, and a bit of Miller's easygoing ragtime sensibility can be heard in Leon Redbone.
But Miller, to quote Donald Sutherland's description of John Milton in *Animal House,* does not speak well to our generation. That's not just because the vaudeville arrangements of his 1920s recordings will strike most modern-day listeners as quaint. It's also because the blackface minstrel tradition—which was just part of the scene in Miller's hey-day—strikes us as distasteful.
Miller began recording for OKeh in the mid-1920s, and made his most important singles for the label at the end of the decade with accompaniment by the Georgia Crackers, which included both Tommy and Jimmy Dorsey. The minstrel tradition faded drastically in popularity after 1930, although Miller did record for Bluebird in 1936, and continued to perform in minstrel shows to dwindling crowds through the early '50s. — *Richie Unterberger*

Minstrel Man From Georgia / Feb. 6, 1996 / Columbia/Legacy ✦✦✦✦
God knows what this is doing in Legacy's Roots N' Blues series; it's a long way from Blind Willie McTell and Bukka White to this. Anyway, this has 20 of his OKeh sides from the late '20s, including a "Lovesick Blues" that served as the model for Hank Williams' hit with the same song in 1949. The Georgia Crackers accompany Miller on every cut, with a cast including Tommy & Jimmy Dorsey (present on every track), Jack Teagarden, and Gene Krupa. More of historical interest and musical significance than anything else, with a thorough sleeve note from country music authority Charles Wolfe. — *Richie Unterberger*

Roger Miller

b. Jan. 2, 1936, Fort Worth, TX, **d.** Oct. 25, 1995, Los Angeles, CA
Guitar, Vocals / Honky Tonk, Nashville Sound/Countrypolitan
Roger Miller is best known for his humorous novelty songs, which overshadow his considerable songwriting talents, as well as his hardcore honky tonk roots. After writing hits for a number of artists in the '50s, Miller racked up a number of hits during the '60s which became not only country classics, but popular classics, as well.
Miller was born in Fort Worth, TX, but raised in the small town of Erick, OK, by his aunt and uncle, following the death of his father and his mother's debilitating sickness. Initially, he was attracted to music by hearing country over the radio, as well as his brother-in-law, Sheb Wooley. By the time he was ten, he earned enough money picking cotton to buy himself a guitar. At the age of 11, Wooley gave him a fiddle and encouraged him to pursue a performing career. Miller completed the eighth grade and left school to become a ranch-hand and rodeo rider. Throughout his adolescence, he played music in addition to working the ranch. Soon, he was able to play not only guitar and fiddle, but also piano, banjo, and drums.
In 1956, he joined the Army during the Korean war. Miller was stationed in South Carolina, where he met the brother of Jethro Burns who arranged an audition at RCA Nashville for him. Early in 1957, Miller left the army and auditioned for Chet Atkins at RCA. The session was unsuccessful and he spent a year as a bellhop at a Nashville hotel. While in Nashville, Miller met George Jones and Pappy Dailey, who introduced him to Don Pierce, an executive at Mercury Records. Pierce signed Miller and had him cut three songs. Roger's first single, "Poor Little John," disappeared without a trace. Following the failure of his first single, Miller continued to work at the hotel and tour with other musicians—he played fiddle with Minnie Pearl for a short time, then he became the drummer for Faron Young. After a few months, he was signed as a songwriter for Tree Music Publishing and stopped performing as a supporting musician. Instead of playing music, he became a fireman in Amarillo, TX. The abandonment of performing was short-lived, however—within a few months, he became the drummer for Ray Price's Cherokee Cowboys.
In 1958, Price recorded Miller's "Invitation to the Blues" and it went to No. 3. It was soon followed by three other successful versions of his songs—Faron Young's "That's the Way I Feel" and Ernest Tubb's "Half A Mind" both went Top Ten, while Jim Reeves had a No. 1 hit with "Billy Bayou." That same year, George Jones recorded "Tall Tall Trees" and "Nothing Can Stop My Love," which he had written with Miller; neither of the songs were hits. The following year, Reeves had a hit with another one of Roger's songs, "Home."
Since his songwriting career was flourishing, Miller decided it was again time to try to become a performing artist as well. He recorded a few tracks for Decca which weren't successful and then he signed to RCA Records. "You Don't Want My Love," one of his first singles for the label, reached No. 14 in early 1961, followed by the Top Ten "When Two Worlds Collide" later that summer.
Miller wasn't able to immediately follow the songs with another hit single. Two years later, "Lock, Stock and Teardrops" scraped the charts and he left the record label.
Around that time, Roger moved to Hollywood began appearing regularly on "The Jimmy Dean Show" and "The Merv Griffin Show," two of the most popular television programs in the country. His guest spots

showcased his new style—instead of concentrating on hardcore country, he had developed a willfully goofy persona, singing silly novelty songs. He signed a record contract with Smash Records and released his first single for the label, "Dang Me," in the summer of 1964. It was an immediate smash, vaulting to No. 1 and spending six weeks at the top of the charts; it also crossed over into the pop charts, peaking at No. 7. "Chug-A-Lug" followed a few months after it, reaching No. 3 on the country charts and No. 9 on the pop charts. At the end of the year, "Do-Wacka-Do" was released, becoming a No. 15 hit. Roger began 1965 with his best-known song, "King of the Road." The single spent five weeks at the top of the country charts and became his biggest pop hit, peaking at No. 4. Its accompanying album, *The Return of Roger Miller*, was another crossover success, also peaking at No. 4 on the pop album charts and going gold. Miller was at his peak in 1965. Every song he released that year—"Engine Engine No.9," "One Dyin' and a Buryin'," "Kansas City Star," "England Swings"—reached the country Top Ten and at the end of the year, his *Golden Hits* album went Top Ten; it would eventually go gold. In the summer of 1965, he released *The Third Time Around*, a record that leaned toward his honky tonk roots; it peaked at No. 13.

After the watershed year of 1965, Roger Miller's career dipped slightly. Although other artists were still having hits with his songs—Eddy Arnold took "The Last Word in Lonesome Is Me" to No. 2—Miller had trouble breaking the Top 40 following the No. 5 hit "Husbands and Wives" in early 1966. He continued to record throughout the late '60s, but fewer and fewer of the songs were becoming hits. Occasionally, he would record the songs of emerging songwriters, whether it was Bobby Russell's "Little Green Apples" (No. 6, 1968) or Kris Kristofferson's "Me and Bobby McGee" (No. 12, 1969). Toward the end of the decade and beginning of the '70s, he began to concentrate on honky tonk, although he still made his trademark novelties.

During the '70s, he recorded sporadically, preferring to concentrate on his hotel chain, appropriately called King of the Road. "Tomorrow Night in Baltimore," released in the spring of 1971, was his biggest hit of the decade, climbing to No. 11. Early in the decade, he wrote songs for Walt Disney's animated adaptation of *Robin Hood*—he also provided a voice for the rooster in the film—as well as the movie *Waterhole Three*. In 1973, he left Smash/Mercury for Columbia Records. He spent four years at Columbia and only his debut single for the label, "Open Up Your Heart," was a hit, peaking at No. 14. Miller didn't record much during the '80s—his biggest hit was "Old Friends," recorded with Willie Nelson and Ray Price. In the mid-'80s, he wrote the music for *Big River*, a Broadway adaptation of Mark Twain's works. Both the play and Roger's music were critically acclaimed and enormously popular. *Big River* won seven Tony Awards and two of those went to Miller, for Best Musical and Outstanding Score. *Big River* would be the last major work of Roger Miller's career. In 1991, he was diagnosed with throat cancer and he died a year later. After his death, his legacy remained strong, as each new generation of country singers found songs in his catalog to cover and reinterpret. —*Stephen Thomas Erlewine*

☆ **Golden Hits** / 1965 / Smash ✦✦✦✦✦
Years before Waylon Jennings and Willie Nelson grew their hair long, Miller took country to the counterculture with these hipster twists on the Nashville sound. No tunesmith in Music City had ever tossed off songs like "Dang Me," "King of the Road," "Chug-A-Lug," and "Engine Engine No.9." No one has since. —*Dan Cooper*

★ **Best of Roger Miller, Vol. 1: Country Tunesmith** / 1991 / PolyGram ✦✦✦✦✦
Downplaying his humorous muse in favor of showing off his skill as a straightahead country writer, these 21 tracks (including some strongly Ray Price-influenced fare from 1957) were either written or co-written by Miller. It's well worth the money to hear his own versions of such standards as "Invitation to the Blues," "Half a Mind," and "Don't We All Have the Right." —*Dan Cooper*

★ **The Best of Roger Miller, Vol. 2: King of the Road** / Aug. 4, 1992 / Mercury ✦✦✦✦✦
Although more comprehensive, it's also a more diffuse version of *Golden Hits*. —*Dan Cooper*

☆ **King of the Road** / 1995 / Mercury Nashville ✦✦✦✦✦
Over the course of three discs, the box set *King of the Road* contains every essential item Roger Miller ever recorded. Unfortunately, the compilation isn't a consistent one—although there are more great songs than weak ones, there are still too many lesser numbers to make the set a truly essential purchase. All of the necessary items are available on Mercury's two-volume *Best of Roger Miller* collection (*Country Tunesmith* and *King of the Road*), which are leaner, more consistent collections that are preferable to this slightly padded three-disc box. —*Thom Owens*

Ronnie Milsap

b. Jan. 16, 1944, Robbinsville, NC
Piano, Vocals / Country-Pop
Ronnie Milsap was one of the major figures of country music in the '70s,

developing a hybrid of country and pop that brought the genre to a larger audience. Milsap was born to a hillbilly family in Robbinsville, NC, and was raised by his father and grandparents following his parents' divorce. Ronnie was born blind from congenital glaucoma and when he was five began attending the Governor Moorhead School for the Blind. When he was seven, his instructors noticed his extraordinary musical talents and he began to study classical music formally with his music teacher, violinist Wallace Greaves. At the time, Milsap's favorite composers were Bach and Mozart; he also enjoyed listening to country and bluegrass. He studied under Greaves for eight years. A single year after he began learning the violin, Milsap was declared a virtuoso. He had also mastered the piano and not much later the guitar and a variety of other stringed instruments, as well as various woodwinds. Eventually, he became interested in rock 'n' roll music and while still in school formed his first rock band, the Apparitions. He briefly attended Young Harris Junior College in Atlanta where he studied pre-law. Though he was awarded a comprehensive scholarship to Emory University, Milsap decided to become a full-time musician; his first professional gig was as a member of J.J. Cale's band in the early '60s.

In 1965, Milsap started his own band and four years later, after having an R&B hit with "Never Had It So Good" on Scepter, moved to Memphis to become a session musician. There he frequently worked for Chips Moman and can be heard playing keyboards on Elvis' "Kentucky Rain" and singing harmony on the King's "Don't Cry Daddy." When not doing session work, Milsap and his backing group were the house band at TJ's Club. In 1970, Milsap began recording on the Chips label and had a pop hit with "Loving You Is a Natural Thing." Following its success, he signed with Warner Brothers and in 1971, he released his eponymous debut. Two years later, Milsap moved to Nashville in hopes of jump-starting his flagging career. In Nashville, he became a client of Charley Pride's manager Jack D. Johnson. Within a year, he signed to RCA Victor, which is where he would remain for the bulk of his career. "I Hate You," his first single for RCA, reached the country Top Ten in the summer of 1973. The following year, he had three No. 1 hits in a row—"Pure Love," "Please Don't Tell Me How the Story Ends," and "(I'd Be) A Legend in My Time," which was a cover of Don Gibson's classic.

Milsap had a handful of Top Ten hits in 1975 and but in late 1976, he became a genuine star when he began a string of six No. 1 hits in a row with "(I'm A) Stand By My Woman Man." In turn, that string of hits begat a remarkable run where Milsap didn't leave the Top Ten for 15 straight years. During that time, he had a number of pop crossover hits, beginning with 1977's No. 16 pop hit, "It Was Almost like a Song." Between 1980 and 1982, Milsap had ten more consecutive No. 1 hits including the crossover hits "Smoky Mountain Rain," "No Gettin' Over Me" and "Any Day Now." Milsap had yet another string of uninterrupted No. 1 hits between 1985 and 1987, when racked up eight consecutive No. 1 singles. He had his last No. 1 hit in 1989, when "A Woman in Love" spent two weeks on the top of the charts. In total, he had 35 No. 1 singles.

In the early '90s, Milsap's commercial appeal began to decline—after 1992, he wasn't able to break into the country Top Ten. Nevertheless, he continued to record. In 1992, he left RCA and signed to Liberty where he recorded *True Believer*, which failed to yield any major hits. Despite his decline in popularity, Milsap continued to record and perform successfully throughout the '90s. —*Sandra Brennan*

● **Greatest Hits** / 1980 / RCA ✦✦✦✦
This is a solid, albeit random, assessment of Milsap's first seven years in country music. Mainstream country is featured, with "Pure Love" and "(I'm A) Stand by My Woman Man," but Milsap really shines on the elaborate and challenging arrangements of "(I'd Be) A Legend in My Time," "It Was Almost like a Song," and "Let's Take the Long Way Around the World." One previously unreleased track is here: "Smoky Mountain Rain." —*Tom Roland*

One More Try for Love / 1984 / RCA ✦✦✦
In his effort to expand the boundaries of country, Milsap pushes the edge harder here than in any other album. The electronically altered vocals in the tracks "She Loves My Car" and "Suburbia" have a winning effect—tasteful, not overdone. —*Tom Roland*

Greatest Hits, Vol. 2 / 1985 / RCA ✦✦✦✦
Juxtaposed to the first *Greatest Hits* package, this one nicely displays the evolution of a motivated risk-taker. Milsap redefines the outer limits of the commercial country format with his soul- and/or rock-inflected singles "(There's) No Gettin' over Me," "Lost in the Fifties Tonight," and (most dramatically) "Stranger in My House." —*Tom Roland*

Greatest Hits, Vol. 3 / 1991 / RCA ✦✦✦
Greatest Hits, Vol. 3 collects the bulk of Ronnie Milsap's late '80s hits, including "Happy, Happy Birthday Baby," "How Do I Turn You On?," "Snap Your Fingers," "Where Do the Nights Go," "Button Off My Shirt," "A Woman In Love," and "Stranger Things Have Happened." Although it bypasses some of his hits ("In Love," "Houston Solution," "Are You Lovin' Me Like I'm Lovin' You") at the expense of lesser-known material ("L.A.

to the Moon"), the collection remains a good sampling of Milsap's final round of Top Ten hits. — *Thom Owens*

True Believer / Jun. 7, 1993 / Liberty ✦✦✦
If only the whole album had the energy of the John Hiatt title track (not to mention the wit of the Hoss Allen intro), Milsap's Liberty debut would have been a record to reckon with. — *Dan Cooper*

● **Essential Ronnie Milsap** / 1995 / RCA ✦✦✦✦
This album isn't necessarily a definitive collection—Milsap simply had too many big hits to fit on a single-disc compilation—but it does come close. Many of his biggest hits are included on *Essential*, as well as a handful of obscurities, including album tracks and lesser-known hits. Consequently, the compilation is a nice cross-section that offers a good representation of Milsap's sound, even if it doesn't come close to being a definitive retrospective. — *Thom Owens*

Patsy Montana (Ruby Blevins)

b. Oct. 30, 1914, Hot Springs, AK, d. 1996
Vocals / Cowboy
Patsy Montana is the first woman in country music to have a million-seller, "I Want to Be a Cowboy's Sweetheart" in 1935. For more than 25 years she was a mainstay on Chicago's WLS National Barn Dance. In the '30s and '40s she was the sweetheart of many a cowpoke, appearing in Westerns on the silver screen. Boy, could she yodel. — *David Vinopal*

● **The Cowboy's Sweetheart** / 1988 / Flying Fish ✦✦✦✦
These are late recordings by the Western radio star. The title track, from 1935, was the first million-selling female country vocal performance. — *Mark A. Humphrey*

John Michael Montgomery

b. Jan. 20, 1965, Danville, KY
Vocals / Contemporary Country, New Traditionalist
Even though his music leaned closer to pop music than most honky tonkers, John Michael Montgomery belonged to the movement of new country traditionalists in the early '90s. Montgomery was born to a guitar-playing father and a mother who played the drums. He made his debut at age five during one of his parents' concerts. Montgomery began playing in local bands at age 15, and when his parents divorced two years later, he began playing in a group with his father and brother. Montgomery dropped out of high school, but later returned to get his GED. He first gained notice while playing at the Austin City Saloon in Lexington, KY. By 1991, he had signed with Atlantic Records.

Montgomery's debut, *Life's a Dance*, was released in 1992 to positive reviews and strong sales, climbing into the Top Five on the country album charts and the Top 30 on the pop album charts. In 1993 it went platinum and produced several hits, including the title cut and "I Love the Way You Love Me," which became a No. 1 country and a moderate pop hit as well. His second album, *Kickin' It Up*, came out in 1994 and contained the chart-topper "I Swear," which remained No. 1 for over a month. *Kickin' It Up* reached No. 1 within a month of its release; it quickly went multi-platinum, as well. "I Swear" was named Single of the Year by the Country Music Association, which also gave him their Horizon Award. In the spring of 1995, he released his eponymous third album. — *Sandra Brennan*

Life's a Dance / 1992 / Atlantic ✦✦
Montgomery's baritone lends itself well to the romantic songs, ensuring his success in the heartthrob-heavy country field of the early '90s. That he also does some competent Oklahoma swing counts in his favor. — *Brian Mansfield*

● **Kickin' It Up** / Jan. 25, 1994 / Atlantic ✦✦✦✦
As the title suggests, Montgomery kicks up the tempos and reveals a stronger country-rock bent. He still leans heavily on contemporary ballads ("I Swear," "Rope the Moon"), but proves just as capable on the brawnier songs. — *Michael McCall*

John Michael Montgomery / Mar. 28, 1995 / Atlantic ✦✦✦✦
It doesn't really matter that *John Michael Montgomery* replicates the formula of its hit predecessor, *Kickin' it Up*. Even though it has the same country-pop ballads, slick country-rock and honky tonk numbers that made *Kickin' It Up* a monster commercial success, the record doesn't sound dull or repetitive. Most of the album's success is due to the clean, commercial production, which makes even the weak material entertaining. — *Stephen Thomas Erlewine*

George Morgan

b. Jun. 28, 1925, Waverly, TN, d. Jul. 7, 1975
Guitar / Traditional Country
Morgan started his career as a smooth country crooner and grew more down-home country as the years passed. He enjoyed his greatest success early, when he scored seven chart hits in 1949. He was a Grand Ole Opry mainstay until his death, and introduced his daughter Lorrie to the stage. — *Michael McCall*

American Originals / 1977 / Columbia ✦✦✦✦
All of his famous hits, including "Candy Kisses" and "Room Full of Roses," are featured, although not necessarily in their original form. Contrary to the album title, a few of these songs are 1959 remakes of earlier hits. — *Michael McCall*

● **Room Full of Roses: The Best of George Morgan** / 1996 / Razor & Tie ✦✦✦✦
Room Full of Roses contains a generous selection of George Morgan's hits from the late '40s and '50s, all in their original versions, making it the definitive retrospective. — *Stephen Thomas Erlewine*

Lorrie Morgan (Loretta Lynn Morgan)

b. 1960
Vocals / Traditional Country, Contemporary Country
Although she spent most of her life singing, Lorrie Morgan didn't become a star until the early '90s, when she scored a string of Top Ten country hits. Lorrie Morgan is the daughter of Grand Ole Opry star George Morgan. She made her professional debut at age 13 on the Opry, where her rendition of "Paper Roses" received a standing ovation. When her father died of in 1975, she took over his band and began leading the group through various club gigs. Within a few years, she disbanded the group. In 1977, Morgan was a runner-up in the Miss Nashville Beauty pageant, and from there went on to play with the Little Roy Wiggins band. She then became a receptionist and demo singer at Acuff-Rose, where she also wrote songs. She signed with Hickory Records in 1978 and had one minor hit single; the following year she moved to MCA and had another minor hit with "I'm Completely Satisfied," an electronically dubbed duet with her late father. She began touring Nashville nightclubs and opened for a number of acts, including Jack Greene, Billy Thunderkloud, and Jeanie Seely. She also toured as a duet partner with George Jones and then spent two years as part of the Opryland USA bluegrass show and as a guest singer on TNN's *Nashville Now.*

In 1984, Morgan scored a minor hit with "Don't Go Changing." That year she became the youngest singer ever to join the *Grand Ole Opry*. She married Keith Whitley in 1986 and two years later moved to RCA, the label Whitley was signed to. That year, she had a Top 20 hit, "Trainwreck of Emotion." Morgan's popularity was just blossoming and had just scored a major hit with "Dear Me" when Whitley died suddenly in 1989. Though devastated, she continued to work and that year her album *Leave the Light On* went gold. In 1990 she had her first No. 1 single, "Five Minutes," along with several other Top Ten hits. *Something in Red*, her second album, was released in 1991; it went platinum and spawned the No. 1 single "What Part of No." Morgan's third album, *Watch Me*, was released on RCA's BNA subsidiary in 1992; it went gold within a year of its release. Morgan released *Merry Christmas from London* (1993) and *War Paint* (1994), before she issued *Greatest Hits* in 1995. She released her fifth studio album, *Greater Need*, in 1996. — *Sandra Brennan*

Leave the Light on / 1989 / RCA ✦✦✦✦
Included are "Trainwreck of Emotion" and other belters. She is hailed by some as the "new Tammy Wynette." — *Mark A. Humphrey*

Something in Red / 1991 / RCA ✦✦✦
Morgan backs off the sad songs for her second album—a wise move. (She went through the first part of her life known as George Morgan's daughter; she wouldn't want to spend the rest of it as Keith Whitley's widow.) Instead she concentrates on laidback country and ballads like the title track, which is about the dress colors during different stages of a woman's life. Dolly Parton duets on "Best Woman Wins." — *Brian Mansfield*

● **Watch Me** / Oct. 1992 / RCA ✦✦✦✦
Morgan's second and third albums each improved on the last. *Watch Me* contains more good songs than the first two combined, including "I Guess You Had to Be There" and "From Our House to Yours," but not "What Part of No" or the remake of Bonnie Tyler's 1978 hit "It's a Heartache." — *Brian Mansfield*

War Paint / May 10, 1994 / BNA ✦✦
● **Greatest Hits** / Oct. 1995 / BNA ✦✦✦✦
As the title implies, *Greatest Hits* contains all of Lorrie Morgan's biggest hits. Morgan's albums tend to be slightly inconsistent, yet her singles have been quite strong. Consequently, *Greatest Hits* is useful both for the casual and the dedicated fan—by featuring nothing but singles, it is her most entertaining album. — *Stephen Thomas Erlewine*

Greater Need / Jun. 1996 / BNA/RCA ✦✦✦

Gary Morris

b. Dec. 7, 1948, Fort Worth, TX
Vocals / Country
An artist who refuses to be categorized, Morris has explored a variety of country sounds—acoustic folk, rock-edged commercial songs, romantic ballads—but also accepted a couple of roles on Broadway, including the

physically demanding part of Jean Valjean in *Les Miserables*. Born and raised in Texas, Morris got his "break" by working on Jimmy Carter's 1976 election campaign. For his efforts, he got a chance to play for some influential members of the Country Music Association at a Presidential function, and when his demo tape crossed the desk of Warner's executive Norro Wilson, Wilson remembered him immediately and signed him to a recording deal. Frustrated by the restrictions inherent in the marketing of modern music, Morris refuses to compromise his musical integrity, and some of his work has thus fallen between the cracks. But few country artists—if any—have been able to match Morris for his vocal strength and clarity. —*Tom Roland*

● **Hits** / 1987 / Warner Bros. ✦✦✦✦
Morris may have the best "pipes" in country music, but he works so hard at showcasing them that most of his studio albums are bogged down by ballads. This collection includes the best of those ballads ("The Love She Found in Me," "100% Chance of Rain"), plus his best overall material ("I'll Never Stop Loving You," "Baby Bye Bye," "Velvet Chains"), which he seemingly undervalues. For those who appreciate such things, it also includes a sampling of his Broadway work, with a song from *La Boheme.* —*Tom Roland*

Greatest Hits, Vol. 2 / 1990 / Warner Bros. ✦✦✦✦
Greatest Hits, Vol. 2 contains most of Gary Morris' biggest hits from the mid-'80s that didn't make his first compilation, including "Why Lady Why," "Between Two Fires," "Second Hand Heart," and the duet with Lynn Anderson, "You're Welcome to Tonight." —*Thom Owens*

Moon Mullican

b. Mar. 29, 1909, Corrigan, Polk County, TX, **d.** Jan. 1, 1967, Beaumont, TX
Piano / Instrumental, Traditional Country, Bluegrass
A piano-pounding honky tonk man, born and raised deep in the heart of East Texas, Aubrey "Moon" Mullican is said to have had a significant musical influence on Jerry Lee Lewis, among others. Throughout the Depression and war years, he cut his ivory teeth on Western swing, most notably as vocalist and piano player in Cliff Bruner's Texas Wanderers. In 1946, he signed with the emerging independent powerhouse King Records. A performer of wide-ranging tastes, Mullican was comfortable singing straight country, treacly pop, or White boy boogie. Indeed, many of his King sides, cut with Black producer Henry Glover, jumped to the beat of hardcore R&B. —*Dan Cooper*

Sings His All-Time Greatest Hits / 1958 / King ✦✦✦✦
On CD, it's a budget-line reissue, but it includes "I'll Sail My Ship Alone," "Pipeliner's Blues," and "Cherokee Boogie." —*Dan Cooper*

★ **Moonshine Jamboree** / 1993 / Ace ✦✦✦✦✦
The best available compilation, this import CD includes "I'll Sail My Ship Alone," the one bona fide smash hit of Mullican's underappreciated career, and 22 lesser successes or hits that never were. —*Dan Cooper*

Moon's Rock / Bear Family ✦✦✦
This draws from Mullican's later years, after his career had gone into commercial decline. —*Dan Cooper*

Seven Years to Rock: The King Years, 1946-56 / Western ✦✦✦✦
Not a hits compilation, it's still a good sampling of Mullican in his boogie phase. His take on Tiny Bradshaw's "Well, Oh Well" is required listening for anyone who thinks Elvis invented the hillbilly/R&B cover. —*Dan Cooper*

Anne Murray

b. Jun. 20, 1946, Spring Hill, NS
Ukulele, Vocals / Country-Pop
Nova Scotia-born Anne Murray built her musical influences from the pop sounds that her parents listened to (Rosemary Clooney, Perry Como) and the Top 40 sounds that AM New York radio stations piped into Canada (Buddy Holly, Elvis Presley, Brenda Lee).
Originally she intended to work as a physical education instructor, but she continued to pursue an interest in music. Turned down for a spot on a national TV show called "Singalong Jubilee," she received a call from the show's producer two years later. He offered her a chance to make records, and when she agreed, she found herself with a million-selling crossover single in 1970, "Snowbird."
Murray was frequently at odds with the trappings of success—she even performed barefoot in Las Vegas—and when she got married in 1975, she seemingly dropped out of the business. With her family established, she started working in 1978 with a producer, Jim Ed Norman, who returned her to prominence with "Walk Right Back" and the million-selling follow-up "You Needed Me."
Throughout the late '70s and early '80s, Murray successfully walked the line between country and pop with a rich alto voice and a knack for romantic material. Admirably, she continues to insist that no matter how high or low her career goes, her family in Toronto is her top priority. —*Tom Roland*

● **Greatest Hits** / 1980 / Liberty ✦✦✦✦
It covers Murray's first decade in the limelight, beginning with "Snowbird" and concluding with "Could I Have This Dance?," a track from the 1980 movie *Urban Cowboy.* It ranges from the folky "Danny's Song" to her cover of The Beatles' "You Won't See Me," but the middle-of-the-road approach is quite obvious. —*Tom Roland*

Greatest Hits, Vol. 2 / 1989 / Liberty ✦✦✦✦
With her country base firmly established, Murray grew restless in the early and mid-'80s, very much desirous of conquering the pop market. It never quite happened, though she made a nice stab at it in her duet with Dave Loggins, "Nobody Loves Me like You Do." She may not be country in the classic sense, but good music is good music and it's hard not to like "Time Don't Run Out on Me" or "Now and Forever (You and Me)." —*Tom Roland*

Now & Forever / 1994 / EMI ✦✦✦✦
This three-disc box contains an excellent booklet and 64 freshly remastered tracks, with a generous helping of alternate mixes, live recordings, and previously unreleased material, including several early, pre-fame nuggets. —*Roch Parisien*

The Best . . . So Far / 1994 / EMI ✦✦✦✦
A serviceable 20-song distillation of the biggest hits from the box set. However, here's the kicker: the single disc includes "Over You," a new-old track from the vaults (released as a single) which is not included in the box set. So if you want to have it all . . . —*Roch Parisien*

Willie Nelson (Willie Hugh Nelson)

b. Apr. 30, 1933, Abbott, TX
Bass, Guitar, Vocals / Traditional Country, Progressive Country, Outlaw Country
A lot of people, including lovers of country music, hadn't heard of Willie Nelson until 1975, the year that an old Roy Acuff song titled "Blue Eyes Crying in the Rain" made him famous to the multitudes and led to the first of his five Grammy awards. During the two previous decades, though, he had written hundreds of quality songs, played thousands of honky tonks, and perfected his vocal style, which many think ranks among the best of any kind of popular American music. His "outlaw" and anti-establishment image, which now seems old hat, nearly twenty years after its creation, was not an act but the real thing. His abundance of talent allowed him to back up this image; there's only one Willie Nelson.
After a stint as a country DJ on a Fort Worth, TX, radio station, Nelson played bass with the Ray Price band, and Price recorded his "Night Life," now a country standard. Faron Young then cut "Hello Walls" and Patsy Cline, "Crazy" and "Funny How Time Slips Away": Nelson had made his reputation as a premier songwriter. (Though he never sang them as such, many of his songs are natural crossovers. Frank Sinatra, Perry Como, Stevie Wonder, and Bing Crosby are a few of the stars who have recorded his songs.) He then borrowed members of Price's band and started on the road. Despite reasonable success, only when he moved back to Texas from Nashville did his singing start getting the attention it deserved. In this period before "Blue Eyes Crying in the Rain," he recorded three albums, including *Shotgun Willie* and *Phases and Stages*, a concept album about a broken marriage, telling the point of view of both the husband and the wife. Nelson ignored the prevalent "Nashville Sound" lushness and succeeded.
Starting in 1975, Nelson reached the top, in the process melding country and "hip" music while turning millions of younger listeners into fans. His *Red-Headed Stranger*, a concept album about the Old West, hit No. 1, as did *Wanted: The Outlaws*, with Waylon Jennings, Jessi Colter, and Tompall Glaser. The Outlaws' national tour following this album created an explosion of interest in country music. Nelson, now a superstar, recorded a number of hit singles ("Remember Me," "Good-Hearted Woman," and others) before joining with Waylon Jennings in 1978 for *Waylon and Willie*, an album that quickly sold a million and locked both singers into the outlaw image for years. *Stardust*, a hit album of popular songs, showcased Nelson's versatility.
In 1979, Nelson showed his acting talent in the well-received movie, *Electric Horseman* (with Robert Redford and Jane Fonda); *Honeysuckle Rose* was released a year later, drawing praise for Nelson's acting. The film's soundtrack album was another hit. The early '80s brought more superstardom, with "On the Road Again" and "Angel Flying Too Close to the Ground."
Nelson's contributions to country music are enormous. His unsurpassed vocal style, his tasteful and subtle guitar playing, his introduction of country music to millions of new listeners, his sophisticated yet real song compositions: these all show us what a unique and incomparable talent is Willie Nelson. And his Farm Aid benefits show us that his heart is where his music is. —*David Vinopal*

☆ **Shotgun Willie/Phases & Stages** / 1974 / Mobile Fidelity ✦✦✦✦✦
Although Willie Nelson's two albums for Atlantic Records—*Shotgun Willie* and *Phases & Stages*—were among his most unsuccessful records

commercially, they were groundbreaking, pivotal releases that rank among his finest and most introspective works. Musically, both albums straddle the lines between outlaw country, folk, and traditional pop—they are innovative, introspective works that sounded unlike his previous work. Additionally, both records are concept albums, with each of the songs intertwining to tell a story. *Shotgun Willie* is about a legendary outlaw; *Phases and Stages* is about a divorce, with the first side taking the perspective of the male, the second taking the female viewpoint. Neither album produced big hits, but they are some of the strongest efforts Willie Nelson ever made, making this single-disc collection an excellent bargain. —*Stephen Thomas Erlewine*

☆ **Red Headed Stranger/Sound in Your Mind** / 1975 / Columbia ✦✦✦✦✦
Recorded in Texas, Nelson's sparsely produced concept album about the old West subverted the old ways in Nashville and made country converts of hippies everywhere. In fact, it did more than that, as "Blue Eyes Crying in the Rain" became one of the unlikeliest Top 40 hits in pop music history. —*Dan Cooper*

☆ **Stardust** / 1978 / Columbia ✦✦✦✦✦
The record label didn't want Nelson to do this project, inspired partially by the death of pop crooner Bing Crosby. Standard material—"Moonlight in Vermont," "All of Me," "Don't Get Around Much Anymore"—is arranged by Booker T. Jones (of "Green Onions" fame) and recorded in Nelson's inimitable style in Emmylou Harris's house. —*Tom Roland*

Sings Kris Kristofferson / 1979 / Columbia ✦✦✦
No one does it better, Janis Joplin notwithstanding. —*Michael McCall*

San Antonio Rose / 1980 / Columbia ✦✦✦

★ **Greatest Hits (& Some That Will Be)** / 1981 / Columbia ✦✦✦✦✦
This capsulizes Nelson's first five years in the spotlight, with lots of classics: "On the Road Again," "Blue Eyes Crying in the Rain," "Heartbreak Hotel" (a duet with Leon Russell), as well as the smartly produced "My Heroes Have Always Been Cowboys." —*Tom Roland*

Half Nelson / 1985 / Columbia ✦✦✦

★ **Nite Life: Greatest Hits and Rare Tracks, 1959-1971** / 1989 / Rhino ✦✦✦✦✦
A compilation of material Nelson wrote and recorded while he was trying to launch a career as a professional songwriter during the '60s. At this time, he also made two albums and several singles for Liberty, and many recordings for RCA. These songs, including some rarities, are compiled for this flawless single-disc collection. *Nite Life* runs through all of the songs other performers had hits with and made standards, including the title tracks, "Crazy," "Funny How Time Slips Away," and "Hello, Walls." Not only does it have the songs that established Nelson's reputation, the disc shows that even early in his career, he was creating eclectic, far-reaching music that never stayed within the boundaries of traditional country. —*Stephen Thomas Erlewine*

Who'll Buy My Memories . . . / 1992 / Columbia ✦✦✦✦
Better known as *The IRS Tapes*, this 25-song collection of solo voice and guitar numbers is equal parts dark and scintillating, but all parts are unadorned. —*Dan Cooper*

Across the Borderline / 1993 / Columbia ✦✦✦

The Early Years / Feb. 15, 1994 / Scotti Bros. ✦✦✦
Those who enjoyed Willie Nelson at his most unadorned on the *IRS Tapes* might also enjoy hearing the bare-bones arrangements of *The Early Years*. The 14 tracks on *The Early Years* were recorded by Nelson as songwriter demos in the early '60s, just before he signed with Liberty. At this point, Nelson was considered more of a songwriter than a performer. Accordingly, there is a sparse feel to most of these performances, which sometimes feature nothing more than his voice or guitar. Not that there's anything especially wrong with that. Willie re-recorded several of these tunes for Liberty and RCA, and one could argue that the arrangements were sometimes less sympathetic than the minimal backing on these tapes. While the demo ambience could be said to add warmth and character, one should also be aware that these aren't the most polished performances; perfunctory arrangements, flat production, and the occasional bum vocal phrase are also found. But fans of Nashville country without the syrup should find something to like here. It includes an early version of "I Hope So," a country hit for Nelson in 1969, and "Undo The Right," which would be a Top Ten country hit for Johnny Bush in 1968. —*Richie Unterberger*

☆ **The Early Years: The Complete Liberty Recordings Plus More** / May 3, 1994 / Liberty ✦✦✦✦✦
Not only a fine compilation, it was a gutsy move. Nelson's 1962-64 sessions for Liberty Records, the first label to sign him as an artist, have never been held in high regard by his fans. On many cuts, the strings were poured on so thick even Eddy Arnold would have protested. But if one dispenses with prejudice and gives this two-CD box set an open-minded listen, there's a wealth of fine work to appreciate among the 61 singles, album cuts and alternate takes. And no matter the production—lush or spare—his songwriting is a continual joy. Besides the famil-

iar (including a riveting, pre-Liberty version of "Night Life" that opens the set), are any number of near-forgotten songs that would have been another writer's best work. Excellent liner notes are provided by Joseph F. Laredo, who deserves credit for not pretending the strings aren't there. —*Dan Cooper*

A Classic & Unreleased Collection / 1995 / Rhino ✦✦✦
Originally released as a mail-order-only release through the Home Shopping Network, the three-disc set compiles a selection of unreleased and rare material recorded between 1957 and the mid-'80s. Considering that all of the set is composed of rarities, the "classic" in the title is a little dubious. Nevertheless, the music throughout the box is fine and occasionally excellent. Opening with Nelson's first independently-released single, the set runs through a number of music-publishing demos he made for Pamper Music, unreleased Atlantic recordings, a complete unreleased live album (*Live at the Texas Opry House*) from 1974, the unreleased *Sugar Moon* from the mid-'80s, a handful of tracks from the scrapped record *Willie Alone* and, finally, *Willie Sings Hank Williams*, another unreleased album from the '80s. Since it covers such a large time-frame, it isn't surprising that the set features a bit of everything that made Nelson famous—his Western swing and honky tonk roots, as well as his fondness for pop standards, jazz, country-pop, and folk. Even though there is music on the box that would please the casual fan, *A Classic and Unreleased Collection* remains a treasure chest for collectors, who will find plenty of rough gems within the set. —*Stephen Thomas Erlewine*

☆ **Revolutions Of Time, The Journey 1975-1993** / 1995 / Columbia/Legacy ✦✦✦✦✦
Compiling material from Willie Nelson's later career, the box set provides a through overview of the singer's most popular recordings, as well as some of his most obscure. Divided into three thematic discs—*Pilgrimage*, *Sojourns*, *Exodus*—the box contains most of his hits from the era, including selections from *The Red Headed Stranger* and *Stardust*, which are featured on *Pilgrimage*. *Sojourns* concentrates on his duets, while *Exodus* is filled with songs from the late '80s and early '90s. It doesn't round up all of his best songs of the era—there are still several gems hidden away on the original albums—but it does provide an effective and thoroughly entertaining portrait of Nelson's later career. *Revolutions of Time* could be all that the casual fan needs to hear from Nelson's later career, and every country fan should be familiar with much of these songs. —*Stephen Thomas Erlewine*

The Essential Willie Nelson / Aug. 1, 1995 / RCA ✦✦✦✦
Willie Nelson didn't have many hits while he was on RCA Records, but the majority of them, including some selected rarities, are collected on *The Essential Willie Nelson*. —*Stephen Thomas Erlewine*

Mickey Newbury

b. May 19, 1940, Houston, TX
Guitar, Vocals / Progressive Country
Along with fellow songwriters such as Kris Kristofferson, Willie Nelson, and Tom T. Hall, Mickey Newbury helped revolutionize country music in the '60s and '70s. He brought broader musical influences coupled with frank, emotional depth, while at the same time never losing respect for tradition. Newbury married country music with the haunting spirit of pure poetry to create an impressive collection of introspective, emotionally complex songs like those of Leonard Cohen or even William Blake (a writer Newbury was turned on to when stationed in England during a stint in the Air Force). The fact that many of his songs became hits for singers from Don Gibson to Elvis Presley was proof that the industry and the public were hungry for a change.

Like many of his generation, however (such as his friend Townes Van Zandt), Newbury is better known as a songwriter than as a singer. Newbury has recorded 15 albums over a nearly 30-year period—right up to 1994's *Nights When I Am Sane*—but his soft, beautiful tenor voice has rarely reached the charts.

Newbury spent his teens in Houston, TX, absorbing a wide range of musical styles, learning to play guitar, and writing poetry, which he began reading in local coffeehouses. Folk music was on the rise at the time, and he soon turned to writing songs. He joined the Air Force in 1959, where he first met Kris Kristofferson, who became a lifelong friend. After his discharge Newbury ended up in Nashville. He wrote songs, knocked on doors, and hung out with fellow musicians such as Kristofferson, Willie Nelson, Tom T. Hall, Harlan Howard, and Waylon Jennings, who were also just getting started. In 1966 Don Gibson had a Top Ten hit with Newbury's "Funny Familiar Forgotten Feelings"; that was followed by Kenny Rogers ("Just Dropped In"), Eddy Arnold ("Here Comes the Rain, Baby"), and Andy Williams ("Sweet Memories"), and Newbury's career was off and running.

Newbury's first album was "Harlequin Melodies" for RCA, followed by "Looks Like Rain" for Mercury, which contained his initial versions of two of his most enduring songs, "San Francisco Mabel Joy" (which he's recorded several times more) and "33rd of August." He earned a contract with Elektra in 1970, and released a string of superb albums that included "Heaven Help the Child," "I Came to Hear the Music," and the acoustic "Live at Montezuma Hall"; the latter was paired with a re-release of "Looks like Rain." These contained such songs as "Cortelia Clark" (about a blind street singer), the snazzy rock and roller "Dizzy Lizzy," and "Heaven Help the Child," based to some degree on Heming-way's life story. In 1972 Newbury had a Top 30 hit with "American Trilogy," a suite-like arrangement of "Dixie," "Battle Hymn of the Republic," and "All My Trials." The song later became a major hit for Elvis Presley and a standard in his repertoire. Newbury recorded three albums for ABC/Hickory in the late '70s, and was inducted into the Nashville Song-writer's Hall of Fame in 1980, but he soon became something of a recluse. He gave up concert touring, and only released two albums in the 1980s. In 1994 he resurfaced with *Nights When I Am Sane*, an acoustic album recorded live with guitarist Jack Williams. He currently lives in Oregon, still performs occasionally at festivals, and still, he says, writes plenty of new songs.

Since he's been out of the spotlight for more than a decade, though, and his catalog is largely out of print, he's little known in contemporary country circles. People familiar with his work, however, recognize New-bury as one of country music's most inspired and moving artists. — *Kurt Wolff*

● **Frisco Mabel Joy** / 1971 / Elektra ✦✦✦✦
Elvis Presley took Newbury's "American Trilogy" as his own, but the deeply felt original is here, along with some other excellent songs by a songwriter who has long deserved far more recognition than he has received, and who turns out to be an affective singer as well. — *William Ruhlmann*

The Best of Mickey Newbury / 1991 / Curb ✦✦
Curb's *The Best of Mickey Newbury* has a misleading title. Not only are many of his best-known songs not included, neither are his best-known versions. Instead, it has a handful of his famous songs—including "She Even Woke Me Up to Say Goodbye" and "An American Trilogy"—in slick, overly-polished versions that only give a hint of his talents. — *Thom Owens*

Juice Newton (Judy Kay Newton)

b. Feb. 18, 1952, Lakehurst, New Jersey
Guitar, Vocals / Country-Rock
Juice Newton was part of the first wave of country singers raised on rock, folk-rock, and singer-songwriters, which is evident from her hit singles. "Angel of the Morning" and "Queen of Hearts," her two crossover hits, have country-pop arrangements but their roots are in '60s pop and new wave roots rock, respectively. That's why she managed pop crossover hits in the early '80s and also why she was able to sustain country success throughout the decade.

Although Newton was born in New Jersey, she was raised in Virginia. As she entered high school, her mother gave her a guitar, prompting her infatuation with folk music. After graduating from high school, she attended Foothill College in Los Altos Hills, CA, where she continued to play folk in coffeehouses. During this time, she met Otha Young, a fellow guitarist and songwriter. The two formed a folk-rock band called Dixie Peach and began playing bars around northern California.

Dixie Peach only lasted a year, but they did gain a local following while they were active. After the band broke up, Newton and Young formed Juice Newton & Silver Spur, which had more country leanings than Dixie Peach. They were also more successful. Their fan base was large enough to convince the band to go to Los Angeles and try to land a record contract. In 1975, Juice Newton & Silver Spur signed to RCA Records and released an eponymous debut, which spawned the minor hit single "Love is a Word" in early 1976. Later that year, the group released *After the Dust Settles*, which didn't attract much attention, and RCA dropped them after its release. The band signed with Capitol Records, releasing *Come to Me* in 1978. Like its predecessor, the album was more or less ignored, causing the Silver Spur to disband.

Though Silver Spur had broken up, Juice Newton and Otha Young continued to work together. Newton still had a contract with Capitol and the pair immediately began working on her solo debut. The result, *Juice*, was released in early 1981 and it quickly became a crossover hit. The first single from the record, "Angel of the Morning," reached No. 4 on the pop charts and on the country charts, it peaked at 22. "Queen of Hearts" was a bigger hit, reaching No. 2 on the pop charts and No. 14 on the coun-try charts. "The Sweetest Thing (I've Ever Known)," the third single taken from *Juice*, was her biggest country hit, peaking at No. 1; on the pop charts, it hit No. 7. *Juice* would eventually go platinum.

Newton's follow-up album, *Quiet Lies*, was released in the spring of 1982. It was also a hit, spawning the pop Top Ten "Love's Been A Little Bit Hard on Me" and the No. 2 country hit "Break It To Me Gently." The album won a Grammy for Best Country Vocal Performance, Female; it also went gold by the end of the year. *Dirty Looks*, her third solo album,

was released in 1983. The record marked the first time Newton failed to crack either the pop or country Top 40.

In 1984, she switched labels, signing with RCA. Juice's first album for the label, *Can't Wait All Night*, was a transitional album, seeing her move away from pop and beginning to concentrate on country. *Old Flame*, released in 1985, was her country breakthrough, spawning the hits "You Make Me Want to Make You Mine," "Hurt," and the duet with Eddie Rabbitt "Both to Each Other (Friends & Lovers)," which all went to No. 1; the album had three additional Top Ten hits—"Old Flame," "Cheap Love," and "What Can I Do With My Heart."

Old Flame happened to be Newton's only major country hit. Its fol-low-up, 1987's *Emotion*, only yielded one Top Ten hit, "Tell Me True." In 1989, she released *Ain't Gonna Cry*, which featured the single "When Love Comes Around the Bend," which barely scraped the Top 40.

Ain't Gonna Cry turned out be Juice Newton's last album. She aban-doned country and began performing showy mainstream pop, which she performed in nightclubs. Throughout the '90s, she continues to perform live concerts without recording any new material. — *Stephen Thomas Erlewine*

Juice / 1981 / Capitol ✦✦✦✦
Juice was Juice Newton's breakthrough album, sending her into not only into the country Top Ten, but also to the top of the pop charts. The key to her success was how her country-pop not only drew from country roots, but also '60s AM pop, folk-rock, and roots rock. For instance, the country production on "Angel of the Morning" can't disguise its soft-rock roots. Similarly, "Queen of Hearts" simply replicates Dave Edmunds' version from *Repeat When Necessary*, down to the vocal inflections and guitar breaks. But Newton's version is slicker, which appealed both to country and pop radio. Throughout *Juice*, Newton straddles the line between country and pop, playing to both sides of the market. As it happened, she appealed to both. As an album, *Juice* has its weak moments, but she sings well throughout the record and when she has the right mate-rial—as on the hit singles—the results are highly entertaining. — *Stephen Thomas Erlewine*

Quiet Lies / 1982 / Capitol ✦✦✦✦
This album assured Newton three country hits (the first three tracks) as she found her way back to the country-rock sound she seems to do best. Her choice of covers works better this time as well. Her Brenda Lee net-ted her a hit, and her Gene Pitney cover wasn't bad either. — *Jim Worbois*

● **Greatest Hits** / 1984 / Capitol ✦✦✦✦
All of Juice Newton's big hits from the early '80s, including "Angel of the Morning," "Queen of Hearts," and "Love's Been A Little Bit Hard on Me," are collected on the single-disc set. — *Thom Owens*

Old Flame / 1986 / RCA ✦✦✦✦
Out of all of Juice Newton's albums, *Old Flame* has the strongest country roots and influences. Newton is still equally informed by rock and pop—after all, she doesn't sing hardcore honky tonk on the album, she sings somewhat roots country-pop. However, *Old Flame* proves that she can perform this material with conviction. Most of the production on the record is too slick and indicative of its time, but the singles—as well as Newton's singing—remain effective. — *Thom Owens*

The Nitty Gritty Dirt Band

Progressive Bluegrass, Country-Rock
Founded in California during 1965, the Nitty Gritty Dirt Band has lasted longer than virtually any other country-based rock group of their era. Younger contemporaries of the Byrds, they played an almost equally important role in the transformation from folk-rock into country-rock, and have been an influence on such bands as the Eagles and Alabama. The Nitty Gritty Dirt Band's beginnings lay with the New Coast Two, a folk duo consisting of Jeff Hanna (guitar, vocals) and Bruce Kunkel (gui-tar, washtub bass), formed while both were in high school in the early '60s. By the time the duo were college students, they were having infor-mal jams at a Long Beach, CA, guitar shop called McCabe's. It was there that they met Ralph Barr (guitar, washtub bass), Les Thompson (vocals, mandolin, bass, guitar, banjo, percussion), Jimmie Fadden (harmonica, vocals, drums, percussion) and Jackson Browne (guitar, vocals). This lineup became the Nitty Gritty Dirt Band in late 1965, and began playing jug band music at local clubs. At that time, Southern California was undergoing a musical renaissance, courtesy of the folk-rock movement, and the Nitty Gritty Dirt Band fit in with these other folkies-turned-rock-ers. Browne left after a few months to pursue a solo career, and was replaced by John McEuen (banjo, fiddle, mandolin, steel guitar, vocals), the younger brother of the group's new manager, Bill McEuen. With the elder McEuen's guidance, the group landed a recording contract with Liberty Records and released their debut album, *The Nitty Gritty Dirt Band*, in April of 1967. Their first single, "Buy for Me the Rain," became a modest hit and got the band some television appearances.

A second album, *Ricochet*, released seven months later, was a critical success but a commercial failure. The group now found itself at an impasse over the issue of whether to go electric. During the dispute,

Kunkel, who wanted to add an electric guitar to their sound, exited the lineup. He was replaced by Chris Darrow (guitar, fiddle). Ironically, by mid-1968 the group had gone electric, and also added drums to their sound. Their first electric album, *Rare Junk*, released in June of 1968, was also a commercial failure. The band was barely working, a far cry from their success of a year earlier. The band persevered, however, and released *Alive!* in May of 1969. The album was another commercial disaster, and the Nitty Gritty Dirt Band closed up shop soon after.

The members scattered for several months, but six months later the group was back for another try; the new lineup included McEuen, Hanna, Fadden, Thompson, and Jim Ibbotson (guitars, accordion, drums, percussion, piano, vocals). They returned to their record company with a demand for control over their recordings and the record company agreed. Bill McEuen became the group's producer as well as its manager. The first result of this new era in the Nitty Gritty Dirt Band's history was *Uncle Charlie and His Dog Teddy*, issued in 1970. Rooted tightly in their jug band sound, the album had a country feel but no trace of the vaudeville and novelty numbers that had appeared on their earlier records. The album yielded what is the group's best-known single, their cover of Jerry Jeff Walker's "Mr. Bojangles," and suddenly, the band had a following bigger than anything they'd known during their brief bout of success in 1967. Their next album, *All The Good Times*, released in early 1972, had an even more countrified feel.

By 1972, several rock bands, most notably the Byrds and the Beau Brummels, had gone to Nashville seeking credibility from the country music community there, only to be received poorly by that community and to have their resulting work ignored by the press and public. At the suggestion of manager Bill McEuen, however, the Nitty Gritty Dirt Band went to Nashville in 1972 and recorded a selection of traditional country numbers with the likes of Roy Acuff, Earl Scruggs, Mother Maybelle Carter, and other members of country and bluegrass music's veteran elite. Some of the veteran Nashville stars were skeptical and suspicious at first of the bandmembers and their amplified instruments, but the ice was broken when they saw how respectful the band was toward them and their work, and their music, as well as how serious they were about their own music. The resulting triple album, *Will the Circle Be Unbroken*, released in January of 1973, became a million-seller and elicited positive reviews from both the rock and country music press. The band had, by now, eclipsed the competition as a "cross-over" act, reaching country and bluegrass audiences even as their rock listeners acquired a new appreciation for musicians such as Acuff and Carter. The Nitty Gritty Dirt Band succeeded with *Will the Circle Be Unbroken* because they were willing to meet country and bluegrass music on the terms of those two branches of traditional music, rather than as rock musicians.

During the year and a half that followed the success of *Will the Circle Be Unbroken*, Les Thompson left the group, reducing the Nitty Gritty Dirt Band to a quartet. Their next album, *Stars and Stripes Forever*, issued in the summer of 1974, was a peculiar live album, mixing concert performances and dialogue. Following one more original album, *Dream* (1975), the group received its first retrospective treatment, a triple-LP compilation entitled *Dirt Silver and Gold*, issued late in 1976. Jim Ibbotson left the line-up at around this time, and was replaced initially by session player Bob Carpenter. The remaining trio of Jeff Hanna, John McEuen, and Jimmie Fadden shortened the band's official name to the Dirt Band. In this incarnation, the group became a much more mainstream, pop-rock outfit with a smoother sound, with Jeff Hanna guiding them as producer. Their records were far less eccentric, although they continued to be popular. The band's next albums were decidedly more laid back than previous records, and didn't attract nearly as much attention. *An American Dream*, released in 1980, did relatively well, as did *Make a Little Magic* (1981). By 1982, however, they were back to their country roots, renamed the Nitty Gritty Dirt Band, and Jim Ibbotson was playing with them again. *Let's Go*, released in the middle of 1983, heralded their return to country music, as a largely acoustic album. In 1984, after 17 years with Liberty/UA/Capitol, they switched labels to Warner Bros., and that same year made some headlines as the first American rock band to tour the Soviet Union. Their Warner albums sold well, but by the end of the 1980s the group was moving between labels.

In 1989, both as a reflection of the changing times, and as though to make sure that everyone got the point that the band was once again mining its country roots, they made *Will the Circle Be Unbroken 2* for MCA/Universal Records, reuniting with surviving country and bluegrass veterans from the original album and adding a whole roster of new players, including Johnny Cash, Chris Hillman, and Ricky Skaggs. This album won the Grammy for Best Country Vocal Performance (duo or group) and the Country Music Association's Album of the Year Award in 1989. By this time, the Dirt Band was working in their field alongside any number of country/bluegrass crossover artists whose career paths were made easier by that first record, including John Hiatt, Mary Chapin Carpenter, and Rosanne Cash. Their next several albums saw them never veering very far from their country/bluegrass roots. The group continues to record a new album every year or so, most recently a new concert

album, *Live Two-Five*, celebrating their 25th anniversary as a band, and the self-explanatory *Acoustic. —Bruce Eder*

Uncle Charlie & His Dog Teddy / 1970 / Liberty ✦✦✦✦
This is the album that gave them a career. Their laidback mix of country and California folk gave a breezy feel to well-selected songs, including their million-selling version of Jerry Jeff Walker's "Mr. Bojangles."
—Michael McCall

★ **Will the Circle Be Unbroken** / 1972 / EMI America ✦✦✦✦✦
The influence of this two-disc set, which brought the previously pop-oriented Nitty Gritty Dirt Band together with some of the seminal names in country music, is incalculable. Mother Maybelle Carter, Earl Scruggs, Doc Watson, Roy Acuff, and others sat down with a bunch of longhairs, found common ground on the best of old-time country music, and changed the direction of popular music. Two decades on, it still sounds great. *— William Ruhlmann*

Stars & Stripes Forever / 1974 / Beat Goes On ✦✦✦
Whatever your preconceptions of the Nitty Gritty Dirt Band, this record will blow them away. One minute they are doing one of their early hits, the next reminiscing about the '50s and covering the Jive 5. They mix Hank Williams, Buddy Holly, and the "Sheik of Araby." This is an incredibly fun live album. *—Jim Worbois*

20 Years of Dirt . . . / 1986 / Warner Bros. ✦✦✦
20 Years of Dirt: The Best of the Nitty Gritty Dirt Band traces the development of the band from a pop outfit with folk and country edges into a contemporary country band. Their version of "Mr. Bojangles" remains memorable, as does "American Dream"; other tracks are sturdy, middle-of-the-road, '80s Nashville. *— William Ruhlmann*

More Great Dirt (Best, Vol. 2) / 1989 / Warner Bros. ✦✦✦
Tight harmonies and infectious arrangements are the staple of this compilation. "I've Been Lookin'," "Fishin' in the Dark," and "Baby's Got a Hold on Me" are the musical equivalent of a good book—you can't put 'em down. *— Tom Roland*

Will the Circle Be Unbroken, Vol. 2 / 1989 / Universal ✦✦✦
This easily won the Country Music Association's Album of the Year Award, thanks to a stellar cast that includes John Denver, Johnny Cash, the Carter Family, Bruce Hornsby, Ricky Skaggs, Chris Hillman, Roger McGuinn, Rosanne Cash, Steve Wariner, Roy Acuff, Chet Atkins . . . you get the message. Tracks were all recorded in one "take," with no overdubs, making the outstanding musicianship particularly noteworthy. Atheists beware: there's a lot of gospel. *—Tom Roland*

Acoustic / May 31, 1994 / Liberty ✦✦✦
Mighty professional sounding when compared to Uncle Charlie, but after more than 25 years as music pros, they still sound best when at their most casual, as they are here. *—Michael McCall*

The Oak Ridge Boys

Country-Pop, Country Gospel
Over the course of their long career, the Oak Ridge Boys became a country music institution. The vocal group has gone through a number of personnel changes over the years, but the sound of the group has remained the same—the band has never strayed from their gospel-inflected country-pop.

The Oak Ridge Boys began as a gospel group named the Oak Ridge Quartet in 1945. In 1949, Bob Weber purchased the rights to the group's name from lead singer Wally Fowler and ascribed it to his group, the Cavalry Quartet. The Oak Ridge Quartet remained together through the mid-'50s, becoming one of the top gospel groups in America. Smitty Gatlin later created a new Oak Ridge Quartet after purchasing the name from the deeply indebted Weber. Gatlin decided to steer the group towards secular success and changed their name to the Oak Ridge Boys in 1961. Although they had changed their name and were concentrating on commercial material, the group continued to sing gospel music. In the late '60s, the Oak Ridge Boys underwent an image makeover, growing their hair long and singing almost nothing but pop-oriented material. In the early '70s, they gradually incorporated more gospel back into their repertoire and in 1970, they earned a Grammy for "Best Gospel Performance" for their song "Talk About the Good Times."

In 1973, the group's core lineup—Duane Allen (lead vocals), Joe Bonsall (tenor), William Lee Golden (baritone), and Richard Sterban (bass)—had fallen into place and they made their first entry in the country charts with a cover of Johnny Cash's "Praise the Lord and Pass the Soup." The following year they signed to Columbia. Although "The Baptism of Jesse Taylor" earned them another Grammy that year, the Oak Ridge Boys nearly disbanded due to financial difficulties. In 1977, the group decided to switch over completely to secular music, beginning with the hit singles "Y'All Come Back Saloon" and "You're the One." Almost immediately, the Oak Ridge Boys became a fixture in the country Top Ten; for the next eight years, they had a string of 25 Top Ten singles, including 13 No. 1 hits. In 1978, they had their first No. 1 single with

"I'll Be True to You." In 1981 the Oaks had their biggest hit with the crossover hit "Elvira."

By the late '80s the group's momentum began to slow down. They still had Top 40 hits, but they no longer dominated the Top Ten, as they did in the early '80s. In 1987, William Golden, who had been with the group since 1964, was fired by the rest of the group who believed that his burly appearance and long beard no longer fit their image. The Oaks' backup guitarist and singer Steve Sanders replaced him, and the group quickly returned to the Top Ten. Over the next three years, the group had four No. 1 hits, including "It Takes a Little Rain (To Make Love Grow)," "Gonna Take a Lot of River," and "No Matter How High." In 1990, their comeback slowed down. One more Top Ten hit, "Lucky Moon," followed in 1991, but the group had all but disappeared from the country charts by the end of 1992. The Oak Ridge Boys continued to tour and record throughout the mid-'90s. — *Sandra Brennan*

Greatest Hits, Vol. 1 / 1980 / MCA ✦✦✦✦
Earliest package of hits, with gospel roots showing on material like "Y'All Come Back Saloon." — *Cub Koda*

Fancy Free / 1981 / MCA ✦✦✦✦
This is their best-selling album, thanks to the presence of "Elvira." Each of The Oaks gets a turn at the lead part, although Duane Allen is easily best suited to that role. Includes some quasi-folk and straightahead country, but the best track is the obligatory gospel tune "I Would Crawl All the Way (To the River)." — *Tom Roland*

● **Greatest Hits, Vol. 2** / 1984 / MCA ✦✦✦✦
This covers the Oaks at their peak, with repetitive, singalong choruses predominating in "American Made," "Love Song," and "Everyday." The delicate "I Guess It Never Hurts to Hurt Sometimes" is a nice change of pace, but why did MCA hold out "Bobbie Sue" until *Greatest Hits 3?* — *Tom Roland*

Monongahela / 1987 / MCA ✦✦✦✦
Though *Heartbeat* was recorded after the dismissal of William Lee Golden, this is the first album in which replacement Steve Sanders was involved from beginning to end in the recording process. Harmonies are understandably more soulful—and more in tune—and the project is generally more uplifting. It includes "Gonna Take a Lot of River." — *Tom Roland*

Greatest Hits, Vol. 3 / 1989 / MCA ✦✦✦✦
This contains "Gonna Take a Lot of River," "Take Pride in America," "This Crazy Love," and other hits from the mid- and late '80s. — *AMG*

Mark O'Connor

b. Aug. 5, 1961
Fiddle / Instrumental, Progressive Country, Bluegrass
Born and raised in Seattle, WA, O'Connor was always a bit out of sync with his teenage peers. Understandably so, since he was winning fiddle contests and had even mapped out a sketchy career path. O'Connor moved to Nashville in 1983, already a former sideman for jazz violinist Stephane Grappelli, a job that allowed him to play the stage at Carnegie Hall. At the time O'Connor arrived in Music City (the post-*Urban Cowboy* era), fiddle was hardly in vogue, and it took a couple of years for him to make his mark. Finally, in 1985, the Nitty Gritty Dirt Band used him in its single "High Horse," thanks to that work, O'Connor's phone number became a popular one with country record producers. Over the next five years he played on 450 albums, including such stellar projects as *Trio* by Dolly Parton, Linda Ronstadt, and Emmylou Harris; *Always & Forever* by Randy Travis; *Killin' Time* by Clint Black; and *Loving Proof* by Ricky Van Shelton. Despite his success, O'Connor gave up session work to concentrate on his own solo career, in the process providing a new focus on Nashville's studio players while simultaneously building a reputation for himself with the general public. — *Tom Roland*

Soppin' the Gravy / 1981 / Rounder ✦✦✦
This is a good collection of mainly traditional Texas fiddle music. — *Brian Mansfield*

Championship Years / 1990 / Country Music Foundation ✦✦✦✦
O'Connor at his earliest and most traditional, these recordings were made during his National Fiddling Championships competitions and were made between 1975 and 1984. — *Brian Mansfield*

The New Nashville Cats / 1991 / Warner Bros. ✦✦✦✦
With an incredible lineup of Nashville's very best musicians, this package covers a wide range of musical territory, from bluegrass to the blues, with plenty of stellar pickin'. Ironically, this mostly instrumental album won a vocal Grammy when Vince Gill, Ricky Skaggs, and Steve Wariner teamed with O'Connor on "Restless." — *Tom Roland*

Heroes / 1993 / Warner Bros. ✦✦✦✦
O'Connor performs with his favorite fiddlers from a variety of styles, including Jean-Luc Ponty, Johnny Gimble, Vassar Clements, Pinchas Zukerman, and L. Shankar, among others. The set features "The Devil Comes Back to Georgia," a sequel to Charlie Daniels 1979 hit "The Devil Went Down to Georgia." — *Brian Mansfield*

● **Retrospective** / Rounder ✦✦✦✦
This is a chronological overview of O'Connor's first six Rounder albums. — *Brian Mansfield*

K.T. Oslin (Kay Toinette Oslin)

b. 1942
Vocals / Country-Pop
During the late '80s, K.T. Oslin had a string of hit singles with her pop-inflected modern country. Most of Oslin's material was directed at, in the words of her breakthrough single, "80's Ladies." Which meant, her songs were about modern women and were recorded with modern equipment, including synthesizers. For a brief time, she was one of the most popular singers in country music, earning four No. 1 singles and two platinum albums. However, her fall from the top was as quick as her rise—by the mid-'90s she still had a large cult following, but was no longer able to have a Top 40 single.

An Arkansas native, K.T. Oslin was the daughter of a singer and a paper-mill foreman. Her father died when she was five, causing her mother to abandon her singing career and begin working as a medical lab technician. After moving around the South for a while, Oslin and her mother settled in Houston, TX. Later she studied drama at Jacksonville, TX, Junior College before forming a folk trio with Guy Clark and David Jones in the '60s. She later paired up with Frank Davis and began recording an album in Los Angeles; it was never released, and she returned to Houston without Davis. Oslin began appearing in musical productions including Carol Channing's National Touring Company's production of *Hello Dolly!* after she returned to Texas. She went on to appear in the Betty Grable Broadway company version of the play in New York. She remained in the Big Apple for a while, appearing in other shows, singing commercial jingles, and doing session work.

In 1974, Oslin began writing songs. Eventually, she sent a demo tape to Dianne Petty at SESAC. Petty helped Oslin sign to Elektra, where she recorded a minor hit debut single, "Clean Your Own Tables," in 1981. Meanwhile, country singers Gail Davis and Dottie West had chart success with two of Oslin's songs. In 1984, Oslin appeared on a public radio broadcast with several established stars, and her song "Come Next Monday" was recorded by Judy Rodman. Two years later, Oslin felt ready to make her own bid for stardom. After borrowing $7,000, she showcased herself in Nashville. Harold Shedd, Alabama's producer at the time, was in the audience, and he helped get her signed to RCA. Oslin's first album, *'80s Ladies*, debuted in the country Top 15 in 1987, becoming the highest-charting debut album for a female since Loretta Lynn's in 1964. The album's title track reached the Top Ten, and Oslin hit No. 1 with its follow up single, "Do Ya." Oslin's successful streak lasted through 1989; in those two years, she recorded three albums, had four other Top Ten hits and won a Grammy for Best Female Country Vocal Performance for "Hold Me." Both her first and second album, *This Woman*, went platinum and her third album, *Love in a Small Town*, went gold. Oslin released the compilation *Greatest Hits: Songs from an Aging Sex Bomb* in 1993. — *Sandra Brennan*

Love in a Small Town / 1990 / RCA ✦✦✦✦
Oslin built this loosely defined concept album from ten years of song, including the first one she wrote. Oslin sings of the guises romance wears in a small southern town. *Love in a Small Town* also contains a low-key version of the 1946 standard "You Call Everybody Darling" and a cover of Mickey And Sylvia's "Love Is Strange." Oslin's coyness isn't always flattering, and the arrangements sometimes border on a new countrypolitan, but those moments are rare. On most of *Small Town*, Oslin displays her best assets: her worldly sensibility and complex maturity. — *Brian Mansfield*

● **Greatest Hits: Songs From An Aging Sex Bomb . . .** / Apr. 27, 1993 / RCA ✦✦✦✦
A compilation of Oslin's biggest hits from the late '80s, featuring the No. 1 singles "Do Ya," "I'll Always Come Back," "Hold Me," and "Come Next Monday," as well as seven other songs, including her three other Top Ten hits, "80's Ladies," "Hey Bobby" and "This Woman." — *Thom Owens*

Buck Owens (Alvis Edgar Owens)

b. Aug. 12, 1929, Sherman, TX
Guitar, Trumpet, Saxophone, Vocals / Traditional Country, Bakersfield Sound
Buck Owens, along with Merle Haggard, was the leader of the Bakersfield Sound—a twangy, electrified, rock-influenced interpretation of hardcore honky tonk that emerged in the '60s. Owens was the first bona fide country star to emerge from Bakersfield, scoring a total of 15 consecutive No. 1 hits in the mid-'60s. In the process, he provided an edgy alternative to the string-laden country-pop that was being produced during the '60s. Several generations of musicians—from Gram Parsons in the late '60s to Dwight Yoakam in the '80s—were influenced by his music, which became one of the blueprints for modern country. Owens learned to play guitar when he was a teenager in Arizona. He dropped out of

high school in ninth grade, to work on the farm to help his family, but also spent a significant amount of time learning how to play the guitar. By his late teens, he was playing gigs in honky tonks and clubs around Phoenix. When he was 19 years old, he married Bonnie Campbell, who was also a country singer. The couple moved to Bakersfield, CA, in 1951 and divorced two years later. Shortly after the move, he had his own band. Between 1954 and 1958, Owens played guitar on a number of Capitol country records produced by Ken Nelson, including some by Tommy Collins, Faron Young, and Wanda Jackson. Occasionally, he did sessions at the local Bakersfield studio Lu-Tal, run by Lewis Talley. Owens made his first solo recordings at Talley's studio in 1956, cutting ten songs for an independent label called Pep. The singles—including two rockabilly sides released under the name Corky Jones—were unsuccessful, yet they attracted the attention of many country music business insiders.

Owens continued to play regularly in Bakersfield clubs. Eventually, Columbia Records expressed interest in signing him to a record contract. Faced with competition, Capitol signed Buck as a recording artist in February of 1957. Owens' initial singles were country-pop numbers which sank without a trace upon their release. Hurting financially, Buck moved to a suburb of Tacoma, WA, to work at a radio station, KAYE, in January 1958. In the fall of 1958, Owens had another session for Capitol Records, but this time he was allowed to use a steel guitar and a fiddle. "Second Fiddle" was released as a single and became a hit, climbing to No. 24 on the country charts.

"Under Your Spell Again," the fall 1959 follow-up to "Second Fiddle," broke the doors open for Buck. Climbing to No. 4, the single began a streak of Top Ten singles that ran more or less uninterrupted into the '70s. After "Under Your Spell Again" became a success, Owens moved back to Bakersfield. That winter, guitarist Don Rich became Buck's fiddler and lead guitarist; throughout the next decade, Rich would be Owens' primarily collaborator. During 1960, he had two Top Ten hits, "Above and Beyond" and "Foolin' Around." Owens and Rich began touring the country together in the spring of 1961, playing with pickup bands in each honky tonk they visited. Soon, the pair began playing electric Fender Telecasters instead of acoustic guitars, which gave their music a bright, punchy twang. This change was evident in Buck's two Top Ten hits in 1962, "Kickin' Our Hearts Around" and "You're for Me." Instead of being the shuffling honky tonk numbers that had been Buck's signature, the songs were bright, driving tracks in 2/4 that showed a hint of rock 'n' roll influence. By the beginning of 1963, Owens had begun to assemble his own band, featuring a drummer, bassist, and a pedal steel guitarist. One of the first bassists for the band was Merle Haggard, who named the group the Buckaroos.

Buck Owens' first No. 1 single, "Act Naturally," arrived in the spring of 1963. "Act Naturally" elevated Buck from a successful singer into stardom, starting a streak of 15 consecutive No. 1 singles. Its follow-up single, "Love's Gonna Live Here," became his biggest hit, spending 16 weeks at No. 1. Owens' success had spearheaded the national acceptance of the Bakersfield Sound. The Bakersfield artists updated honky tonk, standing in direct contrast to the smooth country-pop of Nashville, and the freshness of its sound made Owens one of the biggest stars in popular music in the mid-'60s. He was playing hundreds of shows a year, selling thousands of records, and he launched his first television series, *Buck Owens' Ranch*, in 1966. At the peak of its popularity, the half-hour music show appeared in 100 markets. Buck began to branch out musically in 1968, adding more textures, tempos, and stylistic flourishes to his music. Though he only had one No. 1 hit in 1968, all but one of his singles from that year reached the Top Five. The following year, Owens opened a state-of-the-art, 16-track recording studio in downtown Bakersfield. Capitol allowed him to record himself and several other artists at the studio; the label would merely press and package the records.

While Buck Owens had a dedicated country following, he also had picked up a number of rock fans as well. Not only did the Beatles cover "Act Naturally" on their 1965 *Help!* album, but in the fall of 1968, Buck headlined and sold out two concerts at the rock 'n' roll venue, Fillmore West. In the summer of 1969, Buck Owens' second television show—a country version of the popular sketch comedy *Laugh-In* called *Hee Haw*—premiered. Owens and vocalist/guitarist Roy Clark were hired as co-hosts. Initially, the show was just a summer replacement for *The Smothers Brothers Comedy Hour*, but it was so successful that CBS scheduled it for the fall. As *Hee Haw* became more popular, so did Buck Owens. In the span of just over a year—December 1969 to February 1971—Capitol released no less than three new studio records and six reissues from Owens. During that time, he continued to chart in the Top Ten with regularity.

At the beginning of 1971, Owens signed what would turn out to be his last contract with Capitol; according to its terms, he would record for the label for another four years and five years after his contract expired, he would gain ownership of all of his Capitol recordings. Throughout 1971, he continued to have Top Ten hits. That year, CBS cancelled *Hee Haw*, and the show moved into syndication, where it became even more popular. By 1973, it had been so successful that it forced *Buck Owens' Ranch*

off the air. In the spring of 1972, he had his final No. 1 single as a solo artist, the ballad "Made in Japan." His career began to slide after that—it took him over a year to reach the Top Ten again with "Big Game Hunter."

In July of 1974, Don Rich, Buck's longtime guitarist, died in a motorcycle crash, which sent Owens into a deep depression. Though he had one more Top Ten hit that fall with "Great Expectations," he had trouble breaking the Top 40 in the years following Rich's death. Owens' contract with Capitol expired in 1975 and he moved to Warner Brothers, where he began recording in Nashville. Appropriately, his music began to sound more like country-pop than the hard-edged Bakersfield sound he had become famous for, because he relinquished creative control of his records to the producers. Buck's record sales had significantly declined, but *Hee Haw* remained popular. In 1980, Owens ended his contract with Warner and drastically cut back his concert schedule. Even though he was semi-retired, he continued to tape *Hee Haw* until 1986.

Buck Owens was out of public view for the early and mid-'80s, which is when a new generation of country singers was developing. Like Owens in the '60s, they stood in opposition to the pop-inflected country of Nashville, building their sound on the Bakersfield country of Owens and Merle Haggard. One of the leading new traditionalists, Dwight Yoakam, persuaded Buck Owens to join him on a re-recording of Buck's 1972 song "Streets of Bakersfield." Released in the summer of 1988, "Streets of Bakersfield" became a major hit, reaching No. 1; it was the first time since 1972 that Owens had a No. 1 hit. Its success spurred Buck back into the recording studio, where he made a new album called *Hot Dog*. It was a moderate success and it re-energized Owens. Buck assembled a new version of the Buckaroos and embarked on a small tour and another record.

Buck Owens didn't record or perform frequently in the '90s, but his classic Capitol recordings began to appear on compact disc; they hadn't been in print since 1980, when he gained control of the tapes from Capitol. Furthermore, Buck's influence continued to reverberate throughout country music, as well as some quarters of rock 'n' roll. —*Stephen Thomas Erlewine*

Country Hit Maker #1 / 195 / Starday ✦✦✦
Pre-Capitol material, half of this album consists of Owens' very early recordings like "Sweethearts in Heaven" and "There Goes My Love" (covered later by Highway 101), which show his developing vocal style. It's a little more down-home than his later stuff. The other half consists of covers of Owens' later material by other artists. —*George Bedard*

On The Bandstand / 1963 / Sundazed ✦✦✦
One of Buck's rootsier '60s Capitol albums, including only one hit ("Kickin' Our Hearts"), and giving plenty of instrumental and vocal space to the rest of the band. It's not as heavy on original material as some of his other Capitol LPs, including numbers by Wanda Jackson, Willie Nelson, Leadbelly, and John D. Loudermilk, as well as an arrangement of "Orange Blossom Special." The CD reissue adds two cuts from a 1963 Top 20 duet single he recorded with Rose Maddox. —*Richie Unterberger*

I Don't Care / 1964 / Capitol ✦✦✦

Together Again/My Heart Skips a Beat / 1964 / Capitol ✦✦✦
It includes his covers of "Truck Drivin' Man," "A-11," and "Hello Trouble." —*George Bedard*

I've Got a Tiger by the Tail / 1965 / Capitol ✦✦✦✦
The title track is included, plus some great ballads, such as "Cryin' Time." These '60s Capitol albums are not just mish-mashes, like many C&W albums of the period; they're well thought out, usually including a vocal or two by Don Rich (one of C&W's unsung heroes), or the deep-voiced bass player Doyle Holly, and a fiddle or steel-guitar instrumental by Don or Tom Brumley, respectively. —*George Bedard*

Before You Go/No One But You / 1965 / Sundazed ✦✦✦
When it comes to Owens' mid-'60s Capitol LPs, there really isn't much to choose between them. If you like his Bakersfield sound, you'll like all of them; if you're trying to zero in on just one or two collections, you'd be better off with greatest-hits surveys, because the individual albums sound rather interchangeable to the non-enthusiast. This has the usual competent original material and accomplished guitar picking, paced by the No. 1 title track, with occasional instrumentals thrown in for a change of pace. The CD reissue adds a couple of instrumental bonus cuts from his 1966 album, *The Buck Owens Songbook*. —*Richie Unterberger*

☆ **Live at Carnegie Hall** / 1989 / Country Music Foundation ✦✦✦✦✦
This album contains 21 tracks, the debut concert (March 25, 1966) of Buck & The Buckaroos in its entirety, and features such songs as "Waitin' in Your Welfare Line," "I've Got a Tiger by the Tail," and more. This is Owens at his best. —*AMG*

☆ **The Buck Owens Collection (1959-1990)** / 1992 / Rhino ✦✦✦✦✦
Spanning three discs, *The Buck Owens Collection* is the most comprehensive compilation ever assembled on one of the founders of the Bakersfield sound. Although his earliest recordings aren't included, all of his greatest Capitol hits are present, as is his 1988 duet on "Streets of Bakersfield" with Dwight Yoakam and its follow-up single, "Hot Dog."

The box is a necessary purchase, simply because it presents all of Buck's biggest hits in one place. There might not be many rarities on *The Buck Owens Collection*, but with an artist as consistent as Buck, all you need is on this essential set. —*Stephen Thomas Erlewine*

★ **Very Best of Buck Owens, Vol. 1** / 1994 / Rhino ✦✦✦✦✦
This compilation contains a great deal of Buck's most essential songs, including "Under Your Spell Again," "Act Naturally," "I've Got A Tiger By the Tail," and "Waitin' In Your Welfare Line." The set runs from 1959 to 1971, picking up a good cross-section of his biggest hits along the way. The compilation is a perfect introduction and what songs it doesn't cover are readily available on *The Very Best of Buck Owens, Vol. 2.* Of course, listeners that want the most comprehensive set available should invest in the triple-disc box set, *The Buck Owens Collection.* —*Stephen Thomas Erlewine*

☆ **Very Best of Buck Owens, Vol. 2** / 1994 / Rhino ✦✦✦✦✦
This collection contains all the essential Owens songs the first volume didn't cover, including "Above and Beyond," "Love's Gonna Live Here," "My Heart Skips A Beat," "Cryin' Time," "Buckaroo," and "Big in Vegas." Like its predecessor, the collection spans from 1959 to 1971, and features an excellent cross-section of his biggest hits along the way. Not only is it a perfect supplement to *The Very Best of Buck Owens, Vol. 1,* the compilation works as a good introduction, even though the first collection is a better choice for a new fan. Of course, listeners that want the most comprehensive set available should invest in the triple-disc box set, *The Buck Owens Collection.* —*Stephen Thomas Erlewine*

Lee Roy Parnell

Guitar / Country

Singer-songwriter and slide guitarist Lee Roy Parnell sings with a Texas-style Western swing enlivened with just a hint of blues. In addition to having a string of Top Ten singles of his own, Parnell has written songs for artists as diverse as Sweethearts of the Rodeo, Jo-El Sonnier, and David Wills & Johnny Lee.

The son of a travelling medicine-show musician, Parnell was influenced early on by Bob Wills. Raised on his parents' ranch, Parnell made his debut singing "San Antonio Rose," on Wills' radio show in Fort Worth. As a teenager, he drummed in a local band, but he switched to guitar shortly after he joined the group. Following high school, Parnell moved to Austin, TX, and toured for the next dozen years. Eventually, he settled down and married, and got a job selling ads at a local radio station.

In the early '70s, Parnell visited Nashville, but returned to Austin without signing to a record company. However, he soon signed a publishing contract with Welk Music. One night, Parnell was playing in a local cafe and was heard by Tim Dubois, the head of Arista Records, who signed the aspiring singer to the label. Parnell released his eponymous debut album in 1990 and the record yielded three minor hits. Released in 1992, Parnell's second album, *Love Without Mercy,* produced the number two smash "What Kind of Fool Do You Think I Am." Following its success, he had four consecutive Top Ten hits—"Love Without Mercy," "Tender Moment," "On the Road," and "I'm Holding My Own." The latter two were taken from his third album, which was released in the fall of 1993. During 1994, Parnell slipped from the Top Ten, but he continued to chart in the country Top Ten. In the spring of 1995, he bounced back to the Top Ten with "A Little Bit of You," which was taken from his fourth album, *We All Get Lucky Sometimes.* —*Sandra Brennan*

Lee Roy Parnell / 1990 / Arista ✦✦✦✦
Hard-rocking country soul, complete with horn section, this album was produced by Barry Beckett, whose experience at Muscle Shoals means he knows how to make this kind of record. —*Brian Mansfield*

● **Love Without Mercy** / 1992 / Arista ✦✦✦✦
For his second album, Parnell dropped the horns and gave his slide guitar a bigger role. He was a Texas rocker disguised by a pedal steel, but the album produced three Top Ten hits—"Love Without Mercy," "What Kind of Fool Do You Think I Am," and "Tender Moment." —*Brian Mansfield*

On the Road / Oct. 26, 1993 / Arista ✦✦✦
More roots-rocking road music, though not as perfectly realized as *Love Without Mercy.* The title track and "I'm Holding My Own" were hits, and Parnell sang with Brooks & Dunn's Ronnie Dunn on the Hank Williams standard "Take These Chains from My Heart." —*Brian Mansfield*

We All Get Lucky Sometimes / 1995 / Career ✦✦✦
On *We All Get Lucky Sometimes,* Lee Roy Parnell tempers his mixture of country, R&B, blues, and rock 'n' roll somewhat with a subdued production, designed to attract the attention of country radio. Even when his music is slightly tamed, Parnell turns in a fine effort, filled with enough true grit to satisfy his fans. —*Stephen Thomas Erlewine*

Dolly Parton (Dolly Rebecca Parton)

b. Jan. 19, 1946, Locust Ridge, TN
Banjo, Guitar, Vocals / Traditional Country, Contemporary Country
It's difficult to find a country performer (except, of course, for Elvis Pres-

---

Beginnings: Hillbilly, Old-Time, and String-Band Music

If your experience of country music has consisted of playing the latest Garth Brooks or Barbara Mandrell CD, you'll be needing to set aside considerable time to listen to and appreciate the original country music— but it will be time well spent. Though this music from the '20s can be an acquired taste, depending on what you're accustomed to hearing, the enthusiasm, charm, and simplicity of the music and its performers will transport you back to a decade when country music was facts-of-life music, no more and no less.

The band names give a fair taste of the early performers and of their zest for playing: Gid Tanner and the Skillet Lickers, Al Hopkins and the Hill Billies, the Aristocratic Pigs, the Possum Hunters, the Fruit Jar Drinkers (Uncle Dave Macon's band), the Gully Jumpers, and the Dixie Clodhoppers, all string bands that flourished in the late '20s. The fiddle was the dominant instrument in the beginning; Texan Eck Robertson, who cut six songs for Victor in 1922 (including the classic "Sally Gooden"), is credited with the first recording in country music. The standard repertoire ranged from drinkin'-and-cuttin'-up songs to minstrel/medicine-show standards to gospel and spiritual numbers—something for everyone.

But by no means were hillbilly bands the only show in town in the '20s, nor the fiddle the only instrument: old-time music featured guitars (including the Hawaiian slide guitar), banjos, mandolins, and harmonicas, which soon backed up singers as diverse as Buell Kazee and Bradley Kincaid (folksingers) on one hand and Vernon Dalhart (a reformed opera singer) on the other. It was Dalhart who had the first country hit—"The Prisoner's Song," a 1924 million-seller. In the late '50s and early '60s, hillbilly/old-time/string-band music was rediscovered by the folkniks who, in listening to the New Lost City Ramblers, resurrected the popularity of country music's original genre. — *David Vinopal*

---

ley) who has moved from country roots to international fame more successfully than Dolly Parton. Her autobiographical single "Coat of Many Colors" shows the poverty of growing up one of 12 children on a run-down farm in Locust Ridge, TN. At 12 years old she was appearing on Knoxville television; at 13 she was recording on a small label and appearing on the Grand Ole Opry; at present she has to her credit hit albums, hit singles, hit movies, and a TV variety show.

Her 1967 hit "Dumb Blonde" (which she's not) caught Porter Wagoner's ear, and he hired Parton to appear on his television show, where their duet numbers became famous. By the time her "Joshua" reached No. 1 in 1970, Parton's fame had overshadowed the boss', and she had struck out on her own, though still recording duets with him. Between those duets and her recent one with Ricky Van Shelton came a lot of stardom.

Parton's debut on the silver screen was in the 1980 hit *9 to 5* with co-stars Lily Tomlin and Jane Fonda; Parton's *9 to 5 and Odd Jobs* album was released with the film. *The Best Little Whorehouse in Texas* brought further fame, or notoriety, two years later; in 1984 she and Sylvester Stallone starred (and in fact sang a duet) in *Rhinestone.* "Tennessee Homesick Blues," from the film's soundtrack, earned Parton another Grammy nomination. Since then she has appeared in *Steel Magnolias* as a small-town gossipy beautician, and in *Wild Texas Wind,* a made-for-TV thriller-melodrama co-starring Ray Benson, leader of Asleep at the Wheel, a Western swing band. The critics have told us that she can act, but can Parton sing? Yes, and very well, in spite of the reputation created by her movies, her cheesecake image, and her many forays into pop music. She can still be pure country when she wants, all tinsel aside. Try listening to "Coat of Many Colors," "Jolene," "But You Know I Love You," and "Tennessee Homesick Blues." Parton is a woman of considerable talents, country singing chief among them. —*David Vinopal*

Just Because I'm a Woman / 1968 / RCA Victor ✦✦✦✦
It's a measure of how impressed producer Bob Ferguson must have been with Parton that he (and possibly Porter Wagoner in the background) made no attempt to crowd her with strings or choruses on her first RCA album. In fact, it's almost frightening to hear how fully realized her talent was in 1968. —*Dan Cooper*

The Best of Dolly Parton / 1975 / RCA ✦✦✦✦
She projects an admirable child-like sense of hope and positivism, which

is matched to some degree by her thin, girlish vocal quality. It translates well in her pre-Hollywood, unencumbered productions, notably "Coat of Many Colors," "Love Is like a Butterfly," and "The Bargain Store." — *Tom Roland*

9 to 5 and Odd Jobs / 1980 / RCA ✦✦✦✦
Dolly Parton has never been an album's artist, and RCA has always been adept at shoving poorly organized products onto the market (look how they've treated Elvis Presley). Hence, though she is an important country figure, most of Parton's albums are hard to recommend. This one contains the title hit, plus a few other Parton originals and a version of Woody Guthrie's "Deportee" among its eight tracks. But that's enough to put it a notch above most of Parton's RCA catalog. — *William Ruhlmann*

Greatest Hits / 1982 / RCA ✦✦✦✦
This is a good sampling of Parton's work in the first few years that she deliberately chased a crossover career in Hollywood. The country-pop stuff might offend purists, but it still gets the toe tappin'. "Hard Candy Christmas" and her updated version of "I Will Always Love You" (both from *The Best Little Whorehouse in Texas*) show her growth as an interpreter. — *Tom Roland*

Collector's Series / 1985 / RCA ✦✦✦
This is a well-programmed selection of Parton's RCA hits, among them "Jolene," "Coat of Many Colors," and "Me and Little Andy." — *William Ruhlmann*

Real Love / 1985 / RCA ✦✦✦
A lot of critics would push this one aside, perhaps with good reason since she turned over much of the creative control on the project to David Malloy. But Malloy set out to highlight the bright, bubbly facet of her personality, and he succeeded. — *Tom Roland*

The World of Dolly Parton, Vol. 1 / 1988 / Monument ✦✦✦✦
This captures young Parton on Monument Records circa 1967, just before she hooked up with Porter. — *Dan Cooper*

The World of Dolly Parton, Vol. 2 / 1988 / Monument ✦✦✦✦
Included is more from the Monument catalog. — *Dan Cooper*

White Limozeen / 1989 / CBS ✦✦✦✦
Parton moved to Columbia in the late '80s and started paying more attention to her recordings, the best of which is this album. It's produced by Ricky Skaggs, who brought in such fast-picking cronies as Bela Fleck and Jerry Douglas, and used more of Parton's own songs than usual. The result is an unusual consistency and a musical revitalization for the singer. — *William Ruhlmann*

Eagle When She Flies / 1991 / Columbia ✦✦✦
She confirms that she's fully returned to the country fold, and is rewarded with her first million-selling album that wasn't a greatest-hits package. The title song is a powerful female anthem. — *Michael McCall*

★ **The RCA Years 1967-1986** / May 25, 1993 / RCA ✦✦✦✦✦
The long-overdue box set turns out to be a cursory two-CD set that cheats on her better early years in favor of latter-day hits. Still, it's the best retrospective available, and it emphasizes her stature as a truly significant songwriter, which is easy to forget in the shadow of her Daisy Mae in Hollywood image. — *Michael McCall*

The Essential Dolly Parton / Mar. 28, 1995 / RCA ✦✦✦✦
The Essential Dolly Parton has a good cross-section of her early hits and her latter-day countrypolitan numbers. It isn't as thorough as the double-disc RCA years, but it provides a good introduction to the most popular portion of her career. — *Thom Owens*

Johnny Paycheck (Don Eugene Lytle, Donny Young)

b. May 31, 1938, Greenfield, OH
Bass, Guitar, Guitar (Steel), Vocals / Traditional Country, Country-Rock
The first that many people ever heard of Johnny Paycheck was in 1977, when his "Take This Job and Shove It" inspired one-man wildcat strikes all over America. The next time was in 1985, when he was arrested for shooting a man at a bar in Hillsboro, OH. That Paycheck is remembered for a fairly amusical novelty song and a violent crime (for which he spent two years in prison) is a shame, for it just so happens that he is one of the mightiest honky tonkers of his time.

Paycheck was performing in talent contests by the age of nine, and riding the rails as a drifter by the time he turned fifteen. After a Navy stint landed him in the brig for two years, he arrived in Nashville, where he performed in the bands of Porter Wagoner, Faron Young, Ray Price, and George Jones. He recorded several singles under the name Donny Young, then, in 1965, cut his first sides as Johnny Paycheck for the Hilltop label. A year later, he and gadfly producer Aubrey Mayhew started the Little Darlin' label, for which Paycheck recorded his greatest work. Marked by Lloyd Green's knockout steel guitar and Paycheck's broad, resonant vocals (not to mention his sense of humor) his Little Darlin' records of the 1960s have since become cult favorites.

After splitting with Mayhew (and after running his life into the gutter) Paycheck made a celebrated comeback on Epic in the 1970s. "Take This

Job and Shove It" was the most famous result, though ballads like "She's All I Got" and "Someone To Give My Love To" are far more indicative of his stylistic range. — *Dan Cooper*

Johnny Paycheck at Carnegie Hall / 1966 / Little Darlin' ✦✦✦✦
Despite the title and the photo of Paycheck in black-tie garb, this debut album is actually a Nashville studio product. But what a hopped-up product it is, making most mid-'60s honky tonk sound like Jim Nabors with steel guitar. — *Dan Cooper*

Jukebox Charlie / 1967 / Little Darlin' ✦✦✦✦
One of the all-time great honky tonk singers before his bad habits got the better of him, he included two of the greatest country songs ever—"Apartment No.9" and "Touch My Heart," both written by Paycheck. — *George Bedard*

Again / 1970 / Certron ✦✦✦
Post-Little Darlin', but still Mayhew-produced, he keeps right on kicking. Included is "Living the Life of a Dog," a hilarious romp that probably had multiple meanings for Paycheck. — *Dan Cooper*

Take This Job & Shove It / 1978 / Epic ✦✦✦
His big '70s novelty hit and an uneven selection of tunes are included, but it's worth having for "Colorado Kool-Aid"—a sort of Red Sovine-from-hell recitation on the subject of barroom etiquette. — *George Bedard*

Bars, Booze & Blondes / 1979 / Little Darlin' ✦✦✦

Extra Special / 1982 / Accord ✦✦✦✦
A budget-line release, it features a handful of characteristically bizarre honky tonk recorded in the 1960s around the same time he was recording for Little Darlin'. — *Michael McCall*

● **Biggest Hits** / 1983 / Epic ✦✦✦✦
Heavy on the late-'70s outlaw sound, this is where to find the original "Take This Job and Shove It" on CD. — *Dan Cooper*

Webb Pierce

b. Aug. 8, 1926, West Monroe, LA, **d.** Feb. 24, 1991
Guitar, Vocals / Traditional Country, Honky Tonk
Webb Pierce was one of the most popular honky tonk vocalists of the '50s, racking up more No. 1 hits than similar artists like Hank Williams, Eddy Arnold, Lefty Frizzell, and Ernest Tubb. For most of the general public, Pierce—with his lavish, flamboyant Nudie suits—became the most recognizable face of country music, as well as all of its excesses; after all, he boasted about his pair of convertibles lined with silver dollars and his guitar-shaped swimming pool. For all of his success, Pierce never amassed the reputation of his contemporaries, even though he continued to chart regularly well into the '70s. Webb's weakness for gaudy displays of his wealth, as well as his reluctance to break away from hardcore honky tonk, meant that he had neither the support of the industry, nor the ability to sustain the ever-changing tastes of a popular audience. Nevertheless, he remains one of the cornerstones of honky tonk, both for his success and his artistic achievements.

As a child in West Monroe, LA, Pierce became infatuated with Gene Autry films and his mother's hillbilly records, particularly those of Jimmie Rodgers and various Western swing and Cajun groups. He began to play guitar before he was a teenager. At the age of 15, he was hired as a singer by Monroe's KMLB. During World War II, Pierce enlisted in the Army. While he was in the service, he married Betty Jane Lewis; their wedding was in June of 1942. After he was discharged, Webb and his wife moved back to Monroe, but by 1944 he moved to Shreveport. Getting a job at Sears Roebuck, Pierce began singing on radio stations, night clubs, and dances with Betty Jane. At first, they were featured on an early morning radio show on KTBS, while they would perform in the evening at clubs. It took them five years before they were noticed by the industry. In 1949, the California-based 4 Star Records signed the duo under separate recording contracts. Webb signed under his own name, while his wife was signed for duets with her husband under the name Betty Jane and Her Boyfriends. However, success didn't come to the duo—it only came for Webb; in the summer of 1950, the couple divorced.

In late 1949, Pierce accepted a spot on the "Louisiana Hayride," a radio program on KWKH that was instrumental in launching the careers of many country artists. Webb began to assemble a band of local Shreveport musicians, which included pianist Floyd Cramer, guitarist/vocalist Faron Young, bassist Tillman Franks, and vocalists Teddy and Doyle Wilburn. The Wilburns and Franks all wrote songs, which provided the basis for Pierce's initial set list. Pierce also founded a record label called Pacemaker, and Ark-La-Tex Music, a publishing company, with Horace Logan, the director of the Lousiana Hayride. On Pacemaker, Pierce made several records between 1950 and 1951. They weren't designed to be big sellers—they were created with the intent of attracting radio play around Louisiana. In 1951, he was able to get out of his 4-Star contract and Decca Records signed him immediately. Webb's second single, "Wondering," became his breakthrough hit, climbing to No. 1 early in 1952. After the single became a hit, Pierce left Louisiana for Nashville, where he met and married his second wife, Audrey Greisham. In June of 1952, he had his second No. 1 single with "That Heart Belongs to Me." The following September, the Grand Ole Opry needed to fill the vacancy left by the firing of Hank Williams, so they invited Pierce to join the cast. After Williams' death, Pierce became the most popular singer in country music. For the next four years, every single he released hit the Top Ten, with a total of ten reaching No. 1, including "There Stands the Glass" (1953), "Slowly" (1954), "More and More" (1954), and "In the Jailhouse Now" (1955).

Pierce and Opry manager Jim Denny formed Cedarwood Music, a music publishing company, in 1953; later, the pair would invest in radio stations together. Their business ventures were not looked upon kindly by the Opry superiors and they began pressuring the duo to cease any outside interests. At the same time, Pierce was growing tired of being confined to the Grand Ole Opry—he thought wasn't being treated with the respect a star of his stature deserved and he wanted to be able to partake in the lucrative financial rewards that came with touring. Webb left the Opry in 1955 and began appearing on "Ozark Jubilee," a television program on the ABC network. After "Ozark Jubilee" completed its run in 1956, he returned to the Opry, but left for good the following year.

Pierce continued to have hits until the end of the '50s, but he did take a significant dip in popularity after rock 'n' roll's arrival in the late '50s. Nevertheless, Pierce stayed on the charts, primarily because he kept in close touch with DJs across the country, which meant that he was able to keep his streak of 34 consecutive Top Ten hits running into 1957. For a while, Pierce tried to keep up with rock 'n' roll, covering the Everly Brothers and recording pseudo-rockabilly numbers. Once those proved unsuccessful, he stuck with honky tonk and he continued to rack up Top Ten hits right through 1964.

By 1965, the country-pop leanings of the Nashville Sound had pushed honky tonk from the top of the country charts. Pierce remained a star, but he simply didn't have many big hits in the latter half of the '60s—the most notable was "Fool Fool Fool" in 1967. Since his music had faded from the spotlight, he became known for his excessive lifestyle. Instead of indulging in intoxicants, Webb indulged in material items. Pierce had Nudie Cohen, a Hollywood tailor famous for his custom-made flamboyant clothing, line two Pontiac convertibles with silver dollars. He built a guitar-shaped swimming pool at his Nashville home. The swimming pool became a popular tourist attraction—nearly 3,000 people visited it each week—causing his neighbors, led by Ray Stevens, to file a legal suit against Pierce in order to prevent visitors from coming into their neighborhood.

Throughout the '70s, Pierce continued to record, but most of his income came from his highly lucrative financial investments. Webb left Decca Records in 1975, making a handful of records for Plantation Records that didn't experience much chart success. His last hit came in 1982, when his duet on "In the Jailhouse Now" with Willie Nelson scraped the bottom of the country charts.

Despite all of his success, Webb Pierce was never inducted into the Country Music Hall of Fame during his lifetime; it's likely that the members never forgave him for his rejection of the Grand Ole Opry and the Nashville industry. Webb Pierce died of pancreatic cancer on February 24, 1991. Just months before his death, he didn't receive enough votes to be inducted into the Hall of Fame. Nevertheless, his career stands as one of the most successful in the history of country music. —*Stephen Thomas Erlewine*

☆ **The Wondering Boy (1951-1958)** / 1990 / Bear Family ✦✦✦✦✦
For the devout, Germany's Bear Family offers a 4-CD boxed set of Pierce's primal honky tonk, a total of 113 songs by one of the seminal post-war country artists, including duets with Kitty Wells, Red Sovine, and the Wilburn Brothers. This is the best sound quality and presentation available of this influential music. —*Mark A. Humphrey*

Sands of Gold/Sweet Memories / 1993 / Mobile Fidelity ✦✦✦✦
Oo-ooh, what a little remastering can do. Two Nashville Sound LPs from the downside of Pierce's career feature Webb singing more of other people's hits than his own. But reissued Mofi-style, Pierce and the echo chamber sound great. —*Dan Cooper*

★ **Webb Pierce: King of the Honky-Tonk: From the Original Master Tapes** / 1994 / Country Music Foundation ✦✦✦✦✦
No one ever accused Pierce of being a singer's singer; nevertheless, his classic country oeuvre is totally individualistic, which is really more important. Any fan of '50s fiddle-and-steel honky tonk will want this collection, which features such Pierce immortals as "There Stands the Glass," "Slowly," a rollicking 1954 remake of Jimmie Rodgers' "In the Jailhouse Now," and the to-the-point "Honky Tonk Song." The latter is one of several cuts from the pen of a young Mel Tillis. —*Dan Cooper*

Sandy Posey

b. 1947, Jasper, AL
Vocals / Country-Pop
Despite having several moderate hits in both the country and pop charts, Sandy Posey was never fully embraced by either audience and is far

from being a household name. Posey relocated to Memphis in her teens, where she secured a job as a receptionist in a local studio. Eventually she was given a chance to sing backup during recording sessions, which led to work at several other studios in Memphis and Nashville—where her clear voice was perfectly suited for the ultra-slick Nashville "countrypolitan" sound of the day. MGM records signed her at age 18 to a solo deal on the strength of her demo recording of "Born a Woman," and despite her country roots and the country feel of her material, MGM marketed her as a pop singer—in retrospect, a wise decision. "Born a Woman" and "Single Girl" became her first two hits (both reached No. 12 in the pop charts in 1966). Since both songs were written by Martha Sharp, it was mistakenly reported during this time that Sandy Posey was a pseudonym assumed by Sharp for recording purposes. Posey had two more pop hits with the Top 40 "What a Woman in Love Won't Do" and the No. 12 "I Take It Back." By 1968, Posey's woman-as-a-helpless-victim themes were decidedly out of touch with the times and the hits stopped coming. She went into semi-retirement.

She returned in 1970 for phase two of her career—"the country years." She signed to Columbia Records where she had another string of hits—this time in the country charts, including the Top 20 Vietnam War-inspired "Bring Him Home Safely to Me," the slightly risque "Why Don't We Go Somewhere and Love" (a minor hit in 1975), "Happy Birthday Baby," and "Don't" (both Top 40). She moved to Monument Records in 1976 and later to Warner Brothers where she hit again with a series of oldies revivals—the Chordettes' "Born to Be With You" and a medley of "Love, Love, Love" and "Chapel of Love." Her last hit was in 1979 with "Love Is Sometimes Easy." In 1983, she signed to the independent label Audiograph and released her final solo album. Since then, she has stayed busy as a session singer and infrequently tours with her husband, Wade Cummings, an Elvis impersonator. —*Chris Woodstra*

● **Best of Sandy Posey** / 1996 / Collectibles ✦✦✦✦
The Best of Sandy Posey is a 14-track collection covering Posey's first recording period for MGM, including the classic forgotten hits "Born a Woman," "Single Girl," and "I Take It Back"—oddly, all three peaked at No. 12. Posey's mid-'60s songs, almost all depicting a woman helpless without—or alternately, trapped with—"her man," were slightly out-of-touch at the time and are artifacts now, but the slick pop-country arrangements have a timeless charm. Posey would have later success in the country charts in the '70s but unfortunately, those hits are not represented here. Though the album appears to be a straight reissue of MGM's *The Best of Sandy Posey*, this package actually expands on it by three tracks. —*Chris Woodstra*

Ray Price (Ray Nobel Price)

b. Jan. 12, 1926, Perryville, TX
Guitar, Vocals / Traditional Country, Country-Pop, Honky Tonk
Ray Price has covered—and kicked up—as much musical turf as any country singer of the postwar era. He's been lionized as the man who saved hard country when Nashville went pop, and vilified as the man who went pop when hard country was starting to call its own name with pride. Actually, he was—and still is—no more than a musically ambitious singer, always looking for the next challenge for a voice that could bring down roadhouse walls.

Price spent most of his youth in Dallas. It was there, circa 1949, that he cut his first record for Bullet at the famous Jim Beck studio. In 1951, he was picked up by Columbia, the label for which he would record for more than twenty years. After knocking around in Lefty Frizzell's camp for six months or so (his first Columbia single was a Frizzell composition) Price befriended Hank Williams. The connection brought him to the Opry and profoundly affected his singing style. After Hank died, Price starting stretching out more as a singer and arranger. His experimentation culminated in the 4/4-bass driven "Crazy Arms," the country song of the year for 1956. The intensely rhythmic sound he discovered with "Crazy Arms" would dominate his—and much of country in general's—music for the next six years. To this day, people in Nashville refer to a 4/4 country shuffle as the "Ray Price beat." Heavy on fiddle, steel, and high tenor harmony, his country work from the late '50s is as lively as the rock 'n' roll of the same era. Price tired of that sound, however, and started messing around with strings. His lush 1967 version of "Danny Boy," and his 1970 take on Kris Kristofferson's "For the Good Times," were, in their crossover way, landmark records. But few of his old fans appreciated the fact. For the last twenty-five years, Price's career has been an often awkward balancing act in which twin Texas fiddles are weighed against orchestras. —*Dan Cooper*

Talk to Your Heart / 1958 / Columbia ✦✦✦✦
A great collection of "weepers," honky tonk, and Western swing numbers from the '50s, it includes several songs by Floyd Tillman. Featured is "I'll Keep on Loving You," "Deep Water," "I Gotta Have My Baby Back," and "I'm Tired." This is a real "Texas-flavored" record by a honky tonk master. —*George Bedard*

Night Life / 1963 / CBS ✦✦✦
Probably the first C&W "concept" album, Willie Nelson penned the title track plus other 3 AM classics—tied together by the masterful steel guitar of Buddy Emmons. —*George Bedard*

The Best of Ray Price / 1976 / Columbia ✦✦✦✦
This compilation presents the highlights of Price's string-laden years. "For the Good Times" is one of the most mature singles ever recorded. "She's Got to Be a Saint" has gotten lost over the years. —*Tom Roland*

San Antonio Rose / 1980 / CBS ✦✦✦✦
Fans of Ray Price or Bob Wills won't want to miss Price's 1961 album, *San Antonio Rose: A Tribute to the Great Bob Wills.* Price, who acknowledged Wills as a primary influence, became the first of many to devote an album to covering the songs of the renowned master of Southwestern dance music. Price recorded the album in a nine-hour period, utilizing many of Nashville's best musicians, including guitarist Grady Martin, fiddler Tommy Jackson, pedal steel specialist Jimmy Day, and pianist Pig Robbins (in one of his first Nashville sessions). Also sitting in on acoustic guitar was a new Music City arrival, a little-known songwriter named Willie Nelson, who had just been hired to crank out songs for Price's publishing company. The record finds Price crooning with smooth, easy richness while the band lets it fly. —*Michael McCall*

★ **The Essential Ray Price (1951-1962)** / 1991 / CBS ✦✦✦✦✦
A not-completely-accurate title, this 20-track compilation excludes a few later necessities like "Night Life" and "For the Good Times." The important stuff from Price's hard-country heyday is all here, however, from the teetering rise-and-fall of "Crazy Arms" (the first of a thousand country songs to employ a walking bassline and modified swing beat, which became known as the "Ray Price shuffle") to Harlan Howard's "Heartaches by the Number." The fake stereo that marred earlier reissues of his '50s material is happily absent here. This is essential country music. —*Brian Mansfield & Mark A. Humphrey*

Charley Pride

b. Mar. 18, 1938, Sledge, MS
Guitar, Vocals / Traditional Country, Country-Pop
With 36 No. 1 hits under his belt, Charley Pride, who is Black, has helped prove how little race matters to the majority of country music fans. It's taken a long time to understand that, though. His first single., "Snakes Crawl at Night," was released without publicity photos, as some in the industry feared listeners would automatically reject a Black country singer. Since then, according to the *Book of Lists*, Pride's 12 gold albums in the US, combined with 30 gold and 4 platinum internationally, place him in the top 15 all-time record sellers. His easygoing singing style and easy-to-listen-to voice show why these honors have come his way. From picking cotton in his native Mississippi, Pride ended up working in a smelting plant in Montana, after a stint as a semi-pro baseball player. At the suggestion of Red Sovine, Pride moved to Nashville, where he was signed by Chet Atkins of RCA. In 1966, "Just Between You and Me" brought Pride a Grammy nomination and national fame. At the end of the '60s and the early part of the '70s, he had five No. 1s in a row, including "All I Have to Offer Is Me" and "Is Anybody Goin' to San Antone?" Numerous awards came in 1971 and 1972, with many more hits following, among them "She's Too Good to Be True," "Kiss an Angel Good Mornin'," and "Night Games." Pride's warm baritone voice and relaxed style made him the highest-selling act for RCA since Elvis Presley. His No. 1 album in 1980, *There's a Little Bit of Hank in Me*, showed why he is called Country Charley. —*David Vinopal*

● **The Best of Charley Pride** / 1969 / Curb ✦✦✦✦
Pride sang in a Hank Williams-influenced voice that yielded some of the best performances of the late '60s and early '70s. —*Mark A. Humphrey*

The Best of Charley Pride, Vol. 2 / 1972 / RCA ✦✦✦✦
Perhaps because RCA wanted to leave no doubts about Pride's country heritage, his early career mined the standard three-chord structure almost exclusively. As with the first volume, this set does that, but in "Kiss an Angel Good Mornin'" his performance is a notch or two above the previous package. —*Tom Roland*

The Best of Charley Pride, Vol. 3 / 1977 / RCA ✦✦✦✦
To be honest, Pride sounds a bit bored with some of this material. But "Mississippi Cotton Pickin' Delta Town" is practically a page out of his life. By the way, the cover art, with its rope script and blue-jeans-and-patches sports suit, is so '70s it's camp. —*Tom Roland*

Greatest Hits / 1981 / RCA ✦✦✦✦
Pride seems a little uninvolved with some of the material, but when he lets loose—as in "When I Stop Leaving (I'll Be Gone)" —he's absolutely convincing. —*Tom Roland*

Charley Sings Everybody's Choice / 1982 / RCA ✦✦✦✦
Dumb title, but it's an excellent album. Producer Norro Wilson revitalized Pride's career by bringing out the Memphis soul that rests in the shadows of his country veneer. —*Tom Roland*

Eddie Rabbitt　(Edward Thomas)

b. Nov. 27, 1941, Brooklyn, NY
Guitar, Vocals / Country-Pop
One of country music's most innovative artists during the late '70s and early '80s, Rabbitt has made contributions to the format that have often gone overlooked. Especially in songs like the R&B-inflected "Suspicions" and the rockin' "Someone Could Lose a Heart Tonight," Rabbitt challenged the commonly recognized creative boundaries of the idiom. Hailing from Brooklyn and New Jersey, Rabbitt moved to Nashville in 1968. Though it took a few years to get his recording career off the ground, he paid the rent through songwriting, authoring Elvis Presley's "Kentucky Rain" and Ronnie Milsap's "Pure Love."
Signing with Elektra Records' newly established country division in 1975, Rabbitt made recordings that were decidedly country—mostly uptempo material, like "Two Dollars in the Jukebox" and "Drinkin' My Baby (Off My Mind)"—with thick, inimitable harmonies, most of them overdubbed by Rabbitt himself. Driven in part by then-associates David Malloy and Even Stevens, Rabbitt's records became "progressively progressive," well into the late '80s. At that time, his country shuffle "On Second Thought" demonstrated a return to more traditional sounds. —*Tom Roland*

The Best of Eddie Rabbitt / 1979 / Elektra ✦✦✦✦
Strong melodies are enhanced by Rabbitt's searing harmonies. The instruments are "hotter" in the final mix than in other productions from the same period, so even the mainstream country fare is a little different from that of his mid-'70s contemporaries. —*Tom Roland*

Loveline / 1979 / Elektra ✦✦✦
Fellow reviewers will cringe at this choice, but it displays Rabbitt at his most daring. Lots of R&B influence—even a bit of a "disco" feel on a couple of tracks—inspired melodies and unusual chord progressions throughout. Lyrically lightweight, but hey, this is music not poetry. —*Tom Roland*

Horizon / 1980 / Elektra ✦✦✦
This is Rabbitt's rockabilly release. "I Love a Rainy Night" and "Drivin' My Life Away" set the pace for side one: Sun-inspired, guitar-based productions, heavy on the echo. Side two is a bit ballad-heavy, though most of the tracks stand up well individually. "That's Just The Way It Is" is something of a forerunner for "Someone Could Lose a Heart Tonight." —*Tom Roland*

★ **All Time Greatest Hits** / Mar. 12, 1991 / Warner Bros. ✦✦✦✦✦
It covers Rabbitt's most commercially productive period. "Drivin' My Life Away," "I Love a Rainy Night," and "Step by Step" were all Top Ten pop hits, in addition to hitting No. 1 country. "Drivin'" and "Rainy," in fact, were million-sellers. —*Dan Cooper*

Boots Randolph　(Randolph III, Homer Louis)

b. 1925, Paducah, KY
Trombone, Saxophone / Instrumental, Country-Pop, Jazz Instrumental Pop, Bluegrass
Tenor saxophonist Randolph has been a very influential instrumentalist within the country field, with his peak years in the '60s. Randolph switched from trombone to tenor sax in high school, and played in local combos in Evansville in the '40s and '50s. He scored with "Yakety Sax," a novelty work co-written by James Rich, and was signed to RCA by Chet Atkins. His playing was and is quite simple; pleasant melodies, catchy themes, and occasional use of vocal effects have made up his signature style. He became a featured session musician and did many "countrypolitan" (country MOR) dates, placing 13 albums on the charts in the '60s and '70s. —*Ron Wynn*

Boots Randolph's Yakety Sax / 1963 / Monument ✦✦✦✦
Nashville session tenor saxman doing what he does best on a rocking set. —*Bill Dahl*

Sentimental Journey / 1973 / Monument ✦✦✦
Nice stuff. More jazz-influenced country than country-tinged jazz. —*Ron Wynn*

● **Greatest Hits** / 1976 / Monument ✦✦✦✦
This country saxman shows his versatility. —*Bill Dahl*

Collin Raye　(Floyd Collin Wray)

Vocals / Contemporary Country, New Traditionalist
Singer-songwriter Collin Raye's blend of Western swing, rockabilly, country-rock and sentimental ballads brought him a string of hit singles in the early '90s. As a child in Arkansas, Raye grew up listening to Bob Wills, Waylon Jennings, Buddy Holly, and Johnny Horton. His mother was a well-known local country singer who performed with such stars as Johnny Cash, Carl Perkins, and Elvis Presley, and she sometimes brought Collin and his brother Scott up on stage to sing harmony. Billing himself as Bubba, Collin and Scott founded the country-rock Wray Brothers Band in the late '70s and moved out West to perform. The Wray Brothers

made their recording debut on CIS in 1983 and had some chart success with their first single "Reason to Believe." Over the next four years, the Wrays released a number of singles on different record labels, but had no real success until 1987, when they had a Top 50 hit with "You Lay a Lotta Love on Me." Following the single's success, the band broke up.

After the Wrays disbanded, Collin began performing on his own in Nevada clubs. In 1991, he signed to Epic and released his solo debut, *All I Can Be*. Raye's first single, "All I Can Be (Is a Sweet Memory)," reached the country Top 40 but it was his second single, "Love, Me," that made him a star. "Love, Me" climbed to No. 1 in early 1992 and stayed at the top of the charts for three weeks, kick-starting a string of Top Ten hits that ran for a number of years. Raye's second album, *In This Life* (1992), went gold and produced three hits, including "Somebody Else's Moon." He released his third album, *Extremes*, in 1994 and it went gold by the end of the year, spawning the Top Ten hits "Little Rock," "Man of My Word," and "My Kind of Girl." In 1995, Raye released his fourth solo album, *I Think About You*, which went gold within a few months of its release. —*Sandra Brennan*

All I Can Be / Dec. 1990 / Epic ✦✦
In This Life / Aug. 25, 1992 / Epic ✦✦✦
The soft-focus, yet rugged, album art helped to establish Raye as the heartthrob his silky smooth tenor makes him out to be. Inside, it's an even smoother mix than *All I Can Be*, with Raye indulging his tendencies at every turn, including a revival of the Everly Brothers' make-out classic "Let It Be Me." The hit "I Want You Bad (And That Ain't Good)" put some sweat and muscle into Raye's image, but even the trucker song, "Latter Day Cowboy," sounds like it was written for the women back home. The album also includes "In This Life," a No. 1 hit; "Somebody Else's Moon"; and "That Was a River." —*Brian Mansfield*

● **Extremes** / 1994 / Epic ✦✦✦✦
Tired of the balladeer image "Love, Me" and "In This Life" had tagged him with, Raye set out to show that he was made of stronger material. The first single, the rollicking "That's My Story," was a Lee Roy Parnell tune that Raye roared through. *Extremes*, as its title suggested, caromed recklessly from that type of song to, of course, ballads—but "Little Rock," about a recovering alcoholic, and "Dreaming My Dreams with You," earlier cut by Waylon Jennings, were two of the most powerful recordings of Raye's career. —*Brian Mansfield*

I Think About You / 1995 / Epic ✦✦✦✦
After attempting a somewhat rougher approach with *Extremes*, Collin Raye returned to his smooth ballad stylings on *I Think About You*. Though he still sings the occasional honky tonk raver, the high points on his fourth album come when he slows the pace down. *I Think About You* does suffer from a few bland tracks, but the album does demonstrate why Raye was one of the most popular country singers of the mid-'90s. —*Stephen Thomas Erlewine*

The Red Clay Ramblers

Old-Time
One of the most authentic of the string-band revival groups, the Red Clay Ramblers perform traditional Appalachian folk music, contemporary compositions, and mixed genres with such talent and authority that for years they have been considered among the best of the modern revivalists of string-band music. The Chapel Hill, NC-based quintet includes Tommy Thompson (banjo, vocals), Jim Watson (guitar, mandolin, vocals), Mike Craver (piano, harmonium, vocals), Jack Herrick (bouzouki, guitar, harmonica, bass, cello, flute, harmonium, vocals), and Clay Buckner (fiddle, harmonica, vocals). The Ramblers reach their widest audience through their work scoring and performing in off-Broadway productions, something they have been doing since 1975. One of their most highly acclaimed albums is from their score of Sam Shepard's *A Lie of the Mind*. —*David Vinopal and Sandra Brennan*

● **Twisted Laurel/Merchants Lunch** / 1991 / Flying Fish ✦✦✦✦
Two of the Red Clay Ramblers' best albums—*Twisted Laurel* (1976) and *Merchant's Lunch* (1977)—are collected on this outstanding two-fer CD. This is the sound of the band coming into its own. —*Thom Owens*

Jerry Reed (Jerry Reed Hubbard)

b. Mar. 20, 1937, Atlanta, GA
Guitar / Instrumental, Progressive Country, Bluegrass
Before there were *Smokey and the Bandit I & II, Gator, W. W. and the Dixie Dance Kings*, and *BAT 21*, there was Jerry Reed—a guitarist and singer-songwriter whose musical talents have now been overshadowed by his roles on the silver screen. Reed first made his reputation as a hot studio guitarist. More fame came when Elvis Presley made hits of two Reed compositions, "Guitar Man" and "US Male." In 1970 his "Amos Moses" reached No. 1, resulting in a Grammy. Three other Reed singles reached No. 1: "When You're Hot, You're Hot," "Lord, Mr. Ford," and "She Got the Goldmine (I Got the Shaft)." His fast-playing, fast-talking performances have shown Reed to be a man of many talents. —*David Vinopal*

When You're Hot You're Hot / 1971 / RCA ✦✦✦✦
Wild and loose, this is Reed's best album. —*Dan Heilman*

Best of Jerry Reed / 1972 / RCA ✦✦✦✦
It features several key hits ("Amos Moses," "Guitar Man," "When You're Hot, You're Hot") and some crackling instrumentals. Alimony-payers looking for "She Got the Goldmine (I Got the Shaft)" will be disappointed, however. It's not here. —*Dan Cooper*

● **The Essential Jerry Reed** / Aug. 1, 1995 / RCA ✦✦✦✦
The Essential Jerry Reed contains over 20 of the singer-songwriter's greatest hits, from "Amos Moses" to "East Bound and Down," hitting the No. 1s "When You're Hot, You're Hot," "Lord, Mr. Ford," and "She Got the Goldmine (I Got the Shaft)." In addition to the hits, there's a handful of obscurities, but it remains the best single overview of Reed's career. —*Thom Owens*

Jim Reeves (James Travis Reeves)

b. Aug. 20, 1924, Galloway, TX, **d.** Jul. 31, 1964, outside Nashville
Guitar, Vocals / Country-Pop, Nashville Sound/Countrypolitan
Gentleman Jim Reeves was perhaps the biggest male star to emerge from the Nashville Sound. His mellow baritone voice and muted velvet orchestration combined to create a sound that echoed around the world and has lasted to this day. Detractors will call the sound country-pop (or plain pop), but none can argue against the large audience that loves this music. Reeves was capable of singing hard country ("Mexican Joe" went to No. 1 in 1953). From 1955 ("Bimbo") through 1969, Reeves was without exception in the charts, country and/or pop—an amazing fact in light of his untimely death in an airplane accident in 1964. "Four Walls" (1957) and especially "He'll Have to Go" (1957) solidified the reputation of Reeves as the Crooner of Country. After his death a near-cult developed, and songs of his released after his death actually outsold his previous hits, with six No. 1 hits coming in a three-year period following his burial. (These include "I Guess I'm Crazy," "Is It Really Over?," and "Blue Side of Lonesome.") Hits in the '70s continued, with "Angels Don't Lie" and "Don't Let Me Cross Over." Through technical wizardry he had duet hits in the early '80s: "Take Me in Your Arms and Hold Me" with Deborah Allen, and "Have You Ever Been Lonely?" with his smooth-singing female counterpart of the plush Nashville Sound, Patsy Cline, who also perished in an airplane crash, in 1963. —*David Vinopal*

☆ **He'll Have to Go & Other Hits** / 1960 / RCA ✦✦✦✦✦
There may have been other country crooners as smooth, but no one else in his era had the hand-in-glove marriage of great songs and appropriate "countripolitan" production. This brief collection doesn't contain all of his biggest hits, but the most essential singles—"He'll Have to Go," "Four Walls," "Billy Bayou," and "Anna Marie," among others—are included. —*Mark A. Humphrey*

Live at the Grand Ole Opry / 1987 / Country Music Foundation ✦✦✦

★ **Four Walls—The Legend Begins** / Aug. 1991 / RCA ✦✦✦✦✦
Four Walls—The Legend Begins collects 20 songs Jim Reeves recorded between 1953 and 1957, including his earliest hits, "Mexican Joe," "Bimbo," "According to My Heart," and "My Lips Are Sealed." —*Stephen Thomas Erlewine*

★ **Welcome to My World: The Essential Jim Reeves Collection** / 1993 / RCA ✦✦✦✦✦
A double disc box set that offers an overview of his entire career, even if its balance is a bit uneven. Beginning with his early '50s hits, the box runs through most of his biggest hits, concentrating on his smooth countrypolitan '60s hits. Though fans of his early honky tonk material will feel that side of Reeves is overlooked, *Welcome to My World* is the best overall Reeves retrospective available. —*Stephen Thomas Erlewine*

The Essential Jim Reeves / Aug. 1, 1995 / RCA ✦✦✦✦
The Essential Jim Reeves runs through 20 of Reeves' biggest hits, throwing in a couple of rarities along the way. It's by no means definitive, but it offers a good introduction to his countrypolitan sound. —*Stephen Thomas Erlewine*

Gentleman Jim 1955-1959 / Bear Family ✦✦✦✦
This four-disc set, has Reeves' first ventures into pop as well as some of his best country performances of such favorites as "Am I Losing You?," "Just Call Me Lonesome," "According to My Heart," and others. A discography accompanies the set. —*AMG*

Charlie Rich

b. Dec. 14, 1932, Forest City, AK, **d.** Jul. 24, 1995
Piano, Vocals / Traditional Country, Country-Pop, Rockabilly, Nashville Sound/Countrypolitan
Charlie Rich was simultaneously one of the most critically acclaimed and most erratic country singers of the post-World War II era. Rich had all the elements of being one of the great country stars of the '60s and '70s, but his popularity never matched his critical notices. What made him a critical favorite also kept him from mass success. Throughout his career, Rich willfully bent genres, fusing country, jazz, blues, gospel,

rockabilly, and soul. Though he had 45 country hits in a career that spanned nearly four decades, he became best-known for his lush, Billy Sherrill-produced countrypolitan records of the early '70s. Instead of embracing the stardom those records brought him, Rich shunned it, retreating into semi-retirement by the '80s.

Charlie Rich began his professional musical career while he was enlisted in the US Air Force in the early '50s. While he was stationed in Oklahoma, he formed a group called the Velvetones, which played jazz and blues and featured his fiancée, Margaret Ann, on lead vocals. Rich left the military in 1956, and he began performing clubs around the Memphis area, playing both jazz and R&B; he also began writing his own material. Rich managed to land a job as a session musician for Judd Records, which was owned by Judd Phillips, the brother of Sun Records founder Sam Phillips. Around this time, saxophonist and Sun recording artist Bill Justis heard Charlie play at the Sharecropper Club and asked the pianist to write arrangements for him. Sam Phillips saw Rich perform with Justis at a club gig and asked him to record some demos at Sun Studios. Phillips rejected the resulting demos, claiming they were too jazzy. After absorbing some Jerry Lee Lewis records Justis gave him, Rich quickly returned to Sun and became a regular session musician for the label in 1958, playing and/or singing on records by Lewis, Johnny Cash, Justis, Warren Smith, Billy Lee Riley, Carl Mann, and Ray Smith. He was also writing songs, including "Break Up" for Jerry Lee Lewis, "The Ways of a Woman in Love" for Johnny Cash, and "I'm Comin' Home" for Carl Mann, which was later cut by Elvis Presley.

In August of 1958, Rich released his first single, "Whirlwind," for the Sun subsidiary Phillips International. Throughout 1959, he recorded a number of songs at Sun, though only a handful were actually released. Rich didn't have a hit until 1960, when his third Phillips International single, "Lonely Weekends," became a Top 30 pop hit. However, none of its seven follow-up singles were a success, though several of the songs would become staples in his set, including "Who Will the Next Fool Be?," "Sittin' and Thinkin'," and "Midnight Blues." In the early '60s, Rich's career remained stalled. He left Sun Records in 1964, signing with Groove, a newly-established subsidiary of RCA. His first single, "Big Boss Man," was an underground, word-of-mouth hit, but its Chet Atkins-produced follow-ups all stiffed. On Groove, he jazzily interpreted standards, but he also performed a handful of originals, including "Tomorrow Night" and "I Don't See Me in Your Eyes Anymore." Groove went out of business by the beginning of 1965, leaving Rich without a record contract.

Under the direction of Shelby Singleton, Smash Records signed Charlie Rich early in 1965. Singleton and Rich's producer Jerry Kennedy encouraged the pianist to emphasize his country and rock 'n' roll leanings. The first single for Smash was "Mohair Sam," an R&B-inflected novelty number written by Dallas Frazier. "Mohair Sam" became a Top 30 pop hit, but none of its follow-ups were successful. Again, Rich changed labels, moving over to Hi Records where he recorded straight country, but none of his singles for the label made any impression on the country charts.

Despite his lack of consistent commercial success, Epic Records signed Charlie Rich in 1967, mainly on the recommendation of producer Billy Sherrill. Sherrill helped Rich refashion himself as a Nashville-based, smooth, middle-of-the-road balladeer. At first, the singles were only moderately successful—"Set Me Free" and "Raggedy Ann" charted in the mid-40s in 1968—but persistence paid off in the summer of 1972, when "I Take It On Home" rocketed to No. 6. "I Take It On Home" set the stage for Rich's big breakthrough into the mainstream, 1973's *Behind Closed Doors*. The title track from the record became a No. 1 hit early in 1973, crossing over into the Top 20 on the pop charts. Following the success of *Behind Closed Doors*, RCA re-released "Tomorrow Night" and it reached the Top 30, but it was "The Most Beautiful Girl," the proper follow-up to his first No. 1 single, that established him as a star. "The Most Beautiful Girl" spent three weeks at the top of the country charts and two weeks at the top of the pop charts. *Behind Closed Doors* won three awards from the Country Music Association that year: Best Male Vocalist, Album of the Year, and Single of the Year for the title track. The album was also certified Gold, Rich won a Grammy for Best Country Vocal Performance, Male, and he also took home four ACM awards.

After "The Most Beautiful Girl," No. 1 hits came quickly—"There Won't Be Anymore" (re-released from his RCA sessions), "A Very Special Love Song," "I Don't See Me in Your Eyes Anymore" (also from RCA), "I Love My Friend," and "She Called Me Baby" (RCA) all topped the country charts, and several of the songs also crossed over into the pop charts. Mercury began re-releasing his Smash recordings and two of them—"A Field of Yellow Daisies" and "Something Just Came Over Me"—became minor hits. All of this success led the CMA to name him Entertainer of the Year in 1974.

Rich didn't quite dominate the charts in 1975 as he did the previous year, but he did have three Top Five hits: "My Elusive Dreams," "Every Time You Touch Me (I Get High)," and "All Over Me," plus the Top Ten "Since I Fell For You." Even though he was at the peak of his popularity,

Rich had begun to drink heavily, causing considerable problems offstage. His destructive behavior culminated at the CMA ceremony for 1975, when he presented the award for that year's Entertainer of the Year. Instead of reading the name of the winner, he set fire to the certificate that named the new winner, who happened to be John Denver. Fans and industry insiders were outraged, and Rich had trouble having hits throughout 1976—none of his singles cracked the Top 20.

The slump in his career couldn't be completely attributed to Rich's behavior. His records had begun to sound increasingly similar, as he and Sherrill were working over the same territory they began exploring in 1968. There were exceptions—such as 1976's acclaimed gospel record, *Silver Linings*—but it took Rich until 1977 to break back into the Top Ten with the No. 1 "Rollin' with the Flow." Early in 1978, he signed with United Artists and throughout that year, he had hits on both Epic and UA. Rich worked with Larry Butler at UA, a producer that had a similar style to Sherrill. Epic continued to have hits, as "Beautiful Woman" reached the Top Ten in the summer and a duet with Janie Fricke, "On My Knees," became his last No. 1 hit that fall. "I'll Wake You Up When I Get Home," taken from the Clint Eastwood movie *Every Which Way But Loose*, was a No. 3 hit early in 1979; it would be his last Top Ten single.

Rich struggled to have a big hit throughout 1979, but none of his singles were anything more than a minor success. In 1980, he switched labels to Elektra, resulting in the No. 12 single "A Man Just Don't Know What a Woman Goes Through" in the fall of that year. One more Top 40 hit followed—"Are We Dreamin' the Same Dream" early in 1981—but Charlie Rich decided to remove himself from the spotlight. For over a decade, Rich was silent, living in semi-retirement and only playing the occasional concert. He returned in 1992 with *Pictures and Paintings*, a jazzy record produced by journalist Peter Guralnick and released on Sire.

Pictures and Paintings received positive reviews and restored Rich's reputation, but it would be his last record. Charlie Rich died from a blood clot in his lung in the summer of 1995, when he was travelling to Florida with his wife Margaret Ann. — *Stephen Thomas Erlewine*

Set Me Free / 1968 / Koch ◆◆◆◆
Set Me Free was Charlie Rich's first album for Epic Records and the first record he ever cut with Nashville producer Billy Sherrill. Previously, Rich's producers hadn't known what to do with his eclectic style, although his sessions for Smash came close to capturing all sides of his personality. With Sherrill, Rich had a producer whose musical tastes were nearly as eclectic as his own, and that is captured on the freewheeling, diverse sounds of *Set Me Free*. Purists may be uncomfortable with Sherrill's lush production—he sets Rich's voice in a bed of strings, keyboards, horns, and backing vocals. Consequently, the sound of *Set Me Free* is laid back and relaxed; occasionally, Rich sounds *too* relaxed, as if he didn't connect with the material. Although there are a handful of poor songs and half-hearted performances on the record, *Set Me Free* has an overall tone lacking on Rich's previous records that makes up for the assorted weaknesses. The songs come from a variety of sources, ranging from country and blues to jazz and pop, but they're all given a cohesive Nashville production by Sherrill, which is what makes *Set Me Free* one of Rich's best, most consistent albums. — *Stephen Thomas Erlewine*

☆ **Fabulous Charlie Rich** / 1969 / Koch ◆◆◆◆◆
This album follows the same formula as its predecessor *Set Me Free*, but to more successful results. For starters, there's a more consistent set of material—these are songs that Rich can really sink his teeth into, as evidenced by the beautiful, melancholic "Life Has Its Little Ups and Downs" (written by his wife, Margaret Ann) and his own "Sittin' and Thinkin'." Furthermore, the core of each song—from the blues of "July 12, 1939" and "Bright Lights, Big City" (which is done essentially as a Jimmy Reed medley, performed in the style of Ray Charles) to the soulful "I Almost Lost My Mind" and the country-pop stylings of "San Francisco Is a Lonely Town" and "Love Waits for Me"—are more apparent, thanks to Sherrill's relatively trimmed-down production. There are still strings, vocal choruses, and horns, throughout the album, but Sherrill has incorporated them into Rich's style more effectively. Occasionally, there is a fairly uninspired number, but *The Fabulous Charlie Rich* does capture the eclectic nature of Rich's music better than the great majority of his albums, even if the sumptuous production will make it less palatable for country purists. — *Stephen Thomas Erlewine*

Boss Man / Aug. 1970 / Epic ◆◆◆◆
Charlie Rich and Billy Sherrill reached a peak with *The Fabulous Charlie Rich*, creating a perfect middle ground between Rich's rootsier tendencies and Sherrill's country-pop leanings. Like many of Rich's records, it didn't sell and that might have been one of the reasons its follow-up, *Boss Man*, was their weakest effort to date. Although there are quite a few high spots and the album essentially follows the same formula as their previous efforts, the material isn't consistent, alternating between bluesy shuffles and country weepers; both styles range from the brilliant to the boring. What's even worse is the fact that Rich sounds uninspired himself, giving competent but unenthusiastic performances. There's enough prime material to make *Boss Man* an enjoyable listen, particu-

larly for Rich fans that know that he rarely comes up with consistent albums. However, it didn't have the spark of *The Fabulous Charlie Rich*, nor did it have the immaculate sheen of *Behind Close Doors*, the country-pop masterpiece that followed *Boss Man*. Nevertheless, *Boss Man* has enough fine songs to make it an essential purchase for true Rich fans. *—Stephen Thomas Erlewine*

☆ **Behind Closed Doors** / 1973 / Epic ♦♦♦♦♦
Charlie Rich had been heading toward full-blown country-pop on his previous Epic records, but *Behind Closed Doors* is where Billy Sherrill pulled out all of the stops and created a heavily orchestrated, pop-oriented album. It's to Rich's credit that he never sounds like he's drowning amidst the grand production and layers of instruments—in an odd way, he thrives. While this album doesn't have the casual eclecticism that distinguished all of Rich's past recordings, it is an expertly crafted album. All of the material, from the hit singles ("Behind Closed Doors," "The Most Beautiful Girl," "I Take It on Home") to the album tracks, are classy songs, designed to appeal to a maturing country audience. Furthermore, the arrangements expertly walk the line between pop and schmaltz—the sound of *Behind Closed Doors* is *the* sound of early '70s countrypolitan and numerous artists used the record as a template for their own style. Rich made better, grittier records, but the combined collaborative effort of the vocalist and Sherrill resulted in a seamless, influential work. *—Stephen Thomas Erlewine*

Greatest Hits / 1976 / Epic ♦♦♦♦
This focuses on his biggest hits ("Behind Close Doors," "The Most Beautiful Girl") though not necessarily the most representative work. Ignore the cheesy production, however, and you'll hear his vocals as utterly sublime. *—Dan Cooper*

American Originals / 1989 / Columbia ♦♦♦♦
Essentially the same material as the Epic *Greatest Hits*, it adds the almost claustrophobically intimate version of "Since I Fell for You." *—Dan Cooper*

Pictures and Paintings / 1992 / Sire ♦♦♦♦
Charlie Rich's comeback album *Pictures and Paintings*—which would turn out to be his final recording—is one of his most rewarding records. It is a stripped-down, relaxed album that captures Rich running through a mixture of covers, originals, and new versions of his classics, like "Don't Put No Headstone on My Grave." It's one of the few albums he made that captures all facets of his talent, featuring jazzy playing, bluesy singing, and simple, straightforward country. *—Stephen Thomas Erlewine*

★ **The Complete Smash Sessions** / Aug. 4, 1992 / Mercury ♦♦♦♦♦
The Complete Smash Sessions contains everything that Charlie Rich recorded and released for Smash during the mid-'60s. Many of these songs foreshadow the music Elvis Presley would make during his comeback in 1968, as well as the country-pop of the early '70s. Skillfully mixing rock, blues, R&B, country, and soul, Rich was at the top of his form when he made this music. He may have only had one hit during this period—"Mohair Sam" reached No. 21 in 1965—but his tenure at Smash remained one of his most fruitful and creative periods. *—Stephen Thomas Erlewine*

★ **Lonely Weekends: Best of the Sun Years** / Mar. 19, 1996 / AVI ♦♦♦♦♦
We will never really know what Charlie Rich could have ultimately produced in the studio given free reign; there's no Charlie Rich jazz album, no Charlie Rich solo boogie woogie album, no fully realized Charlie Rich gospel album. For the few years that producer Billy Sherrill got him to sit still long enough to be pigeonholed into the countrypolitan movement, the "Silver Fox" hits that ultimately graced all his obituaries came out one after another, like pre-packaged sausages being fitted into their restrictive casings but giving us only a small taste from Rich's diverse musical menu. But if you really want to get in on the ground floor and experience some of the wide variety and depth of the man's prodigious talents, here's exactly where you go to get straight. All the early hits like "Lonely Weekends," "Sittin' and Thinkin'" and "Who Will the Next Fool Be" are aboard, along with several stereo tracks remixed from the original multi-track masters for the first time ever with sparkling sound. Sam Phillips pretty much let Rich do whatever he wanted to do, cutting everything from great heartfelt ballad material, slick rockers, and classics that skirted all sides of the musical terrain to attempts at being commercial that were awkward that to hear them today will make even the staunchest Sun fan wince in discomfort. That's why this comp's so refreshing—no filler, no dumb stuff, just the best tracks from a five- or six- year period when Rich was one of the last glimmers of hope for Sun, starting his recording career just about the time that Jerry Lee's career was in tatters and Johnny Cash was getting ready to leave the label. Compiler and Sun expert Colin Escott just picks the cool ones and gives an overview on the inside that's right on target. Charlie Rich was one very talented man and here's where you find some of his best. *—Cub Koda*

The Sun Sessions / 1996 / Varese Vintage ♦♦♦♦
A concise collection of the best material that Rich recorded for Sun in the late '50s and early '60s for those who only want a single disc's worth, rather than the lengthier Sun retrospectives that have been available on import. This has all of his key singles from the era ("Lonely Weekends," "Who Will the Next Fool Be," "Midnight Blues," "Philadelphia Baby"), as well as some choice B-sides and other hard-to-find tracks. The harder-rocking cuts show that Rich could be a convincing rockabilly singer, while the bluesier sides show his versatility and sensitivity. *—Richie Unterberger*

Riders in the Sky

Beginning each performance with their trademark greeting "Mighty fine and a great big Western 'Howdy,' all you buckaroos and buckarettes," Riders in the Sky simultaneously paid tribute and poked gentle fun at classic B-movie cowboy songs from the '40s and '50s, particularly the songs of Roy Rogers and Gene Autry. During the '70s and '80s, the Riders built a strong cult following in America, especially on college campuses.

The Riders in the Sky are comprised of Ranger Doug (born Douglas B. Green; lead singer), Woody Paul (born Paul Chrisman; fiddle, vocals), and Too Slim (string bass, guitar, accordion). Before forming the band, the Michigan-born Ranger Doug was a member of Bill Monroe's Bluegrass Boys and was a country music journalist, editing the *Country Music Foundation Press* and the *Journal of Country Music*. Prior to joining the Rangers, Woody Paul played fiddle with Loggins and Messina and Too Slim was a member of Dickey Lee's band, in addition to being a songwriter. The trio formed in the mid-'70s, playing a weekly gig at a local Nashville nightclub. Their residency led to a job with TNN's *Tumbleweed Theater*. Between 1983 and 1986, the group hosted the cable television show. In the early '80s they also signed to Rounder and released five albums. In 1985, the Riders in the Sky appeared in *Sweet Dreams*, the film biography of Patsy Cline. The group signed to MCA in 1987, releasing their first album for the label—*Riders Radio Theater*—a year later. The record was a success, which led to the band hosting *Riders Radio Theater* on National Public Radio. They recorded two more albums with MCA and in 1991 moved to Columbia where they recorded the children's album *Harmony Ranch*. This led to a CBS-TV Saturday-morning television show which ran for one season. In 1991, Ranger Doug received a Wrangler Award from the Cowboy Hall of Fame for his 1990 song "The Line Rider" and received it again in 1993 for co-writing "The First Cowboy Song" with Gary McMann. The Riders in the Sky continued recording and touring through the mid-'90s. *—Sandra Brennan*

Cowboys In Love / 1994 / Epic ♦♦♦♦
Putting the skits aside for the time being, the Riders focus largely on their underrated musical ability. Ranger Doug shows off his sublime baritone on several Western-style love songs, including an exquisite duet with Emmylou Harris on "One Has My Name, the Other Has My Heart." The instrumentals, especially Woody Paul's expert fiddling, are superb, as is the spirited take with guests Asleep at the Wheel on "I'm a Ding Dong Daddy from Dumas." *—Michael McCall*

● **Best of the West Rides Again** / Rounder ♦♦♦♦
These 25 tracks were culled from their first five Rounder albums, over an hour's worth of music in all. *—Mark A. Humphrey*

Jeannie C. Riley (Jeannie Carolyn Stephenson)

b. Sep. 19, 1945, Anson, TX
Vocals / Gospel, Country-Pop
Tom T. Hall's song about small-town hypocrisy did a lot for his reputation, but it also made Jeannie C. Riley a star. "Harper Valley P.T.A." sold 6 million copies, went gold as far away as Australia, and in 1968 brought a Grammy to its singer. Other hits followed, including "The Girl Most Likely," but nothing was going to match her initial success. Riley eventually moved to gospel. *—David Vinopal*

Harper Valley P.T.A. & Other Greatest Hits / Rhino ♦♦♦♦
Jeannie C. Riley's biggest hits are compiled on *Harper Valley P.T.A. & Other Hits*, including, of course, the title track and several lesser hits. *—Thom Owens*

Tex Ritter (Woodward Maurice Ritter)

b. Jan. 12, 1905, Murval, TX, d. Jan. 2, 1973, Nashville, TN
Guitar, Vocals / Traditional Country, Cowboy
Father of TV's John Ritter ("Three's Company"), Woodward Maurice "Tex" Ritter was a college-educated Broadway performer long before he rode into the sunset as a singing cowboy of the silver screen. *Song of the Gringo* in 1936 started a movie career that was to last through nearly 60 horse operas. As one of the first artists to sign with the newly-created Capitol label, in 1942 Ritter recorded enough hits ("There's a New Moon Over My Shoulder," "Deck of Cards," "Boll Weevil") to make him one of the better-selling country singers in the '40s. Nothing before or after matched the theme song of *High Noon*, starring Gary Cooper. This movie

did what all the "B" Westerns couldn't—it made Ritter a national star. —*David Vinopal*

Country Music Hall of Fame / 1991 / MCA ✦✦✦✦
Pure Texan, Ritter was grittier than most of Hollywood's singing cowboys and nearer the roots of western song. His 1935-39 sides are here. —*Mark A. Humphrey*

● **Capitol Collectors Series** / Feb. 17, 1992 / Capitol ✦✦✦✦
Ritter spent more than three decades with Capitol, and the 25 songs (including the great "Rye Whiskey" and "Blood on the Saddle") on this well-annotated set feature Ritter's yelping theatricality at its best. —*Michael McCall*

Marty Robbins (Martin David Robbins)

b. Sep. 26, 1925, Glendale, AZ, **d.** Dec. 8, 1982, Nashville, TN
Guitar, Vocals / Country, Nashville Sound/Countrypolitan
No artist in the history of country music has had a more stylistically diverse career than Marty Robbins. Never content to remain just a country singer, Robbins performed successfully in a dazzling array of styles during more than thirty years in the business. To his credit, Robbins rarely followed trends, but often took off in directions that stunned both his peers and fans. Plainly Robbins was not hemmed in by anyone's definition of country music. Although his earliest recordings were unremarkable weepers, by the mid '50s Robbins was making forays into rock music, adding fiddles to the works of Chuck Berry and Little Richard. By the late '50s, Robbins had pop hits of his own with teen fare like "A White Sport Coat." Almost simultaneously, he completed work on his *Hawaiian Songs of the Islands* album. In 1959, Robbins stretched even further with the hit single "El Paso," thus heralding a pattern of "gunfighter ballads" that lasted the balance of his career. Robbins also enjoyed bluesy hits like "Don't Worry," which introduced a pop audience to fuzztone guitar in 1961. Barely a year later, Robbins scored a calypso hit with "Devil Woman." Marty Robbins also left a legacy of gospel music and a string of sentimental ballads, showing that he would croon with nary a touch of hillbilly twang.

Although it is fashionable to criticize such diversity, Robbins was not simply a dabbler. The truth is he was possessed of a superb voice and the ability to adapt it to an unprecedented range of styles. It also didn't hurt that most of Robbins's biggest hits were his own compositions. Robbins literally established trends, then, while others swarmed in to capitalize, he moved on to other pursuits. If you already know some of Robbins' music, choose a different phase to sample. There is bound to be some aspect you haven't heard. If you are unfamiliar with any of it, the new CBS sampler covers more than a quarter of a century of his career and can be used as a smorgasborg to help define your preferences. There is a lot to enjoy here. —*Hank Davis*

Hawaii's Calling Me / 1963 / Bear Family ✦✦✦
Take a complete look at Robbins' Hawaiian period on these 28 tracks. —*Hank Davis*

☆ **All-Time Greatest Hits** / 1972 / Columbia/Legacy ✦✦✦✦✦
Released in 1972, the double-album/single-CD *All-Time Greatest Hits* remains one of the best compilations ever assembled on Marty Robbins. Featuring 20 tracks—including most of his big hits—there are very few essential tracks missing from the collection. As an introduction, this relatively concise compilation is a bit more manageable than the double-disc *Essential Marty Robbins* and, therefore, is more attractive to neophytes. —*Stephen Thomas Erlewine*

☆ **Rockin' Rollin' Robbins** / 1985 / Bear Family ✦✦✦✦✦
The jewel of Bear Family's exhaustive Robbins reissue project, the title does not lie. He shakes and rattles in fine style on "That's Allright," "Maybelline," "Singing the Blues," and 14 other good rockin' numbers. Much of this material appeared on a 1956 album of the same name, which is many country LP collectors' Holy Grail. —*Dan Cooper*

★ **The Essential Marty Robbins: 1951-1982** / 1991 / Columbia ✦✦✦✦✦
Beware of greatest-hits compilations by Marty Robbins. He had a long and unusually varied career. There are certain phases that will appeal to not everyone's taste (e.g., early hillbilly era 1951-54; pop-rock 1954-58; gunfighter ballads; calypso; sentimental ballads). This collection contains 50 tracks on two CDs or cassettes, including 16 digitally remastered songs that hit No. 1. —*Hank Davis*

Country 1951-1958 / 1991 / Bear Family ✦✦✦✦
Listeners charmed by his pre-*El Paso* country have a motherlode to explore in this five-disc boxed set filled with dewy-eyed weepers (his earliest recordings), his rockabilly (he cut the first cover of "Maybellene"), ancient country-folk accompanied solely by acoustic guitar ("The Dream of the Miner's Chill"), Hawaiiana ("Aloha Oe"), and a handful of his country-pop outings arranged by Ray Conniff. —*Mark A. Humphrey*

★ **The Story of My Life: The Best of Marty Robbins** / 1996 / Columbia/Legacy ✦✦✦✦✦
18-song collection of his biggest chart hits from 1952-65. Some serious

fans may claim that it's way too cursory, but for most who want just one Robbins disc, it'll do pretty nicely. —*Richie Unterberger*

Under Western Skies / Feb. 1996 / Bear Family ✦✦✦✦
Bear Family's four-disc set *Under Western Skies* collects all of Marty Robbins' Western and cowboy-themed albums from the '50s and '60s. For the hardcore collector, there's plenty of interest here, but the material is too specialized to appeal to any but diehard fans. —*Stephen Thomas Erlewine*

Jimmie Rodgers (James Charles Rodgers)

b. Sep. 8, 1897, Meridan, MS, **d.** May 26, 1933, New York, NY
Banjo, Guitar, Vocals / Traditional Country
In 1927 Ralph Peer, an RCA talent scout, placed an ad offering auditions for local hillbilly talent. The results exceeded his wildest expectations: on August 1st and 2nd he recorded the Carter Family, and two days later, a gaunt, ex-railroad man, Jimmie Rodgers. His brass plaque in the Country Music Hall of Fame reads, "Jimmie Rodgers' name stands foremost in the country music field as *the man who started it all.*" This is a fair assessment. The "Singing Brakeman" and the "Mississippi Blue Yodeler," whose six-year career was cut short by tuberculosis, became the first nationally known star of country music and the direct influence of many later performers such as Hank Snow, Ernest Tubb, Hank Williams, Lefty Frizzell, and Merle Haggard. Rodgers sang about rounders and gamblers, bounders, and ramblers—and he knew of what he sang. At age 14 he went to work as a railroad brakeman, and on the rails he stayed until a pulmonary hemorrhage sidetracked him to the medicine show circuit in 1925. The years with trains harmed his health but helped his music. In an era when Rodgers' contemporaries were singing only mountain and mountain/folk music, he fused country (hillbilly), gospel, jazz, Black blues, Appalachian soul, pop, cowboy, and folk; and many of his best songs were his compositions, including "TB Blues," "Waiting for a Train," "Travelin' Blues," "Train Whistle Blues," and his 13 blue yodels. He was the first musician inducted into the Hall of Fame, in 1961.

Although Rodgers wasn't the first to yodel on records, his style was distinct from all the others. His yodel wasn't merely sugar-coating on the song, it was as important as the lyric, mournful and plaintive or happy and carefree, depending on a song's emotional content. His instrumental accompaniment consisted sometimes of his guitar only, while at other times a full jazz band (horns and all) backed him up. Country fans could have asked for no better hero/star—someone who thought what they thought, felt what they felt, and sang about the common person honestly and beautifully. In his last recording session, Rodgers was so racked and ravaged by TB that a cot had to be set up in the studio, so he could rest before attempting that one song more. No wonder Jimmie Rodgers is to this day loved by country music fans. —*David Vinopal*

☆ **First Sessions** / Jan. 1991 / Rounder ✦✦✦✦✦
The opening volume in Rounder's mammoth eight-disc Jimmie Rodgers reissue series presents his earliest, and in some cases, most tentatively performed material from 1927 and 1928. Rodgers quickly makes the leap from raw, engaging singer to emphatic, distinctive artist, and midway through has established a singular sound and riveting delivery, with his trademark yodel, and mastery of blues inflection. These cuts include the signature track "Blue Yodel," plus other classics such as "In the Jailhouse Now," "Treasures Untold," and "Memphis Yodel," as well as "The Brakemen's Blues." Things would never be the same for Rodgers, and these were the songs that helped make him an institution. —*Ron Wynn*

☆ **The Early Years 1928-29** / Feb. 1991 / Rounder ✦✦✦✦✦
The second disc in the Jimmie Rodgers series covers 1928 and 1929, the years in which Rodgers solidified his stature as a premier performer. These 16 tracks saw him doing both his brilliant solo yodeling blues and also working with bands on some cuts. "Desert Blues" featured Rodgers backed by a group with cornet, clarinet, tuba, and piano among the instrumentation. Steel guitarist John Westbrook provided tingling accompaniment on "I'm Lonely and Blue," "My Carolina Sunshine Girl," and "Blue Yodel No. 4." But once more, it's such cuts as "Daddy and Home," "You and My Old Guitar" and "Never No Mo' Blues" that are the triumphs, with Rodgers simply wailing, singing and yodeling, displaying the emotional clout and memorable style that turned these numbers into anthems. —*Ron Wynn*

☆ **On the Way Up 1929** / Mar. 1991 / Rounder ✦✦✦✦✦
This third Jimmie Rodgers disc in the eight-CD line covers arguably his greatest year, 1929. Rodgers scored huge hits doing popular novelty cuts like "Frankie and Johnny," and railroad numbers like "Train Whistle Blues," and continued cutting yodeling tunes, as well as cowboy songs and bawdy blues. The 17 cuts include the marvelous "Everybody Does It in Hawaii," with Weldon Burkes on ukulele and Joe Kapo on steel, and the memorable "Hobo Bill's Last Rides." The session also contains alternate takes of "The Land of My Boyhood Dreams" and "Frankie and Johnny." Rodgers was now ably mixing identities and personas, alternating between yodeling blues singer, railroad narrator and carefree cowboy. —*Ron Wynn*

★ **Riding High 1929-1930** / Apr. 1991 / Rounder ✦✦✦✦✦
Jimmie Rodgers was enjoying the fruits of his labors in 1929 and 1930, the years covered on this fourth CD in Rounder's historic eight-disc retrospective series. The 17 numbers highlighted here were done either during his final 1929 session or in the next year. They're primarily yodeling blues tunes, with Rodgers backed by guitarist Billy Burkes. There are two versions of "Anniversary Blue Yodel (Blue Yodel No. 7)," "Mississippi River Blues" and "Why Did You Give Me Your Love?," as well as stark, marvelous numbers like "She Was Happy Till She Met You," "A Drunkard's Child," and "Why Should I Be Lonely." This set also includes Rodgers working with Lani McIntire's Hawaiians on two tunes and with Bob Sawyer's Jazz Band on the finale, "My Blue-Eyed Jane." —*Ron Wynn*

☆ **America's Blue Yodeler 1930-31** / May 1991 / Rounder ✦✦✦✦✦
This fifth set of vintage Jimmie Rodgers performances included some spectacular collaborations. While neither sounded fully comfortable, the meeting of Rodgers and Louis Armstrong on "Blue Yodel No. 9" is a landmark date in music annals with two immortals finding a way to make seemingly disparate styles mesh on a short tune. Armstrong's wife at the time, Lil Hardin, accompanied the pair on piano. Rodgers also teamed frequently with Lani McIntire's Hawaiians on this set, often on throwaway tunes that Rodgers' vocals made enjoyable. There's another collaboration with a blues artist, this time Clifford Gibson, on "Let Me Be Your Side Track," a great bawdy/innuendo number. Rodgers was paired with the Carter Family on two wonderful classic country numbers, the heartbreak tune "Why There's a Tear In My Eye" and the gospel song "The Wonderful City." —*Ron Wynn*

☆ **Down the Old Road 1931-32** / Jun. 1991 / Rounder ✦✦✦✦✦
This CD features songs with Jimmie Rodgers working in fresh formats as producer Ralph Peer attempted to break a sales slump. Rodgers recorded with the Louisville Jug Band on "My Good Gal's Gone Blues" and teamed with the Carter Family again in both Kentucky and Texas in 1931. They made four songs together, but three were unissued until after Rodgers' death. They're pleasant and often nicely sung, but not among either artist's finest. Rodgers teamed with steel guitarist Cliff Carlisle and guitarist Wilber Ball on three songs, with Rodgers adding ukulele backing. The final four cuts saw Rodgers return to his trademark railroad numbers and yodeling blues in 1932. For the most part, these weren't great tunes, as they show Rodgers experimenting and finally opting to do comfortable, familiar material rather than try new things. —*Ron Wynn*

☆ **No Hard Times, 1932** / Jul. 1991 / Rounder ✦✦✦✦✦
Although he was nearing the end, Jimmie Rodgers kept going in 1932, turning out several sterling numbers; among them were the dynamic "Blue Yodel No. 10" and riveting "No Hard Times" and "Long Tall Mama Blues," with Oddie McWinders on banjo. Rodgers also displayed his affection for his mother on "Mother, the Queen of My Heart" and the interesting confessional number "I've Only Loved Three Women." Rodgers teamed effectively with guitarist Slim Bryant on "Prairie Lullaby," "Miss the Mississippi and You," and "In The Hills of Tennessee," and once more sang frankly and movingly about his illness on "Whippin' That Old T.B.," although it wasn't as triumphant as "The T.B. Blues." —*Ron Wynn*

☆ **Last Sessions, 1933** / Aug. 1991 / Rounder ✦✦✦✦✦
Illness ravaged Jimmie Rodgers during his final days, as he attempted to record as much as possible. There's an eerie quality to such tunes as "The Yodeling Ranger," "Years Ago," and "Somewhere Down The Line," as it's evident that Rodgers was far from top vocal form. But despite the shortness of breath, lack of range and weak quality, he could still deliver emotionally gripping performances. The earlier cuts on the disc, "Blue Yodel No. 13," "Dreaming With Tears In My Eyes," and "I'm Free (From the Chain Gang Now)," have a hypnotic finality and edge, even when his vocals falter. Rodgers died 48 hours after he finished his final song, not turning in a particularly great performance, as might be expected. But his accomplishments had long ago established him as one of the most memorable performers in American music annals. —*Ron Wynn*

The Singing Brakeman / Bear Family ✦✦✦✦
The Singing Brakeman is a six-disc set that compiles every song that Jimmie Rodgers ever recorded. It covers the same ground as Rounder's eight-disc set, but Bear Family's set condenses the material into six CDs and adds a large booklet that features a thorough discography and biography. Although it has the same material, *The Singing Brakeman* has a more scholarly approach—the discs are designed not as a casual listening experience, but an intense, concentrated listen. In the end, however, it's neither superior nor inferior to Rounder's series. No matter how they are presented, Rodgers' recordings constitute essential listening. —*Stephen Thomas Erlewine*

Johnny Rodriguez

b. Dec. 10, 1952, Sabinal, TX
Guitar, Vocals / Traditional Country, Country-Pop
Johnny Rodriguez was a singing stagecoach driver at the Alamo Village

when Bobby Bare and Tom T. Hall heard him, brought him to Nashville, and made him one of Hall's Storytellers. He was born in Sabinal, TX, 90 miles north of the Mexican border. It was his country-music loving older brother, Andres, who bought seven-year-old Rodriguez his first guitar. As a teen, he was an altar boy, a letterman, and captain of the football team. His father died of cancer when he was 16, and afterward Rodriguez began getting into trouble. By the time he was 18, he had been jailed four times. While he was in prison, a Texas Ranger called Joaquin Jackson heard the young man sing. Impressed, Jackson directed the attention of promoter Happy Shahan toward the vocalist. Shahan booked shows for the 19-year-old Rodriguez at the Alamo Village Amusement Park in Bracketville upon his release.

During the summers of 1970 and 1971, he worked as a stagecoach driver. Soon after joining Tom T. Hall's Storytellers, Hall helped him sign a solo contract with Mercury Records. Rodriguez's first single, "Pass Me By (If You're Only Passing Through)," reached the Top Ten in early 1973, beginning a string of 15 consecutive Top Ten hits that ran into 1977. When he signed with Epic in 1979, his career was entering a period of decline, but Rodriguez continued to have Top 40 hits into the mid-'80s, highlighted by the Top Ten singles "Foolin'" and "How Could I Love Her So Much," which both charted in 1983. In 1987, he signed with Capitol Records. His first single for the label, "I Didn't (Every Chance I Had)," reached No. 12 late in 1987, but none of his subsequent singles made the Top 40 and he left the label in 1989. In 1993, he signed with Intersound and released *Run for the Border*. —*Sandra Brennan & David Vinopal*

● **Greatest Hits** / 1976 / PolyGram ✦✦✦✦
A comprehensive overview of a Latino country singer who never achieved the stardom he merited. —*Ron Wynn*

You Can Say That Again / Jul. 1996 / Hightone ✦✦✦
Quite possibly the strongest release Johnny Rodriguez has offered since his heyday of the late '70s and early '80s, *You Can Say That Again* captures his honky tonk roots perfectly. Rodriguez alternates between honky tonk standards and new tunes written in the tradition. Not all of the new songs are fit to stand in comparison to the classics, but Rodriguez's sweaty energy and gritty, soulful vigor make *You Can Say That Again* a joy. —*Thom Owens*

Kenny Rogers (Kenneth Donald Rogers)

b. Aug. 21, 1938, Houston, TX
Bass, Guitar, Vocals / Country-Pop
Kenny Rogers was a star before he was Kenny Rogers. As a member of the First Edition (and the New Christy Minstrels before that), he shared in some million-sellers, among them "Reuben James" and "Ruby, Don't Take Your Love to Town," an excellent Mel Tillis song about a disabled veteran. But superstardom lay ahead for this Texan with the rasp of mellow. If superstardom can be counted, then count 48 major music awards, one at a time, and he's still not done.

His experience with the two previous pop groups had prepared him well: he knew the easy-listening audience was out there, and he supplied them with well-done middle-of-the-road songs with a country flavor. Having gone solo, in 1976 Rogers charted with "Love Lifted Me." But it was with an outstanding song by writer Don Schlitz, "Lucille," that his star shot upward. The rest (as they say) is history: award-winning duets with Dottie West and Dolly Parton, 12 TV specials, another song-of-the-year with "The Gambler," "Daytime Friends," "Coward of the County," "We've Got Tonight," "Crazy," "Lady" (his first pop No. 1), etc., etc., etc.

And that's just the *musical side* of Kenny Rogers. In 1980 the made-for-TV movie "The Gambler" blasted the competition, followed quickly by "Coward of the County," then enough sequels to "The Gambler" to get him to Roman numeral IV. In music and in television and in movies, Kenny Rogers puts the "super" back in superstar, enough so as to have his own private 18-hole golf course on his spread outside Nashville. —*David Vinopal*

● **Greatest Hits** / 1980 / EMI America ✦✦✦✦

25 Greatest Hits / 1987 / EMI America ✦✦✦✦
This two-CD set includes much the same material as *Greatest Hits*, but also has "Daytime Friends," "Love or Something like It," and "Love Will Turn You Around." —*Dan Cooper*

Greatest Hits / MCA ✦✦✦
His First Edition hits and more. —*Bil Carpenter*

Roy Rogers (Leonard Slye)

b. Nov. 5, 1911, Cincinnati, OH
Guitar, Vocals / Acoustic Blues, Electric Blues
Roy Rogers eventually outdrew Gene Autry, his fellow Republic Studio star, at least at the box office. Autry won the battle of the records (his *Silver-Haired Daddy of Mine* alone sold over five million copies). Rogers, in spite of his excellent voice and superior yodel, is perhaps best known musically as the founder of what's generally considered to be among the best vocal group ever to grace country music—the Sons of the Pioneers.

Rogers, Bob Nolan, and Tim Spencer began as a trio (the Pioneers) in 1933, changing to their more famous name a year later, when Hugh Farr, with his swing-style fiddle and bass voice, joined. When Rogers, who was to become known as "King of the Cowboys," left for the silver screen in 1938, the six-piece group in a sense went with him, appearing in scores of his movies through 1949.

Over the years the Sons of the Pioneers recorded hundreds of Western-flavored songs, many of which other Western groups also recorded (for example, "Ghost Riders in the Sky," "Empty Saddles"), but two classic songs written by Bob Nolan, "Cool Water" and "Tumblin' Tumbleweeds," elevated the Sons above the competition. In addition, because of the sophisticated musical arrangements, the intricate instrumentals, and the complicated vocal harmonies, the Sons of the Pioneers have for the past 60 years remained at the top of the scale, against which all subsequent country vocal groups must measure themselves. Happy trails to you, Dale and Roy. —*David Vinopal*

Tribute / 1991 / RCA ✦✦✦

● **Country Music Hall of Fame Series** / 1992 / MCA ✦✦✦✦
When Gene Autry got into a contract dispute with Republic Pictures in 1937, the studio replaced him with Sons of the Pioneers member Len Slye, whose name they changed to Roy Rogers. These Decca tracks, which range from 1934 to 1942, cover Rogers' output just before he became "King of the Cowboys" with the release of *Ridin' Down the Canyon*. Two of these cuts were recorded with the Sons of the Pioneers; the rest are solo. —*Brian Mansfield*

Billy Joe Royal

b. 1945, Valdosta, GA
Vocals / Country-Pop, Pop-Rock
Best-known for his pop-rock hit "Down in the Boondocks," Billy Joe Royal had a long career that saw him shifting his attentions toward country music in the '80s. Although he never had a hit as large as "Down in the Boondocks," he racked up a number of hit country singles over the course of the 1980s. Royal was born into a family of musical entertainers and debuted on his uncle's radio show at the age of 11. The following year, he learned to play steel guitar and joined the Atlanta Jubilee at age 14, performing with Joe South, Jerry Reed, and Ray Stevens, among several other artists. Royal had his own rock band during high school and was regularly singing around Atlanta when he was 16. In 1962, he recorded an independent single which went unnoticed. Three years later his former radio colleague Joe South contacted him with a song, which he wanted Royal to sing as a demo in hopes that Gene Pitney would record it. Royal flew to Atlanta and recorded "Down in the Boondocks" inside the studio's septic tank, which had been converted into an echo chamber. The demo ended up at Columbia, and they signed Royal to a six-year deal. The song became Royal's breakthrough single, reaching No. 9 on the pop charts and making the vocalist into a teen idol. Following the success of "Down in the Boondocks," Royal had a string of lesser hits, including the Top 40 pop singles "I Knew You When," "I've Got To Be Somebody," and "Cherry Hill Park." By the end of the decade, Royal's star waned, and he became a regular performer in Vegas and Lake Tahoe. He also did a bit of acting on television, in feature films, and commercials. In 1978, he recorded a cover of "Under the Boardwalk" for Private Stock Records and scored a minor hit.

During the early '80s, Royal worked on establishing himself as a country artist, but had trouble finding a label. In 1984, Royal finally got a break when he recorded Gary Burr's "Burned Like a Rocket" on an Atlanta label, Southern Tracks. It was in turn picked up by Atlantic Records, who signed Royal to the label. The single became a hit and reached the country Top Ten in early 1986. For the next two years, he had a string of Top 40 hits, breaking into the Top Ten in late 1987 with "I'll Pin a Note on Your Pillow." In 1989, he released the album *Tell It Like Is* and the title cut became his biggest hit, peaking at No. 2. The album itself stayed in the Top 15 for over a year. In 1989, he was inducted into the Georgia Music Hall of Fame. By 1990, Royal's style of pop-inflected country had been replaced by neo-traditional honky tonk at the top of the charts, and his popularity declined. He continued to have minor hits into 1992 and he continued to tour into the mid-'90s. —*Sandra Brennan*

● **Greatest Hits [Columbia]** / 1989 / Columbia ✦✦✦✦
Can't go wrong with this one, featuring his two biggies, "Down in the Boondocks" and "Cherry Hill Park." —*Cub Koda*

Greatest Hits [Atlantic] / 1991 / Atlantic ✦✦✦
Billy Joe Royal's *Greatest Hits* on Atlantic contains the biggest country-pop hits from the '80s, including his debut country hit, "Burned Like a Rocket." —*Thom Owens*

Best of Billy Joe Royal / Pair ✦✦

Sawyer Brown

Contemporary Country
Country-rockers Sawyer Brown got their big break with a victory on the

nationally syndicated TV talent show "Star Search." The band had its origins 1979, when lead guitarist Bobby Randall came to Nashville with the intention of starting a band. While working in Don King's band, he met drummer Joe Smyth; a year later, they teamed up with bass guitarist Jim Scholten, lead vocalist/rhythm guitarist Mark Miller, and keyboardist Hobie Hubbard. After Don King stopped touring in 1981, the band members decided to continue performing, naming themselves Sawyer Brown in tribute to the Nashville street where they used to rehearse.

Sawyer Brown toured the country for two years before their agent asked them to make a video in Nashville, which turned out to be an audition for the television contest "Star Search." The band performed on the show and wound up earning $100,000. The subsequent publicity helped them land a contract with Capitol/Curb in 1984. Later that year, they released their self-titled debut album and had a Top 20 hit with their debut single "Leona." The following year, the band had its first No. 1 hit with their second single "Step That Step," a song written by Miller. This led to two more major hits, and by the year's end, they became the first band to receive the Country Music Association's prestigious Horizon Award.

Despite their initial success, Sawyer Brown experienced a backlash after 1986 from many country radio stations who found their music a bit too slickly produced. By 1987, their singles had plummeted to the bottom half of the charts, until "This Missin' You Heart of Mine" became a No. 2 hit in early 1988. Their next major hit came in 1989 with "The Race Is On." The album it was pulled from, *The Boys Are Back*, did equally well on the charts. During the low spots, Sawyer Brown honed their live act with plenty of touring. In late 1991, they burst back onto the country music scene with *The Dirt Road*, which produced two Top Five hits. Following its release, the group enjoyed their greatest period of success, as they produced a string of Top Ten hits that ran into the mid-'90s. —*Sandra Brennan*

Cafe on the Corner / 1992 / Capitol ✦✦✦✦
By *Cafe on the Corner*, the members of Sawyer Brown had essentially given up on being rock 'n' rollers and revealed themselves to be a pretty decent country band. "Cafe on the Corner" paints a graphic picture of small-town desolation, but these guys are smart enough to avoid preaching: most of the album reflects the marvels of love. The rock 'n' roll sneaks back in on the last two cuts, but by then it's too late to matter. A album filled with good songs, it also includes a great one (Mac McAnally's "All These Years"). —*Brian Mansfield*

The Dirt Road / Jan. 6, 1992 / Liberty ✦✦✦
The band's robust work ethic makes it into these songs about simple life and small-town values, and Mark Miller controls a tendency to over-sing them, maybe because he believes them. Miller's heart is still filled with clichés like "Burning Bridges (On a Rocky Road)," but the sleaze in his voice is convincing on "Ruby Red Shoes," which has to be a song of lust for Judy Garland. —*Brian Mansfield*

● **Greatest Hits 1990-1995** / 1995 / Curb ✦✦✦✦
A solid retrospective of Sawyer Brown's career highlights, featuring nearly all of their biggest hits. —*David Jehnzen*

Jack Scott (Jack Scafone Jr.)

b. Jan. 24, 1936, Windsor, Ontario, Canada
Guitar / Rock & Roll, Traditional Country, Rockabilly
Jack Scott sounded tough, like someone you wouldn't want to meet in a dark alley unless he had a guitar in his hands. When he growled "The Way I Walk," wise men (and women) stepped aside. Despite his snarling rockabilly attitude, Scott hailed from Ontario, Canada, and grew up near Detroit, developing a love for hillbilly music along the way. His first sides for ABC-Paramount in 1957 exhibited a profound country-rock synthesis, and after moving to the Carlton label, Scott hit the charts the next year with the tremulous ballad "My True Love," backed by his vocal group, the Chantones. Flip it over, however, and you have the hauling rocker "Leroy," all about some wacked-out tough guy who's content to remain behind the bars of his local jail.

Scott's pronounced emphasis on acoustic guitar distinguishes atmospheric rockers like "Goodbye Baby," "Go Wild Little Sadie," "Midgie," and "Geraldine." But his principal pop success came with tears-in-your-beer country-based ballads—"What in the World's Come Over You" and "Burning Bridges" were massive smashes on Top Rank in 1960, and he recorded an entire album's worth of Hank Williams covers for the firm the same year.

Scott continued to vacillate between cowboy crooner and rough-edged rocker throughout the '60s, recording for Capitol and Groove. He still occasionally turns up on the oldies circuit, and he still looks and sounds like a man you seriously don't want to mess with. —*Bill Dahl*

Scott on Groove / 1989 / Bear Family ✦✦✦✦
The music on *Scott on Groove* was recorded after Jack Scott's hit-making era on Capitol was finished. Scott recorded for Groove in the early '60s. During this time, he was trying to refashion his sound into a rock 'n' roll/rockabilly direction. Not all of the attempts were successful, but the set is

interesting for dedicated fans, but they would probably rather acquire this material on the more comprehensive box set, *Classic Scott.* —*Stephen Thomas Erlewine*

Classic Scott / Bear Family ✦✦✦✦
Bear Family's *Classic Scott* is a four-disc, 138-track box set that contains all of Jack Scott's recordings for Capitol from the '50s, as well as a selection of material he recorded for smaller, independent labels like Groove in the early '60s. While the set is far too comprehensive for casual fans, it is ideal for collectors and worth their investment. —*Stephen Thomas Erlewine*

● **Greatest Hits** / Curb ✦✦✦✦
Curb's *Greatest Hits* was the only American Jack Scott compilation available in the mid-'90s, after Capitol pulled its *Collector's Series* from the market. Although *Greatest Hits* only has 11 tracks—including a recently-recorded version of "Running Scared"—it has the essential big hits ("My True Love," "Goodbye Baby," "Burning Bridges," "Leroy," "The Way I Walk," "What in the World's Come Over You") and is a serviceable collection, even if it is frustratingly brief. —*Stephen Thomas Erlewine*

Scud Mountain Boys

Alternative Country-Rock
The cult popularity of Uncle Tupelo and its spinoff groups Wilco and Son Volt has opened the doors for what's become an entire new generation of musicians who grew up in the punk-rock generation but have found genuine connection with traditional country music—especially as interpreted through Gram Parsons, who's more or less the granddaddy of country-rock. The Scud Mountain Boys—Joe Pernice, Stephen Desaulniers, Bruce Tull, and Tom Shea—clearly fit into this camp.

The band originally played electric rock 'n' roll under the name the Scuds. Pernice, Desaulniers, and Tull formed the group in Northampton, MA, in 1991, and they gained a respectable local following. But the band-members soon tired of hauling equipment around, and found they much more enjoyed the after-show get-togethers playing acoustic country songs around the kitchen table at home. Finally they decided to haul the kitchen table to a club. Finding the response positive, they've kept with the new format.

The band's debut album, *Pine Box* (originally just a cassette release), features slow, intensely quiet originals alongside covers of '70s pop-country songs such as "Gypsies, Tramps and Thieves" and "Please, Mr., Please." It was literally recorded live around the kitchen table. Their second album, *Dance the Night Away*—which added a couple of rock songs from their Scuds days into the mix again—came out on Chunk Records in 1995, and national interest in the band grew quickly. In early 1996 they were signed to Sub Pop, and the label released the band's third album in less than two years, *Massachusetts.* —*Kurt Wolff*

Dance the Night Away / 1995 / Chunk ✦✦✦✦
Dance the Night Away, one of two albums the Scud Mountain Boys released in 1995 (*Pine Box* was the other), is a quiet but immediately compelling collection of 13 original songs plus two covers—one being the Jimmy Webb pop classic "Where's the Playground, Susie," which is likely the most reverent version of the song this side of Glenn Campbell's. —*Kurt Wolf*

● **Massachusetts** / Apr. 1996 / Sub Pop ✦✦✦✦
In just a short time, the Scud Mountain Boys have risen from relative obscurity (two 1995 albums for indie label Chunk) to a well-earned spot on the Sub Pop roster. The Boys' new album, *Massachusetts,* is once again a quiet, mostly acoustic collection of soft-spoken songs based around spare country rhythms and laidback, whisperlight melodies. *Massachusetts* is more down-to-earth than the faux-hillbilly rambling poems of Palace Music, but also far less Americana-ized than Son Volt or any of the No Depression hangers-on. The sudden national attention seems not to have spooked the Scuds, and so while *Massachusetts* feels better crafted than the band's previous two albums—more mature in terms of songwriting—it retains the easy-going, kitchen-table spirit that marked the band's earlier work. This is music that moves slowly but grows on you quickly. —*Kurt Wolff*

Jeannie Seely

b. Jul. 16, 1940, Pennsylvania
Vocals / Country-Pop
A Pennsylvanian who started performing on the radio at age 11, Jeannie Seely is associated almost as strongly with her duet partners—Porter Wagoner, Ernest Tubb, and Jack Greene—as she is with her own music. Her first single, "Don't Touch Me," won her a Grammy in 1967, and she continued to have charting hits for the next 11 years. Most of her material came from fellow country songwriter (and eventual husband) Hank Cochran. She has been a cast member of the Grand Ole Opry since 1967. —*Brian Mansfield*

● **Greatest Hits on Monument** / 1993 / CBS ✦✦✦✦
Seely recorded her hits for four labels—Decca, MCA, Columbia, and

Monument—and much of that material is currently out of print. These Monument recordings document only about the first three years of her career, but they include some great records, especially "Don't Touch Me," "I'll Love You More (Than You Need)," and the brutally fatalistic "It's Only Love." —*Brian Mansfield*

Billy Joe Shaver

b. Corsicana, TX
Guitar, Vocals / Outlaw Country
Billy Joe Shaver never became a household name, but his songs—including "Good Christian Soldier," "Willie the Wandering Gypsy and Me," and "I Been to Georgia on a Fast Train"—became country standards during the '70s and his reputation among musicians and critics didn't diminish during the next two decades.

One of the best synopses of Billy Joe Shaver's upbringing is his own song, "I Been to Georgia on a Fast Train." When he sings that "my grandma's old-age pension is the reason that I'm standing here today," he ain't kidding. The "good Christian raising" and "eighth grade education"—not to mention being abandoned by his parents shortly after being born, working on his uncle's farms instead of going to high school, and losing part of his fingers during a job at a sawmill—are all part of his life story. "I got all my country learning," he sings, "picking cotton, raising hell, and bailing hay."

Shaver did a quick turn in the Navy and worked a series of nowhere jobs (including the one in the sawmill) before trying his luck in Nashville. After several back and forth trips between Texas and Tennessee that gained him no response, he appeared one day in 1968 in Bobby Bare's Nashville office, where he convinced Bare to listen to him play. Bare ended up giving him a writing job.

Shaver recorded one song for Mercury, "Chicken on the Ground," which went nowhere, but soon his songs began to see the light thanks to Kris Kristofferson ("Good Christian Soldier"), Tom T. Hall ("Willie the Wandering Gypsy and Me"), Bare ("Ride Me Down Easy") and, later, the Allman Brothers ("Sweet Mama") and Elvis Presley ("You Asked Me To"). Shaver's real breakthrough, though, came in 1973 when Jennings recorded an album composed almost entirely of Shaver's songs, *Honky Tonk Heroes*—largely considered the first true "outlaw" album.

Shaver's debut album was *Old Five and Dimers Like Me,* produced by Kristofferson and released by Monument (Kristofferson's label) in 1973. Along with the title track, it contained the now-classic Shaver songs "Willie the Wandering Gypsy and Me" and the aforementioned "I Been to Georgia on a Fast Train." Shaver switched to MGM a year later, but no album materialized. "Raising hell" was, as he had sung, part of his lifestyle at the time, and it kept him out of sight for a couple years. In 1976 Shaver resurfaced with *When I Get My Wings* on Capricorn, and followed it up a year later with *Gypsy Boy.* Johnny Cash recorded Shaver's "I'm Just an Old Lump of Coal (But I'm Gonna Be a Diamond Some Day)" in 1978, a song Shaver wrote just after he chose to give up drugs and booze and turned to God for help. Religious references do crop up in his songs, but they never dominate the emotions or get in the way of the earthy rhythms and melodies.

Shaver switched labels again, this time to Columbia, in 1980, and recorded three more albums during the next decade: *I'm Just an Old Lump of Coal . . . But I'm Gonna Be a Diamond Some Day, Billy Joe Shaver,* and *Salt of the Earth.* The latter was produced by Shaver with his son, Eddy, who has played on every Billy Joe record since *Old Chunk of Coal* (he also toured in Dwight Yoakam's band in the 1980s). After a few more years out of the spotlight, Billy Joe returned once again in 1993, this time recording under the name Shaver. *Tramp on Your Street,* released on Zoo/Praxis, featured Eddy on lead guitar and Billy Joe's own raspy but loveable voice, and coming out during a time when hunky hat acts were the new flavor in Nashville, it was quickly recognized as one of the strongest and hardest country records to hit the shelves in many years. Shaver toured regularly over the next couple of years, and recorded a live album for Zoo, *Unshaven,* in 1995, but was dropped by the label a year later. He's currently signed to Justice Records.—*Kurt Wolff*

Old Five and Dimers Like Me / 1973 / Monument ✦✦✦✦
His hillbilly charm glows on the autobiographical title tune and the rest of his one-of-a-kind songs. —*Michael McCall*

When I Get My Wings / 1976 / Capricorn ✦✦✦
Here's proof that his blend of sawdust-floor honkers and spiritually endowed ballads were in place from the start. —*Michael McCall*

I'm Just an Old Chunk of Coal / 1981 / Columbia ✦✦✦✦
Again, he combines straight-from-the-soul spirituals like the title cut with some of the most colorful honky tonk ever written, including "Fit to Kill and Going Out in Style" and "Saturday Night," as well as an astounding "Ragged Old Truck," in which he begins by contemplating suicide before deciding all he needs is a good, hard night on the town. —*Michael McCall*

Billy Joe Shaver / 1982 / Columbia ✦✦✦
As with the title, this is his most straightforward collection of Texas soul music. It includes a few remakes of earlier classics. —*Michael McCall*

Tramp on Your Street / Aug. 10, 1993 / Zoo ✦✦✦✦
His rawest setting comes courtesy of his guitar-slinging son, Eddie Shaver, who gooses his old man in all the right places. Then, on the more introspective tunes, the father dispenses his hard-earned wisdom in unforgettable fashion. It's a true classic. —*Michael McCall*

● **Restless Wind: The Legendary Billy Joe Shaver 1973-1987** / Oct. 1995 / Razor & Tie ✦✦✦✦
This album covers the highlights of Shaver's acclaimed career effectively, providing a fine introduction to the distinctive, idiosyncratic singer-songwriter. —*Thom Owens*

Jean Shepard

Bass, Vocals
Few country singers—let alone female country singers—working since the 1950s have produced as large a body of enduring work as Jean Shepard. Her voice is pure country—accent on both words. Born in Oklahoma, she grew up in southern California, where Hank Thompson discovered her. She had her first Top Ten hit in 1953, and her last almost exactly 20 years later. In between, she cut one great record after another, mostly on Capitol Records. Nearly all of them crackle, no matter the topic, with honky tonk angel spunk. Born in Oklahoma, Shepard grew up in the area surrounding Bakersfield, CA. As a teenager, she began her musical career by playing bass in the Melody Ranch Girls, an all-female band formed in 1948. Hank Thompson discovered Shepard a few years after the group formed. Impressed by her talents, he helped her set up a record deal at Capitol Records, where she worked with Thompson's producer Ken Nelson. Shepard's first chart appearance was in 1943 as a duet partner with Ferlin Husky, with "A Dear John Letter" and its sequel, "Forgive Me John." Jean and Ferlin toured the country following their hit singles. In 1955, she had her first solo Top Ten single, "A Satisfied Mind," which was backed by the No. 13 hit "Take Possession." Later in the year, she had another Top Ten hit with "Beautiful Lies"/"I Thought of You." Her streak of hit singles led to an invitation to join the Grand Ole Opry in 1956. That same year, she joined Red Foley's Ozark Jubilee and recorded *Songs of a Love Affair*, arguably the first concept album in country music history. Its 12 songs—which were all written by Shepard—depict a marriage torn apart by a love affair; one side of the album is written from the dissolution of a romance.

For nearly ten years after the release of "Beautiful Lies," Jean wasn't able to get a song into the Top Ten. In fact, she had only two Top 40 hits during that period—"I Want to Go Where No One Knows Me" (No. 18, 1958) and "Have Heart, Will Love" (No. 30, 1959). She continued to record and tour—she was even named the Top Female Singer of 1959 by *Cash Box*—but nothing was breaking through to the public. This was primarily because she was a hardcore honky tonk singer in a time that country-pop was ruling the charts. In 1963, her husband Hawkshaw Hawkins died in the same plane crash that killed Patsy Cline. The following year, she returned to the Top Ten with "Second Fiddle (To an Old Guitar)." The song began a string of hits for Jean. Although many of them failed to chart in the Top 20, she racked up 15 Top 40 hits between 1965 and 1970, including the Top Ten hits "I'll Take the Dog" (a duet with Ray Pillow, 1966), "If Teardrops Were Silver" (1966), and "Then He Touched Me" (1970).

Shepard's hits continued throughout the '70s, though as the decade wore on she hit the Top 40 with less and less frequency. Her last hit single was 1978's "The Real Thing," which peaked at No. 85.

During the '80s and '90s, Jean Shepard didn't record but she continued to perform at the Grand Ole Opry and tour, particularly in the UK, where she had a strong fan base.—*Dan Cooper & Stephen Thomas Erlewine*

This is Jean Shepard / 1959 / Capitol ✦✦✦✦
One of her earlier LPs is strong on her voice and is a steel-friendly West Coast production. It includes her spry, proto-feminist "Two Whoops and a Holler." —*Dan Cooper*

● **Honky Tonk Heroine** / Dec. 1995 / Country Music Foundation ✦✦✦✦
At a time when most of her contemporaries were heading down the country-pop route, Jean Shepard was one of the few female honky tonk singers to stay true to the genre in the '50s and '60s. The definitive *Honky Tonk Heroine: Classic Capitol Recordings, 1952-1962* is a terrific anthology of her peak years. Most of her biggest hits are included, as are a handful of rarities that should delight casual fans as much as dedicated fans. —*Stephen Thomas Erlewine*

T.G. Sheppard (Bill Browder, Brian Stacy)

b. Jul. 20, 1944, Humboldt, TN
Guitar, Vocals / Country
Sheppard headed off to Memphis after high school, getting involved in

the record business on several different levels. He tried recording as a pop artist, and even signed with Atlantic Records under the name Brian Stacy, opening shows for the Beach Boys. A few years later, he took a job with a Memphis record distributor, then ended up in record promotion, where the job entailed calling radio stations and trying to persuade them to play his company's records. In that capacity for RCA, he helped break Elvis Presley's "Suspicious Minds," Perry Como's "It's Impossible," and John Denver's "Take Me Home Country Roads." After "going independent," he came across a demo tape of "Devil in the Bottle." He tried to talk a number of artists into doing the song, and when no one was interested, he decided to do it himself. Then a number of record labels said no as well, although Motown's fledgling country division, Hitsville Records, said yes. Primarily a recitation, "Devil" went to No. 1 in 1975, but within three years, the company folded, and Sheppard's career was in limbo. Connecting with record producer Buddy Killen, he signed with Warner Bros., and starting in 1979, the two churned out some of country's best-crafted singles over a four-year period. Sheppard gradually moved away from recitations and grew significantly as a vocalist, though the press often ignored his achievements. He changed producers several times in the mid-'80s and, after a divorce in 1987, took a couple of years off for personal reflection. When he returned, Sheppard found it difficult to regain his earlier momentum. —*Tom Roland*

Slow Burn / 1983 / Warner Bros. ✦✦✦
This album has its weak moments, but Sheppard's performance is stronger than in previous albums. He's more confident, probably understands the craft of singing a little better, and—this being his first outing with record producer Jim Ed Norman—the arrangements don't bury him. —*Tom Roland*

● **The Best of** / 1992 / Curb ✦✦✦✦
You'll have to look for this one at used-record stores. A sampler released only to radio, it covers the half-dozen years up to and including "I Loved 'Em Every One." Some of the performances are a little stiff but it lends appreciation for his improved, later work. —*Tom Roland*

Ricky Skaggs

b. Jul. 18, 1954, Cordell, KY
Banjo, Fiddle, Guitar, Mandolin, Vocals / Traditional Bluegrass, Traditional Country, Progressive Country
For someone still in his thirties, Ricky Skaggs has already produced a career's worth of music. At age seven he appeared on TV with Flatt and Scruggs; at 15 he was a member of legendary Ralph Stanley's bluegrass band (with fellow teenager, the late Keith Whitley). None of the contemporary stars, male or female, has better credentials than Ricky. The term "multi-talented" lacks the power to characterize this extraordinary singer and instrumentalist. Not only can he sing and pick with the best in progressive country, his broad and deep experience in traditional music separates him from the crowd. In the estimation of many, he is without peer as a combination vocalist and instrumentalist (guitar, mandolin, fiddle, banjo). After playing with Ralph Stanley for three years, Ricky moved on to progressive bluegrass bands, the Country Gentlemen and J. D. Crowe and the New South. With his own band, Boone Creek, he mixed the old and the new, adding Django Rheinhardt. Ricky took Rodney Crowell's place in Emmylou Harris's Hot Band in 1977, and the band's excellent *Roses in the Snow* album showcased Ricky's versatility. Two No. 1 hits came out of his *Waiting for the Sun to Shine* self-produced album (1981), and the awards started arriving.

Skaggs is largely responsible for a back-to-basics movement in country music. He showed many that a bluegrass tenor with impeccable taste and enormous talent can sell traditional country, at a time when pop music has invaded the land of rural rhythm. His remake of Bill Monroe's "Uncle Pen," for example, was the first bluegrass song since Flatt And Scruggs' the "Ballad of Jed Clampett" to reach No. 1 in the charts. —*David Vinopal*

Sweet Temptation / 1979 / Sugar Hill ✦✦✦✦
With sweet vocals by then-boss Emmylou Harris, Skaggs' first solo effort (not counting the Boone Creek project) is equal parts bluegrass and Harris-styled new traditionalism. —*Dan Cooper*

Waitin' for the Sun to Shine / 1981 / Epic ✦✦✦
His first album after signing with Epic Records, this one took Skaggs into the mainstream, in effect beginning the new-traditionalist movement. It has a simple, mountain approach, with lots of remakes and Skaggs' mournful vocal tones. The best cut is the plaintive title track. —*Tom Roland*

Highways & Heartaches / 1982 / Epic ✦✦✦✦
Long a sideman or supporting vocalist in previous situations, Skaggs wasn't quite comfortable with his role as a lead vocalist when he signed with Epic Records. Thanks to a year of touring and greater support from his record label (when Epic signed him, the company honestly didn't think he'd sell more than 100,000 copies of his debut for the company), he had greater confidence vocally the second time around. And the material's more upbeat. —*Tom Roland*

Family & Friends / 1982 / Rounder ✦✦✦
Skaggs' last breath of pure bluegrass was recorded with help from the Whites, guitarist Peter Rowan, dobroist Jerry Douglas, and others. Included are two songs by Carter Stanley, one by Bill Monroe, and some fine examples of Appalachian gospel, including a stunning a cappella trio vocal on "Talk About Sufferin." —*Brian Mansfield*

Country Boy / 1984 / Epic ✦✦✦✦
Every one of Ricky Skaggs' albums is a pickin' festival and a country delight. Not only is this one no exception, but it also includes Bill Monroe's "Wheel Hoss" with Monroe himself picking along on mandolin, which earns it a listing here. If you like this album, you'll probably like every other one Skaggs has made. —*William Ruhlmann*

● **Live in London** / 1985 / Epic ✦✦✦✦
This is the one Skaggs album to own if you can only have one. Because it's a live recording, the picking is just that much more exciting, and the album serves as an unofficial best-of, its highlights including "Heartbroke," "Uncle Pen," and a version of "Don't Get Above Your Raising" that features noted country fan Elvis Costello. —*William Ruhlmann*

Carl Smith

b. Mar. 15, 1927, Maynardsville, TN
Guitar, Vocals / Traditional Country, Honky Tonk
For the first five years of the '50s, this Opry headliner was one of country's biggest stars, going on to rack up nearly three dozen hits in the decade. Although he could sing great honky tonk, Smith discovered that his country ballads sold so well he soon specialized in them. His second release for Columbia, "Let's Live a Little," was a huge hit, followed by "If Teardrops Were Pennies" and "Mr. Moon." In 1953 three singles reached No. 1: "Hey Joe," "Satisfaction Guaranteed," and "Trademark." He branched out from Nashville with two movies, and his *Country Music Hall* TV program was broadcast coast-to-coast in Canada in the mid-'60s. In his quarter-century with the Columbia label, Smith sold over 15 million records. Both he and his wife Goldie Hill retired early to their horse farm in Tennessee. Smith was "Mr. Country" in the '50s. —*David Vinopal*

★ **The Essential Carl Smith (1950-1956)** / 1991 / Columbia/Legacy ✦✦✦✦✦
Twenty tracks, including his early hits, appear from this smooth and soulful country vocalist who was popular in the '50s. If you like Hank Williams and Lefty Frizzell and the '50s fiddle and steel sound, give this a try. —*Richard Lieberson*

Connie Smith

b. Aug. 14, 1941, Elkhart, IN
Guitar, Vocals / Country, Christian Rock
You rarely hear the name Connie Smith mentioned in the same breath with Patsy Cline, Loretta Lynn, Tammy Wynette, or Dolly Parton. But poll Nashville's old guard as to who the great female country singers of all time have been, and Connie's name will show up near the top every time. Many, in fact, would put her there without the "female" qualifier. Listening to Smith can be emotionally exhausting. One song blows you off your barstool, the next tears a hole in your heart, and the third sends you crying to the chapel. A Cinderella story to boot, young housewife Smith was discovered by Bill Anderson in 1963 at a talent contest in small town Ohio. Her debut RCA single, released a year later, was the Anderson-penned "Once A Day." A No. 1 smash, it made Smith an instant superstar, the one thing the shy singer has never really wanted to be. In the late 1970s, she dropped out of the business completely, but has recently re-emerged on the Nashville scene, her pipes as strong as ever. —*Dan Cooper*

☆ **Connie Smith** / 1965 / RCA Victor ✦✦✦✦✦
Cut in Music City, Smith's first LP (which includes "Once a Day") features her blowing through the Nashville Sound production like a down-home Streisand fronting the Lennon Sisters. —*Dan Cooper*

Soul of Country Music / 1968 / RCA Victor ✦✦✦
More of the same unearthly sound, but this has Smith covering—at times burying—other singers' hits. Her version of Rex Griffin's "The Last Letter" is almost literally to die for. —*Dan Cooper*

Back in Baby's Arms / 1969 / RCA ✦✦✦✦
If any Thomas ever doubted Smith's religious convictions (which are as much a part of her story as her voice is) one listen to this LP's "How Great Thou Art" should take care of that mistrust. —*Dan Cooper*

★ **The Essential Connie Smith** / Apr. 1996 / RCA ✦✦✦✦✦
This is the only thorough compilation of her '60s hits for RCA, featuring all of her Top Ten hits, including the No. 1 "Once A Day," and a selection of her lesser-known material. —*Thom Owens*

Greatest Hits on Monument / CBS ✦✦✦✦
Smith in the '70s has too much syrupy production. —*Dan Cooper*

Darden Smith

Guitar, Vocals / Blues-Rock, Contemporary Country
Named for a local rodeo rider, Darden Smith grew up in Austin, TX, and placed two singles, "Little Maggie" and "Day after Tomorrow," on the country charts in 1988. His untitled major-label debut was released in 1988 on Epic. In 1989, he teamed up with British songwriter Boo Hewerdine of the Bible pop band to record *Evidence*, which expanded his following beyond the country market. Smith's second solo album, *Trouble No More*, appeared in 1990. —*William Ruhlmann*

Native Soul / 1986 / Watermelon ✦✦✦
A fine debut album. Nanci Griffith sings harmony vocal on "Two Dollar Novels." Lyle Lovett sings harmony on five songs. This one's a gem. Smith is just breaking out and developing his style. —*Chip Renner*

● **Darden Smith** / 1988 / Epic ✦✦✦✦
Darden's big-label debut features three cuts off of his *Native Soul* album. This time the production is better, with strings and extra vocals. Nanci Griffith and Lyle Lovett back him, along with Roland Denney and Paul Pearcy. All of his songs are strong and the playing is dead-on. It's a keeper. —*Chip Renner*

Trouble No More / 1990 / Columbia ✦✦✦
A strong album, not as diverse as *Darden Smith*, but as good. Contains "Midnight Train," "Frankie & Sue," "Trouble No More," "Fall Apart at the Seams," and the list goes on. With two songs co-written by buddy Boo Hewerdine. —*Chip Renner*

Hank Snow (Clarence Eugene Snow)

b. May 9, 1914, Liverpool, Nova Scotia, Canada
Guitar, Vocals / Traditional Country
Canada's greatest contribution to country music, for over forty years Hank Snow has been famous for his "travelling" songs. It's no wonder. At age twelve he ran away from his Nova Scotia home and joined the Merchant Marines, working as a cabin boy and laborer for four years. Once back on shore, he listened to Jimmie Rodgers records and started playing in public, building up a following in Halifax. His original nickname, the Yodeling Ranger, was modified to the Singing Ranger when his high voice changed to the great baritone it is today. And great his voice is—great enough for him to record on the same label, RCA, for forty-five years. In 1950, the year he became an Opry regular, his self-penned "I'm Moving On" (the first of his many great travelling songs) became a smash hit, reaching No. 1 and remaining on the charts for 40 weeks. "Golden Rocket" (also 1950) and "I've Been Everywhere" (1962), two other hits, show his life long love for trains and travel. But he was as much at home with two other styles, the ballad and the rhumba-boogie. Among his many great ballads are "Bluebird Island" (with Anita Carter, of the Carter Family), "Fool Such As I," and "Hello, Love" a hit when Snow was 60 years old.

Still appearing regularly on the Opry, Snow shows that his incredible voice has suffered no loss of quality over the last half-century. And he still proves what a tasteful, understated guitar stylist he is. To show you his impact on the business, in 1963 the nation's disk jockeys voted "I'm Moving On" as their favorite all-time country song. With small stature and huge voice, Snow is a country traditionalist who has given much more to the business than he's taken. His output of over 100 albums gives a sense of his importance to country music history. —*David Vinopal*

The Singing Ranger: 1949-1953 / 1989 / Bear Family ✦✦✦✦
This album contains every song Hank Snow recorded for RCA in the beginning of his career. Not only are career-making songs like "I'm Movin' On," "Marriage Vow," and "The Rhumba Boogie" included, but so are unreleased songs and alternate takes. For diehard Hank Snow fans, this first volume of *The Singing Ranger* series is the most essential of the three. —*Stephen Thomas Erlewine*

★ **I'm Movin' on & Other Country Hits** / 1990 / RCA ✦✦✦✦✦
I'm Movin' On & Other Hits doesn't have all the hits Hank Snow had over the course of his career, but it has 20 essential tracks from the early '50s. These are the songs that made his career and while he had decades worth of other hits, this disc gives you an accurate sense of what Snow accomplished. —*Stephen Thomas Erlewine*

The Singing Ranger, Vol. 2 / 1990 / Bear Family ✦✦✦✦
Running from 1953 to 1958, this four-disc box set contains everything Hank Snow recorded during those five years, including all the hits and outtakes. Again, the set is not for the fairweather fan—there's plenty of brilliant music here, but its very scope makes it appealing only to completists, who will find much to treasure. —*Stephen Thomas Erlewine*

The Thesaurus Transcriptions / 1991 / Bear Family ✦✦✦✦
This five-disc box set contains 138 radio transcriptions that Hank Snow cut during the early '50s, when he was one of the biggest stars in country. Many of these songs were never recorded in the studio and Snow is in superb voice throughout the set. It's not a set for neophytes or casual

fans, but those diehard fans and historians willing to invest in such a mammoth box will find it fascinating. — *Stephen Thomas Erlewine*

My Early Country Favorites / 1996 / RCA ♦♦
The material on this compilation isn't bad at all, featuring Snow on some of his more traditional performances. The problem is in the packaging—there are only ten tracks, there's absolutely no annotation, and the sound quality is substandard, with noticeable surface noise throughout. The music is all right, but there's got to be better ways to get it. — *Richie Unterberger*

The Singing Ranger, Vol. 3 / Bear Family ♦♦♦♦
Singing Ranger, Vol. 3 picks up where the second box set left off and presents the final recordings Hank Snow ever made. The box is extremely lengthy, running a total of 12 discs and spanning all of his '60s work, and contains less first-rate material than Bear Family's other three box sets, but it remains necessary for completists. — *Stephen Thomas Erlewine*

Collector's Series / RCA ♦♦♦
This is a haphazard collection. Out of the eight tracks, four of the selections weren't hits for Snow and one track, "(Now and Then There's) A Fool Such As I," is Snow reciting portions of his autobiography over a string-laden instrumental. — *Stephen Thomas Erlewine*

The Sons of the Pioneers

Cowboy
The Sons of the Pioneers are the definitive Western music group. In the '30s, they set the style and sound of Western music, from the look of the Hollywood cowboy to the sound of the three-part harmonies. Throughout the '40s, the band was the most popular act in country music and their reign lasted for over a decade, with their popularity only beginning to slip in the early '50s, when honky tonk and countrypolitan pop dominated the attention of the record-buying public. Nevertheless, the Sons of the Pioneers continued to exist in varying incarnations well into the '90s.

The roots of the Sons of the Pioneers lie with Roy Rogers, who was originally known as Len Slye (he changed his name when he left the group to star in movies in 1937). Rogers was singing with the Rocky Mountaineers in California and recruited Bob Nolan as a singing partner through a radio advertisement. After Nolan joined, so did one of his friends, a fiddler called Bill "Slumber" Nichols. However, Nolan didn't stay with the group long, because money was growing short; he was replaced by Tim Spencer. Rogers, Nichols, and Spencer left the Rocky Mountaineers shortly after the addition of Spencer, joining the International Cowboys. That too was short-lived, and the trio formed their own group, the O-Bar-O Cowboys.

The O-Bar-O Cowboys toured around the Southwest without gaining much of a following. By the summer of 1933, Nichols left the band and became a golf caddie. Rogers left in the fall of the year, becoming part of the California-based Texas Outlaws, which was led by Jack Lefevre; the group had a regular show on the Hollywood radio station KFWB. At the same time, he began playing with Nolan and Spencer in separate sessions. Soon, the pair joined the Texas Outlaws. Nolan had been writing songs, as had Spencer, and the radio station happened to hear their original material. The station was impressed and offered Nolan, Spencer, and Rogers their own spot and named the group the Pioneer Trio. After they were given a regular spot, the trio decided to expand their lineup to include a fiddler called Hugh Farr and changed their name to the Pioneers. Before their first radio appearance in March of 1934, the station's announcer claimed on the air that since the group was too young to be pioneers, they should be called sons of the pioneers. The name stuck and the group became regulars at the radio station and in local concerts. The band made some recordings for the Standard Recording Company at the end of the year which were pressed on 78s and sent to radio stations across the US.

At the end of 1934, Hugh Farr's brother Karl was added to the lineup as a guitarist. After he joined the band, the group's sound was firmly in place. The Sons of the Pioneers had a swinging beat, jazz inflections, smooth harmonies, yodels, and pop-tinged song structures. They developed a stage act that featured stylized adaptations of Western staples like rope tricks. Soon, they became a popular act across America. In early 1935, the group joined the roster of Decca Records, one of the first artists the new label signed. They also inked a deal with Columbia Pictures to appear in movies, beginning with *The Old Homestead*, which starred Charles Starrett; between 1935 and 1941 they were in 31 movies, all of which starred Starrett.

Tim Spencer left the group in 1936, following a major argument after the Texas centennial; he was replaced by Lloyd Perryman. The following year, they signed a deal with Columbia Records, recording their first session in October of 1937. Within a few months, Roy Rogers left the group to pursue a solo career. Pat Brady replaced Rogers in the beginning of 1938. That year, they toured the country and made a series of recordings for NBC's Orthacoustic Transcription series. For the next few years, the Sons of the Pioneers continued to tour, record, and make movies, becoming one of the most popular groups in America. In 1941, Spencer

rejoined the band. Later that year, the band renewed their union with Roy Rogers, appearing in a series of films with him for Republic Pictures; Rogers and the Sons of the Pioneers would make movies at Republic until 1948.

After World War II arrived, Perryman and Brady joined the service; they were respectively replaced by Ken Carson and Deuce Spriggens, who was later replaced by George "Shug" Fisher. In 1945, when Brady returned from the war, they signed with RCA Victor, where they stayed for nearly 25 years. For the rest of the decade, the Sons of the Pioneers had a steady stream of hits for the label. Their initial records for RCA featured the work of many Nashville sidemen, including guitarist Chet Atkins, who would later produce the group's records. Tim Spencer left the group for a second and final time in 1949, due to vocal problems; he was replaced by Ken Curtis. That same year, Bob Nolan grew tired of performing and left the group; he was replaced by Tommy Doss.

In the early '50s, the Sons of the Pioneers became increasingly pop-oriented. Not only did they accompany everyone from Perry Como and the Fontaine Sisters to opera singer Ezio Pinza, their records began to feature overt pop techniques in their production, including the presence of heavy strings.

By the mid-'50s, the Sons of the Pioneers had passed the peak of their popularity. They would continue to perform and record, but their lineup was anything but steady for the next four decades. Ken Curtis left the group in 1952, becoming an actor; his best-known role would be Festus in the television show *Gunsmoke*. Dale Warren replaced him. In 1958, Hugh Farr left the group; in 1962, his brother Karl died unexpectedly. Karl was replaced in the group by Roy Lanham. Luther Nallie joined as the group's lead singer in 1968. Following his addition, the lineup was stable for nearly a decade as the group was led by Lloyd Perryman. Perryman died in 1977 and the leadership of the band was assumed by Dale Warren. In the '80s, their activity slowed somewhat, but the Sons of the Pioneers continued to perform. — *Stephen Thomas Erlewine*

☆ **Columbia Historic Edition** / 1982 / CBS ♦♦♦♦♦
This group wrote the book on dreamy, close-harmony crooning to panoramic vistas. Leader Bob Nolan supplies poetic lyrics, and Hugh and Karl Farr provide the Django Reinhardt/Stephane Grappelli-inspired accompaniment. Archetypal sounds from the '30s. — *Mark A. Humphrey*

Vol. 3 / 1987 / Bear Family ♦♦♦♦

Vol. 4 / 1987 / Bear Family ♦♦♦♦
This final volume in the series contains 16 tracks recorded at the end of the '40s, some of which are released here for the first time. — *AMG*

★ **Country Music Hall of Fame** / 1991 / MCA ♦♦♦♦♦
The Sons of the Pioneers' *Country Music Hall of Fame* contains 16 of the group's classic recordings for Decca, which span from the '30s into the early '50s. Nearly every one of the band's biggest hits and most famous songs, including "Tumbling Tumbleweed," "Ride Ranger Ride," and "Cool Water," are featured on the compilation, making it both a definitive retrospective and an excellent introduction. — *Stephen Thomas Erlewine*

Empty Saddles / MCA ♦♦♦♦
All of the Pioneers' '30s-era compilations are fine, but this includes Bob Nolan's darkest and most beautiful song, "Blue Prairie." — *Mark A. Humphrey*

Southern Pacific

Country
Stu Cook, John McFee, Tim Goodman, David Jenkins, and Kurt Howell formed this group in mid-1983. Southern Pacific's rock 'n' roll past dogged the group's reputation. Keith Knudsen and John McFee were former members of the Doobie Brothers (McFee had played alongside Huey Lewis in a band called Clover), original lead vocalist Tim Goodman had recorded a solo album, and Stu Cook performed in Creedence Clearwater Revival. Even when Goodman left the band, they replaced him with another ex-rocker, former Pablo Cruise vocalist David Jenkins. They did have one member with strong country roots: Kurt Howell played keyboards for Crystal Gayle. Southern Pacific signed with Warner, and released a strong debut album in 1985, though the media continually questioned the band's commitment to country. The group plied a danceable brand of country, and hit a high point with their 1988 album *Zuma*, which included their biggest single, "New Shade of Blue." Eventually, Southern Pacific left country music to pursue a pop career. — *Tom Roland*

● **Greatest Hits** / 1991 / Warner Bros. ♦♦♦♦
Why this group never quite made "the big time" remains a mystery. The material's sometimes two-step-able, sometimes kick-ass, and in "New Shade of Blue," they out-Eagled the Eagles. — *Tom Roland*

Red Sovine (Woodrow Wilson Sovine)

b. Jul. 17, 1918, Charleston, WV, **d.** Apr. 4, 1980, Nashville, TN
Guitar, Vocals / Traditional Country
Though he had a long, distinguished career in country music, singer-songwriter and guitarist Red Sovine is best remembered for his earnest,

funny and at times highly sentimental odes to the lives of the American trucker. Born to an impoverished family, Sovine was inspired as a child by WCHS radio musicians Buddy Starcher and Frank Welling. Sovine and his childhood friend Johnnie Bailes joined Jim Pike's Carolina Tar Heels and performed as the Singing Sailors. It was not a particularly successful venture and Sovine later became a factory worker in Eleanor, WV. Eventually Sovine became a middle manager with the company. He also continued to put on a local radio show while his friend Johnnie went on to form the Bailes brothers.

Bailes continued to encourage Sovine to return to music, and in the late '40s, Sovine finally began pursuing a radio career again. He landed a job at KWKH, Shreveport, but they gave him an early morning spot and his performances went unnoticed. This was frustrating and he was ready to quit the business when Hank Williams helped him get a better position at WFSA Montgomery, AL, where he soon developed a large following. With Williams' help, Sovine landed a contract with MGM Records in 1949.

Over the next four years, Sovine recorded 28 singles, mostly honky tonks, that didn't make much of a dent on the charts but did establish him as a solid performer. When not recording, Sovine starred on Shreveport's "Louisiana Hayride." In the early '50s, Webb Pierce, one of his fellow "Louisiana Hayride" performers, began having a string of Top Ten country hits. Pierce convinced Sovine to lead his Wondering Boy band and then helped get Red signed to Decca in 1954. Sovine continued recording but had no hits until he did a duet with Goldie Hill, "Are You Mine?," which peaked in the Top 15 in 1955. The following year, he had his first No. 1 when he duetted with Webb Pierce on George Jones' "Why Baby Why." Also in 1956, Sovine had two other Top Five singles, which gave the singer a boost of confidence. Late in 1956, he had a brief stint on the Grand Ole Opry and then he left to work on the Philip Morris Caravan tour. After producing close to 50 sides with Decca by 1959, Sovine signed to Starday and began touring the club circuit as a solo act. It took him five years to produce a hit for the label with "Dream House for Sale," which reached No. 22 in 1964—nearly eight years after his last hit.

In 1966, Sovine at last found his niche when he recorded "Giddy-up Go," his very first spoken-word truck driver song. The single spent six weeks atop the country charts and even crossed over to become a minor pop hit. Subsequent truck-driving hits included the ghost story "Phantom 309" and the tearjerking tale of a crippled child's CB-radio relationship with caring truckers, "Teddy Bear," which spent three weeks at the top of the country charts in 1976. He followed "Teddy Bear" with "Little Joe," the tale of a blinded trucker and his devoted canine friend. Sovine died in 1980 after suffering a heart attack while driving his van. — *Sandra Brennan*

The Best of Red Sovine / Starday ✦✦✦✦
Although it doesn't have many tracks, *The Best of Red Sovine* contains all his big hits and is an excellent introduction to one of the kings of truck-driving songs. — *Thom Owens*

The Statler Brothers

Traditional Country, Country-Pop
Brothers Harold and Don Reid (Phil Balsey and Jimmy Fortune round out the present quartet) have been the kings of country groups since the mid-'60s. The brothers, who began as a gospel quartet in 1955, made it big in 1965 with "Flowers on the Wall," a pop and country hit. In spite of competition from other groups over the years (the Oak Ridge Boys, Alabama, the Judds), the Statler Brothers have pretty much remained in the traditional country mold while winning every award in sight, over 400 in all. Their distinct sound is unmistakable, nostalgic, and unique. Hits include "You Can't Have Your Kate and Edith Too," "Elizabeth," "Class of '57," and "I'll Go to My Grave Loving You." In 1991, their television show quickly became the highest-rated weekly series on TNN. — *David Vinopal*

★ **The Best of the Statler Brothers** / 1975 / Mercury ✦✦✦✦✦
Released in 1975, Mercury's *The Best of the Statler Brothers* is a concise and entertaining run-through of the group's biggest hits of the early '70s, including the Top Ten hits "The Class of '57," "Do You Remember These," and "Bed of Rose's." — *Thom Owens*

The Best of the Statler Brothers, Vol. 2 / 1980 / Mercury ✦✦✦✦
A follow-up to their prior greatest-hits release, this compilation features their late '70s hits like "Do You Know You Are My Sunshine," "The Official Historian on Shirley Jean Berrell," and "How to Be a Country Star." — *Ron Wynn*

★ **Flowers on the Wall: The Essential Statler Brothers** / Mar. 1996 / Columbia/Legacy ✦✦✦✦✦
The Statler Brothers started their recording career at Columbia Records and cut eight albums for the label in five years, scoring eight country singles chart entries, including the Top Ten hits "Ruthless," "You Can't Have Your Kate and Edith, Too," and the pop Top Ten crossover "Flowers on the Wall." This 18-track compilation also includes standards like "The Wreck of the Old '97," "Green Grass," and "Oh Happy Day," and one previously

unreleased track, "Half a Man," which, despite having been recorded two years later, sounds like the logical follow-up to "Flowers on the Wall." The influence of the Statlers' employer, Johnny Cash, is apparent, especially on "Hammer and Nails," on which he appears. At this early stage, without losing the sound of the classic country quartet, the Statlers also sang pop, folk, and gospel well. The only complaint to be made about this set is that, in the CD age, a running time of 42:15 is short for a compilation. But nothing essential is missing. — *William Ruhlmann*

Gary Stewart

b. May 28, 1945, Letcher County, KY
Bass, Guitar, Piano / Traditional Country, Country-Rock
While much of what passes for contemporary country music these days sounds like reheated Eagles and Lynyrd Skynyrd, what's really annoying is what a youth-driven market it has become, leaving many great country performers of the '60s and '70s out in the cold. This is especially irritating when considering the career of Gary Stewart, one of the greatest of the hardcore honky tonk school who, at his peak in the mid- to late '70s, could write and sing circles around just about any contemporary country star you can mention. A native of Florida, Stewart escaped a lifetime of working in an airplane factory in the late '60s by pitching some songs he'd written to soon-to-be RCA country label honcho Jerry Bradley. At the time, Stewart (who was composing with his friend Bill Eldridge) didn't aspire to more than being an in-demand Nashville songwriter, but after a couple of years writing with some success, and through Bradley's continued intercession, he was given the opportunity to record on his own. With his huge, vibrato-laden tenor voice (which sounds a bit like Jerry Lee Lewis'), Stewart, with the inestimable help of songwriter Wayne Carson, released 1975's *Out Of Hand*, one of the finest honky tonk records of all time. Paced by the hit "She's Actin' Single (I'm Drinkin' Doubles)," Gary Stewart was quickly becoming a country music star.

Although he composed songs for traditional Grand Ole Opry stars (Cal Smith, Hank Snow), Stewart himself never emulated the traditional values espoused by the Nashville establishment; as one of his song titles stated he was more of a "flat natural-born good-timin' man." He hung out (and caroused plenty) with Southern-rock musicians, using them on his albums at a time when this was still considered radical. He was a renegade, unwilling to play the Nashville game, and his increasing success provided him with the autonomy he needed to do his own thing. However, this generally meant conspicuous excess, especially when it came to substance abuse. Still, from 1975 through 1980, Stewart's recorded work is mostly excellent, with a high point coming in 1977 with the release of *Your Place or Mine*. A hard-driving slice of aggressive honky tonk, it was a rollickingly good piece of work, not the equal to *Out Of Hand*, but as important an assertion of Stewart's independence from the machinations of country music's star-making machinery. There were problems, however: Stewart was too country for rock audiences and too rock for country audiences, and that limited his broader appeal.

In 1980, he released *Cactus and a Rose*, with considerable help from Southern-rock vets Gregg Allman, Dickey Betts, Mike Lawler, and Bonnie Bramlett. It was a fine record, but attracted only Stewart's core audience, and at this point in his career, that simply wasn't enough. Suddenly it seemed as if his desire and creativity vanished. He hooked up with Dean Dillon and made a couple of terrible two-good-ol'boy records that made the redneck rowdiness of Hank Williams, Jr., sound philosophical by comparison. Not long afterwards, Stewart returned to Florida and stopped recording. After his alcoholism and drug use pretty much cancelled out a large part of the '80s, Stewart returned, clean and sober, with a strong comeback record, *Brand New*, in 1988. It wasn't the Gary Stewart of old, but it was a respectable record, and it was enough to propel a comeback that continues with his recent *I'm A Texan*. Considering that most folks had given him up for dead, this was a remarkable turn of events. His heyday was in the '70s, but Gary Stewart deserves to be celebrated for his considerable talent, tenacity, and influence. — *John Dougan*

☆ **Out of Hand** / 1975 / HighTone ✦✦✦✦✦
Stewart's best album and one of the greatest honky tonk records ever recorded, *Out of Hand* has "Drinkin' Thing," "She's Actin' Single (I'm Drinkin' Doubles)," and "I See the Want To In Your Eyes," as strong a grouping of songs as on any Stewart record. Few, if any, country performers have made a better hard honky tonk record (although Joe Ely came the closest). If you get tired of the songs about drinking and want something a little less self-pitying and uplifting, this won't be for you, but a true fan of country music better own this. — *John Dougan*

Your Place or Mine / 1977 / RCA ✦✦✦✦
If anything has hurt this record since its release, it's that some of the tracks ("Rachel" and "Broken Hearted People") sound a bit pro forma, and the drinking songs sound a little tired. But the best tracks (the title cut and "Ten Years of This") are as good as anything on *Out of Hand*. The record's diamond is Stewart's version of Rodney Crowell's "Ain't Living Long Like This," which he sings as if his life depended on it. It's a truly

transcendent moment, perhaps Stewart's best single moment on record (although his vocal on the title track comes pretty close). One of the great hard country records of all time, *Your Place or Mine* (though few will admit it) is one of the records that contemporary country artists borrow from shamelessly. —*John Dougan*

☆ **Greatest Hits** / 1981 / RCA ✦✦✦✦
A little on the short side (ten tracks), but with 50% of them coming from either *Out of Hand* or *Your Place or Mine*, this is as filler-free and succinct a career summation of Stewart available. Ironically, much of this sounds similar to what has made Garth Brooks and his ilk millionaires many times over, and Stewart (who was truly ahead of his time) was nearly forgotten. No one ever said life (especially in the music business) was fair, but a few spins of this and you will soon understand that nearly 20 years later, Stewart still stands taller than virtually all of the country performers making a mint from imitating his style. A perfect place to start. —*John Dougan*

Brand New / 1988 / HighTone ✦✦✦
Stewart ends a lengthy recording hiatus, showing a newfound maturity while tackling songs that are still rife with tortured self-revelation. His voice has lost little of its edge. —*Michael McCall*

★ **Gary's Greatest** / 1992 / HighTone ✦✦✦✦✦
Featuring material recorded from 1973 to 1990—including songs from both his RCA and HighTone days—*Gary's Greatest* has 17 of Stewart's best songs and is an excellent introduction to the underappreciated singer-songwriter. —*Thom Owens*

I'm a Texan / Oct. 15, 1993 / HighTone ✦✦✦
More impassioned than ever, Stewart continues to excel at raw-boned honky tonk and revved-up country-rock. The songs don't all live up to his treatment, but when they do, as on "Honky Tonk Hardwood Floor" or the inviting "Come on In," he reveals the timidity that undercuts the new traditionalists of the modern country era. —*Michael McCall*

Doug Stone

Vocals / Traditional Country, Contemporary Country
Doug Stone's sensitive Deep South baritone has made him one of country's premier romantic balladeers. This Georgian can sing hard traditional country and easy country with equal ease. For years diesel mechanics was his day job, and he hated it. This dissatisfaction carries over into his music and his stage presence, which presents him as distant and alone; he knows what he's singing about. With the release of his first album, his record company announced the dawning of a new "Stone Age." They weren't far off, as acceptance from country's female-dominated audience was almost immediate; his second album, 1991's *I Thought It Was You*, overdid the self-pity but yielded a couple of hits, including the title cut. "I'd Be Better Off (In a Pine Box)" was his breakthrough song. Shortly before the release of his third album, *From the Heart*, in 1992, 35 years of Southern fried food sent Stone under the surgeon's knife for quadruple bypass surgery. —*Brian Mansfield & David Vinopal*

More Love / 1983 / Epic ✦✦✦
With "Addicted to a Dollar," balladeer Stone stakes his claim for "hot country" status alongside all his Nashville peers. —*Dan Cooper*

Doug Stone / 1990 / Epic ✦✦✦✦
"I'd Be Better Off (In a Pine Box)" is a towering expression of self-pity that most singers could spend a career trying to top. If Stone never bested his performance on his debut, he came close with ballads like "In a Different Light" and "My Hat's Off to Him," becoming a genuine heartthrob in the process. —*Brian Mansfield*

I Thought It Was You / 1991 / Epic ✦✦✦
Self-pity has always played an integral role in country music, but it's more effective a song at a time, not spread over an entire album. Unlike some harder-voiced honky tonkers who funnel their emotions into cathartic country blues, Stone seems to wallow in sorrow. His ex is showing him up; his kid's growing up too fast; his new wife's walking out on him and telling him to shut up as he slams the door. This guy's favorite honky tonk even gets turned into a fern bar. —*Brian Mansfield*

From the Heart / 1992 / Epic ✦✦✦

The First Christmas / Apr. 1992 / Epic ✦✦✦
Given the number of songwriters in Nashville, it's surprising the town hasn't produced more Christmas songs. *The First Christmas* gets a bunch of them, though. Songs like "An Angel Like You" play off Stone's romantic-balladeer image, and "When December Comes Around" would sound great any time of year. "Sailing Home for Christmas" depicts the irony of soldiers celebrating the coming of "peace on earth" while stationed on a battleship. —*Brian Mansfield*

● **Greatest Hits, Vol. 1** / 1995 / Epic ✦✦✦✦
Greatest Hits, Vol. 1 does an effective job of chronicling all of Stone's biggest hits from the early '90s. Most of his Top Ten hits are featured, including the No. 1 singles "In A Different Light," "A Jukebox With A Country

Song," "Too Busy Being In Love," and "Why Didn't I Think of That." —*Thom Owens*

George Strait

b. May 18, 1952, Pearsall, TX
Guitar, Vocals / Traditional Country, Western Swing, Contemporary Country
Out of all the new country singers to emerge in the early '80s, George Strait stayed the closest to traditional country. Drawing from both the honky tonk and Western swing traditions, Strait didn't refashion the genres; instead, he revitalized them for a new decade. In the process, he became one of the most popular and influential singers of the decade, sparking a wave of neo-traditionalist singers from Randy Travis and Dwight Yoakam to Clint Black, Garth Brooks, and Alan Jackson.

Strait was born and raised in Texas, the son of a junior high school teacher who also owned and operated a ranch that had been in the Strait family for nearly hundred years. When George was a child, his mother left the family, taking her daughter but leaving her sons with the father. During his childhood, he would spend his weekdays in town and his weekends on the ranch. Strait began playing music as a teenager, joining a rock 'n' roll garage band.

After his high school graduation in the late '60s, George enrolled in college but he soon dropped out and eloped with his high school sweetheart Norma. In 1971, Strait enlisted in the Army; two years later, he was stationed in Hawaii. While in Hawaii, he began playing country music, initially with an Army-sponsored country band called Rambling Country. They played several dates off the base under the name Santee. Strait left the army in 1975, returning to Texas with the intent of completing his education. He enrolled in Southwest Texas State University at San Marcos, where he studied agriculture. While he was studying, he formed his own country band, Ace in the Hole.

Ace in the Hole made a few records for the independent Dallas-based label D in the late '70s, but they never went anywhere. Toward the end of the decade, Strait attempted to carve out a niche in Nashville, but he failed since he lacked any strong connections. In 1979, he became friends with Erv Woolsey, a Texas club owner that had formerly worked for MCA Records. Woolsey had several MCA executives come down to Texas to hear Strait. His performance convinced the company to sign him in 1980.

"Unwound," George's first single, was released in the spring of 1981 and climbed into the Top Ten. The follow-up, "Down and Out," stalled at 16, but "If You're Thinking You Want a Stranger (There's One Coming Home)" reached No. 3 in early 1982. The song sparked a remarkable string of Top Ten hits that ran well into the '90s. During that time he had an astonishing 31 No. 1 singles, beginning with 1982's "Fool Hearted Memory."

Throughout the '80s, he dominated the country singles charts and his albums consistently went platinum or gold. Strait rarely abandoned hardcore honky tonk and Western swing—toward the beginning of the '90s, his sound became a little slicker, but it was only a relative change. George was also one of the few '80s superstars to survive the generational shift of the early '90s that began with the phenomenal success of Garth Brooks. In 1992, he made his first movie, *Pure Country*, which featured him in the lead role. George released a four-disc box set career retrospective, *Strait Out of the Box*, in 1995. By the spring of 1996, it had become one of the five-biggest selling box sets in popular music history. *Blue Clear Sky*, his 1996 album, debuted on the country charts at No. 1 and the pop charts at No. 7. —*Stephen Thomas Erlewine*

Right or Wrong / 1983 / MCA ✦✦✦
The title track is vintage Bob Wills, and much here draws from similar swinging Southwestern roots. —*Mark A. Humphrey*

Strait Country/Strait from the Heart / 1983 / MCA ✦✦✦
Two early albums appear in one. The first and arguably the best of the '80s crop of Haggard-indebted hats, Strait has never much wavered from a Western-swing tinged, honky tonk base. —*Mark A. Humphrey*

☆ **Does Fort Worth Ever Cross Your Mind** / 1984 / MCA ✦✦✦✦✦
Included are hardcore country shuffles, sudsy weepers, and swinging stompers. This is '80s "nu-traditional" country at its finest and most heartfelt. —*Mark A. Humphrey*

Something Special / 1985 / MCA ✦✦✦✦
Schmaltzier than some, it's still consistent with Strait's work. —*Mark A. Humphrey*

★ **Greatest Hits** / 1986 / MCA ✦✦✦✦✦
A good overview of Strait's MCA chartbusters from the early '80s, it includes "Right or Wrong," "Amarillo by Morning," "You Look So Good in Love," "Fool Hearted Memory," "A Fire I Can't Put Out," "Let's Fall to Pieces Together," and several other hits. —*Mark A. Humphrey*

☆ **Greatest Hits, Vol. 2** / 1987 / MCA ✦✦✦✦✦
Greatest Hits, Vol. 2 picks up George Strait's string of hits in 1984 and has ten of his biggest singles from the mid-'80s, including "Does Fort Worth Ever Cross Your Mind," "The Fireman," "The Chair," "Nobody In

His Right Mind Would've Left Her," "It Ain't Cool to Be Crazy About You," "Ocean Front Property," and "All My Ex's Live in Texas." —*Stephen Thomas Erlewine*

Pure Country / 1992 / MCA ✦✦✦

The soundtrack to the movie of the same name starring George Strait himself. The songs are a little larger than life if you are a Strait fan, but very nice nevertheless. Some were put together just for this movie. "Where the Sidewalk Ends" and "The King of Broken Hearts" stand out, but the version of "I Cross My Heart" recorded here is just one great song. —*Michael Erlewine*

☆ Strait Out of the Box / Sep. 12, 1995 / MCA ✦✦✦✦✦

George Strait was one of the few country singers of the '80s that kept hardcore country alive, whether it was honky tonk, Western swing, or his forte, balladry. *Strait Out of the Box* is the definitive chronicle of his career, containing all 31 of his No. 1 singles, as well as 11 other hits, 19 album cuts, and 11 rare cuts. Over the course of the four discs, Strait proves that he defined the new traditionalist movement of the decade and left behind an impressive body of great recordings. For fans of both Strait and country music, *Strait Out of the Box* is essential listening. —*Stephen Thomas Erlewine*

Blue Clear Sky / Apr. 1996 / MCA ✦✦✦✦

Country's most consistent traditionalist, George Strait, scores again with *Blue Clear Sky,* one of the best albums of his 15-year career. Strait apparently made the best of a recording break afforded by last year's four-CD retrospective, *Strait Out of the Box,* which has become the third best-selling box set in history, following those by Bruce Springsteen and Led Zeppelin. *Blue Clear Sky* shows off Strait's range with a well-chosen sweep of material. "Rockin' in the Arms of Your Memory" and "I'd Just as Soon Go" prove that well-written, mainstream adult ballads can carry an insinuating strength when performed with the subtle grace of a master. On "Need I Say More," Strait reveals, again, that he's also a wonderful jazz-tinged crooner. "I Ain't Never Seen No One Like You" swings with the joyful ease of a youngster on a backyard set, and "Do the Right Thing" gives Strait the chance to show casually that he can navigate an eccentric meter, masking how difficult the inventive arrangement might have been for a lesser vocalist. Strait, an experienced calf-roping competitor, also includes "I Can Still Make Cheyenne," the best of the recent spate of songs about rodeo riders. Instead of creating a deadly dramatic situation or joking about the macho manner of the lifestyle, the song uses a telephone call between a struggling rider and his lover to convey the dreams, the fears, the financial hardships and the difficulties of life on the road that surround the sport. Just like the singer, the song relies on quietly reserved emotion to convey enormously important sentiments. —*Michael McCall*

Marty Stuart

Mandolin, Vocals / Traditional Bluegrass, Country-Rock
Fusing honky tonk with a gritty rockabilly backbeat and a fondness for bluegrass, Marty Stuart became one of the most popular country performers of the early '90s. Stuart was as well-known for his edgy music as he was for his flamboyant, glittery Nudie suits—he was the only performer of his era to wear the gaudy outfits. Throughout the early '90s, he racked up a string of Top 40 hits.

The Mississippi-born Stuart was a child prodigy on guitar and mandolin. By the age of 12 he had played with the Sullivans, and by age of 13, he had joined Lester Flatt's band as a guitarist. Although he was becoming a professional musician, Stuart continued his schooling via correspondence courses and graduated from high school in 1975 at age 17. In 1973, Stuart became Flatt's mandolin player after Roland White left the band. Soon he was also singing lead vocals and harmonies. Stuart remained with Flatt until 1978, when the aging musician disbanded the group because of his failing health. Following the group's breakup, Stuart began working with Doc and Merle Watson. A year later he married Johnny Cash's daughter Cindy and was invited to join his father-in-law's band; he played with Johnny until 1985.

In 1982, Marty Stuart released his first solo effort, *Busy Bee Cafe,* to positive reviews. The album, which appeared on Sugar Hill, featured an all-star lineup of backup musicians including Cash, Earl Scruggs, the Watsons, and Carl Jackson. Stuart left Cash's band for a full-time solo career in 1985. That year, he released an eponymous solo album on Columbia Records. The album yielded four minor hits, including the Top 20 "Arlene." Later in 1986, his marriage with Cindy Cash disintegrated and he was dropped from Columbia. Afterward he went back to Mississippi and rejoined the Sullivans. While he was gone, Columbia released two more of his songs, "Mirrors Don't Lie" and "Matches," which both became moderate hits in 1988. The following year, Stuart's luck changed and he signed with MCA.

Stuart's first album for MCA, *Hillbilly Rock,* generated several hit singles, including "Don't Leave Her Lonely Too Long" and the title track, which became his first Top Ten hit. Stuart's second album, *Tempted,* was his breakthrough album, producing the Top Ten hit singles "Little

Things" and "Tempted." Late in 1991, Stuart duetted with Travis Tritt on the No. 2 hit, "The Whiskey Ain't Working." The following year, the two singers embarked on the popular "No Hats Tour." Also in 1992, Stuart released *This One's Gonna Hurt You* and had two Top Ten hits and three additional Top 20 singles. Marty joined the Grand Ole Opry in 1993 and then released a fourth album, *Love and Luck.* In 1995, he released the compilation, *Marty Stuart Hit Pack.* —*Sandra Brennan*

This One's Gonna Hurt You / 1992 / MCA ✦✦✦

Stuart starts by relating how he received Hank Williams, Sr.'s blessing in a dream. With covers of Charlie Pride's "Just Between You and Me" and Ol' Mae Belle's "High on a Mountain Top," he makes you believe. But the most retro stuff gets too hamfisted to keep *This One's Gonna Hurt You* on the same level as *Tempted.* —*Brian Mansfield*

● Marty Stuart Hit Pack / 1995 / MCA ✦✦✦✦

Marty Stuart Hit Pack has all of Stuart's big hits from the late '80s and early '90s, including the Top Ten singles "Hillbilly Rock," "Little Things," "Tempted," and "Burn Me Down." —*Thom Owens*

Honky Tonkin's What I Do Best / Jun. 18, 1996 / MCA ✦✦✦

The title is a little misleading—honky tonkin' may be what Marty Stuart does best, but he doesn't limit himself to straight honky tonk. Stuart likes to twist things around, adding in bluegrass flourishes and hints of mad, twangy rockabilly. And that stylistic diversity is what makes *Honky Tonkin's What I Do Best* engaging. Sure, Stuart's voice remains a bit thin and indistinctive, but he pours his heart into the songs, which is what makes this one of his best records. Though there are the occasional weak spots, his sustained energy and passion elevate the performances into something special. —*Thom Owens*

Sweethearts of the Rodeo

Contemporary Country
Drawing from country-rock, bluegrass, and pop, the Sweethearts of the Rodeo—Janis Oliver Gill and Kristine Oliver Arnold—made a series of records in the late '80s and early '90s that received positive reviews, particularly for their harmonies, and earned them a dedicated cult following. Janis and Kristine Oliver were both born and raised in Manhattan Beach, CA, and influenced by the Byrds and Poco. The sisters began performing country and bluegrass music in high school and then played various clubs along the California coast—Kristine sang leads while Janis harmonized and played guitar. In 1973, the sisters began calling themselves Sweethearts of the Rodeo after the Byrds album of the same name, and began moving their music toward county-rock. Emmylou Harris spotted the sisters and their band at a Long Beach bluegrass festival; following a Sweethearts of the Rodeo club performance, Harris invited them to sing in one of her shows. The appearance with Harris led to the Sweethearts opening for acts like Willie Nelson, Poco, and Pure Prairie League. The latter band featured Vince Gill and Leonard Arnold, who would later marry Janis and Kristine, respectively. Not long after their weddings, the sisters stopped performing in favor of raising kids. The Gills moved to Nashville in 1983, where Vince began work on his career. Soon after he signed to RCA, producer Steve Buckingham encouraged Janis to continue with her own career. When the Arnolds moved to Nashville, the sisters resumed their act. The Sweethearts of the Rodeo got their first big break in 1985 when they won the prestigious Wrangler Country Showdown. While participating in the talent contest, the sisters were one of the showcased acts, which gained the attention of Columbia Records; by the end of the year, they had signed with the label. In 1986, the duo scored a Top 30 hit with their debut "Hey Doll Baby." Their second single, "Since I Found You," hit the Top Ten, and "Midnight Girl" hit the Top Five. The Sweethearts released their second album, *One Night, One Time,* in 1988 and had two Top Five hits, "Satisfy You" and "Blue to the Bone." In 1990, they released a third album, *Buffalo Zone,* which was followed two years later with *Sisters,* their last record for a major label. In 1993, they signed with Sugar Hill and released *Rodeo Waltz.* —*Sandra Brennan*

● Sweethearts of the Rodeo / 1986 / CBS ✦✦✦✦

These California sisters gone to Music City, feature good vocal harmony on contemporary, rock-tinged country. —*Mark A. Humphrey*

Rodeo Waltz / 1993 / Sugar Hill ✦✦✦

This album is refreshingly open, and the soft Nashville production provides a fine background for the sweet vocal harmonies. "Jenny Dreamed of Trains," "Get Rhythm," and "Broken Arrow" are standout cuts. —*Richard Meyer*

Beautiful Lies / Aug. 1996 / Sugar Hill ✦✦✦

B.J. Thomas (Billy Joe Thomas)

b. Aug. 7, 1942, Houston, TX
Vocals / Gospel, Country-Pop, Pop-Rock
B.J. Thomas straddled the line between pop-rock and country, achieving success in both genres in the late '60s and '70s. At the beginning of his career, he leaned more heavily on rock 'n' roll, but by the mid-'70s, he had turned to country music, becoming one of the most successful country-

pop stars of the decade. Thomas began singing while he was a child, performing in church. In his teens, he joined the Houston-based band the Triumphs, who released a number of independent singles that failed to gain any attention. For the group's last single, Thomas and fellow Triumph member Mark Charron wrote "Billy and Sue," which was another flop. After "Billy and Sue," Thomas began a solo career, recording a version of Hank Williams' standard "I'm So Lonesome I Could Cry" with producer Huey P. Meaux. Released by Scepter Records in early 1966, the single became an immediate hit, catapulting to No. 8 on the pop charts. Although he had a series of moderate follow-up hits, including a re-release of "Billy and Sue," Thomas failed to re-enter the Top Ten until 1968, when "Hooked On A Feeling" became a No. 5 hit. The following year, he scored his biggest hit with Burt Bacharach and Hal David's "Raindrops Keep Fallin' On My Head," taken from the hit film *Butch Cassidy and the Sundance Kid*. It was followed by a string of soft-rock hits in the next two years, including "Everybody's Out of Town," "I Just Can't Help Believing," "No Love At All," and "Rock and Roll Lullaby," which featured guitarist Duane Eddy and the vocal group the Blossoms.

After "Rock and Roll Lullaby," Scepter Records went out of business and B.J. Thomas headed to Paramount Records. At Paramount, Thomas had no hits, prompting the singer to pursue a new country-pop direction at ABC Records. "(Hey Won't You Play) Another Somebody Done Somebody Wrong Song," his first single for ABC, became his second No. 1 record on the pop charts, as well as establishing a country career for the vocalist. For the next decade, he continued to have hits on the country charts, with a couple of songs—most notably "Don't Worry Baby"—crossing over into the pop charts. During this period, he switched record companies at a rapid pace, but it did nothing to slow the pace of his hits. Thomas hit his country peak in 1983 and 1984, when he had the No. 1 hits "Whatever Happened to Old Fashioned Love" and "New Looks From an Old Lover," as well as the Top Ten hits "The Whole World's In Love When You're Lonely" and "Two Car Garage." Throughout the '80s, B.J. Thomas recorded a number of hit gospel records for Myrrh concurrently with his country hits. At the end of the '80s, the hits began to dry up for Thomas, but he continued to tour and put out the occasional country and gospel record in the '90s. *— Stephen Thomas Erlewine*

● **Greatest Hits [Rhino]** / 1990 / Rhino ✦✦✦✦
A fine 18-song collection that features all of B.J. Thomas' greatest hits, from "I'm So Lonesome I Could Cry" through "Hooked On A Feeling" to "(Hey Won't You Play) Another Somebody Done Somebody Wrong Song," *Greatest Hits* is the definitive retrospective of his career. *— Stephen Thomas Erlewine*

More Greatest Hits / Sep. 12, 1995 / Varese Saraband ✦✦✦✦
Picking up where Rhino's *Greatest Hits* collection left off, Varese's *More Greatest Hits* doesn't have any of the big hit singles, but it is ideal for those listeners that want to dig a little deeper into B.J. Thomas' extensive catalog. *— Thom Owens*

Hank Thompson (Henry William Thompson)

b. Sep. 3, 1925, Waco, TX
Guitar, Vocals / Traditional Country, Western Swing, Honky Tonk
Country Hall of Famer Hank Thompson has had chart hits in five different decades. Between Bob Wills and Asleep at the Wheel, there was Thompson in his Brazos Valley Boys, keeping the sound of Western swing alive. His swing music and well-written honky tonk songs produced 21 Top 20 charters from 1949 and 1958. His signature song, "The Wild Side of Life" (1952), was his biggest hit, prompting Miss Kitty Wells to defend bar-life females in "It Wasn't God Who Made Honky Tonk Angels." Much of his best music was set in the dim lights and thick smoke of the honky tonk, with such hits as "Hangover Tavern," "On Tap, in the Can, or in the Bottle," "Smokey the Bar," "A Six-Pack to Go," and "Honky Tonk Girl." While music tastes changed during his career, he kept on touring world wide with his band, keeping true honky tonk and Western swing in the public's ear. He's often seen on Ralph Emery's *Nashville Now* TV show. *—David Vinopal*

Country Music Hall of Fame Series / 1992 / MCA ✦✦✦✦
These 1968-1978 recordings from Dot Records document a past-his-prime Thompson still capable of turning out good singles when the Nashville Sound didn't smother him. *—Brian Mansfield*

● **Vintage** / 1996 / Capitol ✦✦✦✦
Vintage contains nearly all of the essential items from Hank Thompson's salad days at Capitol Records, including his signature song, "The Wild Side of Life." Featuring almost 20 tracks, it's the closest thing to a definitive retrospective yet assembled. *— Thom Owens*

Mel Tillis

b. Aug. 8, 1932, Pahokee, FL
Guitar, Vocals / Traditional Country
Though he stutters when he speaks, Mel Tillis is downright eloquent in his singing and superb songwriting ("Ruby, Don't Take Your Love to

Town" and "Detroit City," a huge hit for Bobby Bare). Over 500 of his songs have been covered by the likes of Faron Young, Kenny Rogers, folksinger Burl Ives, and Webb Pierce. Among his recordings that hit No. 1 are "Good Woman Blues," "Heart Healer," "Coca-Cola Cowboy," and "Southern Rains." As an actor he's appeared in *W. W. and the Dixie Dance Kings* and *Uphill All the Way* (1986) with Roy Clark. His winning personality and sense of humor lead him to regular TV appearances. *—David Vinopal*

American Originals / 1989 / CBS ✦✦✦✦
American Originals compiles material from Tillis' brief time at Columbia Records. He was with the label at the beginning of his career, and while he was there, he primarily recorded his own material. *American Originals*, though too brief at ten tracks, gives a good sense of his developing talents. *— Thom Owens*

● **Greatest Hits** / 1991 / Curb ✦✦✦✦
Featuring a selection of his late '70s and early '80s hits—including the No. 1 hits "Coca Cola Cowboy," "Lying Time Again," "Southern Rains," "Your Body Is an Outlaw," "New Patches," and "Blind In Love"—Curb's *Greatest Hits* is a serviceable, but not thorough, retrospective that does work as an effective introduction to Mel at the height of his popularity. *— Thom Owens*

Pam Tillis

b. 1957, Plant City, FL
Vocals / Contemporary Country
Like several other children of famous fathers, Pam Tillis overcame several obstacles to establish herself as an individual artist, not simply as the daughter of country vocalist Mel Tillis. Eventually, she earned her own identity, which led to a string of country hits in the early '90s. Like her father, Tillis is a singer-songwriter and actress. Tillis was raised in Nashville where she made her debut on the Grand Ole Opry stage at the age of eight. As a child she took classical piano lessons and began playing guitar at age 12 by watching an instructional show on television.

Tillis made her professional debut during a talent contest at Nashville's Last Chance Saloon when she was a teenager. Being raised in Nashville, Tillis had a natural affinity for country music, but she also found herself drawn to other genres. When she was a teenager, she was a rebel, partying too hard and generally running wild. At the age of 16, she suffered a nearly fatal car crash that left her face so badly shattered that she had to undergo painful reconstructive surgery for the next five years. Tillis persevered and enrolled in the University of Tennessee. While attending the university, she founded the High Country Swing band and performed in a folk duo with Ashley Cleveland. In 1976, she dropped out of school to become a songwriter, taking a job at her father's Sawgrass Music publishing house. Barbara Fairchild recorded one of her early tunes, "I'll Meet You on the Other Side of Morning."

Eventually, Tillis wanted to find her own musical identity, so she formed the Pam Tillis Band and moved to San Francisco. Once in San Francisco, she changed the group's name to Freelight and the band became an experimental free-form jazz and rock outfit. In 1978, she went back to Nashville and became a backup singer for her dad. Soon, she fronted her own R&B band. Pam continued to write songs, providing pop singers like Gloria Gaynor and Chaka Khan with successful songs. Tillis made her own recording debut in 1983, releasing *Beyond the Doll of Cutey* on Warner Bros. A year later, she had her first charting single with "Goodbye Highway," which inched its way to No. 71. It would be another two years before she reappeared on the charts with the moderate hit, "Those Memories of You." Throughout the latter half of the '80s, she had a string of minor country hits. During this time, she also wrote commercial jingles, wrote songs for Tree Publishing, and performed in Las Vegas. In 1987, Tillis was nominated for Best New Female by the Academy of Country Music.

For a brief time at the turn of the decade, Tillis flirted with pop music, but she decided to return to her country roots in 1990, when she signed with Arista Records. "Don't Tell Me What to Do," her first single for the label, catapulted to No. 5, becoming her first genuine hit. For the next few years, she had a steady stream of hit singles, highlighted by "Maybe It Was Memphis," which reached No. 3 in early 1992. In 1992, she released *Homeward Looking Angel* and in 1993, it too went gold. In 1994, her album *Sweetheart's Dance* reached the country Top Ten and earned her the Country Music Association's prestigious Female Vocalist of the Year award. In 1995, she released *All of This Love*. *—Sandra Brennan*

Put Yourself in My Place / 1991 / Arista ✦✦✦✦
The album that established Tillis as a performer in her own right has a traditional country base cut with bluegrass, folk, and rock. It all creates the same sort of mixed breed she sings about in "Melancholy Child": "You take a black Irish temper, some solemn Cherokee, a Southern sense of humor, and you got someone like me." Her characters are the awkward dancers of "I've Seen Enough To Know": bruised, tentative, and needing to be cajoled back to love. Even the throwaway songs are of a

high standard; the best ones ("Maybe It Was Memphis," "Don't Tell Me What to Do") are truly enticing. —*Brian Mansfield*

Homeward Looking Angel / 1992 / Arista ✦✦✦

● **Pam Tillis Collection** / Feb. 1, 1994 / Warner Bros. ✦✦✦✦
Before hitting big with Arista Records and "Don't Tell Me What to Do," Tillis had recorded rock-influenced country for Warner Bros. She had minor success with the likes of "There Goes My Love" and "These Memories of You," but what makes *Collection* interesting is early versions of "One of Those Things" and "Maybe It Was Memphis," as well as a version of "Five Minutes," later a hit for Lorrie Morgan. —*Brian Mansfield*

Sweetheart's Dance / Apr. 26, 1994 / Arista ✦✦✦✦
Producing herself for the first time (along with Steve Fishell), Tillis found the magic blend of Nashville Sound, California country-rock, and post-Beatles pop. She released the heady "Spilled Perfume" as her first single, but the riches of *Sweetheart's Dance* go much deeper: the Bo Diddley/Tejano rhythms of "Mi Vida Loca (My Crazy Life)," the lilting waltz of "In Between Dances," and a playfully romantic title cut. A charming album without a bad cut, *Sweetheart's Dance* ranks with the best of Trisha Yearwood, Wynonna Judd, and Carlene Carter. —*Brian Mansfield*

All Of This Love / Nov. 7, 1995 / Arista ✦✦✦

Floyd Tillman

b. Dec. 8, 1914, Ryan, OK
Guitar, Vocals / Traditional Country, Honky Tonk
This Hall of Famer is probably best known for writing "It Makes No Difference Now," a country classic that he sold to Jimmie Davis for $300 in 1938, only to watch it become a hit for Davis, Bob Wills, Bing Crosby, Gene Autry, and others. In the late '40s he had recording hits with his self-penned "Slippin' Around" and "I Love You So Much It Hurts." His Western swing/honky tonk mixture and his easy vocal delivery have made him a much-imitated performer, and for good reason. —*David Vinopal*

● **Country Music Hall of Fame Series** / 1991 / MCA ✦✦✦✦
Tillman had his biggest hits in the late '40s while recording for Columbia, but these World War II–era sides for Decca show him as a leader of a Texas dance band that's not afraid to mix it up with some jazz playing. Moon Mullican plays piano on a number of these sides. —*Brian Mansfield*

☆ **The Best of Floyd Tillman** / CBS ✦✦✦✦✦
It contains his classics, such as "Slippin' Around" and "Gotta Have My Baby Back." Wait for this one; with Columbia reissuing much of its vintage country material, this stuff has got to appear on CD in some form. —*Richard Lieberson*

Aaron Tippin

b. 1958, Pensacola, FL
Vocals / Contemporary Country, New Traditionalist
Aaron Tippin was part of a new traditionalist wave of honky tonk singers in the '90s. Tippin's music was among the rootsiest of the new traditionalists, but that didn't stop him from becoming massively popular—his singles regularly charted in the Top Ten and his albums went platinum.

Tippin was raised on a 120-acre family farm in South Carolina; his chief influences include Jimmie Rodgers, Hank Thompson, and Lefty Frizzell. At age ten, he began playing guitar and soon after began performing in local groups. At age 20, he was working as a commercial pilot, but switched to music before obtaining his Airline Transport Rating. During the early '80s, he wrote songs for various Nashville publishing outfits. In 1986, he permanently moved to Nashville, where he eventually became a staff writer at Acuff-Rose. He also tried to land his own recording contract, to little success. Eventually, a demo tape of his arrived at RCA, who offered him a contract.

Tippin's debut single, "You've Got to Stand for Something," reached the Top Ten in 1991 and was followed by an album of the same name. The album spawned two other minor hit singles and peaked at No. 25 on the country charts. *Read Between the Lines*, his second album, was released in 1992 and contained his first No. 1 single, "There Ain't Nothing Wrong with the Radio." *Read Between the Lines* climbed to the Top Ten and crossed over to the Top 50 on the pop album charts. It went platinum in 1993 and produced two more hits, including the Top Five "I Wouldn't Have It Any Other Way." In 1993, Tippin released his third album, *Call of the Wild*, which went gold four months after its release. Tippin's fourth album, *Lookin' Back at Myself*, appeared the following year. *Tool Box*, his fifth album, was released in 1995. —*Sandra Brennan*

You've Got to Stand for Something / 1991 / RCA ✦✦✦✦
This exciting hardcore country comes from a man whose previous blue-collar experience as a farm hand, welder, pilot, and truck driver made him a publicist's dream. It includes the singles "You've Got To Stand for Something," "I Wonder How Far It Is Over You," and "She Made a Memory out of Me." —*Brian Mansfield*

Read between the Lines / 1992 / RCA ✦✦✦✦
A good follow-up by this popular hatless hillbilly contains "There Ain't Nothin' Wrong with the Radio," "I Wouldn't Have It Any Other Way," "My Blue Angel," and more. —*Mark A. Humphrey*

Call of the Wild / Aug. 1993 / RCA ✦✦✦
Though he was still capable of singing up a storm and cranking out great grooves, some of Tippin's song choices were hillbilly silly. Of course, they were also the singles, which had names like "Honky Tonk Superman" and "Working Man's Ph.D." —*Brian Mansfield*

● **Lookin' Back at Myself** / Nov. 8, 1994 / RCE ✦✦✦✦
Lookin' Back At Myself has a good cross-section of Aaron Tippin's biggest hits and best songs, making it an excellent introduction. —*Thom Owens*

Tool Box / Nov. 21, 1995 / RCA ✦✦✦
Aaron Tippin's *Tool Box* ranks among his finest work, as the singer explores slightly new territory. In addition to his trademark honky tonk, barroom ravers, there are a number of soulful ballads that demonstrate the full range of Tippin's talents. —*Stephen Thomas Erlewine*

Merle Travis

b. Nov. 29, 1917, Rosewood, KY, **d.** Oct. 20, 1983, Tahlequah, OK
Guitar / Instrumental, Traditional Country, Bluegrass
As a guitarist and songwriter, Travis is unsurpassed in the business; he's one of the few to have an instrumental style named after him—"Travis picking"—putting him in the elite company of Earl Scruggs and the Carter Family. Travis learned his distinctive 3-finger-style guitar from fellow Kentuckians Mose Rager and Ike Everly (father of Phil and Don), and he transferred the banjo roll to the guitar. Travis style uses the thumb to play the bottom notes of a chord individually, while playing the melody on the higher strings with the index finger and occasionally the third finger. The result is a constant motion and flow of the lower notes, while the melody floats on the top. The influence of this style can't be overstated: super-picker Chet Atkins has acknowledged his debt to Travis.

Before the war, Travis was a member of two important bands, the Georgia Wildcats and the influential Browns Ferry Four, with Grandpa Jones and the Delmore brothers, Alton and Rabon. After his discharge from the Marine Corps, he had numerous hits, self-written or with others, including "Divorce Me C.O.D.," "So Round, So Firm, So Fully Packed," "Smoke, Smoke, Smoke that Cigarette," "Dark as a Dungeon," and "Sweet Temptation." In 1947 he wrote and recorded "Sixteen Tons" and watched Tennessee Ernie Ford eight years later make it perhaps the blockbuster hit in the history of country music. Country music is so much richer thanks to multi-talented Merle Travis. —*David Vinopal*

Walkin' the Strings / 1960 / Capitol ✦✦✦✦
Although originally issued on LP in 1960 (it was reissued on CD in 1996), these 22 songs were actually recorded in the late '40s and early '50s for Capitol's *Electrical Transcription* series. This showcases Travis' fingerpicking abilities at their best, on unaccompanied acoustic vocal and instrumental numbers; most of the material is original, with a few standards by the likes of Stephen Foster and Georgia Tom Dorsey. —*Richie Unterberger*

★ **The Merle Travis Story**—24 Greatest Hits / 1989 / CMH ✦✦✦✦✦
Although *The Merle Travis Story*—24 Greatest Hits consists of re-recordings from the late '70s, it gives a better sense of why Travis was important than Rhino's *The Best of Merle Travis*. Unlike Rhino's set, CMH concentrates on Travis' guitar playing, which is why he was an important musician. Therefore, it gives a far better sense of why the guitarist was a revered, influential artist than the vocal hits of Rhino's collection, even if the music was recorded late in his career. —*Thom Owens*

The Best of Merle Travis / 1990 / Rhino ✦✦✦✦
Rhino's *The Best of Merle Travis* may contain all of his big chart hits, but it's a misleading collection. Instead of focusing on Travis' revolutionary playing, the set runs through his hits and novelty songs, which all emphasize his vocals. Therefore, it isn't quite as comprehensive—or essential—as it initially appears. The album hints at his greatness, but never shows why Travis' playing was so groundbreaking. —*Thom Owens*

Folk Songs of the Hills [expanded] / 1996 / Capitol ✦✦✦✦
In 1946, Capitol approached Travis with the idea of cutting a folk album, and although he wasn't an especially folk-oriented artist, he agreed to give it a go. Although the resulting 1947 record (released as a 78-rpm album) didn't sell well, it was a respectable effort performed by Travis on solo acoustic guitar. Folksy introductions embellish the songs, which include standbys like "John Henry" and "Nine Pound Hammer." Travis added a few songs of his own penned in the folk style, and one of these, "Sixteen Tons," would prove to be his most famous composition, reaching No. 1 when it was covered by Tennessee Ernie Ford in the 1950s. The CD reissue combines the eight songs from the 1947 release with four songs from the Capitol *Electrical Transcription* series that were added to the batch when the album was reissued as *Back Home* in 1957; it also

adds a song from the 1946 sessions that was previously unreleased in the US, "This World Is Not My Home." —*Richie Unterberger*

Randy Travis (Randy Traywick)

b. May 4, 1959, Marshville, NC
Guitar, Vocals / Contemporary Country, New Traditionalist
Like the Beatles in rock, Randy Travis marks a generational shift in country music. When his *Storms of Life* came out in 1986, country music was still wallowing in the post-*Urban Cowboy* recession, chasing elusive crossover dreams. Travis brought the music back to its basics, sounding like nothing so much as a perfect blend of George Jones and Merle Haggard. He became the dominant male voice in country until the rise of "hat acts" like Garth Brooks and Clint Black, releasing seven consecutive No. 1 singles during one stretch. He won the CMA's Horizon Award in 1986 and was the association's Male Vocalist of the Year in 1987 and '88.

Randy Travis was born and raised in North Carolina, in a small town outside of Charlotte. Travis' father encouraged his children to pursue their musical inclinations, as he was a fan of honky tonkers like Hank Williams, George Jones, and Lefty Frizzell. Randy began playing guitar at the age of eight and within two years, he and his brother Ricky had formed a duo called the Traywick Brothers. The duo played in local clubs and talent contests.

Both of the brothers had a wild streak, which resulted in Ricky going to jail after a car chase and Randy running away to Charlotte at the age of 16. While he was in Charlotte, he won a talent contest at Country City USA, a bar owned by Lib Hatcher. Hatcher was impressed by Travis and offered him a regular gig at her bar, as well as a job as a cook.

For several years, he sang and worked at Country City. He still had trouble with the law in his late teens. At his last run-in with the police, the judge told him if he saw Travis again, he should be prepared to go to jail for a long time. Randy was released into the care of Hatcher. In a short time, Hatcher became Travis' manager and the pair began to concentrate on his career. Joe Stampley helped Randy land a contract with Paula Records in 1978. The following year, Travis released two singles under his given name; one of them, "She's My Woman," scraped the bottom of the country charts.

In 1982, Travis and Hatcher moved to Nashville, where she managed the Nashville Palace nightclub while he sang and cooked. Within a couple of years, the pair independently released his debut album under the name Randy Ray; the record was called *Randy Ray Live* and sold primarily in the Nashville Palace.

Thanks to Hatcher's persistent efforts and the *Randy Ray Live* album, Warner Brothers signed Randy in 1985 and suggested that he change his performing name to Randy Travis. "On the Other Hand," his first single for the label, was released in the summer of that year and climbed to No. 67. Despite its lackluster performance, radio programmers were enthusiastic for Travis, as evidenced by the No. 6 placing of "1982," which was released late in the year. "1982" was followed by a re-release on "On the Other Hand" in the spring of 1986. This time, the song hit No. 1.

Storms of Life, Travis' full-fledged debut album, was released in the summer of 1986 and became a huge success, eventually selling over three million copies. Travis was the first country artist to go multi-platinum; before his success, most country artists had difficulty achieving gold status. With his mass appeal, he set the stage for country music's crossover success in the early '90s. However, Travis dominated the late '80s. The last two singles from *Storms of Life,* "Diggin' Up Bones" and "No Place Like Home," hit No. 1 and 2, respectively. "Forever and Every, Amen"—the first single from Randy's second album, 1987's *Always & Forever*—began a streak of seven straight No. 1 singles that ran through 1989. *Always & Forever* was more successful than his debut, reaching No. 19 on the pop charts and going quadruple platinum; it also earned him the CMA's award for Male Vocalist of the Year. *Old 8X10* (1988) and *No Holdin' Back* (1989) weren't quite as successful as their predecessors, but they still spawned No. 1 singles and both went platinum.

Travis was still at the top of his form in the beginning of the '90s, starting the decade with his biggest hit, "Hard Rock Bottom of Your Heart." However, his hold at the top of the charts began to slip after Clint Black and, in particular, Garth Brooks. Nevertheless, Randy never fell away completely—his albums continued to go gold and he usually could crack the Top Ten. *Wind in the Wire,* a soundtrack to his television special released in 1992, marked his first unsuccessful album—none of the singles broke the Top 40. *This is Me,* released in 1994, was a successful comeback to the top of the charts, featuring "Whisper My Name," his first No. 1 hit in two years. In 1996, Travis released *Full Circle.* —*Brian Mansfield & Stephen Thomas Erlewine*

☆ **Storms of Life** / 1986 / Warner Bros. ◆◆◆◆◆
His first and best album features astonishing Lefty Frizzell-style pipes, excellent material, and sympathetic production. Easily the most impressive country debut of the '80s, it includes "1982," "On the Other Hand," "Diggin' up Bones," and "No Place like Home." —*Mark A. Humphrey*

Always & Forever / 1987 / Warner Bros. ◆◆◆◆
This one stayed at the top of the country charts for ten months and sold five million copies. Well, of course he was huge. If you had songs as good as "Forever and Ever, Amen" you'd be a star too. —*Brian Mansfield*

Old 8x10 / 1988 / Warner Bros. ◆◆◆◆
Almost on a par with *Storms of Life, Old 8x10* lacks the monster hits of his debut but wears just as well. When Travis sings of love, he doesn't mean romance; there's a permanence in his voice that sounds like settling down. The album contains "Honky Tonk Moon," "Deeper than the Holler," and "Is It Still Over?" —*Brian Mansfield*

No Holdin' Back / 1989 / Warner Bros. ◆◆◆◆
Featured are "Hard Rock Bottom of Your Heart," "Somewhere in My Broken Heart," and "He Walked on Water." —*AMG*

Heroes and Friends / 1990 / Warner Bros. ◆◆◆
This duets album includes the obvious influences (George Jones, Conway Twitty, Tammy Wynette) as well as a few surprises (B.B. King, Clint Eastwood). The Jones song, "A Few Ole Country Boys," and the title track were hit singles. —*Brian Mansfield*

High Lonesome / 1991 / Warner Bros. ◆◆◆
With young whippersnappers like Clint Black and Garth Brooks breathing down his neck, Travis realized he needed to be more than just a pretty voice. On *High Lonesome* he proved he could write, too, helping pen five of the album's ten songs, including "Forever Together" for his manager-turned-wife Lib Hatcher, and "I'm Gonna Have a Little Talk," sung a cappella with Take 6. It also includes "Better Class of Losers," written with Alan Jackson. —*Brian Mansfield*

Wind in the Wire / 1992 / Warner Bros. ◆◆

★ **Greatest Hits, Vol. 1** / Sep. 15, 1992 / Warner Bros. ◆◆◆◆◆
When Travis finally got around to releasing a greatest-hits collection, he realized he had almost enough material for two albums. So, adding two new songs to each, he put them out simultaneously. Volume one gets the edge for including those first two hits, "1982" and "On the Other Hand"; the best of the new songs, "If I Didn't Have You"; and the shattering "Reasons I Cheat," which proved as early as 1986 that Travis could write 'em as well as sing 'em. —*Brian Mansfield*

☆ **Greatest Hits, Vol. 2** / Sep. 15, 1992 / Warner Bros. ◆◆◆◆◆
Eleven more Travis classics are included here, among them "Diggin' Up Bones," "Forever and Ever, Amen" and a fabulous remake of Brook Benton's "It's Just a Matter of Time." The new songs are "Look Heart, No Hands" and "Take Another Swing at Me." —*Brian Mansfield*

This Is Me / 1994 / Warner Bros. ◆◆◆◆
The vanity project *Wind in the Wire* excepted, Travis hadn't released an album of new music in three years, and some people were wondering what had happened to the man who started the neo-traditionalist boom. *This Is Me,* which included the wildly funny "Before You Kill Us All" and a stunning song called "Whisper My Name" that synthesized countrypolitan with gospel, silenced most of the questioners and showed the young whippersnappers what all the fuss had been about in the first place. —*Brian Mansfield*

Full Circle / Aug. 1996 / Warner Bros. ◆◆◆◆

Travis Tritt

b. 1963
Guitar, Vocals / Contemporary Country
Travis Tritt was one of the leading new country singers of the early '90s, holding his own against Garth Brooks, Clint Black, and Alan Jackson. He was the only one not to wear a hat and the only one to dip into bluesy Southern-rock. Consequently, he developed a gutsy, outlaw image that distinguished him from the pack. Throughout the early '90s, he had a string of platinum albums and Top Ten singles, including three No. 1 hits.

Tritt fell in love with music as a child, teaching himself how to play guitar when he was eight and beginning to write songs when he was 14. Travis was determined to have a musical career but his parents didn't encourage him to follow his instincts. His mother didn't mind that he wanted to perform, but she wanted him to sing gospel; his father was afraid there was no money in singing. When he was 18, he tried to settle down, work, and have a family but he was unsuccessful—he was married and divorced twice before he was 22. He continued to play music while working various jobs, including one at an air-conditioning company. The company's vice-president was a guitarist who gave up hopes of a musical career and he urged Tritt to follow his dreams. Travis quit his job and began pursuing a career full-time.

In 1982, Tritt began his pursuit by recording a demo tape at a private studio which was owned by Danny Davenport, who happened to be an executive at Warner Bros. Davenport heard the vocalist's songs and was impressed, deciding to take Travis under his wing. For the next several years, the pair recorded demo tapes while Tritt played the honky tonk circuit. The singer was developing a distinctive sound, adding elements of country-rock and Southern-rock to his honky tonk. Part way through in 1989, Warner Bros.' Nashville division signed Tritt and his debut album, *Country Club,* appeared in the stores in the spring 1990. It was preceded by the Top Ten hit, "Country Club." Upon the release of his debut album, Travis entered the first ranks of new country singers. His next two singles, "Help Me Hold On" and "I'm Gonna Be Somebody," hit No. 1 and 2 respectively. "Put Some Drive In Your Country," which had a clear rock and roll influence, stalled at No. 4, since radio programmers were reluctant to feature such blatantly rock-derived music.

Despite his success, the Nashville music industry was hesitant to embrace Tritt. His music and stage show owed too much to rock and roll, and his image didn't conform with the behatted legions of new male singers. Nevertheless, Travis had a breakthrough success with his second album, 1991's *It's All About to Change.* Prior to its release, he had hired manager Ken Kragen, who also worked with Lionel Richie, Trisha Yearwood, Kenny Rogers, and We Are the World. Kragen helped market Tritt in a way that appealed to both country fans and a mass audience, sending *It's All About to Change* into multi-platinum territory.

T-R-O-U-B-L-E, Tritt's third album, was released in 1992. Although it didn't match the success of *It's all About to Change,* it had the No. 1 single "Can I Trust You With My Heart" and went gold. Travis bounced back to in 1994 with *Ten Feet Tall & Bulletproof,* which went platinum, spawned the No. 1 single "Foolish Pride," and marked his highest position, No. 20, on the pop charts. His 1995 compilation *Greatest Hits*—From the Beginning went platinum within six months of its release. —*Stephen Thomas Erlewine*

Country Club / 1990 / Warner Bros. ✦✦✦
Tritt proclaimed his influences early with "Put Some Drive in Your Country," which paid homage not only to Roy Acuff and George Jones but to Hank Williams, Jr. and Duane Allman as well. It was the lowest-charting single off Tritt's debut, but it sold him a ton of albums. Radio programmers preferred the ambitious "I'm Gonna Be Somebody" and the ballads "Help Me Hold On" and "Drift off to Dream." —*Brian Mansfield*

It's All About to Change / 1991 / Warner Bros. ✦✦✦✦
Better production means ballads like "Anymore" sound bigger and rockers like "Bible Belt" (with Little Feat) and a cover of bluesman Buddy Guy's "Homesick" rock harder. Tritt brought in Marty Stuart for a duet on "The Whiskey Ain't Workin'" and revived "Here's a Quarter (Call Someone Who Cares)" as a catchphrase. —*Brian Mansfield*

T–R-O-U-B-L-E / 1992 / Warner Bros. ✦✦✦
Tritt's covers of Buddy Guy ("Leave My Girl Alone") and Elvis Presley ("T-R-O-U-B-L-E") are nice touches and show deeper roots than the Gary Rossington co-write ("Blue Collar Man") or the last album's Little Feat remake. Beyond that, *T-R-O-U-B-L-E* is almost indistinguishable from *It's About to Change:* a good novelty song masquerading as more, a couple of ballads with big flourishes, and a large helping of Southern. That's a good formula, granted, but it still sounds like a formula. —*Brian Mansfield*

Ten Feet Tall & Bulletproof / 1994 / Warner Bros. ✦✦✦✦
Tritt's most personal album is the one in which he feels most comfortable with his Southern-rock/outlaw mantle. ("Outlaws like Us," in fact, features the voices of Hank Williams Jr. and Waylon Jennings.) Tritt poked fun at his own foibles in the title track and co-wrote "Wishful Thinking" and "No Vacation from the Blues" with Lynyrd Skynyrd's Gary Rossington. "Wishful Thinking" and "Foolish Pride" are ballads that rival "Anymore" for power and Skynyrd and Bob Seger for production values. —*Brian Mansfield*

● **Greatest Hits**—From the Beginning / Sep. 12, 1995 / Warner Bros. ✦✦✦✦
Greatest Hits—From the Beginning features 15 of Travis Tritt's biggest hits, including "Country Club," "Help Me Hold On," "Here's a Quarter (Call Someone Who Cares)," and "Tell Me I Was Dreaming." Although there are a couple of hits missing, nothing essential has been overlooked and it's a first-rate introduction. —*Stephen Thomas Erlewine*

Restless Kind / Aug. 27, 1996 / Warner Bros. ✦✦✦✦
Under the direction of Don Was, Travis Tritt turns in one of his leanest and easily his grittiest country record yet with *Restless Kind.* Cutting back the country-rock flourishes that have always distinguished his sound, Tritt opts for twangy guitars, wailing fiddles, Dobros, and unaffected guts vocals. Mirroring the stripped-down instrumentation, the song selection is straightahead honky tonk, rockabilly and traditional country. Tritt benefits immeasurably from this approach—he has never sounded so alive. Actually, he has never sounded so purely country. —*Thom Owens*

Ernest Tubb (Ernest Dale Tubb)

Guitar, Vocals / Traditional Country, Honky Tonk
The incomparable Ernest Tubb ("E.T." to all who knew him) became a legend as much for what he was personally as for the half-century career that stretched from his first radio date in 1932 to his death in 1984. Though other singers with better voices and more raw musical talent have come and gone, none has inspired greater love of the fans over six

decades. Along with such performers as Jimmie Rodgers, Roy Acuff, Bill Monroe, Hank Williams, Lefty Frizzell, and George Jones, E.T. is country music personified. Tubb was among the first of the honky tonk singers and the first to achieve national recognition. His first recording was "The Passing of Jimmie Rodgers," a tribute to his hero. His long association with Decca began with "Blue Eyed Elaine" in 1940. Three years later his self-penned "Walkin' the Floor Over You," a country classic, was a hit, leading to the Opry, movie roles, and stardom. In 1947 he opened his Nashville record store and began the "Midnight Jamboree," which followed the Opry on WSM and advertised the shop while showcasing stars and those on the rise. Over the years, Tubb toured widely with his Texas Troubadours, pressing the flesh with fans after shows that featured his many hits, including "Slippin' Around," "Two Glasses Joe," "Tomorrow Never Comes," "Drivin' Nails in My Coffin," "Rainbow at Midnight," "Let's Say Goodbye Like We Said Hello," and "Driftwood on the River." In 1975, after 35 years with Decca/MCA, he was let go, the allegiance of company executives not matching that of his multitude of fans. Because of a lung disease Ernest Tubb had to rest in pain on a cot between takes, ending his career just as his hero Jimmie Rodgers had 50 years earlier. Quoting one of his album titles, Tubb left a legend and a legacy. —*David Vinopal*

★ **Country Music Hall of Fame** / 1987 / MCA ✦✦✦✦
This set focuses on Tubb's early influential recordings (only three tracks came from the '50s, and only two from the '60s), and its "historical correctness" is a mixed blessing. Had the CMF programmed this with something of the "historic sweep" applied to its Monroe set, they could have given us a more entertaining and varied representation of one of country's most beloved legends. — *Mark A. Humphrey, Rock & Roll Disc*

Live 1965 / 1989 / Rhino ✦✦✦✦
Live 1965 wasn't intended to be a special show, but in a way that's why it is. The album was recorded in 1965 on one of Ernest Tubb's many concerts that year and it captures him in his element, joking with the audience and running through a selection of his greatest hits. Though the performance certainly isn't raucous, it's engaging and the disc functions as a valuable historical document. —*Stephen Thomas Erlewine*

Let's Say Goodbye Like We Said Hello / Bear Family ✦✦✦✦
This five-disc boxed set of Tubb's 1947-1951 recordings (all 115 of them) is arguably "most of the best" of E. T., including his hillbilly jive exchanges with Red Foley. —*Mark A. Humphrey*

Yellow Rose of Texas / Bear Family ✦✦✦✦
Beginning right where *Let's Say Goodbye Like We Said Hello* ended, the five-disc set *Yellow Rose of Texas* contains 150 songs that Ernest Tubb recorded for Decca Records in the '50s, beginning in 1954 and finishing at the end of the decade. Though the set is ideal for a collector, the sheer comprehensive nature of the box makes it difficult for anyone but diehard fans or historians to enjoy. —*Thom Owens*

Tanya Tucker (Tanya Denise Tucker)

b. Oct. 10, 1958, Seminole, TX
Vocals / Country-Rock, Contemporary Country
Tanya Tucker had her first country hit in 1972 when she was just 13 years old. Over the next two decades, Tucker became one of the few child performers to mature into adulthood without losing her artistry. Over the course of her career, she developed a remarkably long streak of Top Ten and Top 40 hits.

Born in Seminole, TX, much of Tucker's childhood was spent moving throughout the Southwest with her family, as her father moved from town to town pursuing construction jobs. At the age of six, Tanya began taking saxophone lessons; two years later, she decided she wanted to sing. When she was eight, she made an auspicious debut, performing a few songs onstage with Mel Tillis. Before the show, Tucker saw Tillis sitting alone in a car and she approached the vocalist, asking him about singing for a career. He asked her to sing and was so impressed with her talent that he asked her to perform with him that evening. A year after the concert, Tanya convinced her father that she was serious about becoming a professional singer and he decided that the family would help her achieve her dream. After appearing on the "Lew King Show" in 1969, Tucker and her family moved to Las Vegas, where she performed regularly. Eventually, she recorded a demo tape that gained the attention of songwriter Dolores Fuller, who sent it to producer Billy Sherrill. At the time, Sherrill was the head of A&R at CBS Records. He was impressed with the demo tape and he signed the 13-year-old vocalist to Columbia Records. Sherrill initially planned to have Tucker record "The Happiest Girl in the Whole USA," but she passed on the tune, choosing "Delta Dawn"—a song she heard Bette Midler sing on "The Tonight Show"—instead. Released in the spring of 1972, the song became an instant hit, peaking at No. 6 on the country charts and scraping the bottom of the pop charts.

At first, Columbia Records tried to downplay Tucker's age, but soon word leaked out and she became a sensation—her second single, "Love's the Answer," also became a Top Ten hit later in 1972. Tucker's third single "What's Your Mama's Name" became her first No. 1 single in the spring 1973. Two other No. 1 hits—"Blood Red and Goin' Down" and "Would You Lay with Me (In a Field of Stone)"—followed within a year of the release of "What's Your Mama's Name," establishing her as a major star. In 1975, Tanya Tucker switched labels, signing with MCA Records. At MCA, she had a string of hit singles that ran into the late '70s. During this time, Tucker gained the reputation of being rather wild. It was a difficult time not only for her personal life, but her professional career, as she tried to branch out into pop music. In 1978, she decided to radically change her image and crossover to rock in 1978 with her *T.N.T.* album. Despite the controversy over the album and its sexy cover, the album went gold the following year. Later that year she made her acting debut in a television movie, "The Rebels." By the end of the '70s, her sales were declining—in 1980 she only had two hits. Also in 1980, she recorded a few singles with Glen Campbell, with whom she was romantically linked. None of the songs, including "Why Don't We Just Sleep on It Tonight," made much of an impression on the charts. In addition to recording, she also continued her film career, making her feature film debut in *Hard Country*. She switched to Arista Records in 1982, where she had three hits in late 1982 and 1983, highlighted by the Top Ten "Feel Right." In 1984 and 1985, she had no hits and she left the label by the end of 1985 to sign with Capitol Records. In early 1986, she returned with "One Love at a Time," which rocketed to No. 3. For the rest of the decade, she had a constant stream of Top Ten hits, including four No. 1 hits. Her success continued in the early '90s, even though she could no longer reach the Top Ten regularly by 1995. *—Sandra Brennan*

★ **Greatest Hits** / 1978 / MCA ✦✦✦✦✦
No matter how far Tucker's come the last 20 years, it all comes back to "Delta Dawn," "What's Your Mama's Name?," and the other hillbilly-gothic hits of her youth. Producer Billy Sherrill is best known for his work with George Jones and Tammy Wynette, but how he turned an underage, waifish Southwestern homegirl into a singer is surely his most notable career achievement. *—Dan Cooper*

The Best of Tanya Tucker / 1982 / MCA ✦✦✦
Later '70s material for the blooming of a belter, honky tonk style. *—Mark A. Humphrey*

Greatest Hits [Liberty] / 1989 / Liberty ✦✦✦✦
Tanya Tucker, undergoing her second coming as a commercial country queen, appears here with her 1986-1991 hits. *—Mark A. Humphrey*

Can't Run from Yourself / Sep. 28, 1992 / Liberty ✦✦✦
Edgier and more consistent than *What Do I Do with Me, Can't Run from Yourself* runs the range of Tucker's abilities, from the slow-blues burn of Marshall Chapman's "Can't Run from Yourself" to the wistful melancholy of Hugh Prestwood's "Half the Moon." A rollicking duet with Delbert McClinton on "Tell Me About It" is matched by the fine romance of "Two Sparrows in a Hurricane"; which one you like best will depend strictly on personal preferences. Switch one song on each side, and you've got a side of rockers and a side of ballads. *—Brian Mansfield*

Greatest Hits 1990-1992 / 1993 / Liberty ✦✦✦✦
As the title says, *Greatest Hits 1990-1992* contains all of the biggest hits Tanya Tucker had in the early '80s, including the No. 2 singles "Down to My Last Teardrop," "(Without You) What Do I Do With Me," "Some Kind of Trouble," and "Two Sparrows In A Hurricane," among others. *—Stephen Thomas Erlewine*

Shania Twain

Vocals / Contemporary Country
Encouraged by her parents to pursue a musical career, Ontario native Shania Twain began singing in musical productions at a northern Ontario resort. Recruiting friend Mary Bailey as a manager, she traveled to Nashville to record demos. When it reached an A&R rep at Mercury, he signed the country singer to a contract. Twain's self-titled album debut was released in 1993. Her second album, *The Woman in Me*, appeared two years later; it eventually went double platinum and broke the record for most weeks at No. 1 on the country charts. *—John Bush*

Shania Twain / Apr. 20, 1993 / Mercury ✦✦✦
● **The Woman In Me** / 1995 / Mercury ✦✦✦✦
Shania Twain's second album broke down the doors of stardom for the singer, selling over four million copies by the beginning of 1996. Like many country artists of the mid-'90s, Twain's music combined country conventions with mainstream rock flourishes, creating a sound that appealed to both audiences. *The Woman in Me* isn't necessarily flawless product—the material is a bit inconsistent, and the music plays it a bit too safe—but it all sounds convincing, thanks to the dynamic charisma of Shania Twain. *—Stephen Thomas Erlewine*

Conway Twitty (Harold Lloyd Jenkins)

b. Sep. 1, 1933, Friars Point, MS, **d.** Jun. 5, 1993, Branson, MO
Guitar, Vocals / Traditional Country, Nashville Sound, Countrypolitan
Adored by his fans and respected by his peers in Music City, Conway

Twitty was in many respects the consummate country star. Though with his rhinestones and sideburns he never looked the part, he was also something of a modernist. His knack for singing in a downhome voice laced with bedroom intimacy allowed adult themes to enter country music, without offending conservative listeners. Conway made "going country" sound like growing up.

Twitty did most of his real-life growing up across the river in Helena, AR. Drafted by Uncle Sam and the Philadelphia Phillies both, he started singing in earnest while stationed in Japan. Back home, he knocked around the local nightclubs, mostly singing Elvis-type rockabilly. He changed his name to Conway (after Conway, AR) Twitty (after Twitty, TX), cut a few unissued sides for Sun, and a few that were issued by Mercury. Finally, in 1958, his immortal MGM recording of "It's Only Make Believe" blasted to the top of the pop charts and made Conway Twitty a rock 'n' roll star. After the usual round of follow-up hits, Bandstand appearances, teen exploitation flicks, and waning popularity, Twitty officially "went country" in 1965. Three years later he scored the first of his more than fifty No. 1 country hits with "Next in Line." Another chart-topper, released in 1970, was "Hello Darlin'," the song that would forever be known as his signature tune. An unstoppable hitmaker, both on his own and through his famous duets with Loretta Lynn, Twitty was still going strong when he died at the age of 59. His sudden passing, sad though it was, was nowhere near as depressing as the ugly estate battle that ensued. *—Dan Cooper*

★ **Greatest Hits, Vol. 1** / 1972 / MCA ✦✦✦✦✦
Every one of these songs were Top Ten hits and this 1972 package goes a long way to explain Twitty's appeal. There's not a weak track on this record and smaller hits like "I Wonder What She'll Think About Me Leaving?" and "Image of Me" are every bit as good as the monster hits. *—Jim Worbois*

Greatest Hits, Vol. 2 / 1976 / MCA ✦✦✦
Greatest Hits, Vol. 2 is a fine summation of Conway's early '70s hits, including "You've Never Been This Far Before," "There's A Honky Tonk Angel (Who'll Take Me Back In)," and "I See the Want To in Your Eyes," among others. *—Thom Owens*

Number One's [MCA] / 1982 / MCA ✦✦✦✦
After moving from rock 'n' roll to country, Twitty remained sensitive to criticism he might not be serious, rarely deviating from the standard three-chord country song for about his first decade in the format. This package, which selects material almost randomly from 1975-81, does a good job of showing a Twitty more willing to experiment, particularly with the soulful "Don't Take It Away" and the dramatic "I May Never Get to Heaven." *—Tom Roland*

☆ **20 Greatest Hits** / 1987 / MCA ✦✦✦✦✦
20 Greatest Hits covers a large portion of Conway Twitty's biggest hits, from "Hello Darlin'" to "Red Neckin' Love Makin' Night," making it an excellent retrospective and introduction. *—Stephen Thomas Erlewine*

Number One's: The Warner Brothers Years / 1988 / Warner Bros. ✦✦✦
This greatest-hits set shows (with the exception of "The Rose") an artist in command of his own performance, with a clear grasp on quality material and a strong sense of powerful arrangements. *—Tom Roland*

Greatest Hits, Vol. 3 / 1990 / MCA ✦✦✦
Greatest Hits, Vol. 3 runs through Conway Twitty's big hits from his second stint at MCA Records in the late '80s. The collection includes the Top Ten hits "Julia," "I Want To Know You Before We Make Love," "That's My Job," "Goodbye Time," "Saturday Night Special," "I Wish I Was Still In Your Dreams," and "She's Got a Single Thing In Mind." *—Stephen Thomas Erlewine*

☆ **Silver Anniversary Collection** / 1990 / MCA ✦✦✦✦✦
25 hits from Twitty's work for MCA and Warner Bros. are contained on this album, from "Guess My Eyes Were Bigger than My Heart" (1966) to "She's Got a Single Thing in Mind" (1989). It's an excellent introduction to one of the most popular singers in country music history. *—AMG*

The Best of Conway Twitty, Vol. 1: The Rockin' Years / 1991 / Poly-Gram ✦✦✦✦
This album contains all of the recordings he made for Mercury Records in the late '50s, when he was trying to follow in the footsteps of Elvis. Naturally, there's a lot of rockabilly on the collection—which he did very well—as well as some ballads that hint at his future country career. In between are some of his very best moments, including "It's Only Make Believe," "Mona Lisa," "Is a Bluebird Blue," and "Lonely Blue Boy." *—Stephen Thomas Erlewine*

☆ **The Conway Twitty Collection** / 1994 / MCA ✦✦✦✦✦
A stellar four-disc box set that contains every essential track he ever recorded. Beginning with some early recordings—including a cut from when he was a pre-teen—the set runs through every hit from 1958's "It's Only Make Believe" to 1993's "I'm the Only Thing (I'll Hold Against You)." Several rarities are scattered throughout, but the real treasure is the simple fact that this compilation contains most of his Top Ten hits, including

his duets with Loretta Lynn. It is a lasting testament to his considerable talents. —*Stephen Thomas Erlewine*

Ian Tyson

Guitar, Vocals / Country
The male half of the early '60s folk group Ian & Sylvia, Ian Tyson had retreated from performing and recording after the duo disbanded in the mid-'70s to become a rancher in the foothills of southern Alberta, Canada. He quietly returned to music-making in the 1980s, releasing a series of albums that dwelled on highly detailed songs about the concerns of the working cowboy.

Tyson was born in Victoria, British Columbia. As a child he was involved in rodeo, not music—he didn't learn to play the guitar until he was recovering from rodeo-related injuries. In the late '50s, he began performing as a folk singer. In 1961, he met singer-songwriter Sylvia Fricker and the two musicians began performing together; they would marry three years later. Shortly after their initial meeting, Ian & Sylvia went to New York and signed to Vanguard Records; they also signed a management deal with Albert Grossman, the man responsible for promoting Bob Dylan and Peter, Paul & Mary.

Ian & Sylvia and their band, Great Speckled Bird, became popular on the folk scene and released their self-titled debut album in 1962. In 1963, they released *Four Strong Winds*. The title track, which was written by Tyson, became a folk standard; other important Tyson originals include the plaintive "Someday Soon" and "Summer Wages." Ian & Sylvia successfully recorded together through the mid-'70s. The duo began hosting a television show, "Nashville North," in the early '70s and this became the "Ian Tyson Show" when the two split up in the middle of the decade.

After Ian & Sylvia's breakup, Tyson signed to A&M Records and recorded *Ol'Oen*. He temporarily retired from recording in 1979 to work his ranch in Alberta. Tyson recorded *Old Corrals and Sagebrush* in 1983 for Columbia, and it was a critical success. In 1984, he toured with Ricky Skaggs and also released an eponymous album. Tyson released a third album, *Cowboyography*, two years later. It won Tyson several awards from the Canadian Country Music Association, including Male Vocalist of the Year, Album of the Year, and Single of the Year for "Navajo Rug." He was also awarded the prestigious Juno for Country Male Vocalist of the Year. Tyson has since continued his distinguished recording career.

In 1991, he released another popular Canadian album, *And Stood There Amazed*, which contained the hits "Springtime in Alberta" and "Black Nights." He was inducted into the Canadian Country Music Association's Hall of Honor in 1989, and three years later, he and Sylvia were inducted into the Juno Awards Hall of Fame. —*Sandra Brennan and Michael McCall*

I Outgrew the Wagon / 1989 / Stony Plain ◆◆◆◆
This is the best of his series of homegrown albums on what he calls "cowboy culture." Included are simple, unadorned songs affectionately examining rural life on the Canadian plains. —*Michael McCall*

● **Eighteen Inches of Rain** / 1994 / Vanguard ◆◆◆◆
Tyson emerges from Canada to record an album with producer Jim Rooney in Nashville. The basic charms and wise observations remain, but are brought into focus without detracting from the raw appeal of Tyson's purposefully casual style. —*Michael McCall*

Ricky Van Shelton

b. 1952
Guitar, Vocals / Contemporary Country
Noted for his rich baritone voice, Ricky Van Shelton became an overnight country music sensation in the late '80s—between 1987 and 1994, he had over 13 No. 1 hits. Van Shelton was raised in Grit, Virginia and grew up listening to gospel music. As a teen, he was interested in pop music and had little interest in country music until his brother convinced him to become lead vocalist in his country group. The brothers' band played local clubs at night. By day, Van Shelton worked as a pipe fitter and gas station attendant. After his wife got a job in Nashville, he moved to the city in the mid-'80s; shortly after his arrival, he began playing local clubs. In 1986, he signed with Columbia Records.

Van Shelton's debut single, the title track from his album *Wild Eyed Dream*, hit the Top Ten, beginning a streak of Top Ten hits that ran for several years. During this time, he had No. 1 hits with "Somebody Lied" (1987), "I'll Leave This World Loving You" (1988), "From a Jack to a King" (1989), and "I've Cried My Last Tear for You" (1990). In 1991, he and Dolly Parton had a chart-topper with "Rockin' Years." Van Shelton's first four albums went platinum. By the mid-'90s, his popularity had slipped somewhat, and he had trouble cracking the country Top 40. Despite his declining record sales, he remained a popular concert attraction. —*Sandra Brennan*

Wild-Eyed Dream / 1987 / CBS ◆◆◆
This debut from this country hunk balladeer, with occasional thumpin' at the hop, contains "Working Man Blues," "Crime of Passion," and more. —*Mark A. Humphrey*

Loving Proof / 1988 / CBS ◆◆◆◆
Here are stabs at rockabilly alongside the ballads in which Shelton excels. Some of the songs on the album are "From a Jack to a King" and "Hole in My Pocket." —*Mark A. Humphrey*

RVS 3 / 1990 / CBS ◆◆◆
The third album puts out more sounds in the winning Shelton formula, such as "I Still Love You," "I've Cried My Last Tear for You," "Oh Pretty Woman," and more. —*Mark A. Humphrey*

Backroads / 1991 / CBS ◆◆◆◆
When he's not trying to be Roy Orbison (as he did on 1990's *RVS 3*), it's easy to see that Van Shelton's a fine singer. And this is a fine record—so fine it's tempting to hunt for signs of listener manipulation. But Van Shelton balances the self-pity of songs like "After the Lights Go Out" with the uptempo punch of stuff like "Call Me Up." So even though Van Shelton recycles "Rockin' Years," the duet from Dolly Parton's *Eagle When She Flies*, just call it good taste, sit back, and enjoy. —*Brian Mansfield*

● **Greatest Hits Plus** / 1992 / CBS ◆◆◆◆
Despite rocking hits like "Wild Man" and "I Am a Simple Man" (or even the new cover of Elvis Presley's "Wear My Ring Around Your Neck"), Ricky Van Shelton's greatest-hits collection shows that he's made his best records as a balladeer raised on stone-country gospel. For proof, just listen to "Just As I Am," "I'll Leave This World Loving You" or "Keep It Between the Lines." —*Brian Mansfield*

Porter Wagoner

Vocals / Country-Pop
Porter Wagoner, the Thin Man from West Plains, MO, is a case of an artist often ahead of his time who has always appeared hopelessly behind the times. He's among the most immediately recognizable figures in country music, largely due to his exploiting TV—and flashy costumes—a good 20 years before the video boom. And while he's forever perceived as the man who tried to hold Dolly Parton back from pop success, he was also responsible, in many ways, for putting her in a career position where the issue could even arise. As for his music, since signing with RCA in 1952 he has produced a wealth of superb hard country, and just as much of the most wretchedly oversentimentalized tripe you'll ever want to hear. The latter, of course, is half the reason we love him.

Wagoner was born in West Plains, Missouri. As he grew up, he fell in love with the country music he heard over the radio, teaching himself guitar so he could sing and play along with them. When he was a teenager, he landed a job at a local market, where he would frequently sing when business was slow. The owner believed that Porter's singing was actually helping the store's reputation, so he arranged to sponsor a local radio show that would feature the fledgling vocalist.

Throughout the late '40s, Wagoner was singing on the local West Plains radio station. Eventually, a Springfield radio station called KWTO offered Porter a show in 1951. Around the same time, Red Foley was beginning his *Ozark Jamboree* program, which was based in Springfield and broadcast both on KWTO and national television. Foley brought Wagoner onto his show, which helped the young vocalist land a record contract with RCA Records in 1954. Later that year, his first single "Company's Comin'" hit the Top Ten. It was followed in the spring of 1955 with "A Satisfied Mind," which stayed at No. 4 for four weeks. At the end of the year he released "Eat, Drink, and Be Merry (Tomorrow You'll Cry)," which climbed to No. 3 in early 1956. In 1957, he joined the Grand Ole Opry and moved to Nashville, where he formed his backing band, the Wagonmasters. For the rest of the '50s, Porter continued to record, but he never broke the Top Ten again. It would take another television show for him to return to the top of the charts. In 1961, he began hosting his own television show, which was syndicated out of Nashville. It was the most popular country show of the '60s, growing from 18 stations in 1961 to over a hundred stations in the early '70s. Wagoner often sang with Norma Jean, a new female singer he introduced to the country audience, on these programs. The look of Porter's television show defined country music for much of America's general public during the '60s, although his music rarely departed from traditional country.

In 1967, Norma Jean was fired from the show and replaced with Dolly Parton, who was then an unknown singer. Not only did exposure on Wagoner's program kick-start Dolly's career, it provided a boost for Porter's as well. Parton was enormously popular on the show and their first joint single, "The Last Thing on My Mind," rocketed to No. 7 at the beginning of 1968. The song launched a string of Top Ten hits that ran more or less uninterrupted until 1975, when the duo stopped working together. In 1968, the Country Music Association named the duo the Vocal Group of the Year; the CMA would award them Vocal Duo of the Year in 1970 and 1971, as well.

Although the duo of Wagoner and Parton was successful, it wasn't stress-free. Porter continued to have solo hits during the late '60s and early '70s, though none of them were as big as his songs with Dolly. Furthermore, he resented her attempts at a solo career; on her part, she felt musically restrained by him. The tensions culminated in late 1974, when she parted ways with Wagoner. RCA issued two singles in 1975 and 1976, and both of the songs—"Say Forever You'll Be Mine" and "Is Forever Longer Than Always"—hit the Top Ten. The pair would continue to duet sporadically over the next decade, highlighted by the No. 2 hit, "Making Plans," from 1980. After Parton and Wagoner separated in 1975, Porter continued to film his TV show and to chart singles, but all of his hits were minor. In 1976, he retired from touring, choosing to concentrate on producing at his own studio, Fireside. Wagoner sued Parton in 1979 over various contractual problems; the suit was settled out of court the following year. For the first few years of the '80s, Porter had several minor hits, but he stopped recording in 1983. In 1981, his television show went off the air. Throughout the '80s and '90s, he earned his living through various businesses and investments, performing occasionally. —*Dan Cooper & Stephen Thomas Erlewine*

Satisfied Mind / 1956 / RCA Victor ✦✦✦✦
This is a common vinyl sampling of Porter's raw-boned early sound. The title cut, from 1955, was his first No. 1 hit. It also has "Company's Comin'," in which he makes the arrival of dinner guests sound as exciting in the current context as logging onto the Internet. —*Dan Cooper*

Confessions of a Broken Man / 1966 / RCA Victor ✦✦✦✦
Not the coolest of the cool among you can hear the aforementioned "Skid Row Joe" without a lump rising in your throat to interrupt your laughter. —*Dan Cooper*

● **The Best of Porter Wagoner** / 1966 / RCA ✦✦✦✦
The Wagonmasters could drive as hard as any backup band of the day, and this set shows it on cuts like "Y'all Come (You All Come)." Meanwhile, good ol' Porter could be as morbid as any singer of his day. Witness "Misery Loves Company," "Green, Green Grass of Home," and "Skid Row Joe." —*Dan Cooper*

The Cold Hard Facts of Life / 1967 / RCA Victor ✦✦✦
Good, straightahead country is one reason to hunt for this LP. The other reason is the album cover—a near-consensus choice as the hillbilly graphics howler of all time. Write to your congressman to get this back in print as is. —*Dan Cooper*

The Thin Man From West Plains [box set] / 198 / Bear Family ✦✦✦✦
It seems a little snooty, this otherwise exemplary four-CD box set. One can't help noticing that it cuts off at approximately the same time Porter became famous for hawking laxative on TV. —*Dan Cooper*

● **Pure Gold** / 1991 / RCA ✦✦✦✦
This low-budget CD is the pick title until RCA sees fit to give him a legitimate reissue set. Actually, it's a pretty decent glimpse at the many moods of career-peak Wagoner. And yup, its got "Skid Row Joe." —*Dan Cooper*

★ **The Essential Porter Wagoner and Dolly Parton** / Jun. 1996 / RCA ✦✦✦✦✦
All of Porter and Dolly's biggest hits, plus a couple of interesting obscurities, are included on this definitive single-disc collection. —*Thom Owens*

Billy Walker

b. Jan. 14, 1929, Ralls, TX
Guitar, Vocals
A native of West Texas, active on the Grand Ole Opry to this day, Billy Walker emerged from the talent-rich Dallas scene of the late '40s and early '50s. After a brief stint on Capitol, he was signed to Columbia in 1951 at almost exactly the same time as Ray Price. For awhile, Walker, Price, and Lefty Frizzell were all recording at the legendary Jim Beck studio in Dallas, which did for '50s honky tonk what the Sun Studio in Memphis did for rockabilly. Nevertheless, Walker enjoyed his greatest success ten years later in Nashville, where the studio sound was perhaps more suited to his smooth tenor voice. —*Dan Cooper*

● **Billy Walker's Greatest Hits** / 1963 / Columbia ✦✦✦✦
Early-'60s Nashville sound, though always with Walker's voice agreeably front and center, it contains "Charlie's Shoes" and a take on Willie Nelson's "Funny How Time Slips Away." —*Dan Cooper*

Cross the Brazos at Waco / 1993 / Bear Family ✦✦✦✦
Here's the usual exhaustive, prestigious, and expensive package (six CDs and a book) from Germany's Bear Family, the best roots music reissue company in the world. Covering the years 1949 to 1965, the set chronicles Walker's career from his initial, tentative Capitol cuts through his entire career on Columbia. —*Dan Cooper*

Greatest Hits on Monument / Columbia ✦✦✦
Not Walker's most compelling material, but it does include "A Million to One," a No. 2 hit for him in 1966. —*Dan Cooper*

Billy Walker's Greatest Hits, Vol. 2 / Columbia ✦✦✦✦
It's noteworthy for "Cross the Brazos at Waco," Walker's 1964 quasi-sequel to Marty Robbins' "El Paso," and a terrific version of the Harlan Howard/Walker tune "Down to My Last Cigarette." —*Dan Cooper*

Clay Walker

Vocals / Contemporary Country
Clay Walker, a native of Beaumont, TX, had performed his country act throughout the South, Midwest, and Canada before he began a regular gig in his hometown. When Giant Records President James Stroud heard Walker sing, he signed him on the spot and produced the debut himself. His first single "What's It to You," hit No. 1 on the *Billboard* charts in 1993, as did "Live Until I Die" and "Dreamin' with My Eyes Open." *If I Could Make a Living* appeared in late 1994. —*John Bush*

Clay Walker / 1993 / Giant ✦✦✦✦
Clay Walker is another country music product from Beaumont, TX (others include George Jones, Mark Chestnut, Doug Supernaw, and Tracy Bird) who has broken into the Nashville music scene. Walker has a high-energy voice and a growl that reminds you of Conway Twitty. The highlights of his first album include "What's It to You?," his first No. 1 hit, and "Live Until I Die." Other featured songs include "The Silence Speaks for Itself" and "White Palace." —*Larry Powell*

● **If I Could Make A Living** / Sep. 27, 1994 / Giant ✦✦✦✦

Hypnotize the Moon / Oct. 17, 1995 / Giant ✦✦✦
Clay Walker's *Hypnotize the Moon* is his most assured, cohesive album to date. Walker shines on both polished, contemporary ballads and gritty traditional country, and his consistently excellent performance is what carries the album over the weak spots. —*Stephen Thomas Erlewine*

Jerry Jeff Walker (Paul Crosby)

b. Mar. 16, 1942, Oneonta, NY
Guitar, Vocals / Progressive Country
Jerry Jeff Walker is best known as the writer of "Mr. Bojangles," an enduring pop classic he wrote at the beginning of his career after meeting a street singer named Bojangles in a New Orleans drunk tank. He's also strongly associated with the progressive ("outlaw") country scene that centered around Austin, TX, in the '70s and included such figures as Willie Nelson, Guy Clark, and Townes Van Zandt.

Ironically, however, Walker is not a native Texan. He was born Ronald Clyde Crosby in upstate New York and recorded his first several albums while living in New York City. He didn't move to Austin until 1971, but he's remained a major figure in the area ever since.

Walker first recorded with the folk-rock group Circus Maximus for Vanguard in 1967. The band split after its second album, and Walker signed with Atco and released his first solo album, *Mr. Bojangles*, in 1968. His version of "Bojangles" never hit it big, but the Nitty Gritty Dirt Band's rendition made the Top Ten of the pop charts in 1971.

Walker lived briefly in Key West, FL, in 1970, but soon found himself in Austin. In 1972 he signed with MCA and released a self-titled album that included his version of Guy Clark's "L.A. Freeway." His best-known album, however, was *Viva Terlingua*, which he recorded in 1973 in the tiny Texas town of Luckenbach with the Lost Gonzo Band. The album went gold, and it's his biggest-selling album to date.

Walker was a hard partier throughout much of his career (his friends called him "Jacky Jack"), and this reputation became part of his identity. He's since cleaned up his act—in part thanks to his wife, Susan, whom he married in 1974—and he's continued to record steadily into the 1990s. He released a couple albums on Elektra/Asylum in the late '70s, but remained mostly with MCA until his 1982 album *Cowboy Jazz*—a record that became his last for any major label. In 1985, however, he showed the industry he could live without their help and released the first of a series of self-made cassettes, *Gypsy Songman*, many of which he sold via a mailing list that has grown to more than 40,000 strong. In 1987 Walker worked out a deal with Rykodisc to release his CDs, but he still sells the cassettes himself through his own company, Tried & True Music.

In 1991 and 1992 Walker hosted the weekly TV show, *The Texas Connection*, on TNN. In 1993 he returned to Luckenbach for an anniversary recording that became the album *Viva Luckenbach!* Walker's birthday is a major celebration in Austin every March, when he plays several shows in different local clubs and theaters. —*Kurt Wolff*

Mr. Bojangles / 1968 / Rhino ✦✦✦✦
Walker's debut introduced his dry vocals and narrative songwriting style, with support from many session musicians, the most notable of whom were Ron Carter and David Bromberg. The influence of Dylan and other singer-songwriters of the time is felt fairly strongly on this extremely low-key release (especially on the seven-minute "Desolation Row"-like "The Ballad of the Hulk"), but Walker favored the country and folk side of folk-rock much more than the rock side. The title track, taken into the Top Ten by the Nitty Gritty Dirt Band, remains his most famous song. The CD reissue includes the original mono single version of "Mr. Bojangles" and its flipside, as well as liner notes with comments on both songs by Jerry Jeff himself. —*Richie Unterberger*

Driftin' Way of Life / 1969 / Vanguard ✦✦✦✦
A beautifully simple album of country-flavored original songs, mostly from the point of view of the sentimental roustabout, this great record

sounds as though the players just went in, knocked it off, and hit the road. —*Richard Meyer*

● **Great Gonzos** / 1991 / MCA ✦✦✦✦
Great Gonzos is a good cross-section of Jerry Jeff Walker's biggest hits and best-known songs. It's not definitive, but it's a good introduction. —*Thom Owens*

Dale Watson

b. Oct. 7, 1962
Guitar, Vocals
Dale Watson is a singer/guitarist who writes and plays original material in the tradition of '50s and '60s honky tonk—which makes him something of an outsider in the '90s country music market. He was born in Alabama, but moved with his family to Pasadena, TX, just outside of Houston, when he was a teenager, and considers Texas his home. His early musical inspiration came from his father, a singer and guitarist, and his brother Jim, who gave him his first music lessons. Watson began writing songs at age 12, and recorded his first at age 14. By the time he graduated from high school, he was performing locally. He spent the next seven years playing the clubs and honky tonks around Pasadena.

In 1988, Watson moved to Los Angeles, seeking the Bakersfield sound of Buck Owens and Merle Haggard, two of his major inspirations. His friend, singer-songwriter Rosie Flores, had encouraged him to relocate there. He soon landed a gig at Los Angeles' Palomino Club, playing guitar in the house band at the club's weekly "barn dances." He also had a small role in the movie *Thing Called Love*, starring River Phoenix.

Watson recorded two singles for Curb, "One Tear at a Time" and "You Pour It On," which were released in 1990. He also contributed one track to volume three of the Los Angeles country compilation *A Town South of Bakersfield*, released in 1992. That same year he moved to Nashville, where he worked as a staff writer for Gary Morris Music, a publishing company. Eventually, however, he settled in Austin, TX. He landed a recording deal with HighTone Records, who released Watson's debut album, *Cheatin' Heart Attack*, in 1995. Watson and his band, Lone Star, released a follow-up, *Blessed or Damned*, in 1996. —*Kurt Wolff*

● **Cheatin' Heart Attack** / 1995 / Hightone ✦✦✦✦
Watson's hearty, down-to-earth honky tonk makes *Cheatin' Heart Attack* one of the most exciting country debuts this side of Junior Brown's *12 Shades of Brown*. Watson and his band Lone Star burn through 14 no-nonsense songs that prove the genre can be vital and fun at the same time. Watson's voice is pure, deep, and strong, and his songs feature guitar and pedal steel prominently. He's a veteran of the Texas honky tonk circuit, which shows in his sharp arrangements on songs like "List of Reasons," "Holes in the Wall," and "Nashville Rash"—the latter mixing heartfelt commentary on the current country market with a smart sense of humor. —*Kurt Wolff*

Blessed or Damned / 1996 / ✦✦✦
Blessed or Damned pretty much picks up where Watson's 1995 debut, *Cheatin' Heart Attack*, left off. He pines for "A Real Country Song" on modern radio, sings praises for his adopted state on "That's What I Like About Texas" (a good-natured duet with Johnny "Whiskey River" Bush), and wonders at the fate of his chosen musical genre on the moving title track. Watson may have no surprise ace in the hole on *Blessed or Damned*, but it's nonetheless a solid hand of fresh, invigorating material. —*Kurt Wolff*

Doc Watson (Arthel Watson)

b. Mar. 2, 1923, Deep Gap, NC
Banjo, Guitar, Vocals / Old-Time, Traditional Country
In this half of our century there have been three preeminently influential guitar players: Merle Travis, Chet Atkins, and Arthel "Doc" Watson, a flat-picking genius from Deep Gap, NC. Unlike the other two, Watson was middle-aged before gaining any attention. Since 1960, though, when Watson was recorded with his family and friends in Folkways' *Old Time Music at Clarence Ashley's*, people have remained in awe of this gentle blind man who sings and picks with a pure and emotional authenticity. The present generation, folkies, and country pickers alike, including Ricky Skaggs, Vince Gill, the late Clarence White, Emmylou Harris, and literally hundreds of others, acknowledge their great debt to Watson. Watson has provided a further service to country/folk by his encyclopedic knowledge of many American traditional songs. While Merle Travis and Chet Atkins started on acoustic guitars and moved to electric, before Watson's "discovery" during the folk revival in the early '60s, he played electric in a local all-purpose band that played current rock, swing, country, and of course folk music. He gained recognition gradually, first from the *Clarence Ashley* album, which led to a rave performance at the Newport Folk Festival in 1963. Folkways soon recorded an album of Watson, followed in 1964 by a series of albums by Vanguard, nearly one a year through the decade. No sooner had interest in folk music waned than Watson was back in great demand because of the three-disc *Will the Circle Be Unbroken*, a watershed album in 1972 that was created by The

Nitty Gritty Dirt Band. It featured Watson, Merle Travis, Roy Acuff, and a Who's Who of country greats. Merle, Watson's son and a talent in his own right, began appearing with his father regularly. The result was good enough for them to win two Grammys for traditional music, in 1973 and 1974. Father and son played beautiful music together for over fifteen years, until Merle died on the family farm in 1985, the sad victim of a tractor accident.

Watson continues with his appearances, showcasing his beautiful voice, his great instrumental talent, and his mastery of traditional material. He is an American treasure. —*David Vinopal*

☆ **The Doc Watson Family** / 1963 / Smithsonian/Folkways ✦✦✦✦✦
The most traditional performances of Watson and such family members as fiddler Gaither Carlton, this is as authentic as country music gets. —*Mark A. Humphrey & David Vinopal*

Live Duet Recordings 1963-1980 / 1963-1980 / Smithsonian/Folkways ✦✦✦✦
Any time two greats who admire each other and are musically compatible team together, the results are usually mutually beneficial. That was true for Bill Monroe and Doc Watson, whose spirited union on this 17-song disc is a sampler of American musical styles. They ripped through bluegrass, folk, blues, spirituals, mountain tunes, work songs, reels, and breakdowns. Monroe's mandolin and Watson's guitar playing were masterful, wondrous, and performed without any trace of self-indulgence. Their vocals were also delivered with ease, fluidity and conviction, the product of two performers completely at ease with themselves and only interested in spotlighting the material. —*Ron Wynn*

☆ **Doc Watson** / 1964 / Vanguard ✦✦✦✦✦
His first Vanguard album features warm vocals, influential guitar, harmonica, and old-time banjo. —*Mark A. Humphrey*

Treasures Untold / 1964 / Vanguard ✦✦✦✦
These Newport Festival performances include four guitar duets with Clarence White. —*Mark A. Humphrey*

☆ **Southbound** / 1966 / Vanguard ✦✦✦✦✦
Watson's second Vanguard album is the debut of son Merle on second guitar. —*Mark A. Humphrey*

Ballads from Deep Gap / 1967 / Vanguard ✦✦✦
Featured are fine traditional songs, old ballads, and more. —*Mark A. Humphrey*

Old-Timey Concert / 1967 / Vanguard ✦✦✦
These wonderful performances feature Fred Price and Clint Howard. —*Mark A. Humphrey*

Doc Watson on Stage (Featuring Merle Watson) / 1971 / Vanguard ✦✦✦
A fine live album, it includes Watson's son Merle. —*Mark A. Humphrey*

★ **The Essential Doc Watson** / 1986 / Vanguard ✦✦✦✦✦
Drawn from performances at the 1963 and 1964 Newport Folk Festival performances, *The Essential Doc Watson* is a concise introduction to one of the greatest guitarists in country and folk music. —*Thom Owens*

Vanguard Years / Nov. 14, 1995 / Vanguard ✦✦✦✦
Four-CD, 64-song collection drawn principally from Doc's Vanguard releases of the 1960s and early 1970s (tapping his solo LPs and performances at the 1963 and 1964 Newport Folk Festival). This was Doc's best period recording-wise, and certainly you couldn't hope for a better document of his virtuosity, as the guitarist covers all manner of American folk and blues styles over the course of the set. It's too much, however, for listeners who aren't big fans; Vanguard's *Essential Doc Watson* is a more economical survey. If you *are* a big fan, though, you'll be especially interested in the 16 previously unreleased performances. Comprising the whole of disc four, these are mostly taken from live duets with Merle Travis or Doc's son, Merle Watson. —*Richie Unterberger*

Watson Family Tradition / Rounder ✦✦✦✦
Featured are austere beauty, ancient ballads, and rough string-band sounds. Joining in are mother Annie Watson, wife Rosa Lee Watson, father-in-law Gaither Carlton, brother Arnold Watson, and son Merle Watson. The unpolished roots of Doc Watson. —*Mark A. Humphrey*

Gene Watson

b. Oct. 11, 1943, Palestine, TX
Guitar, Vocals / Traditional Country
Though he can sing honky tonk, Gene Watson has made a reputation for performing soulful ballads in the classical country tradition. After working as an auto-body man, he finally had success with "Love in the Hot Afternoon," which as a single and as his debut album did well in 1975. His hits have been steady since then, with "Farewell Party," "Got No Reason Now for Going Home," "Nothing Sure Looked Good on You," and "Memories to Burn." Watson is a vocal stylist of considerable talent. —*David Vinopal*

Greatest Hits [MCA] / 1986 / MCA ✦✦✦✦
MCA's *Greatest Hits* collection fills in the gaps left by Curb's *Greatest*

Hits collection, featuring such '80s hit singles as "What She Don't Know Won't Hurt Her," "Fourteen Carat Mind," and "You're Out Doing What I'm Here Doing Without." —*Thom Owens*

Back in the Fire / 1989 / Warner Bros. ✦✦✦
His comeback album is rife with Watson's trademark hard balladeering. —*Mark A. Humphrey*

● **Greatest Hits [Curb]** / 1990 / Curb ✦✦✦✦
This is a solid collection of '70s hits by this unpretentious, terribly under-rated country singer. The key track is "Farewell Party," a deceptive, near-trance-inducing honky tonk number that delivers an emotional knock-out at precisely the moment many country songs wimp out. —*Dan Cooper*

Kitty Wells (Muriel Deason)

b. Aug. 30, 1918, Nashville, TN
Guitar, Vocals / Traditional Country, Honky Tonk
One of the few country stars born in Nashville, Kitty Wells had a string of hits from the '50s to the early '70s that earned her the title "Queen of Country Music." She made her radio debut on Nashville's WSIX, where she met her future husband, Johnnie Wright of Johnnie and Jack. She began touring as part of Johnnie and Jack's show; Wright gave her the stage name, taken from a folk song called "I'm A-Goin' to Marry Kitty Wells." Wells recorded unsuccessfully for RCA before switching to Decca, where she hit with 1952's "It Wasn't God Who Made Honky Tonk Angels," a response to Hank Thompson's "The Wild Side of Life." Its controversial pre-feminist lyrics, which blamed unfaithful men for creating unfaithful women, paved the way for Loretta Lynn and Tammy Wynette and established Wells as the first major female country star. Wells recorded a number of answer songs and remakes, but she has top-notch original material as well, including some of Harlan Howard's earliest hits.

Wells began singing as a child, learning guitar from her father. As a teenager, she sang on a local radio station with her sisters, who performed under the name the Deason Sisters. The group began singing on the station in 1936. The following year, she married Johnny Wright. Shortly after their marriage, Wells and Wright began performing together, along with his sister, Louise Wright; they called themselves Johnny Wright and the Harmony Girls. Jack Anglin, Louise's husband, joined the group in 1939, and they renamed the band the Tennessee Hillbillies, which would eventually evolve into the Tennessee Mountain Boys.

Anglin was drafted into the army in 1942. Following his departure, Wright and Wells performed as a duo; it was at this time that she adopted her stage name, Kitty Wells. When Anglin returned from the army, he and Wright formed a duo, Johnny and Jack. Kitty would tour with the duo, occasionally performing backup vocals. In 1946 and 1947, the duo had a regular spot at the Grand Ole Opry and Wells rarely performed with them. However, she did sing with the pair when they joined the "Louisiana Hayride" in 1948.

The "Louisiana Hayride" helped Johnny and Jack land a record contract with RCA Records in 1949. That same year, Kitty recorded some gospel tracks—featuring Johnny and Jack as instrumental support—for RCA, but they were unsuccessful. Following those recordings, Wells was more or less retired for the next few years. In 1952, Paul Cohen, an executive at Decca Records, approached Kitty to record "It Wasn't God Who Made Honky Tonk Angels." Wells recorded the song and it became a smash hit, reaching No. 1 in the summer and staying in that position for six weeks. Later in 1952, she joined the Grand Ole Opry.

"It Wasn't God Who Made Honky Tonk Angels" was followed by "Paying for That Back Street Affair," a response to Webb Pierce's "Back Street Affair." The single reached No. 6 in the spring of 1953, helping to establish a permanent place at the top of the charts for Wells. For the rest of the '50s, she hit the Top Ten with regularity, racking up a total of 23 Top Ten hits. In the early '60s, her career dipped slightly, but she continued to have Top Ten hits frequently. During the late '60s and '70s, Wells' streak of hits evaporated, but she managed to have a string of minor hits and remained a popular concert attraction.

In 1974, Wells was inducted into the Country Music Hall of Fame, and with good reason. During the '80s, her activity slowed—in addition to running a museum outside of Nashville, she toured with her husband Johnnie and frequently appeared on the Grand Ole Opry. In 1991, Kitty Wells was given a Lifetime Achievement Award from the Grammys. —*Brian Mansfield & Stephen Thomas Erlewine*

★ **Country Music Hall of Fame Series** / 1991 / MCA ✦✦✦✦✦
This 16-track overview is hardly complete (Wells issued more than 400 singles for MCA between 1952 and 1973), but it's got the essentials: "It Wasn't God Who Made Honky Tonk Angels," "I Can't Stop Loving You," "Heartbreak USA," etc., all sung with the thin Tennessee vibrato that made Wells famous. —*Brian Mansfield*

Queen of Country [box set] / Bear Family ✦✦✦✦
The Queen of Country is an exhaustive four-disc box that covers all of Kitty Wells' recordings for RCA and Decca between 1949 and 1958. For the diehard fan, it's an essential collection, but the casual fan will find its thoroughness overwhelming. —*Stephen Thomas Erlewine*

Dottie West

b. Oct. 11, 1932, McMinnville, TN, **d.** Sep. 4, 1991
Guitar, Vocals / Country-Pop
Dottie West had a successful career singing music that ranged from traditional to country-pop to TV commercials. "Here Comes My Baby" was a huge hit for her in 1964 and led to a Grammy. She appeared in movies, wrote more than 400 songs, made commercials, recorded hit duets with Jim Reeves, Don Gibson, and Kenny Rogers ("A Lesson in Leaving"), and was a country beauty queen. In 1991, while en route to the Opry, where she was a member of the regular cast, she was killed in an auto accident. For the two previous years, she had gone through personal bankruptcy and had seen her personal belongings auctioned off by the IRS. A happier end should have come to this veteran performer. She is missed. —*David Vinopal*

Special Delivery / 1979 / United Artists ✦✦✦
With her career revitalized by the duets with Kenny Rogers, West takes a new tack. Her "Country Sunshine" is replaced with country-funk and a touch of melancholy. —*Tom Roland*

● **Essential Dottie West** / Jan. 30, 1996 / RCA ✦✦✦✦
Featuring 20 of her best songs, *The Essential Dottie West* lives up to its title. All of her biggest singles—not only solo hits like "Country Sunshine" and "Paper Mansions," but also her duets with Don Gibson ("Rings of Gold" and "There's A Story (Goin' Round") and Jim Reeves ("Love Is No Excuse")—are included, making this the one definitive compilation. —*Stephen Thomas Erlewine*

Speedy West

b. Jan. 25, 1924, Springfield, MO
Pedal Steel Guitar / Traditional Country, Instrumental Country
One of the greatest virtuosos that country music has ever produced, Speedy West bridged the Western swing and rockabilly eras with eye-popping steel guitar. Besides contributing to literally thousands of country sessions, West cut many of his own instrumentals, as a solo act and with his guitarist partner Jimmy Bryant. Adept at boogie, blues, and Hawaiian ballads, West played with an infectious joy and daring improvisation that, at its most adventurous, could be downright experimental. It's doubtful whether anyone could collect all of Speedy's solos under one roof, but it was his sessions of the 1950s and early 1960s—especially those with Jimmy Bryant—that found his genius at its most freewheeling and dazzling. —*Richie Unterberger*

Steel Guitar / 1960 / Capitol ✦✦✦
A twin album to the set released by his partner Jimmy Bryant at the same time (*Country Cabin Jazz*), both featuring the same bands. Twelve virtuosic steel guitar showcases, ranging from frenetic boogie to Hawaiian-like tranquil moods. —*Richie Unterberger*

Steel Guitar From Outer Space / 1989 / See For Miles ✦✦✦
Together with the 1960 *Steel Guitar* LP, this is West at his peak. This compilation gets the nod not because of superior quality, but because of sheer quantity—24 tracks, half from rare '50s singles, the other half comprising the entirety of his 1963 album *Guitar Spectacular*. The appeal of these skyrocketing boogies and swing tunes is not at all limited to country fans; even in the 1990s, it sounds quite advanced and cutting-edge. —*Richie Unterberger*

● **Stratosphere Boogie** / 1995 / Razor & Tie ✦✦✦✦
The 16-track *Stratosphere Boogie: The Flaming Guitars of Speedy West and Jimmy Bryant* collects highlights from the duo's early '50s records, picking out selected album tracks and singles. It's an excellent retrospective, demonstrating the depth of their mind-bending instrumental genius. —*Thom Owens*

Keith Whitley

b. Apr. 1, 1955, **d.** May 9, 1989
Guitar, Vocals / Progressive Country, New Traditionalist
Keith Whitley's legacy looms large over the country music landscape. A talented new country singer and songwriter, Whitley was just beginning to emerge as a superstar at the time of his death in 1989. Throughout the next decade, his reputation as both a performer and writer continued to grow, as other artists had hits with his songs and posthumous recordings climbed into the Top Ten.

Born and raised in Kentucky, Whitley began singing as a child, winning a talent contest at the age of four. When he was eight years old, he learned how to play guitar and within a year he was singing on a Charleston, WV-based radio station. Whitley formed his first band at the age of 13, playing nothing but straight bluegrass. A few years later, he formed the Lonesome Mountain Boys with his high school friend, Ricky Skaggs. The Lonesome Mountain Boys primarily played Stanley Brothers songs and soon became a popular attraction.

In the late '60s, Ralph Stanley was looking to re-form his band after the death of his brother and partner, Carter. He was so impressed with Whitley and Skaggs, he asked them to join his Clinch Mountain Boys group. The duo accepted the offer immediately and began appearing with the band in 1970. Whitley stayed with the Clinch Mountain Boys for two years, recording a total of seven albums, including 1971's *Crying from the Cross* which was named the Bluegrass Album of the Year.

In 1973, Whitley left the group. For two years, he drifted through various other bands, including acts that played country, not bluegrass. He returned to the Clinch Mountain Boys in 1975 and stayed with them for another two years. During his second tenure with the band, he made five albums. In 1978, Keith joined J.D. Crowe's band the New South. Whitley recorded three albums with the New South between 1978 and 1982, which vacillated between bluegrass and straight country.

Whitley began a full-fledged solo career after leaving the New South in 1982. Signing with RCA Records, he released his debut album, *Hard Act to Follow*, in 1984. A record of pure honky tonk, it didn't attract much of an audience. The following year, he released *L.A. to Miami*, a more commercial affair which spawned the No. 14 single "Miami, My Amy." After that single peaked early in 1986, he had three back-to-back Top Ten hits—"Ten Feet Away," "Homecoming '63," and "Hard Livin'." Late in 1986, he married Lorrie Morgan.

Although *L.A. to Miami* was a success, its slick production didn't please Whitley. In 1987, he recorded a follow-up to the record that sounded exactly the same as its predecessor. Unsatisfied with the musical direction of his new effort, Whitley convinced RCA to allow him to scrap the completed album and have him work on another record with a new producer, Garth Fundis. *Don't Close Your Eyes* was the result. Released in the spring of 1988, the album solidified Keith's commercial standing. The first three singles from *Don't Close Your Eyes*—"Don't Close Your Eyes," "When You Say Nothing At All," and "I'm No Stranger to the Rain"—were all No.1 hits.

Things may have been going smoothly on the surface for Keith Whitley, but behind the scenes he was being torn apart by alcoholism. On May 9, 1989, he suffered from a fatal case of alcohol poisoning; he was 34 at the time of his demise. Just before his death, he completed his fourth album, *I Wonder Do You Think of Me*. The record was released shortly after his death and its first single, which was the title track, reached No. 1, as did its follow-up, "It Ain't Nothin"; another single from the album, "I'm Over You," reached No. 3 in 1990. During the '90s, RCA repackaged and re-released many of Whitley's recordings—including several unreleased songs—in various compilations. Lorrie Morgan recorded an electronic duet, "Til a Tear Becomes a Rose," with her late husband in 1990; it peaked at No. 13. In 1994, a tribute album to Whitley was released. *—Stephen Thomas Erlewine*

Hard Act to Follow / 1984 / RCA ♦♦
Whitley's first album has some hints of brilliance, but it suffers from uneven material and unfocused production. *—Thom Owens*

L.A. to Miami / 1985 / RCA ♦♦
Whitley's first mainstream country album is nice but not as strong as his later work. *—Mark A. Humphrey*

Don't Close Your Eyes / 1988 / RCA ♦♦♦♦
More heartfelt. Artist and producer focus on good songs and piquant performances. *—Mark A. Humphrey*

★ **I Wonder Do You Think of Me** / 1989 / RCA ♦♦♦♦♦
Recorded shortly before his death, the bounty of drinking songs provides a morbid weight to a generally excellent collection. *—Mark A. Humphrey*

☆ **Greatest Hits** / 1990 / RCA ♦♦♦♦♦
Whitley started singing bluegrass with Ralph Stanley, drew great inspiration from Lefty Frizzell and Merle Haggard, and developed an incomparably smooth, melismatic vocal style. He is the best balladeer of his generation. *—Mark A. Humphrey*

Kentucky Bluebird / 1991 / RCA ♦♦♦
This is a posthumous collection of previously unreleased performances. *—Mark A. Humphrey*

● **Essential Keith Whitley** / Jun. 18, 1996 / RCA ♦♦♦♦
The Essential Keith Whitley is an excellent single-disc retrospective of the late country singer-songwriter, including such classic songs as "I Wonder Do You Think of Me," "If You Think I'm Crazy Now," "I'm Losing You All Over Again," and "Miami, My Amy." Although it concentrates on his earlier recordings, it is still the best, most comprehensive collection assembled on the tragically short-lived country star. *—Thom Owens*

Slim Whitman (Otis Dewey Whitman Jr.)

b. Jan. 20, 1924, Tampa, FL
Guitar, Vocals / Traditional Country, Country-Pop
Once known as "America's Favorite Folksinger," Slim Whitman was

more famous in Europe than in the US for the majority of his career. In the States, he is best known for his early '50s hit singles like "Love Song of the Waterfall," "Indian Love Call," and "Singing Hills." Whitman is an excellent yodeler and is known for singing mellow, romantic, and clean-cut songs. As a child, Slim Whitman became infatuated with music and he learned to yodel listening to Montana Slim and Jimmie Rodgers records. At age 17, he married 15-year-old Geraldine Crist, a preacher's daughter. The newlyweds moved to a 40-acre farm south of Jacksonville, FL, where Whitman worked as a meat packer. As he was working in the plant, he suffered an accident, during which he lost two fingers on his left hand. After the accident, he began working in a Tampa shipyard. During World War II, he served in the US Navy aboard the *USS Chilton*. It was there he learned to play guitar.

Following the war, he returned to the shipyard and joined a Class C baseball team for the Orange Belt League, the Plant City Berries. Whitman remained with the team through 1948 and then began building a singing career at several Tampa radio stations. Eventually, he created a backup band, the Variety Rhythm Boys.

Whitman got his first big break after Colonel Tom Parker—who was managing Eddy Arnold at the time—heard him singing on radio station WFLA. Parker landed Whitman a contract with RCA by the end of 1948. RCA suggested that the vocalist change his first name to "Slim" and Whitman reluctantly complied with their request. Whitman's first single, "I'm Casting My Lasso Towards the Sky," was released in early 1949; the tune became his theme song. Whitman made his national debut on the Mutual Network's Smokey Mountain Hayride in the summer of 1949. The following year, he joined the "Louisiana Hayride." Despite his national exposure, Whitman's career wasn't making much of an impact and he was forced to take a job as a part-time mailman.

In the early '50s, Whitman signed to Imperial Records and released a cover of Bob Nolan's "Love Song of the Waterfall," which became his breakthrough hit, peaking at No. Ten on the country charts. Slim's follow-up single, "Indian Love Call," made him a star. It peaked at No. 2 on the country charts and crossed over into the pop Top Ten. Both sides of his next single—"Keep It a Secret"/"My Heart Is Broken in Three"—were also major hits and he continued to have a string of Top Ten hits into the mid-'50s. In 1955, his title song for the film *Rose-Marie* became his breakthrough hit in England, where it stayed at No. 1 in the pop charts for eleven weeks. Following its success, Whitman joined the Grand Ole Opry. Whitman then went to Britain in 1956 and became the first country singer to play the London Palladium. Throughout the late '50s and early '60s, he had a string of British hits, including "Tumbling Tumbleweeds," "Unchain My Heart," and "I'll Take You Home Again Kathleen."

Although he was experiencing great success in the UK, Whitman's career was in neutral in the US. After 1954's "Singing Hills," he had only two Top 40 hits in the course of a decade. In 1965, he bounced back into the country Top Ten with "More Than Yesterday." For the next few years, he had a series of minor country hits, including "Rainbows Are Back in Style" (1968), "Happy Street" (1968) and "Tomorrow Never Comes" (1970). When Imperial became part of United Artists in the early '70s, Whitman switched to the parent label and remained with them until 1974, when he retired from regular recording. Throughout the early '70s, he continued to have minor hits.

In 1979, Whitman filmed a television commercial to support Suffolk Marketing's release of a collection of his greatest hits. On the strength of the commercials, Suffolk's *All My Best* sold four million records, becoming the best-selling television-marketed album in history. After its success, Suffolk released *Just for You* in 1980 and *The Best* in 1982.

Whitman signed to Cleveland International in 1980. Between 1980 and 1984, he had a small run of minor hits, highlighted by 1980's No. 15 hit, "When." In the late '80s, Whitman returned to television-marketed albums, releasing *Slim Whitman—Best Loved Favorites* on Heartland in 1989 and *20 Precious Memories* on Progressive Music in 1991. During the early '90s, Whitman didn't record frequently, but he continued to tour successfully, particularly in Europe and Australia. *—Sandra Brennan*

● **The Best of Slim Whitman (1952-1972)** / 1990 / Rhino ♦♦♦♦
Over its 17 tracks, *The Best of Slim Whitman (1952-1972)* runs through all of his Top Ten hits—from "Love Song of the Waterfall" to "Something Beautiful (To Remember)"—adding significant hit singles like "Cattle Call," "The Twelfth of Never," and "Rainbows Are Back In Style." Out of all the Whitman collections, nothing surpasses this one for selection and sound—it's the definitive compilation. *—Thom Owens*

The Wilburn Brothers

Traditional Country
As members of the larger Wilburn Family group (mother, father, elder brothers, sister), nine-year-old Teddy (b. 1931) and ten-year-old Doyle (1930-1982) appeared on the Opry in 1940; 13 years later, when they had grown up, they became part of the Opry's regular cast. With Jim and Jesse McReynolds and Bobby and Sonny Osborne, the Wilburns continue the tradition of brother duets in country music. Their wide choice

of material is shown by the traditional "Knoxville Girl," a hit in 1959, and the more modern sound of "Hurt Her Once for Me" (1966). —*David Vinopal*

Carefree Moments / 1962 / VL ✦✦✦
Their sometimes slick Nashville Sound recordings and tendency to double-track the vocals sometimes obscure the fact that these guys are one of the great brother duets in C&W. When they keep it straight, as in the rockabilly-esque "Cry Baby Cry" here, they can hold their own with anyone. —*George Bedard*

● Retrospective / MCA ✦✦✦✦
This nice overview of the Wilburn Brothers' smooth Decca hits of the '50s and '60s features 12 songs. —*Mark A. Humphrey*

Don Williams

b. May 27, 1939, near Plainview, TX
Guitar, Vocals / Traditional Country, Country-Pop
With his laidback, straightforward vocals and large, imposing build, Don Williams came to be known as "the Gentle Giant." That nickname was bestowed on him in the early '70s, when he began a string of countrypolitan hits that ran into the early '90s. Williams was never known as an innovator, but his ballads were immensely popular—in the course of his career, he had a total of 17 No. 1 hits.

Williams began playing guitar when he was child, learning the instrument from his mother. As a teenager, he played in a variety of country, rockabilly, folk, and rock 'n' roll bands. After completing high school, he formed his first band with a friend called Lofton Kline. Williams and Kline recruited another singer, Susan Taylor, and formed the Pozo-Seco Singers, a folk-pop group, in 1964. The following year, the band signed a contract with Columbia Records. In 1966, the Pozo-Seco Singers had a pop hit with "Time," which climbed into the Top 50. For the next two years, they had a series of minor hits, highlighted by two Top 40 hits in late 1966, "I Can Make It with You" and "Look What You've Done." The group stayed together until 1971.

After the Pozo-Seco Singers disbanded, Williams decided to pursue a career as a songwriter in Nashville, since he wasn't convinced that he was suited for a solo career. He signed with Jack Clement's Jack Music, Inc., initially just as a songwriter. By the end of 1972, he had signed with JMI as a solo artist, releasing "Don't You Believe" as his debut. The song went nowhere, but "The Shelter of Your Eyes" climbed to No. 14 at the beginning of 1973. For the next year, Williams scored a string of minor hits before he had his 1974 breakthrough, "We Should Be Together," which reached No. 5. The single led to a contract with ABC/Dot.

"I Wouldn't Want to Live If You Didn't Love Me," his first single for ABC/Dot, reached No. 1 in the summer of 1974. The single launched a string of Top Ten hits that ran more or less uninterrupted until 1991—between 1974 and 1991, only four of his 46 charting singles didn't make the Top Ten. Instead of reaching the top of the charts with his original material, most of his big hits were covers of other songwriters, including John Prine, Bob McDill, Dave Loggins, and Wayland Holyfield.

During the '70s, Don Williams became the most successful country artist in the world. His country-pop not only crossed over into the American pop mainstream, it also gained him a large following in England and Europe. In addition to his Top Ten hits, Williams won several country music awards, highlighted by the Country Music Association naming him Male Vocalist of the Year in 1978, the same year his No. 1 single "Tulsa Time" was named Single of the Year. In the late '70s, he began acting, appearing primarily in the films of his friend Burt Reynolds, including *W.W. and the Dixie Dancekings* and *Smokey and the Bandit II.*

In the early '80s, Williams slowed down the pace of his career slightly, as he was suffering from back problems. Nevertheless, the hits continued to come and many of his singles reached No. 1. In 1986, he left MCA Records—who had acquired the ABC label while he was recording for it—signing with Capitol. The change in labels didn't affect his career at all, as he continued to hit the Top Ten with regularity. In 1987, he underwent back surgery, which cured his problems.

Williams signed with RCA Records in 1989. Initially, he continued to have hits, but his streak came to an end in early 1992, following his last Top Ten single, "Lord Have Mercy on a Country Boy." Although he continued to perform in the mid-'90s, he had effectively retired to his Nashville farm. —*Stephen Thomas Erlewine*

Don Williams, Vol. 1 / 1973 / MCA ✦✦✦✦
Don Williams' first album as a country singer was originally released on Cowboy Jack Clement's JMI label before being snapped up by ABC-Dot the following year. There were four hits on this record; not a small feat for any artist much less on the first try. Over the years Williams has made some fine records but none better than this. —*Jim Worbois*

Best of Don Williams, Vol. 2 / 1979 / MCA ✦✦✦✦
This album is so good, it will whet one's appetite for all the records from which these songs were taken. Williams has a laidback sound that no one has been able to imitate or copy. —*Jim Worbois*

I Believe in You/Especially for You / 1981 / MCA ✦✦✦
Two early (1980-1981) collections for the price of one, includes the gem "Lord, I Hope this Day Is Good." —*Hank Davis*

Prime Cuts / 1981 / Capitol ✦✦✦✦
Williams released four greatest-hits albums for MCA, so this is the fifth of his career. The R&B flavor of "Heartbeat in the Darkness" shakes up his approach. Much of the remainder is a thing of sparsely scored beauty. —*Tom Roland*

Best of Don Williams, Vol. 3 / 1984 / MCA ✦✦✦✦

Cafe Carolina / 1984 / MCA ✦✦✦
Williams has a very identifiable core sound, but occasional subtle differences can seem like major alterations. Here he recruits sax player Jim Horn, and while Horn doesn't play on every track, his mere presence provides a fresh change. —*Tom Roland*

★ 20 Greatest Hits / 1987 / MCA ✦✦✦✦✦
The best thing about Don Williams is that it's so hard to peg him in a country music era. Hits like "Amanda," "You're My Best Friend," "I Believe in You," and "Good Ole Boys like Me," all present in this collection, are so understated it's as if they float on top of Nashville history. —*Dan Cooper*

Hank Williams (Hiriam King Williams)

b. Sep. 17, 1923, Mount Olive, AL, d. Jan. 1, 1953, Oak Hill, WV
Guitar, Vocals / Traditional Country, Honky Tonk
Hank Williams is the father of contemporary country music. Williams was a superstar by the age of 25; he was dead at the age of 29. In those four short years, he established the rules for all the country performers that followed him and, in the process, much of popular music. Williams wrote a body of songs that became popular classics, and his direct, emotional lyrics and vocals became the standard for most popular performers. Hank lived a life as troubled and reckless as that depicted in his songs.

When he was eight years old, Williams was given a guitar by his mother. His musical education was provided by a local blues street singer, Rufus Payne, who was called Tee Tot. From Tee Tot, Hank learned how to play the guitar and sing the blues, which would come to provide a strong undercurrent in his songwriting. Williams began performing around the Georgiana and Greenville areas of Alabama in his early teens. His mother the family to Montgomery, AL, in 1937, where she opened a boarding house. In Montgomery, Hank formed a band called the Drifting Cowboys and landed a regular spot on the local radio station, WSFA, in 1941. During his shows, Williams would sing songs from his idol, Roy Acuff, as well as several other country hits of the day. WSFA dubbed him the Singing Kid and Williams stayed with the station for the rest of the decade.

Williams met Audrey Mae Sheppard, a farmgirl from Banks, AL, in 1943 while he was playing a medicine show. The following year, the couple married and moved into Lilly's boarding house. Audrey became Hank's manager just before the marriage. By 1946, Williams was a local celebrity, but he was unable to make much headway nationally. That year, Hank and Audrey visited Nashville with the intent of meeting songwriter/music publisher Fred Rose, one of the heads of Acuff-Rose Publishing. Rose liked Williams' songs and asked him to record two sessions for Sterling Records, which resulted in two singles. Both of the singles—"Never Again" in December, 1946 and "Honky Tonkin'" in February, 1947—were successful and Hank signed a contract with MGM Records early in 1947. Rose became the singer's manager and record producer.

"Move It On Over," released later in 1947, became Hank Williams' first single for MGM. It was an immediate hit, climbing into the country Top Five. By the summer of 1948, he had joined the "Louisiana Hayride," appearing both on its tours and radio programs. "Honky Tonkin'" was released in 1948, followed by "I'm a Long Gone Daddy." While neither song was as successful as "Move It On Over," they were popular, with the latter peaking in the Top Ten. Early in 1949, he recorded "Lovesick Blues," a Tin Pan Alley song initially recorded by Emmett Miller and made popular by Rex Griffin. The single became a huge hit upon its release in the spring of 1949, staying at No. 1 for 16 weeks and crossing over into the pop Top 25. Williams sang the song at the Grand Ole Opry, where he performed an unprecedented six encores. He had become a star.

Hank and Audrey had their first child, Randall Hank, in the spring of 1949. Also in the spring, Hank assembled the most famous edition of the Drifting Cowboys, featuring guitarist Bob McNett, bassist Hillous Butrum, fiddler Jerry Rivers, and steel guitarist Don Helms. Soon, he and the band were earning $1,000 per concert and were selling out shows across the country. Williams had no fewer than seven hits in 1949 after "Lovesick Blues," including the Top Fives "Wedding Bells," "Mind Your Own Business," "You're Gonna Change (Or I'm Gonna Leave)," and "My Bucket's Got a Hole in It." In addition he had a string of hit singles in 1950—including the No. 1s "Long Gone Lonesome Blues," "Why Don't

You Love Me," and "Moanin' the Blues," as well as the Top Tens "I Just Don't Like this Kind of Livin'," "My Son Calls Another Man Daddy," "They'll Never Take Her Love from Me," "Why Should We Try," and "Nobody's Lonesome for Me." That same year, Williams began recording a series of spiritual records under the name Luke the Drifter.

Williams continued to rack up hits in 1951, beginning with the Top Ten hit "Dear John" and its No. 1 flip-side, "Cold Cold Heart." That same year, pop vocalist Tony Bennett recorded "Cold, Cold Heart" and had a hit, leading to a stream of covers from such mainstream artists as Jo Stafford, Guy Mitchell, Frankie Laine, Teresa Brewer, and several others. Hank had also begun to experience the fruits of crossover success, appearing on the Perry Como television show and being part of a package tour that also featured Bob Hope, Jack Benny, and Minny Pearl. In addition to "Dear John" and "Cold, Cold Heart," Hank had several other hits in 1951, including the No. 1 "Hey, Good Lookin'" and "Howlin' at the Moon," "I Can't Help It (If I'm Still In Love With You)," "Crazy Heart," "Lonesome Whistle," and "Baby, We're Really in Love," which all charted in the Top Ten.

Though his professional career was soaring, Hank Williams' personal life was beginning to spin out of control. Before he became a star, he had a mild drinking problem, but it had been more or less controlled during his first few years of fame. However, as he began to earn large amounts of money and spend long times away from home, he began to drink frequently. Furthermore, Hank's marriage to Audrey was deteriorating. Not only were they fighting, resulting in occasional separations, but Audrey was trying to create her own recording career without any success. In the fall of 1951, Hank was on a hunting trip on his Tennessee farm when he tripped and fell, re-activating a dormant back injury. Williams began taking morphine and other pain killers for his back and quickly became addicted.

In January of 1952, Hank and Audrey separated for a final time and he headed back to Montgomery to live with his mother. The hits were still coming fast for Williams, with "Honky Tonk Blues" hitting No. 2 in the spring. In fact, he released five more singles in 1952—"Half As Much," "Jambalaya," "Settin' the Woods on Fire," "You Win Again," and "I'll Never Get Out of This World Alive"—which all went Top Ten. In spite of all of his success, Hank turned completely reckless in 1952, spending nearly all of his waking hours drunk and taking drugs, while he was frequently destroying property and playing with guns.

Williams left his mother in early spring, moving in with Ray Price in Nashville. In May, Audrey and Hank were officially divorced. She was awarded the house and their child, as well as half of his future royalties. Williams continued to play a large number of concerts, but he was always drunk during the show, or he missed the gig altogether. In August, the Grand Ole Opry fired Hank for that very reason. He was told that he could return once he was sober. Instead of heeding the Opry's warning, he just sank deeper into his self-destructive behavior. Soon, his friends were leaving him, as the Drifting Cowboys began working with Ray Price and Red Rose no longer supported him. Williams was still playing the "Louisiana Hayride," but he was performing with local pickup bands and was earning reduced wages. That fall, he met Billie Jean Jones Eshlimar, the 19-year-old daughter of a Lousiana policeman. By October, they were married. Hank also signed an agreement to support the baby—who had yet to be delivered—of one of his other girlfriends, Bobbie Jett, in October. By the end of the year, Williams was having heart problems and Toby Marshall, a con-man doctor, was giving him various prescription drugs to help soothe the pain.

Hank Williams was scheduled to play a concert in Canton, OH, on January 1, 1953. He was scheduled to fly out of Knoxville, TN, on New Year's Eve, but the weather was so bad he had to hire a chauffeur to drive him to Ohio in his new Cadillac. Before they left for Ohio, Williams was injected with two shots of the vitamin B-12 and morphine by a doctor. Williams got into the backseat of the Cadillac with a bottle of whiskey and the teenage chauffeur headed out for Canton. The driver was stopped for speeding when the policeman noticed that Williams looked like a dead man. Williams was taken to a West Virginian hospital and he was officially declared dead at 7:00 AM on January 1, 1953. Hank Williams had died in the back of the Cadillac, on his way to a concert. The last single released in his lifetime was "I'll Never Get Out of This World Alive."

Hank Williams was buried in Montgomery, AL, three days later. His funeral drew a record crowd, larger than any crowd since Jefferson Davis was inaugurated as the President of the Confederacy in 1861. Dozens of country music stars attended, as did Audrey Williams, Billie Jean Jones, and Bobbie Jett, who happened to give birth to a daughter three days later. "I'll Never Get Out of This World Alive" reached No. 1 immediately after his death and it was followed by a number of hit records throughout 1953, including the No. 1s "Your Cheatin' Heart," "Kaw-Liga," and "Take These Chains from My Heart."

After his death, MGM wanted to keep issuing Hank Williams records, so the label took some of his original demos and overdubbed bands onto the original recording. The first of these, "Weary Blues from Waitin'," was

a hit but the others weren't quite as successful. In 1961, Hank Williams was one of the first inductees to the Country Music Hall of Fame. Throughout the '60s, Williams' records were released in overdubbed versions featuring heavy strings, as well as reprocessed stereo. For years, these bastardized versions were the only records in print and only in the '80s, when his music was released on compact disc, was his catalog restored to its original form. Even during those years when only over-dubbed versions of his hits existed, Hank Williams' impact never diminished. His songs have become classics, his recordings have stood the test of time, and his life story is legendary. It's easy to see why Hank Williams is considered by many as the defining figure of country music. *—Stephen Thomas Erlewine*

★ **40 Greatest Hits** / 1978 / Polydor ♦♦♦♦♦
Over the course of two CDs, *40 Greatest Hits* runs through all of Hank Williams' essential songs, presented in their original, undubbed versions. It is the perfect place to start listening to Williams. *—Stephen Thomas Erlewine*

☆ **I Ain't Got Nothin' But Time, December 1946**—August 1947 / Jan. 1985 / Polydor ♦♦♦♦♦
In 1985, after years of cheesy overdubs and haphazard hits compilations, Polydor, with the aid of Colin Escott and Hank Davis, made a commitment to present Williams' music in its original form and in chronological order. The result was an eight-volume series, with each volume containing a mixed bag of hit singles, outtakes, demos, and/or radio transcriptions. If the Hillbilly Shakespeare has worked his way into your blood, you'll want all eight volumes. If you're content with the performances that made him famous, this and the seven companion pieces will probably seem like overkill. In any case, this first volume includes "Honky Tonkin'" and "Move It on Over," and a spooky gospel number called the "Battle of Armageddon." *—Dan Cooper*

☆ **Lovesick Blues, August 1947**—December 1948 / Feb. 1985 / Polydor ♦♦♦♦♦
Volume Two of the chronological series features "Lovesick Blues," the song that made him a superstar. *—Dan Cooper*

☆ **Lost Highway, December 1948**—March 1949 / Jan. 1986 / PolyGram ♦♦♦♦♦
The third in this series, with his 1948-49 material. *—Hank Davis*

☆ **I'm So Lonesome I Could Cry, March 1949**—August 1949 / Feb. 1986 / Polydor ♦♦♦♦♦
By this point, Williams is revealing the fissures in his soul through songs like "I'm So Lonesome I Could Cry," "I Just Don't Like this Kind of Living," and a chilling demo number called "We're Getting Closer to the Grave Each Day." *—Dan Cooper*

☆ **Long Gone Lonesome Blues, August 1949**—December 1950 / Jan. 1987 / Polydor ♦♦♦♦♦
Long Gone Lonesome Blues is the fifth volume of Polydor's series of complete Hank Williams recordings. *—Stephen Thomas Erlewine*

☆ **Hey, Good Lookin', December 1950**—July 1951 / Feb. 1987 / Polydor ♦♦♦♦♦
Hey, Good Lookin' is the sixth volume of Polydor's series of complete Hank Williams recordings. *—Stephen Thomas Erlewine*

☆ **Let's Turn Back the Years, July 1951**—June 1952 / Mar. 1987 / Polydor ♦♦♦♦♦
This is the seventh volume of Polydor's series of complete Hank Williams recordings. *—Stephen Thomas Erlewine*

☆ **I Won't Be Home No More, June 1952**—September 1952 / Apr. 1987 / Polydor ♦♦♦♦♦
The last volume in the chronological series is almost painfully poignant in its sense of desolation. It includes "Take These Chains from My Heart," "You Win Again," and "Your Cheatin' Heart." *—Dan Cooper*

Rare Demos: First to Last / 1990 / Country Music Foundation ♦♦♦♦
This CD features 24 publisher's demo recordings containing Williams' earliest performances, originally released on *The First Recordings* and *Just Me and My Guitar*. *—AMG*

☆ **Original Singles Collection . . . Plus** / 1992 / PolyGram ♦♦♦♦♦
The title of *The Original Singles Collection . . . Plus* is slightly misleading. Although PolyGram marketed the three-disc, 84-song set as a complete collection, it doesn't feature all of the singles Hank Williams released during his lifetime. Several singles Williams released under the pseudonym "Luke the Drifter" as well as all of the duets he cut with Audrey Williams aren't present. Despite these handful of songs, *everything* else is included in their original, undubbed versions and are presented in the best sound possible. For a fan that wants all the essential songs without springing for the eight disc series of complete recordings, *The Original Singles* collection is invaluable. *—Stephen Thomas Erlewine*

Health & Happiness Shows / 1993 / Mercury ♦♦♦♦
The double-disc set *Health & Happiness Shows* collects eight complete radio shows that Hank Williams recorded in 1949, when his career was just taking off. Throughout the collection, Williams sounds energetic and

vibrant, even during his between-song stage patter, which is nearly fascinating as the music. It's a set that is designed for collectors, but even casual Williams fans will find much to treasure on the *Health & Happiness Shows. —Stephen Thomas Erlewine*

Hank Williams, Jr. (Randall Hank Williams)

b. May 26, 1949, Shreveport, LA
Guitar, Vocals / Traditional Country, Country-Rock
Hank Williams, Jr.'s 1966 recording of "Standing in the Shadows (Of a Very Famous Man)" told us how tough it is to be the son of country music's greatest legend. Up to this point, this enormous talent in his own right had made something of a career of doing his father's old songs, and doing them well. When in the mid-'70s he embarked on his own musical journey, with his own sound of country, country/rock, and rockabilly, he attracted a following that would have astonished even his famous father. In 1975 he left Nashville for Alabama to prepare the *Hank Williams Jr. and Friends* album, the first of his unique Southern-rock albums. In spite of a terrible climbing accident in Montana, Williams went on to bigger and more frequent hits. When "My Rowdy Friends" reached No. 1 in 1981, it was his sixth chart-topper. In the late '80s he was the biggest draw of any country music star or act, packing them in coast to coast, to the degree that he had eight albums on the *Billboard* charts simultaneously. Like his father, Williams is a cult figure, enjoying the limelight created by his own talent and opening for Monday Night Football over the past three years. —*David Vinopal*

☆ **Hank Williams Jr & Friends** / 1975 / Polydor ✦✦✦✦✦
The breakthrough record of Williams' career. On his first mature record (made in his mid-20s), Williams teamed with Southern-rockers Charlie Daniels, Toy Caldwell (Marshall Tucker Band), and Chuck Leavell (Allman Brothers Band), among others, for a session that opened his musical vistas to folk, blues, and rock, and incidentally introduced his mature persona in songs like "Stoned at the Jukebox" and "Living Proof." —*William Ruhlmann*

14 Greatest Hits / 1976 / Polydor ✦✦✦✦
Williams was a good, if conventional, country singer during the early years covered in this anthology (1966-1974). It includes 11 of his first 12 Top Ten hits, among them the No. 1s "Eleven Roses" and "All for the Love of Someone." —*William Ruhlmann*

Family Tradition / 1979 / Warner Bros. ✦✦✦
Williams returned to the upper reaches of the country charts with this album, his "outlaw" image, and songs like the title track, a No. 4 hit. —*William Ruhlmann*

Rowdy / 1981 / Warner Bros. ✦✦✦
In 1981, Hank Williams, Jr., was one of the hottest acts in country music, starting the year with this album, which spawned the No. 1 hits "Texas Women" and "Dixie on My Mind" and the striking "Are You Sure Hank Done It This Way." —*William Ruhlmann*

★ **Hank Williams Jr's Greatest Hits** / 1982 / Warner Bros. ✦✦✦✦✦
The biggest hits of Hank Williams, Jr., 1979-82, are among the best country music of the time: hard, tough, and (in the manner of one of country's great eccentrics) weird. —*William Ruhlmann*

Major Moves / 1984 / Warner Bros. ✦✦✦
Williams topped the country charts with this album, largely on the strength of the raucous "All My Rowdy Friends Are Coming over Tonight," though the title track and the caustic "Attitude Adjustment" were also hits. —*William Ruhlmann*

Greatest Hits, Vol. 2 / 1985 / Warner Bros. ✦✦✦✦
A well-chosen hits collection covering 1983 to 1985, including "Leave Them Boys Alone" and "All My Rowdy Friends Are Coming Over Tonight." —*William Ruhlmann*

Greatest Hits, Vol. 3 / 1989 / Warner Bros. ✦✦✦✦
This chronicles Williams' ongoing '80s success, 1985-1989, featuring the No. 1 hits "I'm for Love," "Ain't Misbehavin'," "Mind Your Own Business," and "Born to Boogie." —*William Ruhlmann*

America (The Way I See It) / 1990 / Warner Bros. ✦✦✦
Williams plays political commentator on this, a collection of his best revenge fantasies, reasons for America's problems, and the theme from Monday Night Football. The album includes the survivalist anthem "A Country Boy Can Survive" and "Don't Give Us a Reason," an open letter to Saddam Hussein. —*Brian Mansfield*

Maverick / Oct. 1991 / Capricorn ✦✦✦
Williams' first album for the revived Capricorn label rocks harder than usual, even while he's evangelizing for country music. A good chuck of *Maverick* sounds like a cross between a roaring drunk and a Penthouse letter. There's also a great ghost story ("Cut Bank, Montana") and a really dumb novelty song ("Fax Me a Beer"). There's probably not a soul on earth who could pull off "Come on Over to the Country" but Hank—it's corny and obvious about everything country music wishes it was. But

every time the slide guitar kicks in, he makes it all come true. —*Brian Mansfield*

The Bocephus Box: Hank Williams, Jr., Collection '79-92 / 1992 / Capricorn ✦✦✦✦
A box set covering much the same turf as the Warner Bros. greatest-hits volumes, it does have additional outtakes and live cuts for the completist to enjoy. —*Dan Cooper*

The Best of, Vol. 1: Roots and Branches / Aug. 4, 1992 / Mercury ✦✦✦✦
The title is a bit of a ringer here, as these are the songs Hank Jr. charted with through the mid-'60s to mid-'70s, before his reincarnation as Bocephus, the outlaw country-rocker, brought him mega-success. However, this 20-track compilation makes for interesting listening to hear how he evolved to his present style. — *Cub Koda*

Greatest Hits, Vol. 1 / Sep. 21, 1993 / Capitol/Curb ✦✦✦

Kelly Willis

Vocals / Progressive Country
Kelly Willis became a critical favorite in the early '90s with her edgy, rockabilly-inspired country. Raised in Annandale, VA, Willis began performing when she was 16 years old, joining her boyfriend Mas Palermo's rockabilly band. After she joined, the group became Kelly and the Fireballs, and they began playing the Washington, DC, club circuit. They gained a following, but no record industry recognition, so Palermo decided to move the band, including the teenaged Willis, to Austin, TX, in late 1987. Kelly's parents were not pleased by her move, but they agreed to help her if she would attend college in Texas. She did, but it was only two classes at a community college.

Once in Austin, the Fireballs remained together six months and then disbanded. Palermo began honing his songwriting skills while Willis began taking guitar lessons from David Murray, who was impressed by her demo tape.

Eventually, Murray would join Willis and Palermo's new band Radio Ranch. The band also included steel guitarist Michael Hardwick and bassist Brad Foreman. It didn't take long for Radio Ranch to build up a big following in Austin, but they didn't get their big break until 1987, when singer-songwriter Nanci Griffith attended one of their performances. Impressed by Willis' singing, Griffith told her producer, Tony Brown, about the young vocalist. Radio Ranch held a showcase at Nashville's famed Blue Bird Cafe and Brown attended. Like Griffith, he was impressed by Willis' talent and signed her to MCA immediately. The result was the acclaimed 1990 debut album *Well Traveled Love*. Although it was critically acclaimed, it didn't receive much airplay. Her second album, *Bang Bang*, came out in 1991. For both albums, she and Radio Ranch have toured extensively. In 1992, she had a cameo in Tim Robbins' film *Bob Roberts*. In 1993, she released her eponymous third album. —*Sandra Brennan*

Well Traveled Love / 1990 / MCA ✦✦✦
On her debut, this Austin country-rocker sings Texas-steel tunes and roisterous rockers with spirited assurance, but there's a natural tremble in her voice that makes her sound dangerous yet vulnerable. Willis is one of the few country singers with the disarming beauty to become a true sex symbol, and if she's the feminine response to all the hat acts, that's fine. —*Brian Mansfield*

● **Bang Bang** / 1991 / MCA ✦✦✦✦
Willis' idea of country comes from female rockabillys like Janis Martin and Wanda Jackson and from the blues-influenced Texas crowd she runs with in Austin. *Bang Bang* reflects that influence in the blistering tempos of "Too Much To Ask" and "Standing by the River," the Tex-Mex groove of "The Heart that Love Forgot," and an absolutely incendiary version of Joe Ely's "Settle for Love." —*Brian Mansfield*

Kelly Willis / 1993 / MCA ✦✦✦✦
Where Willis' first two albums occasionally turned into showcases for her musicians, *Kelly Willis* emphasizes concise, twangy pop songs over barn-burners. Willis sings a mandolin-propelled cover of Marshall Crenshaw's "Whatever Way the Wind Blows" and blends her voice with two members of Jellyfish on "One More Night." She also dips into Nashville's back catalog with a version of the Kendalls' 1977 "Heaven's Just a Sin Away." —*Brian Mansfield*

Bob Wills & His Texas Playboys

b. Mar. 6, 1905, Kosse, TX, **d.** May 15, 1975, Fort Worth, TX
Fiddle, Vocals / Western Swing
Bob Wills' name will forever be associated with Western swing. Although he did not invent the genre singlehandedly, he did popularize the genre and changed its rules. In the process, he reinvented the rules of popular music. Bob Wills and his Texas Playboys were a dance band with a country string section that played pop songs as if they were jazz numbers. Their music expanded and erased boundaries between genres. It was also some of the most popular music of its era. Throughout the '40s, the

band was one of the most popular groups in the country and the musicians in the Playboys were among the finest of their era. As the popularity of Western swing declined, so did Wills' popularity, but his influence is immeasurable. From the first honky tonkers to Western swing revivalists, generations of country artists owe him a significant debt, as do certain rock and jazz musicians. Bob Wills was a maverick and his spirit infused American popular music of the 20th century with a renegade, virtuosic flair.

From his father and grandfather, Wills learned how to play mandolin, guitar and, eventually, fiddle, and regularly played local dances in his teens. In 1929, Wills joined a medicine show in Fort Worth, where he played fiddle and did blackface comedy. At one performance, he met guitarist Herman Arnspiger and the duo formed the Wills Fiddle Band. Within a year, they were playing dances and radio stations around Fort Worth. During one of the performances, the pair met a vocalist called Milton Brown, who joined the band. Soon, Brown's guitarist brother Durwood joined the group, as did Clifton "Sleepy" Johnson, a tenor banjo player.

In early 1931, the band landed their own radio show, which was sponsored by the Burris Mill and Elevator company, the manufacturers of Light Crust Flour. The group rechristened themselves the Light Crust Doughboys and their show was being broadcast throughout Texas, hosted and organized by W. Lee O'Daniel, the manager of Burris Mill. By 1932, the band were stars in Texas but there was some trouble behind the scenes—O'Daniel wasn't allowing the band to play anything but the radio show. This situation led to the departure of Milton Brown; Wills eventually replaced Brown with Tommy Duncan, who he would work with for the next 16 years. By late summer 1933, Wills, aggravated with a series of fights with O'Daniel, left the Light Crust Doughboys and Duncan left with him.

Wills and Duncan relocated to Waco, TX, and formed the Playboys, which featured Wills on fiddle, Duncan on piano and vocals, rhythm guitarist June Whalin, tenor banjoist Johnny Lee Wills, and Kermit Whalin, who played steel guitar and bass. For the next year, the Playboys moved through a number of radio stations, as O'Daniel tried to force them off the air. Finally, the group settled in Tulsa, where they had a job at KVOO.

Tulsa is where Bob Wills and the Texas Playboys began to refine their sound. Wills added an 18-year-old electric steel guitarist called Leon McAuliffe, pianist Al Stricklin, drummer Smokey Dacus, and a horn section to the band's lineup. Soon, the Texas Playboys were the most popular band in Oklahoma and Texas. The band made their first record in 1935 for the American Recording Company, which would later become part of Columbia Records. At ARC, they were produced by Uncle Art Satherley, who would wind up as Wills' producer for the next 12 years. The bandleader had his way and they cut a number of tracks that were released on a series of 78s. The singles were successful enough that Wills could demand that steel guitarist Leon McAuliffe—who wasn't on the first sessions due to ARC's abundance of steel players under contract—be featured on the Playboys' next record, 1936's "Steel Guitar Rag." The song became a standard for steel guitar. Also released from that session was "Right or Wrong," which featured Tommy Duncan on lead vocals.

Toward the end of the decade, big bands were dominating popular music and Wills wanted a band capable of playing complex, jazz-inspired arrangements. To help him achieve his sound, he hired arranger and guitarist Eldon Shamblin, who wrote charts that fused country with big band music for the Texas Playboys. By 1940, he had replaced some of the weaker musicians in the lineup, winding up with a full 18-piece band. The Texas Playboys were breaking concert attendance records across the country, filling out venues from Tulsa to California and they also had their first genuine national hit with "New San Antonio Rose," which climbed to No. 11 in 1940. Throughout 1941 and 1942, Bob Wills and the Texas Playboys continued to record and perform and they were one of the most popular bands in the country. However, their popularity was quickly derailed by the arrival of World War II. Tommy Duncan enlisted in the Army after Pearl Harbor and Al Stricklen became a defense plant worker. Late in 1942, Leon McAuliffe and Eldon Shamblin both left the group. Bob enlisted in the Army late in 1942, but he was discharged as being unfit for service in the summer of 1943, primarily because he was out of shape and disagreeable. Duncan was discharged around the same time and the pair moved to California by the end of 1943. Wills revamped the sound of the Texas Playboys after World War II, cutting out the horn section and relying on amplified string instruments.

During the '40s, Art Satherley had moved from ARC to OKeh Records and Wills followed him to the new label. His first single for OKeh was a new version of "New San Antonio Rose" and it became a Top Ten hit early in 1944, crossing over into the Top 15 on the pop charts. Wills stayed with OKeh for about year, having several Top Ten hits, as well as the No. 1s "Smoke on the Water" and "Stars and Stripes on Iwo Jima." After he left OKeh, he signed with Columbia Records, releasing his first single for the label, "Texas Playboy Rag," toward the end of 1945. In 1946, the Texas Playboys began recording a series of transcriptions for Oakland, California's Tiffany Music Corporation. Tiffany's plan was to

syndicate the transcriptions throughout the Southwest, but their goal was never fulfilled. Nevertheless, the Texas Playboys made a number of transcriptions in '46 and '47, and these are the only recordings of the band playing extended jams. Consequently, they are close approximations of the group's live sound. Though the Tiffany Transcriptions would turn out to be important historical items, the recordings that kept Wills and the Playboys in the charts were their singles for Columbia, which were consistently reaching the Top Five between 1945 and 1948; in the summer of 1946, they had their biggest hit, "New Spanish Two Step," which spent 16 weeks at No. 1.

Guitarist Eldon Shamblin returned to the Playboys in 1947, the final year Wills recorded for Columbia Records. Beginning in late '47, Wills was signed to MGM. His first single for the label, "Bubbles in My Beer," was a Top Ten hit early in 1948, as was its follow-up, "Keeper of My Heart." Though the Texas Playboys were one of the most popular bands in the nation, they were beginning to fight internally, mainly because Wills had developed a drinking problem that caused him to behave erratically. Furthermore, Wills came to believe Tommy Duncan was demanding too much attention and asking for too much money. By the end of 1948, he had fired the singer.

Duncan's departure couldn't have come at a worse time. Western swing was beginning to fall out of public favor, and Wills' recordings weren't as consistently successful as they had been before—he had no hits at all in 1949. That year, he relocated to Oklahoma, beginning a 15-year stretch of frequent moves, all designed to find a thriving market for the band. In 1950, he had two Top Ten hits—"Ida Red Likes the Boogie" and "Faded Love," which would become a country standard; they would be his last hits for a decade. Throughout the '50s, he struggled with poor health and poor finances, but he continued to perform frequently. However, his audience continued to shrink, despite his attempts to hold on to it. Wills moved throughout the Southwest during the decade, without ever finding a new home base. Audiences at dance halls plummeted with the advent of television and rock 'n' roll. The Texas Playboys made some records for Decca that went unnoticed in the mid-'50s. In 1959, Wills signed with Liberty Records, where he was produced by Tommy Allsup, a former Playboy. Before recording his first sessions with Liberty, Wills expanded the lineup of the band again and reunited with Tommy Duncan. The results were a success, with "Heart to Heart Talk" climbing into the Top Ten during the summer of 1960. Again, the Texas Playboys were drawing sizable crowds and selling a respectable amount of records.

In 1962, Wills had a heart attack that temporarily debilitated him, but by 1963, he was making an album for Kapp records. The following year, he had a second heart attack which forced him to disband the Playboys. After the second heart attack, he performed and recorded as a solo performer. His solo recordings for Kapp were made in Nashville with studio musicians and were generally ignored, though he continued to be successful in concert.

In 1968, the Country Music Hall of Fame inducted Bob Wills and the following year the Texas State Legislature honored him for his contribution to American music. The day after he appeared in both houses of the Texas state government, Wills suffered a massive stroke, which paralyzed his right side. During his recovery, Merle Haggard—the most popular country singer of the late '60s—recorded an album dedicated to Bob Wills, A Tribute to the Best Damn Fiddle Player, which helped return Wills to public consciousness and spark a widespread Western swing revival. In 1972, Wills was well enough to accept a citation from ASCAP in Nashville, as well as appear at several Texas Playboy reunions, which were all very popular. In the fall of 1973, Wills and Haggard began planning a Texas Playboy reunion album, featuring Leon McAuliffe, Al Stricklin, Eldon Shamblin, and Smokey Dacus, among others. The first session was held on December 3, 1973, with Wills leading the band from his wheelchair. That night, he suffered another massive stroke in his sleep; the stroke left him comatose. The Texas Playboys finished the album without him. Bob Wills never regained consciousness and he died on May 15, 1975 in a nursing home. Wills was buried in Tulsa, the place where his legend began. — Stephen Thomas Erlewine

☆ **Bob Wills Anthology** / 1973 / Columbia ✦✦✦✦✦
These 24 essential songs from the '30s and '40s, in chronological order, show the evolution of one of American pop's most eclectic and adventuresome dance bands, the Texas Playboys. It is a cornerstone of any inclusive pop collection. — Mark A. Humphrey

For the Last Time / 1974 / United Artists ✦✦✦
Wills and the Texas Playboys reunited for the last swinging session of his life. Sitting in on fiddle and vocals is one of his biggest fans: Merle Haggard. — Dan Cooper

Columbia Historic Edition / 1982 / Columbia ✦✦✦
Fun and funky '30s sides. — Mark A. Humphrey

Fiddle / 1987 / Country Music Foundation ✦✦✦
The 20 tracks on this album, seven of which are released here for the first time, feature Wills performing in a variety of styles, from traditional old-time fiddle music to jazz and the blues. The recordings were made

between 1935 and 1942. —*AMG*

★ **Anthology 1935-1973** / 1991 / Rhino ✦✦✦✦
The only comprehensive retrospective of Bob Wills and the Texas Play-boys, the double-disc set *Anthology 1935-1973* contains material from every label the Playboys recorded for and features the hit version of each of Wills's most famous songs, including "Right or Wrong," "Time Changes Everything," "Corrine, Corrina," "New San Antonio Rose," "Take Me Back to Tulsa," "Cherokee Maiden," "Roly-Poly," "Stay A Little Longer," "Big Beaver," "Bubbles in My Beer," "Faded Love," and many others. It's the rare compilation that functions both as a definitive overview and an excellent introduction. —*Stephen Thomas Erlewine*

Country Music Hall of Fame Series / 1992 / MCA ✦✦✦✦
This set contains Western swing recordings made by Wills from 1955-1967, including such hits as "With Tears in My Eyes," "Cornball Rag," "Texas Two Step," and many more. —*AMG*

The Essential Bob Wills & His Texas Playboys / Aug. 25, 1992 / Columbia/Legacy ✦✦✦✦
A basic 20-track primer to some of the Western swing master's best sides. Acknowledged classics like "Steel Guitar Rag," "Take Me back to Tulsa," and "Stay a Little Longer" are all here, with the players and arrangements that made Wills and his Texas Playboys legends in country music. —*Cub Koda*

Longhorn Recordings / 1993 / Bear Family ✦✦✦✦
These mid-'60s Dallas sessions feature Wills in both large band and small rootsy combo settings. —*Dan Cooper*

☆ **Tiffany Transcriptions, Vols. 1-9** / Rhino ✦✦✦✦✦
In 1946, Bob Wills and the Texas Playboys began recording a series of radio transcriptions for Oakland, CA's Tiffany Music Corporation. Tiffany's plan was to syndicate the transcriptions throughout the Southwest, but their goal was never fulfilled. Nevertheless, the Texas Playboys made a number of transcriptions in '46 and '47, and these are the only recordings of the band playing extended jams. Consequently, they are close approximations of the group's live sound. The Tiffany Transcriptions weren't released until the '80s, when the Kaleidoscope label issued a multi-volume set of all of the sessions. These were later reissued by Rhino in the '90s. Available in nine individual volumes, every disc of the Tiffany Transcriptions illustrates the depth and breadth of the Texas Playboys and is one of the few recordings that captures all of their eclectic talents intact. —*Stephen Thomas Erlewine*

Johnnie Lee Wills

b. 1912, Texas, d. 1984
Banjo / Western Swing
Johnnie Lee Wills was younger brother to legendary Bob Wills and a member of the original Texas Playboys, the most famous Western swing band in history. Wills was a talent in his own right, playing tenor banjo in the Light Crust Doughboys, which became the Playboys and finally the Texas Playboys. When business was good, Bob Wills started a satellite band called Johnnie Lee Wills and his Boys. They had two hits, "Rag Mop" and "Peter Cottontail." And when business got bad, Johnnie Lee Wills retired and operated Tulsa's Stampede as well as a popular Western clothing shop. —*David Vinopal*

● **Reunion** / 1978 / Flying Fish ✦✦✦✦
Bob Wills' brother remained in Tulsa in the '30s and led a band that became a training ground for dozens of Western swing sidemen; many of the best are reunited here, in what were to be his last recordings. —*Charles S. Wolfe*

Michelle Wright

b. Jul. 1, 1961, Morpeth, Ontario, Canada
Vocals / Country
A native of Ontario, Canada, Michelle Wright grew up listening to the sounds of '60s soul from nearby Detroit radio stations. Both her parents were country musicians. and Wright followed in their footsteps as a teenager. A major star in Canada (she replaced k.d. lang as the nation's favorite native female country singer), she has yet to rise to those heights in the US. —*Brian Mansfield*

● **Michelle Wright** / 1990 / Arista ✦✦✦✦
With her husky, cigarette-deep voice, Wright sounds like nothing so much as a young Lacy J. Dalton on her American debut. There's some straight country here ("The Dust Ain't Settled Yet"), but more often than not, Wright's singing R&B material with steel guitars. Not only does she sing the stuff, she knows how: drop her voice two octaves on "Not Enough Love to Go 'Round," and she's Barry White. —*Brian Mansfield*

Now & Then / 1992 / Arista ✦✦✦
Wright made a mainstream move with *Now & Then*, downplaying the R&B and remaking herself as a sleek, sultry version of Lorrie Morgan. It paid off, too: she had her first real hits in the US with "Take It Like a Man" and "He Would Be 16," a tear-jerking ballad dealing with the regrets of giving an illegitimate child up for adoption. Her Nudie jackets

and black bodysuits made her a video favorite, too. The music's not as distinctive here as on *Michelle Wright*, but the hits hold up nicely. —*Brian Mansfield*

For Me It's You / Aug. 27, 1996 / Arista ✦✦✦✦

Tammy Wynette (Virginia Wynette Pugh)

b. May 5, 1942, Tupelo, MS
Guitar, Vocals / Traditional Country, Nashville Sound/Countrypolitan
In many ways, Tammy Wynette deserves the title of the First Lady of Country Music. During the late '60s and early '70s, she dominated the country charts, scoring 17 No. 1 hits. Along with Loretta Lynn, she defined the role of female country vocalists in the '70s.

After her father, who was a musician, died when she was just eight months old, Wynette was raised on her grandparents' home in Mississippi; her mother moved to Birmingham, AL, to do military work. As a child, Tammy taught herself to play a variety of instruments left behind by her father. When she was a teenager, she moved to Birmingham to be with her mother. At 17, she married her first husband, Euple Byrd, and set to work as a hairdresser and beautician. The marriage was short-lived, but it produced three children within three years. By the time her third child was born, the couple were divorced.

Tammy's third child had spinal meningitis, which meant she had several expensive medical bills to pay. In order to gain some extra money, she began performing in clubs at night. In 1965, she landed a regular spot on the television program the *Country Boy Eddie Show*, which led to appearances on Porter Wagoner's syndicated show. The following year, she moved to Nashville, where she auditioned for several labels before producer Billy Sherrill signed her to Epic Records.

"Apartment #9," Wynette's first single, was released late in 1966 and almost broke the country Top 40 early in 1967. It was followed by "Your Good Girl's Gonna Go Bad," which became a big hit, peaking at No. 3. The song launched a string of Top Ten hits that ran until the end of the '70s, interrupted by three singles that didn't crack the Top Ten. After "Your Good Girl's Gonna Go Bad" was a success, "My Elusive Dreams" became her first No. 1 in the summer of 1967, followed by "I Don't Wanna Play House" later that year.

During 1968 and 1969, Tammy had five No. 1 hits—"Take Me to Your World," "D-I-V-O-R-C-E," "Stand By Your Man" (all 1968), "Singing My Song," and "The Ways to Love a Man" (both 1969). In 1968, she started a relationship with George Jones, which would prove to be extremely stormy. Beginning in 1971, Wynette and Jones recorded a series of duets—the first was the Top Ten "Take Me"—which were as popular as their solo hits. However, the marriage was difficult and the couple divorced in 1975; they continued to record sporadically over the next two decades.

Throughout the '70s, Tammy Wynette racked up No. 1 hits. In the early '80s, her career began to slow down. Although she still had hit singles, she didn't reach the Top Ten as easily as she did in the previous decade. That trend continued throughout the rest of the decade and into the '90s. Even though she didn't have as many hits as she had in the past, Tammy remained a respected star and a popular concert attraction. —*Stephen Thomas Erlewine*

Your Good Girl's Gonna Go Bad / 1967 / Epic ✦✦✦✦
Her unmatched first album proves why she's the greatest female C&W "heart" singer. —*George Bedard*

☆ **Greatest Hits** / 1969 / Epic ✦✦✦✦✦
This follows Wynette's trail of tears right out of the chutes on classics like "Stand by Your Man" and "D-I-V-O-R-C-E." Producer Billy Sherrill's less-than-light touch never found a better instrument to work with than her voice. —*Dan Cooper*

Kids Say the Darndest Things / 1973 / Epic ✦✦✦
Wynette and Sherrill join forces for a concept album, including "Listen, Spot," "My Daddy Doll," "Buy Me a Daddy," and "Too Many Daddies." Sound funny? It is. Except "Too Many Daddies" will still rip your heart out. —*Dan Cooper*

Greatest Hits, Vol. 3 / 1975 / Epic ✦✦✦
The best reason to include this package is to simply say that one greatest-hits album from Wynette just isn't enough. The lyrical and musical themes here are much the same as in the first package, but the quiet determination of "Til I Get It Right" and the pure celebration of "My Man (Understands)" help broaden the picture of Wynette just a little. —*Tom Roland*

★ **Anniversary: 20 Years of Hits** / 1987 / Epic ✦✦✦✦
"Stand by Your Man" and "D-I-V-O-R-C-E" speak for themselves. But not to be overlooked are the less honored likes of "Apartment No.9," her debut hit, written by Johnny Paycheck; and "Your Good Girl's Gonna Go Bad," in which her freedom (instead of little J-O-E's tears) are at stake. Also included are three duets with George Jones. —*Dan Cooper*

Tears of Fire: the 25th Anniversary Collection / Nov. 3, 1992 / Epic ✦✦✦✦

Tears of Fire: 25th Anniversary, a three-disc box set covering Wynette's entire career, contains most of her hits as well as rarities and oddities like her lead vocal on KLF's "Justified and Ancient." It's hard to fault a collection that includes such classics as "Stand by Your Man" and "D-I-V-O-R-C-E," but casual fans might want to stick with the single disc *Anniversary—20 Years of Hits* collection. —*Thom Owens*

Super Hits / Mar. 19, 1996 / Epic ✦✦✦✦

A no-frills, ten-song disc running under 29 minutes, *Super Hits* should be purchased only at a discount price by a newcomer to Tammy Wynette who wants to get an idea of her music. That said, the set contains her three biggest hits, "I Don't Wanna Play House," "D-I-V-O-R-C-E," and "Stand by Your Man," five other No. 1 hits, and two more that made the Country Top Ten between 1967 and 1976. Strictly speaking, these are not Wynette's ten biggest hits, but they constitute a good sampling of her most popular work. —*William Ruhlmann*

Trisha Yearwood

Vocals / Contemporary Country
The daughter of a prominent Georgia banker, Trisha Yearwood exploded onto the country scene in the early 1990s with her chart-topping smash single "She's in Love with the Boy." That single kick-started a string of hit singles and albums that established Yearwood as one of the most popular country performers of the '90s.

Though born in Monticello, Georgia, Yearwood spent most of her childhood growing up on a 30-acre farm. As a young teen, she idolized Elvis. While in school she would occasionally participate in talent shows and jam with local club bands. She enrolled in Nashville's Belmont College in 1985 and graduated with a music business degree. Before graduating, she did a two-year internship at MTM Records. She enjoyed the work and moved to Nashville in 1987 where she began hanging out with such developing artists as Garth Brooks.

For a while Yearwood worked as a demo singer and then began singing back-up for Garth Brooks; during this time, Brooks promised her that if he became successful, he would help her career. She also worked with Pat Alger and it was while singing with him at a local bar that she was discovered by producer Garth Fundis, who got her a showcase. This led to her signing with MCA Records. Her debut single came out in 1990 and its success was followed by ten others that included "That's What I Like About You," which appeared on her self-titled first album. She was then scheduled to become Brooks' opening act. It soon became apparent that Yearwood was not prepared to handle a tour of that magnitude and as a result, she fired her manager and then signed on with Ken Kragen, who managed Lionel Richie and Kenny Rogers. The switch in management resulted in success. Both her next two albums *Hearts in Armor* (1992) and *The Song Remembers When* (1993) provided her with a respectable string of hits, and in 1994, she again hit No. 1 with "XXXs and OOOs (An American Girl)." In 1995, she released her fourth album, *Thinkin' About You.* —*Sandra Brennan*

Trisha Yearwood / 1991 / MCA ✦✦✦✦

This impressive debut brought everybody to lend a hand: Vince Gill, Mac McAnally, keyboardist Al Kooper, and more. Garth Brooks co-wrote two songs and helped sing one, the tentatively tender "Like We Never Had a Broken Heart." Yearwood's more at home with blue-collar romance than sweltering Texas nightlife, but her big Georgia range lets her sing just about anything, from the ballad "When Goodbye Was a Word" to Pat McLaughlin's saucy "That's What I Like About You." —*Brian Mansfield*

★ **Hearts in Armor** / Sep. 1, 1992 / MCA ✦✦✦✦✦

Take away the bluesy hit "Wrong Side of Memphis," and this is practically an emotional diary of Yearwood's divorce (which happened just as she hit the big time). In light of that event, "Nearest Distant Shore" and "Hearts in Armor" assume devastating significance and the cover of Emmylou Harris' "Woman Walk the Line" couldn't be more appropriate. As before, she's got the big-name backup singer—Harris, Don Henley, Vince Gill, and Garth Brooks—but not one steals the spotlight. *Hearts in Armor* is strictly Yearwood's show, and she's marvelous in it. —*Brian Mansfield*

The Song Remembers When / 1993 / MCA ✦✦✦✦

Yearwood shares common ground with peers Nanci Griffith and Mary-Chapin Carpenter by walking the line between country, folk, and pop, appealing to those who elevate the song above category limitations. Yearwood doesn't write her own material, but she and producer Garth Fundis have impeccable taste, securing contributions from the likes of Rodney Crowell, Willie Nelson (both also guest on backing vocals), and Matraca Berg. Ballads are Yearwood's forte: pure, sweet, sparsely rendered gems like "One In A Row" and "Lying To The Moon." —*Roch Parisien*

Thinkin' About You / 1995 / MCA ✦✦✦

Everybody Knows / Aug. 27, 1996 / MCA ✦✦✦

Trisha Yearwood firmly enters middle age with *Everybody Knows,* a collection of ballads and country-pop. Even when she kicks the tempo into high gear, Yearwood and her band lay back, easing the beat along instead of pushing it. Similarly, the country-pop is engaging and relaxed, gently winning you over. But the heart of the album lies in her ballads, which are appropriately theatrical and grandiose—it's big music with big melodies. The quality of the songs is a little uneven, but Yearwood continues to improve as a singer, which means she brings conviction even to the lackluster material on *Everybody Knows.* —*Thom Owens*

Dwight Yoakam

b. Oct. 23, 1956, Pikeville, KY
Guitar, Vocals / Country-Rock, Bakersfield Sound, New Traditionalist
With his stripped-down approach to traditional honky tonk and Bakersfield country, Dwight Yoakam helped return country music to its roots in the late '80s. Like his idols Buck Owens, Merle Haggard, and Hank Williams, Yoakam never played by Nashville's rules; consequently, he never dominated the charts like his contemporary Randy Travis. Then again, Travis never played around with the sound and style of country music like Yoakam. On each of his records, he twists around the form enough to make it seem like he doesn't respect all of country's traditions. Appropriately, his core audience was composed mainly of roots-rock and rock 'n' roll fans, not the mainstream country audience. Nevertheless, he was frequently able to chart in the country Top Ten, and he remained one of the most respected and adventurous recording country artists well into the '90s.

Born in Kentucky but raised in Ohio, Yoakam learned how to play guitar at the age of six. As a child, he listened to his mother's record collection, honing in on the traditional country of Hank Williams and Johnny Cash, as well as the Bakersfield honky tonk of Buck Owens. When he was in high school, Dwight played with a variety of bands, playing everything from country to rock 'n' roll. After completing high school, Yoakam briefly attended Ohio State University, but he dropped out and moved to Nashville in the late '70s with the intent of becoming a recording artist.

At the time he moved to Nashville, the town was in the throes of the pop-oriented Urban Cowboy movement and had no interest in his updated honky tonk. While in Nashville, he met guitarist Pete Anderson, who shared a similar taste in music. The pair moved out to Los Angeles, where they found a more appreciative audience than they did in Nashville. In Los Angeles, Yoakam and Anderson didn't just play country clubs—they played the same nightclubs as punk and post-punk rock bands like X, the Dead Kennedys, Los Lobos, the Blasters, and the Butthole Surfers. What Yoakam had in common with rock bands like X, the Blasters, and Los Angeles was similar musical influences—they all drew from '50s rock 'n' roll and country. In comparison to the polished music coming out of Nashville, Dwight's stripped-down, direct revivalism seemed radical. The cowpunks, as they were called, that attended Yoakam's shows provided an invaluable support for his fledgling career.

Yoakam released an independent EP, *A Town South of Bakersfield,* in 1984, which received substantial airplay on Los Angeles college and alternative radio stations. The EP also helped him land a record contract with Reprise Records. Dwight's full-length debut album, *Guitars, Cadillacs, Etc., Etc.,* was released in 1986 and was an instant sensation. Rock and country critics praised it and it earned airplay on college stations across America. More importantly, it was a hit on the country charts, as its first single, a cover of Johnny Horton's "Honky Tonk Man," climbed to No. 3 in the spring, followed by the No. 4 "Guitars, Cadillacs" in the summer. The album would eventually go platinum.

Hillbilly Deluxe, Dwight's 1987 follow-up, was equally successful, spawning four Top Ten hits—"Little Sister," "Little Ways," "Please, Please Baby," and "Always Late with Your Kisses." In 1988, Yoakam had his first No. 1 hit with "Streets of Bakersfield," a cover of a Buck Owens song recorded with Buck himself. It was the first single off his third album, *Buenas Noches from a Lonely Room,* which continued his streak of Top Ten hits. "I Sang Dixie," the album's second single, went to No. 1 and "I Got You" reached No. 5. In 1989, Yoakam released a compilation album, *Just Lookin' for a Hit,* which went gold. "Long White Cadillac," taken from the collection, stalled at No. 35 in the fall of 1989.

Although his 1990 album, *If There Was a Way,* didn't have as many Top Ten hits, it was a major success—it was his first album since his debut to go platinum. *This Time,* released in the spring of 1993, was an even bigger hit, spawning three No. 2 singles—"Ain't That Lonely Yet," "A Thousand Miles from Nowhere," and "Fast As You"—and going platinum. After its release, Yoakam was silent for two years, returning in the summer of 1995 with *Dwight Live,* which didn't set the charts on fire. In the fall of that year, he released his sixth album, *Gone,* which went gold by the spring of 1996, although it didn't produce any major country hits. —*Stephen Thomas Erlewine*

Guitars, Cadillacs, Etc., Etc. / 1986 / Reprise ✦✦✦✦

Who would have guessed when this album was released, with its uncompromisingly basic, honky tonk approach, that it would not only be a success but would help move the country music industry back from its crossover ways of the early '80s to a new renaissance based on its most traditional sounds? Maybe Yoakam, who doggedly stuck to that approach and wrote a bunch of songs that fit in with covers like Johnny Horton's "Honky Tonk Man." —*William Ruhlmann*

Hillbilly Deluxe / 1987 / Reprise ✦✦✦
This album essentially follows the same formula as *Guitars, Cadillacs, Etc., Etc.* and is just slightly less successful than Yoakam's breakthrough debut. The record is quite enjoyable—not only are updated honky tonk originals like "Little Ways" first-rate, but so are covers like Elvis Presley's "Little Sister" and Lefty Frizzell's "Always Late (With Your Kisses)." So the problem with the album lies in the fact that it doesn't move forward significantly, it is just Yoakam treading water. It's an enjoyable record, yet it still ranks as a minor work in his canon. —*Thom Owens*

Buenos Noches from a Lonely Room / 1988 / Reprise ✦✦✦✦
The first five cuts constituted a cold-blooded cycle that ran from possessive love to murderous rage with alarming quickness. The rest was subsequently a letdown but still gave Yoakam a couple of big hits in "I Sang Dixie" and "Streets of Bakersfield," a duet with Buck Owens. —*Brian Mansfield*

★ **Just Lookin' for a Hit** / 1989 / Reprise ✦✦✦✦✦
A strong singles collection with a typically sarcastic title, paced by duets with K.D. Lang on Gram Parsons' "Sin City" and with Buck Owens (a match made in heaven) on "Streets of Bakersfield." —*William Ruhlmann*

☆ **If There Was a Way** / 1990 / Reprise ✦✦✦✦✦
Yoakam's strongest studio album to date, with 14 songs (Nashville's standard is ten). Includes the classic Yoakam/Roger Miller collaboration "It Only Hurts When I Cry." —*Brian Mansfield*

La Croix D'Amour / 1992 / Reprise ✦✦✦✦
An international-only compilation, *La Croix D'Amour* is worth searching out for its rarities: two songs that appeared on other collections (Elvis Presley's "Suspicious Minds" and The Grateful Dead's "Truckin'") and four new tracks, among them covers of The Beatles' "Things We Said Today" and Them's "Here Comes the Night." —*Brian Mansfield*

☆ **This Time** / 1993 / Warner Bros. ✦✦✦✦✦
Heartbroke fool that he is, Dwight Yoakam knows all the words for loneliness. He doesn't let up once he starts on the self-pity binge of *This Time*: he begins as the devastated lover and winds up 11 songs later the desolate loner. Musical traditionalist that he is, he knows all the styles, too, from Buck Owens' Bakersfield country ("This Time") to Gene Pitney's mini-soundtracks ("A Thousand Miles from Nowhere") to rock's spite fantasies ("Fast as You"). He knows so many that *This Time* sounds more like a collection of individual songs than the single-minded work that it is. He understands them, too: That's why Yoakam gets good mileage from campy gimmicks like the ooh-wah background vocals on "Pocket of a Clown." There's plenty of hardcore country here—"This Time," "Home for Sale," "Lonesome Road"—but the best stuff allows for Yoakam's pop roots, too. —*Brian Mansfield*

Dwight Live / May 23, 1995 / Reprise ✦✦
Gone / Nov. 1995 / Reprise ✦✦✦
With *Gone*, Dwight Yoakam continued to push the boundaries of country music, adding elements of rock 'n' roll, Tex-Mex, Stax R&B, strings and even sitar to his already eclectic Bakersfield country. However, what makes *Gone* distinctive is the directness of the songwriting. For the first time, Yoakam has written the majority of the album alone and the results are riveting. He is able to fuse together disperate elements into an emotional and daring whole. Ten years into his career, Dwight Yoakam remains one of country's most exciting and restless talents. —*Stephen Thomas Erlewine*

Faron Young (Sheriff)

b. Feb. 25, 1932, Shreveport, LA
Guitar, Vocals / Traditional Country, Honky Tonk
Versatile, Faron Young is. In his younger days known as "the Hillbilly Heartthrob," he has managed to remain in the public eye for nearly 40 years, due to his musical talent, his entertaining personality, his numerous TV appearances (especially on Ralph Emery's *Nashville Now* show), and his many side interests, which have included movie acting and publishing. Young began *Music City News*, country music's dominant monthly magazine. In 1951 Young signed with Capitol, and because of two quick hits ("Have I Waited Too Long" and "Tattle Tale Eyes") he became an Opry regular within the year. The next two years he spent in the army, entertaining the troops at home and abroad. His first major success came with "I've Got Five Dollars and It's Saturday Night" (1956), rounding out the '50s with "Sweet Dreams" and "Country Girl" (1959). In 1961 "Hello Walls," a Willie Nelson composition, became Young's best-known hit. He continued to sell well, singles and albums alike, through the '60s and '70s, with "Wine Me Up," "Another You," and "Crutches." Young's strong, clear voice has been a perfect vehicle for his upbeat, let's-

have-some-fun material. He's in the same league with Jimmy Dean in wit, candor, and downright entertainment as a guest on TV talk shows. The audience gets the feeling that in his life Young has followed the suggestion of "Live Fast, Love Hard, and Die Young" (a 1955 hit for him), except for the dying part, though no doubt he'd come up with some pun about even that, too. —*David Vinopal*

★ **Live Fast, Love Hard: Original Capitol Recordings,1952-1962** / Oct. 1995 / Country Music Foundation ✦✦✦✦✦
Faron Young was one of the most popular honky tonk stars of the '50s and *Live Fast, Love Hard: Original Capitol Recordings, 1952-1962* is an excellent overview of the peak of his career. Featuring his big hits like "If You Ain't Lovin' (You Ain't Livin')" as well as more obscure tracks (a radio transcription of "Three Days"), the album is the most thorough and listenable single-disc retrospective ever assembled on Young. For honky tonk fans, it's an essential listen. —*Stephen Thomas Erlewine*

The Classic Years 1952-62 / Bear Family ✦✦✦✦
Swashbuckling Louisiana honky tonk, much of Faron Young's early work on Capitol is marked by an undertone of grinning lasciviousness. That's not a bad thing, given how many of his industry pals completely hid their wolfishness behind apple-pie lyrics. In any case, Bear Family has here collected the entirety of Young's Capitol output on five CDs. Besides the swaggering stuff ("If You Ain't Lovin'," "Live Fast, Love Hard, Die Young," and the amazing "Alone with You") one can hear the hit version of "Sweet Dreams" he cut seven years before Patsy Cline's. It comes with a beautiful 48-page book. —*Dan Cooper*

Various Artists

Are You from Dixie?: Great Country Brother Teams of the 1930s / RCA ✦✦✦✦
The title is truth in advertising. Excellent sides and spellbinding harmony vocals from the Delmore Brothers, the Monroe Brothers, the Blue Sky Boys, the Dixon Brothers, the Allen Brothers, and the Lone Star Cowboys. —*Richie Unterberger*

Best of Austin City Limits: Country Music's Finest Hour / 1996 / Columbia/Legacy ✦✦✦
From its inception in the mid-'70s until the late '90s, "Austin City Limits" was the premier country music television show in America. What distinguished the show from its competition was its emphasis on performance—each show spotlights one or two showcase artists, plus various guest artists, who are allowed to play whatever they want. The result was a freewheeling, eclectic, and passionate music show unlike any other. *The Best of Austin City Limits: Country Music's Finest Hour* collects 16 highlights from the show's long, illustrious history, and as expected, some of the biggest names in country music are involved. From Merle Haggard ("Silver Wings," 1978) and George Jones ("He Stopped Loving Her Today," 1985) to Asleep at the Wheel ("Boogie Back to Texas," 1987) and Alison Krauss ("Baby, Now That I've Found You," 1995), the album has a wide selection of first-rate artists and stellar performances that hint at the rich legacy of the show. In fact, if there's anything wrong with the disc it is the fact that it feels incomplete, even though it includes such luminaries as Willie Nelson, Tammy Wynette, Waylon Jennings, k.d. lang, Mary Chapin Carpenter, Dwight Yoakam, the Mavericks, the Judds, Charlie Daniels, and Patty Loveless. There's no fault with any of these selections, indeed, but after the disc is finished, you're waiting for the sequel. —*Thom Owens*

Billboard Top Country Hits: 1959 / 1990 / Rhino ✦✦✦✦✦
Each volume of this series contains the Top Ten country hits of that year. This volume contains Johnny Cash's "Don't Take Your Love to Town," George Jones' "White Lightning," Johnny Horton's "The Battle of New Orleans," and more. —*AMG*

Billboard Top Country Hits: 1960 / 1990 / Rhino ✦✦✦✦✦
This features Jim Reeves' "He'll Have to Go," Marty Robbins' "El Paso," Hank Locklin's "Please Help Me, I'm Falling," and other hits. —*AMG*

Billboard Top Country Hits: 1961 / 1990 / Rhino ✦✦✦✦✦
This features Patsy Cline's "I Fall to Pieces," Jimmy Dean's "Big Bad John," and other Top Ten hits from 1961. —*AMG*

Billboard Top Country Hits: 1962 / 1990 / Rhino ✦✦✦✦✦
It features Patsy Cline's "She's Got You," Hank Snow's "I've Been Everywhere," Claude King's "Wolverton Mountain," and other top hits from 1962. —*AMG*

Billboard Top Country Hits: 1963 / 1990 / Rhino ✦✦✦✦✦
Included are Johnny Cash's "Ring of Fire," Buck Owens' "Act Naturally," and Ned Miller's "From a Jack to a King," among other early-'60s favorites. —*AMG*

Billboard Top Country Hits: 1964 / 1990 / Rhino ✦✦✦✦✦
This volume in the series contains George Jones' "The Race Is On" and Roger Miller's "Dang Me," among other hits. —*AMG*

Billboard Top Country Hits: 1965 / 1990 / Rhino ✦✦✦✦✦
Featured are Eddy Arnold's "Make the World Go Away" and Roger Miller's "King of the Road." —*AMG*

Billboard Top Country Hits: 1966 / 1990 / Rhino ✦✦✦✦✦
This volume includes David Houston's "Almost Persuaded," Loretta Lynn's "You Ain't Woman Enough," and Jack Greene's "There Goes My Everything." —*AMG*

Billboard Top Country Hits: 1967 / 1990 / Rhino ✦✦✦✦✦
It includes David Houston and Tammy Wynette's duet "My Elusive Dream" and Wynn Stewart's "It's Such a Pretty World." —*AMG*

Billboard Top Country Hits: 1968 / 1990 / Rhino ✦✦✦✦✦
This volume contains such hits from 1968 as Merle Haggard's "Mama Tried," Tammy Wynette's "Stand by Your Man," Jeanne C. Riley's "Harper Valley PTA," and Johnny Cash's "Folsom Prison Blues." —*AMG*

Billboard Top Country Hits: 1986 / 1986 / Rhino ✦✦✦
Rhino's most recent set of Billboard country anthologies begin at 1986 and show through its lineup just how much things have changed since then in country circles. Ricky Skaggs, John Conlee, Lee Greenwood, T.G. Sheppard, and T. Graham Brown are not exactly factors in the 1990s, while Exile is hanging on for dear life. Both Tanya Tucker and Dan Seals have seen better days. Only Hank Williams, Jr., and Steve Wariner currently matter, and Wariner is doing better tunes now than "Life's Highway." —*Ron Wynn*

Billboard Top Country Hits: 1987 / 1987 / Rhino ✦✦✦
The 1990s have seen country continue to evolve, and the second volume in Rhino's latest anthology line demonstrates the changes once more. There are cuts from the Forester Sisters, O'Kanes (defunct), Highway 101 (now with a new lead vocalist), and holdovers Hank Williams, Jr., and Steve Wariner. It begins with Randy Travis' superb "Forever and Ever, Amen" and includes Rosanne Cash's sublime "This Is the Way We Make a Broken Heart." These compensate for another Exile song. —*Ron Wynn*

Billboard Top Country Hits: 1988 / 1988 / Rhino ✦✦✦
The third volume in Rhino's latest country series towers over the previous two, reflecting both improved songwriting and performance level. Only Earl Thomas Conley's "What I'd Say" dips slightly, while such songs as "Streets of Bakersfield" from the duo of Dwight Yoakam and Buck Owens, Keith Whitley's "When You Say Nothing at All," and Randy Travis' "I Told You So" and "Set 'Em Up Joe" are all fabulous cuts, as are Tanya Tucker's "Strong Enough to Bend" and Highway 101's "Cry, Cry, Cry." —*Ron Wynn*

Billboard Top Country Hits: 1989 / 1989 / Rhino ✦✦✦✦✦
While country ranks as the No. 1 radio format and is arguably the nation's most popular adult form, Rhino's anthology series of No. 1 hits certainly provides ample food for thought regarding what types of songs have been genuine hits: Eddie Rabbitt, Shenandoah, and Eddy Raven had No. 1 hits in 1989. The disc's saving grace comes from Patty Loveless, Randy Travis, Keith Whitley, Highway 101, and Steve Wariner, while it is filled out by Ronnie Milsap and a decent Dolly Parton cut. —*Ron Wynn*

Billboard Top Country Hits: 1990 / 1990 / Rhino ✦✦✦✦✦
The fifth and final volume in the latest Rhino country anthology line concludes things in 1990. Once more, many of the No. 1s offer reason to stop and ponder the condition of contemporary country radio. Shenandoah, Paul Overstreet, Dan Seals, and Mike Reid are not bad, but all of them are as close to MOR and folk as country. Randy Travis, Patty Loveless, and Holly Dunn also scored No. 1 hits, as did Lorrie Morgan. Joe Diffie is a lot closer to country than many of these acts, and Alabama is almost hard-core honky tonk next to Shenandoah. —*Ron Wynn*

☆ **The Bristol Sessions** / 1991 / Country Music Foundation ✦✦✦✦✦
It's common knowledge that Ralph Peer's recording session in Bristol, TN, launched the careers of the Carter Family and Jimmie Rodgers, but as this double CD proves, they weren't the only worthwhile musicians to turn up. In fact, Peer recorded 21 other acts, including the Stoneman Family and Blind Alfred Reed in what turns out to be an amazing display of rural talent and the birth of country music. —*William Ruhlmann*

Cattle Call: Early Cowboy Music and Its Roots / 1996 / Rounder ✦✦✦✦✦
The first of a four-volume history of cowboy music, this collection of 14 songs from 1925-60 was compiled with an eye for illustrating the roots of the style, as heard in songs from sources that date before the commercialization of the form. It covers a fair amount of territory, including stars like Jimmie Rodgers, Tex Ritter, Tex Owens, and the Sons of the Pioneers; early women performers in the style, Patsy Montana and the Girls of the Golden West; early cowboy film singers Ken Maynard and Ray Whitley; and even the Mexican sounds of Trio Los Pancho. Like the entire series, each track is annotated with thorough notes about the history of the songs and the performers. —*Richie Unterberger*

☆ **Columbia Country Classics, Vol. 1: Golden Age** / CBS ✦✦✦✦✦
This five-volume set contains 128 of the greatest country music recordings in Columbia's vaults, which span the genre from its beginnings. Each volume (available separately or as a set) contains major country art-

ists. This first volume contains 27 landmark recordings by the artists that made them famous, such as Roy Acuff's "Wabash Cannonball" and the Carter Family's "Will the Circle Be Unbroken"—16 artists in all. —*AMG*

Common Thread: The Songs of the Eagles / 1994 / Warner Bros. ✦✦
In a benefit album for Don Henley's pet project, Walden Pond, a number of the biggest stars in contemporary country music come together to pay tribute to the influence the Eagles had on country and rock. Ironically, all of the interpretations on *Common Thread* are more pop-rock oriented than the original versions, making the album a well-intentioned but pointless exercise. —*AMG*

Country Music Classics, Vol. 1 (1950's) / 1990 / K-Tel ✦✦✦
How can you account for a whole decade on one disc? It's not easy, and K-Tel didn't quite do it. There are some classics on this disc like Patsy Cline ("Walking After Midnight"), Kitty Wells ("It Wasn't God Who Made Honky Tonk Angels"), and Hank Williams ("Jambalaya"). Overall, this isn't a bad disc, it's just that it was too much time to cover on one disc. —*Jim Worbois*

Country Music Classics, Vol. 3 (1965-70) / 1984 / K-Tel ✦✦✦
If you fondly remember country music before it went "uptown" in the '70s, this disc is one you'll enjoy. Some of the highlights include Tammy Wynette's classic "Stand by Your Man," David Houston's "Almost Persuaded," and Leon Ashley's original version of "Laura (What's He Got That I Ain't Got)," later done by Marty Robbins. Not all the tracks are classics, but there are no duds here either. —*Jim Worbois*

Country Music Classics, Vol. 13 (Late 70's) / 1991 / K-Tel ✦✦✦✦✦
This disc is certainly representative of what was happening in country music in the late '70s, but I don't know if anyone would call any of these tracks "classics." Okay for what it is. —*Jim Worbois*

Country Music Classics, Vol. 14 (1940's) / 1993 / K-Tel ✦✦✦✦✦
While this is a nice disc, it is by no means a complete representation of the entire decade, though it does show what diverse styles the term country music covered in the '40s. There is Western swing from Bob Wills, cowboy music from the Sons of the Pioneers, bluegrass from Bill Monroe, and Merle Travis doing music from the hills of Kentucky. There's something for everyone on this disc. —*Jim Worbois*

Country Music Classics, Vol. 16: 1955-60 / 1993 / K-Tel ✦✦✦✦✦
Overall, a pleasing disc with many of country music's biggest names from the period represented. —*Jim Worbois*

Country Music Classics, Vol. 17 (1960-1965) / 1993 / K-Tel ✦✦✦✦✦
Aside from the fact that "The Race Is On" is not the hit version but one George Jones remade at a later date, there are some nice things on this disc, including the hit versions of two Willie Nelson originals (Patsy Cline's "Crazy," and "Night Life" by Ray Price). —*Jim Worbois*

Don't Fence Me In: Western Music's Early Golden Era / Feb. 1996 / Rounder ✦✦✦✦✦
ion with his son, tenor saxophonist Gene Ammons, is a high point. Singer Helen Humes is showcased on 16 stomps and ballads, pianist Jay McShann (often with vocalists Jimmy Witherspoon or Walter Brown) has 24 songs, and Eddie "Cleanhead" Vinson (on alto and vocals) is heard in a variety of settings on 30 selections. In addition there are nine tunes featuring R&B pianist/singer Professor Longhair; four songs apiece from singers Julia Lee, Myra Taylor, and cornetist Rex Stewart; 12 pieces from Buddy Rich's bebop big band; and ten by trumpeter Cootie Williams, including the Willis "Gator" Jackson R&B hit "'Gator Tail." As if that were not enough, the seventh disc has previously unreleased alternate takes from Ammons, Humes, McShann, Vinson, Cootie, and two "new" numbers by pianist Mary Lou Williams. The 80-page booklet with notes from several writers, including Dan Morgenstern) is definitive. Since this is a limited-edition release, it should be acquired as soon as possible; there are literally dozens of musical highlights. —*Scott Yanow*

★ **Hillbilly Fever, Vol. 5** / 1995 / Rhino ✦✦✦✦✦
If you're a big country-rock fan, you're probably familiar with most of the work on this compilation. But if you're not, it's a good introductory survey of the genre; or, if you are, but aren't passionate enough about the style to actively collect country-rock recordings, it may satisfy more basic needs. Focusing exclusively on music from country-rock's heyday in the late '60s and early '70s, it has cuts by most of the leading lights of the scene, including the Flying Burrito Brothers, the International Submarine Band, the Byrds, the Everly Brothers, Poco, Nitty Gritty Dirt Band, Michael Nesmith, New Riders of the Purple Sage, and into the mid-'70s (briefly) with Pure Prairie League and Marshall Tucker. There are also off-the-beaten-track songs by Linda Ronstadt and Bob Dylan, as well as country-rock outings by name acts who weren't primarily affiliated with the style, such as the Lovin' Spoonful, the Youngbloods, and Delaney & Bonnie. It's a good mix of the familiar and the unfamiliar, though it doesn't include important work in the field by Buffalo Springfield, the Grateful Dead, the Beau Brummels, and Rick Nelson, mostly because of licensing restrictions. —*Richie Unterberger*

☆ **Hillbilly Music: Thank God!, Vol. 1** / 1989 / Bug ✦✦✦✦✦
An excellent double-disc compilation of country music from the late '40s to the mid-'50s, featuring Buck Owens, Merle Travis, Faron Young, Tennessee Ernie Ford, and more. — *William Ruhlmann*

The Kings of Country Music / Oct. 1995 / Ranwood ✦✦✦
Twenty big country hits (some of which were rock 'n' roll hits as well) from the 1950s, including smashes by Johnny Cash, Carl Perkins, Hank Williams, Hank Snow, Jim Reeves, George Jones, Don Gibson, Marty Robbins, Ernest Tubb, and Tennessee Ernie Ford. Nothing here is rare, but for those who are just looking for a decent sampler of popular male-sung country from the 1950s, this will do fine. — *Richie Unterberger*

The Legendary Women of Country Music Sing Their Original Hits / 1996 / Ranwood ✦✦✦

The Nashville Sound . . . Owen Bradley / Feb. 1996 / Decca ✦✦
Producer Owen Bradley is undoubtedly one of the most important figures in Nashville country music. This skimpy ten-song sampler, however, is not the best way to appreciate his legacy. Certainly some of the performances are pivotal classics (Brenda Lee's "I'm Sorry," Patsy Cline's "Crazy"), but it's so short that it's virtually over as soon as it starts. Also, a couple of the standards here (Kitty Wells' "It Wasn't God Who Made Honky Tonk Angels," Red Foley's "Chattanoogie Shoe Shine Boy") are not the original versions, but remakes. — *Richie Unterberger*

The Okeh Western Swing / Columbia Special Products ✦✦✦✦✦
These recordings from the early days of Western swing feature such legends as Hank Penny, Adolf Hofner, the Light Crust Doughboys, Bob Wills, and others. — *AMG*

Outlaws — Super Hits / 1996 / Columbia ✦✦✦
This is a budget-line collection that does an adequate job of summing up the attitude, if not the actual sound, of late-'70s outlaw country. Part of the problem is that the album concentrates solely on artists that recorded for Columbia and its affiliated labels. Therefore, a few major outlaw artists — including Billy Joe Shaver and Tompall Glaser — aren't included at all, while others, like Waylon Jennings, have misrepresentative tracks. Furthermore, several artists that have only a tangential relationship with outlaws — such as Johnny Cash and Merle Haggard, who were more responsible for inspiring the movement than actually being part of it — are given numerous tracks. Still, *Outlaws*—*Super Hits* is enjoyable for what it is — a brief, cheap ten-track sampler with a few good songs. Certain songs are stone-cold outlaw classics — such as Willie Nelson's "Blue Eyes Crying in the Rain," David Allan Coe's "Long Haired Redneck," and Haggard & Nelson's duet, "Pancho and Lefty" — while others are just classics (Johnny Paycheck's "Take This Job and Shove It," Johnny Cash's "Ring of Fire" and "Folsom Prison Blues"). And that just means that although this isn't a definitive outlaw compilation, it's still an enjoyable listen. — *Stephen Thomas Erlewine*

☆ **Ragged But Right** / RCA ✦✦✦✦✦
This seminal collection of early country highlights all influences and spotlights premier string bands from the '30s. Marvelous sound. — *Ron Wynn*

Saddle Up!: The Cowboy Renaissance / 1996 / Rounder ✦✦✦
Fourteen songs performed by cowboy revivalists, spanning 1973-1992. As is the case with most records that aim to preserve and revive a style, it just doesn't compare to the earlier stuff, in passion or originality. It does, however, contain work by several of the most popular performers working the field, such as Ian Tyson, Michael Martin Murphey, and Riders in the Sky; there's also Willie Nelson, with his seminal "Red Headed Stranger." — *Richie Unterberger*

Songs of the West / 1993 / Rhino ✦✦✦✦✦
This "definitive collection of cowboy songs" covers both famous and obscure odes to the high lonesome plains by Gene Autry, Roy Rogers, Tex Ritter, Marty Robbins, Slim Pickens, Bob Wills, and others. Spanning the 1930s to the present, the 72-track, four-CD collection is broken into four separate thematic discs. Vol. 1 features "Cowboy Classics" like "Back in the Saddle Again," "Mule Train," and "Happy Trails." The real find here has to be the ultradramatic narrative by Walter Brennan describing the "Gunfight at the O.K. Corral." Vol. 2, "Silver Screen Cowboys," features tunes from Hollywood Westerns; Vol. 3 is devoted exclusively to performances by the kingpins of the genre, Gene Autry and Roy Rogers. The final disc is perhaps the most fun of the batch, presenting movie and television themes like "Bonanza," "Gunsmoke," "The Good, the Bad, and the Ugly," and "Rawhide." The box comes with a 60-page color booklet that includes detailed essays, photos, and reproductions of movie posters. — *Richie Unterberger*

Stampede! Western Music's Late Golden Era / 1996 / Rounder ✦✦✦✦✦
The third installment of Rounder's four-volume cowboy music series contains the songs most likely to be familiar to the general listener: Tex Ritter's "High Noon," Vaughn Monroe's "Riders in the Sky," Marty Rob-

bins' "El Paso," Johnny Western's "The Ballad of Paladin," Eddy Arnold's "Cattle Call." Taken from the years spanning 1945-1960, it presents the form at its most pop-oriented, but it's not less enjoyable for that. Filling out the 14-track set are numbers by the likes of Elton Britt, Jimmy Wakely, and the Sons of the Pioneers (one of whose tracks is the theme to one of the definitive cowboy western films, *The Searchers*). — *Richie Unterberger*

☆ **The Sun Country Years: 1950-1959** / Bear Family ✦✦✦✦✦
This collection, available only as ten LPs, contains classic performances from the beginning of rock 'n' roll, many of which are now available for the first time. Among the artists on the set are Hardrock Gunther, Jerry Lee Lewis, Charlie Feathers, Johnny Cash, Warren Smith, Jack Clement, Carl Perkins, and others. A 128-page booklet accompanies the set. — *AMG*

Super Hits of 1995 / Mar. 19, 1996 / Epic ✦✦✦
Actually, 1995 was not that good a year in country music for the Epic and Columbia labels of Sony Music, and some of the labels' biggest hits, such as Collin Raye's "One Boy, One Girl," are not included in this ten-song compilation. But some of the best country hits of the year, among them Joe Diffie's "Pickup Man," James House's "This Is Me Missing You," Rick Trevino's "Bobbie Ann Mason," Mary-Chapin Carpenter's "House of Cards," and Ty Herndon's "What Mattered Most" are included, which makes this a reasonable sampler of the year, at least from one major label's perspective. — *William Ruhlmann*

Tulare Dust: Tribute to Merle Haggard / 1994 / Hightone ✦✦✦✦✦
This tribute to Merle Haggard collection is just great. Any fan of contemporary singer-songwriters will want this CD because the lineup includes Peter Case, Iris DeMent, Barrence Whitfield, Katy Moffatt, Dave Alvin, and Marshall Crenshaw, not to mention producer Tom Russell. All the songs are presented straight, and they all jump out of the speakers as wonderful examples of from-the-heart, rough-and-ready songwriting. Also, as with all good tunes, you'll find yourself humming along. — *Richard Meyer*

☆ **Urban Cowboy [O.S.T.]** / 1980 / Asylum ✦✦✦✦✦
It includes Joe Walsh, Bob Seger, Boz Scaggs, and Dan Fogelberg, so it's obviously not strictly a country album. But the soundtrack is important because it symbolizes the country trend that grew, then faded, in the early '80s (a case can be made that J.R. Ewing had a lot more influence on the fad than the film *Urban Cowboy*). Most of the country tracks here lean toward MOR. — *Tom Roland*

☆ **Wanted! The Outlaws** / 1996 / RCA ✦✦✦✦✦
The term "outlaw" had been bandied about after Jennings' 1972 hit "Ladies Love Outlaws," but it didn't permanently gel until the release of the album *Wanted! The Outlaws* in 1976. The songs in this packaged product weren't new — the album contained previously released material by Nelson, Jennings, Glaser, and Jennings' wife, Jessi Colter (who had hit the charts a year earlier with "I'm Not Lisa"). But it marked the industry's recognition of the changing times, and as the centerpoint of a campaign to publicize Nashville's new "progressive" breed it worked like a charm. It quickly became the first country album to sell more than a million copies, and it boosted the careers of all involved. In 1996, RCA reissued *Wanted! The Outlaws* on CD for the first time, adding one new Waylon and Willie recording (a lively reading of Steve Earle's "Nowhere Road") and nine "lost" tracks. But "lost" isn't really correct: Like the original 11 selections, such songs as Waylon's "Slow Movin' Outlaws" and Willie's "Healing Hands of Time" have been previously released. They do, however, sweeten the package, making this 20th anniversary edition a decent (though by no means definitive) sampler of outlaw country. — *Kurt Wolff*

● **Western Swing, Vol. 1** / Old Timey ✦✦✦✦✦
Includes such artists as Bob Wills, Harry Choates, Bill Boyd, Milton Brown, and the Lightcrust Doughboys, among others. — *AMG*

Western Swing, Vol. 2 / Old Timey ✦✦✦✦✦
This second volume features Jimmie Revard, the Tune Wranglers, W. Lee O'Daniel, and others, including several artists who appeared on the first album. — *AMG*

Western Swing, Vol. 3 / Old Timey ✦✦✦✦✦
This album features several artists who appeared in the preceding volumes, plus such additions as the Modern Mountaineers, Brown's Brownies, and Spade Cooley. — *AMG*

Western Swing, Vol. 5 / Old Timey ✦✦✦✦✦
This album features music recorded during the '30s by the Universal Cowboys, Buddy Jones, Bob Skyles, Ocie Stockard, the Farr Brothers, the Nite Owls, and others. — *AMG*

Western Swing, Vol. 6 / Old Timey ✦✦✦✦✦
This features Buddy Duhon & Harry Choates, Johnny Tyler, Don Churchill, Johnnie Lee Wills, T. Texas Tyler, Pee Wee King, Jerry Irby, Easy Adams, Webb Pierce, and other '40s and '50s stars. — *AMG*

BLUEGRASS

Of all the sub-styles within country music, bluegrass is the most distinctly different. The average country music fan who might listen to five average country songs—one each from honky tonk, country-rock, Western swing, country pop, and bluegrass—most likely would label the first four generically as "country" while specifying the last as "bluegrass." Despite common roots, bluegrass and mainstream country diverged during WWII, bluegrass following a path of tradition that has changed relatively little in the last half-century, in sharp contrast to country music's many paths that over the years have continually led into numerous and often far-flung musical territories.

In the early '40s, country and bluegrass parted company, country moving on to honky tonk, Western swing, rockabilly, and electrified instruments, with bluegrass remaining closer to its roots, especially to the string-band music of the '20s and '30s. Among these traditional string bands (at the time called "hillbilly") were Gid Tanner and the Skillet Lickers, the Possum Hunters, the Georgia Wildcats, and many others, most of whom played traditional music in bands of three to six performing on guitars, fiddles, banjos, mandolins, and unamplified steel guitars (dobros) — instruments that were eventually adopted as the standard bluegrass configuration. While it's clear that bluegrass evolved from these bands, it remained for the great Bill Monroe (accurately called the "Father of Bluegrass"), with his band the Blue Grass Boys, to refine the old sound. The music itself does a much better job than words in showing how Monroe transformed this old music from a Model T to the bluegrass Cadillac V-8, with overdrive: no listener can mistake Mainer's Mountaineers, Roy Hall and His Blue Ridge Entertainers, or any other early '40s string band with Bill Monroe's Blue Grass Boys of the same period.

In 1945 Monroe formed the classic bluegrass band: Lester Flatt, guitar and vocal lead; Earl Scruggs, instrumental lead with the reinvented banjo; Chubby Wise, fiddler and cowriter of "Orange Blossom Special"; Cedric Rainwater, standup bass; and Bill. "Kentucky Waltz" and "Footprints in the Snow" were hits, and Monroe and his Boys were wildly popular. Though the term bluegrass wasn't commonly used until ten years later, the bluegrass sound attracted enough attention among country musicians to create numerous competitors to the Blue Grass Boys, by 1950 including Flatt & Scruggs (they had left Monroe after three years), Reno and Smiley, the Stanley brothers, Jim & Jesse, the Osborne brothers, and the Lilly brothers, to name only the prominent bluegrass bands from the "classical" period. Though none of these bands were Monroe soundalikes, they shared

characteristics that have come to define bluegrass: the standard instruments (listed above) played acoustically, with the five-string banjo dominating; alternating instrumental solos (as in jazz bands); close harmony, whether with two, three, or four parts; and a tempo generally much faster than mainstream country's. These are only general characteristics, though, not rules, and they often have been ignored, even by the most conservative of traditional bluegrass bands; Bill Monroe allowed an accordion in early recordings, and that music was still bluegrass. Further, it's difficult to specify a characteristic content of bluegrass songs. To cite two extreme examples, Jim and Jesse in 1965 recorded an album of Chuck Berry songs (Berry Pickin'), while the Boston-based Charles River Boys bluegrassed the Fab Four in Beatles Country, also in the '60s. And both albums sound bluegrass—not classical bluegrass, but bluegrass nonetheless. Bluegrass and country often have shared the same song repertory, though bluegrass bands have shown more reticence at accepting the latest musical fads than have many of their country cousins.

But like mainstream country, bluegrass itself has evolved into sub-styles. These changes were all but assured when urban audiences discovered bluegrass during the urban folk-revival of the late '50s and early '60s. The nation may not have been prepared for Jethro Bodine, Granny, Ellie May, and TV's "Beverly Hillbillies," but they positively embraced the Flatt & Scruggs background music, as witnessed by "The Ballad of Jed Clampett" in 1963 becoming the first bluegrass song to hit No. 1 in the country charts. Then followed "Foggy Mountain Breakdown" by Earl Scruggs in the popular Bonnie and Clyde movie and "Dueling Banjos" in Deliverance. Bluegrass music, and especially the five-string banjo, had become so popular with a new and huge urban audience that traditional bluegrass had to make way for variations. Bluegrass was divided: traditional bluegrass remained, for the lovers of the pure, original sound; and progressive bluegrass (often called "newgrass") was created. The rules for newgrass were more relaxed, allowing electric instruments, rock songs, and whatever else creatively fit within the confines of this new and malleable term. Newgrass doesn't mean worse, it just means different. The top-notch newgrass bands (Seldom Scene, Country Gentlemen, J. D. Crowe and the New South, New Grass Revival) by and large are vocally and instrumentally on the same plane as the traditional bluegrass bands. There's room for both. —*David Vinopal*

Eddie Adcock

Banjo / Progressive Bluegrass

Among the major-league talent that emerged from the folk music boom of the late '50s were the Country Gentlemen, a DC-based quartet that introduced bluegrass to a generation of city folks and college students, people who had never heard of Flatt & Scruggs or Bill Monroe or the Stanley Brothers. The Gentlemen, in playing the old bluegrass standards but playing them "different," were in a sense the first newgrass group. Eddie Adcock was the band's banjo player and he was a player of distinction—his style was as innovative as Don Reno's. Adcock's considerable talent spread to other stringed instruments when he left the Gentlemen in 1970 and began exploring new musical genres. Eddie Adcock remained one of the most popular musicians in bluegrass. Adcock was born and raised in Scottsville, VA. He bought his first banjo as a child and began performing with his brother Frank shortly afterward. The duo would sing in local churches and radio stations based in the nearby Charlottesville. In his teens, he played in a band called the James River Playboys and worked at a theater in his hometown, where he had the

opportunity to see major country artists of the day, including Wilma Lee and Stoney Cooper. At the age of 14, he left home after a family crisis and supported himself through semi-professional boxing. For the next seven years, he boxed and played music at nights.

Eddie Adcock didn't begin his professional musical career until 1953, when he joined Smokey Graves and his Blue Star Boys, who had a regular show at a radio station in Crewe, VA. His exposure with Graves led to jobs with other musicians, including Mac Wiseman, Bill Harrell, and Buzz Busby. Between 1953 and 1957, he floated between different bands. Bill Monroe offered a job to Adcock in 1957, and he played with the Blue Grass Boys for a short time—Monroe had to let him go because the band simply wasn't earning enough money to employ him. Adcock returned to working day jobs but that was short-lived. After he started working in a sheet metal factory, Jim Cox, John Duffery, and Charlie Waller asked him to join their new band, the Country Gentlemen.

The Country Gentlemen became one of the most popular and respected bluegrass bands of the late '50s and '60s, as well as one of the most progressive. They expanded the repertoire of bluegrass bands to include contemporary country, folk, and rock songwriters, most notably

Bob Dylan; usually they added this material at the urging of Adcock. The Country Gentlemen rode to popularity in the late '50s as part of the folk boom and continued to be one of the most popular bluegrass-folk bands in the country throughout the '60s.

At the end of the '60s, Adcock began to feel constrained by the Country Gentlemen. He wanted to experiment with different musical genres, which he felt the band wasn't willing to do. Consequently, he quit the Gentlemen and moved to California, where he formed a country-rock band called the Clinton Special. While he performed with the group he used the pseudonym Clinton Codack. The band recorded only one single, "Just As You Are I Love You /Blackberry Fence," which was released on MGM Records; the A-side of the single was featured in the 1971 film *The Horsemen*.

After the Clinton Special fell apart, Adcock headed back east, where he formed another group, II Generation with Bob White, A.L. Wood, Wendy Thatcher, and Jimmy Gaudreau, who used to play with the Country Gentlemen. II Generation's lineup changed frequently during the '70s but it gelled around 1974 when Martha Hearon joined the group. Hearon played guitar for the band and wrote a good share of its material; she also married Adcock soon after she joined. II Generation was active throughout the '70s, releasing a handful of albums on the Rome, Rebel, and CMH labels.

Adcock and Hearon disbanded the group in 1980 and moved to Tennessee, where they formed a trio called Talk of the Town with bassist Missy Raines. In the mid-'80s, Adcock launched a solo career, releasing a series of cassette-only collections on CMH. In the '90s, he began releasing albums on compact disc, as well as performing with an all-star bluegrass outfit called the Masters. After nearly 40 years in the music business, Eddie Adcock remained as popular as ever, touring around the world. —*Stephen Thomas Erlewine and David Vinopal*

● **Talk of the Town** / 1987 / CMH ✦✦✦✦
Backed by four women, Eddie is at his best here. The album features nice vocals. —*Chip Renner*

And His Guitar / 1988 / CMH ✦✦✦
Just Eddie and his guitar, no backup, and a very clean sound. Chet Atkins- and Merle Travis-influenced. —*Chip Renner*

Red Allen

Guitar, Vocals / Bluegrass
Appalachia-born Red Allen had a voice that personified the "high lonesome sound" of traditional bluegrass music. During the '50s he developed a strong fan base which he retained through numerous recordings and festival appearances over the next four decades. Allen was born in Perry County, KY, and grew up influenced by the music of such performers as Charlie Monroe. After serving two years in the US Marine Corps, the 19-year-old Allen moved to Dayton, OH, in 1949. Many other musicians—including Frank Wakefield, the Osborne Brothers and Noah Crase—also relocated to Ohio, and Allen and these musicians frequently played together for local clubs and the radio.

In 1954, Allen made his recording debut on an independent Kentucky label. Later he joined the Osborne Brothers and the group became a mainstay on the "Wheeling Jamboree." The band began recording on MGM, which is where they made such classics as "Ruby" and "Wild Mountain Honey." Allen stayed with the Osbornes until 1958 and then left music for a time. In 1959, he moved to Washington, DC, where he formed the Kentuckians with fiddler Frank Wakefield; over the years, the group included musicians like Bill and Wayne Yates and David Grisman.

In 1967, Allen moved to Nashville to temporarily replace a recuperating Lester Flatt in Flatt & Scruggs. The next year he and J.D. Crowe founded the Kentucky Mountain Boys and began recording, as well as playing at the Lexington, KY, Holiday Inn. In 1969, Allen went back to Dayton and formed a band with his four teenaged sons. As Red Allen and the Allen Brothers, they began playing the "Wheeling Jamboree" and recording for King Bluegrass and Lemco. Throughout the '70s, Allen toured America and Europe, usually playing bluegrass and folk festivals. A decade later, Allen recorded two albums for Folkways. He continued to play clubs and festivals near Dayton until his death from cancer in 1993. —*Sandra Brennan*

Red Allen & Frank / 1991 / Smithsonian/Folkways ✦✦✦

Red Allen and the Kentuckians / 1991 / County ✦✦✦✦

● **The Osborne Brothers and Red Allen** / Rounder ✦✦✦✦

Dave Apollon

b. 1898
Instrumental, Mandolin / Bluegrass
On the mandolin, Dave Apollon was, in a word, a virtuoso. The late Jethro Burns (of Homer and Jethro) said that Dave Apollon was the best that he had ever heard, and he ought to know, for Burns himself was the best mandolin player of the last quarter-century. Born in Russia, Apollon made many recordings, the first in 1932, and became a celebrity through

them and through his movies. He was to the mandolin what Benny Goodman was to the clarinet. —*David Vinopal*

Mandolin Virtuoso / Yazoo ✦✦✦✦
A ragtime/vaudeville mandolin maestro. —*Mark A. Humphrey*

Mike Auldridge

Dobro Guitar / Instrumental, Bluegrass
Mike Auldridge is generally considered one of the masters of bluegrass dobro. Raised in Kensington, MD, Auldridge began playing guitar at 12, banjo at 16, and dobro at 17. In 1954 he made his first appearance on a local radio station, playing in a band with his brother Dave. In 1967, he graduated from the University of Maryland and became a commercial artist; he continued to play dobro occasionally at local clubs. In 1969 he joined the New Shades of Green. Within a year, the bluegrass group had gained a stong following and Auldridge was considered an innovator in the relatively new field of bluegrass dobro.

Auldridge became a member of the Seldom Scene in 1971, but he still did session work, playing on albums by such artists as Emmylou Harris, Jonathan Edwards, Linda Ronstadt, and Jimmy Arnold. He also recorded several solo albums, including *Dobro* (1972) *Blues and Bluegrass* (1974), and *Eight-String Swing* (1982). Auldridge teamed up with singer/mandolin player Lou Reid and bassist T. Michael Coleman in 1989 for the album *High Time*. Also in 1989 he released a solo album, *Treasures Untold*. Auldridge continued to play concerts and record as a session musician in the '90s. —*Sandra Brennan*

● **Dobro/Blues and Bluegrass** / 1974 / Takoma ✦✦✦✦
Two of Mike Auldridge's early '70s albums, *Dobro* and *Blues & Bluegrass*, are combined on this single disc, which provides an excellent introduction to the dobroist. —*Thom Owens*

Mike Auldridge / 1976 / Flying Fish ✦✦✦✦
On this one, the bluegrass dobroist is joined by apt accompanists. —*Mark A. Humphrey*

Slidin' Smoke / 1979 / Flying Fish ✦✦✦
On this mellow album, Auldridge (dobro) and Newman (steel guitar) add a touch of jazz to their bluegrass sound. —*AMG*

Austin Lounge Lizards

Traditional Bluegrass
The Austin Lounge Lizards are a country bluegrass band out of Austin. The Lizards are Hank Card (guitar, vocals), Conrad Deisler (guitar, mandolin), Tom Pittman (banjo, pedal steel, vocals), Michael Stevens (bass, vocals), and Tim Wilson (mandolin, fiddle, vocals). After the first album, Paul "Tex" Sweeney (mandolin) and Kirk Williams (bass, vocals) replaced Stevens and Wilson. They are known for the humor in their songs and live shows. The group's first album, *Creatures from the Black Saloon*, was released in 1984.—*Chip Renner*

● **Creatures from the Black Saloon** / 1984 / Watermelon ✦✦✦✦
Imagine tradition-steeped Texas swing fused to Monty Python, and you have an idea what's in store with the Austin Lounge Lizards. The Lizards can serve up the tastiest country licks imaginable while at the same time trashing every old West cliche/tradition in the book. The group's debut *Creatures from the Black Saloon* revealed such classics as "The Car Hank Died In,", "Kool Whip" (Devo meets the Bonzo Dog Band), and "Saguaro" (wailing pedal steel and mock heroic baritone rendering the tale of a twerpy urban cowpoke duelling a gang of desperado cacti—and losing). —*Roch Parisien*

The Highway Cafe of the Damned / 1988 / Watermelon ✦✦✦✦
Another good, solid, humor-packed CD featuring "The Highway Cafe of the Damned," "Industrial Strength Tranquilizer," "Ballad of Ronald Reagan," and more. —*Chip Renner*

Lizard Vision / 1991 / Flying Fish ✦✦✦
This very funny album was a Grammy nominee. It features the hit "Jesus Loves Me." —*Chip Renner*

Small Minds / 1995 / Watermelon ✦✦✦
The Lizards offer up a sly collection of country/R&B-flavored songs that range from a commentary on the singer's intelligence in "Shallow End of the Gene Pool" to "Truckload of Art," which blows New York's elitist art attitude all over the road. The playing is greasy and dynamic. These guys know how to play no matter how much genre hopping they do. One imagines that these songs function best in a crowded smoke-filled bar, but it is a testament to the Austin Lounge Lizards that such ephemeral material stands up on record. —*Richard Meyer*

Bashful Brother Oswald (Beecher Kirby)

b. Sevier County, TN
Banjo, Dobro Guitar, Guitar / Old-Time
For nearly 60 years, Bashful Brother Oswald was one of the most influential and talented dobro players in country music. For the majority of his career, Oswald was the dobroist for Roy Acuff's Smoky Mountain

Boys. During his five years with the band, he became the leading dobroist in country music, as well as one of the most popular members of the band. Over the course of his career, Oswald released only a handful of solo recordings, but he left behind enough recordings to illustrate why he was one of the most influential musicians of his era.

Bashful Brother Oswald (born Beecher Ray Kirby) was the son of an Appalachian musician. As a child, Oswald learned how to play dobro and banjo, as well as sing gospel music. When he was a teenager, he began playing square dances with various country groups. During the day, he worked in a Knoxville cotton mill. In the late '20s, Oswald moved to Flint, MI, to work in a Buick factory. After the Great Depression hit, he lost his job and he became a musician at the radio station WFDF. Because Hawaiian music was very popular, the station manager decided to feature it prominently during regular programming, thus inspiring Oswald to buy his first steel guitar. In 1933, Oswald performed at the Chicago World's Fair and found himself greatly influenced by the wide variety of music he heard at the fair. The following year, he went to Knoxville and began playing dobro with several different bands including Acuff's Crazy Tennesseans. Oswald became a permanent member of Acuff's band after the singer was invited to join the "Grand Ole Opry" in the late '30s, replacing the group's dobroist Clell Summey.

As a vocalist, Oswald gained recognition for singing a few lines on Acuff's classic "Precious Jewel" (1940) and on "Wreck on the Highway" (1942). Acuff named the dobroist "Brother Oswald" in a little ruse to convince audiences that he was the brother of the band's singer, Rachel Veach; the fiddler intended to obscure the fact that Veach was a single, unmarried woman. The dobroist happily complied in creating the Bashful Brother Oswald character. In 1943, Oswald began wearing a floppy mountain hat, tattered overalls, and enormous shoes, and he adopted a braying horse laugh. The cartoonish character became a favorite of audiences almost immediately and it stayed popular throughout Oswald's career.

Oswald continued performing and recording with Acuff until the '80s, but the dobroist began a solo career in the '60s. During that decade, he began working as a session musician and released a few albums of his own on Starday Records, beginning with 1962's *Bashful Brother Oswald*. In the early '70s, the Nitty Gritty Dirt Band had Oswald perform on their 1972 hit album, *Will the Circle Be Unbroken*. Also in 1972, guitarist and dobro player Tut Taylor produced Oswald's *Brother Oswald* album for Rounder Records. Oswald made three more albums for Rounder after *Brother Oswald*. In the late '70s, he began playing in the Opryland theme park with former Smoky Mountain bandmate Charlie Collins. During the 1980s, Oswald continued performing with Collins at the Opryland and Acuff at the Opry. Following Acuff's death in 1992, Oswald and Charlie Collins earned a regular slot on the Opry's main stage. —*Sandra Brennan*

● **Brother Oswald** / 1972 / Rounder ✦✦✦✦
Roy Acuff's dobroist since the '30s, in a pleasant set of Hawaiian-inspired old-time country songs. —*Mark A. Humphrey*

Byron Berline

b. 194_
Fiddle / Instrumental, Bluegrass
Like his contemporary Vassar Clements, fiddler Byron Berline expanded the sonic possibilities of bluegrass, adding elements of jazz, pop, blues, rock, and traditional country to the genre. In addition to being a popular solo act, he performed as a session musician on a number of popular albums, including records by the Flying Burrito Brothers, Stephen Stills, the Dillards, Gram Parsons, the Nitty Gritty Dirt Band, Emmylou Harris, Kris Kristofferson, and James Taylor.

Berline learned to play fiddle from his father, an old-time fiddler, and from family friend Frank Mitchell. He attended the University of Oklahoma on a football scholarship, but his football career ended when he broke his thumb during the first season; after his accident, he became a noted javelin thrower. Berline also continued playing music with a campus folk group. In 1963 the Dillards played a concert on the University of Oklahoma campus. A friend of Berline's arranged an audition for him with Doug Dillard. Dillard was impressed and invited the young fiddler to join them for a number. After this meeting, Berline joined the Cleveland Country Ramblers while he was still a student. In 1964 he appeared on the Dillards' *Pickin' and Fiddlin'* and won the National Fiddle Championship in Missoula, MO. Berline played the Newport Folk Festival in 1965, where he met Bill Monroe, who asked him to join the Blue Grass Boys in the future. In 1967 Berline graduated with a B.A. in education, but instead of becoming a junior high school coach, he joined the Blue Grass Boys; his first appearance with the band was a show at the Grand Ole Opry. Six months after he joined Monroe's band, he was drafted into the US Army.

Just before Berline was discharged in 1969, Doug Dillard invited the fiddler to join the Dillard and Clark Expedition. He remained with Dillard and Clark until 1971, when the group disbanded. While with them,

he played sessions for a number of other artists, including the Flying Burrito Brothers' debut album, *The Gilded Palace of Sin*. After the breakup of Dillard and Clark, Berline played with the Dillard Expedition.

In 1970 Berline scored the ABC television movie *Run Simon Run*, the first of many films he would score. In 1971 he toured with a revamped version of the Flying Burrito Brothers. After the tour, Berline and fellow Burritos Roger Bush and Kenny Wertz—who also joined the group specifically for the 1971 tour—formed the Country Gazette. For the next four years he played with the Gazette. During this time he continued session work, appearing on albums by Gram Parsons, Bert Jansch, Ian Matthews and Southern Comfort, and Bill Wyman.

In 1975 Berline left Country Gazette and moved to Los Angeles to concentrate on songwriting, session work, and scoring films. Later that year he founded Sundance with Dan Crary, Jack Skinner, John Hickman, Allen Wald, and Skip Conover. The lineup changed the next year, when Vince Gill and Mark Cohen joined the band. Sundance recorded one eponymous album for MCA in 1976 before disbanding. In the late '70s Berline recruited Crary and Hickman for a tour of Japan. After the tour the trio recorded three albums for Sugar Hill. While the trio was active, Berline founded the L.A. Fiddle Band.

In 1980 Berline founded the production company BCH with Crary and Hickman and released a solo album, *Outrageous*, on Flying Fish. In 1981 the L.A. Fiddle Band released an eponymous solo album for Sugar Hill. Berline worked on Chris Hillman's 1984 album *Desert Rose* and an album of duets with Hickman in 1986. Two years later Berline, Crary, and Hickman changed the name of the trio to BCH and added bassist Steve Spurgin to their lineup. The new incarnation of BCH released *Now They Are Four* on Sugar Hill in 1988. BCH added mandolinist/guitarist John Moore in 1990 and renamed itself California. The group released their first album, *Traveler*, in 1992; later that year the International Bluegrass Music Association named the band the "Instrumental Group of the Year." —*Sandra Brennan*

● **And the L.A. Fiddle Band** / 1980 / Sugar Hill ✦✦✦✦
Put together three fiddles and some great acoustic bluegrass music and you have *Byron Berline & the L.A. Fiddle Band*, a great album. Guests are Vince Gill and John Hickman. —*Chip Renner*

Outrageous / 1980 / Flying Fish ✦✦✦
Berline has a strong cast featuring Dan Crary, Albert Lee, James Burton, and John Hickman. —*Chip Renner*

Berline, Hickman, Crary / 1981 / Sugar Hill ✦✦✦✦
Nice songs: "Bonapart's Retreat," "Turkey in the Straw." —*Chip Renner*

Night Run / 1984 / Sugar Hill ✦✦✦
Fine bluegrass. Pistol Pete, Forked River, Berline, Dan Crary, and John Hickman will knock you out. —*Chip Renner*

Double Trouble / 1986 / Sugar Hill ✦✦✦✦
Berline and John Hickman feed off each other's talents. Very smooth. —*Chip Renner*

Fiddle and a Song / 1995 / Sugar Hill ✦✦✦
Fiddle and a Song is another first-rate album from fiddler Byron Berline, featuring guest contributions from Earl Scruggs, Bill Monroe, Vince Gill, and other musicians. —*AMG*

Norman Blake

b. Mar. 10, 1938, Chattanooga, TN
Dobro Guitar, Fiddle, Guitar, Mandolin, Vocals / Bluegrass
Although he is proficient with a variety of stringed instruments, Norman Blake is famous for his acoustic guitar skills—he was one of the major bluegrass guitarists of the '70s. Blake came into view in the late '60s, when he began performing as a sideman with artists as diverse as June Carter and Bob Dylan. During the '70s, he began a solo career which quickly became one of the most popular and musically adventurous within bluegrass. He continued recording and performing—occasionally with his wife, Nancy—well into the '90s.

Blake began playing music professionally when he was 16 years old, joining the Dixieland Drifters as a mandolinist in 1954; the group debuted on "Tennessee Barn Dance," a radio show based in Knoxville. After two years, he left the band and became a member of the Lonesome Travelers, which was led by banjoist Bob Johnson. By the end of the '50s, the Lonesome Travelers had added a second banjoist, Walter Forbes, and had made two records for RCA. Although he joined Hylo Brown and the Timberliners in 1959, Blake continued to perform with Johnson. The next year he also became a member of June Carter's touring band.

In 1961 Blake was drafted into the Army, where he was stationed in Panama. While he was in the service he formed a band called the Kobbe Mountaineers. The band became a popular attraction and was voted the best band in the Caribbean Command. In 1962 Blake recorded *12 Shades of Bluegrass* with the Lonesome Travellers while he was on leave. He was discharged from the Army the next year and moved to

Nashville, where he joined Johnny Cash's band. That same year, he married Nancy Short and settled in Chattanooga, TN.

For the next few years he played with Cash, both on recordings and concerts. In 1969 Bob Dylan hired Blake to play on his country-rock album, *Nashville Skyline*, providing the guitarist a whole new audience. That audience expanded even further when he became Cash's main guitarist on the singer's television show. Cash's program featured a wide array of musical guests, who were often impressed with Blake's talents. Kris Kristofferson asked him to join his touring band and Blake did so, playing both guitar and dobro; he also played on several of Kristofferson's records. Blake also played on several of Joan Baez' records, including her hit version of "The Night They Drove Old Dixie Down."

After his folk and country-rock experiments, Blake returned to his bluegrass roots in 1971 when he joined John Hartford's band, Aeroplane, which also featured fiddler Vassar Clements. Aeroplane fell apart quickly, but Blake stayed with Hartford for a year and a half. In 1972 Norman recorded his first solo album, *Back Home in Sulphur Springs*, which began a long relationship with Rounder Records. — *Kurt Wolff*

Back Home in Sulphur Springs / 1972 / Rounder ✦✦✦
Norman Blake and Tut Taylor (dobro), basic and pure. — *Chip Renner*

Blackberry Blossom / 1974 / Flying Fish ✦✦✦
Norman and Nancy Blake. A little less bluegrass with the addition of Nancy Blake's cello. — *Chip Renner*

The Fields of November / 1974 / Flying Fish ✦✦✦✦
A first-class album. Tut Taylor, Charlie Collins, and Nancy Short come up strong. Features "Greycoat Soldiers," "Last Train to Poor Valley," and "The Fields of November." — *Chip Renner*

Old and New / 1975 / Flying Fish ✦✦✦
This fine collection of Blake's music was chosen by Blake himself. — *AMG*

Live at McCabe's / 1976 / Takoma ✦✦✦
Very good record features "Nine Pound Hammer" and "Arkansas Traveler." Good sound. — *Chip Renner*

Whiskey Before Breakfast / 1976 / Rounder ✦✦✦
Blake's best. He and Charlie Collins let their guitars do the talking. Perfect. — *Chip Renner*

Norman Blake and Red Rector / 1976 / County ✦✦✦
On these 12 cuts, Blake and Red Rector (on mandolin) are backed by Charlie Collins and Roy Huskie, Jr. — *Chip Renner*

Rising Fawn String Ensemble / 1979 / Rounder ✦✦✦
More memorable acoustic instrumental work. — *Hank Davis*

Full Moon on the Farm / 1981 / Rounder ✦✦✦
This album features Norman Blake and the Rising Fawn String Ensemble—James Bryan, Charlie Collins, and Nancy Blake. It has a nice, well-rounded feeling. — *Chip Renner*

● **Original Underground Music** / 1982 / Rounder ✦✦✦✦
Original Underground Music from the Mysterious South includes deceptively simple acoustic string music featuring multiple mandolins, mandolas, cellos, fiddles, and guitars for a hauntingly beautiful yet old-timey feel. — *Hank Davis & Chip Renner*

Nashville Blues / 1984 / Rounder ✦✦✦
Blake's vocals give this one more of an old-timey bluegrass feel. — *Hank Davis*

Lighthouse on the Shore / 1985 / Rounder ✦✦✦
Norman teams up with Nancy Blake, James Bryan, and Tom Jackson. Features "Hello Stranger," "President Garfield's Hornpipe," and "Wildwood Flower." — *Chip Renner*

Blake and Rice / 1987 / Rounder ✦✦✦✦
Underrated but sprightly, these two fleet-fingered acoustic-guitar flatpickers flex their chops in these 14 cuts. — *Mark A. Humphrey*

Blake and Rice #2 / 1990 / Rounder ✦✦✦
More hot licks and backporch singing. — *Mark A. Humphrey*

The Bluegrass Album Band

Bluegrass
The Bluegrass Album Band was a bluegrass supergroup formed in 1980. Originally, the band featured J.D. Crowe, Doyle Lawson, Tony Rice, Bobby Hicks, and Todd Phillips. All of the members were known as progressive bluegrass musicians, but the Bluegrass Album Band was designed to showcase the traditional side of their talents. Their first album, *The Bluegrass Album*, was intended as a one-shot project, but it proved so successful the group recorded four other albums over the course of the decade. Over the years, the lineup of the Bluegrass Album Band shifted, but Crowe, Lawson, and Rice remained its core members. The group's final album, *The Bluegrass Album, Vol. 5: Sweet Sunny South*, was released in 1989 and featured Crowe, Lawson, Rice, Vassar Clements, Jerry Douglas, and Mark Schatz. — *Thom Owens*

The Bluegrass Album, Vol. 1 / 1981 / Rounder ✦✦✦✦
The debut from this superstar bluegrass band featuring Tony Rice, J.D. Crowe, Doyle Lawson, Bobby Hicks, Todd Phillips, and Jerry Douglas. A superstar bluegrass band. — *Chip Renner*

The Bluegrass Album, Vol. 2 / 1982 / Rounder ✦✦✦
The Bluegrass Album Band's second record reiterates all of the strong points of their debut—the group's interaction and harmonies are so natural, they're breathtaking. — *Thom Owens*

The Bluegrass Album, Vol. 3 (California Connection) / 1983 / Rounder ✦✦✦
On their third album, the Bluegrass Album Band adds some more country-rock to the mix, in the form of the Flying Burrito Brothers' "Devil in Disguise," but they largely stick to bluegrass classics from the likes of Bill Monroe and Flatt & Scruggs. Like the group's two previous albums, *California Connection* is filled with graceful, stunning musicianship that continues to astonish after several listens. — *Thom Owens*

Bluegrass Album, Vol. 4 / 1984 / Rounder ✦✦✦
They get tighter as they go along. Any one of these records is gonna get you movin'. — *Chip Renner*

The Bluegrass Album, Vol. 5: Sweet Sunny South / 1989 / Rounder ✦✦✦

The Bluegrass Compact Disc / Rounder ✦✦✦✦
A full, classic bluegrass album. — *Chip Renner*

● **The Bluegrass Compact Disc, Vol. 2** / Rounder ✦✦✦✦
A collection of the group's first four releases. There are 21 songs in all. — *Chip Renner*

The Bluegrass Cardinals

Traditional Bluegrass
During the '70s and '80s, the Bluegrass Cardinals were one of the premier bluegrass bands in America, noted for performing both contemporary and traditional bluegrass with tight, intricate vocal harmonies and dynamic, precise musicianship. Banjoist Don Parmley and his then 15-year-old son David founded the Cardinals in 1974. Before that, Don had played banjo for "The Beverly Hillbillies" and had been a part of the Golden State Boys and the Hillmen; both bands featured the Gosdin Brothers.

The Bluegrass Cardinals formed in 1974. Two years later, the group—which featured Mike Hartgrove, Norman Wright, John Davis, and Dale Perry in addition to the Parmleys—moved from California to Virginia, where they recorded their eponymous debut album for Briar. The next year the Bluegrass Cardinals recorded *Welcome to Virginia* on Rounder. The group signed to CMH Records in 1978. Over the next five years the Bluegrass Cardinals released five albums for the label, in addition to touring America and Europe and appearing on the Grand Ole Opry and their "Ralph Emery Show."

In 1991 Don and David Parmley left the group and recorded *Parmley and McCoury* with Del McCoury and his sons Ronnie and Robbie. Later, after some solo work, David Parmley performed in Continental Divide with Scott Vestal. — *Sandra Brennan*

Welcome to Virginia / 1977 / Rounder ✦✦✦

Livin' in the Good Old Days / 1978 / CMH ✦✦✦
Twelve solid songs. — *Chip Renner*

Cardinal Soul / 1979 / CMH ✦✦✦
Early sound. Good. — *Chip Renner*

Live and on Stage / 1980 / CMH ✦✦✦✦
The double album has 29 songs. — *Chip Renner*

Sunday Mornin' Singin' / 1980 / CMH ✦✦✦
One of your better gospel albums. — *Chip Renner*

● **Cardinal Class** / 1983 / Sugar Hill ✦✦✦✦
A very good, solid, tight album. The Cardinals at their best. Highly recommended. — *Chip Renner*

Home Is Where the Heart Is / 1984 / Sugar Hill ✦✦✦
A good mix of music. Jerry Douglas guests. — *Chip Renner*

Ginger Boatwright

Guitar, Vocals / Traditional Bluegrass
Ginger Boatwright (born Ginger Kay Hammond) is a talented bluegrass musician who has become especially popular on the festival circuit. Boatwright is known for her keen flat-picking. She learned to play guitar while attending the University of Alabama, Birmingham, on a double scholarship in the mid-'60s. In 1966 she was attending a concert by Grant Boatwright when he invited her onstage to play. After the concert, they formed a duo; eventually, her cousin Dale Whitcomb joined the group.

In 1969 Ginger was six credits shy of obtaining her B.A. in history and sociology when she was diagnosed with cancer. The treatment for the cancer prevented her from graduating and becoming a probation officer in Birmingham. Consequently, she turned to a professional musical career—her trio with Boatwright and Whitcomb became Red, White & Blue(grass). Around this time she also married Boatwright. Ginger was still playing with the Red, White & Blue(grass) when she signed to GRC Records as a solo act in 1972. Her first successful single, "The Lovin's Over," was a relatively successful bluegrass hit. Red, White & Blue(grass) signed with Mercury in the mid-'70s. Simultaneously, Ginger signed to the label as a solo act. None of her records for Mercury gained much attention, nor did any of the band's records. In 1979 the group disbanded and she divorced Grant.

After the breakup of Red, White & Blue(grass), Ginger Boatwright and banjo player Susie Monick formed the all-female bluegrass group the Bushwhackers, along with bassist April Barros and fiddler Ingrid Reese. The Bushwhackers began playing the college circuit and released their eponymous debut in 1980. In 1981 the group broke up, and Boatwright was prepared to quit the music business when Rodney Dillard informed her that his brother Doug was putting together a new band. She joined the group in 1982 and continued playing with Doug Dillard into the mid-'90s. —Sandra Brennan

● **Fertile Ground** / 1991 / Flying Fish ✦✦✦✦
An excellent album. Ginger Boatwright brings her great vocals from the Red, White & Blue(grass) Band. She gets better with age. —Chip Renner

Boone Creek

Progressive Bluegrass, Traditional Bluegrass
Boone Creek was the first band Ricky Skaggs led after his apprenticeship with Ralph Stanley, Country Gentlemen, and J.D. Crowe & the New South. Skaggs formed the band in 1977, when he was only 23 years old. Even though he was quite young, he had already played with some of the most respected musicians in bluegrass, playing both traditional bluegrass with Stanley and progressive newgrass with the Country Gentlemen and Crowe. With Boone Creek, Skaggs wanted to create a music that approached traditional bluegrass with a progressive attitude. To achieve this sound, he added electric guitar, drums, and piano to the traditional bluegrass lineup.

Boone Creek released their eponymous debut in 1977. It was quickly followed by *One Way Track* in early 1978. After the release of *One Way Track*, Skaggs broke up the group and joined Emmylou Harris' Hot Band. Skaggs achieved solo success after leaving Harris in the early '80s. —Stephen Thomas Erlewine

Boone Creek / 1977 / Rounder ✦✦✦
A fine album with great picking. —Chip Renner

● **One Way Track** / 1978 / Sugar Hill ✦✦✦✦
Jerry Douglas and Ricky Skaggs are outstanding. Tight, well-played bluegrass, including "In the Pines." —Chip Renner

Alison Brown

Banjo / Bluegrass
A Harvard graduate who quit a fast-track career as an investment banker to dedicate herself to music, Brown came to prominence as a standout member of Alison Krauss' Union Station band and later as musical director for Michelle Shocked. Her instrumental albums are melodic and graceful and manage to sound both accessible and adventurous. She wrote all but one song on her first three albums, and her compositions owe more to the influence of David Grisman (who produced her debut) and Bela Fleck than to Earl Scruggs or Alan O'Bryant. —Michael McCall

Simple Pleasures / 1990 / Vanguard ✦✦✦
Her all-instrumental debut instantly earned respect among progressive acoustic music fans. Produced by David Grisman, and feaaturing guests Mike Marshall and Alison Krauss, Brown weaves cello, flute, and congas into her hybrid string sound, and she maintains an innate elegance amid the tricky arranging. —Michael McCall

Twilight Motel / 1992 / Vanguard ✦✦✦✦
Produced by Mike Marshall, Brown moves in several new directions, showing off the breadth of her talent while keeping the composition at the center of her playing. Jazzier, yet also more relaxed, than her debut. Maura O'Connell provides vocals on a traditional Irish song. —Michael McCall

● **Look Left** / 1994 / Vanguard ✦✦✦✦
Brown criss-crosses the globe sonically, taking on Cajun, Celtic, Native American, and Australian Aboriginal music with characteristically relaxed proficiency. —Michael McCall

Quartet / 1996 / Vanguard ✦✦✦
Alison Brown scales back her supporting group on *Quartet*, but she doesn't abandon her trademark rootsy eclection. Although the songs are based in bluegrass and folk traditions, what stands out more than anything else on the album is how accomplished and jazzy Brown's playing has become—it is the instrumental sections that make the album a rewarding listen. —Thom Owens

Vassar Clements

b. Apr. 25, 1928, Kinard, SC
Fiddle / Traditional Bluegrass
Combining jazz with country, Vassar Clements became one of the most distinctive, inventive, and popular fiddlers in bluegrass music. Clements first came to prominence as a member of Bill Monroe's band in the early '50s, but he never limited himself to traditional bluegrass. Over the next four decades, he distinguished himself by incorporating a number of different genres into his style. In the process, he became not only one of the most respected fiddlers in bluegrass, he also became a sought-after session musician, playing with artists as diverse as the Monkees, Hank Williams, Paul McCartney, Michelle Shocked, Vince Gill, and Bonnie Raitt.

Clements taught himself to play fiddle at the age of seven. Soon afterward, he formed a band with two of his cousins. By the time he was 21, Clements' skills were impressive enough to attract the attention of Bill Monroe. Monroe hired the young fiddler, and Clements appeared on the "Grand Ole Opry" with the mandolinist in 1949. The next year the fiddler recorded his first session with Monroe.

For the next six years Clements stayed with Monroe's band, occasionally leaving for brief periods of time. In 1957, he joined Jim and Jesse's Virginia Boys and stayed with the band for four years. In the early '60s, Clements was sidelined for a while as he suffered from alcoholism. By the end of the '60s he was rehabilitated, and he returned to playing in 1967. That year he moved to Nashville and began playing the tenor banjo at a residency at the Dixieland Landing Club. In 1969 he toured with Faron Young and joined John Hartford's Dobrolic Plectorial Society. The band only lasted ten months, and after its breakup, Clements joined the Earl Scruggs Revue; he stayed with that band for a year.

Clements began playing sessions in 1971, appearing on albums by Steve Goodman, Gordon Lightfoot, David Bromberg, J.J. Cale, and Mike Auldridge over the next two years. In 1972 he was featured on the Nitty Gritty Dirt Band's hit album *Will the Circle Be Unbroken*, which helped establish him as a country and bluegrass star. Clements capitalized on the record's popularity in 1973 when he released his first solo album, *Crossing the Catskills*, on Rounder Records and began touring the festival and college circuits. That same year he appeared on a number of albums, including the Grateful Dead's *Wake of the Flood*, Jimmy Buffett's *A White Sports Coat and a Pink Crustation*, and Mickey Newbury's *Heaven Help the Child*.

In 1974 Clements signed with Mercury Records, releasing two albums for the label—*Vassar Clements* and *Superbow*—the next year. That same year, he appeared in the bluegrass supergroup Old and in the Way, which also featured Jerry Garcia, David Grisman, Peter Rowan, and John Kahn. He also had a cameo role in Robert Altman's film *Nashville* in 1975. In 1977, Clements released albums for two different labels—*The Vassar Clements Band* on MCA Records and *The Bluegrass Session* on Flying Fish. It would be four years before he released another solo album. During that time he toured constantly and appeared on numerous albums. Clements reappeared in 1981 with *Hillbilly Rides Again* and *Vassar*, both released on Flying Fish.

During the '80s and '90s Clements continued to record sporadically, but he cut numerous sessions for other artists and played numerous concerts every year. In 1995 Clements reunited with Old and in the Way, who released *That High Lonesome Sound* in 1996. —Stephen Thomas Erlewine

Crossing the Catskills / 1973 / Rounder ✦✦✦✦
Tasty fiddling from one of the finest. —Mark A. Humphrey

● **The Bluegrass Sessions** / 1977 / Flying Fish ✦✦✦✦
The title tells the truth. —Mark A. Humphrey

Nashville Jam / 1979 / Flying Fish ✦✦✦
As you may guess from the title, this album features a lively jam session with many greats in bluegrass music. —AMG

Vassar / 1980 / Flying Fish ✦✦✦
This album features Clements strutting his stuff on jazz fiddle with sympathetic backing from his band. Clements is one of the very best on his instrument, and the album showcases his talent. —AMG

Grass Routes / 1991 / Rounder ✦✦✦
This recent album shows why Clements is one of the greatest fiddlers in modern country music. —Mark A. Humphrey

Once in a While / 1993 / Flying Fish ✦✦✦
Violinist Vassar Clements has demonstrated the improvisatory link between bluegrass and jazz, and this was another example of the two styles' affinity. Clements' soaring phrases and adept solos were right at home on such standard jazz tunes as "Perdido," "Cherokee," and "Sonnymoon for Two," but he didn't stray far from his favorite breakdown riffs or signature country sound. The results were the kind of loose, joyous jam date where labels meant nothing, and musicianship rather than genre ruled. —Ron Wynn

Bill Clifton

b. 1931, Riderwood, MD

Guitar, Autoharp, Vocals / Traditional Bluegrass, Traditional Country

Few people have contributed as much to the preservation and performance of traditional bluegrass music as Bill Clifton. Clifton was born William Marburg to a wealthy family in Riverwood, MD. As a child, he became fascinated by the hillbilly music he heard on the radio. Around 1950, he adopted the stage name Bill Clifton and began performing on the radio and in public. During his college years at the University of Virginia, Clifton formed a trio called the Dixie Mountain Boys with folk singers Paul Clayton and Dave Sadler. In 1952, the group made their first recordings, which largely went unheard. Following these recordings, the trio added banjoist Johnny Clark and began playing more traditional bluegrass music. The Dixie Mountain Boys signed a contract with Blue Ridge Records and also appeared on the radio show "Wheeling Jamboree." While there Clifton befriended the Stanley Brothers and A.P. Carter. After a brief stint in the military, Clifton began recording for both Starday/Mercury in the late '50s. Over the course of seven years, he released five albums for the label.

In 1963, Clifton and his family moved to England for four years. While in Europe, he played many local clubs. In 1967, he obtained an administrative position in the Peace Corps and spent three years in the Philippines. While there, he visited Australia and New Zealand, recording an album with the Hamilton County Bluegrass Band in the latter country. Clifton went back to England, occasionally returning to the US to record; he also kept recording in Europe. In 1972 he returned briefly to America to play his first bluegrass festival circuit. Encouraged by the experience, Clifton began visiting the US more frequently, and he began to record more regularly, signing a contract with County Records. On his third album for the label, he formed a band called the First Generation with mandolinist Red Rector and banjoist Don Stover. After the album's release, the trio toured the bluegrass circuit for the remainder of the 1970s. In the early '80s, Clifton and his family moved to Mendota, VA, where he worked as a businessman. However, Clifton continued to perform at bluegrass festivals and occasional concerts into the '90s. *—Sandra Brennan*

★ **The Early Years (1957-1958)** / Jun. 15, 1992 / Rounder ♦♦♦♦♦
Bill Clifton was one of bluegrass' finest guitarists and also an underrated vocalist. He was especially gripping on slow, aching tunes like "Lonely Heart Blues" or gospel numbers like "I'm Living the Right Life Now" and "When You Kneel at Your Mother's Grave." Clifton's late-'50s singles were collected on this CD, featuring him working alongside such musicians as Curley Lambert on mandolin and Johnny Clark on banjo, as well as fiddler Tommy Jackson, Ralph Stanley on banjo, and Gordon Terry on fiddle. These songs are light-years away from the polished, intricate newgrass and contemporary bluegrass sounds of the 1980s and '90s. The harmonies, leads, solos, and arrangements reflect simpler, more innocent times, but don't lack intensity or musical quality. *—Ron Wynn*

The Country Gazette

Progressive Bluegrass

One of the most influential bluegrass acts of the '70s—as well as one of that decade's most popular country artists in Europe—Country Gazette blended bluegrass with country-rock and, in the process, sowed the seeds for the newgrass movement of the '80s. The Los Angeles-based band was originally formed in 1971 by fiddler Byron Berline, bassist Roger Bush, and banjoist Billy Ray Latham, who had all played with Dillard and Clark. The trio added guitarist Herb Pedersen, who was quickly replaced by Alan Munde. Shortly after the band's formation, Berline and Bush played on the Flying Burrito Brothers' *Last of the Red Hot Burritos* album, which turned out to be the last album the group would release before breaking up; they would reunite later in the decade. Berline and Bush convinced guitarist Kenny Wertz to join Country Gazette during the Burritos sessions, and after the Burritos' dissolved, the trio toured as Country Gazette and finished recording the band's debut, *A Traitor in Our Midst*.

A Traitor in Our Midst was released on United Artists in 1972. During the summer of that year, Country Gazette played gigs at Disneyland and soon landed opening spots for Steve Miller, Crosby and Nash, and Don McLean, which indicated that the group was aiming for a more rock-oriented audience. Later that year they recorded and released the *Live in Amsterdam* album. Their second studio album, *Don't Give Up Your Day Job*, appeared in 1973. After its release, the band switched labels, signing with the European-based Ariola, who released *Bluegrass Special* later in 1973. As the location of their record label indicated, the band was more popular in Europe than America.

In 1975 Byron Berline left the band and formed Sundance; Roger Bush left that same year. The next year Country Gazette added guitarist/mandolinist/vocalist Roland White to their lineup and released *Live*. After its release, the band added fiddler Dave Ferguson and released *Out to Lunch* on the American independent label Flying Fish; in Europe, the

album was called *Sunnyside of the Mountain*. After the recording of *Out to Lunch*, Wertz left the band. Two albums—1977's *What a Way to Earn a Living*, which was recorded with Berline, not Ferguson, and 1979's *All This and Money Too*—followed on Ridge Runner.

American and Clean and *America's Bluegrass Band* appeared on Flying Fish in 1981 and 1982, respectively. The group disbanded after the release of *America's Bluegrass Band*, but in 1983 they re-formed. The reunited lineup featured Roland White, banjoist Alan Munde, bassist Mike Anderson, and dobroist Gene Wooten. For the next five years, the band toured America and Europe. Country Gazette broke up for a second and final time in 1988. Roland White joined the Nashville Bluegrass Band after the group's split. *—Stephen Thomas Erlewine*

Out to Lunch / 1977 / Flying Fish ♦♦♦
On this album, one of the best of the progressive bands plays some fine newgrass. *—AMG*

● **Hello Operator . . . This Is Country Gazette** / 1991 / Flying Fish ♦♦♦♦
Keep on Pushing / 1991 / Flying Fish ♦♦♦
Fourteen great bluegrass cuts with Alan Munde. The Country Gazette's 20th year. *—Chip Renner*

The Country Gentlemen

Progressive Bluegrass, Traditional Bluegrass, Bluegrass

The Country Gentlemen expanded the definition of "bluegrass"—they were progressive bluegrass before the term existed. The Gentlemen came along with the first wave of the folk-music revival in the late '50s and quickly made a name for themselves as a band who could not only play traditional material straight but who also brought Bob Dylan and contemporary country material into the genre. Because of their exceptional singing and virtuoso instrumentals, the Gentlemen attracted a broad audience, ranging from traditional country-bluegrass fans to folk and soft-rock lovers.

Formed in Washington, DC, on July 4, 1957, the original lineup of the Country Gentlemen featured guitarist/vocalist Charlie Waller—who has led the band through all of its numerous incarnations—mandolinist/vocalist John Duffey, banjoist Bill Emerson, and bassist Tom Morgan. Waller had spent time with a number of country string bands in the early '50s, most notably Buzz Busby's band the Bayou Boys, which also featured Emerson. After the Bayou Boys suffered a car crash in early 1957, Waller and Emerson put together a group to fulfill the band's regular gig at a Virginia spot while various members were recovering. That replacement band evolved into the Country Gentlemen.

For the first two years of their existence the Country Gentlemen went through numerous lineup changes. In 1959 they settled on a permanent lineup, with banjoist Eddie Adcock and bassist Tom Gray joining a band that already included Waller and Duffey. This lineup secured a contract with Starday Records and released a handful of single sand one album, *Traveling Dobro Blues*. After their Starday recordings, the group moved to Folkways, where they released three albums, including their breakthrough *Country Songs Old and New*. After their stint at Folkways, the group moved to Mercury in 1963, where they released *Folk Session Inside*. The next year they began a long association with Rebel Records.

During the '60s the Country Gentlemen built up a dedicated fan base in America through constant touring. Although their lineup shifted rapidly—after Gray's 1964 departure, they went through several bassists before settling on Ed McGlothlin—their sound stayed pretty much the same. At the end of the '60s, the core lineup began to splinter. Duffey left in 1969; he was replaced by Jimmy Gaudreau. The next year, both Adcock and McGlothlin left the lineup. In 1971 the second classic lineup of the Country Gentlemen—featuring Waller, a rejoined Bill Emerson, mandolinist Doyle Lawson, and bassist Bill Yates—fell into place and they stayed together for two years. For the next 20 years various lineups of the Country Gentlemen, which were led by Waller, remained popular on the bluegrass festival circuit. *—Stephen Thomas Erlewine & David Vinopal*

★ **Country Songs Old and New** / 1960 / Smithsonian/Folkways ♦♦♦♦♦
This is a reissue of the 1960 Folkways album that launched their career. Includes "The Little Sparrow," "The Long Black Veil," "Under the Double Eagle," and 13 other classic cuts. A magic album. *—Michael Erlewine*

Award Winning Country Gentlemen / 1972 / Rebel ♦♦♦♦
Outstanding session. *—Ron Wynn*

One Wide River / 1987 / Rebel ♦♦♦
Nice, but not so energetic or ambitious as other releases. *—Ron Wynn*

Folk Songs and Bluegrass / 1988 / Smithsonian/Folkways ♦♦♦♦
Another essential '60s release. *—Ron Wynn*

☆ **Sit Down Young Stranger** / 1988 / Sugar Hill ♦♦♦♦♦
A tremendous date; brilliant playing by Mike Auldridge. *—Ron Wynn*

River Bottom / 1989 / Sugar Hill ♦♦♦♦
Great solos and harmonies, excellent compositions. *—Ron Wynn*

Sugar Hill Collection / 1995 / Sugar Hill ✦✦✦✦
As the title suggests, *Sugar Hill Collection* compiles the highlights from
the Country Gentlemen's recordings for the independent label Sugar
Hill. Although these were made later in their career, the group sounds as
good as they ever have. — *Thom Owens*

Sound Off / Rebel ✦✦✦
Good, with a more contemporary sound. — *Ron Wynn*

Cox Family

With their pure harmonies and fusion of traditional and progressive
bluegrass that blended gospel, country, rock, and bluegrass, the Cox
Family created their own niche in bluegrass. Though they had been play-
ing their music at country fairs, festivals, concert halls, and on national
radio and television shows (including the "Grand Ole Opry," "Louisiana
Hayride" and "Riders Radio Theater") for more than two decades, the
Coxes did not make it into the mainstream until hooking up with Alison
Krauss in the '90s.

Willard Cox is both the band's founder and the family patriarch. Born
and raised in Cotton Valley, LA, he spent most of his life involved with
music, as did his wife Marie, whom he met while she and her sisters
were performing around Louisiana. Willard and Marie had three children—Sidney, Evelyn, and Suzanne. All of the children were musically
inclined but learned most of their skills on their own, since their father
had little patience with formal teaching. The Cox Family started out playing informally at home.

The Cox Family went professional in the mid-'70s and began performing on the festival and fair circuit. The group continued to tour America—particularly in the South—throughout the '70s and '80s. During this
time, they never cut a record. The Cox Family didn't record until 1993,
when they released *Everybody's Reaching for Someone* on Rounder
Records. The next year, several of Sidney Cox's songs appeared on Alison
Krauss' albums *I've Got That Old Feeling* and *Everytime You Say Goodbye*. Krauss helped the band record their second album, *I Know Who
Holds Tomorrow*, in 1994; the album won a Grammy Award in 1995 for
Best Bluegrass Album. Also in 1995 the Cox Family released their third
album, the Krauss-produced *Beyond the City*. Like its predecessor, it was
nominated for a Grammy as Best Bluegrass Album. — *Sandra Brennan*

Everybody's Reaching Out for Someone / Apr. 1, 1993 / Rounder ✦✦✦

● **Beyond the City** / 1995 / Rounder ✦✦✦✦

Just When You're Thinking It's Over / Jul. 1996 / Elektra ✦✦✦
The Cox Family's major-label debut *Just When You're Thinking It's Over*
combines popular standards from writers like Hank Williams, Sr., and
Barrett Strong and Norman Whitfield, plus contemporary writers like
Lee Roy Parness and Larry Gatlin. As always, the Coxes sound as rich,
pure, and timeless as the hills themselves, yet invigoratingly modern. A
few of the tracks falter a bit—Del Shannon's "Runaway" doesn't quite
translate to the bluegrass medium—but that doesn't prevent the album
from being a wonderful demonstration of the group's prodigious talents.
— *Thom Owens*

J.D. Crowe and the New South

Banjo, Vocals / Progressive Bluegrass
Banjoist J.D. Crowe was one of the most influential progressive bluegrass
musicians of the '70s. Initially influenced by Earl Scruggs, as well as rock
'n' roll and the blues, Crowe worked his way through several bands during the '60s, developing a distinctive instrumental style that melded
country, bluegrass, rock, and blues. Crowe didn't receive national exposure until the early '70s, when he formed the New South, but after the
release of the band's eponymous debut in 1972, he became a fixture on
the bluegrass scene for the next 20 years.

Born and raised in Lexington, KY, Crowe picked up the banjo when he
was 13 years old, inspired by one of Flatt & Scruggs' performances on the
Kentucky Barn Dance. After that show, he regularly attended the duo's
performances, sitting down in the front row to study Scruggs' revolutionary picking. Soon, Crowe was playing with various groups in Kentucky,
including an outfit that also featured Curley Parker and Pee Wee Lambert. The young banjo player frequently played on local radio stations
and that is where he got his first major break in 1956. Jimmy Martin was
driving through Lexington when he heard Crowe on the radio station
and was so impressed with what he heard, he drove to the station and
asked him to join his band, the Sunny Mountain Boys. Crowe immediately accepted and began touring with Martin. While he was in the
Sunny Mountain Boys, J.D. didn't stick to a strict bluegrass set list—he
often added rock 'n' roll songs to his repertoire.

After spending six years with Martin, Crowe left the Sunny Mountain
Boys in 1962 to pursue a solo career. For a while, he played Lexington
bars and hotels, developing a new, progressive direction for bluegrass
which incorporated stronger elements of folk, blues, and rock. In the
mid-'60s, he formed the Kentucky Mountain Boys with Red Allen and
Doyle Lawson, which released their first album, *Bluegrass Holiday*, in

1968 on Lemco Records. The Kentucky Mountain Boys had a varied repertoire, but played solely acoustic instruments. Two other records followed—*Ramblin' Boy* and *The Model Church*—before the group broke
up in the early '70s.

Following the disbandment of the Kentucky Mountain Boys, J.D.
Crowe formed the New South, which was the most revolutionary bluegrass outfit of its time. Originally, the band consisted of guitarist Tony
Rice, mandolinist Ricky Skaggs, dobroist Jerry Douglas, and fiddler/bass-
ist Bobby Sloan, and they played a wildly eclectic brand of bluegrass on
electric instruments. When they released their debut, *J.D. Crowe & the
New South* in 1975 on Rounder Records, it caused an instant sensation—it marked a genuine turning point in the sound of the genre. All of
the musicians in the original lineup of the New South were acclaimed
and they would later go on to popular solo careers—in fact, most of them
had left within a few years of the debut. By the end of the decade, the
band featured guitarist/vocalist Keith Whitley, mandolinist Jimmy Gaudreau, fiddler Bobby Slone, and bassist Steve Bryant.

During the '80s, the New South featured an ever-revolving lineup, as
former members came back for guest appearances and Crowe discovered fresh, developing talents—the group became known as a source for
new musicians that would later go on to individual success. In 1980,
Crowe formed the Bluegrass Album Band with Tony Rice, Bobby Hicks,
Doyle Lawson, and Todd Phillips. The Bluegrass Album Band toured and
recorded sporadically throughout the course of the decade, always to
great critical and popular acclaim. J.D. continued with the New South
until 1988, when he decided to retire from the road. Following his decision, he appeared at special, one-shot concerts—including a tour with
Tony Rice—but he concentrated on studio work, particularly producing
records for developing bands. — *Stephen Thomas Erlewine*

☆ **J. D. Crowe and the New South** / 1975 / Rounder ✦✦✦✦✦
A very influential trailblazing album of "young blood" in bluegrass, it
features Ricky Skaggs and Tony Rice. — *Mark A. Humphrey*

My Home Ain't in the Hall of Fame / 1978 / Rounder ✦✦✦
Crowe, on banjo and baritone, moves closer to country in the company
of Keith Whitley and Doug Jernigan. — *Mark A. Humphrey*

Somewhere Between / 1981 / Rounder ✦✦✦✦
A hard-country album with lovely ballads, it features Lefty Frizzell-style
vocals from Keith Whitley. — *Mark A. Humphrey*

Live in Japan / 1982 / Rounder ✦✦✦
Spirited performances with Keith Whitley and the great mandolinist
Jimmy Gaudreau. — *Mark A. Humphrey*

Straight Ahead / 1986 / Rounder ✦✦✦
More or less traditional bluegrass, with Sam Bush on mandolin and Jerry
Douglas on dobro. — *Mark A. Humphrey*

★ **FlashBack** / 1994 / Rounder ✦✦✦✦✦
FlashBack is a first-rate retrospective of J.D. Crowe's groundbreaking,
innovative career and an excellent way to get acquainted with all aspects
of his music. — *Thom Owens*

Doug Dillard

b. Mar. 6, 1937, Salem, MO
Banjo, Guitar, Vocals / Traditional Bluegrass
Doug Dillard's music blends bluegrass, country-rock, and pop. Throughout his long and varied career, Dillard was one of the leading banjoists in
country and bluegrass music, pioneering a distinctive instrumental style.
Doug was raised in Salem, MO,, where he and his younger brother Rodney began playing bluegrass music together in grade school. From the
mid- to late '50s, the brothers appeared on the Ozark Mountain Boys'
radio program, "The Ozark Jubilee." In 1958 Doug and Rodney recorded
two singles—"Doug's Breakdown"/"My Own True Love" and "Mama
Don't 'Low"/"Highway of Sorrow"—for K-Ark Records. Between 1958
and 1960, the duo played with three bluegrass bands—the Hawthorn
Brothers, the Lewis Brothers and Joe Noel and the Dixie Ramblers. In
1962 the brothers formed the first incarnation of the Dillards with Mitch
Jayne and Dean Webb.

The Dillards headed to California in 1962. Less than a week after their
arrival, Jim Dickson saw them jamming with the Greenbriar Boys at the
Ashcroft and signed the group to Elektra. After the Dillards inked their
deal with Elektra, they were hired to appear on the "Andy Griffith Show"
as the slightly demented hayseeds the Darling Family. In 1963 Doug and
Rodney joined with Dean Webb, Glen Campbell, and Tut Taylor to form
the Folkswingers. The group released two albums of string-band music
for World Pacific during the mid-'60s. In 1966 Doug played with ex-Byrd
Gene Clark and the Gosdin Brothers on their self-titled collaboration. In
1967 he and Rodney played on the soundtrack for *Bonnie and Clyde*;
they performed all of the music except the theme song, "Foggy Mountain
Breakdown." Also in 1967 Doug left the Dillards to form a duo with Gene
Clark.

Dillard and Clark released their debut album, *Fantastic Expedition*,
in 1968. The duo were supported by a band that included guitarist

Bernie Leadon, bassist David Jackson, and dobro/mandolin player Don Beck. Ex-Byrd drummer Michael Clarke joined Dillard and Clark on their first tour and second album, 1969's *Through the Morning, Through the Night.* Clark left the band in 1970. Dillard continued with the group, renaming them Dillard and the Expedition. However, he left the band in 1971; the remaining members became Country Gazette.

In 1971 Dillard formed a new band, Dillard and the Country Coalition, but he went solo by the end of the year. His first solo effort was the soundtrack for *Vanishing Point.* In 1973 and 1974, Dillard released two albums for 20th Century Records, *Dueling Banjos* and *Douglas Flint Dillard*—You Don't Need a Reason to Sing. During this time he also did session work. In 1977 he recorded *Glitter-Grass from the Nashwood Hollyville Strings* with his brother Rodney and John Hartford. The next year Doug released his third solo album, *Heaven,* which was produced by Rodney. After the release of *Heaven,* he formed the Doug Dillard Band, which featured fiddler Byron Berline. In 1979 Doug, Rodney, and Berline appeared in the film *The Rose.* In 1980 he returned to Salem to record a reunion album with the Dillards. That year Dillard also worked on the soundtrack of *Popeye.* During the '80s and '90s Doug Dillard continued to record and play live concerts; occasionally, he reunited with his brother Rodney. —*Sandra Brennan*

Heaven / 1979 / Flying Fish ◆◆◆
A gospel album featuring Dan Crary, Byron Berline, John Hartford, and Herb Pedersen. It includes an excellent cover of "Turn Your Radio On." —*Chip Renner*

● **Jackrabbit** / 1980 / Flying Fish ◆◆◆◆
A live album from the Telluride Bluegrass Festival, with guests Sam Bush and Byron Berline. —*Chip Renner*

What's That? / 1986 / Flying Fish ◆◆◆
A solid album. —*Chip Renner*

The Dillards

Progressive Bluegrass, Bluegrass
During the '60s the Dillards helped bring bluegrass to a wider audience, both through their records and their appearances on television and film. For the next three decades the band continued to perform in various incarnations. All the while they remained one of the most popular bluegrass bands in America.

Brothers Doug and Rodney Dillard formed the core of the original lineup of the Dillards. The brothers were born and raised in Salem, MO; Doug was five years older than Rodney. While they were attending grade school, the brothers began playing bluegrass together—Doug played the banjo, Rodney played the guitar. From the mid- to late '50s the brothers appeared on the Ozark Mountain Boys' radio program "The Ozark Jubilee." In 1958 Doug and Rodney recorded two singles—"Doug's Breakdown"/"My Own True Love" and "Mama Don't 'Low'"/"Highway of Sorrow"—for K-Ark Records. Between 1958 and 1960 the duo played with three bluegrass bands—the Hawthorn Brothers, the Lewis Brothers, and Joe Noel and the Dixie Ramblers. In 1962 the brothers formed the first incarnation of the Dillards with Mitch Jayne and Dean Webb.

The Dillards headed to California in 1962. Less than a week after their arrival, Jim Dickson saw them jamming with the Greenbriar Boys at the Ashcroft and signed the group to Elektra. After the Dillards inked their deal with Elektra, they were hired to appear on the "Andy Griffith Show" as the slightly demented hayseeds the Darling Family. In 1963 the Dillards released their first album, *Back Porch Bluegrass.* That same year Doug and Rodney joined with Dean Webb, Glen Campbell, and Tut Taylor to form the Folkswingers, a side project that released two albums of string-band music for World Pacific in the mid-'60s.

In 1964 the Dillards released *Live . . . Almost!* By the time the album was released, the group had amplified their instruments, which angered the purists that formed the core of the American bluegrass audience. Nevertheless, the group developed a strong fan base. In 1965 they released *Pickin' and Fiddlin',* which featured fiddler Byron Berline. Two years later Doug and Rodney played on the soundtrack to *Bonnie and Clyde.* After completing the soundtrack, Doug left the band to form the Dillard and Clark Expedition with former Byrd Gene Clark. He was replaced by banjo player Herb Peterson, and the group recorded their fourth album, *Wheatstraw Suite.*

Wheatstraw Suite was released in 1968 and featured an increasingly adventurous musical approach by the Dillards, as did its follow-up, 1970's *Copperfields.* On these two albums the Dillards added drums and steel guitar and began covering rock and folk songwriters like Bob Dylan, Lennon and McCartney, Gordon Lightfoot, John Prine, and Tim Harden. Although neither record was a commercial success, the albums opened the doors for progressive bluegrass bands in the '70s. In 1971 the Dillards had a minor pop hit with "It's About Time" and opened for Elton John on his first American tour. The next year they released *Tribute to the American Duck* on Poppy . The group didn't release another album until 1977; by that time the lineup had changed drastically—it now featured Rodney Dillard, banjoist Billy Ray Lathum, bassist Jeff Gilkinson,

drummer Paul York, and steel guitarist Buddy Emmons. In 1977 the Dillards released two albums, *The Dillards vs. the Incredible L.A. Time Machine* and *Glitter-Grass from the Nashwood Hollyville Strings;* the latter featured John Hartford and a reunion between Rodney and Doug. In 1980 Flying Fish released *Homecoming and Reunion,* a documentary of the band's reunion in Salemat the "Dillard Day" celebration August 8, 1980. In 1980, the group released *Mountain Rock.* After completion of the album, Paul York retired from performing and the Dillards restructured their lineup; by the end of the year, the group consisted of Rodney Dillard, Joe Villegas, Eddie Ponder, and Peter Grant. The next year the band played a handful of concerts, but soon Rodney turned his attention to his new group, the Rodney Dillard Band.

Throughout the '80s the Dillards were inactive, but the original lineup occasionally reunited. The Rodney Dillard Band regularly plays at Silver Dollar City in Branson, and the Doug Dillard Band is a popular attraction on the bluegrass and folk circuit. —*Sandra Brennan*

Decade Waltz / 1979 / Flying Fish ◆◆◆
On this album one of the most important bands in the development of country-rock returns to its beginnings. —*AMG*

Homecoming and Family Reunion / 1979 / Flying Fish ◆◆◆
This is a pleasant album of several Dillard generations live at a picnic. —*Mark A. Humphrey*

★ **There Is a Time (1963-70)** / 1991 / Vanguard ◆◆◆◆◆
This is a 29-track retrospective of their influential 1963-1970 Elektra recordings of urban bluegrass. —*Mark A. Humphrey*

Let It Fly / 1991 / Vanguard ◆◆◆
These recordings were produced by Herb Pedersen of the Desert Rose Band. —*Mark A. Humphrey*

Jerry Douglas

Dobro Guitar / Progressive Bluegrass
As one of the premiere dobro players in bluegrass, new acoustic, and country music, Jerry "Flux" Douglas has toured and recorded with everyone from Emmylou Harris, Ricky Skaggs, and the Nitty Gritty Dirt Band to mandolin sensation David Grisman and banjo innovator Bela Fleck. Douglas' albums as a leader fully exploit the dobro's resonant guitar sound. His aggressive touch and incredibly fast finger picking and deft use of the steel bar gives the instrument a bright, cutting tone quality that adds to the breathless intensity of the new-acoustic music he creates. Born in Warren, OH, Douglas was eight years old when his father, a bluegrass musician, introduced him to the dobro. Douglas became further fascinated with the instrument upon hearing Josh Graves play the instrument at a 1963 Flatt & Scruggs concert. By the time he was 16, Douglas had been playing in his father's band for a number of years. That year they played at a festival alongside the Country Gentlemen who were impressed with the youth's playing and invited him to join the band for the rest of the summer. Later Douglas worked with J.D. Crowe and the New South as well as David Grisman, and Boone Creek with Ricky Skaggs.

In 1978, Douglas made his solo debut for Rounder with *Fluxology.* His next album for Rounder, *Tennessee Fluxedo,* came out two years later. He began playing and recording with the Whites in 1983. He eventually left to focus on his solo career and do session work. During the '80s, he became one of the most popular session musicians in Nashville.

Douglas became one of the first performers to sign to the MCA Master Series in 1986. He recorded three albums for the label. Of these, 1989's *Plant Early* is the most notable because it marked a change toward a calmer, more textured direction for Douglas. In the early '90s Douglas and guitarists Albert Lee and Tal Farlow embarked upon a European tour for the National Council of Traditional Arts.

Douglas has won numerous awards for his work including a Grammy for Best Country Instrumental Performance in 1983. In the '90s Douglas began producing other artists and making regular appearances on the TNN show "American Music Shop." In 1993, Douglas, guitarist Russ Barenberg, and bassist Edgar Meyer released the Sugar Hill album *Skip, Hop and Wobble.* —*Sandra Brennan & Linda Kohanov*

Fluxology / 1979 / Rounder ◆◆◆
A good bluegrass album with Tony Rice, Darol Anger, Todd Phillips, and Ricky Skaggs. —*Chip Renner*

Fluxedo / 1982 / Rounder ◆◆◆
A smoother sound, which has become his trademark with Strength in Numbers. Featuring Sam Bush, Bela Fleck, the Whites, Mark Shatz, and Russ Barenberg. —*Chip Renner*

Under the Wire / 1986 / MCA ◆◆◆
Though all of his releases are dobro tours de force, this is a sophisticated ensemble album with some of the best players in the new acoustic realm, including Mark O'Connor, Russ Barenberg, Bela Fleck, and Sam Bush. With seven of the ten tracks written by Douglas, the album is also a tribute to his inventive compositional style. —*Linda Kohanov*

Everything Is Gonna Work Out Fine / 1987 / Rounder ✦✦✦✦
Fluxology and *Fluxedo* on one CD—a great value from the master of the dobro. —*Chip Renner*

● **Slide Rule** / 1992 / Sugar Hill ✦✦✦✦
His finest release hits the jackpot. Featuring Sam Bush, Alison Krauss, Tim O'Brien, Maura O'Connell, Stuart Duncan, Artie McGlynn, and others, this album is produced to perfection. Highly recommended. —*Chip Renner*

Dry Branch Fire Squad

Traditional Bluegrass
The Dry Branch Fire Squad is a modern bluegrass band committed to keeping the old-time Appalachian traditional music alive. This southern Ohio bluegrass group is fronted by Ron Thomason, a mandolinist and comedian. Thomason grew up in Russell County, VA. He received a B.A. from Ohio University in 1967 and spent many years working as a high school English teacher and administrator in the Springfield area, where he also played in a local bluegrass band with Frank Wakefield. He went on to spend a year touring with Ralph Stanley's Clinch Mountain Boys.

Thomason formed the Dry Branch Fire Squad in 1976, after he spent time with Lee Allen's Dew Mountain Boys. The earliest incarnation of the band included guitarist John Baker, banjo player Robert Leach, and bass player John Carpenter. Two years later Mary Jo Leet became the group's vocalist.

During the late 1970s, the Fire Squad recorded three independent albums and then signed with Rounder. They were joined by bassist Dick Erwin and banjoist John Hisey, who would remain with the band for the next ten years. During that time the Dry Branch Fire Squad became favorites on the festival circuit. Over the years the band has undergone many personnel changes, but they always remained committed to preserving the old mountain sounds. —*Sandra Brennan and David Vinopal*

Long Journey / 1972 / Rounder ✦✦✦✦
Old timey—in a modern way. Very good. —*Chip Renner*

Born to Be Lonesome / 1978 / Rounder ✦✦✦
Good. Featuring Kenny Baker, Bobby Osborne. A nice cover of "Brand New Tennessee Waltz." —*Chip Renner*

Fannin' the Flames / 1982 / Rounder ✦✦✦
Very nice album. —*Chip Renner*

Fertile Ground / 1983 / Rounder ✦✦✦✦
Very good. "Devil Take the Farmer" and "Bonaparte Crossing the Rhine." —*Chip Renner*

● **Good Neighbours and Friends** / 1985 / Rounder ✦✦✦✦
Tight mountain harmonies on 14 cuts. A must-have. —*Chip Renner*

Buddy Emmons

b. Jan. 27, 1937, Mishawaka, IN
Bass, Piano, Guitar (Steel), Vocals / Instrumental, Bluegrass
Buddy Emmons is among Nashville's elite as one of the finest steel guitar players in the business. Born in Mishawaka, IN, Emmons first fell in love with steel guitars at age 11 when he received a six-string lap steel guitar as a gift. As a teen, he enrolled at the Hawaiian Conservatory of Music in South Bend, IN, and began playing professionally in Calumet City and Chicago at 16. In 1956 Emmons went to Detroit to fill in for Walter Haynes during a performance with Little Jimmy Dickens, and soon afterward he was invited to join the Dickens' Country Boys. He appeared with them a few times on the "Grand Ole Opry" and recorded a few singles that included "Buddy's Boogie" (1957). He also recorded a pair of solo singles for Columbia, "Cold Rolled Steel" (1956) and "Silver Bells" (1957).

In the late '50s Emmons also began playing occasionally with Ernest Tubb's band on "Midnight Jamboree." In 1963 he began a five-year stint with Ray Price and his Cherokee Cowboys. In 1965 Emmons teamed up with fellow steel player Shot Jackson to record *Steel Guitar and Dobro Sound* for Nashville Records. This led the two to create the Sho-Bud Company, which sold an innovative steel guitar that used push-rod pedals. In 1969 Emmons joined Roger Miller's Los Angeles-based band as a bass player. When not touring with Miller, he did session work for a variety of artists. He quit Miller's band in 1973 and signed a solo contract with Flying Fish Records, where he released several albums in the late '70s. After 1978 Emmons began playing for a number of labels, notably Step One Records, where he and Ray Pennington occasionally collaborated with some of Nashville's finest side-men as the Swing Shift Band. In 1993 Emmons began touring with the Everly Brothers. Throughout the '90s, he continued to do session work. —*Sandra Brennan*

● **Steel Guitar Jazz** / Sep. 1963 / Mercury ✦✦✦✦

Sings Bob Wills / 1976 / Flying Fish ✦✦✦
This album features some of the best pickers in Nashville, with Pig Robbins and Johnny Gimble. —*AMG*

Buddies / 1977 / Flying Fish ✦✦✦
Two of the best session players in Nashville play some fine country jazz. —*AMG*

Minors Aloud / 1979 / Flying Fish ✦✦✦
Here, jazz-guitar great Breau teams with steel master Emmons for an album of lively music. —*AMG*

Buddy and Lenny / Flying Fish ✦✦✦✦
Country meets jazz as two super-pickers, Buddy Emmons and Lenny Breau (pedal steel and electric guitar), collide on this very creative and innovative album. —*Hank Davis*

Flatt and Scruggs

Traditional Bluegrass
Probably the most famous bluegrass band of all time was Flatt and Scruggs and the Foggy Mountain Boys. They made the genre famous in ways that not even Bill Monroe, who pretty much invented the sound, ever could. Because of a guitar player and vocalist from Tennessee named Lester Flatt and an extraordinary banjo player from North Carolina named Earl Scruggs, bluegrass music has become popular the world over and has entered the mainstream in the world of music.

Like so many other bluegrass legends, Flatt and Scruggs were graduates of Bill Monroe's Blue Grass Boys. Because of the unique sound they added ("overdrive," one critic called it), Monroe felt let down after Flatt's quality vocals and Scruggs' banjo leads left in 1948. Quickly the two assembled a band that in the opinion of many was among the best ever, with Chubby Wise on fiddle and Cedric Rainwater on bass; a later band, with Paul Warren on fiddle and Josh Graves on dobro, was equally superb. With so many extraordinary musicians and the solid, controlled vocals of Flatt, it's no wonder the Foggy Mountain Boys was the band that brought bluegrass to international prominence. From 1948 until 1969, when Flatt and Scruggs split up to pursue different musical directions, they were *the* bluegrass band, due to their Martha White Flour segment at the Opry and, especially, their tremendous exposure from TV and movies.

Lester Flatt and Earl Scruggs were originally brought together by Bill Monroe in 1945, when they joined a band that also featured fiddler Chubby Wise and bassist Cedric Rainwater. This quintet created the sound of bluegrass and helped bring it to national recognition through radio shows, records, and concerts. After three years with Monroe, Flatt left the mandolinist behind in 1948 and Scruggs followed his lead shortly afterward. The duo formed their own band, the Foggy Mountain Boys. Within a few months, they recruited ex-Blue Grass Boy Rainwater, fiddler Jim Shumate, and guitarist/vocalist Mac Wiseman. Initially, the band played on radio stations across the South, landing a record contract with Mercury Records in late 1948. Over the next two years, they toured the US constantly, played many radio shows, and recorded several sessions on Mercury. One of these sessions produced the original version of "Foggy Mountain Breakdown," which would become a bluegrass standard.

In 1951 Flatt and Scruggs switched record labels, signing with Columbia Records. The band now featured mandolinist/vocalist Curly Seckler, fiddler Paul Warren, and bassist Jake Tullock. Where the careers of other bluegrass and hard country acts stalled in the early and mid-'50s, the Foggy Mountain Boys flourished. One of their first singles for Columbia, "Tis Sweet to Be Remembered," reached the Top Ten in 1952, and in 1953, the Martha White Flour company sponsored a regular radio show for the group on WSM in Nashville. In 1955 the band joined the Grand Ole Opry. The following year, they added a dobro player called Buck Graves to the lineup.

Flatt and Scruggs reached a new audience in the late '50s, when the folk music revival sparked the interest of a younger generation of listeners. The duo played a number of festivals targeted at the new breed of bluegrass and folk fans. At the same time, country music television programs went into syndication, and the duo became regulars on these shows. In the summer of 1959, Flatt and Scruggs began a streak of Top 40 country singles that ran into 1968—their chart performance was directly tied to their increased exposure. The duo's popularity peaked in 1962, when they recorded the theme song to the television sitcom "The Beverly Hillbillies." The theme, called "The Ballad of Jed Clampett," became the first No. 1 bluegrass single in early 1963, and the duo made a number of cameos on the show.

"The Beverly Hillbillies" began a streak of cameo appearances and soundtrack work for Flatt and Scruggs in television and film, most notably with the appearance of "Foggy Mountain Breakdown" in Arthur Penn's 1968 film *Bonnie and Clyde*. With all of their TV, film, and festival appearances, Flatt and Scruggs popularized bluegrass music more than any other artist, even Bill Monroe. Ironically, that popularity helped drive the duo apart. Scruggs wanted to expand their sound and pushed Flatt to cover Bob Dylan's "Like a Rolling Stone" in 1968, as well as landing concert appearances in venues that normally booked rock 'n' roll acts. Flatt wanted to continue in a traditional bluegrass vein. The opposing forces came to a head in 1969 and the duo parted ways. Flatt formed a traditional bluegrass band, the Nashville Grass, while Scruggs assembled a more progressive outfit, the Earl Scruggs Revue.

Throughout the '70s, both Flatt and Scruggs enjoyed successful solo careers. In 1979, the duo began ironing out the details of a proposed reunion album, but they were scrapped upon Flatt's death on May 11, 1979. Scruggs retired in the '80s. In 1985, Flatt and Scruggs were inducted into the Country Music Hall of Fame. *—Stephen Thomas Erlewine and David Vinopal*

Songs of the Famous Carter Family / 1961 / Columbia/Legacy ✦✦✦
Depression-era country/folk performed bluegrass style. *—Mark A. Humphrey*

Flatt and Scruggs at Carnegie Hall! / 1962 / CBS ✦✦✦
This is a highly influential "folk-boom" concert album . *—Mark A. Humphrey*

Live at Vanderbilt University / 1964 / Columbia Special Products ✦✦✦
Featured is a performance from the early '60s. *—AMG*

☆ **Foggy Mountain Banjo** / 196_ / CBS ✦✦✦✦✦
The album that secured their standing among folk-music enthusiasts in the 1960s, it focuses on Scruggs' instrumental prowess as well as his sharp interplay with dobroist Josh Graves, fiddler Paul Warren, and Flatt's flat-picking guitar. The album also features drummer Buddy Harman, whose appearance shocked purists. *—Michael McCall*

The Golden Era 1950-55 / 1977 / Rounder ✦✦✦
Classic Columbia performances. *—Mark A. Humphrey*

Columbia Historic Edition / 1982 / CBS ✦✦✦
Wonderful '50s recordings, it includes some rarities. *—Mark A. Humphrey*

☆ **20 All Time Great Recordings** / 1983 / CBS ✦✦✦✦✦
Three-part gospel-style harmonies, breakneck banjo, flinty Americana, and "a bubblin' crude" are the cornerstone collection of bluegrass at its best. *—Mark A. Humphrey*

Mercury Sessions, Vol. 1 / 1987 / Rounder ✦✦✦✦
These 1948-1950 recordings were done by the banjo whiz and baleful vocalist who took Bill Monroe's music a step further. *—Mark A. Humphrey*

Mercury Sessions, Vol. 2 / 1987 / Rounder ✦✦✦✦
More great 1948-1950 recordings, including the original "Foggy Mountain Breakdown." *—Mark A. Humphrey*

☆ **1949-1959** / 1992 / Bear Family ✦✦✦✦✦
Four CDs filled with the very best Flatt & Scruggs tunes during their peak years. A Bear Family import with superb liner notes, and music beyond compare. *—Michael Erlewine*

Don't Get Above Your Raisin' / 1992 / Rounder ✦✦✦
Flatt's song became a back-to-basics anthem when Ricky Skaggs waxed it about 1981. The original is here, along with other greats from the '50s. *—Mark A. Humphrey*

☆ **1959-1963** / 1992 / Bear Family ✦✦✦✦
Although the material covered on the five-disc box set *1959-1963* isn't as innovative as the music on Bear Family's first Flatt & Scruggs box, *1949-1959*, it's quite nearly as good. During these five years, the duo brought bluegrass into the mainstream and this collection shows why. Over the set's 129 tracks—which includes a wealth of unreleased material and alternate takes, most notably the complete Carnegie Hall concert from December of 1962—Flatt & Scruggs run through a selection of originals and standards, including some re-recorded versions of their earlier Mercury hits. They might not sound quite as lively as they did a decade earlier, but this remains classic bluegrass. *—Thom Owens*

★ **The Complete Mercury Sessions** / Aug. 4, 1992 / Mercury ✦✦✦✦✦
The integral early recordings of this seminal bluegrass band. Included is their classic "Foggy Mountain Breakdown," "Roll in My Sweet Baby's Arms," "Old Salty Dog Blues," and others. It's indispensable for bluegrass fans. *—Michael McCall*

1964-1969, Plus / Feb. 1996 / Bear Family ✦✦✦✦
Bear Family's third box set of Flatt & Scruggs material is necessary for completists and historians, but it doesn't have the revelatory spark of the first box, nor the crossover appeal of the second. There is plenty of enjoyable music on the set, but the completist approach—all of the released studio recordings are included, plus alternate takes and unreleased tracks—makes listening to the box somewhat difficult. Nevertheless, for diehard Flatt & Scruggs fans, *1964-1969, Plus* is as essential a purchase as the first two Bear Family boxes. *—Thom Owens*

Josh Graves

Dobro Guitar / Traditional Bluegrass
For more than five decades, legendary Josh Graves (born Burkett Graves) has been one of the major forces in keeping the unique sounds of the dobro guitar vital and alive in both country and bluegrass music. Born

and raised in Tellico Plains, TN, he was only nine when he heard Cliff Carlisle, of the Carlisle Brothers performing a few Jimmie Rogers tunes with the dobro. Graves loved the sound and became close friends with Carlisle. Still, Graves spent much of his early career as a bass player.

In 1942 Graves joined the Pierce Brothers and began playing in Gatlinburg. Later he played with Esco Hankins and Mac Wiseman before becoming a part of the Wheeling Jamboree with Wilma Lee and Stoney Cooper. Graves remained with Wilma and Stoney through the mid-'50s. During a performance with the Coopers at the Grand Ole Opry, Graves made a big impression upon Lester Flatt and Earl Scruggs, who invited him to join their Foggy Mountain Boys. Initially he was again a bass player, but about a month after joining, Scruggs and Graves worked out a way to use Scruggs' innovative three-finger banjo picking style on the dobro. In the late '50s, acoustic instruments were out of favor, due to the popularity of rock 'n' roll. The survival of the dobro as an important instrument in country can largely be attributed to Graves, who alternately electrified audiences with a red-hot picking style and then cooled them down with a bluesy, sweet mellowness. Graves remained a primary member of the Foggy Mountain Boys until they disbanded in 1969. Afterward, he joined Flatt's Nashville Grass and did session work on the side. In 1971 he began playing with Earl Scruggs Review; three years later, he decided to go solo.

Graves first solo effort was *Alone at Last* on Epic. He also continued session work—playing with artists like Charlie McCoy, J.J. Cale, Steve Young, and Kris Kristofferson—and collaborating with other musicians, such as his 1975 duet album with Jake Tullock, *Just Joshing*. He continued in a similar vein through the 1980s and the '90s. Graves teamed up with such greats as Kenny Baker, Eddie Adcock, and Jesse McReynolds in 1989 to form the Masters and release an eponymous album. *—Sandra Brennan*

● **King of the Dobro** / 1982 / CMH ✦✦✦✦
This is the man who created bluegrass-style dobro with his bluesy hound-dog slide playing. *—Mark A. Humphrey*

The Puritan Sessions / Rebel ✦✦✦✦
Longtime fiddler Kenny Baker appears in an uncharacteristic role as a finger-style guitarist in a delightfully low-key set of tunes and songs with dobroist (and sometime-singer) Graves. *—Mark A. Humphrey*

David Grisman

b. 1945
Mandolin / Swing, Bluegrass
David Grisman is one of the finest mandolin players in bluegrass history and is credited with creating a hybrid of jazz, folk, and bluegrass dubbed by critics as "new acoustic." Grisman calls it "dawg music."

Grisman was born and raised in Passaic, NJ. By the time he was a teen he could play a variety of instruments including the mandolin, the piano, and the saxophone. He later attended New York University and about this time began playing in different folk groups. Among them was the Even Dozen Jug Band. Grisman graduated from the university in the mid-'60s and moved to San Francisco, where he began moving away from his bluegrass roots toward rock 'n' roll. He joined Peter Rowan's Earth Opera and with them recorded their debut album in 1968 on Elektra. The group disbanded by the end of the year, and Grisman became a session player and sideman until 1973, when he joined Rowan and Jerry Garcia in Old and in the Way. Among the other group members were fiddler Vassar Clements and bassist John Kahn. The group released its debut album on Rounder. Grisman and Rowan also belonged to Muleskinner, a bluegrass band, in 1973.

In 1974 Grisman founded the Great American Music Band featuring Richard Greene and bassist Taj Mahal. He recorded his first solo effort, *The David Grisman Rounder Album*, in 1976 and shortly afterward founded the David Grisman Quintet. The Quintet recorded a self-titled album in 1976 and then came out with *Hot Dawg* in 1979 for Warner Brothers. The band frequently appeared at jazz clubs and opened for several major rock bands. When Stephane Grappelli toured America, he appeared with the Grisman Quintet. By 1980 the Quintet was made up of Grisman, guitarist/fiddler Mark O'Connor, bassist Rob Wasserman, violin and string player Darol Anger, and mandolinist Mike Marshall. That year the new lineup released *Quintet '80* for Warner Brothers.

In 1982 Grisman, Herb Pedersen, and Jim Buchanan teamed up to create "supergrass," a new kind of bluegrass music which can be heard on their Rounder album *Here Today*. Afterward the trio broke up. When not playing with his own group, Grisman would appear on the albums of others such as Judy Collins, John Sebastian, James Taylor, Dolly Parton, Bela Fleck, and Alison Brown. In 1983 he released *Dawg Jazz/Dawg Grass*, and followed it up with a holiday album, *Acoustic Christmas*, for Rounder. In 1985 he began recording for Zebra Acoustic, debuting with the album *Acousticity*.

Grisman continues to explore the possibilities of contemporary mandolin music on his albums and those of others, and through performing. Among his most interesting endeavors are 1987's *Svingin' with Svend,* with Svend Asmussen for Zebra, the Grammy-nominated *Dawg '90* for Acoustic Disc, and *Garcia/Grisman* (1991) for Acoustic Disc. In 1992 he appeared with Herb Pedersen, Jim Buchanan, Jim Kerwin, Red Allen, and Garcia on the album *Bluegrass Reunion.* In 1996 he appeared with the reunited Old and in the Way and released his own *DGQ-20. —Sandra Brennan*

★ **The David Grisman Quintet** / 1977 / Rhino ✦✦✦✦✦
This is a creative and adventurous session by this jazz-bluegrass group. —*Hank Davis*

Hot Dawg / 1979 / A&M ✦✦✦✦
With Stephane Grappelli and a Django-esque sound. —*Hank Davis*

Early Dawg / 1980 / Sugar Hill ✦✦✦
Bluegrass meets jazz. —*Hank Davis*

Mondo Mando / Jul. 7, 1981-Jul. 16, 1981 / Zebra ✦✦✦✦
A 1981 date that finds Grisman's "dawg music" synthesis at its peak. This had acoustic bluegrass compositions, but the band members ventured into other areas as well. They played with improvisational elan, yet had a loose, relaxed country-folk attitude. —*Ron Wynn*

Mandolin Abstractions / 1983 / Rounder ✦✦✦
Modern mandolin playing in a variety of acoustic settings, it's hot and driving at times, but also melodic and haunting, and occasionally abstract and eerie. This is challenging yet pleasant music with guest Andy Statman. —*Hank Davis*

Home Is Where the Heart Is / 1988 / Rounder ✦✦✦
A more traditional country and bluegrass album than his "dawg" sessions, Rounder issued this Grisman session in 1988. He's playing with J.D. Crowe, Ricky Skaggs, and Doc Watson, among others. There's little jazz here, but there are some superb bluegrass, country, and folk selections, plus marvelous playing. —*Ron Wynn*

Dawganova / 1995 / Acoustic Disc ✦✦✦
On *Dawganova*, Grisman and his quintet add Latin and bossa nova rhythms and melodies to their distinctive blend of bluegrass, folk, and jazz; the results are energetic, and usually quite successful. —*Stephen Thomas Erlewine*

DGQ-20 / Jul. 1996 / AD ✦✦✦

Hot Rize

Progressive Bluegrass, Traditional Bluegrass
The eclectic Colorado progressive-bluegrass band Hot Rize can also play traditional, jazz, and rock; as part of their stage act they become Red Knuckles and the Trail Blazers and, in good fun, parody hardcore '50s country music. The band came together in 1976 and was named after the secret ingredient of Martha White Self-Rising Flour, the product Flatt & Scruggs promoted early in their careers. The band members are Tim O'Brien on lead and harmony vocals, mandolin, and fiddle; Pete Wernick on banjo and harmony vocals; and Charles Sawtelle on bass guitar, guitar, harmonies, and lead vocals. Mike Scap departed in 1976 and was replaced by bass player, guitarist, and vocalist Nick Forster, who also became their emcee. This lineup remained intact until the band broke up in 1992. The band recorded its self-titled debut album for Flying Fish in 1979, which featured a blend of traditional and new material. Their second album, *Radio Boogie*, came out in 1981. A year later, alter egos Red Knuckles and the Trail Blazers recorded their own album, *Hot Rize Presents Red Knuckles and the Trail Blazers.* In 1984, Hot Rize released a terrific bluegrass concert album largely comprised of traditional hits. The band moved to the independent Sugar Hill label in 1985 and released *Traditional Ties*, an album featuring songs written by band members Tim O'Brien, Pete Wernick, and the band's technical assistant, Frank Edmonson. The band released another album in 1987, and in 1991 released another Red Knuckles album, *Shades of the Past.* Their final album, *Take It Home*, came out in 1992; since then O'Brien and Wernick have gone on to pursue solo careers. —*Sandra Brennan*

Hot Rize / 1979 / Flying Fish ✦✦✦✦
Debut album. Very good. Featuring Tim O'Brien and Pete Wernick. —*Chip Renner*

Radio Boogie / 1981 / Flying Fish ✦✦✦✦
No sophomore highjinks on this release. Solid album, highly recommended. —*Chip Renner*

In Concert / 1984 / Flying Fish ✦✦✦
Good live presentation. —*Chip Renner*

● **Untold Stories** / 1989 / Sugar Hill ✦✦✦✦
It all comes together on this CD, Tim O'Brien's swan song. —*Chip Renner*

Jim and Jesse (Jim and Jesse McReynolds)

Traditional Bluegrass
One of the great bluegrass bands in history, brothers Jim (b. 1927) and Jesse (b. 1929) McReynolds and their Virginia Boys remained at the top

The Banjo

With the possible exception of pedal steel guitar, the banjo is that one instrument most identified with country music, especially bluegrass music. Beginning as a four-stringed fretless instrument, the banjo became much more versatile with an added fifth string (the shorter "drone" string). In the South after the Civil War, banjos of many configurations — some with four strings (the tenor and plectrum banjo), others with five strings (since the '20s the country banjo) — were plentiful; in fact, in the '20s the banjo/fiddle combination formed the basis of country music instrumentals.

Uncle Dave Macon, the first real star of the Opry, in the '20s played five-string in the old style, often called frailing, clawhammer, or simply "thumping." In this style, the backs of the fingernails pick out the melody, while the thumb catches the drone string, thus creating a regular beat and rhythm. (Grandpa Jones is no doubt the most famous living player of the frailing banjo.)

Although the banjo didn't die out in the '30s, the many guitar/mandolin duets put it on the back burner for the decade. String bands, precursors to Bob Wills and other Western swing bands of the '40s, used the tenor banjo for volume and rhythm. Meanwhile, a banjo picker from North Carolina, Charlie Poole, had developed his own style of playing, three-finger picking instead of frailing; he was in fact paving the way for another North Carolinian, Earl Scruggs, who may not have invented the banjo but certainly reinvented it. Bill Monroe's Blue Grass Boys, formed in 1939, were without a five-string banjo until 1942, when Dave "Stringbean" Akeman added his frailing style to the band. But it wasn't until 1945, when Earl Scruggs joined the Blue Grass Boys, that what is now known as bluegrass banjo was invented.

It's nearly impossible to overstate the effect of Earl Scruggs on banjo playing. Live audiences gaped and gasped in disbelief when they heard the flood of careful notes that rolled off Earl's fingers. Many banjo pickers who rose to prominence admit to giving up the old style the same night they heard the new "Scruggspicking" style on the Grand Ole Opry. This new sound absolutely dominated, in large part because of Scruggs's signature songs "Foggy Mountain Breakdown" (recorded with Flatt and the Foggy Mountain Boys around 1951 and later the chase music for the movie Bonnie and Clyde) and "The Ballad of Jed Clampett" (on TV's "Beverly Hillbillies"). Further reinforcement came in the form of "Dueling Banjos" in the weirdly memorable version from the 1973 film Deliverance.

Though Earl Scruggs will rightly be remembered as the reinventor of the banjo, other musicians, all beholden to Earl, have taken the instrument in yet different directions: Buck Trent electrified it; Bill Keith invented the chromatic/melodic style; and Bela Fleck adds jazz, classical, and other difficult-to-label influences. — *David Vinopal*

by changing with the times. Starting as a traditional brothers duet, Jim on guitar and Jesse on mandolin showed their versatility by following country's changing tastes, moving to country-folk when necessary to keep a road band going. Whatever style they played (including *Berry Pickin' in the Country*, an album of bluegrass versions of Chuck Berry tunes), they retained a pure country core, due in no small part to Jim's pure, high tenor and Jesse's virtuoso, cross-picking mandolin playing.

Raised in Virginia, Jim and Jesse were born into a musical family. Their grandfather Charles McReynolds was a fiddler who had recorded a single for Victor in 1927 with the Bull Mountain Moonshiners. The brothers learned to play a number of stringed instruments while they were children, occasionally playing local dances and events as teenagers. However, the duo didn't begin playing professionally until they were in their 20s and Jim left the Army—by this point, Jim was playing guitar and Jesse played mandolin. In 1947, they landed a daily 15-minute spot on a local Norton radio station. For the next few years, they played on a variety of Southern radio stations, securing a regular spot on Augusta, Georgia's WGAC in 1949. After staying at the station for a year, they moved to the Midwest, where they played stations in Iowa and Kansas without gaining much of a following. In 1951, they relocated to Middletown, OH, where they had a regular spot at WPFB. While they were at the station they cut ten songs with vocalist Larry Roll under the name the Virginian Trio; the records didn't gain much attention. For the remainder of 1951 and much of 1952, Jim and Jesse played at a variety of radio stations throughout the country. Finally, in 1952, the group secured a major label deal with Capitol Records. However, their career was interrupted when Jesse was drafted into the Army to serve in the Korean War. After he was discharged in 1954, he rejoined Jim, who was still playing the Tennessee Barn Dance in Knoxville, TN. For the rest of the decade, they played radio and television stations across the country—including ones in Alabama, Georgia, and Florida—building up a fan base. During this time, their band, the Virginia Boys, included such musicians as fiddler Vassar Clements and banjoist Bobby Thompson. In 1958, they recorded a handful of sides for Starday Records.

Martha White Mills Flour Company became Jim and Jesse's sponsors in 1959; the duo was the company's second major sponsorship, following Flatt & Scruggs. In 1961, they debuted at the Grand Ole Opry; three years later, they became members of the Opry. Jim and Jesse switched record labels in 1962, signing with Epic Records. The change in labels resulted in success for the duo, as "Cotton Mill Man" became their first charting country single in the summer of 1964. For the next few years, they continued in a straight bluegrass direction, scoring the occasional hit. In the late '60s, Jim and Jesse adopted a more country-oriented direction, which resulted in their biggest hit singles, including the No. 18 "Diesel on My Tail."

In 1970 Jim and Jesse re-signed to Capitol Records, and the first album they released under their new contract featured electric instruments. However, the duo quickly returned to a traditional bluegrass sound, since a bluegrass revival had gripped the attention of many country fans and college students across the United States. For the next two decades, the duo was a staple on the bluegrass festival scene, and they recorded for a variety of independent labels, including CMH, Rounder, and their own Old Dominion and Double J labels. In 1982, they had a minor hit single with "North Wind," which was recorded with Charlie Louvin. —*Stephen Thomas Erlewine & David Vinopal*

☆ **Bluegrass Special** / 1963 / Epic ✦✦✦✦✦
A bluegrass classic, it has many of their most popular songs. —*Richard Lieberson*

Jim and Jesse Saluting the Louvin Brothers / 1969 / Epic ✦✦✦
Here are the best of the duo's recordings with electric country, rather than bluegrass accompaniment. —*Richard Lieberson*

Jim and Jesse Story: 24 Greatest / 1980 / CMH ✦✦✦✦
Featured are remakes of some of their best-known tunes. —*Richard Lieberson*

Music Among Friends / 1991 / Rounder ✦✦✦✦
A celebration of this bluegrass duo's 25 years on the Grand Ole Opry includes guest appearances by Bill Monroe, Emmylou Harris, Porter Wagoner, and others. —*Mark A. Humphrey*

★ **Jim and Jesse: 1952-1955** / 1992 / Bear Family ✦✦✦✦✦
Twenty stunning performances for the Capitol label (their first label) feature hand-in-glove harmonies and Jesse's unique banjo-influenced mandolin. —*Mark A. Humphrey*

Bluegrass and More / Bear Family ✦✦✦✦
Bluegrass & More is a comprehensive multidisc box set that includes all of the material, including alternate takes and unreleased tracks, from Jim & Jesse's prime years for Epic Records in the '50s. There's plenty of fine music on the set, but it is primarily of interest for completists and historians—casual fans should stick with the single-disc *Jim and Jesse: 1952-1955*. —*Thom Owens*

The Johnson Mountain Boys

Traditional Bluegrass
During the 1980s the Johnson Mountain Boys were contemporary masters of traditional bluegrass music who revitalized the genre by remaining faithful to the old styles while keeping the songs fresh and original. The band was founded in the suburbs of Washington, DC, by vocalist/banjoist/guitarist Dudley Connell. The original band consisted of Connell, banjoist Richie Underwood, mandolinist David McLaughlin, fiddler Eddie Stubbs, and Larry Robbins on bass. The personnel changed over the years, but the group's sound remained consistent.

The Johnson Mountain Boys made their recording debut with a single for Copper Creek in late 1978; an EP soon followed and helped build a loyal audience in the Washington, DC, area. They became festival favorites after the release of their self-titled album for Rounder. Their second album, *Walls of Time*, came out in 1982 and featured Connell, McLaughlin, Stubbs, and vocalist/banjoist/mandolinist Tom Adams. This lineup recorded four albums for Rounder during the early '80s. During that time, the band toured America, Canada, and England. In 1988, the Johnson Mountain Boys announced that they planned to retire after a farewell concert in Lucketts, VA. Two years later, the Boys reunited briefly to play two festivals. Eventually, the band became an active per-

forming outfit in the early '90s and the group released a new album, *Blue Diamond*, for Rounder in 1993. —*Sandra Brennan*

☆ **Working Close** / 1983 / Rounder ✦✦✦✦✦
Dudley Connell's chilling, high-lonesome lead vocals were only one of the delights of this militantly traditional, young bluegrass band. Any of their albums are among the best bluegrass of recent decades. —*Mark A. Humphrey*

● **Favorites** / 1987 / Rounder ✦✦✦✦
Favorites features a terrific cross-section of highlights from the Johnson Mountain Boys' early-'80s Rounder albums and is the perfect introduction to their traditionalist bluegrass. —*Thom Owens*

Let the Whole World Talk / 1987 / Rounder ✦✦✦
More great wailin'! —*Mark A. Humphrey*

Requests / 1988 / Rounder ✦✦✦
This is an eclectic album by the short-lived but brilliant quintet. —*Mark A. Humphrey*

At the Old Schoolhouse / 1989 / Rounder ✦✦✦
This is wonderful live and traditional bluegrass from their farewell tour. —*Mark A. Humphrey*

Bill Keith

b. Dec. 20, 1939, Brockton, MA
Banjo / Instrumental, Bluegrass
Bill Keith has had great impact on modern banjo playing, particularly in the direction of "newgrass." He even has a picking style informally named after him.

Born in Brockton, MA, Keith began taking banjo lessons with guitar instructor Phil Cooper. Before that, he had learned to play piano and ukulele. During adolescence he played in a few Dixieland bands, but by the late '50s became interested in folk music after listening to such inspirational artists as Pete Seeger and Earl Scruggs. Using instruction books, the Amherst college student began learning their two different styles. Eventually Keith began developing his own unique style, which has since become known as the melodic (or chromatic) or "Keith" picking style. This distinct technique was born of his desire to play fiddle melodies on his instruments. In 1958 Keith teamed up with fellow Amherst student Jim Rooney and began playing at local coffeehouses and on campus. Eventually they hooked up with promoter Manny Greenhill; with his assistance they founded the Connecticut Folklore Society, which sponsored a series of campus concerts throughout New England.

After graduation and a brief stint in the US Air Force Reserve, Keith began learning to make banjos with Tom Morgan. Later he, Rooney, mandolin player Frank Wakefield, and guitarist Red Allen formed the Kentuckians. In 1963 Greenhill had Earl Scruggs contact Keith and help him lay out the tablature for Scruggs' instructional book *Earl Scruggs and the 5-String Banjo*. Later that year Keith and his former Amherst classmate Dan Bump developed a new kind of tuning peg that was adopted by Scruggs. In the mid-'60s Keith joined Bill Monroe's Blue Grass Boys, where he was listed as Brad Keith. He left the band after only eight months to do more session work and by the year's end had joined Jim Kweskin's Jug Band, where he would stay for four years. After that he played with the Blue Velvet Band. He abandoned the banjo for a while in 1968 to become a pedal steel guitarist. In 1970 Keith moved to Woodstock, NY, and spent a year teamed up with Jonathan Edwards. He then went on to work with Judy Collins. He and longtime cohort Rooney toured together in both the US and in Europe during the '70s and '80s, with Keith developing a particularly large following in France. Back home in Woodstock, Keith began playing banjo for the Woodstock Mountain Review, a rather informal group that has been performing together occasionally since the '70s.

In 1977, Keith worked briefly as a columnist for *Frets* magazine. Later, in 1989, Keith, Rooney, Eric Weissberg, and Kenny Koseck re-formed their old band, calling it the New Blue Velvet Band. When not playing with them, Keith sometimes plays with other bands. —*Sandra Brennan*

● **Something Auld, Something Newgrass, Something Borrowed** / 1976 / Rounder ✦✦✦✦
Catch Tony Rice, David Grisman, Jim Rooney, Tom Grey, Vassar Clements, Ken Kasek, and Al Jones on this album. The bluegrass is top-notch, and Bill Keith struts his stuff. —*Chip Renner*

The Kentucky Colonels

Bluegrass
The progressive bluegrass band the Kentucky Colonels had a short but legendary career during the folk revival of the late '50s and early '60s. The band was formed in the early '50s by brothers Roland and Clarence White, who were born in Lewiston, ME, and raised in Los Angeles. The band originally contained the two brothers, another brother, Eric, and sister Joann and played country music, but they changed to bluegrass in 1954. When Joann dropped out, the three brothers began billing themselves as the Three Little Country Boys and appeared on local television

after winning first prize in a talent contest. In 1958 Arkansas native Billy Ray Lathum became their banjo player, and dobro player Le Roy Mack joined the band the next year. Lathum's arrival allowed Roland White to switch to mandolin, his instrument of choice.

As the Country Boys, the group recorded their first single, "I'm Head over Heels in Love with You," for Sundown. They began appearing on "Town Hall Party" and "Hometown Jamboree" and recording on Gene Autry's label. Bassist and banjoist Roger Bush joined the band in 1961 after Eric White dropped out to marry. The Boys then recorded *Songs, Themes and Laughs from the Andy Griffith Show* for Capitol. Before the year was out, Roland White was drafted and left the band for two years, leaving the band without a mandolinist. The group cut its first album on Briar, which disliked the band's moniker and suggested a series of names, the best of which was the Kentucky Colonels.

In 1963 fiddler Bobby Sloane joined the Colonels and Roland returned. By this time, the Colonels had begun to gather a following through their US tours, and they appeared at both the UCLA and Newport Folk Festivals in 1964. The band recorded several albums on the World Pacific label and appeared in the movie *The Farmer's Other Daughter*. The band really took off musically when fiddler Scott Stoneman replaced Sloane, but it broke up in 1965. —*Sandra Brennan*

★ **Long Journey Home** / 1964 / Vanguard ✦✦✦✦✦
These great recordings from a 1964 live performance at the Newport Folk Festival feature Clarence White and many others, including duets with Doc Watson. —*Richard Lieberson & Mark A. Humphrey*

☆ **Appalachian Swing!** / 1964 / Rounder ✦✦✦✦✦
With bluegrass guitarist Clarence White. —*Richard Lieberson*

Alison Krauss

Fiddle / Progressive Bluegrass, Traditional Bluegrass
Alison Krauss helped bring bluegrass to a new audience in the '90s. Blending bluegrass with folk, Krauss was instantly acclaimed from the start of her career, but it wasn't until her platinum-selling 1995 compilation, *Now That I've Found You*, that she became a mainstream star. Between her 1987 debut *Too Late to Cry* and *Now That I've Found You*, she matured from a child prodigy to a versatile, ambitious, and diverse musician and, in the process, made some of the freshest bluegrass of the late '80s and early '90s.

When she was five years old, Krauss began taking classical violin lessons. She soon tired of the regimen of classical playing and began performing country and bluegrass licks. At the age of eight she began entering talent contests in and around her native Champaign, IL. Two years later she had her own band. In 1983, when she was 12, she won the Illinois State Fiddle Championship, and the Society for the Preservation of Bluegrass in America named her the Most Promising Fiddler in the Midwest. In 1985, Krauss made her recording debut on an album, playing on a record made by her brother Viktor, Jim Hoiles, and Bruce Weiss. The album was called *Different Strokes* and appeared on the independent Fiddle Tunes label. Later that year she signed with Rounder Records. She was 14 years old at the time.

Too Late to Cry, Alison's debut album, appeared in 1987 to very positive reviews. The album was recorded with Krauss' backup band, Union Station, which featured guitarist Jeff White, banjoist Alison Brown, and bassist Viktor Krauss; the next year the group won the Society for the Preservation of Bluegrass in America's National Band Championship contest. In 1989 Krauss and Union Station released *Two Highways*, which was nominated for the Grammy Award for Best Bluegrass Recording. Although the album didn't win the award, her next album, 1990's *I've Got That Old Feeling*, did. The success of *I've Got That Old Feeling* was unprecedented for bluegrass acts in the '80s, and it laid the groundwork for Krauss' breakthrough in the '90s. By this time, the Union Station's lineup had more or less settled—it now featured mandolinist Adam Steffey, banjoist/guitarist Ron Block, bassist Barry Bales, and guitarist Tim Stafford; Stafford later left the group and was replaced by Dan Tyminski.

In 1992 Alison Krauss and Union Station released *Every Time You Say Goodbye*, which featured a typically eclectic array of material—everything from "Orange Blossom Special" to the Beatles' "I Will" and Shawn Colvin's "I Don't Know Why." The album appeared in the country charts, and Krauss' videos were shown on Country Music Television. *I Know Who Holds Tomorrow* was released in 1994 and was even more successful. But it was the 1995 compilation *Now That I've Found You: A Collection* that made Krauss a star. The album reached No. 2 on the country charts and—even more remarkably—went into the pop Top Ten and sold over a million copies. Its success confirmed her status as bluegrass' leading light in the '90s. —*Stephen Thomas Erlewine*

Too Late to Cry / 1987 / Rounder ✦✦✦
Alison Krauss may have recorded *Too Late to Cry* when she was only 14 years old, but her sound was already well developed and astonishingly accomplished. Throughout the album, she demonstrates a mastery of bluegrass, singing and playing with a distinctive grace. It's an impressive

debut, but it would pale in comparison to the albums that followed. —*Thom Owens*

Two Highways / 1989 / Rounder ✦✦✦
Earlier recordings of a fine young singer and fiddler, this time with Union Station. —*Mark A. Humphrey*

I've Got That Old Feeling / 1990 / Rounder ✦✦✦✦
There's a sweet voice, fine fiddling, and a tight plaintive band on this breakthrough bluegrass/country/pop album that produced the first music video for bluegrass. —*Mark A. Humphrey*

Every Time You Say Goodbye / 1992 / Rounder ✦✦✦✦
On *Every Time You Say Goodbye*, Alison Krauss continued to expand the boundaries of bluegrass without ever abandoning its roots. Krauss combines contemporary folk covers (such as Shawn Colvin's "I Don't Know Why") with more traditional material, interpreting both in fresh, inventive ways. She plays and sings beautifully throughout the album, proving that she is the most progressive, exciting bluegrass musician of the '90s. —*Thom Owens*

I Know Who Holds Tomorrow / 1994 / Rounder ✦✦✦
I Know Who Holds Tomorrow isn't as consistently engaging as *Every Time You Say Goodbye*, but that's only a relative term—from any other artist, this would be a masterpiece. From Krauss, it's another reliably wonderful collection of jaw-dropping fiddling and breathtaking singing. —*Thom Owens*

★ **Now That I've Found You: A Collection** / Feb. 7, 1995 / Rounder ✦✦✦✦✦
Alison Krauss had been recording a decade before she gained stardom, but when she did, she became a star in a big way. *Now That I've Found You: A Collection*, a retrospective of her ten-year recording career for Rounder, became the surprise hit of 1995, rocketing to No. 2 on the country charts and into the Top Ten on the *pop* charts, which is remarkable for a musician who had never captured the attention of a mass audience. It may have been a surprising success, but it also was deserved. Krauss was arguably the leading bluegrass musician of the late '80s and early '90s, pushing the music into new directions without losing sight of its roots. *Now That I've Found You* does a splendid job of chronicling her career, hitting all of the highlights and making a new listener eager to seek out her albums. —*Stephen Thomas Erlewine*

Doyle Lawson and Quicksilver

Traditional Bluegrass, Cowboy
Doyle Lawson is considered one of the premier bluegrass mandolin players by his peers; his bluegrass-gospel band Quicksilver is equally respected. Lawson was born in Kingsport, TN, and became interested in bluegrass when he was five. During his youth, Lawson listened to such greats as the Stanley Brothers, Flatt and Scruggs, and Bill Monroe. It was the latter who inspired young Lawson to learn the mandolin. He borrowed his first one at age 11 from a member of his father's gospel quartet; Lawson eventually taught himself the five-string banjo and guitar as well. Neighbor Jimmy Martin became a mentor to Lawson, who was also influenced by Red Rector, Paul Williams, Frank Wakefield, and Bobby Osborn. In 1963 Lawson began playing banjo with Martin's Sunny Mountain Boys. Seven months later, he moved to Louisville to play with different groups. He became a part-time guitarist with J.D. Crowe in 1966 and eventually joined his Kentucky Mountain Boys as a mandolin player. Lawson made his recording debut with Red Allen and bassist Bobby Slone on *Bluegrass Holiday* and subsequently recorded two albums with Crowe.

In 1971, Lawson joined the Country Gentlemen and toured Japan with them the following year. He remained with the band for several years and recorded ten albums with them. Lawson recorded an album of mandolin instrumentals, *Tennessee Dream*, in 1977; the album also featured Jerry Douglas, J.D. Crowe, and Kenny Baker. In 1979, Lawson put his band Quicksilver together with banjo player Terry Baucom, guitarist Jimmy Haley, and electric-bass player Lou Reid. In 1980, Quicksilver released its self-titled debut album and followed it up with *Rock My Soul*. In 1981 *Quicksilver Rides Again*, featuring Jerry Douglas, Mike Auldridge, and Sam Bush, came out. They also released a successful gospel album, *Heavenly Treasures*, which proved an even bigger seller. Quicksilver's next album finally appeared in 1985 and featured both bluegrass and gospel tunes. In 1986, an entirely new band behind Lawson recorded *Beyond the Shadows;* the new players were Scott Vestal on banjo, Curtis Vestal on electric bass (shortly replaced by Ray Deaton), and Russell Moore on guitar. In 1987, Lawson and the band released an a cappella gospel album, *Heaven's Joy Awaits*. Between 1987 and 1991, Lawson and Quicksilver, which continually changed personnel, released seven albums. —*Sandra Brennan*

● **Rock My Soul** / 1981 / Sugar Hill ✦✦✦✦
Not a flaw on the album. —*Chip Renner*

The Gospel Collection 1 / 1990 / Sugar Hill ✦✦✦✦
The best way to have their gospel music is with this collection. Highly recommended. —*Chip Renner*

My Heart Is Yours / 1990 / Sugar Hill ✦✦✦✦
As good as *Rock My Soul*. First-class bluegrass. —*Chip Renner*

Never Walk Away / 1995 / Sugar Hill ✦✦✦
This album is crystal clear from the first notes of the Buck Owens tune "Rosie Jones" to the end of "Ancient History." It is a tight ensemble album where the instrumental playing is all the more impressive for being excellent but not showy. Strong songs include "Jealous," "In the Gravel Yard," and "Your Crazy Heart." There's nothing groundbreaking here, just a solid rootsy bluegrass band album, and that's not bad. —*Richard Meyer*

There's a Light Guiding Me / Feb. 20, 1996 / Sugar Hill ✦✦✦✦
Doyle Lawson and Quicksilver are among bluegrass music's most heavenly harmonizers, as they prove once again in the timeless music featured in *There's a Light Guiding Me*. Largely a cappella, and completely focused on spirituals, these songs will fill the soul with warmth. No matter what one believes, this music—just like that of spiritual singers from Tibet, Hungary, Pakistan, or Cambodia—strikes a resonant chord deep within. —*Michael McCall*

The Lilly Brothers

Traditional Bluegrass
The Lilly Brothers, Everett and B., played old-time/bluegrass music together for more than three decades. They may be best remembered in New England, where they were nearly a fixture in the downtown Boston music scene, most notably at the Hillbilly Ranch from the early '60s through 1980.

Charles Everett and Michel Burt Lilly were born three years apart (B. is the eldest) in Clear Creek, WV. Everett plays the mandolin, banjo, and fiddle while B. plays guitar; both brothers sing. Early influences include the Delmore Brothers, the Callahan Bros., and the Monroes. The Lillys debuted in 1938 singing old-time country on a West Virginia radio station. They initially billed themselves as the Lonesome Holler Boys. Later they added a banjo and became a bluegrass group. In 1939 they began performing regularly at the newly established WKLS in Beckley. After that they spent a few years at various Southern stations playing in such groups as the Smiling Mountain Boys and Red Belcher's Kentucky Ridge Runners. They made their recording debut in 1948 while working with the latter group at WWVA. They remained at the station through 1950, whereupon they returned home after a heated fight with Belcher over money. From there the Lillys split up for a time, with Everett becoming a mandolin player and tenor with Flatt and Scruggs' Foggy Mountain Boys. Everett remained with them through early 1952, when he left to join his brother, fiddler Tex Logan, and exceptional banjo picker Don Stove in Boston. They got their first job playing on WCOP's "Hayloft Jamboree "and from there hit the local club circuit.

The Lilly Brothers recorded fairly frequently on different labels, including Event, Prestige International, and Folkways during the 1950s. Between 1958 and 1959, Everett spent another year with Flatt and Scruggs while Don Stover did a bit of touring with other bands. But for that, the Lilly Brothers remained intact through 1970. In addition to playing downtown Boston, they played the local festival circuit and were instrumental in the development of urban bluegrass. In the early '70s, Everett's son was killed in a car crash, causing him and his wife Joann to leave Beantown and return to West Virginia. B. Lilly came down a while later to help Everett host a local television show, but eventually returned to the city. After 1971 Everett would join the band and perform at festivals during the summers and occasionally recorded with them. The Lilly Brothers' career was chronicled in the 1979 documentary *True Facts in a Country Song*, which was first shown at the West Virginia State Culture Center. —*Sandra Brennan*

Bluegrass Breakdown / 1963 / Rounder ✦✦✦
Great 1964 performances. —*Mark A. Humphrey*

★ **Early Recordings** / 1971 / Rebel ✦✦✦✦✦
These driving, late-'50s performances have breathtaking banjo from Don Stover and hand-in-glove vocal harmonies. It is one of the best bluegrass albums ever. —*Mark A. Humphrey*

Jimmy Martin (James Henry Martin)

b. 1927, Sneedville, TN
Guitar, Vocals / Traditional Bluegrass, Bluegrass
Blessed with a great tenor voice, this traditional bluegrass singer and guitarist mastered his craft as lead vocalist for Bill Monroe's Blue Grass Boys for much of 1949-1951 and again in 1952-1953. Martin's vocals and his dynamic guitar playing complemented Monroe perfectly, and in the opinion of many, Martin was the finest lead singer and guitarist Bill Monroe ever had. In 1951, between stints with Monroe's band, Martin joined the Osborne Brothers, forming the Sunny Mountain Boys. Though this association lasted only until 1955, Martin has used this band

name up to the present. In keeping up such high standards over the years, Martin has hired numerous major-league musicians, including banjo players J.D. Crowe, Bill Emerson, Vic Jordan, and Alan Munde, and mandolin player Paul Williams, all of whom subsequently made it big in bluegrass. Jimmy Martin is required listening for anyone with more than a passing interest in bluegrass.

Jimmy Martin was born and raised in the Cumberland Mountains of East Tennessee. As a teenager, he fell in love with Bill Monroe's music, which inspired him to pursue a career as a singer. He began working at radio stations around Morristown, TN, to gain experience; he also worked as a housepainter to make ends meet. At the age of 22 he auditioned in Nashville for Monroe's band to replace Mac Wiseman and he successfully passed the audition. For the next four years, Martin stayed with Monroe, recording 46 sides for Decca Records. In 1951, Martin briefly sang with Bob Osborne, which was captured on a series of singles for King Records. At the same time he was a member of the Monroe side project, the Shenandoah Valley Trio, which cut several songs for Columbia.

Martin split from Monroe for good in 1954, joining Bobby and Sonny Osborne's duo as a lead singer. He stayed with the Osbornes for about a year, recording several sessions for RCA-Victor. Martin left the brothers the next year, taking the band name Sunny Mountain Boys—which had previously been used by the Osborne Brothers—with him. In the spring of 1956, Martin signed with Decca Records and made his first solo recordings. Through his solo records and performances on the Grand Ole Opry and the Louisiana Hayride, Martin helped bring bluegrass into the mainstream. This was primarily because he concentrated on bluegrass that focused on the vocals, not the instruments. Within two years, he began charting in the country Top 40, beginning with the No.14 single "Rock Hearts." Throughout the '60s, he had the occasional hit single and became a staple of the bluegrass festival circuit.

Over the years, Martin's Sunny Mountain Boys hosted a wealth of new musical talents, including Doyle Lawson, Bill Emerson, Clarence "Tater" Tate, Paul Williams, Alan Munde, and J.D. Crowe. Although the lineup of the band changed constantly, the quality of the musicians remained high throughout his career.

In 1971, Jimmy Martin sang "I Saw the Light" and "Sunny Side of the Mountain" on the Nitty Gritty Dirt Band's *Will the Circle Be Unbroken*, which helped increase his audience. Martin parted from Decca Records in 1974, signing with Starday/Gusto Records shortly after his departure. He stayed at Gusto for nearly a decade, releasing six albums during his tenure at the label. After Gusto went out of business in the '80s, Martin began his own record label, King of Bluegrass, which reissued his classic Decca recordings. Martin continued to perform concerts and bluegrass festivals into the '90s. —*Stephen Thomas Erlewine & David Vinopal*

★ **You Don't Know My Mind (1956-1966)** / 1990 / Rounder ✦✦✦✦✦
This is a Monroe band veteran with astonishing high pipes and a penchant for blending bluegrass and honky tonk. These are great bands, great songs, and classic 1956-1966 Decca sides. —*Mark A. Humphrey*

Jimmy Martin and the Sunny Mountain Boys / 1994 / Bear Family ✦✦✦✦
The six-disc set *Jimmy Martin & the Sunny Mountain Boys* contains all of the classic recordings the group made for Decca Records in the late '50s and '60s. For the collector, it's an ideal investment, but most fans will find that the set is simply too exhaustive for their tastes. —*Thom Owens*

The McCoury Brothers

Traditional Bluegrass
Del and Jerry McCoury pursued individual careers in bluegrass before the Pennsylvania-born siblings teamed up for the 1987 Rounder album, *The McCoury Brothers*. Older brother Del had played banjo before switching to guitar and singing lead with Bill Monroe's Blue Grass Boys in 1963-1964. He subsequently led his Dixie Pals and recorded for both Rounder and Rebel. Jerry sang and played bass with Red Allen and the Kentuckians, as well as with Don Reno and Bill Harrell. The McCoury Brothers' sole album together to date is a wonderful close-harmony exposition of bluegrass, rooted in the "brother duo" tradition. —*Mark A. Humphrey*

The McCoury Brothers / 1987 / Rounder ✦✦✦✦
Jerry and Del McCoury fit together like hand-in-glove on these fine performances. —*Mark A. Humphrey*

Del McCoury

b. Feb. 1, 1930
Guitar, Vocals / Traditional Bluegrass
For more than three decades Del McCoury's voice has been the epitome of the "high lonesome sound." Among the most distinguished practitioners of traditional bluegrass, McCoury has won almost every award given by the International Bluegrass Music Association. McCoury (born Delano Floyd McCoury) was raised in Bakersville, NC. In 1941 he and

his family moved to Glen Rock, PA, where he got his start as a five-string banjo picker with Keith Daniels and the Blue Ridge Ramblers as a teen. Later he played with Jack Cooke's Virginia Mountain Boys in Baltimore. McCoury got his first big break in 1963, when Bill Monroe hired the Virginia Mountain Boys to play a few New York gigs. Monroe was impressed by the young banjo player and invited him to join his Blue Grass Boys. Shortly after accepting Monroe's offer, McCoury became the group's lead vocalist and took up rhythm guitar. In early 1964 he recorded a single with Monroe and a month later returned home to marry.

After his marriage, McCoury and fiddler Billy Baker spent three months in California playing with the Golden State Boys. Upon his return back east, McCoury began playing and recording with the Shady Valley Boys. McCoury left the group in 1967 and founded the Dixie Pals with Bill Emerson, Wayne Yates, and Billy Baker. McCoury and his Dixie Pals, which underwent several membership changes, played together for more than 20 years and recorded on Rounder, Revonah, Leather, and Rebel. McCoury began calling the group the Del McCoury Band in 1987.

Featuring his sons Ronnie on mandolin and Robbie on banjo along with fiddler Tad Marks and bass player Mike Brantley, the Del McCoury Band's popularity soared when Lance LeRoy, Lester Flatt's ex-manager, began to manage them. As of 1996, the lineup for the band included McCoury and sons along with fiddler Jason Carter and bassist Mike Bub. —*Sandra Brennan*

Live in Japan / 1980 / Copper Creek ✦✦✦
A live concert with excellent performances and strong material, the recording nevertheless leaves something to be desired. —*Brian Mansfield*

Don't Stop the Music / 1988 / Rounder ✦✦✦✦
The title track is a George Jones song. The album includes diverse and often bluesy material and fine performances. —*Mark A. Humphrey*

★ **Classic Bluegrass** / 1991 / Rebel ✦✦✦✦✦
Rebel label recordings from the '70s by the man who sometimes sounds more like Bill Monroe than Monroe himself. Stunning, pure, high-lonesome pipes and mountain bluesy songs. Beautiful. —*Mark A. Humphrey*

Blue Side of Town / May 15, 1992 / Rounder ✦✦✦✦
Named for his version of the Patty Loveless hit "The Blue Side of Town," McCoury covers Steve Earle's "If You Need a Fool" and Arthur "Big Boy" Crudup's "That's Alright Mama." When it comes to song choice, he may be the most well-rounded man in bluegrass. —*Brian Mansfield*

☆ **Deeper Shade of Blue** / 1993 / Rounder ✦✦✦✦✦
A classic from the word go, McCoury's love affair with blues is never more explicit than here, where songs with titles like "Cheek to Cheek with the Blues," "A Deeper Shade of Blue," and "The Bluest Man in Town" are the order of the day. Never a purist when it comes to songs, McCoury covers Kevin Welch's "True Love Never Dies," Willie Nelson's "Man with the Blues," and the Jerry Lee Lewis hit "What Made Milwaukee Famous." His version of Lefty Frizzell's "If You've Got the Money Honey" is downright piercing. —*Brian Mansfield*

Bill Monroe
(William Smith Monroe, Father of Bluegrass Music)

b. Sep. 13, 1911, Rosine, KY, d. Sep. 9, 1996, Springfield, TN
Fiddle, Guitar, Mandolin, Vocals / Traditional Bluegrass, Bluegrass
Bill Monroe was the father of bluegrass. He invented the style, invented the name and, for the great majority of the 20th century, embodied the art form. Beginning with his Blue Grass Boys in the '40s, Monroe defined a hard-edged style of country that emphasized instrumental virtuosity, close vocal harmonies, and a fast, driving tempo. The musical genre took its name from the Blue Grass Boys, and Monroe's music has forever defined the sound of classical bluegrass—a five-piece acoustic string band, playing precisely and rapidly, switching solos, and singing in a plaintive, high lonesome voice. Not only did he invent the very sound of the music, Bill Monroe was the mentor for several generations of musicians. Over the years, Monroe's band hosted all of the major bluegrass artists of the '50s and '60s, including Flatt and Scruggs, Reno and Smiley, Vassar Clements, Carter Stanley, and Mac Wiseman. Though the lineup of the Blue Grass Boys changed over the years, Monroe always remained devoted to bluegrass in its purest form.

Monroe was born into a musical family. His father had been known around their hometown of Rosine, KY, as a step-dancer, while his mother played a variety of instruments and sang. His uncle, Pendelton Vanderver, was a locally renowned fiddler. Both of his older brothers, Harry and Birch, played fiddle, while his brother Charlie and sister Bertha played guitar. Bill himself became involved with music as a child, learning the mandolin at the age of ten. After the death of his parents while he was a pre-adolescent, Bill Monroe went to live with his Uncle Pen. Soon Bill was playing guitar in his uncle's band at local dances. During this time, Monroe met a local blues guitarist called Arnold Shultz, who became a major influence on the budding musician. When Bill Monroe turned 18,

he moved to East Chicago, IN, where his brothers Birch and Charlie were working at an oil refinery. Bill also got a job at the Sinclair oil refinery and began playing with his brothers in a country string band at night. Within a few years they performed on the "Barn Dance" on WLS Chicago, which led to the brothers' appearance in a square dance revue called the "WLS Jamboree" in 1932. The Monroes continued to perform at night, but Birch left the band in 1934. Ironically, it was just before the group landed a sponsorship of the Texas Crystals Company, who made laxatives. Charlie and Bill decided to continue performing as the Monroe Brothers.

The Monroe Brothers began playing in other states, including radio shows in Nebraska, Iowa, and both North and South Carolina. Such exposure led to record label interest, but the Monroe Brothers were initially reluctant to sign a recording contract. After some persuasion, they inked a deal with RCA-Victor's Bluebird division and recorded their first session in February 1936. One of the songs from the sessions, "What Would You Give in Exchange," became a minor hit, and the duo recorded another 60 tracks for Bluebird over the next two years.

In the beginning of 1938, Bill and Charlie parted ways, with Charlie forming the Kentucky Pardners. Bill assembled his own band with the intention of creating a new form of country that melded old-time string bands with blues and challenged the instrumental abilities of the musicians. He moved to Little Rock, where he formed the Kentuckians, but that band was short-lived. He then relocated to Atlanta, where he formed the Blue Grass Boys and began appearing on the "Crossroad Rollies" radio program. Monroe debuted on the Grand Ole Opry in October 1939, singing "New Muleskinner Blues." It was a performance that made Monroe's career, as well as establishing the new genre of bluegrass.

In the early '40s Monroe and the Blue Grass Boys spent some time developing their style, often sounding similar to other contemporary string bands. The most notable element of the band's sound was Monroe's high, piercing tenor voice and his driving mandolin. The Blue Grass Boys toured with the Grand Ole Opry's road shows and appeared weekly on the radio. Between 1940 and 1941, Monroe cut a number of songs for RCA-Victor, but wartime restrictions prevented him from recording for several years. The classic lineup of the Blue Grass Boys fell into place in 1944, when guitarist/vocalist Lester Flatt and banjoist Earl Scruggs joined a lineup that already included Monroe, fiddler Chubby Wise, and bassist Howard Watts. This is the group that supported Monroe when he returned to the studio in 1945, recording a number of songs for Columbia. Early in 1946 he had his first charting hit with "Kentucky Waltz," which climbed to No. 3; it was followed by the No. 5 hit "Footprints in the Snow."

Throughout 1946 the Blue Grass Boys were one of the most popular acts in country music, scoring hits and touring to large crowds across America. At each town the band would perform beneath a large circus tent they set up themselves; the tent would host a variety of other attractions, including Monroe's baseball team, which would play local teams before the concert began. During the late '40s, the Blue Grass Boys remained a popular act, landing five additional Top 20 singles. Numerous other acts began imitating Monroe's sound, most notably the Stanley Brothers.

Flatt and Scruggs left the Blue Grass Boys in 1948 to form their own band. Their departure ushered in an era of stagnation for Bill Monroe. Monroe left Columbia Records in 1949 because they had signed the Stanley Brothers, who he felt were simply imitating his style. The next year he signed with Decca Records, who tried to persuade Monroe to attempt some mainstream-oriented productions. He went as far as cutting a few songs with an electric guitar, but he soon returned to his pure bluegrass sound. At these sessions he did meet Jimmy Martin, who became his supporting vocalist in the early '50s. Throughout the '50s—indeed, throughout the rest of his career—Monroe toured relentlessly, performing hundreds of shows a year. In 1951 Monroe opened a country music park at Bean Blossom, IN; the venue featured performances from a number of bluegrass acts. Monroe suffered a serious car accident in January 1953, which sidelined his career for several months. The next year Elvis Presley performed Monroe's "Blue Moon of Kentucky" at his one and only Grand Ole Opry appearance, radically reworking the arrangement; Presley apologized for his adaptation, but Monroe would later perform the same arrangement at his concerts.

Bill Monroe released his first album, *Knee Deep in Bluegrass*, in 1958, the same year he appeared on the country singles chart with "Scotland"; the No. 27 single was his first hit in more than a decade. However, by the late '50s his stardom was eclipsed by Flatt and Scruggs. Monroe was not helped by his legendary stubbornness. Numerous musicians passed through his band because of his temperament and his quest for detail. He rarely granted press interviews, and he would rarely perform on television; he even canceled a concert at Carnegie Hall because he believed the promoter, Alan Lomax, was a communist. In the '60s Monroe received a great career boost from the folk music revival, which made him popular with a new generation of listeners. Thanks to his new manager, ex-Greenbriar Boys member Ralph Rinzler, Monroe played bluegrass festivals across the US, frequently on college campuses. In 1967 he founded his own bluegrass festival, the Bill Monroe Bean Blossom Festival, at his country music park, which continued to run into the '90s.

In 1970 he was inducted into the Country Music Hall of Fame and the next year, into the Nashville Songwriters Association International Hall of Fame. Throughout the '70s he toured constantly. In 1981, Monroe was diagnosed with cancer and underwent successful treatment. After his recovery, he resumed his busy touring schedule, which he kept into the '90s. In 1991 he had a double coronary bypass, but he quickly recovered and continued performing and hosting weekly at the Grand Ole Opry. In 1993 the Grammies gave Monroe a Lifetime Achievement Award. —*Stephen Thomas Erlewine*

Live at the Opry: Celebrating 50 Years on the Grand Ole Opry / 1989 / MCA ✦✦✦
Recorded live in 1989, Monroe has by this time turned over a majority of lead vocal turns to guitarist Tom Ewing. But the music proves how vibrant and aggressive Monroe's mandolin skills remain. It also features one fantastic cut from a 1948 Opry date. —*Michael McCall*

Columbia Historic Edition / 1989 / CBS ✦✦✦✦
Columbia Historic Edition has a nice selection of ten songs that Bill Monroe cut for Columbia in the early '40s, including "Kentucky Waltz," "Blue Yodel No. 4 (California Blues)," and "Bluegrass Special." Several hits are missing and there are several compilations released in the '90s that cover the same ground more thoroughly, but this record remains an enjoyable listen. —*Thom Owens*

☆ **Bluegrass 1950-1958** / 1990 / Bear Family ✦✦✦✦✦
This superb four-CD box set from Bear Family (import) offers the most comprehensive collection of Bill Monroe ever assembled. The liner notes are beautifully done—pictures, discography, the works. A second box covering the period from 1959 on is also available. —*Michael Erlewine*

Cryin' Holy unto the Lord / 1991 / MCA ✦✦✦✦
An all-gospel album propped up with some stellar guests, it includes Ricky Skaggs, Ralph Stanley, the Osborne Brothers, Jim & Jesse McReynolds, and Mac Wiseman. —*Michael McCall*

Mule Skinner Blues / 1991 / RCA ✦✦✦
On these 1940-41 recordings of the earliest and loosest bluegrass band, Monroe is wearing his blues, old-time, and even swing influences on his sleeve. —*Mark A. Humphrey*

★ **Country Music Hall of Fame** / 1991 / MCA ✦✦✦✦✦
This is a brilliant overview of one of the great originators and synthesists of 20th-century music on these 16 selections from 1950-1988. This is classic music with a consistent vision and varied accompanists. —*Mark A. Humphrey*

☆ **Bluegrass 1959-1969** / 1991 / Bear Family ✦✦✦✦✦
This, the companion set to the above, comprises over 100 tracks on four CDs, including such hits as "The Long Black Veil," "Midnight on the Stormy Deep," "Big River," "Dusty Miller," and many other Monroe favorites, and also several recordings released here for the first time. —*AMG*

☆ **The Essential Bill Monroe (1945-1949)** / 1992 / Columbia/Legacy ✦✦✦✦✦
A two-disc set of all the "classic" Blue Grass Boys material (the band with Flatt and Scruggs), this is the music that defined bluegrass. —*Mark A. Humphrey*

Live Recordings 1956-1959 / 1993 / Smithsonian/Folkways ✦✦✦
The 27 numbers presented here offer Monroe in more intimate settings, including workshops, jam sessions, and live performances where he's casually swapping yarns, offering anecdotes, and displaying the blistering, yet folksy and down-home style that's made him a musical legend. His group included a number of marvelous players and future stars, such as Del McCoury, Peter Rowan, Bill Keith, and Tex Logan. Monroe was also playing with brothers Charlie and Birch. This is 75 minutes of breakdowns, folk tunes, railroad and work songs, such classics as "Blue Grass Stomp" and "Blue Moon of Kentucky," and many others performed in a loose, next-door neighbor atmosphere. —*Ron Wynn*

Live Duet Recordings 1963-1980 / 1993 / Smithsonian/Folkways ✦✦✦
Live Duet Recordings 1963-1980 contains a good cross-section of live performances from a variety of different settings and years. What's remarkable is how consistent the quality of the disc is—no matter where he is or whom he's playing with, Bill Monroe sounds energetic and lively. —*Thom Owens*

☆ **The Music of Bill Monroe** / 1994 / MCA ✦✦✦✦
A four-disc set covering his entire career from 1936 to 1994, this is a meticulously remastered and researched four hours and 20 minutes of music and features important recordings from seven decades of recordings for RCA, Columbia, Decca, and MCA. It's an exceptional box set, put together with great care and knowledge, and it's essential for any fan of bluegrass or traditional country music. —*Michael McCall*

☆ **16 Gems** / 1996 / Columbia/Legacy ✦✦✦✦✦
Sony's decision to use 16 alternate takes for the double-CD *Essential* collection was disagreeable to some completists. That omission is rectified by *16 Gems*, which makes all 16 of the official versions of those tunes available on CD, and creates a useful adjunct to the *Essential* set for collectors. On its own merits, it's hardly dismissable, with an appeal not limited to Monroe obsessives. Spanning 1945-49, it includes such notable cuts as "Kentucky Waltz" and "Blue Grass Special." —*Richie Unterberger*

The Nashville Bluegrass Band

Progressive Bluegrass, Traditional Bluegrass
The Nashville Bluegrass Band is made up of several excellent musicians who are more interested in preserving their group sound than showing off their individual expertise. The band favors a traditional, earthy sound that has led some critics to call them the band that "put the blues back in bluegrass." But while favoring a traditional sound, they often play more contemporary tunes. The Nashville Bluegrass Band was founded by guitarist Pat Enright, banjo picker Alan O'Bryant, mandolin player Mike Compton, and acoustic bassist Mark Hembree. North Carolina native O'Bryant came to Nashville in the mid-'70s, where he did session work with such artists as Bill Monroe, Doc Watson, and John Starling. O'Bryant is also a songwriter whose tunes have been recorded by several major artists, including "Those Memories of You." An Indiana native, Enright began playing with the popular bluegrass band Phantoms of the Opry while living in San Francisco in the early 1970s. He too went to Nashville in 1974 and there met O'Bryant, and they teamed up and were soon playing clubs. In 1978, Enright moved to Boston and joined Tasty Licks. The following year he returned to Music City and recorded with the Dreadful Snakes and Bela Fleck. Compton hails from Mississippi and moved to Nashville in 1976, where he teamed up with banjo picker Hubert Davis. Compton's style is influenced by Bill Monroe and blues player Robert Johnson. He, O'Bryant, and Enright began playing clubs together. Hembree comes from Wisconsin and first gained experience with the Monroe Doctrine, whom he joined in 1977. He came to Nashville in 1979 to work with Bill Monroe, spending five years as a Blue Grass Boy. He met Compton as he and the Dreadful Snakes were recording *Snakes Alive*.

The Nashville Bluegrass Band came together in 1985 and released *My Native Home*, which featured fiddle player Blaine Sprouse, for Rounder. Bela Fleck produced the album. Before the year's end, fiddler Stuart Duncan, a session player and sideman from California who had just moved to Nashville, joined the band. In 1986, NBB became the first bluegrass group to tour China. The following year they released another Fleck-produced album for Rounder, *Idle Time*, and before the end of 1987 released a bluegrass-gospel album, *To Be His Child*. In 1988, they toured the Middle East and Bangladesh for the Arts America program. Later that year, they were involved in a terrible bus accident near Roanoke, VA; Mark Hembree was so badly hurt that he had to leave the band. Mark Compton, whose mandolin was broken in the accident, soon left the group, as well. They were eventually replaced by bassist Gene Libbea and mandolin player Roland White. The Nashville Bluegrass Band toured Western Europe in 1990 and also released *The Boys Are Back in Town* on Sugar Hill. Two more albums followed, including the excellent, Grammy-winning *Waiting for the Hard Time to Go* (1993). —*Sandra Brennan*

My Native Home / 1985 / Rounder ✦✦✦✦
A flawless album. One of their best. —*Chip Renner*

Idletime / 1987 / Rounder ✦✦✦
This hits on all cylinders with 12 tight songs. Has the classic "The Train Carryin' Jimmie Rodgers Home." —*Chip Renner*

To Be His Child / 1987 / Rounder ✦✦✦✦
A gospel album. Good. —*Chip Renner*

The Boys Are Back in Town / 1990 / Sugar Hill ✦✦✦✦
Very well performed, highly recommended. These vocals are on the mark. Produced by Jerry Douglas. —*Chip Renner*

● **Waitin' for the Hard Times to Go** / 1993 / Sugar Hill ✦✦✦✦

Unleashed / Oct. 1995 / Sugar Hill ✦✦✦
The new CD from the all-star Nashville Bluegrass Band is a jaunty, highly musical collection of contemporary tunes with a few traditional numbers thrown in for good measure. The bluegrass and light gospel singing is very agreeable, unforced and as always with this band, it seems completely natural. Too often this style of country singing is adopted but not lived in. Not the case here. This is a very strong album. Instrumentalists trade licks back and forth with casual authority. Some of the highlights are "I Got a Date," "Tear My Stillhouse Down," and "The Doorstep of Trouble." —*Richard Meyer*

The New Grass Revival

Progressive Bluegrass
The New Grass Revival, formed in 1972 by four former members of the Bluegrass Alliance, flourished in a decade when numerous groups took traditional bluegrass and changed it to varying degrees. The group was

successful enough to have its name become a generic label: "newgrass." The band's image, with long hair and occasionally electrified instruments, as well as its musical material, contrasted greatly with standard (traditional) bluegrass like that played by Bill Monroe, Ralph Stanley, the Lilly Brothers, and Lester Flatt's band. In terms of longevity, popularity, and exposure, the Revival, with its hip reputation, was perhaps the most successful in competition against II Generation, Seldom Scene, the Country Gentlemen, and others. The origins of the New Grass Revival lay in the Bluegrass Alliance, which Sam Bush (vocals, fiddle, guitar, mandolin) and Courtney Johnson (banjo, vocals) joined in 1970. At the time, the Alliance also featured bassist Ebo Walker and fiddler Lonnie Peerce. Within a year after Bush and Johnson's arrival, Curtis Burch (dobro, guitar, vocals) joined the band. In 1972 Peerce left the band, and the remaining members decided to continue under a new name—the New Grass Revival. The band released their eponymous debut, *Arrival of the New Grass Revival*, later that year on Starday Records.

After the release of their debut, Walker parted ways with the band and the group replaced him with Butch Robbins, who was with the band for only a short time. He was replaced by John Cowan, an Evansville, IN, native. This lineup was stable throughout the '70s, recording a number of albums for Flying Fish Records. As their name suggested, the New Grass Revival never played traditional bluegrass—all of the members brought elements of rock 'n' roll, jazz, and blues to the group's sound. Consequently, certain portions of the bluegrass community scorned them, but they also gained a devoted following of listeners who believed they were moving the genre in a new, fresh direction.

In 1981 Johnson and Burch left the band, claiming they were tired of touring. Bush and Cowan replaced them with banjoist Bela Fleck and mandolinist/guitarist Pat Flynn. The New Grass Revival moved to Sugar Hill Records in 1984 and released their first album featuring the new lineup, *On the Boulevard*. Two years later the band signed with EMI Records and released an eponymous album, which proved to be their breakthrough into the mainstream. Two of the singles from the album—"What You Do to Me" and "Ain't That Peculiar"—were minor hits on the country charts, and Fleck's showcase "Seven by Seven" was nominated for a Grammy for Best Country Instrumental. *Hold On to a Dream*, released in 1987, was just as successful as its predecessor, featuring the hits "Unconditional Love" and "Can't Stop Now," which both nearly made the Top 40. In 1989, the New Grass Revival released their third major-label album, *Friday Night in America*, which was another commercial success. "Callin' Baton Rouge" became their first Top 40 single, followed by the No. 58 hit "You Plant Your Fields." Even though the band was more popular than ever, Sam Bush decided to pull the plug on the group after the releaase of *Friday Night in America*. Bush became a session musician and Fleck went on to a very successful and respected solo career. —*Stephen Thomas Erlewine and David Vinopal*

Fly Through the Country / 1975 / Flying Fish ✦✦✦✦
This first version of New Grass was not so polished as their second era, but they had good chemistry. You've gotta love "These Days," "Skippin,'" "All Night Train," and "Fly Through the Country." —*Chip Renner*

Too Late to Turn Back Now / 1977 / Flying Fish ✦✦✦
Recorded live at Telluride, CO, with guests J. Hartford and Peter Rowan, this one has a good-time feel. —*Chip Renner*

When the Storm Is Over / 1977 / Flying Fish ✦✦✦
This exciting music comes from one of the best groups in bluegrass. —*AMG*

Barren County / 1979 / Flying Fish ✦✦✦✦
The first incarnation of this band was never better than on this one. Strong songs and vocals. —*Chip Renner*

Commonwealth / 1981 / Flying Fish ✦✦✦✦
The best of their newer era, with guests Leon Russell, Sharon White, and Kenny Malone. The cover of Hartford's "Steam Powered Aereo Plane" is great. —*Chip Renner*

On the Boulevard / 1984 / Sugar Hill ✦✦✦✦
An overlooked CD with a couple of standout tracks. Played beginning to end, this one will leave you fulfilled. —*Chip Renner*

New Grass Revival / 1986 / EMI America ✦✦✦✦
A solid release, and a great cover of Peter Rowan's "Revival." Pat Flynn shows some good songwriting on "In the Middle of the Night," "Lonely Rider," "Sweet Release," and "How Many Hearts." Sam Busit and John Cowan come together well on T. Moore's "Saw You Runnin." —*Chip Renner*

Hold to a Dream / 1987 / Capitol ✦✦✦
A good use of drums on this one. It worked. Standout tracks include "Looking Past You," "Unconditional Love," "Metric Lips," and the title track. —*Chip Renner*

Friday Night in America / 1989 / Capitol ✦✦✦
Their last album covers John Hiatt's "Angel Eyes," Jesse Winchester's "Let's Make a Baby King," and Bela Fleck's "Big Foot." Hot! These guys will be missed. —*Chip Renner*

● **Best of New Grass Revival** / Mar. 8, 1994 / Liberty ✦✦✦✦
Best of New Grass Revival is a first-rate, 18-track collection of the band's biggest hits of the late '80s, plus a number of significant album tracks. It's the perfect way to get acquainted with the group. —*Thom Owens*

Old and in the Way

Traditional Bluegrass
Old and in the Way was a one-shot bluegrass band whose legacy lasted far longer than the band. Led by Grateful Dead member Jerry Garcia (banjo, vocals), the band also featured David Grisman (mandolin, vocals), Vassar Clements (fiddle), Peter Rowan (guitar, vocals), and John Kahn (bass). Garcia formed the band in 1973 as a way to revisit his bluegrass roots and demonstrate his affection for the music. To round out the lineup, he recruited Clements and Kahn, as well as Grisman and Rowan, West Coast session musicians who had previously played together in the band Muleskinner. Taking their name from an old bluegrass standard, Old and in the Way played a handful of gigs, most of them at the Boarding House in San Francisco. An album, also called *Old and in the Way*, was culled from these shows and released in 1973 on the Grateful Dead's own record label, Round. The record combined standards and Rowan originals, which later became standards. Although the album was the only one the lineup recorded, the members continued to play together in various permutations over the next two decades, and the record continued to sell steadily. The group reunited after Garcia's death in 1995, releasing a second album, *That High Lonesome Sound*, in early 1996. —*Stephen Thomas Erlewine*

★ **Old and in the Way** / Oct. 1973 / Grateful Dead ✦✦✦✦✦
This release was one of the greatest things to happen to bluegrass music, in that it exposed a whole new audience to bluegrass music and acoustic music. —*Chip Renner*

That High Lonesome Sound / Feb. 20, 1996 / Acoustic Disc ✦✦✦✦
Twenty-three years after the first album *Old and in the Way* came the second, an amazing development for a group that existed for only nine months and about 30 gigs in 1973. *That High Lonesome Sound*, like its predecessor, *Old and in the Way*, was drawn from the group's stand at the Boarding House in San Francisco in October 1973. And like that release, it combined traditional bluegrass material, in this case standards like "Orange Blossom Special" and "Uncle Pen," with interpolations from the world of rock 'n' roll ("The Great Pretender") and new originals that touched on contemporary issues (Peter Rowan's "Lonesome L.A. Cowboy," a comment on the Southern California country-rock scene of the time). *Old and in the Way* was a great crossover album, largely because the bandmembers had enjoyed careers in rock, especially banjo player and singer Jerry Garcia, moonlighting from his day job in the Grateful Dead. What was less well known was that the group had real roots in the music, as Neil V. Rosenberg pointed out in the second album's liner notes. Four of the five members had experience in bluegrass, and two had been members of Bill Monroe's Blue Grass Boys. Old and in the Way was a hybrid, but it was far more bluegrass than rock. —*William Ruhlmann*

Osborne Brothers

Progressive Bluegrass, Traditional Bluegrass, Bluegrass
The Osborne Brothers were one of the most popular and innovative bluegrass groups of the post-war era, taking the music into new directions and gaining a large audience. Among their most notable achievements are their pioneering, inventive use of amplification, twin harmony banjos, steel guitars, and drums—they were the first bluegrass group to expand the genre's sonic palette in such a fashion.

Bobby and Sonny Osborne were born in Hyden, KY, but raised in Dayton, OH. As children, their father instilled a love for traditional music. Bobby picked up the eletric guitar as a teenager, playing in various local bands. A few years after his brother began playing the guitar, Sonny picked up the banjo. In 1949, Bobby formed a duo with banjoist Larry Richardson. The pair was hired by a West Virginian radio station and stayed in the state for a while, eventually hooking up with the Lonesome Pine Fiddlers. During their stay with the Fiddlers, they helped change the group's sound to bluegrass and made four singles for Cozy Records. Bobby Osborne left the band in the summer of 1951, forming a band with Jimmy Martin that fell apart shortly after its inception. After making a one-shot single, "New Freedom Bell," with his siblings Louise and Sonny, he joined the Stanley Brothers for a short while before being drafted into the army.

Sonny spent some time with Bill Monroe's Blue Grass Boys in the early '50s, appearing on several sides on Decca Records. He also cut some covers of popular Monroe and Flatt & Scruggs songs for the budget label Gateway. After Bobby returned from the army, he and Sonny formed a band. Initially, they supported Jimmy Martin on his RCA session while they had their own spot on a Knoxville radio station. In 1956, they joined the "Wheeling Jamboree"; they would stay with the radio program for four years. In March of that year, Red Allen joined the brothers—four months after his arrival, they recorded their first session for MGM records. For the next year, they toured and recorded, steadily gaining a large audience. In the spring of 1958, "Once More" became a No. 13 hit on the country charts. Its success helped push the band into the mainstream.

Shortly after the success of "Once More," Allen left the band and the Osbornes filled his vacancy with a string of musicians and vocalists, including Johnny Dacus and Benny Birchfield. The duo stayed with the "Wheeling Jamboree" and MGM Records into the early '60s. The Osbornes became the first bluegrass act to play a college campus in 1960, when they played Antioch College in Yellow Springs, OH. That appearance ushered in a new era for bluegrass, creating a new, younger audience for the music.

The Osbornes left MGM in 1963, signing with Decca Records. On their mid-'60s records for Decca, the duo began experimenting more with their music, adding piano, steel guitar, and electric instruments to their music. Their adventurousness made them more accessible to a mass audience, as their string of late-'60s and early-'70s hit singles proves. Although their experimentation angered many bluegrass traditionalists, the Osbornes were the only bluegrass group to consistently have country hits during this time, even if all their singles were only minor hits.

In 1975, the Osbornes left Decca but continued to play the Grand Ole Opry and bluegrass festivals across America. Later in the '70s, the duo returned to a more traditional sound. Throughout the '80s and '90s they stuck to this sound, playing concerts and festivals frequently and recording albums for CMH, RCA, Sugar Hill, and Pinecastle. Forty years after their formation, the Osborne Brothers remained an active act in the mid-'90s. — *Stephen Thomas Erlewine*

From Rocky Top to Muddy Bottom / 1977 / CMH ✦✦✦
This album contains such cuts as "We Could," "Love Hurts," "Rocky Top," and more. — *AMG*

The Bluegrass Collection / 1978 / CMH ✦✦✦✦
Recorded in 1978, *Bluegrass Collection* is the Osborne Brothers' tribute to the fathers of bluegrass—Bill Monroe, Flatt & Scruggs, and the Stanley Brothers. The duo throws in nice, but unremarkable, remakes of their older hits as well, making the album a pleasant exercise in nostalgia. — *Thom Owens*

Bobby and His Mandolin / 1981 / CMH ✦✦✦
This nice album features sprightly mandolin renditions of traditional fiddle tunes. — *Mark A. Humphrey*

Hillbilly Fever / 1991 / CMH ✦✦✦
Recorded in 1991, *Hillbilly Fever* might not live up to the standards of the Osborne Brothers' earliest and best recordings, but it's a fun listen that shows the duo still has life in them, nearly 40 years after their formation. — *Thom Owens*

Bluegrass 1956-68 [box] / 1995 / Bear Family ✦✦✦✦
Bluegrass 1956-68 is a multidisc box set that contains everything the Osborne Brothers recorded between those years. During that time they recorded for two major labels, MGM and Decca Records. All the songs the duo released on those two labels, plus alternate takes and unreleased tracks, are included on the box. With all of that material, the set is simply too large for anyone but historians and completists to enjoy. Nevertheless, there's lots of wonderful music on the collection and anyone with the patience (and the funds) to invest in the box will not be disappointed. — *Thom Owens*

Greatest Bluegrass Hits / CMH ✦✦✦
This is a good "favorites" collection. — *Mark A. Humphrey*

☆ **The Osborne Brothers** / Rounder ✦✦✦✦✦
Great vocal harmonies and tightly woven banjo-mandolin conversations come together on this, the best early material from 1959-1963. — *Mark A. Humphrey*

★ **Best of the Osborne Brothers** / MCA ✦✦✦✦✦
Their 1963-1967 Decca hits blend smooth bluegrass with then-contemporary country production. A unique sound, it's radical for its time. — *Mark A. Humphrey*

Reno and Smiley

Traditional Bluegrass
Don Reno, Red Smiley, and the Tennessee Cut Ups were a bluegrass band of such high quality that they gave serious competition to Flatt and Scruggs in the '50s. Don Reno, an unsurpassed master of the banjo, played for Bill Monroe in 1948, replacing Earl Scruggs. With a smooth and mellow baritone, Red Smiley made a perfect partner to Don, singing lead to Don's high harmony part. Don's incredible talent carried over to guitar playing and songwriting. Among his compositions are the exquisite "Emotions," as well as "Feuding Banjos," the unforgettable song in the film *Deliverance*, co-written with Arthur "Guitar Boogie" Smith. You don't know the five-string banjo if you haven't heard Don Reno. Reno and Smiley grew up in rural North Carolina, and both played with the

Morris Brothers at different times in their formative early years. Both served in the Army during World War II, and after they were discharged, they played in a variety of country bands—Reno even did a stint with Bill Monroe after Earl Scruggs left the Blue Grass Boys in 1948—before they met in December 1949. Both musicians were recruited by fiddler Tommy Magness to play in his band, the Tennessee Buddies. In the summer of 1950 the pair began playing duets. After cutting a few singles with Magness for King Records (they were eventually released on Federal) in the spring of 1951, they left the fiddler and began working with Toby Stroud's Blue Mountain Boys in Roanoke, VA. In the fall of that year the pair formed their own band, the Tennessee Cut Ups.

Initially Reno and Smiley found it difficult to land jobs in Virginia and South Carolina. Nevertheless, they cut several sides for King early in 1952. Before those singles were issued, the duo had already split up, simply because they couldn't find work. Once the records did appear, they sold fairly well and King's owner, Syd Nathan, convinced the duo to continue recording, even if they weren't actively performing. For the next three years they made assorted records for King while Reno played with Arthur "Guitar Boogie" Smith and Smiley worked as a mechanic. On the first batch of recordings, they were supported by musicians like Jimmy Lunsford and Tommy Faile. By November of 1954, they were allowed to use their longtime backing musicians, fiddler Mack Magaha and bassist John Palmer.

In the spring of 1955 Reno and Smiley reunited as a performing duo and soon landed a regular gig on WRVA's "Old Dominion Barn Dance." Within a year they were secured a daily morning television show in Roanoke, as well as various shows for a station in Harrisonburg, VA. The pair made a handful of recordings for Dot in 1957, but they continued their relationship with King until 1964, recording a wealth of material.

At the end of 1964 Reno and Smiley parted ways. Red Smiley had been suffering from diabetes, and he no longer wanted to travel; he continued to do the television show in Roanoke, but he toured only occasionally. By the spring of 1968 he had completely retired. Don Reno played with a few bands before teaming up with Bill Harrell in 1966—Harrell would be his first true partner since Smiley, but he wouldn't be his last. For nearly two decades, Reno remained active in the bluegrass community, cutting numerous records and playing with a variety of collaborators. — *Stephen Thomas Erlewine and David Vinopal*

● **Early Years 1951-59** / 1994 / King ✦✦✦✦

Tony Rice

Guitar / Traditional Bluegrass
Innovative guitarist Tony Rice is a master flat-picker who combines elements of bluegrass, jazz, and classical music to create a unique acoustic sound. The Virginia-born Rice was raised in California and started out playing bluegrass with his father and brothers Larry and Wayne. When he was just starting out, Rice was influenced by such West Coast masters as Roland and Clarence White of the Kentucky Colonels, Ry Cooder, and Chris Hillman. In 1970 he began playing with the Kentucky-based Bluegrass Alliance and next with the progressive Crowe's New South. He stayed with the latter band through the mid-'70s and then left to join the highly innovative David Grisman Quintet, which played string music with a classical and jazz twist. Rice began his solo career in 1977 and released an eponymous debut album on which he not only played guitar, but also sang with a surprisingly soulful voice that itself was a mixture of traditional, pop, and folk inflections. He released two more solo albums, *Acoustics* and *Manzanita*, and then formed the Bluegrass Album Band with Bobby Hicks, Doyle Lawson, and Todd Phillips. The band recorded five albums in the early '80s.

In 1980, Rice formed the Tony Rice Unit, with whom he played his innovative "spacegrass" jazz interpretations of modern folksongs by such artists as Ian Tyson, Joni Mitchell, and Gordon Lightfoot. This music can be heard on such critically acclaimed albums as 1984's *Cold on the Shoulder*, which he recorded for Rounder. Later, Rice cut two albums with Norman Blake and then had a reunion album with his brothers. In 1993, he cut a traditional bluegrass album for Rounder titled *Tony Rice Plays and Sings Bluegrass*. This album featured covers of Bill Monroe classics as well as those of Flatt & Scruggs, the Stanley Brothers, and Bob Dylan, and was nominated for a Grammy. — *Sandra Brennan*

● **Devlin** / Rounder ✦✦✦✦
Devlin collects a selection of material from his Rounder albums of the '70s and '80s, making it a perfect introduction to his music. — *Thom Owens*

Peter Rowan

Guitar, Vocals / Progressive Bluegrass
Peter Rowan was one of the most popular cult bluegrass artists of the '80s, cultivating a devoted, international cult fan base through his independent records and constant touring. A skilled singer-songwriter, Rowan also yodels, plays stringed instruments and the saxophone. He was born in Boston, MA. Since his parents and many of his relatives

were musicians, it seemed only natural that Rowan too would become one. When he was a teenager, Rowan frequently hung out at the Hillbilly Ranch, where he heard such bluegrass and old-time bands as the Lilly Brothers. He also enjoyed listening to the blues.

Rowan formed the Tex-Mex band the Cupids while he was in high school. The Cupids became a popular New England attraction and independently released a single. Rowan attended Colgate University for three years during the '60s and then decided to become a professional musician. In 1963 he joined the Cambridge-based Mother Bay State Entertainers as a mandolin player and singer, appearing on one Elektra album, *The String Band Project*. In 1964, after performing with Jim Rooney and Bill Keith, Rowan became a rhythm guitarist and lead singer with Bill Monroe and his Blue Grass Boys. He remained with them through 1967, when Rowan left to join mandolinist David Grisman in the folk-rock band Earth Opera. The group recorded a couple of albums and toured (frequently opening for the Doors) until the early '70s. One of the albums, *The Great Eagle Tragedy* (1969) produced a minor hit single, "Home to You."

While with Monroe and Earth Opera, Rowan had begun to write and co-write songs, some of which were used in both bands. After leaving Earth Opera, Rowan became a part of Sea Train, a rock-fusion band whose records were produced by George Martin. Rowan left the band in 1972 to form the Rowan Brothers with siblings Chris and Lorin. They recorded one eponymous album for Columbia. After the Rowan Brothers disbanded, Rowan recorded *Old and in the Way* with Grisman, Jerry Garcia, Vassar Clements, and John Kahn.

In 1974 Rowan, Grisman, Clarence White, and Richard Greene formed Muleskinner, a bluegrass band. Muleskinner released one album and then disbanded. Rowan then reunited the Rowan Brothers; the reunited group played together until the early '80s. Meanwhile, Rowan began playing rock and bluegrass with Mexican Airforce, which featured accordion player Flaco Jimenez. In the mid-'80s, he and Jiminez again reteamed to record *Flaco Jimenez and Peter Rowan Live Rockin' Tex-Mex* in London for the English Waterfront label.

Rowan founded the Nashville-based Wild Stallions in 1983. Throughout the '80s and '90s, Rowan continued to work with a variety of musicians and tour as a solo act. Rowan's tunes have been recorded by such artists as the New Riders of the Purple Sage ("Panama Red"), George Strait ("Dance Time in Texas"), Michael Martin Murphy ("Land of the Navajo"), and Ricky Skaggs ("You Make Me Feel like a Man"). — *Sandra Brennan*

Peter Rowan / 1978 / Flying Fish ✦✦✦
The solo debut album of this bluegrass vocalist features an original mixture of styles and backing from Flaco Jimenez, Richard Greene, and Tex Logan. — *AMG*

Medicine Trail / 1980 / Flying Fish ✦✦✦
Tex-Mex bluegrass and contemporary styling come from this virtuoso original. — *AMG*

The Walls of Time / 1981 / Sugar Hill ✦✦✦
This release is hard to put a finger on. The music takes on a feel more like that of the Old and in the Way band, yet seems to be missing the "something special" that project had. — *Chip Renner*

Red Hot Pickers / 1984 / Sugar Hill ✦✦✦
Peter Rowan is backed by Richard Greene (fiddle), Tony Trischka (banjo), Andy Statman (mandolin), and Roger Mason (bass). This is a lively, well-played album. — *Chip Renner*

The First Whippoorwill / 1985 / Sugar Hill ✦✦✦
A good album. Rowan stacks the deck with Sam Bush, Bill Keith, Richard Greene, Buddy Spicher, and Roy Huskey, Jr. — *Chip Renner*

● **New Moon Rising** / 1988 / Sugar Hill ✦✦✦✦
Tight album. Rowan is backed by the Nashville Bluegrass Band. Maura O'Connell sings harmony vocals on "Meadow Green" and Jerry Douglas is featured on dobro. This release set the tune for some real good music. — *Chip Renner*

Dust Bowl Children / 1990 / Sugar Hill ✦✦✦
A very good album. It is all acoustic, featuring Peter Rowan alone on guitar, mandola, and vocals. This grows on you. — *Chip Renner*

All on a Rising Day / 1991 / Sugar Hill ✦✦✦✦
An all-around fine release. Rowan picks up where he left off on *Dust Bowl* but improves on the idea with some great backup musicians—Stuart Duncan; Sam Bush; Jerry Douglas; Alison Krauss; Roy Husky, Jr.; Alan O'Bryant; and Edgar Meyer. Twelve solid songs. Highly recommended! — *Chip Renner*

Seldom Scene

Progressive Bluegrass
Old-fashioned has never been a word used to describe Seldom Scene's take on bluegrass. Since their inception in 1971, the Washington, DC-based Seldom Scene has remained a driving force in "newgrass" and is considered among the finest modern bands around. This is not surpris-

ing, as the Seldom Scene membership has included some legendary musicians. All but one of the five original members were long-time professionals who got together just to have a little musical fun a couple of times a week. The band's founder, John Duffey, had spent 12 years as a charter member of the Country Gentlemen. A rather flamboyant character onstage, he is noted for playing amazing solos on the mandolin, dobro, and guitar, and for his powerful, exceptionally flexible voice. Banjoist Ben Eldridge was a veteran of Cliff Waldron's New Shades of Grass, as was Mike Auldridge, who is considered among the top three dobro players in the world. These three distinguished (each has won numerous individual awards as well as group awards) musicians are the band's core and remained together through the mid-'90s. Other charter members included former Country Gentleman Tom Gray, and John Starling, a former army surgeon and the only member never to have played professionally.

By the summer of 1971 the group was touring on the bluegrass festival circuit and soon found themselves quite popular on the East Coast. Club dates, more touring, and albums followed, but despite their success, the Seldom Scene adamantly remained an independent band and did not sign with a major record label. The original lineup of the Seldom Scene recorded seven albums for Rebel Records in the first half of the '70s. In 1977 Starling left and was replaced by Phil Rosenthal; in 1986 Rosenthal was replaced by Lou Reid. Also in 1986 Gray was replaced by electric bassist T. Michael Coleman. Starling returned to the Seldom Scene in 1993, replacing Reid in the band's lineup. By 1995 Starling had left again; he was replaced by Moondi Klein.

In addition to playing festivals and recording, the Seldom Scene have also made television appearances on such shows as "Nashville Now" and "Entertainment Tonight." In 1996 the Seldom Scene's lineup fractured, as half the group left to form Chesapeake. The remaining members continued performing under the band's original name. — *Sandra Brennan*

15th Anniversary Celebration / Feb. 1981 / Sugar Hill ✦✦✦✦
A 20-song live CD with Duffey, Auldridge, Mike Reid, Eldridge, and Gray. A must for fans, with special guests galore—Emmylou Harris, Ricky Skaggs, Linda Ronstadt, John Starling, Tony Rice, Jonathan Edwards, and others. — *Chip Renner*

● **Best of Seldom Scene, Vol. 1** / 1987 / Rebel ✦✦✦✦
The Best of Seldom Scene, Vol. 1 contains a sampling of the band's best songs from their first four albums and gives a good sense of what the band is about. — *Thom Owens*

Scenic Roots / 1990 / Sugar Hill ✦✦✦
With *Scenic Roots*, Seldom Scene returned to their traditional bluegrass roots. Although the music occasionally sounds forced, much of it is lively and wonderful, making the disc a worthwhile purchase for longtime fans, even if it isn't the place to start with this perennial bluegrass favorite. — *Thom Owens*

Scene 20: 20th Anniversary Concert / 1991 / Sugar Hill ✦✦✦
For their 20th anniversary, Seldom Scene held a concert and invited all of the former members of the group to join them on stage. Everyone turned up and the results are captured on the splendidly entertaining *Scene 20: 20th Anniversary Concert*. Seldom Scene runs through a wide variety of material, playing everything from traditional bluegrass numbers to Wilson Pickett's "In the Midnight Hour." For fans of the group, this album is an unexpected and totally delightful treat. — *Thom Owens*

Larry Sparks

Vocals / Traditional Bluegrass
One of the finer lead singers in contemporary bluegrass, Larry Sparks filled in with Ralph Stanley's band after the great Carter Stanley died in 1966. He went on to head the traditional bluegrass group the Lonesome Ramblers, who earned a large following of fans.

Sparks was born and raised in Lebanon, OH, and began learning to play guitar as a child. In his teens, Sparks played in bluegrass, country, and rock bands. In 1966 he cut his first bluegrass single for Jalyn and then began his association with the Stanley Brothers' Clinch Mountain Boys. He recorded five albums with the band and stayed through 1969. After that he formed the Lonesome Ramblers and began recording on the Pine Tree label. Later they recorded with Old Homestead and Starday. Among the tunes he is most associated with are "Brand New Broken Heart," "Green Pastures in the Sky," "I Can't Go On Loving You," and especially the standard "Love of the Mountains."

During the latter half of the '70s through the '80s, Sparks recorded on several different labels, most notably Robert Trout's King Bluegrass label. One of his better albums is his tribute to Hank Williams. After the mid-'80s, he began recording less frequently and eventually moved to Richmond, IN. He continues to perform on the bluegrass circuit, where he is regarded as one of the premiere bluegrass players and one who is dedicated to preserving the traditional styles of the Stanley Brothers. — *Sandra Brennan & David Vinopal*

Larry Sparks Sings Hank Williams / 1977 / Rebel ✦✦✦✦
A minor classic. Honky tonk meets bluegrass. —*Mark A. Humphrey*

The Best of Larry Sparks / 1983 / Rebel ✦✦✦✦
A fine traditional bluegrass singer. —*Mark A. Humphrey*

★ **Classic Bluegrass** / 1989 / Rebel ✦✦✦✦✦
Classic Bluegrass collects the highlights of Larry Sparks' early albums, which were recorded for a variety of different labels. The compilation hits all the high points of the records, providing a definitive retrospective of his career, as well as an excellent, concise introduction to one of bluegrass' best singers. —*Thom Owens*

The Stanley Brothers

Traditional Bluegrass, Bluegrass
If you even think you know bluegrass, you have to know Ralph (b. 1927) and Carter (b. 1925) Stanley, the Stanley Brothers. Parallel to Flatt And Scruggs and Bill Monroe's Blue Grass Boys, though not with their renown, were Virginians Ralph and Carter, mountain boys who took those mountains and their traditions and their songs and wove them into a traditional bluegrass sound of utter purity, simplicity, and astonishing beauty. Their first band, formed around 1947, played more of a mountain-folk music reminiscent of the old string bands, changing to their style of ultra-traditional bluegrass when Bill Monroe's band became popular. Even on their recordings in the early '50s, the Stanleys' unmistakable sound is there, with guitarist Carter singing lead and banjo player Ralph singing tenor harmony. In the opinion of many, Carter possessed the best lead voice in bluegrass history—rich, emotional, and (in the best sense of the word) lonely. He took a happy song and sang it sad; he took a sad song and sang it sadder. And Ralph's unworldly mountain tenor matched his brother's voice perfectly, soaring above and often lightening the emotional load of the lyrics, creating a duet unsurpassed in country history.

Ralph and Carter were born into a musical family—their father sang and their mother played banjo. As teenagers the brothers began performing around their hometown. After graduating from high school, the siblings both served in the army during World War II. Carter was discharged before Ralph. When he returned to the States he got a job singing in Roy Sykes' Blue Ridge Mountain Boys. He quit the group as soon as Ralph returned from the army in October 1946, and the brothers formed a band, the Clinch Mountain Boys.

The Stanley Brothers had a regular gig at WNVA Norton for a few months; then they moved to the Bristol, TN-based WCYB, where they appeared regularly on the "Farm and Fun Time" program. They gained quite a following, and they soon signed a contract with the Rich-R-Tone label. The Stanleys made their first records early in 1947, the same year they began playing various radio stations in the South, including ones in North Carolina, Louisiana, and Kentucky. The brothers and their five-piece Clinch Mountain Boys were developing their style, moving from traditional string band sounds to a Bill Monroe-inspired bluegrass style. During the late '40s and early '50s, several well-respected musicians passed through the band, including Curly Lambert, Pee Wee Lambert, Chubby Anthony, and Bill Napier. After recording ten songs for Rich-R-Tone, the Stanley Brothers were signed to Columbia in 1948. For the next three years they stayed with Columbia, producing 22 songs that became bluegrass classics. For a brief time in 1951the Stanley Brothers broke up. Carter sang with Bill Monroe and made a handful of records with the father of bluegrass. Ralph was sidelined for several months after a car crash. The break was brief, and the band was back together before the end of the year.

In the summer of 1953 they left Columbia for Mercury Records. During the mid-'50s, they made a series of recordings that expanded their boundaries, as they played gospel, honky tonk, instrumentals, and a number of original songs.

At the end of the decade, the Brothers left Mercury and signed to both Starday and King, moved to Live Oak, FL, and began playing the Swannee River Jamboree. In the early '60s they played a number of television shows and concerts throughout the South and recorded numerous records. However, the duo began to suffer financial problems beginning in 1961, which meant they couldn't afford to retain a whole band. Nevertheless, the Stanley Brothers continued to tour, playing clubs and various bluegrass festivals. However, they rarely left the South, and their career suffered. They recorded for a number of smaller labels after leaving King, though none of the records sold much. In 1966 Carter Stanley became seriously ill, and on December 1 of that year, he passed away, only 41 years old.

Ralph Stanley continued performing with a new lineup of the Clinch Mountain Boys. For the next three decades he performed with various new lineups of the band, playing festivals and clubs and recording numerous records. —*Stephen Thomas Erlewine and David Vinopal*

Hymns and Sacred Songs / 1959 / King ✦✦✦
These sacred sides are lovely. —*Mark A. Humphrey*

Everybody's Country Favorites / 1959 / King ✦✦✦
Features "Sweeter than the Flowers," "Shenandoah," "I'm a Man of Constant Sorrow," and other hits. —*AMG*

Long Journey Home / 1961 / Rebel ✦✦✦
From the '60s, it's great as always. —*Mark A. Humphrey*

Columbia Sessions #2 / 1982 / Rounder ✦✦✦
More wonderful early performances. —*Mark A. Humphrey*

★ **Angel Band: The Classic Mercury Recordings** / 1995 / Mercury Nashville ✦✦✦✦✦
Angel Band collects the bulk of the Stanley Brothers' mid-'50s recordings, when they were expanding their sound slightly. Although it isn't always straight bluegrass, it shows how versatile and talented the Stanleys were. It's an essential purchase for a bluegrass collection. —*Thom Owens*

★ **Complete Columbia Recordings** / Mar. 1996 / Columbia/Legacy ✦✦✦✦✦
While this doesn't have the two alternate takes that surfaced on the nearly identical Bear Family collection *(1949-1952)*, this does have all 22 of the sides they officially released on Columbia, and will be much easier to find in the US. It's classic bluegrass of great historical importance, featuring mostly original compositions. —*Richie Unterberger*

Ralph Stanley (Ralph Edmond Stanley)

b. Feb. 25, 1927, Stratton, VA
Banjo, Vocals / Traditional Bluegrass, Hillbilly
After brother Carter died in 1966, Ralph Stanley was quick in hiring talented Larry Sparks (to handle Carter's leads) and fiddler Curly Ray Cline. In the years since, the Clinch Mountain Boys have undergone numerous changes in band personnel, but Stanley has kept his standards high, over the years hiring Ricky Skaggs, Keith Whitley, Roy Lee Centers, Jack Cooke, and others. As of this writing, the band is still much in demand, with a full schedule year-round. —*David Vinopal*

Pray for the Boys / 1990 / Rebel ✦✦✦
Sacred performances with the Clinch Mountain Boys. —*Mark A. Humphrey*

● **Saturday Night and Sunday** / 1992 / Freeland ✦✦✦✦
Ralph Stanley and the Clinch Mountain Boys demonstrated their facility on this release, doing 15 bluegrass numbers on the first disc and 16 gospel cuts on the second. The guest roster included Dwight Yoakam, Emmylou Harris, Vince Gill, the Waller and Sizemore Brothers, Ricky Skaggs, Tom T. Hall, Judy Marshall, Patty Loveless, Bill Monroe, Alison Krauss, Jimmy Martin, and Curly Ray Cline. The music was wonderful on each disc, and there were no compatibility problems on any collaboration. —*Ron Wynn*

Back to the Cross / Aug. 15, 1992 / Freeland ✦✦✦
Like Bill Monroe, Ralph Stanley maintains his skills and spirit into the 1990s, still singing and picking classic bluegrass. He joined Freeland in 1992, and appropriately made his label debut a gospel session with the Clinch Mountain Boys. You wouldn't expect any surprises, and there weren't any; nor were there low points. The CD contained 12 wonderful renditions of traditional hymns and praise songs performed with the humility, grace, and down-home artistry that has always characterized Ralph Stanley's music. —*Ron Wynn*

☆ **Bound to Ride** / Rebel ✦✦✦✦✦
This legendary singer and banjoist's most atavistic performances include claw-hammer banjo and terrific wailing Baptist banshee vocals on old-time songs. —*Mark A. Humphrey*

Carl Story

b. May 29, 1916, **d.** Mar. 30, 1995
Fiddle, Vocals / Gospel, Traditional Bluegrass
Fiddler Carl Story has been a key figure in the development of gospel bluegrass music during his six-decade career.

Story was born to musically inclined parents and from them learned much about playing guitar and fiddle. Though his parents played traditional and square dance music, young Story was most interested in the more modern sound of such groups as the Carolina Ramblers. In the early '30s, he moved to Lynchburg, VA, and began hosting a radio show. In 1935 he returned home, where he played with several musicians and eventually he and teenage banjoist Johnnie Whisnant moved to Spartanburg to play in the Lonesome Mountaineers. From there the two founded the Rambling Mountaineers, a part-time group that was sponsored by Scalf's Indian River Medicine. Eventually the band became a full-time venture. The Rambling Mountaineers played at various radio stations and made the occasional record until Story left to become a fiddler for Bill Monroe and his Blue Grass Boys. In 1943, he left them and joined the navy. Following his discharge from the navy, Story reassembled the Rambling Mountaineers with Jack and Curley Shelton, Hoke Jenkins, and Claude Boone. As they moved from radio station to station, the membership changed, and many of the members such as Tater Tate and the Brewster Brothers went on to become important figures in bluegrass. Story and his group began recording secular and gospel songs for Mercury in 1947. He remained with the label until 1952. He moved to Columbia the following year and recorded over a dozen singles. Although his music was close to bluegrass, Story's band did not become a full-fledged bluegrass group, complete with banjo, mandolin, and sometimes the dobro, until 1957. Eventually, the Mountaineers signed to Starday, with whom they recorded for many years. Between the late '50s and the early '70s, Story and his group became veritable fixtures on the bluegrass festival circuit. During the '60s, Story recorded primarily with Starday, but sometimes also recorded for various smaller companies, including Scripture, Sims, and Songs of Faith. He began recording less frequently during the '70s, but still continued touring. When things were slow, Story worked as a deejay at WSEC Greenville, SC. Things continued in a similar vein through the '80s and the '90s. —*Sandra Brennan*

● **16 Greatest Hits** / Starday ✦✦✦✦

Tony Trischka

Banjo / Progressive Bluegrass
The avant-garde banjo stylings of iconoclastic Tony Trischka have inspired a whole generation of progressive-bluegrass musicians; he is not only considered among the very best pickers, he is also one of the instrument's top teachers and has written numerous instructional books and teaching videotapes and cassettes.

A native of Syracuse, NY, Trischka's interest in banjo was sparked by the Kingston Trio's "MTA" in 1963. Two years later, he joined the Down City Ramblers; he remained with them through 1971. While he performed with the band, he also studied at Syracuse University; he eventually earned a B.A. in fine arts. Trischka made his recording debut on *15 Bluegrass Instrumentals* with the band Country Granola in 1971. At the same time, he was also a member of Country Granola. In 1973, he began a two-year stint with Breakfast Special. Between 1974 and 1975, he recorded two solo albums for Rounder, *Bluegrass Light* and *Heartlands*. All three of these groups gave Trischka the opportunity to develop the experimental, free-style playing. He recorded one more solo album for Rounder in 1976, *Banjoland*, and then went on to become musical leader for the Broadway show *The Robber Bridegroom*. Trischka toured with the show in 1978, the year he also played with the Monroe Doctrine.

Beginning in 1978, Trischka began playing with artists such as Peter Rowan, Richard Greene, and Stacy Phillips, as well as by himself. In the early 1980s, he began recording with his new group Skyline. In 1981, he recorded *Fiddle Tunes for Banjo* with Bill Keith and Bela Fleck. Skyline recorded its first album for Flying Fish in 1983. Subsequent albums include *Robot Plane Flies over Arkansas* (solo, 1983), *Stranded in the Moonlight* (with Skyline, 1984), and *Hill Country* (solo, 1985). From 1986 through 1988, Trischka was named Banjo Player of the Year by *Frets* magazine. In 1984, he performed in his first feature film, *Foxfire*. Three years later, he worked on the soundtrack for *Driving Miss Daisy*. Trischka produced the Belgian group Gold Rush's *No More Angels* in 1988. The next year, Skyline recorded its final album, *Fire of Grace*. He was also featured on the BBC-TV series "Voice of America—History of the Banjo" and recorded the theme song for "Books on the Air," a popular National Public Radio show. He continues his affiliation with the network and has appeared on Garrison Keillor's "Prairie Home Companion," "Mountain Stage," "From Our Front Porch," and other radio shows.

While he still recorded solo albums in the '80s and '90s, Trischka recorded sessions with a wide variety of performers ranging from Peter Rowan to the Violent Femmes. Since 1973, he has been publishing instructional manuals through Oak Publishing. These include *Masters of the Five String Banjo* (1983), which he co-wrote with Peter Wernick. In addition to his cassette tapes and videotapes, Trischka occasionally teaches private students and holds week-long workshops, including the Puget Sound Guitar Workshop and the National Guitar Workshop in Connecticut. —*Sandra Brennan*

Robot Plane Flies over Arkansas / 1983 / Rounder ✦✦✦
An early release that spotlights Trischka's banjo skills. A progressive album. —*Chip Renner*

Hill Country / 1985 / Rounder ✦✦✦
A traditional bluegrass album. —*Chip Renner*

● **Dust on the Needle** / 1988 / Rounder ✦✦✦✦
A good collection of Trischka's six Rounder albums, featuring Sam Bush, Marc O'Connor, and David Grisman. —*Chip Renner*

Frank Wakefield

Mandolin / Instrumental, Bluegrass
One of the chief experimenters with the mandolin, Frank Wakefield played straight bluegrass with a number of well-known bands, including Red Allen and the Greenbriar Boys. Wakefield was born into a musical family in Emory Gap, TN. By age eight, he already knew how to play har-

monica, guitar, and bass. In 1950, his family moved to Dayton, OH, and soon afterward Wakefield took up the mandolin and formed the gospel-oriented Wakefield Brothers with sibling Ralph, who played guitar. In 1951, the brothers made their first radio appearance in Dayton.

After the duo split up, Frank Wakefield teamed up with Red Allen to form Red Allen & Frank Wakefield and the Kentuckians. They remained partners through 1972, although the musicians did occasionally pursue side projects. It was with Allen that Wakefield mastered the banjo and dobro. They recorded occasionally through the 1950s, releasing singles on Wayside and PM Records. Wakefield moved with Allen to Washington, DC, in 1960 and began offering private mandolin lessons; his star pupil was a young David Grisman.

Wakefield joined the Greenbriar Boys in 1965 and remained with them through 1970. He founded the Good Ol' Boys and in 1971 recorded *The Frank Wakefield Band* for Rounder. He recorded *Pistol Packin' Mama* for United Artists in 1974 with Don Reno, Jerry Garcia, Dave Nelson, and Chubby Wise. At first the album credits went to him, Nelson and the Good Ol' Boys, but financial difficulties caused the album to be withdrawn, and it wasn't re-released until 1993. Since 1975 Wakefield has performed with his eponymous band and other musicians, most notably Bill Monroe. He also continues to teach and has released an instructional video. —*Sandra Brennan & David Vinopal*

● **Frank Wakefield with Country Cooking** / Rounder ✦✦✦✦
A fine bluegrass album. Wakefield is backed by Country Cooking, featuring Peter Wernick, Tony Trischka, Russ Barenberg, and Kenny Kosek. —*Chip Renner*

Pistol Packin' Mama / Round ✦✦✦✦
Wakefield and David Nelson (New Riders) give a more San Francisco sound to this album, with Jerry Garcia producing "Ashes of Love," "Dim Lights, Thick Smoke," and "Glendale Train." All excellent. —*Chip Renner*

Clarence White

b. Jun. 7, 1944, Lewiston, ME, **d.** Jul. 14, 1973, Palmdale, CA
Guitar / Traditional Bluegrass, Country-Rock
Clarence White was a gifted guitarist who was one of the pioneers of country-rock in the late '60s. Although he died young, his work with the Byrds and the Kentucky Colonels, among others, remained celebrated among country-rock and bluegrass aficionados in the decades following his death. Born in Maine but raised in California, White began playing the guitar at an early age, joining his brothers' band, the Country Boys, when he was just ten years old. The band eventually evolved into the Kentucky Colonels. Clarence left the Colonels in the mid-'60s, becoming a session musician; he played electric guitar on many rock and pop albums. He also began playing with the duo of Gib Gilbeau and Gene Parsons in local California clubs. Gilbeau and Parsons frequently worked with the Gosdin Brothers, so the duo was able to land a cameo appearance for White on the *Gene Clark and the Gosdin Brothers* album. Around the same time, Clarence recorded a solo album for Bakersfield International which the label didn't release.

In 1968, White joined Nashville West, which also featured Gene Parsons, Gib Gilbeau, Sneaky Pete Kleinow, Glen D. Hardin, and Wayne Moore. Nashville West recorded an album for Sierra Records, but the record didn't appear until 1978. White was invited to join the Byrds in the fall of 1968. Roger McGuinn was rebuilding the Byrds' lineup after the departure of Chris Hillman and Gram Parsons, who went on to form the Flying Burrito Brothers. Clarence White fit into the revamped Byrds' country-rock direction. He played on the group's untitled album, which spawned the single "Chestnut Mare." While he was with the band, he continued to work as a session musician, playing on Randy Newman's *12 Songs* (1970), Joe Cocker's eponymous 1969 album, and the Every Brothers' *Stories We Could Tell* (1971), among others.

Once the Byrds disbanded in 1973, Clarence White continued his session work and joined Muleskinner, which also featured David Grisman, Peter Rowan, John Guerin, Bill Keith, John Kahn, and Richard Greene. Muleskinner only released one album, which appeared later in 1973.

After the Muleskinner record was finished, White played a few dates with the Kentucky Colonels and began working on a solo album. He had only completed four tracks when he was killed by a drunken driver while he was loading equipment onto a van; he died on July 14, 1973. Following his death, several posthumous albums of his work with the Kentucky Colonels and the Byrds appeared, as did various albums that featured his playing, including Jackson Browne's *Late for the Sky* and Gene Parsons' *Kindling*. —*Stephen Thomas Erlewine*

● **And the Kentucky Colonels** / 1964 / Rounder ✦✦✦✦
Clarence White & the Kentucky Colonels includes 1964-1967 live performances that are musts for bluegrass guitar enthusiasts. White was a member of the Byrds and a session player for Linda Ronstadt and the Everly Brothers. —*Richard Lieberson*

Kentucky Colonels: Live in Sweden (1973) / 1976 / Rounder ✦✦✦
A good live show. Clarence White is at his best, performing with the White Brothers. —*Chip Renner*

Mac Wiseman

b. May 23, 1925, Waynesboro, VA
Guitar, Vocals / Traditional Bluegrass

If a poll were conducted to find the most popular bluegrass artists, on the list would be a number of groups but only one name unassociated with a particular band. And that would be Mac Wiseman, who over the years has been famous for his clear and mellow tenor voice. Though Wiseman has recorded with many of the great bands, including those of mountain singer Molly O'Day, Flatt and Scruggs, Bill Monroe, and the Osborne Brothers, his great voice has always kept a separate identity of its own. His material has ranged from the old ("Jimmy Brown the Newsboy," "I'll Be All Smiles Tonight") to the new ("You're the Best of All the Leading Brands," "A Million Million Girls," "If I Had Johnny's Cash and Charley's Pride"). Wiseman's command of traditional material has made him much in demand by bluegrass and folk fans alike.

Wiseman was born in Cremora, VA, and grew up influenced by traditional and religious music and such radio stars as Montana Slim Carter. Wiseman started out working as a radio announcer in Harrisonburg in 1944. At the same time he worked as a singer with Buddy Starcher. He later formed his own group and continued performing with others, including Molly O'Day and Flatt & Scruggs, through the '40s. In 1949, he recorded a single, "Travelin' Down This Lonesome Road," with Bill Monroe. By the 1950s, Wiseman was leading his own band again.

Possessing one of the best tenor voices of bluegrass, Wiseman differed from Monroe and Flatt and Scruggs in that he usually sang alone with little or no harmonizing. His band also employed two fiddles to play contemporary songs such as Speedy Drise's "Goin' like Wildfire," and adaptations of standards such as the Carter Family's "Wonder How the Old Folks Are at Home," and Mac and Bob's "Tis Sweet to Be Remembered." During this period, Wiseman continued working on the radio and founded the Country Boys, a band that featured such pioneering musicians as Eddie Adcock and Scott Stoneman. With the Country Boys, Wiseman recorded many popular local singles.

Wiseman had his first national Top Ten hit with his version of "The Ballad of Davy Crockett"; the song's success steered Wiseman away from bluegrass and more towards pop and country. In 1957, Wiseman began recording for Dot; he had a few major successes for the label with such songs as "Jimmy Brown the Newsboy." He moved to Capitol Records in 1962. During his tenure at Capitol, he recorded both country and bluegrass tunes. Wiseman began working for Wheeling's WWVA "Jamboree" in 1965. That year Wiseman began to play at bluegrass festivals; over the next three decades, he would become one of the most popular performers on the circuit. In 1968, he had a minor hit with "Got Leavin' on Her Mind" for MGM.

Wiseman moved to Music City in 1969 and signed with RCA Victor. His first—and only—hit for the label was the Top 40 novelty tune "If I Had Johnny's Cash and Charley's Pride." While at RCA, he also recorded three well-received bluegrass albums with Lester Flatt. From the mid-'70s on, Wiseman concentrated on bluegrass music. He became a fixture at bluegrass festivals and released a series of records on independent labels that ran into the '90s. In 1992, Wiseman narrated the documentary *High Lonesome*, a chronicle of bluegrass music. In 1993, he was inducted into the Bluegrass Hall of Fame. —*Sandra Brennan and David Vinopal*

Country Music Memories / 1976 / CMH ✦✦✦
This has a slightly different sound than other albums; more country than bluegrass. —*Chip Renner*

● **The Mac Wiseman Story** / 1976 / CMH ✦✦✦✦
The best of Mac Wiseman. A good place to start. —*Chip Renner*

Essential Bluegrass Album / 1979 / CMH ✦✦✦
Classics on a double album. These old salts play like spring chickens. Highly recommended. —*Chip Renner*

Mac Wiseman Sings Gordon Lightfoot / 1979 / CMH ✦✦✦
Well done. Belongs in the collection of any Gordon Lightfoot fan. —*Chip Renner*

Classic Bluegrass / 1987 / Rebel ✦✦✦
Very good. Bluegrass at its best. —*Chip Renner*

Greatest Bluegrass Hits / 1989 / CMH ✦✦✦✦
A good collection. —*Chip Renner*

Early Dot Recordings, Vol. 3 / 1992 / County ✦✦✦✦

Twenty Greatest / ✦✦✦
This features "Wabash Cannonball," "Poison Love," "Love Letters in the Sand," and other hits. —*AMG*

Various Artists

☆ **24 Greatest Bluegrass Hits** / CMH ✦✦✦✦✦
Here are the bluegrass greats, ranging from Bill Monroe to Flatt and Scruggs and the Osborne Brothers. —*David Vinopal*

☆ **Appalachian Stomp: Bluegrass Classics** / 1995 / Rhino ✦✦✦✦✦
Like many Rhino compilations, this is geared more to the novice or the casual fan than the aficionado, but that's not a criticism. If someone wants a basic primer of the bluegrass sound past and present that manages to be accessible and avoid unduly clichéd track selection, this 18-song compilation fits the bill well. Most of the biggest names are here (Bill Monroe, Flatt & Scruggs, the Dillards, the Stanley Brothers, the Kentucky Colonels, J.D. Crowe, Ricky Skaggs, Alison Krauss), as are some of the genre's top standards ("Blue Moon of Kentucky," "Orange Blossom Special," "Uncle Pen," "Foggy Mountain Breakdown"). The inclusion of Flatt & Scruggs' "The Ballad of Jed Clampett," Eric Weissberg & Steve Mandell's "Dueling Banjos," and the Nitty Gritty Dirt Band's "Will the Circle Be Unbroken" may rankle purists, but it clears the path to listeners who are only familiar with the idiom through these songs, and may find a lot more that they'll like on the less overexposed performances on this anthology. —*Richie Unterberger*

Bluegrass Breakdown / 1992 / Vanguard ✦✦✦
This album, which features the work of such artists as Bill Monroe, the Stanley Brothers, the Dillards, and the Greenbriar Boys, was recorded at the Newport Folk Festival in 1963-1965. —*AMG*

Bluegrass Masters / 1996 / Vanguard ✦✦✦✦✦
The title doesn't lie—this disc has 21 tracks by three of the best acts in the field (Bill Monroe, Flatt & Scruggs, and Jim & Jesse McReynolds), recorded live at the 1965 and 1966 Newport Folk Festivals. The sound and performances are good, and each act presents some familiar favorites—the McReynolds offer "Dueling Banjos" and "Sugarfoot Rag," Monroe does "Shady Grove" and "Cotton-Eyed Joe," and Flatt & Scruggs play "Orange Blossom Special," "Foggy Mountain Chimes," and "The Ballad of Jed Clampett." A youthful Peter Rowan, then a guitarist with Monroe, does a duet vocal with the bandleader on "Walls of Time." —*Richie Unterberger*

Early Mandolin Classics, Vol. 1 / 1989 / Rounder ✦✦✦✦✦
This fascinating glimpse into multiethnic mandolin music in the '20s and '30s features recordings from ragtime and blues to Ukrainian bands and, of course, hillbillies. —*Mark A. Humphrey*

Hand Picked: 25 Years of Bluegrass on Rounder Records / Oct. 1995 / Rounder ✦✦✦
Over the course of two CDs, *Hand Picked—25 Years of Bluegrass* runs through Rounder Records' back catalog, featuring selections from Ricky Skaggs, Bela Fleck, Alison Krauss, David Grier, Del McCoury, David Grisman, and others. The album gives a good portrait of Rounder's artists, as well as a good sense of bluegrass during the '70s, '80s, and '90s, if not a thorough history. —*Stephen Thomas Erlewine*

Here Today / 1988 / Rounder ✦✦✦
Hot mandolin-led newgrass by David Grisman with guests Herb Pedersen, Jim Buchanan, and others. —*Hank Davis*

Legends of Bluegrass, Vol. 1 / CMH ✦✦✦
This album, like each of the other cassettes in the series, contains 16 hits by the greatest names in bluegrass music, in this case by such legends as Dan Reno, Mac Wiseman, Eddie Adcock, Lester Flatt, Jim & Jesse, the Osborne Brothers, and others. —*AMG*

Mountain Music: Bluegrass Style / 1991 / Smithsonian/Folkways ✦✦✦✦✦
This classic reissue features performances by Don Stover, Earl Taylor, Chubby Anthony, Tex Logan, and others. —*Richard Meyer*

New Bluegrass Way / Jul. 25, 1995 / Polygram ✦✦✦
Country legend Hank Williams is paid tribute on this album by bluegrass artists like Ronnie McCoury of the Del McCoury Band, Terry Eldridge from the Osborne Brothers, and Ernie Thaker (formerly lead singer of the Clinch Mountain Boys). —*Jonathan Ball*

Rounder Banjo / 1988 / Rounder ✦✦✦✦✦
An extensive catalog of banjo music featuring Snuffy Jenkens, J.D. Crowe, Bela Fleck, Tony Trischka, and many more. —*Chip Renner*

Rounder Bluegrass, Vol. 1 / 1987 / Rounder ✦✦✦✦✦
Highly recommended. The best bluegrass money can buy! —*Chip Renner*

Rounder Bluegrass, Vol. 2 / 1988 / Rounder ✦✦✦
A collection of fine music. —*Chip Renner*

Rounder Fiddle / Rounder ✦✦✦✦✦
A loaded album featuring a wide range of fiddle music by Ricky Skaggs, Eddie Stubbs, Alison Krauss, Vassar Clements, and Byron Berline. More than 60 minutes of music. —*Chip Renner*

Rounder Guitar: Acoustic Guitar / 1988 / Rounder ✦✦✦✦✦
Rounder Guitar—Collection of Acoustic Guitar is a fine compilation of flat- and finger-pickin' acoustic guitar featuring Tony Rice, Mark O'Connor, Norman Blake, Dan Crary, and others. —*Chip Renner*

FOLK

In its widest possible application, "folk music" refers to music composed and performed by amateurs and passed down in an oral tradition devoid of formal training. In this sense, folk music is not only the ballads that derive from the Scots and the Irish and that have descended from the Appalachian Mountains, it is also the rural blues of the Mississippi Delta and the drum-heavy music of northwestern Africa, not to mention any other tribal or traditional genres.

In the 20th century in the US, however, the definition of folk music has tended to narrow over time, as other musical styles have encroached on it. Thus, though the Carter Family was an obvious influence on Woody Guthrie, and though they played their traditional music on acoustic instruments and sang it with untrained voices, we think of them as country musicians, not folk ones. Woody Guthrie, however, is resolutely categorized as folk, even though he introduced two main innovations to the form: first, he moved to the city, and second, he wrote his own songs.

It is probably the second factor that's the most important. By the early post-WWII era, Guthrie's songs were getting pop treatments in the hands of the Weavers, and by the mid-'50s, two distinct camps had sprung up, both of whom benefited from the boomlet of popular interest in folk music that lasted roughly from the 1955 Weavers comeback concert at Carnegie Hall (after years of blacklisting) to the summer day in 1965 when Bob Dylan turned up on stage at the Newport Folk Festival with an electric guitar in his hands.

The first camp followed in Guthrie's footsteps, writing their own songs and singing them in some approximation of Guthrie's Oklahoma accent. This camp tended to be more political and artistic, and most of them were individuals. Dylan was the most prominent of them, though Phil Ochs, Tom Paxton, Dave Van Ronk, and many others were included The second camp followed in the footsteps of the Weavers, singing the songs of others (including many of the Child ballads, but also songs written by those in the first camp) in sweet harmonies and clearly enunciated phrases. This camp tended to be apolitical and entertainment-oriented, and most of them were singing groups. Peter, Paul, and Mary were preeminent in this camp, along with the Kingston Trio, the Limeliters, and others. Joan Baez started in the second camp and gradually moved to the first.

After 1965, the first camp merged with pop and rock 'n' roll, especially the "sensitive singer/songwriter" school of the early '70s, and the second camp retreated into a nostalgic past. By the end of the '70s the folk boom was over, but folk music remained healthy, continuing to flourish in the places it always had—in hundreds of small clubs spread across the US and Europe and at dozens of summer festivals. A new crop of singer/songwriters was emerging, and if they didn't have the clear road to national recognition enjoyed by their '60s forebears, they were nevertheless gradually able to build up reputations on a viable circuit, record their own tapes, and even eventually move up to independent labels like Flying Fish and Rounder.

You will find in the listings that follow, therefore, records by the old hands (many of them reissued on CD in recent years) and a healthy sampling of those younger artists operating in what is now, as perhaps it always should have been, a highly decentralized field. It's likely that many of those names will be unfamiliar, but the reader is encouraged to try out a recording or two by the new folk acts and to keep an eye out for their appearances in local venues. That's where folk music lives today. — *William Ruhlmann*

Pat Alger

Guitar, Vocals / Folk

Pat Alger, who is among the most successful country songwriters of the late '80s and early '90s, comes from a folk background, and that colors the unusually thoughtful, articulated songs he writes. He first turned up on record himself playing guitar and singing with the loosely constructed Woodstock Mountains Revue on the album *More Music from Mud Acres* in 1977. He was a co-author of the song "Ocracoke Time," which appeared on the Revue's third album, *Pretty Lucky*, in 1978, as well as "Old Time Music" on its fourth album, *Back to Mud Acres*, in 1981, and the sole author of "Southern Crescent Line" on the same album. But Alger really began to gain recognition as a songwriter with the release of Nanci Griffith's third album, *Once in a Very Blue Moon*, in 1985. Alger co-wrote the title song, which reached the country charts in 1986. He was also heard from on Griffith's fourth album, *The Last of the True Believers*, in 1986, for which he co-wrote the song "Goin' Gone." (He also played guitar on the album and did its graphics.) Alger was co-author of the title song on Griffith's 1987 album, *Lone Star State of Mind*, and that song became a Top 40 country hit. In 1988, Kathy Mattea's version of "Goin' Gone" hit the top of the country charts. In 1990, Mattea took Alger and Fred Koller's "She Came from Fort Worth" to No. 2.

It's no surprise, then, that when Alger came to record his debut album, *True Love and Other Short Stories*, in 1991, he was able to call on the help of the cream of the young Nashville writers and performers. Trisha Yearwood, Nanci Griffith, Mary Black, Ashley Cleveland, Kathy Mattea, and Lyle Lovett all turn up, though Alger himself is the focus, singing his best-known songs. "No one sings or plays Pat Alger like Pat Alger himself," Griffith writes. — *William Ruhlmann*

● **True Love and Other Short Stories** / 1991 / Sugar Hill ✦✦✦✦
This country/folk songwriter sings his own versions of such hits as "Lone Star State of Mind" and "Goin' Gone." Guests include Nanci Griffith and Kathy Mattea. — *William Ruhlmann*

Seeds / 1994 / Sugar Hill ✦✦✦

Eric Andersen

b. Feb. 14, 1943, Pittsburgh, PA
Guitar, Harmonica, Vocals / Folk, Singer-Songwriter

Eric Andersen has maintained a career as a folk-based singer-songwriter for 30 years. In contrast to such peers as Tom Paxton and Phil Ochs, Andersen's writing has had a romantic/philosophical/poetic bent for the most part, rather than a socially conscious one, though one of his best-known songs, "Thirsty Boots," has as its background the Freedom Rides of the early '60s. (The song has been recorded by Judy Collins and others.) After emerging from the Northeast folk-club circuit, Andersen began to record in 1965 with *Today Is the Highway*. His second album, *'Bout Changes and Things*, contained some of his most accomplished writing, including the highly poetic "Violets of Dawn," "Thirsty Boots," and "I Shall Go Unbounded." All were sung in Andersen's flexible tenor (he shaded toward a baritone later), backed by rapid, intricate fingerpicking. In the late '60s and early '70s, Andersen experimented with country, pop, and rock music, settling on an amalgamation by the time of his masterpiece *Blue River* in 1972. This was also his most commercially successful album, but Andersen, like friends Leonard Cohen and Townes Van Zandt, was always too serious-minded for the mainstream. In the '70s and '80s, he recorded sporadically while playing folk clubs around the US and especially in Europe, where he took up residence. His newest recording is the remarkable *Ghosts upon the Road*, in which he reflects ruefully on the '60s. — *William Ruhlmann*

Today Is the Highway / 1965 / Vanguard ✦✦✦

'Bout Changes and Things / 1966 / Vanguard ✦✦✦✦
The best early Andersen. Includes "Violets of Dawn" and "Thirsty Boots." — *William Ruhlmann*

Tin Can Alley / 1968 / Vanguard ✦✦✦✦
This record, which contains "Hello Sun" and "Rollin' Home," is one of his

most solid early albums. It begins and ends with the title cut played by a great junkyard band. —*Richard Meyer*

A Country Dream / 1969 / Vanguard ✦✦✦

Avalanche / 1969 / Warner Brothers ✦✦✦

Eric Andersen / 1970 / Warner Brothers ✦✦✦

Stage / 1973 / CBS ✦✦✦

★ **Blue River** / 1973 / Columbia ✦✦✦✦✦
One of the best folk/rock singer-songwriter albums of the early '70s. —*William Ruhlmann*

Be True to You / 1975 / Arista ✦✦✦

Sweet Surprise / 1976 / Arista ✦✦

Ghosts upon the Road / 1989 / Gold Castle ✦✦✦

Stages: Lost Album / Mar. 1991 / Columbia/Legacy ✦✦✦✦

Lili Aûel

Vocals
Once named best unsigned artist in the New York Music Awards, Aûel has been a fixture on the New York City songwriter's scene since 1979, performing at most of the major venues there. She combines blues, Caribbean, and jazz influences in original material that is powerful and honest. —*Richard Meyer*

Laughed Last / 1994 / Palmetto ✦✦✦✦
This album is marked by beautiful production and arrangements that never call undue attention to themselves. Lili Aûel's singing is relaxed and expressive. In a style reminiscent of Phoebe Snow, Aûel stakes out a personal territory. The title song and "Let Her Go" are particularly strong cuts. Recommended. —*Richard Meyer*

Joan Baez

b. Jan. 9, 1941, Staten Island NY
Guitar, Vocals / Folk, Singer-Songwriter
The most accomplished interpretive folksinger of the '60s, Joan Baez has influenced nearly every aspect of popular music in a career still going strong after more than 30 years. Baez is possessed of a once-in-a-lifetime soprano, which, since the late '50s, she has put in the service of folk and pop music as well as a variety of political causes. Starting out in Boston, Baez first gained recognition at the 1959 Newport Folk Festival, then cut her debut album, *Joan Baez*, released in December 1960. The record was made up of 13 traditional songs, some of them Child ballads, given near-definitive treatment. A moderate success on release, the album took off after the breakthrough of *Joan Baez—Vol. 2*, released a year later, and both albums became huge hits, as did Baez's third album, *Joan Baez in Concert*. Each album went gold and stayed in the bestseller charts more than two years.

From 1962 to 1964, Baez was the popular face of folk music, headlining festivals and concert tours and singing at a variety of political rallies, including the August 1963 March on Washington led by Dr. Martin Luther King, Jr. During this period, she began to champion the work of folk songwriter Bob Dylan, and gradually her repertoire moved from traditional material toward the socially conscious work of the emerging generation of '60s artists like him.

In the late '60s and early '70s, Baez moved toward country and rock music and also began to write her own songs, culminating in the gold-selling *Diamonds and Rust* in 1975. Since then, while her recording career has gradually declined, she has maintained her status on the concert circuit and her commitment to social issues. —*William Ruhlmann*

☆ **Joan Baez** / 1960 / Vanguard ✦✦✦✦✦
Revelatory first album features Baez singing traditional folk songs. —*William Ruhlmann*

Joan Baez in Concert, Vol. 1 / 1962 / Vanguard ✦✦✦✦

Joan Baez in Concert, Vol. 2 / 1963 / Vanguard ✦✦✦
A superb follow-up to *Part 1*, with some more interesting material. —*Bruce Eder*

5 / 1964 / Vanguard ✦✦✦
A good folk set, from a variety of sources. —*Bruce Eder*

Farewell, Angelina / 1965 / Vanguard ✦✦✦
Baez moves toward contemporary work, with songs by Donovan and Woody Guthrie. She sings four songs by Bob Dylan, including the title track. —*William Ruhlmann*

Noel / 1966 / Vanguard ✦✦✦✦
An album of stately beauty, Baez' pure, soaring soprano is accompanied by a consort of recorders and viols, lute, harpsichord, baroque organ, winds, strings, and percussion. Her rendition of the "Coventry Carol" is stirring, and Baez pours her heart into "The Carol of the Birds." Considering Baez's politics, one would never know she recorded this album in the Vietnam War era. —*Decibel Dennis MacDonald*

Joan / 1967 / Vanguard ✦✦✦
Ornate, heavily orchestrated versions of other people's songs. Over-produced, but quite beautiful. —*Bruce Eder*

Any Day Now / 1968 / Vanguard ✦✦✦
Any Day Now is an all-Dylan album that includes a definitive performance of "Love Is Just a Four-Letter Word." —*William Ruhlmann*

● **The First Ten Years** / 1970 / Vanguard ✦✦✦✦
A nearly perfect cross-section of her most enduring work, both traditional and contemporary. —*Bruce Eder*

Come from the Shadows / 1972 / A&M ✦✦✦
After recording for the folk label Vanguard for more than a decade, Baez moved to A&M. On this label debut, she maintained her interest in country music, recording in Nashville with some of the city's session aces. She also continued to dedicate herself to radical politics, from her set opener "Prison Trilogy," which pledged, "We're gonna raze the prisons to the ground," to the closer, John Lennon's "Imagine." In between were her call on Bob Dylan to return to protest music ("To Bobby") and her sister Mimi Farina's touching tribute to Janis Joplin, "In the Quiet Morning." —*William Ruhlmann*

Hits the Greatest & Others / 1973 / Vanguard ✦✦✦
An alternate cross-section of Baez' Vanguard music, including her monster hit "The Night They Drove Old Dixie Down." —*Bruce Eder*

Where Are You Now, My Son? / 1973 / A&M ✦✦✦
Not only is this *not* the place to start listening to Joan Baez, this is the album that separates the true fans from the, um, fellow travelers. Side 2 is taken up by the title song, a musical account of Baez' trip to Hanoi over Christmas of 1972, complete with the sound of US bombs falling on the city. Side 1, on the other hand, contains one of Baez' best original songs, "A Young Gypsy," and two by her sister, "Mary Call" and "Best of Friends." —*William Ruhlmann*

★ **Diamonds and Rust** / 1975 / A&M ✦✦✦✦✦
Baez' peak as a songwriter (title track) and folk/rock interpreter, singing songs of Jackson Browne, John Prine, and Bob Dylan. —*William Ruhlmann*

Joan Baez in Concert / 1976 / Vanguard ✦✦✦
A vibrant concert recording with a radiant sound, humor, and topicality. —*Bruce Eder*

The Best of Joan Baez / 1977 / A&M ✦✦✦✦
Emotionally charged songs from her '70s albums on A&M. Not early Baez, this album of touching songs is probably too commercial for die-hard folk fans. Excellent. —*Michael Erlewine*

Honest Lullaby / 1979 / Portrait ✦✦✦
On her second album for CBS' Portrait label (and her last new album in the US for eight years), Baez was given a full-scale pop-rock production by veteran Barry Beckett and the studio band in Muscle Shoals, AL. The result, on songs that range from "Let Your Love Flow" to "Before the Deluge," is accessible but not particularly memorable '70s-style pop. If you always wanted to know what the words to "No Woman, No Cry" are, however, this is the place to find out. —*William Ruhlmann*

Very Early Joan Baez / 1983 / Vanguard ✦✦✦
A masterful raid on the vault, recapturing the purity and simplicity of her debut recording. —*Bruce Eder*

Live Europe 83: Children of the Eighties / 1983 / Ariola ✦✦✦✦
While Baez declined to record again in the US unless she could get on a major label, she did make several live albums in Europe in the interim. This is the best of them, mixing old favorites like "Farewell, Angelina" with new originals like her heartfelt "For the Children of the Eighties." (Import) —*William Ruhlmann*

Recently / 1988 / Gold Castle ✦✦✦✦
Baez returned to US record shops with a vengeance, delivering her interpretations of songs by Dire Straits, Johnny Clegg, U2, and Peter Gabriel, performers whose political consciousness had been formed by listening to old Joan Baez albums. And on the title track, a stunning original, she boldly answered ex-husband David Harris' downbeat memoir of the '60s, "Dreams Die Hard," as well as other '80s revisionists. —*William Ruhlmann*

Rare, Live and Classic / Sep. 1993 / Vanguard ✦✦✦✦
Spanning three discs, the box set *Rare, Live and Classic* is an odd mix of Baez' best-known songs and rarities. For the hardcore collector, there are plenty of interesting items here, including previously unreleased duets with Bob Dylan, Donovan, Bill Wood, and Jeffrey Shurtleff, but for the casual fan, there's too much material; they would be better off with her original albums or single-disc compilations. —*Stephen Thomas Erlewine*

Cathy Barton and Dave Para

Barton is a protege of Roy Acuff, Jimmy Driftwood, and Grandpa Jones. A master of the frailing banjo style, she has twice won the Tennessee old-time banjo championship. She introduced the hammered dulcimer to the Walnut Valley festival at Winfield. She holds a masters degree in folklore. Para, playing with old-time performers, has developed a great repertoire of traditional songs and stories, and a fantastic stage presence that carries over into their recordings. They have befriended many old-time musicians, encouraging them to join in both performing and recording. Many of their recordings include other Folk-Legacy artists, Missouri old-time fiddlers, and Bob Dyer (the Bard of Boonville). Cathy, Dave, and Bob are currently working on a project of collecting and recording Civil War songs from the Midwest. Parson's great six- and 12-string guitar work, coupled with Barton's banjo, dulcimer, and autoharp, and their fine harmony singing make these recordings a listening treasure. —*Don Stevens*

● **For All the Good People: A Golden Ring Reunion** / Folk-Legacy ✦✦✦✦

Wendy Beckerman

Guitar, Vocals / Singer-Songwriter
New Jersey native Wendy Beckerman came to the Greenwich Village songwriters community in 1989 and has gone on to become a regular performer on the Northeast coffeehouse circuit. —*Richard Meyer*

By Your Eyes / 1992 / Great Divide ✦✦✦
On her debut release, Wendy Beckerman offers a well paced collection of 14 of her direct and poetic songs. Her clear voice is well served by the all-acoustic band and supporting harmonies. Standout tracks include "Lion's Mane," "If I Ask for Love," and "Now Is the Dream." —*Richard Meyer*

● **Marina's Owl** / 1994 / Great Divide ✦✦✦✦
Beckerman has grown a lot since her debut. The songwriting shows that she has a very strong sense of melody and a widening range of subject matter. "The Weasel" is a harrowing and funny song about infidelity and one's place in the crowd. "Blue as My Darlin'" is a potential country hit, an adorable, yet insightful, character study. One wishes the production and arrangement were a little more distinctive, because the songs are strong and varied enough to benefit from it. —*Richard Meyer*

Cindy Lee Berryhill

Guitar, Vocals / Singer-Songwriter, Alternative Pop-Rock, Folk-Rock
Berryhill is a folk-rock singer-songwriter who, although one hates to say it, plays better on paper than on record. Those who bemoan the decline of fresh singer-songwriter talent in the mainstream have to admire her obvious respect for classic singer-songwriter values, and her determination to present them in a present-day context that doesn't merely ape the sound of the '60s and '70s. She has the desirable liberal and feminist politics, and is conscious of delivering these with a sense of humor. But her vocals and songwriting, not to mention that sense of humor, are not top-flight enough to make her more than a minor performer, if a periodically engaging one.

Berryhill has always identified herself with the alternative rock scene, playing in a punk rock band before going solo, and supporting such acts as Billy Bragg, the Smithereens, the Proclaimers, and X. Her music usually owes as much to folk as rock, though. The San Diegan's 1987 debut, *Who's Gonna Save the World*, may be her best simply because it is her most straightforward. Then as now, she was most effective, ironically, at her most basic and serious. Her talking-blues and satirical numbers are not funny or biting enough, and when she adopts a jiving vocal tone, the results are much more awkward than when she just sings.

Berryhill does not lack ambition, moving to New York City in the late '80s to become part of the "anti-folk" scene. It wouldn't be accurate to say that this hurt her career, as the movement wasn't wide enough to be perceived as a failure. But it didn't do much for her either, although former Patti Smith guitarist (and Suzanne Vega producer) Lenny Kaye produced her second album.

Moving back to Southern California in the '90s, she went for a much more unusual sound on 1994's *Garage Orchestra*, enlisting help from musicians who had worked with the San Diego Symphony and the Harry Partch Ensemble. Again, the combination looks more interesting than it sounds, though the ambition is certainly laudable. *Straight Outta Marysville* settles between the extremes, going back to a folkier sound while retaining a wider range of instrumentation than the standard folk-rock unit. —*Richie Unterberger*

● **Who's Gonna Save the World?** / 1987 / Rhino ✦✦✦✦
A reasonably strong debut of a sassy and confident folk-rocker, ranging from rabble-rousing anthems to straight country-folk-rock to playing for laughs. "Looking Through Portholes" and the uncommonly pastoral "Cellaigh Green" are among the best. The more playful narratives are less successful. —*Richie Unterberger*

Naked Movie Star / 1989 / Rhino ✦✦✦✦
This quirky, Los Angeles-based folkie, aided by a folk-rock production courtesy of Lenny Kaye, comments on life in Hollywood, Donald Trump,

and other subjects with a sometimes flip, sometimes self-deprecating attitude. —*William Ruhlmann*

Garage Orchestra / 1994 / Cargo/Earth Music ✦✦✦
Straight Outta Marysville / 1996 / Cargo/Earth Music ✦✦✦

Theodore Bikel

b. Mar. 2, 1924, Vienna, Austria
Guitar, Vocals / Yiddish, Israel, Middle East
Singer, guitarist, song collector, and author Theodore Bikel came to New York in 1955 and was soon an integral part of the folk scene in this country. Speaking17 languages, Bikel was popular in the early and mid-'60s performing the songs of many countries, but particularly those of Israel. —*Michael Erlewine*

● **Sings Yiddish Theatre** / 1991 / Bainbridge ✦✦✦✦
Sings Yiddish Theatre and Folk Songs was originally released in the '60s on Elektra. This 1991 reissue features the original liner notes, complete with Yiddish lyrics and English translations for all 16 tracks, by one of the Yiddish theater's best-known actors. It also features the arrangements of maestro Dov Seltzer. —*Phil Fink*

Tony Bird

b. Malawi
Guitar, Vocals / Folk
Malawi-born Tony Bird was effecting a mixture of modern Western musical styles with traditional African ones ten years before Paul Simon was heard on mbaqanga. Though his excellent '70s recordings went ignored, the surge of interest in African pop in the late '80s got him back in the studio for *Sorry Africa* (Philo 1135) in 1990. —*William Ruhlmann*

● **Bird of Paradise** / 1978 / Columbia ✦✦✦✦
Tony Bird's first album anticipated Paul Simon's fusion of African music and Western folk-pop by ten years. On this, his second album, he combines thoughtful lyrics about such African concerns as apartheid with celebrations of the continent's flora and fauna, using music that evokes both African and US/UK folk styles. —*William Ruhlmann*

Sorry Africa / 1990 / Philo ✦✦✦
Twelve years after his last album, Bird's social commentary is more anguished ("Athlone Incident"), his political statements more plaintive ("Sorry Africa"), and his celebratory songs more fervid ("Mango Time"). He remains the only songwriter honestly taking on the issue of what it means to be White and African. —*William Ruhlmann*

Luka Bloom (Barry Moore)

b. May 23, 1955, Ireland
Guitar, Vocals / Singer-Songwriter
Before making his American debut, Barry Moore recorded three albums in Ireland. Perhaps because his brother is the revered Irish singer Christy Moore, he changed his name to Luka Bloom—Luka is taken from Suzanne Vega's song, Bloom from James Joyce's *Ulysses*. With his literate, melodic, original songs and impassioned live performances, Bloom earned a devoted following in the New York area, which led to his record contract with Reprise. While he can occasionally suffer from over-worked lyrics and a cloying cuteness, Bloom is one of the best post-punk folk performers and songwriters. —*Stephen Thomas Erlewine*

● **Riverside** / Feb. 1990 / Reprise ✦✦✦✦
Expatriate Irishman Luka Bloom cloaks his Celtic folk songs in furious strumming on his "electro-acoustic" guitar, added instrumentation, and echo effects on everything, but he is still a folkie, blowing up his feelings to heroic proportions, whether it's the autobiography of "The Man Is Alive" or the romantic fantasy of "An Irishman in Chinatown." But the content is less convincing than the expression, which is more a characteristic of rock than folk. It isn't that Bloom has much to say, it's that he's so passionate about saying it: he's more Bono than Bob Dylan. Maybe it's an Irish thing. —*William Ruhlmann*

The Acoustic Motorbike / Jan. 1992 / Reprise ✦✦✦✦
Having made his mark in America and moved back home to Ireland, Luka Bloom attempted to incorporate some of the spirit of the country where he spent four years into his Irish folk-rock, covering LL Cool J's "I Need Love" and the Elvis Presley hit "Can't Help Falling in Love." But in his own songs, he didn't go much beyond such surface aspects of the US as Elvis and rap, preferring to devote himself to vague, cliched lyrics of love and longing (some of them not so much rapped as recited), once again set for the most part against his aggressive guitar strumming, various acoustic instruments, and a bottom provided by an Irish bodhran, sometimes played by his brother, Christy Moore. While Bloom's second album expanded somewhat on his first record's stylistic range and maintained its urgency, it lacked the debut's exuberance. Bloom was getting more serious, when what he needed to do was to get more substantive. —*William Ruhlmann*

Turf / Jun. 14, 1994 / Reprise ✦✦✦
A portrait of the Irishman as an American neo-folkie. Having experimented with extra instrumentation on his first two albums, Luka Bloom made a man-with-guitar record his third time out, the better to emphasize his songs, which combine a strong folk traditionalism—one is called "Black Is the Colour (of My True Love's Hair)"; another describes an encounter with a mermaid—with an Amer-Irish social concern. ("Freedom Song" mixes the stories of political activists from each country; "Background Noise" is a tale of violence applicable anywhere, even if it refers to the Irish Troubles.) All of this makes for a more focused record than Bloom's second album, although his debut remains his most satisfying effort. —*William Ruhlmann*

David Blue (S. David Cohen)

b. 1941, Providence, RI, d. Dec. 2, 1982, New York, NY
Vocals / Singer-Songwriter, Folk-Rock
Born in Providence, RI, as S. David Cohen (a name he returned to for one of his albums), David Blue was a member of the folk singer-songwriter community of Greenwich Village in the '60s and a friend of Bob Dylan. (He recounts this period of his life in Dylan's movie *Renaldo and Clara*.) Blue made several albums for Elektra, Reprise, and Asylum in the '60s and '70s, and is best remembered for his songs "I Like to Sleep Late in the Morning" and "Wanted Man" (recorded by the Eagles). — *William Ruhlmann*

● **David Blue** / 1966 / Asylum ✦✦✦✦
Blue's debut album features the first recording of his remarkable "Grand Hotel" and other well written folk/rock songs. — *William Ruhlmann*

Nice Baby and the Angel / 1973 / Asylum ✦✦✦✦
Blue is joined by an all-star California cast (Dave Mason, Graham Nash, David Lindley, and Glenn Frey) for this excellent '70s singer-songwriter collection, which includes "Outlaw Man." — *William Ruhlmann*

Com'n' Back for More / 1975 / Asylum ✦✦✦✦
Blue takes a more jazz/rock approach here, using members of the crony group the Los Angeles Express, whose employer, Joni Mitchell, makes an appearance, as does Blue's old crony, Bob Dylan. — *William Ruhlmann*

Hugh Blumenfeld

b. 1958
Guitar, Vocals / Folk
Brooklyn-born but now residing in Connecticut, Hugh Blumenfeld was a mainstay in the late '80s Greenwich Village scene, an associate editor and contributor of songs to the *Fast Folk Musical Magazine*, winner of the Kerrville New Folk Competition, featured performer on Christine Lavin's *On a Winter's Night* compilation, and the first artist signed to the new 1-800- Prime-CD label. He has a Ph.D. in poetry but doesn't let that get in the way of honest songwriting. —*Richard Meyer*

The Strong in Spirit / 1987 / Grace Avenue ✦✦✦✦
Blumenfeld's first collection contains some of his signature tunes including "Brothers," "Sailing to the New World," and "Rising Moon." Its simple production showcases his intimate vocal style very well. —*Richard Meyer*

Barehanded / 1991 / Grace Avenue ✦✦✦

● **Mozart's Money** / 1996 / 1-800-Prime CD ✦✦✦✦
Hugh Blumenfeld's third album is his strongest so far. Titled *Mozart's Money*, it was produced by David Seitz with a radio-ready sound that is never overbearing. For any who have heard Blumenfeld's two earlier albums and found them a little on the safe side, do take the time to check this record out. He delivers his songs with the confident assurance of someone who knows he has made a quantum leap in his singing dynamics and the consistent focus of his songwriting. Blumenfeld takes on a wide range of subjects, beginning with a humorous musing about where all the money Mozart's work earned has gone, since it certainly didn't go to the composer. There is wonderful vocal support throughout from Lucy Kaplansky, Madwoman in the Attic, and Judith Zweiman. The arrangements are distinctive and make no concessions to a folk audience, although the singer-songwriter nature of the material will still probably still appeal to that audience. "Talking Island" sounds as if he dropped in on the Turtle Island Quartet, "What If You Do Nothing" sounds as if Blumenfeld is channeling Steve Goodman, while "Mr. Rain," an ode to Kurt Cobain, rocks out and hammers the hook into your head with a great guitar part and Blumenfeld's strongest vocal yet. —*Richard Meyer*

Oscar Brand

b. Feb. 7, 1920, Winnipeg, Manitoba, Canada
Guitar, Vocals / Folk, Singer-Songwriter
Oscar Brand is one of the stalwart American folksingers, writers, and interpreters. Over the course of his career he has released 93 albums. He roamed the country with Woody, concertized with Leadbelly, promoted folk of all kinds like Pete Seeger, and has hosted the Folk Song Festival on New York's WNYC for 50 years. Many of his recordings contain parodies on single subjects such as holidays, car songs, or political satire. He is well known for his many collections of bawdy songs. Generally the recording style is simple: Brand and his guitar and a few backup players. Brand's records are totally directed toward the songs. —*Richard Meyer*

● **Best of Oscar Brand** / 1975 / Tradition ✦✦✦✦

Brandywine Singers

From 1962 through 1965 the Brandywine Singers were one of the hottest acts on the college folk circuit. Then life, the Vietnam War, and other careers intervened. The Brandywines re-formed in 1992 with original members Rick and Ron Shaw and Les Clark, joined by multi-instrumentalist, multi-talented Taylor Whiteside. The result is pure magic, folk music as we remember it in its popular heyday and still able to send chills up and down one's spine. Folk favorites, beautifully sung, played, and arranged, spiced with a couple of originals. —*Allan Shaw*

World-Class Folk / 1993 / Folk Era ✦✦✦✦
Here's the group you've never forgotten and never can forget. —*Mike Fleischer*

David Bromberg

Dobro Guitar, Fiddle, Guitar, Mandolin / Blues, Singer-Songwriter
Often referred to as a musician's musician throughout his career, Bromberg has spent almost as much time being a sideman to people like Bob Dylan and Jerry Jeff Walker as he has fronting his own band. Session credits for albums by Tom Paxton and Jerry Jeff Walker started getting Bromberg attention in the mid-'60s, and he began making the transition from sideman to frontman in the early '70s, when he was signed to record for Columbia Records.
The key to appreciating Bromberg is to realize he has an equal passion for blues, folk, country and western, bluegrass, and rock 'n' roll. This diverse range of influences is reflected on all his recordings for Columbia, Fantasy, and Rounder, and in his performances as well. His musical eclecticism over the years may have cost him some fans, but a typical Bromberg concert can be a musical education. —*Richard Skelly*

● **David Bromberg** / 1971 / Columbia ✦✦✦✦
David Bromberg was already a well known folk instrumentalist before this album proved he is also a top-notch songwriter and an appealing vocalist. The styles mix folk, blues, rock, and jug band music, and the songs alternate from the painfully sensitive ("Sammy's Song) to the ribtickling "The Holdup," which was co-written by George Harrison. — *William Ruhlmann*

Wanted Dead or Alive / 1974 / CBS ✦✦✦
Backing musicians include several members of the Grateful Dead, as well as Andy Statman on mandolin and tenor sax. Some of Bromberg's strongest and best-loved material can be found here, including "The Holdup," "Danger Man," "Send Me to the 'Lectric Chair," "The New Lee Highway Blues," and Bob Dylan's "Wallflower." —*Roundup Newsletter*

Midnight on the Water / 1975 / Columbia ✦✦✦
A big-band blowout album with guest appearances by Bonnie Raitt, Linda Rondstadt, and Emmy Lou Harris, it features "The Joke's on Me" and "Don't Put that Thing on Me." —*Richard Meyer*

How Late'll Ya Play 'Til? / 1976 / Fantasy ✦✦✦
Bromberg's band, with two horns and a fiddle player, is capable of playing just about any style of popular music, and most of them are here on a double album, half recorded in the studio and half live. (Fantasy has also issued the two discs separately.) The standout inclusion is Bromberg's "Will Not Be Your Fool," which became his onstage showstopper. —*William Ruhlmann*

Bandit in a Bathing Suit / 1978 / Fantasy ✦✦✦
A lot of hot playing, including Pink Anderson's "Travelin' Man" and "If You Don't Want Me Baby." —*Richard Meyer*

Sideman Serenade / 1990 / Rounder ✦✦

Brothers Four

Folk
The band was formed in 1958 by four University of Washington students (Bob Flick, Michael Kirkland, John Paine, and Richard Foley) who met in a fraternity. The group signed to Columbia in 1959 and immediately hit the charts with "Greenfields." From 1961 to 1963, they toured over 300 college campuses and in 1961 performed on the Academy Awards Show. The Brothers also made TV appearances on "The Ed Sullivan Show," "The Pat Boone Chevy Showroom," and "Mitch Miller's Singalong." They recorded their last Columbia album in 1967. —*David Szatmary*

● **Best Of** / Apr. 1996 / Vanguard ✦✦✦✦

Greg Brown

Guitar, Vocals / Folk, Singer-Songwriter
With his sandpaper-coarse but sensitive baritone, Greg Brown offers

keen insights into the realities and foibles of modern life, tinged with a hefty dose of common sense. He is the son of an electric guitar-playing mother and a Pentecostal preacher and was raised listening to gospel music in rural Iowa. He began singing around age 18 in New York, where he ran hootenannies at Gerdes Folk City. A year later he began writing for Buck Ram (of Platters fame) and his production company. After that he worked with a band for a few years and eventually returned to Iowa to marry. There, he worked for the Iowa Arts Council where he performed for children, mentally challenged people, and hospital patients. It was at this time that he learned to adapt to any situation. He also played in many Midwestern coffeehouses and clubs. From there he worked with Garrison Keillor on the "Prairie Home Companion" live radio program. It was an exciting period for Brown, who enjoyed performing with a wide variety of musicians. Writing with Keillor also proved an interesting, edifying experience.

In 1985 his debut album, *In the Dark with You*, met widespread critical acclaim. The next year he released *Songs of Innocence and Experience*, William Blake's poetry set to music. The album featured BeauSoleil founder Michael Doucet on fiddle. With his own songwriting, Brown expresses many moods in a variety of styles. Many of his compositions are filled with vivid imagery, as in songs such as "Just a Bum" or "Wild Geese" from his first album. Many of his songs tell stories, both humorous and sad. In 1993 he and East Coast folksinger Bill Morrisey teamed up to record the tradition-based album *Friend of Mine*. In addition to recording folk albums for adults, Brown has recorded an intelligent children's album, *Bath Tub Blues*, featuring songs he wrote with elementary school students. —*Sandra Brennan*

In the Dark with You / 1985 / Red House ✦✦✦
Humorous and sardonic reflections on domestic life and aging, from a journeyman folksinger. —*William Ruhlmann*

● **One More Goodnight Kiss** / 1986 / Red House ✦✦✦✦
Brown's best collection of touching, funny, small-town songwriting. —*William Ruhlmann*

One Big Town / 1989 / Red House ✦✦✦
Brown turns his eye outward and views the world cynically on "America Will Eat You." —*William Ruhlmann*

Dream Cafe / 1992 / Red House ✦✦✦

Poet Game / 1994 / Red House ✦✦✦
This release is somber and streetwise, with more political undertones than his previous CDs. The simple "1964 Dodge" is a powerful song about the impending destruction of faith in America after the Kennedy assassination; and it does not even mention the event. Production is simple, and in a few cases one would have liked a bit more thought given to the instrumental arrangement; but still this is a fine stripped-to-the-bone album by a premier contemporary writer. —*Richard Meyer*

The Live One / Oct. 11, 1995 / Red House ✦✦✦✦
On this concert disc recorded at JR's Warehouse in Traverse City, MI, we get to hear Brown's commanding, but relaxed, solo performances of some of his old and new songs. His gravelly voice is remarkably expressive, especially when he is conveying the humorous side of some serious subject. He includes covers of Richard Thompson's "1952 Vincent Black Lightning" and Van Morrison's "Moondance." This is very informal recording, with bits of tuning and chit-chat. The songs, of course, carry the day. "Spring Wind" is heartbreaking and lovely, as is his classic "Canned Goods." —*Richard Meyer*

Richard Buckner

Vocals
A husky-voiced country/folk singer-songwriter very much in the mold of the Lubbock, TX, school of mavericks including Butch Hancock, Terry Allen, and Jimmie Dale Gilmore. Buckner is actually based in San Francisco, but the Lubbock connection is no accident. His debut album, *Bloomed*, was recorded in Lubbock with producer Lloyd Maines, who has also worked with Hancock, Allen, Joe Ely, and Uncle Tupelo. Maines himself plays several instruments on the record, and Buckner's band is fleshed out with several other Texas musicians, including Hancock (who adds a harmonica cameo) and accordion player Ponty Bon.

Buckner's principal following, however, is with the alternative rock, not the country, audience. Like Allen and Hancock, the guitarist's work is based in rootsy country traditions, but his lyrics are far too personal and ambitious for those who think of country music as virtually synonymous with Nashville. So, like those Lubbock musicians, he tends to appeal to open-minded rock fans, or adventurous general music fans, more than country ones. The alternative rock thread is strengthened by Buckner's leadership of a San Francisco country-rock band, the Doubters (who do not appear on his album), and a support slot on a Son Volt tour in early 1996. Appearing on a small Texas independent label, his album won good critical notices, and his signing to a major company shortly afterward probably means that both rock and country listeners will be much more widely exposed to him in the future. —*Richie Unterberger*

Bloomed / 1994 / Dejadics ✦✦✦
Buckner's debut is an accomplished but subdued affair with hardly a trace of rock. The emphasis is on his rich but weary vocals and sober tales of romance and restlessness, with dignified backup by such esteemed regionals as Lloyd Maines (who produced) and Ponty Bon. Very much in the vein of Butch Hancock, but much more ordinary at this point, without the eccentricity and boisterousness that characterizes much of Hancock and fellow Lubbockite Terry Allen's work. —*Richie Unterberger*

Sandy Bull

b. 1941, New York, NY
Guitar / Folk, Folk-Rock
Long before Ry Cooder, Leo Kottke, Richard Thompson, and others were impressing us with their ability to hop from genre to genre, Sandy Bull glided from classical and jazz to ethnic music and rock 'n' roll with grace and verve on his first two albums. Accompanied by renowned jazz drummer Billy Higgins, Bull produced some of the first extended instrumental compositions for guitar that incorporated elements of folk, jazz, and Indian and Arabic-influenced dronish modes. Not "rock" by any stretch of the imagination, it's nevertheless easy to see that it could have had an influence on the rock musicians who began incorporating eclectic and Middle Eastern sensibilities into their music a few years later. After his debut, Bull expanded his arsenal from the acoustic guitar and banjo to include oud, bass, and electric guitar. After his second album, however, his recordings were less focused and less impressive. In the '70s, he dropped out of music altogether due to drug problems, although he began recording again in the late '80s. —*Richie Unterberger*

Fantasias for Guitar and Banjo / Aug. 1963 / Vanguard ✦✦✦
Bull's debut is most notable for the side-long cut "Blend," a 22-minute track on a folk (more or less) album in the days when that just wasn't done outside of classical and jazz records. The second side features imaginative interpretations of traditional gospel and Southern mountain tunes, as well as a work by German composer Carl Orff. —*Richie Unterberger*

● **Inventions for Guitar and Banjo** / 1965 / Vanguard ✦✦✦✦
On his second and best album, Bull added more instruments and a bit of electricity. The centerpiece of the record is "Blend II"; like "Blend" from his first album, it is a melange (somewhat more electric in tone) of folk, jazz, and the Middle East, this time 24 minutes' worth. Also included on this 54-minute LP are two versions (electric and acoustic) of a Bach passage, a composition from the 14th century (Guillaume de Machaut's "Triple Ballade"), and Luiz Bonfa's "Manha de Carnival." A heavily reverbed (with drums), extended version of Chuck Berry's "Memphis, Tennessee" closes the set with an unexpected blast of rock 'n' roll. —*Richie Unterberger*

Jane Byaela

Guitar, Vocals / Folk, Singer-Songwriter
A New York-based singer-songwriter of the '80s and '90s, Byaela's sound crosses between the purity and perfection of Judy Collins and the quirkiness and drama of Suzanne Vega, without ever imitating either. Byaela is a classically trained guitarist, and her songs are all characterized by a virtuoso's command of her instrument and rich tonal colorations amid their intimacy. —*Bruce Eder*

Burning Silver / 1994 / 1-800-Prime CD ✦✦✦
Jane Byaela's second album continues the deeply revealing confessional songwriting which marked her first fine album. Producer David Seitz has recorded her with exceptional clarity. Jane plays the intricate classically inspired guitar and viola parts. The title song is one of the strongest, though many others will be deeply affecting to the listener if they are willing to take some time with this record. —*Richard Meyer*

● **On the Edge** / Spark ✦✦✦✦
An especially pleasing all-acoustic record, soaring artfully and plunging bluesily along on a beguiling and stylized roller-coaster ride that is twice as interesting and three times more honest than Suzanne Vega's best work. —*Bruce Eder*

Andrew Calhoun

Vocals / Urban-Folk, Singer-Songwriter
Andrew Calhoun is a Chicago-based singer-songwriter with a sly but deeply reverent view of life. He released two albums on Flying Fish and recently founded Waterbug Records. —*Richard Meyer*

● **Hope** / Waterbug ✦✦✦✦
This album finds Calhoun in fine form. He is humorous in the face of domestic disaster in "Better Get a Lawyer," and passionate in "I Love You All the Time." His rich voice lends a traditional sound to all he does, but his songs are rooted in a modern poetic sensibility that is uncluttered and powerful. —*Richard Meyer*

Isla Cameron

Vocals

Isla Cameron was one of a quartet of key figures in England's postwar folksong revival—and to give a measure of her importance, the other three were Ewan MacColl, A.L. Lloyd, and Alan Lomax. Her public singing career began quite by accident—she was a member of a theater workshop run by Joan Littlewood, who was then the wife of Ewan MacColl (1915-1989), when she and MacColl met backstage. They began a long friendship and professional relationship, and MacColl helped secure Cameron's first recording, an unusual unaccompanied performance of "The Fair Flower of Northumberland," which was released as a 78 rpm disc by EMI in the early '50s. Cameron became one of the most popular woman folksingers of her day and performed regularly in clubs throughout the British Isles. She had a special affinity for songs from Dorset and Somerset, having grown up there.

Cameron had always set her sights on an acting career in addition to her singing, and in the late '50s she began appearing in movies as well as on stage—she played small roles in *Room At the Top* (1958), *The Innocents* (1961), and *Nightmare* (1963), and a somewhat larger part in *The Prime of Miss Jean Brodie* (1969). Cameron was to have played an on-screen role in John Schlesinger's *Far From The Madding Crowd* (1967), but her scenes were cut. It was no matter, however, for her most important contribution to that film was as music advisor to Schlesinger and composer Richard Rodney Bennett. She chose the songs heard in the film, recruited the other folk artists who worked on the movie, including Fairport Convention alumni Trevor Lucas and fiddler Dave Swarbrick, was responsible for the recording of the folksongs on the soundtrack album, and did the singing for Julie Christie in the film. Cameron continued to record into the mid-'60s, expanding her repertory to include modern material by Bob Dylan, Kurt Weill, and Bertolt Brecht. Her pioneering work in the '50s paved the way for such figures as Sandy Denny and Fairport Convention, and opened English folk music to a wider audience.

Cameron seldom sang in public after the mid-'60s, however, as acting became more the focus of her life. She died in an accident in her home in 1980. —*Bruce Eder*

Cliff Carlisle

Guitar, Vocals

During the '30s, country singer/yodeler/guitarist Cliff Carlisle rivaled Gene Autry as the era's most popular and prolific recording artist. He recorded more than 300 singles for almost all of the major labels, including Gennett, Bluebird, ARC, and Decca. In addition to his Jimmie Rodgers-style yodeling, Carlisle was one of the pioneers of using the Hawaiian guitar in country music. As a singer, he was known for his tendency to sing bluesy, double-entendre-filled songs such as "The Girl in the Blue Velvet Band." At the end of the decade he branched out into crooning cowboy songs and more sentimental tunes in addition to his typical bawdy novelty fare. The latter he occasionally recorded under the alias "Bob Clifford." In the mid-'30s, he and his brother Bill began recording together. By 1936 his son Tommy was singing with them and became known as Sonny Boy Tommy. During the '40s, Cliff and Bill worked together periodically on radio stations throughout the South and in recording studios. In 1946 they scored their biggest hit as a duo with the Top Five "Rainbow at Midnight" on the new King label. Cliff eventually retired around 1950 but turned to recording albums for independent labels after his music became popular again during the folk revival of the '60s. —*Sandra Brennan*

● **Volume 1-2** / Old Timey ✦✦✦✦

Born in 1904 in Mt. Eden, KY, Cliff Carlisle was raised in tobacco country. He drew on songs he heard growing up and wrote a number of his own incorporating themes of the old West. His style is up-tempo, with a lot of yodeling and Hawaiian guitar licks. He performed on the radio in the '30s and with his brother. These LPs collect his rare original recordings. —*Richard Meyer*

Slaid Cleaves

Vocals / Singer-Songwriter

Cleaves is an Austin-based singer-songwriter by way of Maine and is a winner of the 1992 Kerrville Folk Festival's New Folk competition. His rootsy songs have a folk and honky tonk feel to them which, combined with his honest delivery, reminiscent of Peter Case, make them easily accessible. —*Richard Meyer*

Promise / 1990 / Rock Bottom ✦✦✦

The Promise contains 13 straightforward solo performances. These are melodic songs of romantic longing. —*Richard Meyer*

★ **Life's Other Side** / 1992 / Play Hard ✦✦✦✦✦

This simply produced CD contains songs of wandering and wanderers. Many of the lyrics have an underlying theme of mystery. "Willie in the Wind" is one of the highlights. —*Richard Meyer*

For The Brave and Free / 1993 / Slaid Cleaves ✦✦✦✦

The songwriting here is darker than the previous two releases. Like Springsteen's *Nebraska*, this album is comprised of sparse, sketched-out stories. The band is simple and tight. —*Richard Meyer*

Judy Collins

b. May 1, 1939, Seattle, WA

Guitar, Keyboards, Vocals / Folk, Singer-Songwriter, Folk-Rock

Judy Collins was one of the major interpretive folksingers of the '60s. A child prodigy at classical piano, she turned to folk music at the age of 15 and released her first album, *A Maid of Constant Sorrow*, in 1961 when she was 22. That album and its follow-up, *The Golden Apples of the Sun*, consisted of traditional folk material, with Collins' pure, sweet soprano accompanied by her acoustic guitar playing. By the time of *Judy Collins No.3*, she had begun to turn to contemporary material and to add other musicians. (Jim, later Roger, McGuinn tried out his first arrangements of "The Bells of Rhymney" and "Turn, Turn, Turn" on this album, before using them with the Byrds.)

Collins' musical horizons were expanded further by 1966 and the release of *In My Life*, which added theater music to her repertoire and introduced her audience to the writing of Leonard Cohen; it was one of her six albums to go gold. Her first gold-seller, however, was 1967's *Wildflowers*, which contained her hit version of "Both Sides Now" by the then-little-known songwriter Joni Mitchell.

By the '70s, Collins had come to be identified as much as an art song singer as a folksinger and had begun to make a mark with original compositions. Her best-known performances cover a wide stylistic range: the traditional gospel song "Amazing Grace," the Stephen Sondheim Broadway ballad "Send in the Clowns," and such songs of her own as "My Father" and "Born to the Breed."

Collins recorded less frequently after the end of her 23-year association with Elektra Records in 1984, though she made two albums for Gold Castle. In 1990 she signed with Columbia Records and released *Fires of Eden*, her 23rd album. —*William Ruhlmann*

Maid of Constant Sorrow / 1961 / Elektra ✦✦✦

Collins' talent is to sing these traditional chestnuts without prissiness. Her phrasing has enough strength to stand up to the "Prickle Bush" and give in to "Wild Mountain Thyme." —*Richard Meyer*

Golden Apples of the Sun / 1962 / Elektra ✦✦✦

Collins takes on such diverse repertoire as Gary Davis' "Twelve Gates to the City," "Crow on the Cradle," and her setting of "Golden Apples of the Sun." —*Richard Meyer*

3rd Album / 1963 / Elektra ✦✦✦

Having established herself as one of the foremost interpreters of traditional material, Collins did the same for contemporary folk songwriters on this album, which mixed standards with pristine covers of compositions by Dylan, Bob Gibson, Pete Seeger, Ewan MacColl, and Shel Silverstein. With Jim McGuinn arranging and playing second guitar and banjo, this album, which included a fine version of Seeger's "Turn! Turn! Turn!," had a clear (if overlooked) influence on the folk-rock he pioneered with the Byrds a couple years later. —*Richie Unterberger*

Judy Collins' Concert / 1964 / Elektra ✦✦✦

On this live set recorded at Town Hall in New York in 1964, Collins stirs up the audience with a rich mixture of traditional and contemporary covers, including Billy Ed Wheeler's "Coal Tattoo" and Paxton's "Ramblin' Boy." —*Richard Meyer*

5th Album / 1965 / Elektra ✦✦✦✦

Collins took a major stride forward with this fine, consistent album, tailoring both her material and arrangements to reflect contemporary changes shaking folk and folk-rock. Features stellar interpretations of songs by several major '60s songwriters (Dylan, Eric Andersen, Phil Ochs, Gordon Lightfoot, Malvina Reynolds, Richard Farina), and first-rate accompaniment by some of the day's finest folk and folk-rock musicians, including Eric Weissberg, Bill Lee, Danny Kalb, John Sebastian, and Richard Farina (although no drums are present). —*Richie Unterberger*

In My Life / 1966 / Elektra ✦✦✦✦

Collins, who by this point has moved from the acoustic renderings of traditional folk ballads to more extensive instrumentation and the work of contemporary folk writers, takes another step here, turning to tasteful string arrangements by Joshua Rifkin and adding theater music from *Threepenny Opera* and *Marat/Sade* to the Bob Dylan covers. She also starts covering Leonard Cohen ("Suzanne," "Dress Rehearsal Rag"). —*William Ruhlmann*

Wildflowers / 1967 / Elektra ✦✦✦

Passionate and filled with memorable passages. Includes her hit "Both Sides Now" and her first major original composition, "Since You Asked." Leonard Cohen's "Priests" has not appeared elsewhere. —*Bruce Eder and William Ruhlmann*

Who Knows Where the Time Goes / 1968 / Elektra ✦✦✦
Rock and country leanings are found on this album featuring guitarists James Burton and Stephen Stills. Includes the hit "Someday Soon" and Collins' own brilliant "My Father." —*William Ruhlmann*

Recollections / 1969 / Elektra ✦✦✦✦
Collins sings "Tomorrow Is a Long Time," "Early Mornin' Rain," and "Winter Sky." This is a best-of compilation. —*Richard Meyer*

● **Colors of the Day: Best of Judy Collins** / 1972 / Elektra ✦✦✦✦
The biggest hits of her early career, well chosen. —*Bruce Eder*

True Stories and Other Dreams / 1973 / Elektra ✦✦✦
Collins at her most political, saluting Che Guevara, among others. Elaborately produced and well sung. —*Bruce Eder*

Judith / 1975 / Elektra ✦✦✦
A soaring collection of songs from the Depression, '70s Broadway ("Send in the Clowns"), and modern C&W. —*Bruce Eder & William Ruhlmann*

☆ **So Early in the Spring . . .** / 1977 / Elektra ✦✦✦✦✦
So Early in the Spring, the First 15 Years. Double-album best-of covering the years 1961 to 1976; the place to start and also some of the best singing in contemporary folk music. —*William Ruhlmann*

Fires of Eden / 1990 / CBS ✦✦✦✦
A graceful, personal, and finely crafted work that crosses between art song and folk music. —*Bruce Eder*

Live At Newport / 1994 / Vanguard ✦✦✦
A compilation of material recorded at the 1959, 1963, 1964, and 1966 Newport Folk Festivals; it would have been nice if they'd documented what year each song was recorded. In any case, it does reflect Collins' artistic growth during this period, from an interpreter of strictly traditional fare to more contemporary material by Bob Dylan, Richard Farina, and others. Highlights include her versions of "Turn, Turn, Turn," "Blowin' In The Wind," "Hey, Nelly Nelly," "Get Together," and "The Great Silkie," which has the same melody the Byrds used for "I Come and Stand at Every Door" on their *Fifth Dimension* album. All of the songs are previously unreleased, except "The Greenland Whale Fisheries," a duet with Theodore Bikel. On some tracks Collins is accompanied on upright bass by Bill Lee and on second guitar by Steve Mandell or Eric Weissberg. A nice if not essential addition to the Collins catalog. —*Richie Unterberger*

Phil Cooper and Margaret Nelson with Paul Goelz

This Illinois-based duo has released about a dozen recordings and tours constantly. Their work is marked by an intelligent and sensitive reading of traditional songs from all over the Celtic, English, and American map. Cooper is an assured guitarist who uses many alternate tunings to effectively support the songs. Nelson contributes bodhran, doubek, spoons, and understated vocals. On their many albums, Cooper and Nelson are joined by other instrumentalists, but they retain their identity as a duo no matter what. —*Richard Meyer*

● **What Fond Delight** / 1995 / Porcupine ✦✦✦✦

Cornerstone

A group of five musicians with musical roots in Florida, Virginia, Texas, and upstate New York can add up to only one thing: a bluegrass band with a solid folk base that does stunning original material. That's what Cornerstone, based near Ithaca, NY, is all about. Led by banjo player-songwriter Chris Stuart, Cornerstone is made up of vocalist-fiddler Dee Specker, mandolinist-fiddler Rick Manning, bassist Dana Paul, and virtuoso guitarist Tim Wallbridge. This fusion of musicians from old-timey and bluegrass traditions makes for a special sound, one that features twin fiddles on some cuts, Cajun accordion on others, Irish harp, and even the traditional five-piece bluegrass band lineup. The vocals are stunning, the feelings real, the instrumental backup exactly right for each tune. —*Allan Shaw*

● **Out of the Valley** / 1994 / Folk Era Productions ✦✦✦✦
Cornerstone is a bluegrass sensation, and *Out of the Valley* clearly proves it. —*Mike Fleischer*

Elizabeth Cotten
b. 1893, Syracuse, NY, d. Jun. 29, 1987, Syracuse, NY
Guitar / Folk
Elizabeth Cotten has influenced the finger-picking style of every guitarist who tried it since she began performing publicly in the '50s. Cotten worked as a domestic for the Charles Seeger family (whose children included Pete, Peggy, and Mike) in Washington, DC, and was persuaded by Mike Seeger to take up performing at the age of 60. The song "Freight Train," which she wrote when she was 12, became a Top Five hit in the UK and is now a standard. She recorded several albums for Folkways in the '50s and '60s, displaying her remarkably dexterous style, which (like stride piano playing) mixed a strong rhythmic backing with precisely, yet

delicately, picked melody work. She continued to perform until shortly before her death in her mid-90s. —*William Ruhlmann*

★ **Folksongs and Instrumentals with Guitar** / 1958 / Smithsonian/Folkways ✦✦✦✦✦
This first LP collection by a widely influential guitarist includes her classic "Freight Train." —*William Ruhlmann*

Freight Train and Other Folk Songs / 1989 / Smithsonian/Folkways ✦✦✦✦
Reissue of recordings of this National Heritage Award-winning Piedmont guitarist. A model for finger-pickers. —*Barry Lee Pearson*

Mike Cross
Fiddle, Guitar / Folk
Mike Cross is a gifted musician (guitar and fiddle) who started playing late in life. He is known for his high-energy live shows. His songwriting styles lean toward folk, country, and Gaelic. —*Chip Renner*

Carolina Sky / 1975 / Sugar Hill ✦✦✦
Another well done studio album of Cross' energetic songs, played with a crack band. —*Richard Meyer*

Irregular Guy / Sugar Hill ✦✦✦
A solid collection of instrumental rave-up and fun songs from this multi-instrumentalist, it includes "Carolina Calling" and the tongue-twisting "Directions." —*Richard Meyer*

● **Prodigal Son** / Sugar Hill ✦✦✦✦

Live and Kickin' / Sugar Hill ✦✦✦✦
Cross mixes country, folk, bluegrass, and Scots/Irish music, playing fiddle and guitar and singing on material ranging from spirited dance tunes to off-the-wall novelties. He is thus best heard in a live setting. —*William Ruhlmann*

Best of the Funny Stuff / Sugar Hill / ✦✦✦
The title says it. "The Great Strip Poker Massacre," "The Scotsman," and "Dear Boss" are high points. —*Richard Meyer*

Erik Darling and Border Town
b. Sep. 25, 1922, Baltimore, MD
Banjo, Vocals / Folk
Erik Darling was an important influence on the folk scene in the late '50s and early '60s. Inspired by the Weavers, in the '50s he formed the Tunetellers, later called the Tarriers. Darling left that group to replace Pete Seeger in the Weavers, staying with them from 1958 through 1962. He then formed the Rooftop Singers (see separate entry in this section). His solo album *True Religion* for Vanguard influenced younger folksingers in the '60s. —*Michael Erlewine*

● **True Religion** / 1961 / Vanguard ✦✦✦✦
Darling performs on banjo and six- and 12-string guitar. He has good command of the idiom on such tunes as "Moanin' Dove" and "Blackeyed Susan." —*Richard Meyer*

The Possible Dream / 1975 / Elektra ✦✦✦
Featuring guest Patricia Street. —*Michael Erlewine*

Border Town at Midnight / Folk Era ✦✦✦
This group is setting new trends. —*Mike Fleischer*

Iris Dement
Guitar, Vocals / Singer-Songwriter
Iris DeMent's spare, haunting songs and powerful, yet innocent, voice have earned her considerable attention from critics and peers. DeMent grew up in a strongly religious family in Arkansas and sang gospel songs from an early age. A few years after finishing high school in California, DeMent moved to Kansas City and attended two semesters of college, but her newfound obsession with songwriting took precedence over her studies. She played open-mike nights and talent shows for two years before moving to Nashville, where she met songwriter Gene Levine. Levine advised her to send a demo to producer Jim Rooney, who helped DeMent sign with Rounder Records and produced her debut album, *Infamous Angel.* DeMent returned to Kansas City as her audience grew slowly but steadily, and a copy of her album found its way to Warner Brothers. DeMent signed with the label after ensuring that she would retain artistic control of her music, and Warner re-released *Infamous Angel* in 1993. Her second album, *My Life,* was released in 1994. —*Steve Huey*

● **Infamous Angel** / 1992 / Philo ✦✦✦✦
Do you remember hearing Emmylou Harris for the first time? That amazing heartbreak contained in every cracked note? Well, she is now joined in the ranks of Angeldom by newcomer Iris DeMent (in fact, Emmylou joins us in welcoming her, adding her harmonies to the sweet "Mama's Opry". Most are originals, gems one and all, poignant remembrances, wry observations, and lovely portraits, with titles like "Hotter than Mojave in My Heart" and "50 Miles of Elbow Room." She embodies

everything that's wonderful about traditional country music, incorporating bluegrass, gospel, blues, and a bit of swing. —*Ladyslipper*

My Life / 1993 / Warner Brothers ✦✦✦✦
Since her beautiful debut record on Philo, Iris DeMent has graduated to the majors with her style intact. She has a confessional spirit and maintains her perspective as a free thinker. The album is dedicated to her father, and it is lovely throughout. These are songs that sound as if they've always been around. —*Richard Meyer*

Sandy Denny

b. Jan. 6, 1948, London, England, **d.** Apr. 21, 1978, London, England
Guitar, Piano, Vocals / Folk-Rock, British Folk
Maddy Prior, Jacqui McShee, and June Tabor all give her a run for her money, but the late Sandy Denny remains the pre-eminent British folk-rock singer. In addition to recording several albums of her own, Denny was an integral force behind the best work of the most respected British folk-rock band of all, Fairport Convention, and also contributed mightily to recordings by the Strawbs and Fotheringay. It's impossible for words to fully evoke the haunting, spectral presence of her powerful and penetrating alto voice, which seemed to bring the mythology of English moors and folktales to life in contemporary settings.

Denny was studying to be a nurse when she began to pursue music seriously in the mid-'60s, partially at the encouragement of the then-struggling Simon & Garfunkel, whom she met when they were still unknown. She was also friendly with the American folk singer Jackson Frank and recorded a couple of his songs on her first album (now available as *The Original Sandy Denny*). While this solo acoustic recording was her most traditional folk effort, it showed considerable potential, which she came closer to realizing on the 1967 album she recorded as a member of the Strawbs. This found her singing with fuller folk-rock arrangements and included her first recorded composition, "Who Knows Where the Time Goes." The song gave Sandy her first international recognition when Judy Collins recorded it in 1968.

Denny was tapped to replace Judy Dyble in Fairport Convention in 1968 and is prominently featured on their late-'60s albums *What We Did on Our Holidays*, *Unhalfbricking*, and *Liege and Lief*. These are recognized not only as Fairport's best work, but as some of the finest British folk-rock records of all time. Although Denny shared the lead vocal chores with other members of the group, it was her singing that highlighted the best tracks, such as "Tam Lin," "Fotheringay," and "Autopsy" (the last two of which she wrote).

Denny left Fairport Convention in 1970, and while both she and Fairport would produce some worthwhile work in the future, it's fair to say that neither band nor singer would reach the same peaks again. She formed the short-lived Fotheringay, which included her future husband, Trevor Lucas, on guitar, but which disbanded after one album. (A planned second LP was never completed.) She recorded a few solo albums for Island in the '70s that sometimes suffered from unsympathetic over-production and weak material, though the highlights are worth hearing. There was also an unremarkable album of oldies covers that she helped out with as a member of the Bunch, a British folk supersession of sorts that also included Richard Thompson. When mainstream rock listeners heard her voice in the '70s, however, it was usually not on her own records, but as a guest vocalist on Led Zeppelin's "The Battle of Evermore." Much of the best of Denny's later solo work, oddly, is found on live and BBC recordings, some of which surfaced on the box set *Who Knows Where the Time Goes?* (Others appear on the bootleg *Dark the Night*.) While Denny was a first-rate folk-rock singer, she usually didn't mesh well with mainstream rock or hard rock arrangements, and the live work usually framed her vocals in more appropriately sparse settings. She joined Fairport again for a while in the mid-'70s, appearing on the 1975 album *Rising for the Moon*, but the reunion didn't really excite either the participants or the audiences, and she left for good in 1976. Her final LP, *Rendezvous*, came out in 1977; the following year, she died from injuries sustained in a fall down a flight of stairs. —*Richie Unterberger*

All Our Own Work / 1968 / Pickwick ✦✦✦

Sandy Denny / 1970 / Saga ✦✦✦

North Star Grassman and the Ravens / 1971 / Hannibal ✦✦✦
Some second thoughts and re-approaches to older work. —*Bruce Eder*

Sandy / 1972 / A&M ✦✦✦✦
Those seeking initiation into the ranks of Denny fans may consult listings for Fairport Convention and Fotheringay. Also try this solo album, which features many of the same players (Richard Thompson, Dave Swarbrick, etc.) and contains a good collection of Denny originals, along with her rendition of Dylan's "Tomorrow Is a Long Time." —*William Ruhlmann*

Rendezvous / 1977 / Hannibal ✦✦✦
Stylistically varied, if not so fresh as her album *Sandy*. —*Bruce Eder*

Sandy Denny and The Strawbs / 1985 / Hannibal ✦✦✦
Pre-Fairport Denny with a British bluegrass band that later moved into progressive rock (without her). Her voice and a moody rendition of her classic "Who Knows Where the Time Goes" make it worthwhile. —*Bruce Eder*

Who Knows Where the Time Goes [Box Set] / 1986 / Hannibal ✦✦✦✦
This magnificently produced multi-disc box set presents a complete portrait of Sandy Denny, the haunting singer; the melodic, mournful songwriter; and the mesmerizing bandleader of Fairport Convention and Fotheringay. Much of the material is previously unheard, but it's all of a piece with Denny's accomplished work on her solo albums and in her groups. The album makes the case for Denny as a major folk artist. —*William Ruhlmann*

● **The Best of Sandy Denny [Best of Box]** / 1989 / Hannibal ✦✦✦✦
A concise collection of key tracks and an excellent introduction. —*Bruce Eder*

Original Sandy Denny / 1991 / Trojan ✦✦✦
Denny's first recording, originally released in 1967, is her most traditional effort. Backed only by her own acoustic guitar, Denny's voice is assured, pure, and powerful. The album features traditional folk staples like "This Train," "Make Me a Pallet On Your Floor," and "Pretty Polly," as well as covers of Tom Paxton's "Ramblin' Boy" and "Milk and Honey." There are also a couple of songs by the obscure American songwriter Jackson Frank, one of which she would soon perform with Fairport Convention ("You Never Wanted Me"). Although this has little of the folk-rock cross-pollination that Denny would soon master with Fairport and others, it is still an impressive LP that shows her voice in as haunting and commanding form as her more renowned recordings. —*Richie Unterberger*

Dark The Night [Bootleg] / 1995 / Nixed ✦✦✦✦
Excellent not just by bootleg standards, but by any standards, this 73-minute disc assembles unreleased demos and BBC sessions from 1966, 1972, and 1973. Two BBC performances from 1966, and seven demos from the same year, show Denny at her purest and most traditional, her voice accompanied only by acoustic guitar. These early cuts are similar to the obscure *Original Sandy Denny* album (also recorded around 1966) in showcasing her amazing high, soaring vocals on a mixture of traditional material and contemporary folk songs. What's more, the sound quality is excellent, at least as good as the official *Original Sandy Denny*; only one song from that album is performed on this disc, which also includes Sandy covering unexpected tunes like Dylan's "It Ain't Me Babe" and folkie Jackson Frank's "Blues Run the Game." The 1972-73 BBC sessions, in stellar quality, feature Denny originals from the period and a couple of jazz/pop covers with basic, straightforward arrangements. As Denny's solo albums often suffered from over-production, these performances actually benefit from the sparseness. Closing the CD are two odd but atmospheric pieces from the obscure 1972 soundtrack *Pass of Arms*. It might not be that easy for everyone to find, but Sandy Denny fans need this disc—it not only fills in important gaps, but stands up well against her best solo releases. —*Richie Unterberger*

Hazel Dickens

b. West Virginia
Vocals / Folk
One of 11 children of a West Virginia preacher, Hazel Dickens has recorded self-penned songs of deep conviction, delivered with rough-edged passion. A country singer too raw for Nashville, Dickens is generally pegged a folksinger, albeit one without a dulcet warble. She's more akin to Sara Carter than to Joan Baez. Dickens also has been placed in the bluegrass camp, though one suspects her labor activism and feminism make much of her company there uneasy. Twenty years ago, her album with Alice Gerrard, *Hazel and Alice* (Rounder), was a cult classic that inspired, among others, Emmylou Harris. Her anthemic "They'll Never Keep Us Down" appeared in the award-winning documentary *Harlan County, USA*. Dickens' solo albums for Rounder are uniformly excellent, the title of one (borrowed from Woody Guthrie) neatly summarizing her work: *Hard Hitting Songs for Hard Hit People*. This is a woman Guthrie would've loved as a kindred spirit. —*Mark A. Humphrey*

Hard Hitting Songs / 1980 / Rounder ✦✦✦
Hard Hitting Songs for Hard Hit People is a very good record that deals wit the out-of-work, down-on-his-luck, average American. It features Nancy and Norman Blake, Tony Trischka, Ross Barenberg, James Bryan, Matt Glaser, Barry Mitterhoff, and Buddy Spicher. —*Chip Renner*

★ **By the Sweat of My Brow** / 1983 / Rounder ✦✦✦✦✦
A great record that which features "By the Sweat of My Brow," "Old and in the Way," "The Ballad of Ira Hayes," and "Your Greedy Heart." —*Chip Renner*

Hard to Tell the Singer from the Song / 1987 / Rounder ✦✦✦✦
Dickens covers Dylan's "Only a Hobo" and Dallas Frazier's "California Cottonfields." Jerry Douglas, Pat Enright, Roy Husky, Ross Barenberg, and Mike Compton back her up. —*Chip Renner*

Connie Dover

Keyboards, Vocals / Folk
A resident of Missouri, Connie Dover is the stunning singer with the American Irish group Scartaglen. She became interested in British and Irish music in the '70s but started out playing bluegrass. She got involved in the Kansas City Irish music scene and joined Scartaglen in the early '80s. The '90s have brought a blossoming solo career. *—Steve Winick*

Somebody / 1991 / Taylor Park Music ◆◆◆◆
A triumphant solo debut, *Somebody* features a backing band made up of members of Silly Wizard, Capercaillie, and the Boys of the Lough. Dover treats traditional Scottish, Irish, and American material, along with medieval and contemporary songs. It's one of the most impressive albums of this sort to come from the US. *—Steve Winick*

★ **Wishing Well** / 1994 / Taylor Park ◆◆◆◆◆
This one improves upon *Somebody,* with many of the same accompanists and styles represented. Dover's soaring voice is lovely and pure, and the arrangements are lively and interesting. *—Steve Winick*

Nick Drake

b. Jun. 19, 1948, Burma, d. Nov. 25, 1974, Worchestershire, UK
Guitar, Vocals / Singer-Songwriter, Folk-Rock, British Folk
A singular talent who passed almost unnoticed during his brief lifetime, Nick Drake produced several albums of chilling, somber beauty. With hindsight, these have come to be recognized as peak achievements of both the British folk-rock scene and the entire rock singer-songwriter genre. Sometimes compared to Van Morrison, Drake in fact resembled Donovan much more in his breathy vocals, strong melodies, and the acoustic-based orchestral sweep of his arrangements. His was a much darker vision than Donovan's, however, with disturbing themes of melancholy, failed romance, mortality, and depression lurking just beneath, or even well above, the surface. Ironically, Drake has achieved a far greater stature in the decades after his death, with an avid cult following that grows by the year.

Part of Drake's failure to attract a mass audience was attributable to his almost pathological reluctance to perform live. It was at a live show in Cambridge, however, that a member of Fairport Convention saw Drake perform, and recommended the singer to producer Joe Boyd. Boyd, already a linchpin of the British folk-rock scene as the producer for Fairport and the Incredible String Band, asked Drake for a tape, and was impressed enough to give the 20-year-old a contract in 1968.

Drake's debut, *Five Leaves Left* (1969), was the first in a series of three equally impressive, and quite disparate, albums. With understated folk-rock backing (Pentangle bassist Danny Thompson plays bass on most of the cuts), Drake created a vaguely mysterious, haunting atmosphere, occasionally embellished by tasteful baroque strings. His economic, even pithy, lyrics hinted at melancholy; yet any thoughts of despair were alleviated by the gorgeous, uplifting melodies and Drake's calm, measured vocals. *Bryter Layter* (1970) was perhaps his most upbeat effort, featuring support from members of Fairport Convention and traces of jazz in the arrangements. On some cuts, the singer-songwriter, remarkably, dispensed with lyrics altogether, offering only gorgeous, orchestrated instrumental miniatures that stood well on their own.

Neither album sold well, and Drake, already a brooding loner, plunged into serious depression that often found him unable to make music, work, or even walk and talk. He managed to produce one final full-length work, *Pink Moon* (1972), a desolate solo acoustic album that ranks as one of the most naked and bleak statements in all of rock. He did record a few more songs before his death, but no more albums were completed, although the final sessions (along with some other fine unreleased material) surfaced on the posthumous compilation *Time of No Reply.*

Drake's final couple of years were marked by increasing psychiatric difficulties, which found him hospitalized at one point for several weeks. He had rarely played live during his days as a recording artist, and at one point declared his intention never to record again, although he wished to continue to write songs for others. (It's been reported that French chanteuse Francoise Hardy recorded some of Drake's songs, but she hasn't released any.) On November 26, 1974, he died in his parents' home from an overdose of antidepressant medication; suicide has been speculated, although some of his family and friends dispute this.

In the manner of the young romantic poets of the 19th century who died before their time, Drake is revered by many listeners today, with a following that spans generations. Baby boomers who missed him the first time around found much to revisit once they discovered him, and his genuine loneliness speaks directly to contemporary alternative rockers who share his sense of morose alienation. *—Richie Unterberger*

Five Leaves Left / 1969 / Hannibal ◆◆◆◆
Nick Drake's debut album skillfully augments his haunting folk-based songs with tasteful string arrangements that accentuate the gorgeous melancholy of his music. *—Stephen Thomas Erlewine*

Bryter Layter / 1970 / Hannibal ◆◆◆◆
While the strings on Nick Drake's second album are more prominent, they rarely take away from the impact of his music, which is significantly less sad on this record. However, *Bryter Layter* isn't lighthearted—it's a reflective piece of music that gains power from its own introspection. *—Stephen Thomas Erlewine*

Pink Moon / 1972 / Hannibal ◆◆◆◆
Nick Drake strips away all of the excess instrumentation of his first two albums, keeping only the bare essentials. The result is a stark, brilliant album of despair, loneliness, and alienation that is startling in its emotional power. *—Stephen Thomas Erlewine*

★ **Fruit Tree** / 1986 / Hannibal ◆◆◆◆◆
Multi-disc album contains the complete works of this enigmatic British singer-songwriter. *—William Ruhlmann*

Time of No Reply / 1986 / Hannibal ◆◆◆
A collection of ten previously unreleased tracks recorded between 1968 and 1974, the songs on *Time of No Reply* rank with Nick Drake's finest work. *—Stephen Thomas Erlewine*

Way to Blue: An Introduction to Nick Drake / 1994 / Hannibal ◆◆◆
Sixteen tracks from three of his studio albums and the *Time Of No Reply* collection, compiled by Drake's producer, Joe Boyd. Of course the music is excellent, but Drake's albums stand so well on their own that this collection of piecemeal offerings hardly works as the best way to experience his distinctively haunting brand of folk-rock. *—Richie Unterberger*

Tanworth-in-Arden 1967/68 / Bootleg ◆◆◆

Judy Dunaway

Urban-Folk
From rural Mississippi, Dunaway uses balloons, bottle brushes, and standard instruments for songs about monsters, nudity, death, and immigration. Her songs range in style from rock to salsa to country to blues to noise, suspended over irregular rhythms and forms that often incorporate free improvisation. This is experimental but not at all self-indulgent. *—Richard Meyer*

Judy Dunaway / 1990 / Lost ◆◆◆◆
The remarkable variety here is typified by "Missionary Kid" and "El Norte." *—Richard Meyer*

Cliff Eberhardt

Guitar, Vocals / Folk, Singer-Songwriter, Folk
New York-based singer-songwriter Cliff Eberhardt combines a hoarse, expressive voice with a dynamic guitar style for some of the most moving music to be heard in the "new folk" music of the '80s and '90s. Though his debut album released in 1990, *The Long Road,* shows how stirring he can be, *The Songwriters Exchange,* a compilation made ten years earlier, shows he's been good for a long time. *—William Ruhlmann*

The Long Road / 1990 / Windham Hill ◆◆◆◆
The debut from one of the best of the new crop of folksinger-songwriters. *—William Ruhlmann*

● **Now You Are My Home** / 1993 / Sanachie/Cachet ◆◆◆◆
On his second release, Pennsylvania-born Eberhardt gets closer to the energy of his live sound with this well-produced album. He is joined by Patty Larkin, John Gorka, and Nanci Griffith. The collection is engaging all the way through to the driving "Make Me Believe." *—Richard Meyer*

Mona Lisa Cafe / 1995 / Shanachie ◆◆◆

Ed's Redeeming Qualities

Folk
Quirky, contemporary folk trio. Singing of distributor caps, lawn darts, and guys named Bob, Ed's Redeeming Qualities is responsible for two cleverly amusing albums that transcend genre limitations. Sharing vocals are violinist/guitarist Carrie Bradley, ukulele ace Dan Leone, and bongos/clarinet man Neno Perrotta (who also shakes a mean jar of rice). The San Francisco-based ERQ debuted on Flying Fish Records with *More Bad Times* in 1990 (the set is dedicated to Dom Leone, writer of "Buck Tempo," who died before its release), and encored with *It's All Good News,* another delightfully off-the-wall 1991 collection. *—Bill Dahl*

● **More Bad Times** / 1990 / Flying Fish ◆◆◆◆
Creative, low-fi folk with a silliness that is almost, but not quite, cloying. Humorous lyrics, with instruments like xylophones, ukuleles, and a coffee can. *—Robert Gordon*

It's All Good News / 1991 / Flying Fish ◆◆◆

Ramblin' Jack Elliott

b. Aug. 1, 1931, Brooklyn, NY
Guitar, Vocals / Folk
Ramblin' Jack Elliott, who has been playing folk music since the '40s, is

an important link between Woody Guthrie (Elliott's dominant influence) and the folk artists of the '60s and after. A repository of folk-blues, cowboy songs, and early country, an archivist, and an excellent performer. — *William Ruhlmann*

Sings the Songs of Woody Guthrie / 1960 / Prestige International ✦✦✦✦

Elliott interprets many of the most popular items in the Guthrie repertoire, including "So Long," "This Land Is Your Land," "Pretty Boy Floyd," "Talking Dust Bowl," and "Philadelphia Lawyer," on the LP that is most representative of his role in popularizing the work of his hero. It's been combined with another early-'60s Prestige album, *Ramblin' Jack Elliott*, on Fantasy's *Hard Travelin'* CD reissue. — *Richie Unterberger*

Ramblin' Jack Elliott / 1961 / Prestige ✦✦✦

A solidly traditional set of interpretations of standards like "The Cuckoo," "Rollin' in My Sweet Baby's Arms," "East Virginia Blues," and "Railroad Bill," as well as occasional blues covers ("Candyman," "San Francisco Bay Blues"). John Heard (second guitar) and Ralph Rinzler (mandolin) help out occasionally on this set, which has been combined with another early-'60s Prestige album, *Sings the Songs of Woody Guthrie*, on Fantasy's *Hard Travelin'* CD reissue (with one song, "I Love You So/I Got a Woman," omitted for space reasons). — *Richie Unterberger*

★ The Essential Ramblin' Jack Elliott / 1970 / Vanguard ✦✦✦✦✦

Elliott was the complete folksinger of the '60s, singing and yodeling traditional material derived from folk, country, and blues sources and (especially) carrying on the tradition of Woody Guthrie. This two-pocket set, some of which is taken from a 1965 concert, provides a representative sampling of his repertoire and style. — *William Ruhlmann*

Sings Woody Guthrie and Jimmie Rodgers / 1976 / Monitor ✦✦✦

Elliott devotes one side each to his two chief influences, re-creating Guthrie standards such as "Grand Coulee Dam" and "I Ain't Got No Home" as well as Rodgers' favorites like "T for Texas" and "Waitin' for a Train." Not coincidentally, he brings out the similarities between them. — *William Ruhlmann*

Hard Travelin' / 1989 / Fantasy ✦✦✦✦

Elliott's early-'60s Prestige LPs *Sings the Songs of Woody Guthrie* and *Ramblin' Jack Elliott* are combined onto a single 77-minute disc on this CD reissue, with one song ("I Love Her So/I Got a Woman") deleted for space reasons. It's not as good as hearing Guthrie himself, and may strike contemporary listeners as a bit tame and dated. Elliott played an important role in the '60s folk revival as a popularizer of Guthrie's songs and style, though, and this is one of the best places to hear him at his best, on both Guthrie covers and interpretations of various traditional and blues songs. — *Richie Unterberger*

Country Style / Prestige ✦✦✦

Elliott knows how to tell a story, as we hear on this album, which has him interpreting "Wabash Cannonball," "Wreck of the Old 97," and "Lovesick Blues." — *Richard Meyer*

Alejandro Escovedo

Guitar, Vocals / Progressive Country

Alejandro Escovedo's family tree includes former Santana percussionist Pete Escovedo and Pete's daughter, Sheila E (also Prince's former drummer and later a pop star). He began his music career with the Nuns, a mid-'70s punk band based in San Francisco. He co-founded the cowpunk band Rank and File in 1979, which moved to Austin, TX, in 1981 after a stint in New York City. The band released *Sundown* on Slash Records; shortly after, Escovedo left to form the True Believers with brother Javier. The band recorded two albums for EMI (the second was never released, a fact that eventually caused the band to break up in 1988) and toured the country, often as an opening act for Los Lobos. Escovedo released a solo album, *Gravity*, in 1992 on Watermelon Records, uniting his wide variety of styles; the album was produced by Stephen Bruton of Bonnie Raitt's band. — *John Bush*

● Gravity / 1992 / Watermelon ✦✦✦✦

He's got a sandpaper quality to his voice that gives credibility to these songs, many of which have an edge of danger or desperation. This is guitar-based music enhanced by dramatic arrangements making use of orchestral touches and a rockin' band. "Broken Bottle" is like a beautiful chamber work. — *Richard Meyer*

Thirteen Years / 1994 / Watermelon ✦✦✦✦

The Austin singer-songwriter reaches deep once again, adding triple violins, harp, and cello to his palette of movingly introspective material. Overall, the expanded lineup provides for plenty of tonal space. Before the mood ever gets maudlin, Escovedo cranks up the volume with guest guitarist Charlie Sexton for "Losing Your Touch," a playful rocker that could have come from the Replacements/Paul Westerberg camp. With the exception of this track, "Mountain of Mud," and the John Cougar-ish "The End," *Thirteen Years* keeps to fragile, graceful interiors. — *Roch Parisien*

With These Hands / Jun. 18, 1996 / Rykodisc ✦✦✦

Alejandro Escovedo's third solo album, *With These Hands*, is his most direct, straightforward collection to date. Stripping away some of the ambitious musical eclecticism that characterized his earlier records, Escovedo sticks with rock 'n' roll and country-rock, and the results are frequently bracing. The songs bear his trademark cutting lyrical bite, and they are brought alive by the lean attack of his band, which helps bring alive the meanings of the songs. Both Escovedo's incisive songwriting and his passionate performing make *With These Hands* a roots-rock record that matters. — *Stephen Thomas Erlewine*

John Fahey

b. Feb. 28, 1939, Cecil County, MD

Guitar / Instrumental, Bluegrass, Folk

One of acoustic music's true innovators and eccentrics, John Fahey has been crucial in expanding the boundaries of the acoustic guitar over the last few decades. His music is so eclectic that it's arguable whether he should be defined as a "folk" artist. In a career that has seen him issue several dozen albums, he's drawn from blues, Native American music, Indian ragas, experimental dissonance, and pop. His good friend Dr. Demento has noted that Fahey "was the first to demonstrate that the finger-picking techniques of traditional country and blues steel-string guitar could be used to express a world of nontraditional musical ideas—harmonies and melodies you'd associate with Bartok, Charles Ives, or maybe the music of India." The more meditative aspects of his work foreshadowed new age music; yet Fahey plays with a fierce imagination and versatility that outshines any of the guitarists in that category. His idiosyncrasy may have limited him to a cult following, but it also ensured that his work continues to sound fresh.

Fahey was a colorful figure from the time he became an accomplished guitarist in his teens. Already a collector of rare early blues and country music, he made his first album in 1959, ascribing part of it to the pseudonymous "Blind Joe Death." Only 95 copies of the LP were pressed, making it a coveted collector's item today. (In the '60s, Fahey would re-record the material for wider circulation.) In college, he wrote a thesis on Charley Patton (an exotic subject at the time). Yet Fahey did not perform publicly for money until the mid-'60s, after his third album.

Fahey's early albums for Takoma in the mid-'60s laid out much of the territory he would explore. His instrumentals, filtering numerous genres of music into his own style, evoked haunting and open spaces. At times they could be soothing and plaintive; at other times they were disquieting, even dissonant. The more experimental aspects of his material even foreshadowed psychedelia in their lengthy improvisations (some cuts lasted as long as 20 minutes), use of Indian modes, unpredictable stylistic shifts, and overall eerie strangeness. His persona as a weirdo of sorts was amplified by his bizarre and lengthy song titles and liner notes. He also employed odd guitar tunings that continue to exert an overlooked influence on contemporary musicians to this day.

Fahey remained consistently popular on a cult level through the mid-'80s. His most commercially successful efforts, oddly, were probably his Christmas albums, which are among the more interesting holiday records of any genre. For a time he ran the Takoma label, where he was instrumental in starting the career of Leo Kottke (who owes much of his stylistic inspiration to Fahey), as well as promoting lesser-known talents like Robbie Basho. He was a catalyst in other subtle ways, helping to form Canned Heat by introducing Al Wilson (who played on a Fahey album in 1965) to Bob Hite, and rediscovering Delta bluesman Bukka White with his friend Ed Denson.

Fahey sold Takoma to Chrysalis in the mid-'70s but continued to record regularly and tour (though his live performances were erratic). In 1986, he contracted Epstein-Barr syndrome, a long-lasting viral infection that, combined with diabetes and other health problems, sapped his energy and resources. Although the Epstein-Barr virus was finally overcome, the mid-'90s found him living in poverty in Oregon, where he paid his rent by pawning his guitar and reselling rare classical records. The appearance of a major career retrospective on Rhino, *Return of the Repressed*, in 1994 boosted his profile to its highest level in years. Now in his mid-50s, he still plays, is writing a book of memoirs, and is hopefully preparing a return to active recording. The Fahey discography is dauntingly large and diverse; the neophyte is advised to start with the two-disc *Return of the Repressed* or search for the Takoma LPs (which have, unfortunately, become hard to find). — *Richie Unterberger*

★ The Transfiguration of Blind Joe Death / 1959 / Takoma ✦✦✦✦✦

This is the definitive work by this influential acoustic guitar master. — *William Ruhlmann*

Vol. 3: Dance of Death and Other Plantation Favorites / 1965 / Takoma ✦✦✦

One of Fahey's less eccentric early efforts, featuring relatively straightforward instrumentals showcasing his deft fingerwork and occasional keening slide. Blues, ragtime, and Appalachian influences come to the fore on this even-toned collection, with occasional excursions into dark and somber territory, as on the closing track "Dance Of Death." Also includes an adaptation of "Poor Boy," taken from Bukka White, whom Fahey rediscovered with Ed Denson in the early '60s. — *Richie Unterberger*

John Fahey, Vol. 4 / 1966 / Takoma ✦✦✦
Also known as *The Great San Bernardino Birthday Party And Other Excursions*, this hodgepodge of tracks from 1962 to 1966 nevertheless stands as Fahey's most, well, far-out work. The 19-minute "The Great San Bernardino Birthday Party" anticipated elements of psychedelia with its nervy improvisation and odd guitar tunings, and other tracks broke ground for acoustic guitar with their unsettling moods and dissonances, even using backwards tapes. — *Richie Unterberger*

Voice of the Turtle / 1968 / Takoma ✦✦✦✦
Like some of Fahey's other projects in the '60s, this was actually recorded/assembled over a few years, primarily composed of duets with various other artists (including overdubs with his own pseudonym, Blind Joe Death). One of his more obscure early efforts, it's both listenable and wildly eclectic, going from scratchy emulations of early blues 78s and country fiddle tunes to haunting guitar-flute combinations and eerie ragas. "A Raga Called Pat, Part III & IV" is a particularly ambitious piece, its disquieting swooping slide and brief bits of electronic white noise reverb veering into experimental psychedelia. Most of this is pretty traditional/acoustic in tone, however, though it has the undercurrent of dark, uneasy tension that gives much of Fahey's '60s material its intriguing combination of meditation and restlessness. — *Richie Unterberger*

Old Girlfriends and Others / 1992 / Varrick ✦✦✦

● Return of the Repressed: Anthology / 1994 / Rhino ✦✦✦✦
It could be argued that this 42-song double CD, covering Fahey's work from the early '60s to the early '90s, is too piecemeal, drawing from no less than 20 albums, many of which work well on their own. It could also be argued, with equal validity, that very few listeners, even Fahey fans, own all or even most of these records. On those grounds, this well-chosen retrospective must be judged a winner, working as well as an entity as his best albums. Features extensive liner notes by Fahey's longtime friend Barry ("Dr. Demento") Hansen and comments on the songs by Fahey himself. — *Richie Unterberger*

Mimi Farina

b. Apr. 30, 1945, California
Vocals / Folk
Mimi Farina, Joan Baez's younger sister, first got into performing professionally in partnership with her husband, novelist and songwriter Richard Farina, whom she married in 1963. Singing harmony, the couple released two remarkable albums on Vanguard, *Celebrations for a Grey Day* in 1965 and *Reflections in a Crystal Wind* (1966), before Richard was killed in a motorcycle accident. Mimi Farina was 21.

She subsequently released an album of the duo's outtakes, *Memories*. (The two albums made during Richard's lifetime were reissued as a best-of two-fer.) In the late '60s, Farina, based in California, worked with a satiric improvisational acting group and began to write her own songs. She re-emerged on record in 1971 on *Take Heart*, a duo album with Tom Jans that included her tribute song to Janis Joplin, "In the Quiet Morning." (This and other songs of hers were also recorded by her sister.)

In the '70s, Farina founded Bread and Roses, a charity organization devoted to putting on musical performances in hospitals and prisons. Several of the organization's annual benefit concerts, featuring some of the biggest names in folk and popular music, have been recorded and released. In 1985 Farina finally released a solo album, appropriately entitled *Solo*, and undertook a national tour. — *William Ruhlmann*

● Solo / 1985 / Philo ✦✦✦✦

Hit Songs, Vol. 1 [Portugal] / Monitor ✦✦✦

Hit Songs, Vol. 2 [Portugal] / Monitor ✦✦✦

Richard and Mimi Farina

Folk-Rock
Richard Farina was a noted counterculture author and folksinger in the early '60s. Married for a time to folksinger Carolyn Hester, he was an early intimate of Bob Dylan, and in fact recorded a collectible album with Dylan (playing under the pseudonym "Blind Boy Grunt") and Ric Von Schmidt in 1963. After marrying Joan Baez' sister Mimi, he formed a folk-rock duo that released two acclaimed albums in the mid-'60s. Unlike folk-rock figureheads like the Byrds, the Farinas were far more firmly rooted in folk than rock.

Their recordings effectively flavored their material (mostly written by Richard) with jangling electric guitars and a rhythm section, ably assisted by such session players as guitarist Bruce Langhorne (who also played on Dylan's first electric recordings), bassist Felix Pappalardi, and harmonica player John Hammond. The Farinas themselves also played guitar, autoharp, and dulcimer. Least successful with blues, they recorded

some effective Appalachian-flavored material, and several excellent bona fide midtempo folk-rockers and ballads. Their best songs effectively balanced world-wise, sardonic observations with good-natured, melodic optimism. The Farinas' promising career ended prematurely with the death of Richard in a motorcycle accident on his birthday in 1966. His novel of the same year, *Been Down So Long It Looks Like Up to Me*, became a cult favorite. Since Richard's death, Mimi Farina has sporadically recorded and performed as a solo act. — *Richie Unterberger*

Celebrations for a Grey Day / 1965 / Vanguard ✦✦✦
The duo's debut effectively laid out their approach: Appalachian-like instrumentals that put the dulcimer to the fore alternate with strong contemporary folk compositions, which are by turns mournful and high-spirited. The world-weary "Reno Nevada" (a part of Fairport Convention's repertoire in their early days) is the duo's best song. — *Richie Unterberger*

Reflections in a Crystal Wind / 1965 / Fontana ✦✦✦
Basically a continuation of the first album with a slightly more electric feel, finding Richard developing deeper insight and a subtler touch. — *Richie Unterberger*

Memories / 1968 / Vanguard ✦✦✦
A posthumous collection of odds and ends, this actually holds considerable appeal for anyone who likes their pair of fully realized albums. The 12 songs include a few studio outtakes, a few solo turns by Mimi on compositions written by Richard but incompletely recorded at the time of his death, a couple of performances from the 1965 Newport Folk Festival, and a couple of Joan Baez tracks from sessions for an aborted album Richard was producing with her. These leftovers are generally up to the standard of the two "real" albums, especially "The Quiet Joys of Brotherhood" (covered by Fairport Convention) and "Morgan the Pirate" (a farewell to Bob Dylan, according to the sketchy liner notes). The two cuts by Baez (that Richard wrote or co-wrote), especially the compellingly melancholy "All the World Has Gone By," are excellent, leading one to wonder if the projected album they came from would have been one of Baez' best. These may be leftovers, but it's a worthwhile collection, nonetheless. — *Richie Unterberger*

● Best of / 1971 / Vanguard ✦✦✦✦
While a 26-song double album is not ordinarily recommended as the best introduction to such a short-lived act, the Farinas' work was so consistent that it makes sense to pick up this compilation, which combines *Celebrations For a Grey Day* and *Reflections in a Crystal Wind*. — *Richie Unterberger*

Sally Fingerette

Guitar, Piano, Vocals / Singer-Songwriter
Ohio-resident Sally Fingerette has a polished style for her personal songs. She tours on her own and with the Four Bitchin' Babes. Her consistently well-produced solo albums have many lovely songs, most notably "Home is Where the Heart Is." — *Richard Meyer*

● Unraveled / 1990 / Amerisound ✦✦✦✦
A woman of many identities, she's also known as one of the 4 Bitchin' Babes, and should be considered Shawn Colvin's stylistic soul sister. Her ten original songs explore the landscape of relationships, whether it's enjoying the nostalgia of an old flame ("Smilin' Boy"), realizing the nature of love for a child ("The Return"), or the lament for one's parents ("He Loved Her So"/"The Ballad of Harry and Esther"). The treatment is tender, the music beautiful, and the voice warm and inviting. — *Ladyslipper*

Five Chinese Brothers

Folk
The Five Chinese Brothers are not Chinese or brothers. What they are is a five-piece band that plays a combination of folk, rock, and country. The New York-based band is made up of Tom Meltzer (lead vocals, acoustic guitar), Paul Foglino (bass), Charlie Shaw (drums), Neil Thomas (accordion, piano, vocals), and Kevin Trainor (lead guitar, vocals). — *Chip Renner*

● Singer, Songwriter, Beggarman, Thief / 1992 / 1-800-Prime CD ✦✦✦✦
After some remixing of their indie cassette and the addition of a few tracks, Five Chinese Brothers have released their first album after ten years on the New York scene. Tom Meltzer and Paul Foglino handle the writing separately, though their styles complement each other so well you'd think they were a team. These songs have open-hearted humor and the performances are tight but animated with a very live feeling. This is a great record that captures the fun of the band live but with the precision of a studio. Not a bad cut on this record; it's a must have. — *Richard Meyer*

Shiney Brite/Santa Claustrophobia / 1994 / 1-800-Prime CD ✦✦✦

Stone Soup / Aug. 1, 1995 / 1-800-Prime CD ✦✦✦
This, the second Five Chinese Brothers CD, doesn't have quite the irrepressible drive and bite of their first disc, but this one is still so good that

it's not a fair comparison. The standout song is "Mole in the Ground." Tom Meltzer's elastic voice adds the right amount of energy and edge to the FCBs' sound. Like *Singer, Songwriter, Beggarman, Thief,* you ought to play this until it is part of you. —*Richard Meyer*

Folk Like Us

Folk
Folk Like Us is a traditional band featuring Debra Bagwell (flute, piccolo, pennywhistle, recorder, piano), Johnny Carlisle (guitar, five-string banjo), Doug Reid (fiddle), David Shaw (string bass, tenor banjo), Mark Shelton (hammer dulcimer, bodhran bones, snare drum, spoons), Dave Yonley (fiddle), and special guest Beth Shelton on oboe. —*Chip Renner*

● **Spring Dance** / 1992 / North Star ✦✦✦✦
A fine collection of reels, polkas, jigs, and traditional standards. If you enjoy traditional instruments played to perfection, pick up this CD. —*Chip Renner*

Stephen Foster

b. Jul. 4, 1826, **d.** Jan. 13, 1864
Instrumental, Vocals
Composer of minstrel songs and popular household melodies which eventually became part of the American folk tradition. Essentially self-taught, he entered a partnership with E.P. Christy, who maintained exclusive initial performance rights to his songs. Foster composed approximately 200 songs with relatively simplistic piano or guitar accompaniments. Productions by Foster included the state songs of Kentucky and Florida ("My Old Kentucky Home" and "Old Folks at Home," respectively) as well as "Jeanie with the Light Brown Hair," "Oh! Susanna," and "Old Black Joe." —*Keith Johnson*

Favorite Songs / 1994 / Allegretto ✦✦✦
● **Songs of** / Columbia/Legacy ✦✦✦✦

Fotheringay

Folk-Rock, British Folk
A short-lived offshoot of Fairport Convention, featuring key member and leader Sandy Denny. A second album was planned but never completed; tracks from it turn up on the triple-CD Denny anthology *Who Knows Where the Time Goes.* This is far more interesting and beguiling than their work with Fairport Convention, especially the Bob Dylan songs, but it lacks Fairport's precision and focus. —*Bruce Eder and William Ruhlmann*

● **Fotheringay** / 1970 / Hannibal ✦✦✦✦
Also featured are Trevor Lucas and Jerry Donahue, both of whom eventually joined Fairport when Denny rejoined. The album is a close relative of Denny's other solo and group work and features several of her flowing ballads, showcasing her lovely voice. A footnote, but a pleasing one. —*Bruce Eder and William Ruhlmann*

Jackson C. Frank

Guitar, Vocals
One of the most interesting and enigmatic cult figures of '60s folk, Jackson Frank's reputation rests almost solely upon one hard-to-find album from the mid-'60s. A stronger composer than a singer, he nonetheless had an appreciable influence on many more famous performers of the decade, including Paul Simon, Sandy Denny, and Nick Drake.

Trauma and misfortune have dogged Frank throughout his life. When he was 11, a fire in his elementary school killed many of his classmates and left him with burns over most of his body. He eventually recovered, learned to play the guitar, and hung around the early-'60s New York coffeehouse scene with John Kay, later of Steppenwolf. A large insurance settlement enabled him to travel to England after he turned 21, and it was there that he made most of his impact.

Frank shared a London flat with fellow American expatriates Paul Simon and Art Garfunkel, who were briefly based there in the mid-'60s before their first hit, "The Sounds of Silence." Simon, then a struggling folk singer-songwriter himself, was impressed enough to produce Frank's self-titled album, released in the UK only. While Frank's voice was tremulously earnest, the quality of the compositions was often impressive, with a reflective, melancholic air that most likely influenced Simon, Al Stewart (who made his recording debut on one of the LP's tracks, "Yellow Walls"), and Nick Drake (who covered one of the songs, "Here Come the Blues," on late-'60s home tapes that have been extensively circulated as a bootleg).

Frank's album was well received in British folk circles, and several of his songs made their way into the repertoire of his friend Sandy Denny, who recorded a couple, "Milk and Honey" and "You Never Wanted Me," on her own debut LP. (She also recorded a version of "You Never Wanted Me" with Fairport Convention, and a 1966 demo of "Blues Run the Game" appears on her *Dark the Night* bootleg.) Frank, however, was unable to come up with a similar quality of material for a follow-up. This, combined with stage fright, depression, and an end of the funds from the insurance settlement that had enabled him to travel in high style, meant that he returned to the States in 1969 without releasing another album.

Based in Woodstock, NY, Frank continued his songwriting, but family and depression problems resulted in homelessness by the mid-'70s. For most of the next two decades, Frank lived on the streets or hospitals, too discouraged to contact old friends and family. He was further hobbled by arthritis, inappropriate medication for his mental problems, and a shooting incident that left him legally blind in his left eye. In the mid-'90s, a sympathetic folk fan, Jim Abbott, helped Frank regroup by gaining more appropriate medical assistance and settling back in Woodstock, where he resumed songwriting and occasionally performs. A 1995 profile in *Dirty Linen* magazine effectively "rediscovered" the missing legend, and legendary vintage recordings were finally issued on CD in 1996. —*Richie Unterberger*

● **Blues Run the Game** / 1996 / Mooncrest ✦✦✦✦
Ten songs from Frank's legendary (and rare) self-titled mid-'60s album, including "Blues Run the Game," "Here Come the Blues," "Milk and Honey," and "You Never Wanted Me," as well as five previously unreleased tracks from 1975. The '60s tracks are perhaps not as stunning as some have been led to believe, sounding a bit naive and dated, but at their best they have an appealingly moody, troubadour feel. The songs from the '70s, also performed solo on acoustic guitar, are surprisingly worthwhile; similar in quality to the ones from the previous decade, they're very much of a piece with his '60s work. —*Richie Unterberger*

Kinky Friedman (Richard Friedman)

b. Oct. 31, 1944, Palatine, TX
Vocals / Country-Folk
Outrageous, irreverent, but nearly always thought-provoking, Kinky Friedman wrote and performed satirical country songs during the '70s and has been hailed as the Frank Zappa of country music. He was born Richard F. Friedman, the son of a professor at the University of Texas, in Palestine, TX, who raised his children on the family ranch, Rio Duckworth. Before coming to music, Friedman graduated from the U of T with a psychology degree. While studying there, he founded his first band, King Arthur and the Carrots —a group that poked fun at surf music—and recorded a single in 1966. After graduating, he served three years in the Peace Corps and was stationed in Borneo, where he worked as an agricultural extension worker. By 1971 he had founded Kinky Friedman and His Texas Jewboys. In keeping with the group's satirical nature, each member had deliberately un-pc names such as Little Jewford, Big Nig, Panama Red, Rainbow Colors, and Snakebite Jacobs. Friedman got his break through Commander Cody, who called attention of Vanguard Music to the acerbic young performer in 1973. That was the year he and his group made their debut album, *Sold American,* featuring John Hartford and Tompall Glaser in Nashville. The title track barely made it into the charts, where it remained for a while, but Friedman did attract enough attention to be invited to the *Grand Old Opry.* In 1974 he recorded a self-titled album for ABC Records. It was produced by Willie Nelson; and he, Waylon Jennings, and Glaser performed along with Friedman. Among the album's best-known tracks is his response to anti-Semitism, "They Ain't Making Jews like Jesus Anymore." In the mid-'70s, Friedman and his band began touring with Bob Dylan's Rolling Thunder Revue. In 1976 he made his third album, *Lasso from El Paso,* featuring Dylan and Eric Clapton. The Texas Jewboys disbanded three years later and Friedman moved to New York, where he played at the Lone Star Cafe. In 1983 he released *Under the Double Ego* for Sunrise Records. It was his last recording to date and since then Friedman has turned toward writing. He has not only been a critic for *Rolling Stone* magazine, he has also become a mystery writer of tales such as *Greenwich Killing Time, A Case of Lone Star* and *Frequent Flyer,* all of which feature a Jewish country singer turned Greenwich Village private eye named "The Kinkster." —*Sandra Brennan*

Sold American / 1973 / Vanguard ✦✦✦✦
A renegade figure who often stresses the outrageous. The title song is a gem. Part of the '70s country/folk/rock wave. —*Hank Davis*

● **Lasso from El Paso** / 1976 / Epic ✦✦✦✦
Of the many albums that grew out of Bob Dylan's *Rolling Thunder Revue,* this must be the strangest. Friedman has a husky voice and an off-kilter sense of humor best captured on the live-from-the-revue track "Sold American." Also notable for a version of the Bob Dylan outtake "Catfish." —*William Ruhlmann*

Old Testaments and New Revelations / 1992 / Fruit of the Tune ✦✦✦
Kinky Friedman, backed by his faithful combo the Texas Jewboys, brings old-time swing to Hollywood with plenty of satire on *Old Testaments and New Revelations.* Social satire from a Jewish perspective is Friedman's forte, and this generous live recording blends classics like "We Refuse the Right to Refuse Service to You" with a whole new set of barbed hooks. —*Roch Parisien*

Jim Gaudet

Vocals / Singer-Songwriter
Albany-based singer-songwriter Jim Gaudet began writing in his 30s after a long hiatus playing in the local Lost Country Ramblers and building a family life. Now he tours the Northeast, performing his own witty and heartfelt material. Before the release of *It's a Colorful Life*, Gaudet released three independent cassettes. —*Richard Meyer*

It's a Colorful Life / 1994 / Primero ✦✦✦✦
This 15-track CD offers a combination of studio and live cuts that offer a strong selection of his material. He has songs of social awareness like "In Real Life" and the lighthearted "Phone in My Car." This is essentially a solo direct to two-track record with occasional fiddle and harmonies. —*Richard Meyer*

Jane Gillman

Dulcimer, Guitar, Harmonica, Vocals / Folk, Singer-Songwriter
Gillman is a DC-based singer-songwriter who performs nationally in a play about Woody Guthrie. She plays guitar, harmonica, and dulcimer and is known for her well-crafted songwriting. —*Richard Meyer and Chip Renner*

Pick It Up / 1970 / Green Linnet ✦✦✦
A great debut album. Gillman plays some good cross-picking guitar and is backed by Lyle Lovett and Mark O'Connor. —*Chip Renner*

● **Jane Gillman** / 1980 / Green Linnet ✦✦✦✦
A beautifully produced album. Mary-Chapin Carpenter, Marcy Marxer, Lucy Kaplansky, John Gorka, Nina Gerber, and Seamus Egan back Gillman up. There is something about her vocals that catches you. Gillman's songwriting is topnotch, especially on songs such as "Listen to the Thunder," "Three Quarters," and the contemporary folk view of romance in the pop '60s, "Song on the Radio." —*Chip Renner*

Steve Goodman

b. Jul. 25, 1948, Chicago, IL, d. Sep. 20, 1984
Guitar, Vocals / Singer-Songwriter
Chicago-based singer-songwriter Steve Goodman made a number of excellent albums on Buddah, Asylum, and his own Red Pajamas Records before his death from leukemia. His best-known song was "The City of New Orleans," which was a hit for Arlo Guthrie and was recorded by many others. —*William Ruhlmann*

Steve Goodman / 1972 / Buddah ✦✦✦✦
The debut of a great new songwriter. —*William Ruhlmann*

Somebody Else's Troubles / 1973 / Buddah ✦✦✦
This is another great mixture of ballads ("The Dutchman") and fun songs ("Somebody Else's Troubles"). —*Richard Meyer*

Jessie's Jig and Other Favorites / 1975 / Asylum ✦✦✦
Included are Michael Smith's "Spoon River," "Door Number Three," and the rave-up "Mama Don't Allow." —*Richard Meyer*

Unfinished Business / 1987 / Red Pajamas ✦✦✦
Released after Goodman's death from leukemia, it contains "A Fool Such as I," "My Funny Valentine," and "The Whispering Man." A sweet, more subdued collection. —*Richard Meyer*

Words We Can Dance To / 1976 / Asylum ✦✦✦
A good collection of mostly Goodman originals, along with rockers like "Tossin' and Turnin'." —*Richard Meyer*

Say It in Private / 1977 / Asylum ✦✦✦✦
A full-blown studio affair with chestnuts like "Is It True What They Say About Dixie?" and wonderful originals, including "The Twentieth Century Is Almost Over." —*Richard Meyer*

Hot Spot / 1980 / Asylum ✦✦✦
He may have been trying to be more mainstream with this LP but the great "Sdrawkcab klat (Talk Backwards)" shows that his sense of fun can rise to new heights. —*Richard Meyer*

Artistic Hair / 1983 / Red Pajamas ✦✦✦✦
Goodman achieved artistic control with this album, featuring his "City of New Orleans" and other classics. —*William Ruhlmann*

Best of the Asylum Years, Vol. 1 / 1988 / Red Pajamas ✦✦✦✦

Best of the Asylum Years, Vol. 2 / 1989 / Red Pajamas ✦✦✦

Affordable Art / 198_ / Red Pajamas ✦✦✦
This one features "A Dying Cub Fan's Last Request" and "Watchin' Joey Glow." —*William Ruhlmann*

★ **No Big Surprise: Anthology** / 1994 / Red Pajamas ✦✦✦✦✦

John Gorka

Guitar, Vocals / Folk, Singer-Songwriter
This perceptive, husky-voiced singer-songwriter spent the early '80s hustling around the Northeast folk circuit, then won the Kerrville Folk Festi-

val's New Folk Award in 1984. He has since recorded four albums. —*William Ruhlmann*

● **I Know** / 1987 / Red House ✦✦✦✦
Still some of his best work, it includes "Blues Palace," "Downtown Tonight," and "Down in the Milltown." —*Richard Meyer*

Land of the Bottom Line / Jun. 8, 1992 / Windham Hill ✦✦✦✦
This is a long record filled with a full range of Gorka's romantic and story songs. He states his case as an outsider forced to meet the mainstream with the title cut and confronts his demons on "Raven in the Storm." More sentimental tracks are "The One That Got Away" and "Love Is Our Cross to Bear." "Mean Streak" is gritty and shows that Gorka can howl when he wants to. —*Richard Meyer*

Jack's Crows / Dec. 8, 1992 / High Street ✦✦✦
The songwriting is particularly strong on this album. His ballad of the Marines and his father demonstrates how he can handle the most sentimental subjects well. "Silence," the first cut, is a crystalline beauty, and "Where the Bottles Break" is a rockin' song about personal convictions and the real estate business. —*Richard Meyer*

Temporary Road / Dec. 8, 1992 / High Street ✦✦✦

Out of the Valley / May 10, 1994 / High Street ✦✦✦
On this, Gorka's fifth album, he continues the steady stream of bluesy and lyrical songs. Produced by John Jennings, this CD has a larger, more filled out sound than any release since his debut. His songwriting has remained consistent in quality and style. —*Richard Meyer*

Between Five and Seven / Aug. 1996 / HST ✦✦✦
On *Between Five and Seven* John Gorka opens up his sound somewhat, touching on contemporary pop and rock without losing his confessional folk foundation. The result can be frustrating at times—occasionally, the production obscures the simple beauty of his melodies—but overall, the album is another winner from Gorka, one of the finest songwriters of the '90s. —*Thom Owens*

Davey Graham

Guitar, Vocals / Folk, British Folk
One of the most eclectic guitarists of the '60s, Graham's mixture of folk, blues, jazz, Middle Eastern sounds, and Indian ragas was an important catalyst of the British folk scene. Like Sandy Bull and John Fahey—two folk-based guitarists with a similar taste for genre-bending experimentation—Graham could not be said to be a rock musician. But like Bull and Fahey, he shared the eagerness of the '60s psychedelic rockers to stretch out and incorporate unpredictable influences into his music. While he wasn't much of a singer, Graham's taste in material was broad and shrewd, encompassing blues, ragas, Joni Mitchell, Charles Mingus, and the famous instrumental "Anji," which Graham recorded in 1962, way before the more famous versions by Bert Jansch and Simon & Garfunkel . Besides cutting several albums of his own work in the '60s with sympathetic, low-key rhythm sections, he recorded with traditional folk singer Shirley Collins and British blues father Alexis Korner. Graham recorded only sporadically after the '60s, although he performed with the renowned acoustic guitar wizards Stefan Grossman and Duck Baker. —*Richie Unterberger*

The Guitar Player . . . Plus / 1963 / See For Miles ✦✦✦✦
Graham established himself as one of the most innovative players in acoustic music with his 1963 debut, *The Guitar Player*. With this album, Graham became one of the first folk guitarists to fuse traditional virtuosity with cross-currents from contemporary jazz and blues. Accompanied by drummer Bobby Graham (a top British sessionman who played on many British Invasion rock records, including several by the Kinks), Davey invigorates pop and traditional standards, as well as compositions by Sonny Rollins, the Adderleys, and Ray Charles. Neither jazz nor folk, Graham displays eclectic bounce that was quite visionary for its time, and remains fresh today; in his subsequent '60s recordings, he would branch out into Middle Eastern and psychedelic sounds as a natural extension of his experimental bent. As a significant bonus, the 1992 CD reissue of this album includes the three tracks from his rare 1962 EP *3/4 A.D.* One of these is the original version of "Anji," which was reworked by Simon & Garfunkel on one of their early albums; another features British blues-rock godfather Alexis Korner on second guitar. —*Richie Unterberger*

● **Folk, Blues, and All Points in Between** / 1985 / See For Miles ✦✦✦✦
Side one includes the entirety of his 1965 album *Folk, Blues and Beyond;* side two features seven tracks from three of his late-'60s LPs. The 1965 record was probably his most accomplished, as Graham handled blues, jazz, and Northern African music with aplomb. His other '60s recordings were more erratic, but the highlights gathered here matched his 1965 work, peaking with the original "No Preacher Blues," his folk-jazz cover of Joni Mitchell's "Both Sides Now," and the Indian-influenced "Blue Raga." —*Richie Unterberger*

Clive Gregson and Christine Collister

Folk, Singer-Songwriter, Folk-Rock

Clive Gregson and Christine Collister were the most moving UK folk-rock duo to emerge since Richard and Linda Thompson. Gregson (b. Jan 4, 1955) was the founder of Any Trouble, a rock quartet, in Manchester in 1975. The band's sound, and Gregson's songwriting and singing, reminded some of Elvis Costello, and Any Trouble was signed by Stiff, Costello's label. The band made several well-remembered but poor-selling albums, then split up. Gregson made a solo album, *Strange Persuasions,* in 1985, then hooked up with Collister. Gregson first introduced Collister into Richard Thompson's band (Gregson was backup guitarist at the time); then they began performing as a duo. The duo's first release was a homemade tape sold at gigs, later released as *Home and Away.* It was followed by their first formal album, *Mischief,* in 1988, and by *Change in the Weather* in 1990. *Love Is a Strange Hotel,* released later the same year, was an album of cover versions of Gregson and Collister's favorite songs. Their songs, all written by Gregson, are wry tales of the ins and outs of love, sung in Collister's heartbreaking voice. *— William Ruhlmann*

Strange Persuasions / 1985 / Compas ✦✦✦
Strange Persuasions came out in England in 1985, but had never been released in North America. After leaving Any Trouble, Gregson made a name for himself in the US as a member of Richard Thompson's band and half of the Gregson and Collister duo. Now his refreshingly varied CD will let us know what we have been missing. Some tracks sound like big Los Angeles pop productions with a dash of Squeeze thrown in, while others, "Jewel in Your Crown," for example, offer his sophisticated ballad writing. Perhaps this is what Ralph McTell would have sounded like had he chosen a more produced musical road; the melodies are often rooted firmly in the late-'60s and '70s folk singer-songwriter genre. While there is nothing revelatory here, *Strange Persuasions* is a good solid album. *—Richard Meyer*

Home and Away / 1986 / Flying Fish ✦✦✦✦
A collection of songs recorded during an early acoustic tour in 1986. The duo runs through new originals, some songs from Gregson's Any Trouble days, and a few well-chosen covers in a warm, intimate setting. *— Chris Woodstra*

Mischief / 1987 / Rhino ✦✦✦✦
Clive Gregson's songs treat romance with ironic charm. "We're Not Over Yet" is a compendium of reasons why they ought to be over, and "Everybody Cheats on You" is about more than romantic infidelity. Christine Collister gives the songs a depth that keeps them from being a bit too glib and clever, as do the folk-pop arrangements. *— William Ruhlmann*

● **A Change in the Weather** / 1989 / Rhino ✦✦✦✦
The self-insight continues in Gregson's lyrics, but the concerns are expanded. Collister does a fine job covering "Tryin' to Get to You." *—William Ruhlmann*

Love Is a Strange Hotel / 1990 / Rhino ✦✦✦
A departure from the expansive arrangements of the previous two albums, *Love Is a Strange Hotel* is a low-key acoustic collection of covers. Even unlikely choices, like Aztec Camera's "How Men Are" and 10cc's "Things We Do for Love," are pulled off in their own charming way. *— Chris Woodstra*

Welcome to the Workhouse / 1990 / Special Delivery ✦✦✦✦
Welcome to the Workhouse is a collection of Gregson's home demos and outtakes, and while most albums of this sort appeal only to the diehard fans, this one stands out as one of his finest moments. The recordings span 1980 to 1985 and provide a good bridge between his work with Any Trouble and his partnership with Christine Collister. *—Chris Woodstra*

The Last Word / 1992 / Rhino ✦✦✦
Gregson and Collister have perfected their now classic sound. Their extraordinary harmonies have never sounded better on Gregson's moody songs mixing folk, jazz, country, and blues. *—Chris Woodstra*

People and Places / 1995 / Compas ✦✦✦
One hears more of Elvis Costello and Richard Thompson's influence on this release. Still, the songs are strong and the production crisp, with enough unusual dynamics to keep you listening. His literate lyrics are short domestic stories told in a generally straightforward way ("Mary's Divorce" or "My Eyes Gave the Game Away"). The Ralph McTell comparison still stands, and it's meant as a compliment. *—Richard Meyer*

Carousel of Noise / 1995 / Gregsongs ✦✦✦

I Love This Town / Aug. 20, 1996 / Compass ✦✦✦✦

Stefan Grossman

b. Apr. 16, 1945
Guitar
Stefan Grossman is a student of the folk, blues, and ragtime styles of the

Reverend Gary Davis (with whom he studied) and a variety of other performers. He has become a virtuoso guitarist, as is demonstrated by numerous recordings and concert appearances. *— William Ruhlmann*

● **Yazoo Basin Boogie** / 1970 / Shanachie ✦✦✦✦
Yazoo Basin Boogie compiles 22 tracks from Stefan Grossman's early-'70s albums for Transatlantic Records. These songs are primarily instrumental delta blues, ragtimes, and country tunes—it's old-timey music at its best. Grossman also offers a detailed background of the music in his liner notes, making the package not only entertaining, but educational. It's an excellent way to become familiar with his style. *— Thom Owens*

Shining Shadows / 1988 / Shanachie ✦✦✦✦
Shining Shadows offers another solid collection of Grossman's stirring guitar instrumentals. *— William Ruhlmann*

Guitar Landscapes / 1990 / Shanachie ✦✦✦
Guitar Landscapes offers a diverse collection of blues, jazz, country, and folk. Grossman's skill is evident on every track—he weaves subtle, inventive phrases throughout the album. If he can be faulted for anything, it's that the songs are occasionally *too* subtle, drifting into the background. Nevertheless, there is plenty of wonderfully evocative music on *Guitar Landscapes,* making it a necessary listen for his fans. *— Thom Owens*

Arlo Guthrie

b. Jul. 10, 1947, Coney Island, NY
Guitar, Vocals / Folk, Singer-Songwriter, Folk-Rock
Like his father, Woody Guthrie, Arlo Guthrie has carved out a career as a folksinger and songwriter with a social conscience who leavens political messages with humor. Though Woody Guthrie was hospitalized for much of Arlo's youth, the youngster nevertheless grew up in a musical community that included Pete Seeger, Leadbelly, and Cisco Houston. He learned to play the guitar at age six and was performing in coffeehouses by his late teens.

Guthrie's early fame was based on his anti-establishment shaggy-dog story in song, "Alice's Restaurant," actually a comic monolog about the singer's troubles with the police and the draft board that was extremely timely when it appeared on record in 1967. *Alice's Restaurant* became Guthrie's only gold record, but he made a series of folk-rock records through the '70s, filling them with his own songs and those of his contemporaries, notably Steve Goodman's "The City of New Orleans," which in 1972 became Guthrie's sole hit single.

Guthrie's commercial fortunes, like those of most folkies, declined by the end of the '70s, and he made his last album for Warner Bros. in 1981. Since then he has launched his own label, Rising Son, which has reissued his Warner albums and released his new recordings. He continues to tour extensively and to work for such causes as environmentalism. *— William Ruhlmann*

☆ **Alice's Restaurant** / 1967 / Reprise ✦✦✦✦✦
In 1967, when this LP came out, it was totally radical, directly political, and so deliciously funny that it deflated a great deal of the seriousness of the growing anti-war movement. In this one stroke Guthrie established himself as more than the son of the famous man and major star. "Motorcycle Song" and "Chillin' of the Evening," are highlights of side two. *—Richard Meyer*

Arlo / 1968 / Rising Son ✦✦✦
On this LP Guthrie continues his monologue with an extended "Motorcycle Song" and other originals. *—Richard Meyer*

Running Down the Road / 1969 / Reprise ✦✦✦

Washington County / 1970 / Reprise ✦✦✦
This album is more homey and roots flavored, with cuts like "Valley to Pray" with Doc Watson, and "Lay Down Little Doggies." It's a good relaxed effort. *—Richard Meyer*

Hobo's Lullaby / 1972 / Rising Son ✦✦✦✦
It contains his hit version of "City of New Orleans" and "1913 Massacre." *—Richard Meyer*

The Last of the Brooklyn Cowboys / 1973 / Rising Son ✦✦✦
A strong collection, it has good versions of "Ramblin' Round," "Gypsy Davey," "Love Sick Blues," and "Gates of Eden." *—Richard Meyer*

Together in Concert / 1975 / Reprise ✦✦✦✦
Separately and together, Arlo Guthrie and Pete Seeger delight in a live setting. *— William Ruhlmann*

Amigo / 1976 / Rising Son ✦✦✦✦
An excellent, rocking collection including Guthrie's adaptation of "Guabi, Guabi," a song about Victor Jara, and a knockabout cover of the Rolling Stones' song "Connection." *— William Ruhlmann*

The Best of Arlo Guthrie / 1977 / Reprise ✦✦✦✦
This includes "Alice's Restaurant," the equally comic "Motorcycle Song," "Coming into Los Angeles," and "City of New Orleans." *— William Ruhlmann*

● **Precious Friend** / 1982 / Reprise ✦✦✦✦
A second excellent collection by Pete Seeger and Arlo Guthrie, veterans from two generations. — *William Ruhlmann*

Mystic Journey / Feb. 1996 / Rising Son ✦✦✦

Woody Guthrie

b. Jul. 14, 1912, Okemah, OK, d. Oct. 3, 1967, Queens, NY
Harmonica, Vocals
Woody Guthrie was the most important American folk music artist of the first half of the 20th century. Coming out of Oklahoma, Guthrie had firsthand knowledge of the dustbowl diaspora chronicled in John Steinbeck's novel *The Grapes of Wrath*. In fact, Guthrie wrote his own version of the story in a song called "Tom Joad." By the time he gained recognition in the '40s, Guthrie had written hundreds of songs, many of which remain folk standards to this day. When he was interviewed by Alan Lomax for the Library of Congress in March 1940, Guthrie punctuated his reminiscences by singing "So Long, It's Been Good to Know You," "Dust Bowl Blues," "Do-Re-Mi," "Pretty Boy Floyd," "I Ain't Got No Home," and other songs. He later wrote "Pastures of Plenty," "The Grand Coulee Dam," and his masterpiece, "This Land Is Your Land." He was also an author (*Bound for Glory*) and a newspaper columnist.

Guthrie made some recordings for RCA in 1940, but much of his work was issued on the small Folkways label. Meanwhile, in the late '40s and early '50s, versions of his songs became hits for such artists as the Weavers. By then, Guthrie himself was in physical decline, suffering from Huntington's chorea, a hereditary neurological disorder. But during his long illness, Guthrie's influence spread to the next generation, fostering the folk boom of the late '50s and early '60s. Not only is Bob Dylan unimaginable without him, but large segments of popular music are permanently affected by his concerns as a songwriter and his approach to the form. Guthrie also composed a body of children's music toward the end of his performing career in the early '50s, when he was raising a family with his wife Marjorie. The songs, many sung from a child's point of view, have been covered and performed extensively since. — *William Ruhlmann*

Sings Folk Songs / 1962 / Smithsonian/Folkways ✦✦✦✦
Guthrie sings traditional material here, with Leadbelly and others. — *William Ruhlmann*

☆ **Library of Congress Recordings, Vols. 1-3** / 1964 / Rounder ✦✦✦✦✦
A multi-disc set of songs and conversations from 1940. — *William Ruhlmann*

☆ **Library of Congress Recordings, Vol. 1** / 1964 / Rounder ✦✦✦✦✦
Woody, the singer and storyteller, in his historic recordings from 1940 for Alan Lomax, explains the origins of many of his tunes including "Pretty Boy Floyd," "Goin' Down that Road Feelin' Bad," and "So Long It's Been Good to Know You." These are wonderfully relaxed sessions, just Woody and his guitar. — *Richard Meyer*

★ **Dust Bowl Ballads** / 1964 / Rounder ✦✦✦✦✦
His classic Okie songs, "Talking Dust Bowl Blues," "Do-Re-Mi," and more. — *William Ruhlmann*

☆ **This Land Is Your Land** / 1967 / Smithsonian/Folkways ✦✦✦✦✦
The title track and some of the Columbia River songs. — *William Ruhlmann*

Tribute to Woody Guthrie: Highlights from Concerts / 1972 / Warner Brothers ✦✦✦✦
Woody Guthrie died on Oct 3, 1967. Tribute concerts to him were organized at Carnegie Hall in New York in January 1968 and at the Hollywood Bowl in Los Angeles in September 1970. This double-record set presents highlights from both shows and is notable for a rare Bob Dylan performance and a collection of Guthrie songs sung by others of his children (literally and figuratively): Arlo Guthrie, Judy Collins, Odetta, Richie Havens, Tom Paxton, Pete Seeger, and more. — *William Ruhlmann*

Struggle / 1976 / Smithsonian/Folkways ✦✦✦✦
This album features Woody Guthrie, Cisco Houston and Pete Seeger playing political songs including "The Dying Miner," "Ludlow Massacre," and "Union Burying Ground." It's an energetic album. — *Richard Meyer*

Columbia River Collection / 1988 / Rounder ✦✦✦
An intelligent reconstruction of Guthrie's Columbia River songs, including "Grand Coulee Dam" and "Pastures of Plenty." — *William Ruhlmann*

Kristen Hall

Guitar, Vocals / Folk, Singer-Songwriter
Atlanta-based singer-songwriter Kristen Hall has built a strong reputation in folk circles with her infectious, Indigo Girls style of acoustic folk-rock. Her raspy-voiced delivery of highly personal lyrics are the center of attention and often accompanied only by acoustic guitar. While her first album, *Real Life Stuff*, released independently, consisted of minimalist arrangements of nearly demo quality, subsequent releases (1991's *Fact and Fiction* and 1994's *Be Careful What You Wish For*) have been bigger

productions, featuring high-profile guests such as Emily Saliers of Indigo Girls, Cindy Wilson of the B-52's, and Jules Shear. — *Chris Woodstra*

Real Life Stuff / 1990 / Dog Gone ✦✦✦
An outstanding independent release from this Atlanta-based singer-songwriter. Her debut, a self-produced low-key folk album centered around Hall's raspy voice and guitar, gives the blueprint for her later releases. Well worth seeking out. — *Chris Woodstra*

● **Fact and Fiction** / 1991 / High Street ✦✦✦✦
This mainly acoustic album ranges from introspective ballads to catchy upbeat folk-rock anthems. Hall's world-weary voice, both rough and delicate, tells reflective tales of yearning and love lost while retaining an uplifting spirit. Guests include Emily Saliers (Indigo Girls) and Cindy Wilson (B-52's). — *Chris Woodstra*

Be Careful What You Wish For / 1994 / High Street ✦✦✦✦
Kristen Hall has a gutsy voice that never sounds forced. The rocking guitar-based arrangements have a sound not unlike some of John Hiatt's recent records. These are very personal songs, some with political centers such as "Proud Man," sung with commitment and deep emotion. The opening cut, "Cry Tomorrow," sets the tone of the album; she maintains the drive and quality to the end. — *Richard Meyer*

Butch Hancock

b. Jul. 12, 1945, Lubbock, TX
Guitar, Vocals / Singer-Songwriter, Country-Folk
An obscure, legendary Texas songwriter whose work has been covered by Jerry Jeff Walker and Joe Ely, Hancock has a gift for wordplay and nuance. The songs become gradually more accessible as the tentative voice-and-guitar approach is replaced by surprisingly full folk-rock settings and assured singing. — *William Ruhlmann*

Firewater / 1981 / Rainlight ✦✦✦
Off-the-cuff versions of Butch's classics are here, including "The Wind's Dominion," and "If You Were a Bluebird." The band includes Jimmy Dale Gilmore. — *Richard Meyer*

Yella Rose with Marce Lacouture / 1985 / Rainlight ✦✦✦
This album has a rather big band with occasional horns, congas, accordion, and Marce Lacouture songs on the title cut. A good one. — *Richard Meyer*

● **Own and Own** / 1989 / Sugar Hill ✦✦✦✦
This compilation is culled from Hancock's many albums on his own Rainlight label from 1978 to 1987 (plus four tracks from 1989). — *William Ruhlmann*

Live in Australia / 1990 / Virgin ✦✦✦
An energetic live album of duets by Hancock and Gilmore, it was recorded in Sydney in 1990. The Flatlander hit "Dallas" is here with other ragged but right cuts from these musical pals. — *Richard Meyer*

Eats Away the Night / 1995 / Sugar Hill ✦✦✦✦
Hancock's first produced studio album for a national label not compiled from his previously released Rainlight Records LPs. In many ways, Hancock set his style down with his very first self-produced album, *West Texas Waltz*. All the elements from that period remain—the Dylanesque vocal sound, his love of wordplay, and a deep feeling for the stories that make up an individual's life. The warm sound of this album makes it easier for newcomers to get past his dry voice, and the inclusion of his hit "If You Were a Bluebird" will help a new audience locate him properly in the contemporary Texas songwriting scene. The band is tight and steps back enough to let Hancock's stories and personality shine through. — *Richard Meyer*

No Two Alike / Rainlight ✦✦✦✦
This 14-tape series (available by subscription only) is a document of six nights at the Cactus Cafe, where Butch performed with a host of great guests and never repeated a song. — *Richard Meyer*

Tim Hardin

b. Dec. 23, 1941, Eugene, OR, d. Dec. 29, 1980, Los Angeles, CA
Guitar, Vocals / Folk, Singer-Songwriter, Folk-Rock
A gentle, soulful singer who owed as much to blues and jazz as folk, Tim Hardin produced an impressive body of work in the late '60s without ever approaching either mass success or the artistic heights of the best singer-songwriters. When future Lovin' Spoonful producer Erik Jacobsen arranged for Hardin's first recordings in the mid-'60s, Tim was no more than an above-average White blues singer, in the mold of many fellow folkies working the East Coast circuit. By the time of his 1966 debut, however, he was writing confessional folk-rock songs of considerable grace and emotion. The first album's impact was slightly diluted by incompatible string overdubs (against Hardin's wishes), but by the time of his second and best LP, he'd achieved a satisfactory balance between acoustic guitar-based arrangements and subtle string accompaniment. It was the lot of Hardin's work to achieve greater recognition through covers from other singers, such as Rod Stewart (who did "Reason to

Believe"), Nico (who covered "Eulogy to Lenny Bruce" on her first album), Scott Walker (who sang "Lady from Baltimore"), Fred Neil ("Green Rocky Road" has been credited to both him and Hardin), and especially Bobby Darin, who took "If I Were a Carpenter" into the Top Ten in 1966. Beleaguered by a heroin habit since early in his career, Hardin's drug problems became grave in the late '60s; his commercial prospects grew dimmer and his albums more erratic, although he did manage to appear at Woodstock. His end was not a pretty one; due to accumulated drug and health problems, as well as a scarcity of new material, he didn't complete any albums after 1973 and died of a drug overdose in 1980. —*Richie Unterberger*

Tim Hardin 1 / 1966 / Verve ♦♦♦
Hardin's official debut introduces a vocalist and composer of some talent, most effective on the gentle confessional tunes and least effective on the blues. Occasionally it suffers from inappropriate ornamental string arrangements, but it includes some of his finest compositions, including "Reason To Believe," "How Can We Hang On to a Dream," and "Don't Make Promises." —*Richie Unterberger*

Tim Hardin 2 / 1967 / Verve ♦♦♦
Probably his best single album, on which he eschews blues nearly entirely and forges a distinctive, folk-rock voice, occasionally embellished by tasteful full arrangements. "Lady Came From Baltimore," "Red Balloon," and especially "If I Were a Carpenter" rank among his best and most famous songs. —*Richie Unterberger*

This Is Tim Hardin / 1967 / Edsel ♦♦♦
Hardin's very earliest recordings from approximately 1964, not issued until the late '60s, when he had achieved some success with his albums for Verve. Accompanied by nothing besides his own guitar, Hardin's arrangements are far sparser and bluesier than his folk-rock work for Verve. Over half of the ten tracks are traditional blues numbers like "Hoochie Coochie Man" and "House of the Rising Sun," and even the four originals (one co-written by future Holy Modal Rounder Steve Weber) are in a very similar straight blues style. The material isn't nearly as distinctive as the best of Hardin's work, but the performances rank with Dave Van Ronk's and Fred Neil's as the best White blues/acoustic folk to emerge from the early-'60s Greenwich scene. Indeed, Hardin covers Neil's "Blues on the Ceiling" here.) The hollow, reverbed, one-man-sitting-alone-in-an-empty-room production gives this album a haunting, somber feel (though not to its detriment). While not as good as Fred Neil's similar material from this era, it's still well worth tracking down. —*Richie Unterberger*

Live in Concert / 1968 / Polydor Chronicles ♦♦♦♦
Originally titled *Tim Hardin 3*, this set was recorded live in 1968 with a backing band comprised primarily of jazz musicians. The support crew is a bit tentative—it's evident that they hadn't played much with Hardin, and in places the tempo comes close to breaking down. It's still a good, effective performance; Hardin is in good voice (a condition which apparently couldn't be counted on, even in his early days), and on the songs that had already been released on his first two albums, the arrangements vary from the recorded versions in interesting fashions. *Live in Concert* includes renditions of most of his best early compositions ("If I Were a Carpenter," "Red Balloon," "Reason to Believe," "Misty Roses," "Lady Came from Baltimore," "Black Sheep Boy"), and half a dozen Hardin originals that didn't make it onto his first pair of albums. The best of these is the Lenny Bruce tribute, "Lenny's Tune," which Nico covered on her first solo album (where it was retitled "Eulogy to Lenny Bruce"). The 1995 CD reissue of this album adds three previously unreleased bonus tracks from the same concert. —*Richie Unterberger*

Tim Hardin 4 / 1969 / Verve ♦♦

● **Hang On to a Dream: The Verve Recordings** / Feb. 22, 1994 / Polydor ♦♦♦♦
Double-CD set of 47 tracks that Hardin recorded for Verve between 1964 and 1966. His expressive, blues-inflected vocals and confessional songwriting are heard on covers and famous compositions like "If I Were a Carpenter," "Lady Came from Baltimore," and "Reason to Believe." The compilation includes every studio recording that Hardin released on the Verve label, as well as two alternate takes and 15 previously unreleased tracks. —*Richie Unterberger*

● **Reason to Believe** / PolyGram ♦♦♦♦
The great early work of this top-flight '60s singer-songwriter includes the title track, "If I Were a Carpenter," and "Misty Roses." —*Kenneth M. Cassidy and William Ruhlmann*

Jack Hardy

b. 1948
Guitar, Vocals / Folk, Singer-Songwriter

Jack Hardy has been a central figure in folk music since his arrival in Greenwich Village in 1978. Instrumental in founding the Songwriter's Exchange, the SpeakEasy Musician's Co-op, and *the Fast Folk Musical Magazine*, Hardy has released nine albums domestically on his Great

Divide label. Considered a writer's writer, he is known for politics in his songs, Americanized Irish influences, and a preoccupation with mythological imagery, mixed with New York folk 'n' roll. —*Richard Meyer*

Mirror of My Madness / 1976 / Great Divide ♦♦♦♦
New York urban folk-rock period. It includes "The Tailor" and "Go Tell the Savior." —*Richard Meyer*

Landmark / 1980 / Great Divide ♦♦♦
This album shows Hardy's Irish influence and some of his best work, including "The Tinker's Coin," "Orphan from Madrid," and "The Inner Man." —*Richard Meyer*

● **White Shoes** / 1982 / Great Divide ♦♦♦♦
A brilliant collection of songs by this husky-voiced founder of New York's "Fast Folk" movement. —*William Ruhlmann*

The Cauldron / 1984 / Great Divide ♦♦♦
Politically charged and neo-traditional originals, adeptly performed. —*William Ruhlmann*

The Hunter / 1986 / Great Divide ♦♦♦
An excellent example of Hardy's various lyric preoccupations includes "Dublin Farewell" and "The Changing Wind." —*Richard Meyer*

Civil Wars / 1994 / Great Divide ♦♦♦
These songs describe civil wars of all sorts—political, domestic, and artistic. Highlights are "The 111th Pennsylvane" and "Double Edged Sword." Recorded direct to DAT, the album has an intimate, immediate mood that is perfectly suited to these often very personal songs. —*Richard Meyer*

Kim and Reggie Harris

From school programs to major folk festivals and huge concert halls, from Chicago Stadium to church social halls, Kim and Reggie Harris have been delighting audiences for years. Their songs are in the spirit of Phil Ochs, Richie Havens, Bob Dylan, and David Roth. The central message is one of hope, love, and unity done with musicality and vocal power that compel attention. This husband-wife team sparkles on everything from traditional spirituals and "Underground Railroad" songs to stunning originals and interpretations of well known material. —*Allan Shaw*

In the Heat of the Summer / Folk Era Productions ♦♦♦♦
This is a musical message that everyone can join. —*Mike Fleischer*

Richie Havens (Richard Pierce Havens)

b. Jan. 21, 1941, Brooklyn, NY
Guitar, Vocals / Folk, Singer-Songwriter, Folk-Rock

Born in the Bedford-Stuyvesant section of Brooklyn, Richie Havens moved to Greenwich Village in 1961 in time to get in on the folk boom then taking place. Havens had a distinctive style as a folksinger, appearing in such clubs as the Cafe Wha? His guitar set to an opening tuning, he would strum it while barring chords with his thumb, using it essentially as percussion while singing rhythmically in a gruff voice for a mesmerizing effect. Havens was signed to Douglas Records in 1965 and recorded two albums that gained him a local following. In 1967, the Verve division of MGM Records formed a folk section (Verve Forecast) and signed Havens and other folk-based performers. The result was Havens' third album, *Mixed Bag*. It wasn't until 1968 and the *Something Else Again* album, however, that Havens began to hit the charts—actually, Havens' fourth, third, and second albums charted that year, in that order. In 1969 came the double album *Richard P. Havens 1983*. Havens' career benefited enormously from his appearance at the Woodstock festival in 1969 and his subsequent featured role in the movie and album made from the concert in 1970. His first album after that exposure, *Alarm Clock*, made the Top 30 and produced a Top 20 single in "Here Comes the Sun." These recordings were Havens' commercial high-water mark, but by this time he had become an international touring success. By the end of the '70s, he had abandoned recording and turned entirely to live work.

Havens came back to records with a flurry of releases in 1987: a new album, *Simple Things;* an album of Bob Dylan and Beatles covers; and a compilation. In 1991 Havens signed his first major-label deal in 15 years when he moved to Sony Music and released *Now*. —*William Ruhlmann*

Mixed Bag / 1967 / Verve ♦♦♦♦
Havens' first major-label album, and his best, featuring his distinctive interpretations of such songs as Dylan's "Just Like a Woman" and the scathing anti-war anthem "Handsome Johnny." (It should be noted that, while it is his best overall collection, *Mixed Bag* is a also characteristic album; if you like it, you'll probably like other Havens records, which adopt much the same style.) —*William Ruhlmann*

Collection / 1987 / Rykodisc ♦♦♦
A compilation of Havens' '60s and early-'70s material. It leaves out some of his signature material but it does include his version of "Here Comes the Sun." —*William Ruhlmann*

● **Resume: Best of Richie Havens** / 1993 / Rhino ✦✦✦✦
Havens' output has been so extensive that picking tunes for a single-disc anthology would be a difficult task for any label. Rhino has done a respectable job in compiling 17 selections, although there was no material from the LPs *Stonehenge* or *1984*, and while he certainly performed them his way, neither Ray Charles' "Drown in My Own Tears" nor Billie Holiday's "God Bless the Child" were among Havens' best songs. By comparison, "Handsome Johnny," "Freedom," "Here Comes the Sun," "The Klan" and "Just Like a Woman" had a strength and power that came partly from being ideally suited for Havens' style. This isn't the comprehensive or qualitative anthology Havens deserves, but it is a decent hits collection. —*Ron Wynn*

Cuts to the Chase / 1994 / Forward ✦✦✦

Margo Hennebach

Synthesizer, Piano, Vocals
Margo Hennebach served as a backup musician for many of Greenwich Village's established singer-songwriters in the '80s. She also performed as a member of the group Idle Rumors. Now she is on her own, touring nationally, and has released an album of her own. —*Richard Meyer*

Margo Hennebach / 1994 / 1-800-Prime CD ✦✦✦✦
On her eponymous release, Margo effectively performs the songs that have made her a favorite of fans of the traditionally oriented contemporary song. A trained musician, Hennebach arranged the vocals and instruments with a classical feel that never weighs down the essence of her songs. Her very clear voice floats over the music in a way that is similar to many Celtic singers. —*Richard Meyer*

Judy Henske

b. Chippewa Falls, WI
Vocals / Folk, Folk-Rock
Success is a matter of luck as well as talent. Given different circumstances, Henske could certainly have been a much bigger star than she was. Instead she's a hazily remembered figure, known, if at all, for some recordings that faintly prefigured folk-rock, and for tangential associations with more famous performers. Her strong, bold, and versatile delivery would have been well-suited for the folk-rock era; her timing was just a bit off.

Before beginning her solo career, Henske worked with ex-Kingston Trio member Dave Guard in the Whiskeyhill Singers in the early '60s. Soon she was recording under her own name for Elektra. *High Flying Bird* is the best of her Elektra efforts, anticipating folk-rock with full arrangements that featured drums (by top session musician Earl Palmer), guitars, and bass. Certainly someone in the Jefferson Airplane must have heard a copy, as the group recorded the title track at their first studio session in 1965.

A stay at Mercury later in the '60s presented her as an all-around entertainer, capable of folk, pop, blues, and Broadway, all backed by middle-of-the-road production. Henske wasn't bad at this, but one got the feeling that her truest talents were being under-utilized. She finally got her chance to blossom on the 1969 LP *Farewell Aldebaran*, a collaborative effort with Jerry Yester that appeared on Frank Zappa's Straight! label (an association that probably arose because Henske and Zappa were both managed by Herbie Cohen). The album was a wildly eclectic, impressive effort that showcased an astonishing range of vocal delivery on Henske's part, and owed more to psychedelic music than folk (the Henske-Yester project and LP is detailed in a separate entry). That proved to be a one-shot, and aside from an effort as a member of the band Rosebud, Henske has not been heard from since. —*Richie Unterberger*

Judy Henske / 1963 / Elektra ✦✦✦✦

High Flying Bird / 1964 / Elektra ✦✦✦
Henske sings with a full-throated, bluesy style reminiscent of Mama Cass on her best album, which was one of the first contemporary folk records to use a rhythm section (including Earl Palmer on drums). Highlighted by the title track, a moody, soaring ballad that was covered by Jefferson Airplane. —*Richie Unterberger*

Little Bit of Sunshine . . . Little Bit of Rain / 1965 / Mercury ✦✦✦
Henske seemed to be trying to be all things to all people on this mid-'60s release. In the manner of a White Nina Simone, she tackles soul ("Any Day Now"), showtunes, the Gershwins, and brassy blues with gusto, as if to prove her versatility. Her rich vibrato is genuinely first-rate, but it would have been a better idea to stick with more contemporary soul and folk-rock all the way than play the all-around entertainer; this is the material from the album that holds up reasonably well today, while the more "adult" stuff is gratingly dated. The record is notable for her interpretation of two Fred Neil songs (the title track and "The Other Side of This Life") when the cult singer-songwriter was just emerging as a performer. A frustratingly spotty effort from a talented artist who never fully came into her own. —*Richie Unterberger*

● **The Death Defying Judy Henske** / 1965 / Reprise ✦✦✦✦

Carolyn Hester

b. 1937, Waco, TX
Guitar, Vocals / Folk
An important, if marginal, figure of the early '60s folk revival, Hester's early albums were produced by music legends Norman Petty (who had produced Buddy Holly's best work), Tom Clancy, and John Hammond, without making a wide impact. Her first Columbia album is notable for one of the first appearances of Bob Dylan on record (playing harmonica). Singing traditional material with a high voice in the manner of Joan Baez and Judy Collins (though with less command), she was married for a time to fellow folkie Richard Farina, and drifted out of the music business after the mid-'60s. In the '80s, she was a mentor for budding talent Nanci Griffith (whose vocals have been compared to Hester's), and appeared on Griffith's *Other Voices, Other Rooms* album. —*Richie Unterberger*

● **Carolyn Hester** / 1962 / Columbia/Legacy ✦✦✦✦
An album, in retrospect, more important for the accompanying musicians than Hester herself. Hester delivers a solid, somewhat precious set of traditional material in the early-'60s Greenwich Village folk mode. One of the first LPs of the scene to use a full band, it also features guitar by future Dylan accompanist Bruce Langhorne, bassist Bill Lee (who played on many other folk albums of the era by Ian and Sylvia and others), and Dylan himself, who contributed harmonica to a few tracks shortly before he made his own Columbia debut. The CD reissue adds a couple of bonus alternate takes. —*Richie Unterberger*

Anne Hills

Banjo, Guitar, Autoharp, Vocals / Folk, Singer-Songwriter
A mainstay on the folk circuit, Anne Hills has recorded with Priscilla Herdman and Cindy Mangsen and on her own. Originally from Chicago, Hills is known for her clear, expressive singing. —*Richard Meyer*

Woman of a Calm Heart / 1978 / Flying Fish ✦✦✦

October Child / 1993 / Flying Fish ✦✦✦✦
This is a collection of fellow-Chicagoan Michael Smith's songs. Peter Erskine's arrangements are respectful of the songs' carefully crafted lyrics. One of the great benefits of this CD is the chance to hear some of Smith's less well-known songs, including "Disappearing Heart." —*Richard Meyer*

● **Angle of the Light** / 1995 / Flying Fish ✦✦✦✦
Anne Hills has finally made an album that lives up to her promise. Her voice has gotten progressively stronger and more flexible, and her writing has grown more detailed and evocative. On this release, she comes across as a thoughtful romantic with a mature, compassionate view of how each of us must work to fit in the world. Her abstract "Follow That Road" directs how to find her, but more listeners will find some of their own past in her direction. Hills has come to terms with some part of herself when she sings "Today let me eat, Today let me breathe, Today let me speak with a friend, Today let the sun shine down on my head, 'Til moon light shines on me again, It's enough to live." —*Richard Meyer*

Tish Hinojosa

Guitar, Piano, Vocals / Folk, Tex-Mex, Singer-Songwriter
In the liner notes to her album *Homeland*, Tish Hinojosa writes of a dilemma she faced as she began to emerge as a singer-songwriter. She writes of " . . . wondering how my love for my parents' humble Mexican heritage and language would mix with idealistic images of a musical future." Hinojosa has fashioned her blend of cultures into a compelling voice in American music. Typically a Tish Hinojosa album or concert moves effortlessly from songs of loves forgotten and family struggles remembered, of eloquent cries against injustice and playful evocations of sawdust dance floors, of the rolling endless highways of the Southwest to the struggles of the disenfranchised.

Hinojosa was born Leticia Hinojosa in San Antonio to a large blended family, went to parochial school, listened to the songs of her parents as well as the Beatles and Woodstock, and began her musical career doing jingles and recording for a small Tejano label before leaving Texas for Taos. In the spectacular beauty of northern New Mexico, she further honed her art and recorded an EP featuring three original songs. Nashville was her next stop.

Although she worked steadily—touring, doing demo work, even recording a successful single, "I'll Pull You Through," for Curb Records—she never felt that she could find her niche in Music City. She says, "Nashville requires a delicate balance. I began to see that incorporating aspects of my ethnic heritage into my music was a problem, at least at that time (early '80s)."

In 1985 Hinojosa returned to New Mexico where she recorded an independent cassette, *Taos to Tennessee*. The recording features some of her compositions that would later appear on *Homeland*, her 1989 A&M/ Americana major label debut. Finding the opportunity for work limited as a Taos-based artist, she moved to Austin in the summer of 1988. She rapidly became an integral part of the vibrant Austin musical scene by making many club appearances but also standing tall for her social concerns by being a willing participant in benefits for migrant farmworkers. Her concern for the dangers of picking pesticide-laced crops was also evident in her song "Something in the Rain," a moving account of the tragedy of unsafe crop-spraying practices told through the eyes of a small boy. Hinojosa also has a loyal following overseas, and her touring itinerary often includes stops in Amsterdam and Scandinavia as well as the more familiar confines of clubs in Houston, Cambridge, and Taos.

The highpoint of her recording career so far is the 1992 album *Culture Swing* on Rounder Records. This is an essential album in the classic folk tradition of Baez and Dylan. With all of the songs written by Hinojosa, *Culture Swing* is a singer-songwriter tour-de-force that bridges the folk and country idioms. The 1994 album *Destiny's Gate* carries on the Hinojosa tradition in the vein of *Culture Swing.*

Recently Hinojosa has produced a couple of theme albums on the Rounder label: a collection of border songs, *Frontejas* (1995) and a bilingual album designed for kids, *Cada Nino (Every Child)* (1996). —*Alonso Jasso and Michael Erlewine*

Homeland / 1989 / A&M ✦✦✦✦
Her first album and a clear harbinger of what is to come. With most songs written by Hinojosa herself, she has her own sound and style. Outstanding songs are "The Border Trilogy," "Voice of the Big Guitar," "Who Showed You the Way to My Heart," "Let Me Remember," and "Amanecer." —*Michael Erlewine*

★ **Culture Swing** / Aug. 27, 1990 / A&M ✦✦✦✦✦
With a voice that rivals Joan Baez' and a sense of humor all her own, Tish Hinojosa is proof that really great singer-songwriters still appear from time to time. Each generation has but a few perfect folk albums, and *Culture Swing* (all songs are written by Hinojosa) is one of these—an instant classic. —*Michael Erlewine*

Memorabilia Navidena / 1991 / Watermelon ✦✦✦

Aquella Noche / 1991 / Watermelon ✦✦✦
A largely Spanish album, it balances traditional Mexican songs with her own romantic, clear-eyed originals. This was recorded live at Austin's Waterloo Icehouse the week of Cinco de Mayo 1991. —*Michael McCall*

Taos to Tennessee / 1992 / Watermelon ✦✦✦✦
Recorded in 1987, *Taos to Tennessee* predates the more successful *Culture Swing*, but shows the same kind of style and clarity. She wrote six of the 12 songs on this album and most are outstanding, including the gorgeous "Prairie Moon," "Taos to Tennessee," "Amanecer," "Who Showed You the Way to My Heart," and "Let Me Remember." The Peter Rowan song "Midnight Moonlight" is also very fine. Singer-songwriter Hinojosa is a treasure. —*Michael Erlewine*

Destiny's Gate / 1994 / Warner Brothers ✦✦✦
Hinojosa continues to move into the mainstream with *Destiny's Gate* without losing the magic of *Culture Swing*. With a beautiful voice reminiscent of Joan Baez and Emmylou Harris, she seems to have perfected her unique blend of Mexican folk and country music. "I Want to See You Again" stands out as one of her finest songs. —*Chris Woodstra*

Frontejas / 1995 / Rounder ✦✦✦
Not your standard album release, but a theme recording. This is a collection of border songs sung in Spanish, some written by Hinojosa, some by others. The inspiration for this collection was her apprenticeship with Don Americo Paredes, the anthropologist, border historian, and professor emeritus at the University of Texas at Austin. Hinojosa writes "In a series of sessions I listened and enriched my soul with 'corridos' (ballads that tell stories, news, or history), love songs, and anecdotes of the borderland where he was raised and where my family's roots lie deeply embedded. These sessions continue still, and the knowledge I receive is a precious resource from which I'll always draw." A number of these songs involve assistance from the likes of Flaco Jimenez, Ray Benson, Peter Rowan, and others. This makes for enjoyable listening but Hinojosa is not as creative and fiery as on an album like *Culture Swing*. —*Michael Erlewine*

Cada Nino (Every Child) / 1996 / Rounder ✦✦
A theme album. Not for us old folks, but11 bilingual songs (English/Spanish) for kids. With titles like "Barnyard Dance," "Music Scale," and "Always Grandma," these really are for children. Although sung in Hinojosa's clear and vibrant voice, they are too cutesy for most of us. Kids will like this. —*Michael Erlewine*

Dreaming from the Labyrinth / May 1996 / Warner Brothers ✦✦✦
Dreaming from the Labyrinth (Hinojosa's second for Warner Bros.) is more what comes to mind with the word "traditional." Hinojosa was born in Texas to Mexican immigrant parents, and her multicultural upbringing is a defining characteristic of her acoustic folk music (she sings in both Spanish and English, for example), as is her association with the current folk and country scene in Austin. Hinojosa's music, however, is often so sweet and nice around the edges that it becomes a turn-

off. The songs on *Labyrinth* are as pretty as Hinojosa's voice, but there's no dirt under the fingernails, which is exactly what makes the music of Lucinda Williams, for instance (another Austin-based artist), so vibrant and alive. —*Kurt Wolff*

Robin Holcomb

b. 1954, Georgia
Piano, Vocals / Urban-Folk, Singer-Songwriter
This Georgia-born singer-songwriter, composer, pianist, and poet incorporates elements of gospel, blues, R&B, and rock in her music. Holcomb has had a varied background in chamber music, ethnomusicology (including performing in a Javanese gamelan ensemble), musical theater, and work with her husband, Wayne Horvitz, on the New York downtown avant-garde experimental scene. After attending the University of California at Santa Cruz, she and Horvitz moved to New York before settling in Seattle in 1988. —*AMG*

● **Robin Holcomb** / Nov. 19, 1990 / Elektra ✦✦✦✦
The songs are arty, piano-based, spooky, and very sensual. "Deliver Me" is particularly fine. —*Richard Meyer*

Rockabye / Sep. 8, 1992 / Elektra ✦✦✦

The Holy Modal Rounders

Folk, Folk-Rock
The Holy Modal Rounders were almost the very definition of a cult act. This isn't a case of a group that would be described by such cliches as "if only they got more exposure, they would certainly reach a much wider audience." Their audience was small because their music was too strange, idiosyncratic, and at times downright dissonant for mainstream listeners to abide. What makes the Rounders unusual in this regard is that they owed primary allegiance to the world of acoustic folk—not one that generates many difficult, arty, and abrasive performers.

The Holy Modal Rounders were not so much a group as a changing aggregation centered around the two principals, Peter Stampfel and Steve Weber. When the pair got together in 1963, the intention was to update old-time folk music with a contemporary spirit. As Stampfel told *Folk Roots* in 1995, "The Rounders were the first really bent traditional band. And the first traditionally-based band that was not trying to sound like an old record." They weren't the only musicians in New York thinking along these lines, and Stampfel and Weber contributed heavily to the first recordings by a similar, more rock-oriented group, the Fugs.

The Rounders began recording in the mid-'60s for Prestige as an acoustic duo. Even at this early stage, they were not for everybody. Although clearly accomplished musicians, and well-versed in folk traditions, they were determined to subvert these with off-kilter execution and strange lyrics that could be surreal, whimsical, or just silly. They outraged folk purists by simply changing melodies and words to suit their tastes on some of their cover versions of old standards; Stampfel once wrote in the liner notes that "I made up new words to it because it was easier than listening to the tape and writing words down."

On their 1967 LP *Indian War Whoop*, Stampfel and Weber added other musicians, including playwright Sam Shepard on drums (Shepard also wrote some material). The resulting chaos was as exasperating as it was inspiring, but both material and performance improved on 1969's *Moray Eels Eat the Holy Modal Rounders*. This addled combination of folk and psychedelia was their most inventive work and featured their most famous song, "If You Wanna Be a Bird" (which was used on the *Easy Rider* soundtrack).

The haphazard style of the Rounders perhaps militated against any sort of stable lineup (Jeff Baxter, later to play with Steely Dan and the Doobie Brothers, was one of the musicians that passed through the group briefly in the '60s). *Good Taste Is Timeless*, in the early '70s, was engineered in Nashville by legendary Elvis Presley guitarist Scotty Moore and generated one of their most renowned songs, "Boobs a Lot." Shortly afterwards, Stampfel and Weber separated for a time, although they reunited in 1976 for *Alleged in Our Own Time* on Rounder. By this time the Rounders were more of a concept than an ongoing group, and 1979's *Last Round* was recorded with various musicians that had been part of the group at some point. *Goin' Nowhere*, billed just to Stampfel and Weber, was their last recorded joint partnership.

Stampfel has been much more visible as a solo recording artist than Weber, acting as a key contributor to Michael Hurley's critically lauded *Have Moicy!* in 1976. He's been recording on his own since the mid-'80s, sometimes with the Bottlecaps, in a fashion that keeps the spirit of the Holy Modal Rounders alive without sounding embarrassingly revivalist. —*Richie Unterberger*

Holy Modal Rounders / 1964 / Rounder ✦✦✦✦

Indian War Whoop / 1967 / ESP ✦✦✦✦
Comic, absurdist folk with Peter Stampfel as ringleader. —*William Ruhlmann*

● **The Moray Eels Eat the Holy Modal Rounders** / 1969 / Elektra ✦✦✦✦
Like a psychedelic folkie fusion of the Fugs and the Mothers of Invention, this ranks as one of the best "acid folk" albums. This sprawling, demented LP includes "Bird Song," which was featured on the *Easy Rider* soundtrack. —*Richie Unterberger*

Last Round / 1978 / Adelphi ✦✦✦
More madness, with "Pink Underwear" and "Romping Through the Swamp." —*William Ruhlmann*

Cisco Houston

b. Aug. 18, 1918, Wilmington, DE, **d.** Apr. 29, 1961
Guitar, Vocals / Folk
An associate of Woody Guthrie, with whom he made many recordings, Houston scored a hit single with "Rose, Rose, I Love You" in 1951. He was a popular folk interpreter until his death from cancer. —*William Ruhlmann*

● **900 Miles and Other Railroad Ballads** / 195 / Smithsonian/Folkways ✦✦✦✦

Sings Songs of the Open Road / 1968 / Smithsonian/Folkways ✦✦✦✦
This Woody Guthrie sidekick sings Guthrie's songs and traditional tunes. —*William Ruhlmann*

Ian and Sylvia

Folk, Folk-Rock
One of the most popular acts of the early-'60s folk revival, Canadian duo Ian Tyson (b. 1933) and Sylvia Tyson (b. 1940) made several fine albums that spotlighted their stirring harmonies on a mixture of traditional and contemporary material. While these recordings can seem a tad earnest and dated today, they were overlooked influences upon early folk-rockers such as the Jefferson Airplane, the We Five, the Mamas and the Papas, and Fairport Convention, all of whom utilized similar blends of male/female lead/harmony vocals. They were also inspirations to fellow Canadian singer-songwriters such as Neil Young, Joni Mitchell, and Gordon Lightfoot. Like most acoustic folkies, after the mid-'60s they moved into folk-rock and country-rock, though the results were less impressive than their early work. Tyson took up folk music in his 20s while convalescing from a rodeo injury, and teamed up with Fricker after moving to Toronto in the late '50s. In 1960 they moved to New York, where they were signed by Albert Grossman, famous for managing Bob Dylan and Peter, Paul, and Mary. Their self-titled debut (1962) began a successful series of recordings for Vanguard, on which they helped expand the range of folk by adding bass (sometimes played by Spike Lee's father, Bill) and mandolin to Ian's guitar and Sylvia's autoharp. Just as crucially, they ranged far afield for their repertoire, which encompassed not just traditional folk ballads, but bluegrass, country, spirituals, blues, hillbilly, gospel, and French-Canadian songs. Ian and Sylvia were among the first to cover songs by Dylan, Lightfoot, Joni Mitchell, and Phil Ochs, and also began writing material of their own. Although original compositions were never at the forefront of their early LPs, a couple of them would become very influential indeed. Tyson's "Four Strong Winds" would be covered by the Searchers and (in the '70s) Neil Young, and Fricker's "You Were On My Mind," given a far poppier treatment by the We Five, became one of the first big folk-rock hits. By 1966 Ian and Sylvia had started to rely primarily on original material, and had begun to use electric instruments. While some of these tracks were outstanding, generally their folk-rock lacked the focus and consistency of their acoustic recordings. In the late '60s, they would take stabs at country-rock and straight country music, even hooking up with young producer Todd Rundgren for the 1970 album *Great Speckled Bird*. The quality of their records, and the size of their audience, declined steadily after they ended their association with Vanguard in 1967. In the '70s, they split up, professionally and personally (they had married in 1964). Both have since pursued solo careers. Tyson's was far more successful, as he moved into country music, recording albums of songs with cowboy and rodeo themes that received much popular and critical acclaim in Canada. —*Richie Unterberger*

Ian and Sylvia / 1962 / Vanguard ✦✦✦
Ian and Sylvia's debut album is their most standard affair, and indeed a fairly typical folk recording for the era, with such traditional warhorses as "Rocks And Gravel" (also recorded, but not released, by Dylan during this time), "C.C. Rider," and "Handsome Molly." What makes the pair distinctive is their superb vocal dueting, a case of the sum being greater than its parts. Blended, they cancel each other's weaknesses and give the material great freshness and vigor. Ian's guitar and Sylvia's autoharp are backed by stellar playing from guitarist John Herald and string bassists Bill Lee and Art Davis. —*Richie Unterberger*

Four Strong Winds / 1964 / Vanguard ✦✦✦✦
Ian and Sylvia hit their stride on their second LP, which features the first in a line of talented second guitarists (John Herald) they would use to augment their original guitar-autoharp-bass lineup. The album features an assortment of largely traditional material unsurpassed in its time,

encompassing bluegrass, spirituals, gospel, hillbilly, the French-Canadian standard "V'la l'Bon Vent," a British prison song, and two tunes from the Cecil Sharp collection of Southern mountain folk songs of British origin. Two of the most impressive cuts, however, are contemporary compositions. One is their version of Bob Dylan's "Tomorrow Is a Long Time," one of the first obscure Dylan tunes to be committed to vinyl. The title cut, an Ian Tyson original, would prove to be the duo's first song to influence rock musicians, as the Searchers covered it shortly afterwards with a reverent version that was quite close to the original; Neil Young revived it in the late '70s. —*Richie Unterberger*

Northern Journey / 1964 / Vanguard ✦✦✦
The duo continue to fill out their sound on another collection of mostly traditional material, with John Herald (guitar), Monte Dunn (mandolin and guitar), and Eric Weissberg and Russ Savakus (bass) backing Ian and Sylvia's own guitar and autoharp. The few originals stand out much more than the traditional updates on this LP; Tyson's "Four Rode By" and "Some Day Soon" clearly point toward his future C&W/cowboy direction, and Fricker's "You Were on My Mind" remains their best (and best-known) song. —*Richie Unterberger*

Early Morning Rain / 1965 / Vanguard ✦✦✦
Side one continues in the eclectic folkie style of the earlier albums, containing only one original (Tyson's "Marlborough Street Blues"). The other cuts include the fine Gordon Lightfoot title track, a Johnny Cash cover ("Come In Stranger") that heralded their increasing interest in country and western music, one of their finest interpretations of a bona fide traditional warhorse ("Nancy Whiskey"), and "Darcy Farrow," a fine obscure composition that could pass for a traditional standard (written for the duo by an unknown Californian singer-songwriter pair). Side two, however, with the exception of one traditional tune and another Lightfoot cover, is composed entirely of originals. The most notable of these is Tyson's "Song for Canada" (written with Pete Gzowski). A bittersweet plea for greater communication between French- and English-speaking Canadians, it could just as well be heard as a comment on any sort of deteriorating relationship. —*Richie Unterberger*

Play One More / 1966 / Vanguard ✦✦✦
Ian and Sylvia rely mostly on original material for the first time on this erratic record. For the first time, they employ full modern arrangements on four of the tracks, which sometimes works (their cover of "24 Hours from Tulsa") and sometimes doesn't (unfortunately for them, on one of their best compositions, "The French Girl"). They also cover songs by Phil Ochs and Scott McKenzie, and their own tunes range from solid numbers in their proven contemporary folk style ("Short Grass") to mediocre. Future Cream producer Felix Pappalardi plays bass. —*Richie Unterberger*

So Much for Dreaming / 1967 / Vanguard ✦✦✦
Ian and Sylvia's adjustment to folk-rock was sometimes fine, sometimes awkward, and this is another inconsistent, though generally worthwhile, effort. Highlights include "Circle Game," one of the very first recorded covers of a Joni Mitchell composition. Tyson's "Wild Geese" and "Child Apart" count as some of their better unheralded tunes, and the occasional muted orchestration works well on "Circle Game" and the melancholy title track. On the other hand, the attempts at blues are abominable, the traditional ballads anachronistic, and some of the material (especially Fricker's) undistinguished. —*Richie Unterberger*

● **Greatest Hits** / 1987 / Vanguard ✦✦✦✦
This compilation (CVSD 5/6) captures much of their best work. Do not confuse it with the identically titled Vanguard album 73114, which includes only half the material found on this set. —*William Ruhlmann*

Long Long Time / 1994 / Vanguard ✦✦✦
After leaving Vanguard in 1967, Ian and Sylvia spent the next few years recording in a much more countrified style for MGM, Ampex as figureheads of the band Great Speckled Bird, and Columbia. This compilation—ironically on Vanguard—draws from five albums they released between 1967 and 1971. While the duo's ambitions to expand their artistic horizons were admirable, the fact is that they were much more effective as eclectic folkies than country-pop-folk-rockers. The harmonies remained intact, but the material (mostly original) is often humdrum, the arrangements sometimes lackadaisical. A few cuts, like "Salmon in the Sea" and "Last Lonely Eagle," are reasonably strong; the highlights are the 1967 versions of "Hang on to a Dream" and "Reason to Believe," among the first Tim Hardin covers ever recorded. —*Richie Unterberger*

Live at Newport / 1996 / Vanguard ✦✦✦
Divided about equally between material from their appearances at the 1963 and 1965 Newport Folk Festivals, these 14 tracks present concert versions of many of the duo's best songs, including "You Were on My Mind," "Someday Soon," "Song for Canada," and "Four Strong Winds." Eric Hord adds lead acoustic guitar on the 1963 cuts; Rick Turner does the same on the ones from 1965. Ian and Sylvia recorded studio versions of all of the songs on their '60s Vanguard albums, which makes this disc

a sort of souvenir that's essential only for big fans, although the sound and performances are decent. —*Richie Unterberger*

Incredible String Band

Folk, Folk-Rock, British Folk
Hippie mystics or cosmic fools? In the late '60s the Incredible String Band mixed folk and psychedelia in ways that could be innovative, irritating, or both. Folk was always more prominent than the psychedelic, though, for the ISB's two mainstays, Scottish singer-songwriters Robin Williamson (b. 1943) and Mike Heron (b. 1942).

Williamson, who had occasionally played with fellow Scotsman Bert Jansch before Jansch established himself as a solo act, began the Incredible String Band with Clive Palmer in the mid-'60s. (Palmer owned the Incredible Folk Club in Glasgow, hence the Incredible String Band.) The jug band duo was soon joined by Mike Heron, and as a trio they recorded their debut for Elektra in 1966. Though the debut is tame in comparison with later outings, the group's ambitious blend of British folk, American folk, and miscellaneous exotic influences was already evident. The influence of the contemporary music of the '60s was felt in the fairytale ambience of the songwriting and the melismatic, almost raga-like, vocals, traits that would both charm and annoy listeners, depending upon individual tastes.

Soon after the LP's release, this iteration of the band broke up. Palmer, whose contributions to the first LP were marginal in any case, traveled to India; Williamson took off for Morocco. Williamson returned from North Africa while Heron was touring as a solo act, and the pair reunited for the second Incredible String Band album, *The 5000 Spirits or the Layers of the Onion* (1967). Psychedelic influences were apparent in the music as well as the title, and these cosmic ambitions would be pushed further on *The Hangman's Beautiful Daughter*, which is usually cited as their most innovative album. In the UK it was also their most successful, reaching No. 5.

The Williamson-Heron era is seen as the ISB's peak. In the late '60s, Christina McKenzie and Rose Simpson joined, and the music became less concise and more airy-fairy. At least The Incredible String Band could not be accused of standing still. Some of their later records were considerably more rock-oriented, and the 1970 album *U* was performed with a mime troupe when it was presented onstage.

But like an overdose of chocolate (or of acid, for that matter), the Incredible String Band's charm began to wilt. The fantasy world detailed by the ISB seemed increasingly silly and trivial. The ISB didn't have much straight pop appeal, which consigned them to a much smaller audience, especially in the US, where they were known only to underground cultists. They did gain an unlikely fan in Led Zeppelin's Robert Plant, who once credited them (in a Led Zeppelin tour booklet) as having inspired his band's occasional digressions into folk (though it must be said that these don't sound a whole lot like the Incredible String Band).

With some further musical chairs in personnel, the Incredible String Band continued releasing albums through the mid-'70s. Williamson and Heron had begun separate recording careers in the early '70s, and it was little surprise when the increasingly anachronistic group dissolved. Williamson has had a much more active solo career than Heron, releasing a few solo albums and attaining a higher American profile after moving to Los Angeles. —*Richie Unterberger*

The Incredible String Band / 1966 / Rykodisc ✦✦✦
As much a showcase for individual performances as group ones, the ISB's debut was their most traditional effort, though Williamson and Heron modernized traditional British Isles music with their whimsical songwriting and vari-pitch vocals. It also has minor contributions from guitarist Clive Palmer, who would leave the group after this album. —*Richie Unterberger*

5,000 Spirits or the Layers of the Onion / 1967 / Elektra ✦✦✦✦
For their second album, the ISB officially reduced to the duo of Mike Heron and Robin Williamson. Lumped in with the psychedelic movement, that categorization was probably more due to the trippy cover graphics, the occasional Indian influences, and the whimsical, sometimes fantasy-ridden lyrical images than the music. It's more like a slightly cosmic version of traditional British folk than psychedelic rock. Although their next album, *The Hangman's Beautiful Daughter*, is usually considered their most adventurous, some listeners may find this to be the more accessible effort. It also features what is probably Williamson's best-known song, "First Girl I Loved" (also familiar via Judy Collins' cover version, "First Boy I Loved"). —*Richie Unterberger*

● **Hangman's Beautiful Daughter** / 1968 / Hannibal ✦✦✦✦
The ISB's most ambitious album, with Williamson and Heron employing an arsenal of unusual instruments (sitar, gimbri, pan pipe, oud, chahanai, and more), and Dolly Collins adding a couple of the more dignified arrangements. It's usually considered their most important effort by critics, but there were also traces of the sprawling, occasionally grating lack of focus that would increasingly come to characterize their work. —*Richie Unterberger*

Wee Tam / 1969 / Elektra ✦✦✦
Mixing English and American folk with what we now call "world music," the multi-instrumental Scottish duo of Robin Williamson and Mike Heron achieve a whimsical, delicate style that has never been duplicated. It reaches a peak here with such songs as "You Get Brighter." (*Wee Tam* is sometimes packaged with the simultaneously released *The Big Huge*, which is also recommended.) —*William Ruhlmann*

Relics of the Incredible String Band / 1970 / Elektra ✦✦✦✦
The ISB's prolific output makes a compilation a virtual necessity, and this two-record set selects wisely from the seven albums the group released in the US between 1967 and 1970. From Robin Williamson's "First Girl I Loved" (covered by Judy Collins) and "Way Back in the 1960s" (recorded in 1967), to Mike Heron's "Air," and "This Moment," the ISB's eclectic, fanciful acoustic style is well portrayed. —*William Ruhlmann*

No Ruinous Feud / 1973 / Edsel ✦✦✦
The ISB began to change its approach in 1971, cutting back on its sometimes open-ended song structures and adding a rock rhythm section to selected tracks. But it wasn't until this album that everything came together, resulting in a delightful collection of songs that range from reggae to light pop, along with the traditional folk styles that had always been the group's strong suit. —*William Ruhlmann*

Burl Ives

b. Jun. 14, 1909, Jasper County, IL, **d.** Apr. 13, 1995
Guitar, Vocals / Folk
Ives traveled as an itinerant handyman throughout the US after a brief stay at New York University. He became a working actor and performed concerts of folk ballads. He published several songbooks and an autobiography, *Wayfaring Stranger*. —*David Szatmary*

★ **Wayfaring Stranger** / 1959 / CBS ✦✦✦✦✦
This is traditional folk from the smooth-sounding Ives; it includes "On Top of Old Smokey," "Roving Gambler," and "Green Broom." —*David Szatmary*

Bert Jansch

b. Nov. 3, 1943, Scotland
Guitar, Vocals / Folk, Folk-Rock, British Folk
One of the most important figures in contemporary British folk, Bert Jansch brought an unsurpassed combination of virtuosity and eclecticism to the acoustic guitar, both as a solo act and a key member of Pentangle. Also a talented songwriter and affecting (if gruff) vocalist, he wrote dark and sparse material that recalled the folkie side of Donovan, though he was much less pop-oriented than the psychedelic pop troubadour. Incorporating elements of blues, American folk, and British Isles traditional music into his playing, his influence was not only immense in the British folk scene, it extended to the rock world. Neil Young and Jimmy Page, two electric guitar gonzos who often turn to acoustic picking as well, have acknowledged Jansch as a major influence. Young went as far as to tell *Guitar Player* that Jansch did for the acoustic guitar what Jimi Hendrix did for the electric. A revered elder statesperson in the UK, he has escaped widespread notice in the States. He has all the prerequisites for a large cult following on the order of Nick Drake—another musician whose work contains definite echoes of Jansch.

Born in Scotland, Jansch vagabonded around the UK and Europe for a while before basing himself in London in the early '60s. He made an impact on the city's folk community with his guitar skills and original songwriting, singing his own compositions at a time when Dylan was just beginning to make that practice widespread in folk circles. Friend and fellow folk singer Ann Briggs helped Jansch get a contract with Transatlantic, a small British folkie label. Recorded on a single microphone and a borrowed guitar at Jansch's apartment, it immediately established him as a major force in British folk. Consisting almost entirely of original compositions, the brooding, plaintive album showcased his dextrous fingerpicking. "Needle of Death," inspired by the heroin-related death of a friend, may still be his most famous composition.

Jansch graduated to a real studio for his second album, *It Don't Bother Me*. That LP featured some contributions from guitarist John Renbourn, and the pair recorded a joint effort in the mid-'60s as well, *Bert and John*. Soon Jansch and Renbourn were playing together as part of Pentangle, one of the greatest folk acts of the '60s. Pentangle, also featuring vocalist Jacqui McShee and the rhythm section of Danny Thompson and Terry Cox, was very much a group effort. Of all the group members, however, Jansch was probably the most important, writing the best original material, singing occasional lead vocals, and recording some enthralling guitar tandems with Renbourn.

Jansch's increasing involvement (and eventual commercial success) with Pentangle did not mean an end to his solo career, although Pentangle got first priority in the late '60s and early '70s. *Nicola*, from 1967, was a pretty good attempt to commercialize his sound with poppier material and some fuller studio arrangements. *Birthday Blues* in 1969 was more like his early folk recordings and included instrumental support by some members of Pentangle. *Rosemary Lane* (1971) is acclaimed by fans as one of his finest.

Jansch's first decade of recording attracts the lion's share of interest from listeners. But he's continued to record, his instrumental skills intact, although his best compositions date from the early part of his career. He also played in re-formed versions of Pentangle in the '80s and '90s. *—Richie Unterberger*

Bert Jansch / 1965 / Transatlantic/Demon ◆◆◆◆
Recorded with a portable tape player on a borrowed guitar in the kitchen of his London flat, the impact of Jansch's debut has been somewhat blunted by time, but it was a vastly influential work. His masterful acoustic picking, which blended elements of traditional British folk, blues, and jazz, inspired not just other folk players, but rockers who frequently used acoustic guitars. Specifically, Jimmy Page and Neil Young have gone on record as noting their heavy debts to Jansch's early folk music. Jansch was also a talented songwriter, and all but one of the 15 tracks on his debut were original compositions. (The set closes with his version of the instrumental "Angie," originally performed by fellow British folk guitarist Davy Graham, and popularized by Paul Simon.) Jansch sounds quite close to early Donovan with his Scottish inflections, though Bert is darker and less pop-oriented; indeed, Donovan recorded a couple of early Jansch tunes and wrote a couple of songs directly inspired by Bert ("Bert's Blues" and "House of Jansch"). Jansch reflects a rambling, beatnik sort of lifestyle with his compositions on this album, which includes one of his most famous tunes, the somber "Needle of Death" (about the heroin-induced death of a friend). In 1993 this LP and Jansch's third album *(Jack Orion)* were combined onto one CD reissue. *—Richie Unterberger*

It Don't Bother Me / 1965 / Transatlantic/Demon ◆◆◆
Basically an extension of his 1965 debut, Jansch's second album is perhaps a bit lighter in mood and doesn't boast quite as strong material, although it's nearly in the same league. Includes one of his most explicitly political songs ("Anti-Apartheid"), his first recording with John Renbourn ("Lucky Thirteen," a Renbourn original), and his first use of banjo on record ("900 Miles"). The Demon reissue of this album adds four bonus tracks, a couple of songs cut around this time that appeared only on the obscure Transatlantic LP *Box Of Love—The Bert Jansch Sampler Vol. 2* in 1972, and the two vocal tracks from Jansch's mostly instrumental 1966 album with John Renbourn, *Bert And John. —Richie Unterberger*

Jack Orion / 1966 / Transatlantic/Demon ◆◆◆
After presenting almost all-original sets on his first two albums (albeit originals that sometimes borrowed heavily from traditional folk themes), Jansch opted to devote all of his third LP to traditional folk numbers. His future Pentangle partner John Renbourn joins Bert on four of the eight songs. Highlights include the ten-minute title track (whose length was a real oddity on contemporary folk albums of the time) and a cover of "Nottamun Town" (whose melody Dylan lifted for "Masters Of War"). Not as original as Bert's first two LPs, the guitar and vocal work on these adaptations was still as influential on the '60s folk world as anything else in Jansch's catalog. *—Richie Unterberger*

Nicola / 1967 / Demon ◆◆◆
Jansch's third solo album is perhaps too lightly dismissed by both folk critics and the artist himself. Bowing slightly to commercial pressures, he allowed orchestration to be used on five of the 12 tracks. Actually, the orchestrated cuts aren't that bad at all, and the remainder are pretty much in keeping with the character and high standard of his other '60s work. Nine of the12 cuts are Jansch originals and ably display his nimble guitar work, incorporation of blues and traditional British Isles folk influences into a contemporary style, and his Donovan-esque vocals. For the first and only time, Bert played both electric and acoustic guitars on this LP; it's also his first work to feature drumming. Some of the orchestrated numbers, especially "Woe Is Love, My Dear," were actually deemed to have potential as singles. That didn't happen (the cut "Wish My Baby Was Here" would have been a better choice in any event), but that doesn't take away from their fey, period charm. *Nicola* and Jansch's 1969 release *Birthday Blues* were combined on one CD for a 1993 reissue. *—Richie Unterberger*

Birthday Blues / 1969 / Demon ◆◆◆◆
It's no accident that Jansch's 1969 album sounds like a modified version of Pentangle. Jansch was a member of the great British folk-rock group at the time of this album's release, which was produced by Shel Talmy (who also worked with Pentangle). And he's backed by the Pentangle's sterling rhythm section of Danny Thompson (bass) and Terry Cox (drums), with occasional touches of harmonica (played by British blues singer Duffy Power), alto sax, and flute. The effect is akin to hearing an unbalanced Pentangle, with no John Renbourn on dueling guitar or Jacqui McShee on vocals. That's not at all a bad thing—Jansch was one of the group's main motors and can still be a compelling writer and performer. All of the cuts on this LP are originals, showing Jansch leaning a

little more toward bluesy styles than usual, though the mood is predominantly British folk. It's a pleasant effort but not his best work, either as a solo performer or within a group. *Birthday Blues* and Jansch's release *Nicola* have been combined on one CD for a 1993 reissue. *—Richie Unterberger*

Moonshine / 1973 / Reprise ◆◆◆

Avocet / 1979 / Charisma ◆◆◆

● **Best of** / 1980 / Shanachie ◆◆◆◆

Sketches / 1990 / Temple Music ◆◆◆

● **Ornament Tree** / Nov. 1990 / Capitol ◆◆◆◆

Victor Jara

d. Sep. 14, 1973
Vocals / Folk, Singer-Songwriter
Victor Jara was the main proponent of the Chilean New Song movement, which brought a political consciousness to native folk music in Chile, much as the "protest" singers of the '60s did to US folk music. A national figure, he was closely associated with the Allende government of the early '70s and was murdered by the military junta that took over Chile in 1973. *— William Ruhlmann*

● **Unfinished Song** / 1990 / Redwood ◆◆◆◆
Jara's expressive, vibrant singing shows why he was the leading light of the South American New Song movement as well as a significant political figure. This compilation includes not only original political songs but traditional Chilean folksongs and even an adaptation of Malvina Reynolds' "Little Boxes." The album's 23 tracks, taken from various sources, provide a thorough view of Jara's broad talent. (Also recommended: Monitor Records' four-volume series of Jara recordings.) *— William Ruhlmann*

Michael Jerling

Guitar, Vocals / Folk
A Chicago native, Jerling has developed an urban style with the feel of country-blues. He is an excellent guitar player and singer-songwriter, and his songs are full of strong imagery. "The Long Black Wall" has become one of his signature pieces. *—Richard Meyer and Chip Renner*

Blue Heartland / 1988 / Moonlight ◆◆◆
Including "The Long Black Wall" and "Road House." *—Richard Meyer*

● **My Evil Twin** / 1992 / Shanachie ◆◆◆◆
Jerling has a way with words that can paint a picture in your mind's eye. "Take Me to Juarez" is a classic tale; also worthwhile are "Breakdown," and the title cut. "Before the Country Moved to Town" features Robin and Linda Williams singing nice background vocals. All in all, this is a good label-debut album, with great songs and great production. *—Chip Renner*

New Suit of Clothes / 1994 / Shanachie ◆◆◆
This collection has more bluesy-based ballads than Jerling's previous CD. The playing, including guest appearances by John Sebastian and Peter Ostroushko, is clean and unobtrusive, allowing Jerling's warm baritone to serve his sophisticated lyrics well. *—Richard Meyer*

Josh Joffen

Vocals / Urban-Folk
Brooklyn-born Josh Joffen has recorded often for *The Fast Folk Musical Magazine.* He released an album with songwriter David Roth (they each have one side). Joffen won the Kerrville New Folk Competition in 1987. *—Richard Meyer*

Josh Joffen W/ David Roth / 1987 / 6 of 1 ◆◆◆◆
Joffen highlights are "Video Arcade" and "Chain of Love." David Roth faves are "Rising in Love" and "Fireflies." *—Richard Meyer*

Si Kahn

Guitar, Vocals / Folk
A Southern activist and political songwriter, Kahn is known for his direct community work and his articulate writing. *—Richard Meyer*

● **Home** / 1980 / Flying Fish ◆◆◆◆
This album features songs in a mixture of styles, from gentle pastoral to hard-edged political, by a singer-songwriter who is also a union organizer. *—AMG*

● **Doing My Job** / 1982 / Flying Fish ◆◆◆◆
This album features politically aware, sensitive songs. *—AMG*

Good Times and Bedtimes / 1993 / Rounder ◆◆◆

In My Heart / 1994 / Philo ◆◆◆
A solo live recording made in concert in Holland (April 1993), it contains songs from his large repertoire performed with great intimacy. *—Richard Meyer*

Paul Kaplan

Harmonica / Urban-Folk

Chicago native Paul Kaplan now resides in Amherst, MA, with his two daughters. In addition to appearing on various Folkways records and contributing songs to *Fast Folk*, Kaplan has compiled three Phil Ochs albums for that company, and edited the 1982 *Fast Folk* songbook. —*Richard Meyer*

● **Life on This Planet** / 1982 / Hummingbird ✦✦✦✦
It contains his signatures, "Call Me the Whale" and "Henry the Accountant." —*Richard Meyer*

The King of Hearts / 1985 / Hummingbird ✦✦✦
This concert of new material, recorded live at the SpeakEasy club in Greenwich Village in 1985, features his beautiful song "The King of Hearts," as well as some great audience participation on "I Had an Old Coat." This album really captures the atmosphere of a more traditional NY singer-songwriter in the mid-'80s. —*Richard Meyer*

Robert Earl Keen, Jr.

Guitar, Vocals / Folk

Singer-songwriter Robert Earl Keen, a native of Bandera, TX, began playing the guitar as a diversion from journalism classes at Texas A&M. To fend off boredom, he and neighbor Lyle Lovett jammed together and, on Sunday mornings, sitting on the front porch in their underwear, serenaded churchgoers across the street from Keen's house. As Keen's songwriting talent blossomed and he began to make a name for himself in Austin, Lovett recorded one of his songs, as did Nanci Griffith, Joe Ely, and Kelly Willis, providing a springboard for a solo career. His most accomplished album is 1994's *Gringo Honeymoon*. —*Steve Huey*

● **No Kinda Dancer** / 1984 / Philo ✦✦✦✦
A well-crafted debut, not one bad song. "Armadillo Jackal and This Old Porch," co-written by Lyle Lovett and Nanci Griffith singing harmony. —*Chip Renner*

The Live Album / 1988 / Sugar Hill ✦✦✦✦
Good sound, new material, good stories, plus audience interaction make this worthwhile. Featuring great mandolin and fiddle by Johnathan Yadkin and a nice cut of "I Would Change My Life." —*Chip Renner*

West Textures / 1989 / Sugar Hill ✦✦✦
Well produced, with Jerry Douglas on dobro and a cover of the Koller/Silverstein song "Jennifer Johnson and Me." —*Chip Renner*

A Bigger Piece of Sky / 1993 / Sugar Hill ✦✦✦
This album contains the radio hit "Jesse with the Long Hair," which soundslike the Bob Dylan tune "Tangled Up in Blue," as well as more of Keen's rough and tumble story-songs. —*Richard Meyer*

Number 2 Live Dinner / Mar. 19, 1996 / Sugar Hill ✦✦✦

Steve Key

b. Brooklyn, NY
Folk

Key was born in Brooklyn, NY, and raised in San Francisco, CA. He later returned to New York City and joined the *Fast Folk* crowd. He hosted a radio show on WFUV-FM in New York. He now resides in Washington, DC, has issued the DC compilation *Capitol Acoustics*, and is involved in the Washington folk community. Key is a polished performer whose well crafted songs are full of deep imagery and emotion. —*Chip Renner*

Between Trains / 1970 / Local Folkel ✦✦✦
Key's debut album is a rich collection of well-written stories that were greatly influenced by his NYC lifestyle. —*Chip Renner*

Record Time / 1980 / Local Folkel ✦✦✦✦
Key's songs represent the best of the suburban homespun genre in contemporary folk. The title cut of this CD is a recommended example. —*Richard Meyer*

● **New Hope** / 1990 / Local Folkel ✦✦✦✦
This release is more upbeat than his first. Every song is strong. The title song could be an anthem for the '60s generation. —*Chip Renner*

Kingston Trio

Folk

Bob Shane (b. 1934), Nick Reynolds (b. 1933), and Dave Guard (b. 1934, d. 1991) formed the Kingston Trio in California in 1957. For the next ten years the group was perhaps the most popular in folk music, starting with their hit version of the traditional song "Tom Dooley," which topped the charts in 1958. The trio adapted traditional songs and novelties to their exuberant style, which filled nightclubs and then concert halls. Critics, especially in folk music, objected to the inauthenticity of their approach, but they popularized folk music to millions who might never have heard it otherwise. They racked up seven gold albums by 1964, paving the way for Joan Baez; Peter, Paul & Mary; Bob Dylan; and others.

Guard left in 1961 and was replaced by John Stewart; and the group disbanded completely in 1967, its music in popular decline. But Shane put together a new Kingston Trio in 1973 that has performed and recorded sporadically since. Much of the group's Capitol Records output from the early '60s has recently been reissued on CD. —*William Ruhlmann*

The Kingston Trio / 1958 / Capitol ✦✦✦
The debut album of the most popular act in the folk boom of the late '50s. This contains their No. 1 hit "Tom Dooley," Dave Guard's "Scotch and Soda," "Wreck of the 'John B'," and others. A massive hit, it spent almost four years on the best-seller charts. —*William Ruhlmann*

The Kingston Trio at Large / 1959 / Capitol ✦✦✦
Perhaps the Trio's best-selling album (15 weeks at No. 1), this contains their hilarious "M.T.A.," the lovely "Scarlet Ribbons," and several Dave Guard originals. —*William Ruhlmann*

★ **Capitol Collectors Series** / 1990 / Capitol ✦✦✦✦✦
Here's a well-chosen 20-track compilation containing all 17 of the Trio's hit singles. —*William Ruhlmann*

Live at Newport / 1994 / Vanguard ✦✦✦
The Kingston Trio had just become superstars when they performed this 12-song set at the Newport Folk Festival. Including well-known features of their repertoire, it's a good-sounding and well-executed performance, but necessary only for major fans. —*Richie Unterberger*

The Capitol Years / 1995 / Capitol ✦✦✦✦
A mammoth four-CD, 107-song box set of their most famous and commercially successful work, recorded for Capitol between the late '50s and mid-'60s. All of the big hits are here, as well as key album cuts and a whopping 33 previously unreleased studio and live tracks. Collectors will appreciate the inclusion of rarities by related groups like Dave Guard and the Calypsonians (a pre-Kingston Trio outfit), Dave Guard and the Whiskeyhill Singers (Guard's post-Kingston outfit, also featuring Judy Henske), and the Cumberland Three (John Stewart's pre-Kingston group), as well as the awesomely detailed 48-page insert. But this is way too much for anyone but the fanatic. It's interesting to hear the Kingstons' now-obscure versions of songs that would become hits many years later by other artists, like "Sloop John B," "The First Time (Ever I Saw Your Face)," "Seasons in the Sun," "It Was a Very Good Year," and (most incredibly) "Let's Get Together." But for all its historical significance, the execution is usually far too sterile and whitebread to appeal to contemporary listeners, unless it's on purely nostalgic grounds. —*Richie Unterberger*

"Spider" John Koerner

b. Aug. 31, 1938, Rochester, NY
Guitar, Harmonica, Vocals / Blues

Korner was a major force in the '60s folk community around Minneapolis. His Vanguard album *Running, Jumping, Standing Still,* recorded with Tony Glover and David Ray, was a seminal album of American folk and blues played by urban players. —*Richard Meyer*

● **Nobody Knows the Trouble I've Been** / 1970 / Red House ✦✦✦✦
This album contains classics from the American songbag like "Cotton Eyed Joe," "The Leatherwing Bat," "Froggy Went A-Courting" and "Shenandoah." Koerner sings and plays (12-string guitar) with a casual authority that brings this material to life brilliantly. The music jumps out of the speaker so effortlessly you can appreciate the fun and dark side of these old songs. *Nobody Knows the Trouble I've Been* is an excellent example of contemporary interpretations that don't treat the songs like academic artifacts. "The Leatherwing Bat," for example, is a courting song that sounds cute and innocent in most interpretations. Koerner brings out, and seems to delight in, the licentious innuendo as each verse leads to the advice that for a girl to catch the boy she should keep him up both day and night. Blood, love, and murder are at the heart of many songs so familiar that we have forgotten to even listen anymore while we sing along. A record like this is a wake-up call to all interpreters. The fact that it was impeccably recorded live to two-track in one day with great musicians only adds to its reputation. —*Richard Meyer*

Raised by Humans / 1992 / Red House ✦✦✦✦
Produced in the same style as *Troubles,* this includes some Koerner originals as well as driving, jubilant versions of "The Titanic" and "The Fox and the Boll Weevil." —*Richard Meyer*

Stargeezer / May 21, 1996 / Red House ✦✦✦
This is the standard brew of endearingly clever originals and energetic covers that fans have come to expect from Spider John Koerner. There aren't any standout songs, but the entire album has a relaxed, welcoming vibe that makes it quite a pleasant listen. —*Thom Owens*

Leo Kottke

b. Sep. 11, 1945, Athens, GA
Guitar

Kottke is considered (along with John Fahey) one of the finest virtuoso finger-picking guitarists on the music scene. The two worked closely in the '70s, playing and producing some of the most innovative solo guitar playing of that period. Kottke and Fahey influenced Preston Reed and Michael Hedges, both of whom have carried on their vision in the years since. —*Chip Renner*

6 & 12 String Guitar / 1969 / Rhino ✦✦✦✦
Kottke's debut came about after he sent a cassette to John Fahey's Takoma label. Not surprisingly, it recalls Fahey's work in a number of respects: the synthesis of numerous influences from blues, pop, classical, and folk styles, the weirdly titled instrumentals, even the tongue-in-cheek liner notes. Kottke's brand of virtuosity, however, is more soothing and easy on the ear than Fahey's. Establishing much of the territory Kottke was to explore throughout his career, this release was also one of his most popular, eventually selling over 500,000 copies. —*Richie Unterberger*

Circle Round the Sun / 1970 / Symposium/Bay Street ✦✦✦
This is a good, hard-to-find record. —*Chip Renner*

Ice Water / 1974 / Beat Goes On ✦✦✦
Kottke adds vocals, drums, bass, dobro, and steel guitar for a unique Kottke sound. —*Chip Renner*

Leo Kottke / 1976 / Chrysalis ✦✦✦
Very good guitar playing. —*Chip Renner*

Leo Kottke 1971-1976: Did You Hear Me? / 1976 / Capitol ✦✦✦
This album contains early and influential acoustic hot licks from this fleet guitarist. —*Mark A. Humphrey*

Balance / 1979 / Beat Goes On ✦✦✦
Good guitar work, featuring "Embryonic Journey" and Buddy Holly's "Learning the Game." —*Chip Renner*

Guitar Music / 1981 / Chrysalis ✦✦✦
Twelve solid guitar instrumentals. —*Chip Renner*

My Father's Face / 1989 / Private Music ✦✦✦
Funky songs and staccato picking make this a very good album. —*Mark A. Humphrey*

● **Essential** / 1991 / Chrysalis ✦✦✦✦
Guitarist Leo Kottke has earned a reputation as a premier finger-picker, slide master, and 12-string virtuoso. The proof is in this 22-track, 70-minute collection, culled from five albums released between 1976-83. —*Roundup Newsletter*

Great Big Boy / 1991 / Private Music ✦✦✦✦
Kottke sings on this record to good effect. Features Lyle Lovett and Margo Timmons. —*Chip Renner*

Jim Kweskin and His Jug Band

Folk
Jim Kweskin's Jug Band, including Bill Keith, Geoff Muldaur, Maria D'Amato (later Muldaur), and others, came out of Cambridge, MA, in 1963 with a combination of old-timey country music, bluegrass, and ragtime, and became the major '60s proponents of jug-band style. It never caught on in a big way, but it was fun while it lasted. —*William Ruhlmann*

● **Greatest Hits** / 1990 / Vanguard ✦✦✦✦
Washboards, kazoos, novelty songs, and general hilarity combine to make some of the most delightful, foolish music of the '60s. The jug band craze was small and short lived, but Kweskin and his band— which included Maria D'Amato, soon to marry bandmember Geoff Muldaur—were its premier act, and this double set captures much of their whimsical style. —*William Ruhlmann*

Peter LaFarge

b. 1931, d. 1965
Vocals / Folk
Singer-songwriter Peter LaFarge was the son of Pulitzer Prize-winning author Oliver LaFarge and, like his father, a spokesman for Indian rights. His involvement in the Korean War, where he was decorated five times, served as the inspiration for his best-known song, "Ballad of Ira Hayes," about a Pima Indian who was at the battle of Iwo Jima in World War II but suffered in the post-war world. After a career as a rodeo cowboy, LaFarge turned to folksinging in the late '50s and was part of the *Broadside* magazine/Folkways Records community in New York in the early '60s, recording several albums devoted to cowboy songs and Native American concerns. Johnny Cash took "Ira Hayes" to No. 3 in the country charts in 1964. LaFarge died of a stroke the following year. —*William Ruhlmann*

As Long As the Grass Shall Grow / 1968 / Smithsonian/Folkways ✦✦✦✦
Surprisingly, this collection of songs about what we now call Native Americans does not include LaFarge's best-known song, "The Ballad of Ira Hayes." But the singer-songwriter, who was a Native American himself, still manages to turn in one of the most thorough and moving examinations of the sorry history of White deception and aggression ever recorded. He gives his songs a dramatic, near-spoken delivery, making the messages all the more convincing. —*William Ruhlmann*

● **On the Warpath/As Long as the Grass Shall Grow** / 1992 / Bear Family ✦✦✦✦

Patty Larkin

Guitar, Vocals / Folk
Boston-based folk artist Patty Larkin is a talented singer-songwriter and guitarist with a large New England following. She considers herself a musical adventurer and writes songs designed to invite audiences to share her journeys. She began recording in the mid-'80s for Philo Records. Her compositions are known for their depth, sensuality, and introspection. Proficient on acoustic, electric, and slide guitar, her playing style has been compared to Bonnie Raitt's. Since 1991 Larkin has been recording for High Street Records. Though her strongest following remains in New England, she is a favorite on folk circuits throughout the US. —*Sandra Brennan*

Step into the Light / 1985 / Philo ✦✦✦✦
Fine debut album. —*Chip Renner*

I'm Fine / 1987 / Philo ✦✦✦✦
Fairly stunning production by Darleen Wilson, who also engineered and mixed this Boston-area artist's second release; buy it for the title cut alone. Patty's fine, as is her voice, which has seasoned and grown richer. Included is the blues sound of "Pucker Up." —*Ladyslipper*

In the Square: Live / 1990 / Philo ✦✦✦

● **Tango** / 1991 / High Street ✦✦✦✦
Most polished of her releases—backed by John Gorka and Darol Anger. Very mature. —*Chip Renner*

Angels Running / 1993 / High Street ✦✦✦
Patty Larkin's second High Street album shows remarkable artistic growth. Larkin's redoubtable musical facility that has made her so well known is evidenced here, as is her wit. Seamless production of Ben Wisch supports Larkin's new soaring songs. The first track, "Who Holds Your Hand," is a good example in that it is romantic, intense, and definitely moving, but you couldn't say that it rocks. Her lyrics are more deeply poetic and her delivery more fluid than on earlier projects. —*Richard Meyer*

Strangers World / 1995 / High Street ✦✦✦
Patty Larkin has really grown as a lyricist. These introspective songs are more sensual and mysterious than previously. Relationships are still the main subject, and she examines them in finer detail. Produced by John Leventhal, this CD is warm, spacious, and inviting, using dramatic dynamics to serve up a consciously artistic sound. Bruce Cockburn, Shawn Colvin, and Jonathan Brooke all make contributions to this lush recording. —*Richard Meyer*

Christine Lavin

Guitar, Vocals / Folk, Singer-Songwriter, Folk
Christine Lavin emerged from the crowded New York City songwriter scene of the '80s with a style that distinguished her from her peers. First of all, her songs were overwhelmingly concerned with contemporary romantic mores (that scary, uncertain world of "relationships" and "commitments" and "biological clocks"). Second, while her takes on this subject could sometimes be sentimental or maudlin, more often they were humorous. "If You Need Space, Go to Utah" was the first track on her first recording, a 1983 EP called *Husbands and Wives*, later reissued as *Another Man's Woman*. By 1984 Lavin had released her first full-length album, *Future Fossils*, which included both her serious and comic numbers, notably "Damaged Goods" (what people start to feel like after enough failed relationships) and "Don't Ever Call Your Sweetheart by His Name" (how difficult it is to remember people's names after enough failed relationships). In 1986 Lavin signed with Rounder's Philo label, and since then she has recorded regularly, also touring extensively and building up a wide following.

Lavin has made a point of promoting the work of her contemporaries, notably on such collections as *When October Goes* and *Buy Me, Bring Me, Take Me, Don't Mess My Hair!!! (Life According to Four Bitchin' Babes)*. —*William Ruhlmann*

Future Fossils / 1984 / Philo ✦✦✦✦
A bright, wry, and earthy collection of her early songs. A great introduction. —*Bruce Eder*

● **Beau Woes (and Other Problems of Modern Life)** / 1986 / Philo ✦✦✦✦
From undoubtedly the sharpest wit in the contemporary folk scene, this is a splendidly entertaining, lively, honest, and eclectic album. It includes her clever "Biological Time Bomb"; her song for all those athletically challenged, "Ballad of a Ballgame"; the more serious "Gettin' Used to

Leavin'" with veteran folkie Eric Andersen, her spoof on "Camping"; and other humorous and cynical vignettes. —*Ladyslipper*

Good Thing He Can't Read My Mind / 1988 / Philo ◆◆◆◆
Both satire and good folk music fill this album, and there's even a duet with Livingston Taylor. —*Ladyslipper*

Attainable Love / 1990 / Philo ◆◆◆
Here are ten more serio-comic songs that debunk, explore, and create the myths of contemporary romance; includes "Shopping Cart of Love" and "Sensitive New Age Guys," as well as the somewhat more serious "Victim/Volunteer," "The Kind of Love You Never Recover From," and the title song. There's a straightforward acoustic production from this insightful observer/commentator. —*Ladyslipper*

Buy Me Bring Me Take Me: Don't Mess My Hair!!! Life According to Four Bitchin' Babes . . . / 1991 / Philo ◆◆◆◆
This is more than just a best-of-sampler of four of the best contemporary folksinger-songwriters. This live album presents a cohesive group as well as soloists performing material that ranges in subject matter from romance to vacation troubles, and in mood from heartbreaking to side-splitting. It will make you want to hear each of the singers on her own, but it will also make you hope they tour together more often. — *William Ruhlmann*

Compass / 1991 / Philo ◆◆◆
For years her specialties have been droll commentary on the foibles of the modern world and the people in it, and what are sometimes more somber observations on heartbreak's variations. Her eye just gets sharper, and in this collection the two get mixed a bit more—irony informs the love songs, and the funny songs are just a touch more pointed than before. —*Roundup newsletter*

Live at the Cactus Cafe: What Was I Thinking? / 1993 / Philo ◆◆◆

Please Don't Make Me Too Happy / 1995 / Shanachie ◆◆◆◆

Leadbelly (Huddie William Ledbetter)

b. Jan. 20, 1888, Mooringsport, LA, **d.** Dec. 6, 1949, New York, NY
Guitar, Piano, Accordion, Vocals / Acoustic Country Blues
Leadbelly was the first blues musician to achieve fame among White audiences. For this reason alone, and more for the sheer novelty of his career as an ex-convict-turned-singer than for any recognition of his abilities, he was the first bluesman to be treated as a major media figure in the mainstream press.

Huddie Ledbetter was born on January 20, 1888, not far from the Texas border. He remained in school until he was 12 or 13. He was a precocious child, serious and ambitious beyond his years. Ledbetter was surrounded by a multitude of influences growing out of the post-slavery/post-Reconstruction era of the late 19th century, including blues, spirituals, and minstrel songs. By the time he was 14 he was known for his ability with the guitar and his way with a song. He played before audiences on most Saturday nights at parties and square dances in the area around Mooringsport, LA, but before he was far into his teens, he was attracted to the red-light district in Shreveport. Apart from the women, however, the district's main attraction to the teenager was its music. He was married by the first decade of the 20th century, but the marriage didn't last. The music, however, did, with an important new wrinkle—Ledbetter switched from the six-string to the 12-string guitar, a pivotal decision in the development of his own career. He was already performing songs of his own and adapting others during the 1890s. He first picked up a song known as "Irene" sometime in the first decade of the 20th century, and as "Goodnight, Irene" it became one of Leadbelly's best-known songs.

Sometime around 1915 he made the acquaintance of Blind Lemon Jefferson, from whom he learned slide guitar. Despite some months of working together, Ledbetter was left behind by Jefferson, a result of his inability to stay clear of the law. In 1917 he was arrested for shooting a man and sentenced to 30 years in prison. On the Shaw State Prison Farm in Texas, Leadbelly's singing and guitar playing made him one of the more popular prisoners. He was released in 1925 after he played for visiting Texas Governor, Pat Neff, and requested a pardon. The pardon was signed by Neff on virtually his last day in office.

Leadbelly, as he was now known professionally, tried working regular jobs for the remainder of the '20s, but was never able to stay far from the rambling life that had led him into trouble in the previous decade. In 1930 he was convicted in Louisiana of assault with intent to commit murder and sentenced to 30 years in the Louisiana State Penitentiary at Angola. It was there, in 1933, that he met John Lomax, an ambitious researcher for the Library of Congress, who was traveling through the South with his son Alan, collecting blues and other authentic American music. Leadbelly was well known within the prison, and it was inevitable that he would meet the Lomaxes. Leadbelly dazzled them with his singing, playing, songwriting; and Lomax recognized in his new discovery a talent that was very different from the makers of the commercial "race" records of the period. Leadbelly was released in 1934 with help from John Lomax and began an extended relationship with him and his

son, serving as driver and valet while making recordings and preparing plans for concerts. It was Lomax's intention to make Leadbelly and—as his manager and "discoverer"—himself into stars. On the positive side, this resulted in Lomax trying to get Leadbelly to record virtually every song he knew, an impossible task given the sheer range of music to which he'd been exposed since the 1890s, but one that resulted in dozens upon dozens of sides for the Library of Congress, cut on Lomax's relatively crude "portable" recording unit, and later many attempts at commercial recording as well. On the negative side, however, it resulted in exploitation of Leadbelly, who appeared in photos and on stage in striped prison uniforms, and whose violent past was emphasized along with his musical abilities. The result was a flurry of publicity that brought Leadbelly some exposure in the White community but also gave the impression that he was a captured savage. It would have been demeaning for any man, but was especially so for Leadbelly, and ultimately it was not terribly profitable for Lomax. The copyrights that he signed his name to as Leadbelly's songwriting "collaborator" ultimately proved to be worth a small fortune, but he quickly discovered that sensationalistic press didn't necessarily translate into large paying audiences. Moreover, Leadbelly quickly grew beyond Lomax's ability to control him, and later rebelled at their relationship. And Lomax found out as early as 1935, after Leadbelly's first commercial recording sessions for the American Record Company, that Leadbelly's brand of blues was of virtually no interest to Black audiences, who had already moved to more modern sounds. Ironically, the ARC sides contain some of Leadbelly's best music; brought into a real recording studio for the first time, he took to the new environment like a natural, his voice booming larger than life and his guitar captured more crisply than ever before.

Leadbelly moved to New York City and split with Lomax, although they remained close. It was in New York that Leadbelly found some success, reaching a small but dedicated following of White listeners, mostly consisting of folk song enthusiasts and members of the city's uniquely Bohemian intelligentsia. He did some sessions for Musicraft and Bluebird, but his major activities during the early '40s were with Moe Asch, the founder of Folkways Records.

Leadbelly's music at any phase of his career was startling. but his sound also evolved, a process made all the more vivid by the many different versions of his songs that he recorded across his career. By the early '40s, he began to develop a consciousness that prefigured the topical songwriters of the early '60s. This was all pretty strong stuff in the middle of World War II. And yet Leadbelly also did programs and concerts for children, and those recordings were among the most successful that Moe Asch recorded.

Leadbelly never gave up hope that he might become a star in the music world. He recognized enough that was special in his life story that he even tried to interest Hollywood in signing him up. That didn't work, although a visit to California did result in a short-lived contract with Capitol Records in 1944, yielding a dozen sides.

Soon, however, he began developing health problems. Leadbelly continued working into 1949, but it was too early for the folk revival boom that would have embraced him. He played his last concert at the University of Texas on June 15 of that year. The recording of that concert is very poignant; as he leaves the stage, he promises to come back, vowing to get well now that he has a new doctor. Instead, he was hospitalized a month later and died in New York on December 6, 1949. Two years later his one-time proteges the Weavers had a million-selling hit with their recording of "Goodnight Irene," starting the whole folk-song revival, and six years later England's Lonnie Donegan had a hit with a version of "Rock Island Line," a song that Leadbelly adapted and brought to modern audiences.

Leadbelly's place in blues history is a peculiar one, unassailable as a source for much of the country-blues repertory, and a major contributor to the folk music revival of the '50s, but virtually non-existent in terms of his effect upon the commercial blues market. —*Bruce Eder*

Includes Legendary Performances Never Before Released / Mar. 21, 1952 / Columbia ◆◆◆◆
While one should always be suspicious about how "legendary" material can be that was originally withheld from circulation, there's little that Leadbelly did that isn't worth hearing. That holds true here. —*Ron Wynn*

☆ **Library of Congress Recordings [2 LPs]** / 1966 / Elektra ◆◆◆◆◆
These powerful performances date from 1939-43 when Ledbetter had moved to New York City after his years in prison. He was a fluid performer, and his command of his trademark 12-string guitar is evident. Recorded by John and Alan Lomax, these sessions include "Boll Weevil," "The Titanic," "Tight Like That" and "Henry Ford Blues." —*Richard Meyer*

Good Mornin' Blues (1936-1940) / 1969 / Biograph ◆◆◆◆
Wonderful mid-'30s and early-'40s material from Leadbelly, including some of his finest and most colorful blues tunes and good folk numbers as well. —*Ron Wynn*

Bourgeois Blues: Golden Classics, Pt. 1 / 198 / Collectibles ◆◆◆

Leadbelly Sings Folk Songs / 1990 / Smithsonian/Folkways ✦✦✦✦
Leadbelly was a consummate song stylist but not necessarily a blues artist, although he certainly could deliver the blues with earnestness and authority. His forte was taking all types of songs, whether they were simple, filled with chilling metaphors, funny stories, or tragic events, and making them unforgettable personal anthems. That's what he does on all 15 cuts on *Leadbelly Sings Folk Songs*, teaming with such fellow greats as Woody Guthrie, Cisco Houston, and Sonny Terry. Leadbelly made many great albums with Folkways; this was certainly among them. —*Ron Wynn*

Sings Folk Songs / 1990 / Smithsonian/Folkways ✦✦✦✦
Included are '40s Folkways recordings with Woody Guthrie, Cisco Houston, and Sonny Terry. —*Mark A. Humphrey*

Alabama Bound / 1990 / RCA ✦✦✦✦
Sixteen of the sides that Leadbelly cut for Victor's Bluebird label in the summer of 1940, many backed by the Golden Gate Singers. The mix of blues with a gospel chorus doesn't always work, although "Pick a Bale of Cotton," "Rock Island Line," and "Midnight Special" are appealing, and there are Leadbelly solo covers of "Roberta," "Easy Rider," and "New York City." —*Bruce Eder*

☆ **Gwine Dig a Hole To Put the Devil In** / 1991 / Rounder ✦✦✦✦✦
An excellent sampling of material from Leadbelly's early Library of Congress sessions, including versions of some of the first songs he ever learned, "Green Corn" and "Po' Howard," his song to Governor Neff that helped secure his release from a Texas prison in 1925, his first recorded version of "If It Wasn't for Dickie" (later transformed into "Kisses Sweeter than Wine")—the master of which is, alas, somewhat damaged—and "C.C. Rider." —*Bruce Eder*

Let It Shine on Me / 1991 / Rounder ✦✦✦✦
The third volume of Leadbelly's incredible Library of Congress sessions includes several searing spiritual numbers, among them "Down in the Valley to Pray," "Must I Be Carried to the Sky," "Run Sinners" and "You Must Have That Religion, Hallaloo." The CD begins with an informative interview/performance segment that features Leadbelly answering questions about his life and stylistic influences, then demonstrating techniques and recounting the origins of particular songs. The disc also contains an interesting rendition of "When I Was a Cowboy" and the topical tunes "Mr. Hitler," "The Scottsboro Boys" and "The Roosevelt Song." Leadbelly's mournful, moving and authoritative vocals, plus his sometimes surging, sometimes reflective guitar playing, were never more moving or appealing than during the Library of Congress sessions. —*Ron Wynn*

☆ **Midnight Special** / 1991 / Rounder ✦✦✦✦✦
The earliest of Leadbelly's surviving Library of Congress recordings, from 1934, in surprisingly good sound. This is where it all started, and the power and sheer kinetic energy of these songs remain undiminished more than 60 years later. Includes "Irene," "Midnight Special," and "Matchbox Blues." —*Bruce Eder*

Leadbelly ("Irene Goodnight") / 1992 / Blues Encore ✦✦✦✦
The best anthology on Leadbelly to date—unfortunately, it's also a bootleg from Italy, where this material is considered fair game. Includes an excellent overview of Leadbelly's work from the '30s to his final concert in 1949 ("Goodnight Irene"), with recordings from the Victor and ARC sessions as well. Excellent transfer, sketchy notes, decent sessionography. —*Bruce Eder*

Complete Studio Recordings, Vols. 4-5 / 1994 / Document ✦✦✦✦
These two European bootlegs cover a lot of material available elsewhere on legitimate American releases, but between them, they also contain the complete Leadbelly Capitol recording sessions of 1944, which have never surfaced on CD. The quality is superb, and the material is unique as the last commercial sides that Leadbelly ever cut. —*Bruce Eder*

Kisses Sweeter Than Wine / 1994 / Omega ✦✦✦✦
NOTE: This is actually a Weavers double-CD, and if you buy it for the Leadbelly material, make sure that it has the third bonus disc with his stuff. A dozen songs cut by Leadbelly for Musicraft in 1947—not mentioned in any discography—and forgotten for the next 46 years, all found on tapes in the label owner's garage when he moved to Florida. The singing is good, the material is unique, and it includes his last recording of "If It Wasn't for Dickie," the Irish folk song that Leadbelly taught the Weavers and that they turned into "Kisses Sweeter than Wine." —*Bruce Eder*

Nobody Knows the Trouble I've Seen, Vol. 5 / Mar. 30, 1994 / Rounder ✦✦✦✦
This is another excellent installment in Rounder's reissue of Leadbelly's Library of Congress recordings. —*AMG*

Pickup on This / Mar. 30, 1994 / Rounder ✦✦✦✦
Like the other volumes that came before it, *Pickup on This* is full of wonderful music and interviews from Leadbelly's Library of Congress recordings. —*AMG*

The Titanic, Vol. 4 / Mar. 30, 1994 / Rounder ✦✦✦✦
Later Leadbelly Library of Congress recordings, from 1939-43, including several children's songs and quasi-biographical and topical material, including "Mister Tom Hughes' Town." —*Bruce Eder*

Leadbelly's Last Sessions / 1995 / Smithsonian/Folkways ✦✦✦
Four CDs containing the best part of Leadbelly's only recordings on magnetic recording tape, which allowed him to stretch his songs to their usual length for the first time on record. The clarity of the recording, the presence of the between-song comments, and the selection of material make this a seminal part of any serious collection. —*Bruce Eder*

Goodnight Irene / 1996 / Tradition ✦✦✦✦
The date of these recordings is unclear, and the sleeve is not of much help. The liner notes identify them as being taped in 1943 and 1944, while the back cover confidently refers to a 1939 date (though it seems much more likely that they were made in the '40s). At any rate, these are very good performances, with Leadbelly in fine voice. Most are performed solo on his 12-string guitar, although Sonny Terry and Josh White make cameos on one track each. "Goodnight Irene," "New Orleans" (essentially the same song as "House of the Rising Sun"), "John Hardy," and "When I Was a Cowboy" are all among the most famous tunes that he helped to popularize. But at a mere 28 minutes, this is pretty short. —*Richie Unterberger*

Leadbelly In Concert / 1996 / Magnum ✦✦✦✦
Leadbelly's final concert from June 15, 1949, reissued on CD at last. The sound is very clean, the fidelity excellent, and the recording indispensable. —*Bruce Eder*

Where Did You Sleep Last Night / Feb. 20, 1996 / Smithsonian/Folkways ✦✦✦
The first of Folkways Records-founder Moses Asch's original Leadbelly releases, from the best existing sources and remastered using the best mid-'90s technology, with some notable outtakes. The results are startlingly good, with an overall crisp sound and surprising delicacy in both the audio texture and Leadbelly's playing and singing, which is usually lost on the inferior reissues that have appeared on some of this work. —*Bruce Eder*

★ **King of the 12-String Guitar** / 199 / Columbia/Legacy ✦✦✦✦✦
One of the greatest collections of Leadbelly's '30s work, and his best commercial sides, done for ARC in 1935. It isn't quite complete, however, and one should also own the earlier Columbia Records CD, *Leadbelly*, as a companion. —*Bruce Eder*

Convict Blues / Aldabra ✦✦✦✦
Convict Blues collects a number of recordings he made for the American Record Corporation in 1935, which were, for the most part, never released. These 16 tracks are straight blues songs, delivered with passion. While it's not as essential as his Folkways or Library of Congress recordings, there's a wealth of terrific music here. —*Thom Owens*

Congress Blues / Aldabra ✦✦✦✦
Congress Blues collects a batch of folk songs that Leadbelly recorded in the early '40s. There is wonderful music here, to be sure, but it is available on better collections from Folkways and Rounder. —*Thom Owens*

Golden Classics: Pt. 2 (Defense Blues) / Collectibles ✦✦✦
Rather thin at ten songs, of indeterminate origin, but the material is very strong, including "Defense Blues," "Jim Crow," and a short version of "Midnight Special." —*Bruce Eder*

Gordon Lightfoot

b. Nov. 17, 1938, Orillia, Ontario
Guitar, Piano, Vocals / Folk, Singer-Songwriter, Folk-Rock
Canadian Gordon Lightfoot first began to gain recognition in the mid-'60s as a songwriter when his compositions "For Lovin' Me" and "Early Morning Rain" became hits for Peter, Paul and Mary, and Marty Robbins topped the country charts with "Ribbon of Darkness." Lightfoot's own style was understated, his tasteful folk arrangements topped by a gentle burr of a voice. His albums began to appear in 1966, but it was not until the start of the '70s that he became a big success as a performer, scoring in 1970 with *Sit Down Young Stranger*, which contained his hit "If You Could Read My Mind," a song with a typically flowing melodic line and gently poetic lyrics.

Thereafter, the first half of the '70s were his. Lightfoot hit a peak in 1974 with *Sundown*, which went to No. 1, as did the title song when released on a single. Lightfoot was caught by the popular decline of folk-based music in the latter half of the '70s and has performed and recorded less frequently since, sometimes trying to conform to perceived commercial trends without success. But concert appearances in the early '90s confirmed that he remains an engaging performer and that his catalog of original songs is hard to match. —*William Ruhlmann*

Lightfoot / Mar. 1966 / United Artists ✦✦✦✦
Lightfoot was already 27 at the time of his solo debut, which might have accounted in part for the unusually fully developed maturity and confi-

dence on this recording, in both his songwriting and vocals. Contains some of his best compositions, including "Early Mornin' Rain," "I'm Not Sayin'," "The Way I Feel," "For Lovin' Me," and "Ribbon of Darkness." At this point Lightfoot was still including some covers in his repertoire, and he handles numbers by Phil Ochs ("Changes"), Ewan MacColl ("The First Time Ever I Saw Your Face"), and Hamilton Camp ("Pride of Man") well. The whole album is included on *The United Artists Collection.* —*Richie Unterberger*

The Way I Feel / Apr. 1967 / United Artists ✦✦✦✦
Lightfoot had used additional guitar and bass on his debut, but for his second LP he went for a fuller band sound, using a couple of the noted Nashville sessionmen (Charlie McCoy and Ken Buttrey) who had played on Bob Dylan's *Blonde on Blonde.* The result was a brighter and more accessible sound, with the country elements more to the fore. The songs weren't quite as impressive as his first batch, but they were still very good, highlighted by the epic "Canadian Railroad Trilogy" and an electrified remake of "The Way I Feel." The whole album is included on *The United Artists Collection.* —*Richie Unterberger*

Did She Mention My Name? / Jan. 1968 / United Artists ✦✦✦✦
Every '60s singer-songwriter of note expanded their instrumental approach as time went on, and Lightfoot was no exception. For his third album, he worked with John Simon (who would handle the Band and Big Brother), and occasionally used low-key orchestration. Though a tad more erratic than his earlier efforts, his songwriting remained remarkably consistent. His characteristically bright, uplifting outlook became more diverse as well, allowing for the chilling "Black Day in July" (written in response to the 1967 Detroit riots), the odd "Pussywillows, Cat-Tails" (an unusual and successful detour into baroque orchestral pop), and the ambiguous sobriety of "Does Your Mother Know?" The whole album is included on *The United Artists Collection.* —*Richie Unterberger*

Back Here on Earth / Nov. 1968 / United Artists ✦✦✦
After the mild experimentation of *Did She Mention My Name?*, *Back Here on Earth* was a retrenchment of sorts, recorded in Nashville with a three-piece acoustic lineup and a more countrified approach. It's not quite as outstanding as his first three albums, lacking highlights on the order of "Early Mornin' Rain" or "Black Day in July." Lightfoot never offered weak material on his United Artists efforts, however, and *Back Here on Earth* is still a very solid set, certainly worth acquiring if you like his other UA LPs. And all of the UA studio LPs, of course, are available on the two-disc *The United Artists Collection.* —*Richie Unterberger*

Sunday Concert / 1969 / Beat Goes On ✦✦✦
Recorded at a March 1969 concert in Toronto, this holds more interest than the usual live album because about half of the songs are Lightfoot compositions that had not been previously recorded in the studio. Accompanied by Red Shea on lead guitar and Rick Haynes on bass, he also mixed old favorites like "I'm Not Sayin'" and "Canadian Railroad Trilogy" with the new material on this set, which has good (though not outstanding) sound. These then-new songs aren't among his classics but are up to the general high standard of his '60s work, with the socially conscious "The Lost Children" and the poetic "Leaves of Grass" standing out as lyrical highlights. This is the only one of Lightfoot's '60s United Artists albums that is not included on *The United Artists Collection;* the UK CD reissue includes his 1966 debut, *Lightfoot.* —*Richie Unterberger*

Sit Down Young Stranger / 1970 / Reprise ✦✦✦✦
Lightfoot's Reprise albums are always tastefully constructed, with their careful finger-picking, restrained rhythm sections, and subtle string arrangements serving as a bed for the singer's sturdy baritone. What distinguishes the albums is the quality of Lightfoot's songwriting, and this one, featuring the title track as well as "Approaching Lavender" and "If You Could Read My Mind," has the best overall selection. —*William Ruhlmann*

Summer Side of Life / 1971 / Reprise ✦✦✦
This extraordinary release doesn't have big hits on it but contains some of his finest songwriting, from the political song "Miguel" to the wistful songs about divorce, "Same Old Loverman" and "Talking in Your Sleep," to the joyous "Cotton Jenny." Highly recommended. —*Richard Meyer*

Sundown / 1974 / Reprise ✦✦✦✦
Lightfoot's commercial peak came with this album, which topped the US charts, containing both the No. 1 title song and the Top Ten hit "Carefree Highway." But songs like "Somewhere USA" and "High and Dry" are textured, catchy folk/rock on a par with the better known tunes. —*William Ruhlmann*

Gord's Gold / 1975 / Reprise ✦✦✦

Summertime Dream / 1976 / Reprise ✦✦✦
Due to Lightfoot's tendency to re-record his hits when preparing compilations (the warning "caveat emptor" applies to the two volumes of *Gord's Gold)*, this is the only place to find the original version of his No. 2 "Wreck of the Edmond Fitzgerald." —*William Ruhlmann*

Waiting for You / 1993 / Reprise ✦✦✦

★ **Gordon Lightfoot: The United Artists Collection** / Oct. 5, 1993 / EMI ✦✦✦✦✦
This double CD contains all four of the Toronto singer-songwriter's '60s studio albums. (The live LP *Sunday Concert*, not included here, was also released in the '60s.) On these records, his resonant vocals, lyrical ambition, and melodic strengths produced as close a rival to Bob Dylan as Canada ever fashioned during that decade, and foreshadowed work by other major Canadian singer-songwriters of the late '60s, such as Joni Mitchell, Neil Young, and Leonard Cohen. "Early Mornin' Rain" (covered by fellow Canadian folkies Ian and Sylvia), the folk-rock protest number "Black Day in July," the epic "Canadian Railroad Trilogy," and his cover of Ewan MacColl's "The First Time Ever I Saw Your Face" are present and are among the most popular tracks Lightfoot has issued. Featuring both acoustic and folk-rock recordings, this neatly bundles Lightfoot's early work into a listenable and fairly inexpensive package. —*Richie Unterberger*

Larry Long with the Children of Okemah

Folk
Contemporary singer and songwriter Larry Long had a mission: to take Woody Guthrie's music back to the Dust Bowl balladeer's hometown. Okemah, OK, had spent about 40 years with its jaw set against its most famous native son. Decent folk there called him a Communist and said a determined "NO" when the Guthrie family proposed a kind of museum at the decaying homeplace back in the '70s. "It would just attract hippies," said the decent folk who knew this Woody was just trouble. Long's gentle subversion was to teach Guthrie's songs to the kids of Okemah and encourage them to make up their own songs in Guthrie's kid-friendly idiom. The results were recorded at a local theater by the Flying Fish label, and now Okemah's water tower proudly proclaims the town as "Home of Woody Guthrie." —*Mark A. Humphrey*

● **It Takes a Lot of People . . .** / 1988 / Flying Fish ✦✦✦✦
It Takes a Lot of People (Tribute to Woody Guthrie) was recorded by Long and his young friends at the Crystal Theater in Okemah, OK, Guthrie's hometown. When they are singing Guthrie songs or reading from Guthrie's works, the tribute works beautifully. Long's own children's material is somewhat less successful. —*William Ruhlmann*

Rod MacDonald

b. 1949
Guitar, Harmonica, Vocals / Urban-Folk
Connecticut-born MacDonald has performed internationally, and many of his songs have been adapted as standards by the contemporary folk/songwriter community. With his pure emotive tenor and stirring, catchy tunes, MacDonald is one of the most appealing singer-songwriters to emerge in the '80s. Add thoughtful lyrics that touch on a variety of political and social issues, and you have a remarkable artist deserving a much wider public. MacDonald has contributed more than 20 songs to *The Fast Folk Musical Magazine,* in addition to his solo releases. —*Richard Meyer and William Ruhlmann*

No Commercial Traffic / 1983 / Cinemagic ✦✦✦✦
"On the Road to NY Town" should not be missed. —*Richard Meyer*

● **White Buffalo** / 1985 / Mountain Railroad ✦✦✦✦
Greenwich Village in the mid-'80s was an unparalleled meeting place for the contemporary generation of songwriters. The group of writers who were drawn there and worked in the various clubs and co-ops that made up the scene have gone on to form the core of this country's important singer-songwriters. Gadfly Records has had the good sense to reissue Rod MacDonald's 1985 album *White Buffalo.* It was originally released in a slightly different form by Autogram in Germany in 1985, then in Canada on the McDisk label with the current tracks and an organ overdub, then again on CD by Brambus in Switzerland with a few extra cuts. Now finally *White Buffalo* is available in the US. MacDonald was one of the most active and dynamic of the Greenwich Village performers at that time, and this record accurately represents how he sounded in the clubs. Recorded live in the attic studio of bassist Mark Dann after a sold out two-night stand at the SpeakEasy (the important club in the village then), these sessions feature terrific, tight playing, the late Howie Wyeth on drums, John Kruth on banshee mandolin, Dann on bass, and MacDonald on guitar and harmonica. His classics "Song of My Brothers," "Blues for the River," "The Aliens Came in Business Suits," "Water," "Cross Country Waltz" and other superb tunes are all here. They are melodic, thoughtful, and fun songs with great hooks; the ballads are bittersweet and haunting. Of his four albums to date, this one is his most consistent and true to his onstage sound. —*Richard Meyer*

Highway to Nowhere / 1992 / Shanachie ✦✦✦

Man on a Ledge / 1994 / Shanachie ✦✦✦
Rod has put together another set of original songs with his longtime musical partner Mark Dann. They cover the wide range of romance, pol-

itics, and fun rhythm tunes. "The Song for Czechoslovakia" and "Grapes on the Vine" are two standout tracks. —*Richard Meyer*

John Martyn (Iain McGeachy)

b. 1949, Glasgow, Scotland
Guitar, Vocals / Folk, Singer-Songwriter
Though not well known by mainstream audiences, Scottish singer-songwriter/guitarist John Martyn has a large cult following and is a favorite among contemporary music critics. His music has been influential in determining the direction of modern folk, moving it away from strictly acoustic traditions by infusing it with powerful rock, blues, and jazz influences.

Born in Scotland, but raised in Surrey, England, Martyn is the son of musically talented parents. His mentor, folk artist Hamish Imlach, helped Martyn launch his career at age 17. While playing in London, Martyn came to the attention of Island Records founder Chris Blackwell, who signed him to his recently created label. Martyn was the first White soloist to get an Island contract. His first album, *London Conversation* (1968), filled with blues and jazz-colored songs, was one of the first to break away from the acoustic folk that was then popular. His next release, *Tumbler*, was even jazzier. Though barely 20, Martyn was already being compared to Bob Dylan, who was also experimenting with electric folk. He and his new wife, singer Beverly Kutner, released two easy-going albums in the early '70s. The first, *Stormbringer*, was recorded live at Woodstock and featured a number of highly respected American musicians. It was in the early '70s that Martyn's well-publicized alcoholism surfaced. His favorite drinking buddy was jazz bassist Danny Thompson, who appeared on Martyn's ironically titled fifth album, *Road to Ruin* (1970). Martyn continued to develop his distinctive style of acoustic guitar playing and a unique, slurred singing style, in which he treated his voice as an instrument.

By the mid-'70s, Martyn's music began rapidly moving away from folk towards a rock and jazz fusion. His alcoholism also rapidly progressed and led to the destruction of his marriage at the decade's end. In 1977 he recorded two of his finest albums, including *One World,* which contained many subtle references to his personal troubles. He didn't record again until 1980. That year's release, the Phil Collins-produced *Grace and Danger*, offered deeply personal and painful insights into the death of the marriage. Later in 1980 he left Island and signed with WEA for two rock albums, *Glorious Fool* and *Well Kept Secret*. He also began touring extensively. He continued recording and touring through 1988, eventually returning to Island Records. Though his music reflected his newfound happiness, his alcoholism again took over. Thanks to a physician's ultimatum, Martyn was finally able to clean himself out and resumed his career in 1990 with *The Apprentice*. He has since continued to record and perform with a voice that is even stronger, and an octave lower, than it was in his youth. —*Sandra Brennan*

The Road to Ruin / 1970 / Island ✦✦✦
Martyn's wife Beverly is the vocalist. South African saxophonist Dudu Pukwana is on three tracks. This is folk mixed with new age musings. Excellent musicianship. By now it is rare, both musically and as a collector's item. —*Michael G. Nastos*

One World / 1977 / Island ✦✦✦✦
This virtuoso British guitarist and innovator mixes the music world of folk, blues, and fusion with some surprising results. Guests include Jamaican trombonist Rico, Steve Winwood, and fusioneers Hansford Rowe and Morris Pert. String arrangements are by Harry Robinson. For aficionados, a must-buy; for novices, it's a good one to try. —*Michael G. Nastos*

● **Sweet Little Mysteries: The Island Anthology** / 1995 / Island ✦✦✦✦

David Massengill

Dulcimer, Guitar, Vocals / Folk, Singer-Songwriter
New York-based David Massengill has been involved in folk music, particularly the New York Fast Folk community, for over two decades. Renowned as a writer of songs noted for their universal themes and their faithfulness to American folk traditions, he has also earned a reputation as an excellent guitarist and hammer dulcimer player, in addition to being a top-notch storyteller. Massengill released two independent cassettes, *Great American Bootleg Tape* in 1987 and *Kitchen Tape* in 1987, that both received rave reviews throughout the folk community. He has since signed with Flying Fish Records, releasing *Coming Up for Air* in 1992 and *Return* in late 1995.—*Sandra Brennan*

★ **Great American Bootleg Tape** / 1986 / Bowser Wowser ✦✦✦✦✦
Massengill assembled this tape himself, using tracks recorded for Stash Records' *Cornelia Street* collection, *The Fast Folk Musical Magazine*, and the video of the Folk City 25th-anniversary concert. The result is the single most impressive folk-based song collection of the decade. Massengill's lyrical facility is the most astounding to appear since that of Elvis Costello; he can be wickedly funny and deeply touching in the same line,

and his imagination seems unlimited. By rights, this should be on all lists of the best albums of the '80s. (Write to David Massengill, 179 E. 3rd St., Apt. 20, NY, NY 10009.) —*William Ruhlmann*

The Kitchen Tape / 1987 / Bowser Wowser ✦✦✦
More varied and novelty-oriented than *The Great American Bootleg Tape*, this collection of demos (recorded on a Sony Walkman) nevertheless shows the range in Massengill's mastery of the English language even more extensively than the earlier tape. His guitar, dulcimer, and harmonica are clean (except for an occasional fire engine or street noise caught on the tape). —*William Ruhlmann & Chip Renner*

Coming up for Air / 1992 / Flying Fish ✦✦✦✦
Massengill's first studio album. He does a great job on several old songs like "Fairfax," "My Name Joe," and some new material. Producer Steve Addabbo, who has produced Suzanne Vega, manages to bring out the best in the music. Long overdue, but well worth it! —*Chip Renner*

The Return / Oct. 31, 1995 / Plump ✦✦✦

Iain Matthews

b. Jun. 1946, Lincolnshire, England
Guitar, Vocals / Folk, Singer-Songwriter, Folk-Rock, British Folk
Ian Matthews (now spelled Iain to reflect his Celtic roots) has had a widely varied and complex recording career. He began as the lead singer for Fairport Convention after a short stint as the vocalist for a London-based surf band, Pyramid, in 1966. During Fairport's 1969 *Unhalfbricking* sessions, he decided to leave due to growing musical differences with the band. After making his first solo album, *Matthews Southern Comfort*, he released two albums with a band of the same name. They had a hit with a version of "Woodstock."

Matthews left in 1971 for a second chance at a solo career, releasing two fine folk-rock albums for Vertigo. He then formed Plainsong while finishing the contractual obligation album *Journey from Gospel Oak*, one of his finest recorded moments despite the conditions. Plainsong released one critically acclaimed album on Elektra and then disbanded while recording the second. His stay at Elektra ended after two more acclaimed, yet overlooked, country-folk albums— *Valley Hi* (1973) and *Some Days You Eat the Bear Some Days the Bear Eats You* (1974). He began experimenting in different styles for the rest of the '70s, often with uninspired and unsuccessful results. He did, however, have a US Top Ten hit in 1978 with "Shake It" from the *Stealin' Home* album.

The '80s were a relatively slow period for Matthews. Recording intermittently, he spent a few years as an A&R man for Island and later worked for Windham Hill. He relocated permanently to the US in the late '80s. The '90s found him reviving his solo career, signing with Watermelon Records, and returning to his folk-rock roots. Plainsong reunited in 1993, releasing two more albums. Matthews has since formed another group, Hamilton Pool, for one album. —*Chris Woodstra*

Matthews Southern Comfort / 1969 / Decca ✦✦✦

Second Spring / 1969 / Elektra ✦✦✦

1 2 3 Too Good / 1970 / MCA ✦✦

Later That Same Year / Dec. 1970 / Line ✦✦✦

If You Saw Thro' My Eyes / Jan. 1971 / Vertigo ✦✦✦✦
After leaving Southern Comfort, Matthews reunited with Fairport Convention members Richard Thompson and Sandy Denny and made one of his finest albums. Though the material and playing are superior to his previous work, it was unfortunately overlooked at the time. With his follow-up, *Tigers Will Survive* on CD (German import only), this is a must-have for fans. —*Chris Woodstra*

Tigers Will Survive / Nov. 1971 / Vertigo ✦✦✦
Recorded during two different periods broken up by a US tour, his follow-up to *If You Saw Through My Eyes* lacks the focus of its predecessor. Still worthwhile if only for "Morning Star," one of Matthews' most beautiful originals. —*Chris Woodstra*

Journeys from Gospel Oak / 1972 / Mooncrest ✦✦✦✦
Billed as a contractual obligation record by the artist, *Journeys from Gospel Oak* is easily as good as Matthews' best work. It is most assuredly a companion piece to Plainsong's *In Search of Amelia Earhart* (an album loosely based on the disappearance of Amelia Earhart), this time loosely based on the night Hank Williams died. This album includes such solid tracks as Gene Clark's "Polly," "Bride 1945" by Paul Siebel, and the haunting Jimmy Webb tune "Met Her on a Plane." A strong (but often overlooked) record and well worth the effort it takes to find a copy. —*Jim Worbois*

Valley Hi / 1973 / Elektra ✦✦✦✦
Often regarded as his best solo album, *Valley Hi* finds Matthews combining his folk-rock expertise with producer Mike Nesmith's country leanings. Highlights include the Nesmith penned "Propinquity" and Jackson Browne's "These Days." —*Chris Woodstra*

Some Days You Eat the Bear Some Days the Bear Eats You / 1974 / Elektra ✦✦✦

His final LP recorded for Elektra continues in the country spirit of *Valley Hi* with a stronger pop sensibility. Includes a brilliant rendition of Tom Waits' "Old 55" and a tribute to Hank Williams, "A Wailing Goodbye." —*Chris Woodstra*

Hit and Run / 1976 / Columbia ✦✦

Stealin' Home / 1978 / Rockburgh ✦✦

This album features Matthews' highest-charting single, "Shake It," which (along with two others) was written by John Boylan, an underappreciated songwriter of the late '70s. While not one of Matthews' stronger records, it is pleasant overall. —*Jim Worbois*

Siamese Friends / 1979 / Rockburgh ✦✦

Discreet Repeat / 197 / Rockburgh ✦✦

This is a nice cross-label compilation which features some of his best work (stuff recorded for Vertigo, Elektra, and Mooncrest) as well as some of his least interesting work. If you are a fan of Matthews, you likely own all these records already. If not, this compilation will help you decide which areas of his career you will need to concentrate on in order to build your Ian Matthews collection. —*Jim Worbois*

Spot of Interference / 1980 / Rockburgh ✦✦✦

Matthews makes an attempt at new wave and power-pop on this 1980 album. Surprisingly, he pulls it off quite well. Not his strongest work but certainly of interest to fans. Jules Shear's "Driftwood from Disaster" and the Wilde-Ainsworth's (later the Rembrandts) "I Survived the '70s" stand out. —*Chris Woodstra*

Moods for Mallards / 1983 / Shanghai ✦✦

Shook / 1983 / Teldec ✦✦

Walking a Changing Line / 1988 / Windham Hill ✦✦✦

On this, the first vocal album for Windham Hill, Matthews pays tribute to the songwriting of Jules Shear. While the song selection is first-rate as always, the typical Windham Hill musical indulgences take away from the enjoyment of this disc. Worthwhile for curious fans of Matthews or Shear. —*Chris Woodstra*

Pure and Crooked / 1990 / Gold Castle ✦✦✦

● **Best of Matthews' Southern Comfort** / 1992 / MCA ✦✦✦✦

A fine 16-track collection drawing from Matthews' first solo effort and the two Matthews' Southern Comfort albums. Includes the band's hit version of "Woodstock." —*Chris Woodstra*

● **The Soul of Many Places** / 1993 / Elektra ✦✦✦✦

The Soul of Many Places compiles the best moments from Matthews' recording high point for Elektra (1972-1974). Featuring selections from *Valley Hi, Some Days You Eat the Bear . . .*, and Plainsong's *The Search for Amelia Earhart*, this is the best introduction to Matthews' finest work (all currently out-of-print in the US). The inclusion of non-LP tracks makes this essential for fans as well. —*Chris Woodstra*

Orphans and Outcasts, Vol. 1 / 1993 / Dirty Linen ✦✦✦

An exceptional collection of demos, rarities, and outtakes from Matthews' '70s period, it is essential for fans. —*Chris Woodstra*

Skeleton Keys / May 18, 1993 / Rhino ✦✦✦

Dark Ride / 1994 / Watermelon ✦✦

Orphans and Outcasts, Vol. 2 / 1994 / Dirty Linen ✦✦✦

Volume 2 of the series, essentially a demos collection of the late '70s/ early '80s material, is more interesting than the actual albums of the time. Fans of Matthews' folkie early-'70s albums who couldn't connect with this somewhat misdirected phase of his career should find this much more enjoyable. —*Chris Woodstra*

Scion / 1995 / Band Of Joy ✦✦✦

Wall Matthews

Guitar, Percussion, Piano / Folk

Wall Matthews is a composer, performer, and teacher who is accomplished on guitar, piano, and African percussion. As composer in residence for dance at Connecticut College, Wall has an ongoing involvement with modern dance. He has composed numerous dance scores that have been performed by the Paris Opera Ballet, the Royal Danish Ballet, the Nikolai-Louis Company, and the Limon Company. —*Chip Renner*

● **Riding Horses** / 1988 / Clean Cuts ✦✦✦✦

Matthews goes from new age to new acoustic on this release. Seven selections from his *Solo Piano and Guitar* appear on this CD. His guitar playing is up there with the best acoustic guitar players. —*Chip Renner*

Gathering the World / 1991 / Clean Cuts ✦✦✦

This is not like other Matthews albums—he goes from delicate guitar work to Pygmy chants to African music. Female vocals are a nice touch for a Wall Matthews album. Those with eclectic tastes will enjoy this. —*Chip Renner*

The Heart of Winter / Clean Cuts ✦✦✦

Here are 14 gentle solo acoustic guitar renditions of traditional carols. —*Roundup Newsletter*

Tom May

Guitar, Vocals, Whistle (Instrument)

Working out of the heartland of America, Omaha, NE, Tom May hosts "River City Folk," syndicated by American Public Radio to more than 200 stations. The TV version of the show is broadcast by Americana Cable and is this country's only televised folk music program. May himself is the epitome of the balladeer, singing his own songs and those of others with warmth, humor, and accessibility. He's performed with most of this continent's better known folk musicians and across the world. May is also an accomplished guitar and Irish pennywhistle player. —*Allan Shaw*

● **Coming Home** / Vignette ✦✦✦✦

The sweep and grandeur of America is captured by this quintessential balladeer. —*Mike Fleischer*

Mary McCaslin

Banjo, Guitar, Vocals / Singer-Songwriter, Folk

As a singer-songwriter who wrote story-songs combining elements of country, folk, and pop, Mary McCaslin was one of the most appealing contemporary folk performers of the '70s. As a country-folk singer working totally outside of the Nashville sphere, singing of prairies and Old West images in almost mythic terms, her audience was confined to the folk circuit (though within that boundary, it was very wide). Yet her ability to appeal to rock and pop listeners helped pave the way for country-folk-pop stars like Nanci Griffith and Mary-Chapin Carpenter, although her influence in this area has remained relatively unacknowledged.

Born in Indiana, McCaslin moved to Southern California with her family at a young age. Inspired both by country narrators like Marty Robbins and singer-songwriters like Joni Mitchell, she recorded her first album, *Goodnight, Everybody*, for Barnaby in 1969. At this point her repertoire consisted entirely of covers; she didn't begin writing until her 20s, coming up with one of her signature tunes, "Way out West," on her second try. That composition would be the title track of her first Philo album, recorded after a brief liaison with Capitol.

Way out West was the first of three albums that she made for Philo in the '70s, featuring her finely wrought songs, strong upper-register vocals, and sympathetic, fully arranged accompaniment. Two of the tracks that attracted widest notice were her acoustic interpretations of two Beatles songs ("Things We Said Today" and "Blackbird"), which were not only among the few truly fine folk renditions of Lennon-McCartney tunes, but among the best Beatles covers ever attempted. Her Philo era is recognized as her artistic peak, although she maintained her presence on the folk scene with albums for Mercury (*Sunny California*, 1979) and Flying Fish (*A Life and a Time*, 1981). She also did a duo album with her husband, guitarist and songwriter Jim Ringer, in the late '70s.

Surprisingly little was heard from McCaslin in the '80s. Ringer (from whom she separated in 1989) became very ill, and her family problems put her songwriting on hold; she once estimated that she wrote only three songs between 1981 and 1989. 1994's *Broken Promises* was her first album in 13 years. —*Richie Unterberger*

Way Out West / 1974 / Philo ✦✦✦✦

This was the album that established McCaslin as a major folk performer. Her interpretive skills are in evidence on covers of "Let It Be" and Randy Newman's "Living Without You," but most of the set was devoted to original material, showing her to be an impressive songwriter (if not quite as impressive a singer). The title track and "San Bernardino Waltz" are standouts, the latter being probably her most famous song. —*Richie Unterberger*

● **The Best of Mary McCaslin** / 1990 / Philo ✦✦✦

The best of her '70s material, taken from her first three solo albums. Many strong originals and two excellent Beatle covers ("Things We Said Today" and "Blackbird") that remain among the best folk interpretations of Lennon/McCartney compositions. —*Richie Unterberger*

Ed McCurdy

b. 1919, Willow Hill, PA
Guitar, Vocals / Folk, Singer-Songwriter

Singer-songwriter Ed McCurdy dropped out of college to make a career as a folksinger. In the late '40s he learned guitar, put together a folk repertoire, and began performing on radio and TV in Canada. By the early '50s he was known in the US, and he made NYC his home in 1954. Throughout the '60s McCurdy was a mainstay of the folk scene and a pacesetter for the younger '60s folksingers. —*Michael Erlewine*

● **When Dalliance Was in Flower** / 195 / Elektra ✦✦✦✦

There are four volumes to this series on which McCurdy delves into fun, racy, and indelicate songs about love. Accompanied on some of the cuts by Alan Arkin, these are generally polite versions of ribald tunes. This set, along with many similar records by Oscar Brand, covers a lot of scatalogical ground. — *Richard Meyer*

Kate and Anna McGarrigle

Folk

Kate (b.1946) and Anna (b.1944) McGarrigle are Canadian songwriting sisters whose work first received international recognition in 1974 when Linda Ronstadt recorded Anna's "Heart Like a Wheel" as the title song to one of her albums. The sisters were signed to Warner Brothers and recorded *Kate and Anna McGarrigle*, an album of deeply felt (sometimes deeply funny) songs with a homey, eclectic folk backing and tart, striking vocals. It was widely hailed. Its two follow-ups seemed rushed, though they contained some good songs. In 1981, the sisters (having left Warner) recorded *French Record* for Joe Boyd's Hannibal label, and it showed considerable charm. *Love Over and Over*, in 1982, marked a move toward rock that cheered fans but also turned out to be their last album for almost a decade.

In the meantime, they raised families and ventured out every now and then to play a few rapturously received dates, especially in the Northeast. At one of these in the late '80s, they said they'd been working on a musical with producer Roma Baran. That project never came to fruition, but in 1990 they returned to the record racks with *Heartbeats Accelerating.* — *William Ruhlmann*

★ **Kate and Anna McGarrigle [Carthage]** / 1975 / Hannibal ✦✦✦✦✦
This album was *Melody Maker*'s pick for Best Record of 1975, and it's hard to argue with that choice when you listen to the tart harmonies and solo singing on one of the best songwriting collections ever. From Anna's famous "Heart Like a Wheel" to Kate's bouncy "Kiss and Say Goodbye," the songs paint a deeply felt, highly detailed portrait of life and romance. A revelation when it was released and a classic today. — *William Ruhlmann*

Dancer with Bruised Knees / 1977 / Hannibal ✦✦✦

Pronto Monto / 1978 / Warner Brothers ✦✦✦

French Record / 1980 / Hannibal ✦✦✦
Many McGarrigle fans cite this as their favorite, even if they don't speak French. The Canadian-based sisters are expressively at home in the country's other language, and this may be the most musical of their albums. — *William Ruhlmann*

Love Over and Over / 1983 / Polydor ✦✦✦
The first English-language record the sisters had done in several years found them rocking harder (Mark Knopfler of Dire Straits was a prominent guest star), but the layoff had also given them time to write a strong set of songs that found new things to say about love and motherhood. — *William Ruhlmann*

Heartbeats Accelerating / 1990 / Private Music ✦✦✦
Eight years later, the McGarrigles have adopted a more new-age sound, with extensive synthesizer programming. The sound may be lush and modern, but the sentiments are still deeply felt, and the observations remain laser-sharp. — *William Ruhlmann*

Loreena McKennitt

Harp, Vocals

When Loreena McKennitt released her first album, *Elemental*, in 1985, listeners thrilled to her delicate renditions of mythic tales and poems and especially to her virtuoso harp playing; what was most amazing about that album, however, was that McKennitt had been playing the harp only two years at the time of its release. McKennitt, who grew up in rural Manitoba, Canada, studied classical piano for ten years, took five years of voice training, and had extensive stage and theater experience. From her first album onwards, McKennitt has sought to explore the British (and especially) Celtic tradition in its most lyrical and haunting manifestations. A literate and engaging musician, she has set the poems of Yeats, Tennyson, and Blake to song, while branching out from her British preoccupations to experiment with tinctures of jazz and eastern music. — *Leon Jackson*

● **The Visit** / 1992 / Warner Brothers ✦✦✦✦
McKennitt's breakthrough album, using exotic and fascinating popworld music fusion sounds. It's creeping even further away from Celtic roots, but in equally interesting directions. — *Steve Winick*

The Mask and Mirror / 1994 / Warner Brothers ✦✦✦✦
On this extraordinary album McKennitt leaves behind the occasionally precious seriousness of her previous records and offers up a gypsy-like mix of original songs and traditional music. She is searching for an understanding of spirit in the modern world by traveling the world musically and, as the diary entries in the booklet show, in person. There is no sense in the album of cultural carpetbagging. It is beautifully written and performed. — *Richard Meyer*

Elemental / Quinlan Road ✦✦✦
McKennitt's first album features mostly traditional songs and light, open arrangements. This is her best album for folksong fans. — *Steve Winick*

Parallel Dreams / Quinlan Road ✦✦✦
This album marks a shift for McKennitt from traditional material toward songs she wrote herself. Guitarist and co-producer Brian Hughes also makes his first appearance. — *Steve Winick*

To Drive the Cold Winter Away / Quinlan Road ✦✦✦
Featuring Christmas carols, this album was recorded in various churches, giving it a somewhat cavernous sound. — *Steve Winick*

Ralph McTell

b. Dec. 3, 1944, Farnborough, England
Guitar, Harmonica, Vocals / Folk, Singer-Songwriter, British Folk
British singer-songwriter Ralph McTell is one of those artists whose career has been defined by the success of a single song. That song is "Streets of London," in which the narrator takes a companion complaining of loneliness through London's backstreets, pointing out the army of poor and wretched who are truly lonely. McTell recorded the song on his second album, *Spiral Staircase*, in 1969, but it wasn't until he re-recorded it in 1974 that it became a No. 2 UK hit. He has continued to make albums, has become associated with the Fairport Convention family of musicians, and has appeared on British TV, especially on children's shows. — *William Ruhlmann*

★ **You Well-Meaning Brought Me Here** / 1971 / ABC ✦✦✦✦✦
This record includes McTell's "Streets of London," which has by now become a genuine folk song—lots of people don't know he wrote it. Sadly, its portrait of what we now call the homeless is even more relevant in these times than it was in the early '70s. Happily, this album, gorgeously but simply produced by Gus Dudgeon, almost lives up to its most memorable track. — *William Ruhlmann*

Slide Away the Screen / 1979 / Warner Brothers ✦✦✦
Slide Away the Screen, originally released in 1979, represents one of McTell's finest recorded moments with backing by several friends from Fairport Convention. The CD reissue restores the full title (*Slide Away the Screen and Other Stories*) and rounds out the album by including five additional tracks from the recording sessions. — *Chris Woodstra*

● **From Clare to Here** / May 21, 1996 / Red House ✦✦✦✦

Collection of His Love Songs / Castle ✦✦✦
As the title suggests, this 23-track disc collects some of Ralph McTell's best songs pertaining to matters of the heart. While he is best remembered for songs dealing with social and political concerns, especially for "Streets of London," this collection offers an interesting alternate view of the artist with a subject he's equally capable of pulling off. Presumably due to licensing problems, McTell had to re-record a few of his early songs, but that shouldn't detract from the album—the remakes are faithful to the originals. — *Chris Woodstra*

Best Of Ralph McTell / Castle ✦✦✦
While the material covered on this collection doesn't give the complete picture—several albums are not represented—this 24-track "best of" does hit quite a few highlights. "Streets of London" is here, but in one of its many re-recorded forms. — *Chris Woodstra*

Richard Meyer

Guitar, Vocals / Folk, Singer-Songwriter
Singer-songwriter Richard Meyer has been at the center of the Greenwich Village scene since the early '80s, producing concerts and radio programs, editing *Fast Folk Musical Magazine* for many years, and developing a strong body of work. He is a comprehensive artist, producing, arranging, and writing. — *Bill McCauly*

Laughing/Scared / 1987 / Old Forge ✦✦✦
Meyer's folk/rock debut sometimes has an almost rockabilly exuberance, even when he's dealing with the "scared" side of his lyrical dichotomy. And then there are those songs, such as "All My Ex-Girlfriends (Are Married)," in which singer and listener are laughing and shivering at the same time. Still, Meyer remains able to assure us there's "No Reason to Cry" with a song that's one of those hit-single shoulda-beens. A fine, varied collection. — *William Ruhlmann*

The Good Life! / 1992 / Shanachie ✦✦✦✦
Meyer's second release is solid throughout. He has a very good group helping out—Rex Fowler, Mark Dann, Lucy Kaplansky, Andrew Hardin, Lisa Gutkin, Margo Hennebach, and Barry Mitterhoff. This is not the kind of CD that jumps out at you; it just grows on you. — *Chip Renner*

● **Letter from the Open Sky** / 1994 / Shanachie ✦✦✦✦
Richard Meyer has made an artistic breakthrough with this, his third album. The curious song structures and intricate productions are well crafted. The seven-minute title cut is driven by mandolins, harp, and drums; "Century's End" (a song of the Holocaust's last survivor) uses minor-key violin lines to emphasize the lyric. Meyer is joined on "Blind

Music Map

Folk-Rock

Early '60s Folkies		British Invasion Groups
Bob Dylan (acoustic); Peter, Paul & Mary		The Beatles, The Searchers, The Animals

American Folk-Rock Groups
The Byrds, The Beau Brummels, Bob Dylan (electric), The Blue Things

Commercial L.A. Folk-Rock
The Mamas & the Papas,
Sonny & Cher, The Turtles

Early '60s Folkies Go Electric
Fred Neil, Gordon Lightfoot,
Phil Ochs, Ian & Sylvia, Donovan,
Richard & Mimi Farina

New York Folk-Rock Groups
The Lovin' Spoonful,
Simon & Garfunkel

**California Folk-Rockers
Gone Psychedelic**
Jefferson Airplane, Love,
Buffalo Springfield

Late '60s British Folk-Rockers
Fairport Convention, Pentangle,
Nick Drake

Singer-Songwriters
Neil Young, Joni Mitchell,
Tim Buckley, Jackson Browne,
Carole King, Paul Simon

October" by Katy Moffatt in a cinematic, romantic, travelogue duet. Meyer covers a lot of political and romantic ground in this hauntingly arranged album. —*Bill McCaully*

Walt Michael

Guitar, Harmonica, Mandolin, Dulcimer (Hammer) / Folk
Bluegrass musician Walt Michael was born and raised in Maryland. He first became aware of bluegrass while working as a student volunteer in West Virginia and developed a passion for the sounds of the Appalachians. Although he is an accomplished musician—he can play harmonica, guitar, and mandolin—he is best known for his work on the hammer dulcimer, which he has been playing since 1971. As a seminarian, Michael began performing at coffee houses and, with Jim Albertson on guitar and Lew London on banjo, he formed the Bottle Hill Band. During its years of activity (1972-1977) the Bottle Hill Band toured extensively, released two albums, and developed a distinctive "new grass" sound. When the Bottle Hill Band dissolved in 1977, Michael joined Tom McCreesh and Harley Campbell to form Michael, McCreesh, and Campbell. The band recorded two albums and toured Europe before breaking up. Once again Michael found himself alone, and this time he chose to lead his own band, naming it Walt Michael and Co. His recordings with Walt Michael and Co. have seen his ability on the dulcimer reach a new stage of confidence and maturity, and many consider them his best work to date. —*Leon Jackson*

Music for Hammer Dulcimer / 1983 / ✦✦✦
Early work. One of the finest hammer dulcimer players out there. —*Chip Renner*

The Good Old Way / 1985 / FH ✦✦✦✦
Highly recommended. —*Chip Renner*

● **Step Stone** / 1986 / Flying Fish ✦✦✦✦
Twelve solid songs. His best work. —*Cub Koda*

Chad Mitchell

Vocals
During the '60s, Chad Mitchell (and the Chad Mitchell Trio) had a permanent place in the nation's Top 40 charts. Chad's performing has lost ranking in the years since he "retired" as an active musician. This time he's a solo, and the tunes he's chosen for his return to singing include numbers by such respected songwriters as Dave Mallett, David Massengill, Nancy Griffith, and Tom Russell. —*Allan Shaw*

● **At the Bitter End** / 1962 / Kapp ✦✦✦✦

Hugh Moffatt

Guitar, Vocals / Folk, Singer-Songwriter
Singer-songwriter Hugh Moffatt was born in Fort Worth, TX, and learned to play piano and trumpet as a boy. He was influenced by the Sons of the

Pioneers, whom he heard on the radio. In high school Moffatt performed in band, specializing in big-band swing music. During the late '60s, he moved to Houston, where he listened to blues, learned to play guitar, and joined the pop band Rollin' Wood. In 1971 he moved to Austin and performed folk and country music at two clubs a night. In 1973 he headed for Washington, DC, but paused in Nashville, and after seeing Stringbean and Marty Robbins perform at the *Grand Ole Opry* decided to stay and try writing songs. As a songwriter, he was heavily influenced by Kris Kristofferson and later Ed Penney, who became his mentor. In 1974, Ronnie Milsap recorded Moffatt's "Just in Case" and scored a Top Five hit. Two years later, Moffatt signed with Chappell Music. In 1977 he signed a recording contract with Mercury and had a minor hit with his debut single "The Gambler," but his second single went nowhere and he was dropped. In 1978, Joe Sun recorded Moffatt's "Old Flames (Can't Hold a Candle to You)," his most famous song. In 1980, Dolly Parton recorded it and had a No. 1 hit. Several artists had success with Moffatt's songs during the early '80s, including Lacy J. Dalton with "Wild Turkey," Alabama with "Words at Twenty Paces," and Johnny Rodriguez with "How Could I Love Her So Much." Around that time, Moffatt founded the four-piece band Ratz, who recorded a five-song EP in 1984, *Puttin' on the Ratz*. Moffatt and his parents paid for the first 1,000 copies. He cut some solo tracks in 1986 with the help of a friend who had recently inherited some money. The following year he signed with Philo/Rounder and, using some of his unreleased tracks, completed *Loving You*. Most of the songs were written or co-written by Moffatt. In 1989 he released Troubadour and then cut *Dance Me Outside* (1991) with his sister Katy. His songs have also been covered by Bobby Bare, Jerry Lee Lewis, and Alabama. —*Sandra Brennan*

Loving You / 1987 / Philo ✦✦✦✦
A very good debut album with solid songwriting. Russ Barrenberg and Jerry Douglas back up Moffatt. —*Chip Renner*

● **Troubadour** / 1989 / Philo ✦✦✦✦
Highly recommended. Moffatt's songwriting is at its best. —*Chip Renner*

Dance Me Outside / 1992 / Philo ✦✦✦
Siblings Hugh and Katy Moffatt have pursued different musical roads over the years. Hugh has established himself in Nashville as a songwriter and folk-influenced singer, while Katy has leaned in a more overt country direction. This is their first full collaboration, and it showcases Hugh's troubadour-like rich baritone and poetic lyrics and Katy's dynamic country vocals and passionate songs. The top-notch backing musicians include Buddy Emmons (steel guitar, dobro), Tim O'Brien (mandolin), Stuart Duncan (fiddle), and Albert Lee (lead guitar on two songs). —*Roundup Newsletter*

Katy Moffatt

Guitar, Vocals / Folk
Katy Moffatt hasn't had mainstream success, but with her unique blend

of country, rock, blues, and folk, has gathered a devoted following of fans and colleagues. Her brother is noted country songwriter Hugh Moffatt. She was born in Fort Worth, TX, and started out singing Leonard Cohen's "Dress Rehearsal Rag" in a local coffeehouse. In 1969, while studying at St. John's College in Santa Fe, she sang in the movie *Black Jack*. After making the film, she dropped out of school and moved to Corpus Christi, TX, to work at a TV station, and also sang with a local blues band. Soon after Hurricane Celia destroyed the station, she moved to Austin and then to Colorado. She got a job singing on a Denver radio station in 1973 and became locally popular, and in 1975 she signed with Columbia Records. Columbia released her more rock-oriented debut *Katy* a country album, but one of the singles, "I Can Almost See Houston from Here," still became a low-level country hit. Columbia released her second album, *Kissin' in the California Sun* (1977), as a pop album while Moffatt opened for such performers as Charlie Daniels, Warren Zevon, Muddy Waters, and Steve Martin and toured with guitarist Leo Kottke. The next year she worked with Willie Nelson and Andrew Gold. In 1979 she appeared with Poco at an Los Angeles club and then with John Prine at the Palomino. This led to tours with Jerry Jeff Walker and J.D. Southern and then a tour with the Allman Brothers the next year. In 1981 she sang with Tanya Tucker, Lynn Anderson, and Hoyt Axton. She continued in a similar vein until 1983, when she signed with Permian Records. Label president Chuck Robinson valued her distinctive style and set her up with producer Jerry Crutchfield, a partnership that spawned three impressive singles, including "This Ain't Tennessee and He Ain't You" (1984). Even though none of them charted above the Top 70, she was nominated as the ACM's Female Vocalist of the Year in 1985. In the mid-'80s her label folded and she moved to Philo/Rounder. She made a duet album, *Dance Me Outside*, with her brother Hugh in 1991 and has done duet work with Tom Russell, Mary Flower, and Rosie Flores. Moffatt debuted at the Wembley Festival in England in 1990. Two years later she snagged roles in the films *Honeymoon in Vegas* and *The Thing Called Love*. —*Sandra Brennan*

Walkin' on the Moon / 1976 / Philo ✦✦✦✦
Moffatt's album is not over-produced. It features her on vocals and acoustic guitar and Andrew Harden on vocals and guitar. Moffatt co-wrote with Tom Russell and covers three of her brother Hugh Moffatt's songs. Nice job on "Walkin' on the Moon." —*Chip Renner*

Kissin' in the California Sun / 1978 / CBS ✦✦✦
A nice album. Features Dickie Betts, Chuck Leavell (Sea Level), the Allman Brothers rhythm section, and the Muscle Shoals horn section. —*Chip Renner*

Child Bride / 1990 / Philo ✦✦✦
A startling departure from last year's introspective and acoustic *Walkin' on the Moon*. — *Mark A. Humphrey, Rock and Roll Disc*

Indoor Fireworks / 1992 / Red Moon ✦✦✦

★ **The Evangeline Hotel** / 1993 / Philo ✦✦✦✦✦
The first thing to be aware of is that this album was briefly released with a different cover and title—*The Greatest Show on Earth*. Be assured it is the same album, and a great one it is, too. Many of the tracks were co-written with Tom Russell, who produced the CD. Andy Hardin plays great parts, as usual, and it's all held together by some of the most open and honest-sounding vocals among contemporary songwriters. —*Richard Meyer*

Bill Morrissey

Guitar, Harmonica, Vocals / Folk
Since 1984 Bill Morrissey has released four albums of original songs that have startled and delighted the following he's built up in touring around the Northeast. By the second one, *North*, he'd been picked up by the Philo division of Rounder. Morrissey sings in a surprisingly flexible deep voice (somewhat reminiscent of Leon Redbone's croak, but more supple). His songs are full of humor and pathos, expressed in keenly observed details. This is small-town life, sometimes desperate, sometimes hopeful, but always presented in new, unexpected ways. — *William Ruhlmann*

North / 1986 / Philo ✦✦✦✦
Morrissey's New England country accent and self-deprecating humor make it easy to miss the bite in many of his songs, which have a Hemingwayesque understatement both in their sly, sidelong observations and their matter-of-fact presentation. In fact, Morrissey is a taste well worth acquiring for anyone seeking perceptive songwriting and the occasional dry laugh. — *William Ruhlmann*

★ **Standing Eight** / 1989 / Philo ✦✦✦✦✦
His third release may just be his best yet. If there's anything about Morrissey that becomes wearing, it may be his croak of a voice, which might be more than many can take. Still, he has a wryness and toughness of character that make his tales of hard-won love seem fresh and devoid of cliché and melodrama. *Standing Eight* may also be seen as Morrissey's super session. But this is clearly Morrissey's show from start to finish, and he's wise enough to give his famous pals the slack they need to con-

tribute some tight, winning performances (Shawn Colvin's especially good on "She's That Kind of Mystery.") —*John Dougan*

Inside / 1992 / Philo ✦✦✦
Great production, great arrangements, and perfectly honed lyrics bring a timeless sense to these short stories of rootlessness and love. "Long Gone," "Robert Johnson," and "The Man from Out of Town" are key songs. Morrissey has matured so that these songs sound as if they have always been with us. —*Richard Meyer*

Friend of Mine / Apr. 1, 1993 / Philo ✦✦✦

Night Train / 1994 / Philo ✦✦✦✦
His style has really matured, and this album contains another solid, thoughtful set of story songs. The sound on this album is more stripped down, as basic as a Lou Reed record and just as effective. —*Richard Meyer*

You'll Never Get to Heaven / Apr. 1996 / Philo ✦✦✦

Geoff Muldaur

b. Pelham, NY
Guitar
Muldaur grew up just outside NYC in Pelham, NY. He plays country-blues guitar. Muldaur was a member of Jim Kweskin's Jug Band. —*Chip Renner*

● **Sleepy Man Blues** / 1963 / Prestige ✦✦✦✦
Great covers of Blind Willie Johnson's "The Rain Don't Fall on Me," Bukka White's "Good Gin Blues," and Sleepy John Estes' "Drop Down Mama." —*Chip Renner*

Geoff and Amos / Dec. 1978 / Flying Fish ✦✦✦
On this album, two artists who were prominent in folk music during the '60s sing and play a variety of lively material. —*AMG*

Blues Boy / 1979 / Flying Fish ✦✦✦
This solo album features fine blues singing from Muldaur. —*AMG*

Comer "Moon" and Deborraha Mullins

Moon and Deborraha perform regularly at the Ozark Folk Center in Mountain View, AR. Usually performing as a duo, they also have a group—Sassafras. Moon has won many guitar contests. Deborraha, in addition to being one of the most beautiful women in music, has one of the most beautiful voices. She plays guitar and bowed psaltry to Moon's banjo and guitar. On their recordings, as in their performances, they make you feel as though you are sitting in their parlor. Their choice of old songs is beautiful. —*Don Stevens*

● **River of Memory** / Comer Mullins ✦✦✦✦

Fred Neil

b. 1937, St. Petersburg, FL
Guitar, Vocals / Folk, Singer-Songwriter, Folk-Rock
Moody, bluesy, and melodic, Fred Neil was one of the most compelling folk-rockers to emerge from Greenwich Village in the mid-'60s. His albums showcased his extraordinarily low, rich voice on intensely personal and reflective compositions, sounding like a cross between Tim Buckley and Tim Hardin. His influence was subtle but significant; before forming the Lovin' Spoonful, John Sebastian played harmonica on Neil's first album, which also featured guitarist Felix Pappalardi, who went on to produce Cream. The Jefferson Airplane featured Neil's "Other Side of This Life" in their concerts and dedicated a couple of songs ("Ballad of You and Me and Pooneil" and "House at Pooneil Corner") to him. On the B-side of Orbison's "Crying" is Neil's "Candy Man," one Orbison's bluesiest efforts. Stephen Stills has mentioned Neil as an influence on his guitar playing. Most famously, Nilsson took Neil's "Everybody's Talkin'" into the Top Ten as the theme to the movie *Midnight Cowboy*.

For all his tangential influence, Neil himself has remained an enigmatic, mysterious figure. His recorded output was formidable but sparse. His drumless debut, *Little Bit of Rain* (which did have additional instruments), is one of the best efforts from the era in which folk was just beginning its transition to folk-rock. The bluesiest of his albums, it contained some of his best songs, including the title track, "Other Side of This Life," and "Candy Man." His true peak was his follow-up, *Fred Neil*, which made a full transition to electric instruments. Less bluesy in tenor, it featured "Everybody's Talkin'," as well as an equal gem in "The Dolphins."

Neil's subsequent slide into obscurity was strange and quick. *Sessions*, from 1968, was a much more casual and slapdash affair that included some instrumental jamming. Always a recluse, he retreated to his home in Coconut Grove, FL, after achieving cult success, and hasn't released anything since a live album in 1971. His current obscurity is enforced by an absence of domestic compact-disc reissues of his best work, a situation that should be rectified. —*Richie Unterberger*

Bleecker and MacDonald / 1964 / Elektra ✦✦✦✦
Neil's Greenwich village coffeehouse roots are in strongest evidence on this album (later retitled *Little Bit of Rain*). The drummerless (but not entirely acoustic) LP is also his bluesiest recording. The uniformly strong tracks include "Other Side of This Life" and "Candy Man." —*Richie Unterberger*

● **Very Best of Fred Neil** / 1986 / See For Miles ✦✦✦✦
It doesn't include any of his Elektra tracks, but this is a good compilation of his Capitol work, including all of the 1967 album *Fred Neil* (which featured Stephen Stills) and four tracks from his follow-up LP *Sessions*. Contains "Everybody's Talkin'," "Green Rocky Road," and the beautiful "The Dolphins." —*Richie Unterberger*

The New Christy Minstrels

Folk
A ten-member choral group organized by Randy Sparks in 1961, the New Christy Minstrels were among the most popular performers on the clean-cut, fresh-faced, earnest, fun-loving side of the folk music boom. If all those clichés don't sound like what '60s folk music was all about, it's because the scruffy, "authentic," critical, politically oriented side of the folk music boom turned out to be more influential. But the Christys' side was initially more successful; between 1962 and 1965, the group placed eight albums on the Top 100 best-seller charts by cheerily singing songs like "That Big Rock Candy Mountain." After that, times changed, and such original members as Barry ("Eve of Destruction") McGuire left, but the group continued until the end of the decade. Other members of the troupe at one time or another included Gene Clark and Kenny Rogers. —*William Ruhlmann*

☆ **Presenting: The New Christy Minstrels** / 1962 / Columbia ✦✦✦✦✦
Presenting: The New Christy Minstrels, the Christys' first album, was also the closest founder Randy Sparks came to his conception of a modern folk chorus singing such American standards as "Nine Hundred Miles" and "That Big Rock Candy Mountain." The original group contained some excellent solo and ensemble singers, and the overall impact is of full, warm harmony with an unabashedly sunny outlook. —*William Ruhlmann*

★ **Ramblin' Featuring Green, Green** / 1963 / Columbia ✦✦✦✦✦
The Christys scored their biggest seller with their fourth album, which also contained their biggest hit single, Barry McGuire's "Green, Green." The album was also their artistic high-water mark. Their arrangements were never more stirring and their singing never lustier, as Barry Kane and McGuire made their marks as soloists. —*William Ruhlmann*

The New Christy Minstrels' Greatest Hits / 1966 / CBS ✦✦✦✦
Decent folk-pop like "Green, Green" (sung by Barry McGuire), grouped with pure-pop choir versions of "Downtown." An honest anthology. —*Bruce Eder*

● **The Very Best of the New Christy Minstrels** / 1996 / Vanguard ✦✦✦✦
An admirably succinct, 12-song distillation of their most popular cuts, including the massive hit "Green, Green," and the modest chart singles "Saturday Night," "Today," "This Land Is Your Land," and "Silly Ol' Summertime." The rest is mostly whiter-than-White cover versions of folk/pop staples like "Wimoweh," "Flowers on the Wall," and "Kisses Sweeter than Wine" that make the hit versions (by the Tokens, Statler Brothers, and Jimmie Rodgers, respectively) sound authentically raucous in comparison. —*Richie Unterberger*

The New Lost City Ramblers

Old-Time
During the folk boom of the late '50s and early '60s, the NLCR introduced the authentic string-band sound of the '20s and '30s, in the process educating a generation that had never heard this uniquely American sound of old-time music. While maintaining music with a social conscience, they added guts and reality to the folk movement, performing with humor and obvious reverence for the music.

Mike Seeger, John Cohen, and Tom Paley in 1958 modeled their band after groups like the Skillet Lickers, the Fruit Jar Drinkers, and the Aristocratic Pigs, choosing a name in keeping with the past. When Tracy Schwarz replaced Paley in 1962, The Ramblers added solo songs from the Appalachian folk repertoire, religious and secular, educating a large segment of the American population about traditional music. Folkways recorded the NLCR on five albums in the early '60s, making the Ramblers famous and leading to TV appearances, successful tours, and appearances at the Newport Folk Festival. A songbook with 125 of their songs came out in 1964 and sold well.

The NLCR served at least three important purposes: they brought real folk music to a huge audience, they entertained us well with their highly entertaining acts, and they led us to rediscover the original music on which they had based their band. In the early '70s the group broke up. Tracy Schwarz went on the road with his wife and then his son, gradually leaning toward Cajun squeezebox music; Mike Seeger toured with his

wife, Alice, and did many solo spots; and John Cohen continued playing in another string band, while making award-winning documentaries about the old music. —*David Vinopal*

20th Anniversary Concert: Live at Carnegie Hall / 1987 / Flying Fish ✦✦✦
This is a nicely spirited celebration of a band that was longer-lived than many of its old-time role models. —*Mark A. Humphrey*

★ **Early Years (1958-1962)** / 1991 / Smithsonian/Folkways ✦✦✦✦✦
These influential revivalists of old-time string-band music played it straight, but with spirit and a keen ear for the music's inherent humor. —*Mark A. Humphrey*

The Now St. George

Conceived from the English folk-rock scene of the '60s that spawned Steeleye Span and the Fairport Convention and nurtured in the DC folkscene that gave the world Mary Chapin Carpenter, the New St. George is at once a look ahead at where folk music is going and a look back at where it has been. Their avant-traditional style is equally at home rocking 16th-century Breton jigs and band member-penned originals. This award-winning band is made up of Jennifer Cutting (keyboards, accordion, arrangements), Juan Dudley (drums), Bob Hitchcock (acoustic and electric guitars, mandolin, vocals), Rico Petrucelli (bass), and Lisa Moscatiello (guitar, bouzouki, whistle, vocals). They follow in the long tradition of musicians using modern instruments with diverse musical influence to play ancient songs and melodies. It's a little jazz, a little rock, a little classical, a little folk, a little Morris dance music, and a whole lot of the New St. George. —*Allan Shaw*

● **High Tea** / Folk Era Productions ✦✦✦✦
It's whirling, hard-hitting, sensual, exotic. —*Mike Fleischer*

Penny Nichols

b. Dec. 26, 1947
Guitar, Vocals / Folk
Penny Nichols, with a background as a composer and vocal arranger, has worked as a backup singer for a wide variety of R&B and rock acts, including Jimmy Buffett, Arlo Guthrie, Art Garfunkel, Suzi Quatro, and Donna Summer. She received a platinum record with Jimmy Buffett and a Grammy nomination. Nichols is one of the new lights in the modern folk scene, and her songs are living proof that all the great folk songs were not written 60 years ago. "Pioneer Woman" and "New Moon Refugees" are on their way to becoming modern folk classics. You can catch her live at any number of folk festivals, and her most recent album, *All Life Is One*, is mandatory listening for all folk-music fans. —*Michael Erlewine*

Penny's Arcade / 1968 / Buddah ✦✦✦
This debut album sold more than 50,000 copies. Hard to find. —*Michael Erlewine*

● **All Life Is One** / 1990 / Penny Nichols' Music ✦✦✦✦
Includes "Pioneer Woman" and "New Moon Refugees." —*Michael Erlewine*

Songs of the Jataka Tales / 1994 / KKI ✦✦✦

Northeast Winds

The influence of the Irish in all of New England is as strong as the sailing traditions in the state of Maine. Combine the music of those two groups and the result is Northeast Winds, an Irish band that takes advantage of its proximity to the sea. The band's lineup includes Taylor Whiteside, Emery Hutchins, and Allan McHale. —*Allan Shaw*

● **On Tour** / 1994 / Folk Era ✦✦✦✦
A musical travelogue, it has plenty of frequent listener miles. —*Mike Fleischer*

Tim O'Brien

Bouzouki, Guitar, Mandolin, Vocals / Singer-Songwriter
A Colorado resident formerly of the band Hot Rize, Tim O'Brien has begun to make solo records that cross catagories of folk, country, and rock, all performed with enthusiasm and virtuosity. —*Richard Meyer*

Take Me Back / 1988 / Sugar Hill ✦✦✦✦
Mollie and Tim O'Brien's vocals blend perfectly. A masterpiece. —*Chip Renner*

Odd Man In / 1991 / Sugar Hill ✦✦✦✦
This album rocks the borders of country, folk, and pop. The songs are smart and ironic. There is great playing throughout. "Lonely at the Bottom" is a really good track. —*Richard Meyer*

Oh Boy! O'Boy! / 1993 / Sugar Hill ✦✦✦
More gospel-pop than *Odd Man In*, this record with his band the O'Boys lets us hear O'Brien run down Dylan's "When I Paint My Masterpiece,"

the bluegrass spiritual "Church Steeple," and the ancient "The Farmer's Cursed Wife." —*Richard Meyer*

★ **Away Out on the Mountain** / 1994 / Sugar Hill ✦✦✦✦✦
If you ever wished you could hear brand new music with the conviction and flawless vocal work of the classic Everly Brothers recordings, this album by brother and sister Mollie and Tim O'Brien is for you. The cuts are mostly contemporary gospel-bluegrass-sounding tunes with an A.P. Carter and Leadbelly song tossed in. There is not a misplaced note. —*Richard Meyer*

Phil Ochs

b. Dec. 19, 1940, El Paso, TX, d. Apr. 9, 1976, Far Rockaway, NY
Guitar, Vocals / Folk, Singer-Songwriter, Folk-Rock
Singer-songwriter Phil Ochs was a self-described "singing journalist" when he began performing in New York in the early '60s. Like Bob Dylan, the rival who always outpaced him, Ochs made his reputation singing topical protest songs. He stayed with them much longer than Dylan (and indeed would never really abandon them), but eventually he, too, would follow Dylan into electric music and more personal, abstract, and romantic compositions. Ochs came off as a perennial second-best to critics during his heyday. It was only after his tragic tailspin and eventual death that he was properly appreciated as one of the most sincere and humane songwriters of his day, whether detailing political atrocities or more poetic concerns.

Ochs moved from Ohio to New York in the early '60s, and was soon a prolific writer of the topical, left-leaning protest songs then in vogue. His initial recording efforts, heard on compilations for Broadside, Folkways, and Vanguard, were rather dry and instantly dated. By the time he made his Elektra debut in 1964 with *All the News That's Fit to Sing*, Ochs was finding his own voice—more melodic than Dylan (if not as lyrically innovative), its strident accusations tempered by a warm delivery and underlying compassion. With second guitar by Danny Kalb (later of the Blues Project), his first album was highlighted by "Power and the Glory" and "Bound for Glory," as well as an adaptation of Edgar Allan Poe's "The Bells." The similar follow-up *I Ain't Marching Any More* (1965) gave the anti-war movement two rallying calls with the title track and "Draft Dodger Rag," along with a moving civil-rights piece, "Here's to the State of Mississippi."

Ochs addressed all manner of anti-war, civil rights, labor, and social justice issues on his first albums, the best of which was *In Concert* (1966). Ochs' social criticism was deepening in acuity, as heard on "Cannons of Christianity," "Cops of the World," and the satirical "Love Me, I'm a Liberal." But he also began to move into nonpolitical subjects with equal or greater effect, as on "There But for Fortune" and "Changes," his most famous love song.

In Concert was Ochs' final acoustic album. He'd already moved into electric rock with a fine (though flop) single-only version of "I Ain't Marching Anymore." In 1967, he broke from his acoustic folk troubadour image with a vengeance, leaving Elektra for A&M and moving to Los Angeles. There he plunged into baroque folk-rock, with mixed results. Some of the tracks on his late-'60s A&M records are among the best he ever did, especially the devastating social apathy parody "Outside a Small Circle of Friends." On others, he seemed to be overreaching or straining for highbrow poetry. The L.A. session production sometimes enhanced his musical settings, but the more elaborate and pretentious arrangements worked against the material just as often.

Ochs hadn't forsaken his political commitments, appearing at the violence-riddled 1968 Democratic convention in Chicago. By 1969's *Rehearsals of Retirement*, some weariness and disenchantment with idealism were beginning to seep into both his compositions and his singing. The problems became more acute with 1970's facetiously titled *Greatest Hits*, when the standard of his material began to drop noticeably.

Although it wasn't foreseen at the time, *Greatest Hits* was his last studio album. Ochs did remain active, recording a live LP (initially released only in Canada) that excited controversy with its strange mix of original songs and unexpected covers of old rock 'n' roll tunes by Elvis Presley and Buddy Holly, performed in a gold lamé suit. The '50s revival act was received poorly by an audience accustomed to a folkie troubadour, but that was among the least of Ochs' obstacles. His well of original compositions had run dry, and he was developing severe alcohol and psychological problems. In a mysterious mugging incident in Africa, his voice was permanently damaged.

Ochs did record a couple of flop singles in the early '70s, but by the middle of the decade he was largely inactive and afflicted with serious depression. In early 1976, he hanged himself at his sister's suburban home. —*Richie Unterberger*

All the News That's Fit to Sing / 1964 / Hannibal ✦✦✦
All the News That's Fit to Sing is his bittersweet debut and is a vital and topical album of its time. —*Bruce Eder and William Ruhlmann*

I Ain't Marching Anymore / 1965 / Carthage ✦✦✦✦
A strident, searching, and haunting echo of the '60s. —*Bruce Eder*

Phil Ochs in Concert / 1966 / Elektra ✦✦✦✦
It's since been revealed that some or all of these tracks were not "in concert" at all, but recorded in the studio, with audience noise dubbed on afterwards. Nevertheless, this is Ochs' finest acoustic album. As a lyricist, he was moving from the singing journalist mode to more abstract symbolism, but still attacked US imperialism, knock-kneed bleeding hearts, and even organized religion with an uncompromising sensitivity. Some haunting, wistful ballads transcended topical concerns entirely, including the beautiful love song "Changes" and "There But for Fortune" (a British hit for Joan Baez). —*Richie Unterberger*

★ **Pleasures of the Harbor** / 1967 / A&M ✦✦✦✦✦
Moving from his acoustic base to elaborate musical arrangements, Ochs also turns largely away from his topical material to more lyrical and poetic songs, though the caustic "Outside a Small Circle of Friends" and the apocalyptic "The Crucifixion" clearly retain his social and political focus. —*William Ruhlmann*

Tape from California / 1968 / A&M ✦✦✦
A somewhat manic production, highlighted by reasonably successful straightforward rock (the title track) and one of the great '60s anti-war songs, "The War Is Over," a perfect combination of droll commentary with jaunty backing. Most of the rest of the tracks fall into the over-orchestrated malaise that, to a lesser degree, afflicted *Pleasures of the Harbor*. —*Richie Unterberger*

Rehearsals for Retirement / 1969 / A&M ✦✦✦
Ochs' final album to feature top-notch original material continued his move to poetic abstraction, as can be guessed from titles like "William Butler Yeats Visits Lincoln Park and Escapes Unscathed." The L.A. session musician production values resulted in indifferent arrangements that were downright bland at worst. In hindsight, the muted tone of much of the material contained some seeds of Ochs' loss of boisterous idealism. More to the point, it doesn't have as many outstanding songs as his other '60s albums, though the standard of writing remained fairly solid. The *Live in Vancouver 1968* CD contains higher-charged acoustic versions of six of the songs, and many listeners may find these interpretations superior. —*Richie Unterberger*

Phil Ochs's Greatest Hits / 1970 / Edsel ✦✦✦
Not really his greatest hits (the title was intended as irony). This is his final, troubled studio album, and a good companion to *Gunfight at Carnegie Hall*. —*Bruce Eder*

Gunfight at Carnegie Hall / 1975 / Mobile Fidelity ✦✦✦✦
Most unusual. Ochs does Elvis and Buddy Holly songs to an angry audience and plays out his own internal conflicts at the same time. —*Bruce Eder*

Chords of Fame / 1976 / A&M ✦✦✦✦
A fine collection on vinyl only, but worth having for the liner notes. Note that this out-of-print double LP is the only album to combine Ochs' Elektra work (1964-1966) with his A&M work (1967-1970). The two CD samplers cover the same ground separately. —*Bruce Eder and William Ruhlmann*

A Toast to Those Who Are Gone / 1987 / Rhino ✦✦✦
Fourteen previously unreleased demos, all of excellent fidelity; while no dates or sources are given for these sessions, an educated guess would put them in his earliest, most topical period, circa 1964-65. Most of these feature just Ochs and acoustic guitar, and sound as strong as the material officially released on his first Elektra LPs. The other, equally fine cuts seem to date from a later period, and show him delving into intensely personal, non-political concerns. —*Richie Unterberger*

War Is Over: The Best of Phil Ochs / 1988 / A&M ✦✦✦
Not his best by a longshot, but a cross-section of his better A&M recordings. —*Bruce Eder*

The Broadside Tapes 1 / 1989 / Smithsonian/Folkways ✦✦✦
This album of previously unreleased songs was recorded casually in the 104th St. offices of *Broadside* magazine. They were intended as demos for transcription but are in fact quite good performances. —*Richard Meyer*

There and Now: Live in Vancouver / 1990 / Rhino ✦✦✦✦
Definitive Ochs (along with *Gunfight at Carnegie Hall*). A "lost" 1968 concert featuring his most beloved songs. The real "best-of." —*Bruce Eder*

Live at Newport / Mar. 12, 1996 / Vanguard ✦✦✦
A dozen songs from Ochs' performances at the 1963, 1964, and 1966 Newport Folk Festivals. Four of these cuts were previously available on the *Newport Broadside* and *Evening Concerts, Vol. 1* anthologies, but the rest were previously unreleased. While all of these songs are available on his studio albums, Ochs was in good form for these shows, so these are good supplementary versions. Especially noteworthy are the 1966 tracks; four of the five songs would appear in far more elaborately produced arrangements on his *Pleasures of the Harbor* and *Tape from California* albums. These solo acoustic performances are interesting contrasts, put-

ting the voice and the lyrics at the forefront, in the best unplugged tradition. —*Richie Unterberger*

Maura O'Connell

Vocals / Folk, Irish, Singer-Songwriter

Maura O'Connell embodies many paradoxes: lead singer for De Danann, she was not a traditional Celtic singer; a resident of Nashville, she is not American; collaborator with New Grass Revival, she is not a bluegrass pilferer. Nevertheless, O'Connell has made a name for herself on two continents as a superb singer. O'Connell was born and raised in County Clare, Ireland, where she began singing at an early age. Involvement in the folk club scene led to an invitation from Celtic traditionalists De Danann to join their ranks. Her involvement with De Dannon resulted in the recording of *Star Spangled Mollie*, a clear indication of interest in trans-Atlantic culture. O'Connell then began to collaborate with members of New Grass Revival, and in particular with Bela Fleck, who produced several of her tracks. Together with Fleck and others, she recorded *Just in Time* and made the decision to settle in Nashville. Since then, she has released *Helpless Heart*, *Blue is the Colour of Hope*, and *Real Life Story*, each registering a move toward a pop synthesis. —*Leon Jackson*

Just in Time / 1988 / Philo ♦♦♦
This album, produced by Bela Fleck with string arrangements by Edgar Meyer, is one of O'Connell's cleanest and most uncluttered releases. Her voice sounds beautifully free; while some of her recordings sound forced, this one is relaxed and natural. This album demonstrates why she is often compared with Mary Black. The album's band is an all-star affair with Jerry Douglas, Bela Fleck, Mark O'Connor, and Nanci Griffith contributing. Maura O'Connell can be given credit here for picking up Paul McCartney's "I Will" seven years before Alison Krauss. —*Richard Meyer*

● **Helpless Heart** / 1989 / Warner Brothers ♦♦♦♦
Irish interpretive singer O'Connell has suffered from the inability of her record company to figure out whether she's a folkie, a country singer, or a pop artist. Meanwhile, she keeps singing her heart out, cherrypicking the work of such writers as Paul Brady, Nanci Griffith, Linda Thompson, and others. If you already own the albums those writers have made, maybe she's redundant. However, great songs still benefit greatly from being performed by great singers, and if you're looking for a sympathetic sampler of the best of today's songwriters, here it is. —*William Ruhlmann*

A Real Life Story / 1991 / Warner Brothers ♦♦♦

Blue Is the Colour of Hope / 1992 / Warner Brothers ♦♦♦
This charmingly eclectic album may be O'Connell's best. Working with producer Jerry Douglas, O'Connell finds sympathetic accompaniment on all these songs, whether it's the piano and arco bass on the gently painful "So Soft Your Goodbye," the small-combo swing on "Love to Learn," or the full-band acoustic pop on "Still Hurts Sometimes." Though O'Connell records albums by Nashville stalwarts like Pat McLaughlin and Tom Kimmel, her ear for a wider range of material makes *Blue Is the Color of Hope* such a joy. "Bad News at the Best of Times," by rockers Paul Carrack and John Wesley Harding, is a real find, and O'Connell's cover of Mary-Chapin Carpenter's "It Don't Bring You" is simply gorgeous. —*Brian Mansfield*

Stories / Oct. 1995 / Hannibal ♦♦♦

Odetta (Odetta Gordon)

b. Dec. 31, 1930, Birmingham, AL
Guitar, Vocals / Folk

Starting out in classical voice training, Odetta crossed over to folk just before she turned 20. Teaching herself to play the guitar, she began singing in coffee houses in the early '50s. Her appearances with Pete Seeger and Harry Belafonte helped establish her as a major talent. She began recording solo albums in the late '50s and has been active ever since. She sings in a deep, husky voice with great control and clarity. —*Michael Erlewine*

And the Blues / 1962 / Legacy ♦♦♦♦
One of the outstanding figures of the '60s folk boom, she always featured more than a few blues songs in her vast repertoire, so this album, recorded for Riverside in 1962, was a natural step. The vocal style and instrumental backing recall the classic blues of the '20s and '30s. Twelve tunes are here, including "Oh, Papa," "How Long Blues," and "Make Me a Pallet on the Floor." —*Roundup Newsletter*

At Town Hall / 1962 / Vanguard ♦♦♦
This thankfully-back-in-print classic contains "Carry It Back to Rosie," "Freedom Trilogy," "Children's Trilogy," and 13 other great songs from folk, blues, spiritual, and work song repertoires . . . all grounded in dignity, strength and resistance. —*Ladyslipper*

● **The Essential Odetta** / 1989 / Vanguard ♦♦♦♦
This two-fer includes "No More Auction Block for Me," "If I Had a Hammer," "When I Was a Young Girl," and more. —*Ladyslipper*

The Old-Time Radio Gang

Based in Maine, the Old-Time Radio Gang recreate the early days of electronic communication when live radio emanated from every small-town station in North America. There's no homogenized "country Top 40 format" sound here, just four singers and pickers who love the music and have taken the time and trouble to recreate it in its natural setting. From novelty tunes to gospel favorites, inspirational songs to ballads, Allan "Mac" McHale, Russ Miller, Dick Monroe, and Smokey Valley have it all. —*Allan Shaw*

Old Country Radio Songs / 1988 / Folk Era ♦♦♦
Country music as it was and as it should be. —*Mike Fleischer*

● **When Roses Bloom Again** / 1991 / Folk Era ♦♦♦♦

The Old-Time Music Group

The Old-Time Music Group from southwestern Ohio is one of the few groups still performing the old folk songs in the old-time way. Nothing pretentious, this is fun music played by a group of people just playing to entertain us and themselves. The leader of the group, Ed Simpkins, plays banjo, guitar, and harmonica, and the rest of the band play fiddle, autoharp, dulcimer, bass, and tipple. They have played at the Appalachia Folk Festival and are regulars at the Tennessee Fall Homecoming. This is what folk music is all about. —*Don Stevens*

● **The Songs at Mother's Knee** / Jim Dawg ♦♦♦♦

The Oyster Band

Folk, British Folk

A British folk-rock band of the late '80s and early '90s, specializing in contemporary dance rhythms (played by a rock rhythm section), yet retaining a traditional English folk flavor. Members are John Jones (melodeon, accordion), Ian Telfer (fiddle, viola, concertina), Alan Prosser (guitar, mandolin), Chopper (bass), and Russell Lax (drums). —*William Ruhlmann*

Wide Blue Yonder / 1987 / Cooking Vinyl/Polydor ♦♦♦
The Oysters turn in some highly political material here, leading off with "The Generals Are Born Again" and covering Billy Bragg's "Between the Wars," but the love songs are just as fervent, notably "The Oxford Girl." It all barrels along at quick tempos, with much intricate playing and full-voiced singing; this is stirring stuff. —*William Ruhlmann*

● **Ride** / 1989 / Cooking Vinyl/Polydor ♦♦♦♦
"New York Girls" is a rollicking square-dance workout about prostitutes, which asks the musical question, "Can you dance the polka?" On the same album, the Oysters cover New Order's electro-rock "Love Vigilantes." And, somehow, it all sounds like English folk music. —*William Ruhlmann*

From Little Rock to Leipzig / Feb. 22, 1991 / Rykodisc ♦♦♦
With their infectious music and dance beats, it stands to reason the Oyster Band would be terrific live. They are, and it shows here, on a collection of their best originals plus such wide-ranging covers as Phil Ochs' "Gonna Do What I Have to Do" and the old Bobby Fuller hit "I Fought the Law." —*William Ruhlmann*

Trawler / 1995 / Cooking Vinyl ♦♦

Tom Paley

Banjo, Vocals

Everyone remembers Paley from the New Lost City Ramblers. While now living in England, he has continued to advance traditional music throughout the world, and has recorded with many traditional artists, including Jean Ritchie and Peggy Seeger. In recent years, Paley has added traditional Scandinavian music to his repertoire. His latest release on Mirimac, is with his son, Ben. A fine source of unusual traditional music. —*Don Stevens*

● **On a Cold Winter Night** / Marimac ♦♦♦♦

Sandy and Caroline Paton

Sandy and Caroline are the owners of Folk Legacy Records. In that capacity they have brought us some of the best traditional folk musicians in America. Most of the Folk-Legacy LPs are still available. In addition to bringing us other musicians, and outstanding collections like *The Golden Ring* and *Sharon Mountain Harmony* anthologies, they have made numerous terrific recordings themselves. Recording together or with other Folk-Legacy artists, they have brought us traditional songs rarely heard in any other venue. All of these recordings should be a part of any folk collection. —*Don Stevens*

● **New Golden Ring, The "Five Days Singing," Vol. 1** / Folk-Legacy ♦♦♦♦

● **New Golden Ring, The "Five Days Singing," Vol. 2** / Folk-Legacy ♦♦♦♦

Ellis Paul

Violin, Keyboards, Vocals
Originally from Maine, Paul is now one of the most highly regarded of the early-'90s generation of singer-songwriters to come out of the Boston area. He won the 1994 New Folk competition at the Kerrville Folk Festival and has been a regular on the national touring circuit. His songs are finely drawn, often romantic stories. —*Richard Meyer*

Say Anything / 1993 / Black Wolf ✦✦✦✦
Produced by Bill Morrissey, *Say Anything* provides a good introduction to Paul's music. Geoff Bartley, Johnny Cunningham, and the Story provide some of the very tasteful support. "Conversations with a Ghost," "Just the Jester Fool," and "New Light in Your Halo" are some of the key tracks on this fine debut CD. —*Richard Meyer*

★ **Stories** / 1994 / Philo ✦✦✦✦✦
Stories is a step forward for Paul. The lush and understated arrangements frame his detailed lyrics. Ballads like "Don't Breathe" and "Here She Is" are lovely, and placed alongside the uptempo songs "All Things Being the Same" and "Autobiography of a Pistol," make this a strong, well balanced album. —*Richard Meyer*

Tom Paxton

b. Oct. 31, 1937, Chicago, IL
Guitar, Vocals / Singer-Songwriter
Though he has never achieved widespread popular success, Tom Paxton has proven to be one of the most talented and certainly the funniest of the topical folksinger-songwriters who emerged in the '60s. Born in Chicago, Paxton moved to Oklahoma when he was ten. After earning a BFA at the University of Oklahoma in 1959, he joined the army, which gave him the experiences recounted in one of his best early satiric songs, "The Willing Conscript." After leaving the service, he moved to New York City. His first national release was *Ramblin' Boy* on Elektra in 1965. His songs were recorded by a variety of fellow performers, including Peter, Paul and Mary and Judy Collins. Paxton recorded seven albums for Elektra through 1971, two of which, *The Things I Notice Now* and *Tom Paxton 6*, reached the charts. He switched to Reprise Records for three albums, two of which, *How Come the Sun* and *Peace Will Come*, also made the charts. Since then he has recorded for Private Stock, Vanguard, Flying Fish, Mountain Railroad, and his own Pax label. Paxton has continued to write satiric topical material over the years, from "I'm Changing My Name to Chrysler" (an attack on the government bailout of the auto giant) to "Little Bitty Gun," which mocked Nancy Reagan. But his songs can also be scathingly serious, such as his account of "The Death of Stephen Biko," and romantically touching, such as "The Last Thing on My Mind." Recently Paxton has recorded more children's music and penned books for children. —*William Ruhlmann*

Tom Paxton 6 / 1970 / Elektra ✦✦✦✦
The best of Paxton's Elektra albums came toward the end of his tenure with the label and featured an above-average collection of trenchant originals. "Whose Garden Was This" remains a masterpiece on ecology, while "Forest Lawn" is one of Paxton's funniest songs ever. —*William Ruhlmann*

The Paxton Report / 1980 / Mountain Railroad ✦✦✦
An unusually high quotient of comic/political material makes this one of his most scathing collections. "I Am Changing My Name to Chrysler" nails its subject perfectly. —*William Ruhlmann*

Even a Grey Day / 1983 / Flying Fish ✦✦✦✦
This collection is filled with Paxton's more serious, romantic, and thoughtful songs, some of them re-recordings of '60s favorites. The overall mood is unusually somber, but the album is unusually moving, too. —*William Ruhlmann*

● **A Paxton Primer** / 1986 / Pax ✦✦✦✦
One of the frustrating things about Tom Paxton is his tendency to scatter his best material across his many albums, a couple of gems per record. This makes him a prime candidate for a "best-of," and though these are re-recordings, they are the artist's own choices, issued on his own label. This is the compilation that covers the most ground and therefore the one to look for. (74 East Park Place, East Hampton, NY 11937) —*William Ruhlmann*

Herb Pedersen

b. Apr. 27, 1944, Berkeley, CA
Banjo, Guitar / Folk
Pedersen is a member of the Desert Rose Band. He is a skilled studio musician, equally adept on the guitar and banjo. He has released several solo albums and appeared on countless projects. —*Chip Renner*

● **Lonesome Feeling** / Sugar Hill ✦✦✦✦
A very fine blend of bluegrass and country. Sugar Hill lets Pedersen shine. —*Chip Renner*

Southwest / 1976 / Epic ✦✦✦
A solid album featuring David Lindley, Mike Post, Larry Carlton, Josh Graves, Al Perkins, Jim Gordon, and some fine backing vocals by Linda Ronstadt and Emmylou Harris. (Out of print.) —*Chip Renner*

Sandman / 1977 / Epic ✦✦✦
The same backups as on the *Southwest* album, with the additions of Lowell George and Dolly Parton. This album is out of print, but worth the search. —*Chip Renner*

Pentangle

Folk, British Folk
Were Pentangle a folk group, a folk-rock group, or something that resists classification? They could hardly be called a rock 'n' roll act; they didn't use electric instruments often, and were built around two virtuoso guitarists, Bert Jansch and John Renbourn, who were already well-established on the folk circuit before the group formed. Yet their hunger for eclectic experimentation fit into the milieu of late-'60s progressive rock and psychedelia, and much of their audience came from the rock and pop worlds, rather than the folk crowd. With Jacqui McShee on vocals and a rhythm section of Danny Thompson (bass) and Terry Cox (drums), the group mastered a breathtaking repertoire that encompassed traditional ballads, blues, jazz, pop, and reworkings of rock oldies, often blending different genres in the same piece. Their prodigious individual talents perhaps ensured a brief lifespan, but at their peak they melded their distinct and immense skills to egg each other on to heights they couldn't have achieved on their own, in the manner of great rock combos like the Beatles and Buffalo Springfield.

When Pentangle formed around late 1966 or early 1967 (accounts vary), Jansch and Renbourn had already recorded one album together (*Bert and John*), and done some solo recordings as well. Jansch was more inclined toward blues and contemporary songwriting than Renbourn, who was stronger in traditional British folk music. Jacqui McShee, whose bell-clear, high singing set the standard (along with Sandy Denny) for female British folk-rock vocals, began rehearsing with the pair. After a false start with a forgotten rhythm section, Thompson and Cox—who had been working with Alexis Korner—were brought in to complete the quintet.

Pentangle's first three albums—*The Pentangle* (1968), the double LP *Sweet Child* (1968), and *Basket of Light* (1969)—are not only their best efforts, but arguably their only truly essential ones. With Shel Talmy acting as producer, the band rarely took a misstep in its mastery of diverse styles and material. Thompson and Cox gave even the traditional folk ballads a jazz swing and verve; the guitar interplay of Jansch (who was also a capable singer) and Renbourn was downright thrilling, each complementing and enhancing the other without showing off or getting in each other's way. McShee's beautiful vocals, though not as emotionally resonant as those of her close counterpart Sandy Denny's, were an underappreciated component of the band's success with the pop audience.

And Pentangle *were* very popular for a time, at least in England, where *Basket of Light* made No. 5, and "Light Flight" was a small hit single. They introduced some electric guitars on their early-'70s albums, which generally suffered from weaker material and a less unified group effort. The original lineup broke up in 1973; Jansch and Renbourn (who had never really abandoned their solo careers) continued to record often as soloists and remained top attractions on the folk circuit. Thompson joined John Martyn for a while and has remained active as a session musician, in addition to recording some work of his own for the Hannibal label. The original group reunited for the reasonably accomplished *Open the Door* album in the early '80s, and other versions of the group recorded and toured throughout the '80s and '90s, usually featuring McShee and Jansch as the sole remaining original members. —*Richie Unterberger*

The Pentangle / 1968 / Reprise ✦✦✦
A thrilling debut, which saw five virtuosos creating a progressive folk album that added up to more than the sum of its parts. Divided between traditional and original material, highlights included their arrangement of "Bruton Town" and the seven-minute instrumental "Pentangling." —*Richie Unterberger*

Sweet Child / 1968 / Reprise ✦✦✦
A double album, one comprised of studio recordings, the other of a 1968 concert. No other Pentangle LP covered as much ground as this one, which included original material, Scottish folk songs, jazz, and blues, as well as instrumentals and numbers which spotlighted McShee, Jansch, and Thompson as soloists. "In Time" is a sparkling guitar duel between Jansch and Renbourn that ranks as one of the highlights in both of their careers. —*Richie Unterberger*

Basket of Light / 1969 / Edsel ✦✦✦✦
Although *Sweet Child* is usually cited as the group's high-water mark, *Basket of Light* finds them at their most progressive and exciting. Highlights of this album—which actually reached the Top Five in the

UK—include the buzzing jazz dynamics of "Light Flight," their moving rendition of the traditional folk song "Once I Had a Sweetheart," their reinvention of the girl-group smash "Sally Go Round the Roses," and "Springtime Promises," one of their finest original tunes. —*Richie Unterberger*

● **Essential, Vol. 1** / 1986 / Transatlantic ✦✦✦✦
● **Essential, Vol. 2** / 1986 / Transatlantic ✦✦✦✦
A Maid That's Deep in Love / 1987 / Shanachie ✦✦✦✦
Much of this nine-track compilation is lovely, notably McShee's haunting singing and Jansch's finger-picking. But a more complete picture is provided by the two volumes of *Essential* Pentangle on Transatlantic in the UK, which may be found in US record racks. —*William Ruhlmann*

Live at the BBC / Nov. 1995 / Band Of Joy ✦✦✦✦
Taken from sessions and concerts held in 1969, 1970, and 1972, these 14 tracks aren't necessary supplements to their official releases from the same period—the arrangements are pretty close to the studio takes. But big Pentangle fans might like to have this, capturing the group playing live at its peak, with many songs from the *Sweet Child* and *Basket of Light* albums, a couple offered in two versions. All songs are Pentangle originals; the five from 1972, unsurprisingly, aren't in the same league as ones of earlier vintage. The group plays well, and the sound is excellent; the renditions of "Light Flight" and "In Time" are highlights. —*Richie Unterberger*

Peter, Paul, and Mary

Peter, Paul, and Mary were the most popular folk group of the '60s. Put together by manager Albert Grossman in 1961, Peter Yarrow (b. 1938), Paul Stookey (b. 1937), and Mary Travers (b. 1937) carried on in the tradition of the Weavers, mixing old folk songs with many newly written ones, especially those of the new crop of socially committed songwriters of the early '60s. Though their musical approach embraced clear enunciation and carefully shaded harmonies over the more "authentic" approach of other singers of the time, they were distinguished from such competitors as the Kingston Trio, the Limeliters, and the Chad Mitchell Trio by their seriousness and their ties to political causes.

They were also enormously popular, scoring 19 hit singles (six of which hit the Top Ten) and 11 hit albums (eight of which went gold) between 1962 and 1970. Most of their songs were written by others, their biggest hits including "Leaving on a Jet Plane" (a John Denver composition that helped establish him as a solo artist), "Blowin' in the Wind," and "If I Had a Hammer" (a song written by Weavers Pete Seeger and Lee Hays), but they could also write their own, as proven by Yarrow's "Puff the Magic Dragon" and Stookey's co-composition "I Dig Rock and Roll Music." The latter was a satire that accurately described their musical dilemma as the '60s wore on (popular music was becoming much more rock-oriented than they felt comfortable with).

The group split in 1970, leading to three moderately successful solo careers. But they reformed in 1978 and have maintained a steady performing and recording schedule since. —*William Ruhlmann*

Peter, Paul, and Mary / 1962 / Warner Brothers ✦✦✦
Their debut, and their purest studio album. —*Bruce Eder*

Moving / 1963 / Warner Brothers ✦✦✦

In the Wind / 1963 / Warner Brothers ✦✦✦

In Concert / 1964 / Warner Brothers ✦✦✦
This definitive collection highlights Paul Stookey's comedic talents and features the expected hits plus "Single Girl," a surprisingly early feminist song. —*Bruce Eder*

See What Tomorrow Brings / 1965 / Warner Brothers ✦✦✦

A Song Will Arise / 1965 / Warner Brothers ✦✦✦

The Peter, Paul, and Mary Album / 1966 / Warner Brothers ✦✦✦
This 1966 album was produced by Albert Grossman, with supporting players including Mike Bloomfield, Al Kooper, Paul Butterfield, and others. It includes "The Other Side of This Life" and a cover of Jimmy Rodgers' 1957 hit "Kisses Sweeter than Wine." —*Roundup Newsletter*

Album 1700 / 1967 / Warner Brothers ✦✦✦

Late Again / 1968 / Warner Brothers ✦✦✦
A classic album from 1968, *Late Again* inspired girls to iron their hair and guys to grow goatees in emulation of their heroes: Peter, Paul, and Mary. Songs include "Too Much of Nothing," "I Shall Be Released," and "Reason to Believe." —*Roundup Newsletter*

Peter, Paul and Mommy / 1969 / Warner Brothers ✦✦✦✦
This classic children's album by the beloved trio includes "Puff (The Magic Dragon)," "The Marvelous Toy," "Going to the Zoo," "Mockingbird," and other favorites. —*Ladyslipper*

● **Ten Years Together: Best of Peter, Paul and Mary** / 1970 / Warner Brothers ✦✦✦✦
Exactly what the title says. This is a good companion to *In Concert*. —*Bruce Eder*

Reunion / 1978 / Warner Brothers ✦✦✦
Much underrated, with a hauntingly beautiful version of Bob Dylan's "Forever Young." —*Bruce Eder*

Flowers and Stones / 1990 / Gold Castle ✦✦✦
This 1990 release, the 16th of their career, retains the intimacy of a traditional PP&M recording, while adding an improvisational character. Featuring 14 titles, it includes originals plus covers of songs by Bob Dylan, Tom Paxton ("Yuppies in the Sky"), and other contemporary writers. It's a must for fans. —*Ladyslipper*

Pierce Pettis

Guitar, Vocals / Folk, Singer-Songwriter

An excellent songwriter who was probably first heard by most people when Joan Baez covered his "Song at the End of the Movie" on her *Blowin' Away* album in 1979. Pierce Pettis put out his independent album, *Moments*, in 1984, and has since been releasing albums on Windham Hill. —*William Ruhlmann*

Moments / 1987 / Small World ✦✦✦✦
Containing the title cut, "Grandmother's Song," and "St. Paul's Song," this is his first album, and still his best. —*Richard Meyer*

● **While the Serpent Lies Sleeping** / Jan. 15, 1992 / Windham Hill ✦✦✦✦
The keen observations in Pettis' songwriting gain force from the caught-in-the-throat emotionalism of his singing. As befits this record label, the instrumental settings are somewhat busy in a new-age way. But where the drum and keyboard programming leave off, a strong contemporary folk album remains, especially on "Legacy," in which Pettis confronts the conflicts of his Southern heritage. —*William Ruhlmann*

Chase the Buffalo / 1993 / High Street ✦✦✦
On *Chase the Buffalo*, Pettis shows a great deal of growth as a writer and studio performer. His other releases have had some high points, but on this CD, Pettis' politics and Southern gothic-folk style are integrated better. His writing is more consistent and stands up to his mature and controlled vocals. The production by David Miner is also more focused than before. This is an album worth tracking down. —*Richard Meyer*

Utah Phillips

Guitar, Vocals / Folk

Phillips is an entertaining (and just plain fun) singer-songwriter and guitarist in the traditional style. Famous for his jokes, hobo and railroad songs, and sound effects, he is a well-known and popular performer on the folk and concert circuit. —*Michael Erlewine*

Good Though / 1968 / Philo ✦✦✦✦
This 1973 Philo album includes a mix of Phillips' originals with traditional tunes like "Cannonball Blues," the notorious "Moose Turd Pie," and "Wabash Cannonball." —*Roundup Newsletter*

● **I've Got to Know** / 1991 / Alcazar ✦✦✦✦

Plainsong

Folk-Rock

A quartet formed by Ian Matthews in 1972 with Andy Roberts, Bob Ronga, and Dave Richards. They released *In Search of Amelia Earhart* the same year to critical praise but little commercial success. While working on their follow-up, the more country-oriented *Plainsong III*, Ronga quit and Matthews and Richards were unable to agree on the direction the band would take musically. They disbanded before the album's completion. In 1993, a revived interest in the band inspired a new studio album, *Dark Side of the Room*, as well as a BBC recording of a promotional tour from 1972. In 1994 the band released *Voices Electric*. —*Chris Woodstra*

● **In Search of Amelia Earhart** / 1972 / Elektra ✦✦✦✦
The theme of this album is loosely based on the disappearance of Amelia Earhart and features four tunes penned by Matthews, including the spooky "For the Second Time" and "Call the Tune." Matthews also shows his ability to pick top-notch material by covering Paul Siebel's "Louise," the Jim and Jesse classic "Diesel on My Tail," and Rick Cunha's "Yo Yo Man" (a song Cunha attempted to chart a year later). —*Jim Worbois*

Dark Side of the Room / 1993 / Line ✦✦✦

On Air—Original BBC Recordings / 1993 / Band Of Joy ✦✦✦✦

Voices Electric / 1994 / Watermelon ✦✦

Polka Dogs

Folk

The band consists of John Millard (banjo, vocals), Tina Kiik (accordion), Colin Couch (tuba), Ambrose Pottie (drums), and Tom Walsh (trombone). The band was formed in 1987 as the pit band for a Toronto musical (*Kensington Sons et Lumières*). They play a type of polka music with a banjo. —*Chip Renner*

Polka Dogs / 1991 / Aural Traditions ✦✦✦✦
A strange record: it starts out as polka and ends like rock 'n' roll—Alabama-Starspangled-Washboard Band meets the Red Clay Ramblers. Unique release. —*Chip Renner*

John Prine

b. Oct. 10, 1946, Maywood, IL
Guitar, Vocals / Singer-Songwriter
He's from the Bob Dylan school of talented folkies who like to play with words. But unlike most Dylanites, Prine also evokes the sly, dry humor of Woody Guthrie, and his broken-hearted laments are not chauvinistic and only seldom wallow in self-pity. If he's never made one album as great as prime Dylan, that's because he isn't Dylan; he makes great albums that flaunt his own personality, not the personality of his inspirations. —*John Floyd*

☆ **John Prine** / 1971 / Atlantic ✦✦✦✦✦
A revelation upon its release, this album is now a collection of standards: "Illegal Smile," "Hello in There," "Sam Stone," "Donald and Lydia," and, of course, "Angel from Montgomery." Prine's music, a mixture of folk, rock, and country, is deceptively simple, like his pointed lyrics, and his easy vocal style adds a humorous edge that makes otherwise funny jokes downright hilarious. —*William Ruhlmann*

Diamonds in the Rough / 1972 / Atlantic ✦✦✦
John Prine's second album is a cut below his first, only because the debut was a classic and the follow-up is merely terrific. "Sour Grapes" shows Prine's cracked sense of humor and "Souvenirs" his sentiment. *Diamonds In the Rough* demonstrates that Prine has enduring talent. —*William Ruhlmann*

Sweet Revenge / 1973 / Atlantic ✦✦✦✦
A bold and brilliant stab at (almost) straight country, it tempers Prine's cynical streak with the tone of a jaded humorist and social commentator. —*John Floyd*

Common Sense / 1975 / Atlantic ✦✦✦
A brash album, it's full of aggressive rock rhythms and morose tunes. Even the Chuck Berry cover "You Never Can Tell" is shot full of melancholy. —*John Floyd*

Prime Prine / 1976 / Atlantic ✦✦✦✦
Atlantic Records' compilation of John Prine's first four albums was good for its time (and became his only gold record) but has been superseded by Rhino's *Great Days* anthology. —*William Ruhlmann*

Bruised Orange / 1978 / Asylum ✦✦✦✦
Despite some brilliant songs, Prine's follow-up albums to his stunning debut were uneven until this, his fifth, produced by his friend Steve Goodman. Here, Prine's always finely tuned sense of absurdity once again collides with his ability to depict pain sympathetically for a whole album, typified by "That's the Way That the World Goes 'Round," a neat statement of his philosophy, and "Sabu Visits the Twin Cities Alone," perhaps the best depiction of life on the road in the entertainment business. —*William Ruhlmann*

Pink Cadillac / 1979 / Oh Boy ✦✦✦

Storm Windows / 1980 / Oh Boy ✦✦✦
A relaxed effort, it's defined by straightforward love songs and subdued vocals. Modest but quite nice. —*John Floyd*

Aimless Love / 1984 / Oh Boy ✦✦✦
John Prine moved to his own independent label, Oh Boy, after stints at Atlantic and Asylum (later, he acquired his Asylum albums and reissued them on Oh Boy). On this label debut, he is under no commercial pressures, but that seems to make him more low-key, less striking. "The Oldest Baby in the World," "Somewhere Someone's Falling in Love," and "Unwed Fathers" are good examples of his new sweetness, which is as winning as, if less impressive than, his witty older songs. —*William Ruhlmann*

German Afternoons / 1986 / Oh Boy ✦✦✦
Another straight country set, but unlike *Sweet Revenge*, this is a sleepytown stroll, highlighted by some beautiful ballads and snappy accompaniment by the New Grass Revival. —*John Floyd*

Live / 1988 / Oh Boy ✦✦✦✦
With years of experience playing club dates, John Prine has evolved into a very entertaining live performer, and this album, originally a double-LP and now a single CD, presents him at his intimate best, telling funny stories and performing his most impressive material in unadorned arrangements. —*William Ruhlmann*

The Missing Years / Sep. 1991 / Oh Boy ✦✦✦✦
Prine took five years between his ninth studio album and this, his tenth—enough time to gather his strongest body of material in more than a decade. From the caustic "All the Best" to the cliche compilation "It's a Big Old Goofy World," Prine's gifts for emotional revelation and off-the-wall humor are on display in abundance, and he's aided by excel-

lent production (courtesy of Heartbreaker Howie Epstein) and strong backup musicians. *The Missing Years* won the 1991 Grammy Award for Best Contemporary Folk Album. —*William Ruhlmann*

★ **The Great Days: John Prine Anthology** / Aug. 17, 1993 / Rhino ✦✦✦✦✦
Prine's career has been rich but scattered, and *Great Days* gathers almost all of his finest moments, providing a comprehensive introduction to one of the best songwriters of the past 20 years. —*Stephen Thomas Erlewine*

John Prine Christmas / 1994 / Oh Boy ✦✦✦
An eight-song EP of new and old works with a holiday theme. Knowing John Prine's sense of humor, you can expect that much of this is not to be taken straight, so when he sings of "Christmas in Prison" or, in the live version of the romantic kiss-off "All the Best" starts talking about nailing the trains to the dining room table, you find you're in for a Christmas celebration unlike any other. —*William Ruhlmann*

Lost Dogs and Mixed Blessings / Apr. 4, 1995 / Oh Boy ✦✦✦
John Prine's follow-up to his comeback album, *The Missing Years*, is more of the same in terms of freeing up Prine's idiosyncratic muse and marrying the result to Howie Epstein's top-flight production sound. Fans of the early Prine may find that sound overproduced, but the songs never get lost, and with Prine's typically humorous, off-center view of the world (song titles include "Humidity Built the Snowman" and "He Forgot That It Was Sunday"), it's the songs that count. Actually, this is not quite as strong a collection of material as *The Missing Years*, but it has its moments. —*William Ruhlmann*

Willis Alan Ramsey

Guitar, Vocals / Singer-Songwriter
Few artists have sustained a devout cult following from only one album as Willis Alan Ramsey has. In a way, it's understandable. Ramsey's 1972 self-titled debut, on Denny Cordell's Shelter label, contained some real gems: "Satin Sheets," "Ballad of Spider John," "Painted Lady," and "Muskrat Love," a song that became a huge hit for Captain & Tennille. —*Rick Clark*

Willis Alan Ramsey / 1972 / DCC ✦✦✦✦
One of the great (and sadly overlooked) albums of the '70s, Willis Alan Ramsey's self-titled debut had great impact among Austin's progressive country-folk songwriters. Although best known as the writer of "Muskrat Love," which Captain and Tennille took to the Top Ten, Ramsey's muse was rooted much deeper in American lore and folk music. Influences from Robert Johnson to Jimmie Rodgers to Woody Guthrie can be felt if not actually heard on these 11 highly original tracks. Unfortunately Ramsey, a unique talent with a clear and idiosyncratic artistic vision, hasn't been heard from since. —*Tom Graves*

Blind Alfred Reed

Fiddle, Vocals / Folk
This West Virginia singer-songwriter and fiddler was one of Ralph Peer's discoveries on the legendary 1927 Bristol field trip that unearthed the Carter Family and Jimmie Rodgers. Reed was one of those uniquely Southern contradictions, both reactionary and progressive in his songs. "How Can a Poor Man Stand Such Times and Live?" echoed the sentiments of the rural poor, who tasted none of the Roaring Twenties prosperity (a myth for all but a privileged few). "Why Do You Bob Your Hair, Girls?" invoked Biblical sanctions against flappers. Topical commentary of this sort was rare in early hillbilly recordings; Reed's contemporaries usually pruned a branch from the folk tree or swiped a page from Mom's Victorian songbook. Incongruously, Reed was a protest singer-songwriter out of time and place. Ry Cooder revived a couple of his songs in the '70s, the decade of Rounder's reissue of several Reed performances. —*Mark A. Humphrey*

● **How Can a Poor Man Stand Such Times and Live** / 1920 / Rounder ✦✦✦✦
This is '20s hillbilly social commentary, both reactionary ("Why Do You Bob Your Hair, Girls?") and progressive ("How Can a Poor Man Stand Such Times and Live") from this West Virginia singer and fiddler. It's austere and engaging. —*Mark A. Humphrey*

John Renbourn

Guitar / Folk, British Folk
Guitarist John Renbourn is one of the fathers of contemporary British folk music and is one of the finest fingerstyle players in the world. A founder of the seminal group Pentangle, Renbourn's music fuses British and Celtic folk with blues, jazz, British early music, classic guitar, and Eastern styles.
Born and raised in Torquay, England, Renbourn began playing guitar as a teen. At first he was into skiffle, a style that became popular as the folk music revival was beginning. An instructional book, *How to Play Guitar* by Rory McKuen, introduced Renbourn to the music of many American folk artists and he began to research them. In 1964, he began

studying classical guitar at the George Abbot School in Guildford. Two years later he was playing folk music in Soho, where he met many other musicians, including Paul Simon, Davey Graham, and most importantly, Bert Jansch, a guitar player whom Renbourn greatly admired. Renbourn and Jansch were roommates for a while; during impromptu sessions they noticed how much in synch they were and how easy it was to play together. Both men had fledgling recording careers at the time. Renbourn performed on Jansch's second album and afterward they teamed up formally to record *Bert and John.*

In 1967 the two founded Pentangle and remained together through 1978. Renbourn, as with the other group members, continued to release such solo albums as *The Hermit* and *The Black Balloon.* He formed the John Renbourn Group in the '80s and began adding East Indian percussion and jazz woodwinds to his music. Around the mid-'80s, he teamed up with guitarist Stefan Grossman and embarked upon a series of world tours. The two also recorded a few albums before Renbourn went on to found the ensemble Ship of Fools and play music with a stronger Celtic influence. He continues to tour alone and with other guitarists including Grossman, Larry Coryell, and Isaac Guillory. He also occasionally reunites with Jansch and sometimes tours with Scottish storyteller Robin Williamson. *—Sandra Brennan*

Faro Annie / 1972 / Reprise ✦✦✦
Renbourn focuses more on his bluesy side here, making for an interesting, though not representative, portrait of the artist. *—Chip Renner*

The Hermit / 1977 / Shanachie ✦✦✦
Exceptional acoustic guitarist John Renbourn recorded this solo release shortly after Pentangle disbanded. Inspired by lute music, it includes "Goat Island," "Caroline's Tune," the title track, and eight others. *—Roundup Newsletter*

A Maid in Bedlam / 1977 / Shanachie ✦✦✦✦
A superb collection of traditional songs and Renaissance dances, it features the sublime voice of his Pentangle mate Jacqui McShee. *—Michael P. Dawson*

The Black Balloon / 1979 / Shanachie ✦✦✦
A collection of ayres, danceries, a pastoral fantasia, and an abstract fantasia. *—Chip Renner*

The Enchanted Garden / 1980 / Shanachie ✦✦✦
His follow-up to *Maid in Bedlam* has multi-instrumentalist John Molineux replacing fiddler Sue Draheim. *—Michael P. Dawson*

Live in America / 1981 / Flying Fish ✦✦✦
An excellent double album on one CD, it features the *Enchanted Garden* lineup. *—Michael P. Dawson*

Live in Concert / 1985 / Shanachie ✦✦✦✦
Live solos and duos with Stefan Grossman include a couple of Charles Mingus compositions. *—Michael P. Dawson*

The Three Kingdoms / 1986 / Shanachie ✦✦✦
A ragtime-jazz-folk collaboration. A very mellow guitar album. *—Chip Renner & Michael P. Dawson*

Ship of Fools / 1988 / Flying Fish ✦✦✦
Featured are flutist Tony Roberts, guitarist Steve Tilston, and singer Maggie Boyle. *—Michael P. Dawson*

● **Wheel of Fortune** / 1994 / Flying Fish ✦✦✦✦
On this lush, warm, digital recording, done live in Chicago in May 1993, we hear the onstage collaboration of two masters of Celtic instrumental music and songs, traditional and contemporary. There is little obvious performance, just music made by two men who love their material; consequently, they have an exceptionally relaxed way of playing. *—Richard Meyer*

Snap a Little Owl / Shanachie ✦✦✦
Snap a Little Owl features another fine batch of Renbourn's ragtime-laced duets. *—Michael P. Dawson*

Malvina Reynolds

b. 1900, d. 1978
Vocals / Folk, Singer-Songwriter
A topical songwriter who came to prominence in the '60s when she was at an age at which most people retire, Malvina Reynolds is best known as the author of the satirical song "Little Boxes," which was Pete Seeger's only pop singles hit in 1964. She also wrote "What Have They Done to the Rain," a hit for the Searchers in 1965. Her songs also have been covered by Joan Baez, Judy Collins, and others. Reynolds herself recorded for Columbia (*Malvina Reynolds Sings the Truth*), Folkways (*Another Country Heard From*), and her own Cassandra label. She also wrote children's songs and material for the TV show *Sesame Street. —William Ruhlmann*

Malvina / 1972 / Cassandra ✦✦✦✦
Reynolds is best known for Pete Seeger's versions of her compositions, songs like "Little Boxes" and "What Have They Done to the Rain." The

first is included on this collection, along with 11 other uncompromisingly political songs that mark Reynolds as one of the great topical songwriters of the '60s. She has other excellent albums (including a long out-of-print Columbia LP), but this is a good place to start. *—William Ruhlmann*

Jean Ritchie

b. Dec. 8, 1922, Viper, KY
Dulcimer, Vocals / Folk, Singer-Songwriter
Singer, songwriter, song collector, dulcimer player, and author. Jean Ritchie, who was born in the heart of the Cumberland Mountains of Kentucky, was raised in the folk music of that area. She has been active in preserving and performing traditional mountain ballads and songs. She eventually moved to the New York City area and achieved a national reputation throughout the '50s and '60s, singing solo voice, or with the mountain dulcimer. A number of Ritchie albums are still available from Smithsonian/Folkways recordings. *—Michael Erlewine*

● **The Most Dulcimer** / Flying Fish ✦✦✦✦
Over the years, she has made about 40 albums. They all have had some dulcimer accompaniments, but people looking through the record bins always study the record jackets bemusedly and sooner or later ask the question: "Which one has the most dulcimer?" So . . . here it is. It includes Diane Hamilton, John McCutcheon, Mike Seeger. *—Ladyslipper*

Maggie and Terre Roche

Folk, Singer-Songwriter
A duet from deepest New Jersey, this pair of folkies debuted with one well-produced record but didn't hit their stride until they found a freer sound and a third sister, forming the Roches. *—Bruce Eder*

● **Seductive Reasoning** / 1975 / Columbia ✦✦✦✦
A very well-produced folk-rock album that is unexceptional but clearly sung and harmonized, very pleasant in its modest way. *—Bruce Eder*

The Roches

Folk, Singer-Songwriter
Maggie, Terre, and Suzy Roche harmonize magnificently and share a quirky sense of humor that informs their songs. Most of the time it works, and their music is always interesting to listen to. *—Bruce Eder*

● **The Roches** / 1979 / Warner Brothers ✦✦✦✦
An extraordinary debut record with ringing, soaring harmonies rubbing up against a beautiful and spare instrumental sound. A powerful piece of work. *—Bruce Eder*

Nurds / 1980 / Warner Brothers ✦✦✦
If you love to laugh, you'll love this group and everything they record, including this album. Featured songs include "The Death of Suzzy Roche," "Factory Girl," "This Feminine Position," "My Sick Mind." *—Ladyslipper*

Keep on Doing / 1982 / Warner Brothers ✦✦✦
This is a comeback after their bizarre second album. *—Bruce Eder*

Another World / 1985 / Warner Brothers ✦✦✦
Their most unabashedly lyrical album. A bracing work that, alas, isn't as daring as their debut. *—Bruce Eder*

A Dove / 1992 / MCA ✦✦✦✦
An update from the singing sisters finds them living in the urban jungle and overcoming romantic expectations in favor of self-reliance, though not without regret and not, thank God, without moments of humor and absurdity. For the most part, the trio's folkie past has given way to a rock-pop approach on this album. *—William Ruhlmann*

Can We Go Home Now / 1995 / Rykodisc ✦✦✦

Stan Rogers

b. 1949, d. 1983
Bass, Vocals / Folk
Stan Rogers came from Hamilton, Ontario, a six-foot-four poet who started out as a rock bassist before turning to folk music. With his rich voice, he used his music to call to life all of the wonder and mysticism of his native Canada. His singing is occasionally mistaken for that of Gordon Lightfoot, but it's huskier and earthier than Lightfoot's, and his repertoire—made up of song cycles drawn from throughout Canada—is also more tradition-oriented and more mystical. Rogers died in a fire aboard an Air Canada flight in Cincinnati, OH, in June 1983, leaving behind a half-dozen albums. *—Bruce Eder*

From Fresh Water / 1984 / FOC ✦✦✦
The final Stan Rogers album, mixed and mastered after his death, is a dazzling array of songs devoted to the Great Lakes region and the rest of inland Canada. Some of the environmental sensibilities are bitter, and the politics, as with all his work, defiantly Canadian. *—Bruce Eder*

● **Fogarty's Cove** / 1976 / FCM ✦✦✦✦
A dozen songs of and about Nova Scotia, mostly about the sea, and all but one written by Rogers. They successfully capture not only a people but their sense of time and beauty. Rogers' baritone has traditional acoustic backing (guitar, violin, flute, etc.). —*Bruce Eder*

Northwest Passage / 1981 / FCM ✦✦✦
Precisely what its title indicates—a collection of material from and about the vast western expanse of Canada, filled with robust singing and melodies that are practically part of the landscape. —*Bruce Eder*

Between the Breaks . . . Live! / FCM ✦✦✦
A superb concert album, without a weak moment in any of its nine songs. The highlight is Rogers' rendition of Archie Fisher's "The Witch of Westmoreland," which opens the disc, although it is hard to get past Rogers' own "The Flowers of Bermuda" without having it run through your head for days. The upbeat, ebullient mood of the performances is also rather infectious. —*Bruce Eder*

Rooftop Singers

Folk
Founded by Weaver alumnus and banjo player Erik Darling in 1962, the Rooftop Singers included guitarist Bill Svanoe and vocalist Lynne Taylor. The group, active in concerts and festivals in the early '60s, was most known for their 1963 nationwide hit "Walk Right In." —*Michael Erlewine*

Walk Right In! / 1965 / Vanguard ✦✦✦
● **The Best of Rooftop Singers** / 1992 / Vanguard ✦✦✦✦

David Roth

Vocals / Inspirational
A songwriter's songwriter, Roth combines a keen social sensibility with dazzling musical ability and a strong voice to produce songs that are performed by dozens of other top musicians. He's been recorded by the likes of Christine Lavin, Anne Hills, and Tom Chapin. His appearances have ranged from singing the national anthem in front of a sold-out Chicago Bulls/New York Knicks game to intimate house concerts and innumerable workshops to singing for the United Nations' 40th anniversary celebration. —*Allan Shaw*

Rising in Love / 1993 / Folk Era ✦✦✦
● **Digging Through My Closet** / 1994 / Folk Era Productions ✦✦✦✦
Remember the name David Roth, because you'll never forget the songs. —*Mike Fleischer*

Tom Rush

b. Feb. 8, 1941, Portsmouth, NH
Guitar, Vocals / Folk, Singer-Songwriter
Tom Rush came up in the Cambridge folk scene of the early '60s, playing folk-blues on a series of albums for Prestige Records, then moved to Elektra, and by the late '60s was interpreting the work of such upcoming writers as Joni Mitchell and James Taylor. By the early '70s, he was mixing his own songs on albums for Columbia. In recent years, Rush has become something of a folk packager, putting together road shows that include some of the newer folk performers. —*William Ruhlmann*

Got a Mind to Ramble / 1963 / Prestige/Folklore ✦✦✦
An acoustic 1963 session, from Rush's Cambridge folk/blues days. Much of this is White acoustic revival blues, but there are detours on selections like Merle Travis' "Nine Pound Hammer," Rush's own "Duncan and Brady," and the instrumental "Mole's Moan," which was written by Maria Muldaur. The album has been combined with another 1963 LP, *Blues, Songs and Ballads*, on Fantasy's expanded CD reissue of *Blues, Songs and Ballads*. —*Richie Unterberger*

Blues, Songs and Ballads [original LP] / 1963 / Prestige ✦✦
Consisting mostly of traditional blues covers, this early acoustic effort has a weaker selection of material than the *Got a Mind to Ramble* LP, which was cut at the same May 1963 sessions. Both *Got a Mind to Ramble* and the original *Blues, Songs and Ballads* album have been combined for Fantasy's expanded CD reissue of *Blues, Songs and Ballads*, which is the recommended alternative to the original LP. —*Richie Unterberger*

Take a Little Walk with Me / 1966 / Elektra ✦✦✦
● **The Circle Game** / 1968 / Elektra ✦✦✦✦
Rush managed an undistinguished career in the early '60s as a folkie who performed old blues and rock 'n' roll tunes until he changed gears on this album and turned to the songs of a group of then-unknown contemporary songwriters: Joni Mitchell, James Taylor, and Jackson Browne. That was impressive in 1968, but even today Rush's versions of songs like "Something in the Way She Moves" and the title track hold up well against those of their now-famous composers. And Rush's own songs, among them "No Regrets," are up to their standard. —*William Ruhlmann*

Tom Rush / 1970 / Columbia/Legacy ✦✦✦
Wrong End of the Rainbow / 1970 / Columbia ✦✦✦✦
Fellow songwriters such as James Taylor and Jesse Winchester continue to be represented here, but the focus is on Rush's own compositions, notably the title track and "Merrimac County," and the result is one of the strongest albums in the style of the early-'70s soft-rock singer-songwriters. —*William Ruhlmann*

Merrimack County / 1972 / Columbia ✦✦✦
Ladies Love Outlaws / 1974 / Columbia ✦✦✦
New Year / 1982 / Night Light ✦✦✦
Late Night Radio / 1984 / Night Light ✦✦✦
Blues, Songs and Ballads [expanded CD version] / 1989 / Fantasy ✦✦✦
A 23-song collection combining two albums that Rush recorded in 1963 (*Got a Mind to Ramble* and *Blues, Songs and Ballads*) onto a single CD. Rush plays acoustic guitar, accompanied only by Fritz Richmond on washtub bass, on a selection of almost exclusively traditional material; the only track penned by Rush himself is the opener, "Duncan and Brady." This anthology is definitive early-'60s Cambridge coffeehouse music, which means that it's a bit quaintly dated, but also that it's Sunday-morning listening in the good sense of the term. Rush plays accomplished acoustic guitar and sings with calm authority, though he's no one's ideal bluesman (or even ideal White bluesman). The traditional blues covers, which dominated the original *Blues, Songs and Ballads* LP (now the second part of this CD), can sound pretty callow; the folkier ones work better, one highlight being the instrumental "Mole's Moan," penned by a young Maria Muldaur. —*Richie Unterberger*

Tom Russell Band

Folk, Singer-Songwriter
Tom Russell is a NY-based singer-songwriter who has co-written songs with Nanci Griffith, Peter Case, Ian Tyson, Sylvia Tyson, Katy Moffatt, and Dave Alvin. His band features Andrew Hardin (guitar), Fats Kaplin (pedal steel, fiddle, and accordion), Billy Troiani (bass), and Charles Caldarola (percussion). The sound varies from country to Tex-Mex to rock. —*Chip Renner*

Road to Bayamon / 1988 / Philo ✦✦✦✦
A great CD, with songs full of images. Songwriters do not get much better. This contains a great cover of Tom Waits' "Downtown Train." —*Chip Renner*

Poor Man's Dream / 1990 / Philo ✦✦✦
This CD is as good as *Road to Bayamon*. The songs might even be more polished. "Blue Wing," "Veterans Day," and "Navajo Rag" are all classics. Russell co-writes with Nanci Griffith, Kathy Moffatt, and Ian Tyson. —*Chip Renner*

Hurricane Season / 1991 / Philo ✦✦✦
A solid performance, and the band clicks. Features a great song about Bill Haley's demise, plus Russell co-writes with Peter Case, Bob Neuwirth, Sylvia Tyson, and Dave Alvin. —*Chip Renner*

Cowboy Real / 1992 / Philo ✦✦✦
A real nice cowboy/Western release featuring new and old Tom Russell favorites. Russell scales down the production on "Navajo Rug," "Gallo Del Cielo," and an old Hardin and Russell song, "Zane Grey." —*Chip Renner*

● **The Rose of the San Joaquin** / Oct. 1995 / HighTone ✦✦✦✦
Russell has grown consistently in the course of his many albums into one of the most articulate singer-songwriters on the country side of the tracks. His efforts with Barrence Whitfield and earlier incarnations of the Tom Russell Band have the guitar work of Tom's longtime partner Andrew Hardin. On this record, however, Russell and producers Dave Alvin and Greg Leisz (same as the Flores CD) have chosen to create a more linear feel to the album, with each song set feeling as if it takes place in the border town Russell has been so good at describing. Each song is a miniature film soundtrack, with characters clearly drawn. "The Sky Above and the Mud Below" is one of the key tracks that with its slow tempo and plain-spoken telling truly brings the listener a sense of despair in the middle of nowhere. It is ominous in the way it builds to the inevitable conclusion, as potent after repeated listening as the tragic ending in Russell's earlier *Gallo del Ciello*. On the other hand, "Out in California" celebrates lust and longing of a different and no less universal loneliness for that girl with the red dress. "Somebody's Husband, Somebody's Son" (with Peter Case and Dave Alvin) is a hobo's waltz. The album has some soft lovers' ballads, "Hand Carved Heart" and "Strawberry Moon." The liner notes include Russell's reminiscence about the appearance and subsequent disappearance of a long-lost relative that is perfectly in keeping with the tone of the album's songs. He has carved out a place for himself as a compelling storyteller, and this is one of his strongest albums of the '90s. —*Richard Meyer*

Buffy Sainte-Marie

b. Feb. 20, 1941, Saskatchewan, Canada
Guitar, Vocals / Folk, Singer-Songwriter, Folk-Rock, Folk

Buffy Sainte-Marie has enjoyed a long career that has seen her rise to stardom on the folk circuit and try her hand at country, rock, soundtrack themes, acting, activism, and children's television. For most listeners, she remains identified with the material she wrote and sang for Vanguard in the mid-'60s. Her songs that addressed the plight of the Native American, particularly "Now That the Buffalo's Gone" and "My Country 'Tis of Thy People You're Dying," were the ones that generated the most controversy. Yet she was also skilled at addressing broader themes of war and justice ("Universal Soldier") and romance ("Until It's Time for You to Go"). She was also a capable interpreter of outside material, although her idiosyncratic vibrato made large-scale commercial success out of the question.

Sainte-Marie was born to Cree Indian parents and adopted by a White family. Signed to Vanguard, she was one of the folk scene's more prominent rising stars in the '60s, and certainly the only widely heard performer articulating Native American viewpoints in song. Much of her best material from this era, however, gained its greatest commercial inroads via cover versions. "Universal Soldier" was one of Donovan's first hits. "Until It's Time for You to Go," perhaps her best composition, was covered by numerous pop singers, and became a big British hit for Elvis Presley in the early '70s. "Cod'ine," one of the few '60s songs to explicitly address the dangers of drugs, was covered by Californian rock bands Quicksilver Messenger Service and the Charlatans.

Sainte-Marie didn't pigeonhole herself as a folkie, though, recording in Nashville in the late '60s in attempts to break into the country market. In the '70s, she would make some rock records, including one (1971's *She Used to Wanna Be a Ballerina*) with contributions from Ry Cooder and Crazy Horse. These country and rock outings were far less successful, both commercially and artistically, than her early folk efforts.

But Sainte-Marie was never as reliant on selling units as most musicians. She kept busy with a long-running stint on *Sesame Street*, performing benefits for and organizing on behalf of Native Americans, and composing for movies (she won an Oscar for the theme to *An Officer and a Gentleman*, co-written with her husband, producer Jack Nitzsche). She hadn't made an album for 15 years before issuing *Coincidence and Likely Stories* in 1992. —*Richie Unterberger*

☆ **It's My Way!** / 1964 / Vanguard ✦✦✦✦✦
This is one of the most scathing topical folk albums ever made. Sainte-Marie sings in an emotional, vibrato-laden voice of war ("The Universal Soldier," later a hit for Donovan), drugs ("Codeine"), sex ("The Incest Song"), and most telling, the mistreatment of Native Americans, of which Sainte-Marie is one ("Now That the Buffalo's Gone"). Even decades later, the album's power is moving and disturbing. —*William Ruhlmann*

Many a Mile / 1965 / Fontana ✦✦✦

Little Wheel Spin / 1966 / Vanguard ✦✦✦✦
Recorded in 1966, this classic album reveals the roots of Buffy's musical career, the folk and protest songs that revolutionized the '60s. Drawing on a repertoire of traditional European ballads with more than a hint of irony, she also introduces "My Country 'Tis of Thy People You're Dying," probably the first recording to confront White America on its racism towards Native Americans. It includes acoustic and electric guitar accompaniment, plus mouthbow. —*Ladyslipper*

Fire and Fleet and Candlelight / 1967 / Vanguard ✦✦✦

I'm Gonna Be a Country Girl Again / 1968 / Vanguard ✦✦
And, one hopes, she'll *never* be a country girl again. Sainte-Marie went to Nashville to record this album, with help from such session vets as Grady Martin, Floyd Cramer, and the Jordanaires. As expected, it doesn't jell that well, although it's not as poor as you might fear. Sainte-Marie's strengths, though, are best amplified by folk material; her vibrato isn't suited for Nashville country. Predictably, the best songs are the ones which most recall her early folkie work. "Now That the Buffalo's Gone," like several of her better songs, touches upon Native American issues, and the stark, somber "Tall Trees in Georgia," a solo acoustic guitar piece, seems like a refugee from an earlier album. —*Richie Unterberger*

Illuminations / 1970 / Vanguard ✦✦

● **The Best of Buffy Sainte Marie [Double]** / 1970 / Vanguard ✦✦✦✦
Sainte-Marie pursued a variety of musical styles, from folk to country to experimental rock, and all are represented on this wide-ranging double-record compilation. It doesn't all work, but there are some terrific songs, among them the Native American lament "My Country 'Tis of Thy People You're Dying," the romantic "Until It's Time for You to Go," and a musical adaptation of a passage from a Leonard Cohen novel, "God Is Alive, Magic Is Afoot." (Beware of the abbreviated version, Vanguard 73113.) —*William Ruhlmann*

She Used to Wanna Be a Ballerina / 1971 / Vanguard ✦✦✦

Quiet Places / 1973 / Vanguard ✦✦
You know you're in trouble when the first track roars in like a Tina

Turner tune, as Buffy unsuccessfully plays her hand at ballsy bar-band rock 'n' boogie. Actually, most of the rest of the album eschews this approach in favor of more expected singer-songwriter territory, but this still makes for an unimpressive effort, with unsuitably mainstream rock production values hovering over much of the content. Sainte-Marie mixes her own compositions with covers of songs by Joni Mitchell, Randy Newman, and Carole King, but the only real highlight of the record is the final tune, the reflective and haunting ballad, "The Jewels of Hanalei." —*Richie Unterberger*

Coincidence and Likely Stories / 1992 / Chrysalis ✦✦✦

Claudia Schmidt

Dulcimer, Guitar, Harmonium, Vocals / Folk
A folksinger with an impressive vocal range, Schmidt has recorded both as a solo artist and with Sally Rogers. —*Mark A. Humphrey*

Midwestern Heart / 198_ / Flying Fish ✦✦✦
Fine singing is accompanied by dulcimer, pianolin, and guitar. —*AMG*

Claudia Schmidt / 198_ / Flying Fish ✦✦✦
This is the debut album from this critically acclaimed songwriter and performer. —*AMG*

● **Claudia Schmidt and Sally Rogers** / 1991 / Red House ✦✦✦✦
This CD features some fine dulcimer and guitar work, along with vocals that will thrill you. Many of the songs deal with social problems facing today's generation. —*Chip Renner*

Essential Tension / Red House ✦✦✦
Her most personal statement to date, this 1991 release of all original material communicates an introspectiveness that clearly marks a period of profound growth and change for the artist. Her voice has a powerful new edge and, with its incredible three-octave range, has never been more expressive. The album reflects a greater maturity as both a composer and a poet in love with the sound and meaning of language. —*Ladyslipper*

While We Live / 1991 / Red House ✦✦

David Schnaufer

Dulcimer / Folk
David Schnaufer is a transplanted Texan now residing in Nashville, TN. His mountain dulcimer playing is legendary, making him one of the premier dulcimer session men in Nashville. He has joined up with Paul Kirby, John Golemon, Will Goleman, Dave Kennedy, and Sam Polano in the band the Cactus Brothers. —*Chip Renner*

Dulcimer Player / 1989 / Smithsonian/Folkways ✦✦✦✦
This is one of the finest mountain dulcimer albums you will ever find. Schnaufer goes all out with the help of Mark O'Connor and the Cactus Brothers. This album is more polished and uptempo than *Dulcimer Deluxe*. —*Chip Renner*

● **Dulcimer Player Deluxe** / 1990 / Smithsonian/Folkways ✦✦✦✦
This is a combination of his first two releases, *Dulcimer Deluxe* and *Dulcimer Player*. —*Chip Renner*

Dulcimer Deluxe / Smithsonian/Folkways ✦✦✦
A fine collection of old standards and traditional music. —*Chip Renner*

Dulcimer Sessions / Smithsonian/Folkways ✦✦✦
David Schnauffer's most recent dulcimer release continues his pioneering work on the instrument, this time featuring collaborations with guitarists Mark Knopfler and Albert Lee, blues vocalist Toni Price, and Norteno star Santiago Jimenez. As always, Schnaufer's playing is brisk, exciting, and energetic, his rippling lines and fast pace shattering myths about what can and can't be played on the dulcimer. He not only matches Lee and Knopfler, but meshes with Price and Santiago just as smoothly. —*Ron Wynn*

Mike Seeger

b. Aug. 15, 1933, New York, NY
Banjo, Fiddle, Guitar, Mandolin, Autoharp, Vocals / Folk
Seeger is a great musician in traditional folk music. He has done more to preserve and to perpetuate old-time music than any other person. Seeger has "discovered" more traditional musicians than anyone else. He has mastered every old-time musical instrument. As performer, collector, teacher, lecturer, and producer he has earned respect and admiration. Take every opportunity to see and hear him. —*Don Stevens*

Oldtime Country Music / 1962 / Rounder ✦✦✦✦
Here's solo material from this multi-instrumentalist and founder of the New Lost City Ramblers. —*Mark A. Humphrey*

American Folk Songs for Christmas / 1989 / Rounder ✦✦✦✦
Lovers of traditional serious folk music will enjoy this double-CD set, which features everything from earnestly untrained a cappella perfor-

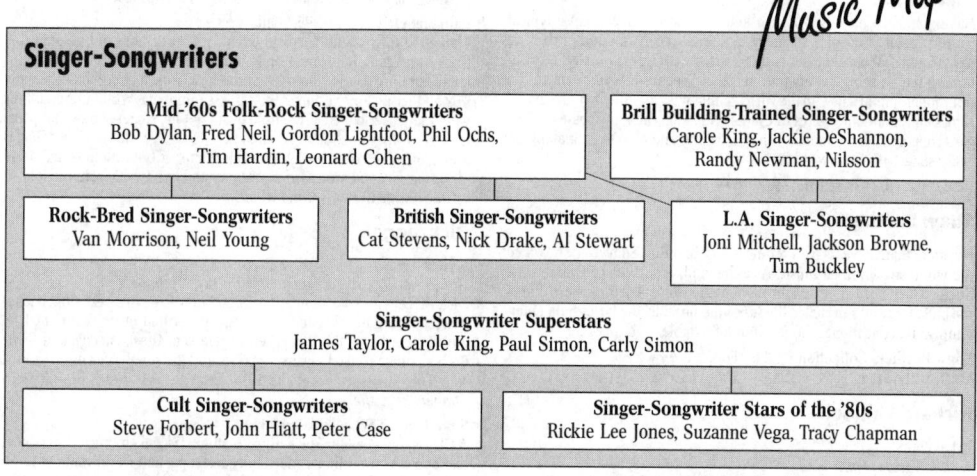

Music Map

Singer-Songwriters

Mid-'60s Folk-Rock Singer-Songwriters
Bob Dylan, Fred Neil, Gordon Lightfoot, Phil Ochs,
Tim Hardin, Leonard Cohen

Brill Building-Trained Singer-Songwriters
Carole King, Jackie DeShannon,
Randy Newman, Nilsson

Rock-Bred Singer-Songwriters
Van Morrison, Neil Young

British Singer-Songwriters
Cat Stevens, Nick Drake, Al Stewart

L.A. Singer-Songwriters
Joni Mitchell, Jackson Browne,
Tim Buckley

Singer-Songwriter Superstars
James Taylor, Carole King, Paul Simon, Carly Simon

Cult Singer-Songwriters
Steve Forbert, John Hiatt, Peter Case

Singer-Songwriter Stars of the '80s
Rickie Lee Jones, Suzanne Vega, Tracy Chapman

---

mances to a whole array of acoustic instrumentation, including mandolin, dulcimer, guitar, psaltery, autoharp, banjo, and so forth. — *Rick Clark*

● **Come All You Tenderhearted** / June Appal ♦♦♦♦
● **Music From the True Vine** / Mercury ♦♦♦♦

Peggy Seeger

b. Jun. 17, 1935, New York, NY
Dulcimer, Banjo, Guitar, Vocals / Folk
The half-sister of Pete Seeger and widow of Ewan MacColl, Peggy Seeger has carved a niche for herself writing and singing folk ballads, especially with a feminist slant. Many of her albums are collaborations with her husband and other British folk artists. — *William Ruhlmann*

At the Present Moment / 1973 / Rounder ♦♦♦♦
This album collects some of Seeger's best material, some that she sings with her husband, Ewan MacColl. The most striking song remains "I'm Gonna Be an Engineer," which encapsulates most of what the women's movement has been saying for the past 20 years. — *William Ruhlmann*

● **Folkways Years, 1955-92: Songs of Love and Politics** / 1992 / Smithsonian/Folkways ♦♦♦♦
For more than 35 years Peggy Seeger has been a dominant figure in the folk song movement in the United States and England. As a member of the famous Seeger family, she was raised in a musical environment. This collection focuses on themes of love and politics. It includes titles that have reached millions—such as "First Time Ever I Saw Your Face" and "Gonna Be an Engineer"—and highlights her brilliant and subtle musicianship and fine songwriting. In addition to solo work, this anthology features Seeger's collaborations with various family members, most notably her late husband and singing partner, Ewan MacColl. In her notes accompanying this release, Peggy reflects on her career and comments on the songs, providing us with a history and context for each. — *Roundup Newsletter*

Familiar Faces / Redwood ♦♦♦♦

Peggy Seeger / Riverside ♦♦♦
This is a beautiful collection of old songs and ballads performed solo. Part of what makes this LP so great is the youthful sound of Seeger's voice and her understanding of the material, much of which has the dark overtones that make so many traditional songs haunting, such as the "Waggoner's Lad." — *Richard Meyer*

Pete Seeger

b. May 3, 1919, New York, NY
Banjo, Vocals
Pete Seeger probably has had a greater influence on the development of modern folk music than any other single individual. The son of musicologist Charles Seeger, he began playing the banjo in his teens, soon turning to the five-string version that would become his trademark. He hooked up with Woody Guthrie in the late '30s, and the two formed the politically oriented Almanac Singers with several other folksingers to promote unions and condemn fascism. He was a cofounder of such organizations as People's Songs and People's Artists. In 1948 he formed the folk group the Weavers, which scored massive hits with "Tzena, Tzena, Tzena," Leadbelly's "Goodnight Irene," and "On Top of Old Smokey" before losing its record contract and bookings during the Communist

witch-hunts of the '50s. Seeger refused to testify before the House Unamerican Activities Committee and was charged with contempt of Congress, winning his case in 1962. By that time, he had made numerous solo albums for Folkways and more Weavers albums for Vanguard. In 1961, he signed to Columbia Records, staying with the label until the end of the decade. Seeger was a major force at the Newport Folk Festivals and a promoter of upcoming talent. His marathon-length concerts included Spanish songs, African songs, Negro worksongs, new protest songs, and old folk songs, sometimes with rewritten lyrics. And he got everyone singing along, often in multi-part harmony. Seeger's own songs, sometimes adaptations from other sources, became hits for others: "If I Had a Hammer" for Trini Lopez and Peter, Paul, and Mary; "Turn! Turn! Turn!" for the Byrds—but he was also known for his hit version of Malvina Reynolds' "Little Boxes," for "We Shall Overcome," for "Guantanamera," and for dozens more. In 1969 Seeger launched the sloop Clearwater and formed a group to help clean up the Hudson River. He maintained a busy appearance schedule, much of it given over to benefits for a variety of causes. — *William Ruhlmann*

American Industrial Ballads / 1957 / Smithsonian/Folkways ♦♦♦♦
This collection demonstrates Seeger's interest in and respect for workers of all stripes. It's a wonderful record. — *Richard Meyer*

☆ **We Shall Overcome** / 1963 / Columbia ♦♦♦♦♦
We Shall Overcome: The Complete Carnegie Hall Concert shows that Pete Seeger was at his apex as a performer and as an influential figure in the surging folk movement when John Hammond turned on the Columbia Records tape machine to capture this performance. Out flowed stories, traditional songs, covers of songs by new songwriters like Bob Dylan, and lots more. Seeger was perfectly in tune with his audience as well, and in the acoustic wonder of the hall, the harmonies were well captured. Columbia cut the tape down to a single disc in 1963, but this reissue, running over two hours on compact discs, presents the full concert for the first time. Anyone wondering what it is that has put Seeger at the forefront of folk music for the better part of his life need only hear this to understand. — *William Ruhlmann*

Broadsides / 1963 / ♦♦♦♦
Pete Seeger's fearless, clearly articulated voice and spare, accurate guitar and banjo playing are presented here in the service of a collection of songs published in early editions of *Broadsides*, the topical song magazine, among them Malvina Reynolds' "From Way Up Here" and the civil rights anthem "We Shall Overcome." — *William Ruhlmann*

Broadsides Ballads, Vol. 2 / 1964 / Smithsonian/Folkways ♦♦♦♦
Seeger turns to the new generation of topical folksingers on this follow-up to the first *Broadsides* collection, leading with Malvina Reynolds' best-known song, "Little Boxes," and including the work of Bob Dylan, Tom Paxton, Peter LaFarge, and Phil Ochs. — *William Ruhlmann*

★ **The World of Pete Seeger** / 1973 / Columbia ♦♦♦♦♦
An excellent two-disc compilation of Seeger's Columbia years, this album contains 20 songs, most of which will be familiar to Seeger fans and folk enthusiasts in general. There's far more valuable Seeger on Columbia, but it's good to have "Turn! Turn! Turn!" as sung by its adapter and "If I Had a Hammer" as sung by its coauthor, not to mention such Seeger concert staples as "Guantanamera" and "Last Night I Had the Strangest Dream." — *William Ruhlmann*

Singalong Demonstration Concert / 1980 / Smithsonian/Folkways ✦✦✦✦

Having reached his 60s, Seeger asked Folkways to document a typical concert "before my voice, memory, and sense of rhythm and pitch were too far gone." What they got is this 25-track, two-record boxed set containing the amazing variety and depth of Seeger's repertoire, from the traditional "John Henry" to the African lullaby/story "Abiyoyo" to Charlie King's anti-nuke tune "Acres of Clams." But what most impresses is Seeger's rapport with an audience that is willing and able to sing along on every song. — *William Ruhlmann*

Pete / Apr. 16, 1996 / Living Music ✦✦✦

Shaw Brothers

For more than 30 years twin brothers Rick and Ron Shaw have travelled the world sharing their music, As a duo and as part of the Brandywine Singers, they have appeared throughout the world. Their music is that of the balladeer and storyteller, the tunes memorable, the lyrics both entertaining and educational, the result unforgettable. — *Allan Shaw*

● **Shaw Brothers Collection** / 1986 / Folk Era ✦✦✦✦
Music with variety, spice, and life. — *Mike Fleischer*

Richard Shindell

b. Lakehurst, NJ
Guitar, Vocals / Folk
Born in Lakehurst, NJ, Shindell began his musical career in college in Bethlehem, PA, where he was the lead guitar player in the infamous Razzy Dazzy Spasm Band (which also included John Gorka). Shindell began writing songs in earnest in 1986. He was also featured on Christine Lavin's 1991 compilation *When October Goes* (Rounder). Shindell earned an MA in theology from Union Theological Seminary in 1991 but says he has no intention of joining the priesthood. — *William Ruhlmann*

● **Sparrow's Point** / 1992 / Shanachie ✦✦✦✦
A strong debut release. Shindell's songwriting is intense at times ("Sparrow's Point," "The Courier," "On the Sea of Fleur de Lis"). His "Kenworth of My Dreams" is the classic blue-collar truck-driver song, and the title song should not be missed, either. "Are You Happy Now" is the most commercial song—very strong. This is an up-and-coming artist you should check out. — *Chip Renner and Richard Meyer*

Blue Divide / 1994 / Shanachie ✦✦✦
While not as startlingly original as *Sparrow's Point*, Shindell's second CD is still far better than the work of his many contemporaries. His political songs, "Arrowhead" and "Fishing," make their points as affecting stories well told rather than by posturing. Never one to shy away from difficult subjects, the "Ballad of Mary Magdalene" is a masterful casting of one of religion's pivotal relationships; that by implication says a great deal about the confused state of human affairs. The playing and singing are all first-rate. — *Richard Meyer*

Paul Siebel

Guitar, Vocals / Country-Rock, Singer-Songwriter, Folk-Rock
Despite the undeniably high quality of his songs—which have been covered by the likes of Linda Ronstadt, Bonnie Raitt, Ian Mathews, and Waylon Jennings—Paul Siebel is far from being a household name. Within folk circles and among songwriters, however, his two albums—*Woodsmoke and Oranges* (1969) and *Jack-Knife Gypsy* (1971)—are legendary. Siebel was born in Buffalo, NY. Inspired by Hank Williams and Hank Snow, he taught himself to play guitar while in his teens. By the early '60s, after serving in the military, he began playing folk clubs, eventually moving to Greenwich Village, where he found support in the coffeehouse circuit. In 1969, a collection of demos he made with David Bromberg caught the attention of Elektra Records owner, Jac Holzman, who offered him a modest recording deal (reportedly he was only given enough money to finance four three-hour recording sessions). The resulting album, *Woodsmoke and Oranges*, was met with critical praise from the media including *Rolling Stone* magazine. Despite the attention, the album and its equally praised follw-up, *Jack-Knife Gypsy*, sold disappointingly little. Aside from a live album released in 1981, *Live at McCabes*, Siebel hasn't recorded since. — *Chris Woodstra*

☆ **Woodsmoke and Oranges** / 1970 / Elektra ✦✦✦✦✦
Fans of Linda Ronstadt, Bonnie Raitt, or Ian Matthews records from the '70s will know some of these tunes already. Let their interpretations stand only as your introduction to this fine songwriter. While his style may not be as polished or commercial as any of the people who covered him, this is a fine batch of songs that deserve to be heard. — *Jim Worbois*

Jack-Knife Gypsy / 1971 / Elektra ✦✦✦
The first record may have drawn listeners for the opportunity to hear Siebel originals of songs they knew from elsewhere. This record does not have that same kind of pull but is every bit as good. His strong sense of

melody and storytelling style paved the way for such current songwriters as Butch Hancock and Robert Earl Keen. — *Jim Worbois*

★ **Paul Siebel** / Oct. 31, 1995 / Philo ✦✦✦✦✦
Though known mainly through others' interpretations of his songs (Ian Matthews, Linda Ronstadt, Bonnie Raitt), Paul Siebel's first two albums for Elektra are prime examples of the New York folk scene of the early '70s and easily among the scene's finest moments. While these albums were sadly overlooked at the time by all but his singer-songwriter peers and critics, they have since reached near-legendary status. *Paul Siebel* is a long-overdue collection of the high points of both albums, featuring *Woodsmoke and Oranges* in its entirety and five tracks from the followup, *Jack-Knife Gypsy*. — *Chris Woodstra*

Dick Siegel

b. New Jersey
Guitar, Vocals / Singer-Songwriter, Blues Jazz, Ballads
Dick Siegel earned a reputation as one of Michigan's best singer-songwriters during the '70s and '80s. Siegel never had much of an opportunity to record until the '90s, when he released *Angels Aweigh* and *Snap!* Both albums received positive reviews and the songwriter won the Best New Folk Artist award at the 1991 Kerrville Folk Festival. — *Stephen Thomas Erlewine*

● **Snap** / 197_ / Schoolkids ✦✦✦✦
A CD reissue of a late-'70s/early-'80s album. Siegel embraces blues, jazz, and pop structures in an interesting, arresting, and clever manner reminiscent of Mose Allison. A four-piece horn section backs up the vocal trio. The Kevin O'Connell Trio, George Bedard on guitar, and Mike Blanchard on tenor sax are featured. There are ten cuts, all Siegel originals. Standouts are "Razzle Dazzle," "Angelo's," and "What Would Brando Do?" — *Michael G. Nastos*

Live / 1990 / Schoolkids ✦✦✦

Angels Aweigh / 1994 / Schoolkids ✦✦

Shel Silverstein

b. 1932, Chicago, IL
Guitar, Vocals
Silverstein originally gained fame as a cartoonist and satirist for *Playboy* magazine. His satirical songs first found a national audience with Johnny Cash's "A Boy Named Sue," Loretta Lynn's "One's on the Way," and Doctor Hook's interpretations of several of Silverstein's best, including "Sylvia's Mother" and "Cover of the Rolling Stone." Silverstein's own recordings have earned him a deserved cult following. — *Cub Koda*

● **Inside Folk Songs** / 1962 / Atlantic ✦✦✦✦
A hilarious collection of folk songs by the gravel-voiced humorist. — *David Szatmary*

Shel Silverstein / 1967 / Cadet ✦✦✦
A very strong album. — *Chip Renner*

Freakers Ball / 1972 / CBS ✦✦✦
A very humorous and satirical collection of music. — *Chip Renner*

The Great Conch Train Robbery / 1979 / Flying Fish ✦✦✦✦
Silverstein is joined by Sam Bush, Josh Graves, John Hartford, Roy Husky, Benny Martin, Pig Robbins, Joe Stuart, and Amos Garrett. A great, funny album. — *Chip Renner*

Lynn "Chirps" Smith

Fiddle, Vocals
Smith played mandolin with the Indian Creek Delta Boys. Since then he has befriended dozens of old-time musicians, both learning from and teaching them fiddling techniques. He has played with many old-time musicians and groups, including the Volo Bogtrotters. He performs and records alone and with groups across the country. — *Don Stevens*

● **Prairie Dog and Other Fiddle Tunes From The Midwest** / Marimac ✦✦✦✦

Michael Smith

Guitar, Vocals / Folk
Smith lives in Chicago and is best known for writing "The Dutchman," popularized by Steve Goodman. His recent work has included the score for the Steppenwolf Theater Company's Broadway production of *The Grapes of Wrath*. Other recordings include a live coffeehouse album, the long out-of-print *Juarez*, which, strictly speaking, is not a Michael Smith album, but an electric band performing his songs with other singers. — *Richard Meyer*

Time / 1994 / Flying Fish ✦✦✦
After years of having two excellent but short Michael Smith albums (eight songs each on LP, combined on one Flying Fish CD), containing his signature songs the "Dutchman" and "Spoon River," it's great to have a new collection. This is a solo album of Smith's impassioned singing and

authoritative rhythmic guitar playing. The songs are, like all Smith's work, detailed pieces of poetry. "Lady Susquahanna" and "Time Is Moving in the Hallways" are two of the 15 strong tracks. —*Richard Meyer*

● **Michael Smith and Love Stories** / Flying Fish ✦✦✦✦
This CD compiles Smith's two solo albums for the Flying Fish label on one disc. It has all his signature tunes, including "Three Monkies" and "Dead Egyptian Blues." A writer's writer, he is highly recommended. —*Richard Meyer*

The Song Project

Urban-Folk
The Song Project was a group formed in the late '70s/early '80s in Greenwich Village, with various lineups through the years. During an Italian tour in 1985, members Lucy Kapbinsky, Tom Intondi, Martha Hogen, and Frank Christian recorded an album. They covered the work of Village writers as well as their own. —*Richard Meyer*

The Song Project / 1985 / Folkstudio ✦✦✦✦
The sonic quality is not state of the art here, but the performances are, and the fact that this is the only Song Project material aside from the few *Fast Folk* cuts makes this an important record. Good liner notes by Dave Van Ronk. —*Richard Meyer*

Rosalie Sorrels

b. 1933, Idaho
Guitar, Vocals / Traditional Folk
Sorrels is a collector and performer of traditional American folk songs, but in all her music, traditional and original, there is a deeply personal vein. Sorrels' music is about loss and survival; when she was 16, she had an illegal abortion; when she was 17, she gave up a child for adoption; she married and had five children, left her husband and struggled to raise her family alone, and then saw her eldest child take his own life; finally she suffered a cerebral aneurysm in 1988. Through all her suffering, Sorrels has found solace in her ability to make music, an ability that has enraptured audiences for years.

Sorrels' musical career began in the '60s, when, as a way of alleviating the tedium of domestic life, she took a class on American folk songs while living in Salt Lake City. Work for that class resulted in her first album, *Folk Songs of Utah and Idaho*. Her albums since then have been a mix of traditional and original material, always sung with great passion and personal feeling; they have become increasingly autobiographical. —*Leon Jackson*

Always a Lady / 1976 / Green Linnet ✦✦✦✦
Stories and confessions by a great and legendary folksinger. —*Richard Meyer*

Travelin' Lady Rides Again / 1978 / Green Linnet ✦✦✦✦
Here is a good album of road songs and tales of love and lost love performed either in a honky tonk style or as country weepers. —*Richard Meyer*

Be Careful There's a Baby . . . / 1990 / Green Linnet ✦✦✦
It's for those loved ones who are expecting a Little Person to join their household soon—they'll need to learn lullabies, soothing *and* hostile ("Baby Rocking Medley") and stories ("Mehitabel and Her Kittens"); those with children, so they can be reminded just why they had them in the first place; those who don't have any kids, and need an excuse to gloat; and yourself, because you deserve the best. Warm, alternately whimsical and serious, Rosalie introduces many of the songs with personal observations and stories (great liner notes, too), and makes clear her opinion that children and motherhood *are* sacred, but to be chosen, not required. The album includes an emotional reading of Marge Piercy's "Right to Life." —*Ladyslipper*

● **Report from Grimes Creek** / 1991 / Green Linnet ✦✦✦✦
This release is the culmination of a career and of a remarkable life. As reflected in thoughts and recollections of the log cabin in Utah in which she grew up and now again lives, Sorrels weaves a tale, through song and story, of home, roots, and rural western America. Poignant and articulate. —*Ladyslipper*

What Does It Mean to Love? / 1994 / Green Linnet ✦✦✦
In her notes for this album Rosalie Sorrels says, "This album started out to be a children's album, but in making it I have come to think of it as a conversation between an old woman (me) and a child." A very accessible but personal record. —*Richard Meyer*

Bill and Eileen Spencer

Bill writes songs that sound as if they have been handed down for generations. He has been a friend and tutor to many musicians and groups in central and southern Ohio. He and Eileen have helped get several festivals started in the area. Bill is a manufacturer of, and player on, the mountain dulcimer. —*Don Stevens*

● **Roses and Old Walnut** / Central ✦✦✦✦

Bill Staines

Banjo, Guitar, Vocals
A popular performer, New Englander Bill Staines is known for his terrific fingerstyle guitar playing and yodeling. His song "The Roseville Fair" was covered by Nanci Griffith. —*Richard Meyer*

● **Tracks and Trails** / 1991 / Philo ✦✦✦✦
On this studio album, Staines mixes traditional songs like "Peter Amberly," in which we get to hear the melody Dylan used in "I Pity the Poor Immigrant," with another dozen of his comforting originals, enhanced by delicate arrangements. —*Richard Meyer*

Stampfel and Weber

Folk
Peter Stampfel and Steve Weber are the founding members of the Holy Modal Rounders. Some of their albums together have been billed as "Stampfel and Weber," perhaps for contractual reasons or to distinguish them from the Rounders' albums that featured a larger band. — *William Ruhlmann*

Going Nowhere Fast / 1981 / Rounder ✦✦✦✦
Properly speaking, this is a reunion album by the Holy Modal Rounders, which is the name Peter Stampfel and Steve Weber used for their folk duo when they formed it in the early '60s. The group eventually expanded and went electric, then disbanded. This album is a return to form in more ways than one, restricted to Weber's guitar and Stampfel's banjo and fiddle, plus their squeaky, enthusiastic vocals. It blends folk standards and novelty tunes, as the early Rounder albums did, and, like them, is an off-the-wall gem. — *William Ruhlmann*

Peter Stampfel and the Bottle Caps

Former Holy Modal Rounder Peter Stampfel founded the Bottle Caps in 1981 to provide a folk-rock backup to his zany collection of novelty songs. They have recorded several albums for Rounder. — *William Ruhlmann*

Peter Stampfel and the Bottle Caps / 1986 / Rounder ✦✦✦
Stampfel remains a folkie eccentric, and the main difference between his '80s band and his '60s one (the Holy Modal Rounders) is that the later one rocks harder and more of the material is original. But much of the act still consists of novelties, and it's never quite clear whether Stampfel is celebrating or parodying his sources. — *William Ruhlmann*

● **People's Republic of Rock 'n' Roll** / 1989 / Homestead ✦✦✦✦
Stampfel hasn't quite turned pro on this album, but the band is a lot tighter than usual, which only makes the result funnier in songs such as "Bridge and Tunnel Girls" and "Bigfoot Stole My Wife." — *William Ruhlmann*

Jody Stecher and Kate Brislin

Stecher has recorded with Alasdair Fraser from Scotland, Krishna Bhatt from India, and with many of America's best traditional musicians. Brislin has played with many west coast groups. Stecher plays mandolin, guitar, fiddle and banjo. Brislin plays banjo and guitar. Both are terrific vocalists, and as a duet are unbeatable. —*Don Stevens*

● **Blue Lightning** / 1990 / Rounder ✦✦✦✦
Based in Seattle, this duo has the ability to perform contemporary as well as traditional songs with a singular relaxed authority. —*Richard Meyer*

Steeleye Span

Folk, Folk-Rock, British Folk
Aside from Fairport Convention, Steeleye Span was the most successful and enduring British folk-rock band. The parallels between the bands are numerous: both updated traditional British folk material with rock arrangements, both featured an excellent female lead singer (Sandy Denny for Fairport, Maddy Prior for Steeleye Span), both frequently employed multi-part harmonies, and both mixed original and traditional songs. Although Fairport was more innovative in their early days, Steeleye Span was arguably the more interesting band after 1970, when personnel changes had gutted the original Fairport lineup. Steeleye Span, too, would undergo numerous personnel changes, even at their peak. Prior was the constant factor that gave the group something of a recognizable identity at all phases of their journey.

One thing that differentiated Steeleye Span from their counterparts was that Fairport came to traditional folk from a rock background, whereas Steeleye traveled in the opposite direction. The original lineup, formed around the beginning of 1970, included guitarist Terry Wood, who had been in a traditional Irish folk group called Sweeney's Men (with Andy Irvine). The supple-voiced Prior had been in a folk duo with guitarist Tim Hart. The impetus for Steeleye Span's formation, ironically, came from ex-Fairport Convention bassist Ashley Hutchings. Hutchings wanted to keep pursuing the traditional folk direction ploughed by Fairport on the 1969 album *Liege and Lief*, and left Fairport to join forces with Prior, Hart, Terry Woods, and Gay Woods (Terry's wife) to anchor the first incarnation of Steeleye Span.

This lineup lasted for only one album, with the Woods leaving for Doctor Strangely Strange; Terry Woods would eventually resurface with the Pogues in the '80s. He was replaced by Martin Carthy, one of the most respected guitarists on the English folk circuit. Carthy's abdication of acoustic folk for electric (if drumless) folk-rock apparently caused much consternation within the purist English folk community, a kerfuffle that is hard to understand (at least from an American perspective), given that Dylan had already successfully fought that battle in the mid-'60s. While Steeleye Span played folk music, they had no aversion to playing it loud, and this version of the band proved that it was possible to create an energetic ruckus without a drummer.

Both Hutchings and Carthy, by far the most famous members of the group, left around the end of 1971. This sort of defection would have crippled most acts. Yet Steeleye Span not only persevered, but entered their most commercially successful phase. Tim Hart was once quoted as saying that the group wanted to "put traditional music back into current musical language—to make folk music less esoteric." They were aided in doing so by new bassist Rick Kemp, who became Maddy Prior's husband. In 1973, they finally added drums to the band, becoming a true folk-rock act after years of ramping up.

One asset to Steeleye Span's unusual durability (in the face of the revolving door of players) was their open-minded approach to contemporary influences. They covered oldies (and well) by Buddy Holly, the Four Seasons, and Phil Spector. David Bowie and Peter Sellers made cameo appearances on their albums in the mid-'70s. They occasionally acted in plays (in which they also performed musically as a group). They covered Brecht-Weill songs. Some of their work was produced by Mike Batt, whose primary credential was masterminding the Wombles, a British kiddie-rock group.

Steeleye Span finally had a British chart hit in 1974 with the Christmas song "Gaudette." In 1975 they had a huge (by folk-rock standards) smash with "All Around My Hat," which reached the UK Top Five. In the US, they were consigned to cult status. They picked up some airplay on open-minded FM stations, but got their widest exposure as an opening act during a Jethro Tull tour. The onslaught of punk and new wave weakened any prospects for continued chart success at home. In 1977 they took on more traditional elements with the return of Martin Carthy and the addition of John Kirkpatrick on accordion, but they finally split the following year.

Not for good, however. In a final parallel with Fairport Convention, they decided to reunite periodically while pursuing their own projects. Other studio albums appeared, and the group sometimes performed at festivals or even toured, though with enough irregularity to make it confusing to determine whether they were "together" again. A devoted following makes it possible for them to be received warmly by cult audiences whenever the mood suits them to play live again. Carthy has enjoyed the most notable solo career of the Steeleye Span alumni, continuing to command great respect among British folk listeners. Maddy Prior's most notable outside endeavors have been her duo recordings with fellow British folk singer June Tabor. —*Richie Unterberger*

Hark the Village Wait / 1970 / Shanachie ✦✦✦
Their debut, with a smoother and more traditional sound than later albums. The only album to feature the original lineup. —*Bruce Eder and Steve Winick*

Ten Man Mop / 1971 / Shanachie ✦✦✦
This album features a more traditional folk sound. —*Steve Winick*

Please to See the King / 1971 / Shanachie ✦✦✦
The group solidifies its lineup and sharpens its sound. Fiddler Peter Knight and the well-known singer and guitarist Martin Carthy joined the band on this album. —*Bruce Eder and Steve Winick*

Below the Salt / 1972 / Shanachie ✦✦✦✦
Fine renditions of traditional ballads, songs, and tunes. —*Steve Winick*

Parcel of Rogues / 1973 / Shanachie ✦✦✦
It's increasingly tinged with hard rock sounds. —*Steve Winick*

● **Now We Are Six** / 1974 / Beat Goes On ✦✦✦✦
High-energy folk that rocks hard despite three throwaway numbers. Their best. —*Bruce Eder*

All Around My Hat / 1975 / Shanachie ✦✦✦
More rock 'n' roll versions of folk songs. —*Steve Winick*

Live at Last / 1978 / Chrysalis ✦✦✦
Steeleye's only live album, recorded at their farewell concert, features Martin Carthy and John Kirkpatrick. —*Steve Winick*

Tempted and Tried / 1989 / Shanachie ✦✦✦
The reformed group's most recent work. An impressive return, complete with videos; their best album since reforming in the mid-'80s. —*Bruce Eder and Steve Winick*

● **Spanning the Years** / 1995 / Chrysalis ✦✦✦✦
A 35-song, two-CD best-of, moving from their earliest 1970 recordings through the early '90s. The emphasis is properly on their '70s work, and accordingly the first disc is more essential, though the second part also has merit. With lengthy liner notes by Maddy Prior, it's an excellent survey of the group and may serve the needs of listeners who aren't devoted fans. —*Richie Unterberger*

John Stewart

b. Sep. 5, 1939, San Diego, CA
Guitar, Vocals / Folk, Singer-Songwriter, Adult Contemporary, Folk
John Stewart first gained recognition as a songwriter when his songs were recorded by the Kingston Trio. In 1960 he formed the Cumberland Three, which recorded three albums for Roulette. The following year, he joined the Kingston Trio, replacing Dave Guard, and stayed with them until 1967. His song "Daydream Believer" was a No. 1 hit for the Monkees at the end of that year. Stewart traveled with Senator Robert Kennedy on his 1968 presidential campaign, an experience that affected him deeply. In 1969 he released his classic *California Bloodlines*, the first of seven solo albums to reach the charts through 1980. Stewart found his biggest commercial success with the Top Ten album *Bombs Away Dream Babies* and its single "Gold" in 1979. He released several of his albums and albums by others on his Homecoming label starting in the '80s. —*William Ruhlmann*

● **California Bloodlines/Willard Minus 2** / 1969-1970 / Bear Family ✦✦✦✦
This German import contains some of Stewart's most powerful work. *California Bloodlines* offers 12 original tunes backed by Nashville's finest studio musicians. *Willard Minus 2*, though not so powerful as *Bloodlines*, still features many great songs (two tracks missing from the original) and a good cast of musicians. Highly recommended. —*Chip Renner*

Lonesome Picker Rides Again / 1971 / Warner Brothers ✦✦✦
Good collection of music, with more energy than his first two records. —*Chip Renner*

Sunstorm Live 1972 / 1972 / Bear Family ✦✦✦
Featuring Russ Kunkel, James Burton, Buddy Emmons, and brother Michael Stewart. Contains the song "Kansas Rain." A good, solid release. —*Chip Renner*

Cannons in the Rain/Wingless Angel / 1973-1975 / Bear Family ✦✦✦✦
In this two-fer (*Cannons in the Rain/Wingless Angels*) the *Wingless Angels* release is the stronger collection, featuring Robert "Waddy" Wachtel on guitar and a guest appearance by John Denver. *Cannons...* is a nice collection of ballads and folk-rock. —*Chip Renner*

Complete Phoenix Concerts / 1974 / Bear Family ✦✦✦✦
A great collection of live music covering Stewart's first five albums. —*Chip Renner*

Trancas / 1984 / Affordable Dreams ✦✦✦
Stewart's electric guitar is nicely backed by touches of strings, drums, keyboards, and synthesized sounds. This album is positive in content and easy listening. —*Chip Renner*

The Last Campaign / 1985 / Homecoming ✦✦✦
Influenced by Robert Kennedy's campaign for president, the songs paint a tapestry of America. Very good. —*Chip Renner*

Secret Tapes '86 / 1986 / Homecoming ✦✦✦
An 80-minute tape featuring songs recorded in Stewart's studio. Includes "California Bloodlines," "Chilly Winds," "Cheyenne," "The River." A must for any serious collector. —*Chip Renner*

Secret Tapes II / 1986 / Homecoming ✦✦✦
Another collection, featuring "A Grace of Rain," "Seven Angels," "Tears of the Sun," "Quarter Moon on the Golden Gate," and "Irresistible Targets." Another must-have for the serious collector. —*Chip Renner*

Punch the Big Guy / 1987 / Cypress ✦✦✦✦
An exceptional release. Stewart stands out on electric guitar with minimal backup. Bela Fleck, Sam Bush, and Pat Flynn (New Grass Revival), along with Roseanne Cash, Edgar Meyers, Brent Rowan, and others add just enough, but do not take away from Stewart's sound. Great job on "Runaway Trains." A classic. —*Chip Renner*

Neon Beach / 1991 / Line ✦✦✦
Over 60 minutes of great live music, featuring some old and new favorites: "Angels with Guns," "Lady Came from Baltimore," "Seven Angels," "Gold Medley," and "Bad Rats." Stewart's talking between songs is insightful. —*Chip Renner*

Deep in the Neon: Live at McCabe's / Jun. 1991 / Homecoming ✦✦✦
Deep in the Neon—Live at McCabe's features just Stewart and Dave Batti and 16 well-performed songs. The audience is into the show, and Stewart plays an easy and relaxed, quiet set. —*Chip Renner*

● **Turning Love into Gold: The Best Of** / 1995 / Polydor ✦✦✦✦

The Story

Vocalist/guitarist/pianist Jonatha Brooke met vocalist Jennifer Kimball at Amherst College, where both were English majors. They later relocated to Boston and shopped their demo around until they received an independent release of their first album, *Grace in Gravity*. Elektra signed the duo and issued *The Angel in the House* in 1993. *—John Bush*

● **Grace in Gravity** / 1992 / Green Linnet ✦✦✦✦
The interweaving, intuitive harmonies of the Story's Jonatha Brooke and Jennifer Kimball are mesmerizingly beautiful. Add a top-notch, sympathetic band (guitarist Duke Levine, bassist Mike Rivard, keyboardist Alain Mallet, and drummer/producer Ben Wittman) and a bunch of probing, emotional songs, and the result is this heartfelt release. Folk-pop music of the highest calibre and a great live act. *—Roundup Newsletter*

Angel in Our House / 1993 / Asylum ✦✦✦
Here are more intricate harmonies from the Story's Boston-based duo. The level of jazz influence and art music has been increased to good effect. It's not as accessible as *Gravity* but is quite good. *—Richard Meyer*

Tamarack

From its Ontario base, Tamarack has been exploring Canada's history through song for more than 15 years. This popular trio, dubbed the "Peter, Paul, and Mary of Canada," travels their land, singing about the fishermen and farmers, whalers and wilderness guides, trappers and tourists, immigrants and natives, and passing Americans. Tamarack is made up of founding member James Gordon, Alex Sinclair, and Carole LeClaire. The first two are from Ontario, and Carole adds the rich maritime music tradition to the mix. Lots of good songs and some unusual views of the history of North America. *—Mike Fleischer*

Frobisher Bay / 1993 / Folk Era ✦✦✦

● **Fields of Rock and Snow** / Jul. 1993 / Folk Era Productions ✦✦✦✦

Tamarack on the Grand / Folk Era ✦✦✦

Eric Taylor

Guitar, Vocals / Folk, Singer-Songwriter
Although a Georgia native, Eric Taylor found fame in Texas, where his folksinging influenced both Lyle Lovett and Nanci Griffith (both of whom have recorded his songs). Taylor got a ride to Houston in 1970 and after seeing Lightnin' Hopkins and Townes Van Zandt was convinced to stay. He emerged from the Houston folk scene of the '70s with Van Zandt and Guy Clark; despite local fame, his full-scale national debut on Watermelon Records wasn't released until August 1995. The self-titled album (produced by Iain Matthews and Mark Hallman) included backing vocals from Lovett and help from many Texas musicians. *—John Bush*

Shameless Love / 1981 / Featherbed ✦✦✦✦
Every song is good on this album. The acoustic guitar blends with Taylor's voice, and Nanci Griffith sings nice harmony on several songs. This is a recommended album for the singer-songwriter's fans. *—Chip Renner*

● **Eric Taylor** / 1995 / Watermelon ✦✦✦✦
Eric Taylor has become something of a legendary reclusive songwriter by way of Nanci Griffith's recordings. Regarded as a writer's writer, this is Taylor's first commercial release. The lyrics are detailed short stories in the vein of Michael Smith. Taylor always seems to respect the human dignity of his characters. Produced by Iain Matthews, this album has a clean, intimate, modern country sound which never gets in the way of the singer. Highlights are "Deadwood," "Visitors from Indiana," and "Hemingway's Shotgun." *—Richard Meyer*

Art Thieme

Banjo, Guitar, Vocals
Thieme is a one-man skiffle band. His main instruments are guitar and banjo, but he plays everything from the saw to the jew's harp to the nose flute, as well as another dozen or so weird gadgets. None of them, however, is as weird as his sense of humor. *—Don Stevens*

★ **On the Wilderness Road** / Folk Legacy ✦✦✦✦✦

Aileen and Elkin Thomas

Folk
A Texas-based duo, the Thomases bid fair to become the South's answer to Ian and Sylvia, with a robust mix of folk and country sounds and clean, pleasing voices that meld beautifully. *—Bruce Eder*

Arise, We Must Be Growing / Shantih ✦✦✦✦
A gorgeous collection of material, alternately upbeat, sentimental, and serious, with Charlie Daniels sitting in on guitar and bass. A sweet and low-keyed mid-'80s folk/country gem. *—Bruce Eder*

Artie Traum

b. 1943
Banjo, Guitar, Vocals / Folk, Singer-Songwriter
Artie Traum is a singer-songwriter based in Woodstock, NY. Born in the Bronx, he followed his brother Happy into folk music in the early '60s in the New York area, taking guitar lessons from jazz artists. He and his brother formed the folk-rock group the Children of Paradise in the mid-'60s and, after Happy's departure, they changed their name to Bear and recorded an album for Verve/Forecast. Traum moved to Woodstock in 1967 and has worked as a record producer and written film soundtracks. He has also recorded albums with his brother and with the Woodstock Mountain Revue. *—William Ruhlmann*

● **Life on Earth** / 1974 / Rounder ✦✦✦✦
A fine album with Pat Alger, featuring "Is There Life on Earth," "Girls of Montreal," and "Riptide." *—Chip Renner*

From the Heart / 1980 / Rounder ✦✦✦✦
Traum and Pat Alger were meant to play together. Highlights include "Gambling Man," "City Lights," and "Screwin' It Up." *—Chip Renner*

Cayenne / 1986 / Rounder ✦✦✦✦
Artie Traum is a fine acoustic guitarist, but this release is more a showcase for his technical skills than a thoughtful or gripping effort. The 12 numbers are so short (none longer than four minutes) that frequently all Traum can do is present an opening melody, improvise briefly, and complete the track. The numbers are mostly on the light/impressionistic side, creating an atmosphere close to background caliber. *—Ron Wynn*

Letters from Joubee / 1993 / Shanachie ✦✦✦

View from Here / Feb. 20, 1996 / Shanachie ✦✦✦
Artie Traum's second foray into jazz is less of a new age-oriented effort than its predecessor, *Letters From Joubee*. It is a confident, highly produced effort that can be classified as "contemporary jazz," which is to say that it is an eclectic mix taking in everything from a cover of Stevie Wonder's "Superwoman" to tunes with a Latin feel like "Abracadabra" and even several vocalists, best-known among them Michael Franks. Playing steel- and nylon-string acoustic guitars, Traum takes the melody lines and a lot of solos on a series of engaging songs, leaving room for accompanists like David Sancious and Warren Bernhardt, notably on "Ferry To Panarea," which is closer to a straight-ahead jazz number. If this keeps up, Artie Traum will have to be moved out of the Folk section. *—William Ruhlmann*

Happy Traum

b. 1939
Banjo, Guitar, Vocals
Happy Traum is a singer-songwriter based in Woodstock, NY, who served as editor of *Sing Out!* magazine for three years and runs Homespun Tapes, a company that sells instructional tapes narrated by well-known folk and rock musicians for aspiring musicians. Born in the Bronx, Traum attended the High School of Music and Art, where he took up music and was drawn into the folk music boom of the late '50s. He was a member of the New World Singers and formed a folk-rock band in the mid-'60s called the Children of Paradise with his brother Artie, Eric Kaz, and others. He moved to Woodstock in 1967. Traum conducted one of the first interviews Bob Dylan granted after the 1966 motorcycle accident, and in October 1971 he recorded several tracks with Dylan that appeared on *Bob Dylan's Greatest Hits, Volume II.* He has made solo albums, records with his brother, and recordings with the Woodstock Mountain Revue. *—William Ruhlmann*

Doubleback / 1971 / Capitol ✦✦✦
A nice album featuring Artie Traum, Bill Keith, Amos Garrett, Eric Kaz, Billy Sanford, and Buddy Spicher. *—Chip Renner*

Hard Times in the Country / 1975 / Rounder ✦✦✦✦
Artie Traum, Paul Butterfield, Roly Salley, Arlen Roth, Pat Alger, and Jim Rooney blend nicely. Great covers of "Blow Your Whistle," "Freight Train," and "Penny's Farm." *—Chip Renner*

Relax Your Mind / 1976 / Kicking Mule ✦✦✦
Traditional fingerpicking guitar styles. Good covers of "John Henry" and "Worried Blues." *—Chip Renner*

● **Bright Morning Stars** / 1980 / Greenhays ✦✦✦✦
A fine collection of music and friends makes this special. With Pat Alger, Merle Watson, John Sebastian, Richard Manuel, Maria Muldaur, and Artie Traum. *—Chip Renner*

Bucket of Songs / 1983 / Shanachie ✦✦✦
This pleasing collection of covers and instrumentals is performed with some of the Mud Acres Gang, Andy Robinson, Pat Alger, and Rolly Sally. This is a compilation up to earlier Kicking Mule LPs. *—Richard Meyer*

Ed Trickett

Dulcimer, Guitar, Vocals
Ed is known as a song interpreter. On his day job, he is a professor of psychology. He looks for the hidden truths in songs and sings them to us in a manner that gives new meaning to old songs. Usually playing guitar and singing in a very gentle manner, he is also an accomplished piano player. He has recorded alone, with Anne Mayo Muir and Gordon Bok, and others. —*Don Stevens*

● **On a Day Like Today** / Folk-Legacy ✦✦✦✦

Greg Trouper

Guitar, Vocals / Singer-Songwriter
This Brooklyn-based singer-songwriter has had his songs covered by many other artists, including Maura O'Connell and Tom Russell. He collaborates and writes in Nashville but remains in NY. His style is commercial but driving. It's guitar-based '60s folk-rock with a '90s sensibility and thoughtfulness. He's a great performer of his own tunes. —*Richard Meyer*

Everywhere / 1992 / Black Hole ✦✦✦✦
Songwriter Greg Trouper's independent CD with his band the Flatirons contains great examples of his thoughtful commercial style. Key tracks here are the title cut, "Ireland," and "Blind Spot." —*Richard Meyer*

Sylvia Tyson

Guitar, Autoharp, Vocals
From her days as half of the Canadian folk duet Ian and Sylvia to today's career as a solo performer, Sylvia Tyson has lost none of the singing power and songwriting muscle that made her a household word. Collaborations with Tom Russell, Colleen Peterson, and Shirley Eikhard have simply added to her strengths. On this, her first album in several years, Sylvia returns to her rightful spot as a respected performer and songwriter. —*Allan Shaw*

Gypsy Cadillac / Folk Era ✦✦✦✦
Here's a new vehicle for fans to ride in. —*Mike Fleischer*

Dave Van Ronk

b. Jun. 30, 1936, Brooklyn, NY
Guitar, Vocals / Singer-Songwriter
Guitarist, singer, songwriter, and native New Yorker Dave Van Ronk has inspired, aided, and promoted the careers of numerous singer-songwriters who came up in the blues tradition. Most notable of the many musicians he's helped over the years is Bob Dylan, whom Van Ronk got to know shortly after Dylan moved to New York in 1961 to pursue a life as a folk/blues singer.

Van Ronk's recorded output over the years is healthy, but he's never been as prolific a songwriter as some of his friends from that era, like Dylan or Tom Paxton. Instead, the genius of what Van Ronk does lies in his flawless execution and rearranging of classic acoustic blues tunes.

Born June 30, 1936, in Brooklyn and raised there, Van Ronk never completed high school. He left home for Greenwich Village as a teenager. Van Ronk's recording career began in 1959 with *Ballads, Blues and a Spiritual* on the Moses Asch's Folkways label. He took his inspiration from Odetta, who encouraged the then-merchant seaman to play the classic jazz music that he was so keenly interested in.

Van Ronk, an expert finger picker, was influenced as a vocalist by Bing Crosby and Louis Armstrong. Although he had a short-lived folk-rock band called the Hudson Dusters in the mid-'60s, the bulk of Van Ronk's recordings are solo acoustic affairs. His 1967 album for Verve Forecast, *Dave Van Ronk and the Hudson Dusters*, is worthy of reissue on compact disc for its sound qualities and for the statements it makes about American society in the '60s.

Often regarded as the grand uncle of the Greenwich Village coffeehouse scene, the self-effacing Van Ronk, an engaging intellectual and voracious reader, would be the first to tell you that there were others, like blues and folk singer Odetta, who were around Greenwich Village before him. As the blues and folk boom bloomed into the '60s, Van Ronk became part of an inner circle of musicians who then lived in Greenwich Village, including then up and coming performers like Bob Dylan, Tom Paxton, Phil Ochs, Ramblin' Jack Elliott and Joni Mitchell.

Van Ronk's reputation wasn't solid, however, until he began recording for Prestige in the first half of the '60s. These recordings allowed him to tour the US and perform at major folk festivals like Newport.

Different recordings of Van Ronk's serve different purposes. To check out Van Ronk the songwriter, pick up *Going Back to Brooklyn* (Gazell Productions, 1985), which was his first all-original album, containing only his own songs; for students of Van Ronk's complex guitar technique, pick up *Dave Van Ronk*, a compact disc reissue of two earlier Prestige albums, *Dave Van Ronk, Folksinger* and *Inside Dave Van Ronk*. Another

compilation, *The Folkways Years, 1959-1961*, is available from Smithsonian/Folkways in Washington, D.C.

Van Ronk continues to record, and the Alcazar Records label released *From . . . Another Time and Place* in 1995. He continues to be a favorite at large folk festivals throughout the US, Canada, and Europe. —*Richard Skelly*

And the Ragtime Jug Stompers / 1960 / Mercury ✦✦✦
This wild and unrestrained collection of blues, jazz, and blues standards makes Van Ronk's *Red Onion* album sound positively subdued. The rave-up of "Everybody Loves My Baby" is an acoustic equivalent of garage bands-to-come for sheer energy. You can tell that he loves these tunes; and in the notes, Van Ronk says he had been planning to start a jug band since 1958. (There is no © date on this LP.) —*Richard Meyer*

Sings the Blues / 1961 / Verve Forcast ✦✦✦
Like the LP *Just Dave Van Ronk*, this is a mostly solo collection, though his approach is a bit more aggressive. He more deliberately uses the rough qualities of his voice to take on the characters that populate the songs. Some of the best of these elastic performances are "Dink's Song," "Hesitation Blues," and "Come Back Baby," which every budding guitarist in the '60s was obliged to learn. —*Richard Meyer*

With the Red Onion Jazz Band / 1963 / Prestige ✦✦✦✦
Most people think of Van Ronk as a folk singer, and that is the community he has been most a part of, but he has always thought of himself as a jazz singer. On this album from his early career he shows why. Van Ronk offers up exuberant performances of "Cake Walkin' Babies from Home" and "Ace in the Hole." There are some solo guitar songs such as Son House's "Death Letter Blues," and even a Bob Dylan tune, "If I Had to Do It All Over Again, I'd Do It All Over You." This record and its others which have not made the jump to CD are hard to find, but they're well worth picking up. —*Richard Meyer*

Just Dave Van Ronk / 1964 / Mercury ✦✦✦✦
Solo guitar and vocal interpretations of blues and traditional standards. Van Ronk's understated guitar style is perfect for these intimate performances. His naturally rough voice allows him to sing these songs believably, without any ethnic affectation or false energy. —*Richard Meyer*

Dave Van Ronk and the Hudson Dusters / 1967 / Verve Forcast ✦✦✦✦
The sound on this album is reminiscent of the New York folk-rock band the Blues Project. It begins with a ragged rendition of the Hollywood Argyles' "Alley Oop" and ranges from that doo wop chestnut to Joni Mitchell's "Chelsea Morning and Clouds" to "Romping Through the Swamp." More familiar Van Ronk territory is covered also, with reprise performances of "Dink's Song" and "Cocaine." Van Ronk always brings his enthusiastic roar to his material and makes it his own. His rendition of "Swing on a Star" is but one example. The Hudson Dusters seem to be a combination electric jug band, folk orchestra, and bubblegum band, as on "Mr. Middle." A strange collection. —*Richard Meyer*

● **Inside Dave Van Ronk** / 1969 / Fantasy ✦✦✦✦
This CD reissue includes both the 1962 album of the same name and the *Folksinger* LP (recorded around the same time), encompassing 25 tracks in all. It is certainly Van Ronk's most enduring work and one of the few relics of the early-'60s traditional folk boom that holds up well today. With the possible exception of Bob Dylan (whom Van Ronk and his wife helped immensely when Dylan was a struggling unknown in New York), Van Ronk was the finest interpreter of traditional folk tunes of that time, with a big bear of a voice that was both anguished and tender. One of the few White folkies who could sing acoustic blues without embarrassment, Van Ronk was also an accomplished acoustic guitar picker. Instrumentally and vocally, he brought an intensity to his covers that made the songs his own. Of the two albums on this CD, *Inside* has the edge because of its more varied instrumentation, including 12-string guitar, dulcimer, and autoharp (*Folksinger* has only vocals and guitar). Dominated by classics like "Motherless Child," "Silver Dagger," "Poor Lazarus," and "Fixin' To Die," this also has an arrangement of "He Was a Friend of Mine" that Van Ronk learned from Dylan, who apparently claimed the traditional song as his own at the time. —*Richie Unterberger*

☆ **Folkways Years (1959-1961)** / 1991 / Smithsonian/Folkways ✦✦✦✦✦
Van Ronk sums up this album well with his own notes. "I never really thought of myself as a 'folksinger' at all. Still don't. What I did was to combine traditional fingerpicking guitar with a repertoire of old jazz tunes." On this album Van Ronk covers folk and blues songs such as "Hesitation Blues," "Twelve Gates to the City," and Spike Dreiver's "Moan." —*Richard Meyer*

Hesitation Blues / Big Beat ✦✦✦✦
Good compilation of 16 songs from three '60s Prestige LPs (*Folksinger, In the Tradition*, and *Inside Dave Van Ronk*) that probably represent his peak as a recording artist. Most of the songs appear on the 25-track Fantasy CD *Inside Dave Van Ronk*, which repackages his first and third LPs together, and remains a better first purchase. —*Richie Unterberger*

Going Back to Brooklyn / 1985 / Gazell ✦✦✦
This is an album unusual in that it contains only Van Ronk originals. It's a solo album and it's great to hear his irreverent tunes, such as "Losers," "Tantric Mantra," and "Zen Koans Gonna Rise Again," as well as the bittersweet "Another Time and Place." —*Richard Meyer*

Townes Van Zandt

b. March 7, 1944, Fort Worth, TX
Guitar, Vocals / Folk, Country-Rock, Singer-Songwriter
Townes Van Zandt's music doesn't jump up and down, wear fancy clothes, or beat around the bush. Whether he's singing a quiet, introspective country-folk song or a driving, hungry blues, Van Zandt's lyrics and melodies are filled with the kind of haunting truth and beauty that you know instinctively. His music comes straight from his soul by way of a kind heart, an honest mind, and a keen ear for the gentle blend of words and melody. He can bring you down to a place so sad that you feel you're scraping bottom, but just as quickly he can lift your spirits and make you smile or raise a chuckle.

Despite his warm, dusty-sweet voice, as a singer Townes has never had anything resembling a hit in his nearly 30-year recording career; he's had a hard enough time simply keeping his records in print. Nonetheless he's widely respected and admired as one of the greatest country and folk artists of this generation. The long list of singers who've covered his songs includes Merle Haggard and Willie Nelson (who had a No. 1 country hit with "Pancho and Lefty" in 1983), Emmylou Harris, Jimmie Dale Gilmore, Nanci Griffith, Hoyt Axton, Bobby Bare, the Tindersticks, and the Cowboy Junkies.

Van Zandt is a Texan by birth and a traveler by nature. His father was in the oil business, and the family moved around a lot, which accounts for his sometimes vague answers to questions of where he "comes from." He spent a couple of years in a military academy and a bit more time in college in Colorado before dropping out to become a folksinger.

Van Zandt moved to Houston and got his first paying gigs on the folk music circuit there in the mid-'60s. He played clubs like Sand Mountain and the Old Quarter (where in 1973 he recorded one of his finest albums, *Live at the Old Quarter*, released four years later), and he met singers such as Guy Clark (who became a lifelong friend and frequent road partner), Jerry Jeff Walker, and blues legend Lightnin' Hopkins, who's had a large influence on Van Zandt's guitar playing.

Another Texas songwriter, Mickey Newbury, saw Van Zandt in Houston one night and soon had him set up with a recording gig in Nashville (with Jack Clement producing). The sessions became Van Zandt's debut album, *For the Sake of the Song*, released in 1968 by Poppy Records. The next five years were the most prolific of Townes' career, as Poppy released the albums *Our Mother the Mountain*, *Townes Van Zandt*, *Delta Mama Blues*, *High, Low and In-Between*, and *The Late, Great Townes Van Zandt*.

Van Zandt moved to Nashville in 1976 at the urging of his new manager, John Lomax. He signed with Tomato Records and in 1977 released *Live at the Old Quarter*, a double album—and the first of several live recordings—that contained many of his finest songs. In 1978 Tomato released *Flyin' Shoes;* players on that album included Chips Moman and Spooner Oldham.

Van Zandt didn't record again for nearly a decade, but he continued to tour. He moved back to Texas briefly, returning to Nashville in the mid-'80s. During the early '80s both "If I Needed You" and "Pancho and Lefty" became country radio hits. In 1987 he was back in business with his eighth studio album, *At My Window*, which came out on his new label, Sugar Hill. By this time Townes' voice had dropped to a lower register, but the weathered, somewhat road-weary edge to it was as pure and expressive as ever. Two years later Sugar Hill released *Live and Obscure* (recorded in a Nashville club in 1985), and two more live albums (*Rain on a Conga Drum* and *Rear View Mirror*) appeared on European labels in the early '90s. In 1990, he toured with the Cowboy Junkies, and he wrote a song for them, "Cowboy Junkies' Lament," which appeared on the group's *Black Eyed Man* album.

Sugar Hill released *Road Songs* in 1994, on which Van Zandt covered songs by Lightnin' Hopkins, Bruce Springsteen, and the Rolling Stones all recorded off the sound board during recent concerts. At the end of that year, Sugar Hill released *No Deeper Blue*, his first studio album since 1987.

In the late '80s, he was working on re-recording 60 of his songs for a planned career retrospective for Tomato Records. The collection, however, has yet to be released. —*Kurt Wolff*

For the Sake of the Song/First Album / 1968 / Poppy ✦✦✦
The original versions of the title track, "Sad Cinderella," and "Waitin' Around to Die." An essential album for anyone interested in contemporary songwriting. (Originally released in December 1968 by Poppy Records as *For the Sake of the Song* was reissued under the title *First Album* by Rhino Records in 1993.) —*Richard Meyer*

Our Mother the Mountain / 1969 / Tomato ✦✦✦✦
Featured are small-band performances and another set of Van Zandt's intimate songs. —*Richard Meyer*

Townes Van Zandt / 1969 / Tomato ✦✦✦
On his third album, Townes Van Zandt recut three trucial tracks from his debut album, "For the Sake of the Song," "Waiting Around To Die," and "I'll Be Here in the Morning." It was some indication of the obscurity in which he remained enveloped, but no indication of the quality of his work. As usual, his closely observed lyrics touched on desperate themes, notably in the mining ballad "Lungs," but they were still highly poetic, especially the album-closing "None But the Rain," which reflected on a failed relationship. Van Zandt's finger-picking was augmented by spare arrangements, usually featuring one added instrument for color, such as a fiddle or flute. (Originally released by Poppy Records in 1969, *Townes Van Zandt* was reissued by Tomato Records in 1989.) —*William Ruhlmann*

Delta Momma Blues / 1971 / Tomato ✦✦✦
Townes Van Zandt's dour viewpoint found more expression on his fourth album, its most characteristic song being "Come Tomorrow," on which he looked forward to how lonely life would be when his lover left. Even "Brand New Companion," which hailed the arrival of a lover, was done as a blues. "Here's to feeling good," he sang in "Only Him or Me," then added, "Here's to feeling bad." But, as usual, what made so compelling was that, in songs like "Rake" and "Nothin'," he painted despair so vividly. (Originally released by Poppy Records in 1971, *Delta Momma Blues* was reissued by Tomato Records in 1989.) —*William Ruhlmann*

High, Low and in Between / 1972 / Rhino ✦✦✦✦
The lead-off track, "Two Hands," is an uptempo gospel number featuring piano and backup vocals. Van Zandt returns to religion in the country waltz "When He Offers His Hand," sings rock 'n' roll with a harmony vocal on "Standin'," tries a martial beat worthy of Johnny Cash on the gambling story song "Mr. Gold and Mr. Mudd." The musical variety makes *High, Low and in Between* a more interesting listen than Van Zandt's previous work, but what makes it his best album since his debut is the quality of the songs, especially "You Are Not Needed Now" and "To Live Is to Fly." (Originally released by Poppy Records in 1972, *High Low And In Between* was reissued by Tomato Records in 1989.) —*William Ruhlmann*

The Late, Great Townes Van Zandt / 1972 / Tomato ✦✦✦✦
On his sixth album in five years, Townes Van Zandt seemed to be getting less prolific, but his songwriting craft only improved. Van Zandt rerecorded yet another track from his debut album, "Sad Cinderella," and did three cover tunes, including one by main influence Hank Williams. But among the remaining seven new originals were "Pancho and Lefty," a sly Western story song about two outlaws, and "If I Needed You," among his most telling romantic statements. The two songs would become valuable copyrights for Van Zandt, and they made this oddly titled album one of his best, which was good since, as it happened, it would be his last release for five years. (Originally released by Poppy Records in 1972, *The Late, Great Townes Van Zandt* was reissued by Tomato Records in 1989.) —*William Ruhlmann*

★ **Live at the Old Quarter (Houston, Texas)** / 1977 / Tomato ✦✦✦✦✦
Townes Van Zandt is one of the most impressive songwriters to emerge in the '70s, and his extensive catalog is sufficiently consistent to be recommended in its entirety, once the listener has acquired a taste for his spare, dry delivery and gallows humor. The place to get that taste is on this live disc (originally a two-LP set), which features the best of Van Zandt's early songs, including "If I Needed You" and "Pancho and Lefty." —*William Ruhlmann*

Flyin' Shoes / 1978 / Rhino ✦✦✦
His songs are a bit overburdened by production, but the writing is still great. —*Richard Meyer*

At My Window / 1987 / Sugar Hill ✦✦✦✦
Van Zandt's first album after a long layoff found him in a more accessible musical setting, courtesy of producers Jack Clement and Jim Rooney, with his striking lyrical observations intact. Van Zandt's qualities are sometimes subtle, and this is an album that gets better every time it's listened to. —*William Ruhlmann*

Live and Obscure / 1989 / Sugar Hill ✦✦✦
Recorded after Van Zandt returned to Nashville in 1985, this album has some of the chestnuts and some obscure material played to an adoring crowd. —*Richard Meyer*

Rear View Mirror / 1993 / Sundown ✦✦✦

The Nashville Sessions / 1993 / Tomato ✦✦✦
When Poppy Records went bankrupt in 1973, it left Townes Van Zandt with two unreleased albums. One was *Live At The Old Quarter, Houston, Texas*, which was released by Tomato, Poppy's successor, in 1977. The other was a studio recording that languished for 20 years until being

issued by Rhino/Tomato in 1993 under the title *The Nashville Sessions*. By that time, Van Zandt had put ten of its 12 songs on such albums as *Live At The Old Quarter, Flyin' Shoes, At My Window,* and *Live and Obscure.* Since six of them turned up on his next studio album, *Flyin' Shoes, The Nashville Sessions* acted as a kind of rough version of that album. Otherwise, one might have suspected that the songs came from before Van Zandt's sixth album, *The Late, Great Townes Van Zandt,* since they seemed to have more in common with his fifth album, *High, Low and in Between.* One of the two previously unheard songs, "Upon My Soul," was similar to the uptempo gospel tunes on that album. One also might have suspected that the songs could be outtakes from the fifth and sixth albums, since they were not quite up to the quality of those records. — *William Ruhlmann*

Roadsongs / 1994 / Sugar Hill ✦✦✦
Here we have one of the great troubadour songwriters on the road performing the songs he admires in his own ragged but right style. It's interesting to hear how these songs sound so much like Townes Van Zandt songs. Key tracks are "Automobile Blues," "Racing in the Streets," and "My Starter Won't Start," one of four Lightnin' Hopkins covers. — *Richard Meyer*

No Deeper Blue / 1995 / Sugar Hill ✦✦✦

Rain on a Conga Drum: Live in Berlin / Nov. 7, 1995 / MMS ✦✦✦✦
This 18-track, 63-minute import disc was Townes Van Zandt's third live album, recorded in October 1990. It shared eight selections with his first, *Live At The Old Quarter, Houston, Texas,* and five with his second, *Live and Obscure.* Distinguishing this set were some interesting covers, including Lightnin' Hopkins' "Short-Haired Woman Blues" and the Rolling Stones' "Dead Flowers," a long, funny story concerning the composition of Van Zandt's most famous song, "Pancho and Lefty," and the otherwise unrecorded original "Catfish Song," a typically poetic and downcast Van Zandt composition. If you didn't have any of Van Zandt's other albums, discovering material like "If I Needed You," "To Live Is to Fly," and "Tecumseh Valley" would be a revelation. — *William Ruhlmann*

Loudon Wainwright III

b. Sep. 5, 1946, Chapel Hill, NC
Guitar, Vocals / Singer-Songwriter
Loudon Wainwright, III, is a singer-songwriter with a humorous, confessional style that has made him a concert favorite and moderately successful recording artist, with almost a dozen albums to his credit. He had a fluke pop hit with "Dead Skunk" in 1973. — *William Ruhlmann*

Album 1 / 1970 / Atlantic ✦✦

Album 2 / 1971 / Atlantic ✦✦✦

Album III / 1972 / Columbia/Legacy ✦✦✦
Wainwright's directly autobiographical songs are both brutally honest and extremely funny. Usually he plays alone, but here he gets a full folk/rock backup, which brings out the pop implications of his music. His fluke hit "Dead Skunk" is here, and so is "Red Guitar," about the destruction of one. — *William Ruhlmann*

Attempted Moustache / 1973 / Columbia ✦✦✦

Unrequited / 1975 / Columbia ✦✦

T Shirt / 1976 / Arista ✦✦✦

Final Exam / 1978 / Arista ✦✦✦

A Live One / 1979 / Rounder ✦✦✦✦
Wainwright is well served by this collection of samples of his live work, which doubles as the best of his '70s material, with songs like "Whatever Happened to Us," "Nocturnal Stumblebutt," and "Clockwork Chartreuse." — *William Ruhlmann*

Fame and Wealth / 1983 / Rounder ✦✦✦
Bitterness and regret become bigger factors in Wainwright's albums in the '80s. This collection shows tremendous personal insight, continuing passion for children (Wainwright may have written more about children than any contemporary singer-songwriter), and a brave humor, holding out against the little defeats of middle age. — *William Ruhlmann*

I'm Alright / 1984 / Rounder ✦✦✦✦

More Love Songs / 1986 / Rounder ✦✦✦✦

Therapy / 1989 / Silvertone ✦✦✦

★ **History** / 1992 / Charisma ✦✦✦✦✦

Career Moves / Jan. 1993 / Virgin ✦✦✦✦
As both a career summary and introduction, the live set *Career Moves* is a delight. Sparkling with the humor that drives Wainwright's concerts, the album features 24 first-class songs showing what a witty, gifted songwriter he is. It's great fun and arguably his best album. — *Stephen Thomas Erlewine*

One Many Guy (1982-86) / 1995 / Music Club ✦✦✦✦

Grown Man / Oct. 1995 / Virgin ✦✦✦

Watersons

Folk
A singing family from Yorkshire, England, the Watersons have been performing and recording unaccompanied harmony singing for years. Martin Carthy married into the family and appears on many of the recordings. If you like a cappella, four-part harmony singing of folk material, you can't do better than this group. — *Steve Winick*

Watersons / 1966 / Topic ✦✦✦
The Watersons was a strong follow-up to *Frost and Fire,* featuring a greater variety of songs. — *Steve Winick*

Yorkshire Garland / 1966 / Topic ✦✦✦
Again, this has variety of songs, but all of them come from Yorkshire. — *Steve Winick*

Bright Phoebus / 1972 / Trailer ✦✦✦
Lal and Mike Waterson recorded this without their other siblings. It features traditional and pop songs, and is worth seeking out. — *Steve Winick*

● **For Pence and Spicey Ale** / 1975 / Shanachie ✦✦✦✦
This lovely album, almost entirely a cappella, was first released by the Watersons in 1975. It is considered by many to be their finest recording and includes the participation of Martin Carty in addition to family members. This reissue also includes some later solo Waterson recordings that feature others helping out. This record sounds like the back room of an old pub in its charming immediacy. You really get a sense of the fun it is to sing these old songs with affection and respect. — *Richard Meyer*

Sound, Sound Your Instruments of Joy / 1977 / Topic ✦✦✦
On this one, they return to one of their first loves: hymns and carols. — *Steve Winick*

True Hearted Girl / 1977 / Topic ✦✦✦
Lal and Norma Waterson, known unofficially as "the Waterdaughters," perform traditional songs solo and in harmony. — *Steve Winick*

Mike Waterson / 1977 / Topic ✦✦✦
Mike Waterson's solo recording features big ballads and other wonderful traditional songs. — *Steve Winick*

Frost and Fire / Elektra ✦✦✦✦
The original LP, a recording of seasonal songs, remains one of their greatest accomplishments. The CD re-release, featuring tracks from *Sound, Sound Your Instruments of Joy,* is indispensable. — *Steve Winick*

The Weavers

Folk
Pete Seeger, Lee Hays, Fred Hellerman, and Ronnie Gilbert formed the Weavers in 1948 to sing folk music in harmony. The group got its big break at a two-week gig at the Village Vanguard in New York City at Christmas 1949; the gig lasted six months. The Weavers were signed to Decca and scored a double-sided hit in the summer of 1950 with "Tzena, Tzena, Tzena," which went to No. 2, and "Goodnight Irene," which topped the charts for 13 weeks, one of the biggest hits of the first half of the century. More hits followed through 1952, but then the Weavers fell afoul of the Communist scare of that decade, and their career declined precipitously. They came back, however, at a Carnegie Hall concert in 1955 that is remembered as the birth of the late-'50s/early-'60s folk boom. They toured and recorded successfully for Vanguard. Seeger left in 1958, replaced by a succession of good musicians: Frank Hamilton, Bernie Krause, and Erik Darling. In 1963 the Weavers (with Seeger and his replacements onstage) staged a reunion and farewell at Carnegie Hall. There was a final reunion and farewell of the original four at the hall in 1980. In addition to their considerable musical accomplishments, the Weavers are remembered as popularizers of folk music and as the inspiration for a whole generation of folk performers. — *William Ruhlmann*

☆ **The Weavers at Carnegie Hall** / Dec. 1956 / Vanguard ✦✦✦✦✦
The Weavers made a dramatic comeback from the McCarthy era at their 1955 Christmas Eve Carnegie Hall concert, immortalized here. Many of the songs are from the pop-star days—"Kisses Sweeter Than Wine," "Goodnight Irene"—but backed only by guitar and banjo, they are fresh and stirring. — *William Ruhlmann*

Greatest Hits / 1957 / Vanguard ✦✦✦✦
This is an excellent double-disc compilation of this group's more directly folk-related work from the mid-'50s to the mid-'60s. Note, however, that these are not the original Weavers' recordings of their hits. — *William Ruhlmann*

Together Again / 1984 / Loom ✦✦✦
After years apart, the Weavers played together one last time at—where else?—Carnegie Hall in November 1980. Lee Hays was ailing (he would die the following year), but the show still transcended nostalgia, demonstrating their individual and collective talents and proving they were still a seminal folk ensemble. — *William Ruhlmann*

★ **The Best of the Weavers** / 1987 / MCA ◆◆◆◆◆
The recording career of the Weavers falls into two categories: pre-black-list and post-blacklist. In their pre-blacklist days, they recorded for Decca (now MCA), and their adaptations of folk songs were backed by orchestras and choruses. Frequently, these songs (notably "Goodnight Irene") were giant pop hits. This two-album set captures 24 examples of this quasi-folk pop style, and though the group's singing is excellent, the arrangements, intended to modernize the material, now sound quaintly dated. —*William Ruhlmann*

☆ **Wasn't That a Time** / Sep. 1993 / Vanguard ◆◆◆◆◆
Wasn't That a Time! is a treasure for serious Weavers fans. Featuring 87 songs on its four discs, including several unreleased numbers, the box set is designed for devoted fans; the liner notes are filled with anecdotes and photos that provide a good portrait of the group. For some casual fans, it might be a bit too much, but *Wasn't That a Time!* is a fitting tribute to the seminal folk group. —*Stephen Thomas Erlewine*

Kisses Sweeter Than Wine / 1994 / Vanguard/Omega ◆◆◆◆
This two-disc live set is drawn from vintage concerts by the original Weavers from the early to mid-'50s. It captures them at the height of their fame and during the chilly era of McCarthyism. It's a good example of how the political leanings (perceived or real) of the performers color essentially neutral material. The performances themselves sound immediate and not at all dated. It's great to hear the vocal blend and commitment to a world of songwriting rarely equaled since the Weavers broke up. Ford Hellerman, who compiled this album from a variety of previously unreleased sources including concerts at Town Hall, has left in many of the song's introductions and comments among the group. The hits are here in new versions that stand up well to the "standard" versions. There are 11 songs never released in any form on Weavers records. As an added bonus and not mentioned on the package anywhere is the inclusion of a third CD of previously unreleased material by Leadbelly recorded in 1947. He performs a dozen driving blues songs, including "Howard Hughes," "Hangman's Blues," and "Black Betty," and it sounds great. —*Richard Meyer*

Dick Weissman

Banjo, Guitar
Before Bela Fleck and Tony Trischka began experimenting with jazz on the banjo, Dick Weissman was a master. He has stretched the boundaries of the folk idiom; his most recent features bluegrass icons Tim and Molly O'Brien and jazz saxophonist Bob Rebholz. All originals too. —*Allan Shaw*

New Traditions / Folk Era ◆◆◆◆

Gillian Welch

Guitar, Vocals / Singer-Songwriter
Gillian Welch is a singer-songwriter from Los Angeles who mixes elements of country, folk, and bluegrass with simple, straightforward lyrics. She was raised in Los Angeles and became interested in music through her parents, who composed music for TV shows and contributed a great deal to "The Carol Burnett Show." Welch learned to play drums, piano, ukulele, and guitar as a child, but didn't really experience a musical epiphany until she attended college in Santa Cruz during the mid-'80s. She discovered a local bluegrass group called Harmony Grits, from whom she learned a great deal about the music's traditions, and began writing songs. Her efforts coalesced on her 1995 debut, the aptly titled *Revival*. —*Steve Huey*

● **Revival** / Apr. 1996 / Geffen ◆◆◆◆
Gillian Welch's debut album, *Revival*, looks to be one of the strongest artistic introductions of the year. Produced by T Bone Burnett, *Revival* could be lifted from some long lost Depression Era folk recording. Welch sings with a focused austerity, bypassing any modern conceits to concentrate on songs about the rudiments of life: survival, heartbreak, struggle, honesty, natural beauty. The closest thing to decadence comes when a dying man asks that his still be burned down, turning to ash the bane of his life. The closest thing to optimism comes in a song about a fragile mountain flower's ability to endure the elements. Welch may be accused of losing herself in the styles of the past; her music evokes the primitive yet aesthetically timeless work of the Carter Family and the Stanley Brothers. But such an argument becomes empty when hearing the deep passion, and compassion of Welch's songs. From the astringent quality of her voice to the bare beauty of her melodies to the resourceful moodiness of guitarist David Rawlings, Welch comes on like a rare and precious talent with a vision so set and strong that it can't be denied. —*Michael McCall*

Harry and Jeanie West

Years ahead of the folk revival Harry and Jeanie West were singing and recording beautiful traditional folk songs. They are as well known for dazzling instrumentals as for beautiful harmonizing and selection of

songs. They specialize in "heart of mine" songs and sing gospel in the old-time way. In addition to collecting vintage instruments, they operate an instrument business, concentrating on hand-picked vintage instruments. —*Don Stevens*

● **Smoky Mountain Ballads** / Esoteric ◆◆◆◆

Cheryl Wheeler

Guitar, Vocals / Folk
Wheeler is a gifted songwriter and singer. Her song "Addicted" was a hit by Dan Seals. —*Chip Renner*

● **Cheryl Wheeler** / 1986 / North Star ◆◆◆◆
Her debut album features her hit "Addicted," and is more rock 'n' roll than her other albums. If you like the rest, add this to the collection. —*Chip Renner*

Circles and Arrows / 1990 / Capitol ◆◆◆◆
Wheeler shines on this CD. Guests include Mark O'Connor, Jerry Douglas, Jonathan Edwards, and Billy Joe Walker. Every song is a winner, especially "Northern Girl," "Aces," and "I Know This Town." —*Chip Renner*

Half a Book / 1991 / Cypress ◆◆◆

Driving Home / 1993 / Philo ◆◆◆
On *Driving Home* Cheryl Wheeler has finally got the natural-sounding production that her material needs. Her melodies are highly ornamented and shine through. The distinctive nature of her voice is never overshadowed by synthesized sound as on previous albums. The material is often humorous, as in "Don't Forget the Guns," commercially romantic, as in "Silver Lining," and heartwarmingly beautiful, as in "Arrow." This is an excellent album. —*Richard Meyer*

Mrs. Pinocci's Guitar / Oct. 17, 1995 / Philo ◆◆◆

Josh White

b. Feb. 11, 1908, Greenville, MS, **d.** Sep. 5, 1969
Guitar, Vocals / Folk, Folk-Blues
Most blues enthusiasts think of Josh White (Jr.) as a folk revival artist. It's true that the second half of his music career found him based in New York playing to the coffeehouse and cabaret set and hanging out with Burl Ives, Woody Guthrie, and fellow transplanted blues artists Sonny Terry and Brownie McGhee. When I saw him in Chicago in the '60s his shirt was unbuttoned to his waist à la Harry Belafonte and his repertoire consisted of folk revival standards such as "Scarlet Ribbons." He was a show business personality—a star renowned for his sexual magnetism and his dramatic vocal presentations. What many people don't know is that Josh White was a major figure in the Piedmont blues tradition. The first part of his career saw him as apprentice and lead boy to some of the greatest blues and religious artists ever, including Willie Walker, Blind Blake, Blind Joe Taggert (with whom he recorded), and Blind Lemon Jefferson. On his own, he recorded both blues and religious songs, including a classic version of "Blood Red River." A fine guitar technician with an appealing voice, he became progressively more sophisticated in his presentation. Like many other Carolinians and Virginians who moved north to urban areas, he took up city ways, remaining a fine musician if no longer a down-home artist. Like several other canny blues players, he used his roots music to broaden and enhance his life experience, and his talent was such that he could choose the musical idiom that was most lucrative at the time. —*Barry Lee Pearson*

Jazz Ballads / 1986 / Rykodisc ◆◆◆◆
This is a tribute to Josh White, Sr. —*Michael Erlewine*

Jazz, Ballads and Blues / 1986 / Rykodisc ◆◆◆

● **Blues Singer 1932-1936** / Feb. 6, 1996 / Sony/Legacy ◆◆◆◆
The suave and debonair blues sex symbol in his earliest and purest period, when the Piedmont influence was at its peak in his playing. This is strong stuff, eons away from the collegiate crowd-pleasing folkie stuff he engaged in during the '60s: "Milk Cow Blues," "Lazy Black Snake Blues," and "Silicosis Is Killin' Me" are acoustic solo blues of a consistently high quality, and there are a few religious tunes thrown in to spotlight the other side of White's early recording activities. —*Bill Dahl*

★ **The Legendary Josh White** / MCA ◆◆◆◆◆
This is a two-record set that has a good sampling of White's major songs. —*Michael Erlewine*

Taylor Whiteside

Guitar, Violin, Accordion, Vocals / Singer-Songwriter
This singer-songwriter has his feet firmly planted in the rich musical roots of his native New England, so much so that it's often hard to tell a Whiteside original from a tune that's been around for centuries. A member of the Brandywine Singers and Northeast Winds, Taylor is also in demand as a soloist and studio musician. —*Allan Shaw*

● **Martin Greigh and Other New England Favorites** / 1992 / Folk Era ✦✦✦✦
While Taylor Whiteside may not be a household name, with the captivating *Martin Greigh and Other New England Favorites*, he displays a rare songwriting talent that carefully and seamlessly blends traditional with modern. —*Mike Fleischer*

David Wilcox

Guitar, Vocals / Folk, Singer-Songwriter
The moody, thoughtful songs of David Wilcox are as complex and haunting as his exquisite guitar playing. Among the most popular of the contemporary American folk artists, his style has been compared to both James Taylor and Nick Drake. Subjects for songs range from deeply personal introspection to heartache to anger to sharp humor to newfound joy with family life. Wilcox is an innovative guitarist who loves experimenting with different tunings and with his specially designed capos that cover only part of the strings. He prefers finger-picking but occasionally uses a flatpick.

For someone with as much skill on guitar as Wilcox demonstrates, it could be inferred that he has been practicing hard since childhood, but in truth, he didn't learn to play until he was attending Antioch College in Ohio during the '70s. According to Wilcox it was a young woman playing her guitar in a stairwell who inspired him to begin toying with open tunings. Joni Mitchell's music had great influence on Wilcox, and it was with her songs that he taught himself to play. Other influences include John Martyn, Nick Drake, and Richie Havens. The stairwell woman taught him a few songs, and he also took four formal lessons from a classical guitarist. He dropped out of school for a while to work a series of odd jobs, but eventually returned. Later he moved to Asheville, NC, where he played the regional clubs and bars. He recorded his debut album, *Nightshift Watchman*, for the independent label Song of the Wood. A performance at Nashville's Bluebird Cafe in the late '80s led to his signing with A&M in 1989. After three albums with A&M—*How Did You Find Me Here* (1989), *Home Again* (1991), and *Big Horizon* (1994)—he was dropped from the label. In 1996, he released *East Asheville Hardware*, a collection of previously unreleased live tracks for the Koch label.

Though he frequently tours the US and has earned consistent critical acclaim for his work, Wilcox' reputation remains largely word-of-mouth. He continues to live in Asheville. —*Sandra Brennan*

Nightshift Watchman / 1987 / Song of the Wood ✦✦✦
This debut release shows his earliest work. Worth a listen. —*Chip Renner*

How Did You Find Me Here / 1989 / A&M ✦✦✦✦
Nice songs that, although sometimes sad, are all solid on this sophomore release. —*Chip Renner*

Home Again / 1991 / A&M ✦✦✦
A little more mature and better produced. —*Chip Renner*

Big Horizon / Feb. 8, 1994 / A&M ✦✦
● **East Asheville Hardware** / Feb. 20, 1996 / Koch ✦✦✦✦
For all the recordings they may do, folkies earn their living on the road, and David Wilcox has been doing that long enough to have developed a repertoire of crowd-pleasers that are not the sort of thing he likes to put on his more sober, earnest studio albums. Comic, bawdy, whimsical, sentimental, touching, these songs are in essence novelty material, and it is one of the characteristics of novelty songs that, like jokes, they are at their best the first time you hear them. But now that David Wilcox has been dumped by A&M after failing to go platinum with three albums, he's back to living off the land, and so here are his previously unrecorded live favorites (a few of them written by other people), from Chuck Brodsky's "Blow 'Em Away," a justification for (or maybe just a celebration of) drive-by shootings, to "Mango," perhaps the most straight-spoken song of romantic disappointment since Nilsson's "You're Breakin' My Heart." Physical characteristics ("Top of My Head," "Boob Job"), current events ("Barbie"), and religion ("Carpenter Story") all make appearances, along with a pleasant if aimless nine-minute story song called "Johnny's Camaro," and then there's "Levi Blues," which is about what happens when you put a new pair of jeans in the washing machine with your other clothes. The funny thing is, this album of throwaways may be David Wilcox's best album. It's certainly his most immediately enjoyable. —*William Ruhlmann*

Dar Williams

Guitar, Vocals / Singer-Songwriter
Dar Williams has become a major force on the New England folk scene. An idiosyncratic songwriter who writes folk songs from a unique, often insightful perspective, Williams takes pains to avoid the coy and the quirky; her songwriting and performing style has been compared to that of Joni Mitchell and Joan Baez but with a few acidic and, at times, hilarious twists.

She was born in Mount Kisco, NY, but raised in Chappaqua, the daughter of medical writer/editor Gray Williams and Marian Ferry, an active figure in Planned Parenthood. Her parents were educated at Yale and Vassar, respectively. Raised in a decidedly liberal arts atmosphere, Williams began studying guitar at age nine and wrote her first song at eleven. In high school she was interested in athletics, but an ankle injury led her to audition for the musical *Godspell*. She became active in drama and by her senior year, after composing more music and writing plays, considered herself a playwright. She blames an "existential crisis" at age 16 for her creativity and sharp sense of humor.

In her sophomore year at Wesleyan College in Connecticut, Williams spent a few months in Berkeley, CA, where she wrote songs and performed at the Plough and Stars. After earning a B.A., she moved to Boston in 1990 to find a career in the arts; she dabbled in everything from directing plays and operas to performing. By the year's end she was stage manager for the Opera Company of Boston. She also began taking voice lessons, and it was her teacher, Jeannie Diva, who encouraged Williams to try the coffeehouse circuit. Williams tried hard, especially between late 1992 and early 1993, but things didn't pan out, so she abandoned Boston for the relaxed folksy, artsy atmosphere of Northhampton, MA.

After several self-released cassettes, Williams made her proper debut in 1993 with the independent *Honesty Room* to considerable critical acclaim for both her beautiful soprano voice and her lovely, intriguing songs. She signed the following year with Razor and Tie Records, who reissued the album. Her second album, *Mortal City* (1995), has been similarly praised. She performs on the college and coffeehouse circuit and has been winning rave reviews for festival appearances, including the Newport Folk Festival and the Mississippi River Music Fest in St. Louis, since 1994. In the mid-'90s, an opening spot for Joan Baez increased her exposure. —*Sandra Brennan*

Honesty Room / 1993 / Waterbug ✦✦✦✦
On this, her first official release, Dar Williams' writing successfully explores life from unusual points of view: a child excited that the babysitter is coming, a pair of punk angels in heaven, and Mark Rothko's paintings. While this worthwhile album has some band productions, it is primarily a songwriter's record. —*Richard Meyer*

● **Mortal City** / Jan. 23, 1996 / Razor & Tie ✦✦✦✦
Mortal City, Dar Williams' second album, is as direct and affecting as her first. Even with a stellar supporting cast—John Prine, Cliff Eberhardt, the Nields, and Lucy Kaplansky—Williams manages to keep the focus on her beautiful songs, which are overflowing with detail, melody, and poetic imagery. —*Thom Owens*

Lucinda Williams

b. Jan. 26, 1953, Lake Charles, LA
Guitar, Vocals / Folk, Singer-Songwriter, Folk-Rock, Alternative Country-Rock
Lucinda Williams isn't the kind of artist who caves in easily. Faced with label executives and producers who want to shape her music into cleancut, radio-friendly rock or country numbers—no doubt with someone like Bonnie Raitt in mind—Williams has time and again proven herself to be as stubborn as she is talented. She's released a mere four albums (and one EP) since her debut on Folkways in 1979, partly because she had such a hard time finding a label whose demands don't get in the way of the music as she hears it.

Raised under the intellectual nurture of her father—poet, critic, and English lit professor Miller Williams (a buddy of Tom T. Hall)—Lucinda spent her youth on the ramble from one college burg to another in the American South, as well as Mexico City and Santiago, Chile. She was singing and playing by the time she was 12, when Dylan's *Highway 61 Revisited* had seeped into her psyche, and later found inspiration in the raw Delta blues of singers like Skip James, Bukka White, and Robert Johnson. By the early '70s she was playing shows of her own, mixing folk-inspired originals and traditional material. She traveled before landing in Austin in 1974 at the height of the cosmic cowboy era. Next she tried Houston and became part of a folk scene there that included Nanci Griffith, Lyle Lovett, and Townes Van Zandt. In 1978 she spent an afternoon in the Jackson, MS, R&B studio Malaco, and the result was her 1979 debut for Folkways, *Ramblin' on My Mind*, a collection of traditional blues and country standards. A year later she recorded *Happy Woman Blues* in Houston. This time all the songs were originals, and they featured a full band of acoustic guitar, fiddle, pedal steel, bass, and drums. Both albums have since been reissued on Smithsonian/Folkways.

It was eight years, however, until Williams' third album, *Lucinda Williams*, recorded for the indie-rock label Rough Trade. In the meantime she had lived back and forth between Houston and Austin before moving to Los Angeles in 1984. She'd been courted by several labels, but always held out for creative control. In the end she won it, and her Rough Trade album immediately stood out for its integration of traditional folk, country, and blues influences into a rock 'n' roll format. The album featured "The Night's Too Long," "Passionate Kisses," and "Changed the Locks" and marked a more rock-oriented direction for Williams. Her guitarist and co-producer on that album, Gurf Morlix, has become a vital part of her music, recording and touring with her ever since. In 1989 Rough Trade released the EP *Passionate Kisses*, which included four additional songs, three of which were live radio broadcasts. An ill-fated association with RCA followed, but again Williams was unhappy with the results, and left the label before releasing anything. Her next album, *Sweet Old World*, didn't emerge until 1992, and again it was on an indie label, Chameleon. Well worth the wait, it was again rich with Williams' hearty, twangy voice and solid, Southern-inflected rock 'n' roll originals. Since then Williams has switched labels again, this time to American Recordings. —*Kurt Wolff*

Ramblin' / 1979 / Smithsonian/Folkways ✦✦
In one afternoon at the Malaco Studios in Jackson, MS, in 1978, Lucinda Williams laid down all the tunes on this natural, relaxed album, which still has an underlying drive and soulfulness. The instrumentation is bare, with Williams playing six- and 12-string guitar and John Grimaudo adding supportive second guitar fills. Many of these songs will be instantly familiar: "Motherless Children," "Great Speckled Bird" and "Make Me a Pallet on Your Floor." She brings her own fluid interpretation to each one, never forcing the blues. —*Richard Meyer*

Happy Woman Blues / 1980 / Smithsonian/Folkways ✦✦✦
Happy Woman Blues is a complete departure from her previous album, *Ramblin'.* On this 1980 set, Lucinda Williams turns to her own material with the same soft strength she previously brought to the blues. *Happy Woman Blues* is captivating from the first verse of "Lafayette" on through to the end of the album. A Tex-Mex influence is strong, but it never sounds like an artificially adopted style. Her band gives full, unobtrusive support. —*Richard Meyer*

Lucinda Williams / 1988 / Rough Trade ✦✦✦✦
One of the most exciting recording artists to emerge in the second half of the '80s, Williams combined a recklessly passionate lyrical style with an exuberant, energetic performing approach to achieve this stunning result—an infectious album full of compelling songs. —*William Ruhlmann*

Passionate Kisses / 1989 / Chameleon ✦✦✦
This EP contains Williams' signature tune, "Passionate Kisses," along with four other radio performances and studio outtakes. Well worth having. —*Richard Meyer*

● **Sweet Old World** / 1992 / Chameleon ✦✦✦✦
Lucinda Williams graduated from her near-solo blues album to this 1990 full band electric folk-rock set, and it is a beautiful one to hear. She has an ear for strong hooks; "Six Blocks Away," the leadoff track, has the same simplicity and depth as her signature tune, "Passionate Kisses." Williams is assisted on these songs by Benmont Tench, Byron Berline, and Jim Lauderdale, among others. The solidly produced sound is arranged to allow Williams' distinctive voice to float above it all, as on the great "Sweet Old World." —*Richard Meyer*

Robin and Linda Williams

Folk
Singers/songwriters Robin and Linda Williams were regulars on Garrison Keillor's "A Prairie Home Companion" radio show. Some of their songs have been recorded by Emmylou Harris, Kathy Mattea, and Michael Martin Murphey. Their harmonies are smooth and well matched. Their musicianship is tight and well crafted. —*Chip Renner*

Harmony / 1981 / June Appal ✦✦✦
Very hard to find, but it should be in your collection. —*Chip Renner*

● **Close As We Can Get** / 1984 / Flying Fish ✦✦✦✦
Perfect in all ways. "The Leaving Train" is one of their best songs. As good as *All Broken Hearts.* —*Chip Renner*

Nine 'Til Midnight / 1985 / Flying Fish ✦✦✦
A very good live album featuring gospel, traditional country, and contemporary songs. —*Chip Renner*

All Broken Hearts Are the Same / 1988 / Sugar Hill ✦✦✦✦
With top-notch songwriting and smooth vocals, this features Jerry Douglas, Stuart Duncan, and T. Michael Coleman. —*Chip Renner*

Rhythm of Love / 1990 / Sugar Hill ✦✦✦
These 12 songs are all good. Features guests Jerry Douglas and Stuart Duncan. —*Chip Renner*

Turn Toward Tomorrow / 1993 / Sugar Hill ✦✦✦
Produced by John Jennings, this collection of primarily Robin and Linda songs is held together by great economical band arrangements. Weepers like "When the Last Tear Falls" and "Chain of Pain" are given an uptempo treatment so we don't have to get too torn up about life's hardships. "Lying to the Moon" brings the CD to a peaceful close. —*Richard Meyer*

Robin and Linda Williams and Their Fine Group Live / 1994 / Sugar Hill ✦✦✦
Recorded while on tour in Holland, this album finds Robin and Linda

Williams in a more basic band setting. It lets the strength of their vocals come through better than on some of their slicker studio records. The highpoint comes with "The Devil Is a Mighty Wind." —*Richard Meyer*

Victoria Williams

Guitar, Vocals / Singer-Songwriter, Folk-Rock, Alternative Country-Rock
During the late '80s and early '90s, singer-songwriter Victoria Williams recorded two critically acclaimed albums, featuring her distinctive, lyrical songwriting. Occasionally her thin voice can be a little shrill; yet her music is consistently complex, drawing from folk, pop, gospel, and country. At times, Williams' lyrics can be slightly cloying, but more often, she writes rich, detailed narratives.

After the release of 1990's *Swing the Statue!,* Williams was diagnosed with multiple sclerosis. She had no money or insurance to pay for her expensive hospital bills. Her dire situation led to a bunch of her musician friends assembling a relief fund for her; the fund led to the 1993 tribute album *Sweet Relief,* which featured 14 artists covering her songs. The proceeds were donated to Williams, as well as the Sweet Relief Musicians Trust Fund, designed to help musicians who, like Victoria Williams, have no health insurance. After the album was a success, her two records were reissued by Geffen. During this time, Williams went into remission. She released her third album, *Loose,* in 1994. —*Stephen Thomas Erlewine*

Happy Come Home / 1987 / Geffen ✦✦✦
This debut LP by Victoria Williams is as wonderful as it is eclectic. Van Dyke Parks' arrangements give the collection a carnival feel, while Anton Fier's pop productions never let this become anything close to an ordinary singer-songwriter album. But how could it, with Williams' elastic vocals and trippy lyrics? This is a great record to play when anyone says that all L.A. pop albums are slick and sanitized. —*Richard Meyer*

● **Swing the Statue** / 1990 / Rough Trade ✦✦✦✦
Victoria Williams' second album was her most accomplished set of folk-rock, featuring the remarkable "Summer of Drugs." —*Stephen Thomas Erlewine*

Loose / 1994 / Mamoth ✦✦✦✦
What a great collection. Victoria Williams has put together a fine-tuned tight but loose band, as expressed in the title. Her folk-rock Carol Channing voice is perfectly suited to the arrangements, some of which were written by Van Dyke Parks, and include players such as Greg Cohen, Peter Buck, and Don Heffinton. Her originals are quirky and beautiful. Williams' choice of covers is also refreshing. She does a heartbreaking take on "What a Wonderful World" and revives the psychedelic chestnut "Nature's Way," making it her own. *Loose* is a wonderful album, full of life. —*Richard Meyer*

This Moment: Live In Toronto / Nov. 7, 1995 / Atlantic ✦✦✦
Recorded on the *Loose* tour, Victoria Williams' live album *This Moment: Live in Toronto* demonstrates the depths of her songwriting talents. Performing with a sympathetic folk-rock supporting band, Williams runs through her catalog, playing nearly all of her fans' favorite songs. She is in fine voice, turning in an impassioned performance, but the best thing about the record is how all the songs play off each other. Unlike her other records, there is no filler on *This Moment,* which makes the album a perfect introduction to her rich talents. —*Stephen Thomas Erlewine*

Robin Williamson and His Merry Band

Between 1966 and 1974 Robin Williamson was one half of the Incredible String Band, but his career did not founder after ISB's demise, although it might be said to have taken a few quirky turns, including collaboration on a spy novel and the publication of a bizarre semi-autobiography. Away from these literary avocations, Williamson formed the Far Cry Ceilidh Band with Stan Schnier and Mark Simos, but never made it to the recording studio. In 1976, Williamson met harpist Sylvia Wood, and together with Chris Caswell and Jerry McMillian, they formed Robin Williamson and His Merry Band. Between 1977 and 1979 they released three albums: the highly traditional *Journey's Edge* in 1977, *American Stonehenge* in 1978, and *A Glint at the Kindling* in 1979, which featured the epic historical cycle, "Five Denials on Merlin's Grave." After the breakup of the Merry Band, Williamson started to tour solo, offering highly ambient sets dominated by traditional stories set to song. Releases of this period include *Songs of Love and Parting* and the dedicated folklorist's *Legacy of the Scottish Harpers.* Williamson's concern with the British bardic tradition also manifested itself in several books and tapes containing spoken renditions of traditional tales. Subsequent projects have seen prolific Williamson recording tapes and discs of music for children and pouring his energies into environmental projects for the Scottish Wildlife Trust. —*Leon Jackson*

Journey's Edge / 1977 / Edsel ✦✦✦
This album features an unusual blend of baroque, traditional, and contemporary music played by Robin Williamson, one of the founders of the Incredible String Band. —*AMG*

● **American Stonehenge** / 1978 / Flying Fish ✦✦✦✦
This album is perhaps Williamson's most generally accessible, featuring his late-'70s touring band on a variety of humorous and pastoral Williamson originals. — *William Ruhlmann*

Glint at the Kindling / 1979 / Flying Fish ✦✦✦
This album features a blend of rock, jazz, and Celtic music from a popular band. — *AMG*

Music for the Mabinogi / 1984 / Flying Fish ✦✦✦

Kate Wolf (Kathryn Louise Allen)

b. Jan. 27, 1942, San Francisco, CA, **d.** Dec. 10, 1986
Piano, Guitar / Folk, Singer-Songwriter
Although she was a significant presence on the folk scene in the late '70s and mid-'80s, it's difficult to categorize Kate Wolf as a folk performer (though that is ultimately the broad category that suits her best). Although she largely employed acoustic instrumentation, she really owed more to the contemporary singer-songwriting movement than folk-based traditions. While it's easy to imagine her music appealing to fans of, say, Joni Mitchell, she never made the slightest impact on the rock audience, and barely drew from rock elements at all in her own work. Her music also had a strong country flavor, though not of the Nashville variety. Her fusion of country, folk, and singer-songwriter influences helped point the way for later country-folk-pop performers such as Nanci Griffith and Mary-Chapin Carpenter.

The appeal of Wolf's music is broad—folk, pop, and rootsy country fans can all find something to like—yet elusive. Her songs are not necessarily striking upon first listen, and her body of work, if taken more than an album at a time, can be described as rather heterogeneous. Her style tends to grow on listeners over time, as Wolf is not about flash. Her songs, characterized by a strong narrative thread, are about the ebb and flow of adult life, in terms that are neither overly sentimental nor mundane. She describes family, romance, and the rural life of her native Northern California with fine (though not studious) detail, projecting a sort of reserved sensitivity with her lower-than-average vocals. Hers is a voice of wisdom, comfort, and independence. If those aren't the most exciting things around, there are few other performers who convey such consistent warmth and dignity, making listeners she never met personally feel as if they were hearing letters from a friend.

Wolf didn't get her recording career going until the mid-'70s, by which time she was well into her 30s. Before emerging as a solo artist, she had headed the band Wildwood Flower (who backed her on her first two albums) and organized folk concerts and festivals in Northern California. Very much a self-starter, her first two albums were released on her own Owl label; thereafter, her catalog was handled by Kaleidoscope.

Over the next few years, Wolf built a strong following on the folk circuit with a series of fairly similar and remarkably consistent albums. Her recordings always benefited from first-rate instrumental support from various small bands; guitarist Nina Gerber was her most important associate in this regard. Wolf was still at her peak when her life was cut short by leukemia in 1986.

Rhino Records has reissued all of Wolf's albums on CD; in addition to the five studio discs, there are several collections of live and previously unreleased material. Neophytes are advised to start with the two-CD *Gold in California* set, a career-spanning retrospective of some of her best songs. — *Richie Unterberger*

Back Roads / 1976 / Rhino ✦✦✦✦
Wolf's debut album introduced an approach that would, in most essential respects, vary little over the next decade: gentle, slightly mournful country/folk songs with a strong narrative voice, and a semi-rural Californian ambience with the frequent evocation of golden, natural landscapes. Even at this stage, Wolf stood out from the pack with her restrained, tasteful vocals, sincere compositions that avoided maudlin cliches, and careful, almost diligent, arrangements. — *Richie Unterberger*

Lines on the Paper/Backroads / 1977 / Rhino ✦✦✦
Wolf's second album indicated that there weren't going to be any significant changes in her style. At the same time, it also gave notice that she was an extraordinarily consistent performer with a deep catalog of original compositions. More reflective song-stories about family and life passages, sensitively but not sappily performed. — *Richie Unterberger*

Safe at Anchor / 1979 / Rhino ✦✦✦
While at this point you knew what to expect from a Kate Wolf album, it would be inaccurate to call her work formulaic. Her musical arrangements didn't vary all that much, but each of her compositions was carefully constructed and performed with commitment. That's true of all of the songs here, with occasional tracks (such as "Early Morning Melody") emerging as true standouts. — *Richie Unterberger*

Close to You / 1981 / Rhino ✦✦✦
Wolf's arrangements got a little more complex on this album, with occasional string arrangements and drum tracks. "Leggett Serenade" especially sounds like an attempt to craft a track with more pop/adult con-

temporary appeal. Largely, though, it's the same dependable sparsely arranged, strong material, with support from Nina Gerber, Tony Rice, Norton Buffalo, and Darol Anger. — *Richie Unterberger*

Give Yourself to Love, Vol. 1 & 2 / 1983 / Rhino (Kaleidoscope) ✦✦✦✦
A worthy live supplement to her studio albums, as many of the songs were previously unrecorded. Taken from shows in 1982 and 1983, it features both Wolf compositions and covers of songs by Sandy Denny, John Stewart, Jim Ringer-Mary McCaslin, Robin Williamson, and others. This is identical to the intitial Kaleidoscope release of *Give Yourself to Love,* though the Rhino CD adds an unnecessarily confusing "Vol. 1 & 2" to the title. — *Richie Unterberger*

Poet's Heart / 1985 / Rhino ✦✦✦✦
Wolf's final studio album found her continuing to capably explore pretty much the same musical territory she always had, perhaps with a slightly heavier heart and somewhat more acute lyricism. She was still looking for new ways to modify her core approach, making imaginative use of dobro and steel guitar player Mike Auldridge and Celtic harpist Kim Robertson. — *Richie Unterberger*

● **Gold in California, Vol. 1 & 2** / 1986 / Rhino (Kaleidoscope) ✦✦✦✦
Featuring 20 songs from 1975 to 1985, this is the definitive Kate Wolf retrospective, compiled by the singer herself shortly before her death. For most listeners, it will serve as *the* Kate Wolf album to own, assembling the best of her somewhat similar albums in one place (and for those who want more, Rhino has reissued her entire catalogue). Every one of these titles was previously released, with the exception of a version of Alice Stuart's "Full Time Woman." This is identical to the intitial Kaleidoscope release of *Gold in California,* though Rhino CD adds "Vol. 1 & 2" to the title. — *Richie Unterberger*

The Wind Blows Wild / 1988 / Rhino ✦✦✦
A posthumous collection of previously unreleased studio outtakes and live performances spanning 1979 to 1986. This may be the most marginal entry in the Kate Wolf discography, but that doesn't mean it's bad. The arrangements are more sparse than most of her other records, and the compositions are up to her usual standards, though not among her very finest ones. — *Richie Unterberger*

Evening in Austin / 1989 / Rhino (Kaleidoscope) ✦✦✦
Recorded for PBS' "Austin City Limits," program in November 1985, this CD includes the entire concert (only 25 minutes were broadcast on TV). Wolf presents good interpretaions of 14 songs spanning her career, sticking mostly to original material, although four covers are also present, including a Robin Williamson tune and the '60s folk-rock warhorse "Let's Get Together." It has a couple of songs that weren't released on any of her records, but it's mostly for serious fans, as is the accompanying video of the event (available seperately). — *Richie Unterberger*

Looking Back at You / 1994 / Rhino ✦✦✦
Ten live songs, performed at various venues in Southern California between 1977 and 1979 (several at a club in Santa Monica, a couple for a public radio show in Los Angeles, and one at the San Diego Folk Festival). These tracks are notably sparse, featuring little besides Wolf's vocals and guitars (by Wolf and accompanists). The approach is different enough from her studio work to make this worth hearing, especially as it includes both original songs and unexpected covers of compositions by Leonard Cohen, Jackson Browne, Tom Paxton, and Utah Phillips. — *Richie Unterberger*

Breezes / 1995 / Gadfly ✦✦✦
Gadfly Records has released a new album of material recorded in 1973. The hallmarks of Wolf's later work are evident: her breathy intimate vocals and the mid-tempo tunes about delicate connections and the human spirit. This album is stripped down, totally acoustic, with assistance from David Coffin and Lionel Kilberg. The somber quality that makes so many of her recordings seem timeless can be heard on "There Are No Medals for Loneliness" and "Help." "You Can't Go Back," however, is a real spirit lifter. — *Richard Meyer*

Woodstock Mountain Revue

Woodstock Mountain Revue is a loose, informal affiliation of folk-based musicians who live near Woodstock, NY, and record occasionally for Rounder Records. Their first album (at which time they had not yet adopted their name) was *Mud Acres*—Music Among Friends. It was recorded in 1972 and featured Happy Traum, Artie Traum, Maria Muldaur, John Herald, Eric Kaz, Jim Rooney, Bill Keith, Tony Brown, and Lee Berg. Their second album, 1977's *More Music from Mud Acres,* was credited to "Woodstock Mountains," and featured the Traums, Herald, Rooney, Keith, and Berg, plus Pat Alger, Eric Andersen, Rory Block, Paul Butterfield, Roly Salley, John Sebastian, and Paul Siebel. Their third album, 1978's *Pretty Lucky,* was the first to be credited to Woodstock Mountain Revue, which was defined as an eight-member group consisting of the Traums, Herald, Rooney, Keith, Alger, Solley, Larry Campbell, and Caroline Dutton, with special guest Cyndi Cashdollar. — *William Ruhlmann*

Mud Acres: Music Among Friends / 1972 / Rounder ✦✦✦✦
With Happy and Artie Traum, Bill Keith, Maria Muldaur, Eric Kaz, Jim Rooney, John Herald, Tony Brown, and Lee Berg. Their first release, just sittin' and pickin'. Very informal. —*Chip Renner*

● **Woodstock Mountains** / 1977 / Rounder ✦✦✦✦
Woodstock Mountains (More Music from Mud Acres) features Pat Alger, Happy and Artie Traum, Eric Andersen, Lee Berg, John Butterfield, John Herald, Bill Keith, Jim Rooney, Roly Salley, John Sebastian, and Paul Siebel. This album brought it all together! Their peak. —*Chip Renner*

Pretty Lucky / 1978 / Rounder ✦✦✦
Overshadowed by the first Mud Acres album. —*Chip Renner*

Back to Mud Acres / 1981 / Rounder ✦✦✦
Featuring Happy and Artie Traum, Pat Alger, Larry Campbell, John Herald, Bill Keith, Jim Rooney, Roly Salley, Cyndi Dollar. Nice, but something was missing. —*Chip Renner*

Glenn Yarbrough

b. Jan. 12, 1930
Vocals
From his days as the singing mainstay of the Limeliters through a long solo career that's seen its share of hits, Glenn Yarbrough has been a respected interpreter of folk and popular music. He's had a top hit in "Baby, the Rain Must Fall" and his interpretation of "Seven Daffodils" is the benchmark against which love songs are measured. From his days in a boys choir through today, Glenn's powerful voice has rung with lusty conviction about all that he cares about. —*Allan Shaw*

● **Bramble and the Rose** / Folk Era ✦✦✦✦
With Holly Yarbrough and fingerpicking guitar champion Muriel Anderson. —*Allan Shaw*

Various Artists

American Impressionist Songwriters / 1993 / Waterbug ✦✦✦
This collection of songs represents the work of many of the American singer-songwriters coming up these days. While the impressionist tag implies more lyrical adventure than one actually hears, it is a good ambitious category to begin filling. Some of the best cuts are "The Deerhunter" by Doyle Carver and "Jack's Belted Galoways" by Diane Zeigler. —*Richard Meyer*

☆ **Anthology of American Folk Music, Vol. 3** / 1966 / Smithsonian/Folkways ✦✦✦✦✦
This is an invaluable set of three double albums of songs, ballads, and social music recorded in the field in the late '20s and early '30s. Clarence Ashley and the Carters are represented here, as are Dick Boggs, Blind Lemon Jefferson, and Uncle Dave Macon. Classic songs include "I Wish I Was a Mole" by Bascomb Lunsford, "Spikedriver's Blues" by John Hurt, and "Wagoner's Lad" by Buell Kazee. The historical importance of this set, issued originally in 1952, cannot be overestimated. This is folk music as heard before it became touched by the word business. These recordings are sonically primitive but have far more energy than so many modern recordings. —*Richard Meyer*

Been in the Storm So Long / 1990 / Smithsonian/Folkways ✦✦✦✦✦
This is a truly wonderful collection of spirituals, folk tales, and children's stories recorded in the early '60s on Johns Island, SC. How much the Gullah culture of the islands is an antebellum US survival and just how it links with its Caribbean cousins isn't clear. What is clear is the beauty and importance of this recompilation of two old Folkways albums (3841 and 3842), with new notes. —*John Storm Roberts*

Ben & Jerry's Newport Folk Festival 88 / Alcazar ✦✦✦✦✦
Vanguard Records used to record the Newport Folk Festivals of the early '60s for some seminal albums displaying the quality of folk artists of the time. Alcazar has done much the same for the revived festival, and this disc spotlights a range of talent, from veterans of the '60s festival to figures who emerged during the hiatus, and to new folkies. —*William Ruhlmann*

Big Times in a Small Town: The Vineyard Tapes / 1993 / Philo ✦✦✦
This CD has highlights of the first annual Martha's Vineyard Singer-songwriter retreat. Sponsored by Christine Lavin, it was recorded live at the Wintertide Coffeehouse. Standout cuts are Jonatha Brooke's "Dog Dreams," Pierce Pettis' cover of Mark Heard's "Nod over Coffee," and James Mee's title cut. —*Richard Meyer*

Bread & Roses Festival 1977 / 1979 / Fantasy ✦✦✦✦✦
This two-record set chronicles the October 1977 benefit concert for Mimi Farina's Bread & Roses organization, which brings music into prisons and hospitals. A broad range of folk-related artists, including Joan Baez, Jackson Browne, Pete Seeger, and Arlo Guthrie, among many others, turns this into a brilliant songwriting showcase. —*William Ruhlmann*

Bread & Roses Festival 1979 / 1980 / Fantasy ✦✦✦✦✦
The lineup for the 1979 festival was even broader than the 1977 one, including the Chambers Brothers and Chick Corea, plus the Roches, Graham Nash and David Crosby, and many more. But the folk theme still runs through all the wonderful music. —*William Ruhlmann*

Bringing It All Back Home, Vol. 2 / 1994 / Legacy ✦✦✦
These two CDs contain performances taken from Happy and Artie Traum's radio shows, broadcast over WAMC in Albany, NY, in the late '80s. Both CDs are uniformly good and feature earthy immediate performances from Rick Danko, David Wilcox, Dianne Zeigler, John Herald, and Maria Muldaur. The artists all really let their hair down. Some favorite cuts include Maria Muldaur's "New Orleans," and John Hall's solo version of his hit "Still the One." These are good solid records. —*Richard Meyer*

The CooP: February 1982 / Feb. 1982 / CooP ✦✦✦✦
The CooP's debut issue combined the work of established folk figures such as Ed McCurdy and Dave Van Ronk (who contributed the hilarious "Jersey State Stomp") with up-and-coming performers like folk-blues guitarist Frank Christian, Ilene Weiss, David Massengill (whose "Fairfax County" turned up on a Roches album later in the year), and Suzanne Vega (whose "Cracking" would be recorded three years later for her debut album). —*William Ruhlmann*

The CooP: April 1982 / Apr. 1982 / CooP ✦✦✦✦
Highlights of this issue include "Small Town on the River," by Bill Morrissey, who later recorded four albums on Rounder Records; "I'm Talking to You," by Shawn Colvin, later a Grammy-winning folk artist on Columbia Records; and perhaps the most impressive song of the new folk movement of the time, David Massengill's epic "The Great American Dream." —*William Ruhlmann*

The CooP: May 1982 . . . / May 1982 / CooP ✦✦✦✦
*The CooP—*May 1982, The Political Song Revisited. A thematic album featuring Matt Jones' version of *CooP* editor Jack Hardy's Civil War story, "Incident at Ebenezer Creek," Sherwood Ross' humorous "I Sliced Pastrami for the CIA and Found God," and a duet between Steve Forbert and Jack Hardy on Woody Guthrie's "This Land Is Your Land." —*William Ruhlmann*

The CooP: June 1982 . . . / Jun. 1982 / CooP ✦✦✦✦
*The CooP—*June 1982, Traditional Music Revisited. Actually, humorous music revisited is more like it, what with the first appearance of future Philo recording artist Christine Lavin on her "Regretting What I Said . . . ," and David Massengill's "The Eunuch's Lament." Also included is Suzanne Vega's "Gypsy," later to appear on her second A&M album, five years hence. —*William Ruhlmann*

The CooP: September 1982 / Sep. 1982 / CooP ✦✦✦✦
An especially strong collection recorded live at SpeakEasy and including Suzanne Vega's "Knight Moves," Rod MacDonald's "Sailor's Prayer," George Gerdes' "The Policeman Is My Friend," and Jack Hardy's "The Children." —*William Ruhlmann*

The CooP: February 1983 . . . / Feb. 1983 / CooP ✦✦✦✦
*The CooP—*February 1983, 1st Anniversary! Standouts here are Tom Paxton performing his Nancy Reagan parody, "Little Bitty Gun," Suzanne Vega's "The Queen and the Soldier," future editor and Shanachie recording artist Richard Meyer's "Jive Town," and then-editor Jack Hardy's Central American topical song "Porto Limon." —*William Ruhlmann*

The CooP: May 1983 . . . / May 1983 / CooP ✦✦✦✦
Appropriately, this album contains a contribution from *Broadside* magazine founder Sis Cunningham, and the other highlights include Michael Jerling's Vietnam vets song "Long Black Wall" and Fred Small's "Everything Possible." —*William Ruhlmann*

The CooP: June 1983—Love Songs / Jun. 1983 / CooP ✦✦✦✦
Suzanne Vega (who seems to have recorded much of her first two albums for *The CooP*) contributes "Some Journey," while Richard Meyer presents what will be the title track of his debut album, "Laughing/Scared." John Gorka, who now records for Windham Hill, makes his first appearance with "Downtown Tonight." —*William Ruhlmann*

Cornelia Street: Songwriter's Exchange / 1980 / Stash ✦✦✦✦
Re-released in 1991 with additional tracks on CD. From the late '70s on, there was a weekly meeting of the many contemporary Greenwich Village songwriters. This compilation album spotlights some of the fine work from that time and is a precursor to *The Fast Folk Musical Magazine.* —*Richard Meyer*

Fast Folk Magazine, Vol. 1 #1 / 1984 / Fast Folk ✦✦✦✦✦
This first issue of the renamed record/magazine features Eric Andersen's "The Girls of Denmark," Suzanne Vega's future Top Ten hit "Tom's Diner," John Gorka's "I Saw a Stranger with Your Hair," and Christine Lavin's "Don't Ever Call Your Sweetheart by His Name." —*William Ruhlmann*

Fast Folk Magazine, Vol. 1 #2 / 1984 / Fast Folk ✦✦✦✦
Pete Seeger turns up on this edition, as do such other folk veterans as Oscar Brand, Sammy Walker, and Jim Glover (of Jim and Jean). Among the new generation, Shawn Colvin contributes "I Don't Know Why," and

Rod MacDonald sings the anthem like "Every Living Thing." —*William Ruhlmann*

Fast Folk Magazine, Vol. 1 #4 / 1984 / Fast Folk ✦✦✦✦✦
Subtitled: *Live at the Bottom Line*. On January 28, 1984, the Fast Folk cooperative staged the first of what would be an annual concert series presenting the best of the songs that had appeared so far on the records. The result is an essential greatest-hits album that makes the case for a folk-music renaissance in the early '80s. —*William Ruhlmann*

Fast Folk Magazine, Vol. 1 #6 / 1984 / Fast Folk ✦✦✦✦✦
Subtitled: *The Blues*. "Traditional" is the author of the majority of these folk-blues cuts, which are performed by the likes of John Hammond, Dave Van Ronk, and some less illustrious but equally talented musicians. —*William Ruhlmann*

Fast Folk Magazine, Vol. 1 #8 / 1984 / Fast Folk ✦✦✦✦✦
Subtitled: *Women in Song*. This exceptional album leads off with Nanci Griffith and also includes Shawn Colvin and Christine Lavin. Among the less well known names, the duo Palmer and Bragg turn in the impressive "Bayonne" and Megan McDonough contributes "A Lesson in Every Good-Bye." —*William Ruhlmann*

Fast Folk Magazine, Vol. 2 #8 / 1985 / Fast Folk ✦✦✦✦✦
A new batch of singer-songwriters gets their first exposure in this release, among them Lyle Lovett, Buddy Mondlock, and Cindy Lee Berryhill. —*William Ruhlmann*

Fast Folk Magazine, Vol. 2 #10 / 1985 / Fast Folk ✦✦✦✦✦
Tom Paxton returns in this album, along with a large number of folksingers who have gone on to greater recognition, among them Pierce Pettis, David Mallett, Greg Brown, Bob Franke, Schooner Fare, and Cliff Eberhardt. All of them recorded at SpeakEasy. —*William Ruhlmann*

Fast Folk Magazine, Vol. 3 #3 / 1986 / Fast Folk ✦✦✦✦✦
Lyle Lovett, Aztec Two Step, Steve Gillette, and Tom Russell are the stars of this issue, but also note Tom Intondi's stirring "Straight from the Heart" and the Folkano version of Pierce Pettis' "Moments." —*William Ruhlmann*

Fast Folk Magazine, Vol. 3 #4 / 1986 / Fast Folk ✦✦✦✦✦
Subtitled: *Boston One*. This issue is notable for the first recorded appearance anywhere of Tracy Chapman (singing "For My Lover"), but also as a representative sampling of Boston folk music, much of it on a par with the New York scene *Fast Folk* usually chronicles. —*William Ruhlmann*

Fast Folk Magazine, Vol. 3 #6/7 / 1986 / Fast Folk ✦✦✦✦✦
Subtitled: *Live at the Bottom Line*. Double-pocket souvenir of the third annual Fast Folk Revue show, recorded May 10, 1986, it is once again a best-of, containing the most impressive songs from *Fast Folk* over the previous year, highlights including the heartbreaking Irish emigration ballad "Kilkelly" and the sidesplitting "Railroad Bill," written and sung by Andy Breckman, whose day job is head writer for "Late Night with David Letterman." —*William Ruhlmann*

Fast Folk Magazine, Vol. 3 #10 / 1986 / Fast Folk ✦✦✦✦
Richie Havens is here in this release, as is Michelle Shocked (that's right, another debut). Buddy Mondlock and Fred Small return, too. —*William Ruhlmann*

Fast Folk Magazine, Vol. 4 #5/6 / 1988 / Fast Folk ✦✦✦✦✦
Subtitled: *The 6th Anniversary Issue*. Nicknamed "the flag album" for its cover, this double album features such *Fast Folk* regulars as David Massengill, Jack Hardy, Rod MacDonald, and Richard Meyer, plus old friends like Dave Van Ronk and Eric Andersen, new stars like Christine Lavin and Michelle Shocked, and guest Suzanne Vega, whose "The Marching Dream" is unavailable elsewhere. —*William Ruhlmann*

Fast Folk Magazine, Vol. 4 #9 / 1989 / Fast Folk ✦✦✦✦✦
Subtitled: *Los Angeles*. Fast Folk goes bicoastal for an album featuring Peter Case, Victoria Williams, and Milo Binder. —*William Ruhlmann*

Fast Folk Magazine: Songs of Tradition / 1986 / Fast Folk ✦✦✦
This compilation is an exceptional collection of contemporary singer-songwriters who know all the traditional rules enough to enhance or break them. Josh Joffen's "Pontchatrain"-inspired "Girl from the Great Divide" is a riveting revision; Paul Kaplan's "Johnny of Hazelgreen" is lilting and delicate; Nikki Matheson turns in a haunting "Star of the County Down." One side of this album is in English; the other ranges from Italian to Yiddish. The garage-band version of "500 Miles" is a classic. —*Richard Meyer*

Folk Classics / 1989 / CBS ✦✦✦✦✦
Though one thinks of Elektra and Vanguard as the main record labels of the folk revival, the giant Columbia Records also made some inroads into the field, signing up not only Bob Dylan but also a wide range of folkies, from Pete Seeger to the New Christy Minstrels. This 15-track compilation delves deeper into the Columbia vault for tracks by Leadbelly and Burl Ives, but its focus is on '60s performers—the Brothers Four, Carolyn Hester, Malvina Reynolds. Many of them, like Dylan, are John Hammond signings. The focus of the album is scattered, but the selection is excellent, and Columbia was long overdue to examine its folk archives. —*William Ruhlmann*

Folk Masters / 1993 / Smithsonian/Folkways ✦✦✦
This 22-cut sampler culled from the "Folk Masters" radio show series reflects the program's openness—bluegrass, klezmer, classic gospel, Western swing, mountain music, blues, Cajun, and traditional jazz are represented, as well as international styles and conjunto. It is a quick musical education and one that should forever shatter stereotyped notions about what does and does not constitute folk music. —*Ron Wynn*

☆ **Greatest Folksingers of 60s** / 1972 / Vanguard ✦✦✦✦✦
Not only was Maynard Solomon's Vanguard Records one of the major folk labels of the '60s (having the prescience to pick up Joan Baez early on, and then recording the cream of the singer-songwriters thereafter), but it also had the rights to record and release material from the Newport Folk Festival, giving it access to several artists who were not signed to the label. As a result, this double-packet compilation features songs by nearly every major folk figure of the decade, from the Weavers to Jose Feliciano, with Vanguard artists such as Buffy Sainte-Marie, Eric Andersen, and Odetta sharing space with Elektra's Phil Ochs and Judy Collins and Columbia's Bob Dylan. Listen to this one record and you'll know what the '60s folk revival sounded like. —*William Ruhlmann*

The Greatest Songs of Woody Guthrie / 1972 / Vanguard ✦✦✦✦✦
This 23-track, 70-minute disc, assembled from recordings dating from the '50s and the '60s, is by now a historical document tracing the kinds of interpretations offered by the first generation of folksingers to be influenced by Guthrie, some of whom were his contemporaries. For the most part, the singers, who include the Weavers, Odetta, Ramblin' Jack Elliot, Cisco Huston, and Joan Baez, offer covers of Guthrie favorites that are sweeter and more conventional than the originals. Thankfully, they are interspersed with a handful of tunes featuring Guthrie himself. —*William Ruhlmann*

Have Moicy! / 1976 / Rounder ✦✦✦✦✦
The various members of the Holy Modal Rounders are a sneaky bunch of folks with a tendency to turn up on record in a variety of guises, which is only a partial explanation of why, with three artists credited on the cover, this album is really the brainchild of one who is unmentioned: Rounder cofounder Peter Stampfel. And as with his other manifestations (see the Holy Modal Rounders, Stampfel & Weber, and Peter Stampfel & the Bottle Caps), this is a collection of folk, blues, country, and rock novelties, some of which are ridiculously funny. A Rounder by any other name is still a hoot. —*William Ruhlmann*

Legacy: A Collection of New Folk Artists / 1989 / Windham Hill ✦✦✦✦✦
Although only a few of them managed to break through to national attention, a generation of important folk talents appeared during the '80s, playing clubs and festivals and recording for *The Fast Folk Musical Magazine* and self-financed records sold at gigs. In 1989, Windham Hill noticed and copied the *Fast Folk* formula, presenting some of the best—David Massengill, Cliff Eberhardt, Bill Morrissey, John Gorka, and others—on this 15-track disc and even signing a few of them to contracts. The result is a stunning showcase of talent that will shock anyone who thinks good folk music disappeared around 1970. —*William Ruhlmann*

The Music of Kentucky: Early American Rural Classics 1927-37, Vols. 1 & 2 / 1995 / Yazoo ✦✦✦✦
Many rural fiddlers, guitarists, and banjo players from the state of Kentucky were taped while the recording industry was in its infancy. This interesting and valuable two-volume set, numbering 53 songs in all, presents a wide-ranging set of old-timey folk styles, by artists who are known only to scholars in the field. Much of the material is taken from the famed Bristol sessions of the late '20s, and late-'30s field recordings by renowned folklorist Alan Lomax. The roots of much modern country, folk, and even blues can be heard in these heartfelt, occasionally stirring performances of great conviction, religious or otherwise. It's not just a history lesson and is a lot more accessible to modern-day listeners than many would assume. —*Richie Unterberger*

The Real Music Box: 25 Years of Rounder Records / Oct. 1995 / Rounder ✦✦✦
Within the discount, ugly-duckling packaging of *The Real Music Box: 25 Years of Rounder Records* lie nine CD swans worth several hundred times their weight in superficial music-industry gold records. Since 1970, Massachusetts-based Rounder has been a stalwart sanctuary of various musics at the root of what has recently been labeled "Americana." The retrospective is segmented into four thematic two-disc sets, each offering a staggering 30 to 50 tracks where legendary names rub shoulders with bright young Rounder talent. On *Hills of Home* (folk), Woody Guthrie and Leadbelly hang out with Rory Block and Alison Krauss; while *Hand-Picked* (bluegrass) highlights the likes of J.D. Crowe & the New South, Tony Trischka, and Bela Fleck. *Deep Blue* (blues) captures a wide range of shades, from Professor Longhair and Champion Jack Dupree to Clarence "Gatemouth" Brown and the Holmes Brothers. *Louisiana Spice*

stews up a gumbo of New Orleans R&B, cajun, and zydeco, including Dirty Dozen Brass Band, Zachary Richard, and Boozoo Chavis. A final bonus disc captures 23 random Rounder samples, including psych-folk from the Holy Modal Rounders, Brave Combo's polka party, Jonathan Richman's childlike whimsy, and the Chicano rock of the Blazers. In some respects, this disc is the most satisfying of all just for its sheer breadth of scope. In all, a living, breathing, vibrant roots music encyclopedia. —*Roch Parisien*

Songs of Jack Hardy, Vol. 1: Of the White Goddess / 1995 / Beacon ✦✦✦
New York songwriter Jack Hardy has been honored by this tribute compilation made up of Boston-based Beacon Records' Celtic artists and some from New York. Some interpretations differ radically from Hardy's own arrangements, which of course is a compliment. The album is cohesive because the songs are primarily Hardy's Irish-inspired ones, although it is not always clear that the performers understand the tunes. The real treats are the cuts by the Roches and Lucy Kaplansky if only because they seem more sensitive to the lyrics. Another plus is Hardy's own previously unreleased late-'70s outtake of "An Bael Bocht" ("The Poor Mouth"). —*Richard Meyer*

Songs of the Civil War / New World ✦✦✦
Released around the time of the PBS series on the Civil War, this collection offers tunes of that period performed by Kate & Anna McGarrigle, Kathy Mattea, Richie Havens, Waylon Jennings, and Sweet Honey in the Rock. It's a celebratory but wistful sounding collecton. —*Richard Meyer*

Tribute to Bob Dylan, Vol. 1 / 1991 / Sister Ruby ✦✦✦
Sister Ruby Records, a small label based in Tucker, GA, has begun putting together cover versions of Dylan songs by local and nationally known singer-songwriters. The first volume includes Michelle Malone's performance of "I'll Be Your Baby Tonight," Kristen Hall's "It Ain't Me Babe" and the Indigo Girls' dramatic version of "Tangled Up in Blue." While these are generally pretty true to the style of the originals, listening to them reminds one of the breadth of Dylan's writing and often sends the listener back to the originals. —*Richard Meyer*

Tribute to Bob Dylan, Vol. 2 / 1994 / Sister Ruby ✦✦✦✦
Like the first volume, this record contains a dozen of the key Bob Dylan songs performed by other contemporary singer-songwriters. The geographical scope has widened a bit on this second volume and includes some key performances by Ellis Paul; a soulful "All Along the Watchtower," Richard Shindell's version of "Love Minus Zero (No Limit)," and a compelling cover of the coal-mining ballad "North Country Blues." —*Richard Meyer*

Tribute to Guthrie/Leadbelly:... / 1988 / Smithsonian/Folkways ✦✦✦✦✦
Tribute to Guthrie and Leadbelly: A Vision Shared. This album was organized as a benefit to help the Smithsonian buy the Folkways Records catalog. The performers, mostly rock-based pop stars influenced by folk music, present their interpretations of Guthrie and Leadbelly songs, with varying results. The best, however, is very good, and that includes Bob Dylan doing "Pretty Boy Floyd," Willie Nelson's "Philadelphia Lawyer," and Taj Mahal's "The Bourgeois Blues." —*William Ruhlmann*

Tribute to Woody Guthrie: Highlights from Concerts / 1972 / Warner Brothers ✦✦✦✦
Woody Guthrie died on Oct 3, 1967. Tribute concerts to him were organized at Carnegie Hall in New York in January 1968 and at the Hollywood Bowl in Los Angeles in September 1970. This double-record set presents highlights from both shows and is notable for a rare Bob Dylan performance and a collection of Guthrie songs sung by others of his children (literally and figuratively): Arlo Guthrie, Judy Collins, Odetta, Richie Havens, Tom Paxton, Pete Seeger, and more. —*William Ruhlmann*

★ **Troubadours of British Folk, Vol. 1: Unearthing the Tradition** / Nov. 21, 1995 / Rhino ✦✦✦✦✦
Rhino's *Troubadours of British Folk* series, encompassing three volumes, four decades, 49 songs, and almost as many performers, is a model genre retrospective. For those who want a representative collection of the style's highlights, it covers virtually all of the major performers and innovators of British folk, represented by their best-known (and usually best) songs. For those who want an introduction/guide to the form, it's equally useful, serving as an excellent foundation to build upon if you're motivated to seek out more albums by these performers after an initial taste. Vol. 1 covers the mid-'50s to the early '70s, encompassing skiffle (Lonnie Donegan), elder statespersons (Ewan MacColl), virtuoso guitarists (Davy

Graham, Bert Jansch, Martin Carthy), traditional singers (Jean Redpath, Shirley & Dolly Collins), singer-songwriters (Donovan), and early efforts by the major players of British folk-rock (Fairport Convention, Pentangle, the Incredible String Band, Steeleye Span). Then there are names which are virtually unknown these days in the States, like the Young Tradition, Anne Briggs, and Wizz Jones. Along with some expected classics (Fairport's "Fotheringay," Donegan's "Rock Island Line," Jansch's "Needle of Death") are some rare coveted treasures, like MacColl's "Dirty Old Town" (eventually covered by the Pogues) and Graham's "Angi" (popularized by Simon & Garfunkel). The liner notes, with quotes from many of the artists and extensive commentary, are great, as they are for each volume of the series. —*Richie Unterberger*

★ **Troubadours of British Folk, Vol. 2: Folk into Rock** / Nov. 21, 1995 / Rhino ✦✦✦✦✦
All of the cuts on this volume hail from what is commonly considered the golden age of British folk-rock, 1969-75. Virtually all of the major players, including Fairport Convention, Nick Drake, Roy Harper, Ralph McTell, Steeleye Span, and Richard Thompson, are represented by some of their most famous tracks. Not as renowned, but of near-equal importance, are the contributions by Shirley Collins, Fotheringay, Amazing Blondel, Lindisfarne, Mr. Fox (by far the most obscure name on the set), and the surprise inclusion of Traffic, represented by "John Barleycorn." It may be that big British folk-rock fans are already familiar with most or all of this. But you can't fault the content: this is the cream of the crop of a vital strain of both folk and rock, though it wasn't nearly as popular in the States as the UK —*Richie Unterberger*

★ **Troubadours of British Folk, Vol. 3: An Evolving Tradition** / Nov. 21, 1995 / Rhino ✦✦✦✦✦
The final volume of the series covers the mid-'70s to the mid-'90s, emphasizing traditional acts who pepped things up with a bit of electricity and eclecticism (Silly Wizard, Mouth Music), acoustic guitarists (Nic Jones, Dick Gaughan, Martin Simpson), "rogue" folkies who merged traditional sounds with influences from modern rock, world music, and punk (Billy Bragg, Oyster Band), and esteemed veteran singers (Richard Thompson, June Tabor, Maddy Prior). If this collection doesn't seem as essential to many listeners as the first two volumes, that may be because these artists (mostly still in their primes at the time of this reissue) are still forging their place in history. But few would deny that they are certainly some of the most significant British folk performers of recent times. Those wishing to catch up on the evolution of British roots music in the '80s and '90s will find this a handy primer, especially as that scene is for the most part little known in the US —*Richie Unterberger*

● **Troubadours of the Folk Era, Vol. 1** / Apr. 21, 1992 / Rhino ✦✦✦✦✦
Some of the tunes include Woody Guthrie's "This Land Is My Land," Dave Van Ronk's "Cocaine Blues," Ramblin' Jack Elliott's "San Francisco Bay Blues," and the Holy Modal Rounders' "Mister Spaceman." —*Roundup Newsletter*

★ **Troubadours of the Folk Era, Vol. 2** / Apr. 21, 1992 / Rhino ✦✦✦✦✦
Here are some of the performers and their signature songs on which the '60s folk revival was based. Pete Seeger's rendition of "Turn, Turn, Turn" and Tim Hardin's "Reason to Believe" remind the listener that contemporary performances have a vital history. Other strong cuts are "There but for Fortune" by Phil Ochs, and "Who Knows Where the Time Goes" by Judy Collins. —*Richard Meyer*

★ **Troubadours of the Folk Era, Vol. 3** / Apr. 21, 1992 / Rhino ✦✦✦✦✦
These group performances represent some of the more commercial releases of the folk revival. Beginning with Leadbelly's "Goodnight Irene" performed by the Weavers and the hit "Tom Dooley" by the Kingston Trio, continuing through to recordings by Jim Kweskin's Jug Band, this collection demonstrates how more "authentic" and "traditional" folk songs were sanitized and popularized for mass consumption. It's an interesting reminder of how essentially neutral material can take on political weight due to the actions of the performers themselves, as in the case of the Weavers. —*Richard Meyer*

Woody Guthrie/Leadbelly ... / Smithsonian/Folkways ✦✦✦✦✦
Woody Guthrie/Leadbelly—Folkways Original Vision. This collection of recordings made between 1940 and 1947 was assembled as a complement to the album *A Tribute to Guthrie and Leadbelly: A Vision Shared* (Columbia OC 44034), on which various country, folk, and rock stars covered the Guthrie and Leadbelly songs. The result is an excellent sampler, made all the more potent when heard in contrast with the Columbia album. —*William Ruhlmann*

CELTIC

There is in me (faint memory of a smile)
The soul of a shivery old cat —
Let the wood-grey body be wounded, beaten,
Whatever be at it, it will live.

These words, written in the 14th century by the Welsh bard Dafydd ap Gwylim, express the unquashable endurance of the Celtic cultures of Europe. Through centuries of oppression, of systematic attempts by foreign occupiers to destroy Celtic cultural identity, their expressive arts have continued to develop and to spawn new and emergent forms. It is a supreme and fitting irony that we consider English folk music under the rubric of "Celtic and British Isles" music.

The term "Celtic" in its most rigid sense refers to languages: to Irish, Manx, and Scots Gaelic, and to Welsh, Cornish, and Breton Brythonic. However, what we think of as Celtic music is performed by both Celtic speakers and speakers of English and French, in the Celtic homelands in the British Isles, Ireland, Brittany and the diaspora that spans the globe from Australia to America. It is defined here as music that has sprung from the ancient, ever-developing musical tradition of the Celtic homelands.

There are various levels of "professionalism" and "traditionality" among performers of this music. The tradition continues of amateur musicians and singers who watch and listen to their elders, gradually learning to express themselves within the medium of traditional musical performance. On the other hand, a renewed interest in traditional music since the '60s has created an international demand for newer groups influenced by classical, folk, jazz, and pop music. The result is a musical system with many genres and styles, ranging from unaccompanied singing or solo playing to highly structured arrangements of folk ensembles and to rock 'n' roll bands belting out jigs and reels with a vicious backbeat.

The standard of musicianship in this music is extraordinarily high. This is due partly to the important role of music in the cultural and national identities of the countries and ethnic groups in question, partly to vigorous systems of musical competition leading to national championships for each instrument. The high standard of performance, combined with the multifarious genres and styles considered in this section, lead to a problem of sorts: there are a huge number of good records to buy and limited space for us to guide you to them. This section concentrates somewhat on the newer, revival acts, which have a broader appeal than strictly traditional approaches. Many of these groups list their traditional sources in the notes to their albums, giving the interested listener leads for further listening.

This, then, is but a tip of the old cat's tail, a vantage point from which to begin your own explorations of the rich realms of Celtic and English folk music. *— Steve Winick*

The Albion Band

Originally used as a name to credit the musicians hired to accompany Shirley Collins in 1971, the Albion Band later became a group in their own right. Bass player Ashley Hutchings, who had previously founded and left both Fairport Convention and Steeleye Span, is the driving force behind this group. The members use acoustic and electric instruments to create a folk-rock sound something like Fairport Convention's, but usually more typically English in character. They have existed as the Albion Band, the Albion Country Band, and the Albion Dance Band. *— Steve Winick*

Rise up Like the Sun / 1978 / Carthage ◆◆◆

Battle of the Field / 1989 / Carthage ◆◆◆◆
Recorded in 1973 and released in 1976, this lovely album was the band's debut as a separate entity. *— Steve Winick*

● **Songs From the Shows** / 1990 / Road Goes on Forever ◆◆◆◆
A pastiche of concert and studio recordings from The Albion's words-and-music presentations from 1977 to 1989, it's a nicely crafted program, pleasantly strung together. *— Danny Carnahan*

Live in Concert / 1993 / Windsong ◆◆◆◆
Combining material from two BBC radio concerts, one in 1977, one in 1982, this is classic material from two of the band's most exciting periods, blending traditional music with pop. *— Steve Winick*

Captured / 1994 / HTD ◆◆

Martin Allcock

Dulcimer, Banjo, Bass, Bouzouki, Guitar, Accordion, Keyboards, Vocals
A former member of the Bully Wee Band, Allcock took his multi-instrumental talents into Fairport Convention in the mid '80s. *— Steve Winick*

Maart / 1990 / Woodworm ◆◆◆◆
Featuring traditional and original songs, Maart plays everything under the sun, cooking up a well-balanced folk-rock stew. *— Steve Winick*

Altan

Ireland's most electrifying current group features fiddles, flute, bouzouki, and guitar in driving and precise arrangements of dance tunes, along with airs and songs by the stunning Mairead Ni Mhaonaigh. The band began as a duo, Ni Mhaonaigh on vocals and fiddle and her husband, Frankie Kennedy, on flute. They have added accompanists and lead players to the group over the last decade and now exist as a five-piece band. Altan explores the music of their Ulster and Donegal heritage—as well as some from further afield—with uncompromising senstivity and innovative flair. Each of their recorded projects has surpassed its predecessors, a truly amazing accomplishment. *— Steve Winick*

Ceol Aduaidh / 1983 / Green Linnet ◆◆◆
Like Altan, this album is by Mairead Ni Mhaonaigh (fiddle and vocals) and Frankie Kennedy (flute). It also includes Ciaran Curran, still an Altan member, on cittern. Synthesizers are added by Eithne Ni Bhraonain, who would later become a pop sensation as Enya. Like all recordings by these spectacular musicians, this one is an excellent piece of work. *— Steve Winick*

Altan / 1987 / Green Linnet ◆◆◆
This album is technically credited to Mairead Ni Mhaonaigh and Frankie Kennedy, but it's clearly the first step in Altan's development into a tight band. It's full of beautiful, fiery music, a little less dense and powerful than the later recordings. *— Steve Winick*

Horse with a Heart / 1989 / Green Linnet ◆◆◆
This album was evidence that Altan would become the best Irish traditional band in the world. *— Steve Winick*

The Red Crow / 1990 / Green Linnet ◆◆◆

Harvest Storm / 1992 / Green Linnet ◆◆◆◆
Harvest Storm represents one of the group's best—a true necessity. *— Steve Winick*

● **The First Ten Years: 1986-1995** / 1995 / Green Linnet ◆◆◆◆

Blackwater / 1996 / Virgin ◆◆◆
Altan's major label debut, *Blackwater* is yet another step in the group's continuing evolution from a traditional Irish folk band to something truly unique and special. Without abandoning their Celtic roots, Altan has updated their material to include various worldbeat and folk influ-

ences—which are all grafted to a flawless selection of traditional Irish ballads, jigs, and reels. *Blackwater* manages to push forward while retaining its roots and that, in a nutshell, is why the group is an important band. —*Thom Owens*

Ar Log

Ar Log formed in 1976, more or less at the drop of a hat, to represent Wales at a Celtic music festival after the original Welsh entry withdrew at the eleventh hour. Less a band than an accident, they referred to themselves as the band-for-hire, and so came by their Welsh name Ar Log (literally, on hire). The band caught the wave of Celtic revivalism while adding their own distinctively Welsh sound to the scene, most notably through their adoption of the Welsh triple harp. The band has been through innumerable membership changes since David Burns (mandolin, guitar, bodhran, vocals), Iolo Jones (fiddle, recorder), Dafydd Roberts (triple harp, flute), and Gwyndaf Roberts (knee harp, clarsach) came together. Since the 1980s the band (greatly expanded) has gone into semi-retirement, preferring to confine its touring activities to Wales, but continues to record albums. —*Leon Jackson*

Ar Log / 1978 / Dingles ✦✦✦
This debut is full of great singing and playing, if still a little rough. —*Steve Winick*

● **Ar Log II** / 1981 / Dingles ✦✦✦✦
Smooth vocal harmonies and powerful virtuoso playing make this their best. —*Steve Winick*

Ar Log III / 1982 / Dingles ✦✦✦
Very similar in style, presentation, and quality to *Ar Log II*, it features gentle electric bass accompaniment. —*Steve Winick*

Meillionen / 1982 / Dingles ✦✦✦
This all-instrumental release of tunes for dancing features Ar Log's classically tinged arrangements, as well as new sounds like accordion and keyboards. Ar Log did not consider *Meillionen* a regular Ar Log album, but rather a special project. —*Steve Winick*

Pedawar / 1985 / Ar Log ✦✦✦
Pedwar is Welsh for four; this fourth Ar Log release (not counting the *Meillionen* project) is very much like its predecessors, highly orchestrated but still sprightly. —*Steve Winick*

Ar Log V / 1988 / Sain ✦✦✦

Dan Ar Bras

Guitar, Vocals
A truly great acoustic and electric guitarist, and a good singer as well, Ar Bras is the guitar wizard in many of Alan Stivell's arrangements. He has also had a long and productive solo career. —*Steve Winick*

Douar Nevez / 1977 / Hexagone ✦✦✦
A Breton rock concept album, it relates the story of Ys, the Breton equivalent of Atlantis. —*Steve Winick*

● **Allez Dire a la Ville** / 1978 / Hexagone ✦✦✦✦
A well-crafted pop album with Celtic leanings, this foregrounds Ar Bras' electric guitar and voice, as well as several songs written by poet Xavier Grall. —*Steve Winick*

Acoustic / 1985 / Green Linnet ✦✦✦✦
These highly personal compositions have a Celtic feel. —*Steve Winick*

Les Iles de la Memoire / 1992 / Keltia Musique ✦✦✦

Reve de Siam / 1992 / Keltia Musique ✦✦
This is a soundtrack album that includes Ar Bras's guitar as well as John Kirkpatrick on accordions and concertinas. —*Steve Winick*

Arcady

A Galway band, Arcady features several former members of De Danann, as well as fine singing by Frances Black. —*Steve Winick*

● **After the Ball** / 1991 / Shanachie ✦✦✦✦
This features traditional Irish tunes, sentimental ditties, and one French song from Brittany. —*Steve Winick*

Frankie Armstrong

b. Jan. 13, 1941, Workington, Cumbria (UK)
Vocals
One of the most powerful voices in English folksong, Armstrong has been part of Ewan MacColl's Critic's Group. Her solo albums are all worth listening to. —*Steve Winick*

Birds in the Bush / 1966 / Topic ✦✦✦✦

Out of Love, Hope and Suffering / 1974 / Bay ✦✦✦
Serious, humorous, and bawdy songs and ballads are featured. —*Steve Winick*

Musical Instruments of England and the Celtic Countries

Bagpipes — Bagpipes are found all over the world. In its simplest form, a bagpipe consists of an air reservoir (or bag), a chanter (a pipe fitted with a double reed), and an inflation device for the bag. It may also be fitted with one or more drones (pipes that sound a single continuous note). Scottish Highland pipes, called "warpipes" in Ireland, have a mouth pipe to inflate the bag, three drones, and a nine-note fingered chanter. In the lowlands of Scotland and the north of England, mellow-toned, bellows-blown smallpipes are the norm. In Ireland, the Uillean pipe, the world's most complex bagpipe, reigns supreme. It consists of a bellows, a bag, a two-octave chanter, three drones, and three regulators (keyed drones controlled by the player's wrist) that can play short rhythmic bursts of any of a number of chords as accompaniment to the chanter.

Free Reeds — Named after their metal reeds, which are free to vibrate on three sides, these instruments include the harmonica and various squeezeboxes. The harmonica (or "moothie" in Scotland) is popular all over Britain and Ireland, owing to its affordability and small size. The melodeon (or diatonic accordion) is a squeezebox with one, two, or three rows of buttons tuned to different diatonic scales. The accordion can be the familiar piano-keyed instrument or a melodeon whose rows are tuned a half-step apart, creating a chromatic instrument. In general, chromatic-button accordions are the most popular in Ireland, melodeons are the most popular in England, and piano accordions are the most popular in Scotland, but all forms are played in all countries. The concertina is a squeezebox of hexagonal cross-section, whose buttons are spread over both ends.

Woodwinds — The whistle is a metal tube with either a wooden fipple or a plastic mouthpiece, with fingerholes like a recorder. The flute, either wooden or metal, was popular originally in Ireland but is beginning to find popularity elsewhere as well. The bombarde, a high, piercing oboe, is one of the national instruments of Brittany.

Strings — The fiddle, or violin, is popular everywhere in Europe. The harp is a very important instrument, historically speaking, to the Celtic countries; it is still the national symbol of Ireland. Celtic harps are smaller and have fewer strings than the familiar concert harp, and have no pedals. Fretted, plucked, and strummed strings like guitars, banjos, and mandolins have become important to the folk revival, both as accompaniment to singing and as solo instruments. The bouzouki, a Greek instrument imported to Irish music, and the cittern, a revived Renaissance instrument, as well as mandolas and mandocellos, also grace the music frequently.

Percussion — Anything handy may be knocked together as percussion, but the most common are spoons and bones, which can become amazingly precise, rhythmically speaking, in the right person's hands. In Ireland, the bodhran, a goatskin on a wooden frame, is the drum of choice, and this has spread all over the Celtic lands. In Scotland, side drums and snare drums are used, mostly in military music. —*Steve Winick*

Frankie Armstrong: Songs and Ballads / 1975 / Topic ✦✦✦
Classic old ballads are included. —*Steve Winick*

★ **And the Music Plays So Grand** / 1981 / Briar ✦✦✦✦✦
A live performance of traditional and contemporary songs, held in Sweden in 1978, is captured on this wonderful album. —*Steve Winick*

I Heard a Woman Singing / 1984 / Flying Fish ✦✦✦
The traditional and original songs on this album address women's issues. —*Steve Winick*

Auffret, Anne, and Yann-Fanche Kemener

Harp, Vocals
Anne Auffret is a singer and harp player with an angelic voice who specializes in religious music and hymns. Yann-Fanche Kemener is one of the most important Breton singers of the current generation. It was

largely through his influence that many younger people became interested in Breton songs. His name is sometimes spelled Jean-Francois Quemener. — *Steve Winick*

● **Roue Gralon Ni Ho Salud** / 1994 / Keltia Musique ✦✦✦✦
The two unearthly voices and the gentle ring of the harp make this an album of rare beauty. — *Steve Winick*

Barely Works

This English dance band draws on eclectic instrumentation and influences to create stimulating and original music. — *Steve Winick*

Don't Mind Walking / Green Linnet ✦✦✦
This punchy and upbeat album features accordion, brass, drums, guitar, and vocals. — *Steve Winick*

Barley Bree

Vocals
An Irish-Canadian act, Barley Bree sounds a lot like the Clancy Brothers and Tommy Makem. — *Steve Winick*

● **No Man's Land** / Shanachie ✦✦✦✦
Consistently well-played and sung, overbrimming with nostalgia, this is the group's best album. — *Steve Winick*

Barry Margaret with Michael Gorman

An Irish tinker of high renown, Barry possessed a remarkable, strong voice and a unique, untutored banjo style. — *Steve Winick*

● **Her Mantle So Green** / 1994 / Topic ✦✦✦✦
Cork streetsinger Barry and Sligo fiddler Gorman were among the aristocracy of the 1950s London-Irish music scene. Gorman was superb, but Barry was the queen of the come-all-ye's, whether in "The Wild Colonial Boy" or the title-song, or comic songs like "The Bicycle Race." This CD has their classic Topic recordings, including an EP with Seamus Ennis, and it's one degree more than essential. — *John Storm Roberts, Original Music*

Folk Songs (Ireland) / Smithsonian/Folkways ✦✦✦✦
Barry sang some of her best material on this album. — *Steve Winick*

Barzaz

Barzaz is one of Brittany's most innovative bands, producing unmistakably Breton music on instruments that are recent imports to the Breton scene. Jean-Michel Veillon's wooden flute, Gilles Le Bigot's guitar, Alain Genty's fretless bass, and David Hopkins' bamboo flutes and percussion are a perfect foil for Yann-Fanch Kemener's vocals, the one truly traditional aspect of Barzaz's sound. — *Steve Winick*

Ec'honder / 1989 / Excalibur ✦✦✦
Both slow, meditative songs and quicker dance songs fill this debut disc. — *Steve Winick*

● **Den Kozh Dall** / 1992 / Keltia Musique ✦✦✦✦
A fuller, more confident sound is achieved, and some dark and moody arrangements created. — *Steve Winick*

The Battlefield Band

The Glasgow-based Battlefield Band is one of Scotland's foremost folk-revival bands. Their older albums are quite traditional in style and content, but their later ones are tinged with pop. Along the way, they were among the first bands to incorporate the sounds of electric keyboards and the great Highland bagpipe into a folk-pop setting. — *Steve Winick*

Battlefield Band: Scottish Folk / 1976 / Arfolk ✦✦✦
Battlefield Band's first recording features Alan Reid, Brian McNeill, and Ricky Starr. They sing and play pretty arrangements of tunes and songs from the Scottish tradition. — *Steve Winick*

Battlefield Band 2 / 1977 / Arfolk ✦✦✦
This third album had the same year and lineup as their second, and a very similar title. However, it features different material and was released on a different label. It also features three guests who add three different types of bagpipes to Battlefield's sound. Buy it if you can find it. — *Steve Winick*

At the Front / 1978 / Topic ✦✦✦✦
A brilliant older album, it features the singing of Jamie McMenamy (later of Kornog) and Pat Kilbride. — *Steve Winick*

Stand Easy / 1979 / Topic ✦✦✦
This fine release was their first to feature a Highland piper (Duncan MacGillivray) as a band member. — *Steve Winick*

Home Is Where the Van Is / 1980 / Temple Music ✦✦✦✦
Their first US release, this excellent album introduces Ged Foley, later of the House Band. It is also the first to feature Brian McNeill's excellent songwriting, and achieves a very nice balance between their traditional roots and their modern sensibilities. — *Steve Winick*

The Story So Far / 1982 / Flying Fish ✦✦✦
A compilation of some of their older material, it includes rare tracks.

There's a Buzz / 1982 / Temple Music ✦✦✦
The same line-up as *Home Is Where the Van Is* gives a less compelling performance. — *Steve Winick*

Anthem for the Common Man / 1984 / Temple Music ✦✦✦
Alistair Russell replaces Foley, Dougie Pincock replaces MacGillivray. They begin to experiment more with electronics and with new sounds and rhythms. — *Steve Winick*

On the Rise / 1986 / Temple Music ✦✦

Music in Trust / 1986 / Temple Music ✦✦✦
With Alison Kinnaird (harp) and Robin Morton (concertina), this music from a TV soundtrack about historic places in Scotland is mostly lovely and subdued instrumental music. — *Steve Winick*

Celtic Hotel / 1987 / Temple Music ✦✦✦
The last and best trip to the studio for the band's longest-lived lineup, this album is one of their best. It features almost exclusively original material based on Scottish traditions. — *Steve Winick*

★ **After Hours** / 1987 / Temple Music ✦✦✦✦✦
This compilation of material from Battlefield's Temple Records releases is probably the place to start listening. — *Steve Winick*

Music in Trust 2 / 1988 / Temple Music ✦✦✦
More good soundtrack music. — *Steve Winick*

Home Ground Live / 1989 / Temple Music ✦✦✦
Captured live in the highlands, the band performs old favorites and new. — *Steve Winick*

The Battlefield Band's Hi-Light / 1991 / Tonn Mor ✦✦✦
A good set comes from the new lineup, caught live in the Scottish Highlands. — *Steve Winick*

New Spring / 1991 / Temple Music ✦✦✦
This new lineup finds Pincock replaced by veteran piper Iain MacDonald and McNeill, one of the band's founders, replaced by 17-year-old whiz kid John McCusker. They still make equally fine music. — *Steve Winick*

Quiet Days / 1992 / Temple Music ✦✦✦
The follow-up to *New Spring* finds the group still indulging in mostly original music based on Scottish roots. — *Steve Winick*

★ **Opening Moves** / 1993 / Topic ✦✦✦✦✦
This CD combines most of the material from *At the Front* with extra tracks taken from *Battlefield Band* and *Stand Easy*. It's the essential compilation of Battlefield's Topic period. — *Steve Winick*

Derek Bell

Piano, Harp, Oboe
Best known as the harpist with the Chieftains, Derek Bell periodically records solo albums that allow his instrumentals to take center stage, backed by fellow Chieftains on whistle, bodhran, and fiddle. — *Bruce Eder*

Carolan's Receipt / 1992 / Shanachie ✦✦✦
Bell's tribute to 17th-century harpist Turlough Carolan, backed by the New Irish Chamber Orchestra. — *Bruce Eder*

Ancient Music for the Irish Harp / 1992 / Claddagh ✦✦

● **Carolan's Favorite** / Shanachie ✦✦✦✦
Probably Bell's best and most mystical album, a subdued and varied account of Turlough Carolan's music. — *Bruce Eder*

Derek Bell's Musical Ireland / Shanachie ✦✦✦
A more general look at Irish music spanning numerous periods in various styles. — *Bruce Eder*

Peter Bellamy

b. Sep. 8, 1944, Bournemouth, Dorset, England, d. Sep. 24, 1991
Vocals
Bellamy was one of the English folk revival's greatest voices. In the early days of 1965 he moved to London, where he met up with Royston Wood and Heather Wood, and the three got a regular gig at a club whose name they would eventually adopt—the Young Tradition. In flamboyant costumes, with witty presentation, and with the startling power of Bellamy's voice backed by his companions, they entertained a lot of audiences, recorded a pair of albums, gained a reputation for excellence, and were still unable to make a living as performers. In 1969 they broke up. As Bellamy would later point out, they became important and influential, even legendary, after they had ceased to exist.

In 1970 the idea first struck Bellamy to set the poems of Kipling to music. This fascination with Kipling continued until Bellamy's death, resulting in no fewer than five albums of Kipling songs. Also in the '70s, Bellamy composed *The Transports*, a ballad opera in the mold of Ewan MacColl's work, and recruited such people as Martin Carthy, Nic Jones, A. L. Lloyd, and Cyril Tawney to record it. It was released as an album in 1977 and also had several stage runs in England. During the '70s and

'80s, Bellamy was trying to find an audience wider than the traditional folk crowd, so he cut back on the traditional songs in his shows, turning them into multimedia historical presentations. But traditional singing was in Bellamy's blood, and the beginning of the '90s found him performing mostly a traditional repertoire once again, with the exuberant enthusiasm he had always been known for. Bellamy felt there was a lack of appreciation for the music to which he had devoted his life. More than once he commented on how countless performers have ditched traditional music for other forms of "folk" music. Some, he felt, did it for money, something he no doubt understood but regretted. More often, though, he expressed regret that interest in traditional song was simply on the wane, not only with audiences, but with performers as well. He always acknowledged that his own unwillingness or perhaps his inability to compromise had led to the demise of the Young Tradition. Perhaps, some 22 years later, it helped lead to his own; in September 1991, Peter Bellamy took his own life. All Peter Bellamy recordings are recommended. —*Steve Winick*

Peter Bellamy Sings the Barrack-Room Ballads of Rudyard Kipling / 1974 / Green Linnet ✦✦✦
Bellamy performs songs of Rudyard Kipling. —*Steve Winick*

Tell it Like it Was / 1975 / Trailer ✦✦✦
Over the ten years previous to this release, Bellamy had been writing tunes to traditional words and words to traditional tunes. This release showcased some of the results. —*Steve Winick*

☆ **The Transports** / 1977 / Free Reed ✦✦✦✦✦
Bellamy's masterpiece ballad opera starred himself and other influential folk singers. —*Steve Winick*

★ **Both Sides Then** / 1979 / Topic ✦✦✦✦✦
Traditional songs of England, Ireland, and America, sung in Bellamy's amazing voice and accompanied by guests such as Louis Killen and Dave Swarbrick, are simply beautiful. —*Steve Winick*

Songs An' Rummy Conjurin' Tricks / 1991 / Fellside ✦✦✦✦
Recorded live a scant nine months before his death, this album is an excellent example of Bellamy's charm as a live performer. —*Steve Winick*

Mary Bergin

Flute (Wood), Whistle (Instrument)
Mary Bergin is a member of a musical family from Dublin. She learned to play the tin whistle as a child and was all-Ireland champion in her teens. Not primarily a performer, she teaches whistle and makes Uillean pipes and flutes. —*Steve Winick*

Mary Bergin / 1979 / Shanachie ✦✦✦✦

★ **Feadoga Stain** / 1979 / Shanachie ✦✦✦✦✦
Bergin is joined by members of De Danann, who accompany her through an outstanding display of tunes and talent. —*Steve Winick*

Feadoga Stain 2 / 1993 / Shanachie ✦✦✦✦
We waited 14 years for another solo album, and it's worth it. —*Steve Winick*

The Black Family

This talented singing family features Mary Black, who gained recognition with the group De Danann and then broke through to great fame on her own, as well as Frances Black, whose work with Arcady seems sure to catapult her to similar success. Their brothers Martin, Michael, and Shay round out the group. —*Steve Winick*

★ **The Black Family** / Dara ✦✦✦✦✦
One of the best albums of Irish singing you'll find, this features old ballads, sea shanties, and contemporary numbers all together. —*Steve Winick*

Mary Black

b. May 22, 1955, Ireland
Vocals
Mary Black is a performer equally at home singing traditional Irish folk tunes and contemporary music including blues, rock, jazz, country and soul. She was born into a musical family, the daughter of a fiddler and a singer. She started out professionally with her brother and sister in Dublin nightclubs and then performed with General Humbert, a folk group, until 1982, when she released her eponymous solo debut. The album made it to the Top Five on the Irish album charts and won the Irish Independent Arts Award for Music. At the invitation of Alec Finn, Black joined the band De Danann. A week later, she took part in the recording of *Song of Ireland* with them. She remained with De Danann for three years. In 1984, Black helped produce and sang back-up on the *Black's Family Favourites* album. She was still performing with De Danann when she launched her solo career with the Declan Sinnott-produced largely pop album *Without the Fanfare*. Many of the tracks went gold, and for both 1987 and 1988 she was named Best

Female Artist in the Irish Rock Music Awards Poll. Black's music crossed the Atlantic in 1990, when her 1989 album *No Frontiers*, debuted in the US and climbed to the Top 20 of the New Adult Contemporary charts. It was also a top seller in Ireland. That year Black began a successful concert tour of Japan. Though her music is firmly based in Irish tradition, Black is interested in performing all kinds of music. Her first influences included Sandy Denny and the Fairport Convention. Other influences include Billie Holiday, Aretha Franklin, and Bonnie Raitt. —*Sandra Brennan*

Mary Black / 1983 / Gifthorse ✦✦✦
Mary Black's sound is a perfect blend of pop, jazz, and traditional Celtic. Known to many for her work as vocalist for the famous De Danann band, her style is sometimes contemporary, and at other times, as on her beautiful rendition of "Anachie Gordon," the most traditional essence. It's for all you folkies who don't think you like pop music. —*Ladyslipper*

● **Collected** / 1984 / Gifthorse ✦✦✦✦
This 1986 album contains both previously released and unreleased material; many traditional songs with Irish instrumentation (Uillean pipes, bouzouki, fiddle, sitar, etc.), including a beautiful Gaelic ballad and "She Moves Through the Fair." —*Ladyslipper*

Without the Fanfare / 1985 / Gifthorse ✦✦✦
This album by this indescribably wonderful vocalist has leavings and separations as a theme: "Ellis Island," "As I Leave Behind Neidin," plus the plaintive "Crow on the Cradle." —*Ladyslipper*

By the Time It Gets Dark / 1987 / Gifthorse ✦✦✦
Mary Black exhibits diverse musical interests and a broad vocal range on her latest recording, *By the Time It Gets Dark*, making this a must-buy for Black fans and Celtic music lovers in general. With a voice that has the depth of a poet's passion, Black captures and synthesizes both the folk sound of Ireland and today's pop sounds, creating a Celtic sound that is ancient and timeless. Black explores the range of her emotion in the folk-like "School Days Over" and "Leaving the Land," expressing a passion that can't be explained by the lyrics alone. "Sparks Might Fly" exhibits Black's contemporary music side, with its spicy jazz melody. She is accompanied by a mostly acoustic band that matches her stunning skills. —*MusD*

No Frontiers / 1989 / Gifthorse ✦✦✦
Mary Black's strong vocals take hold of you on this CD, along with the strong producing and guitar work of Declan Sinnott. Features Noel Bridgeman, Garvan Gallagher, Pat Crowley and Carl Garaghty. Black shines on past the point of rescue on the lighthearted "Carolina Rua" and the "Moving Hearts Sounding Another Day." —*Chip Renner*

Babes in the Woods / 1991 / Gifthorse ✦✦✦✦
An exquisite collection of music. Mary Black's vocals are at their best. Declan Sinnott produced the album and plays on it. Includes a fine cover of Joni Mitchell's "The Urge for Going." —*Chip Renner*

The Holy Ground / Apr. 1993 / Gifthorse ✦✦✦
. . . The Holy Ground offers a number of contemporary folk songs, along with a sprinkling of traditional songs. Guitars, bass, fiddles, percussion, and a number of traditional instruments round out the instrumentation. The treat, though, is her voice. To listen to Black's voice is to hear an Ireland thick with stories, dripping with emotion, and full of life. —*MusD*

Bleizi Ruz

One of Brittany's top bands, Bleizi Ruz blend traditional accordion and bombarde playing with the newer sounds of electric guitars, bass, and drums. —*Steve Winick*

En Concert / 1991 / Escalibur ✦✦✦
A live album featuring innovative instrumentals and traditional and original songs. —*Steve Winick*

Hent Sant Jakez / 1993 / Shamrock ✦✦✦
With guests like Spain's La Musga–a and Leilia, Ireland's Desi Wilkinson, and Brittany's Laurent Jouin, Bleizi Ruz perform music relating to the pilgrimage from France to Santiago, Spain. —*Steve Winick*

● **Coz Lizoriou-Klask Ar Plac'h** / Pluriel ✦✦✦✦
Two albums on one CD make for a lot of good, solid, instrumental music. —*Steve Winick*

Blowzabella

Blozabella was formed in the early '80s by a group of musicians studying instrument making. The idea was to make traditional dance music based on the use of melody accompanied drones. Original members included Sam Palmer and Cliff Stapleton (hurdy-gurdies), and Dave Roberts (melodeons, piano). Over the years they evolved into a highly electric band featuring Andy Cutting (melodeons, percussion), Nigel Eaton (hurdy-gurdies, cello, percussion), Jo Freya (vocals, tenor saxophone, clarinet), Paul James (saxophone, bagpipes, rauschfeife, percussion), and Jon Swayne (saxophone, bagpipes). Their music has been influenced by Middle Eastern, Irish, and Bulgarian music. —*Steve Winick and Chip Renner*

Blowzabella / 1982 / Plant Life ✦✦✦
Subtitled "Traditional Dance Music," this album is intended for dancing,
and the notes include dance instructions as well as detailed descriptions
of their instruments. The music is mostly French, with English music taking second place. — *Steve Winick*

In Colour / 1983 / Plant Life ✦✦✦
Like their first album, this live follow-up includes mostly French music
played on bagpipes, hurdy-gurdy, melodeon and woodwinds. It's got
great energy and verve, and also has dancing instructions included.
— *Steve Winick*

● **Bobittyshooty** / 1984 / Plant Life ✦✦✦✦
The Blowzabella boys began to foreground their own compositions on
this LP. Spirited and enjoyable, this is one of their best. — *Steve Winick*

Vanilla / 1990 / Green Linnet ✦✦✦✦
You'll hear all types of European influences on this CD. Not for the faint
of heart; only fans of the eclectic need apply. — *Chip Renner*

The Bothy Band

This groundbreaking band of the '70s folk revival includes pipes, flute,
fiddle, guitar, and more, plus the unbelievable singing voice of Triona Ni
Dhomhnaill. — *Steve Winick*

1975: The First Album / 1975 / Green Linnet ✦✦✦✦
The brilliant 1975 debut featured fiddler Tommy Peoples. — *Steve Winick*

★ **Old Hag You Have Killed Me** / 1976 / Green Linnet ✦✦✦✦✦
An electrifying set, *Old Hag* features some of Bothy Band's strongest
material and best performances. It marks the debut of Kevin Burke as a
member. — *Steve Winick*

Out of the Wind into the Sun / 1977 / Green Linnet ✦✦✦
Perhaps their weakest album, this is still very much worth hearing. It features more synthesizer and electric piano than before, and marked an
era when the band was uncertain of its future. — *Steve Winick*

After Hours (Live in Paris) / 1979 / Green Linnet ✦✦✦
The Bothy Band are back at their peak on this live farewell album. Some
of their greatest hits are reprised, and some new material is introduced
in a concert context. — *Steve Winick*

★ **Best of the Bothy Band** / 1988 / Green Linnet ✦✦✦✦✦
Intricate arrangements, lovely singing, and powerful rhythms make this
an absolute must. — *Steve Winick*

La Bottine Souriante

Quebec's traditional music is a blend of French and Irish styles. This is
Quebec's top folk ensemble, incorporating fiddle, accordion, and guitar.
— *Steve Winick*

Les Epousailles / 1981 / Gamma ✦✦✦
Lots of good material. — *Steve Winick*

Y a Ben du Changement / 1982 / Gamma ✦✦✦
This sounds much like Les Epousailles. — *Steve Winick*

Je Voudrais Changer d'Chapeau / 1989 / Rounder ✦✦✦
This won a Juno award in Canada, and it brilliantly mixes diverse styles
ranging from folk to Cajun to French to country. The group shares vocal
duties, and their exuberant harmonies, spirited arrangements, and rousing uptempo themes are uniformly appealing throughout. Despite structural and linguistic differences, La Bottine Souriante's music has elements that fans of many American idioms should recognize and admire.
— *Ron Wynn*

● **Jusqu'aux P'tites Heures** / 1991 / Mille Pattes ✦✦✦✦
La Bottine have melded with a brass quartet to become a driving Quebec
folk orchestra. — *Steve Winick*

Chic'n' Swell / Green Linnet ✦✦✦
A strong followup to their earlier albums. — *Steve Winick*

La Traversee de l'Atlantique / Green Linnet ✦✦✦✦
Their most Irish-sounding album has a bodhran player adding to the distinctly Canadian percussion of heavy boot-tapping. — *Steve Winick*

Robin Huw Bowen

Harp
Bowen is the greatest exponent of the Welsh triple harp. He has been a
member of the group Mabsant as well as a solo musician. — *Steve Winick*

Cyfarch y Delyn (Greet the Harp) / 1988 / Sain ✦✦✦
A collection of beautiful airs and dances is played by Bowen on solo
harp. — *Steve Winick*

● **Telyn Berseiniol fy Ngwlad (The Sweet Harp of My Land)** / 1991 /
Flying Fish ✦✦✦✦
More of the same, this CD features two tracks from Cyfarch Y Delyn as
bonus tracks. — *Steve Winick*

The Boys of the Lough

This folk-revival group features members from England, Ireland, and
Scotland, led by the great Shetland fiddler Aly Bain. — *Steve Winick*

● **The Boys of the Lough** / 1973 / Shanachie ✦✦✦✦
This debut album is particularly brilliant because of Robin Morton and
Dick Gaughan's contributions. — *Steve Winick*

Second Album / 1973 / Rounder ✦✦✦
Live album. Good sound quality. — *Chip Renner*

Lochaber No More / 1975 / Philo ✦✦✦
This is another excellent album of dances, airs, and songs. — *Steve Winick*

Live at Passim's / 1975 / Philo ✦✦✦
A great early album, still with Morton. — *Steve Winick*

Wish You Were Here / 1978 / Flying Fish ✦✦✦
These are live-performance recordings of the traditional Irish group's
Shetland Islands tour. — *AMG*

Regrouped / 1980 / Flying Fish ✦✦✦
This album features traditional Celtic folk music in a variety of styles,
from airs and hornpipes to reels, a capella ballads, and jigs. — *AMG*

To Welcome Paddy Home / 1986 / Shanachie ✦✦✦
The tragic death of guitarist Tich Richardson left the band short and
shocked for a while, but they bounced back beautifully on this album.
— *Steve Winick*

Far from Home / 1986 / Shanachie ✦✦✦
Highly recommended. — *Chip Renner*

Farewell and Remember Me / 1987 / Shanachie ✦✦✦
One of their finest records. — *Chip Renner*

Sweet Rural Shade / 1988 / Shanachie ✦✦✦
Includes their top three releases. — *Chip Renner*

The Fair Hills of Ireland / 1993 / Sage Arts ✦✦✦
The boys celebrate their 25th anniversary with this excellent studio
album. — *Steve Winick*

Live at Carnegie Hall / Sage Arts ✦✦✦
A good live album. The crowd is into the show. — *Chip Renner*

Brass Monkey

Brass Monkey were a most unusual and appealing English folk group.
Composed of Martin Carthy (guitar, mandolin, vocals), John Kirkpatrick
(squeezeboxes, vocals), Howard Evans (trumpet, fluegelhorn, vocals),
Martin Brinsford (saxophone, mouth-organ, percussion) and, depending
on the date, either Roger Williams or Richard Cheetham (trombone),
they were a powerful and commanding group. Unfortunately, these very
busy musicians were unable to find enough time for the band to continue. — *Steve Winick*

Brass Monkey / 1971 / Rare Earth ✦✦✦✦
This was the band's majestic debut album, featuring Carthy and Kirk-
patrick's singing backed by the innovative combination of instruments.
— *Steve Winick*

See How it Runs / 1986 / Topic ✦✦✦
A worthy successor, this features more bold and brassy arrangements of
traditional songs. — *Steve Winick*

★ **Complete Brass Monkey** / 1993 / Topic ✦✦✦✦✦
A CD re-release of all the Brass Monkey material, it's thoroughly indispensable and is the one to buy. — *Steve Winick*

Anne Briggs

b. Sep. 29, 1944, Toton, Nottinghamshire, England
Bouzouki, Guitar, Vocals
Both a singer of traditional songs and a songwriter, Briggs was an influence on many important revival singers—June Tabor, Maddy Prior,
Sandy Denny, Jacqui McShee, Christy Moore, and others—before she
gave up performing for a quieter life. Her lovely voice and accompaniments on guitar and bouzouki still sound fresh and vital. — *Steve Winick*

Anne Briggs / 1971 / Topic ✦✦
The Time Has Come / 1971 / CBS ✦✦✦
★ **Classic Anne Briggs** / 1990 / Fellside ✦✦✦✦✦
This CD re-release captures all of her recordings for Topic between 1964
and 1971. Almost every folk song she recorded is here, making this an
absolute must. — *Steve Winick*

Robin Bullock

Fiddle, Guitar, Mandolin
Multi-instrumentalist Robin Bullock is a bluegrass-turned-Celtic string
wizard. He is currently a member of the group Helicon. — *Steve Winick*

- **Green Fields** / 1993 / Dorian Discovery ✦✦✦✦
Bullock plays Celtic instrumentals on cittern, guitar, and other instruments and uses the studio to its fullest effect. —*Steve Winick*

Joe Burke

b. Mar. 16, 1884, Philadelphia, PA, d. Jun. 9, 1950, Upper Darby, PA
Accordion
One of Ireland's best-known accordion players, Burke comes out of the great Galway squeezebox tradition. —*Steve Winick*

The Tailor's Choice / 1983 / Green Linnet ✦✦✦
Burke plays mostly boxwood flute. Maire Ni Chathasaigh joins him on harp. —*Steve Winick*

Happy to Meet and Sorry To Part / 1986 / Green Linnet ✦✦✦
This trio album with Michael Cooney and Terry Corcoran features pipes, accordion, guitar, and singing. —*Steve Winick*

- **Traditional Music of Ireland** / Green Linnet ✦✦✦✦
Recorded in 1972 and 1973, this album was released in 1983. A truly classic accordion album, it has impressive lift and verve. —*Steve Winick*

Kevin Burke

Fiddle
The most fluid and mesmeric fiddler playing Irish music, Burke has been a member of Patrick Street and the Bothy Band. —*Steve Winick*

If the Cap Fits / 1978 / Green Linnet ✦✦✦
This showcases Burke's amazing talents. —*Steve Winick*

Promenade / 1979 / Green Linnet ✦✦✦
With Michael O Dhomhnaill, it's not to be missed. —*Steve Winick*

- **Eavesdropper** / 1981 / Green Linnet ✦✦✦✦
Kevin and Jackie Daly show amazing empathy for one another's playing—a true musical union. —*Steve Winick*

Portland / 1982 / Green Linnet ✦✦✦✦
Another fine display, it includes Michael O Domhnaill. —*Steve Winick*

Up Close / 1984 / Green Linnet ✦✦✦✦
A gem, it features guests like Matt Molloy, Joe Burke, and the Murphy family of harmonica players. —*Steve Winick*

Open House / 1992 / Green Linnet ✦✦✦✦
An astounding disc comes from Burke and his band. —*Steve Winick*

Celtic Fiddle Festival / 1993 / Green Linnet ✦✦✦✦
This magnificent fiddle album also stars Johnny Cunningham and Christian LeMaitre of Kornog. —*Steve Winick*

Buttons and Bows

This group is made up of Jackie Daly, along with brothers Seamus and Manus McGuire on fiddles. —*Steve Winick*

The First Month of Summer / 1987 / Green Linnet ✦✦✦
More of a good thing. —*Steve Winick*

Ian Campbell

Vocals
Ian Campbell and the Ian Campbell Folk Group were Britain's favorite folk performers, bar none, during the '60s. Based in Birmingham, they featured singers Ian and Lorna Campbell of Aberdeen as well as Dave Swarbrick and Dave Pegg, later of Fairport Convention. Their arrangements are somewhat dated today, but with their rousing guitar, banjo, and fiddle accompaniments, some songs still sound fresh, and Swarbrick in particular was ahead of his time. —*Steve Winick*

Across the Hills / 1964 / Transatlantic ✦✦✦
A good general Campbell album. —*Steve Winick*

- **Coaldust Ballads** / 1965 / Transatlantic ✦✦✦✦
These mining songs are mostly from the Northeast. —*Steve Winick*

The Singing Campbells / 1965 / Topic ✦✦✦
Ian and Lorna, plus their sister Winnie, their parents Dave and Betty, and their friend Bob Cooney play unaccompanied traditional songs, including old ballads and modern street songs. —*Steve Winick*

Tam O'Shanter / 1968 / Xtra ✦✦✦
Ian Campbell alone performs songs by Robert Burns. —*Steve Winick*

Capercaillie

Featuring accordion, fiddle, whistles, and guitar along with an array of electronics, Capercaillie makes new Scottish folk music. —*Steve Winick*

Crosswinds / 1984 / Green Linnet ✦✦✦
This is the great 1987 debut release that introduced Karen Matheson's angelic vocals—soaring above mystical backgrounds—to the American public. These Scottish musicians move effortlessly from highly charged gigs and reels to serene, spellbinding ballads in both Gaelic and English,

in a style that has been described as early Clannad crossed with Silly Wizard. Instruments include accordion, recorder, whistles, bouzouki, guitar, fiddles, basses, and percussion. —*Ladyslipper*

- **Sidewaulk** / 1989 / Green Linnet ✦✦✦✦
Donal Lunny's production and the band's skill make this collection of driving, syncopated tunes and songs very exciting indeed. —*Steve Winick*

Get Out / Jul. 1996 / Green Linnet ✦✦✦✦
Get Out is a cross-section of traditional Celtic music and funk-inflected British music. The album is split between live tracks and remixed older releases, including "Coisich a Ruin," which was a Top 40 hit. That mean's *Get Out* is nearly a Capercaillie "greatest hits" collection—it features their most familiar material, although not in their most familiar versions. Nevertheless, the album offers a good sampling of the group's material and works as a solid introduction to the group. —*Thom Owens*

Danny Carnahan

Fiddle, Guitar, Vocals
Danny Carnahan and Robin Petrie have enjoyed a fruitful partnership since the 1970s, when they first began to perform folk and experiment with a widening variety of world musical styles. Carnahan and Petrie met while students at the University of Califorinia at Irvine and soon began to play together, he on guitar and subsequently fiddle; she on recorder and later the hammered dulcimer. While Petrie gave up on music to become a potter, Carnahan embraced Irish and Scottish music, teaming up with Chris Caswell and recording two albums. Then, in 1980, Petrie rejoined Carnahan, and the two of them began to play a music that was at once very Celtic and very American; the results were heard on 1984's *Two for the Road*. There followed *Journeys of the Heart*, also released in 1984, and *Continental Drift*, released in 1987. In 1988 the band decided to change from the Celtic fringe toward a more synthetic sound, one less derivative and more coherent. Their release in 1989 of *No Regrets* was welcomed as a refreshing departure and a new chapter in the annals of the band. —*Leon Jackson*

- **Journeys of the Heart** / 1984 / Celtoid ✦✦✦✦
One of the best recordings of traditional and original Irish and Scottish material from an American act, this features Carnahan's voice and instruments backed by Petrie on a few tracks. —*Steve Winick*

Two for the Road / Flying Fish ✦✦✦
Another great set of tunes and songs, this features more participation by Petrie. —*Steve Winick*

No Regrets / DNA ✦✦✦✦
Mostly contemporary folk-style material with a Celtic flavor, this is a new direction for the duo. It works well. —*Steve Winick*

Liz Carroll

Fiddle
A fantastic Irish fiddler from Chicago, Liz Carroll has been a member of Cherish the Ladies and of the Green Fields of America. She's also part of one of the greatest Irish trios performing today, along with Billy McComiskey and Daithi Sproule. Her solo work also deserves attention. —*Steve Winick*

Friend Indeed: Irish Fiddle and Piano / 1978 / Shanachie ✦✦✦
Carroll's light and quick but firmly accented fiddling is backed by Marty Fahey's better-than-average piano on this, her first solo album. —*Steve Winick*

Kiss Me Kate: Irish Fiddle and Accordion / 1978 / Shanachie ✦✦✦
Carroll is joined by button-accordion player Tommy Maguire for some tight duo playing that predicts her later work with Billy McComiskey. —*Steve Winick*

Liz Carroll / 1988 / Green Linnet ✦✦✦✦
Accompanied by guitarist Daithi Sproule, she wrote some of these powerhouse tunes by herself. —*Steve Winick*

★ **Trian** / 1992 / Flying Fish ✦✦✦✦✦
Carroll and Billy McComiskey play as one on this utterly brilliant recording, and Daithi Sproule's accompaniment and singing are as good as it gets. This is the best Irish trio there is. —*Steve Winick*

Trian II / Nov. 21, 1995 / Green Linnet ✦✦✦✦

Martin Carthy

b. May 21, 1940, Hatfield, Hertfordshire, England
Guitar, Vocals
Martin Carthy is one of the pioneers of the folk revival that swept Britain in the early '60s. As a singer, he has introduced many beautiful and moving traditional songs to audiences worldwide. As a guitarist, he's credited with helping to invent a style of accompaniment prevalent in British folk music. He has created many songs from shreds and patches of traditional material, fragments that were too beautiful to be discarded. Others he

has created out of whole cloth. For all this he has been called "the best-known urban revival singer in England," and, more succinctly, "a living legend." In 1965 Martin recorded his first album. He was accompanied by fiddler Dave Swarbrick, who played with the Ian Campbell folk group, at the time one of Britain's most successful folk acts. Carthy and Swarbrick soon became fast friends and musical accomplices, and they toured and recorded together from 1966 to 1969. They were one of the most important folk revival acts in Britain. Since that time, Martin has been a member of many groups, including one of the first and one of the last line-ups of the enormously successful folk-rock outfit Steeleye Span, the first line-up of the less successful Albion Country Band, the excellent and innovative group Brass Monkey, and the a capella singing family the Watersons (of which he remains a member). Recently he and Dave Swarbrick re-cemented their musical partnership. — *Steve Winick*

Martin Carthy / 1965 / Fontana ✦✦✦
Carthy's debut album, while a bit rudimentary by his later standards, sounds remarkably good 30 years later. — *Steve Winick*

Second Album / 1966 / Topic ✦✦✦
Carthy and Swarbrick start sounding more comfortable together on this fine album. — *Steve Winick*

Byker Hill / 1967 / Fontana ✦✦✦✦
Carthy and Swarbrick become a fully integrated musical personality. The title track is simply astounding. — *Steve Winick*

But Two Came By / 1968 / Fontana ✦✦✦
Carthy and Swarbrick first received equal billing on this album, a fine collection. — *Steve Winick*

Prince Heathen / 1969 / Fontana ✦✦✦
Another astounding title track is put together from traditional fragments by Carthy. — *Steve Winick*

Because It's There / 1971 / Rounder ✦✦✦
Carthy and his pal John Kirkpatrick left a two-year stint in the folk-rock group Steeleye Span in 1978, then teamed up again for this album. Wonderful, brassy arrangements feature trumpeter Howard Evans and predict Carthy's work with Brass Monkey. — *Steve Winick*

Crown of Horn / 1971 / Rounder ✦✦✦
Carthy's guitar gets a real workout on songs like "The Bonny Lass of Anglesey" and "Old Tom of Oxford." Included is really impeccable playing and singing. — *Steve Winick*

Out of the Cut / 1971 / Rounder ✦✦✦✦
The trio of Carthy, Kirkpatrick, and Evans are back for this album, one of Carthy's very best. — *Steve Winick*

Sweet Wivelsfield / 1971 / Rounder ✦✦✦
Carthy goes it alone, on his first album without Swarbrick. The result is quite good. — *Steve Winick*

Right of Passage / 1988 / Topic ✦✦✦
This set is good, but not as stunning as we might expect after a six-year hiatus in which to work up material. — *Steve Winick*

Life and Limb / 1991 / Green Linnet ✦✦✦✦
Singer/guitarist Martin Carthy and fiddler Dave Swarbrick, stars of the British folk circuit in the '60s, are reunited on a fine '90s set. It has fleet and passionate playing. — *Mark A. Humphrey*

Skin and Bone / May 1992 / Green Linnet ✦✦✦✦
A new studio album from the re-formed (though not reformed) Carthy/Swarbrick team is finally here. It's full of class and grace. — *Steve Winick*

★ **The Collection** / 1993 / Green Linnet ✦✦✦✦✦
The tracks on this compilation were picked by Martin himself from his solo recordings. — *Steve Winick*

Mike Casey

Dulcimer
A native of North Carolina, Casey has adapted Irish banjo and mandolin techniques to the Appalachian dulcimer. Along the way, he's learned to play flute in the East Galway style. — *Steve Winick*

Hourglass / 1992 / Celtic Trader ✦✦✦✦
This lovely disc features Casey's delicate dulcimer and wooden flute backed by several guests. — *Steve Winick*

Ceolbeg

Ceolbeg is an impressive Scottish band for the '90s featuring Highland bagpipes, harp, flute, and other traditional instruments next to drums, bass, and keyboards. It's all held together by the voice and guitar of singer-songwriter Davy Steele. — *Steve Winick*

/ 1990 / Greentrax ✦✦

● **Unfair Dance** / 1993 / Greentrax ✦✦✦✦
This one features some breathtaking modern arrangements of traditional songs and new material. — *Steve Winick*

Seeds to the Wind / Greentrax ✦✦✦
More polished and confident than their first album, this established Ceolbeg as one of Scotland's most important recording folk groups. Traditional and original songs alternate with excellent instrumentals. — *Steve Winick*

Cherish the Ladies

This group started with a concert series produced by the Ethnic Folk Arts Center in New York City. The theme was young women in traditional Irish music. Out of that series grew an ensemble of women musicians, fronted by flute player Joanie Madden, that is one of America's great Irish music groups. — *Steve Winick*

★ **The Back Door** / 1992 / Green Linnet ✦✦✦✦✦
Their first album as an ensemble is also one of the finest American Irish records ever. It features dance music, airs, and songs sung by Cathy Ryan. — *Steve Winick*

Out and About / May 1993 / Green Linnet ✦✦✦
This followup to *The Back Door* is another marvelous display of tight group playing and soloing. Johnny Cunningham produced it. — *Steve Winick*

Cherish the Ladies' Artists / 1995 / Shanachie ✦✦✦✦

The Chieftains

The original traditional Irish folk band, as far as anyone who came of age in the '70s is concerned, the Chieftains' sound is built principally around the sound of Paddy Moloney's pipes. It is an other-worldly sound, entirely instrumental, and the Chieftains have done more over the 20 years since they first emerged (several years after the recording of their debut album, *Chieftains I*) to reintroduce the sound of pipes, bodhran, and whistle to the world outside of Ireland than any other group of musicians. Their breakthrough to an audience beyond the ranks of Irish music enthusiasts came with the group's appearance on the soundtrack to Stanley Kubrick's movie *Barry Lyndon* (their "Women of Ireland" became a radio hit, and led to extensive further film work). Since the late '70s, their albums have settled into an effective but less-than-fully-inspired mode of creativity as the group has sought to add new wrinkles to an old repertory without repeating itself. — *Bruce Eder*

The Chieftains 1 / 1964 / Shanachie ✦✦✦
A rather tame debut album, exploring what was truly unknown territory during the mid '60s. Better things would follow. — *Bruce Eder*

The Chieftains 2 / 1969 / Shanachie ✦✦✦
More fully developed and secure sound, with Moloney stepping out in front and the rest of the group forming up nicely. — *Bruce Eder*

The Chieftains 3 / 1971 / Shanachie ✦✦✦✦
The group's first great record, a haunting trip through an Ireland of song, story, and legend. — *Bruce Eder*

The Chieftains 4 / 1973 / Shanachie ✦✦✦✦
The record that broke the group with college audiences in the mid '70s—this is elegant, wistful, and ethereal in equal measures. — *Bruce Eder*

The Chieftains 5 / 1975 / Shanachie ✦✦✦

Bonaparte's Retreat / 1976 / Shanachie ✦✦✦
The group's attempt to merge their traditional sound with a progressive form, and only partly successful—overdone and overambitious, but still worth hearing. — *Bruce Eder*

Chieftains Live! / 1977 / Shanachie ✦✦✦
An older lineup performs a rousing live set. — *Steve Winick*

The The Chieftains 7 / 1977 / CBS ✦✦✦
This is a boisterous and exuberant traditional album. — *Steve Winick*

The Chieftains 8 / 1978 / CBS ✦✦

Boil the Breakfast Early / 1980 / CBS ✦✦✦

☆ **The Chieftains 10: Cotton-Eyed Joe** / 1981 / Shanachie ✦✦✦✦✦
The Chieftains, masters of traditional Celtic music, play with vibrant energy as well as smooth cohesion. On this release, they traverse 11 tunes, including "The Christmas Reel," "Manx Music," "My Love Is in America," and the title track. — *Roundup Newsletter*

Ballad of the Irish Horse / 1985 / Shanachie ✦✦✦
Quite a concept album—songs devoted to the Irish horse and its importance and role in legend and history. — *Bruce Eder*

Irish Heartbeat / 1988 / Polydor ✦✦✦
Van Morrison sings traditional Irish songs with The Chieftains. — *Steve Winick*

Chieftains Celebration / 1989 / RCA ✦✦✦
This release features the traditional Chieftains instrumentation with the addition of drums, guitars, sax, didgeridoo, and cello. The Chieftains perform a medley of Scottish dance tunes, a double jig, a drinking song, a Van Morrison title (with Van M. himself), and a few vocals. — *MusD*

Reel Music: The Film Scores / 1991 / RCA ✦✦✦
The collected film tracks by the group, which constitute their most famous work to the public at large. A generous collection. —*Bruce Eder*

☆ **The Bells of Dublin** / Oct. 1991 / RCA ✦✦✦✦✦
Joined by Nancy Griffith, the Irish group presents a superb concert, blending folk and country music. Well recorded and well photographed. —*Bruce Eder*

Another Country / 1992 / RCA ✦✦✦✦
A classic for lovers of good and heartfelt music played with joy. This has Paddy Moloney and the Chieftains combining forces with one of the best assemblages of country musicians. A diverse group it definitely is, stretching from Ricky Skaggs to Don Williams to Colin James running into Willie Nelson and Chet Atkins in a cornucopia of audio delight. From the opening joy of "Happy to Meet," crossing the musical streets to "Heartbreak Hotel," to the romping joy shown by the players in "Cotton-Eyed Joe" and "Cunla," this CD is a never-ending country grab-bag of musical mastery. The players seem to be a unit that has been down the long, hard road of wire-fenced stages in cheap bars together, honing skills that arrive at fruition here. —*Bob Gottlieb*

Irish Evening / 1992 / RCA ✦✦✦
Guests are Nanci Griffith and Roger Daltrey. —*Steve Winick*

● **The Best of the Chieftains** / Jan. 14, 1992 / Columbia/Legacy ✦✦✦✦
Twelve favorites come from Ireland's foremost cultural ambassadors. —*Roundup Newsletter*

Long Black Veil / 1995 / RCA Victor ✦✦✦✦
With *Long Black Veil*, the Chieftains attempted a mainstream pop crossover by recording with rock and pop stars from the Rolling Stones and Sting to Van Morrison and Sinead O'Connor. Instead of changing their sound to accommodate the talents of their guests, the band plays it straight. As always, their performance is superb; what is surprising is how well the pop stars sing Celtic material. None of the guest singers sound displaced or uncomfortable, which is largely due to the sympathetic performances of the Chieftains. In fact, the pairings work so well that *Long Black Veil* doesn't sound like an effort to broaden their audience; rather, it sounds completely natural. —*Sara Sytsma*

The Clancy Brothers

The Clancy Brothers are a family of singing Irish expatriates who have been important figures in re-popularizing their native music in North America and are still among the most internationally renowned Irish folk bands. Some even credit the band as important figures in starting the folk revival of the '50s and '60s. Tom, Pat and Liam Clancy were born in Carrick-on-Suir, County Tiperrary, Ireland, to a family of nine, all of whom were musically inclined. Tom and Pat emigrated to New York around the early '50s to become actors. Liam and his friend Tommy Makem, born in Keady, County Armagh, the son of noted balladeer Sarah Makem, came to the US in 1956. Before Liam emigrated, he had founded a dramatic society and had put on a play, taking over the direction, producing, and set design himself. He had also acted at the famed Gaiety Theatre in Dublin. Both he and Makem also hoped to have acting careers in New York. The Clancy Brothers with Tommy Makem (as they were first billed) came together to sing fund-raising concerts for the Cherry Lane Theater and at the Guthrie benefits. Foregoing the stereotypical maudlin Irish ballads in favor of lusty party songs, traditional American and Irish folk songs, and even protest tunes sung in close harmony and performed most theatrically, the Clancys soon became popular folk performers around Greenwich Village. In the mid-'50s, Pat founded Tradition Records so the Clancys and Makem could begin recording. Early recordings include "The Rising of the Moon" and "Come Fill Your Glass with Me."

By recording and touring often, the Clancys continued to become more and more popular in Eastern and Midwestern clubs, but it was their debut on the "Ed Sullivan Show" in 1961 that brought them national exposure. Originally scheduled to only play three minutes, they ended up playing for 16 minutes and became an instant national sensation and soon signed a major contract with Columbia Records. The Clancys continued recording and performing together through 1969. That year Makem left to pursue his solo career. In 1975, Liam departed; he and Makem were replaced by brother Bobby Clancy and their nephew Robbie O'Connell. Since then, the original members have occasionally regrouped for reunion concerts. Tom Clancy died in 1990, but the band continues on. —*Sandra Brennan*

By the Rising of the Moon / 1959 / Tradition ✦✦✦
Their first album, recorded in Kenneth S. Goldstein's kitchen with Tommy Makem, is free from some of the hokeyness of later efforts. —*Steve Winick*

● **Greatest Hits** / 1973 / Vanguard ✦✦✦✦
This set was recorded with Lou Killen, a famous singer of Northumberland folksongs and sea chanties. Killen and The Clancys make an inter-

esting combination; it's a record worth getting and features more Scottish material than is common for The Clancys. —*Steve Winick*

Live! / 1982 / Vanguard ✦✦✦✦
With nephew Robbie O'Connell, from Waterford City, this is another indication of their skill at handling the audience. —*Steve Winick*

Aiofe Clancy

Vocals

The daughter of Bobby Clancy, one of the Clancy Brothers, Aiofe is a fine singer in her own right. She has sung in folk clubs and concert halls from Ireland to Australia, and now lives in the US. —*Steve Winick*

It's About Time / 1994 / Rego ✦✦✦
An impressive debut that features Clancy singing songs old and new. He's accompanied by some great Irish musicians. —*Steve Winick*

Liam Clancy

Guitar, Vocals

One of the original three singing Clancy Brothers, Liam later went off with Tommy Makem as a duo, and then on his own as a solo act. —*Steve Winick*

The Dutchman / Shanachie ✦✦✦
Mostly sad, slow songs fill this solo album. —*Steve Winick*

● **Liam Clancy** / Vanguard ✦✦✦✦
A classic old album of Irish songs in Clancy's gentle style, it's an excellent introduction to this artist. —*Steve Winick*

Clannad

Clannad bridged the gap between traditional Celtic music and pop. Usually their results were an entrancing, enchanting form of pop that managed to fuse the disparate elements rather seamlessly. Such fusions have earned the band an international cult of fans.

Taking their name from the Gaelic word for "family," Clannad formed in 1970 when the Brennan family—Maire (vocals, harp), Ciaran (vocals, guitar, bass, keyboards), Pol (guitar, percussion, flute, vocals)—began playing at their father Leo's tavern with two of their uncles, Padraig Duggan (guitar, vocals, mandolin) and Noel Duggan (guitar, vocals). Soon afterward, the group began playing folk festivals in Ireland. They released their self-titled first album in 1973; yet the band didn't earn any wide-spread success until they toured Germany in 1975. Maire's sister, Enya, joined the group in 1979, yet left in 1982, just as the group was beginning to come into some pop success in the UK. Clannad recorded the theme song for the television program "Harry's Game"; the single hit number five on the charts and won the band an Ivor Novello Award. The band recorded the soundtrack to the television production "Robin of Sherwood" in 1984; it won a British Academy Award for best soundtrack the next year. Clannad's success continued in 1986, when U2's Bono was featured on the Top 20 hit "In A Lifetime." The band continued to release albums into the 1990s, building their pop following without losing their folk audience. —*Stephen Thomas Erlewine*

Clannad / 1973 / Philips ✦✦✦
From a latter-day vantage point, the group's first album is probably too pop-oriented for traditionalists, but too traditional in feel for those who were attracted to the group by their pop-oriented later recordings. For those listeners without any particular preconceptions, it's an invigorating blend of Irish traditional folk with modern influences. More than any of their subsequent albums, this debut bears the influence of the eclectic, jazzy edge of Pentangle, particularly in the fat double bass lines; Maire Brennan's high, pristine vocals show an affinity with Pentangle's Jacqui McShee as well. Maire's harp and Paul Brennan's flute, however, give the music a strong Irish stamp. Singing mostly in Gaelic, occasionally in English, the scope of the material is quite varied, the arrangements and vocals vastly pretty and melodic. The cover of Tim Rose's "Morning Dew" that concludes the album is one of the best versions ever of this oft-covered folk-rock tune. —*Richie Unterberger*

Clannad 2 / 1974 / Shanachie ✦✦✦✦
Clannad 2 features crisp and subtle arrangements. —*Steve Winick*

Dulaman / 1976 / Shanachie ✦✦✦
It is the exquisite voice of Maire Ni Bhraonain that centers the vocal harmonies, and her harp playing that provides the focal point for the instrumental arrangements. The repertoire consists of traditional Gaelic songs that they infuse with an uptempo, improvisational, yet precise and delicate musicianship. —*Ladyslipper*

Clannad in Concert / 1978 / Shanachie ✦✦✦
Spectacular lead singer Maire Ni Bhraonain is Enya's sister, but if you didn't know that, you might deduce it when you hear their styles. In fact the entire ensemble consists of close relatives to these two. This album affords a rare opportunity to hear this ensemble in person—almost. (Really do it if you ever have the chance. Included is "Fairies Hornpipe,"

"Off to California," "Down by the Sally Gardens," and many Gaelic tunes. —*Ladyslipper*

Crann Ull / 1980 / Shanachie ✦✦✦
This 1980 recording from Dublin's Tara Records contains pure traditional Gaelic and Irish material, impeccably performed, naturally revolving around Maire's heavenly voice. It's one of the last straight-forward, all-acoustic albums Clannad recorded before they embarked on their experimentations with more contemporary sounds. —*Ladyslipper*

● **Fuaim** / 1982 / Atlantic ✦✦✦✦
This 1982 release (the only one with Enya) contains the beginnings of their ingenious blending of contemporary modes with the traditional; you will hear intermittent touches of synthesizer, clarinet, sax, electric guitar, and percussion. That, coupled with these six-part genetic harmonies, makes this a must for every Enya and Clannad fan. —*Ladyslipper*

Magical Ring / 1983 / Tara ✦✦✦
The best Clannad record is now available again. This exceptional album shows to great advantage the many sides of this venerable Irish group, and features the gorgeous choral feast of "Theme from Harry's Game," one of their "hits." Recorded in 1983, *Magical Ring* includes a half-dozen originals and four traditional tunes, sung in the uniquely majestic and timeless manner of Clannad's lead vocalist, Maire Ni Bhraonain. Slow, yearning pieces alternate with lively folk-inspired ballads, some laced effectively with rock elements, while the hauntingly mesmerizing "Newgrange" is filled with strumming guitars and a low bass-drum rhythm that springs open with the many colors of the rainbow. *Magical Ring* is bound to become a personal favorite for many. —*Backroads Music/Heartbeats*

The / 1984 / Tara ✦✦✦

Macalla / 1985 / RCA ✦✦✦✦
Macalla is one of Clannad's strongest albums. The songs are mainly mid-tempo or slower, and combine the poignant beauty of Irish balladry with the immediacy of a rock band line-up. Traditional Irish instruments come and go, along with touches of sax and on "In a Lifetime," soulful guest vocals by fellow Irishman Bono of U2. *Macalla* is a well-rounded album of melodic folk pop, infused with that beautiful warm sadness that seems to pervade Irish music and culture. —*Backroads Music/Heartbeats*

Sirius / 1987 / RCA ✦✦

● **Pastpresent** / 1989 / RCA ✦✦✦✦
Pastpresent is an anthology spanning five Clannad albums from 1982 to the present. The full range of the band's styles is presented here, from the gorgeous a capella song that opens the album, to slick pop-rock, acoustic guitar ballads, Irish folk strains, and sophisticated power-pop crunch. Along the way we are treated to a lyrical harp and flute instrumental, several songs sung in Gaelic, and two new pieces (recorded in part at Peter Gabriel's Real World Studios) designed to make this retrospective a collector's item. *Pastpresent*, clocking in at 65 minutes, succeeds in offering an overview of the many faces of this seminal Irish group. —*Backroads Music/Heartbeats*

Anam / 1990 / Atlantic ✦✦✦✦
Anam has primarily an acoustic sound, with the ongoing variety of 12 tracks covering vast musical terrain. Fans of Loreena McKennitt and Enya (one-time Clannad member) will also appreciate the subtle harmonies and vocal clarity of Maire Brennan. The domestic version has two extra tracks: "In a Lifetime," a duet with Bono of U2 which was previously heard on *Macalla;* and "Harry's Game," a longtime favorite from the classic *Magical Ring.* —*Backroads Music/Heartbeats*

Banba / 1994 / Atlantic ✦✦✦
Clannad continues in the trend of the last few albums with their latest release, *Banba*. Though certainly a pop effort, the Celtic influences are still present, this time in a more subdued, low-key production. —*David Jehnzen*

Clannad Themes / 1995 / Celtic Heartbeat ✦✦✦
There's only so much passion you can wring from a collection of film and TV theme songs. The cover of Joni Mitchell's "Both Sides Now" (from the Blake Edwards movie "Switch"), all cuddly synths and dewy vocals (Maire Brennan duetting with Paul Young), is very pleasant. Of marginally more substance is "Ancient Forest," from the British TV series "Robin of Sherwood," and "Theme From Harry's Game," the first Gaelic song to become a top ten hit in the UK (1982). It also earned a Billboard World Music Award and a Grammy nomination and has kept Clannad in soundtrack gravy ever since. —*Roch Parisien*

Lore / Sep. 19, 1995 / Atlantic ✦✦✦✦

Clishmaclaver

Maryland-based duo Jennifer Culley and Brooke Parkhurst specialize in Irish, American, and Scottish songs sung in bright harmonies. They have both studied singing with Irish ballad-singer Frank Harte. —*Steve Winick*

Hearing Double / Bright Phoebus ✦✦✦
Two beautiful voices treat a number of Irish ballads, English laments, and American hymns. A backing band that includes Billy McComiskey (accordion) and Myron Bretholz (bodhran) adds punch. This is an impressive debut. —*Steve Winick*

● **Roots Entwined** / Bright Phoebus ✦✦✦✦
Parkhurst and Culley display talent, feminist sensibilities, and good humor on their second album. There's a lot of Scottish and American material here, sung with skill. On this album, the backing band is all-female, and equally excellent. —*Steve Winick*

Jack and Charlie Coen

Flute, Vocals
These two musicians, formerly of Woodford, County Galway, emigrated to New York in the '50s. Both have played whistle and flute, though Jack now concentrates on flute and Charlie on concertina. Charlie Coen, also a fine singer, is known in Irish music circles simply as "Father Charlie," since his day job is serving the Church as a priest. —*Steve Winick*

The Branch Line / 1977 / Green Linnet ✦✦✦✦
This is a 1992 re-release of a classic 1977 Topic album. With reels, jigs, hornpipes, flings, and polkas, by each musician solo and by the pair of them, this is real traditional Irish music at its best. —*Steve Winick*

Michael Coleman

Fiddle
Michael Coleman (1891-1945) of Killavil, County Sligo, is one of the seminal figures in Irish and Irish-American traditional music. He came to the United States in 1914 and became a successful performer of Irish music in vaudeville and variety theaters across America. He settled in New York City, where Irish music was in great demand. Between 1921 and 1944 he did many 78 rpm recordings of fiddle music that even today exert a great influence on players both here and in Ireland. Coleman's recorded material is one of the reasons why the Sligo fiddle style and tune repertoire predominate in much Irish and Irish-American fiddling. Many of Coleman's classic recordings have been re-released on albums. —*Steve Winick*

★ **Michael Coleman 1891-1945** / 1992 / Gael-Linn/Viva Voce ✦✦✦✦✦
This stunning double-CD release features 48 of Coleman's hugely influential sides, as well as a booklet over 100 pages long with fascinating accounts of Coleman and his music. It's the best Coleman compilation available. —*Steve Winick*

Shirley Collins

b. Jul. 5, 1935, Hastings, Sussex, England
Vocals
Shirley Collins, though almost unknown in the United States, was an immensely important figure in Britain's early-'60s folk revival and the golden age of British folk-rock in the late '60s and early '70s. She is one of British folk's most golden-throated vocalists and one of its most eclectic, handling traditional fare, Renaissance music, and folk-rock. Any discussion of her recordings must also note the important contributions of her non-singing sister, the late Dorothy Collins, who was co-billed on several albums. Dorothy, who played keyboards, also devised the arrangements for the albums of Renaissance-influenced folk that the pair released to high critical acclaim in the late '60s.

Shirley actually made her first album in 1959 for Folkways. For a time she was a companion of noted folklorist Alan Lomax, whom she accompanied on trips through the American South that produced some of the most widely praised field recordings of traditional American folk music. In 1964, she helped point the way for a more eclectic approach to British folk music by recording with guitar wizard Davey Graham on the album *Folk Roots, New Routes*.

Collins made her true mark when she teamed with sister Dolly to offer several albums of medieval-based folk music. The most widely hailed effort in this direction was 1969's *Anthems in Eden*, a suite of sorts combining traditional material and original instrumental interludes. The 1970's follow-up, the similar *Love, Death & the Lady*, was just as good; both albums appeared on the Harvest label, a company most noted for its British progressive/underground rock acts. The affiliation wasn't as unlikely as it might appear, for Collins had already helped direct British folk-rock acts such as Pentangle to traditional folk material. Therefore, it wasn't a total surprise to find her turning up in bonafide folk-rock groups, particularly as she had married Ashley Hutchings, a key early member of both Fairport Convention and Steeleye Span. With Hutchings, she sang in a couple of the mid-'70s' most traditionally oriented British folk-rock outfits, the Albion Country Band and the Etchingham Steam Band. —*Richie Unterberger*

Folk Roots, New Routes / 1964 / Decca ✦✦✦✦
Collins appears with Davy Graham, a fantastic guitarist. —*Steve Winick*

The Sweet Primeroses / 1967 / Topic ♦♦♦
Her sister, Dolly Collins, adds portative pipe organ to Shirley's voice and banjo. —*Steve Winick*

● **Anthems in Eden** / 1969 / Harvest ♦♦♦♦
Considered a landmark recording in some circles, this was constructed as a concept album of sorts. The suite-like flow of Renaissance-period material (sung by Shirley) was linked by instrumental passages. Dolly Collins' intricate arrangements, executed with the help of David Murrow of the Early Music Consort, displayed her virtuosity on pipe organ. The duo's next album, *Love, Death & the Lady* (1970), was equally noteworthy; *Anthems in Eden* is recommended as the first purchase because it is regarded by the folk community as a pivotal release. —*Richie Unterberger*

Love, Death and the Lady / 1970 / Harvest ♦♦♦♦
More outstanding arrangements of medieval fare, given emotional resonance by Shirley's outstanding interpretations and Dolly's dignified, haunting arrangements for an ensemble featuring Christopher Hogwood on harpsichord, Pentangle drummer Terry Cox on percussion, and Dolly herself on organ and piano. Just as impressive as *Anthems in Eden*, although not as widely discussed. —*Richie Unterberger*

No Roses / 1971 / Antilles ♦♦♦
This features a truly impressive folk-rock backing band, later to become the Albion Band. —*Steve Winick*

Seamus Connolly

Fiddle
Seamus Connolly has won all-Ireland fiddle titles a whopping ten times. He has also been a judge at the same competition, a solo musician, and a teacher. Currently, he teaches traditional Irish music at Boston College, and tours and records when he can. —*Steve Winick*

Notes from My Mind / Green Linnet ♦♦♦
This brilliant debut established his reputation among listeners as a master performer. It is slightly marred by weak sound in places, but the musicianship is impeccable. Guests include Liam O'Flynn (uilleann pipes) and Tommy Hayes (percussion). —*Steve Winick*

● **Here and There** / Green Linnet ♦♦♦♦
Connolly's second album surpasses his first. Robust sound is a big improvement, and the tunes are unusual and exciting. Accompanists include Mick Moloney and Tommy Hayes. —*Steve Winick*

The Copper Family

Farmers, shepherds, carters, and innkeepers, the Coppers have sung for at least 200 years in the same Sussex village, in a style reflecting the tradition of pub bard on Saturday, church choir on Sunday. —*John Storm Roberts*

Coppersongs / 1988 / EFDSS ♦♦♦♦
Four generations of this most important of English singing families continue, delightfully, an unusually pure example of living tradition. —*John Storm Roberts*

Arthur Cormack

Vocals
Arthur Cormack won the 1983 Gold medal in Gaelic singing at the national competition, the highest accolade for a Scottish Gaelic singer. He was only 18 years old at the time. Since then, Cormack has continued to sing Gaelic songs and has released two albums. —*Steve Winick*

Nuair Bha Mi Og: Gaelic Songs by the Mod Gold / 1984 / Temple Music ♦♦♦
Accompanied by members of The Battlefield Band and by Alison Kinnaird, Cormack uses his naturally strong voice to great effect. —*Steve Winick*

● **Ruith Na Gaoith** / Temple Music ♦♦♦♦
Many of the same accompanists and some new ones join Cormack for his second album. Like his first, this one is restrained and tasteful. The arrangements are a bit more contemporary in sound, making it just a bit more accessible. —*Steve Winick*

Craobh Rua

Craobh Rua is a relatively new band from Northern Ireland that performs stirring music on uilleann pipes, fiddle, banjo, guitar, and vocals. Their greatest success has been in Scotland, where their albums and live shows have been accepted warmly and heartily by both fans and influential musicians. They could be one of the groups to watch in the future. —*Steve Winick*

Not a Word About It / 1990 / BTB ♦♦♦
Craobh Rua's debut album has real verve in the instrmental passages, but the vocal selections are less forceful. —*Steve Winick*

The More That's Said, the Less the Better / 1992 / BTB ♦♦♦♦
Both the playing and singing convey the group's passion. —*Steve Winick*

The Critic's Group

This folksong discussion group led by Ewan MacColl eventually began recording albums as singers. They included Frankie Armstrong and John Faulkner. All are well worth hearing. —*Steve Winick*

The Female Frolic / 1968 / Argo ♦♦♦
Featured are songs addressing women's issues. —*Steve Winick*

● **Waterloo-Peterloo** / 1968 / Argo ♦♦♦♦
Here are songs of laborers and soldiers. —*Steve Winick*

As We Were A-Sailin' / 1970 / Argo ♦♦♦
This collection of sea songs features MacColl himself. —*Steve Winick*

Tony Cuffe

Guitar, Vocals
Tony's voice, whistle, and guitar are as wonderfully expressive alone as they were when he sang with Ossian. —*Steve Winick*

When First I Went to Caledonia / 1988 / Iona ♦♦♦♦
These beautiful selections are beautifully done. —*Steve Winick*

John and Phil Cunningham

Fiddle, Guitar, Accordion, Keyboards
John, an outstanding Scottish fiddler, was a founding member of Silly Wizard. Phil, an equally impressive accordionist, joined after the group lost its original accordion player. Though known best for their work with the Wizard, John and Phil have a few other records available. —*Steve Winick*

● **Against the Storm** / 1980 / Shanachie ♦♦♦♦
Scottish pipe tunes, Irish reels, and haunting slow airs fill this lovely album. —*Steve Winick*

Thoughts from Another World / 1981 / Shanachie ♦♦♦
His first solo album, an impressive debut, includes Celtic and American tunes. —*Steve Winick*

Fair Warning / 1983 / Green Linnet ♦♦♦♦
Great fun from John Cunningham. Quicksteps and reels rub shoulders with slower, more haunting pieces. —*Steve Winick*

Airs and Graces / 1984 / Green Linnet ♦♦♦♦
This Phil Cunningham solo outing uses not only accordion but great whistle playing and moody synthesizer sounds to make this an outstanding recording. —*Steve Winick*

★ **The Palamino Waltz** / 1988 / Green Linnet ♦♦♦♦♦

Tom Dahill

Fiddle, Vocals
Tom Dahill grew up in Irish neighborhoods in St. Paul, MN, where he met many old-time Irish musicians. He learned to play the fiddle and to sing from such figures as Terence "Cuz" Teahan and Pat Hill. He has been a member of several bands and has toured extensively in the US and Ireland. —*Steve Winick*

Irish Music from St. Paul to Donegal / Flying Fish ♦♦
● **Ragged Hank of Yarn** / Flying Fish ♦♦♦♦
Glenn Walker Johnson adds Irish harp and whistle. Dahill's singing is still less than thrilling, but this record is saved by its unusual selection of songs. —*Steve Winick*

Jackie Daly

Accordion
Daly is one of Ireland's top accordion players and has been a member of De Danann, Buttons and Bows, Arcady, and Patrick Street. —*Steve Winick*

● **Buttons and Bows** / 1984 / Green Linnet ♦♦♦♦
Dance tunes, from the Celtic lands as well as Scandinavia, appear in impressive arrangements. —*Steve Winick*

Shaun Davey

Shaun Davey is a classical composer from Belfast whose work frequently features traditional motifs and instrumentation. He is best known for several compositions that feature the uilleann bagpipe, perhaps the only bagpipe refined enough to sit in with a symphony orchestra. —*Steve Winick*

★ **The Brendan Voyage** / 1991 / Tara ♦♦♦♦♦
The Brendan Suite was Davey's first work for orchestra. It is based on the journey of a sixth-century monk who may have been the first European in America. The uilleann pipes, played by Liam O'Flynn, represent the

boat. This innovative work, combining classical and traditional folk music, made Davey's reputation. —*Steve Winick*

Pilgrim / Tara ✦✦✦
Featured are selections from the Lorient Festival Suite, composed for 1983's Interceltic festival in Lorient, Brittany. This one features orchestra, Welsh choirs, Scottish pipe bands, Galician bagpipes, Breton bombardes, and, of course, Liam O'Flynn. —*Steve Winick*

Granuaile / Tara ✦✦✦✦
This one features orchestra, Liam O'Flynn's pipes, and Rita Connolly's singing. The songs and music, all written by Davey, tell the story of a 16th-century outlaw noblewoman. —*Steve Winick*

Meg Davis

Vocals
American-born singer Meg Davis now spends a lot of time in Ireland, where she sings with Joe Burke's trio. —*Steve Winick*

Claddagh Walk / 1990 / Lismor ✦✦✦
Davis' voice treats some lovely songs, and the arrangements are classy and clean. —*Steve Winick*

De Danann

De Danann began by producing vibrant arrangements of the traditional music of Galway and Kerry, two of Ireland's musically rich counties. Influenced by both the instrumental sound of the Chieftains and the more vocal-dominated sound of Planxty, this band built a name for itself in the wake of the Chieftains' rise to international fame. Its members, especially the support singer, have come and gone with dizzying regularity, so that many of the greatest musicians in Ireland, including Frankie Gavin, Johnny Moynihan, Johnny McDonagh, Jackie Daly, Martin O'Connor, Dolores Keane, Mary Black, and Maura O'Connell, have passed through its ranks. They've also changed the spelling of the name over the years; they go by either De Danann or De Dannan. —*Steve Winick*

De Danann / 1976 / Decca ✦✦✦✦
Their debut features singer Dolores Keane. —*Steve Winick*

Star-Spangled Molly / 1978 / Shanachie ✦✦✦
This time, the singer du jour is Maura O'Connell, and the theme is Irish-American music of the '20s. —*Steve Winick*

The Mist Covered Mountain / 1980 / Shanachie ✦✦✦✦
One of their strongest albums instrumentally, this release also features the singing of Tom Phaidin and Sean O Conaire. —*Steve Winick and Bruce Eder*

A Jacket of Batteries / 1983 / Green Linnet ✦✦✦
This album features many new members but achieves remarkable continuity of sound with De Danann's previous albums. —*Steve Winick*

Song for Ireland / 1983 / Sugar Hill ✦✦✦✦
Mary Black contributes the stunning vocals that have made her famous, and the instrumentals have even more energy than usual. —*Steve Winick*

Anthem / 1985 / Dara ✦✦✦
On this album, the band has lots of former members back on board, including Delores Kean. Jackie Daly and Martin O'Connor both play accordion, and Mary Black sings a few songs. The band's name changed spelling between the two covers of this LP. —*Steve Winick*

Selected Jigs Reels & Songs / 1988 / Shanachie ✦✦✦
This one features Johnny Moynihan's singing and bouzouki. —*Steve Winick*

★ **The Best of De Danann** / 1991 / Shanachie ✦✦✦✦✦
Probably as good a way as any to start off, with the most popular cuts from the group's albums. —*Bruce Eder*

1/2 Set in Harlem / 1991 / Green Linnet ✦✦✦
They blend their traditional music with gospel, klezmer, and other styles. —*Steve Winick*

Ballroom / Green Linnet ✦✦✦
Featured are music-hall songs sung by Dolores Keane, along with more great instrumentals. —*Steve Winick*

Johnny Doherty

Fiddle
A Donegal Traveler, John Doherty was one of the great masters of his own region's traditional fiddle style. —*Steve Winick*

Bundle and Go / Green Linnet ✦✦✦✦
This collection of excellent field recordings was made by Allen Feldman and Eamonn Doherty. —*Steve Winick*

Mickey Doherty

Fiddle
For perspective on all the revivalist "Celtic" music around, here is an

undisputed master of Irish tradition. Mickey Doherty was one of the great names of Donegal fiddling and storytelling. —*John Storm Roberts*

Gravel Walks / 1949 / Irish Folklore Commission ✦✦✦✦
These superb recordings, his first, were made pretty much by happenstance during a 1949 field trip. —*John Storm Roberts*

Tom Doherty

Melodeon
Born in Donegal, Ireland, Tom Doherty learned to play the melodeon in the early '20s. He traveled to find work, first to Scotland and England, and then to the US, where he settled in Brooklyn. All the while, he kept alive the now rare tradition of Irish melodeon, playing for dances, parties, and sessions. —*Steve Winick*

Take the Bull by the Horns / Green Linnet ✦✦✦✦
Well into his 70s, Doherty recorded his first solo album. Backed by many great younger musicians, including his daughter, he achieves a refreshingly light and experimental approach. —*Steve Winick*

Johnny Doran

Pipe
An undisputed grand master of Irish tradition. Doran, a traveler from Clare, was heir to a major family tradition of pipers and a true original. He was a major influence on Willy Clancy. —*John Storm Roberts*

The Bunch of Keys / Irish Folklore Commission ✦✦✦✦
This tape includes the handful of recordings he made for the Irish Folklore Commission in the mid-'40s. —*John Storm Roberts*

Dubliners

Irish musician and folklorist Mick Moloney calls the Dubliners "the bearded Bohemians of the Irish folk scene." They had a gritty, urban image that contrasted with some of the prettier origins of other bands. Although they're still around today, their great recordings were made years ago, with singer Luke Kelly and banjo player Barney McKenna. —*Steve Winick*

Live at the Albert Hall / 1969 / Starline ✦✦✦
An early live set shows what all the fuss was about. —*Steve Winick*

● **20 Original Greatest Hits** / 1978 / Chyme ✦✦✦✦
You can't go wrong with this compilation; it spans about ten years of the Dubliners. —*Steve Winick*

Milestones / 1995 / Tansatlantic ✦✦✦✦

Best Of / Feb. 13, 1996 / K-Tel ✦✦✦

A Parcel of Rogues / Arc ✦✦✦✦
Out of all The Dubliners' original albums, this one shines the brightest. —*Steve Winick*

Seamus Ennis

Pipe, Vocals
A folklorist, singer, storyteller, and performer on uillean pipes and tin whistle, Ennis was one of the pioneering figures in Irish folklore. His fluency in English and every dialect of Irish and Scottish Gaelic made him an excellent cultural ambassador, telling translated Gaelic tales and playing venerable tunes to English audiences with a flair that revealed the genius hidden in folklore. —*Steve Winick*

Forty Years of Irish Piping / 1974 / Green Linnet ✦✦✦
A musical biography, it plots the development of his playing and was compiled by Pat Sky. —*Steve Winick*

● **Feidlim Tonn Ri's Castle** / 1977 / Claddagh ✦✦✦✦
On *Feidlim Tonn Ri's Castle, or the King of Ireland's Son*, he tells a long Gaelic heroic folktale in English, with music on his pipes and whistle. It's literally wonderful. —*Steve Winick*

The Wandering Minstrel / 1977 / Green Linnet ✦✦

● **The Best of Irish Piping** / Aug. 15, 1995 / Passport ✦✦✦✦

The Wandering Minstrel / Green Linnet ✦✦✦

Meredydd Evans

Vocals
A tutor at the University of Bangor, Wales, Meredydd Evans studied Welsh folk songs. He became quite influential, and his singing and teaching can be heard today in the repertoire of many Welsh folk groups. —*Steve Winick*

Traditional / Tradition ✦✦

● **Welsh Folksongs** / Smithsonian/Folkways ✦✦✦✦
Unaccompanied performances of many songs. Evans' beautiful voice floats. —*Steve Winick*

John Faulkner

Bouzouki, Guitar, Vocals
Better known as the former husband and singing partner of Dolores Keane, John Faulkner is also a formidable talent in his own right. He was a member of Ewan MacColl's Critics' Group in the '60s, and continues to perform today. He sings and plays several instruments. —*Steve Winick*

Nomads / 1992 / Clo-Iar Connachta ✦✦✦
Featuring a seven-track "concept side" concerning the Highland clearances in Scotland, Faulkner is joined by many friends, including Dolores Keane. —*Steve Winick*

● **Kind Providence** / Green Linnet ✦✦✦✦
Faulkner plays every instrument, including guitar, bouzouki, fiddle, and hurdy-gurdy. He also sings many lovely songs on this excellent album. —*Steve Winick*

Figgy Duff

Playing traditional folk with elements of rock, Figgy Duff was founded in the mid-'70s by Noel Dinn, with Pamela Morgan, David Panting, Philip Dinn, and Arthur Stoyles. The band's self-titled debut appeared on Phonodisc in 1981. Nine years later, their sophomore album, *Weather the Storm*, was released. *After the Tempest* (1991) and *Downstream* (1993) followed, but Noel Dinn died of cancer in mid-1993. —*John Bush*

Figgy Duff / 1980 / Hagdown ✦✦✦✦
Their debut is their folkiest outing. —*Steve Winick*

After the Tempest / 1984 / Celtic Music ✦✦✦
Their second album features a lot of great music, traditional and new. —*Steve Winick*

Weather the Storm / 1989 / Hypnotic ✦✦✦
Powerful pop music with Celtic roots. —*Steve Winick*

Downstream / 1993 / Hypnotic/A&M ✦✦✦✦
Downstream completes a four-album evolution for Newfoundland's Figgy Duff. The group's first two releases consisted entirely of traditional Celtic offerings; 1990's *Weather the Storm* introduced their first original recordings; now this latest consists entirely of songs written by core members Noel Dinn and Pamela Morgan. It may be an oversimplification—but still a reasonable benchmark—to think of Figgy Duff as a Celtic Cowboy Junkies. —*Roch Parisien*

● **A Retrospective 1974-1993** / 1996 / Amber/EMI ✦✦✦✦

The Fisher Family

Children of a Gaelic speaker and occasional singer from the isle of Barra and a Glasgow police inspector who sang choral music, opera, and music-hall songs, the Fishers have become respected traditional and contemporary folksingers. Archie Fisher sings the old songs as well as writing his own, Ray sings the old ballads in a magnificent voice, and Cilla, with her husband Artie Tresize, performs both traditional and contemporary music as well as a large repertoire of children's music. The siblings occasionally unite for tours or special appearances, but most of their recorded material is separate. —*Steve Winick*

The Fisher Family / 1965 / Topic ✦✦✦✦
In 1965, when this was recorded, Cilla was barely a teenager. Still, she makes valuable contributions along with Archie, Ray, and her sisters Joyce, Audrey, and Cindy. The guitar accompaniments by Archie are little more than simple strumming, but the singing is wonderful. This is a real collector's item. —*Steve Winick*

Archie Fisher

Guitar, Vocals
Singer-songwriter and guitarist Archie Fisher has created many Scottish folk standards such as "Will Ye Gang, Love," "Men O'Worth" and "Mally Lee." He is a member of the Fisher family, a group of highly respected folksingers who occasionally regroup for performances. Fisher's style has been compared to that of Martin Carthy and Dick Gaughan. —*Sandra Brennan*

Archie Fisher / 1968 / Celtic Music ✦✦✦
Released in 1968, this first album shows off Fisher's gentle voice and guitar accompaniments. —*Steve Winick*

● **The Man with a Rhyme** / 1976 / Folk Legacy ✦✦✦✦
More gentle singing and guitar make this his best. —*Steve Winick*

Off the Map / 1986 / Snow Goose ✦✦✦
Archie Fisher's singing and guitar are wedded to Garnet Rogers' fiddle and flute. —*Steve Winick*

Will Ye Gang, Love / Green Linnet ✦✦✦✦
Fisher was one of the first good Scottish folk guitarists, and this shows off both his guitar playing and his singing. —*Steve Winick*

Winston Fitzgerald

Fiddle
Winston "Scotty" FitzGerald was a pioneer recording artist of Scottish fiddle music in Cape Breton Island, Nova Scotia. His influence on maritime Canadian music is similar to that of Michael Coleman on Irish-American music. —*Steve Winick*

● **Classic Cuts** / 1992 / Breton Books and Music ✦✦✦✦
This CD compilation brings together 22 medleys of breathtaking Scottish fiddle music. —*Steve Winick*

Finbar and Eddie Furey

Pipe
The sons of fiddler Ted Furey from Ireland, Finbar and Eddie rose to fame in the '60s. Finbar is a flamboyant and forceful uillean piper who won his first all-Ireland championship at the age of 15, while Eddie is a singer and guitarist. They have been members of the Furey Brothers and Davey Arthur, but their most charming recordings are the ones they did as a duo. —*Steve Winick*

Finbar and Eddie Furey / 1968 / Transatlantic ✦✦✦
A good set of tunes and songs, it includes Irish and Scottish songs and dance tunes. —*Steve Winick*

● **Best of Finbar and Eddie Furey** / 1991 / Harp ✦✦✦✦
Here is one of the few currently available collections of early Finbar And Eddie. —*Steve Winick*

Irish Pipes of Finbar Furey / Nonesuch ✦✦✦
A modern piper, sometimes with guitar or flute. —*David L. Mayers*

Dick Gaughan

Guitar, Vocals
Gaughan is one of the finest singers and guitarists on the Scottish scene, and has put his talents to both traditional music and contemporary political material. —*Steve Winick*

☆ **No More Forever** / 1972 / Leader ✦✦✦✦✦
His first album is all traditional and wonderful. —*Steve Winick*

Coppers and Brass / 1977 / Green Linnet ✦✦✦
Originally released in 1977, this is a brilliant all-instrumental set of guitar tunes. —*Steve Winick*

Gaughan / 1978 / Topic ✦✦✦✦
This CD re-release features all of the excellent 1978 album *Gaughan*, plus four sets from *Coppers and Brass* and two from his guest spots on the High Level Ranters album *Bonnie Pit Laddie*. —*Steve Winick*

● **A Handful of Earth** / 1981 / Green Linnet ✦✦✦✦
Another fine album. "Song for Ireland" is a classic. Features Brian McNeill, Phil Cunningham, and Stewart Isbister. Voted Album of the Decade of the '80s by *Folk Roots* magazine, *A Handful of Earth* is Gaughan's best blend of traditional and contemporary songs. —*Chip Renner & Steve Winick*

A Different Kind of Love Song / 1983 / Folk Freak ✦✦✦
The sound of this import CD is stellar. There is a chilling song, "Prisoner 562," a song to make you "think again." I can't fault a thing on this one. Buy it. —*Chip Renner*

Frankie Gavin

Fiddle, Flute
Frankie Gavin comes from Connemara. He is best known as De Danann's fiddle player, but he also plays the flute and records solo records. —*Steve Winick*

● **Up and Away** / 1983 / Gael Linn ✦✦✦✦
He plays mostly flute on this album, but also fiddle and even accordion. He is backed by Ringo McDonagh's bodhran and Charlie Lennon's piano, and gives a great performance. —*Steve Winick*

Frankie Goes to Town / 1991 / Green Linnet ✦✦✦✦
A superb album of fiddling is backed by Alec Finn's bouzouki and Charlie Lennon's piano. —*Steve Winick*

Irish Fiddle and Bouzouki / 1991 / Shanachie ✦✦✦
This is a live-in-the-studio, one-session album, recorded with Alec Finn (bouzouki) in Greenwich village during a De Danann tour. The players are relaxed, and the tunes flow nicely. —*Steve Winick*

Hugh Gillespie

Fiddle
Hugh Gillespie was a Donegal man who emigrated to New York, where he joined a community of Irish musicians. A fantastic fiddler, he was soon well known and began recording 78s in the late '30s. —*Steve Winick*

Classic Recordings of Irish Traditional Fiddle Music / 1978 / Green Linnet ✦✦✦
The tracks on this fine disc have been collected from Gillespie's 78-rpm recordings. Listen for echoes of Michael Coleman. —*Steve Winick*

The Goadec Sisters

Three sisters from rural Brittany, the Goadecs are acclaimed as the greatest of Brittany's traditional singers to make it onto recordings. —*Steve Winick*

● **Moueziou Bruded a Vreiz** / 1975 / Keltia Musique ✦✦✦✦
The CD re-release of a classic 1975 LP, this record contains both sad ballads and songs for dancing. —*Steve Winick*

Great Big Sea

A rollicking young band from Newfoundland, Canada, Great Big Sea plays music derived from Irish and English traditions. —*Steve Winick*

Great Big Sea / 1993 / NRA Productions ✦✦✦
This is a debut album of upbeat, fun music. —*Steve Winick*

The Green Fields of America

Mostly a touring ensemble, Green Fields has included many of the very finest musicians on the Irish-American scene. —*Steve Winick*

The Green Fields of America: Live in Concert / 1989 / Green Linnet ✦✦✦✦

● **Live in Concert** / 1989 / Green Linnet ✦✦✦✦
A fine showcase of a lot of talent, it includes Mick Moloney, Seamus Egan, Eileen Ivers, Robbie O'Connell, and Jimmy Keane. —*Steve Winick*

Gwerz

Erik Marchand's startling voice and Soig Siberil's guitar work helped Gwerz become one of Brittany's best-known bands. —*Steve Winick*

Musiques Bretonnes de Toujours / 1985 / Dastum ✦✦✦
Despite interesting arrangements, this isn't as masterful as the second album. —*Steve Winick*

● **Au Del** / 1987 / Escalibur ✦✦✦✦
It's their best album. —*Steve Winick*

Gwerz Live! / 1992 / Gwerz Pladenn ✦✦✦✦
This one was recorded live during a reunion concert in 1992. It features live versions of their most popular songs. —*Steve Winick*

Tim Hart and Maddy Prior

A young duo from St. Albans who founded Steeleye Span with Ashley Hutchings and Gay and Terry Woods, most of their influence on the music scene has been with that band, but their solo albums are also classics. —*Steve Winick*

Folk Songs of Olde England, Vol. 1 / 1968 / AdRhythm ✦✦✦
Simple accompaniments with guitar, banjo, and dulcimer grace two volumes of top-flight renditions of traditional songs. —*Steve Winick*

● **Summer Solstice** / 1971 / Shanachie ✦✦✦✦
This album features fuller, more mature arrangements. —*Steve Winick*

Folk Songs of Olde England, Vol. 2 / 1976 / Mooncrest ✦✦✦
Here is more of what made *Vol. 1* a classic. —*Steve Winick*

Frank Harte

Vocals
A source of traditional songs among folk-revival singers, Harte has collected thousands of songs and has published a book and several albums of Dublin street songs. —*Steve Winick*

Dublin Street Songs / 1967 / Topic ✦✦✦
Included are classic ballads as well as humorous pieces, recorded with Alf Edwards on concertina. —*Steve Winick*

● **And Listen to My Song** / Ram ✦✦✦✦
Broadside ballads of old Dublin feature Donal Lunny on bouzouki and Bertram Levy on concertina. —*Steve Winick*

Through Dublin City / Topic ✦✦✦
Just Harte, unaccompanied. —*Steve Winick*

Joe Heaney (Seosaimh O'Heanaæ)

Vocals
A magnificent singer in both Gaelic and English, Heaney sings in *sean-nos*, the ornamented style of traditional Irish song. —*Steve Winick*

● **Joe and the Gabe** / 1979 / Green Linnet ✦✦✦✦
Heaney's remarkable voice is joined by the flute, whistle, and fiddle playing of Gabe O'Sullivan, for a fine cross-section of Galway music and song. —*Steve Winick*

O Mo Dhuchas / Gael Linn ✦✦✦
All unaccompanied, all Gaelic, this is for really hardcore fans. —*Steve Winick*

The High Level Ranters

A Northumbrian group, they formed in the late '60s, featuring Alistair Anderson, Tom Gilfellon, Johnny Handle, and Colin Ross. The High Level Ranters were very regionally oriented, with lovely songs in broad Geordie dialect and tunes identified with the region. —*Steve Winick*

High Level / 1971 / Trailer ✦✦✦
They first perfected their arrangements on this album. —*Steve Winick*

A Mile to Ride / 1973 / Trailer ✦✦✦✦
With beautiful singing from Handle and Gilfellon, and subtle but rousing work on the tunes, this disc comes highly recommended. —*Steve Winick*

● **Bonny Pit Laddie** / 1975 / Topic ✦✦✦✦
A double album of songs about the lives of coal miners, it's very well-done, with guest appearances by Dick Gaughan and Harry Boardman. —*Steve Winick*

Noel Hill

Concertina
The concertina in Irish music is associated with County Clare. Noel Hill is certainly one of Clare's best-known concertina players, and one of the best in Ireland. —*Steve Winick*

The Irish Concertina / 1982 / Shanachie ✦✦✦
Backed by Charlie Lennon's piano, Hill plays jigs, reels, hornpipes, and airs. The dry little squeezebox never sounded better. —*Steve Winick*

● **Noel Hill and Tony MacMahon** / Shanachie ✦✦✦✦
Along with ace accordionist Tony MacMahon, Hill played three evenings in a pub in County Cork in October 1985. The sessions were taped and a live album produced. It's the kind of album that makes you wish you'd been there. —*Steve Winick*

Horslips

The first group in Ireland to mix electric rock with traditional music, their early albums are the most interesting for Celtic music fans. —*Steve Winick*

Happy to Meet, Sorry to Part / 1973 / Atco ✦✦✦✦
This is raw and raunchy folk-rock with fiddle, banjo, and flute along with electric guitars, bass, and drums. Traditional songs and Tull-like rockers are included. —*Steve Winick*

● **The Tain** / 1974 / Atco ✦✦✦✦
A concept album that relates the story of Tain Bo Cuailgne, Ireland's great medieval epic. —*Steve Winick*

House Band

This excellent British group features Ged Foley (voice, guitar, Northumbrian pipes), Chris Parkinson (vocals, melodeon), and John Skelton (flutes, whistles, bombardes). They specialize in blending traditional English, Scottish, and Breton music with other sounds, traditional and contemporary. —*Steve Winick*

Word of Mouth / 1988 / Green Linnet ✦✦✦
Ged Foley's vocals are a bit dreary on this record, but the fresh and inspired instrumentals make it more than worth having. —*Steve Winick*

● **Stonetown** / 1991 / Green Linnet ✦✦✦✦
Same story, but the vocals pick up just a bit. The instrumentals are still the group's strength. —*Steve Winick*

Paul Huellou

Vocals
Paul Huellou is well known in his native Brittany, where he has become one of the foremost singers of the Breton music tradition. —*Music of the World*

Songs from Brittany / Music of the World ✦✦✦
This recording features Mr. Huellou (vocals), J. Pol Huellou (flutes), Paddy Keenan (pipes), Brendan Fahy (guitar), and Pascal Segart (violin). —*Music of the World*

The Irish Rovers

This quintet started out in the late '50s (curiously, by way of Canada) and by the mid-'60s were a popular folk ensemble on television on two continents. Although their work, exuberant and boisterous, with relatively little scholarship and lacking a traditional sound, became less fashionable with the ascent of groups like the Chieftains, the Irish Rovers continue to have a devoted core following. —*Bruce Eder*

The Unicorn / 1971 / MCA ✦✦✦
The single most popular record that the Irish Rovers ever made, their cover of Shel Silverstein's slyly written "The Unicorn" stands apart from the more straightforward material on this album, which is devoted to good times, family, and religious differences, and other significant elements of Irish song. —*Bruce Eder*

● **Irish Rovers' Greatest Hits** / 1981 / MCA ✦✦✦✦
The record to start with to get to know the Irish Rovers, even though it isn't representative of their full range of material. —*Bruce Eder*

The Boys Come Rolling Home / 1994 / Potato/Attic ✦✦✦
Some of the modern studio flourishes that graced previous albums have been pared back to a more rootsy, folk-pub feel. So while the Rovers can turn over such charming, good-natured fare as "Killiburn Brae" in their sleep, one can at least find something to inspire the hoisting of a pint and a hearty sing-along. —*Roch Parisien*

Eileen Ivers

Fiddle
A fiddle virtuoso, Eileen Ivers was born in New York City to parents who had both immigrated from Ireland. She began to play fiddle at the age of eight, and learned to play from Martin Mulvihill, the great fiddler and teacher from County Limerick. Between the ages of 11 and 19, she won eight all-Ireland championships, culminating in the senior championship in 1984. She has been a member of Cherish the Ladies, the Green Fields of America, Chanting House, and even Hall and Oates' band. —*Steve Winick*

● **Traditional Irish Music** / 1994 / Green Linnet ✦✦✦✦
Tradition and innovation go hand in hand on Ivers' surprising, fresh, and impeccably played solo recording. —*Steve Winick*

Eileen Ivers / Green Linnet ✦✦✦
Eileen Ivers, on her debut album, *Eileen Ivers*, shows remarkable inventiveness while still standing on the firm ground of traditional Irish music. From folk to rock and Ireland to Africa, Ivers spices up contemporary, traditional, and original tunes with guitar, saxophone, zither, viola da gamba, and Hammond organ. This is serious fun. The beautiful tune "Nagh Seola" becomes a jazz ballad duet. On "Pachelbel's Frolics," Ivers deconstructs this classical piece into a driving hoedown. A more talented, adventurous musician on the Irish music scene would be hard to find. —*MusD*

Dafydd Iwan

Vocals
Dafydd Iwan has been a tireless activist in attempting to revitalize Welsh language and culture. He is also a marvelous singer and songwriter, with many recordings to his credit. —*Steve Winick*

Yma O Hyd / 1993 / Sain ✦✦✦
This CD features tracks from two albums Iwan recorded with the band Ar Log. It contains almost the entirety of *Rhwng Hwyl A Thaith* (1982) and *Yma O Hyd* (1983). It's stirring stuff, but it's mostly lost on non-Welsh speakers. —*Steve Winick*

● **Canueuon Gwerin** / 1993 / Sain ✦✦✦✦
Iwan's renditions of traditional songs are played with punchy, pop-tinged arrangements. —*Steve Winick*

The Johnstons

The Johnstons rose to prominence in Dublin in the late '60s. Formed by Luci, Adrienne, and Michael Johnston, the group featured harmony singing with guitar accompaniment. Eventually Michael left the group and was replaced by Mick Moloney (vocals, mandolin, banjo) and Paul Brady (vocals, guitar). This four-piece band became extremely popular in Ireland and toured the world, starting off the careers of both Moloney and Brady. Unfortunately, their albums are equally split between innovative treatments of traditional material and fairly derivative covers of American folk/pop. Look for the traditional stuff! —*Steve Winick*

The Johnstons / 1968 / Mercury ✦✦✦✦
This excellent debut is full of the good stuff. —*Steve Winick*

The Barleycorn / 1969 / Transatlantic, Ltd. ✦✦✦
More great ballads and songs are here. —*Steve Winick*

● **Transatlantic Years** / 1992 / Transatlantic/Demon ✦✦✦✦
This anthology is about equally split between their traditional material and their arrangements of Joni Mitchell, Gordon Lightfoot, Leonard Cohen, etc. It's a great way to get a feel for the group. —*Steve Winick*

Nic Jones

Guitar, Vocals
Jones, one of the best English singers and guitarists in folk music, had a relatively short career before being paralyzed in an auto accident. His albums are all worth buying. —*Steve Winick*

● **Ballads and Songs** / 1970 / Trailer ✦✦✦✦
This debut album established him as one of the best. —*Steve Winick*

Nic Jones / 1971 / Trailer ✦✦✦
It's a beautiful follow-up to *Ballads and Songs*. —*Steve Winick*

The Noah's Ark Trap / 1977 / Shanachie ✦✦✦
A few guests join him to fill out the arrangements. —*Steve Winick*

Penguin Eggs / 1980 / Shanachie ✦✦✦✦
Even better than *The Noah's Ark Trap,* many critics consider this his best. —*Steve Winick*

Ron Kavana

Banjo, Guitar, Mandolin, Vocals
A singer, songwriter, and guitarist, Kavana took the Irish music world by storm a few years ago with the group Alias Ron Kavana. His solo recording is the place to start for folk music lovers. —*Steve Winick*

● **Home Fire** / 1991 / Green Linnet ✦✦✦✦
Angry, impassioned, gritty singing. Wild, boisterous, irreverent playing. Excellent musicianship, songwriting, and production. It adds up to one heck of an album. —*Steve Winick*

Dolores Keane and John Faulkner

An English husband and Irish wife in a harmonious (though temporary) partnership, she sings with an angel's voice, while he sings and plays guitar, bouzouki, and fiddle. —*Steve Winick*

There Was a Maid / 1978 / Claddagh ✦✦✦✦
After she left De Danann, Keane recorded this lovely solo album, accompanied by another band, Reel Union. —*Steve Winick*

Brokenhearted I'll Wander / 1979 / Green Linnet ✦✦✦✦
Featured is Reel Union, a band including pipes and fiddle, as backup. A truly gorgeous album, this is Keane and Faulkner's best work. —*Steve Winick*

Farewell to Eireann / 1980 / Green Linnet ✦✦✦
Poignant emigration ballads are here, including the lovely "Galway Bay." —*Steve Winick*

Sail Og Rua / 1983 / Green Linnet ✦✦✦
These are mostly Gaelic songs, with guests that include Keane's aunt Sarah, a well-known traditional singer. —*Steve Winick*

★ **Dolores Keane** / 1988 / Round Tower ✦✦✦✦✦

James Keane

Accordion
James Keane was well known as an accordion player in his native Dublin before he emigrated to New York. He is the brother of Sean Keane, fiddler with the Chieftains. —*Steve Winick*

That's the Spirit / 1994 / Green Linnet ✦✦✦
Features some of New York's best musicians backing Keane's robust button-box. —*Steve Winick*

● **Roll Away the Reel World** / Green Linnet ✦✦✦✦
Brother Sean joins James on this classic album. —*Steve Winick*

Kelly/O'Brien/Sproule

James Kelly is a Dubliner by birth and one of the best Irish fiddlers anywhere. Paddy O'Brien is a fine accordionist from County Offaly. Daithi Sproule of Derry city is one of the best guitarists in Irish traditional music and a great singer. All three are based in the US, although this trio, which called itself Bowhand, no longer performs together. —*Steve Winick*

● **Spring in the Air** / Shanachie ✦✦✦✦
Tight trio playing from this extremely talented group makes this a fine listen if traditional tunes are your bag. Sproule's two songs are also beautiful. —*Steve Winick*

Pat Kilbride

Guitar, Vocals, Cittern
A virtuoso cittern and guitar player and an excellent singer and songwriter, Pat Kilbride is one of the most dynamic solo performers in Irish music. He was a member of the Battlefield Band for a brief time in the '70s, then moved to Belgium and eventually Brittany, where he performed in a more pop-oriented group. In the '90s, Kilbride's a New Yorker and plays music both solo and with the Kips Bay Ceili Band. —*Steve Winick*

Rock and More Roses / 1989 / Flying Fish ✦✦✦✦
This extra-length CD and cassette includes the entirety of Kilbride's 1980 *Rock and Roses* album, along with six tracks of instrumental music recorded in 1986 and 1987. It's brilliant and a bargain to boot. —*Steve Winick*

Undocumented Dancing / 1992 / Green Linnet ◆◆◆
This album has everything that made *Rock and More Roses* great, plus Kilbride's original songs. —*Steve Winick*

● **Loose Cannon** / 1995 / Green Linnet ◆◆◆◆
Kilbride starts this set off with the muscular and funky "The Working Man." This is Celtic music with a more modern touch than is often heard. Musicians Denny McDermott, Mike Visceglian, and Larry Campbell, who are one of New York's premier rhythm sections, put a polish and tightness into these songs that is bracing. Augmented by Lucy Kaplansky's vocals and Jerry Sullivan's uillean pipes, Kilbride has produced a great allbum that showcases the wide range of his writing and interpretive talent. —*Richard Meyer*

Kips Bay Ceili Band

This New-York based quartet features Pat Kilbride (vocals, guitar, cittern), John Whelan (button accordion, keyboards), Steve Missal (drums, percussion, vocals), and Richard Lindsey (bass). They perform original and traditional folk, rock 'n' roll, and Irish music. —*Steve Winick*

Digging In / 1993 / Green Linnet ◆◆◆
Included are some powerful tracks and some lightweight ones. See them live instead. —*Steve Winick*

John Kirkpatrick

Melodeon
A fine melodeon player, Kirkpatrick has been a member of Steeleye Span. He is a champion of English music and dance and also heads a Morris dance team. —*Steve Winick*

The Rose of Britain's Isle / 1974 / Topic ◆◆◆
Included are lovely material and lovely performances with Sue Harris. Harris, Kirkpatrick's wife, sings and plays the oboe, and also heads a dance team. —*Steve Winick*

★ **Plain Capers: Morris Dance Tunes** / 1976 / Free Reed ◆◆◆◆◆
A pioneering effort at producing an acoustic yet modern setting for Morris dance music, *Plain Capers* features such guests as Sue Harris (oboe, hammered dulcimer) and Martin Carthy (guitar). Impeccably researched and performed, this album is a delight. —*Steve Winick*

Shreds and Patches / 1977 / Topic ◆◆◆
This is an excellent follow-up with Sue Harris. —*Steve Winick*

● **Going Spare** / 1978 / Free Reed ◆◆◆◆
Of these all-original songs and tunes, some are weird and hilarious. —*Steve Winick*

Kornog

Brittany's greatest instrumentalists team up with Scottish singer and instrumentalist Jamie McMenamy (previously of the Battlefield Band) for an unbeatable combination. —*Steve Winick*

Kornog / 1983 / Escalibur ◆◆◆
The debut album overlaps in material with *Premiere* but is still worth having. —*Steve Winick*

● **Premiére** / 1984 / Green Linnet ◆◆◆◆
Live in Michigan, this features the ambiance of a live album, plus some great Scottish ballads. This is Kornog's best album. —*Steve Winick*

Ar Seizh Avel / 1985 / Green Linnet ◆◆◆
This is a pretty album of traditional and original tunes and songs. —*Steve Winick*

Christine Kydd

Guitar, Vocals
Christine Kydd is a singer and guitarist based in Edinburgh. She performs traditional and contemporary songs, both solo and as a duo with Janet Russell. —*Steve Winick*

● **Heading Home** / 1993 / Fellside ◆◆◆◆
An excellent album, mostly of slow, pensive folksongs. Kydd's rich, full voice is worth seeking out. —*Steve Winick*

Sam Larner

b. 1878, d. 1965
Vocals
The fens, farms, and fishing ports of East Anglia were among the richest lodes of southern English traditional songs, and Larner one of the finest East Anglian source singers. He was a fisherman from the age of 12, but his repertoire went far beyond sea songs or the standard broadside ballad fare. —*John Storm Roberts*

● **Now Is the Time for Fishing** / 1994 / Musical Traditions ◆◆◆◆
This classic comes from perhaps the finest of all English source singers. Larner (1878-1965) was at sea much of his life, but his repertoire was extremely varied. These recordings from 1959 and 1960 are a wonderful

mix of songs both famous and less known, with reminiscence, rhymes, and sea lore (once a Folkways LP of the same title). —*John Storm Roberts, Original Music*

A Garland for Sam / Topic ◆◆◆◆
Splendid notes amplify splendid music. —*John Storm Roberts*

Grey Larsen and Andre Marchand

Fiddle, Flute, Guitar, Piano, Vocals
Grey Larsen is a well known American flute and concertina player. He has played with Malcolm Dalgliesh and with the group Metamora. Andre Marchand is one of Quebec's most important folk revival figures. His vocals, guitar, and tapping feet were among the ingredients in La Bottine Souriante. —*Steve Winick*

The Orange Tree / 1993 / Sugar Hill ◆◆◆◆
Larsen and Marchand explore their Irish and French Canadian roots on this album. The material is marvelously played and sung, and mostly upbeat and fun. —*Steve Winick*

Donal Lunny

Bouzouki, Guitar
Guitar and bouzouki player Donal Lunny is one of the pioneers of the Irish folk music revival. His first group, he told me, "was a very close imitation of the Clancy Brothers, [who] used to go to sessions every weekend in a pub called Pat Downing's in Prosperous, where there were some traditional musicians. As there was no other accompanist, I had sort of carte blanche with my guitar. So I used to go there and play all night, play tunes, reels, and jigs, and whatever on my guitar. I'm sure I was dreadful at the beginning. It improved as time went on, and I got involved in different groups in Dublin." One of those groups, Emmet Spiceland, also included Mick Moloney, now a champion of American-Irish music. In 1972, Christy Moore came home to Ireland to record an album. Lunny says, "He decided to collect musicians together. So he assembled whatever it was, eight or nine musicians, and we recorded *Prosperous*. And it just felt so good to everyone that we just said, 'Well, jeez, of course, yeah. Of course . . . let's form a band.' At the time, I was making jewelry, making a living at that, if you like, and it just stopped. Planxty started, and I never had time to do anything else since." In 1975, Lunny left Planxty to join a group that never got off the ground. His career, however, bounced back nicely: "the Bothy Band was in existence at that point, not as the Bothy Band, but as an ensemble I think was known as 1691. I joined them, and we became the Bothy Band, and off we went." Lunny toured with the Bothy Band and recorded four albums with them. When they broke up, it was back to Planxty and eventually to Moving Hearts: "Some of the most enjoyable moments I've had in the last 10 years have been with Moving Hearts. That did actually spring straight from the last version of Planxty. I wanted Planxty to sort of gear up, get a rhythm section in. Christy was interested in pressing on, so Moving Hearts started. That was an exciting time for me, both on stage and in the studio, because it was the first time I had to deal with bass and drums on an ongoing basis." Since Moving Hearts, Lunny has been more active as a producer than as a musician, producing records by many of the top groups in Ireland and Scotland. Look for his name as musician or producer, and you're sure to be buying an exciting, high-quality album. —*Steve Winick*

Donal Lunny / 1987 / Gael Linn ◆◆◆

Mac-Talla

In 1993, producer Robin Morton asked a group of extraordinary talents in the field of Scottish Gaelic music to get together and record. This led to their creation of a working, touring group. The members are singers Arthur Cormack, Eilidh MacKenzie, and Christine Primrose, and instrumentalists Blair Douglas (keyboards, accordion) and Alison Kinnaird (Scottish harp, cello). —*Steve Winick*

Mairidh Gaol Is Ceol / 1994 / Temple ◆◆◆
Brilliant performers sing and play some fine Gaelic material on this disc. Sad songs of parting rub shoulders with upbeat *puirt-a-beul*, or mouth music intended for dancing. —*Steve Winick*

Ewan MacColl

b. 1915, d. 1989
Vocals
Ewan MacColl may well have been the most influential person in the current British folksong revival. From his early manhood until his death in 1989, he remained passionately committed to folksong, though not exclusively; he was also a poet, playwright, organizer, activist, songwriter, husband, and father. MacColl was born in Scotland in 1915. His father was a lowland man who spoke Scots English, his mother a highlander who spoke Gaelic. Both of his parents were singers. MacColl left school at 14 to busk and act in the streets and was quickly discovered by the

BBC. Soon he was not only singing but also writing programs for the radio. He founded the first folk club in England, the Ballads and Blues Club, as well as the Critics' Group, an influential early singing group that included such singers as Frankie Armstrong, Anne Briggs, and John Faulkner. He himself was one of the foremost interpreters of traditional songs ever recorded. The most ambitious project he undertook was to record a representative sampling of Professor Francis James Child's English and Scottish popular ballads. While his early repertoire was mainly of street songs and traditional material, he has always also been an important songwriter. Most impressive was his competence in producing expressions that had appeal for all levels of society; his songs have been covered by performers as diverse as Dick Gaughan, the Pogues, Roberta Flack, and Elvis Presley, and many have been collected in several versions from the oral tradition. They range from savage political satire to tender love songs and are supremely effective at producing the desired emotions. Beyond his activities as a singer and songwriter, MacColl was an actor and a playwright. In 1947, George Bernard Shaw commented, "Apart from myself, MacColl is the only man of genius writing for the theatre in England today." His playwrighting and songwriting joined seamlessly in his "radio ballads," radio plays that bordered on ballad operas. Many of his most lovely and best-remembered songs were written for these plays, some of which have been released in album form. MacColl was married to Peggy Seeger, herself a singer of folk songs (and half-sister to American icon Pete Seeger). Together MacColl and Seeger, sometimes accompanied by their children, who are also skilled musicians and singers, have recorded quite a few albums as well. Many of MacColl's albums are out-of-print products of long-defunct record companies. Some, however, are readily available. All, like MacColl himself, are important factors in the history of the folk revival, to be cherished by all who encounter them. This great singer made many, many albums over many years. All of them are recommended for fans of great singing, though some may be a bit specialized (i.e., unaccompanied singing in broad Scots dialect) for some listeners. —*Steve Winick*

English/Scottish Popular Ballads / 1956 / Riverside ✦✦✦✦
This nine-album set, edited by Kenneth S. Goldstein and performed by MacColl and A.L. Lloyd, is the first systematic attempt to record a representative sampling of the Child canon of ballads in a traditional British singing style. It is important for academic reasons, but more so for those who simply love the English-language ballad. The disc features exquisite performances by MacColl and Lloyd. —*Steve Winick*

The Wanton Muse / 1968 / Argo ✦✦✦
Included are bawdy and sexually suggestive songs. —*Steve Winick*

The Angry Muse / 1968 / Argo ✦✦✦
A good collection of protest songs. —*Steve Winick*

★ **Black and White** / 1990 / Green Linnet ✦✦✦✦✦
A compilation of 20 important tracks. The album works well as an introduction, though it will undoubtedly lead you to further listening. —*Steve Winick*

Real MacColl / 1993 / Topic ✦✦✦✦
A CD reissue of tracks recorded during the '50s and '60s, the arrangements are somewhat dated, but the singing is marvelous. —*Steve Winick*

Scots Street Songs / Riverside ✦✦✦
This is urban folksong at its best. —*Steve Winick*

Eilidh Mackenzie

Vocals
Eilidh MacKenzie is a Gaelic singer who has won the gold medal at the national music competitions. —*Steve Winick*

Eideadh Na Sgeulachd (The Raiment of the Tale) / 1992 / Temple Music ✦✦✦
This CD features traditional and original songs in Gaelic. Some are sung unaccompanied; some feature excellent backup musicians. —*Steve Winick*

Talitha MacKenzie and Martin Swan

Vocals
The former lead singer of Mouth Music, this American-born doyenne of Scottish Gaelic singing has performed sea chanties, waulking songs, and *puirt-a-beul*, the Gaelic term for nonsense songs intended as accompaniment for dancing. —*Steve Winick*

Solas / 1994 / Shanachie ✦✦✦
Starting from a multilayered treatment of a Hebridean waulking song nestled in electronics, this solo release by the Mouth Music alumnus keeps getting better—until the deadly halfway point, when the disc doesn't so much run out of steam as abandon its smarts. The best cuts show how the eccentricities and earthiness of Celtic music lend themselves to various traditional and avant-garde marriages, like "Sein O," which embeds a clipped-syllable *puirt-a-beul* lyric in a bogle rhythm introduced by a hair-raising sample of Huun Huur Tu's Tuvan throat

singing. But the disastrous ode to positive thinking, "Owen's Boat," belongs in a TV movie, and "Chi mi na Morbheanan/JFK" uses St. Jack soundbites about fighting tyranny without a trace of irony—hallowing our descent into Southeast Asia. Decent songs follow, but try fighting your way back. —*Bob Tarte*

● **Mouth Music** / Rykodisc ✦✦✦✦
Truly a remarkable, innovative, mesmerizing synthesis of the traditional Gaelic singing style called "*puirt-a-beul*" or "mouth music," with African rhythms and modern keyboard technology. MacKenzie is the vocalist on this intense material, which she discovered when she traveled to Edinburgh to study Scottish and ancient Gaelic culture in depth; Swan is the instrumentalist and arranger (except on one that MacKenzie arranged). They say it's a matter of finding a strong rhythm that complements the traditional song structures, and then creating some kind of tension or powerful or surprising harmonic context. They've certainly accomplished just that. —*Ladyslipper*

Tony MacMahon

Accordion
Tony MacMahon is an excellent button accordion player from Miltown Malbay, County Clare, a noted center for traditional music. Among his influences were Joe Cooley and Sonny Brogan among accordionists, as well as piper Willie Clancy, fiddler Bobby Casey, and singer and piper Seamus Ennis. —*Steve Winick*

Traditional Irish Accordion / Shanachie ✦✦✦✦
MacMahon's solo album is a great listen, and a frequently consulted reference work among other accordionists. —*Steve Winick*

Catherine-Ann Macphee

Vocals
MacPhee, an extremely talented Gaelic singer from Barra, rose to fame with Edinburgh's well-known 7:84 theatre, with whom she sang and acted in various shows. Her acivities with the theatre brought her exposure and many requests for a recording. She has since become a recording artist to meet that demand. —*Steve Winick*

● **Canan Nan Gaidheal (The Language of the Gael)** / 1987 / Greentrax ✦✦✦✦
A fascinating collection of work, play and protest songs in Scottish Gaelic, this album features MacPhee's beautiful voice accompanied by members of the group Ossian. —*Steve Winick*

Chi Mi'n Geamhradh (I See Winter) / 1991 / Greentrax ✦✦✦
MacPhee's voice treats more wonderful songs in Gaelic. —*Steve Winick*

Malicorne

Malicorne founder Gabriel Yacoub, taking his inspiration from the French/Celtic explorations of Alan Stivell and Dan Ar Bras as well as the British folk/rock of Steeleye Span, led his crew in producing rich, haunting arrangements of the folk music of France, Brittany, and francophone Canada. The band's later recordings feature original compositions and more contemporary instrumentation while retaining a traditional flavor. —*Michael P. Dawson*

Malicorne [Hexagone] / 1974 / Hexagone ✦✦✦
Their debut is more acoustic and folky than their later works, and just as terrific. —*Steve Winick*

Malicorne Two / 1975 / Hexagone ✦✦✦
Malicorne's second album is much like their first: solid and well-played arrangements of traditional material, folkier than their later outings. —*Steve Winick*

Almanach / 1976 / Hexagone ✦✦✦✦
This beautifully packaged album consists of seasonal songs and music from around France and is Malicorne's most consistently excellent album. —*Steve Winick*

Malicorne IV / 1976 / Hexagone ✦✦✦
This excellent album features some stirring songs with orchestral arrangements. —*Steve Winick*

Quintessence / 1977 / Antigon ✦✦✦
This is a compilation of tracks from Malicorne's early albums. —*Steve Winick*

L'Extraordinaire Tour de France d'Adelard Rousseau / 1978 / Ballon ✦✦✦
This concept album follows a Compagne, the French equivalent of a Freemason, through his rite of passage, a tour of France. Dan Ar Bras guests. —*Steve Winick*

En Public à Montreal / 1979 / Ballon ✦✦✦✦
Malicorne's live album features material from their albums as well five new tracks. A set of French-Canadian reels drives the Montreal audience wild. —*Steve Winick*

Bestiare / 1979 / Ballon ✦✦

● **Legende: Deuxiéme Epoque** / 1991 / Hannibal ✦✦✦✦
Legende is an anthology gleaned from five albums by a group touted for all the best reasons as "France's answer to Fairport Convention." From 1973 on, Malicorne mined and expanded France's folk ballad tradition with good songs, alluring singing, both arcane and ultra-modern instruments, and oddball studio tricks that worked in their favor. Their music is so melodically rich that it won't matter if your command of French doesn't get you through a Folger's commercial. —*Roundup Newsletter*

Trio Erik Marchand

Vocals
Erik Marchand, formerly of the group Gwerz, is a powerful singer of Breton songs. His trio came into being when accompanist Thierry Robin discovered that the oud, or middle eastern lute, could reproduce the unusual intervals of traditional Breton vocal music. Soon the duo had recruited Hameed Khan, a tabla player, to round out their Breton-Arabic fusion. —*Steve Winick*

● **Chants du Centre-Bretagne "An Henchou Treuz"** / 1990 / Ocora ✦✦✦✦
The first outing by this innovative trio blends Middle Eastern rhythms and melodic improvisation with old Breton ballads. —*Steve Winick*

Tri Breur / 1991 / Silex ✦✦✦
With more of the same, Marchand's startling voice is joined by Yann-Fanch Kemener on one track. —*Steve Winick*

Cathal McConnell and Len Graham

Flute, Vocals
Cathal McConnell is a singer and flute player from the North of Ireland. He has been a member of the Boys of the Lough for many years. Len Graham is a folk revival singer of great renown. He fronts the group Skylark. Both are all-Ireland champions. —*Steve Winick*

● **On Lough Erne's Shore** / 1989 / Flying Fish ✦✦✦✦
The Boys of the Lough's whistle and flute player performs traditional Irish music. —*AMG*

For the Sake of Old Decency / 1992 / Sage Arts ✦✦✦
This was recorded live in concert in Pittsburgh. It's a nice cross-section of the repertoires of two of Ireland's important singers and musicians. —*Steve Winick*

Andy McGann

Andy McGann is a legendary name in New York Irish music circles. He has influenced some of this generation's best musicians. In his younger days, he played with Michael Coleman, probably the most important fiddler that ever recorded. Since then, he's remained at the top of the field for traditionalists. —*Steve Winick*

It's a Hard Road to Travel / Shanachie ✦✦✦✦
This album makes it obvious why McGann is revered as the top fiddler of the Bronx. A robust, almost classical tone combines with an easy grace and fluttering ornaments for a distinctive and masterful sound. Paul Brady's guitar accompaniments bring out the best. —*Steve Winick*

McGann/Reynolds

See Andy McGann for notes on this fine fiddler. Paddy Reynolds is from County Longford, Ireland, and emigrated to the US in the late '40s. He and McGann lived close to one another and played together throughout the '50s. Although their individual styles are quite different, they accommodate one another so well that they become an extremely tight duo. —*Steve Winick*

Traditional Music of Ireland / Shanachie ✦✦✦
Simple, major key jigs, reels, and hornpipes fill this tight duet album. Paul Brady accompanies on guitar. —*Steve Winick*

Seamus and Manus McGuire

Celtic
The McGuire brothers are two of Ireland's great fiddle players who rarely tour internationally. They can be heard on several grand recordings, though, including those by Buttons and Bows. Daithi Sproule is a distinguished Gaelic singer and guitarist now living in the US. He has played with several great bands, including Skara Brae and Altan. —*Steve Winick*

● **Carousel (with Daithi Sproule)** / 1984 / Gael Linn ✦✦✦✦
They breeze through reels, waltzes, and jigs, and Sproule sings three lovely songs in Gaelic. —*Steve Winick*

The Wishing Tree / 1995 / Green Linnet ✦✦✦

Joe and Antoinette McKenna

Joe McKenna is a piper, and his wife Antoinette (nee Bergin) is a singer

and harp player. Both hail from Dublin, where Joe learned to play pipes from Leo Rowsome and other members of the famed Pipers Club. —*Steve Winick*

● **Irish Pipes and Harp** / 1974 / Shanachie ✦✦✦✦
Their recording debut, this one features two songs by Antoinette and lots of dance music from Joe. It's all impeccably played. —*Steve Winick*

Magenta Music / 1975 / Shanachie ✦✦

At Home / Shanachie ✦✦✦
The McKennas and accompanists Mick Moloney and Irene Herrmann explore some sensitive slow airs as well as songs and dance music. —*Steve Winick*

Farewell to Fine Weather / Shanachie ✦✦✦
Here are more songs and tunes in fairly conservative folk-revival style. —*Steve Winick*

Brian McNeill

Fiddle, Guitar, Mandolin, Violin, Vocals
Brian McNeill was involved in the Edinburgh folk scene in the '70s, when he formed the Battlefield Band with Alan Reid. Although he originally specialized in the fiddle, and is still a superb fiddle player, he is also a multi-instrumentalist of amazing breadth and a songwriter of the first order. His solo works, both before and after leaving Battlefield at the end of 1990, are varied in content but consistent in quality. —*Steve Winick*

Monksgate / 1978 / Greentrax ✦✦✦
McNeill's friends, including members of the Battlefield Band, perform a rousing set of instrumental selections. —*Steve Winick*

Busker and the Devil's Only Daug / 1979 / Temple Music ✦✦✦
This one includes both traditional and original numbers, and is populated by guests like Cilla Fisher and Battlefield personnel. More excellent original songs and tunes, plus a few staples of the busker's repertoire. —*Steve Winick*

Unstrung Hero / 1985 / Temple ✦✦✦✦
McNeill gives us an album of completely original tunes and songs, on which he sings and plays violin, viola, guitar, mandolin, mandocello, bouzouki, cittern, tenor banjo, concertina, xylophone, hurdy-gurdy, synthesizers, acoustic and electric bass, and drums. —*Steve Winick*

Horses for Courses / 1993 / Greentrax ✦✦✦
This album is by the duo of McNeill and Tom McDonagh. McDonagh's Irish songs and string-picking back up McNeill's usual slew of instruments. Dick Gaughan guests on voice, guitar, and synthesizer. It's entertaining and solid, but not as amazing as some of McNeill's solo work. —*Steve Winick*

● **The Back o' the North Wind** / Greentrax ✦✦✦✦
A brilliant, historical labor of love, this solo outing is the musical half of his daring and exquisite stage show tying together Scots and American history through the stories of five very different emigrants, both willing and reluctant. McNeill is a truly great songwriter, and this album includes some of his best work. —*Danny Carnahan*

Ed Miller

Vocals
An Edinburgh native living in Texas, Miller has earned a reputation as one of North America's best Scottish singers. He's also earned a Ph.D. in Folklore from the University of Texas. —*Steve Winick*

● **Scottish Voice** / 1993 / Wellfield ✦✦✦✦
Miller's commanding vocal presence and impeccable taste in songs make this his most enjoyable album. —*Steve Winick*

Home and Away / Folk Legacy ✦✦✦
Miller sings excellent and moving renditions of songs associated with Scotland's folk revival. Songwriters include Robert Burns, Adam MacNaughton, Matt Armour, Mary Brooksbank, Nancy Nicholson, Hamish Henderson, Ian Sinclair, and Miller. —*Steve Winick*

Border Background / Folk Legacy ✦✦✦

Molard/Molard/Pellen

This trio is made up of Jacky and Patrick Molard, who have been members of Gwerz and Pennou Skoulm, and Jacques Pellen, an innovative guitarist. —*Steve Winick*

Triptyque / 1993 / Gwerz Pladenn ✦✦✦
Jacky Molard plays fiddle, mandolin, and guitar; his brother Patrick plays bagpipes; and Pellen holds it all together on guitar. This is an impressive album of experimental Breton music. —*Steve Winick*

Matt Molloy

Flute
Matt Molloy of Ballaghadereen, County Roscommon, Ireland, is one of the standards against whom Irish flute players are measured. His charac-

teristically strong blow and robust tone make him a powerful addition to any session. He was an original member of the Bothy Band in the '70s, then joined Donal Lunny in the reformed Planxty when the Bothy Band broke up. After his stint in Planxty, he replaced Mick Turbridy in the Chieftains, Irish music's most famous instrumental group. With them, he's toured the world, from China to the US. Along the way he's recorded several solo, duo, and trio projects, and settled down as a pub owner in County Mayo. —*Steve Winick*

Matt Molloy with Donal Lunny / 1984 / Green Linnet ✦✦✦
Molloy plays reels and airs as no one else can. —*Steve Winick*

Contentment Is Wealth / 1985 / Green Linnet ✦✦✦
This album pairs Molloy with fellow Chieftains member Sean Keane for some amazing flute and fiddle duets. Arty McGlynn accompanies on guitar. —*Steve Winick*

Matt Molloy with Tommy Peoples and Paul Brady / 1985 / Green Linnet ✦✦✦✦
A 1985 release of 1977 studio sessions, it includes fiddler Peoples and guitarist and singer Brady joining Molloy for unbelievably fiery trio playing. —*Steve Winick*

Stony Steps / 1987 / Green Linnet ✦✦✦
Molloy again demonstrates his amazing virtuosity. —*Steve Winick*

Heathery Breeze / 1988 / Shanachie ✦✦✦✦
Molloy's flute is once again backed only by Donal Lunny's guitar, bouzouki, and synthesizer. —*Steve Winick*

● **Music at Matt Molloy's** / Jan. 22, 1993 / Real World ✦✦✦✦
Live music comes from the locals at Matt Molloy's pub in County Mayo, Ireland, in which Molloy himself plays flute. It's one of the better recordings of "live-in-the-pub" style Irish music anywhere. —*Steve Winick*

Moloney O'Connell and Keane

Mick Moloney came to the US in 1973, and soon met fiddler Eugene O'Donnell. Seamus Egan was only four years old at the time, but he grew up to be one of the country's finest young Irish musicians. —*Steve Winick*

There Were Roses / 1986 / Green Linnet ✦✦✦
This also has a brilliant title track. Fiddler Liz Carroll guests. —*Steve Winick*

● **Kilkelly** / 1988 / Green Linnet ✦✦✦✦
The title track is an absolute classic. —*Steve Winick*

Mick Moloney

Banjo, Guitar, Mandolin, Vocals
Moloney is one of the most active members of the Irish-American musical community. In the '60s he played with the Johnstons, one of the most important early revival bands. A singer, instrumentalist, and folklorist, Moloney hails from Limerick but now lives in Philadelphia, where he recently earned his Ph.D. in folklore with a brilliant dissertation on Irish music in America. —*Steve Winick*

We Have Met Together / 1973 / Green Linnet ✦✦✦
An interesting first solo album, it includes traditional and modern songs and tunes. —*Steve Winick*

● **With Eugene O'Donnell** / 1978 / Green Linnet ✦✦✦✦
A beautiful album, it includes lovely songs and tune arrangements. Derry-born O'Donnell is king of slow airs and set dances on the fiddle. —*Steve Winick*

Strings Attached / 1980 / Green Linnet ✦✦✦✦
His only all-instrumental recording features his mastery of tenor banjo and mandolin as well as guitar and bouzouki accompaniments. —*Steve Winick*

Uncommon Bonds / 1984 / Green Linnet ✦✦✦
Classic Irish and Irish-American material with Eugene O'Donnell. —*Steve Winick*

Christy Moore

Guitar, Vocals
Founder of Planxty and Moving Hearts, Moore has also had an important solo career and has played both traditional music and folk-tinged pop music. —*Steve Winick*

Prosperous / 1971 / Tara ✦✦✦
Guests include Andy Irvine, Liam O'Flynn, Donal Lunny, and Kevin Conneff. It's a collector's item, mainly because it was the album that spawned Planxty. —*Steve Winick*

Live in Dublin / 1978 / Tara ✦✦✦
Christy at his best on this better-than-average live album. —*Chip Renner*

The Iron Behind the Velvet / 1978 / Tara ✦✦✦
His band on this one includes Moore's brother Barry, aka Luka Bloom. —*Steve Winick*

The Time Has Come / 1983 / Green Linnet ✦✦✦
A great solo effort, it features traditional and political songs. —*Steve Winick*

Ride On / 1984 / Green Linnet ✦✦✦✦
A powerful CD featuring "Ride On," "City of Chicago," "Lisdoonvarna," and "Among the Wicklow Hills." This one is so good it can make his other good ones seem weak. —*Chip Renner*

Ordinary Man / 1985 / Green Linnet ✦✦✦
A notch below *Ride On*. Featuring "Delirium Tremens," "Reel in the Flickering Light," and "Quiet Desperation." —*Chip Renner*

Nice 'n' Easy / 1986 / PolyGram ✦✦✦
This import contains "Sacco & Vanzetti," "Nancy Spain," and "Lanigan's Ball." —*Chip Renner*

Unfinished Revolution / 1987 / Warner Brothers ✦✦✦
Very good. Contains "Biko Drum," "A Pair of Brown Eyes," and the title track. Produced by Donal Lunny. —*Chip Renner*

The Christy Moore Folk Collection / Tara ✦✦✦
A hard-to-find collection of Moore's early works. Buy it if you see it. —*Chip Renner*

● **Christy Moore [Polydor]** / Polydor ✦✦✦✦
This is a terrific album of traditional songs and ballads. —*Steve Winick*

Moving Hearts

This Irish folk-rock group of the first half of the '80s had a lineup including Brian Calnan, Keith Donald, Donal Lunny, Christy Moore, Eoghan O'Neill, and Davy Spillane. It was the forerunner of such groups as the Pogues, the Mekons, and the Oyster Band and mixed a traditional approach (they played acoustic instruments, such as bodhran and uillean pipes, as well as electric ones) with a contemporary repertoire, some of it socially conscious material. For example, *Moving Hearts* in 1981 included "Hiroshima, Nagasaki, Russian Roulette." The second album, *Dark End of the Street*, was internationally hailed.

The band's talented lineup had trouble staying together, and *Live Hearts* in 1983 was their last real album, though *The Storm* in 1985 was an interesting instrumental collection. The band's influence has been extensive, and Christy Moore has gone on to a successful solo career. —*William Ruhlmann*

● **Moving Hearts** / 1981 / Green Linnet ✦✦✦✦
This compilation album features Hearts standards such as "Hiroshima, Nagasaki, Russian Roulette" and "McBrides," as well as a version of Jackson Browne's "Before the Deluge" that turns it into an Irish folk song. —*William Ruhlmann*

Mulhaire/Connolly/Coen

Accordionist Martin Mulhaire, fiddler Seamus Connolly, and flute player Jack Coen all come from the east Galway/east Clare region of Ireland. They all now live in America. —*Steve Winick*

☆ **Warming Up** / 1993 / Green Linnet ✦✦✦✦✦
Masterful performances by all three musicians and their accompanist, Felix Dolan, make for a fine album of straight-out Irish instrumental music. —*Steve Winick*

Brendan Mulvihill

Fiddle
Brendan Mulvihill is the son of influential fiddler and music teacher Martin Mulvihill. His unique style and fine technique have contributed to the success of the group the Irish Tradition, as well as to his separate work. —*Steve Winick*

● **Morning Dew** / 1993 / Green Linnet ✦✦✦✦
Mulvihill shares the billing on this release with Donna Long, a gifted pianist and harpsichord player. Together they extend the boundaries of Irish music. —*Steve Winick*

Flax in Bloom / Green Linnet ✦✦✦
Mulvihill is backed by Mick Moloney's guitar and banjo on this album of traditional fiddle tunes. His tone and flamboyant style are undeniable, but his innovative ornaments may distract fans of traditional fiddling. —*Steve Winick*

Martin Mulvihill

Fiddle
Martin Mulvihill, a fiddler who came from Limerick, Ireland, to the Bronx, had a major impact on Irish music in the eastern US. It was not so much his playing that influenced others as his teaching; Mulvihill ran a highly successful Irish music school and even went on the road to other cities to teach Irish music to interested youth. Many of the good and great young players studied with Mulvihill. —*Steve Winick*

Irish Music: The Living Tradition / Green Linnet ✦✦✦

• **Traditional Irish Fiddling from County Limerick** / Green Linnet ✦✦✦✦
There's nothing flashy or fancy here, just solid and spirited playing from Mulvihill and his accompanist, Mick Moloney. —*Steve Winick*

Denis Murphy

Fiddle
Denis Murphy and Julia Clifford are from the area of County Kerry, Ireland, known as Sliabh Luachra. They are brother and sister, both students of the fiddle master Padraig O'Keeffe. —*Steve Winick*

★ **The Star Above the Garter** / 1992 / Shanachie ✦✦✦✦✦
This re-release of an early-'60s album shows the richness and variety of Kerry's musical tradition through the repertoire of these talented siblings. —*Steve Winick*

Phil, John, and Pip Murphy

The late Phil Murphy and his sons John and Pip hail from County Wexford, Ireland. They are among the best-known harmonica players in the Irish tradition. —*Steve Winick*

• **Trip to Cullenstown** / 1991 / Claddagh ✦✦✦✦
Sprightly tunes are played on various harmonicas. —*Steve Winick*

Na Fili

This important trio set an early high standard for group playing on pipes, fiddle, and whistle. —*Steve Winick*

• **An Ghaoth Aniar: The West Wind** / 1969 / Mercier ✦✦✦✦
The playing is augmented by explanations of the tunes and songs right on the record. —*Steve Winick*

Farewell to Connacht / 1971 / Outlet ✦✦✦
Here's another fine Na Fili album. —*Steve Winick*

Na Fili 3 / 1972 / Outlet ✦✦✦
Featured are several religious songs sung in Gaelic. —*Steve Winick*

Mairead Ni Dhomhnaill

Fiddle, Vocals
Maighread Ni Dhomhnaill of Donegal is one of Ireland's finest traditional singers. She was a member of Skara Brae with her siblings Triona Ni Dhomhnaill and Micheal O Dhomhnaill. She takes most of her songs from the Donegal tradition, many from her own family. —*Steve Winick*

Mairead Ni Dhomhnaill / 1976 / Gael Linn ✦✦✦
As fine as her sister's solo album, this features some excellent musicians backing Mairead (as she then spelled her name) on fiddle, concertina, guitar, whistle, and keyboards. —*Steve Winick*

• **Gan Dha Phingin Spre (No Dowry)** / 1991 / Gael Linn ✦✦✦✦
Fifteen years later, Maighread is back with a new way to spell her name and a new way to arrange her songs: '90s-style. Smooth production and arrangements by Donal Lunny make this a winner. —*Steve Winick*

Maire Ni Chathasaigh

Harp, Vocals
Considered one of Ireland's finest clarsach (harp) players, Ni Chathasaigh is also a fine singer in Gaelic and English. —*Steve Winick*

• **The New-Strung Harp** / 1985 / Temple Music ✦✦✦✦
Ni Chathasaigh shows off all her talents, particularly that of arranging dance tunes on the harp. —*Steve Winick*

The Living Wood / Black Crow ✦✦✦
The first album to feature both Maire Ni Chathasaigh and her husband Chris Newman features mostly traditional tunes and songs, lovingly arranged. —*Steve Winick*

Out of Court / 1991 / Old Bridge Music ✦✦✦
With Ni Chathasaigh's husband, Chris Newman, an eclectic talent on the guitar, they make lovely and lively instrumental music. —*Steve Winick*

Triona Ni Dhomhnaill

Harpsichord, Vocals
A member of Skara Brae and the Bothy Band, Ni Dhomhnaill always seems to be part of an interesting musical outing. Her clear singing voice and harpsichord playing are an asset to any lineup. —*Steve Winick*

Triona / 1975 / Green Linnet ✦✦✦✦
This solo album features some of her loveliest recorded songs, some in English and some in Gaelic, with accompaniment by some of Ireland's greatest players. —*Steve Winick*

Chris Norman

Flute
Chris Norman is a classically trained flute player from Canada now living in the Baltimore area. He plays with the world music group Helicon and the early music ensemble the Baltimore Consort. —*Steve Winick*

• **Man with the Wooden Flute** / 1992 / Dorian ✦✦✦✦
Norman's sweet-toned flute leads a rousing set of tunes from Britain, Ireland, the US, and Canada. —*Steve Winick*

Beauty of the North / 1994 / Dorian ✦✦✦
This time, Norman and friends concentrate on tunes from Quebec and Maritime Canada. It's beautiful playing, somewhat classical in sound. —*Steve Winick*

Screaming Love / 1995 / Dice ✦✦

Nowell Sing We Clear

This four-man group features John Roberts, Tony Barrand, Fred Breunig, and Steve Woodruff. They perform traditional English songs of the Christmas season. —*Steve Winick*

• **Nowell Sing We Clear** / 1977 / Front Hall ✦✦✦
Mid-winter carols sung by Roberts and Barrand and accompanied by Breunig (fiddle) and Woodruff (accordion).Tasty vocal harmonies and a spirit of joy fill this one. —*Steve Winick*

Second Nowell / 1981 / Front Hall ✦✦✦
Here are more carols in Roberts' and Barrand's trademark style. —*Steve Winick*

Nowell Sing We Clear, Vol. 3 / 1985 / Front Hall ✦✦✦
Mostly new material, it has a few new versions of previously recorded songs. —*Steve Winick*

A Pageant of Mid-Winter Carols, Vol. 4 / 1988 / Front Hall ✦✦✦
This CD introduces Andy Davis (who replaces Steve Woodruff). It features mostly fresh versions of songs that the group has recorded before. —*Steve Winick*

• **The Best of Nowell Sing We Clear** / 1989 / Front Hall ✦✦✦✦
This picks the best tracks from the first three albums. It's a great introduction to the group. —*Steve Winick*

Paddy O'Brien

Accordion
Paddy O'Brien was a giant in the world of traditional Irish music. In 1954, he recorded three 78s that highlighted his own style of buttonbox playing, a style that allowed him to graft the full range of keys and ornaments from traditional fiddle playing to his accordion. There are few accordionists in Irish music today who have not been influenced by this innovative and inspired style of playing. Seamus Connolly, O'Brien's partner, is one of the top Irish fiddlers in the world. He teaches Irish music at Boston College. —*Steve Winick*

Stranger at the Gate / 1988 / Green Linnet ✦✦✦✦
O'Brien's button accordion is backed by Daithi Sproule's sensitive guitar. —*Steve Winick*

Robbie O'Connell

Guitar, Vocals
This nephew of the world-famous Clancy Brothers is also a fine folksinger and a respected songwriter. —*Steve Winick*

• **Close to the Bone** / 1982 / Green Linnet ✦✦✦✦
O'Connell's gentle voice and guitar perform traditional songs. It's quite a treat. —*Steve Winick*

Love of the Land / 1989 / Green Linnet ✦✦✦
These mostly original songs prove he's a fine songwriter. —*Steve Winick*

Never Learned to Dance / Green Linnet ✦✦✦
Featured is O'Connell's voice and guitar on new original songs. Some of the tracks are serious and some funny, but all are fine work. —*Steve Winick*

Eugene O'Donnell

Fiddle
This native of Derry city now lives in the Philadelphia area. He is a master of slow airs and set dances on the fiddle. —*Steve Winick*

• **Slow Airs and Set Dances** / Green Linnet ✦✦✦✦
An excellent showcase of O'Donnell's talents. His fiddle weeps and sings. —*Steve Winick*

3 Way Street / Green Linnet ✦✦✦
Egan's flute and banjo fit in perfectly with O'Donnell's fiddle and Moloney's voice, guitar, and strings. Tracks go from delightful to devastating. —*Steve Winick*

Liam O'Flynn

Pipe, Wind
An uilleann piper from County Kildare, O'Flynn was a founding member of

Planxty. An innovative performer, he has recorded with pop, folk, and classical musicians and on film soundtracks in varied styles. —*Steve Winick*

Liam O'Flynn / 1988 / WEA ✦✦✦
O'Flynn's piping is backed by former members of Planxty, among others. —*Steve Winick*

Fine Art of Piping / 1991 / Celtic Music ✦✦✦
This solo album shows off O'Flynn's amazing talents. —*Steve Winick*

● **Out to an Other Side** / 1993 / Tara ✦✦✦✦
O'Flynn's most eclectic album, this one features solo tracks as well as folk revival and orchestral arrangements. —*Steve Winick*

Jerry O'Sullivan

Pipe

Jerry O'Sullivan is one of the United States' finest uillean pipers. He won the all-Ireland piping championship in 1979, and since then has played at major Irish events up and down the east coast and spent several years in County Clare honing his piping skills still further. He has appeared on several film soundtracks, including *Far and Away*. —*Steve Winick*

The Invasion / Green Linnet ✦✦✦
For him, music is a social force, a thing to be shared with friends. This is reflected on his solo album, which features several of his musical pals, including Joanie Madden (flute), Eileen Ivers (guitar), and Seamus Egan (flute, banjo, whistle). —*Steve Winick*

Ossian

Formed in the mid '70s, Ossian became one of Scotland's best-loved folk revival bands. Members have included fiddler John Martin, highland bagpipe virtuoso Iain MacDonald, composer and multi-instrumentalist Billy Jackson, and singer and guitarist Tony Cuffe. The group broke up after Cuffe and Jackson moved to the US. The other members have remained prominent on the Scottish folk scene. —*Steve Winick*

St. Kilda Wedding / 1978 / Iona ✦✦✦
Featured is Billy Ross singing in English and Gaelic. —*Steve Winick*

Seal's Song / 1981 / Iona ✦✦✦
Singer Tony Cuffe shines on this lovely, lovely album. —*Steve Winick*

Dove Across the Water / 1982 / Iona ✦✦✦
Another beautiful album, this one features compositions by Billy Jackson and Tony Cuffe as well as traditional material. —*Steve Winick*

Borders / 1984 / Iona ✦✦✦✦
Every tune and song is gorgeous on this masterpiece. —*Steve Winick*

Light on a Distant Shore / 1986 / Iona ✦✦✦
Lots of compositions by Billy Jackson presage his later composition work. Wonderful playing and singing make this another fine effort. —*Steve Winick*

● **Best of Ossian** / 1995 / Iona ✦✦✦✦

Niamh Parsons

Vocals

Niamh Parsons is a fine singer from Ireland. Her roots are traditional, but she sings in a variety of styles. —*Steve Winick*

● **Loosely Connected** / 1995 / Greentrax ✦✦✦
A lovely showcase for Parsons' voice, this album features some traditional and folk material from Ireland, along with some contemporary material with pop and country leanings. Her singing is very much worth hearing. —*Steve Winick*

Patrick Street

Veterans of a lot of old, great bands like Planxty, the Bothy Band, and De Danann got together in the mid-'80s to form Patrick Street. The most consistent members are Kevin Burke, Jackie Daly, Andy Irvine, and Arty McGlynn. —*Steve Winick*

Patrick Street / 1986 / Green Linnet ✦✦✦
Much lighter, airier, and less intense than a lot of Irish music, it's a style that fits the artists well. —*Steve Winick*

All in Good Time A / 1986 / ✦✦✦✦
The four original recording members are back as a cohesive band for another excellent outing. —*Steve Winick*

No. 2 Patrick Street / 1988 / Green Linnet ✦✦✦
Here's another thoroughly enjoyable album. —*Steve Winick*

● **Irish Times** / 1990 / Green Linnet ✦✦✦✦
The addition of pipes and another fiddle makes for a fuller sound on this, their best work. —*Steve Winick*

Tommy Peoples

Fiddle

An electrifying fiddler from Donegal, Tommy Peoples has converted

more than one person to the religion of Irish traditional music. A member of the Bothy Band in 1975, he was the propulsive fiddler that powered that group's landmark first album. He also has some magnificent solo work. —*Steve Winick*

● **The Iron Man** / 1995 / Shanachie ✦✦✦✦
This features extremely strong fiddling backed by Daithi Sproule's guitar. A set of Donegal strathspeys steals the show. —*Steve Winick*

High Part of the Road / Shanachie ✦✦✦
Shortly after his stint with the Bothy Band, Peoples recorded this masterful solo album. Even on his slower tunes, his rolls are lightning flurries of notes. He's backed by Paul Brady, who was then Ireland's premiere guitar accompanist. —*Steve Winick*

The Plankerdown Band

This fine folk-rock band from the Canadian province of Newfoundland features former members of Figgy Duff. —*Steve Winick*

Jig Is Up / 1993 / Pigeon Inlet ✦✦✦
An all-instrumental debut album, this features fresh and vibrant arrangements of tunes from the Newfoundland tradition, which includes English and Irish heritage. —*Steve Winick*

Planxty

This band grew out of the sessions that produced Christy Moore's album *Prosperous*. Originally, it featured Moore, Donal Lunny, Andy Irvine, and Liam O'Flynn. This line-up made two albums in 1973 before Lunny went off to join the Bothy Band. His replacement was Johnny Moynihan, a former member, with Irvine, of Sweeney's Men. This line-up recorded the next Planxty LP in 1974, after which Moore left the group. Planxty recorded no more albums before they broke up in 1975. In 1979 the group was back together and recording albums with new members until 1983, when they evolved into Moving Hearts. —*Steve Winick*

★ **Planxty** / 1973 / Shanachie ✦✦✦✦✦
This stunning 1973 debut features arrangements of traditional songs and tunes with both punch and subtlety. —*Steve Winick*

The Well Below the Valley / 1973 / Shanachie ✦✦✦✦
Perhaps not quite as compelling as the debut album, it's still a treasure. —*Steve Winick*

Cold Blow and the Rainy Night / 1974 / Shanachie ✦✦✦✦
Lunny is replaced by Johnny Moynihan of Sweeny's Men and De Danann fame. —*Steve Winick*

The Planxty Collection / 1976 / Shanachie ✦✦✦
Just a notch below *Well Below the Valley*. Well produced. —*Chip Renner*

● **After the Break** / 1979 / Tara ✦✦✦✦
With brilliant tunes and songs, it features Matt Molloy. —*Steve Winick*

The Woman I Loved so Well / 1980 / Tara ✦✦✦
Some of the fire is gone from their arrangements, but a few of the songs are their best ever. —*Steve Winick*

Words and Music / 1983 / Shanachie ✦✦

Plethyn

A group from Wales that bases its harmony singing style on the Plygain carol tradition, Plethyn features the lovely voice of Linda Healy. —*Steve Winick*

Drws Agored / 1991 / Sain ✦✦✦
Bright harmonies and simple accompaniment make this a pleasant listen. The words are in Welsh, but there are some English translations in the booklet. —*Steve Winick*

Maddy Prior

Singer Maddy Prior gained a following in England's folk clubs as a member of a duo with Tim Hart. In the late '60s, she recorded several albums with Hart. After meeting Ashley Hutchings at a folk festival, Prior and Hart joined Steeleye Span, the highly acclaimed electric folk group that Prior still fronts today. Along the way, she has been part of another duo with June Tabor, called Silly Sisters. She has also recorded several albums solo and with her husband, Rick Kemp. —*Steve Winick*

Carols and Capers / 1991 / Park ✦✦✦
Prior is joined on this release by the Carnival Band, an early music-style instrumental group, for Renaissance arrangements of Christmas carols. —*Steve Winick*

Year / 1993 / Park ✦✦✦✦
Year features a few traditional songs, plus a suite of songs written by Prior about the passing of the year. —*Steve Winick*

Hang up Sorrow and Care / Feb. 27, 1996 / Park ✦✦✦
Maddy Prior teams up again with the Carnival Band, this time for a set of love and drinking songs. *Hang Up Sorrow & Care* is subtitled "A Cure for

All Melancholy, being a collection of the Wit and Philosophie of Old Simon the Ring." Adapted by the band, the songs come from the 17th and 18th century and combine romantic laments with tavern celebrations and dance tunes. Except for a few "electric modern guitars" here and there, the instrumentation is as traditional as the lyrics, but the music would retain its celebratory mood in any age. *— William Ruhlmann*

● **Summer Solstice** / Shanachie ✦✦✦✦
This heralded British folk release by Prior and Hart led to the creation of Steeleye Span. It includes "Three Drunken Maidens," "Fly Up My Cock," "Bring Us in Good Ale," "Sorry the Day I Was Married," and nine others. *—Roundup Newsletter*

Silly Sisters / Shanachie ✦✦✦✦
This is an exquisitely wonderful duet album of traditional English songs. Though the lyrics aren't the most progressive, these two outstanding British vocalists create perfect harmonies, plus a few fine solos. A better blend of voices is hard to find. It includes "My Husband's Got No Courage in Him" and "The Seven Joys of Mary." *—Ladyslipper*

Jean Redpath

b. Apr. 28, 1937, Edinburgh, Scotland
Vocals
Blessed with a sweet, but slightly roughened mezzo-soprano as gentle as mist and haunting as the Highlands, Jean Redpath is one of the definitive interpreters of Scottish traditional songs. She is also a noted folk music ethnographer who has played an important role in the reconstruction of nearly forgotten Scottish songs and has been a lecturer at Scotland's Stirling University since 1979, and has also lectured regularly at Weslyan University, CT, and other prominent institutions, including Harvard.

She was born outside Edinburgh. Her father played hammered dulcimer and her mother was well versed in Scottish oral history, most of which was passed from mother to daughter via songs. Her mother passed on the music to each of four daughters. Knowledge of the ancient songs proved useful while Redpath was attending the School of Scottish Studies at the University of Edinburgh and had begun formal research into her native ballads and compositions. She emigrated to New York in 1961, where she began singing in Greenwich village coffeehouses. Redpath also gave formal concerts at events such as the Lincoln Center's Mostly Mozart Festival and soon became an extremely popular performer on the folk circuit. Not only did they love her unique, sensitive voice, audiences were also impressed by her knowledge about the more than 400 songs in her repertoire and the fascinating insights about the music that Redpath offered during her concerts. In 1963, she sang for the first time at the new School of Social Research and this led her to sign with Elektra, where she recorded through 1975, when she switched to the Vermont-based Philo label. With them she has become one of folk music's most prolific recording artists. One of her most notable achievements has been an ongoing project to record all of the songs written by Scotland's poet laureate Robert Burns. Out of 22 planned volumes, only seven were completed, due to the death of producer Serge Hovey. Other well-known Redpath series include a compilation of Scottish songs written by women, including *Lady Nairne* (1986).

In addition to recording and performing live, Redpath has also appeared on such radio programs as "Morning Pro Musica" on Boston's WGBH public radio station. Between 1974 and 1987 Redpath was also a regular on Garrison Keillor's "Prairie Home Companion" radio show. *—Sandra Brennan*

The The Jean Redpath Scottish Ballad Book / 1964 / Elektra ✦✦✦
These Scottish ballads are beautifully done. *—Steve Winick*

Laddie Lie Near Me / 1967 / Elektra ✦✦✦
Laddie Lie Near Me features another solid batch of Scottish interpretations. *—Steve Winick*

★ **Frae my ain Countrie** / 1973 / Folk Legacy ✦✦✦✦✦
The Songs of Robert Burns / Philo ✦✦✦
This ambitious multivolume set aims at recording all of Burns' songs, with authentic accompaniment. *—Steve Winick*

Sue Richards

Harp
Sue Richards specializes in Scottish and Irish material on the Celtic harp. She is well-known to audiences in the DC area and beyond as a three-time American Scottish harp champion and as a member of Ceoltoiri (Celtic music) and Ensemble Galilei (early music). *—Steve Winick*

Grey Eyed Morn / 1991 / Maggie's Music ✦✦✦
Richards plays mostly Scottish tunes, along with a few Irish and Welsh pieces. Guests include Bonnie Rideout (Scottish fiddle) and members of Ceoltoiri. *—Steve Winick*

● **Morning Aire** / Maggie's Music ✦✦✦✦
This one's split equally between Irish and Scottish material. Billy McComiskey (accordion, concertina) and Myron Bretholz (bodhran) add

an Irish touch to arrangements. It's wonderfully played all-round. *—Steve Winick*

Bob Roberts

Accordion
The accordion was an important British folk and popular instrument from the mid-19th century on, and very much a sailor's instrument. Roberts, who worked on sailing cargo wherries much of his life, was a fine melodeon player and a singer with a very wide repertory. *—John Storm Roberts*

Songs from the Sailing Barges / Topic ✦✦✦✦
Includes a hilarious epic about a North Sea oilrig; "The Grey Hawk," of Renaissance origin; and "The Foggy Dew," in an Eastern English version. *—John Storm Roberts*

Loeiz Ropars

Vocals
Loeiz Ropars is one of the fathers of the Breton music revival. In the early '40s, he became interested in revitalizing the kan ha diskan, a special kind of call-and-response singing used to accompany dances. He made himself a part of the post-war reawakening of Breton cultural identity. His background of peasant life and his involvement in the the "Cercle Celtique" or Celtic cultural association, of Poullaouen led him to the idea of creating a new type of event for Breton music and dancing. It would be like the community-based fest-noz, or night party, except that it would bring people together from different parts of Brittany. His idea, the "new-style" fest-noz, is the most important type of folk music event in Brittany today. *—Steve Winick*

● **Kan Ha Diskan** / 1992 / Keltia Musique ✦✦✦✦
This is an album of pure, unaccompanied vocals. It's melodically and rhythmically catchy, and sung with enthusiasm by Ropars and his partners. Still, the inaccessibility of the language makes this a release for diehard fans of Breton music. For those diehard fans, it's a treasure. *—Steve Winick*

Leo Rowsome

Pipe
Leo Rowsome was one of the most influential pipers of his generation, indeed of all time. He came from a long line of Wexford pipers but lived himself in Dublin, where he taught many of the current generation of pipers. He died in 1970. *—Steve Winick*

★ **The King of the Pipers** / Shanachie ✦✦✦✦✦
Originally released on Dublin's Claddagh label in the '60s, this classic is now available again on CD. Rowsome's open-piping style flows beautifully. *—Steve Winick*

Classics of Irish Piping / Topic ✦✦✦✦
The Irish uillean pipes are less austere than the Scots'; the pipes play chords as well as drone and melody, much like a concertina with a drone. This gives the songs a familiar structure to go with the entrancing sound, which is also warmer than in the Scots' pipes. Rowsome was not only a master piper (he was a teacher at 16) but a master craftsman as well, and his own pipes were never equalled in his lifetime. This stunningly beautiful recording is a monument to a remarkable musician. *—Carl Hoyt*

Janet Russell

Vocals
From Buckhaven in Fife, Scotland, Janet Russell is one of the finest voices in contemporary Scottish folk. Steeped in traditional song but also fond of songwriting, Russell stresses the unity of old and new songs. *—Steve Winick*

Gathering the Fragments / 1988 / Harbourtown ✦✦✦
The emphasis on Russell's debut is on powerful arrangements of contemporary Scottish songs, with a few older gems thrown in. *—Steve Winick*

Ben Sands

Guitar, Mandolin, Vocals
Ben Sands is a member of the Sands Family of County Down. He specializes in singing gentle love songs, both traditional and contemporary. He also plays guitar and mandolin. *—Steve Winick*

Take Your Time / 1993 / Spring ✦✦✦✦
Unlike his brothers Tommy and Colum, Ben Sands is not a prolific songwriter, so this album is full of songs written by others, including traditional songs. Most are gentle love songs with an easy, uplifting feeling. *—Steve Winick*

Colum Sands

Bass, Vocals
A member of the Sands Family of Co. Down, Colum Sands is a fine

singer and an inspired songwriter, much like his brother Tommy. —*Steve Winick*

● **March Ditch** / 1991 / Spring ✦✦✦✦
Colum's songs are full of hope, irony, humor, and political consciousness. His singing is accompanied by members of the Sands family, among others. —*Steve Winick*

Scartaglen

Scartaglen is a four-piece Kansas City band that plays traditional Irish music. The members of the band include Connie Dover (vocals, keyboards), Michael Dugger (vocals, fiddle, guitar, banjo), Roger Landes (bouzouki, mandolin, guitar, bodhran), Kirk Lynch (uillean pipes, tinwhistle, guitar, bouzouki), and Rebecca Pringle (fiddle). —*Chip Renner*

The Middle Path / 1986 / Castle Island ✦✦✦
A very good album featuring great vocals—a totally satisfying sound. —*Chip Renner*

● **Last Night's Fun** / 1992 / City Spark ✦✦✦✦
Their finest release to date. Everything about their music has matured to the point that I feel Scartaglen is one of the finest Celtic bands on the scene to date. Highly, highly recommended. —*Chip Renner*

Shanachie

A quintet from Germany, Shanachie have spent a lot of time in Miltown Malbay, County Clare. There, in a pub called the Ocean View, they've learned to play Irish music better than many Irish bands do it. —*Steve Winick*

Ocean View / 1990 / Errigal ✦✦✦
A debut album full of verve, they do sound a bit stilted in the vocal department, but the playing is quite good. —*Steve Winick*

● **Second Home** / 1993 / Airborne ✦✦✦✦
The playing's more polished and—even better—they've imported singer Olga Vaughan from Ireland. It's a truly impressive album. —*Steve Winick*

Sharon Shannon

Fiddle, Accordion
Sharon Shannon is a young, gifted accordion player from Galway. Her pared-down, speeded-up and rocked-out approach to traditional music appeals to other artists as much as it does to her fans. It earned her a place in the Waterboys and in Christy Moore's band before she toured Europe and the US with her own successful band. —*Steve Winick*

● **Sharon Shannon** / Jul. 1, 1993 / Philo ✦✦✦✦
Shannon and band breeze through some great material with amazing virtuosity. This one'll keep your toes tapping for weeks. —*Steve Winick*

Out the Gap / 1995 / Green Linnet ✦✦✦

Soig Siberil

Guitar
An innovative guitarist, Soig Siberil has been a member of many great Breton bands, including Kornog, Gwerz, Den, Pennou Skoulm and Kemia. —*Steve Winick*

Digor! / 1993 / Gwerz Pladenn ✦✦✦✦
Siberil's rhythm guitar skills are matched by his beautiful lyrical lead abilities, and his compositions are equally captivating. Many styles and moods are explored. The band includes flute, percussion, banjo, bagpipes, mandolin, fiddle, and bass along with the guitars, which keeps everything interesting and fresh. —*Steve Winick*

Sileas

Patsy Seddon and Mary McMaster are Sileas (pronounced she-liss). Both of them sing and play the Celtic harp. Their music features both the standard nylon-strung acoustic harp and the bright-sounding camac electroharp. —*Steve Winick*

Delighted with Harps / 1987 / Green Linnet ✦✦✦
This is a pretty collection of traditional melodies and songs. Material includes dance music, airs, and songs in both Scots and Gaelic. —*Steve Winick*

Beating Harps / 1987 / Green Linnet ✦✦✦
More fine tracks include one original composition by Seddon. —*Steve Winick*

● **Harpbreakers** / 1990 / Lap Wing ✦✦✦✦
Sileas continue their trend of playing top-quality Scottish and Irish music on harps. They also keep up the lovely singing. —*Steve Winick*

Silly Sisters

Steeleye Span's Maddy Prior and folk diva June Tabor teamed up in 1976

for the first Silly Sisters album. It was more than a decade before they followed it up with a second, but both recordings feature a gorgeous melding of Prior's clear, brassy soprano with Tabor's darker tones. —*Michael P. Dawson*

★ **Silly Sisters** / 1976 / Shanachie ✦✦✦✦✦
Maddy Prior and the then little-known June Tabor teamed to keen a delightful lark of an album. An enduring minor piece with many, many of the English folk revival's best players, it's whimsical and spirited. —*Mark A. Humphrey*

No More to the Dance / 1988 / Shanachie ✦✦✦✦
A new masterpiece by these two vocalists, whose harmonies do truly sound like they are of a family, breaks new ground for traditional music. It features innovative textures with touches of Eastern European harmony, and constantly shifting combinations of western, eastern, modern, and traditional instruments (Chinese flutes, soprano sax, Celtic harps by the women of Sileas, and bagpipes). Very highly recommended! —*Ladyslipper*

Silly Wizard

Generally considered the world's finest performers of traditional and contemporary Scottish music—and with good reason. Silly Wizard's music is at once driving and sensitive, powerful and poignant, at times hypnotic, often humorous, with sensitive group interplay and virtuoso-level musicianship, particularly from brothers Phil (accordion, keyboards, whistles, guitar, vocals) and Johnny (fiddle) Cunningham. Their repertoire includes centuries-old instrumental dance music along with traditional and contemporary narrative ballads: tales of joy and woe, of men and women, of time and travel, of love and loss. Silly Wizard is not just another folk music group; they rank with the greatest creators and performers from any country from any time.

Several members of the group, particularly the Cunningham brothers and vocalist Andy Stewart, have made solo and duo recordings and have performed and recorded with other artists, primarily Scottish traditionalists. These recordings are also well worth investigating, but get the Silly Wizard stuff first. —*Niles J. Frantz*

Silly Wizard / 1976 / Xtra ✦✦

Caledonia's Hardy Sons / 1978 / Shanachie ✦✦✦
Stewart's voice is sweeter and more innocent on this early album than on later works. —*Steve Winick*

So Many Partings / 1980 / Shanachie ✦✦✦
This is another great early set. —*Steve Winick*

● **Wild and Beautiful** / 1981 / Shanachie ✦✦✦✦
A brilliant set, it featurestsome great original songs by Andy and some breathtaking tunes from the Cunninghams. —*Steve Winick*

The Best of Silly Wizard / 1985 / Shanachie ✦✦✦
Really only the best of their Shanachie releases, it's still a great compilation. —*Steve Winick*

☆ **Live Wizardry** / 1988 / Green Linnet ✦✦✦✦✦
This two-for-one bargain captures a brilliant live set in 1988, at the culmination of their career. —*Steve Winick*

Skara Brae

Skara Brae is a vocal quartet that features Michael O Dhomhnaill and his sisters Triona and Mairead Ni Dhomhnaill of Rann na Feirste in Donegal and Daithi Sproule from Derry city. —*Steve Winick*

Skara Brae / Shanachie ✦✦✦✦
Michael and Triona went on to form the Bothy Band, and Daithi became a fine solo artist and a member of groups like Altan, but this was their first recorded effort (made in the early '70s) of beautifully performed Gaelic songs. The four vocalists are skillfully backed by guitar from Micheal and Daithi and harpsichord from Triona. —*Steve Winick*

J. Scott Skinner

b. 1843
Fiddle
James Scott Skinner, born in 1843, was already playing by 1855. Skinner was no folk artist, but a virtuoso of a drawing-room style that drew from both the folk and classical traditions. —*John Storm Roberts*

The Strathspey King / Topic ✦✦✦✦
These extraordinary recordings link us with a style first formed about 150 years ago, and a musical idiom not just dead but unjustly forgotten. —*John Storm Roberts*

Skolvan

One of the top bands on the Breton dance music scene, Skolvan use fiddle, bombarde, guitar and more to create rousing and intricate arrangements of Breton music. —*Steve Winick*

★ **Come to the Dance** / 1991 / Keltia Musique ✦✦✦✦✦
Guest vocalists Yann-Fanch Kemener and Marcel Guilloux add another dimension to this excellent album of dance music. —*Steve Winick*

Skylark

Skylark is an excellent group featuring Len Graham of Antrim, one of Ireland's great singers, along with Gerry O'Connor's fiddle and Garry O'Briain's mandocello and guitar. —*Steve Winick*

Skylark / 1972 / Shanachie ✦✦✦
Skylark's first album, featuring Andrew McNamara's accordion, is dance music, along with singing by Graham's rich voice. —*Steve Winick*

2 / 1974 / Capitol ✦✦✦

● **All of It** / 1979 / Green Linnet ✦✦✦✦
Several guests add fullness to the arrangements; otherwise, it's more of the same good thing. —*Steve Winick*

Daithi Sproule

Guitar, Vocals
A former member of the group Skara Brae, Daithi Sproule of Derry city now lives in Minneapolis. He is one of Irish music's greatest guitar accompanists, and also a fine singer in English and Gaelic. He currently performs part-time in the groups Trian and Altan. Although his guitar accompaniment and vocals have been featured on many albums, he has not recorded much as a solo artist. —*Steve Winick*

★ **Heart Made of Glass** / Green Linnet ✦✦✦✦✦
Simply a stunning debut, this is the kind of album that will never be last year's model. Liz Carrol and Peter Ostroushko help create simple, beautiful arrangements for ten songs and two instrumentals featuring Sproule's unparalleled voice and guitar. —*Steve Winick*

Andy M. Stewart

Bouzouki, Guitar, Vocals
The lead singer of Silly Wizard, Stewart has also had an impressive career on his own and with Manus Lunny, who backs his vocals with expert playing of bouzouki and guitar. —*Steve Winick*

By the Hush / 1982 / Green Linnet ✦✦✦✦
This excellent solo album was the winner of *Melody Makers'* Folk Album of the Year award in 1983. —*Steve Winick*

Fire in the Glen / 1986 / Shanachie ✦✦✦
This album features Stewart along with Phil Cunningham and Manus Lunny. It's a fine piece of work. —*Steve Winick*

● **Dublin Lady** / 1987 / Green Linnet ✦✦✦✦
A masterpiece and a must for Celtic music fans, it includes Manus Lunny. —*Steve Winick*

Songs of Robert Burns / 1990 / Green Linnet ✦✦✦
Anybody with a fondness for Burns' poetry should hear this album. The renditions are stirring and beautiful, even if the arrangements are a little weaker than Lunny's usual. —*Steve Winick*

At it Again / 1990 / Green Linnet ✦✦✦
With Manus Lunny. It's not as fantastic as *Dublin Lady,* but is still a fine record. —*Steve Winick*

Man in the Moon / 1994 / Green Linnet ✦✦✦
Credited to Stewart as a solo artist, this one features Gerry O'Beirne handling much of the accompaniment and production work. With some great songs, plus a few sappy ones, it's a beautiful album on balance. —*Steve Winick*

Alan Stivell

Bagpipes, Harp, Vocals
New age/worldbeat performer Alan Stivell relies chiefly on the ethereal sounds of the Celtic harp for his sound, but incorporates bits of many other cultures' musics, including the Middle East, Africa, China, South America, and even American rock 'n' roll. Stivell grew up in the French region of Breton, where his father built Celtic harps as a hobby and introduced his son to the instrument at a young age. Stivell's music covers a wide range of moods, from the new age sounds of *The Mist of Avalon* and *Harpes du Nouvel Age* to the "Celtic rock" style of *Again,* which features guest performances from more rock-oriented artists Kate Bush and the Pogues' Shane MacGowan. —*Steve Huey*

From Celtic Roots / 1974 / Fontana ✦✦✦
Featured is Irish, Scottish, and Welsh music as well as Breton, with an electric folk-rock band. —*Steve Winick*

In Dublin / 1975 / Fontana ✦✦✦
This nice little live album features folky and electric arrangements of traditional music. —*Steve Winick*

● **E Langonned** / 1976 / Fontana ✦✦✦✦
Stivell's finest acoustic band performs traditional and original material. —*Steve Winick*

Journee a la Maison / 1978 / Rounder ✦✦✦
Stivell's arrangements here are tinged with jazz and pop, but it's still very Breton. —*Steve Winick*

Legend / 1984 / Celtic Music ✦✦✦
Based on the ancient Irish invasion legends, this album is atmospheric and new age in feeling. —*Steve Winick*

David Surette

Bouzouki
David Surette is a well known performer on the New England contradance and Celtic music scene. He has played and recorded with many of the area's finest acoustic musicians. —*Steve Winick*

● **Back Roads** / 1993 / Madrina Music ✦✦✦✦
Surette's guitar, mandolin, and bouzouki playing are quite impressive on this disc. The range of tunes includes traditional music from New England, Ireland, Scotland, Sweden, France, Canada, Brittany, and Appalachia as well as original Surette compositions. All in all, it's impeccable and full of surprises. —*Steve Winick*

Dave Swarbrick

Fiddle
This fiddler is best known for his partnership with Martin Carthy and his participation in groups like the Ian Campbell Group and Fairport Convention. He also has many excellent solo albums to his credit. —*Steve Winick*

● **Rags, Reels and Airs** / 1967 / Polydor ✦✦✦✦

Swarbrick / 1976 / Transatlantic ✦✦✦✦
Swarb's first solo album features old buddies from his Ceilidh band days as well as Martin Carthy and Fairport Convention. It includes a lot of good slower tunes, plus a few slower tunes. —*Steve Winick*

Swarbrick 2 / 1977 / Transatlantic ✦✦✦
Really a continuation of *Swarbrick,* it has the same personnel and producer. Swarbrick even wears the same shirt for the cover photo! —*Steve Winick*

Lift the Lid and Listen / 1978 / Sonet ✦✦✦
This continues the trend started on his first few albums. —*Steve Winick*

Sweeny's Men

Celtic
An early and important Irish group that influenced both the acoustic and the electric folk revival, it featured Andy Irvine, later of Planxty and Patrick Street, Johnny Moynihan, later of Planxty and De Danann, and Terry Woods, later of Steeleye Span and the Pogues. —*Steve Winick*

1968 / 1968 / Transatlantic ✦✦✦✦
Mostly traditional songs appear on this great collector's item. —*Steve Winick*

● **The Legend of Sweeny's Men** / 1988 / Demon ✦✦✦✦
The best of Sweeny's Men and a good place for introduction to the band. —*Steve Winick*

June Tabor

b. Dec. 31, 1947, Warwick, England
Vocals
June Tabor is probably the finest female traditional British folk singer of the late 20th century—if not the best British folk singer of her time, period. What links her to Britain's traditions are the chilling and emotional qualities of her voice. What links her to the British present is her fine taste in material, arrangements, and backing musicians, along with a willingness to try different things and interpret work by contemporary songwriters. Tabor's first high-profile project was a duet album with Steeleye Span's Maddy Prior in the 1970s. (The duo dubbed themselves the Silly Sisters for the occasion). An all-star cast of some of the leading lights of the British folk scene supported the singers, including Martin Carthy, Nic Jones, and Andy Irvine. For her own albums and tours she has worked with outstanding guitarists, most notably Jones and Martin Simpson. She's also tread into folk-rock waters with Fairport Convention (with whom she's guested onstage) and the Oyster Band (with whom she collaborated on a 1990 album). Her 1994 album, *Against the Stream,* found her still at her peak, interpreting both traditional tunes and efforts by modern-day composers, including Elvis Costello and Richard Thompson. —*Richie Unterberger*

Airs and Graces / 1976 / Shanachie ✦✦✦✦
This album features mostly traditional songs, as well as Eric Bogle's now-classic " . . . And the Band Played 'Waltzing Matilda'" in its first recorded version. —*Steve Winick*

Ashes and Diamonds / 1977 / Green Linnet ✦✦✦
The overall sound on the American CD re-release of this 1977 album is a bit dated, but lovely singing from Tabor and Nic Jones' guitar make this a treat. —*Steve Winick*

● **A Cut Above** / 1980 / Topic ✦✦✦✦
This one, featuring Martin Simpson on guitar, consists of more brilliant renditions of traditional songs. —*Steve Winick*

Abyssinians / 1983 / Shanachie ✦✦✦
Few people can wrap vocals around a folk melody the way June Tabor does. Here, she breathes life into "The Month of January," "A Smiling Shore," "I Never Thought My Love Would Leave Me," and seven more. —*Roundup Newsletter*

Some Other Time / 1989 / Hannibal ✦✦✦✦
English folksinger sings American popular ballads. A lovely album from a lovely vocalist. —*Michael G. Nastos*

Freedom and Rain / 1990 / Rykodisc ✦✦✦
Tabor teams up with one of Britain's leading folk-rock outfits, the Oyster Band, with fairly successful results, although it won't be the favorite of June's most traditionally-minded fans. She takes all the lead vocals on these fully electrified arrangements. The material is certainly varied, including both traditional numbers and covers of contemporary folk and rock tunes by Richard Thompson, Si Kahn, the Pogues, Billy Bragg, and the Velvet Underground. —*Richie Unterberger*

☆ **Angel Tiger** / 1992 / Green Linnet ✦✦✦✦✦
One of the more intelligent and beautiful albums released in 1992 was June Tabor's *Angel Tiger*. Since her last album as one of the Silly Sisters, Tabor has released increasingly sophisticated collections of contemporary and traditional songs. The arrangements are spare and classical in their construction, and her voice is always the dominant, most impressive instrument. Her choice of material is impeccable, including covers of Bob Franke's "Hard Love" and Elvis Costello's "All This Useless Beauty." *Angel Tiger* is more an art song cycle than a pop album. —*Richard Meyer*

Against The Streams / 1994 / Green Linnet ✦✦✦✦
Tabor works best in sparse settings, and *Against the Streams* backs her vocals with arrangements that manage the difficult feat of being both minimal and imaginative. Accordion, bass, and strings create a dignified backdrop for her fine interpretations of a variety of traditional and contemporary material. The Elvis Costello ("I Want to Vanish") and Richard Thompson ("Pavanne") covers got the most attention, but they aren't necessarily the highlights of the set, which includes renditions of songs by less famous composers such as Ian Telfer and Bill Caddick. —*Richie Unterberger*

Taillevent

Taillevent is a group of amateur singers who came together during a 1990 workshop on sailors' songs in Sarzeau, Brittany, France. Since then, they have ventured forth to entertain in bars and pubs with traditional maritime shows. —*Steve Winick*

En Revenant du Large / Taillevent ✦✦✦
Ernest and energetic, if unpolished, this album is loads of fun and a great collection of maritime music from Brittany. —*Steve Winick*

The Tannahill Weavers

Folk
The Tannahill Weavers occupy a unique position among the groups on the Scottish folk scene. Stalwarts Roy Gullane and Phil Smillie have surrounded themselves with a rotating cast of great musicians. Their music, which uses the highland bagpipe, flute, and fiddle as its melodic core, is tighter, more intense, and harder-driven than the Battlefield Band, Silly Wizard, or other of their contemporaries. Despite their mostly acoustic sound, they're the closest thing to a rock and roll band in intensity and attitude that the Scottish traditional music scene has to offer. —*Steve Winick*

Are Ye Sleeping Maggie / 1976 / Plant Life ✦✦

Old Woman's Dance / 1978 / Plant Life ✦✦✦
An excellent early effort, it features Alan Macleod's highland pipes. —*Steve Winick*

Tannahill Weavers / 1979 / Green Linnet ✦✦✦✦
A classic album of Scottish folk music, it features fiddle, bagpipe, and flute. —*Steve Winick*

Tannahill Weavers 4 / 1982 / Green Linnet ✦✦✦
Another classic, this one features some favorites of their concert repertoire. —*Steve Winick*

Passage / 1984 / Green Linnet ✦✦✦
The Weavers add electric guitarist Bill Bourne for an excursion into electric folk. —*Steve Winick*

Land of Light / 1986 / Green Linnet ✦✦✦
Back to a mostly acoustic sound, this is a solid Tannahill album. —*Steve Winick*

Dancing Feet / 1987 / Green Linnet ✦✦✦✦
This album finds the Weavers as energetic as in the days of their classic early albums. —*Steve Winick*

★ **Best of 1979-1989** / 1989 / Green Linnet ✦✦✦✦✦
A great compilation, this is the place to start. —*Steve Winick*

Cullen Bay / 1990 / Green Linnet ✦✦✦
Fiery and ferocious, they're up to their old ways once again. —*Steve Winick*

Mermaid Song / 1992 / Green Linnet ✦✦✦
Their arrangements are beginning to sound a little formulaic, but there's great material and fine performances here. —*Steve Winick*

Capernaum / 1994 / Green Linnet ✦✦

Cyril Tawney

Vocals
Cyril Tawney has been a mainstay of the English folk scene for many years. He is well known both as an interpreter of traditional material and as an excellent songwriter. His songs have been sung by many other folk revival performers, further enhancing his reputation. He is strongly associated with his native region of Devon and Cornwall, and has recorded much material from that part of southern England. The years he spent in the Royal Navy also make him a natural interpreter and writer of sea songs. —*Steve Winick*

Outlandish Knight / 1965 / Polydor ✦✦✦
Tawney performs versions of some of the "big ballads," the narrative songs that are an important part of England's folk poetry. —*Steve Winick*

Children's Songs from Devon and Cornwall / 1969 / Argo ✦✦

Mayflower Garland / 1970 / Argo ✦✦✦
This contains both traditional and original songs, and was recorded in honor of the 350th anniversary of the sailing of the Mayflower. —*Steve Winick*

In Port / 1972 / Argo ✦✦✦✦
Original Tawney songs focusing on the sea fill up this album. Many of his best-known songs appear on this album, including "Sally Free and Easy," "The Grey Funnel Line," and "The Ballad of Sammy's Bar." —*Steve Winick*

I Will Give my Love / 1973 / Argo ✦✦✦
Tawney returns on this album to the traditional songs of southwestern England. —*Steve Winick*

● **Sally Free and Easy** / 1990 / Neptune ✦✦✦✦
Included are fresh interpretations of some of the material from *In Port*, plus new songs. —*Steve Winick*

Seamen Bold / 1993 / Neptune ✦✦✦
Traditional and original songs of the sea are here. —*Steve Winick*

Little Boy Billee / 1993 / Neptune ✦✦✦
Tawney lends his voice and guitar to more children's songs. —*Steve Winick*

Scan Tester

b. 1887, **d.** 1972
Accordion
Accordionist Scan Tester was that great rarity, a southern English traditional instrumentalist who was repeatedly recorded. —*John Storm Roberts*

I Never Played too Many Posh Dances / 1990 / Topic ✦✦✦✦
The music here, all from the late '50s to mid-'60s, includes solos (including some traditional Sussex fiddle), duets, and group numbers. Included is wonderful music, a very thorough job, and a unique record of the range and style of a pub-cum-village-hop musician. It's not to be missed by any lover of English traditional music. —*John Storm Roberts*

The Russell Family

Micho, Pakie, and Gussie Russell, three brothers from the town of Doolin, County Clare, were among the smoldering coals that fed the Irish folk revival. Micho in particular, through extensive touring and sharing of his music and songs, was an important link between the essentially urban folk revival and the roots of Irish rural music. His death in 1994 in an auto accident saddened all lovers of Irish music. —*Steve Winick*

★ **The The Russell Family** / Mar. 1993 / Green Linnet ✦✦✦✦✦
A classic album of traditional tunes and songs in rural style, this is a wonderful CD for lovers of the older Irish traditional music. —*Steve Winick*

Carol Thompson

Harp, Vocals

Carol Thompson is an American harpist of Anglo-Welsh background. She performs traditional music on the neo-Celtic harp, the classical pedal harp, and the fascinating Welsh triple harp. —*Steve Winick*

The Enchanted Isles / 1989 / Dorian ✦✦✦

Thompson's first CD recording finds her playing a variety of airs on a variety of harps. It's one of the finest solo harp discs available, for quiet times and moods. —*Steve Winick*

● **Carolan's Welcome** / 1993 / Dorian ✦✦✦✦

Thompson is back, this time with friends Billy McComiskey (accordion, concertina), Jack Coen (wooden flute) and Darcy Fair (neo-Celtic harp). Her repertoire includes more dance music on this one, making it both uplifting and gentle. —*Steve Winick*

Kathryn Tickell

Bagpipes, Fiddle

A young virtuoso on the Northumbrian bagpipes and fiddle, Tickell was named official piper to the Lord Mayor of Newcastle-upon-Tyne in 1984. She is the first person to hold that title in over 150 years. —*Steve Winick*

On Kielder Side / 1984 / Saydisc ✦✦✦✦

This excellent collection of English and Celtic tunes comes from Tickell and her small band. —*Steve Winick*

★ **Kathryn Tickell Band** / 1991 / Black Crow ✦✦✦✦✦

Sizzling contemporary arrangements of traditional material fill this album. —*Steve Winick*

Steve Tilston

Guitar, Vocals

This married couple from England (Tilston) and Ireland (Boyle) are one of the most compelling acts in this genre of music. His songwriting, singing, and guitar work are excellent, and her singing of traditional songs and her instrumental work are likewise impressive. —*Steve Winick*

☆ **Swans at Coole** / 1989 / Capitol ✦✦✦✦✦

An absolutely beautiful album of guitar music, this features traditional tunes played in a classical vein. —*Steve Winick*

★ **Of Moor and Mesa** / 1992 / Green Linnet ✦✦✦✦✦

An extremely well-balanced album, this features beautiful traditional songs sung by Boyle and equally lovely original songs written and sung by Tilston. Accompaniments on guitar, flute and other instruments help make this a joy to hear. —*Steve Winick*

Tri Yann

This band is the most important exponent of urban folk-rock from Brittany. Over the years, their music has ranged from punchy acoustic arrangements of traditional songs to rock 'n' roll based on the Breton and Gallo traditions. —*Steve Winick*

An Naoned / 1972 / Kelenn ✦✦

This debut album is energetic and fun, but rather rudimentary. —*Steve Winick*

Dix Ans Dix Filles / 1973 / Kelenn ✦✦

Getting there, but it's still a bit undisciplined. —*Steve Winick*

Suite Gallaise / 1974 / Marzelle ✦✦✦

Their best acoustic album is full of bouncy energy. —*Steve Winick*

La Decouverte ou l'Ignorance / 1976 / Marzelle ✦✦✦✦

An excellent album, this was their first to use electric guitars, drums, and other rock instruments in a mostly folk setting. —*Steve Winick*

Les Filles des Forges / 1977 / Marzelle ✦✦✦

Early double-album compilation. —*Steve Winick*

Urba / 1978 / Marzelle ✦✦✦

Tri Yann continued their exploration of folk-rock on this album about urbanization in Brittany. —*Steve Winick*

An Heol a Zo Glaz / 1981 / Marzelle ✦✦✦

Another good collection of folk-rock tunes and songs, this one features a suite about Breton resistance to a French nuclear power plant. —*Steve Winick*

● **Si Mort a Mors** / 1982 / Philips ✦✦✦✦

This excellent double-album compilation covers the first ten years or so, without overlapping *Les Filles des Forges*. —*Steve Winick*

Cafe du Bon Coin / 1983 / Marzelle ✦✦✦

More of an electric feel is brought to this album. The band is still excellent. —*Steve Winick*

Belle et Rebelle / 1990 / Marzelle ✦✦✦

Breton folk-rock for the '90s. —*Steve Winick*

Le Vaisseau de Pierre / Marzelle ✦✦✦

A sort of rock opera on CD, this features a new lineup and a real rock 'n' roll sound. —*Steve Winick*

Paddy Tunney

Vocals

A magnificent singer and lilter from County Fermanagh in Ulster, Paddy Tunney has a huge repertoire of songs and is a singer of consummate skill. He has many recordings, but most are hard to find and out of print. —*Steve Winick*

Stone Fiddle / Green Linnet ✦✦✦✦

This cassette contains 11 songs from the Fermanagh region where Tunney was reared. If you like unaccompanied singing, this is perfect. —*Steve Winick*

Jean-Michel Veillon

Flute, Whistle (Instrument)

Jean-Michel Veillon was a child prodigy on the bombarde, that piercing woodwind characteristic of Breton music. Later in life, he became interested in Irish music, particularly the wooden flute, which was not played in Brittany. Through his exemplary work with groups like Galorn, Kornog, Barzaz, Den and Pennou Skoulm, Veillon has made the wooden flute an acceptable instrument in the Breton tradition. —*Steve Winick*

★ **E Koad Nizan** / 1993 / Gwerz Pladenn ✦✦✦✦✦

Accompanied by the best musicians Brittany has to offer, Veillon plays the flute in a lovely, lilting style. This is the first album ever to focus on Breton music played on the wooden transverse flute, and it's a landmark for that reason. However, buy it simply because it's wonderful. —*Steve Winick*

The Voice Squad

Fran McPhail, Phil Gallery and Gerry Cullen are the Voice Squad, a three-part harmony singing group from Ireland. —*Steve Winick*

Good People All / 1993 / Shanachie ✦✦✦

Lovely ballads in an easy, flowing a cappella style fill this recording. —*Steve Winick*

● **Many's the Foolish Youth** / Jan. 30, 1996 / Passport ✦✦✦✦

John Whelan & Eileen Ivers

A great button accordion player, Whelan has won the all-Ireland championship on the instrument six times, and the all-Britain seven. His playing is exciting and fresh, if not strictly traditional. Ivers is his match, having won the all-Ireland fiddle titles seven times herself. —*Steve Winick*

● **Fresh Takes** / Green Linnet ✦✦✦✦

Accompanied by Mark Simos and Triona Ni Dhomhnaill, Whelan and Ivers tear into some wonderful tunes, using consistently fresh and newfangled arrangements to keep the album interesting. —*Steve Winick*

Chris Wood And Andy Cutting

Fiddle

This English duo play the fiddle and melodeon. Cutting has been a member of Blowzabella. —*Steve Winick*

Lisa / 1992 / RUF ✦✦✦

This is a debut album of quirky charm. —*Steve Winick*

● **Live at Sidmouth** / 1995 / RUF ✦✦✦✦

Tri Yann

This band is the most important exponent of urban folk/rock from Brittany. Over the years, their music has ranged from punchy acoustic arrangements of traditional songs to rock 'n' roll based on the Breton and Gallo traditions. —*Steve Winick*

An Naoned / 1972 / Kelenn ✦✦

This debut album is energetic and fun, but rather rudimentary. —*Steve Winick*

Dix Ans Dix Filles / 1973 / Kelenn ✦✦

Getting there, but it's still a bit undisciplined. —*Steve Winick*

Suite Gallaise / 1974 / Marzelle ✦✦✦

Their best acoustic album is full of bouncy energy. —*Steve Winick*

La Decouverte ou l'Ignorance / 1976 / Marzelle ✦✦✦✦

An excellent album, this was their first to use electric guitars, drums, and other rock instruments in a mostly folk setting. —*Steve Winick*

Les Filles des Forges / 1977 / Marzelle ✦✦✦

Early double-album compilation. —*Steve Winick*

Urba / 1978 / Marzelle ✦✦✦

Tri Yann continued their exploration of folk-rock on this album about urbanization in Brittany. —*Steve Winick*

An Heol a Zo Glaz / 1981 / Marzelle ✦✦✦
Another good collection of folk-rock tunes and songs, this one features a suite about Breton resistance to a French nuclear power plant. —*Steve Winick*

● **Si Mort a Mors** / 1982 / Philips ✦✦✦✦
This excellent double-album compilation covers the first ten years or so, without overlapping *Les Filles des Forges*. —*Steve Winick*

Cafe du Bon Coin / 1983 / Marzelle ✦✦✦
More of an electric feel is brought to this album. The band is still excellent. —*Steve Winick*

Belle et Rebelle / 1990 / Marzelle ✦✦✦
Breton folk-rock for the '90s. —*Steve Winick*

Le Vaisseau de Pierre / Marzelle ✦✦✦
A sort of rock opera on CD, this features a new lineup and a real rock 'n' roll sound. —*Steve Winick*

Various Artists

The Best of the Irish Folk Festivals / Green Linnet ✦✦✦✦✦
The Best of the Irish Folk Festivals—The Seventies features over 60 minutes of live music from DeDanann, Clannad, Liam O'Flynn, Mick Hanly, Dolores Keane, John Faulkner, Jackie Daly, and Eddie and Finbar Furey. The recordings are from the Irish Folk Festivals held in West Germany. —*Chip Renner*

The Big Squeeze / 1988 / Green Linnet ✦✦✦✦✦
Nine of the finest accordion players are presented on *The Big Squeeze: Masters of Celtic Accordion* collaboration featuring Joe Burke, Phil Cunningham, Jackie Daly, James Keane, Jimmy Keane, Billy McComiskey, Sean McGlynn, Paddy O'Brie, and John Whelan. —*Chip Renner*

Bothy Ballads / Tangent ✦✦✦
This recording from the School of Scottish Studies of Edinburgh University has solid documentation. The bothies of northeastern Scotland were basically dormitories for unmarried farm labor, which became music incubators. Here are instrumental jigs, diddling (mouth music), ballads old and new on themes heroic and pretty, all in the Anglophone lowland tradition. —*John Storm Roberts*

☆ **A Celebration of Scottish Music** / 1988 / Temple Music ✦✦✦✦✦
This compilation features the Battlefield Band, Cilla Fisher, and other great players and singers. —*Steve Winick*

Celtic Folk Festival / 1982 / Calig ✦✦✦✦
Recorded at two Dutch folk festivals in the early 1980s, this has good performances by some of the biggest names in British Isles traditional folk/folk-rock, including Clannad, Andy Irvine, the Tannahill Weavers, Silly Wizard, and Battlefield Band. The program's rounded out by three lesser-known acts from Brittany (Kornog, Dan Ar Bras, and Sonerien Du). Material, sound, and performance are good, and while it may not be the first place you should stop to check out the artists, it's a good addition for those building a deep Celtic collection. Incidentally, the Clannad tracks were recorded during their first performances with then-14-year-old Enya in the lineup; the Silly Wizard cut is one of the few recordings of the group with Dougie McLean. —*Richie Unterberger*

The Celts Rise Again / 1990 / Green Linnet ✦✦✦✦✦
Green Linnet shows off its stable of Celtic artists, and it's our gain—featuring 18 tracks by Altan, Capercaillie, John & Phil Cunningham, Andy Irvin, Matt Molloy, and Robbie O'Connell. Great sampler. —*Chip Renner*

Feed the Folk / Temple Music ✦✦✦✦✦
Featuring tracks by the Chieftains, the Battlefield Band, Fairport Convention, Steeleye Span, Martin Carthy, Paul Brady, and others; all proceeds go to charity. —*Steve Winick*

The Fiddler and His Art / Tangent ✦✦✦
This presents examples of five regional styles played by seven of Scotland's finest musicians in recordings ranging from the '30s on. An enormously valuable recording, it is enhanced by admirable notes and delightful packaging. —*John Storm Roberts*

☆ **Flight of the Green Linnet** / 1988 / Rykodisc ✦✦✦✦✦
Flight of the Green Linnet—The Next Generation is a first-class collection of Scottish, Irish, and British music featuring Relativity, Silly Wizard, Capercaillie, the Chieftains, Patrick Street, the Tannahill Weavers, and many more. Seventy minutes of excellent music and song. A favorite. —*Chip Renner & Steve Winick*

Folk Songs of Britain: Songs of Courtship / 1970 / Topic ✦✦✦✦✦
These ten volumes were organized by themes from a huge body of field recordings by Peter Kennedy, Alan Lomax, Hamish Henderson, and several other collectors over a period of some 15 years (and originally issued, though long deleted, on the Caedmon label). Some performers (the Copper brothers of Sussex, Jeannie Robertson, and Sean Ennis) are familiar source singers; others are totally unknown. All are outstanding and authentic artists. Together they present an unprecedentedly full picture of a rich but cohesive tradition. —*John Storm Roberts*

☆ **Heart of the Gaels** / 1992 / Green Linnet ✦✦✦✦✦
A follow-up to *The Celts Will Rise Again*, this 18-track sampler of Celtic music features over 70 minutes of Altan, Patrick Street, the Tannahill Weavers, Dick Gaughan, Matt Malloy, Sean Keane, Andy Irvine, and others. —*Scott Bultman*

Melodeon Greats / Topic ✦✦✦
Featured are pre-1920 recordings of Scots polkas, reels, jigs, marches, and the like in early 20th-century urban popular style, mostly with piano accompaniment. —*John Storm Roberts*

The Rights of Man: Concert for Joe Doherty / 1991 / Green Linnet ✦✦✦✦✦
The Rights of Man: The Concert for Joseph Doherty is a great collection of music from the Feb 24, 1990, benefit in NYC for political prisoner Joseph Doherty. Celtic Thunder, Cherish the Ladies, Seamus Connolly, Seamus Egan, Eileen Ivers, Jimmy Keane, Pat Kilbride, Donal Lunny, Robbie O'Connell, and John Whelan are featured. Highly recommended. —*Chip Renner*

Waulking Songs / Tangent ✦✦✦
Besides the Gaelic waulking (cloth-fulling) songs, there are pipe reels, mouth music, laments, pibroch, a hymn, and even a Fenian song. —*John Storm Roberts*

CAJUN

Zydeco and Cajun are the premier cultural expressions of the spirited and hardy people of southwest Louisiana. While the two styles have some similarities, they are also quite different.

Cajun music as we know it today can be traced back to early Acadian, French, Creole, and Anglo-Saxon folk songs. These early ballads and lullabies—typically concerned with troubles and hard times—were often sung a cappella. For the most part, they were performed at home and passed down orally from generation to generation; however, the singers of these traditional songs were eventually accompanied by simple instrumentation.

Cajun music is of course meant for dancing—one-step, two-step, and waltzes. Traditionally, the Cajun dance ("Fais-do-do" in Cajun) was the major social function in Cajun society. The principal instrument in Cajun music is the diatonic accordion, preferably in the key of C. Although it is a German instrument, the Cajun people adopted it in the 1870s. To a lesser degree, the fiddle is also a favorite instrument in Cajun music. Early Cajun bands featured both of these instruments as well as a triangle to keep the rhythm. Acoustic guitars were added to the lineup by 1920, then, three decades later, steel, electric guitars, and sometimes drums. Although Cajun music has changed somewhat over the years and has been influenced by other styles of music—notably country and blues—it has remained a distinctive style.

The first Cajun record was Joe Falcon's "Allons à Lafayette" from 1928. Although the style was recorded only sporadically for several decades, Iry Le Jeune, Harry Choates, Nathan Abshire, Lawrence Walker, Leo Soileau, and Vin Bruce had become influential Cajun artists by the middle of the 20th century. While the music's popularity continued to grow within Louisiana, it didn't enter the spotlight nationally until the mid-'80s, riding on the coattails of the Cajun food explosion. Today several traditional and contemporary Cajun artists—including Dewey Balfa, Zachary Richard, and Beausoleil — tour nationally and internationally.

Compared to Cajun music, zydeco music has a much shorter history. Like Cajun music, the dominant instrument is the accordion, but unlike Cajun music, zydeco adds electric bass, horns, and sometimes keyboards. In a nutshell, zydeco is creole (Black) dance music of southwest Louisiana that blends Cajun music with R&B and soul. The word "zydeco" is actually a bastardization of an early zydeco song, "L'Haricots Sont Pas Salés" (The Snap Beans Aren't Salted). The first Black-French recordings were made in 1928 by Amadé Ardoin, an accordion player who played in the Cajun style. However, the music we know as zydeco today didn't begin to evolve—at least on record—until the mid-'50s, when Clifton Chenier and Boozoo Chavis made their initial recordings.

Like Cajun music, zydeco didn't achieve national popularity until 1980, buoyed somewhat by Rockin' Sidney's surprise hit "My Toot Toot." By the '90s, several zydeco artists were signed to major labels, including Terrance Simien, Boozoo Chavis, Buckwheat Zydeco, and Rockin' Dopsie. —Jeff Hannusch

Nathan Abshire

b. 1915, **d.** 1981
Accordion, Vocals / Cajun
Abshire, the best-known accordionist of the modern era, played more of a honky tonk style of Cajun music, one often heard in the barrooms and dancehalls of Louisiana. Abshire's playing and singing were strongly rooted in the blues. Along with the legendary Iry LeJeune, Abshire is credited with restoring the accordion to its former prominence in Cajun music after World War II. His 1949 O.T.-label hit "Pine Grove Blues" became his signature song, and its bluesy barroom bark epitomizes the best rough-edged Cajun honky tonk. Abshire recorded extensively and often appeared at folk festivals with the Balfa Brothers. —*Jeff Hannusch and Mark A. Humphrey*

Cajun Social Music / 1990 / Smithsonian/Folkways ◆◆◆◆
A summit meeting of Cajun stars yields outstanding renditions of classics and originals. —*Ron Wynn*

● **The Best of Nathan Abshire** / 1991 / Swallow ◆◆◆◆
With "The Good Times Are Killing Me" emblazoned on his accordion case, Abshire embodied the Cajun musician's ethos. There are 20 two-steps and waltzes here, some with the Balfa Brothers. Includes a remake of the great "Pine Grove Blues" and a heartfelt "Tramp sur la Rue" with wailing vocals. —*Mark A. Humphrey*

Ardoin and Fontenot

Fiddle, Accordion / Cajun, Creole
Accordionist Alphonse "Bois Sec" ("dry wood") Ardoin (b.1914) grew up idolizing his legendary uncle, Amédée Ardoin, as did fiddler Canray Fontenot (b.1922). Ardoin and Fontenot began playing together in their youth, though they were unrecorded until the '70s. Their music is a still-strong reflection of the early Cajun/Creole traditions, with an added burst of bluesiness in Fontenot's fiddling. —*Mark A. Humphrey*

Musique Creole / Arhoolie ◆◆◆◆
The haunting music on this album shaped modern Cajun/zydeco music. —*Jeff Hannusch*

Amédée Ardoin

b. 1896, **d.** 1941
Accordion, Vocals / Blues, Cajun
Although he recorded some of the purest early Cajun records, Amédée Ardoin (his name has also been spelled Amadie or Amade) was a French-speaking Black singer/accordionist who was popular with both Cajun and Creole audiences. His crying, high-pitched vocals were the model for much that came later in Cajun music, as was his empathetic squeezebox playing. Ardoin's recordings with fiddler Dennis McGee are noteworthy not only because they are among the first racially integrated folk recordings, but also for an emotional/artistic integrity to which traditionalists like the Savoy-Doucet band continue to aspire. —*Mark A. Humphrey*

★ **His Original Recordings** / Mar. 1983 / Old Timey ◆◆◆◆◆
Accordionist Amédée Ardoin was the first Black recording artist in the Cajun style. Though most of the tracks show virtually no difference from White Cajun music, other numbers like "Blues de la Prison" make him the first zydeco recording artist. The style's complex roots are symbolized by the fact that all these recordings were made with White fiddler Dennis McGee. —*John Storm Roberts, Original Music*

☆ **The Roots of Zydeco** / 1995 / Arhoolie ◆◆◆◆◆
Amede Ardoin was arguably the founder of zydeco music, incorporating blues into French folk. The songs on this collection were recorded in 1930 and 1934. Though the sound might be a bit harsh for some—these were taken from 78s, after all—these are important recordings, and they continue to sound fresh and vital. —*Stephen Thomas Erlewine*

● **Louisiana Cajun Music, Vol. 6** / Old Timey ◆◆◆◆
This is a stunning collection of 14 of his 30 recordings. (Ardoin also appears on several Cajun compilations, such as *J'Etais au Bal*—Vol. 1.) —*Mark A. Humphrey*

First Black Cajun Recording Artist / Arhoolie ◆◆◆
Violinist Dennis McGhee is featured on this 14-track album, which contains recordings from 1929, 1930, and 1934. —*AMG*

The Balfa Brothers

Fiddle, Guitar / Cajun

The Balfa Brothers (Les Freres Balfas) helped keep traditional Cajun music alive in the '60s, when it was in danger of disappearing. The sons, three of a family of six, were born to a poor southwest Louisiana share-cropper, from whom they learned about traditional Cajun lore and culture. Fiddler Dewey Balfa was heavily influenced by players such as J.B. Fusilier, Leo Soileau, Harry Choates, and Bob Wills. He and his brothers Rodney, who sang and played guitar and harmonica; Will, the second fiddler; Harry, the accordion player; and Burkeman, who played triangle and spoons, began playing informally at family parties and local gatherings during the '40s. They achieved enough local popularity to play up to eight dances a week at local dance halls. The Balfas were later joined by neighbor Hadley Fontenot on accordion. They made their recording debut in 1951 with "La Valse de Bon Baurche" and "Le Two Step de Ville Platte," which were captured on a home recorder and released as a 78 single. Dewey Balfa went on to a solo career playing with numerous Cajun artists and recording on such labels as Khoury, Kajun, and Swallow.

In 1967 Dewey, Rodney, Will, and his daughter Nelda, along with Fontenot formed the Balfa Brothers and began spreading the Cajun sound throughout Europe and at folk festivals across the US. In 1968 they played for the Olympics Festival in Mexico City. They made their first professional recording, "Le Valse de Bambocheurs/Indian on a Stomp," in 1967 for Swallow. This led to an album, *Balfa Brothers Play Traditional Cajun Music,* also on Swallow. Another album followed. In 1972 the Balfas appeared in the Les Blank documentary *Spend It All,* which introduced a new generation to the lively Cajun sound. That year they also recorded *The Cajuns* on Sonet and another for Swallow, *The Good Times Are Killing Me,* which included the soundtrack for the documentary of the same name. Although most of their musical focus was on tradition, the Balfas were not averse to trying more modernized Cajun songs with a nightclub orchestra comprised of Dewey, Rodney, accordion player Nathan Menard, fiddler Dick Richard, J.W. Pelsia on steel guitar, Austin Broussard on drums, and Rodney's son Tony on bass guitar.

Things went well for the band until February 1979, when Rodney and Will were killed in a car wreck. The next year, Dewey's wife died of trichinosis. Despite the tragedy, Dewey and the orchestra (with a few personnel changes) continued to play as the Balfa Brothers, for Dewey believed that music created as strong a fraternal bond as did blood. His band proved him right when they kept the name Balfa Brothers after his death in 1992. Through them, his rich and valuable legacy of Cajun music carries on. *—Sandra Brennan*

● **Play Traditional Cajun Music, Vols. 1 & 2** / 1987 / Swallow ✦✦✦✦
From the '60s recordings that helped launch the Cajun revival, these are still stirring performances . *—Mark A. Humphrey*

J'ai Vu le Loup, le Renard et la Belette / 1988 / Rounder ✦✦✦✦
The Balfa Brothers' long heritage in traditional Cajun music has never been exemplified better than on this 13-cut CD recorded in 1975. There were mostly short songs (only one song longer than four minutes), which were predominantly uptempo dance numbers with some two-steps, waltzes, and romantic pieces as well as an interesting version of "Casey Jones." The session was produced and recorded by Gerard Dole and was originally issued on the Cezame label in France. True believers and purists couldn't find a better example of the vintage sound anywhere. *—Ron Wynn*

Let's Get Cajun / Flying Fish ✦✦✦
These modern Cajun sounds are played by the young Balfa Brothers. *—Jeff Hannusch*

Dewey Balfa

b. 1927, d. 1992

Fiddle / Cajun, Zydeco

The son and grandson of Cajun fiddlers, Dewey Balfa played fiddle in a relaxed, yet spirited, style and inspired much of the best of the Cajun revival. A gentle and gracious man, he was passionate about his culture and was a father figure and guiding light for Cajun music. With his brothers, he helped introduce this music to the world at the Newport Folk Festivals of the '60s, and won renewed attention and support for Cajun music in Louisiana. He died in 1992—*Mark A. Humphrey*

Souvenirs / 1987 / Swallow ✦✦✦✦
A low-key but excellent effort from the late king of Cajun fiddle. *—Jeff Hannusch*

Cajun Legend / Swallow ✦✦✦
Featured are such artists as Tracy Schwartz, Robert Jardell, and other friends of Balfa on this album's 21 tracks. *—AMG*

● **Fait a la Main** / Swallow ✦✦✦✦
These 21 tracks compiled from two '80s Swallow albums offer a fine

introduction to the fiddling of one of the architects of the Cajun music revival. Balfa sings four songs, but instrumentals carry the day here, most of them standards of the Cajun repertoire ("Grand Mamou," "La Jolie Blonde," "Les Flumes d'Enfer"). Balfa's lead fiddle is seconded (and thirded) by the father-son duo of Tracy and Peter Schwartz. A disciple of Nathan Abshire, Robert Jardell, holds down the accordion chair. Homespun and heartfelt, this set exudes the generosity of spirit of a rare man who has inspired many younger musicians. — *Mark Humphrey, Roundup Newsletter*

Beausoleil

Cajun, Zydeco

The formation of Beausoleil, one of the best known and most highly respected Cajun bands in the world, is due to fiddler Michael Doucet's desire to keep the unique southern Louisiana culture and music from extinction. But while Beausoleil originated to help preserve his Cajun musical heritage, over the years the band has also been known for innovation. They are continually adding spice from other musical genres, including jazz and Caribbean. In this way, Beausoleil keeps the music vital and contemporary.

Doucet was born and raised in Cajun country, surrounded by the old French songs that comprise the basis of the music. But from the time of his birth to adulthood in the '60s, Cajun culture began to disappear. Young Doucet, thinking Cajun music antiquated and passé, began his musical career playing rock with New Orleans influence. He began getting into folk-rock towards the end of the '60s and even tried singing a few of his numbers in French. It was a song from the British folk group Fairport Convention, "Cajun Woman," that resparked his interest in his native music. He went to France and England in 1973 just before he was to enter grad school in the US. He ended up staying many years, studying with Scottish fiddle great Barry Dransfield, who eventually introduced him to Richard Thompson. Later Doucet credited Thompson for influencing his own compositions. The young fiddler's stay in France also had a profound influence. There he saw that the roots of Cajun were still very much alive. The old songs were still sung, and he heard their centuries-old influence in newer folk songs. It made him realize how modern Cajun music was in comparison. In the mid-'70s Doucet joined Coteau, an improvisational folk music-based French group that was known as the Cajun equivalent to the Grateful Dead. After a time with them, he returned to the US, determined to immerse himself in Cajun musical history. A grant from the National Endowment for the Arts supported him as he located the nearly forgotten early composers and performers of Cajun music.

Armed with many traditional Cajun songs, Doucet formed Beausoleil with some of the finest Cajun musicians, Dennis McGee, Dewey and Will Balfa, Varise Connor, Canray Fontenot, and Bessyl Duhon. Their band name literally means "good sun" and is a reference to a fertile region in Nova Scotia. In the 17th century, French-speaking Acadians lived in the Canadian province until conflicts with the French and British forced them to migrate to Louisiana, where they became called Cajuns. Beausoleil cut its first record in 1976 and released it only in France. They made their American debut the following year with *The Spirit of Cajun Music.* It was an eclectic work, illustrating the many musical styles from which Cajun music is derived. Between then and the early '90s, Beausoleil released over a dozen albums. Some are traditional, while others are more experimental. In 1988 Doucet received the first annual Clifton Chenier Award as the finest musician in French-speaking Louisiana. Since 1985 the band has been nominated for numerous Grammy awards. They have played on movie soundtracks such as *The Big Easy, Passion Fish,* and *Belizaire the Cajun.* They have played at jazz and folk festivals around the world and have also appeared on numerous television shows ranging from CNN's "Showbiz Today" to "Austin City Limits" to "Late Night with Conan O'Brien." Beausoleil also performs regularly on public radio, most notably on Garrison Keillor's "Prairie Home Companion." Keillor has hailed them as the "best Cajun band in the world." They have performed with Mary Chapin Carpenter and opened for the Grateful Dead.

In the mid-'90s the lineup for Beausoleil included Doucet's brother David on guitar, Acadian accordion player Jimmy Breaux, Al Tharp on bass/banjo and fiddle, percussionist Billy Ware, and drummer Tommy Alesi. Doucet and other bandmembers periodically record solo albums such as Doucet's *Beau Solo. —Sandra Brennan*

Bayou Boogie / 1987 / Rounder ✦✦✦
A fine modern Cajun collection, it includes "Cajun Dead" at full tilt. *—Jeff Hannusch and Mark A. Humphrey*

Allons ...Lafayette / 1988 / Arhoolie ✦✦✦
This is a more traditional sound as compared with the group's other albums. *—Jeff Hannusch*

● **Hot Chili Mama** / 1988 / Arhoolie ✦✦✦✦
It's the perfect blend of Cajun, zydeco, and rock 'n' roll. *—Jeff Hannusch*

Bayou Cadillac / 1989 / Rounder ✦✦✦

Those who define everything in strict, inflexible color terms consider all Black South Louisiana sounds zydeco and all White sounds from that region Cajun. However, Beausoleil, an obviously White group, opens this release with a signature zydeco tune, Clarence Garlow's "Bon Temps Roulet." Quite simply, they're unaware of this "rule," violating it repeatedly. They include entertaining remakes of "Bo Diddley" and "Iko Iko" in the title medley and cover Big Joe Williams' "Baby Don't Go," doing them just as effectively as "Couchon de Lait" and "Flammes d'Enfer." While they sometimes venture a bit afield, as with the concluding "Island Zydeco," much of Beausoleil's fare artfully crosses genres and successfully combines divergent influences and material. This disc should satisfy audiences regardless of idiomatic preference. — *Ron Wynn*

Live from the Left Coast / 1990 / Rounder ✦✦✦

This is an excellent example of this popular group's live sound. — *Jeff Hannusch*

Déjá Vu / 1991 / Swallow ✦✦✦

Included are leader Michael Doucet's musical concoctions. — *Jeff Hannusch*

Cajun Conja / Sep. 1991 / Rhino ✦✦✦

A 1991 Grammy nominee. — *Mark A. Humphrey*

Parlez-Nous á Boir and More / Oct. 1991 / Arhoolie ✦✦✦

The best of their Arhoolie albums has a taste of the modern sound. Traditional Cajun/zydeco zip with rock and ethno-synergistic overtones. — *Jeff Hannusch and Mark A. Humphrey*

☆ **Cajun and Creole Music** / Music of the World ✦✦✦✦✦

This recording combines the great masters of the Creole music tradition with the internationally acclaimed Cajun group Beausoleil. This Library of Congress Award-winner belongs in every Cajun lover's collection. — *Music of the World*

Vin Bruce (Ervin Bruce)

Guitar, Vocals / Cajun

Known as the "King of Cajun Singers," this native of Cut Off, LA, born Ervin Bruce, first recorded for Columbia in 1951, where he found some success with the ballad "Dans la Louisianne." A decade later this singer/ guitarist was recording for Floyd Soileau's Swallow label, where he scored a hit with "Jole Blon" (at least the third go-round for "the Cajun national anthem"). Bruce currently resides in Galliano, LA, and is widely respected in Louisiana for his country-tinged Cajun traditionalism. — *Jeff Hannusch and Mark A. Humphrey*

● **Greatest Hits** / 1979 / Swallow ✦✦✦✦

Recorded by one of the pioneers of Cajun music, these early-'60s sides are a mix of traditional songs and French interpretations of country hits. — *Jeff Hannusch*

Cajun Country / 1979 / Swallow ✦✦✦

A good country-tinged album featuring "Dog" Guidry on fiddle, Harry Anselm on guitar, and Eldridge "Johnny" Comeaux on steel guitar. — *Chip Renner*

Buckwheat Zydeco (Stanley Dural)

b. 1947, Lafayette, LA
Accordion, Keyboards / Cajun, Zydeco

Accordionist Buckwheat Zydeco has done much to introduce the spicy southern Louisiana music to the world. Born Stanley Dural, Jr. in Lafaytte, LA, he showed little interest in Creole culture. Though his father wanted him to learn the accordion, Dural, associating it with fuddy-duddy polkas and other uncool kinds of music, instead took up piano at age four and by age nine had gone professional. He got his nickname in childhood after a popular character from the "Little Rascals" film shorts. He founded his first band, Buckwheat and the Hitchhikers, in 1971. An R&B band with 15 members, they became locally popular over the next four years. Dural left the group and the music business in 1975 to rest and reconnoiter. A while later he popped up playing organ with Clifton Chenier's Red Hot Louisiana Band. Chenier became Dural's mentor, teaching him about Creole music and culture. Most importantly, he taught Dural to respect the accordion. By 1979 Dural had learned the instrument and left Chenier's band to form Il Sont Partis. They got their first major break in the mid-'80s when a New York critic sent some of their tapes to Chris Blackwell, the founder of Island Records. Dural became the first zydeco artist to sign with a major label. His first album, *On a Night Like This*, came out in 1987 and was a hit with critics. Buckwheat Zydeco's subsequent work is known for its rough-edged, exciting danceability. Though based in tradition, it contains enough modern influence to keep it contemporary. — *Sandra Brennan*

★ **100% Fortified Zydeco** / 1985 / Black Top ✦✦✦✦✦

This mid-'80s effort is Buckwheat Zydeco's best, as the material recorded is more inventive. The sound is great, and the song selection is superior. — *Jeff Hannusch*

On a Night Like This / 1987 / Island ✦✦✦

Not bad, but still not as good as his Black Top or Rounder work. — *Jeff Hannusch*

Turning Point / 1988 / Rounder ✦✦✦

This is a good sampling of modern zydeco. — *Jeff Hannusch*

Menagerie: The Essential Zydeco Collection / Mango ✦✦✦

This good compilation includes some of the best tracks of one of today's top zydeco artists. — *AMG*

Chubby Carrier (Roy Carrier)

Accordion, Vocals / Cajun, Zydeco

Louisiana-born Carrier got his training with Terrance Simien and the Mallet Playboys, going on to form his first band in 1990. Although his music is steeped in tradition, Carrier adds an original twist with a heavy reliance on rock 'n' roll rhythms and electric guitar solos. — *Cub Koda*

★ **Boogie Woogie Zydeco** / 1991 / Flying Fish ✦✦✦✦✦

One of the best albums in the genre, this is loaded to the brim with great songs and performances. Highlights include the title track, "Bernadette," "Good for the Goose," and "Young Creole Man." It's infectious beyond belief! — *Cub Koda*

Hadley J. Castille

Fiddle, Vocals

Vocalist, composer, and fiddler Hadley J.Castille has been a prolific performer since learning music from his uncle as a boy in the Opelousas, LA, area. Castille's song "200 Lines: I Must Not Speak French" won the '92 Cajun Music Association Heritage Award, and he's made several fine releases for Cajun labels. — *Ron Wynn*

200 Lines: I Must Not Speak French / 1991 / Swallow ✦✦✦

Hadley J. Castille's award-winning composition, plus several other instrumentals, originals, and covers, including a strong rendition of Nathan Abshire's "Nathan's Blues." — *Ron Wynn*

● **Cajun Swamp Fiddler** / 1993 / Swallow ✦✦✦✦

Fiddler and vocalist Hadley J. Castille plays and sings vintage French and Cajun material, mostly his sometimes comical, sometimes autobiographical originals, like the award-winning "200 Lines: I Must Not Speak French." That song is one of 16 on this CD, which is a treat. Castille and the Louisiana Cajun Band perform both his own traditional tunes "Panique et Lodie" and "Cyprien et Marie" and covers of Austin Pitre's "Chere Joue Rouge" and Nathan Bashire's "Nathan's Blues." Excellent and undiluted Cajun material. — *Ron Wynn*

Along the Bayou Teche / Swallow ✦✦✦

This album consists of Cajun vocal music with fiddle accompaniment. — *AMG*

Boozoo Chavis

b. Oct. 23, 1930, Lake Charles, LA
Accordion, Vocals / Zydeco

Chavis supplied the first-ever zydeco hit in 1954 with "Paper in My Shoe." Unfortunately, he was in musical semi-retirement for three decades, but he returned with a bang in the mid-'80s. His many great albums underline his traditional but rocking zydeco style. — *Jeff Hannusch*

Louisiana Zydeco Music / 1986 / Maison de Soul ✦✦✦✦

This is a zydeco masterpiece and a down-home foot-stomper. — *Jeff Hannusch*

● **Paper in My Shoe** / 1987 / Ace ✦✦✦✦

If it hadn't been for the fact that he quit playing for three decades, Boozoo Chavis might have been one of the great names of zydeco. His recent renaissance presumably prompted this reissue of the early sessions he made, in often chaotic conditions, for the small local Goldband label. This was the Black bayou sound unselfconscious, local, and pure. It's still wonderful. — *John Storm Roberts, Original Music*

★ **Zydeco Trail Ride** / 1989 / Maison de Soul ✦✦✦✦✦

This collects his best sides from the Maison de Soul label. Whoop-ti-yo cover and bootin' sounds to match. — *Jeff Hannusch and Mark A. Humphrey*

The Lake Charles Atomic Bomb / 1990 / Rounder ✦✦✦

Boozoo Chavis vaulted to fame in zydeco circles during the mid-'50s, when his gritty, anthemic "Paper in my Shoe" helped get the fledgling zydeco industry off the ground. The 14 tracks on this 1990 anthology showcase a younger, more vocally spry and dynamic Chavis, singing short, simple two-step tunes and zydeco/blues hybrids. There wasn't anything intricate or complicated about pieces like "Hamburgers and Popcorn," "Oh Ho She's Gone," and "Telephone Won't Ring." They were either anguished heartache songs, novelty tunes, or wailing uptempo pieces, and Chavis didn't vary his approach, attack, or treatment. But they were direct, honest, and often memorable. It's good to have them available on one anthology. —Ron Wynn

Boozoo Chavis / 1990 / Elektra/Nonesuch ✦✦✦
Still bluesy and rockin' in the '90s, this was part of the celebrated *American Explorer* series. —Mark A. Humphrey

Boozoo, That's Who! / 1993 / Rounder ✦✦✦
Boozoo Chavis was singing zydeco long before it got widespread exposure outside Louisiana. He's never bothered to tap into trends or vie for crossover dollars. The 14 cuts on this release are primarily vintage zydeco numbers, though he also does an occasional novelty song like "Billy Goat Number Three." These are sizzling two-steps, waltzes, and driving zydeco numbers, with Chavis' aging but still effective vocals leading the way. —Ron Wynn

C.J. Chenier

b. Sep. 28, 1957, Port Arthur, TX
Accordion / Zydeco
C.J. Chenier may no longer be under his father Clifton's shadow, but he is certainly following in his illustrious footsteps as one of the hottest, most recognizable zydeco artists in the world. Like his father, Chenier is constantly perfecting zydeco, helping it to stay up with contemporary tastes, infusing it with an unparalleled raucous energy that commands listeners to get up and dance.

He was born Clayton Joseph Chenier and raised in Port Arthur, TX. His father, who lived in Lafayette, LA, was constantly touring, so Chenier saw him only a couple of times per year. Since zydeco back then was a Louisiana phenomenon and seldom received radio airplay, C.J. had little exposure to his father's music. When he did hear it, he considered it strange and old fashioned. Chenier started piano lessons in the third grade. The following year he took up the saxophone, playing in bands and contests until earning a music scholarship for Texas Southern University. At that time, Chenier was most interested in performers such as the Commodores, Kool & the Gang, James Brown, John Coltrane, and Miles Davis.

Hot Ice was his first band, a Top 40 outfit. He played sax, keyboards, and flute and sang backup. By the late '70s Chenier was seriously considering a career in R&B or soul, but his father had other plans, calling his son in 1978 and asking him to join the Red Hot Louisiana Band as a replacement for sax player John Hart. Though C.J. knew none of the songs, he joined his father. It took over a year for Chenier to really understand the Cajun beat. Around 1983, the ailing Clifton began teaching C.J. to play the accordion to prepare him to take over the band. Though having the band continue with his son was Clifton's dream, he never forced C.J., and much of what his son learned from him came from observation rather than formal instruction. During many performances, the elder Chenier was too ill to finish and his son began taking over. Clifton Chenier died in 1987, and it only seemed natural to C.J. that he play his father's music. A week after his father's burial, Chenier began accepting bookings for the band. —Sandra Brennan

● **Hot Rod** / Oct. 30, 1990 / Slash ✦✦✦✦

Clifton Chenier

b. Jun. 25, 1925, Opelousas, LA, d. Dec. 12, 1987, Lafayette, LA
Accordion, Vocals / Cajun, Zydeco
Clifton Chenier was a master Louisiana musical chef of the highest order. On a good night, with a crowd in high spirits, Chenier's musical gumbo had Cajun two-steps and waltzes sitting right next to slow blues or a scorching rendition of "Bon Ton Roulet," which was Clifton's version of Louis Jordan's "Let the Good Times Roll" sung in French. The musical hybrid that he helped to create—zydeco, or "zodico," its spelling variant and superior phonetic pronunciation—is as rich and as deep as the area from which it sprang. Chenier may not have invented the form—an accordion-driven, blues-inspired variant of Cajun music played for dancing—but he helped give it shape and define the form as we know it today. In his own words, "What I did was to put a little rock 'n' roll into the zydeco to mix it up a bit. You see, people been playing zydeco for a long time, old style, like French music. But I was the first one to put the pep to it." Chenier had taken a backwoods art form, mixed it up with rock 'n' roll, country, R&B, and blues, put a heavier beat to it, and brought this spicy gumbo concoction to the world. Of course, it also helped that he put this Creole hybrid over with personality to spare, singing and playing with a high-energy approach that made the music damn near impossible to ignore.

Chenier was born in 1925 near Opelousas, LA, to a sharecropping family who played music on the side. Early inspirations for him included his father, John Chenier, who played accordion and fiddle, and his guitar-playing uncle, Maurice "Big" Chenier, as well as local player Izeb Laza, who gave him his first accordion. But the musician who really turned Clifton's head was Amédée Ardoin, the first Black Creole musician to play the blues on an accordion. Ardoin was the Charlie Pat-

ton of the music, king of the Louisiana dance music being dispensed as far back as 1928—then called French lalas—making the sounds on the front porch, loose, rough, and informal. The accordion was usually accompanied by a triangle, a washboard, and a fiddle. It was homegrown music, based on the two-steps and waltzes of Cajun music, and when Ardoin became the first to put blues licks to ancient French melodies, a livelier version of the form immediately existed. Once Clifton heard Ardoin's records, he was hooked; here was dance music elastic enough to change, update, and expand its vocabulary. At the same time that Chenier was learning Ardoin's lively versions of the old French-Cajun dance tunes, Chenier learned his very first tune on the accordion, the Joe Liggins jump blues hit, "The Honeydripper."

By the age of 17 Chenier was working weekend gigs in nearby Lake Charles, with his older brother Cleveland playing the rubboard. Their good-time party music was perfectly suited for the numerous "joys" (little dance halls, which were usually nothing more than shacks) that dotted the coastal region, and they worked a lot at their uncle "Big" Chenier's club. Soon the duo expanded, and by the early '50s, Clifton had his first electric band together, the Hot Sizzling Band (aka the Hot Sizzlers), a perfect description of the sound that the seven-piece combo was laying down. With electric guitar, piano, tenor saxophone, bass, and drums fleshing out the sound of the two Chenier brothers, this was clearly a long way away from a triangle player tinging along with a squeeze box in the backyard. How Clifton came to make records in 1954 in California is still a matter of speculation. But the conventional wisdom is that Beaumont, TX, bluesman Clarence Garlow—who had been booking Chenier at his Bon Ton Drive Inn for three years—put in the good word to Los Angeles record man J.R. Fullbright. Legend has it that when Garlow put the telephone up to Clifton's amplifier and J.R. heard the sound of the music, he told Clarence, "I'm coming to get him."

With Fullbright behind the controls, Chenier and his band cut seven sides at a Lake Charles radio station. The first single issued ("Louisiana Stomp") kicked up enough noise on J.R.'s Elko label that four more sides from the session were quickly issued on Post, an Imperial subsidiary.

By the next year, Fullbright had hooked Chenier up with Specialty Records in Hollywood; the 1955 sessions that he cut for the label are where his success story—and that of the music—truly begins. A session in Los Angeles was set up with Bumps Blackwell (who would later produce Little Richard) in charge. Legend has it that Blackwell pulled half the band off the session to give greater focus to Chenier's accordion. A quick listen to the two sessions reveals that this appears to been have a track-by-track decision; some tracks feature the full band, and players drift in and out of the lineup on other tracks, while most are just Chenier and the rhythm section vainly trying to keep up with him on boogie woogie instrumentals. But Chenier's first Specialty single—"Ay Te Te Fee" and "Boppin' the Rock," released a month after it was cut—became a left field R&B charter, moving enough copies to get him booked on package shows with the likes of Etta James and Jimmy Reed. But rock 'n' roll was also coming in strong, and with Richard's "Tutti Frutti" outselling everyone else in the Specialty catalog *combined*, Chenier suddenly found himself without a recording contract. He quickly signed for a short stint with Chess, resulting in two excellent singles, and a couple of years later became a part of Crowley, LA, producer Jay Miller's stable, recording for his Zynn label between 1958 and 1960.

Meanwhile, Chenier stayed a hot road attraction, playing all through Texas and Louisiana for dances, picnics, and nightclubs. It was after relocating to Houston's Frenchtown quarter in 1960 that his next (and longest) recording partnership came about. A young California-based folklorist and record label owner was in town, and after Lightnin' Hopkins hooked the two of them up, Chenier was quickly signed to Chris Strachwitz' fledgling Arhoolie label.

Not that everything was always an easy road to travel between the two men. Strachwitz wanted to keep the music as close as possible to the rubboard, drums, and accordion format of the old-time French lala material, while Clifton wanted to rip through a set of the tunes that people danced to on a live gig. Though Chenier stayed with Strachwitz for several albums and singles into the '70s, he was also recording during the same period for Floyd Soileau's Bayou label, with both men later leasing material to labels like Bell and Blue Thumb. In addition to Arhoolie and Bayou, Chenier would also record for Crazy Cajun, Blue Star, GNP Crescendo, Jin, Caillier, Maison de Soul, and his final stop, Alligator Records, in 1982.

After the release of the Arhoolie albums, Europe came a-calling, and in 1969 Chenier was bowling over crowds on the American Folk Blues Festival tour, staying overseas and adding extra play dates to his already crowded calendar. By the '70s, Chenier and his Red Hot Louisiana Band seemingly covered the globe.

Unfortunately, by the dawn of the following decade, Chenier was a very sick man. Diagnosed with diabetes and with a road schedule that was unrelenting, Chenier's failing kidneys that needed dialysis treatment every third day and a partially amputated foot started to take a toll. In 1984 he played the White House, but his health finally gave out on December 12, 1987. — *Cub Koda*

Zodico Blues and Boogie / 1955 / Specialty ◆◆◆◆
Clifton Chenier's mid-'50s singles for Specialty were among his rawest and simplest; they were short ditties with rippling accordion and gritty vocals on top and driving rhythms and surging instrumental accompaniment underneath. That's the formula displayed on this 20-cut presentation of Chenier's early work, where he was often backed by guitarists Phillip Walker or Cornelius Green (Lonesome Sundown), with his brother Cleveland handling rubboard duties. This is Chenier in his stylistic infancy, building and nurturing what ultimately became a signature sound. — *Ron Wynn*

Bayou Blues / 1970 / Specialty ◆◆◆◆
Bayou Blues compiles a selection of 12 tracks Clifton Chenier cut for Specialty Records in 1955, including the original versions of "Boppin' the Rock," "Eh, Petite Fille," "I'm On My Way," and "Zodico Stomp." It may not be a definitive retrospective, but it's an entertaining and necessary sampler of Chenier at the beginning of his career. — *Thom Owens*

Out West / 1974 / Arhoolie ◆◆◆◆
Special guests Elvin Bishop and Steve Miller join Chenier for an excellent outing blending blues and rock influences with zydeco. Chenier's vocals are tough and convincing; Bishop and Miller, along with saxophonist Jon Hart, are outstanding. — *Ron Wynn*

In New Orleans / 1979 / GNP ◆◆◆
In New Orleans was recorded in the late '70s with one of Clifton Chenier's classic bands, which featured his brother on washboard, saxophonist John Hart, and guitarist Paul Senegal, among others. The album is textbook Chenier—it rocks and rolls, wails and shouts. It may be a typical record for the king of zydeco, but that means it's very, very enjoyable. — *Thom Owens*

Live! / 1985 / Arhoolie ◆◆◆
The 19 selections on this disc were done in the early '80s, when Chenier was past his romping prime but still keeping the zydeco engine running. He has done them all before on other releases, but keeps them entertaining and enjoyable through sheer will and personality. — *Ron Wynn*

Sings the Blues / 1987 / Arhoolie ◆◆◆
Lots of great accordion and unique vocals from the blues side of the bayou. — *Jeff Hannusch and Mark A. Humphrey*

Bogalusa Boogie / Jul. 1987 / Arhoolie ◆◆◆
Backed by a fuller band on this release, he sounds great. Here's the hottest of the red-hot Louisiana bands, and they're feelin' frisky. — *Jeff Hannusch and Mark A. Humphrey*

Live at St. Mark's / 1988 / Arhoolie ◆◆◆
Live at St. Mark's captures a rollicking concert performed in San Francisco. Chenier leads the band through a blend of zydeco and blues, singing with gusto and spice all along. Furthermore, he plays to the audience, telling jokes and stories that give the album a special, intimate feel. With all the wonderful music and joy that *Live at St. Mark's* radiates, there's little question that it is one of Chenier's finest live albums. — *Thom Owens*

☆ **60 Minutes with the King of Zydeco** / 1988 / Arhoolie ◆◆◆◆◆
Zydeco at its best, it compiles his greatest hits from the Arhoolie label. — *Jeff Hannusch*

★ **Zydeco Dynamite: The Clifton Chenier Anthology** / 1993 / Rhino ◆◆◆◆◆
Clifton Chenier was to zydeco what Elvis Presley was to rockabilly, only more so—the genre's founding father and tireless ambassador. Rhino has done an admirable job of collecting the accordionist's important work for this two-disc, 40-track set, harking back to a wonderfully chaotic "Louisiana Stomp" that he waxed in Lake Charles, LA, in 1954 for J.R. Fullbright's tiny Elko label. Whether you're in the market for one zydeco collection to summarize the entire genre or ready to delve deeply into the legacy of the idiom's pioneer, this is precisely where to begin. — *Bill Dahl*

Harry Choates

b. 1922, d. 1951
Fiddle / Cajun
Choates' 1946 recording of "Jole Blon" presented a simple traditional waltz, sung in Cajun French and played with few frills. Yet it became a national hit, was covered (in English) by Roy Acuff and others, and became as essential to any Cajun music performance as "The Star-Spangled Banner" is to a baseball game. "Jole Blon" was actually atypical of the frenetic Choates, whose Western-swing-tinged fiddling was jazzier than that of any Cajun before or since. Choates was also a passable singer who punctuated his songs with an energetic "Eh, hah hah!" in the manner of Bob Wills. Hard drink and fast living got the better of Choates, who died in an Austin jail in 1951. Disparaged by Cajun purists, he is the Acadian that Western swing enthusiasts find most approachable. — *Mark A. Humphrey*

● **Jole Blon** / 1979 / 'D' ◆◆◆◆
The title cut has become the "Cajun national anthem." Includes many other great fiddle-led Cajun tunes. — *Jeff Hannusch*

Five-Time Lobster / 1990 / Krazy Kat ◆◆◆
A followup to "Jole Blon" and 13 other performances, it includes the Hank Williams-inspired "Cat'n' Around." It has a rough sound but great music, blending Cajun, swing, and honky tonk. — *Mark A. Humphrey*

His Original 1946-1949 Recordings / Arhoolie ◆◆◆
Sixteen performances by the man dubbed "the Godfather of Cajun Music." Includes his swingin' takes on such standards as "Allons . . . Lafayette" and "Grand Mamou." — *Mark A. Humphrey*

Clark and Duhon

Cajun
Accordionist Oct Clark and fiddler Hector Duhon formed the Dixie Ramblers in 1930, performing in contests alongside Nathan Abshire and Amedee Breaux. In the '80s they hooked up with fiddler Michael Doucet and his brother, guitarist David Doucet. — *Liz Opoka*

Old-Time Cajun Music / Arhoolie ◆◆◆◆
Old-time Cajun music played right. — *Jeff Hannusch*

Bruce Daigrepont

b. 1959
Accordion, Vocals / Cajun
An admitted child of the Cajun revival, Daigrepont began regarding Cajun music as something other than the music of his grandparents' generation only when he heard such young Turks as Michael Doucet and Zachary Richard in the '70s. Ironically, this singer and accordionist developed a style somewhat more traditional than that of his mentors. Writing his own material and fronting a tight band, Daigrepont has earned both the approval of his elders and the respect of his peers. — *Mark A. Humphrey*

● **Stir up the Roux** / 1988 / Rounder ◆◆◆◆
While Daigrepont is aware of other sounds like rock and country, he integrates their edge and sensibility into his work without losing or deserting the basic Cajun mode. The 10 tunes on this release are predominantly driving, uptempo pieces with his frenetic accordion and infectious vocals setting the pace, backed by a sharp band that includes tremendous fiddler Waylon Thibodeaux. Daigrepont makes no lyrical concessions, but the color and flair of his singing should overcome any hesitancy non-French speakers might have about the material. It's certainly up-to-date, but also thoroughly steeped in the old ethic. — *Ron Wynn*

Coeur des Cajuns / 1989 / Rounder ◆◆◆
Bruce Daigrepont's second album for Rounder is even more traditionally Cajun than his award-winning first effort. The title track and other works such as "Les Mains du Bon Dieu," "Acadie a la Louisiane," and "Laissez Moi Tranquille" present tales of Cajun life and times ranging from struggles to triumphs, and are sung with power, earnestness, and verve. His accordion playing is equally assertive. — *Ron Wynn*

Petit Cadeau / May 2, 1994 / Rounder ◆◆◆

John Delafose

b. 1939
Accordion, Vocals / Zydeco
Delafose's driving but down-home zydeco is indebted to Clifton Chenier but reaches back to African-tinged Creole roots. He played sporadically while farming, before committing to music with a family-based band that included sons Tony on drums (now bass) and John Jr. on washboard. A fine singer and fiery accordionist, Delafose's unique traditionalism is a refreshing counterweight to the more R&B and funk-tinged zydeco bands. — *Mark A. Humphrey*

Heartaches and Hot Steps / 1984 / Maison de Soul ◆◆◆◆
Explosive arrangements, powerhouse vocals and accordion playing, and good band support make this a first-rate contemporary zydeco date. — *Ron Wynn*

● **Joe Pete Got Two Women** / 1988 / Arhoolie ◆◆◆◆
Delafose's best contains his popular saga of Joe Pete. Zydeco fundamentalism from this singer/accordionist, and his music clearly echoes African hypnotic grooves. — *Jeff Hannusch and Mark A. Humphrey*

Pere et Garcon Zydeco / 1992 / Rounder ◆◆◆
While zydeco and Cajun-influenced hybrids have been the norm in many circles during the '80s and '90s, John Delafose and the Eunice Playboys have remained true to the classic style. This session features predominantly hardcore material, emphasizing the two-steps, waltzes, and French lyrics at the heart of zydeco/Cajun. Delafose and his son Geno alternate lead vocals and accordion support, each singing and playing with vigor, conviction, and authenticity. The band backs them with equal

electricity, and while such tunes as "Watch That Dog," "Morning Train," and "Go Back Where You Been" are lyrical departures, they are as fully in the zydeco framework as "Mon Coeur Fait Mal" or "Grand Mamou." —*Ron Wynn*

Michael Doucet

Fiddle, Vocals / Cajun

Since the mid-'70s, Doucet has been one of the dominant figures of the Cajun music revival, respected for his scholarship and admired for his showmanship. On the one hand Doucet dredges up ancient Cajun tunes with medieval French roots, and on the other plays flamboyant fiddle with Beausoleil. Singer and fiddler Doucet has also performed and recorded with the more purely traditional Savoy-Doucet Cajun Band. He is as passionate about Cajun tradition as he is eager to drop-kick it into the 21st century, and for that reason Doucet has earned the applause of both purists and plebians who just wanna boogie. —*Mark A. Humphrey*

Christmas Bayou / 1986 / Swallow ✦✦✦
Cajun fiddler extraordinaire and leader of Beausoleil, Michael Doucet is backed by swamp-guitar whiz Sonny Landreth, accordionist Pat Breaux, and others on this unique assortment of French fare and rollicking instrumental versions of "Deck the Halls" and "Auld Lang Zyne" (sic). —*Decibel Dennis MacDonald*

And Cajun Brew / 1988 / Rounder ✦✦✦✦
Sometime Beausoleil member Michael Doucet heads a different type of ensemble in Cajun Brew. The band is a fusion/rock/pop group, and this release begins with a reworking of "Wooly Bully" and includes covers of "Hey, Good Looking" and "Louie Louie." The roster includes flamboyant, stirring guitarist Sonny Landreth, whose blues-rock leanings are quite evident. As if aware that there might be questions about allegiances, the group's song roster contains such numbers as "Un Autre Soir Ennuyant" and "Like A Real Cajun" alongside the covers. While they sometimes blur or hedge their focus, there is enough Cajun flavor in the arrangements, performances, and instrumentation to keep purists from grumbling, while joyful rock/pop remakes aim for a wider audience. —*Ron Wynn*

Le Hoogie Boogie: Louisiana French Music for Children / 1992 / Rounder ✦✦✦

● **Bayou Deluxe: The Best of Michael Doucet and . . .** / 1993 / Rhino ✦✦✦✦
This is an excellent collection of some of the best tracks from a leader in the Cajun music revival. —*AMG*

Joseph Falcon

b. 1900, d. 1965
Accordion / Cajun

One of the pioneers of Cajun music, Falcon made the first commercial Cajun recording, *Lafayette ("Allons . . . Lafayette")*, with his wife Cleoma in 1928. Cleoma's simple guitar and emotive singing, driven by Joe's crying accordion, was an instant hit in Cajun country, foisting a regional stardom on the team, who recorded for Columbia, Decca, Bluebird, and Okeh in the '30s. Cleoma's death in 1941 and changes in listeners' taste (the accordion was out, the fiddle in) led Falcon away from performing, though he and his second wife, Theresa, fronted a band in the years before his death. Falcon's early recordings are among the enduring classics of the Cajun genre. —*Mark A. Humphrey*

★ **Live at a Cajun Dance** / 1988 / Arhoolie ✦✦✦✦✦
Perhaps the best live Cajun album of all time, this was recorded near the end of Falcon's career in the early '60s. —*Jeff Hannusch*

File

Accordion / Cajun

A fun, contemporary Cajun/zydeco dance band, File's influences include Zachary Richard and Beausoleil. They have recorded Cajun zydeco standards but also delve into other genres for variety (namely their brilliant version of Richard Thompson's "Two Left Feet"). —*Liz Opoka*

● **Cajun Dance Band** / Oct. 1987 / Flying Fish ✦✦✦✦
This is the debut album by one of the more popular contemporary Cajun bands. —*Jeff Hannusch*

Two Left Feet / 1990 / Flying Fish ✦✦✦✦
Excellent dancehall music. —*Jeff Hannusch*

Allen Fontenot

Fiddle, Vocals

Allen Fontenot is one of the best-known fiddlers in Cajun music. Fontenot always loved the fiddle and made his own on several occasions out of such materials as a ukulele, cigar boxes, bow and arrow sets, and wire. His grandfather, also a fiddler, bought him his first real one when Fontenot was 15. After working for several years as a bill collector, Fontenot founded the five-piece Country Cajuns in the early '70s. The first members were concertina player Leroy Veilloa, guitarist Hudson Dauzat, drummer Darrel Brasseaux, and bass player John Scott. They recorded a few singles and played at the Jazz and Heritage Festival. The Country Cajuns also appeared regularly on a Sunday morning radio show and made their feature film debut in 1975 in Charles Bronson's *Hard Times*. They have also appeared on the television shows "Good Morning America" and "Austin City Limits." When not playing with the band, Fontenot worked as a popular deejay in Slidell, LA. In the late '70s, he opened the Cajun Bandstand in Kenner, LA, which served authentic Cajun cuisine and showcased authentic Cajun music; he and his band frequently played there until he sold the club in 1982. Fontenot's work can be found on the Great Southern, Antilles, and Delta labels. —*Sandra Brennan*

Jole Blon and Other Cajun Honky Tonk Songs / Jan. 1980 / Great Southern ✦✦✦✦

Hackberry Ramblers

Cajun

Started by a group of teenagers in 1930, the Hackberry Ramblers went on to become the most popular and influential Cajun band of the '30s. Fiddler Luderin Darbone (b. 1913) led this accordionless Cajun band with as many as three supporting guitarists. Their recordings featured songs in both French and English, and their music was deeply influenced by the jazzy Western swing string-bands of Texas. In a sense, the Hackberry Ramblers were the first "hybrid" Cajun musicians, reflecting the impact of records and radio on an isolated regional culture. Despite long periods of inactivity, Darbone and a revived Hackberry Ramblers continue to appear at folk festivals across America. —*Mark A. Humphrey*

Early Recordings: 1935-1948 / 1988 / Old Timey ✦✦✦✦
No accordions here: this strain of Cajun music includes fiddles and guitars. —*Jeff Hannusch*

● **Cajun Boogie** / Jun. 1992 / Flying Fish ✦✦✦✦
As they sing on the theme song that opens this CD, the Hackberry Ramblers "play you some music and try to make you smile" with their infectious brand of hoedown music. By and large the Hackberry, LA, band succeeds on this album, which features original members Glen Croker (guitar) and Luderin Darbone (fiddle). Since 1933, they've been blending Cajun, country, and Western swing music with touches of blues and pop. Croker and Darbone recorded this in their 80s, but they haven't lost their manic energy and taste for get-down party sounds. Besides presenting several of their own compositions, they cover tunes by Bob Wills, Ray Price, and Howlin' Wolf. This CD features guest fiddle by zydeco star Michael Doucet on four tracks, as well as a guest vocal by country star Rodney Crowell on "Old Pipeliner." —*Richie Unterberger*

Doug Kershaw (Douglas James Kershaw)

b. Jan. 24, 1936, Tiel Ridge, LA
Fiddle / Country, Cajun

Cajun country fiddler Kershaw emerged from the steamy South Louisiana swampland with his own wildly energetic approach on the violin. He is widely recognized as a Cajun music pioneer. Paired with his brother as Rusty and Doug, he first hit the country charts in 1955 for Hickory with "So Lovely Baby." In 1961 the pair issued the original "Louisiana Man" and "Diggy Liggy Lo," both solid country sellers and now the songs perhaps most vividly associated with the manic violinist. While Kershaw sawed his fiddle like a man possessed, his solo career took off during the '70s, although his popularity was never properly reflected by the charts. —*Bill Dahl*

The Cajun Way / 1969 / Warner Brothers ✦✦✦
Kershaw's first calling card is very good. —*Jeff Hannusch*

Louisiana Man / 1971 / Warner Brothers ✦✦✦
Contains the infamous title-track hit and several other goodies. —*Jeff Hannusch*

★ **The Best of Doug Kershaw** / Aug. 8, 1989 / Warner Brothers ✦✦✦✦✦
This compilation of Kershaw's '60s/'70s Warner Bros. sides features "Everly Brothers-on-the-bayou" vocal harmonies, Doug Kershaw's fiddle, and crisp Nashville production. —*Mark A. Humphrey*

Rusty Kershaw

Guitar, Vocals

The younger brother of Doug Kershaw, Russell "Rusty" Kershaw hasn't enjoyed as much success operating on his own as he has performing with brothers Doug and Sammy Kershaw. He released an LP on Domino in 1992. —*Ron Wynn*

- **Cajun in Blues Country** / 1970 / Cotillion ✦✦✦✦
Rusty's best Cajun LP as a leader includes both solid vocals and first-rate playing. —*Ron Wynn*

Shorty LeBlanc (Vorris LeBlanc)

Accordion / Cajun
LeBlanc is best remembered as the accordionist on the bluesy "Sugar Bee" by Cleveland Crochet and his Hillbilly Ramblers, which climbed to No. 80 in the *Billboard* Hot 100 in early 1961. LeBlanc's performance was Cajun accordion played to sounds such as amplified blues harmonica. Sidney Brown was an accordion maker and repairer who scored a regional hit with "Pestauche ah Tante Nana" ("The Peanut Song.") —*Mark A. Humphrey*

- **Best of Two Cajun Greats** / 1987 / Swallow ✦✦✦✦
Shorty Le Blanc and Sidney Brown are two lesser-known but great Cajun artists. These are their best sides waxed for Swallow. —*Jeff Hannusch*

Eddie LeJeune

d. Aug. 26, 1993
Accordion / Cajun
For over three decades, Eddie LeJeune has ranked among the liveliest and best of the Cajun accordionists and singers. The son of Iry LeJeune, one of the most important post-WWII-era Cajun artists, Eddie began playing music as a child. He and the Morse Playboys, fiddler Lionel Leleux, and guitar player Hubert Maitre, have an international following for their brilliant renditions of traditional Cajun tunes. LeJeune's repertoire also includes many of his father's most famous songs. —*Sandra Brennan*

- **Cajun Soul** / 1988 / Rounder ✦✦✦✦
Although he had been singing traditional, evocative Cajun music for many years, Eddie LeJeune didn't record an album for a general label until his 1988 date. He made the most of his opportunity, singing with abandon, fervor, and intensity on 15 tunes. Some, such as "Jolie Blon" (a CD-only cut), are familiar efforts; others have some country flavor but are Cajun through and through. The backing, which includes assistance from the great D.L. Menard on guitar and LeJeune's own spicy accordion, never veers from its straight Cajun path and is quite invigorating. The lack of thematic and musical variety might be a detriment to the session's appeal outside Cajun circles, but within them it's a winner. —*Ron Wynn*

It's in the Blood / 1991 / Rounder ✦✦✦
Eddie LeJeune's 1991 Rounder release continued to build his reputation among those who hadn't heard his contributions to efforts by such greats as D.L. Menard. While LeJeune was a steady, occasionally intriguing vocalist, he was a super instrumentalist. His accordion solos and fills add extra bite to these songs, and while the 15 numbers are predominantly basic Cajun, he demonstrates on "The Happy Hop" the ability to do credible rock and pop. The close, tight backing of the Morse Playboys provides additional spark to the session. —*Ron Wynn*

Le Trio Cadien / 1992 / Rounder ✦✦✦✦
When three Cajun music greats and virtuosos team, it seems inevitable that they would make a superb recording. *Le Trio Cadien* wasn't quite that magical, but it was certainly first-rate. D.L. Menard's vocals and guitar work are at their usual fervent peak, while Eddie LeJeune provides some swaying, rocking accordion and poignant, moving vocals. Ken Smith takes the spotlight on "Bayou Pon Pon" and "Blues de Port Arthur." There's very little wrong with this album, and plenty that's excellent. Only the air of casual intimacy rather than charged intensity kept this from being one of those unforgettable summit meetings. Instead, it's more like a wonderful get-together. —*Ron Wynn*

D. L. Menard (Doris Menard)

Guitar, Accordion, Vocals / Cajun
One of the purest examples of Cajun music around today, the sound of D. L. Menard and the Louisiana Aces harks back to the genre's ground-floor days and has changed very little in style over the years. Menard's impassioned vocals (largely sung in French) have invited comparisons to country legend Hank Williams. —*Cub Koda*

- **Cajun Saturday Night** / 1985 / Rounder ✦✦✦✦
"The Cajun Hank Williams" appears in Nashville with Ricky Skaggs, Jerry Douglas, and others. No one can imitate Menard or the great sounds on this album. —*Jeff Hannusch and Mark A. Humphrey*

No Matter Where You at, There You Are / 1988 / Rounder ✦✦✦
Although most of the songs on this release are two-steps and/or waltzes, Menard also sings such country-flavored numbers as "The Little Black Eyes," "I Went to the Dance Last Night" and "The Heart of the City." His voice rings with clarity, conviction, and intensity, whether doing heartache tunes, bittersweet narratives, or exuberant dance numbers.

Menard's vocals get an additional boost on several tunes from the hot accordion of Eddie LeJeune. —*Ron Wynn*

Nathan and the Zydeco Cha-Chas

Accordionist and bandleader Nathan Williams symbolizes the new breed among zydeco and Cajun artists. He speaks and plays French songs wonderfully, but can also handle R&B, blues, and pop. —*Ron Wynn*

Steady Rock / 1989 / Rounder ✦✦✦
Nathan Williams has emerged near the head of the class among contemporary zydeco artists. This release features mostly zydeco-tinged versions of blues and R&B tracks, although the cuts "Zydeco Joe" and "Everything on the Floor" are closer in structure and arrangements to straight zydeco. But Williams' voice, flair, and energy, coupled with his band's ability to keep the beat moving, help him retain a sizable following among Louisiana music purists, yet also branch out and do material that could gain attention from less knowledgeable fans. It is fiery, enjoyable music, produced with a modern sensibility and performed in vintage fashion. —*Ron Wynn*

Your Mama Don't Know / Oct. 1990 / Rounder ✦✦✦
Nathan Williams continued his string of solid releases with this 1991 date. It includes good pop and R&B tracks like "Outside People" and "Don't Burn No Bridges," plus vibrant traditional material such as "El Sid O's Zydeco Boogaloo" and "Mardi Gras Zydeco." Williams sings with zest, drive, and non-stop intensity, while the band shows once more why they're considered the tightest unit working in the genre. There aren't any surprises or low points, just a consistently fine set spotlighting the best group in '90s zydeco. —*Ron Wynn*

- **Follow Me Chicken** / 1993 / Rounder ✦✦✦✦
While Nathan Williams has generally been more contemporary in his song selection, approach, and performance style on the zydeco circuit, he's also proficient doing traditional French tunes and two-steps. He shows on this album that he can handle the demands of older material with fine performances on "Tout Partout Mon Passe" and "Elle Est Jolie," a French cover of Stevie Wonder's "Isn't She Lovely." But Williams remains the champion of churning, blues and R&B-flavored numbers, and the band rips through "Zydeco Road," "Follow Me Chicken," and "One Track Mind," as well as the more low-key "I Need Someone to Love Me" and "I'm in Love." Williams' vocals and whirling accordion lines punctuate the music of modern zydeco's finest group. —*Ron Wynn*

Creole Crossroads / Oct. 3, 1995 / Rounder ✦✦✦

Queen Ida

Accordion / Cajun, Zydeco
Queen Ida was the first female accordion player to lead a zydeco band. Favoring a 31-button accordion, she is noted for her melodic playing, and for focusing on the treble side of her instrument, which makes her style similar to Mexican playing styles. Like many other zydeco artists of the '80s, her music was well grounded in Creole traditions, but she also integrates Caribbean, Cajun (with the addition of a fiddle to her Bon Temps Zydeco Band), blues, and other genres. She came to music rather late in life.

Born Ida Guillory to a musically talented family in Lake Charles, LA, she learned to play accordion from her mother. Her family moved to Beaumont, TX, when she was 10, and eight years later to San Francisco. Her first language is French. But while music was important to Guillory, during her young adult years while busy raising her family, she performed only for social occasions. She briefly attended nursing school but left during her first pregnancy. When her children were all school-aged, she became a part-time bus driver. As the children grew, Guillory's friends began more strongly encouraging her to perform publicly.

In the early '70s, she began performing with the Barbary Coast Band and with the Playboys. She was in demand not only because of her talent, but also because female accordion players were a rarity. She got her stage name in 1975 during a Mardi Gras celebration in the Bay Area. There she was formally crowned "Queen of the Zydeco Accordion and Queen of Zydeco Music." The following year she and her band played at the Monterey Jazz and Blues Festival. She also signed to GNP/Crescendo Records, a Los Angeles-based jazz label.

Despite her popularity, Queen Ida never felt music was stable enough to support her children and so continued bus driving until her youngest daughter went to school. After that Ida began touring more frequently. In 1978, John Ullman became her agent. He helped make her internationally known. In 1979 she was nominated for a Bay Area Music Award. Though Taj Mahal won it, Ullman arranged a two-week European tour for her. She continued recording and touring through the '80s. Because she feels she and the band sound best live, most of her albums are recorded while she tours.

In 1988 Queen Ida toured Japan, becoming the first zydeco artist to do so. She toured Africa the following year for the State Department and in 1990 went to Australia and New Zealand. Queen Ida has appeared in one feature film, *Rumblefish*, and a documentary about Louisiana music, *J'ai Ete au Bal*. She has also performed on television shows ranging from "Austin City Limits" to "Saturday Night Live." For many, Queen Ida is not only an excellent musician, she is also a fine example of how a determined middle-aged woman can still find success in a youth-obsessed culture. —*Sandra Brennan*

Caught in the Act / 1985 / GNP ✦✦✦
Live from San Francisco, CA. It includes classics "Jole Blon," "Don't Mess with My Tu Tu," and Nick Lowe's "Half a Boy, Half a Man." Rollicking zydeco. —*Michael G. Nastos*

In San Francisco / 1988 / GNP ✦✦✦✦
A Grammy Award-winning, live, and potent album, with Al Rapone on accordion. —*Michael G. Nastos*

★ **Cookin' with Queen Ida** / 1989 / GNP ✦✦✦✦✦
She cooks up a hearty menu of traditional zydeco and Cajun harmony, blending in blues, reggae, and more, on this 1989 release. It includes "Hard Headed Woman" and "C'est Moi," her personal lament about life on the road. —*Ladyslipper*

Band on Tour / GNP ✦✦✦✦
Band on Tour was the winner of the 1982 Grammy Award for best ethnic/traditional folk album. —*Ladyslipper*

Zachary Richard

b. Sep. 8, 1950
Guitar, Accordion, Vocals / Rock, Cajun, Zydeco
Cajun rebel Zachary Richard has been offering his zesty, unique fusion of traditional Cajun, zydeco, rock, and New Orleans blues since the early '70s. Though not well known outside of Louisiana, Canada, and France, Richard, along with Michael Doucet and others, has been a key figure in the revitalization of Cajun music. He has also been a longtime social activist, using his lyrics to promote Cajun pride and solidarity in the face of long-standing injustice and prejudice. This activism originally somewhat alienated Richard from conservative traditional Cajun artists and from audiences unprepared for the underlying kick of his punchy party music.

A full-blooded Cajun, Richard can trace his family tree straight back to Acadia, where his ancestors lived for 200 years before the British forcibly exiled them in the mid-1700s. During the '50s and '60s, Cajun culture, due to prejudice, was on the decline. Richard's parents did little to instill cultural pride in their son and even refused to speak their native French. While earning a B.A. at Tulane University in New Orleans during the late '60s, Richard began his longtime campaign on behalf of the Cajuns. The eclecticism of his own music reflects his personal tastes. Early influences included Ray Charles, Professor Longhair, Howlin' Wolf, Little Walter, Muddy Waters, the Byrds, and Bob Dylan.

He went to New York in the early '70s and signed with Elektra Records to produce a country-rock album. Largely due to Elektra's merger with Warner at that time, the album was never released. He went back to Louisiana to further hone his musicianship. At that time he played piano, accordion, and guitar. With a little tutoring from Clifton Chenier, the accordion became Richard's favorite instrument. He, his cousin Michael Doucet, and Kenneth Richard teamed up in 1974 to form the Bayou Drifter Band and play a mixture of Cajun and rock that they called "swamp rock." The new style didn't catch on in Louisiana, but it was extremely popular in Canada. With socially conscious lyrics penned and performed in French, Richard's music found particular favor in politically charged Quebec, where the secession movement was gaining momentum. He remained in Canada through the early '80s and earned several gold records. Richard also spent time in France learning more about folk music. He returned to Louisiana around 1981 and suddenly found that Cajun culture and music had become a national fad. He formed a new group and dove right in. In the late '80s, Richard signed with Rounder and released a pair of albums, *Mardis Gras Mambo* and *Zack's Bon Ton* (1990). After that he signed a major contract with A&M. His debut album with the label, *Women in the Room*, featured some of the best session men in music. —*Sandra Brennan*

Live / 1970 / Arzed ✦✦✦
An exciting live performer, he's at his best here. —*Jeff Hannusch*

Allons Danser / 1980 / Arzed ✦✦✦
A foot-tapper all the way. —*Jeff Hannusch*

★ **Looking Back** / 1985 / Arzed ✦✦✦✦✦
The greatest hits from this important artist. —*Jeff Hannusch*

Mardi Gras Mambo / 1989 / Rounder ✦✦✦✦
Zachary Richard blends Cajun with classic R&B on this set, paying homage to the link between Louisiana's Mardi Gras heritage and its other musical styles. He does spirited and convincing versions of "Iko Iko," "Big Chief," and "Down on Second Street," while including "Creole Lullaby," and scoring with "Moi Connais Pas" and "Ton Ton Gris-Gris." Richard has expert assistance from the Bon Ton Playboys, plus a guest vocal

corps, and he handled production chores himself, This isn't a crossover project but a unified one that demonstrates the intrinsic links between all Louisiana genres. —*Ron Wynn*

Zack's Bon Ton / 1990 / Rounder ✦✦✦
Zachary Richard has been among Cajun music's finest performers during the '80s and '90s, and this late-'80s session is one of his finest. The 12 tracks include hot versions of "Jolie Blonde," "La Valse de Grande Riviere," and "Ma Petite Fille Est Gone." Richard also demonstrates his country proficiency with a heady cover of Johnny Horton's "The Battle of New Orleans," as well as "Big River" and "Take Me Deep (Song For C)." The Bon Ton Playboys include outstanding musicians in fiddler Rufus Thibodeaux, saxophonist Pat Breaux, and keyboardist Craig Lege, with Richard doubling on Acadian accordion, harmonica, and acoustic guitar in addition to doing leads. This is alternately spicy and reflective material, providing a good look at Cajun music's past, present, and future. —*Ron Wynn*

☆ **Women in the Room** / 1990 / A&M ✦✦✦✦✦
Zach's writing comes together on this release with his most powerful songs to date. "No French, No More" is a sad tale about how teachers denied the Cajun people the use of their language. "Who Stole My Monkey" is a knock-you-out fun song. A very diverse release. Highly recommended. —*Chip Renner*

Bayou des Mystées / 1991 / Arzed ✦✦✦
His traditional album. —*Jeff Hannusch*

Snake Bite Love / Sep. 8, 1992 / A&M ✦✦✦
This CD stands up as an energetic *tour de force*. It carries a high head easily with some of the best songwriting and singing to come out of the Louisiana scene that has included Sonny Landreth's *South of I-10*, and Richard's own *Women in the Room*. For this record he has culled some of the best people from the southern Louisiana music scene (Brian Stoltz, Doctor John, the Dirty Dozen Brass Band, and Daryl Johnson to name a few) to take part in this fine blending of zydeco, Cajun, rock, and country. The only bother with this CD is that you can't sit and listen to it, you are compelled to get up and move. Try to sit and contemplate while "Dancing at Double D's" is spinning. Listen to the heartfelt vocals and the exposed emotions of "Cote Blanche Bay" or "Sunset on Louisianne," and feel the love and hurt from his voice come coursing through your body. —*Bob Gottlieb*

Rockin' Dopsie

b. Feb. 10, 1932
Accordion, Vocals / Cajun, Zydeco
If Clifton Chenier was the king of zydeco music, Rockin' Dopsie (pronounced *doopsie*), with his unequaled proficiency on the button accordion, was its crown prince. Like Chenier, Dopsie was devoted to preserving the old French songs that form the basis of zydeco. He was born Alton Rubin in Carencro, LA, a small town near Lafayette. He spent much of his childhood picking cotton and working in the cane fields. His father played accordion and performed at local weekend house parties. He frequently brought young Rubin along. His father gave him his first small accordion when Rubin was 14. He then told his son that he must teach himself. A lefty, Rubin played the accordion upside down, learning tunes off the radio. It didn't take long before he began playing parties and gaining a reputation as an even better musician than his father. Alton eventually moved to Lafayette and began performing in blues clubs in the '50s with his cousin Chester Zeno on washboard. During the day, Rubin worked as a hod carrier. He took his stage name from a Chicago dancer who had come to perform in Lafayette. Like his namesake Doopsie, Rubin also had a reputation as an excellent hoofer. Later the accordion player was given the name Rockin' to describe his lively playing. Over the years, Rockin' Dopsie performed zydeco in clubs and, despite Chenier's advice, continued working day jobs, eventually becoming an electrical contractor.

Through the '50s and '60s, Dopsie occasionally recorded with independent labels. He recorded his debut album with Sam Charters for Sweden's Sonet label. Over the next decade Dopsie recorded five more albums for the label. He began touring Europe twice annually in 1979. It wasn't until well into the '80s that Dopsie's music began garnering attention back home. His US career got a big boost in 1985 when he recorded "That Was Your Mother" with Paul Simon on the latter's landmark *Graceland* album. Later Dopsie would also record with other pop singers, including Cyndi Lauper and Bob Dylan. He has also done television commercials and appeared in a few films, including *Delta Heat*. He continued performing and recording until his death in 1993. His son David Rubin has become a noted metal washboard player, and his other son, Alton Rubin, Jr., is a drummer. Both sons performed in their father's band. —*Sandra Brennan*

Big Bad Zydeco / 1988 / GNP ✦✦✦✦
Hot Louisiana R&B/zydeco from one of its most popular modern practitioners. —*Hank Davis*

Good Rockin' / 1988 / GNP ✦✦✦
Upbeat and spirited zydeco. —*Hank Davis*

● **Louisiana Music** / 1991 / Atlantic ✦✦✦✦
The jumping Atlantic debut by Rockin' Dopsie and the Zydeco Twisters has a killer dance blend of rootsy zydeco full of grit, funk, and soul with pedal-to-the-metal rhythms. Tunes include "I'm in the Mood," "Keep a Knockin'," "The Things I Used to Do," "Zydeco Two Step," and six others. —*Roundup Newsletter*

Rockin' Sidney

b. 1938
Organ, Guitar, Harmonica, Accordion / Soul, Cajun, Zydeco
Sidney Simien began playing guitar and harmonica before discovering accordion. (He also played organ in Lake Charles lounges.) He cut his first demo in 1958 and worked the zydeco circuit in Louisiana and Texas before the unlikely 1985 success of "My Toot Toot" (a term of endearment, "my special one") made Rockin' Sidney a star and "Toot Toot" a Grammy winner and the first zydeco record to get extensive pop, rock, and country air play. —*Mark A. Humphrey*

● **My Toot Toot** / 1986 / Maison de Soul ✦✦✦
Rockin' Sidney had the biggest zydeco release of all time—"My Toot Toot"—and it has enjoyed many subsequent covers. Some of this release is unfortunately unacceptable, as it includes updated covers, but he rises above it most of the time. —*Jeff Hannusch*

Roddie Romero

Accordion, Vocals / Cajun
This zydeco-Cajun accordionist's first effort, *The New Kid in Town*, was produced by Rick Lagneaux, the keyboardist with the Wayne Toups Band. Romero was nominated as the Best New and Upcoming Act by the Cajun French Music Association. —*Liz Opoka*

● **New Kid in Town** / Swallow ✦✦✦✦
Much of this music sounds alike, but Romero's definitely one to watch. —*Jeff Hannusch*

Marc Savoy

b. 1940
Accordion / Cajun
Savoy labels himself a "crusader" for Cajun culture and, as such, is ranked at the top of the revivalists who followed the Balfa Brothers' example and championed pure Cajun music. Savoy's dedication to the music includes building Cajun accordions at his workshop in Eunice, LA, as well as playing the music and discussing its background at festivals around the world. He and his wife Ann (singer and guitarist with the Savoy-Doucet Cajun Band and author of the excellent *Cajun Music: A Reflection of a People*) were the subject of Les Blank's PBS documentary, *Marc and Ann*. In September 1992 Savoy received the prestigious Heritage Award from the National Endowment for the Arts. —*Mark A. Humphrey*

Oh What a Night / 1988 / Arhoolie ✦✦✦✦
This album's excellent dance music proves that not only is Savoy an accomplished accordion maker, he can play one, too. —*Jeff Hannusch*

Savoy-Doucet Cajun Band

Fiddle, Guitar, Accordion / Cajun
The Savoy-Doucet Cajun Band is a group with not one, but two missions: to play outstanding music, and to keep Cajun free of external influences. With its peerless lineup, it succeeds well in both respects. Savoy is not only one of the nation's leading accordionists, he is also a master craftsman and makes the instruments he plays. Doucet, when not fronting for the popular group Beausoleil, plays fiddle, while Savoy's wife, Ann, plays guitar. —*Leon Jackson*

Two Step d'Amadé / Arhoolie ✦✦✦✦
This is the kind of acoustic music you used to hear only at Cajun houseparties. Very spirited and a timepiece, it's a glorious tribute to Cajun pioneer Amédée Ardoin. —*Jeff Hannusch*

● **Live!** / Arhoolie ✦✦✦✦
Any album featuring Michael Doucet's fiddle playing is a treat. But here in the bare-bones company of Marc Savoy on accordion, Anne Savoy on acoustic guitar and vocals, and string bassist Billy Wilson on seven tracks performing live before enthusiastic dancers, we get a slice of the real thing without the commerical studio overlay. Featuring 18 tracks that total more than76 minutes' running time, this one's a delightful toe-tapper every note of the way. —*Cub Koda*

Terrance Simien

Accordion, Vocals / Cajun, Zydeco
Terrance Simien and his band, the Mallet Playboys, have built upon the

legacy of the late Clifton Chenier. Simien has worked with Paul Simon and has co-written and performed a song with actor Dennis Quaid for the film *The Big Easy*. *Billboard* magazine rated Simien and the Mallet Playboys as one of the top 10 performance acts of 1987. —*Liz Opoka*

Zydeco on the Bayou / 1992 / Restless ✦✦✦✦
A modern zydeco artist whose songs aren't yet in an essential category. More rock than zydeco, but lots of energy nonetheless. —*Ron Wynn and Jeff Hannusch*

Jo-El Sonnier

b. 1946
Guitar, Accordion, Vocals / Country, Progressive Country, Cajun
In the late '80s, when the folks in Nashville realized country consisted of more than the Tennessee-Texas axis, they started looking for new sounds. One of the best was that of Cajun accordionist Jo-El Sonnier, who had kicked around for a number of years, gaining a reputation as a "musician's musician." Sonnier initially caused a major fuss in Nashville and a minor one elsewhere, though his songs—a blend of Cajun music, twangy guitars, and New Orleans R&B—briefly added a touch of spice to country radio.
Sonnier was born the son of French-speaking sharecroppers near Rayne, LA. He was raised in extreme poverty, often attending school barefoot and with a rope holding up his pants. Many of his early years he went go to the cotton fields with his parents. Music was an early joy for Sonnier, who began playing his much older brother's battered accordion at age three. He began performing on the radio when he was six. He then began playing Cajun music in local clubs, making his recording debut at age 13. He remained a local sensation through his mid-'20s occasionally recording for regional labels. He moved to California to try for a solo career but ended up doing session work. He moved to Nashville in the mid-'70s and continued playing backup and writing songs. After six years he had yet to become popular and returned to Louisiana so bitterly disappointed that he almost stopped playing. It was Merle Haggard who gave Sonnier his badly needed break when he hired him to work as his opening act on a few road shows.
In 1982 Sonnier and his wife went back to California where, thanks to the help of friends, including guitarist Albert Lee, he began putting on solo shows in Los Angeles. He recorded *Cajun Life* for Rounder in 1984 and that year garnered his first Grammy nomination. In 1987 he signed with RCA and, though encouraged to continue recording pure Cajun material, began exploring country, rock, and pop influenced music. The result was *Come on Joe* (1988), an acclaimed album that contained several Top 20 country hits, including "Tear Stained Letter." He signed to Capitol-Nashville in the early '90s. Though few would dispute his expertise and versatility on the accordion, for some reason, Sonnier's career has not taken off. —*Brian Mansfield and Sandra Brennan*

Cajun Life / 1975 / Rounder ✦✦✦
Jo-El Sonnier, like Jimmy C. Newman, has found a comfortable middle ground between traditional Cajun and contemporary country music, working both styles and achieving a measure of commercial and aesthetic success in each. This session accents the Cajun side, although it includes competent pop/country material as well. Besides the autobiographical title track, Sonnier demonstrates his roots facilty on "Yes Yeux Bleu," "Jolie Blon," and "Les Grands Bois." Sonnier has gone on to become a bigger name in country, but this earlier date will appeal to both lovers of vintage material and those unaware of his solid Cajun skills and background. —*Ron Wynn*

● **Come on Joe** / 1987 / RCA ✦✦✦✦
Sonnier's French-Cajun accent brings new life to songs by Randy Newman, Richard Thompson, Moon Martin, and Dave Alvin. Steve Winwood takes an organ solo on a cover of Slim Harpo's "Raining in My Heart." Cajun-tinged contemporary country with a rock edge and intelligent songs, it is the best of Sonnier's Nashville work. —*Brian Mansfield and Mark A. Humphrey*

Have a Little Faith / 1990 / RCA ✦✦✦
The emphasis here is on ballads, as Sonnier discovers John Hiatt and delivers penetrating versions of his "Have a Little Faith" and "I'll Never Get over You." The album also includes a remake of Iry LeJeune's 1945 "Evangeline Special" and a straight-country single in "If Your Heart Should Ever Roll This Way Again." —*Brian Mansfield*

Tears of Joy / 1991 / Liberty ✦✦✦
In the Cajun/pop/country mold of his RCA albums. —*Mark A. Humphrey*

The Complete Mercury Sessions / 1992 / Mercury ✦✦✦✦
Fifteen fine '70s country songs are here, including the aching "Blue Is Not a Word." —*Mark A. Humphrey*

Rufus Thibodeaux

b. 1934
Fiddle / Cajun
Thibodeaux is the consummate Cajun fiddle session player and side-

man. He worked at Jay Miller's Crowley studios in the '50s, playing various stringed instruments on everything from blues to rockabilly and touring with Bob Wills and George Jones. But he is best known for a long association as sideman to Jimmy C. Newman. —*Mark A. Humphrey*

● **The Cajun Country Fiddle of . . .** / 1987 / La Louisianne ✦✦✦✦
This album demonstrates the emotive style of one of the premier Cajun fiddlers. —*Jeff Hannusch*

Wayne Toups

Accordion / Cajun
A native of Crowley, LA, Toups began playing accordion at age 14. Like Zachary Richard, Toups is noted for his flamboyance and rock-derived rhythms. Not high on any purist's list of faves, Toups is nonetheless a great crowd pleaser. —*Mark A. Humphrey*

★ **Zydecajun** / 1985 / Mercury ✦✦✦✦✦
When rock meets Cajun, it must be Zydecajun. —*Jeff Hannusch*

Johnnie Can't Dance / 1990 / Mercury ✦✦✦✦
Uptown zydeco. Slick, with strong rock and Western-swing elements, and a touch of swamp-pop as well. —*Hank Davis*

Zydeco Force

A good contemporary zydeco band led by bassist Robby Mann Robinson. The group began performing in 1987, and combines jazz, blues, and R&B influences in their performances of zydeco originals and French classics. —*Ron Wynn*

Zydeco Push / 1993 / Maison de Soul ✦✦✦
Zydeco Force is caught between trying to extend their popularity with pop covers and then verifying their credentials doing Clifton Chenier's "I'm on the Wonder" and Lightnin' Hopkins' "12-String Boogie." As a result, an air of confusion reigns, and they seldom sound either comfortable or creditable. —*Ron Wynn*

Various Artists

☆ **Alligator Stomp, Vol. 1** / 1990 / Rhino ✦✦✦✦✦
Alligator Stomp is a stellar collection of zydeco, featuring stars and lesser-known musicians. The disc is filled with great, rollicking music—there simply isn't a weak moment on the disc, and it provides an excellent introduction to one of America's most distinctive musics. —*Stephen Thomas Erlewine*

Cajun & Zydeco Classics / Jun. 18, 1996 / Rhino ✦✦✦✦✦
Cajun & Zydeco Classics is an excellent budget-line sampler of some of the biggest names in contemporary cajun music, including Buckwheat Zydeco, Rockin' Sidney, Boozoo Chavis, Beausoleil, and Queen Ida. Although the disc is brief, there are no weak tracks on the compilation and it offers a terrific introduction to the musical genre. —*Stephen Thomas Erlewine*

Cajun Music 1928-1941 / Country Music Foundation ✦✦✦
Containing 25 historic tracks, some of which are extremely rare, it includes such artists as Leo Soileau, Nathan Abshire, Rayne-Bo Ramblers, Joseph Falcon, and many other legends in Cajun music. The album has been digitally remastered and comes with a booklet in English with French translation. —*AMG*

Cajun Social Music / 1987 / Smithsonian/Folkways ✦✦✦✦✦
Field recordings from various Cajun groups, they were recorded in the '60s. —*Jeff Hannusch*

Cajun Spice / 1989 / Rounder ✦✦✦✦✦
This is a generous (over 60 minutes) sampling of great Cajun and zydeco music from artists who have recorded for the Rounder label during the last two decades. —*Jeff Hannusch*

Le Trio Cadien / 1992 / Rounder ✦✦✦✦
When three Cajun music greats and virtuosos team, it seems inevitable that they would make a superb recording. *Le Trio Cadien* wasn't quite that magical, but it was certainly first rate. D.L. Menard's vocals and guitar work were at their usual fervent peak, while Eddie LeJeune provided some swaying, rocking accordion and poignant, moving vocals during his numbers. Ken Smith was a superior instrumentalist, taking the spotlight on "Bayou Pon Pon" and "Blues de Port Arthur." There's very little wrong with this album, and plenty that's excellent. Only the air of casual intimacy rather than charged intensity kept this from being one of those unforgettable summit meetings. Instead, it's more like a wonderful get-together. —*Ron Wynn*

☆ **Louisiana Cajun, Vol. 1 1989** / Rounder ✦✦✦✦✦
This first of two 1989 Rounder anthologies spotlighting traditional Cajun music from the mid-'60s began with a great group, the Balfa Freres. This

was among the finest and most intense of the founding Cajun bands, characterized by wonderful harmonizing, intense leads and great fiddle backing. Others on this anthology were Austin Pitre & the Evangeline Playboys, a hard-driving, upbeat unit, and the venerable Edius Nacquin, in his 70s when he cut the anthology's final four tracks and still an energetic, distinctive singer. The selections were recorded as part of several field sessions initiated by the Newport Folk Foundation from 1964 through 1967. —*Ron Wynn*

☆ **Louisiana Cajun, Vol. 2** / Rounder ✦✦✦✦✦
The second of two superb Cajun anthologies issued by Rounder in 1989 featured 13 more selections by vintage artists. Like its predecessor, the featured artists sang exclusively in French, performed waltzes, two-step tunes, quadrilles, and traditional material with a country flavor, using primarily fiddle/accordion backing. The opening five cuts spotlighted vocalist and fiddler Canray Fontenot teaming with accordion player Alphonse "Bois Sec" Ardoin. The middle section blends a modern country flavoring and looser rhythmic style, while the final cuts by Adam and Cyprien Landreneau on vocals, fiddle, and accordion are early indications of an evolving modernism and spirited Cajun sound emerging in the late '60s. All the songs on both anthologies were recorded by the Newport Folk Foundation during three field trips in the mid-'60s. —*Ron Wynn*

The Mardi Gras Indians Super Sunday Showdown / Mar. 1, 1992 / Rounder ✦✦✦✦✦
The diversified strains that comprise New Orleans "Indian" and Mardi Gras music were spotlighted on this anthology. It included vibrant instrumental contributions from the Rebirth Brass Band, spicing up classic jazz, as well as the hoodoo blues of Dr. John, the swamp boogie and soul of Champion Jack Dupree, more sophisticated but equally lowdown stylings from Willie Tee and John Mooney, and the fiery sound of such groups as Bo Dollis & the Wild Magnolias and Monk Boudreaux & the Golden Eagles. The eight songs ranged from "Shoo-Fly" to "Oops Upside Your Head" and "Meet de Boys on the Battlefront." It was a delightful session offering the best of the old and recent in New Orleans material. —*Ron Wynn*

Zydeco Blues 'n' Boogie / 1989 / Rykodisc ✦✦✦
The 13 songs here are mostly stomping pieces, although they also include some two-step and waltz pieces. It's modern material and reflects the influence of other things like blues, rock, and soul. The songs were originally done for the Lanor and Cooking Vinyl labels in 1989 and 1990, then issued to Rykodisc for this compilation. It's a good way to gauge where zydeco was at that point in '89 and '90 and where it was heading. —*Ron Wynn*

The Zydeco: Early Years, Vol. 1 / Arhoolie ✦✦✦✦✦
This exceptional collection includes some interesting early tracks from Clifton Chenier, Clarence Garlow, and Herbert Sam. —*Jeff Hannusch*

Zydeco Live!, Vol. 1 / 1989 / Rounder ✦✦✦✦✦
Contained is great material from two of South Louisiana's best zydeco artists: Boozoo Chavis and Nathan Williams & the Zydeco Cha-Chas. —*Jeff Hannusch*

Zydeco Live!, Vol. 2 / Rounder ✦✦✦
Contemporary zydeco band John Delafose and the Eunice Playboys split the bill with the more traditional Willis Prudhomme and the Zydeco Express on this 12-cut live session recorded in 1989 at Richard's Club in Lawtell, LA. Delafose's vocals and musical style include healthy infusions of steamy blues and R&B, particularly on such tracks as "I Done Got Over It" and "Gotta Find My Woman." But they didn't ignore the basic zydeco beat either, showing on "Poor Man Two Step" that they could burn in a straighter setting. Prudhomme's group played lots of waltz items, as well as a nice rendition of Boozoo Chavis' classic "Paper in My Shoe." This was surging, undiluted dance music, sung and played for audiences unafraid to express their exuberance. —*Ron Wynn*

Zydeco Shootout at El Sid O's / Oct. 1990 / Rounder ✦✦✦
Lafayette, Louisiana's major nightspot, El Sid O's, was the scene for this 13-cut anthology highlighting six of the newer bands on the zydeco circuit. The roster included Zydeco Force, with its pop-rock/blues mix interspersed within the zydeco style, the more traditional sound of Warren Cesar and Creole Zydeco Snap, Lynn August's pronounced R&B motif blended with vintage French music, and the nonstop energy of Pee Wee and the Zydeco Boll Weevils. With no song longer than five minutes and groups alternating performances, the anthology provided room for comparisons and showed which bands (Cesar, the Weevils, Jude Taylor and the Burning Plants) were the most entertaining among those working the zydeco halls during the early '90s. —*Ron Wynn*

WORLD

Any book with a single chapter on "world music" runs straight into a very basic problem. You can tell it like it really is, from the perspective of the proverbial "musical Martian," giving a balanced picture of styles (99 percent of which are totally unknown to Americans,) or you can wildly distort reality and produce something your public can relate to. The latter course is the only reasonable one in a book like this, but the result is a little like a supermarket with three shelves: "soup," "pretzels," and "everything else."

Even if you simply divide the world into the West and the Rest, ignoring the fact that a good deal of Western music ends up in the World category, we're looking at one chapter devoted to at least 85 percent of the world's music. There is obscure stuff, of course — like Chinese music, which is relevant to a mere one-fifth of the world's population (a bit more than that, if you count the millions of overseas Chinese). Or Indian music, with not one but two major classical traditions, three "universal" religions, and many more regional ones. And Latin America has 33 nations, two major languages, and styles that have transformed the whole rhythmic basis of popular music in the United States. And if international influence rather than numbers is the issue, there's Cuba: an island of ten and a half million people whose sounds beat out the US for enduring influence on other cultures.

Just as no chapter (and no book and no ten-volume series) can really offer more than a drop in the ocean of world music, there's no way I can pretend to sum things up in a few hundred words. Instead I've decided to point out a few hidden confusions and traps in the American (and therefore this chapter's) concept of the subject.

The most important of these is the major difference between what I like to call "other people's music" and the intercultural experiments of Western musicians, whether it's Yehudi Menuhin playing with Ravi Shankar, Art Blakey playing with Solomon Ilori, or Annababoula mixing various Middle Eastern styles with various Western idioms. Though these mixes have recently come to be called "world beat," they're really Western styles with non-Western elements, just as willow-pattern Delft china was Dutch plates with Chinese motifs.

This would be a lot more obvious if almost every music in the world didn't stem from a mix of other music, very frequently from different cultures. There may be a couple of Amazonian nose-flute players and a didgeridoo virtuoso in central Australia who was never influenced from outside, but that really isn't the way most music works, and the richest cultures are usually the most mixed (United States, Balkans, Latin America, India). On this level, pretty much all music is crossover music.

"Other people's music" is in fact most of the music that exists. This would be more obvious if the US weren't so large, so geographically isolated, and so musically deprived. I know somebody who did a survey of recordings on sale in an open-air market in Abidjan, the capital of Ivory Coast. There were local recordings. There were recordings from other African countries. There was soul. There was jazz. There was French pop. There was the Beatles. There was US country music (lots of it, though stressing Jim Reeves). There was New York salsa. There were several kinds of Cuban music. There was more, which I've forgotten. All of this in a stall next to a woman selling yams. I defy anybody to find an equivalent range of music in your average US mall.

We also tend to overestimate our influence on the rest of the world. So it comes as a bit of a surprise to learn that, while the rest of the world has consumed US music quite freely for the last half century, Cuba and Argentina have been overwhelmingly more influential internationally over the last 75 years or so. Over the long term, the powerhouse has been the Middle East, which gave both Asia and the West most of their musical instruments.

One reason for listening to "world music" is because it's most of the music there is. The second reason—and most important—is because it's enriching beyond belief. World beat can be nifty, but the real thing can strike like lightning—it can raise the hair on the nape of your neck. It wasn't some worldbeat recording (or Xavier Cugat) that really launched the Latin takeover in the US in 1930; it was a recording of "The Peanut Vendor" by a genuine Cuban band. And the same is true for individuals. I've known people whose entire lives have been changed by the revelation of Cuban or Indian music (or, in my case, calypso-and-blues-and-flamenco-and-Arabic music all at once). So, welcome to "other people's music" in all its many-splendored glory. — *John Storm Roberts*

WORLDBEAT

Mickey Hart

b. Sep. 11, 1943
Drums / Ethnic Fusion, Worldbeat
Mickey Hart is a drummer, an ethnomusicologist, and an author. He joined the Grateful Dead as its second percussionist in 1967. In 1970, Hart left the Dead and cut the solo album *Rolling Thunder* in 1972, featuring various members of the Dead. Hart returned to the band in 1974.

Hart's musical activities outside the Dead have been extensive. In 1976, the Dead's Round Records label released *Diga* by the Diga Rhythm Band, an early experiment in worldbeat fusion put together by Hart. His interaction with drummers from around the world sparked an abiding interest in the role of the drum in other cultures—and a steadily expanding curiosity about non-Western musics. 1979 and 1980 saw the release of two albums of music from the film *Apocalypse Now*, much of it contributed by Hart. In 1983, Hart released albums under the heading *The World*. These began with a reissue of *Diga Rhythm Band* (an album by Babatunde Olatunji produced by Hart). Then came a series of albums of music Hart had recorded around the world. In 1989 Hart released *Music to Be Born By*, an album based on the heartbeat of his son in the womb,

and 1990 saw the simultaneous release of Hart's first book, *Drumming at the Edge of Magic*, and an album, *At the Edge*. In 1991, another book and disc, both called *Planet Drum*, appeared. Both albums made the upper reaches of the new age and world music charts. — *William Ruhlmann & Bob Tarte*

Rolling Thunder / 1972 / Grateful Dead ◆◆◆
This is the nearest thing to a conventional pop-rock album Mickey Hart ever made. It features Grateful Dead members Bob Weir, Jerry Garcia, and Phil Lesh, as well as other San Francisco rock musicians, and contains early versions of the Dead songs "Playing in the Band" and "Greatest Story Ever Told." — *William Ruhlmann*

Däfos / 1983 / Rykodisc ◆◆◆◆
An established audiophile classic for its thrilling, nearly overpowering sonics, this percussion-based journey to a mythical country features Brazilian percussionist Airto Moreira and vocalist Flora Purim. — *Bob Tarte*

Music to Be Born By / 1989 / Rykodisc ◆◆◆
Hart plays off the sound of a pre-natal heartbeat to create a soothing ambient recording. — *William Ruhlmann*

At the Edge / 1990 / Rykodisc ◆◆◆
Sounds like we're at the edge of the rainforest on this atmospheric recording that uses a variety of unusual instruments and employs such

musicians as Jerry Garcia, Babatunde Olatunji, Airto Moreira, and Zakir Hussain. — *William Ruhlmann & Bob Tarte*

★ **Planet Drum** / Dec. 1991 / Rykodisc ◆◆◆◆◆
A dazzling all-percussion workout with plenty of muscle and deep grooves, it features many of the world musicians from *At the Edge*, and is loosely tied to Hart's book of the same name. — *Bob Tarte*

Mickey Hart's Mystery Box / Jun. 1996 / Rykodisc ◆◆◆◆
With *Mickey Hart's Mystery Box*, the former Grateful Dead drummer no longer makes worldbeat that is academic and theoretical in its approach. Instead, he shapes his rhythms and drones into actual pop songs, complete with identifiable hooks and melodies. It manages to not alienate world music while it appeals to a whole new set of listeners, which is quite a difficult trick to pull off, indeed. — *Thom Owens*

Yamantaka / Celestial Harmonies ◆◆◆
This collaboration, recorded in 1982 at the Grateful Dead Studios, combined Hart with the composers and performers of the *Tibetan Bells* series. Since *Yamantaka* is the Tibetan god of the dead and lord of the underworld, you might guess that the tone of this release is dark and otherworldly, with music played on unusual and invented percussive instruments that seem to build and appear almost from out of nowhere. — *Backroads Music/Heartbeats*

Mouth Music

Worldbeat

● **Mouth Music** / Jan. 18, 1991 / Rykodisc ◆◆◆◆
This intriguing blend of puirt a beul (traditional Gaelic vocal music intended for dancing) has African and other drumming styles plus the requisite drum machine and synths, resulting in the world's first Irishroots house music. — *Bob Tarte*

Mo-Di / 1993 / Rykodisc ◆◆◆
Mouth Music got their first CD across on the strength of an unlikely conceit, the bouncy marriage of Celtic and African music. Even though half that disc was sequenced instrumental filler, the tracks that worked forced one to rethink the relationship to the reel. But this time around, the yawning synth quotient is boosted at the expense of the unexpected, and innovative genre splicing is abandoned in favor of generic dance tunes with occasional Gaelic lyrics and a few broad Africanisms. — *Bob Tarte*

Shorelife / 1995 / Rykodisc ◆◆◆◆
Percussion, synthesizer and some torchy and spicy voices cast *Shorelife* by Mouth Music as the pop sound for the 21st century. The future is Mouth Music, and the sound is a compelling techno-pop-funk. The vocals, sometimes Enya-like, spin words of silken threads over the sharpedged, post-industrial, dance club music, creating a harmony of man and machine. This is entrancing music that will bring you up and get you dancing. — *MusD*

Outback

Worldbeat
Outback's ebullient, accessible, yet highly irregular style could be described as "tribal new-acoustic." The group is anchored by two multi-instrumentalists, Graham Wiggins and Martin Craddick, who in 1988 met by chance in Oxford and began playing as a duo all over England. A former jazz pianist, Wiggins taught himself to play the didgeridoo (sometimes spelled *didjeridu*), an Australian aboriginal wind instrument made of a hollowed-out wooden tube. Through the use of various techniques (including circular breathing), the instrument produces an earthy, gritty, and at times almost electronic sound. Curiously enough, Wiggins' didgeridoo takes on a folksy quality similar to the resonant twang of a mouth harp when combined with Craddick's acoustic guitar and mandolin strummings. After the success of their first international release *Baka*, the two refined and expanded upon this unusual sound by adding the talents of Sagar N'Gom on West African percussion and Ian Campbell on drums. Outback's latest release, *Dance the Devil Away*, also features French fiddle player Paddy LeMercier. — *Linda Kohanov*

● **Baka** / 1990 / Hannibal ◆◆◆◆
Acoustic guitarist Martin Craddick makes a strong team with Graham Wiggins, whose axe of choice is the Australian aboriginal instrument, the didjeridu. Wiggins' unorthodox techniques on this instrument—which generate percussive patterns as well as animal barks—finds their equal in Craddick's narrative instrumental style. — *Bob Tarte*

Dance the Devil Away / 1991 / Hannibal ◆◆◆
An expanded Outback adds violin, synthesizer, and all sorts of drums to the mix, giving this album a more complete sound. The percussion and acoustic guitar form a nice wall of sound with Wiggins' didgeridoo slicing out and hypnotizing the listener. — *Bob Tarte & Chip Renner*

3 Mustaphas 3

Worldbeat
The 3 Mustaphas 3 pratfell onto the burgeoning worldbeat scene from out of nowhere in 1986—or from Szegerely, somewhere in the Balkans, if you believe their press releases. According to Mustapha mythology, the Balkan Beat Boys first sharpened their musical teeth at the Crazy Loquat Club under the guidance of Uncle Patrel Mustapha Bin Mustapha. Then, seeking broader horizons, they stole away one night, accompanied by their favorite refrigeration equipment, to seek world success from a UK base. The Mustaphas' humor has been a double-edged scimitar, however. In the beginning it allowed them to introduce difficult music to unsuspecting audiences new to the worldbeat sound. But the burlesque that initially forwarded their agenda also worked against them by threatening to consign the group to the purgatory of novelty act. An increasing emphasis on solid musicianship, plus their collaboration with revered African performers like Stella Chiweshe, have begun to win the band the critical respect they deserve. And no one else makes a crash course in world music so much fun. — *Bob Tarte*

Shopping / 1987 / Shanachie ◆◆◆
Egyptian film music is a major influence here in the fezsters' first fulllength release. But don't miss the hilarious Mustaphas rap tune "Fiz'n" or the terrific cover of Moroccan artist Najat Atabou's searing "Shouffi Rhirou." — *Bob Tarte*

Heart of Uncle / 1989 / Rykodisc ◆◆◆◆
A convincing tour of world-capital backstreets, it features crisp arrangements of an Indian film-music classic ("Awara Hoon") plus forays into taarab, benga, klezmer, merengue, Bulgarian vocal music, and more. — *Bob Tarte*

★ **Soup of the Century** / 1990 / Rykodisc ◆◆◆◆◆
Stung by allegations that they're nothing but a "joke band," the Mustaphas cook up their hardest set yet, recorded live in the studio with minimal overdubbing. Look for mind-boggling genre fusions plus molten clarinet and electric bazouki breakouts. — *Bob Tarte*

Friends, Fiends & Fronds / 1991 / Omnium ◆◆◆◆
A portrait of the artists as an evolving concept is presented in this collection of singles, B-sides, and remixes. It is worth its weight in premium goat's cheese for the two versions of their masterpiece "Linda Linda" and a pair of brand new songs. — *Bob Tarte*

Yothu Yindi

Guitar, Drums, Keyboards, Didjeridu / Ambient, Worldbeat, Aboriginal, World General
Yothu Yindi are a fusion group in every sense of the word. This multiracial Australian band (the name means Mother Child) blends native and white sounds and sentiments. Yothu Yindi were founded in 1986, the year of Australia's bicentennial, and from that time until now they have practiced a highly politicized and nationalistic form of music making. Drawing from sounds as diverse as the didgeridoo and the electric guitar, and finding great thematic inspiration in Bob Marley, Yothu Yindi sing for cultural harmony and aboriginal integrity. Their albums include *Homeland Movement, Tribal Voice* (1992), and *Freedom* (1993). — *Leon Jackson*

Tribal Voice / 1992 / Hollywood ◆◆◆◆◆
● **Freedom** / 1994 / Hollywood ◆◆◆◆◆

Zap Mama

Zap Mama is an all-female a cappella quintet founded by Zaire native Marie Daulne. Daulne's father, a white Belgian, was killed during the revolution of 1960 while her mother was pregnant with her, so the remainder of the family fled to the forests and found refuge with a tribe of pygmies. Daulne was raised primarily in Europe, but when she heard a recording of traditional pygmy music at age 20, she decided to return to Africa to learn about her heritage. She was trained in pygmy onomatopoeic vocal techniques before returning to the West to found Zap Mama. Her group blends world music styles from all over the globe with little, if any, instrumental or percussive backup other than what group members can do with their voices and bodies. Their 1993 debut, *Adventures in Afropea I*, became the biggest-selling non-compilation album in the history of Luaka Bop Records, helped in part by an opening slot on that summer's 10,000 Maniacs tour. A year later, they released a follow-up, *Sabsylma*. — *Steve Huey*

● **Adventures In Afropea 1** / 1993 / Warner Bros. ◆◆◆◆
Warner Brothers presents this exciting, innovative, dynamic group of five women from Brussels. They are new to the States, but already extremely well-received in Europe. Led by Marie Daulne, they weave their polyphonic, polyrhythmic harmonies displaying the strength and brilliance of unaccompanied voices. The songs, inspired by traditional African and European melodies, celebrate the richness and diversity of these cultures. The album incorporates Central African Pygmy chants and their unique yodels and clicks, the ululating sounds of a Syrian harem, and anti-apartheid chants, as well as songs from Zaire, Tanzania, France, and Spain. — *MusD*

Worldbeat Collection

Anthology of Chant / 1995 / Celestial Harmonies ✦✦✦✦✦
In recent years, the popularity of Les Mysteres Des Voix Bulgares and, more particularly, the Benedictine Monks has brought devotional chanting to a mass audience. *Anthology of Chant* doesn't have enough marketing muscle behind it to match the sales figures of the aforementioned artists. But the artists assembled for the collection will certainly appeal to anyone who got their first taste of the music through the more famous Bulgarian or Spanish ensembles. The diversity here would certainly be hard to match, including chants by Tibetan monks, Armenian and European choirs, a Native American peace pipe prayer, a Turkish ney flautist, and a security guard at the Taj Mahal. All of the pieces share qualities that are both soothing and inspirational. —*Richie Unterberger*

Native Wisdom: World Music of the Spirit / Feb. 27, 1996 / Narada ✦✦✦
This double disc set collects music from all over the globe in an attempt to offer an introduction to world music. Though any effort like this is bound to be incomplete, the album does indeed offer an effective introduction to broad array of musics. Neophyte listeners would be well-served by the collection, since it lets them sample a variety of styles. —*Stephen Thomas Erlewine*

Africa Fete '94 / 1994 / Mango ✦✦✦
The latest songs and styles from Africa and the Caribbean are on display via this eight-track anthology, with tracks culled from recent Mango albums. Baaba Maal's "Hamady Bogle" is one of several recent compositions capitalizing on the "bogle" dance sensation, while Haiti's prime group, Boukman Eksperyans, are represented with two numbers, "Tande M Tande" and "Kouman Sa Ta Ye," that accent their contemporary sound. Benin's Angelique Kidjo and Senegal's Ismael Lo complete the set, which should inspire anyone within earshot to attend an actual Africa Fete festival performance. —*Ron Wynn*

Diga Rhythm Band / 1976 / Grateful Dead ✦✦✦✦
Grateful Dead drummer Mickey Hart has long been a proponent of student of world music. He produced this 1976 all-percussion outing, which is a compelling and powerful recording that draws in the listener with its spellbinding rhythms. —*Jeff Tamarkin*

Global Dance Music Experience / 1994 / SBK ✦✦✦
Dance music in the '90s has gotten faster and more diverse and has both gone underground and infiltrated the mainstream. This 11-cut anthology spotlights pop, rap, and club stars, featuring tracks performed in the fashion that clicked with dance audiences—lengthy, remixed, and highly produced. Some are basic soul-R&B or gospel-influenced vocals placed into a dance production; others are strictly dance-club tracks, with the beats and arrangement as important, if not more so, than the vocal. Jon Secada's "Just Another Day" is a pop cut remixed for clubs, and Guru's "Trust Me" with N'Dea Davenport sounds like a new song in its "Mackintosh club mix." —*Ron Wynn*

Global Meditation / Relaxation Company ✦✦✦✦✦
This splendid set of four CDs is also available individually. Because of careful editing, each piece flows perfectly into the next. The best are the uplifting trance of "A Habibi Ouajee Tallel Allaiya" by the Master Musicians of Jajouka in the *Harmony and Interplay* CD, the spirited, almost R&B Japanese Buddhist chant "Hannya-Shingyo" from Kyoto, and the pleading soulfulness of the Norwegian song "Heiemo Og Nykkjen" in the *Voices of the Spirit* CD, the mysterious shamanic drumming on the Irish bodhran by Glen Velez, and the fascinating recombining of rhythms and melodies in the Santeria ceremony "Yemaya," its power descending from the blue of the sea in *The Pulse of Life* CD, and the strangeness of the droning "A Cool Wind Is Blowing" played on the Armenian duduk, an oboe made from apricot wood in the *Music from the Heart* CD. —*"Blue" Gene Tyranny*

Manifestation: Axiom Collection II / 1993 / PolyGram ✦✦✦
The second compilation of Axiom artists showboats the label's aggressive aggregate of traditional formats and urban innovation, including a mind-bending "Tarab Dub" transmuted from Nicky Skopelitis' *Ekstasis*, the "Kora in Hell Mix" of a cut by Foday Musa Suso's griot dance band Mandingo, plus reality shifts by Material, Praxis, the Master Musicians of Jajouka, Bahia Black, and Turkish saz-ist Talip Ozkan. Redeeming *Manifestation* from the particularly painful rung of Purgatory reserved for ambitious anthologists is the fact that many musicians guest on one another's compositions, resulting in a big fat holistic ambience bolstered by Bill Laswell's genre-straddling bottomless pit production. This is the sound of psychedelia to come. —*Bob Tarte*

☆ **Passion Sources** / Jan. 29, 1993 / Real World ✦✦✦✦✦
A superb sampler of passionate world music on Peter Gabriel's Real World label concentrates on Asia and Africa. —*Myles Boisen*

World Beat Explosion / 1988 / Shanachie ✦✦✦
Rai, South African reggae, and Arabic music are among the idioms presented on this 1988 sampler, which contained eight songs and spot-lighted artists then slowly building audiences. Since its release, 3 Mustaphas 3 and Ofra Haza have become more widely known, while Dissidenten and Ashwin Batish have also gained more European fans, and Alpha Blondy has become arguably reggae's most popular African artist. The songs were pulled from various Shanachie albums and remain available on those discs as well as this anthology. —*Ron Wynn*

AFRICA

Angelique Kidjo

Vocals / Worldbeat, Africa, Afro Pop
Angelique Kidjo is the spitfire of African pop. Though many critics and African music aficionados disdain the Benin-born artist's slickly-produced sound, a funky blend of electronic dance music, native Benin rhythms, and a touch of voodoo (she is both an animist and a Catholic), as too commercial and westernized, the iconoclastic, feminist-oriented, and thoroughly modern Kidjo refuses to alter her style to suit them, and has become a crossover success on the world music scene, finding popularity in many American dancehalls with such songs as "Batonga" and "We-We" from her 1991 album *Logozo* (produced by Galdo of Miami Sound Machine fame for Mango).

She was born, one of nine children, in Ouidah village. Her father is a musician; while her mother, a clothing merchant, was the director and producer of a large African ballet troupe. Kidjo got her start dancing and singing at age six. One of her older brothers had his own band and introduced her to late '60s pop artists such as the Stones, the Beatles, Hendrix, Santana, James Brown, and Aretha Franklin. Kidjo herself has eclectic taste in music and listens to everything from jazz to rock to Arabic to Pakistani music. As a girl, she would sing church music, but then at age 15 began singing pop tunes. Following the tragic death of 17-year old Togoan singer Bella Bellow in 1973, Kidjo wrote her first song as a tribute. While still in high school, she began playing in Sphinx, a local band that became quite popular and won several contests.

In 1980, Kidjo followed the advice of Cameroonian composer Ekambi Brillant, and moved to Paris. While there, she enrolled in music school where she received formal training in classical, French song, and jazz. She then studied under jazz singer Joy Kane for two years. This jazz training has had great effect on Kidjo's singing; with her low, powerful voice, her rhythm and precision. In 1984, she joined a Radio France tour and visited different West African countries, returning afterward to wax a second album in Holland. In 1989, Kidjo opened for her idol, Miriam Makeba, in South Africa. Soon after recording a third album in Paris, Kidjo came to the attention of Island Records helmer Chris Blackwell. She signed to the label and began recording her breakthrough album, *Logozo*, with Galdo. It is a distinguished album featuring such world-renowned jazz and fusion artists as Beninois keyboardist Wall Badarou, Zairian guitarist Ray Lema, Galdo on percussion, and a guest appearance by Branford Marsalis. Her next album, *Aye*, was produced by pop producer David Z who has worked with such artists as Prince and Jody Watley. Though she is fluent in eight languages including English, French, German, Nago, Yoruba, and Swahili, she prefers to record in her native Fon, saying that she is more interested in evoking emotion from her listeners through the strong natural rhythms of the language. Translations appear in the liner notes for those interested in the content of the songs. —*Sandra Brennan*

● **Logozo** / 1991 / Mango ✦✦✦✦✦
State-of-the-art production and mainstreamed African dance beats are poised to propel this talented singer from Benin to international pop stardom. Branford Marsalis, Ray Lema, and Manu Dibango contribute. —*Bob Tarte*

Aye / 1994 / Mango ✦✦✦
Angelique Kidjo has alienated some musicians and fans who want her to do traditional African music rather than mix and match her slashing delivery with rock, R&B, and pop elements and arrangements. But Kidjo doesn't want to do a strictly African date. She recorded five numbers at Paisley Park studios, and they reflect the punchy guitar and synth-dominated Minneapolis sound. The other five tunes were recorded in London, with both a dance-soul flavor and nice horn backing and arrangements. Kidjo hasn't done a sellout album, despite singing in English on some cuts (another move designed to anger some of the hardcore). Rather, she's trying to link all her interests and do a respectable pop effort with some African elements. —*Ron Wynn*

Africa Collection

Juju Roots / 1994 / Rounder ✦✦✦
This anthology covers the foundation sounds that blossomed into the ultra-sophisticated, highly electric juju style that became an international sensation in the '80s. The earlier styles were less intricate and more singular in their performance modes, as documented by the 16 tracks here. They illustrate the influence of guitar-band highlife and

show how palmwine artists, whose songs were backed by listeners striking bottles, cigarette tins, or palmwine calabashes with nails or knives, were juju's forerunners. The genre was also influenced by American and European musical styles, such as country, Hawaiian guitar bands, and British ballroom dance orchestras. The disc's sound quality and extensive liner notes are also a plus for another of Rounder's masterful international music anthologies. —*Ron Wynn*

Out of Africa / 1988 / Rykodisc ✦✦✦✦✦
A good continental selection, it includes Senegal's Youssou N'Dour, South Africa's Mahotella Queens, Nigeria's juju master Ebenezer Obey, and Rochereau. —*J. Poet*

Algeria

Chaba Fadela (Fadela Zalmat)

Vocals / Ethnic, World-Arab, Rai, Algeria, Africa
Chaba Fadela grew up in a squalid Oran neighborhood near the city's theater and early on made it her goal in life to perform on stage. She made a name for herself as both as an actress (scandalizing Algeria with her television portrayal of a loose woman in the film *Djalti*) and as a rai performer (scandalizing Algeria with her upbeat, synthesized songs of love and passion). Her 1979 single, "Ana Ma M'lali Ennoum" (I Don't Care About Sleep Any More), was a decided hit and is regarded as the quintessential pop-rai cut. Shortly thereafter she stepped out of the limelight to marry fellow rai singer, Mohamed Sahraoui, returning in 1983 to active recording as part of a wife-husband duo. In that year the couple recorded "N'Sel Fik" which was a huge hit, as was their 1990 album, *Hana Hana*. —*Leon Jackson*

Hana Hana / 1978 / Mango ✦✦✦✦✦
On this album, backed by a more modern sythesizer sound and pristine French production, the Queen and King (her husband Sahraoui is here also) of rai unite for a series of solid duets. —*Bob Tarte*

● **You Are Mine** / 1988 / Mango ✦✦✦✦✦
"N'sel Fik," by Fadela and her husband Sahraoui, is the biggest Algerian hit in the country's history. The rest of the tracks here aren't bad either. —*J. Poet*

Cheb Kader

Vocals / World-Arab, Rai, Algeria, Africa
The Elvis of rai music, Kader features a potent hybrid—emotional Arabic vocals and melodies set against contemporary rock percussion and production. —*Hank Davis*

Cheb Kader / Blue Silver ✦✦✦✦
Like both Ahmed Fakroun and Cheb Mami, Kader tends to upset rai snobs, who regard him as too poppish (as if electronic rai weren't born of such crossovers). In reality, he's good. His rhythms are a little harder and more funk-oriented than most mainstream raisters, and his backings include very effective rock guitar and gorgeous Maghrebi fiddle. —*John Storm Roberts, Original Music*

El Awama / Michel Lévy Prod. ✦✦✦
Two rai recordings from major stars, and they could hardly (within the same substyle) be more different. Kader is a young France-based whizkid whom producer Lovy found when Mami got drafted. He's an attractive singer, though a little lightweight, and his style (backings in any event) is heavily but effectively influenced by rock, reggae, and so on. Khaled and Zahouania are both superb singers, but what completes the ecstasy-quotient of this particular album is that the electronics are ditched in favor of the classic spike-fiddle and percussion. —*John Storm Roberts, Original Music*

● **From Oran to Paris** / Shanachie ✦✦✦✦✦
This odd hybrid of emotional Arabic vocals and melodies is set against contemporary rock production. —*Hank Davis*

Cheb Khaled (Khaled Brahim)

Vocals / Rai, Algeria, Africa
Cheb Khaled led the generation of rai performers who emerged in the wake of rai-pop pioneers Bellemou Messaoud and Belkacem Bouteldja. Khaled was the son of a police officer and grew up in Oran. His earliest musical influences were Umm Kalthum and Farid el-Atrache although he was also indebted to such European performers as Piaf, Aznavour, and Jacques Brel. Khaled started his performing career in the traditional way, singing at weddings and circumcisions; his big break came in 1985, when he was recognized as Algeria's official "King of Rai" at an Oran musical festival. The following year, he performed at a major musical festival in Paris. Khaled once said that his only contract was "with God," but in 1991, he signed a major recording deal with a Polygram subsidiary, Barclay. His album, *Khaled*, released in 1992, sold more 100,000 copies and included the smash hit, "Didi." His next album, *N'ssi Nssi*, of 1993 was used as the soundtrack for the movie *1-2-3 Soleil* and earned

African Music

There's no way to write coherently about the music of a continent covering 52 independent nations, between 800 and 1600 languages (depending on your definition), and at least five major cultural groupings. The confusions inherent in this kind of diversity are many, but a few stand out. Some of the confusion stems from the fact that African music has been both influential and influenced. The direct or indirect influence on new-world popular music has been varying, but all of it, "White," "Black," or "Latin," has at least a touch of Africa. And the compliment has been returned. African music has always been (and remains) essentially local, but African musicians have always drawn from elsewhere: for over a thousand years from Islam, for over a couple of hundred years from Europe, over half a century from the Americas, somewhat (and increasingly) from US African-American styles and reggae, greatly in the past from US country music, and enormously from Cuba and Latin New York.

More confusion results from the Western stereotype that associates drums with African traditional music. In reality, western Nigeria (for example) has a dozen or so 20th-century urban styles for voices and percussion alone, and at least one of these outshines in popularity all the Nigerian musicians known to the West.

There's another confusion of immediate importance to this listing of African recordings. Different circumstances have led to noticeably different levels of "Africanness" in contemporary pop styles. At the most "African" level, there's what happens when a whole culture falls in love with an overseas influence, as the Congolese did with Cuban music. Sophisticated individual bands sometimes develop styles with an abnormally high proportion of overseas influence (Fela Kuti, Manu Dibango). When expatriate musicians form bands to play the music of their homeland, as did Osibisa in London, they come under different influences and produce a different mix. Different yet again are groups combining expatriate African musicians with Europeans, like the Germano-Ghanaian "Burger-Highlife" bands in Germany. Lastly, famous musicians with a local or expatriate African audience (N'Dour, Ade, many others) have recently been trying to "cross over" internationally, with still different results.

All this tends to mislead newcomers to African music. At first, naturally enough, people tend to like music that's not too foreign, which means very American-influenced. So we latch onto individual musicians with a strong American element and assume, usually incorrectly, that Africans think as much of them as we do. The result is that Fela or Manu Dibango get described as "African superstar" when they are not by any means the superstars of their own countries and are pretty much unknown elsewhere in Africa. (In fact, the only musicians with a real pan-African appeal are the big names of soukous, and even they don't have any noticeable following in South Africa.)

All of which means that if you want to explore African music, albums by Fela or the recent big-label recordings of Youssou N'Dour make handy vehicles for starting the journey. But if that's as far as you go, you haven't even landed yet. — *John Storm Roberts*

the singer an award in France for that year's best soundtack. Always a provocative and colorful character—he drinks, smokes, and has a live-in lover—Khaled makes his home in France and tends to avoid returning to Algeria for fear of drawing fundamentalist wrath upon his family and friends. —*Leon Jackson*

● **Kutche** / 1989 / Intuition ✦✦✦✦✦
Though its heart is in the right place, even the best Algerian rai usually suffers from a less than state-of-the-art synthesizer sound. Not so here. Collaboration between Paris-based keyboard-whiz Safy Boutella and one of rai's most powerful voices sets tough standards for other discs. —*Bob Tarte*

Young Khaled / 1994 / MDE ✦✦✦
This is a reminder of what the fuss was about, before rai joined the other five-minute wonders. You can hear the reworking of tradition in the long songs with the free-rhythm openings before the percussion kicks in (even if the backing is synth and not oud) and realize where Khaled came from and where he was going before the world-beat

surfers and global-village marketeers sucked him in. —*John Storm Roberts, Original Music*

Cheb Mami

Accordion, Keyboards, Vocals / Rai, Algeria, Africa
Mami was one of the first "Chebs" to be heard in the West when rai music came out into the open in 1985-86. Known as the Prince of Rai, he presented a clean-cut, fashionable image consistent with the Paris scene, but maintained a rootsy stance on his first few recordings. —*Myles Boisen*

Prince of Rai / 1989 / Shanachie ✦✦✦
Unlike most rai, this disc features live musicians, including a wailing Arabic fiddle guaranteed to raise goose bumps. —*J. Poet*

● **Let Me Rai** / 1990 / Priority ✦✦✦✦✦
Recorded in Los Angeles using session musicians, this album is more Western, but retains enough Algerian influence to keep things interesting. It includes a couple of interesting reggae-rai fusions. —*J. Poet*

Bellemou Messaoud

Bass, Trumpet / Rai, Algeria, Africa
Bellemou Messaoud was born in 1947 in the town of Ain Temouchent. His earliest showcase was the local town brass band. In the mid-'60s, Massaoud made a musical breakthrough by taking the traditional rai instrumental lineup of the berouka, guellala, karkabou, and t'bar and adding to it the electric guitar, bass, and quarter tone trumpet to create modern pop-rai. Massaoud, who played many of these instruments himself (especially the trumpet), scandalized both the polite establishment and also more traditional rai performers, such as Cheikha Remitti, with his sounds, if not with his sentiments. In 1975, he collaborated with the other leading pop-rai pioneer, Belkacem Bouteldja, in the recording of "Ya Rayi." Several younger performers began their careers in Massaoud's band, thus leading to his being dubbed the Father of Rai. —*Leon Jackson*

● **Le Pére du Rai** / World Circuit ✦✦✦✦✦
Messaoud was not only an early pop-rai luminary but a man with the bizarre but ultimately successful notion of using a trumpet in Maghrebi music. This release, with new vocalist Cheb Ourrad Houarri, features a basically acoustic band consisting of accordion, guitar, keyboards, and rhythm. —*John Storm Roberts*

Cheikha Remitti

Vocals / Rai, Algeria, Africa
Easily the best-known and most colorful rai singer in the world, Cheikha Remitti was born Saadia in the small town of Relizane in Oranie. She was orphaned at an early age and as a young woman, made her daily bread by working as a dancer with a group of sheiks who performed rural music in the streets of Oran. She subsequently began to sing, performing husky and sensuous songs about the hard living and hard loving of the Algerian poor. Such songs were not new; indeed, they were a traditional feature of Algerian women's private wedding celebrations, but Remitti was one of the first to make the songs public and commercially viable, eschewing all the protocols of decency in singing of physical passion and lust. At first by word of mouth, Remitti's fame began to spread; she gained her name after buying her fans round after round of drinks to the call of "remettez" (fill them up) in a bar she happened upon during a rain storm. Remitti recorded her first records in 1936 and had to suffer criticism from the more orthodox of Muslims as well as the colonial French rulers and later from the Marxist government of post-Independence Algeria, although she had sung in support of the latter during their long struggle for national self-determination. Nevertheless, Remitti remained popular during her long years of active performing and recording. She enjoyed a revival of interest in the 1990s. —*Leon Jackson*

● **Ghir el Baroud** / Michel Levy ✦✦✦✦✦
This stunning new recording appears from the Bessie Smith of rai. Aside from the sheer splendor of the performance, its flute-and-percussion backing is the "missing link" between urban styles like chaabi and the electronic rai of the new generation. The emotional charge of this anti-establishment music comes with a subdued humor, but the overriding effect is of power. —*John Storm Roberts*

Algeria Collection

Algeria (Sahara) / EMI ✦✦✦
This is strong tribal music. —*David L. Mayers*

Rai in Algeria / Artistes Arabes ✦✦✦✦✦
Good stuff, it features four artists, Abdelhak and Zahouni, Mami, and Zahouania. Striking is the lead-off, a sensational cut from Cheb Mami backed by sax (terrific) and strings (innocuous) as well as the usual keyboards and percussion. The distinctly grouchy notes, by an Algerian musicologist of the older generation, are long on background but lack data on the artists. —*John Storm Roberts*

☆ **Rai Rebels** / 1988 / Earthworks ✦✦✦✦✦
Virgin's collection goes beyond the obvious rai heavies, though it includes Fadela's "N'sel Fik" yet again. Here is the great Chaba Zahouania and a particularly fine newcomer, Houari Benchenet, who gets a great deal of mileage out of mixing the older harmonium sound with his electronics—plus Sahraoui, Khaled, and Hamid. Adequate sound and rather ragged editing on this wonderful music. —*John Storm Roberts*

☆ **Rai Rebels, Vol. 2: Pop Rai & Rachid Style** / 1989 / Atlantic ✦✦✦✦✦
The anthology includes selections from Cheb Zahouzni, Cheb Khaled, Chaba Zahouania, etc. An excellent intro to the East African pop sound of rai. —*Ron Wynn*

Benga

Daniel Owino Misiani

Guitar / Benga, Africa, Kenya
D.O. Misiani, the king of Kenya's "Benga" pop music, is an energetic and varied guitarist. His band Shirati Jazz is also featured on *The Nairobi Beat* (Rounder 5030) with other important Benga groups, and it's good to see him getting his due in the world-music explosion of the '80s and '90s. —*Myles Boisen*

★ **Benga Blast** / 1990 / Atlantic ✦✦✦✦✦
Flashy Zairians get the press, but Misiani's Shirati Band skips the hyper-kinetic overkill for a straightforwardness that updates what John Storm Roberts calls the Kenyan plain-man style. This compilation of '80s material is chock full of more goodness than even the best soukous CDs. No gimmicks, no machines, no excuses for missing this.—*Carl Hoyt, Original Music*

Shirati Jazz / Globestyle ✦✦✦✦✦
The Shirati Jazz release is a really outstanding collection of the Benga heavies' early recordings, with founder Misiani. There's no date given here, but it sounds like the mid-'70s. The album consists of yet more recordings from a fine and influential band. —*John Storm Roberts*

Burundi Collection

The Master Drummers of Burundi / Arion ✦✦✦✦✦
Why do some tiny countries produce more kinds of soul-snaring music than others ten times their size? The most striking music on the Ocora recording is the eerily beautiful whispered singing that accompanies the inanga zither. But even the more common East African sounds—the delicacy of the sanza, the almost-human musical bow, the crisp acridity of the spike-fiddle—seem to reach a peak of eloquence in this moon-mountain land. The master drummers were once royal musicians and they preserve a courtly tradition that has vanished in too many African countries. —*John Storm Roberts*

Music from the Heart of Africa: Burundi / Nonesuch ✦✦✦
Music for enanga (zither) and other tribal music. —*David L. Mayers*

Cameroon

Francis Bebey

b. 1929, Douala, Cameroon
Guitar, Vocals / Neo-Traditional, Cameroon, Africa
A composer, guitarist, and novelist from Cameroon, Bebey has combined Latin American, Western (pop and classical), and African elements into his compositions. —*J. Poet*

Akwaaba: Francis Bebey / 1986 / Original Music ✦✦✦✦✦
In this 1985 release, composer/guitarist/singer/author Bebey used finger-piano, African flute, percussion and electric bass to draw on the whole range of African music today: traditional vocal styles (including an extraordinary "double-voice" technique), Ghanaian flute, soukous bass lines. A critic at the *Boston Herald* called *Akwaaba* "one of the most amazing and beautiful records I have ever heard." —*John Storm Roberts, Original Music*

Amaya / 1987 / Ozileka ✦✦✦
In a sequel to and amplification of Bebey's 1986 *Akwaaba, Amaya* uses instruments ranging from balafon and sanza to synthesizer and acoustic piano, all played by Bebey in wide pieces reworking or taking off from traditional melodies and procedures. The emotional range is wide, with cuts as deep as *Akwaaba*, and cuts charming and poppish. —*John Storm Roberts, Original Music*

● **1962-1994: Nandolo** / Original Music ✦✦✦✦✦
Francis Bebey's Pygmy flute and finger-piano recordings are as original as anything in African music, yet his gently satirical or romantic palm-wine-guitar-backed songs are permanent hits in Africa. The album is a retrospective, combining re-mastered tracks from three decades of recordings, with several cuts recorded specifically for this CD. —*John Storm Roberts, Original Music Congo (Brazzaville)*

Diblo Dibala (Lokoto)

b. 1954

Guitar / Soukous, Africa, Congo (Brazzaville)

Dibala began playing guitar when he was 12. By the time he was 15 he almost beat Franco, Zaire's top guitarist and band leader, in a guitar duel, and Franco offered Diblo a job in his band. Dibala became Zaire's top session player and arranger, playing and composing material on over 60 albums by other artists. In 1979 Kanda Bongo Man lured Diblo away from Franco; the band relocated to Paris where their success can be traced in large part to the fiery solo work he has contributed to Bongo Man's albums. In 1968 Dibala left Kanda to form Loketo with singer Aurlus Mabele. *—J. Poet*

Super Soukous / 1989 / Shanachie ✦✦✦✦✦

This was the buzz-record, only patchily available, that drew the attention of US buffs to Dibala, a sparkling guitarist. On this, his first solo recording, he was backed by zouk keyboard heavy Ronald Rubinel as well as by Loketo itself. No-frills punch is the watchword. *—John Storm Roberts*

Soukous Trouble / 1990 / Shanachie ✦✦✦

● **Extra Ball** / 1991 / Shanachie ✦✦✦✦✦

Loketo's swansong as a group is their most highly charged, hook-filled release yet, with dazzling guitar pyrotechnics from Diblo Dibala and friends. *—Bob Tarte & J. Poet*

Les Tetes Brulees

Guitar, Vocals / Africa, Bikutsi, Cameroon

Les Tetes Brulees (the name means the hot heads or the burnt heads, but implies, more pointedly, the mind-blown) are truly hard to miss in a crowd. The five-man lineup sport neatly torn t-shirts, elaborate dots-and-bars body paint over most of their skin, retro mirror shades, Afro mohawks, huge sneakers, and trademark day-glo book bags that they wear through their electrifying stage shows. The brain child of journalist turned musician Jean-Marie Ahanda, the well-named band blew the minds of many in hard-to-shock Cameroon. Les Tetes garnered international attention to match their local fame after members appeared in two documentaries: *Man No Run,* which recorded their first tour of France, and *Bikutsi Water Blues,* which featured band guitarist Zanzibar discussing the politics of water in Cameroon. Less welcome was the scrutiny turned on the band after Zanzibar died in 1989. Suggestions of murder and sorcery tainted the air for some time, but the band rallied, added a keyboard player, and have since returned to recording and touring. Beyond the body paint and scandal, Les Tetes' music is somewhat less adventurous, being composed largely of high-energy bikutsu and riff-driven randomness. What truly sets Les Tetes apart is their attempts to bring a punk mentality to a highly traditional art form. *—Leon Jackson*

★ **Hot Heads** / Apr. 1991 / Shanachie ✦✦✦✦✦

This exciting, electric "new wave" band from Cameroon is funky and punky. *—Myles Boisen*

Bikutsi Rock / 1992 / Shanachie ✦✦✦

Cameroon's "hotheads" sweeten their sound with the Mory Kante Group's horn section and multilayered vocals by Charlotte Mbango. This comes across less like African punk than like a Gold Coast funk and soukous experiment. *—Bob Tarte*

Camaroon Collection

Music of the Baka Pygmies / Auvidis ✦✦✦

This is top music from the Cameroons. There is one particular track that features young girls singing and slapping the water. *—David L. Mayers*

Congo (Brazzaville) Collection

Ba Benzele Pygmies / Barenreiter Musicaphon ✦✦✦

This is excellent, vigorous storytelling, with beautiful polyphonic singing, women singing into one-note flutes. *—David L. Mayers*

Banda Polyphony / Philips ✦✦✦

Featured are fascinating polyphonic horn, and flute, and vocal ensembles. *—David L. Mayers*

Bayaka: The Extraordinary Music of the BaBenzele Pygmies / 1995 / Ellipsis Arts ✦✦✦✦✦

The strength of Ellipsis Arts releases is the impeccable taste with which the music is selected and packaged, making their collections of traditional music from around the world closer to "coffee-table records" than ethnographic surveys. *Bayaka* is their most lavish creation to date, a full-size hardcover book of spectacular photos and articulate text by Louis Sarno, who has lived among the BaBenzele of the western Congo basin for the past decade. The coffee-table concept extends to the accompanying CD as well. Rather than scholarly excerpts, it's a seamless panorama in which pygmy voices fade in and out to reverberate amid animal calls and forest ambiance. And what music! These are pristine stereo recordings of performances so precise and spirited they stand beside the best of

current music in any genre. Those who aren't bothered by studio manipulations will find both the material and the presentation stunning—the ultimate ambient music. Those who are would do well to search out the pygmy volume of Ellipsis Arts' *Musical Expeditions* series, which serves up raw field recordings no less glorious. *—Ted Greenwald*

☆ **Echoes of the Forest: Music of the Central African Pygmies** / 1995 / Ellipsis Arts ✦✦✦✦✦

Currently the definitive release of pygmy music, this CD brings together outstanding recordings by three men who have written most of what we know about the people of the forest: Colin Turnbull, Jean-Pierre Hallet, and Louis Sarno. By offering three distinct portraits of pygmy bands in northeast Zaire (Turnbull and Hallet) and the western Congo basin (Sarno), this album conveys the uniqueness and breadth of the pygmy singing better than any other. Like other releases in Ellipsis Arts' *Musical Expeditions* series, it's packaged in a beautifully designed CD-sized 64-page clothbound book that includes high-quality photos and substantial commentary by the three ethnographers. Some of Turnbull's contributions are duplicated on the Lyrichord collection, but this is a well-rounded sampling of his recordings of the Mbuti pygmies, including the extraordinary "girl's echo song" in which entrancing fragments of dense harmony break off suddenly as the singers listen for an echo. Hallet's recordings, previously unreleased, include excellent examples of Efe violin, flute, and thumb-piano playing. (A portion of the sale of each CD goes to his charitable foundation, the Pygmy Fund.) Sarno's tapes capture a darker, more intense side of pygmy life exemplified by mangissa and ejengi, secret BaBenzele rituals of exorcism and possession. For an introduction to pygmy music, culture, and life, there's no better option. *—Ted Greenwald*

The Mbuti Pygmies of the Ituri Rainforest / 1992 / Smithsonian/Folkways ✦✦✦✦✦

Colin Turnbull's and Francis S. Chapman's late-'50s field recordings are among the most captivating examples of traditional pygmy music. Folkways released two LPs of them, one devoted entirely to the Mbuti pygmies, the other giving a side each to the forest people and their villager neighbors. This CD collects all of the pygmy material from the earlier two volumes—too much for one sitting, perhaps—and presents them in pristine re-mastered form. The disc begins in a Mbuti camp where small groups sing rounds and play homemade flutes; moves to a Bantu village for raucous ritual observances; and then returns to the forest for private meditations on musical bow (a hunting bow plucked and held to the mouth) and the fireside evening reveries of the sacred molimo. *—Ted Greenwald*

Music of the Rainforest Pygmies / 1992 / Lyrichord ✦✦✦✦✦

Another reissue of Colin Turnbull's recordings, this one comes from 1961. Song types are more varied than his Folkways collection because selections include the Mbuti influence on music of neighboring peoples. It contains a delightfully baffling Twa pygmoid rendition of "(Oh, My Darling) Clementine," presented to Turnbull as a very old and sacred song. *—Bob Tarte*

Musique Centrafricaine / Auvidis ✦✦✦

This is the best overview of various tribal musics throughout the Central African Republic. It includes music from the following peoples: Azande, Babinga, Bagandou, Bianda, Bofi, Broto, Dakpa, Isongo, Linda, and Ndokpa. *—David L. Mayers*

Polyphony of Deep Rainforest: Music of Pygmy in Ituri / Victor ✦✦✦

The Japanese liner notes make it difficult to determine the particulars of these 1983 recordings by Yamashiro Shoji and Ohashi Tsutomu, except that they were made in the same region as Turnbull's and Hallet's. The performances are ragged bordering on listless, but they do add a number of unfamiliar songs and, in providing a contrast to more adept performances, shed some light on Mbuti style. *—Ted Greenwald*

UNESCO Collection: The Music of the BaBenzele Pygmies / Barenreiter Musicaphon ✦✦✦✦✦

The first cut, a fascinating one-man hocket for voice and nose flute, became the inspiration for Herbie Hancock's updated arrangement of "Watermelon Man" on the *Headhunters* album. This adapted yodel shows up throughout the album in a variety of settings, often propelled by drums and enmeshed with unison lines sung by men, women, or children, at times exuberant, at others contemplative. It differentiates this group from others whose music is commercially available, making this rare release well worth searching out. *—Ted Greenwald*

Ethiopia

Mahmoud Ahmed

Vocals / World Fusion, Ethiopia, Africa

Mahmoud Ahmed is a well-dressed elder statesman of Ethiopian popular music, leading the field for over 20 years at home, and even making concert appearances in the US. He is a master vocalist in the highly ornamented East African style and is known for inducing the uninhibited shaking of "eskeukta" on the dance floor. *—Myles Boisen*

★ **Ere Mela Mela** / 1986 / Hannibal ✦✦✦✦✦
Ere Mela Mela: Modern Music from Ethiopia is a dark and brooding mix of '60s San Francisco rock ambience with Ethiopian modality. It's driven by bluesy sax riffs and Ahmed's passionate vocals. —*Bob Tarte*

Era Era / Hannibal ✦✦✦✦✦
This band was way ahead of its time, with a kind of Cushitic precursor of Algerian rai with echoes of the soul sound documented in *Africa Dances* back in the early '70s. It's a stunning release then and now. —*John Storm Roberts, Original Music*

Aster Aweke

Vocals / Africa, Ethiopia, Mali
Aster Aweke was born in 1961 in the city of Gondar. The child of a well-connected family of civil servants, she began to drift into the musical world in 1974 and by 1977 was singing with a variety of groups around Ethiopia, under the influence of Bezunesh Bekele. After a while she decided to go it alone and soon thereafter received the financial backing of Ethiopia's leading musical entrepreneur, Ali Tango. In 1978 Aweke began a short stint with the celebrated Roha Band, but cut short her collaboration to leave the country as it descended into chaos. After a period of wandering she settled in Washington, DC, where she performs. Aweke is notable for her incredible voice and has been frequently compared with Aretha Franklin. Listeners can decide for themselves on any number of CDs she has recorded. —*Leon Jackson*

● **Aster** / 1989 / CBS ✦✦✦✦✦
If Aretha Franklin had been born in Ethiopia, she might have grown up to be Aster Aweke. The singer mixes jazz, soul, funk, and Ethiopian strains to produce a form that's made her a superstar back home and a fast-rising talent in the US. American soul music has been a force in Ethiopia since the '60s, so Aweke's fervent vocalizing should ring a bell with most listeners. —*J. Poet*

Kabu / 1990 / CBS ✦✦✦
The second effort of this amazing Ethiopian songwriter and vocalist has more of an Afro-pop musical sound, with the exception of the haunting love ballad, "Kabu," which means "sacred rock" and employs a slow marimba for both rhythm and melody . . . simply lovely. Backed up on other cuts by a variety of percussion instruments, horns, keyboards, and acoustic bass, Aster's voice is again rich and enchanting. Lyrics are translated in the liner notes. Also included are several traditional Ethiopian songs with contemporary arrangements. —*Ladyslipper*

Aster Aweke / Triple Earth ✦✦✦
Aside from a couple of voice-and-krar-lute duets as relief, here one of Ethiopia's leading singers mostly fronts an Anglo-Amharic Afrosoul ensemble—no new concept, as owners of *Africa Dances*, let alone *Mahmoud Ahmed*, are aware. It's exhilarating stuff from a very fine vocalist. —*John Storm Roberts, Original Music*

Ethiopia Collection

Ethiopia 2: Music of the Desert Nomads / Tangent ✦✦✦
Very interesting vocal selections, love songs, work songs for hauling water, and trance music are all included. —*David L. Mayers*

Ethiopia 2: Music of the Cushitic Peoples / Barenreiter Musicaphon ✦✦✦
Ethiopia II: Music of the Cushitic Peoples of Southwest Ethiopia, Baren Reite offers interesting selections of a tribal people—especially the Gidole flute ensemble. The vocal techniques are interesting as well. —*David L. Mayers*

Ethiopia 3 [Eritrea] / Tangent ✦✦✦
This comes from the outstanding collection recorded by Jean Jenkins of London's Horniman Museum in the '60s. This third volume includes Afar and Rashaia music, and also music of a large number of settled peoples, including songs to lyres, milking songs, dance music, etc. The recording quality is fair, and there are adequate (though rather general) notes. —*David L. Mayers*

Music of Ethiopia, Vol. 3 / Barenreiter Musicaphon ✦✦✦✦✦
The baganna, the magnificent "harp of David," here on *Music of Ethiopia—Three Chordophone Traditions*, plays its essential role as accompaniment to songs of meditation. The krar, known as the devil's instrument, is used to accompany love and topical songs. The masinqo, a spike fiddle of a type common in Africa, as well as the Middle East and the Balkans, is heard in music for weddings and other social gatherings. All are played on this album by exceptional musicians. —*John Storm Roberts*

Jewish Liturgies of Ethiopia / Inedit ✦✦✦✦✦
Though their own legends make the Falasha, or Ethiopian Jews, descendants of the Queen of Sheba, the oldest solid records go back to the 14th century AD, and the oldest scholarly guesstimate goes to the 4th. Whichever, their liturgical music is very different from both local secular forms and Ethiopian Orthodox Christian liturgy. There are

parts of Sabbath offices, wedding prayers, and circumcision songs. —*John Storm Roberts*

Gambia

Alhaji Bai Konte

b. 1920, West Gambia, d. 1983
Kora / Kora, Africa, Gambia
Traditional kora player from the Gambia, Konte is an elder of the West African pop generation and the father of Dembo Konte. —*Myles Boisen*

● **Kora Melodies: Music from Gambia, West Africa** / 1979 / Rounder ✦✦✦✦✦
Alhaji Bai Konte is an African music master able to fit a traditional instrument and sensibility into a contemporary framework. Konte plays the kora, a 21-stringed harp, with such rhythmic virtuosity and wide-ranging ability that he negates questions of language and adaptability. His 14-cut disc features everything from a 58-second fragment, "Tuning Kora," to a spectacular six-minute-plus triumph, "Cedo." During the disc, he demonstrates the properties, appeal and charm of the kora, sometimes going through uptempo pieces that accent his speed, other times probing and exploring an ancient number in a manner that showcases his knowledge of and reverence for vintage African music. —*Ron Wynn*

Simbomba / 1979 / Red House ✦✦✦
These are kora-playing brothers-in-law, one Senegalese, one Gambian. Both are fine musicians—Dembo (the son of the great Alhaji Bai Konte) is one of the best-known kora virtuosi—who toured very successfully together and separately. Their first joint album, made on the eve of their 1987 British tour, was excellent. *Simbomba*, recorded at the end of it, is marginally better. —*John Storm Roberts, Original Music*

Mandingo Griot Society

Africa, Gambia
Foday Musa Suso is a Mandingo (West African tribe) griot (hereditary musician and cultural curator) who can trace his hereditary lineage back to the first performer on the 21-string kora lute. After a traditional apprenticeship in Africa, he came to the US in 1977 and formed the Mandingo Griot Society to bring his native sounds to a new, receptive audience. The group included Adam Rudolph (who recently appeared on Hassan Hakmoun's *Gift of the Gnawa* CD) and had featured jazz trumpeter Don Cherry as a guest, anticipating world-music fusion many years before the worldbeat era. —*Myles Boisen*

● **Watta Sitta** / 1985 / Celluloid ✦✦✦✦✦
This is another great kora electrification project. Watta Sitta bravely attempts to mold an international dance-music sound around Muso's African harp, while Herbie Hancock provides moral support. —*Bob Tarte*

Foday Musa Suso

Drums, Vocals, Kalimba / Kora, Africa, Gambia
Foday Musa Suso is a master musician with one foot on the dance floor and one foot in the villages of Africa. Suso was born in Gambia to a distinguished family of griots (musician storytellers) that can trace their line back almost a thousand years. He has been tireless in his efforts to spread African music and culture to all corners of the globe. On his solo recordings, and as a member of his Mandingo Griot Society, he plays traditional African folk music. On his Mandingo records he leads an electro funk fusion band that can rock the house with the best rap, funk, and house groups. He's played extensively with Herbie Hancock (that's his kora on "Rockit") and frequently collaborates with Bill Laswell on various Afro-fusion experiments. —*J. Poet*

The Dreamtime / 1969 / CMP ✦✦✦
On *The Dreamtime* he presents us with a selection of traditional vocal and instrumental tunes, characterized by lively dancing kora patterns played over solid bass lines, with much use of repetition, creating an almost hypnotic effect. On some pieces Suso multi-tracks himself, adding, in places, the raspy voice of the nyanyery (a one-string violin), talking drums, kalimba (thumb piano) and karinyan (metal scraper). The kora provides a delightful alternative to more familiar stringed instruments. —*Backroads Music/Heartbeats*

Hand Power / 1969 / Flying Fish ✦✦✦✦✦
This is a solo album of traditional Gambian acoustic music. —*J. Poet*

New World Power / 1981 / Axiom ✦✦✦
Suso continues his Afro-funk experiments with Bill Laswell and other members of New York's Downtown Art-Rock Mafia. —*J. Poet*

● **Mandingo Griot Society** / Flying Fish ✦✦✦✦✦
Musa Suso, a kora player from Gambia, joins a contemporary rhythm section for this African-flavored fusion music. —*AMG*

Gambia Collection

Musics of Fouta-Djalon / Playasound ✦✦✦
Fouta-Djalon, in North Guinea, is home to groups with a strong griot tradition. This collection includes string and flute ensembles, a rare type of transverse flute, balafon, and of course various forms of song. —*David L. Mayers*

Ghana

Mustapha Tettey Addy

b. 1943
Drums, Vocals / Africa, Ghana
Part of a drumming family, Ghana's Mustapha Tettey Addy eventually became its most famous member. He was initiated into ritual drumming and dancing by his father, a fetish priest. Addy became "dadefoiakye," the head of the ritual drummers, after his father's death. He was a full-time member of the Ghana Dance Ensemble during the '60s, and also loosely associated with the Institute of African Studies at the University of Ghana. Widespread travels throughout West Africa in the early '70s alerted Addy to other styles and techniques, which he utilized when he formed his group Ehimono in '74. Addy toured Europe several times in the '70s, then returned there in the '80s, this time mainly as a teacher. A master of complex, intricate, and intense rhythms, Addy's superb '70s and '80s recordings *Master Drummer Vol. 1* and *Master Drummer Vol. 2* are essential, while his 1990 release *Come and Drum*, with his son Abdul Rahman Kpany Addy and two German musicians, aims at simplifying and breaking down tricky rhythms without destroying the music's essence. —*Ron Wynn*

● **Master Drummer from Ghana** / Lyrichord ✦✦✦✦✦
Addy, a Ga from Accra, spent many years learning the major traditions of other groups as well as such recent developments as kpanlogo, a style developed by Accra teenagers in the '60s. It has good technical quality and adequate notes. —*John Storm Roberts*

Obo Addy

b. 1936
Percussion, Drums, Vocals / Worldbeat, Africa, Ghana
Obo Addy may be the most widely traveled member of this celebrated Ghanian family. Like his brothers, Obo Addy got his early training from his father, a fetish priest, who immersed him in the drumming, dancing, and singing of traditional music. Addy started on the gong, then moved to the drums, playing at ritual occasions and later bigger gatherings. He joined Joe Kelly's band in 1954, learning to play Western music for highlife audiences in hotels and nightclubs. Addy switched groups in 1959, becoming a member of the Builder's Brigade Band, one of Kwame Nkrumah's state ensembles. He toured the country extensively, and two years later was invited to join the Farmer's Council of Ghana, a band that helped educate farmers across the nation using a combination of music, cinema, and drama. Addy learned how to package and present traditional music in a multimedia context to live audiences, and eventually the show Edzo was unveiled before Nkrumah. Addy became the Farmers' Band's deputy leader by 1962, heading the traditional troupe that operated within the overall group framework. This enabled him to champion traditional values, yet also understand and absorb changes in both society and the music.

Nkrumah was overthrown in 1966, but Addy formed a band to headline at the newly opened Continental Hotel near the airport. He again blended traditional drumming and contemporary music. After working briefly with the Ghana Broadcasting Band, Addy decided he wanted to save and publicize vintage drum and dance traditions. He took a job at the Arts Council, honed his compositional skills and continued exploring fusions of the old and the new. Addy helped formed Anansi Krumian Soundz, a band that exclusively used traditional instruments. Upon returning from a 1972 Arts Council visit to Israel, Addy joined with his brothers to form Obuade (Ancient). This group won universal acclaim and an invitation to perform at the '72 Munich Olympics, becoming extremely popular worldwide. For three years, Addy performed extensively, winning plaudits for his shows and teaching skills. The Addy brothers moved to Seattle in 1977, creating a new group, Ablade, that led to radio and television opportunities, as well as teaching and performing jobs. Obo Addy spun off his own band in 1981, Kukrundu, cutting two albums in '83 and '84 on the Avocet label, and spending more time composing. He issued two albums in '86, one spotlighting traditional Ghanian music on cassette, the other a contemporary effort titled *African-American*. With interest growing in traditional African material, Obo Addy gained more stature and fame as the '80s ended. He formed a smaller band in '88 Okropong, and soon after released *Okropong: Traditional Music of Ghana*, while reissuing *Born in the Tradition*. —*Ron Wynn*

● **Okropong** / 1989 / Earthbeat! ✦✦✦
On *Okropong* he presents several traditional songs sung in a vigorous call and response style to the accompaniment of many African hand drums and gongo bells. Also included are two original instrumentals featuring lively melodies played on a soft-toned wooden xylophone. Obo Addy multi-tracks himself to create his complex drum orchestra and chorus, playing all the instruments on all but one cut on this dynamic and highly rhythmic album. —*Backroads Music/Heartbeats*

● **The Rhythm of Which a Chief Walks Gracefully** / 1994 / Earthbeat! ✦✦✦✦✦
Obo Addy uses expressive percussion, engaging melodies, and studio wizardry to paint a rich picture of his native Ghana on *The Rhythm of Which a Chief Walks Gracefully*. Addy combines his masterful performances on African hand drums and xylophone with vocals from Jim Cheek and Gary Harris on flutes. The compositions spring from Addy's thoughts and remembrances of his homeland and expectedly cover a range of emotions. But even in sadness the pieces sound joyful, owing to Addy's optimistic perspective on life. Nature sounds provide a natural texture and background to many pieces. —*MusD*

The African Brothers Band

Highlife, Africa, Ghana
Ghana's African Brothers Band has thrived and survived through three decades of social and political transition and turmoil throughout their homeland. They have reigned supreme atop the highlife hierarchy almost since their inception. They're currently led by Nana Kwame Ampadu the Third, and record at Ambassador studios in Kumasi. A couple of years ago, they did their first shows in England since 1984. The African Brothers emerged as superstars in 1967, with their first hit "Ebi Tie Ye." They were part of the new highlife sound that fused rock and reggae bits into a tight, multiple guitar front line, accenting lyricist and leader Nana Ampadu's exhaustive, metaphor-driven sermons drawn from stories of the animal kingdom. They have several releases available on the international market, plus many other cassette-only items not sold outside Ghana. —*Ron Wynn*

● **Me Poma** / 1984 / Rounder ✦✦✦✦✦
The African Brothers Band has been around a while now—its leader, Nana Ampadu, was a pioneer in developing a local Afrobeat which he calls Afrohili. Soul-funk touches in the rhythm section, classic sweet-sour highlife vocals, guitars and horns, some tasty though unobtrusive organ—it's a good example of what's happening in a style that's been strangely ignored lately. —*John Storm Roberts*

Kakraba Lobi

Xylophone / Neo-Traditional, Africa, Ghana
Kakraba Lobi, who comes from a family of xylophonic virtuosi, is one of a large and growing number of African musicians who expand traditional music from within besides teaching it at university level. —*David L. Mayers*

Xylophone Player from Ghana / Tangent ✦✦✦
On this deeply satisfying recording, Lobi plays mostly his own compositions and arrangements of traditional material, supported by percussionist Mustapha Tettey Addy. —*David L. Mayers*

E.T. Mensah & Tempos Dance Band
(Emmanuel Tetteh Mensah)

Highlife, Africa, Ghana
Mensah has had the longest reign of any of African music's self-crowned kings. The King of Highlife made his first records in 1952 and was an instant success with his Latin- and Caribbean-inspired danceband style. He played in England in 1953 and toured West Africa steadily in the '50s and '60s. In the '70s, the sweet and swinging sounds of highlife were drowned out by a profusion of new styles, but Mensah's influence was still strongly felt. —*Myles Boisen*

● **All for You** / 1986 / Retro ✦✦✦✦
This highlife pioneer from Ghana merged the rhythms of calypso, Latin, and local tradition to establish the first African supergroup. —*J. Poet*

Day by Day / 1987 / Retro ✦✦✦
Here is another stunning collection from Mensah and the Tempos. —*J. Poet*

Ghana Collection

Giants of Danceband Highlife / 1990 / Original Music ✦✦✦✦✦
In their palmy days, E.T. Mensah's '50s Tempos were the most influential band in West Africa. Here are four of their most charming early hits. The Ramblers—one of the hottest bands of the '60s—and the Uhurus were both jazz-oriented. The Ramblers stuck to straightahead dance music; Uhuru experimented, with phenomenal results, in the early '70s. This

was the cutting edge of highlife in its time, and its extinction was a real loss. —*John Storm Roberts*

Heavy on the Highlife! / 1991 / Original Music ✦✦✦✦✦

Guinea

Bembeya Jazz National

Jazz, Guinea, Africa
Legendary band formed in Beyla in 1961 by Aboubacar Camara, who was killed in a car crash in 1973. They became the state band in 1966, recording a series of classic albums. Their instrumentation consists of electric guitars (including renowned virtuoso Sekou Diabate), horns, percussion, and vocals, with 15 to 25 musicians at various points in their history. Their stylistic range includes traditional Guinean music, soukous, rumba, and others. Owing to foreign policy restrictions, they were unable to tour extensively outside the country until the mid-'80s, when they made a name for themselves in the West. They are regarded by many as one of the finest African bands ever. —*Steve Huey*

● **Wa Kele** / Sonodisc ✦✦✦✦✦
Bembeya Jazz National, one of the oldest and greatest of all Sahelian bands, was the inspiration for more famous groups (Les Ambassadeurs among them). Alas, none of their superb music from the '70s is currently available, but the '80s material is almost as good. Like any working band they keep up with the trends (at times too much so). But they're still one of the freshest of all Sahelian bands despite the commercial pressures that have so damaged Youssou N'dour and other big names. Instead of hunting transitory international glory, they've stuck to their glorious mix of swooping Afro-funk and hot Afro-Cuban, sparked by the otherworldly guitar of Sekou "Diamond Fingers" Diabate. —*John Storm Roberts*

Regarde Sur le Passe / Syliphone ✦✦✦
. . . And speaking of Bembeya Jazz, here is a CD from 1982, a time when Guinean nationalism was in full swing and the restrictions of the hardline gov't had been slightly relaxed. The music was not so much a product as an expression of cultural identity. Mixing the ever-present Cubanisms with a very strong traditional element makes the band at this period less smooth and more emotive, with an undisguised fervor for the re-emerging Africanism of the time. Balafon and guitar, horns and percussion—by now a familiar blend, but never less than fresh and new (including some nasty funk and a mind-blowing neo-Robert Fripp guitar solo!). —*Carl Hoyt, Original Music*

Sekouba Diabate

Bass, Guitar / Guinea, Africa
"Diamond Fingers" Diabate is the virtuoso lead guitarist for Bembeya Jazz. —*Steve Huey*

Le Destin / Popular African Music ✦✦✦
Not Sekou "Diamond Fingers" Diabate, but very close. Sekouba was a young singer with Bembeya Jazz when the collapse of Guinea's Marxist government brought the dissolution of that fabulous state-sponsored band. As the money dried up the instruments disappeared, and the musicians went back to kora, balafon, and n'goni. The result is the same languid groove and sleepy funk without a horn section (though a very tasteful synth drum is used). It's another fabulous CD from my second-favorite label. —*Carl Hoyt, Original Music*

Sona Diabate

Guitar, Vocals / Guinea, Sahelian, Africa
Sona Diabate comes from an extensive family of hereditary griot musicians from Guinea that includes many of the biggest names in traditional West African music. She is a particularly gifted singer who, as part of her occupation, must memorize vast amounts of oral history and compose "praise songs" to important figures and benefactors. She has also performed as a singer and guitarist with the band Les Amazones de Guinea. —*Myles Boisen*

● **Girls of Guinea** / 1988 / Shanachie ✦✦✦✦✦
Two female vocalists and a pair of intertwining acoustic guitars weave in and out of the deep recesses of the heart in an urgent appeal to traditional values. Recorded live to two-track tape with acoustic guitar backing by guitar master Sekou Diabate and background singing from Les Amazones, this stirring set of vaguely Western-sounding songs bristles with passion and immediacy. —*Bob Tarte & Myles Boisen*

Kankele-Ti / Shanachie ✦✦✦✦✦
Here's a stunning album from a member of the famous Amazones de Guinea, singing mostly her own compositions here. Like the other Amazones offshoots, this is very different from the band itself: it's fairly traditional in tone, with the delicate richness of three guitars—one of whom is played by her brother Sekou, the famous lead guitarist of Bembeya National Jazz, no less. —*John Storm Roberts, Original Music*

Jali Musa Jawara (Diawara)

b. 1961, Northern Guinea
Guitar, Harp, Vocals / Guinea, Sahelian, Africa
Jali Musa Jawara, the half-brother of African pop star Mory Kante, performs traditional Manding songs of West Africa, praising important citizens and delivering well-intentioned advice. His glittering kora (multistringed gourd harp) is the centerpiece of gentle folk groups that include the marimba-like balafon, guitar, and a characteristic West African vocal chorus. —*Myles Boisen*

Soubindoor / 1988 / Mango ✦✦✦
Guinean pop musician Jawara returns to his roots with a folk ensemble built around kora (Mandikan harp), balafon (marimba), guitar, and soaring high-energy vocals. —*Bob Tarte*

★ **Yasimika** / May 1991 / Hannibal ✦✦✦✦✦
This new US release was first issued in France in 1983. Two koras, a balafon, and a splendid female chorus backing Jawara's lead make for a deserved best-seller among Africans in France. This is contemporary-traditional Mandingo music, purely and wonderfully performed and admirably recorded. —*John Storm Roberts*

Ivory Coast

Aicha Kone

Africa, Ivory Coast
Poro Dance / 1994 / Tamaris ✦✦✦
Kone, a local star since the 1970s, has a warm voice à la Zaire's Mpongo Love and Togo's Bella Bellow, but she's emphatically her own woman. Unlike most Ivorians, she sings in Bambara—not French—to backings that span charming acoustic guitar, punchy soukous and quirky kwela. She was virtually ignored in the West for decades but produced two CDs in a year. —*John Storm Roberts, Original Music*

Kenya

Orchestra Virunga

Soukous, Africa, Kenya
Samba Mapangala left Zaire and settled in Kenya in the late '70s. He first led a soukous band of Zairian musicians called Les Kinois (Kinshasa Boys). When they broke up, he looked for local talent and formed Virunga, a group that takes soukous and adds Kenya's benga beat, as well as Western rock and blues influences. —*J. Poet*

● **Virunga Volcano** / 1990 / Earthworks ✦✦✦✦✦
This disc, with Samba Mapangala, compiles the band's early hits, including "Malako," the tune that made them famous. —*J. Poet*

Feet on Fire / 1991 / Stern's Africa ✦✦✦
At the end of Virunga's sold-out European tour, the band went into a London studio to document their sound. The band carries a hard-hitting horn section, but their sound remains true to their African roots. —*J. Poet*

Kenya Collection

Kenya Dry / 1990 / Original Music ✦✦✦✦✦
Three takes on the seminal but totally unknown early Kenyan acoustic-guitar styles underlay all that was to come in the next 30 years: '40s and '50s rural music in regional languages, Swahili-language rural songs, and some exceedingly rare early big-city music from Nairobi, from Inkspots imitation to Cuban inspiration. This is one of those collections that arouse a heady combination of ecstasy and amazement. The music is wonderful—real people stuff—but what also amazes people who have discovered it is the variety. Neither Zaire nor benga had imposed any orthodoxy, and pretty much anything went deliciously. —*John Storm Roberts*

The Nairobi Sound / 1993 / Original Music ✦✦✦✦✦
This is still the only release covering the '60s pre-benga electric guitar, and the acoustic material fills the gap between Kenya Dry and the more recent British releases. Both the acoustic and electric sounds back then—before soukous took over the world—were strongly local and idiosyncratic, and this set offers a side of each (including the original version of "Malaika," which Miriam Makeba once turned into an international hit). —*John Storm Roberts*

Madagascar

Tarika Sammy

Madagascar, Africa
Probably the most notable contemporary Malagasy group to achieve international exposure in the 1990s, Tarika Sammy update traditional

and regional sounds of their country in invigorating ways. Dressed up in full-bodied arrangements without sounding slick, the group employ zithers and hand-drums in addition to more modern instruments. The songs also deal with contemporary concerns like drought, cattle rustlers with automatic weapons, and even Madagascar's national transportation system. For most listeners, the most appealing elements of the group's sound are the mellifluous vocals of the two sisters who sing much of Tarika Sammy's material.

Tarika Sammy was formed by Samoela Andriamalalaharijaona in 1983 in Antananarivo, the capital of Madagascar. The group had a floating lineup (tracks by some versions appear on compilation albums) until 1991, when Tina Norosoa Raharimalala and her sister Hanitra joined as singers. This arrangement was recommended by Ian Anderson, a longtime figurehead of the British folk and roots music scene (as editor of *Folk Roots* and a BBC DJ) who married Hanitra. After some well-received recordings, Tarika Sammy changed into Tarika in the mid-'90s with the departure of Samoela Andriamalalaharijaona. *—Richie Unterberger*

● **Balance** / 1994 / Green Linnet ✦✦✦✦✦
More oriented toward contemporary, original material than their debut (*Fanafody*), though still sung entirely in Malagasy. Characterized by effervescent vocals and arrangements, it strikes a rare, even balance between traditional and contemporary regional African music without sounding strained. *—Richie Unterberger*

Madagascar Collection

Madagasikara One / 1986 / GlobeStyle ✦✦✦✦✦
Madagasikara One: Current Traditional Music of Madagascar features the rapid, tumbling accordion styles and the sound of the valiha box-harp that typify the airy music of the Malgasy Republic. It also contains selections by master flutist Rakotofrah and the out-of-place military-band troupe Tsimialona Volambita. *—Bob Tarte*

☆ **Madagasikara Two** / 1986 / GlobeStyle ✦✦✦✦✦
Island-accented township jive, Trio FA's irresistible accordion jam, and a pair of African outreach cuts by rising star Rossy testify to the richness of island culture. The diversity and uniqueness of this material is impressive. *—Bob Tarte*

Mali

Fanta Damba

b. 1938
Guitar, Vocals / Kora, Mali, Africa
Born into a griot family, Damba started recording in the 1960s, becoming one of the top interpreters of Mali's various traditions and a star by the end of the decade. In 1975, she formed her own group, often being accompanied by her two daughters. She retired from public performance in 1985 as a legend. *—Steve Huey*

Mamadou Magadji / Esperance ✦✦✦✦✦
Fanta Damba is a peerless singer in the classical Malian vein, a vocalist of power, restraint, and subtlety with centuries of Afro-Islamic tradition behind her. *—John Storm Roberts*

Mory Kante

b. 1950, Kissidougou, Guinea
Vocals / Kora, Mali, Sahelian, Africa
Along with Salif Keita, Mory Kante was an early member of the seminal Rail Band of Bamako, joining as a singer when he was in his teens. After a stint as lead vocalist, he left the band to form his own theatrical troupe, which included dozens of performers and his brother Jali Musa Jawara. In the '80s he became an international pop star, exploring neo-traditional Manding music on the kora, as well as club-ready dance mixes. His "Yeke Yeke" became the biggest-selling African release to hit the European pop charts. *—Myles Boisen*

10 Cola Nuts / 1986 / Barclay ✦✦✦
After early success in his native Guinea, Kante moved to Paris where he began making waves with his blend of funk, rock, and traditional African sounds. This disc is short (25 min.), but compelling. *—J. Poet*

● **Akwaba Beach** / 1987 / Barclay ✦✦✦✦✦
The first single from *Akwaba Beach*, "Yeke Yeke," was a major European dance hit for Kante in 1987. Dismissed by some for his heavy dance beat, Kante's crossover sound is a perfect way to ease your ears into the joys of African pop. *—J. Poet*

Touma / 1990 / Mango ✦✦✦✦✦
A breakthrough release, it features an international band with guest stars Carlos Santana and Ray Phiri, but the unsung heroine is backing vocalist Djanka Diabate, who showers spice on Mory's cool. *—Bob Tarte*

Salif Keita

b. Djoliba
Vocals / Afro Pop, Mali, Africa
Salif Keita was born in Mali into a family that can trace their roots back to Soundjata Keita, the warrior king who founded the Malian Empire in 1240. Keita was born an albino (a bad omen), and his family frowned upon his choice of a musical career. When he refused to follow a traditional path of study, Salif's father disowned him and he was left to wander the streets of Bamako, Mali's capitol. After years of singing on street corners and in small clubs, Keita landed a job as vocalist for the Super Rail Band, a government-sponsored group that was gaining national fame with their mixture of traditional and Western (especially Cuban) music. Mali is one of the northernmost states in Black Africa, and has always been a cultural melting pot, with Arabic, French, Spanish, and regional ethnic groups contributing to a unique musical and cultural mixture. In the Rail Band, Keita met guitarist Kante Manfila, another musician with an international pop vision, and together they pursued their vision of a Cuban/Zairean/Malian fusion. In 1973, the duo left the Rail Band and joined Les Ambassadeurs Internationaux, where their stylistic hybrid began to earn them an international reputation. As Les Ambassadeurs became more successful, they also became more aware of their roots and, as the Arabic influences of their culture crept back into the music, they developed one of Africa's most hypnotic sounds.

In 1987 Keita left the Ambassadeurs to pursue a solo career in Paris. With the cream of that city's African session players, he recorded *Soro*, the international hit that brought him to the attention of Island Records, who now record his music for international distribution. *—J. Poet*

Soro / 1987 / Mango ✦✦✦✦✦
This album propelled Keita into the front ranks of the international scene. *—J. Poet*

Ko-Yan / 1989 / Mango ✦✦✦
A cabaret touch invades this Parisian production, which blends straightahead Afro-pop and punk with lacy electronic ornamentation. *—Bob Tarte*

Amen / 1991 / Mango ✦✦✦✦✦
Produced by Joe Zawinul (Weather Report), this set is more international in scope, with guest shots by Carlos Santana and Wayne Shorter adding to its commercial appeal. *—J. Poet*

● **The Mansa of Mali . . . A Retrospective** / 1994 / Mango ✦✦✦✦✦
The ten cuts on this anthology range from the late-'70s "Mandjou," with its stinging guitar riffs, throbbing organ, and gorgeous sax backing, to the spectacular "Souareba," in which Keita's vibrant vocals are backed by electric drums and synthesizers, plus "Tenin," from the LP *Ko-Yan.* This was produced by Joe Zawinul and included his contributions on keyboards, assistance from the great Antillean bassist Etienne M'Bappe, and appearances by many other African music superstars. The anthology covers Keita's three Mango releases, plus the LP *L'Enfant Lion.* While it's not a substitute for the complete LPs, those unaware of Keita's vocal mastery will hopefully be persuaded to get the complete package by this fine sampler. *—Ron Wynn*

Kante Manfila

b. 1947
Guitar, Vocals / Mali, Africa
Manfila was born into a jali family and played balafon and guitar as a child. He joined Les Ballets Africains, moved to Bamako during the '60s and joined the Rail Band, which featured Salif Keita and Mory Kante at the time. He and Keita moved over to Les Ambassadeurs in the early '70s, beginning a fruitful collaborative relationship. Both pursued solo careers in the '80s, with Manfila moving to Paris and recording in both small, traditional groups and big dance bands. *—Steve Huey*

● **Kankan Blues** / 1991 / African Music ✦✦✦✦✦
This is a stunning record. Ace Afro-Frankfurter Gunter Gretz went to Manfila's hometown of Kankan and recorded him and various relatives, including balafonist Balla Balla. As you'd expect of a family of griots, there's magnificent traditional singing here, along with acoustic and electric guitar and superb balafon. Gretz's notes are both eccentric and very revealing, with a long account of the sundry hazards of field recording. *—John Storm Roberts*

Diniya / Esperance ✦✦✦✦✦
Diniya is OK, as is Soro and many other Afro-Parisian productions since the "world music" boom. Not a patch on Manfila's older recordings: far too much hit-hunting paraphernalia, from Synclavier to synth to the usual Afro-zouk horns. Manfila sings beautifully, as do the backup singers, and there are certainly splendid moments. *—John Storm Roberts*

Oumou Sangare

b. 1968
Guitar, Vocals / Afro Pop, Mali, Africa
In 1990, Wassoulou singer Sangare became a superstar in West Africa

with *Moussolou*, which sold an astonishing 250,000 copies (many more were likely pirated). She received much of her attention for writing and singing lyrics that specifically addressed concerns of women in modern West African society, such as the conflict between marriage and personal freedom; not a shocking subject in the Western world, perhaps, but a pioneering one for the popular music of the region. Western listeners who can't understand the lyrics will be drawn in by her mellifluous vocals and smooth, circular compositions, which use full arrangements without sounding over-produced. Both traditional instruments and electric guitars/basses are prominently used on her 1993 release *Ko Sira*, her most widely available recording in the US. —*Richie Unterberger*

Moussolou / "Women" / 1989 / World Circuit ♦♦♦
This traditional recording (produced by Ibrahim Sylla, who turned the knobs for Salif Keita's international breakthrough *Soro*) was West Africa's biggest seller in 1989. Sparkling kora (African harp), driving percussion, and a stunning multitracked voice, often recalling an African version of the Shirelles, makes this one a winner. —*J. Poet*

● **Ko Sira** / 1993 / World Circuit ♦♦♦♦♦
A strong set of all-original material that has its cake and eats it too. With unobtrusive electric guitar and bass blending in with more traditional instrumentation like flute and djembe, it's both more accessible to modern audiences than traditional African instruments, and not as pop- and dance-oriented as much contemporary African music. The focus remains on Sangare's gliding singing (thickened by a couple of female backup singers) and the music's looping (but not laid-back) grooves. —*Richie Unterberger*

Mauritius Collection

Segas de l'Ile Maurice / Piros Disques ♦♦♦
At last there's a new sega collection with the idiosyncrasy, tacky lilt, and small-town bounce of the style at its best. The singers are of Indian background, but that fact makes no odds stylistically. Tune after tune is backed by the typical sega backwards-waltz beat. It's irresistible after all these years. —*John Storm Roberts*

Morocco

A. Doukali & A. Belkayat

Morocco
Abdelhadi Belkayat and Abdelwahab Doukali, leaders of the first wave of big-time Moroccan pop music, both began singing in the '60s. Both were inevitably influenced by Egypt, and indeed spent time there. But neither simply "went Egyptian," and both in fact ended up international stars. In very broad terms, Belkayat is reminiscent of Egypt's Abdel Hali Hafez. Doukali is a more dramatic singer with lusher and slightly more adventurous backings. —*John Storm Roberts*

★ **A. Belkayat & A. Doukali** / Disque Arabe ♦♦♦♦♦
They make a terrific pairing on a super CD. —*John Storm Roberts*

Aisha Kandisha's Jarring Effects

Morocco
Starting in the late '80s as a traditional Shabee dance band, this quintet became one of the few North African acts to successfully merge traditional and modern sounds and technology on their electrifying 1990 debut. In addition to haunting violins, mandolins, guitars, and mesmerizing Arabic vocals and chanting, the album used electronic tinkering and turntable DJing, aided by the post-production work of the Swiss producer Pat Jabbar. Their 1992 followup, *Shabeesation*, was produced by Bill Laswell (who contributed bass), and featured appearances by Omar Ben Hassan of the Last Poets and Parliament-Funkadelic keyboardist Bernie Worrell. For all that, it was a disappointment, relying much more heavily on thumping modern electronic dance rhythms. —*Richie Unterberger*

● **Aisha Kandisha's Jarring Effects** / 1990 / Barraka El Farnatshi ♦♦♦♦
One of the most exciting blends of traditional North African music with up-to-the-minute influences like dub reggae and hip-hop scratching. Sounding like a traditional Moroccan jam that has been somehow trapped in an arty, rattling echo chamber, this is one of few contemporary African pop albums that uses state-of-the-art production techniques to augment indigenous music instead of subsume it. —*Richie Unterberger*

Abdelhadi Belkhat

Morocco, Africa
El-Kamar El-Ahmar / 1994 / Tichkaphone ♦♦♦
Belkhyat-built high-octane vocals, Egyptian-derived strings setting off oud or khanoun interspersions, rubato to the max, an occasional cut with an unnamed woman singer, into a Moroccan sound. No discoid or Europop trimmings, but a sound of great self-assurance and integrity with an odd grandeur and sweep to it. —*John Storm Roberts, Original Music*

Hassan Hakmoun

Vocals / Morocco, Africa
● **Gift of the Gnawa** / 1991 / Flying Fish ♦♦♦♦♦
Moroccan musician Hakmoun's compelling vocals and sintar (lute) playing rides the tide of Adam Rudolph's fierce tabla foundation. Joined by Don Cherry's trumpet and Richard Horwitz on nay (flute), they produce an intensely evocative fusion. —*Bob Tarte*

Moroccan Gnawi Songs / Apr. 1991 / World Music Institute ♦♦♦
Hakmoun, a singer/dancer now living in the US, performs music and songs from the Afro-Moroccan trance ceremonies of the Gnawi people. Some of the songs are for solo voice accompanied by sintir lute, the rest have multitracked performances. —*John Storm Roberts, Original Music*

Zahar / 1992 / Knitting Factory Works ♦♦♦
On *Gift of the Gnawa*, Moroccan vocalist/sintar player Hassan Hakmoun combined traditional North African music and jazz by enlisting Don Cherry, Adam Rudolph, and Richard Horwitz to the cause. Zahar's Moroccan-roll fusion is more subversive yet, but Hakmoun's thrash accompanists aren't the equal of his former jazz partners. Bill McClellan raises an unholy clatterdom on drums when focused brutality would be to the point, and Anthony Michael Peterson's Zani Diabate-flavored fuzz guitar feels oddly outdated for such a forward-looking meld. It's easy to enjoy the rawness and spontaneity, but if blending Moroccan trance music with numbness-inducing Western sonics is the intention, how about a session with My Bloody Valentine instead? —*Bob Tarte*

Trance / 1993 / RealWorld/Caroline ♦♦♦♦♦
From the Hendrix-in-a-fez riff of "Bania" to the fuzz-box nirvana of "Challaban," *Trance* asserts psychedelic sovereignty over Moroccan sensibilities that hippie hash-heads once claimed as their own music base. Twenty-five years ago, Hakmoun's high-amplification drone would have blown Cream out of the stadium, but its thrills-per-wattage ratio today depends on whether or not you're willing to let bygone eras be bygones—or how ardent you are about wanting to hear Gnawa music done boggle style on two cuts. One experiment that reaps great dividends is an a cappella duet between Hakmoun and Carole Rowley on "The Sun is Gone," where the two baptize one another in mutually unreachable longing until Hakmoun finally falls below the horizon, his voice narrowed to a *rhaita-like rasp*—the one great idea on this disc that isn't clogged with electronics. —*Bob Tarte*

Cheikh Salah

Morocco, Africa
☆ **Arabo-Andalusian Music** / Buda Musique ♦♦♦♦♦
The late Cheikh Salah led one of the finest modern orchestras, playing North African classical music based on forms brought by refugees from the great music school of Cordoba at the collapse of Muslim Spain. This is pure and authentic style, superbly sung and backed by a small ensemble of local instruments. Dismal notes, short measure for a steep price, but the superb music more than compensates. —*John Storm Roberts*

Morocco Collection

☆ **Master Musicians of Jajouka [Morocco]** / 1972 / Adelphi ♦♦♦♦♦
A field recording of hypnotic Moroccan oboe, string, and drum ensembles made famous by Brian Jones (Rolling Stones). —*Myles Boisen*

Moroccan Music: Pan-Islamic Tradition / Lyrichord ♦♦♦♦♦
This album features powerful music-flutes, double-reed oboe, drums, and chanting. —*David L. Mayers*

Rwayes Anthology: Berber Songs & Music ... / Inedit ♦♦♦
Rwayes Anthology: Berber Songs and Instrumental Music from the Sous Region is included in a large and highly recommended series from Morocco on the Inedit series of recordings put out in France by the Maison des Cultures du Monde. —*David L. Mayers*

Mozambique Collection

Mozambique Two / 1995 / Globestyle ♦♦♦♦♦
The music on these 1989 recordings is both wonderful and varied: timbila, a one-note-shawm ensemble, choirs including Afro-Luso-Arab women's choruses (strongly Luso, vocally, which the notes ignore), a mbube-influenced group, Shangaan acoustic guitar, and several fine urban-influenced pieces on local or homemade instruments. The notes match up, too. —*John Storm Roberts*

Nigeria

Admiral Dele Abiodun

b. Bendel State, Nigeria
Guitar, Vocals / Juju, Africa, Nigeria
"Admiral" Dele Abiodun has had a steady music career of approximately

20 years. As a singer, composer and guitarist, Abiodun is considered to be one of the best juju musicians. He started his music career at a young age, dropping out of school and moving to Ghana to study music and to find a job. In Ghana he played the bass for several different highlife bands, but in 1969 he decided to go out on his own and he formed his own band called Sweet Abby and the Tophitters. The year following the formation of the band, Abiodun created a new style and used that in many of his performances. The new style of music that was created is known as Adawa, which in translation means Independent Being. After the introduction of the Adawa style, Abiodun and his band released several LPs and singles. In 1981 Abiodun released the hit album Beginning of a New Era and in 1983 he released another hit album titled Ma Se'Ke. In more recent times, Abiodun and his band have released two albums almost back to back. In 1985 they released Confrontation, which is a mini-LP, and in 1986 they released Oro Ayo in Nigeria. —AMG

● **Prince of Juju** / Shanachie ✦✦✦✦✦
Abiodun himself says his style is a mix of juju and highlife. That isn't too obvious, except at times in the guitar work, and perhaps in a more driving approach than is the juju norm. But he's the latest big name in Lagos, and it's easy enough to see why from this collection of several of his latest big-sellers. —*John Storm Roberts, Original Music*

King Sunny Ade (Sunday Adeniyi)

Guitar, Drums, Vocals / Juju, Africa, Nigeria
Ade was born to a royal family in the Yoruba tribe, but like many musicians, he dropped out of (grammar) school and left home in search of fame and fortune. Ade's first gig was with the highlife band Moses Olaiya and his Rhythm Dandies, but he was increasingly drawn to juju, which traces its roots back to various forms of traditional Yoruba guitar playing that includes but is not limited to Christian "Aladura" church music and a Nigerian "blues" form. In the '20s, as cheap gramophones became available in Nigeria, players added elements drawn from American country music, Hawaiian and Cuban folk music, and the British music hall tradition. I.K. Dairo is known as the father of modern juju; he added electric guitars, accordion, and bass guitar to the music's folky style, while Ebenezer Obey added pedal steel and other African and modern touches. Ade formed his first juju group, the Green Spots, in 1967. In 1974, tired of the hassles common to the Nigerian music industry, Ade formed his own record company and has since released over 40 albums and countless singles and EPs for both the home and international markets. Island Records promoted him in the States as the "African Bob Marley," but after pumping millions into Ade's organization they admitted defeat and dropped him from the label in 1984. Ade's juju is heavy on the guitars (usually six guitars, each playing different lead lines), and the band produces a shimmering tidal wave of rhythm (live gigs use seven or more percussionists) and melody that's soothing and energetic at the same time. —*J. Poet*

● **Juju Music** / 1982 / Mango ✦✦✦✦✦
The first of Ade's international releases on Mango, this is the classic record that made North American and British fans aware of the richness of African music. —*J. Poet*

Synchro System / 1983 / Mango ✦✦✦✦✦
High-tech sound and some electronic instruments give this an international appeal. —*Myles Boisen*

Aura / 1984 / Mango ✦✦✦
This mid-'80s recording has studio gloss, but still delivers. Included is harmonica work by Stevie Wonder. —*Myles Boisen*

Live Juju Live / 1988 / Rykodisc ✦✦✦
An entire set (70+ minutes) captures some of the live power of Ade and his band, recorded in 1988. —*J. Poet*

The Return of the Juju King / 1988 / Mercury ✦✦✦
More contemporary grooves come from Ade's own label. —*Myles Boisen*

E Dide (Get Up) / 1995 / Mesa ✦✦✦
Like King Sunny Ade's previous albums, *E Dide (Get Up)* is an infectious collection of juju, featuring a wild array of percussion, intertwining guitars, and talking drums. —*Sara Sytsma*

Master Guitarist, Vol.2 / African Songs ✦✦✦
Here's early Ade, from his Green Spot days—strongly guitar-oriented and more solidly rooted in the classic juju sound than much of his later work. But already, especially with the second, late-Green Spots-era album, Ade was beginning to stand out, the cool, crystal-clear style starting to move toward his later individuality. At the same time, it was still firmly within what was already becoming a guitar-oriented juju tradition. —*John Storm Roberts, Original Music*

Segun Adewale & His Superstars

Juju, Africa, Nigeria
Adewale was a willing participant in the juju boom of the early '80s, with an eclectic mix of Nigerian and Western styles he dubbed "yo-pop." He

never made the splash that Obey or King Sunny did, but he produced a couple of exciting, distinctive albums in his heyday. —*Myles Boisen*

Ojo Je / 1988 / Rounder ✦✦✦
Adewale's second US release amplifies the juju tradition with heavy rock touches in the guitar work and a heavy, rolling bass guitar that coexist with the percussion on pretty much even terms. Which, of course, is how the style moves onward—feeding on influences from all over. —*John Storm Roberts, Original Music*

● **Play for Me** / 1988 / Rounder ✦✦✦✦✦
Adewale's juju style is less guitar-centered than that of other, more popular Nigerian groups. The vocal harmonies are a major attraction here, as are the tracks in apala style, with just vocals and throbbing drums. Some English lyrics. —*Myles Boisen*

Barrister (Sikiru Ayinde)

b. 1948, Lagos, Nigeria
Percussion, Vocals / Fuji, Africa, Nigeria
Sikiru Ayinde, better known to his fans as Barrister, is the first and foremost practitioner of Fuji music. Fuji, which has no real connection with Japanese music, has been slightingly referred to as "Juju without the guitars," and there is a grain of truth to this: it consists of intense Yoruba drumming, over which are layered Muslim-inflected lyrics. Barrister's outfit, the Supreme Fuji Commanders, consists of 25 performers, and their stage show is a blend of powerful drumming and praise song lyrics. —*Leon Jackson*

● **More Fuji Garbage** / 1991 / Globestyle ✦✦✦✦
Take Nigerian juju, strip it down to its rhythmic essentials, discarding everything else but atmospheric bursts of Hawaiian guitar and Barrister's incantatory voice, and you've got the meanest, leanest sound this side of rap. —*Bob Tarte*

Fuji Garbage / Globestyle ✦✦✦
Barrister is perhaps the greatest name in fuji, a splendid Yoruba percussion style that surfaced in the mid-'60s. This new recording has the expected wonderful drumming and singing, along with splendidly idiosyncratic pedal steel and synth—an irony, since fuji was in part a reaction against juju's adoption of Western instruments. —*John Storm Roberts, Original Music*

I.K. Dairo (Isaiah Kehinde Dairo)

b. 1931, Kwara State, Nigeria
Guitar, Accordion, Drums, Vocals / Juju, Africa, Nigeria
Considered by many to be the "father of juju" for his many innovations. One story has it that his lifelong love of music stemmed from a drum that his father, a carpenter, made for him in his youth and that accompanied him wherever he went. In early adulthood, Dairo tried earning a living as a barber, a construction worker, and a cloth merchant, among other jobs. Dairo sat in with early juju bands at night, led by musical pioneers Ojoge Daniel and Oladele Oro. In the mid-'50s he formed his own group, the ten-member Morning Star Orchestra, which gained fame later as the Blue Spots.

Though highlife was the most popular form of band music in West Africa at the time, Dairo and his band released a long succession of influential singles that, by the end of the Nigerian Civil War in 1970, helped establish juju as the premier Nigerian sound. Dairo changed the tenor of juju by introducing the accordion and talking drums to the orchestra and singing in a variety of regional dialects, which widened the rural appeal of the music. When his appeal began to wane at the end of the '70s, he gave up performing, turning first to managing clubs and a hotel in Lagos, then to a ministry in the Cherubim and Seraphim church movement. In 1990 he recorded his first album in 15 years with a re-formed Blue Spots band. —*Bob Tarte*

★ **Juju Master Mbe** / 1990 / Original Music ✦✦✦✦✦
The Glory Years / 1991 / Original Music ✦✦✦✦✦
I.K. Dairo, the most influential juju master ever, borrowed the style's gorgeous vocal sound from the harmonies of local Nigeria's indigenous Christian churches, and paved the way for the synth of Sunny Ade by introducing the one-row accordion. These are the early 1960s recordings that made him the king overnight: jaunty accordion, plus splendid guitar, soaring vocals, great percussion. (A declaration of interest: I produced this CD for my own company and wrote the notes). —*John Storm Roberts*

I Remember / 1991 / Music of the World ✦✦✦✦✦
One of the founding fathers of Nigerian juju returns after a 15-year retirement from the music business. The accordion anchor to his sound is a charming antidote to over-produced, technology-heavy pop. —*Bob Tarte*

Fela Anikulapo Kuti

b. 1938
Guitar, Piano, Horn, Keyboards, Saxophone, Vocals / Afro-Beat, Africa
Fela Kuti was born the son of a strict minister father and a mother

named Funmilayo, who went on to become one of Nigeria's leading feminists. Fela was a problem child in grammar school, and by the age of 16 he was singing in a highlife band, much to the chagrin of his parents. Upon the death of his father, Fela convinced his mother to send him abroad to study music. He landed in London in 1957 where he studied trumpet, got married, and formed his first band, Koola Lobitos. In 1963, Fela and the band moved back to Nigeria and began experimenting with various stylistic innovations ranging from highlife to jazz to soul. In 1968, after hearing the music of James Brown (through cover versions played by the band of Geraldo Pino from Sierra Leone), Fela added funk to his mixture and called it "Afrobeat." In 1969 he took his band on an extended US tour, where a month's residence in Los Angeles brought him in contact with the Black Panthers and other American Black Nationalist groups. He attended consciousness-raising groups, read widely in Black and African history, and returned to Nigeria with a militant gleam in his eye. Between 1970 and 1977 Fela released over 30 albums of incendiary African agit-pop that took the Nigerian government to task for corruption, brutality, and mismanagement. In 1977 the government responded by burning Fela's living quarters and nightclub to the ground; Fela was jailed and tortured. On his release, he continued to make records that made the government squirm as much as they made the common folk dance. As his reputation grew, Fela added more and more musicians and dancers, until his troupe grew to a revue of some 80 people. Although most of his recent music has been rather perfunctory in nature, his '70s classics stood out in the African pop landscape. —*J. Poet*

● **Fela's London Scene** / 1970 / Makossa ◆◆◆◆◆
A superb early-'70s album of funky Afro-pop, it's one of his most successful efforts at blending Nigerian music with James Brown-style soul grooves. —*Myles Boisen*

Army Arrangement [Orig. version] / 1985 / Celluloid ◆◆◆
One of the tunes that got Fela in trouble with Nigeria's military government, it's a hard-hitting bit of rhythmic agit-pop. This (Celluloid 6615) was also released in an inferior remixed and overdubbed version aimed at the dance-club market under the same title on Celluloid 6109. Be sure to read the small print. —*J. Poet*

Vols. 1 & 2 / 1987 / Ced ◆◆◆
This is a two-album anthology on EMI (France) of Kuti's Nigerian hits from the early to mid-'70s, when he was at the height of his lyrical and musical powers. —*J. Poet*

The Best of, Vols. 1 & 2 / 1990 / Oceana ◆◆◆
This is a nice overview of Kuti's incendiary recordings for the Celluloid label. —*Myles Boisen*

The Lijadu Sisters

Africa, Nigeria
Kehinde and Taiwo Lijadu are a rarity in the African music scene—liberated twin sisters who share the spotlight on smooth close harmonies and command a sharp, inventive backing band. —*Myles Boisen*

★ **Double Trouble** / 1984 / Shanachie ◆◆◆◆◆
Apala is just one of many Yoruba street-popular styles for voices and percussion. Among the others is a women's equivalent called waka. And waka is the strong local root that makes the Lijadu Sisters' pop style blossom. Not only is their singing rich with its glorious choral sound, but the electric bass line and guitars are equally balanced by Yoruba percussion. A very fine recording, outclassing many of those with more famous names. —*John Storm Roberts*

Prince Nico Mbarga (Nicholas Mbarga)

b. 1950, Abakaliki, Nigeria
Guitar, Vocals / Panco, Highlife, Africa, Nigeria
With his band, Rocafil Jazz, Prince Nico scored the biggest African hit ever. His 1976 triumph was a song called "Sweet Mother" and its appeal (13 million copies sold) was largely due to Mbarga's pan-African mix of Cameroonian, Nigerian, and Zairian styles. Despite his multi-instrumental talents and ownership of his own record label, Prince Nico has not been able to sustain his success, and seems fated to go down in history as a one-hit wonder. —*Myles Boisen*

● **Aki Special** / 1987 / Rounder ◆◆◆◆◆
Mbarga plays panco, a style from East Nigeria that borrows from reggae, funk, soukous, highlife, and more. This CD collects most of the tracks from Mbarga's two Rounder albums, *Sweet Mother* and *Free Education*. —*J. Poet*

Sweet Mother / Rounder ◆◆◆◆◆
More Nigerian highlife, this one with touches of music from neighboring Cameroon—not too surprising, since Mbarga himself and his band of the period were both half-Cameroonian. The title track, a smash in its time, remains a song of great charm. —*John Storm Roberts, Original Music*

Ebenezer Obey

b. 1942, Idogo, Western Region, Nigeria
Guitar, Drums, Vocals / World Fusion, Juju, Africa, Nigeria
Since the 1960s, Ebenezer Obey has been one of the most popular, prolific, and influential musicians in Nigeria, releasing over fifty albums, developing juju style, and conducting an informal and highly creative campaign against his competitors in the musical world. Obey's first band, the International Brothers, was formed in 1964, and played a slow and music composed of layered guitars and Yoruban percussion sounds. Always a cultural and religious traditionalist, Obey worked within the praise song mold, vaunting both Christianity and the various heads of state for whom he played. But while his lyrics were traditional, his musical direction was highly innovative. In an effort to rise above his competition, Obey began to develop new musical "systems," adding as many as 20 new musicians to his ensemble at a time, extending the length of his album tracks, and pumping out hit after hit. A stylish and bluesy guitarist whose music had been contagious in Nigeria for years, Obey finally enjoyed international success in 1980 with *Current Affairs.* —*Leon Jackson*

Je Ka Jo / 1983 / Virgin ◆◆◆◆◆
His first international release on Virgin UK is a shimmering masterpiece of hypnotic polyrhythmic madness. —*J. Poet*

★ **Juju Jubilee** / 1985 / Shanachie ◆◆◆◆◆
Obey and Sunny Ade are the kings of juju, and for 20 years each has tried to top the other by adding more guitars, more singers, pedal steel licks, and so forth. This compilation, Obey's first US release, collects Obey's best-selling singles and album tracks from the early '80s. —*J. Poet*

Get Yer Jujus Out / 1989 / Rykodisc ◆◆◆
This is how juju music should be—live and full of "juice." More than 75 minutes of juju's polyrhythmic madness by one of the genre's inventors. —*Myles Boisen & J. Poet*

Solution / Sterns ◆◆◆◆◆
In *Solution*, Ebenezer Obey cut back on choral singing modifications to allow for even more Zairian borrowings in his guitar playing on what some aficionados claim is his best album for some time. —*John Storm Roberts, Original Music*

Babatunde Olatunji

Traditional Drumming, Percussion / World Fusion, Africa, Nigeria
Olatunji came to the US in the early '60s to study medicine, but when a group of African expatriates he put together to combat homesickness took off, he became one of the first African musicians to make a major impact on the American market. —*J. Poet*

★ **Drums of Passion** / 1959 / CBS ◆◆◆◆◆
This set came out on vinyl in 1959 and stayed on the charts for several years, an amazing feat for a record of traditional chanting and drumming. Olatunji's success allegedly sparked John Coltrane's interest in African culture, and the music has lost none of its power over the years. —*J. Poet*

☆ **Drums of Passion: Invocation** / 1988 / Rykodisc ◆◆◆◆◆
The first in a pair of releases that featured percussionist Olatunji showcasing his celebrated multi-rhythmic style in a fresh context. Olatunji was adding African beats to jazz and R&B dates back in the '60s, and does roughly the same thing on this date, fueling careening, expansive tracks that are long enough to incorporate everything from singers to numerous drummers playing traps, congas, shakers, and all manner of drums. It's infectious and among the best blends of traditional and contemporary African and American elements. —*Ron Wynn*

Drums of Passion: The Beat / 1989 / Rykodisc ◆◆◆◆◆
Percussionist Olatunji was championing African music long before anyone devised the worldbeat marketing strategy. His 1989 recording *Drums of Passion: The Beat* updated his classic *Drums of Passion* concept, adding rock and pop energy and instrumentalists to the wall of multiple rhythms. The idea clicks, and Olatunji's African beats are contrasted by Airto Moreira's Latin percussion, Mickey Hart's bombastic presence, and such special guests as Carlos Santana and Bobby Vega. —*Ron Wynn*

Nigeria Collection

The Igede of Nigeria / 1989 / Music of the World ◆◆◆◆◆
Most Nigerian collections focus on three or four dominant ethnic groups, so these late-'70s albums from the central Benue State would be welcome even if they weren't intrinsically so worthwhile. Particularly interesting are some Christian hymns in traditional style, but there is also a wide range of tradition-based music old and new. —*David L. Mayers*

Juju Artists: '30s to '50s / 1930-1950 / Rounder ◆◆◆◆◆
The earliest juju music evolved from the West African palmwine guitar style and went through many changes before emerging as a potent world

music phenomenon in the hands of Sunny Ade. This is a superb "roots" collection, as well as one of a very few non-import compilations of African 78-rpm recordings. The scholarly notes are a plus. —*Myles Boisen*

Yoruba Street Percussion / 1992 / Original Music ✦✦✦✦✦
The true stars of West Nigerian pop music are the percussionists, who mix Islamic singing, local drumming, and Afro-Cuban feedback in endless permutations of voices and drums. Here are five different styles, all 20th century, all true street music, all different, all recorded for the local market in the '60s. Percussive offshoots of juju are joined by very early fuji, apala, sakara, the Latin-tinged agidigbo, and waka, the women's music. —*John Storm Roberts*

Senegal

Pascal Diatta

Guitar / Senegal, Africa
Diatta is a guitarist who sings backup vocals for Mane, his wife. He was raised in an orphanage and twice attempted to build his own guitar after becoming interested in music. He was eventually given one. After serving in the Army, he decided to develop his talent and came up with his own unique style of guitar playing. When he married Mane, the two became a duo, playing on radio and in ceremonies around the country. He was reluctant to record until 1989 because he had been swindled out of proper payment by a record company, but he did, and eventually wound up touring the UK. —*Steve Huey*

● **Simnade** / Rogue ✦✦✦✦✦
This is an outstanding recording by a fine woman singer and a man who developed his own acoustic guitar style, avoiding any conscious influence from outside. (Unconscious influences, of course, are a different issue.) This is the real thing, by a local hero of the southern Casamance recorded (extremely well) on location. Altogether, it's exceptional acoustic guitar, and more evidence that African acoustic guitar is alive and highly creative, even if the local record industries have blinders. —*John Storm Roberts*

Ismael Lo

Guitar, Harmonica, Vocals / Afro Pop, Senegal, Mbalax, Sahelian, Africa
Senegalese guitarist, harmonica player and singer Ismael Lo is a rising star of world music. With his smooth multi-textured voice and low-key folky style, he and his 12-piece band play strong, complex, percussion-laden mbalax songs that discuss important topics in Senegal ranging from racism and respect to immigration.

He was born into a Muslim family in Rufisque, Senegal, the son of a Senegalese father and Nigerian mother. His first few years were spent in Niger. His father had two wives and between them they had 18 children. Lo is the only one who became a musician. He loved music from an early age and got his start playing a homemade one-string guitar. Early American influences included Otis Redding, Wilson Pickett, and Etta James, and he learned their songs by listening to the radio. At first he only played for the joy of it and never considered performing, but then an older brother, who owned a club, asked him to play on a local television show, "Tele Variety." Lo said no the first time, and continued to study decorating and painting at a trade school, but a few months later he reconsidered and appeared on the show. He was an instant hit and this inspired him to think about performing full-time. One week later, Lo again appeared on the show and was paid $300 for his work.

In 1979, singer-songwriter Omar Pene invited Lo to play in his popular group Super Diamono de Dakar, a band that played mbalax-blues, a mixture of Cuban and Senegalese rhythms. Lo, with his talent for guitar playing and songwriting, quickly established himself as a key figure in the band and soon became the second lead singer, backup singer and rhythm guitarist. By the early '80s he found himself wanting to launch a solo career, but felt like he would leave a gaping hole in the band that could destroy it. In 1984, the pressure became too much and he left for Spain to do some painting. He began recording as a solo artist upon his return. His first albums included *Xalat, Xiff, Natt,* and *Gor Sayina.* All but the latter were produced by Ibrahima Sylla. They are hard to find in the Americas, but an updated version of one song from *Gor Sayina,* "Ale Lo," can be heard on Lo's 1992 self-titled album on Mango. —*Sandra Brennan*

● **Ismael Lo** / 1992 / Mango ✦✦✦✦✦
Moody guitar finger-picking and Dylanesque harmonica playing kick off this attractive pop amalgam of American and Manding folk styles, which ultimately shifts into straightahead mbalax. —*Bob Tarte*

Baaba Maal

Guitar, Vocals / Afro Pop, Senegal, Sahelian, Africa, Club-Dance
Baaba Maal stands out among Senegalese performers, in that he hails from Fouta Toro in the far north of the country. Unlike the dominant wolof music of Dakar and the south, Maal's fula music leans on Malian and Guinean traditions in its emphasis on lyricism and melody rather than rhythm and beat. Maal's music runs the gamut from very traditional acoustic material through mild rock and reggae-inflected cuts. His lyrics, likewise, range from mystical hymns and Muslim spiritual leaders all the way to political songs addressing the poor treatment of his fellow inhabitants in northern Senegal. —*Leon Jackson*

★ **Baaba Maal, Mansour Seck & Djam Leelii** / 1989 / Mango ✦✦✦✦✦
Baaba Maal and Mansour (Thione) Seck, two of Senegal's biggest pop stars, return to their roots (and the roots of the blues, from the sound of it) on this beautifully hypnotic picking session, which also features Djam Leelii. Two guitars, accented by a bit of African percussion and some tasty electric fills by Aziz Dieng, produce pure magic. —*J. Poet*

Djam Leelii / 1989 / Mango ✦✦✦
Baaba Maal is special even by Sahelian standards in that he runs an electric band, but is also a fine acoustic guitarist who spent some years with a traditional group. This splendid recording combines some cuts from a semilegendary two-acoustic-guitar cassette with some rediscovered tracks by an early version of his electric band. Both are magnificent, and the contrast of this often stark sound is a fine contrast with the Sona Diabate album listed under Guinea. —*John Storm Roberts, Original Music*

Baayo / 1991 / Mango ✦✦✦
Solid African pop aimed at the Senegalese market has few concessions to European taste. —*J. Poet*

Wango / Syllart ✦✦✦✦✦
Senegal's Maal borrows from reggae, funk, and Tuculeur traditions for his take on international pop. *Wango* is one of his strongest efforts. —*J. Poet*

Youssou N'Dour

b. 1959, Dakar, Senegal
Drums, Vocals / Senegal, Mbalax, Africa, Nigeria
The father of mbalax, a jumping, complicated blend of African, Caribbean, and pop rhythms, Youssou N'Dour is a Senegalese performer who is proud to be constantly evolving and perfecting his music. While he seeks to appeal to a worldwide audience, he also remains true to his cultural roots, and where many other West African performers emigrate to Paris to record and be closer to the European music scene, he is content to remain in Dakar and record out of his modern Studio Xippi so he can remain near his family and biggest fans. Though he spends considerable time touring every year, he tries to set aside at least three months annually to be at home with his wife and three kids.

N'Dour has been performing since he was 12 and early on became famous after joining the Star Band de Dakar. Later he left them to found Etoile de Dakar. A few years later he moved on to found Super Etoile. For a while he did live and record in Paris, but then returned to Senegal. A singer with a wide vocal range, N'Dour's earliest work was noted for a high clear wailing sound, as can be heard on Peter Gabriel's 1986 hit single "In Your Eyes," the song that gained N'Dour international recognition. In the mid-'90s, N'Dour began singing more quietly in a lower range, a change he attributes to a broader base of life experience. Before, he concentrated on live performances, but as he has been doing more studio work, N'Dour is into experimenting and exploring the full extent of his vocal range, as can be heard on his 1994 album *The Guide (Wommat).* —*Sandra Brennan*

Immigrés / 1988 / Earthworks ✦✦✦
Though he was already one of the biggest names in Sahelian pop when it was made back in the 1980s, this album was a good part of what put him on the international map. On their way away from their earlier Cuban sound, N'Dour and Super Etoile did a nice job of marrying Sahel and soul, despite some rather pointless synthesizer. And, of course, by now this one is part of recent musical history—almost a classic, in fact. And yes, it's disgracefully short. —*John Storm Roberts, Original Music*

The Lion / 1989 / Virgin ✦✦✦
N'Dour's big crossover album has several English-language songs. It's good, but not great work. —*J. Poet*

★ **Set** / 1990 / Virgin ✦✦✦✦✦
The title tune became the anthem of Senegalese youth in 1990. This is the first album N'Dour hasn't re-recorded for the international market. It's very African and his best recorded work to date. —*J. Poet*

Eyes Open / 1992 / 40 Acres & A Mule ✦✦✦
N'Dour's ongoing quest for a truly global African pop spurs his smoothest—you might say most homogenized—disc yet, one that basks in assimilation and transformation. He is becoming to mbalax what Milton Nascimento is to Brazilian, which means a gain in sophistication but a certain loss of directness. —*Bob Tarte*

Djamil / Celluloid ✦✦✦
N'Dour has become one of the biggest names in Sahelian pop, certainly in the eyes of non-African enthusiasts. *Djamil* is a collection of previ-

ously unreleased cuts (unreleased in France, anyway) from 1984 and 1985. On one level, you know what to expect. But most of the numbers here are less synthesized, more straightforward—and at the same time quite rich, with excellent horns as well as the usual very individual singing. —*John Storm Roberts, Original Music*

Orchestre Baobab

Bass, Clarinet, Guitar, Drums, Saxophone, Vocals / Senegal, Afro-Cuba, Africa
The Orchestre Baobab is composed of Barthelemy Atisso (guitar), Baroune N'Diaye (sax), Sedat Li (bass), Laye Nboub (vocals), Rodolphe Gomis (vocals), and founder Balla Sidibe (vocals), with Issa Cissoko (horn), Peter Oudu (clarinet), Thione Seck (vocals), and Ndiouga Dieng (vocals), who were added soon after formation. Formed in 1970, they became the resident band at the Baobab Club for seven years, which was their glory period. After the club changed ownership, the band played at a couple of other clubs, but the unsatisfactory arrangements led to their departure for Paris in 1978. Things did not go well there either, as there was virtually no publicity. They moved to Marseilles, where there was a larger Senegalese community, but when their situation failed to improve, they returned to Senegal to find popular tastes moving away from dance bands and towards the mbalax of Youssou N'Dour. They were reluctant to abandon their Cuban-influenced sound, but wanted to bring in new influences, and personnel shifts began, with only Balla Sidibe left from the original lineup. In 1985, trying to recapture a sense of direction, Sidibe called his musicians together and made something of a comeback, incorporating more percussion and better lyrics. They were somewhat successful for the rest of the '80s, but nothing approaching the earlier days. —*Steve Huey*

● **Pirate's Choice** / 1982 / World Circuit ✦✦✦✦✦
Too many current releases are hit-hunting hybrids truly deserving of the vile "Afro-pop" label, which overshadow the superb music made in Africa by Africans for Africans. This charming recording from 1982 is the real thing, driving, delicate, and wholly African. It is much of the Afro-Parisian stuff on the market as fresh-squeezed orange juice is to lukewarm Kool-aid. —*John Storm Roberts*

Toure Kunda

Senegal, Djabadong, Africa
Toure Kunda was formed in Senegal by Amadou Tilo Toure to provide singing and drumming accompaniment to the djabadong ceremonies of their native region. To some, djabadong sounds much like reggae, so when Amadou Tilo and his three brothers moved to Paris in the '70s, it seemed natural for them to experiment with a djabadong/reggae fusion. As their popularity increased, the brothers Toure added electric guitars, keys, and more percussion, finally hiring more musicians from Africa and the French Caribbean. After the death of Amadou Tilo the band reorganized and went on to become one of the top commercial attractions in France with their winning mix of reggae, rock, funk, and traditional Senegalese rhythms. —*J. Poet*

Casamance au Clair de Lune / 1984 / Celluloid ✦✦✦
This is an acoustic set of traditional tunes from Senegal. —*J. Poet*

Live / 1984 / Celluloid ✦✦✦✦✦
One of the few live albums that lives up to its name, it's worth its hefty import (French) price. All their early hits appear in extended versions, recorded before an adoring crowd that pushes the musicians to their limits. It is also available as a single CD. —*J. Poet*

E'mma Africa / 1985 / Celluloid ✦✦✦✦✦
The first hit album from the brothers Toure includes "E'mma," one of the most irresistible of African pop tunes. —*J. Poet*

1983-1984 / 1986 / Celluloid ✦✦✦✦✦
This CD compilation contains most of *Amado Tilo* and *Casamance au Clair de Lune*. —*J. Poet*

Karadindi / 1988 / Celluloid ✦✦✦
There are lots of catchy, danceable hits on this good African pop release, with growing rock and funk influences. —*J. Poet*

● **Salam** / 1990 / Trama ✦✦✦✦✦
The brothers Toure still use traditional material, but there's more funk and a more commercial edge to the production in evidence; this import recording (on the French label Trama) is very user-friendly to non-African ears. —*J. Poet*

Sierra Leone Collection

African Elegant / 1992 / Original Music ✦✦✦✦✦
Freetown, Sierra Leone's capital, early developed a charming, calypso-like Creole-language palmwine guitar music. The style's undisputed king was Ebenezeer Calendar, whose Maringar band (acoustic guitar, tuba, percussion) ruled the roost for 30 years. His gentle, extraordinarily catchy hits, on the order of "Jollof Rice" and "Arriah Baby," dominate this

unique collection. Also present are several recordings by the Kru seamen who first developed the guitar style that was to travel via Ghana to the world, as well as some Mandingo and Mende groups with wonderfully eccentric brass playing. —*John Storm Roberts*

Somalia Collection

Jamiila: Songs from a Somali City / 1987 / Original Music ✦✦✦✦✦
Somali popular music has almost never been recorded, yet it has a rich musical culture whose Afro-Islamic ingredients have Swahili, Italian, and Indian garnishes. These delightful performances from 1984 include songs for the oud and flute, acoustic guitar, and guitar with slightly batty electronic organ (replacing the old portable harmonium). It is an authentic grassroots sound, with its unselfconscious mix of tradition and gadgetry, and the street-corner hipness of a music that's strictly a neighborhood affair. —*John Storm Roberts*

South Africa

African Jazz Pioneers

South Africa, Africa
The Pioneers, founded in the '80s, play '50s and '60s South African jazz, attempting to recreate the fun of that era's live performances. Led by sax player Ntemi Piliso, a seasoned marabi star, the group is composed of both veteran marabi players and younger musicians who have picked up the style. —*Steve Huey*

● **Sip 'n' Fly** / 1994 / Flame Tree ✦✦✦✦✦
Mavens of the great days of jazz-tinged kwela remember those mellow, driving days with a mix of love and awe. Both emotions will be revived by this run-don't-walk collection of revivalists, young and old. The classic rhythms of kwela and sax-jive live on, the brass and sax solos are sensational and there's even a really successful little bit of rap. —*John Storm Roberts, Original Music*

Live at the Montreux Jazz Festival / Celluloid ✦✦✦
There's jazz, and there's "township jazz," meaning jazz-influenced dance music, and then there's a township jazz, pretty much a fifty-fifty blend, that is the world's only really solidly based non-US jazz idiom. The Pioneers play this third wonderful style, and last year they blew their audience away in two appearances in Switzerland. This recording lets you hear them do it. —*John Storm Roberts, Original Music*

Boyoyo Boys

Vocals / Mbaqanga, South Africa, Africa
This group would perhaps be unknown outside of South Africa had they not come to the attention of the great rock 'n' roll swindler, Malcolm McClaren, who took their hit single "Puleng" and adapted it for his own production, "Double Dutch." McClaren came to blows with the Boys after refusing to share the royalties from his single. Only after a lengthy legal struggle did the group receive their due. Out of court and on stage, the Boyoyo Boys offer an ebullient music, consisting of chanted, bouncing rhythms. The group suffered a tragic blow in 1984 with the slaying of their drummer, but with their next album, proved to the world that they were *Back in Town*. —*Leon Jackson*

● **Back in Town** / 1987 / Rounder ✦✦✦✦✦
The Boyoyo Boys, among South Africa's premier township ensembles, had to regroup following the 1984 slaying of drummer Archie Mohlala. They took some time before regrouping for this smashing comeback set in 1987. The ten tracks on this CD were prototype Boyoyo Boys material; all were three-minute, steaming workouts with punchy guitar lines, torrid sax and funky bass/drum interplay, everything linked by rousing group vocals and harmonies. Despite being only a 30-minute disc, it doesn't qualify as a ripoff item. —*Ron Wynn*

Tj Today / Aug. 1989 / Rounder ✦✦✦✦✦
The Boyoyo Boys, a four-member South African ensemble, offered boiling-hot examples of 1980s township music on this ten-cut disc. As saxophonists Lukas Pelo and Thomas Phale provided a mix of outside riffs and funky, bluesy licks, bassist Vusi Xhosa laid down booming lines, with guitarist Vusi Nkosi skittering, flickering and riding the waves atop the beat. The songs were short, catchy, hook-laden workouts, done at fever pitch. A bonus was violinist Noise Khanyile, whose sawing, spiraling solos turned several selections into bubbling, explosive triumphs. —*Ron Wynn*

Johnny Clegg (Juluka/Savuka)

Ethnic Fusion, Africa, Mbaqanga, South Africa
Johnny Clegg was the founder and chief songwriter of Juluka, South Africa's first interracial and intercultural rock 'n' roll band. For the first year and a half, Juluka played mostly in Black areas where Whites didn't see them, but as they became more popular they often risked their lives (literally) to play the kind of music they loved. Clegg met Sipho (See-poe)

Mchunu, a "formidable guitarist," when they were both 17. They formed a strong musical and personal bond and in 1976 cut an album of Zulu ethnic songs under the name of Juluka ("sweat"). The next albums added elements of South African folk, rock, funk, and Zulu street guitar. By 1979 they had a Zulu-rock, South African folk-fusion band with six members (three White and three Black) and a platinum album. Juluka's success helped break down the racial barriers that separated musical styles, and before they disbanded in 1985 they even had a Top 40 hit in Europe with "Scatterlings of Africa," a poignant tribute to the African diaspora.

As the political situation heated up in the late '80s, Clegg returned with another interracial band called Savuka ("we have arisen"), this time writing and singing highly political material. After a tumultuous tour of South Africa and western Europe, Savuka inked a worldwide deal with EMI International (Capitol in the US). —*J. Poet*

African Litany / 1982 / Priority ◆◆◆
Juluka's second release with Johnny Clegg, the first album by an integrated rock band in South Africa, went gold in three months. This first single, "Impi," was based on a Zulu war chant and was considered a call to revolution by people in the know. —*J. Poet*

Ubuhle Bemvelo / Jan. 1982 / Priority ◆◆◆
Juluka's follow-up to *African Litany* is a selection of traditional Zulu folk songs done in a rock 'n' roll style. —*J. Poet*

Scatterlings / Oct. 1982 / Warner Bros. ◆◆◆
A good Juluka set, it features "Scatterlings of Africa" and "Simple Things." —*Scott Bultman*

● **Third World Child** / 1987 / Capitol ◆◆◆◆◆
"Asimbonanga (Mandela)" is an anthem already adopted by Joan Baez and others, while the title tune devastatingly discusses what it's like to be asked to "walk in the dreams of the foreigner." —*William Ruhlmann*

Cruel, Crazy, Beautiful World / 1989 / Capitol ◆◆◆
By his third album with Savuka, Clegg had adopted some Los Angeles production techniques, such as those booming drums, perhaps in an attempt to meet the marketplace. But the message is still there: "Woman Be My Country" brilliantly examines Clegg's conflicting feelings about his homeland, while the title song expresses his alternating realism and optimism: "It's your world, so live in it!" —*William Ruhlmann*

★ **The Best of Juluka** / 1991 / Rhythm Safari ◆◆◆◆◆
This is a good summary of Clegg's work with Juluka. —*Scott Bultman*

Johnny Clegg & Juluka Collection / 1996 / Putumayo ◆◆◆◆
Compiling a majority of the highlights of Johnny Clegg and Juluka's long and acclaimed career, this single-disc collection not only offers a perfect introduction to their music, but it also stands as one of the definitive testaments of worldbeat music in the '80s. —*Stephen Thomas Erlewine*

Dollar Brand

Piano, soprano sax, flute, cello, composer / South Africa, Africa
A gifted player, excellent on ballads and able to combine African rhythms and a jazz sensibility in a totally original manner. He began playing piano at seven, and was part of the superb group the Jazz Epistles with Hugh Masekela. This band made the first genuine South African jazz record in 1960. Brand, now known as Abdullah Ibrahim, left South Africa with his wife Sathima Bea Benjamin in 1962 and moved to Zurich. He met Duke Ellington there, who arranged a recording session with him in 1963 and then two years later sponsored an appearance by him at the Newport Jazz Festival. Brand played with Elvin Jones in 1966, toured Europe as a soloist and played in groups with such musicians as Don Cherry, Gato Barbieri and Johnny Gertze. He converted to Islam in 1968. After a return to South Africa and some extensive recording sessions in 1976, Ibrahim moved permanently to New York. He formed his septet Ekaya in 1983. —*Ron Wynn*

● **African Marketplace** / Dec. 1979 / Elektra ◆◆◆◆◆
This is one of Abdullah Ibrahim's most colorful band recordings. With a 12-piece group that includes altoist Carlos Ward, trombonist Craig Harris and bassist Cecil McBee along with some lesser-known names, Ibrahim performs eight folklike originals that pay tribute to his life growing up in South Africa. "The Homecoming Song," "Anthem for the New Nation" and especially "The Wedding" (a beautiful hymn) are particularly memorable. —*Scott Yanow*

Good News from Africa / Enja ◆◆◆◆◆
Wonderful 1973 album that accents and celebrates his African roots, yet also has superior solos and arrangements in a jazz vein. Ibrahim plays flowing, graceful phrases at times; other times, he ranges over the keyboard and is an aggressive, attacking stylist. Bassist and percussionist Johnny Dyani is masterful, both as an accompanist and adding extra colors to pieces with vocals and bells. —*Ron Wynn*

Ladysmith Black Mambazo

Vocals / Africa, Mbube, South Africa
Ladysmith Black Mambazo was founded by Joseph Shabalala in 1974.

They've cut 29 albums over the past 14 years, but the group did not become well known outside of South Africa until Paul Simon asked them to perform on *Graceland.*

Shabalala was born into a poor family that lived on a White man's farm near the town of Ladysmith. There were eight children in the Shabalala family, and, as the oldest boy, it was Joseph's duty to take care of the family after his father died.

Shabalala's first musical experience, save for a bit of fooling around on the guitar, came with a choral group called the Blacks. Shabalala eventually took over leadership of the group and became its main composer.

The Blacks won most of the local vocal competitions and became the most popular Zulu vocal group, but Shabalala felt that something was missing. "I had been hearing a voice inside me," Shabalala said. "I didn't know it, but it was the voice of God." When the voice told him to fast, Shabalala obeyed, and on his fast, he had a vision of a new kind of vocal music. Shortly thereafter he became a Christian. Taking the choral music he heard in the Christian church, he combined it with the Zulu tradition to create his own style.

When the Blacks refused to take part in Shabalala's experiments, he formed Ladysmith Black Mambazo. The group consists of seven bass voices, an alto, a tenor, and Shabalala singing lead. Even if you don't speak Zulu, when they hit a low rumbling note, you can literally feel the power of their voices in your body.

"In Zulu singing there are three major sounds," Shabalala explains. "A high keening ululation; a grunting, puffing sound that we make when we stomp our feet; and a certain way of singing melody. Before Black Mambazo you didn't hear these three sounds in the same songs. So it is new to combine them, although it is still done in a traditional style. We are just asking God to allow us to polish it, to help keep our voices in order so we can praise Him and uplift the people." —*J. Poet*

Induku Kethu / 1984 / Shanachie ◆◆◆
This group can be heard at its most direct and unadorned on this collection, with Joseph Shabalala leading the ensemble through some swooping vocal harmonies and the group's unique stop-and-start call-and-response sequences. (In Zulu.) (Also recommended: The religious collection *Ulwandle Oluncgwele.*) —*William Ruhlmann*

Inala / 1986 / Shanachie ◆◆◆
Here's a release from one of the top modern groups in the style usually called *mbube* or *iscathamiya*, the soul-shaking vocal sound that stems equally from traditional Azanian choral music, US gospel, and the Inkspots—a group whose importance goes far beyond its contribution to Paul Simon's *Graceland* album. These, of course, are straight, no Simon . . . —*John Storm Roberts, Original Music*

Shaka Zulu / 1987 / Warner Bros. ◆◆◆◆◆
In the wake of their participation on his *Graceland* album, Paul Simon produced this Ladysmith album, their most accessible work for Western ears, which is pristinely recorded and sung partially in English. —*William Ruhlmann*

● **Classic Tracks** / 1990 / Shanachie ◆◆◆◆◆
This is a selection of tunes from Ladysmith's many South African albums. —*J. Poet*

Two Worlds One Heart / 1990 / Warner Bros. ◆◆◆
A great album that joins the vocal traditions of North America and South Africa, it includes collaborations with George Clinton, Ray Phiri (*Stimela* and *Graceland*), and gospel star Marvin Winans. —*J. Poet*

liph' iqiniso / 1994 / Shanachie ◆◆◆
The seventh Shanachie release by the premier South African a cappella group is both short (36 minutes) and decisive. The ten selections feature their trademark layered vocals, shimmering harmonies and producer/lead vocalist Joseph Shabbala's transcendent singing rising over the backgrounds. The tracks don't feature any spotlight numbers, but each has sections with memorable exchanges and appealing leads. If anything, the group's customary excellence has led fans to take them for granted. These aren't their finest cuts, but they're not far from them. —*Ron Wynn*

Thuthukani Ngoxolo (Let's Develop in Peace) / 1996 / Shanachie ◆◆◆
Thuthukani Ngoxolo (Let's Develop in Peace), as the title suggests, is a rallying call from Ladysmith Black Mambazo for world peace and genuine understanding. But, as well-intentioned as they are, lyrics rarely matter with music like this—the harmonies and polyrhythms are so enchanting, you tend to become mesmerized and just groove along on the sound. *Thuthukani Ngoxolo (Let's Develop in Peace)* doesn't offer anything out of the ordinary for Ladysmith Black Mambazo, but compared to nearly any other group, the record is quite extraordinary. —*Leo Stanley*

Best of Ladysmith Black Mambazo / Music For Little People ◆◆◆◆
It is only fitting that Ladysmith Black Mambazo introduced the world to the beauty and intricacy of Black South African harmony singing, the extraordinary style known generically as mbube. Ladysmith has been

the preeminent mbube group for some 20 years. Each track on this collection is a unique musical moment which reveals Ladysmith Black Mambazo's special genius and the breathtaking beauty of their deep, rich harmonies. —*MusD*

Sipho Mabuse

Vocals / Pop, Mbaqanga, South Africa, Africa
Former Harari member, Mabuse has gone on to enjoy considerable success with his effortless synthesis of soul, pop, and the township jive known as mbaqanga. —*Leon Jackson*

Harari / 1981 / A&M ♦♦♦♦♦
A solid but unhappily out-of-print album, it's from the pop band Mabuse and Harari led in the mid-'70s. —*J. Poet*

Burn Out / 1985 / CBS ♦♦♦
This EP introduced Europe and America to Mabuse. The title track is an African dance-pop classic and worldwide hit. CBS sold several thousand copies of this one to American dance clubs in 1985, but they were unable to get it to cross over to the pop market. —*J. Poet*

● **Sipho Mabuse** / 1987 / Virgin ♦♦♦♦♦
One of the first African pop records to get wide US distribution, it contains "Burn Out" and several other tracks from the South African album of the same name; again, the market wasn't ready. —*J. Poet*

Chant of the Marching / 1989 / Earthworks ♦♦♦
Another South African take on funk, rock, and Zulu pop, it has many tracks in English. —*J. Poet*

Mahlathini

b. 1937
Vocals / Mbaqanga, South Africa, Africa
Simon Nkabinde Mahlathini (nicknamed "the Lion of Soweto") came to international attention via the 1985 sampler *The Indestructible Beat of Soweto.* He began to tour internationally with female singers The Mahotella Queens, although he has been playing and singing his brand of mbaqanga (Zulu pop music, heavily influenced by traditional singing styles) since the early '60s. Mahlathini started singing on street corners, graduated to men's choral music, and went on to form his own smaller group in the mid-'60s. When he "went electric" in the mid-'70s, his new sound caused a sensation, and much controversy. With the Mahotella Queens supplying their dynamic backing vocals and fancy dance routines (think of a South African version of the Supremes) and Mahlathini's primal groaning filling the air, you don't have to understand the language to get the message, although the group has occasionally recorded in English. Another part of Mahlathini's success is the backing supplied by West Nkosi and the Makgona Tsohle Band. "'Makgona Tsohle' means 'Jack-of-all-trades,'" says Nkosi. "Our mbaqanga is a blend of traditional styles with modern instruments, a music anyone can relate to." —*J. Poet & William Ruhlmann*

● **The Lion of Soweto** / 1987 / Earthworks ♦♦♦♦♦
This compilation introduced Mahlathini to the rest of the world. Primal, growling mbaqanga (with backing vocals by the Mahotella Queens), it prompted many critics to call Mahlathini the "Howlin' Wolf of South Africa." —*J. Poet*

Thokozile / 1988 / Earthworks ♦♦♦
Another exemplary outing from Mahlathini and the Mahotella Queens, this is a kwela-like swing to the arrangements. —*J. Poet*

Paris: Soweto / 1989 / Polydor ♦♦♦
More of Mahlathini and the Mahotella Queens was recorded in Paris at the end of their first post-*Graceland* tour. More produced and glossier than their Shanachie recordings, with a slight concession to the international dance market in the rhythms, it's still not lacking in musical and vocal firepower. —*J. Poet*

Rhythm & Art / 1990 / Shanachie ♦♦♦♦♦
Included is more Zulu and accordion jive from Mahlathini and the Queens, with several songs in English. —*J. Poet*

The Lion Roars / 1991 / Shanachie ♦♦♦
Mbaqanga was in disfavor when Paul Simon's *Graceland* rekindled interest in the form. This is a late-'80s reunion album that shows Mahlathini and the Queens have lost none of their fire. —*J. Poet*

Mbaqanga / 1991 / Verve ♦♦♦
This 1992 album found itself way up there on the Billboard charts, signifying the worldwide recognition that this South African group is finally enjoying, deservedly. Joyful harmonies, spiced with guitars, saxophone, penny whistle, and intense drumming characterize their rhythmic style. —*Ladyslipper*

You're Telling Tales / Shanachie ♦♦♦♦♦
Yes, again . . . .Still, even with mbaqanga coming out of our ears there's room for one more good one, and this is pleasing stuff. The Lion sings a lot as well as growling, and the backing band plays a smooth but

extremely effective version of the South African semirural sound, with splendid soloing by fiddle and accordion. —*John Storm Roberts, Original Music*

Mahotella Queens

Mbaqanga, South Africa, Africa, Jive
The Queens, often heard in concert and on record with deep-voiced "groaner" Simon Mahlathini, represent the South African township style with absolute perfection. Established in 1964 as a session harmony group, they came to prominence in the '70s with their tough vocal style and rock-solid mbaqanga backing band. Some of the original Queens have toured the States with Mahlathini recently, displaying their sprightly dancing and gutsy harmonies to appreciative Western audiences. They are also heard to great effect on the collection album *Soweto Never Sleeps*—Classic Female Zulu Jive (Shanachie 43041) with other sister groups. —*Myles Boisen*

★ **Izibani Zomgqashiyo** / 1986 / Shanachie ♦♦♦♦♦
Striking harmonies in the Mbube style come from four women of South Africa's best female vocal group. They sing in Zulu, with the very upbeat backing of Mbaqanga music: an electric guitar with machine-gun licks of paired notes, whizzing up and down the fretboard; bass notes of rapid counter-melodies played high up in the instrument's register. The content of their material is not overtly political, since it would be banned and the musicians probably jailed if it were, but it reflects the strength and indomitability of their spirits. —*Ladyslipper*

Marriage Is a Problem / Jun. 1991 / Shanachie ♦♦♦
Very danceable and upbeat, it's certain to lift any dragging spirits. —*Ladyslipper*

Women of the World / 1993 / Shanachie ♦♦♦
Although usually heard backing the groans and surging vocals of Mahlathini, the Mahotella Queens can certainly perform on their own. A working unit since 1964, they show on this new release that their harmonies and leads deserve attention on their own. There are celebratory praise songs such as "Africa" and the title track, numbers done in both their traditional language and English, a wonderful remake of Bob Dylan's "I Shall Be Released," and the potent message tracks "Homeless" and "I'm Not Your Good Time Girl." —*Ron Wynn*

Rhythm and Art / Shanachie ♦♦♦
Already widely known and recognized for high-energy stage shows and soaring vocals, this female trio (back after their temporary retirement, and now just three) and male vocalist have revolutionized the South African pop scene. On this 1990 album the group performs five new compositions and two English versions of their most popular songs; it includes what could be the most incredible version of a gospel song, "God Is on Your Side," ever recorded. Again, don't expect overtly political lyrics, but be prepared to be swept away by the sheer power of this release. —*Ladyslipper*

Miriam Makeba

b. Mar. 4, 1934, Johannesburg, South Africa
Vocals / Protest, South Africa, Africa
Born in Johannesburg, South Africa, she played with the Black Mountain Brothers from 1954 to 1957. In 1959 she met Harry Belafonte, who brought her to the States and groomed her career. Makeba's Black Nationalist position in the late '60s led to public backlash, which did not overcome until the '80s. —*Bil Carpenter*

☆ **Evening with Belafonte/Makeba** / 1965 / RCA ♦♦♦♦♦
A '60s album of folk music. —*Bil Carpenter*

● **Pata Pata** / 1983 / Esperance ♦♦♦♦♦
Do you wonder why recordings by this vocalist from South Africa are becoming so rare? This limited-quantity import contains "a multifaceted repertoire that knocks down walls, bridges, barriers, and transforms a dozen different languages into a universal tongue." Her daughter Bongi does backup vocals; it includes several originals such as "Amampondo," "West Wind," and "Ngoma Kurila," plus the Tanzanian folktune "Malaika," and other writers' works. The CD contains four extra songs. —*Ladyslipper*

The World of Miriam Makeba / 1986 / RCA ♦♦♦
Included is material in Spanish, English, and African languages; songs include "Forbidden Games," "Dubula," "Pole Mze," and "Tonados de Media Noche." —*Ladyslipper*

Sangoma / 1988 / Warner Bros. ♦♦♦♦♦
Makeba's comeback album, her first US release in almost a decade, is a beautiful collection of traditional South African songs with spare production values that highlight the power of Makeba's vocals. This is an excellent set of Xhosa folk songs she learned as a child. —*J. Poet & Bil Carpenter*

Miriam Makeba / 1989 / RCA ♦♦♦
The first American album from Makeba is anout-of-print classic. —*J. Poet*

Eyes on Tomorrow / Jun. 11, 1991 / Polydor ✦✦✦

This 1991 release features some very special guest artists: Nina Simone, Dizzy Gillespie, and Hugh Masekela. Freedom is the absolute theme on this internationally recorded album (Johannesburg, Brussels, Bologna, NYC), with a very upbeat and dedicated spirit. Nina Simone collaborates with Miriam on a song well known in Simone's repertoire: they combine the traditional African "Thulasizwe" with "I Shall Be Released." Rich, resonating backing vocal choirs throughout. —*Ladyslipper*

Africa / Oct. 1991 / Jive/Novus ✦✦✦✦✦

This 1991 compilation encompasses several recordings from Miriam's early US career, from 1960-1965, yet the content and arrangements sound fresh and timely. It includes works from her collaborations with Harry Belafonte, and former-husband Hugh Masekela, with spare instrumental backup—guitar, percussion—and a lovely backup chorus . . . 23 songs in all. —*Ladyslipper*

● **The Best Of . . .** / ✦✦✦✦✦

There are classics and there are Classics. The Skylarks recordings were and are Classics, the setting in which Makeba's unparalleled voice shone most brightly (aided, let's remember, by the almost equally fine Dorothy Masuka). This stuff is pure heaven, with or without Spokes Mashiyane sitting in on penny-whistle: the greatest moments of the greatest women's sound in Africa. —*John Storm Roberts, Original Music*

The Click Song / Esperance ✦✦✦✦✦

This is a classic: her first long-playing album, recorded with the Belafonte Folk Singers. It includes her well-known songs "The Click Song," "Mbube," another version also known as "Wimoweh," "House of the Rising Sun," "Iya Guduza," which triple tracks her voice and was probably the first multiple recording in Zulu, the humorous "One More Dance," and others, performed in Xhosa, Swazi, Zulu, and English. —*Ladyslipper*

Welela / Mercury ✦✦✦

This dynamic 1989 release contains songs in both English and African dialects, including a reinterpretation of her classic "Pata Pata," which means "Touch, Touch," as well as "African Sunset, Soweto Blues." —*Ladyslipper*

Dorothy Masuka

Vocals / Jazz, South Africa, Africa, Zimbabwe

Dorothy Masuka was born in Rhodesia but received her schooling in South Africa and chose to stay there after graduating in order to pursue a musical career. She started out in a show called *African Jazz and Variety*, with Miriam Makeba, Hugh Masekela, and others, imitating American jazz greats like Ella Fitzgerald. With the full-blown emergence of Apartheid in Rhodesia, she moved to London where she lived for many years, performing on one occasion at Wembley during Harold Wilson's election campaign. Masuka went back to Rhodesia in 1965 but left again and did not return until 1980. Masuka's musical style is known as mabira: a fusion of swing and Zulu melodies, sung with great force and intensity. Her earlier songs, and most notably "Kutheni Zulu," were hard-edged and political, but she has since chosen to de-emphasize polemics in favor of poetics. Masuka's songs in the 1990s are upbeat and chipper. A veteran performer now, with more than 40 years of performing and touring under her belt, she is finally enjoying celebrity status in the world music world and hopes to crown her career by attaining the financial security that most African performers still lack. —*Leon Jackson*

● **Pata Pata** / 1991 / Mango ✦✦✦✦✦

This Zimbabwean woman has a beautiful, flowing voice and is backed up by other female vocalists and a "typical" Afro-pop band—twangy finger-picked electric guitar, steady percussion with lots of hand claps, keyboards and horns, yielding a tribal, hypnotic effect, some of it great for dancing . . . this is her first worldwide album release. —*Ladyslipper*

Mbongeni Ngema

Guitar, Fluegelhorn, Keyboards, Vocals / South Africa, Africa

Ngema wrote and performed *Woza Albert*, an anti-apartheid comedy/drama that got rave reviews when it toured the US in 1984. Along with Hugh Masekela, Ngema wrote *Sarafina*, a musical drama that told the story of a day in the life of a South African township as seen through the eyes of a group of high school children. —*J. Poet*

★ **Sarafina [Original Cast Album]** / 1988 / RCA ✦✦✦✦✦

The songs express the conflicting feelings of hope, terror, love, and struggle of life under the gun. —*J. Poet*

Time to Unite / 1988 / Mango ✦✦✦

Songs of struggle and liberation, featuring the cast of *Sarafina*. —*J. Poet*

Dudu Pukwana

b. Jul. 18, 1938, Port Elizabeth, South Africa, d. Jun. 28, 1990, London, UK

Sax (Alto) / Avant-Garde, South Africa, Africa

A fiery, inspirational alto saxophonist, Dudu Pukwana's wailing leads

and indomitable spirit brilliantly fused township jive, free music, and honking R&B. Pukwana actually began on piano, taking lessons from his father at the age of ten. He joined Tete Mbambisa's Four Yanks as a teen in the late '50s after the family moved from Port Elizabeth to Cape Town, South Africa. He also started learning saxophone from Nick Moyake, and listening to imported American jazz and R&B records. Chris McGregor invited Pukwana to join the Blue Notes, an integrated band in the early '60s. He'd eventually depart his homeland with the rest of the band, settling temporarily in Switzerland, then later in London. Pukwana stayed with McGregor's groups until 1969, when he joined Hugh Masekela's Union of South Africa in America. After they disbanded in 1970, Pukwana returned to England and formed his own band. They were initially Spear, and later Assegai. Pukwana also worked with Keith Tippett's Centipede, Jonas Gwangwa, Traffic, the Incredible String Band, Gwigwi Mrwebi, Sebothane Bahula's Jabula, Harry Miller's Isipingo, and the Louis Moholo Unit. Pukwana recorded with Mrwebi in 1970, and made two albums with Assegai before founding a new edition of Spear in 1972. He also played that year on Masekela's *Home Is Where The Music Is* Chisa session. The new Spear, which included Mongezi Feza, Moholo and Miller, plus Bixo Mngqikana, made some excellent albums, among them *In The Townships* and *Flute Music* before they disbanded in 1978. Pukwana formed the big band Zila, recorded with them, and continued heading the group until his death of liver failure in 1990. Sadly, none of Pukwana's sessions are available in America on CD. —*Ron Wynn*

In the Townships / Aug. 25, 1973-Nov. 10, 1973 / Earthworks ✦✦✦

An excellent recording with Feza, Louis Moholo, and Harry Miller. —*Michael G. Nastos*

● **Diamond Express** / 1975 / Freedom ✦✦✦✦✦

An early-'70s recording of this saxophonist, with the late trumpeter Mongezi Feza, in their last meeting before Feza died of pneumonia. Squeaky sax and ensemble in an unabashed mood. South African free jazz. —*Michael G. Nastos*

Zila / 1981 / JIKA ✦✦✦✦

A live date at the 100 Club in London, with a larger ensemble and great soloists. —*Michael G. Nastos*

In the Townships / Earthworks ✦✦✦

Exciting Afro-pop, fusion, and jazz set led by the frenetic saxophonist who was a premier soloist among the class of expatriate South African musicians. Pukwana leads a crew of fellow exiles through songs that both celebrate and commemorate their background, with lots of dashing solos and flashy rhythms as well. —*Ron Wynn*

South Africa Collection

★ **Indestructible Beat of Soweto** / 1986 / Shanachie ✦✦✦✦✦

This anthology of South African artists surprised everyone by becoming a best seller. It introduced worldbeatniks to Ladysmith Black Mambazo, Mahlathini, and Moses Mchunu, and paved the way for Paul Simon's *Graceland*. Winner of *The Village Voice*'s Jazz and Pop Poll for Best Record of 1987, it's an essential sampler of modern African styling, a revelation and a joy. —*J. Poet & Hank Davis*

Izibani Zomgqashiyo / 1989 / Shanachie ✦✦✦✦✦

One of the lively, hip, funky Mgqashiyo rhythm's hottest exponents is this group of five women from Southern Africa, mostly around Soweto, who have been together since 1964. They were voted the 1975 Radio Bantu Best Group of the Year. At times, they are also accompanied by their male "groaners" (Robert Mbazo Mkhize, Potatoes Mazambane, and Joseph Mthimkhulu) and a super band. —*"Blue" Gene Tyrany*

Music of Africa / Kaleidophone ✦✦✦

The most outstanding contribution to documenting African musics is the *Sound of Africa* series by Hugh Tracey. That entire collection can be found only in particular college libraries and homes of collectors, but the ten-volume *Music of Africa* is available on the Kaleidophone label. It includes separate volumes on strings, reeds (mbira), drums, flutes and horns, xylophones, guitars (two volumes), and volumes on the music of Rhodesia, Tanzania, and Uganda. —*David L. Mayers*

Rhythm of Resistance: Music of Black South Africa / Earthworks ✦✦✦

This is a broad survey of South African styles collected by filmmaker Jeremy Marre on a documentary shoot—good variety but not on a par with many collections released since then. —*Myles Boisen*

Singing in an Open Space / 1990 / Rounder ✦✦✦✦✦

This set of Zulu semirural music from 1962 to 1982 is perhaps the best South African release in the current glut. None of it is traditional (as the above-average notes rightly point out, the word is routinely misused). All of it—voices, guitars, fiddles, harmonicas—is far more intense than the usual city sounds. —*John Storm Roberts*

Siya Hamba / 1989 / Original Music ✦✦✦✦

Two faces of '50s Azanian music appear here, from recordings by Hugh

Tracey of the International Library of African Music. The first side covers a wide range of rural sounds, including some amazing harmonica (dances with vocals and strange hyperventilations, bluesy solos); concertina; an entirely unexpected piece backed by autoharp; and various wonderful country guitar styles. Side two is a session of small-town dance music from the jazz- and jump blues-influenced kwela period, with some terrific women singers. —*John Storm Roberts*

Sudan

Abdel Aziz el Mubarak

Vocals, Oud / Sudan, Africa

Abdel Aziz was almost fated to become a performer: the child of a musical family who lived in an area noted for its music (Medani), he got an early start on the ladder of fame, as an angel-voiced school boy. He began singing for Sudanese radio in the early '70s and in 1975 enjoyed his first big hit with "Laih Ya Galbi Laih" (Why, My Heart, Why?). Abdel Aziz plays oud and sings, as do many Sudanese musicians, but he is anything but constricted by local sounds, happily blending traditional and Western musical forms. He toured England in 1987-1988 to great acclaim. —*Leon Jackson*

Abdel Aziz el Mubarak / 1987 / Globestyle ✦✦✦✦✦
Mubarak is one of Sudan's most popular bandleaders, a man who combines Western influences (including reggae) with his country's age-old Muslim traditions. —*J. Poet*

Songs from the City / World Circuit ✦✦✦✦
Here's two versions of the splendid Sudanese sound, the most Arabic of all the Afro-Islamic idioms. Salim is backed by oud, percussion, and the small portable harmonium so popular in India. Mubarak substitutes an accordion for the harmonium. Salim is the more consciously traditional in feel, Mubarak the more powerful. But neither album is to be missed (though it would be nice if somebody recorded Mubarak with his usual, larger and more syncretic band). —*John Storm Roberts, Original Music*

● **Straight from the Heart** / World Circuit ✦✦✦✦✦
Mubarak was featured on an earlier release with a small group, but this is a better release: Mubarak as the Sudanese hear him, backed by a ten-piece group including accordion and saxophones. A fine live recording (made at a London concert), it shows off one of the most exciting and least known of the Afro-Arab pop idioms. —*John Storm Roberts*

Hamza El Din

Lute / World Fusion, Africa, Neo-Traditional, Sudan

One of the first African musicians to gain widespread international recognition, Hamza El Din is a Sudanese master of the oud, or the fretless lute. Western listeners are as likely as not to have been exposed to his work via the Grateful Dead, who have played with him onstage occasionally. (El Din also helped arrange the Dead's tour of Egypt.) He has played an integral role in modernizing Nubian music, using his work to both evoke and tell stories of Nubian life. El Din was originally trained to be an engineer, but changed direction and enrolled in the Middle Eastern School of Music, where he began to compose his own songs. On a fellowship to study Western classical music in Rome, he met American Gino Foreman, who exposed Hamza's work to Joan Baez and Bob Dylan. This resulted in a contract with Vanguard. His mid-'60s album, *Al Oud—Instrumental and Vocal Music From Nubia*, was one of the first "world" music recordings to achieve wide exposure in the West. In the second half of the 1960s, El Din spent much of his time in America, living in guitarist Sandy Bull's apartment for a while. Taking a series of teaching positions in various American locations, he also found time to record a Nonesuch album in 1968, *Escalay*, that is considered one of the best recordings of Nubian music. *Eclipse* is his most notable post-*Escalay* record, raising his profile in the US when it was issued on CD by Rykodisc. —*Richie Unterberger*

Al Oud / 1965 / Vanguard ✦✦✦✦
His second album is similar in tone to his debut, featuring original compositions based on Nubian folk traditions, masterful oud playing, and soothing vocals. Serene and haunting, this was among the first world music to make an international impact. —*Richie Unterberger*

★ **Escalay: The Water Wheel** / 1968 / Nonesuch ✦✦✦✦✦
Extensive selections of a unique style of music personally developed by the soloist-vocalist on oud and tar. *Escalay: The Water Wheel—Oud Music of Nubia* is the recording that brought El Din's Nubian traditions to the attention of many in the West—an ethnomusicological classic. —*Myles Boisen & David L. Mayers*

Eclipse / 1978 / Rykodisc ✦✦✦✦✦
These meditatively paced traditional songs are by a master of Sudanese music. Hamza's deep, smoky voice is accompanied by the oud—and by a precursor to the lute—and by the compelling use of a simple Nubian frame drum called the tar. This is a beautiful, even lush recording of El Din's latest oud mastery. —*Bob Tarte & Myles Boisen*

A Song of the Nile / JVC ✦✦✦
A beautiful introduction to Nubian culture of Sudan, for many Hamza is a true hero of world music. He introduced this deep tradition to people all over Europe, the US, and Asia. Music from the Horn of Africa has a very powerful pull. The most beautiful recordings are on the Museum Collection of West Berlin. These recordings by Robert Gotlieb feature stunning performances from the Blue Nile region. —*David L. Mayers*

Abdel Gadir Salim

Vocals, Oud / Merdoum, Sudan, Africa

In a country where nationalist lyrics have been the norm and governmental repression the standard response, Abdel Gadir Salim has stood out as a charismatic, yet resolutely non-political, musician: vibrant, successful, innovative, and widely admired. Abdel Gadir was born in Dilling, in the far west of this country, but started out by writing and performing distinctly urban songs that sounded as if they belonged in Khartoum. He studied both classical European and Arabic music at the Khartoum Institute of Music and started playing oud at the suggestion of a friend. In the early 1970s, he moved away from his city sound and turned back toward the musical culture of his own Kordofan province, playing regional folk songs and celebrations of Kodorfan. Sudan is often called the bridge between Arabia and Africa, and Abdel Gair has taken it as his mission to fuse Arabic and African sounds of the country, taking musical scales and motifs from the former and wild percussion from the latter. The lyrics to his songs (he rarely writes the words himself) address any number of themes ranging from traditional love ballads to educational polemics, although he is always careful to avoid antagonizing the Islamic government. Abdel Gadir sometimes likes to sing alone, but more often than not he keeps the company of his seven-piece backing band, the All-Stars, who count the virtuoso saxophonist Hamid Osman Abdalla among their ranks. A successful musician who has appeared on radio and television, recorded in England, and toured widely, Abdel Gadir still manages to divide his time creatively between music and heading a Sudanese school in Chad. —*Leon Jackson*

● **Nujum Al-Lail/Stars of the Night** / 1989 / Shanachie ✦✦✦✦
This silky-voiced Sudanese bandleader delivers a strong set of swaying music highlighted by the gentle alto saxophone of Abdel Hadi. Included is "A'Abir Sikkah," a successful attempt to meld reggae with a local village rhythm. —*Bob Tarte*

The Merdoum Kings Play Songs of Love / 1992 / World Circuit ✦✦✦
Backed by the All Stars, a seven-piece band with an understated but compelling orchestral sound, Abdel Gadir returns with more lush music from the Sudan. The complex layering of instruments and medium-boil tempos suggests the effortless flow of a juju all-nighter. —*Bob Tarte*

Tanzania

Mlimani Park Orchestra

Tanzania, Africa

Formed in 1978 by twelve musicians under the sponsorship of Tanzania Transport and Taxi Drivers' Association. Core performers included vocalists Ilassani Bitchuka and Muhiddin Maalim, guitarist Abel Balthazar, and bandleader/guitarist/saxophonist/arranger Michael Enoch, who recently retired from performing due to illness. These musicians had been in Nuta Jazz and helped form Dar International. They won the national music contest in 1982 and had a long string of hits over the next few years, changing their sponsorship to that of the Dar Development Corporation in 1983. In 1985, several members, including Bitchuka, formed International Orchestre Safari Sound, which stole Mlimani Park's thunder until Bitchuka decided to return a few years later. —*Steve Huey*

● **Sikinde** / Line ✦✦✦✦✦
This is a great compilation of '80s recordings. A big group and, thanks to the flexibility of cassette (Tanzania has no record industry), it lays out at length in fine style. Expensive, but not to be missed on any account—a rare-to-unique release with great horns, real-thing strength, and an absence of worldbeat slickness. —*John Storm Roberts*

Sungi / African Music ✦✦✦
Mlimani Park on their first European tour, this is a stripped-down 12-man version with a front line of two trumpets and two saxes (the full band is a 30-piece), and with overdubs on only one cut. The resulting sound is less rich, but as tight and joyous as "live" recordings tend to be, even in the studio. As a bonus, the group's original lead singer, Hassani Bitchuka, is back after a decade. —*John Storm Roberts, Original Music*

Remmy Ongala

Guitar, Vocals / Tanzania, Africa

Ongala, who became interested in music as a child through his father, unfortunately lost both his parents at age nine. He joined a youth band called Bantu Success at age 17 as a drummer and singer, leaving in 1966 due to familial objections. Two years later, he reentered music as a guitarist, influenced by Franco and Slim Abdullah, and played with several groups, including Success Mwachame, Mickey Jazz, and Uganda's Grand Mika Jazz. He then moved to Tanzania and joined Orchestre Makassy, which also featured ex-OK Jazz guitarist Fan Fan. Ongala went solo in 1980 and formed the first incarnation of Matimila, developing the band into its current alignment of three guitars, sax, trumpet, bass, and drums. They play a number of Zairean roots styles and have grown quite popular both in Tanzania and on the international circuit, recording for Peter Gabriel's WOMAD label on several occasions. —*Steve Huey*

Songs for the Poor Man / 1990 / Real World ✦✦✦
This Tanzanian take on soukous is as restrained as the Zairian form is hedonistic. Ongala's songs on social themes are delivered with winning conviction. —*Bob Tarte*

Mambo / 1991 / Real World ✦✦✦✦
Backed by Orchestre Super Matimila, Ongala trades the laidback soukous of his first US release for political songs—in English and Swahili—whose directness recalls Nigeria's Fela Anikulapo Kuti and includes touches of contemporary Latin music and a shot of rhythm & blues. —*Bob Tarte*

● **Nalilia Mwana** / Womad ✦✦✦✦✦
Life gets very confusing in East Africa. Ongala is Congolese by origin, and his group consists mostly of expatriate Zairians. Not that the sound is soukous: it's a mix of truly Tanzanian elements with early-'70s boucher. The results are highly individual—and, given that contemporary Tanzanian bands just don't get recorded, not to be passed up. —*John Storm Roberts*

Tanzania Collection

African Moves, Vol. 1 / Jan. 1987 / Rounder ✦✦✦✦
This CD has soukous from Tabu Ley Rochereau, juju from Ebenezer Obey, and highlife from African Brothers, as well as other artists. —*J. Poet*

Music of Zanzibar: Taarab 2 / 1988 / GlobeStyle ✦✦✦✦✦
The vocal approach is borrowed from Indian film music, the instrumentation from Arabic orchestras, and the rhythms from Latin America—but the music's heart is as large as its influences. Deliciously cornball in the best pop-music sense, it's from Zanzibar (now part of Tanzania). —*Bob Tarte*

Music of Zanzibar: Taarab 3 / 1990 / GlobeStyle ✦✦✦✦✦
This is a collection of hits by some of Zanzibar's best taarab bands, including supergroups Ikhwani Safaa Musical Club and Culture Musical Club. —*J. Poet*

Tunisia

Hassan Elgharbi

Africa, Tunisia
Enchanted Kanun / CDDA ✦✦✦✦✦
Elgharbi, Tunisia's leading player of the kanun zither, is a major virtuoso. In 1976 he won the grand prize at Iran's prestigious Shiraz Music Festival. Here he plays the piece that gained him the prize, along with various other improvisations on traditional modes and personal compositions (one backed by a bassist!). The CD winds up with a couple of recordings by an Egyptian virtuoso of the early 20th century. —*John Storm Roberts*

Uganda

Geoffrey Oryema

Guitar, Vocals / Africa, Uganda
Oryema came from a highly musical family: his father, a government minister, played the nanga, while his mother was the director of the Ugandan national dance troupe, the Heart Beat of Africa. His grandfathers and uncles were also musicians and storytellers. Oryema learned to play the nanga, guitar, thumb piano, and flute as a teenager, but his progression was interrupted when his father was abducted and murdered by Idi Amin's government, and, perceiving the danger that the remaining family was in, Geoffrey was smuggled into Kenya in a car. He soon moved to Paris, drawing on traditional folklore and the theme of exile for his subject matter, and found a large East African (and a small Western) following. Oryema recorded his debut album with Peter Gabriel and Brian Eno and contributed a track to the Leonard Cohen tribute album, *I'm Your Fan*. —*Steve Huey*

Exile / 199_ / Atlantic ✦✦✦
Oryema plays the nanga, a zither described as having seven strings, though some have one string that runs seven times across the instrument, making them hell to tune. This is half of a terrific CD—wonderful except when Brian Eno and co. get in on the act and undercut it. You can

program out the well-meaning-but-blah bits—unless you disagree anyway, in which case all is well. —*John Storm Roberts, Original Music*

● **Beat the Border** / Oct. 1, 1993 / Real World ✦✦✦✦✦
This highly creative mix of Ugandan songs and laidback rock should have been a disaster, since the genres meet on the field of ambient dreams—a woozy terrain amply littered with the rainsticks of fallen warriors. But ex-pat Ugandan Oryema neither tries mainstreaming African sources to fit rock fissures nor piles extra beats and instruments on the heads of reluctant Western forms. Instead, like any good ambient technician, he subjugates every other element to the service of applying textures so palpably rich you wish you could drizzle them over sauteed vegetables. Just to prove it's not all dial twiddling, he kicks in with first-rate songwriting to boot. —*Bob Tarte*

Samite

Flute, Piano, Vocals / Neo-Traditional, Africa, Uganda
Singer and multi-instrumentalist Samite is a little like Francis Bebey in that he overdubs both his own voice and various African and Western instruments (including the big East African litungu lyre, finger piano, and flutes). While he has a slight, slight folky edge in places and is not a strong solo singer, his overdubbed polyphonic vocals and most of his instrumental work is gorgeous. —*John Storm Roberts*

● **Abaaba Bakesa** / 1992 / Shanachie ✦✦✦✦
Abaaba Bakesa—Dance, My Children, Dance offers joyful, endearing, traditional-based songs performed on marimba, kalimba (finger piano), and litungu (Ugandan harp). Samite's mellifluous vocals exert a powerful charm. It's recommended for listeners with children. —*Bob Tarte*

Pearl of Africa Reborn / 1992 / Shanachie ✦✦✦
Fuller instrumentation and punchier production than his first release help embed firmly in memory these bright pop songs derived from Ugandan stories. Musicians from Senegal, the US, and Barbados join the avuncular Samite in a loving tribute to his mother that's perfect for families everywhere. —*Bob Tarte*

Uganda Collection

The Kampala Sound: 1960s Ugandan Dance Music / 1988 / Original Music ✦✦✦✦✦
It's a unique recording, since the national shipwreck caused by Idi Amin's policies sank the Uganda dance-music scene almost before it got going. These kicking, charming cuts from 1964-1968 are backed by Kenyan and Zairian as well as Ugandan musicians. But the mellow vocal sound is unique, and some of the numbers here deserve to be pan-African classics. —*John Storm Roberts*

West Africa

Ali Farka Toure

b. 1939
Guitar, Vocals / Africa, Mali
One of the most internationally successful West African musicians of the last decade, Ali Farka Toure has been described as "the African John Lee Hooker" so many times that it's probably beginning to grate on both Toure's and Hooker's nerves. There is a lot of truth to the comparison, however, and it isn't exactly an insult. The guitarist, who also plays other instruments such as calabash and bongos, shares with Hooker (and similar American bluesmen like Lightnin' Hopkins) a predilection for low-pitched vocals and mid-tempo, foot-stomping rhythms, often playing with minimal accompaniment., Toure's delivery is less abrasive than Hooker's, and the general tone of his material somewhat sweeter. Widespread success on the order of Hooker will probably not be in the offing, though, as Toure sings in several languages, and only occasionally in English. As he once told *Option*, his are songs "about education, work, love, and society." If he and Hooker sound quite similar, it's probably not by conscious design, but due to the fact that both draw inspiration from African rhythmic and musical traditions that extend back many generations., Toure was approaching the age of 50 when he came to the attention of the burgeoning world music community in the West via a self-titled album in the late '80s. Since then he's toured often in North America and Europe, and recorded frequently, sometimes with contributions from Taj Mahal and members of the Chieftains. 1994's *Talking Timbuktu*, on which he was joined by Ry Cooder, was his most well-received effort to date. It was also proof that not all Third World-First World collaborations have to dilute their non-Western elements to achieve wide acceptance. — *Richie Unterberger*

★ **Ali Farka Toure** / 1988 / Mango ✦✦✦✦✦
At first blush you think you're hearing American Delta blues—then the Malian-language vocals kick in. This starkly beautiful acoustic guitar has tasty calabash and bongo percussion. —*Bob Tarte*

The River / Jan. 1990 / Mango ✦✦✦✦✦
Toure's second release expands his adventuresome blues-based approach, with a harmonica, sax, and native violin beefing up the sound on several cuts. —*Bob Tarte*

African Blues / Feb. 1990 / Shanachie ✦✦✦
This is a compilation of formative import recordings from this West African bluesman. —*Myles Boisen*

Source / Nov. 1991 / Hannibal ✦✦✦✦✦
African guitarist Ali Farka Toure's previous releases were wonderful mixes of traditional language and rhythms being supported by contemporary concerns, instrumentalists, and producers. His most recent session features his working band backing Toure in a series of impassioned, animated tunes that are done in both his native tongue and English. The similarity between Toure's sparse playing and percussive writing and early blues songs has been noted. What also deserves mention is the cohesive qualities his band have and the way his electric and acoustic playing, with its light, frilly air, fills in the spaces underneath his vocals easily. —*Ron Wynn*

Talking Timbuktu / 1994 / World Circuit ✦✦✦
Guitarist Ali Farka Toure has repeatedly bridged the gap between traditional African and contemporary American vernacular music, and this release continues that tradition. The CD features him singing in 11 languages and playing acoustic and electric guitar, six-string banjo, njarka, and percussion, while teaming smartly with an all-star cast that includes superstar fusion bassist John Patitucci, session drummer Jim Keltner, longtime roots music great Ry Cooder (who doubled as producer), venerable guitarist Gatemouth Brown, and such African percussionists and musicians as Hamma Sankare on calabash and Oumar Toure on congas. —*Ron Wynn*

Timbarma / World Circuit ✦✦✦
Here's one of two recent releases of the great Malian acoustic guitarist, both typical. As usual, he plays a style rooted in traditional kora music, but shaded by blues and other guitar techniques from "outside." On one level Farka's work has links with both the "new age" of Fanta Sacko and traditionally based composers in other countries. But as Farka fans know, the results are very special. This one has English notes, though they're not very informative. —*John Storm Roberts, Original Music*

West Africa Collection

Musique d'Afrique Occidentale / Vogue ✦✦✦✦✦
An excellent sampling from West Africa, it includes xylophones, women's chorus, flutes, drums, and musical bow. This particular recording has had a profound effect on many of my friends as an introduction to African music. It's out of print, but worth searching for. —*David L. Mayers*

Zaire

M'bilia Bel

b. Jan. 10, 1959, Kinshasa, Zaire
Vocals / Soukous, Zaire, Africa, Congo (Brazzaville)
Bel's career took off in the mid-'80s when she sang alongside Tabu Ley on a number of recordings and tours, also recording solo albums at the same time. After her first child was born, she took some time off and decided to part company with Ley, making one last album with him in 1987. She moved to Paris and hooked up with guitarist Rigo Star, who composed and arranged much of her material. Most of her lyrics revolve around themes of adult love, which has proven controversial on some occasions. She toured the US, UK, and West Africa from 1989 to 1990, drawing enthusiastic crowds. More recently, she has taken to experimenting within the traditional rumba-soukous framework, mixing in rap and other elements, with mixed results. —*Steve Huey*

Bameli Soy / 1987 / Shanachie ✦✦✦✦✦
This album, by one of Africa's top female vocalists, is replete with Congolese rhythms, harmonies, percussion, and energetic joyousness. —*Ladyslipper*

● **Phénomène** / Melodie Makers ✦✦✦✦✦
Bel sang for years with Rochereau and went out on her own in 1988. Bameli Soy presents her in the Rochereau days. The marvelous *Phénomène* was the first fruit of her artistic freedom and it's wonderful, with ace arranger Rigo Star's work framing her sensuous style without making it soupy. And given how well her style and voice blended with the benign drive of Afrisa International, as Bameli Soy attests, her solo success was against considerable self-competition. —*John Storm Roberts*

8/10 Benedicta / Sonodisc ✦✦✦
Soukous guitar is inherently pretty, and Zairian women singers have always sung dovelike. The continuing transformation of Bel into Kinshasa-pop diva works by accentuating these qualities rather than departing from or adding to them, and therefore works wonderfully. This is, in

fact, as enchanting a record as *Phénomène*, flowering lushly and organically out of its native soil. —*John Storm Roberts, Original Music*

Franco (L'Okanga La Ndju Pene Luambo Makiadi)

b. 1938, Sona-Bata, Zaire, d. Oct. 1989
Guitar / Soukous, Zaire, Africa, Congo (Brazzaville)
After World War II, Kinshasa (the capitol of what is now Zaire) became a bustling city where the popular music of Ghana (highlife), Cuba (rumba), and various local groups simmered down into the folkloric form of pop known as soukous. Franco, "the Sorcerer of the Guitar," was the leader of the TPOK Jazz Band, the most influential and popular band in Africa's modern history. A natural guitar talent, Franco joined Ebengo Dewayon's Watam band while in his early teens, cutting his first guitar solo record, "Bolingo Na Ngai Beatrice," at the tender age of 13. He formed the first edition of TPOK at the age of 15, and the group dominated the charts from that moment until Franco's death in 1990. —*J. Poet*

20ème Anniversaire / 1976 / African Music ✦✦✦
A two-record (French import) set released to celebrate Franco's 20th year in the music business, it's a good buy if you can find it. —*J. Poet*

● **Franco & His All Powerful TPOK Jazz** / 1984 / Makossa ✦✦✦✦✦
One of the master's last big hits, "Tres Impolie," has a catchy chorus, great guitar fireworks, and a relentless groove. —*J. Poet*

Originalité / 1987 / Retro ✦✦✦
Remastered from original 78-rpm singles cut between 1956 and 1959, these are the hits that established Franco (and TPOK Jazz Band) as Africa's reigning guitar god. —*J. Poet*

Still Alive / Koch International ✦✦✦
Recorded in Holland in 1987, two years before Franco's death, sound quality aside, this is far superior to any of his studio LPs. It has a joyousness, a . . . something I've not heard on other recordings; the dynamics and timbres shift from mood to mood as the songs progress; it's far more adventurous than any Diblo disc for example (some of it sounds positively West African!). Though the sound is not perfect, the live mixing is excellent. —*Carl Hoyt, Original Music*

Mario/Les "On Dit" / Esperance ✦✦✦✦✦
These contain pieces of two earlier LPs. "Mario" was a hit of hits, and for good reason: this is the medication as prescribed throughout, with the plaintive sax and rumba-era backup vocal sound that both Franco and Rochereau recently re-adopted. —*John Storm Roberts, Original Music*

Live in Europe / Esperance ✦✦✦
No performance location is listed on what might have been Franco's last European tour. Which matters less is that there aren't huge differences (crowd enthusiasm aside) from his records. Still, live performance almost always has a little extra intensity, and as a different sort of bonus there's a fine, unusual (for Franco) song called "Miguel." —*John Storm Roberts, Original Music*

Franco & TPOK Jazz 1980/1981 / Sonodisc ✦✦✦
With a gentler, more earthy Caribbean influence than the later Afro-zouk ventures, Franco and OK Jazz glorified and personified the roots of the rumba, and certainly carried it to a new peak (especially in adding the faster second part, the sébène). Sam Mangwana is an extraordinary singer on his own wonderful albums, and the legendary sessions on this CD (including "Cooperation") are, for once, just that. —*Carl Hoyt, Original Music*

Kanda Bongo Man

b. 1955, Inongo, Zaire
Guitar, Vocals / Soukous, Zaire, Africa, Congo (Brazzaville)
Paris-based Kanda Bongo Man has concocted a winning soukous formula that has sold thousands of records, but his path to stardom has been long and hard. Prior to his move to France in 1979, the Bongo Man spent decades playing in Kinshasa soukous groups, and even after arriving in Europe, he supplemented his musical earnings by working in a Paris glass factory. Together with guitarists Diblo Dibala and (yes, you read right) Rigo Starr, he began to put together a souped-up dance music based on soukous. His 1981 release *Lylole* took him out of the factory and into the big time. Subsequent hits, *Kwassa Kwassa* and *Zing Zong*, assured the world of his international status. —*Leon Jackson*

Non Stop Non Stop / 1985 / Globestyle ✦✦✦✦✦
Kanda sticks with the small-combo format that stood the style in such good stead when it was at its most creative. In addition, these guys have a strong sense of where the music has come from a more intelligent approach to the newer influences than many of their coevals. —*John Storm Roberts, Original Music*

★ **Amour Fou/ Crazy Love** / 1988 / Hannibal ✦✦✦✦✦
Sharp soukous from two Paris albums. Diblo Dibala's agile guitar is a real plus on this American debut. —*Myles Boisen*

Kwassa Kwassa / 1989 / Hannibal ◆◆◆
More dance-floor fun comes from this very uptempo and infectious Zairian pop. —*Myles Boisen*

Kanda Bongo Man / 1990 / Globestyle ◆◆◆◆◆
Early hits by one of the hottest new wave soukous bands, it features lead guitarist Diblo Dibala (see Loketo). —*J. Poet*

Zing Zong / 1991 / Hannibal ◆◆◆
Kanda's latest ups the pleasure quotient a notch to achieve absolute delirium. Effervescent vocals ride the crest of lead guitarists Dally Kimoko and Nene Tchakou. —*Bob Tarte*

Soukous in Central Park / 1993 / Hannibal ◆◆◆
The Man's Central Park gig pretty much sums up the pros and cons of contemporary big-name soukous. It dances on non-stop with the idiom's patented driving prettiness, beguiling as all-get-out but without peaks and valleys, in a steady-state hyper-competence that never sags but never builds. These guys can play endlessly without effort or attention: in fact, if they went home their instruments would just keep on trucking all by themselves. —*John Storm Roberts, Original Music*

● **Amour Fou** / ◆◆◆
In part because he believes in keeping his groups down to a reasonable sound, Kanda Bongo Man's recordings all have something of the feel of the great pre-soukous period of Zairian music. Fad-hounds will be interested, and many others relieved, to note further evidence that the disco-bomp that has recently shackled Zairian rhythm sections is on the way out. —*John Storm Roberts, Original Music*

● **Sai-Liza** / Hannibal ◆◆◆◆◆
The recording that introduced the kouassa-kouassa dance has been a runaway smash in Paris and Africa. Unsure why this has been one of the biggest hits in quite a while? Try Diblo on lead guitar, Lokassa ya Mbongo backing him up, and Pablo Lubadika on bass guitar, all of them in top form. Add KBM's admirable liking for a small tight group—aside from those mentioned, there's only synth, drum, and a two-voice backup vocal group. Kanda Bongo Man is one musician who almost always deserves the semi-adulation Western buffs have given him. —*John Storm Roberts*

Sam Mangwana

Vocals / Zouk, Soukous, Zaire, Africa, Congo (Brazzaville)
This former singer with Rochereau and Kanda Bongo Man has added elements of soca and zouk into his high-octane soukous style. —*J. Poet*

● **Aladji** / 1978 / Shanachie ◆◆◆◆◆
This album, containing hits from several African albums, was one of the hottest African dance compilations of the late '80s. —*J. Poet*

Maria Tebbo / 1995 / Stern's African Classics ◆◆◆◆◆
These two LPs from 1978 and 1979 have a pan-African virtuosity as yet unmatched. One album has no horns and shimmers through the gentlest dance music you ever heard. The other is slightly more international, from the trenchant "Affaire Disco" with its Willie Colon bone sound to the smash "Waka Waka." —*Carl Hoyt, Original Music*

Canta Mozambique / PAM ◆◆◆
Mangwana is the only singer to have worked with both Franco and Rochereau, and is one of the finest and most influential soukousards ever to have failed to achieve stardom. The compilation shows him at an early peak and makes a nifty contrast with the Maquisards. The core of the PAM release is an obscure mini-album first issued on 1983. Also included are songs from an Abidjan release of 1982. —*John Storm Roberts, Original Music*

For Ever / Syllart ◆◆◆
Here's one of two brilliant Franco CDs, with 15 years between them. Listening to the pair together underlines the enormous and highly personal talent of Franco, as well as his ability to bring out the best in other musicians while turning fashionable elements to his own purposes. "For Ever," ironically, was Franco's last issued recording. Despite rumors of AIDS, his own guitar was as brilliant as ever, whether slashing in the mid-range solos he loved or teasing the beat behind the superb Mangwana. As always, there are the bows to fashion—here, zouk horn players whose riffs sound more effective against the soukous guitar than they ever do these days in their own music. —*John Storm Roberts, Original Music*

Tabu Ley Rochereau (Tabu Pascal)

b. 1940, Bundundu, Zaire
Vocals / Africa, Congo (Brazzaville)
Tabu Ley (Rochereau), with Franco, is the father of modern African pop. His band, Africa International, was a leading innovator and changed the way Congolese (and later Zairian) music was played. In an interview with Ronnie Graham, later reprinted in Graham's *Guide to Contemporary African Music* (Da Capo, 1988), Tabu Ley spoke at length about his life and music. "Tabu is my father's name; Ley is my father's

father's name. Rochereau is a name I got in grammar school. During a French history lesson I was the only one who knew the names of Napoleon's generals; the rest of the class was punished because of it. They teased me and called me Rochereau, but I liked the sound of it and kept it as my artistic name." Rochereau learned sacred and secular music at the Catholic grammar school he attended, although he'd been singing at home since he was a child. At the age of 14, he wrote his first hit, "Besama Muchacha," which was recorded by L'African Jazz, the band of Le Grande Kalle, the greatest bandleader of the '40s, '50s, and '60s. Because Rochereau was underage, the songwriting credit was taken by Kalle. When Rochereau finished high school, Kalle gave him a job as a singer with L'African Jazz, and the first tune he wrote for them, "Kelia," made Rochereau an instant success. In 1965 Rochereau left Kalle to form African Fiesta with Docteur Nico, another Kalle alumnus. Since then, Rochereau has led the pack in musical innovations and creative drive. He's written more than 2000 songs for himself and other artists, and recorded more than a hundred albums, with almost every new release bringing a new facet of his creativity to the fore. He's added Latin, jazz, soul, and disco elements to his music. His organization is a fertile training ground for other musicians, who have gone on to fame and fortune (including Sam Mangwana and Mbilia Bel). —*J. Poet*

Tabu Ley / 1967 / Shanachie ◆◆◆
At his best, Rochereau is still irresistible, a master at the effortless, laid-back ease that has been the trend since the mid-'70s. This contains some of his best cuts from the early '80s. —*John Storm Roberts, Original Music*

Omana Wapi / 1976 / Shanachie ◆◆◆◆◆
Picked by *The Village Voice*'s Robert Christgau as one of the greatest albums of the '80s, this historic collaboration teams Rochereau with Franco, Zaire's greatest singer and guitarist, for one of the few "super-sessions" worthy of the title. —*J. Poet*

Man from Kinshasa / 1991 / Shanachie ◆◆◆
In a nod to contemporary logic, the Zairian master gets behind a drum machine. With another nod to roots, he dares accordion-driven soukous on one of the many highlights here, including "Tour Eiffel." —*Bob Tarte*

● **Babeti Soukous** / Plan 9/Caroline ◆◆◆◆◆
There is an infinity of projects more worthwhile than yet another recording by Zaire's most-recorded name. But this is a fine performance with touches probably never heard from Rochereau before, along with such felicities as his new focus on solo rather than ensemble horns. It's excellent, except for the silly DJ and "live recording" conceit. —*John Storm Roberts, Original Music*

Papa Wemba (Shungu Wembadia)

b. 1953, Kasai, Zaire
Guitar, Vocals / Soukous, Zaire, Africa, Congo (Brazzaville)
Stylish, suave, and singularly talented, Papa Wemba has become as much a fashion icon as a pop star. Wemba served his musical apprenticeship listening to Cuban dance music and, later on, to Otis Redding. He got his musical break with the ubiquitous ZLL before going on to pursue his own projects. Now based in Paris, Wemba looks toward Japan for both corporate support and clothes styles. An extremely articulate individual, Wemba eschews the Soukous label, insisting that he is *sui generis* and simply performs to be danced to. In Wemba's music one finds no heavy funk/R&B overlays and no horns—at most, some bluesy flashes in the scintillating guitar work. Just a sparkling glittering interplay of guitars, drums, and voices that doesn't let up. —*John Storm Roberts and Leon Jackson*

La Voyageur / 1992 / Earthbeat! ◆◆◆◆◆
This is the American debut by one of the continent's most arresting vocalists, who is loathe to let a syllable escape his throat without first gift-wrapping it in brightly colored knots. Compositions hurl themselves from soukous to mbube, dashing against the rocks only during flirtations with mellow rock and jazz—but his amazing cockcrow of a voice continually triumphs. —*Bob Tarte*

★ **L'Esclave** / Gitta ◆◆◆◆◆
This recording, a massive hit for a full six months when it first came out, testifies to a driving Zairian style that other big names have neglected in favor of more laidback sounds. —*John Storm Roberts*

Amour Kilawu / Esperance ◆◆◆◆◆
This collaboration with Viva La Musica (a band of ZLL alumni) is among his very best from the mid-'80s. The collaboration with Modogo (full title: *Papa Wemba, Modogo Gian Franco Ferre and Viva la Musica: Nouvelle Generation ... Paris*) is an outstanding example of how they moved the basic sound forward a notch for the '90s. —*John Storm Roberts*

Papa Wemba w/ Modogo / Esperance ◆◆◆◆◆
Much of Wemba seemed to exemplify the blustery, overproduced Afro-Parisian sound that so overvalues the trendy. But, and this is a big BUT, this is a great LP. No horns, no synth, no kwassa kwassa, just the laidback

hipness that has come to be expected from Zaiko Langa Langa and its satellites. —*John Storm Roberts*

Zaiko Langa Langa

Bass, Guitar, Conga, Vocals / Soukous, Zaire, Africa, Congo (Brazzaville)
ZLL is one of the key groups of the Congolese New Wave: a nebulous coalition of up to 20 musicians who have thoroughly updated soukous by infusing it with an almost electric energy. Their key innovation has been to remove the horn section that had until recently defined Congolese music. The result is a much raunchier and more youthful sound. ZLL—the name is a contraction of Zaire of Our Elders—has spawned a veritable family of offsprings, the so-called "Clan Langa Langa," including Papa Wemba, Bozi Boizana, and the groups Zaiko, WaWa, Langa Langa Stars, Choc Stars, Anti-Choc, and many more. —*Leon Jackson and Myles Boisen*

Langa Langa F.D. / 1990 / Celluloid ♦♦♦
This is one of the few non-import CDs available. —*J. Poet*

Avis de Recherche / 1995 / Stern's Africa ♦♦♦
Zaiko (the seminal youth-quake band of the '70s, home to Wemba et al.) is a hydra—splitting into equally lethal offshoots while still retaining not just vigor but enthusiasm and relevance. Though now stripped of all "names" (due to past defections), Zaiko has (can it be?) improved—expanding its groundbreaking two-part guitar assault into three and even four sections of ever more divine permutations. There's more variety than ever and no crossover fantasies.—*Carl Hoyt, Original Music*

● **Sentiment Bimi** / Bono Music ♦♦♦♦♦
This is a showcase for a founding member/lead singer of Zaire's mother-of-most-bands. This 1988 session has all the trademarks—remorseless, soaring guitar jams, kicking trap drums that had by then absorbed the early-'80s disco-bomp into something a lot more integral and effective. The first side here is a hefty medley of songs associated with Bimi. —*John Storm Roberts, Original Music*

Zaire-Ghana / Retroafric ♦♦♦♦♦
Formed in 1969, Zaiko dropped the more overt Cuban references and horn sections of the early giants of Zairean music, Franco, Rochereau, Kale, and Nico, in favor of a faster, guitar, voice- and snare drum-driven style. The seben, the improvised instrumental section at the end of Zairean songs, took on a new, supercharged exuberance as the guitars intertwined over the chattering snare reminiscent of the march-tinged drumming in a New Orleans brass band. This is not just an important document of a seminal band at its peak in 1976, but a rip-snorting great time! —*Carl Hoyt, Original Music*

Songo-Fiele / Sonodisc ♦♦♦
Here's one take on the Zaiko phenomenon, the great youth-quake band formed in 1970 which helped set the tone for today's soukous. Zaiko goes for a deeply layered, multipercussion sound with a tremendous swing which is anything but desperately trendy. *Songo-Fiele* has plenty of hints of non-zouk outside influences (relatively rare in soukous) and a very well-produced warm sound. —*John Storm Roberts, Original Music*

Zaire Collection

Afrique En Or / Lusafrica ♦♦♦
A pleasing collection, it has (despite the pan-African title) a decent cross-section of modern Zairian rumba. Wenge Musica, Diblo, Lokassa and Pepe Kalle (though his contribution is an instrumental, a major silliness given his extraordinary voice) anchor a line-up that sets up the lesser lights very well. There is some fine stuff here: more than enough to make up for the always tedious Koffi Olomide. —*Carl Hoyt, Original Music*

Belle Epoque / 1994 / RetroAfric ♦♦♦
All RetroAfric Recordings are a must, but this is plain stunning—super-classic proto-soukous from the days before it became a job for professionals, back when they played with joy and love. Two 1970 Kinshasa cuts, plus four in Tanzania with Remi Ongalla's Makassi and three early Somo Somo numbers, all remind us why this stuff transformed the music of a continent. —*John Storm Roberts, Original Music*

Roots of OK Jazz / 1994 / Cramworld ♦♦♦
These delicious mid-'50s recordings would be entirely irresistible even if they weren't also history in the making, being that their common factor is the presence of the great Franco—along, on many of them, with other founding members of the great OK Jazz orchestra. —*John Storm Roberts, Original Music*

Tombe Ditumba Music of the Luba Shankadi of Shaba / Fonti Musicali ♦♦♦
This fine traditional CD from eastern Zaire was recorded in the early '70s and compiled for width rather than depth, with a good range of music, vocal and instrumental, fine recording and documentation. The pieces seem selected for musical attractiveness (in the outside listener's

terms) as well as authenticity, giving them emotional as well as intellectual resonance. —*John Storm Roberts, Original Music*

Upper Uele: Mangbetu / Fonti Musicali ♦♦♦
The Mangbetu of northeastern Zaire have a highly original and varied musical culture built on interaction with widely differing local groups. Though percussion is central, their horn bands, thumb-piano, harp music, and singing are all choice. But what puts the cap on many of these tracks is a lively sense of the people behind the sounds: laughter, apparent badinage, life happening. —*John Storm Roberts, Original Music*

Urban Music In Kinshasa / Ocora ♦♦♦
There's a whole music out there that never gets onto disc: the music of the locations, Africa's equivalents of the barrio. There are sometimes acoustic imitations of electric guitar, but it often sucks the "new" music right back to the roots, adapting it to whatever instruments are around. One of these late-'70s groups uses accordion, the others amplify finger-piano. Soukous this ain't. Deep Kinshasa it emphatically is. —*John Storm Roberts, Original Music*

The Sound of Kinshasa: Guitar Classics from Zaire / 1982 / Original Music ♦♦♦♦♦
Included are Zairian classics from the acoustic '50s to the soukous '70s, from an example of the great Shaba acoustic tradition and a gorgeous biguine in a forgotten style, to biggies such as OK Jazz and early-empire bakuba. Every cut is crème de la crème, and they're arranged chronologically so you can hear the style grow from acoustic to electric two decades later—by which time it was profoundly influencing music all across Black Africa. —*John Storm Roberts*

Zambia Collection

From the Copperbelt: Zambian Miners Songs / 1989 / Original Music ♦♦♦♦♦
If you're into country-blues, Mwenda Jean Bosco, or roots in general, this is for you. The remarkable guitarists of the '50s Zambian copper mines were mostly wandering minstrels who roamed from mine to mine, criss-crossing the border between Zambia and Katanga and forming part of a guitar movement that has always been incorrectly credited to East Zaire alone. There's an enormous variety here, from rugged, rootsy stuff to the beginnings of an urban-influenced sound with US and South African as well as Congolese elements. —*John Storm Roberts*

Zimbabwe

Bhundu Boys

Jit, Africa, Zimbabwe
The Bhundus built up a national following in Zimbabwe by taking the more traditional guitar styles of chimurenga (made popular by Thomas Mapfumo), adding some English-American-style finger-picking and a heavy disco-like bass drum beat, and playing with a lilting, rhythmic swing that's part highlife and part soukous. They call their hybrid "jit." In 1986 the Bhundu Boys put out their first record; when Scottish booker Gordon Muir heard it, he called Zimbabwe and flew the Bhundu Boys to the UK for a tour that became a year-long residence. With music industry heavies like Elvis Costello and Madonna touting them to the press, the Bhundus were soon under contract to Warner Brothers International (Island in the US). Influenced by the Rolling Stones and soukous as well as the traditional music of their native Zimbabwe, the Bhundu Boys are one of Africa's most ass-kicking guitar bands. —*J. Poet*

★ **Shabini** / 1986 / Disque Afrique ♦♦♦♦♦
An earlier album with a relatively under-produced sound, this exciting music from Zimbabwe features guitars, bass, keyboard, and percussion. —*Hank Davis*

Tsvimbodzemoto / 1987 / Disque Afrique ♦♦♦
Their second album is another great recording that mines the roots of Zimbabwe and serves them up with plenty of dazzling rock guitar. —*J. Poet*

True Jit / 1988 / Mango ♦♦♦♦♦
Their international debut is considered "watered down" by some purists, but it'll still knock-your-socks-off, with a fuller sound and some English lyrics. —*J. Poet & Hank Davis*

Pamberi / 1990 / Mango ♦♦♦
This is highly melodic and rhythmic music from Zimbabwe. —*Hank Davis*

Stella Chiweshe

Vocals, Hosho / Neo-Traditional, Mbira, Africa, Zimbabwe
Together with Amai Muchena and Beulah Diego, Stella Chiweshe is one of the few women to break into the almost exclusively male world

of mbira music. She studied under her uncle and began to perform at weddings, funerals, and political meetings, gradually earning a reputation as a forceful and exemplary musician.

The mbira is a sacred instrument, and Chiweshe is insistent that there is a spiritual dimension to the experience of playing; on stage she sometimes even enters a trance-like state. Nevertheless Chiweshe has encountered a certain amount of flak for her introduction of the mbira into a secular and popular arena. Still, she remains immensely popular in Zimbabwe, having released more than 20 singles and several albums. Although currently based in Germany, Chiweshe still tours and performs in Africa with her Earthquake Band. *—Leon Jackson*

● **Ambuya/Ndzyozvo** / 1988 / Globestyle ◆◆◆◆◆
As you can hear on the last four tracks of this CD, Chiweshe experiments with a fusion of rock and traditional Zimbabwean styles. (This import version includes material from the *Ndzyozvo* EP that the Shanachie version does not.) *—J. Poet*

Thomas Mapfumo

b. 1945, Marondera, Zimbabwe
Guitar, Vocals / Chimurenga, Africa, Zimbabwe
Thomas Mapfumo made revolutionary changes in Zimbabwe's pop-music scene by recording a song for which he'd written his own music. Before Mapfumo, songs in the traditional style were always based on tunes that had been handed down for generations. Mapfumo's music, chimurenga ("music of struggle"), became popular during the civil war against White minority rule, but his popularity made the government unhappy. In 1977 he was sent to a prison camp for subversion. To obtain his release, Mapfumo agreed to perform for the ruling party, but at the concert he sang only his most revolutionary songs. "I told them that since I'd been in detention, I didn't have time to write new ones."

Mapfumo grew up in the country, went to a British colonial school, and worked as a herd boy, watching over the cattle. After hearing the Beatles and Wilson Pickett in the early '60s, Mapfumo taught himself guitar and started a band that played pop music from African countries as well as Beatles, Rolling Stones, funk, and soul.

Mapfumo left Western music behind to form the Acid Band. Their first album, *Hokoyo* ("Beware"), contained the songs that led to Mapfumo's detention. After Zimbabwe's liberation in 1978, Mapfumo formed Blacks Unlimited and released *Gwindingwe Rine Shumba* (Lion in the Bush), a joyous celebration of his country's independence.

Jumbo Van Renen, the president of Earthworks Records, arranged to put out Mapfumo's music in England; when Van Renen later became CEO of Island Records in the UK, he signed Mapfumo again, this time to an international recording contract. *—J. Poet*

Ndangariro / 1983 / Hannibal ◆◆◆
Given all the trivia thrown up by the "world music" and reggae fads, one approaches this recording with gloom, but its mix of traditional and contemporary work. Mapfumo's ability to weave originality out of references from Zimbabwean tradition to rasta reggae is the foundation of one of Africa's most individual personal idioms. *—John Storm Roberts, Original Music*

Indangariro / 1984 / Shanachie ◆◆◆
These were done shortly after the Zimbabwean independence and still have that youthful fire. *—Myles Boisen*

★ **Chimurenga Singles** / 1984 / Shanachie ◆◆◆◆◆
The early hit singles by Mapfumo and Blacks Unlimited, these classic sides were recorded during the civil war; their musical and lyrical content completely revamped the face of pop music in Zimbabwe. *—J. Poet*

Corruption / 1989 / Mango ◆◆◆
Mapfumo's first international release has more stunning guitar, and the title tune is sung in English to a calypso-like beat. A joyful mix of innovation and traditional roots, it is great dance music. *—J. Poet & Myles Boisen*

Chamunorwa / 1991 / Mango ◆◆◆
Sidestepping his characteristic flinty sound, Mapfumo digs in deep with extended trance-inducing grooves propelled by thundering bass-drum heartbeats. *—Bob Tarte*

Shumba: Vital Hits of Zimbabwe / 1991 / Earthworks ◆◆◆
An anthology of Mapfumo's hits from the late '70s and early '80s, it includes most of *Gwindingwe Rine Shumba*, an album released by Mapfumo to celebrate Zimbabwe's independence. *—J. Poet*

Zimbabwe Collection

Viva! Zimbabwe: Dance Music from Zimbabwe / 1983 / Hannibal ◆◆◆◆◆
Post-liberation pop, it has generous samplings of jit, soukous, chimurenga, and other styles. *—J. Poet*

ASIA

Burma Collection

Birmanie: l'Art de la Harpe/The Art of the Harp, Musiques de l'Asie Traditionnelle / Playa Sound ◆◆◆
An entire album of music for Asia's only surviving harp, the saung gauk, accompanied by the si and wa time markers. *—Terry Miller*

Birmanie: Musique d'Art / 1981 / Ocora ◆◆◆
The first fine recording ever issued of Burmese music, this 1981 triple album includes harp, flute, hsaing waing ensemble, pattala (xylophone), and songs, all played by professional performers. *—Terry Miller*

Music of Myanmar / World Music Library ◆◆◆
As with all currently available recordings of Myanmar (Burmese) music, this album features members of an outstanding professional, government-sponsored troupe playing both ensemble and solo pieces. Related to this is *Hsaing Waing of Myanmar*, World Music Library (KICC 5162), which also includes both ensemble and solo examples. *—Terry Miller*

Cambodia Collection

Cambodge/Cambodia: Musiques de l'Exil/Music of the Exile / VDE-Gallo ◆◆◆
Although this includes "imperfect" performances, it is a valuable document of music-making in the Khao-I-Dang refugee camp in Thailand from 1980 and by Cambodian-Americans in Maryland from 1983-84. *—Terry Miller*

Cambodia: Royal Music/Cambodge: Musique Royale / Auvidis-Unesco ◆◆◆
Recorded before 1975 at the palace in Phnom Penh, this album includes several different ensembles and a solo for the "crocodile" zither. Related to this is *Les musiques du Ramayana, Vol. 2: Cambodge* (Ocora C 560015) recorded in 1964 in Paris. *—Terry Miller*

Music of Cambodia: The Sam-Ang Sam Ensemble / World Music Institute ◆◆◆
Songs and instrumental selections recorded in concert by wedding and mohori ensembles under the leadership of Dr. Sam-ang Sam, the foremost authority on Cambodian music. Related is *Cambodian Mohori: Khmer Entertainment Music* (World Music Institute, WMI 015, cassette) and *Silent Temples, Songful Hearts: Traditional Music of Cambodia* (World Music Press, WMP-008, cassette), which accompanies a book of the same title. *—Terry Miller*

Vol. 2: Cambodia / 1971 / Ocora ◆◆◆
This album is a recording of a 1964 performance of the *Reamker* or *Khmer Ramayana* by the Cambodian Royal Ballet. *—John Storm Roberts*

Homrong / 1991 / Real World ◆◆◆◆◆
This classical performing troupe lacks refinement but is one of the few groups to survive the Khmer Rouge revolution, and so is commendable for keeping the tradition alive. Featured are classical vocals plus oboe, xylophone, flute, violin, percussion, and so forth. *—Myles Boisen*

Musicians of the National Dance Company of Cambodia: Homrong / Real World ◆◆◆
This recording documents the renaissance of classical music in modern Cambodia. Recorded in 1990 in England by the first touring company of court musicians since the 1975 holocaust. *—Terry Miller*

Royal Music of Cambodia / Philips ◆◆◆
This long piece comes from a pinpeat orchestra, wooden-keyed xylophones predominating with gongs. Various smaller ensembles and mohori orchestra. *—David L. Mayers*

China

Guo Brothers & Shung Tian

World Fusion, Asia, China
The Guo Brothers (Guo Yue and Guo Yi) come from a musical family, and distinguished themselves as young woodwind players in official Chinese orchestras. After leaving China, their musical horizons have broadened, but still reflect the austerity and poise of their native traditions. *—Myles Boisen*

Yuan / 1990 / Virgin ◆◆◆◆◆
These young brothers put some new twists into traditional Chinese music with these gorgeous recordings of an accessible small group. *—Myles Boisen*

Lu-Seng Ensemble

Asia, China
Shantung . . . / Nonesuch ◆◆◆◆◆
These peaceful melodies from the Lu-Sheng Ensemble are excellent

examples of folk and classical music played on sona (oboe), drum and cymbals, sheng, cheng, t'unti, nan'hu, and ti-tzu. Truly the people's music, it's not Westernized. —*Myles Boisen & David L. Mayer*

Li Xiantang

Asia, China

Art of the Qin / Ocora ♦♦♦♦♦
Li's performance of compositions from 223 to 1937 highlights the transcendence of styles and eras typical of the seven-stringed qin zither (and indeed Chinese music as a whole). Bizarre, maybe, but as a bassist, I'm fascinated by the qin. Not only are some new basses like a vertical version of it, but Li's techniques provide a wonderful model, from the delicate, breathy slides of the rare "Fisherman's Song" to the vigor of "Flowing Waters." —*Carl Hoyt, Original Music*

China Collections

China / Barenreiter Musicaphon ♦♦♦
This is a varied and very beautiful set, recorded in mainland China, of classical compositions for stringed instruments—pipa, qin, and zheng—plus one for xiao bamboo flute and qin. The pieces are all several hundred years old (dates are often disputed). The musicians are of different generations and reflect several approaches to their tradition. The notes and illustrations are, as always, admirable. —*John Storm Roberts*

China: Music of the Pipa / Nonesuch ♦♦♦
Folk and classical instrumentals on the four-string Chinese lute by master Lui Pui-Yuen. —*Myles Boisen*

Chinese Turkestan/Xinjian Uighur Music / Ocora ♦♦♦
This is music from the Mideast/Asia interface. Though ruled by China, Uighur and Dolan are Muslim, and their music (despite Asian influences more obvious in the look of its instruments than in its sound or structure) is a highly individual descendant of the Arabo-Persian nexus. A superb recording of instrumental and vocal pieces, it has very full notes. —*John Storm Roberts*

Hong Kong: Instrumental Music / Auvidis ♦♦♦
This is a re-release of an old *Musical Atlas* album mostly devoted to solo music, notably (though not solely) to stringed instruments: pipa lute, butterfly harp, and ch'in zither are all represented along with various wind instruments, all in particularly fine performances. The term "classical" may be unsuited to the Chinese tradition, but this is art music, old and new, of high order. —*John Storm Roberts*

Music from the People's Republic / 1989 / Rounder ♦♦♦
An update on traditional songs (from the 1976 *People's Republic*) uses pre-revolution folk instruments. —*Myles Boisen*

☆ **Spring Night on a Moonlit River** / Nonesuch ♦♦♦♦♦
Spring Night on a Moonlit River—Music of the Chinese offers beautiful Chinese classical music, featuring the soulful sounds of the seven-string ch'in. —*Myles Boisen*

India

Balachander

India, Asia

Born on January 18, 1927, in Madras, Dr. S. Balachander was a key figure in Carnatic classical music. His vina playing was exquisite but he also played a range of other instruments to various degrees of mastery including tabla, harmonium, mridangam, shehnai, dilruba and sitar. He started out, like many instrumentalists, as a vocalist and by the age of six he was on the concert stage. Between the age of 12 and 16 he gave concert recitals on a Hindustani instrument, the sitar. During the '60s his work was put before the public by Richard Bock's World Pacific label. Through albums such as *Magic Music of India* (World Pacific 1426) and *Sounds of the Veena* (WPS 21436)—the latter with the flautist N. Ramani—and later *The Music of India* (Nonesuch Explorer H-72003) he became one of the best-known Carnatic instrumentalists in the US. His work has also appeared on labels such as Bharat Records, EMI India, Oriental, and Polydor. His death in Bhilai on April 15, 1990, was a great loss to Carnatic music. Often controversial, sometimes confrontational, he enriched the field immeasurably. —*Ken Hunt*

● **Veena Virtuoso** / Mar. 1982 / World Music Library ♦♦♦♦♦
Recorded in March 1982 in Tokyo, this selection presents two Tyagaraja kritis with mridangam and tanpura accompaniment. Fulsome notes in Japanese. Skimpy notes in English. —*Ken Hunt*

Raga Malahari / JVC ♦♦♦
Recorded in March 1974, this Japanese release comes with even less information in English. Good music prevails. —*Ken Hunt*

Nikhil Banerjee

Sitar / India, Asia

Calcutta-born Nikhil Banerjee (1931-1986) was one of the most distinctively voiced sitarists to emerge after the Second World War. After learning initially from his father, Jatindra Nath Banerjee, he was accepted as a student by Allauddin Khan. Later he studied with Allauddin Khan's son, the sarod maestro Ali Akbar Khan. He is, after Vilayat Khan and Ravi Shankar, the greatest sitarist of the immediate post-War years, and since him, only Rais Khan has proven himself worthy of carrying the crown. —*Ken Hunt*

The Hundred-Minute Raga: Purabi Kalyan / 1982 / Raga ♦♦♦
Accompanied by Swapan Chaudhuri on tabla, this recording stems from a concert recital given in Berkeley, CA, in October 1982. Length is no guarantee of success but Nikhil Banerjee's lengthy performance truly is never less than memorable. —*Ken Hunt*

Live: Berkeley 1982 / 1982 / Raga ♦♦♦
This extensive raga—"Misra Kafi"—shows Banerjee at his best (especially since it was recorded in the second part of the concert). It's a very fine digital recording. —*John Storm Roberts*

● **Immortal Sitar of Pandit Nikhil Banerjee, Ragas: Purabi Kalyan, Zila-Kafi, Kirwa** / 1986 / Chanda Dhara ♦♦♦♦♦
This is one of the best and unfortunately last recordings of Banerjee, the incomparable sitarist. His beautiful rendering of "Purabi Kalyan," a combined raga, expresses with restraint the peaceful and devout mood of this twilight raga through an original melody. Another combined raga ("Zila-Kafi") is next, played with liberal development of the romantic mood. The concluding South Indian raga, "Kirwani," begins in a mood of devotion and develops into a fast Jhala. —*"Blue" Gene Tyranny*

Lyrical Sitar / 1991 / Chhanda Dhara ♦♦♦
Nikhil Banerjee had a magic touch and a sweet voice on the sitar. This recording regrettably is undated—a common characteristic with Banerjee's recorded work. It contains "Nat Bhairab," "Mishra Khamaj," and an unnamed folk melody from the Baul tradition of Bengal. He is accompanied by Anindo Chatterjee on tabla. —*Ken Hunt*

Raga Patdeep / Sonodisc ♦♦♦
Both his sense of musical architecture and the influence of Ali Akbar Khan can be heard clearly in the extended development of this evening raga. —*John Storm Roberts*

Ashwin Batish

Guitar / Fusion, Asia, Indian Diaspora

Ashwin is a dynamic younger member of the Batish family, who brought their rich musical heritage from India to Santa Cruz, CA, where they run a cassette-only label and tape-duplicating service. He is a nimble and energetic performer on the sitar, recording with his father, Pandit Shiv Dayal Batish, as well as with various fusion musicians and renowned tabla-master Zakir Hussain. —*Myles Boisen*

● **Sitar Power** / 1987 / Shanachie ♦♦♦♦♦
This is the logical extension of Indian-music flirtations with the Beatles and the Rolling Stones. High-energy raga rock! —*Myles Boisen*

Asha Bhosle

Vocals

Sister of the most influential voice of India, Lata Mangeshkar, Asha Bhosle was born September 8, 1933. In April 1942 her father Dinath Mangeshkar died, causing upheaval in the family, which moved from Pune to Kolhapur and in turn to Bombay. Around the age of ten she apparently sang her first film song in the Marathi film *Majha Bal*. Asha Bhosle has since sung in virtually every Indian language, in Russian and Malay, has sung Rabindra Sangeet (the songs of Bengali poet Tagore), has sung with the bhangra group Alaap, the Indian rap act Baba Sehgal and Boy George, the former lead vocalist of the British pop group Culture Club. Cassette compilations and recyclings of her work are numerous.

To commemorate her 60th birthday in 1993, for example, EMI India released three cassette sets of her work—the set of devotional material *Bala Main Bairagan Hoongi* (STHVS 65107), a set of non-film ghazals by composers such as Ghulam Ali, R.D. Burman and Nazar Hussain called *The Golden Collection Memorable Ghazals* (STHV 63173/4), and *The Golden Collection: The Ever Versatile Asha Bhosle* (STHV 62197/62200), a 44-song anthology of popular film hits. To no small degree, her success can be attributed to her versatility. She has successfully sung in many different voices and in many different styles. —*Ken Hunt*

Sizzling Hits / 1989 / EMI India ♦♦♦
Proof that the art of album titling has not been lost, this volume is a catch-all of songs to tempt the completist, but little else. —*Ken Hunt*

● **Duets Forever**—Asha Bhosle & Mohd. Rafi / EMI India ♦♦♦♦♦
EMI India's industriousness at producing thematically linked compila-

tions is demonstrated with this collection of male and female duets garnered from films such as *Batwara, Razia Sultan,* and *Neela Akash.* —*Ken Hunt*

Rare Gems—Mukesh & Asha Bhosle / EMI India ✦✦✦✦
An alternative anthology series. —*Ken Hunt*

Sheila Chandra

Vocals / Vocal, Ambient, Indo-British, Indi-Pop, Asia, Indian Diaspora
One of the most unusual and successful singers of the '80s and '90s that has attempted to fuse the music of non-Western cultures with Western pop, Chandra began recording as a teenager in Monsoon. Of Indian ancestry, but born and raised in Britain, Chandra took lead vocals in the band, which pursued a sort of new wave-tinged raga-rock along the lines of George Harrison's explorations on Beatles tracks like "Love You To." The combination yielded an album and an unexpected British hit single, "Ever So Lonely," in the early '80s. Chandra, however, felt limited by the label's pressures for more commercial product, and signed to a small indie label, Indipop, which she felt would offer more freedom for her explorations as a solo artist.

In the mid-'80s, Chandra was astonishingly prolific, releasing five solo albums over a period of about two or three years that drifted away from the Asian dance-pop of Monsoon into a more personal sort of world fusion. Chandra also began to write much of her own material, usually in collaboration with producer and husband Steve Coe; Coe had also helped produce, write, and perform the music in Monsoon with Martin Smith, who also assisted on Chandra's early solo records. Indian instruments were still usually employed, and electronic rhythm tracks still sometimes used to guarantee some measure of danceability and pop-rock appeal. But with increasing frequency, Chandra was pushing herself beyond the parameters of pop-rock with wordless pieces of both melismatic singing and percussive mouth noises, ambitious song cycles, interwoven overdubbed vocal tracks, and a 27-minute track based around a raga. (Her mid-'80s Indipop albums have been reissued in the US by Caroline.) Chandra truly matured as an artist, however, with her albums for Peter Gabriel's Real World label (distributed in the US, again, by Caroline). As proof that adulthood doesn't have to mean tamer and more mainstream product, these found Chandra achieving a true world fusion that drew from Indian ragas, elements of British folk, Middle Eastern chants, sophisticated studio overdubs, and more vocal percussion compositions, the last of which bordered on the downright experimental.

Chandra and Coe were now almost solely responsible for the music (Martin Smith no longer being an active participant), constructing drone-like instrumental textures to suitably complement Chandra's oft-wordless singing. Pop and rock were hardly factors anymore; Chandra was primarily interested in extending the limits of vocal expression, whether applied to Indian, Spanish, or Islamic forms, or the kind of material that could find a suitable home in the repertoire of June Tabor or Laurie Anderson. These recent works have firmly established Chandra as one of the principal boundary jumpers of contemporary music, but she's not a dilettante, and she imbues her music with a haunting, spiritual grace. —*Richie Unterberger*

Out on My Own / 1984 / Caroline ✦✦✦
Chandra's debut still reflects the pop-rock influence of Monsoon, particularly in the dance-oriented rhythm tracks. Indian instruments dominate the arrangements, though, and a few songs foreshadow her future direction of multi-track vocal experimentations, particularly "From a Whisper . . . to a Scream." —*Richie Unterberger*

Quiet / 1984 / Caroline ✦✦✦✦✦
This was truly the album where Chandra broke away from the pop structures underlying much of Monsoon's work. Beginning to write much of her material (in collaboration with Martin Smith and producer Steve Coe), the dance rhythms of her debut were virtually eliminated, although the emphasis on Indian instrumentation remained intact. The music simultaneously incorporated elements that were both more traditional and more free-form than her previous work. Traditional in the sense that she drew upon Indian vocal styles such as spoken bols; free-form in that there were no lyrics, just wordless vocalizations, often overdubbed numerous times. Divided into ten tracks with a single title ("Quiet 1," "Quiet 2," etc.), the suite-like piece remained cognizant of modern technology and outside musical influences, without being overwhelmed by them. In most crucial respects, the album outlined the approach she has taken to her idiosyncratic brand of world music ever since. —*Richie Unterberger*

The Struggle / 1985 / ✦✦✦
For her third album, Chandra staked out a midpoint between the pop-dance stylings of Monsoon and the more personal, less song-oriented material of her second record, *Quiet.* Electronic rhythm tracks were usually used to back the acoustic and Asian instruments, and the material consisted of discrete tracks, rather than a lengthy song cycle. It's an ambitious fusion of Western pop and Indian/Asian music, but within the context of Chandra's entire career, it's one of her less impressive efforts. —*Richie Unterberger*

The Music of India

The music of India has enjoyed a worldwide explosion since coming into vogue in the psychedelic '60s. Most Indian musicians come from musical families and begin study from an early age at the knee of a father or uncle. In the classical tradition (the majority of recordings available in the US are by North Indian classical musicians), music is a prestigious, life-long pursuit where sustained solo expression figures prominently. Centuries-old scales called ragas serve as the basis for extended improvisation in small groups, typically involving a tabla drummer and tambura player, whose ethereal drone reinforces the mood of the raga for the lead instrumentalist.

Popular lead instruments in the North Indian school are the multi-stringed sitar, sarod, sarangi, and santour, and woodwinds—bamboo flute and shehnai. A double-reed oboe is sometimes heard in larger ensembles. The voice is also featured in both North and South Indian classical forms—in the South the dominant art music is the Carnatic style, which emphasizes highly ornamented improvisation based on long melodies of folk, sacred, and classical origin. Common instruments in the South are the stringed vina

and violin, often used in larger groups with singers and a variety of percussion—the double-headed mridangam, clay-pot drum, and tambourine. In recent years, Western instruments—mandolin, guitar, clarinet, piano, and even the saxophone—have been embraced by younger innovators and incorporated into the classical tradition (though not without protest).

India also has a rich legacy of regional folk music; religious songs of various sects; theatrical epics involving mythology, dance, and music; pop forms; and of course an extremely prolific film-music industry, just beginning to be appreciated abroad. Recordings offered by American companies are just the tip of the iceberg—go to an Indian market in a major city and you will find a bewildering array of national styles, most on inexpensive cassettes. —*Myles Boisen*

Nada Brahma / 1985 / Caroline ✦✦✦
Originally released as a limited edition of only 5,000 copies, Chandra continued to develop an eclectic approach on this album, particularly on the 27-minute title track, which is based around one raga and employs several vocal styles, Indian and otherwise. On this cut in particular, Chandra explores some of the percussive, wordless vocal techniques that she would explore in greater depth on subsequent releases. The remaining four tracks are in the main more pop-conscious, occasionally adding electronic beats; the moody closing number "In Essence" is one of her better efforts along these lines. —*Richie Unterberger*

☆ **Silk 1983-1990** / 1991 / Shanachie ✦✦✦✦✦
A career retrospective of one of the innovators of the British Indi-pop style, this album contains moody and danceable hits collected from various '80s releases. *Silk* combines classical Indian music and Western pop into exotic club-dance music. —*Bob Tarte & Myles Boisen*

● **Weaving My Ancestors' Voices** / 1992 / Caroline ✦✦✦✦✦
Although Chandra had been recording for over a decade when this was released, this may be the album where she truly found her creative voice. Most vestiges of the pop-dance-rock rhythms of Monsoon, and some of her early albums, are absent. Chandra is now a virtuoso of the voice, offering almost avant-garde presentations of vocal gymnastics on "Speaking in Tongues." More often, though, she presents explorations of various musical cultures: India, of course, but also Irish folk, a Spanish lullaby, and Islamic singing. The spiritual quality of the material is enhanced by the drone-like textures of much of the music, devised by Chandra and her writing/production partner, Steve Coe. —*Richie Unterberger*

Zen Kiss / 1994 / Real World ✦✦✦✦✦
This is pretty much of a piece with her previous album (*Weaving My Ancestor's Voices*), continuing her eclectic forays into the forms and feelings of various Western and non-Western genres, and resuming her most avant-garde projects with her a cappella clucking/chanting of "Speaking in Tongues" (parts three and four). It's not a redundant repetition of the territory laid out on *Weaving My Ancestor's Voices.* It's more an extension of the mood, Chandra delving more deeply into June Tabor-styled British folk vocals in particular. —*Richie Unterberger*

Hariprasad Chaurasia

Flute, Wind Instruments / India, Asia
The classical flute player Hariprasad Chaurasia established his name with a collaborative suite of ragas with Shivkumar Sharma and Brijb-

hushan Kabra named *Call of the Valley* in 1967. Born in 1937 in Allahabad in Uttar Pradesh, Hariprasad Chaurasia studied with Annapurna Devi. Although she is popularly known as Ravi Shankar's first wife, word of mouth has her as a highly accomplished teacher and, especially, surbahar player. Hariprasad Chaurasia is also the bearer of one of the least fortunate album titles: *Nothing but Wind* (Oriental ORI/AAMS CD 121), an apparent victim of flatulent prose. —*Ken Hunt*

● **Rag Kaunsi Kanhra** / 1989 / Nimbus ✦✦✦✦✦
This sensuous evening raga for the bamboo bansuri flute was recorded with tabla by Sabir Khan. —*Myles Boisen*

Flutist / 1990 / Chhanda Dhara ✦✦✦
A studio recording made in Ludwigsburg in Germany featuring a lengthy rendition of "Raga Mian Ki Malhar" with tabla by Fazal Qureshi. —*Ken Hunt*

Venu / Apr. 1990 / Rykodisc ✦✦✦
Credited to Hariprasad Chaurasia and Zakir Hussain, this recording by Mickey Hart of the Grateful Dead dates from December 1974 and was recorded in Fairfax, CA. It consists of the early morning raga "Ahir Bhairav." For comparison seek out his studio rendition of the same raga on the album *Rag Ahir Bhairav* (Nimbus NI 5111), released in 1988 and recorded in 1987. —*Ken Hunt*

Raga Jait / 1993 / Navras ✦✦✦
A live recording made in London in June 1990, according to Hariprasad Chaurasia in the notes, this raga is the only one which is sung or played in both the morning and evening: In the morning, "Jait" is based on a morning melody known as raga "Vibhas," and in the evening the raga is based on a very well known evening raga, "Marwa." —*Ken Hunt*

Dagar Brothers

Vocals / India, Dhrupad, Asia
In the field of contemporary dhrupad singing, the Dagar Brothers are legends. Since there have been a succession of Dagar Brothers, a little chronology may help to tell them apart. The family had been court musicians in Indore. In 1936 Nasiruddin Khan Dagar died at the age of 41. His eldest sons, Moinuddin and Aminuddin, continued the family tradition of singing dhrupad and were responsible for introducing this austere, stately form to Western ears. In 1966 Moinuddin died and Nasir Zahiruddin Dagar (1933-) and Nasir Faiyazuddin Dagar (1934-1989) took over. It was their work in particular that made such an enormous mark on Indian music lovers. —*Ken Hunt*

Rag Kambhoji / 1989 / Music of the World ✦✦✦
This recording also features the two brothers. Completing the ensemble are Mohan Shyam Sharma on pakhawaj and Wasifuddin and Mussarat Dagar (another daughter of Nasir Faiyazuddin Dagar) on tanpura. The notes announced it as "the first recording of Dhrupad vocal music ever released on an American label." A strong performance of a night raga. —*Ken Hunt*

● **Chant Dhrupad** / 1989 / Auvidis ✦✦✦✦✦
This album offers two selections from the two brothers recorded at an unspecified date but from the context of the notes presumably within a year or so of Nasir Faiyazuddin Dagar's death on Feb. 7, 1989. They perform "Raga Bageshri" and "Raga Bhatiyar." —*Ken Hunt*

Dhrupad / Barenreiter Musicaphon ✦✦✦✦✦
This is a strong performance by Moinuddin and Aminuddin Dagar singing in Dhrupad style. —*David L. Mayers*

Raga Miyan Ti Todi / Jecklin ✦✦✦
This recording made in 1988 features Nasir Zahiruddin and Nasir Faiyazuddin Dagar. On it they are accompanied by Wasifuddin and Nilofar Dagar (the son and daughter of the younger of the two brothers) on tanpura and Mohan Shyam Sharma on pakhawaj (a double-headed barrel drum). —*Ken Hunt*

Zakir Hussain

Percussion, Concertina, Drums, Tabla / World Fusion, Ambient, India, Asia
Born March 9, 1951, in Bombay, India, Zakir Hussain is son to Alla Rakha and brother to Fazal Qureshi. He has played in a variety of different contexts including strict Hindustani classical music and East-West collaborations. In this later context, he has worked with Shakti, a group consisting of the English guitarist John McLaughlin, the violinist L. Shankar, and ghatam and mridangam player T.H. "Vikku" Vinayakram. The finest of the three Shakti albums was *Handful of Beauty* (1977). He also worked with Mickey Hart of the Grateful Dead on several projects: *Hart's Rolling Thunder* (1972), *Diga Rhythm Band* (1976 reissued in 1988); Coppola's *Apocalypse Now* film soundtrack; Hart's *At the Edge* (1990); and *Planet Drum* (1991), for which Hart received a Grammy the following year. His tabla playing has graced many, many soloists' work in the fields of classical music and Western popular music. —*Ken Hunt*

Making Music / Dec. 1986 / ECM ✦✦✦
World fusion-jazz group falls short of its great potential. With guitar star John McLaughlin. —*Michael G. Nastos*

● **Tabla Duet** / 1988 / Chhanda Dhara ✦✦✦✦
This release reversed the usual order placing son before father in the billing. A riveting performance with Sultan Khan accompanying on sarangi. Exemplary musicianship all round. —*Ken Hunt*

Memorable Tabla Duet / 1991 / Chhanda Dhara ✦✦✦
A live recording from the Liederhall in Stuttgart in 1988 with Sultan Khan on sarangi. —*Ken Hunt*

Brij Bhushan Kabra

Guitar / India, Asia
The guitar is a recent foreign introduction to the world of Hindustani music. Its best known exponent is Brij Bhushan Kabra. During the '60s he was involved in the making of two significant albums through which he came to a wide international audience. The more important of the two was *Call of the Valley*, a collaboration with santoor maestro Shivkumar Sharma and flautist Hariprasad Chaurasia. The second was *Two Raga Moods on Guitar* (World Pacific WPS 21452). Describing him on the sleeve of *Call of the Valley* in 1968, G.N. Joshi wrote, "Brij Bhushan Kabra hails from Jodhpur and took to guitar playing about ten years ago under the guidance of Ali Akbar Khan. His proficiency and skill in producing Indian classical music on a Western instrument have received acclamation from critics and listeners alike." It was the start of a long and illustrious career. —*Ken Hunt*

Lure of the Desert / 1990 / EMI India ✦✦✦
A suite of pieces, apart from track titles, devoid of information except that Kashinath Mishra accompanies on tabla. —*Ken Hunt*

Exotic Sounds on Guitar / Oriental ✦✦✦
One of the first recordings by Brij Bhushan Kabra which set a trend for information-free releases. Zakir Hussain is the tabla player. —*Ken Hunt*

● **Raga Puriya Alap** / Celluloid ✦✦✦✦✦
In this reissue of a 1983 recording, this amazing slide guitarist not only makes spontaneous and spontaneous melodic inventions but also evokes surprising new sounds from his instrument. A tremolo-inflected cry, a stream of fire rising into space will suddenly turn into a heartfelt, personal sigh. Confident statements underlined by strong rhythms soon follow. "Raga Puriya," played at sunset, is a meditation on renunciation, subtle and complex to play. Serious listening will be highly rewarded. —*"Blue" Gene Tyrrany*

Ustad Ali Akbar Khan

b. 1922, Shivpur, Bangladesh
Sitar, Sarod / Classical, India, Asia
Born in the village of Shivpur, Bangladesh in 1922, Ustad Ali Akbar Khan is acknowledged as being one of the great Indian musicians. He is the son of Padma-Vibhusan Acharya Allauddin Khan, perhaps the greatest musician in recent times in the school of North Indian music. Taught from the age of three by his father, Khan learned a variety of instruments including voice, drums, and of course sarod—his primary instrument. For 20 years, Ali Akbar Khan kept a rigorous training schedule of some 18 hours per day!

In 1995, he made his first Western recording during a visit to the US at the request of violinist Yehudi Menuhin. In the mid-'60s, Khan moved to the US where he has lived and worked ever since. He first opened the Ali Akbar College of Music in San Rafael, CA, in 1967, where he is still active recording today in the '90s.

Khan has produced some incredible recordings. His well-known *Signature Series* are still available. These now legendary recordings were made for the Connoisseur Society in the '60s and represent the musician at the top of his form. These are spiritual exercises as well as music. Ali Akbar Khan is a teacher and composer as well as a performer. He has a loyal following throughout the world. —*Michael Erlewine*

Artistic Sound of Sarod / 1985 / Chhanda Dhara ✦✦✦
Accompanied by Swapan Chaudhuri on tabla, this is a perfect example of what a master can do. The album focuses on "Raga Basant Mukhari with Jogia." —*Ken Hunt*

Journey / Aug. 1990 / Triloka ✦✦✦
On *Journey*, Khan displays both his instrumental prowess and his inventiveness in fusing Western musical idioms with Indian sensibilities. The album consists entirely of original material, with clearly discernible chord changes and strong melodies—Journey is a daring statement by a brilliant artist. —*Backroads Music/Heartbeats*

Signature Series, Vols. 1 & 2 / 1990 / Ammp ✦✦✦✦✦
His long-unavailable 1967 recordings for the Connoisseur Society were the gateway to raga for many Americans. More than that, these are examples of one of the great schools of Hindustani classical music. Among the first of the Connoisseur series to be reissued, these and all his recordings

are essential. *Volume 1* has ragas "Chandranandan," "Gauri Manjari," "Jogiya Kalingra"; *Volume 2*, ragas "Medhavi," "Khammaj," "Bhairavi Bhatiyar w. Ragmala." — *John Storm Roberts*

Plays Alap a Sarod Solo / May 5, 1992-May 6, 1992 / Alam Madia ✦✦✦✦
Ali Akbar Khan Plays Alap is a landmark. A highly ambitious undertaking, it focuses on the first movement of a raga performance, the invocation known as alap. To call it the prelude to the kiss that is a raga would capture its sensuality and evoke its intention more poetically but this is dense, intellectual stuff. Disc one focuses on "Raga Shri" and a thumristyle reading of "Pilu Baroowa." "Iman Kalyan" (Iman is a variation of "Yaman") occupies all of the second disc. During the alap the musician gently probes, at first using no more than three notes played in different sequences. Gradually Ali Akbar Khan draws in the raga's other notes to convey its soul. Words like perfection get bandied about so let's err on the side of litotes and say that this album of Ali Akbar Khan's is a consummate piece of work. — *Ken Hunt*

Rag Manj Khammaj & Rag Misra Mand / 1994 / AMMP ✦✦✦✦✦
When Ali Akbar Khan was still young he would help Nikhil Banerjee prepare for the arduous study regime of Allauddin Khan, who was Ali Akbar Khan's father as well as Nikhil Banerjee's guru. Years later Ali Akbar Khan would play with the sitarist some nine years his junior and this sarod-sitar jugalbandi is an example of the heights they could achieve as this unexpected unearthing proves. It has a rare, essential beauty. Evidently his clandestine visits paid off handsomely. — *Ken Hunt*

Morning Visions / 1995 / AMMP ✦✦✦
David B. Jones recorded these performances between 1963 and 1974 for the Signature Series, but the two morning ragas that make up *Morning Visions* were never released during the first incarnation of the series. It features "Mian Ki Todi" and "Sindhu Bhairavi." Eloquence personified. Mahapurush Misra is on tabla. Music as sacrament. — *Ken Hunt*

★ **Duet** / RSM ✦✦✦✦✦
A near-perfect example of the classical duet, this superb live concert features star violinist L. Subramaniam and tabla drummer Zakir Hussein. — *Myles Boisen*

Salamat Ali Khan

Vocals / India, Asia
Two brothers from Pakistan (Nazakat is now dead) who challenged and inspired each other to great vocal heights in a stirring duet form usually heard in Indian music. Salamat has gone on to record as a soloist. — *Myles Boisen*

Salamat & Nazakat Ali Khan / 1988 / Hannibal ✦✦✦✦
These are classical vocal duets in the uplifting Khayal tradition. — *Myles Boisen*

Salamat Remembers Nazakat / 1992 / Magnasound ✦✦✦
Here too Salamat Ali Khan appears with his sons, Sharafat Ali and Shafqat Ali. For variety Sultan Khan plays sarangi and Asad Ali Khan harmonium. Nayan Ghosh plays tabla. Three khyals set in "Marwa," "Madh Kalyan," and "Chandrakauns," and a thumri set in "Mishra Pilu" make up the selection. Released in the days before many record companies had realized the value of comprehensive explanatory booklet notes, this recording contains no details apart from basic personnel and track information. — *Ken Hunt*

● **Raga Gunkali/Saraswati/Durga** / Nimbus ✦✦✦✦✦
Here he appears with his sons Sharafat and Shafqat with Ghulam Abbas Khan on tabla. Recorded in December 1990, this was a historic recording marking the debut of Shafqat Ali on disc—he opens with a lovely rendition of "Raga Gunkali," a morning raga elsewhere found in the recorded repertoire of Bade Ghulam Ali Khan but otherwise seldom heard. "Saraswati" is an opportunity for Sharafat Ali Khan to shine with his father. The final selection gives each a turn to solo or support. An exceptional disc. — *Ken Hunt*

Sultan Khan

Sarangi / India, Sarangi, Asia
A much in demand soloist and accompanist. He obtained his first international platform during the 1974 Dark Horse tour with Ravi Shankar and George Harrison. Thereafter he steadily built such a reputation that by 1985 he was recruited to work on the soundtrack to Richard Attenborough's *Gandhi.* Sultan Khan's sensitivity on the sarangi, stylistically quite different from better-known players such as Ram Narayan and Sabri Khan, brought him increased demand as an accompanist and principal soloist. He has recorded as a soloist for a variety of labels including Audiorec, CBS (India), Chhanda Dhara, Moment, Navras and many others. His specialty is as an accompanist for vocalists such as Girija Devi, Shobha Gurtu and Mehdi Hussan. — *Ken Hunt*

Singing Sarangi of Sultan Khan / 1988 / Chhanda Dhara ✦✦✦
Zakir Hussain accompanies on tabla. Good performances of "Kaunsi

Kanada," "Chandra Madhu," and "Mishra Tilang." The album also includes a tabla solo piece lasting a few seconds short of ten minutes. — *Ken Hunt*

Rag Bhupali, Rajasthani Folk Song In Rag Bhup Mand / 1991 / Moment ✦✦✦✦✦
A slow lyrical performance on the sarangi expressing love and sadness begins "Rag Bhupali," one of the oldest and simplest of ragas, and the exposition develops into exciting virtuosic exchanges between Khan and the famous Zakir Hussain on tabla. Perhaps the nicest surprise this album offers is the warm, sweet Rajasthani folk song, which is alternately sung and then played on the sarangi, beautifully varied but never overdone by Khan and Hussain, who actually provide a decrescendo section at the end instead of simply stopping. — *"Blue" Gene Tyrany*

● **Sarangi** / 1992 / Navras ✦✦✦✦✦
A sublime concert performance from Kensington Gore in London in 1990 with accompaniment by Shaukat Hussain Khan on tabla. Consummate musicianship. He delivers renditions of "Raga Jaijaiwanti" and "Raga Mishra Shivranjani." One of the ten best Indian classical releases of 1992. — *Ken Hunt*

Saptrang / 1993 / Audiorec ✦✦✦
A fine studio recording with Zakir Hussain. Featured pieces are "Gurjari Todi," a ragamala or garland of ragas (medley) and "Bhairavi." — *Ken Hunt*

Raga du Début de la Nuit / 1993 / Adès ✦✦✦✦✦
Well-played night ragas are always special and this hour-long exposition of "Raga Yaman" is exceptional. Recorded in January 1993, this one showcases the skills of one of the tabla's most riveting exponents, Zakir Hussain. — *Ken Hunt*

Ustad Sultan Khan

Sarangi / Classical, India, Asia
Along with his contemporary Ram Narayan, Ustad Sultan Khan is one of a handful of Indian classical musicians keeping the sound of the sarangi alive. This archaic instrument is bowed, with the performer sliding his fingernails along the melody strings; the many sympathetic strings vibrating in harmony produce a haunting drone accompaniment. — *Myles Boisen*

★ **Sarangi: The Music of India** / 1975 / Rykodisc ✦✦✦✦✦
Remixed CD reissue of an earlier vinyl album released on Grateful Dead drummer Mickey Hart's short-lived 360° label. Recorded in December 1974 while Sultan Khan was on the Dark Horse tour with Ravi Shankar and George Harrison. Sultan Khan plays "Raga Bageshree" and a thumri most eloquently. — *Ken Hunt*

Ustad Vilayat Khan

Sitar, Surbahar / India, Asia
Vilayat Khan, one of the greatest Hindustani musicians of the century, was born in Gouripur in East Bengal (later Bangladesh) in August 1922. (Various other dates are strewn throughout the literature but that is the date that he confirmed in 1993.) His grandfather, Imdad Khan (1848-1920), and his father Enayat Khan (1894-1938)—Vilayat Khan gives the spelling Inayat Khan—were famed musicians in their lifetimes and Vilayat and his younger brother Imrat Khan inherited their musicality. Their gharana is known as the Imdadkhani gharana after their grandfather.

Vilayat Khan studied initially with his father. On his father's death in 1938 his training became the responsibility of his mother, Bashiran Begum, his grandmother, Bande Hussain Khan, and his maternal uncle, Wahid Khan. Around the same period Vilayat Khan began recording 78s. Peculiarly it is reported that he had to cope with odious comparisons with his father. Gradually he developed a style which, while acknowledging his kinsfolk's contribution, spoke with his own distinctive voice. His most outstanding contribution to his gharana's tradition is the evolution of what is known as a vocal style, or gayaki ang, on sitar. To some degree this is a term of convenience. Other contemporary musicians were striving to develop instrumental styles which more closely resembled the human voice—it was after all the goal of all instrumentalists to mimic as far as possible the human voice—and Vilayat Khan did not have a monopoly in this endeavor, whatever some commentators have claimed. That is not to detract from his achievement, which was considerable and caused a sensation.

Vilayat Khan's strides in compensating for the sitar's shortcomings were immense. His career has been marked by a regally consistent musical quality. An outspoken critic of low standards, he has maintained levels of personal integrity that on occasion have earned him the disfavor of the establishment. Little of his work has been in any context other than the strictly classical one although he worked with Satyajit Ray on the soundtrack to the film *Jalsaghar* and the Ismail Merchant/James Ivory film *The Guru.* He might be summed up as a keeper—not a quencher—of the flame. — *Ken Hunt*

Indian Classical Music / 1989 / Nataraj Music ✦✦✦
This performance of unspecified date during the 1980s finds him in the company of tabla player Sabir Khan. They present a 45-minute rendition of "Raga Desh." A pleasing performance. —*Ken Hunt*

Sitar [1994] / 1994 / Navras ✦✦✦
This concert recording from London's Royal Festival Hall in December 1993 consists of an extended reading of the early evening raga "Hameer." Once again Sabir Khan accompanies on tabla. —*Ken Hunt*

Night at the Taj / 1994 / EMI India ✦✦✦✦
The CD reissue of a classic jugalbandi performance, as ever given the combination, featuring the intriguing combination of sitar and surbahar. —*Ken Hunt*

● **Raga Bhairavi** / India Archive Music ✦✦✦✦✦
There is something particularly captivating about Vilayat Khan's sitar voicings. His alluringly playful style is thick with deep and subtle variations. His rendering of the much recorded late-morning raga Bhairavi combines the tranquil depth of classical interpretations with the lighter sentimentality of the semi-classical thumri. Hidayat Khan is on tanpura. —*Raissa St. Pierre, Original Music*

Sitar / India Archive Music ✦✦✦✦
If you wish to inaugurate a new label with an auspicious event there can be little better way than having Vilayat Khan. "Raga Bhairavi" is a studio interpretation from April 1989 performed solo. A landmark performance, it sends shivers up the spine. It would be an auspicious place to begin a lifetime's love of the man's music. —*Ken Hunt*

Lata Mangeshkar

b. Sept. 28, 1929, Indore, India
Vocals / India, Asia
Any account of popular Indian music must start with Lata Mangeshkar. While it is not possible to more than list the most important playback singers, Mangeshkar, because of her stature, merits detailed attention. Lata Mangeshkar has been active in all Indian popular and light classical music, having sung ghazals, bhajans, and pop. She is the supreme voice of popular Indian music, an Indian institution. Her importance rests not solely with her prodigious output. Many of her performances are considered timeless and undatable, although her voice has matured over the years. In effect she sang the soundtrack for millions of Indians' lives. Until the 1991 edition, when her entry disappeared, the *Guinness Book of Records* listed her as the most recorded artist in the world with not less than 30,000 solo, duet, and chorus-backed songs recorded in 20 Indian languages between 1948 and 1987. By 1990 she supposedly had worked on over 2,000 film soundtracks as a playback singer—meaning she pre-recorded the songs to which the films' leading ladies lip-synched.

Dinanath Mangeshkar, her father, owned a theatrical company and was a classical singer, a disciple of the Gwalior school, and gave her singing lessons from around the age of five. She also studied with Aman Ali Khan Sahib and later Amanat Khan. Her God-given musical gifts meant that she could master the vocal exercises effortlessly on first pass and from early on she was recognized as being highly gifted musically. Also in the family were brother Hridaynath, a music director, and sisters Meena, Asha (the famed Asha Bhosle), and Usha. Hridaynath's soundtrack included *Lekin . . .* , released in 1990 which, keeping it a family affair, placed Lata Mangeshkar well to the fore. Usha also became a playback singer. Only Asha Bhosle's career can compare in any way with her sister's award-strewn output, although by 1994 reports were appearing to the effect that Asha Bhosle had overtaken her big sister's output. Lata Mangeshkar began work as playback singer in the 1940s and grew to become the most famous playback singer of the century. She received her first proper credit under her own name in actor/director Raj Kapoor's 1949 film *Barsaat* (the soundtrack from which forms a third of the *Barsaat/Aah/Aag* album on EMI India CD PMLP 5188). She would sing for every major actress, including Geeta Bali, Nanda, Nargis, Nimmi, Nutan, Padmini, Sadhana, and Meena Shorey. The sheer volume of recording activity makes any examination of her life and works impossible in such a confined space. —*Ken Hunt*

● **Hits in the 80's** / 1990 / EMI India ✦✦✦✦✦
Subtitled "Duets by Lata Mangeshkar," this anthology includes work with S.P. Balasubramanyam (the title track from "Maine Pyar Kiya" and "Tere Mere Beech Mein" from *Ek Duuje Ke Liye*), Nitan Mukesh, and Kishore Kumar. A good representative collection of songs but left waif-like, like most Hindi film collections, to fend for themselves since sleeve notes would be a frivolous luxury. —*Ken Hunt*

Memorable Duets / 1994 / EMI India ✦✦✦
Lata is the unchallenged queen of the offscreen Indian film playback singers. Here she is paired with Hemant Kumar, Manna Dey and Talat Mahmood, just three of many males who have played second uvula to her. The wild-and-wooly, anything-goes aspects of *filmi* music are certainly a joy, but Lata is a wonderful singer, as this collection amply attests. —*John Storm Roberts, Original Music*

Shraddhanjali, Vol. 2 / 1995 / EMI ✦✦✦
Her second volume of tributes to Indian film music's "Immortals." Here she pays tribute to Mukesh, Mohd. Rafi, Hemant Kumar, Geeta Dutt, and Parul Ghosh. This double set is a far better introduction than many of the label's recyclings and theme albums. Although her spoken introductions in Hindi are not translated, listen and marvel at the lavish scale and sweep of her film songs. She helped to define one of the most popular musical genres in the world. —*Ken Hunt*

In Her Own Voice / EMI India ✦✦✦✦✦
Any selection of Mangeshkar's work must be entirely subjective and arbitrary because of the scale of her achievement. This three-volume set mixes hits and dialogue explaining aspects of her career in Hindi. It opens appropriately with "A Flash from Lekin . . . " —*Ken Hunt*

Najma

Vocals / Indo-British, Asia, Indian Diaspora
Najma Ashtar, a beautiful and talented young woman born in England of Indian parentage, seems bound for stardom in our world music-conscious age. She sings traditional lyrics of the Urdu-language poets primarily, backing the complex poetry with a contemporary musical palette that includes pop, jazz, and popular Indian music. Recently she has branched out to include qawwali, Indian ragas, and Western sources in her repertoire, always keeping her sensuous music close to its roots. —*Myles Boisen*

★ **Qareeb** / 1989 / Shanachie ✦✦✦✦✦
This beguiling album showcases the ethereal, haunting music of this stunning Indian vocalist based in Great Britain. With power and grace, she mixes ancient Indian ghazals (short romantic poems) with original melodies in an "Indipop" style, combining traditional and Western instrumentation. An album of great immediacy and impact, it offers an arresting new musical experience. —*Ladyslipper*

Atish / 1990 / Shanachie ✦✦✦✦✦
Atish is Urdu for "fire," and this extension of ideas first explored on *Qareeb* burns with the flame of inspiration. This follow-up album (which contains English vocals) is a liquid, sensual blend of jazz, pop, rock, and various Indian vocal styles exploring the complexity and pitfalls of love. —*Bob Tarte & Myles Boisen*

Ram Narayan

b. Dec. 25, 1927, Udaipur, India
India, Sarangi, Asia
For many connoisseurs of Indian classical music, Ram Narayan's name is synonymous with his chosen instrument, the sarangi, and he has justly earned himself an international reputation. Narayan has recorded for a great many labels but most of his early work is now out of catalogue—work on labels such as Amigo, Nonesuch, and Stil. His daughter, Aruna Narayan Kalle, is also a proficient sarangi player and performs sarangi duets with her father as well as performing as a sarangi soloist. —*Ken Hunt*

Rag Bhupal Tori & Rag Patdip / 1987 / Nimbus ✦✦✦
This session produced memorable performances of, respectively, a morning and an afternoon raga. Bliss. —*Ken Hunt*

★ **Rag Lalit** / 1989 / Nimbus ✦✦✦✦✦
The same Dec. 1987 session that gave rise to *Rag Bhupal Tori & Rag Patdip* produced a magical performance of the dawn raga "Lalit." Over 73 minutes, Ram Narayan coaxes out phrase after phrase to set the senses tingling. Quoted on the back of this CD, Yehudi Menuhin spoke for many people when he said, "I cannot separate the sarangi from Ran Narayan, so thoroughly fused are they, not only in my memory but in the fact of this sublime dedication of the great musician to an instrument which is no longer archaic because of the matchless way he had made it speak." Others may have left space for a breath. That have would been the only difference. —*Ken Hunt*

Volume 1 / 1989 / Ocora ✦✦✦
This recording was made in December 1978 with Suresh Talwalkar on tabla. This rewarding album is divided into two parts exploring "Raga Purya Kalyan," revealing its vinyl past. —*Ken Hunt*

Rag Shankara & Rag Mala in Jogia / 1990 / Nimbus ✦✦✦
Ram Narayan is the best-known virtuoso of the sarangi and this recording was made in December 1989. His performance of the night raga "Rag Shankara" is ideal for the night hours. —*Ken Hunt*

Sarangi: the Voice of 100 Colors / Nonesuch ✦✦✦
This album offers excellent performances on the sweet sarangi, a bowed-string instrument. —*David L. Mayers*

Shankar

Violin, Vocals
Shankar, a violinist, singer and composer, teaches Indian Classical styles by incorporating them into Western musics. He has worked with many Western musicians, including Peter Gabriel, Yoko Ono, Bruce Springs-

teen, Phil Collins, Talking Heads, and Lou Reed. He first began vocal lessons at the age of two, violin lessons at five, and drumming lessons at seven. After receiving a doctorate in ethnomusicology, he co-formed (with British composer Caroline) a pop-rock group in 1982, the Epidemics. The band has released three albums: *The Epidemics, Do What You Do,* and *Eye Catcher.* The two also work in an Indian quartet with Shankar's father, V. Lakshminarayana, and his sister, Gana Rao. The group's four albums are *Panca Nadai Pallavi, Galaxy, Nobody Told Me,* and *Soul Searcher.* Shankar also co-founded Shakti with John McLaughlin; the two released *Shakti, Handful of Beauty,* and *Natural Elements.* His two solo albums are *Touch Me There* (produced by Frank Zappa) and *Who's to Know. —John Bush*

● **Raga Aberi** / 1995 / Music of the World ✦✦✦✦✦
The South Indian violin virtuoso, L. Shankar, presents a dazzling rendition of a traditional raga in untraditional terms. He plays in a rhythm cycle of 4-3/4 beats, difficult enough to maintain, let alone be as musically creative as these three. The energy is consistently high, and there are a lot of solos by each musician, as well as deftly coordinated unison passages. —*Original Music*

Lakshiminarayan Shankar

b. 1950
Violin, Vocals / World Fusion, Jazz-Fusion, India, Asia
Sister-in-law to Ravi Shankar, mother-in-law to L. Subramaniam, Lakshmi Shankar is a remarkable singer. As a young girl she fell under the spell of dance and, encouraged by her forward-thinking mother, she studied Bharat Natyam dancing. She married the scriptwriter Rajendra Shankar, an elder brother of Ravi Shankar, and joined Uday Shankar's artistic circle during the early '40s. Ill-health forced her to give up dancing but, for us, this had the joyful effect of catalyzing her singing career. Around 1946-47 she worked on the historic adaptation of Pandit Nehru's *Discovery of India,* a work that prompted Nehru to say, "The ballet's better than my book." In the 1960s she recorded an album called *The Voice of Lakshmi Shankar* for World Pacific. Since then she has recorded widely in varying capacities and styles including Tamil folk songs, Hindu devotional songs of all sorts, film work (including the soundtrack to *Gandhi*) and for television documentaries. Her work appears on many labels including EMI India and RCA. —*Ken Hunt*

● **Who's to Know** / Nov. 1980 / ECM ✦✦✦✦✦
This is more like it. Genuine Indian classical ragas, though the somber quality robs session of vitality. —*Ron Wynn*

Vision / Apr. 1983 / ECM ✦✦✦
Jan Garbarek (ts) has some good solos. —*Ron Wynn*

Song for Everyone / Sep. 1984 / ECM ✦✦✦✦
One of Shankar's best. —*Ron Wynn*

Les Heures Et Les Saisons / 1987 / Ocora ✦✦✦
These recordings capture her in full flight. —*Ken Hunt*

Nobody Told Me / 1990 / ECM ✦✦✦
Exquisite recording, moments of beauty. —*Ron Wynn*

Soul Searcher / 1991 / Axiom ✦✦✦
1991 date with special guest Peter Gabriel. Decent, occasionally surprising. —*Ron Wynn*

Evening Concert / Ravi Shankar Music Circle ✦✦✦
Lakshmi Shankar has a heavenly voice, sweet and clear. The "Khyal in Raga Dhaani" is in a blues-like pentatonic scale and the romantic Thumri are delivered in an innocent, direct, lyrical melodiousness. The bhajan "Gopala," by the 16th-century poet Nidhiram, is totally engaging in its pleading yet devotional quality, with Shankar beginning at a high point right from the onset. "Janama Marana," by the saint/poetess of the 16th century, Mirabai, who gave up her life as a queen for devotion to Lord Krishna, has a loving, serious quality. It is a thoroughly enjoyable album. —*"Blue" Gene Tyrany*

Songs of Devotion / Auvidis ✦✦✦
Shankar sings mostly religious bhajans and semi-classical thumri in the khayal style, accompanying herself on the swaramandal zither—a relation to the santur.—*John Storm Roberts*

Ravi Shankar

b. 1920
Sitar, Sarod, Surbahar / Classical, India, Asia
Born on April 7, 1920, at Varanasi near Benares in West Bengal into an orthodox, well-off Brahmin family, Rabindra Shankar Chowdery's father, Shyam Shankar, was employed as a diwan (minister) by the Maharajah of Jhalawar. By the age of 13, Ravi Shankar was going along on every tour of his brother Uday Shankar's Compaigne de Danse et Musique Hindou (Company of Hindu Dance and Music). At the All-Bengali Music Conference in December 1934 he met the multi-instrumentalist Allauddin Khan. Precisely when Allauddin Khan was born is uncertain. People hazard dates in the 1860s around 1862 but in later years he himself gave

his age haphazardly. He would transform many musicians' lives but he had an incalculable effect on Ali Akbar (his son), Annapurna Devi (his daughter), and Ravi Shankar.

Allauddin Khan joined Uday's troupe as its principal soloist around 1935-36. In 1938 Ravi Shankar gave up a potential career as a dancer and went to study with Allauddin Khan in Maihar. In 1939 he began giving public recitals and came out of training at the end of 1944. Until 1948 he based himself in Bombay and gave programs all over India. He toured and wrote for films and ballet. Around this time he began his recording career with a small session for HMV (India). Work for All India Radio followed—as music director from February 1949 to January 1956 in New Delhi. Concurrently, his international star was on the rise. In 1954 he performed in the Soviet Union. In 1956 he played his debut solo concerts in Western Europe and the US. Within a decade he would be the most famous Indian musician on the planet. Within two decades he would become probably the most famous Indian alive. His English-language autobiography, *My Music, My Life* (1969), is still one of the best general introductions to Hindustani music.

Ravi Shankar is not one-dimensional. Apart from pursuing a career as a classical performer, he has also experimented outside this field. For this reason he has attracted criticism from purists. Some of this, especially during the Beatles era, undoubtedly had an element of jealousy to it: some was certainly warranted, because Ravi Shankar did take many chances. In fact, that was one of the things that kept his music exciting. To use a cricketing image—baseball would be wholly inappropriate—Ravi Shankar's batting average has remained high throughout a long and illustrious career. —*Ken Hunt*

★ **Ragas** / 1973 / Fantasy ✦✦✦✦✦
A less-than-perfect recording, this double-album is still an impeccable document of inspired raga duets by the masters Ravi Shankar and Ali Akbar Khan. —*Myles Boisen*

Raga Parameshwari / 1976 / Capitol ✦✦✦
A full raga cycle, it features his best tabla drum accompanist, Alla Rakha. —*Myles Boisen*

Shankar Project: Tana Mana / 1987 / Private Music ✦✦✦
This new age-oriented project isn't traditional classical sitar music. —*Myles Boisen*

Inside the Kremlin / 1988 / Private Music ✦✦✦
This is a collaboration with The Russian Folk Ensemble, Chorus, and Orchestra. —*Myles Boisen*

Golden Jubilee Concert / 1990 / Chhanda Dhara ✦✦✦✦
A double CD recorded in London in early 1990. Appearing on this recording is his late son Shubho Shankar on sitar and the late Durga Lal on pakhawaj (a barrel drum). Four ragas are featured: "Jhinjhoti," "Khamaj," "Bihag," and "Pancham Se Gara." —*Ken Hunt*

Farewell, My Friend / 1992 / EMI India ✦✦✦
During the 1950s Ravi Shankar collaborated with Satyajit Ray on a trilogy about a Bengali boy's life. It broke the mold and created the first real buzz about an Indian cinematic work internationally. Coming home from the studio in April 1992 he learned of the film director's death and with Ray on his mind he completed this album named after a novella by Rabindranath Tagore. "Raga Rajya-Kalyan" is a raga of his own creation deserving of, and destined for, wider performance. "Raga Pahadi Jhinjhoti" evokes his guru, Allauddin Khan. The title track completes the album. Directly inspired by Ray's death, it quotes the *Pather Panchali* theme (the first in the film trilogy). One of his best studio recordings of the '90s. —*Ken Hunt*

Concert For Peace / 1995 / Moment ✦✦✦
Released to celebrate Ravi Shankar's 75th birthday, this double disc was recorded at the Royal Albert Hall in London in 1993. Accompanying the sitar master are sarod player Partho Sarathy and Zakir Hussain on tabla. Delightful! —*Jonathan Ball*

In Celebration—the Highlights / Jun. 18, 1996 / Angel ✦✦✦✦✦
In Celebration—the Highlights pulls the most essential items from Ravi Shankar's four-disc box set, presenting his finest moments on a concise collection that acts as an excellent introduction to the master Indian musician. —*Thom Owens*

The Genius of Ravi Shankar / CBS ✦✦✦
Another worthy effort from Shankar's period of worldwide fame. —*Myles Boisen*

★ **The Sounds of India** / CBS ✦✦✦✦✦
A CD reissue of an important introduction to Indian music, this release is one of the few recordings featuring Chatur Lal on tabla and N.C. Mullick on tanpura. Notes are by the American composer Alan Hovhaness. —*Ken Hunt*

Ravi Shankar / Capitol ✦✦✦
This is one of the best recordings of this excellent sitar player. —*David L. Mayers*

Music of ... / Ocora ✦✦✦
Ravi Shankar, of course, is not just a major proponent of cultural inter-change, but (as sometimes seems to be overlooked these days), a musi-cian equalled only by Ustad Ali Akbar Khan in his generation, a major influence on younger Indian players, and a profound and far-ranging exponent of the Hindustani sitar tradition. —*John Storm Roberts, Original Music*

Pandit Ravi Shankar (Sitar) / EMI ✦✦✦
Recorded in June 1986 in Paris, this focuses on "Raga Puriya Kalyan" and a dhun entitled "Man Pasand" (literally, "That which is the favorite of the mind") which acts as a compendium of folk styles from Uttar Pradesh, Punjab, and Bengal. Kumar Bose plays tabla on this underappreciated recording. —*Ken Hunt*

Ravi Shankar / Deutsche Grammophon ✦✦✦✦
Released around 1993, this limited-edition triple CD reinstated to cata-logue three of the most interesting releases in Ravi Shankar's career. The first source is *East Greets East*, a trail-blazing collaboration between Indian and Japanese musicians dating from 1978. Straddling it and the second CD is the album *Ragas Hameer & Gara* from 1979. The middle CD completes that album and adds *Raga Jogeshwari* from 1980. These last two albums are also available individually as Music India (CDNF 010 and 009 respectively). Completing the trilogy is one of Ravi Shan-kar's finest ever studio albums, *Homage to Mahatma Gandhi & Baba Allauddin* from 1981, also available as Music India (CDNF 119). The only thing weakening this compilation is its German-only text, a curios-ity in some senses since the original Deutsche Grammophon/Polydor releases carried English (and French) texts. —*Ken Hunt*

Raga Mishra Piloo / EMI India ✦✦✦
Ravi Shankar and Ali Akbar Khan were not pioneers of the art of jugal-bandi in Hindustani music. But their jugabandhis set new heights and in the 1950s their jugabandhis reached new heights of popularity. One commentator in 1957 ascribed its popularity as "due essentially to the Ali Akbar Khan-Ravi Shankar combination." Others explored the sarod-sitar combination—Ishtiaq Ahmad and Illyas Khan, Bahadur Khan and Nikhil Banerjee—but it reached its apogee with Ali Akbar Khan and Ravi Shan-kar. This 1960s jugalbandi shows the famous flower in full bloom. It con-tains a 56-minute interpretation of "Raga Mishra Piloo" with tabla accompaniment by Alla Rakha and Zakir Hussain. —*Ken Hunt*

Shivkumar Sharma

Dulcimer / India, Asia
Shivkumar Sharma is one of the truly great visionaries in the Hin-dustani classical music firmament. His popularity has created a knotty problem for his admirers. Popularity has led to a demand for recordings by him, to a degree that having a Shivkumar Sharma album acts like a kind of validation for a label. Consequently the market is flooded with his recordings. His playing is consummate, therefore he is unlikely to produce a piece of work that is below par, which makes selecting a short-list even more difficult.

Sharma's story is one of dedication. He was born in January 1938 in Jammu Kashmir. His father, Uma Dutt Sharma, asked him to pursue the development of the Kashmiri santoor. Being a dutiful son he obeyed and persevered despite private reservations. Though its Persian relative, the santur, had associations with Persian and Iranian classical music, elevat-ing the Indian instrument to the classical concert platform was widely viewed as folly in conservative quarters. But Shivkumar Sharma per-sisted, experimented, restrung, and reconfigured his instrument. His first major santoor recital took place in Bombay in February 1955, but it took, he reckons, until the 1970s to finally silence the querulous, "the die-hard connoisseurs of the music, musicologists and purists." Parallel with his development of the santoor he worked as a tabla player (he accompanied acts as diverse as the renowned Punjabi folksinger Surinder Kaur and sitar maestro Ravi Shankar), and his understanding of tabla playing and rhythm has immeasurably enhanced his performance style and stage-craft. —*Ken Hunt*

★ Rag Madhuvanti & Rag Misra Tilang / 1987 / Nimbus ✦✦✦✦✦
Shivkumar Sharma is accompanied on this album by Zakir Hussain. Nimbus' importance as the first CD pressing plant in Britain meant that its recording wing had developed a keen and early appreciation of the technology and potential of CD production. A beautiful, sensitively played pairing. —*Ken Hunt*

Raga Purya Kalyan / 1996 / World Network ✦✦✦
Sharma is a virtuoso of the santur, a hammered dulcimer of a kind found all the way from western China to Hungary. But he's more than simply a virtuoso player. He's the man who introduced it from the purely folk tra-dition to the classical canon and gave it a whole technical vocabulary as he did so. Zakir Hussain, who's well-known in the new age-cum-cross-over world, is a genuinely brilliant classical tabla player. Here the two of them perform—delightfully—a piece combining two ragas, one medita-tive and one somewhat romantic. —*John Storm Roberts*

Colours of 100 Strings / EMI India ✦✦✦
Until Sharma brought it into the classical canon quite recently, India knew the santur largely as a Kashmiri folk instrument. On this recording he plays an extended "Rag Vachaspati" and a shorter piece, based on a Rajasthani folk form, that creeps into the classical canon. —*John Storm Roberts*

Shringar / Real World ✦✦✦✦✦
Ragas for sarod and violin in the southern Carnatic tradition were recorded in concert by two brothers (Shivakumar and Sridhar) from the younger generation of musicians. "Raga Bageshri" is a late-night raga, while the extremely popular "Bhairavi" is played at any time of the day. Here they are both given somewhat contemplative renderings that focus on spiritual depth rather than technique. —*John Storm Roberts*

Parween Sultana

Vocals / India, Asia
Parween Sultana was born in Gowgong in Assam in 1950. She was steeped in the lore and lives of the great musical masters by her father, Janal Ikramul Majib, a classical music devotee and a great admirer of Bade Ghulam Ali Khan. From an early age her father would take her to music festivals. "I come from a very conservative Muslim family and Muslims are very, very conservative," she told me in 1991. In spite of this, her father encouraged her dawning interest in singing. It led in time to the much frowned-upon practice of singing in public. She debuted on stage at the age of nine. In 1965 she recorded her first EP for EMI India, and in 1967 her first LP for the same label. She trained with Chinmoy Lahiri for ten years before failing health necessitated him suggesting a replacement in the Bombay-based Dilshad Khan. She balked at this ini-tially, only accepting him as her guru in August 1974. They married on August 26, 1975. Since then they have each pursued solo careers parallel to their duo work. An adjunct of her classical work is her occasional moonlighting in the Indian film industry. She has, for example, sung for the soundtracks of *Ashary, Kudrat*, and *Pakeezah*. —*Ken Hunt*

Rare Melodies / 1990 / EMI India ✦✦✦
A good mixture of different vocal styles—a khyal rounded off by a tarana, another khyal and a thumri—served up with tabla or tabla and harmonium accompaniment. —*Ken Hunt*

De l'Aube a la Nuit / 1991 / Auvidis Ethnic ✦✦✦
Translating as "From Dawn Until Night," this album presents nine pieces in a bhajan, tarana or thumri style performed as solos or duos. —*Ken Hunt*

Duologue in Raga / 1992 / Magnasound ✦✦✦
According to the booklet notes, Parween Sultana first performed one of the pieces on this album—"Raga Ragashree"—as a young girl on the stage of Sadarang Sangeet Sammelan in Calcutta. It presents, as is usual with their recorded work, interwoven solo and duo performances. —*Ken Hunt*

● Khayal Se Bhajan Tak, Vol. 1 / 1994 / EMI India ✦✦✦✦
A good introduction to Sultana's and Khan's work. Each performs a solo piece before concluding with a duet khyal. The introductory volume in a four-volume series. —*Ken Hunt*

Khayal / Esperance ✦✦✦
Khayal developed (like the European romantic movement) to reassert the primacy of expressiveness over rules that are too rigid; lyricism, free-dom, improvisation, and virtuosity are its hallmarks. Sultana and Khan, perhaps the most highly regarded of India's younger singers, perform both solos and duets in a recording that is, at times, breathtaking. —*John Storm Roberts*

From Dawn to Dusk / Auvidis ✦✦✦
Sultana and Khan perform in the expressive khayal style. —*John Storm Roberts*

Raga Rageswari, Raga Hamsadwani, Bhajans / Oriental ✦✦✦✦✦
This is a married musical duo, a "jugabandhi" par excellence. The clarity of line of perfectly complementary soprano and tenor voices, the emo-tional depth, and the sheer rollercoaster-ride thrill of their musical devel-opment is exceptional even in the richness of Indian music. Parween Sul-tana has the distinction of singing in musical festivals of both the North and South to sold-out audiences. — *"Blue" Gene Tyrany*

Live from Pune Music Festival / Alurkar ✦✦✦✦✦
Two pieces by the reigning queen of khayal, "Raag Gujri Todi" and "Raag Jaunpuri." Restrained (almost too much so) in the earlier passages, as she builds her performance Sultana begins to sparkle, singing with strength and joyousness. An incidental charm of uncensored live performance, occasional asides, a chuckle, even a cleared throat, only add to the imme-diacy of the recording. —*John Storm Roberts*

Live from Savai Gandharva Music Festival, Pune '92 / Alurkar Music House ✦✦✦
Recorded live, this brings together a 49-minute performance of "Gujari Todi" and a 20-minute performance of "Jaunpuri." Both are textbook dis-plays of Parween Sultana's classical maturity. —*Ken Hunt*

India Collection

Asia Classics 1 / Luaka Bop/ Warner Bros. ◆◆◆
Madras has been underrepresented when it has come to Western *filmi* anthologies, most of which have zoomed in on Bollywood's clique of playback vocalists. Largely, a peep at the world of the Madras-based playback singer S.P. Balasubramanyam (alternatively spelled S.P. Balasubramaniam), this is a first-rate introduction to the Anand's magpie-eyed blending and borrowing tendencies. Any musical sound or genre is fair game. —*Ken Hunt*

Bhangra Power / Multitone ◆◆◆
Bhangra, a new fusion idiom built from a Punjabi folk form by Indo-Brit teenagers for their own communal purposes, is not quite like anything from India itself. Punjabi percussion, electronics, and vocals from all quarters blend splendidly with enormous vitality to form that quite rare phenomenon, a truly teenage music. The groups on this album span the style riotously. —*John Storm Roberts*

Carnatic Music / Barenreiter Musicaphon ◆◆◆
A very fine recording, it involves vocals by Semmangudi Srinavasa Aiyar, the vina player K.S. Narayanaswami, and mridangam player Palghat Ragu. They perform two kritis by Muttuswami Dikshitar, one of the three founders of Carnatic music, along with two raga medleys. Major musicians (this series is bizarre in its reluctance to treat performers as individual artists rather than carriers of a style), excellent notes, and recording by John Levy. —*John Storm Roberts*

Flutes of Rajasthan / Playasound ◆◆◆
A revised and expanded edition of a 1977 vinyl release, this album focuses on the region's various flute styles. Featured instruments are nar (an end-blown flute), satara (twin separate flutes played together), and pawa (a double-necked flute, on one pipe of which the melody is played, on the other the drone). —*Ken Hunt*

★ **Golden Voices From the Silver Screen, Vol. 1** / GlobeStyle ◆◆◆◆◆
Western compilations have tended to focus on *filmi* songs with quirky and gimmicky arrangements. GlobeStyle's three volumes have their fair share of those but as a primer for Western audiences the trilogy remains unbeatable. After all, once the ears are attuned to the nuances and variation available in the quirky and the straight an appreciation of *filmi* can develop. There are matchless compilations with extensive notes which explain the context of this music. —*Ken Hunt*

★ **Golden Voices From the Silver Screen, Vol. 3** / GlobeStyle ◆◆◆◆◆
Western compilations have tended to focus on *filmi* songs with quirky and gimmicky arrangements. GlobeStyle's three volumes have their share of them but theirs are a balanced selection revealing the genre's grandeur. —*Ken Hunt*

Inde Centrale/Traditions Musicales des Gond (Central India/Musical Traditions of) / 1990 / VDE-Gallo ◆◆◆◆◆
India is the homeland for more than 40 million "tribals," aboriginals or indigenous peoples, whose ancestors lived there before the Aryans arrived in approximately 1500 BC. Many of these people live in the more inhospitable forests and mountain regions or work as hunters, farmers; some have become "outcast" Hindus. There are about four or five million Gond who speak an unwritten Dravidian language, and this recording is primarily of the Gond who live in Bastar, the southernmost district of Madhya Pradesh. Many of their villages show characteristics of megalithic civilization with menhir grave monuments and enormous stone slabs that serve as roofs and fences. There is a wide variety of songs presented here: a drumming "Rain Dance"; the fascinating "l'Escorte de la Mariée" ("Bridal Escort") for antiphonal chorus of friends and family wishing her farewell as she makes a strange noise like weeping; the joyous "Pani Mali Gala Jai" ("The Rainshowers Pour Down"); and a heartfelt "Ode to Bastar" sung in elegant Halbi by a famous poet met on a deserted mountain road on the hottest day of the year. —*"Blue" Gene Tyrany*

☆ **Indian Classical Music** / Caprice ◆◆◆◆◆
This standout set of two LPs covers several different approaches to both of the major classical traditions. Young sitarist Debu Chaudhuri takes a strongly traditional approach. So does S. Balachander, the greatest Carnatic vina player of the older generation. Bhimsen Joshi, too, sings khayal and thumri with more austerity than vocalists like Parveen Sultana. Lastly, flutist Hariprasad Chaurasia and santurist Shivkumar Sharma play Vivaldi and Bach in performances that are airy and playful, while in no way less serious. —*John Storm Roberts*

Carnatic Music of the South / Barenreiter Musicaphon ◆◆◆
Two artists dominate here. Three vocal pieces (two kritis and a ragamalika, or garland of ragas) are sung by Semmangudi Srinavasa Aiyar. An improvisation for vina on five ragas, plus a demonstration of the vina's tuning, is played by K.S. Narayanaswami, who also accompanies the vocals. Excellent notes, photos, and recording by John Levy. —*John Storm Roberts*

Classical Vocal and Instrumental / Barenreiter Musicaphon ◆◆◆
It introduces some of the major strains of Indian classical and religious music, and presents typical music of the two major Indian classical traditions. —*John Storm Roberts*

Southern Dance & Theatre Music / Barenreiter Musicaphon ◆◆◆
Introducing some of the major strains of Indian classical and religious music, the theatrical dance forms covered are women's bharata natyam and men's kathakali. —*John Storm Roberts*

Vedic Recitation & Song / Barenreiter Musicaphon ◆◆◆
Vedic chant is thought to be the oldest extant form of psalmody, preserved unchanged over thousands of years by extremely strict and complex instruction. These recitations and incantations, the heart of Hindu ritual, have endured as an unchanging constant in all the richness and variety of Indian music as a whole. —*John Storm Roberts*

Musical Appreciation / 1992 / Music Today ◆◆◆
This three-volume set is an excellent introduction to Hindustani vocal and instrumental music, introducing the concepts and instruments step-by-step. A full script is provided for visual reference. Disc one presumes no knowledge of the Hindustani musical cosmos. It opens with a section called "Silence, Sound and Musical Sound." Next the voice and the main instruments are introduced. Then there is an explanation of the technical terms swara and raga—swara is generally translated as something like tonal register because it can be more fluid than the fixed pitch of a musical note in Western art music. Disc two expands on the concept of raga. Disc three introduces a few of the more popular vocal styles that are set in ragas—dhrupad, khyal, and thumri—and gives pointers on listening and appreciating a performance. Much of the music is drawn from other volumes on the Music Today label and uses performances by Kishori Amonkar, Iqbal Bano, Hariprasad Chaurasia, Zahiruddin & Wasifuddin Dagar, Gangubai Hangal, Pandit Jasraj, Bhimsen Joshi, Amjad Ali Khan, Bismillah Khan, Imrat Khan, Mallikarjun Mansur, Rajan & Sajan Mishra, Shahid Parvez, Dr. N. Rajam, Shruti Sadolikar, Ravi Shankar, Shivkumar Sharma, and Padma Talwalkar. A small team of house musicians augments these recordings. As an educative tool, this set is the best primer on the market. —*Ken Hunt*

North Indian Classical Music, Vol. 1 / Barenreiter Musicaphon ◆◆◆
This is perhaps the finest of all Musicaphon's Eastern collections for coverage, accessibility, quality of performance, and being concise. The first album is devoted to vocal styles. The performers best known in the West are probably vocalist Lakshmi Shankar and flutist Hariprasad Chaurasia, but they hardly outshine their colleagues, if at all. Splendid notes are included by producer Manfred Junius, who also plays surbahar, and whose inside/outside perspective adds considerably to the venture. —*John Storm Roberts*

North Indian Folk Music / Auvidis ◆◆◆◆◆
This is a really fine glimpse into an enormously rich musical culture. Aside from their very great instrinsic merits, many of these recordings—among them a bhajan by a wandering monk, a shahnai solo, an episode from the *Ramayana*—give a feeling for the popular equivalents of music more familiar in their classical aspect in the West. —*John Storm Roberts*

Vocal Music of Rajasthan / 1992 / World Music Library ◆◆◆
One of two companion volumes exploring the world of two of the musician castes of Rajasthan. Traditionally they would perform their music for patrons of either Muslim or Hindu persuasion, whether the Rajput princes or Brahmins. Musical themes may be sacred or profane, religious or secular. Their instrumental music features folk or regional versions of the sarangi and shehnai. Musically their repertoire of songs and tunes is very interesting for its contribution to the debate about the origins of classical ragas since much of their repertoire is bedded in ragas. —*Ken Hunt*

Bangladesh: Les Garo de la Forêt de Madhupar / 1994 / Ocora ◆◆◆
The Garo are a people of Tibeto-Burman origin whose stronghold was the far west of the Meghalayan plateau known as the Garo Hills. These ancestral lands have increasingly been forfeited due to external pressures. This music is a mixture of ritual and social forms. Their cultural roots mean that stylistically this may be very different from people's usual expectations of Indian music. —*Ken Hunt*

Indonesia

Gamelan Sekar Tunjung

Asia, Indonesia (Java)

☆ **The Music of K.R.T. Wasitodiningrat** / 1992 / CMP ◆◆◆◆◆
This landmark LP recording presents gorgeous compositions in classical Javanese forms by the great artist and teacher known as "Pak Cokro." The gamelan is heard throughout, with solo instruments coming to the fore, and several works have Wasitodiningrat's characteristic multipart vocals. Performed by Gamelan Sekar Tunjung in Yogyakarta, it is

directed by Djoko Waluyo and is available from the American Gamelan Institute, Box 5036, Hanover, NH 03755-5036, USA. —*"Blue" Gene Tyrany*

Idjah Hadidjah

Vocals / Jaipongan, Asia, Indonesia (Java)

Idjah Hadidjah is the gorgeous voice of Gugum's' Jugala group, an outstanding female singer from a whole generation who avoided Western and Indian influences in favor of a distinctive regional sound. —*Myles Boisen*

★ **Tonggeret** / 1987 / Elektra/Nonesuch ✦✦✦✦✦
An Indonesian delight, this exotic document comes from one of Sunda's most popular jaipongan singers. —*Myles Boisen*

Euis Komariah

Vocals / Jaipongan, Asia, Indonesia (Java)

Jaipongan Java / 1990 / Globestyle ✦✦✦
Euis' frail and plaintive vocals are adrift in a landscape of jagged gamelan percussion and rhythms. It's capricious, moody, inspired, and dosed with shots of wit. —*Bob Tarte*

● **The Sound of Sunda** / 1990 / Globestyle ✦✦✦✦✦
Western vocal harmonies combine with music-box-style gamelan-derived instrumentation in a highly recommended recording of torch songs in the popular degung genre. Playing the part of heart-wrenched lovers, the entwining yearnings of Euis and Yus Wiradiredja recall the best and most soulful American male-female pop duets. —*Bob Tarte*

Jugala Orchestra / Globestyle ✦✦✦
On the island of Sunda in the 1970s, a new popular style emerged that was entirely based on older local forms and instruments, yet appealed to the young, and eventually to Indonesians on the other islands as well. Komariah, produced by a (perhaps the) creator of jaipongan, is a fine, slightly pop-oriented singer. She sings covers of the Jugala cassette label's major hits over the years. Here's wonderful music and admirable notes. —*John Storm Roberts, Original Music*

Nasidaria Group Semarang

Asia, Indonesia (Java)

☆ **Keadilan** / Piranha ✦✦✦✦✦
This is a truly wonderful recording. The all-woman Nasidaria is a supergroup by Javanese standards, with 32 cassette releases under their belts. This is yet another of the great Muslim crossover sounds, with Indian and Arabic (including contempo-Cairo) influences, but also a sound totally its own. Traditional Qasidah was epic poetry accompanied by percussion and response singing. Indonesian Muslims use the form as a kind of Islamic calypso of social and topical comment, and Nasidaria added synth, guitars, and so on, along with Indian drumming, *filmi* touches, and all the usual wonderful stuff. —*John Storm Roberts*

Indonesia Collection

Bali: Gamelan & Kecak / Elektra/Nonesuch ✦✦✦✦✦
A good contemporary survey of major traditional Balinese styles, it has lots of variety. —*Myles Boisen*

Balinese Contemporary Music / Barenreiter Musicaphon ✦✦✦
These early-to-mid-'80s recordings give examples of the gamelan gong kebyar in the villages of Pinda and Sawan—both centers of the most widespread contemporary Balinese gamelan sound. Kebyar is one of those few forms that develop out of tradition with little or no outside influences (a much more common procedure than is sometimes realized). The music is splendid and the documentation and photos are, as usual, outstanding. —*John Storm Roberts*

Flute & Gamelan of West Java / Tangent ✦✦✦
Recordings by the National University group of Jakarta feature Indonesia's best-known flute player, Sulaeman. The first side is devoted to music for bamboo flute accompanied by kacapi zither. The gamelan pieces are played by a group half-a-dozen strong, in the coastal style. —*John Storm Roberts*

Gamelan Music from Seloatu-Bali / Archive ✦✦✦
This is a dramatic, shimmering, precise, and exciting gamelan. —*David L. Mayers*

Gamelan Semar Pegulingan Saih Pitu: The Heavenly Orchestra of Bali / Sep. 1991 / CMP ✦✦✦✦✦
Semar Pegulingan gamelans were originally royal ensembles and used a seven-tone scale. Later, various different ensembles with the same name developed, all of them pitched higher and with a brighter, more delicate sound than gong gede. This group is one of the few remaining seven-tone Semar Pegulingan gamelans. Its music seems almost weightless, slower and less insistently virtuosic than modern styles. —*John Storm Roberts, Original Music*

Gamelan Semar Pegulingan: Gamelan Music from Sebatu / Nonesuch ✦✦✦
Here is an excellent recording of a full, rich, classical gamelan. —*David L. Mayers*

☆ **Golden Rain: Balinese Gamelan Music** / Nonesuch ✦✦✦✦✦
An introduction to the exciting Balinese kebjar style, it also includes a long excerpt from the gripping ritual drama known as ketjak (monkey chant). —*Myles Boisen*

Java: Historic Gamelans / Philips ✦✦✦
Some old, rare, varied, and interesting types of gamelans are here. —*David L. Mayers*

Javanese Court Gamelan . . . / Nonesuch ✦✦✦✦✦
Javanese Court Gamelan from the Pura Paku Aleman, Jogjakarta offers some extended stately and beautiful pieces by a very traditional Central Javanese gamelan. —*David L. Mayers & Myles Boisen*

Javanese Music from Surinam / Lyrichord ✦✦✦
Most Asian culture in the Caribbean is India-derived, but Surinam was once Dutch-ruled, and it was to Indonesia that the colonial authorities looked for indentured labor. Venra Gillis documented Suriam-Javanese traditions. This is essentially gamelan music, but there are very considerable differences between Javanese and Surinamese versions of similar forms. —*John Storm Roberts*

☆ **Music from the Morning of the World** / Jun. 17, 1988 / Elektra/Nonesuch ✦✦✦✦✦
This combines two classic Nonesuch albums to offer a good survey of gamelan music from Bali, along with the famous monkey chant ritual. —*Myles Boisen*

Music of Indonesia, Vol. 1: Songs Before Dawn / 1991 / Smithsonian/Folkways ✦✦✦
Though you wouldn't think it from the Western obsession with gamelan, Java has a wealth of "contemporary" and more or less syncretic popular styles, many of them with strong Muslim elements and influences from the Middle East and India. This is a splendid set in a lavish and altogether admirable vein. The first of the trio is devoted to gandrung banyuwangi, which has links with ancient religious beliefs, but is performed by professionals as party music with a female singer who also dances with the guests, backed here by two violins, gongs, and percussion. —*John Storm Roberts*

Music of Indonesia, Vol. 2: Indonesian Popular Music / 1991 / Smithsonian/Folkways ✦✦✦✦✦
Vol. 2 includes commercial recordings of Muslim dangdut, kroncong, and langgam jawa. These slick and street-wise popular music groups demonstrate individualistic approaches influenced by Indian film music, European folk, and Western pop. —*Myles Boisen & John Storm Roberts*

Music of Indonesia, Vol. 3: The Outskirts of Jakarta / 1991 / Smithsonian/Folkways ✦✦✦
The third, and a favorite, is real local street music of the capital, Jakarta—a mix of Chinese and Indonesian elements, which paradoxically sounds quite Muslim. —*John Storm Roberts*

Music of Indonesia, Vol. 4: Music of Nias & North Sumatra [va] / 1992 / Smithsonian/Folkways ✦✦✦
Another slap-in-the-face collection of startlingly bright music in the Smithsonian *Music of Indonesia* series, this one spotlights the rich diversity of a small region of the westernmost archipelago. The frenetic Toba and Karo peoples' gong and vernacular oboe recordings are impressive enough. But the unaccompanied hoho vocal music of the men of the island of Nias steals the show, crafting deeply resonant wells of sound from a four-tone scale—simultaneously funereal and lusty. It was meticulously recorded and documented. —*Bob Tarte*

Panji in Lombok, Vol. 1 / Barenreiter Musicaphon ✦✦✦
Panji was a person—the legendary Prince Panji of myths and classical poems, the ideal hero in search of a bride. Lombok, the second largest of the Sunda Islands, lies very close to Bali and has many Balinese inhabitants. But this is incidental. Instrumental music to Panji dance-dramas on Lombok comes mostly from the majority Sassk. It is delightful, accessible, and extremely varied, including metallic and wooden xylophones, gongs, lutes, oboes, spike fiddle, and a variety of percussion. This recording involves mostly smaller groups. —*John Storm Roberts*

☆ **Street Music of Java** / 1989 / Original ✦✦✦✦✦
Featured are three major street-popular idioms. Kroncong, a seductive music for fiddle, ukulele, and guitar, is thought to have originated under Portuguese influence as far back as the 17th century. Dangdut is a newer style, with strong Muslim influences (including Egyptian film music). The street versions here are based on the percussion that gives it its name. Langgan Jawa is a regional form of kroncong with stronger musical links to other local styles. Also included is some village ronggeng and a guitar-backed style called melayu that crosses local, Latin, and Indian influences. —*John Storm Roberts*

The Sultan's Pleasure / Music of the World ✦✦✦✦✦
Here are recordings of courtly music from the Sultan's palace, where the classical tradition is maintained and developed. Made during the ceremonial performances associated with the Sultan's birthday, they include several of the 18 different royal gamelan sets. —*John Storm Roberts*

Sunda [West Java] / Philips ✦✦✦
Gamelan music and music for small kecapi suling ensemble is featured on this album. —*David L. Mayers*

Iran Collection

☆ **Classical Music of Iran . . .** / 1991 / Smithsonian/Folkways ✦✦✦✦✦
The *Classical Music of Iran: The Dastgah Systems* collection of classical Iranian music performances was recorded before the 1979 Iranian revolution drove many accomplished players into exile. Extensive liner notes add to the appeal of this historic document. —*Linda Kohanov*

Japan

Japanese Koto Consort

Japan, Asia

Japanese Koto Consort / Lyrichord ✦✦✦✦✦
These are very fine recordings of sokyoku, instrumental music for koto, shamisen, and shakuhachi, two of them accompanying vocals. Though the instruments are a lot older, these ensembles took hold during the Edo period when a new mercantile class was having a profound effect on what had until then been mostly a courtly and religious tradition. The notes are sparse but fairly informative, the duration chintzy even for an LP reissue, but the music delightfully combines authenticity and accessibility. —*John Storm Roberts*

Shoukichi Kina

Guitar, Vocals / Japan, Asia

Shoukihi Kina is a folk-rock performer from Okinawa Japan. He came to prominence in the 1970s, performing songs protesting the American occupation of Okinawa during the Vietnam war. Using his own nightclub as a base, Kina and his band performed on electric sanshin, bass, and drums. Kina's song "Haisai Ojisan" was covered by the band FFKT and scored a hit. Kina has collaborated with slide guitarist Ry Cooder on *Bloodline* and has also recorded *Paradise* and, with Champloose, a live concert from 1977, *The Music Power from Okinawa*. —*Leon Jackson*

The Music Power from Okinawa / 1991 / Globestyle ✦✦✦✦✦
Delirious, high-spirited ditties shelter a tough sense of nationalism, cultural identity, and opposition to colonialism—hence Bob Marley's admiration for Kina, captured here in a 1972 live recording, which is deliciously ragged. A pair of bonus studio tracks demonstrate the power of Okinawan pop at full hi-tech tilt. —*Bob Tarte*

● **Asia Classics 2: Peppermint Tea House** / 1994 / Warner Bros. ✦✦✦✦✦
Silent-dog-whistle aficionados will relish the relentless female vocalists of Shoukichi Kina's band. Thank heavens for the balancing testosterone-pumping energy of Shoukichi himself, whose emergence holds back until the third cut to insure a dramatic entrance. And why not? As the intensely engaging songs here prove, Kina is the indisputable godfather of Okinawan pop, the inventor of a genre that combines elements of local folk music, Japanese-style vocals, Western instrumentation, and Kina's axe, the plucky sanshin banjo—augmented on several cuts by Ry Cooder's electric guitar. —*Bob Tarte*

Kodo

Japan, Asia

Heartbeat Drummers of Japan / 1985 / Sheffield Lab ✦✦✦
This authentic Japanese Taiko-drum ensemble sometimes adds modern and/or Western touches to their thunderous drumming repertoire. —*Myles Boisen*

Kohachiro Miyata

Japan, Asia

Shakuhachi: the Japanese Flute / 1976 / Elektra/Nonesuch ✦✦✦
These five solo pieces were recorded in 1976 by one of Japan's leading shakuhachi players. All are parts of the standard repertoire, and most are meditative in nature. The music is magnificent, the recording excellent, and the notes exemplary in their combination of clarity and information. It's short measure at 34+ minutes. —*John Storm Roberts*

Tadashi Tajima

Japan, Asia

Traditional Chamber Music / 1994 / Auvidis/SAGA ✦✦✦
Tajima plays the shakuhachi flute, the ideal instrument for these honky-

oku, pieces handed down through the centuries as "blowing meditation." By contrast, the voice is pre-eminent in the chamber music of the Nihon No Oto Ensemble (though there is one honkyoku played in, as far as can be told, quite a different style than Tajima). The singer slides, jumps, and stretches around the texts while the instruments (koto zither, shakuhachi, and biwa and shamisen lutes) accent, comment and agree in glorious slow-motion synchronization. —*Carl Hoyt, Original Music*

Kinshi Tsuruta

● **Kinshi Tsuruta/Katsuya Yokoyama** / Ocora ✦✦✦✦✦
This reissue of a fine, austere set of solo performances by two masters of their respective instruments was recorded almost 20 years ago. Tsuruta sings an episode from the Heike epic in a declamatory Buddhist-influenced style to his own percussive Satsuma-biwa lute. Yokoyama performs four pieces for shakuhachi: two on Buddhist concepts, the others inspired by cranes and the love-songs of deer. —*Original Music*

Satsuma-biwa / Ocora ✦✦✦
The satsuma-biwa, a type of lute, has its own traditions and repertoire. The energetic and percussive style featured in the music composed for this instrument appeared in 16th-century South Kyusu, whose then-ruler wrote its first lyrics. Tsuruta, one of the major living interpreters of satsuma-biwa, sings three contrasting songs here. The music is exemplary; the notes are brief but adequate. —*John Storm Roberts*

Japan Collection

☆ **Bell Ringing in the Empty Sky** / Nonesuch ✦✦✦✦✦
This is haunting, quieting, evocative solo shakuhachi bamboo flute by Goro Yamaguchi. *Bell Ringing in the Empty Sky—Japan Shakuhachi Music* offers two lengthy selections. —*David L. Mayers*

☆ **Flower Dance: Japanese Folk Melodies** / Nonesuch ✦✦✦✦✦
Ten ancient folk tunes—lullabies, drinking songs, dances, and so forth—feature the Noday family performing on shamisen and koto (both stringed instruments), plus percussion and bamboo flute. —*Myles Boisen*

Gagaku: Imperial Court Music [Japan] / Lyrichord ✦✦✦✦✦
This is a long-overdue reissue of a magnificent recording and performance by the majestic Kyoto Imperial Court Music Orchestra. The "gagaku" (refined, elegant, or correct music) style is an amalgam of various court musics from India, China, and Korea from as long as 1500 years ago. Because of the continued support, Gagaku music may be heard today much as it sounded a millennia ago. Included are classics such as "Etenraku" (music of divinity), the masterpiece "Manzairaku," for the majestic dance of four persons in bird costumes, the sword dance "Embu," and "Hassen," the music of the crane dances. Also included are the dragon dance "Nasori"; "Goshoraku," with tones based on the five Confucian principles; music to the Indian bird "Karyobin"; and the opening prelude "Irite." —*"Blue" Gene Tyranny*

Japan: Semi-Classical & Folk Music / EMI ✦✦✦
Good recordings of nagauta, koto, and shakuhachi are enhanced by especially good selections of folk music. —*David L. Mayers*

Japan 11: Gagaku / Barenreiter Musicaphon ✦✦✦
Featured is dramatic and beautiful ensemble music for the court. —*David L. Mayers*

Kabuki & Traditional Music of Japan / Nonesuch ✦✦✦✦✦
This is a nice recording of Japan's dramatic but austere theater music. —*Myles Boisen*

Kagura: Shinto Ritual Music / Hungaraton ✦✦✦✦✦
Kagura is the general word for Shinto practices associated with music and song. As this recording documents, that covers a wide range: an invocation from the ancient shamaness tradition, festival dances of various kinds, folk drama on mythological themes, and court ceremony. A wide range of recordings is enhanced by admirable recording and very thorough notes. —*John Storm Roberts*

Koto Music of Japan / 1978 / Bescol ✦✦✦✦✦
Stately art music for the resonant Japanese zither is played in solo or ensemble settings. —*Myles Boisen*

Noh Play/Recitation to Biwa / Barenreiter Musicaphon ✦✦✦
Lyrical Noh choral drama, developed in the late 14th century and largely unchanged since, consists mainly of recitative and song. Included is *Hagoromo*, one of a class of plays concerning romantic and nature spirits. Also included is an example of a pre-Noh-play narrative tradition. —*John Storm Roberts*

O-Suwa-Daiko Drums / Auvidis ✦✦✦✦✦
Originally used in Shinto rituals, and later as military music, the complex percussion ensembles of the Suwa valley use other instruments only as garnishes. As privileged audiences in the US have recently discovered, this is one of the great percussion traditions of the world, overwhelming even on record. —*John Storm Roberts*

Shinto Music / Barenreiter Musicaphon ✦✦✦
Shinto music goes back to the 4th century, but it was much reworked in the mid-19th century. Here are religious dance-songs and other music, including both wind and stringed instruments. —*John Storm Roberts*

Traditional Vocal & Instrumentals / Elektra/Nonesuch ✦✦✦
A nice variety of Japanese singing and instrumental styles coming from the traditional Ensemble Nipponia. —*Myles Boisen*

Korea

Samulnori
....
Asia, Korea (North)

Record of Changes / Feb. 1988 / CMP ✦✦✦
Included is contemporary-traditional ritual song and percussion. Salumnori is a young group that composes (or re-creates) compositions stemming from ancient Korean ceremonial music, arranged and played by 20th-century Koreans. As such, it is part of a quite widespread attempt to adapt tradition to modern life and beliefs. —*John Storm Roberts*

Park Sang Won
....
Asia, Korea

The Kayagum: Korea, Vol. 1 / Disques Esperance ✦✦✦✦✦
Park's technique on the 12-string kayagum is formidable. —*Myles Boisen, Roots & Rhythm*

Korea Collection

Kolam: The Masked Play / Barenreiter Musicaphon ✦✦✦
This is the music of Sri Lanka's majority ethnic group. Kolam, more like a masquerade than a drama in the European sense (involving dance, mime, and highly elaborate costumes), belongs mainly to three villages in southern Sri Lanka, and even there it is dying out. This recording includes songs and music for the dance sections, and comes with outstanding notes and photos of the intricately beautiful masks and costumes. —*John Storm Roberts*

Korean Music / Philips ✦✦✦
Prominent on this album are the oboe-like hyangpiri played in small court ensemble and the taegum flute, both expressive and virtuosic. —*David L. Mayers*

☆ **P'Ansori: Korea's Epic Vocal Art & Instrumental** ... / Elektra/Nonesuch ✦✦✦✦✦
Although difficult for Westerners, the p'ansori vocal style featured on this album is highly regarded in Korea, and singer Kim So-Hee is a national treasure. —*Myles Boisen*

Laos Collection

Lam Saravane/Khen Music / Ocora ✦✦✦
In the lam, performed at various important village occasions, male and female vocalists sing a kind of competitive love song in which he charms and she exposes the shallowness of his charm. A performance of delicate strength, it is backed by flute and khen (bamboo) mouth-organ. To this performance by one of the great women lam singers is added a number of solo pieces for khen. The performances are fine, the recording is excellent, and the notes are good. —*John Storm Roberts*

Laos / Barenreiter Musicaphon ✦✦✦
This is an admirable introduction to the varied classical and village idioms of this musically rich nation, with its ancient Indian as well as Chinese and Southeast Asian elements. Included are several varied pieces for the khene, a bamboo mouth organ that is the precursor to the Chinese cheng, and various classical orchestras, some dominated by strings, some by xylophones, one (in a *Ramayana* epic) by oboe and percussion. Included are fine photos which are nonetheless slighter in notes than is usual for this series. —*John Storm Roberts*

Laos: Musique pour le Khene/Lam Saravane / Ocora ✦✦✦
This double recording offers an entire disc of solo khene and another of a regional genre from the south—from Saravane province—accompanied by khene and flute. —*Terry Miller*

Laos: Musiques du Nord, Musiques de l'Asie Traditionnelle, Vol. 2 / Playa Sound ✦✦✦
The only album from Laos to offer music from the north, it includes classical music from the former palace at Luang Prabang, khap toom (the local repartee genre from Luang Prabang), and examples of Puan, K'mu, and Hmong musics. Related to it is *Musique des Hmong du Laos: Cour d'Amour et Culte des Ancetres*, Societe francaise de productions phonographiques-Paris (SFPP) 8-2911. —*Terry Miller*

Laos: Traditional Music of the South / UNESCO-Auvidis ✦✦✦
A reissue of a 1973 recording with uncorrected (and often misinformed) annotations, the music is nonetheless of interest, including solo khene

mouth organ, lam singing, and an excerpt of the buffalo sacrifice ceremony by uplanders from the Vietnamese-Lao border. —*Terry Miller*

Music from Southern Laos Played by Molam Lao / Nimbus ✦✦✦
This recently issued recording features Lao musicians living in France and offers a good survey of styles from southern Laos. —*Terry Miller*

Southern Laos: Traditional Music / Philips ✦✦✦
Featured is music for khenes (mouth organ), singer, pi-phat orchestra, wedding orchestra, buffalo sacrifice, gong with singer. It is exciting and interesting. —*David L. Mayers*

Thailand: Lao Music of the Northeast / Lyrichord ✦✦✦
This album offers pre-modernized singing and instrumental music, including mouth organ, lute, metal-can bodied fiddle, and vertical log xylophone. —*Terry Miller*

The Flower of Isan/Isan Slete: Songs and Music from North-East Thailand / GlobeStyle/Ace ✦✦✦
An excellent anthology of traditional music for local instruments and several types of lam recorded by teachers from the School of Dramatic Arts in Roi-et. Also from Roi-et but featuring more modernized music, is *Instrumental Music of Northeast Thailand* (World Music Library, King Record Co., KICC 5124), and *Mo Lam Singing of Northeast Thailand* (World Music Library, KICC 5123), featuring famous singer Chawiwan Damnoen and khene master Thongkham Thaikla, but without the usual male vocalist/partner. —*Terry Miller*

Music of Laos / World Music Institute ✦✦✦
Recorded in New York, this album combines the talents of National Heritage Award winner Mr. Khamvong Insixiengmai, Ms. Thongkhio Manisone, and their khene and phin (lute) player, Khamseung Syhanone. —*Terry Miller*

Malaysia Collection

An Anthology of South-East Asian Music: Music of the Senoi of Malacca / Barenreiter Musicaphon ✦✦✦
This album, along with two others—*The Negrito of Malacca* (BM 30 L 2562) and *The Protomalayans of Malacca* (BM 30 L 2563), all collected and written by eminent scholar Hans Oesch, present field recordings of three upland minority groups from the interior of Malaysia. These are believed to represent some of the earliest layers of music living on our planet. —*Terry Miller*

Musiques & Traditions du Monde, Malaisie: Musique Traditionnelle / CBS ✦✦✦
Recorded in the most traditional areas—Kota Bharu and Trengganu—these selections represent dance, theatre, and court musics. —*Terry Miller*

Musiques de l'Asie Traditionnelle: Malaisie / Playa Sound ✦✦✦
The most comprehensive collection of lowland Malay music, this album includes nine selections of the Malay, two of the Indians, two of the Chinese, and four from Insular Malaysia (Borneo). —*Terry Miller*

UNESCO Collection: The Music of Malaysia / Barenreiter Musicaphon ✦✦✦
Going back to 1969, this first-to-be-published anthology remains eminently useful, covering as it does palace, theatrical, and dance music with excellent notes by Mubin Sheppard. —*Terry Miller*

Mongolia Collection

Instrumental Music from Mongolia / Tangent ✦✦✦
Mongolian flutes and stringed instruments (including the beautiful two-stringed horse's-head fiddle) are mostly used to back singers. Here one hears them mostly solo, and very beautiful they are. (Also amazingly accessible to American ears: this is not one for ethnologists alone.) Good brief notes by Jean Jenkins of the Horniman Museum, who also did the recording. —*John Storm Roberts*

Mongolian Folk Music / Hungaraton ✦✦✦
In a world with ever more fine recordings of once-unobtainable music, this two-CD collection of 1967 recordings by a Hungarian ethnomusicologist remains almost *hors concours* (even from Jean Jenkins' Tangent set). Superb recording quality does justice to a very wide selection of vocal and instrumental pieces that are remarkable in their beauty and variety (three different musical subcultures). One song is also remarkable in its almost spookily Scots-Irish sound. English notes are included. —*John Storm Roberts*

Virtuosos from the Mongol Plateau / King Records ✦✦✦
Virtuosos is the right word for these members of the National Ensemble of Folk Song and Dance. Most beautiful are the long-song vocals of Namdzilin Norovbanzadan, whose sound the liner notes aptly describe as a shining metallic tone. The double-tone singing and jaw-harp playing of Gundenbiliin Yavgaan and moriin zuur (horsehead fiddle) of Tsendiin Batcuulin are equally fine. Superb recording. —*John Storm Roberts*

Nepal Collection

Folk Music of Nepal / 1994 / King ✦✦✦
This volume presents a variety of settings of vocal and instrumental music. A good collection, it does not compare with the regrettably out-of-print *Musician Castes in Nepal* LP collection edited by Mireille Helffer and released in 1969 by the Paris-based Musee de l'Homme label. (Folkways released three volumes of material from Nepal. These comprise *The Gaines of Nepal* (4078), *Music of a Sherpa Village* (4320), and *Songs and Dances of Nepal* (4101), but it is to Mireille Helffer's collection that one should turn if exploring the vinyl legacy of Nepal.) —*Ken Hunt*

Pakistan

Nusrat Fateh Ali Khan

b. Oct. 13, 1948, Lyallpur , Punjab Province, Pakistan
Vocals / Ambient, Pakistan, Qawwali, Asia
Without doubt the most important qawwal is Nusrat Fateh Ali Khan & Party—Party is a generic term for a qawwali ensemble but is also used in Sikhism and to describe some classical music ensembles, for example, shehnai maestro Bismillah Khan and Party.

Dubbed Shahen-Shah-e-Qawwali (the Brightest Star in Qawwali), Khan made his first recording in 1973 in Pakistan and a number of early EMI (Pakistan) albums jointly billed him with his uncle Mubarak Ali Khan. Since these mainly cassette albums were undated and numerous, it is difficult to place them in any more accurate chronological sequence than catalogue number order. Between 1973 and 1993 his recorded output could only be described as prodigious, with more than 50 album releases to his name on numerous Pakistani, British, American, European, and Japanese labels. Heavily over-recorded, blighted with a rash of poppy remix albums or albums with Westernized instrumentation or arrangements, his recorded work is a mire to suck in the uninitiated and their money. Converts, however, do not escape scot-free. Although some releases hint at their nature with coded titles such as *Volume 4 Punjabi* (Oriental Star CD SR013) from 1990 or *Ghazals Urdu* (Oriental Star CD SR055) from 1992, the chosen language and style is frequently a matter of conjecture or uncertainty. While the Western market is saturated with his work, the Indian market is supersaturated, and his recorded output is in danger of overwhelming any sense of taste.

Real World was the label largely responsible for Khan's breakthrough into a non-Indian audience. It was their marketing skills and the platform provided by the WOMAD organization which introduced him to Westerners. *Musst Musst* (Real World CD RW 15), released in 1990, was a deliberate attempt to target the White market with its non-traditional arrangements, yet it seems positively cherubic beside later abominations. "All these albums are experiments," he told me in 1993. "There are some people who do not understand at all but just like my voice. I add new lyrics and modern instruments to attract the audience. This has been very successful." Success, however, bred indifference to the virtues and values of the original music. Many find the remix albums, the Western and youth-market releases a source of despair: buyer beware remains the watchword. When singing his traditional work he remains peerless. Many, including myself, regret the dilution of his talent that has occurred with his "experiments." However, in 1994, reportedly tired of unauthorized releases, he took greater control of both his business affairs and his concert and recording activities. —*Ken Hunt*

Mustt Mustt / 1990 / Atlantic ✦✦✦
This was one of several attempts to extend Nusrat Fateh Ali Khan's popularity outside the strict world of qawwali, a light classical Islamic music. The album's title track opens and closes the album. Typifying the album's approach, at its spine is a funk bass track over which he croons. The upshot is all bone and no marrow. The pure schlock of "Nothing Without You" gives one the sense of outrage provoked by an animal pacing in a cage. There were worse experiments to come. Disco- and bhangra-inflections, infantile sound effects and samples, and the Party turned into the qawwali equivalent of chick vocals. —*Ken Hunt*

Day, Night, Dawn, Dusk / 1991 / Shanachie ✦✦✦
An uninspired collection from EMI Pakistan's archives but a convenient taster of his style owing to its widespread availability in the West. The early Real World material is far superior as an introduction, just as available and served up better. —*Ken Hunt*

☆ **Shahbaaz** / 1991 / Real World ✦✦✦✦✦
This shows Kahn taking chances with tradition, pushing his dynamic voice and ensemble to new expressive heights. —*Myles Boisen*

Shahen-Shah / Apr. 1991 / Atlantic ✦✦✦
Four lengthy selections of Sufi devotional music were recorded with an impassioned chorus and accompaniment. —*Myles Boisen*

★ **Devotional Songs** / 1992 / Real World ✦✦✦✦✦
A well-deserved favorite. Its opener, named "Allah Hoo Allah Hoo" (although the piece is neither fixed in shape nor lyric), became a rallying cry for early qawwali converts but it is an enormous crowd pleaser and a sort of greatest hit. —*Ken Hunt*

Love Songs / 1992 / Real World ✦✦✦✦✦
The complement to *Devotional Songs*, and one that set the West's qawwali taste buds buzzing. Like *Devotional Songs* it had been a cassette release before its 1992 CD reissue. —*Ken Hunt*

Traditional Sufi Qawwalis, Vols. 1 & 2 / 1993 / Navras ✦✦✦✦✦
Recorded live in London in December 1989, this four-volume series (available separately) is an exemplary illustration of the sort of repertoire the listener would hear at a qawwali concert where the audience is made up largely of Muslims of Asian descent or Indians of other religions. (Khan tends to adjust his repertoire and performance style to take account of the style of venue, the devotional situation—for example, his presence at a Sufi shrine—or the composition of his audience.) —*Ken Hunt*

Ilham / 1993 / Audiorec ✦✦✦
Released in 1993 but consisting of material recorded some 15 years before, *Ilham* (*Revelation*) is exclusively in Khan's mother tongue, Punjabi. He has recorded other albums in the same language, but this one has a special significance for me since I wrote the booklet notes. —*Ken Hunt*

The Last Prophet / 1994 / Realworld ✦✦✦
Nusrat's recent Western releases seemed only okay. His latest, however, is the finest qawwali recording in years, by one of the greatest qawwali singers, and certainly the most impassioned. This is just simply perfection—musically speaking—and the notes aren't bad in their nontechnical way. —*John Storm Roberts, Original Music*

Live in Paris, Vols. 1 & 2 / 1992 / Ocora ✦✦✦
There is no single greatest singer of qawwalis, the ancient Sufi songs that have become central to popular religion and popular music in Pakistan. But if there were, his name would be Khan. He inherits a family tradition of qawwali singing going back several centuries, and in live performances like this concert he can be emotionally devastating. —*David L. Mayers*

En Concert a Paris / Ocora ✦✦✦✦✦
This five-volume series—each disc is available singly—covering two concerts (the first two volumes date from November 1985, the rest from March 1988) is, in a word, magnificent. For those who wish to dive headlong, it captures the man's magic better than any other recording on the Western market. Exemplary packaging and notes in French and English. —*Ken Hunt*

Magic Touch / Oriental Star ✦✦✦
This anthology of sometimes good, mostly too blatantly commercial, mixes of material by Nusrat Fateh Ali Khan, polarizes taste. Love it or leave it. But there are far worse pains that can be inflicted in the name of qawwali. Producer Bally Sagoo is actually very good at his job and you do not want to hear the competition. A taste of Bally Sagoo's can be sampled (all puns intended) on Bally Sagoo *On the Mix—The Story So Far*, released on Star or Mango depending on the territory, a various-artists collection. —*Ken Hunt*

Live in Paris, Vols. 3-5 / Ocora ✦✦✦

Sabri Brothers

Pakistan, Qawwali, Asia
The Sabri Brothers, Haji Ghulam Farid (or Fareed) Sabri (1930-1994) and Haji Maqbool Ahmed Sabri (also born in Kalyana in East Punjab, on October 12, 1945), were taught music by their father, Ustad Haji Inayat Sen Sabri. The family claims descent from Mian Tansen, one of the greatest and most legendary Hindustani musicians of all time. The musically gifted Tansen was a musician in the court of Akbar and is credited with miraculous powers of enchantment. Maqbool Ahmed Sabri formed his first party of qawwals at the age of 11; soon afterward in 1956 his elder brother (who had been singing with Kallan Khan's qawwal and party) joined him and the Sabri Brothers came about. Their career was marked by brotherly squabbles followed by periods of each doing solo work. The duo created a body of recorded work, consistent in quality, but more traditional than Nusrat Fateh Ali Khan's recorded work. Ghulam Farid Sabri's funeral in Karachi was attended by an estimated 40,000 mourners. Haji Maqbool Ahmed Sabri continues to carry the torch. —*Ken Hunt*

Qawwali: Sufi Music from Pakistan / 1978 / Nonesuch ✦✦✦
The first Pakistani Sufi record issued in the US is a fine example of full-throated qawwali. —*Myles Boisen*

The Pakistan: The Music of the Qawal / 1990 / Audivis ✦✦✦✦✦
Uncredited anywhere but in the booklet, this UNESCO collection consists of four performances by the Sabri Brothers. The opening piece is an allegory in ghazal form (a light classical poetic form) on, as Alain Daniélou's notes put it, "the emotions of love and the transitory aspects of the world." Amen apart from pointing out that qawal is an alternative spelling. —*Ken Hunt*

Pakistan: The Music of the Qawal / 1990 / Auvidis/UNESCO ✦✦✦
Uncredited anywhere but in the booklet, this volume consisted of four performances by The Sabri Brothers. The opening piece is an allegory

in ghazal form (a light classical poetic form) on, as Alain Danielou's notes put it, "the emotions of love and transitory aspects of the world." Amen apart from pointing out that qawal is an alternative spelling. —*Ken Hunt*

Ya Habib / 1990 / Plan 9/Caroline ♦♦♦♦♦
Magical moments captured for posterity. —*Ken Hunt*

★ **Qawwali Masterworks** / 1993 / Piranha ♦♦♦♦♦
A trawl through the archives of EMI Pakistan, the label which released their domestic product for decades, produced this double-CD set of vintage Sabri material. The concluding piece, a 14-minute rendition of two Sufi themes titled "Posida Posida" ("Discreetly, Discreetly"), demonstrates the power of their poetic vision. —*Ken Hunt*

Pyar Ke Morr: Live in U.K. Vol. 1 / 1993 / Oriental Star Agencies ♦♦
A word to the wise. Such releases are omnipresent and, while they fuel theories about the male drive to collect, they add little of spiritual or aesthetic value to the debate. —*Ken Hunt*

Pakistan Collection

Baloutchistan: Musiques d'Extase et de Guérison / 1989 / Ocora ♦♦♦
An album of "Ecstasy and healing musics" from the Baluchi, a people who occupy the western half of Pakistan and southeastern Iran, and whose music straddles the Indian and Iranian modal system. —*Ken Hunt*

Doli—Wedding Songs / Sirocco ♦♦♦
This selection of songs drawn from the EMI Pakistan archives is the popular rather than musicological face of the tradition. The artist represented to the nigh-exclusion of all others is the great playback singer Noor Jehan. The incidence of mehndi (henna) in its song titles alludes to the henna body decoration ceremonies associated with nuptial celebrations found throughout the subcontinent. —*Ken Hunt*

☆ **Treasures of Pakistan** / Playasound ♦♦♦♦♦
Excellent examples of music for sarinda and sarangi fiddles as well as the rabab lute, extremely well recorded on location. As a nice touch, the producer is Kudzi Erguner, a Turkish musician, rather than the usual Western ethnomusicologist (not the first—Deben Bhattacharya's recordings are remembered with nostalgia—but still too rare). Brief but cogent notes are included. —*John Storm Roberts*

Philippines Collection

Music of the Magindanao / Smithsonian/Folkways ♦♦♦
These are examples of gongs used in a gamelan-like ensemble; also with Jew's harps, flutes, vocal chants, boat lute, and percussion beams. —*David L. Mayers*

Sri Lanka Collection

Maha Pirit: the Great Chant / Jecklin ♦♦♦
One part of a new series from Switzerland, this album is particularly important because all attention to Buddhist chant has focused on Tibetan and Zen traditions. The material comes from the '70s recordings of ethnomusicologist Wolfgang von Laade, founder of the Music of Man Archive. —*David L. Mayers*

Singhalese Music . . . / Barenreiter Musicaphon ♦♦♦
Singhalese Music—Singing & Drumming is the music of Sri Lanka's majority ethnic group. The first recording is mostly religious folk, with a side devoted to unaccompanied vocals, including various agricultural songs. The second consists of drumming with and without vocals; notable are part of the "heavenly elephant" dance and the fine drum duet. —*John Storm Roberts*

Sufi Collection

☆ **Islamic Music of Asia** / Inedit ♦♦♦♦♦
This is Muslim music from Pakistan, India, Malaysia, and Indonesia. Here is a call to prayer from Pakistan, a qawwal from India and one from Pakistan (Sabri Brothers); a Pakistani ghazal; a Malaysian maulidd; and a salawat dulang, a two-singer vocal contest special to Indonesia. An admirable idea makes for fine music. —*John Storm Roberts*

Thailand

Saman Hongsa & Group
Thailand, Asia

Isan Slete / Globestyle ♦♦♦♦♦
Modern songs and music from northeast Thailand are sung by a husband-and-wife team with traditional ties and instruments but a modern attitude (and an electronics shop). The instrumentals, including kaen, xylophone, panpipe, and lute, are played by traditionalists rather than

village musicians. Exhilarating music and fine notes are included. —*John Storm Roberts*

Thailand Collection

Ceremonial Music of Thailand: Music for Sacred Rituals and Theatre / Pacific Music Co., Tao ♦♦♦
This includes music similar to most Thai recordings, but is packaged to have a new-age spin. —*Terry Miller*

Classical Music of Thailand / World Music Library ♦♦♦
Although the musicians in this album are highly skilled, nearly half of the recording is devoted to solos on one instrument—the jakhe "crocodile" zither. The remaining selections have one major flaw: the khruang sai ensemble is missing the khlui flute, a problem akin to leaving out the second violin in a recording of string quartets. A Thai source says that the flute player failed to appear at the recording studio, but this did not deter the recording team. As with most other King issues, the notes are minimal and unreliable. —*Terry Miller*

The La Hu Nyi of Thailand / Barenreiter Musicaphon ♦♦♦
Featured is music of a minority group living in North Thailand, Burma, Laos, and part of China's Yunnan province. Unlike in Thailand as a whole, the bamboo mouth organ is a major instrument here and heavily represented. The examples on this recording include music for a New Year's dance and for a lunar festival, mostly for mouth organ. Also here are love songs, some accompanied by lute. —*John Storm Roberts*

Music of Chieng Mai / Auvidis ♦♦♦
Chieng Mai shows clearly the influences that have shaped Thai music as a whole: Chinese, Khmer (and thus Indian, Laotian, and Burmese). This graceful and well-annotated CD from the UNESCO *Musical Atlas* series presents three idioms: a xylophone-led regional orchestra, a monastic group in which lutes dominate, and an ensemble with fiddles, zither, and percussion. —*David L. Mayers*

Royal Court Music of Thailand / Smithsonian-Folkways ♦♦♦
Issued in conjunction with the 1994 Festival of American Folklife but recorded in 1993 in Thailand by musicians of the Fine Arts Department, this recording features works by Thai royalty, both living and deceased. Besides the outstanding performances, there is variety of sound since piphat mai khaeng (hard mallet), piphat mai nuam (soft-mallet), krueng sai, and mahori ensembles are used. —*Terry Miller*

Shiva's Drum: Spiritual Music from the Beginning of Time / Pacific Music Co., Tao ♦♦♦
This includes music similar to most Thai recordings, but is packaged to have a new age spin. —*Terry Miller*

Siamese Classical Music, Vols. 1-5 / Marco Polo ♦♦♦
Each CD presents splendid performances by top-notch musicians of the most important Thai classical repertory. The only limitation is that the notes are meager, especially in Gaston's reluctance to express anything, including titles, in Thai, making identification difficult. The most controversial aspect is the several recordings made on reconstructed "historical" ensembles, the instrumentation of at least one being disputable. —*Terry Miller*

Thailand: The Music of Chieng Mai / EMI ♦♦♦
Here are three lengthy complete pieces by piphat orchestra (ceremonial orchestra of monastery), an old Thai ensemble with fiddles, zither, flute, and percussion. —*David L. Mayers*

Tibet

Ache Lhamo
Tibetan, Asia

Tibetan Musical Theatre / Esperance ♦♦♦
Ache Lhamo is a form of traditional theater that has been very popular at all Tibetan social levels since it developed in the 15th century, but pretty much unknown to the world at large. Members of the India-based Tibetan Institute of Performing Arts perform scenes from an early libretto, accompanied by the traditional drums and cymbals. —*John Storm Roberts*

Karma Kagyu Institute
Tibetan, Asia

Chenresik / Karma Kagyu Institute ♦♦♦♦♦
An authentic version of the Tibetan Buddhist ritual to Chenresik, the Bodhisattva of Compassion. This complete version of the classic ritual chant practice also includes the remarkable "Calling the Guru from Afar" written by the First Jamg"n Kongtrül Lodr" Thaye. Produced at the Karme Thegsum Choyang Studio with authentic personnel, this is the actual ritual as it has been practiced for hundreds of years in Tibet. —*Michael Erlewine*

Tibet Collection

Gyoto Monks: Tibetan Tantric Choir / 1987 / Windham Hill ✦✦✦✦✦
This was astonishingly recorded—as if you are sitting right next to or among the singers. The profound liturgical chanting is also astonishing...at times the monks are coordinating not only rhythm and extraordinary overtone singing, but the very micro-pulses of the vocal waveforms are exactly in sync, precisely as if they were one voice guided by a universal computer. The first chant is from the *Guhyasamaja Tantra, Chapter II*, and the second, "Melody for Mahakala," is interrupted with dramatic instrumental sections played by an ensemble of skull drum, small bell, several pairs of cymbals, a pair of conch shells, two long copper horns, a pair of short bone trumpets, and several large drums struck with sticks. — *"Blue" Gene Tyrany*

Ladakh: Songs & Dances from Western Highlands / Nonesuch ✦✦✦
Lovely folk songs and instrumentals comes from the highlands of central Tibet. — *David L. Mayers*

Music of Tibet: Tantric Ritual / Anthology ✦✦✦
An excellent example of a chord-like vocal phenomenon in this type of chanting, it has extensive notes. — *David L. Mayers*

Shartse College of Ganden Monastery / 1978 / Bridge ✦✦✦✦✦
Three extended pieces by monks of the Geluppa (Dalai Lama) sect of Tibetan Buddhism, two a cappella, and one with a full ritual orchestra—cymbals, handbells, conch shells, long and short trumpets, drums, etc. One of these pieces is the song of the great Tibetan saint Tsongkhapa to the Buddha, and the other two involve the dharma protectors Setab and the fierce Yamantaka. — *Michael Erlewine*

Tantras of Gyütö / 1978 / Nonesuch ✦✦✦✦✦
Two extended pieces by monks of the Geluppa (Dalai Lama) sect of Tibetan Buddhism. These monks from the Gyütö Tantric college (some 40 monks) chant from two of the most profound Tibetan texts, the one dedicated to the deity Guhyasamaja (*Sangway Düpa*), which is concerned with the self-existing sacredness of the universe; and the other, dedicated to the fierce dharma protector Mahakala—Tibetan Buddhism's chief protector. — *Michael Erlewine*

Tibet: Musiques Sacrées / Ocora ✦✦✦✦✦
This album was recorded in Nepal at Tibetan Buddhist monasteries of the Geluppa and Nyingmapa sects. Most of the cuts are Geluppa, including part of the Chòd—a cleansing ritual. Other sections include the assembly call (with conch horns), prayer wheel, prostration rites, and more. A second group of tracks includes a ritual to Vajrayogini—a major female deity in Tibetan Buddhist practice. Various ritual instruments (thigh-bone trumpets, hand drums, cymbals, oboes, etc.) are heard. — *Michael Erlewine*

Tibetan Buddhism: Ritual Orchestra & Chants / Nonesuch ✦✦✦
Extracts from music for three rituals were played in 1973 by the magnificent ensemble of shawms, trumpets, and percussion of Khampagar Monastery. The recording opens with an invocation to Padmasambhava, who brought Buddhism to Tibet from India. Then follows two rites associated with Mahakala, who removes impediments to enlightenment. New notes by producer David Lewiston are included. — *John Storm Roberts, Original Music*

Tibetan Buddhist Chant / 1994 / King ✦✦✦
Parts of the Kalacakra Offering chants are performed by monks of the Nyamgyal Monastery, headquarters of the Dalai Lama's Geluppa sect. As so often with King's World Music Library, the details given in the English notes are a little confusing, but these recordings were definitely made in a Tokyo recording studio—as the technical quality attests. — *John Storm Roberts, Original Music*

Tibetan Ritual Music / Lyrichord ✦✦✦✦✦
A rare recording of an entire Tibetan ritual from the Nyingmapa monastery of Dehra Dun. Divided into three parts, each of which has both chanting and music for metal horns and trumpets as well as oboes and drums. Nominally an invocation to the goddess Yeshiki Mamo, though the notes overstate the shamanistic elements involved. — *Carl Hoyt, Original Music*

Tuvalu

Shu-de
....
Asia, Tuvalu

Voices from the Distant Steppe / 1994 / Real World ✦✦✦
With their extraordinary harmonic-whistle vocal techniques, Tuvans could well be the next sampling craze. From the Central Asian country reputedly settled by the descendants of Genghis Khan, folk group Shu-de accompany songs derived from shamanistic rituals with instruments whose sounds are as irreproducible as the vocals, including two-stringed *igil* fiddle and *doshpuluur* lute, a particularly articulate *khomus* jaw's harp, and a variety of drums and rattles. The wildness of these songs

evokes centuries of accommodation to a demanding landscape, but tongue-twister "Durgen Chugaa" goes even further to verify prehistoric associations with a Popeye the Sailor cult. — *Bob Tarte*

Tuvalu Collection

☆ **Tuva: Voices Center of the of Asia** / 1990 / Smithsonian/Folkways ✦✦✦✦✦
Not only are there 33 examples here of some of the most impressive vocal techniques in the world (including chordal throat-singing), with some almost equally remarkable instrumental work, but the notes, though cheaply produced, are extremely thorough. — *John Storm Roberts & Myles Boisen*

Vietnam

Tran Quang Hai
....
Vietnamese, Asia

Landscape of the Highlands / 1985 / Music of the World ✦✦✦
Original compositions for the dan tranh, a sixteen-string zither from Vietnam. The mesmerizing sound of this instrument combined with the virtuosity of Tran Quang Hai make this a unique and very special recording. — *Music of the World*

● **Dreams & Reality** / Playasound ✦✦✦✦✦
Tran Quang Hai, a virtuoso of the dan tran zither as well as many other instruments, is also a well-known author and researcher. Singer Bach Yen started her professional life as a Saigon pop singer before she went to Paris to study voice. Both have been working for years outside Vietnam: Bach Yen sings in Hebrew and several European languages as well as Vietnamese, and Tran Quang Hai's playing shows clear, though intermittent signs of influence by European harp playing. As you'd expect, their performances are colored by these experiences in a personal way that is rather different from the customary intercultural cross-fertilizations. — *John Storm Roberts*

Phong Nguyen Ensemble
....
Vietnamese, Asia

Music of Vietnam / World Music Institute ✦✦✦✦✦
As musician and ethnomusicologist, Phong Nguyen is one of the major international figures of Vietnamese music. Here he joins other expatriate musicians (including the 77-year-old master of the dan nguyet lute, Nguyen Cia Cam) to perform a wide range of traditional and contemporary music. (These recordings were made at two WMI concerts in New York City.) Excellent recording, notes, and production as always with the World Music Institute. — *John Storm Roberts*

Vietnam Collection

Ca Tru & Quan Ho / Auvidis ✦✦✦
Included are two traditional forms from North Vietnam. Ca Tru is a rather delicate women's art-music form based on codified modes, rhythms, and ornamentations, and accompanied by various combinations of lute, zither, flute, and percussion. The equally beguiling but notably more robust quan ho songs, a form for young men and women, also has a traditional repertory but is often improvised. In this recording, made in Hanoi in 1976, they are backed by wind and stringed instruments but without percussion. — *John Storm Roberts*

Eternal Voices / 1994 / New Alliance ✦✦✦
These are superb recordings by an ensemble of major US-resident Vietnamese musicians. Directed by Phong Nguyen, five singers and ten musicians present gorgeous performances of just about all the major traditional forms. The notes are wonderful, the packaging exceptional. — *John Storm Roberts, Original Music*

Eternal Voices: Traditional Vietnamese Music in the United States / New Alliance ✦✦✦
Recorded by master musicians living in the United States, this anthology of 22 items ranging from folk songs, theatre music, chanted poetry, and instrumental modal improvisations, this album includes the most extensive explanatory booklet written on Vietnamese music. — *Terry Miller*

From Rice Paddies and Temple Yards: Traditional Music of Vietnam / World Music Press ✦✦✦
This cassette tape accompanies a book by the same title in which the author, Dr. Phong Thuyet Nguyen, introduces a series of Vietnamese folk and play songs designed for school use. — *Terry Miller*

Instrumental Music of Vietnam / World Music Library ✦✦✦
The King Record Co. team spent a few days in Hanoi in March 1991, and produced four albums, two traditional and two of musicians trained at the Hanoi Conservatory playing modernized traditional music and new "ethnic" compositions inspired by Socialist arts policies in eastern

Europe and China. Both this album and *String Instruments of Vietnam* (KICC 5121) consist of this sort of music. While some new compositions are interesting, the performances of "traditional" music lack the spices (nuances) that give Vietnamese music its individuality. Related to this, and including many of the same pieces played by the same musicians, are *The Music of Vietnam, Volume 1.1* and *1.2* (Celestial Harmonies 13082-2 and 13083-2), as well as *Vietnam: Reviving a Tradition* (Playa Sound PS 65116). None of these albums has expert annotations either. —*Terry Miller*

Music from Vietnam / Caprice ✦✦✦
An anthology that includes "modernized ethnic music" from Hanoi as well as hat cai luong music from the south, hat quan ho antiphonal songs from near Hanoi, hat cheo theatre of the north, and hat chau van possession ritual music, there is at least a full range of traditional and modern music. Recorded one month before the arrival of the King Record Co. team and using many of the same musicians. —*Terry Miller*

The Art of Kim Sinh / World Music Library ✦✦✦
Cai luong is a theatre of southern Vietnam and unlike cheo, tuong, and water puppet theatres is not supported by the Vietnamese government. Musician Kim Sinh, however, caught the ears of the recording team. While traditional and interesting, he is a northerner performing a "foreign" southern genre. —*Terry Miller*

The Tradition of Hué / Barenreiter Musicaphon ✦✦✦
This covers musical idioms from central Vietnam. The *Hué* album devotes a side to several forms of court music, and another to ritual and entertainment music. It includes pieces for a wide range of wind, string, and percussion groups, with fine notes and photos. —*John Storm Roberts*

Vietnam: Traditional Folk Theatre, Hat Cheo / Auvidis ✦✦✦
Recorded in Vietnam by Dr. Tran van Khe about 1978 before other researchers were allowed into the country, this album presents music and songs of the northern cheo theatre. Related to this is *Vietnamese Folk Theatre: Hat Cheo*, recorded in 1991. —*Terry Miller*

Vietnam: Traditions of the South / Auvidis ✦✦✦
Recorded by, and performed in part by Dr. Tran van Khe, this album presents a series of modally improvised solos on the 17-string dan tranh zither and in two cases, with dan ty ba pear-shaped lute. —*Terry Miller*

CARIBBEAN

Bahamas

Joseph Spence

b. Aug. 1910, Andros, Bahama, d. Mar. 18, 1984
Guitar, Vocals / Bahamian, Caribbean
Born on the island of Andrus in the Bahamas, Spence created an idiosyncratic (and inimitable) guitar style rife with percussive and improvisatory vamps around staid hymns and such "square" standards as "Coming in on a Wing and a Prayer." He was a folk guitarist's Thelonious Monk, and his growling vocal counterpoint and surprising inventions are one of folk music's great delights. —*Mark A. Humphrey*

● **The Complete Folkways Recordings (1958)** / 1958 / Smithsonian/ Folkways ✦✦✦✦✦
Just when the aspiring folk guitarist thought mastering "Freight Train" was a feat, along came this mind-boggler! These are Spence's most influential recordings; field-quality sound but stunning music. —*Mark A. Humphrey*

Happy All the Time / 1964 / Carthage ✦✦✦
Waxed for Elektra in 1964, this has better sound than the Folkways recordings and offers some of Spence's most percussive playing. —*Mark A. Humphrey*

The Real Bahamas, Vol. 1 / 1965 / Nonesuch ✦✦✦
The recordings on *The Real Bahamas in Music and Song, Vol. 1* date from 1965 and feature Spence accompanying members of the family of his sister, Jenny Pindar. They may be available on CD. In any event, the Folkways, Elektra, and Arhoolie albums are pretty much "the essential" Spence. —*Mark A. Humphrey*

The Real Bahamas, Vol. 2 / 1965 / Nonesuch ✦✦✦
This second volume of a two-volume set may be available on CD. —*Mark A. Humphrey*

Living on the Hallelujah Side / 1987 / Rounder ✦✦✦
Bahamian guitarist/vocalist Joseph Spence's humming, flailing, sensational singing and playing combined secular flair and spiritual fervor in a manner close to that of the brilliant Blind Willie Johnson and Rev. Gary Davis. This set of 1970s performances, reissued on CD, included evocative renditions of "A Closer Walk With Thee," "More and More With Jesus," and "When The Saints Go Marching In," plus equally arresting

versions of "Irene Goodnight" and the holiday ditty "Santa Claus Is Comin' to Town." Spence was incapable of self-indulgence or fakery; his lines, phrasing, riffs, and solos are enchanting, while his vocal effects and accompaniment often come close to surpassing his playing. This was simply magical material, the kind that comes only from the genuine originals. —*Ron Wynn*

Bahamian Guitarist / 1990 / Arhoolie ✦✦✦
His Boston concert (1971) is included, plus informal recordings. Spence chortles at his twists on tradition. Carter Family purists should lend an ear to "Will the Serpent Be Unbroken." —*Mark A. Humphrey*

Bahama Collection

Bahamian Songs, Vol. 1 / 1951 / ART ✦✦✦✦✦
This out-of-print album by Blake Higgs (no relation to the blues player of the same name) is quite hard to find. Higgs plays with a small acoustic folk group, but his timeless music makes an indelible impression. He wrote several tunes, including "Pretty Boy" and "Love Alone" (the story of King Edward's abdication), which became standards during the '60s folk revival. —*J. Poet*

Caribbean Collection

☆ **Calypso Breakaway** / 1990 / Rounder ✦✦✦✦✦
This disc centers on some of the best Decca calypsos of the late '30s. Here are the songs and singers that sparked the calypso boom in the US. They include Beginner, Lion, Radio, Invader, Caresser, Tiger, and Atilla. The notes are not very informative, but the transcriptions are good. —*Don Hill*

Calypso Pioneers: 1912-1937 / 1989 / Rounder ✦✦✦✦✦
Companion CD to a prior Rounder anthology devoted to classic calypso, these 16 cuts present formative songs from 1912-1937. The music is still emerging from a confluence of American dance band sounds, African and Afro-Latin rhythms, plus Caribbean social situations and influences. As carnival became an entrenched celebration within the Caribbean community, the songs composed to be performed during that time came to be known as calypso. The anthology includes early performances by such calypso heroes as Atilla the Hun, Wilmouth Houdini, Phil Madison, Julian Whiterose, and Sam Manning. Vocal styles, instrumental backing, lyrics, arrangements, and production are quite unsophisticated and uneven on the early cuts, but a sound and unified approach began to appear in the middle section and is quite evident by the final numbers. —*Ron Wynn*

☆ **Caribbean Island Music** / Nonesuch ✦✦✦✦✦
I recorded this material on my first field trip in 1971. Many of these recordings are still unique: Jamaican country mento, digging songs, and nine-night songs; a Haitian acoustic merengue group; Dominican merengues, salves, tonadas, drum groups, and the English-language Mummies later featured in the British *Repercussions* TV/video series. —*John Storm Roberts*

Caribbean Revels / Smithsonian ✦✦✦✦✦
Both rara and gaga are exuberantly documented here through street recordings of both traditional and trumpet-led examples. Joyous stuff from a beleaguered people. —*John Storm Roberts*

Island Carnival: Music of the West Indies / Elektra/Nonesuch ✦✦✦✦✦
More a sampler of the spectrum of West Indian music than a spotlight on reggae or modern sounds. It does have some reggae, but also includes rock, vocals, and more traditional island styles, mainly artists, sounds and performers steeped in classic West Indian genres. Celebrating the carnival festival. —*Ron Wynn*

☆ **Salt & Tabasco** / Mango ✦✦✦✦✦
A good anthology that blends soca, reggae, Afro-Cuban, and Latin selections. Includes the Cuban group Los Van Van, plus Arrow and others. —*Ron Wynn*

☆ **Under the Coconut Tree** / 1984 / Original Music ✦✦✦✦✦
This is a really nice CD of long neglected Anglo-Caribbean music from these two islands. The music from Tortola in the British Virgin Islands includes "The Spanish Merchant," a fine creolized British ballad that is beautifully sung with the relaxing sounds of the surf in the background; the "Butcher Boy" sung as a duet; and a nice version of the sea shanty, "Captain, Where's Your Cargo?" The music from Grand Cayman includes several other fine sailor's songs and "The Devil's Dream," a Scots-Irish fiddle tune, among others. —*Don Hill*

Costa Rica Collection

Calypsos: Afro-Limonese Music of Costa Rica / Lyrichord ✦✦✦✦✦
Like Panama, Costa Rica has a substantial minority of English-speaking inhabitants. These pieces—mostly calypsos, after a terrific percussion comparsa—were recorded in the Costa Rican port city of Puerto Limón. They have a spread from wonderful to tentative, but this is pure street-

Caribbean Music Styles

Biguine—Throughout the long history of the biguine, the dominant sound has been that of the clarinet and trombone, both solo and as a duet, and, while the phrasing often recalls New Orleans jazz, the overall sound is unmistakably Caribbean. The signature sound of the biguine is the interplay between the clarinet and trombone, which can still be heard today throughout the Antilles musical milieu, from the most traditional music to the music of the cadence era or the pop sounds of today's zouk. Any contemporary music that uses biguine as its base, even that which ventures as far off as contemporary jazz, is considered "biguine moderne." The classic music of carnival in the Antilles is an uptempo version of the biguine rhythm, called "biguine vide."

Cadence—A constantly changing style that evolved primarily among the islands of Guadeloupe, Martinique, Dominica, and Haiti. The cadence era was exciting and extremely fertile, requiring musicians of only the highest calibre, who could master not only Antilles pop styles like biguine and Creole mazurka but also those of Haiti and the other neighboring islands. The cadence years saw the evolution of the pop influences that embellish the rootsier foundation of today's Antilles musicians, allowing for expression in an internationally familiar musical language: electric instruments, riffing horn sections, trapset drums, topical lyrics, and specific stylings of rock music, reggae, soca, American Black music, and more. In addition to Les Aiglons, this was the heyday of big bands like La Perfecta, Typical Combo, La Selecta, Les Maxels, Les Léopards, Les Vikings de la Guadeloupe (whose co-leader, Pierre-Edouard Decimus, went on to create Kassav' at the end of the decade), and Gordon Henderson's Exile One of Dominique. Recordings from this era, while fascinating and enjoyable, often suffer from out-of-tune instruments and sub-par recording quality. Cadence led directly into the early '80s and the rise of zouk, and it was the musicians schooled in cadence who were the first zouk stars. The major catalyst behind the emergence of zouk was the desire to produce a new Caribbean music that treated the multifaceted music of the Antilles to the state-of-the-art recording technology of the Paris studios.

Chouval bwa—A rural Martiniquan style of music that evolved as accompaniment to the "manege" (or carousel). Originally featuring a large drum like a bass drum, hand drums, and ti bwa, chouv' was led by melodic instruments like accordion, bamboo flute, and wax-paper/comb-type kazoos. One young artist, Claude Germany, is attempting to carry on the traditional form of chouval bwa, while others have updated it minimally (by the addition of electric bass) or dramatically (as in the case of zouk chouv', which features an array of electric instruments, including synthesizer). Chouval bwa is Creole for the French term "cheval bois," meaning "wooden horse."

Compas—Haitian dance music, started by Nemours Jean-Baptiste in the '50s, known first as compas-direct.

Gwo ka—The various indigenous rhythms of Guadeloupe are played on a two-drum family of hand drums called gwo ka. Gwo ka music is rhythm-driven by the two drums and is often accompanied by a mounted stick or bamboo log hit with sticks called a ti bwa. The drummers lead the way for dancers, and usually there is singing accompaniment. Gwo ka has been an underlying element of zouk from day one, and, in fact, Kassav's first album was entitled Love and Ka Dance. Anzala and Ti Celeste (or Ti Seles) are two gwo ka artists still recording today, the latter sticking to the roots while the former has electrified his sounds.

Road March—Chosen at the carnival in Trinidad, this is the most popular song of the year. —Gene Scaramuzzo

music, presenting a range of singers and styles mostly old and unaffected by commercial recordings. Very unspecific notes, disgracefully short measure even for an LP, let alone CD, but very rare music that is charming. —John Storm Roberts

French Antilles

Les Aiglons

Zouk, Caribbean, French Antilles
A classic Guadeloupian band of the '70s cadence era who, like nearly all bands of the period, were influenced by the Haitian music that literally overwhelmed the Antilles from the late '50s to the early '80s. Les Aiglons held the record for the most sales of a record (*Cuisse-La*) of any Antilles band until the overwhelming success of Kassav' with *Zouk-La Se Sel Medikamen Nou Ni* in 1985. The band broke up quietly after their 1987 release, *Bon'm La*, but two members resurfaced in the summer of 1988 as a more commercial project called Love Stars. —Gene Scaramuzzo

● Bonm La / Debs ◆◆◆◆◆
While zouk went pop and funk, the new-biguine band Les Aiglons hewed to a sound almost classic. They relied on supertight, crisp arrangements and voicings to carry a basic dance message. But there was also constant variety there—check out the way the female coro's relationship to the leads is quite different in every track. A Latin impresario once described the salsa group's job as "come out smoking and kick ass." That's how Les Aiglons saw it in this album from the mid-'80s. —John Storm Roberts, Original Music

Alphonso et son Orchestre Antillais

Zouk, Caribbean, French Antilles
A biguine artist who represents the classic form of the biguine as it evolved through the war years. —Gene Scaramuzzo

● Vive La Biguine / Disques Festival ◆◆◆◆
Alphonso, who spent time in Stellio's band, went on to found perhaps the last of the groups playing the classic clarinet-and-trombone biguine, a sound a bit like New Orleans jazz but with lilt instead of stomp (and without the trumpet). It was one of the most enchanting of all Caribbean styles, and this was one of the great bands. —John Storm Roberts, Original Music

Anzala

Gwo Ka, Caribbean, French Antilles
One of the preeminent stars of the Guadeloupian music called "gwo ka," featuring two-hand drums of the same name. In an effort to compete with the zouk market, Anzala has released a couple of successful records that add electric instruments to the basic drum and vocal gwo ka sound. —Gene Scaramuzzo

● Se Roule Moin Ka Roule / 1983 / Henri DEBS ◆◆◆◆◆
This early-'80s effort features the rawer gwo ka for which he is most famous. —Gene Scaramuzzo

Batako (Patrick Parole)

Zouk, Caribbean, French Antilles
Band led by Guadeloupian guitarist Patrick Parole, who plays strongly in the Haitian mini-jazz-band guitar style. Because of this, Batako records continue to be among the more Haitian-sounding and thus stand apart from formula zouk efforts. —Gene Scaramuzzo

● Chiraj / 1988 / Henri DEBS ◆◆◆◆◆
Parole's release was one of the best of what has, admittedly, not been a particularly inspiring period for zouk. It's mellow but not soupy, with a nice Creole tinge to some of the melodies, a lot of Haitian influence (what goes round comes round), and such passing felicities as a neat trumpet solo. It's evidence that zouk's recent pop orientation doesn't necessarily mean triviality. —John Storm Roberts

Jocelyne Beroard

Vocals / Zouk, Caribbean, French Antilles
Martiniquan lead singer for Kassav' whose popularity soared in 1986 because of her endearing stage personality and her convincing vocals on Kassav' classics like "Pa Bisouin Pale" and "Move Jou." —Gene Scaramuzzo

★ Siwo / 1987 / Georges DEBS ◆◆◆◆◆
This lead female vocalist from Kassav' sings zouk love ballads better than anyone. Backed by the group Kassav', this is an excellent zouk classic. Import. —Robert Leaver & Gene Scaramuzzo

Milans / 1991 / CBS ◆◆◆
Her second solo effort was a formula success pleasing all but those who wished to hear her break new ground. —Gene Scaramuzzo

Bwa Can'non

Cadence, Caribbean, French Antilles
An extremely interesting Martiniquan band in that their records present the complete range of music to be found in the Antilles repertoire: cadence, biguine, quadrille, Creole mazurka, calypso, merengue . . . everything but zouk. —Gene Scaramuzzo

Amour Passion / 1986 / Solo Gammes ◆◆◆◆◆

Henri Debs

Clarinet, Saxophone / Caribbean, French Antilles
A Guadeloupian entrepreneur who began his career as a biguine artist and gained renown as the creator of a style dubbed "biguine kombas." Currently he is best known for his studio in Point . . . Pitre, Guadeloupe, known sometimes as Studio Zouk La Terreur. As a former musician, he is more involved in the production of the Debs stable of stars than most record producers, especially his brother Georges who owns the now-defunct Georges Debs label out of Martinique. With his background and resources, he occasionally indulges himself by performing and releasing compilations of classic Antilles music, usually a bit on the overly sentimental side. (Also see "Max et Henri.") *—Gene Scaramuzzo*

● **30th Anniversary** / Debs ✦✦✦✦
Henri Debs is an old-hand singer/guitarist as well as record executive. This album with Severin, another veteran vocalist, has an odd mix of Antillean and salsa musicians (Hector Zarzuela and Mauricio Smith, e.g.). But the results are fresh beyond expectation. Frisky horn arrangements and a strong creole feel make this more interesting to us than Kassav' and its clones. *—John Storm Roberts, Original Music*

Georges Decimus

Bass, Vocals / Zouk, Caribbean, French Antilles
Two early solo efforts by one of the founders of Kassav'. After more than a decade with Kassav', Georges went off in 1990 to form his own band, called Volt-Face. *—Gene Scaramuzzo*

☆ **La Vie** / 1982 / Moradisc ✦✦✦✦✦
Recorded during the highly experimental phase of Kassav', it featured the prototype formula soon adopted by the group and by zouk artists in general. *—Gene Scaramuzzo*

★ **Nwel** / 1983 / Liso Musique ✦✦✦✦✦
This classic is another example of the experimental phase of Kassav'. *—Gene Scaramuzzo*

Kassav' / Celluloid ✦✦✦

Pierre-Edouard Decimus

Zouk, Caribbean, French Antilles
The founder of Kassav' and the father of zouk. Look under Kassav' and Soukoue Ko Ou for further information on Decimus. *—Gene Scaramuzzo*

Waya Se Sa Ki Peyi La / 1983 / Liso Musique ✦✦✦
Waya Se Sa Ki Peyi La/Carnaval Ave le Roi et la Reine is a typical early carnival effort. *—Gene Scaramuzzo*

● **Love & Ka Dance** / Chancy ✦✦✦✦✦
This early US release is basically a version of Kassav's first recording with material in English for a national US market, issued in 1980 by Chancy. Not the least bizarre element is a cover with a monochrome photo woman wearing not much aside from a bunch of chains, riding a gwo ka. The overt reference is probably supposed to be slavery, but the S-M subtext can't be accidental. Either way it's wildly unsuited to the music. *—John Storm Roberts, Original Music*

Jacob Desvarieux

Guitar / Zouk, Caribbean, French Antilles
One of the three founding members of Kassav', Desvarieux credits the title cut from *Banzawa* as being the spark that touched off the zouk explosion. *—Gene Scaramuzzo*

☆ **Banzawa** / 1983 / Georges DEBS ✦✦✦✦✦
After listening to the title cut (and the entire album), there will be no question in one's mind as to why this set off the zouk craze. *—Gene Scaramuzzo*

★ **Yelele** / 1984 / Georges DEBS ✦✦✦✦✦
As with all solo Kassav' efforts, these albums include participation by all members of the band. Among the more than two dozen Kassav'-related records released since 1979, *Yelele* and *Gorée*, duo efforts by Desvarieux and Georges Decimus, are among the absolute cream of the crop. *—Gene Scaramuzzo*

Oh Madiana / 1985 / Georges DEBS ✦✦✦
Perhaps I'm getting to be a fogy before my time, but I can't find any new zouk to touch this 1985 gem from my favorite Kassavite. Besides the adjective-boggling title track, this album has Desvarieux's tremendously influential arrangements and extensive use of traditional percussion—including the Antillean Ka drum! *—Carl Hoyt, Original Music*

Djo Dezormo

Vocals / Biguine Vide, Caribbean, French Antilles
One of the most unusual of all the contemporary artists of Martinique, Dezormo is best known for being one of the few singers of "angaje"

(political/social-commentary) lyrics, always releasing his records at carnival time in order to add some spice to the festivities. From the separatist community of Rivière-Pilote, Dezormo is a political activist in a country not known for activism. His commentaries have included everything from local politics to French presidential candidate Jean-Marie Le Pen. His Carnival 1990 "Voici les Loups" (Here Come the Wolves), a huge success, pictured Europe as a wolf devouring Martinique, alluding to a European Community agreement that will soon allow citizens of any member country to buy land in any other member country, which includes by default Martinique and Guadeloupe. Brother of biguine moderne artist Michel Godzom, Dezormo also loves biguine, Creole mazurka, and waltz, always incorporating these styles into his music. *—Gene Scaramuzzo*

● **Sa Pe Change** / 1988 / Solo Gammes ✦✦✦✦✦
The Creole lyrics are a barrier to understanding his clever messages, but fortunately the fine music carries the day. *—Gene Scaramuzzo*

Ethnikolor

Traditional, Caribbean, French Antilles
One of the surprise hits of the 1991 carnival and indicative of the growing revival of interest in classic Antilles pop music. The brainstorm of Martiniquan "living legend" Ronald Rubinel, the Ethnikolor discs feature a Who's Who of Antilles artists ranging from Kassav' members to biguine moderne clarinetist Michel Godzom to chouval bwa stars Marce Pago and Dede St. Prix. *—Gene Scaramuzzo*

Bel Biguine / 1991 / New Deal ✦✦✦
The Carnival 1991 release featured two long medleys, one a biguine, the other a Creole mazurka, much in the spirit of the early-'80s Soukoue Ko Ou Carnival releases but with more of a live feeling. *—Gene Scaramuzzo*

★ **La Fête Antillais Continue . . . , Vol. 2** / 1992 / New Deal ✦✦✦✦✦
The Carnival 1992 release was even better, covering a wider range of Antilles sounds and including a rootsy, percussive tribute to the late Eugene Mona. *—Gene Scaramuzzo*

Fal Frett

Biguine Moderne, Caribbean, French Antilles
One of the best of the contemporary jazz bands from the French Antilles, a small list that also includes artists like Lucien Joly, Caraibes Jazz Ensemble, and the West Indies Jazz Band. *—Gene Scaramuzzo*

Cha Pastiche / 1985 / Celluloid ✦✦✦

Gilles Floro

Zouk, Caribbean, French Antilles
One of the star crooners of the "zouk love" style, Floro produces hit after hit. Every album contains chartbusters, not only the ones listed below. *—Gene Scaramuzzo*

● **Pa Pawol Anle, A** / Liso Musique ✦✦✦✦✦
Here's one of many zouk superstars that the US has yet to discover. Floro, like Kassav's Naimro, both a vocalist and keyboard-player, was one of the creators of lovers' zouk, without lurching into sappiness like some. This recording is enriched by strong biguine and compas touches in among the zouk, and by Floro's own jazz-influenced playing. *—John Storm Roberts, Original Music*

Michel Godzom

Clarinet / Biguine Moderne, Caribbean, French Antilles
One of the great biguine moderne artists of Martinique (an all-encompassing term that includes any contemporary styles using biguine as the basis). Clarinetist Godzom is a great experimenter, exploring the limits of biguine, mazurka, quadrille, and waltz, usually hitting solidly on the mark as he did on the albums listed below. *—Gene Scaramuzzo*

● **10éme Anniversaire** / 1991 / Solo Gammes ✦✦✦✦✦

Simon Jurad

Vocals / Zouk, Caribbean, French Antilles
Simon Jurad is one of the few Martiniquan musicians who can be found playing live somewhere on the island almost every night of the week, his gigs including everything from tourist bar/lounge performances to hip zouk shows. His career began in the cadence era, so as both singer and musician he has a wealth of experience under his belt. Jurad's biggest strength is his consistent ability to write catchy, musically interesting songs, although contractual complications have prevented him in recent years from being able to credit himself as songwriter on his albums. *—Gene Scaramuzzo*

Faut Pas Faire / 1986 / Melodie Makers ✦✦✦

★ **Mama** / 1989 / Georges DEBS ✦✦✦✦✦

Glorye La Te A / 1991 / Akatoto ✦✦✦

Kali

Banjo / Folklore, Caribbean, French Antilles
Kali began his professional music career in what many consider to have been Martinique's finest reggae band, Sixième Continent, which hit big with a 12-inch single called "Reggae Dom-Tom." In the late '80s Kali picked up a century-old family heirloom, a banjo, and began exploring roots music of a different nature—music of the Martiniquan capital St. Pierre that was destroyed at the beginning of the century by the eruption of Mount Pelée. He can often be heard contributing his banjo to zouk and traditional projects alike, from recordings by Pier Rosier and Ze Top to Max Ransay and the latest by Malavoi. —*Gene Scaramuzzo*

Racines, Vols. 1-2 / 1989 / Hibiscus ✦✦✦✦✦
This is a charming re-exploration of the classic forms of Antilles music. The vocalist and banjo player perform neo-traditional biguine moderne. —*Gene Scaramuzzo*

Live Au New Morning / 1991 / Hibiscus ✦✦✦
A live recording of classic Antilles music, it helped put Kali on top of the list of Martiniquan roots music artists. —*Gene Scaramuzzo*

★ **Roots** / 1991 / Philips ✦✦✦✦✦
These are the best cuts from Kali's first three albums. —*Gene Scaramuzzo*

Kali / Affirmations ✦✦✦
A simple recording yet harmonically stunning, especially on the a cappella numbers, as well as quite woman-identified . . . or, as their press release says, "a rich vocal texture and lyrics that express concern for the quality of relationships on our planet—humans and the earth, women and men, life and death; celebrating those that are mutually enhancing and questioning those that are not." —*Ladyslipper*

Kassav'

Guitar, Drums, Keyboards, Vocals / Zouk, Afro Pop, Caribbean, French Antilles
The zouk scene evolved from a studio project by Guadeloupian Pierre-Edouard Decimus, who had moved to Paris in the late '70s following an extremely successful career as co-leader of the legendary cadence band Les Vikings de la Guadeloupe. Enlisting the services of his brother Georges and Paris studio wizard Jacob Desvarieux, himself a Guadeloupian, Decimus began to forge a new sound that treated Antilles musical traditions to the state of the art recording technology available in Paris. By 1984 the three had settled on a stable lineup of musicians and singers (now representing both Guadeloupe and Martinique), had made their first live performance (in Guadeloupe), and had achieved their first massive radio success with "Banzawa" from a Desvarieux solo album.

Parties in the Antilles are called "zouks," and since Kassav's new records were the music of choice at the zouks, their music came to be called "zouk music." By 1985 nearly every Antilles musician was jumping on the zoukwagon and a whole new style of music was born.

Supported by a horn section, two dancers, extra keyboard, drummer, and percussion, the core of Kassav' is Jocelyne Beroard, Jacob Desvarieux, Jean-Philippe Marthely, Patrick St. Eloi, Jean-Claude Naimro, and until recently, Georges Decimus (who recently quit the band to pursue a career with a new group; Pierre-Edouard comes and goes at whim, never performing live but often resurfacing as a songwriter). Through the release of *Majestik Zouk*, the band has released ten studio albums and one live album. Each bonafide member of the band has also released solo albums that include support by the entire band. In fact, since 1987, all re-pressings of the back catalog of solo releases have had the name Kassav' added to the cover in bold letters. Add various carnival projects under the pseudonyms Soukoue Ko Ou and Turbo II, and the total number of Kassav'-related albums approaches 30. The early releases were certainly experimental in nature as Desvarieux and the Decimus brothers searched for the right mix of musicians and musical elements. The best of the solo and carnival efforts can be found under the discography entries for the particular band member or carnival project. It's indisputable that much of the most dramatic groundbreaking occurred on the early- to mid-'80s solo releases. Of the official Kassav' albums, all are interesting in that they provide a view into the development of what became the zouk sound. The formula from which the whole Antilles zouk scene evolved had kicked in by the sixth release, so from there on specific preferences are merely a matter of personal taste. —*Gene Scaramuzzo*

Eva / 1982 / 3A ✦✦✦✦✦
This, their fourth album, was the first with the touch of total greatness. —*Gene Scaramuzzo*

Passeport / 1983 / Sonodisc ✦✦✦
This is precisely the sound that made zouk so influential—a modified Haitian beat, Stevie Wonder-style keyboards, and heaps of traditional gwo ka percussion—surprising when you consider the techno-monster the style has become. Includes two songs from *Oh Madiana*. —*Carl Hoyt, Original Music*

Zouk

When zouk music from the French Antilles islands of Guadeloupe and Martinique exploded onto the international music scene in the mid-'80s, attention was again focused on a part of the Caribbean that hadn't been heard from musically since the popularity of the biguine in the early 20th century. Created in the late '70s by a small clique of Guadeloupian musicians residing in Paris, zouk presented a mélange of global influences that touched millions in the French-speaking African diaspora, subsequently acting as a catalyst for an exciting mid-'80s period of musical experimentation.

Zouk truly draws its power from the rich musical heritage of Africa and the Caribbean. In its bubbly, light, loping beat can be heard elements from Guadeloupe, Martinique, Dominica, and Haiti, with dashes thrown in from Paris, Zaire, Antigua, Trinidad, Cuba, Puerto Rico, and the Dominican Republic. With so many influences, it's not surprising that popular zouk can range from highly percussive, driving dance music to slow ballads that hover dangerously close to French disco and cabaret singing. —*Gene Scaramuzzo*

Aye / 1984 / Georges DEBS ✦✦✦
One of the earlier LPs by the now almost late, great zouk powerhouse, *Aye*, from 1984, has the US influence wrapped around the swinging (loping would be a good word) Antillean beat. —*Carl Hoyt, Original Music*

An-Ba-Chen'n La / 1985 / Georges DEBS ✦✦✦✦✦
Kassav's output has always intriguingly tended to veer before the roots and funk sides of their mix. *An-Ba*, the one that cemented the band's position as the biggest deal pretty much anywhere on the Afro-French circuit, returned to the individual approach and general hang-loose joviality of the earlier salsa-based style at its best. It was also a very highly worked album: "thanks also to . . ." brass, string, and synthesizer types outnumbered the basic band. —*John Storm Roberts, Original Music*

Kassav' aux Zenith / 1987 / Georges DEBS ✦✦✦
Kassav' is a variable band, capable of great music but too prone to lapse into an overslick funk typical of any pickup group of session-men (which is how they began life). These tending to be studio-oriented faults, it's perhaps not surprising that this live concert recording was one of the most genuinely exciting Kassav' sessions ever recorded. —*John Storm Roberts*

Vini Pou / 1987 / CBS ✦✦✦
Ironically, the first to receive widespread distribution in the States was one of their weaker efforts. —*Gene Scaramuzzo*

● **Zouk Is . . .** / 1989 / Greensleeves ✦✦✦✦✦
A superb greatest-hits collection comes from the top band. —*Robert Leaver*

Edith Lefel

Vocals / Zouk, Caribbean, French Antilles
A Martiniquan zouk singer whose sparkling strong voice graced many records by Lazair, Simon Jurad, Kassav', and others before she attempted her own record. —*Gene Scaramuzzo*

● **La Klé** / 1988 / Georges DEBS ✦✦✦✦✦
It was a huge success, even though (or because) Lefel opted to sing in the weak, rather wimpy vocal style that was the rage of late-'80s zouk-love. —*Gene Scaramuzzo*

Moci / Sonodisc ✦✦✦✦✦
Lefel's Big One is big indeed. It's not just that she's one of zouk's finest and most varied singers or that it's staggeringly long for a pop CD. It's that everybody's here on one cut or another, from neo-traditionalist banjoist Kali and harmonica-man Pier Rosier to Malavoi's string section to just about all the reigning pop-zouk names (Rubinel is musical director). The results are an odd mix. There's lots of splendid stuff: memories of pre-zouk Antillo-salsa, and Martiniquan string-band music, and solos ranging from Kali's banjo to Rubinel's fine acoustic piano. And lots of mega-pop lover's zouk. The splendid stuff is—well, splendid. —*John Storm Roberts, Original Music*

Love Stars

Zouk, Caribbean, French Antilles
A Guadeloupian "zouk love" studio project involving three singers, two of whom were original members of Les Aiglons. As with many Henri Debs productions, it includes a star-studded cast. —*Gene Scaramuzzo*

Ipokrit / 1988 / Henri DEBS ✦✦✦
This album is, in fact, excellent, and particularly notable for fine solo sax

rather than the usual ensemble riffs, as well as for a pleasingly batty edge and plenty of verve. —*John Storm Roberts*

● **Yo Malade/Jane** / 1989 / Henri DEBS ✦✦✦✦✦

De Plus Belle / 1992 / Henri DEBS ✦✦✦

La Maafia

Compas, Caribbean, French Antilles

A Martiniquan band led by drummer, singer, and songwriter Jean-Michel Cabrimol, and one of a handful (including Diapason, Filpak, and Nouvelle Galaxie), that specializes in playing a Martiniquan version of classic Haitian mini-jazz. La Maafia's albums are typically a balance of uptempo dance numbers and slow ballads graced by flute. It's certainly not formula zouk but very popular, nonetheless, because of the longtime Antillean love of Haitian music. —*Gene Scaramuzzo*

★ **Mama Afrika** / 1988 / JMC ✦✦✦✦✦

Exquisite Antilles funk jazz (a Martinquan version of Haitian compas) features flute, sax, trumpet, and conga. —*Robert Leaver*

Malavoi

Zouk, Folklore, Caribbean, French Antilles

Led by Martiniquan pianist Paulo Rosine, Malavoi has been recording since the late '60s. The original band featured a horn section and consisted mainly of Latin music enthusiasts. The band added a string section in the late '70s and recorded a superb album of charanga-style music that included percussion by Dede St. Prix. Only this one album captured the brief period when Malavoi had both a horn section and a string section; the horns left soon afterward. An anthology of hits from this era is now available on the Hibiscus label release *L'Autre Style.*

The albums listed below are among the best of the band as it exists today, presenting a varied repertoire of "Creolized" European dance forms like the quadrille, mazurka, and waltz along with strong elements of biguine and charanga. Pipo Gertrude, who replaced longtime Malavoi vocalist Ralph Thamar in late 1987, appears on *Jou Ouve* and *Souche* (which is not listed because it's not among their best), as well as the group's latest. The *Live au Zenith* album features Thamar. —*Gene Scaramuzzo*

Gram e Gram / 1982 / Georges DEBS ✦✦✦

Zouel / 1983 / Georges DEBS ✦✦✦

When it comes to string-band arranging, this one has the kitchen with faucets. Lush is the word—the calorie count has to be enormous, but the cream is real and rich, the chocolate dark and gorgeous. Ralph Thamar sings. Vocalist Marijose Alie, who has been listening to the Brazilians with good results, is featured on one cut. Seriously, the uptempo numbers swing mightily, the traditional ones update perfectly (great quadrille), and the slow ones, by the very splendor of their richness, simply obliterate the usual sub-bolero plod. Oh yes, demon bass and dynamite piano too. —*John Storm Roberts*

La Case ... Lucie / 1987 / Blue Silver ✦✦✦

After some ill-received forages into zouk on their previous album, Malavoi have decided to stick with the mellow, delicate sound that crosses Cuban charanga with earlier Martiniquan stras. Not that they're in any time warp—there are some quite effective synthesizers in spots, and a lot of kick in the rhythm section. A couple of cuts don't make it, including the title track. But five elegant successes out of seven ain't bad, and it's always nice to hear from the French Antilles' more neglected idioms. —*John Storm Roberts, Original Music*

● **Live au Zenith** / 1989 / Blue Silver ✦✦✦✦✦

A classic 1987 concert from this large orchestra, "String Creole music" featuring Edith Lefel on vocals. —*Robert Leaver*

Malavoi: L'Autre Style / 1992 / Hibiscus ✦✦✦✦✦

Malavoi (along with Kassav') is one of the "national" treasures of the French Antilles. Playing largely pre-zouk styles, including a good dose of salsa, and featuring a guitar-less front line, their sound is less punchy than zouk but with a lot more swing. Trying to catalog the profusion of styles on this record would give me a headache, so . . . this is for everyone tired of zouk, but who wished they weren't. —*Carl Hoyt, Original Music*

La Belle Epoque / Hibiscus ✦✦✦

Malavoi is the tradition-bearer of the Martiniquan stringband tradition. The string section's sweetness is floribundantly attested to by this compilation from the days when Ralph Thamar was singing lead. —*John Storm Roberts, Original Music*

Eugene Mona

d. Aug. 1991

Flute / Zouk, Caribbean, French Antilles

This legendary bamboo flutist, songwriter, and performer was an extremely creative musician who, on the one hand, was a keeper of the flame of rural music traditions and who, on the other hand, was not afraid to experiment with the addition of contemporary sounds. He set the stage onto which later came Dede St. Prix, Marce Pago, Pakatak, and others. Mona died in August of 1991. —*Gene Scaramuzzo*

Temoignage / 1989 / Hibiscus ✦✦✦

This live album features raw roots music. —*Gene Scaramuzzo*

Blan Manje / 1991 / Hibiscus ✦✦✦✦✦

Recorded nearly five years after *Temoignage*, *Blan Manje* is a percussive/electric treat. —*Gene Scaramuzzo*

● **Mona, Vols. 1 & 2** / 1992 / Hibiscus ✦✦✦✦✦

This '70s anthology is a must for any fans of Dede and Marce. —*Gene Scaramuzzo*

Pakatak

Zouk, Chouval Bwa, Caribbean, French Antilles

This Martiniquan tambour group under the leadership of Krisyan Jesophe has been around for a long time, though members change. —*Gene Scaramuzzo*

● **Chouval Bwa** / Pakatak ✦✦✦✦✦

It's a fine example of this band's work. —*Gene Scaramuzzo*

Pa Fe Wol / Hibiscus ✦✦✦

The charming "tambour" group Pakatak is proof that there's still great zouk out there. Their trick is to keep the contempo-funk fun-and-games with plenty firmly rooted. The Carnival roots here include super flute and clarinet by leader Krisyan Josephe (who also sings, plays small percussion and programs the digitalia), and three tradition-based drummers. —*John Storm Roberts, Original Music*

Plastic System Band

Biguine Vide, Caribbean, French Antilles

An approximately 80-piece carnival street band that consists of horns, stiltwalkers, and dozens of percussionists playing on plastic drums and ti bwa. In the Martiniquan carnival tradition, their recordings are medleys of everything from French nursery songs to popular zouk songs to the myriad of Antilles carnival songs. These recordings give a superb introduction to Martiniquan carnival music. *Bel Je* includes both songs found on the "Kalot Kannaval" 12-inch single. —*Gene Scaramuzzo*

Kalot Kannaval / 1988 / Solo Gammes ✦✦✦

★ **Bel Je** / 1991 / Plastic System Band ✦✦✦✦✦

Pier' Rosier

Vocals / Zouk, Caribbean, French Antilles

A Martiniquan singer of traditional music who went the zouk route in 1985 with a first-rate group of Paris-based musicians calling themselves Gazoline. Artistic differences between Rosier and the band led to their breakup in late 1987, so Rosier went on to form his own handpicked band of underlings, which he named Gazolinn'. His entire catalog, with both bands, is worth hearing, strong on chouval-bwa-influenced rhythms and providing some of the most serious hard-edged "zouk chire" this side of Kassav' (in terms of technical and songwriting excellence). The Shanachie Records anthology is a fine introduction and includes many of the best of Rosier's collaborations with the original Gazolinn'. —*Gene Scaramuzzo*

Le Bidongaz / 1989 / Cyclonn' ✦✦✦✦✦

A friend describes *Bidongaz* as "Gazolinn's Kraftwerk album"—a good line with a good deal of truth. Rosier's idiosyncrasy, however, still flashes plentifully from the technology like lightning from a storm cloud. —*John Storm Roberts, Original Music*

★ **Zouk Obsession** / 1990 / Shanachie ✦✦✦✦✦

Among the top Zouk groups on the worldbeat circuit. This 1990 release of their greatest hits spotlights the great Pier' Rosier. —*Ron Wynn*

Ultra Light / Sonodisc ✦✦✦✦✦

Rosier is one of the more interesting of the zoukistes, and here is some actual evidence. Neither lover's zouk nor raunchy, this album cultivates an air of sophisticated steaminess that will make you want to pull your baby onto the dance floor. Besides going up and down every street in zouk-land, Gazolin' strays into soukous (with some help from Diblo) as well as sega. Rosier also plays a mean harmonica when called upon. —*John Storm Roberts, Original Music*

Ronald Rubinel

Keyboards / Zouk, Caribbean, French Antilles

Aside from Michel Alibo, there is no Antilles musician with a longer list of musical credentials, both live and on record, than Ronald Rubinel. He was a staple of touring Haitian bands in the '70s, who was heard adding rare keyboard parts to soukous recordings by Loketo and the other superstar Zairian bands. In the Antilles, he was a cadence star in the '70s and a zouk star in the '80s through to today. He is also the catalyst behind Martinique's most exciting carnival creation of the past two years, Ethnikolor. Besides playing on nearly as many zouk releases as the members of the Zouk Allstars, he has released a handful of his own recordings, always featuring a Who's Who of Antilles stars. *Bal Boutche* may be the best introduction. —*Gene Scaramuzzo*

Tilda / 1987 / Georges DEBS ✦✦✦

Zoulou / 1987 / Georges DEBS ✦✦✦

● Bal Boutche / 1989 / Georges DEBS ✦✦✦✦✦

Dede St. Prix

Flute, Drums / Chouval Bwa, Caribbean, French Antilles
A hand drummer, bamboo flutist, and songwriter, St. Prix is one of the rootsmen of Martinique. After stints as a percussionist in many local bands (including E+, Malavoi, and Pakatak), he formed his own band, Avan Van, in the early 80s and has never looked back. His pioneer efforts were in the melding of zouk sounds with a rural musical tradition called chouval bwa. As a songwriter he has lent his efforts to a variety of projects, reaching a pinnacle with an extremely funky cut called "Amazon" that appeared on Joelle Ursull's *Black French* album. *Mi Se Sa*, reissued on Mango Records, is the most electric and not the most indicative of the total recorded output of St. Prix, even though it's likely to be the easiest to find. —*Gene Scaramuzzo*

● Mi Se Sa / 1988 / Mango ✦✦✦✦✦
Altogether successful at putting over a classical chouval bwa, it's freshened but not threatened by the contemporary touches. —*John Storm Roberts*

Lerdou / CBH ✦✦✦
Martinique fights back, or St. Prix goes zouk—at the time, a big shock for fans of pure chouval bwa, and anybody who had his earlier flute-and-percussion recording. So after the trauma subsides, what's the verdict? In a word, mixed. A couple of bland tracks are offset by several that blend traditional and zouk elements very effectively (after all, zouk simply built on tendencies already present in both islands). —*John Storm Roberts, Original Music*

Tanya St. Val

Vocals / Zouk, Caribbean, French Antilles
The darling of the French Antilles music scene, St. Val's records benefit from strong support by the best the islands have to offer. Her voice is hefty, much in the way of Grace Slick, and her interpretations are always convincing. She is definitely deserving of her star status. —*Gene Scaramuzzo*

● Tamboo / 1987 / Henri DEBS ✦✦✦✦✦
This 1986 album was the rocket that propelled St. Val from the semi-obscurity of backup singing to stardom. Though this last has to be chalked up as a negative, Tamboo—like St. Val herself—is full of charm and bounce. —*John Storm Roberts, Original Music*

Ti Seles (Celeste)

Gwo Ka, Caribbean, French Antilles
Basic gwo ka drums and singing but a real standout because of Seles' authoritive voice, beautiful singing, and occasional use of very melodic sax. —*Gene Scaramuzzo*

Ti Celeste / 1984 / Henri DEBS ✦✦✦
This is an excellent recording of traditional gwo ka percussion and vocals. —*Robert Leaver*

● Virus La / Wirem ✦✦✦✦✦
Singer Ti Seles has the reputation as both a gwo ka traditionalist and a modernizer of the form. His "Hommage ... Robert" (a gwo ka legend) is rootsy drumming, and his voice is always deep and rural. But for several tracks he adds synth and piano, very successfully, in a quite effective adaptation of zouk to the far more local Guadeloupian sound of gwo ka. —*John Storm Roberts*

Joelle Ursull

Vocals / Zouk, Caribbean, French Antilles
★ Miyel / 1988 / CBS ✦✦✦✦✦

Black French / 1990 / CBS ✦✦✦
Included is a collaboration with none other than French bad-boy Serge Gainsbourg. The Gainsbourg/Ursull duet "White and Black Blues" took Europe by storm in the summer of 1990, but it's the Dede St. Prix composition, "Amazon," that makes the album worth buying. —*Gene Scaramuzzo*

Francky Vincent

Piano / Zouk, Caribbean, French Antilles
Probably the best way to get acquainted with this master of suggestive lyrics is through the recent anthology on Declic Records, although the

other one listed may still be in print. Vincent's album jackets and music are often downright hilarious, although the clever wordplay will be lost on non-Creole-speaking listeners. The reason his records are listed as being of high interest is that instrumentally his music is superb, featuring sparkling production, ringing instruments, and creative songwriting. On e of the true talents of the Antilles. —*Gene Scaramuzzo*

15 Ans Dèjà . . . (Braguette d'Or) / 1989 / Bleu Caraibes ✦✦✦

● Coquinement Zouk / 1991 / Declic 100% ✦✦✦✦✦

Ze Top

Zouk, Caribbean, French Antilles
This first-class gathering of musicians casts a witty, irreverent look at zouk and Antilles music in general. —*Gene Scaramuzzo*

Ka Dance / 1991 / Hibiscus ✦✦✦✦✦
This record came out at carnival time 1991 and is already one of the classics. It will probably remain available for years to come. —*Gene Scaramuzzo*

Zouk Allstars

Zouk, Caribbean, French Antilles
The Zouk Allstars are Dominique Gengoul, Jean-Luc Alger, Frederic Caracas, and Charles Maurinier, four young musicians who have made an indelible mark on Antilles music of the '80s and early '90s. To call them prolific is a gross understatement; pick up any ten zouk albums, and it's likely that one or more of their names will appear on at least seven as producers and/or instrumentalists. Solo projects include studio groups like Karata, Mazout', Champagn', and Lazair. The crystal clarity of their production, the funkiness of their playing, and their ceaseless creativity are the reasons behind their popularity. —*Gene Scaramuzzo*

An Nou Swe / 1987 / Moradisc ✦✦✦✦✦

● Vol. 2 / 1988 / Moradisc ✦✦✦✦✦

Top Niveau / 1989 / Moradisc ✦✦✦

French Antilles Collection

Antilles d'Aujourd'hui / 1978 / Festival ✦✦✦
Undoubtedly the best, it's probably the only collection of Antilles music circa mid- to late '70s. Included are cuts from many of the biggest names of the era, usually their most popular songs. This collection confirms what was said earlier about the diverse talents of Antilles musicians, presenting everything from cadence and Haitian compas to biguine, Creole mazurka, and calypso. It still occasionally surfaces in Paris record stores. —*Gene Scaramuzzo*

☆ Dance! Cadence! / 1985 / GlobeStyle ✦✦✦✦✦
This classic is a wonderful look at cadence, biguine moderne, ti kannot, (kalenda), and early zouk by the likes of Eugene Mona, Georges Decimus, and Michel Godzom. —*Gene Scaramuzzo*

Generation Zouk, Vols. 1-3 / New Deal ✦✦✦✦✦
It's arguably the best of the collections of radio hits, but please refer to the *Planète Zouk* record entry to read more on this. The New Deal/Carrere label features some of the best music made in the Antilles, and whoever was responsible for compiling these collections (which feature artists from all labels) showed typical good taste. —*Gene Scaramuzzo*

Planète Zouk, Vols. 1 & 2 / 1991 / Declic100% ✦✦✦✦✦
An abridged version of *Volume 1* was reissued as *Planet Zouk: The World of Antilles Music (Rhythm Safari)*, and there are plans to do the same soon with *Volume 2*. These are compilations of radio hits from a variety of record labels (circa 1988-1991) from Paris and the French Antilles. The cuts feature samples from a Who's Who of Antilles greats, from Kassav', Dede St. Prix, Malavoi, and Ronald Rubinel to lesser-known but also accomplished artists like Edith Lefel, Ralph Thamar, Eric Virgal, and Experience 7. Many good songs can be found here, from the biguine tinges of Thamar's "Polisson" to the underlying soukous feeling of Experience 7's "Goudjoua." Eric Virgal's "Pa Fe Mwen la Pen" is a fine example of zouk-love, while Edith Lefel's lead vocal on her co-composition with Ronald Rubinel ("Sensation") shows the best melding of zouk with American soul sounds, an oft-made attempt that is rarely successful. The fact that these are all radio hits implies a common thread that runs throughout the set of music: strong on formula, weak on experimentation. This is a "safe" set of music, which features good songs but few surprises and few moments of pure zouk ecstasy. —*Gene Scaramuzzo*

☆ Zouk Attack / 1992 / Rounder ✦✦✦✦✦
This zouk anthology features such outstanding zouk groups as Pier' Rosier and Gazoline, Love Stars, Typical, and Tatiana and Zouti, but sounds just a bit smooth in many places. It's a reminder that zouk was and is a roots-oriented pop sound, and as such has a soft center as well as frenetic edges. —*Ron Wynn*

Zoukollection, Vols. 1-3 / 1988 / Hibiscus ✦✦✦✦✦
Although much the same argument can be made for these compilations (released 1988-90) as for the above *Planète Zouk* discs, the difference is that these are mostly all artists from the Hibiscus label, a stable of unusual artists who are much more involved in experimentation and a return to classic forms like biguine, ti kannot, etc. — *Gene Scaramuzzo*

Haiti

Boukman Eksperyans
....
Bass, Guitar, Vocals / Jazz, Afro Pop, Haiti, Caribbean
Boukman Eksperyans announce their radicalism in their name, an allusion to Boukman the slave who initiated the island's 1804 independence uprising. Always aware that freedom and culture go hand in hand, this ten-member band sing in the sporadically outlawed creole tongue and blend African religious motifs and street slang into a wild, syncretic celebration of Haitian voodoo culture. To sing out so boldly in Haiti, however, is to invite repression; although the band's "Wet Chenn" ("Remove the Chains") won first place in a 1989 musical contest, their 1992 entry was banned. In an environment torn apart with military unrest and governmental crackdowns, Boukman Eksperyans are regarded as a radical threat. Thus, their 1990 song, "Kem Pa Sote," was banned from Haitian airwaves. — *Leon Jackson*

● **Vodou Adjae** / 1991 / Mango ✦✦✦✦✦
The vaudou revival was barely perceptible in BE's first recording: compare the international choral sound or its pan-Afro drumming to the neo-Africanism of the roots. BE's main influences are lover's zouk and rock guitar. But this is an attractive recording in Haiti's new-wave genre, with eclectic French, zouk, and US elements and political agenda. — *John Storm Roberts, Original Music*

Kalfou Dangare / 1992 / Mango ✦✦✦✦✦
The release of their first album on Mango Records marked Boukman Eksperyans as Haiti's most successful and creative musical voice. With "Kalfou Danjere," Boukman picks up the threads of lakou spirituality and sharp political commentary, blending them with the infectious rhythms, soaring guitars and hypnotic vocals that earned *Vodou Adjae* a Grammy Award nomination. — *Mango*

Coupé Cloué (Gesner Henry)
....
Guitar, Vocals / Haiti, Caribbean
An enigmatic guitarist and singer, Coupé Cloué acquired this nickname (translated as "kickout") from his prowess on the soccer field. He is famous, or rather notorious, for his lyrics containing sexual double-entendre, long "raps" ranging from risqué to romantic, and social satire. His "compas mamba" (peanut compas) seems very African, with a guitar style resembling West African highlife and the use of Cuban bongo drums and bamboo tubes played with sticks in addition to the standard conga and drum kit. Appearing on many album covers wearing African clothing, Coupé Cloué, with his shaved head, cuts a striking figure. This may explain why he was given the title "Le Roi" (the king) when he played in the Ivory Coast, West Africa, in 1975. Of all the electric Caribbean bands, Coupé Cloué has the strongest African sound, which shows the strength of his roots, for he claims he never heard African music before his 1975 trip. — *Richard Lieberson*

● **The World of** / 1979 / Mini ✦✦✦✦✦
Coupé Cloué's always had the capacity to beguile all over again, however many recordings he issues. But this 1979 release has to be one of the man's very finest. Every track is catchy to the max, egg-full of the jaunty charm that defines Haitian mini-jazz, and rich in simply wonderful guitar. — *John Storm Roberts*

L'essentiel Coupé Cloué / Mini ✦✦✦
Gesner Henry (Coupé Cloué) runs one of the prettiest guitar bands on either side of the Altantic, though Tabou Combo's hit-hunting has kept C.C. out of the international spotlight. Here are the interlocking guitars, roosty percussion, and chatty vocals which make Coupé in general, and this mid-'70s collection in particular, one of our undisputed faves. — *Carl Hoyt, Original Music*

Live / Melodie Makers ✦✦✦
Thankfully, Coupé Cloué's gentle guitar hot springs only bubble more spaciously in this recent (though undated) onstage recording. Unique in his slow-paced, very African-sounding compas, leader Gesner Henry here comes across as a combination of Franco and Barry White. — *Carl Hoyt, Original Music*

The Preacher / Mini ✦✦✦
Here are eight classic '70s cuts and "Myan Myan." — *Robert Leaver*

Sociss [With Terio Select] / Marc's ✦✦✦✦✦
Sociss (from the late '70s?) is decently recorded, and a favorite musically speaking. This is unpretentiously but outstandingly catchy three-guitar band stuff, gentle and rippling but still with a kick, and there are very

few Haitian recordings that really overshadow these guys, particularly in their good-humored creole genre. — *John Storm Roberts*

Les Shleu Shleu
....
Mini Jazz, Caribbean, Haiti
Shleu-Shleu, the Haitian forerunner of what in NYC became Ska-Shah No.1, was one of the great bands. Their combination of swing and delicacy was one reason, but from this distance what stands out from that pre-funk era is their strong Creole flavor, not just in the melodies but in the wonderful solo sax, a style no longer heard. Here's a question: given the Congo touch in the guitars, who was influencing whom? — *John Storm Roberts*

● **Les Shleu Shleu** / 1978 / Dada's ✦✦✦✦✦
Unmistakably creole, yet still quite cosmopolitan with its jaunty sax and Congolese-style guitar, Haitian music of this period (1978) had an influence only more remarkable for the fact that Haiti is only half of a small island. Bands like Shleu Shleu played more for love than money. It certainly sounds that way. — *John Storm Roberts*

Ce La ou Ye / 1990 / Mini ✦✦✦
Early-'70s classic mini-jazz. — *Robert Leaver*

6éme Anniversaire / Feb. 1990 / Mini ✦✦✦
Shleu-Shleu, the Haitian forerunner of what in NYC became Ska Shah No.1, was one of the great bands. Their combination of swing and delicacy was one reason, but from this distance what stands out from that pre-funk era is their strong creole flavor, not just in the melodies but in the wonderful solo sax, a style no longer heard. Here's a question: given the Congo touch in the guitars, who was influencing whom? This reissue bears a 1990 copyright date, but it sounds like the '60s or very early '70s. — *John Storm Roberts*

Pionniers / 1991 / Melodie Makers ✦✦✦
A new, different band has a modern sound with soukous-like guitar and full horn section. — *Robert Leaver*

Tabou Combo
....
Haiti, Caribbean
Formed in the Port-Au-Prince suburb of Petion-Ville by the Chancy brothers, Albert on bass and Adolphe on guitar, this young band won the Radio Haiti mini-jazz competition in 1968. They relocated to Brooklyn in 1971, and their song "New York City," which spoke of the difficulty of life in exile, reached No. 1 on the Paris pop charts in August 1975. They competed with Ska-Shah for top band honors in the '70s and '80s and fought "musical duels" similar to the Weber Sicot / Jean-Baptiste Nemours battles of the '50s and '60s.

An irresistible live band, Tabou Combo takes Haitian compas to the widest of audiences. From their regular appearances in the '80s at the famous Zenith Theatre in Paris, to an audience of 20,000 in New York's Central Park, to the Jazz and Heritage Festival in New Orleans, in football stadiums throughout the Caribbean, and on the turntables of the top DJs, this band makes people dance.

Influenced by funk and soul in their adopted home, Tabou took on the likeness of the Commodores on the covers of their late-'70s releases. They even made a demo tape with hopes of a Motown contract. Their desire to reach the Black US market remains unsatisfied, but they should be proud that popular musicians such as Kassav' from the Antilles/Paris and Wilfrido Vargas from the Dominican Republic have absorbed their music. — *Richard Lieberson*

★ **8éme Sacrement** / 1974 / Mini ✦✦✦✦✦
The CD is from 1974, which some regard as the band's golden age. Back then it was essentially a guitar band (with accordion to link back to Nemours), with a perfect blend of drive and simplicity. "New York City," the biggest Haitian hit of all time, is featured on this live album. — *John Storm Roberts*

Any Antilles / 1989 / Traditional Crossroads ✦✦✦
New sound. Ultimate Haitian dance music. — *Robert Leaver*

Live au Zenith / 1989 / Esperance ✦✦✦
The band's relative recent success outside its core community led to hit-hunting that marred its 1989 release. Happily, however, there's little of it in this Zenith set, recorded at a gig in Paris. This double album (also available on video) has plenty of zouk influence, but on the whole it's a return to the band's '80s sound at its best. — *John Storm Roberts*

Haiti Collection

Caribbean Revels: Haitian Rara & Dominican Gaga / 1978 / Smithsonian/Folkways ✦✦✦✦✦
Rara and Gaga are basically the same thing—vaudou-related Easter parade music using (traditionally) African-derived single-note shawms, and—quite often these days—trumpets and saxes as well as percussion. Gaga is distinct from rara to the extent that the Haitian minority in the Dominican Republic has developed its own traditions. Both branches

are exuberantly documented here through street recordings of both traditional and trumpet-led examples. —*John Storm Roberts, Original Music*

☆ **Konbit Burning Rhythms of Haiti** / A&M ✦✦✦✦✦
Filmmaker Jonathan Demme compiled this sharp package of classic (and rarely heard) Haitian music from 1957 to the present; most tracks came from the last half of the '80s and contain potent political sentiments, not to mention potent dance rhythms. —*Myles Boisen*

Jamaica

Jolly Boys

Banjo, Guitar, Bongos, Kalimba / Mento, Jamaica, Caribbean
The Jolly Boys are the foremost performers of mento, the ribald, witty first cousin of Jamaican reggae. Like reggae, mento is marked by a shuffling, syncopated guitar strum, an irreverent attitude, and a lazy, swaying danceability. Unlike reggae, mento has no sacramental roots, nor does it strain after profundity. Instead, mento makes a religion of sexual braggadocio, drinking, and good times. The Jolly Boys have been composing and performing mentos for decades; indeed, they used to perform for Errol Flynn when he stayed at his Jamaican villa. Their sound is derived from rhythmic bongo playing, along with solos by the banjo and kalimba (finger piano). Two representative discs are *Pop 'n' Mento* and *Sunshine 'n' Water*. —*Leon Jackson*

● **Pop 'n' Mento** / 1989 / Rykodisc ✦✦✦✦✦
Mento is one of the rhythms that went into the mix that became reggae. The Jolly Boys (the youngest of whom is 50-plus) have been playing their acoustic brand of double-entendre, crowd-pleasing mento for decades. Included are traditional faves like "Big Bamboo," "Shaving Cream," "River Come Down," and "Back to Back (Belly to Belly)." —*J. Poet*

Beer Joint & Tailoring / Jan. 1991 / First Warning ✦✦✦
The Jolly Boys play mento, an acoustic forerunner of styles such as reggae and ska. Their first two albums garnered incredible press and worldbeat/NPR radio support. This third release, recorded live to DAT in rural Jamaica by BBC personality Andy Kershaw, properly captures their infectious spirit. Tunes include "Tenement Yard" and "We Want More Money." —*Roundup Newsletter*

Jamaica: Roots of Reggae / Lyrichord ✦✦✦

Panama

Denyse Plummer

Vocals / Caribbean, Trinidad
Enlisted by Phase II Pan Groove steelband arranger Len "Boogsie" Sharpe in 1986 to sing his band's Panorama entry, Plummer began making a name for herself as a calypsonian. In 1988, with yet another Len "Boogsie" Sharpe pan tune, "Woman Is Boss," she arrived at the National Calypso Monarchy finals and also won the Calypso Queen crown. Since then she has taken the Calypso Queen crown a total of four times and has won the World Calypso crown three times. Blessed with a strong voice and always an outstanding composition, Plummer makes records that are fresh and exciting. —*Gene Scaramuzzo*

★ **The Boss** / 1988 / Weldon's ✦✦✦✦✦
Included is "A Nation Forges On" and "Woman Is Boss." —*Gene Scaramuzzo*

Still the Boss / 1989 / Boss ✦✦✦
It includes "Together Right Here" and "The Champ." —*Gene Scaramuzzo*

Victory / 1990 / Oscar's ✦✦✦✦✦
A 12-inch EP with "DJ Fever" and "The Message," it brought Plummer her third Calypso Queen crown. "DJ Fever" was a much-welcomed tribute to the DJs worldwide who push soca. —*Gene Scaramuzzo*

Carnival Killer / 1991 / Dynamic Sounds ✦✦✦
The title track brought her yet another Calypso Queen crown, her fourth. —*Gene Scaramuzzo*

Trinidad

Arrow

Vocals / Soca, Party Soca, Calypso, Trinidad, Caribbean
From Montserrat, Arrow got his start as a first-class calypsonian in the traditional Trinidadian style but soon began exploring ways to bring the music to an international level. Always an innovator, he played around with mixing elements of cadence, salsa, and American R&R guitar into his music. In 1983 he experienced his first pan-Caribbean success, "Hot Hot Hot" (a song that later became an international hit). Since then he has branched out to include a wider array of world music elements, from hip-hop to the sounds of various African nations, while concentrating on lyrics that act predominantly as a vehicle to drive the music to a higher

Compas

Haitian bandleader Nemours Jean-Baptiste coined the phrase "compas direct" in the '50s to refer to his style of music. *Compas* means "musical measure" in Spanish, and *direct* refers to the absence of a third chord. Although similar to merengue, compas has a more driving rhythm; its moderate tempo is paced by a steady bass, which anchors the drum and cowbell percussion.

The instrumentation changed from a big band with a full horn section to the smaller "mini-jazz" combos of the later '60s and '70s, who introduced electric guitars and trap drums while retaining the solo saxophone (most typically, the alto sax) and sometimes the accordion. Compas now had a less direct meaning and became a generic term to refer to the Haitian style or, more specifically, rhythm. New York City became home to the top compas bands as the immigrant community grew. Compas spread to Miami, Montreal, Paris, and throughout the Caribbean, especially Guadeloupe and Martinique.

In exile, compas has been influenced by soul and funk and more recently by zouk, a popular dance music inspired by Haitian compas. —*Robert Leaver*

frenzy. A late-'80s contract with Island/Mango Records has made him the soca artist most widely distributed and most easily available in the States. His 1992 release, *Zombie Soca*, was notable for including three songs with social commentary lyrics. Unlike those of most calypsonians, Arrow's early releases, including those preceding the Island/Mango albums, are still easily available. —*Gene Scaramuzzo*

Instant Knockout / 1980 / Charlie's ✦✦✦✦✦
From his heavily cadence-flavored period, it features the original version of the social commentary, "Bills." —*Gene Scaramuzzo*

Hot Hot Hot / 1983 / Arrow ✦✦✦✦✦
An exciting album not only for the title cut, it still features social commentary; every song is great. —*Gene Scaramuzzo*

Heat / 1984 / ✦✦✦
This album is also called *Rush Hour*. —*Gene Scaramuzzo*

Soca Savage / 1984 / Arrow ✦✦✦
This early Arrow album includes two major dance hits, "Party Mix" and "Columbia Rock," one of soca's best Latin fusion tunes. —*J. Poet*

Knock Dem Dead / 1988 / Mango ✦✦✦
This disc continues Arrow's fusion experiments and includes Zulu soca, Latin soca, and heavy metal soca courtesy of guitar ace Chris Newland. —*J. Poet*

O'la Soca / 1989 / Mango ✦✦✦
Hot tracks and exuberant, though sometimes irritating vocals. A remix of his 1989 *Massive* album. —*Ron Wynn*

Massive / 1989 / ✦✦✦✦✦
It was remixed as *O La Soca* on Mango. —*Gene Scaramuzzo*

Soca Dance Party / 1990 / Mango ✦✦✦
Arrow's latest exploration of Caribbean rhythms includes an excursion to Guadaloupe entitled "Zouk Me." —*J. Poet*

★ **Hot Soca Hot** / 1990 / Arrow ✦✦✦✦✦
This outstanding anthology of hits was put together by the man himself (unlike other Arrow anthologies), and therefore features what he knows is the best. —*Gene Scaramuzzo*

Zombie Soca / 1992 / Arrow ✦✦✦
This is an outstanding album by Arrow, including the superb dancehall soca "Wine Yuh Body." Complete with several remixes, social commentaries, and a total of 70 minutes of music, this is the best Arrow album to come along in a while. —*Gene Scaramuzzo*

Outrageous / Arrow ✦✦✦
Continuing with a bit of social commentary, it still jams hard with tunes like "Pressure" and "Physical." —*Gene Scaramuzzo*

Black Stalin

Soca, Party Soca, Social Commentary, Trinidad, Caribbean
Stalin is the master of socially conscious lyrics combined with infectious soca dance music, and is a revered legend in T&T (the Trinidad & Tobago style). Song topics range from local concerns like support for the steel drums and calypsonians to concerns of African and Caribbean unification, with occasional global topics like the litany against world leaders in "Burn Dem." Between 1967 and 1992 Stalin has been a finalist contender for the coveted National Calypso Monarchy crown 16 times, winning it four times. —*Gene Scaramuzzo*

Caribbean Man / 1979 / Makossa ✦✦✦✦✦
This album brought him his first Calypso Monarchy crown with "Caribbean Unity" and "Play One." —*Gene Scaramuzzo*

Wait Dorothy Wait / 1985 / Charlie's ✦✦✦
This 12-inch single was backed with "Ism Schism"; these two songs brought him his second crown. —*Gene Scaramuzzo*

I Time / 1987 / B's ✦✦✦
Included is "Burn Dem," the most internationally known of any Stalin composition. It brought him his third crown. —*Gene Scaramuzzo*

★ **Roots Rock Soca** / 1991 / Rounder ✦✦✦✦✦
Black Stalin has been among Trinidad's most popular soca and calypso musicians since 1979, when he won his first National Calypso Monarch crown. He has satisfied audience demands for joyous party material while also producing some incendiary, uncompromising protest material. Rounder collected 11 Stalin gems on this anthology, which has been recently been released on CD. Such numbers as "Caribbean Unity," "Black Man Music," and "Burn Dem" have a pronounced Afro-Latin bent, showing soca's ties with Latin jazz and Afro-Cuban rhythms. Material done in the late '80s has a faster pace, and Stalin begins including more synthesized backbeats and contemporary arrangements. —*Ron Wynn*

The Bright Side / 1991 / Straker's ✦✦✦
A great album, it will go down in history for including his first hit with party lyrics, "Ah Feel to Party." The song brought him his fourth crown. It's excellent from beginning to end. —*Gene Scaramuzzo*

Help / Straker's ✦✦✦
The title cut is rather whiney, but is left in the dust by superb cuts like "Black Man Killing Black Man," "Kaiso" and "Wey de Wok." —*Gene Scaramuzzo*

Rebellion / Ice ✦✦✦
There are more cuts than necessary on this first Ice Records release for Stalin, but there is a core of songs here that would have made an excellent normal-length LP. —*Gene Scaramuzzo*

Blueboy (Superblue)

Vocals / Soca, Party Soca, Social Commentary, Trinidad, Caribbean
Blueboy may very well be the most loved of T&T's calypsonians. After dominating the Road March competition in the early '80s, a difficult bout with personal problems removed him for a while from the big leagues. His triumphant return in 1991 (as "Superblue") was met with overwhelmingly positive response by a public that had been truly empathetic during his "lost years." In both 1991 and 1992 Superblue was so far ahead in the Road March competition that his ultimate victories were pronounced long before Carnival Tuesday, but in 1993 he even exceeded this feat by writing the most popular road march ever (in terms of votes tallied), "Bacchanal Time." Look under Blueboy for the best of his earlier efforts, but consider both albums as Superblue to be essential listening. —*Gene Scaramuzzo*

★ **Soca in the Shaolin Temple** / 1980 / Charlie's ✦✦✦✦✦
This is a classic early-'80s album. —*J. Poet*

Thundering Soca / 1984 / CCP ✦✦✦
Soca with a hard rock edge. —*J. Poet*

Caribbean Magic / 1988 / B's ✦✦✦
The still-embattled Blueboy managed to come through with hints of his past grandeur with this album, which includes "Ding Ding" and "Look the Devil Deh." —*Gene Scaramuzzo*

Poom Poom / 1990 / ✦✦✦✦✦
After 1990, Blueboy began going by the name Superblue. —*Gene Scaramuzzo*

10th Anniversary / 1991 / Charlie's ✦✦✦
A soca masterpiece, it contains the 1991 Road March, "Get Something and Wave." —*Gene Scaramuzzo*

Burning Flames

Soca, Trinidad, Caribbean
From Antigua, this band represents the epitome of the high-energy, multiple-influenced, synthesizer-driven soca bands of some of the other soca islands. Years of tourist gigs and a stint as backup band for Montserrat calypsonian Arrow laid the groundwork for their solo debut . . . total domination of the Antigua carnival in 1986 with *Stiley Tight*. Elements of rock, funk, reggae, cadence, zouk, and more, put to frenetic tempos of amphetamine-like proportion, were the trademark of this band until 1989's "Workey Workey," a funky, zoukish second-line that was an international sensation. They zouked it out further in 1990 with "Chook and Dig" and shortly afterward were anthologized on a Mango release, *Dig*, although the remixing done for the record worked to the detriment of each cut. They have taken Antigua Road March almost every year since 1985. —*Gene Scaramuzzo*

● **Me Na Freard** / 1989 / BF ✦✦✦✦✦
Many songs from this album, including "Workey Workey," were selected and remixed for Mango's *Dig* anthology. —*Gene Scaramuzzo*

Mek E Bark / 1990 / BF ✦✦✦
More hit songs were selected and remixed for *Dig*, this time including "Chook and Dig." —*Gene Scaramuzzo*

Dig / 1991 / Mango ✦✦✦
Remixes of some of the band's best late-'80s output surprisingly deemphasize the frenzied tempos that made them famous. —*Gene Scaramuzzo*

Hard Fu Ded / Dr. G Prod ✦✦✦
"De Donkey" took 1992 Road March honors, initiating a donkey craze that exploded a few months later at the 1993 T&T Carnival. —*Gene Scaramuzzo*

Brigiding Biff / BF ✦✦✦
Every kind of liquid imaginable was being tossed around at Antigua Carnival 1993 because of "Wet Down," the Road March winner from this LP. —*Gene Scaramuzzo*

Calypso Rose

Vocals / Soca, Party Soca, Calypso, Social Commentary, Trinidad
Rose has won more national and international awards than any other calypsonian save for Sparrow and Kitch. The title of the National Calypso King Competition had to be changed to National Calypso Monarchy Competition as a result of her being the first female to ever take the crown (in 1978). Her material is often feminist in nature, and the music is much in the style of Antigua's Swallow . . . heavy on the cowbell and horn section. It is no exaggeration to say that every album by Rose is worth hearing. —*Gene Scaramuzzo*

Trouble / 1984 / Straker's ✦✦✦✦✦
One of calypso's small number of women performers and the only female Carnival "King," she has a strong message of Black pride and feminist consciousness, often turning in scathing criticisms of the way men treat women. This album is one of her best. —*J. Poet*

● **Pan in Town** / 1985 / Straker's ✦✦✦✦✦
This one is among her best; it includes "Huttam Pullam," "Put It on the Table," and "Turn on the Pressure." —*Gene Scaramuzzo*

Stepping Out / 1986 / Straker's ✦✦✦
The songs that appear on this album were documented in the outstanding calypso film *One Hand Don't Clap*. —*Gene Scaramuzzo*

Soca Explosion / 1988 / Straker's ✦✦✦
This above-average album from one of soca's top singers is especially notable for a really fine Indo-calypso (an old calypso tradition that has produced many fine songs) in "Indian Baccanal," and a rare and welcome bonus: lots of solo horn to freshen the backings. —*John Storm Roberts*

Soca Diva / Ice ✦✦✦
Her first album away from the Straker label in more than a decade is a perfect collection of social commentary, always from an amused but experienced perspective. —*Gene Scaramuzzo*

Chalkdust

Vocals / Soca, Social Commentary, Trinidad, Caribbean
An extremely dedicated social commentator, and schoolteacher, Chalkdust predominantly limits his lyrics to local concerns, with a point of view that often forces Trinidadians to look within themselves for the causes and answers to the country's problems. He has won the Monarchy crown five times since 1976, most recently in 1993 for "Kaiso in Hospital" and his remarkably timely surprise song at the Monarchy Finals, "Misconceptions." A kaiso legend, but probably not very accessible to those with a passing interest in calypso. —*Gene Scaramuzzo*

● **Total Kaiso** / 1989 / Straker's ✦✦✦✦✦
"Chauffeur Wanted" is a scathing indictment against the prime minister of the time, a song that brought Chalkdust the National Calypso Monarchy crown in 1989. —*Gene Scaramuzzo*

Field Marshall of the People's Army / 1990 / ✦✦✦

Visions / Straker's ✦✦✦
The 1993 T&T Carnival raged in controversy over new styles of music entering the calypso/soca scene. Chalkdust's finger-pointing "Kaiso in Hospital" was widely accepted as the "official" viewpoint on the matter, even if a bit extreme in its accusations. One of Chalkie's best LPs ever, it included other great commentaries like "The Acid Test" and "Stickman's Lament." —*Gene Scaramuzzo*

Charlie's Roots

Party Soca, Trinidad, Caribbean
A T&T brass band that had been popular for years prior to the emergence of one of their lead singers, David Rudder, as a solo calypsonian in 1986.

In that year Rudder won both the Road March and the National Calypso Monarchy crown. In 1988 another Charlie's Roots lead singer, Chris "Tambu" Herbert, began a three-year domination of the Road March as a solo artist. Despite the solo careers of the two, they remain to this day as singers for Charlie's Roots, although as of 1988 they began to release albums under their own names, with the band listed as backup artists. Albums are still released occasionally under the group's name. Sire Records reissues Rudder's music with Charlie's Roots in nice packages that are more available than the original releases. Their tendency to mix songs from different years may confuse those who wish to familiarize themselves with Rudder as a developing artist. —*Gene Scaramuzzo*

★ **The Hammer** / 1986 / Charlie's ✦✦✦✦✦
The album that made Rudder a legend was released under the Charlie's Roots name. It won him the title of Road March King, King of Carnival, and Best New Artist, a feat unprecedented in calypso. —*J. Poet*

10th Anniversary / 1987 / Charlie's ✦✦✦
It features Rudder again, this time with "Dedication" and "Calypso Music." This album, along with the previous year's "Bahia Gyal," was reissued on Sire Records as *This Is Soca—Vol. 1.* —*Gene Scaramuzzo*

☆ **Total Party** / 1992 / Charlie's ✦✦✦✦✦
This album, which features Rudder on "Savannah Party," was one of the finest releases from Carnival 1992. —*Gene Scaramuzzo*

Crazy

Reggae, Soca, Trinidad, Caribbean
As number 2 he certainly tries harder. There is perhaps no artist in T&T who more consistently composes a party masterpiece aimed at the Road March and yet loses time and again, usually placing second. Best known internationally for his Indian soca success, "Nani Wine," he has actually been responsible for many huge hits, including "Ain't Bong for You" (from 1984), "Drive It" (1988), "Gimme More" (from 1990), and "Penelope/Party Now Start" (from 1992). Only once, in 1985, did he win the Road March, with "(Suck Me) Soucouyant." For all-out party soca, any record by Crazy will do. —*Gene Scaramuzzo*

New Directions / 1984 / ✦✦✦
It contains two great songs for the road, "Ain't Bong for You" and "Soca Tarzan." —*Gene Scaramuzzo*

Soucouyant / 1985 / Trinity ✦✦✦
This is another three-song "LP" from Crazy. A soucouyant is a Trinidadian spirit that can suck the life out of you, but Crazy is so pumped up on soca energy that he taunts the apparition with one of the great double-entendre lines of the '80s, "Suck Me, Soucouyant." —*J. Poet*

★ **Nani Wine** / 1989 / Trinity ✦✦✦✦✦
The title song, written by Superblue, is an infectious Indian soca response to Drupatee's "Mr. Bissessar" from the year before, and is Crazy's most well-known song. —*Gene Scaramuzzo*

Crazymania / 1992 / JW Productions ✦✦✦✦✦
Most music lovers of T&T agree that "Penelope" from this LP could have been the Road March if it hadn't advised "if you can't find a woman, take a man." —*Gene Scaramuzzo*

Let's Go Crazy / JW Productions ✦✦✦
"Paul" from this LP got banned from Children's Carnival but it only opened the door for another great tune, "Jump Up and Wail," to jump into the battle for the Road March race. —*Gene Scaramuzzo*

Craziah Than Ever. . . / JW Productions ✦✦✦
On first listen it may be a lesser LP than others by Crazy, but nonetheless contains three hits during Carnival 1994: "Dis Is How," "OPP in the Party," and "La La Lay La La Lo." —*Gene Scaramuzzo*

Duke (Mighty)

Vocals / Soca, Social Commentary, Trinidad, Caribbean
A legendary calypsonian for his unduplicated feat of winning the calypso Monarchy four years in a row. Considered one of the major figures in calypso, Duke releases albums that are always of interest. He never fails to deliver a party soca for the Road March competition but has only once captured it (in 1987 with "Is Thunder"). His topics range from party lyrics to global concerns, addressing only on rare occasions something of local concern. —*Gene Scaramuzzo*

Calypso Forever / 1983 / Straker's ✦✦✦✦✦
Duke (aka Mighty Duke) is one of calypso's founding fathers; this is one of his best efforts from the early '80s. —*J. Poet*

● **Yesterday, Today and Tomorrow** / 1987 / Lem's ✦✦✦✦✦
It contains the 1987 Road March, "Is Thunder." —*Gene Scaramuzzo*

Party for Yuh Life! / 1989 / JW Productions ✦✦✦
"Yahhhhhhh" was among the hottest songs of 1989. —*Gene Scaramuzzo*

The Phung-Uh-Nung Sweet / 1992 / Straker's ✦✦✦
The title cut and "Rocket in Yuh Pocket" are worth hearing. —*Gene Scaramuzzo*

Calypso and Steelband Music of the Caribbean

Recordings of calypso (whose more uptempo contemporary form is called "soca," from the words *soul* and *calypso*) feature a fairly standard formula of programmed drums and rhythm section, calypso guitar, occasional lead or tenor pans (steel drums), horns, and a syncopated bass guitar that gives the music its true soul. While the lyrical content and cleverness will differ dramatically from song to song, a calypso album will typically include some songs strong on lyrics and some that put lyrics secondary to a strong dance beat. The best of the lot are undoubtedly those that combine infectious dance beats with thoughtful or timely messages.

A discussion of Trinidad & Tobago calypso/soca wouldn't be complete without mention of the steel drum (simply called a "pan" in the islands). For decades, the steel bands, large and small, waited to hear the annual crop of new music and then selected their favorite to arrange and perform during carnival. Since the mid-'80s, however, there has been a growing trend for steelband arrangers to write an original song and record it as soca, with a calypsonian singing. This has added exciting new music to carnival that very often features virtuoso lead or tenor panplaying. In Carnival '92 there were a remarkable dozen popular tunes written by steelband arrangers. —*Gene Scaramuzzo*

Explainer

Vocals / Soca, Social Commentary, Trinidad, Caribbean
A severely underrated calypsonian who rarely makes it to the Monarchy finals but who nearly always releases an album of interest. His albums are always a talented mix of social commentary and (often risqué) party tunes. —*Gene Scaramuzzo*

Nature / 1982 / Charlie's ✦✦✦✦✦
Mostly songs about sex and romance, they're told with much humor and compassion. —*J. Poet*

The Awakening / 1984 / B's ✦✦✦✦✦
"Caribbean Change" was one of the best commentaries on the unrest caused by foreign intervention in the Caribbean (Grenada, Cuba, etc.). —*Gene Scaramuzzo*

Dedicated to You / 1985 / B's ✦✦✦
Explainer is very political, and one of the few soca singers who can tell a tale from the women's perspective. Featured is "Lunch Time," an amusing celebration of oral sex. —*J. Poet*

★ **Positive Vibrations** / 1989 / Vista ✦✦✦✦✦
One of the few calypsonians to date to have his past work anthologized, this disc provides a taste of all the styles of lyrical commentary that make Explainer great. —*Gene Scaramuzzo*

Tongue / 1991 / Charlie's ✦✦✦
Especially good, it includes the party hit "Curfew Jam," as well as one of the first soca tunes ever written about a love affair between a calypsonian and his hand. —*Gene Scaramuzzo*

Rebound / Charlie's ✦✦✦
This is a superior album from the (mostly not very inspired) mid- to late '80s. Explainer is on the ball in songs about compulsive gambling, lubricious dancing, and the sins of big-shots and governments. But the top song, lyrically and melodically, is titled "Is Horse." —*John Storm Roberts, Original Music*

Francine (Singing)

Vocals / Party Soca, Social Commentary, Trinidad, Caribbean
A calypsonian who rarely plays a major role in carnival but who often makes a good commentary on some local issue. 1988's "Carnival Controversy" and 1989's "Sing for the Judges" show her to be unafraid to speak out against the T&T government, and these in fact represent two albums that would provide a good introduction to her music. —*Gene Scaramuzzo*

She/Chinaman / 1984 / ✦✦✦
A 12-inch single with funky soca, it featured steel drum lead that livened up Carnival 1984. —*Gene Scaramuzzo*

● **Reaching Out** / 1988 / Straker's ✦✦✦✦✦
"Cultural Controversy" was a major commentary of 1988. —*Gene Scaramuzzo*

Dedication / 1989 / Straker's ✦✦✦
"Sing for the Judges" was mentioned above, but "Soca Do That" is also a fine tune from 1989, although admittedly it was not among the biggest hits. —*Gene Scaramuzzo*

Gabby (Mighty)

Vocals / Trinidad, Caribbean
Gabby is undoubtedly Barbados' finest calypsonian as he has proved again and again in the past dozen years. —*Gene Scaramuzzo*

● **Boots** / 1984 / Ice ✦✦✦✦✦
This hard-hitting anti-war commentary deplores the use of tax money for a costly acquisition of boots for the military. It had a particularly strong impact coming as it did in the same year as the invasion of nearby Caribbean island Grenada. —*Gene Scaramuzzo*

Soca Trinity / 1993 / Ice/Ras ✦✦✦
There are six songs by Gabby on this collection also including 1993 tunes by Bajan calypsonians Grynner and Bert "Panta" Brown. "Pow Pow (Arm the Police)" was his forceful solution to addressing the growing crime problem in Barbados. —*Gene Scaramuzzo*

Gypsy

Trinidad, Caribbean
Gypsy is one of the outstanding calypsonians of T&T who annually since 1988 has won the National Extempo Calypso crown, a competition in which contestants must compose lyrics on the spot. He has had a roller-coaster career that has reached the extremes of peaks and valleys. His "Sinking Ship: SS Trinidad" from his classic 1986 release was considered by most to be the crowning blow that brought on the downfall of the PNM government, which had been in power for nearly 30 years. Despite his triumph, he lost out that year to David Rudder's "Bahia Gyal/The Hammer." Somewhat bitter (a 1987 calypso, "Sing Ram Bam," sarcastically refers to the "inane" lyrics of Rudder's "Bahia Gyal"), and further embattled by other career setbacks, he has nonetheless gone on to compose outstanding calypsos each year. Any album by Gypsy is recommended. —*Gene Scaramuzzo*

★ **The Action Too High** / 1986 / MRS Productions ✦✦✦✦✦
This classic features the aforementioned "The Sinking Ship." The title cut is also one of the most danceable commentaries ever written in soca style concerning the drug problem. —*Gene Scaramuzzo*

We Need More Love / 1987 / J&M ✦✦✦
This is one of the best albums from the sometimes uninspired second half of the '80s. Gypsy, who is consistently good and consistently underrated, devotes one side to party and topical lyrics. The title track is a tearaway, but a top cut is "Sing Ram Bam," which has a classic calypso melody and nice acid guitar punctuations. —*John Storm Roberts*

I Believe in You / 1990 / MRS Productions ✦✦✦
A true calypsonian who comments on the issues of the times, Gypsy sings on the previous year's incident, in which toilet paper was thrown at him during a live performance, and on the terrible new "Value Added Tax," in "No VAT." He boogies down in "Gimme the Thing." It's another great album. —*Gene Scaramuzzo*

Bad Behavior / 1992 / MRS Productions ✦✦✦
Here's another first-rate offering. —*Gene Scaramuzzo*

Kitch (Lord Kitchener)

Vocals / Party Soca, Social Commentary, Trinidad, Caribbean
Kitch is, along with the Mighty Sparrow, the most well-known of any calypsonian of T&T. With a career spanning over four decades, he has an extremely large catalog of annual releases, complicated further by an unknown number of anthologies and reissues. Amazingly, none are bad. Several anthologies of pre-soca-era material are listed below as starters, along with a handful of the best annual releases from the soca era, beginning with the early-'80s release, *Kitchener Goes Soca*, in which he dramatically demonstrated that he was more than capable of keeping abreast of any latest musical fashion. —*Gene Scaramuzzo*

Goes Soca / 1980 / Charlie's ✦✦✦
This was one of the first hit soca albums. —*J. Poet*

Kitchener Goes Soca / 1981 / Charlie's ✦✦✦
There is no denying that Kitch is the master here as he picks up the tempos and delivers some of the best soca tunes of the day. It includes "Soca Jean" and "Kitchener It Bon Down." —*Gene Scaramuzzo*

★ **Roots of Soca** / 1984 / Charlie's ✦✦✦✦✦
This album doesn't have a single second-rate song on it and was one of the high points of Carnival 1984. —*Gene Scaramuzzo*

Master at Work / 1985 / Kalico ✦✦✦✦✦
"Soca Misinterpretation" may very well be the best party song Kitch has written in the '80s, aided by a fantastic echoed mix courtesy of arranger Leston Paul. —*Gene Scaramuzzo*

The Grand Master / 1987 / B's ✦✦✦
It includes "Pan in A Minor," a huge hit among the steelbands in 1987 and more than enough reason to search out this album. —*Gene Scaramuzzo*

A Musical Excursion / 1990 / ✦✦✦
Though he shows occasional signs of his age in his latest, Kitchener is still in there swinging. The songs and singing style are pretty much as they were in his prime, though slightly hampered by high-energy, but overly predictable standard soca arrangements. —*John Storm Roberts, Original Music*

The Honey in Kitch / 1992 / MCA ✦✦✦
The popularity of "Bee's Melody" among the steelbands in 1992 may have even surpassed their enthusiasm in 1987 for Kitch's "Pan in A Minor." —*Gene Scaramuzzo*

Klassic Kitchener, Vol. 3 / 1994 / Ice ✦✦✦
Ironically, this set of early soca is the best of the Kitchener collections so far. First, it has all his major songs of the '70s, including the great "Pan in A Minor." Second it shows him contriving, like no other calypsonian of his generation, to move into the new idiom while keeping the freshness and variety of the old one. As a bonus, it's the only example extant of soca's early panache. —*John Storm Roberts, Original Music*

King of Calypso / Melodisc ✦✦✦✦✦
This collection from one of the pioneers of calypso reaches back to the hits of the '40s and early '50s for classics like "Black & White," "Life Begins at 40," and "Short Skirts." —*J. Poet*

Spicy Delight / Melodisc ✦✦✦
More early Kitch, it leans toward the bawdy tunes that first made him popular. —*J. Poet*

Longevity / JW Productions ✦✦✦
Unbelievably, "Mystery Band" from this LP was an even bigger success than "Bee's Melody" from 1992. —*Gene Scaramuzzo*

Still Escalating / JW Productions ✦✦✦
This LP came out early in a short carnival season during which there were very few early releases. It may explain why two otherwise average songs, "Earthquake" and "No Wuk for Carnival," were such big hits. —*Gene Scaramuzzo*

Klassic Kitchener / Ice ✦✦✦
A several-volume set, it includes high-quality versions of the original hit songs by Kitchener from the beginning of his career to the onset of the soca era in the late '70s. —*Gene Scaramuzzo*

Classic Carnival Hits / Ice ✦✦✦
Between them, Lord Kitchener and the Mighty Sparrow have written 18 road marches between 1956 and 1994. Nine of the ten written by Kitch are included on this wonderful collection. —*Gene Scaramuzzo*

Melody (Lord)

Vocals / Calypso, Trinidad, Caribbean
Another of the legends of calypso who died just at the end of the '80s. Responsible for many classic songs. —*Gene Scaramuzzo*

● **Through the Looking Glass** / 1960 / Cook ✦✦✦✦✦
Melody gained fortune, if not fame, by writing hits for Harry Belafonte, including "Momma Look at Boo Boo." This early-'60s album contains some of his biggest hits, including "Si Senior," an early Latin-influenced calypso, which Belafonte recast as "Sweetheart from Venezuela." —*J. Poet*

I Man / 1979 / Charlie's ✦✦✦
This was Melody's first crack at soca, just a year after Maestro and Shorty started the ball rolling. A classic, it still sounds great. —*Gene Scaramuzzo*

Lola / 1982 / B's ✦✦✦
A strong soca effort from 1982, it shows him rocking just as hard as the young turks. —*J. Poet*

Sparrow (Mighty) (Singer Francisco)

b. Jul. 9, 1935, Grandroy Bay, Grenada
Vocals / Calypso, Trinidad, Caribbean
Mighty Sparrow has been one of calypso's most popular performers since he began winning regional competitions in the mid-'50s. His jovial, ebullient style was applied to both the titillating romantic comedies that are calypso's staple diet, and more topical fare about regional politics, human rights, and Russian satellites. In the 1990s he enlisted the production skills of Eddy Grant for *Dancing Shoes*, and Grant's Ice label reissued many of his vintage sides. —*Richie Unterberger*

25th Anniversary / 1980 / Charlie's ✦✦✦✦✦
A double-record set released to celebrate 25 years of calypso classics, it features "Wanted: Dead or Alive," a worldwide pop hit later covered by the Manhattan Transfer. —*J. Poet*

The Greatest / 1983 / Charlie's ✦✦✦
There are no bad Sparrow records, but some are better than others,

including this masterpiece from 1983. It includes a critique of inflation, "Capitalism Gone Mad," as well as "Phillip My Dear," a nasty account of what "really" happened when that stranger crept into Queen Elizabeth's bedroom. —*J. Poet*

Vanessa / 1984 / B's ✦✦✦
The title track is an ode to the "nasty" Miss America, Vanessa Williams. —*J. Poet*

★ **King of the World** / 1984 / B's ✦✦✦✦✦
Included is the classic "Doh Back Back," a hopelessly infectious soca that brought Sparrow the Road March title. —*Gene Scaramuzzo*

Party Classics 1 & 2 / 1985 / Charlie's ✦✦✦
The aforementioned two volumes of '50s through '70s hits by Sparrow were redone in a soca style. Titles like "Jean & Dinah" and "Mr. Walker," which appear on *Volume I*, are surely known by most of the world. The biggest hit, though ("Congo Man"), was on *Volume 2*. —*Gene Scaramuzzo*

A Touch of Class / 1986 / B's ✦✦✦✦✦
Another classic, it includes "Coke Is Not It," "Ah Fraid De AIDS" and "Invade South Africa," all performed to killer soca beats. This is one of the most topical of Sparrow's '80s releases. —*Gene Scaramuzzo*

Hot Like Fire / 1992 / Rohit ✦✦✦
In a move that brought enough controversy to enliven conversations for the next year, Sparrow re-entered the Monarchy competition in 1992 with "Both of Them" from this album. He won, but that's another story. —*Gene Scaramuzzo*

● **Vol. 1** / Ice ✦✦✦✦✦
Well, yes, of course, it's run-don't-walk time. This baker's dozen of songs revealed Sparrow as the greatest calypsonian of the post-WWII era, and arguably of all recorded time —"Jean and Dinah," "Sparrow Come Back Home" and "Obeah Wedding" are perhaps the biggest gems, but nothing here is less than a diamond of the purest ray serene. —*John Storm Roberts, Original Music*

Vol. 4 / 1994 / Ice ✦✦✦✦✦

Dancing Shoes / Ice ✦✦✦
An all-around good LP, it shines for "More the Merrier," which takes a jab at calypsonian Shorty for his holier-than-thou criticism of Sparrow's 1992 tale of debauchery, "Both of Them." —*Gene Scaramuzzo*

All in the Game / Charlie's ✦✦✦
Sparrow's latest is mixed. During the first two tracks the man tries to disguise himself as a purveyor of standard party-hearty. The last cut on side one brisks up with a tribute to his old adversary, Melody. Side two has a splendid French/creole double-entendre number and a call to "document pan" that are vintage Sparrow. If only somebody would put out a retrospective. —*John Storm Roberts, Original Music*

Machel Montano

Vocals / Party Soca, Social Commentary, Trinidad, Caribbean
The youngest calypsonian to ever reach the National Monarchy finals (in 1986 at the age of 11), Montano has consistently put out above average material. It wasn't until 1991 that he repeated the level of success of 1986, though, with "1st in De Party" and the repatriation sentiment of "Take Me Back." —*Gene Scaramuzzo*

● **Too Young to Soca?** / 1986 / Macho ✦✦✦✦✦
Montano was only 11 years old when he burst on the scene with this fine EP. —*J. Poet*

One Step Ahead / 1991 / Straker's ✦✦✦
This is probably his best since "Too Young . . . " —*Gene Scaramuzzo*

Obstinate (King)

Vocals / Party Soca, Social Commentary, Trinidad, Caribbean
One of Antigua's best calypsonians, a frequent winner of the Monarchy competition. —*Gene Scaramuzzo*

● **Obstinate** / 1987 / Greenbay ✦✦✦✦✦
Included are two uptempo party tunes, "Voyier y Montez" (in a zouk style) and "Jam Band Beat" (a Road March contender). —*Gene Scaramuzzo*

Murder With An Attitude / Charlo's ✦✦✦
The melodic, bubbling "Jumbie" from this LP proved to be a big hit for Obstinate. —*Gene Scaramuzzo*

Leston Paul

Vocals / Party Soca, Trinidad, Caribbean
One of just a handful of arrangers who are responsible for nearly the entire yearly crop of records coming out of T&T. Most years he releases an album that includes his versions of the songs from that year that he enjoyed the most. —*Gene Scaramuzzo*

● **Soca Invasion** / 1985 / B's ✦✦✦✦✦
Check the back of any soca album from the early '80s on and you're likely to find him credited with keyboards, drum programs, and arrangements. On this instrumental recording he introduces his version of several standards which include Arrow's "Tiny Winey," Merchant's "Rock It," and Crazy's "Socouyant." —*J. Poet*

Penguin

Vocals / Party Soca, Social Commentary, Trinidad, Caribbean
Penguin has consistently produced first-rate records during his career but has never repeated the level of popularity he enjoyed in the early '80s. —*Gene Scaramuzzo*

Touch It / 1984 / B's ✦✦✦✦✦
In 1984, with this album, he dominated the Road March competition with "Sorf Man" (although he lost out to Sparrow) and took the Monarchy crown with "We Livin' in Jail" and "Sorf Man." —*Gene Scaramuzzo*

Protector

Vocals / Soca, Party Soca, Social Commentary, Trinidad, Caribbean
Among the top of the list of underrated calypsonians, Protector has yet to release a bad record. He delivers plenty of good party soca but is also very skilled at social commentary (local and global) and has several times made it to the Monarchy finals. Any Protector album is recommended. —*Gene Scaramuzzo*

Simply Beautiful / 1985 / Charlie's ✦✦✦
This EP lives up to its name, featuring the killer "Spanish Party" and the slow, funky tale of unrequited love, "Charmaine." —*Gene Scaramuzzo*

Going Places / 1989 / Straker's ✦✦✦
Included is the excellent commentary on today's youth, "Young-Restless." —*Gene Scaramuzzo*

● **Total Protection** / 1990 / Straker's ✦✦✦✦✦
The superb "Crossover Sweet" is enough reason to look for this album, but the whole package is another fine offering from this talented calypsonian who is somewhat unknown outside T&T. —*Gene Scaramuzzo*

David Rudder

b. 1953
Vocals / World Fusion, Soca, Calypso, Trinidad, Caribbean
Rudder has become perhaps soca's most visible performer, and one of the few on a major American label. Rudder began singing in 1965 as a member of a group called the Solutions. He began heading his own group in 1970, doing pop and soul songs, then turned to soca in the late '70s, working with the great Kitchener before joining Charlie's Roots in 1980 as a replacement for lead vocalist Chris "Tambu" Herbert. Rudder finished third in the Road March competition for Carnival '85, then in 1986 became one of the few performers to win the Young King and Calypso Monarch titles. Rudder has gotten heavy criticism from calypso traditionalists for his incorporation of R&B, blues, funk, and rock elements into his soca compositions, but his popularity has increased to the point that he's appeared at international jazz and blues festivals as well as carnival and soca events. —*Ron Wynn*

★ **Haiti** / 1988 / Sire ✦✦✦✦✦
In terms of Road March power, 1988 was Rudder's finest moment, with "Bacchanal Woman" and the superb social commentary, "Panama." The title cut was a remarkable ode to Caribbean unity. Sire reissued this album with cuts from the previous two years under the same title, *Haiti*. —*Gene Scaramuzzo*

☆ **1990** / 1990 / Sire ✦✦✦✦✦
A concept album from the king of contemporary soca, it details the international struggle against racism with particular emphasis on South Africa. —*J. Poet*

Frenzy / 1992 / Lypsoland ✦✦✦
"Knock Them Down" and "Stiff Waist Man" were popular, but "De Long Time Band," with its unusual percussion and old-time sound, is a song that will long be remembered. —*Gene Scaramuzzo*

Ministry of Rhythm / Lypsoland ✦✦✦
A fine LP throughout, it features one of his biggest hits ever, a commentary on the state of affairs in T&T presented through the image of the steel band controversy of '92, "Dus' in Deh Face." The CD version includes a bonus rhythm track. —*Gene Scaramuzzo*

Shadow

Bass / Soca, Party Soca, Social Commentary, Trinidad, Caribbean
There are many calypso lovers who await Shadow's annual release more than that of any other calypsonian. Like Stalin and just a handful of others, Shadow is a totally unique calypsonian; there is no other like Shadow. Since 1974 and his landmark composition "De Bassman," he has never failed to deliver some of the toughest basslines, most infec-

tious grooves, and most original compositions of anyone in the Caribbean. On top of all this, he has a low, authoritative voice that lends an air of truth and finality to all he sings. His social and political commentaries are delivered in such a clever way (and propelled as they are by his unique soca beat) that the messages often sink in subliminally, a testimony to his unique lyrical skills. With this in mind, how does one narrow down his nearly 20 records to a handful of recommendations? —*Gene Scaramuzzo*

De Bassman / 1974 / ✦✦✦✦✦
This legendary album brought Shadow to fame. —*Gene Scaramuzzo*

If I Coulda I Woulda I Shoulda / 1979 / Charlie's ✦✦✦
A particularly outstanding album from this era of Shadow's career, it features a raw sound worth hearing and is quite different from the Shadow of today. —*Gene Scaramuzzo*

Return of De Bassman / 1984 / Straker's ✦✦✦
This is the end of an era for a particular raw sound to Shadow's music. As always, there's a killer mix of hits like "More Music," "Snakes," and the title cut. —*Gene Scaramuzzo*

High Tension / 1988 / Straker's ✦✦✦✦✦
This represents the epitome of Shadow's late-'80s recorded output. "Tension" was a killer in the Road March arena, yet was in serious competition with two other songs from this same album, "Bad Boy Peter" and "Garden Want Water" (with sexual tension in all three). "Crazy Computer" was a favorite in the tents, giving Shadow four hit songs in one year. —*Gene Scaramuzzo*

★ **Columbus Lied** / 1991 / Shanachie ✦✦✦✦✦
Shadow is one of the few calypsonians who has been anthologized on an American label. This recent release presents eight of the best of his songs from 1988 through 1990, a landmark period in his career. —*Gene Scaramuzzo*

Winston Bailey Is the Shadow / 1992 / Kisskidee ✦✦✦
There is a decidedly different approach on this album. Only one song, "Hard Head," was Road March bound. Neither "Soucouyant," the superb commentary on AIDS, nor the late-bloomer "Music" (aka "Dingolay") were typical uptempo grooves, showing that Shadow can hit no matter how far he strays from formula. —*Gene Scaramuzzo*

Moods of the Shadow / Kisskiddee ✦✦✦
It's hard to single out any one song as the best on this LP, which delivers outstanding soca, reggae, and funk. —*Gene Scaramuzzo*

Dingolay / Kisskiddee ✦✦✦
"(Pak Pak) Pay de Devil" and the rapso "Poverty Is Hell" were the two most popular songs of Carnival 1994. Shadow's exclusion from the Calypso Monarchy Finals was the scandal of the year. —*Gene Scaramuzzo*

Shandileer (brass band)

Party Soca, Trinidad, Caribbean
A T&T brass band that consistently produces party hits, although some years the songs tend to sound alike. You can't go wrong with their releases. —*Gene Scaramuzzo*

● **Happy** / 1988 / ✦✦✦✦✦
It was a serious Road March contender in 1988. —*Gene Scaramuzzo*

Do What You Want / 1991 / Sorrell ✦✦✦
Another highlight in their bid for Road March, it includes "Do What You Want" and "We Pushin'." —*Gene Scaramuzzo*

De Pong/The Donkey Dance / Sorrel ✦✦✦
Although the lesser of the two donkey songs for 1993, this one certainly added fever to "doin' the donkey." —*Gene Scaramuzzo*

Shorty (Lord)

Vocals / Soca, Social Commentary, Trinidad, Caribbean
The founding father of soca music who, along with Maestro, brought a new image to calypso at the end of the '70's, and he still occasionally releases records as Ras Shorty I. He became involved in the jam and wine controversy of '92 which made him the butt of Sparrow's '93 calypso, "The More the Merrier." —*Gene Scaramuzzo*

● **Soca Explosion** / 1978 / Charlie's ✦✦✦✦✦
This is the ultimate classic. —*Gene Scaramuzzo*

Collection / 1985 / Carotte ✦✦✦
This wonderful anthology covers Shorty's scandalous early career of extremely suggestive calypsos, including a handful of cuts from *Soca Explosion*. The sound quality is rather poor, unfortunately. —*Gene Scaramuzzo*

Superblue

Hard Bop, Trinidad, Caribbean
Named after a Freddie Hubbard tune. All-star band led by trumpeted

arranger Don Sickler. Plays mainstream, post-bop blue note-type material. —*Michael G. Nastos*

★ **Superblue** / Apr. 1988 / Blue Note ✦✦✦✦✦
Top-flight octet includes Bobby Watson (alto sax), Roy Hargrove (trumpet), Mulgrew Miller (piano). This group should have gotten more mileage out of its fine 1989 release. —*Ron Wynn*

Superblue 2 / Apr. 24, 1989-Apr. 25, 1989 / Blue Note ✦✦✦
Nice followup with revamped personnel features Wallace Roney (trumpet), Ralph Moore (tenor sax), Rene Rosnes (piano), and holdovers Bobby Watson (alto sax), Don Sickler (trumpet, conductor) impressive. —*Ron Wynn*

Bacchanal Time / Ice ✦✦✦
Although the rest of the cuts are less exciting, the title cut ranks as the ultimate pastiche of commands, countdowns, and song hooks. —*Gene Scaramuzzo*

Flag Party / Ice ✦✦✦
The very late arrival of this disc for Carnival 1994 prevented Superblue from achieving his fourth consecutive Road March victory. In fact, in T&T this album was rush-released in a plain white sleeve under the subtitle "The Late but Great '94 Album." —*Gene Scaramuzzo*

Swallow

Vocals / Party Soca, Trinidad, Caribbean
Antigua's undisputed party master who pleases everyone from the Caribbean to NYC to Toronto with cowbell- and horn-driven soca. Talented beyond compare, able year after year to compose infectious hooks with catchy lyrics. There's not a bad release by Swallow throughout his long career. —*Gene Scaramuzzo*

Subway Jam, Pace Yourself / 1981 / Charlie's ✦✦✦
Swallow specializes in party jams, usually without any social or sexual message beyond "Have a good time." "Subway Jam," the title tune, is an all-time soca anthem. —*J. Poet*

Party in Space / 1983 / Charlie's ✦✦✦
The title track of this great party album has Sally Ride jammin' to the soca beat with her fellow astronauts and a sacerful of aliens. —*J. Poet*

● **First Take** / 1984 / Charlie's ✦✦✦✦✦
This one will leave you breathless; it includes "Flagwoman," "Town Mash Down," and "Satan Comin' Down." —*Gene Scaramuzzo*

Hit Man / 1987 / Charlie's ✦✦✦
This is one of the best albums from the second half of the '80s. Swallow's 1987 "Hit Man" is notable for a very fine kick-em-up about the Brooklyn carnival. —*John Storm Roberts*

☆ **Swallow on the Streets of Brooklyn** / 1988 / Charlie's ✦✦✦✦✦
"Fire in the Backseat" had everyone moving in 1988. —*Gene Scaramuzzo*

Steam / 1990 / Charlie's ✦✦✦
The title cut was another gem. —*Gene Scaramuzzo*

Tambu (Chris Herbert)

Conga, Vocals / Party Soca, Social Commentary, Trinidad, Caribbean
This Charlie's Roots singer began his solo career after fellow Charlie's Roots singer David Rudder's successful attempt in 1986. Tambu succeeded in capturing the Road March title three years in a row with basically the same song recycled, as well as making it to the Monarchy finals each of those years. Tambu is a good singer and, despite the fact that he recycles song ideas, capable of writing very catchy choruses. His pursuit of a music degree at Berklee has kept him out of the '92 through '94 T&T Carnivals. —*Gene Scaramuzzo*

● **Culture** / 1988 / Sire ✦✦✦✦✦
The title cut was somewhat of an anthem during Carnival 1988, calling for the preservation of T&T's unique cultural achievements like steelband, limbo, calypso, and East Indian tassa drumming, although it was "This Party Is It" that captured the Road March. —*Gene Scaramuzzo*

The Journey / 1989 / Lypsoland ✦✦✦
Road March number two was "Free Up" from this album. —*Gene Scaramuzzo*

The Cry / 1990 / Lypsoland ✦✦✦
"No No We Eh Going Home" and "Let's Do It" brought Tambu his third Road March victory and again brought him to the Monarchy finals. —*Gene Scaramuzzo*

Reach Out / 1991 / Lypsoland ✦✦✦
Ironically, "Rant and Rave" and "Not Me Is the Music" from this album were two of Tambu's better songs, but they were crushed in the Road March competition by Superblue's "Get Something & Wave." —*Gene Scaramuzzo*

Trinidad Collection

Big Drum Dance, Carriacou [West Indies] / Smithsonian/Folkways ✦✦✦
Very few musical traditions enjoy such thorough documentation as the Big Drum Dance of Carriacou. Recorded in the 1950s, this was the first album of Big Drum songs. It includes a wide variety of "nation" dances (thought to be songs from specific West African and West Central African ethnic groups) such as Cromanti (Carriacou's "first" nation), Moko, Congo, etc. It also includes Creole songs such as bongo, chiffond, manbongo, and hallecord. The notes are excellent except that none of the drummers or singers are identified. However, two of Carriacou's greatest performers of the 20th century are on this album: May Fortune sings as lead chantwell on "Congo." That selection probably has Sugar Adams (May Fortune's husband) playing the lead or cutter drummer. Sugar Adams sings in his western Sudanic style on "Chamba" and on "Bongo."
—*Don Hill*

Calypso Season / 1989 / Mango ✦✦✦✦✦
This is a fine collection full of unintended ironies. Most of it is in fact soca, balanced between names (Baron, Tambu, Sparrow) and unknowns (All Rounder). But there are two old-calypso cuts with acoustic guitar by Roaring Lion, and one by classic steelband the Desperados—and all three strike like a cool breeze in a crowded dancehall. Still and all, the soca cuts are just fine in their own affably shallow way. Whoever selected this lot had fine ears (pity Mango couldn't have spared the time or the bucks for at least some kind of notes, fer crine out loud). —*John Storm Roberts*

Calypsos from Trinidad / 1991 / Arhoolie ✦✦✦✦
A favorite CD of the classic 1930s calypso recordings, this stresses calypsos about the labor troubles in the Trinidadian oil fields in 1937. Many beautiful and poignant songs are included such as the Growling Tiger's "The Gold in Africa" (about Italy's invasion of Ethiopia), "Money Is King" (about the depression), Executor's "Shop Closing Ordinance," the Roaring Lion's "Bargee Pelauri," Atilla's "Commission's Report" (about a British report of the riot of the striking oil field workers), and Radio's "Sedition Law" (about the censorship of calypso). —*Don Hill*

Carnival Jump-Up / Feb. 1989 / Delos ✦✦✦✦✦
Anthology featuring various steel-bands from Trinidad and Tobago. All recordings were made on location, and it includes songs by Amoco Renegades, Carib Tokyo, Neal and Massy Trinidad All-Stars, etc. Sterling sound. —*Ron Wynn*

Double Entendre Soca / Rounder ✦✦✦✦✦
Soca rivals "slack" dancehall reggae and vintage "hokum" blues for great risque material. That's the theme linking the seven songs featured on this anthology. The CD includes sassy, suggestive hits from Shadow, Poser, and particularly Bally, whose "Gimme Piece" leaves absolutely nothing to the imagination. Each tune has catchy melodies and throbbing arrangements, showing soca's musical punch and hypnotic grooves. There aren't any weak links, and only limited distribution and publicity prevents soca from rivaling reggae as the prime Caribbean musical import. —*Ron Wynn*

Heart of Steel: Steelbands of T&T / Flying Fish ✦✦✦✦✦
Modern steelbands from Trinidad and Tobago. Little duplication with other anthologies, and it's also better produced. More instructive than inspirational. —*Ron Wynn*

☆ **Heat in de Place: Soca from Trinidad** / 1990 / Rounder ✦✦✦✦✦
A wonderful collection of modern soca tunes, with a good mix of topical and sociopolitical selections. —*Ron Wynn*

Jazz 'n' Steel from Trinidad & Tobago / Delos ✦✦✦✦✦
Another anthology, this one featuring the Rudy Smith Trio & Annise Hadeed Quartet. It features steelbands that combine improvisational flair and eclectic approach. —*Ron Wynn*

Pan Champs, Vol. 1 / Blue Rhythm ✦✦✦✦✦
This was drawn from a series of steelband cassettes issued in Trinidad, and recorded in the various Panyards just before Carnival. The first release has cuts from the Solo Harmonites, Phase II Pan Groove, Amoco Renegades (including a splendid "Pan in A Minor"), and Catelli Trinidad All Stars. The second has the Carib Tokyo All Stars and American Stores Exodus, as well as more from Phase II and Renegades. —*John Storm Roberts*

☆ **Pan Classics** / Blue Rhythm ✦✦✦✦✦
Literally! Augmented by piano from time to time, four of Trinidad's most popular steelbands play Handel, Johann Strauss, Vivaldi and even Wagner. Grandiose, but an authentic local phenomenon, and the groups here—Samaroo Jets, Solo Harmonites, Tropical Angel Harps, and Trinidad Cement Ltd Skiffle Bunch Steel Orchestra—are no flash-in-the-pan. —*Don Hill*

☆ **Rebel Soca: When the Time Comes** / Shanachie ✦✦✦✦✦
Unlike reggae, soca plays not a Messianic-rebellious role in Trinbago society, but a pragmatic reformist one. The three weakest tracks here seem attempts to justify a basically inappropriate concept. The rest, ranging from good to terrific, are from mainstream soca commentators from Stalin and Nelson to Ras Iley and Red Plastic Bay. —*John Storm Roberts*

☆ **Say What? Double Entendre Soca** / 1990 / Rounder ✦✦✦✦✦
Anthology featuring contemporary soca and calypso musicians from Trinidad who specialize in songs containing sexual innuendos and explicit/implicit messages. The roster includes Shadow, Bally, Monarch, Poser, etc. —*Ron Wynn*

Soca Music from Trin / 1990 / Rounder ✦✦✦✦✦
Outstanding numbers by seven contemporary calypsonians were spotlighted on this 1990 disc, one of two Rounder issues that year featuring various soca stars. Shadow took honors with a pair of selections, one the roaring "Tension," the other more humorous "Garden Want Water." Another sizzling tune was Singing Francine's "Soca Do That," as well as Johnny King's "Wet Me Down" and Bally's "Shaka Shaka," which now sounds lyrically dated, but retains a potent musical punch. —*Ron Wynn*

☆ **This Is Soca** / 1987 / Sire ✦✦✦✦✦
This two-record set makes for a fine introduction to soca/calypso. The first record is David Rudder's strong 1987 effort, while the second is a compilation of hits, including Stalin's "Burn Dem." —*J. Poet*

Trinidad 1912-1941 / Harlequin ✦✦✦✦✦
This is a mixed bag of enchanting music and cuts only a collector could love. Pretty much all—and all the best—material is instrumental, with gems ranging from charming Venezuelan-influenced string-band to a superb piano solo by George Cabral. The preceding spate of reissues has swept up most of the treasures already, though the Lion is on form. —*John Storm Roberts, Original Music*

Trinidad Carnival / 1989 / Delos ✦✦✦✦✦
Various steelbands recorded live at the 1989 Trinidad Carnival, issued on Delos' Caribbean subsidiary label. Fine sound. —*Ron Wynn*

Wind Your Waist / 1991 / Shanachie ✦✦✦✦✦
A fine selection of soca dance hits by Arrow, Shadow, and Kitch, it includes Tambu's 1987 anthem, "This Party Is It." —*J. Poet*

Champion Steelbands of Trinidad / Cook ✦✦✦
Early tuned-pan orchestras from Trinidad, including the Katzenjammers, the Highlanders, the Facinators, Ellie Manette's Invaders, and the Girl Pat Steelband. —*Don Hill*

Drums of Trinidad: Tribal Rhythms from Carriacou / Cook ✦✦✦
This album has six Carriacouan Big Drum rhythms on side two. They're called "rhythms" although the Spanish word "toque" better conveys the sense of rhythm since each toque evokes a particular mood or an ancestral spirit. These recordings were made at Beryl McBurnie's Little Carib Theatre in Port of Spain, Trinidad. The group consisted of six drummers, not the traditional three, and there is no guarantee that all the drummers are born Carriacouans. (Trinidad has a definable Carriacouan minority and in its own small way the music of Carriacou has effected the music of Trinidad and, of course, vice versa.) —*Don Hill*

Folk Music of Carriacou / Egrem ✦✦✦
The recordings were made by Cuban ethnomusicologists in 1982 and 1983. Side one contains Big Drum songs while side two has quadrille and string band selections (calypso, waltz, and parang or Christmas songs). Most performers are identified except Lucien Duncan on some of the Big Drum recordings made in Six Roads village. The notes are good but some of the titles of the selections are misidentified: for example, the Temne song is actually a Cromanti ("Kromantin"). —*Don Hill*

Tamboo-Bamboo, Bongo & the Belair / Cook ✦✦✦
This is just what the title suggests, traditional Afro-Trinidadian music. —*Don Hill*

The Big Drum & Other Ritual & Social Music of Carriacou / Folkways ✦✦✦
This contains four Big Drum songs as well as hymns, a ballad, and quadrille, and lancers dance music. There is wedding music, funeral music, and carnival music (including calypso, steelband, string band, and traditional speeches). The recordings were made in 1970 and 1971 and the album contains a short monograph, giving an overview of the culture and the social and seasonal context of the songs. Participants are recognized by name and are freely quoted or otherwise referenced in the monograph. —*Don Hill*

US Virgin Islands

Blinky & the Roadmasters

Caribbean, US Virgin Islands

Crucian Scratch Band Music / 1990 / Rounder ✦✦✦✦✦
Blinky & the Roadmasters offer a 1990s variation on the classic Crucian (St. Croix) style. They feature a frontline with two alto saxophonists interacting with an electric guitarist and banjo or ukelele player. The rhythm

section blends electric bass with congas and other percussion devices. The feel and sensibility, as well as the vocal arrangements and style, combine the floating flavor of classic calypso with the modern intensity and improvisational flavor of rock, plus Afro-Latin rhythmic elements. Such songs as "Ay Ay Ay" and "Labega's Carousel" have a folk wit and irony. Blinky & the Roadmasters are also an excellent musical unit, cohesive, funky and entertaining. —*Ron Wynn*

EUROPE

Albania Collection

Folk Music of Albania / Topic ✦✦✦
Sandwiched between Yugoslavia and Greece, part Christian and part Muslim, Albania is a tiny land with a rich and ancient musical culture. These are fine recordings by A.L. Lloyd of songs, dances, and instrumentals, among them bagpipe, flutes, and lutes. Given the country's beleaguered history, the vocals include many epic ballads, old and new. —*John Storm Roberts*

Vocal & Instrumental Polyphony / Chant du Monde ✦✦✦
An absolutely stunning recording, Albanian singing (unlike Bulgarian, which is gorgeous but in the South Slav mainstream) really is mysterious. Very ancient—it's thought to trace right back to ancient Illyria—and individual, though with Islamic elements and occasional reminders of the Epirot idiom of North Greece (all the examples here are from the south). —*John Storm Roberts*

Austria Collection

Lieder u. Jodler aus den Bergen / Koch International Corp. ✦✦✦✦✦
Alpine yodeling is one of humanity's most remarkable vocal techniques, and commercial "Jodlerlieder" are worthy of much more attention than they get. Some of the best stuff is on ill-documented collections like this one, which mixes some outstanding "Jodler" with pretty zither playing. —*John Storm Roberts*

Zauerli: Yodel of Appenzell / Auvidis ✦✦✦
This recording was done by Hugo Zemp. —*David L. Mayers*

Bulgaria

Mystère des Voix Bulgares

World Fusion, Bulgaria, Europe
The Mysterious Voices of Bulgaria belong to the National Radio and Television Chorus, the premier women's choir popularized worldwide through the efforts of ethnomusicologist Marcel Cellier. His recordings, issued on various import labels before appearing on Nonesuch, made a big splash in western Europe and the US, cultivating vast new audiences for the group's dramatic adaptations of folk singing styles. Their spine-chilling harmonies, punctuated by whoops and quavers, are presented in full choral arrangements and smaller groups—duos and trios—with and without instrumental backing. —*Myles Boisen*

★ **Le Mystère des Voix Bulgares** / Nonesuch ✦✦✦✦✦
The record that started the boom, this is an excellent introduction to the thrilling Bulgarian women's choir. —*Myles Boisen*

Le Mystère des Voix Bulgares, Vol. 3 / 1991 / PolyGram ✦✦✦
When the first volume in this series was released in 1975 it created a sensation, as Western European and North American audiences fell in love with the dazzling dissonant harmonies of the all-female Bulgarian State Radio And Television Choir. *Volume 2*, released in 1987, included pieces by other choirs, while *Volume 3* divides itself among four groups, including the original State Choir and the mesmerizing Trakia Choir. Bulgarian folk music, with its roots in Central Asia, heavily features diaphonic singing, a technique in which two voices (solo or choral) track each other in intervals that are both startling and enchanting to Western ears. Along with yodels, yelps and harmonies that shift back and forth between sweet consonance and bracing dissonance, the choirs produce an earthy style of vocal music full of power, passion and a strange beauty. While it may puzzle and challenge the mind, the body wakes up and the heart rejoices. —*Backroads Music/Heartbeats*

Cathedral Concert / 1994 / Polygram ✦✦✦✦✦

Ivo Papasov & His Orchestra

World Fusion, Bulgaria, Wedding, Europe
This very popular Bulgarian bandleader is a fierce clarinetist known for brilliant improvisations and blazing interpretations of all manner of Balkan melodies. His Bulgarian Wedding Band has caused a sensation, particularly among younger Bulgarians, with its blending of traditional music and high-octane Western rock, delivered at the upper limits of speed and volume. —*Myles Boisen*

Orpheus Ascending / 1989 / Hannibal ✦✦✦
An energetic debut of this thrilling Bulgarian clarinetist and wedding band leader. —*Myles Boisen*

★ **Balkanology** / 1991 / Hannibal ✦✦✦✦✦
This surpasses the *Orpheus Ascending* album on every count. Simply amazing. —*Myles Boisen*

Trio Bulgarka

The three female vocalists in the Trio Bulgarka—Yanka Rupkina, Styanka Boneva, and Eva Georgieva—have also performed and recorded with the Sofia Radio Choir, who can be heard on the famous series *Le Mystère des Voix Bulgeres* albums. The trio's performances, understandably, place considerably greater weight on the harmonic and solo vocal skills of each member. Several respected Bulgarian musicians accompany them on the tracks of their album, *The Forest Is Crying*, which was co-produced by Joe Boyd (producer of Fairport Convention and R.E.M.). The Trio Bulgarka are also a part of the group Balkana, have made well-received tours with the Radio Choir, and recorded a few tracks with rock singer Kate Bush. —*Richie Unterberger*

● **The Forest Is Crying** / 1988 / Hannibal ✦✦✦✦✦
With help from a half-dozen Bulgarian musicians (although there are occasional a cappella and solo tracks), the trio perform 18 traditional folk songs. The emotional vocals and astonishing harmonics will appeal to anyone who likes the more renowned *Le Mystère des Voix Bulgares* albums. The approach here may be sparser and have less elaborate vocal arrangements, but it's none the less powerful for that. —*Richie Unterberger*

Bulgaria Collection

Balkan: Mysterious Voices of Bulgaria / Virgin ✦✦✦✦✦
These film soundtrack recordings, mostly original music, offer a departure from the *Mystère des Voix Bulgares* repertoire. —*Myles Boisen*

Bulgarian Musical Folklore / Balkanton ✦✦✦✦✦
The Hungarians aside (most of the time), Eastern European record companies are vague to hopeless about distinguishing between genuine village music, more-or-less tarted-up People's Ensembles, and semi-folknik groups—which, of course, means that recordings like this are normally a very mixed bag. The balance on this particular CD is mostly tipped toward authenticity, and the variety is fine. There's some really super bagpipe and double-reed playing, and, though the singers are often a bit too professional, they all out-sing the overly hyped and wimpy Trio Bulgarka to a fare-thee-well. The notes are rotten on detail but somewhat informative in general. —*John Storm Roberts*

Bulgarian Village Singing . . . / 1990 / Rounder ✦✦✦✦
In *Bulgarian Village Singing—Two Girls Started to Sing*, the roots of the commercially acclaimed Bulgarian "mystery" vocals are explored in this field recording of harvest, wedding, and ritual songs of remote villages. A vibrant document of a vanishing musical form, it features extensive helpful liner notes. —*Bob Tarte*

Byelorussia / Auvidis ✦✦✦
This wonderful recording covers a relatively small area, but a particularly rich one. The extraordinary Slavic contrapuntal choral music is here in pure form, along with other songs, plus fiddle, pipe, and other instrumentals. —*John Storm Roberts*

Macedonian Songs & Dances / Nonesuch ✦✦✦✦✦
A nice variety of singing, from solo to choirs, from the Turkish-influenced region of Pirin-Macedonia. —*Myles Boisen*

Music of Bulgaria: Balkana / 1987 / Hannibal ✦✦✦✦
Ten of Bulgaria's leading professional musicians illustrate the breadth of Bulgarian traditional music. It includes the unmistakable vocal sound of Trio Bulgarka and the exhilarating flute-and-bagpipe romps of Traki-iskata Troika (the Thracian Trio). —*Bob Tarte*

☆ **Village & Folk Music of Bulgaria** / Nonesuch ✦✦✦✦✦
This combines two of the best Nonesuch collections into one unbeatable folk music document. —*Myles Boisen*

Village Music of Bulgaria . . . / 1968 / Nonesuch ✦✦✦
Recordings from four major Bulgarian regions, each with its own captivating style of singing and accompaniment, are featured on this album, *Village Music of Bulgaria—A Harvest, a Shepherd, a Bride*. This is the real thing. —*Myles Boisen*

Corsica Collection

Corsica: Religious Music . . . / 1989 / Auvidis ✦✦✦✦✦
Among the most neglected of idioms are the oral religious traditions of Europe, and particularly western Europe. *Corsica—Religious Music of the Oral Tradition* offers recordings of an ancient polyphonic church style from the remote village of Rusiu that are probably unique: certainly nothing is quite like them (some Sardinian singing is loosely sim-

ilar). The outstanding a cappella music is backed by outstanding notes. —*John Storm Roberts*

Czechoslovakia Collection

Czechoslovakia / Planett ✦✦✦
This is kind of a generic release, as you'll gather from the fact that it really has no discernible title. But the music is nice enough. What you get is a series of regional groups and singers that smack overmuch of your standard overarranged National Folk Ensemble but which contain some signs of local roots. Among them are some more-than-just-agreeable performances. It badly needs a few rude boors to give it more zip and vulgarity, but it's very amiable. —*John Storm Roberts*

Songs & Dances from Czechoslovakia / Argo ✦✦✦
With panpipes, fiddles, string orchestras, and vocals—interesting selection. —*David L. Mayers*

Estonia Collection

Folk Music of Estonia / Melodiya ✦✦✦
These two LPs are field recordings culled from material collected over almost half a century. They cover everything from signal-horns to dance groups variously involving fiddle, concertina, and the kannel zither, along with vocals in both the ancient runo-song and "new" melodic forms. The notes are in English, too. —*John Storm Roberts*

Finland

Konsta Jylha

Fiddle / Finland, Europe
Before his death, fiddler Jylha attained the status of a national icon for his folk compositions. Closely associated with the Kuastinen-based Folk Music Institute, Jylha recorded many fiddle classics, including perhaps his best-known piece, the "Konstan parempi valsi." Together with his band, he recorded *Purpurilimannit Finnish Folk Music, Vol. 1.* —*Leon Jackson*

Master Fiddler / Finnish Folk Music Institute ✦✦✦
Jylha became an icon of the Finnish folk revival. A fiddler whose groups also played popular music for village hops, he was both authentic and versatile. Side one is devoted to superlative traditional playing backed by accordion. Side two, a 1971 concert, has fine but more familiar playing. —*John Storm Roberts*

Eino Tulikari

Kantele / 1994 / Finnish Folk Music Institute ✦✦✦
Like the Alpine zither or the African finger-piano, the kantele zither—the "national instrument" of Finland—is a reminder that genuine rural traditions aren't all raunch and fireworks. Eino Tulikari was the greatest 20th-century kantele player, and this brilliant recording deserves a place in the world music Top 100 rather than the obscurity in which it languishes. —*John Storm Roberts, Original Music*

Varttina

Vocals / Finland
Varttina reflect a catchy and winning synthesis of tradition and innovation in Finnish folk circles. This all-female vocal quartet work mostly with distinct folk materials from the Russian borderlands, yet give them a novel twist. Varttina eschew not only the traditional folk costume of their predecessors, but also the traditional assumption that women should sing unaccompanied. With a strong instrumental backing group, Varttina give the folk materials a home-grown feminist twist. Starting out as a youth ensemble in the '80s, Varttina have coalesced behind leader Sari Kaarinen to become on Finland's best-selling folk groups. —*Leon Jackson*

● **Oi Dai** / 1994 / Green Linnet ✦✦✦✦✦
Once a 15-member chorus with pipes and girth to rival the Bulgarian women's choirs, this formerly traditionalist Finnish chorale slimmed to a four-woman brat-pack to deliver a bracing disc of speed-folk. Reportedly, one in every hundred people in Finland bought a copy when it was released in 1991. The nightmarish joy of bright, unison singing, and merry-go-round tempos pays off in surprising Finno-Ugric lyrics. Who would guess that the cheerful chipmunks of "Marilaulu" darkly fantasize, "The old hags nag with their jaws clanking. I should cut out their tongues and fill up their mouths with hot tin"? —*Bob Tarte*

Seleniko / Green Linnet ✦✦✦
A sassy, pop-smart disc produced by Hijaz Mustapha, in which the women tear through Ingrian rune chants, ancient wedding songs, and centuries-old village insults like there's no yesterday, twisting odd-metered 13/8 or 5/8 snips of history into maddeningly affecting jump-rope jingles. As defeated sounding violin, accordion, sax, even a tin whis-

tle burble along behind them, the four-headed, single-voiced mutant offspring of ABBA kicks its heels in a giddy blurring of the chaste and libidinous with results that often transcend novelty-act status. —*Bob Tarte*

France Collection

☆ **Chansons de la Belle Époque** / Music Memoria ✦✦✦✦✦
France's Café concert style under its various names was as rooted in the urban working class as in English music hall, but it reached further into cafe society and produced international stars as the London music hall never did. Here are some great early moments—major stars like Yvette Guilbert and Mistinguett and huge hits like Bruant's original "Auprés de Ma Blonde," but mostly earlier and more obscure names like Paul Lack, who influenced Chevalier and Felix Mayol (a song about the *maxixe,* a Brazilian dance introduced at the same time as the tango but without the staying power). The notes are rotten. —*John Storm Roberts*

Greatest Classics of the Musette Waltz 1930-1945 / Frémeaux ✦✦✦✦✦
French musette accordion (with its very strong Italian roots) was until very recently a grossly neglected splendor of 20th century urban music. *Greatest Classics of the Musette Waltz 1930-1945* is a superb compilation— not surprisingly, since its artists were a mini-generation-and-a-half of giants: nine of them in all, from a vieille garde represented by Charles Péguri and Émile Vacher to the phenomenal Gus Viseur, who played musette with the best besides helping to create the accordion-jazz style called manouche. Gorgeous music, wonderful mastering, fine notes. —*John Storm Roberts*

Georgia (Republic)

Rustavi Choir

Georgian Choir, Georgia (Republic), Europe
The Rustavi Choir is an all-male vocal group, the best known of the many ensembles now active in the Georgian Republic (formerly USSR). Their traditional repertoire encompasses many Georgian regions and is largely polyphonic, with rich intertwining melodic lines and dramatic vocal effects. —*Myles Boisen*

● **Georgian Voices** / 1989 / Elektra/Nonesuch ✦✦✦✦✦
A soulful representation of the distinctive Georgian vocal chorus sound, it's similar to Bulgarian music, with a different sense of drama. —*Myles Boisen*

Georgia (Republic) Collection

Georgia 1 / Barenreiter Musicaphon ✦✦✦
Here is religious polyphonic music with surprising and strange harmonies: "yodeling." —*David L. Mayers*

Georgia Work Songs and Religious Songs / Ocora ✦✦✦
Georgia is home to ancient polyphonic traditions and an epicenter where ancient Asian and southern European cultures met. It has also benefited from considerable isolation: one amazing, hocketed piece here is sung only in one village. This is an essential and often eerily beautiful recording. —*David L. Mayers*

Greece

Sotiria Bellou

Vocals / Greece, Rembetiko, Europe
Bellou is best known for her collaboration with Vassilis Tsitsanis in the 1940s, when her incredible voice sung of tragic woes. —*Leon Jackson*

40 Sotiria Bellou / 1988 / Lyra ✦✦✦
Nineteen selections by this rembetika star commemorate her 40 years as a renowned singer. The sound is very good, so these must be recent, instead of vintage, recordings. Compared to her more impassioned early songs the material is a little on the light and delicate side, but even if this CD doesn't persuade you to make a marathon run to the bottom of a bottle of ouzo it's still a great rembetika without the scratches and grit. It is an important contribution to the small world of authentic Greek music on CD. —*Myles Boisen, Roots & Rhythm*

★ **Sotiria Bellou** / Margo ✦✦✦✦✦
Fourteen vintage recordings come from one of the most highly regarded female rembetiko singers. —*Roots & Rhythm*

Kalamatiana/Syrta

Greece, Europe
☆ **Kalamatiana/Syrta** / EMI India ✦✦✦✦✦
EMI's huge Demotic Anthology was a treasury and it's wonderful to see a CD version starting. These were not village recordings but very fine performances by professionals close to the roots, with traditional backings.

Among those splendidly present are singers Iota Lidia, Rosa Abatsi, Yoryos Nakos (superb, underrated), Papasideres, and clarinetists Karakostas and Malliaras. —*John Storm Roberts*

Iota Lidia

Greece, Europe

Mega Souxe / EMI India ✦✦✦✦✦
She was at her considerable peak in the urban music called laika and the country-based dimotika, which varied as much as anything in their instrumentation (bouzouki plus accordion equals laika, clarinet plus fiddle equals dimotika, in a justified oversimplification). The songs here, of whatever idiom, are gems of the point where Europe and the Middle East intersected. —*John Storm Roberts*

Iorgos Mangas

Clarinet, Vocals / Greece, Europe

Mangas is one of Greece's leading folk musicians. A professional wanderer, he divides his time between outdoor festivals and Athens nightclubs. —*Leon Jackson*

New Urban Greek Folk Music for Dancing & Listening / 1987 / Globestyle ✦✦✦
Incredible pop clarinetist. —*Myles Boisen*

● **Iorgos Mangas** / Globestyle ✦✦✦✦✦
Mangas is a fine clarinetist in the dimotiki tradition, which long since left the villages to play a role more like US country music. His first solo album is a fusion music with accordion from the urban laika style, various traditional instruments, electric guitar from the pop idiom, and rembetika touches. It's not a new mix, but this band does it well. —*John Storm Roberts*

Poly Panou

Greece, Europe

Mega Souxe / EMI India ✦✦✦✦✦
By Panou's time, the earlier styles of laika and dimotiki had coalesced into something mainstream but still very Greek. Panou arguably outsings Lidia by a hair on this superb CD. —*John Storm Roberts*

Bassiles Perpiniades

Greece, Rembetiko, Europe

Bassiles Perpiniades / Margo ✦✦✦✦✦
Fourteen selections by a bouzouki performer appear on the acclaimed Margo rembetiko series. —*Roots & Rhythm*

S. & N. Gatsos Xarchakos

Greece, Europe

Rembetiko / CBS ✦✦✦
The CD contains 13 of the songs issued on the Greek import two-LP set. This is excellent contemporary Greek music. —*Roots & Rhythm*

Y. & Y. Sarris Xintaris

Greece, Rembetiko, Europe

Songs from the "Dawn Song in the Minor" / Minos ✦✦✦
Contemporary rembetika from this Greek TV series features 23 selections by Tsisanis, Vamvakaris, and others, performed by modern ensemble. —*Myles Boisen, Roots & Rhythm*

Greece Collection

Clarinet Virtuosi of Greece / 1980 / Disques Cellier ✦✦✦
Traditional clarinet field recordings. —*Myles Boisen*

☆ **Folk Music of Greece** / Topic ✦✦✦✦✦
Rural Greek music is commonly divided into the Mountains and the Islands. This collection opens with a variety of mainland music, including some splendid clarinet as well as the usual impassioned and highly decorated vocals. The second side focuses on the very different styles of the Aegean Isles, stressing fiddle and lute as well as the ancient Balkan bagpipe. —*John Storm Roberts*

Greek Folk Dances / Monitor ✦✦✦
A series of recordings of various Greek dance ensembles, it has superb variety throughout the series. —*Myles Boisen*

☆ **Greek-Oriental Rembetika** / Arhoolie ✦✦✦✦✦
This is a wonderful introduction to one of the great 20th-century urban musics. Not only does it include both famous names (Papasideris and Abatsi, who are widely reissued elsewhere) and names otherwise entirely obscure, but it has excellent notes in English. It's even more important now that the Greek EMI recordings have become so hard to find. —*John Storm Roberts*

☆ **Rembetica** / Rounder ✦✦✦✦✦
This is a welcome collection, especially since the Folklyric LP is now history. There are some musical and conceptual cavils, but each is more than balanced by a strength. Some of the cuts are far from their singers' best, and the Papaioannis piece is plain unworthy. But there's a great deal of fine music from unfamiliar as well as familiar artists (including the first recorded bouzouki solo—check out the "Moonlight Sonata" piano!). —*John Storm Roberts*

Gypsy

Muzsikas (Marta Sebestyen)

Vocals / Ethnic, World Fusion, Gypsy, Hungary, Klezmer, Europe
The diminutive Marta Sebestyen is a giant of Hungarian music, leading the folk revival field and also experimenting with pop forms. Her strong and expressive voice is often backed by the Muzsikas, a young group who have revived interest in a number of Hungarian ethnic styles with their energetic, traditional performances. Marta also records with other folkloric ensembles such as Vujicsics. —*Myles Boisen*

★ **Prisoner's Song** / 1988 / Hannibal ✦✦✦✦✦
A dark and powerful statement of life in a Cold War climate is explored through traditional Hungarian songs and instruments. Marta Sebestyen's amazingly evocative voice connects with the medieval sound of the hurdy gurdy and the sting of Mihaly Sipos' Gypsy violin. —*Bob Tarte*

Blues for Transylvania / 1990 / Hannibal ✦✦✦
Their second domestic release, also with Sebestyen, is part celebration and part commemoration of a troubled history. This recording explores the traditional music of the Romanian region of Transylvania (taken from Hungary after World War I). Even the fast and furious songs have a meditative quality. This is another outstanding release from one of Europe's premier folk ensembles. —*Bob Tarte & Myles Boisen*

Marta Sebestyen with Muzsikas / Hannibal ✦✦✦✦✦
This lovely solo effort by the premier Hungarian singer again features her performing group Muzsikas. —*Myles Boisen*

Hungary

Vujicsics

Traditional Bluegrass, Hungary, Europe

★ **Vujicsics** / 1988 / Hannibal ✦✦✦✦✦
Stunning instrumental wizardry and undiluted Slavic songs from southern Hungary. *Vujicsics* features Marta Sebestyen and others. —*Myles Boisen*

Serbian Music from Southern Hungary / 1989 / Hannibal ✦✦✦
Serbian Music from Southern Hungary is another landmark recording of vibrant Hungarian music from the Hannibal label. Vujicsics is a traditional music ensemble with roots in the leading Hungarian conservatories, but they sure don't sound like a bunch of scholars—this collection of songs and dance tunes will have you whirling so fast you just might lose your borscht if you're not careful. Technically their repertoire is not Hungarian but Serbian, belonging to a distinct ethnographic area spanning Hungary and Yugoslavia, with a slightly crazed sound relying on rapid tempos and odd rhythms. The presence of singer Marta Sebestyen (also with Muzsikas) is a bonus—add this to your must-have list. Included are twelve selections for concertina, accordion, bass, clarinet, flute, violin, guitar, vocals, and more. —*Roots & Rhythm*

Hungary Collection

Gypsy Folk Songs / Quintana ✦✦✦
Despite its importance in Hungarian tradition, the music Gypsies play and sing for each other is much rarer on record than, say, Australian Aboriginal. Here are solo voices, and also some songs backed by remarkable guitar. None of it is professional, and much is less than polished, but it has all the emotional reality the tearoom czardas lack. By contrast, the notes are an outrage: titles in three languages and names of performers but zero other information. —*John Storm Roberts*

Hungarian Folk Music, Vol. 1 / Hungaraton ✦✦✦
Hungarian Folk Music from Szek is a collection on three LPs. Szek, in Transylvania, is now in Romania, but was Hungarian when this material was recorded in 1940. At the time it was remarkably isolated even by local standards, and its music was unknown when Laszlo Lajtha recorded it. These recordings give evidence of an extremely pure local idiom, where even the Gypsy musicians were influenced by the professionalized music of the cities. Some of the recordings were done in the local Hungarian Radio studio and are of much better quality than the field recordings of the time. A 60-page booklet gives background and specific notes, photos, and extensive transcriptions. —*John Storm Roberts*

Hungarian Folk Music, Vol. 2 / Hungaraton ✦✦✦
Hungarian Folk Music—Vol. 2 (The North) contains recordings from the northern Magyar tradition, made both in north Hungary and south Slovakia. Most are unaccompanied ballads, but there are also some very fine instrumental cuts, including small string groups, bagpipes, flute, and clarinet. There are 64 pages of notes with photos and transcriptions as part of this singularly handsome boxed set. —*John Storm Roberts*

Musique Populaire Hongroise, Ocora 54 / EMI ✦✦✦
A good selection with panpipes, *Musique Populaire Hongroise, Ocora 54. Rich and Varied Old Music-Songs, Music* is a very moving lamentation. (See also Romania.) —*David L. Mayers*

Italy Collection

The Bagpipe in Italy / Lyrichord ✦✦✦
Bagpipes, of course, are extraordinarily widespread throughout the world. But Italy, it's fair to say, is not one of the areas most buffs would identify as pipes heaven. Wrong, as this album licensed from the superb Italian Albatros collection reveals. Here are pipes small and pipes huge, mostly from the Mezzogiorno, but including two examples from the north and one from Zardinia. Also included are thorough photocopied notes, a big plus. —*John Storm Roberts*

Corsica: Chants Polyphoniques [Polyphonic Chants] / 1987 / Harmonia Mundi ✦✦✦✦✦
Highly ornamented religious and secular poetical chants come from a local group of singers (E Voce Di U Cumune—The Voice of the Community), most of whom do not read music, yet sing remarkably complex traditional styles with a raw, warm energy. Harmonies are often in ancient parallel fifths, in natural non-"trained" modal tuning, at times sliding into place with emotion. Sometimes several voices ornament together and a glorious chord emerges from the midst. This is truly moving and honest music. —*"Blue" Gene Tyranny*

☆ **Folk Music of Calabria** / Barenreiter Musicaphon ✦✦✦✦✦
The new Musicaphon CDs are all remarkable for the quality of their documentation (here, a 70-page English booklet is filled with photos as well as admirable text). This one is also the most remarkable so far for the quality of its material. Italian traditional music, with its range of influences from French to Berber, is staggeringly rich and varied. That Calabria—the toe of the Italian boot—is as rich as any, the music here amply proves. Extraordinary bagpipe music, ancient and magnificent polyphonic singing, accordion, shepherd's pipe, on and stunningly on. —*John Storm Roberts*

Italian Folk Music, Vol. 1 / Smithsonian/Folkways ✦✦✦
Italian Folk Music—Vol. 1 (Piedmont, Emelia, Lombardy) features nice songs and small instrumental ensembles with clarinets, and accordion. —*David L. Mayers*

Polyphonies of Sardinia / Chant du Monde ✦✦✦✦✦
If Italian traditional music is the richest in western Europe, Sardinian is some of the most extraordinary, mingled with Arabic and ancient Berber as well as mainland influences. Except for one track, the music here is an amazing four-voice a cappella polyphonic idiom with an improvising lead on a two-voice bass of extraordinary deep vocalizations unlike anything heard from Europe or the Mediterranean. The last track is a more orthodox song to guitar and jaw-harp. The effect of this interpolation is a little odd: one could use either more variety or a total concentration on the one form. —*John Storm Roberts*

Sicily / Argo ✦✦✦
These selections are short but there's a great variety of folk music, some surprising and raucous, some plaintive and charming. —*David L. Mayers*

Norway

Mari Boine Persen

Drums, Vocals / Norwegian, Europe
Lead vocalist for a band that shares her name, Mari Boine has become the spokeswoman for the music and culture of the Sami: inhabitants of the Laplands of northern Scandanavia. Representing a distinct and indigenous culture, Sami music is composed of aphoristic song phrases known as "joiks." Brief and compelling, the joiks convey a holistic world view in which humans live in harmony with their environment. Joiks are thus sacred as well as secular entertainment and play a part in community rituals. With her group, Mari Boine has fused Sami music with African drum beats and electronic backing to produce a sound that is politically engaged, environmentally aware, and spiritually vibrant. —*Leon Jackson*

★ **Gula Gula** / 1989 / Real World ✦✦✦✦✦
Gula Gula means "Hear the Voices of the Foremothers," and many of the songs here are reflective of an oppressed woman's rage and determination to succeed. Titles include "Vilges Suola" (or "White Thief"), "Balu

Badjel Go Vuoittan" (or "When I Win Against Fear"), "Eadnan Ba'kti" (or "To Woman"), and "Oppskrift for Herrefolk" (or "Recipe for a Master Race"). Sung in Sa'mi, with English translations, the label is Peter Gabriel's, designed to promote world music. —*Ladyslipper*

Norway Collection

Nordisk Sang / 1991 / New Albion ✦✦✦
A collection of starkly beautiful Norwegian songs that blends the ancient hardingfele violin and an eschatological synthesizer on the same disc without a bump, thanks to the unnerving clarity of solo vocals in a class with the Latvian Dzintars and Bulgarian mystere recordings. Bottomless as a mountain lake, Pernille Anker's amazingly flutelike voice on "Bla Tonar Fra Lom" is matched by Kirsten Braten Berg's dark gift of narrative on the runic "Heiemo Og Nykkjen." Besides Hans Brimi's violin, Irish-plaintive one moment, Gypsy-fierce the next, skyblown reeds and keyboards inhabit 19 sparse, mostly traditional compositions. —*Bob Tarte*

Nordic Folk Instruments / Caprice ✦✦✦
The Nordic countries are—by northern European standards—remarkably rich in instrumental music. No fewer than 24 instruments, indigenous and naturalized, are presented in this admirable album, from the simple birchbark through flutes, fiddles, zithers, to accordions and guitar. A lavish illustrated booklet has an English translation. —*John Storm Roberts*

Portugal

Francisco Fialho
....

Portugal, Europe
● **Best of Fado** / Arc ✦✦✦✦
It isn't that, of course, but Fialho is a really fine singer in the somewhat starker Coimbra vein, and the duo backing (Alfredo Marceneiro and Fernando Farinha) are also right on the money. Included are lots of saudade and all the fixings, in fact. —*John Storm Roberts*

Fernanda Maria
....

Portugal, Europe
Fado . . . Fados! / Arion ✦✦✦
One of the younger artists in the pure Lisbon fado vein, Fernanda Maria adds to the traditional saudade a predilection for more uptempo numbers, sometimes accompanied by accordion and/or triangle as well as the classic guitars of fado itself. Ever less Lisbon fado being available, this is one to celebrate. —*John Storm Roberts*

Carlos Paredes
....

Guitar / Instrumental, Portugal, Europe, Bluegrass
The Portuguese guitar is a 12-string instrument with double courses (string pairs) and a small body, similar in tone to the mandolin or Greek bouzouki. Its penetrating sound is championed by Carlos Paredes, a sensitive, even shy performer who balances tradition and spontaneous invention. His original approach was likened to the freshness of Ornette Coleman by bassist Charlie Haden, who is himself a minor cultural hero in Portugal. —*Myles Boisen*

● **Dialogues** / 1990 / Antilles ✦✦✦✦
This collaboration with jazz bassist Charlie Haden is a marvel of sensitive string playing. —*Myles Boisen*

Guitarra Portuguesa / Mar. 1990 / Elektra/Nonesuch ✦✦✦
The old-fashioned crystalline beauty of this instrument has made Paredes an overnight sensation. —*Myles Boisen*

Fernando Machado Soares
....

Guitar, Vocals / Portugal, Europe
● **The Fado of Coimbra** / 1994 / Auvidis Ethnic ✦✦✦✦✦
Coimbra fado, an idiom as obscure and as splendid as any in Europe (and for centuries, the heritage of that city's university students), has a pure and impassioned classicism unique in my experience. Vocals and guitar backings are ravishing beyond power to describe. The fact that a handful of examples have begun to appear after years of drought is perhaps a proof of salvation by works. —*John Storm Roberts, Original Music*

Coimbra Fado / Ocora ✦✦✦
Coimbra fado, for centuries the heritage of that city's university students, has a pure and impassioned classicism that is unique. Vocals and guitar backings are both ravishing beyond power to describe or even suggest. The fact that this is the only example available is proof of the doctrine of the Cosmic Fall. —*John Storm Roberts*

Portugal Collection

Anthology of Portuguese Music / Smithsonian/Folkways ✦✦✦
Nice, simple, and heartfelt songs are sung by various women, as well as instrumental music. —*David L. Mayers*

Romanian Collection

Reflections of Romania . . . / Nonesuch ✦✦✦✦✦
Reflections of Romania combines the best this musically rich country has to offer—rough Gypsy peasant songs contrasted with polished ensemble work. —*Myles Boisen*

Russia

Valia & Aliocha Dimitrievitch

Russia, Europe

The Russian Gypsies / Disc AZ ✦✦✦✦✦
Russian Gypsy music—12 by Valia and Aliocha, and eight from the Matrioschka Ensemble. —*Roots & Rhythm*

Alem Kassimov

Russia, Europe

● **Azerbaijan Mugams** / Melodiya ✦✦✦✦✦
Although it was a Soviet republic, the music of Azerbaijan has a strong Middle Eastern sound related to neighboring Turkey and Iran. This album presents the tremendously powerful and acrobatic singer Alim Gasymov in front of a traditional three-piece ensemble, doing two side-long "mugam" suites. —*Myles Boisen, Roots & Rhythm*

Two Mugam / Inedit ✦✦✦
Azeri art music is one of the lesser known of major idioms within the Mideastern/Islamic tradition. Of the two mugam (loosely, modes) for tar lute, spike fiddle, and daf frame drum performed here, the 51-minute "Mugam rast" is overwhelmingly the major work with its 19 vocal and instrumental sections. An excellent performance, it is a fine recording with passable notes. —*John Storm Roberts*

Russia Collection

Journey to the USSR / Chant du Monde ✦✦✦
Unparalleled in their scope, the six CDs in this collection cover both instrumental and vocal music in, respectively (and at times illogically), Russia, Ukraine, and Bielorussia; Uzbekistan; Kirghizistan, Azerbaijan, and Turmenistan; North Caucasus; the Volga/Urals region; and Siberia. The musical range is just as wide: from wonderful, authentic music to the kind of pseudo-folk ensemble ruined by unsuitable arrangements from some party hack of a third-rate composer. It's worth it, though, for the good stuff. —*John Storm Roberts*

Music of the Tundra & Taiga / Inedit ✦✦✦
A rare collection of the music of Russian Asian groups, bordering on Mongolia: notably the Burait, but also Tungus, Yakuts, Nenets, and Nganasans. Some of the vocal styles are extremely impressive, but the most extraordinary cuts are of jaw-harp playing, almost a parody of electronic music. This has been a very elusive release, but one hopes less so in the future. —*John Storm Roberts*

Women's Songs from Old Russia / Inedit ✦✦✦
These songs are, in fact, from the women's choirs of three villages, one in the far north, a second a little south of Moscow, and the third (settled by exiles) near Lake Baikal. As obvious as the common roots of this ancient idiom are the differences between the three groups. But, whatever the level of complexity, all are grassroots versions of the great Slavic choral sound. —*John Storm Roberts*

Serbia Collection

Serbia: Pastoral Dances and Melodies / Auvidis ✦✦✦✦✦
A splendid recording of non-vocal music recorded in the '70s, it is divided by instrument: violin trio, bagpipes small and large, ditto flutes, and one of those irresistible local brass bands—a very fine one, both lyrical and marginally comic. The notes are very thorough (sometimes to the point of irrelevance), the recording quality is remarkable by any standards, but the music is simply superlative. —*John Storm Roberts*

Slavic Collection

Eastern Carpathian Traditional Music / Quintana ✦✦✦
These recordings made in Ukrainian areas that were once part of Hungary have the strengths and weaknesses of a seriously imperiled tradition. The music (including Gypsy and Jewish material) is enormously rare. The performances are sometimes limited, though some of the instrumentals are charming. —*John Storm Roberts*

Spain

Paco de Lucia

Guitar / World Fusion, Flamenco, Contemporary Flamenco, Spain, Europe

One of the leading flamenco guitarists of the late 20th century, Paco de Lucia was born in Algeciras, began to study guitar at the age of 12, and at 14 won first prize in a major flamenco competition. He achieved national status with the release of his *Entre Dos Aguas* in 1974. De Lucia was greatly inspired by a trip to Brazil and upon his return began a series of innovative developments in flamenco guitar style, based on new rhythms derived from the bossa nova. In addition to leading his own sextet, de Lucia enjoyed a long and creative partnership with leading flamenco singer, El Camaron de la Isla. Other musicians with whom he has worked include Chick Corea, John McLaughlin, Al di Meola, and, in 1989, tenor Placido Domingo. —*Leon Jackson*

Fabulosa Guitarra De Paco De Lucia / 1984 / Verve ✦✦✦
Amazing solos and playing throughout. —*Ron Wynn*

Entre Dos Aguas / 1986 / Polydor ✦✦✦✦✦
Any and all of his albums have a great blend of traditional elements and virtuoso playing. —*Ron Wynn*

Solo Quiero Caminar / 1986 / Polydor ✦✦✦
Beautiful, wonderful playing. —*Ron Wynn*

★ **Sirocco** / 1987 / Polydor ✦✦✦✦✦
At times, flamenco phenomenon de Lucia has branched out into jazz, bossa nova, and Cuban mixes. Here, however, he plays essentially solo compositions based on pure flamenco, though with a virtuosity and reach that belong in a concert hall rather than in the traditional settings. —*John Storm Roberts*

☆ **Live . . . One Summer Night** / Polydor ✦✦✦✦✦
Ranges from sentimental to animated. —*Ron Wynn*

Gipsy Kings

World Fusion, Ethnic Fusion, Flamenco, Spain, Europe

The Gipsy Kings are largely responsible for bringing the joyful sounds of progressive pop-oriented flamenco, called *Sevillana* in Spain, to the world. The band started out in Arles, a village in southern France during the '70s when brothers Nicolas and Andre Reyes, the sons of renowned flamenco artist Jose Reyes, teamed up with their cousins Jacques, Maurice, and Tonino Baliardo, whose father is Manitas de Plata. They originally called themselves Los Reyes and started out as a gypsy band traveling about playing weddings, festivals, and in the streets. Because they lived so much like gypsies, the band adopted the name the Gipsy Kings. Later, they were hired to add color to posh parties in St. Tropez. Popularity did not come to Los Reyes right away and their first two albums attracted little notice. At this point the Gipsies played traditional, albeit passionate flamenco music punctuated by Tonino's precise guitar playing and Nicolas' exceptional voice. Though they had devoted fans, they still had yet to gain wider recognition until 1986 when they hooked up with visionary producer Claude Martinez, who could see that the Kings had the makings of a world-class band.

Thanks to Martinez, the Kings began to relax a bit and take on a more contemporary edge, combining their traditional songs with sounds from the Middle East, Latin America, North Africa, a hint of rock, and their inimitable joy. It was, in a music industry filled with flamenco purists who resisted any kind of change, a very daring move, and many felt the Gipsy Kings would fall flat and disappear. But the nay-sayers were wrong. In 1987, they released "Djobi Djoba" and "Bamboleo" on an independent label and scored two smash hits in France. Their success led them to sign with Sony Music and release their eponymous debut album later that year. Again, they had tremendous sales in France and then found their album was appearing on the Top Ten album charts in 12 European countries including England, which is traditionally unreceptive to international music. In the late '80s, the Gipsy Kings debuted in the US at a New York New Music Seminar. This led them to sign to Sony in America. In 1989, they were invited to perform at the inaugural ball for George Bush, but they chose to return home to rest and be with their families. Later that year, they held an SRO concert at the Royal Albert Hall, where the Gipsy Kings hobnobbed with some of the world's biggest pop stars, including Elton John and Eric Clapton. To top off their great year, the Kings' debut album spent 40 weeks on the US charts and went gold, becoming one of the few all-Spanish albums to do so. —*Sandra Brennan*

★ **Gipsy Kings** / Feb. 1988 / Elektra ✦✦✦✦✦
Their US debut is an especially dynamic introduction to the sound of the Spanish Gypsy ensemble. —*Myles Boisen*

Allegria / Jul. 1989 / Elektra ✦✦✦
This album features raw, early recordings from this Gypsy family. Very authentic. —*Myles Boisen*

Luna De Fuego / Aug. 1989 / Philips ✦✦✦
Both sides of this album run continuously as though in a live perfor-mance, but there is no audience apparent. What background noise there is sounds like group interaction and is not intrusive, rather it adds to the feeling of excitement and fiery authenticity. It is recommended for all those who like to dig a little deeper into "overnight successes," and for those who have any interest in flamenco and/or gypsy music. —*Roots & Rhythm*

Mosaique / Nov. 1989 / Elektra ✦✦✦
Less traditional than the first, this has some drums, synthesizer, and other pop music trappings. —*Myles Boisen*

Este Mundo / Jul. 1991 / Elektra ✦✦✦

Los Reyes / 1994 / FNA ✦✦✦

Love & Liberte / 1994 / Elektra/Nonesuch ✦✦✦✦✦

Greatest Hits / 1995 / Columbia ✦✦✦✦✦

Tierra Gitana / Feb. 27, 1996 / Nonesuch ✦✦✦

Best Of The Gipsy Kings / Nonesuch ✦✦✦✦

Prey / Simmons ✦✦✦

Pepe Habichuela

Guitar / Flamenco, Spain, Europe

A Mandeli / 1983 / Hannibal ✦✦✦✦✦
Guitarist Habichuela, born into a well-known flamenco clan in 1944, wears two hats. Under one, he is an eminent traditionally oriented gui-tarist. Under the other, he has recorded with Don Cherry and with North African musicians. Several tracks on this album are traditional: on others he works with electric bass, percussion, and even lute. Either way, he's dazzling. —*John Storm Roberts*

Ketama

Guitar / Flamenco, Worldbeat, Spain, Europe
Dubbed the exemplary musicians of the "New Spain," Ketama were the darlings of the Spanish media during the 1980s, with their "flameco cool" sound. Ketama was formed by members of two prominent gypsy families, the Carmonos and the Sotos, and took its name from a village in Morocco renowned for its hashish production. The brothers Carmona, their cousin Jose Miguel, and Jose Soto scored a decided hit with their 1987 album *Ketama* as well as with the follow-up, *Y Es Ke Me Kambiao Los Tiempos*. They have collaborated with the great Malian kora player, Toumani Diabate, and with British bass player Danny Thompson. —*Leon Jackson*

● **Ketama** / 1987 / Hannibal ✦✦✦✦✦
The funk-fusion-flamenco of Ketama is by now a very well-established style. To the Andalucian root, this young trio adds Cuban and vaguely disco touches, but also what sounds remarkably like Indian passages (presumably from lute, since there's no Indian instrument in the credits). The results are interesting but less than 100% successful—mostly because the flamenco underpinnings are hardly virtuosic. —*John Storm Roberts*

Pastora Pavón

b. 1890

Vocals / Flamenco, Spain, Europe
Doubtless the greatest female flamenco singer to have recorded, Pastora Pavón, or "the Girl of the Combs," was born to a gypsy family in Seville in 1890. Successful from her youth, she performed in Madrid, Seville, and Bilbao with such artists as Manuel Valle, Antonio Chacon, brother Tomas, and husband Pepe Pinto. —*John McCord, Roots & Rhythm*

Niña de los Peines, La / 1989 / Chant du Monde ✦✦✦✦✦
One of the greatest 20th-century artists in any style, Pastora Pavón—"The Girl with the Combs"—was largely ignored in Spain during her lifetime because she refused to make the compromises that led to the big time. If flamenco is one of the great popular idioms, she was its Bessie Smith or Umm Kulthum. —*John Storm Roberts*

Spain Collection

Basque Songs & Dances / Lyrichord ✦✦✦
These choral songs (music for flute and drums) are an unexpected sound from Spain. —*David L. Mayers*

Early Cante Flamenco (1934-1939) / Folk Lyric ✦✦✦
It includes the classic "La Niña de los Peines." These are historic record-ings. —*David L. Mayers*

Gypsy Folk Songs / Hungaraton ✦✦✦
Flamenco aside, genuine Gypsy music has not been much recorded, so this CD reissue of a wonderful—and long-vanished—double album is welcome indeed. This is Gypsy-to-Gypsy a cappella singing, as opposed to semi-pro village-hop, let alone Budapest-restaurant "Gypsy" groups.

European Music

As the small list here suggests (even allowing for the fact that Great Britain and Ireland are taken care of in the Celtic and British Isles section), the reaction against Euro-centrism can go too far. True, Eastern Europe has recently been "discov-ered," with much harrumphing from the marketing depart-ments, but even here the proportion of derivative to authentic is notably out of whack. But the traditional music of western Europe is not only extraordinarily varied (perhaps most star-tlingly so in the case of Italy), much of it comprises the other major root of New World styles of all kinds. Spain isn't so badly off, though the focus is exclusively on flamenco. Portugal is beginning to surface. Greece is beginning to take an interest in its roots. But the rest is — almost everywhere — silence. While there are plenty of revivalists, less than a dozen recordings of true traditional French singers ever existed and all but two are now deleted. Germany is not so badly off, thanks only to an active regional commercial industry: German ethnomusicolo-gists no sooner hatch than they fly south to Africa and beyond, like so many geese in winter. —*John Storm Roberts*

Particularly remarkable are examples with a specialized form of "dou-ble-bassing" mouth-music under a solo vocal. One-hundred minutes of music are enriched by a thorough booklet of notes. —*John Storm Rob-erts*

☆ **The Young Flamencos** / Nov. 22, 1991 / Hannibal ✦✦✦✦✦
Devoted to the various young fusion flamenco types: Pata Negra, Ket-ama, and some less-known groups. Purist buffs become hypertensive over this stuff. It is interesting, not necessarily good (most of the singing is plain weak), but then some really lousy performances form part of important stylistic change. —*John Storm Roberts*

Sweden

Filarfolket

Sweden, Europe

● **1980-1990** / Amalthea ✦✦✦✦
This 19-cut retrospective was taken from the eclectic unit's recordings on the Amalthea label. —*Roots & Rhythm*

Smuggel / Amalthea ✦✦✦
Filarfolket continue to use Swedish folk music as a starting point for their own blend of music. "Tuffepolskan," "Karnevalspolska," "Polska Lucumi," "Tartan," "Rockan," and others are included. —*Roots & Rhythm*

Sweden Collection

Suede/Norvege; Musique des vallées scandinaves / 1993 / Ocora ✦✦✦
An anthology of 31 short, pristinely recorded traditional tunes from the valleys of Sweden and Norway. Material ranges from ancient shepherd's songs, medieval ballads, and various dance and work songs, to intrigu-ing miniatures called stav or stev that immortalize quick snapshots of the daily grind. Most compositions are not unexpectedly stately and measured, including a delicate, staccato bagpipe performance by Per Gudmonson, who helped rescue this Norwegian instrument from histor-ical obscurity. Best of all are songs in the vein of "Gyris Anders Svit," whose wild 2+4+3 rhythm scheme and eccentric quarter-tone modali-ties bring pagan overtones closer to the surface than most other West European musics. —*Bob Tarte*

Switzerland Collection

Jüüzli: Muotatal Jodel / Chant du Monde ✦✦✦
This is one of the very few available recordings of the true mountain jodel (as opposed to commercial recordings of jodler, which are regional popular songs). As such, it is essential to a European collection. —*John Storm Roberts*

Ukraine Collection

Music of the Tatar People / Tangent ✦✦✦
This is music of both the Muslim majority and Orthodox minority of Tatars, mostly unaccompanied vocals (including remarkable duets and trios), but with examples of a local copper pipe, jaw harp, and violin. It is a remarkable documentation of one of the obscure frontiers between Europe and Asia that are home to so much superlative music. —*John Storm Roberts*

Ukraine / Auvidis ✦✦✦
Like just about all of the series, this reissue of the old UNESCO *Musical Atlas* (which was designed for non-academic listeners) has a fine balance of authenticity and variety. The multifarious splendors of Slavic choral singing are very well-represented, but there's also plenty of splendid instrumental work. —*John Storm Roberts*

Ukrainian-American Fiddle & Dance . . . / Folk Lyric ✦✦✦
Ukrainian-American Fiddle & Dance Music—1926-1934—Vol. 1 contains reissues of historic recordings. —*David L. Mayers*

Yugoslavia

Jova "Besir" Stojilkovic

Yugoslavia, Europe

Blow "Besir" Blow / 1988 / Globestyle ✦✦✦✦✦
True heavy metal music is delivered by Stojilkovic and his raucous brass band, Brass Orkestar. Incredibly dynamic performances of festival and wedding standards seem constantly on the verge of dissolving into chaos. —*Bob Tarte*

Yogoslavia Collection

Folk Music of Yugoslavia / Topic ✦✦✦
Given Yugoslavia's ethnic diversity and geographical position, the variety of its music is hardly surprising. Here is open-throated singing in the magnificent Slavonic choral style, decorated vocals of Balkan-Turkish ilk, ancient diaphonic duets, Gypsy songs, clarinet/violin duos, and solos for bagpipes, one-string fiddle, flute, and other ancient instruments—all of it superb. —*John Storm Roberts*

Islamic Ritual Music from Yugoslavia . . . / Philips ✦✦✦
Islamic Ritual Music from Yugoslavia—Zikr of the Rufai Brotherhood offers strange, ecstatic, trance-like music. —*David L. Mayers*

LATIN CONTINUUM

Argentina

Astor Piazzolla

b. 1921, d. Jul. 5, 1992
Accordion / Opera, Tango, Argentina, Latin Continuum
Often referred to as the originator of the "nuevo tango," Piazzolla was an Argentine visionary who endured the wrath of many of his countrymen for adapting their national dance to his own modern ends. A soulful and accomplished performer on the accordion-like bandoneon, Piazzolla's many recordings have placed him as a leading international composer. Besides his own hand-picked groups, he recorded with a mix of jazz and classical players in the US. —*Myles Boisen*

Sur / 1987 / Milan ✦✦✦
Despite battles with repressive governmental heads that eventually forced him into exile, Piazzolla's recordings enjoyed worldwide impact. *Sur* was among his final releases; he wrote it shortly after returning from exile as a score for a French air film titled *Sur*, blending short songs with involved orchestral works and even some rock and pop elements ("Dando del Tartamudo," for example). But like almost all his material, the CD's real appeal and beauty was hearing Piazzolla's evocative, lush bandoneon solos and the way they were incorporated into various arrangements and songs. —*Ron Wynn*

The New Tango / 1988 / Atlantic ✦✦✦✦✦
An interesting, uneven, but often lush and beautiful collaboration between tango master Piazzolla and vibist Gary Burton. Each went out of their way to accommodate the other, with the results being more complementary than challenging. Still, it yielded several enticing selections. —*Ron Wynn*

La Camorra: La Soledad de la Provocacion Apasiona / Mar. 1990 / American Clave/Pangaea ✦✦✦

★ **Tango: Zero Hour** / Apr. 23, 1992 / Pangaea ✦✦✦✦✦
Astor says it's his best—he's right. This is the perfect haunting, passionate recording from the master of the new tango, with his best group. —*Myles Boisen*

The Vienna Concert / Aug. 7, 1992 / Messidor ✦✦✦
The late Piazzolla's *nuevo tango* was one of the most remarkable musical fusions of the past 30 years: a combination of traditional tango rhythms, lyrical melodies, and 20th-century harmonies and compositional techniques. The result was bracing, incredibly dramatic music that managed to be intensely romantic without lapsing into sentimentality. There was nothing else quite like it. Astor Piazzolla left a legacy of remarkable recordings: one of the best was this 1983 Vienna Opera House concert. —*Roundup Newsletter*

The Late Masterpieces / 1993 / American Clave ✦✦✦✦✦
Few musicians have ever remained so identified with a singular style, yet made as many innovations within it as Astor Piazzolla. Piazzolla experimented with jazz, rock, and pop themes, recorded with Gary Burton and Kip Hanrahan, varied tango's harmonic options, and expanded its melodic sources. He was a brilliant bandoneon player, getting from the extremely restrictive four-keyboard instrument new tones, phrases, and lines that had not even been considered, let alone executed. American Clave's three-disc retrospective covering Piazzolla's entire label work merits its title; the opening volume alone, *Tango: Zero Hour*, reaffirms it. —*Ron Wynn*

Rough Dancer & the Cyclical Night / 1993 / American Clave/Pangaea ✦✦✦
Along with *Tango: Zero Hour*, this is one of his crowning achievements, nostalgic yet uncompromisingly modern. —*Myles Boisen*

The Lausanne Concert / Jul. 13, 1993 / Milan ✦✦✦
Piazzolla was nearing the end of his distinguished career when he performed this concert in Switzerland in 1989; he divided it between playing classic material and debuting compositions. The first half was devoted to songs from the '50s to the late '80s, while the second portion featured new material titled "Tango Nuevo, Nuevo." Each section was marked by swaying, hypnotic bandoneon solos with full lines, elegant melodies and romantic passages. This wasn't issued until a year after Piazzolla's death; it's a wonderful reminder of his greatness. —*Ron Wynn*

Bandoneon Sinfonico / 1996 / Milan ✦✦✦
Bandoneon Sinfonico documents a concert Astor Piazzolla gave in July of 1990, where the the godfather of tango gave a standard performance of his repertoire and was supported by the Athens Colours Orchestra and conductor Manos Hidjidakis. What makes the concert notable is that it happened to be the last concert Piazzolla ever gave, so it is a special release for diehard fans, and even casual listeners will be surprised by how vital Piazzolla sounds toward the end of his career. —*Thom Owens*

Concierto para Bandoneon / Nonesuch ✦✦✦
This recording with a classical orchestra is Piazzolla's apotheosis. For years he has been turning a dance form into an art music. Here he essentially crosses into the regional conservatory style called national music. —*John Storm Roberts*

Love Tanguedia / WEA Latina ✦✦✦
Featured are highlights from Piazzolla's work on two films, *South* and *Enrico IV*. An interesting fusion of tango, classical, jazz, and pop, it includes "Tanguedia III." —*Roundup Newsletter*

New Tango / Atlantic ✦✦✦
Astor paired with jazz vibraphonist Gary Burton on this beautiful, if not representative, recording. —*Myles Boisen*

Five Tango Sensations / Elektra ✦✦✦
Contemporary tangos with the Kronos Quartet which are surprisingly well-suited the modern string-quartet format. —*Myles Boisen*

Tango del Angel / Sonodisc ✦✦✦✦✦
South Americans have never been afraid of string sections, as both Piazzolla and Brazil's Antonio Jobim attest. Many cuts on this compilation show off the king of nuevo tango's delight in romantic, and even lush, string writing. Others feature his Quinteto Nuevo Tiempo. Relatively rare for Piazzolla, some tracks also contain vocals, by Jorge Sobral. —*John Storm Roberts, Original Music*

Live / American Clave ✦✦✦
This is a concert by the guru of New Tango, recorded in Vienna in 1983. The repertoire includes three of his favorite pieces, "Verano Porteno," "Invierno Porteno," and his unofficial signature tune, "Libertango." Piazzolla is at his best working, as he does here, with a quintet and thus free of the temptation to pop-neo-classical string-writing, which has sometimes led him into areas perilously close to film-soundtracks (Piazzolla was the first choice for the *Last Tango in Paris* soundtrack). —*John Storm Roberts, Original Music*

Bolivia Collection

Instruments and Music of Bolivia / Smithsonian/Folkways ✦✦✦
Raucous, strong, sometimes discordant music, it still has great dignity and charm. —*David L. Mayers*

Brazil

Alcione

b. 1947, Sao Luis, Maranhao
Vocals / Brazil, Latin Continuum
A former schoolteacher from the northern state of Maranhao, Alcione Nazar is strongly identified with samba but excels at regional styles and ballads as well. —*Terri Hinte*

Fogo da Vida / RCA ✦✦✦✦✦
Afro-Brazilian singer Alcione is more of a belter than most Brazilian women vocalists, and solidly rooted in the carnival sambas de enredo. It's no coincidence that the solo instrument often chosen to balance her in this fine recent release is a trombone: of all her contemporaries, she's the nearest thing to The Big Mamas of Black US music. —*John Storm Roberts, Original Music*

● **Personalidade** / Philips ✦✦✦✦✦
An exciting sampling of her work, it includes "Etelvina Minha Nega" (composed by her father Joao Carlos), the dreamy ballad "Amantes da Noite," and the anthemic "Nao Deixe o Samba Morrer." —*Terri Hinte*

Leny Andrade

Vocals / Samba, Brazil, Latin Continuum
A carioca (native of Rio de Janeiro), Andrade has been called Brazil's First Lady of Jazz, but she is a masterful interpreter of the great Brazilian composers, classic and contemporary. —*Terri Hinte*

● **Cartola 80 Años** / 1987 / Pandisc ✦✦✦✦✦
In this 1987 recording, Andrade's husky contralto and the beautiful songs of the samba composer Cartola make an inspired pairing. The arrangement on this album was done by keyboardist Gilson Peranzzetta. —*Terri Hinte*

Roberto Baden-Powell
(de Aquino, Roberto Baden-Powell)

b. Aug. 6, 1936, New York, NY, **d.** Aug. 1, 1966, New York, NY
Guitar / World Fusion, Brazil, Latin Continuum
Among Brazil's finest, most expressive guitarists, perhaps the strongest rhythmic player to emerge from the blend of Iberian baroque and West African/Latin influences. Powell's albums have had authenticity, beauty, and transcendent elegance, and he's demonstrated complete command of guitar and knowledge of jazz, flamenco, and classical genres. —*Ron Wynn*

Tristeza on Guitar / Jun. 1, 1966-Jun. 2, 1966 / Verve ✦✦✦
A superb Brazilian guitarist and a superb jazz album without the usual pop trappings. —*Myles Boisen*

● **Solitude on Guitar** / Dec. 10, 1971-Dec. 11, 1971 / Columbia ✦✦✦✦✦

The Frankfurt Opera Concert 1975 / May 1975 / Tropical Music ✦✦✦
Baden-Powell, a renowned guitarist in a nation of guitarists, here plays both solo and in trio, and which you prefer will depend on whether you more value rhapsodic freedom or focused tightness. Either way this is a celebrated recording by a phenomenal artist, and long unavailable. —*John Storm Roberts, Original Music*

Estudos / 1975 / Verve ✦✦✦
Beautiful, expressionistic playing from a Latin player. —*Ron Wynn*

Jorge Ben

b. 1940
Guitar, Vocals / Samba, Brazil, Latin Continuum
Born in 1940, this carioca singer and guitarist devised an ingenious synthesis of samba and pop rhythms that helped earn him many worldwide hits, notably the oft-covered "Mas Que Nada." —*Terri Hinte*

Benjor / 1990 / WEA Latina ✦✦✦
Ben's most recent outing lacks the punch of his Brazilian-label releases. —*Ron Wynn*

★ **Personalidade (Best of Brazil)** / Feb. 5, 1991 / Verve ✦✦✦✦✦
Truly a best-of collection, it includes "Mas Que Nada," "Pais Tropical," "Oba, L Vem Ela," and "Taj Mahal," which years later was transmogrified into Rod Stewart's megahit "Do Ya Think I'm Sexy?" —*Terri Hinte*

Luiz Bonfá

b. 1922
Guitar / Brazil, Latin Continuum, Brazilian Jazz
From Rio de Janeiro, Bonfá was already well-established as a composer and guitarist when he was invited to contribute to *Black Orpheus*. He was both progenitor and popularizer of the bossa-nova style. Famous for writing "Manha de Carnaval" and "Samba de Orfeu," he worked with Stan Getz on bossa-nova recordings of the '60s. —*Terri Hinte & Michael G. Nastos*

● **Non-Stop to Brazil** / Apr. 17, 1989-Apr. 18, 1989 / Chesky ✦✦✦✦✦
Recent but classic jazz-bossa is played by one of its defining spirits. The elusive Bonfá, an important influence on US jazz-bossa who has pretty much vanished, is superbly evanescent in style. The recording expresses the close links of bossa nova and jazz. Bonfá is joined for a trio of tracks by NY guitarist Gene Bertoncini. —*John Storm Roberts*

That Bonfa Magic / 1991 / Milestone ✦✦✦✦✦
This recording is one of the first results of a licensing deal with the Caj

label with a focus on the acoustic guitar, in its most gracefully jazz- (and ecological-effects)-tinged. The Bonfá release has the largest number of backup artists. —*John Storm Roberts, Original Music*

Gilberto Gil

b. 1942, Salvador, Bahia
Guitar, Vocals / Brazilian Pop, Brazil, Latin Continuum
An important Brazilian vocalist, composer, and political activist who has been on the cutting edge of Afro-Latin music over at least three decades. Gil was a pioneer in utilizing everything from reggae to rock in his music. He is idolized by many American rockers and was one of a wave of musicians signed by US labels in an attempt to reap the worldbeat harvest. Gil is an outstanding and charismatic vocalist. —*Ron Wynn*

★ **Realce** / 1978 / Elektra ✦✦✦✦✦
A good example of how Gil mixes it all up: recorded in Los Angeles with a Brazilian/American cast, this 1978 session combines Gil's unique samba-rock-funk fare with a Portuguese version of Bob Marley's "No Woman, No Cry." —*Terri Hinte*

Acoustic / 1994 / Atlantic ✦✦✦✦✦
Classic Gil: lilt, falsetto, tropicalia guitar, the works, in a splendid "live-in-studio" recording before an audience that seems to have upped his wattage considerably. It's hard to see why Brazilians of all people bother with reggae beats, but the opener here could almost make one a convert: as music should, it overrides mere cerebrality with sheer joie de vivre. And so it goes from there on in. —*John Storm Roberts, Original Music*

Live in Tokyo / Braziloid ✦✦✦
Brazilian musicians and studios are fond of backup arrangements quite as mushy as anything the US industry can provide, so live albums of Brazilian performers tend to be a lot more satisfying than studio gigs. That's certainly true of this release compared with his earlier Braziloid album. A punchy backup band does wonders for his attractively laidback style. —*John Storm Roberts, Original Music*

Joao Gilberto

b. Jun. 1931, 1931, Bahia, Brazil
Guitar, Vocals / Bossa Nova, Brazil, Latin Continuum
Vocals, guitar, composer. One of the greatest Brazilian singers of all time. It would be difficult to overestimate the influence of Joao Gilberto on Brazilian music. "Everything he did, and does," Caetano Veloso remarked, "illuminates the past and the future of the music in Brazil."
　Gilberto electrified Brazil with his 1958 recording of Jobim's "Chega de Saudade." Just a few years later the colossal hit "The Girl from Ipanema," which he recorded with then-wife Astrud and saxophonist Stan Getz, precipitated the worldwide bossa-nova phenomenon.
　Gilberto is generally recognized as the architect of bossa nova: he condenses samba polyrhythms into his syncopated, thoroughly original guitar style, while his cool, caressing, utterly free vocals define intimacy and swing. —*Terri Hinte*

The Boss of the Bossa Nova / Oct. 19, 1962 / Atlantic ✦✦✦
● **Amoroso/Brasil** / Nov. 17, 1976-1980 / Warner Bros. ✦✦✦✦✦
Two of the influential Joao Gilberto's LPs (*Amoroso* and *Brasil*) are combined on this single CD. The former session is pretty definitive with Gilberto interpreting four of Antonio Carlos Jobim's compositions (including "Wave" and "Triste") and four other songs (highlighted by "Besame Mucho," "Estate" and an odd 31-bar rendition of "'S Wonderful"). The strings (arranged by Claus Ogerman) are unnecessary but Gilberto proves to be in prime form. The later album also has its moments of interest (including a Brazilian version of "All of Me") and finds Gilberto backed by Johnny Mandel arrangements and assisted by singers Caetano Veloso, Gilberto Gil, and Maria Bethania. Overall there is not much variety throughout this gently swinging program but these are a pair of Gilberto's better post-1970 recordings. —*Scott Yanow*

The Legendary Joao Gilberto / Nov. 1990 / World Pacific ✦✦✦✦
A 1990 compilation of Gilberto's alluring bossa-nova recordings (1958-1961), contains a generous 75 minutes of music. At the time of its original release, it changed the musical landscape of Brazil and beyond. —*Terri Hinte*

Joao / Dec. 22, 1992 / Verve ✦✦✦✦
Recent but classic jazz-bossa is played by one of its defining spirits. Vocally, Gilberto is in fine muttering form, communicating intensely with somebody in his breast pocket, and his guitar is as delicate as ever. This recording expresses the close links of bossa nova and jazz. *Joao* has Clare Fisher arranging and on some cuts playing keyboards, along with one of those saccharin string-sections even the most avant-garde Brazilians love. —*John Storm Roberts*

★ **Joao Gilberto** / PolyGram ✦✦✦✦✦
Minimalist Joao (guitar and percussion) for maximal intimacy: "As always," comments Arto Lindsay in his notes, "his music is defined as much by what it leaves out as by what is there." —*Terri Hinte*

Desafinado / Saludos Amigos ◆◆◆◆

Samba's kick-back ebullience has always seemed more attractive than the muttering ellipses of bossa nova. But these (presumably early—zilch data) recordings remind one once again just how great was Gilberto's talent, up-the-sleeve vocal style and all. Classics all, from the super-familiar "Desafinado" to the favorite, "O Pato," with its quirkily enchanting backing. —*John Storm Roberts, Original Music*

Antonio Carlos Jobim

b. Feb. 2, 1927, **d.** Dec. 8, 1994

Guitar, Piano, Vocals / Bossa Nova, Brazil, Latin Continuum

Without question one of the greatest 20th century popular music composers in any idiom, Antonio Carlos Brasileiro de Almeida Jobim has an unprecedented impact on Brazilian, American, and world music. His music mixes the romantic and the ugly, and is alternately lyrical, urbane, harmonically and rhythmically sophisticated, as well as melodically rich and striking. Above all, it's extraordinarily beautiful. His style avoids jarring effects and mixes simple, evocative lyrics with syncopated melodic figures and subtle chord progressions. Jobim persuaded Odeon Records, where he was music director, to record Joao Gilberto performing his composition "Chega de Saudade." The recording helped launch a reshaping of the samba into the bossa nova. This was popularized in America by Stan Getz and Charlie Byrd with their album *Jazz Samba* in 1962. The album included Jobim's composition "Desafinado," which was later recorded by Coleman Hawkins. Jobim and Gilberto later appeared with Getz, Byrd, and Dizzy Gillespie at a Carnegie Hall concert in 1962. Astrud Gilberto's recording of his composition "The Girl from Ipanema" with Stan Getz on tenor sax later was a No. 1 pop hit. The bossa nova was enormously popular in the '60s, and many other jazz musicians recorded in the style. Jobim recorded as a leader for Verve and A&M in the '60s, CTI, Discovery, and Columbia in the '70s; Warner Bros., Verve, and Polydor in the '80s; and Verve in the '90s. His list of hit compositions includes "Wave," "Corcovado," "Aguas de Marco," "Felicidade," "Once I Loved," "Dindi," "One Note Samba," and "Triste." Vocalist, pianist, and arranger Tom Ze has emerged as one of Jobim's finest interpreters, but many others from Frank Sinatra to Wayne Shorter have recorded his compositions. Jobim's also done albums with Sinatra, Nelson Riddle, and Claus Ogerman's orchestras, Gal Costa and Elis Regina among others. —*Ron Wynn and Terri Hinte*

Wonderful World of Antonio Carlos Jobim / Sep. 1965 / Musicraft ◆◆◆

1986 reissue featuring noted Brazilian vocalist and composer Antonio Carlos Jobim, backed by the Nelson Riddle Orchestra. It's a showcase for Jobim's songs, sensual style, and charismatic voice, plus Riddle's always-impressive arrangements. This was originally issued in 1978. —*Ron Wynn*

Wave / May 22, 1967-Jun. 1, 1967 / A&M ◆◆◆

★ **Elis and Tom** / 1974 / Verve ◆◆◆◆◆

A perfect record: Brazil's beloved cantora Elis Regina singing an all-Jobim program, accompanied by the composer, who also joins her for several duets, notably his masterpiece "Aguas de Marco." —*Terri Hinte*

Urubu / Nov. 1976 / Warner Bros. ◆◆◆◆

This beautiful 1976 session features Claus Ogerman's incomparable string arrangements. In fact, half the album is orchestral-only; on the other half, Jobim sings such gems as "Correnteza," co-written by Bonfá. —*Terri Hinte*

Terra Brasilis / 1980 / Warner Bros. ◆◆◆◆

Once again teaming with arranger Claus Ogerman on this 1980 double album, Jobim reworks many of his classic compositions, including "Dindi," "One Note Samba," and of course "The Girl from Ipanema." —*Terri Hinte*

Man From Ipanema / Nov. 21, 1995 / Verve ◆◆◆◆◆

★ **Girl from Ipanema: The Antonio Carlos Jobim Songbook** / Jan. 1996 / Verve ◆◆◆◆◆

The Art of / Verve ◆◆◆

Recent release covering Jobim material issued on Verve's import label. It includes lush ballads, more celebratory tunes, and his romantic, poetic love material. —*Ron Wynn*

Margareth Menezes

Vocals / Brazil, Latin Continuum

Brazilian vocalist Margareth Menezes is an international star and was for a few years her country's top musical export, known for her powerful voice and commanding stage presence. A native of Bahia, she originally aspired to be an actress. One of Menezes' first tours was with Gilberto Gil, for which this first time she had ever seen other parts of her country. She got her big break as a singer in 1989 when David Byrne hired her as his opening act and she embarked upon a world tour. The tour made her a star, but her career was nearly eclipsed by a series of bad managers, and

many of the sometimes difficult details of touring. Menezes also believes that her career was subtly undermined by racial discrimination and the difficulties for Black artists such as herself to get their records adequately promoted. In the mid-'90s, a much more savvy Menezes began her bid for a comeback and in 1995 released *Luz Dorado*. As of early 1995, she was still looking for new management and a new support team as she prepares to tour Europe and the US. —*Sandra Brennan*

● **Kindala** / 1991 / Mango ◆◆◆◆◆

One of the most versatile and energetic new voices on the world music scene. This follow-up to her chart-topping debut, *Elegibo*, offers similar strong songs and deft arrangements. It features both a duet with reggae star Jummy Cliff and her interpretation of a song by Haiti's Boukman Ekspyeryans. —*Mango*

Milton Nascimento

b. 1942

Guitar, Piano, Vocals / World, MPB, Brazil, Latin Continuum

Milton Nascimento grew up in the small town of Tres Pontas in Minas Gerais, and retains a strong identity as a mineiro (i.e., resident of Minas). Since making his recording debut in 1967, Nascimento has enjoyed broad international acclaim as a singer and composer; he's also been a favored collaborator of many American artists, notably Wayne Shorter, Pat Metheny, and Paul Simon. Nascimento's songs incorporate influences as diverse as the Beatles, Gregorian chants, American jazz, African rhythms, bossa nova, and mineiro folk music, and address both the personal and political. A singer of uncommon emotional power whose plaintive tenor can soar to an otherworldly falsetto, he is "the Voice of Brazil" for audiences around the world. —*Terri Hinte*

● **Minas** / 1975 / A&M ◆◆◆◆◆

Milton's debut American release. Includes famous tunes "Carvo e Canela" and "Nada Sera Como Antes," with Herbie Hancock, Wayne Shorter and Raul Souza, Tonin Ho, Airto Moreira, Roberto Silva. An important document. —*Michael G. Nastos*

Geraes / 1976 / Odeon ◆◆◆

Stylistically and emotionally a counterpart to *Minas*, *Geraes* (an obsolete spelling of "Gerais") includes some of Nascimento's most haunting melodies, as well as a powerful duet with Chico Buarque, "O Que Ser (A Flor da Pele)." —*Terri Hinte*

Missa dos Quilombos / 1982 / Verve ◆◆◆

Quilombos were settlements established by runaway slaves during the Portuguese colonial period. Nascimento's mass (recorded in 1982) "celebrates the death and resurrection of the Negro people in the death and resurrection of Christ." It was banned by the Vatican. —*Terri Hinte*

☆ **Sentinela** / Nov. 7, 1990 / Verve ◆◆◆◆◆

Folk themes with sacred overtones: this 1980 session is one of the most spectacular examples of how Nascimento weaves many threads into his music. The title track is an unforgettable duet with Nana Caymmi. —*Terri Hinte*

A Barca dos Amantes (Ship of Lovers) / Mar. 8, 1991 / Polydor ◆◆◆

A decade or so ago, Nascimento was listed, not very prominently, on a Shorter release. Times change . . . . The style is somewhere between jazz-influenced Brazil and straight Latin-jazz, but as you'd expect, the dominant force is the sparkling talent of Nascimento himself. —*John Storm Roberts, Original Music*

Amigo / Jun. 25, 1996 / Warner Bros. ◆◆◆

Amigo is a pleasant, but unengaging, live album from Milton Nascimento. All of his best-known songs are featured, but the elaborate musical support—featuring a full orchestra and a children's chorus—dilutes the impact of the music. Nevertheless, there's enough fine moments to make it a worthwhile listen for Nascimento's dedicated fans. —*Thom Owens*

Elis Regina

Vocals / World Fusion, Latin Folk, Brazil, Latin Continuum

Arguably the greatest female singer Brazil has ever produced, Elis Regina was born in the southernmost state of Rio Grande do Sul. A drug overdose in 1982 took her life at the height of her popularity and artistic powers. —*Terri Hinte*

Arte de Elis Regina (Art of Elis Regina) / 1975 / Fontana ◆◆◆

This 1975 best-of is a well-rounded portrayal of Regina's rich artistry, including hits like "Madalena" and "Arrastao" and her definitive performances of songs by many of Brazil's most important composers. —*Terri Hinte*

Personalidade (Best of Brazil) / Oct. 1989 / Philips ◆◆◆

Contemporary Afro-Latin and Brazilian music from a rising star. Regina has a lighter, more sensual sound, but it's grounded in the tougher, less optimistic rhythms and sounds of its '80s and '90s composer/performer class. She's also a harsher, more assertive singer than the sentimental vocalists like Astrud Gilberto. —*Ron Wynn*

Elis Por Ela / 1993 / WEA Latina ✦✦✦✦
This best-of collection features live and studio recordings from her middle and late albums. It contains five tracks from the live *Saudade do Brasil*, four tracks from *Live at Montreux*, and five studio tracks, notably a resuscitated (finally) version of "Beguine Dodoi," whose mastering was horrifically botched on the US release of *Essa Mulher*. It includes complete Portuguese lyrics. —*David Rumpler*

★ **Saudade do Brasil** / ✦✦✦✦✦
This well-recorded, two-CD set catches Regina in extremely outgoing and expressive form. Highlights include inventive reworkings of classics such as Nascimento's "Cançao da America," (complete with Andean flutes and percussion). The most daring piece is Ary Barroso's "Aquarela do Brasil." Here the '50s standard is superimposed on Native Indian tribal chanting, giving new meaning to the song's lyric, "Brazil, my Brazilian Brazil." This is one of her greatest recordings, though not a first choice for the unacquainted. Complete Portuguese lyrics are included. (Note: disc one was released in the US in 1992 on Tropical Storm as *That Woman*. A 1991 Tropical Storm release entitled *Elis por Ela* includes three cuts from disc two, but omits the remaining seven.) —*David Rumpler*

Elis Especial / ✦✦✦
Classic early material is accompanied by an uncredited, relentlessly swinging piano trio. The sound quality could be better (it was recorded in 1968), but by the end of the first song you won't care anymore — you'll be blissfully tapping your foot. —*David Rumpler*

☆ **Transversal do Tempo** / ✦✦✦✦✦
This is one of Regina's most passionate recordings — an excellent example of her artistry and integrity. Her voice conveys deep anger and sadness, even as the music is uplifting and inspiring. It includes complete Portuguese lyrics. —*David Rumpler*

Brazil Collection

Afro Brasil / 1988 / Philips ✦✦✦✦✦
Verve's international division issued a four-disc anthology series of Brazilian music covering selections mostly from the '70s and '80s, plus a few things done in 1990. The 18 tracks compiled for *Afro Brasil* spotlight the rhythms and sounds from Bahia, the most African section of Brazil. The influence of the Candomble and Macumba religions, coupled with the sounds of samba, reggae, and the afoxes and bloco afros genres, are displayed by such artists as Caetano Veloso, Nana Vasconcelos, the Bushdancers, and the lush vocals of Margareth Menezes and Beth Carvalho. This is the modern Afro-Brazilian sound, captured in stark, digital glory. —*Ron Wynn*

Afro-Brazilian Religious Songs / Lyrichord ✦✦✦
The album is an outstanding overview of the music of the Fon/Yoruba-derived religions of Salvador in northeastern Brazil, a religious center nicknamed "the Rome of the Africans." The pieces were recorded over eight years during the ceremonies themselves. —*John Storm Roberts*

Amazonia: Cult Music of Northern Brazil / Lyrichord ✦✦✦
This album features the Afro-Brazilian religious music of Amazonia, which is very different from that of the Bahian version mostly because it mixes Amerindian ingredients with its Yoruba elements. Though most of the music on the album is religious, there are a couple of splendid examples of Carimbo by a local band. —*John Storm Roberts*

Asa Branca: Accordian Forró from Brazil / Rykodisc ✦✦✦
Forró, a song form combining elements of Portuguese and Indian language and rhythm, became popular in Brazil during the '70s and '80s. The accordion-driven music was spotlighted on a 1990 CD issued by Rykodisc that presented 19 examples of recent forró songs done by top Brazilian artists. Forró, as performed by this group, sways, rises, dips, and keeps shifting its mood as the song continues. It's not as romantic as the samba, but forró has its charms. —*Ron Wynn*

Batucada Brazileira / Parrot ✦✦✦✦✦
Rio carnival aside, Brazil is full of African-derived percussion. Batucada descends directly from the social dances permitted slaves once a week; batucada is dynamite percussion music. This release focuses on batucadas for drums leavened by the whistles beloved also of African drum choirs, passages of fine cavaquinho (a small guitar), and manic, squeaky-squeak cuica friction drum. Maddeningly generic packaging, but this really is the best Brazilian percussion release I've met these many years, with technical quality as sparkling as the drumming. —*John Storm Roberts*

☆ **Black Orpheus . . .** / 1990 / Fontana ✦✦✦✦✦
The prodigious talents of Antonio Carlos Jobim, Vinicius de Moraes ("Felicidade"), and Luiz Bonfa ("Manha de Carnaval") were introduced to the world on this unforgettable soundtrack. —*Terri Hinte*

☆ **Bossa Nova**—Trinta Anos Depois (Thirty Years Later) / Verve ✦✦✦✦✦
Carmen Miranda was a fad here. The bossa nova was a revolution. Here's what the originators made of it: A collection of early Brazilian recordings that is not just a great listen, but a salutary reminder about a music that has attracted a lot of nonsense talk. Bossa nova—the authentic, real, genuine stuff—was from the start strongly jazz-oriented and heavily pop in musical aesthetic. Here to prove it are some names known to US Brazil fans—Caetano Velosa, Elis Regina, Joao Gilberto, Toquinho—along with all sorts of other legends. —*John Storm Roberts*

☆ **Bossa Nova Brasil** / 1991 / Philips ✦✦✦✦✦
A good various-artists sampler of the modern Brazilian sound, including cuts from contemporary artists like Jorge Ben and Gilberto Gil. —*Ron Wynn*

Brasil / PolyGram ✦✦✦
A sampler with cuts from some of the label's prime modern artists, such as Milton Nascimento, Gal Costa, Caetano Veloso, Ney Matogrosso, and Emilio Santiago. —*Ron Wynn*

Brazil: Roots-Samba / 1989 / Rounder ✦✦✦✦✦
Real Rio samba sounds like this fine small-group, bunch-of-friends-in-a-corner-bar samba, mostly with the little cavaquinho guitar well to the fore, as well as the usual jubilant percussion. Some of these groups sound professional, some semi-professional, but they're all pretty close to the street. Personally, I'd trade an hour of the trendies for ten minutes of this stuff any time. —*John Storm Roberts*

☆ **Brazil Classics: Beleza Tropical** / Oct. 1989 / Fly/Sire ✦✦✦✦✦
The first of a three-volume set, compiled by David Byrne, it gives gringos a chance to pick up on the salacious sounds that've been going on in Brazil. Fans of Talking Heads' later work or Paul Simon's African excavations will enjoy these well-done sets. —*John Floyd*

Brazil Classics 2: O Samba / Jan. 1990 / Luaka Bop ✦✦✦✦✦
Compiler David Byrne has better taste than most US concocters of Brazilian compilations. I prefer *O Samba* over the previous *Beliza Tropical* because I have a strong preference for the samba-based artists over the more eclectic types (e.g. Gil and Nascimento) on Beleza. But a few small cavils aside, Byrne's choices of cuts are all excellent. —*John Storm Roberts*

Brazil Classics 3: Forró, Etc. / 1991 / Luaka Bop ✦✦✦✦✦
This is the third volume in the *Brazil Classics* series. —*AMG*

☆ **Brazil Forró: Music for Maids and Taxi Drivers** / 1989 / Rounder ✦✦✦✦✦
This is a textbook anthology, capturing the sound of Brazil's newest music form forró, a style that's more rhythmically aggressive and stimulating than any of their recent genres. Well-packaged and well-produced, and with excellent sound and a nice cross-section, *Brazil Forró* features Jos, Orlando, and Toinho de Alagoas, among others. —*Ron Wynn*

Brazil Is Back / 1989 / Braziloid ✦✦✦✦
A variable compilation with some newish names and some famous ones, it was originally designed to introduce a label now defunct. Some cuts are terrific, notably a fine choro by Paulo Moura. Some are good examples of work by major artists, from de Vila to Gil via Bethania. The much-hyped Obina Shock is more interesting than good (a case of disco-funk fever). The residue is mostly Brazilian supermarket pop. —*John Storm Roberts*

Brazil Today, Vol. 2 / 1985 / PolyGram ✦✦✦✦✦
A sampler focusing on Brazilian music in the mid-'80s. The second of a two-part series originally issued in 1985. —*Ron Wynn*

Brazil: The Sound World of the Bororo Indians / Auvidis ✦✦✦
This recording may be an indicator of the future of world music. Collected here are field recordings from a small tribal group, which up until recently may have been regarded as "primitive." They have a remarkably rich mythology and cosmology, with which their music is intimately connected. This digital recording covers both specifically religious and more secular songs and dances. What really shows is the attention to music and nature being intertwined. —*David L. Mayers*

Bresil: Musiques Du Haut Xingu / Ocora ✦✦✦
Included are interesting long horns, animal songs, and flutes. Fascinating people are fast disappearing. —*David L. Mayers*

Bresil 88 / Buda Musique ✦✦✦
This is an attractive anthology with a largely samba-based feel. Some cuts are by artists known in the US—Jorge Ben, Milton Nascimento, Elis Regina, and Gilberto Gil—but more who are at least as good though less famous are here: Jovelina Perola Negra, Maria Creuza, Marcos Valle, Wando, Filo, and more. —*John Storm Roberts*

Forró / Rounder ✦✦✦✦✦
Talk about entirely different . . . Forró was the first Brazilian music I ever heard, back in the '50s when I was a London schoolkid and my father brought 78s back from business trips. It's a wonderful, punchy, and totally surprising accordion-and-percussion sound from the plains of the Northeast, totally unlike anything you've heard from Brazil. No major artists of the Luiz Gonzaga status here, but several contemporary groups that stick to the jaunty mainstream sound. If you don't know forró, you owe yourself. —*John Storm Roberts*

Music of Mato Grosso: Brazil / Smithsonian/Folkways ✦✦✦
Especially interesting for animal calls and eight-foot long flutes. From the Xingu area. —*David L. Mayers*

Nordeste Brasil / 1992 / Philips ✦✦✦
The variety of sounds and themes from Brazil's Northeast corridor were spotlighted on this 21-cut volume, one of the four issued in 1992 by Verve's Phonogram division. They covered songwriters, vocalists, instrumentalists, and material ranging from the late '60s to the mid-'80s. There are forró and accordion cuts, ballads, protest music, light romantic fare, and driving, aggressive sounds. Some names, such as Elis Regina, Gilberto Gil and Milton Nascimento, are world music superstars today. Others, such as Gal Costa, Beth Caravalho, and Luis Gonzaga, Jr., do not have the reputations that their performances show they deserve. Gerald Seligman once again provides excellent notes. —*Ron Wynn*

☆ **Sambas Enredo de Sempre** / ✦✦✦✦✦
This "all-time greatest carnival sambas" collection features some of the most memorable "theme sambas" written during the past 35 years, and offers a variety of singing styles and band arrangements. The overall production and recording quality is excellent. Highlights include rare samba de enredo performances by Clara Nunes, Martinho Da Vila, and Roberto Ribeiro, the highly regarded puxador (lead singer) of the Imperio Serrano school. —*David Rumpler*

Cape Verde Collection

Cape Verde Islands: The Roots / Playasound ✦✦✦✦✦
This 1990 recording of the Afro-Lusitanian tradition of Cape Verde leans heavily toward the Portuguese end of the Verdean spectrum; mornas and coladeiras for cavaquinho and viola (guitar family), and funanas for accordion and metal scraper—all radiating the nostalgic melancholy the Portuguese call saudade. Of special interest, on the more Afro end, is a song for the rare cimboa spike fiddle. —*John Storm Roberts*

Chile Collection

Amerindian Ceremonial Music of Chile / Philips ✦✦✦
This music for panpipes, consisting of lengthy selections, represents a curing ceremony of a shamaness. —*David L. Mayers*

☆ **Hispano-Chilean Metisse Traditional Music** / Auvidis ✦✦✦✦✦
From the re-released *UNESCO World Atlas* series, this is almost the only recording of Hispano-Chilean traditional music. Included are religious music, including parade-dances influenced by the Andean Indians, various types of guitar-accompanied ballads, harp-backed cuecas, and more. Thorough notes are included, though the English translation is eccentric and in a couple of places positively cryptic. —*John Storm Roberts*

Traditional Music of Chile / Command ✦✦✦
This music is for guitarron, accordion, guitars, and singers—mestizo music. —*David L. Mayers*

Columbia

Joe Arroyo   (Alvaro Jose Arroyo Gonzalez)

b. Nov. 1, 1955, Cartagena, Columbia
Vocals / Salsa, Columbian, Latin Continuum
Arroyo is Columbia's best-known salsa singer. He began singing when he was only eight, performing in a topless bar, and at 16 joined the prestigious Fruko y sus Tesos. In 1981, he formed La Verdad. His great popularity lies in the way he has managed to fuse a medley of Caribbean sounds together including soca, reggae, merengue, and compas. —*Leon Jackson*

● **Fuego** / Fuentes ✦✦✦✦✦
Arroyo had become a major favorite among European salsa buffs, and a considerable success on the Latin concert circuit. Novelty aside, the reason is that while he adheres to a tight but pretty standard salsa sound, he uses all sorts of Colombian rhythms (including cumbia), thus giving his universality strong local roots. —*John Storm Roberts*

16 Exitos / Fuentes ✦✦✦

Lisandro Meza

Columbian, Vallenato, Latin Continuum, Indian Classical
Mandamas, El / 1986 / RCA ✦✦✦
The greatest accordionist/bandleader and all-round maestro of vallenato is both sophisticated and true to what is, at its best, very much a roots music. It's amazing how many changes he can ring on what is theoretically a fairly simple idiom. His playing is sharp, bluesy, and humorous at once, and there are touches of blissful acoustic guitar. —*John Storm Roberts, Original Music*

Pa'l Mundo / 1996 / Faisan ✦✦✦✦✦
The vallenato accordion groups from the Caribbean coast of Colombia

are just wonderful: driving, downhome, and eccentric. Meza is about the best-known vallenato accordionist, and this re-issue remains my favorite Meza recording ever. Its pearl is his wonderful take on Garcia Marquez' most famous novel, "Cancion Para Una Muerte Anunciada," which would have been one of his finest recordings even without the associations. Out of 19 tracks, almost a dozen have to rate as among Meza's best. —*John Storm Roberts*

● **15 Exitos** / Fuentes ✦✦✦✦✦
They call a recording *15 Hits* when nothing better comes to mind, but in Meza's case any 15 songs would qualify. Gutsy singing, percussion boiling over, and jaunty accordion combine to make this one of the great feel-good albums. —*John Storm Roberts, Original Music*

De Fiesta por el Mundo / Fuego ✦✦✦
This is a wonderful musician, a man who manages to be both sophisticated and true to what is still very much a roots music. Subtler than Ochoa and more varied (especially in the accordion), he's a little lighter on the roots, but totally and knowingly within the tradition. This particular CD is mostly quartet, but with such added trimmings as nifty old-Carib sax and gorgeous acoustic guitar in a cut or two. —*John Storm Roberts, Original Music*

Estas Pillao / Faisan ✦✦✦

Sabanero Mayor / Sonolux ✦✦✦
A couple of recent Meza recordings have been disappointingly low-energy ones. On this he's back on form, his endearingly plain-man voice and chunkily elegant accordion a perfect mix, and a particularly good coro, often with the ravishing sharp, plena-like edge that women's voices give such choruses. And of course the mix of rhythms (no cumbia-after-cumbia for Meza) and the sudden brilliantly individual take on vallenato melody, running on a phrase or so past the logical stopping place, or just plain quirky—in this case "El Santo Cachon" and "La Nube." —*John Storm Roberts, Original Music*

Cancion Para Una Muerte Anunciada / Toboga ✦✦✦
This riff on a famous novel is just part of what makes Meza the finest vallenato musician extant. He takes the Marquez story and reworks it back into a small-town drama with brilliance, setting it to a melody that is amazingly sophisticated without ever going beyond tradition. An unacknowledged classic, this. —*John Storm Roberts*

Linda Conjunto with Carmen Rivero Vera

Columbian, Latin Continuum
A Bailar la Cumbia / CBS ✦✦✦
This is a re-release of a very fine band from the '50s. Vera is a fine singer in the semiplaintive, semihumorous cumbia vein, and the mambo-inflected band (two trumpets, two saxes) is with her all the way. Fine as some of the new Colombian salsa groups are, the cumbia bands have much more regional flavor, and this one is a classic. —*John Storm Roberts*

Columbia Collection

☆ **Cumbia Cumbia** / 1989 / World Circuit ✦✦✦✦✦
Running from the '50s to the '80s, these cuts perfectly showcase the most charming of Latin American music—a kind of musical equivalent to the poetry of Edward Lear. —*Carl Hoyt, Original Music*

Cumbia Cumbia Cumbia / Fuentes ✦✦✦
The old cumbias that can be found primarily on records issued in Colombia on the Discos Fuentes label are important to mention. This is the best choice. —*David L. Mayers*

Fiesta Vallenat / 1986 / Shanachie ✦✦✦✦✦
Fiesta Vallenata: Colombian Dance Music is a non-stop orgy of uptempo accordions and a sure cure for the blues. —*Myles Boisen*

Cuba

Desi Arnaz

b. Mar. 2, 1917, Santiago, Cuba, d. Nov. 2, 1986
Vocals
To most of the public, Desi Arnaz is known as the lovable, temperamental Ricky Ricardo, husband of Lucille Ball in the 1950s (in real life and on screen) on one of the most successful television series of all time, *I Love Lucy*. Within the industry, he's known as one of the forces behind Desilu Productions. Yet before he became an international star, he was known primarily as a musician, not an actor or as an executive. It was Arnaz who may have done more to popularize the conga in the US than any other figure, leading an orchestra that mixed Latin-Cuban music with big-band pop, and putting it over to the masses with his irresistibly good-natured, melodramatic vocals. He's attracted far less critical acclaim than more ambitious Latin-American hybrids like Machito, the Dizzy

Gillespie Orchestra of the late '40s, or his one-time mentor Xavier Cugat, but his recordings contain a surprising amount of shake-em-loose verve.

Born in Santiago, Cuba, Arnaz moved to Miami in his teens, and began to work as a conga player, singer, and guitarist. For six months, he apprenticed with Xavier Cugat's orchestra, and then split to form a band of his own. He made his first sides as a bandleader around 1940 with his La Congra Orchestra, and his New York shows created enough of a buzz to get him a stage role in a musical by Richard Rodgers and Lorenz Hart, *Too Many Girls*, in 1939. He repeated his *Too Many Girls* role on screen, leading to a Hollywood career and his marriage to comedienne Lucille Ball.

After serving in the Army during World War II, Arnaz focused on music for the rest of the '40s, cutting quite a few infectious sides for Victor between 1946 and 1949. Certainly some of his accented routines could be corny, but he and his orchestra could also whip up a storm on tracks like "Babalu" and "El Cumbanchero," achieving his avowed goal of combining the rhythm of Machito with the melody of Andre Kostelanetz. After recording his last session for Victor in 1949, Arnaz refocused his attention on Hollywood, putting his musical career on permanent back burner after becoming one of television's first superstars with *I Love Lucy*. —*Richie Unterberger*

● **Babalu** / 1996 / RCA ✦✦✦✦✦
Twenty tracks primarily his 1946-49 prime, mostly paced by Arnaz himself on vocals, with some instrumentals and occasional pieces for female singers Jane Harvey, Elsa Miranda, and Amanda Lane. Sure, this is sometimes corny, but more often it's invigorating Latin big-band pop, Arnaz' conga and quasi-operatic vocals to the forefront. Those who dismiss this as Cuban rhythms watered down for American consumption are missing the essential point: It's *fun* stuff that's usually overflowing with joie de vivre, as a listen to "Babalu," "Carnival in Rio," "Quizas, Quizas, Quizas," "Guadalajara," and "El Cumbanchero" will confirm. —*Richie Unterberger*

● **The Best of Desi Arnaz: The Mambo King** / Jun. 18, 1996 / RCA ✦✦✦✦✦
The Best of Desi Arnaz: The Mambo King is the definitive compilation of Arnaz's hit-making peak, featuring all of his biggest hits plus some lesser-known tracks that are just as interesting and entertaining. —*Thom Owens*

Don Azpiazu & His Havana Casino Orchestra

Cuba, Latin Continuum
Don Azpiazu was until recently a forgotten giant. This was the band whose 1930 "Peanut Vendor" not only became a huge national hit, launching a decade of rumbamania, it was also the first US recording of an authentic national Latin style (in other words, Latin music, not US music to a Latin rhythm, like the '20s tangos). Equally important, Azpiazu's "Peanut Vendor" introduced to the US all those Cuban percussion instruments we now take for granted. His second recording, "Green Eyes," was the first example of true crossover with a North American vocalist. More important yet, this was simply a very fine band indeed, by the standards of its own or any other day. —*John Storm Roberts*

Don Azpiazu & His Havana Casino Orchestra / 1991 / Harlequin ✦✦✦✦✦

Batacumbele

New York Salsa, Cuba, Latin Continuum
A hot Afro-Cuban outfit that rivals any today. Their name comes from the bata drum from Africa plus the "cumbia" rhythms of montuno and mambo, which evolved from tribal dance. —*Michael G. Nastos*

● **Con Un Poco De Songo** / 1981 / Disco Hit ✦✦✦
This is a recording by one of the most adventurous, interesting, and—more simply—best bands extant. The story is told by the instrumentation, which includes one trumpet, baritone sax, flute, clarinet, bata drums, and cuatro. Which translates into a sound drawing from a very wide range of traditions, mixing charanga and conjunto and the rest in a more varied way than the standard orquesta sound. —*John Storm Roberts*

★ **In Concert Live at the University of Puerto Rico** / 1988 / Montuno ✦✦✦✦✦
This is hot and heavy Latin/Afro/Cuban music from this stellar 20-plus-piece band. It mostly includes traditional themes extended with improvisation. This is one you cannot live without. —*Michael G. Nastos*

Cachao (Israel "Cachao" Lopez)

Latin Pop, Salsa, Tropicalia, Cuba, Latin Continuum
Cuban bassist Cachao is credited as the man who created mambo music. He spent most of his 76 years living in Cuba where he was a prominent jazz sideman who specialized in Afro-Cuban dance music. He eventually made it to the US and lived in Miami almost nine years with little or no

recognition, due in part to his extreme modesty. He was first introduced to the world by actor/ filmmaker Andy Garcia, who was born in Cuba but raised in Miami, via his 1993 documentary *Cachao... Como Su Ritmo No Hay Dos*. The film earned glowing reviews, especially for the music. On January 16, 1993, Cachao played a sold-out Radio City Music Hall in New York to considerable acclaim. In March of 1995, Cachao earned a Grammy for his album *Master Sessions, Vol. 1*. —*Sandra Brennan*

Cachao Y Su Descarga '77, Vol. 1 / May 1978 / Sony ✦✦✦
One of the greatest Cuban bassists (and the bass is what pegs all that superb rhythmic interplay), Cachao has played with all the greatest names in his time. Alas, the personnel of this superlative '60s recording isn't given, but greatness is everywhere present. And not just greatness in the splendid tres playing, the brilliant trumpet, and singing, and on and on, but richness and variety. The numbers range from extremely Afro-centric pieces to classic son ("Tres Lindas Cubanas," and the delights along the way include a rare-as-hen's-teeth clarinet solo of enormous charm. Quintessential about sums it up . . .). —*John Storm Roberts, Original Music*

● **Master Sessions, Vol. 1** / 1994 / Cresecent Moon/Epic ✦✦✦✦✦
Too often when historical forms (think danzón, son, rumba) are given note-for-note renderings, they end up museum pieces. Doesn't happen here, though. Of course, it doesn't hurt at all that Cachao has had a hand in the development of almost every significant modern Latin style (think mambo, chachachá, descarga). —*Original Music*

From Havana & New York / Caney ✦✦✦✦✦
Yes, well, this Spanish compilation of recordings made in 1957 and 1961 respectively is just stunning. The Havana sides are part of the general descarga ("jam-session") ferment that hit Cuba in the mid-'50s. The New York set, a logical extension of the idea, mixes Clark Terry and other jazzmen with Cuban musicians in about the most even típico/jazz balance I've heard. —*John Storm Roberts, Original Music*

Celia Cruz

Vocals / Salsa, Tropicalia, Cuba, Latin Continuum
For over 40 years Celia Cruz has been the reigning queen of Latin Music, and while there are up-and-comers—such as La India—vying for her throne, she shows no signs of abdicating just yet. She was born the youngest of four children in Barrio Santo Suarez, a district of Havana, Cuba, and even as a child was a gifted singer. She grew up in the '30s, when Cuban culture, music, and its legendary nightlife flourished. Even back then, the island recording industry was strong and as a girl the lively music—a blend of native, African, European, and American jazz rhythms—inspired her. Though her father wanted her to become a teacher, Cruz was determined to become a singer and enrolled in Cuba's Conservatory of Music in 1947. Afro-Cuban Paulina Alvarez, the first singers she ever saw perform with an orchestra, was Cruz's earliest inspiration. Though she learned a lot about music at the Conservatory, Cruz has had little voice training. She deliberately eschewed it because she believed that she was already so steeped in authentic Cuban music that formal instruction was irrelevant.

Cruz started out singing the rather downbeat protest songs of the African-Cubans, but realizing that the songs didn't sell, she began singing a happier style of music, guaracha. Her first real break came in 1950 when she was hired to sing with one of Cuba's biggest bands, La Sonora Matancera. Though still inexperienced, she wowed audiences with her charisma, and strong—though they would become even more powerful in years to come—vocals. She made her recording debut with the band in early 1951 and sang such hits as "Cao Cao Mani Picao" and "Mata Siguaraya." The band developed a tremendous following in Latin America, where they were nicknamed "Cafe Con Leche." As the decade progressed, Cuban music became a worldwide phenomenon, thanks to such performers as Tito Puente, Perez Prado, Cachao, and even Desi Arnaz, and these opened doors for Cruz and La Sonora Matancera. She soon gained an enormous international reputation.

In 1960, as she and the band were touring and recording in Mexico, the US blockade against Cuba tightened, and her country was thrown into chaos. The band decided not to return to the island, and though Cruz never planned on it being a permanent situation, she never was able to go back. Eventually Cruz became a US citizen and signed a contract to work at the Hollywood Palladium. Things didn't work out due to trouble with her papers, so Cruz went to New York City to work at the Palladium. In 1961, she married Pedro Knight, the lead trumpeter with La Sonora Matancera. He quit the band to become her full-time manager. She was at the Palladium when mambo music became popular and though she frequently sang with other artists, like Machito and Mario Bauza, Tito Puente was one of her favorites. He founded a band for her in 1966 and they began recording with Tico Records. Though she has long since left Puente's band, they still perform together and tour frequently, especially in Europe. The two recorded eight albums (*Cuba y Puerto Rico Son* and

Quimbo Quimbumbia were the first two), but they were never big sellers.

During the mid- to late '60s, the newly created salsa music was beginning to gather an audience. Cruz signed to Vaya Records, the sister label of Fania, the biggest label in salsa music, and began to sing with many of the early salseros such as Oscar D'Leon, Cheo Feliciano, Hector Rodriguez, and others. She made her mark in the genre and in the early '70s had her first gold album, *Celia and Johnny,* with Fania VP Johnny Pacheco. She then became part of the Fania All-Stars. This band became one of the leaders in salsa music and contained such major stars as Bobby Cruz, Pacheco, Ismael Quintana, Mongo Santamaria, Willie Colon, and Hector Lavoe. The band debuted at the MIDEM convention in Cannes and were the hit of the gathering. Soon they became popular all over Europe. After their European tour the All-Stars recorded a live album in New York and Puerto Rico. While Cruz and the others were international stars, they had trouble breaking into US markets, something she attributes to this country's pop radio stations' notorious bias against songs lacking English lyrics. Still she continued a heavy touring schedule abroad through the '80s. Cruz visited Africa many times, where Latin music is especially popular in Senegal, Kenya, and Zaire. When the film *The Mambo Kings* came out in the early '90s, it caught the interest of a wider US audience. Around this time, Cruz was given her own star on Hollywood's Walk of Fame and was awarded an honorary doctorate from Yale. *— Sandra Brennan*

Homenaje a Los Santos / Mar. 8, 1994 / Polydor ♦♦♦
This a wonderful early recording consisting of songs to and around the spirits of lucumi/santeria, and backed by dance-type bands. It's an interesting Cuban subgenre, with wonderful singing, variable but sometimes superb backings. *—John Storm Roberts, Original Music*

De Nuevo / Vaya ♦♦♦
By this, their sixth collaboration, Cruz con Pacheco has become sort of like arroz con pollo. Standouts here are the classic guarachas, "El Agua de Bonga" and "Barin Barin," along with the closing "Historia de una Rumba." Cruz remains incredible: age cannot stale nor custom wither. *—John Storm Roberts, Original Music*

Brillante / Vaya ♦♦♦♦♦
Cruz's second coming first linked her with Johnny Pacheco's very traditional sound, then with others including, among the most interesting, Willie Colon. This anthology features many of the biggest hits from both the Pacheco and Colon collaborations: "Cucala," "Usted Abuso," "Toro Mata," "Reina Rumba," "Quimbara," "A Papa," "Vamos a Guarachar," "Vieja Luna" and "No Aguanta Mas." *—John Storm Roberts, Original Music*

● **Celia Cruz Y La Sonora Matancera** / Sony ♦♦♦♦♦
The greatest living female exponent of one of the greatest and most influential improvising vocal traditions is brought together with one of the finest of all the glorious Cuban trumpet-led conjuntos. This compilation contains some of the best of all their early recordings, which is saying something. In case you have others, here's the track list: "Burundanga," "Juancito Trucupey," "Tuya y Mas que Tuya," "La Sopa en Botella," "Tu Voz," "Caramelo," "Nuevo Ritmo Omolenko," "Contentosa," "El Yerbero Moderno," "Ritmo," "Tambo y Flores," "Dile Que Por Mi No Tema," "Pa'La Paloma," "El Rock and Roll," "Vallan Vallende," "Melao de Caña," and "Pepe Antonio." *—John Storm Roberts, Original Music*

Nostalgia Tropical / Orfeon ♦♦♦
This is a wonderful early recording. It's not just Celia with Matancera, but includes other Sonora Matancera hits from the '50s. *—John Storm Roberts, Original Music*

The Winners / Charly ♦♦♦♦♦
Cruz with Willie is just about as sure a thing as Celia with Johnny (Pacheco). Surer, maybe, since C&J have made far more recordings than C&W. Celia Cruz is the nearest thing to an icon in contemporary salsa, and since she reaches at least two generations, you can bet on this reaching at least the Top Three, if not the zenith. *—John Storm Roberts, Original Music*

Beny More

Vocals / Sonero, Cuba, Latin Continuum
Venerated by buffs of the '50s Cuban sound, Beny More was, like New York's Tito Rodriguez, not only a dynamic sonero but a fine, fine bolero singer. He was also a big deal as a bandleader fronting full-throated mambo bands. The first Cuban artist to have his own TV show, he was, as far as I know, the only Cuban singer to have an entire book written about him. *—John Storm Roberts*

★ **The Most from Beny More** / 1976 / BMG ♦♦♦♦♦
Even though this reissue lacks documentation except for titles, his biggest '50s hits are a basic item for your collection. Worth every cent and more. *—Ned Sublette & John Storm Roberts*

Historia Del Carnaval De Brasil, 1902-1952, Vol. 2 / 1994 / RCA Tropical ♦♦♦
"El Barbaro del Ritmo" was one of the greatest singers of Cuba's '50s golden age: not only a dynamic sonero but a fine bolero singer. He also ran a dynamite big band in high-energy mambo style, as this fine collection amply proves: Everybody who was anybody blew their socks off in it at one time or another, and somewhere the palm trees are still swaying from the impact. *—John Storm Roberts, Original Music*

Y Hoy Como Ayer / BMG ♦♦♦

El Inigualable / Discuba ♦♦♦
Even though this reissue lacks all documentation except titles, it's worth every cent and more. *—John Storm Roberts, Original Music*

Mambo Numero Uno / Discos Habanos ♦♦♦

Homenaje Postumo a Joseito Fernandez / Mediterraneo ♦♦♦
Beny More, one of the very greatest improvisers of Cuban singing, remains a demi-god to all Latino Cuban-music buffs; it is baffling that so few Anglo aficionados have picked up on him. This '50s set, dedicated to the composer of the international hit "Guajira Guantanamera" (no, not Pete Seeger), is mostly sones and totally superb (in every respect except recording quality, which is ho-hum-minus). It even has a couple of superb charanga cuts—rare as hen's teeth. Cuban-music-wise, if you don't know More you're faking it, so why not come in out of the cold? *—John Storm Roberts, Original Music*

Orquesta Reve

Latin Pop, Progressive Big Band, Salsa, Latin Folk, Cuba, Latin Continuum
Named for its charismatic leader, Elio Revé, Orquesta Revé mixes urban son with a very distinctive regional son variant (changui) that is indigenous to the Guantanamo region at the very eastern tip of Cuba. Changui uses percussion originally designed for religious ceremonies, which no doubt gives the music an added power and seriousness. Revé not only plays fine music, he also writes hard-hitting lyrics that address Cuban social and political issues. Orquesta Revé's music is rhythmic and very danceable. They can be heard on *La Explosion del Momento.* *—Leon Jackson*

● **La Explosion Del Momento!** / 1989 / Real World ♦♦♦♦♦
Hot Latin jazz with good horn chants and choral vocals. Twelve tracks, four pieces written by Revé Matos and Juan Carlos Alfonso. *—Michael G. Nastos*

Suave Suave + 3 / Discos Habanos ♦♦♦♦♦
One of Cuba's three or four finest modern bands is a fine example of the hot mix of flute-and-fiddle charanga with trombones—in this case heavier on the trombones then shared by several contemporary Cuban bands. Revé is hot enough to sear steak, and a super mix of classic and new (the singing style re-creates the high nasality of the golden age). The band's also notable for a brilliant pianist. This is fire-and-filigree in an idiom that's one of the most amazing survivals-by-adaptation in new world dance music. *—John Storm Roberts*

Perez Prado

d. Dec. 4, 1983
Piano / Salsa, Mambo, Latin Continuum
Dubbed the King of Mambo at the height of his fame, Cuban bandleader/arranger Perez Prado was instrumental in creating the sound. Starting in the 1940s, he blended the music of his native country with elements of big band jazz to form an infectious and extremely danceable hybrid. First coming to notice as the pianist/arranger in the Cuban big band Orquesta Casino de la Playa, Prado's popularity spread to Mexico, Latin America and, in the '50s, the US. Because his two No. 1 hits, "Cherry Pink and Apple Blossom White" and "Patricia," were as much (or more) pop as mambo, Prado is sometimes unfairly remembered as an easy listening instrumentalist. In fact, the bulk of his material was comprised of hot dance tunes highlighting bursts of shrill horns, busy bongoes, and, at times, ghostly organ. His irresistible, propulsive rhythms swung with great verve and humor, punctuated by shouts and grunts from various bandmembers. One of the most popular Latin musicians and bandleaders of his time, both in Latin America and the US, his innovations were also widely appreciated by jazz fans and musicians. He was largely forgotten by the American audience after 1960, but remained active until his death in 1989. *—Richie Unterberger*

"Prez" / 1958 / RCA ♦♦♦♦♦
This was the album that brought Perez Prado, the King of the Mambo, into the American mainstream. On the record, he rearranged pop hits to fit the Latin dance idiom, adding a few genuine mambos for good measure. Though the album wasn't pure mambo, it was simply delightful music, and it illustrated how to bring world music to a broader, popular audience. The CD reissue includes five bonus tracks. *—Stephen Thomas Erlewine*

Havana 3 AM / 1971 / BMG ✦✦✦✦✦
This is instrumental big-band-jazz-mambo, including a mini-version of the Latin-jazz suite, a big thing in Cubop and as dead as the dodo now. Maynard Ferguson contributed the fine lead trumpet. There's terrific piano and arrangements by PP (his way of setting brass against winds was nonpareil). —*John Storm Roberts, Original Music*

Que Rico Mambo! / 1982 / BMG ✦✦✦
Perez Prado had some huge hits with trivial numbers. But he was also a mambo innovator à la Machito, swing voicings (with a strong Stan Kenton influence) to the Cuban roots, and his sound was extremely distinctive. A retrospective like this one, which includes most of his best material and little junk, belongs in any well-rounded collection. —*John Storm Roberts, Original Music*

Dance Date with . . . Perez Prado / 1994 / Polydor ✦✦✦
The '50s are generally considered to be Prado's peak, but the 1964-68 tracks on this compilation sound just as lively. There are some faint modern touches (mambo covers of "The James Bond Theme" and "Goldfinger"), but basically this is Prado as he sounded during his prime. "Cayetano" has some wonderfully off-key blaring horns, and "Estoy Acabando" has a bubblegum organ reminiscent of ? & the Mysterians. Major drawback is the short running time (only eight songs are included). —*Richie Unterberger*

★ **Mondo Mambo: Best of** / 1995 / Rhino ✦✦✦✦✦
Twenty tracks from the '50s and early '60s. Includes the chart-toppers "Cherry Pink and Apple Blossom White" and "Patricia," but most of the album is given over to sassy, even frenetic at times, mambo dance tunes that rank among the most popular and infectious Cuban pop ever produced. —*Richie Unterberger*

Go Go Mambo / Tumbao ✦✦✦✦✦
This is a wonderful cross-section of Perez Prado's early recordings (1949-1951). It runs from the best of his classic mambos (e.g. "Caballo Negro") to the totally unmamboid but brilliant pop hit, "Cerezo Rosa," and includes a good deal of rare material (check "Pianola"). It was once fashionable to be sniffy about this band. Big mistake: it was a major influence on the best of Cubop and vice versa. —*John Storm Roberts, Original Music*

Arsenio Rodriguez

b. Aug. 30, 1911, Guira de Macurijes, Matanzas, Cuba, **d.** Dec. 31, 1971, Los Angeles, CA

Guitar / Conjunto, Cuba, Latin Continuum
Rodriguez was blinded at age three when kicked in the face by a horse. The Marvelous Blind One, as he was fondly referred to, changed the course of Afro-Cuban dance music when he became the first to utilize the conga drum in a dance band in 1937. His son montuno sound was first heard in 1944, four years after he formed his trumpet conjunto. Considered one of Cuba's best composers and tres guitarist, he left Cuba in 1952 for New York City. —*Max Salazar*

Cuban Counterpoint: History of the Son Montuno / 1992 / Rounder ✦✦✦✦✦
The son montuno, a somewhat more Afro-Cuban subset of the Afro-European creole son, is a basic rhythm (the most compelling of all) in all forms of Cuban music and salsa. This is a mega-must overview, ranging from field recordings of rural guitar-and-percussion to Celia Cruz, Arsenio Rodriguez, and just about every great name in one of the world's great musics. —*John Storm Roberts, Original Music*

A Todos los Barrios / Jun. 1992 / RCA ✦✦✦✦✦
Oh, glory—music from the greatest period of one of the greatest names in classic Cuban conjunto. This is the long-overdue re-release of René López's great 1974 compilation. The original recordings date from 1946-1950. The length is shabby, even for a former LP, and the CD is totally without information beyond titles. But music of any sort—certainly Cuban music—simply does not come more classic than this. —*John Storm Roberts, Original Music*

● **Afro Cuban Classic** / Ansonia ✦✦✦✦✦
From Cuba comes the extremely talented artist and composer, Arsenio Rodriguez. This album was also reviewed by Peter Watrous of the *New York Times*: "'Afro Cuban Classic,' it says simply on the back cover, and this isn't hype. Mr. Rodriguez, a blind Cuban who played the tres, led a terrific band in the '50s and '60s and was an excellent songwriter as well, having written, among other tunes, the standard, 'Bruca Manigua.' Mr. Rodriguez was known as a master of Afro-Cuban music and the disk is loaded with different types of rhythms, ostinatos and riffs that are kicked off by his insistent yet graceful figures." —*Roundup Newsletter*

Arsenio Rodriguez y Su Conjunto / Ansonia ✦✦✦✦✦
This CD version of two albums from his New York period brings together just about all of his material currently available. —*John Storm Roberts*

Sabroso y Caliente / Antilla ✦✦✦
One of the greatest names in classic Cuban conjunto, he is said to have brought both the conga drum and the smoky-sounding tres guitar into the conjunto, and with introducing the mambo rhythm from the religious cults. He was also an important composer, and hired all the major names of his time. This CD is totally without information beyond titles, but the sound is pure Arsenio. —*John Storm Roberts, Original Music*

Vol. 2 / Ansonia ✦✦✦
Singer/tres-player Rodriguez was rightly called the father of all conjunto music, and many of his compositions have become salsa standards. The recordings of his greatest era are all out of print, but this later album gives enough of an idea of the man to fill the gap almost completely. —*John Storm Roberts, Original Music*

Silvio Rodriguez

Guitar, Vocals / Nueva Trova, Cuba, Latin Continuum
A modern Cuban pop musician, Rodriguez's sound is utterly beautiful, passionate, hip, and melodic. Even without subtitles, this is compelling music. —*Hank Davis*

● **Dias y Flores** / 1988 / Hannibal ✦✦✦✦✦
Silvio Rodriguez, one of Cuba's finest guitarists, tried to link the music in his homeland with newer styles from Latin America on 1975's *Dias Y Flores*, issued on compact disc in 1988 by Hannibal. The results were both intriguing and uneven; the playing was always impressive, but sometimes the vocals seemed unfocused or rambled, with Rodriguez and company trying to fit their work into styles they weren't thoroughly familiar with. But most of this is gripping, magical material, particularly the sections where Rodriguez's guitar and the rhythms laid down by Leoginaldo Pimentel, Ignacio Berroa, Norberto Carrillo, and Daniel Aldama converge. —*Ron Wynn*

Nico Saquito

Guitar / Cuba, Latin Continuum
One of Cuba's most famed guitarists, Nico Saquito founded the guaracha style, renowned for its four-line stanzas and humorous lyrics. He was born in Santiago de Cuba in 1901 and began to gain popularity for his compositions by the age of 15. He gave up a career in baseball to join the Castillo Quartet and spent ten years with the band, touring around the country. Returning to Santiago to form the Guaracheos de Oriente, he eventually took that group to tour Venezuela in 1950. He stayed for ten years, until the Revolution forced him to return to Cuba. Saquito spent most of his later years playing in Havana, where Cuba's national record company recorded him in 1982, playing with el Quarteto Patria and el Duo Cubano (two of the country's best groups). That performance, released on World Circuit as *Good-bye Mr. Cat*, proved to be his only American release. Nico Saquito died later that year. —*John Bush*

● **Good-Bye Mr. Cat** / 1982 / World Circuit ✦✦✦✦✦
Saquito was the driving force of the great son trio Los Guaracheros de Oriente. He last recorded in 1982, backed by some truly wonderful string-picking. His voice had faded slightly—after all, he was in his eighties. But both he and his backup have a rarely surpassed charm and flair. Down-home without raunch, masterly without flash, this is some kind of perfection. —*John Storm Roberts, Original Music*

Sexteto Habanero

Bass, Guitar, Percussion, Vocals / Sonero, Cuba, Latin Continuum
At the beginning of the 20th century, three Cuban musicians formed Trio Oriental to perform the folk music that hailed from the west of the island. The trio later added members, changed their name to Sexteto Habanero, and became the first and most influential performers of son, a vivid Afro-Spanish fusion of musical styles. Son consists of two stylistic levels. The first level (African in origin) is a rumba rhythm over which a variety of percussionists improvise. The second level (deriving from Spain) is provided by a combination of three string guitars known as tres and a makeshift bass. Spanish lyrics are sung over the instruments in traditional decima form with rhymed octosyllabic lines. During the 1920s, Sexteto Habanero were the definitive son band of cuba. Their music is featured on two compilations: *Cuban Counterpoint: History of the San Montuno* and *Cuba—El son es la mas sublime*, as well as *The Roots of Salsa*. —*Leon Jackson*

● **Sexteto Habañero** / Tumbao ✦✦✦✦✦
Tumbao is a Swiss label that's turned up with this reissue with some previously unavailable classic sides. This is one of the greatest of the great son groups of the '20s. —*Ned Sublette*

Son Cubano / Tumbao ✦✦✦
The perfect tart is a balance of strawberries, cream, and short pastry. The perfect small-music group is a balance of voices, trumpet, guitars, and percussion—in short, an Afro-Cuban sexteto or septeto performing sones of the great inter-war years. The Sexteto Habanero was one of the two or

three greatest of all, and these 1924-1927 recordings caught them in their early prime. This is what they play in Heaven when the Andeans and the Burmese put down their harps. *—John Storm Roberts, Original Music*

Bebo Valdes

b. 1918, Quivican, Cuba
Piano / Latin Continuum, Afro-Cuban Jazz

★ **Bebo Rides Again** / Nov. 1994 / Messidor ◆◆◆◆◆
This CD is both historic and quite exciting. Bebo Valdes (father of Chucho, the leader of Irakere) was one of the giants of Cuban jazz and popular music until he fled the country in 1960. Amazingly enough he had not recorded since living peacefully in Sweden. This recording is also significant in that it is one of the first times that Cuban exiles had recorded with Cubans still living under Castro (guitarist Carlos Emilio Morales and percussionist Amadito Valdes). Paquito D'Rivera (who organized this set) deserves a lot of credit for its success but Bebo Valdes is the real star. He composed eight new selections in the 36 hours before the recordings began although he was 76 years old at the time! Although Valdes claimed that with the lack of sleep and excess of writing (he also arranged ten of the 11 songs) his fingers felt a bit stiff, he plays quite well throughout the very enjoyable music. The final results are full of strong melodies, stirring rhythms, exciting ensembles and lots of variety. The instrumentation differs on each track with plenty of solo space for D'Rivera (on both alto and clarinet), trombonist Juan-Pablo Torres (who takes "Veinte Anos" as a duet with Valdes), trumpeter Diego Urcola and the pianist. The percussionists work together quite well behind the lead voices and every selection is well worth hearing. This is one of the finest Afro-Cuban jazz recordings of recent times. Highly recommended. *—Scott Yanow*

Cuba Collection

Caliente = Hot / 1977 / New World ◆◆◆◆◆
Five fine NYC roots groups re-create classic idioms from Afro-Cuban drumming through plena to the pure conjunto and sones sound: The Pleneros de la 110th Street, Julito Collazo, Hector Rivera y Su Conjunto, Sexteto Criollo Puertorriqueno, and the Sepeto Son de la Loma. *—John Storm Roberts*

Cuban Dance Party / Jun. 1991 / Rounder ◆◆◆◆◆
This second of three 1990 volumes devoted to past and present Afro-Cuban music included fiery contemporary songs from Irakere and Los Van Van, and vintage tunes by Estrellas Cubanas, Orquesta Orestes Lopez, and Isaac Oviedo and his Family. The modern numbers include jazz, rock, and pop influences backed by riveting Afro-Cuban beats; the older pieces spotlight both classic rhythms and the spirit and customs they represent, providing a direct link with traditional African and Iberian religion and culture. *—Ron Wynn*

Cuba Classics 1: Canciones Urgentes / Warner Bros. ◆◆◆◆◆
This anthology, compiled by David Byrne, consists of various tracks by Silvio Rodriquez, one of the leaders of Cuba's nueva trova (new song) movement. *—Ned Sublette*

Cuba Classics 2: Dancing with the Enemy / 1988 / Luaka Bop ◆◆◆◆◆
Peter Watrous at the *New York Times* gave this one the number-two spot on his Ten Best of 1991 list. These are obscure recordings mostly, the majority from the '60s and '70s. *—Ned Sublette*

Cuba Classics 3 / 1992 / Warner Bros. ◆◆◆◆◆
This album is more forward-looking. Buy with confidence. *—Ned Sublette*

☆ **Cuban Counterpoint** / 1992 / Rounder ◆◆◆◆◆
This 22-track anthology issued by Rounder in 1992 covered the wide-ranging son montuno idiom and its diverse, yet related forms. It included segments from the '20s to the '70s; there were Spanish vocal arrangements and ensembles, polyrhythmic African percussion, linguistic elements of each, and material that sometimes sounded like the songs heard in saloons and cantinas on the Mexican border, and other times like the bustling jam sessions heard in East Coast clubs. The songs were mostly short (none longer than 3.5 minutes) and included several contributions from the great bandleader Arsenio Rodriquez as well as cuts by Sexteto Habanero, Benny More, and the Cachao All Stars featuring El Nino Rivera. It was exhaustively annotated as well. *—Ron Wynn*

Dances of the Gods / Ocora ◆◆◆◆◆
Here's something crucial for percussion buffs: field recordings covering all the major religious traditions (lucumi, arara, palo monte, tambor yuka, abakwa, transplanted Haitian), along with a couple of street rumbas (guaguancó and columbia). More of the latter would have been nice, and the notes are a bit confused on relationships between denominations. But this is still essential stuff. *—John Storm Roberts*

Routes of Rhythm, Vols. 1 & 2 / 1988 / Rounder ◆◆◆
Volume 1 is subtitled *Carnival of Cuban Music* and the second volume is subtitled *Cuban Dance Party*. (See Isaac Oviedo for Volume 3.) *—AMG*

Salsa

In 1974 salsa became a household word in the Hispanic communities. It was first heard when Cuba's Ignacio Pineiro's Sexteto Nacional introduced his tune "Echale Salsita" at the 1932 Chicago World's Fair. Salsa, the Spanish word for spicy sauce, was uttered when dancers urged bandleaders to swing the music. The word lay dormant until 1962, when Seeco Records released Joe Cuba's Stepping Out album, which was vocalist Jimmy Sabater's tune "Salsa y Bembe." Salsa's boost to national recognition occurred after Cal Tjader's 1964 recording of "Soul Sauce" (Salsa del Alma), which received airplay on jazz, R&B, and Latin-music programs across the United States. It achieved international acceptance after the fiery music of the Fania All-Stars and the bands of Larry Harlow, Johnny Pacheco, Ray Barretto, Eddie Palmieri, Orchestra Broadway, La Sonora Poncena, Willie Rosario, El Gran Combo, the Willie Colon/Ruben Blades combination, and Tito Puente modernized the Afro-Cuban sound in the '70s. *—Max Salazar*

Dominican Republic

Jossie/Patrulla Esteban

Merengue, Latin Continuum, Dominican Republic

Noches de Copas / TTH ◆◆◆
Esteban has chalked up some hefty hits over the last few years on a mix of tearaway vocals, humor, and a tight, tight band. Patrulla 15 put merengue and salsa romantica together in a terrific album with salsa fire, merengue's manic joviality and the richness of the best Latino pop. Which is why they survived the merengue decline so successfully. *—John Storm Roberts, Original Music*

● **Los Exitazos de . . .** / TTH ◆◆◆◆◆
The dominance of merengue in the early '80s gave way to another trend in contemporary salsa, the blending of romantic themes with hot backings, and arrangements that use both salsa and bolero voicings (which used to be very different styles). In Acariciame, Patrulla 15 put it all together in a terrific album with salsa fire, merengue's manic joviality and the richness of the best Latino pop. *—John Storm Roberts, Original Music*

Tatico Henriquez

Latin Continuum, Dominican Republic

● **20 Exitos** / Bachata ◆◆◆◆◆
Henriquez, like the other great names of last-generation accordion-quartet merengue típico, stood out only on quality, not style, from the guys who came into town on Sunday to play for dimes. The craggy rural voice, the punch of the accordion, the drive of the tambora drum, the slashing guira scraper, are all (marvelously) as close to the roots as you can get. *—John Storm Roberts, Original Music*

Homenaje a . . . / Kubaney ◆◆◆◆◆
These rural merengues and mangulinas come from one of the true greats of the genre, with a sharp country voice and an accordion style to match. I've recorded this kind of merengue in the field, and the only difference isn't stylistic, it's Henriquez's tightness, in-tuneness and general making-it-sound-the-way-it's-meant-to. There's even a marimbula (what the Jamaicans call a rumba-box) in there. He was no naïf, but he wasn't just close to the roots, he was the roots. *—John Storm Roberts, Original Music*

Johnny Ventura

Merengue, Latin Continuum, Dominican Republic

Y Su Combo / Kubaney ◆◆◆◆◆
With the rise of the merengue new wave, Ventura, once the hippest of the salsa-merengueros, has become something of a Grand Old Man—an elder statesman à la Tito Puente. Here are the original versions of some of his greatest hits going back a couple of decades, including "El Pinguino" and "El Problema de Ramon." This stuff holds up. *—John Storm Roberts*

Dominican Republic Collection

Afro-Dominican Music from San Cristóbal / Smithsonian Folkways ◆◆◆
Recorded and with good notes by Morton Marks. The best of the rural Afro-Dominican recorded material. *—John Storm Roberts*

Bachatazos, Vol. 1 / Jose Luis ◆◆◆
Bachata Rosa, though pretty enough, was basically the pop sound you'd

expect from a big hit. The music in this first-of-its-kind compilation is the real bachata, the small-town guitar-based music that grew from Dominican backyard barbecues of the same name. It's mostly bolero-based, but its influences (other than local) are enormously varied: from classic trios to Mexican to Puerto Rican. —*John Storm Roberts*

Stripping the Parrots: Essential Merengue / 1995 / Corason ✦✦✦
It's hard to beat the loony rural merengue of the Dominican Republic, which may or may not add a splendidly manic solo sax style bouncing off the accordion. This is a great introduction from five bands, four of them accordion-centered, the fifth a bachata guitar group. All have that real rural sound, jaunty, repetitive, and exhilaratingly unpretentious. (The title comes from the Spanish name of the style—it's all in the notes.) —*John Storm Roberts*

Ecuador

Karu Nan

Ecuador, Latin Continuum

Chimbaloma / 1994 / Tumi ✦✦✦
Ecuadorian music of any kind is rare on record, as is Andean music not by new age-tinged PC middle-class bands with Quechua names. These guys are all peasants and craftsmen living in the village of Chimbaloma, and—polished though they are—they have real roots. —*John Storm Roberts, Original Music*

Ecuador Collection

Music of the Jivaro / Smithsonian/Folkways ✦✦✦
This is the music of an interesting jungle tribal people. —*David L. Mayers*

Mexico

Los Alegres de Teran

Mexico, Latin Continuum

Triunfadores del Norte / CBS ✦✦✦
This hugely popular norte¤o group was introduced to Anglos by Chris Strachwitz's reissues. The basic sound here is the gentle older duo/trio style, in which accordion and bajo sexto are underpinned by electric bass, but not traps. As in most of the Alegres' many recordings, however, the core unit is joined on-and-off by mariachi backings. —*John Storm Roberts*

El Golpe Traidor / CBS Latino ✦✦✦
Here's a hugely popular norteno group. The basic sound here is the older duo/trio style, in which accordion and bajo sexto are underpinned by electric bass, but not traps. Unlike many of the Alegres' many recordings, the core unit is joined here by solo sax rather than mariachi trumpet, which gives this release a more down-home sound than some of the Alegres' recordings. —*John Storm Roberts, Original Music*

● **Canijas Viejas** / CBS Latino ✦✦✦✦✦
This enormously popular norteno group was introduced to Anglos by the indefatigable Chris Strachwitz. This record is the one the Latinos buy. The basic sound here is the gentle older duo/trio style, in which accordion and bajo sexto are underpinned by electric bass, but not traps. As in most of the Alegres' many CBS recordings, however, the core unit is joined by on-and-off mariachi trumpets, harps, and such. —*John Storm Roberts, Original Music*

Lola Beltran

Mexico, Ranchera, Latin Continuum

La Grande . . . / Peerless ✦✦✦
Lola Beltran has claims to be the greatest woman singer in the high-octane pop-ranchera style. The Beltran CD has a wide range of superb songs. Perhaps the finest is one, somewhat out of her main line, called "Pelea de Gallos"; there's also a "Caballo Blanco" which is worth comparing with Jimenez's original. —*John Storm Roberts*

Hermandos Vega

Mexico, Latin Continuum

Esto Es Puro Norteno / 1994 / Dos coronas ✦✦✦
. . . Pure Norteno indeed: clean and crisp and classic, with punchy, mellow accordion and all the fixins. There's a notably fine bass player, too. The Brothers Vegas recently took top honors at the Arizona Battle of the Norteno Bands. —*John Storm Roberts, Original Music*

Pregoneros Del Puerto

Mexico, Latin Continuum

● **Music of Veracruz** / 1985 / Rounder ✦✦✦✦✦
Entrancing, often ethereal songs from Los Pregoneros del Puerto, play-ing music from Veracruz. The most immediately striking characteristic is the harp playing of Gonzalo Mata. His strumming, swirling lines are punctuated by tremendous singing from Jose Gutierrez and equally effective harmonizing. Likewise, the guitar interplay and percussive support add depth to the setting. While this isn't as rhythmic or percussive as other Latin music genres, it has widespread harmonic and melodic appeal. The songs are short (none longer than 3 1/2 minutes), but performed with enough vigor to get and hold your attention. —*Ron Wynn*

Sones Jarochos / 1990 / Rounder ✦✦✦✦
The sones of the harp-led groups of Vera Cruz are a lot more complex than norteno music both rhythmically and in playing style, and arguably even more impassioned. Los Pregoneros del Puerto are an old-established professional group with a regional base, so they are both authentic and virtuoso, which is by no means always the case. With superb music and very full notes with lyrics and translations, it rates four stars at least. —*John Storm Roberts*

Lucha Reyes

Mexico, Latin Continuum

● **Exitos** / BMG ✦✦✦✦✦
Not much is known about Reyes except what one hears; she was a powerful ranchera singer with a fresh and natural style nearer to the grassroots than most later singers. The original copyright of this collection is 1964 but she both sounds and looks earlier. Perhaps she was, like most, a singer/filmstar, but both her singing and the instrumental backing date from a simpler time. —*John Storm Roberts*

Mexico Collection

Fiestas of Chiapas & Oaxaca / Nonesuch ✦✦✦
This is an excellent selection, ranging from church music to brass band, small string ensemble, solo singer, and guitar. David Lewiston must be highly commended for this brilliant recording, now available on CD. —*David L. Mayers*

Indian Music of Northwest Mexico / Canyon ✦✦✦
Indian Music of the Northwest Mexico: Tarahumara—Warihio—Mayo features lovely, gentle music, including matachin dance with five violins, pascola with harp, violin, and rattles. —*David L. Mayers*

Mexique: Musique Traditionnelles / Ocora ✦✦✦
This is a good introduction to traditional music from Mexico. —*David L. Mayers*

Modern Maya: Indian Music of Chiapas / Smithsonian/Folkways ✦✦✦
Soulful and plaintive music, it was recorded at various fiestas, with violins, harps, and guitars. —*David L. Mayers*

Music of the Tarascan Indians / Smithsonian/Folkways ✦✦✦
Included is some fine guitar and violin music, chirimias and flutes from one of the most musically interesting areas of Mexico. —*David L. Mayers*

Tejano Roots: Orquestas Tejanas: The Formative . . . / 1992 / Arhoolie ✦✦✦✦✦
These are small combos and orchestras which played for the more formal dances. Some are slick, some very primitive, with varying arrangements. There's a much more urban sound to these. The time period covered is 1946-66. — *Cliff Martin*

Tex-Mex Border Music, Vol. 1: An Introduction / 1970 / Folk Lyric ✦✦✦✦✦
This LP anthology on the Folk Lyric spans 14 volumes of various Mexican border music, the titles of the first five of which are listed here. —*AMG*

Yaqui Dances / Smithsonian/Folkways ✦✦✦
Haunting, enchanting, and beautiful music, it has violin and guitar. —*David L. Mayers*

Panama

Rubén Blades

b. Jul. 16, 1948, Panama City, Panama
Guitar, Vocals / Salsa, New York Salsa, Tropicalia, Latin Soul, Latin Continuum, Panama, United States

Rubén Blades is a voice of power in the worlds of both music and politics: a leading salsa musician and a radical critic of Latin American dictatorships. He was born in Panama City to singer/pianist Anoland Blades and a police officer Rubén Blades, Sr. He credits his paternal grandmother, a vegetarian Rosicrucian/spiritualist who practiced yoga, for instilling in him a lifelong passion for truth and justice by introducing him to Hollywood films and US culture. During the '50s, Blades and his friends loved American rock 'n' roll, spending many hours perfecting the songs even though they didn't understand the English lyrics. Eventually,

Blades learned English and in 1963 sang it in his brother's pop band. His infatuation with North American culture abruptly ended when a violent conflict erupted between Panama and the US over the flying of the Panamanian flag beside the American flag over a Canal Zone high school. The skirmish left 21 dead and injured 500 of Blades' countrymen. Disillusioned, the young singer turned his interest toward Latin music and sang only in Spanish. Early Latin influences included Joe Cuba and Ismael Rivera.

In 1966, Blades became a singer with Conjunto Latino and then sang with Los Salvajes del Ritmo until 1969 while studying law at the University of Panama. While there, Joe Cuba invited Blades to sing with his band, but he declined, preferring to finish his schooling first. Shortly thereafter, military turmoil forced the temporary closure of the school, leading Blades to visit New York. There he recorded *De Panama a Nuevo York* with Pete Rodriguez. Blades composed all but one of the songs on the album. He then returned to the university where following graduation in 1974, Blades worked as a lawyer for the Bank of Panama. He then helped rehabilitate convicts before returning to New York to work in the mailroom at Fania Records.

At the suggestion of a mutual acquaintance, bandleader Ray Barretto auditioned Blades in the mailroom as a replacement for Tito Allen. Blades debuted with Barretto's band that summer at Madison Square Gardens. He then appeared on Barretto's 1975 eponymous album; afterward Barretto left to form a new band and Blades renamed the old group Guarare. Blades gained widespread recognition when he composed and performed "El Cazangero" for Willie Colon on Colon's album *The Good, the Bad, and the Ugly.* The song earned Blades the *Latin NY* magazine's "Composer of the Year" award in 1976. He continued performing with Colon and the Fania All-Stars through 1978. At the same time he began writing songs for himself and other artists including Ricardo Ray, Ismael Miranda, Cheo Feliciano, and Tito Puente. In 1978, working in conjunction with Colon, Blade} recorded *Siembra*, which has become the bestselling salsa album ever and continues to set the standard for the genre. Blades' subsequent albums continue to be enormously popular and demonstrate his increasing willingness to explore other musical traditions without compromising the integrity of his Latin American roots. The 1985 *Escenas* featured Linda Ronstadt and Joe Jackson, while the smash hit *Nothing But the Truth*, numbered Elvis Costello, Lou Reed, and Sting.

In addition to his musical career, Blades has also actively pursued an acting career, making his feature film debut in 1985's *Crossover Dreams.* Subsequent films include *Critical Condition, The Milagro Beanfield War*, and *The Two Jakes.* Blades also headlined a British television documentary, *The Return of Rubén Blades*, and it was here that he first mentioned his political aspirations. A recurrent theme in his recordings and performances is the need for Latin Americans to transcend national barriers and unite as a people. Blades ran in the Panamanian presidential election in 1994 to gain a solid second place. *—Leon Jackson and Sandra Brennan*

Bohemio y Poeta / 1979 / Fania ✦✦✦
This release was a transition between Blades' post-Willie Colon sound and the '80s *Seis del Solar.* The salsa sounds predominate much of the time, and there's a Cuban classic in among his own compositions. But keyboards and vibes (presumably from Louie Ramirez, who did some of the arranging) point to a new dispensation in the offing, with their (here, at least, very successful) fusion edge. *—John Storm Roberts*

Buscando America / 1984 / Elektra ✦✦✦✦✦
A masterful concept album (the title means "searching for America"), it spins hard-hitting tales of Latino strife and American injustice. This album includes some of his most gorgeous ballads. *—John Floyd*

Escenas / 1985 / Elektra ✦✦✦
There's a lot going on here, aside from Blades' agreeable duet with Linda Ronstadt and the Joe Jackson solo, which got the press. Besides, pianist Ricardo Marrero has long been on many "most-underrated" lists. *—John Storm Roberts, Original Music*

Crossover Dreams / 1986 / Elektra ✦✦✦
An album of salsa music prominently featuring the work of Ruben Blades, who also starred in the 1985 film. *—William Ruhlmann*

Antecedente / 1988 / Elektra ✦✦✦
Although sung in his native tongue, his return to exuberant, dance-oriented salsa breaks through all language barriers. *—John Floyd*

★ **Ruben Blades y Son del Solar...Live!** / Mar. 20, 1990 / Elektra ✦✦✦✦✦
A smoldering set, it was recorded live with his 11-piece band, Son del Solar, who romp and stomp for over an hour. Perfect for parties. *—John Floyd*

Doble Filo / Fania ✦✦✦
Stylistically, this Blades release goes back to his professional roots with a backup band with the two-trombone lineup beloved of his first best musical buddy, Willie Colon. It's vintage Blades in several senses: intelli-

gent but (in salsa terms) fairly mainstream—no musical barriers trodden down. On the other hand, there's outstandingly intelligent treatment of that mainstream (and some tributaries of it). *—John Storm Roberts, Original Music*

Panama Collection

Street Music of Panama / 1988 / Original Music ✦✦✦✦✦
Panamanian music is among the most exciting in the whole Afro-Latin area. On the Afro end are the voices-and-drums tamboritos, sung and played superbly here by groups of young women. The fiddle-and-percussion cumbia and guitar-backed mejorana are both real Creole idioms, whose Spanish and African elements are both crucial. Then there's the carnival music of the diablitos, and oddest of all, the howling gritos of the midnight hours. This is the real thing, taped before the tradition began to fade. It is also the only album devoted to this wonderful idiom, and capped by a charming piece of Choco Indian flute playing. *—John Storm Roberts*

Paraguay Collection

Chiriguanos of Paraguay / Nonesuch ✦✦✦
This is bright, lively music played on guarani harps, sometimes with singing. *—David L. Mayers*

Peru

Huayno Music of Peru
· ·
World Fusion, Peruvian, South America
Huayno is the popular music of the Indians from the Andean mountain regions of Peru. Many of these indigenous people have left their homes to find employment in Lima and other cities, bringing back a cross-fertilizing element of urban culture and music to their villages. *—Myles Boisen*

★ **Huayno Music of Peru, Vol. 1** / 1989 / Arhoolie ✦✦✦✦✦
The popular huaynos of Peru go back hundreds of years and come in all sorts of forms, from village square to (relatively) bigtime pop. Part Spanish, part Indian, they are almost nothing like the better-known Latin forms in feeling or rhythm. As this superlative collection shows, the truly popular versions are almost hypnotically beguiling. *—David L. Mayers*

Inti-Illimani
· ·
Peruvian, Latin Continuum
A six-piece South American folk group with ethnic instrumentation. *—Michael G. Nastos*

● **Imagination** / 1984 / Redwood ✦✦✦✦✦
Andean folkloric instrumental music; 14 tracks with the emphasis on joy and light. *—Michael G. Nastos*

Leyenda / Jan. 1990 / CBS ✦✦✦
Inti-Illimani's assortment of wind, string, and percussion instruments, in collaboration with the two master guitarists, has now yielded a world music recording which celebrates unity in diversity while managing to communicate the deep-rooted commitment to freedom and human rights at the core of Inti-Illimani's music. *—Backroads Music/Heartbeats*

Palimpsesto / Redwood ✦✦✦
Also a good representation of their work. *—Michael G. Nastos*

Sukay
· ·
Peruvian, South America
Sukay specializes in Peruvian music of the Andes Mountains. Led by the Badouxes, musicologists from San Francisco, these are storytellers with romantic presence. *—Michael G. Nastos*

● **Music of the Andes** / 1978 / Flying Fish ✦✦✦✦✦
Traditional music of Peru, Argentina, Ecuador, and Bolivia. Music of wooden panflutes is most prevalent. Led by Edmond and Quentin Badoux, who play Peruvian traditional music. Beautiful. *—Michael G. Nastos*

Mama Luna / Flying Fish ✦✦✦
This one-woman, two-man trio presents lovely Ecuadorian, Peruvian, and Bolivian music featuring notched bamboo flutes, pan pipes, and charangos or Andean guitars, with lead vocals by Quentin Howard (a woman). Some contemporary material with Spanish lyrics is included in addition to their trademark traditional instrumentals; so this, their fifth release, should appeal to an even broader audience. *—Ladyslipper*

Peru Collection

Ayllu Sulca: Music of the Incas / Lyrichord ✦✦✦
This is music for harp, two violins, quena flutes, mandolin, and percus-

sion, recorded in Ayacucho, in the Quechua heartland. This family group combines village ruggedness with a certain musical "sophistication," to an unusual and mostly very striking effect. It's more interesting than the rather over-polite groups that get most of the running when it comes to Andean music—often on the basis of political correctness rather than real musical distinction. —*David L. Mayers*

Fiestas of Peru: Music of the High Andes / Nonesuch ✦✦✦
With flutes, harps, guitars—this is festive music. —*David L. Mayers*

Flutes and Strings of the Andes / 1984 / Music of the World ✦✦✦
This is an outstanding recording from an area almost entirely represented on record by imitators rather than source musicians. It casts a fairly wide net, with examples for voices, flutes, strings, and percussion from three provinces. Track by track, the music is marvelous, and the cassette is admirably programmed for diversity as well as authenticity. Good notes, too, for a cassette. —*John Storm Roberts*

☆ **Huayno Music of Peru, Vol. 1** / 1989 / Arhoolie ✦✦✦✦✦
The popular huaynos of Peru go back hundreds of years and come in all sorts of forms, from village square to (relatively) bigtime pop. Part Spanish, part Indian, they are almost nothing like the better-known Latin forms in feeling or rhythm. As this superlative collection shows, the truly popular versions are almost hypnotically beguiling. —*David L. Mayers*

Indian Harps / Playasound ✦✦✦
The Indios took to the Spanish harp with enthusiasm and creativity, building a dozen regional variants and styles. This particularly beguiling release covers Mexico, Venezuela, Colombia, Paraguay, and Peru. The range is from wonderfully fiery street groups to virtuoso concert performers. —*David L. Mayers*

Mountain Music [Peru] / Smithsonian/Folkways ✦✦✦
Here is a most interesting and comprehensive collection of Peruvian music—Quechua and mestizo. —*David L. Mayers*

Mountain Music of Peru, Vol. 1 / 1986 / Smithsonian/Folkways ✦✦✦
What makes a satisfactory national compilation is obviously to some extent a question of ideology. This one is superb as an overview and introduction. It ranges from shepherd pipe, solo voice, and carnival music, to popular huaynos from the towns. Unlike the plethora of middle-class groups with a political agenda that beclutter the field, this one does music that is real and superb, as are John Cohen's notes. Parts were released in 1966, but 15 minutes has been added for this re-release. —*John Storm Roberts*

Puerto Rico

El Gran Combo

Piano / Salsa, Tropicalia, Puerto Rico, Latin Continuum
Led by Puerto Rican pianist-composer-arranger Rafael Ithier, which was the Rafael Cortijo y su Combo in 1959. Since the '70s El Combo has become a top seller and sells out performances. —*Max Salazar*

● **Nuestra Música** / 1971 / Combo ✦✦✦✦✦
El Gran Combo is a perennial sellout on pure tight mainstream salsa alone—mainstream in the contemporary sense, which includes a lot of Puerto Rican tinge. Here they carry the Boricua sound especially far, with an album rich in plena, bomba, and even jibaro riffs and rhythms. They're also pretty funny guys: the jibaro-style "No Hay Cama Pa' Tanta Gente" rings a very cute change on the standard let's-mention-everybody. —*John Storm Roberts*

Boogaloos Con . . . / 1972 / Gema ✦✦✦
Coming from the band's very early days, this is the genuine '60s Real Thing. The album has a lot of straight salsa in the Combo's typical downhome sound. It was arranged by pianist/leader Ralph Ithier and features Andy Montanez on lead vocals. —*John Storm Roberts*

Latin-Up / 1973 / Combo ✦✦✦
The title cut of the band's newest release is a sort of a boogalu in spots. As was and is customary, this album has a lot of straight salsa as is typical of the Combo's sound, arranged by Ralph Ithier. —*John Storm Roberts*

Innovations / Cmo ✦✦✦
A more mainstream album, this—and therefore a good way to find out what's so special about these fellows. One thing is a tendency to surprising little touches like a sudden soprano sax solo. But the most important ingredients are bedrock: a fine, flexible, individual singer in Charlie Aponte, intelligent leadership by Rafael Ithier. —*John Storm Roberts, Original Music*

Romantico . . . Sabroso / Cmo ✦✦✦
Here's more from one of the island's finest salsa groups. EGC, of course, is a little mellower, as befits an institution. —*John Storm Roberts, Original Music*

Bailando Con el Mundo / Combo ✦✦✦
They bring to the mainstream a particularly mellow approach to vocals,

ensembles and solos alike (though not always—check out the powerful opener to the anniversary CDs here). All of which informs and warms their two most recent releases, *Gracias* and the pricey but unusually good-value 30th-anniversary double CD. Can it really be five years since their quarter-century? —*John Storm Roberts, Original Music*

Willie Rosario

b. May 6, 1930, Cuomo, Puerto Rico
Percussion / Salsa, Puerto Rico, Latin Continuum
Arriving in New York City from Puerto Rico in 1948, Rosario was moved by Tito Puente's drumming ability at the Palladium Ballroom. He began his percussion studies and made his pro debut with Johnny Sequi's band in 1953. When Sequi moved to Puerto Rico, Rosario took over the band and today it is among the most popular salsa and Latin jazz aggregations in Latin America. —*Max Salazar*

● **Roaring Fifties** / Sonotone Latino ✦✦✦✦✦
Percussionist Rosario moved back to Puerto Rico in the '70s, but he came up in NYC. He once said his influences were the likes of Tito Rodriguez and Herbie Mann, not the Cubans. He also said, "I like clean music, music that has definition." Put those two elements together and you have a dynamite big-band sound: crisp, elegant, and driving. Call it timelessly classic, but this band plays as freshly as if they'd only just invented the sound. —*John Storm Roberts*

La Sonora Poncena

Salsa, Puerto Rico, Latin Continuum
One of Puerto Rico's most popular orchestras, which was founded by Quique Lucca in 1954 in Ponce, Puerto Rico. La Poncena is directed by Lucca's son, the brilliant composer, arranger, and keyboardist, Papo, born in 1950. Papo Lucca's career started in 1964 when he became the band's pianist. At the moment, La Poncena is among the top five salsa and Latin jazz bands in Latin music. —*Max Salazar*

● **On the Right Track** / Inca ✦✦✦✦✦
Sonora Poncena is one of the best bands around—and not just in Puerto Rico, though that's where it's based. With the possible exception of pianist Papo Lucca, these aren't names—just a very tight, fresh group with the ability to make a tradition-based sound brand new. Listen to the sudden trumpet duet in "Odiame" and rejoice. —*John Storm Roberts*

Puerto Rico Collection

Grandes del Cuatro / Leon ✦✦✦✦✦
A tremendous recording of a little-known member of the American guitar family, the four-string Venezuelan cuatro, fronting five small guitar-and-percussion combos in a variety of styles: mainly Venezuelan folkloric, but including the occasional bossa and jazz number. The playing is even more manically virtuosic than flamenco, echoes of which surface here. Andean touches are also prevalent. —*Carl Hoyt, Original Music*

Music of Puerto Rico 1929-1946 / Harlequin ✦✦✦✦✦
This is a very fine set of recordings, mostly string groups, mostly from the mid-'30s. Many of them are by New York-Puerto Rican groups in the fashionable Cuban idioms of the time—boleros, sones, and so forth—by major composers like Pedro Berrios and Rafael Hernandez. These have a lot of charm, but the gems are a handful of truly Puerto Rican forms: seises, aguinaldos, and plenas. A major bonus is a two-clarinet-lead danza. The only bummer: the greatest of all early pleneros, Canario, appears just once, playing a commercial bolero. —*John Storm Roberts*

Return on Wings of Pleasure: Pedro Padilla y su Conjunto / Rounder ✦✦✦
This mellow group from Puerto Rico was recently recorded. —*David L. Mayers*

South America Collection

Anthology of Central & South American Indians / Smithsonian/Folkways ✦✦✦
Here's a good sampling from Yaquis in the north all the way to Tierra del Fuego. —*David L. Mayers*

Arpa Instrumental / Kubaney ✦✦✦
This is a very fine and varied instrumental collection despite the maddening lack of information, the ubiquitous "Alma Llanera," and the cheesecake cover. There are 14 pulsing, melancholic, sentimental Andean harp songs reflecting various influences from Spanish to Trinidadian (plus a fine duet for harp and pan). —*David L. Mayers*

In Praise of Oxala & Other Gods . . . / Nonesuch ✦✦✦
In Praise of Oxala & Other Gods—Black Music of South America is festive music from Colombia, Ecuador, and Brazil. —*David L. Mayers*

United States

Willie Colon

b. Apr. 28, 1950, Bronx, NY

Trombone, Vocals / Jazz, Salsa, New York Salsa, Latin Soul, Latin Jazz, Latin Continuum, United States

A hero in Latin America and one of the major names in contemporary Latin music, Willie Colon has been a major bandleader, composer, producer, vocalist, and trombonist since the early '60s. He began playing trumpet at 12, then switched to trombone at 14. Colon began music studies while he directed a 14-piece group the Latin Jazz All-Stars. His first professional group used a two-trombone frontline in homage to Eddie Palmieri. Colon signed with Fania at 17, and his debut album was *El Malo*. He quickly scored hits with the singles "Jazzy" and "I Wish I Had a Watermelon." Vocalist Hector Lavoe, also a Puerto Rican, was Colon's lead vocalist and worked with him until the mid-'70s.

Colon helped introduce non-Cuban musical influences and players into the Latin music and Latin jazz mainstream. His albums have been famous for their multi-cultural blends. Colon has drawn from African children's songs, Brazilian, Cuban, Caribbean, and Panamanian numbers. He featured Panamanian cuatro (ten-string) player Yomo Toro on the hit single "La Murga." Ntozake Shange later used the single "Che Che Cole" in her production of "for colored girls who have considered suicide when the rainbow is enuf." It was adapted from a Ghanaian children's song. Colon's songs addressed everything from street crime to politics. He used the Puerto Rican "bomba" rhythm, jazz, and even featured Sha Na Na guitarist Elliott Randall on one cut.

Throughout the '70s and '80s, Colon expanded his musical options and experimented. He gave the reins of his band to Lavoe at one point, then brought Rubén Blades in to team with him. Colon wrote a salsa ballad for a New York television production in the late '70s. He began collaborating with the great vocalist Celia Cruz in the late '70s, and produced a pair of successful Blades albums. Colon won musician, producer, arranger, and trombonist of the year in 1978 from *Latin New York*'s readers poll, and repeated as Musician of the Year in 1981, while also winning Album of the Year for *Fantasmas*. Colon maintained his hectic pace during the '80s. He worked with Ismael Miranda, Lavoe, Cruz and Blades. Colon's '82 album with Blades, *Canciones del Solar de los Aburriodos*, won a Grammy. He visited Europe for the first time in the '80s, and formed a new band. Both Blades and Lavoe went their separate ways, while Colon continued his idiomatic fusions. He recorded songs by Jacques Brel, Carole King, and Mark Knopfler, did a big band date, produced albums with soca and Haitian rhythms, recorded songs by Brazilian composers Caetano Veloso and Wally Salomao, and his own lyrics became more overtly political and satirical. Colon produced albums for Lavoe and Cruz in the late '80s, while also having an international club hit with the single "Set Fire to Me."

Colon was one of several prominent Latin stars involved with David Byrne's controversial but hugely successful Latin music album. He viewed the conflict with a bemused attitude, freely admitting Byrne was no Latino or salsero master, but also acknowledging that neither he nor Celia Cruz had the clout to get on Warner Bros. at that point. Despite his involvement at every level of the music business and international stature, Colon doesn't have an album listed in the Schwann catalog. His numerous Fania releases are available from Latin music stores. —*Ron Wynn and Max Salazar*

Guisando / 1969 / Fania ✦✦✦
His third album has, for trivia buffs, his second-favorite cover. Colon was 20 at the time, and this is still the funky, riotous, sometimes mildly ragged and chaotic sound of his early days. The hallmarks are exuberance, humor, innovation, lots of Colon compositions and, as a bonus, the fine piano of the band's African-American pianist, Mark Diamond. —*John Storm Roberts*

★ **The Good, the Bad, the Ugly** / 1975 / Fania ✦✦✦✦✦
This classic recording is by one of the most creative heads in New York salsa. In 1975 *The Good...*, a New Directions release after Colon got fed up with the two-trombone sound, was the evidence that he could reach beyond his youthful sound into an idiom both wider and deeper. It was also the last album with Hector Lavoe, who had decided to stay a teen idol. *The Big Break, Asalto Navideno*, and this album in their different ways were pinnacles of early- to mid-'70s salsa. —*John Storm Roberts*

Vigilante / 1983 / Fania ✦✦✦
The 1983 *Vigilante*, the last recording Colon made with his longtime singer Lavoe, has three substantial cuts with the classic Colon sound. The title song, sung by Colon, is more experimental and a less successful one. The title track also includes both rock and jazz soloing. —*John Storm Roberts, Original Music*

Canciones del Solar de los Aburridos / 1983 / Fania ✦✦✦
The Colon/Blades partnership produced the tightest combinations of musical creativity and lyrical intensity in recent salsa. This 1981 album

is among their finest: ominous harmonies, meaningful lyrics, tradition shot with experimentation: constant surprise and constant pleasure. —*John Storm Roberts, Original Music*

Color Americano / 1990 / Discos CBS International ✦✦✦
Alone among the big names that came up in the late '60s, Colon is always fresh, because he's always trying to make music rather than hits. In his latest album he relies on his own ever-better singing and on a good deal of excellent sax (uncredited) to enrich his usual fine sense of melody and lyrics, and a gutsy mainstream-original instrumental approach. —*John Storm Roberts, Original Music*

Singers of the Cibao / 1994 / Vaya ✦✦✦✦
Two of the biggest influences on Colon were traditional Puerto Rican music and the two-trombone sound created by bandleader Mon Rivera. In this wonderful 1975 attempt to revive Rivera's career, both elements get a full workout. It was one of Colon's warmest albums and was rewarded by almost immediate oblivion. So it's a real joy to see it revived in its turn. —*John Storm Roberts, Original Music*

Asalto Navideno / Fania ✦✦✦
A groundbreaking early-'70s recording, *Asalto Navideno* was a Christmas album, and Christmas is the time when the old jibaro mountain sound comes briefly into its own. Colon hired cuatro player Yomo Toro and gave him a leading role, launching him on a new career. A major album, it includes one of Colon's finest Panamanian-flavored early hits, "La Murga." —*John Storm Roberts*

Especial No 5 / Sonotone Latino ✦✦✦
One half of this album was recorded in Colombia, the other in New York. Neither is Colon at his best, in our view, but for the record here it is. —*John Storm Roberts, Original Music*

Honra y Cultura / Discos CBS International ✦✦✦
Though the adulation given Colon's early recordings is fully justified, it has the unfortunate side-effect of blinding people to his equally fine recent recordings. Yet aside from the fact that he'd turned himself into an excellent and very individual singer, the recordings he made just before his political ambitions took over are by any measure outstanding. The 1991 *Honra y Cultura* reverted to Colon's historic passion for Puerto Rican music, featuring cuatro player Yomo Toro in two compositions by the great jíbaro singer Ramito. But as always, the references—not just jíbaro, but touches of both rap and toasting, jazz, on and on—were unified by an overall vision combining passion and humor. —*John Storm Roberts, Original Music*

Metiendo Mano / Fania ✦✦✦✦✦
Salsa history in the making: the album in which Willie Colon introduced Rubén Blades to the wider world. An obvious classic, given Blades' subsequent history, but it's also a gorgeous album with Yomo Toro on two tracks (one playing guitar), the great pianist Sonny Bravo on two cuts, and ace percussion with Milton Cardona and Nicky Marrero. —*John Storm Roberts*

☆ **The Big Break/La Gran Fuga** / Fania ✦✦✦✦✦
Colon's third album is the clearest early sign of his individuality, with a Ghanaian children's song, the first of his Panamanian-influenced numbers, and a prophetic venture into Brazilian rhythms. —*John Storm Roberts*

Tiempo Pa' Matar / Fania ✦✦✦
Colon, one of the most creative heads of the '60s, has retained the same restlessness and inquiring mind, and the same ability to come up with music both beguiling and intelligent. (Check out the use of the female *coro* in "Volo" on this album.) With fine vocals and fine musicians, who would dare claim to spot all the stylistic sideglances under the surface of this subtle and enchanting album? —*John Storm Roberts*

El Malo / Fania ✦✦✦✦✦
El Malo was Colon and Hector Lavoe's first recording, made in 1967 when Colon was a mere 17 years old. Every number's a killer: "Jazzy," "Juana Pena," "Borinquen," "El Malo." *Plus* boogalu! —*Carl Hoyt, Original Music*

Joe Cuba (Gilberto Calderon)

New York Salsa, Tropicalia, Latin Continuum, United States

Cuba's music career started with La Alfarona X in 1950. In 1955 the Joe Cuba Sextet came into being and his vibraharp sound caught on. In 1962, when the group recorded "To Be with You" for Seeco Records, the band began to soar to popularity because of Nick Jimenez's arrangements and the vocals of Cheo Feliciano and Jimmy Sabater. When the boogaloo era arrived, the majority of the popular New York bands were put out of work. The Cuba sound changed with its recordings of "El Pito" and "Bang Bang"; it not only sold millions but enabled the Cuba sextet to enjoy the No. 1 spot in the Latin music world along with the Eddie Palmieri Orchestra. —*Max Salazar*

● **Joe Cuba Sextet** / Tico ✦✦✦✦✦
The '50s and '60s cusp saw a last flowering of the bilingual, Cubop-inflected, often vibraphone-led quintet sound. Puente was one of its heav-

ies, but in New York at least, the tradition was maintained into the pachanga and even boogalu era of the '60s by Joe Cuba. Jaunty mambo, soupy English-lyric boleros, Latin-jazz or neo-tipico; this was an archetypal Latin New York sound. —*John Storm Roberts*

HMA Salsa

Latin Folk, Latin Continuum, United States
Jazz orchestra. The Hispanic Musician Association of Los Angeles Big Band is a repertory orchestra that plays hip Afro-Cuban music. New to national audiences. Worth your attention. —*Michael G. Nastos*

★ **California Salsa** / Apr. 24, 1992 / Sea Breeze ✦✦✦✦
Fine West Coast band with an excellent feel for what this music brings to jazz and vice versa. A group/collective to watch and listen to. —*Michael G. Nastos*

California Salsa II / 1994 / Dos Coronas ✦✦✦
This is a big band like the classic mambo groups, with three lead singers. Justo Almerio, Alex Acuna, and Poncho Sanchez guest-star, but the other folks are just dynamite musicians. The arrangements are swirling, rich and brassy, and the solos range from blow-you-down to stunning. —*John Storm Roberts, Original Music*

Noro Morales

b. Jan. 4, 1911, Puerto de Tierra, Puerto Rico, d. Jan. 16, 1964
New York Salsa, Latin Continuum, United States
Morales was in New York in 1935, and played briefly with the bands of Alberto Socarras and Augusto Coen before establishing the Brothers Morales (Noro-Humberto-Esy) orchestra in 1939. The 1942 Decca 78 "Serenata Ritmica" gave Morales instant recognition. During the decade of the '40s, his and Machito's band was the most popular in NYC. —*Max Salazar*

● **His Piano and Rhythm** / Ansonia ✦✦✦✦✦
Like so many of the big names of the '40s, Morales went from enormous popularity to total oblivion. Which is a major pity, since he was very important in the early days of New York salsa as a main creator of a quintet style that blended jazz with classic Cuban piano. This late-period album documents both the brillance and the prolixity of a musician long overdue for a reassessment. —*John Storm Roberts*

Johnny Pacheco

b. Mar. 25, 1935, Santiago de los Caballeros, Domin
Flute, Percussion, Saxophone / Salsa, Latin Continuum, United States
Pacheco relocated to New York during the late '40s. In high school he learned to play sax, percussion, and flute. In September 1959, he left Charlie Palmieri's flute and strings orchestra to organize his own. With his first recording, *Pacheco y su Charanga*, released by Alegre Records in 1961, three tracks, "Oyeme Mulata," "El Guiro de Macorina," and "Que le Pasa a mi Mama," changed the sound of music throughout Latin America and ushered in the "Pachanga" (a strenous dance) era which faded out in 1964. Pacheco and attorney Gerald Masucci founded the Fania label in 1964 and with its first LP #325 (Pacheco's birthdate), kicked off the yet unborn salsa era in New York City. —*Max Salazar*

● **Que Suene la Flauta** / 1962 / Alegre ✦✦✦✦✦
Pacheco's first avatar was as a flutist, first with Charlie Palmieri's groundbreaking 1959 charanga, then—until he switched to conjunto in 1964—with his own flute-and-fiddles group. Though the band followed Cuban models (far too closely, some Cuban musicians grumbled), his own style was very distinctive, tougher, and less flowing than his Cuban rivals, and his wildly successful band benefited also from a very fine singer in Elliot Romero. "Alto Songo," from this album, was one of his personal classics. —*John Storm Roberts, Original Music*

Compadres / Fania ✦✦✦
This early-'70s classic was among the finest of all Cuban-derived New York tipico salsa recordings. Even then, Conde was one of the great soneros of the Big Manzana, and Pacheco already knew all there was to know about getting the last snap, crackle, and pop out of a conjunto. It's one of a great band's great moments. —*John Storm Roberts, Original Music*

Early Rhythms / Mpl ✦✦✦
Pacheco has never run a mambo-type big band. Yet here he is, fluting away like Johnny-Begone in front of full brass and sax sections. This is Pacheco freelancing, in about 1962, with what was essentially Machito's band. It's an unusual disc, with fine flute, and great Rene Hernandez arrangements. —*John Storm Roberts, Original Music*

Charlie Palmieri

b. 1927, New York, NY, d. 1988
Piano / Latin Jazz, Latin Continuum, United States
Charlie Palmieri was a child prodigy as a pianist and was among Latin jazz's flashiest, most flamboyant stylists. His playing was alternately aggressive and mellow, percussive, then very supportive and low-key. He began studying piano at seven, and eventually attended Juilliard. Palm-

ieri played dances at 14 and turned professional at 16. He started his group "El Conjunto Pin Pin" in 1948, and played piano for Pupi Campo, Tito Puente, Tito Rodriguez, Bicentico Valdes, and Pete Terrace before forming his Charanga Duboney group in 1958. They recorded in the '60s for United Artists and Alegre. Palmieri helped initiate the charanga (flute and violin band) explosion of the early '60s. He was music director for the Alegre All Stars on a series of descarga (jam session) albums, working with such stars as Johnny Pacheco, Willie Rosario, and Cheo Feliciano. They spawned a growth industry as other Latin labels like Tico and Fania established their own all-star groups to compete. Palmieri formed the Duboney Orchestra in the mid-'60s, replacing the violin and flute with three trumpets and two trombones. He temporarily moved to RCA from Alegre, but returned and recorded some albums in the the popular R&B/latin "boogaloo" style. One for Atlantic was produced by Herbie Mann. Palmieri survived a near mental breakdown in 1969, and was hired by Tito Puente to be musical director for his "El Mambo de Tito Puente" TV program. Palmieri began a parallel career in the '70s as a cultural historian and lecturer on Latin music and history, and subsequently taught courses at various New York institutions. He added organ to his band in the '70s, and continued recording on Alegre before switching to Coco. There were subsequent albums on Tipica, Cotique, then Alegre again. He was featured on the 1979 British television film *Salsa*. Palmieri moved to Puerto Rico in 1980, remaining there until 1983. He'd planned a concert in Puerto Rico with his brother Eddie, but suffered a severe heart attack and stroke while back in New York organizing the event. After his recovery, Palmieri returned to the Latin music wars with a small combo in 1984. He played with Ralphy Marzan and Joe Quijano, and co-led the band Combo Gigante with Jimmy Sabater. Palmieri made his first trip to England in 1988, but suffered another heart attack upon his return to New York. This time he didn't recover. Charlie Palmieri left a legacy of masterful albums in various Latin pop and jazz styles. Unfortunately most of them aren't available on CD, except through Latin or international music specialty stores. —*Ron Wynn and Max Salazar*

Adelante Gigante / Alegre ✦✦✦✦✦
Eddie Palmieri always said his elder brother was the better player, and by the time of his death, Charlie Palmieri was well enough known outside the barrio to get an obituary in the *New York Times*. This classic mid-'70s album has all his usual taste, talent, classic piano (and in a couple of places organ) along with his favorite lead singer, Vitin Aviles, and a tight band. —*John Storm Roberts*

● **Impulsos** / Mpl ✦✦✦✦✦
The late Charlie P. was a greater pianist than his brother, as deeply musical, as universally loved, and with far more sense. He picked musicians by talent not fame, and they blew their hearts out for him. This mid-'70s session has the swing, as hot as EPs but more benign. —*John Storm Roberts*

Lou Perez

b. Jun. 21, 1928, New York, NY
Guitar, Drums, Vocals / Salsa, Latin Continuum, United States
Born to Puerto Rican and Cuban parents. Perez is a most underated musician in that very few people know of his musical genius. He's a composer and cracker-jack arranger who began studying music in 1945. He has recorded 15 albums, all for dancers only. What makes Perez special is his rich imagination, which is evident in three outstanding LPs. Movie star Patrick Swayze became a star after dancing to Perez's "De Todo un Poco" in the box office hit *Dirty Dancing*. A Lou Perez album is a collector's item. —*Max Salazar*

● **Para la Fiesta Me Voy** / Recomar ✦✦✦✦
When the charanga sound first hit New York in 1959, one of the earliest and finest groups to form was launched by pianist Lou Perez. This album became an instant hit and has remained an underground classic, little known but highly prized by the aficionados. It's a reminder of just what a fine mix was produced by Cuban delicacy and NYC drive at their best. —*John Storm Roberts, Original Music*

Daniel Ponce

b. 1953
Percussion / World Fusion, Latin Jazz, Latin Continuum, United States
Latin percussionist whose presence and magnetism is inspirational of its own accord. Primarily a conga player who leads contemporary Latin-jazz dance oriented bands. A premier, in-demand sideman. —*Michael G. Nastos*

NY Now! / 1982 / Celluloid ✦✦✦
First album. Musicians include Paquito (sax), Olufemi (keyb), Ignacio Berroa (d), Bill Laswell (b), and Michael Beinhorn (k). Seven pieces are by conga-man Ponce. There is a bit of a contemporary edge, but all is in the Latin spirit. —*Michael G. Nastos*

★ **Arawe** / 1987 / Antilles ✦✦✦✦✦
Ponce is a charismatic conga player as hot as any. There are six pieces here, five written by Ponce, played by mostly nine- to ten-piece bands

with one quintet cut. Ponce gets help from notables Yomo Toro, Nicky Marrero, Steve Turre, Isidro Bobadilla, Law Soloff, and Vernon Reid. —*Michael G. Nastos*

Chango Te Llama / 1991 / Mango ✦✦✦✦✦
The large ensemble is burning hot. This is an excellent companion to *Arawe*. Ponce wrote three selections. There is lots of vocalist Tito Allen and saxophonists Mario Rivera and Dave Snachez. —*Michael G. Nastos*

Tito Rodriguez

b. Jan. 4, 1923, San Juan, Puerto Rico, d. Feb. 28, 1972, New York, NY
Guitar, Vibraphone, Vocals / New York Salsa, Latin Continuum, United States
Rodriguez came to New York in 1939, where he sang with the orchestras of his brother Johnny Rodriguez, Enric Madriguera, Caney, Xavier Cugat, Noro Morales, and José Curbelo. Rodriguez formed a quintet in 1947 and enlarged it in 1948 to a trumpet conjunto. In 1963 his recording of "Inolvidable" in Argentina sold 1,000,500 copies throughout Latin America. —*Max Salazar*

● **Un Retrato de . . .** / Total Recordings ✦✦✦✦✦
The great TR was, of course, part of the New York mambo troika of which Puente and Machito were the other members. A fine singer of both mambo and romantic material, he ran a band as fiery as any. Here are "Mama Guela" and "Yambu" in the former vein, and the monster hit "Cuando Cuando" in the latter, as well as much more. This is a major re-release. —*John Storm Roberts*

Uptempo / Tico ✦✦✦✦✦
An interesting cut-out of relatively unfamiliar Rodriguez mambos, cha cha chas, and such, it includes his version of "El Manicero." Rodriguez was a major heart-throb, and his albums always had plenty of schmaltz. With big-band bolero seeming like a major waste of a rhythm section, it's good to have the hotter stuff unsullied. —*John Storm Roberts*

Venezuela

Julio Jaramillo

Vocals / Venezuelan, Latin Continuum
Sentimental de America / Fonodisco ✦✦✦✦✦
The delightful popular music of Venezuela—particularly in its elegant older forms—is particularly hard to find. Jaramillo was a fine singer whose backings included harp, guitar and occasional fiddles and/or accordion. This was a style that, while definitely pop rather than traditional, owed little or nothing to any outside source (with the notable and obvious exception of the Argentine tango). —*John Storm Roberts, Original Music*

Collección de Pasillos / Discolando ✦✦✦
A mid-'70s recording, this is elegant, delicate, and very Venezuelan singing with guitar-led backings to match. Jaramillo had an international name at times, but this is far more local than the pan-Latin trio music of groups like Los Panchos. It would be nice to see this kind of classic sound rediscovered. —*John Storm Roberts*

● **En Puerto Rico** / Suaritos ✦✦✦✦✦
The delightful older popular music of Venezuela and Ecuador—particularly in its elegant older forms—is particularly hard to find. Jaramillo, an Ecuadorian by birth who lived many years in Venezuela, was a fine singer whose backings included trios led by harp, guitar, and occasional accordion (lots of elegant accordion here, plus some harp-leads). This enchanting deleted LP consists of boleros and valses. But the treatment makes them a particularly satisfactory mix of pan-Latin and local. —*John Storm Roberts, Original Music*

Pastor Lopez

Venezuelan, Latin Continuum
En Mexico / Discolando ✦✦✦
Lopez became a big-time exponent on the heartthrob end of contemporary cumbia, but he started real rootsy. The band here has horns along with its accordion, but this is still a great small-town sound, and Lopez himself is super. —*John Storm Roberts*

● **Vacaciones Tropicales** / Grupo Velvet ✦✦✦✦✦
Lopez hangs out in the heartthrob end of contemporary cumbia, and in records like this both he and his backup group achieve just the right balance of its various elements. The heartbreak is short of maudlin, and effectively set off by the styles' inherently jaunty quality. Vacaciones contains plenty of Lopez's three-beers-down musings on life, women, and how it's not his fault his heart is broken. Palo Santo provides a crisp and upbeat backing with a highly unusual and effective harp-and-brass frontline. This is now probably out-of-print. —*John Storm Roberts, Original Music*

Maria Rodriguez

Vocals / Venezuelan, Latin Continuum
Tremenda, La / World Circuit ✦✦✦
Rodriguez came out of the Venezuelan street comparsa, became a Cuban-style pop singer in the '40s, and then went home to teach and sing the traditional comparsas and joropos. On this admirable first album by a new British label, she is backed by a classic quartet of mandolin, cuatro, guitar, and maraccas, and a few more beautiful sounds. —*John Storm Roberts*

Venezuela Collection

Folk Music from Venezuela / Reportage ✦✦✦
Side one of this cassette is devoted to a semipro revivalist—or at least preservationist group, which performs fulias and other forms from all over Venezuela in a pretty authentic style. Side two is given over to field recordings of all three types of Venezuelan music—Euro-Venezuelan, Afro-Venezuelan, and Indian. Particularly fine is some of the drumming, but the string groups playing for joropos are also a rarity. Outstanding notes, for a cassette. —*John Storm Roberts*

Music of Venezuela / Zu-Zazz ✦✦✦✦✦
A very fine set of recent recordings by amateur and semi-professional groups, with a focus on stringed instruments—violin as well as members of the huge family of Latin guitars and mandolins. Many of the styles included are available on commercial recordings, but not on the whole in such grassroots idioms, nor with such excellent notes. This album is also available in the US on the High Water label. —*John Storm Roberts & Myles Boisen*

Venezuela: Musique Folklorique / Ocora ✦✦✦
A favorite recording of Venezuelan music, this sampler contains a wonderful overview of musical traditions and is recommended highly. —*David L. Mayers*

MIDDLE EAST

Afghanistan Collection

Afghanistan Folk Music, Vol. 2 / Lyrichord ✦✦✦
A very interesting selection of vocal and instrumental folk music. —*David L. Mayers*

Afghanistan Songs of the Pashai / 1990 / Le Chant du Monde ✦✦✦
A new and expanded edition of an earlier Chant du Monde LP consisting of vocal and instrumental performances collected between December 1970 and December 1971. The Pashai are an agrarian people who raise livestock and crops. Much of this album consists of sung poetry. —*Ken Hunt*

Music of Afghanistan [Argo] / Argo ✦✦✦
A fine selection of vocal and instrumental music. —*David L. Mayers*

Music of Afghanistan / Barenreiter Musicaphon ✦✦✦
A cultural crossroads, Afghanistan's music has elements from India as well as Iran, Turkey, and even Russia and ancient Greece. Here is a piece in Farsee, of clear Persian inspiration; pieces with apparent links to ancient Europe; and Indian-style drumming. Here are vocals, percussions, varied pipes, and lutes. This is one of Musicaphon's finest recordings. —*John Storm Roberts*

Arabic

Simon Shaheen

b. 1955, Tarshiha, Galilee
Violin / Arabic, Egypt, Middle East
A virtuoso on the oud as well as the violin, Shaheen is equally adept at performing traditional Arabic music and Western classical styles. Born in the village of Tarshiha in northern Galilee, he learned his craft initially from his father. At the same time, Shaheen also studied Western classical music, graduating from the Jerusalem Music Academy in 1978. Two years later, he moved to New York where he continued his studies at the Manhattan School of Music. In addition to his performances worldwide, Shaheen teaches oud and violin, composes for theatrical productions, and produces recordings. —*Linda Kohanov*

The Music of Mohamed Abdel Wahab / 1990 / Axiom ✦✦✦
Cairo was once a major movie-making capital, and Wahab invented the soundtrack sound that still influences how we think about Egyptian music. Oud dervish Simon Shaheen, backed by an energetic orchestra and chorus, interprets some of the composer's most intoxicating pieces. —*Bob Tarte*

● **Turath (Heritage): Masterworks of the Middle East** / 1992 / CMP
✦✦✦✦✦
This rarity is a very welcome one: a really outstanding classical recording by a quartet of young musicians. Shaheen, an excellent oud-player
and violinist, is joined by fine nay quanun and percussion in a recital of
classic and contemporary works in the linked Arabic and Ottoman-Turk-
ish tradition. — *John Storm Roberts*

Arabic Collection

Arabian Music: Maquam / Philips ✦✦✦
Featured are very fine performances on oud. — *David L. Mayers*

Archives of Arabian Music, Vol. 1 / Ocora ✦✦✦
These early acoustic recordings from Egypt, Syria, and Lebanon are
especially important release given the enormous outside pressures on
and changes in Middle Eastern music since these recordings were made.
The quality of the remastering as well as the notes are an additional
plus. — *John Storm Roberts*

Sung Poetry / Auvidis ✦✦✦
In most cultures the distinction between recitation and song, poem and
lyric, is not nearly as distinct as in the West. Many great poems of the
Middle East are still sung, and cantatas or song-cycles with particular
structures are the backbone of the Andalus classical tradition, whether
in Syria or the Maghreb. The examples here are in Turkish, Farsi, and
Arabic. — *David L. Mayers*

Egypt

Mohamed Abdel Wahab

Vocals / Classical, Egypt, Middle East
As a singer and an influence on Egyptian music during its renaissance,
Abdel Wahab was equaled only by Umm Kulthum. But while she was a
traditionalist to the core, Abdel Wahab believed in learning from Western music. Yet he too was a musical nationalist, renewing rather than
diluting Egyptian tradition. Starting from a highly traditional sound as a
teenager, he gradually moved into a highly varied (and internationally
popular) film-based repertoire. But besides contributing to the pop
world, he introduced more fundamental elements, such as long instrumental passages, a major element in his work. — *John Storm Roberts*

● **Vol. 1 (1920-1925)** / 1970 / Artistes Arabes ✦✦✦✦✦
This set of Wahab's earliest recordings is an event of supreme importance. It's also superb—and as a double bonus, it has fine notes (translated into English) by a man who knew him most of his artistic life.
— *John Storm Roberts*

Vol. 10 (1939) / 1971 / Artistes Arabes ✦✦✦✦✦
The most recent in this ongoing series dedicated to Egypt's greatest 20th-
century singer/composer consists of music from a film, *Youm Said*. This
is an early work, perhaps his first soundtrack. Both Abdel Wahab's singing and the accompaniments (despite a little accordion and piano here
and there) were mostly far more traditional than his later movies. This
was a significant transition period. — *John Storm Roberts*

Cleopatra / 1991 / Soutelphan ✦✦✦
Abdel Wahab and Umm Kulthum, king and queen of 20th-century Egyptian music, also epitomized opposing approaches. While Kulthum was
traditionalist to the core, Abdel Wahab believed in learning from Western music. Yet he too (as this mid-period recording shows) was nothing if
not a musical nationalist, using new ideas and practices to refresh rather
than to dilute ancient tradition. — *John Storm Roberts*

Mohaued Abdel Wahab A~habib Al-Uaghoul / Cairophon ✦✦✦
This second of two classic recordings, done a quarter-century after its
predecessor, shows Abdel Wahab's consistent development of long
instrumental passages, a major element in his work, as well as the splendid singing of his maturity. — *John Storm Roberts, Original Music*

Amina

Egypt, Middle East

Yalil / 1989 / Mango ✦✦✦✦✦
Egyptian motifs tangle with hot Parisian production styles in the service
of pouty-voiced diva Amina, who knows the power of sexy exotica over
the feet of continental clubgoers. This is an intriguing experiment in widening North African pop. — *Bob Tarte*

Asmahan

Egypt, Middle East
Asmahan, sister and co-star of the great Farid al Atrash, has been called
the only voice that can be compared with Umm Kulthum's, but with (as
one Arab expert put it) more "tenderness and femininity." A master of the
traditional sound, she was also on the cutting edge of the film-oriented
and to some extent Western-oriented 1940s "new music," and some of

her most unforgettable songs were in that vein. Her brother sings with
her on many of her recordings. Asmahan's fame was increased by her
(not very) private life. During World War II she was reputed to be a triple
if not quadruple agent, and the more heated Cairene gossip even claimed
her fatal car accident was courtesy of the British Secret Service! — *John
Storm Roberts*

★ **Asmahan & Farid** / 1970 / Baidaphon ✦✦✦✦✦
Farid al Atrache is one of the great names in 20th-century Egyptian pop-
ular music. Asmahan had one of the greatest voices of '30s and '40s pop.
Both were stars of Egypt's musical cinema. This set of their '40s hits
charmingly recalls an era of experiment and eccentricity. — *John Storm
Roberts*

Aleik Salat Allah / 1980 / Artistes Arabes ✦✦✦
The AAA recording—which atypically has English notes—covers rather
the same ground, though with more of Asmahan's early classic or neo-
traditional recordings along with the crossover film material. — *John
Storm Roberts*

Early Recordings / Club du Disque Arabe ✦✦✦
In her early days (from which these splendid recordings date) she
worked brilliantly within the tradition-based mainstream of her time,
usually with small ensembles of local wind and string instruments.
— *John Storm Roberts*

Les Chansons Eternelles / EMI India ✦✦✦✦
Asmahan was something of a legend in her time. A star of musical films
in the '30s and '40s, Like all the music—above all, the film music—of the
period, her recordings were tugged back and forth between nationalism
and internationalism. In either vein, she was wonderful. — *John Storm
Roberts*

Baidaphon / ✦✦✦✦
Farid al Atrache, of course, is one of the great names in 20th-century
Egyptian popular music. Asmahan had one of the great voices of 1930s
and '40s pop. Both were stars of Egypt's musical cinema. This set of their
1940s hits charmingly recalls an era of experiment and eccentricity.
— *John Storm Roberts*

Farid al Atrache

b. 1915, d. 1974
Vocals / Egypt, Middle East
This singer/instrumentalist/composer was notable for a deep voice with
an evocative quality of poignancy, the fact that within the pop field he
sang in styles regarded as "authentic" in both Egypt and the Levant, and
above all for his extensive use of the oud. He was born in Syria, but
moved to Egypt with his mother, when he was around nine years old.
Atrache was part of a musical family: His mother, "Aliyah," supported the
family by singing, and his sister, Asmahan, appeared with him in many
movies. Aside from his singing prowess, Atrache was a virtuoso oud
player: he studied the instrument at Cairo's Institute of Arab Music and
in fact began his professional career accompanying an older singer.
Atrache revived the dying use in concert of improvised instrumental
solos (tagasim) as part of a longer piece, by lengthening the instrumental
introductions to his songs and building tagasim into them. Through
recordings of his concerts he thus became the most famous oud player in
the Arab world and earned the nickname "King of the oud." — *John
Storm Roberts*

Awal Hamsa / Cairophon ✦✦✦
This 1972 release was one of Atrache's very finest, both instrumentally
and vocally. Following his usual custom in live performances, he opens
with oud, and proceeds by a smooth sequence to the main business of
the evening, his singing. — *John Storm Roberts*

Takasim Oud / Voice of Lebanon ✦✦✦
This compilation consists of a taqasim out of the introductions to various
vocal recordings, complete with audience response. The recording quality is variable, the music splendid. This is one not only for lovers of Middle Eastern music, but for lovers of fine string playing of all kinds. — *John
Storm Roberts*

● **Addi Errabi** / Voice of Lebanon ✦✦✦✦✦
This 1973 live recording is thought by many to be his finest, and is certainly a splendid example of his way of building oud taqasim into his
performances. It is certainly typical of his concerts in its progression
from solo oud to Atrache's tenderly stark vocals, all punctuated by an
equally typical passionate audience response. — *John Storm Roberts*

Aziza Galal

Egypt, Middle East
Wal Tekeina Netkabel Sawa / EMI ✦✦✦
Behind her spectacles, Morocco-born, Cairo-based Galal clearly has no
pop-star glitz in her appearance or her art, but she is one of the finest living singers in the Egyptian vein. She seeks flexibility rather than flash
and purity rather than richness of tone, and her accompaniments impec-

cably vary the now classic string sound with unobtrusive modern touches. —*John Storm Roberts*

Abdel Halim Hafez

b. 1929, d. 1977
Vocals / Egypt, Middle East
Despite a fairly short career, singer/movie-actor Hafez was one of the most influential Egyptian stars of the '50s and '60s. His mellow, resonant voice, subtle vocal style and notably clean intonation marked him out, along with a liking for long, seemingly endless musical phrases. When Mohamed Abdel Wahhaab switched from singing to composition, Hafez pretty much stepped into his shoes. Born in 1929, Abdel Halim studied at Cairo's Institute of Arabic Music and the Higher Institute for Theatre Music, and began his career teaching and playing oboe before taking aim at vocal stardom. His first hit came in 1951, and he soon signed a contract with Abdel Wahhaab to sing his songs and appear in his films. During the 1960s, he started to sing colloquial poetry more colorful and meaningful and nearer to popular folk song than ordinary pop songs, and his work on these lines had a significant influence on popular song in general. He cofounded a film company and the Saut el-Fann record label in the early '60s, and remained a major star until he died in 1977 of Bilharzia, which he had caught as a child and which had begun to affect him intermittently from 1955 onward. —*John Storm Roberts*

Mawood / 1994 / Soutelphan ♦♦♦
Hafez is in typical mellow, yearning voice here, backed by electric guitar (effective) and sax along with the usual oud, qanun, and string section etc. This is quintessential Egyptian mainstream pop without silly frills, much enhanced by the live audience. —*John Storm Roberts*

Kariat al-Fengan / Soutelphan ♦♦♦
A concert recording by a major star of the post-World War II generation. Like Lebanon's Fairuz, Hafez fronts settings that range from the now-traditional chorus and strings-and-percussion orchestra to various groups with heavy overseas influences. But his own style and the melodies he sings are both quintessentially Egyptian. —*John Storm Roberts*

● Ala Hasb Weddad / Soutelphan ♦♦♦♦♦
A concert recording by a major star of the post-World War II generation. Like Lebanon's Fairuz, Hafez fronts settings that range from the now-traditional chorus and strings-and-percussion orchestra to various groups with heavy overseas influences. But his own style and the melodies he sings are both quintessentially Egyptian. —*John Storm Roberts*

Hanan

Vocals / Egypt, Middle East
Hanan is the only female artist to successfully break into the male-dominated world of Al-jil pop music. A heterodox representative of a socially marginal music, Hanan began her musical career within the very fortress of tradition, singing with the Arab Music Institute Ensemble. Her big break came with the single "Beima" (Smile). She can be heard on innumerable cassettes, including *Besma* (I'm Listening). —*Leon Jackson*

● Ghanni / Slam ♦♦♦♦♦
Is Hanan still queen of Al-jil music, that sometimes rowdy, sometimes hyper-pop Egyptian equivalent of rai? The bounce and the new-generation sound are still there along with her real singing talent, but in the years since she first surfaced on cassettes she's moved subtly toward the Egyptian pop mainstream. It's inevitable, probably—and not a criticism: merely an observation about a very attractive recording. —*John Storm Roberts, Original Music*

Haluwa / Slam ♦♦♦
Hanan is one of the finest singers on the younger Egyptian scene. There's less Euro-pop on this than on the earlier Slam releases, more strongly Egyptian material, plus a few splendid oddities, such as an intro that sounds vaguely like Astor Piazzolla. —*John Storm Roberts*

Umm Kulthum

b. 1904, d. 1975
Vocals / Operettas, Egypt, Middle East
Without question the best-known 20th-century Middle Eastern singer, Umm Kulthum went from performing in the villages of the Egyptian delta to international stardom as great as virtually any Western pop artist. She first sang in public as a child with her father, an imam who performed religious songs at local celebrations, and was so popular that in 1922 the family moved to Cairo so she could try for commercial success. Though her style struck Cairenes as overly rural, her first recordings in 1924 and 1925 did well because her years singing in small villages and towns had built her a larger audience outside Cairo itself than most singers. By 1928 she was the most popular singer in Egypt, and during the '30s her work on radio and in films brought her international fame. From 1937 until shortly before her death she gave a live broadcast concert on the first Thursday of every month heard by millions of listeners.

Umm Kulthum started out with a repertoire of traditional and mostly religious songs she had learned as a child. During the late '20s and the '30s she moved to new and more virtuoso romantic material, and in the '40s and '50s she adopted her best-known repertoire, a mix of colloquial, populist material, and neo-classical compositions. But her style was always marked by her early involvement with religious material: clarity of diction and stress on syntax and meaning were at its core, and the varied renderings of individual lines for which she was famous were designed to increase understanding of her texts as well as to give musical pleasure. During the '60s and '70s Umm Kulthum became an important public figure, a symbol of authentic Egyptian and Arab culture, member of commissions on the arts and president of the musicians' union. After Egypt's defeat in the 1967 war with Israel she gave benefit concerts throughout the Arab world to earn money for the depleted Egyptian treasury. —*John Storm Roberts*

Umm Kulthum, Vol. 1: 1926 / Artistes Arabes ♦♦♦
Umm Kulthum's incredible first recordings are backed by the traditional small groups that later grew into positive orchestras. Notes in English are a rare bonus. —*John Storm Roberts*

Hajrik / Sono Cairo ♦♦♦

★ El Atlaal / Sono Cairo ♦♦♦♦♦
Umm Kulthum is among the greatest singers of the 20th century. She's been called the Bessie Smith of Egypt, and for stark passion she was all of that. But she was also much more. She found a way of moving traditional music into the contemporary mainstream without dilution or compromise, and achieved a popularity unparalleled by any singer anywhere. *Al Atlaal* is typical of Kulthum at her prime, shortly after the LP form allowed her to record songs the way she sang them live—at length and in depth. —*John Storm Roberts*

Rubayeat el-Khayyam / Sono Cairo ♦♦♦
This CD, recorded live in concert near the start of the LP era, is typical of Kulthum in her prime. Her voice, always instinct with power and subtlety, still has a youthful lightness, and the backings retain small-group freshness and depth. —*John Storm Roberts*

Faat el-Mi'ad / Sono Cairo ♦♦♦
In *Faat el-Mi'ad*, a concert recording from her later years while not changing her own style, she acknowledged contemporary Egyptian musical developments in accompaniments with far from classic but fascinating elements: notably some sensational tagassim for saxophone. —*John Storm Roberts*

In the Old Tradition / Sono Cairo ♦♦♦
This cassette, one of a set of three, brings together the '20s recordings of the queen of Islamic song. Made in her young days, backed by a small traditional group, they have a freshness that transcends the poor recording quality, and a depth that foreshadows the days when she would reign supreme from Pakistan to Morocco. —*John Storm Roberts*

Hakam Alena al-Hawa / Sono Cairo ♦♦♦
The last recordings by one of the greatest singers of our century, anywhere. Kulthum was rooted in the Egyptian earth, but she touched millions throughout the entire Muslim world for 30 years and more. Towards the end her arrangements became a little less starkly classic (in this case with some fine organ-playing). But she herself never changed and never faltered. —*John Storm Roberts*

Zalamouni el-Nass / Cairophon ♦♦♦
Umm Kulthum was a singer who needed an audience, and her live recordings always excel over her studio ones. Two cuts here come from concerts in (probably) the late '50s. The single studio cut dates from a little earlier. —*John Storm Roberts*

Musicians of the Nile

Egypt, Middle East
The Musicians of the Nile are an international performing troupe of professional musicians from the Luxor area. Using only folk instruments, this group keeps the traditions of upper Egypt alive. —*Myles Boisen*

★ From Luxor to Isna / 1989 / Real World ♦♦♦♦♦
This is a first-class collection of Arabic folk music from Egypt from the country's premier touring group. Strictly traditional drums, strings, reeds, and songs from the desert. —*Myles Boisen & J. Poet*

Musicians of the Nile, Vols. 1 & 2 / Ocora ♦♦♦
The music of contemporary Egypt has come a long way from the villages of the Egyptian Nile. But its roots are in the flutes, the oboes, the two-stringed fiddles, and impassioned vocalism and drumming of a peasant culture with strong Gypsy roots, in which popular and classical met. —*David L. Mayers*

Ali Jihad Racy

b. 1943, Lebanon
Clarinet, Flute / Egypt, Middle East
An accomplished multi-instrumentalist, Racy has done much to promote

an appreciation for Middle Eastern music in the West. Born in Lebanon, Racy came to the US in 1968, where he earned his Masters and Doctorate degrees from the University of Illinois before accepting a position as Professor of Ethnimusicology at UCLA. His recordings for various labels provide a showcase for his mastery of the flute-like nay and the clarinet-like mijwiz, as well as the stringed instruments oud and buzuq, both important to Middle Eastern styles. Racy is currently working on a book tentatively titled *The Art of Ecstasy in Arab Music.* —*Linda Kohanov*

Jazayer / 1989 / Earthbeat! ✦✦✦✦✦

Originally recorded by the Grateful Dead's Mickey Hart in 1979, this collection features traditional and contemporary Middle Eastern dance music performed with great spirit and skill by Racy in collaboration with the members of Jazayer, an American ensemble of Middle Eastern music enthusiasts. —*Linda Kohanov*

Ancient Egypt: a Tribute / Lyrichord ✦✦✦

This musical tribute to ancient Egypt was originally composed in 1978 for the King Tutankhamun exhibit at the Seattle Art Museum. It was inspired by the artistry of the ancient treasures and the religious symbolism of the Egyptian Book of the Dead, which suggested titles of the compositions. Only traditional Near Eastern instruments were used in making this recording, like the nay, salamiyyah, buzuq, mijwiz, mizmar, and others. —*MusD*

● Taqasim / Lyrichord ✦✦✦✦✦

Taqasim (the plural of taqsim) are extended, non-metrical instrumental improvisations. This collection of three such pieces features Simon Shaheen on oud and Racy on buzuq, offering a rare opportunity to hear the sublime, at times feverish, interactions of two virtuoso performers. —*Linda Kohanov*

Ihab Tawfi

Egypt, Middle East

Ikmini / Slam ✦✦✦

This is the cassette from which Island extracted the cut "Masakeen." Tawfi's a fine singer, with a sound locally enough rooted (along with the hip version of local rhythms) to subdue and turn to good purpose the international-pop garnishes. At its best, the newer Egyptian sounds approach rai in intensity, and surpass it in variety. —*John Storm Roberts*

Egypt Collection

Cairo Tradition / Auvidis ✦✦✦

All the music on *Cairo Tradition: Taqasim & Layali* is played by members of the Takht ensemble under the aegis of the Cairo conservatory. There's a lot of excellent kanun zither playing, both solo and under the layali, vocal improvisations on a maqam. There are also admirable oud and nay solos. It's a core recording, all in all. —*David L. Mayers*

Music of Egypt: Upper & Lower / Rykodisc ✦✦✦

The Grateful Dead's Mickey Hart recorded these pieces in 1978, having happened across the music during a tour. The first four are from the Aswan area, the last two are fine instrumentals, one for a mizmar oboe group, the other for tar with a darabukka backing. —*David L. Mayers*

☆ From Luxor to Isna / 1989 / Real World ✦✦✦✦✦

This is a first-class collection of Arabic folk music from Egypt from the country's premier touring group. Strictly traditional drums, strings, reeds, and songs from the desert. —*Myles Boisen & J. Poet*

☆ Hitlist Egypt / 1990 / Mango ✦✦✦✦✦

A hard-hitting overview of a variety of gritty, hardworking Egyptian pop, it mixes elements of bazaar culture with Eurodisco technocraft. The disc is divided equally between uptown and street styles. It contains "Elli Shatr Enhaa Tgannen," the naughty newlywed rap that had Cairo's elders blushing. —*Bob Tarte & Myles Boisenl*

Iran

Karimi/Musavi

Iran, Middle East

Masters of Traditional Music, Vol. 2 / Ocora ✦✦✦

A reissue of 1979 recordings, the CD is entirely devoted to a fine recording of duets by singer Mohammad Karimi and Musavi on nay. It's extremely good technically. —*John Storm Roberts*

Faramarz Payvar

Dulcimer (Hammer) / Iran, Middle East

Faramarz Payvar is an important composer and conservator of Persian classical music, leading his touring ensemble on the 72-string santur (hammer dulcimer). Various other string instruments are featured in this group, as well as the zarb drum and soloist Khatereh Parvaneh, a prominent female vocalist. —*Myles Boisen*

● Faramarz Payvar Ensemble / 1974 / Nonesuch ✦✦✦✦✦

Iran has arguably been the world's most important musical culture. It links us with ancient Greece, and is at the root of both Arabian and Indian (and thence Southeast Asian) classical idioms. Santurist Payvar's ensemble brought together some of Iran's finest classical musicians in the group and solo performances for santur zither, kamancheh fiddle, tar lute, and zarb percussion, with—a rare treat—a fine woman singer, Khatereh Parvaneh. —*John Storm Roberts*

Manoochehr Sadeghi

Vocals / Iran, Middle East

Sounds of the Santur / IER ✦✦✦

The Iranian santur is the progenitor of a great sweep of instrumentals from China to south-central Europe, and a major classical instrument in its own right. Sadeghi is one of the recognized younger leaders of the renaissance in the instrument, whose tradition was being gradually lost. Here he plays two dastgahs (essentially, suites), one of them also played on the nay by Hossein Omoumi. —*John Storm Roberts*

Dariush Tala'i
with Mohammad Musavi & Majid Kian

Iran, Middle East

Masters of Traditional Music, Vol. 1 / 1979 / Ocora ✦✦✦

This reissue of the classic 1979 recording is devoted to instrumentals for tar (Dariush Tala'i), nay (Mohammad Musavi), and santur (Majid Kiani). All are outstanding, but the nay playing is simply breathtaking. It is superb music and the notes give plenty of general background but are totally lacking in properly attributed track information. —*John Storm Roberts*

Iran Collection

Music of Iran, Vol. 1 / Barenreiter Musicaphon ✦✦✦

This recording is of music for solo kamantche, voice with tar, and solo sehtar. —*John Storm Roberts*

Music of Iran, Vol. 2 / Barenreiter Musicaphon ✦✦✦✦✦

Here is a good range of music from renowned musicians of several generations: dumbek solo, piece for santur, mathnavi mystical poem in a mode like one used in Indian devotional chant, nay flute solo, and tar and kamantche duet. —*John Storm Roberts*

Musique Persane/Persian Music / Ocora ✦✦✦

Music from the culture at the root of both Arabic and Indian classical music. This re-release of a deleted 1971 recording consists of two contrasting suites (so to speak), one in Dastgah Mahu, the other in Dastgah Segah, for a group consisting of oud, santur, tar, kamantche, nay, and tumbak. (The seven Dastgah are the basic modal structures of Iranian music.) —*John Storm Roberts*

Iraq

Munir with Mohamed Elkassabgi Bachir

Iraq, Middle East

Munir Bachir & Mohamed Elkassabgi / CDDA ✦✦✦

An oud virtuosi of two generations and two traditions, Munir Bachir is perhaps the finest living player in the great Iraqi school. In the Geneva concert featured in this record, he plays both traditional modes and looser, more personal improvisations of marked Spanish influence. The great Egyptian player Elkassabgi both composed for and accompanied Umm Kulthum in her early glory days: his solos here, mostly from the '30s, are drawn from 78s originals. —*John Storm Roberts*

● In Concert / Inedit ✦✦✦✦✦

Here are oud virtuosi of two generations and two traditions. Munir Bachir is perhaps the finest living player in the great Iraqi school. In this Paris concert he concentrates on the high-classical tradition in four maqamaat. —*John Storm Roberts, Original Music*

Islam Collection

☆ Holy Quran: Surat Yusuf / Oriental ✦✦✦✦✦

Orthodox Islam has always viewed music with ambivalence, if not downright disapproval. Yet the recitation of the Holy Koran and the call to prayer form the aesthetic bedrock of all the music of the Islamic world. The late Sheikh Mahmoud Khalil El Houssary, a former head of the Al Azhar Mosque in Cairo, here recites Surat Yusuf, the Koranic story of Joseph (no coat of many colors, but the pit and the fat and lean kine are there). —*John Storm Roberts*

Prayer and Religious Incantation / Barenreiter Musicaphon ✦✦✦

This is a particularly fine recording of prayers, muwashaat (hymns), and other religious material. Druze, Sunni, and Shiite: music of the mosque, not of the mystical sects. Despite the ambivalence and intermittent hostility of Islam to music, this is not only beauty of a high order but the sound that underlies all other vocal idioms of the whole Islamic world. —*John Storm Roberts*

Israel Collection

Le Folklore Israelien / Atoll ◆◆◆◆◆
Not field recordings, these are instead a mix of traditional and traditional-style songs, of which the best-known is perhaps "Hava Nagila." Many are performed by the Effi Netzer Singers. Also featured are Ianit, Lahakat Hanachal, Luci Arnon, and Danny Granot. —*John Storm Roberts*

Treasury of Immortal Performances / 1966 / RCA ◆◆◆◆◆
This is a set of three albums each by a different cantor (Josef Rosenblatt, Samuel Vigoda, and Moshe Koussevitsky). Released in 1966, this boxed set repackaged recordings from as early as 1928 and includes a booklet on the cantors. The Koussevitsky portion has been re-released on CD (Israel Music ICD 5002) with two additional tracks, while the Rosenblatt portion (Israel Music ICD 5001) has three bonus tracks. —*Phil Fink*

The Very Best of Israel / 1990 / CBS ◆◆◆◆◆
This compilation covers material from CBS Israel's vaults, spanning 40 years of Israeli folk and light popular music. —*Phil Fink*

Israel: Forty Years / Atoll ◆◆◆◆◆
This anthology is doubly welcome for its wide view of Israeli popular music. Here are rock-disco-influenced idioms (very interesting); straight rock; the more traditional but equally fine Central European sound of the Effi Netzer Singers, the sonic chicken soup of the Kibbutz Folk Singers, and several other styles to boot. Very varied, very unfamiliar, and mostly very good. —*John Storm Roberts*

Jewish

Giora Feidman

Clarinet / Jewish, Israel, Klezmer, Middle East
Argentine-born and Israeli-based, Giora Feidman has become the leading interpreter and performer of Eastern European klezmer. Despite his classical training with the Israel Philharmonic Orchestra, Feidman's clarinet playing is unrestrainedly and emphatically eclectic. —*Leon Jackson*

Jewish Soul Music: 20 Jewish Tunes / 1989 / Hed Arzi ◆◆◆◆◆
This release features both live and studio recordings from the early '70s, digitally remastered on CD. It's a virtual greatest-hits by this greatest of Klezmers. —*Phil Fink*

David "Dudu" Fisher

Vocals / Yiddish, Israel, Middle East
One of Israel's leading male vocalists, Fisher has recorded numerous albums in Hebrew, ranging from showtunes (he played Jean Valjean in the Tel Aviv production of *Les Miserables*) to Chassidic and Hebrew versions of '60s classic rock tunes. —*Phil Fink*

● **Mamma Loshen (Mother Tongue)** / 1992 / Helicon ◆◆◆◆◆
Fisher sings 22 of the greatest Yiddish songs ever written. —*Phil Fink*

Ofra Haza

Vocals / Disco, Ethnic, Israel, Middle East
By the early '80s, Ofra Haza was already a popular teen singer-songwriter in Israel, before she exploded onto the international scene with a glossy album of ancient Yemenite songs updated for the nightclub set. Since then, pop sensibilities have overshadowed the Jewish traditions in her music, and she has even applied her gorgeous, sensual singing to English-language chart attempts. —*Myles Boisen*

Fifty Gates of Wisdom: Yemenite Songs / 1987 / Shanachie ◆◆◆
A fusion of ethnic world music and pop, *Fifty Gates of Wisdom* by Ofra Haza provides a colorful listening experience. Percussion instruments play a predominant role in these Yemenite Jewish songs because traditionally, percussion instruments were the only way of getting around a Muslim ban on music. The contemporary arrangements give the beautiful and expressive voice of Ofra Haza a traditional yet thoroughly modern setting. Some of the instrumentation includes drums, congas, wood and metal percussion instruments, Yemenite tin and tamabala, strings, flute, oboe, bassoon, clarinet, and French horn. —*MusD*

Shaday / 1988 / Sire ◆◆◆◆◆
This CD made Haza a household name throughout Europe because it was her first to sell millions of copies there, earning her the nickname "the Israeli Madonna." She combines Hebrew, Yemenite, and English in prayers and original compositions with a driving European dance beat. Included are the international hits "Im Nin Alu" and "Galbi" (later made famous after rap stars Eric B. & Rakim sampled it for one of their hits).

It's also available domestically on Sire with bonus remixes of the above tracks. —*Phil Fink*

● **Desert Wind** / 1989 / Sire ◆◆◆◆◆
Most of the songs on Haza's 1990 release, which fittingly coincides with her first US concert tour, are sung partially in English; but the content is still about the Yemenite Jewish community, Yemenite tradition, and peace in the Middle East, with the imagery and rhythm of the desert an integral part of the music. "Fantamorgana," a tribute to her mother and other Yemenite Jews who were persecuted and banished to Yemen's desert, includes the voice of her mother chanting in Arabic. The time's ripe for this sort of world music to gain a foothold in the arena of commercial recognition and success. —*Ladyslipper*

Kirya / 1992 / Shanachie ◆◆◆
Her most recent album heralds a return to the style of her *Fifty Gates of Wisdom* album (and her return to the Shanachie label). Guided by producer Don Was (the B-52's, Bonnie Raitt, Bob Dylan), the album offers a unique contemporary groove and Haza's striking vocals (here in Aramaic, Hebrew, and English). Guests include Lou Reed. —*AMG*

The Klezmatics

Clarinet, Trumpet, Violin, Drums / Israel, Klezmer, Middle East
The Klezmatics stand at the crossroads of the past and the present; they perform traditional numbers but give them a decidely modern twist by adding layers of wild improvisation, changing tempos, and novel instrumentation. Group leader Frank London insists that this is not a break from the philosophy of klezmer but simply an extension of its capacity to absorb and accommodate new sounds. Their *Rhythm & Jews* contains old numbers by Naftule Brandwein as well as original material. —*Leon Jackson*

Rhythm & Jews / Dec. 1990 / Flying Fish ◆◆◆
A bebop attack meets Middle Eastern angst in this klezmer on a hot bed of coals irresistible to anyone with a sympathetic foot in eastern Europe—or who's willing to be swept away by gale-force brass and woodwinds sliced apart by blistering drums. This is music so overpowering one has to listen one song at a time, stop the CD player, then stare out into space marveling at the all and everything these fierce New Yorkers encompass. Klezmer purists may scowl at the unrestrained passion of the solos, but Naftule Brandwein has rarely been as open and raw as on this arrangement of "Araber Tants," in which Alicia Svigals' MIDI violin gives one new appreciation for the emotive possibilities of synthesizers. —*Bob Tarte*

● **Shvaygn + Toytt** / 1991 / Piranha ◆◆◆◆◆
Unafraid of shameless schmaltz when it suits the cause of raising an aorta-busting ruckus, these New Yorkers recognize the bent nature of the tunes they cover, playing up the hokey woodblock percussion on the galloping "Tantst Yidelekh" or altering the last verse of "Ale Brider" (We're All Brothers) to "We're all gay, like Jonathan and King David." Making fun of tradition can be a means of honoring the past—but lest we still think they're sentimentalists at heart, the Klezmatics uncork a healthy dose of rage in an anarchic rendition of the Israeli song "Bilvovi" that will send the relatives running from the room. —*Bob Tarte*

The Klezmorim

Israel, Klezmer, Middle East
Hailing from Berkeley, CA, the Klezmorim are a revival band who specialize in playing the traditional Jewish music known as klezmer that flourished in Eastern Europe. —*Leon Jackson*

● **East Side Wedding** / Flying Fish ◆◆◆◆◆
Among the best of US klezmer revivalists—the first album here was the recording that arguably sparked the idiom's entire rediscovery. Included are Rumanian, Greek, Serbian, Russian, and US pieces. The wedding has what the notes call the "Turkey in the Straw" of eastern Europe, "Yoshke Yoshke." It includes a reminder of just how open Balkan musical frontiers were, since it's called taksim—the Arabic word for a free-rhythm improvisation, which presumably got into Jewish music via Turkey and the Balkans or some similar route. A minor plus for the visually minded is a charming cover by cartoonist R. Crumb of Cheap Suit Serenaders fame. —*John Storm Roberts, Original Music*

First Recordings (1976-1978) / Arhoolie ◆◆◆
From the best of the new Klezmer bands comes an admirable effort by young musicians to capture the sound and feeling of the classic Yiddish music. It was recorded in Berkeley, CA, in 1976 and 1978. —*Cliff Martin*

Dave Tarras

Clarinet / Jewish, Israel, Klezmer, Middle East
David Tarras was born in Russia at the end of the 19th century and in his youth absorbed the laws of both Judaism and klezmer clarinet playing. Extolled for the second, he was reviled for the first, and suffered from the growing waves of anti-Semitism that swept across Eastern Europe at the

dawn of the 20th century. Although Tarras enjoyed a considerable reputation as a clarinetist, he could not abide the pressures of Russian life, and in 1921 he emigrated to America. Arriving at Ellis Island, NY, his baggage was fumigated and his clarinet ruined, but his will to play music survived. Tarras managed to become one of the best respected klezmer musicians in America, widely known for graceful, soaring music with its powerful evocation of shtetl life. But Tarras not only played with traditional ensembles, he also played for the theater, in big bands, and for radio commercials. —*Leon Jackson*

● **Yiddish-American Klezmer Music** / Yazoo ✦✦✦✦✦
This much-welcome CD provides a capsule history of one of the most important American klezmorim via a 36-page biography keyed to 78-sides, radio transcriptions, and theatrical performances that zoom from cartoon-soundtrack joy to delicate waltzes. Klezmer clarinetist Tarras may not have taught Benny Goodman to swing, but his breakthrough style had a profound effect on American pop. Bandmate Ziggy Ellman brought the Yiddish influence on jazz out into the open via Goodman's "And the Angels Sing," and where would the Andrew Sisters be without "Bay mir bistu sheyn?" Highly recommended. —*Bob Tarte*

Jewish Collection

Hassidic Tunes of Dancing and Rejoicing / Smithsonian/Folkways ✦✦✦✦✦
A delicious album, it includes music for clarinets and percussion; a charming dance for clarinet, trumpet, and accordion; a great deal for voices, including some fine "mouth music." Strong Balkan and eastern European influences are here, of course, but also a few are reminiscent of the western European ballad tradition. These field recordings are backed by extensive notes and photos. —*John Storm Roberts*

Israeli Chassidic Song Festival / Hed Arzi ✦✦✦✦✦
These "cast" recordings have been released annually on cassette and vinyl since the first festival in 1968. Many of the tunes first released on these albums have passed into the public's consciousness as though they had been written hundreds of years ago. —*Phil Fink*

Jewish Music / Philips ✦✦✦
It includes religious chants from the Mediterranean-Middle Eastern area from Gibraltar and Morocco to Turkey and Yemen. —*David L. Mayers*

London School . . . / 1991 / Holyland ✦✦✦✦✦
One of the finest recordings of Chassidic music, it's performed by a boys choir and conducted by Yigal Calek. —*Phil Fink*

A Time for Music, Pt. 5 / 1992 / HASC ✦✦✦✦✦
This live two-CD recording features the king of American Chassidic music, Mordechai Ben David, as well as performances by other greats in the American Chassidic music field. —*Phil Fink*

Kurdistani Collection

Kurdish Music / Barenreiter Musicaphon ✦✦✦✦✦
Ethnically and culturally united though they are, the Kurds of the mountainous region that is split between Iran, Iraq, Turkey, and the Soviet Union are also a part of the great Islamic Middle Eastern cultural block. The music here—all superbly performed—includes flute solos and duets (the Kurds, a pastoral mountain people, have no stringed instruments) and songs epic and romantic, as well as a Soviet Kurdish dance piece. —*John Storm Roberts*

Kurdish Music [Philips] / Philips ✦✦✦
Dramatic and exciting music is included on this excellent recording. —*David L. Mayers*

Kurdistan / Auvidis ✦✦✦
Though they are spread across several Middle Eastern countries, the Kurds are very much a cultural entity and their music a recognizable subset of the general regional idiom, with strong links to Persian tradition and a particular liking for the Dorian mode. The Kurds are also traditionally nomadic: they have relied largely on shepherd's pipes and the human voice (though they have adopted stringed instruments from their neighbors over time). —*John Storm Roberts*

Kuwait Collection

Stars of Kuwait, Vol. 1 / Buzaidphone ✦✦✦✦✦
In the late '80s, Kuwait developed a whole new take on mainstream Arabic pop, in which a bunch of fresh new singers fronted groups not only with standard string sections, but also with novelties ranging from Greek bouzouki to the only Arab piano playing to use the bottom half of the keyboard. Most of the important names are here: Rabab, Nawaal, Adul Karim Kader, and others. Lots of range stylistically, from at least a couple of mini-generations. The singing aside, the Kuwaitis are into a lot of intriguing instrumental stuff including occasional gorgeous solo fiddle. —*John Storm Roberts*

Nubia

Ali Hassan Kuban
....
Vocals / Nubian, Egypt, Middle East
Ali Hassan Kuban is a master singer and popularizer of Nubian music, a typically vocal expression native to the border region of Egypt and Sudan. In the mid-'50s, Kuban added electric guitars, keys, a horn section, and percussion to his music, fusing traditional songs of love with uptempo pop instruments in a Western-influenced mix. His group appeals to old and young alike. —*Myles Boisen & J. Poet*

★ **From Nubia to Cairo** / 1980 / Shanachie ✦✦✦✦✦
These traditional wedding and love songs of southern Egypt have propulsive drumming, clapping, and strings, R&B influenced horn charts, and Farfisa-like electric organ underpinning Kuban's arid vocals. A true masterpiece. —*Myles Boisen & J. Poet*

Saudi Arabia

Mohamed Abdu
....
Saudi Arabia, Middle East

● **Mohamed Abdu** / Saut el Jazira ✦✦✦✦✦
Currently one of the big names of Saudi popular music, Abdu is squarely in the mainstream. Here you get three long songs from a concert appearance. Vocally he sounds like Abdel Halim Hafez, though his voice is more sinewy. Instrumentally there are touches of updating—occasional keyboards, electric guitar, and the like. But the orchestra, and particularly the strongly Egyptian string sound, would mostly fit fine behind Umm Kulthum in her later days. —*John Storm Roberts*

Evening with . . . / Duniaphon ✦✦✦
The young Mohamed Abdo is perhaps Saudi Arabia's favorite singer. This concert recording presents him in typical form, with a youthful style that still (like pretty much all Gulf music) sticks very close to tradition. Within the general Middle Eastern ambit, this is a very different idiom from those of Egypt or Lebanon, having strong Persian, Indian, and even African links. —*John Storm Roberts, Original Music*

Inti El-Hawa / Saut el Jezira ✦✦✦✦✦
This is gorgeous: not just his singing, but the extensive and extremely imaginative string section. Indeed the arrangements in general work splendidly within a basically classic mold. And Abdu, though not a particularly outstanding voice, is a fine and subtle singer. —*John Storm Roberts, Original Music*

Ettab
....
Saudi Arabia, Middle East

The Very Best of Ettab / Relax-In ✦✦✦✦✦
Afro-Saudi Ettab is terrific. Like most Saudi singers she doesn't get as contemporary as, say, the Egyptians. But she's a vocalist of both power and charm. Moreover, her backings add to the mainstream strings all sorts of effective garnishes, from accordion to keyboards, that contrive to be at once goofy and effective. —*John Storm Roberts*

Sudan Collection

Sounds of Sudan / 1990 / World Circuit ✦✦✦✦✦
Included is Arabic pop music by Abdel Aziz el Mubarak, Abdel Gadir Salim, and Mohamed Gubara. —*J. Poet*

Sufi

Kudsi Erguner
....
b. 1952, Istanbul
Flute / Sufi, Lebanon, Turkey, Middle East
The haunting sound of the flute-like nay is literally in Erguner's blood. Born in Istanbul, he is the oldest son of Ulvi Erguner, considered to be Turkey's last great master of the instrument and the man responsible for perserving traditional Turkish music during the period of cultural upheaval at the end of the Ottoman Empire. Kudsi Erguner expanded upon his father's role by spreading Turkish music through the world. Moving to Paris in 1975, he opened a school for Turkish music. He has since recorded several beautifully produced albums of Sufi music and contributed his talents to scores for plays and films, including Peter Brook's acclaimed production of the *Mahabharata* epic. —*Linda Kohanov*

Turkey: Art of the Ottoman Tanbur / 1989 / VDE ✦✦✦✦✦
Kudsi Erguner recorded this album featuring alternating solo performances by two modern masters of the tanbur, Abdi Coskun and Fahreddin Cimenli. The tanbur is the most commonly used lute-like instrument

in Turkish art music. The musicians here fully exploit the rich, sonorous timbre of the instrument, which can be either plucked or bowed. —*Linda Kohanov*

● **Sufi Music of Turkey** / 1990 / CMP ✦✦✦✦✦
This is a powerful recording of Middle Eastern music. Kudsi plays nay with Mahmoud Tabrizi Zadeh, adding the scintillating sounds of the santur (a type of hammer dulcimer) and the sensual melodies of the kemantche (a bowed string instrument). Bruno Caillat also plays zarb and tabla. —*Linda Kohanov*

Whirling Dervishes from Turkey / 1991 / Arion ✦✦✦
Another fine performance of Sufi music from Kudsi, collaborating this time with some traditional singers and instrumentalists who perform a Mevlevi Whirling Dervish ceremony. —*Linda Kohanov*

Sufi Flutes / JVC ✦✦✦
Despite Islam's ambivalent attitude to music, Koranic recitation are at the heart of the music religious incantations of the Islamic world. The Sufi mystical brotherhoods use music and dance to induce religious ecstasy, one of many reasons why they are suspect in the eyes of orthodox theologians. In this CD you get the pure religious sound in its pristine form, and instrumental preludes to Sufi ceremonies are played on the nay flute backed by percussion, in a style close to classical music (the Sufis were in fact guardians of the Middle Eastern classical tradition for a while). As a plus, there are English notes for a change. —*John Storm Roberts*

Sufi Collection

Classical and Religious Music / Barenreiter Musicaphon ✦✦✦
The Mevlevi Sufi mystical sect that Westerners call the Dancing Dervishes place particular stress on music and dance as spiritual exercises—above all a ritual representing the movement of the heavenly bodies. There is an extract from a Mevlevi ritual here, along with ghazals, hymns, and pieces for oud, santur, kanun, and several other instruments. The fine photos and notes are more musically detailed than is usual even for Musicaphon releases. —*David L. Mayers*

Syria

Souheil Arafeh

Middle East, Syria

Magic Touch / Byblos ✦✦✦
Arafeh uses a mix of traditional instruments and styles with occasional modernisms (drum rhythm, electric organ), in what amounts to an instrumental suite evocative of various provincial towns and other places in Syria. The result is a kind of program music building on tradition, which is relatively unfashionable in modern Arabic music but really very attractive. —*John Storm Roberts*

Omaya Orchestra/Chorale

Andalus Classical, Middle East, Syria

Raska al Samah/Waslat Mouachahat / Byblos ✦✦✦
Syrian andalus classical music differs from its Maghrebi cousin not just in that it has ancient Byzantine elements but because Syrian orchestras have been more willing to borrow ensemble string voicings from the West. These two vocal suites are typical and splendid, opening with a fine kanoun solo and sung magnificently throughout. —*John Storm Roberts*

Turkey

Erkose Ensemble

Turkey, Middle East

Tzigane: Gypsy Music of Turkey / 1992 / CMP ✦✦✦✦✦
Remarkably full and emotionally compelling, these pieces arise from modest folk instrumentation with an orchestral sweep. Most selections consist of medleys beginning with impressive improvisations called taksim on kanun (zither), clarinet, oud (lute), or kaman (zither). Songs resemble an inspired cross between Jewish klezmer stylings and Egyptian music. —*Bob Tarte*

Talip Ozkan

Percussion, Lute, Vocals / Turkey, Middle East

Mysteries of Turkey / 1988 / Music of the World ✦✦✦✦✦
The mysterious and exotic sound of the saz, a long-necked lute, is the focus of this recording. Talip Ozkan, a master musician from Turkey, presents traditional songs and dances from his homeland with this unique instrument. Both solo saz and accompanying vocal selections are featured on this recording. —*Music of the World*

The Dark Fire / 1992 / Axiom ✦✦✦
Buzzing, stinging forays into medieval Turkish music by Ozkan, the master of the saz (a member of the lute family played with a cherrywood plectrum), are accompanied by stark frame-drum and wooden spoon percussion. Fierce performances brim with slurred runs, angular melodies, and fractal-shaped riffs. —*Bob Tarte*

● **The Art of the Tanbur** / 1994 / Ocora ✦✦✦✦✦
Cemil Bey was the most famous composer of instrumental art music in the late Ottoman Empire, whose notes compare to Johann Sebastian Bach. These pre-World War I recordings are documents without parallel, and remarkably well-recorded. Ozkan, a virtuoso of the saz lute, turns here to another lute and takassinm to the classical Turkish repertoire. The result is meditative music whose apparent timelessness is in reality molded by a musical sensibility both steeped in tradition and intensely contempoarary. If Cemil Bey is Turkey's Bach, Julian Bream was the Ozkan of the European lute. —*John Storm Roberts, Original Music*

Turkey Collection

Masters of Turkish Music / 1990 / Rounder ✦✦✦✦✦
This scholarly (though very entertaining) collection of Turkish 78s is divided evenly between classical vocal music and various instrumental recordings, all demonstrating sophisticated musicianship. —*Myles Boisen*

Sharki: Love Songs of Istanbul / 1992 / CMP ✦✦✦✦✦
Here is the first-ever collection of sharki music recorded with traditional instruments. Dating back to the 18th century, sharki is a dark and bluesy offshoot from Turkish classical music lamenting the decline of the Ottoman Empire, and Sipahi conveys deep recesses of collective sorrow with her subdued vocal delivery. The eight-piece Kudsi Erguner ensemble adds colorful accompaniment. It is tightly focused, starkly arranged, and emotionally compelling. —*Bob Tarte*

NORTH AMERICA

Arctic Collection

Arctic Circle / Ocora ✦✦✦✦✦
This is a very important recording, done by the scholar Jean Malaurie. It includes Inuit chants and drums from Thule to the Bering Strait. —*David L. Mayers*

Canada

Canada: Jeux Vocaux des Inuit [Inuit du Caribou, Netsilik et Igloolik] / 1989 / Ocora ✦✦✦✦✦
Ninety types of gestures and games are mostly sung by two people facing each other, sometimes alternating arm movements, sometimes holding shoulders, crouching, drop to heels and then standing up. They make throat sounds, pant, quack like ducks, and make other noises, with half of the games telling a story. Some songs are made by two women with their heads side by side singing into a basin, or alternately by one woman singing into metal bowls which act as a resonator. Some games are based on single words repeated in a sequencing pattern drawn from a story without the whole story ever being told. There are stories of fish, dogs, a woman who counts the stars to find out how many children she will have, but the stars are covered by cloud and fog. There are games to make your friend laugh, and to imitate the sound of zero degree weather. It is enjoyable for the sound of the songs and fascinating for the sheer variety, and the depth of their poetry, and philosophy of experience. — *"Blue" Gene Tyrany*

The Copper Eskimo Tradition / 1994 / Auvidis/UNESCO ✦✦✦
Though they never sang outdoors (in case the spirits stole the words and thus the life of the singer), song accompanied every ritual, social or even commercial transaction of the Copper Eskimo. Though the traditional songs have largely been forgotten now, this fine reissue of the old UNESCO musical Atlas compensates somewhat. —*John Storm Roberts, Original Music*

Canada: Vocal Games of the Inuits / Ocora ✦✦✦
As for Native American traditions from the North, this is perhaps the top recording. Included are Caribou, Netsillik, and Igloolik. These examples of voice imitating sounds of nature are mind-blowing. —*David L. Mayers*

Native American Collection

Pow Wow Songs: Music of the Plains Indians / 1975 / New World ✦✦✦
This 1975 collection of social and ceremonial music of the Great Plains Indians mostly focuses on intertribal music from southern groups,

mostly Oklahoman, although there are five cuts of northern plains music. Most of the selections involve groups singing at a powwow in Skiatook, OK. Here are war dance songs, contest songs for straight dancers and fancy dancers, a Sioux flag song, a Vietnam song, and grass dance songs. —*John Storm Roberts*

Inuit Games and Songs / Auvidis ✦✦✦✦✦
A recording like this was my introduction to ethnic music, and the sonic complexity and communal nature of the breath games have had a tremendous impact on my musical thinking. In addition to the games, this CD contains goose imitations, a shamanic song, and a very rare piece for Inuit violin. Good, if not too extensive, notes. —*Carl Hoyt, Original Music*

Night and Daylight Yeibichei / Indian House ✦✦✦
Perhaps the best recording of Navajo elders singing healing songs; it will make the walls of your home tremble. —*David L. Mayers*

PACIFICA

Australia

David Blanasi
....
Didjeridu / Australia, Pacifica

Bamyili corroboree / 1994 / Grevillea ✦✦✦
A fine but frustrating tape, the music is more involving than any other Aboriginal recording, but there are zero notes and what is gleanable is confusing. Though the title suggests a range of music, it is apparently all by one singer, backed by a small chorus, percussion and what the UK distributor calls a didgeridoo but sounds more like a bull-roarer. —*John Storm Roberts, Original Music*

Australia Collection

Aboriginal Sound Instruments / AIAS ✦✦✦
This is more than a mere demonstration, because almost all the tracks are performances, with singing where relevant. All are, of course, musicologically important. Most involving for non-academics are the eerily beautiful didgeridoo tracks. The booklet includes the cultural background, thorough notes on individual tracks, and transcriptions of all examples. —*John Storm Roberts*

Australia: Aboriginal Music / 1992 / Auvidis - Unesco ✦✦✦✦✦
A good overview of the many varieties of Aboriginal music, it also includes many selections of the more rarely heard women's music. Included are mysterious vocal trillings across distances in the "Rain Dreaming" ceremony, an ancient tale of two drowning girls in "Women's Wu-ungka Songs," melisimatic vocalizations like North Indian music in the "Wongga Dance Songs," and wonderful rhythmic inventions in the "Stingray, Dolphin, Curlew and Shark Songs." The excellent notes were written by the recordist Alice M. Moyle. —*"Blue" Gene Tyrany*

Australia: Songs of the Aborigines and Music of Papua, New Guinea / Lyrichord ✦✦✦✦✦
This is a reissue of interesting field recordings of two distinct Aboriginal cultures—particularly, the Malkari "Centipede" and "Snake" songs; the Bunggul dance songs "Seagull" and "Spider," with their rhythmically innovative didgeridoo accompaniments; the haunting Gizra People's flute piece announcing the coming of the Southeast winds during the rainy season; the surprising sudden dissonances of the "Two Flutes" piece; and the evocative "Magician Song" sung by magicians and their initiates while preparing potions. —*"Blue" Gene Tyrany*

☆ **Djambidj: An Aboriginal Song Series** / AIAS ✦✦✦✦✦
Clan-song series like *Djambidj* constitute an important musico-poetic form with strong spiritual and ritual significance. Two singers are accompanied by didgeridoo and percussion. This, along with *Goyulan: The Morning Star*, are the only recordings of complete Aboriginal song series. The accompanying very substantial monographs include transcriptions and translations as well as detailed background notes. Crucially for its quality, it is a real collaboration between the main singer and an ethnomusicologist. —*John Storm Roberts*

Music of the Torres Strait / AIAS ✦✦✦
Like Native Americans, Aborigines have developed a range of new music as well as drawing on an expansion of their own resources (including intertribal styles) borrowing from other traditions. The two cassettes covering traditional and modern idioms illustrate the process and its results in changing old styles or evolving new ones. There is an excellent booklet of notes. —*John Storm Roberts*

Songs of Aboriginal Australia / Smithsonian/Folkways ✦✦✦
Included are vocal songs and didgeridoo music. —*David L. Mayers*

Songs from the Kimberleys / AIAS ✦✦✦
This is one in a series of three sets in the outstanding collection issued by the Australian Institute of Aboriginal Studies. The Kimberleys area of Western Australia offers a quite different tradition. It comes with substantial booklet. —*John Storm Roberts*

Songs from North Queensland / AIAS ✦✦✦
One in a series of three sets in the outstanding collection issued by the Australian Institute of Aboriginal Studies, it contains examples of both traditional music and more syncretic styles from a town in North Queensland and comes with a substantial booklet. —*John Storm Roberts*

Songs from Yarrabah / AIAS ✦✦✦
This, too, contains examples of traditional music and more syncretic styles from a town in North Queensland, but offers in greater detail one stylistic area in the region covered more generally by the North Queensland album. —*John Storm Roberts*

Songs of the Northern Territory / AIAS ✦✦✦
This camp and corroboree singing was recorded in 1962-1963 in a wide range of locations in Australia's vast Northern Territory. Most of the music is ceremonial. These tapes are a remarkably thorough exploration of a series of interlocking cultures. The 60-page accompanying illustrated booklet goes into great detail about the individual tracks and background. —*John Storm Roberts*

Hawaii

Sol Hoopii
....
Guitar (Steel) / Hawaii, Pacifica
The most celebrated steel guitarist of the Hawaiian golden age was undoubtedly Sol Hoopii, who first came to the mainland as a stowaway in 1919. I believe he is the only performer to appear on every Hawaiian slide compilation, where liner notes typically describe him with a single word—"hot." Most of his 78s (over 200!!) were recorded in Los Angeles, where he enjoyed great popularity in such clubs as the Hula Hutt and Seven Seas. He appeared in many movies, toured the country advancing his highly rhythmic slide techniques, and left his stamp on an entire generation of lap steel and pedal steel guitarists in the emerging C & W style. —*Myles Boisen*

Master of the Hawaiian Guitar, Vol. 1 / 1987 / Rounder ✦✦✦
Sol Hoopii was most certainly a guitar master, and his facility, inventiveness, phrasing, and harmonic ideas were many years ahead of their time. You can hear ideas Hoopii formulated on these 16 songs, which were recorded between 1926 and 1930, repeated on countless Western swing, dobro, country, and folk sessions. Rounder recently reissued this first of two fine collections from 1977 on CD. The remastering fully accents the creativity and richness of Hoopii's solos. Even if the harmonies and vocals on such cuts as "Alekoki" and "Hilo" don't bowl you over, it's impossible not to be impressed by Sol Hoopii's instrumental talents. —*Ron Wynn*

★ **Master of the Hawaiian Guitar, Vol. 2** / 1988 / Rounder ✦✦✦✦✦
This second anthology featuring songs from the great Hawaiian guitarist Sol Hoopii moves from the late '20s into the '50s, and shows Hoopii extending his technique and displaying his jazz style. Hoopii's voicings, speed, riffs, accompaniment, and solos are varied and unpredictable over the 16 songs, and often are the saving grace compensating for lightweight lead vocals and sleep-inducing harmonizing. The latest numbers feature fiery guitar displays, with Hoopii particularly spectacular on "Kohala March" and the concluding "Honolulu March." His influence looms large, even among people who don't know his name but hear the influence of his playing through others. —*Ron Wynn*

Hawaii Collection

Hawaiian Guitar / Yazoo ✦✦✦
The most agile dazzlers of the 78-rpm era are a slide guitarist's dream come true. —*Myles Boisen*

Hawaiian Steel Guitar, Vol. 2 / 1976 / Arhoolie ✦✦✦
Features Hawaiian, cowboy, and vaudeville slide experts. —*Myles Boisen*

☆ **Hula Blues** / 1971 / Rounder ✦✦✦✦✦
Another great sampling of top Hawaiian and stateside sliders features some with a country beat. —*Myles Boisen*

Kanak Songs: Feast & Lullabies / Chant du Monde ✦✦✦
The culture of the New Caledonian Kanaks east of Australia varies from island to island and community to community (the 60,000 Kanaks speak at least 20 languages), yet the music has a good deal of underlying cohesion. The examples here, including a remarkable recitative speech and many swirling songs to percussion, were mostly recorded on the main

island of Grande Terre. The music comes with the usual thorough notes. —*John Storm Roberts*

Na Mele O Paniolo / Hawaii State Foundation ✦✦✦
The local cowboys and their 19th-century predecessors from Mexico were major catalysts in Hawaiian music. This recent project (recorded in the mid- and late '80s by the Hawaii State Foundation of Culture and the Arts) offers performances of traditional material performed by several groups from several islands, most of them with ranch connections. Included are very fine recordings and an excellent booklet. —*David L. Mayers*

Vintage Hawaiian Music, Vol. 1 / 1989 / Rounder ✦✦✦
Vintage Hawaiian Music—Steel Guitar Masters (1928-1934) contains the earliest Hawaiian 78 rpm recordings. With its companion volume of singers, they are important historical documents. Both volumes are treasures. —*Myles Boisen*

☆ **Vintage Hawaiian Music, Vol. 2** / 1989 / Rounder ✦✦✦✦✦
Very early Hawaiian 78 rpm recordings, *Vintage Hawaiian Music—Great Singers 1928-1934* has a companion volume of steel guitar. Both of these important historical documents are treasures. —*Myles Boisen*

New Zealand

Inia Te Wiata

Pacifica, New Zealand

Waiata Maori / Waikiki ✦✦✦
The Maori people are known for their joyous communal singalongs known as waiata. This album provides a good example. —*AMG*

Polynesia Collection

Bastille Celebrations in Polynesia / Arion ✦✦✦
It was recorded in Polynesia by Gérard Krémer. —*AMG*

Samoa Collection

Samoan Songs: Historical Collection / Barenreiter Musicaphon ✦✦✦
This outstanding recording brought together Samoan recordings of great rarity. Three were recorded before World War I, three in 1940, and the rest in the mid- and late '60s. They include dance songs, war songs, and topical songs of various sorts, including political ones. Music of enormous importance is underpinned by Musicaphon's thorough notes. —*John Storm Roberts*

REGGAE

"Reggae music is boring; it all sounds the same."

Those are fighting words in the torpid back alleys of Kingston, because nowhere on the face of the earth is there more recorded output per capita than on this Isle of Springs, where literally hundreds of 7-inch singles are released each week, in a staggering variety of styles. It started as the '60s dawned, when steamy-hot and ripe-for-revolution JA was about to oust its British master, and the music (ska) drove the engine of change—double-time, frenetic, and as unyielding as a fully loaded cane truck on a hairpin turn. Ska turned to the half-time lope of rock steady for a couple of years, producing some of the most lyrical and lasting musical mementos of the century, songs of freedom that will be chanted by sufferers I-ternally. Then reggae burst on the scene in 1968, and the world has never stopped listening.

Reggae is as close to a universal music as this receding century has—with superstars like Bob Marley, Peter Tosh, Jimmy Cliff, Toots and the Maytals, and other touring pioneers; with the cult classic movie "The Harder They Come" and a soundtrack that has never stopped selling; with the success of the annual Sunsplash extravaganzas in Montego Bay and their touring counterparts from Japan, Europe, and North America; and with major American labels turning gold and platinum with artists such as Ziggy Marley and Shabba Ranks.

Check it! Maori, Tongan, and Fiji Islanders put aside age-old battles to form a reggae band called Herbs; a Japanese boy toasts (raps) in the rattle-blasted patter of a Kingston speed-rapper; Havasupai Indians at the foot of the Grand Canyon regard Marley as a prophet and display his picture in their homes; Poland's top ethnic fiddler joins a Twinkle Brother for a Polski hoedown/dub showdown, while at the shipyards in Gdansk, 10,000 people (most in red, gold, and green clothing) cheer an eight-hour reggae festival; and Aboriginals form a protest group whose chosen rhythm of resistance is reggae, calling themselves No Fixed Address. Reggae is triumphant, the irresistible heartbeat call to consciousness, the call of the Los Angeles rioters—"No Justice, No Peace!" It is a call that can be as deep and spooky as a bad dream; as lopey and leering as Red Foxx after hours; ethereal and eternal—the true new Psalms; as understated as a pause and as robust as a rocket. This is the music of the Movement of Jah People, future folk who know God is a living man and paradise is right here right now. It is Jah love made manifest, not fe de weakheart, and definitely not boring. — *Roger M. Steffens*

Abyssinians

Reggae, Jamaica, Caribbean
Dreadly serious purveyors of praise-filled Rastafarian religious music, this superb trio began by writing and recording "Satta Massagana" in 1969. The song became a heavily covered standard. Although their output has been spotty, the group is still active. —*Roger Steffens*

● **Forward** / 1982 / Alligator ✦✦✦✦
"Satta" and other hymns for the hearticle are included. —*Roger Steffens*

Satta Massagana / Heartbeat ✦✦✦
The Abyssinians were one of the greatest of rasta-reggae groups, and the title song under various spellings became an anthem. Though the version here isn't quite up to the original single, it and the rest of the music here make up a must-have classic even if you have the LP, since four rarities have been added. —*John Storm Roberts, Original Music*

Laurel Aitken

Vocals / Ska
Though born in Cuba, Laurel Aitken played a pivotal role in helping break Jamaican music internationally. He moved to Jamaica from Cuba in the '50s, then came to England in the '60s. Aitken's recording "Boogie in My Bones" was the first Jamaican single issued in England in 1958. Aitken's debut Bluebeat label release "Boogey Rock" was released two years later. More importantly, his evolution from an imitative R&B vocalist to a premier ska and reggae singer influenced many ska, bluebeat, and reggae vocalists. Aitken recorded hundreds of singles, ranging from incendiary protest to sentimental romance and crass sexual innuendo. He continued performing with his band the Full Circle well into the '80s. —*Ron Wynn*

● **Rasta Man Power** / ROIR ✦✦✦✦

Dennis Alcapone

b. Aug. 6, 1947, Clarendon, Jamaica
Vocals / Ska, Deejay
Dennis Smith (aka Dennis Alcapone) became a dominant toaster/DJ during the early '70s, using a similiar style to U-Roy, though not as fast nor as clever. Alcapone worked with such top producers including Prince Tony and Keith Hudson. Alcapone also recorded for many labels including Studio One and Treasure Isle. Alcapone's popularity began to dip when toasters praising Jah and decrying political, social, and moral injustices began winning the audience's hearts and minds rather than those doing comedic and novelty tunes. Alcapone moved to England, but also found the going there tough. Despite teaming with Bunny Lee on such records as "Investigator Rock" and "Six Million Dollar Man," Alcapone was a nonfactor by the end of the '70s. —*Ron Wynn*

● **Forever Version** / 1971 / Heartbeat ✦✦✦

● **Universal Rockers** / 1992 / RAS ✦✦✦✦
Toaster/DJ Dennis Alcapone was at his humorous, barbed, and bizarre best on this collection of '70s material. His style was often a near mirror imitation of Big Youth's, but he was also at his performing peak during this period. —*Ron Wynn*

Guns Don't Argue / Oct. 1995 / Jamaican Gold ✦✦✦

Bob Andy

Vocals / Reggae
An early member of the mid-'60s Paragons of "Tide Is High" fame, Bob Andy has written some of Jamaica's most lasting songs such as "Desperate Lover" and "Feeling Soul." With Marcia Griffiths, he hit the UK Top Ten in the early '70s. Andy is a strong, lyrical singer of powerful love songs and incisive social statements. His "Fire Burning" became one of 1992's most-used rhythms. —*Roger Steffens*

● **Retrospective** / 1986 / Heartbeat ✦✦✦✦
A fine overview of a sorely overlooked reggae vocalist, composer, arranger, and session singer. —*Ron Wynn*

Song Book / 1988 / Studio One ✦✦✦✦
These are among Coxsone Dodd's most important albums ever, with virtually every cut a classic. —*Roger Steffens*

Horace Andy

b. Jamaica
Vocals / Reggae
An animated, often compelling vocalist, Horace Andy's tenor delivery was featured on many '70s reggae hits. These included "Love of a Woman" and "You Are My Angel." He made his recording debut in the mid-'60s, then left the music scene to sharpen his skills. Upon his return in 1970, Andy's popularity rose as he recorded for Studio One, Crystal, Santic, Randy's, Ja-Man, Channel One, and Jackpot. Andy later moved to America, and established his own label. A prolific composer as well as singer, Andy scored an

international hit in 1980 when Tapper Zukie produced "Natty Dread a Weh She Want." It was recorded during a brief return trip to Jamaica. Andy's issued several albums and LPs during the '80s and '90s, the most recent being *Rude Boy* for Shanachie in 1993. — *Ron Wynn*

● **In The Light/In The Light Dub** / 1995 / Blood & Fire ✦✦✦✦

Best of Horace Andy / Liberty ✦✦✦

Aswad

Reggae
Despite a series of dramatic fluctuations in popularity, the reggae trio Aswad is one of Britain's most enduring and, many say, greatest roots band. Originally a quintet comprising George "Ras Levi" Oban, Angus "Drummie Zeb" Gaye, Brinsley "Dan" Forde, Courtney Hemmings, and Donald "Benjamin" Griffiths, Aswad (the name means "black" in Arabic) had a unique sound composed of jazz/funk, soul, and fusion layered over a rock steady reggae beat. Dub versions of such singles as "Back to Africa" were quite popular in West London dance clubs then and by 1976, Aswad had such a reputation that visiting Jamaican artists such as Dennis Brown, Black Uhuru, and Bob Marley employed them as a backup band. Over the latter part of the '70s through the '80s, Aswad underwent many stylistic changes. The group had great early success with such tunes as "Back to Africa," "Three Babylon," and the innovative "Warrior Child," a song that originally played a key role in *Babylon*, a feature film that starred founding member of Aswad Brinsley Dan, a native of Guyana who was once a child actor for BBC TV.

Their first album was far more jazz-oriented than their second album, *Hulet*. In between these two albums Courtney Hemmings was replaced by Tony "Gad" Robinson. Producer/manager Michael "Reuben" Campbell also joined them. They often gave concerts in conjunction with such British new-wave bands as the Police and Elvis Costello. Critics were not thrilled by the group, considering them pale imitations of real reggae music, this despite the fact that they still had a large devoted fan base who knew better. By the early '80s, they had signed to CBS and released *New Chapter* (1982). Unfortunately, reggae's popularity in England was declining; this coupled with inadequate marketing strategy (something that has plagued the band's albums since their debut) caused the album to receive little fanfare, even though it was critically acclaimed. The following year they released *New Chapter on Dub* for Mango, a small, independent label. Interestingly, this version sold more copies than the original. By this time they had pared themselves down to a trio and with no commercial breakthrough in sight, they reverted to their original style and returned to their old haunts where on their Simba label they recorded such early dancehall tunes as "Bubblin'" and "Kool Noh." Eventually the group made another bid for the mainstream market, this time as pop artists covering versions of others' songs. When that didn't work, it was back to their old style. The strategy worked and gave Aswad a No. 1 hit with "Don't Turn Around." Aswad is an excellent concert band, and though they have yet to reappear on the charts, they continue to perform and record. In 1994 they released the self-produced *Rise and Shine*. As of 1995, Aswad was made up of Forde, Drummie Zeb, and Tony Gad. — *Sandra Brennan*

Aswad / 1976 / Mango ✦✦✦
Their leadoff album that established the group's sound. — *Ron Wynn*

New Chapter / 1981 / CBS ✦✦✦✦
Aswad made its debut on Columbia's British division with this release. It marked a musical shift as keyboardist Tony Gad (also known as Tony Robinson) moved to bass, replacing George Oban. The songs were well produced and exuberantly performed, while there was a good mix between fiery uptempo tunes and passionate love songs. — *Ron Wynn*

A New Chapter of Dub / 1982 / Mango ✦✦✦
Fine dubs of songs from the *New Chapter* album. — *Ron Wynn*

Live and Direct / 1983 / Mango ✦✦✦
This compiles several group favorites. A solid live outing. — *Ron Wynn*

Rebel Souls / 1984 / Mango ✦✦✦✦
Good covers of Marvin Gaye and Toots Hibbert classics. — *Ron Wynn*

To the Top / 1986 / Mango ✦✦✦✦
Contains the wonderful single "Bubbling" and good vocal harmonies. — *Ron Wynn*

Distant Thunder / 1988 / Mango ✦✦✦
A crossover album geared toward a nonreggae audience. — *Ron Wynn*

● **Crucial Tracks: The Best of Aswad** / 1989 / Mango ✦✦✦✦
The best collection for both fans and novices. — *Ron Wynn*

Buju Banton (Mark Myrie)

b. 1973
Vocals / Reggae, Dancehall, Club/Dance
During the early '90s, young dancehall DJ Buju Banton exemplified almost everything that many critics hated about ragga music. With harsh, sexually explicit lyrics, he seemed to encourage nihilism and violence. Still, by 1992, when he was only 19, Banton was one of Jamaica's biggest

dancehall acts with several chart toppers that included such singles as "Bogle" and "Love Me Browning/Love Black Woman." Later that year he started an international firestorm of controversy with "Boom Boom Bye Bye," a song strongly advocating violence and death for Jamaica's "batty boys" (homosexuals). The song spawned protests from gay-rights organizations in Jamaica and New York, and many questions arose concerning the Jamaican and Rastafarian attitudes toward homosexuality. Mercury Records, the major label that had just signed Banton, insisted he write a statement about the song. While he stated that he was not trying to cause violence, Banton did not apologize for his feelings about homosexuality, citing the Bible and his religious beliefs as a basis for his feelings.

Perhaps realizing that his negative music would not find a great market outside the Jamaican context, or perhaps just having matured, he has undergone a gradual but tremendous transformation since his early releases. After becoming a Rastafarian, his music developed a new social consciousness and was more about love rather than sex. He has become an ardent supporter of AIDS education programs, having started Project Willy to help AIDS-afflicted children. He also released his country's first song promoting condoms, "Willy (Don't Be Silly)," from his 1993 album *Voice of Jamaica;* he used the proceeds from the single to help fund his cause. Banton has also turned to educating the island youth about the importance of religion.

Buju Banton was born Mark Myrie, youngest of fifteen children, on Salt Lane, a slum outside Kingston that had no running water. His parents were direct descendants of the independent, rebellious Maroons who fought hard against the British to preserve their freedom. His nickname Buju (meaning breadfruit, a moniker given to chubby children like him) is a reminder of his heritage. Much later he took the last name Banton, a word for talented storytellers, after a favorite performer, Burro Banton. At age 13, Banton took up the mike to become a sound-system DJ. Not long afterward, he began recording. In 1995, the new Banton released the album *Til Shiloh* and changed the face of dancehall music. Instead of relying on synthesized and computer-generated music, he brought back a studio band complete with horns. Most dramatic were the songs such as the haunting tribute to Jamaican's working poor, "Murderer," released as a single in January 1994, a powerful condemnation of exploitational sex, gun culture, and violence in dancehall music. It was inspired by the shootings deaths of up-and-coming ragga artists Panhead and Dirtsman. The song topped the charts and spawned many imitators. It even inspired some area sound systems to stop playing gun songs. — *Sandra Brennan*

Voice of Jamaica / 1993 / Mercury ✦✦✦
Growling, gravelly voiced toaster Buju Banton's recent Mercury release contains entertaining slack material, such as "Good Body" and "Willy (Don't Be Silly)," and respectable social commentary with "Deportees (Things Change)" and "No Respect." But Banton is not that creative or imaginative a wordsmith, and once the delivery wears thin, the lightness of his sentiments becomes acute. The single "A Little More Time" features a great, soulful vocal from the criminally underrated Beres Hammond. For the most part, this is competently produced and performed majorlabel dancehall. — *Ron Wynn*

● **'Til Shiloh** / 1995 / Loos Cannon ✦✦✦✦
Buju Banton's second album *'Til Shiloh* displays a more mature songwriter than that of his 1993 debut, *Voice of Jamaica*. On *'Til Shiloh*, Banton explores a variety of subjects, ranging from social commentary and Rastafarian culture to love songs. Similarly, the music is diverse, taking in dancehall, ska, and reggae, as well as an acoustic number, "Untold Stories," that strongly suggests Bob Marley's "Redemption Song." Throughout the record, Buju Banton justifies his position as one of the leading reggae stars of the mid-'90s. — *Stephen Thomas Erlewine*

Mr. Mention / Fader ✦✦✦
This set concentrates on love and romance, with Banton's ideas falling into the arch-traditional vein on such songs as "Love Black Woman," "Love How the Gal Dem Flex," and "Love Me Brownin'." While he avoids the easy vulgarity that plagues several of his comrades, Banton's heavy-voiced quips lack the flexibility, speed, tonal color, or creativity of several top toasters, and he seldom discusses anything other than his sexual desires or abilities, except his proficiency on the microphone. Within that limited universe, a couple of the CD's cuts are interesting. But thus far, it's hard to understand why he's so popular based on the content of his recordings. — *Ron Wynn*

Beenie Man (Moses Davis)

Vocals / Raggamuffin, Ragga
Born Moses Davis, Beenie ("small") Man grew up in the Kingston, Jamaica, ghetto of Waterhouse. He was a child prodigy on the dancehall circuit, first performing at age five and releasing his debut album, *The Invincible Beenie Man: Ten Year Old Boy Wonder*. However, it took until age 21 for Beenie to release his first international album, *Blessed*, which came out in the US in 1995 and featured the hit "Slam." — *Steve Huey*

● **Blessed** / 1995 / Island Jamaica ✦✦✦✦
Beenie Man's first international album *Blessed* proves why the young reggae star is one of the most popular ambassadors of dancehall in the world. Featuring hit singles like "World Dance" and "Blessed," the album is an infectious, danceable collection that never makes any deep lyrical statements—even though Beenie Man does make a couple of stabs at philosophical and political insights on a couple of songs—but is carried by a set of deep bass grooves and Beenie Man's dynamic charisma. —*Stephen Thomas Erlewine*

Big Youth

Percussion, Vocals / Reggae, Deejay
Though most would call longtime toaster Big Youth a DJ, he prefers to think of himself as an "inspirator," one who calls his audiences towards a higher Jah consciousness of love, clean living, and commitment to building society up rather than tearing it down with slackness and violence. During the early '70s, he was the most popular toaster in Jamaica. He was born Marley Buchanan in the same hospital where his mother, a Christian preacher, was born. His father was a policeman for 39 years. With such a background, Big Youth's conversion to Rastafarianism created considerable tension with his family, particularly his mother (eventually, after seeing all the good that came of his music, she reconciled with her son and they have a fine long-distance relationship). He got his nickname shortly after leaving high school to learn the auto mechanic's trade. Because he was younger, the others called him "Youth." It was a close friend from downtown Kingston who teasingly began to call him "Big Youth," because Buchanan was a large boy.

As a performer he got his start working with the Mightyness Emperor Lord Tippertone sound system, located on Princess Street in Kingston, at night while working by day as a porter. He then worked for a time with Gregory Isaacs and Jimmy Rodway and first gained notice singing on Errol Dunkley's "Movie Star" and "The Black Cinderella" during the early '70s. Before hitting the big-time, Big Youth worked with a variety of producers including Joe Gibbs, Derrick Harriott, and Gussy Clark, who produced his debut album. He also worked with Prince Buster and Keith Hudson, who gave Big Youth his first two hits, including his Hudson-produced tribute to the current fad for Honda S. 90 motorcycles, "S.90 Skank." With Hudson, Big Youth recorded a number of successful songs. At one point he had seven simultaneous chart entries with five of them in the Top Ten. His style and uplifting message inspired many subsequent artists, including Bob Marley, who in turn called Big Youth his favorite toaster. In the late '70s, Big Youth formed his own record label and has since continued recording and performing steadily. Considered the founder of Jah music, Big Youth remains committed to singing songs that have real meaning and frequently aims his music at youth, encouraging them to avoid all drugs and alcohol and to turn to God instead. He also strongly supports the education of youth. —*Sandra Brennan*

Screaming Target / 1973 / Trojan ✦✦✦✦
Excellent toasts and fine instrumental versions of reggae classics by Dennis Brown, Gregory Isaacs, and others. —*Ron Wynn*

Dreadlocks Dread / 1975 / Frontline ✦✦✦✦
An outstanding set of early material, with the spotlight on their compositional prowess. —*Ron Wynn*

★ **Natty Cultural Dread** / 1976 / Trojan ✦✦✦✦✦
A definitive early-period album from this reggae toaster. A must for every reggae lover. —*Michael G. Nastos*

● **Everyday Skank: The Best of Big Youth** / 1980 / Trojan ✦✦✦✦
A tremendous anthology containing early, out-of-print singles and album cuts. —*Ron Wynn*

Live at Reggae Sunsplash / 1984 / Genes ✦✦✦
High-energy live performances of Big Youth's greatest hits are backed by the Soul Syndicate. —*Roger Steffens*

A Luta Continua / 1985 / Heartbeat ✦✦✦
Songs of the '80s worldwide struggle—sung, not toasted. —*Roger Steffens*

Black Uhuru

Reggae, Dub
By 1992, Black Uhuru (Black Sounds of Freedom) had gone through six distinct incarnations, the only common factor being Duckie Simpson, their dreadly serious harmonist and sometime composer. Founded in the mid-'70s, the group hit its key period in the early '80s with a charismatically scowling lead singer named Michael Rose, who remade his classic "Dreadlocks Coming..." as "Guess Who's Coming to Dinner." A fearsome prowler onstage with a Far East style of roots warbling, Rose was often touted as the "next Bob Marley," an observation that has ruined the career of many a lesser performer. The militancy of the group was enhanced by an African-American woman with a Master's degree from Columbia University, Puma Jones, whose wavy-armed dancing and high, chromatic harmonies echoed the communal gatherings she had witnessed while working in Mama Africa. Add to this the essential underpin-

Reggae Styles

DJ — Over a dub track, rappers (called toasters) chant lyrics of topical concerns. The form began live at sound system dances, eventually leading to recordings of toasts on disc. Major figures include U-Roy, Big Youth, I Roy.

DANCEHALL — Dancehall developed in the '80s as "raggamuffin," a hybrid style featuring a DJ or "sing-jay" half-singing, half-rapping with often bawdy ("slack") themes. The musical structure is rooted in reggae though the rhythms, played by drum machines, are considerably faster. By the '90s dancehall crossover was common with many gangta-rappers incorporating dancehall rhythms and its rapid-fire toasting. Major dancehall figures include Yellowman and Shabba Ranks.

DUB — Instrumental reggae. Pure dub is a rhythm track with special effects including altered bits of vocal. From the early-'70s, nearly all Jamaican singles would feature the vocal version on the A-side and a dub instrumental version of the same song on the B-side. Major figures include Mad Professor, King Tubby, and Augustus Pablo.

LOVERS ROCK — Primarily a UK-fostered style, lovers rock is a secular form of reggae. Divorced from reggae's lyrical emphasis on social justice and Rasta, lovers rock instead deals with mainly romantic concerns. John Holt and Maxi Priest are major figures in lovers rock.

RAGGA — Ragga is a term used when dancehall reggae is incorporated into other genres, most notably hip-hop and R&B. Ragga and dancehall are essentially interchangeable terms for the same music, but reggae audiences and critics tend not to use ragga, while pop audiences do.

SKA — Jamaica's first indigenous music, ska is a double-horn-driven amalgam of R&B shuffle, Nyabinghi, calypso, Afro-Cuban, pocomania, jazz, and rock 'n' roll. Important players include: Skatalites, Byron Lee, Prince Buster, Toots & the Maytals, Desmond Dekker, and Laurel Aitken. Duke Reid and Coxsone Dodd played prominent roles in the music's development as producers.

nings of rhythm twins Sly & Robbie, who were considered equal members of the group while Rose was aboard, and you have the quintessential reggae lineup of the post-Marley era and reggae's first-ever Grammy winners. However, internal problems and dissatisfaction with their record label broke up that lineup. But 1986's *Brutal*, featuring new lead singer Junior Reid, revealed a surprisingly strong resolve to continue. Eventually, visa problems sidelined Reid and Puma died of cancer, and in full circle the three original members came together to take the group to a new level. The current lineup is composed of solo star Don Carlos (whose style is hauntingly similar to Reid's and Rose's), Duckie Simpson, and former Wailing Soul Garth Dennis, showing that the concept could be successfully molded to fit almost anyone willing to give voice to these Black sounds of freedom and righteous indignation. —*Roger Steffens*

★ **Sinsemilla** / 1980 / Mango ✦✦✦✦✦
An outstanding set that helped break them in the States. —*Ron Wynn*

Black Sounds of Freedom / 1981 / Shanachie ✦✦✦
A reissued remix of the early *Love Crisis* album. —*Ron Wynn*

Guess Who's Coming to Dinner / 1981 / Heartbeat ✦✦✦
A reissue of a fine album, *Showcase*. —*Ron Wynn*

☆ **Red** / 1981 / Mango ✦✦✦✦✦
This album is a landmark release, one of the great reggae sessions of the '80s. —*Ron Wynn*

Tear It Up / 1982 / Mango ✦✦✦
A strong live date, though an overly familiar selection. —*Ron Wynn*

Chill Out / Dec. 1982 / Mango ✦✦✦✦
Superb Sly and Robbie backing—dark, haunting, and bare. —*Roger Steffens*

The Dub Factor / 1983 / Mango ✦✦✦
A great dub date. —*Ron Wynn*

Reggae Greats / 1985 / Mango ✦✦✦
An adequate collection of past hits. —*Ron Wynn*

Brutal / 1986 / RAS ✦✦✦
Black Uhuru's late-'80s trio didn't garner as much crossover attention or publicity as earlier editions, but were equally outstanding from a content and performance standpoint. While Sly Dunbar and Robbie Shakespeare's production embraced the computerized mode, Junior Reid's lead vocals were as dynamic and explosive as those of former lead singer

Michael Rose, and the occasional leads and sparkling harmonies of Puma Jones and Ducky Simpson were expertly incorporated into the mix. *Brutal* included strong message tracks, good love/romantic fare, and a fine spiritual number, "Dread in the Mountain." —*Ron Wynn*

Brutal Dub / 1986 / RAS ✦✦✦
This dub version of Black Uhuru's 1986 *Brutal* benefited from a great mixing job by Scientist, whose snaking patterns and boosting of Robbie Shakespeare's bass illuminated the appeal of the original production and songs. Guitarists Frank Stepanek and Daryl, plus rhythm guitar ace Willie Lindo and synthesizer master Tyrone Downie, played brilliantly, and percussion and horn support was seamlessly integrated. Even those who find dub unappealing or distracting should be hooked by this fine release. —*Ron Wynn*

★ **Liberation: The Island Anthology** / Sep. 21, 1993 / Mango ✦✦✦✦✦
With new remastering and carefully chosen tracks, this two-disc anthology is essential for fans and newcomers alike. A perfect starting point. —*Chris Woodstra*

Alpha Blondy (Seydou Kone)

b. Jan. 1, 1953, Dimbokora, Cote d'Ivoire
Vocals / Reggae, Africa, Ivory Coast
Hailing from the Cote d'Ivoire, Alpha Blondy is among the world's most popular reggae artists. With his 12-piece band Solar System, Blondy offers a reggae beat with a distinctive African cast. Calling himself an African Rasta, Blondy creates Jah-centered anthems promoting morality, love, peace, and social consciousness. With a range that moves from sensitivity to rage over injustice, much of Blondy's music empathizes with the impoverished and those on society's fringe. Blondy is also a staunch supporter of African unity and to this end, he sings to Moslem audiences in Hebrew and sings in Arabic to Israelis. Some of his best known songs include "Cocody Rock," "Jerusalem," and "Apartheid Is Nazism."

He was born a member of the Jula tribe in Dimbokoro and named Seydou Kone after his grandfather. His grandmother Cherie Coco raised him. He was always a rebellious child and for this, Coco named him "Blondy," her unique pronunciation of the word "bandit." When he started performing professionally, he took on the name Alpha (the first letter in the Greek alphabet) so his name literally translates to "first bandit." Though he grew up listening to African folkloric music such as yagba and gumbe, his primary musical influences were such Western bands as Deep Purple, Pink Floyd, Hendrix, the Beatles, Creedence Clearwater Revival, and soul artists like Otis Redding. Later Bob Marley's music tremendously affected Blondy. Though he wanted to become a musician, his family expected him to become a respectable English teacher. He studied English at Hunter College in New York, and later in the Columbia University American Language Program. Outside of class, he would play music in Central Park and in Harlem clubs, where occasionally house bands would let him sing his Bob Marley covers in French, English, and various West African languages. One night, record producer Clive Hunt heard Blondy sing and invited him to record six songs. Unfortunately, Hunt absconded with the tape. Shortly afterward, he returned to the Ivory Coast where he was arrested for threatening the ambassador at the New York Ivorian embassy because the diplomat felt that Blondy's English was too good for him to be an Ivorian native. While at the police station, Blondy's temper again flared and he slapped a policeman (after the cop slapped him first). He spent a week in jail and then stayed briefly at the Bingerville Asylum in Abidjan, where he was declared reasonably sane and released. Soon afterward, he began honing his songwriting and performing skills. Later, he dedicated an album to the patients of Bingerville.

Blondy got his big break from a friend, Fulgence Kass, an employee of Ivory Coast Television who helped him land a spot on the "Premiere Chance" talent show. Singing three of his own tunes plus Burning Spear's "Christopher Columbus," the young artist was a hit with the audience. Blondy then hooked up with producer G. Benson who recorded his eight-song debut album *Jah Love* in a single day. The most popular song, "Brigadier Sabari," was an account of Blondy's run-in with an Abidjan police street raid in which he was nearly beaten to death. It was the first time a West African artist had dared to mention random police brutality in public. After releasing the album, he and the newly formed Solar System band signed to EMI. They recorded his second album *Cocody Rock!!!* in Paris in 1984. Later he returned to Tuff Gong to record his third album, *Jerusalem* (1986). By the release of his 1987 album *Revolution*, Blondy had established himself as an international artist. Three years before he had been voted the number one artist by a Radio France international poll. His popularity continues to grow, and he continues steadily releasing albums. His 1992 album *Masada* was released in over 50 countries around the world and went double-gold in France. —*Sandra Brennan*

Jerusalem / 198 / Shanachie ✦✦✦
Blondy sings in Arabic, Hebrew, French, English, and many African languages in an effort to reach as many people as possible. On this disc, one of his most popular titles, he's backed by the Wailers (sans Bob Marley) for a simmering, roots-heavy session. —*J. Poet*

Jah Glory / 1985 / Moya ✦✦✦✦
Alpha Blondy's smash-hit 1983 first album with an all-local band, the Natty Rebels, had all the accessibility and directness that made him an international star. Two cuts are agreeable reggae in English, the rest is Afro-reggae and a lot more interesting for that. In some ways Blondy's music is typical of the Ivory Coast: light, accomplished, and geared to a regional rather than local audience. Though the notes don't tell you so, *Cocody Rock!!!* is a re-release of Blondy's 1984 second album, recorded in Paris and Kingston with a mix of African and Jamaican musicians (plus Kassav's Jocelyne Beroard on backup vocals). Pre-superstar Blondy, it has the freshness you'd expect from somebody pretty much just starting out. He sure believes in touching all bases. Besides its so-so title song, *Apartheid* has something for both Muslims and Christians as well as a hilarious cut claiming Ivory Coast's ultra-conservative president as a rasta. —*John Storm Roberts*

Apartheid Is Nazism / 1987 / Shanachie ✦✦✦✦
This is Blondy's most militant statement, and a continent-wide hit. —*J. Poet*

Cocody Rock!!! / 1988 / Shanachie ✦✦✦✦
This is Blondy's bestselling album. —*J. Poet*

The Prophets / 1989 / Capitol ✦✦✦✦
Blondy's first international release under a new worldwide contract with EMI is as soulful and militant as past efforts, with an added gloss to the production that may win new listeners. —*J. Poet*

Cocody Rock!!! / Aug. 1989 / Shanachie ✦✦✦

● **The Best of Alpha Blondy** / 1990 / Shanachie ✦✦✦✦
This disc lives up to its title with hits like "Jerusalem," "Cocody Rock," and "Apartheid Is Nazism." —*J. Poet*

Yami Bolo (Rolando Mclean)

Vocals
International star Yami Bolo has been recording and performing "Jah-centered" cultural reggae since the '80s. Bolo believes that he has been divinely called to make himself and his entourage soldiers of the Almighty on a mission to spread their message of love, peace, and hope to the world with their performances and recordings. He is particularly interested in uplifting-the-youth songs that warn against violence, such as "Gun War." Born Rolando McLean, Yami Bolo's earliest musical influence was church music; he began performing at age 11. He got his big chance when he hooked up with Sugar Minott and his Youth Promotion organization. Minott was impressed by Bolo's sincerity and eventually allowed him to record special promotions for traveling DJs—none of the many tracks he recorded with Minott were ever released. While associated with Minott, the adolescent Bolo would spend much time hanging out at Jamaican studios listening to roots beats and learning about recording. Later, Bolo performed with Stur-Mas and Third World. As an independent artist, Bolo signed with Techniques in the mid-'80s and released three singles. He then went on to cut one LP with Junior Delgado and another with Augustus Pablo before recording the solo CD *He Who Feels It Knows It* for Heartbeat in 1989. In the early '90s, he was signed with Taxi records and also to Paisley Park Records as a songwriter. —*Sandra Brennan*

● **Ransom** / Shanachie ✦✦✦✦

Ken Boothe

b. 1948, Kingston, Jamaica
Vocals / Reggae, Rock Steady
Legendary producer Coxsone Dodd dubbed Boothe "Mr. Rock Steady" in the mid-'60s and this hard-belting crooner had some of that genre's biggest hits. His career has spanned the past 30 years, in a style rooted in the Jamaican fundamentalism called "pocomania" and mixed with a touch of Otis Redding. His cover of Bread's "Everything I Own" hit No. 1 on the UK pop charts in the mid-'70s. Born in Trenchtown, Jamaica, Boothe was first known for singing soulful ska. An exceptionally handsome youth, Boothe was a teenage heartthrob while he himself was still a teen. He got his start at age 15 when Dodd paired him up with Stranger Cole to form the ska-beat duo Stranger and Ken. They had some success, most notably the songs "World's Fair" and "All Your Friends." It was when rock steady music evolved that Boothe really found his niche. Still working with Dodd, he had major local hits with "Just Another Girl," and "Moving Away." In the early '70s, he hooked up with producer Lloyd Charmers and became popular in both Jamaica and the UK With a smooth, at times sentimental style (it has also been compared to that of Wilson Pickett) that appealed to a wide audience ranging from young teens to the more conservative, older middle-class Jamaicans, Boothe is credited with helping reggae music gain acceptance as a valid style. Following major success with "Everything I Own" in 1974, Boothe had another major, but not quite as successful, hit with "Crying over You." Afterward, Boothe's career began to fade, though he has continued performing through the mid-'90s. —*Roger Steffens & Sandra Brennan*

● **Live Good** / 1978 / United Artists ✦✦✦✦
Coxsone sessions include the hits "Moving Away," "Live Good," and "Thinking." —*Roger Steffens*

Call Me / Rohit ✦✦✦
One of reggae and Jamaican music's finest pure singers. —*Ron Wynn*

Brigadier Jerry

Vocals / Reggae, Deejay

A speed-rapping pioneer, "Briggy" was the featured toaster of the Jah Love sound system run by an uptown Rasta organization called the Twelve Tribes, which counted Bob Marley among its membership. His raps are invariably cultural, not slack (bawdy), and he ruled the mid-'80s DJ clashes in Jamaica. —*Roger Steffens*

● **Jamaica Jamaica** / 1985 / RAS ✦✦✦✦
Toaster/DJ Brigadier Jerry moves from praise to political and dancehall tunes. The eight tracks include the lightweight throwaway "Three Blind Mice," more substantial "Kushunpeng" and "Armadiddeon Style," reverent "Jah Jah Move" and "Give Thanks and Praise," and the powerful "Everyman a Me Brethren." Jerry is a no-nonsense toaster who seldom does novelty numbers or emphasizes speed and verbal facility at the expense of his message. Only the set's brevity (less than 40 minutes) works against it, as it ends just when Brigadier Jerry has generated some momentum. —*Ron Wynn*

Dennis Brown

b. 1957, Kingston, Jamaica

Vocals / Reggae, Lovers Rock, Dancehall, Jamaica, Caribbean, Ragga

Often referred to as "Emmanuel, the Crown Prince of Reggae," Dennis Brown was Bob Marley's favorite singer. He was 13 when his career began, recording initially (and typically) for Coxsone Dodd, scoring big with a cover of "No Man Is an Island" (the Impressions) in 1968. In the '70s he made a series of exciting albums for Joe Gibbs and had a UK hit with his classic "Money in My Pocket." From 1977 to 1982 he recorded for Joe Gibbs, in his peak period producing such classics as "Revolution," "Have You Ever Been Lonely (Have You Ever Been Blue)," "The Promised Land," and "Sitting and Watching." A live album was cut in Montreux in 1979, a year after he was featured in the film *Heartland Reggae*. With a no-nonsense, straightahead style, Brown is capable of wrapping a love song in a crooning caress or inciting a crowd (as he did memorably at the 1983 Sunsplash in Montego Bay) to uncontrolled hysteria. He continues to be one of Jamaica's classiest and most riveting performers. —*Roger Steffens*

Super Hits / 1972 / Trojan ✦✦✦✦
Although only a complete reggae novice would need any convincing, here's a set that displays the lyrical mastery and soulfulness that have made Dennis Brown a legend since his days as a youthful star. —*Ron Wynn*

20 Classic Reggae Tracks / 1985 / Meteor ✦✦✦✦
Another excellent collection intended for the casual or novice buyer rather than the hardcore fan, but it's an opportunity to get some seminal Dennis Brown material on one CD. Otherwise, grab the entire albums from which these songs were culled to get their full and accurate context. —*Ron Wynn*

Hold Tight / 1986 / Live & Learn ✦✦✦
Since he was a child star in Jamaica, Dennis Brown's golden voice has been among the island's most evocative and striking, regardless of lyrical content or musical setting. This mid-'80s album featured him doing gorgeous love ballads and probing message tracks with sensitive, laid-back production. Al Campbell joined him on "I've Got Your Number," a fine performance that saw both vocalists soaring and uniting on a convincing tune. This fell in the above-average category by Brown's standards, which meant that by most other singers' criteria, it was excellent despite the brevity (35 minutes). —*Ron Wynn*

Brown Sugar / 1986 / RAS ✦✦✦
No Dennis Brown disc is ever completely worthless, but some are sure a lot better than others. This one is perilously close to forgettable, mainly because there are only seven cuts (clocking in at just over 33 minutes) and Brown often coasts along, letting his great voice recite the melody and conclude the song with little effort. When he chooses to extend himself, as on "Can't Keep a Good Man Down" or "All Over the World," you hear the vocal flourishes, soulful ardor, and skill that have stamped him a reggae legend. Otherwise, you get nicely crafted, pro forma performances. —*Ron Wynn*

Greatest Hits / 1988 / Rohit ✦✦✦✦
An arguable title, but no problems otherwise. —*Ron Wynn*

Inseparable / 1988 / VP ✦✦✦✦
Simply stunning. —*Ron Wynn*

My Time / Jan. 1989 / Rohit ✦✦✦
Keeps things at a generally high level. —*Ron Wynn*

Good Vibrations / May 1989 / Rohit ✦✦✦
A harder edge and tone. —*Ron Wynn*

Unchallenged / 1990 / VP ✦✦✦✦
The songs, production, and arrangements on this album are all first-rate. —*Ron Wynn*

Over Proof / 1991 / Shanachie ✦✦✦
Uniformly excellent. Exuberant, passionate vocals. —*Ron Wynn*

Victory Is Mine / 1991 / RAS ✦✦✦
No reggae vocalist surpasses Dennis Brown's glorious skills. Brown, like Gregory Isaacs, does so much recording that even his worst albums will have some good and at least one great cut. This session includes a skillful remake of "Sea of Love" and has stirring romantic material, plus competent, though not great, roots and message tunes. With Brown, you'll never get anything less than solid vocals; the trick is whether he sings up or down to the material. On this one, the ratio of stirring to detached performances makes it well worth hearing. —*Ron Wynn*

Blood Brothers / 1994 / RAS ✦✦✦
Gregory Isaacs and Dennis Brown are among reggae's greatest pure vocalists and personalities, and each has recorded numerous albums. Thanks to a lack of specific discographical information, it's tough to tell the vintage of these Flabba Holt-produced sessions. The duo divide writing credits and the spotlight. The disc's best cuts include the title track, the soothing "Closer Than a Friend" and "True Love Is Hard to Find," the slashing "Hard Labor," and the reverential "Give Thanks to the Father." While it's far from groundbreaking, it's a decent example of their prowess. —*Ron Wynn*

★ **Love Hate: The Best of Dennis Brown** / Jul. 1996 / VP ✦✦✦✦✦
Love Hate: The Best of Dennis Brown is an adequate but incomplete retrospective of Brown's lengthy career. Although it gives a fair representation of Brown's sound, it only includes a handful of hits like "Money in My Pocket" and omits a number of other important tracks. Nevertheless, the collection is useful as a starting point, even if it doesn't provide a definitive retrospective. —*Leo Stanley*

Burning Spear (Winston Rodney)

Reggae, Dub

Winston Rodney took his stage name from Jomo Kenyatta, hero of Kenyan independence. The Spear, as he is called, first recorded in 1969 for Coxsone Dodd. Those productions, collected six years later on a pair of Studio One albums, were lean, mysterious, and way ahead of their time. A similar sound would sweep Jamaica in the late '70s and be dubbed the "Rockers" style. Not meeting much initial success, Spear retreated to his rural home in St. Ann's, in the hills of North Coast Jamaica. Eventually he returned in 1975 as part of a self-named trio for producer Jack Ruby. This time the world woke up, and Spear was recognized as a major figure. After two albums Spear dismissed his backing trio, journeyed to London, and cut one of the most astonishing live reggae sets ever for Island, for whom he recorded until 1980. That same year, he was featured unforgettably in an a cappella performance of "Jah No Dead" in the reggae movie *Rockers*. Since then he has skipped through several major and minor labels, returning in 1990 to Island.

Spear is one of those artists whose style is so immediately recognizable that those who like him from the start seem to have followed his every move with joy. He is similar to a trance singer, especially in his horn-lofted live performances, whirling around the stage with arms outstretched, a dreadlocked dervish chanting of dark carnal nights of captivity and imminent deliverance. By the end of his best shows he has often repeated phrases in delicious delirium, reaching the higher heights that is reggae and Rasta's promised land. Without question, Spear is one of reggae's greats. —*Roger Steffens*

★ **Marcus Garvey** / 1975 / Mango ✦✦✦✦✦
A reggae cornerstone, this is the most focused and musically exhilarating tribute to Marcus Garvey, a recurring theme in his music. —*John Floyd*

Garvey's Ghost / 1976 / Mango ✦✦✦
This is a pulsating dub version of his album *Marcus Garvey*. —*John Floyd*

Man in the Hills / 1976 / Mango ✦✦✦✦
This nearly repeats the success of his debut, through a wide-ranging array of topics and a sturdy groove. —*John Floyd*

☆ **Live** / 1977 / Mango ✦✦✦✦✦
Aswad backs Spear's solo debut, one of reggae's greatest live sets ever. —*Roger Steffens*

★ **Harder Than the Best** / 1979 / Mango ✦✦✦✦✦
A magnificent career overview, it includes every highlight from Spear's canon, the best songs from otherwise turgid albums. —*John Floyd*

Hail H.I.M. / 1980 / Radic ✦✦✦
Burning Spear was among the most exciting and charismatic vocalists to emerge from the initial group of '70s reggae performers, but he wasn't as versatile nor able to transcend linguistic and cultural barriers as easily as Bob Marley. His message tracks were unrelenting in their indictments

and uncompromising in their views about what constituted justice and progress. This album had no American distribution and was only available briefly as an import. It contains the typical undiluted, furious leads on such cuts as "Columbus," "Follow Marcus Garvey," and "Cry Blood Africans." —*Ron Wynn*

Farover / 1982 / Heartbeat ✦✦✦✦
Some superb compositions and searing vocals. —*Ron Wynn*

The Fittest of the Fittest / 1983 / Heartbeat ✦✦✦✦
Taut production, memorable leads from Winston Rodney. —*Ron Wynn*

Resistance / 1984 / Heartbeat ✦✦✦✦
A great pairing of Rodney vocals and horn section. A Grammy nominee, this boasts the added bonus of a wonderful nonpolitical piece, "Love to You." —*Ron Wynn*

People of the World / 1986 / Slash ✦✦✦
A nice debut on a major label not known for reggae. This release also includes eclectic material and a female horn section. —*Ron Wynn*

Mek We Dweet / 1990 / Mango ✦✦✦✦
Spear makes a triumphant return to the label where he started his career, at least from a worldwide perspective. —*Ron Wynn*

Jah Kingdom / 1992 / Mango ✦✦✦✦
A powerful, timely, and timeless album with the deep-in-the-Land-of-Look-Behind roots consciousness and spirituality that only Spear can deliver. Simply some of his finest tracks in recent years, including a cover of the Grateful Dead classic "Estimated Prophet." "A compelling and highly spititual tour de force." —*The Beat*

The World Should Know / 1993 / Heartbeat ✦✦
★ **Chant Down Babylon: The Island Anthology** / Jun. 18, 1996 / Island ✦✦✦✦✦
Spanning two compact discs and over 30 songs that cover his career at Island Records, *Chant Down Babylon: The Island Anthology* is the definitive Burning Spear collection, featuring all of his classic songs, plus a bevy of essential rarities, including 12-inch mixes and dub versions. While the original singles and album tracks are classics, the rare dub and 12-inch mixes are nearly as essential, since Burning Spear's dub mixes were as influential, if not more so, than the original versions. Since *Chant Down Babylon* showcases both sides of his talents, it is the definitive retrospective—it's a necessary item for any reggae library. —*Leo Stanley*

Don Carlos & Gold

Reggae
A founding member of Black Uhuru and an outstanding "sweet" vocalist, Don Carlos has been an international reggae star since the '70s. He's recorded for Roots, Greensleeves, Negus Roots, RAS, Empire, and several other labels as a solo performer and recorded with the group Gold. Carlos, Rudolph Dennis, and Derrick Simpson were the original Black Uhuru, but this trio made only one single for Top Cat, "Folk Song," before disbanding. Carlos rejoined Black Uhuru along with Dennis for the CD *Now* in 1990. Their most recent release was *Iron Storm* for Mesa in '94. —*Ron Wynn*

● **Just a Passing Glance** / 1972 / RAS ✦✦✦✦
One of reggae's finest "sweet" vocalists, Don Carlos' earnestness and sincerity overcome occasionally overwrought and sentimental material. He was more forceful on the message cuts. —*Ron Wynn*

Charlie Chaplin

Deejay / Reggae
Conscious and comical are the words that best describe DJ Charlie Chaplin. He is among the most respected toasters in Jamaica, noted for speaking out against slackness and violence in his music. —*Sandra Brennan*

Cry Blood / 1991 / RAS ✦✦✦
Whether singing or toasting, Charlie Chaplin is one of reggae's most versatile performers. This CD includes a clever reggae adaptation of an old B.B. King tune retitled "Singin' the Blues" and a less successful cover of Hammer's "U Can't Touch This" called "Don't Touch Crack." Chaplin also offers a take on James Bond with "License to Kill," his thoughts on contemporary romance with "Modern Girl" and some other notions on life and love. His vocals and interaction with backup singers are engaging, while his verbal quips are often thoughtful and catchy. —*Ron Wynn*

● **20 Super Hits** / Sonic Sounds ✦✦✦✦
Toaster/DJ Charlie Chaplin dispenses wit and wisdom on a variety of subjects on this anthology covering his most popular singles. Most were done for small Jamaican labels, with sound and production quality varying. —*Ron Wynn*

Johnny Clarke

b. Jan. 1955, Bull Bay, Jamaica
Vocals / Reggae
Johnny Clarke, though not well-known outside of Jamaica, was the

island's most popular reggae artist during the '70s. Born in Bull Bay, Jamaica, Clarke was a naturally gifted singer who started out in his late teens after winning a local talent contest. He recorded his debut single, "God Made the Sea and Sun," for producer Clancy Eccles. He then recorded "Everyday Wondering" for Rupie Edwards. Unfortunately, Edwards did not bother to put Clarke's name on the label. Wanting to have his name publicized, the young singer next hooked up with Bunny Lee to record "None Shall Escape the Judgment in This Time." Originally the song was to be sung by Earl Zero, but after a session at Duke Reid's Treasure Isle Studio, Clarke came up with his own version of the song and it was this recording that became a hit. When Rupie Edwards saw that his former artist was becoming hot, he found the rhythm track for a Clarke song, "Everyday Wondering," added new lyrics, and released it in Britain as "Irie Feelings," where it made it to the Top Ten to become the first internationally popular reggae song. Clarke was voted Jamaica's best vocalist five years running.

Some of his best-known songs include "Move Out of Babylon Rastaman," "Jah Jah We Are Waiting," "Roots Natty Congo," and "Rebel Soldiering." As with all of Lee's performers at that time, Clarke was expected to constantly record not only original material, but also covers of others' work. He recorded a cover of Marley's "No Woman, No Cry" and had a major Jamaican hit—Marley had been prevented from releasing the single himself for contractual reasons. A rift between Clarke and Lee in the late '70s led to Clarke leaving Lee to work with different producers. Though Clarke continues to perform and record original tunes and covers, he has yet to attain the popularity he found during his Bunny Lee years. —*Sandra Brennan*

Enter into His Gates / 1975 / Attack ✦✦✦✦
These mid-'70s tracks were mixed by virtuoso King Tubby. —*Roger Steffens*

● **20 Massive Hits** / 1985 / Striker Lee ✦✦✦✦
A superb and soulful vocalist, Johnny Clarke never sounds less than inspired on this anthology. The cuts range from evocative to commonplace, the lyrics from enlightening to cliched, humorous to vulgar. —*Ron Wynn*

Reggae Archives / 1991 / Gong Sounds ✦✦✦
An up-to-the-second production brings well-deserved exposure to the mellifluous Mr. C. It's a real winner with 16 cuts. —*Roger Steffens*

Authorised Rockers / Jul. 26, 1991 / Frontline ✦✦✦✦
Another great pure singer, adept at soul, reggae, or lovers-rock styles. —*Ron Wynn*

Jimmy Cliff (James Chambers)

b. 1948, St. Catherine, Jamaica
Vocals / Soul, Reggae
The first artist in Lesley Kong's groundbreaking Beverly's label stable in 1962, Jimmy Cliff has been a figure of major influence in the internationalization of Jamaican music for thirty years. Bob Dylan called Cliff's late-'60s hit "Vietnam" the best protest song he ever heard. Hearing that same tune led Paul Simon to travel to Kingston, book the same rhythm section, engineer, and studio, and record "Mother and Child Reunion," the first Yankee reggae song ever. Despite a number of ska hits and an Island Records contract in 1967, it wasn't until he was recruited to act in Perry Henzell's rollickingly hypnotic film *The Harder They Come* that Cliff achieved true stardom. He sang a number of his own compositions in the movie, including "Many Rivers to Cross," "Sitting in Limbo," and the title track, three standards that helped make the soundtrack album one of the biggest sellers in reggae history. The follow-up albums, however, were generally unfocused, their spotty material spoiling Cliff's bid to become reggae's main exponent, a gap rushed into and filled brilliantly by Bob Marley. By 1976, Cliff had regrouped and enlisted Wailers tutor Joe Higgs to be his bandleader. A yearly stream of albums followed, with songs as good as anything he ever recorded ("Beyond the Boundaries," "Bongo Man"); and Cliff became a mainstay on the international festival and touring circuit, achieving huge fame in places like Nigeria, where he keeps a second home. Cliff's style is a high, almost gospel plaint, with a keen rhythmic sense that echoes Africa as well as R&B. A concert film, *Bongo Man*, was released around 1980, as Cliff looked unsuccessfully for the proper vehicle to follow up the worldwide penetration of *The Harder They Come*. Cliff, a father figure to several generations of young musicians, can still be counted on to deliver thoroughly professional shows and recordings. —*Roger Steffens*

Wonderful World, Beautiful People / 1970 / A&M ✦✦✦✦
Contains the Cliff anthem "Vietnam." —*William Ruhlmann*

★ **The Harder They Come** / 1972 / Mango ✦✦✦✦✦
Jimmy Cliff starred in this gritty film about street life in Kingston, Jamaica. The album is a brilliant compilation of early reggae music, and Cliff's own songs. "You Can Get It If You Really Want It," "Many Rivers to Cross," "The Harder They Come," and "Sitting in Limbo," are among the best of a very good lot. —*William Ruhlmann*

Struggling Man / 1973 / Mango ✦✦✦✦
Although not as well regarded or as vocally spectacular as *The Harder They Come*, this was nevertheless some outstanding early Jimmy Cliff material. The title cut was especially strong, and there were also some good ballads. —*Ron Wynn*

Hanging Fire / 1987 / CBS ✦✦✦
Cliff has long since been eclipsed by other reggae stars, but this later release shows him effectively mixing his own quick-step version of the music with general pop trends. — *William Ruhlmann*

Reggae Greats / 1991 / Mango ✦✦✦
This is a good overview of his hits, including "Vietnam," "The Harder They Come," "Many Rivers to Cross," and "Struggling Man." —*Scott Bultman*

Breakout / Jun. 23, 1992 / JRS ✦✦✦
This session tried to strike a balance between commercial concessions and stylistic integrity. There were cuts with drum tracks and synthesizers, and others, like "War a Africa," with its simple rhythm backing, and a redone "Stepping Out of Limbo," in which Cliff sounds almost as energized as on past numbers. He does include some strong political and message tracks, notably "Shout for Freedom," "I'm a Winner," "Peace," and "True Story." The final results are mixed; there's much to admire about the lyrics, and Cliff's voice hasn't lost much quality or fire, but this pales beside classic Cliff material. —*Ron Wynn*

Dave and Ansel Collins

Rock Steady
An enjoyable trivia question of reggae history, Dave and Ansel Collins had one of the first international reggae hits in 1971 with "Double Barrel." One of the most unlikely fluke successes of the era, it went to No. 1 in the British pop surveys, and then No. 22 in the US pop charts, although most American listeners were probably unaware that the duo hailed from Jamaica. Kicking off with unforgettable, heavily reverbed, basically incomprehensible boasting ("I am the magnificent!" being the only readily discernible phrase), the track then locked into a tight, rock steady groove highlighting rinky-tink piano lines and swelling organ. More echoing, infectiously silly boasts and exhortations to "work!" pushed the cut along, with a brief digression into a chord sequence nicked from Bob Dylan's "Lay Lady Lay."

That's a tough act to follow, and Dave and Ansel Collins were destined to be a one-shot in the US, although they did make the British Top Ten one more time with the less remarkable "Monkey Spanner." Winston Riley played a strong hand in the duo's recordings, producing and writing all of their material. Dave Collins' exact role remains mysterious; he is only credited as a backing vocalist in the latest reissue of the pair's vintage recordings (perhaps he was the boaster on "Double Barrel"?). Keyboardist Ansel Collins has played in the Upsetters and Jimmy Cliff's band at various points, and has also been an active session musician, contributing to recordings by Black Uhuru, the Mighty Diamonds, Barrington Levy, and many others. —*Richie Unterberger*

● **Double Barrel: Original Yard Classics** / 1995 / RAS ✦✦✦✦
Twelve songs from the early '70s, more often than not instrumentals, but also including some straight vocal numbers. Nothing's nearly as impressive as "Double Barrel," unfortunately. For the most part these are good-natured but tame and simplistic ditties, with the cheesy piano and organ parts highlighted in the mix. Includes their other big hit (at least in the UK), "Monkey Spanner," though the actual high point (other than "Double Barrel") is a rendition of Gene Chandler's soul-pop hit "Groovy Situation," here retitled "That Girl." This 1995 reissue is not to be confused with another album released under the title *Double Barrel* back in the '70s. —*Richie Unterberger*

Culture

Reggae
This outstanding vocal trio has been hailed as prophetic visionaries and since their inception in the mid-'70s, Culture has been an influential group, calling Jamaica's poor to rise up in peace and fight against oppression. At the center of Culture is chief songwriter and leader Joseph Hill, who started out his career as a solo singer and guitarist. On stage, he is the fiery one, energetic and charismatic, while Albert Walker and Roy "Kenneth" Dayes are ice-cool and steady.

They came together in 1976 in St. Catherine's Parish where Hill was born and raised. Hill, along with cousins Albert Walker and Roy Sylvester Dayes, formed their first group, the African Disciples, the same year. Dayes adopted the name Kenneth to honor his old friend Kenneth Richards. Shortly after they formed, the trio came to the attention of producer Joe Gibbs, who invited them to audition at his studio. The Disciples sang several songs for Gibbs, most of them written by Hill, who had begun composing tunes at age 14. It was a powerful session, and Gibbs grabbed the songs without signing the group to a contract and set the naive threesome to recording. Some of the songs they sang at the audition included

"Get Ready to Ride the Lion to Zion," "Two Sevens Clash," and "Calling Rasta for I," songs that would appear on their first two albums along with "Baldhead Bridge" and "Love Shines Brighter."

Eventually they left Gibbs. Their first album, *Two Sevens Clash*, came out the following year. The recording session featured such artists as Sly Dunbar, Robbie Shakespeare, Bingy Bunny, Bobby Marquis, and others. It was Bingy Bunny and Blacka Morewell who suggested the Disciples change their name to Culture. The album, released during a time when reggae music was at a crossroads, is credited for having helped to guide the genre towards new directions, and for Culture that direction was to spread a more aggressive political message. An excellent example of their political bent can be heard on the title track of their 1982 Heartbeat album, *Lion Rock*, a powerful call to African Jamaicans to throw off the cultural chains placed upon them by the Anglo colonialists.

But while considered militant, Culture does not advocate violence as means of enacting change. Like many Rastafarians, they promote the use of ganja, but find other, harder drugs such as cocaine destructive, not only to users, but to society as a whole. As chief songwriter, Hill is inspired by many things, from current political events to the sounds of nature when he is out in the country meditating. The music of others also moves him, and Hill has rather eclectic taste, ranging from reggae to American country music. Throughout their long, distinguished careers, Culture has gone on to influence and work with many of reggae's greats. —*Sandra Brennan*

★ **Two Sevens Clash** / 1978 / Shanachie ✦✦✦✦✦
The landmark debut, with gorgeous vocals, concise rhythms, and tough and properly impassioned heart, makes this a cornerstone of any reggae collection. —*John Floyd*

Cumbolo / 1979 / Shanachie ✦✦✦✦
A classic, almost on par with *Two Sevens*, it utilizes similar themes and is sung with similar amounts of passion. —*John Floyd*

International Herb / 1979 / Shanachie ✦✦✦✦
The politics have subsided just a notch, but this is still a beauty. —*John Floyd*

Lion Rock / 1982 / Heartbeat ✦✦✦
An exemplary '80s session with Hill in top form. —*Ron Wynn*

Nuff Crisis / 1988 / Shanachie ✦✦✦✦
Topical, passionate, and, as always, beautifully sung. —*Ron Wynn*

Too Long in Slavery / 1989 / Frontline ✦✦✦✦
Here is a decently compiled collection of their output up to *Cumbolo*. —*John Floyd*

● **Strictly Culture: The Best of Culture 1977-1979** / 1995 / Music Club ✦✦✦✦

Desmond Dekker (Desmond Dacres)

b. 1943, Kingston, Jamaica
Vocals / Ska, Rock Steady
One of the most identifiable voices of rock steady, Desmond Dekker is a seminal figure in the development of reggae music and was once one of Jamaica's most popular figures. In the US, he is still best remembered for the 1969 Top Ten hit "Israelites" that he recorded with his band, the Aces. It was a chart topper in England and was the first gold record ever issued in Jamaica. In the US it was presented as a novelty song since few could understand the meaning of the puzzling lyrics, which are actually a cry against the oppression and brutal conditions daily faced by most modern-day African-Jamaicans. The lyrics "Get up in the morning, bake beans for breakfast. Get up in the morning, same thing for breakfast" are a sly reference to slaving, meaning that most have to get up early so they can slave away for a little bit of money.

Desmond Dekker was born Desmond Dacres in Kingston. By the time he was in his early teens, Dekker knew that he wanted to sing, but getting a contract in the early '60s was difficult. The main producer in Kingston back then was Leslie Kong, who produced the early records of giants Jimmy Cliff and Derrick Morgan. Kong, who would only infrequently seek out new talent, eventually agreed to give Dekker a chance after Dekker literally pushed his way into Kong's office and demanded an audition. With studio keyboardist Theophilus "Easy Snappin" Beckford playing along, Dekker proceeded to sing his "Honor Your Father and Your Mother." Beckford was deeply impressed as were the others who made him sing it several times. He also sang "Madgie," another of his songs. After that, he was given a rehearsal date and a recording time. The recording session included such distinguished players as Morgan, Cliff, Frank Coslo, Eric Morris, and Andy and Joey to wax the songs he had auditioned. Kong correctly predicted that "Honor Your Father and Your Mother," the A-side of the single, would be a hit. While waiting for the single's release, Dekker returned to his day job where he met a young coworker, Bob Marley, another aspiring musician. Dekker then introduced Marley to Kong. Both Dekker and Marley's singles came out about the same time, but it was Dekker who hit the jackpot. His next single was the gospel-inflected "Sinners Come on Home/Labor for Learning." Working with Kong, Dekker created a number of classic tracks that continue to be recorded by others today including "Rude Boy Train," "Intensified," and "Pretty Africa."

While he and Kong had been pretty tight throughout the decade, in the late '60s things changed when Kong began focusing most of his attention on producing the new sensation from Barbados, Jackie Opel, shorting the old guard on recording time. Bob Marley finally got fed up and moved to work with Coxsone Dodd. Eventually, Dekker left as well, joining instead Duke Reid. On the day he was to record with Reid, Kong showed up and begged him to return. Dekker recorded "Get Up Adina" and "King of Ska" with his backup band, the Aces. They had international success with "007," a song credited with shaping the direction of future rock steady music. The song reached the top of Jamaican charts and peaked at No. 15 on the UK charts. In 1968, Dekker's song "Intensified" won the Jamaica Festival song competition. Following the success of "Israelites," Dekker left his Aces and toured as a solo act. Solo successes include "A It Mek," a song he wrote about his little sister. Later he had another smash hit with his cover of Jimmy Cliff's "You Can Get It if You Really Want." As reggae music began to overshadow rock steady through the '70s, Dekker's popularity began to fade a bit. By the late '70s, his career was revitalized by the British ska-revival. He signed to Stiff Records and recorded two albums, including 1980's *Black and Dekker*, but since then has only infrequently recorded. —*Sandra Brennan*

Black and Dekker / 1980 / Stiff ✦✦✦✦
A fierce ska version of "Israelites" sets the tone and tempo for this release that came at the crest of the UK 2-Tone revival, initiated by such bands as the English Beat and the Specials. Not meant to take the place of the originals, these punk-intense versions of a half-dozen of Dekker's biggest hits are cleverly arranged, meticulously (albeit loosely) performed, and shed not a single nostalgic tear, not when the music remains this fresh. —*Bob Tarte*

Compass Point / 1981 / Stiff ✦✦✦
Proof positive that Dekker had a potentially vital future along with his accomplished past, this Robert Palmer-produced release brings state-of-the-art studio craft and a global sensibility to a set of strong new Dekker tunes. Rich, varied, and mature, this should have had more impact, but it came a few crucial years too early for the world music boom. —*Bob Tarte*

★ **Rockin' Steady: The Best of Desmond Dekker** / 1992 / Rhino ✦✦✦✦✦
His unmistakable voice is irrevocably tied to the rock steady era—not a question of limitation but the versatility the times demanded. Dekker could be light as a sigh in the strangely portentous "Fu Manchu," wax comic in "Licking Stick," or summon enough raucousness to blow down a picket fence ("Warlock"). At his most righteous he never succumbed to preachiness, shifting instead into an otherworldly eccentricity that shaped an outstandingly memorable body of work, including one of the most transcendent records in anybody's canon, the still-jarring "Israelites." —*Bob Tarte*

Chaka Demus (John Taylor)

Vocals / Reggae, Dancehall
Deejay Chaka Demus (born John Taylor) did have a brief, fairly unsuccessful solo career, but it was after he teamed up with singer Pliers (born Everton Banner) that he became part of an international sensation. The two teamed up in 1991 after sharing the stage at a reggae show in Miami. Produced by Sly & Robbie, the duo record together in the studio, smoothly alternating between sung and spoken lines (typically such artists record their parts on separate tracks). In 1993, Chaka Demus and Pliers hit the big time with the international hit "Murder She Wrote." The following year, they had a No. 1 hit on the British charts with "Twist & Shout." —*Sandra Brennan*

● **Reggae Dance Hall Sensation** / 1970 / Rohit ✦✦✦✦
A contemporary dancehall star, Chaka Demus' music is neither compelling nor very original. It is extremely popular, and you can hear the hip-hop and rock influences within this conventional pop-reggae material. —*Ron Wynn*

Ruff This Year / 1993 / RAS ✦✦✦✦

Dillinger (Lester Bullocks)

Vocals / Reggae, Deejay
Lester Bullocks aka Dillinger was a seminal stylist in DJ/toaster circles during the '70s. His blazing, witty, and irreverent style, sometimes comedic, sometimes tragic or poignant, was featured on many singles as he moved from simply recyling Big Youth and U-Roy's style and developed his own gripping approach. Dillinger began as a disc jockey on Prince Jackie and El Brasso's sound systems during the early '70s. He enjoyed his first hit with "Freshly" in 1974, cutting it for Yabby U. Later came singles for Augustus Pablo, Joe Joe Hookim, and Coxsone Dodd. Dodd issued the LP *Ready Natty Dreadie* in '75 and '76, establishing Dillinger as a star, while Kim issued the second album containing the classics "Cocaine in My Brain" and "Crank Face," a superb duet with Trinity. Dillinger tried to

repeat the formula with "Marijuana in My Brand," which did reasonably well. But as audience interests shifted during the '80s, Dillinger's fortunes plummeted. He eventually left music, but returned with "Say No to Drugs" in 1990. —*Ron Wynn*

● **Cocaine** / 1983 / Charly ✦✦✦✦
Dillinger's "Cocaine" remains an all-time anthem. It's without question the high point on an otherwise erratic album, one whose rambling qualities accurately reflect Dillinger's entire career. The songs are great one moment and utterly forgettable the next. —*Ron Wynn*

Clement "Coxsone" Dodd

One of the most important producers in the history of reggae music, Clement "Coxsone" Dodd was a vital figure in the journey of Jamiacan popular music from ska through rock steady and early reggae, on par with Duke Reid and Lee Perry. Dodd got his start in the Jamaican scene by operating sound systems in the '50s, beginning to record discs at the end of the decade, and opening the first black-owned Jamaica studio in 1963. Exact details of who he produced, and when, in the '60s are sketchy, as they are for most vintage reggae music, but it's agreed that there were very few early reggae performers of consequence who did not record for Dodd at one point. While he has worked with stars like Burning Spear, Sugar Minott, Frankie Paul, Brigadier Jerry, and Niney the Observer, his best work is considered to have been laid down during the rock steady era; many of the tracks he produced during this time have been "versioned" ever since. —*Richie Unterberger*

● **Musical Fever 1967-1968** / 1989 / Trojan [UK] ✦✦✦✦
A double CD of 28 rock steady tracks produced by Dodd during the late '60s. Most of these were very obscure; the only well-known names are organist Jackie Mittoo and a young Niney the Observer, recording as Winston Holness. A few of the cuts are little more than basic instrumental grooves, but mostly this is top-notch, and fairly diverse, rock steady. The best attributes of the style are captured in the easy, shuffling grooves, ethereal organs, and dreamy horn lines that anchor nearly all of the songs. The tracks featuring vocal harmony groups make the connection between early reggae and American soul music explicit. —*Richie Unterberger*

Mikey Dread

Vocals / Reggae
Mikey Dread changed the face of Jamaica radio (albeit briefly) in the late '70s with a postmidnight weekend program of weird sound effects, dub-wise mixing techniques, and almost no talk for hours. Of course he was fired. His cave-deep voice has a narrow range, but on record it penetrates to the core of heartfelt and conscious concerns. A tour with the Clash exposed him to US audiences a decade ago, and constant reissues and new material have kept him in the public eye. —*Roger Steffens*

● **Dread at the Controls** / 1979 / Trojan ✦✦✦✦
Mikey Dread made his recording debut with this 1979 session, and it was a good, but tentative one. His toasting was functional and his compositions occasionally arresting. —*Ron Wynn*

Beyond WW3 / 1981 / Heartbeat ✦✦✦✦
Mikey Dread was at his toasting best on this '81 session, peppering his commentary with fiery topical references and quips. Producer Scientist provided swirling electronic backing and multitracked sonic support, and this was among the most influential reggae-meets-punk/new-wave LPs of its day. —*Ron Wynn*

Don Drummond

Trombone / Ska
A magnificent trombonist, Don Drummond ranks with Roland Alphonso, Jackie Mittoo, Tommy McCook, Rico, and Dean Fraser. Drummond's meaty, fluid trombone solos graced numerous singles in the '60s, and prior to that he'd been a first-rate jazz player. Drummond was educated at the Alpha Catholic Boys Home and School, where he later served as an instructor. Drummond, like Alphonso, was in the original Skatalites. He was among the first major musicians to publicly embrace Rastafarianism, and such singles as "Far East" and "Addis Ababa" reflected that faith. Sadly, Drummond became mentally unstable following the mid-'60s murder of his common-law wife. He was committed to Kingston's Belle Vue asylum where he died in 1969. —*Ron Wynn*

● **Best of Don Drummond** / 1989 / Studio One ✦✦✦✦
A collection highlighting some of the most popular material Don Drummond and the Skatalites performed during the ska era. There's little thematic variety, but it's a good anthology of early Jamaican music. —*Ron Wynn*

Lucky Dube

Vocals / Reggae, Africa
Lucky Dube, with his trademark military beret, sings powerful songs call-

ing for social reform, freedom, and God's love. With his onstage charisma, broad vocal range, exuberant Zulu-inspired dancing, and lively rapport with his audience, Dube's concerts are an unforgettable experience. In his native South Africa, Dube had one of his country's biggest selling albums, *Slave*, and he has been the first South African reggae artist to have international success. He was also the first Black performer to have a song, "Together As One," to get airplay on the segregated South African White radio stations, eventually making it onto the White record charts.

Dube (pronounced DOO-bay) was born in Ermelo, a town near Johannesburg, to a single mother and was raised by his grandmother and other close relatives. He was his mother's first child and she named him Lucky, because she had never thought she would ever be able to have children. As a child, Dube seldom saw his mother and spent his youth being shuffled between his grandmother, an aunt, and an uncle. It was a rootless existence and he grew up feeling that he and his siblings never had a real home. Dube grew up in apartheid South Africa during the '60s and '70s, and he didn't learn that there were other ways of living until he began visiting other more free African countries later in life. Regardless of his lack of formal training in politics, Dube's songs are infused with awareness that cries out for interracial unity and strongly protests injustice, false prophets, and self-righteousness, as can be heard in such numbers as "War and Crime," the first track on his *Prisoner* album.

Dube began singing in local bars, in church, and at school when he was eight years old; his earliest musical influence was the South African singer Steve Kekhana. While in high school, he and three friends decided to form a band. Too poor to buy instruments, Dube and his friends asked wealthy townsfolk for donations. When that failed, he wrote a stage play and managed to earn just enough from local performances to buy one guitar. Elated, he named the band Skyway, to signify that now that they had a guitar, the sky was the limit. They performed a kind of rock music together for two years (but did not record), and then Dube joined the Love Brothers, a mbaqanga band led by Richard Siluma, who later became his manager. Dube then launched a solo career as an mbaqanga singer.

Greatly influenced by the reggae of Bob Marley and Peter Tosh (to whom many critics compare Dube's singing style), Dube hesitated to sing it because he believed South Africans were not ready to hear its message. He didn't make the switch until he got his first recording contract around 1979. As a recording artist, Dube plays many of the instruments himself and arranges his own music, a remarkable feat considering he can neither read nor write music.

At the time he was just getting started, Dube encountered considerable resistance from his mother, who had dreamed he would become a doctor or lawyer and not an irresponsible musician. She was so strongly opposed to his choice that she refused to speak to him for a long time. Early on in his recording career he waxed a special plea to her with the mbaqanga song "Dear Mother." It helped a little, but she still refused to communicate and would not attend the televised ceremony in which Dube received his first gold record for the song. They eventually became more reconciled after he began buying her gifts and her own house. Despite the tension, Dube understands her fears that he would end up as impoverished as she, a domestic worker, was. Fortunately, his talent, international superstar status, and continued good luck seem to dictate that this will not be the case. — *Sandra Brennan*

Slave / 1990 / Shanachie ✦✦✦
Here's another strong statement of militant "sufferation," liberation, and love. — *J. Poet*

● **Prisoner** / 1991 / Shanachie ✦✦✦✦
This is one of the best efforts from the South African reggae superstar, whose vocal style owes much to Peter Tosh. Dube is one of the finest post-Marley singer-songwriters in the reggae field. — *J. Poet*

House of Exile / 1992 / Shanachie ✦✦✦✦
The latest refinement of Dube's sound features his toughest songwriting yet and several numbers with the expanded version of his band, the Slaves. — *Bob Tarte*

Captured Live / Shanachie ✦✦✦
This intense live recording captures Lucky Dube's charismatic force as none of his studio discs do—plus he's backed by a hot horn section. — *Bob Tarte*

Clancy Eccles

Vocals
Though not nearly as well known as Duke Reid or Coxsone Dodd, producer and sometimes vocalist Eccles made a lot of rock steady in the late '60s and early '70s, much of it on his Clandisc label. As a singer, Eccles had started recording back in the late '50s, when he cut some ska for Dodd. After bouncing around the ska and early reggae scene for a while, he became more active in the studio in the late '60s, overseeing tracks by Alton Ellis, Joe Higgs, Beres Hammond, and several less famed artists. Not as distinctive as the works of Reid or Dodd, Eccles' oeuvre nonetheless included some solid and enjoyable material that contributed to the peak of the rock steady movement. His greatest achievement took place

outside of the studio. In the early '70s, he organized a traveling stage show to contribute to the successful campaign of Jamaican socialist politician Michael Manley. — *Richie Unterberger*

● **Presents His Reggae Review** / 1990 / Heartbeat ✦✦✦✦
A 16-track survey of Eccles productions played by Alton Ellis, Beres Hammond, Eccles himself, and several other artists, recorded at West Indies Records in the late '60s and early '70s. It's not the most top-rank rock steady compilation, and some of the cuts are fairly generic. But it's solid, highlighted by the floating silkiness of Ellis' "Feeling Inside" and Eccles' own "The Revenge," with its enhancing female harmonies. — *Richie Unterberger*

Eek-A-Mouse (Ripton Hylton)

Reggae, Jamaica, Caribbean
Born Ripton Hylton, this "six-foot-six above sea level" toaster was named after a race horse. The Mouse's Far Eastern "bong-gong-giddy-mem-giddy-hoy" style set the pace for many early-'80s imitators. His sing-jay lyrics run the gamut from wildly funny to terrifying and touching. A master of stagecraft, his witty costumes range from Mexican caballero to Samurai warrior and help keep him touring successfully into the '90s. — *Roger Steffens*

Wa-Do-Dem / 1982 / Shanachie ✦✦✦✦
The classic innovative title track and autobiographical material make this a major debut. — *Roger Steffens*

● **Mouseketeer** / 1984 / Shanachie ✦✦✦✦
Definitive toasting from Eek-a-Mouse. This LP included the definitive "Star, Daily News or Gleaner," in which he examined the bitter rivalry between Jamaica's newspapers, and the entertaining "How I Got Me Name," for all those interested in his origins. — *Ron Wynn*

Eek a Nomics / 1988 / RAS ✦✦✦
This includes good songs in "Calamity," "Lies," and "Rich and Famous," plus more conventional dancehall offerings "The Freak" (with both the regular and a dance version) and "Oh Me Oh My." Eek-a-Mouse's yells, upper register squeals, and other trademarks are evident on other cuts like "Do Me" and "Goon-a-Goon." While not breaking new ground, Eek-a-Mouse offered his fans a good group of dance and love numbers, with an occasional lyric insight available as well. — *Ron Wynn*

U-Neek / 1991 / Island ✦✦✦

● **The Best of Eek-a-Mouse** / Shanachie ✦✦✦✦
A strong anthology collecting Eek-a-Mouse's most clever and popular cuts from the early '80s. — *Ron Wynn*

Alton Ellis

Vocals / Reggae, Ska, Rock Steady, Jamaica, Caribbean
One of Jamaica's first singers, the silken-smooth Alton Ellis made his first hit "Muriel" in 1959 as part of a duo with Eddie Perkins. Producer Coxsone Dodd oversaw a string of subsequent successes. Eventually Ellis, seeing little financial remuneration, left for Coxsone's archrival Duke Reid and his Treasure Isle label. Tunes like "Dance Crasher," "Cry Tough," and "Girl, I've Got a Date" gave Reid his first chance to pass Dodd in the popular mind as Jamaica's heaviest studio and sound system.

By 1966 the red-hot double-time ska beat had given birth overnight to a much slower, hiccupping rhythm dubbed "rock steady," and it was Alton who was to be its midwife. "One evening in the studio," Alton recalls, "the bass man didn't show up. So Jackie Mittoo, the keyboardist, had to play the bass pattern on the piano with his left hand, but he couldn't hold it steady, and we all thought the line was so fresh and nice. When the bass player turned up next time, Jackie insisted that he play what Jackie was playing with his left hand. That's how rock steady was born; we called it so that night." Coxsone lured Alton back, and by 1968 Alton was the undisputed King of rock steady with shots like "Willow Tree," "I'm Just a Guy," and "Sitting in the Park," often highlighted with his trademark yelp of "Looka here now!" Again, the money failed to follow the hits, and somewhat disillusioned, Alton spent several years in the US and Canada before pulling up stakes and moving permanently to England in 1973. Scores of songs were issued steadily, cementing his reputation as one of the most consistent reggae artists around. By 1984 he was celebrated internationally for his 25 years in show business, making a pair of critically acclaimed appearances at Jamaica's Sunsplash festival in 1983 and 1985. From 1989 on, he has been releasing compilations on his own Alltone label of his early masterpieces, and he even recorded *Man from Studio One*, a new 12-inch for Coxsone in 1991. One of the real gentlemen of reggae, Alton is a satisfying and scintillating singer, one of Jamaica's extraordinary gifts to the world, right up there with Bob Marley. — *Roger Steffens*

Best of Alton Ellis / 1988 / Coxsone ✦✦✦✦
A great cross-section of mid-'60s covers sound far better than the originals, along with self-penned classics. — *Roger Steffens*

Legendary Alton Ellis / 1990 / Alltone ✦✦✦✦
Ska, rock steady, and early reggae singles include the essential "Cry Tough" and "Dance Crasher." — *Roger Steffens*

Alton and Hortense / 1990 / Heartbeat ✦✦✦

The brother/sister duo of Alton and Hortense Ellis were among Jamaica's more intriguing combinations. This outstanding CD collected several rare singles by each singer, with only one duet number, their marvelous rendition of "Breaking Up Is Hard to Do." Hortense Ellis was best on soul covers; she turned Billy Stewart's "Sitting in the Park" and Tyrone Davis' "Can I Change My Mind" inside out, using the role-reversal ploy to recast them as statements of female anguish rather than male uncertainty. Alton Ellis moves from the spiritual tone of "Lord Deliver Us" to the heartache of "When I'm Down" and "Can't Get Used to Loving You," then becomes emphatic on "Wide World" and closes on a reflective note with "The Picture Was You." An extremely attractive set of classic rockers and lovers' rock reggae. —Ron Wynn

★ **Cry Tough** / 1993 / Heartbeat ✦✦✦✦✦

This 20-track collection features the finest moments from one of Jamaica's great vocalists. Concentrating mainly on his strong mid-'60s rock steady material, this serves as the best introduction for newcomers. Longtime fans will also be pleased with the inclusion of rare takes from the long lost Treasure Isle Sessions. Essential for any lover of reggae or rock steady. —Chris Woodstra

Ethiopians

Reggae, Ska

The Ethiopians were an important group in the evolution of reggae music. Founded in 1966, they were a tough act combining rudeness with righteousness and performed an early, exciting version of rock steady. Originally, the Ethiopians were a trio comprising Leonard "Sparrow" Dillon, Stephen Taylor, and Aston Morris. Dillon was the founding member. Around 1964, Dillon's new friend Peter Tosh helped him launch a solo career with producers Lee Perry and Coxsone Dodd. He had just released a hit single, "Ice Water," when he heard Taylor and Morris singing on a street corner and invited them to sing backup for him. They did so and then planned to launch their own career. Still when Dillon suggested they all get together, Taylor expressed interest while Morris, a songwriter and guitarist, was reticent. He eventually agreed and after many rehearsals, Dillon took them to Studio One to record three songs including "Live Good." Morris left them after that.

The Ethiopian's distinctive sound is characterized by sweet, close, at times mournful, harmonies that speak of the social injustice and racism that has plagued the island's Africans since colonial times. Dillon wrote many of their songs and claims that very few of them are based on his experiences. Rather he finds inspiration by observing other people. Occasionally he wrote love songs, but he never felt comfortable singing them. Following their first recording session, the two performed a bit and then Dillon went back to construction work until his latest employer, contractor Lee Robertson, heard him singing one of his songs at work. He loved it, and after Dillon convinced him that he knew all about making records, agreed to finance a new single. The result, "Train to Skaville," became the Ethiopians' breakthrough hit. It was so popular that they had trouble producing enough disks to satisfy the public. Among their most famous songs are the reggae standard "The Whip" (the first reggae tune to contain percussion; he used three bottles to make the distinctive clicking sounds) and their 1968 career single "Everything Crash."

The Ethiopians hit a rocky stretch when they went broke. With no received royalties, and unable to afford to record, Taylor took a side job at a gas station. He was crossing the street one day to make change when he was killed by a van. Dillon and friends were having a party at the time and had been expecting Taylor to bring some booze. The bad news was a terrible shock, and Dillon took a hiatus from music for a while. Eventually he and Aston Morris got together and revived the Ethiopians and continued recording and performing through the '70s. Afterward, they continued to release new versions of some of their greatest hits, as can be heard on such albums as *Owner fe de Yard* (1994). —Sandra Brennan

Engine '54: Let's Ska and Rock Steady / 1968 / Jamaican Gold [West Indies] ✦✦✦✦

Their debut album, far more rock steady than ska, recorded with Tommy McCook and the Supersonics. It's excellent, consistent stuff from the prime of rock steady, with seductively cooing harmonies and falsettos; few if any other acts brought '60s soul and Jamaican rhythms together with such entrancing results. The CD reissue adds a Lee Perry production ("Love and Respect") and an updated version of "Train to Ska-Ville." —Richie Unterberger

Slave Call / 1977 / Heartbeat ✦✦✦✦

★ **Ethiopians** / 1986 / Trojan ✦✦✦✦✦

These 21 songs from 1966 to 1972 give the best available overview of a major Jamaican duo. —Roger Steffens

Owner fe de Yard / 1994 / Heartbeat ✦✦✦✦

For the sound of the classic reggae sound, nothing will ever match the music that came out of Coxsone Dodd's Studio One in the '60s, '70s, and '80s. The 15 tracks on this superb anthology spotlight the Ethiopians, one of

Jamaica's most consistent vocal groups, thanks largely to the tremendous leads of Leonard Dillon. Whether singing love tunes, protest songs, soul covers, or in patois, Dillon turned each number into a shimmering, radiant masterpiece. Dodd's production lacked the multitrack sophistication, computerized synth-backing, and other colorations that are now routine. Instead, he relied on the brilliance of individual musicians. —Ron Wynn

Majek Fashek (Majekodunmi Fasheke)

Guitar, Vocals / Reggae, Africa, Nigeria

Beneath the reggae melodies of Nigerian artist Majek Fashek runs a powerful river of ecstatic African rhythms filled with pounding talking drums and complex percussion designed to call the listener to free his or her mind. In Africa, Fashek is considered not only one of the primary reggae performers, he is also a mystic prophet and rainmaker. In concert, he has become known as a flamboyant, versatile performer who seamlessly integrates a variety of musical styles amid wild dancing and antics with his guitar, which include playing it with his teeth. Born Majekodunmi Fashek (meaning "the oracle speaks the truth") in Benin City, he was raised listening to kpangolo music, a traditional music close to reggae. He was also later influenced by the music of Bob Marley and Jimmy Cliff, but his very first musical inspiration was East Indian music. He claims his tendency to sing songs of freedom and personal consciousness came through a revelation, and though he speaks of Jah, he does not consider himself a Rastafarian, nor a part of any other world religion. Rather, he sees himself as representing a prisoner of conscience, and the spiritual leaders of the world have become his guides, not his gods. To him, formalized religion keeps people focusing on their differences and prevents true unification of the races.

While still in school, he formed the band Jah Stix and eventually they began playing clubs in Lagos. In 1988, Fashek became a solo act and remained in Lagos. It was there that he gained his reputation as a rainmaker. It happened during a severe drought in Nigeria. He saw dark clouds one day and it inspired "Send Down the Rain," a metaphorical song calling for blessings. He performed it one night during an outdoor concert and while playing a cloudburst poured down and broke the dry spell. They called him the Rainprophet; he went on to play it in other dry areas, and every time rain fell—sometimes so heavily that it caused flooding. He later sang a song, "Free Mandela," Soon afterward, Mandela was freed from South African prison. His fans, attributing this in part to Fashek, called him "The Visionary," and so his reputation spread through Nigeria. The song "Send Down the Rain" and his cover of Marley's "Redemption Song" both became big hits from his hot-selling African debut album *Prisoner of Conscience* (1989). —Sandra Brennan

Prisoner of Conscience / 1989 / Mango ✦✦✦

Heavily influenced by Marley—Fashek sounds more like the reggae avatar than Ziggy—this batch of Nigerian-flavored "skanking" is startlingly redeemed by the brilliant "Send Down the Rain," which took on near-incantatory intensity on Fashek's tours across the drought-stricken continent. —Bob Tarte

● **Spirit of Love** / 1991 / Interscope ✦✦✦✦

Seamlessly blending elements of juju with reggae, Fashek turns from imitator to innovator in a disc with so much clear-eyed enthusiasm and vision you'd think reggae was his personal invention. "Majek Beware" is the most powerful reggae song in years, awash in talking drums, jungle chants, and shamanistic lead vocals. —Bob Tarte

Dean Fraser

b. Aug. 4, 1957

Horn, Sax (Alto) / Reggae, Dancehall

Sax player Dean Fraser has been tearing up horn sections on innumerable reggae singles, working with some of Jamaica's legends, including Bob Marley and the Wailers, since 1978. He is considered one of Jamaica's finest brass players and has developed an international following for his sultry jazz-toned reggae music. He was born Dean Ivanhoe Fraser in Kingston and began playing the clarinet at the National Volunteers' Youth Organization community club at age 12. At age 15, his teacher, Babe O'Brian, taught him the saxophone. Fraser formed his first band, the Sonny Bradshaw 7, around 1978. It was rising reggae star Jacob Miller who helped Fraser become popular. At the time, Miller would occasionally jam with Fraser and band while they were performing at the Sheraton. He took a liking to Fraser's song "Take Five," and so took the young sax player to the studio. Fraser had recorded an earlier single, "Blue Moon." Unfortunately, a labeling mistake on the "Take Five" single named the talented new artist Jah Devon instead of Dean Fraser. That problem was rectified on all his subsequent work. In the mid-'90s, he released *Dean Plays Bob* and *Dean Plays Bob, Volume II*, as a tribute to the music of his longtime idol Bob Marley. —Sandra Brennan

● **Sings and Blows** / 1989 / Shanachie ✦✦✦✦

Dean Fraser's most exciting and spirited instrumental release. His solos were nicely played, the production wasn't too elaborate, and there was a good balance between improvisational and popular concerns. —*Ron Wynn*

Dean Plays Bob / RAS ✦✦✦✦

Eddy Grant (Edmond Montague Grant)

b. Mar. 5, 1948, Plaisance, Guyana
Synthesizer, Guitar, Vocals / Ethnic Fusion, Pop-rock
Grant was a member of the London group the Equals during the '60s; after they broke up, he established Coach House Studios in London in 1973 and founded the Ice Records label in 1974. He made records throughout the late '70s, gaining a following in the UK In 1982, he hit big with "Electric Avenue" in the US. While Grant has not been able to repeat the success of "Electric Avenue" in the US, he remains popular in other countries. —*Stephen Thomas Erlewine*

Walking on Sunshine / 1979 / Ice ✦✦✦
The title cut was a monster hit, while "Living on the Frontline" and "The Frontline Symphony" were also gems. —*Ron Wynn*

Killer on the Rampage / 1982 / Portrait ✦✦✦✦
In his Barbados recording studio, Eddy Grant doesn't play reggae music so much as dance-oriented music with thoughtful lyrics. His big US hit, "Electric Avenue," had a new-wave beat and a message about poverty. The rest of his album is also toe-tapping and timely. —*William Ruhlmann*

● **Walking on Sunshine: The Best of Eddy** / 1989 / Parlophone ✦✦✦✦

Barefoot Soldier / 1990 / Enigma ✦✦✦
A popular term in the '90s is "world music," which is as good as any for Grant's bouyant sound, matched to the tough anti-apartheid message of the album's hit "Gimme Hope Jo'anna." —*William Ruhlmann*

Albert Griffiths and the Gladiators

Reggae
A harmony group fronted by Griffiths, whose high-pitched, slightly nasal voice gave them an instantly identifiable sound influenced by the Wailers and the Techniques in the '60s. Still active after 25 years. —*Roger Steffens*

● **Trenchtown Mixup** / 1976 / Virgin ✦✦✦✦
Captured at their peak with some of their most representative compositions, this includes "Hello Carol" and "Thief in the Night." —*Roger Steffens*

On the Right Track / 1989 / Heartbeat ✦✦✦
Their best '80s effort, with assistance from members of The I-Tones. —*Ron Wynn*

Valley of Decision / Heartbeat ✦✦✦
Albert Griffiths is one of the most inspiring voices in reggae today, and he goes way back: producer Chris Wilson remembers hearing the Gladiators' classic "Hello Carol" in Kingston in 1968. This is his fifth Heartbeat release, recorded in Kingston, with a band including drummer Leroy "Horsemouth" Wallace, star of the reggae cult-film classic *Rockers*. —*Roundup Newsletter*

Marcia Griffiths

Vocals / Reggae, Dancehall
Jamaica's longest-running and perhaps biggest female vocalist ever. Griffiths began as a teenager in Coxsone's Studio One, racking up hit after hit, then joined with paramour Bob Andy as Bob and Marcia for the Top Five UK pop hit "Young, Gifted and Black." She formed The I Threes to back Bob Marley's international tours and recordings from 1974-1980 and scored a massive international hit with "Electric Boogie" in the '80s. Despite a few '70s Rasta tunes like "Stepping out of Babylon," she is known primarily for her strong, smooth-as-mousse love songs and captivating live performances. —*Roger Steffens*

● **Naturally** / 1978 / Shanachie ✦✦✦✦
Ten of her greatest early hits are here, seven written by Bob Andy. —*Roger Steffens*

Steppin' / 1979 / Shanachie ✦✦✦✦
Stirring leads from a wonderful singer. —*Ron Wynn*

Marcia / 1988 / RAS ✦✦✦
This session wasn't a strict reggae effort; Griffiths did a straight soul version of "Don't Let Me Down" and a quasi-jazz/pop turn on "Blue Skies." But when Griffith turned to reggae, she was as captivating as ever. Her duet with Bunny Clark, "It's Not Funny," was beautifully performed on both sides, while "Trenchtown Rock" and "I'm Leaving" were the type of unadorned, from-the-heart singing that's sorely lacking in contemporary reggae and a lot of urban music. —*Ron Wynn*

Carousel / 1990 / Mango ✦✦✦
It's always worth hearing her sing, but the album is not essential. —*Ron Wynn*

H.R. (Ras Hailu Gabriel Joseph I)

Vocals / Hardcore Punk
Iconoclastic, enigmatic, and angst-ridden are words used to describe former front man for the punk/thrash-metal group Bad Brains, H.R. (Ras Hailu Gabriel Joseph I). A devout Rastafarian, H.R.'s songs, a seamless blend of singing, rap, and African chanting, demand social and economic equality and an end to oppression and racism. He got his start with the Washington, DC-based Bad Brains, and sang with them through the '80s. H.R. periodically left to pursue his own career, returning only to make a few quick bucks. He infused their music with his own brand of reggae rhythms, which they called "rasta-core," but grew disillusioned because fans were more interested in their hardcore sound than the message of love he was trying to convey. Compared to the rough-edged, riotous energy of the Brains, H.R.'s reggae was mellower, as can be heard in his late '80s album *Singin' in the Heart* (SST), which he recorded in between Bad Brains' *I Against I* and *Quickness*. H.R. left the band for good in 1989 and has since worked on developing his solo career. —*Sandra Brennan*

● **The H.R. Tapes '84-'86** / 1988 / SST ✦✦✦✦

Half Pint

Vocals / Reggae, Dancehall
Important roots rocker whose 1985 release "Cost of Living" ("there are more sellers than buyers") was a career-making single. Mick Jagger has covered him, and Sunsplashes have starred him. Impassioned delivery, great voice, conscious poetry mark him as a long-termer. —*Roger Steffens*

● **Victory** / 1986 / RAS ✦✦✦✦
While typed in some quarters as strictly a dancehall artist, Half Pint is actually an above-average vocalist who's made several commendable message and protest tunes alongside the lighter uptempo material. This disc includes the solid "Cost of Living" to open the session, before moving into a predominantly romantic vein. "She's Mine," "Desperate Lover," and "Night Life Lady" are the top tracks from that perspective, although he takes one trip through harder territory with the final selection, "I Don't Like It." It's more vocally attractive and less produced and predictable than some later Half Pint albums. —*Ron Wynn*

Beres Hammond

Vocals / Soul, Reggae, Dancehall
Beres Hammond is one of reggae's great soul singers though for much of his 20 years he has only been known for the most part in his native Jamaica. Hammond's style harkens back to the Rastafarian sounds of the '70s that center on a strong melody coupled with socially conscious lyrics and intricate harmonies.

He was born Beresford Hammond in the province of St. Mary in Annotto Bay. Early on, Hammond became intensely interested in the ska/reggae sounds of such performers as Peter Touch and soulful singer Alton Ellis—who would become one of the "fathers" of rock steady music. Following grade school, he dropped out. Already a talented singer, he found himself particularly drawn to the music of Leroy Sibbles of the Heptones and Ken Boothe, another favorite, after Ellis, his primary influence. Though island music was his prime inspiration, Hammond also loved the R&B, and jazz frequently played by his father who had an enormous and varied record collection. His favorite R&B singers included Sam Cooke, Otis Redding, and later Marvin Gaye.

Hammond got his own start between 1972 and 1973. His first break came when he wandered into auditions for a Merritone Amateur show. During the audition, Hammond sang about a dozen songs in radically different genres; he believed the judges liked his voice. This led him to record a soul version, in the style of Alton Ellis, of "Wanderer." Hammond became the lead singer of Zap Pow in late 1975. "The System," recorded on Mango in 1978, was their known single.

While with Zap Pow, he launched his solo career; his first solo album *Soul Reggae* was released in 1976 on the Aquarius label and produced by longtime friend Willie Lindo. It was a big success, but when the label suggested he release a single off it, Hammond insisted that they leave the album intact and so returned to the studio to cut a new track. The ballad "One Step Ahead" stayed at No. 1 for over 14 weeks. In 1978, Joe Gibbs produced Hammond's second single, "I'm in Love," and it, too, became a chart topper. By 1979, the strain of performing and recording with the group and managing his own career was too much, so he left Zap Pow. Though he had two chart hits and a top-selling album by then, Hammond saw very little money from the sales. He decided to curtail his solo work concentrating instead on more profitable session work. He soon demonstrated a knack for singing and arranging harmony parts. Eventually he returned to Gibbs and cut the album *Just a Man*. It did well and produced a couple of hit singles, but again he made no money. It turned out that while Gibbs was a fine producer, he had a reputation for flooding the market with the songs of one artist. Not wanting to continue the saturation, Hammond again stopped recording for one year. He recorded his next album in 1981 with Willie Lindo. It was first released on Dynamics and titled *Comin' at You*.

Around this time, he and four others formed Tuesday's Children. They never recorded, but audiences loved their close harmonies, and the band was quite successful as a live act. Other group members included Calmon Scott (who wrote the reggae standard "One Teacher, One Preacher") and Ferris Walters. Hammond also continued with his session work. In 1985, he recorded another album, *Let's Make a Song*, on Brotherhood, a label he founded with a good friend. Hammond then decided to start his own label, Harmony House, with no partners just so he could always have a home base. His debut single, "Groovy Little Thing," was a substantial hit. Lindo recorded his next single, "What One Dance Can Do," and it became one of his biggest hits not only in Jamaica, but also abroad. He followed with an eponymous CD on Lindo's label.

In 1987, Hammond was in the process of recording a new album on his own label when he was attacked, tied up, and robbed in his own home. Blaming the attack on his sudden fame, Hammond headed for New York to stay with family, out of the public eye for the next three years. Around 1989, he and Lindo, who had come to New York to recuperate from a nervous breakdown, recorded the crossover album of ballads *Have a Nice Weekend*, but did not release it until after he recorded *Resistance* in Jamaica following Hurricane Gilbert. In 1990, he returned to Jamaica determined to turn his life around. He ended up at Penthouse Records and during the session, spontaneously created "Tempted to Touch"—a song inspired by the sight of a beautiful girl in shorts he'd seen sashaying about the studio that day—with producer Donovan Germain. It became an enormous hit in Jamaica, New York City, and even England. He then returned home to record the album *Love Affair* with Germain.

At long last, Hammond found himself a hot property when the album produced several more major hits including "Is This a Sign" and "Respect to You Baby." Following the success of these first Penthouse recordings, Hammond has recorded prolifically and released compilations of earlier tracks; one such compilation is *Soul Reggae and More* on VP. In 1995, Hammond recorded *In Control* on Elektra, an excellent blend of ballads and socially conscious reggae targeted toward an international audience. —*Sandra Brennan*

● **Live & Learn Presents: Beres Hammond & Barrington Levy** / 1991 / Live & Learn ◆◆◆◆
Beres Hammond and Barrington Levy rank among reggae's greatest pure vocalists, and this eight-track CD presents five Levy numbers. Hammond is more soulful, while Levy is more vocally flexible and spirited. Levy does playful fare such as "Some Girls Are Trouble" and political/topical material like "Juggling Soldier," although the emphasis is clearly on entertainment rather than relevance. "Sho-Be-Do-Sho" showcases Levy's verbal facility, and "Strictly Rocker" features his classic reggae sound. Hammond's "Never Let Go" and "I Will Follow You" are gloriously sung, powerful performances, while "When the Grass Is Green" falters lyrically, but Hammond's evocative singing elevates it. —*Ron Wynn*

Putting up Resistance / Aug. 1996 / RAS ◆◆◆◆
Beres Hammond's *Putting up Resistance* is a more consistent effort than several of his mid-'90s releases. There are still problems with the album—a few of the songs are filler, RAS provides no information about the sessions and the recording quality is occasionally substandard—but Hammond's wonderful vocals more than make up for these shortcomings. —*Stephen Thomas Erlewine*

Love from a Distance / Aug. 1996 / VP ◆◆◆
By the middle of the '90s, Beres Hammond had settled on a predictable pattern for his albums, and *Love from a Distance* is no different from any of his previous few releases. That is both for better and for worse. Hammond is one of the finest and most soulful reggae vocalists, so it is a pleasure to simply hear him sing. However, the production is careless and the songs are uneven, which makes the record a frustrating listen. Still, tracks like "Sweet Lies" and "Take Time to Love," which features guest vocals by Shaggy, are first-rate and there are enough strong songs to satisfy fans, even though there's not enough to win him new ones. —*Stephen Thomas Erlewine*

The Heptones

Reggae, Rock Steady
The legendary lead vocals of Leroy Sibbles and the close harmonies of Earl Morgan and Barry Llewellyn are what made the Heptones one of the finest, most important reggae trios of the '60s and '70s. During the '60s, the Heptones played a key role in the transition between ska and rock steady. Sibbles, Morgan, and Llewellyn, all natives of Kingston, grouped up in the early '60s, naming themselves the Hep Ones. It didn't take long for people to change the pronunciation to the much cooler Heptones. They first began recording at Caltone, cutting a very strange adaptation of "The William Tell Overture." The next year Coxsone Dodd signed them to his Studio One. Under his guidance, they honed their harmonies, and Sibbles began to improve his naturally formidable songwriting skills. They had their first real hit in 1966 with "Fattie Fattie." Songs prior to that

include "Party Time," "Only Sixteen," and "Triple Girl." One of their biggest hits was "Pretty Looks Isn't All." The Heptones remained with Dodd and Studio One through 1971. By then, Sibbles, who had also worked as a talent scout, arranger, and production assistant, began chafing under Dodd's control. He tired of feeling more like an oppressed laborer expected to churn out songs in the same old style rather than a vital, creative artist interested in expanding the new genre's horizons. It resulted in a bitter split between Sibbles and Dodd. Fortunately for the Heptones, they were at the height of their popularity and could choose among many producers, deciding on producer Joe Gibbs. It was a good move, and they began gaining an even bigger following. They worked with other producers such as Pablo and Rupie Edwards until 1973 when they teamed up with Lee "Scratch" Perry, the one producer with the skills to update their sound without losing touch with the rootsiness that made them so popular. Their first album with Perry, *Party Time*, which contained new versions of many of their best Studio One tracks, gained them international popularity. In 1977, Sibbles left the trio to launch a very successful solo career. Naggo Morris replaced him, and though the group has continued on, they have yet to regain their previous popularity. —*Sandra Brennan*

Night Food / 1973 / Mango ◆◆◆
Night Food features the Heptones' trademark wonderful harmonies and some of their finest material. —*Ron Wynn*

Party Time / 1973 / Mango ◆◆◆◆
Sizzling. One of the first reggae vocal groups to hook Americans. —*Ron Wynn*

★ **Book of Rules** / 1976 / Island ◆◆◆◆◆
The title track is transcendent poetry. This album includes brilliant updates of classics such as "Fatty Fatty," "I've Got the Handle," and "Mama Say." —*Roger Steffens*

Better Days / 1981 / Rohit ◆◆◆
Top-flight singing. —*Ron Wynn*

Joe Higgs

Percussion, Vocals / Reggae, Jamaica, Caribbean
The "godfather of reggae music," teacher of Bob Marley and the Wailers, the Wailing Souls, and dozens of other Trenchtown youths, Higgs is also known as the "Jazz Connection" for Jamaican music. He became one of Jamaica's first indigenous stars in the late '50s, helping turn R&B covers into a new kind of music called ska. In the mid-'70s, he was Jimmy Cliff's bandleader on worldwide tours. His career continues into its fourth decade with regularly released albums showcasing his sharp-shock style and vocal daring. —*Roger Steffens*

● **Life of Contradiction** / 1975 / Vulcan ◆◆◆◆
Remakes of big '60s hits include "There's a Reward" and "Song My Enemy Sings." —*Roger Steffens*

Triumph / 1985 / Alligator ◆◆◆
Smashing, defiant vocals from a legendary figure, done during the brief time Alligator was involved in reggae. —*Ron Wynn*

Family / 1988 / Shanachie ◆◆◆◆
This is an unpretentious charmer by the man who taught Marley and the Wailers to sing. Almost everything works—above all a terrific version of the old chestnut "Day O" and a delicious comment on gossips called "Mother Radio." Notable, aside from Higgs himself, are the standout solo sax and harmonica playing, but the whole album is plain no-frills-satisfying. —*John Storm Roberts, Original Music*

Blackman Know Yourself / 1990 / Shanachie ◆◆◆◆
Wonderful in every aspect. —*Ron Wynn*

Justin Hinds & Dominoes

Reggae
This sugarcane-sweet country/gospel trio (begun in 1964) spotlighted the inimitable round warmth of leader Justin Hinds. Their music is marked by themes of righteousness often cloaked in hoary folk sayings. The ska revival in the UK in 1980 renewed interest in the group, although Hinds remains a recluse in the North Coast bush and rarely leaves Jamaica. —*Roger Steffens*

Jezebel / 1976 / Mango ◆◆◆
Well sung and well produced. —*Ron Wynn*

● **Just in Time** / 1979 / Mango ◆◆◆◆
Hot leads, piercing harmonies. —*Ron Wynn*

Travel with Love / 1984 / Nighthawk ◆◆◆
Eight perfectly beautiful mid-tempo country croonings are here. —*Roger Steffens*

Know Jah Better / 1992 / Nighthawk ◆◆

John Holt

Vocals / Lovers Rock
The father of lovers rock (non-Rasta, nonpolitical reggae rhythm in ser-

vice of the ultimate emotion), Holt is a founder of the Paragons and the songwriter of some of the biggest hits of the '60s in Jamaica, such as "On the Beach" and "Wear You to the Ball," as well as a consistently interesting smooth-voiced interpreter of US and UK pop hits. Still active, he finally got his payday when Blondie covered his "Tide Is High." —*Roger Steffens*

● **A Love I Can Feel** / 1970 / Bamboo ✦✦✦✦
Fine Coxsone productions from the early '70s are here. —*Roger Steffens*

Sweetie Come Brush Me / 1980 / Volcano ✦✦✦
This mid-'80s career reviver includes "Ghetto Queen," backed by the Radics. —*Roger Steffens*

I Roy

Vocals / Reggae, Deejay
A reggae toaster and original rapper, I Roy uses quick wit and sharp rhythms to make modern poetry in a stylish roots-skank mode. —*Michael G. Nastos*

● **Truth & Rights** / 1975 / Grounation ✦✦✦✦
Horns, organ, and a rhythm section by Sly & Robbie. Top-drawer toasting. —*Michael G. Nastos*

Musical Shark Attack / 1976 / Virgin ✦✦✦✦
This album features "Semi-Classical Natty Dread" and "Tribute to Marcus Garvey." —*Michael G. Nastos*

Ijahman (Trevor Sutherland)

Guitar, Vocals / Reggae, Dub
Folk poet Trevor Sutherland, under the nom de chanteur Ijahman Levi, has since the late '70s issued yearly compilations of (generally) acoustic, lengthy meditations of Jah, repatriation, and the healing power of love, occasionally abetted by his wife, Madge. Soft, subtle, sensuous—he's a one-of-a-kind balladeer in an otherwise electrified music. —*Roger Steffens*

Haile I Hymn [Chapter 1] / 1978 / Mango ✦✦✦✦
Four extended tracks epitomize spiritual longing; it includes "Jah Heavy Load" and "I'm a Levi." —*Roger Steffens*

● **Are We a Warrior** / 1979 / Mango ✦✦✦✦
The title track and "Moulding" are two of reggae's most haunting meditations ever. —*Roger Steffens*

Inner Circle

Reggae
Inner Circle has been playing their own brand of rock/pop-influenced reggae since the early '70s. While lacking much of the raw, rough edges that make their rootsier Rasta-brothers great and sometimes inaccessible to mainstream audiences, the music of Inner Circle could be classified as "reggae lite," still rocking steady and focused on typical reggae issues such as Jah-love, social consciousness, and the healthful qualities of the collie weed, but done in a way to invite mass appeal.

Inner Circle was founded by brothers, Ian and Roger Lewis, along with three other musicians in 1968. They found early popularity and made a good living playing in North Coast hotel lounges. In the early '70s the three other players, Cooper, Coore, and Daly, left to found their own group, Third World. That is when moderately popular solo artist Jacob Miller joined the Lewis brothers. A devout Rastafarian, he changed the direction of the band. Soon they all had dreadlocks and began playing covers of popular reggae hits. They also wrote their own songs that became noted for both their earnestness and catchy pop tunes. Reggae purists may have turned up noses at Inner Circle's music, but international audiences loved it and they became quite popular, especially in the US. During the mid-'70s, Inner Circle recorded a bit with the American disco band KC and the Sunshine Band. In 1980, Davis was killed in a traffic accident and Inner Circle came apart. The Lewis brothers went to Miami to open their own studio. Eventually they re-formed the band with new lead singer Carlton Coffey and in the early '90s had success with "Sweat (A La La La La Long)." They then came back even more strongly with the song "Bad Boys," which became a major hit after Fox Television selected it as the title of their new reality-series "Cops." —*Sandra Brennan*

Black Roses / 1986 / RAS ✦✦✦

One Way / 1987 / RAS ✦✦✦✦
Inner Circle found surprising pop success with the single "Bad Boys," which became the theme song for Fox's television show "Cops." The original version is on this 1987 CD, spotlighting Carlton Coffie's exuberant lead vocals, which don't match Jacob Miller's anthemic quality but are energetic and competently delivered. There's a decent mix of soul and rock influences integrated within the core reggae sound, and guitarist Michael Sterling has some solid riffs and licks on several cuts. They also deliver a pair of first-rate message songs, "Champions" and "Keep the Faith," which are lyrically superior to "Bad Boys," despite lacking its catchy groove. —*Ron Wynn*

● **The Best of Inner Circle: The Capitol Years 1976-1977** / Aug. 24, 1993 / The Right Stuff ✦✦✦✦
Before they were fluke pop stars, Inner Circle recorded a series of solid reggae singles in the '70s; the best of these are compiled on this 14-track collection, which draws from their two Capitol albums. Anyone who was turned on to the group through "Bad Boys" should continue their exploration here. —*Stephen Thomas Erlewine*

Gregory Isaacs

Vocals / Soul, Reggae, Jamaica, Caribbean
Nobody sings a love song quite like Gregory Isaacs, reggae music's "Cool Ruler." His voice is languidness personified, insinuating itself around snatches of rhythm like a duppy through a canefield. There's no insistence here, more an intimation. His is the voice of lullabies and laments and loneliness, of indignation and sufferance, of soothing and seething. Few singers in Jamaica have had as many hits as he, few his impressive durability. A recent issue of the *Reggae Directory* was devoted entirely to a discography of Isaacs, listing more than 400 releases in the past twenty years. Recording initially in the late '60s as part of the Concordes, he cut his first solo disc, "Another Heartache," for WIRL, the label founded by one-time Jamaican prime minister Edward Seaga. Almost immediately, Gregory decided to establish his own labels, Cash and Carry and African Museum, and produce himself. On his third album, *Extra Classics*, he found his own voice on such laidback laments as "Mr. Cop" and "Rasta Business," and most especially "Loving Pauper." The follow-up, *Mr. Isaacs*, joined him with Sly & Robbie and the Heptones and gave the world the four Ss: "Sacrifice," "Slavemaster," "Smile," and "Storm." As an example of the respect other artists accord Gregory, on the *Soon Forward* album he is backed by the voices of Junior Delgado, Dennis Brown, and Leroy Sibbles. The *Cool Ruler* collection continued the streak of classics, which culminated in 1983's *Night Nurse*, one of his all-time best-sellers. Throughout the '80s, Gregory released more music than any other artist of the time, sometimes offering six singles in the space of a week. Many of them were critically and commercially successful, such as "Rumours" and "Private Beach Party." Throughout his career, though, he has had frequent and well-publicized run-ins with the law, contributing to his image as the ultimate rude-boy artist, with his head in the clouds and his feet in the street. Ultimately, though, as Gregory says, "Only love can win the war!" —*Roger Steffens*

Mr. Isaacs / 1982 / Shanachie ✦✦✦
Inherent in the best of reggae is a kind of laidback kick, and a sly creativity that almost sneaks by you. Both are in abundant evidence in this 1982 album. Isaacs and his backup band consistently appear to be hewing to a pretty orthodox line—and as consistently import a subtle and entirely appropriate series of original twists. Check out, for example, the melody line of "Sacrifice," or the whole concept and execution of "Story Book Children." —*John Storm Roberts, Original Music*

★ **Night Nurse** / 1982 / Mango ✦✦✦✦✦
Isaacs' strongest vocal performance and most memorable album. This is essential lovers rock. —*Chris Woodstra*

Out Deh / 1983 / Mango ✦✦✦
Almost as brilliant vocally as *Night Nurse*, despite its erratic songs. —*Ron Wynn*

All I Have Is Love / Feb. 1983 / Trojan ✦✦✦
First-rate vocals, and great coproduction by Isaacs and Alvin Ranglin. —*Ron Wynn*

Gregory Isaacs Live: Reggae Greats / 1984 / Mango ✦✦✦
A decent but not exhaustive compilation. —*Ron Wynn*

Red Rose for Gregory / 1988 / RAS ✦✦

Sly and Robbie Present Gregory Isaacs / 1988 / RAS ✦✦✦✦
Gregory Isaacs has recorded so often and for so many labels, it's both difficult and almost impossible to label anything other than individual compositions as his finest work. But this early-'70s session for Sly and Robbie's Taxi label certainly ranks among his finest full LPs. There were no flimsy soul or pop covers, and Isaacs sang with clarity, depth, verve, and confidence, whether covering "Slave Driver," ripping through "Soon Forward" and "Going Downtown," or embellishing "Motherless Children." There were no unnecesssary or exaggerated mannerisms, and his voice and range were at their peak. The CD includes both vocals and versions, and also has a bonus track in the 1987 single "I'm Coming Home." —*Ron Wynn*

Call Me Collect / 1990 / RAS ✦✦✦
When given good songs and arrangements, Gregory Isaacs has always made solid music, and when he's gotten great material, he's turned in definitive performances. The songs on this session are excellently produced by Fatis and include first-rate bass/drums interaction and support from Sly Dunbar and Robbie Shakespeare, plus synthesized assistance from Clive Hunt that's neither rigid or obtrusive. Isaacs wrote nine of the ten numbers, and there's a good blend of urgent love songs and one or two spirited protest numbers. Isaacs can still croon, moan and sigh with

the best of Jamaica's wailers, and this contains several above-average numbers in that style. —*Ron Wynn*

● **Cool Ruler; Soon Forward Select** / 1990 / Frontline ✦✦✦✦
A good twin set, pairing past releases. —*Ron Wynn*

Dancing Floor / 1990 / Heartbeat ✦✦✦
The excellent digital production fully captures his vocal quality. —*Ron Wynn*

My Number One / 1990 / Heartbeat ✦✦✦
A thorough compilation of past hits, plus rare cuts and remixes. —*Ron Wynn*

State of Shock / 1991 / RAS ✦✦

Love Is Overdue / 1991 / Heartbeat ✦✦✦
Love Is Overdue shows Isaacs to be still soulful and as vibrant as ever. —*Ron Wynn*

The Best of Gregory Isaacs, Vols. 1 & 2 / 1992 / Heartbeat ✦✦✦✦
Gregory Isaacs, the "Cool Ruler," bears an apt nickname. His vocals drip with a laidback sexuality that mirror the romantic yearnings of his lyrics. Songs like his big hit, "My Number One," function both as direct come-ons and catchy tunes. But he also reveals a more socially conscious side on songs like "Border." Both songs are included in this 20-track collection, which features drummer Sly Dunbar, bassist Robbie Shakespeare, saxophonist Dean Fraser, and other stellar reggae musicians. —*Roundup Newsletter*

Pardon Me! / 1992 / RAS ✦✦✦✦
Few of Isaacs' recent recordings have proven more satisfying than this ten-track release issued in 1992. *Pardon Me* not only had the classic guitar/horn section underpinning, but featured Isaacs singing with the care, confidence, and earnestness that marked his finest early work for Mango. Other than an occasional tendency to crunch his words, Isaacs was soulful on the love songs, defiant on the protest numbers, and totally in command throughout. The finest songs included "Mister Cop," with a good toast from Macka B, "Pride and Dignity," "Judge and Jury," and the title cut. There was also an entertaining remake of Leadbelly's "House of the Rising Sun." —*Ron Wynn*

Unlocked / 1993 / RAS ✦✦

Dance Hall Don / 1994 / Shanachie ✦✦✦
Shanachie contributed to the Gregory Isaacs record glut with this 12-track disc pairing the erstwhile "Cool Ruler" with a variety of toasters on dancehall tunes. But these weren't simply "slack" or vulgar numbers; the remix of "Downpressor," as well as "Wailing Rudie," "Wanted," and "Jailhouse," packed some lyrical punch, while "Heartical Don" and "In My Nest" were nicely produced and strongly sung. The guest toaster roster included Nardo Ranks, Ninja Man, Major Damage, Bounty Hunter, and General TK. While nothing here leaped out, there was plenty that didn't wilt after a second or third listen. —*Ron Wynn*

Looking Back / Jun. 18, 1996 / RAS ✦✦✦
Looking Back is an informative 14-track collection covering most of Gregory Isaacs' finest moments. It may not be a definitive retrospective or feature all of best songs, but it has the truly necessary items and functions as an excellent introduction to his music. —*Thom Owens*

Israel Vibration

Reggae
Israel Vibration consists of three young men who met in a polio rehab center. Their voices are among the holiest of Jamaican trinities. Dr. Dread of RAS Records arranged their reunion following a mid-'80s period of breakup, and reggae fans have been thanking him ever since. Ever soulful, ever sure, their voices are so close to the roots you can hear the earth itself in their blending. Roots exemplaire. —*Roger Steffens*

● **Forever** / 1991 / RAS ✦✦✦✦
The flowing "Reggae on the River" celebrates some of America's most famous reggae locales; a satisfying and sultry collection. —*Roger Steffens*

Why You So Craven / 1991 / RAS ✦✦✦
Containing "Highway Robbery" and a great title track, this formative album was produced by Junjo and engineered by Scientist. —*Roger Steffens*

Dub the Rock / 1995 / RAS ✦✦✦
Mixed under the direction of Jim Fox, *Dub the Rock* is the dub version of Israel Vibration's hit album, *On the Rock.* —*Stephen Thomas Erlewine*

Free To Move / Aug. 1996 / RAS ✦✦✦
Free to Move continues Israel Vibration's streak of winning albums, offering another collection of soulful, socially aware reggae. Occasionally, the album sounds a bit too similar to its predecessor, *On the Rock,* but since that sound is so fine, it doesn't really matter. The record is an intoxicating listen on its own terms, filled with spiritual messages and deep grooves. —*Leo Stanley*

The Itals

Reggae
Since the mid-'70s, the Itals have been dedicated to keeping roots-reggae alive. They are a harmony trio noted for their strong voices, close harmonies, and sharp Rasta lyrics that stress cultural consciousness; even their few love songs are written from that perspective.

The first incarnation of the group was founded by lead singer/head songwriter Keith Porter and Ronnie Davis. Originally known as the Westmorlites (both Porter and Davis were raised in Westmorland), the band included such other members as Roy Smith, Lee White, and Lloyd Ricketts. The Westmorlites stayed together long enough to record one single, "Hitey Titey," on the Studio One label and then Davis left to sing leads with the Tennors, another successful early harmony band. From there, Davis went on to become a distinguished solo artist with several albums and over thirty 45s to his credit. Porter also embarked upon a solo career and recorded for several different Kingston producers including Clancy Eccles, but eventually he tired of the scene there and returned to the country, where he performed with different groups on the hotel circuit and in small local clubs.

Eventually, Porter decided to record again and returned to Kingston where he ran into Davis. The latter had just written a new tune, "Won't You Come Home," and asked if Porter could provide some lyrics. Porter enthusiastically agreed, returned to the country, and two days later returned with "In a Dis Ya Time." Porter and Davis recorded the 45, but the track was credited to Porter (on a subsequent reissue, the song was credited to the Itals). The two made the single without thinking about reforming a group, but two producers, including Lloyd Campbell, liked what they heard and suggested they stay together. The success of "In a Dis Ya Time" persuaded the two to remain together, with Lloyd Ricketts rejoining them a short time later. This was during the mid-'70s, and the Itals released many 45s on several different labels. Some of their best, including "Time Will Tell," "Don't Wake the Lion," and "Temptation," were released on Spiderman. The taut backing of the Roots Radics can be heard on several of these tracks, many of which have been gathered by their primary label Nighthawk and released as *Early Recordings 1971-1979.* The Roots Radics went on to play on the Itals' earliest albums, such as their debut *Brutal Out Deh* (1981). Shortly after the release of their 1983 album *Give Me Power,* the Itals embarked upon their first US tour.

In the mid-'80s, they had some legal trouble when a Cleveland-based reggae group, I-Tal, sued them for stealing their name. As there was ample proof that the Itals had been recording and performing first, they didn't have much of a case and the Jamaican group came out on top. The Cleveland band subsequently changed their name to I-Tal USA. In 1985, the Itals released their *Rasta Philosophy,* and again proved to be a consistently strong group with such tracks as "Don't Blame It on Me" and "No Call Dread Name." Not long after it came out, Lloyd Ricketts was sent to prison and was replaced by solo artist David Isaacs, who had recorded many singles and had a couple of albums released in Jamaica and the UK. At first he was only a temporary replacement, and then Isaacs was to become their opening act for their next US tour, but as Ricketts was unable to legally enter the US, Isaacs became a permanent member. —*Sandra Brennan*

● **Brutal out Deh** / 1982 / Nighthawk ✦✦✦✦
The powerhouse reggae trio is in fine form on this, their debut outing. —*Ron Wynn*

Give Me Power! / 1983 / Nighthawk ✦✦✦
Intense and energized. —*Ron Wynn*

Cool and Dread / Nighthawk ✦✦✦✦
Nicely sung. A fine set of compositions. —*Ron Wynn*

Early Recordings 1971-1979 / Nighthawk ✦✦✦✦
Groundbreaking records that brought this trio initial recognition. —*Ron Wynn*

Winston Jarrett

Vocals / Reggae
He came to Kingston to sing with his idol, Alton Ellis, whose voice is very similar to Jarrett's. Joining the Flames in the mid-'60s to back Ellis, he soon branched out on his own to record a series of albums which often feature Marley and Ellis covers, and self-penned ghetto plaints as evocative as Bosch paintings. —*Roger Steffens*

● **Kingston Vibrations** / 1991 / RAS ✦✦✦✦
Strong, forceful, and rootical. —*Roger Steffens*

Linton Kwesi Johnson

b. 1952 Chapelton, Jamaica
Vocals / Dub Poetry, Club/Dance
"I coined the phrase dub poetry because I was trying to argue that what the DJs in Jamaica were actually doing is poetry—improvised, spontaneous, oral poetry." Johnson's initial recorded work, *Dread Beat an' Blood*

(recorded in the UK in 1978), provided an entirely different way to look at Caribbean rhythms and life, and had a major impact on Jamaican poet/performers like Mutabaruka, Michael Smith, and Oku Onuora. Johnson had emigrated with his family to England in 1963, eventually receiving an honors degree in sociology from the University of London. He joined the British arm of the Black Panthers in 1970, where he began writing poetry and reciting it publicly. His topics were revolutionary in both content and style—using Jamaican patois to reflect the realities of immigrant life in the ghettos of Britain. *Forces of Victory*, his second album, was a musical novel about oppression and confrontation, backed by the machine-gun force of Dennis Bovell's Dub Band. The follow-up *Bass Culture* expanded Johnson's themes to include meditations on the relationship of art to its audience, and was followed by *LKJ in Dub*, an instrumental version of his most powerful sessions. *Making History*, released in the Orwellian year of 1984, broadened his rhythmic horizons and added a pan-Caribbean flavor to his sound. A live album, summing up his career to date, came out the following year, after which Johnson claimed he had retired. But in 1991, he made a well-received return to the scene with *Tings and Times*, another multirhythm outing of indignant rhymes. Taking stage in a porkpie hat and modest demeanor, Johnson's understated performances belie the power of his carefully observed imagery and uncompromising calls for change. He is one of the true internationalizers of the form, a musical Marxist with upheaval on his mind. *—Roger Steffens*

Dread Beat An' Blood / 1977 / Frontline ◆◆◆◆
Debut album with political statements about racism and inequality. A powerful forum. *—Michael G. Nastos*

★ **Forces of Victory** / 1979 / Mango ◆◆◆◆◆
Johnson's best studio date. Many of his finest numbers, recorded for the first time. *—Michael G. Nastos*

Bass Culture / 1980 / Mango ◆◆◆
A studio date, with this rapper at his best. *—Michael G. Nastos*

LKJ in Dub / 1980 / Mango ◆◆◆◆
Desert-island dub. Johnson's better early material, with vocals deleted. All instrumental, all outstanding. *—Michael G. Nastos*

In Concert with the Dub Band / 1985 / Shanachie ◆◆◆
A fine live show and a good introduction. *—Michael G. Nastos*

Tings An' Times / 1991 / Shanachie ◆◆◆
A wonderful reunion between Johnson and Bovell, plus several brilliant compositions. *—Ron Wynn*

Ini Kamoze

Vocals / Reggae, Club/Dance, Ragga
For Ini Kamoze, the road to success has been arduous and he has undergone many substantial changes musically and physically since he burst onto the music scene in 1983 with his highly successful eponymous debut album for Island. Known as "The Hotstepper," Kamoze advocates change through what he calls "intelligent and constructive militancy" rather than random acts of violence.

Kamoze made his recording debut in the early '80s with a 12" single "Trouble You a Trouble Me" on Taxi and found immediate success. He then began touring as part of the Taxi Connection International Tour with Yellowman and Half Pint. During this time, Kamoze was 6 feet tall, reed-thin, and appeared too frail to contain his powerful stage presence. He followed up his first album success with *Pirate*, but the recording received mixed reactions and wasn't as successful. Kamoze then retaliated with several hit singles recorded on his Slekta label. One of the biggest hits from this period was "Shocking Out," which was eventually picked up by the RAS label in 1988. In 1985, Kamoze had greater success with *Settle with Me*, which produced such hits as "C all the Police" and "Taxi with Me." By 1988, Kamoze's successes became intermittent and his career erratic. Kamoze suddenly disappeared from the music scene. He returned with a new, more aggressive image in 1994, signing to Sony and exploding back into the charts with "Here Comes the Hotstepper." The song made its debut on the compilation reggae album *Stir It Up* from Columbia, and then showed up on the soundtrack of Robert Altman's feature film *Pret-A-Porter*. Produced by Salaam Remi, it was released as a single in 1995 and spent two weeks at the top of *Billboard's* Hot Singles Chart, and nearly four months appearing on various other charts. Kamoze made a video for the song and with his beefy, well-muscled physique and long dreadlocks, no longer fit the description of the liner notes on his 1983 debut album that characterized him as a "pencil-thin . . . . disentangled . . . . six-foot vegetarian." With the success of his new single, Kamoze was now a gangster and began a series of promotional tours in LA. At this point, Kamoze refuses to categorize his music and remains open to singing a variety of songs from different sources. *—Sandra Brennan*

★ **Ini Kamoze** / 1984 / Island ◆◆◆◆◆
Essential to the understanding of early-'80s roots, it's simply brilliant. *—Roger Steffens*

Here Comes the Hotstepper / 1995 / Columbia ◆◆◆◆
The title track of *Here Comes the Hotstepper* was Ini Kamoze's big pop crossover hit. Also featured on the soundtrack to *Ready to Wear*, the song lifts a line from "Land of 1000 Dances" and places it on an infectious dancehall beat—it's a great single that deserved to be a huge hit. The rest of the album isn't as strong, but there enough first-rate tracks to make it enjoyable for most fans of the single. *—Stephen Thomas Erlewine*

Byron Lee

Vocals / Soca, Ska, Party Soca, Trinidad, Caribbean
Jamaican artist who, with his band the Dragonnaires, is always a part of T&T carnival both as a live performer and through his annual release of cover versions of the year's most popular tunes. In the '90s he has begun to release his own tune each year, and has been one of the strongest proponents of Jamaican dancehall-influenced soca. *—Gene Scaramuzzo*

Tiney Winey / 1985 / Dynamic Sounds ◆◆◆◆
The first recording of "Tiney Winey," a song written by Arrow but set aside as second-rate, it was one of the huge hits of the Caribbean in 1985. Arrow went on to record the song in 1988. *—Gene Scaramuzzo*

Soca Engine / Jun. 25, 1996 / DY ◆◆◆
Highlighted by the laidback grooves of "Weakness for Sweetness" and "Chutney Bachannal," Byron Lee's *Soca Engine* doesn't keep a consistent mood throughout its course, but when it does find the right tone, it is as good as any of his previous fourteen albums. *—Thom Owens*

Dancehall Soca / Dynamic Sounds ◆◆◆
A huge hit, it was written and sung by Preacher. *—Gene Scaramuzzo*

Carnival Fever / Dynamic Sounds ◆◆◆
Salty lyrics, fiery performances. *—Ron Wynn*

De Music Hot Mama / Dynamic Sounds ◆◆◆
Bombastic vocals and great tunes. *—Ron Wynn*

● **Soca Bacchanal** / Dynamic Sounds ◆◆◆◆
Hot tunes and fine leads make *Soca Bacchanal* one of Lee's finest recorded moments. *—Ron Wynn*

Soft Lee / Dynamic Sounds ◆◆◆
Soft Lee effectively combines soca, soul, and reggae. *—Ron Wynn*

Barrington Levy

b. Apr. 30, 1964
Vocals / Reggae, Dancehall
Though veteran performer Barrington Levy is closely associated with dancehall music, he considers himself a straight reggae man committed to using his powerful lyrics and music to promote Rastafari's message of universal love and peace. Instead of drawing his inspiration from anger, frustration, and lust like many '90s-style dancehall performers, Levy bases his songs on his observations of the daily lives and travails of ordinary people.

A native of Kingston, Levy spent much time as a youth in the countryside of Clarendon. It is in the surrounding hills that he developed his signature riff, which some call the Blue Mountain yodel. He learned to do it by experimenting with different vocalizations and bouncing them off the mountainsides. As a youth, his biggest influence was Dennis Brown, but he also liked the music of US artists such as Sam Cooke. He started playing a little guitar at age nine, and was performing in dance halls at age 14 in Mighty Multitude, a band he formed with his cousin Everton Dacres, with such locally based sound systems as Burning Spear Stereograph. During these early performances, his singing was often informally recorded and sent to places in England and the US. His first single was "A Ya We Deh," but his first major hit was "Collie Weed," produced by Junjo Laws for Jah Guidance. This was followed up by such successes as "Twenty-One Girls Salute" and "Mind Your Mouth." In 1983, Levy made a big splash in Great Britain with "Under Mi Sensi," a tune that spent 12 weeks topping their charts. He later performed this pro-marijuana song on the British children's television show *Number 73*. The tune for "Under Mi Sensi" is said to have become the basis for one of reggae's biggest songs "Under Mi Sleng Teng," that is primarily credited to Wayne "Jammy" Smith. Though Levy came up with the melody, he has received no royalties. In the early '90s, Levy scored a major recording contract with the US label MCA and has since been gaining an international following. *—Sandra Brennan*

Teach Me Culture / 1983 / Profile ◆◆◆
Barrington Levy's earlier material doesn't have the sophisticated production of his recent releases, but was more lyrically varied and intense. This nine-track set presents Levy doing the rich, powerful, traditional reggae that made him a legend in the '70s and early '80s. The menu includes the anguished "To Love Someone" and "Lonely Man," the prophetic title cut and the poignant "Jah Is with Me." While these songs often invoke a melancholy note or bittersweet mood, there's nothing dispirited or solemn about Levy's soaring vocals and vigorous delivery. *—Ron Wynn*

Barrington Levy / 1984 / Clock Tower ✦✦✦✦
Barrington Levy, one of reggae's golden voices, straddles the fence between dancehall and roots material on his major label debut. Levy is better suited to love tunes and traditional material than the busy, hip-hop-influenced contemporary dancehall sound, but he still manages to sound interested when doing songs like "Work," "Vice Versa Love," and "Go There." But those aware of Levy's glorious, swirling style and incandescent voice will be more pleased by his remake of the classic "Under Me Sensi," the powerful "Murderer," and "Nothing's Changed," tunes that showcase his vocal might rather than his ability to incorporate it into a sea of production gimmicks. —*Ron Wynn*

● **Broader than Broadway: The Best of ...** / 1990 / Profile ✦✦✦✦
This is a fine collection of his best hits of the '80s. —*Roger Steffens*

Prison Oval Rock / 1991 / RAS ✦✦✦
Reggae fans knew about Levy's vocal brilliance early in his career, especially his dynamic roots material and equally fervent love ballads and romantic tunes. The ten tracks on this RAS set are from that period, when he was among the great crooners and pleaders in reggae. If you want anger and venom, there's the slashing fury of "Robber Man" and the title cut; those who prefer sensuality and suggestiveness will devour "Good Loving" and "Mary Long Tongue," while the religious zealots can delight in "Please Jah Jah." —*Ron Wynn*

Divine / 1994 / RAS ✦✦✦
While Barrington Levy continues to soak up the publicity riches from his recent MCA set, RAS RAS reminds everyone of his greatness in more conventional reggae settings with several discs showcasing him away from trendy dancehall productions. This ten-track set has some nods to the present, notably an inspired remake of Del Shannon's "Runaway," although it's credited to someone called "S. Crook." The real gems are his brilliant covers of Ken Boothe's "Silver Words" and John Holt's "Darling I Need Your Loving." This is the kind of urgent, convincing material on which Levy made his reputation. —*Ron Wynn*

Duets / 1995 / RAS ✦✦✦
The great reggae vocalist Barrington Levy engages a number of other singers—including Beenie Man, Cutty Ranks, Bounty Killer, and Spragga Benz—on a series of duets on the appropriately titled *Duets*. Unfortunately, the material isn't always as strong as the singers, but there are several killer cuts on the record. —*Stephen Thomas Erlewine*

J.C. Lodge

Vocals / Reggae
With her classic girlish pop voice, J.C. Lodge helped bankrupt producer Joe Gibbs when he failed to pay songwriter's royalties to Charley Pride for J.C.'s million-selling cover of "Someone Loves You, Honey." In the late '80s, her "Telephone Love" became a massive, long-lasting international hit penetrating the dancehalls as well as radio stations. She seems poised for a genuine breakthrough in the '90s by piecing rock, reggae, and soul into a highly seductive mosaic. —*Roger Steffens*

● **Revealed** / 1985 / RAS ✦✦✦✦
J.C. Lodge's teasing, lithe sound has made her one of the '90s' top female reggae singers; her coy, suggestive leads have proven quite potent commercially. This nine-track session was recorded before she became a star, and while there's a preponderance of synthesizers and electronic backing, it's less busy and heavily produced than her recent material. Lodge is mostly creditable, although the cover of "You Can't Hurry Love" is disposable, and "You Can Dance" and her version of the Bee Gees' "To Love Somebody" strictly generic. But "Stick By Me," "Stalemates," and "You Make Me Shine" demonstrate the potential other producers have since tapped. —*Ron Wynn*

Tropic of Love / 1992 / Tommy Boy ✦✦✦
Her debut for a major label has both high and low points. Contains the smash "Telephone Love." —*Ron Wynn*

To the Max / 1993 / RAS ✦✦✦✦

Love For Seasons / Aug. 1996 / RAS ✦✦✦
Recorded with Mad Professor, *Love for Seasons* captures the more experimental tendencies of J.C. Lodge. Throughout the record, Lodge and the Mad Professor delve deeply into dub reggae, occasionally surfacing for relatively straightforward reggae numbers. In the process, the team creates a hypnotic, trancelike groove that exemplifies nearly all the best qualities of dub-influenced reggae. —*Leo Stanley*

Mad Professor (Neil Fraser)

Percussion, Drums, Vocals / Reggae, Dub Poetry, Dub, Jamaica, Caribbean
Born in Guyana, South America, but later transplanted to southeast London, Mad Professor used a hand-built mixer, echo, and effects machine to gradually transform his four-track home studio Ariwa into a bastion of dub-reggae. Although he uses computers and effects, his music empha-

sizes roots and culture, much like the music of his idol, Lee "Scratch" Perry.
Mad Professor's first release, *Dub Me Crazy Part 1*, appeared in 1981. (Two more volumes followed in the series.) *Black Liberation Dub*, a later series with two parts, followed. The greatest hits compilation *It's a Mad, Mad, Mad, Mad, Mad, Mad, Mad Mad Professor* spans the years 1981-94. All albums are available through RAS Records. Also, he has remixed Massive Attack and the Orb, among others. —*John Bush*

Dub Me Crazy / 1982 / Amwa ✦✦✦
On his own small British Label lurks the most sonically (and electronically) creative producer of the age. The Mad Professor's own albums, while still clearly reggoid, mix in a vision like George Clinton on astrodust and an approach to sampling, synth, and so on that makes other electron-maniacs sound like nice little old ladies playing hymns. Macka is a little more conservative, though still pretty ionospheric, what with the synth balafon and Martian belly drums. —*John Storm Roberts, Original Music*

Escape to the Asylum of Dub: Dub Me Crazy Pt. 4 / 1983 / RAS ✦✦✦
These 1983 sessions are his most traditional dub, but they point the way to the craziness to come. Many female vocalists are heard here. —*Myles Boisen*

★ **Who Knows the Secret of the Mad Professor** / 1987 / RAS ✦✦✦✦✦
More creative instrumentation and plenty of dub madness make this album a unique offering in a sometimes overdone field. —*Myles Boisen*

Captures Pato Banton / 1988 / RAS ✦✦✦✦
This collaboration with Jamaican singer Pato Banton is typically mind-expanding, with more pop intent and extending vocal tracks. —*Myles Boisen*

Science and the Witchdoctor / May 1989 / RAS ✦✦✦
The professor's treatment of reggae backing tracks is most inspired on side two. Wild keyboards abound. —*Myles Boisen*

Recaptures Pato Banton / Jul. 1989 / RAS ✦✦✦
This collaboration with Jamaican singer Pato Banton is typically mind-expanding, with more pop intent and extending vocal tracks. —*Myles Boisen*

Psychedelic Dub / 1990 / RAS ✦✦✦
More craziness, with guest appearances by singer Macka B and the legendary trombonist Rico. —*Myles Boisen*

Hijacked to Jamaica: Dub Me Crazy Pt. II / 1991 / RAS ✦✦✦
Part II of the *Dub Me Crazy* series was actually done in Jamaica, rather than in the Professor's England home. —*Myles Boisen*

At Checkpoint Charlie / ROIR ✦✦✦
MP meets the German reggae band Puls der Zeit for crazy times. —*Myles Boisen*

Bob Marley (Robert Nesta Marley)

b. Feb. 6, 1945, St. Ann, Jamaica, d. May 11, 1981, Miami, FL
Guitar, Vocals / Reggae, Jamaica, Caribbean
Born of a middle-aged, White father and a teenage Black mother, Robert Nesta Marley transcended the humility of his rural beginnings to become not only a million-selling artist and stadium-filling entertainer but—more importantly—a nearly religious figure whose pleas for brotherhood and justice achieved universal anthemic status.
He began singing professionally at 16 with his self-penned "Judge Not!" It and its follow-up were not successful, and he returned to his ghetto neighborhood of Trenchtown to be tutored by Joe Higgs, a recording artist who coached promising youngsters like Marley, Bunny Livingstone, and Peter Tosh (who would become the Wailers). Signed in 1963 to Coxsone Dodd's influential, pacesetting Studio One, the Wailers saw their first release, "Simmer Down," become an instant No. 1 hit. During the next two-and-a-half years, the group recorded over a hundred songs, and at one point in 1965 held five of the Top Ten slots on the Jamaican charts.
Forming their own label, Wail 'n' Soul'm, in 1966, the Wailers continued a series of local hits, with little financial remuneration. Following an album with Leslie Kong (*Best of the Wailers*), they hooked up with the oddball producer, Lee Perry, and produced an amazing series of singles that are collected under a variety of names and remain their finest hour.
In 1972, Island Records prez Chris Blackwell signed the Wailers, but after two albums the group broke up, leaving Marley at the head of the band, to which he added a female backing trio, the I Threes. By 1975, Marley had gone clear as a revolutionary standard bearer, the inheritor of the '60s activist energy and hippie ganja enlightenment. Almost assassinated in 1976 in Kingston, Marley was given the UN Peace Medal on behalf of 500 million Africans in 1978 for his humanitarian achievements. He headlined a Peace Concert that same year in Jamaica, uniting the warring factions in the Kingston slums. But his greatest honor came when he was invited to headline the Zimbabwe Independence Celebrations in 1980. He outdrew the Pope in Milan, fathered eleven children by seven women,

sold tens of millions of records worldwide, left a $30 million estate, wrote "the new Psalms," and died at 36 of melanoma. — *Roger Steffens*

Soul Rebels / 1970 / Trojan ✦✦✦✦
Bare, haunting Lee Perry productions with the Wailers echo into eternity. — *Roger Steffens*

☆ **African Herbsman** / 1973 / Trojan ✦✦✦✦✦
Here are sixteen Perry tracks, brilliant late-'60s classics that may be the best work of the Wailers trio ever. "Put It On," "Sun Is Shining," "Small Axe," and "Brain Washing" are standouts. — *Roger Steffens*

☆ **Catch a Fire** / Jan. 1973 / Tuff Gong ✦✦✦✦✦
This was the first Wailers album on Island, their first with a real budget, their first international success. It is very nearly the birth of international reggae music—songs include Peter Tosh's "Stop That Train" and Marley's "Concrete Jungle," "Kinky Reggae," and "Stir It Up." — *William Ruhlmann*

☆ **Burnin'** / Feb. 1973 / Tuff Gong ✦✦✦✦✦
Another extraordinary collection of songs with the Wailers, featuring the vocal blend of Marley, Peter Tosh, and Bunny Livingstone on such songs as "Get Up, Stand Up," "I Shot the Sheriff," and "Burnin' and Lootin.'" The last album to feature the original group. — *William Ruhlmann*

☆ **Natty Dread** / 1975 / Tuff Gong ✦✦✦✦✦
Adding a female vocal trio, Marley proved himself up to the task of carrying on without Tosh and Livingstone, delivering the memorable songs "Lively Up Yourself," "No Woman, No Cry," and "Them Belly Full (But We Hungry)." — *William Ruhlmann*

Live / 1975 / Tuff Gong ✦✦✦✦
One of the great live albums of all time, this collection demonstrated not only Marley's charismatic presence as a leader, but also the power and subtlety of the Wailers as a band. It's one live recording that captures the feel of the concert perfectly. — *William Ruhlmann*

Rastaman Vibration / 1976 / Tuff Gong ✦✦✦✦
Marley's breakthrough American album finds him discovering new polyrhythms while continuing to turn out powerful new songs, among them the title tune, "Who the Cap Fit" and "War." — *William Ruhlmann*

Birth of a Legend / 1977 / Epic ✦✦✦✦
These 20 songs were originally issued on the late-'70s LPs *Birth of a Legend* and *Early Music;* this puts all of them on one CD, with the addition of liner notes on the Wailers' early years by Marley biographer Timothy White. Great heart and energy on these harmony-filled early ska stompers and soul ballads, and about half of these tracks are not included on the more comprehensive early Wailers retrospective *One Love*, making this a recommended addition to the library of both Wailers and general early ska/reggae fans. — *Richie Unterberger*

Kaya / Jan. 1978 / Tuff Gong ✦✦✦
Here are laidback ganja meditations, love songs, plus "Running Away," which tells the critics he hasn't gone soft. — *Roger Steffens*

☆ **Babylon by Bus** / Feb. 1978 / Tuff Gong ✦✦✦✦✦
Arguably the most powerful live album in reggae's history, it was recorded with the Wailers at various international stops over a three-year period and demonstrates how Marley remade his music constantly, especially in performance. — *Roger Steffens*

Survival / 1979 / Tuff Gong ✦✦✦
Perhaps Marley's most militant statement, its bare-boned production put many off at first, but it returned him to the political realm in powerful fashion. "One Drop," "So Much Trouble," and "Babylon System" are among his best. — *Roger Steffens*

Uprising / 1980 / Tuff Gong ✦✦✦✦
The last album Marley released in his lifetime, this collection is one of his most impassioned, especially the acoustic folk song that closes it, "Redemption Song." — *William Ruhlmann*

Confrontation / Sep. 1983 / Tuff Gong ✦✦✦
This posthumous collection of singles and newly created tracks was based on work Marley left behind. It includes "Buffalo Soldier." — *Roger Steffens*

★ **Legend** / 1984 / Tuff Gong ✦✦✦✦✦
This well-chosen 14-track greatest hits collection serves as an excellent introduction to the definitive reggae musician. Songs like "No Woman, No Cry" and "I Shot the Sheriff" remain among Marley's most moving efforts. Start here. — *William Ruhlmann*

Soul Revolution 1 & 2 / 1988 / Trojan ✦✦✦✦
This is a thoughtful repackaging of 14 of the best Perry vocal sessions plus the only "legitimate" Wailers dub album ever, with four bonus tracks. — *Roger Steffens*

Reggae Greats / 1989 / Mango ✦✦✦
A good, although not formidable, compilation. — *Ron Wynn*

☆ **One Love at Studio One** / 1991 / Heartbeat ✦✦✦✦✦
This is the only Studio One collection pressed from the unaltered master tapes. There are 40 tracks, many never before available, including a 1965

rehearsal and several alternates. It is essential 1963-1966 Bunny, Bob, and Peter. — *Roger Steffens*

Talkin' Blues / 1991 / Tuff Gong ✦✦✦
This live broadcast during the band's first US tour in 1973 is an amazing testament to Marley's power. It's a soul-tingling treat to hear Marley, Peter Tosh, and Joe Higgs . . . harmonizing on these early Wailers' classics as the Barret brothers and the rest of the Wailers lay down an earthshaking reggae rhythm. — *J. Poet, Rock & Roll Disc*

☆ **Songs of Freedom** / Oct. 6, 1992 / Tuff Gong ✦✦✦✦✦
A limited-edition four-CD box set, concentrating on rarities instead of hits. This approach paints a full picture of Bob Marley as an artist, so *Songs of Freedom* is perfectly suited to a listener willing to spend the money on a box set as an introduction to an artist (even though they will still need to own the greatest hits collection *Legend*, because most of the famous versions of his hits are not included here). For Marley's devoted fans, *Songs of Freedom* is essential for the abundant rarities, including a stunning 12-minute acoustic medley. — *Stephen Thomas Erlewine*

Natural Mystic: The Legend Lives On / May 23, 1995 / Island ✦✦✦✦
Where *Legend* concentrated on singles, its sequel *Natural Mystic: The Legend Lives On* is a collection of album tracks. Consequently, it isn't cohesive as *Legend*—most of these songs work better in their original context, since Bob Marley created albums that were carefully constructed and sequenced. Since it contains a fair share of gems, *Natural Mystic* will be a reasonable way to supplement the greatest hits collection for casual Marley fans, but it doesn't quite convey the depth of his talents the way the original albums did—or *Legend* itself, for that matter. — *Stephen Thomas Erlewine*

One Love / Heartbeat ✦✦✦✦

Ziggy Marley and the Melody Makers

Reggae
Raised in the studio, these four children of Bob and Rita Marley (Ziggy, Stephen, Sharon, and Cedella) are third-generation professionals. Their debut album was named after a song Bob wrote for them years earlier ("Children Playing in the Streets"), and now all four have become composers. "We are here to complete Bob's mission," says Ziggy, and they have had stupendous early success, becoming the first reggae group to top the US R&B singles chart with "Tumbling Down" and already winning two Grammies. Their material is revivifying modern roots music, with an occasional nod to dancehall in Stephen's attitude-rich speed-rapping. — *Roger Steffens*

Play the Game Right / 1985 / Capitol ✦✦✦
An interesting concept, but underdeveloped potential. — *Ron Wynn*

Hey World / 1986 / EMI America ✦✦✦
Establishing a style, sound, concept, and direction. — *Ron Wynn*

Time Has Come . . . The Best of Ziggy Marley and the Melody Makers / 1988 / EMI America ✦✦✦
A compilation of his formative material. Not his finest period but interesting nonetheless. — *Ron Wynn*

One Bright Day / 1989 / Virgin ✦✦✦
An excellent followup album that helped cement Ziggy's popularity. — *Ron Wynn*

● **Conscious Party** / Aug. 1989 / Virgin ✦✦✦✦
A pivotal release, with special guest Keith Richards. — *Ron Wynn*

Jahmekya / 1991 / Virgin America ✦✦✦
Possibly his best overall release, it didn't enjoy the same impact as other material. — *Ron Wynn*

Joy and Blues / Jun. 1993 / ✦✦
Free Like We Want 2 B / 1995 / Elektra ✦✦

Larry Marshall

Vocals / Disco, Reggae
Despite being an energetic, convincing, and very soulful vocalist, Larry Marshall's not well known except among the reggae faithful. He's both a superb romantic balladeer and excellent message and roots vocalist. Marshall's single "Nanny Goat" was among the early transitional tunes signaling the music's evolution from rock steady to reggae. He cut his first single at Studio One in the mid-'60s; it was later remade by Clancy Eccles. Later came sessions for the Prince Buster and Top Deck labels, then a return to Studio One where he attained stardom. He eventually became an engineer as well as vocalist at the label. He's since recorded for various companies, among them Heartbeat and King's Music. — *Ron Wynn*

Come Let Us Reason / 1992 / King's Music ✦✦✦
Larry Marshall is another wonderful singer completely forgotten in the dancehall blitz. His romantic laments and soul numbers are masterful, while his social/protest tunes are equally memorable. The recording dates are uncertain, since this label evidently does not value comprehensive session information, but the feel, sound, and sensibility are basic '70s

reggae, and the production and mastering provide enough '90s sheen to keep it from sounding dated. —*Ron Wynn*

● **Presenting Larry Marshall** / Jan. 15, 1992 / Heartbeat ✦✦✦✦
A fine ballad stylist and effective uptempo singer, Larry Marshall is an obscurity to all except the reggae faithful. This is a nice album featuring more recent material. —*Ron Wynn*

Freddie McGregor

Vocals / Reggae, Dancehall
"Little Freddie" joined the Clarendonians at the age of seven in 1963 and hasn't stopped singing since, first for Coxsone Dodd's Studio One, through the Soul Syndicate in the late '70s, then as his own producer in the '80s. *Bobby Bobylon* became one of the finest productions in Dodd's history, compiling a decade's worth of unreleased tracks into Freddie's masterpiece. Equally at home in lovers rock or Rasta roots, composer/singer McGregor is consistently satisfying. —*Roger Steffens*

Come on Over / 1984 / RAS ✦✦✦
The soulful, jubilant voice of Freddie McGregor was equally outstanding on every track from this mid-'80s session. The gem of the set was the soothing "Go Away Pretty Woman," but McGregor also ventured into topical material with "Stand Up and Fight" and "Brotherman" and spicy romantic ballads like "Rhythm So Nice" and "Shirley Come on Over." It was short, sweet, and to the point, and performed minus the slack lyrics and gun imagery that are now almost mandatory on dancehall material. —*Ron Wynn*

Across the Border / 1984 / RAS ✦✦✦
Freddie McGregor's wondrous, soulful voice and engaging delivery are sometimes wasted on this mid-'80s album, issued on CD in 1992. The title track, as well as the hard-hitting message cuts "War Mongers," "Freedom, Justice & Equality," and the lyrically naive "Love Will Solve the Problems," address issues and offer McGregor a worthy forum for his glorious singing. But he's sorely tested by the cover of "Guantanamera," which was a silly pop hit and sounds even sillier in a reggae version. "Freddie" and "Work to Do Today" have awkward arrangements and vapid lyrics, forcing McGregor to waste energy and intensity trying to make them palatable. This wasn't one of his most consistent releases, but McGregor never coasts or plods on a session, even on tepid tunes. —*Ron Wynn*

All in the Same Boat / 1986 / RAS ✦✦✦
Freddie McGregor has shown repeatedly that he's a vocal master in any reggae context; he can deliver searing indictments and prophetic themes, tearful laments or moving tributes, and even maintain his integrity on the silliest pop covers. This CD has several first-rate selections, and there aren't any dumb cuts or fluff tunes that waste his skills. Even if you think the lyrics of "Somewhere" or "Jah Is the Don" may be trite or overly optimistic, McGregor's vocals will make you sit up and take notice. Why he's not as well respected outside reggae's annals as Gregory Isaacs or Dennis Brown remains a puzzle; Freddie McGregor is a fine all-around vocalist. —*Ron Wynn*

Big Ship / 1988 / Shanachie ✦✦✦✦
A fine reissue of a classic session. —*Ron Wynn*

★ **Sings Jamaican Classics** / 1991 / VP ✦✦✦✦✦
Excellent vintage tracks brilliantly sung by one of reggae's all-time greats. —*Ron Wynn*

Jamaican Classics, Vol. 3 / Jul. 1996 / VP ✦✦✦✦
Jamaican Classics, Vol. 3, offers an entertaining but frustratingly incomplete overview of Freddie McGregor's career, including songs like "Everything Crash" and "Danger in Your Eyes," but missing a number of other hits. Still, this disc is a good sampler of McGregor's sound. —*Leo Stanley*

☆ **Bobby Bobylon** / Heartbeat ✦✦✦✦✦
His overall best, the product of a decade's work, is sung over nothing but classic Coxsone rhythms. —*Roger Steffens*

Meditations

Reggae, Meditation, Caribbean
The Meditations have been in and out of reggae music since the '70s spreading their Rastafarian message of unity and love for all humankind regardless of race. Despite the many social and political changes in the world since their inception, the group has stayed true to their message and continue to play largely roots music.

The Meditations are Ansel Cridland (who during his solo efforts has used different last names including Meditation, Scandal, and Linkers), Winston Watson, and Danny Clarke, all of whom write songs. Before joining the group, Cridland had been lead singer for the Linkers, while Watson and Clarke both got their starts in gospel music. It was Clarke who named the Meditations. Like many other bands of their era, the Meditations were heavily influenced by American R&B. The Impressions, the Temptations, and Jimmy Cliff were particularly influential to the group. In 1976, they recorded their debut album, *Message from the Meditations*.

Though most of the album was produced by Dobby Dobson, Cridland produced one track and another was produced by JoJo Hookum. The album was successful in both Jamaica and the US with such classic tracks as "Woman Is like a Shadow," "Tricked," and "Running from Jamaica." In late 1978, following their second album, *Wake Up!*, the group hooked up with Lee "Scratch" Perry, who had been very impressed with the harmonies on "Running from Jamaica." In early 1979, they began doing backup work for Bob Marley. They produced a few singles during this time, including "Miracles" on Marley's Tuff Gong. As backup singers, the Meditations worked with such artists as Jimmy Cliff, Gregory Isaacs, and the Congoes. In 1980, the band used the knowledge gained from Perry and Marley to self-produce their *Guidance* album. In 1983 they released the album *No More Friend* and followed with an extensive promotional tour in the US and a hits package for Shanachie in 1984. They also released a 12-inch single, "Quiet Woman/Reggae Crazy."

Both Watson and Clarke liked working in the US, but Cridland wanted to be back in Jamaica, so they split up. Cridland, using different names, began recording singles such as "Lookout Lookout" (under the name Ansel Meditation), while Watson and Clarke continued to record and tour as the Meditations. The two made one album, *For the Good of Man*, in 1988. In 1992, Ansel rejoined the group and they recorded *Return of the Meditations* and launched a new tour. Their 1994 album, *Deeper Roots (Best of the Meditations)*, contains songs done by the individual members as singles. —*Sandra Brennan*

● **Greatest Hits** / 1984 / Shanachie ✦✦✦✦
Just as it says, here are two sides of pleasing meditations. —*Roger Steffens*

Deeper Roots: The Best of The Meditations / Mar. 30, 1994 / Heartbeat ✦✦✦✦
The Meditations have long been a premier reggae trio, equally spectacular on urgent protest tunes, danceable uptempo tunes, love songs, or novelty cuts. This 20-track collection features excellent '70s and '80s cuts, notably the emphatic "Wake Up," "What a Bam Bam" and "No Peace," plus the sensual "Quiet Woman" and "Woman Like a Shadow." Their sound is neither aggressive nor passive, and retains its appeal regardless of tempo. Those unaware of reggae's long harmony trio tradition should start with the Meditations; they've had few equals. —*Ron Wynn*

The Melodians

Rock Steady
The Melodians are among the rock steady greats and have provided reggae music with some of its most enduring hits including "Swing and Dine," "Too Young to Fall in Love," and their monster hit "Rivers of Babylon." The Melodians got their start when they were still teens as a trio comprised of lead singers Tony Brevette and Brent Dowe backed up with the sweet harmonies of Trevor McNaughton; Renford Cogle, who did not sing, but penned, co-penned, and arranged their best songs, is also a legitimate, important member of the group.

All of the Melodians were born and raised near Greenwich Town, and it was the burg's local singing contest that brought them together in 1963. They won the competition, and this led them to a recording session for Coxsone Dodd at Studio One, where they recorded four songs: only one, "Lay It On," made any real chart impact. After that the Melodians began recording for Duke Reid's Treasure Isle, and it is with Reid that their career took off, with three fast hits, including "Expo 67." They had steady success with Treasure Isle, but left after a monetary dispute and moved to the High Note label, where Sonia Pottinger became their new producer. Another steady stream of hits, including their classic "Little Nut Tree" emerged. With their mellow tones and sweet harmonies, the Melodians became one of the chief proponents of lovers rock. After a brief attempt at producing themselves, they teamed up with producer Leslie Kong and his Beverly label in 1969. "Sweet Sensation" was one of their biggest hits from this period. Following Kong's death in 1971, the Melodians performed for almost every major studio in Jamaica. They did, however, stay far away from Studio One. Unfortunately, things had changed and the Melodians, while not unsuccessful, were unable to rekindle the fire of their earlier careers and so went their separate ways in the mid-'70s. Of the three singers, Brent Dowe had the most success, but the other two did all right as well. The Melodians regrouped in the '90s as part of the roots revival and continue to perform and record. They are particularly popular in Japan. —*Sandra Brennan*

★ **Sweet Sensation** / 1976 / Mango ✦✦✦✦✦
Sweet Sensation is the finest collection of the trio's soulful rock steady. This showcases the period of 1969-1971, when the Melodians found their greatest success, thanks in part to Leslie Kong's brilliant production. Includes the anthemic "Rivers of Babylon," their international hit. —*Chris Woodstra*

Pre-Meditation / 1986 / Sky Note ✦✦✦✦
"Swing and Dine" and "Don't Get Weary" make this an exemplary collection of the rock steady style. —*Roger Steffens*

Irie Feeling / 1990 / RAS ✦✦✦

The Melodians were a superb rock steady vocal group, and they smoothly made the transition to reggae on this session. Despite the faster pace and different rhythmic patterns, the Melodians' harmonies and vocals were just as smooth and convincing, whether they were doing party cuts, love songs, or message tracks. The most passionate tunes were the title cut, "You Don't Need Me," and "Hold on Tight," while they stoked the spiritual fires on "Down Here in Babylon" and "Jah Reggae" and had a good time with "Get Up and Dance" and "Push a Little Harder." One of the best discs in RAS' entire reggae collection. —*Ron Wynn*

Swing and Dine / 1992 / Heartbeat ✦✦✦✦

Rather than the customary single lead contrasted by twin harmonies, the Melodians divided lead duties between Tony Brevette and Brent Dowe, with Trevor McNaughton harmonizing with the singer who wasn't featured on a particular track. This outstanding 16-track collection includes their biggest hits for Treasure Isle. The threesome glided along atop skipping, light rhythms provided by such bands as the Gaytones, Lyn Taitt and the Jets, the Soul Syndicate, and Tommy McCook and the Supersonics. The Melodians primarily did poignant love tunes, although they could also handle evangelical or political material. The set features such classics as "Little Nut Tree," "Hey Girl," "You Don't Need Me," and "Love Is a Doggone Good Thing." It's also thoroughly annotated and superbly mastered. —*Ron Wynn*

Michigan and Smiley

Reggae

Papa Michigan and General Smiley were among the first dual-toasters on the Jamaican scene. Beginning in the late '70s while still in school, the humorous duo (Smiley got his name because he never smiles) scored immediately with "Rub a Dub Style" and "Nice up the Dance," two ubiquitous songs on the dancehall circuit. "One Love Jam Down" became a popular anthem, and 1982's "Diseases" established them as major stars, especially at the annual Sunsplash festivals. They broke up in the late '80s, although occasional attempts at reunions have been made recently. —*Roger Steffens*

Sugar Daddy / 1986 / RAS ✦✦✦

Michigan and Smiley are reggae's best toaster duo. Their voices are similar enough to make their unison lines flow, yet there is enough difference to make their separate verbal improvisations effective. There are some strident social and message tracks among the ten on this album, including "Pass It to the Church," "The System," "Blackness Awareness," and "Give the Children a Helping Hand." "Here We Go Again" mixes political, comedic, and religious themes, while the title track, "A Who?" and "Queen of the Minstrel" aren't quite as specific in their targeting but are prime examples of their wordplay and slick blending of sung and spoken lines. —*Ron Wynn*

● **Rub-A-Dub Style** / 1992 / Heartbeat ✦✦✦✦

General Smiley and Papa Michigan helped to pioneer the DJ duo format in reggae. Trading rhymes over versions of crucial roots-reggae songs, they've created ripples of excitement in Jamaican dance halls. Their talent for wordplay energizes tracks like "Rub a Dub Style" and "Nice up the Dance," both of which were massive hits on the island. Find out why with this welcome reissue, produced by Clement "Coxsone" Dodd. —*Roundup Newsletter*

The Mighty Diamonds

Reggae

The most consistent and long-running vocal trio in Jamaican musical history, consisting of the judge (Judge), the jester (Bunny), and the prophet (Tabby, the lead singer). Possessing one of the most achingly pure voices on earth, Tabby croons mini morality plays, limning life on the island of suffering with the precision of a microscope. They are best known for the reggae classics "Pass the Koutchie," "Country Living," and "The Right Time." —*Roger Steffens*

★ **Right Time** / 1976 / Shanachie ✦✦✦✦✦

The right album at the right time, it has the right musicians, the right mix, and the right things to say. —*Roger Steffens*

Indestructible / 1982 / Alligator ✦✦✦

The only release that was issued and licensed on Alligator Records. —*Ron Wynn*

The Roots Is There / 1982 / Shanachie ✦✦✦

Well done. —*Ron Wynn*

Struggling / 1985 / RAS ✦✦✦

Although it says 1985 on the back of this CD, it might as well be the early '70s, for the Mighty Diamonds stick to the principles that guided vintage reggae. They're still singing devout praise songs, defiant protest tunes, and infrequent but moving love ballads. The Diamonds wrote seven of the ten tracks, and also cover three fine Al Campbell originals, including the dynamic "Reggae-Lution." The production blends contemporary and classic touches. If you've had problems in determining where the hip-hop and pop ends and the reggae begins in current material, you'll have no such problems with the Mighty Diamonds. —*Ron Wynn*

Reggae Street / 1987 / Shanachie ✦✦✦

A fine, funky knockout. —*Ron Wynn*

The Real Enemy / Jul. 1987 / Rohit ✦✦✦

The title track is another memorable message piece. —*Ron Wynn*

Get Ready / 1988 / Rohit ✦✦✦

Nice harmonies, but the leads vary in energy and quality. —*Ron Wynn*

Go Seek Your Rights / Jul. 1990 / Frontline ✦✦✦

The title cut is among the best message tracks. —*Ron Wynn*

Jacob Miller

Bass, Vocals / Reggae

One of reggae's brightest lights, Miller was abruptly snuffed out in a car crash in 1980, at which time he had become more popular than Marley among the in-crowd. Huge, bubbling, and boyish, Jacob blew spliff smoke in the face of authority (literally) and demanded that "we jam all night until daylight." His songs are timeless testaments to Jah and the healing power of herb. His loss is immense. —*Roger Steffens*

Jacob "Killer" Miller / 1978 / RAS ✦✦✦

"Shaky Girl" and "Forward Ever," backed by the Fatman riddim section of the Lewis Brothers, peg Jacob's stuttering style for all time. —*Roger Steffens*

● **Reggae Greats** / 1984 / Mango ✦✦✦✦

These are the true greatest hits. —*Roger Steffens*

Collector's Classics / 1988 / RAS ✦✦✦✦

Although they've enjoyed pop success in the post-Jacob Miller era, Inner Circle has never been the same since his death. This is a comprehensive anthology featuring Miller's powerful, captivating voice at its finest. —*Ron Wynn*

Lincoln Sugar Minott (Sugar Minott)

Vocals / Raggamuffin

Penning hit after hit for two decades, Minott is not only one of dancehall reggae's all-timers, but also a mentor to two generations of young stars developed by his Youth Promotions organization. Timely and touching, Minott at his best is utterly irresistible, as enticing as his nickname. —*Roger Steffens*

● **Slice of the Cake** / 1984 / Heartbeat ✦✦✦✦

Including "Buy out the Bar," "Level Vibes," and "No Vacancy," this is all killer, no filler. —*Roger Steffens*

Extra Hot / 1986 / RAS ✦✦✦

"Herbman Hustling" and other '80s standouts are here. —*Roger Steffens*

Sugar & Spice / 1990 / RAS ✦✦✦

There are only seven Minott vocals on this album, and the best ones are on "Ain't Nobody Move Me" and "Don't Know Why I Love You." He injects energy and passion into "Herbman Hustling" and "Love of Jah," but isn't as forceful or convincing. The ten-track set includes three dub numbers, with "Rub a Dub Dub" proving the most musically interesting, and "Herbsman Hustling Dub" the least successful. Minott seldom makes a completely worthless record. This one has some pleasant songs and entertaining moments, but falls far short of being one of his best. —*Ron Wynn*

Collector's Collection, Vol. 1 / Jul. 1996 / Heartbeat ✦✦✦

Collector's Collection, Vol. 1, is a compilation of rarities and obscurities from Sugar Minott's lengthy career. Most of the songs are outtakes from the late '70s and early '80s, when Minott was inventing the form of reggae that became known as dancehall. While these aren't the songs that defined the genre, the grooves will be pleasantly familiar to anyone well-acquainted with Minott's released material and, for them, this collection is essential. Casual fans can safely pass it by, however. —*Leo Stanley*

Jackie Mittoo

Organ, Piano, Keyboards, Vocals / Reggae, Pop

A recording organist for the Skatalites at the age of 15, Jamaica-born Jackie Mittoo also played with Bob Marley, Jimmy Cliff, and Johnny Nash. He moved to Toronto in 1968 when he was 20 years old and began recording; "Wishbone" became a hit in Canada. Mittoo later released a self-titled album in 1978 and *The Keyboard King* (1979). —*John Bush*

● **Jackie Mittoo: Anthology of Reggae Collector's Series, Vol. 4** / 1978 / United Artists ✦✦✦✦

● **Tribute** / 1995 / Heartbeat ✦✦✦✦

Featuring 31 songs, *Tribute* is a wonderful selection of organist Jackie Mittoo's work. The music on the album illustrates his diversity, as he switches between reggae, soul-jazz, and Memphis-style R&B. —*Stephen Thomas Erlewine*

Pablo Moses (Pablo Henry)

Vocals / Reggae

Pablo Moses burst onto the reggae scene in 1975 with the puzzling song "I Man a Grasshopper" from his debut album *Revolutionary Dream*. The song title refers to the title character of the then-popular television series "Kung Fu," though it tells the story of a drunken ex-cop who turns in a ganja-smoking singer. It was an enormous hit in both Jamaica and England, but Moses himself remained fairly unknown.

He was born Pablo Henry in the rural Manchester part of Jamaica. Except for two years spent in New York City, he remained a country boy until his desire to perform became too strong. Moses got his start performing with informal school bands. He and chum Don Prendes eventually formed the Canaries, which remained his backup group, and began performing at talent shows. They also auditioned for Duke Reid and at Dodd's Studio One with little success. Following the success of "Grasshopper," Moses released a few more singles, including "We Should Be in Angola," but for some reason, they did better in England than they did in Jamaica. The song "Give I Fe I Name" was an exception. *Revolutionary Dream* was acclaimed, but it brought him little profit and Moses decided to back off from the music scene for a while. During this time, he spent two years studying at the Jamaica School of Music. It was there that he gathered a new group of musicians and began performing at nightclubs, theaters, and on campus. They also made a television show that was quite popular in Jamaica. In 1980, Moses returned to reggae with *A Song* (1980), an innovative album produced by Moses and Geoffrey Chung that was recorded in Jamaica using the island's finest session players and then remixed in London. The result was a multilayered blend of roots and sophisticated international reggae that many consider Moses' masterpiece. Chung then produced a follow-up, *Pave the Way*. He continues recording through the '90s. *—Sandra Brennan*

★ **A Song** / 1980 / Mango ✦✦✦✦✦
This is a masterpiece of forward-looking sophistication from a roots perspective. *—Roger Steffens*

In the Future / 1983 / Alligator ✦✦✦
Always reliable and dependable—frequently electrifying. *—Ron Wynn*

Reggae Greats / 1984 / Mango ✦✦✦
A decent collection. *—Ron Wynn*

Tension / 1985 / Alligator ✦✦✦
This second album on Alligator Records tops the first. *—Ron Wynn*

Live to Love / 1988 / Rohit ✦✦✦
A capable production, first-rate vocals. *—Ron Wynn*

We Refuse / Nov. 1990 / Profile ✦✦✦
Updated, forthright, and to the point. *—Ron Wynn*

Judy Mowatt

Vocals / Reggae

Starting as lead singer for the Gaylettes in the mid-'60s, Judy Mowatt has been one of reggae's leading female vocalists for a quarter century with no signs of diminishment. Originally planning to become a preacher, Mowatt possesses one of the most sweetly powerful voices in Jamaica, an instrument she places in the service of Rastafarian and feminist causes above all else. After a series of local hits for her group or under the temporary pseudonym of Juliann, Mowatt became an international celebrity by helping form the I Threes, Bob Marley's backup singers, in 1974. When Marley built Tuff Gong, his own studio in Kingston, in 1977, Mowatt's seminal album *Black Woman* was the first to be recorded there. Considered by many critics to be the finest female album ever made in Jamaica, Mowatt wrote nearly all its tracks (Freddie McGregor and Bob Marley wrote the others). The title track and "Sisters Chant" are two ethereally beautiful cuts that encapsulate women's concerns everywhere and have achieved the status of anthems. Following Bob Marley's death, Mowatt has carved out a successful solo career, releasing a series of carefully crafted albums of canny originals and clever covers ("Grooving" and "Sing Our Own Song") that have solidified her forefront position in reggae's pantheon. *—Roger Steffens*

★ **Black Woman** / 1980 / Shanachie ✦✦✦✦✦
The debut by this former Bob Marley backup vocalist blends touching romanticism with impassioned feminism and religious Rastafarian fervor. *—John Floyd*

Only a Woman / 1982 / Shanachie ✦✦✦
Wonderful vocals, fine production, and a quiet but discernible edge. *—Ron Wynn*

Hugh Mundell

Vocals / Reggae, Protest

Vocalist Hugh Mundell made some stirring records during the late '70s and early '80s, particularly the landmark *Africa Must Be Free by 1983*.

Unfortunately, Mundell didn't live to see South Africa eliminate apartheid. He was killed in a shooting incident in the early '80s. *—Ron Wynn*

● **Africa Must Be Free by 1983** / RAS ✦✦✦✦
Hugh Mundell's protest masterpiece proves the highlight of this otherwise good but conservatively produced LP. *—Ron Wynn*

Junior Murvin

Guitar, Vocals / Reggae

A high-pitched alto verging on falsetto distinguishes this languid singer from his peers. "Police and Thieves," produced by the wacky genius Lee Perry, is a prophetic standard that Murvin himself has rewritten several times in various versions. *—Roger Steffens*

● **Police and Thieves** / 1977 / Mango ✦✦✦✦
Here is a mid-'70s golden age of reggae masterwork. *—Roger Steffens*

Mutabaruka

Vocals / Dub Poetry

Just above his forehead, poet Mutabaruka has a strip of white hair that bisects his jet-black locks. That is the only white thing about this revolutionary writer whose "Every Time I 'Ear Dis Sound" burst through the mellow reggae of the early '80s like a bullet from an AK-47. Performings sans shoes and shirt, Muta's deep-voiced uncompromising rants make his a unique, almost fearsome figure whose melding of poetry and dub music make him seem akin to an Old Testament prophet saying "Listen—or else!" *—Roger Steffens*

● **Check It!** / 1983 / Alligator ✦✦✦✦
This brilliant debut from Jamaica's hardest dub poet is essential listening. *—Roger Steffens*

Outcry / 1984 / Shanachie ✦✦✦
There's more militant poetry with a rock-hard beat. *—Roger Steffens*

The Mystery Unfolds / 1986 / Shanachie ✦✦✦
Poems with more highly orchestrated backing are featured. *—Roger Steffens*

Any Which Way . . . Freedom / 1989 / Shanachie ✦✦✦
His first release in three years was as potent, abrasive, and defiant as any of the prior dates. *—Ron Wynn*

Blakk Wi Blak . . . Kkk / 1991 / Shanachie ✦✦✦
Strong, assertive, but nothing new. *—Ron Wynn*

Melanin Man / 1994 / Shanachie ✦✦✦✦

Johnny Nash

b. Aug. 19, 1940, Houston, TX
Vocals / Soul, Reggae, Pop-rock

Johnny Nash experienced his first chart success in 1958 with the No. 23 hit "A Very Special Love." By the end of the '60s, Nash had begun recording in Jamaica and formed his own record labels, Joda and Jad. He became one of the first artists to bring reggae into the pop mainstream, with the 1968 No. 5 hit "Hold Me Tight," 1972's No. 1 "I Can See Clearly Now," and a 1973 No. 12 version of Bob Marley's "Stir It Up." *—Rick Clark*

● **I Can See Clearly Now** / 1972 / Epic ✦✦✦✦
This is West Indian music for a pop audience, rhythmic and melodic. Nash helped open the mass-market doors to reggae. The title song and "Stir It Up" are winners. *—Hank Davis*

The Reggae Collection / 1993 / Epic ✦✦✦
Nash was the first American singer to incorporate reggae rhythms, and as such deserves a lot of credit for paving the way for the acceptance of bonafide Jamaican performers. His own pop-soul-reggae concoctions, though, were often rather watery in comparison to the real thing. This brings together 20 of the reggae-style tracks he cut between 1968 and the mid-'70s, including his hits "Hold Me Tight," "Cupid," and "Stir It Up"; the version of "I Can See Clearly Now" is an alternate take. This leans too heavily on his 1972-75 Epic material without enough of his late-'60s work; the small hit "You Got Soul" is missing, and the delightfully light and soaring "Hold Me Tight" towers over most everything else here. Almost half the tracks were previously unreleased or previously unavailable in the US. *—Richie Unterberger*

Sonny Okosuns

b. 1947, Benin City, Nigeria
Guitar, Vocals / Reggae, Africa, Nigeria

With 16 African album releases to his credit—many of them gold—Nigeria's Sonny Okosuns is one of the continent's most enduringly popular performers. Okosuns caught the pop music bug via Elvis and the Beatles, forming his first band, the Postmen, in 1964. In the early '70s, he helped usher in a back-to-African-roots trend with a stylistic mix of Western pop and local highlife he called "ozzidi." He later broadened it to include the rapidly spreading gospel of reggae. His diversity has kept him from being pigeonholed. He was featured in *Black Star Liner*, a 1983 anthology of

African reggae, and more recently appeared on the anti-apartheid *Sun City* EP produced by Steve Van Zandt. His albums typically feature vocals in English as well as the Nigerian Ishan language. —*Bob Tarte*

● **3rd World** / 1981 / OTI ✦✦✦✦
This is one of his best African records. —*J. Poet*

Which Way Nigeria? / Feb. 1983 / Jive Afrika ✦✦

Liberation / 1984 / Shanachie ✦✦✦
Afro-reggae Okosun sometimes tends to Top 40 glibness, but at his best he's a significant member of the Nigerian new wave, with its pan-Africanism and its constant feedback between the New World and electronic juju. —*John Storm Roberts, Original Music*

African Soldiers / 1991 / Profile ✦✦✦✦
Okosuns expands his music, moving away from a predominantly reggae-based music by adding highlife, funk, soca, and some punchy horn chants. —*J. Poet*

Togetherness / Tangent ✦✦✦

Johnny Osbourne

Vocals / Reggae
A 25-year career that shows no sign of letting up, from soulful reggae to a massive dancehall catalog. With his warm voice filled with conviction and yearning, he's one of the island's best, especially on standards like "Ice Cream Love," "Water Pumping," and countless rub-a-dub singles. —*Roger Steffens*

★ **Truth and Rights** / 1980 / Heartbeat ✦✦✦✦✦
With backup from Freddie McGregor and Jennifer Lara, this is one of Coxsone Dodd's most righteous and impressive outings. —*Roger Steffens*

Water Pumping / 1983 / Greensleeves ✦✦✦✦
The title track remains a reggae dancehall classic. Otherwise, the material ranges from soulful to tepid, although Osbourne is seldom less than first-rate vocally. —*Ron Wynn*

Rougher Than Them / 1989 / VP ✦✦✦
A standout, whether singing fast or slow. —*Ron Wynn*

Cool Down / 1989 / VP ✦✦✦
An expert with reggae, soul, or even quasi-pop. —*Ron Wynn*

Augustus Pablo (Horace Swaby)

Organ, Synthesizer, Piano, Keyboards, Vocals, Melodica / Reggae, Dub Poetry, Dub
The name hasn't gained the international recognition of Bob Marley's, but Augustus Pablo (Horace Swaby) is one of reggae's legitimate legends, a pioneer who flipped the genre completely upside down. Along with producer King Tubby, Pablo almost singlehandedly invented dub, wherein reggae's fat bass and popping drums are twisted and contorted until they crack like bullwhips and rumble like syncopated earthquakes. This is instrumental music—voices will emerge from the supple rhythms only to trickle into an echo-shrouded void, forsaking their contribution to the bedrock grooves. And Pablo's haunting splashes of melodica (which at times conjure images of Ennio Morricone's Sergio Leone soundtracks) give his music a sound that is immediately identifiable and as singular as anything Marley managed. As a youngster, Swaby hung around Kingston's jostling recording studios, watching the masters. There he met the original Augustus Pablo—the Upsetters keyboardist Glen Adams—who invented the name and played the melodica, the odd instrument that gave reggae its "Far East" sound. Adams moved to the States in 1971 and left the concept to Swaby, who began recording in 1972. Pablo released a string of brilliant singles over the next five or so years on his Rockers label. The best of those singles are collected on *Original Rockers;* his best early album is *King Tubby Meets the Rockers Uptown* (1976). His more recent work has only occasionally matched the breathtaking innovation of the old stuff. Only the 1981 *East of the River Nile* has equaled his early triumphs. But he's still at it, occasionally striking a balance between the technical wizardry of his Tubby years and the slick production style of modern reggae. The results aren't always great but they are always interesting. —*John Floyd & Roger Steffens*

Rebel Rock Reggae: This Is Augustus Pablo / 1973 / Heartbeat ✦✦✦
Augustus Pablo formed his mysterious dub style on these early sessions, with Lee Perry producing and the best reggae session players backing. —*Myles Boisen*

King Tubby Meets the Rockers Uptown / 1976 / Shanachie ✦✦✦✦
A personal favorite, it features Robbie Shakespeare and members of Bob Marley's band. —*Myles Boisen*

★ **East of the River Nile** / 1977 / Shanachie ✦✦✦✦✦
Many regard this as Pablo's masterpiece, a superlative blending of earthy dub techniques with floating melodic lines in an exotic, oriental mode. —*Myles Boisen*

Original Rockers / 1979 / Shanachie ✦✦✦
Yet another heavy early work. —*Myles Boisen*

Rockers Meet King Tubby Inna Fire House / 1981 / Shanachie ✦✦✦
Another early gem, *Rockers Meet King Tubby Inna Fire House* shows the influence of dub pioneer King Tubby. —*Myles Boisen*

Earth's Rightful Ruler / 1983 / Shanachie ✦✦✦✦
Top session players and some vocal assistance from Hugh Mundell, Delroy Williams, and others makes this an early classic. —*Myles Boisen*

Rising Sun / 1986 / Shanachie ✦✦✦
This 1985 effort is a little slicker than others, but still worthwhile. —*Myles Boisen*

Eastman Dub / 1988 / RAS ✦✦✦
Pablo extends his musical arsenal to include xylophone and various keyboards in addition to his trademark melodica. —*Myles Boisen*

Rockers International Showcase / 1991 / Rykodisc ✦✦✦
This compilation of Pablo tracks gives a nice cross-section of his work. —*Myles Boisen*

Blowing with the Wind / Jun. 1991 / Shanachie ✦✦✦
One of his newest recordings, it has a Far Eastern sound reminiscent of *East of the River Nile*. —*Myles Boisen*

Heartical Chart / 1994 / RAS ✦✦✦
Although not as elaborate a producer as King Jammy, Scientist, or the Mad Professor, Pablo's skillful use of space, electronics, and floating melodica runs remain extremely popular among the dub faithful. The set's 13 tracks, released domestically in 1991, feature Pablo on bass, piano, and synthesizer, joined by Chinna Smith on guitar, percussionist Skully Simms, bassists Denny Thompson and P. McLean, and drummers Pow Creary and Santa Davis. The best tracks nicely mix a lean, "roots" rock sound, sparse production, and a gentle yet firm rhythmic bounce. —*Ron Wynn*

● **Classic Rockers** / 1995 / Island ✦✦✦✦
A collection of Augustus Pablo's best productions, *Classic Rockers* includes King Tubby and Pablo's collaboration "King Tubby Meets the Rockers Uptown." —*Stephen Thomas Erlewine*

Lee "Scratch" Perry

Percussion, Vocals / Reggae, Dub, Jamaica, Caribbean
The "bumpity riddim" of Lee Scratch Perry, Jamaica's most outrageous producer, percolates like an aural gallop through a mine field in a hailstorm. Why is he named "Scratch"? "Because," he cackles, "all things start from Scratch. So check it out—who am I?" Whenever a dub track is shattered by an earthshaking shriek from the ninth dimension, whenever a glossolalia-quick burst of word salad blurts over an acid-tinged assault of bass and drums, whenever a "Croaking Lizard" grunts toward some "Roast Fish and Cornbread"—chances are great that the diminutive Mr. Perry has had his flexible fingers in it. Starting as an assistant to Coxsone Dodd as he struggled to begin his seminal Studio One in the mid-'50s, Perry soon was mixing, arranging, and engineering sessions. Shortly after, he was producing and singing as well. By the late '60s he had established a series of labels under the Upsetter umbrella and forged one of the most critical links in the chain of reggae's worldwide successes by joining his studio band with Bob Marley, Peter Tosh, and Bunny Livingston (the Wailers). The result was a pair of crucial albums that have never stopped selling since 1970—*Soul Rebels* and *African Herbsman*—re-released all over the world in dozens of different titles, most notably Trojan's recent vocal and dub triumph called *Soul Revolution Vol. I and II,* an absolutely essential Wailers compilation and a triumph of early reggae minimalism. Perry suffers from a combination of glossolalia (speaking in tongues) with phrases like "wizzy wizzy" for "wisdom," and "graphalalia" (filling every available surface with writing). He's a beat poet number ten, the original speed-rapper whose Black Ark studio became home to a myriad noteworthy '70s artists who were discovered by, or whose careers were revivified by, Perry's take-no-prisoners production techniques. These singers included the Heptones (the essential "Party Time" album), Big Youth, the Mighty Diamonds, Max Romeo ("War Ina Babylon"), Gregory Isaacs, Delroy Wilson, U-Roy, I Roy, Junior Murvin ("Police and Thieves"), and Dillinger, to name a tiny fraction. As the '80s dawned, artists from Paul McCartney to the Clash beat a path to the graffiti-scrawled door of Perry's Black Ark in Kingston. During periods of controlled madness in the past decade, Perry toured Europe with a stage lineup similar to Marley's, right down to the three female backup singers. Recently, he married an allegedly titled Swiss woman and began spending half of each year in the Alps. His music is unmistakable still: wacky, wondrously histrionic, and persistent as a jackhammer to the brain. Long may he rave! —*Roger Steffens*

Roast Fish Collie Weed & Corn / 1976 / VP ✦✦✦✦
A fairly typical all-Jamaican effort, it was done at Perry's Black Ark studio (before he burned it down). —*Myles Boisen*

Mystic Miracle Star / 1982 / Heartbeat ✦✦✦
These long rambling excursions of recent vintage were recorded with a White band. —*Myles Boisen*

History, Mystery, & Prophesy / 1984 / Mango ✦✦✦
More contemporary rantings. —*Myles Boisen*

● **Reggae Greats** / 1984 / Mango ✦✦✦✦
These Perry productions feature the Heptones, Junior Murvin, Max Romeo, Prince Jazzbo, and the upsetter himself—fairly straightforward but brilliant song settings. —*Myles Boisen*

Some of the Best / 1986 / Heartbeat ✦✦✦✦
Perry, of course, was behind the creation of Bob Marley and the Wailers, whose great "Duppy Conqueror" is here. But this highlights his Upsetters—a generic label for groups that over time involved almost all the idiom's most creative musicians. It's tough to exaggerate Perry's influence over the years; despite some omissions, this album suggests why. —*John Storm Roberts, Original Music*

Time Boom X De Devil Dread / 1987 / On U Sound ✦✦✦
Finally there's a producer as manic as Perry. Adrian Sherwood's (pre-sampler days) cut-and-paste dub approach keeps pace with Scratch's stream-of-preconsciousness ramblings, making his rants not only seem palatable, but lending them the appearance of bonafide songcraft. Much credit goes to the ultratough instrumental backing by the Dub Syndicate plus sweet female vocals by Ak a Bu on two great cuts. Techno-Perry is at top form. —*Bob Tarte*

Scratch Attack / 1988 / Clock Tower ✦✦✦
Two albums appear on one CD—the imaginative *Chapter 1* and the dubbed-out *Blackboard Jungle Dub* session, from Perry's own Black Ark studio. —*Myles Boisen*

Chicken Scratch / 1989 / Heartbeat ✦✦✦
Mid-'60s material with the Upsetter from Studio One—Perry is the featured vocalist on singles with the Wailers, Rita Marley, the Skatalites, and more. —*Myles Boisen*

From the Secret Laboratory / 1990 / Mango ✦✦✦
Produced by modern dub master Adrian Sherwood, Perry presides regally over a crew of Jamaican, English, and American players. —*Myles Boisen*

Lord God Muzick / 1991 / Heartbeat ✦✦✦
This recent dementia was recorded with the Upsetters after a European tour and dedicated to his new European and American fans . . . hmm! —*Myles Boisen*

The Upsetter and the Beat / 1992 / Heartbeat ✦✦✦
Having dabbled in the uncertainty principle for so long, it was only a matter of time before Perry threw himself into entropy. The hope is that this found-object poetry vaguely juxtapositioned over recycled Coxsone Dodd-produced Studio One instrumental tracks is a Hugo Ball attempt at transcending the limitations of language and not the twilight of a brilliant career. It sets a new benchmark standard for sheer annoyance value, always an important consideration with any Perry purchase. —*Bob Tarte*

Pinchers (Delroy Thompson)

Vocals / Reggae, Dancehall, Ragga
Delroy Thompson may be named after a pair of pliers, but there's nothing mechanical about his soothing, melodic dancehall singing style. Going against the genre's grain, Pinchers does not chant slackness, but seeks to elevate, educate, and entertain, although "Agony," his trademark, walks a fine line between the profane and the profound. —*Roger Steffens*

● **Pinchers Meets Sanchez** / VP ✦✦✦✦

Maxi Priest (Max Elliot)

Vocals / Urban, Lovers Rock
Born Max Elliot in Manchester, England, in 1962, Maxi Priest changed his name when he converted to Rastafarianism. He stumbled into a career in reggae when he was discovered while building sound systems. Since then, Maxi Priest has become one of the '80s great crossover success stories, making chart-toppers on both sides of the Atlantic. A pleasant, easygoing vocal manner coupled with a sexy stage presence have yielded consistent hits—including a cover of "Some Guys Have All the Luck" in 1987, and Cat Stevens' "Wild World" in 1988. Though he initially sang straight, ultraslick lovers rock, the '90s have found him dabbling in dancehall with impressive results. In 1990, he scored a No. 1 pop hit in the US with "I Just Want to Be Close to You" and a Top Ten with "Set the Night to Music," a duet with Roberta Flack. *Man with the Fun*, released in 1996, contained another hit, "That Girl," featuring Shaggy. —*Roger Steffens*

You're Safe / 1985 / Charisma ✦✦✦

Intentions / 1986 / Capitol ✦✦

Maxi Priest / 1988 / Virgin ✦✦✦✦
This bends the reggae/pop equation back toward the crossover side. —*Ron Wynn*

Bonafide / Jun. 1990 / Charisma ✦✦

● **The Best of Me** / 1991 / Charisma ✦✦✦✦

Fe Real / 1992 / Charisma ✦✦

Man with the Fun / 1996 / Virgin ✦✦✦
Man with the Fun showcases Maxi Priest's talent for shaping reggae, dancehall, and soul into a distinctly pop-oriented and commercial amalgam. *Man with the Fun* happens to be one of Priest's better efforts, simply because the quality of the production and songwriting is uniformly first-rate throughout the record. Of course, there are quite a few mediocre tracks, but the smooth sounds of Priest's voice and the seamless production holds your interest until the album arrives at high points like Maxi's duet with Shaggy, "That Girl." —*Leo Stanley*

Prince Buster (Cecil Bustamante Campbell)

Vocals / Ska
Cecil Bustamanate Campbell aka Prince Buster was among Jamaica's first international stars. His singles were outrageous, sexist, hilarious, widely influential, and inspirational. A onetime boxer, Prince Buster began working as a combination sound engineer and bouncer for Coxsone Dodd. His claims to be ska's inventor, making him the Jamaican equivalent of Jelly Roll Morton for exaggerated importance, but Buster certainly helped popularize it. After parting company with Dodd, Buster established his own sound system, label, and record store. His first recording session yielded the anthemic original "Oh Carolina" by the Folks Brothers. Buster soon had multiple labels operating: Wild Bells, Voice of the People, and Buster's Record Shack. His singles were distributed on the Blue Beat label in England, and Buster's fame rose while such hits as "Al Capone" and "Madness" exploded. His talking/toasting records, filled with lewd imagery and vivid language, proved enormously popular. Buster doubled as a prolific performer and busy recording executive in the '70s, cutting sessions with Dennis Brown, Big Youth, John Holt, and Alton Ellis, among others. He reissued his old records, churned out compilations, bought record stores, and built a huge empire. Buster stopped performing in the late '70s, then returned to the stage in the late '80s. He was still cutting fresh tracks as recently as 1992. —*Ron Wynn*

★ **Fabulous Greatest Hits** / 1980 / Melodisc ✦✦✦✦✦
This is arguably the set to get if you're unaware of Prince Buster's charms. There are several outlandish, outrageous numbers spiced by Prince Buster's madcap toasting and energetic presence. —*Ron Wynn*

Prince Far I

Percussion, Vocals / Reggae, Deejay
With a voice deeper and more darkly shaded than a mid-ocean trench, Prince Far I rapped tales of eccentrics like Bedward, "the Flying Preacher," and prophesied the holocausts of these "last days," before being murdered in his bed at the close of the '80s. —*Roger Steffens*

Voice of Thunder / 1981 / Trojan ✦✦✦
This showcases his earthshaking vocals, conscious lyrics, and sharp backing tracks. —*Myles Boisen*

Cry Tuff Dub Encounter 4 / 1983 / ROIR ✦✦✦
A heavily dubwise adventure with the Arabs, this was one of the first Jamaican efforts to use English avant-garde musicians. —*Myles Boisen*

Musical Revue / 1989 / ROIR ✦✦✦
He appears with his celestial band, the Suns of Arqa, on this rare live recording from 1982. —*Myles Boisen*

★ **Black Man Land** / 1990 / Frontline ✦✦✦✦✦
This reissue of his penetrating vocal raps appeared on the Virgin/Caroline label. —*Myles Boisen*

Dubwise / 1992 / Frontline ✦✦✦
More Virgin/Caroline recordings were reissued, with an emphasis on spacey dub mixes. —*Myles Boisen*

Shabba Ranks (Rexton Rawlston Fernando Gordon)

Vocals / Rap, Reggae, Raggamuffin, Dancehall, Club/Dance
During the '90s, Shabba Ranks was the reigning king of reggae-rap, a combination of Jamaican dancehall and New York hip-hop filled with X-rated slack lyrics. As a performer, Shabba is known for his high-energy, hypersexual shows. With unabashed ambition to become a trendsetter, sex symbol, and innovator of Jamaican music, Shabba Ranks does not shy away from blatant commercialism in his music, and is more interested in providing listeners with a good-time than raising their consciousness. Born in the hilly countryside of St. Ann's Parish, Shabba spent much of his youth growing up amid the violence of West Kingston. Early inspirations included deejays such as Charlie Chaplin and Yellowman, but his idol was DJ Josey Wales. Blessed with a powerful baritone voice and a knack for rhyme, Shabba started out at age 14 during the early '80s. At first he performed under the name CoPilot, which appeared on his first single "Heat Under Sufferer's Feet." Later he chose Shabba after two gangsters with the same name died. Shabba did not begin to make a real name for himself until the mid-'80s, after he began working with some of Jamaica's biggest producers. His unpredictable energy on and off stage made him a

hit on the dancehall circuit, and soon Shabba was in demand all over the West Indies. Soon he even eclipsed Yellowman, Ninjaman, and Johnny P as the biggest DJ around with such hits as "Roots and Culture," "Live Blanket," and his smash single, "Wicked in Bed." Between 1989 and 1991, Shabba released 50 singles and has since toured Europe, Asia, and the US. He is particularly popular in Japan and in England where two of his albums, *Golden Touch* and *Rappin' with the Ladies*, earned him a six-figure income. In the early '90s, he made a three-album deal with Epic/Sony. He has had considerable crossover success with three Top Ten R&B hits—"House Call (You Body Can't Lie to Me)," "Mr. Lover Man," and "Slow and Sexy"—as well as several other minor hits. —*Sandra Brennan*

● **As Raw As Ever** / 1991 / Epic ◆◆◆◆
This is an X-rated hip-hop reggae crossover that won a Grammy. —*Roger Steffens*

Rough & Ready, Vol. 1 / Jul. 14, 1992 / Epic ◆◆◆◆
Shabba Ranks kept the slack dancehall coming with this follow-up to *As Raw As Ever*. His thick, patois-laced delivery scored a pop hit with "Mr. Loverman," a song that basically defined the CD. If you didn't get it the first time around, you sure understood it after hearing "Bad & Wicked," "Ca'an Dun," and "Gal Yuh' Good," among others. —*Ron Wynn*

X-tra Naked / Oct. 6, 1992 / Epic ◆◆◆◆
Shabba Ranks landed another pop hit on his third album to hit the charts over a two-year span. "Slow and Sexy" peaked at No. 33, providing ample momentum for another collection of sex cuts and come-ons. Ranks did include "Rude Boy" and "Two Breddrens," but otherwise, the focus stayed completely in the bedroom. —*Ron Wynn*

Rough & Ready, Vol. 2 / 1993 / Epic ◆◆◆
Yet another sex-heavy dancehall collection from Shabba Ranks, whose superlewd material rivals the pedantic ramblings of X Clan and other Islamic/Afrocentric rappers in its utter lack of thematic variety. Not only were almost all the songs alike, but Ranks seemed like he was recycling the raps and beats as well. —*Ron Wynn*

No Competition / 1993 / Critique ◆◆◆
Deejay/toaster Shabba Ranks enrages reggae traditionalists and delights contemporary dancehall audiences with his fast-paced, sexually explicit commentary and quips. This 14-song set included not only Ranks but several other equally sassy dancehall stars such as Cocoa Tea, Laddy G, Deborah Glasgow, Cutty Ranks, Snagga, Krystal, E.T. and less suggestive veterans J.C. Lodge and the great Freddie McGregor. Ranks teamed with different performers on most cuts. Other than Cutty Ranks' hard-hitting "Wealth," there wasn't much sociopolitical material on this session. Instead, it was a showcase for dancehall, offering fans a primer of styles, sounds, and themes. —*Ron Wynn*

Ras Michael & the Sons of Negus

Reggae, Nyahbinghi
Negus is a title of Ethiopian Emperor Haile Selassie, the Almighty God of the Rastafarian movement, and none pays him more eloquent homage than Ras Michael and his group. This is the beat of the heart, based on the original "instrument of ten strings," the hand-beaten drum. On *Dadawah* in 1975, Michael took a religious ceremonial gathering as the basis for an album of elegant poetry and raw, visceral power. Later, eschewing minimalism, such works as *Promised Land Sounds* added electronics and produced a primeval psychedelia without compare in Jamaican history. This is the sound of the Roots Church in the 21st century, highly charged hymns for humanity's future survival. —*Roger Steffens*

Rastafari / 1975 / Top Ranking ◆◆◆◆
More Rasta gospel music includes the essential "None a Jah Jah Children No Cry" and "Mr. Brown." —*Roger Steffens*

Promised Land Sounds / 1980 / Lions Gate ◆◆◆
Four extended Nyabinghi jams sound like the Grateful Dead meeting *2001*. —*Roger Steffens*

Rally Round / 1985 / Shanachie ◆◆◆
Here are more Rasta standards from their primary musical spokesman. —*Roger Steffens*

★ **Dadawah** / Trojan ◆◆◆◆◆
The best Rasta testament from the '70s, spin it and become a "Man in the Hills." —*Roger Steffens*

Tony Rebel (Patrick Barrett)

Vocals / Dancehall, Ragga
Tony Rebel sings a peaceful, roots-oriented form of dancehall music designed to inspire his audience to take a more positive approach to life and social change. Rebel is a Rastafarian, but rather than simply creating serious, philosophical tunes, he infuses his music with a lighthearted, liberal-leaning dose of humor. Prior to becoming a recording artist in the '90s, he spent 14 years playing the local dancehall circuit. Examples of his uplifting approach to dancehall can be heard on his 1993 album *Vibes of Time*. —*Sandra Brennan*

● **Rebellious** / 1992 / RAS ◆◆◆◆
Tony Rebel's recent Stateside release on Columbia/Chaos doesn't match the quality or depth of this earlier session recorded in Jamaica. Although there's still plenty of trendy "computerized" underpinning, Rebel's toasts aren't quite as fast, or as obsessed with sex. Indeed, such songs as "Working Man" and "Rainbow People," with guest appearances from Ken Bob and Half Pint, respectively, are moving, strongly performed message pieces. "God of Abraham" takes the melody of an old R&B song and recasts it as the foundation for expressive praises to Jah. Even the love tunes are romantic rather than lustful. —*Ron Wynn*

Junior Reid

Vocals / Reggae
Junior Reid found himself in a difficult spot when he joined Black Uhuru in 1986. He replaced Michael Rose, who had become quite popular as a longtime Uhuru contributor. Though essentially a good vocalist, Reid's style was so close to Rose's he didn't establish his own identity. The group also suffered compositional difficulties and personal crisis during Reid's tenure. Puma Jones left and was replaced by Olafunke. They also didn't always get quality material or support from Sly and Robbie during this period as well. Reid departed in '90, and has since been struggling as a solo artist to fulfill his considerable potential. —*Ron Wynn*

● **Long Road** / 1991 / Cohiba ◆◆◆◆
Junior Reid has been unable to attain consistent stardom, despite being among reggae's better vocalists. This was his finest LP, marked by tremendous singing and both strong romantic and effective roots/message material. —*Ron Wynn*

Listen to the Voices / 1996 / RAS ◆◆◆
Junior Reid's *Listen to the Voices* is a typical collection of his genre-expanding dancehall, but it is too inconsistent to warrant the attention of anyone but his fans. —*David Jehnzen*

Max Romeo and the Upsetters

Disco, Reggae
Max Romeo was a performer who managed to rise above the rudest of beginnings (recording-wise) to become one of the first Rastaman singers to record a series of deeply spiritual and socially conscious roots songs. He was born Maxwell Smith in Kingston and first became famous for his raunchy late-'60s hit "Wet Dream," containing suspiciously suggestive lyrics concerning a man in bed with his woman. The song was a runaway hit in Great Britain until older people began listening to it closely and banned it. Though Romeo publicly claimed the song was about a leaky roof, the ban remained. This did not stop the song from making it to the British Top Ten thanks to its popularity among London's rebellious young skinheads. With that success under his belt (as it were), Romeo released a few more similarly themed "novelty" tunes such as "Wine Her Goosie" and "Pussy Watch Man" with only modest success. As the '70s progressed, Romeo underwent a few profound spiritual changes. By the time he teamed up with production wizard Lee Perry in the mid-'70s, he had become a committed Rastaman and was singing visionary songs praising Jah and calling the sufferahs to social consciousness and culture. Songs from this period include "Let the Power Fall," "Pray for Me," "Every Man Ought to Know," and "Black Equality." With Perry, Romeo recorded his magnum opus, *War Ina Babylon* (1976), with the Upsetters. Though Romeo penned or co-penned most of the songs and sang all of the songs, most of the album's success has been attributed to the genius of Perry, and many consider this one of his finest albums ever. Romeo continued recording singles with Perry for a short while afterward, but then the two had a falling out and split up. Since then though, he continues to record and perform. Romeo has yet to find the perfect niche for his silky, haunting voice and earnest style. —*Sandra Brennan*

● **War Ina Babylon** / 1976 / Mango ◆◆◆◆
This is one of Lee Perry's most perfect '70s productions, especially on the chilling title track and "One Step Forward." —*Roger Steffens*

Reconstruction / 1978 / Mango ◆◆◆◆
Several stirring vocal performances, even on otherwise shaky numbers, made this an above-average vehicle for Max Romeo. —*Ron Wynn*

Roots Radics

Reggae
The key studio band of the '80s in Jamaica, they've recorded with everyone from Gregory Isaacs (his greatest, *Night Nurse*) to Bunny Wailer (*Rock & Groove*). With Dwight Pinkney on finger-picked guitar, Flabba Hold on wicked punchy bass, Style Scott on hard metronomic drums, and Bingy Bunny on precise rhythm guitar, along with Steelie on scintillating keyboards, they set the standard for a decade of increasing, unceasing, international penetration of Jamaican music. —*Roger Steffens*

● **World Peace III** / 1992 / Heartbeat ◆◆◆◆
Lots of singing is here, with a great Garvey song, "International Hero." It's the culmination of two decades' work in the studios. —*Roger Steffens*

Shaggy

Dancehall, Club/Dance, Ragga

A resident of Brooklyn, Shaggy exploded onto the American reggae and dance scenes in 1995 with the gold single "Boombastic," following the massive worldwide success (except in the US) of the smash "Oh Carolina." Shaggy began his career as a dancehall vocalist in Brooklyn, but joined the Marines as a way to pay the bills. On weekends, he traveled from Camp LeJeune in North Carolina back to his hometown to perform, but this routine was interrupted by the Gulf War, in which Shaggy was called upon to drive a tank through an Iraqi mine field. Shortly after the war, Shaggy cut "Oh Carolina," a new version of a popular ska song, and had a global smash with the help of producer Sting Intl. and vocalist and compatriot Rayvon. Americans never caught on to this single, but that was not to be the case with "Boombastic," which went gold even before the album of the same name was released. The follow-up single, "Summertime," was a hit as well, and Shaggy's career was well on its way. *—Steve Huey*

Pure Pleasure / Aug. 24, 1993 / Virgin ♦♦♦
Shaggy's debut contained several numbers reminiscent of Yellowman in prime slack mode; these included "Lust," "Bedroom Bounty Hunter," "All Virgins," "Love How Them Flex," and "Bun Me." Some were more explicit than others, but none required any imagination to determine Shaggy's intentions and desires. He teamed with Rayvon on two tracks and Sylva on another, but only on "Give Thanks and Praise" and the bonus CD cut "Follow Me" was there any attempt to move the lyric emphasis beyond or off a hardcore sexual focus. Shaggy's heavy-voiced style was less patois-dominated and easier to understand than Shabba Ranks, but otherwise seldom varied from standard dancehall. *—Ron Wynn*

★ **Boombastic** / 1995 / Virgin ♦♦♦♦♦
Boombastic confirmed Shaggy's status as one of the most popular dancehall acts of the '90s, and for good reason—the record is a infectiously entertaining collection of deep, funky grooves that celebrate good times. Featuring the major hit title track, the album also sports a great guest appearance by Grand Puba on "Why You Treat Me So Bad," as well as a hot duet with singer Wayne Wonder on "Something Different." Despite a silly cover of "Day O," *Boombastic* keeps the funky reggae coming and is Shaggy's best album to date. *—Stephen Thomas Erlewine*

Leroy Sibbles

Bass, Vocals / Reggae, Ragga

Both a wonderful vocalist and fine bassist, Leroy Sibbles initially gained fame as the lead singer for the Heptones. The trio began at Caltone, then became stars when they moved to Studio One in 1966. They were accomplished at both rock steady and reggae, and Sibbles' wondrously soulful leads and excellent compositions were augmented by his smooth, hypnotic bass lines that were reproduced on numerous Heptones' knockoffs and versions. Unfortunately, a once musically profitable relationship soured, and the Heptones left Studio One under bitter circumstances in 1971. Sibbles has since enjoyed a successful solo career, but retains his bitterness towards Dodd and Studio One. He remained with the Heptones a couple more years, and their 1973 LP *Party Time* was an international reggae favorite. *—Ron Wynn*

● **Mean While** / Attic ♦♦♦♦

Garnett Silk

Vocals / Dancehall, Ragga

Singer Garnett Silk was regarded as the next successor to Bob Marley, and indeed his meteoric rise to stardom spoke of much promise. Unfortunately, a freak accident abruptly ended the life of the developing young performer. Though not yet as adept at singing and songwriting as Marley, Silk's passionate, socially conscious reggae, with its basis in R&B and rock, was a cry for peace and love in a genre increasingly filled with references to guns and violence. A versatile singer, he was equally at home with roots music, lovers rock, classic reggae, and even soul hits from the '70s.

Born in Manchester parish in the mid-'60s, Silk, billing himself as "Bimbo," started out as a DJ. He recorded his first song, "Ram Dance Master," in 1985, but it was never released. The song was followed by the Callo Collins-produced "Problem Everywhere." He reverted to his given name in 1990 and began singing rather than rapping. Working with producer Derrick Morgan, he began recording albums such as *Tony Rebel Meets Garnett Silk in a Dancehall Conference* (released in the US by Heartbeat Records). Silk's big break came in 1992 with a large string of hits recorded on various labels. These hits included "Seeing Zion" (on Black Scorpio) and "Fill Us up with Your Mercy" (on Penthouse). Performing and recording so much—in 1994, he had released dozens of 7-inch singles in Jamaica—took its toll on Silk, and rumors that he was using drugs and suffering from physical exhaustion abounded. He eventually took a six-month break from recording and performing. Even then his popularity did not abate, and he began to develop an international following. He increased that audience with stellar performances at the Sunsplash and the Sunfest gatherings. He had also just signed to a major

label in the US. In light of his pacifistic songs, it is ironic that a gun caused his death. According to the Jamaican press, he had borrowed two guns from his attorney after his home had been robbed. Someone was showing Silk how to use the gun when it accidentally went off; the bullet struck a small gas tank which instantly exploded, killing Silk and his mother, and severely burning two of his brothers. *—Sandra Brennan*

● **In a Dancehall Conference** / 1994 / Heartbeat ♦♦♦♦
Two scorching hot dancehall artists are presented both solo and in tandem on this 19-cut anthology, which offers the latest in the idiom's conventions. Garnett Silk has a booming, yet engaging and soulful voice, which he can also lower effectively. Tony Rebel is in the harsh, attacking, booming class alongside Buju Banton. While they're similar in their abilities to dominate an arrangement, there's enough disparity to make their duets delightful, particularly the memorable "Help the Poor and Needy." The anthology also contains seven decent-to-fine dub tracks, the best being "Prisoner's Dub" and "Killer Dub." *—Ron Wynn*

Sister Carol (Carol East)

Vocals / Reggae, Dancehall

The music of Rastawoman Sister Carol carries a potent message to younger listeners, urging them to take the high road and work for lasting, peaceful change. Since the early '80s, she has also been a driving feminist force in a genre still dominated by male performers.

Born Carol East and raised to age 14 in the ghettos of Kingston, she grew up influenced by a variety of musical styles ranging from traditional reggae to R&B to gospel to jazz to rock. She still draws her diverse musical background in her music to help reach out to international audiences. Her family emigrated to Brooklyn to look for work when Sister Carol was a young teen. Carol went on to earn a degree in education at City College, NY. She came to music in 1981 after meeting Brigadier Jerry. They met just before she gave birth. He had a tremendous effect on her and shortly after having the child, she began singing and writing songs patterned after those of Jerry. By 1982 she had waxed her first two singles, "Black Cinderella" and "Jamaica Little Africa." Her first album, *Liberation for Africa*, had a limited release through Serious Gold. Her career got a real boost when she appeared in a couple of Jonathan Demme films—*Something Wild*, in which she sang "Wild Thing" during the closing credits, and *Married to the Mob*. While recording her next two albums, *Black Cinderella* and *Jah Disciple*, Sister Carol began producing her own singles on her Black Cinderella label. In Jamaica some of these singles were released on the Fameous and Spiderman labels. An early highlight was a recording of Marley's "Screwface" that she did with Judy Mowatt, who produced it and released it in Jamaica on her Ashandan label. In New York the song came out on Jah Life. As a producer, Sister Carol likes to try and record things and have them released on major labels to ensure that the songs reach as many listeners as possible. She tried this with her 1995 album *Call Mi Sister Carol*, but had no success. It was eventually picked up and released by the highly respected Heartbeat. For Sister Carol, who is still best known as a DJ, the album carries the same strong messages about changing sexism, avoiding violence and the nonspiritual/medicinal use of drugs, and of encouraging self-respect and spirituality, but with a wider variety of styles designed to appeal more directly to the younger audiences, while still appealing to her longtime fans. Though many differentiate between dancehall and reggae, to Sister Carol it is all part of the same force. *—Sandra Brennan*

Mother Culture / 1991 / RAS ♦♦♦
Sister Carol mixed love tunes, defiant message tracks, and hip-hop-influenced toasts/raps on this collection. "Shackles" and "Mother Culture," as well as "Mandela's Release," were aggressive, striking political tunes, while "Tight Spot" was in the rap/reggae groove just emerging in the early '90s. "Lovers Rock Style" and "The Music Nice" were romantic numbers, though not as sensual or soothing as they would be in the hands of a Sandra Cross. Sister Carol's tone and delivery belied her tough, independent style. There were no weak or compliant qualities in her music, even when the lyrics might suggest otherwise. *—Ron Wynn*

Lyrically Potent / Jun. 18, 1996 / Heartbeat ♦♦♦♦
As the title suggests, Sister Carol takes a hard-hitting, no holds barred approach on *Lyrically Potent*. Even though there are a lot of messages in the lyrics, the music hasn't been ignored—it is a dynamic fusion of reggae and hip-hop, featuring deep, loping grooves. Occasionally, the album bogs down with undistinguished songs, but for the most part, *Lyrically Potent* is an explosive listen. *—Thom Owens*

● **Jah Disciple** / 1989 / RAS ♦♦♦♦
Sister Carol emphasized truth and rights over sex and love on this session issued by RAS in 1989. She had harsh words for outer-space exploration, internal African problems, and rude boys who disrupt social affairs, while recalling an earlier, more enjoyable time on "Remember When" and calling for respect and dignity from an ignorant male on "A No Me Name Peggy." Her toasts were slower and paced differently than the rapid-fire dancehall mode; the arrangements and backing combined

electronic and acoustic instrumentation, and there was more than a trace of vintage reggae in her style and sound. —*Ron Wynn*

Skatalites

Reggae, Ska

Ska was Jamaica's first indigenous creation, a compelling mix of fast R&B, Rastafarian African rhythms, and Afro-Cuban percussion highlight. This double-time delight ruled Jamaica from 1962 to 1966, and none played it more convincingly than its creators, the Skatalites. Led by a mentally disturbed, world-class trombonist named Don Drummond, the Skatalites were composed of the top instrumentalists on the island at the time: Tommy McCook, Roland Alphonso, and "Ska" Campbell on tenor sax; Lester Stering on alto; Karl Bryan on baritone; "Dizzy Johnny" Moore and Baba Brooks on trumpet; Lloyd Brevett on bass; Lloyd Knibbs on drums; Jackie Mittoo on piano; and Lyn Tait and Jah Jerry on guitar. This is a roster of Jamaica's musical gods, the foundation of all that would come out of this tiny land of two million people to influence the entire world of music for the next 30 years. Rock steady, reggae, rockers, dub—all are merely tempo reworkings of the skipping ska beat.

It is remarkable, then, to note that the Skatalites existed for a mere 14 months. As 1965 dawned, Drummond murdered his wife, and was put away in "de Bellevue" mental hospital, where he died a couple of years later. The band then broke up into several different lineups, most notably Tommy McCook and the Supersonics, and the Soul Brothers. Their rhythm slowed in 1966 to the rock steady, a twin result of Drummond's loss and a torpid, steamy summer during which people no longer wanted to dance as frenetically as they had before. But ska underwent periodic revivals, most notably among British skinheads in the late '60s; Northern British two-tone skanksters in 1980; and massive movements in the '80s in places as far afield as Brussels, Tokyo, and California. Today, ska has achieved a permanent place in the world's beats as alive, fresh, and exciting as rock 'n' roll. Yet even now no interpretation sounds more compelling than the original Studio One recordings made by its masters, the Skatalites. —*Roger Steffens*

Ska Authentic / 1967 / Studio One ✦✦✦✦
Early '60s ravers include "Lee Oswald" and "Bridge View" (any Studio One Skatalites collection is worth owning). —*Roger Steffens*

● **Scattered Lights** / 1984 / Alligator ✦✦✦✦
Recorded from 1962 to 1965 for Justin Yap's Top Deck, it features some of the final shots of Don Drummond. —*Roger Steffens*

Sly and Robbie

Reggae

Drummer Sly Dunbar and bassist Robbie Shakespeare have been reggae's pre-eminent production team since the early '70s. Besides appearing on countless sessions, they patented the "Taxi" sound; a clean, less choppy style with Shakespeare's bass lines augmented by Dunbar's use of syndrums, which added a different sound to the reggae mix. This helped bring more electronic and production effects (detractors viewed them as gimmicks) into reggae and created changes in style, tone, and emphasis that have continued nonstop. The duo's produced sessions by Gregory Isaacs, Black Uhuru, Grace Jones, Joan Armatrading, Bob Dylan, Ian Dury, the Mighty Diamonds, and many, many others. They've also issued many compilations and sessions featuring their productions as the highlight, and Dunbar's cut solo dates for Front Line and Mango. —*Ron Wynn*

A Dub Experience—Reggae Greats / 1984 / Mango ✦✦✦✦
Here's a good sampling of dub from this in-demand rhythm duo on this installment of Island/Mango's *Reggae Greats* series. —*Scott Bultman*

Language Barrier / 1985 / Island ✦✦✦
Sly and Robbie team with producer Bill Laswell for an edgy dub set. Guests include Herbie Hancock, Bob Dylan, Afrika Bambaataa, and Manu DiBango. —*Scott Bultman*

● **Rhythm Killers** / 1987 / Island ✦✦✦✦
This is another session with Bill Laswell. The all-star guest lineup includes Bootsy Collins, Bernie Worrell, Bernard Fowler, Henry Threadgill, Nicky Skopelitis, Shinehead, and Pat Thrall. It features a killer version of the Ohio Players, hit "Fire," with funky Bootsy Collins grooves throughout the album. —*Scott Bultman*

Padlock / Island ✦✦✦
It features the track "Peanut Butter," with Gwen Guthrie. —*AMG*

Millie Small

Vocals / Urban

Jamaican teenager Millie Small stunned the music business by reaching No. 2 in the US, and No. 1 in the UK, with "My Boy Lollipop" in 1964. Recorded in England with British session musicians backing Millie's childlike, extremely high-pitched vocals, it was the first (and indeed, one of the few) international ska hits and remains one of the biggest-selling reggae or ska discs of all time. Perceived as a one-shot novelty artist from the start because of her unusual, almost screeching vocals (which actually owed a lot to Shirley Goodman, of the '50s New Orleans R&B duo Shirley & Lee), she only made the Top 40 one more time, with the "My Boy Lollipop" soundalike "Sweet William." —*Richie Unterberger*

● **My Boy Lollipop** / Combo ✦✦✦✦
Besides the megasmash title track, this compilation of uncertain origin includes 17 other mid-'60s recordings, including her only other hit of any size, "Sweet William." Arranged by respected early reggae musician Ernest Ranglin, Millie's immediately identifiable high-pitched voice paces some fairly hot ska numbers, as well as quite a few New Orleans R&B classics given the ska treatment. —*Richie Unterberger*

Leroy Smart

Vocals / Reggae, Dancehall

A master at love songs and roots material, Leroy Smart has been on the reggae scene since the early '70s. He was raised in Kingston's Alpha Catholic Boys Home, and began recording in the early '70s. Smart worked with such producers as Gussie Clarke, Joe Joe Hookin, and Bunny Lee while gaining fame for a flamboyant performance style and exceptionally anguished delivery and penetrating vocal manner. Smart's smashing voice often seemed about to collapse from anxiety and earnestness in mid-song. He's maintained his popularity through the '70s, '80s, and '90s, never scoring any crossover or international hits, but retaining his pull with the notoriously fickle Jamaican audience. —*Ron Wynn*

● **Dread Hot in Africa** / 1988 / Burning Sounds ✦✦✦✦
Piercing, poignant, and topical fare from a legitimate reggae great. Leroy Smart's cutting delivery and wailing leads are as moving and hypnotic as those of Dennis Brown, Gregory Isaacs, Freddie McGregor, or any other better-known superstar. —*Ron Wynn*

Slim Smith

Vocals / Reggae

In the '60s, Slim Smith was one of the lead singers of the seminal Techniques, then went on to form (with Jimmy Riley) the Uniques. Often compared to Curtis Mayfield (his major influence), Smith never achieved the financial rewards his extensive, big-selling output deserved. He died tragically in the early '70s when he punched his fist through a glass door in frustration and bled to death before he could summon help. One of Jamaica's most venerated and gifted interpreters, virtually everything he cut is worth owning, particularly if your tastes run to Impressions-style harmonics. —*Roger Steffens*

● **Born to Love** / 1979 / Heartbeat ✦✦✦✦
It includes the eternal "You Don't Care" and the oft-versioned "Rougher Yet." —*Roger Steffens*

Steel Pulse

Reggae

One of Bob Marley's favorite bands, Steel Pulse became one of reggae's most successful bands in the late '70s and early '80s. After releasing their debut album, *Handsworth Revolution* (1978, Mango), and its successors, *Tribute to the Martyrs* and *True Democracy* (both for Elektra) in the early '80s, with their blend of straightahead reggae, flamenco, and Euro-pop containing potent pleas for social reform, critics and fans alike hailed them as Marley's successors. By the late '80s, Steel Pulse was making a blatant bid toward a commercial sound and lost its unique edge. However, in 1995 the band abandoned attempts to cross over to mainstream markets and returned to their roots with the album *Vex*.

The original members of Steel Pulse—David Hinds on keyboards, bassist Ronald "Stepper" McQueen, guitarist Basil Gabbidon, and Selwyn Brown—all hail from the Birmingham ghettoes of Handsworth, England. Their families were immigrants from the West Indies. Growing up in poverty, they were victimized by colonialist-racist attitudes that kept them from being accepted in the highly stratified British society. They found some solace and considerable cultural pride in the island music they grew up with, including calypso, mento, ska, bluebeat, and eventually reggae during their boyhood in the '60s. One of the biggest influences back then was Burning Spear (Winston Rodney), considered the father of the Rastafari music movement in Britain, from whom they heard the radical messages and philosophies that later shaped their own music. As teens, such music attuned them to the many sociopolitical problems faced by their people in England and abroad while simultaneously buoying their spirits. The band first came together in early 1975 at the suggestion of McQueen, their bassist. None of them really knew how to play, but their sincere desire drove them to practice extensively, so they taught each other the basics. Even then, they were driven to create something enjoyable yet socially conscious. A little later they recruited drummer Steve "Grizzly" Nisbett, Phonso Martin on percussion, and vocalist Michael Riley. Steel Pulse spent the next three years honing their sound, playing covers of songs by Burning Spear, Bob Marley, the Gladiators, and others, while looking for places to play.

Finding gigs back then was difficult. The owners of British Black clubs found reggae music and Rastafarians, with their radical, anti-authoritarian ideas and penchant for smoking ganja, subversive and inflammatory, and would not let the band perform. The band did not really get their break until the birth of the punk movement. The punk and new-wave bands loved Steel Pulse, and the group opened for such acts as the Clash, Generation X, the Stranglers, XTC, and the Police. The latter two bands had a great influence on Steel Pulse and taught them to articulate their music, making it precise and professional. During performances, the band would wear wild, highly symbolic clothing to show their defiance. McQueen would wear tails and a bowler to symbolize British bureaucracy; Riley dressed as a vicar, while Martin dressed as an 18th-century footman. Such statements endeared them to the punks.

Steel Pulse first signed with Island Records and recorded their first three albums, all of which were produced and engineered by Jamaican born Karl Pitterson. Pitterson had worked extensively with Bob Marley and the Wailers, Peter Tosh, and Bunny Wailer. He felt a deep connection to the music of Steel Pulse; he not only helped make their music stronger and even more authentic, he also was behind their most successful albums. By 1980, against the advice of Island Records execs, Steel Pulse decided to head for the US. The band was surprised to find that they had somehow already developed a large, devoted following in the States. Soon Steel Pulse began trying in earnest to bring reggae music to an international audience, but thanks largely to Marley's message of love, audiences began preferring a less militant reggae and again, Steel Pulse found themselves without a real niche until 1981 when they headlined Reggae Sunsplash in Montego Bay. A successful live album from Elektra came from that concert, and the band once again enjoyed a high profile. In 1982, Elektra released their *True Democracy* album in the States where it garnered considerable acclaim; it had flopped in England two years before. Two years later, they released *Earth Crisis*, an album containing a more progressive sound. The album was produced by Jimmy Haynes, and two original members, Gabbidon and McQueen, had been replaced. They have since had several different guitarists, including Carlton Bryan. Alvin Ewen became their new bass player. Unfortunately, Haynes's obsession with studio perfection led to the slightly disappointing *Babylon the Bandit*. Despite losing some of the older fans, it did win Steel Pulse a Grammy in 1986. It did poorly on the charts, and Elektra terminated their contract. Two years later, they signed to MCA and came out with a blatant commercial effort, *State of Emergency*. The album bombed. They made another attempt at mainstream success in 1991 with *Victims* and again sales did poorly.

A new live album from a Paris performance, *Rastafari Centennial: Live in Paris, Elysee, Montmarte*, was a turning point for Steel Pulse. The fans' positive response to the band's older material helped remind them of their original vision and set them back on course. They recorded *Vex* in 1994, and true to their determination to get more in touch with their roots, recorded it on Jamaica. While they have returned more to their original style, Steel Pulse also continue to try to keep their sound relevant to contemporary tastes and issues. As of 1994, the basic lineup consisted of Hinds, Selwyn Brown, and Steve Nisbett. —*Sandra Brennan*

Handsworth Revolution / 1978 / Mango ✦✦✦
Another among several unforgettable numbers penned and performed by Steel Pulse during their tenure on Island. The LP as a whole was just a shade below *Babylon the Bandit*. —*Ron Wynn*

Tribute to the Martyrs / 1979 / Mango ✦✦✦
Tribute is perhaps their most deeply felt album to date, mixing political militancy with the desire for Rastafarian repatriation. One of the best by one of Bob Marley's favorites. —*Mango*

● **True Democracy** / 1982 / Elektra ✦✦✦✦

Reggae Greats / 1984 / Mango ✦✦✦
With their rock-style guitar work and punklike energy, Steel Pulse have been one of the most consistently innovative reggae bands of the last 15 years. —*Mango*

Babylon the Bandit / 1986 / Elektra ✦✦✦✦
Biting, frequently riveting protest material from Steel Pulse. The title track is one of several anthemic numbers punctuated by the remarkable David Hinds. Only Aswad compares to them among British reggae bands, and they've never produced any roots or political tracks superior to routine Steel Pulse material. —*Ron Wynn*

Steely and Clevie

Reggae
The Sly and Robbie of contemporary '90s dancehall, Wycliffe "Steelie" Johnson and Cleveland Browne are the in-house rhythm programmers from studios like Jammy's, Techniques, Powerhouse, Redman, and Gussie Clarke's Music Works. Those they have backed include Gregory Isaacs,

Frankie Paul, Maxi Priest, Freddie McGregor, and Grammy winner Shabba Ranks. Highly digital. —*Roger Steffens*

● **Twenty-First Century Sound Clash** / 1988 / VP ✦✦✦✦

Third World

Reggae
Third World is a band that some reggae purists disdain because they dare to deliberately cross over to other genres to popularize their music for international mainstream audiences. Despite the critics, Third World remains one of most enduring and popular Jamaican bands in the world. Unlike many Jamaican reggae bands, comprising hungry street kids with raw talent, no formal musical training, and only their passion and drive to spur them to the top, the members of Third World come from the Kingston middle class.

The band was founded in 1973 by Stephen "Cat" Coore and Michael "Ibo" Cooper. Cooper is a policeman's son, while Coore's father was a deputy prime minister who also taught music. Both Coore and Cooper received formal musical training at Forster Davis School of Music and Kingston's Royal School of Music, respectively. Each also had solo and group experience on the Kingston reggae circuit. Cooper and Coore met while playing for Inner Circle. Other charter members include Richard Daley, Milton Hamilton (another Inner Circle veteran), Irwin "Carrot" Jarrett (a veteran percussionist with considerable concert and television production experience), and Cornel Marshal. From the start, the band was meant to be self-contained, a rarity back then. Third World did this so they could perform wherever they wanted rather than constantly scrambling for musicians or a sound system to support their singing.

They made their debut at the 1973 Jamaican Independence Celebration. Though they performed steadily around Kingston, they had trouble finding a studio willing to record them because most of the studios also ran the sound systems. In 1974, Third World went to London, released their debut single "Railroad Track," and signed to Island Records. Their first album came out in 1975. It received critical accolades, and later that year Third World opened for Bob Marley on his UK summer tour. That year Marshall was replaced by William Stewart. Though the title track of their second album, *96 Degrees in the Shade* (1977), has become a reggae classic, the second album only sold moderately, yet it is considered to be one of their finest albums. Their third album, *Journey to Addis*, finally broke through to a bigger audience thanks to the R&B staple "Now That We Found Love," which Third World sang with a sophisticated blend of pop, funk, and reggae riddims. The song, an international Top Ten hit, provided listeners the opportunity to sample the new Jamaican sound in a familiar aural environment. Third World released three more albums through Island, but began feeling that they were standing too much in the shadow of the label's star act, Marley, and so moved to Columbia in the early '80s. In 1979, William Clarke replaced Milton Hamilton on bass. Their first four albums did quite well in the US and the UK with the single "Hooked on Love" from *Rock the World* (1981), making it to the Top Ten on the British charts. During the early '80s, Third World began working closely with Stevie Wonder, who in 1982 penned and recorded another crossover hit with the group, "Try Jah Love."

In response to critics, Third World justifies its forays into different genres as a means to keep the genre from stagnating. In making it accessible to wider audiences, they are also thereby making new inroads for their messages and making it music for the common people the world over. They are credited for being the first reggae act to add funk and to use a synthesizer. They were also instrumental in popularizing dub poetry, which in turn became the basis for dancehall, a form the band has increasingly embraced since the mid-'80s. Their 1985 album for Mercury, *Sense of Purpose*, marked their first foray into American hip-hop. Their 1992 album, *Committed*, was primarily a dancehall album though the title track spent time on the R&B charts. —*Sandra Brennan*

● **96 Degrees in the Shade** / 1977 / Mango ✦✦✦✦
The album that cemented their stateside popularity. —*Ron Wynn*

Rock the World / 1981 / CBS ✦✦✦
Well-meaning, this juggles R&B, pop, and reggae. —*Ron Wynn*

All the Way Strong / 1983 / CBS ✦✦✦
Teetering on the pop tightrope. —*Ron Wynn*

Reggae Greats / Mar. 1985 / Mango ✦✦✦
A decent place to start on reggae's longest-lasting pop ensemble. —*Ron Wynn*

Sense of Purpose / Apr. 1985 / CBS ✦✦✦✦
A-1 production and arrangements. —*Ron Wynn*

You've Got the Power / 1989 / CBS ✦✦✦
Some above-average ballads and social cuts. —*Ron Wynn*

● **Reggae Ambassadors: 20th Anniversary Collection** / Oct. 5, 1993 / Mercury ✦✦✦✦
While they didn't make groundbreaking albums, this pop-reggae outfit found a great deal of success with their ultra-smooth, mainstream singles. This two-disc anthology may be too much for the casual listener but

the more ambitious will want to start here. All of the essential tracks are here combined with some fine live performances. —*Chris Woodstra*

Tiger (Norman Jackson)

Vocals / Dancehall, Calypso, Trinidad, Caribbean

Tiger burst onto Jamaica's early dancehall scene in 1985 and for the next four years produced a steady stream of popular songs including his first hit "No Wanga Gut." He was born Norman Jackson and claims that it was his fans who nicknamed him Tiger in the mid-'80s. A rather eccentric character, Tiger's lyrics are noted for their witty, offbeat attitude that he punctuates with his trademark growl and other strange vocalizations. In the late '80s, Tiger became involved in drugs and he seemed to have hit a creative lull. He dropped out of music for a while, but returned to performing and recording in the early '90s, signed to Chaos, and has since begun to reclaim the popularity that was once his. —*Sandra Brennan*

● **Me Name Tiger** / 1987 / RAS ◆◆◆◆
"No Wanga Gut" and "Puppy Love" anchor his US debut. —*Roger Steffens*

Bam Bam / 1988 / RAS ◆◆◆◆
Peripathetic toaster/DJ Tiger first began attracting attention on the international circuit with this 1988 release. It featured frenetic verbal thrusts, quips, and commentary, performed over a skeletal musical framework with authentic drums rather than rhythm machines, both acoustic and electric keyboards and occasional guitar/bass in support. Harold "Papa Biggs" McLarty and Doctor Dread stripped down the backgrounds and let Tiger's verbal acrobatics carry the day on such tracks as "Carbon Copy," "Bam Bam," "Nominee," and "Presto." —*Ron Wynn*

Brand New Style / Jul. 18, 1995 / RAS ◆◆◆
Produced by "Papa Biggs" McCarty, this album by Tiger continues in his trademark style. While nothing on the album quite measures up to his 1986 hit "No Wanga Gut," *Brand New Style* shows Tiger as one of the standout artists in '90s reggae. —*Jonathan Ball*

Toots and the Maytals

Reggae, Ska

The Maytals were key figures in reggae music. Comprising leader Frederick "Toots" Hibbert, Nathaniel "Jerry" Mathias/McCarthy, and Raleigh Gordon, all natives of Kingston, the Maytals are said to have been the first group to use the word "reggae" in a song title with their Leslie Kong-produced "Do the Reggay."

Formed in the early '60s when ska was hot, the Maytals had a reputation for having strong, well-blended voices and a seldom-rivaled passion for their music. Hibbert's soulful style led him to be compared to Otis Redding. They first recorded with producer Clement "Coxsone" Dodd and the resulting album, *Hallelujah*, offered a blend of gospel-style vocals and soul sung to a horn-driven Jamaican beat. They were popular from the start, but after recording a few sides with Studio One, they left Dodd in favor of Prince Buster. With him, they soon gained a bigger Jamaican following and also became popular in Great Britain. The Maytals began working with Byron Lee in 1966. Hits from this era include "Dog War," "Daddy," and "Broadway Jungle." That year Lee and his Dragonaires backed the Maytals at the premiere Jamaican Festival Song Competition. Their song, "Bam Bam," won the contest and began their rapid ascent to real stardom. Occasionally, the Maytals would record with other producers, who perhaps to keep from having to pay royalties, would put different band names on the labels such as the Vikings, the Royals, and the Flames. The Maytals were reaching the height of their popularity toward the end of 1966 when Hibbert was arrested for smoking and possessing ganja and was sent to prison for 18 months. Fortunately, the other two Maytals, who were best friends with Hibbert and realized that they could not possibly re-create their unique sound with another front man, waited for him. When Hibbert was released, the band started working with legendary producer Leslie Kong. This was a time of transition in Jamaican popular music and ska was being replaced by the angry, violent music of Rude Boys, and this in turn was becoming reggae. The Maytals changed accordingly, but still kept that soul and gospel-influenced sound that made them unique. While in prison, Hibbert had honed his songwriting skills. Their first Kong single "54-46 That's My Number," a reference to Hibbert's prison number, recounted his experiences and suggested that he was jailed on a trumped-up charge because he was a Rastafarian. It became a huge hit in both Jamaica and England and has since become a rock steady standard. Other major songs from this time include the scathingly funny "Monkey Man," and "Sweet and Dandy," which provided the Maytals with a second win at the 1969 Festival song Competition. One of their all-time great hits, "Pressure Drop," was on the soundtrack of the definitive reggae film *The Harder They Come*. By 1971, they had not only become the biggest act on the island, they were also (thanks to signing with Chris Blackwell's Island Records) international stars. Then Leslie Kong died. They moved on to producer Byron Lee, and though the hits continued, things began to slow down. It was Lee who renamed them Toots and the Maytals. Hibbert and the group broke up in 1981. From there Hibbert began

working with producers Sly Dunbar and Robbie Shakespeare. He had international success through the '80s. Hibbert created a new Maytals in the early '90s and continues touring the world. —*Sandra Brennan*

★ **Funky Kingston** / 1973 / Mango ◆◆◆◆◆
This is the album that brought Toots' soul-infused testifying to American audiences. Forget about this being a great reggae album; this set transcends categorization. —*John Floyd*

Reggae Got Soul / 1976 / Mango ◆◆◆◆
Among his landmark releases, this album wasn't quite as magnificent as *Funky Kingston*, but still contained plenty of explosive numbers and Otis Redding-influenced leads from Toots Hibbert. —*Ron Wynn*

Reggae Greats / 1984 / Mango ◆◆◆
It's skimpy, but this one offers an adequate smattering of essentials, including their first hit, "54-46 Was My Number," "Funky Kingston," and "Sweet and Dandy." —*John Floyd*

Toots in Memphis / 1988 / Mango ◆◆◆◆
Recorded with a slew of Memphis studio pros, Toots pays homage to the power of Southern soul with sterling covers of "I Can't Stand the Rain," "Knock on Wood," "Love and Happiness," "Hard to Handle," and six others. This is an amazing return to form. —*John Floyd*

★ **Time Tough: Anthology** / Jun. 18, 1996 / Island ◆◆◆◆◆
Featuring over 40 songs and spanning the entire length of the group's career, the double-disc set *Time Tough: Anthology* contains every essential song by Toots and the Maytals, from early ska material to reggae classics like "Pressure Drop" and "Funky Kingston." Not only are all of their best-known singles included in the collection, but so are prime album tracks, rare singles, and three unreleased tracks that hold their own with nearly everything else on the collection. *Time Tough* is not only the perfect introduction to Toots and the Maytals' groundbreaking career, it is the only compilation to put their career in focus and feature the best songs. It's an essential item for any reggae collection. —*Stephen Thomas Erlewine*

Do the Reggae / Attack ◆◆◆◆
Sixteen cuts from their early days, when the Maytals were perfecting their sound, it includes some rare early material. —*John Floyd*

Andrew Tosh

Vocals / Reggae

Eldest son of the late Wailer Peter Tosh, Andrew made his debut at his father's funeral in 1987, wowing the mourners with his physical and vocal similarities to Peter. Two promising albums later, Andrew was looked upon as one of conscious reggae's greatest hopes. A tour with the Wailers in 1991 solidified his live reputation. With strong material, he could fill his famous father's shoes in a manner similar to that of Ziggy Marley. —*Roger Steffens*

● **Make Place for the Youth** / 1989 / Tomato ◆◆◆◆
Self-penned minidramas showcase his promising growth. —*Roger Steffens*

Original Man / 1994 / Heartbeat ◆◆◆
While they seldom blunder or even do anything questionable, Heartbeat's decision to update Andrew Tosh's late-'70s Tomato album *Original Man* is mystifying. Instead of re-releasing the old album in remastered form, they've totally remixed the tracks, putting Tosh's voice into a new musical situation with a dancehall sound that doesn't fit the lyrics. In addition, there are eight new dub tracks for an album that wasn't that scintillating the first time out. A couple of the dubs have good production, but this really isn't very moving or interesting. While Tosh tries hard, and the song "Poverty Is a Crime" was a strong one, there wasn't enough on the album to merit this deluxe repackaging and remixing job. —*Ron Wynn*

Peter Tosh (Winston Hubert McIntosh)

b. Oct. 9, 1944, Jamaica, d. Sep. 11, 1987, Kingston, Jamaica
Organ, Guitar, Vocals, Melodica / Reggae, Jamaica, Caribbean

In the early Wailers lineup, Winston Hubert McIntosh (Peter Tosh) stood apart from the other members not only because of his six-foot-plus height but because of his boasty-boy attitude. He was known as the "stepping razor" after a song Joe Higgs had written, and his knife-sharp temper could whittle many a bad man down to size. But he had a soft, extremely humorous side as well, as evidenced in his frequent wordplay: he complained about the "crime ministers who shit in the House of Represent-a-Thief" and called America "A-*sada*-ca, because there is nothing merry about it." Tosh joined up with Bunny Wailer and Bob Marley in 1962, and they rehearsed nearly two years before they made their Studio One debut with "Simmer Down." Tosh played guitar, melodica, piano, and organ on many of their early tracks and even played behind American pop star Johnny Nash's Columbia Records sessions in the late '60s, when Nash had hired the Wailers as songwriters. By 1973, Tosh felt the need to pursue a solo career because of the mass of material he had written and his dissatisfaction with Island Records boss Chris Blackwell. *Legalize It* was his debut in 1976, remaking many of his earlier Jamaican recordings and giving the marijuana movement its most potent anthem in the title track, which Tosh would perform not once but twice in his '70s live concerts. A firm opponent of the hypocritical "shitstem," Tosh was a favorite target of Babylon's legal forces. Police in Jamaica beat him nearly to death on at least three occasions, and he bore the scars till his death. *Equal Rights*, 1977's follow-up, provided a key line that echoed 15 years later in the mouths of LA rioters: "I don't want no peace, I want equal rights and justice!" The Rolling Stones, impressed by Tosh's ferocious and unflinching posture, signed him to their fledgling label and released *Bush Doctor* in 1978, another series of hymns and harrangues. *Mystic Man* (1979) and *Wanted: Dread & Alive* (1981) kept a militant attitude while trying to cross over to the mainstream that Marley had conquered, without achieving anything near Marley's success. Following 1983's *Mama Africa* and a live album from that tour, Tosh disappeared for four years, seeking advice from traditional medicine men in Africa and trying to extricate himself from various recording agreements when he found his records released in South Africa against provisions in his contracts. In 1987, shortly after the release of *No Nuclear War*, Tosh was assassinated at his home in Kingston. Only one of the three gunmen responsible was arrested; he was sentenced to hang after a brief trial. Like Marley, Tosh left at least ten children and no will. A brilliant documentary *Peter Tosh: Red X-Stepping Razor* was released in 1992, and there is hope that at least one more album will come out of the vaults. *—Roger Steffens*

Legalize It / 1976 / CBS ✦✦✦✦
Tosh cut this album after leaving the Wailers, but used virtually the entire Wailers band (minus Bob Marley) to do it. His "Legalize It," a plea about marijuana with a twist ("I'll advertise it"), is still winning. *— William Ruhlmann*

★ **Equal Rights** / 1977 / CBS ✦✦✦✦✦
Tosh's most political album includes his own version of "Get Up, Stand Up," as well as the chilling "Stepping Razor." The music, anchored by Sly and Robbie, is as tough as the lyrics. *—William Ruhlmann*

Bush Doctor / 1978 / Trojan ✦✦✦
"Creation" is Genesis set to music; "Moses" continues the story; "Don't Look Back" teams Tosh with Jagger. This is an appealing collection. *—Roger Steffens*

Wanted Dread & Alive / 1981 / EMI America ✦✦✦
Great Binghi roots-rave on "Rastafari Is," plus the gorgeous ballad "Fools Die" and other mixed pleasures. *—Roger Steffens*

Mama Africa / 1983 / EMI America ✦✦✦✦
A strong collection, it has the hit "Johnny B. Goode" and remakes of "Maga Dog" and "Stop That Train." *—Roger Steffens*

No Nuclear War / 1987 / EMI America ✦✦✦
His valedictory album has "Lesson in My Life," strangely foreshadowing his murder by a "friend." *—Roger Steffens*

The Toughest / 1996 / Heartbeat ✦✦✦✦
Tosh's roots were intertwined with Bob Marley's, and like Marley, his very earliest efforts had much more to do with ska than the reggae popularized by the Wailers. That doesn't mean that Tosh's earliest work wasn't very enjoyable and accomplished, although the spiritual and political concerns had yet to surface. This is a near-complete, 19-song retrospective of his Studio One recordings, two-thirds of which were produced by Coxsone Dodd in the mid-'60s, the remainder by Lee Perry at some later point. Exact source documentation is vague: some if not all of the Dodd tracks were certainly Wailers discs, not Tosh solo outings (some appear on compilations of Bob Marley and the Wailers' '60s material). At any rate, the Dodd sides are good cuts in the ska vein, with some flashes of developing diversity and sophistication: the rock-influenced "Can't You See," "Rasta Shook Them Up" (the first Wailers tune to refer to Rastafarianism), and a cover of the Temptations' "Don't Look Back" (which Tosh would record as a duet with Mick Jagger in 1978). The Lee Perry material, from an uncertain vintage, is much more identifiable as reggae entering its prime. "Rightful Ruler" has an early appearance by U-Roy, and a reverb-soaked version of "Downpresser," which Tosh would recut on his *Equal Rights* album, is the highlight of the disc. *—Richie Unterberger*

Twinkle Brothers

Reggae, Dub Poetry
Norman Grant is the unifying factor in the various lineups of the Twinkles over the past 20 years. Possessing a rootical North Coast sensibility, as opposed to the harder-edged Kingston vibe, the Twinkle Brothers' music is Rastafarian belting at its best. Grant is even a big star in reggae-loving Poland, where he has cut five albums for that market. *—Roger Steffens*

Live at Reggae Sunsplash: Since I Throw / 1984 / Genes ✦✦✦✦
Superb vocals and a representative live set. *—Ron Wynn*

★ **Free Africa** / 1990 / Frontline ✦✦✦✦✦
Grab anything you can find by this tremendous outfit. *—Ron Wynn*

U-Roy (Ewert Beckford)

Vocals / Reggae, Deejay
In the late 60s, Ewart Beckford (U-Roy) almost single-handedly invented the modern DJ rap style in Jamaica by toasting on the sound system of pioneer King Tubby, who was the first engineer to mix reverb and echo effects on deconstructed rhythm tracks. This led directly to the Jamaican peculiarity of having only one song per 7-inch single (the A-side being the vocal, the B-side being the "dub version" or rhythm bed that any local toaster could "skank" over with the events of the day). But U-Roy remains the most trickily tasteful exemplar of the style, due largely to his uncanny choice in tracks over which to toast, creating ad hoc dialogues with the singer, commenting on and responding to the lyrics in such classics of the form as "On the Beach," "Wear You to the Ball," and "Tide Is High," not to mention the royalty-ridiculing '70s scat "Chalice in the Palace," on which he invites the Queen herself to suck on the ganja pipe (chalice). Still active, living in Los Angeles, he is now referred to respectfully as Daddy U-Roy. *—Roger Steffens*

● **Dread in a Babylon** / 1975 / Frontline ✦✦✦✦
It's this veteran rapper's best album, comparable to any in this idiom. *—Michael G. Nastos*

Rock with I / 1992 / RAS ✦✦✦
While not quite as fluid or able to maintain the rapid-fire verbal pace of past sessions, legendary DJ/toaster U-Roy can still spin a powerful, hypnotic yarn. He hasn't lost his fire, religious zeal, or political and cultural convictions, and there are several strong message cuts and/or spiritual laments. But not everything is so heavy; there are also fun tracks where U-Roy demonstrates the flair, inflections, screams, and style that made him a DJ innovator. The sound, arrangements, and production are vintage reggae, with cymbals clashing, thudding bass lines, flickering guitars, and the echo and fades that characterized '70s reggae and dub. He's a venerable warrior, but U-Roy still has plenty to say. *—Ron Wynn*

Bunny Wailer (Neville O'Reilly Livingstone)

Percussion, Vocals / Reggae, Jamaica, Caribbean
Born Neville O'Reilly Livingstone and dubbed Bunny Wailer, this crucial Jamaican singer and songwriter was raised as Bob Marley's brother from the age of nine. As cofounder of the Wailers (along with Peter Tosh), Bunny gave high chromatic shadings to some of the most exhilarating harmonies ever pressed on wax, the equal of the finest work done by their contemporaries, the Impressions. Bunny's "Pass It On" was one of the standout tracks on the final album the Wailers did together as a trio, 1973's *Burning*. Three years later, Bunny released his first solo project, one of reggae's most majestic achievements, the roots classic *Blackheart Man*, which included hymnlike chants with titles like "Dreamland," "Bide Up," and "Rastaman." Bunny's baritone has been showcased in as many as three albums a year, most notably *Struggle* (1980); *Bunny Wailer Sings the Wailers* (1980s collection of covers); *Rock & Groove* (1981 dancehall classics); *Live* (recorded at his first solo concert in Kingston in December 1982); and *Liberation* (1988, consciousness-raiser that is the acknowledged peer of his spectacular debut album *Blackheart Man*). He won a Grammy in 1991 for *Time Will Tell*, a tribute collection of covers of Bob Marley songs. He has toured abroad twice, trying to overcome his reputation as reggae's most reclusive artist, backed by members of the original Skatalites, Sly and Robbie, and the Roots Radics. A spectacular show at NY's Madison Square Garden (1986) has been released on video. Today Bunny is obsessed with reaching the teenage dancehall crowd, attempting to wean them away from the predominant slackness of the form and back to a recognition of the truth and rights that were reggae's original concerns. He also feels the need to continue the work of his late partners, Tosh and Marley, bringing to oppressed people everywhere the twin messages of hope and the faith to carry on. *—Roger Steffens*

★ **Black Heart Man** / 1976 / Mango ✦✦✦✦✦
Maybe his best, certainly a classic. *—Ron Wynn*

Struggle / 1980 / Solomonic ✦✦✦
The title cut is anthemic; everything else is superb. *—Ron Wynn*

Bunny Wailer Sings the Wailers / 1980 / Mango ✦✦✦
As poignant a tribute as you'll ever hear. *—Ron Wynn*

Live / 1983 / Solomonic ✦✦✦✦
Tough to find, but worth the effort. *—Ron Wynn*

Roots Radics Rockers Reggae / 1983 / Shanachie ✦✦✦
A reggae original runs the genre's gamut. *—Ron Wynn*

Marketplace / 1985 / Shanachie ✦✦✦
Entertaining and enriching. *—Ron Wynn*

Protest / 1987 / Mango ✦✦✦
Inspirational. *—Ron Wynn*

Rootsman Skanking / 1987 / Shanachie ✦✦✦
Emphatic vocals. *—Ron Wynn*

Rule Dance Hall / 1987 / Shanachie ✦✦✦
Controversial content, but outstanding. —*Ron Wynn*

Liberation / 1989 / Shanachie ✦✦✦✦
A textbook Wailer outing. —*Ron Wynn*

Time Will Tell / 1991 / Shanachie ✦✦✦
Heartwarming, Grammy-winning remakes of Marley compositions are included. —*Roger Steffens*

Crucial! Roots Classics / 1994 / Shanachie ✦✦✦
This 14-track collection covers 1979-1982; the major themes are Jamaica's wretched political wars and the necessity for radical change. Although Wailer doesn't always specifically address individuals or situations, it's clear from the force and vocal authority that he's discussing the inequities in his homeland. Other than "Baldheaded Woman," these are uplifting, searing tunes demanding that the citzenry stop ignoring evils and unite for change. His voice is clear, urgent, and decisive, never more so than on "Free Jah Jah Children." —*Ron Wynn*

Wailing Souls

Reggae, Dub
If lead singer Winston "Pipe" Matthews sounds like a higher-pitched version of Bob Marley, it may be because he was tutored by the same teacher (Joe Higgs) in the same yard that produced the Wailers. The Souls have gone through many different lineups, but Pipe and his partner Lloyd "Bread" McDonald have survived as a duo, and currently record for Columbia Records. Through most of their history they were one of reggae's only quartets with shimmering harmonies that gave voice to Jamaican folk-sayings and righteous religious rumblings. —*Roger Steffens*

★ **Wild Suspense** / 1979 / Mango ✦✦✦✦✦
These brilliant quartet triumphs echo the harmonic heights of the early Wailers. It's virtually their greatest hits, backed by Sly and Robbie. —*Roger Steffens*

Firehouse Rock / 1980 / Shanachie ✦✦✦
Junjo-produced, with the Radics mixed by Scientist at King Tubby's. What's not to like? —*Roger Steffens*

The Best of the Wailing Soul / 1984 / Empire ✦✦✦✦
These Channel One classics were produced by Jo Jo Hookim and backed by the Revolutionaries. —*Roger Steffens*

Kingston 14 / 1987 / RAS ✦✦✦
The Wailing Souls belong in any short list of great reggae vocal groups, especially in terms of harmonies and songwriting. The compositions on this '87 set are uniformly gripping, finely writtten, and exquisitely performed, despite the fact Winston Matthews, Lloyd McDonald, and Devon Bedford are all complementary singers rather than spectacular leads. But their trading of the spotlight and those shimmering harmonies are so superbly done that this slight defect is totally obscured. The Wailing Souls show those unaware of their skills that they're in the pantheon of great reggae trios. —*Ron Wynn*

All over the World A / 1992 / Chaos ✦✦✦✦
A genre-busting all-star duo debut, it features guest shots from L. Shankar to U-Roy. —*Roger Steffens*

Delroy Wilson

Vocals / Soul, Reggae
A great veteran of the Jamaican vocal scene, Delroy Wilson's been performing and recording since he was 11 years old. His song "Better Must Come" became the theme song for Michael Manley during the 1972 election for Jamaica's prime minister. Wilson's recorded for Studio One, CCAS, Empire, BP, Pioneer, Top Rank, and Vista, among others. He has a vibrant, extremely soulful sound and can also easily handle roots material. —*Ron Wynn*

● **The Best of Delroy Wilson** / 1991 / Heartbeat ✦✦✦✦
Superb soul-tinged reggae from a veteran of the Jamaican music wars. —*Ron Wynn*

Special / 1993 / RAS ✦✦✦
This set included a remake of Wilson's first major hit, "Time Hard," which became the theme song for Michael Manley's first triumphant campaign for Prime Minister in the '70s. While the production has the requisite contemporary touches, it also gives Wilson's full, gritty voice prominence and doesn't overwhelm it with electronic or synthesized studio backdrop. Those unfamiliar with Wilson's early songs will be brought up to speed by the "Medley of Hits," which cleverly incorporates snatches of several early reggae gems. —*Ron Wynn*

Yabby You (Vivian Jackson)

Vocals / Reggae
Yabby You was born Vivian Jackson in a Kingston ghetto. By the time he was 17, Jackson was so malnourished that he had to be hospitalized. He eventually left with severe arthritis and crippled legs. While he could not

work, he had musical talent, and taking his cues from divine inspiration that he feels comes from the sounds of nature around him, and with the help of friends, he founded a harmony trio, the Prophets, in 1972. They made their single debut with "Conquering Lion," a classically styled reggae song with a deeply personal message. They made a few more singles and eventually they all appeared on Jackson's debut album, *Conquering Lion.* Throughout the decade, he recorded frequently on his Prophets labels. He was closely affiliated with King Tubby, whose dubs often appeared on the B-sides of Jackson's singles. It was Tubby who gave Jackson his famous nickname Yabby You. Some of Yabby You's better-known albums from this period include *Deliver Me from My Enemies* (1977) and *Chant Down Babylon Kingdom.* When not recording his own material, Yabby You launched the careers of other new singers including Michael Prophet, Wayne Wade, and Tony Tuff. He also began producing the early recordings of such performers as Willie Williams, Ras I-buna, and Half Pint. A Yabby You-produced recording usually features a distinctive bass line combined with organs, horns, and soaring harmonies that he uses to create a meditative, spiritual atmosphere. He continued recording steadily through the mid-'80s, and then abruptly stopped after a 1985 North American tour with his backup band, the Gladiators. He often needed crutches to perform. After that, he recorded, but nothing was released so in essence, Yabby You disappeared until 1991 when some of those recordings began to emerge. After that, he resurfaced and began releasing new and old material again. —*Sandra Brennan*

Conquering Lion / 1975 / Prophet ✦✦✦
These debut beauties are deliciously menacing and admonitory. —*Roger Steffens*

Deliver Me from My Enemies / 1977 / Prophet ✦✦✦✦
Here is timeless social commentary and Rasta prophecy. —*Roger Steffens*

● **One Love, One Heart** / 1983 / Shanachie ✦✦✦✦
An anthology of some of his greatest hits: what to bring when you summer in the cave of the Dead Sea Scrolls. —*Roger Steffens*

Yellowman (Winston Foster)

Vocals / Reggae, Raggamuffin, Dancehall, Jamaica, Caribbean
Yellowman was one of the hottest toasters in Jamaican dancehalls during the '80s and though his career slowed down toward the decade's end, he has begun to come back in the early '90s with a mellower, slightly less controversial style. It was his rude style, filled with lyrics many consider homophobic and explicitly sexist, that inspired the word "slackness" as a descriptor for some types of dancehall music. But he has always been more than merely vulgar, and careful listening to his lyrics reveals a wicked sense of humor and even a genuine consciousness.

He was born Winston Foster and is an albino, something that made life difficult growing up as albinos are outcasts in Jamaica. Rather than be consumed by this, he became charismatic and outgoing, marketing himself as Jamaica's newest sex symbol. With his witty, blindingly rapid-fire, erotic rap describing his bedroom prowess, he had little trouble convincing his audiences of the early '80s. Soon he was known as "Mr. Sexy." He soon proved himself able to out-slack the rudest toasters in town. This has earned him considerable criticism from those who find much of Yellowman's bawdy repartee irresponsible and damaging even though it is often spoken with tongue firmly in cheek. During the '80s, Yellowman recorded prolifically and in 1982 had 40 records circulating in Jamaica at the same time. With so much music out there, it is not surprising that the quality of the songs varied widely. Much of his best material was produced by Junjo Lawes between 1982 and 1985. At his peak, Yellowman had a contract with CBS Records, New York, and an international following. By the late '80s, he had slowed down considerably. He re-emerged in the '90s with a new style. He was still energetic and sharp, but his dancehall riddims became more melodic and he spoke a little more slowly. Some of his songs have become more conscious as well. —*Sandra Brennan*

Mister Yellowman / 1982 / Shanachie ✦✦✦✦
Yellowman suffers from his reputation, yet in the early '80s he came out with some of the best reggae around—sly, irreverent, and very personal, without the tedious slackness that has marred his recent work. Especially notable is the tremendous production work of Henry "Junjo" Lawes (buy anything with his name on it!), and the incomparable asides from where-is-he-now? co-MC Fathead (Bim!). —*Carl Hoyt, Original Music*

Bad Boy Skanking / 1982 / Shanachie ✦✦✦
Though Yellowman has become tediously slack of late, this 1982 recording shows him in top form, with social commentaries both cryptic and trenchant. Such great tunes as "Can't Stand It," "Tarzan," and the title track are made even greater by the presence of Fathead and his repertoire of sounds from "oink" to "bim." It's an undeservedly neglected classic. —*Carl Hoyt, Original Music*

● **One in a Million** / 1989 / Shanachie ✦✦✦✦
One of the few nonslack albums in his career, this boasts Yellowman's signature rap "Mad over Me" and serious scenarios of guns and fire. —*Roger Steffens*

Party / 1991 / RAS ✦✦✦

Yellowman often sounded casual and mild during this session. He alternated between patois and English, mixed toasting and singing, and even included a surprise cut, "Oldies But Goodies," on which he performed decent covers of such tunes as "Rock Around the Clock." The Roots Radics' rhythm tracks were bright and active, giving him a traditional reggae backdrop with rich bass/guitar interplay and percussive energy. Anyone aware of his reputation will be surprised by these nine tracks' content; none contained anything overtly offensive, and most were simply pleasant, if at times bland, compositions. —*Ron Wynn*

Reggae on the Move / 1992 / RAS ✦✦✦✦

Prayer / 1994 / RAS ✦✦✦

Although he's long been the king of "slack" (vulgar) toasts, Yellowman often sounds serious and less energized on this collection of recent cuts. Such songs as "Prayer," "Crowd Africa," and "Politician" are a long way from the fast-paced, sexually overt material that made his reputation. Even the less political fare isn't delivered with the verbal frenzy or lyrical coarseness that once characterized his music. Yellowman is aided by outstanding background singers Ruddy Thomas and Derrick Barnett, and anyone unfamiliar with past Yellowman might think they had picked up a Mutabaruka disc by mistake at times. —*Ron Wynn*

Various Artists

★ **The Best of Studio One, Vol. 1** / Heartbeat ✦✦✦✦✦

This stunning series is devoted to the voluminous output of Clement Dodd's Jamaican studio. The first two volumes cover the best from the '60s and '70s, from shimmying ska to rock steady. —*John Floyd*

Best of Studio One, Vol. 3: Downbeat the Ruler ... / Heartbeat ✦✦✦✦✦

This third installment features a scalding set of instrumentals, full of crashing cymbals, twisting bass lines, and razor-sharp guitars. —*John Floyd*

Best of the Best, Vol. 1 / 1993 / RAS ✦✦✦✦

While this anthology isn't overloaded with huge hits, it contains several formidable reggae acts, including longtime stars Dennis Brown, Gregory Isaacs, and Sugar Minott, whose numbers are produced in the contemporary synthesizer-dominated mode, but boast excellent lead vocals. Beres Hammond, among the finest pure vocalists of his generation, has a tremendous number, "Putting Up Resistance," which he reworks in collaboration with vintage toaster U-Roy, still among the great verbal ad-libbers. Others on the set include breathy (and slightly overrated) female vocalist J.C. Lodge, popular dancehall talents Yami Bolo, Half Pint, and Frankie Paul, and the energetic Brigadier Jerry and Junior Reid. —*Ron Wynn*

Big Blunts / 1994 / Tommy Boy ✦✦✦✦

The link between reggae and ganja has always been a prominent one, although that's hardly been the sole motivational or compositional force driving the music. But this fine 12-track anthology features some seminal tracks outlining and celebrating that connection; these include the remarkably influential "Under Mi Sleng Teng," both Wayne Smith's original and a remix featuring special guests Cypress Hill and a KRS-One sample, as well as Barrington Levy's spectacular version of "Under Mi Sensi" and extended treatments of the Mighty Diamonds' "Pass the Kutchie" and Rita Marley's "One Draw." Add outstanding numbers from U-Roy, Ninjaman, Sugar Minott, and Frankie Paul and you've got a throbbing, memorable reggae set. —*Ron Wynn*

● **Calling Rastafari** / Nighthawk ✦✦✦✦✦

An excellent anthology, with gems from Culture, Itals, and others. —*Ron Wynn*

● **Clancy Eccles Presents His Reggae Revue** / Heartbeat ✦✦✦✦✦

Sixteen tracks produced by Eccles between 1967 and 1972, including cuts by Alton Ellis, Joe Higgs (as part of a duo with Roy Wilson), Beres Hammond, and Eccles himself, as well as more obscure names. Features the tight rhythm sections, smooth soulful vocals, and bass-heavy arrangements that are among rock steady's chief trademarks. Unusually well produced for a vintage reggae reissue, it was digitally transferred from the original master tapes, with extensive liner notes, comments on each song by Eccles himself, and six previously unreleased outtakes and alternate versions. —*Richie Unterberger*

Club Ska '67 / 1980 / Mango ✦✦✦✦✦

This decent assortment of latter-day ska tracks serves as a nice complement to the label's *Intensified* series. —*John Floyd*

D.J.'s, Pt. 1 / 1994 / RAS ✦✦✦

This first of a two-part collection highlighting big reggae hits from the '80s spotlights toasters, Jamaica's fast-talking, high-speed verbal improvisers who influenced the first generation of African-American rappers. The anthology includes such perennials as Yellowman, Brigadier Jerry, U-Roy, Eek-A-Mouse, and Charlie Chaplin, whose elocution, pacing, and style differ considerably from the new generation's Sanchez, Little Lenny, Johnny P., and Tiger. While no one has done more openly vulgar toasting

in reggae history than Yellowman, such songs as "Girls Guide" by Johnny P. or "Wicked & Wild" by Little Lenny lack the flowing wit vintage toasters such as I-Roy or Big Youth brought to their exaggerated sexual exploits and outlandish narratives. —*Ron Wynn*

Dancehall Classics / RAS ✦✦✦

Reggae producer Jah Screw lacks the visibility of pioneer studio mavens like Coxsone Dodd or Lee Perry, but has enjoyed success in Jamaica; he helped make Barrington Levy a star. This 12-track anthology includes his more recent material, showing Screw's ability to coax outstanding vocal performances from a varied lineup that includes Frankie Paul, Sanchez, Mickey Little, and Bev Love. Screw doesn't emphasize synthesized backing and electronic surroundings as much as some of his comrades, maintaining links with the traditional roots-oriented horn sound. But he doesn't neglect contemporary voicings and studio tricks, giving this set a good balance between past and present reggae values. —*Ron Wynn*

● **Explosive Rock Steady: Joe Gibbs' Amalgamated Label** / 1992 / Heartbeat ✦✦✦✦✦

If ska reflected the clamor for Jamaican independence in the early '60s, rock steady signified the hopeful innocence of a new beginning. It bubbles through the stuttered bass line and pre-reggae skank but primarily in fragile lead vocals and yearning choruses perpetually on the verge of a swoon. Except of course for Lee "Scratch" Perry, whose "Upsetter" signature song bristles with understated menace—and whose pointy producer's ears honed classic performances by Roy Shirley, Errol Dunkley, and the lost-in-the-mists-of-history Overtakers. —*Bob Tarte*

From Kongo to Zion / Heartbeat ✦✦✦✦✦

Vocal and percussion music from Jamaica's four major local religious traditions: Central African-based Kumina, Afro-Christian, Revival Zion, and Rastafari. Splendid music in its own right, this dramatically underlines the diversity of neo-African adaptations in the Caribbean and is a main root of reggae. The notes are unusually good. —*John Storm Roberts*

Go Ska Go / Oct. 17, 1995 / Heartbeat ✦✦✦✦✦

This originally comprised the second disc of the *Ska Bonanza* compilation. Nineteen tracks, including excellent cuts by Bob Marley & the Wailers, Toots & the Maytals, and Don Drummond. It's preferable to buy the *Ska Bonanza* set in one piece rather than opt for one or both of the two discs that were separately issued (the other being *Streets of Ska*) in its place, though. —*Richie Unterberger*

★ **Groove Yard** / Mango ✦✦✦✦✦

If you're looking for a crash course in reggae, this is the place. The biggest names from Island Records with their biggest hits appear on this generous 70-minute set. It includes key songs from Jimmy Cliff, the Melodians, Augustus Pablo, Junior Murvin, and 15 others. —*John Floyd*

Heartbeat Reggae / Heartbeat ✦✦✦✦✦

A tremendous collection, culled from labels on the Heartbeat roster. —*Ron Wynn*

A History of Dub: The Golden Age / 1995 / Munich ✦✦✦

Twelve dub cuts spanning the mid-'70s to the mid-'80s, licensed from the Heartbeat, Greensleeves, and Blood & Fire labels. The range is too perfunctory, and the liner notes too brief, for this to qualify as a benchmark retrospective of the style. It does have cuts by some of the major exponents of dub (Scientist, Lee Perry, King Tubby's, and Augustus Pablo), as well as dubbafied versions of songs by vocal acts lke Culture, Joe Gibbs, and Black Uhuru. —*Richie Unterberger*

A History of Jamaican Vocal Harmony / 1996 / Munich ✦✦✦

As "histories" go, this is scant, with 11 tracks licensed from the Heartbeat, Greensleeves, and Blood & Fire labels, and little in the way of liner notes. For someone who wants just a taste of reggae harmony around, though, it's all right, with cuts by Black Uhuru, the Mighty Diamonds, the Meditations, Culture, the Gladiators, Israel Vibration, the Abyssinians, and others. Of special interest is the Paragons' "Tide Is High," which was covered by Blondie in 1980 for a No. 1 hit. —*Richie Unterberger*

In the Belly of the Whale / 1994 / Shark ✦✦✦

This 13-cut anthology featuring dancehall cuts includes both veterans and challengers. The most notable entry from the venerable side is the Heptones, who reprise their signature song "The Book of Rules" in two settings; one teams them with toaster Shaka Shamba, who provides an entertaining if discursive monologue; the other doesn't have the riveting harmonies of the original but does have an up-to-date musical framework. The great Sugar Minott displays his wonderful voice on "Rub-A-Dub Sound," smoothly mixing soulful urgency and sexual innuendo. Interesting newer acts include Baby Wayne, Glen Ricks, Sugar Black, and Chopper. As with most anthologies, quality varies from track to track, but it's a good overview of contemporary dancehall. —*Ron Wynn*

Intensified!: Original Ska 1962-66 / 1979 / Mango ✦✦✦✦✦

This 16-track disc (part one of two) offers a fine introduction to reggae's roots. Features innovators such as Don Drummond, the Skatalites, and the Maytals. —*Chris Woodstra*

Intensified!: Original Ska, Vol. 2 1963-67 / Mango ✦✦✦✦✦
Part two, *More Intensified* contains some of the better known ska songs from the Ethiopians ("Train to Skaville") and Don Drummond ("Man in the Street"), but its strength lies in the coverage of the often overlooked artists such as Marguerita and Sir Lord Comic. Both volumes of the series offer a good overview of ska. —*Chris Woodstra*

Jahmento Records / 1994 / Hightone ✦✦✦
The bubbling voice of Half Pint gets this anthology off to a rousing start, and the energy level seldom dips through the other 11 cuts. This is driving, surging dancehall, nonpolitical in content and frenetic in pace, production style, and performance, aimed at the hip-hop, dance, and rock audience. The vocals are mostly competent; Edi Fitzroy and Wayne Wonder are above average. But this is more music for dancing and partying than listening, with the beat and production dominant. —*Ron Wynn*

Jammin' / Mango ✦✦✦✦✦
Offering the best-known artists and songs, this 23-track sampler is one of the best single-disc introductions to reggae. —*Chris Woodstra*

A Man & His Music, Vol. 2 / RAS ✦✦✦✦
The synthesizer began to dominate reggae in the '80s, thanks to the massive success of Wayne Smith's "Under Me Sleng Teng." This 13-track set, the second of three highlighting the productions of King Jammy, appropriately begins with "Under Me Sleng Teng," which set the stage for numerous variations. In addition, toasting and vocal styles also changed; they became faster, more slashing, and less soulful in order to better punctuate and accompany the slithering, snaking electric keyboards and synth patterns underneath. While traditionalists bemoaned the dearth of "Praise Jah" songs and de-emphasis on soul singing, the new generation hailed the acrobatics of Tenor Saw, Pinchers, and Pad Anthony. These are the songs that paved the way for the late-'80s and early-'90s hip-hop/dancehall explosion. —*Ron Wynn*

Mojo Rock Steady / 1994 / Heartbeat ✦✦✦✦✦
Jamaican music fans still fondly remember the rock steady era, particularly those who love soulful, evocative ballads and romantic tunes. This 16-cut anthology culled from Coxsone Dodd's seminal Studio One vaults includes magnificent group numbers by the Clarendonians, Gaylads, Bassies, and Minstrels, plus equally impressive solo outings from Hugh Godfrey, Denise Darlington, and Hortense Ellis. There are also strong instrumentals by Roland Alphonso and the Soul Brothers and King Stitt, and Alton Ellis demonstrates his classic soul approach on "Whipping the Prince," aided by the Soul Vendors. Sublime, gorgeous singing from a prime period in Jamaica's rich musical history. —*Ron Wynn*

More Heartbeat Reggae Now! / Heartbeat/Rounder ✦✦✦
Heartbeat's most recent reggae anthology line extends into contemporary territory, including commendable outings by Beres Hammond and Garnett Silk, plus material by dancehall stars Tony Rebel, Frankie Paul, and Baby Wayne (teaming with Dennis Brown). The roots and hard-core contingent will much prefer the tracks by Burning Spear, Rita Marley, Marcia Griffiths, Culture, Gregory Isaacs, and the Abyssinians. The anthology demonstrates how much reggae production, emphasis, and style have changed. An impressive gathering of reggae artists, with one foot in the past and another in the present. —*Ron Wynn*

Musical Feast: Mrs. Pottinger's High Note and Gayfeet Label / 1991 / Heartbeat ✦✦✦✦✦
In contrast to the brittle edges of digital production, these recordings from the back of the Tip-Top Record Shop at 37 Orange Street, Kingston, bask in the kitchen-table warmth of vacuum-tube equipment technology. Sweet, fragile harmonies, bouncing bass lines, and taffy-pull organ phrases contribute to the atmosphere of intimacy, but most of all, label-owner Sonia Pottinger's auteur's touch provides the sense of an unwavering attention to quality. All the hallmarks of a great pop collection are here: a novelty number worthy of an idiot savant (the Gaylads "ABC Rocky Steady"), uncredited cover versions (appropriating both the Beatles and Nat King Cole), an early duff ditty by a future star (Judy Mowatt's "I Shall Sing"), verses to inspire (from Strange Cole's "Let the Power Fall"), and flat-out scorchers like the Conqueror's "Look Pon You" and Ken Boothe's "Say You." —*Bob Tarte*

Nice Up Dance—The RAS Tapes 2 / 1991 / Rykodisc ✦✦✦
This second set of reggae hits issued on CD from the RAS vaults included two classics, Tiger's "Bam Bam" and Paul Blake and Bloodfire Posse's "Get Flat," plus some other super numbers, notably Foxy Brown's reggae remake of Tracy Chapman's "Fast Car" and Little Kirk's variations on Michael Jackson's "Man in the Mirror." The dancehall slant was heavy, with other songs featuring Little Lenny, Johnny P., Sanchez, Tippa Lee & Rappa Robert, and Super Glen, among others. —*Ron Wynn*

Original Club Ska: Best of Studio One / 1990 / Heartbeat ✦✦✦✦✦
Ace Jamaican sessionmen like Tommy McCook, Roland Alphonso, Don Drummond, and Ernest Ranglin have a heavy hand in this decent collection of mid-'60s ska recordings from Studio One. Includes tracks by the Wailers ("Ska Jerk," a takeoff on "Cool Jerk"), the Skatalites, the Gaylads, and others. —*Richie Unterberger*

Real Authentic Sampler, Vol. 3 / RAS ✦✦✦
This recent RAS sampler spotlights current and contemporary reggae, with a mix of styles. The hot team of Chaka Demus & Pliers are dominant on "Ruff This Year," while Tony Rebel sounds far more interesting on "Firing Strong" than on his Chaos LP, and Israel Vibration and Delroy Wilson bring veteran skills and vintage sounds to the program on their cuts. Dean Fraser's version of "Unforgettable" comes dangerously close to background music, but J.C. Lodge's "Love You to the Max" has a good arrangement and nice rhythmic underpinning, while Cocoa Tea does what's expected on "Kingston Hot." Gregory Isaacs and Dennis Brown are creditable, but far from their peak, and Yellowman is thankfully more lyrically restrained than usual on "Reggae on the Move." —*Ron Wynn*

Reggae Classics / 1990 / Dcc ✦✦✦✦✦
A good collection, but most of the selections are available elsewhere. —*Ron Wynn*

Reggae Dance Party / 1987 / RAS ✦✦✦✦✦
Reggae's link to dance was explored on this 11-cut anthology, which featured single vocalists, groups, and an occasional toaster doing cuts celebrating or extolling dance. It included an interesting reworking of "Let the Good Times Roll" by Michigan & Smiley retitled "Reggae Ska," plus the complete ten-minute-plus hit "Get Flat" by Paul Blake & Bloodfire Posse, as well as Gregory Isaacs' superb "Private Beach Party" and Sugar Minott's swaying "Rub a Dub Sound." There was also Wayne Smith's "Teach Me to Dance" and Barrington Levy's "Do the Dance," both novelty numbers made into effective vocal and musical workouts. Black Uhuru's "Great Train Robbery" and Horace Andy's "Elementary" were sociopolitical tracks with a dance beat, and J.C. Lodge's "You Can Dance" explored the steamier side of meeting on the dance floor, as did Don Carlos' "Springheel Skanking." —*Ron Wynn*

● **Reggae Greats: Strictly for Lovers** / Mango ✦✦✦✦✦
A high-caliber review of artists who popularized the "lovers" style. —*Ron Wynn*

★ **Reggae Greats: Strictly for Rockers** / Mango ✦✦✦✦✦
Here is a well-done overview, this time for "rockers" artists. —*Ron Wynn*

Reggae Jamdown—The RAS Tapes / 1990 / Rykodisc ✦✦✦
There are 25 certified reggae hits on this CD anthology culled from RAS' vaults. It's heavy on dancehall selections, but also has several rockers and traditional reggae songs by Dennis Brown, Hugh Mundell, Freddie McGregor, Ijahman, and Israel Vibration. The other numbers feature artists among the hottest dancehall performers: Sugar Minott, Pinchers, Charlie Chaplin, Frankie Paul, Half Pint, and Admiral Tibet. Unlike the sexually oriented material that now dominates dancehall releases, this anthology had a hefty amount of sociopolitical protest material alongside the requisite tunes, like Minott's "Rub A Dub Sound." —*Ron Wynn*

Roof International / 199_ / Producer's Trophy/Hightone ✦✦✦✦
Hightone's expansion into reggae and dancehall continues with this 14-cut anthology. While most songs are the usual party or sex/slack material favored by many dancehall performers, there's also some solid socio-political material. Beenie Man's "If You Live by the Gun" outlines the bleak consequences for those who make their decisions via firearms, while Dread Bob's "Mad City" and Silk's "Man Is Just a Man" manage to communicate effective messages without being polemics. Jigsy King's "My Sound Kill" and "Every Mickle Make a Muckle" score points for the silly song, while Toney Curtis' "If I Follow My Heart" and "Rain from the Sky" are reminiscent of vintage lover's rock and rockers reggae. —*Ron Wynn*

Roots of Reggae, Vol. 1: Ska / Aug. 20, 1996 / Rhino ✦✦✦✦
Roots of Reggae, Vol. 1: Ska captures 17 hits from the late '60s. Many of the genre's classic songs and artists are here—including Prince Buster, Duke Reid, Laurel Aitken, Bunny & Skitter, and Derrick Morgan—but the compilation ignores such major artists as Desmond Dekker. Consequently, *Roots of Reggae, Vol. 1: Ska* can only be seen as a useful sampler, not a definitive overview of original ska. —*Leo Stanley*

Roots of Reggae, Vol. 2: Rock Steady / Aug. 20, 1996 / Rhino ✦✦✦✦
Roots of Reggae, Vol. 2: Rock Steady captures 18 hits from the late '60s. Although the compilers don't follow strict rules about what is and what is not rock steady, many of the genre's classic songs and performances—including the Melodians' "Swing and Dine," the Paragons' "The Tide Is High," and the Duke Reid Group's "Soul Style"—are included on the collection, making it an excellent one-stop introduction to the music. —*Leo Stanley*

Scandal Ska / 1989 / Mango ✦✦✦✦✦
Released as a tie-in with the movie *Scandal*, this 16-cut comp of early-'60s recordings is actually one of the very best ska collections. Includes cuts by Bob Marley, Don Drummond, Desmond Dekker, Jimmy Cliff, Laurel Aitken, and Millie Small, as well as Ernest Ranglin, who contributes a killer instrumental version of "Exodus." —*Richie Unterberger*

Singers, Pt. 2 / 1994 / RAS ✦✦✦
This 14-track compilation, the second in a two-part series, features both great pure vocalists and contemporary performers doing big hits. Gre-

gory Isaacs, Freddie McGregor, and Sugar Minott take vocal honors, with Isaacs gliding atop a synthesized backbeat on "Rumors," and McGregor's lean, soulful leads triumphant on "Across the Border." Black Uhuru's "Dread in the Mountain" strikes a pastoral note, while Half Pint, Pinchers, and Little Kirk bring a contemporary dancehall flavor to their numbers. Kirk's "Child Abuse" is the anthology's best message track, and the set also contains the original version of Inner Circle's "Bad Boys," which later became the theme song for the Fox Network's "Cops." — *Ron Wynn*

★ **Ska Bonanza: The Studio One Ska Years** / 1991 / Heartbeat ✦✦✦✦✦
Forty-one-song, double-CD compilation of '60s ska, produced by Clement S. Dodd, largely (if not totally; the documentation is vague) at Studio One. Most of the big names of ska's vintage era are represented: Bob Marley & the Wailers, the Skatalites, Lee Perry, Don Drummond, Toots & the Maytals, Alton Ellis. Considering that ska's sometimes thought of as a homogenous style, the range of actual sounds and variants is impressive. There's New Orleans R&B derivations, doo-wop-influenced ska, Motownish uptempo struts, soulful slower tunes, and instrumentals. The cuts by the unknowns include pleasurable surprises that match or exceed the ones by the stars; Frank Anderson's tropical instrumental "Wheel and Turn," for instance, or the goofy modern doo wop jive of Chuck Josephs' "Du Du Wap." It isn't necessarily the best ska compilation that could have been concocted; *Scandal Ska*, to name just one, is on the whole a more exciting anthology. It is, however, one of the best of the relatively few available, and thus for the time being merits the highest rating. It's since been divided into two separate compilations, *Streets of Ska* and *Go Ska Go*. But get the original two-disc version if you can, as it's more convenient to have all the tracks and liner notes in one place. — *Richie Unterberger*

Solid Gold: Coxsone Style / 1992 / Heartbeat ✦✦✦
Harder-edged than any of the smooth Studio One reissues, this anthology confirms the growing suspicion that—until something new skanks along—reggae hit its artistic peak some 20 years ago. Songs are tougher than usual too, including versions of "Rivers of Babylon" and the one-stanza-short-of-perfection "Declaration of Rights," plus flinty instruments by Jackie Mitoo and Ernest Ranglin that lead you back to PiL's *Metal Box*. Only quibble: where are the women? With the addition of four new tracks on this reissue, the compilers could have righted past oversights by easily including the sistren. — *Bob Tarte*

★ **The Story of Jamaican Music: Tougher than Tough** / Mango ✦✦✦✦✦
Island Records was the Jamaican music lifeline for curious Americans in the 1960s, bringing us the music of Bob Marley and the Wailers, Toots and the Maytals, Justin Hines, Gregory Isaacs. This marvelous anthology's four discs are chronologically arranged, with the first covering the amalgam of American genres that were absorbed into Jamaican culture: bebop and swing, New Orleans R&B, Chicago and Memphis soul, country, and film soundtracks. The second volume cements reggae's emergence as an evocative love music and voice of the nationalistic/militant Rasta generation. Volumes three and four chronicle reggae's final maturation into a hit form and show the inevitable production uniformities that arise when any style must produce hits for a large audience. This does not claim to be the definitive reggae anthology, so take it for what it is—Island's portrait of reggae's beginnings, growth, and flowering into a prime international style. — *Ron Wynn*

Streets of Ska / Oct. 17, 1995 / Heartbeat ✦✦✦✦✦
Originally the first disc of the double-CD *Ska Bonanza*. Twenty-two tracks from ska's heyday, including numbers by the Skatalites, Lee Perry, Don Drummond, and Roland Alphonso, as well as less famous figures like Chuck Josephs and Frank Anderson. It's better to find the original *Ska Bonanza* than to buy one or both of its halves (the other being *Go Ska Go*) separately, though. — *Richie Unterberger*

This Is Lovers Reggae / 1991 / RAS ✦✦✦✦
Lover's rock was reggae's sentimental, sometimes sappy but often hypnotic end. These were frequently soul or R&B covers, done either by male crooners or innocent-sounding female balladeers. The 12 tracks on this first of two volumes culled from Ariwa's catalog includes Sandra Cross' wonderful cover of "So in Love," Brown Sugar's coy version of Barbara Lewis' "Hello Stranger," and a great remake of Curtis Mayfield's "I'm So Proud" by Kofi. These aren't some of reggae's biggest names, but they acquit themselves well. Another gem is Slim Linton's "Two's Company," a number that nicely balances jealousy and anticipation. — *Ron Wynn*

This Is Lovers Reggae, Vol. 2 / Ariwa ✦✦✦
This second volume devoted to classic lover's rock reggae has two less tunes than its predecessor and includes repeat appearances from Sandra Cross, Kofi, Slim Linton, John McLean, and Robotiks, although this time Just Dale is their featured vocalist. Cross again sounds sublime, as does Kofi on a marvelous reworking of the Emotions' "Don't Ask My Neighbors." Tomorrow's People makes the original Royalettes version of "Gonna Take a Miracle" seem like a cynical, bitter effort by comparison, while Sister Audrey's "My Thing" matches any contemporary dancehall tune in its lyrical boldness and suggestiveness. — *Ron Wynn*

☆ **This Is Reggae Music, Vol. 1** / 1974 / Island ✦✦✦✦✦
First of five essential volumes. You can't have one without the others. — *Michael G. Nastos*

☆ **This Is Reggae Music, Vol. 2** / 1975 / Mango ✦✦✦✦✦
A compilation with Scotty & Lorna Bennett, Arthur Louis, and Desi Young. — *Michael G. Nastos*

☆ **This Is Reggae Music, Vol. 3** / 1976 / Mango ✦✦✦✦✦
A compilation with Junior Murvin, Prince Jazzbo, and Bunny Wailer. — *Michael G. Nastos*

Towering Dub Inferno / 1990 / Rykodisc ✦✦✦
Dub, the stripped-down instrumental covers of prior vocal hits, has long been a favored style in Jamaica. Ryko issued on CD in 1990 a 14-song anthology using great songs that had been previously released on cassette by ROIR. The selections include numbers by the idiom's finest producers, Scientist, Niney the Observer, and the Mad Professor, taking classics originally done by Lee Perry, Prince Far I, and many others. — *Ron Wynn*

Towering Dub Inferno: ROIR Tapes / Rykodisc ✦✦✦✦✦
A powerhouse compilation, with Lee Remy, Scientist, and others. — *Ron Wynn*

Treasure Isle / Heartbeat ✦✦✦✦✦
Duke Reid was among Jamaica's most prolific and innovative producers. His artists combined vintage R&B and soul influences with insights and visions gleaned from their daily experiences. The results were brilliant tunes covering both the end of rock steady and beginning of reggae, and this anthology collects 17 classics by groups and single artists. Highlights include tracks by the Gladiators, Paragons, and Versatiles, and a great tune pairing toaster/DJ legend U-Roy with the Melodians. Phyllis Dilddon, Freddie McKay, Tyrone Evans, and Dave Barker are also prominently featured. A wonderful collection of premier early material from a major Jamaican label. — *Ron Wynn*

Truth and Rights / 1994 / Heartbeat ✦✦✦✦✦
The rockers and lover's rock era is recaptured on this 16-cut anthology featuring vintage songs from many marvelous performers. They include the deceased Jacob Miller, the incomparable Big Youth and Dennis Brown, and other classy, first-rate singers such as Delroy Wilson, Freddie McGregor, the Heptones, and Johnny Clarke. It's great to hear these songs; there won't be another era like it again. — *Ron Wynn*

☆ **Twenty Reggae Classics, Vol. 4** / Trojan ✦✦✦✦✦
Never pass anything from the fertile Trojan vaults and collections. — *Ron Wynn*

Underground and Beyond / 1993 / Mesa ✦✦✦
Contemporary dancehall music continues to embrace many things beside reggae, although that genre remains its primary focus. This 15-cut anthology includes a pair of numbers from Mike Smith that are much more straight hip-hop/rap with a light jazz influence than reggae, although there's plenty of that from the likes of Derrick Parker, Captain Remo, Major Scorpion, and Louis Rankin. The roots end is represented by Yasus Afari's "King Immanuel," and Lilly Melody and Janet Moore showcase soulful, romantic tunes. — *Ron Wynn*

Word Sound 'ave Power: Dub Poets & Dub / Feb. 28, 1994 / Heartbeat ✦✦✦✦
This anthology covers the early dub poets, with tracks from Mutabaruka, Malachi Smith, Glenville Bryan, Nawie Nabble, and others, plus the original versions from the *Dub Poets Dub* recording. It's a chance to revisit a sound that hasn't gotten the recognition it deserves outside Jamaica for its impact in helping boost reggae's popularity, while showing that it hadn't completely lost its social significance or vision. — *Ron Wynn*

WOMEN

"Women's Music" is more about women than it is about music. Formally, "women's music" is the name applied to the songs that were one of the earliest expressions of the feminist cultural network. The folk and protest music traditions—themselves responses to the oppressiveness of the '50s—lingered from the '60s. Feminist and gay liberation movements were gathering speed; and the possibilities of a diverse and visible lesbian communityexploded into reality. Women's bookstores, art by and for women, woman-only space, even new spellings of the words "woman"/"women," minus references to "man"/"men" (womon, womoon, wimmin, womyn), were explored.

Women's music got its start with lesbians. It all began in 1971, with the first two Lesbian-oriented records produced in the US: Maxine Feldman's *Angry Atthis* and Madeline Davis' *Stonewall Nation* (both 45 rpm). The idea of music written, arranged, and played by and for women; the concept of taking a women-only show on the road (as happened with Women on Wheels); the thought of producing, manufacturing, distributing, and promoting music made by women—all caught on like wildfire.

Among the most popular artists of that era was Alix Dobkin, who brought her years of experience as a folksinger to homegrown songs about her new lesbian identity (*Lavender Jane Loves Women*, Women's Wax Works, 1974). Dobkin has recently released a retrospective commemorating her career as a lesbian troubadour (*Love and Politics: A 30-Year Saga* (Women's Wax Works, 1992). Meg Christian's *I Know You Know* (Olivia Records, 1974) was soft and gently Euro-classical, in contrast to her strong butch look; Cris Williamson, fresh from gigging as an interpreter of modern folk, lent her breathtakingly resonant voice to her metaphorical ballads. Williamson's seminal *The Changer and the Changed* (Olivia Records, 1975) remains the best-selling independent album of all time. All three mid-'70s albums, plus the myriad of other music from artists like Deidre McCalla, Ginni Clemmens, Kristin Lems, and Margie Adam, were collected eagerly and played endlessly. These records' very existence, as much as their lyrics, opened up a world of exciting, challenging, and radical contingencies to their mostly lesbian audience.

Other women, whose music was based on more complicated or less mobile modalities (electric, band, multi-instrumental, or chorus, for example), were less well-known but every bit as important in setting precedents. Collective experience was gained from—and great music was played by—BeBe K'Roche, Gwen Avery, Heather Bishop, Linda Tillery, Mary Watkins, Nancy Vogl (Berkeley Women's Music Collective), Robin Flower, Sue Fink, Vicki Randle (now on Jay Leno's "Tonight Show"), and Woody Simmons.

There were also women in the mainstream who, like their women's music counterparts, were learning the business of music. Some of these women subsequently entered the women's music arena, able to teach the essentials to other women—minus the unwanted hierarchal industry politics. June Millington, a rock guitarist, teamed with her bass-playing sister, Jean, and several other women musicians to form Fanny, the first all-women's band to be signed by a major label. Through four successful albums with Warner Brothers, Fanny served notice that women could do more than simply sing. Helen Hooke, of Deadly Nightshade fame, has also been making music for over 20 years, first on the RCA label and currently self-produced. The all-women quintet, Alive!, tore up the jazz world; their two recent Northern California reunion concerts sold out, a testament to the recalled power of their collaboration. Two other mainstream women artists—Bertha, and Goldie and the Gingerbreads—also made significant recordings. There was also a handful of notable women musicians who made music with men, including April Lawton (guitarist with Ramatam) and Tret Fure (lead guitarist with Spencer Davis).

Even before there was women's music, there were women who were determined to be heard, and to have other women's (including lesbians') voices heard. In 1973, ten of these women—some associated with the radical lesbian feminist newspaper *The Furies*—got together in Washington, DC. Through hard work, strong wills, self-denial, and a benevolent Goddess, they were able to record a 45 rpm single of Meg Christian's rendition of "Lady" (Carole King/Gerry Goffin), backed with Cris Williamson's "If It Weren't for the Music." The spirit spread, money was raised, and the newly-born Olivia Records was able to release the aforementioned early discs by Meg Christian and Cris Williamson—along with the tide-turning, innovative, and witty *Lesbian Concentrate*, designed as a response to Anita Bryant's vicious campaign against homosexuals.

For over 20 years now, Olivia has produced lesbian and feminist women's music featuring such artists as Cris Williamson, Deidre McCalla, Lucie Blue Tremblay, Teresa Trull, Nancy Vogl, Mary Watkins, June Millington, Linda Tillery, Dianne Davidson, and Tret Fure (the latter two on the Second Wave label, a division of Olivia). Another record company thatfigured vitally in women's music was Redwood Records, founded in 1972 when Holly Near recorded *Hang in There*, and then known as Redwood Cultural Work. Redwood produced and distributed records, and presented concerts, by dozens of artists—male and female, from many cultures—who sing for peace, justice, feminism, and human rights.

Other individuals and organizations have played roles in the development of the feminist cultural network. The groundbreaking book *Lesbian/Woman*, by Del Martin and Phyllis Lyon, was initially printed amid the tidal wave of post-Stonewall gay activism; following 1991's National Lesbian Conference, Volcano Press reprinted it in a special 20th-anniversary edition (1992). The Naiad Press, founded in 1973 by Donna McBride and Barbara Grier, remains the largest publisher/supplier of lesbian titles in the world.

The National Women's Music Festival (the oldest festival of its kind) and the Michigan Womyn's Music Festival (the largest of its kind) celebrated their 20th anniversaries in 1994 and 1995, respectively. As of 1994, there were at least 15 major festivals of women's music in the South, Alaska, Hawaii, the West Coast, and the East Coast (including Northampton, MA, or "Lesbianville," according to the *National Enquirer*). The Ladyslipper Catalog, the largest listing of lesbian and other women's music products in the world, was founded by Laurie Fuchs nearly 20 years ago, and still functions as an important resource in a rapidly changing industry. *Hot Wire: The Journal of Women's Music and Culture*, widely acknowledged as the most thorough current chronicler of women's music, unfortunately ended production after ten years.

At one time, it was possible to own all the "women's music" that had been recorded. As *The Changer and the Changed* has gracefully aged, women musicians have hit the scene playing all styles including soul, rock, rap, Latin American, jazz, funk, bebop, house music, Caribbean/island, African, reggae, C&W, gospel/hymnal, punk/thrash, folk, R&B, Australian aboriginal, swing, chanty, klezmer, Native American/Canadian, big-band, taiko, and Euro-classical. There are singers, instrumentalists, songwriters, solo acts, backup musicians, duos, trios, dance ensembles, and larger groupings. The Ladyslipper Catalog mentions 68 pages worth of women's music, and one would need hundreds of CDs and cassettes to boast of an up-to-date collection.

Many people think of women's music as an exclusively "White-woman-with-guitar" genre, because some of the movement's pioneers were visible in the established and accepted tradition of folkie-with-guitar. In fact, not all of those pioneers were White, and not all were guitar players; nonetheless, the label "White-women-with-guitar" has stuck to women's music. Simplification and prejudice aside, women's music currently transcends this label, and goes far beyond any specific performer or performance.

Where once only a handful of labels released women's music—Olivia, Redwood, Icebergg, Flying Fish, Ladyslipper—many sisters are doing it for themselves through self-production. Multitudes of local producers, promoters, distributors, managers, booking agents, engineers, and other technicians are facilitating the process. Along with the expansion in roles and realities for women making music, new resources have developed.

In 1986, a group of visionary women agreed that the time had come for a national organization of women's music and culture. In 1987, the Association of Women's Music and Culture (AWMAC) was founded by a steering committee that included performers Deidre McCalla and Sue Fink, festival producer Lisa Vogel (of the Michigan Womyn's Music Festival), record producer/engineer Leslie Ann Jones, and Olivia Records founder and president Judy Dlugacz. AWMAC currently sponsors an annual National Conference in conjunction with the National Women's Music Festival, plus more intimate regional meetings. The organization strives to encourage women's music and culture by assisting its members' networking and education, and by offering members other support services.

Also in 1987, June Millington realized her dream of creating new possibilities for women pursuing careers in music—a dream born of her own frustrating experiences in the male-dominated music industry. Millington founded the Institute for the Musical Arts (IMA), a nonprofit, multicultural teaching and performing-arts organization that trains women in skills that are useful in the music business.

Finally, Women's Music Plus (edited by Toni Armstrong, Jr., one of the founders of Hot Wire) is a comprehensive resource that suggests the levels of competence, complexity, and diversity in women's music and culture. This directory lists performers, live-event and record producers, record labels, record distributors, recording technicians, stage workers, women's choirs and choruses, comedians, dance artists, storytellers, theater artists, cartoonists, festivals, American Sign Language interpreters, artists' representatives, photographers, film/video/television professionals, feminist writers and broadcasters, feminist publishers, periodicals, libraries and archives, bookstores, and other catalogs and directories. Where Northern California was once the exclusive "capital" of women's music—Olivia and Redwood both make their homes in the San Francisco Bay Area, as do AWMAC and the IMA—the Women's Music Plus list spans North America, and in fact the globe.

In summary, women's music is a cultural phenomenon—and more than music. Not all women's music is about lesbians, or stridently feminist, or even about women. But women's music does convey words, ideas, and role models that are supportive of, and culturally relevant to, lesbians. Its broader themes embrace a range of ecofeminist, anti-patriarchal, pro-peace, and humanitarian philosophies.

Women's music and women's culture represents an international movement whose boundaries are constantly being stretched—whose definition is known to many listeners, but can't be adequately written down. One definition of women's music would include all performers who appear at women's music festivals; another definition might simply include all those who do define themselves as participants in women's music. Whatever the definition, it is certain that the existence of women's music and her products nourishes lesbian feminists, heterofeminists, and other open-hearted listeners. —Laura Post

Margie Adam

Guitar, Vocals / Singer-Songwriter

Margie Adam is a singer-songwriter known to the feminist and progressive communities for her blend of passionate love songs, goofball humor, and thoughtful political observation. In the decade spanning the mid-'70s and early '80s, Adam helped to define and expand notions about women's music as an art form, a political force, and an industry.

While performing on university campuses, at festivals, in theaters and clubs, and at the conventions of many major women's organizations (NOW, Women in the Law), Adam created a recorded body of work on her own label, Pleiades Records. Her albums include *Margie Adam, Songwriter* (1976), a solo piano album; *Naked Keys* (1980), recorded live; *We Shall Go Forth!* (1982); and *Here Is a Love Song* (1983).

Highlights of Adam's performance history include the thrilling experience of leading 10,000 women at the National Women's Conference in Houston in singing a three-part harmony version of "We Shall Go Forth!" The song was later placed in the archives of the Political History division of the Smithsonian Institution. In 1980, the National Women's Political Caucus sponsored Adam on the first national concert tour designed specifically to raise funds for feminist candidates. Adam had the honor of headlining a concert at Constitution Hall which coincided with the July 1, 1982, Equal Rights Amendment ratification deadline and which was attended by members of 80 national women's organizations.

In 1984 Adam came off the road for a "Radical's Sabbatical." In the intervening years, she studied piano and voice and returned to college, where she obtained credentials for working in the field of chemical dependency.

To the surprise of many, particularly of Margie Adam herself, she began to write music again, in 1990, after a six-year hiatus. As she developed a new repertoire, Adam made the decision to perform the music in public. Constant requests for a new recording led her to gather together a group of women musicians to record her latest album, *Another Place*, which exemplifies the balance of humor, politics, and passion which is the hallmark of Margie Adam's work. —Laura Post

Songwriter / 1976 / Pleiades ✦✦✦
Of the many moods reflected here, that of a childlike exuberance predominates. Outstanding vocal harmonies are provided by Vicki Randle, Meg Christian, and Cris Williamson. The all-original compositions include "Best Friend (The Unicorn Song)," "Would You Like to Tap Dance on the Moon?," and two exquisite piano solos. —Ladyslipper

Naked Keys / 1980 / Pleiades ✦✦✦
Eleven original solo piano performances. Soothing, drifting, whimsical. This is Margie in some ways at her truest: her medium, her style. Her years at the piano, having this music flow through her, precede and underlie her singing and her songwriting ones. —Ladyslipper

We Shall Go Forth / 1982 / Pleiades ✦✦✦
This contains songs that have been in-concert favorites for years: "Tender Lady," "I'm Not a Service Station," "Baby Child," "Dare to Struggle," "Who Among Us," and the title song. All are original vocal pieces, recorded live. —Ladyslipper

Here Is a Love Song / 1983 / Pleiades ✦✦✦✦
An elegant, beautifully instrumented LP of beautiful swoons and fun songs, it has an extra-hot group of musicians: Jean Fineberg and Ellen Seeling on horns, Vivian Stoll on vibes, Barbara Cobb on bass, Barbara Borden, Susanne Vincenza, Carolyn Brandy, Diane Lindsay, and Michele Sell, who used to play with Frank Sinatra, on harp. —Ladyslipper

★ **Best of Margie Adam** / 1990 / Olivia ✦✦✦✦✦
This late-1990 double-length edition is one of her *Women's Music Classics* collections, chosen from all of Margie's albums to commemorate one of women's music best-selling pianists and songwriters, and the first time Margie's work is available on CD. It includes "Best Friend (The Unicorn Song)," "Tender Lady," "Naked Keys," and 14 more. —Ladyslipper

Another Place / 1993 / Pleiades ✦✦✦✦
A lovely collection of songs, chock-full of her trademark wry and gentle observations on the ways of the heart. Her voice has matured and deepened, and by bringing together some of today's best women's music artists (old and new), she breathes a new, steady life into the scene. —Ladyslipper

Alive

Ballads, Latin Jazz, Post-Bop

Alive is and all-female quintet from San Francisco. Hard swinging, with Latin leanings. As they said in a song, "For lack of a better word, call it jazz." —Michael G. Nastos

★ **Alive!** / Sep. 5, 1979-Sep. 7, 1979 / Urana ✦✦✦✦✦
This all-female group swung like mad and held no punches. All-original contents include three by lead singer Rhiannon and one from Michelle Rosewoman. "City Life" is an absolute knockout. Featured is Barbara Borden on drums, Carolyn Brandy (percussion), Janet Small on piano, Suzanne Vincenza on bass. —Michael G. Nastos

Call It Jazz / May 17, 1981-May 19, 1981 / Alive ✦✦✦
If you love Rhiannon as a vocalist but weren't around when she fronted this ensemble, you'll love this. Recorded at the Great American Music Hall in San Francisco in May 1981, it's dynamite . . . this recording actually preserves that elusive, most magical spirit which Alive! embodied in performance. Produced by Helen Keane. —Ladyslipper

City Life / Nov. 1982 / Alive ✦✦✦✦
"A triumph of human and musical spirit—that is *City Life* at its best. Their individual and collective mastery of idioms—from bebop and ballads to Afro-Cuban and pop—is abundantly evident on this album"—this

quote from their jacket sums it up. The reasons *Alive!* is gaining recognition and respect in the greater jazz world will be no mystery to listeners. — *Ladyslipper*

Altazor

Women's

Formed in 1987, this groundbreaking Latin American ensemble combines the multinational talents of Chilean Lichi Fuentes, Venezuelan Jackeline Rago, Cuban Dulce Arguelles, and Asian-American Vanessa Whang. The group's name comes from the Spanish "alta" (high) and "azor" (hawk), words that suggest the soaring vocal harmonies of the singers as well as the high-flying spirit with which the group's haunting, passsionate music is created. When performing its repertoire of traditional Latin American vocal and instrumental arrangements along with the more socially conscious lyrics of New Song, Altazor employs an impressive range of instruments that includes the quena, tiple, tres, and charango, along with the more familiar flute, mandolin, guitar, and piano. — *AMG*

Altazor / 1989 / Redwood ✦✦✦
With all-acoustic instrumentation—including guitar, mandolin, charango, flutes, congas, and percussion—the songs range from poignant ballads to lively dances, with the group really cutting loose on two instrumental tracks, one of which features a wild guitar and charango duet. — *Backroads Music/Heartbeats*

● **Concurrencia** / Redwood ✦✦✦✦
This spring 1993 release, Altazor's second, promises to be similar to their first, only better. — *Ladyslipper*

Jamie Anderson

Women's

Known for her warm voice and unique, sometimes outrageous songs, Jamie Anderson's music has reached many people. In 1990 and 1991, she was voted Favorite New Performer by readers of *Hot Wire*, an international journal of women's music and culture.

Anderson is a versatile performer who has been touring nationally since 1987, playing everywhere from coffeehouses to concert halls all over the US. In 1990 alone, Anderson performed for audiences in 22 states, and she has been featured at several Women's Music festivals, including Campfest, East Coast Lesbians' Festival, National Women's Music Festival, New England Women's Musical Retreat, Southern Women's Music and Comedy Festival, and West Coast Women's Music and Comedy Festival.

Anderson introduces new listeners to the subtitles of lesbian culture while promoting self-pride and affirmation for other lesbians. — *Laura Post*

★ **Center of Balance** / 1992 / Tsunami ✦✦✦✦✦
Her second release continues with the humorous, pointed material she's become quite known for and contains many of the songs she's performed on tour. Plus her usual array of contemplative and/or weird songs. Vocal assistance is given by Sue Fink, Mimi Baczewska, and Leah Zicari. — *Ladyslipper*

Bad Hair Day / 1994 / Tsunami ✦✦

Family of Friends / Jul. 26, 1994 / Ladyslipper ✦✦✦

Closer to Home / Tsunami ✦✦✦
This is a wonderfully lesbian-identified album filled with warmth, humor, and honesty. Anderson explores topics near and dear to many lesbians. Her voice is sweet; delivery is straightforward; lyrics are direct, thoughtful, and refreshing. — *Ladyslipper*

Heather Bishop

Guitar, Vocals / Folk

Heather Bishop possesses one of those resonant, endlessly expressive voices that make audiences want to sing along and weep at the sheer beauty. What sets Bishop apart is the grounded spiritual energy that infuses all her work, live and recorded. Her career has spanned two decades of spreading her messages—sometimes joyous, sometimes painful, always passionate—in urban US and Canadian centers (Bishop hails from Manitoba), fly-in Yukon villages, festivals, and conferences.

In her teens, Bishop began to study the acoustic guitar; by the late '70s, she was touring North America, building bridges between communities and generations. Although she is an artist who moves easily among genres, Bishop considers herself to be a folk musician who belts out the blues, croons ballads, and delivers stirring political songs.

Old New Borrowed Blue (Mother of Pearl Records, 1992), her ninth album, features remixed/digitally mastered versions of "old" tunes from her five albums for adults, "new" tunes (five, by Canadian women), cuts "borrowed" from artists whom Bishop has admired, and several blues numbers. — *Laura Post*

Grandmother's Song / 1979 / Mother Of Pearl ✦✦✦
The title song on this, Bishop's first release, gives the perspective of a pioneer woman growing old on the prairies. Bishop is also a painter, and she used a beautiful original of her grandmother for the cover art. — *Ladyslipper*

Belly Button / 1982 / BMG/Children's Group ✦✦✦
Rated the top children's album in 1983 by the CBC/Canada's National Radio Network, this is assuredly one of the more delightful kids' LPs around. Some great rock, country, and good-time instrumentation. Bishop produced and mixed. — *Ladyslipper*

I Love Women . . . Who Laugh / 1982 / Mother of Pearl ✦✦✦
This album is the embodiment of a successful transition in style, from a solid blues background to a more rock-oriented, funkier sound. Using an array of synthesizers plus congas and saxophone, Bishop produces strong moods and currents of emotion. Mostly original and clearly woman-identified material. — *Ladyslipper*

★ **A Taste of the Blues** / 1987 / Mother of Pearl ✦✦✦✦✦
This 1987 release is another serving of Bishop's tasty blues, the style for which her voice was obviously created. Sumptuous jacket, fine production, excellent artistry. — *Ladyslipper*

Walk That Edge / 1989 / Mother of Pearl ✦✦✦
Her seventh recording has a simple, down-home flavor, a contemporary folk sound with both country and rock influences. Her lyrics and music are sometimes sassy, sometimes sultry—daring to walk that edge—and sometimes sad and haunting, with images of separations, ghosts from the past, the path not taken. It includes "Let Them Talk," which becomes an affirmation of love between women, and "I'm Not the One," about surviving an abusive relationship, with a driving guitar solo by Sherry Shute. — *Ladyslipper*

☆ **Old New Borrowed Blue** / 1992 / Mother of Pearl ✦✦✦✦✦
This 1992 compilation has two or three selections from each of her albums for adults: *Walk That Edge, A Taste of the Blues, I Love Women Who Laugh, Celebration,* and *Grandmother's Song...*[and] five newly recorded songs, including "Ancient Cry" and "Yes to Life." There's lots of her best work here. — *Ladyslipper*

A Duck in New York City / BMG/Children's Group ✦✦✦✦
Winner of the Gold Parents' Choice Award, and following in the tradition of "Bellybutton" and "Purple People Eater," Bishop's third children's album is much more than a collection of songs—it's the story of the adventures of a country duck in the big city. From a chance meeting with a robot on the street to playing a guitar solo with the Slug Opera, whimsical fantasy abounds. Funny and touching in turns. — *Ladyslipper*

Purple People Eater / BMG/Children's Group ✦✦✦
Heather Bishop decided to focus her considerable talent, wit, and warmth on another kids' album. Opening with a moving rendition of "Ghost Riders in the Sky" complete with female pronouns, she then swings into "The Fairy Song" and the rollicking "The Name Game." Connie Kaldor, Tracy Riley, and Ilena Zaremba contribute inspired backup vocals, and production and instrumentation are highly sophisticated. Recommended for preschool, middle young. — *Ladyslipper*

Celebration / Mother of Pearl ✦✦✦
Includes classic blues covers "Cry Me a River" and "Fever," plus feminist-themed originals. — *AMG*

Blackgirls

Women's / Folk-Pop

Blackgirls, including Eugenia Lee (guitar/vocals), Dana Kletter (piano/vocals), and Hollis Brown (violin/vocals), are a folk-pop band from North Carolina. Their two albums, released on the independent North Carolina label Mammoth Records, were produced by Joe Boyd, the head of Hannibal Records and a noted producer of such folk-rock performers as Fairport Convention. — *AMG*

● **Procedure** / 1989 / Mammoth ✦✦✦✦
Blackgirls are, in reality, three White women from North Carolina who bring together vocal excellence and classical training on a variety of acoustic instruments (strong on violins, no percussion) to create a new folk-punk sound. The melodies reflect their musical background, adding a simple beauty to the thought-provoking lyrics imparted in three-part harmonies. The tempo changes from song to song, from dreamy to jarring, keeping listener interest sparked. Produced by Joe Boyd, known for his work with Fairport Convention, Sandy Denny, and 10,000 Maniacs. Includes "A Visit to the Behaviorist." — *Ladyslipper*

Happy / 1991 / Mammoth ✦✦✦
How to describe the uncategorizable? To compare them thematically and musically to the Indigos, Bush, Mitchell, Roches, and Raincoats does not do justice. But life ain't fair, a fact these girls recognize and (sometimes cheerfully) lament. No simple downer missives of life's and love's lumps, but wistful observations, multilayered declarative chants, honest

(and therefore clever) statements—all with lovely vocals and instrumentation. Produced by Joe Boyd. —*Ladyslipper*

Blazing Redheads

Latin Jazz
All-female septet from California who play upbeat Latin-jazz on the funky side. SF Bay Area darlings. P.S. None is actually a redhead. —*Michael G. Nastos*

★ **Blazing Redheads** / Aug. 11, 1987-Aug. 12, 1987 / Reference ✦✦✦✦✦
Worth getting, it's Latin-jazz, funky, get-down music. —*Michael G. Nastos*

Crazed Women / Dec. 10, 1990-Dec. 12, 1990 / Reference ✦✦✦
Jazzy and percussion-rich, with elements of Latin, R&B, and even rock. Fun and exciting. Joy Julks plays bass on this one. —*Ladyslipper*

Meg Christian

Guitar, Vocals / Folk-Pop, Women's
Meg Christian recorded Olivia's first album and, along with Cris Williamson, brought the whole field of women's music into its golden age. A singer-songwriter with a folk and classical bent, her music tends to be impassioned and filled with intense feelings, and her sound very elegant and restrained. Although she retired from performing during the '80s, her work still looms large among older listeners, and she is revered within the field. —*Bruce Eder*

Face the Music / 1982 / Olivia ✦✦✦
The poignant and reflective lyrics are balanced against an opulent sound. Featuring the supporting talents of Holly Near and Sweet Honey in the Rock. —*Bruce Eder*

Turning It Over / Olivia ✦✦✦✦
Christian's first release since 1977 has love ballads, lovely instrumentals, reflective and humorous tunes. As always, she infuses her music with her "personalness." Yet there is also something new here, a sense of self-recognition that will hit home for many. —*Ladyslipper*

★ **The Best of Meg Christian** / Olivia ✦✦✦✦✦
Here are all of the landmark songs from this remarkable singer-songwriter and her decade-long career. Probably the best introduction to her work. —*Bruce Eder*

From the Heart / Olivia ✦✦✦
Songs of gentle honesty come from one of the founding mothers of women's music, whose recording career spans ten years. This album of beautiful music will warm your spirit in a rare experience of shared intimacy, poignancy, and laughter. —*Ladyslipper*

I Know You Know / Olivia ✦✦✦
The first "produced" women's music record, this has held up with its humor and poignancy, although it may seem dated to some modern ears and sensibilities. —*Bruce Eder*

Kate Clinton

Women's / Comedy
Kate Clinton began performing her political comedy in 1981, the same year as Ronald Reagan. Like Reagan, Kate Clinton has built her success upon breaking the rules. Her fast paced, cutting-edge performance skewers political egos and shreds taboos.

Kate Clinton sees comedy as a bawdy politic. The laughter she evokes is less a machine-gun staccato outburst and more a rolling, building blend of fading fears and connections made. It's hard to be a dominatrix in a kinder, gentler nation, so Kate Clinton's comedy is more stand-with than stand-up, a witty yes in the land of no. Her popularity has been based on a fast-paced, satirical style that focuses on topical world concerns and an affirmative feminist agenda while drawing on her recovering Catholic roots and her years of high school English teaching.

Kate Clinton has emerged as a national force outside those traditionally male-dominated bastions, the comedy clubs. With four self-produced albums on her own WhysCrack label to her credit, *Making Light* (1982), *Making Waves* (1983), *Live at the Great American Music Hall* (1985), and *Babes in Joyland* (1991), Kate has built a wide following in her ten years of performing professionally. —*Laura Post*

Making Light / 1982 / Whyscrack ✦✦✦

Making Waves / 1983 / Whyscrack ✦✦✦

Live at Great American Music Hall / 1985 / Whyscrack ✦✦✦
In her inimitable style, where every breath packs a punch, she relates experiences as a recovering Catholic (coveting her neighbor's wife), sensitively and deeply describes Californians discussing relationships, satirizes personals in papers, sings her song for parthenogenesis, and tells how she answered the question "What do YOU do?" at an S/M workshop. Though her audiences continue to expand at a rapid rate and the types of people she performs for have broadened significantly, she never omits her lesbian material. —*Ladyslipper*

★ **Babes in Joyland** / 1991 / Whyscrack ✦✦✦✦✦
Recorded live in Boston, she draws on her recovering Catholic roots, years of high-school English teaching, and her authority on politics to build laughter of fading fears and connections made. It's hard to be a dominatrix in a kinder, gentler nation, so her comedy is more stand-with than stand-up. —*Ladyslipper*

Catie Curtis

Guitar, Vocals / Urban-Folk, Folk
Boston-based Catie Curtis is noted for her exquisite, powerful voice (often compared to Karla Bonoff) and for writing gentle songs with poignant humanist and feminist messages—always powerful, personal statements that rarely drift into preaching. She usually performs with an acoustic guitar, backed by bass and drums. Her recording debut was 1989's cassette-only *Dandelion* for the independent Mongoose label. Since then she has released *From Years to Hours* (Mongoose, 1991) and *Truth from Lies* (Hear Music, 1995). Curtis remains a favorite on the folk club and festival circuit. —*Sandra Brennan*

Dandelion / 1989 / Mongoose ✦✦✦
Curtis' debut cassette, featuring 12 songs, is not as polished as her *From Years to Hours* CD. Her acoustic guitar work is good, and she uses just enough backup to add to her music without overpowering it. Good effort. —*Chip Renner*

● **From Years to Hours** / 1991 / Mongoose ✦✦✦✦
Curtis shines on her second release, really maturing as a songwriter. Her music is well produced (Darleen Wilson), and her songwriting is intelligent and thought-provoking. "Hole in the Bucket" is the key song on this collection. —*Chip Renner and Richard Meyer*

Truth from Lies / 1995 / Hear Music ✦✦✦
Catie Curtis has taken her personal songwriting to a new depth. With sexual politics never far from the surface, she has crafted some fine lyrics that make her case for individual choice in all things; yet she never gets up on a soap box. The best of these is "Radical"; "I don't feel radical when I kiss you." The production by Darleen Wilson is simple and effective. Curtis' voice has a catch pleasantly reminiscent of Karla Bonoff. —*Richard Meyer*

Dianne Davidson

Guitar, Vocals / Soul, Blues-Rock, Women's
Some of this singer-songwriter's musical talents may have been inherited; her grandmother was an opera singer, and her mother claims Davidson came out of the womb singing. As a child, Davidson even toyed for a while with the piano and saxophone before settling on being a singer and developing her own personal vocal style. Davidson's recording career began at 19 when she produced and recorded her own LP for Janus Records, following a period of belting out soul standards with an eight-piece band. Two more LPs for Janus followed before the label went out of business in 1974. More recently Davidson has been recording for Oakland's Olivia Records. The robust, passionate voice featured on her own albums has also provided backup vocals for Linda Ronstadt and Tracy Nelson. Although Davidson handles the blues, R&B, and pop ballads with skill, her strongest songs are the rousing rockers that allow her to belt out the lyrics loud and clear. —*Laura Post*

● **Breaking All the Rules!** / 1988 / Second Wave ✦✦✦✦
An excellent showcase for Davidson's powerful voice and guitar, highlighted by her loud, raunchy version of Willie Dixon's "Built for Comfort." —*Bruce Eder*

Lea DeLaria

Women's
Lea DeLaria has been a professional lesbian for over ten years, earning a living with her comedy and singing routines. She helped to create San Francisco's Gay Comedy Nights and New York's People Who Are Funny That Way and has uproariously emceed open mics, festival stages, and Gay Pride rallies across the nation, including the 1987 March on Washington for Lesbian and Gay Rights, to a crowd of nearly a million.

You may know her musical comedy about perverts, *Dos Lesbos*, which toured the country for three years (1987-89), or *Girl Friday*, a comedy conceived, written, directed by, and starring Lea, which won the 1989 Golden Gull for Best Comedy Group in Provincetown, where she lives. You may have seen her show, *Lesbo-a-GoGo*, or caught her chatting, late-night, on a recent *Arsenio*.

Lea's high-octane delivery, her gift for spontaneous repartee, and her loud, often-vulgar presence make deliberate inroads into rethinking the stereotyping of lesbians and other women in our society. One of her greatest advantages is that DeLaria is comfortable onstage and, onstage, she is herself. Her muse is lesbian life, gay life, all life.

She careens unabashedly around a stage and into the audience. Nothing is sacred, yet all, somehow, is respected. The targets of her energetic blitz: a gynecology appointment from hell, Bette Davis being born, gay/

lesbian relations, lesbian dating and sex in all their absurdity, straight women tourists in Provincetown, and the occasional gullible patron at her shows. She has been known to wind up on the laps of female audience members; even in a large room, Lea's performances are intimate. And, would you believe her big-voiced presentation of scat/blues and soul? She has recently released *Bulldyke in a China Shop*. —*Laura Post*

● **Bulldyke in a China Shop** / 1994 / ✦✦✦✦

Ani DiFranco

Guitar, Vocals / Urban-Folk

What does androgynous twentysomething new wave folk-punk singer Ani (Ah-nee) DiFranco have in common with feminist author/speaker/activist Gloria Steinem? They both have developed ardent followings through preaching a contemporary commonperson's gospel; they both are charismatic onstage; they both believe in the power of the Revolution Within.

Ani DiFranco is the inadvertent messiah to the "Nose Ring Generation," identified by body piercings, undaunted attitude, and haircuts that would get you fired from the bank: tufted, dyed, and shaven to the scalp. They are spunky, dramatic, and brimming with awareness, bursting with social consciousness unimagined by their forebears at the same age.

Her understated voice powers her unflinching lyrics. She delivers the intensity of Janis Joplin but will never drown in the discontent that she stirs. Her songwriting melds the down-home sensibility of Dolly Parton with the biting energy of metal, with the jittery beat of thrash. The beat used to come from her guitar alone. Now drummer Andy Stochansky joins her gigs.

DiFranco's genuine warmth takes some of the edge off her righteous rage. The unarguable rightness of her vision and the tunefulness of her compositions temper the harsh details of her vignettes.

In her native Buffalo, she briefly attended art school, then enrolled in New York City's New School for Social Research. At the same time playing gigs in bars, she quickly built a strong local following. A West Coast live event producer, Tracye Lawson, had brought a relatively unknown DiFranco to Santa Cruz early in 1993; by the time of DiFranco's return engagement, in the fall of the same year, her audience had multiplied incredibly.

Following startling popularity of her sparely self-produced debut recording, *Ani DiFranco* (Righteous Records, 1990), she generated enough revenue to finance a second album, *Not So Soft*, in 1991. In 1993, she released *Puddle Dive* (Righteous Babe Records), which spent ten weeks on the college charts, providing another quantum leap in the direction of recognition.

Having employed a small posse of session players on *Puddle Dive*, Ani gave the same treatment to some of her older solo material on 1993's *Like I Said/Songs 1990-1991. Out of Range* was released by Righteous Babe Records in 1994.

Upon its release in 1995, *Not a Pretty Girl* earned DiFranco positive reviews in mainstream publications, which helped her expand her audience. *Dilate*, released in the spring of 1996, signaled a shift toward a more textured and produced sound and, in doing so, it earned her new fans. —*Laura Post*

Ani DiFranco / 1989 / Righteous ✦✦
A fine debut from this young songwriter, singer, and guitarist, whose songs and poems are literate, melodic, feminist, well-arranged, and full of imagery. She has a lovely, versatile voice. —*Ladyslipper*

Not So Soft / 1991 / Righteous ✦✦✦
The delivery is sweet and urgent here, giving blood to her poetry and making the listener get active in the listening. She employs a very rich acoustic guitar on most songs, does some beautiful self-harmonizing, and adds some conga drum and dust broom. —*Ladyslipper*

Imperfectly / 1992 / Righteous ✦✦✦✦
With her third album, she achieves a level of intensity that folk-rock rarely reaches. Unflinching in her pursuit of honesty, she strikes sparks incessantly, challenging sexual politics, social conventions, and the meaning of existence, including her own. For the first time, other musicians appear as accompanists to add shadings of viola, trumpet, mandolin. —*Ladyslipper*

Puddle Dive / 1993 / Righteous ✦✦✦✦
On this 1993 release, her most complete effort to date, she goes boldly where no one has gone before, joined at various moments by pianist Ann Rabson from Saffire, the Uppity Blueswomen, virtuoso violinist Mary Ramsey from the folk-rock duo John and Mary, and English harmonica sensation Rory McLeod. An in-your-face lyricist who exposes our hidden thoughts and feelings, she confronts the status quo in sex, psychology, and society by reaching unflinchingly into her experience and personal politics. —*Ladyslipper*

Out of Range / 1994 / Righteous ✦✦✦✦

★ **Not a Pretty Girl** / 1995 / Righteous Babe ✦✦✦✦✦
On *Not a Pretty Girl*, Ani DiFranco stakes out the same territory she has in her previous albums, but she still turns in a number of biting, funny songs. —*Sara Sytsma*

Dilate / May 21, 1996 / Righteous Babe ✦✦✦✦
Ani DiFranco doesn't really expand her sonic palette on *Dilate*, but she doesn't need to. DiFranco racked up a dedicated cult audience on the basis of her conviction. There's not much melody on any of her songs, but there are messages and, thankfully, a fair share of humor. *Dilate* suffers from a bit too much repetition, but when Di Franco lands on a good hook—such as "Superhero" or "Done Wrong"—the results suggest that she could reach a wider audience. —*Thom Owens*

disappear fear

Group / Women's, Folk-Rock,

Beneath the veneer of catchy tunes, popish folk rhythms, and sophisticated harmonies of blood sisters Sonia Rutstein and Cindy Franks beats a heart of hardcore social, feminist consciousness. Born and raised in Baltimore, the sisters formed disappear fear in 1987. As the name implies, they call for unity and an end to injustice, and seek to break down the prejudicial barriers that keep people apart. Rutstein composes most of the songs, and her compositions have been compared to those of Phil Ochs, Joni Mitchell, and Bob Dylan; their harmonies and approach are reminiscent of the Indigo Girls. After three critically acclaimed self-released albums and an EP, disappear fear signed to Philo Records. In 1995 their self-titled album for Philo received a 1995 Gay and Lesbian Alliance Against Defamation Award for Outstanding Album. In June of 1996, they released *Seed in the Sahara*.—*Sandra Brennan*

Echo My Call / 1988 / Refined ✦✦✦
Sonia and Cindy Rutstein are blood sisters with captivating sister-harmonies, and their duo album is characterized by haunting melodies, content that spans the personal to US intervention in Central America, and a soulful, folkbeat delivery. All the material is by husky-voiced lead singer and guitarist Sonia. It is a nice debut. —*Ladyslipper*

● **Live at the Bottom Line** / 1989 / Philo ✦✦✦✦
Primarily live performance, acoustic and vocals from a Nov. 1991 concert at this special NYC club, plus four tracks from *Box of Heaven* and a new studio track. —*Ladyslipper*

Deep Soul Diver / 1990 / Disappear Fear ✦✦✦
With not much more than two voices, a guitar, and a tambourine, this duo has created a surprisingly sophisticated sound. Sisters Sonia and Cindy combine engaging melodies with catchy and thoughtful lyrics. This 1990 album balances emotional sincerity and irreverence in songs like "For Hollywood I Will" and "Sexual Telepathy." —*Ladyslipper*

20% of Heaven / 1994 / ✦✦✦✦

disappear fear / May 28, 1994 / Philo ✦✦✦✦

Seed in the Sahara / Jun. 18, 1996 / Philo ✦✦✦
With the help of former E-Street Band member Roy Bittan, disappear fear creates *Seed in the Sahara*, an album that expands the sonic palette of their folk-rock without making it too sweet or pop-oriented. It's not one of their strongest efforts, but it remains intriguing for most fans. —*Thom Owens*

Alix Dobkin

Vocals / Women's, Political Folk

When Alix Dobkin graduated with a bachelor of fine arts degree in 1962, she headed right for New York City's Greenwich Village, where she initiated a career for herself as a folk singer.

In the early '70s, having discovered women in her life, she released *Lavendar Jane Loves Women* (1973). A positive role model for its clear feminist lyrics, for its unwavering pro-lesbian stance, it set an early standard with its independence of production (her own Women's Wax Works label), as well as for its collective spirit.

Since that time, Alix Dobkin has been the most visible and vocal lesbian feminist in the community. Unlike some performers, Dobkin has shared the process of her life with her audience; unlike most performers, she has been personally available to non-performers after gigs on site, at festivals; and as a lesbian feminist resource doing workshops (on the sexism and misogyny of commercial album art, for example). Like few performers she publicly claimed her own identity, as a Jewish lesbian, and brought music from her culture into her shows.

Twenty years and five albums later, she has, with Ladyslipper Music, released a 30-song cassette and CD, *Love and Politics*, tracing that career and highlighting many of the songs—from *Living with Lesbians, XX Alix, These Women Never Been Better*, and *Yahoo Australia*—which have established her as a foremother of contemporary lesbian culture. The FBI named Dobkin a "troublemaker"; to her peers, she is "Head Lesbian." —*Laura Post*

Xx Alix / 1980 / Women's Wax Works ✦✦✦
Her material just gets better and better. This collection of songs is, as usual, highly personal, concrete, articulate, thoughtful, and thought-provoking. Her originality, observations, and experiences emerge as entities that are simultaneously aesthetic and contentful, vulnerable and solid as a rock. *—Ladyslipper*

These Women / Never Been Better / 1986 / Women's Wax Works ✦✦✦
Ever in a groundbreaking, controversial mode, she will shock her folkie fans with some of these selections. Mixing high-tech sound with unadulterated feminist and lesbian messages, Dobkin joins with Carol MacDonald and Witch to create the honest, scathing "Boy-Girl Rap," "Some Boys," and a country remake of her classic "The Woman in Your Life Is You." Then, switching to her more familiar and still-dear folk style, she delivers "Big Girls," "Crazy Dance," "100 Easy Ways to Lose a Man," and the lovely "These Women." *—Ladyslipper*

Yahoo Australia! Live from Sydney / 1990 / Women's Wax Works ✦✦✦
A *Live from Sydney* concert featuring Dobkin at her best and having fun with her subjects, even as she stridently sings out on any number of political issues. *—Bruce Eder*

★ **Love and Politics: A 30-Year Saga** / 1992 / Women's Wax Works ✦✦✦✦✦
Basically a *Best of Alix* collection, this documents her life in songwriting—and the landmarks of her life that inspired those songs. It's well balanced, with 20 songs spanning 1962-1992: six generic love songs, six specific love songs, six political analysis songs, and two "inspirational," one generic and one specific. In addition to some of everyone's favorites, she includes a brand new recording of the previously unreleased, very controversial "My Lesbian Wars," plus a 1970 pre-lesbian recording of "Shinin' Through." The CD has the complete liner notes and lyrics. *—Ladyslipper*

☆ **Lavender Jane Loves Women** / Women's Wax Works ✦✦✦✦✦
A pioneering lesbian-oriented record with a clever collection of material, such as an interpretation of Dusty Springfield's "I Only Want to Be with You," which holds up well today. *—Bruce Eder*

Living with Lesbians / Women's Wax Works ✦✦✦✦
A surprisingly lively follow-up with earthy, powerful material featuring basic guitar and all-woman backup singing. *—Bruce Eder*

Therese Edell

Women's, Singer-Songwriter
She may be best known as the unofficial Voice of the Michigan Womyn's Music Festival, announcing events between sets from her chair backstage. Her *From Women's Faces* album (1978) reflected her 20s; *For Therese* (1990)—a compilation of Edell's tunes recorded by Women's Music artists as a 40th birthday present to her—is an organic portrait of her 30s, after the influence of her Saturn return. Edell has been a songwriter/composer for over two decades and toured the US between 1978 and 1983, performing her music. Her debut on the Michigan stage was in 1977, oddly enough the same year that she was diagnosed with multiple sclerosis. Since that time, Edell has gone from being athletic, able-bodied, and outspoken to being self-assured, spiritual, and even more outspoken. She is still in love with her partner of 15 years and still cares as much about child abuse, self-abuse, and alcoholism as she did when she sang "Emma" in 1975. *—Laura Post*

● **From Women's Faces** / 1978 / Sea Friends ✦✦✦✦

Ferron

Guitar, Vocals / Women's
In listening to Ferron's music, audiences are allowed to acknowledge the passage of time, people, memories, and hopes through her poetic metaphors. Her familiar vernacular; direct statements; enlightened associations; warm, husky voice; and engaging stage presence have permitted identification with her experiences and her process, her struggles and her wisdom, universal anguish and strength. Beginning in 1986, however, many of her followers began to wonder at and mourn her absence from recording and touring.

Born on June 2, 1952, Ferron grew up in a semi-rural suburb of Vancouver, British Columbia, the eldest of seven children in a working-class family. After leaving home at 15, she scrambled financially, supporting herself by driving a cab, waitressing, shovelling gravel, and packing five-pound bags of coffee in a factory. From her basement, she recorded and distributed *Ferron* (1977) and *Ferron Backed Up* (1978). Since both albums are now out-of-print collector's items, Ferron has decided to re-release much of their material In 1978 Ferron was "discovered" by Gayle Scott, an American living and working in film production in Vancouver, who became Ferron's first and only manager and business partner. Ferron and Gayle collaborated on Ferron's next two studio albums: *Testimony* (Lucy Records, 1980) and *Shadows on a Dime* (Lucy Records, 1984), on which Ferron continued to convey her polished messages of raw truths, through sharply lyrical, soothingly melodic music dealing

with the cyclicity of relationships, questions of survival and identity, and optimism amid fear. Despite a small budget dependent on loans and contributions, in the absence of organized promotion, *Shadows on a Dime* received a four-star rating from *Rolling Stone* magazine.

In October of 1985, Ferron received a Canadian Council Arts Grant, enabling her to take a much-needed year off, ostensibly to write and take voice lessons but also to recover a long-neglected personal life. Recognizing that she would need more than a year to fully heal from the hardships of the road and the vagaries of the business, Ferron remained withdrawn from the spotlight. After the grant money ran out, she earned a living by laboring as a carpenter's assistant and a bartender and by doing daycare. Having reconnected with her physical and spiritual roots and having reaffirmed and redefined her own needs, Ferron has returned to the studio and the stage, having come to a remarkable new peace and with a fresh body of work: *Phantom Center* (Chameleon 1990), *Resting with the Question* (1992), *Not a Still Life* (1992), *Driver* in 1993, and *Polvo* in 1995. *—Laura Post*

★ **Testimony** / 1982 / Redwood ✦✦✦✦✦
Considered her best record, this is a collection of song-poems that run the gamut of deep and intense emotions. *—William Ruhlmann*

☆ **Shadows on a Dime** / 1989 / Redwood ✦✦✦✦✦
Literate songs by one of the best singer-songwriters, on an elaborate follow-up album courtesy of producer Terry Garthwaite, with a special instrumental luster. *—Bruce Eder & William Ruhlmann*

☆ **Phantom Center** / 1990 / Earthbeat! ✦✦✦✦✦
Connecting rich, poetic, archetypal imagery with vibrant musical textures, it is guaranteed to create an immediate emotional impact. Instrumentalists include Barbara Higbie and Novi. *—Ladyslipper*

Resting with the Question / 1992 / Cherrywood Station ✦✦✦✦
Who'd have guessed that Ferron's musical gift could express its poetry through instrumental music as well as through songs with lyrics? Eloquent compositions performed on synthesizer are saturated with emotion: lush, wistful, yearning, haunting, rich, and circular. And you'll probably lapse into thinking you're hearing flutes, classical guitars, strings, piano, and human voices. This is a highly recommended opportunity to experience another dimension of this woman's artistry. *—Ladyslipper*

Not a Still Life / 1992 / Cherrywood Station ✦✦✦✦
This 1992 in-concert album, subtitled *Live at the Great American Music Hall*, contains selections from all her previous releases of vocal music, including her '70s releases *Ferron* ("I Am Hungry") and *Ferron Backed Up* ("Light of My Light," "Call Me Friend," and "Dear Marly"). It includes a couple of selections not on any albums: the concert favorite "I Know a Game," and "Shady Gate." A great retrospective of her songwriting career, and a chance to enjoy her in a more personal way than the studio recordings afford. *—Ladyslipper*

Driver / Sep. 13, 1994 / Warner Brothers ✦✦✦

Polvo / Aug. 1, 1995 / Polygram ✦✦✦

Still Riot / Aug. 27, 1996 / Warner Brothers ✦✦✦

Cathy Fink

Dulcimer, Banjo, Guitar, Vocals / Folk, Children's
Cathy Fink may be best known for the many children's albums she has recorded over the years, but she is also a key figure in feminist-oriented folk and country music. Born and raised in Baltimore, Fink got her professional start at the Yellow Door coffeehouse in Montreal in 1973, at the height of the folk revival. There she became well known for her excellent banjo and guitar playing, as well as her yodeling. The next year she debuted on CBC Canada and has since played in every major North American folk festival. She and Duck Donald teamed up that year and stayed together until the end of the decade. Fink made her recording debut in 1975 with *Kissing Is a Crime* for Likeable Records. Three years later, she and Duck released a self-titled album on Flying Fish; the two released their first children's album, *I'm Gonna Tell*, in 1980. After the breakup with Duck, she moved to Takoma Park, MD, and has immersed herself in the folk, bluegrass, and old-time music scene, playing more than 5,000 concerts. In 1983 she teamed up with Marcie Marxer. In 1985 she recorded *The Leading Role* for Rounder, her first "adult" album in several years, and began producing other artists a year later. In 1988 she moved to Sugar Hill and recorded *Blue Rose*; the next year, Fink and Marxer released a self-titled album. She also produced an album for Great Dreams and, along with Marxer and Si Kahn, released cassette tapes of the best-selling children's books *The Runaway Bunny/Goodnight Moon* for Harper and Row. In 1991 she released a solo album on Sugar Hill and then put together 80 songs to contribute to the Macmillan/McGraw-Hill reading curriculum, a project entitled *A New View* (1992). In 1993 she produced Si Kahn's children's album *Goodtimes and Bedtimes.* *—Sandra Brennan*

Resources in Women's Music

Women's Music is closely associated with two record companies, Olivia and Redwood Records, both of which have figured prominently in the advancement of Women's Music. For 20 years, Olivia (and its sister label, Second Wave Records) has produced the music of such artists as Cris Williamson, Deidre McCalla, Lucie Blue Tremblay, Teresa Trull, Dianne Davidson, and Tret Fure. Redwood Records (now Redwood Cultural Work) was started in 1972 when Holly Near recorded *Hang in There*. Since then, Redwood has produced and distributed records and presented concerts by dozens of artists, male and female, from many different cultures, all of whom sing for peace, justice, feminism, and human rights.

Where once only a handful of labels (Olivia, Redwood, Icebergg, Flying Fish) released Women's Music, many sisters are now doing it themselves, via self-production. Multitudes of local producers, promoters, distributors, managers, booking agents, engineers, and other technicians facilitate the process. Along with the expanded roles and realities for women interested in making music, new resources have clearly developed as well.

Other individuals and organizations have also played leading roles in the development of the feminist cultural network. The groundbreaking book *Lesbian/Woman* by Del Martin and Phyllis Lyon, initially printed following the tidal wave of post-Stonewall gay activism, was reprinted after the 1991 National Lesbian Conference for a special 20th anniversary edition by Volcano Press (1992). And the Naiad Press, founded in 1973 by Donna McBride and Barbara Grier, remains the largest publisher/supplier of lesbian titles in the world.

The Ladyslipper Catalogue, founded by Laurie Fuchs nearly 20 years ago and now containing the largest listing of lesbian and other women's music products in the world, continues to function as an important resource in a rapidly changing industry. *Hot Wire: The Journal of Women's Music and Culture*, widely acknowledged as the most thorough current chronicler of Women's Music, unfortunately ended production after ten years.

At one time, it was possible to own all the "Women's Music" that had ever been recorded. However, as *The Changer and the Changed* has gracefully aged, more and more women musicians playing all styles (including soul, rock, rap, Latin American, soul, jazz, funk, bebop, house music, Caribbean/island, African, reggae, country/western, gospel/hymnal, punk/thrash, folk, R&B, Australian aboriginal, swing, chanty, klezmer, Native American and Canadian, big band, karaoke, taiko, and Euro-classical) have hit the scene. There are singing musicians, instrumentalists, songwriters, solo acts, backup musicians, duos, trios, dance ensembles, and larger groupings. *The Ladyslipper Catalogue* devotes 25 pages to Women's Music listings, and one would have to own hundreds of CDs and cassettes today to boast of having an up-to-date collection.

The National Women's Music Festival (the oldest Women's Music festival) and the Michigan Womyn's Music Festival (the largest Women's Music festival) celebrated their 20th anniversaries in 1994 and 1995, respectively. As of 1993, there are at least 15 major festivals of Women's Music being held throughout the United States: in the South, on the East and West coasts, in Northampton, MA ("Lesbianville," according to the National Enquirer), and in Alaska and Hawaii.

In 1986, a group of visionary women agreed that it was time to form a national organization of Women's Music and Culture. In 1987 the founding Steering Committee—including performers Deidre McCalla and Sue Fink, festival producer Lisa Vogel (Michigan Womyn's Music Festival), record producer/engineer Leslie Ann Jones, and Judy Dlugacz, founder and president of Olivia Records— appointed a bylaws committee to draft governing principles for the nascent Association of Women's Music and Culture (AWMAC). AWMAC, which currently sponsors an annual National Conference in conjunction with the National Women's Music Festival (as well as a number of more intimate regional meetings), strives to encourage and empower Women's Music and culture through networking, education, and support services for its members.

Finally, the comprehensive resource *Women's Music Plus* (edited by Toni Armstrong, Jr., one of the founders of *Hot Wire*) reflects the competence, complexity, and diversity of Women's Music and Culture. Listed are performers, artists in film, video, and television, women's choirs and choruses, record and live event producers, artists' representatives, American Sign Language interpreters, record distributors, stage workers, technicians, feminist press and other writers, feminist broadcasters, photographers, publishers, festivals, periodicals, bookstores, libraries and archives, record labels, catalogs and directories, cartoonists, crafts, comedy, dance, storytelling, and theater. Where northern California was once the exclusive "capital" of Women's Music (Olivia and Redwood both make their homes in the San Francisco Bay Area, as do AWMAC and the IMA), the Women's Music Plus list, although emphasizing North America, virtually spans the globe. —*Laura Post*

● **Grandma Slid Down the Mountain** / 1984 / Rounder ✦✦✦✦
Fink sings, plays, and produces up a storm. Imaginative songs impart good, general, positive values. For ages four to seven. —*Bob Hinkle*

When the Rain Comes Down / 1987 / Rounder ✦✦✦✦
A definitively outstanding children's production by a woman who has been a leader in providing excellent material for kids. First-rate youngsters deserve first-rate music like this. —*Ladyslipper*

Help Yourself / 1990 / Rounder ✦✦✦
A how-to-take-care-of-yourself recording, with Marcy Marxer. Usually such albums are a bit preachy, but this one is much less so. For ages four to seven. —*Bob Hinkle*

● **The Leading Role** / Rounder ✦✦✦✦

Sue Fink

Synthesizer, Vocals / Rock
Sue Fink is a multitalented, multifaceted artist. Brian Wilson (of the Beach Boys) and backup singers for Aretha Franklin and Marvin Gaye have come to her to study voice. Other artists have hired her to produce and arrange their recordings and to write songs. The National Association of Independent Record Distributors (NAIRD) gave *Big Promise*, Fink's first solo album, an award of excellence; the *Washington Post* loved it. While critics acclaim Fink's serious talent, festivals and conferences have also recognized her acute sense of humor by inviting her to emcee their events. Sue Fink grew up in Beverly Hills practicing piano four hours daily. She graduated magna cum laude from UCLA's music department and continued in graduate school there. Fink has sung on television, albums, and at Nixon's presidential inauguration. Fink's professional credits, prior to becoming involved with women's music, include a State Department-sponsored 13-nation tour of Asia with the California Chamber Singers and a singing tour of Europe, Israel, Canada, Hawaii, and the

US with the Roger Wagner Chorale. Fink toured with Meg Christian, playing synthesizer, during the spring of 1984. The next year brought the release of Fink's critically acclaimed techno-synthesizer *Big Promise*, which she toured in collaboration with Diane Lindsay. Fink then started to tour solo; she has performed or emceed at all of the major women's festivals in the US. She also founded the Los Angeles Women's Community Chorus and was featured on CBS Television's "Two on the Town" as the group's energetic conductor. With her humor, heart, and concern, Sue Fink reached new depth as an artist with the R&B ballads of her 1989 release *True Life Adventure*, on her own FrostFire label. Sue Fink was voted favorite songwriter, emcee, and MIDI programmer by *Hot Wire*, the international journal of women's music and culture; her song "Leaping Lesbians" was, as usual, included as an all-time favorite song. Fink played and/or sang on several new recordings by Pam Hall, Jamie Anderson, and Margie Adam. She co-produced, with Jamie Anderson, a compilation entitled *A Family Of Friends* (a modern "Lesbian Concentrate") as a fundraiser to fight the "family values" crusade while demonstrating her own sense of family. Fink, Anderson, Millington, and others co-wrote the title, recorded with a "we are the world" cast of women's music. —*Laura Post*

True Life Adventure / 1989 / Frostfire ✦✦✦
A strong and long-awaited follow-up with a jazzy, torch style, it's sophisticated and polished. —*AMG*

★ **Big Promise** / Ladyslipper ✦✦✦✦✦
From new wave dance to ballads to rock, Fink's polished debut contains strong political statements in a fun and enjoyable manner. —*AMG*

Judy Fjell

Guitar, Vocal / Women's, Singer-Songwriter
Judy Fjell's performing career began as a teenager, when she picked up a guitar at a garage sale, learned a few chords, and began entertaining

folks in her small Montana hometown with favorites from the "Hootenanny" radio program.

In the mid-'70s, inspired by the women's music movement and encouraged by a close poet friend, Fjell began to write songs featuring messages of social change and deeply personal lyrics. With six albums on her own Honey Pie Music label and through private lessons and Music Empowerment Workshops, Fjell travels and inspires in the minstrel tradition. — *Laura Post*

Dance in the Moment / 1988 / Honey Pie ✦✦✦✦
Her famous "Middle-Aged Body (with Teenage Emotions)," the song that speaks for a generation, is preserved on this 1988 album. Her humor helps us keep things in perspective. — *Ladyslipper*

Livin' on Dreams / 1990 / Honey Pie ✦✦✦
Live music, humor, and stories from this Norwegian lesbian singer-songwriter. Her political wit is still finely tuned. — *Ladyslipper*

★ **Love and Justice** / 1991 / Honey Pie ✦✦✦✦✦
This 1991 release is a collection of political songs (plus a few by Malvina Reynolds), which started out a small, simple, available-only-at-concerts project, until folks started clamoring for it to be available more widely. Here it is, in its simple and straightforward essence. Fjell deals with lesbian/gay, peace, environmental, feminist, and labor issues. — *Ladyslipper*

Robin Flower and Libby McLaren

Vocals / Women's
Robin Flower and Libby McLaren have been breaking ground with their novel fusion of Irish, Cajun, bluegrass, and western swing; progressive bluegrass, they call it. In their songs, they yearn for connection with kindred spirits in diverse forms: she-wolves, faraway women, grandmothers, conscientious interveners in cycles of abuse, courageous interveners in larger political dramas, romantic lovers.

Flower's career began with laudatory reviews from the *Village Voice*, *Frets*, and *Billboard*. McLaren had applied her rich keyboards, clear voice, and ear for instrumental interplay to recording, arrangement, and accompaniment for the Roches, Ronnie Gilbert, and Holly Near. Teaming with flatpicker Nancy Vogl, Flower released her first album, *More Than Friends* (Spaniel, 1979). In 1982 came *Green Sneakers* (Flying Fish)and *First Dibs* (Flying Fish, named Best String Band Jazz by N.A.I.R.D.in 1984) and *Babies with Glasses* (Flying Fish, named Best Women's Music Album by N.A.I.R.D. in 1987).

In the the late '80s Flower teamed with the equally committed and competent Libby McLaren, whose pop view has softened Flower's sophisticated, technical approach. Flower and McLaren found that they were both very focused, intent upon hard practice, and unquestioning about the need to collectively arrange and assign instrumental and vocal parts. They split from Nancy Vogl, with whom they had initially believed they would play as a trio. Several talented Bay Area women have accompanied them: fiddler-vocalist Crystal Reeves, harpist Michelle Sell, and guitarist-singer Teresa Chandler.

At the end of the '80s, Flower and McLaren played for diverse audiences: folk—though they were oftimes labelled too progressive or too electric for folk purists—general mainstream, and women's music.

Robin Flower-Libby McLaren's debut recording, *Angel of Change*, was released on Little Cat Records (2468 Hearst Avenue, Oakland, CA 94602.) Plans include a wholly instrumental album and an album more purely folk-styled, perhaps even recorded live in the studio, not over-dubbed. — *Laura Post*

More Than Friends / 1979 / Spaniel ✦✦

Robin Flower and Libby McLaren! / 1989 / Robin Flower & Libby ✦✦✦
This self-produced 1989 cassette features the talents of two of the industry's finest instrumentalist/singer-songwriters. Their lyrics are catchy and relevant, the arrangements tight, and their voices light and sweet. — *Ladyslipper*

● **Babies with Glasses** / Flying Fish ✦✦✦✦
This 1987 release chronicles the development of this instrumentalist/singer-songwriter's new acoustic sound: a mixture of bluegrass with jazz influences and bits of rock and classical strains. — *Ladyslipper*

Mimi Fox

Guitar
Mimi "Fast Fingers" Fox is one of the very few established female jazz guitarists (Emily Remler, Mary Osborne), her passion and technical excellence gracing the albums and performances of Darol Anger, Rhiannon, and Terry Garthwaite. Primarily self-taught, Fox focused early on folk styles until she heard John Coltrane's seminal *Giant Steps* at age 14. Fox's early influences—Aretha Franklin, Dixieland, jazz traditionals—emerge in her evocative interpretations of jazz with swing stylings, blues, Latin, and her forte, bebop.

Against the Grain, Fox's debut release, demonstrated her playful mastery of standards and inspired insight through medleys, convincing established jazz aficionados, awing young fans, and even winning some pop listeners. *Mimi Fox—Live* shows the explosive power of an improvisational approach by a confident artist surrounded by empathic players. — *Laura Post*

● **Against the Grain** / 1987 / Catero ✦✦✦✦

Turtle Logic / Jun. 5, 1991-May 10, 1995 / Monarch ✦✦✦✦
Guitarist Mimi Fox has long been a fixture in the San Francisco Bay area. A fine hard bop-based guitarist with a sound of her own (that sometimes hints a little at Grant Green), Fox is in excellent form throughout this CD. Backed on most selections by a local trio, Fox alternates stimulating originals with such standards as "Night and Day" and "My Romance." This set (recorded at a couple of clubs in 1991-92 and before a live audience in a studio in 1995) concludes with an eight-minute, three-song unaccompanied medley during which Mimi Fox shows off her talents on acoustic guitar. Fine music. — *Scott Yanow*

Tret Fure

Guitar, Vocals
Pop-rocker Fure's personal background is as diverse as her musical talent. Born in Iowa, she grew up in Illinois and in Michigan's upper peninsula; she moved to the west coast to attend the University of California at Berkeley. She began her music-writing career when she was 19 and worked for a time as a vocalist and guitarist for Spencer Davis before combining her music-making skills with those of engineer and producer for Olivia Records, where she engineered, co-produced, and performed on albums for Cris Williamson and June Millington, as well as Olivia's landmark double album, *Meg/Cris at Carnegie Hall*. Her own first (self-titled) solo album was released in 1973 on RCA Records, and shortly thereafter she toured extensively, opening for such groups as the J. Geils Band, Yes, and Poco. After the release of her second album, *Terminal Hold* (Olivia), Fure focused on her solo career. With the appearance of her third album, *Edges of the Heart*, she became firmly established as a leading pop-rock performer with unusual depth and diversity. In *Time Turns the Moon* (Olivia) Fure has continued to pay homage to her roots in folk and rock 'n' roll. — *AMG*

★ **Time Turns the Moon** / 1991 / Olivia ✦✦✦✦✦
One of the best women's music records ever, and one of the finer rock albums of 1990. Assertive and sensitive, tough and reflective, with a sense of humor nearly as prominent as its beat. — *Bruce Eder*

Edges of the Heart / Second Wave ✦✦✦
Not as strong as *Terminal Hold*, but with one seriously sexy number ("Tight Black Jeans"); well worth owning. — *Bruce Eder*

Terminal Hold / Second Wave ✦✦✦✦
Half of this record (mostly one side) rocks beautifully hard and breaks a lot of new ground, with help from Dave Davies of the Kinks and Lou Reed-alumnus Steve Hunter. — *Bruce Eder*

Kay Gardner

Flute / New Age
An internationally known composer of healing music and a pioneer in the women's spirituality movement, Kay Gardner takes the listener on an inspirational journey through the curative and transformative ingredients of music and sound, offering insights into their mysteries and how they may be used in the healing process.

Kay Gardner's many albums on the Ladyslipper label have featured acoustic instrumentation using the principles of droning, toning, mantra, and chant; harmonics/stairway to the spiritual; rhythm as pulse; and melody/heart and soul of music.

Gardner has written for several professional music journals, for women's music and culture publications, and for spirituality pages. She regularly teaches workshops on the healing properties of music and sound at the Omega Institute of Holistic Studies and has been invited to medical schools (including Yale) to present her work. Years of research went into Kay's book, *Sounding the Inner Landscape: Music as Medicine*. In 1994 she released the oratorio *Ourobourosa*, a broad work featuring soloists, a 40-piece orchestra, and a 100-voice chorus. In 1996 she followed with *Drone Zone*. — *Laura Post*

Mooncircles / 1975 / Vrana ✦✦✦
Her earliest instrumental album is a mellow, luscious collection of compositions for her instrument, the flute, with piano and guitar accompaniment. — *Bruce Eder*

Emerging / 1978 / Urana ✦✦

★ **A Rainbow Path** / 1984 / Ladyslipper ✦✦✦✦✦
A multi-year project that embraces medieval and Eastern influences, yet is almost new age in its ambience. This is the closest that any record has gotten to the feel of Van Dyke Parks's classic *Song Cycle*. — *Bruce Eder*

Ocean Moon / 1991 / Urana ✦✦✦✦
Combining all the best from *Mooncircles*—all the instrumental tracks—and *Emerging*—the entire album minus one track, this extra-

long-playing compact disc brings her early classic discography to the technological age. This collection features some of her most important work. — *Ladyslipper*

Amazon / 1992 / Ladyslipper ✦✦✦
Another masterpiece of improvisation brings the full sound and ambience of the Peruvian Rainforest right into your head(set) and heart. Alto flute meditations are blended with her own on-site recordings of birds, tree frogs, rainfall, waterfalls, and pan pipes, which she made when she visited the Amazon River with a women's tour in February of 1992. — *Ladyslipper*

One Spirit / 1993 / Ladyslipper ✦✦✦
This summer 1993 release is like a magical musical trip around the world. The One Spirit duo is a charismatic collaboration between two masters of their instruments—Kay Gardner on flutes, Nurudafina Pili Abena on drums and percussion—performing original and traditional pieces inspired by global musics and rhythms from four continents. You'll travel through Nigeria, Senegal, Peru, Cuba, Brazil, East India, and North America as you undertake this aural journey. It features a cameo appearance by Brooke Medicine Eagle on the Native American-inspired composition entitled "Medicine Eagle." Includes "Mother of Creation," "Dance of Strength," "The Gypsy Kiss," "Silencia," "Carnival," "Asian Sunset," and "Happy Life." Abena plays congas, djembe, quica, dundun, pandeira, balafon, agogo, dumbek, surdo, and rain rattles. — *Ladyslipper*

Ouroboros: Seasons of Life / 1994 / Ladyslipper ✦✦✦✦
The National Women's Music Festival highlighted the premiere performance of *Ouroboros: Seasons of Life*, Kay Gardner's new oratorio. It was performed by six female soloists (ranging in age from eight to 80-something), a 100-voice women's orchestra, and a 50-member women's orchestra, conducted by Nan Washburn from the Women's Philharmonic. The work consists of eight movements, each beginning with a narrative solo, moving to an orchestral interlude and ending with a choral chant. Each movement corresponds with the stages of women's lives as defined by the seasons of the ancient Celtic calendar. This is by far Kay Gardner's most ambitious work to date. — *MusD*

Drone Zone / 1996 / The Relaxation Company ✦✦✦

Fishersdaughter / Even Keel ✦✦✦
Some of Gardner's most fascinating work outside of classical/new age. She recreates folk music in a distinctly woman-centered mode. Not to all tastes, but resounding with a lot of heart. — *Bruce Eder*

Garden of Ecstasy / Ladyslipper ✦✦✦
Her follow-up to *A Rainbow Path* is just as lush and surprising with its medieval and mystical quality. — *Bruce Eder*

Moods & Rituals / Even Keel ✦✦

Avalon / Ladyslipper ✦✦✦
This tape of solo flute meditations was created when Gardner co-led a "women's mysteries" tour in Glastonbury, England, where Brigid, the goddess of wells, flames, oaks, creative arts/music and healing, once dwelled and was worshipped. Remarkably good quality, quieting, and suitable for meditation. — *Ladyslipper*

Ronnie Gilbert

Vocals / Folk
Ronnie Gilbert is no stranger to success or to controversy. Born to working-class, Jewish parents in New York City, she refused to participate in her '40s high school senior play because she was convinced of the racial injustice of the minstrel show theme. In the '50s Gilbert melded her joyous contralto with the voices of Pete Seeger, Lee Hays, and Fred Hellerman in their celebrated group the Weavers, who brought folk rhythms and social activism to the mainstream even while being branded as subversives, in the hysteria of the McCarthy era, and blacklisted.

In 1963, divorced from both her husband and the cultural expectations of a wife, Gilbert was beginning to build a solo singing career when she met Joseph Chaikin, then a young actor/director with a fledgling experimental troupe, the Open Theater. In the '70s Gilbert's career took yet another surprising turn, when she earned an M.A. in clinical psychology and worked as a therapist for a few years.

The '80s saw Gilbert make her debut appearance at the Michigan Womyn's Music Festival, reading a lesbian-themed poem. Gilbert met, was inspired by, and sang with Holly Near, recording *Lifeline* (live, 1983) and *Singing with You* (1986) with Near, and *Harp* (1985) with Near, Arlo Guthrie, and Pete Seeger. Gilbert's debut solo release, *The Spirit Is Free* (1985), was released on the feminist Redwood label; the live *Love Will Find a Way* followed in 1989 on the Abbe Alice label, the collaborative product of a new alliance with manager/partner Donna Korones. In 1990 Gilbert gave the keynote speech at the annual conference of the Association of Women's Music and Culture (AWMAC). Currently, Gilbert is performing her one-woman theater piece on the life of the legendary American labor activator Mother Jones. — *Laura Post*

★ **The Spirit Is Free** / 1985 / Redwood ✦✦✦✦✦
Gilbert retains a strong vocal presence on standards and feminist-oriented originals. A rousing mix of old standards, such as "The Midnight Special," with the new, such as "Mothers, Daughters, Wives." A good start-up album. — *Bruce Eder*

Love Will Find a Way / 1989 / Abbe Alice ✦✦✦
A very honest and representative live album consisting of a dozen numbers drawn from her current repertoire. — *Bruce Eder*

Lifeline / 1983 / Redwood ✦✦✦
A fresh and vibrant concert album with Holly Near, and a repertoire ranging from current topical songs like "Biko" to romantic classics like "Stormy Weather." Followed up by the album *Singing with You*. — *Bruce Eder*

Susan Herrick

Women's, Folk, Jazz, New Age
Her two-and-a-half-octave range voice is equally comfortable with haunting whispers and resonant power. Her melodies innovatively blend folk, jazz, and pop styles; the words she writes offer personal revelation and insight. She is Susan Herrick, singer-songwriter, guitarist, pianist, drummer, and sacred healer.

In 1985, Herrick received a B.S. in music therapy, with emphasis on classical voice and composition. While establishing a private practice as a music therapist, she toured her first independent album, *Loving Me*, an acoustic collection. On the heels of that success came multiple challenges: the breakup of a seven-year relationship and the recalling of sexual abuse. Fortified by her process of self-healing, Herrick released *Truth and the Lie* (1991), on the WATCHfire label that she cofounded with her partner Jessie Cocks. — *Laura Post*

★ **Truth and the Lie** / 1991 / Watchfire ✦✦✦✦✦
A remarkable recording from a remarkable artist and performer. Herrick sings original songs about her childhood sexual abuse, and the discovery and healing process she has undergone as an adult. Her lyrics are full of depth and grace, her voice tender yet strong, her harmonies sweet. Musically the production is excellent. — *Ladyslipper*

Loving Me / 1991 / Susan Herrick ✦✦✦
This is her debut folk recording. While not specifically dealing with recovery issues, there is a strong healing theme—not surprising from a music therapist. — *Ladyslipper*

Soul Chant / 1994 / WFR ✦✦✦✦

Helen Hooke

Fiddle / Women's, Folk, Country
Helen Hooke was first known in her '70s incarnation as the inspired fiddler for the country/feminist/rock touring band, Deadly Nightshade. Deadly Nightshade released *The Deadly Nightshade* and *F & W* on RCA, received press in *Rolling Stone*, the *New York Times*, and *Ms.* magazine as harbingers of feminism, and played alongside feminist luminaries Bella Abzug and Gloria Steinem, and for NOW.

In the mid-'80s, after several more bands and managers, Hooke decided to put out her next album independently: *Verse-Ability* (Montana Blake Productions, 1988). Satisfied with her involvement in the music from beginning to end, drawn to the women's music and culture circuit in which such independent production is possible, she appeared at the 1991 Michigan Womyn's Music Festival and at the 1991 Association of Women's Music and Culture Annual Conference. In 1992 Hooke released *Your Body's A Rocket* (Montana Blake Productions). — *Laura Post*

● **Verse-Ability** / 1988 / Montana Blake Music ✦✦✦✦
The spirit and sound of the groundbreaking '70s feminist rock group Deadly Nightshade are alive and well and dwelling in the music of this former member. Hooke puts forth some of her multi-instrumental best on this self-produced 1988 release, blending electric violin, guitar, synthesizer, accordion, drums, and percussion. The songs take on a personal, heartfelt nature and are testimony to her "live in the moment" attitude. — *Ladyslipper*

Libana

Women's, Folk, Worldbeat
Libana is a unique feminist performing group whose interpretations of ethnic and spiritual woman-themed music from around the globe have been performed at educational institutions, folk/ethnic events, and women's music and culture festivals across North America.

Libana was formed in 1979 when 25 women came together to explore women's music from different genres. At the time, the women's music scene was flourishing, but the 25 women believed that their approach would be different. They wanted to look cross-culturally at music of, by, and about women. The group of 25 has been reduced to eight, though five of the current eight have been performing together since the beginning. Seven albums have been recorded and released, including one from the feminist Ladyslipper label; *Fire Within, Sojourns,* and *Borderland* are on the world music Shanachie label. Despite the changes, Libana's cross-cultural focus has continued to define their music. —*Laura Post*

Handed Down / 1985 / Spinning ✦✦✦
On this 1985 tape, they sing songs from Eastern Europe and the Middle East, with some accompaniment on instruments such as oud, violin, and dumbek. The sound is at times reminiscent of the Bulgarian Women's Choir. —*Backroads Music/Heartbeats*

A Circle Is Cast / 1986 / Spinning ✦✦✦
The 1986 release from this feminist ensemble is a departure from their previous recordings; it represents Libana's spiritual basis of celebrating community and reverence for the rootedness of ritual, the Earth, the nuances of seasons, the solitude of meditation, and the Divine within. —*Ladyslipper*

Sojourns / 1991 / Shanachie ✦✦✦
Sojourns features tunes mainly from the Balkans and the Middle East, sung with joy and conviction to the accompaniment of guitars, violins, and dumbeks. A lively and captivating work full of all kinds of pleasures. —*Backroads Music/Heartbeats*

● **Fire Within** / 1993 / Ladyslipper ✦✦✦✦
The latest release from this 11-woman vocal group again offers a bouquet of traditional tunes from around the world. Notably absent are any songs from the Balkans and the Middle East, which have been heavily featured on previous albums. Instead there are 18 pieces from countries as geographically and culturally diverse as Spain and Hawaii, Sweden and Japan, Kenya and the United States, as well as a couple of original tunes. —*Backroads Music/Heartbeats*

Borderland / 1993 / Shanachie ✦✦✦
Libana, A Women's Chorus, Vol. 1 / Libana ✦✦✦✦
Formed in 1979, this ensemble researches and performs vocal, instrumental, and folk dance music that celebrates women's traditions from a variety of cultures through the ages. This tape, recorded live in concert, celebrates women and nature with primarily Eastern European/Balkan music, plus a little early medieval music and contemporary folk. —*Ladyslipper*

Libana, A Women's Chorus, Vol. 2 / Libana ✦✦✦
Fourteen women's voices celebrate women's work and women's spirit, with songs and dances of Celtic, Jewish, and Slavic origins. Part of it was recorded in concert, part in the studio. —*Ladyslipper*

Laura Love

Bass / Women's, Singer-Songwriter, Vocals
Laura Love is acclaimed in the Northwest music scene as an unparalleled vocalist, bassist, and songwriter. Love's style is a synthesis of inner-city funk and folkish sensibility. One of the most difficult tasks for a musician is to find an apt label for her music; folk/funk, African/Appalachian, and House/Celtic have been bandied about for Laura Love. Whatever you choose to call it, Love's original music is at once fresh and rooted in tradition.

Although a popular headliner in her own right, she has opened for John Lee Hooker, Lyle Lovett, Bo Diddley, Karla Bonoff, and Elayne Boosler and been invited to perform at a number of folk and eclectic music festivals.

Born in Lincoln, NE, Laura Love began her career at 16, singing jazz and pop standards at the Nebraska State Penitentiary. Since then Love has played in a blues-grunge outfit and in a duo, a trio, and the funny feminist foursome Venus Envy. Love has released three albums: *Menstrual Hut* (1989), *Z Therapy* (1990), and *Pangaea* (1993), all on her own label, Octoroon Biography. —*Laura Post*

● **Menstrual Hut** / 1989 / Octoroon Biography ✦✦✦✦
She identifies strongly as a lesbian/feminist woman of color, and her material reflects this consciousness—both original songs and some carefully selected traditional folksongs. To her own guitar accompaniment, she presents, with a voice laden with depth and texture, her song "I'm Your Daughter's Lover"; "Listen to Me," a tribute to Native American women; "W-I-M-M-I-N"; a spectacular rendition of "Wayfaring Stranger"; the title song; and more. —*Ladyslipper*

Z Therapy / 1990 / Octoroon Biography ✦✦✦✦
Love's second release is beautifully produced. She is accompanied by, among others, the Therapy Sisters and Z-Helene Christopher from the Z-Band. Except for "Swing Low, Sweet Chariot," all songs are originals. Several songs impart a world beat, with instrumentation such as cymbals, dumbek, congas, and bongos; Love plays acoustic and bass guitars. —*Ladyslipper*

Pangaea / 1992 / Octoroon Biography ✦✦✦✦
Fabulous, kickin', polished, vibrant—all these words exemplify this 1992 self-produced release. With more than a passing resemblance to Nanci

Griffith's emotional warmth, this is an artist with clear vision, a great band, and a marvelous set of pipes. —*Ladyslipper*

● **The Laura Love Collection** / 1995 / Putamayo ✦✦✦✦

Deidre McCalla

Guitar, Vocals
Said to combine the delivery of Nina Simone with the lyrical insightfulness and social commentary of Phil Ochs, urban singer-songwriter McCalla came of age in New York City during the McDougal Street pop/folk heyday, when artists sought to give musical expression to the nation's unrest. Transplanted now to a new home base in northern California, McCalla continues to tour. Her first two albums, *Don't Doubt It* and *With a Little Luck,* have received numerous New York Music Award nominations. Her LP *Everyday Heroes and Heroines* was produced by Teresa Trull and featured contributions from Mike Marshall, Linda Tillery, and Bonnie Hayes. —*Laura Post*

★ **Everyday Heroes and Heroines** / 1992 / Olivia ✦✦✦✦✦
This 1992 release, beautifully produced by Teresa Trull and Deidre's best yet, again demonstrates this singer-songwriter's exceptional talent with bright, energetic material. —*Ladyslipper*

Don't Doubt It / Olivia ✦✦✦✦
Very hip, contemporary, and danceable, her unique sound is brought out by the superb production skills of Teresa Trull. If you like Cris Williamson or Teresa Trull, you're sure to like McCalla. —*Ladyslipper*

With a Little Luck / Olivia ✦✦✦✦
Her second album is even better than her first, from the irrepressible exuberance of "All Day Always" (bound to become a classic), to her pursuit of a woman in "Would You Like to Dance," to a vocal duet with Teresa Trull that's just too hot for words. —*Ladyslipper*

Carol McComb

Guitar, Vocals / Folk
McComb is a California singer-songwriter whose music ranges from country to folk. —*Chip Renner*

Tears into Laughter / 1989 / Kaleidoscope ✦✦✦✦
McComb's album is very compelling. The sad "Faded Dresden Blues," about the effects of Alzheimer's disease on her grandmother, touches the soul. She is backed by Nina Gerber on acoustic guitar (Kate Wolf's guitar player), Sally Van Meter on dobro (Good Ol' Persons), Laurie Lewis on vocals, and Barbra Higbie on piano. —*Chip Renner*

June Millington

Guitar, Vocals
In 1969 when June Millington began her career as lead guitarist for Fanny—a mainstream all-women band—she recognized that mainstream music was largely inaccessible to women. During the five years in the '70s that Fanny was active, few women made significant establishment recordings.

Through four successful albums with Warner Brothers (*Fanny, Charity Ball, Fanny Hill,* and *Mother's Pride,*) June Millington and Fanny served notice to the rock world that women could do more than simply sing; women could also write and play rock 'n' roll passionately. Yet there were nearly no women technicians supporting either the studio recording process or live tours, and women booking agents, managers, and promoters were few and far between.

In 1975 Millington was asked to play on Cris Williamson's seminal album, *The Changer and the Changed.* It had been a leap from fooling on the ukulele as a child in Millington's native Manila, to rock fluency in California; it was a greater leap between mainstream fame and "women's music." Resonating with the politics of women making music, Millington established her own label, Fabulous Records, and released several albums: *Heartsong* (1981), *Running* (1983), and *One World, One Heart* (1988).

Millington began to conceive of mentorship for women pursuing music and allied professions. The Institute for the Musical Arts (IMA) was her idea of how to empower women, especially women of color, in their pursuit of careers in music, bridging the gap between women in the mainstream and in women's music, and promoting social justice and equality within the music industry and in other social and cultural spheres.

Millington's idea immediately drew some of the most experienced women in the music industry to IMA's advisory boards: Bonnie Raitt, Linda Tillery, Teresa Trull, and Cris Williamson. Today, IMA is a multicultural, nonprofit, national teaching and performing arts organization based in the San Francisco Bay area. Through classes, apprenticeships, and experiences in live performance and studio recording, IMA students gain knowledge and expertise in artist management, concert lighting/sound, entertainment law, instrument/voice development, marketing, music composition, promotion, sound technology, stage management, video, and recording/engineering, the latter of which has resulted in several new albums by up-and-coming artists on the Fabulous Label. —*Laura Post*

Heartsong / 1981 / Fabulous ✦✦✦

Running / 1983 / Fabulous ✦✦✦

★ **One World, One Heart** / 1988 / Fabulous ✦✦✦✦✦

Ticket to Wonderful / Fabulous ✦✦✦✦
This long-awaited 1993 release is the Millington sisters' best work yet. They combine their Phillipine Island roots, elevated lyrics, and a folk-rock sensibility (honed in the '70s with their pioneering work in Fanny, the first all-woman rock band to achieve international prominence) to create a unique worldbeat blend of island consciousness and rocksteady, global rhythms. Original songs range from the upbeat and passionate "Lighting the Night," to the crisp and hauntingly beautiful "Indigo Skies," to the playful "Goin' to Hawaii," to the prayerful "Family (World of Love)." Living up to its title, this album brings a new dimension to the words "soul music." —*Ladyslipper*

Melanie Monsur

Guitar, Piano
Melanie Monsur wants to be known as a composer. Perhaps best recognized for her supple piano accompaniments for the Washington Sisters, June Millington, Ronnie Gilbert, Cheryl Wheeler, Gayle Marie, and Sylvia Kohan, Monsur has also released two albums of original music, *Dragonfly* and *Opus K4.*

She learned piano when she and her siblings took lessons. In adolescence, she rebelled against the rigorous practice of the piano, and took up the guitar. After earning a B.A. in music theory and composition from the University of Massachusetts at Amherst, Monsur got to know folk singer Cheryl Wheeler, which helped her decide to pursue a performing career.

Though Monsur's first live gig had been while she was in eighth grade and she had played at coffeehouses while in high school, she cites the actual start of her professional career as when she joined forces with two men and scrambled between gigs for several years. In 1983 the lure of working with other women musicians drew her to the San Francisco Bay area.

She recorded her first album, *Dragonfly*, in 1987—teaming with a woman engineer and working with a low budget and no producer. Her second album, *Opus K4* (the name of a synthesizer), was recorded live at June Millington's Institute for the Musical Arts (IMA), in Bodega, CA.

In 1991 Monsur moved to New Mexico to write. She has amassed a body of new, Mexican-influenced instrumental piano tunes and travels monthly to New York to perform Persian-influenced music for students of the philospher Gurdjieff. —*Laura Post*

● **Opus K-4** / Melanie Monsur Music ✦✦✦✦
Her second recording features her all-instrumental compositions, performed on Kawai K-4 digital synthesizer. The result is a captivating blend of styles and moods—contemplative and rhythmic, melodic, and just plain lovely. —*Ladyslipper*

Holly Near

Vocals / Women's
Holly Near is one of the most respected singers of our time. She is a consummate entertainer who retains her integrity amid the rise and fall of fads in the music industry. She has recorded 15 albums, selling well over 1.5 million copies. More concerned with peace-making than with hit-making, Near's uncompromising vision has led her to defend originally unpopular causes. For her achievements, she was named Woman of the Year by *Ms.* magazine. She has appeared in the critically acclaimed feature film *Dog Fight* with Lili Taylor and River Phoenix and the television show "L.A. Law." She appears as herself in the film *Emma and Elvis.* Her autobiography *Fire in the Rain . . . Singer in the Storm* (William Morrow), detailing her life as an artist and activist, has been published in paperback after selling 30,000 copies in hardback. With her sister Timothy, Near wrote a musical docudrama that ran through the fall of 1992 as part of the prestigious Mark Taper Forum's season. A 30-minute video featuring live concert footage interspersed with candid background banter and a two-hour video autobiography that includes more than 20 cuts of her music are now available. Near's first children's book, based on her inspiring song, "The Great Peace March," was published by Henry Holt.

Near got her start in a local talent show at the age of seven. She attended UCLA, where she was "discovered," and began to work in film and television: George Roy Hill's *Slaughterhouse 5, Minnie and Moscowitz,* and the Broadway production of *Hair,* popular television shows such as "All in the Family," "Room 222," and "Mod Squad."

Near worked through the '70s and '80s for peace and feminism. She has a passion for Central and Latin America and is one of only a handful

of performers to perform in war-torn El Salvador. She has toured the world as an ambassador of peace and hope.

One of Near's greatest accomplishments is the founding of Redwood Cultural Work. What started 20 years ago as a record label supportive of other artists otherwise marginalized in the music industry, has become a leading multicultural, non-profit arts organization. —*Laura Post*

Hang in There / 1973 / Redwood ✦✦✦

A Live Album / 1974 / Redwood ✦✦✦✦
Her 1974 classic second album, which captures the dynamic quality of her performances, is now back in print. It contains many of the best-loved songs about women. —*Ladyslipper*

You Can Know All I Am / 1976 / Redwood ✦✦✦✦
This is a powerful, sometimes playful, sometimes painful look at the conditions of many kinds of women: in prison, organizing in factories, initiating relationships. More produced than her previous albums, but her voice still sparkles through. —*Ladyslipper*

Imagine My Surprise! / 1979 / Redwood ✦✦✦
A playful, quirky feminist record with elements of jazz, country, and even a little bit of Broadway. —*Bruce Eder*

Speed of Light / 1982 / Redwood ✦✦✦
A lively, snappy follow-up to *Imagine My Surprise!,* with extra pop wrinkles. —*Bruce Eder*

Journeys / 1984 / Redwood ✦✦✦
A handy retrospective, covering Near's first six albums. —*Bruce Eder*

☆ **Don't Hold Back** / 1987 / Redwood ✦✦✦✦✦
Near's party album, a thoroughly pleasing collection of love songs, with guest appearances by Bonnie Raitt and Kenny Loggins. —*Bruce Eder*

Watch Out! / 1989 / Redwood ✦✦✦
Here she collaborates with the West Virginia folk and traditional quartet Trapezoid, well known for their Appalachian instruments and styles, and so enters yet another musical genre, acoustic folk music. —*Ladyslipper*

Singer in the Storm: Life/Music of . . . / 1990 / Chameleon ✦✦✦
This live recording defines what Near is about. Divided between love songs and political statements, it is spirited and well-executed. —*Bruce Eder*

Sing to Me the Dream / 1990 / Redwood ✦✦
★ **Fire in the Rain** / 1993 / Redwood ✦✦✦✦✦
Musical Highlights from the Play "Fire in the Rain" chronicles the Holly Near songs from her autobiographical play. As such, it is in effect a compilation of some of Near's best work, from standards like "I Can't Give You Anything But Love" and "If I Loved You" to feminist and lesbian anthems like "Started Out Fine" and "Simply Love," dating back 20 years and re-recorded. She is in wonderful voice and is accompanied by pianist John Bucchino and occasional strings. This is a good way to sample Near's warm, political, triumphant style. —*William Ruhlmann*

Sky Dances / Redwood ✦✦✦
A 1989 folky, intimate, emotion-filled release, it features Near at her absolute best, singing songs by contemporary writers such as Ferron, Bernice Johnson Reagon, Ruben Blades, Phil Ochs, and Malvina Reynolds. —*Ladyslipper*

Lifeline / Redwood ✦✦✦✦
This is a majestic collaboration of generations and spirits. Ronnie Gilbert was one of the Weavers in the '40s and '50s, a folk group that loudly voiced the progressive and humanist concerns of the American people until the blacklist virtually silenced them, and that won the hearts and devotion of a huge following. This is a live recording from the Great American Music Hall in San Francisco. Styles encompass Broadway, folk, jazz, gospel. —*Ladyslipper*

Singing with You / Redwood ✦✦✦✦
Including both studio and live recordings from this inimitable duo, it also has a medley of old favorites ("Imagine My Surprise," "Something About the Women"); Ruth Pelham's sweet, touching song from the perspective of a child whose parents have divorced, "I Cried"; Ferron's "Kid's Song" from her out-of-print record *Ferron Backed Up;* and a variety of others that relate to social issues, friendship, and love. —*Ladyslipper*

Singer in the Real World / New Dimensions Radio ✦✦✦
Near is not only a talented singer and songwriter but a passionate, humorous, and articulate spokesperson for peace and sanity. On this New Dimensions Radio interview, we hear stories of how her family influenced her creativity and self-expression, stories from her musical career and political work, and her own description of her philosophy of music and life and continuing work and hopes for peace, social justice, and freedom of expression. —*Ladyslipper*

Musical Highlights: Fire/Rain Play / Redwood ✦✦✦
About the release of highlights from her play *Fire in the Rain,* Near says, "While doing the play, audiences kept asking for the cast recording. We didn't have one. The songs were spread out on 15 different recordings made over the last 20 years! A compilation? No, let me record these

songs one last time . . . not like I sang them back then . . . maybe not even how I sing them in the show! I hope you enjoy this recording . . . a celebration of the last 20 years and a reassurance that there are many surprising years yet to come." —*Ladyslipper*

Faith Nolan

Bass, Guitar, Harmonica, Tambourine, Vocals / Women's

Faith Nolan was born in Nova Scotia, a fifth-generation Canadian, in a predominantly Black community. An activist from a musical family, Nolan sings about Canadian Black history and heritage, feminism, and workers' and children's rights. Enhancing her musical abilities is her educational background in theater, opera, and writing and commitment to community work. Nolan is a singer and composer who plays folk guitar sprinkled with funk and reggae; who plays slide guitar, tambourine, and harmonica in the earliest blues traditions; and who speaks the cultural language of African-North American music: spirituals, gospel, and jazz. Nolan's concern for common people is articulated in her albums. —*Laura Post*

● **Freedom to Love** / 1989 / Redwood ◆◆◆◆
One of Nolan's best releases includes an original rock anthem, "I Black Woman"; an incredible rendition of "Strange Fruit," from Billie Holiday's repertoire; the title song, which equates homophobic laws with slavery; Ma Rainey's lesbian song "Prove It on Me"; and more, each with a clear and inspiring message of liberation. It's backed by some of Vancouver's finest musicians. —*Ladyslipper*

Africville / Multi-cultural Women ◆◆◆◆
Focusing on Black women historically and presently, Nolan's original songs give voice to issues and instill a sense of strength, through a variety of styles—blues, jazz, reggae, funk, and African drumming. The title song is about the relocation of the largest Black community in Canada. All accompanying musicians are Black Canadians. —*Ladyslipper*

Sistership / Multi-cultural Women ◆◆◆◆
This album focuses on the struggles and contributions of Black women; some songs relate to sexuality and lesbianism, others to various political struggles. Nolan plays almost every instrument on the album: electric bass, 12-string, six-string, slide guitar, harmonica, and tambourine. —*Ladyslipper*

Parachute Club

Women's, Group

Lorraine Segato (vocals, guitar, percussion) and Billy Bryans (drums, percussion) formed the Parachute Club in 1977 with Margo Davidson (saxophone, percussion, vocals), Lauri Conger (keyboards, synthesizer, vocals), and bassist Steve Webster, all veterans of previous bands. The group's self-titled debut album appeared in 1983, after they had added percussionist Julie Masi and guitarist Dave Gray. Second guitarist Keith Brownstone debuted on 1984's *At the Feet of the Moon*. Two more studio albums followed before the Parachute Club disbanded in 1989: *Moving Thru' the Moonlight* (1985) and *Small Victories* (1986). Lorraine Segato issued a solo album called *Phoenix* the year after the break-up, and *Wild Zone: The Essential Parachute Club* was released in 1992. —*John Bush*

At the Feet of the Moon / 1984 / RCA ◆◆◆◆
The overall production and instrumentation is tight and highly synthesized; the lyrics are political and inspiring. —*Ladyslipper*

● **Wild Zone: Essential Parachute Club** / RCA ◆◆◆◆
This 15-track retrospective contains some of the most incredible, political material this band has ever recorded. —*Ladyslipper*

Phranc

Guitar, Vocals / Folk-Rock

Who knew that little pigtailed Suzy Gottlieb, who was born in 1959 in Southern California and attended 13 years of Hebrew School, would come out as a lesbian separatist, then a punk rocker, then a radical folksinger named Phranc, effective at dissolving prejudice and barriers, and the only lesbian solo artist to perform out to mainstream audiences? Tracing her lyrical roots to Allan Sherman (she has listened to *My Son the Folksinger* since age five), Phranc has toured with the Smiths and the Pogues; appeared in the film *The Fall of Western Civilization* with her band, Nervous Gender; has been interviewed for *People Magazine*; and has released three albums, *Folksinger* (1985, Rhino Records), the campy *I Enjoy Being a Girl* (1989, Island Records), and *Positively Phranc* (1991, Island Records). Experiencing consistent, positive role models; living and working within a disciplined, politically thoughtful collective; and being shown personal tolerance cultivated the inner reserve and confidence necessary for confronting and thriving within the straight world. Though Phranc's early path was often unproductive, sometimes wild, and occasionally self-destructive, she retained a firm commitment to coming out and staying out with her own opinions as well as with her lesbian identity. —*Laura Post*

Folksinger / 1985 / Island ◆◆◆
Phranc's debut of modern acoustic folk with a rock edge includes voice, guitar, and harmonica. —*AMG*

● **I Enjoy Being a Girl** / 1989 / Island ◆◆◆◆
Her pop breakthrough features songs like "Take Off Your Swastika." She doesn't mince words, and her music is just as good as the message. Politics infused with humor and irony. Great cover! —*AMG*

Positively Phranc / 1991 / Island ◆◆◆
Harder and more electric, with a song about Billy Tipton and a wonderful a cappella cover of the Beach Boys' classic "Surfer Girl." —*AMG*

Ranch Romance

Country

● **Western Dream** / 1990 / Sugar Hill ◆◆◆◆
From several opening dates for k.d. lang to their 1990 debut women's festival performances, this four-woman trad-but-rad band has brought their flawless harmonies, driving rhythm, hot instrumentals, and wild yodeling to thousands of new fans around the country. It's perfect for two-stepping or any other partner dancing you'd care to do, as well as feet-stomping and finger-snapping. —*Ladyslipper*

Blue Blazes / 1991 / Sugar Hill ◆◆◆◆
This 1991 release is a hot mix of "regressive country" originals, incorporating acoustic honky tonk, rockabilly, and swing. Characterized by thoughtful, original lyrics, entertaining music, and great arrangements for guitar, fiddle, accordion, and bass, it has been described as" k.d. lang and Patsy Cline meet Bob Wills." —*Ladyslipper*

Flip City / 1993 / Sugar Hill ◆◆◆
The four women/one guy who comprise Seattle's Ranch Romance stir up an unconventional but tasty cocktail with *Flip City*. Guitar, accordion, fiddle, mandolin, and upright bass breed an infectious cross of jazzy swing, bluegrass, Tex-Mex, lonesome prairie ballads, and funky zydeco. —*Roch Parisien*

Bernice Johnson Reagon

Vocals

Though perhaps most widely known as the founder and guiding force of the Washington, D.C.-based women's group Sweet Honey in the Rock, Bernice Johnson Reagon is also a noted political activist, a Distinguished Professor at Washington's American University, and a curator emeritus at the Smithsonian Institution. She also occasionally records solo albums. During the '60s she was a founder of the Student Non-Violent Coordinating Committee Freedom Singers. Before founding Sweet Honey in the Rock in 1973, she was the vocal director of the D.C. Black Repertory Theater. Early musical inspirations for Reagon include the gospel music she heard while attending the Black American Baptist church. The harmonies that surrounded her became the basis for those of her famous group. To Reagon, music is a means of effecting change in society, of instilling a sense of heritage and cultural pride, and of creating solidarity in the face of adversity. For her, music is also the means of uniting people while simultaneously celebrating their differences. In addition to performing with Sweet Honey in the Rock, writing songs, teaching, and acting as curator, she writes books, and makes videos. —*Sandra Brennan*

● **River of Life / Harmony: One** / 1972 / Flying Fish ◆◆◆◆
This incredible a cappella album features Reagon's multi-tracking her own voice, with 12-16 parts in one song! This is a documentation of the several harmony systems she operates with Sweet Honey as well as in her solo efforts. The traditional songs such as "Jacob's Ladder" and "Since I Laid My Burden Down" use the Black congregational harmony system not commonly used in recordings or performances, which generally feature quartet, doo wop, or jazz systems. Other harmony systems are employed in her originals: "I Am a Lady," "Easy Street," "Running." This is another facet of her invaluable contributions in the fields of education, culture, musicology, and history, not to mention listening enjoyment! —*Ladyslipper*

The Songs Are Free / ◆◆◆◆
This is the audio track from the video by the same title, on which she traces the history of communal singing and the repertoire rooted in the Black church—from songs of resistance, courage, and pride to songs of determination and faith—and explores their roles from the Underground Railroad through the civil rights movement into the present. It includes dialogue, instruction, and performance—solo and with the SNCC Freedom Singers and Sweet Honey in the Rock. —*Ladyslipper*

Toshi Reagon

Guitar, Vocals / Folk

Toshi is the daughter of Bernice Johnson Reagon (from Sweet Honey in the Rock). She plays guitar and delivers beautiful soul-laden vocals. —*Chip Renner*

● **Demonstrations** / 1985 / T&R ◆◆◆◆
Not only a "strong voice in a new generation of Black women's music," a really *fine* voice, fine songwriting, and stylistically distinctive musicianship from a woman of diverse and growing talents. Reagon plays electric lead and rhythm guitar, acoustic guitar, drums, and bass, and does lead and background vocals. Co-producer with Reagon and a contributing percussionist and vocalist is Toshi's mom, Bernice Reagon of Sweet Honey in the Rock. The folky and rock 'n' roll-ish numbers here are equally strong. —*Ladyslipper*

Justice / 1992 / Flying Fish ◆◆◆
The material here is mostly original, though she does include a Georgia Sea Island song and Sting's "Walking in Your Footsteps." It was recorded with her famous mother, Bernice Johnson Reagon of Sweet Honey in the Rock, as well as Casselberry-Dupree and Annette Aguilar. —*Ladyslipper*

Rhiannon

Vocals / Jazz
Rhiannon, best known through her ten years as vocalist with the jazz group Alive!, blends classical drama with multicultural street theater, and scat phrasings in her innovative genre of jazz storytelling. Born in the Dakotas, Rhiannon was lured to California by burgeoning lesbian passions. She received support from a mostly dyke audience who came to hear her double-bill with Helen Hooke and Deadly Nightshade. She was introduced to the world of women's music and culture at the First National Women's Music Festival in Champaign, IL, in 1975. Alive! formed soon after, going on to wow jazz clubs across the US for ten years.
Rhiannon has taught voice, has released two cassettes for voice training, has toured with her moving and intensely personal one-woman show "Toward Home" (*Toward Home* was recently released on cassette), and has joined Voicestra, a multicultural, mixed-gender, gay-and-straight all-vocal ensemble orchestrated by longtime friend and collaborator Bobby McFerrin. —*Laura Post*

Loosen up and Improvise / 1986 / Rhiannon ◆◆◆
This vocal stretching and improvisation tape was created by Rhiannon (known to many as the lead singer of Alive!) because many of her vocal students were frequently asking to tape her classes. This tape is the more advanced of the two, for people who already sing, and includes guided physical stretching; rhythmic duets with Rhiannon; call and response; suggestions for developing rhythmic and melodic patterns; and exercises with piano to develop strength, intonation, and improvisation skills. Rhiannon talks you through the exercises and sings with you to open up new ideas. This wonderful and skilled teacher has been developing her own vocal method for over 12 years. If you like to sing, you need this tape. —*Ladyslipper*

Finding Your Voice / 1987 / Rhiannon ◆◆◆
This is geared to those who don't sing yet or who have lost their voices, for whatever the reasons: being "tone-deaf," having been discouraged from it when young, adult children of alcoholics, incest survivors, being shy. For those who want to begin to explore their hidden songs. Using improvisation, Rhiannon leads the listener through body-instrument awareness and alignment, physical music warm-up, breathing exercises, long tones, call and response, and simple duets. Enjoy at home or in your car. —*Ladyslipper*

★ **Toward Home** / 1991 / Ladyslipper ◆◆◆◆◆
With material by Betsy Rose, Janet Small, and Carolyn Brady, Rhiannon shows her stuff. Accompanied by Nina Gerber and Barbara Borden, she displays her range and diversity. —*AMG*

Sweet Honey in the Rock

Women's, A Cappella
The voice as a dominant instrument is finding new favor among music lovers. The group that has been central to this development within the contemporary music scene is a quintet of electrifying vocalists based in Washington, DC, Sweet Honey in the Rock.
Singing unaccompanied except for body and hand percussion instruments, this ensemble of African-American women singers has built a solid international reputation and following. The strength of Sweet Honey lies within its repertoire rooted in the tradition of African congregational choral style and its many extensions. One hears the moan of blues, the power of early 20th-century gospel, echoes of the community quartet, and jazz choral vocalizations freshly tinged with church melodic and harmonic runs. A Sweet Honey in the Rock concert is a transforming experience, drenching audiences with harmonies. The rhythms change, leads change, and women dance: breathtaking music.
The women of Sweet Honey sing fiercely of being fighters, tenderly of being in love, and knowingly of being women. They take their evergrowing audiences through a complex journey of celebration and struggle rooted in the African-American legacy. The concept and leadership of the group rest primarily with Bernice Johnson Reagon, who, as vocal direc-

tor of the DC Black Repertory Theater, founded Sweet Honey in 1973. Reagon began her work as a socially conscious artist in 1961 during the Albany, GA, civil rights movement. The musical and political groundwork set by Reagon is expanded by the other singers who join her on Sweet Honey's stages. —*Laura Post*

Sweet Honey in the Rock / 1976 / Flying Fish ◆◆◆
This album features original compositions and traditional gospel music. —*AMG*

B'lieve I'll Run On (See What the End's Gonna Be) / 1978 / Redwood ◆◆◆
This is the second album of gospel-influenced a cappella vocals, with emphasis on harmonies. Original songs include ones about nuclear proliferation and Jimmy Carter; women who have loved other women as mothers, daughters, sisters, lovers; the experiences of Black women; a couple about strong Black women such as Sojourner Truth and Fannie Lou Hamer. —*Ladyslipper*

Good News / 1982 / Flying Fish ◆◆◆
Recorded live in Washington, DC, in 1981, it includes "Breaths," probably their finest, most breathtaking track ever, a top-notch "circular sharing of historic wisdom, boundless energy and love." —*Ladyslipper*

The Other Side / 1986 / Flying Fish ◆◆◆
Sweet Honey addresses a spectrum of issues with a blend of contemporary, protest, topical, personal, and love songs. Included is "Venceremos (We Will Win)," "Mandiacappella" (a vocal improvisation based on West African drum rhythms), Woody Guthrie's "Deportees," and Bernice Reagon's original "Mae Frances." —*Ladyslipper*

★ **Live at Carnegie Hall** / 1988 / Flying Fish ◆◆◆◆◆
Probably the group's best showcase, playing to their audience in high spirits and with excellent sound. —*Bruce Eder*

☆ **All for Freedom** / 1989 / Music For Little People ◆◆◆◆◆
This is technically a children's album, but it will inspire and be enjoyed by adults and children alike. Drawing on their rich heritage of African musical traditions, Sweet Honey has put together this dynamic and empowering collection of African songs, African stories, and gospel songs, including "Calypso Freedom," "Kumbaya," "Juba," "The Little Shekere," and the title song. —*Ladyslipper*

☆ **Breaths** / 1989 / Flying Fish ◆◆◆◆◆
A CD-only compilation features over an hour of their best tracks from the Flying Fish label. —*AMG*

We All . . . Everyone of Us / 1989 / Flying Fish ◆◆◆
These five Black women need and use nothing more than their voices to create music more complete and moving than a full orchestra. On this 1983 release, which includes favorites "More than a Paycheck" and "Battle for My Life," powerful lyrics join intertwining harmonies which leave a message that haunts you long after the record stops spinning. —*Ladyslipper*

Feel Something Drawing Me On / 1989 / Flying Fish ◆◆◆◆
It's a different album concept from their previous discography, and a unique release. This is an album of sacred music: from Christian gospel songs sung by congregations in the Deep South as well as Liberia, to traditional lullabies, to "Meyango," a West African funeral song. Here they give voice to many of the traditions that their more contemporary music is rooted in, and beautifully document the diverse cultural, spiritual, and artistic powers of sacred song. —*Ladyslipper*

In This Land / Sep. 15, 1992 / Earthbeat! ◆◆◆◆
In the inspired congregational tradition of African-American culture, this 1992 album goes straight to the hearts and souls of our lives, sharing truth, tragedy, comfort, outrage, hope, love, healing, solidarity, and wisdom—and always at the highest levels of beauty and art. —*Ladyslipper*

I Got Shoes / Oct. 1992 / Music for Little People ◆◆◆◆
Brilliant harmonies abound on the a cappella group's second album for children. —*Janet Schnol*

Still on the Journey / 1993 / Earthbeat! ◆◆◆
Sweet Honey in the Rock proves once again that the human voice is a beautiful instrument. This famous a cappella group is thankfully *Still On the Journey*. Steeped in the spiritual and other African-American traditions, *Still on the Journey* offers a full banquet of sound. The songs are of love and living, and of struggling and dying. Sweet Honey sings gospel, folk, and rap songs, all with a message of unity and freedom. The scholarly attention that Sweet Honey shows in this recording is superseded only by the utterly natural arrangements. —*MusD*

Sacred Ground / Nov. 1995 / Earthbeat! ◆◆◆

Linda Tillery

Drums, Vocals / Blues-Rock
Linda Tillery shared the stage with John Mayall and Tiny Tim in the early '70s, before it was fashionable for women to play music alongside of men. Her rock band, the Loading Zone, released a self-named album

on RCA (1969), and Tillery's debut solo disc, *Sweet Linda Divine* (CBS), came out a year later, to enthusiastic reviews and high praise. Around the time that women's music and culture was getting started, Tillery–Tui to her friends–lent her percussive and vocal skills to albums by Mary Watkins and Teresa Trull, eventually playing/singing on 40 albums. Tillery's own second solo effort, *Linda Tillery*, was released on the Olivia label (1978). Tillery collaborated with such female musical powerhouses as June Millington, Deidre McCalla, Barbara Higbie, and Margie Adam, as well as on the Olivia tenth anniversary album, *Meg/Cris Live at Carnegie* (1983). In 1985, Tillery released *Secrets* on her own 411 label; distributed by Redwood Records, it returned her to center stage. In recent years, she has assembled a large band that plays jazzy, funky blues. —*Laura Post*

Shake It to the One That You Love the Best / 1989 / Music For Little People ◆◆◆◆
Shake It to the One That You Love: The Best Play Songs and Lullabies from Black Musical Traditions is another excellent compilation from Music for Little People. —*Janet Schnol*

★ **Secrets** / Redwood ◆◆◆◆◆
A powerful collection of sultry, potent rock and R&B driven by Tillery's forceful voice and personality. —*Bruce Eder*

Topp Twins

Lynda and Jools Topp, identical twins with that eerie twin kinship and an irresistible propensity for finishing each other's sentences, are as different from each other as they are from the stereotypical Kiwi country/western lesbian political theatrical humorists. More physically solid, Lynda has the magnificent yodel. Jools, sparer in size and in conversation, sports a dry sense of humor and comes alive on-stage, pacing their musical sets with her guitar.

Raised on a dairy farm on the North Island of New Zealand, Lynda and Jools milked cows and obtained the "educational certificates that we needed in order to leave school." Taking inspiration from their mother, who used to sing, and a guitar given to them by their brother when they were 11, the Topp Twins got their chance to play and sing at a yearly local shindig. Lynda and Jools later moved to Christchurch, the biggest city on the south island, supporting themselves with blue-collar jobs. They played their first gig to 300 people there. A women's fundraiser followed, as did skits and theater bits for their debut tour in 1979. Touring with Helen Caldicott in New Zealand and with Billy Bragg in England brought them an eclectic, loyal following. They were voted New Zealand's Entertainers of the Year in 1987. Their commissioned theater show was voted best TV performance the same year. —*Laura Post*

No War in My Heart / 1987 / Topp Twins ◆◆◆◆
Their 1987 album juxtaposes biting political satire with beautiful love songs. It includes "President's Men," "Throw Down Your Guns," "Dolly Parton," "The Queen," "Untouchable Girls," and more. —*Ladyslipper*

● **Hightime** / 1992 / Topp Twins ◆◆◆◆
Jools and Lynda Topp, one of the top New Zealand sibling duos, bring their offbeat humor, genetic harmonies, and a unique acoustic guitar sound to this 1992 release. —*Ladyslipper*

Lucie Blue Tremblay

Guitar, Keyboards, Vocals / Folk
Tremblay's music has an intensity that also soothes. The bilingual background of this Canadian-born singer-songwriter has proved a valuable asset, and her keyboard and guitar-playing skills have provided useful accompaniment to her poignant, spellbinding ballads ever since she first arrived on the Canadian music scene in 1984. Her self-titled debut album was voted Top Ten Album of the Year by the Boston Globe in 1986, and in subsequent albums she has continued to turn personal experience into compelling song, with studio recordings being interspersed with concert cuts, and English lyrics alternating with songs in French. Tremblay serenades us with a rich, warm voice that can soar from a throaty purr to strong, crystal tones, her songs combining a soft melodic essence with a depth of feeling that is riveting, particularly in her love songs. Her performing credits include appearances at New York's Carnegie Hall and the Canadian Pavilion at the 1992 World's Fair in Seville, Spain, and she has been heard with James Taylor and Randy Newman on National Public Radio's weekly broadcast "E-Town." —*Laura Post*

☆ **Lucie Blue Tremblay** / 1986 / Olivia ◆◆◆◆◆
Her debut features sweetly sung material in both French and English, although the listener should have no trouble following the emotional content of either. Side one is live; side two is studio-recorded, featuring backing vocals by Cris Williamson, Teresa Trull, Tret Fure, and Deirdre McCalla. —*AMG*

Tendresse/ Tenderness / 1989 / Olivia ◆◆◆
Beautiful love songs, political statements, and traditional folk music show her diversity. These poignant stories are in both French and English. —*AMG*

★ **Transformations** / 1992 / Olivia ◆◆◆◆◆
Another charmed release. Songs are in both English and French, including "Chez Nous," "All Out of Love Tonight," "Homeless," "Sail Away," and "The Guilty One." —*Ladyslipper*

Teresa Trull

Keyboards, Vocals / Country-Pop
Brought up in Durham, NC, where she was steeped at an early age in blues, gospel, and R&B, Trull began her musical career singing gospel in churches, then served as the lead singer in a rock 'n' roll band for several years before joining the East Coast nightclub circuit. Since the release of her first album, *The Ways a Woman Can Be*, in 1977, Trull's gutsy rock 'n' roll vocal style, along with her songwriting and record production talent, has won the fiery-haired singer ever-widening recognition. In particular, Trull's album *Acclaimed*, a collaboration with Barbara Higbie, received high critical praise. Other musicians with whom Trull has performed and recorded include Bonnie Hayes, Dave Sanborn, Andy Narell, Darol Anger, Mike Marshall, Alex DeGrassi, Joan Baez, Linda Tillery, Cris Williamson, Holly Near, and Tracy Nelson. A songwriter of considerable note, Trull co-wrote two songs on the Whispers' gold album *Love for Love*, including the title track, with Roy Obiedo, and her production talents were recognized in 1985 when she was nominated for Best Producer of an Independent Album in the NY Music Awards. Trull's live performances have been said to combine the high power of Nona Hendryx with the irreverent wit of Bette Midler. —*AMG*

★ **A Step Away** / Redwood ◆◆◆◆◆
Trull's best is a high-quality work of hope and joy from this vocalist/keyboardist. —*AMG*

Unexpected / Second Wave ◆◆◆
The women of this dynamic duo show their stuff on this LP as they have been doing on tour around the country. It features an eclectic bunch of styles—country, gospel, ballads—some simple, some fairly produced. Barbara is a pianist extraordinaire; don't miss her LPs on Windham Hill. —*Ladyslipper*

Two Nice Girls

Women's, Folk, Group
Two Nice Girls are a trio of women who play rock with a keen, socially conscious, feminist/lesbian edge. Known for their multi-textured harmonies and versatility, the Girls are at home singing everything from satirical songs to raucous parodies to smooth love songs. —*Sandra Brennan*

● **2 Nice Girls** / 1989 / Rough Trade ◆◆◆◆
They're not two, they're not nice, and they're not girls; they *are* three talented women who make great music together. If you can imagine the layered harmonies and humor of the Roches, blended with vibrant, kaleidoscopic imagery as well as a true women-identified sensibility, you'll have an inkling of the Girls' style. They spoof hetero love, in "I Spent My Last $10 (on Birth Control and Beer)"; they sing unself-consciously of their women lovers. —*Ladyslipper*

Like a Version / 1990 / Rough Trade ◆◆◆◆
This 1990 EP release contains primarily covers of material by artists from Donna Summers to Sonic Youth, Carpenters to Janis Martin! Also included is "I Spent My Last $10," from their debut album. Six songs in all. —*Ladyslipper*

Chloe Liked Olivia / 1991 / Rough Trade ◆◆◆
Funny, kitschy, feisty, smart, brave, sexy, political, warm, or just plain wonderful—all of these qualities are in abundance on their 1991 release, a musical hybrid that transcends the boundaries of most musical genres. From the faux-disco of "Let's Go Bonding," to the smooth-as-Smokey "Swimming in Circles," to "The Queer Song," and "Princess of Power," the Girls have outdone themselves with ten brilliant songs that run their usual range from tender to tongue-in-cheek. —*Ladyslipper*

Nancy Vogl

Guitar, Vocals
Vogl began picking out tunes on a beat-up nylon string guitar when she was 13, then graduated to steel strings when she was 20. She went on to become a founding member (in Berkeley, CA) of one of the first feminist bands and ended up touring nearly every major folk club and university in the US. She released her first solo album, *Something to Go On* (Redwood Records), in 1984. A trip to Nashville two years later produced *Fight Like the Dancer* (Olivia Records), a contemporary mix of country, blues, and swing. Vogl's reflective, challenging, visionary lyrics combine the grace and humor of '40s musical show tunes with the solid power of '70s acoustic rock, and wed the heartbreak of country ballad to the clean-picking fun of folk. —*Laura Post*

Fight Like the Dancer / Olivia ◆◆◆

● **Something to Go On** / Redwood ◆◆◆◆
Vogel is a master of acoustic steel-string guitar-picking. She is a veteran

of women's music tours and recordings. On her first solo effort she has structured one side instrumental, featuring original duets with musical partner Suzanne Shanbaum, and the other side vocal. Her song "Crime of the Century" is an outstanding indictment of homophobia and other oppressions. Her insight into economic, social, and political history infuses the work with an extra intelligence. —*Ladyslipper*

Washington Sisters

Women's, Blues, Gospel, Jazz, Pop, Group
Once upon a time, two little girls stayed up through the night singing every song they knew. Years later, identical twins Sandra and Sharon Washington have taken their late-night ramblings and laughter on the road.

Bold. Joyful. The Washington Sisters bring an uplifting spirit of hope through their two albums, *Understated* (Icebergg Records, 1987) and *Take Two* (Shsawa Music, 1991). The Washingtons have performed hundreds of concerts, including over two dozen appearances at music and cultural festivals in the US and Canada. Their blend of a cappella, jazz swing, blues, gospel, and island rhythms provides a unique basis for their message of peace, women's rights, pride, and cultural diversity. —*Laura Post*

Understated / 1987 / Icebergg ✦✦✦
This debut album of hot sounds by identical twins Sandra and Sharon is full of unique harmonies and special songs: "Breaths," "Sweet Inspiration," "Brown Like Me," and "Find the Spirit." A cappella funk is combined with contemporary pop/folk/jazz and a touch of calypso. It features backup vocals by Linda Tillery and Vicki Randle, and is expertly produced by Teresa Trull. —*Ladyslipper*

● **Take Two** / 1991 / Shsawa ✦✦✦✦
Even better and more stylistically diverse than the harmonizing twins' first album, this follow-up includes blues, jazz, swing, country, and love songs. Produced by Teresa Trull, with backup artists such as Linda Tillery, Melanie Monsur, Nina Gerber, Paul McCandless, John Bucchino, even Trull herself. —*Ladyslipper*

Mary Watkins

Piano / Folk, Progressive Big Band
An eclectic composer who works comfortably in both the classical and jazz traditions, Watkins draws no firm boundaries around any one style. Elements of blues, gospel, county/folk, and pop slip easily into her work, and her versatility as a composer, arranger, pianist, and producer is reflected in the pieces she has composed for symphony orchestras, chamber ensembles, film, and the theater. Born in Denver, Watkins began her formal musical training when she was four, and by the age of eight she was starting to improvise and compose short piano pieces. After receiving a degree in music composition from Howard University in 1972, she performed with jazz combos in the Washington, DC, area, then moved to the West Coast and established her own jazz quartet. Several albums and numerous commissions and awards followed. Notable among Watkins' many compositions are the jazz score for the musical play *Lady Lester Sings the Blues*, based on the life of Lester Young, and "The Revolutionary Nutcracker Sweetie," a jazz adaptation of Tchaikovsky's *Nutcracker* ballet. —*AMG*

Winds of Change / Oct. 16, 1981-Oct. 17, 1981 / Palo Alto ✦✦✦
Large ensemble/orchestral recording done at Herbst Theatre in San Francisco. Watkins plays piano in the spirit of, say, Duke Pearson and Melba Liston. A fine album. —*Michael G. Nastos*

★ **Spirit Song** / 1985 / Redwood ✦✦✦✦✦
Different, perhaps arty. Imaginative. Worth looking for. —*Michael G. Nastos*

The Soul Kings / 1992 / Wenefil ✦✦✦✦
Arranged and interpreted with care and great affection. Watkins treats familiar gospel hymns (in the words of Will Thompson) "softly and tenderly" in a generous attempt to share their healing and soothing qualities with a frenzied and wounded world. Performing solely on her synthesizers and electric pianos, she presents such gems as "Amazing Grace," "Blessed Assurance," "Pass Me Not," "By and By," and "I'll Fly Away." —*Ladyslipper*

Something Moving / Olivia ✦✦✦

Ilene Weiss

b. 1953
Guitar, Vocals / Folk
Weiss is from Philadelphia and now resides in New York City. A very perceptive writer of songs about romantic irony (which have been covered by Anne Hills, Deidre McCalla, Robin Flowers, Marcy Marxer, and Cathy Fink she has been nominated for a BMI Songwriters Award and two New York Music Awards. She is also a contributor to the *Fast Folk Musical Magazine*. —*Chip Renner and Richard Meyer*

● **Outside and Curious** / 1992 / Gadfly ✦✦✦✦
This CD is just Weiss singing and playing guitar. Her vocals and guitar playing are very good. What stands out is her songwriting. Her songs are often filled with humor, but they can make you think. A very good release. —*Chip Renner*

Karen Williams

Vocals
Karen Williams is known as that thin Black lesbian stand-up comic with a lot to say and the gift for saying it in a screamingly funny way. Heads turn at her rapid-paced raps on single motherhood, dating, relationships, celibacy, AIDS, economic inequity, racism, codependency, and whatever topic strikes her fancy. Audiences marvel at her thinking presence, her acute awareness, but it is her attitude—angermasked behind diffidence —that brings her observations home.

Once a model and a serious dancer of African-Haitian and Modern styles, currently a committed Buddhist, Williams considers her non-humorous writing of great sustaining importance. She has acted in a department store TV commercial and in a play on lesbian life.

Born in the Bronx, Williams grew up amidst creative and lively people. Through her eventual relocation to the West Coast, she garnered a panoply of California jokes ("What is tofu anyway? I throw away my old sponges"). Williams debuted in and promoted herself through nightclubs in the San Francisco Bay Area. Interspersed with her international successes as a comic, she is raising two boys, establishing a network for touring women performers, learning French, and lending her organizational skills and political commitment to the Association of Women's Music and Culture, as their president. —*Laura Post*

● **Wild Child at Large** / Yahoo Video ✦✦✦✦
This performance at the 1991 Michigan Womyn's Music Festival has been captured on video, showing her being what she thought would be an easy, satisfying thing to be: an African-American lesbian mother comic. Her ad-lib with the plastic baby "Pookie" will have you in stitches. —*Ladyslipper*

Cris Williamson (Chris Williamson)

Keyboards, Vocals
For the fans who flock to her sold-out concerts and who have bought her 14 albums, Williamson's music and its messages are restorative balms that soothe, enlighten, and inspire. Her timeless classic, *The Changer and the Changed* remains one of the top-selling independent albums of all time and continues to be the best-selling women's music album. An avid environmentalist and humanitarian, Williamson frequently lends her name, talent, and support to causes (such as those involving terminally ill children) that others might consider lost, but to which she brings her special brand of energy and hope. Her "Don't Lose Heart" serves as the theme song for Henry Jaglom's acclaimed motion picture *New Year's Day*, and she has contributed compositions to a variety of other feature films and TV documentaries, including the PBS documentary "Is Anyone Home on the Range?" Williamson also wrote, produced, and narrated the Parents' Choice award-winning sci-fi fable for children, "Lumiere," which is now part of the curriculum of several Montessori schools. A blend of toughness, honesty, and intimacy marks her strongly personal, pop-styled ballads. As a musician, poet, and teacher of "the art of the possible," Williamson creates music that feeds the spirit and calms the soul. —*Laura Post*

Cris Williamson / 1971 / Olivia ✦✦✦✦
A remastered reissue of her first album. Very basic and raw, with veiled hints of things to come. —*Bruce Eder*

☆ **The Changer and the Changed** / 1975 / Olivia ✦✦✦✦✦
The record that set a new standard in the field. Soulful, passionate, and poignant. —*Bruce Eder*

Strange Paradise / 1980 / Olivia ✦✦✦
Musically on par with *Changer and the Changed*, it has more rock 'n' roll influence and some phenomenal synthesizer. Joined by Jackie Robbins, June Millington, and Bonnie Raitt. —*Ladyslipper*

Lumiere / 1982 / Olivia ✦✦

Blue Rider / 1982 / Olivia ✦✦✦✦
Bonnie Raitt guests on this, Williamson's most highly regarded rock album—a successful mix of electric guitars and topical concerns with some very personal lyrics. —*Bruce Eder*

Meg/Cris at Carnegie Hall / 1983 / Second Wave ✦✦✦
This deluxe double volume includes the entire herstory-making Carnegie Hall performance of Nov. 1982, which celebrated her tenth anniversary. The CD is one volume and contains all but two selections. —*Ladyslipper*

Portrait / 1983 / Olivia ✦✦✦
This retrospective, compiled in 1983, is a collection of favorites drawn from her previous albums. —*Ladyslipper*

Snow Angel / 1985 / Olivia ✦✦✦
This is a winter holiday album, with songs for the variety of seasonal holidays. Think of it sort of as a "Cris-Ms." album. —*Ladyslipper*

Wolf Moon / 1987 / Olivia ✦✦✦
This varied selection of songs has a wolf theme running throughout. From "The Run of the Wolf," a poignant dedication to Kate Wolf, to the love song "Home Free" ("no longer the lone wolf . . . ") to the title song, about listening to Wolfman Jack's radio show. —*Ladyslipper*

Country Blessed / 1989 / Second Wave ✦✦✦
Recorded as a duo with Olivia Records' ace-producer Teresa Trull in a somewhat country-fied vein. An especially unusual record that showcases Williamson doing songs of other writers. —*Bruce Eder*

☆ **Prairie Fire** / 1989 / Olivia ✦✦✦✦✦
Her hardest rocker ever, and her cleverest, most pointed collection of songs, covering concerns that range from Native Americans to new age vacuousness. —*Bruce Eder*

★ **Circle of Friends: Cris Live . . .** / 1991 / Olivia ✦✦✦✦
This live recording of the *15th Anniversary of the Changer and the Changed* show, as performed in Berkeley in 1990, brings back the special magic of that remarkable album that influenced so many in the early years. Included are selected highlights from the *Changer*—"Waterfall," "Sweet Woman," "Shooting Star," "Dreamchild," "Sister," "Song of the Soul"—as well as previously unrecorded songs from her early repertoire: "If It Weren't for the Music," "Circle of Friends," "Sisters of Mercy," "Olivia," "Millworker," and "Hey Good Lookin'." —*Ladyslipper*

The Best of Cris Williamson / Olivia ✦✦✦
It's not quite what the title says. The folk material dominates, leaving out some cool and hot rock numbers. —*Bruce Eder*

Various Artists

☆ **A Family of Friends** / Tsunami ✦✦✦✦✦
This 1993 release may be the best sampler of women's music ever created. The title song, an anthem-to-be and a must-have for every women's music lover, is one of the sweetest and most memorable tunes ever composed. As a collaboration, it expresses some of the highest spirit of our lesbian culture. Co-written by Sue Fink, Jamie Anderson, June Millington, Jane Emmer, and Dakota, it is performed by songwriters Sue, Jamie, June and Jane, plus Margie Adam, Deidre McCalla, Cris Williamson, Tret Fure, Sharon Washington, Jean Millington, Susan Herrick, Robin Flower, Monica Grant, Helen Hooke, Mary Watkins, Barbara Borden, and others. There are tracks (many previously released) by the following individual artists: Alix Dobkin (with her previously unreleased "My Kind of Girl"),

Pam Hall, Venus Envy, Yer Girlfriend, OneSpirit (Kay Gardner and Nurudafina Pili Abena), Sue Fink, June Millington, Mimi Baczewska, Laura Berkson, Diane Lindsay, Leah Zicari, Jamie Anderson. Some profits will be donated to a lesbian organization. It is a great introduction for friends and "family" new to women's music, and a classic for the confirmed. —*Ladyslipper*

★ **Michigan Live 85: Womyn's Music Fest** / 1986 / August Night ✦✦✦✦✦
This double album is the definitive sampler of women's music, joyfully reflecting all the richness and diversity of the women's cultural movement at its best. Live performances by Holly Near, Kay Gardner, Alix Dobkin, Ferron, Lucie Blue Tremblay, and others have been superbly engineered into a body of work which flows as beautifully as the landmark festival it commemorates. It is a must for every lover of women's music, and a perfect gift for anyone. —*Ladyslipper*

Peace Camp Sings / Tallapoosa ✦✦✦✦✦
These 38 songs were collected by Sorrel Hays primarily at Greenham Common and Seneca Women's Peace Camps, 1983-1985. Several were recorded later in her living-room studio by Marilyn Ries; some were composed by individuals, some collective efforts, others new lyrics to well-known melodies; sung by a variety of artists. Included is Naomi Littlebear's "You Can't Kill the Spirit," recorded at the Barbara Deming Memorial Service; "We're Shameless Hussies," "My Old Mom's a Lesbo," "Fuck Off Sexist Pigs," "I'm a Dyke," "Ron with the Neutron Bomb," "Rocka My Soul in the Bosom of Sisterhood," "We Are the Weavers," and many more priceless expressions of the strength of womankind. Proceeds go to women's peace camps. —*Ladyslipper*

The Redwood Collection / Redwood ✦✦✦✦✦
This sampler album includes selections by Holly Near, Ronnie Gilbert, Inti-Illimani, "H.A.R.P.," Ferron, Linda Tillery, Mary Watkins, Guardabarranco, Judy Small, and Nancy Vogl—all of whom have records released on the Redwood label. It's great for introducing new audiences to the Redwood roster. —*Ladyslipper*

Voices of Battered Lesbians / MA Coalition ✦✦✦✦✦
This 1990 tape was produced by the Lesbian Caucus of the Massachusetts Coalition of Battered Women Service Groups, created by survivors, and features the experiences of battered lesbians from differing cultural, economic, and racial backgrounds. Opening with Alix Dobkin's "Pitfalls of True Love," it attempts to define abusive behavior and to dispell the myths surrounding what is still a very taboo subject in our communities. It would be helpful for anyone wondering whether her situation should be considered battering, and use for anyone working with battered women. It includes support services numbers, including 1-800-333-SAFE. —*Ladyslipper*

WOMEN IN ROCK

To talk about "women in rock" as a sub-genre of its own is a little peculiar, because women have been a part of every step of rock's evolution. Teen idols, '50s R&B, girl groups, soul, psychedelic rock, British Invasion, singer/songwriters, funk, punk, new wave, rap, you name it—women performers may not have been as numerous as male ones in most instances, but they've always been part of the action, often on center stage. The increased media attention given to women rockers in the '90s results not just from their commercial presence—there have always been women stars—but their increasing assumption of roles that have traditionally been primarily male domains, especially as regards hard-rocking, self-contained bands of females that play their own electric guitars, drums, and basses.

Ascribing a distinct feminine perspective to rock performed by women is opening a minefield of debate. Some critics and listeners, both female and male, insist that women rockers should not be judged for the feminine qualities in their work, but by the quality of the work itself, gender having as little to do with its ultimate value as the color of their shoes. Others insist that appreciation of the feminine elements of their music need to be taken into account, especially when considering that the role of women in both the music business and larger society has been often suppressed, oppressed, and under-represented. It's unquestionable, though, that women have played a larger part in some important rock styles—the '60s girl-group sound, the singer/songwriter movement, and the "riot grrrl" alternative rockers in the '90s—than others, to the degree that some sub-genres are almost defined by their female performers. There could be an entire separate column about women musicians who were instrumental in forming the roots of rock, such as the blues singers of the '20s and hillbilly/country acts like the Carter Family and Rose Maddox. The first to sing in a style that approached or entered rock 'n' roll were R&B singers of the late '40s and early '50s such as Faye Adams, Big Mama Thornton and Big Maybelle; some also played boogie piano, such as Camille Howard. Ruth

Brown and LaVerne Baker, both of whom recorded for the Atlantic label, are usually thought of as the most important women singers participating in the transition from R&B to rock & roll. Women in rockabilly were relatively rare—Sparkle Moore and Janis Martin are names known only to collectors at this point. Yet the best of them, Wanda Jackson, was indeed one of the best rockabilly singers of any kind, with a raspy, saucy delivery that anticipated the raunch of later vocalists like Janis Joplin.

There were a few female teen idols, such as Annette Funicello, although the biggest of them—Connie Francis and Brenda Lee—were such big stars, with such wide demographic appeal, that it's inaccurate to pigeonhole them into the style. But the first type of rock & roll to be identified primarily— solely, actually, as it turned out—with female performers were the girl groups of the early '60s. Acts like the Shirelles, the Shangri-Las, and the Ronettes wed R&B harmonies with pop-conscious melodies, sophisticated orchestral production, and aching, jubilant declarations of young love. Most of the girl groups (and solo singers that adhered to the girl group blueprint, such as Lesley Gore), it must be pointed out, did not write their own material, much of which was supplied by professional songwriters. Some of the most noted of these tunesmiths, though, were female (Carole King, Cynthia Weil, Ellie Greenwich), ensuring a feminine viewpoint in much of the music, even if they did often write with their husbands.

The girl group sound was a big influence on the British Invasion—the Beatles, for instance, recorded tunes by the Shirelles, the Cookies, the Marvelettes, and Little Eva, and Manfred Mann, Herman's Hermits, and the Searchers had big international hits with girl group covers. It's inaccurate to declare, as has sometimes been written, that the British Invasion wiped out the girl group sound—1964, the year the Beatles landed in the States, in fact saw girl groups at a commercial peak. And a few of the British Invasion acts were women that owed prominent debts to the girl group sound, the best of those being Dusty Springfield, Lulu, and Marianne Faithfull. But in a couple of years, the self-contained British acts, as well as folk-rockers and soul belters, had combined to make the bouncier and quainter girl group sound seem passe, as brilliant as many of the girl group records were.

Some of the biggest girl groups emerged from Motown, including the Supremes, the Marvelettes, and Martha & the Vandellas. They would survive the death of the girl group trend, partly because the mainstream of soul music was packed with top-notch women performers, even if they had a smaller slice of the pie than their male counterparts. To list all of the female soul greats would take paragraphs, if not pages; it's enough to note that Aretha Franklin, Carla Thomas, Irma Thomas, Gladys Knight, Mavis Staples, Mary Wells, Maxine Brown, Barbara Lewis, and Ann Peebles (for starters) are among the very best soul singers of any kind. Sometimes they wrote some or much of their own material, but it's not accurate to say that they were necessarily denied songwriting opportunities routinely granted to other soul stars. Top-flight acts like the Temptations, the Jackson 5and Sam & Dave, for instance, wrote little of their own material; even geniuses like Marvin Gaye and Stevie Wonder had to feed into the Motown pipeline of staff songwriting at the outset of their careers. It was rare to find female soul stars who also played an instrument (other than the occasional pianist); guitarist/singer-songwriter Barbara Lynn was a notable exception, and Sly & the Family Stone ran against the pack by prominently featuring women horn players and keyboardists in the backing band.

White rock of the '60s was a pretty guitar-based medium, and it was rare to find women assuming important roles in bands, other than vocal ones, with exceptions like drummers Maureen Tucker (of the Velvet Underground) and Honey Lantree (of the Honeycomb). Several folk-rock groups prominently featured women singers, such as the Mamas and Papas and Sonny & Cher. Two of the biggest California psychedelic groups were instrumental in providing vehicles for female lead singers to perform in a far gutsier, more assertive style than the norm. Grace Slick was not the Jefferson Airplane's sole vocalist, but she sang (and wrote) many of their best songs. The raunchier Janis Joplin, both with Big Brother & the Holding Company and as a solo act, delivered her material in a rasping, bluesy, aggressively sexual style that had been previously unseen in White women rock singers.

Fairly or unfairly, women songwriters were thought of as preferring more confessional, laidback, introspective, and romantic themes than guitar-dominated rock bands. If that was the case, they found their best vehicle in the singer-songwriter movement, which started to gather steam in the late '60s. Some of them were former professional pop songwriters (Jackie DeShannon, Carole King) who yearned to both record their own material and investigate more personal subjects. Others (Joni Mitchell, Janis Ian) moved into the style from folk backgrounds. Often they played instruments as well; almost always, these were guitars (often acoustic) or pianos. The singer-songwriter school peaked commercially in the '70s, yet it continues to spawn performers to this day, some (such as Tracy Chapman) becoming superstars. Kate Bush fused singer-songwriter ethos with elements of progressive rock and new wave to become a huge star in Britain, although she never made it much past cult status in the US. In retrospect, one of the chief achievements of punk rock in the mid-'70s was to shatter the stereotype that assigned women to particular roles and instruments. Many punk bands featured women on electric guitar, bass, and drums, roles which had usually been reserved for men, with rare exceptions such as glam rocker/guitarist Suzi Quatro. Self-contained, all-women rock groups that wrote their own material had been rarities, but bands like the Slits and the Raincoat did much to trash those unwritten rules. What's more, mixed-gender lineups, with women sharing the songwriting, vocal, and instrumental duties with males, also became increasingly frequent. Some of the best first-generation punk/new wave singers—Patti Smith, Deborah Harry, Siouxsie Sioux, a revitalized Marianne Faithful— were women that did much to redefine traditional female rock images, singing about politics, sex, and alienation (sometimes all at once) with forthright, occasionally theatrical abandon.

The edges of punk were rounded off to form new wave, a more easily digestible form of alternative rock that was more palatable to the rock mainstream. Some women with punk, or at least harsher-sounding new wave roots, became superstars, such as Annie Lennox of Eurythmics, Chrissie Hynde (leader of the Pretenders), the Go-Gos, the Bangles, and Deborah Harry of late-period Blondie. Others appropriated some of new wave's fashion sense for music that was at its essence mainstream pop, such as Cyndi Lauper and the biggest

30 Recommended Albums

Ruth Brown, *Best Of* (Rhino)
Wanda Jackson, *Rockin' with Wanda* (Capitol)
Brenda Lee, *Anthology, Vol. 1 & 2* (MCA)
Various Artists, *The Best of the Girl Groups, Vol. 1 & 2* (Rhino)
The Shirelles, *Anthology* (Rhino)
The Ronettes, *Best of the Ronettes* (ABKCO)
The Shangri-Las, *Myrmidons of Melodrama* (RPM)
Irma Thomas, *Sweet Soul Queen of New Orleans: The Irma Thomas Collection* (Razor & Tie)
The Supremes, *Anthology* (Motown)
Jackie DeShannon, *What the World Needs Now . . . ; The Definitive Collection* (EMI)
Dusty Springfield, *The Silver Collection* (Philips)
Aretha Franklin, *30 Greatest Hits* (Atlantic)
Janis Joplin, *Janis box set* (Columbia/Legacy)
Joni Mitchell, *Blue* (Reprise)
Carole King, *Tapestry* (Epic)
Patti Smith, *Horses* (Arista)
The Raincoats, *The Raincoats* (Geffen)
Blondie, *The Platinum Collection* (EMI)
Marianne Faithfull, *Broken English* (Island)
The Pretenders, *The Singles* (Sire)
Madonna, *The Immaculate Collection* (Sire)
Janet Jackson, *Control* (A&M)
Tracy Chapman, *Tracy Chapman* (Elektra)
Bonnie Raitt, *Nick of Time* (Capitol)
Salt-N-Pepa, *Blacks' Magic* (London)
Queen Latifah, *All Hail the Queen* (Tommy Boy)
Hole, *Live Through This* (DGC)
Liz Phair, *Exile in Guyville* (Matador)
Kristin Hersh, *Hips and Makers* (Sire)
PJ Harvey, *To Bring You My Love* (Indigo)

entertainment phenomenon of the late 20th-century bar Michael Jackson, Madonna. Madonna's multiple image changes, and dance-oriented material that titillated with sexual explicitness that usually didn't get truly direct enough to inspire much outrage or censorship, has inspired book-length theoretical treatises.

Attracting both widespread adulation and scorn, it may be that she will be remembered primarily for her persona, rather than her music, as many millions of units as she has shifted.

To generalize, the last two decades have not seen as much redefinition/expansion of the roles of women in R&B/Black pop as in White rock. There were disco divas, of course, like Donna Summer, and the disco production machine still echoes today in contemporary dance music, in which many female singers are little more than figureheads of records constructed around beats, sequencers, and mixes. Urban contemporary singers such as Patti LaBelle and Anita Baker update (some would say dilute) classic soul styles for mellower radio formats and an adult-oriented audience. Janet Jackson made a lot of noise about declaring her creative and emotional independence on her phenomenally successful albums of the late '80s and '90s. But much of her dance/pop/soul appeal could be attributed to her producer/collaborators, and the records could only be judged as adventurous statements in comparison to the tame sex-kitten images and sounds of many other mainstream female R&B singers. Rap, still a male-dominated field nearly a couple of decades after its birth, has been justly accused of frequent over-the-top misogyny. The imbalance has been addressed to some extent by female rappers such as Salt-N-Pepa, Queen Latifah, and MC Lyte.

Mainstream female rockers, it should be noted, are far from unknown; two-fifths of Fleetwood Mac (including two of their three songwriters) were female at the apogee of their '70s success, Heart (fronted by sisters Ann and Nancy Wilson, who also wrote songs and played guitars) played unabashedly radio-friendly guitar rock, and Joan Jett ground out hard pop/rock with enough vague alternative ancestry to ride the riot grrrl bandwagon years after her commercial peak. Melissa Etheridge plays heartland AOR rock that's not so far from Tom Petty territory; Bonnie Raitt, after nearly two decades in the business, became a superstar as she entered her 40s, though the blues flavor of her earliest albums was toned down.

In the eyes of many listeners and critics, however, the true cutting edge of women in rock in the '90s was to be found in the alternative scene. This wasn't a '90s phenomenon, really; women such as Kim Gordon (of Sonic Youth) and Kristin Hersh (of Throwing Muses) had been integral to some of the most popular alternative rock bands of the '80s. In the '90s, the difference was that, following albums like Nirvana's *Nevermind,* this music was being heard by the commercial mainstream, after years of primarily being relegated to cultish audiences and college/noncommercial radio. Thus it came as a surprise to many to suddenly find women fronting, or entirely comprising, assertive guitar-based acts like Belly, the Breeders, and Veruca Salt, although this had really been going on since the punk era. Dozens of overlooked female acts of the '80s, like Salem 66 and Scrawl, missed out on those major-label contracts and national magazine features mostly as a matter of timing, playing alternative guitar rock at a time when its audience was somewhat ghettoized into a college-educated elite frequenting small clubs and independent record stores.

A radical offshoot of the '90s alternative rock scene was formed by the "riot grrrls," who fused punk and metal in the manner of grunge groups, but with a more explicitly feminist stance, and one that sometimes encompassed confrontational politics as well. As with any underground rock movement, even to comment upon, or try to briefly describe, riot grrrl is a controversial act. Some music critics dismiss the groups as much sound and fury signifying little, or worse, as musically inept. Devotees charge that the music's harsh stances and explicit examination of gender roles and emotional abuse are precisely designed to make complacent listeners uncomfortable. Some feminists don't know what to think, debating whether women are proving a point by acting as sluttish and exhibitionistic as any male glam metal band, or just reflecting their own confusion by misguidedly emulating macho rock posturing. L7, Babes in Toyland and 7 Year Bitch are some of the most popular/notorious of these bands. Hole, featuring Courtney Love's anguished wails and

relentless appetite for media attention, are the biggest of all of them. Those who want alternative rock with an avowedly uncompromising and feminine perspective that's more melodic and accessible than the riot grrrls could look to (at the most radio-friendly extreme) Bjork and Sinéad O'Connor. PJ Harvey, also based in the British Isles, offered something more bluesy and rawly produced than those two superstars. Kristin Hersh, in her solo debut away from Throwing Muses, showed a folkier side that made more direct emotional hits than her much more fully produced work with Throwing Muses.

The greatest hope for synthesizing past and present alternative rock and pop elements into a modern, non-exclusionary, feminist-colored vision is singer/songwriter Liz Phair, who scored one of the biggest critical smashes of recent years with her 1993 debut, *Exile in Guyville.* Although she wrote about personal and sexual relationships with unbridled frankness (and occasional profanity), her lyrics were married to compelling guitar riffs, and tempered by a sensitivity and naked emotion akin in spirit to vintage Joni Mitchell. While she hasn't been able to yet match the brilliance of her first album, she probably captured the tenor of young adult identification struggles and gender roles better than any singer-songwriter of the '90s, male or female. *—Richie Unterberger*

Books

Girl Groups: The Story of a Sound, by Alan Betrock (Delilah)
Will You Still Love Me Tomorrow: Girl Groups from the '50s On, by Charlotte Greig (Virago)
She Bop, by Lucy O'Brien (Penguin)
Grrrls: Viva Rock Divas, by Amy Raphael (St. Martin's Griffin)
Angry Women in Rock, Vol. 1 (Juno)

GAY

With the major labels reporting $10 billion in cassette and CD sales, 1993 was a record-breaking year for the international music industry. It was also the biggest year ever for gay music. More new artists emerged, more albums with openly gay themes were recorded and released (most on independent labels), and more gay albums were purchased than ever before in the history of the community. In fact, according to Overlooked Opinions, a national market-research firm, gay and lesbian people buy eight times as many tapes and CDs as the average consumer.

Although gay literature is enjoying popularity, and shows like Angels in America and Kiss of the Spider Woman have had big commercial breakthroughs, gay music has been the poor stepchild of the gay cultural arts. Barbra Streisand, Bette Midler, the Village People, and Taylor Dayne were staples in the musical diets of gay people for years, and mainstream record companies focused on mega-selling album artists, in the process overlooking the needs of the gay community to hear its stories represented in pop music. This critical oversight has pushed an incredible array of diverse artists into the independent record scene. Ten years ago, Romanovsky & Phillips

were just emerging to join Tom Wilson Weinberg in what for years would be the only representation of gay male recording artists in the community. Today, dozens of gay artists and groups are making great albums in the fields of pop, rock, alternative, folk, dance, and Country & Western. Pop music is slowly emerging from the closet!

At the same time, the gay movement is at a crossroads, continuing to define itself and working to represent a widely diverse, constantly evolving population of human beings. There has never been more need—or opportunity—to support music with a specifically gay perspective—music that speaks to the lives of gay people everywhere. And more than ever before, there is good reason to believe that gay people will discover and enthusiastically embrace their own new music and help bring it into the mainstream.

Every movement has its music, and now we are creating our own. With the recent passing of Stonewall 25, we still don't know how far ahead equal rights for gay people may lie, but we can be sure that through all our struggles, the music will be there—for gay men and lesbians, for our families, for straights, and for anyone who will listen to this bold new music.— *Will Grega*

Adult Children Of Heterosexuals

Rock, Cabaret
Part of Boston's Theatre Offensive and founded by members of the legendary United Fruit Company, this hard-edged, co-gender cabaret band entertains in an exciting and provocative way with their blend of high camp and low humor. — *Will Grega*

Adult Children Of Heterosexuals / 1993 / Mcmillan ◆◆◆
"I'm So Hard So I'm So Easy" and "I Never Liked You Anyway," (which is a read up, down, and in every direction) are two of the screamingly hilarious gender-bending romps on this raucous blend of avant-garde jazz, cheesy synths, sax, and vocal ensemble. — *Will Grega*

Tina Benez

Pop-Rock
Benez is a self-styled drag queen goddess, with solid pop smarts, unlimited ambition, chart savvy, and a fervent following all too willing to propel him/her to superstardom. — *Will Grega*

☆ **Glamour Overdose** / 1994 / Benez Popaganda Muzik ◆◆◆◆◆
Benez delivers one of the most wildly original albums of the '90s. "Hitler's Daughter (High Fascist Model)" is a chilling peep into the fascistic (but highly fashionable) future of the world politic. "Glamour Overdose (G.O.D.)" is a scream from start to finish, and is delivered over a highly polished Eurodance/rock track. The vocal samples and overall production are brilliantly tasty, and "Ghost in You" is a phenomenal ballad with an arrangement reminiscent of Ennio Morricone's spaghetti Western film scores. — *Will Grega*

Richard Bone

Synthesizer / Dance-Pop
A founding member of NYC's electronic music scene, Richard Bone started his career by writing music for off-Broadway theater productions (using home-made processors), and has worked with neo-legendaries Lenny Kaye and Reeves Gabrels. In 1980, he joined Shox Lumania, but soon went solo and released a string of singles on Chrysalis Records. He has produced singles for Rubber Rodeo, composed original music for award-winning cable and broadcast television, and has been involved in the music video production of his own work released on the experimental Sony "Video 45's" in the early '80s. — *Will Grega*

● **Quirkwork** / 1992 / Quirkworks Laboratory ◆◆◆◆
Tricky arpeggiated passages, layered vocals, and deft production combine to make these dance-floor friendly tracks a real treat. Tracks include "Last Days of Heaven," "Calling All Cars," and "Eveready Strut." — *Will Grega*

Ambiento / 1994 / Quirkworks Laboratory ◆◆◆◆
Bone's delightful foray into ambient music. Stylized, peppered with fantastic samples and a sense of humor about itself, *Ambiento* serves to humanize the genre. — *Will Grega*

Michael Bonti

Vocals / Folk-Pop
Long Island native with a masterful voice and a gift for writing melodic folk music. — *Will Grega*

Michael Bonti / 1993 / ◆◆◆
This gorgeous melodic acoustic pop weaves social insight ("Quilted City") and downright horny playfulness. — *Will Grega*

Joe Bracco

Pop
Joe Bracco represented one of the best hopes for gay music's future when he sadly died of AIDS in March 1991 at 30 years of age. But thanks to Paul Phillips of Romanovsky & Phillips, Bracco's buoyant performances live on. Phillips took a collection of the late Bracco's rough home recordings and demos and layered them with lush instrumental arrangement enhancements to create a wonderful posthumous tribute to a true pop talent. — *Will Grega*

True to Myself / 1992 / Fresh Fruit ◆◆◆◆
The collection sparkles with Bracco's warm personality, melodic pop-new wave influence and a true gift for lyric writing. "Friend in My Pocket" is a goofy tribute to condom use. These recordings are proof that Joe Bracco was a rare and compelling talent (a new wave Bruce Springsteen), and Paul Phillips is to be commended for bringing Bracco's superlative gift to light. — *Will Grega*

Butt Boy

Ambient, Techno, Leather
Thrust Recordings specializes in music written expressly as sensuous sounds for those serious about leather. This sensual music has the mel-

lowness of new age, the orchestral influence of classical music, the sharp edge of rock, and the futuristic sounds of techno-pop, with a heavy leaning toward early Pink Floyd and the synthesized electronic pop of Jean-Michel Jarre. — *Will Grega*

Feel the Music / 1993 / Thrust ✦✦✦

Already an accomplished composer in video, radio, and theater, Butt Boy brings his sexual music into the private places of the leather community's play places and sets the mood required for a mind trip into the erotic. "Dance of the Whip" builds its swirling sound around the rhythmic pattern of a cracking whip. This is an album that should come with protection. — *Will Grega*

Michael Callen

Vocals / Pop-Rock

Leading AIDS activist Michael Callen single-handedly redefined the public's concept of a person with AIDS after his diagnosis with the disease in 1982 by giving speeches, writing articles, appearing on national television, giving interviews, organizing within the community, campaigning, and singing at a tempo that would exhaust most healthy people. His political efforts have been chronicled in Randy Shilts' classic book, *And the Band Played On*. His musical output is nothing less than amazing, and includes recording two albums as one of the Flirtations (see listing). His debut solo release was recorded six years after he was diagnosed with HIV, had established the PWA Coalition, and testified at congressional hearings on AIDS. — *Will Grega*

★ **Purple Heart** / 1988 / Significant Other ✦✦✦✦✦

Purple Heart is nothing less than the most stunning gay album recorded to date. The album has a pop-rocking set that segues into a more intimate set of six songs with Callen at the piano, and contains the classics "Living in Wartime," "Love Don't Need a Reason," and Callen's ultra-campy reading of "Where the Boys Are." It is a must-have by an outstanding human being and hero to our community with one of the most wondrous voices ever recorded, and about whom Elizabeth Taylor said, "His life is a shining symbol of hope, strength, and courage." — *Will Grega*

Keith Christopher

Vocals / Soul, Pop-Rock

An exceptionally talented vocalist with a wide range and a personable, embraceable quality, Keith Christopher produces music that is melodic, endearing, and just plain thrilling to hear. His songs reflect the emotions and issues of today in a style that is strong and vulnerable, passionate and clear. He has composed special material for the United Nations Environmental Program as well as the Names Project. — *Will Grega*

● **Keith Christopher** / 1993 / Kct Productions ✦✦✦✦

Sublime and gratifying songs reinforce his belief in the power of love as a force for personal growth and physical health. The tracks on this debut are muscular and lush, with hip '90s rhythms that surround his made-for-radio, big, White soul voice. — *Will Grega*

That's What America Means to Me / ✦✦✦✦

David & Jane

Gospel, Pop

David & Jane is a unique combination of a gay man and lesbian woman singing gospel music. They are vanguards in the use of inclusive language, a testimony to their belief in God's love for everyone. Both David and Jane are ministers based in the greater New York City area, and they have been featured at New York City Gay Pride Festivals since 1991. — *Will Grega*

David & Jane . . . Not Ashamed / 1993 / Heifer ✦✦✦

This is jump up on your chair and wave your hands and say hallelujah kind of fun, with first-rate originals ("Standing on the Promises." "Bless It Back," "Rejoice") and stirring covers ("My God Is Real" and "Farther Along"). This collection of glorious songs only goes to prove that God is on our side. — *Will Grega*

Diamond Rose

Folk

With rare honesty and haunting melodies, Diamond Rose writes from the heart. This is an entertaining blend of styles: JayDee is bluesy and playful, Steven Gellman is woeful and bummed; this presents a compelling mix in this diverse acoustic duo. Gellman plays a handmade stringed instrument that has become a trademark of the Diamond Rose sound. The "strumstick," a cross between a banjo, mandolin, and dulcimer, is unique in sound and appearance. — *Will Grega*

This Road Called Life / 1992 / Blue Guitar ✦✦✦

A promising premiere by future killers, Diamond Rose are seriously committed performers who will challenge your perceptions of acoustic music. Steve Gellman's voice, like his lyrics, is powerful and sensitive,

and the group's lyrics consistently achieve a delicate balance between humor and poignancy, while the hypnotic chord changes evoke an R.E.M.-like dreaminess. JayDee's lyrics are laugh-out-loud hysterical, and her voice brings to mind Natalie Merchant; at times fragile, at times sardonic and playful, it is a voice that captures both the depth and whimsy of her lyrics. — *Will Grega*

David Diamond

b. Jul. 9, 1915

Vocals / Contemporary Country

A legend while still in his teens for being a founding member of Berlin ("The Metro," "Sex I'm A . . . ") and racking up numerous gold records, David Diamond discovered that country music was what really saddled his horse. He's a fine producer and writer, gifted with a voice that sounds remarkably like Don Henley of the Eagles, and evokes the whole Southern California country sound of the late '70s. — *Will Grega*

Qowboy / 1993 / 2 Butch 4 U ✦✦✦

Delivered with intelligence and solid pop smarts with slide guitar and California country-rock thrown into the stew, *Qowboy* is a pure country-pop confection by a superb stylist. Diamond balances the release with good-time songs of the Highway 101 honky tonk variety, and cryin' in your beer numbers. Diamond explores the pain of a shattered soul loving too well, losing and bruising: hard stuff that goes down smooth. — *Will Grega*

The Fabulous Pop Tarts

House Music

Two of the busiest men in show business, the Pop Tarts have produced three hit television series (including *The Best of Manhattan Cable* for England's Channel 4), written a book (about Michael Milken!), masterminded the career of supermodel/singer RuPaul, and composed and recorded this 17-song CD—all in the past 12 months! Superachievers of the world! — *Will Grega*

Gagging on the Lovely Extravaganza / 1992 / World of Wonder ✦✦✦✦

Running through smooth dance grooves in Erasure and Pet Shop Boys territory without sounding nearly as alienating as the mass of house music being churned out today, this album speeds you along the freeway of love with no exit ramps. Guest luminaries include Dan Hartman, RuPaul, and Dee-Lite's Lady Kier Kirby. — *Will Grega*

The Flirtations

A Cappella

If there is one group that embodies the state of gay culture today, it's the Flirtations. The Flirtations gained national prominence in the late '80s as the only openly gay-positive a cappella group. Oh, it helped that they had tremendous voices and chose outstanding material. In a few short years, these media darlings became everybody's group of choice as ambassadors of homosexuality the world over. Little could they have known that within five short years of their first Greenwich Village street performance in 1988, they would have appeared on *The Phil Donahue Show*, *Good Morning America*, *Nightwatch*, *MTV News*, and National Public Radio; that they would have gathered rave reviews across the country; and that they would actually be making a living doing what they love most: being gay and singing about it. — *Will Grega*

The Flirtations / 1990 / Significant Other ✦✦✦✦

Their eponymous, fully digital premier contains some of their best-loved material: "To Know Him Is to Love Him," "Something Inside So Strong," "Everything Possible," and "Surfin' USA" camped to perfection. A group like this only comes along once in a lifetime. Between the brilliant harmonies, general silliness, and giddy repertoire, a splendid time is guaranteed for all. The Flirtations have been thrilling audiences with their unique blend of musical artistry, politics, and infectious humor since their first street corner appearance in Greenwich Village in the fall of 1988. — *Will Grega*

★ **Live: Out on the Road** / 1992 / Flirt ✦✦✦✦✦

Stunning, exciting, moving, engrossing, and hysterically funny, this album gives you a front-row seat for the best gay act in America. Recorded in Vancouver in December 1992, *Out on the Road* captures all the excitement of the Flirts' live performances. The album contains Flirts faves "Boy from New York City," "Johnny Angel," "Lesbian Love," "The Homecoming Queen's Got a Gun," and "Living in Wartime." There is a wonderful excitement to hearing the group live, and experiencing the audience interplay and reaction. — *Will Grega*

Ted Fox

Vocals / Folk-Pop

Uplifting, political, and stridently queer! The spirit is reborn in Ted Fox, and it is mighty! He is an out and proud gay man singing songs of defiance and positive self-affirmation. — *Will Grega*

Record Company Addresses

Y'All
235 East 10th Street, Studio G, New York, NY 10003-7666

Benez Popaganda Muzik
c/o William Spring, 353 6th Avenue, 3rd Fl., New York, NY 10014

McMillan Records
8 Westwood Road, Somerville, MA 02143-1518

Longhorn Records
31-65 29th Street #A-6, Astoria, NY 11106

Feather Boa Records
584 Castro Street, Suite 260, San Francisco, CA 94114

Siegerwerke, Inc.
PO Box 14348, San Francisco, CA 94114-0348

Windy City Performing Arts
3023 North Clark #329, Chicago, IL 60657

Worm
2103 Harrison NW, Suite 2414, Olympia, WA 98502

Aboveground Records
PO Box 2233, Philadelphia, PA 19103

Fresh Fruit Records
369 Montezuma #209, Santa Fe, NM 87501

Elliot Pilshaw
PO Box 021616, Brooklyn, NY 11201

Phideaux Xavier
c/o Bloodfish Music, 172 East 4th Street #7E, New York, NY 10009

Scream Sync Production
137 Hollett Street, Scituate, MA 02066-2036

Motta Music
PO Box 1245, Cathedral Station, New York, NY 10025

Paralic
PO Box 20231, New York, NY 10011

Everything Possible
PO Box 1483, Indianapolis, IN 46206-1483

Tommie Saeli
Howling Wolf Records, 75 2nd Avenue #2, New York, NY 10003

Spotted Dog
PO Box 40-0041, Brooklyn, NY 11240-0041

Rob Krikorian
c/o CommonTime Productions, PO Box 1076, Brookline, MA 02146

Dan Martin
PO Box 1575, Canal Street Station, New York, NY 10013

Open Secrets Musicworks
PO Box 132, Old Chelsea Station, New York, NY 10113-0132

Heymanee
1415 Steele Street #3, Denver, CO 80206

Flirt Records
PO Box 421, Prince Street Station, New York, NY 10012-0008

World of Wonder
80 Varick Street #7B, New York, NY 10013

David Diamond
2 Butch 4 U Productions, 1427 Sanborn Avenue, Silverlake, CA 90027

Heifer Records
304 East 38th Street #2C, New York, NY 10016

Diamond Rose
PO Box 0077, Rockville, MD 20848

KCT Productions
230 Riverside Drive #14F, New York, NY 10025

Significant Other, Inc.
PO Box 1545, Canal Street Station, New York, NY 10013

Thrust Recordings
PO Box 29212, Dallas, TX 75229

Quirkworks
PO Box 229, Greenville, RI 02828

Wild Monk Records
147 2nd Avenue #477, New York, NY 10003

One of Us / 1992 / Heymanee ◆◆◆◆
Fox's debut features folkie melodies sung with self-assurance and the social commitment that Peter, Paul, and Mary mined in the '60s heyday of the folk form. The beautifully executed lyrics and the coffeehouse energy make this album well worth a listen, and the sentiment comes through loud and queer. "Sink or Swim," an anthem for our struggle, is the real winner here. — *Will Grega*

Jesse Hultberg

Folk, Pop-Rock
Former mastermind behind cult band 3 Teens Kill 4 steps out (way out) to begin an auspicious solo career. "I Was Raised a Straight Boy (But I'm Not Today)" is used as the theme for cable's "Party Talk" program. — *Will Grega*

☆ **Jesse Hultberg** / 1994 / Wild Monk ◆◆◆◆◆
Whether delivering an acoustic rendering of "If I Can't Have You," or light hip-hopping along a Joni Mitchell buried gem ("The Priest Song"), Hultberg proves himself the master of blending acoustic and high-tech genres. Best song title in a long time: "Am I Raquel Welch Starring in *Fantastic Voyage?*" — *Will Grega*

Grant King

Vocals / Folk-Pop
Grant King's recordings capture surprisingly well the warmth and sensuousness of his incredible live performances. He writes from the heart and never fails to win over audiences, and is and always has been an unflinching and proud gay singer-songwriter. — *Will Grega*

Where to Now / 1992 / Open Secrets Musicwor ◆◆◆
King's easy, James Taylor-like charm oozes out of the tracks on his debut. Some of his more popular performance pieces are here, "To Hold and Be Held" and "Your Roses Came Today." His amazing rhythm guitar work drives "Loving Cup" in a manner reminiscent of Lindsey Buckingham's guitar work with Fleetwood Mac. — *Will Grega*

● **Entitled to Bloom** / 1993 / Open Secrets Musicwor ◆◆◆◆
ETB includes more heartfelt lyrics that are deeply personal, bringing one much closer to the artist. King uses the crystal clarion of his voice to

communicate straight to your heart. Also featured on this tape is King's collaboration with Rob Costin, "James and Me," a sweet song sung from the perspective of an adoring child about the tall, strong, older brother he looks up to, that could well be the most innocently subversive song ever penned by a gay songwriter. — *Will Grega*

Ben & Ellie Kreader

Soul, Synth-Pop
Writer/producer Ben Kreader began singing in college after placing an ad in the *Chicago Reader* for a woman who "smokes at least a pack a day." When nobody responded, he ended up discovering his own voice without the aid of Marlboros. — *Will Grega*

Sink or Swim B/w Blizzard-cassingle / 1993 / Eat Your Wheat ◆◆◆
Kreader's sister, Ellie, takes vocal lead on the first track, "Sink or Swim." Ellie Kreader has a dream voice, a voice with the elasticity and how-dee-do of K.T. Oslin, able to convey every little quirk of emotion. The tracks are dark, rhythmic masterpieces that call to mind early work by Eurythmics. Ben Kreader's voice (he sings "Blizzard") is big, bluesy, and R&B-tinged. These two tracks are from an elaborate multimedia performance Ben presents that involves rear-screen projection, hand-held lights, glowsticks, road flares, flashlights, and pinwheels, and that pulls 17 of his songs into a narrative story line. — *Will Grega*

Rob Krikorian

Vocals / Folk-Pop
Rob Krikorian writes about time and love: how time passes and love heals. Krikorian's voice is perfectly suited to this mellow style of music popularized by Dan Fogelberg and others: contemporary folk for those with a taste for quiet music and with an interest in lyrics/imagery and a sense of humor. — *Will Grega*

Quicksand in the Hourglass / 1990 / Common Time ◆◆◆◆
"Aren't We Born to Dance" is the most direct of this set, alluding to the Stonewall riots. The title song deals with mortality in a particularly moving manner, and "Send in $9.95" takes a jab at televangelists peddling Jesus. *Quicksand* is a lovely, polished work, a gentle disc on which Krikorian conveys a Michael Franks-style easiness and charm. — *Will Grega*

Dan Martin & Michael Biello

Pop

Dan Martin and Michael Biello are the fathers of the newly born gay music scene and are responsible for many new artists coming to light in our community. Martin has written scores for films and videos including *Clones in Love,* winner of the San Francisco Gay & Lesbian Film Festival's top prize for Best Short. His score for Lauren Malkasian's video *The Last Run* is currently being aired on PBS, and his score for Jim Hubbard's *The Dance* (which chronicles Martin and life-partner Michael Biello's relationship) has screened at the Berlin Film Festival, MOMA, and at festivals around the world. He has also written instrumental music for Hazelden Publishing's *Sound Recovery* series of subliminal healing cassettes, and for Erospirit's sexual environments series. Martin is the founder of OutMusic, the organization of lesbian and gay composers, lyricists, and musicians, which produces the only annual festival of gay and lesbian music. He has brought to the stage numerous queer music-theater pieces with Biello, a performing visual artist and Martin's lyricist. — *Will Grega*

Homo Love Song / 1990 / Dan Martin ✦✦✦
On their debut release, the material is riveting, so you don't mind the spare piano/vocal production, though this artist deserves the full treatment. Martin's delivery runs the gamut from downright bratty (when called for) to heartbreakingly tender. This release introduced two gay standards: "Forgive Me," and the much-covered "Hold Me in Your Arms." Compassionate, raunchy, romantic, and beautiful, the songwriting talents of Martin and Biello seem unending. — *Will Grega*

★ **Hu*Man*Be*Ing** / 1992 / Dan Martin ✦✦✦✦✦
From anthems like "You Do Not Know Me" and "Lay Your Burden Down" to the butt-shaking beat of "Drag Dance" and the mechanical dance rhythms of "Strange Now," this album delivers consistent entertainment pleasure. The spiritually uplifting pieces are emotionally ardent songs that resonate in the heart and soul. — *Will Grega*

Tom McCormack

Vocals / Pop-Rock

McCormack represents the best our community has to offer. His outstanding voice, superb writing and production skills, and inspiring artistry embody the future of gay music. — *Will Grega*

Running with Light / 1991 / Spotted Dog ✦✦✦✦
McCormack's debut showcases his more subdued, spiritual side, and contains some devastating songwriting, most notably on "Everything," which *Billboard* called "a warm and affecting ballad of earnest delivery complemented by a stark, piano-dominated arrangement." *Running with Light* speaks with the language of the heart to a contemporary audience that yearns to mine more deeply the power of each person's passionate journey. — *Will Grega*

Rose Colored Glasses / 1993 / Spotted Dog ✦✦✦✦
McCormack uses a rock sound that is an intentional throwback to the '70s sound, at times recalling Billy Joel, Elton John, and Crosby, Stills, Nash and Young. This kick-ass set of astonishing songs includes "I Am Alive," "Here I Am," and current crowd-pleaser, "Falling Down Kind of Love," as he journeys still deeper on his second album into the gray areas of life with stories of money, desire, and identity. — *Will Grega*

★ **Missing** / 1994 / Spotted Dog ✦✦✦✦✦
One gets the feeling that this is the definitive gay album that artists in our community have been trying to write for years. "In Secret," "Don't Tell," and "Love Is Love Is Love" eloquently speak for the collective gay subconscious. — *Will Grega*

Rus McCoy

Vocals / Alternative Pop-Rock

An artist whose ultimate goal is to be an openly gay rock artist who achieves regular airplay on mainstream radio, McCoy was born to write and sing affecting alternative rock. The arrangements soar thanks to Ace, his producer/collaborator, and set him squarely in Simple Minds/ New Order/Depeche Mode territory. — *Will Grega*

☆ **Ace Sessions** / 1991 / Stonewall ✦✦✦✦✦
"Never Tell a Soul" is a synth-pop standout that deals with alienation, self-induced silence, and internalized homophobia. With guitar work that demands striking comparison to U2's Edge, songs like "Happy Birthday, Baby Butch" grab your ears immediately. From ambitious Springsteen-like suites to a sound reminiscent of early Los Angeles new-wave, McCoy hits the mark every time. — *Will Grega*

Bill McKinley

Vocals / Vocal, Pop

It is the rare performer who emerges and is granted instant and universal legendary status, but the sheer power of Bill McKinley's musical gifts

has propelled him into mythic stature in a few short years. He is a showman and artist who possesses that winning combination of show biz savvy and utter naturalness that is the unmistakable mark of the Genuine Article. — *Will Grega*

☆ **Everything Possible** / 1992 / Everything Possible ✦✦✦✦✦
An openly gay performer on the cabaret circuit, McKinley's talent is so electrifying that he deserves his own 76-piece orchestra on call 24 hours a day. Fresh, subtle, and a showcase for astonishing technique, *Everything Possible* is a beautiful gift to the community, and is so stunningly brilliant, it leaves you gasping. A command performance, this is not just an album, it's an arrival. — *Will Grega*

Will McMillan

Vocal, Cabaret

This Sondheim tribute is actually a soundtrack itself, taken from McMillan's one-man show in which he begins as a tuxedoed man and gradually transforms himself into a woman and then back into a man. — *Will Grega*

Will Sings Sondheim / 1992 / McMillan ✦✦✦✦
This is a remarkable album of intelligent and sensitive interpretations of Sondheim classics that span the songwriter's career, up to and including "More," written for the *Dick Tracy* soundtrack. The songs are performed with the reverential emotion and loving restraint of an adoring fan. Entertaining, and a welcome relief from those over-the-top ultra-theatrical Sondheim tributes of late, this is a collection that has been praised by the master himself. — *Will Grega*

Gustavo Motta

Motta's songs have been performed in concerts and cabarets in New York, San Francisco, and Philadelphia during years when he was also staging productions for the Houston Grand Opera, the Washington Opera, Cincinnati Conservatory of Music, and the Metropolitan Opera. Only after testing positive for HIV in 1987, did he devote himself full-time to recording and performing his music in solo concerts and AIDS benefits, and began an effort to ensure that his songs would be preserved and performed. — *Will Grega*

Songs 1963-1993 / 1993 / Motta Music ✦✦✦✦
This abundant tribute to Gustavo Motta, who died in 1993, is a collection of 30 years' worth of intelligent songwriting in traditions that borrow from cabaret, theater, pop-rock, and world influences. Readings by male and female voices lend nuance to the song interpretations, and they all feature Motta himself on piano. Motta's 30-year output reveals a super tunesmith whose songs deserve good homes. — *Will Grega*

Pansy Division

Punk, Alternative Pop-Rock, Punk Revival

A San Francisco band that celebrates deep subculture fringes of gay life, Pansy Division gained mainstream attention when they supported Green Day on their 1994 tour. Consequently, the band became the de-facto leaders of the punk rock "queer-core" movement and developed a small mainstream following. In February 1996, the band released *Wish I'd Taken Pictures.* — *Will Grega*

● **Undressed** / 1993 / Lookout ✦✦✦✦
These sex punks tunefully and loudly wag their penises and preferences about. The most successful track here is a departure for the band, the Byrds-influenced "Boyfriend Wanted." — *Will Grega*

Deflowered / 1994 / Lookout ✦✦✦

Wish I'd Taken Pictures / Feb. 13, 1996 / Lookout ✦✦✦✦

Andrew Paralic

Piano / Jazz

Composer/pianist Andrew Paralic has an extraordinary facility for jazz composition and utilizes an ensemble's supple execution of his Coltrane-like pieces to recreate a mood and era. Paralic is a graduate of Baruch College, and has attended the Berklee College of Music and the Jazz Mobile. — *Will Grega*

Three Tunes / 1993 / Paralic ✦✦✦✦
The pieces on this release were written about reflections of his own gay-ness with titles like "Too Little, Too Late" (about AIDS funding), "Out Tune," and "Finally" (about the total acceptance of his lifestyle by his family). — *Will Grega*

Phideaux

Art-Rock/Progressive-Rock, Celtic Pop

Phideaux Xavier has performed in the New York area since the '80s when he fronted punk-pop combo Sally Dick & Jane. Early 1990 saw the birth of the SunMachine, a sextet consisting of guitar, bass, percussion, flute, violin, cello with three strong singers besides Xavier, whose boyish exuberance and soulful intensity create one irresistible package. — *Will Grega*

Friction / 1993 / Bloodfish ✦✦✦✦

The Celtic pop-poetry and art-rock pieces cast a beautiful, dreamlike spell that charms and disorients at the same time. The surrealistic imagery and elaborate introductions create a strangely unified whole, though the pieces careen stylistically from psychedelic pop to urban dance to dance-pop and sensitive ballads. — *Will Grega*

Elliot Pilshaw

Vocals / Singer, Songwriter

Elliot Pilshaw has been recording as an out gay musician since his debut release in 1982. He is co-founder of the Flirtations, an original cast member of Tom Wilson Weinberg's Ten Percent Review, and founder of Sons & Lovers, a new gay a cappella quintet. Alongside his work in the larger gay community, Pilshaw has been especially active in the Jewish gay and lesbian community. He has performed at the International Conferences of Gay and Lesbian Jews, traveled and performed extensively throughout Israel, and is currently a cantor at Congregation Beth Simchat Torah, New York's gay and lesbian synagogue. — *Will Grega*

Bending the Rules / 1982 / ✦✦✦

His debut release has a fresh sound for a work that was recorded 12 years ago. That just goes to prove that there's something timeless about Pilshaw. On *Bending the Rules*, Lorin Sklamberg and Pilshaw combine musical excellence with social awareness to give us all yet another means to celebrate and affirm the beauty and validity of our lifestyle. Covers include "Millwork" (James Taylor), "Something About the Women" (Holly Near), and a remarkably moving interpretation of Kristin Lem's "How Nice." — *Will Grega*

● **Feels like Home** / 1986 / Icebergg ✦✦✦✦

Teamed with John Bucchino and engaging material, Pilshaw delivers an album that finds its way home into the heart. Weaving together pop, jazz, folk, and Broadway musical styles, Pilshaw has delivered an album of songs that glow with the goodness of gay love, life, and friendship. Provocative lyrics, dazzling piano arrangements, and Pilshaw's breathtaking vocals combine to make this album a landmark of gay men's cultural expression. He sings of liberation without blaming or apologizing, informed by pride and a spirited political intelligence, and John Bucchino provides lush and elegant piano accompaniment. — *Will Grega*

Queer Conscience

Pop

A community activist along with his husband, Rick Cresswell is compelled to get at the greater truths of our struggle for human rights. The couple received a lot of press in 1991 when they participated in a "visibility action" at Boston's Stocks and Bonds bar. In that action, the two were attacked by a uniformed Boston police officer because the couple refused to stop kissing each other. — *Will Grega*

It's a Queer Nation / 1992 / Scream Sync ✦✦✦

QueerCon's debut features militantly queer pop songs from Rick Cresswell and gang that bounce along happily in bubble-gum groovy, '60s melodies and arrangements. Cresswell has a muscular tenor that calls to mind Harry Chapin, and he uses it to put over songs of defiance that deal with shame, rejection, societal indifference, and self-acceptance. — *Will Grega*

● **Back to the Other World?** / 1993 / Scream Sync ✦✦✦✦

Rick Cresswell's supple tenor complements the forthright, unflinching lyrics with gentler determination than on the group's debut. Queer Conscience is committed to pushing a blatantly direct queer agenda with such songs as "Telling Someone" and "The Ballad of Harvey Milk." In "OUTside Information," Cresswell sings about the need to be obviously and visibly queer. With blunt and bruisingly political songs, and a particularly striking album cover collage, this collection will make you want to march. — *Will Grega*

Curtis A. Robertson

Bass, Vocals / Pop-Rock

Fusing wide-ranging influences from Herman's Hermits to Ray Stevens to Randy Newman, Robertson's parodies turn our reverential and taken-for-granted concepts of pop music inside out. — *Will Grega*

Stinkwater & the Page Boys / 1994 / ✦✦✦✦

Deranged set in which Curtis Robertson imagines himself as two groups, one a white-trash country unit, the other a new wave Herman's Hermits. "This Isn't Love in My Eyes (I'm Just Tired)," "Kiss Me Like You Mean It," and "I'm Gonna Hurt to Have to Hate You" are the countrified standouts. — *Will Grega*

Rick Robertson

Vocals / Alternative Pop-Rock

Robertson is blessed with a voice that was made to be recorded, and a gift for writing terrific lyrics that lock into the mood of the musical settings. — *Will Grega*

Six / 1993 / ✦✦✦

These songs are the result of two unique musical collaborations, and both succeed brilliantly at exploring the farther fringes of alternative pop driven by synthesizer technology, detached alienation, and the longings of a man in limbo. The sound of this release calls to mind the Cure, New Order, and Depeche Mode. The moody "For Saturday" is a standout smash, but also check out the Rob Costin collaborations, "Magnificent Man," "The Lover's Tent," and "Carry Me." The ease, power, and poetic language of this release are pure genius, and Robertson may just be our own little psychedelic-era Bob Dylan, a poet and prophet of queerdom. — *Will Grega*

Romanovsky & Phillips

Pop-Rock

Romanovsky & Phillips (R&P) are easily the most popular out-of-the-closet singing duo in history. Having toured extensively in the US, Canada, and Australia, R&P have earned the title of "Ambassadors of Homosexuality." Prolific and long-standing members of the gay music community, R&P have a hysterically comic bent on contemporary gay life. Each of their albums is also peppered with beautifully romantic ballads and sensitive and politically impassioned numbers that give their releases exhilarating balance. Fifties doo wop parodies with silly kazoo solos don't seem out of place beside poignant ballads in the musical world of R&P. As the most successful gay group in the history of our community, R&P have been on the forefront of gay entertainment for over a decade. Since gay people love to hear about nothing more than themselves, these two brilliant young men write about what we couldn't possibly hear enough about, our favorite subject: ourselves. And, why not? Gay people have been so invisibilized in the media and American society, it's about time we Hear Queer. — *Will Grega*

I Thought You'd Be Taller! / 1984 / Fresh Fruit ✦✦✦

This album was the folky beginning of the dynastic duo, and reflects the sound they honed in their humble, hummable beginnings as a San Francisco folk duo in the early '80s. As such, it showcases the wonderful harmony vocal arrangements of their two distinctive voices, and contains their most naive but always charming material. — *Will Grega*

● **Trouble in Paradise** / 1986 / Fresh Fruit ✦✦✦✦

Expertly tuned into gay fascinations and foibles, R&P nail the issues in love and politics right on the head. More classics include "What Kind of Self-Respecting Faggot Am I?," "Wimp," "Homophobia," "Must've Been Drunk," "The Answering Machine Song," and "Don't Use Your Penis for a Brain." This "sounds" like a hit album should sound, and is probably their best-known work. With *Trouble in Paradise*, they grew leaps and bounds above their auspicious debut, and became international gay pop stars. — *Will Grega*

Emotional Rollercoaster / 1988 / Fresh Fruit ✦✦✦

On the third album they changed the formula a little bit and captured the crazy cabaret ambience of their live performances, leaning toward vaudeville. But it's the vaudeville treatment given this album that nearly covers up the fact that R&P have written the most incisive and brilliantly observed lyrics of their career. Classics: "The Sodomy Song," "Give Me a Homosexual," "My Mother's Clothes," and "I've Created a Monster." — *Will Grega*

☆ **Be Political, Not Polite** / 1991 / Fresh Fruit ✦✦✦✦✦

It was three years before R&P managed a follow-up to their record three releases of blatant gay pop music. In the meantime they had become the most successful, beloved, and prolific group in the history of gay music. This album is a feast of R&P at the top of their form. Packed with 15 songs of love, anger, politics, and hope, the duo covers a wide range of subjects from lesbian/gay parents to lesbian/gay teachers, from surviving AIDS to surviving dating. As always, the harmonies are terrific. Classics include "Tango Indigesto," "Queers in the Closet," "When Heterosexism Strikes," and "OH NO I'm in Love (With My Therapist)." — *Will Grega*

Ron Romanovsky

Guitar, Piano, Vocals / Pop-Rock

Of Romanovsky & Phillips, recorded his first solo album in 1992. — *Will Grega*

Hopeful Romantic / 1994 / Fresh Fruit ✦✦✦✦

The music is mostly upbeat and covers a wide variety of musical styles woven together with some of Romanovsky's best vocals ever. At his tenderest, he evokes Don McLean, but in the world of Ron

Romanovsky, a polka party never seems out of place. As a solo artist, Romanovsky ventures into new territory with the Gershwin-esque "A Measure of Sadness," the rock 'n' roll riffs of "The Perfect Crime," and the seductive cabaret-blues of "Baby Take Advantage of Me." — *Will Grega*

Tommie Saeli

Vocals / Alternative Pop-Rock, Glam Rock

Saeli is a retro-rocker, best known as the host of cable's "Gay Dating Game". The rock cello-wielding Saeli (a former go-go dancer at NYC's Pyramid Club) is a hot muscled Italian boy in a pink glitter metallic suit and feather boa, who offsets the sexy Billy Idol growl of his voice with a Yoko Ono-like falsetto that accompanies him in unison on many of his songs. With dazzlingly mind-bending lyrics that blend myth, fantasy, and magic, Saeli weaves a psychedelic spell once he gets that Marc Bolan groove going. — *Will Grega*

Hello / 1993 / Howling Wolf ✦✦✦✦
The crunchy sound of this disc is a throwback to the early-'70s glam rock of gender-benders David Bowie and T. Rex: heavy drumming, hand claps, and football-cheer choruses. It's a hard sound with no guitars, just layers of rock cello and cathedral organ. With the exception of the drumming, the album is a one-man tour de force. "Rock & Roll Queen" evokes Elton John's ripping "Saturday Night's Alright for Fighting." "Michaelangelo Irreducible" is a Motown (Supremes . . . surprised?) takeoff. "Lady of the Well" sports a Moody Blues harpsichord. Take the savage sweetness of John Lennon, add the guts of David Bowie, the flash fame of Nirvana, the magic of Sigfried and Roy and shake . . . don't stir. — *Will Grega*

Joseph Victor Sieger

Synth-Pop, Alternative Pop-Rock

Psychosemipornographic music for the groin, San Francisco's Sieger composes poetic electronic music that reeks of "Rush," leather, and mansweat. With a voice that ranges from pleasing to deranged, his lyrics comprise an incredibly hot journey into the super sexual psyche of master Sieger. — *Will Grega*

☆ **Self-portrait** / 1993 / Siegerwerke ✦✦✦✦✦
This is an absolutely uncompromising, without-a-net performance of over-the-edge, self-ghettoized, gay-sex-obsessed material. This release combines an '80s retro synth-pop sound with touches of '90s techno, and freely mixes rap with balladry, consistently exhibiting an experimental electronic edge. The album also contains a brave a cappella reading of the Village People's "San Francisco (You Got Me)." — *Will Grega*

Doug Stevens & the Outband

Contemporary Country

Doug Stevens and the Outband are consistently winning fans in the gay and straight country music communities. In the short time this band has been together they've played Gracie Mansion, Town Hall in NYC with Joan Rivers, the Rainbow Room at Rockefeller Center, and the 1993 March on Washington. There they were seen by 3 million people around the world on C-SPAN, and millions more on the NBC Evening News affiliates. They have appeared three times on "In the Life", and have played at many two-step dances and concerts on the East Coast and in the Midwest. This thoroughly entertaining and consistent album is produced with sparkling clarity and punch. The pansexual line-up includes the wicked fiddle work of John Cordes and the electrifying lead guitar work of Desiree, who has a strong guest spot as lead vocalist on the self-penned "Cactus Country." — *Will Grega*

★ **Out in the Country** / 1993 / Longhorn ✦✦✦✦✦
The runaway favorite of the year, this pop biography could have been called "Meet Doug Stevens," because Stevens not only writes and sings good songs, he's lived them. The Tupelo, MS, native begins with his tale of kissing boy cousins ("Out in the Country"), and Southern intolerance ("Born in Mississippi"). He then leaves for the big city ("Git While the Gittin's Good"), falls in love ("Sweet Breath of Love"), looks back in anger ("White Trash"), loses his lover when he's diagnosed with HIV ("HIV Blues"), and emerges stronger and renewed of spirit ("Act Up"). The Outband owes much to country-rock crossover traditions like Linda Ronstadt, the Eagles, and Neil Young. On this debut that is nothing less than a gay music cultural milestone, the Outband embodies what the best "country music" should be: rock with an accent. — *Will Grega*

Pussy Tourette

Vocals / Pop-Rock

Beginning as a go-go dancer in San Francisco's teeming underground scene, Tourette was acclaimed the hottest and sauciest act on the city's cabaret scene when she started singing her original compositions live. Touring nationally has helped her develop nothing less than a fanatical following. Five Tourette songs are featured in *Sex Is*, which won the Best Gay Film Award at Berlin's International Film Festival. — *Will Grega*

★ **Pussy Tourette in Hi-Fi** / 1993 / Feather Boa ✦✦✦✦✦
With a gift for self-invention, this fiercest of drag divas constructs the myth and legend of Pussy Tourette while simultaneously deconstructing queer misconceptions. From the New Orleans Dr. John camp of "If I Can't Sell It . . ." to the gritty Led Zeppelin-influenced heavy blues of "Free Pussy," it's clear that Ms. Tourette is not the girl next door. Tourette has a streetwise, gritty gift for blues-rock. "French Bitch" is an instant queer classic (the video has more slaps per minute than any other music video in history). — *Will Grega*

Kiss / 1995 / Feather Boa ✦✦✦

Turtle Creek Chorale

Choral

The Turtle Creek Chorale (TCC) is a Dallas-based male chorus under the direction of Dr. Timothy Seelig. Membership in the TCC currently stands at 200 singing members. The repertoire of TCC can best be described as eclectic, drawing on everything from Bach to Broadway and both sacred and secular works. In 1993, the Chorale made their Carnegie Hall debut. They have also been the focus of the PBS special "After Goodbye: An AIDS Story," chronicling the stages of loss and grief recovery from AIDS by looking at the impact of the disease on the members, families, and friends of the TCC. (The choir has lost 60 members during the past ten years.) Among other luminaries, the TCC has performed for Texas Governor Ann Richards and the Queen of England. This chorale, with their four albums, presents very intelligent song cycle selections. — *Will Grega*

● **From the Heart: Live** / 1990 / Turtle Creek Chorale ✦✦✦✦
For choral music lovers, Turtle Creek is heaven. Each disc is stuffed with over an hour's worth of song. *From the Heart* was voted "Best Choral Recording of 1990" by the readers of the national publication *CHORUS*. Like they say, the turtle only makes progress when he sticks his neck out. Standouts on this gorgeous disc include "Not While I'm Around" (Sondheim), "Pie Jesu" (Webber), and "Bring Him Home" (Boublil). — *Will Grega*

Peace / 1991 / ✦✦✦
A gorgeous feast of choral music, it includes holiday favorites "The First Noel," "White Christmas," "O Holy Night," "What Child Is This?" and "Ave Maria." — *Will Grega*

Testament / 1992 / Reference ✦✦✦
TCC rises to new heights of accomplished, dramatic, downright thrilling sound with punchy orchestral brilliance, all derived from a new sound process called High Definition. Joined by the Dallas Wind Symphony, the combination of chorus and orchestra jump off the disc, and it truly feels as if the performance is taking place in your living room. Focusing on the music of five 20th-century American composers, Ron Nelson, Howard Hanson, Randall Thompson, Aaron Copland, and Leonard Bernstein, *Testament* is a lesson in American history that will revive old-fashioned patriotism. — *Will Grega*

When We No Longer Touch / 1993 / ✦✦✦✦
A transformative work of raw beauty, and a breakthrough in choral recordings, this original piece addresses the stages of grief recovery (denial, isolation, anger, bargaining, depression, acceptance, and hope), and benefits AmFAR. This is an incredibly moving work that is a testament to the strength and resilience of the human heart and soul, and it is based on Peter McWilliams' poems from the book *How to Survive the Loss of Love*. Its blending of wit and sorrow make it a poignant, near-flawless tribute to lost love. — *Will Grega*

Tom Wilson Weinberg

Musicals

As Tom Wilson, before reclaiming the name Weinberg in 1983, he released two albums of original songs, *Gay Name Game* and *All-American Boy*. Wilson Weinberg has traveled and performed extensively, and continues to do so, but in recent years his writing has been focused on musical theater. His new show *Get Used to It* played off-Broadway in 1992, and Wilson Weinberg is now at work on a book musical. He was awarded the honor of being able to write and produce the official CD of *Stonewall 25* in 1994. — *Will Grega*

Don't Mess with Mary / Aboveground ✦✦✦✦
This benefit album (the official CD of *Stonewall 25*) is a disc no gay person should be without. Featuring hard-edged new material with a scorching rock vocal by Jan Tilley, and a fierce reading of the title track performed by drag-diva Tina Benez, these tracks (which even include a dance remix) represent a departure in style for Weinberg, although

Weinberg favorites "Safe Sex Slut" and "Before Stonewall" (from *Ten Percent Revue*) have been specially re-recorded for this project. — *Will Grega*

Ten Percent Revue / Aboveground ✦✦✦
This album is a studio cast recording of the musical revue that had a long run off-Broadway in 1988 and has played in more than two dozen cities. Two men and two women sing such songs as "Flaunting It," "Turkey Baster Baby," and "The Supremes" (a spoof on our highest court). — *Will Grega*

★ **Get Used to It** / Aboveground ✦✦✦✦✦
Joyous, romantic, uplifting, and satirical, Weinberg's cast recording of his latest revue is an incisive and humorous look at the serious gay issues of our time. From the wacky opening number "No Opening Number" to the heartwarming "I'll Call You Lover" through the defiant (but bouncy) "Breaking the Penal Code with You," this is a great gift of one of the most talented members of the gay community, and superb musical theater. — *Will Grega*

Windy City Gay Chorus

Choral
This chorus is a stunning example of the revival of male choral singing in North America. Windy City Gay Chorus' precision, flexibility of style, warmth of color, well-balanced tone, firm diction, and meticulous attention to detail add up to what some have termed the finest male chorus in the country. WCGC is now into its second decade of music making. They have won first place in the Great American Choral Festival, and have received grants based on musical excellence from the National Endowment for the Arts, the Illinois Arts Council and ChorusAmerica. — *Will Grega*

● **Mostly Love** / 1991 / Windy ✦✦✦✦
Accessible and well paced, this tape could convert even the most resolute disparagers of choral music. The work charms, lulls, and ultimately seduces. What really works here is the blending of obscure and familiar material: "The Great Peace March" (Holly Near), "What'll I Do?" (Irving Berlin), and "Where Is Love?" (Lionel Bart) being among the familiar. — *Will Grega*

Don We Now . . . / 1992 / Wcpa ✦✦✦
Tasty selections of Christmas favorites include "Deck the Halls," "Silent Night," and "White Christmas." — *Will Grega*

Worm

Synth-Pop, Folk
Worm is a one-of-a-kind vocal/songwriting duo of twins: a gay brother and a lesbian sister! On their debut release, they tap an analog synth production sound that hearkens back to Yaz and early Eurythmics. The duo blends beautifully balanced harmonies as well as vocal solos that brother and sister trade off. — *Will Grega*

Worm / 1992 / Worm ✦✦✦
With honesty, clarity, and poppy melodic hooks, the Seattle siblings grapple with issues of acceptance, same-sex relationships, justice, coming out, freedom, equal rights, and world peace. Best tracks here are "Woman of the Third Wave" and "Gay Nineties." The wonderful acoustic guitar work of sister Janie is showcased on her contributions while keyboardist Jamie explores synth-pop grooves on his compositions, and that's what works best about this release: it is the ultimate in inclusion. The gay male and lesbian/feminist viewpoints exist side by side as well as merge, and this formula is what it's all about: coming together as brothers and sisters. — *Will Grega*

Y'all

Country
As a lowbrow, southern fried, trailer park Simon & Garfunkel, it is astonishing how well these two men illuminate the gay experience. It is really surprising that they have gotten overwhelming positive and downright affectionate coverage for their stage act (performed by the six-foot-three-inch Jay Byrd in his lucky green dress, and shirtless Steven Cheslik-DeMeyer in beat-up overalls) in both the gay and straight media. Their sound is a mix of rural Americana: gospel, country-western, and bluegrass music performed Hee-Haw style with superb harmonizing. James Dean Jay Byrd is the son of a tent revivalist from Okey-Dokey, TX, and the nephew of a trailer-home salesman/cross-dresser. His pardner Steven is a former corn farmer from Corn Flake, IN, and the seventeenth child of former Catholics. — *Will Grega*

An Evening of Stories & Songs / 1993 / Y'all ✦✦✦
"I Am the Queen of the Rodeo" and "Man Who's Not in My Family Tree" (about grandpa's boyfriend) are knee-slappin' standouts in these homespun tales of rural gay life. All of Y'all's songs are heartfelt originals, from lonely trail-riding tunes, to everybody-join-in hillbilly ditties, to classic-styled gospel numbers. — *Will Grega*

SOUNDTRACKS

The motion picture soundtrack as we know it today dates from the early '40s, although film music itself goes back much further than synchronized sound. Piano and organ accompaniments were played live in theaters from the beginning of the century, and it was in 1916 that Victor Schertzinger wrote the first full orchestral and choral score for a motion picture.

During the '30s, it became customary for record companies to release official recorded versions of songs heard in musical films. Hence, much of the musical history of Fred Astaire's RKO work, in films such as *Top Hat* and *Swing Time*, was captured simultaneously on the Brunswick label (now reissued by Columbia Records). And certain orchestral scores by recognized composers, such as Arthur Bliss' music for Alexander Korda's 1936 science-fiction epic *Things to Come*, found a separate life in the concert hall.

But it wasn't until 1942 that a record company fixed on the notion of recording and releasing the major parts of a full orchestra score. The film was *The Jungle Book*, produced by Alexander Korda and scored by Miklos Rozsa. One piece of Rozsa's, the waltz from his score for the 1942 film *Lydia*, had previously been recorded on a single 78-rpm disc by RCA Records with some success. Shortly after *The Jungle Book*'s release, RCA brought Rozsa to New York to record a suite of the key movements from his new score with the NBC Symphony Orchestra, with a narration of the story provided by Sabu, the star of the film. This set of 78-rpm records, which has since been issued many times, marked the start of the movie soundtrack as a record genre.

The next major development took place in 1945, when MGM established its record label, MGM Records. The studio had originally planned to start the label in 1941, with Tommy Dorsey heading it, but the war intervened with a five-year delay. The first "musical biography" was *Till the Clouds Roll By*, inspired by the life and songs of Jerome Kern. It seemed logical to release eight of the musical highlights from the film in a set of four 78-rpm records, which was precisely what was done, with some modifications to make the songs suitable for release on record. These included the removal of lengthy instrumental breaks and sound effects that were germane to the screen presentation but not to the record.

Till the Clouds Roll By was a success, if not a raging best-seller, but it established the pattern for musical soundtracks. Its release ahead of the film secured radio play for the songs, thus promoting the film, and also made the record-buying public aware of the release of the movie in a way that print advertising alone would not have. Subsequently, with the advent of the long-playing record two years later, studios would release their musicals in reasonably complete form, either on their own labels or under contract to other record companies.

Looking at this history more than 40 years later, one must bear in mind just how important the soundtrack album was to the public. In the days before home video (and the boom in movie memorabilia shops), the soundtrack album was the only piece of a movie a fan could actually own, take home, and enjoy at will, without having to depend on the movie studio or the local theater or, in later years, the television station. Additionally, the early soundtrack albums appeared in the era of radio, before the visual medium completely overwhelmed popular culture, and their impact and importance were much greater at the time.

For the film studios, the soundtrack album (whether devoted to dramatic film scores or musicals) became a major marketing tool, promoting the film by its release weeks ahead of the opening date, securing radio play for the major songs, and promoting the studio's own music-publishing interests. This often led to peculiarities in song and musical lineups. Most movie musical albums, for example, failed to include dance numbers, incidental music, and choral pieces, since these were not hooked to specific singing personalities. Additionally, the running-time restrictions on 78s and early long-playing records required the cutting of extended instrumental breaks, however pleasant.

Finally, there were the peculiarities of the music and movie businesses themselves: Frank Sinatra, who was under contract to MGM Studios for a period of five years and turned in at least one major musical performance on screen during that time (*On the Town*), never appeared on an MGM soundtrack album because he was under exclusive contract to Columbia Records in the '40s. However, the soundtrack album to MGM's 1956 *High Society*, featuring Sinatra, Bing Crosby, and Louis Armstrong, did appear on Capitol Records, where Sinatra was recording in the '50s.

The soundtrack business went along as an adjunct to the movie business until the '60s, when changes began occurring, most notably a splintering of the market. Swept up by the boom in pop and rock and a decline in traditional entertainment and subjects, studios stopped making musicals (except for multimillion-dollar blockbusters) and began demanding a lighter touch in scoring their dramatic films. At the same time, two generations of listeners and fans—one that had grown up when the older films were originally in the theaters, and one that had grown up with them on television—began expressing an interest in the music that had filled their lives.

The business of reissuing soundtracks had existed, particularly where musicals were concerned, since the switch from 78s to long-playing records. But in the early '60s, various labels (most notably Capitol, Decca/London, and Warner Bros.) began commissioning new recordings that made use of the dramatic improvements that had been made in record fidelity and stereo sound. *Gone with the Wind* by Max Steiner, *Ben Hur, El Cid*, and *King of Kings* by Miklos Rozsa, and the *Adventures of Robin* Hood by Erich Wolfgang Korngold were just a few of the scores represented in new recordings, often done under the supervision of their original composers.

By the beginning of the '70s, with the recognition of film's cultural importance (it even became a field of academic study), re-recordings had become common. Producers Peter Munves and George Korngold and conductor Charles Gerhardt brought the first successful extended series of such efforts to RCA Records in the form of the *Classic Film Scores* series, with each volume devoted to a specific composer (e.g., *The Classic Film Scores of Alfred Newman*). The Gerhardt series was ideal for the serious listener and the novice just getting started. Careful attention was paid to the details and nuances of the music itself, and the material was assembled in suites of easily absorbed length.

Meanwhile, on a more intensive level, Elmer Bernstein (himself a major movie composer) had begun a concerted effort to preserve scores and secure rights for the original composers and their estates. As an adjunct to this effort, he made a monumental series of re-recordings in England of vintage film scores in their entirety, through his Film Music Society label.

The '70s and '80s saw a veritable explosion in the field of film music, as a second generation of major screen composers—Elmer Bernstein, Jerry Goldsmith, Leonard Rosenman, Ennio Morricone (whose music for the Clint Eastwood/Sergio Leone "man with no name" Westerns virtually revolutionized that genre)—achieved wide recognition and major composer status. Along with new soundtrack albums, which now seem to accompany virtually every film release, even of the lowest-budgeted picture, re-recordings became still more common using various European orchestras, which work under far less restrictive union rules and for far less money than their American counterparts.

The '80s also saw the establishment of a new kind of soundtrack album, which actually had its roots in the '70s: the rock 'n' roll soundtrack. Films built around rock groups and personalities had been common from the '50s onward (most notably the relatively well-made early films showing the young, lean Elvis Presley; the early British films of Cliff Richard and the Shadows; and the one great work in the genre, the Beatles in *A Hard Day's Night*), but the '70s saw the emergence of the rock soundtrack as a separate screen entity. It began with George Lucas' *American Graffiti*, the soundtrack which, filled with a superbly selected body of rock oldies, was nearly as prominent in the film as any of the actors. The accompanying double album also became a massive seller.

Francis Ford Coppola's *Apocalypse Now*, with its use of '60s hits, moved the formula up a decade and a notch in dramatic intensity, even if its most famous scene involved Wagner's "Ride of the Valkyries" and a helicopter attack. But it was *Fast Times at Ridgemont High*, another film about adolescent life, that brought the formula first used in *American Graffiti* into a contemporary time frame, with an enviable assembly of catchy singles and FM-style hits by contemporary rock artists. From there on, the die was cast: producers saw the path to success with otherwise flawed and conceptually weak movies was simply to license the right rock tracks, and many movies of the '80s and '90s acquired the feel of a jukebox in operation. With varying degrees of success, the specific music involved everything from post-new wave (*I Was a Teenage Zombie*) to such vintage music-and-myth-mixing efforts as Oliver Stone's *The Doors*, where the songs structured the film and occasionally the soundtracks outperformed and outlasted the movies themselves. —*Bruce Eder*

110 in the Shade / RCA ✦✦✦✦✦
Based on an N. Richard Nash play that also became the Katharine Hepburn/Burt Lancaster film *The Rainmaker*, this film was a moderate success in 1963. The Harvey Schmidt/Tom Jones score is not their best but shouldn't be overlooked. Stephen Douglass singing the opening number "Gonna Be Another Hot Day" evokes *Oklahoma!*, clearly an inspiration to this production. —*Marjorie Ellen Ruhlmann*

● **55 Days at Peking** / 1963 / Varese Sarabande ✦✦✦✦✦
One of Dimitri Tiomkin's better '60s scores, with more interesting material than usual and fewer sluggish spots—the one to get. —*Bruce Eder*

Above the Rim / 1994 / Interscope ✦✦✦✦✦
The soundtrack *Above the Rim* is an example of how all soundtracks should sound. Coordinated by Dr. Dre, the record is a virtual catalog of the cutting edge of hip-hop and R&B in 1994, featuring stars as well as unknowns that wind up making a big impression. Every artist turns in a first-rate song, but the real attraction of the record is Warren G.'s hit single, "Regulate," which straddles the line between rap and soul with grace and style. —*Stephen Thomas Erlewine*

Adventures of Robin Hood / 1988 / Varese Sarabande ✦✦✦
A surprisingly dull score (from the 1938 movie) by Erich Wolfgang Korngold—one that he reportedly had a lot of trouble finishing—well and rousingly re-recorded and elevated by its moments of inspiration, which are fewer in number than typical for this composer. —*Bruce Eder*

Against All Odds [O.S.T.] / 1984 / Atlantic ✦✦✦
The soundtrack to this remake of *Out of the Past* is highlighted by the title song, "Against All Odds (Take a Look at Me Now)," a dramatic ballad sung by Phil Collins that topped the charts for three weeks. It also contains songs by Stevie Nicks, Peter Gabriel, Big Country, and Kid Creole and the Coconuts, plus selections from the score by Michel Colombier and Larry Carlton. —*William Ruhlmann*

☆ **Aladdin** / 1992 / Disney ✦✦✦✦✦
Disney's restored winning streak with animated musicals stretched to three with this film, scored (as were its predecessors, *The Little Mermaid* and *Beauty and the Beast*) by Alan Menken, who collaborated both with his usual partner, Howard Ashman (Ashman died before production was completed) and Tim Rice, known as the lyricist on Andrew Lloyd Webber's early musicals. The standout performances, as in the film, are by Robin Williams, playing the Genie, on such songs as "Friend Like Me" and "Prince Ali." The score also contains Peabo Bryson and Regina Bell's hit single, "A Whole New World." (Note that, while early copies of this album contain what some Arabs considered objectional lyrics in the lead-off song, "Arabian Nights," the lyrics have been redone on later copies.) —*William Ruhlmann*

The Alamo / 1960 / Varese Sarabande ✦✦✦✦✦
A famous Dimitri Tiomkin score, which suffers from a lack of melodic invention and fatal passages broken by a few memorable moments. It has its fans, however. —*Bruce Eder*

Alamo Bay / 1985 / Slash ✦✦✦✦✦
One of Ry Cooder's better film scores, though the picture itself vanished into obscurity. Five of the nine pieces are instrumental, and Cooder flavors his distinctly trembling blues guitar with shakuhachi and violin to create moody pieces evoking spare and desolate landscapes that owe as much to the tropics and the desert as the Delta. Also has some routine bar-band blues-rock songs, a country duet between John Hiatt and actress Amy Madigan, and cameo appearances by David Lindley, David Hidalgo and Cesar Rosas of Los Lobos, and Fear vocalist Lee Ving. —*Richie Unterberger*

☆ **Alien** / 1980 / Virgin ✦✦✦✦✦
Jerry Goldsmith's music, recorded under the baton of Lionel Newman, holds up nearly as well as Ridley Scott's 1979 movie, with long, lyrical passages broken up by genuinely unsettling timbral effects. —*Bruce Eder*

American Gigolo [O.S.T.] / 1980 / Polydor ✦✦✦✦✦
Danceable electronic score by Eurodisc master Giorgio Moroder, including "Call Me" by Blondie, which was No. 1 for six weeks. —*William Ruhlmann*

☆ **American Graffiti Soundtrack, Vol. 1** / 1973 / MCA ✦✦✦✦✦
The soundtrack to the George Lucas film about teenage life in a small California town in the early '60s was probably the best thing about the movie, featuring several dozen outstanding early rock 'n' roll hits. There's nothing terribly obscure here—in fact, most of those were big smashes—but it's a good survey of rock's early days, ranging from superstars like Buddy Holly, Chuck Berry, Fats Domino, and the Beach Boys to great one-shots like the Monotones, the Tempos, and Buster Brown. Drawbacks: Wolfman Jack talks over the intros of a few songs, and there are a couple tracks by early-'70s Sha-Na-Na-type revivalists Flash Cadillac. —*Richie Unterberger*

☆ **An American in Paris** [O.S.T.] / CBS ✦✦✦✦✦
An expanded edition of the George Gershwin showcase soundtrack from the 1951 movie, with good sound (especially on the title ballet, re-scored by Saul Chaplin). —*Bruce Eder*

Animal House / 1978 / MCA ✦✦✦
Animal House is a classic frat-house comedy, full of low-brow humor and outrageously entertaining vulgarity. The soundtrack nearly captures that atmosphere on record, even though it has a couple of flaws. The meat of the soundtrack lies in a selection of great rock 'n' roll and R&B oldies, including Chris Montez's "Let's Dance," Bobby Lewis' "Tossin and Turnin'," Paul and Paula's "Hey Paula," and Sam Cooke's "Twistin' the Night Away" and "Wonderful World." No matter how good these tracks are—and they are great—their impact is lessened by the re-recorded oldies from Lloyd Williams ("Shout," "Shama Lama Ding Dong") and John Belushi ("Money," "Louie Louie"), as well as two lightweight Steven Bishop songs and Elmer Bernstein's instrumental "Faber College Theme." While those songs reflect the boozy pleasures of the movie, they don't sound quite as good when isolated on record. Nevertheless, the soundtrack remains a good party—even if its momentum sags occasionally. —*Stephen Thomas Erlewine*

Annie / 1982 / CBS ✦✦✦✦
The soundtrack to John Houston's movie adaptation of the Broadway blockbuster *Annie* is fitfully entertaining, featuring good versions of "Tomorrow," "It's the Hard-Knock Life," and "You're Never Fully Dressed Without a Smile." Even though the glossy production sounds good and most of the vocalists sound good, the soundtrack isn't as consistent or rich as the original cast recording. —*Stephen Thomas Erlewine*

Back to the Future [O.S.T.] / 1985 / MCA ✦✦✦
Huey Lewis and the News scored a No. 1 hit with the typically bouncy "The Power of Love" from this album. Completists will also want to note the appearance of otherwise unavailable tracks by Lindsey Buckingham and Eric Clapton. —*William Ruhlmann*

Bad and the Beautiful / Jun. 18, 1996 / Rhino ✦✦✦✦
Composed and conducted by David Raskin, the soundtrack to *The Bad and the Beautiful* is a subtle, dramatic effort that effectively conveys the drama inherent in the film. Rhino's disc—which is the first time the soundtrack was ever released—includes music that wasn't heard in the original film, as well as extended versions of pieces that were used in the movie. —*Stephen Thomas Erlewine*

☆ **Band Wagon** / CBS ✦✦✦✦✦
Fred Astaire's personality dominates this collection of songs from the musical, and that's a plus. The classic "That's Entertainment" is the best number by far, and Fred carries the rest well. —*Bruce Eder*

Batman Forever / 1995 / Atlantic ✦✦✦
On its surface, *Batman Forever* is the traditional studio-assembled soundtrack, bringing together heavy hitters (U2, the Offspring, Brandy,

Method Man) with cult favorites (PJ Harvey, Massive Attack, Nick Cave) that have little connection. However, the record turns the formula on its ear, creating a dark, hypnotic mood that doesn't let up until the end of the album. It's the first half of the soundtrack that is the most impressive. Beginning with the club-ready T. Rex riffs of U2's Nellee Hooper-produced "Hold Me, Thrill Me, Kill Me, Kiss Me" and segueing immediately into the loose, dirty blues stomp of PJ Harvey's "One Time Too Many" and the seductive pulse of Brandy, the album draws connections between artists that don't seem to have anything to do with each other. What ties nearly everything together is their underlying dark rhythmic pulse—each song has a vague menace that is also sexual. With the notable exceptions of the Offspring, Michael Hutchence, and the Flaming Lips—whose songs are used to deflate the mood—*Batman Forever* is a surprisingly effective, atmospheric record; although only three of the songs are featured prominently in the film, it's even better than the movie. —*Stephen Thomas Erlewine*

Batman [Original Motion Picture Score] / May 1989 / Warner Bros. ✦✦✦✦✦
The best of all the Danny Elfman soundtracks, the "Batman Theme" is familiar to all who've seen the film, but anyone who hasn't listened to the "Finale" is in for a real treat. Without a doubt Elfman has a flair for writing for brass. —*Tavia Hobart*

☆ **Beauty and the Beast** / 1991 / Disney ✦✦✦✦✦
This music by Alan Menken and lyrics by Howard Ashman are positively delightful. While not as good as the *Little Mermaid* score, this album has its moments, such as "Be Our Guest" (in an *A Chorus Line* style). Including both orchestral and vocal selections, it features the talents of Robby Benson, Paige O'Hara, and Angela Lansbury, among others. The album also includes "Beauty and the Beast" as a duet between Celine Dion and Peabo Bryson. —*Tavia Hobart*

Ben-Hur / 1990 / PolyGram ✦✦✦
Miklos Rozsa conducting the Royal Philharmonic Orchestra. This '70s re-recording by the composer of the 1959 movie has a very bright sound and most of the highlights, but lacks the weight of the original recordings. —*Bruce Eder*

☆ **Ben-Hur** / Sony ✦✦✦✦✦
A monumental double CD of Miklos Rozsa's music, assembled from the complete two original albums plus the original film tracks, all cleaned up and properly re-sequenced. —*Bruce Eder*

Benny and Joon / 1993 / RCA ✦✦✦
Scotland's Proclaimers got a belated No. 3 hit with their four-year-old "I'm Gonna Be (500 Miles)" when it was taken up as the theme song of this offbeat romantic comedy. The rest of the soundtrack album features Rachel Portman's score, which emphasizes the movie's whimsical nature. —*William Ruhlmann*

Best of James Bond: 30th Anniversary / 1992 / Capitol ✦✦✦
The Best of James Bond: 30th Anniversary is a limited-edition double-disc set that collects the hit versions of all the James Bond themes, as well as adding an extra disc of unreleased material, featuring commercials and incidental music composed by John Barry. Bond collectors will delight with the rarities, but many listeners will settle for the single-disc version, which just contains the theme songs, including "Goldfinger," "Diamonds Are Forever," "Live and Let Die," "A View to a Kill," and "For Your Eyes Only." —*Stephen Thomas Erlewine*

The Beverly Hillbillies [TV Soundtrack] / 1993 / Columbia/Legacy ✦✦
The "Beverly Hillbillies" television series, which ran from 1962 to 1971, was a situation comedy, not a musical show, other than its famous Flatt and Scruggs theme song. Nevertheless, after three years on the air, the show spun off this album, in which members of the cast, prominently featuring Buddy Ebsen and Irene Ryan, sang songs based on their characters. The result is a novelty with a vengeance. Ebsen, a former musical comedy star, comes off fine, but even fans of the show may not be ready to hear Max Baer sing out about the foibles of life in Beverly Hills. Long out of print, the album was released on CD in 1993 in anticipation of the movie version of the show. —*William Ruhlmann*

Beverly Hills Cop / 1984 / MCA ✦✦✦✦✦
Two million copies of this album were sold within a year of release, which is no surprise, given that it contained such hits as Patti LaBelle's "New Attitude," Glenn Frey's "The Heat Is On," and Harold Faltermeyer's "Axel F." Another notable aspect of the recording is the small-print admission "Contains additional songs that are not in the film." In other words, this is more of a compilation than a soundtrack album per se. It didn't bother anybody, though. —*William Ruhlmann*

☆ **The Big Chill** / 1983 / Motown ✦✦✦✦✦
Motown scored big with this album, which contains ten '60s hits, from Marvin Gaye's "I Heard It Through the Grapevine" to Procol Harum's "A Whiter Shade of Pale," just the sort of thing the yuppie thirtysomethings in the movie loved, and music rediscovered by the audience that saw the film. —*William Ruhlmann*

The Big Easy [O.S.T.] / 1987 / Mango ✦✦✦✦✦
The soundtrack to *The Big Easy* is a dynamite collection of New Orleans R&B, rock 'n' roll, and zydeco, featuring several of the genre's biggest names as well as some lesser-known gems and a respectable track from the film's star, Dennis Quaid. —*Stephen Thomas Erlewine*

Bird / 1988 / Columbia ✦✦✦
This set has the soundtrack of Clint Eastwood's film *Bird*. Arranger Lennie Niehaus managed to isolate Charlie Parker's original alto solos (some from studio sessions and a few from rarer club appearances) and re-recorded them with contemporary bop-based musicians. The effect is rather eerie and generally works, allowing such musicians as pianists Monty Alexander, Barry Harris, and Walter Davis, Jr., bassists Ray Brown, Chuck Berghofer, and Ron Carter, drummer John Guerin, and trumpeters Jon Faddis and Red Rodney to play with Bird. Worth acquiring if only for the novelty value since this setting did not allow Parker the opportunity to react to the other musicians. —*Scott Yanow*

Blue in the Face / Sep. 19, 1995 / Luaka Bop ✦✦✦
Music from the wilds of Brooklyn! Luaka Bop label-head and co-executive producer David Byrne teams up with the late Tejano singer Selena on "God's Child" and with Indian orchestra leader Vijaya Anand on "Happy Suicide," songs that, as their titles suggest, feature Byrne's typically quirky lyrics; Spearhead and Zap Mama perform "To My Ba-Bay!"; the John Lurie National Orchestra declares, "Let's Get Ready to Rhumba"; Astor Piazzolla contributes "Tango Apasionado"; and Lou Reed previews his upcoming *Set the Twilight Reeling* album with the nostalgic "Egg Cream." In and around and through, Danny Hoch, in various guises, contributes spoken-word performances. Who would have thought New York City's least respected borough could be so exotic? —*William Ruhlmann*

The Bodyguard / 1992 / Arista ✦✦✦✦✦
The main draw of *The Bodyguard* soundtrack is the biggest single of all time, "I Will Always Love You" (14 weeks at No. 1!), surrounded by other adult-contemporary/urban-pop songs from Whitney Houston that are equally appealing to fans of her mega-hit. —*AMG*

Border Radio / 1987 / Enigma ✦✦✦
Former Blasters and X songwriter/guitarist Dave Alvin scored this film and brought in his friends—the cream of the early '80s Los Angeles rock scene—to help. Various tracks feature Alvin, fellow X member John Doe, Green on Red, Steve Berlin of the Blasters, and Los Lobos, among others. —*William Ruhlmann*

Born on the Fourth of July / 1989 / MCA ✦✦✦✦✦
The first eight tracks on this disc are rock and pop, including songs from Edie Brickell and the New Bohemians, Don McLean, and the Temptations. The last six are from the pen of John Williams. The music literally haunts you as you watch the movie. It's just as effective here. —*Tavia Hobart*

☆ **Boyfriend** / 1955 / RCA ✦✦✦✦✦
A tribute to the frivolous musicals of the '20s, this tongue-in-cheek entertainment was one of the few successful musicals of its time to originate in Great Britain. It's notable for introducing a 19-year-old Julie Andrews to Broadway. —*William Ruhlmann*

The Breakfast Club / 1985 / A&M ✦✦✦
Anchored by the Simple Minds hit "Don't You (Forget About Me)," this also features tracks by Wang Chung and Jesse Johnson and several good instrumentals by producer Keith Forsey (producer of Billy Idol, Psychedelic Furs). —*Scott Bultman*

Bridges of Madison County / 1995 / Warner Bros. ✦✦✦✦✦
Noted jazz fan Clint Eastwood assembled the soundtrack to his film *The Bridges of Madison County* and it reflects his tastes. Heavy on cool jazz, traditional pop, and crooner Johnny Hartman, the soundtrack is appropriately romantic and keeps a consistent mood throughout the album. —*Stephen Thomas Erlewine*

☆ **Brigadoon** / 1947 / RCA ✦✦✦✦✦
The tale of an 18th-century Scottish village that travels through time and its romantic encounter with two 20th-century visitors became the first major hit written by the team of Alan Jay Lerner and Frederick Loewe. It features "Almost like Being in Love." —*William Ruhlmann*

Bright Lights, Big City / 1988 / Warner Bros. ✦✦✦✦✦
Excellent contemporary dance music on this album, including Prince, New Order, Bryan Ferry, and Depeche Mode, plus a rare song by Steely Dan's Donald Fagen. —*William Ruhlmann*

Brimstone and Treacle / 1982 / A&M ✦✦✦
The better part of this album is given over to songs by the Police and by Sting (who starred in the film), though IRS labelmates the Go-Go's and Squeeze also turn up. —*William Ruhlmann*

Broadway Classics, Vol. 1 / 1991 / MCA ✦✦✦
The choice seems nearly random but this sampler of Broadway songs from Broadway shows originally released on Decca includes everything

from "The Impossible Dream" to "Don't Cry for Me, Argentina." Listen, and then seek out the complete show. — *William Ruhlmann*

A Bronx Tale / 1993 / Epic ✦✦✦
The music from this motion picture consists of period tunes heard in the Bronx and elsewhere in the '50s and '60s, starting, naturally, with homeboys Dion and the Belmonts and running through the Jimi Hendrix Experience. That's quite a stretch, of course, but it is bridged by interludes given over to recreations of the period sound by Cool Change. And from the Cleftones' "Little Girl of Mine" to the Rascals' "A Beautiful Morning," the selections are such classics it's hard to argue with them. Still, without the movie's images to hold them together, the collection seems virtually random. — *William Ruhlmann*

Cabaret [O.S.T.] / 1972 / MCA ✦✦✦✦✦
Liza Minnelli hit a career peak in this film musical, and she dominates the soundtrack, lending personal meaning to such songs as the title track (in which she almost seems to be singing about her mother, Judy Garland). Joel Grey is equally impressive. — *William Ruhlmann*

Cal / 1984 / Mercury ✦✦✦
Mark Knopfler's second album of soundtrack music features the guitarist with his band, Dire Straits, along with tin whistle and mandolin player Paul Brady and uilleann pipes player Liam O' Flynn on a set of atmospheric Irish-tinged instrumentals. The slow, stately rhythms and careful fingerpicking recall the middle sections of calmer Dire Straits songs. — *William Ruhlmann*

☆ **Camelot** / Sep. 22, 1987 / Warner Bros. ✦✦✦✦✦
The Lerner and Loewe music in this film version is sung with passion, if not great control, by Richard Harris and Vanessa Redgrave, and is livelier than the movie. — *Bruce Eder*

☆ **Can Can** / 1974 / Capitol ✦✦✦✦✦
A Cole Porter dalliance set in Paris and featuring a young Gwen Verdon, plus such memorable songs as "I Love Paris" and "It's All Right with Me." — *William Ruhlmann*

Casino [O.S.T.] / Nov. 14, 1995 / MCA ✦✦✦✦✦
The soundtrack to Martin Scorsese's '70s mob epic *Casino* is as oversized as the movie. Assembled by Robbie Robertson, the album runs the gamut from schmaltzy pop to blues and rock 'n' roll, featuring a great assortment of classic tracks and performers. — *Stephen Thomas Erlewine*

Casualties of War / 1989 / Columbia ✦✦✦✦✦
A dark, brooding, and surprisingly restrained work by Ennio Morricone, also more sentimental than his usual standard, and very operatic—parts of it sound like music for a Broadway extravaganza waiting to happen. — *Bruce Eder*

☆ **Chariots of Fire** / 1982 / Polydor ✦✦✦✦✦
Vangelis' Academy Award-winning score to the movie continues to be his most famous album, probably because the theme is immediately recognizable yet quickly lures listeners into a musical world that stands on its own. — *Linda Kohanov*

Chess / 1984 / RCA ✦✦✦✦✦
This is a studio recording made prior to any staged version of the musical, with music by former ABBA members Benny Andersson and Bjorn Ulvaeus and lyrics by Tim Rice about an international chess tournament. A UK Top Ten hit, it includes Murray Head's hit version of "One Night in Bangkok." — *William Ruhlmann*

Cinderella / 1957 / CBS ✦✦✦
Perhaps Rodgers and Hammerstein's most seen but least performed musical, *Cinderella* was written for and played on television, for only one, nontaped time. The typically lovely music and affecting lyrics softened some of the harder aspects of the fairy tale, and Julie Andrews gave a wonderful performance in the title role. This recording features the TV cast and was made a couple of weeks before the broadcast. The score features memorable songs such as "Do I Love You Because You're Beautiful." — *William Ruhlmann*

Cinema Gala: Citizen Kane / Decca ✦✦✦✦✦
Performed by the London Philharmonic Orchestra and National Philharmonic Orchestra. The *Citizen Kane* material isn't as interesting as that on Charles Gerhardt's RCA collection, but the material from *The Devil and Daniel Webster* and *Jason and the Argonauts* is a necessary part of any collection. (Unicorn Records has a still-better rendition of the former that simply has never turned up on CD.) — *Bruce Eder*

☆ **Citizen Kane: Herrmann Film Scores** / Jun. 1974 / RCA ✦✦✦✦✦
Citizen Kane: The Classic Film Scores of Bernard Herrmann is probably the best of the entire series by conductor Charles Gerhardt and the National Philharmonic Orchestra. Every track is worthwhile and memorably played, especially *Beneath the 12-Mile Reef* and the suite from *Citizen Kane*, the latter highlighted by Kiri Te Kanawa's performance of the Strauss-like aria from *Salammbo*. — *Bruce Eder*

☆ **Classic British Film Music** / Silva Screen ✦✦✦✦✦
An essential import recording of several long-neglected English film scores, most notably Ralph Vaughan Williams' "Coastal Command"; the

Irving Berlin

Irving Berlin (1888-1989) was the most successful songwriter of the 20th century. Though, like his contemporaries, he spent the better part of his career writing songs (usually both words and music) to be used in Broadway musicals, he is better remembered for the songs themselves than for the shows (and sometimes films) in which they were introduced. This is because Berlin was a master at the kind of music that flourished from the turn of the century until World War II, shows that were really just collections of production numbers, scenes, and novelty acts (organized vaudeville presentations, really) rather than the story musicals that became prevalent starting with Rodgers and Hammerstein's *Oklahoma!* in 1943. It is also because Berlin, who did not read music and could play the piano in only one key and only on the black notes (he used a special piano with a lever that changed keys for him and employed a musical secretary to notate his compositions), wrote songs, not scores.

But what songs! Out of more than a thousand, a short list would include "Alexander's Ragtime Band" (his first major hit, in 1911), "God Bless America," "A Pretty Girl Is Like a Melody," "Always," "Blue Skies," "Puttin' on the Ritz," "How Deep Is the Ocean?," "Cheek to Cheek," "Let's Face the Music and Dance," "White Christmas," "There's No Business Like Show Business," "I Love a Piano," "What'll I Do?," "Easter Parade," and "Oh, How I Hate to Get Up in the Morning." The last came from one of the two shows Berlin organized and performed in during the two world wars (he can be seen in the film version of the second one, *This Is the Army*).

Berlin became his own song publisher and built and owned a Broadway theater, the Music Box, to house his shows. Perhaps his greatest and his last hit came with the musical *Annie Get Your Gun* in 1946, though he did write three more before retiring in 1962. — *William Ruhlmann*

playing is competent if not always inspired. Kenneth Alwyn and the Philharmonic Orchestra. — *Bruce Eder*

The Classic Rozsa / DRG ✦✦✦✦
Some of Miklos Rozsa's most endearing folk-based classical material. Not in a league with his most heavyweight pieces, but enjoyable and very direct expressions of his love of native Hungarian music. — *Bruce Eder*

Clockers / 1995 / 40 Acres and a Mule ✦✦✦
The soundtrack to Spike Lee's adaptation of Richard Price's drug-dealer/murder drama *Clockers* is alive with first-rank hip-hop and soul artists, accurately reflecting the urban sounds of 1995. From the smooth soul of Seal, Des'ree, and Chaka Khan through the hip-hop/jazz fusions of Buckshot LeFonque to the intense Crooklyn Dodgers (Jeru the Damaja, Chubb Rock, O.C., and DJ Premier), the *Clockers* soundtrack offers a wide variety of style. Nothing on the soundtrack became a hit, but that doesn't mean the album isn't worthwhile. More than most soundtracks, it captures both the spirit of the movie while standing as its own, entirely listenable, entity. — *Stephen Thomas Erlewine*

A Clockwork Orange / 1968 / Warner Bros. ✦✦✦✦✦
Tangerine Dream's soundtrack to Stanley Kubrick's nightmarish adaptation of Anthony Burgess' *A Clockwork Orange* captures the seedy, horrific images of the film perfectly. Twenty years later, the synthesizers might sound a little dated, but the music itself is still supremely eerie, capable of conjuring frightening images on its own—it's nearly as scary as the movie. — *Stephen Thomas Erlewine*

Close Encounters of the Third Kind / 1977 / Varese Sarabande ✦✦✦✦✦
John Williams' score draws too much from Ravel for its own good, but the sound is impressive and the effects are entertaining. — *Bruce Eder*

Club Paradise / 1986 / CBS ✦✦✦
For all intents and purposes, this is a Jimmy Cliff album, which means some high-quality, pop-oriented reggae. On one track, "Seven-Day Weekend," Cliff duets with Elvis Costello (they also wrote the song together), along with the Attractions. — *William Ruhlmann*

Clueless / Jul. 18, 1995 / Capitol ✦✦✦
It's hard to argue with the Muffs' cover of Kim Wilde's "Kids in America," Counting Crows' live "The Ghost in You," Supergrass' "Alright," and an acoustic version of Radiohead's "Fake Plastic Trees." A pair of all-time pop-rock pantheon tracks get covered here to cautious approval—both Cracker and World Party hold their own on more subdued renditions of the Flaming Groovies' "Shake Some Action" and Mott the Hoople's "All

the Young Dudes," respectively. Jill Sobule closes with her wry, deadpan "Supermodel." "I didn't eat yesterday, and I'm not going to eat today, and I'm not going to eat tomorrow . . . 'cause I'm gonna be a supermodel . . ." —*Roch Parisien*

Cocktail / 1988 / Elektra ✦✦✦
The four-million-selling summer party album of 1988, featuring the No. 1 hits "Don't Worry, Be Happy" by Bobby McFerrin and "Kokomo" by the Beach Boys, plus radio hits by Starship, the Fabulous Thunderbirds, the Georgia Satellites, and John Cougar Mellencamp. —*William Ruhlmann*

A Collector's Sondheim / 1985 / RCA ✦✦✦✦✦
A four-LP box-set compilation that gathers material from a variety of Stephen Sondheim scores over the 30 years 1954-1984 (those for which he only provided lyrics are excluded). This is an outstanding, if pricey, sampler that features many rarities and is a must for Sondheim fans. —*William Ruhlmann*

The Color of Money / 1986 / MCA ✦✦✦
Ex-Band songwriter/guitarist Robbie Robertson put together this soundtrack, which allowed him to collaborate with blues master Willie Dixon and jazz master Gil Evans, though it was his collaboration with Eric Clapton that produced the album's hit song, "It's in the Way That You Use It." Also featured: Don Henley, Robert Palmer (three tracks), and B. B. King. —*William Ruhlmann*

The Commitments / Aug. 13, 1991 / MCA ✦✦✦
Alan Parker's film about a Dublin, Ireland, cover band sparked this wildly popular soundtrack of R&B remakes. Male vocalist Andrew Strong shouts like a working-class Michael Bolton, and all three female singers have knelt at the altar of Queen Aretha. The band's competent, as bar bands go, and the songs are good—any album that includes "The Dark End of the Street" and "Slip Away" has to have something going for it. —*Brian Mansfield*

The Commitments, Vol. 2 / 1992 / MCA ✦✦✦
More R&B retreads from Ireland's favorite fictional White-soul band. Seven of the 11 tracks are billed as new recordings, so this is really film leftovers plus some filler. It shows, too—it's a long way down from *Vol. I*'s "I Can't Stand the Rain" to "Too Many Fish in the Seas." —*Brian Mansfield*

Cool Runnings / 1993 / Chaos ✦✦✦
It was inevitable that a comedy about a Jamaican bobsled team would have a reggae soundtrack. What is surprising is that it is so enjoyable in a light, unforced way. Worl-A-Girl note the unlikeliness of Jamaica having a bobsled team; Diana King covers Bob Marley's "Stir It Up"; and Wailing Souls cover Talking Heads' "Wild Wild Life." Best of all (if somewhat redundant), Jimmy Cliff got his first chart hit in 23 years with a cover of the 21-year-old "I Can See Clearly Now," by Johnny Nash. —*William Ruhlmann*

Crooklyn [O.S.T.] / 1995 / MCA ✦✦✦✦✦
Spike Lee's *Crooklyn* is a touching coming-of-age film, set in the early '70s. Appropriately, the soundtrack is crammed with an abundance of smooth soul and gritty R&B from the era. —*Stephen Thomas Erlewine*

Crossroads [O.S.T.] / 1986 / Warner Bros. ✦✦✦
The ersatz blues story of the film gives Ry Cooder leeway to turn in an impressive blues-derived soundtrack featuring Sonny Terry along with his usual collaborators Van Dyke Parks, Jim Keltner, Nathan East, and others. But it's Cooder's guitar playing that highlights the album. —*William Ruhlmann*

The Crow / 1995 / Atlantic ✦✦✦✦✦
Not to be confused with the collection of alternative pop-rock songs, *The Crow: The Original Score* is the hauntingly dramatic, gothic incidental music used in the action/adventure film starring Brandon Lee. The music is frequently powerful and stirring, and works well as an individual entity. —*Stephen Thomas Erlewine*

Dances with Wolves / Aug. 1990 / Epic ✦✦✦✦✦
This majestic John Barry score is slightly underrecorded but very rewarding despite its occasional overreliance on material all too familiar from the *James Bond* movies. —*Bruce Eder*

Dangerous Minds [O.S.T.] / 1995 / MCA ✦✦✦✦✦
Thanks to Coolio's monolithic single "Gangsta's Paradise," the soundtrack to Michelle Pfieffer's urban school drama tore up the charts. Even with a single as powerful as Coolio's masterpiece, the *Dangerous Minds* soundtrack wouldn't have stayed at the top of the charts, selling over three million copies, if there was only one good song on the album. Like many soundtracks of the mid-'90s, *Dangerous Minds* is an expertly crafted urban R&B/hip-hop collection, featuring stellar production and songwriting from a number of the best and most popular artists of 1995. Admittedly, "Gangsta's Paradise" remains the standout, but there's not much disappointing material on the rest of the disc. —*Stephen Thomas Erlewine*

David Shire: Aat the Movies / 1991 / Bay Cities ✦✦✦✦✦
A too-often-overlooked composer gets to play some of his best movie music at the piano, with help from Maureen McGovern. The album

includes material from *Norma Rae, Farewell My Lovely, The Conversation,* and *Return to Oz.* —*Bruce Eder*

Dazed and Confused / 1994 / Warner Bros. ✦✦✦
Dazed and Confused is a lazy comedy about growing up stoned in the '70s. Appropriately, the soundtrack is filled with 8-track anthems, from Black Sabbath's "Paranoid" and Foghat's "Slow Ride" to Sweet's "Fox on the Run." In fact, with its abundance of disposable classics, the music captures the spirit of the decade better than the movie itself. —*Stephen Thomas Erlewine*

Dead Man Walking—Music from and Inspired by the Motion Picture / 1996 / Columbia ✦✦✦
Copying the successful approach taken by director Jonathan Demme on *Philadelphia,* Tim Robbins asked a group of prominent songwriters to contribute newly written songs for the soundtrack of his death-row drama *Dead Man Walking.* The result is this album of "music from and inspired by the motion picture" (which means not all of it was used in the movie). Bruce Springsteen, who won an Oscar and a few Grammies for his *Philadelphia* song, leads things off with "Dead Man Walkin'," which is in the spare style of his *Nebraska* and *The Ghost of Tom Joad* albums. (The song earned Springsteen a second Oscar nomination.) The rest of the lineup is impressive: Johnny Cash (no stranger to prison songs), Suzanne Vega, Lyle Lovett, Eddie Vedder, Tom Waits, Michelle Shocked, Mary-Chapin Carpenter, Steve Earle, and Patti Smith (who did not write her song). The artists turn in characteristic performances of songs with themes drawn from or similar to the film, which is to say they are about crime and punishment; Earle's "Ellis Unit One," for example, is a first-person story of a prison guard. In general, these are not among the artists' better songs, but the album has a consistency of tone and makes many of the same points that the film does. Thus, this is more a companion album to the film than a soundtrack, and in fact a separate album containing the actual score also was released. —*William Ruhlmann*

Dead Man Walking: The Score / Mar. 1996 / Columbia ✦✦✦
"The predominant style that you hear in the score is Pakistani Sufi devotional (Qawwali) chanting . . . ," writes composer and music supervisor David Robbins of the recordings that make up his score for *Dead Man Walking.* Accordingly, the predominant performer is singer Nusrat Fateh Ali Khan. The score album replicates two duets between Khan and Pearl Jam singer Eddie Vedder from the other *Dead Man Walking* soundtrack album, which contained "music from and inspired by the motion picture," but the versions heard here are longer. —*William Ruhlmann*

Dead Presidents [O.S.T.] / Oct. 1995 / Capitol ✦✦✦✦✦
The soundtrack to the Hughes Brothers' tribute to early-'70s blaxploitation gets the sound of the era right, featuring hits by the O'Jays, the Spinners, Isaac Hayes, Al Green, and Harold Melvin and the Blue Notes, among others. The inclusion of Danny Elfman's instrumental theme interrupts the flow of the album, but for the most part, *Dead Presidents* is a first-rate collection of prime soul. —*Stephen Thomas Erlewine*

☆ **Deep Blues** / 1992 / Anxious/Charisma ✦✦✦✦✦
In what amounts to a state-of-the-art field recording, Robert Palmer (author of *Deep Blues,* one of the finest books ever written on the subject) took a 24-track mobile unit into the Delta and came back with ample recorded proof that the low-down, jacketing brand of Mississippi blues is still alive, well, and flourishing. No famous names, just loads of incredible music. With fidelity so true you can hear the beer bottles clinking on the tables, all live blues recordings should sound this exciting. A new standard of excellence. —*Cub Koda*

Deep in My Heart / CBS ✦✦✦✦✦
The Sigmund Romberg material is generally extremely well performed, even by Jose Ferrer, and this collection, from the 1954 movie, is unique in terms of content. —*Bruce Eder*

Desperado [O.S.T.] / 1995 / Epic/Sony ✦✦✦
The soundtrack to *Desperado* (sequel to *El Mariachi*—artist/musician hero in black sports guitar case full of weapons) desperately sought to capture the style of *Pulp Fiction,* with its Latin-flavored, Tarantino-meets-Morricone mood. It partially succeeded, integrating movie dialogue with choice contributions from Los Lobos and uncentered offshoot band Latin Playboys and vintage instrumental kickers courtesy of Link Wray's "Jack the Ripper" and the obscure "Pass the Hatchet" by Roger and the Gypsies. Salma Hayek's steaming "Quedate Aqui" and Dire Straits' "Six Blade Knife" stay in character, but the mood is lost to bombastic blues-rockers by Tito (Larriva of the Cruzados) and Tarantula, Carlos Santana, and one uncharacteristic Los Lobos miscue (the dire "Let Love Reign"). —*Roch Parisien*

Devil in a Blue Dress / 1946-1995 / Columbia ✦✦✦
The music on this CD is taken from the soundtrack of the film *Devil in a Blue Dress,* a drama set in late-'40s Los Angeles. There are representative selections from the era by T-Bone Walker, Jimmy Witherspoon ("Ain't Nobody's Business If I Do"), Duke Ellington, Roy Milton, Wynonie Harris, Pee Wee Crayton, Bull Moose Jackson, Amos Milburn, Memphis Slim, Lloyd Glenn, and even Thelonious Monk (the original version of "'Round

Midnight"). In addition, this CD has the opening and closing theme and one melody from the film by Elmer Bernstein. One of the better jazz/R&B soundtracks. —*Scott Yanow*

Diamonds Are Forever [O.S.T.] / 1972 / EMI America ✦✦✦✦✦
John Barry wrote a big, impressive-sounding score for this 1971 film, which on record comes off as a good follow-up to *On Her Majesty's Secret Service*. —*Bruce Eder*

Dirty Dancing / 1987 / RCA ✦✦✦
This album includes songs from the hit movie—both old favorites (Bruce Channel's "Hey Baby"; "In the Still of the Night," from the Five Satins; and Mickey and Sylvia's "Love Is Strange") and recent ones (Eric Carmen's "Hungry Eyes" and "(I've Had) The Time of My Life," performed by Bill Medley and Jennifer Warnes). "She's Like the Wind" is performed by Patrick Swayze, who played the male lead in the movie. While this may not be "the time of your life," as the album cover advertises, it is a fun collection. —*Tavia Hobart*

☆ **Doctor Zhivago** / 1990 / CBS ✦✦✦✦✦
A lush, beautiful score for an epic film. "Lara's Theme" was the biggest hit from the 1965 movie, but there were enough secondary tunes to turn it into one of the biggest-selling soundtrack albums in history. Glittering and gorgeous. —*Bruce Eder*

★ **Doctor Zhivago** / 1995 / Rhino ✦✦✦✦✦
If you're a big fan of this classic soundtrack, with its grandiose themes and blend of lush orchestration with Russian folklike melodies and instruments, you might want to consider an upgrade to this deluxe CD reissue. Besides including all of the original soundtrack music, it adds over half a dozen outtakes. That's actually not the most significant bonus; more essential is the 28-page booklet, with exhaustive track-by-track annotation, and detailed personal recollections by composer Maurice Jarre himself. —*Richie Unterberger*

Don't Be a Menace to South Central While You're Drinking Your Juice in the Hood / Jan. 1996 / Island ✦✦✦
Don't Be a Menace to South Central While You're Drinking Your Juice in the Hood is a silly spoof of Black urban dramas of the '90s, like *Boyz N the Hood, Menace II Society*, and *Juice*. Appropriately, the soundtrack is a slightly off-center collection of hip-hop and rap-influenced R&B. Not all of the soundtrack works—it's too long, for one thing, and there are too many mediocre cuts—but the songs that are good are first rate, particularly Ghost Face Killah's first solo track. It's just a shame there aren't more than a handful of good songs. —*Stephen Thomas Erlewine*

Dr. No / 1963 / EMI America ✦✦✦
John Barry's "James Bond Theme" from the 1962 movie is the best part of this weakest of the James Bond soundtracks, which otherwise boasts pseudo-Jamaican melodies and a couple of guitar instrumentals. —*Bruce Eder*

Dumb and Dumber [O.S.T.] / 1995 / RCA ✦✦✦
Dumb and Dumber is a surprisingly entertaining hodgepodge of alternative rock (Echobelly, Primitives), mainstream pop, and novelties (Deadeye Dick's "New Age Girl") that is considerably smarter than the movie it supports. —*Stephen Thomas Erlewine*

☆ **Easter Parade** / 1989 / Sony ✦✦✦✦✦
The sound of these 1947 recordings is old, but the assembly of Irving Berlin tunes sung by Fred Astaire, Judy Garland, and Ann Miller is one of the best—especially "Drum Crazy." —*Bruce Eder*

Eddie and the Cruisers [O.S.T.] / 1983 / RCA ✦✦✦✦✦
There was a year's delay before this film, which concerns the mysterious death of a fictional '60s rock star, took off via video and cable TV; but when it did, the soundtrack album, featuring such songs as "On the Dark Side" and "Tender Years," by John Cafferty and the Beaver Brown Band, took off with it. To most, the music sounded like Bruce Springsteen clones, but it was appealing nonetheless. —*William Ruhlmann*

Eddie and the Cruisers 2: Eddie Lives / 1989 / RCA ✦✦
The soundtrack to the sequel for *Eddie and the Cruisers* follows the basic blueprint of John Cafferty's songs for the first film—they're all high-energy, pounding three-chord rock 'n' roll. However, Cafferty wasn't able to come up with a batch of songs as good as "The Dark Side," which leaves the soundtrack as bland and predictable as the movie it was supporting. —*Stephen Thomas Erlewine*

El Cid / 1977 / CBS ✦✦✦✦✦
Rozsa and most listeners agree that *El Cid*, from the 1961 movie, was his last great score. Overall, it is a surprisingly lyrical and sensitive body of music for what was essentially an epic-scale action film—much of the material has been most inventively derived from medieval Spanish and Arab sources, and while the recording has an unfortunate softness to modern ears, the playing is exceptionally polished and the 1962-vintage stereo separation still holds some surprises. —*Bruce Eder*

Empire Records / 1995 / A&M ✦✦✦✦✦
The soundtrack to a movie that was barely released, *Empire Records* is a fine collection of mainstream alternative pop-rock, featuring two hit sin-

Danny Elfman

Since 1980 Danny Elfman has enjoyed modest success as frontman for the eccentric alternative band Oingo Boingo, but an opportunity to score Tim Burton's 1985 film *Pee Wee's Big Adventure* opened up a lucrative career as a composer of TV and film soundtracks. Since then, his credits have included *Batman, Dick Tracy, The Simpsons, Edward Scissorhands, Scrooged, Beetlejuice, Big Top Pee Wee*, and too many more to mention. —*Rick Clark*

gles—the menacing Motown-meets-Bowie pop of Edwyn Collins' "A Girl like You" and the stirring "Till I Hear It from You" from the Gin Blossoms. The rest of the album is hit-or-miss—mostly noticeable for the debut appearance of the Martinis, a new band from former Pixies Joey Santiago and David Lovering—but it is enjoyable, nevertheless. —*Stephen Thomas Erlewine*

☆ **The Empire Strikes Back** / 1980 / Varese Sarabande ✦✦✦✦✦
Here is an album that includes what are probably some of the most overplayed, overused themes in the history of film scores. However, if you can get past the familiarity and actually *listen* to what's there, you'll find another well-written score from John Williams. —*Tavia Hobart*

Even More Dazed and Confused / Oct. 25, 1994 / Medicine ✦✦✦
Even More Dazed and Confused is a collection of songs that are in the same spirit of the *Dazed and Confused* soundtrack. A couple of the selections were used in the film, but they were buried underneath the dialogue. For the most part, the songs included on the album have nothing to do with the movie itself, yet they faithfully replicate the feeling of the film and its soundtrack. —*Stephen Thomas Erlewine*

The Falcon and the Snowman / 1985 / EMI America ✦✦✦✦✦
Pat Metheny and Lyle Mays lent their trademark sound to the sweeping (occasionally orchestral) score of this original soundtrack. David Bowie's vocals are featured on "This Is Not America." —*Scott Bultman*

Fallen Angels / 1993 / Verve ✦✦✦
This is the soundtrack to a six-part cable television series based on detective stories set in Los Angeles in the '40s and '50s. It contains mostly small-band jazz from the Verve Records catalog and features people like Charlie Parker, Stan Getz, Nat "King" Cole, and Billie Holiday. As such, it functions as a neat jazz sampler separate from the series. —*William Ruhlmann*

☆ **Fame** / 1980 / Polydor ✦✦✦✦✦
The film's setting in the New York High School of the Performing Arts provided a frame for one of the most inspiring soundtracks of a film in the '80s. Film star Irene Cara scored with the chart-topping title track and the Top 20 "Out Here on My Own." This soundtrack, most of it by Michael Gore, is a knockout. —*William Ruhlmann*

☆ **Fantasia** / 1991 / Disney ✦✦✦✦✦
One of the best and one of the earliest full orchestral scores available (it was recorded for the 1940 film), featuring Leopold Stokowski and the Philadelphia Orchestra in top form. Avoid the digital re-recording from the '80s at all costs. —*Bruce Eder*

☆ **Far from the Madding Crowd** / 1985 / Sony ✦✦✦✦✦
Possibly the best score written for any English picture since the '40s heyday of Vaughan Williams and William Walton's film work—Richard Rodney Bennett composed a haunting, melodic yet atonal score for this 1967 movie, built on English folk melodies, that lingers long in the listener's memory. James Galway's flute playing is a bonus. —*Bruce Eder*

Faraway, So Close! / Jan. 25, 1994 / SBK ✦✦✦
Director Wim Wenders assembled a modern rock Who's Who for this soundtrack, which includes tracks by U2 (both of which also turn up on their *Zooropa* album), Lou Reed, Nick Cave, Jane Siberry, and Laurie Anderson. The result is a moody, evocative set that works with the film and as a consistent collection of contemporary songs. (Almost half of the album is given over to selections from Laurent Pettitgand's low-key score.) —*William Ruhlmann*

Fast Times at Ridgemont High / 1982 / Elektra ✦✦✦✦✦
The first great rock 'n' roll compilation soundtrack of the '80s, which sold in the millions (justifiably) and gave Jackson Browne a Top Ten hit with "Somebody's Baby." —*Bruce Eder*

● **The Film Music of John Barry** / 1988 / CBS ✦✦✦✦✦
An interesting if predictable compilation, touching most of the key parts of the composer's 1960 output. —*Bruce Eder*

Film Music, Vol. 1: The Collection / 1987 / Virgin ✦✦✦✦✦
A good survey of some of Ennio Morricone's more notable movie themes, spanning the mid-'60s to the mid-'80s. Includes some of his most famous work (from *The Good, the Bad, and the Ugly, The Mission, The Battle of Algiers, Once Upon a Time in the West*, and *Sacco and Vanzetti*), as well as more obscure items like a 1971 BBC TV program.

George Gershwin

In a career tragically cut short in mid-stride by a brain tumor, George Gershwin (1898-1937) proved himself to be not only one of the great songwriters of his extremely rich era, but also a gifted "serious" composer who might bridge the worlds of classical and popular music. The latter is all the more striking, given that, of his contemporaries, Gershwin was the most influenced by such styles as jazz and blues.

Gershwin's first major hit, interpolated into the show Sinbad in 1919, was "Swanee," sung by Al Jolson. Gershwin wrote both complete scores and songs for such variety shows as George White's Scandals (whose annual editions thus were able to introduce such songs as "I'll Build a Stairway to Paradise" and "Somebody Loves Me").

After 1924, Gershwin worked primarily with his brother Ira as his lyricist. The two scored a series of Broadway hits in the '20s and early '30s, starting with Lady Be Good (1924), which included the song "Fascinatin' Rhythm." 1924 was also the year Gershwin composed his first classical piece, "Rhapsody in Blue," and he would continue to work in the classical field until his death.

By the '30s, the Gershwins had turned to political topics and satire in response to the onset of the Depression, and their Of Thee I Sing became the first musical to win a Pulitzer Prize. In the mid-'30s, Gershwin ambitiously worked to meld his show music and classical leanings in the creation of the folk opera Porgy and Bess, with lyrics by Ira and by Dubose Heyward. The Gershwins had moved to Hollywood and were engaged in several movie projects at the time of George Gershwin's death. —William Ruhlmann

---

Anthology has superseded this as the most in-depth retrospective, but this doesn't repeat many of the tracks from that compilation, making for a worthwhile supplement. —Richie Unterberger

Film Music, Vol. 2 / 1988 / Virgin ✦✦✦✦✦
As worthy a collection of Ennio Morricone's pieces as Vol. 1, spanning 1968 to 1986. Like the first installment, it mixes pieces from well-known soundtracks (Once Upon a Time in America, Once Upon a Time in the West, A Fistful of Dynamite, The Mission) with the arcane. Bits of spaghetti western are here, but the emphasis is primarily on his orchestral arrangements, with "Moses' Theme" being one of his most impressive achievements in the idiom. Like Film Music, Vol. 1, it does duplicate a few tracks from Anthology, but is certainly a good compilation on its own terms. —Richie Unterberger

Finian's Rainbow / 1948 / CBS ✦✦✦✦✦
Ella Logan, Donald Richards, and David Wayne starred in this mixture of Southern politics and Irish blarney, which was the most successful of Burton Lane's musicals. —William Ruhlmann

The Firm / 1993 / MCA/GRP ✦✦✦✦✦
Dave Grusin's score for this Sydney Pollack treatment of the John Grisham legal thriller starring Tom Cruise consists of jazzy acoustic piano pieces, a surprisingly low-key yet effective approach. It is augmented with some pop and fusion songs, notably tunes by Jimmy Buffett, Lyle Lovett, and Nanci Griffith, to give a feel of the contemporary Southern locale. —William Ruhlmann

Flashdance [O.S.T.] / 1983 / Casablanca ✦✦✦✦✦
Giorgio Moroder's score for this dance fantasy album turned into a blockbuster (five million copies and counting) due to the title single, sung by Irene Cara, Michael Sembello's "Maniac," and a bunch of other modern dance tracks. —William Ruhlmann

Footloose / 1984 / CBS ✦✦✦✦✦
Footloose was a throwback to '50s rock 'n' roll movies, with a silly plot about a town where it was illegal to dance. It was a major hit, as was its soundtrack, which spent a grand total of ten weeks at No. 1 and selling over seven million copies. It's easy to see why—the album delivers its mainstream pop, anthemic rock, and light dance-pop with style and abundance of hooks. Six of the nine tracks became Top 40 hits and three—Kenny Loggins's bouncy title song, the excellent power ballad "Almost Paradise . . . Love Theme from Footloose" (a duet between Loverboy's Mike Reno and Heart's Ann Wilson), and Deniece Williams' frothy, charming "Let's Hear It for the Boy"—shot into the Top Ten. The sound and production of Footloose has dated badly—there is a reliance on synthesizers and drum machines that instantly announces that the record was made in 1984—but that isn't necessarily a weakness. Not only does it function as a time capsule of a certain moment in pop music history, but many of the songs are catchy enough to transcend their pro-

duction. There's nothing of substance on the Footloose soundtrack, but it's a light, entertaining listen. Sometimes, that can be better than something substantial. —Stephen Thomas Erlewine

Forrest Gump / 1994 / Sony ✦✦✦✦✦
The surprise hit of the 1994 summer movie season traces the life of a half-wit through the major historical events of the '50s, '60s, and '70s, and this soundtrack album is a travelogue of the same period, from Elvis Presley's 1956 hit "Hound Dog" to Bob Seger's 1980 hit "Against the Wind." Like the movie, the soundtrack to Forrest Gump succeeds at repackaging the familiar—in the film, we revisit everything from desegregation and the Vietnam War to the self-centered trends of the '70s, and on the soundtrack, we hear the concurrent hits for the umpteenth time—although, unlike the movie, the soundtrack doesn't trivialize what it recycles. Playing it is basically like listening to an oldies radio station, minus the commercials and annoying DJ patter, but, just like many other song-oriented soundtracks, this is still a miscellaneous collection. That, however, didn't keep it from shooting into the Top Ten as the movie became a blockbuster. The double-CD version contains eight more tracks than the cassette. —William Ruhlmann

Forrest Gump [Original Score] / 1994 / Epic Soundtrax ✦✦✦
Forrest Gump was a sugar lump of a movie, a fact driven home by this album containing Alan Silvestri's saccharine score, all cute little piano high notes and swatches of melody rolling out of the string section. There is also a two-disc soundtrack album containing pop songs heard in the picture. It's music to watch feathers waft in the breeze by, and is therefore appropriate to the film, although it has little value on its own. —William Ruhlmann

Four Rooms [O.S.T.] / 1995 / Elektra ✦✦✦✦✦
The soundtrack to Four Rooms is a collection of kitschy cocktail music, performed by original practitioners like Esquivel and revivalists like Combustible Edison. It's an enjoyable if lightweight album. —Stephen Thomas Erlewine

Four Weddings and a Funeral / Apr. 5, 1994 / London ✦✦✦
Not surprisingly, we have a cornucopia of love songs here, the best of them perhaps being Elton John doing Gershwin on "But Not for Me." (The older rockers get, the more they want to do pop standards.) John also is heard on his own "Crocodile Rock" and "Chapel of Love," and when he's not singing, we are getting remakes of "La La La (Means I Love You)" and "Smoke Gets in Your Eyes." Well, what did you expect from a movie that has four weddings in it? And speaking of the funeral, the album concludes with John Hannah's reading of W.H. Auden at the movie's most solemn moment. Thankfully, the film itself ends on a more up note, and you can always program your CD player to play only the wedding material. —William Ruhlmann

Friday / 1995 / Priority ✦✦✦✦✦
By 1995, R&B and hip-hop artists expended some of their greatest creative energy on soundtracks, turning in compilation albums that frequently were more compulsively listenable and adventurous than soloartist collections. Fridays was no exception. The soundtrack to a lightweight comedy co-written by Ice Cube, the record conveys all the strengths of hit urban radio. Keeping all of the good elements of the format—including the G-Funk of Dr. Dre, old school soul, contemporary R&B and gangsta rap—the record sounds like a "Best of the '90s" collection. —Stephen Thomas Erlewine

☆ **From Russia with Love** / 1975 / EMI America ✦✦✦✦✦
Probably the best of the James Bond scores, with radiant music for strings and startling percussion passages punctuating this recording from the 1963 film. —Bruce Eder

Funny Girl / Aug. 1968 / Columbia ✦✦✦
As a movie, Funny Girl is even more of a Barbra Streisand star vehicle than it was as a Broadway show. The main differences between the cast album and this, the film soundtrack, are that there are fewer songs from the Bob Merrill-Jule Styne score, there is less singing for the leading man, in this case nonsinger Omar Sharif, and Streisand gets to sing two songs actually associated with Fanny Brice (whom she portrays), "I'd Rather Be Blue over You (Than Happy with Somebody Else)" and "My Man." —William Ruhlmann

Funny Lady / 1975 / Bay Cities ✦✦
Barbra Streisand is not known for singing standards, so the chief virtue of this soundtrack to the disappointing sequel to Funny Girl is hearing her singing songs like "Am I Blue." This is not a great virtue, however, especially when you also have to endure the singing of James Caan. —William Ruhlmann

Geronimo: American Legend / 1993 / ✦✦✦
Director Walter Hill hired Ry Cooder to do the score for a movie he describes on the back cover as "a drama about two cultures," and Cooder (with such cronies as David Lindley and R. Carlos Nakai) has delivered an appropriate mixture of sounds identifiably based in Native American music and in nineteenth century American folk music—music for the campfires of both camps, as it were. Cooder is steeped in such styles, and

the result is effective, if not one of his more independent scores. —*William Ruhlmann*

Get Shorty / Oct. 17, 1995 / Antilles ♦♦♦
The soundtrack to Barry Sonnenfeld's hit film adaptation of Elmore Leonard's gangsters-in-Hollywood satire *Get Shorty* is a lot like the movie itself—light and breezy, without much lasting substance. The score is essentially soul-jazz colored in pastels, which sounds nice for a few tracks but soon becomes a bit monotonous. Nevertheless, it sounds very good if taken in moderation, since it is simply too lightweight to be ingested all at once. —*Stephen Thomas Erlewine*

Get Yourself a College Girl / 1964 / CBS ♦♦♦♦♦
A pretty cool soundtrack for a pretty lousy movie. Featured here are the Dave Clark Five, the Standells, the Animals, and Stan Getz. —*Bruce Eder*

☆ **The Ghost and Mrs. Muir** / 1975 / Varese Sarabande ♦♦♦♦♦
Elmer Bernstein conducting the Royal Philharmonic Orchestra. An excellent re-recording, from the 1947 movie, of one of Bernard Herrmann's finest scores, a dark, brooding, romantic work that is lovely and haunting. —*Bruce Eder*

☆ **Giant** / Apr. 12, 1989 / Capitol ♦♦♦♦♦
The best of Dimitri Tiomkin's original soundtrack albums, in a crisp, dense mono that is extremely impressive on CD. This album, from the 1956 movie, is a treat for the ears, and well worth owning. —*Bruce Eder*

☆ **Gigi** / 1958 / Sony ♦♦♦♦♦
One of the finest musical scores ever recorded. A warm, witty, romantic confection highlighted by Andre Previn's spirited conducting, Betty Wand's delectable singing, and Lerner and Loewe's greatest film score. —*Bruce Eder*

Girl 6 / Mar. 19, 1996 / Warner Bros. ♦♦♦♦
Prince compiled the soundtrack to Spike Lee's phone-sex comedy *Girl 6*, using a handful of new tracks from himself and the New Power Generation, as well as several classic Prince-performed and Prince-produced tracks. If anything, the soundtrack sounds like it was recorded in 1986—nearly every song is about sex and they're all driven by funky keyboards or they're smooth soul ballads. Fortunately, all of Prince's new material comes in shooting distance of standards like "Erotic City," "Adore," and "Girls and Boys," as well as Vanity 6's "Nasty Girl." The New Power Generation tracks fall a little flat in comparison, but *Girl 6* is a fine record, ideal for those pining for Prince's mid-'80s heyday. —*Stephen Thomas Erlewine*

Godspell [O.S.T.] / 1973 / Arista ♦♦♦♦♦
A stirring rock-pop score by Stephen Schwartz and a strong lead performance by Victor Garber make a success of this film version of the stage hit emphasizing the religious nature of Christ (as opposed to the secular *Jesus Christ Superstar*). Robin Lamont's rendition of "Day by Day" was a Top 15 hit. —*William Ruhlmann*

Goldeneye [O.S.T.] / 1995 / Virgin ♦♦♦
Apart from the awkward title song, performed by Tina Turner and written by U2's Bono and the Edge, the soundtrack to *Goldeneye*, the first James Bond movie starring Pierce Brosnan, is an enjoyable collection. Most of the disc is devoted to Eric Serra's score, which builds on John Barry's classic Bond theme, developing into a bold, exciting piece of music. "Goldeneye" may be one of the weakest Bond themes, but that doesn't prevent the rest of the record from being as strong as the previous 007 soundtracks. —*Stephen Thomas Erlewine*

Goldfinger / 1964 / EMI America ♦♦♦♦♦
The first of the hit James Bond albums, driven by Shirley Bassey's inimitable performance of the title track. —*Bruce Eder*

☆ **Gone with the Wind** / 1990 / Sony ♦♦♦♦♦
An expanded and remastered edition of the original 1939 track, with much of the echo and distortion removed. —*Bruce Eder*

Good Morning Vietnam / 1987 / A&M ♦♦♦♦♦
Good Morning Vietnam was a comedy/drama starring Robin Williams as an American Army DJ in Vietnam. Appropriately, the soundtrack is filled with oldies—from Louis Armstrong's "What a Wonderful World" and Martha and the Vandellas' "Nowhere to Run" to the Rivieras' "California Sun" and James Brown's "I Got You (I Feel Good)"—punctuated by Williams' manic comic routines. Some listeners will find the routines a bit tedious, but it's a thoroughly entertaining and well-paced collection of oldies that manages to evoke the mid-'60s quite well. —*Stephen Thomas Erlewine*

☆ **The Good, the Bad and the Ugly** / 1988 / EMI America ♦♦♦♦♦
Probably Ennio Morricone's most appealing and enduring Western score—funny, intense, dramatic, and filled with haunting melodies. The CD's stereo separation adds to the fun of this 1967 soundtrack. —*Bruce Eder*

The Gospel at Colonus / 1984 / Warner Bros. ♦♦♦
The original cast recording of the Bob Telson/Lee Breuer musical based on Sophocles' *Oedipus at Colonus* has music written in gospel style and sung by the Five Blind Boys of Alabama and other gospel groups. It is

---

Jerry Goldsmith

Jerry Goldsmith (born in Los Angeles in 1929) is the leading figure in film music of his generation. After starting out in radio, he moved into television and motion pictures in the early '60s, where his instrumental inventiveness and superb melodic sense quickly moved him to the top of his profession. His scores are seldom less than inspired and are always absorbing, whether they are written for thrillers (*The Prize*, "The Twilight Zone" TV series), science fiction (*Logan's Run*), military subjects (*Patton, The Blue Max*), or serious drama (*A Patch of Blue*). —*William Ruhlmann*

---

beautifully produced by Telson, Daniel Lazerus, and the Steely Dan team of Donald Fagen and Gary Katz. —*William Ruhlmann*

The Great Escape / 1963 / Intrada ♦♦♦♦♦
An impressively remastered recording, with a very rich sound, despite a little more hiss than one might like. —*Bruce Eder*

Great Western Themes (With Geoff Love and Orch.) / EMI ♦♦♦♦♦
Twenty-four tracks done with verve but not much insight, highlighted by "The Big Country," "The Big Valley," "Wagon Train," and a creditable version of "The Virginian." —*Bruce Eder*

☆ **Hang 'Em High/Guns for San Sebastian** / CBS ♦♦♦♦♦
Dominic Frontiere's *Hang 'Em High*, from the 1968 film, is a spare, clever score, but Ennio Morricone's *Guns for San Sebastian* (1968) is practically an opera without words—intense, draining, and magnificent. —*Bruce Eder*

★ **The Harder They Come** / 1972 / Mango ♦♦♦♦♦
Jimmy Cliff starred in this gritty film about street life in Kingston, Jamaica. The album is a brilliant compilation of early reggae music, and Cliff's own songs. "You Can Get It If You Really Want It," "Many Rivers to Cross," "The Harder They Come," and "Sitting in Limbo," are among the best of a very good lot. —*William Ruhlmann*

☆ **Bernard Herrmann: Classic Fantasy Film Scores** / ♦♦♦♦♦
Four of Bernard Herrmann's fantasy film scores written for the movies of Ray Harryhausen (*Seventh Voyage of Sinbad*, etc.) and taken from the original film recordings. The sound is a little soft and compressed, which is understandable given its origins, and the representation of *Jason and the Argonauts* here is a bit of a cheat, but the rest of the material has never been excerpted as fully. —*Bruce Eder*

☆ **Bernard Herrmann—Film Fantasy: Cinema Gala** / London ♦♦♦♦♦
Bernard Herrmann—Film Fantasy: Cinema Gala is an extraordinarily fine collection of some of Herrmann's most famous film music, originally well recorded by the composer during the '60s and remixed for a bright sound today. Worth owning just for the suite from *The Day the Earth Stood Still*, but it's all first rate. —*Bruce Eder*

☆ **Bernard Herrmann—Music from the Great Hitchcock Movie Thrillers** / London ♦♦♦♦♦
This collection is a well-programmed and well-performed overview of Herrmann's work in association with Hitchcock. None of the scores is anywhere near complete, but all of the famous movie selections from *Psycho*, *North by Northwest*, *Vertigo*, and *The Trouble with Harry* are represented. —*Bruce Eder*

Hollywood Screen Classics / Chesky ♦♦♦♦♦
Charles Gerhardt conducting the National Philharmonic Orchestra. Chesky has done unexpectedly well with these mostly 1968-vintage recordings. Although the sound is a little compressed compared with Gerhardt's later work, the detail is all there, and the work does have a youthful freshness. Highlights include perhaps the best of all *Gone with the Wind* suites, plus oddities such as the music from *Rashomon*. —*Bruce Eder*

Honeymoon in Vegas / Aug. 11, 1992 / Epic ♦♦♦♦♦
Country singers rule this soundtrack of Elvis Presley covers, which is every bit as flawed, frivolous, and fun as the film from whence it came. While Billy Joel parodies "All Shook Up" and "Heartbreak Hotel," John Mellencamp labors to avoid parodying "Jailhouse Rock," and U2's Bono transforms "Can't Help Falling in Love" into an obsessive parable about hero worship, folks like Ricky Van Shelton and Trisha Yearwood just sit back and sing the things, which at least makes them pleasant after more than one playing. Dwight Yoakam's power-chord-country version of "Suspicious Minds" and Travis Tritt's "Burning Love" rank with their best remakes. Breaking the trend are pop crooner Bryan Ferry, who sings a seductive British soul version of "Are You Lonesome Tonight?" and the usually trustworthy Vince Gill, whose Pat Boone-style rendition of Arthur Crudup's classic blues "That's All Right" cleans up the grammar. —*Brian Mansfield*

Bernard Herrmann

The dean of film composers, Bernard Herrmann was probably the most gifted musician ever to work in films, with barely a note of music to his credit that is not worthwhile. A classically trained composer, Herrmann worked for Orson Welles' Mercury Theatre and the CBS radio network before he went to Hollywood with Welles in 1940. His first two film scores, *Citizen Kane* and *The Devil and Daniel Webster*, were both nominated for Oscars in the same year (Webster won), and he was established from then on. Herrmann worked principally for 20th Century-Fox from the mid-'40s until the end of the '50s, and did brilliant work on such films as *The Ghost and Mrs. Muir, The Day the Earth Stood Still, Beneath the 12-Mile Reef*, and *Journey to the Center of the Earth*. In the '50s and '60s, Herrmann also contributed notably to the success of Alfred Hitchcock's films and wrote inspired scores for early films by Brian De Palma and Martin Scorsese. He died the night he finished work on *Taxi Driver*. —*William Ruhlmann*

Hook [O.S.T.] / 1991 / Epic ✦✦✦✦
A John Williams masterpiece, the emotion he evokes through this music is incredible: it can make you experience what the characters in the movie are feeling—see the menace of Captain Hook, or find your happy thought and fly. One could just sit and listen to it for hours without finding all the little nuances in the music. It includes the vocal selections "We Don't Wanna Grow Up" and "When You're Alone." —*Tavia Hobart*

The Hot Spot [O.S.T.] / 1990 / Antilles ✦✦✦
This score is credited to "The Ultimate Blues Band," and you can't argue with the name when the personnel includes John Lee Hooker and Miles Davis. A moody, slinky, bluesy, jazzy, improvised score that's full of treats. —*William Ruhlmann*

House of Dark Shadows/Night of Dark Shadows / Apr. 1996 / Rhino ✦✦✦
The soundtracks of two early '70s movie spinoffs of the "Dark Shadows" TV series, composed and conducted by Robert Cobert, have been combined by Rhino onto one CD release. Reusing and re-recording some cues and material from the television show, and adding some new pieces, Cobert crafted an ambience that was characteristically spooky and occasionally eclectic, but primarily of interest to the show's considerable cult following. Much of it sounds like standard-issue horror soundtrack fare; things get a little weirder on the eeriest items (like the main theme and "The Possession of Quentin"), with a goofy surfish generic rock instrumental ("David's Radio") tacked on. The deluxe booklet includes 28 pages of photos and information/trivia about the series and the movies. —*Richie Unterberger*

House Party [O.S.T.] / 1990 / Motown ✦✦✦
Not strictly, or even mainly, their album, it does contain the singles "Funhouse" and "Kid vs. Play (The Battle)." Its prime importance was as the soundtrack from an extremely successful film of the same name, which launched the duo into cinematic stardom. —*Ron Wynn*

☆ **How the West Was Won** / 1985 / Sony ✦✦✦✦
This soundtrack, from the 1962 movie, was the most successful Western film album ever issued, and justifiably so—spacious, poignant, and inspired. —*Bruce Eder*

I Was a Teenage Zombie / 1987 / Enigma ✦✦✦✦
An excellent compilation album featuring a Who's Who of the premier roots-rock bands of the '80s: the Fleshtones, the Del Fuegos, the dB's, Dream Syndicate, the Violent Femmes, the Smithereens, Los Lobos, Alex Chilton, the Ben Vaughn Group, and Bob Pfeifer. Want to know what '80s alternative rock sounded like? Just put this album on. —*William Ruhlmann*

Jacques Brel Is Alive and Well [Original Cast] / 1974 / Atlantic ✦✦✦✦
This film version of the musical revue of the songs of Belgian singer-songwriter Jacques Brel retains the pleasure of the stage version of *Jacques Brel Is Alive and Well and Living in Paris* and adds to it by including the author himself on the moving "Ne Me Quitte Pas" (known in English as "If You Go Away"). But the standout performer is Mort Shuman, who, with Eric Blau, also provides the English translations. —*William Ruhlmann*

☆ **Jacques Brel Is Alive and Well [Original Cast]** / 1987 / CBS ✦✦✦✦
This 1968 off-Broadway revue of *Jacques Brel Is Alive and Well and Living in Paris* established an "in-concert" style of presentation for dramatic music that has often been used since. The poetic lyrics of Jacques Brel, expertly translated by Mort Shuman and Eric Blau, lend themselves to this bookless format. Its best-remembered numbers include "Marathon (Les Flamandes)," "Amsterdam," "Carousel (La Valse a Mille Temps)," and

"If We Only Have Love (Quand On a Que L'Amour)." —*Marjorie Ellen Ruhlmann*

Jaws / 1975 / MCA ✦✦✦✦✦
This is an outstanding John Williams score. Almost everyone is familiar with the driving and repetitive main theme, but few would recognize anything else from this score. There's some really good stuff here, and it's worth investigating. —*Tavia Hobart*

☆ **Jerome Robbins' Broadway** / 1989 / RCA ✦✦✦✦✦
A two-disc cast album from Robbins' anthology show, which includes his re-creations of production numbers excerpted from such shows as *On the Town, West Side Story, The King and I, Gypsy*, and *Fiddler on the Roof*. Onstage it was breathtaking; on record it makes for a sort of Broadway's-greatest-hits album, albeit with re-recorded versions. —*William Ruhlmann*

Jimmy Hollywood / 1994 / Atlas ✦✦✦
This Barry Levinson-directed film came and went so quickly that it would have been easy to miss its soundtrack, which is the work of ex-Band guitarist/songwriter Robbie Robertson. Robertson has constructed several excellent soundtracks in the past (*Carney, The Color of Money*), and this is another good one. He himself performs several tunes, and he selects others, including tracks by the Iguanas, Sand Rubies, and Concrete Blonde. A smoky and smokin' set; whatever happened to the movie? —*William Ruhlmann*

☆ **John Williams: Tribute to Spielberg** / CBS ✦✦✦✦✦
This is a must-have for any John Williams fan who hasn't started a collection yet, as some of the scores from which these tracks were taken may be difficult to find. It includes music from the *Indiana Jones* movies, *Empire of the Sun, E.T., Always, Jaws, 1941, Sugarland Express*, and *Close Encounters of the Third Kind*. It's a great representation of some of his finest scores. —*Tavia Hobart*

Jurassic Park / 1993 / MCA ✦✦✦
John Williams' score for what has become the most successful movie of all time is similar to his scores for other popular Steven Spielberg films. He remains firmly in the tradition of the lush, heavily orchestrated score. This is the first horror movie he and Spielberg have collaborated on since *Jaws*, but there is nothing like the threatening theme that helped define that monster movie here. Instead, there is a lot of quiet music, a much more subtle touch, and a wistful theme that runs throughout, although things do come to a boil now and then. —*William Ruhlmann*

Kids [O.S.T.] / 1995 / London ✦✦✦✦✦
Directed by Lou Barlow, the *Kids* soundtrack is an excellent, moody collection of lo-fi indie-rock pleasures. Mainly, it's devoted to Barlow's numerous side projects, most notably the Folk Implosion, who scored a surprise hit single with the eerie "Natural One." There are also two Daniel Johnston songs and a contribution from the frightening noise-rock band Slint, but the real meat of the package lies with Barlow's songs. Alternately introspective and poppy, they rank among his best work. —*Stephen Thomas Erlewine*

King and I / Jun. 11, 1956 / Angel ✦✦✦
The film soundtrack to Walter Lang's *The King and I* is distinguished from the Broadway cast album chiefly by Alfred Newman's expanded orchestrations and by the presence of Marni Nixon in the role of Anna Leonowens. On film, the part was played by Deborah Kerr, but Nixon, one of the best invisible voices in Hollywood (she also ghosted Audrey Hepburn in *My Fair Lady*), is the wonderful singer of songs like "I Whistle a Happy Tune" and "Getting to Know You," sung onstage by Gertrude Lawrence, who died before the film was made. Yul Brynner repeats his performance as the king, and Rita Moreno gets to play Tuptim and sing "We Kiss in a Shadow." This is a Hollywood adaptation done right—bigger and more dramatic than Broadway can be, with a show that benefits from the frills—and makes you wonder why they didn't always do as well. —*William Ruhlmann*

Kings Row / 1979 / Varese Sarabande ✦✦✦✦✦
Charles Gerhardt conducting the National Philharmonic Orchestra. A well-produced, early digital recording of Erich Wolfgang Korngold's 1942 score for the melodrama, capturing the original's majesty. —*Bruce Eder*

☆ **Kiss Me Kate** / 1990 / Angel ✦✦✦✦✦
A two-disc, nonstop, orchestral version of the score of the Cole Porter show, conducted by John McGlinn and featuring the London Sinfonietta. It contains large, instrumental parts of the score not previously recorded. —*William Ruhlmann*

☆ **The Last Emperor [O.S.T]** / 1987 / Virgin ✦✦✦✦✦
Ex-Talking Head David Byrne and actor/composer Ryuichi Sakamoto (who co-starred in the film) each get a side of this beautiful score to Bernardo Bertolucci's Academy Award-winning film, and each took home Oscars and Grammies for their efforts. —*William Ruhlmann*

Last Exit to Brooklyn / Oct. 1989 / Warner Bros. ✦✦✦
Unlike Mark Knopfler's first three soundtracks, his music for *Last Exit To Brooklyn* did not sound like outtakes from Dire Straits sessions, but

instead consisted of fully orchestrated scoring, even if the credit "music performed by Guy Fletcher" suggested that most of the stringlike sound was being made by a synthesizer. Nevertheless, this was Knopfler's most ambitious and accomplished soundtrack, if his least characteristic. — *William Ruhlmann*

☆ **Laura, and Other Soundtracks** … / RCA ✦✦✦✦✦
Laura, and Other Soundtracks by David Raskin and the New Philharmonic Orchestra is a colorful collection of Raskin's film music, from the haunting dark strains of "Laura" and "The Bad and the Beautiful" to his inventive historical setting for "Forever Amber," all well performed. — *Bruce Eder*

A League of Their Own / May 1992 / Columbia ✦✦✦
Various Columbia Records-affiliated pop singers contribute covers of period songs to the soundtrack of this film, which is a tribute to the all-girls baseball league that existed during World War II. James Taylor performs "It's Only a Paper Moon" and "I Didn't Know What Time It Was," making them his own as he frequently does with material he didn't write. Billy Joel recreates Duke Ellington's "In a Sentimental Mood," Art Garfunkel does nicely with "Two Sleepy People," and the Manhattan Transfer apply their jazz vocal abilities to "Choo Choo Ch'Boogie" and "On the Sunny Side of the Street." The song that got the most attention, however, was Carole King's original tune, "Now and Forever," which hit the adult contemporary chart. The album is filled out with music from Hans Zimmer's score, which is appropriate to the film's nostalgic and inspirational themes. (Note that Madonna's No. 1 hit "This Used to Be My Playground," heard in the film, does not appear on this album for contractual reasons.) — *William Ruhlmann*

Leaving Las Vegas / Nov. 28, 1995 / Pangaea/IRS ✦✦✦
Trumpeter and keyboard player Mike Figgis composed a No. 1 jazz album with his score to the film *Leaving Las Vegas*, most of which consisted of low-key, moody jazz pieces, along with five vocal numbers—three standards ("Angel Eyes," "My One and Only Love," and "It's a Lonesome Old Town") sung by Sting with just a piano and acoustic bass accompaniment, one ("Come Rain or Come Shine") by Don Henley, and a song by the neo-rockabilly band the Pallaminos. Oddly, the score was interspersed by excerpts from the film's dialogue. Since Nicholas Cage won an Academy Award for his acting and Elizabeth Shue was nominated, it could be argued that these portions contained at least aural representations of good acting, but the use of spoken-word passages was odd for a soundtrack album (though, come to think of it, it's become increasingly common on cast albums). — *William Ruhlmann*

☆ **Legendary Italian Westerns** / 1990 / RCA ✦✦✦✦✦
These are the performances, more than any other, that Ennio Morricone's reputation was built upon. This 31-track, 73-minute collection draws highlights from nine of his '60s Westerns, leaning especially heavily on *A Fistful of Dollars*, *For a Few Dollars More*, and *Once Upon a Time in the West*. Ranging from hysterical gunfighter ballads to contemporary classical chamber music, it is among the most dramatic and evocative music composed in any idiom. — *Richie Unterberger*

Less than Zero / 1987 / Def Jam ✦✦✦
Rap/metal producer Rick Rubin put together this hard-edged soundtrack, which features rockers Aerosmith, Poison, and Slayer, plus rappers L L Cool J and Public Enemy, though the hit from the album was a remake of Simon and Garfunkel's "Hazy Shade of Winter," performed by the Bangles. — *William Ruhlmann*

Light of Day / 1987 / Blackheart ✦✦✦
Ian Hunter and the Fabulous Thunderbirds turn up on this mainstream rock soundtrack, though it's dominated by the film band, the Barbusters, led by Joan Jett and Michael J. Fox, notably on the Bruce Springsteen title tune. — *William Ruhlmann*

Like Water for Chocolate / Jun. 22, 1993 / ✦✦✦
Leo Brower's score for the highest-grossing foreign film in American history is by turns lushly romantic (and played by an orchestra) and contemporary to the pre-World War II setting of the story in Mexico, with elements of ragtime and norteno styles. In all modes, it helps recall the moods of Alfonso Arau's evocative movie, with its magical realist approach to cooking and romance. — *William Ruhlmann*

The Lion in Winter / 1968 / Varese Sarabande ✦✦✦✦✦
An unusually stark and serious John Barry score, nicely remastered. — *Bruce Eder*

● **Local Hero** / 1983 / Warner Bros. ✦✦✦✦✦
Dire Straits leader Mark Knopfler's intricate, introspective finger-picked guitar stylings make a perfect musical complement to the wistful tone of Bill Forsyth's comedy film, *Local Hero*. This album was billed as a Knopfler solo album rather than an original soundtrack album, with the notation "music . . . for the film." Knopfler brings along Dire Straits associates Alan Clark (keyboards) and John Illsley (bass), plus session aces like saxophonist Mike Brecker, vibes player Mike Mainieri, and drummers Steve Jordan and Terry Williams. The low-key music picks up traces of Scottish music, but most of it just sounds like Dire Straits doing instrumentals,

Erich Wolfgang Korngold

A composer and performer prodigy from an early age, Erich Wolfgang Korngold (born in 1897) was already an established and respected author of operatic and orchestral works by his twenties. He bid fair to be a successor to Richard Strauss when a chance offer to go to Hollywood to supervise the scoring of *A Midsummer Night's Dream* brought him to America. He stayed for over a decade, bringing his skills to bear on some of the most celebrated movies of that period. Beginning with *Captain Blood* in 1935, he was inextricably associated with the intense and rousing music for Errol Flynn's swashbucklers, but he also wrote the landmark dramatic scores to such serious films as *Kings Row* and *Between Two Worlds*. He returned to Europe during the period after WWII and attempted to resume his career in serious music, but he found that tastes and styles had altered too radically and that his work was regarded as archaic. He died in 1957. — *William Ruhlmann*

especially the recurring theme, one of Knopfler's more memorable melodies. Gerry Rafferty (remember him from "Baker Street"?) sings the one vocal selection, "That's the Way It Always Starts." — *William Ruhlmann*

Logan's Run [O.S.T.] / Bay Cities ✦✦✦✦
Jerry Goldsmith's brilliant, witty, often very touching score for this 1976 big-budget science-fiction thriller was easily the best part of the movie, and it has been cleaned up and polished up considerably for this CD reissue. It's the first time this music—a mix of hauntingly lyrical orchestral passages and electronic tonalities—has been properly treated. — *Bruce Eder*

Lost Horizon: The Classic Film Scores of Dimitri Tiomkin / RCA ✦✦✦✦✦
Tiomkin was arguably the least talented of the major composers associated with Hollywood, and a surprising amount of the material here simply doesn't hold up. On the other hand, the 23-minute suite from *Lost Horizon* does, and then some—a radiant pastiche of largely Russian influences that surges and soars brilliantly. Charles Gerhardt conducts the National Philharmonic Orchestra. — *Bruce Eder*

Malcolm X / 1992 / 40 Acres and a Mule ✦✦✦
Composer/conductor Terence Blanchard, better known as one of the Wynton Marsalis-era young jazz traditionalists and an outstanding trumpet player, turns in a score worthy of the scope of Spike Lee's biographical drama. He mixes jazz segments with effective orchestral mood pieces for a series of musical settings in keeping with the heroic sweep of the film. — *William Ruhlmann*

The Man Who Would Be King / Bay Cities ✦✦✦✦✦
This soundtrack, from the 1975 film, was probably Maurice Jarre's best movie music of the '70s, lyrical and powerful. — *Bruce Eder*

☆ **Manhattan** / 1978 / CBS ✦✦✦✦✦
A brisk rescoring of George Gershwin's music for the 1979 Woody Allen film—very pleasant. — *Bruce Eder*

Married to the Mob / 1988 / Reprise ✦✦✦✦✦
Director Jonathan Demme has a talent for compiling terrific soundtrack albums, and this is a good example, featuring Sinéad O'Connor, New Order, Chris Isaak, Debbie Harry, Ziggy Marley and the Melody Makers, Tom Tom Club, the Feelies, and Brian Eno. Quite a mixture, but it all works. — *William Ruhlmann*

Melrose Place: The Music / 1994 / Giant ✦✦✦
It's an alternative-rock collection for the mainstream, but who cares when the pleasures are as great as Urge Overkill's arena-ballad redux "Back on Me" and Aimee Mann's gorgeous pop confection "That's Just What You Are"? Song-for-song it has a higher good-song ratio than most soundtracks, making *Melrose Place* an embarrassingly guilty pleasure. It's almost as fun as the show itself. — *Stephen Thomas Erlewine*

Mo' Better Blues / 1990 / Columbia ✦✦✦
Although the Spike Lee film *Mo' Better Blues* had a somewhat absurd ending, its depiction of the jazz life had its accurate moments and the music was generally quite rewarding. A few of the selections on this soundtrack CD are throwaways or filler but there is also some fine playing by a modern hard-bop quintet consisting of trumpeter Terence Blanchard, Branford Marsalis on tenor and soprano, pianist Kenny Kirkland, bassist Robert Hurst, and drummer Jeff "Tain" Watts. It's sure to be a collector's item someday. — *Scott Yanow*

More Music from the Valley Girl Soundtrack / 1995 / Rhino ✦✦✦
It's unlikely that there will ever be a groundswell of nostalgia for that peculiar hybrid of new wave and bubblegum pop that came into vogue in the early '80s. If you do get a hankering for that stuff, this compilation (which includes tracks that both were and were not included on the origi-

Lerner and Loewe

Alan Jay Lerner (1918-1986) and Frederick Loewe (1901-1988) wrote some of the most stylish, sophisticated theater music of the 20th century. The collaboration didn't come until relatively late in the career of each. New York-born, Harvard-educated Lerner wrote material for radio and for individual performers in the '30s. Loewe, born in Berlin, came to the US in 1924 and gradually worked his way into theater music. The two were introduced in 1942. They scored their first hit, the fantasy *Brigadoon*, in 1947.

The Lerner-Loewe formula was to combine Loewe's lush, melodic music, redolent of Viennese waltz, with Lerner's witty, literate lyrics. This they did in some of the most popular and best-remembered musicals of the '40s, '50s, and '60s, notably *Paint Your Wagon*, *My Fair Lady*, and *Camelot* (plus the film musical *Gigi*). After Loewe's retirement, Lerner wrote with other composers, most successfully with Burton Lane (*On a Clear Day You Can See Forever*). —*William Ruhlmann*

nal *Valley Girl* soundtrack) is pretty representative of that lightweight genre. Bananarama, Culture Club, and Toni Basil are represented with their most popular cuts; Rachel Sweet and Bonnie Hayes are among the lesser-known exponents of the style; Little Girls and Gary Myrick are among the most *unknown* exponents of the style; and the Jam's "Town Without Malice" provides a much-needed blast of credibility. —*Richie Unterberger*

The Most Happy Fella / 1992 / RCA ✦✦✦✦✦
A new Broadway cast recording led by opera singer Spiro Malas. The two-piano arrangement lacks the sweep of the classic original orchestrations but brings out the material in a relatively unadorned fashion that probably works better onstage in the more naturalistic '90s than the original score might. —*William Ruhlmann*

Moviola / 1992 / Epic ✦✦✦
John Barry specializes in lush, romantic, symphonic themes for big-budget motion pictures. Here, he conducts the Royal Philharmonic Orchestra, playing a series of them, from *Born Free* to *Dances with Wolves*. —*William Ruhlmann*

Murder Was the Case / 1994 / Interscope ✦✦✦✦✦
The soundtrack to an 18-minute film inspired by Snoop Doggy Dogg's "Murder Was the Case" provides more thrills than the average hip-hop release. Again, Dre relies on his standard production tricks and crew, introducing a couple of new members to the mix. But the result sounds anything but stale—it ranks alongside *The Chronic*, *Doggystyle*, and *Above the Rim* in terms of quality. In fact, various-artist compilations like *Murder Was the Case* are the ideal vehicle for Dr. Dre—they show his versatility. *Murder* has the harrowing title track from Snoop Dogg, as well as the smooth funk of Warren G and the chilling hard core of "Natural Born Killaz," the first track from Dre's collaboration with Ice Cube. At some point, Dre will need to find some new tricks, but *Murder Was the Case* finds him at the top of his game. —*Stephen Thomas Erlewine*

Music from the Motion Picture Clerks / 1994 / Chaos/Columbia ✦✦✦
In the spirit of *Reservoir Dogs*, the soundtrack to the hip independent comedy *Clerks* is filled with little clips of the movie's dialogue, which only proves how important context is to comedy. In the film, the jokes and pop-culture debates are uproariously funny, but when they're heard outside of the cramped convenience store where the film takes place, they fall flat. And that's also what happens with the songs. With the exception of Alice in Chains' sinewy, acoustic-based "You've Got Me Wrong" (also featured on their *Sap* EP) and Soul Asylum's "Can't Even Tell," none of the songs have much power when separated from the film. Furthermore, there's not much variety—it's all grunge and metal, and none of it is particularly distinctive. Fans of the film will find the *Clerks* soundtrack a fun memento, even if it's a bit tiring. Alternative hard-rock fans will find some of the album entertaining, but will also find it somewhat subpar. —*Stephen Thomas Erlewine*

Music from the Motion Picture Angus / 1995 / Reprise ✦✦✦
The movie itself—an overweight teenager tries to make sense of his angst-ridden life—may have fared poorly with critics, but the soundtrack to *Angus* delivers an invigorating adrenaline rush. Green Day leads the way with "J.A.R.," its latest Jam-induced pop-punk single, while Ash generates a manic handclapping rhythm on "Kung Fu." The Smoking Popes' "Mrs. You and Me" is irresistible; Pansy Division sets a pantheon of acoustic guitars to jingling for "Deep Water"; Weezer punches out "Buddy Holly" companion piece "You Gave Your Love to Me Softly." OK, so the disc was *mostly* a marketing tool for then-current Warner-family releases (Goo Goo Dolls, the Muffs, etc.)—it at least has the good grace to

include performers from other labels, and besides, the exuberance, energy, and wall-to-wall pop hooks set the soundtrack well beyond the movie it serves. —*Roch Parisien*

Music by Erich Wolfgang Korngold / 1991 / DCC ✦✦✦
The granddaddy of all film score re-recordings, this 1962 vintage collection is also one of the best, presenting Korngold's most popular film work in well-chosen excerpts performed by the Warner Brothers Orchestra, conducted by Lionel Newman. Steve Hoffman has done an exceptionally fine job remixing the CD, and even the original insert booklet is re-created. Probably the best recorded version of Korngold's *Adventures of Robin Hood* music, too. —*Bruce Eder*

☆ **Music for a Darkened Theater** / 1990 / MCA ✦✦✦✦✦
A very representative collection of some of Elfman's best work for films and television, it includes music from *Batman*, *Dick Tracy*, *Midnight Run*, even the theme from "The Simpsons," among others. —*Tavia Hobart*

Music from the Films of Audrey Hepburn / 1993 / Big Screen/Giant ✦✦✦
In his liner notes to this collection, Henry Mancini, who wrote five of the 11 selections, makes the case that Audrey Hepburn was the inspiration for his writing for the pictures she starred in, and who is to disagree with him? Certainly, some of Mancini's most memorable work came with his Hepburn movies of the early '60s—*Charade*, *Two for the Road*, and of course, *Breakfast at Tiffany's*. Other pieces here cannot be tied so closely to Hepburn; Frederick Loewe's music for *My Fair Lady* predated her. Still, it is Hepburn's image that comes to mind when one hears Fred Astaire singing "He Loves, She Loves" from *Funny Face*, even if composer George Gershwin died when she was nine. In any case, this compilation makes for a charming listening experience, especially at its end, when Hepburn is heard singing "Moon River." —*William Ruhlmann*

My Family / 1995 / East West ✦✦✦
The soundtrack to the Mexican-American epic *My Family* presents a cross-section of Latin music, ranging from the mambo of Perez Prado and the gritty blues of Los Lobos to the slick modern pop of Mana and the crooning of Juan Luis Guerra. Consequently, the album isn't that cohesive—it's unlikely one person would like every track on the album. Nevertheless, there isn't a weak song on the record, although it's unlikely that a listener that hasn't seen the movie would appreciate every cut, since the end result seems a little schizophrenic. —*Stephen Thomas Erlewine*

Mystery Train / 1989 / Milan ✦✦✦
The soundtrack to Jim Jarmusch's excellent film about various intersecting characters in the underbelly of Memphis is divided between vintage Memphis rock-soul and John Lurie's atmospheric score. The classics by Elvis Presley, Junior Parker, Otis Redding, Roy Orbison, Rufus Thomas, Bobby Blue Bland, and the Bar-Kays are certainly good, though for the most part easily available elsewhere. Most of Lurie's compositions are delicate miniatures built around spare, reverbed guitar lines that evoke a haunted, late-night Delta vista. There are much better tasters of either Memphis rock-soul or John Lurie, but for someone who just wants a bit of the flavor of the movie and isn't worried about building serious collections, it's not bad at all. —*Richie Unterberger*

Naked Lunch / 1992 / RCA ✦✦✦
Ornette Coleman's score for David Cronenberg's film adaptation of William Burroughs's *Naked Lunch* perfectly fits the warped '50s ambience of the movie. In fact, it's stronger than the movie itself. —*AMG*

The Natural / 1984 / Atlantic ✦✦✦
Once again, Randy Newman turns out to be a good choice for scoring a period picture, this time with a more overtly sentimental, romantic theme than *Ragtime*. He shows a mastery of structure and genre that marks him as the successor to his uncles, who spent decades writing film music. —*William Ruhlmann*

Natural Born Killers / 1994 / Interscope ✦✦✦✦
Most soundtracks simply feature the film's incidental music or songs that were heard in the background throughout the movie. Not *Natural Born Killers*. Assembled by Trent Reznor (Nine Inch Nails), the soundtrack to Oliver Stone's brutally warped serial killer saga recreates the hallucinatory feeling of the film. Snatches of dialogue interweave with song fragments and sound effects, creating a harrowing, violent soundscape, where Leonard Cohen occasionally offers a relief of sorts. In fact, Reznor managed to convey the insanity of the movie's lead characters much more effectively than Stone did with the film itself. —*Stephen Thomas Erlewine*

New York, New York [O.S.T.] / 1977 / EMI America ✦✦✦
A movie musical with songs by John Kander and Fred Ebb. They tell the story of the evolution of popular music from the swing era to the singer era and bebop, with reference to the lavish movie musicals of the late '40s. Liza Minnelli sings brilliantly, especially on the title song and on "But the World Goes 'Round," while big-band sax player Georgie Auld handles the music for Robert De Niro. —*William Ruhlmann*

The Nightmare Before Christmas: The Soundtrack / 1993 / Disney
✦✦✦✦✦

Danny Elfman, who has scored many of Tim Burton's imaginative films (*Edward Scissorhands*, his two *Batman* films, etc.), is a perfect musical partner for the somewhat macabre director, and never more so than here, where, in fact, Elfman gets not only to write the music but to play the part of the main character. *The Nightmare Before Christmas* is an animated movie musical about the abduction of Christmas by the denizens of Halloweenland, and Elfman sings the part of Jack, the Pumpkin King. The score is in his usual lush but threatening style (Kurt Weill is his biggest influence), but the highlight is Elfman's singing. Even in his rock band, Oingo Boingo (now merely Boingo), Elfman doesn't get to sing like this. Granted, the soundtrack album inevitably lacks the film's outlandish visuals, but it tells the story on its own, and one is better able to appreciate Elfman's outstanding performance. — *William Ruhlmann*

Nutty Professor [O.S.T.] / Jun. 1996 / Def Jam ✦✦✦✦
The soundtrack to Eddie Murphy's remake of the classic Jerry Lewis film *The Nutty Professor* is a veritable encyclopedia of mid-'90s urban soul and hip-hop, featuring first-rate tracks from Warren G and Slick Rick, among several other stars. It's a consistent, fun collection that keeps the good times rolling. — *Stephen Thomas Erlewine*

Odds Against Tomorrow [O.S.T.] / 1959 / CBS ✦✦✦✦✦
This superb jazz score by John Lewis was later turned into a hit by the Modern Jazz Quartet. It's dark and dynamic, and a classic. — *Bruce Eder*

☆ **Of Thee I Sing/Let 'Em Eat Cake** / 1987 / Columbia ✦✦✦✦✦
The Brooklyn Academy of Music staged concert versions of these two Gershwin political musicals of the '30s, one a sequel of the other, with Michael Tilson Thomas as music director and conductor and a cast including Maureen McGovern, Larry Kert, and Jack Gilford. The result is an exquisite recording that restores valuable Gershwin material to the record racks. — *William Ruhlmann*

☆ **On Her Majesty's Secret Service** / 1969 / EMI America ✦✦✦✦✦
A complex, lyrical John Barry score from the 1969 movie, featuring his greatest song ("We Have All the Time in the World") amid its brilliant instrumentals. — *Bruce Eder*

On a Clear Day You Can See Forever / Jul. 1970 / Sony ✦✦✦
The film version of the Broadway musical *On a Clear Day You Can See Forever* was something of a disaster, but the soundtrack album is better because the focus is on the Burton Lane/Alan Jay Lerner songs and on the primary singer, Barbra Streisand, who has six vocals out of ten selections. Far less impressive is co-star Yves Montand, whose singing voice is as suspect as his English, such that the album is a mixed success. — *William Ruhlmann*

On the Town [Studio Recording] / 1960 / CBS ✦✦✦✦✦
This is a studio re-creation of the 1944 show about three sailors on leave for a day in New York City, featuring original cast members Nancy Walker, Betty Comden, and Adolph Green, plus John Reardon. Comden and Green provided lyrics to this delightful work, and the music is by Leonard Bernstein, who conducts here. In addition to such standards as "New York, New York" and "I Can Cook Too," this version includes a great deal of instrumental dance music. — *William Ruhlmann*

Once Upon a Time in the Cinema / Jan. 30, 1996 / Varese ✦✦✦✦✦
A collection of Ennio Morricone's greatest movie themes—including *A Fistful of Dollars*, *The Good, the Bad and the Ugly*, and *Cinema Paridiso*—are featured on *Once Upon a Time in the Cinema*. Many of Morricone's most memorable moments are featured on these themes, making the disc an effective introduction to one of the great film composers of the 20th century. — *Stephen Thomas Erlewine*

One from the Heart / 1982 / CBS ✦✦✦✦✦
A series of romantic duets by the seemingly unlikely couple of Tom Waits and Crystal Gayle in fact works surprisingly well, bringing out the ballad side of each. The score is heavily integrated into the film and tells its story of love and loss in Las Vegas. — *William Ruhlmann*

Original Music from the Films of Francois Truffaut / 1993 / Milan
✦✦✦

This draws from the soundtracks of five movies by the great French director: *The 400 Blows*, *Love at 20*, *Stolen Kisses*, *Bed and Board*, and *Love on the Run*. Filmed over a period of 20 years (1958-1978), these pictures traced the life and loves of Truffaut's most famous character, Antoine Doinel, who was portrayed in all the movies by Jean-Pierre Leaud. First appearing as a juvenile delinquent in *The 400 Blows*, this tragicomic series follows Antoine as he falls in love, marries, divorces, and becomes a novelist. The music, scored by three separate composers, reflects both the different eras in which the movies were made and the different phases of Antoine's adolescence and adulthood. *The 400 Blows* is bouncy and sentimental; *Love at 20* is lush and symphonic; *Bed and Board*, during which Antoine takes a Japanese lover, is colored by sparse Japanese motifs. The accompanying booklet features a detailed synopsis of the Antoine Doinel saga and thorough liner notes about the scores

Ennio Morricone

Morricone (an Italian composer born in 1928) came out of a mixed jazz and classical background and first started scoring low-budget action/adventure films in the early '60s. His music for Sergio Leone's three Clint Eastwood "man with no name" Westerns brought him to the attention of moviegoers around the world, who appreciated his mix of refined, elaborate scoring (often with chorus as well as full orchestra) and witty, clever humor—all rather like serious comic opera, and eminently listenable. In addition to his work with Leone, Morricone is famous for his music for such films as *The Mission* and has, by his own estimate, scored 600 or more films. — *William Ruhlmann*

and their composers. Francophiles and cinemaphiles alike should get a kick out of this. — *Richie Unterberger*

The Owl and the Pussycat / 1970 / Columbia ✦
The movie represented a comeback for Barbra Streisand after the big-budget disasters of *Hello, Dolly* and *On a Clear Day You Can See Forever*. But the soundtrack album is the lowest charting record of her career, perhaps because she doesn't sing! What she does do is talk—the album consists of dialogue from the movie, endless bickering between Streisand and George Segal, with background music by Blood, Sweat and Tears. — *William Ruhlmann*

Pal Joey: Studio Recording / 1951 / CBS ✦✦✦✦
Rodgers and Hart's *Pal Joey*, with a book by John O'Hara, was a sophisticated, downbeat tale about a gigolo. It may have been a bit too dark for audiences in 1940, when it had a moderate run on Broadway. More than a decade later, Columbia Records' Goddard Lieberson decided to make a studio recording of the show, which included such classic songs as "I Could Write a Book" and "Bewitched, Bothered and Bewildered," with Harold Lang and Vivienne Segal in the main roles. It is *not*, as the album jacket suggests, a "Broadway cast," although, just to confuse matters, the success of this album led to a Broadway revival starring Lang and Segal. — *William Ruhlmann*

The Paper / 1994 / Reprise ✦✦✦
Usually, these days, when a soundtrack album is subtitled, "Music from the Motion Picture," it's a signal that it contains songs featured in the movie, but not the instrumental score, which is indicated by the subtitle, "Original Motion Picture Soundtrack." But just to be confusing, this album of Randy Newman's score to *The Paper* says it contains "Music from the Motion Picture." The music will be familiar to anyone who knows Newman's work, with its sweet strings, ragtime feel, and strong melodies. And it does conclude with a song, "Make Up Your Mind," on which Newman duets with Alex Brown. — *William Ruhlmann*

Paris, Texas / Mar. 14, 1989 / Warner Bros. ✦✦✦
This Ry Cooder score has a spare, evocative sound created by the guitarist, with partners Jim Dickinson and David Lindley. Star Harry Dean Stanton is also heard, providing some of the dialog from the 1984 film. — *William Ruhlmann*

☆ **Patton** / 1970 / PolyGram ✦✦✦✦✦
A stunning, haunting martial score by Jerry Goldsmith. This is possibly the finest military film score ever written. — *Bruce Eder*

Pennies from Heaven [O.S.T.] / 1981 / Warner Bros. ✦✦✦✦✦
Original recordings from the '20s and '30s by Bing Crosby, Helen Kane, Fred Astaire, Rudy Vallee, and others formed the soundtrack to this Steve Martin/Bernadette Peters film. A collection of timeless show tunes, this album is sadly out of print. — *Scott Bultman*

☆ **Peter Gunn [TV Soundtrack]** / 1989 / RCA ✦✦✦✦✦
This was TV's first big-hit music track. The title theme from this series produced by Blake Edwards is one of the finest things Henry Mancini ever wrote. Here is driving, popular jazz, with a beat and style. — *Bruce Eder*

Peter Pan / 1954 / RCA ✦✦✦✦✦
A minor success in 1954, this show owes its persistence in the American consciousness to two television broadcasts. The second (in 1960) was taped for posterity and re-run religiously in the '60s, so the whole baby-boom generation can sing "Tender Shepherd," "I've Gotta Crow," "Never Never Land," "I'm Flying," and "I Won't Grow Up" in a giant chorus. Mary Martin stars as the little boy traditionally played by adult actresses. Betty Comden, Adolph Green, and Jule Styne are among those who contributed to the score. — *Marjorie Ellen Ruhlmann*

Peter Pan [Original Cast] / 1950 / CBS ✦✦✦✦✦
This 1950 version of J.M. Barrie's children's classic predates the more familiar Mary Martin production by four years. Words as well as music

are by Leonard Bernstein in one of his earliest Broadway efforts. It stars Jean Arthur and Boris Karloff. —*Marjorie Ellen Ruhlmann*

Philadelphia / 1993 / Epic ✦✦✦✦✦
Director Jonathan Demme has developed a reputation for assembling especially interesting soundtracks to such previous movies as *Something Wild* and *Married to the Mob*, but he's never gotten quite such high-powered talent to work for him as he has on this collection of songs from Philadelphia. Topping the list, of course, is Bruce Springsteen's Golden Globe and Academy Award-winning gold Top Ten hit, "Streets of Philadelphia" (even if it seems to be as much about homelessness as about AIDS, the movie's subject). But also included is Neil Young's "Philadelphia," arguably a better song, and a new number by Peter Gabriel, "Lovetown." Those are the major contributions, although Spin Doctors do a nice version of Creedence Clearwater Revival's "Have You Ever Seen the Rain?," and Indigo Girls' take on Danny Whitten's "I Don't Want To Talk About It" is equally enjoyable. And there's the excerpt from the opera *Andrea Chenier* by Maria Callas that makes such a striking scene in the movie (minus Tom Hanks' commentary), and a piece of Howard Shore's score. —*William Ruhlmann*

Pins and Needles [O.S.T.] / 1962 / Columbia ✦✦✦
Harold Rome's musical revue *Pins and Needles*, staged by the Cultural Division of the International Ladies Garment Workers Union in 1937, was an unusual mixture of Broadway show music style and '30s union content. It also had a union cast of workers who performed the show on weekends for four years in the late Depression. Twenty-five years later, Rome was back on Broadway with *I Can Get It for You Wholesale*, which inspired Columbia Records to make the first recording of his first show, using a simple piano/guitar/bass/drums backup. Rome sang some of the songs himself, and he brought along a young Barbra Streisand, who was stopping the show as a featured performer in *Wholesale*. Streisand, heard on six of the 15 cuts, was given the comic material for the most part, her "Nobody Makes a Pass at Me" playing up the same angle as her *Wholesale* feature, "Miss Marmelstein." The songs did not give Streisand much of a chance to display her vocal gifts, especially because the romantic material was handled by Rose Marie Jun and Jack Carroll. Carroll sang the show's one hit, "Sunday in the Park," and Jun sang its best-written effort, "Chain Store Daisy." The real star was Rome, and Streisand seemed headed for typecasting. —*William Ruhlmann*

Plan 9 from Outer Space / 1958 / Performance ✦✦✦✦✦
A silly and sublime sound recording from one of the most enjoyably silly sci-fi films ever made. The music cues from this 1959 movie are fine familiar fun; the dialog is a hoot. —*Bruce Eder*

Porky's Revenge! [O.S.T.] / 1985 / Mobile Fidelity ✦✦✦✦
Dave Edmunds produced this album of rockin' tunes featuring a couple of his own, though it's really an album of high-profile ringers: George Harrison, Jeff Beck, Willie Nelson, Robert Plant, and Phil Collins all make appearances, and the result is a rollicking set of songs from the 1985 film that are far above the usual soundtrack effort. —*William Ruhlmann*

● **Powerhouse, Vol. 1** / Mar. 11, 1935-Nov. 11, 1939 / Stash ✦✦✦✦
A 1991 CD reissue featuring material recorded by Raymond Scott and the Raymond Scott Project from the middle and late '30s. It's nicely remastered and well played, although the arrangements and solos aren't among the hottest or most swinging done during the period. —*Ron Wynn*

Pret a Porter (Ready to Wear) / 1994 / Columbia ✦✦✦✦✦
The soundtrack to Robert Altman's attack on the fashion industry is more engaging than the film, thanks to hot R&B hits like Ini Kamoze's "Here Comes the Hotstepper" and Janet Jackson's "'70s Love Groove," as well as new tracks from the Rolling Stones, Sam Phillips, and Terence Trent D'Arby. It's one of the rare pop soundtracks that plays as an album, not as a collection of songs. —*Stephen Thomas Erlewine*

Pretty in Pink / 1986 / A&M ✦✦✦✦✦
The Psychedelic Furs achieved stardom with their re-recorded version of the title track, an old song of theirs, but the soundtrack album also makes a good modern rock sampler, featuring tracks by Orchestral Manoeuvres in the Dark, New Order, Echo and the Bunnymen, and the Smiths, plus the Suzanne Vega/Joe Jackson collaboration "Left of Center." —*William Ruhlmann*

Prince of Tides / 1991 / Columbia ✦✦✦
James Newton Howard's score for Barbra Streisand's *The Prince of Tides* is a delicate, pretty set of repetitive orchestral themes. Indeed, for a soundtrack, it is amazingly consistent in terms of tone, continually employing swelling strings and slowly played piano figures in what sounds more like music for an air freshener commercial than a drama. Streisand sings two songs at the end, neither of them heard as a vocal selection in the actual film. One is the old J. Fred Coots and Sam M. Lewis standard "For All We Know," and the other is the newly written "Places That Belong to You," with music by Howard and lyrics by Alan and Marilyn Bergman in their "The Way Were" mode. Both songs are typically well sung, but the oldie is the better tune. —*William Ruhlmann*

The Princess Bride [O.S.T.] / 1987 / Warner Bros. ✦✦✦✦✦
A charming, low-key instrumental score, appropriate to the funny, wistful tone of the film, by Dire Straits leader Mark Knopfler. —*William Ruhlmann*

The Prisoner [TV Soundtrack] / ✦✦✦
An interesting score with a great title theme by Ron Grainer, but there's too much mood and effect music stuck in for all but hard core fans. —*Bruce Eder*

Providence / 1980 / DRG ✦✦✦✦✦
A lyrical, subtle score by Miklos Rozsa from the 1977 movie—one of his most accomplished and enjoyable pieces of music. —*Bruce Eder*

Pulp Fiction / 1994 / MCA ✦✦✦✦✦
The soundtrack to Quentin Tarantino's darkly funny crime classic *Pulp Fiction* manages to recreate the film's wildly careening sense of style, violence, and humor by concentrating on the surf music that comprises the bulk of the movie's incidental music and adding a few sexy oldies integral to the film's story ("Let's Stay Together," "Son of a Preacher Man," "You Never Can Tell"). Of course, the inclusion of dialogue and Urge Overkill's seductive cover of Neil Diamond's "Girl, You'll Be a Woman Soon" don't hurt either. —*Stephen Thomas Erlewine*

Pure Country / 1992 / MCA ✦✦✦
The soundtrack to the movie of the same name starring George Strait himself. The songs are a little larger than life if you are a Strait fan, but very nice nevertheless. Some were put together just for this movie. "Where the Sidewalk Ends" and "The King of Broken Hearts" stand out, but the version of "I Cross My Heart" recorded here is just one great song. —*Michael Erlewine*

☆ **Quo Vadis** / London ✦✦✦✦✦
A well-produced re-recording of the classic 1951 score by Miklos Rozsa and the Royal Philharmonic Orchestra, with a bright but not too brittle sound and excellent stereo balances. The music itself sounds hokey, but only for having been imitated so many times since 1951. —*Bruce Eder*

Ragtime / 1981 / Elektra ✦✦✦
Randy Newman's first feature-film scoring assignment appropriately came with this turn-of-the-century-with-a-modern-sensibility adaptation of E.L. Doctorow's novel. You might miss Newman's voice (you do get to hear Jennifer Warnes), but his musical style is unmistakable. —*William Ruhlmann*

Reservoir Dogs / 1992 / MCA ✦✦✦✦✦
Only five songs here were featured prominently in Quentin Tarantino's rousing crime film ("Little Green Bag," "Hooked on a Feeling," "I Gotcha," "Stuck in the Middle with You," and "Coconut"), but they include Steven Wright's introductions from the film (separately indexed, thankfully), as well as Tarantino's infamous interpretation of the meaning of Madonna's "Like a Virgin" and Harvey Keitel's monologue on how to rob a jewelry store. In total, that's about 15 to 20 minutes of material. Padding out the rest of the disc are three new songs—"Fool for Love" is very good, "Harvest Moon" passable, and "Magic Carpet Ride" is abominable. After this, the disc has passed the half-hour mark by two minutes. The amount of music you'll actually want to listen to makes it even shorter, but it is a soundtrack you'll want to return to. —*Stephen Thomas Erlewine*

A River Runs Through It / ✦✦✦
Mark Isham's score for this family saga has much the same warm, nostalgic tone as Robert Redford's film. It's a period piece, and there are touches of the '20s here and there, but for the most part, Isham mixes slow, string-filled passages with stately small-group pieces. It makes for good Sunday afternoon background music. —*William Ruhlmann*

The Rocky Horror Picture Show [box set] / 1990 / Rhino ✦✦✦
This 15th Anniversary four-CD box set contains the film soundtrack, the Roxy cast album, a disc of international performances, and a disc of rare tracks by such film principals as Tim Curry and Little Nell. There's also a booklet of photos and such. Pricey, but essential for Rocky fans. —*William Ruhlmann*

☆ **The Rocky Horror Picture Show [Motion Picture Soundtrack]** / 1975 / Rhino ✦✦✦✦✦
It took almost six years for this soundtrack of the all-time midnight movie favorite to go gold, but it is one of the most memorable film scores (and show scores, for that matter) of the '70s, combining old-time rock 'n' roll with campy horror movie clichés. Tim Curry and Meat Loaf star. —*William Ruhlmann*

The Rocky Horror Picture Show [Original Cast Recording] / 1974 / Rhino ✦✦✦
The first American production of this sci-fi/rock 'n' roll pastiche from Britain, presented at the Roxy in Los Angeles and featuring Tim Curry, who originated the starring role of Dr. Frank N. Furter in London. Richard O'Brien's score has passed into legend, but it's still fresh here. —*William Ruhlmann*

Romeo Is Bleeding / 1993 / Verve ✦✦✦
Mark Isham's score for this thriller features low-key traditional jazz (which gets more intense and electronic as it goes along) led by his trumpet and fluegelhorn, mostly muted. Echoes of Miles Davis are everywhere, and the album works as a mood piece separate from the film. Abbey Lincoln and A.J. Croce each contribute one vocal track. — *William Ruhlmann*

Round Midnight Soundtrack / 1986 / Columbia ✦✦✦
This is the official soundtrack from the movie *Round Midnight*. Although tenor saxophonist Dexter Gordon (who is only actually on five of the 11 songs) was past his prime, his realistic acting gained him a nomination for an Oscar. In addition to Gordon, this historic and generally well-rounded album has performances by pianists Herbie Hancock and Cedar Walton, vocalist Bobby McFerrin, bassists Ron Carter and Pierre Michelot, drummers Tony Williams and Billy Higgins, guitarist John McLaughlin, trumpeters Freddie Hubbard and Chet Baker, Wayne Shorter on tenor and soprano, vibraphonist Bobby Hutcherson, and a vocal by Lonette McKee. — *Scott Yanow*

Sarafina! / 1987 / Shanachie ✦✦✦
An abbreviated version of the Mbongeni Ngema musical about South African school children. It was recorded in South Africa before the show's arrival in New York. Cheaply made, but stirring. — *William Ruhlmann*

☆ **Saturday Night Fever** / 1977 / PolyGram ✦✦✦✦✦
One of the biggest-selling albums of all time, this double-disc soundtrack features the Bee Gees hits "Stayin' Alive," "Night Fever," and "How Deep Is Your Love"; Yvonne Elliman's "If I Can't Have You"; and a selection of popular disco hits by Tavares, K.C. and the Sunshine Band, and others. This wasn't only the soundtrack to a film, it was the soundtrack to an era; that era is over, but it's evoked by the music. — *William Ruhlmann*

The Sea Hawk / Varese Sarabande ✦✦✦✦✦
Charles Gerhardt conducting the National Philharmonic. The definitive recordings of the Korngold scores, even more so than his own performances from the Warner Bros. archives. The early '70s sound is opulent, and the CD includes portions of the scores that wouldn't fit on the original long-playing record. — *Bruce Eder*

The Secret Policeman's Third Ball: The Music / Atlantic ✦✦✦✦✦
Above-average rock-performance soundtrack, sparked by a superb duet between Kate Bush and David Gilmour. — *Bruce Eder*

Seven Brides for Seven Brothers / 1954 / CBS ✦✦✦✦✦
An engaging folklike musical, this soundtrack was remastered into stereo for the first time and sounds quite crisp. — *Bruce Eder*

She's Having a Baby / 1988 / IRS ✦✦✦✦✦
A charming collection of modern rock songs based on the themes of marriage and family, including Dave Wakeling's title song (the best thing that came from his brief solo career), XTC's "Happy Families," Kate Bush's "This Woman's Work," and especially the infectious "Apron Strings" by Everything But the Girl. — *William Ruhlmann*

Sherlock Holmes: Classic Themes from 221B Baker / Jun. 18, 1996 / Varese Sarabande ✦✦✦
Sherlock Holmes: The Classic Themes is an odd album. Collecting the musical themes from several Sherlock Holmes films—including *The Private Life of Sherlock Holmes*, *The Seven Percent Solution*, *Young Sherlock Holmes*, and *The Hound of the Baskervilles*—the disc does serve some purpose, since Holmes fanatics will want all of these in one place. However, there isn't any unifying musical theme on the collection: Miklos Rozsa's theme doesn't necessarily complement Stephen Sondheim's songs and neither sit well next to Henry Mancini. Taken as individual pieces, each one works nicely, but the don't gel into a cohesive whole. — *Stephen Thomas Erlewine*

Short Cuts / 1993 / Imago ✦✦✦✦✦
In the movie *Short Cuts*, Annie Ross, a jazz singer (formerly of Lambert, Hendricks and Ross), plays a jazz singer, and Lori Singer, who can play cello, plays her cello-playing daughter. This soundtrack album of "music from and inspired by the film" alternates songs by Ross, many of which appear in the film, with classical music performances by Singer, alone and with a quartet. Although they sound like old jazz standards, most of the Ross songs are newly written pieces, with her singing, playing, and songwriting collaborators including a Who's Who of rockers—Bono and the Edge of U2, Terry Adams of NRBQ, Doc Pomus and Dr. John (who contribute four compositions), Elvis Costello, Iggy Pop, and Michael Stipe of R.E.M. All of them subsume their vocal tendencies to fit into the smoky, late-night ambience of the approach. And Ross, her voice full of knowledge beyond even the sophisticated lyrics, dominates the proceedings. The result is a brilliant album that works well with or without the movie it was constructed to accompany. — *William Ruhlmann*

Show / 1995 / First Night ✦✦✦✦✦
Featuring first-rate tracks from Onyx, Bone Thugs N' Harmony, LL Cool J, Mary J. Blige, 2 Pac, A Tribe Called Quest, the Notorious B.I.G., and a collaboration between Method Man and Redman, the soundtrack to the

Cole Porter

Cole Porter (1891-1964) has been described as the greatest songwriter of the century; he was unquestionably the wittiest. A child of enormous wealth, Porter did not turn his complete attention to songwriting until the '20s, but from then until the end of the '40s, he turned out nearly a show a year, and he even managed three more in the '50s, not to mention a fair amount of work for motion pictures. Porter, who wrote both words and music, had a flair for melody, but his gift for lyrics was unparalleled. Like Irving Berlin, his work of the '30s is better remembered for individual song hits than complete scores, and those songs included "Let's Do It," "You Do Something to Me," "What Is This Thing Called Love?," "Night and Day," "Begin the Beguine," and "Just One of Those Things." An exception to this rule was *Anything Goes* (1934), which, in addition to the title song, included "You're the Top" and "I Get a Kick Out of You." The entire score is brilliant, and the show has been revived on stage and in films frequently.

Porter was severely injured in a riding accident in 1937 and lived in pain for the rest of his life. His work, however, continued largely without interruption. His greatest success came with an adaptation of Shakespeare's *Taming of the Shrew* called *Kiss Me, Kate* in 1948, after which he worked less frequently, though *Can-Can* (1953) and *Silk Stockings* (1955) were notable later hits. — *William Ruhlmann*

rap documentary *The Show* is a good portrait of state-of-the-art mid-'90s hip-hop in all of its diversity. — *Stephen Thomas Erlewine*

☆ **Show Boat** / 1988 / Angel ✦✦✦✦✦
This lavish three-CD studio reconstruction of the original score is more than complete: it includes outtake material cut from the show before the opening and also restores controversial lyrics. This was lovingly and thoroughly put together by John McGlinn, who brought in such opera singers as Frederica von Stade and Jerry Hadley, backed by the London Sinfonietta, and is the most exhaustive rendering of perhaps the most important American musical of the 20th century. — *William Ruhlmann*

☆ **Show Boat [Broadway Score]** / 1928 / Sony ✦✦✦✦✦
This album, originally issued on 78s, presents eight selections recorded by members of the original 1927 Broadway production of the landmark musical, plus Paul Robeson's rendition of "Ol' Man River." (Robeson was in the original London production and the first Broadway revival.) *Show Boat* is the crowning achievement of Jerome Kern's career. It is the prototype for the unified story musicals that followed it, especially after World War II. It begins lyricist Oscar Hammerstein II's series of socially conscious musicals. And its songs, especially in these versions, are unforgettable. Here you also get Helen Morgan singing "Bill" and "Can't Help Lovin' Dat Man." — *William Ruhlmann*

Show Boat: A Collector's Show Boat / 1976 / RCA ✦✦✦
Performances culled from various recordings of *Show Boat*. It leans heavily on a 1956 version featuring Robert Merrill and Patrice Munsel, but also includes 1928 recordings by Paul Robeson and Helen Morgan. — *William Ruhlmann*

☆ **Showstoppers** / 1989 / RCA ✦✦✦✦✦
A collection of 20 songs from Broadway show recordings made between 1909 and 1941. This features such stars as Fanny Brice, Al Jolson, George M. Cohan, Beatrice Lillie, Helen Morgan, Paul Robeson, Eddie Cantor, Ethel Merman, Fred Astaire, Noel Coward, Cole Porter, and Gertrude Lawrence. — *William Ruhlmann*

★ **Sinatra** / 1992 / Reprise ✦✦✦✦✦
This is the two-disc soundtrack to a 1992 television mini-series about the life of Frank Sinatra. There is no musical scoring, and there are no re-recordings. Rather, this is a collection of 30 songs recorded between 1931 and 1979, most by Sinatra, although Bing Crosby, Benny Goodman, and Billie Holiday also make appearances. What is notable about the set is that it is the only album to combine tracks from Sinatra's recordings on Columbia, RCA Victor, Capitol, and Reprise, and thus the only one offering the breadth of his work over a period of 40 years. Of course, it remains a sampler, and there's far more great Sinatra material, but the unique circumstances make this an excellent compilation for the beginner. — *William Ruhlmann*

☆ **Singin' in the Rain** / Sony ✦✦✦✦✦
A towering film score from the 1952 movie made up of some grand tunes of the '30s, climaxing with the extended "Broadway Ballet." — *Bruce Eder*

Singles [O.S.T.] / Jun. 30, 1992 / Epic ✦✦✦✦✦
Although Nirvana isn't included, there's no better introduction to the

Seattle grunge scene than the *Singles* soundtrack. Most of the significant Seattle bands—Pearl Jam, Mudhoney, Alice in Chains, Screaming Trees, Soundgarden, and Mother Love Bone—are featured, as well as Chicago's Smashing Pumpkins, ex-Replacements leader Paul Westerberg, and Seattle native Jimi Hendrix. "State of Love and Trust" is arguably Pearl Jam's finest moment. Westerberg's first songs since the breakup of the Replacements are here; "Dyslexic Heart" and "Waiting for Somebody" are excellent acoustic-based rockers. Mudhoney's "Overblown," an attack on the marketing of the Seattle scene, is the only true grunge song, with pummeling fuzz guitars and whiny vocals. Competing for top song honors are Alice in Chains' grinding "Would?" and Screaming Trees' pop-psychedelic guitar rave-up "Nearly Lost You." An excellent introduction to the alternative rock scene of the '90s. —*Stephen Thomas Erlewine*

Sleeping with the Enemy / CBS ✦✦✦✦✦
A lyrical, moving Jerry Goldsmith score, which soars to elegant heights of wistfulness and menace. —*Bruce Eder*

Sleepless in Seattle / 1993 / Sony ✦✦✦
A collection of romantic pop standards sung by everyone from Jimmy Durante to Carly Simon, the soundtrack to *Sleepless in Seattle* will delight fans of the movie seeking to recapture the magical romance of the film. —*AMG*

☆ **Snow White and the Seven Dwarfs** / 1993 / Disney ✦✦✦✦✦
The re-release of Walt Disney's first full-length animated feature in theaters in 1993 prompted the record division of Disney to put together the first full-length soundtrack CD, timing out at more than 73 minutes and containing most of the film's music. The bulk of it was written by Frank Churchill, with lyrics on such songs as "Whistle While You Work," "Heigh-Ho," and "Some Day My Prince Will Come" by Larry Morey. By now, this music has charmed generations of children, and there's no reason why it won't charm even more. —*William Ruhlmann*

☆ **Some Like It Hot** / 1956 / DRG ✦✦✦✦✦
Soundtrack of Billy Wilder's comedy features Marilyn Monroe's breathy versions of several '20s jazz-pop classics, including a steamy "Running Wild." Out of print, but worth the search. —*Cub Koda*

Something Wild / 1986 / MCA ✦✦✦✦✦
Another brilliant compilation of unusual music handled by director Jonathan Demme. The hit was "Ever Fallen in Love," by Fine Young Cannibals, but the album also includes tracks by David Byrne (one of his earliest Latin American outings), Oingo Boingo, Jimmy Cliff, Jerry Harrison, and New Order, among others. —*William Ruhlmann*

Sondheim / 1985 / Book of the Month Club ✦✦✦
A three-LP box set of newly recorded Sondheim songs, featuring such singers as Cris Groenendaal, Bob Gunton, and Debbie Shapiro and conducted by frequent Sondheim orchestrator Paul Gemignani. The album presents Sondheim's songs outside a theatrical context, in renditions by great singers. A welcome addendum to the Sondheim library. —*William Ruhlmann*

★ **Sondheim: A Musical Tribute** / 1973 / RCA ✦✦✦✦✦
A two-disc recording of a special benefit show held Mar 11, 1973, featuring many of the original performers from Stephen Sondheim musicals, reprising their performances of his songs. Thus, the album is a kind of "Sondheim's Greatest Hits," with the added excitement of being a one-time event. Originally issued as a two-LP set by Warner in 1973, it was reissued by RCA on CD/cassette with previously unreleased tracks. —*William Ruhlmann*

The Soundtrack / 1982 / Full Moon ✦✦✦✦✦
A somewhat unsatisfying orchestral re-recording of Vangelis' original electronic score, but acceptable in the absence of the Vangelis music on record. —*Bruce Eder*

Soundtrack / Sep. 11, 1990 / Warner Bros. ✦✦✦✦✦
Composer Angelo Badalamenti (*Cousins*) set the tone for David Lynch's bizarre television soap with a haunting theme created from electric piano, synthetic strings, and the twangiest guitar this side of Duane Eddy. The love theme, appropriately enough, sounds like a funeral march. (The series' central character was found dead at the beginning of the first episode.) The rest of the music, instantly recognizable to anyone who saw even one episode of the series, borders on fever-dream jazz. Lynch-favorite Julee Cruise sings the only three vocal songs. The music from *Twin Peaks* is dark, cloying, and obsessive—and one of the best scores ever written for television. —*Brian Mansfield*

☆ **The Carl Stalling Project: The Music from Warner Bros. Cartoons 1936-58** / 1990 / Warner Bros. ✦✦✦✦✦
The Carl Stalling Project: Music from Warner Brothers Cartoons is music almost everyone will recognize. Generations of children and adults know Carl Stalling's music, whether consciously or not. This CD collects nearly 80 minutes of Stalling's music from 1936 to 1958. He was a master of making the music fit the animation, using every style of music from the time, including jazz, classical (Wagner, Mendelssohn, and Mozart), big band, children's songs, and Christmas music. An excellent

collection of highly innovative soundtrack music, it's guaranteed to spark all of your cartoon memories. —*Tavia Hobart*

St. Elmo's Fire / 1987 / Atlantic ✦✦✦
St. Elmo's Fire was the definitive Brat Pack movie, following Emilio Estevez, Judd Nelson, Demi Moore, Ally Sheedy, Andrew McCarthy, Rob Lowe, and Mary Stuart Masterston as they tried to sort their life out after college. The soundtrack launched two big hits, "Love Theme from St. Elmo's Fire" and John Parr's "Man in Motion (Theme from St. Elmo's Fire)," but those are the only two memorable pieces of the music on the album. Apart from his "Love Theme," David Foster doesn't manage to write music that stands apart from the movie, which makes the soundtrack a bit of a dull listen when taken on its own terms. —*Stephen Thomas Erlewine*

Stand by Me / 1986 / Atlantic ✦✦✦
Set in the '50s, *Stand by Me* was a touching coming-of-age movie about a group of pre-teen boys. Appropriately, the soundtrack is crammed with early rock 'n' roll hits. The movie may have been nostalgic, but the music on the soundtrack still sounds alive, decades after it was originally recorded. —*Stephen Thomas Erlewine*

☆ **A Star Is Born (Judy Garland)** / CBS ✦✦✦✦✦
This album, from the 1954 movie, has Judy Garland's last musical soundtrack of any note, sounding a little compressed but not severely marred by age. Garland is in fine voice and spirits on the songs themselves, and the notes are about as full and informative as they get. —*Bruce Eder*

Star Trek / 1979 / CBS ✦✦✦✦✦
Jerry Goldsmith's music, alternately eerie and savage, was the best part of the movie. It still holds up. —*Bruce Eder*

Star Trek TV Soundtrack, Vol. 1 / 1990 / Varese Sarabande ✦✦✦✦✦
The first *Star Trek* TV soundtrack includes some of the finest music written for television during the '60s—moody, atmospheric, and very striking, all broken into relatively short cues. Unfortunately, the source tapes haven't held up well, and the quality leaves a lot to be desired. —*Bruce Eder*

Star Trek, Vol. 2 / GNP ✦✦✦✦✦
Far more impressive sonically than the first volume, this consists of cues from two second-season episodes, "Amok Time" and "The Doomsday Machine." It is unexpectedly rewarding. —*Bruce Eder*

☆ **Star Wars** / 1977 / Polydor ✦✦✦✦✦
John Williams at his most ostentatious, a grand Wagnerian-scale soundtrack that deserves credit at least for reviving interest in the classic Hollywood film score. —*Bruce Eder*

Staying Alive [O.S.T.] / 1983 / Polydor ✦✦✦
This sequel to *Saturday Night Fever* lacked the box office clout of the original, and the soundtrack album was likewise a disappointing seller, but it actually contains some of the better Bee Gees work of the '80s, notably the sad ballad "Someone Belonging to Someone." —*William Ruhlmann*

Straight to Hell / 1987 / Enigma ✦✦✦✦✦
This soundtrack to Alex Cox's bizarre Western features British new-wave graduates the Pogues, Joe Strummer, and the MacManus Band (i.e., Elvis Costello). They also appeared in the film. —*William Ruhlmann*

Streets of Fire [O.S.T.] / 1984 / MCA ✦✦✦
Jim Steinman (the melodramatic writer behind Meat Loaf's *Bat out of Hell*) is the author of many of the tracks here, and they have his typical rock 'n' roll *Sturm und Drang*, especially when the backup group consists of members of Bruce Springsteen's E Street Band. Also on hand are the Blasters, Maria McKee, and Ry Cooder. The album's hit single turned out to be Dan Hartman's "I Can Dream About You." —*William Ruhlmann*

Strictly Ballroom / 1992 / CBS ✦✦✦
The Australian film is offbeat, and the soundtrack dances to its own drummer too, with tango and samba rhythms (and heavy drum tracks) added to songs like "Tequila" and other music borrowed from all over, everything from Cyndi Lauper's "Time After Time" to "The Blue Danube," as played by the Bogo Pogo Orchestra. This is a party album. —*William Ruhlmann*

Striptease / 1996 / EMI ✦✦✦
Following the usual formula for major Hollywood releases of the mid-'90s, this mixes golden oldies (by Spencer Davis, the Soul Survivors, Booker T. and the MG's, and the Miracles) with material of more recent vintage by Eurythmics, Blondie, Billy Idol, Prince, Joan Jett, and Billy Ocean, throwing in a non-rock pop ballad by Dean Martin for variety. —*Richie Unterberger*

Subterraneans / 1960 / CBS ✦✦✦✦✦
A very effective, moody jazz score by Andre Previn, featuring Gerry Mulligan and Carmen McRae, which holds up better than the movie for which it was written. —*Bruce Eder*

☆ **The Sullivan Years: Best of Broadway [Original Cast]** / 1992 / TVT ✦✦✦✦✦
This two-disc set collects TV performances of some of Broadway's biggest hits as they were done with original cast members on Broadway. Among the priceless material from shows like *Camelot, West Side Story,* and *My Fair Lady* is a bonus interview with Richard Rodgers and Oscar Hammerstein, II (not on the cassette version). — *William Ruhlmann*

☆ **A Summer Story** / 1950 / CBS ✦✦✦✦✦
Judy Garland's final MGM outing, sparked by her rendition of "Get Happy" and some good Gene Kelly numbers. — *Bruce Eder*

Sunset Park / Apr. 1996 / Elektra ✦✦✦✦✦
Although it appears on the surface to be as pedestrian and formulaic as the movie it supports, the soundtrack to *Sunset Park* shows that it is possible to find something worthwhile within a formula. Like all mid-'90s urban R&B/hip-hop soundtracks, *Sunset Park* is divided between hardcore hip-hop (2 Pac, Ghostface and RZA, Mobb Deep, Onyx), smooth R&B (Aaliyah, Xscape, and MC Lyte), and music that falls between the two categories (Adina Howard, Queen Latifah). What makes the album noteworthy is the consistent quality of the material. Although there are only a handful of genuinely outstanding tracks on the record, the whole thing flows from beginning to end and delivers on its promise, even if it never delivers *more* than it promises. — *Stephen Thomas Erlewine*

Tales from the Hood [O.S.T.] / 1995 / ✦✦✦
In an attempt to replicate the surrealistic violence of the film, the soundtrack to the exploitation horror film *Tales from the Hood* is filled with hard-core gangsta rappers. Predictably, most of the songs on the disc are filled with explicit violence and ridiculous boasts, which wouldn't be so bad if they were all executed with the imagination of the Wu-Tang Clan's "Let Me at Them" or Wu-Tang member Ol' Dirty Bastard's "Ol' Dirty's Back," two tracks driven by spare, razor-sharp beats and lyrics. Most of the rest of *Tales from the Hood* is filled with generic gangsta fare, which means the album will only appeal to the genre's most devoted fans. — *Stephen Thomas Erlewine*

Television's Greatest Hits, Vol. 1 / TVT ✦✦✦✦✦
An uneven but enjoyable compilation of the good, the bad, and the forgettable among TV music themes from the '50s and '60s, with variable sound quality to boot. But it's unique. — *Bruce Eder*

Tex Avery Cartoons / 1993 / Milan ✦✦✦✦
Tex Avery was an animator at MGM during World War II and just after, and his work was characterized by a nonstop, hellzapoppin approach, full of manic energy and wild characters. The scores to his cartoons, by Scott Bradley, had to match Avery's madness, and on these six they do so, helped along by the cartoon dialogue. With the 'toons turning up frequently on Ted Turner's Cartoon Network, the music is newly timely, and Droopy remains a deadpan favorite. — *William Ruhlmann*

The Three Musketeers / 1974 / Bay Cities ✦✦✦
This is Michel Legrand's lush soundtrack to Richard Lester's comic version of the Alexandre Dumas novel. It's some of the most romantic and stirring instrumental music to turn up in a film in years. — *William Ruhlmann*

Threepenny Opera / 1976 / CBS ✦✦✦
A marvelous staging of the Brecht/Weill musical by the New York Shakespeare Festival and a cast headed by Raul Julia. The new translation by Ralph Manheim and John Willett is fresh and highly singable. — *William Ruhlmann*

Threesome / 1994 / Epic ✦✦✦
There are some curious covers on this modern rock compilation. A reformed General Public does the Staple Singers' "I'll Take You There" (and earns a hit single for its trouble), U2 tries Patti Smith's "Dancing Barefoot," Teenage Fanclub appropriates Madonna's "Like a Virgin," and, perhaps most imaginatively, Duran Duran resurrects Steve Harley and Cockney Rebel's "Make Me Smile (Come Up and See Me)." Also featured: originals by Tears for Fears and Bryan Ferry. As usual with such "music from the motion picture" collections, there's a sense of randomness here, but there are enough interesting tracks to keep you listening. — *William Ruhlmann*

Thunderball / 1978 / Capitol ✦✦✦✦✦
John Barry's fourth James Bond score from the 1965 movie shows a little weariness, as some material is repeated and the new stuff isn't always memorable. — *Bruce Eder*

☆ **Till the Clouds Roll By** / CBS ✦✦✦✦✦
This soundtrack is an all-star tribute to Jerome Kern, without the climactic Frank Sinatra "Ol' Man River" but filled with worthwhile performances. — *Bruce Eder*

Tommy [Cast/Orchestra] / 1972 / Rhino ✦✦✦
Lush, orchestrated version of the rock opera, done with Pete Townshend's participation and blessing, and featuring Roger Daltrey, Rod Stewart, Ringo Starr, and Merry Clayton. Pretentious in its proportions and bombast, but often moving if this sound is your cup of tea. — *Bruce Eder*

Miklos Rozsa

Born in Hungary in 1907, Miklos Rozsa is the last surviving veteran of moviemaking's "golden age," having scored his first film in 1936 and his latest in 1984. His early success as a serious composer, working in an idiom inspired by the work of Bartók and Kodaly, gave Rozsa the foundation for his dual career in motion pictures. A post-romantic who never accepted atonalism, his best work—and there is much of it—is derived from the texture of native Hungarian folk songs. He began collecting these as a child, giving him a unique command of orchestral timbre and the most distinctive approach of any composer of his generation.

After working for Alexander Korda's London Films, where he provided the memorable and brilliant scores for *The Four Feathers, The Thief of Baghdad,* and *The Jungle Book,* Rozsa took up residence in Hollywood in the early '40s, and by mid-decade had made his mark in the area of film noir. The rhythmic nature of his music and his facility with dark melodic lines gave a brooding savagery to films like *The Killers* and *The Naked City.* In the '50s he became the master of the religious epic. His sweeping scores for *Quo Vadis, Ben Hur, King of Kings,* and *El Cid* found favor among serious choral groups as well as the public, who devoured his albums (originally on the MGM Records label) including two complete albums of music from *Ben-Hur.*

The end of the studio system, the increasing demand for pop tunes in movie soundtracks, and the general coarsening of film subjects in the '60s didn't serve Rozsa well, and his activity in films declined steeply after 1963. Fortunately, he had his career as a serious classical composer to keep him occupied, and by the '70s, filmmakers such as Alain Resnais (*Providence*), Nicholas Meyer (*Time after Time*), and Carl Reiner (*Dead Men Don't Wear Plaid*) gave him a chance for a satisfying "Indian summer" prior to his retirement in the mid-'80s. —*William Ruhlmann*

Touch of Evil / 1993 / Varese Sarabande ✦✦✦✦✦
Unquestionably one of Henry Mancini's greatest achievements, this score to the classic 1958 Orson Welles film of scandal and intrigue along the Mexican border used a lot of appropriate Latin accents: Afro-Cuban percussion, smoky Tijuana jazz jive, and honky-tonking instrumental jump blues with a strong rock 'n' roll flavor. Both ominous and exuberant in its evocation of temptation and deceit, it attracted the specific praise of no less a critic than Francois Truffaut. —*Richie Unterberger*

Toy Story / Nov. 1995 / Walt Disney ✦✦✦
Randy Newman wrote and sang three songs in his characteristic style for the soundtrack of the first computer-animated children's movie, *Toy Story,* along with a sprightly, stirring score that reflected the film's fun, adventurous spirit. "You've Got a Friend in Me," performed both as a solo by Newman at the start and as a duet with Lyle Lovett at the end (reflecting the theme of emerging friendship between toys Woody and Buzz Lightyear), earned an Oscar nomination; "Strange Things" was a comically ominous song used to express Woody's feelings about being supplanted by Buzz; and "I Will Go Sailing No More" was a wistful lament for Buzz when he made the agonizing discovery that he was a toy, not a space hero. Newman's winning score helped set the mood for the charming film that was a box office champion for Christmas 1995. — *William Ruhlmann*

Trainspotting O.S.T. / Feb. 1996 / EMI Premier ✦✦✦✦✦
Trainspotting concerns the adventures of a group of young, nearly criminal, drug-addicted English friends. The novel, written by Irvine Welsh, became one of the most popular books in the British indie scene in the early '90s and was adapted to film in 1996 by the makers of *Shallow Grave.* Appropriately, an all-star collection of British pop and techno stars—everyone from Blur, Pulp, and Elastica to Leftfield, Primal Scream, and the Underworld—contributed to the soundtrack, which also features a couple of oldies by veteran punk godfathers like Lou Reed ("Perfect Day") and Iggy Pop ("Lust for Life," "Nightclubbing"). The entire soundtrack holds together surprisingly well, as the techno tracks balance with the pop singles. Every song, whether it's Pulp's deceptively bouncy "Mile End" or Brian Eno's lush "Deep Blue Day," is quite melancholy, creating an effectively bleak, but oddly romantic, atmosphere for the entire record. With the exception of the oldies, every song is rare or especially recorded for the soundtrack, and nearly every one is superb. Primal Scream's title track sees them returning to the dub/dance experiments of *Screamadelica* with grace, while Damon Albarn's first solo song, "Closet Romantic," is as good as any of Blur's waltzes. But the finest new song is

Pulp's "Mile End," with its jaunty, neo-dancehall melody and rhythms and Jarvis Cocker's evocative, haunting lyrics. That song, more than anything else on the soundtrack, captures the feeling of the film. *—Stephen Thomas Erlewine*

Trespass: Original Score / 1993 / Sire ✦✦✦✦✦
In the music for *Trespass*, which starred Ice-T and Ice Cube, the disembodied groans of Ry Cooder's guitars combine with Jim Keltner's percussion and Jon Hassell's otherworldly trumpet playing to create a dark, frightening mood. Outside of "King of the Streets," which features film dialogue, and Austin singer Junior Brown's boozy country song "Party Lights," the music here possesses the ambience of an urban street western. This is one of Cooder's scariest scores. *—Brian Mansfield*

Trip [O.S.T.] / 1967 / Edsel ✦✦✦
Before the Electric Flag had recorded their first album or even played live, they composed and performed the soundtrack to *The Trip,* the 1967 psychedelic exploitation film starring Peter Fonda, directed by Roger Corman, and written by Jack Nicholson. This odd but worthwhile relic is entirely instrumental, and as befits the subject matter, wildly eclectic, veering from ragtime and hurdy-gurdy music to basic soul-rock and sweeping, spacey psychedelia and harsh electronics. One of the funkiest snippets, "Flash, Bam, Pow," was later used by Fonda in *Easy Rider.* *—Richie Unterberger*

Trouble in Mind / 1986 / Antilles ✦✦✦
Mark Isham provides the brooding instrumental texture and Marianne Faithfull adds her gravelly chanteuse vocals to the score of this Alan Rudolph film. *—Scott Bultman*

☆ **Twilight Zone, Vol. 1** / 1983 / Varese Sarabande ✦✦✦✦✦
Ignore the slightly compressed sound and take in the eerie, beautifully wrought compositions, every one of them memorable not only from the series but from lots of subsequent use. *—Bruce Eder*

Twin Peaks: Fire Walk with Me / Aug. 11, 1992 / Warner Bros. ✦✦✦
Composer Angelo Badalamenti, who wrote the music for the television series for which this movie served as a "prequel," presents another low-key score mixing after-midnight jazz with ambient sounds, never taken at more than a medium tempo. The mood is dark and languid, appropriate to the unusual tone of the TV show and movie. Jimmy Scott and Julee Cruise contribute eerie vocals to songs with lyrics by director David Lynch. *—William Ruhlmann*

The Unsinkable Molly Brown / 1981 / CBS ✦✦✦✦✦
Debbie Reynolds sparks this homespun early-'60s movie musical version that has proved a favorite over the years. She can be a bit overbearing, but it works, and Harve Presnell sings well. *—Bruce Eder*

Unsinkable Molly Brown [Broadway Cast] / 1960 / Capitol ✦✦✦
Meredith Willson's follow-up to *The Music Man,* about a nouveau riche Colorado mine owner's wife who survives the sinking of the Titanic, is not quite as impressive as its predecessor, but the irrepressible Tammy Grimes does much to make it a success on record. *—William Ruhlmann*

☆ **Urban Cowboy [O.S.T.]** / 1980 / Asylum ✦✦✦✦✦
It includes Joe Walsh, Bob Seger, Boz Scaggs, and Dan Fogelberg, so it's obviously not strictly a country album. But the soundtrack is important because it symbolizes the country trend that grew, then faded, in the early '80s (a case can be made that J.R. Ewing had a lot more influence on the fad than the film *Urban Cowboy*). Most of the country tracks here lean toward MOR. *—Tom Roland*

Vampyros Lesbos: Sexadelic Dance Party / 1995 / Motel ✦✦✦
Around the late '60s, Jess Franco directed three B-movies starring Soledad Miranda that have attracted a following of sorts in the incredibly strange film cult. This is a compilation of music heard in those productions, composed and arranged by Manfred Hubler and Siegfried Schwab, and performed by "the Vampires' Sound Incorporation." It's very much period psychedelic-tinged exploitation soundtrack stuff: fuzzy guitars, occasional odd vocal interjections, jazzy organ runs, sitars for the freak factor, and blaring horn charts. None of these contemporary touches can disguise the fact that this is basically typical gimmicky soundtrack product, altered just enough to be suitable for some mod-psychedelic go-go party-type scenes or seductive encounters. It's just strange enough, though, to find its niche in the exploding easy-listening/space-age pop revival of the mid-'90s. *—Richie Unterberger*

Waiting to Exhale / Nov. 28, 1995 / Arista ✦✦✦
The soundtrack to *Waiting to Exhale* was Whitney Houston's follow-up to the multimillion-selling *The Bodyguard* soundtrack. Although Houston gave a better performance in *Exhale* than *The Bodyguard,* the music on the *Waiting to Exhale* album isn't any noticeably different than that on its predecessor. Featuring a handful of other artists besides Whitney, the soundtrack is devoted to smooth, slick contemporary soul and pop. *—Stephen Thomas Erlewine*

☆ **West Side Story** / 1962 / CBS ✦✦✦✦✦
This film version of the Leonard Bernstein/Stephen Sondheim score of a modern, urban *Romeo and Juliet* spent more weeks at No. 1 in the charts

(54) than any other album in history. It is an effective rendition of the score, featuring Natalie Wood, Richard Beymer, Russ Tamblyn, Rita Moreno, and George Chakiris, and features all of the show's important songs, among them "Something's Coming," "Maria," "Tonight," and "Somewhere." *—William Ruhlmann*

The Western Film World of Dimitri Tiomkin / Unicorn ✦✦✦✦✦
Laurie Johnson conducting the London Studio Symphony Orchestra and the John McCarthy Singers. A brace of long-overdue modern recordings of Tiomkin's best Western music, including a good (but not complete) accounting of his score for *Red River.* *—Bruce Eder*

Western Quintet / Jul. 18, 1995 / DRG ✦✦✦✦
This two-disc set contains five of Ennio Morricone's Western soundtracks. Includes *A Fistful of Dynamite, A Fist Goes West, Campaneros,* and *Blood and Guns,* in their entirety. *—Jonathan Ball*

What's Love Got to Do with It / Jun. 15, 1993 / Capitol ✦✦✦
This is the soundtrack for the Tina Turner film that got Angela Bassett and Lawrence Fishburne Oscar nominations. There's little here that you couldn't get elsewhere in better versions, but if you only want a hint of the music Tina Turner made in various contexts, with and without Ike, this would be a serviceable purchase. Otherwise, get the film and hear the music in the correct setting. *—Ron Wynn*

White Christmas [O.S.T.] / 1954 / Decca ✦✦✦
The oddity about this soundtrack album from the Bing Crosby-Danny Kaye movie musical is that, apparently for contractual reasons, co-star Rosemary Clooney has been replaced on record by Peggy Lee. The Irving Berlin score combines oldies like the title song and "Blue Skies" with a few new ones, such as "What Can You Do with a General." Although successful at the time of its release, the entire production was a throwback to the war years. Today, that doesn't matter, and the soundtrack album serves as a Berlin sampler with the Crosby-Kaye-Lee team performing effectively. *—William Ruhlmann*

☆ **The Wizard of Oz [O.S.T.]** / 1995 / Rhino ✦✦✦✦✦
This two-volume set contains the complete soundtrack to the famous 1939 movie. Remastered and appended to contain previously unreleased song demos, rehearsals, and alternate takes. *—Jonathan Ball*

☆ **The Wizard of Oz** / Sony ✦✦✦✦✦
What else can one say about this bright, tuneful 1939 score—it's a treasure! *—Bruce Eder*

Cast Recordings

Allegro / 1947 / RCA Victor ✦✦✦
Rodgers and Hammerstein were coming off the twin successes of *Oklahoma!* (1943) and *Carousel* (1945) when they produced this, their third Broadway musical. Not surprisingly, the pre-opening box office was record-breaking, but that was all that kept the show going for 315 performances that disappointed audiences. Today, it is remembered for experimental effects that eventually made their way into later musicals, but this cast album (ten songs originally issued as a five-disc 78 rpm set, now a short CD) indicates that it wasn't one of R&H's better scores. Only Lisa Kirk's showstopper "The Gentleman Is a Dope" is really worthwhile. *—William Ruhlmann*

☆ **Annie** / 1977 / CBS ✦✦✦✦✦
One of the biggest Broadway hits of the '70s, this Charles Strouse and Martin Charnin musical based on the *Little Orphan Annie* comic strip charmed audiences with its Depression-era nostalgia and a score that is highlighted by the standard "Tomorrow." *—William Ruhlmann*

☆ **Annie Get Your Gun [Original Cast]** / 1955 / MCA ✦✦✦✦✦
Although this recording does not quite represent the "original Broadway cast" of the 1946 Irving Berlin musical, it's the next best thing, featuring Ethel Merman, Ray Middleton, "and members of the original cast, chorus, and orchestra, under the direction of Jay Blackton." Merman is in fine voice, and the score remains one of Broadway's best collections of songs, from "Doin' What Comes Naturally" to "They Say It's Wonderful" and "Anything You Can Do," not to mention "I Got Lost in His Arms," "The Girl that I Marry," and the showstopping standard "There's No Business like Show Business." *—William Ruhlmann*

☆ **Annie Get Your Gun** / 1966 / RCA ✦✦✦✦✦
This revival of the Irving Berlin show once again stars Ethel Merman and also features Jerry Orbach. It includes the newly written "An Old-Fashioned Wedding." *—William Ruhlmann*

☆ **Anyone Can Whistle** / 1964 / CBS ✦✦✦✦✦
Stephen Sondheim's second complete Broadway score, with a book by Arthur Laurents, was not a success onstage, running only nine performances. But the cast album has kept the show alive, due to such outstanding songs as "There Won't Be Trumpets," "With So Little to Be Sure Of," and the title tune, plus a cast led by Lee Remick and Angela Lansbury. *—William Ruhlmann*

☆ **Anything Goes** / 1987 / RCA ✦✦✦✦✦
This classy 1987 revival features Patti LuPone's spirited interpretations of Cole Porter classics, including the title song, "I Get a Kick Out of You," "You're the Top," and "Blow, Gabriel, Blow." —*Marjorie Ellen Ruhlmann*

Anything Goes / 1989 / Angel ✦✦✦
This is a re-creation of the original 1934 score, not a cast album, put together by John McGlinn and featuring such opera singers as Kim Criswell, Cris Goenendaal, and Frederica Von Stade, along with the London Symphony Orchestra. It is most notable for containing the show's incidental music as well as its famous songs. —*William Ruhlmann*

Assassins [Original Cast Recording] / 1991 / RCA ✦✦✦
Stephen Sondheim's show about presidential assassins is unusual to say the least—which may be why it never got beyond an off-Broadway show-case—but it's filled with brilliant songs. —*William Ruhlmann*

☆ **Barnum [Original Cast]** / 1980 / CBS ✦✦✦✦✦
This musical about the life of the great promoter, with music by Cy Cole-man and lyrics by Michael Stewart, is dominated by Jim Dale's bravura performance in the title role, although Glenn Close, in one of her few musical-comedy appearances, is also featured. — *William Ruhlmann*

☆ **Bells Are Ringing** / 1956 / CBS ✦✦✦✦✦
Book and lyrics by Betty Comden and Adolph Green, music by Jule Style. The recording documents Judy Holliday's genius for musical comedy. "The Party's Over" and "Just in Time" are the most memorable numbers in a clever score. —*Marjorie Ellen Ruhlmann*

☆ **The Best Little Whorehouse in Texas** / 1978 / MCA ✦✦✦✦✦
Tommy Tune staged this rip-roaring, country-style musical, and while you can't see the dance steps on record, Carol Hall's songs accurately express the show's down-home vitality. — *William Ruhlmann*

Beyond the Fringe / Nov. 5, 1962 / Angel ✦✦✦
This British comedy revue, featuring Peter Cook, Dudley Moore, and Jonathan Miller, was a precursor to Monty Python's Flying Circus, with its zany humor, though its satire is somewhat more political and brutal. While some of it is no longer topical, most of it remains hilarious. —*William Ruhlmann*

Blood Brothers / 1988 / RCA ✦✦✦
This is the London revival cast recording of Willy Russell's weepy melo-drama, originally released in England in 1988 at the time of the revival, and released in the US in 1993 to commemorate the opening of the show on Broadway. Russell is steeped in '60s British pop music, and the show is full of catchy songs, though the contrived and dreary subject matter, and the repetitiousness may drive some to distraction. *Blood Brothers* is more than a tearjerker; it suctions tears out of its audience with a vac-uum cleaner. To be fair, there are many who love it for that, and even those who don't will have trouble not humming its score on the way out of the theater. —*William Ruhlmann*

☆ **Boyfriend** / 1955 / RCA ✦✦✦✦✦
A tribute to the frivolous musicals of the '20s, this tongue-in-cheek enter-tainment was one of the few successful musicals of its time to originate in Great Britain. It's notable for introducing the 19-year-old Julie Andrews to Broadway. — *William Ruhlmann*

☆ **Brigadoon** / 1947 / RCA ✦✦✦✦✦
The tale of an 18th-century Scottish village that travels through time and its romantic encounter with two 20th-century visitors became the first major hit written by the team of Alan Jay Lerner and Frederick Loewe. It features "Almost like Being in Love." —*William Ruhlmann*

Brigadoon / 1992 / Angel ✦✦✦
This is a studio recreation of the Lerner and Loewe musical, performed by the Ambrosion Chorus and the London Sinfonietta, conducted by John McGlinn and featuring soloists Brent Barrett, Judy Kaye, Rebecca Luker, John Mark Ainsley, and Frank Middlemass. It is notable for con-taining instrumental music from the score not heard on previous albums (it runs a CD-busting 79 minutes), but is otherwise not a striking version of the show. —*William Ruhlmann*

Bubbling Brown Sugar / 1976 / Amherst ✦✦✦
A musical revue featuring some of the most memorable jazz-age tunes of African-American '30s composers such as Duke Ellington, Eubie Blake, and Fats Waller: "Sophisticated Lady," "Honeysuckle Rose," and more. On record, the show becomes essentially a sampler of that music, and it's effective for that, though the listener should also check out the original versions. —*William Ruhlmann*

Buddy—The Buddy Holly Story [London Cast] / 1989 / Combat ✦✦✦
Buddy—The Buddy Holly Story is the London cast recording of a bio-graphical musical about the rock 'n' roll legend. It contains Holly's great-est hits enthusiastically performed by Paul Hipp, who also performed the role on Broadway. —*William Ruhlmann*

☆ **Bye Bye Birdie** / 1960 / CBS ✦✦✦✦✦
The original Broadway cast album of the Charles Strouse/Lee Adams musical that fictionalizes the impact Elvis Presley's departure for the

Army had on American teenagers. The authors deftly satirize teen life and early rock 'n' roll and provide a typical Broadway musical love story involving Dick Van Dyke and Chita Rivera. Paul Lynde is also a standout, singing "Kids." The other hit of the show is "Put On a Happy Face." —*William Ruhlmann*

☆ **Cabaret [Original Cast]** / 1966 / CBS ✦✦✦✦✦
With a malevolent grin and the words "Willkommen, bienvenue, wel-come," actor Joel Grey established his future as well as the dark tone of this 1966 Tony Award-winning musical. This recording includes a num-ber of songs not in the film version, several performed by the remark-able Lotte Lenya (widow of composer Kurt Weill, whose work clearly influenced the Kander and Ebb score). —*Marjorie Ellen Ruhlmann*

☆ **Camelot** / 1960 / CBS ✦✦✦✦✦
One of the great Lerner and Loewe musicals, based on the King Arthur legend, starring Richard Burton and Julie Andrews. The music is both a Broadway landmark and a delight. Highlights include the title song, "How to Handle a Woman," and "If Ever I Would Leave You" (sung by Robert Goulet). —*William Ruhlmann*

Camelot—London Cast / 1982 / Varese Sarabande ✦✦✦✦
Richard Harris took over the stage role of King Arthur (he played the part in the film) and played it on the road and in revivals. The album is well recorded and includes some music not found on other recordings. —*William Ruhlmann*

☆ **Can Can** / 1974 / Capitol ✦✦✦✦✦
A Cole Porter dalliance set in Paris and featuring a young Gwen Verdon, plus such memorable songs as "I Love Paris" and "It's All Right with Me." —*William Ruhlmann*

☆ **Candide** / 1974 / CBS ✦✦✦✦✦
A complete recording of the revised version of the Bernstein musical (containing some additions to the lyrics by Stephen Sondheim), taken from its most successful theatrical run. Some of Leonard Bernstein's best show music. —*William Ruhlmann*

Candide / 1986 / New World ✦✦✦
A recording by the New York City Opera, based on its 1982 revival of the show, once again with revised music. —*William Ruhlmann*

Carnival [Original Cast Recording] / 1961 / Polydor ✦✦✦✦
Bob Merrill produced his best-loved score for this delicate musical based on the 1953 French film *Lili* about an orphan taken in by a traveling car-nival. Michael Stewart was the lyricist, and the stars included Anna Maria Alberghetti and Jerry Orbach. The title song, "Theme from Carni-val (Love Makes the World Go 'Round)," became a standard. —*William Ruhlmann*

Carousel / 1965 / RCA Victor ✦✦✦✦
The Twentieth Anniversary Lincoln Center revival of the Rodgers and Hammerstein classic, with John Raitt re-creating his original portrayal of Billy Bigelow. He's still in good voice, and the stereo recording is superb. —*William Ruhlmann*

Carousel / 1994 / RCA ✦✦✦✦
This is the original London cast album of the 1993 Royal National The-atre revival starring Michael Hayden and directed by Nicholas Hytner. Hytner takes a far more down-to-earth approach to Rodgers and Ham-merstein's second show, bringing out its more tragic aspects. The effect is to bear it anew. (Hayden only was carried over to the 1994 New York pro-duction.) —*William Ruhlmann*

☆ **Carousel [Original Cast]** / MCA ✦✦✦✦✦
This was Rodgers and Hammerstein's 1945 follow-up to their landmark hit *Oklahoma*. It includes such chestnuts as "If I Loved You" and "You'll Never Walk Alone," as well as John Raitt's soaring vocals. —*Marjorie Ellen Ruhlmann*

☆ **Cats** / 1981 / David Geffen Co. ✦✦✦✦✦
The original London cast album of Andrew Lloyd Webber's musical revue celebrating T.S. Eliot's *Old Possum's Book of Practical Cats*. It con-tains Elaine Paige's UK Top Ten "Memory." —*William Ruhlmann*

☆ **Cats [Original Cast]** / 1983 / David Geffen Co. ✦✦✦✦✦
This is the original Broadway cast album, containing slight musical alter-ations from the earlier London version and, of course, different singers, though it is not very different. This is a two-disc complete version of the show. There is also an abridged, single-disc version, Geffen 2026. —*William Ruhlmann*

● **Celebrate Broadway, Vol. 1—Sing Happy** / 1994 / RCA ✦✦✦✦
The first in a series of compilations of songs from Broadway shows recorded by RCA Victor, this album puts together an hour's worth of what used to be called "eleven o'clock numbers." These were the show-stoppers that woke you up shortly before the end of the show and got you ready to hit the street with a smile on your face. (Though, to tell the truth, some of these are first act finales meant to send you into the lobby anticipating the rest of the evening.) "Blow, Gabriel, Blow," from *Any-thing Goes*, "I've Gotta Crow," from *Peter Pan*, "Oklahoma!" from *Okla-

homa—these are the big, bright Broadway songs audiences have hummed to themselves for generations. The RCA catalog is mixed—not all of these performances are taken from the original casts, and the notes don't make that clear—but this is a good sampler for the casual fan who likes Broadway's stirring songs. — *William Ruhlmann*

Celebrate Broadway, Vol. 2—You Gotta Have a Gimmick / 1994 / RCA ✦✦✦

For this collection, RCA has scoured its vaults for Broadway novelty songs, comic numbers frequently performed in shows by the supporting players that provide a change of pace and some laughs. Songs like "I Cain't Say No," from *Oklahoma!* and "Arthur in the Afternoon" from *The Act* show that being risqué is not a problem, but just as often these songs are just odd: What else to say about the celebratory "Lizzie Borden," from *New Faces of 1952?* That song, from a revue, had no real context in a show, and some of these songs are actually ringers, such as Fats Waller's "Your Feet's too Big" from *Ain't Misbehavin'* and the "Caribbean Plaid" medley from *Forever Plaid*, material not actually written for Broadway. This is an episodic album, to be sure, but you won't get through it without laughing a few times. — *William Ruhlmann*

Celebrate Broadway, Vol. 3—Lullaby of Broadway / 1994 / RCA ✦✦✦✦

Broadway has always had an ability to celebrate itself, and that ability is showcased on the third volume of RCA's anthology series in songs about show business, starting with the title (actually written for the movie musical *Forty-Second Street*, which then became a Broadway musical) and ending, with "There's No Business Like Show Business." In between are songs by Sondheim, Coleman, Styne, Herman, Kern, Yeston, and Kander, all exploring aspects of the biz. As with the other volumes in this series, the caveat is that these songs come from various sources including but not limited to original Broadway cast albums—concert versions, revivals, revues, etc.—but there isn't a performance here that isn't good, and the selection makes a powerful case for Broadway. — *William Ruhlmann*

Celebrate Broadway, Vol. 4—Overtures! / 1994 / RCA ✦✦✦

Overtures introduce Broadway audiences to the music they're going to hear during the course of the evening. Played one after another, they can take on the quality of Muzak, not unpleasant but not compelling. This collection of 12 overtures taken from shows that played on Broadway between the '40s and '80s displays the consistency of style in Broadway music. Much of it is appealing, but then, that's the problem—it's like trying to make a dinner out of appetizers. — *William Ruhlmann*

Celebrate Broadway, Vol. 5—Hello Young Lovers / Jul. 19, 1994 / RCA Victor ✦✦✦

On its fifth Celebrate Broadway compilation, RCA explores love, with the emphasis on variety. Indeed, only somewhat complicated love songs have been chosen here, starting with the title song, from *The King and I*, which is sung by an older woman who is not involved in romance, and including "The Human Heart," from *Once on This Island*, which is about universal love; "My Cup Runneth Over," from *I Do! I Do!*, and "I Still Get Jealous," from *High Button Shoes* by way of Jerome Robbins' Broadway, which concern mature relationships; and "Who Can I Turn To?" from *The Roar of the Greasepaint, the Smell of the Crowd* and "In Buddy's Eyes," from *Follies*, which have a real sense of emotional dependency that comes across as desperate. But then, Broadway has treated love in many ways, from *Show Boat's* fanciful 1927 flirtation, "Make Believe," to *Hair's* knowing 1968 revelation that it's "Easy to Be Hard." So, don't expect to put this album on in preparation for a romantic evening with your companion—it's liable to convince the two of you that you should give it up instead. Though the *Celebrate Broadway* series has made extensive use of performances other than original cast recordings, this compilation goes a little farther, with a full two-thirds of the selections drawn from Off-Broadway, revivals, and concert versions. — *William Ruhlmann*

Celebrate Broadway, Vol. 6—Beautiful Girls / Jul. 19, 1994 / RCA ✦✦✦

This is a case of going with what you've got. Many of Broadway's greatest divas are represented here, including Ethel Merman, Mary Martin, Julie Andrews, Liza Minnelli, and Barbara Cook. But they are not necessarily heard in their most memorable performances because, for example, RCA Victor has rights only to Julie Andrews' appearance in the recent *Putting It Together* rather than her earlier triumphs. And a few great ones, such as Carol Channing, are missing entirely. There's nothing wrong with what's here, of course, but as an anthology of Broadway's leading ladies, *Beautiful Girls* doesn't show its women to their best advantage. — *William Ruhlmann*

☆ **A Chorus Line [Original Cast]** / 1975 / CBS ✦✦✦✦✦

Michael Bennett's 1975 valentine to "gypsies," the dancers who are often treated as so much mobile scenery in Broadway musicals, is sometimes considered to have broken new ground with its frank portraits of talented but frustrated performers. The score by Marvin Hamlisch and Edward Kleban is a favorite of "theater people" everywhere, but was designed to showcase the abilities of dancers rather than singers. Conse-

quently, only the ballad "What I Did for Love" has had a life outside of the show's context. — *Marjorie Ellen Ruhlmann*

City of Angels [Original Broadway Cast] / 1990 / CBS ✦✦✦✦

The original Broadway cast version of a musical set in Hollywood in the '40s, exploring the interaction between a writer of hard-boiled detective novels and his gumshoe hero. Cy Coleman has turned in some low-key, jazzy period music, and David Zippel's witty lyrics are a match for the book, which was written by Larry Gelbart, the man who brought you the TV series "M*A*S*H." — *William Ruhlmann*

City of Angels / Oct. 12, 1993 / RCA ✦✦✦

The London cast recording of Cy Coleman and David Zippel's City of Angels is a virtual carbon copy of the Broadway cast album, though, since that one has a slightly more distinctive cast, it gets the edge. — *William Ruhlmann*

Closer Than Ever [Original Cast] / 1990 / RCA ✦✦✦✦

A follow-up to Richard Maltby, Jr. and David Shire's previous off-Broadway revue, *Starting Here, Starting Now*, featuring two discs' worth of smart songs about the ups and downs of modern life—especially romance. — *William Ruhlmann*

☆ **Company [Original Cast]** / 1970 / CBS ✦✦✦✦✦

Winner of both the Drama Critics Circle and Tony awards in 1970, this show established composer Stephen Sondheim as a demigod of the contemporary musical theater. The story of a bachelor afloat in a sea of the very married was certainly of its time, but it has proven to have enduring appeal, as has Sondheim's deliciously tongue-twisting libretto. — *Marjorie Ellen Ruhlmann*

Crazy for You / 1992 / Capitol ✦✦✦✦

Broadway's 1992 Tony winner for Best Musical is a show that borrows Gershwin songs primarily from *Girl Crazy*, but also from some of the Hollywood musicals of the '30s. You've heard the songs before, but they're freshly, enthusiastically presented here, and there's enough of the show's book in the lengthy CD to get a sense of the new context. Harry Groener and—especially—Jodi Benson shine in the starring roles. — *William Ruhlmann*

Crazy for You / Nov. 9, 1993 / RCA ✦✦✦

This is the London cast recording of "the new Gershwin musical comedy" *Crazy for You*, which repeated its New York success by winning the Olivier Award for Best Musical. The album is similar to the American recording, though the American West accents affected by the British actors are a bit less certain and the cast is slightly less distinctive. — *William Ruhlmann*

Curtain Up! Overtures of the American Musical Theater / 1993 / Met ✦✦✦✦

It is traditional in the theater that musicals begin with instrumental medleys of the show's songs, probably because that allows everyone time to get in their seats. But some of these orchestral pieces are quite accomplished. In some cases (Cy Coleman's *On the Twentieth Century* is an example) they provide as much as you need of a show. So, here are 16 Broadway musical overtures in 64 minutes, gathered by the Metropolitan Opera Guild to lead off its series of Broadway compilations. First, appropriately, is John McGlinn's 1988 restoration of *Show Boat*, and we have music by most of the greats of the American theater, including George Gershwin, Richard Rodgers (note how differently he writes for Lorenz Hart and for Oscar Hammerstein II), Irving Berlin, Leonard Bernstein, Jule Stein, and Stephen Sondheim. One might quibble and note that Cole Porter, Jerry Herman, Jerry Bock, John Kander, and Andrew Lloyd Webber are missing, but what's here is terrific. — *William Ruhlmann*

☆ **Damn Yankees [Original Cast]** / 1955 / RCA ✦✦✦✦✦

The Faust legend is retold, in sports terms, as a baseball fan sells his soul so his team can win the pennant. Starring Gwen Verdon and Ray Walston. The score is by Richard Adle and Jerry Ross. Highlights are: "Whatever Lola Wants," and "Heart." — *William Ruhlmann*

Do I Hear a Waltz? / 1965 / Sony Classical ✦✦✦✦

With music by Richard Rodgers and lyrics by Stephen Sondheim, based on the Arthur Laurents play *The Time of the Cuckoo* (which also served as the basis for the Katharine Hepburn movie *Summertime*). It was not a big success, though some of the songs do reflect the talent that created them, especially the humorous "What Do We Do? We Fly!" — *William Ruhlmann*

Do Re Mi / Jan. 1961 / RCA ✦✦✦

Jule Styne's follow-up to *Gypsy*, was this sendup of the music business, starring Phil Silvers, fresh from his years on TV's "Sgt. Bilko," and Nancy Walker. Other principals were lyricists Betty Comden and Adolph Green, and writer/director Garson Kanin. With all that proven talent, the show should have been better, and as it was, it wasn't a total flop—it got good reviews and ran for about a year, though it closed at a loss. The score proves to have been one of Styne and Comden/Green's less successful ones, with the one memorable song being "Make Someone Happy," though the irrepressible Silvers, one of the great clowns of the era,

Cast Recordings

The truth is that the Broadway musical does not travel well. Conceived as a combination of comedy, drama, song, and dance for one of those thousand-seat theaters that sit on a handful of streets in midtown Manhattan, the Broadway musical, if it is successful, immediately gets translated into a variety of forms into which it doesn't really fit. A road version may travel the country, playing before abbreviated sets in much larger theaters. A film version may appear that, even if it doesn't alter the work in other ways, somehow looks less impressive on film than it does when you're in the theater. Why is it easy to accept that a person onstage may just burst into song, when it looks silly on celluloid? Maybe the stages are the real dream factories—in movies, things are just too realistic. And then, of course, there are the cast albums, which, in a sense, are the farthest-removed translations of Broadway musicals. Here are a few songs, but no story, no dance. The volatile chemistry of opposing art forms that gives birth to the musical simply isn't present. A cast album is a souvenir, but no more to be confused with the real thing than a three-inch model of the Statue of Liberty you can buy at Battery Park.

And yet Broadway musicals have been the spawning ground for some of the most important popular music of the 20th century. In the first few decades of this century, when most people heard new songs by obtaining the sheet music and playing them themselves, Broadway introduced America to most of its new music. Musicals then were often what we would now call revues, developed out of vaudeville and really just collections of individual scenes and songs. But the country's best songwriters—George M. Cohan, Irving Berlin, George Gershwin—were devoting their efforts to the Broadway stage. Despite this dominance, only occasionally was anything resembling an "original Broadway cast" recording made. Recordings had limited popularity, especially after the start of the Depression, when record sales fell precipitously, and while Broadway served as a source for pop songs, usually they were recorded by other singers. One reason for this, of course, was that the record industry's main format—the 78 rpm single—allowed for two songs, each no more than about three minutes in length. "Albums" (bound collections of several 78s) were rarities, though *Show Boat*, for example, appeared in this form a year after it hit Broadway in 1927. But *Show Boat* was different in many ways. For one thing, it told a single, unified story, and the songs were mostly integrated into the plot.

By the '40s, the style set by *Show Boat* became the norm for most shows, especially after *Oklahoma*. At the same time, CBS developed the 33 1/3 rpm, long-playing record, and CBS president Goddard Lieberson recognized the Broadway cast album to be ideal for the new medium. As a result, cast albums frequently became big hits. From 1945 to 1965, *Song of Norway* (1945), *Carousel* (1945), *Kiss Me, Kate* (1949), *South Pacific* (1949), *Three Little Words* (1950), *Guys and Dolls* (1951), *The Music Man* (1958), *My Fair Lady* (1958), *Flower Drum Song* (1959), *The Sound of Music* (1959), *Camelot* (1961), *Carnival* (1961), and *Hello Dolly!*

(1964) all hit No. 1 on the Billboard album charts. The peak of popularity came in the late '50s and early '60s. Then came the rock 'n' roll era, and Broadway show music (like many other pre-rock styles) was swept into a marginalized pop category. Only *Hair* (1968), a rock pastiche, got to the top of the charts, and most cast albums sold modestly.

Stephen Sondheim, the acknowledged master of the Broadway musical in the '70s and '80s, has enjoyed no genuinely successful cast albums, though his song "Send in the Clowns (from *A Little Night Music*) has become a standard. Andrew Lloyd Webber, on the other hand, has largely bucked the trend, starting with his *Jesus Christ Superstar*, of which the pre-stage studio version went to No. 1 in 1970. Webber has gone on to enjoy million-selling hit cast albums for *Evita, Cats*, and *Phantom of the Opera*. Alain Boublil and Claude-Michel Shonberg have also sold a respectable number of copies of *Les Miserables*. These are the exceptions, however. For the most part, not only is the Broadway cast album no longer a commercial sure shot, it may not even get made. It used to be that the week after a show opened and good reviews indicated a hit, the cast would be in a recording studio to get the album out fast. Today, it may be six months before a cast album appears. Recent cases in point include *The Will Rogers Follies* and *The Secret Garden*, both of which opened in the spring of 1991, with their cast albums not available until December. And *Grand Hotel* was at the conclusion of its two-year run before a cast album appeared, by which time it was impossible to append the word "original," since one of the principal actors had died. If this is what happens with big hits, you can imagine how things are for less successful shows.

In spite of all this, there is probably more recording of show music going on now than at any time in the past. Archivists such as John McGlinn, John Mauceri, and Thomas Z. Shepard are hard at work restoring full scores of vintage shows and presenting them in new studio recordings with classically trained singers, further blurring a line between musical and opera already grown fuzzy enough as opera companies have incorporated musicals like *Sweeney Todd* and *South Pacific* into their repertoires. In addition, a plethora of small labels—First Night, Bay Cities, DRG—have taken up the task of recording shows with limited popular appeal, while the majors are digging into their vaults and reissuing long-out-of-print cast albums on compact disc. And then, of course, people keep writing musicals, and audiences keep going to them. How much worry can we have for the musical when we look to the 1992-1993 Broadway season and see on the horizon a version of *Jekyll and Hyde* that already has a cast album out, as well as Lloyd Webber's musical, *Sunset Boulevard*? Even if the original Broadway cast album is the souvenir of a great evening (as it's always been) and no longer the blockbuster seller it was 30 years ago, it's still the repository of some of the best music of yesterday and today.
—*William Ruhlmann*

makes a strong impression. (Originally released in 1961, this cast album was reissued on CD in 1994 with extensive liner notes by theater historian Steven Suskin.) —*William Ruhlmann*

Dreamgirls [Original Cast] / 1981 / David Geffen Co. ✦✦✦✦
This rags-to-riches story of an African-American '60s girl group was a 1981 success for director/choreographer Michael Bennett, in part due to speculation about its possible similarity to the real-life rise of the Supremes. The score by Henry Krieger and Tom Eyen deliberately evokes the pop and R&B sounds that are the play's subject matter. Jennifer Holliday's rendition of "And I Am Telling You I'm Not Going" stopped the show and began her musical career. —*Marjorie Ellen Ruhlmann*

Evening with Frank Loesser / 1992 / DRG ✦✦✦
This disc contains performances associated with three Frank Loesser shows—*Guys and Dolls, The Most Happy Fella*, and *How to Succeed in Business Without Really Trying*. Loesser has a good, sometimes gruff voice and puts the material across well while accompanying himself on piano. These are early versions—lyrics changed and songs were replaced before these scores got to Broadway—so this is in a sense an album for Broadway scholars, though mere fans will have a good time, too. The material from *The Most Happy Fella*, dating from three years before the actual production, features Maxene Andrews of the Andrews Sisters and is previously unreleased. —*William Ruhlmann*

Evita [London Cast] / 1978 / MCA ✦✦✦
The two-disc pre-stage studio recording by Andrew Lloyd Webber and Tim Rice, billed as "an opera" about Argentine political figure Eva Peron, was a massive UK hit, reaching No. 4, with Julie Covington's "Don't Cry for Me, Argentina" hitting No. 1 and Barbara Dickson's "Another Suitcase in Another Hall" reaching the Top 20. —*William Ruhlmann*

☆ **Falsettoland** / 1990 / DRG ✦✦✦✦✦
Original off-Broadway cast album from William Finn's sequel to his previous off-Broadway show, *March of the Falsettos*, and one of the most impressive musical scores in years, a fact confirmed when the combined shows came to Broadway under the title *Falsettos* and won a Tony for best score. —*William Ruhlmann*

☆ **The Fantasticks [Original Cast]** / 1960 / Polydor ✦✦✦✦✦
Overwhelmingly the world's longest-running musical, it debuted May 3, 1960, at the Sullivan Street Playhouse in Greenwich Village. Boy meets girl, boy loses girl, boy gets girl in the end. The simple and utterly charming score by Tom Jones and Harvey Schmidt includes "Try to Remember," "Soon It's Gonna Rain," and "They Were You." —*Marjorie Ellen Ruhlmann*

☆ **Fiddler on the Roof** / 1964 / RCA ✦✦✦✦✦
Original Broadway cast recording of Sheldon Harnick and Jerry Bock's massively successful musical based on Sholem Aleichem's stories about poor Russian Jews at the turn of the century, starring Zero Mostel, who

gets to sing such songs as "Tradition," "If I Were a Rich Man," and "To Life." One of the great musicals of all time, this album was a Top Ten, gold-selling hit. (Note: This edition is a 1986 CD reissue containing two previously unreleased tracks. The still-in-print cassette version, RCA 1005, does not contain these new songs.) — *William Ruhlmann*

Fiddler on the Roof [Original London Cast] / 1984 / CBS ✦✦✦✦
This is the original London cast recording and features Israeli actor/singer Topol in the starring role of Tevye. Topol has since gone on to play the part on film and in a Broadway revival, which means his version is by now more familiar than that of the role's originator, Zero Mostel. Topol's Tevye is notably less comic than Mostel's, but he brings great warmth to his performance, and this, not the film soundtrack, is his definitive rendition. — *William Ruhlmann*

Finian's Rainbow [Original Cast] / 1960 / RCA ✦✦✦
Revival of the 1947 musical by E.Y. Harburg and Burton Lane. The story is too complicated by half, but that doesn't matter on record, and the music is some of Lane's best. The songs include "How Are Things in Glocca Morra?," "Look to the Rainbow," "Old Devil Moon," and "If This Isn't Love." — *William Ruhlmann*

Fiorello! [Original Broadway Cast] / 1989 / Capitol ✦✦✦✦
Based on the life and times of New York City's most beloved mayor, Fiorello La Guardia. This show won the 1959 Pulitzer Prize for drama, a rare feat for a musical. It was the first success for the composer/lyricist team of Jerry Bock and Sheldon Harnick, and was Tom Bosley's Broadway debut in the title role. — *Marjorie Ellen Ruhlmann*

Five Guys Named Moe / Jul. 1992 / Columbia ✦✦✦
This Original Broadway Cast Recording is a good example of the kind of music that can be vital and exciting in a theater and redundant on disc. *Five Guys Named Moe* is a musical revue with the thinnest of story lines, the music for which is taken from the repertoire of jump blues star Louis Jordan, who filled the R&B charts with songs like "Is You Is Or Is You Ain't My Baby" and "Choo Choo Ch'Boogie" in the '40s and '50s. It makes for a delightful theater going experience, but on record it has to compete with Jordan's originals, and it doesn't. Also, this show originated in the West End, and there is a London Cast album that is virtually identical. — *William Ruhlmann*

Flower Drum Song [Original Cast] / 1961 / CBS ✦✦✦✦
Rodgers and Hammerstein return to a theme that had served them well in both *The King and I* and *South Pacific*: misunderstanding and reconciliation between individuals of differing cultural backgrounds. This 1958 musical revolved around the meeting of old and new worlds in San Francisco's Chinatown. *Flower Drum Song* has a serviceable score but is not the team's most exciting. The novelty "I Enjoy Being a Girl" is more often excerpted than the lovely and overlooked "Love Look Away." — *Marjorie Ellen Ruhlmann*

Follies / 1971 / Capitol ✦✦✦
Stephen Sondheim's show about aging follies girls remains one of his greatest scores. This Broadway cast recording is somewhat abbreviated, even though the 1989 CD reissue includes previously unreleased material. — *William Ruhlmann*

★ **Follies—In Concert [Studio Cast]** / 1985 / RCA ✦✦✦✦✦
This performance, recorded live at New York's Avery Fisher Hall, features a dream cast singing Stephen Sondheim's ambitious and fascinating score. With Barbara Cook, George Hearn, Mandy Patinkin, Lee Remick, Betty Comden, Adolph Green, Liliane Montevecchi, Elaine Stritch, Phyllis Newman, and Carol Burnett, among others. — *Marjorie Ellen Ruhlmann*

Follies / 1987 / Encore ✦✦✦
A two-disc London cast recording of the complete score as revised by Sondheim for a West End production. This includes newly written songs. — *William Ruhlmann*

42nd Street [Original Cast] / 1977 / RCA ✦✦✦✦
In a reversal of usual practice, producer David Merrick turned to the 1933 movie musical for this stage musical, which uses Harry Warren and Al Dubin's venerable songs—such as "You're Getting to Be a Habit with Me," "We're in the Money," "Lullaby of Broadway"—and the chorus-girl-becomes-a-star storyline. The result was new and exciting, almost 50 years later. Stars Tammy Grimes and Jerry Orbach. — *William Ruhlmann*

☆ **Funny Face** / 1980 / Smithsonian ✦✦✦✦✦
A reconstruction of the 1927 George and Ira Gershwin musical, using period recordings by Fred and Adele Astaire, various orchestras, and even a couple of piano recordings by George Gershwin himself. — *William Ruhlmann*

Funny Girl / 1964 / Capitol ✦✦✦
The Jule Styne/Bob Merrill musical about Ziegfeld Follies comedienne Fanny Brice became a star vehicle for Barbra Streisand—her first and last starring role on Broadway. It also provided her with some of the best material of her early repertoire: "I'm the Greatest Star," "People," and

"Don't Rain on My Parade." This album went gold and reached No. 2. — *William Ruhlmann*

Funny Thing Happened on the Way [Original Cast] / 1962 / Bay Cities ✦✦✦
A Funny Thing Happened on the Way to the Forum, Stephen Sondheim's first musical as both composer and lyricist, was a delightful comedy hit set in ancient Rome and starring Zero Mostel. It included "Comedy Tonight," one of the great opening numbers in Broadway history. This is a reissue of the original Broadway cast recording. — *William Ruhlmann*

George M! [Original Cast] / 1968 / CBS ✦✦✦
Joel Grey's second triumph on Broadway (after *Cabaret*) was this musical biography of George M. Cohan, who ruled the Great White Way at the turn of the century. Unlike the Jimmy Cagney movie, the show pulled no punches, but what really mattered were the Cohan songs, including his biggest hits, "Over There" and "Give My Regards to Broadway." A young Bernadette Peters played Cohan's sister. — *William Ruhlmann*

☆ **Gigi [Original Cast]** / 1974 / RCA ✦✦✦✦✦
A Broadway version of the film musical by Alan Jay Lerner and Frederick Loewe, this recording is notable for a cast that includes Alfred Drake and Agnes Moorehead and introduces four new songs, including the cynical and witty "The Contract." — *William Ruhlmann*

Girl Crazy / 1990 / Asylum ✦✦✦
A non-stage restoration of the original 1930 show by George and Ira Gershwin, conducted by John Mauceri and featuring Lorna Luft, Judy Blazer, and Frank Gorshin. — *William Ruhlmann*

Godspell [Original Cast] / 1974 / Arista ✦✦✦
Stephen Schwartz's reverent musical based on the St. Matthew gospel actually opened off-Broadway (which is where it stayed) before the Broadway version of *Jesus Christ Superstar*, to which it was a kind of response. As a piece of theater, *Godspell* was much more successful, running more than five years. This cast album appeared several years into the run, but it effectively captures the show's rock/pop score and Schwartz's re-reading of the Bible into the American vernacular (he had done much the same with Leonard Bernstein on *Mass*). — *William Ruhlmann*

The Gospel at Colonus [Original Cast] / 1988 / Nonesuch ✦✦✦
This is a little complicated. Bob Telson and Lee Breuer's musical, which mixes gospel music sung by gospel singers with Sophocles' *Oedipus at Colonus*, was originally performed off-Broadway, and a cast album was released. A year later, it was videotaped for the PBS series "Great Performances," and that is the version heard on the album reviewed here. Then three years later, it opened on Broadway. But there's no Broadway cast album. Got that? Okay. This version is similar to the one above (in fact, one track is taken from that recording), but it is a little looser, and in gospel music that's all to the good. — *William Ruhlmann*

Grand Hotel / 1992 / RCA ✦✦✦
It took years for this Tommy Tune musical to reach disc, during which time one of the leads, David Carroll, died (he is remembered in a club performance of one of the songs, included as a bonus track). But most of the rest of the principals—Liliane Montevecchi, Karen Akers, Michael Jeter—are here, making the most of this musical adaptation of the famous movie about a hotel in Berlin in the '20s. The score, by Robert Wright and George Forrest, with significant additions by Maury Yeston, is not the show's strong point (the staging and choreography were what made it a hit), but it gives a good sense of the story and is true to the original source. — *William Ruhlmann*

The Grass Harp / 1971 / Painted Smiles ✦✦✦
This Kenward Elmslie/Claire Richardson musical, based on a novel by Truman Capote, was a flop, but it is notable for Barbara Cook's outstanding starring role performance. — *William Ruhlmann*

Grease / 1994 / RCA Victor ✦✦✦
For this Broadway revival of the 1972 show, Jim Jacobs and Warren Casey's score has been reorchestrated and a genuine oldie has been added, the Skyliners' "Since I Don't Have You." But *Grease!* is still the same shallow pastiche of '50s high school references, still unsure whether it wants to celebrate or satirize. The new cast sings with gusto (including star Rosie O'Donnell, who is more comedienne than vocalist), but this still isn't much of a show. — *William Ruhlmann*

Greenwillow / 1960 / CBS ✦✦✦✦
The original Broadway cast recording of the Frank Loesser musical (perhaps his least well known, but still imbued with his musical talent), starring Anthony Hopkins. — *William Ruhlmann*

☆ **Guys and Dolls [Original Cast]** / 1951 / MCA ✦✦✦✦✦
Frank Loesser's brilliant musical version of the stories of Damon Runyon was a massive hit, running 1200 performances, and this original Broadway cast album shows why, with songs like "The Oldest Established," "A Bushel and a Peck," "Luck Be a Lady," and "Sit Down You're Rockin' the Boat," sung by a cast including Stubby Kaye, Sam Levene, Robert Alda, and Vivian Blaine. — *William Ruhlmann*

Gypsy [Original Cast] / May 1959 / CBS ✦✦✦✦
This tribute to burlesque was a star vehicle for Ethel Merman. The score by Jule Styne and Stephen Sondheim includes the Merman standard "Everything's Coming Up Roses," and the song that is invariably used to introduce anything having to do with the strip tease, "Let Me Entertain You." —*Marjorie Ellen Ruhlmann*

☆ **Hair [Original Cast]** / 1968 / RCA ✦✦✦✦✦
The appearance of "The American Tribal Love Rock Musical" on Broadway in April of 1968 had an effect not unlike the arrival of the motion picture *Woodstock* two years later. *Hair* helped to popularize and, ultimately, to trivialize the "counterculture" it sought to celebrate. But the Gerome Ragni/James Rado/Galt MacDermot score remains one of the most appealing artifacts of the "Age of Aquarius." —*Marjorie Ellen Ruhlmann*

Hello Again / Jun. 28, 1994 / RCA Victor ✦✦✦
Michael John La Chiusa's off-Broadway 1994 musical *Hello Again*, based on Arthur Schnitzler's play La Ronde, contains ten two-character scenes chronicling sexual encounters in different decades of the 20th century—"The Soldier and the Nurse" in scene two, "The Nurse and the College Boy" in scene three, "The College Boy and the Young Wife" in scene four, etc. As such, it is an ambitious undertaking and necessarily episodic. Onstage, there may have been many unifying visual elements, but on record, the sung-through scenes pass by quickly and sketchily, simultaneously full of deep feeling and passion, yet not presented in enough detail to convey those emotions fully to the listener. Though there are nods to musical styles across the century, much of the music is in a post-Sondheim musical recitative style: It's a musical because the dialogue is sung, not because there are real songs, which means it loses more in mere audio form than a standard musical might. A talented effort, then, but relatively inaccessible. —*William Ruhlmann*

Hello, Dolly! [Original Cast] / 1964 / RCA ✦✦✦
Jerry Herman's musical (with book by Michael Stewart) based on Thornton Wilder's *The Matchmaker* was one of the last great old-style musicals and a massive hit. Even today, its songs (including the title track, "Before the Parade Passes By," and "So Long Dearie") are so memorable most people can hum them. Herman used a turn-of-the-century, major-chord, big-melody approach, effectively kidded and overcome by Carol Channing in the title role. It's precisely because Channing doesn't quite have the range for these melodies that she's able to express the character so well (an effect lost in the Barbra Streisand movie version, though Streisand has no trouble expressing character in other ways). And the supporting cast, including Charles Nelson Reilly, Eileen Brennan, and David Burns, is ideal. —*William Ruhlmann*

Hello, Dolly! / 1967 / RCA ✦✦✦
This is the recording of the cast that took over the show more than three years into its run, with Pearl Bailey and Cab Calloway in the lead roles. Though less accomplished than the original, it is notable for Bailey's individual interpretation of Dolly. Bailey was sadly underrecorded during her career, and this is a highlight of what little there is. —*William Ruhlmann*

☆ **House of Flowers [Cast Recording]** / 1955 / Sony ✦✦✦✦✦
With a score by Truman Capote and Harold Arlen and a cast that included Pearl Bailey and Diahann Carroll (in her stage debut), this had the elements of a great show. They're best heard on this cast album in such songs as "A Sleepin' Bee" and "Two Ladies in de Shade of de Banana Tree," which bring out the show's Caribbean flavor. It was a flop onstage for reasons too complicated to explain here, but the soundtrack is very much a hit. —*William Ruhlmann*

How to Succeed in Business ... / 1961 / RCA
Frank Loesser's satire on the business world, *How to Succeed in Business without Really Trying*, is as meaningful today as ever. Starring Robert Morse and Rudy Vallee, it features such highlights as "The Company Way" and "I Believe in You." It's overdue for a revival, but this original cast album is probably unbeatable. —*William Ruhlmann*

I Can Get It for You Wholesale / 1962 / Sony ✦✦✦
Harold Rome's musical about the garment trade, *I Can Get It for You Wholesale*, has long been remembered for the Broadway debut of 19-year-old Barbra Streisand, who played the part of a secretary and sang a song about it, "Miss Marmelstein." This is due not only to her obvious talent, but also to the mediocre nature of the rest of the show, a charmless tale of an unscrupulous businessman played by Elliott Gould. —*William Ruhlmann*

I Do! I Do! / 1966 / RCA ✦✦✦✦
The main draws to this two-character musical are the two stars: Mary Martin and Robert Preston. *I Do! I Do!* traces 50 years of a marriage, and the show's relative banality is overcome by the strong performances of the principals, as well as the quality of the Tom Jones score, which includes the standard, "My Cup Runneth Over." —*William Ruhlmann*

☆ **Into the Woods [Original Cast]** / 1987 / RCA ✦✦✦✦✦
Stephen Sondheim and James Lapine's re-telling of children's stories is an intricate, moving show that works on many levels. The music and lyrics are among Sondheim's best (which is to say, the best there are), and the performances, especially those of Bernadette Peters and Chip Zien, are outstanding in this original Broadway cast recording. —*William Ruhlmann*

Into the Woods [London Cast] / 1991 / RCA ✦✦✦
An excellent recording of the Sondheim classic. —*William Ruhlmann*

☆ **Jacques Brel Is Alive and Well [Original Cast]** / 1987 / CBS ✦✦✦✦✦
This 1968 off-Broadway revue of *Jacques Brel Is Alive and Well and Living in Paris* established an "in concert" style of presentation for dramatic music that has often been used since. The poetic lyrics of Jacques Brel, expertly translated by Mort Shuman and Eric Blau, lend themselves to this bookless format. Its best-remembered numbers include "Marathon (Les Flamandes)," "Amsterdam," "Carousel (La Valse a Mille Temps)," and "If We Only Have Love (Quand On a Que L'Amour)." —*Marjorie Ellen Ruhlmann*

Jelly's Last Jam / 1992 / Mercury ✦✦✦
The good news is that Gregory Hines, playing the part of Jelly Roll Morton in this successful Broadway musical, creates a full-bodied character and performs it with conviction and gusto. His Jelly is proud, impressive, and ultimately tragic. The bad news is that he is also fictional: Writer-director George C. Wolfe has distorted Jelly Roll Morton's true story to tell a fable about African-American assimilation and the evolution of jazz. Unfortunately, Luther Henderson's musical adaptation does to Morton's music what Wolfe does to his life, and the result will be frowned upon by jazz fans, even though it conforms to Broadway conventions. —*William Ruhlmann*

☆ **Jesus Christ Superstar [Original Cast]** / 1970 / MCA ✦✦✦✦✦
Writers Andrew Lloyd Webber and Tim Rice set several precedents with this album. First, it is a pre-stage studio version, and it topped the US charts upon release. Second, it is the first show to successfully put rock music in a theatrical context (*Hair* is really a pop/show-music pastiche, not rock). Third, it is a "sung-through" musical without spoken dialog, technically an operetta. Fourth, though musicals had turned more serious at this point, writing a show about Jesus Christ from the point of view of Judas was about as daring as you could get. It succeeds in all ways. In addition to the title song (a No. 14 hit sung by Murray Head), it includes "I Don't Know How to Love Him" by Yvonne Elliman. —*William Ruhlmann*

Joseph & the Amazing Technicolor Dreamcoat / 1993 / Polydor ✦✦✦
Andrew Lloyd Webber's first musical to be based on biblical sources, written in 1967 when he was still a teenager, has taken on greater importance in the wake of his subsequent success. It finally hit Broadway in 1982, and there was a London revival in 1992. This cast album (which is at least the fifth recording) chronicles an American revival production that opened in Los Angeles in February 1993, starring Michael Damian. By now, the short musical has expanded to full length (the CD runs 73 minutes, including the nine-minute discoish "Joseph Megamix" medley), but it remains a rock pastiche with an uncertain tone. Lloyd Webber and lyricist Tim Rice would find their feet with this kind of approach in 1970 when they recorded *Jesus Christ Superstar*, and *Joseph* is still best understood as a dry run for that success. —*William Ruhlmann*

☆ **The King and I** / 1955 / CBS ✦✦✦✦✦
This 1951 Rodgers and Hammerstein triumph is one of those few musical comedies that gives definition to the art form. This original cast recording stars Gertrude Lawrence, for whom the show was written, as well as Yul Brynner. "I Whistle a Happy Tune," "Getting to Know You," and "Shall We Dance?" are among the classics that grace the score. —*Marjorie Ellen Ruhlmann*

The King and I / 1992 / Philips ✦✦✦✦
This is a studio recreation of the Rodgers and Hammerstein musical by the Hollywood Bowl Orchestra, conducted by John Mauceri, with soloists Julie Andrews and Ben Kingsley. Andrews is perfect casting; she restores to the show its true nature as a star vehicle (it was written for Gertrude Lawrence), she embodies the role of the English tutor, and she sings brilliantly. Kingsley brings a contemporary distanced cool to the role of the King of Siam, and the cast is effectively filled out by Lea Salonga and Peabo Bryson (as the lovers who sing "We Kiss in a Shadow"), and by Marilyn Horne (who sings "Something Wonderful"). Mauceri has opted to use the orchestrations developed for the movie version, which gives the score an added sweep and depth. This is the exception to the many opera-singers-doing-a-musical recreations we've been seeing over the last few years. It makes you wish Andrews and company would take it to New York. —*William Ruhlmann*

☆ **Kismet** / 1953 / CBS ✦✦✦✦✦
This adaptation of Edward Knoblock's play about a Baghdad beggar who rises to the rank of Emir in one magical day is notable for its score, adapted by Robert Wright and George Forrest from the music of classical

composer Alexander Borodin (Borodin even won a Tony!), and for the lead performance by Alfred Drake. This cast album was a big hit, reaching No. 4 in the charts, and "Stranger in Paradise" got to No. 2 in a contemporary recording by Tony Bennett. Onstage, the song was a duet between Doretta Morrow and a young Richard Kiley. — *William Ruhlmann*

☆ **Kiss Me Kate [Original Cast]** / 1961 / CBS ✦✦✦✦✦
Cole Porter's most successful show and his most popular score came with this adaptation of Shakespeare's *The Taming of the Shrew*, updated by the addition of a contemporary backstage subplot. Songs such as "I Hate Men," "Too Darn Hot," "Where Is the Life that Late I Led?," and "Always True to You (In My Fashion)" shows that Porter had lost none of his lyrical wit or compositional skill, especially when heard in the voices of a cast led by Alfred Drake and including Lisa Kirk. This cast album spent ten weeks at the top of the album charts in 1949 and stayed in the best-seller lists over a year. The show ran more than a thousand performances. — *William Ruhlmann*

Kiss Me Kate / 1987 / Relativity ✦✦✦
It's scandalous that there hasn't been a Broadway revival of this Porter masterpiece, but at least the Royal Shakespeare Company in England tried it, and here's the result: a cast led by Paul Jones and Nicola McAuliffe enthusiastically enunciating every delicious bit of wordplay, while a full orchestra plays the music beautifully. — *William Ruhlmann*

Kiss of the Spider Woman / 1993 / RCA Victor ✦✦✦
John Kander and Fred Ebb's music for *Kiss of the Spider Woman* tied for the 1993 Tony Award for Best Score with the Who's *Tommy*. The material seems ideal for the longstanding team, which has specialized in writing star vehicles (notably for Liza Minnelli) and have an interest in political themes (*Cabaret*). *Kiss*, which is set in a South American prison and features a prisoner who dreams of a gaudy movie star, would seem to offer them opportunities for both elements. In practice, though Chita Rivera does her best as the title character, this is not on a par with *Cabaret*, which is to say, good but not great Kander/Ebb. (Though it features the major performers from the Broadway cast, this recording is not technically an original Broadway cast recording, but in fact an original London cast recording, since it was made in London at the time of the West End run, prior to the show's coming to Broadway.) — *William Ruhlmann*

☆ **La Cage aux Folles [Original Cast]** / 1983 / RCA ✦✦✦✦✦
Composer Jerry Herman finds much greater depth in this French farce about a club for transvestites in St. Tropez than did the original play or the film, turning it into a virtual proclamation of gay pride ("I Am What I Am"). The score has his typically catchy tunes and slangy lyrics, and it remains touching, perhaps even more so in the age of AIDS. George Hearn is outstanding in the lead role. — *William Ruhlmann*

Lady Be Good! / 1977 / Elektra ✦✦✦✦
A reconstruction of the 1924 George and Ira Gershwin musical featuring period recordings by Fred and Adele Astaire, George Gershwin himself, and others. The songs include "Fascinating Rhythm" and "The Man I Love." — *William Ruhlmann*

Lenny / Blue Thumb ✦✦✦✦
A two-disc version of the Broadway play based on the comedy routines of Lenny Bruce, starring Cliff Gorman. Funny and heartbreaking, the play served as the basis for a film directed by Bob Fosse and starring Dustin Hoffman. — *William Ruhlmann*

☆ **Les Miserables [Original Cast]** / 1985 / David Geffen Co. ✦✦✦✦✦
This is the original London cast recording of the musical by Alain Boublil and Claude-Michel Shonberg and starring Colm Wilkinson. A riveting theatrical experience, the show is somewhat less impressive in a merely aural version, but it remains an excellent souvenir for the millions who have seen this show all over the world. — *William Ruhlmann*

Les Miserables [Complete Sym.] / 1990 / Combat ✦✦✦✦
This is quite easily the most impressive complete symphonic recording of *Les Miserables* on the market. The three-disc set is the entire production, not just the major numbers. The company is an all-star cast taken from productions around the world; and the singers hail from New York, Los Angeles, London, Sydney, and Tokyo. Perhaps the most remarkable performance is from Kaho Shimada of Tokyo in the role of Eponine. Shimada herself speaks virtually no English, but you wouldn't be able to tell by listening to this recording. A simply outstanding set. — *Tavia Hobart*

Let's Face It / 1979 / Smithsonian ✦✦✦✦
A reconstruction of the 1941 Cole Porter musical featuring performances by Danny Kaye and Hildegard. Also included on the album are five selections from *Red, Hot, and Blue!*, a 1936 Porter show with Ethel Merman, and three from *Leave It to Me!*, the 1938 show that introduced Mary Martin. — *William Ruhlmann*

Li'l Abner [Original Musical Comedy] / 1956 / Sony ✦✦✦✦
The Johnny Mercer/Gene de Paul musical captures the arch, sometimes cynical tone of Al Capp's comic strip and contains all those hayseed characters. Songs like "Jubilation T. Cornpone" and "The Country's in the

Very Best of Hands" are much more satiric than anything one normally associates with the '50s, but they certainly don't sound dated today. The cast includes Edith Adams, Stubby Kaye, Tina Louise, and Julie Newmar. — *William Ruhlmann*

A Little Night Music [Original Broadway Cast] / 1973 / CBS ✦✦✦✦
This recording of Stephen Sondheim's musical based on the Ingmar Bergman film *Smiles of a Summer Night* is at least as charming as its source material. Sondheim sets the romantic roundelay of the story to a series of waltzes with lyrics that bring out the ups and downs of "Liaisons," to borrow one song title. "Send in the Clowns" was the show's hit, but it is no more impressive than "The Glamorous Life," "You Must Meet My Wife," or "The Miller's Son." The score is effectively handled by a cast led by Len Cariou, Glynis Johns, Hermione Gingold, and Beth Fowler. — *William Ruhlmann*

A Little Night Music [Original London Cast] / 1975 / RCA ✦✦✦✦
Original London cast album of the Sondheim hit, featuring Jean Simmons (a better singer than Broadway's Glynnis Johns), Hermione Gingold (reprising her Broadway performance), and Joss Ackland. — *William Ruhlmann*

Loesser by Loesser / 1992 / DRG ✦✦✦✦
Composer Frank Loesser (who wrote *Guys and Dolls*, *The Most Happy Fella*, and other Broadway shows as well as many movie songs) was married to actress/singer Jo Sullivan, who starred in *The Most Happy Fella*. In the years since Loesser's death, Sullivan has toured with a concert revue called *The Songs of Frank Loesser*, and this, with Don Stephenson and the Loessers' daughter Emily, is something of a recreation of that show. It features a selection of some of Loesser's best, well sung and played by a small band. As such, it contains such songs as "Heart and Soul" and "Two Sleepy People," along with medleys from Loesser's shows. — *William Ruhlmann*

Lost in the Stars [Original Cast] / Nov. 1949 / MCA ✦✦✦✦
A 1949 musical with an African-American cast, dealing with racial unrest in South Africa. Music by Kurt Weill, words by Pulitzer Prize-winning playwright Maxwell Anderson. Based on Alan Paton's condescending novel *Cry, the Beloved Country*. The score is lovely but not very African. — *Marjorie Ellen Ruhlmann*

☆ **Mame [Original Cast]** / 1966 / CBS ✦✦✦✦✦
Jerry Herman's score hasn't a weak song, and it has some very strong ones, starting with the title tune and including "We Need a Little Christmas" and "If We Walked into My Life." Add a cast headed by Angela Lansbury and a book by Jerome Lawrence and Robert E. Lee (based on the Patrick Dennis novel about a boy and his zany aunt), and you have a big Broadway hit. — *William Ruhlmann*

☆ **Man of La Mancha [Original Cast]** / 1965 / MCA ✦✦✦✦✦
The musical version of Cervantes' *Don Quixote*, *Man of La Mancha* opened inauspiciously in an off-Broadway house in the fall of 1965, moved to Broadway, and became the hit of the 1965-1966 season. The original cast recording, with Richard Kiley in the title role, was a gold-selling hit that stayed on the best-seller charts more than three years, and no wonder, with a Mitch Leigh/Joe Darion score that included the stirring title song and the anthemic "The Impossible Dream." — *William Ruhlmann*

Me and My Girl / 1986 / MCA ✦✦✦✦
A revival/revision of Noel Gay's '30s musical comedy about a Cockney who is heir to an earldom, this Broadway cast album has plenty going for it: Robert Lindsay, who gives a delightful star turn in the main role, and a score including such favorites as "The Lambeth Walk" and "Leaning on a Lamppost." — *William Ruhlmann*

Me and Juliet / 1953 / RCA Victor ✦✦✦
Of Rodgers and Hammerstein's three relative flops, *Allegro*, *Me and Juliet*, and *Pipe Dream*, *Me and Juliet* was the most successful. In fact, it broke even. But after 40 years, the only memorable thing about it remains the song that was already a hit on opening night, "No Other Love," based on a theme Rodgers had previously used in *Victory at Sea*. Rodgers and Hammerstein were trying for a light romantic comedy in the style of Rodger and Hart, but Hammerstein was not Hart, and this wasn't *Pal Joey*. — *William Ruhlmann*

Merrily We Roll Along [Original Cast] / 1982 / RCA ✦✦✦
Stephen Sondheim wrote one of his typically outstanding scores for this show, tracing the lives of a composer and lyricist—backwards. It was a complete flop onstage, but the album proves its quality. This is a 1986 CD reissue of the LP version, containing one song that previously didn't fit. The cassette version lacks the added song. — *William Ruhlmann*

Miss Saigon [Original London Cast] / 1990 / David Geffen Co. ✦✦✦✦
Alain Boublil and Claude-Michel Schonberg's follow-up to *Les Miserables* is another sung-through operetta with a serious theme and a classic source: They have placed *Madame Butterfly* in the waning days of the Vietnam War. Jonathan Pryce stands out as a pimp named the Engineer

in this London cast recording, and the score has the same rock feel as Schonberg's *Les Miserables* music. — *William Ruhlmann*

Mr. Wonderful [Original Cast] / 1956 / MCA ✦✦✦
This Jerry Bock/Larry Holofcener/George Weiss show is remembered today for boosting Sammy Davis, Jr. to stardom. It also featured a young Chita Rivera. — *William Ruhlmann*

Moby Dick / May 11, 1993 / RCA ✦✦✦
Now, here's an oddity. Robert Longden and Hereward Kaye wrote a musical version of *Moby Dick* as it might have been performed by an English girls school and got it on—briefly—in the West End. This cast album was recorded live onstage and, on two discs, is the complete show. Given the apparently satiric setting, you'd expect the result to be funnier than it is: the authors can't seem to decide what their take on the material should be. — *William Ruhlmann*

☆ **The Music Man [Original Broadway Cast]** / 1958 / Capitol ✦✦✦✦✦
The original Broadway cast of Meredith Willson's most successful musical was headed by Robert Preston, who played the part of Harold Hill, a conman who breezes into an Iowa town and tries to sell the inhabitants on non-existent boys band equipment. Willson concentrates on percussive effects and rapid-fire spiels for Preston, though the musical standout is Barbara Cook as Marian the Librarian. Highlights of this perennial hit show include "Seventy-Six Trombones" and "Till There Was You." — *William Ruhlmann*

The Music Man [Studio Recording] / 1991 / Telarc ✦✦✦
Erich Kunzel leads the Cincinnati Pops Orchestra in this concert version of the score, which features more incidental music than previous albums. Timothy Noble is only adequate in the lead role, but Doc Severinsen proves a surprisingly effective Marcellus Washburn on his featured number, "Shipoopi." — *William Ruhlmann*

☆ **My Fair Lady [Original Broadway Cast]** / 1956 / Sony ✦✦✦✦✦
The original Broadway cast recording of Alan Jay Lerner and Frederick Loewe's musical, based on George Bernard Shaw's *Pygmalion*, about the relationship between an elocutionist and a flower girl. This is one of the great musical scores, including "Wouldn't It Be Loverly," "I Could Have Danced All Night," and "On the Street Where You Live," sung by a cast that includes Rex Harrison, Julie Andrews, and Stanley Holloway. The album spent 15 weeks at No. 1 in the charts. — *William Ruhlmann*

My Fair Lady [Original London Cast] / 1975 / CBS ✦✦✦✦
This mega-hit moved into the Drury Lane Theatre in London in April of 1958 with the British stars of the Broadway version intact; hence the original London cast recording is very similar to its more familiar American counterpart. At present this album in CD form is rather less expensive than the original-Broadway-cast CD, and it is far better to have this *My Fair Lady* than none at all. — *Marjorie Ellen Ruhlmann*

My One and Only [Original Broadway Cast] / 1983 / Atlantic ✦✦✦✦
"The New Gershwin Musical" was the subtitle given this musical, but most people knew it as the new Tommy Tune musical, since he starred in it (with Twiggy) and staged and choreographed it (with Thommie Walsh). On record, Tune's personality comes across even if his long legs aren't visible, and the mostly understated arrangements of Gershwin favorites sound newly minted. — *William Ruhlmann*

No, No, Nanette [Broadway Cast] / 1971 / CBS ✦✦✦✦
A revival of a 1925 musical by Vincent Youmans, Irving Caesar, and Otto Harbach, mounted in an essentially faithful style 41 years later with a cast featuring Ruby Keeler and a production supervised by Busby Berkeley. A romantic roundelay with a flapper at its center, it proved a success all over again in the '70s, probably because it still had a score featuring such songs as "I Want to Be Happy" and "Tea for Two." — *William Ruhlmann*

Oh, Kay! / 1978 / Smithsonian ✦✦✦✦
A reconstruction of the 1926 George and Ira Gershwin musical, featuring recordings by Gertrude Lawrence, with George Gershwin playing many of the piano parts. Songs include "Clap Yo' Hands," "Do, Do, Do," and "Someone to Watch over Me." — *William Ruhlmann*

★ **Oklahoma! [Original Cast]** / 1955 / MCA ✦✦✦✦✦
Rodgers and Hammerstein's first collaboration in 1943 created the mold from which most musicals were made for the next twenty-five years. The combination of a serious book, with score and ballet truly subservient to the plot, proved a successful formula, particularly in the hands of this team. Alfred Drake's dreamy "Oh, What a Beautiful Mornin'" and Celeste Holm's "I Cain't Say No" are irresistible. — *Marjorie Ellen Ruhlmann*

Oklahoma! [Broadway Revival] / 1980 / RCA ✦✦✦✦
An excellent Broadway revival of the 1943 Rodgers and Hammerstein show that still ranks among their greatest works, and which gets a hi-fidelity workout here. — *William Ruhlmann*

☆ **Oliver! [Original Broadway Cast]** / 1962 / RCA ✦✦✦✦✦
Lionel Bart's musical version of *Oliver Twist*, Charles Dickens' novel of Industrial Revolution London in the late 19th century, was far more enter-

Jerome Kern

Jerome Kern (1885-1945) is arguably the father of the modern American musical theater. Born in New York of German heritage, he attended the New York College of Music and began to break into Broadway theater during the first decade of the century by having songs of his interpolated into shows. An Anglophile and friend of P. G. Wodehouse, Kern scored his first success with songs inserted into *The Girl From Utah*, a British import, in 1914, including the ballad "They Didn't Believe Me." Breaking away from the European model of waltz music, Kern proved adept at adapting contemporary dance music into his songs as well as producing subtle, inventive ballads. He collaborated with Guy Bolton and, later, Wodehouse on a series of shows presented at the Princess Theater in the middle of the decade, notably *Very Good Eddie*, and continued to score successes into the '20s.

But Kern really entered the history books with *Show Boat* (1927), the first truly modern American musical, with an integrated story and such memorable songs as "Ol' Man River" and "Can't Help Lovin' Dat Man." Like many of his contemporaries, Kern divided his time between Broadway and Hollywood in the '30s, after sound came to the movies, and his movie hits included the Fred Astaire-Ginger Rogers film *Swing Time*, with such songs as "A Fine Romance" and "The Way You Look Tonight" (with lyrics by Dorothy Fields). Kern worked steadily—he wrote or contributed to 37 shows during his career—and was beginning work on *Annie Get Your Gun* when he died suddenly in 1945. He left behind one of the richest catalogs of show music in history. — *William Ruhlmann*

taining than the subject matter would suggest. The show has Dickens' sad story of poverty and crime, but also one of the strongest scores heard on Broadway in the '60s—"I'd Do Anything," "Be Back Soon," "Oom-Pah-Pah," "As Long As He Needs Me"—in fact, it's one hit after another (no wonder this album reached No. 4 in the charts and went gold). And it has the incomparable Georgia Brown too. — *William Ruhlmann*

Once on This Island / 1990 / RCA ✦✦✦✦
A wonderful Caribbean-influenced musical by Lynn Ahrens and Stephen Flaherty. You can't see the fluid staging of Graciela Daniele on this disc, but the music almost makes up for it. — *William Ruhlmann*

Over Here! / Mar. 1974 / Sony Classical ✦✦✦
The Andrews Sisters returned to active duty as a duo in this musical, which bears a certain similarity to the movies they made during World War II, with a score by Richard M. and Robert B. Sherman (who spent most of their career writing for Walt Disney Movies) that apes the polka and boogie-woogie styles of the Andrews' pop hits of the '40s. Unfortunately, it's all a bit too broad and knowing—"The Good-Time Girl" is a warning against venereal disease, and "Wait for Me, Marlena" is a parody of Marlene Dietrich—and doesn't match the era or the material it simultaneously salutes and satirizes. (Originally released in 1974, *Over Here!* was reissued on CD in 1992.) — *William Ruhlmann*

Pacific Overtures [Original Cast] / Jan. 1976 / RCA ✦✦✦
One of Stephen Sondheim's most ambitious works, treating the relations between Japan and the West and, in retrospect, containing some of Sondheim's best songs, among them "Pretty Lady" and "Someone in a Tree." Mako leads a distinguished Asian-American cast. — *William Ruhlmann*

☆ **Paint Your Wagon** / 1951 / RCA ✦✦✦✦✦
Alan Jay Lerner and Frederick Loewe turn their attention to the American West and come up with a story that anticipates the romantic triangle of *Camelot*. On the way, they present one of their best scores, featuring such songs as "They Call the Wind Maria" and "Wand'rin' Star." James Barton stars. — *William Ruhlmann*

The Pajama Game [Original Cast] / 1954 / CBS ✦✦✦✦
This 1954 comedy about organized labor launched Bob Fosse's Broadway career. The jazzy score by Richard Adler and Jerry Ross includes "Steam Heat," "Hernando's Hideaway," and "Hey There." This recording features John Raitt, one of the era's most popular actor/singers. — *Marjorie Ellen Ruhlmann*

Pal Joey—Froman, Beavers & the Broadway Cast / 1952 / Capitol ✦✦✦✦
One of the biggest hits of the 1951-1952 Broadway season was the revival of *Pal Joey*. Capitol got the rights to the cast album, but couldn't use the stars, who had already recorded the score for Columbia, so they substituted with Jane Froman and Dick Beavers, plus the revival cast. They sing wonderfully, however, and with a score this good, how could they miss? — *William Ruhlmann*

Rodgers and Hammerstein

Composer Richard Rodgers (1902-1979) and lyricist Oscar Hammerstein II (1895-1960) had both had extensive careers in Broadway theater music before they scored their first hit together with *Oklahoma!* in 1943. Rodgers first teamed with Lorenz Hart (1895-1943), with whom he scored a series of Broadway successes that began when the team's song "Manhattan" was interpolated into *The Garrick Gaities of 1925.* Rodgers and Hart's shows included *Present Arms* (1928), *On Your Toes* (1936), *Babes in Arms* (1937), and *Pal Joey* (1940), among others, and they are responsible for a slew of song standards including "You Took Advantage of Me," "Dancing on the Ceiling," "There's a Small Hotel," "Where or When," "The Lady Is a Tramp," "My Funny Valentine," "I Wish I Were in Love Again," "Isn't It Romantic," and "Bewitched, Bothered and Bewildered." But Hart's health declined, and Rodgers had sought out Hammerstein prior to his partner's death from pneumonia.

Hammerstein, scion of a theatrical family (his grandfather owned several theaters and wrote shows and his father and brother were also involved in the theater), attended Columbia University, where he wrote college shows with Rodgers. He was a considerable success in the '20s, collaborating with Jerome Kern on *Show Boat* (1927) and also working with Sigmund Romberg, but he went for a long stretch in the '30s without having a hit.

The Rodgers and Hammerstein team returned to the plot-oriented, socially conscious style of *Show Boat* for a series of landmark musicals in the '40s and '50s, notably *Carousel* (1945), *South Pacific* (1949), *The King and I* (1951), and *The Sound of Music* (1959), among others.

Rodgers, who had the luck to work with two of the most gifted lyricists of the century, continued after Hammerstein's death, though without lucking into a third major partner. He wrote music and lyrics to *No Strings* in 1962, and tried working with Stephen Sondheim on *Do I Hear a Waltz?* (1965), but his later work was less successful. —*William Ruhlmann*

Phantom / 1993 / RCA ✦✦✦
Composer/lyricist Maury Yeston (*Nine*) actually began work on this musical version of Gaston Leroux's novel *The Phantom of the Opera* before it attracted the attention of Andrew Lloyd Webber (and before it fell out of copyright). But Lloyd Webber got to the stage first and had a spectacular success with his show, so the Yeston version is doomed always to be known as "the other *Phantom.*" Nevertheless, it has gotten some productions (though not in New York or London), and this "premiere cast recording" reveals it to be a respectable effort, free of the bombast of Lloyd Webber, if not quite the superior treatment claimed in the liner notes. —*William Ruhlmann*

The Phantom of the Opera [Original Cast] / 1987 / Polydor ✦✦✦✦
This is one of Andrew Lloyd Webber's most highly acclaimed productions. The two-disc set comes with a booklet that has not only the lyrics, but also the dialog and stage directions. Sarah Brightman stars as Christine Daae (the heroine) and Michael Crawford as the Phantom. Also available in a one-disc "highlights" version. —*Tavia Hobart*

Pippin [Original Broadway Cast] / 1972 / Motown ✦✦✦✦
The biggest hit of the 1972-1973 season on Broadway, *Pippin* is perhaps better remembered for Ben Vereen's performance and for the choreography by Bob Fosse than for the songs by Stephen Schwartz. The score is not as good as Schwartz's masterpiece, *Godspell*, but nevertheless has an appealing pop style, especially on such songs as "Corner of the Sky" and "Spread a Little Sunshine." —*William Ruhlmann*

Porgy and Bess / 1977 / RCA Victor ✦✦✦
The Houston Grand Opera mounted a revival of George Gershwin's 1935 musical/opera *Porgy and Bess* in July 1976, and brought it to Broadway in September. In November, RCA Victor recorded a full-length cast album of the show, released as a multi-record set in 1977. In 1983, a one-disc abridgement of highlights was released, and this is the CD version of that album, which was reissued in 1993. Unlike recordings that have taken a pop, jazz, or Broadway approach, this one positions *Porgy and Bess* squarely as an opera, with singing that emphasizes musical embellishment over lyrical expressiveness. As such, it is likely to appeal more to opera fans than to show music fans, but the quality of the Gershwin score, from "Summertime" to "I Loves You, Porgy," is unmistakable. —*William Ruhlmann*

☆ **Porgy and Bess [Original Cast]** / 1989 / MCA ✦✦✦✦✦
According to Alan Jay Lerner, "It was the first of its kind and remains to this day the greatest triumph of the modern musical theater." According to noted African-American theater historian Loften Mitchell, it was "a work generally hailed by Whites and disliked by many Negroes." George Gershwin's 1935 "folk opera," with lyrics by Ira Gershwin and Du Bose Heyward, based on Heyward's novel, introduced "Summertime," "I Got Plenty o' Nuttin,'" and "It Ain't Necessarily So." Even if, as Mitchell says, the characters are stereotypical and the story "not as moving as its source," the musical importance of *Porgy and Bess* is undeniable. —*Marjorie Ellen Ruhlmann*

Premiere Collection I / 1993 / MCA ✦✦✦
This 16-track various artists album, a sequel to the 1988 *Premiere Collection* compilation, features everyone—from Placido Domingo to Barbra Streisand—singing some of the more minor entries in Lloyd Webber's catalog. Streisand gets to do "Memory" from *Cats*, probably the closest thing to a hit here, but the album is more interested in resurrecting material from such duds as *Starlight Express* and *Aspects of Love*. The composer told annotator Baz Bamighoye that the latter show's score "will last longer than *Cats* and *[The] Phantom [of the Opera]*. Don't bet on it. —*William Ruhlmann*

Pump Boys and Dinettes [Original Cast] / CBS ✦✦✦✦
An ensemble piece written and performed by John Foley, Mark Hardwick, Debra Monk, Cass Morgan, John Schimmel, and Jim Wann. This was quickly promoted from supper club to off-Broadway, and then to Broadway in 1982. It's a warm, small-scale, country-style celebration of life among the denizens of the Double Cupp Diner and the filling station across the highway, somewhere in the contemporary American South. —*Marjorie Ellen Ruhlmann*

Purlie / 1970 / RCA ✦✦✦✦
This musical comedy adaptation of Ossie Davis' play about a Black preacher who returns to his southern hometown has a boisterous gospel score written by Gary Geld and Peter Udell and also boasts a cast including Cleavon Little, Melba Moore, Linda Hopkins, and Sherman Hemsley. —*William Ruhlmann*

Return to the Forbidden Planet / 1991 / Rhino ✦✦✦✦
What a jumble of sources! This is the original London cast recording of a musical based on the sci-fi movie *Forbidden Planet* and Shakespeare's *The Tempest*, employing pop songs of the '50s and '60s—On record, it's just a bunch of rock oldies—but it's still fun. —*William Ruhlmann*

The Roar of the Greasepaint [Orig. Broadway Cast] / 1965 / RCA ✦✦✦✦
The Roar of the Greasepaint, the Smell of the Crowd is a sequel to Anthony Newly and Leslie Bricusse's previous show, *Stop the World—I Want to Get Off*, with almost as winning a score, largely sung by Newly and Cyril Ritchard. Featuring "Who Can I Turn To (When Nobody Needs Me)." —*William Ruhlmann*

Runaways / 1978 / CBS ✦✦✦✦
Elizabeth Swados conducted this show about teenage runaways, which features a child cast who turn in outstanding performances on some terrific pop-rock material. It's the kind of thing Broadway needs more of. —*William Ruhlmann*

Sarafina! / 1987 / Shanachie ✦✦✦
An abbreviated version of the Mbongeni Ngema musical about South African schoolchildren. It was recorded in South Africa before the show's arrival in New York. Cheaply made, but stirring. —*William Ruhlmann*

Sarafina! / 1988 / RCA ✦✦✦
This is the more complete Broadway cast version of this show, which by November 1988 had turned into the most moving evening in a Broadway theater. Ngema's music captures the newly popular mbaqanga sound of the homelands, and the story paints apartheid in its most glaring colors. —*William Ruhlmann*

She Loves Me [Original Broadway Cast] / 1976 / Polydor ✦✦✦
Sheldon Harnick and Jerry Bock's musical version of *The Shop Around the Corner* was not a stage success (unlike their *Fiddler on the Roof* the following year), but the score has been well remembered in this near-complete recording (originally on two LPs), especially for Barbara Cook's performance. —*William Ruhlmann*

Show Boat [Original Cast] / 1962 / CBS ✦✦✦
Non-stage studio recording featuring John Raitt, Barbara Cook, William Warfield, Anita Darian, Fay De Witt, Louise Parker, and the Merrill Staton Choir, conducted by Franz Allers. Cook is especially impressive (she went on to a stage revival of the show four years later). —*William Ruhlmann*

Show Boat [London Cast] / 1972 / Stanyon ✦✦✦
This well-recorded revival stars Cleo Laine. —*William Ruhlmann*

☆ **Side by Side by Sondheim [Original London Cast]** / 1976 / RCA ✦✦✦✦✦
A two-disc London cast recording of a revue culled from songs written by Stephen Sondheim for such musicals as *A Funny Thing Happened on*

the Way to the Forum, Company, A Little Night Music, Follies, Anyone Can Whistle, Pacific Overtures, Do I Hear a Waltz?, West Side Story, and Gypsy, and more obscure works such as "Evening Primrose" (a TV show), The 7 Percent Solution, and The Mad Show. In anthology and presented starkly, the songs are (if possible) even more impressive than when heard in the shows for which they were written. If there was any doubt that Stephen Sondheim is the greatest talent writing contemporary musicals, this show erased it. — William Ruhlmann

Silk Stockings [Original Broadway Cast] / 1955 / RCA ✦✦✦

Cole Porter based this charming musical on the movie Ninotchka, about a Russian official tempted by the romantic and capitalistic elements of Paris. Hildegarde Neff inhabits the Greta Garbo role, while Don Ameche plays Melvyn Douglas' film part. It isn't one of the great Porter scores, but with lyrics like the ones in "Siberia" and "It's a Chemical Reaction, That's All," it is full of Porter's typical wit. — William Ruhlmann

Sondheim—Putting It Together / 1993 / RCA ✦✦✦

Nominally, this is a sequel to the anthology show Side By Side By Sondheim, which selected some of the composer's songs for individual performance by a small cast in a revue format. In practice, it's closer to Marry Me a Little, which attempted to build a new book show out of existing Sondheim songs. The five characters in Putting It Together are upper-class types having a dinner party, with songs from such Sondheim shows as Company, Follies, and Merrily We Roll Along, which treated such people prominently, interpolated into the proceedings. The songs are terrific, of course, and the cast is talented; this off-Broadway production marked Julie Andrews' return to the theater for the first time in decades. But the story doesn't really work, and the treatment of the material is sometimes odd, as when Christopher Durang finds himself singing "I [You] Can Drive a Person Crazy," originally written for a female trio in Company. Nevertheless, when Andrews takes on "Getting Married Today," it's easy to forgive all. — William Ruhlmann

Sondheim: A Celebration at Carnegie Hall / 1993 / RCA Victor ✦✦✦

This two-CD set is the recording of a benefit concert for Carnegie Hall performed at the hall on June 10, 1992 and featuring the American Theatre Orchestra, conducted by Paul Gemignani, supporting a variety of soloists doing songs written by Stephen Sondheim for Broadway musicals and films. As several anthologies of Sondheim's work and tributes to him have been recorded in the past, the organizers weren't able to find much new in the composer's catalog, and they have settled for sometimes gimmicky arrangements of his familiar songs. Nevertheless, many of the performances are strong, and the stars are many: Glenn Close ("Send in the Clowns"), Madeline Kahn ("I'm Not Getting Married Today"), Patti Lupone ("Being Alive"), Liza Minnelli (the sole new song, "Water Under the Bridge"), and Bernadette Peters ("Not a Day Goes By") are stand-outs, but the cream of Broadway is represented. Also, it's worth noting that, while the album may be a disappointment to diehard Sondheim fans, newcomers not familiar with this material may well be bowled over by its quality. Sondheim is Broadway's top contemporary composer, and this album demonstrates that as well as any. (Also available as a video, which actually works better, given that some of the numbers have strong visual elements.) — William Ruhlmann

Sondheim: a Musical Tribute / 1973 / RCA ✦✦✦

A two-disc recording of a special benefit show held March 11, 1973, featuring many of the original performers from Stephen Sondheim musicals, reprising their performances of his songs. Thus, the album is a kind of "Sondheim's Greatest Hits," with the added excitement of being a one-time event. Originally issued as a two-LP set by Warner in 1973, it was reissued by RCA on CD/cassette with previously unreleased tracks. — William Ruhlmann

The Sound of Music [Original Cast] / Nov. 1959 / CBS ✦✦✦✦

The Sound of Music was a huge hit in 1959 for Rodgers and Hammerstein, and a highlight in the remarkable career of Mary Martin. The book by Howard Lindsay and Russel Crouse was based on Maria von Trapp's autobiography. It's a rather cloying story that involves nuns, Nazis, and seven cute kids, but it has pleased audiences for years. The title song, "Climb Every Mountain," "My Favorite Things," "Do-Re-Mi," "Sixteen Going on Seventeen," and "Edelweiss" all entered the culture through this score. The cast album features Theodore Bikel in the romantic lead, which unfortunately became a non-singing role in the subsequent film. — Marjorie Ellen Ruhlmann

South Pacific / 1986 / CBS ✦✦✦

A studio recording featuring a combination of opera singers (Kiri Te Kanawa, Jose Carreras), jazz singers (Sarah Vaughan), and Broadway singers (Mandy Patinkin), with the London Symphony Orchestra, directed by Jonathan Tunick. — William Ruhlmann

☆ South Pacific [Original Cast] / CBS ✦✦✦✦✦

Adapted from James A. Michener's Tales of the South Pacific and starring Mary Martin and opera star Ezio Pinza, with music and lyrics by Rodgers and Hammerstein, this show enjoyed the largest advance ticket sale ever recorded on Broadway when it opened in 1949. The book inter-

Stephen Sondheim

According to most critics and theater historians, Stephen Sondheim (b. 1930) stands among Broadway show composers and lyricists not only as the greatest of his generation but as the only great one of his generation. There may be many reasons why Broadway has failed to produce consistently great writers to follow the Rodgers and Hammersteins and Lerner and Loewes of the '40s and '50s, but the fact remains that, though he operates without serious competition, Sondheim clearly ranks with such masters, as well as with the Jerome Kerns and Irving Berlins of an even earlier generation.

Sondheim became a mentor of Hammerstein's after befriending the lyricist's son in school, but he got his first big break when he was hired to write lyrics to Leonard Bernstein's score for West Side Story (1957), which turned out to be one of the biggest hits and most memorable works of its time. This led to a lot of lyric-writing work, though Sondheim always wanted to write music as well. Nevertheless, he worked with Jule Styne on Gypsy (1959), another enormous hit, and would later agree to do the same with Richard Rodgers for the unsuccessful Do I Hear a Waltz? (1965).

Before that, however, Sondheim scored his first success as composer and lyricist with A Funny Thing Happened on the Way to the Forum (1962). It was his last hit until Company (1970), a show about contemporary life and mores that did much to revolutionize the Broadway musical and, as Hammerstein's '50s shows had, move it more toward serious and exotic subjects. Since that time, Sondheim's shows have been amazingly daring in terms of subject matter, with unusual musical ideas and stunningly original lyrics. But they have not always been big hits and have marked a time in the theater when Broadway show music became a marginalized art form in terms of popular culture.

Nevertheless, Sondheim's shows of the '70s and '80s are benchmarks of the genre: Follies (1971) brought together aging follies girls for a look at middle-aged American life; A Little Night Music (1973) was based on Ingmar Bergman's film Smiles of a Summer Night and contains Sondheim's sole hit song, "Send in the Clowns"; Pacific Overtures (1976) ambitiously took on the subject of Japanese-American relations; Sweeney Todd (1979) was an operetta based on the British grand guignol tale of a murderous barber; Sunday in the Park with George (1984) was a biography of impressionist painter Georges Seurat; Into the Woods (1987) wove together children's fairy tales with the theories of psychologist Bruno Bettelheim, and Assassins (1991), a short piece about presidential killers. In recent years, Sondheim has turned toward films; he wrote a score for Stavinsky in the '70s, and wrote songs for Madonna in Dick Tracy in 1990. —William Ruhlmann

twines two wartime love stories complicated by American prejudices against Asians. The brilliant score includes "A Cockeyed Optimist," "Some Enchanted Evening," "There Is Nothin' Like a Dame," "I'm Gonna Wash That Man Right Outa My Hair," and "Younger Than Springtime." —Marjorie Ellen Ruhlmann

Starting Here, Starting Now / 1977 / RCA ✦✦✦✦

This celebrated off-Broadway revue serves as a retrospective of the work of Richard Maltby, Jr. and David Shire, a songwriting team that has done just about everything except write a successful Broadway musical. Contemporary mores are examined in a series of songs including the title tune and "What About Today," both previously recorded by Barbra Streisand. — William Ruhlmann

A Stephen Sondheim Evening / 1983 / RCA Victor ✦✦✦✦

Stephen Sondheim must be one of the most anthologized Broadway composers, his shows having been cannibalized into several revues, reconceived musicals, and concert performances. This is a particularly good one. It is a concert featuring a cast of eight, among them Cris Groenendaal, Bob Gunton, George Hearn, and Angela Lansbury, recorded in 1983 and featuring songs written for shows ranging from Sondheim's unproduced first effort, Saturday Night, to what was then his latest, Merrily We Roll Along. Particularly notable are the songs cut from shows, such as "There's Something About a War" from A Funny Thing Happened on the Way to the Forum. The composer himself turns up toward the end to play piano for Lansbury on "Send in the Clowns" and help sing "Old Friends." (The original two-LP set, released in 1983 contained 21 selections. When the album was released on CD in 1994, two songs, "Fear No More" and "You're Gonna Love Tomorrow" were cut to keep the time down to the limits of one CD.) — *William Ruhlmann*

Stop the World, I Want to Get Off! [Original Cast] / 1962 / Polydor
♦♦♦♦
Stop the World, I Want to Get Off!, Anthony Newley and Leslie Bricusse's innovative show, holds up very well after 30 years, due as much to the score as to Newley's singing on such standards as "Gonna Build a Mountain" and "What Kind of Fool Am I?" — *William Ruhlmann*

Sunday in the Park with George [Original Cast] / 1984 / RCA ♦♦♦♦
Stephen Sondheim's musical, imaginatively based on the life of French painter Georges Seurat, is a meditation on life and the creative process, brilliantly realized by Mandy Patinkin and Bernadette Peters. — *William Ruhlmann*

☆ **Sweeney Todd [Original Cast]** / 1979 / RCA ♦♦♦♦♦
A complete, two-disc recording of Stephen Sondheim's *grand guignol* operetta about a barber who cuts things close. This show is a masterpiece full of stirring music and witty, intricate lyrics, lustily delivered by a cast led by Angela Lansbury and Len Cariou. Don't confuse this score with a single-disc "highlights" album also in print. — *William Ruhlmann*

Sweet Charity [Broadway Cast] / 1966 / CBS ♦♦♦♦
Gwen Verdon is the standout performer in this recording of the Cy Coleman/Dorothy Fields score, but consider that the songs she has to sing include "Big Spender," "If My Friends Could See Me Now," and "Where Am I Going?" — *William Ruhlmann*

Take Me Along / Oct. 1959 / RCA ♦♦♦
Based on playwright Eugene O'Neill's sole comedy, *Ah, Wilderness,* the musical *Take Me Along* was mounted on Broadway in 1959 as a vehicle for TV star Jackie Gleason. It ran for a little over a year and lost money, though it has gone into the black since. Robert Merrill's score is only functional, though it does provide showcases for Gleason on such songs as "Single Kid" and "I Get Embarrassed" (a duet with Eileen Herlie). Walter Pidgeon also makes a strong impression and Robert Morse took a big step to stardom playing the juvenile and singing "I Would Die" with Susan Luckey. Nevertheless, *Take Me Along* never competes with the great musicals of the era. — *William Ruhlmann*

They're Playing Our Song [Original Cast] / 1979 / Casablanca ♦♦♦♦
A successful musical with a book by Neil Simon and songs by Marvin Hamlisch and Carole Bayer Sager. It concerns the on-again, off-again relationship between a composer and lyricist. *They're Playing Our Song* has a pop music score characteristic of its time, even to the point of the disco style of some of its songs. Robert Klein and Lucie Arnaz are the principals. — *William Ruhlmann*

☆ **The Threepenny Opera [Original Cast]** / 1954 / Polydor ♦♦♦♦♦
Marc Blitzstein's translation of the Kurt Weill/Bertolt Brecht musical ran for six years off-Broadway and established the work as a major theater piece in the US. This excellent recording not only presents Blitzstein's terrific versions of the songs but also a cast led by Jo Sullivan, Beatrice Arthur, and Lotte Lenya. — *William Ruhlmann*

Unsinkable Molly Brown [Broadway Cast] / 1960 / Capitol ♦♦♦
Meredith Willson's follow-up to *The Music Man,* about a nouveau riche Colorado mine owner's wife who survives the sinking of the *Titanic,* is not quite as impressive as its predecessor, but the irrepressible Tammy Grimes does much to make it a success on record. — *William Ruhlmann*

Weird Romance: Two One-Act Musicals ... / 1993 / Columbia ♦♦♦
Weird Romance: Two One-Act Musicals of Speculative Fiction is the cast album for an off-Broadway production of a couple of mini-shows with music by Alan Menken (who has composed the Disney film musicals *The Little Mermaid, Beauty and the Beast,* and *Aladdin*) and new lyrical collaborator David Spencer, plus book writer Alan Brennert. Both shows are love stories set in science fiction scenarios (one was filmed as a "Twilight Zone" episode). The first, "The Girl Who Was Plugged In" attempts

social criticism in a tale of mechanical transubstantiation, and largely fails; but the second, "Her Pilgrim Soul," which concerns holograms and past lives and is played sincerely, works well and contains two first-rate songs: "Need to Know," a science nerd's explanation of his life; and "A Man," a timely dissection of the male gender by a couple of knowing women. — *William Ruhlmann*

West Side Story / 1985 / Deutsche Grammophon ♦♦♦
Leonard Bernstein conducts his own score on this studio recording, which features opera singers Kiri Te Kanawa and Jose Carreras. The singers somewhat overwhelm the material (and it's more than a little odd that the only person with a Spanish accent is Carreras, who plays Tony, the American Romeo), but the music is magnificent. — *William Ruhlmann*

☆ **West Side Story [Original Cast]** / CBS ♦♦♦♦♦
A fabulous collaboration of Jerome Robbins (concept, direction, choreography), Arthur Laurents (book), Leonard Bernstein (music), and Stephen Sondheim (lyrics). This modern retelling of the *Romeo and Juliet* story debuted on Broadway in 1957. Larry Kert and Carol Lawrence sing the leads magnificently. Bernstein's instrumental ballet music for this show is probably as familiar as its many standout songs: "Maria," "Tonight," "I Feel Pretty," and "Somewhere," among others. — *Marjorie Ellen Ruhlmann*

The Who's Tommy / 1993 / RCA Victor ♦♦♦
The Broadway cast album of *Tommy* (called *The Who's Tommy* presumably to alert Who fans that this really is the stage version of the group's 1969 "rock opera" and not some unrelated *Tommy*) is the best recording of Peter Townshend's song cycle since the Who did the original. Beatles producer George Martin was in the recording booth, and a stellar cast led by Michael Cerveris sings fervently. That's the good news. The bad news is that Townshend has radically re-thought his ideas in 24 years, and rewritten nine songs to reflect his many changes of heart. Artists rarely improve their work by changing it years later, though they frequently succumb to the temptation, and anyone familiar with the original who tries to sing along to this album is in for a rude surprise. The Broadway *Tommy* has been secularized and domesticated; no longer a messiah, he now longs for normality. It's too bad that Townshend didn't have the wisdom to bring *Tommy* to the stage intact. (*The Who's Tommy* tied for the 1993 Tony Award for Best Score.) — *William Ruhlmann*

The Will Rogers Follies [Original Cast] / 1991 / CBS ♦♦♦♦
This original Broadway cast recording of the musical by Cy Coleman, Betty Comden, and Adolph Green (book by Peter Stone), tells the story of the humorist and Ziegfeld Follies star—"a life in revue." Directed and choreographed by Tommy Tune, it won the 1991 Tony Award for Best Musical. On disc, the show's charm comes across, especially when star Keith Carradine is before a microphone. — *William Ruhlmann*

Wonderful Town [Original Broadway Cast] / 1953 / MCA ♦♦♦♦
Leonard Bernstein brings a typical sense of invention and musical ambition to this score, and Betty Comden and Adolph Green their usual street-smart New York lyrics, for a show based on the play *My Sister Eileen* about two siblings struggling in Greenwich Village in the '30s. Rosalind Russell leads a strong cast. — *William Ruhlmann*

☆ **Words and Music** / CBS ♦♦♦♦♦
An all-star (or nearly so) tribute to Rodgers and Hart, and worthwhile for the Judy Garland and Mel Torme numbers. — *Bruce Eder*

Zorba [Original Broadway Cast] / 1968 / Capitol ♦♦♦♦
John Kander and Fred Ebb's score to this musical adaptation of *Zorba the Greek* was less accomplished than their last show, *Cabaret,* and clearly under the influence of *Fiddler on the Roof,* but it is performed in a spirited manner by a cast led by Herschel Bernardi and Maria Karnilova. — *William Ruhlmann*

CHRISTMAS

In 1942, Irving Berlin wrote "White Christmas" for the movie *Holiday Inn*, and while not an overnight success, once the GIs overseas besieged the Armed Forces Radio with requests for this song (sung by Bing Crosby), the top-selling Christmas single of all time was also on its way to becoming the most recorded song of all time. Berlin collected an Academy Award for "Best Song" and the market for Christmas music was now well-established.

One of the great things about Christmas records: there's something for everyone, be it blues, jazz, country, pop, R&B, rock 'n' roll, novelty, or even reggae! While there are probably more sacred Christmas recordings, the emphasis in this chapter is on the secular releases. There may have been more artists recording holiday tunes in the '50s and '60s than in the present, but now we see artists getting together to record Yule classics for worthwhile causes, such as the two A&M CDs, *A Very Special Christmas*, for the Special Olympics. Record labels also continue to release seasonal compilations of artists from their rosters, with mixed results. This idea was first generated (and best executed) by Phil Spector with his 1963 paragon, *A Christmas Gift for You from Phil Spector*. Even though the 45 has gone the way of the 8-track, searching the used record stores, the flea markets, the yard sales, and whatever way one hunts down the elusive Christmas 45, 78 or LP from the past can bring lots of pleasure (I'm especially proud of my 78 of Art Carney doing a beatnik version of "'Twas the Night Before Christmas"). Rhino Records has done the most commendable job of reissuing classic "Cool Yule" 45s on various compilations, and more labels seem ready to enter the Christmas reissue marketplace. Another great way to find buried treasures (there's probably a longer list of artists who haven't recorded a Yule tune than of those who have) is to trade tapes with people who have made it an annual tradition to make a new holiday tape to send to friends and fellow collectors as a combination Christmas card/gift; over the years, I have acquired rarities from all over the world on tape.

With so many holiday treats to choose from, keep in mind that compilations of various artists are often the best way to go, as many artists could not maintain a full album's worth of high-quality material. Here, then, in alphabetical order, are my recommended "Twelve CDs of Christmas." —*Decibel Dennis MacDonald*

Charles Brown: *Please Come Home for Christmas* / King (1961)
James Brown: *Santa's Got a Brand New Bag* / Rhino (1966-70)
Elvis Presley: *Elvis' Christmas Album* / RCA (1957)
Ventures: *The Ventures' Christmas Album* / EMI (1965)
Various: *A Christmas Gift for You from Phil Spector* / ABKCO (1963)
Various: *The Best of Cool Yule* / Rhino (1988)
Various: *Christmas Kisses: Christmas Classics from Capitol's Early Years* (1990)
Various: *Christmas Party with Eddie G.* / Sony (1990)
Various: *Hipster's Holiday: Vocal Jazz and R&B Classics* / Rhino (1989)
Various: *Merry Christmas Baby* / Hollywood
Various: *Santa Claus Blues* / Jass (1988)
Various: *Soul Christmas* / Atlantic (1991)

Johnny Adams

Christmas in New Orleans / 1988 / ACE ◆◆◆
A disappointing effort from "The Tan Canary" who is in fine voice but weighed down with poor arrangements. Adams also stays in control too much, rarely letting that tenor voice take flight. —*Decibel Dennis MacDonald*

Air Supply

☆ **The Christmas Album** / 1987 / Arista ◆◆◆◆◆
The adult-contemporary sounds of the season, from light-rock radio's favorite Australian group. —*David A. Milberg*

Alabama

☆ **Alabama Christmas** / RCA ◆◆◆◆◆
A must for your C&W Christmas, it contains the classic "Christmas in Dixie." —*David A. Milberg*

Herb Alpert & The Tijuana Brass

Christmas Album / 1968 / A&M ◆◆◆◆
A million-seller from 1968. This is an essential part of any Christmas collection, especially their hit version of "The Christmas Song." —*David A. Milberg*

Julie Andrews with Andre Previn

☆ **Christmas Treasure** / 1968 / RCA ◆◆◆◆◆
Orchestra with Andre Previn arrangements that feature Andrews. —*AMG*

Eddy Arnold

Christmas with Eddy Arnold / 1961 / RCA ◆◆◆
This is the immortal "Tennessee Plowboy's" classic Christmas album. First released in 1962, it still sounds great today. —*David A. Milberg*

Joan Baez

☆ **Noel** / 1966 / Vanguard ◆◆◆◆◆
An album of stately beauty as Baez's pure, soaring soprano is accompanied by a consort of recorders and viols, lute, harpsichord, baroque organ, winds, strings, and percussion. Her rendition of the "Coventry Carol" is as stirring as any recorded version I've heard, and Baez pours her heart into "The Carol of the Birds." Considering Baez's politics, one would never know she recorded this album in the Vietnam War era. It's timeless. —*Decibel Dennis MacDonald*

The Beach Boys

The Beach Boys' Christmas Album / Oct. 1964 / Capitol ◆◆◆
What more can you say about this all-time classic? A million-seller from 1964, featuring "Little Saint Nick" and "Man with All the Toys." —*David A. Milberg*

Harry Belafonte

☆ **To Wish You a Merry Christmas** / 1962 / RCA ◆◆◆◆◆
A subdued setting for Belafonte as he is backed by an orchestra and chorus throughout. Traditional fare, including sacred and secular, with two medleys, along with the calypso feel of "Mary's Boy Child" and "A Star in the East." Includes a sung version of Henry Wadsworth Longfellow's "I Heard the Bells on Christmas Day." —*Decibel Dennis MacDonald*

Tony Bennett

☆ **Snowfall: The Tony Bennett Christmas Album** / 1968 / CBS ◆◆◆◆◆
Tony Bennett at his peak in 1968, adding an uncommon style to the common standards of the day. —*David A. Milberg*

David Benoit

☆ **Christmastime** / Oct. 31, 1991 / Blue Moon ◆◆◆◆◆
Pleasant piano stylings. Perfect for meetings under the mistletoe. —*David A. Milberg*

Booker T. & the MGs

In the Christmas Spirit / Oct. 1966 / Atlantic ♦♦♦
Booker T. and the MG's find the groove to come up with funky instrumentals of Yule classics "Jingle Bells," "Silver Bells," and the percolatin' "We Wish You a Merry Christmas." Steve Cropper makes his guitar sing on the down 'n' bluesy "Merry Christmas Baby." *—Decibel Dennis MacDonald*

Boston Camerata
with the Boston Shawm and Sackbut Ensemble

☆ **Noel, Noel! (Noels Francais/French Christmas Music (1200–1600)** / Erato ♦♦♦♦♦
Joel Cohen conducts medieval/renaissance French Christmas music with the Boston Shawm and Sackbut Ensemble. Very fine traditional music. *—Michael Erlewine*

Liona Boyd

☆ **A Guitar for Christmas** / 1989 / CBS ♦♦♦♦♦
Classical guitarist extraordinaire manages to shine once in a while, even when the Muzak production is smothering her in a morass of holiday Velveeta—Richard Clayderman for classical guitar music. *—Rick Clark*

Brave Combo

☆ **It's Christmas, Man!** / 1991 / Rounder ♦♦♦♦♦
Originally recorded for the Japanese market (!), this Denton, TX, "polka band" (they play many styles beyond polka) have recorded one of the funnest, albeit goofiest, seasonal delights you'll ever hear. "O, Christmas Tree" is done as a samba, "The Christmas Song" is performed in the ska style, while "Feliz Navidad" makes your feet want to dance to the cumbia. The traditional "Hanukkah, Oh Hannukah" is turned into a hora and "The Little Drummer Boy" into a wild guaguanco, whatever that is. Brave Combo also add several original songs to the Christmas canon, including the cha cha "It's Christmas," but the CD's high point is the frenzied polka, "Must Be Santa." Highly recommended fun, and danceable too! *—Decibel Dennis MacDonald*

Jack Brokensha with Lenore Paxton

☆ **Holiday Inventions** / 1968 / US Steel ♦♦♦♦♦
One side has vibist Brokensha with pianist Bess Bonnier; other has pianist Paxton and vocalist Robert Chambers. Crystalline chamber Christmas jazz. The album was subsidized by US Steel. *—Michael G. Nastos*

Garth Brooks

Beyond the Season / Aug. 17, 1992 / Liberty ♦♦♦♦
One of the most successful Christmas albums ever, *Beyond the Season* is a varied collection for a country star, even one as "progressive" as Brooks. The tunes range from a gospel version of "Go Tell It on the Mountain" to a song-play where Brooks' songwriters take the roles of animals in the manger. It's about half traditional and half original, with Brooks cowriting the hardest rocking tune, "The Old Man's Back in Town." *—Brian Mansfield*

Charles Brown

★ **Please Come Home for Christmas** / Deluxe ♦♦♦♦♦
These dozen tracks from rhythm & blues singer/pianist Charles Brown are among the most essential Yule tunes ever recorded, including his original, oft-covered "Please Come Home for Christmas" and "Merry Christmas, Baby." Brown's smoother-than-aged-brandy voice is perfectly suited to an intimate evening at home with that special someone beneath the mistletoe. *—Decibel Dennis MacDonald*

James Brown

★ **Santa's Got a Brand New Bag** / 1988 / Rhino ♦♦♦♦♦
Compiled from three Christmas LPs and various singles released by the "Santa of Soul" between 1966-1970, this 16-track collection includes one of JB's most over-the-top screamfests on "Let's Make Christmas Mean Something This Year," while he gets loose and funky with "Soulful Christmas." Others have tried, but nobody can beat the Godfather on his ballad "Sweet Little Baby Boy," and nobody but the "man who put the 'wet' in sweat" can pull off "Santa Claus Go Straight to the Ghetto." This is as essential as it gets. *—Decibel Dennis MacDonald*

Kenny Burrell

☆ **Have Yourself a Soulful Little Christmas** / Oct. 1966 / Cadet ♦♦♦♦♦
Have Yourself a Soulful Little Christmas is recently back in print after its original release on Cadet Records in 1966. Pensive, meditative, precise playing. A must-have, with a definitive jazz hit version of "Little Drummer Boy." *—David A. Milberg & Michael G. Nastos*

The California Raisins

☆ **Christmas with the California Raisins** / Priority ♦♦♦♦♦
From their 1988 claymation CBS-TV special. The cut "Hark" is especially worth hearing. *—David A. Milberg*

The Cambridge Singers

☆ **Christmas Night—Carols of the Nativity** / Collegium ♦♦♦♦♦
The lovely Cambridge Singers as conducted by John Rutter—one of the most brilliant living composers. If you yearn for an elegant Christmas album in the traditional style, this is it. Includes 22 carols. *—Michael Erlewine*

Glen Campbell

☆ **Merry Christmas** / Aug. 19, 1991 / Liberty ♦♦♦♦♦
A great combination of easy-listening and C&W treatments of Christmas standards. *—David A. Milberg*

Larry Carlton

☆ **Christmas at My House** / MCA ♦♦♦♦♦
One of the greatest jazz/rock guitarists of the '80s & '90s provides this classic Christmas guitar album. *—David A. Milberg*

The Carpenters

Christmas Portrait / 1978 / A&M ♦♦♦♦
An essential album for your fireside Christmas. It sold a million in 1978 and contains the classics "Merry Christmas, Darling" and "Have Yourself a Merry Little Christmas." *—David A. Milberg*

An Old Fashioned Christmas / 1978 / A&M ♦♦♦♦
Their second Christmas album. More of the soft sounds of the season, made for mistletoe and someone you love. *—David A. Milberg*

Ray Charles

Spirit of Christmas / 1987 / Columbia ♦♦♦♦
Ray's capable of better than this, but it ain't half bad, either. Freddie Hubbard knocks off a fine solo during the hard-swinging break on "What Child Is This" and Ray almost gets down on "Santa Claus Is Coming to Town." "All I Want for Christmas" is another highlight. The drawback is that for every good cut, there's a throwaway track. But some Ray is a lot better than no Ray at all. *—Rick Clark*

The Chipmunks

Christmas with the Chipmunks / 1962 / EMI America ♦♦♦
Their first Christmas album, with the classic "Chipmunk Song." Great for kids of all ages. *—David A. Milberg*

Christmas Jug Band

Mistletoe Jam / Relix ♦♦♦
Led by multi-instrumentalist/vocalist Dan Hicks, the CJB are best heard in small doses (unless, of course, you truly enjoy the novelty of jug bands). "Somebody Stole My Santa Claus Suit" is the highlight (and can also be found on Rhino's *Bummed Out Christmas* collection). *—Decibel Dennis MacDonald*

Cincinnati Pops Orchestra/Erich Kunzel

☆ **Christmas with the Pops** / Telarc ♦♦♦♦♦
Trim your tree with the full orchestral delights of holiday standards with a true maestro. *—David A. Milberg*

Nat King Cole

☆ **The Christmas Song** / Oct. 27, 1986 / Capitol ♦♦♦♦♦
Cole recorded the definitive version of "The Christmas Song" in 1946, and while this 1960 re-recording is sublime, it's worth seeking out the original. Although there is a heavy-handed use of orchestras and choruses on this record, Cole rises above the dreck with stellar versions of "Adeste Fidelis," "O Holy Night," and more. *—Decibel Dennis MacDonald*

☆ **Cole, Christmas, & Kids** / Sep. 10, 1990 / Capitol ♦♦♦♦♦
More Christmas magic with touching tunes like "The Little Boy that Santa Forgot." *—David A. Milberg*

Mitzie Collins with Roxanne Ziegler
& Glennda Dove

☆ **Nowell** / Sampler ♦♦♦♦♦
Hammer dulcimer, with harp and flute accompaniment. Lesser-known but lovely works done in a creative and bright way. *—Michael Erlewine*

Music Map
Christmas

MEDIEVAL FOLK MUSIC
YULETIDE SONGS

'20s BLUES

'30s JAZZ/BIG BAND

'40s CROONERS & BIG BANDS

Bing Crosby's
"White Christmas"

COUNTRY & WESTERN

Louvin Brothers
Eddy Arnold
Ernest Tubb
Gene Autry

Les Brown   Glenn Miller
Harry James   Guy Lombardo
Frank Sinatra   Andrews Sisters

JAZZ

Louis Armstrong
Miles Davis
Jimmy Smith Collections

'50s POP/NOVELTY

Perry Como
Tony Bennett
Nat King Cole
Spike Jones

ROCK/POP/NOVELTY

Elvis Presley
James Brown
New Kids On The Block
California Raisins

EASY LISTENING

Andy Williams
Johnny Mathis
John Denver

Perry Como

★ **Christmas Album** / 1968 / RCA ✦✦✦✦
A million-seller with an updated version of his 1950 classic "There's No Christmas Like a Home Christmas." —*David A. Milberg*

☆**I Wish It Could Be Christmas Forever** / 1982 / RCA ✦✦✦✦
His fans will delight in this Christmas present. His most recent recording of the sounds of the season. —*David A. Milberg*

Ray Conniff

☆**Christmas Album** / 1962 / CBS ✦✦✦✦
This album, also known as *Merry Christmas to All*, was a million-seller in 1962 and a top-seller for ten years. A good '60s sound-of-the-season timepiece. —*David A. Milberg*

★ **We Wish You a Merry Christmas** / 1962 / Columbia ✦✦✦✦
This is a million-selling album, and includes his hit version of "Silver Bells." —*David A. Milberg*

☆**Here We Come A-Caroling** / Columbia ✦✦✦✦
More classics with the Conniff touch, from 1965. His second-most-popular Christmas album collection. —*David A. Milberg*

Floyd Cramer

☆**We Wish You a Merry Christmas** / RCA ✦✦✦✦
Nashville's most famous pianist recorded and released this in 1967. Great C&W easy-listening. —*David A. Milberg*

Bing Crosby

☆ **Bing Crosby's Christmas Classics** / 1962 / Capitol ✦✦✦✦
This is a reissue of Crosby's 1962 album *I Wish You a Merry Christmas*. Above-standard renditions of famous Christmas standards. —*David A. Milberg*

Christmas Songs / 1990 / Vintage Jazz ✦✦✦
This 75-minute CD is in four parts, including the complete Kraft Music Hall broadcast of December 21, 1944, in which Crosby performs "Adeste Fidelis" and "Jingle Bells"; other performers are included. There are selections from various broadcasts, 1942-46, and a Christmas Eve 1944 Philco Radio Hall of Fame broadcast with the Paul Whiteman Orchestra,

including a performance of "White Christmas." The CD concludes with excerpts from a Christmas 1946 broadcast, including a duet with Skitch Henderson on "The Christmas Song." —*Decibel Dennis MacDonald*

Merry Christmas / MCA ✦✦✦✦
"Der Bingle" in two distinctly different moods: from the solemnity of "Silent Night" and "Adeste Fidelis" (sung in English and Latin) to the playfulness ("gonna have a lotta fun") on "Jingle Bells," with the Andrews Sisters providing some smiles with their "Ji-ji-jingle" vocals. They duet on two more, including "Mele Kalikimaka." Also includes a remake of "White Christmas." —*Decibel Dennis MacDonald*

★ **Bing Crosby Sings Christmas Songs** / MCA ✦✦✦✦
Includes his definitive "White Christmas." —*Michael Erlewine*

Original White Christmas / **Unreleased Studio Masters from Holiday Inn and Blue** / Vintage Jazz Classics ✦✦✦
The musical *Holiday Inn* garnered Irving Berlin an Academy Award for Best Song, "White Christmas." The film version is on this CD, transferred from a radio transcription disc, as "Der Bingle" duets with Marjorie Reynolds on this and a medley of "Happy Holiday/ Let's Start the New Year Right." —*Decibel Dennis MacDonald*

Bobby Darin

25th Day of December / 1961 / Atco ✦✦✦
Give Darin credit for choosing mostly American spirituals for this release, but he would have fallen flat had he not been backed by the Bobby Scott Chorale on "Go Tell It on the Mountain," "Jehovah Hallelujah," and other rousing numbers. On the hymns, however, Darin is lost in syrupy arrangements. —*Decibel Dennis MacDonald*

Danny Davis & The Nashville Brass

Christmas with Danny Davis & the Nashville Brass / RCA ✦✦✦
This album was a Christmas hit in 1970, and the smooth C&W stylings of Christmas standards still sound great after 20 years. —*David A. Milberg*

Doris Day

☆**Christmas Album** / 1964 / CBS ✦✦✦✦
The Doris Day sound of the '60s. Includes a notable new (at that time) Christmas number, "Christmas Present." —*David A. Milberg*

John Denver

Rocky Mountain Christmas / 1975 / RCA ✦✦✦✦
This million-seller is a must! It contains the classics "Aspen Glow" and "Christmas for Cowboys." —*David A. Milberg*

A Christmas Together with the Muppets / 1979 / RCA ✦✦✦
John Denver and the Muppets. The most fun since David Seville & the Chipmunks. Moving renditions of "Have Yourself a Merry Little Christmas" and "We Wish You a Merry Christmas." —*David A. Milberg*

Placido Domingo

☆ **Christmas with Placido Domingo** / 1984 / CBS ✦✦✦✦✦
A perennial favorite. Christmas standards in the great tradition of legendary operatic tenors. —*David A. Milberg*

Fats Domino

Christmas Is a Special Day / Nov. 16, 1993 / The Right Stuff ✦✦✦
It's amazing that 40-plus years after recording "The Fat Man," Fats Domino's voice is virtually unchanged. Hearing that lazy N'awlins drawl on his original "I Told Santa Claus" and "Christmas Is a Special Day" is a delight *despite* the electronic keyboards and rhythm machine used on the latter. Fats romps through other seasonal favorites, "Jingle Bells," "Silver Bells," and "Blue Christmas" among them. Once you get past the rhythm machine (three drummers are credited ?!?), you canenjoy the return of the "Fat Man." —*Decibel Dennis MacDonald*

Michael Doucet with Beausoleil

Christmas Bayou / 1986 / Swallow ✦✦✦
Cajun fiddler extraordinaire and leader of Beausoleil, Michael Doucet is backed by swamp guitar whiz Sonny Landreth, accordionist Pat Breaux, and others on this unique assortment of French fare and rollicking instrumental versions of "Deck the Halls" and "Auld Lang Zyne" (sic)—be prepared to do some two-steppin' and waltzing under the mistletoe when you throw this one on. —*Decibel Dennis MacDonald*

Elmo & Patsy

☆ **Grandma Got Run over by a Reindeer** / CBS ✦✦✦✦✦
Worth buying, if only for the classic title tune. —*David A. Milberg*

John Fahey

Christmas Album / 1975 / Burnside ✦✦✦
Fahey's latest Christmas project includes accompaniment from a small acoustic band. — *Roundup Newsletter*

☆ **Christmas Guitar** / 1989 / Varrick ✦✦✦✦✦
Fahey's studious acoustic guitar explorations of traditional music won him a lot of notoriety in folk circles during the '50s and '60s. *Christmas Guitar* features cuts previously available on other Fahey Christmas albums. Fahey's style is a distinctive blend of blues, folk, and ragtime. Even though his playing sometimes sounds a little too stiff and academic, all of the songs on this collection are wonderfully rendered. —*Rick Clark*

Percy Faith

☆ **Music of Christmas** / 1966 / CBS ✦✦✦✦✦
Hit album with a notable rendition of "Silver Bells." —*David A. Milberg*

● **Christmas Is** / 1989 / CBS ✦✦✦✦
This had its debut at Christmastime 1954. It's a great "time peace" of the decade's sounds of the season. —*David A. Milberg*

Arthur Fiedler

● **Pops Christmas Party** / 1959 / RCA ✦✦✦✦
This album is most famous for the classic version of "Sleigh Ride." —*David A. Milberg*

☆★ **A Christmas Festival** / RCA ✦✦✦✦✦
Fiedler and the Boston Pops are in good form on this holiday album. —*David A. Milberg*

Ella Fitzgerald

● **Ella Fitzgerald's Christmas** / 1967 / Capitol ✦✦✦✦
1968 hit album representing a change in Ella's style after her switch to Capitol. Re-released in 1978 as *Ella Fitzgerald Sings Christmas*. —*David A. Milberg*

☆ **Wishes You a Swinging Christmas** / Polydor ✦✦✦✦✦
Originally released in 1960 as *A Swinging Christmas*, this album is representative of Fitzgerald's Verve label career. —*David A. Milberg*

Scott Fitzgerald

A Child's Music Box Christmas ✦✦✦✦
A recording of Christmas music especially for children, played on music boxes, and woven together with other sounds of the season. —*Backroads Music/Heartbeats*

Old Fashioned Country Christmas ✦✦✦✦
Stir up memories of the perfect Christmas, with the sounds of a jinglebell sleigh ride, chestnuts roasting on the open fire, and Christmas melodies played on music boxes and the old family organ. —*Backroads Music/Heartbeats*

Rita Ford

☆ **Joyous Music Box Christmas** / Music Masters ✦✦✦✦✦
Christmas music played on old music boxes. —*Michael Erlewine*

● **Music Box Christmas** / CBS ✦✦✦✦
This one has been part of the Christmas record scene continuously since 1961. Warm and pleasant sounds for a fireside Christmas. —*David A. Milberg*

Tennessee Ernie Ford

☆ **The Star Carol (Reissue 2)** / Capitol ✦✦✦✦✦
A best-seller for ten years; the sacred sounds of the season never sounded better! —*David A. Milberg*

Frankie Valli & The Four Seasons

Christmas Album / 1967 / Rhino ✦✦✦✦
A reissue of their 1966 best-selling Christmas classic on the Philips label. "Santa Claus Is Coming to Town" is a great rocker. "Joy to the World Medley" is a surprise treat. —*David A. Milberg*

Connie Francis

Christmas in My Heart / 1959 / Polydor ✦✦✦✦
Originally released in 1959. Vintage Connie Francis. —*David A. Milberg*

James Galway

☆ **Christmas Carol** / RCA ✦✦✦✦✦
Galway's magic flute is perfect for a fireside Christmas Eve with the entire family. —*David A. Milberg*

Art Garfunkel with Amy Grant

Animal's Christmas / 1986 / Columbia ✦✦✦✦
One of the best Christmas albums of the '80s, featuring "Carol of the Birds." —*David A. Milberg*

Edward Gerhard

Christmas / Oct. 1991 / Virtue ✦✦✦
A sterling collection of seasonal standards from Gerhard, an acoustic guitar fingerpicking virtuoso from New Hampshire. (He produced and played on Bill Morrissey's *North* album on Philo, and has a solo album of his own, *Night Birds*, also on Virtue.) — *Roundup Newsletter*

Jackie Gleason

☆ **Merry Christmas** / 1956 / Capitol ✦✦✦✦✦
Originally released in 1956, this is the album for Christmas cuddling, in the great tradition of Jackie Gleason instrumental arrangements. —*David A. Milberg*

Merry Christmas / Sep. 10, 1990 / Capitol ✦✦✦
"The Great One" tended to be overly sentimental in the orchestrations he used on his many "mood" LPs, but on this seasonal reissue, the arrangements, while somewhat cloying, somehow work, making this a fine choice for the over-sixty set. His original "Christmas in Paris" is a bittersweet standout. —*Decibel Dennis MacDonald*

Amy Grant

☆ **A Christmas Album** / 1983 / Word ✦✦✦✦✦
Amy's first seasonal offering is still a perennially strong seller, and one of the best contemporary Christmas albums ever recorded. — *Thom Granger*

Home for Christmas / Oct. 6, 1992 / A&M ✦✦✦
A year (1993) after her mainstream success, contemporary Christian's most popular (and controversial) female vocalist is back with a very nice Christmas album—her second such project in her almost 17-year career. There's no rollicking "Baby, Baby" or "Good for Me" in this set, and Grant and her longtime producer Brown Bannister go for a softer, easy-listening, middle-of-the-road sound. —*Edwin Smith, Rejoice*

Al Green

White Christmas / 1986 / Word ✦✦✦✦
Although seasonal albums can be ponderous affairs, Rev. Al Green made sure that wasn't the case on this mid-'80s work. He attacks traditional carols, hymns and holiday material with the same devotion as he does soul anthems and gospel classics. Even if you're not a fan of holiday albums (and I for one am not) this deserves high praises. —*Ron Wynn*

David Grisman

☆**Acoustic Christmas** / 1983 / Rounder ✦✦✦✦✦
The Dawg's new tricks include wayward wanderings amid medieval settings (Respighi airs), swing ("Santa Claus Is Coming to Town"), the light fantastic (a wonderful "Winter Wonderland" like a hail of radiant snowflakes), and an odd, slummy, delightful "Silent Night." Except for the bad duck joke on the mercifully brief "We Wish You a Merry Christmas" and the sax-soggy "White Christmas," the level of music is consistently out of this world. The mood ranges all over the place, but what virtuosity! —*Bob Coltman*

Vince Guaraldi

☆**A Charlie Brown Christmas** / Jan. 16, 1992 / Fantasy ✦✦✦✦✦
The original soundtrack to this annual CBS TV special is one that both children and the child in all of us can enjoy. Aside from the association with the Charles Schulz cartoon characters, Guaraldi's light piano touch makes this a nice CD to throw on when the Christmas party is over. —*Decibel Dennis MacDonald*

Merle Haggard

☆**A Christmas Present** / 1973 / Curb ✦✦✦✦✦
While Hag keeps the mood light with selections such as "Santa Claus and Popcorn" and more traditional fare, he also has some bite with the high and lonesome "Daddy Won't Be Home for Christmas." His matter-of-fact tale about layoffs at the factory, "If We Make It through December," has become timeless in tough times. —*Dennis MacDonald*

John Wesley Harding

God Made Me Do It—The Christmas EP / 1989 / Warner ✦✦✦
On this four-song EP (plus "A Cosy Promotional Chat" with ex-Bonzo Dog Band Viv Stanshall), Harding, apparently at the behest of his label, wrote one seasonal song, the Bob Dylan-inspired "Talking Christmas Goodwill Blues," a free-association acoustic folk ditty. Amusing. —*Decibel Dennis MacDonald*

Emmylou Harris

☆**Christmas Album (Light in the Stable)** / Jul. 1979 / Warner Bros. ✦✦✦✦✦
An album of soaring beauty, as if from angels on high. Neil Young, Dolly Parton, and Linda Ronstadt add harmony vocals to the moving title track, aided by James Burton's electric guitar and Hank DeVito's pedal steel. Beauty beyond belief. Recently reissued on CD. —*Dennis MacDonald*

Michael Hedges with Kelly McGillis

☆**Santabear's First Christmas** / Windham Hill ✦✦✦✦
A story disc. Kelly McGillis narrates a Christmas tale over the lovely acoustic guitar of Hedges. —*AMG*

Tish Hinojosa

Memorabilia Navidenia / 1991 / Watermelon ✦✦✦✦
One does not have to understand Spanish to be moved by the beauty of Hinojosa's voice on "A La Nanita Nana," a traditional Spanish lullaby from "Las Posadas" ("The Inns," a Christmas re-enactment). The remaining tunes are Hinojosa originals, including Spanish and English versions of "Arbolito" (Little Christmas Tree) and "Milagro," recalling the message of peace, hope and love from the Nativity. A release of rare beauty. —*Decibel Dennis MacDonald*

Paul Horn

☆**The Peace Album** / 1988 / Kuckuck ✦✦✦✦
This holiday release from 1988 is by one of the greatest flutists of our time. The exquisite elegance of the music comes partly from the uniquely conceived "multi-flute orchestra," in which Horn is the only musician, adding unusual depth and dimension to the performances of these pieces, ranging from "Silent Night" to "We Three Kings" to "Ave Maria." This Celestial Harmonies release is dedicated to the peace inside each one of us and offers sterling performances throughout. —*Backroads Music/Heartbeats*

Engelbert Humperdinck

☆**Merry Christmas** / Epic ✦✦✦✦✦
This was a hit album in 1980. All the romance of a typical Humperdinck album. —*David A. Milberg*

Inner Voices

Christmas Harmony / 1990 / Rhino ✦✦✦
Four women whose a cappella voices will mesmerize you as they take flight on mostly sacred material, although they do a finger-snappin', sultry version of "Merry Christmas Baby" and "Boogie Woogie Santa Claus" accompanied by sleigh bells. Inner Voices have a fan in Johnny Mathis, who said "I am a fan forever." —*Decibel Dennis MacDonald*

Burl Ives

Have a Holly Jolly Christmas / MCA ✦✦✦✦
An all-time holiday favorite. Includes the classic "Santa Claus is Coming to Town." —*AMG*

The Jackson 5

☆**The Jackson 5 Christmas Album** / 1970 / Motown ✦✦✦✦
One of the greatest holiday albums ever, and that's coming from someone who doesn't care for Christmas LPs. But Michael and company carry off the seasonal bit well, and their versions of these dusty hymns and carols could even charm Scrooge. —*Ron Wynn*

Alan Jackson

☆**Honky Tonk Christmas** / Oct. 12, 1993 / Arista ✦✦✦✦✦
One of the best country Christmas albums, with a smart blend of old and new songs and not a traditional carol in the bunch. Jackson starts off strong with the rocking "Honky Tonk Christmas," then sings a gorgeous duet with Alison Krauss. He adds his voice to a previously taped track by the late Keith Whitley on "There's a New Kid in Town," and does a credible job with Merle Haggard's "If We Make it Through December." Fabulous, save for a silly duet with the cartoon Chipmunks. —*Brian Mansfield*

Mahalia Jackson

☆ **Silent Night (Songs for Christmas)** / 1962 / CBS ✦✦✦✦✦
Whether or not you like sacred music, one cannot help but be moved by the power and passion with which Mahalia Jackson sings "Sweet Little Jesus Boy" and the spiritual "Go Tell It on the Mountain." Her rendition of "Silent Night, Holy Night" is simply inspirational. —*Decibel Dennis MacDonald*

☆ **Christmas with Mahalia Jackson** / Special Music ✦✦✦✦✦
This was the second of her two legendary gospel Christmas albums for Columbia. A worthy companion to her earlier *Silent Night* album. —*David A. Milberg*

Jambalaya Cajun Band

Joyeux Noel / Swallow ✦✦✦
This Cajun band sings six of the fourteen songs included here in French and another five more bilingually. Lyrics are provided for all songs in both French and English, as Jambalaya add some spice to seasonal favorites and include original compositions alongside old traditional Cajun fare, e.g. "Il Est Ne" ("He Is Born," which used to be sung in French Catholic masses). With twin fiddles and pumping accordion, this includes the most rollickin' instrumental of "Joy to the World" you may ever hear. —*Decibel Dennis MacDonald*

The Jets

Christmas with the Jets / 1986 / MCA ✦✦✦
A somewhat charming holiday album by the Minneapolis family group the Jets. But they'd lost their commercial clout some time back, and by now were beginning to sound like one more faded teen troupe. As with most Christmas releases, if you enjoy the genre, you'll find room for one more. —*Ron Wynn*

Evan Johns & His H-Bombs

Please, Mr. Santa Claus / Aug. 23, 1991 / Rykodisc ✦✦✦✦
Put this nine-song mini-album CD in the Christmas stocking of any rock 'n' roll fan. The "crash and burn" guitar style of Johns recalls Santo and Johnny ("Snowed In") and Jimmy Bryant ("Santa's Little Helper"), while his snarly vocals on the title track bring new meaning to "cool yule." Spiced with original instrumentals and a cover of "Telstar," this is a must for Evan Johns fans and those who want a little bite in their yuletide listening. —*Dennis MacDonald*

Etta Jones

Christmas with Etta Jones / Jan. 1991 / Muse ✦✦✦
Well done holiday album featuring the underrated singer Etta Jones putting her spin on traditional Christmas favorites. It's strictly for Christmas music fans, but maintains integrity and jazz connection through fine vocal and instrumental performances, production and song selection. —*Ron Wynn*

Spike Jones

☆ **It's a Spike Jones Christmas** / 1970 / Rhino ✦✦✦✦✦
A real oddity, this features Spike Jones's usual sense of musical humor, with spoofs of holiday standards intermingled with reverently sung Christmas carols by his 25-voice choir. Includes his novelty hit, "All I Want for Christmas Is My Two Front Teeth," and "Jingle Bells" sung in Pig Latin. How curious are you? —*Roundup Newsletter*

The Judds

☆ **Christmas Time with the Judds** / RCA ✦✦✦✦✦
Country Christmas with Wynonna and Naomi Judd. Strong performances. —*AMG*

Peter Kater

☆ **For Christmas** / 1987 / Silver Wave ✦✦✦✦✦
Supper-club piano stylings of familiar holiday songs. Very fine pianist. It works. —*Michael Erlewine*

The Season / Nov. 26, 1991 / Silver Wave ✦✦✦✦
Expanding the scope and repertoire of his previous holiday recording, Kater is joined here by a violin, sax and flute on six traditional and four original Kater compositions, making for another classic recording. —*Backroads Music/Heartbeats*

Stan Kenton & His Orchestra

☆ **Merry Christmas!** / 1961 / Capitol ✦✦✦✦
A hit album. A definite Kenton collectible. —*David A. Milberg*

Kenton's Christmas / Feb. 21, 1961-Mar. 14, 1961 / Creative World ✦✦✦✦
Traditional carols arranged for the Kenton brass and rhythm—no saxes. "O Holy Night," "Angels We Have Heard on High," "O Tannenbaum," "The Holly and the Ivy." Recorded in 1961. — *Roundup Newsletter*

King's College Choir

☆ **O Come All Ye Faithful** / Argo ✦✦✦✦✦
Sixteen traditional carols done by this classic Christmas choir. This is what carols were meant to sound like. —*Michael Erlewine*

The Kingston Trio

☆ **The Last Month of the Year** / 1960 / Capitol ✦✦✦✦✦
An essential part of any Christmas album collection. True Christmas folk songs, from spirituals to Old English rounds. A must! —*David A. Milberg*

Gladys Knight & The Pips

That Special Time of Year / 1971 / Columbia ✦✦✦
A good Christmas album from Gladys Knight and the Pips, a great one if you're a fan of holiday releases. They don't have to fake intimacy since they're a family group, and Knight's voice sounds both sincere and moving on the hymns, carols and seasonal items. Unfortunately, at present it's out of print. —*Ron Wynn*

Lyn Larsen

The Pipes of Christmas / Pro Arte ✦✦✦✦
A large theater organ (Paramount Theater) and Christmas songs add up to a trip to the 1930s. —*Michael Erlewine*

Peggy Lee

☆ **Christmas Carousel** / 1960 / Capitol ✦✦✦✦✦
This is the classic Christmas sound of Peggy Lee during her peak recording years. —*David A. Milberg*

The Lettermen

☆ **For Christmas this Year** / Sep. 10, 1990 / Capitol ✦✦✦✦✦
Here is the early Lettermen sound of 1966. Put a log on the fire, sit back, and enjoy. —*David A. Milberg*

Ramsey Lewis Trio

The Sound of Christmas / 1960-1961 / Chess ✦✦✦
The good half of this classic jazz yule release features just the trio having

a swingin' time with "Here Comes Santa Claus" and "Winter Wonderland," and cookin' on the funky original, "Christmas Blues." The bad half kicks in when Riley Hampton adds a ten-man string section to the last five tunes. —*Decibel Dennis MacDonald*

☆ **More Sounds of Christmas** / MCA ✦✦✦✦✦
Again hampered by strings on too many cuts, on the plus side, this does contain the ultra-cool original, "Eggnog," featuring Lewis on celeste. —*Decibel Dennis MacDonald*

Norman Luboff Choir

☆ **Christmas with the Norman Luboff Choir** / RCA ✦✦✦✦✦
This one debuted in 1964 and made the *Billboard* charts. If you like the choral group sound of the early '60s, you'll love this one. —*AMG*

Madeline MacNeil

☆ **Christmas Comes Anew: Christmas Music with Dulcimers and Singing** / Kicking Mule ✦✦✦✦✦
European and American Christmas songs with the bright voice of MacNeil backed by acoustic guitar, dulcimer, and strings. —*Michael Erlewine*

Henry Mancini

☆ **Merry Mancini Christmas** / RCA ✦✦✦✦✦
Mancini magic at its best, for the holidays. Perfect background music for holiday family get-togethers. —*David A. Milberg*

Barry Manilow

Because It's Christmas / Arista ✦✦✦✦
Christmas classics in the Manilow style. Nestle under the mistletoe with this one. —*David A. Milberg*

Mannheim Steamroller

☆ **Fresh Aire Christmas 1988** / American Gramaphone 1988 ✦✦✦✦✦
A worthy successor to their first *Christmas Album*. —*David A. Milberg*

Mantovani Orchestra

☆ **All-Time Xmas Favorites, Vol. 1 & 2** / Deram ✦✦✦✦✦
Great music to wake up to on Christmas morning. Many cuts taken from his 1953 million-selling album. —*David A. Milberg*

Christmas Carols / London ✦✦✦
This album made the Billboard Top 40 charts for five consecutive years, 1957-1961, with the peak of Number 3 in 1958. —*AMG*

Manzanera & Mac

Christmas the Player / 1989 / Rykodisc ✦✦✦
Christmas carols played on traditional instruments by British street musicians, led by Roxy Music's Andy MacKay. — *Roundup Newsletter*

Wynton Marsalis

☆ **Crescent City Christmas Card** / 1989 / Columbia ✦✦✦✦✦
This elegant Christmas album swings with heart and soul and is certain to be a standard. — *Rick Clark*

The Martin Best Medieval Ensemble

☆ **Thys Yool**—a Medieval Christmas / May 1988 / Nimbus ✦✦✦✦✦
Elegant music. Early Christmas celebrations on original instruments. —*Michael Erlewine*

Johnny Mathis

☆ **Merry Christmas** / 1958 / Columbia ✦✦✦✦✦
Of the several Christmas LPs Mathis has recorded, this one gets the nod. With empathetic arrangements by Percy Faith, it's impossible to say how many babies were born the following season after parents heard Johnny Mathis crooning "The Christmas Song." Smo-o-o-oth! —*Decibel Dennis MacDonald*

Give Me Your Love for Christmas / 1969 / Columbia ✦✦✦
A million-seller featuring the Mathis sound after he returned to Columbia Records from the Mercury label. —*David A. Milberg*

Christmas Eve with Johnny Mathis / 1986 / Columbia ✦✦✦
More romantic sounds of the season, '70s-style, featuring "Christmas Is." —*David A. Milberg*

John McCutcheon

Winter Solstice / 1984 / Rounder ✦✦✦
A collection of hammer dulcimer music for Christmas, Chanukah, and the New Year's season. With help from members of the Washington Bach

Consort and the group Trapezoid, McCutcheon leads a musical journey through many lands and cultures, all in the holiday spirit. —*Roundup Newsletter*

Maureen McGovern

☆**Christmas with Maureen McGovern** / CBS ✦✦✦✦✦
Velvety smooth. Great for Christmas cuddling. —*David A. Milberg*

Jacob Miller

Natty Christmas / 1978 / RAS ✦✦✦
Along with DJ Ray I, Jacob sends up Xmas; "Deck the Halls with Boughs of Collie" sets the pace. —*Roger Steffens*

Mitch Miller

● **Christmas Sing-Along with Mitch Miller** / 1958 / CBS ✦✦✦✦
The first *Sing Along with Mitch* Christmas album. The MOR sound of the '50s. —*David A. Milberg*

☆**Holiday Sing-Along with Mitch Miller** / 1961 / CBS ✦✦✦✦✦
This album made the Billboard Top 40 in both 1961 and 1962. —*AMG*

The Miracles

Christmas with the Miracles / 1963 / Motown ✦✦✦
Recorded in October, 1963, when the Miracles still included Claudette Robinson, Smokey's wife, in the lineup; she sings lead on "Let It Snow." Smokey contributes one original, the mid-tempo "Christmas Everyday," that stands as one of the finest Motown seasonal favorites and one of Smokey's most memorable performances of his long career. —*Decibel Dennis MacDonald*

Jim Nabors

☆**Christmas Album** / 1990 / CBS ✦✦✦✦✦
An easy-listening treat that includes one of the best versions of "White Christmas" ever. —*David A. Milberg*

Willie Nelson

Pretty Paper / 1979 / CBS ✦✦✦✦✦
Worth the price just for the title song. —*David A. Milberg*

New Edition

Christmas All over the World / MCA ✦✦✦✦
A musical Christmas party, featuring the title tune. —*David A. Milberg*

Mojo Nixon & The Toadliquors

Horny Holidays! / Triple X ✦✦✦
Irreverent and raunchy, would you expect anything less from Mojo Nixon? Not for the kiddies or Tipper Gores of the world, this CD is hilarious if you listen to it in the spirit it was recorded (a few trips to the spiked eggnog punchbowl might help). "Mr. Grinch" is a perfect vehicle for Nixon's from-the-gutter vocals, while his original "It's Christmas Time" recalls the Memphis soul-struttin' of Rufus Thomas crossed with Clarence Carter's down 'n' dirty style. "We Three Kings" is turned into a tale of debauchery as Nixon growls "We were drunk for three days straight, feeling like we were Tom Waits." Play this not to be sanctified but to be amused. —*Decibel Dennis MacDonald*

NRBQ

Christmas Wish / Rounder ✦✦✦✦
NRBQ bring a sense of goofy fun to this eight-song mini-album, covering standards in their wacky style and contributing a few originals—Terry Adams' "Electric Train" and Joey Spampinato's "Christmas Wish." The cover photo of NRBQ decked out in their winter pajamas is a real hoot. —*Dennis MacDonald*

Laura Nyro

Christmas and the Beads of Sweat / 1970 / Columbia ✦✦✦
One of her most wonderful early albums; includes "Brown Earth," "When I Was a Freeport and You Were the Main Drag," "Up on the Roof," and more. —*Ladyslipper*

Odetta

☆ **Christmas Spirituals** / 1960 / Alcazar ✦✦✦✦✦
Odetta's husky voice is often stunning, both in her a cappella performances and her songs with accompaniment. Odetta says these songs are traditional spirituals; neither purely African nor purely American, but songs that emerged from the sufferings of slavery. Powerful stuff. —*Dennis MacDonald*

Alexander O'Neal

My Gift to You / 1988 / Tabu ✦✦✦✦
So good I want to play it year 'round. Decent contemporary holiday discs are hard to come by, but Minneapolis' finest soul singer and producers Jimmy Jam and Terry Lewis created a disc that nearly rivals Spector's in concept (all the originals are brilliant) and Elvis Presley's in performance. "Sleigh Ride" is the hardest piece of Xmas funk James Brown never cut, and the brassy treatment given to "Winter Wonderland" would make Sinatra proud. —*John Floyd*

Eugene Ormandy

☆**Glorious Sound of Christmas** / CBS ✦✦✦✦✦
Although they're not credited in the title, this album also features the Mormon Tabernacle Choir. It was a million-seller when it was first released in 1962. —*David A. Milberg*

Greatest Christmas Hits / CBS ✦✦✦
This album also includes the Temple University Choir, combined with the Philadelphia Orchestra for a truly classical Christmas. —*David A. Milberg*

Osmond Family Christmas

Osmond Family Christmas / Curb ✦✦✦✦
Donny and his brothers singing smooth harmonies for the holidays. —*David A. Milberg*

Buck Owens

☆ **Christmas with Buck Owens** / Curb ✦✦✦✦✦
Buck adds fun to the season's festivities when dishing out country corn such as "Santa Looked a Lot like Daddy." The Buckaroos turn in a romping instrumental of "Jingle Bells," and Buck contributes a honky-tonk Christmas classic with "Blue Christmas Lights." —*Dennis MacDonald*

Patti Page

☆**Christmas with Patti Page** / 1956 / Mercury ✦✦✦✦✦
Holiday standards and sacred sounds, as with the hit "Happy Birthday, Jesus." —*David A. Milberg*

Stevan Pasero

☆ **Christmas Classics for Guitar** / Sugo ✦✦✦✦✦
Guitar transcriptions and arrangements of a variety of traditional Christmas fare, folk tunes, and classical compositions. —*Michael Erlewine*

Kim Pensyl

A Kim Pensyl Christmas / 1991 ✦✦✦
This 1989 Christmas release comes from the composer of the popular *Pensyl Sketches*. Kim blends his inimitable piano style with extensive synthesizer orchestrations to produce an album that varies from dynamic uptempo renditions to gentle, introspective colorings. A couple of original pieces complement the selection of traditional Christmas tunes, making this an exciting year-end release. —*Backroads Music/Heartbeats*

Peter Paul & Mary

☆**A Holiday Celebration** / 1988 / Gold Castle ✦✦✦✦✦
This 1988 release contains songs they made famous, such as "Blowin' in the Wind" plus "A Soalin'," "Children Go Where I Send Thee," "O Come O Come Emmanuel," "Light One Candle," "The Cherry Tree Carol," and more; joyfully and elegantly performed live-in-concert, many with full choir and orchestra. —*Ladyslipper*

Michael Petri

☆ **Noel! Noel! Noel!** / RCA ✦✦✦✦✦
Christmas music from one of the world's finest recorder players. Backed by the Westminster Abbey Choir and the National Philharmonic with Martin Neary. —*Michael Erlewine*

The Platters

Christmas with the Platters / PolyGram ✦✦✦✦
Christmas standards with the Platters touch, plus a couple of Buck Ram originals: "Come Home for Christmas" and "Merry Christmas, Baby." —*David A. Milberg*

Elvis Presley

Christmas Album / Nov. 1957 / RCA ✦✦✦✦
From playful takes on "White Christmas" to bluesy, low down readings of "Blue Christmas" and "Santa Claus Is Back in Town," to the straight inter-

pretations of yuletide standards that close it out, there's simply no other Christmas album that sounds quite like this. —*Cub Koda & Rick Clark*

Memories of Christmas / RCA ✦✦✦
Compiled in 1982, this collects some of the King's most-loved Christmas material—"Blue Christmas," "Santa Claus Is Back in Town"—and adds four unreleased versions of seasonal songs, the standout being a sizzling eight minutes of "Merry Christmas, Baby" showing that this boy from Memphis could grind out the blues with the best of 'em. —*Decibel Dennis MacDonald*

Sings the Wonderful World of Xmas / RCA ✦✦✦
The least of the Elvis seasonal releases, notable only for his version of "Merry Christmas, Baby." —*Decibel Dennis MacDonald*

Charley Pride

☆**Christmas in My Home Town** / 1970 / RCA ✦✦✦✦
The title tune was a great Christmas hit. Mellow C&W for the holidays. —*David A. Milberg*

Raffi

☆**Raffi's Christmas Album** / Shoreline ✦✦✦✦
This is an essential collection that's perfect for kids and still enjoyable for adults. —*David A. Milberg*

Lou Rawls

Merry Christmas Ho! Ho! Ho! / Sep. 10, 1965 / Capitol ✦✦✦
Early Lou Rawls at his best, including his hit version of "Little Drummer Boy." —*David A. Milberg*

Leon Redbone

Christmas Island / 1989 / Private Music ✦✦✦
The enigmatic Leon Redbone gives his time-warp treatment to a predictable bunch of Christmas standards. Fans of Redbone's low-key camp style will enjoy this, particularly the duet with Dr. John on "Frosty the Snowman." —*Rick Clark*

Ren & Stimpy

Crock O' Christmas / Sony Wonder ✦✦✦
What hath Nickelodeon begat? Celebrate that shabbiest holiday of the year, Yaksmas Eve, with the hairballing Stimpy and high-strung Chihuahua, Ren, as they trash Christmas classics : "Fleck the Walls," "Cobb to the World," "The Twelve Days of Yaksmas"—you get the idea. Stupidity knows no limits unless, of course, Beavis and Butthead get to release *Huh Huh Holidays.* —*Decibel Dennis MacDonald*

Paul Revere & The Raiders

Christmas Present & Past / 1967 / CBS ✦✦✦
A rocking-great trip back to the, '60s with Mark Lindsay and Paul Revere. An essential oldie-but-goodie. —*David A. Milberg*

Bob Rivers Comedy Corp

☆**Twisted Christmas** / Critique ✦✦✦✦
This is one of the funniest Christmas albums of all time! Essential! Includes the classic "Message from the King." —*David A. Milberg*

Marcus Roberts

Prayer for Peace / 1991 / Jive/Novus ✦✦✦
Outstanding piano solos, so good that even those who loathe holiday music might find it hard to ignore if they give it a listen. Roberts' solo dates have moved more and more back to early styles like stride, ragtime and boogie-woogie, but here he's more contemporary and introspective than reflective. —*Ron Wynn*

Kenny Rogers

☆**Christmas** / Sep. 1981 / EMI America ✦✦✦✦
Kenny Rogers does his thing with old and new Christmas tunes. Just what you would expect. —*AMG*

Rotary Connection

Peace / 1968 / Chess ✦✦✦
A great Christmas present from the '60s, featuring the late Minnie Riperton. —*David A. Milberg*

Royal College of Music Choir/Brass Ensemble

☆**Carols for Christmas** / 1989 / Rykodisc ✦✦✦✦
These 41 carols and hymns are done, for the most part, a cappella. Spacious. Lovely. —*Michael Erlewine*

Royal Philharmonic with David Newman

☆**It's a Wonderful Life; a Christmas Carol ...** / Telarc ✦✦✦✦
Royal Philharmonic with David Newman. Original scores for three of the greatest Christmas films of all time, *It's a Wonderful Life, A Christmas Carol,* and *Miracle on 34th Street.* Restored and recorded in pristine digital sound. —*Michael Erlewine*

Sackville All Stars

☆**Christmas Record** / Mar. 29, 1986-Mar. 30, 1986 / Sackville ✦✦✦✦
Jazz improvisations on standard Christmas tunes. With Milt Hinton on bass, Gus Johnson on drums, Ralph Sutton on piano, and Jim Galloway on soprano saxophone. —*Michael Erlewine*

Mike, Peggy, and Penny Seeger

☆**American Folk Songs for Christmas** / 1989 / Rounder ✦✦✦✦
Lovers of traditional serious folk music will enjoy this double CD set, which features everything from earnestly untrained a cappella performances to a whole array of acoustic instrumentation, including mandolin, dulcimer, guitar, psaltery, autoharp, banjo, and so forth. —*Rick Clark*

Doc Severinsen

☆**Merry Christmas** ✦✦✦✦
"Tonight Show" band treatment of Christmas classics. —*David A. Milberg*

Robert Shaw Chorale

☆**Many Moods of Christmas** / 1962 / Telarc ✦✦✦✦
This is one of the later, and better, Christmas offerings from these performers. —*David A. Milberg*

Harry Simeone Chorale

☆**The Little Drummer Boy** / 1984 / PolyGram ✦✦✦✦
Contains the definitive version of the title song and similar performances of other sounds of the season. Essential. —*David A. Milberg*

Frank Sinatra

☆**The Sinatra Christmas Album** / Nov. 11, 1987 / Capitol ✦✦✦✦
Essential Sinatra Christmas sounds of his Capitol era, with "Christmas Waltz" and "Have Yourself a Merry Little Christmas." —*David A. Milberg*

Christmas Dreaming / 1989 / CBS ✦✦✦
A collection of Sinatra sides cut between 1944 and 1950 to commemorate the season. The refinement of his phrasing and vocal timbre during those years is stunning. Even though his best work was yet to come, this is a worthwhile CD for Sinatra lovers. —*Rick Clark*

Chris Stamey Group

Christmas Time / 1986 / Coyote ✦✦✦
An expanded reissue of the 1986 Coyote LP, this is a popmeister's heaven as ex-dB's Stamey reunites with the dB's on the title track and duets with Wes Lachot on the Badfinger soundalike, "Christmas Is the Only Time (I Think of You)." Cult figure Alex Chilton turns in a fairly straight version of "The Christmas Song" and his "Jesus Christ" (from his last Big Star LP) is here as well. Syd Straw turns in a Phil Spector "Wall of Sound" version of Blondie's "(I'm Always Touched by Your) Presence, Dear"(with the title changed to "Presents"). More ear candy from the dB's, Peter Holsapple and others, and look for that hidden track eighteen! —*Decibel Dennis MacDonald*

The Statler Brothers

☆**Statler Brothers Christmas Card** / 1979 / Mercury ✦✦✦✦
Wonderful stuff, with "I Believe in Santa Claus." —*David A. Milberg*

Doug Stone

The First Christmas / Apr. 1992 / Epic ✦✦✦
Given the number of songwriters in Nashville, it's surprising the town hasn't produced more Christmas songs. *The First Christmas* gets a bunch of them, though. Songs like "An Angel Like You" play off Stone's romantic-balladeer image, and "When December Comes Around" would sound great any time of year. "Sailing Home for Christmas" depicts the irony of soldiers celebrating the coming of "peace on earth" while stationed on a battleship. —*Brian Mansfield*

Barbra Streisand

Barbra's Christmas Album / 1967 / CBS
An essential collection including "Sleep in Heavenly Peace (Silent Night)" and "Jingle Bells." —*David A. Milberg*

Supremes with Stevie Wonder

Merry Christmas/Someday at Christmas / Motown ✦✦✦✦
Contains the classics "Twinkle, Twinkle Little Me" and "Someday at Christmas." Truly supreme wonders. *—David A. Milberg*

Russ Taff

The Christmas Song / Oct. 5, 1992 / Sparrow ✦✦✦
Jazzy, '50s pop vocal and instrumental approach reminds of classic Cole/Sinatra seasonal sets. *—Thom Granger*

Take 6

☆ **He Is Christmas** / Feb. 1992 / Reprise ✦✦✦✦✦
Take 6 makes the sacred Christmas repertoire their own with their unique blend of gospel, jazz and vocal magic. *He Is Christmas* features the original title track along with nine traditional Christmas carols transformed in arrangements by the soul-stirring rhythms and ear-shaking dissonances of the Take 6 fundamental style. Joey Kibble, brother of chief arranger Mark Kibble, joins the sextet for the first tune on the album; and the Yellowjackets provide instrumental accompaniment on "God Rest Ye Merry Gentlemen." *— Erin Ryan*

The Temptations

Christmas Card/Give Love at Christmas / Motown ✦✦✦✦
This two-album CD contains all of their Christmas hits, including "Rudolph the Red-Nosed Reindeer," "Give Love at Christmas," and "Silent Night." *—David A. Milberg*

The Christmas Card / Oct. 1970 / Motown ✦✦✦
The Christmas sound for the "Big Chill Generation," including a great rendition of "Rudolph the Red-Nosed Reindeer." *—David A. Milberg*

Give Love at Christmas / Aug. 1980 / Motown ✦✦✦
A nice holiday package, and arguably the company's best, along with the *Jackson 5 Christmas* album. The group didn't just coast through the carols and hymns, but really injected some energy into them, particularly Eddie Kendricks. *—Ron Wynn*

Dylan Thomas

☆ **A Child's Christmas in Wales** / Caedmon ✦✦✦✦✦
Everyone should hear Dylan Thomas read this lovely prose piece. Enchanting, in the true sense of the word. Also included are Thomas poems such as "Do Not Go Gentle into that Good Night." *—Michael Erlewine*

Eric Tingstad & Nancy Rumbel

☆ **The Gift** / 1989 / Sona Gaia ✦✦✦✦
Tingstad and Rumbel, who have a couple of the best cuts on the *Narada Christmas Collection*, blend a spatial new-age sensibility with straight melodic readings of traditional Christmas music, performed on acoustic string and wind instruments. Sometimes the exquisite technique is a little bloodless, but all in all, very well done. *—Rick Clark*

Randy Travis

☆ **Old-Time Christmas** / Aug. 29, 1989 / Warner Bros. ✦✦✦✦✦
Ten Christmas songs, some old, some new, one by Travis ("How Do I Wrap My Heart for Christmas," written with Paul Overstreet). "God Rest Ye Merry Gentlemen" is outstanding. *—Brian Mansfield & AMG*

Trinity College Choir

☆ **Carols from Trinity** / Conifer ✦✦✦✦✦
Twenty-seven carols (old and new) from renowned Trinity College Choir, with Richard Marlow. Classic and elegant. *—Michael Erlewine*

Travis Tritt

Loving Time of the Year / May 1992 / Warner Bros. ✦✦✦
The harder Tritt rocks on *Loving Time of the Year*, the better he sounds. His Southern-boogie versions of "Winter Wonderland" and "Silver Bells" make a perfect antidote to sleigh-bell burnout. When he tries to be an "interpretive singer" on "Have Yourself a Merry Little Christmas," he falls flat on his face. Elsewhere, Tritt writes the title track while covering two by Buck Owens and one by Sonny James. *—Brian Mansfield*

Bobby Vee

Merry Christmas / 1962 / EMI America ✦✦✦
Not just the standards, but some tasty originals like "A Not So Merry Christmas" in this '60s Christmas time capsule. *—David A. Milberg*

The Ventures

★ **Ventures' Christmas Album** / Oct. 22, 1990 / EMI America ✦✦✦✦✦
This is easily one of my Top Ten favorite Yuletide albums of all time. Recorded in 1965, at the height of the Ventures' popularity, the group takes seasonal classics and with their trademark Mosrite guitars in hand, they adapt the tunes to incorporate hits of the day: "Santa Claus Is Comin' to Town" crossed with "Wooly Bully"; "Frosty the Snowman" with a little "Tequila" thrown in; even the original "Sleigh Ride" reprises the group's smash hit "Walk—Don't Run." Highest recommendation. *—Decibel Dennis MacDonald*

The Whispers

Happy Holidays to You / 1979 / CBS ✦✦✦✦
A hit when it was first released, the title tune is especially good. *—David A. Milberg*

Slim Whitman

Christmas Album / 1969 / EMI America
This is a reissue of an album originally released in 1969. Vintage Slim Whitman for the holidays. *—David A. Milberg*

Roger Whittaker

☆ **Christmas Album** / 1978 / RCA ✦✦✦✦✦
This is the sound of Roger Whittaker at the peak of his career. A worthwhile stocking-stuffer. *—David A. Milberg*

Andy Williams

☆ **Christmas Album** / 1963 / CBS ✦✦✦✦✦
An essential Christmas classic! A million-seller in 1963, and a perennial hit ever since. *—David A. Milberg*

Christmas Present / 1965 / CBS ✦✦✦
This was Andy Williams' second million-selling Christmas album, and with good reason. Here is Andy's sound at its peak. *—David A. Milberg*

Merry Christmas / CBS ✦✦✦
Andy's voice is custom-made for Christmas. Here are 17 tunes crooned by an expert. *—AMG*

Joe Williams

That Holiday Feeling / 1990 / PolyGram ✦✦✦
Dave Pell's Prez Conference was to Lester Young what Supersax is to Charlie Parker. Pell's short-lived group featured harmonized Lester Young solos recreated by three tenors and a baritone; their matchup with singer Joe Williams is quite enjoyable. Since Young was in Count Basie's orchestra when Jimmy Rushing was the vocalist, Joe Williams has a rare opportunity to give his own interpretation to Rushing and Billie Holiday classics like "I May Be Wrong," "You Can Depend on Me," "If Dreams Come True" and "Easy Living." A delightful and swinging date. *—Scott Yanow*

Jackie Wilson

Merry Christmas from Jackie Wilson / 1963 / Rhino ✦✦✦✦
After being out of print for years, this 1963 gem from one of the most exciting R&B entertainers of all time is finally available. Essential. *—David A. Milberg*

George Winston

☆ **December** / 1982 / Windham Hill ✦✦✦✦✦
The mother of all solo instrumental albums, and with good reason. Mixing traditional carols with Pachelbel's Canon and a few originals, Winston produces a solo piano album of unparalleled—and undeniable—beauty. How can music be simultaneously stirring and soothing, relaxed yet exalted? Millions have found the answer here, and an industry has spent more than a decade trying to duplicate it. *—William Ruhlmann*

Frank Yankovic

☆ **Christmas Memories** / Smash ✦✦✦✦✦
This one won a Christmas-music Grammy, and with good reason. You'll love this version of "Blue Christmas." *—David A. Milberg*

Christmas Collections

Acoustic Christmas / 1990 / CBS ✦✦✦
All but two of the dozen tracks were recorded specifically for this compilation: Harry Connick, Jr.'s solo piano rendition of "Winter Wonderland" was cut for the movie *When Harry Met Sally.* . . . Tops on this CD is Rosanne Cash's tender version of "It Came Upon a Midnight Clear,"

accompanied by guitar, violin and mandola. T-Bone Burnett turns in a sparse "God Rest Ye Merry Gentlemen," with sonorous dobro and violin from Jerry Douglas and Mark O'Connor. Shawn Colvin steams things up a bit with a jazzy "Have Yourself a Merry Christmas," but the most unusual track belongs to the unlikely pairing of Poi Dog Pondering with the Dirty Dozen Brass Band: prepare to second-line for their festive version of "Mele Kalikimaka." —*Decibel Dennis MacDonald*

★ **All Star Christmas Jubilee** / Vintage Jazz Classics ◆◆◆◆◆
This 77-minute disc includes two Armed Forces Radio Service Christmas Jubilee shows (1945 and 1947) and other '40s holiday tracks. The Delta Rhythm Boys harmonize on a snippet of "Jingle Bells" before the master of patter and jive, Ernie "Bubbles" Whitman takes over as MC. Count Basie and His Orchestra are the house band for the 1945 show, with guests including Lena Horne on "Silent Night" and a hilarious Christmas jive routine with Whitman and Eddie Green. Duke Ellington and His Orchestra are the backing band for the '47 show, jumping into the festivities with "Ring Dem Blues." The Nat King Cole Trio deliver a smooth take of "The Christmas Song," Perry Como wanders through a "Winter Wonderland" and there are non-Yule selections from other jazz artists. The non-Jubilee selections include four from Frank Sinatra, Kay Starr's "December" and a novelty version of "Jingle Bells" from Mel Blanc & the Sportsmen. Although half a century old, these performances are every bit as entertaining today. Highly recommended. —*Decibel Dennis MacDonald*

☆ **The Alligator Records Christmas Collection** / 1992 / Alligator ◆◆◆◆◆
To get that Christmas party smoking, throw *The Alligator Records Christmas Collection* (Alligator/Warner Music) on the disc player and another log on the fire. The legendary blues label dishes up the goods and turns up the heat with a set of mostly original compositions. Koko Taylor peels wallpaper with "Merry, Merry Christmas"; William Clarke's wailing harp drives "Please Let Me Be Your Santa Claus"; Charles Brown sets the tone with "Boogie Woogie Santa Claus"; and Lonnie Brooks serves the gumbo with "Christmas on the Bayou." For an updated traditional, just try sitting still for Katie Webster's "Deck the Halls with Boogie Woogie." —*Roch Parisien*

Alligator Stomp, Vol. 4—Cajun Christmas / 1992 / Rhino ◆◆◆
If you're throwin' a Yule dance party, I don't know of a better seasonal collection that features two-steps and waltzes. Of the 17 tracks, 15 were licensed from THE Cajun label, Swallow Records. Beausoleil recorded two songs especially for this compilation, the original "Christmas Bayou" and "It Came Upon a Midnight Clear," performed as an instrumental Cajun waltz. Four tracks are drawn from Beausoleil's fiddler/singer/leader Michael Doucet's Swallow *Christmas Bayou* CD, including this CD's closer, "Auld Lang Syne," which starts out traditionally slow before finishing off as a spirited two-step. Other highlights include Belton Richard's versions of "Blue Christmas" and "Please Come Home for Christmas," both sung in Cajun French: Richard's mournful vocals and the accompanying steel guitar give both songs added depth. Caveat emptor: If you hate accordions, fiddles, or just having a good time, do not buy this CD. —*Decibel Dennis MacDonald*

Austin Rhythm and Blues Christmas / 1989 / Epic ◆◆◆
Originally issued on the Austin label in 1983, this rockin' release was reissued with a new cover on Epic in 1986. Standouts include the Fabulous Thunderbird's spirited instrumental "Rockin' Winter Wonderland," and vocalist Kim Wilson pouring his harp and soul into Hop Wilson's "Merry Christmas, Darling." Two of Austin's finest blues divas, Angela Strehli and Lou Ann Barton, turn in smokey and sultry covers of yule classics, but it is bassist/vocalist Sarah Brown who sizzles with her original "My Christmas Is Hung with Tears." —*Dennis MacDonald*

Big Band Christmas / CBS ◆◆◆
Big bands, often with pop vocalists, including Les Brown with Doris Day singing "The Christmas Song," Red Norvo with vocalist Mildred Bailey on "I've Got My Love to Keep Me Warm" and Benny Goodman with Peggy Lee and Art Lund duetting on "Winter Weather." Laster Lanin's arrangement of "Christmas Night in Harlem" is one that'll have you flip, flop and flying, but most of this CD is on the slower, sentimental side. —*Decibel Dennis MacDonald*

☆ **Billboard Greatest Christmas Hits: 1955-1989** / Rhino ◆◆◆◆◆
Billboard Greatest Christmas Hits: 1955–1989 / Vol. 2 features Elvis on "Blue Christmas," Bobby Helms ("Jingle Bell Rock"), and Brenda Lee ("Rockin' around the Christmas Tree"). On the novelty side, this disc has "Grandma Got Run Over by a Reindeer," "The Chipmunk Song," and others. —*Rick Clark*

☆ **Billboard Greatest Christmas Hits: Country** / Rhino ◆◆◆◆◆
Primarily late '40s and late '50s hits, many more novelty than C&W. The Texas Troubadour, Ernest Tubb, hit the charts twice with his 1949 A-side, "Blue Christmas," and then the B-side, "White Christmas" (both are here). Country corn from Tex Ritter, Buck Owens, Eddy Arnold, and others,

alongside Johnny Cash's solemn "The Little Drummer Boy." —*Dennis MacDonald*

☆ **Billboard Greatest Christmas Hits: 1935-1954** / Rhino ◆◆◆◆◆
Some of the biggest seasonal classics are represented on these two discs. *Vol. 1* opens with Bing singing (guess what?) "White Christmas" and runs through Gene Autry's "Rudolph the Red-Nosed Reindeer," "The Christmas Song" (Nat King Cole), "Let It Snow, Let It Snow, Let It Snow" (Vaughn Monroe), the annoying "All I Want for Christmas (Is My Two Front Teeth)" by Spike Jones, and more. —*Rick Clark*

Billboard Greatest R&B Christmas Hits / Rhino ◆◆◆◆
Includes the original version (1947) of "Merry Christmas, Baby" by Johnny Moore's Three Blazers, featuring Charles Brown's smoother-than-brandy vocals; jump-blues from Mabel Scott on "Boogie-Woogie Santa Claus"; vocal group contributions from the Orioles and the Cadillacs; Chuck Berry's "Run Rudolph, Run"; and more. —*Dennis MacDonald*

☆ **Blue Yule—Christmas Blues and R&B Classics** / Rhino ◆◆◆◆◆
A stellar 18-song compilation with many tracks that are not duplicated on other in-print collections. Treasures abound here: rare tracks from John Lee Hooker and Lightnin' Hopkins, Hop Wilson's original "Merry Christmas, Darling" (covered by the Fabulous Thunderbirds on *An Austin Rhythm & Blues Christmas*), Louis Jordan's last recording (1968, "Santa Claus, Santa Claus"), and more. —*Dennis MacDonald*

Bob Hope's Christmas Party / 1945 / Vintage Jazz Classics ◆◆◆
"Command Performances" were half-hour radio programs recorded for the Armed Forces Radio Service and shipped to the WWII troops as 16-inch platters. On this collection there is a humorous sketch from Mel Blanc as "P-P-Private Sad Sack," using the Porky Pig voice; banter with Hope, Bing Crosby, Judy Garland and other celebrities; and musical performances from Dinah Shore, Harry James, Johnny Mercer, and others. Carols performed by Garland, Shore, Crosby and more conclude the CD. —*Decibel Dennis MacDonald*

☆ **Bummed-Out Christmas!** / Rhino ◆◆◆◆◆
Not just for the Scrooge on your holiday list. This album has a rare gem from the Everly Brothers, "Christmas Eve Can Kill You." George Jones is equally mournful on "Lonely Christmas Call" from 1963, but the most powerful track comes from the duo of Johnny & Jon with the deep soul ballad, 1966's "Christmas in Vietnam"—their call-and-response style is textbook Sam and Dave. On the lighter side, there's the Christmas Jug Band (featuring Dan Hicks) to the humorous (Sherwin Linton, "Santa Got a D.W.I.") to the mournful (George Jones, "Lonely Christmas Call"). —*Dennis MacDonald*

☆ **Christmas Album** / CBS ◆◆◆◆◆
A wonderful holiday sampler. Includes Tony Bennett, Frank Sinatra, Andy Williams, Johnny Mathis, and others. —*David A. Milberg*

☆ **Christmas Cheers from Motown** / Motown ◆◆◆◆◆
A hit album from 1973 with great Christmas presents from the Temptations, Diana Ross & the Supremes, Stevie Wonder, and Smokey Robinson & the Miracles. —*David A. Milberg*

☆ **Christmas Classics** / 1989 / Rhino ◆◆◆◆◆
A well-rounded compilation of R&B, rock 'n' roll, pop, and rocking instrumentals (the Ventures and Santo & Johnny). Aretha Franklin is elegant on "Winter Wonderland," while Stevie Wonder and the Supremes represent "The Motown Sound." Roy Orbison is in top form on "Pretty Paper," and Bobby "Boris" Pickett would make the Grinch smile with "Monsters' Holiday." —*Dennis MacDonald*

☆ **The Christmas Collection** / Dec. 12, 1991 / Prestige ◆◆◆◆◆
Devotees of acoustic combo jazz will love *The Christmas Collection*. Every song is a highlight on this Who's Who of jazz giants, featuring Dexter Gordon, Paul Bley, Art Blakey, Charles Mingus, Gene Ammons, Bobby Timmons, Eddie "Lockjaw" Davis, Bill Smith, Don Patterson, and more. There is a continuity from beginning to end that makes this a very playable collection. It's a must! —*Rick Clark*

☆ **Christmas Comedy Classics** / Priority ◆◆◆◆◆
Collectibles by Dancer, Prancer & Nervous—the Singing Reindeer (Stan Freberg, Mel Blanc, and Yogi Yogesson). —*David A. Milberg*

☆ **Christmas Gift Set** / Sep. 16, 1991 / Capitol ◆◆◆◆◆
With tracks from Bing Crosby, Nat King Cole, and Frank Sinatra, this is essential stuff for a nostalgic Noel. Cuddle under the mistletoe or by a warm fireplace with this one. —*David A. Milberg*

★ **A Christmas Gift for You from Phil Spector** / 1963 / Phillies ◆◆◆◆◆
Featuring Phil Spector's "Wall of Sound" in its prime and his early stable of artists, the Ronettes, Crystals, Darlene Love, and Bob B. Soxx & the Blue Jeans, this stands as inarguably the greatest Christmas record of all time. Spector believed he could produce a record for the holidays that would capture not only the essence of the Christmas Spirit but also be a pop masterpiece, standing against any work these artists had already done. He succeeded on every level, with all four groups/singers recording some of their most memorable performances, from Ronnie sounding

sexy as ever on the Ronettes' "I Saw Mommy Kissing Santa Claus" to the playfulness of the Crystals on "Santa Claus Is Coming to Town." The star on top of this Christmas tree, however, is Darlene Love, with her impassioned "Christmas (Baby Please Come Home)." This is the Christmas album by which all later holiday releases have to be judged and it has inspired a host of imitators. It's absolutely essential. (Note: This CD is available separately and as part of the highly recommended four-CD boxed set, *Phil Spector: Back to Mono (1958-1969)* Abkco CD 7118 1991) —*Decibel Dennis MacDonald*

☆ **Christmas Kisses** / Oct. 1, 1990 / Capitol ✦✦✦✦✦
An outstanding 22-track compilation from Capitol's vaults, 1944-1963, covering many styles, from the folk blues of Leadbelly to the entrancing pop vocals of Nancy Wilson. Doo-wop, honky-tonk, piano boogie, and the playful girl group Pop of the Bookends on "Christmas Kisses" all fit in with Les Paul's dazzling display of guitar virtuosity on "Jingle Bells" and the irresistible "Rudolph the Red-Nosed Reindeer Mambo" from Billy May and his orchestra. —*Dennis MacDonald*

☆ **Christmas Memories** / RCA ✦✦✦✦✦
Relive the Christmas sounds of pop singers and artists of the '40s and '50s. —*David A. Milberg*

☆ **Christmas Party with Eddie G.** / 1990 / CBS ✦✦✦✦✦
If there is a more entertaining Christmas compilation than this CD, I have not heard it. This is a party platter that includes international Christmas greetings and amusing comedy bits from old radio in between 17 tracks of R&B, blues, country, exotica, rock, novelty, and more. Most tracks are unavailable elsewhere on CD. From the surf sounds of Untamed Youth to the strains of Monty & Marsha Brown's "Cajun Christmas," this is a nonstop Christmas party. —*Dennis MacDonald*

A Christmas Present for You from Phil Spector / Rhino ✦✦✦✦✦
There is no doubt that Phil Spector's production vision was brilliant. This Christmas album is one of his greatest achievements (which is saying a lot). Features Darlene Love, the Ronettes, Bob B. Soxx & the Blue Jeans, and the Crystals. Spector focuses Christmas through the attitude of early '60s pop magic the way Crosby did for music of the '40s. —*Rick Clark*

☆ **Christmas Rap** / Profile ✦✦✦✦✦
Early rap-masters from the early '80s, including Run D.M.C., Sweet Tee, Surf MCs, Derek B, Dana Dane, Spyder-D, and others! —*David A. Milberg*

☆ **Christmas Rock Album** / Priority ✦✦✦✦✦
Great Christmas hits from Elton John, Foghat, Queen, Beach Boys, Elvin Bishop, Waitresses, and others. Super stuff! —*David A. Milberg*

Christmas Soul Special / Varrick ✦✦✦
This 1982 session brings together many great soul singers of the '60s—Mary Wells, Martha Reeves, Shirley Alston (of the Shirelles), Sam Moore (of Sam & Dave), and Ben E. King—but only Wilson Pickett rises to the occasion with incendiary versions of "Jingle Bells" and "Silver Bells." —*Decibel Dennis MacDonald*

☆ **Christmas with the Canadian Brass** / RCA ✦✦✦✦✦
Christmas favorites performed by this popular brass choir, plus the great organ of St. Patrick's Cathedral. The combination works. Fine traditional arrangements with some modern flavor. —*Michael Erlewine*

Cool Yule / Rhino ✦✦✦✦
Eighteen tracks culled from two out-of-print "Cool Yule" albums, this includes "Santa Claus" by the '60s garage band the Sonics (set to the tune of "Farmer John"); the hilarious R&B novelty "Christmas in the Congo" from the Mar-Keys; Tina Turner's wailing on "Merry Christmas, Baby"; and more essential offerings from James Brown, Solomon Burke, and others. —*Dennis MacDonald*

Cool Yule, Vol. 2 / Rhino ✦✦✦✦
Subtitled "A Collection of Rockin' Stocking Stuffers," this platter delivers with Johnny Preston's humorous rockabilly number "(I Want a) Rock and Roll Guitar" and the girl-group delights of Honey and the Bees "Jing Jing a Ling." The Pacific Northwest's kings of garage rock, the Sonics, turn in an original, "Santa Claus," that cops the "Farmer John" riff and gets their wish list straight: "I want a brand new car / a twangy guitar / a cute little honey / and lots of money." More R&B and R&R from Huey "Piano" Smith, Jack Scott, the Uniques, Gary "U.S." Bonds, and more. Pass the eggnog. —*Decibel Dennis MacDonald*

☆ **Country Christmas, Vol. 1** / RCA ✦✦✦✦✦
Great stuff from the '70s and '80s by Alabama, Charley Pride, Willie Nelson, Razzy Bailey, and others. —*David A. Milberg*

Country Christmas Collection / 1991 / PolyGram ✦✦✦
An uneven collection with a few standouts: Bob Wills & His Texas Playboys turn in a playful "Santa's on His Way" and the more sentimental strains of "When It's Christmas on the Range." Jerry Lee Lewis, an underrated country singer, can break your heart with "I Can't Have a Merry Christmas, Mary, Without You" and George Jones is high and lonesome on "Maybe Next Christmas." Dave Dudley turns his "Six Days on the

Road" into a seasonal treat with "Six Tons of Toys." —*Decibel Dennis MacDonald*

☆ **Creole Christmas** / 1990 / Epic ✦✦✦✦✦
Featuring some of the finest singers of New Orleans, including Aaron Neville, Johnny Adams, Irma Thomas, and more. —*Dennis MacDonald*

December's Eve / RCA ✦✦✦✦
Fireside Christmas sounds from RCA's popular (not rock 'n' roll) artists of the '50s. —*David A. Milberg*

Dr. Demento Presents: Greatest Xmas Novelty CD / 1989 / Rhino ✦✦✦
Dr. Demento's novelty collections are usually in sync with those folks who think *Mad Magazine* is essential reading. Nothing wrong with that, even though this collection is at times overbearingly cute and the humor often too dated to be meaningful or funny for those who didn't remember the songs the first time around. Nevertheless, where else can you find "Grandma Got Run over by a Reindeer," Bob & Doug McKenzie's (of SCTV) "Twelve Days of Christmas," the Barking Dogs, Wild Man Fischer, Weird Al Yankovic, Cheech & Chong, and Stan Freberg on one disc? If *Handel's Messiah* represents the loftier aspects of Christmas, then *Dr. Demento Presents* is the season's whoopee cushion. —*Rick Clark*

☆ **A GRP Christmas Collection** / 1989 / GRP ✦✦✦✦✦
Chick Corea's Elektric Band, Special EFX, Lee Ritenour, David Benoit, Tom Scott, Gary Burton, Mark Egan, and a host of others run through a batch of standards with an inhumanly high level of virtuosity. As with many GRP releases, the state-of-the-art sound tends to take precedence over sparks. Gary Burton's mathematically precise "God Rest Ye Merry Gentlemen" does for jazz what Gentle Giant did for rock. Dave Grusin, Szakcsi, and Lee Ritenour turn in emotive solo performances, and the unique Kevin Eubanks arrangement of "Silver Bells" work well. —*Rick Clark*

☆ **A GRP Christmas Collection, Vol. 2** / GRP ✦✦✦✦✦
If you loved the first one, you'll love this too. —*David A. Milberg*

☆ **God Rest Ye Merry Jazzmen** / 1981 / CBS ✦✦✦✦✦
A compilation of tracks not on any other albums. With Dexter Gordon Quartet, McCoy Tyner (solo), Arthur Blythe Quartet, Heath Brothers, Paquito D'Rivera Duo, and the Wynton Marsalis Quintet in modern and modal settings. —*Michael G. Nastos*

Handel's Messiah—a Soulful Celebration / 1992 / Warner Bros. ✦✦✦✦
Contemporary soul/pop artists, including Patti Austin, Tevin Campbell, Stevie Wonder, Quincy Jones, Take 6, Howard Hewett, and Dianne Reeves, take a pop-song approach to Handel's classic Christmas oratorio. Handel's wonderful melodies are updated with synthesizers, drum machines, and slick pop production from Quincy Jones and Take 6's Mervyn Warren. —*AMG*

☆ **Have Yourself a Jazzy Little Christmas** / Verve ✦✦✦✦✦
This 15-track CD has something for everyone: the smooth vocal styling of Billy Eckstine on "Christmas Eve," the purring Dinah Washington on the seductive "Ole Santa," and Ella Fitzgerald showing her soft and sentimental side on the single, "The Secret of Christmas." Billie Holiday, with help from Benny Carter and Sweets Edison, warms up the punchbowl with "I've Got My Love to Keep Me Warm," while Sister Rosetta Tharpe raises the rafters on her powerful rendition of "O Little Town of Bethlehem." Jimmy Smith and his funky Hammond B3 invigorate "Jingle Bells," but by adding tympani and horns, he totally re-invents "God Rest Ye Merry Gentlemen." —*Decibel Dennis MacDonald*

Have Yourself a Merry Little Christmas / 1989 / Rhino ✦✦✦
A well-intentioned effort with a portion of the proceeds going to some unspecified charity. Eclectic, but ultimately too uneven to make this ecumenical effort a satisfying listen. — *Rick Clark*

☆ **Have a Merry Chess Christmas** / 1989 / Chess ✦✦✦✦✦
A fine cross-section of R&B and blues plus three tracks from the out-of-print 1968 Chess Gospel Christmas album, *A Christmas Dedication*. It includes the Meditation Singers doing a plaintive "Blue Christmas" (not the Elvis classic), '60s soul from the O'Jays and Rotary Connection (featuring the late Minnie Ripperton), Chuck Berry singing "Run Rudolph, Run," a smokey take on "Merry Christmas, Baby," and more. —*Dennis MacDonald*

☆ **Hillbilly Holiday** / 1989 / Rhino ✦✦✦✦✦
To date, the best compilation of Christmas Country ranging from the Louvin Brothers wrapping their harmonies around "It Came Upon a Midnight Clear" to unabashed fun from Hank Snow ("Reindeer Boogie"), Buck Owens, Loretta Lynn, and the downright amusing "Daddy's Drinking up Our Christmas" from Commander Cody. —*Dennis MacDonald*

☆ **Hipsters' Holiday: Vocal Jazz & R&B Classics** / Rhino ✦✦✦✦✦
Typical of Rhino releases, *Hipster's Holiday* has very well laid-out annotation and pictures. This collection covers tracks from 1946 to 1988. Eartha Kitt's "material girl" ode, "Santa Baby," as well as its antithesis in the Miles Davis "Blue Xmas (To Whom It May Con-

cern)," are here, as well as the hyper-scat singing of Leo Watson and Lambert, Hendricks & Ross. Both of the former are also on the CBS *Jingle Bell Jazz* collection, but they sound better here. As with the Jass and Savoy discs, Rhino has drawn from some performances of off-vinyl sources. All in all, this disc sounds cleaner and more detailed than those two releases, primarily due to the more recent vintage of recordings. —*Rick Clark*

Home Alone 2: Lost in New York / 1992 / Fox ◆◆◆
Bruce Springsteen had always sought to re-create Phil Spector's "Wall of Sound" with his E-Street Band (one listen to "Born to Run" is all the proof you need), so when Steven Van Zandt wrote "All Alone on Christmas" for ex-Phil Spector singer par excellence Darlene Love, he also used four other former E-Streeters to back her up on this full-scale production, adding six horns, bells, tambourines and extra percussion to outdo the "Boss" in apeing the "Wall of Sound." The remainder of the CD, unfortunately, is filled with dreck from Bette Midler, Atlantic Starr, even a later (read: subpar) Johnny Mathis tune. Will someone please give Darlene Love her own record? —*Decibel Dennis MacDonald*

Home for the Holidays / RCA ◆◆◆
This nine-song CD is mediocre at best with one gem: Foster and Lloyd's original "Christmas List," a power-popper that recalls Marshall Crenshaw. Other tracks by Clint Black, K.T. Oslin, Keith Whitley, and more. —*Decibel Dennis MacDonald*

Hot Jazz for Cool Nights / 1992 / Music Masters ◆◆◆
Anthology featuring vintage performers doing classic traditional jazz cuts. Earl Hines, Charlie Johnson, Tiny Parham, The Missourians, The Jungletown Stompers and Musical Stevedores are the acts presented. —*Ron Wynn*

☆ **It's Christmas Time Again** / Stax ◆◆◆◆◆
Only the *Soul Christmas* collection of Atlantic beats this compilation of Christmas soul and blues. Rufus Thomas, Mack Rice, and Albert King sound downright salacious, while the Rance Allen Group sanctify "White Christmas" in a way Bing Crosby never could. The Emotions joyously set the record straight with "Black Christmas," and the Staples Singers sermonize in their special fashion with "Who Took the Merry out of Christmas?" Isaac Hayes, the Temprees, and Little Johnny Taylor are also in great form here. —*Dennis MacDonald & Rick Clark*

☆ **Jingle Bell Jazz** / 1989 / CBS ◆◆◆◆◆
Jingle Bell Jazz is a single-CD compilation of two previously released CBS holiday jazz albums, *Jingle Bell Jazz* (1974) and *God Rest Ye Merry Jazzmen* (1985). This disc is loaded with strong performances by Herbie Hancock, McCoy Tyner, Dexter Gordon, Wynton Marsalis, Duke Ellington, Lionel Hampton, Miles Davis, and more. —*Rick Clark, Rock & Roll Disc*

Just in Time for Christmas / 1990 / IRS ◆◆◆
When Phil Spector assembled his stable of artists in 1963 to create the masterpiece, *A Christmas Gift for You from Phil Spector*, he probably did not suspect that other labels would try to imitate his success: this collection shows how bringing together bands from a label's stable can fail miserably. Except for contributions from Squeeze (the quirky "Christmas Day") and the dB's (the powerpop "Home for the Holidays"), this is fairly unnecessary fare. —*Decibel Dennis MacDonald*

★ **Legends of Christmas Past, a Rock 'n' R&B Holiday Collection** / EMI America ◆◆◆◆
A "must" for any cool yule fan, this 20-track CD will delight collectors with nine rare or previously unreleased cuts, including two rockin' tracks from Bill Haley. Lon Chaney, Jr. escapes from the vaults to unleash the playful "Monster Holiday," while Canned Heat boogie down with their original "Christmas Blues" and attempt to make Alvin & the Chipmunks hip on a remake of "The Chipmunk Song." Gorgeous doo wop from the Five Keys and Marvin & Johnny; blues from Amos Milburn and Charles Brown; rock 'n' roll from Jan & Dean and the Belmonts; and more from Eddie Cochran with the Holly Twins, Manfred Mann, others. —*Decibel Dennis MacDonald*

☆ **Lump of Coal** / Oct. 8, 1991 / First Warning ◆◆◆◆◆
These are old holiday standards performed in a punk/new-wave style. Fun and nicely done. —*David A. Milberg*

Mas! A Caribbean Christmas Party / 1992 / Rykodisc ◆◆◆
Christmas releases tend to sound the same, mainly because there's only so many ways to sing shopworn carols and holiday tunes. But here's actually a Christmas alternative; a nine-track CD with Caribbean artists putting their spin on the season. El Gran Combo, Joseph Spence, Lord Nelson and Machel don't distort the traditional meaning of the lyrics, but they certainly bring a fresh quality to their holiday numbers, while performing much more upbeat versions than you'll hear on many rote Christmas discs. —*Ron Wynn*

☆ **Merry Christmas Baby** / King ◆◆◆◆◆
The original issue of this classic was subtitled *Intimate Christmas Music for Lovers*, and with five of the dozen tracks featuring the smoothest of the smooth vocalists, Charles Brown, that subtitle is appropriate. Other King artists represented here are bluesmen Lowell Fulson and Jimmy Witherspoon and Lloyd Glenn on "Sleighride" doing a swinging piano workout. Mabel Scott's original jumping "Boogie-Woogie Santa Claus" can be found here. —*Dennis MacDonald*

☆ **Merry Christmas Baby** / Paula ◆◆◆◆◆
R&B and blues from 15 artists on 23 songs including some re-recordings by Charles Brown and Lowell Fulson. Includes the riveting "Christmas in Vietnam" by deep-soul duo Johnny and Jon. —*Dennis MacDonald*

☆ **Merry Christmas Baby—Romance & Reindeer** / Sep. 30, 1991 / Capitol ◆◆◆◆◆
For that beneath-the-mistletoe mood-setter, this compilation of crooners and pop singers is hard to beat. You'll be put under the spell of sultry sounds from Julie London and Nancy Wilson or the silky soul of Nat "King" Cole. Dean Martin's dreamy "Winter Romance" is here, along with the seductive pairing of Johnny Mercer and Margaret Whiting on "Baby, It's Cold Outside." Twenty-five tracks from 1946-1968. —*Dennis MacDonald*

The Mother of All Flagpole Christmas Albums / Fla ◆◆◆
Culled from three Christmas tapes released by *Flagpole Magazine*, this includes performances recorded in 1990-92 from 21 Atlanta and Athens, GA, bands. Most of the songs are diverse "alternative" originals but there's also a bizarre guitar/sax duet of "Jingle Bells" from the Flat Duo Jets, a cover of Spinal Tap's "Christmas with the Devil" by Allgood, an okay version of the Sonics' "Santa Claus" by the Woggles, "You're a Mean One, Mr. Grinch" from the Labrea Stompers, and more spotty fun. —*Decibel Dennis MacDonald*

The Narada Christmas Collection / 1989 / Narada ◆◆◆
Even though Narada is known as a new-age label, this collection maintains the musical attitude of that genre, while embracing the classier pieces of the Christmas holiday, such as, "What Child Is This," "It Came Upon a Midnight Clear," "O Holy Night," and so forth. Nice, unobtrusive, polite—ultimately the kind of stuff that may teeter a little too close to easy listening for some listeners. —*Rick Clark*

New England Christmastide / North Star ◆◆◆
These 14 Rhode Island performers on folk instruments come from separate musical traditions—sea, Irish, singer-songwriter, classical—with a determination not to leave Christmas to the choirs, orchestras and trumpeters. They have fashioned an unassuming gem: an album full of warm colors and quiet delights... a bounty of beautiful (and unimpeachably traditional) Christmas music, done in ways that are fresh, sprightly, reverent and deeply Christmasy. Recommended. —*Bob Coltman*

Nipper's Greatest Christmas Hits / RCA ◆◆◆
Nipper's Greatest Christmas Hits is a time-warp escape into the '50s world of the Ames Brothers, Roger Whittaker, Dinah Shore, Perry Como, and Arthur Fiedler. —*Rick Clark*

Reggae Christmas / RAS ◆◆◆◆
Here are all your favorite carols with a Rastafarian twist from Eek-A-Mouse, Mighigan & Smiley, Freddie McGregor, and others. —*AMG*

Rhythm & Blues Christmas: 20 Songs / Hollywood
Among the 20 tracks included here are two from Hank Ballard and the Midnighters that alone would be worth the price of admission: "Christmas Time for Everybody but Me" rivals the most testifyin' pleas of King labelmate James Brown, and Ballard turns in another outstanding performance with "Santa Claus Is Coming." While there is some duplication with other in-print collections (especially *Merry Christmas Baby*, on Starday/King), this marks the only CD appearance of many holiday classics from the King vaults. Recommended highly. —*Decibel Dennis MacDonald*

Rock & Roll Christmas / ACE ◆◆◆◆
Reissue of Huey "Piano" Smith and the Clowns' *'Twas the Night before Christmas* album on Ace, with six added tracks from other New Orleans artists. Oddly, the tracks are not identified by artist, but that won't spoil your yule dance party. You can mambo to Smith's "Almost Time for Santa" and do the Popeye to "All I Want for Christmas (Is a Little Bit of Music)." A nutty but danceable party platter. —*Dennis MacDonald*

☆ **Rockin' Little Christmas** / MCA ◆◆◆◆◆
A dozen sides of rock 'n' roll, R&B, girl group (the 1964 "Love for Christmas" by the Gems), and more. "Mambo Santa Mambo" by the Enchanters and "Hey, Santa Claus" by the Moonglows are unbeatable fun. —*Dennis MacDonald*

☆ **Santa Claus Blues** / Jass ◆◆◆◆◆
There isn't a seasonal CD that'll keep the hepcats swingin' more than Santa Claus Blues. Spanning 1925-1971 with a generous 23 tracks, this

includes the gutbucket blues of Lionel Hampton and His Orchestra on "Merry Christmas, Baby," Fats Waller's humorous arrangement of "Swingin' Them Jingle Bells," Jimmy Rushing as the vocalist in Count Basie's Orchestra on "Good Morning Blues (I Want to See Santa Claus)," and a mournful-sounding Victoria Spivey on "Christmas Morning Blues." From the Crescent City there's the title cut from the Clarence Williams Five (with Louis Armstrong and Sidney Bechet), Louis Prima's playful "What Will Santa Claus say (When He Finds Everybody Swingin')," and Louis Armstrong on the last five selections, including "Cool Yule" and "'Zat You, Santa Claus?" This album is highly recommended. —*Decibel Dennis MacDonald*

Scrooged / Arista ◆◆◆
While only a portion of this soundtrack has a yule theme, the duet of blue-eyed soul diva Annie Lennox and the ever-in-style Al Green on "Put a Little Love in Your Heart" sends a message that should be broadcast year-round. Also includes Robbie Robertson's "Christmas Must Be Tonight" and Natalie Cole reprising her father's "The Christmas Song"; surprisingly, she didn't think to turn this into a duet and video with her father. —*Decibel Dennis MacDonald*

Soul Christmas / 1968 / Atlantic ◆◆◆◆
This 1991 reissue includes eight of the original 11 tracks included on the Atco 1968 release (a rare album still worth seeking), with 11 more tracks added from the Atlantic vaults. Few, if any, Christmas compilations are more essential than this one. Otis Redding's performances of "White Christmas" and "Merry Christmas, Baby" are alone worth the price of admission. Clarence Carter's funky "Back Door Santa" and Joe Tex's ballad "I'll Make Every Day Christmas (For My Woman)" are only two more tracks that make this an absolute must-have CD. —*Dennis MacDonald*

In a Christmas Mood—A Swing Era Big Band Celebration / Mobile Fidelity ◆◆◆
Christmas big-band-style, performed by the Starlight Orchestra. The playing is very tight, professional, and true to style, but like Glenn Miller (to whom this collection tips its hat), *In a Christmas Mood* might be too much white bread for certain lovers of jazz. As with all Mobile Fidelity discs, the sound is impeccable. —*Rick Clark*

★ Street Carols / Sep. 1991 / Street Gold ◆◆◆◆◆
Recorded in 1991, this a capella recording has a timeless quality as hand-in-velvet-glove harmonies work their magic on songs new and old, with blasts from the past in Jerry Butler, the Spaniels, and the Chi-Lites, but credit must go to the group Stormy Weather, who not only organized this doo wop project but also sang five of the 15 selections, including the original "Street Carols" that sounds like a lost gem from 1954. David Somerville, ex-lead singer of the Diamonds, does all four vocal parts on "The Last Month of the Year" but the CD peaks with Ronnie Spector's version of Frankie Lymon's "Creation of Love" (with re-worked lyrics to fit the yule theme). —*Decibel Dennis MacDonald*

Sugar Plums: Holiday Treats from Sugar Hill / Sugar Hill ◆◆◆
Most of this CD is imbued with soft, sublime sounds of the season, including Jerry Douglas' double-tracked dobro/guitar rendering of "Away in a Manger," Dan Crary's guitar and sleigh bells version of "What Child Is This?" and the stately bluegrass harmonies of John Starling, Larry Stephenson, and Rickie Simpkins on "Beautiful Star of Bethlehem." Robin and Linda Williams sing Steve Earle's "Nothing But a Child" as if it were a yule folk standard. The all-female Ranch Romance vamp up Elvis' "Santa Bring My Baby Back (To Me)" with sizzling accordion and fiddle, and Red Knuckles & the Trailblazers end the proceedings with a medley that'll make you "n'yuk n'yuk n'yuk." —*Decibel Dennis MacDonald*

Swinging Big Band Christmas / Laserlight ◆◆◆
Of the ten selections included, only a few really swing: the Gene Krupa Trio's (drums/sax/piano) live version of "Jingle Bells" is tops, and the Larry Clinton Orchestra and the Les Brown Orchestra work wonders with Tchaikovsky ("Dance of the Sugar Plum Fairies" and "The Nutcracker Suite," respectively). Otherwise, much is "sweet music" of Guy Lombardo, Jack Teagarden and others. —*Decibel Dennis MacDonald*

The Texas Christmas Collection / Amazing ◆◆◆
Sixteen Texas artists, but only a handful offer a worthwhile performance here. Willie Nelson turns in a delicate version of "Silent Night" while gui-

tarists Eric Johnson and Van Wilks pair up for an acoustic rendering of "What Child Is This?" Jerry Jeff Walker calls his friend up to say he's coming home in "Mason Dixon's on the Line" and Beto & the Fairlanes liven the party up with a salsa instrumental take of "We Three Kings." The real gem in this Lone Star compilation belongs to Long Tall Marcia Ball with her impassioned version of Charles Brown's seasonal chestnut, "Please Come Home for Christmas." —*Decibel Dennis MacDonald*

☆ Traditional Christmas Classics / 1989 / Adventures in Music ◆◆◆◆◆
Why the artists performing on this disc aren't listed on the outside of the package is a mystery. Mel Torme does "The Christmas Song," and there's Bing Crosby's "White Christmas." "Christmas in New Orleans" by Louis Armstrong is easily the highlight on this outing. Easy-listening kingpins Billy Vaughn, LeRoy Anderson, and Roger Williams are here doing their most famous Christmas music contributions. —*Rick Clark*

A Very Special Christmas / A&M ◆◆◆
Recorded to benefit the Special Olympics, this has some of the biggest names in contemporary music, most covering seasonal favorites with mixed success. Outstanding tracks include the Pretenders "Have Yourself a Merry Little Christmas" with Chrissie Hynde giving a touching performance. Run-D.M.C.'s topical "Christmas in Hollis" relies heavily on sampling "Back Door Santa" and may head you toward the dance floor. Alison Moyet's stately version of "The Coventry Carol" is beautifully haunting. Only the "Material Girl," Madonna, embarrasses herself with an overly campy "Santa Baby." —*Decibel Dennis MacDonald*

A Very Special Christmas 2 / Oct. 20, 1992 / A&M ◆◆◆
Although not even half of this CD is outstanding, it was recorded for a worthwhile cause (Special Olympics) and contains some songs I certainly wouldn't want to be without, most notably Tom Petty and the Heartbreakers' "Christmas All Over Again"—this is jingle/jangle pop at its best. Boyz II Men wrap their a capella voices around "The Birth of Christ" and the two "Wall of Sound" standouts, Darlene Love and Ronnie Spector, bring their powerful voices together for the first time on "Rockin' Around the Christmas Tree." Bonnie Raitt duets with Charles Brown on his sexy "Merry Christmas, Baby" while Aretha Franklin shows why she's called the "Queen of Soul" on "O Christmas Tree." —*Decibel Dennis MacDonald*

Warner Bros. Records Presents a Christmas Tradition, Vol. 3 / Warner Bros. ◆◆◆
This CD is worth the price of admission for the Texas Tornados' Farfisa-fueled, accordion-pumped "Rudolph the Red-Nosed Reindeer," one of the best Tex-Mex Christmas party records you'll ever hear. The gospel quartet, the Fairfield Four, sing "The Last Month of the Year" a capella—another standout. Holly Dunn contributes a spirited rendition of "Feliz Navidad" with a lively percussion break and empathetic accordion and Brenda Lee re-does her classic "Rockin' Around the Christmas Tree." —*Decibel Dennis MacDonald*

☆ A Winter's Solstice—Vols. 1 & 2 / Windham Hill ◆◆◆◆◆
This is a superb sampler with 15 artists from the label performing original pieces as well as their own renderings of traditional works. The artists include Hedges, Aaberg, Nightnoise, Dalglish, Ackerman, Stein and Walder, McCandless, Metamora, and Therese Schroeder-Sheker, plus others. In the finest Windham Hill tradition, this is a truly stirring collection. —*Backroads Music/Heartbeats*

☆ Yuletunes / Black Vinyl ◆◆◆◆◆
Inspired by the Beatles Fan Club Christmas EPs and Phil Spector's Christmas LP, popmeisters the Shoes put together this compilation of 16 bands, most relatively obscure, and came up with some pure pop delights. This yule punchbowl is filled with jingley/jangley guitars, Beatlesque melodies and harmonies, Spector "Wall of Sound" sleigh bells, and more to brighten your holiday listening. Standouts are many, including the Shoes' "This Christmas," Bill Lloyd's Marshall Crenshaw-ish "Underneath the Christmas Tree," the Idea's Byrdsy "It's About that Time," and Matthew Sweet's "Baby Jesus." The Cavedogs' "Three Wise Men and a Baby" sounds like an outtake from *The Beatles* (a.k.a. *The White Album*). —*Decibel Dennis MacDonald*

VOCALS

If the human voice is the oldest musical instrument of all, then it's also the most recorded one in the history of the medium itself. In essence, this section reflects how that instrument has been part and parcel of the development of American pop music since recorded performances were being etched into cylinders in Thomas Edison's laboratories.

What we now know as popular or "pop" music started right around the turn of the century. Song publishers were flourishing in a section of New York City known as "Tin Pan Alley," selling sheet music like crazy, while the recording industry was just getting off the ground. Once the sheet music publishers found they needed someone to sing or "plug" that song and make it popular, and the record companies realized that the singer in question could sell a lot of records for them by singing that song, we saw the birth of popular music and the pop singer.

As pop music, even before the advent of rock 'n' roll, took many stylistic twists and turns, so do the artists profiled in this section. If

one rule of thumb may be applied: the pop music we're talking about here predates rock 'n' roll and is of the Tin Pan Alley variety, and the artists profiled belong to all the various offshoots that genre entails. We're covering nearly a century's worth of recordings—from early vaudeville performers like Al Jolson to modern-day artists singing material that clearly falls outside of rock music's several subgenres, and pretty much everything in between. Vocal pop music embraces everything from Rudy Vallee to Barbra Streisand, the Andrews Sisters to Frank Sinatra, and Bette Midler to Tony Bennett. That's a lot of stylistic ground to cover, but the genre itself maps out the same territory, adding decided left-hand turns to include song-and-dance men like Fred Astaire and "international" favorites like Marlene Dietrich and Yma Sumac. Given the current climate of music, one can only wonder what will constitute an entry in this section by the 21st century. As long as people keep singing, the boundaries of vocal/pop music will keep expanding. — *Cub Koda*

Ames Brothers

Vocal

Brothers Ed, Vic, Joe, and Gene Ames formed a group in their native Malden, MA, and scored 23 Top 40 hits between 1949 and 1960. When rock 'n' roll made chart success more and more difficult to attain, they split up, Ed going on to a solo career of his own. — *Cub Koda*

☆ **The Best of the Ames Brothers** / 1958 / RCA Victor ✦✦✦✦
Though their early hits recorded for Coral (now MCA) will probably be anthologized at some point, this one features all their biggest and best: "You, You, You," "The Man with the Banjo," "Melodie d'Amour," "Tammy," and "The Naughty Lady of Shady Lane." Smooth as silk. — *Cub Koda*

● **Best Of: Sentimental Me** / 1995 / Varese ✦✦✦
Featuring 18 songs recorded while the group was signed to Coral and Decca, *Best of the Ames Brothers: Sentimental Me* compiles some of their earliest hits, including "I'm Looking over a Four-Leaf Clover," "Sentimental Me," and "Rag Mop." — *Stephen Thomas Erlewine*

The Andrews Sisters

Vocals / Vocal

This American vocal trio consisted of sisters Patty (b. 1920), Maxine (b. 1918), and LaVerne Andrews (b. 1915–d. 1967). Their tight-knit harmonies were a direct descendant of the groundbreaking work done in the early '30s by the Boswell Sisters, but they soon developed their own successful strain. They sold over 60 million records, cashing in on the boogie-woogie fad of the '40s and becoming wartime favorites with film appearances in *Buck Privates* and *Stage Door Canteen*, among others. They are still the biggest-selling girl group ever. — *Cub Koda*

● **The 50th Anniversary, Vols. 1 & 2** / 1990 / MCA ✦✦✦
A two-volume definitive overview, with their best and most interesting sides from a long and successful career. — *Cub Koda*

Capitol Collectors Series / 1991 / Capitol ✦✦✦
Terrific overview of their mid-'50s output for Capitol, including such songs as "Rum and Coca-Cola," "Boogie Woogie Bugle Boy," "Don't Sit Under the Apple Tree (With Anyone Else But Me)," "Begin the Beguine," and "Beat Me Daddy, Eight to the Bar." — *Stephen Thomas Erlewine*

Harold Arlen

b. Feb. 15, 1905, Buffalo, NY, **d.** Apr. 23, 1986
Vocals

An American songwriting legend and son of a cantor, Harold Arlen was fascinated early in his life with the sound of ragtime. While singing in his

father's synagogue he also played ragtime piano in local Buffalo bands and accompanied silent films. After arranging for the Buffalodians, Arlen moved to New York. His jobs included arranging for Fletcher Henderson, and serving as a rehearsal pianist for radio and theater. A vamp he devised while practicing was later turned into the song "Get Happy," with lyrics from Ted Koehler. Arlen and Koehler wrote eight revues for the Cotton Club, one of which included the anthem "Stormy Weather," first performed by Ethel Waters. Though he moved to Hollywood in the '30s, Arlen kept penning songs for Broadway, working with other lyricists like Dorothy Fields, Les Robin, Johnny Mercer, Yip Harburg and Ira Gershwin as well as Koehler. His list of hits and accomplishments is amazing; they include songs for the films *Take a Chance, Star-Spangled Rhythm, The Sky's the Limit*, and his most famous, *The Wizard of Oz*. Arlen also composed tunes for the films *Earl Carroll Vanities, Rhythm Mania*, and *St. Louis Woman*. The incredible array of unforgettable compositions includes "I've Got The World on a String," "I Gotta Right to Sing the Blues," "The Devil and the Deep Blue Sea," "Come Rain or Come Shine," "It's Only a Paper Moon," and "Over the Rainbow." Numerous jazz artists have recorded his songs, as well as pop performers across the spectrum. Arlen made a few albums as a performer, among them sessions with Duke Ellington and Barbra Streisand. At present only one Arlen album, *Harold Sings Arlen, with Streisand*, is available, and it's not on CD. — *Ron Wynn*

● **Harold Sings Arlen (With Friend)** / 1966 / Vox Cum Laude ✦✦✦

Fred Astaire (Franz Austerlitz)

b. May 10, 1899, Omaha, NE, **d.** Jun. 22, 1987, Los Angeles, CA
Vocals, Dancer / Dancing, Vocal, Swing, Standards

When being rated as a magnificent all-round talent, many people would deem singing the least of Fred Astaire's skills, ranking it well behind dancing and acting. Yet Irving Berlin once said he'd rather hear Fred Astaire sing his compositions than any other vocalist. He was an excellent interpreter of classic American tunes, and could interact with great musicians without being overwhelmed or threatened. Astaire began his professional career as a five-year-old and was starring on vaudeville with his sister Adele until 1916; they equalled that success on the Broadway stage until 1932, when she gave up show business for marriage. George Gershwin penned "Lady Be Good" for them in 1924, and they did his "Funny Face" in 1927 and the Arthur Schwartz/Howard Dietz number "The Band Wagon" in 1931. A role in Cole Porter's *The Gay Divorcée* in 1932 led to a screen test in which the book on Astaire supposedly was "can't act, slightly bald, can dance a little." No matter, he teamed with Ginger Rogers and became the epitome for most Americans (particularly those unaware of or unwilling to consider Bill Robinson) of grace and flair as a dancer. But throughout his extraordinary film, stage, and television career, Astaire made superb recordings. He did transcendent versions of "Lady Be Good," "Fascinating Rhythm," "Dancing in the Dark," "Night and Day," and many, many others. Whether doing songs in theatrical productions or interpreting them in the studio, Astaire brought to every number a quiet charm, casual elegance, and exquisite timing, as well as distinctive enunciation and understated sense of swing. He made outstanding records in the '30s for Brunswick, and Decca in the '40s. The 1953 four-disc set *The Fred Astaire Story* was a collection of songs long associated with him, and featured him backed by an array of session and jazz greats. He also made *Swings and Sings Irving Berlin* during that same period and recorded with Oscar Peterson, Ray Brown, and Charlie Shavers. While his vocal triumphs will never get as much ink as his film and dance exploits, Astaire deserves mention as an important singer in the pre-swing era, with links to, if not a complete foothold in, jazz. —*Ron Wynn and Bruce Eder*

The Irving Berlin Songbook / Dec. 1952 / Verve ✦✦✦

● **Starring Fred Astaire** / 1989 / Columbia ✦✦✦✦
This 36-track album traces Fred Astaire's recordings from June 1935 to September 1940, including his No. 1 hits with "Cheek to Cheek," "I'm Putting All My Eggs in One Basket," "The Way You Look Tonight," "A Fine Romance," "They Can't Take That Away from Me," "Nice Work If You Can Get It," and "Change Partners." In addition to his movie stardom, Astaire was a major recording success in the second half of the '30s, introducing songs that would become standards by some of the great songwriters of the era—Irving Berlin, Jerome Kern and Dorothy Fields, and the Gershwins, especially. These recordings, which are studio efforts, not identical to the same songs in the movies, show Astaire to be as effortless a singer as he is a dancer (and you get to hear the tapping of those famous feet now and then, too). —*William Ruhlmann*

Pearl Bailey

b. Mar. 29, 1918, Newport News, VA, **d.** Aug. 17, 1990, Philadelphia, PA
Vocals / Vocal
Bailey started in show business by winning an amateur contest at age 13. Her eventual move from Washington, DC, to New York City established her as the darling of the cabaret/nightclub circuit. Bailey's languid, bluesy style, with assorted humorous asides and dialogs, only improved with time as movies and Vegas beckoned. In the 1940s and '50s, Bailey was one of the first women to bring salacious lyrics into the mainstream (witness her seduction of Hot Lips Page, "Baby, It's Cold Outside"). She was also the first female rapper (check "Tired"). In her rich, expressive alto, Bailey didn't just sing a song, she lived it and rhythmically talked you through it as few artists had done before or have done since. —*Cub Koda and Bil Carpenter*

The Intoxicating Pearl Bailey / 1956 / Mercury ✦✦✦
Spicy, sing-song storytelling. —*Bil Carpenter*

Pearl Bailey Sings for Adults Only / 1959 / Roulette ✦✦✦✦
Delightfully wicked set of standards done up in the inimitable Pearl Bailey manner, with immaculately swinging support from husband/drummer/bandleader Louis Bellson. —*Cub Koda*

Porgy and Bess / Apr. 30, 1959 / Columbia ✦✦✦
Backed by the Buddy Baker Orchestra. —*Bil Carpenter*

☆ **The Best of Pearl Bailey** / 1961 / Roulette ✦✦✦✦✦
Sassy and outlandish, this anthologizes most (but not all) of Bailey's best sides, including "It Takes Two to Tango." —*Cub Koda*

● **16 Most Requested Songs** / 1991 / Columbia ✦✦✦✦
Her most memorable '40s/'50s pop cuts. —*Bil Carpenter*

Josephine Baker

b. 1906, St. Louis, MO, **d.** Apr. 12, 1975, Paris, France
Vocals / Vocal
After drawing attention to herself with comic dancing in the all-Black chorus line of *Shuffle Along*, Baker became the sensation of Paris during the Jazz Age. Her silvery voice (said to be strong enough in her prime to fill a theater without the use of a microphone), exotic good looks, and energetic manner made her a legend for over a half-century in France, with movies, musicals, revues, and hit records to her credit; however, success eluded her in the US. She was still active in a one-woman show (with a dozen costume changes) in 1975 when she died in her sleep after giving 14 well-received performances. —*Cub Koda*

● **Josephine Baker** / Dec. 1926-Nov. 1936 / DCC ✦✦✦✦
Josephine Baker was much more famous as a cabaret performer, dancer, and personality than as a jazz singer but, as she shows on some of these early recordings, she could swing and improvise when she wanted to. The two-CD set gives one a well-rounded picture of Baker's prime period and a surprising percentage of the songs are jazz standards such as

"Dinah," "I Found a New Baby," "Bye Bye Blackbird," "Blue Skies," "You're Driving Me Crazy," etc. The musicianship of the French bands, which is rather streaky on part of the first disc, greatly improves by the later tracks and Baker is heard at her best throughout. It's a perfect introduction to her singing talents. —*Scott Yanow*

Shirley Bassey

b. Jan. 8, 1937, Tiger Bay, Cardiff, Wales
Vocals / Vocal
The Welsh belter supplied the strident theme song for one of Sean Connery's action-packed James Bond films, *Goldfinger*, in 1965. Bassey had scored a bundle of hits in Great Britain prior to landing the movie theme. Among her later US chart items for United Artists was the title song to another Bond flick in 1972, *Diamonds Are Forever*. —*Bill Dahl*

● **Goldslinger: The Best of Shirley Bassey** / 1995 / EMI ✦✦✦✦

Harry Belafonte

b. Mar. 1, 1927, New York City, NY
Vocals / Vocal, Calypso
The Harlem-born vocalist spearheaded the mid-'50s calypso movement in America, although he started out as a more conventional pop artist. Belafonte's clear diction, pure voice, and strikingly handsome features made him a national sensation when RCA released "Jamaica Farewell" in 1956 and "Banana Boat (Day-O)" the next year. Although much of his subsequent RCA output was calypso-oriented, Belafonte dabbled in everything from blues to Gershwin over the next few years. In addition to his music, Belafonte has starred in several movies, including *Buck and the Preacher* in 1972 and *Uptown Saturday Night* in 1974. His daughter Shari is a successful actress. —*Bill Dahl*

Calypso / 1956 / RCA ✦✦✦✦
His third album, which made him a star. —*Ron Wynn*

☆ **Belafonte at Carnegie Hall** / 1959 / RCA ✦✦✦✦✦
Landmark late-'50s live set. —*Ron Wynn*

Jump Up Calypso / 1961 / RCA Victor ✦✦✦✦
Belafonte was an established all-around entertainer and actor by the time of this album, so it could be seen in a sense as a return to "roots" styles. In any case, it's all-out calypso, with backing by the Trinidad Steel Band, and qualifies as one of his most energetic albums, even getting rambunctious at times. —*Richie Unterberger*

Pure Gold / 1975 / RCA ✦✦✦✦
Another overview/anthology. —*Ron Wynn*

All Time Greatest Hits, Vol. 1 / 1978 / RCA ✦✦✦✦
All Time Greatest Hits collects most of Harry Belafonte's biggest calypso hits, including "Banana Boat (Day-O)." —*Stephen Thomas Erlewine*

★ **All-Time Greatest Hits, Vols. 1-3** / 1987 / RCA ✦✦✦✦✦
The three-volume *All Time Greatest Hits* is the definitive collection. —*Ron Wynn*

Tony Bennett (Anthony Dominick Benedetto)

b. Aug. 3, 1926, New York City, NY
Vocals
Tony Bennett has enjoyed a resurgence of popularity in the late '80s and early '90s that matches his success in the '50s and '60s. He's been the model of consistency, singing with warmth, choosing ideal material, and making excellent albums with their foundation in jazz regardless of lyric content. Bennett's admiration for jazz musicians has often been expressed, and he's said to have modeled his phrasing on Art Tatum's piano technique and delivery on Mildred Bailey's vocal style. He sang while waiting tables as a teenager, then performed with military bands during World War II, and later had vocal studies at the American Theatre Wing School. Comedian Bob Hope noticed him working with Pearl Bailey and made some career suggestions; from them he changed his name from Joe Bari to Tony Bennett. Bennett's initial success came via several Columbia singles in the '50s. These included "Because of You," a chart topper in 1951; "I Won't Cry Anymore"; and a remake of Hank Williams (Sr.)'s "Cold, Cold Heart," which also made it to the No. 1 spot.

Bennett had an impressive run of chart entries, with 24 songs making the Top 40 from 1950 to 1964, and hits for almost 16 consecutive years. "Stranger in Paradise," "Just in Time," "Rags to Riches," and "There'll Be No Teardrops Tonight" were other big '50s hits, and in the early '60s came the signature tune "I Left My Heart in San Francisco," which also won a Grammy, plus "I Wanna Be Around," "The Good Life," and "Who Can I Turn To." Bennett made the transition in the '60s and '70s to an album artist, with 25 LPs making the charts between 1962 and 1972. Robert Farnon provided arrangements for four major ones. Bennett didn't merely churn out hits; he recorded with Count Basie, Duke Ellington, and Woody Herman. In the '70s, he played with Bill Evans and

Jimmy and Marian McPartland. Later came sessions of Rogers and Hart songs with Ruby Braff that yielded two volumes of material.

Bennett took a sabbatical from the recording studios in the '70s and '80s, concentrating on touring, performing, and painting. Columbia filled the void with reissues until his 1986 release *The Art of Excellence*. It primarily featured Bennett with Ralph Sharon's trio, but also included an intriguing duet with Ray Charles. A two-volume 1987 anthology *Tony Bennett/Jazz* featured an unissued track from 1964 with Bennett and Stan Getz. George Benson, Dizzy Gillespie, and Dexter Gordon were guests on the 1987 new album *Bennett and Berlin*. His profile hasn't decreased in the '90s, thanks to the hit album *Perfectly Frank*, devoted to songs popularized by Frank Sinatra, and another album with numbers sung by Fred Astaire. Not only does he continue performing all over the world, Bennett's making new inroads; he appeared on "MTV Unplugged" in 1993. —*Ron Wynn and William Ruhlmann*

The Beat of My Heart / 1957 / Columbia ✦✦✦✦
On only his third full-length, 12-inch LP, Tony Bennett comes up with a concept album, singing against novel percussion arrangements, backed by drummers like Art Blakey, Jo Jones, Chico Hamilton, Billy Exiner, Candido, and Sabu. Several songs feature only drums and flutes. Over this unusual instrumentation, Bennett sings beautifully, giving his usual full-voiced emotion to songs like "Lullaby of Broadway," "Let's Face the Music and Dance," and "Just One of Those Things." This was the first album to give notice that Bennett was more than just another near-operatic, melodramatic pop singer of the early 1950s. Here was a man who had jazz chops, musical imagination, and a sense of swing. He was practically a hipster! —*William Ruhlmann*

Tony's Greatest Hits / 1958 / Columbia ✦✦✦✦
Tony Bennett's first hits collection chronicles his initial seven years as a recording artist, during which he frequently was found in the singles charts. Among this album's 12 selections are nine chart songs: "Because of You" (No. 1 for 10 weeks, 1951), "Cold, Cold Heart" (No. 1 for six weeks, 1951), "Rags To Riches" (No. l for eight weeks, 1953), "Stranger in Paradise" (No. 2, 1954), "There'll Be No Teardrops Tonight" (No. 7, 1954), "Just in Time" (No. 46, 1956), "In the Middle of an Island" (No. 9, 1957), "Ça, C'est l'Amour" (No. 22, 1957), and "Young and Warm and Wonderful" (No. 23, 1958). Also featured is Bennett's noncharting debut single, "Boulevard of Broken Dreams," a tango complete with castanets that first gained him notice. In retrospect, early Bennett is not Bennett at his best—the song selection and arrangements are often so idiosyncratic and gimmicky they border on being novelty material, and Bennett often oversings in a mock-operatic style. But his intonation is always clear, his confidence always apparent. And there remains a historical interest—this is Tony Bennett as pop idol, and he carries it off. —*William Ruhlmann*

Strike Up the Band / 195_ / Columbia ✦✦✦

To My Wonderful One / 1960 / Columbia ✦✦✦

☆ **I Left My Heart in San Francisco** / 1962 / Columbia ✦✦✦✦✦
Along with his producer, Ernest Altschuler, and his arranger/pianist Ralph Sharon, Tony Bennett had been searching for a repertoire and a musical approach beyond his long-gone pop work with Mitch Miller of the early 1950s and his artistically pleasing but commercially dicey jazz work of the mid-to-late '50s. It seemed to be a combination of Broadway songs and other contemporary material, carefully selected and arranged to show off Bennett's now-burnished vocals, which, as he approached the end of his thirties, were starting to be located in a more comfortable range closer to a baritone than a tenor. With this album, they found the key, not only by happening across a signature song in the title track, but also in the approach to songs like "Once Upon a Time," a gem from the flop musical *All American*, and Cy Coleman and Carolyn Leigh's "The Best Is Yet to Come," which Bennett helped make a standard. (Frank Sinatra didn't do it until two years later.) From here on, until the world changed again toward the late '60s, Bennett would not have to feel that he had to compromise his art for popularity, making uptempo singles in an attempt to meet the marketplace while longing to do ballads and swing material instead. *I Left My Heart in San Francisco*, a gold-selling Top Ten hit that stayed in the charts almost three years, demonstrated that he could have it all. (Tony Bennett won two 1962 Grammy Awards for the title song: Record of the Year and Best Solo Vocal Performance, Male.) —*William Ruhlmann*

● **At Carnegie Hall** / 1962 / Columbia ✦✦✦✦
Recorded on June 9, 1962, one week before the release of the *I Left My Heart in San Francisco* album that would catapult Tony Bennett's career into the stratosphere, this concert album effectively sums up his accomplishments so far. Some of the hits—"Stranger in Paradise," "Rags to Riches," "Because of You"—are still on the set list (although drastically rearranged), but clearly he has found his true repertoire in reinventions of older material like "All the Things You Are" (the version here is exquisite) and good choices of new songs—he champions the team of Cy Coleman and Carolyn Leigh, and introduces "San Francisco," which some in the audience already know. (Released as a single in advance of the *San

Francisco* album, it was in the charts already.) And on the album's original four LP sides, Bennett managed to find time for such experiments as an uptempo "Ol' Man River" featuring percussionist Candido, a throwback to his innovative *Beat of My Heart* album. As a consistent demonstration of Bennett's strengths, the album earns its designation as a "pick." More than his greatest hits collections of the '50s and early '60s, it gives a broad sense of Bennett's work, and it does so in the format with which he's most comfortable—live in concert. —*William Ruhlmann*

I Wanna Be Around / 1963 / Columbia ✦✦✦✦
As the studio album follow-up to Tony Bennett's breakthrough record, *I Left My Heart in San Francisco*, *I Wanna Be Around* had a lot to live up to, but since *San Francisco* was a culmination of Bennett's development, not a fluke, *I Wanna Be Around* turned out to be almost on a par with its predecessor. "The Good Life" and "I Wanna Be Around" became Top 20 hits, showing that Bennett had somehow found a line into good new pop material, and there were also some excellent arrangements, courtesy of Marty Manning, including a percussion-and-flute reading of "Let's Face the Music and Dance" that echoed the *Beat of My Heart* album and a nod to the South American trend with Antonio Carlos Jobim's "Quiet Nights (Corcovado)." A worthy successor. —*William Ruhlmann*

This Is All I Ask / 1963 / Columbia ✦✦✦

Who Can I Turn To / 1964 / Columbia ✦✦✦

If I Ruled the World: Songs for the Jet Set / 1965 / Columbia ✦✦✦

★ **Tony's Greatest Hits, Vol. 3** / 1965 / Columbia ✦✦✦✦✦
Tony Bennett's third hits collection isn't only the best of his best-ofs, it's a classic "classic pop" album. Bennett's career hit its second and highest artistic peak in the first half of the 1960s, starting with "I Left My Heart in San Francisco" and continuing through a series of magnificent ballad hits—"I Wanna Be Around," "The Good Life," "This Is All I Ask," "When Joanna Loved Me," "Who Can I Turn To," "If I Ruled the World"—all of which are here, along with such equally impressive album tracks as "Once Upon a Time" and "The Best Is Yet to Come." As a result, this album became Bennett's second gold seller, and it remains the definitive statement of a major pop singer at his zenith. A complete understanding of his work requires a listen to his 1991 box set, *Forty Years: The Artistry of Tony Bennett*. But this 12-song set, covering the years 1962-1965, remains the brightest jewel in his crown. —*William Ruhlmann*

Movie Song Album / 1966 / Columbia ✦✦✦

Rodgers and Hart Songbook / 1973 / DRG ✦✦✦

The Tony Bennett Bill Evans Album / 1975 / Fantasy ✦✦✦

Chicago / 1984 / DCC ✦✦✦

Bennett/Berlin / 1987 / Columbia ✦✦✦

☆ **Jazz** / 1987 / Columbia ✦✦✦✦✦
What a wonderful idea. This is a compilation album ranging across Tony Bennett's early career, from 1954 to 1967, highlighting some of his more adventurous sessions with jazz musicians, including Count Basie, Herbie Hancock, Herbie Mann, Art Blakey, Stan Getz, and others, and featuring jazz standards like "Green Dolphin Street," along with a healthy dose of Duke Ellington compositions. Bennett not only holds his own, he sounds delighted on every track. The ironic thing, of course, is that Columbia frowned on these kinds of side excursions from his pop career in the '50s. Now, all is forgiven, and this proves an unusually imaginative repackaging that illuminates an important part of Bennett's talent and further contributes to his '80s renaissance. (The album contains a previously unreleased 1964 performance of "Danny Boy" featuring Stan Getz. Originally released as a two-LP set, *Jazz* was compressed to a 68-minute CD by excising two tracks.) —*William Ruhlmann*

Astoria: Portrait of the Artist / 1990 / Columbia ✦✦✦✦
Like *The Art of Excellence*, the album that marked Tony Bennett's return to recording in 1986, *Astoria: A Portrait of the Artist* was a nonthematic collection of new and old songs on which Bennett was backed both by his regular trio, led by pianist Ralph Sharon, and the UK Orchestra. Bennett's new songwriting discovery was Charles DeForest, three of whose songs—"When Do the Bells Ring for Me," "Where Do You Go from Love," and "I've Come Home Again"—were included, along with songs by the Gershwins and Jerome Kern, standards like "Body and Soul," and even a re-recording of Bennett's initial Columbia recording, "The Boulevard of Broken Dreams." That recording had come out in 1950, and the point of *Astoria* (which featured a cover photo of the young Bennett in the old neighborhood, with Bennett today standing in the same spot on the back) was to celebrate that 40-year anniversary while looking into both the past and the future, a task it accomplished admirably. —*William Ruhlmann*

☆ **Forty Years: The Artistry of Tony Bennett** / Oct. 7, 1991 / Columbia/ Legacy ✦✦✦✦✦

Perfectly Frank / 1992 / Columbia ✦✦✦✦
Think no one can touch the Chairman on his own turf? Think again. Bennett's tribute is such an obvious move. It's odd that it's taken this long

to materialize. Sinatra has made no secret of his admiration of Bennett, who puts his spin on this collection of Francis Albert classics. In the process, we wind up with Bennett's best in years. — *Steve Aldrich*

Art of Excellence / Mar. 4, 1992 / Columbia ✦✦✦✦
This album marked Tony Bennett's return to recording after half a dozen years, his return to Columbia Records after 14 years, and the beginning of the third stage in his career. Back with the Ralph Sharon Trio and backed by The UK Orchestra, Bennett demonstrated that he had spent his time off from recording gathering a bunch of good songs and refining his singing. The older material, such as "A Rainy Day" and "I Got Lost in Her Arms," were better than the new discoveries, like "How Do You Keep the Music Playing?" and "Everybody Has the Blues," but the new ones weren't bad, and with this album Bennett joined and helped to lead the swelling trend toward classic pop. It became his best-selling album in 15 years. — *William Ruhlmann*

MTV Unplugged / 1994 / Columbia ✦✦✦

Here's to the Ladies / 1995 / Columbia ✦✦✦

Irving Berlin

b. May 11, 1888, Tumen, Siberia, Russia, **d.** Sep. 22, 1989
Show Tunes, Pop
Irvin Berlin was the most successful songwriter of the 20th century. Though, like his contemporaries, he spent the better part of his career writing songs (usually both words and music) to be used in Broadway musicals, he is better remembered for the songs themselves than for the shows (and sometimes films) in which they were introduced. This is because Berlin was a master at the kind of music that flourished from the turn of the century until World War II, shows that were really just collections of production numbers, scenes, and novelty acts (organized vaudeville presentations, really) rather than the story musicals that became prevalent starting with Rodgers and Hammerstein's *Oklahoma!* in 1943. It is also because Berlin, who did not read music and could play the piano in only one key and only on the black notes (he used a special piano with a lever that changed keys for him and employed a musical secretary to notate his compositions), wrote songs, not scores.

But what songs! Out of more than a thousand, a short list would include "Alexander's Ragtime Band" (his first major hit, in 1911), "God Bless America," "A Pretty Girl Is like a Melody," "Always," "Blue Skies," "Puttin' on the Ritz," "How Deep Is the Ocean?," "Cheek to Cheek," "Let's Face the Music and Dance," "White Christmas," "There's No Business like Show Business," "I Love a Piano," "What'll I Do?" "Easter Parade," and "Oh, How I Hate to Get Up in the Morning." The last came from one of the two shows Berlin organized and performed in during the two world wars (he can be seen in the film version of the second one, *This Is the Army*).

Berlin became his own song publisher and built and owned a Broadway theater, the Music Box, to house his shows. Perhaps his greatest and his last hit came with the musical *Annie Get Your Gun* in 1946, though he did write three more before retiring in 1962. — *William Ruhlmann*

★ **Irving Berlin: A Hundred Years** / 1988 / Columbia ✦✦✦✦✦
Issued to commemorate Berlin's 100th birthday, this 21-track compilation of his songs is culled from recordings made primarily in the '30s, though there are also a few from the '40s and '50s. The artists include Connee Boswell, Bing Crosby, Eddie Cantor, Fred Astaire, Benny Goodman, Dinah Shore, Tony Bennett, and Johnny Mathis. — *William Ruhlmann*

The Boswell Sisters

Group / Vocal, Swing, Classic Jazz
The Boswell Sisters were the greatest jazz vocal group prior to Lambert, Hendricks, and Ross 30 years later. Consisting of Connee (1907-76), Martha (1908-58), and Helvetia (1909-88), the trio (which often used Martha on piano) featured hard-swinging choruses and group scatting with numerous key and tempo changes. Connee received all of the solos, but Martha and Helvetia both had very appealing voices, too. The Boswells grew up in New Orleans, where they all learned how to play numerous instruments. The group recorded "Nights When I'm Lonely" (and Connee cut "I'm Gonna Cry") in 1925 and they soon were appearing regularly on Los Angeles radio. The group really got going in 1930 with four recordings for Okeh. They were soon signed to Brunswick, where they recorded regularly during 1931-35. Their records usually featured top jazz soloists (including Bunny Berigan, the Dorsey Brothers, and Joe Venuti) and were often quite exciting. During this period the Boswell Sisters appeared in several films (both shorts and full-length movies) and were a popular radio attraction. They recorded four numbers for Decca in 1936, but by that year all three sisters were married. Martha and Helvetia retired and Connee Boswell (who had been recording solo sides on an occasional basis for several years) went out on her own. A high point was her recordings with Bob Crosby, but otherwise Connee's career (although reasonably satisfying) did not live up to its potential. In the

1950s for a time she had a major role on the television series Pete Kelly's Blues. Ella Fitzgerald always stated that Connee Boswell was her main influence. — *Scott Yanow*

Syncopating Harmonists from New Orleans / 1930-1935 / Take Two ✦✦✦
The Boswell Sisters were the premiere jazz vocal group (along with the early Mills Brothers) of the 1930s. This Take Two CD not only has nine enjoyable (but mostly fairly common) studio recordings from the 1932-35 period but nine numbers from a 1930 radio show and two ("I'll Never Say 'Never Again' Again" and "Lullaby of Broadway") that are taken from a 1935 program. Unfortunately the personnel is not given for the studio sides, but the rarity of the 1930 show (which exclusively features songs not recorded elsewhere by this very appealing group) will make classic jazz collectors want to get this release anyway. — *Scott Yanow*

★ **Boswell Sisters, Vol. 1** / Mar. 19, 1931-Apr. 9, 1932 / Collector's Classics ✦✦✦✦✦
Most vocal groups that attempt to sing jazz instead end up in the genre of middle-of-road pop music. The Boswell Sisters (comprising Connee, Vet, and Martha) were a strong exception, always swinging and, by changing tempos and keys frequently while including some other surprises, performing creative jazz of the early '30s. This Collector's Classics CD unfortunately skips their first seven recordings but then reissues complete and in chronological order 24 of the Boswells' finest performances. With a supporting cast frequently including trumpeters Bunny Berigan and Manny Klein, trombonist Tommy Dorsey and clarinetist Jimmy Dorsey (all of whom receive a generous amount of solo space), the sisters are heard at their best throughout this consistently exciting set. Highlights include "Roll On Mississippi, Roll On," "Shine On, Harvest Moon," "Heebies Jeebies," "River Stay 'Way from My Door," "Put That Sun Back in the Sky," and "There'll Be Some Changes Made." This is an essential acquisition. — *Scott Yanow*

Okay America!: Alternate Takes and Rarities / May 25, 1931-Jul. 19, 1935 / Vintage Jazz ✦✦✦✦

● **That's How Rhythm Was Born** / 1995 / Sony ✦✦✦✦
That's How Rhythm Was Born compiles 20 of the Boswell Sisters' greatest hits of the '30s, including "The Darktown Strutter's Ball" and "Between the Devil and the Deep Blue Sea." All of the tracks feature musical support from the Dorsey Brothers Orchestra. — *Stephen Thomas Erlewine*

Teresa Brewer

b. May 7, 1931, Toledo, OH
Vocals / Vocal, Swing, Pop
Specializing in bright, chirpy melodies, spunky Teresa Brewer was one of the top pop thrushes of the '50s. Raised in Toledo, OH, she was a regular on "The Major Bowes Amateur Hour" as a child. Brewer scored her first huge hit in 1950 at the tender age of 18 with "Music! Music! Music!" and followed it up with an impressive string of smashes for Coral Records that spanned the entire decade. Several of Brewer's mid-'50s hits—Fats Domino's "Bo Weevil," Ivory Hunter's "Empty Arms"—were sanitized R&B covers. Brewer has pursued jazzier directions in recent years, still retaining her youthful vocal delivery. Since marrying producer Bob Thiele in 1972, she has recorded with Duke Ellington, Count Basie, Stephane Grappelli, Ruby Braff, the World's Greatest Jazz Band, and Earl Hines. — *Bill Dahl and Scott Yanow*

● **Best Of: Music! Music! Music!** / 1995 / Varese ✦✦✦✦
The highlights from Teresa Brewer's time on Coral Records are included on *Best of Teresa Brewer: Music! Music! Music!*, as well as her hit version of the title song, recorded for London. — *Stephen Thomas Erlewine*

Hoagy Carmichael (Howard Hoagland Carmichael)

b. Nov. 11, 1899, Blooming, IN, **d.** Dec. 27, 1981, Palm Springs, CA
Piano, Vocals / Vocal, Classic Jazz, Standards
One of the great composers of the American popular song, Hoagy Carmichael differed from most of the others (with the obvious exception of Duke Ellington) in that he was also a fine performer. Such Carmichael songs as "Stardust," "Georgia on My Mind," "Up the Lazy River," "Rockin' Chair," "The Nearness of You," "Heart and Soul," "In the Cool, Cool, Cool of the Evening," "Skylark," and "New Orleans" have long been standards, each flexible enough to receive definitive treatment numerous times. Carmichael, who was supposed to become a lawyer, loved jazz almost from the start, and particularly the cornet playing of Bix Beiderbecke. His first composition, "Riverboat Shuffle," was recorded by Bix and the Wolverines in 1924 and became a Dixieland standard. Hoagy, as a pianist, vocalist, and occasional trumpeter, eventually abandoned law to concentrate on jazz, particularly after recording "Washboard Blues" with Paul Whiteman in 1927. He led a few jazz sessions of his own in the late '20s (including one that interpreted "Stardust" as an uptempo stomp!) but became more popular as a skilled songwriter. By 1935 he was working in Hollywood and he became an occasional character actor, appear-

ing in 14 films including, *To Have and Have Not* and *The Best Years of Our Lives*, generally playing a philosophical and world-weary pianist/vocalist. In the 1940s Carmichael recorded some trio versions of his hits, and in 1956 he cut a full set of vocals while backed by a modern jazz group that included Art Pepper. After that he drifted into semiretirement, dissatisfied with how the music business had changed. His two autobiographies (1946's *The Stardust Road* and 1965's *Sometimes I Wonder*) are worth picking up. —*Scott Yanow*

● **Classic Hoagy Carmichael** / May 9, 1927-Dec. 15, 1987 / Smithsonian ✦✦✦✦
The talented Hoagy Carmichael gained fame in his lifetime for his singing, acting, and to a lesser extent his skills at the piano, but his most important contributions to music were made as a composer. This handsome three-LP box set (which includes a classy 64-page booklet) has recordings of Carmichael's songs from a 60-year period and a wide variety of performers. Programmed more or less in chronological order, the box includes no less than six versions of "Stardust" along with fairly definitive versions of his bigger hits and some obscurities. The music is not strictly jazz, although one gets Bix, Louis Armstrong, the Boswell Sisters, Mildred Bailey, Benny Goodman, Artie Shaw, Billie Holiday, Ella Fitzgerald, Mel Torme, Art Pepper, and even Wynton Marsalis. In addition, there are selections featuring Bob Hope, Kate Smith, Frank Sinatra, Betty Hutton, Bing Crosby, Jane Wyman, Ray Charles (guess which song), and Margaret Whiting along with ten appearances by Carmichael himself. There are many more than its share of classics in this admirable package which is highly recommended to all. —*Scott Yanow*

Stardust and Much More / Nov. 18, 1927-Mar. 1, 1960 / RCA/Bluebird ✦✦✦✦

Hoagy Carmichael Collection / Smithsonian ✦✦✦✦
A definitive, triple-volume set, mostly devoted to others' interpretations of his work, including recordings by Louis Armstrong and the Boswell Sisters. —*Bruce Eder*

Vikki Carr (Florencia Martinez Cardona)

b. Jul. 19, 1941, El Paso, TX
Vocals / Vocal, Pop
After singing in various school functions, local groups, and Pepe Callahan's Mexican-Irish band, Carr began her professional musical career in earnest in the early '60s. Her solo debut was in Reno, supported by the Chuck Leonard Quartet, which led to a record contract with Liberty. While not gathering much attention in the US, her first single ("He's a Rebel") was a hit in Australia and led to numerous television appearances and a spell as a regular on the "Ray Anthony Show." In the late '60s, Carr scored three Top 40 hits, including the No. 3 "It Must Be Him." Her American sales dwindled in the beginning of the '70s. With the release of her 1980 album, *Vikki Carr y el Amor*, Carr gained enormous success in the Latin music world. In 1991 Carr won a Best Latin Pop Album Grammy for her *Cosas del Amor*. —*Stephen Thomas Erlewine*

● **It Must Be Him: The Best of Vikki Carr** / 1992 / EMI America ✦✦✦✦
A 23-track compilation of Carr's '60s singles, it contains her three Top 40 hits, "It Must Be Him," "The Lesson," and "With Pen in Hand." Carr's over-wrought reading of "He's a Rebel" (cut before the Crystals' version) shows how out of touch she was with the pop sounds of her time. Fans of her easy-listening style will appreciate the fine sound, detailed liner notes, and comprehensive discography that round out this collection. —*Rick Clark*

● **The Best** / Discos CBS International ✦✦✦✦
The Best collects a well-chosen cross-section of highlights from Vikki Carr's Latin hits. —*AMG*

June Christy

b. Nov. 20, 1925, Springfield, IL, **d.** Jun. 21, 1990, Los Angeles, CA
Vocals / Vocal, Cool
Although she originally sounded heavily influenced by Anita O'Day, June Christy's cool-toned yet cheerful style grew to be quite individual and popular, being both sensual and nonthreatening. She sang locally in Chicago and then received her big break, replacing O'Day with Stan Kenton's Orchestra in 1945. She had hits with "Tampico," "Shoo-Fly Pie," and "How High the Moon," and her renditions of ballads and novelties helped to keep the Kenton Orchestra going, contrasting with her more experimental and "progressive" works. Christy married tenor saxophonist Bob Cooper, cut her first solo recordings in 1947 and, after Kenton broke up his band in 1948, she had a very successful career. Her series of Capitol records in the 1950s (particularly *Something Cool* and *The Misty Miss Christy*) defined the "cool jazz" singing style and sold quite well. Christy had occasional reunions with Kenton and, even after she drifted into retirement after 1965, she appeared with the bandleader at the 1972 Newport Jazz Festival. Though she came back for one final record in 1977, June Christy will always be associated with the 1950s. —*Scott Yanow*

The Uncollected June Christy with the Kentones (1946) / 1946 / Hindsight ✦✦✦✦
Previously unissued June Christy material from late '40s and '50s with a knockoff unit from Stan Kenton Orchestra. It's designed for completists, as it consists of alternate takes and unreleased cuts that were judged inferior or left over. There's nothing wrong with some of them, but these are not the songs that made Christy famous. —*Ron Wynn*

★ **Something Cool** / 1953 / Capitol ✦✦✦✦✦
June Christy's classic *Something Cool* has been expanded from 11 songs to 24 on this essential CD with two unreleased cuts and six songs only previously out as singles. Christy's attractive "cool" tone was a trademark of jazz in the 1950s, her version of "Something Cool" remains a classic and many of the other numbers are nearly as memorable. Accompanied by Pete Rugolo's Orchestra, Christy is heard at her best on such numbers as "Whee Baby," "You're Making Me Crazy," "Midnight Sun," "A Stranger Called the Blues," "Softly as in a Morning Sunrise," "This Time the Dream's on Me," and "The Night We Called It a Day." —*Scott Yanow*

Duet / May 1955 / Capitol ✦✦✦✦
This set of duets between singer June Christy and pianist Stan Kenton is often quite emotional. Christy's cool sound and careful diction hint at darker feelings than appear on the surface during these ballads, while Kenton provides sparse but effective piano. Emotions and melody are much more significant in this setting than mere chord changes, and this haunting music is surprisingly memorable. —*Scott Yanow*

● **The Misty Miss Christy** / Jul. 26, 1955-May 23, 1956 / Capitol ✦✦✦✦
Singer June Christy is heard in prime form on this set. The reissue CD adds two numbers ("You Took Advantage of Me" and "Intrigue") to the original LP program. Backed by orchestras filled with West Coast jazz all-stars and arranged by Pete Rugolo, Christy is particularly memorable on "I Didn't Know About You," "Day Dream," "Dearly Beloved," and "There's No You." This is one of her finest all-around recordings. —*Scott Yanow*

A Lovely Way to Spend an Evening / 1957 / Jasmine ✦✦✦

Interlude / 195_ / Discovery ✦✦✦

Rosemary Clooney

b. May 23, 1928, Maysville, KY
Vocals / Vocal, Standards
Vocalist Rosemary Clooney remains in the news during the '90s. She's been in the midst of a career revival since the '80s, and was among the artists who performed in 1993 at the White House jazz concert. She was also criticized by Carmen McRae, who cited her as one of the pop artists inaccurately tabbed as a jazz singer by ignorant critics. Clooney's rise to fame in the '50s came on the strength of songs that in many instances were without genuine novelty tunes; she's not a vocal improviser like McRae, Carter, or Sarah Vaughan. She is an excellent lyric interpreter, has fine timing, phrases skillfully and intelligently, and performs with the dramatic quality evident among all great singers. Her background and foundation are jazz, even if her technique doesn't always adhere to rigid jazz scrutiny. Clooney entered amateur events with her sister Betty in Cincinnati, and they sang on radio stations. The duo worked in Tony Pastor's band during the late '40s, then Clooney started as a soloist. She joined the Columbia roster in 1950, and made several hits for them, among them "You're Just in Love," "Beautiful Brown Eyes," "Half as Much," "Hey There," "This Ole House," the No. 1 hit "Come on-a My House"(cowritten by Ross Bagdasarian of Chipmunks fame), and "If Teardrops Were Pennies." Clooney had 13 Top 40 hits in the early '50s, among them duets with Guy Mitchell and Marlene Dietrich. She also appeared in such films as *The Stars Are Singing*, *Here Come the Girls*, *White Christmas*, and *Red Garters* in 1953 and 1954. Clooney recorded with the Benny Goodman Sextet, the Hi-Lo's, and Duke Ellington in the '50s. She moved to RCA in the '60s and recorded with Bing Crosby. There were also dates for Coral, Reprise, and Capitol, among them another session with Crosby. The rock revolution and a decision to spend more time with her family resulted in Clooney's going into semiretirement. She returned in the late '70s, singing with renewed power and confidence while making swing-influenced dates and combo sessions for Concord. She's maintained that relationship through the '80s and '90s, doing standards and repertory albums and demonstrating a resiliency and energy that validate her position among the fine jazz-based vocalists in American music. —*Ron Wynn and Bill Dahl*

Blue Rose / 1956 / Columbia ✦✦✦✦
A moody 1956 collaboration with Duke Ellington, it's well worth seeking out. —*Charles S. Wolfe*

● **Everything's Coming Up Rosie** / 1977 / Concord Jazz ✦✦✦✦

Rosie Sings Bing / Jan. 6, 1978 / Concord Jazz ✦✦✦

Here's to My Lady / Sep. 1978 / Concord Jazz ✦✦✦✦
This CD reissue of Rosemary Clooney's third Concord album (which was originally titled *Here's to My Lady*) is one of her best. Clooney sings ten songs associated with Billie Holiday, and she is in prime form on such

numbers as "I Cover the Waterfront," "Mean to Me," "Comes Love," and a swinging "Them There Eyes." The backup group is quite noteworthy, too: tenor-saxophonist Scott Hamilton, cornetist Warren Vache, guitarist Cal Collins, pianist Nat Pierce, bassist Monty Budwig, and drummer Jake Hanna. Recommended. — *Scott Yanow*

Rosemary Clooney Sings the Lyrics of Ira Gershwin / Oct. 1979 / Concord Jazz ✦✦✦

Sings the Music of Cole Porter / Jan. 1982 / Concord Jazz ✦✦✦

My Buddy / Aug. 1983 / Concord Jazz ✦✦✦

Sings the Music of Harold Arlen / 1983 / Concord Jazz ✦✦✦✦

Sings Ballads / Apr. 1985 / Concord Jazz ✦✦✦

Sings the Music of Jimmy Van Heusen / Aug. 1986 / Concord Jazz ✦✦✦

Girl Singer / Nov. 1991-Dec. 1991 / Concord Jazz ✦✦✦

Still on the Road / 1993 / Concord Jazz ✦✦✦

Dedicated to Nelson / Sep. 27, 1995-Sep. 30, 1995 / Concord Jazz ✦✦✦

Perry Como (Pierino Como)

b. May 18, 1913, Canonsburg, PA
Vocals / Easy Listening
Starting out as a barber in his hometown of Cannonsburg, PA, Como gained national attention with the Ted Weems Orchestra in the mid-'30s. After World War II, he signed with RCA Victor as a solo artist and started amassing hits, 42 of them in the Top Ten between 1944 and 1958. His laidback, laconic delivery and persona served him well when he became the most successful "band singer" in TVs early days, hosting his variety show for over eight years. Changing over to whimsical novelty material, he still had hits when rock 'n' roll started dominating the charts. After a 25-year layoff, Como started performing live again in 1970, to devoted audiences, and has maintained a modest touring schedule to this day. —*Cub Koda*

Legendary Performer / 1976 / RCA ✦✦✦

★ **Pure Gold** / 1984 / RCA ✦✦✦✦✦
The essential greatest-hits package, it has original masters dating from the '40s and '50s. — *Charles S. Wolfe*

All-Time Greatest Hits, Vol. 1 / May 27, 1988 / RCA ✦✦✦✦
Most of Perry Como's greatest hits and most popular tunes are collected on *All-Time Greatest Hits, Vol. 1*, which is designed to appeal to his casual fans. It's not a definitive retrospective, but it has most of the hits that fans would need. —*David Jehnzen*

Harry Connick, Jr.

b. Sep. 11, 1967, New Orleans, LA
Piano, Vocals / Vocal, Swing
For a short time Harry Connick, Jr., was praised for helping to popularize standards among younger fans, and then he caught on so big with the media that his faults became obvious; he has not been taken seriously since in the jazz world. Connick studied music at the New Orleans Center for Creative Arts with Ellis Marsalis and played piano in New Orleans before being signed by Columbia. Emerging as an instrumental pianist with somewhat faulty time but a sincere approach towards playing swing and New Orleans standards, Connick evolved quickly into a singer who based his limited voice closely on the style of Frank Sinatra. He was excellent on the soundtrack of the film *When Harry Met Sally* but then headed a bland big band, essentially hogging the great majority of the solo space himself. He has since recorded in the pop field and had non-musical roles in films, making one doubt his dedication to jazz. Connick's earliest Columbia records are his best. —*Scott Yanow*

Harry Connick, Jr. / 1987 / Columbia ✦✦✦
A versatile, nervy pianist whose gift for rhythmic variation and counter-melody is well displayed on this debut album, especially when he tackles such standards as "Love Is Here to Stay" and "Sunny Side of the Street." — *William Ruhlmann*

20 / 1989 / Columbia ✦✦✦✦
Even more confident and exuberant than his debut, Connick's second album (the title refers to his age) finds him pulling out the stops on Irving Berlin's "Blue Skies" and trying out his limited but earnest vocal style on a few tunes, notably "Do You Know What It Means to Miss New Orleans?" — *William Ruhlmann*

● **When Harry Met Sally . . .** / Jun. 1989 / CBS ✦✦✦✦
The soundtrack that made Connick an MOR star. —*Ron Wynn*

We Are in Love / 1990 / Columbia ✦✦✦
Sentimental, pre-rock pop-oriented music. Nicely done though quite mannered. —*Ron Wynn*

Lofty's Roach Souffle / Apr. 4, 1990-Apr. 22, 1990 / Columbia ✦✦✦

Blue Light, Red Light / Jun. 27, 1991-Jul. 14, 1991 / Columbia ✦✦
His latest, with a slick, large-orchestra format. —*Ron Wynn*

25 / Oct. 2, 1992-Oct. 9, 1992 / Columbia ✦✦✦

She / 1994 / Sony ✦✦

Whisper Your Name / Aug. 29, 1995 / Sony ✦✦

Star Turtle / Jul. 1996 / Sony ✦✦✦

Barbara Cook

b. Oct. 25, 1927, Atlanta, GA
Vocals / Nostalgia
A singer with a warm, light soprano, Barbara Cook became a successful Broadway musical performer in the '50s and '60s. By the '70s, she had moved largely into cabaret singing, at which she was equally successful. Born in Atlanta, she made her professional debut at the Blue Angel nightclub in New York in 1950 and her Broadway debut in *Flahooley* (1951), one of several flops in which she got good notices. Another of these was the original version of *Candide* (1956). Cook finally found a Broadway show with legs when she created the role of Marian the librarian in *The Music Man* (1957). The most successful of several shows in which she appeared in the '60s was *She Loves Me* (1963). By the mid-'70s, she was popular enough to move up to concert halls, and this is reflected in her album *Barbara Cook and Carnegie Hall* (1975). Her more recent accomplishments include her appearance in the special recording *Follies in Concert* (1985), her inclusion in a new studio recording of *Carousel* (1987), and her delightful album of songs associated with Walt Disney children's films, *The Disney Album* (1988). — *William Ruhlmann*

It's Better with a Band / 1986 / Moss Music ✦✦✦
A live recording from Carnegie Hall. Includes a wonderful Leonard Bernstein medley, as well as "The Ingenue," a song written for Cook by Wally Harper and David Zippel. — *William Ruhlmann*

● **The Disney Album** / 1988 / MCA ✦✦✦✦
A dream match: Barbara Cook's warm, optimistic voice singing songs taken from Disney films—"Some Day My Prince Will Come," "A Dream Is a Wish Your Heart Makes," and more. — *William Ruhlmann*

Bing Crosby (Harry Lillis Crosby)

b. May 2, 1904, Tacoma, WA, **d.** Oct. 14, 1977, Madrid, Spain
Vocals / Swing, Standards
A beloved icon whose contributions to American music are so great that they are difficult to describe, Bing Crosby had a major influence on jazz singers. Prior to his rise in the late '20s, most male vocalists (outside of the blues world) were hired as much for their ability to project volume as for anything else. With the exception of Cliff Edwards, few White singers were worth listening to. Bing Crosby's friendly baritone voice and easy sense of swing saved the world from being overrun by Rudy Vallee imitators and boy tenors!

Crosby's main connection to jazz was in his early days. He played drums and sang with jazz groups as a boy. In 1926 he became part of the Rhythm Boys with Al Rinker and the greatly underrated Harry Barris. The colorful trio (one of the few jazz vocal groups) performed regularly with Paul Whiteman's Orchestra during 1926-30 (appearing in the 1930 film *The King of Jazz*), and during this time Crosby had a special solo on a few recordings, inspired by his friends Bix Beiderbecke and Joe Venuti. Crosby, who proved to be a fine scat singer, hit it big singing ballads with Gus Arnheim in the early '30s but always retained a love for jazz, particularly Dixieland. He recorded "St. Louis Blues" with Duke Ellington, teamed up with Louis Armstrong in the films *Pennies from Heaven* (1936) and *High Society* (1956), sang in a Dixieland setting throughout *The Birth of the Blues* (1940), and introduced dozens of songs that became jazz standards. Although he moved beyond jazz by the mid-'30s, Crosby occasionally recorded with top jazz players including Jimmy Dorsey's orchestra, his brother Bob Crosby's Bobcats, Eddie Condon, Woody Herman, Louis Jordan, Eddie Heywood's sextet, and Bob Scobey. —*Scott Yanow*

★ **Bing! His Legendary Years, 1931 to 1957** / Nov. 23, 1931-Dec. 27, 1957 / MCA ✦✦✦✦✦
This four-CD set does a superb job of summing up Bing Crosby's years with Decca. After nine titles from 1931 (which were acquired by Decca later on), the program concentrates on the 1934-57 period and, in addition to the expected hits, all aspects of his career are covered. Despite a few Dixieland-flavored selections, Crosby had largely abandoned jazz by the late '30s, but his phrasing (which was influenced by Louis Armstrong) and appealing voice should be of interest to jazz listeners. In later years his ballads grew in stature while the uptempo performances tended to be less memorable novelties. Although it should be augmented by collections that focus on his recordings of the 1920s and early '30s, this is the definitive Bing Crosby set. —*Scott Yanow*

And Some Jazz Friends / Aug. 8, 1934-May 27, 1942 / GRP ✦✦✦✦
More than most pop singers of his era, Bing Crosby meshed naturally

with the jazz world. This 20-track collection includes collaborations with Louis Jordan, Joe Sullivan, Louis Armstrong, Jack Teagarden, Eddie Condon, Lionel Hampton, Lee Wiley, Woody Herman, Bing's brother Bob, and more. —*Roundup Newsletter*

★ **The Best of Bing Crosby** / 1980 / Decca ✦✦✦✦✦
No single package can hold all of Crosby's hits, but this is a start: original cuts from the '30s and '40s, with many favorites. —*Charles S. Wolfe*

Top o' the Morning: His Irish Collection / Feb. 27, 1996 / MCA ✦✦✦✦
Of the many musical genres Bing Crosby tackled, he probably felt closest to the Irish songs, many of which he must have heard when he was growing up in an Irish-American home. Crosby recorded 25 Irish-themed songs between 1940 and 1952, both traditional and newly written, and they appeared originally on singles, including the gold-selling Top Ten hits "Too-Ra-Loo-Ra-Loo-Ral (That's an Irish Lullaby)," "McNamara's Band," and "Galway Bay." In the LP era, the songs were gathered onto two albums, *When Irish Eyes Are Smiling* and *Shillelaghs and Shamrocks*, the latter becoming a bestseller in 1958. *Top o' the Morning/His Irish Collection*, a 24-track, 72+-minute disc, contains the contents of both those albums, the rarity "Rosaleen," and the original recording of "Too-Ra-Loo-Ra-Loo-Ral," unissued since the 1944 single. Within the Irish context, there are warm ballads and sprightly marches, and Crosby handles them all with ease. —*William Ruhlmann*

The Crooner / Columbia ✦✦✦
These classic Columbia sides from 1928 to 1934 have fine remastering and good notes. —*Charles S. Wolfe*

Sammy Davis, Jr.

b. Dec. 8, 1925, **d.** May 16, 1990
Vocals / Vocal
When Sammy Davis, Jr., died in 1990, the entertainment world lost one of its reigning superstars. The versatile Davis hailed from a showbiz family and started young, tap dancing up a storm in the 1933 featurette "Rufus Jones for President." His uncle headed the Will Mastin Trio along with Sammy and his dad, and they were a popular lounge act during the '40s. Davis signed with Decca as a singer in 1954, charting with "Hey There," but an auto accident that year cost him an eye. "Something's Gotta Give" was a major hit for Davis in 1955, but his recording career took a back seat for a time of cavorting with the Rat Pack, an all-star crew of Las Vegas swingers headed by Frank Sinatra and Dean Martin. They starred en masse in the films *Ocean's Eleven* (1960) and *Robin and the Seven Hoods* (1964). Moving to the Reprise label, Davis scored with the dramatic ballads "What Kind of Fool Am I?" in 1962, "The Shelter of Your Arms" in 1963, and "I've Gotta Be Me" in 1968, but his only No. 1 hit came on a very atypical 1972 effort—the saccharine "Candy Man," a million-seller on MGM. A superstar of Broadway, film, and recordings, Sammy Davis, Jr., earned his ranking as one of America's leading entertainers. —*Bill Dahl*

★ **Greatest Hits 1 & 2** / 1978 / DCC ✦✦✦✦✦
His best, most complete hits package. —*Ron Wynn*

Capitol Collectors Series / Jun. 18, 1990 / Capitol ✦✦✦✦
Fine retrospective of pop- and jazz-flavored cuts. —*Ron Wynn*

Doris Day

b. Apr. 3, 1922
Vocals / Swing
Though better known for her film roles and All-American Girl image, Doris Day was a professional vocalist from her teens and enjoyed pop stardom as a lead singer with the Les Brown Orchestra. Critics still dispute whether she was truly a jazz singer. She was certainly no improviser, but she was effective on light novelty fare and innocent tunes of the '40s and '50s, as with her Oscar-winning hit "Que Sera, Sera (Whatever Will Be, Will Be)." —*Ron Wynn*

The Best of the Big Bands / Nov. 28, 1940-Sep. 14, 1946 / Columbia ✦✦✦
A good collection of Day's hit recordings with Les Brown. —*Ron Wynn*

Day Dreams / 1955 / Columbia ✦✦✦

● **Greatest Hits** / 1958 / Columbia ✦✦✦✦
Day at her most palatable, but not necessarily her best. —*Bruce Eder*

Hooray for Hollywood, Vol. 1 / Jan. 1959 / Columbia ✦✦✦
Soft, pop-oriented material that is well known but not her most inspired repertoire. —*Bruce Eder*

Hooray for Hollywood, Vol. 2 / Feb. 1959 / Columbia ✦✦✦
An acceptable follow-up to the first volume. —*Bruce Eder*

● **16 Most Requested Songs** / Aug. 25, 1992 / Columbia ✦✦✦✦
16 Most Requested Songs contains some, but not all, of Doris Day's biggest hits. Consequently, it's more of a sampler for casual fans than a definitive retrospective, but it still highlights some of her very best performances, including "A Bushel and a Peck," "You Won't Be Satisfied,"

"Till the End of Time," "In Love in Vain," and "Black Hills of Dakota." —*Stephen Thomas Erlewine*

Secret Love [box] / 1995 / Bear Family ✦✦✦✦

Marlene Dietrich (Maria Magdalena Von Losch)

b. 1901, **d.** May 6, 1992
Vocals / Nostalgia, Torch
Probably Europe's most valued export of the late '20s, Dietrich rocketed to fame in the movie *The Blue Angel*. Her vamp blonde hair and corset-and-black-stockings look is still in use today (Madonna, Madeline Kahn's spoof of her in Mel Brooks' *Blazing Saddles*). Dietrich's deep, almost foghorn-like voice served her well into grandmotherhood, delighting audiences all around the world. —*Cub Koda*

The Essential Marlene Dietrich / Sep. 14, 1992 / Capitol ✦✦✦✦

● **Her Complete Decca Recordings** / MCA ✦✦✦✦
Though Dietrich recorded (and re-recorded) many of her best-known tunes for a variety of labels, this compilation catches her in fine form and features an excellent reading of her biggest hit, "Falling in Love Again." —*Cub Koda*

Michael Feinstein

b. 1956
Piano, Vocals / Nostalgia
Michael Feinstein was born in Columbus, OH, and developed an interest in the piano and in show music at an early age. After moving with his family to Los Angeles in 1976, he met Oscar Levant's widow, who introduced him to Ira Gershwin. He was hired by Gershwin in 1977 to help organize the Gershwin archives, and continued to work with the lyricist until Gershwin's death in 1983. In 1984, Feinstein launched a career as a pianist and singer devoted to the music of the '30s and '40s, playing at private parties in the Los Angeles area. He had a seven-month residence at the Mondrian Hotel, during which Liza Minnelli threw a party in his honor (February 1985) that got his name around. In January 1986 he opened at the Algonquin Hotel in New York, where a six-week engagement stretched to 16 weeks. Feinstein's debut album, *Live at the Algonquin*, mixed the songs of Irving Berlin and Oscar Levant with more current material by Stephen Sondheim and Gretchen Cryer. By 1988 he had been signed to Elektra Records, for whom he has recorded a series of albums spotlighting the work of specific composers, as well as a recent children's album. —*William Ruhlmann*

Live at the Algonquin / 1986 / Asylum ✦✦✦
Feinstein in his element. The limitations in his vocal range are made up for by an evident understanding of and enthusiasm for the material, starting with Ray Jessel's "Wanna Sing a Show Tune." —*William Ruhlmann*

● **Pure Gershwin** / 1987 / Asylum ✦✦✦✦
Pure delight. Feinstein's reading of other composers is very, very good, but his feeling for Gershwin (as might be expected from a man who worked with Ira Gershwin for years) is near perfect. Feinstein's piano playing is excellent here, and he relishes every syllable of the words. 'S wonderful. —*William Ruhlmann*

Remember: Michael Feinstein Sings Irving Berlin / 1987 / Asylum ✦✦✦
The first of Feinstein's theme albums, and one of the best. He captures the simple (and at times deceptively clever) sentiment of Berlin with an unadorned approach that brings out the sturdiness of the melodies as well. —*William Ruhlmann*

Such Sweet Sorrow / 1995 / Atlantic ✦✦✦
Michael Feinstein's label debut for Atlantic was a thematic album of sad love songs, but the emphasis was more on the sweet than the sorrow; this was no album of saloon songs like Frank Sinatra's *Only the Lonely*. As often as not, Feinstein simply chose songs of not-yet-requited love, like Cole Porter's "Easy to Love" or Leo Robin and Lewis Gensler's "Love Is Just Around the Corner," while he reflected on love's downs as well as its ups in Johnny Burke and Jimmy Van Heusen's "But Beautiful." Feinstein effectively combined such vintage material with "Wasn't There a Moment," a brand-new Jimmy Webb song, and even "For Love Alone," one of his own, and dug up such lost gems as "Theme from the Bad and the Beautiful," Dory Previn's lyrical setting over David Raksin's theme. And Feinstein made a point of inserting arcane lyrics and other musical treats, such as having a quartet of flutes play Coleman Hawkins' famous saxophone solo during "Body and Soul," making the album a delight for fellow archivists as well as fans of vocal music. —*William Ruhlmann*

Over There / Angel ✦✦

Jose Feliciano

b. Sep. 8, 1945, Lares, Puero Rico
Guitar, Vocals / Vocal, Pop, Soft Rock, Folk-Rock, Club-Dance
Jose Feliciano's virtuoso guitar work and impassioned vocals have been

spotlighted in numerous contexts, notably on his hit adaptation of the Doors hit "Light My Fire." Born in Puerto Rico and blind since birth, Feliciano was raised in New York City. He began his lengthy string of successes on RCA in 1968 with his intimate reworking of "Light My Fire," winning a Grammy for Best New Artist that year. He wrote the theme song for Freddie Prinze's acclaimed TV sitcom "Chico and the Man" and acted in numerous programs. Feliciano continues to perform frequently today. —*Bill Dahl*

Feliciano! / 1968 / RCA ✦✦✦✦
Released at the apex of his popularity, this was Feliciano's most successful album. It reached No. 2, largely on the strength of his only big hit single, "Light My Fire" (which is featured here). Soulful easy listening is an oxymoron, but this is about as close as that fusion gets to reality, with passionate vocals and virtuosic flamenco guitar. Besides "Light My Fire," it's dominated by interpretations of '60s hits like "Sunny" and "California Dreamin'," as well as three Lennon-McCartney tunes. Noted jazz bassist Ray Brown is one of the supporting musicians. —*Richie Unterberger*

● **Encore! Jose Feliciano's Finest Performances** / 1971 / RCA ✦✦✦✦
● **Grandes Exitos de Jose Feliciano** / 1986 / RCA ✦✦✦✦
All-Time Greatest Hits / 1988 / RCA ✦✦✦✦
Included are his versions of "Light My Fire," "California Dreamin'," "Suzy Q." and "Walk Right In." —*AMG*

Eddie Fisher

b. Aug. 10, 1928, Philadelphia, PA
Vocals / Vocal, Pop
A major pop star during the pre-rock '50s, Eddie Fisher's roller-coaster career includes seven million-sellers and two famous ex-wives (actresses Debbie Reynolds and Elizabeth Taylor). The Philadelphia-born Fisher sang with Buddy Morrow's orchestra before getting his big break on Eddie Cantor's radio show in 1949. He started his amazing string of hits for RCA Victor with "Thinking of You" in 1950, quickly developing into a teen heartthrob and peaking in 1953 with the chart-topping "I'm Walking Behind You" and "Oh! My Pa-Pa." Fisher attempted to go with the rock 'n' roll flow in 1955 with "Dungaree Doll," another big hit, but his style was unabashedly pop-oriented, and the rock revolt all but pushed him off the charts. Fisher continues to sing, and his daughter, Carrie Fisher, is a well-known actress and writer. —*Bill Dahl*

● **All-Time Greatest Hits Vol. 1** / 1991 / RCA ✦✦✦✦

Four Freshmen

Vocal, Pop
With their highly advanced concepts of group harmony, the Four Freshmen scored a few hits during the '50s, while deeply influencing the vocal blend of the Beach Boys. Formed at an Indianapolis music conservatory, the Four Freshmen were brought to Capitol Records by jazz bandleader Stan Kenton, and the quartet (Bob Flanigan, brothers Ross and Don Barbour, and Ken Arrair) hit with "It's a Blue World" in 1952. Their top seller was "Graduation Day" in 1956, but six chart items in all by the Four Freshmen don't begin to indicate the influence of their breathtakingly close harmonies on subsequent vocal groups. —*Bill Dahl*

● **Capitol Collectors Series** / Jan. 21, 1991 / Capitol ✦✦✦✦
This is an excellent and well-annotated collection of the best of this '60s harmony group. —*Charles S. Wolfe*

Spotlight on Four Freshmen / Jan. 23, 1996 / Capitol ✦✦✦
The *Capitol Collectors Series* CD has their most popular material; this concentrates on their LP tracks, offering 18 cuts that they recorded between 1954 and 1961. As is par for the course on Capitol's *Spotlight* series, the emphasis is on orchestrated standards. —*Richie Unterberger*

Four Lads

Vocal
Soaring four-part harmonies were this Toronto group's stock in trade, and they parlayed their robust sound into a string of pop hits during the pre-rock era. Signed to Columbia Records as background vocalists in 1950, they harmonized behind Johnnie Ray on his 1951 smash "Cry" before making the most of their own shot in the spotlight with "The Mocking Bird" the next year for Okeh. Led by tenor Bernie Toorish, the Four Lads tallied numerous hits for Columbia, including "Skokiaan" in 1954, the powerful "Moments to Remember" in 1955, and "No, Not Much!" and "Standing on the Corner" in 1956. The Four Lads continued to chart frequently through 1959. —*Bill Dahl*

Moments to Remember / 1955 / Columbia ✦✦✦
Included are more of their melodic early-'50s pop hits and harmonies. —*Hank Davis*

● **16 Most Requested Songs** / 1991 / Columbia ✦✦✦✦
Featuring melodic early-'50s pop hits by this Canadian quartet, it was big-selling, with extremely appealing harmonies. —*Hank Davis*

The Four Preps

Vocal, Pop
While performing at a Hollywood High School talent show in 1956, the Four Preps impressed a Capitol Records producer enough to sign them to a long-term contract. By the end of the year, the wholesome, clean-cut group had their first chart single, "Dreamy Eyes." From 1956 to 1964, the Four Preps (Bruce Belland, Ed Cobb, Marv Ingraham, and Glen Larson) charted 13 times on the Hot 100. As the British Invasion stormed US shores, their popularity withered away, although they continued to record until 1967. —*Stephen Thomas Erlewine*

● **Capitol Collectors Series** / 1989 / Capitol ✦✦✦✦
All the Four Preps you'll ever need, on a 20-track compilation. Every one of their Top 40 hits is here, as are many smaller hits and unfamiliar songs, including their last chart hit, "A Letter to the Beatles." —*Stephen Thomas Erlewine*

Judy Garland

b. Jun. 10, 1922, **d.** Jun. 22, 1969
Vocals / Standards
Immortalized while a teenager in the 1939 film musical *The Wizard of Oz*, Judy Garland also recorded often. Of course, her classic rendition of "Over the Rainbow" from *Oz* was a smash that same year on Decca, and she scored numerous hits during the '40s. By 1954, Garland was recording for Columbia, and her rendition of "The Man That Got Away," from her hit movie *A Star Is Born*, helped to define the Garland mystique. She hosted her own TV variety show in the early '60s and continued to belt out her classic material until her premature death. Daughters Liza Minnelli and Lorna Luft are very talented chips off Garland's brilliant block. —*Bill Dahl*

Judy / 1956 / Capitol ✦✦✦
Judy at Carnegie Hall / 1961 / Capitol ✦✦✦✦
The best of the later Garland, it was recorded live at a 1961 concert. —*Charles S. Wolfe*

● **The Best of the Decca Years, Vol. 1** / 1990 / Decca ✦✦✦✦
Prime early material includes the original "Over the Rainbow," as well as pieces from the '40s, like "The Trolley Song." —*Charles S. Wolfe*

Changing My Tune: Best of the Decca Years, Vol. 2 / 1992 / MCA ✦✦✦✦

Spotlight on Judy Garland / Jan. 23, 1996 / Capitol ✦✦✦✦
Eighteen tracks from her 1955-1960 Capitol recordings, often with orchestral conduction from Nelson Riddle. As expected, standards are the order of the day, the most famous being "That's Entertainment!," "Zing! Went the Strings of My Heart," "Me and My Shadow," and a 1955 version of "Over the Rainbow." —*Richie Unterberger*

Eydie Gorme

b. Aug. 16, 1931
Vocals / Vocal
Usually paired vocally with her husband, Steve Lawrence, Eydie Gorme cashed in on a Latin-flavored dance craze in 1963 with her bubbly "Blame It on the Bossa Nova" for Columbia Records. The Bronx, NY, product signed on as a regular on Steve Allen's "Tonight Show" in 1953, and the next year had her first chart hit with "Fini" on Coral. Moving to ABC-Paramount, Gorme's perky pipes rode the charts with the likes of "Love Me Forever" in 1957 and "You Need Hands" the next year. She married Lawrence, another "Tonight Show" regular, in 1957, and they're a popular TV and concert attraction to this day. —*Bill Dahl*

Eydie Swings the Blues / 1957 / Paramount ✦✦✦
Gorme spreading her jazz wings and digging into a nice selection of pop/ jazz/blues-style material. —*Cub Koda*

● **Eydie Gorme's Greatest Hits** / 1967 / Columbia ✦✦✦✦
Just what the title says, including "Blame It on the Bossa Nova" and her best pop material. —*Cub Koda*

Softly, As I Leave You / 1967 / Columbia ✦✦✦
One of Gorme's best ballad albums, nicely done. —*Cub Koda*

Robert Goulet

b. Nov. 26, 1933, Lawrence, MA
Vocals / Vocal
A robust vocalist whose handsome profile has turned up on countless TV variety programs, Goulet first made an impression while starring on Broadway in *Camelot*. He hit in 1962 on Columbia with "What Kind of Fool Am I?" and in 1964 with "My Love Forgive Me (Amore, Scusami)." Goulet still thrives as an actor and easy-listening crooner. —*Bill Dahl*

● **Greatest Hits** / 1969 / Columbia ✦✦✦✦
Includes "If Ever I Should Leave You" and all the rest. —*Bil Carpenter*

Annette Hanshaw

b. 1910, **d.** 1985
Vocals / Vocal, Classic Jazz

One of the first great female jazz singers, in the late '20s Annette Hanshaw ranked near the top with Ethel Waters, the Boswell Sisters, and the upcoming Mildred Bailey. Unlike her contemporary Ruth Etting, Hanshaw could improvise and swing while also being a strong interpreter of lyrics. She was not quite 16 when she started her recording career, and her recordings (1926-34) included such major jazz players as Red Nichols, Miff Mole, Jimmy Lytell, Adrian Rollini, Joe Venuti, Eddie Lang, Vic Berton, Benny Goodman, Manny Klein, Phil Napoleon, Jimmy Dorsey, Tommy Dorsey, and Jack Teagarden. Billed as "The Personality Girl," Annette Hanshaw (whose trademark was saying "That's all" at the end of her record) soon got tired of show business and retired in 1934, at the age of 23! She lived outside of music for the rest of her life, but fortunately most of her records were reissued on British LPs in the 1970s and '80s. —*Scott Yanow*

★ **Sweetheart of the Twenties** / Oct. 1926-Sep. 8, 1927 / Halcyon ✦✦✦✦✦
Solid collection of Hanshaw's earliest sides, 1926-1928, with superb jazz backing. Import. —*Cub Koda*

The Rare BG 1927-29 / 1927-1929 / Sunbeam ✦✦✦
Features Benny Goodman backing Hanshaw on two Betty Boop-style sides originally issued in the '20s under the pseudonym "Dot Dare." —*Cub Koda*

It Was So Beautiful / 1932-1934 / Halcyon ✦✦✦✦
Superlative collection of Hanshaw's last recordings, with "Say It Isn't So," "Give Me Liberty or Give Me Love," and "I'm Sure of Everything But You" being particular standouts. Import. —*Cub Koda*

Benny Goodman Accompanies "The Girls" / Sunbeam ✦✦✦
Hanshaw shares this compilation album with tracks by Ethel Waters and the Boswell Sisters, but her five tracks here (especially "I Hate Myself" and "Would You Like to Take a Walk?") are major treasures and showcase her at her best. —*Cub Koda*

Phil Harris

b. Jan. 16, 1904, Linton, IN
Guitar, Drums, Vocals / Big Band, Swing

Better known as a longtime actor who made his first film appearance in 1933, Phil Harris was also a successful drummer and singer. Harris played drums with Francis Craig and led his own groups during the '30s, using the song "Rose Room" as a theme. Harris was a regular on Jack Benny's radio show for a decade from 1936-1946 and had his own show with Alice Faye from 1947-54. He had a number of novelty hits in the '40s and early '50s. His jazz value is limited, but his '30s bands did have some good musicians. —*Ron Wynn*

● **Phil Harris** / 194_ / ✦✦✦✦
Some nice recordings from the '40s, before Harris more or less deserted music for an acting career. —*Ron Wynn*

Richard Harris

b. Oct. 1, 1932
Vocals / Vocal, Pop

A veteran actor of the stage and screen, Richard Harris made his pop debut in 1968 with the Jimmy Webb composition "MacArthur Park," one of the most talked-about records of that year. Webb wrote most of Harris' early material, and his songs were perfect for Harris' dramatic delivery. Harris never achieved the success with other writers that he did with Webb, and by the mid-'70s was back to acting full-time. Harris can also be heard in the role of King Arthur on the movie soundtrack of *Camelot*. —*Kenneth M. Cassidy*

His Greatest Performances / 1979 / MCA ✦✦✦✦
This features Harris performing songs—mostly by Jimmy Webb. It includes his two biggest hits, "MacArthur Park" and "Didn't We." —*Kenneth M. Cassidy*

● **Webb Sessions** / 1996 / Raven ✦✦✦✦
Richard Harris' biggest hit, "MacArthur Park," was pulled from *A Tramp Shining*, an album recorded, and largely written, by Jimmy Webb. After its success, the pair teamed up for the follow-up, *The Yard Went On Forever*, which wasn't quite as successful commercially. *The Webb Sessions* combines both albums onto a single disc. —*Stephen Thomas Erlewine*

Al Hibbler

b. Aug. 16, 1915
Vocals / Vocal

This blind pop-jazz singer worked with Duke Ellington's orchestra for eight years before waxing a series of stately pop ballads in the mid-'50s. Hibbler debuted in 1942 with Kansas City pianist Jay McShann's combo for Decca before joining Ellington the next year. Hibbler was on the R&B

charts four times in 1948-51 for major independent labels like Chess and Atlantic, but he signed with Decca and crossed over to the pop lists in 1955, battling Roy Hamilton for top honors on "Unchained Melody." The deep-voiced Hibbler encored with the inspirational "He" and the blues-tinged "After the Lights Go Down Low," retaining his reputation as one of the jazz world's leading vocalists until his death. —*Bill Dahl*

After the Lights Go Down Low / 1956 / Atlantic ✦✦✦
In the post-Decca period, the title track is a remake of the 1956 hit. The backing has a heavier backbeat than earlier efforts. —*Hank Davis*

● **Best of Al Hibbler** / MCA ✦✦✦✦
This contains all his mid-'50s pop such as "Unchained Melody" and "After the Lights Go Down Low," done in his compelling and at times bizarre vocal style, with a big-band backing. —*Hank Davis*

Lena Horne

b. Jun. 30, 1917
Vocals / Swing, Middle-of-the-Road Pop

An ageless beauty and a very appealing personality, Lena Horne was never really a jazz singer as much as a superior pop vocalist, since she does not improvise. Horne started performing when she was six, sang and danced at the Cotton Club as early as 1934, was with Noble Sissle's Orchestra (1935-36), recorded with Teddy Wilson in the late '30s, and sang with Charlie Barnet's big band during 1940-41. She also recorded with Artie Shaw (1941) and made major impressions in the films *Boogie Woogie Dream* (actually a jazz short), *Cabin in the Sky*, and especially *Stormy Weather*. Married to arranger/pianist Lennie Hayton, Horne has been a popular attraction since the 1940s, but her connection with jazz (even when she sings veteran swing standards) is peripheral. A Bluebird compilation of some of her best early recordings is recommended. —*Scott Yanow*

● **Stormy Weather: The Legendary Lena (1941-1958)** / Jan. 7, 1941-Jun. 9, 1958 / Bluebird ✦✦✦✦
A wonderful anthology covering her '40s and '50s show tunes, blues, and ballads. —*Ron Wynn*

Lena Goes Latin / 1963 / DRG ✦✦✦
Vintage Lena Horne set from the early '60s, with backing from the Lennie Layton Orchestra. Horne made a nice adjustment to Latin tempos and rhythms, although there are lots of show biz touches and flourishes as well. She wasn't really doing traditional Latin material; it was more Latinized pop, but she did it with distinction. —*Ron Wynn*

Lena and Gabor / Oct. 11, 1969 / Gryphon ✦✦✦
Collaboration between Horne and guitarist Gabor Szabo, who proved to be one of her most sympathetic accompanists. They made expert duo recordings, with Szabo's delicate, sometimes emphatic playing smoothly accompanying Horne's distinctive vocals. The 1969 session has been reissued on CD. —*Ron Wynn*

Live on Broadway (Lena Horne: The Lady and Her Music) / 1981 / Qwest ✦✦✦✦
A triumphant cast album from 1981 that effectively captured Lena Horne's acclaimed one-woman Broadway show on a two-record set. The album served both as a vinyl autobiography and also as a centerpiece to document her rise to symbolic importance for Black performers. —*Ron Wynn*

At Long Last Lena / Jul. 1, 1992 / RCA ✦✦✦
A package of standards and ballads that showcases her less jazz-oriented side. —*Ron Wynn*

An Evening with Lena Horne / Sep. 19, 1994 / Blue Note ✦✦✦✦
It is difficult not to love Lena Horne. Recorded when she was 77, this live CD finds the ageless singer sounding as if she were 57 at the most (and the photo of her on the cover makes her look 47!). Horne talks the lyrics a little more than in the past, but she cuts loose in spots with power, performs superior standards, takes part of a Duke Ellington/Billy Strayhorn medley as a duet with bassist Ben Brown and is not shy to hold long notes. On six of the songs, 11 horns from the Count Basie Orchestra riff and play harmonies behind her; otherwise Horne is joined by her usual quartet with pianist Mike Renzi and guitarist Rodney Jones. The well-rounded set is Lena Horne's most rewarding recording in years. —*Scott Yanow*

Engelbert Humperdinck (Arnold George Dorsey)

b. 1936, Madras, India
Vocals

Raised in Leicester, England (one of ten kids), Humperdinck started playing saxophone when he was eleven. He claims his singing career was an accident. "I went to a small club in Leister and everyone was getting up and singing. So I got up on stage and sang a ballad—and I got a standing ovation!" Thus encouraged, he went on to then launch a career as a dance-band singer under the name Gerry Dorsey. This was in the middle 1950s. For ten years he struggled for success, but his one single, "I'll

Never Fall in Love Again" went nowhere. He toured with Marty Wilde and even appeared on the UK TV series "Oh Boy." During this time, Dorsey contracted tuberculosis. He hit bottom around 1963.

Then in 1966, Dorsey contacted his former roommate, Gordon Mills. Mills, formerly a singer in the skiffle group Viscounts, had moved on to songwriting (producing top hits for groups like Johnny Kidd and the Pirates) and then to artist management of matinée-idol singers of the likes of Tom Jones.

Mills decided to re-invent Dorsey, gave him the name of the 19th-century classical German opera composer *(Hansel and Gretel)*, and introduced him to the world as the enigmatic balladeer Engelbert Humperdinck. To maintain his mysterious image, he always disappeared after every show—never meeting his fans. This often involved climbing out of bathroom windows and the like. Armed with his new name, a vivid stage presence, rugged good looks, smooth style, and three-and-a-half-octave singing range, Humperdinck broke into full stardom in 1967 with his version of the country song "Release Me." This was followed by "There Goes My Everything" and "The Last Waltz." He remained in the charts until the early '70s and was often the biggest selling artist in the UK. Country music offered Humperdinck a smorgasbord of material for his silky voice. He had many songs in the "Hot 100" and his albums charted time and again in both the UK and US.

He had another huge hit, "After the Lovin'," in 1986 but, for the most part, he has toured the cabaret circuit for the last 27 years. He did a successful album with Gloria Gaynor, *Remember I Love You*, in 1987. He has earned many different awards (Golden Globe, etc.) including some 59 gold records, 17 platinum albums, and various Grammy awards. His can't-buy-these-in-stores compilations are among the favorites of late-night two-minute TV advertisers.

Humperdinck presides over the largest fan club in the world with 250 chapters and some eight million members. Still on the road, he travels with an 18-member group and has added impersonations and comedy skits to his act over the years (imitations of Dean Martin, Elvis Presley, and his archrival, Julio Iglesias, somewhat obscuring his impact as a singer. Still, when he is not goofing around on stage, Humperdinck can sing a ballad like few others. His dynamic range, heartfelt understanding of lyrics, and clarity of exposition make him one of the great ballad singers. He states, "There's always going to be a market for romance and, as long as people come and see me, I'll be there." *—Michael Erlewine*

Release Me / 1966 / Mercury ♦♦♦♦
This is his first album with that initial gold single—"Release Me." The CD has 12 tracks including "There's a Kind of Hush," "This Is My Song," "There Goes My Everything," and "Ten Guitars." This is early Humperdinck, but all the feeling is there. If you can find a copy of this, it is fun to have. Some of these songs appear on the compilations, not always in the original versions. *—Michael Erlewine*

The Last Waltz / 1967 / Parrot ♦♦♦
Humperdinck was discovered in 1967. This is his second album; the year is still 1967. Included here is his chart-topping gold record, "The Last Waltz," plus such Englebert standards as "Two Different Worlds" and "Am I That Easy to Forget." Humperdinck's voice is a touch higher (and thinner) here than the velvet tones we all know so well from his more recent late-night-TV album offers. If you can find this bit of vinyl (or his first album *Release Me*), the photo of Humperdinck on either cover will make the search worth your time. *—Michael Erlewine*

● **Greatest Hits** / 1974 / Polydor ♦♦♦♦

★ **Very Best of Engelbert Humperdinck** / Heartland ♦♦♦♦♦
These are the original songs and they are some of the very best that Humperdinck has recorded—21 velvet-voiced gems. Includes his first three single gold records (original UK chart toppers): "Release Me," "There Goes My Everything," and "The Last Waltz." Other favorite Humperdinck songs like "Two Different Worlds," "Can't Take My Eyes Off You," "After the Lovin'," and "This Is My Song" are there, too. This was available from Heartland Music via those late-night TV offers. Yup (gulp), I bought it and have never been sorry. *—Michael Erlewine*

Julio Iglesias

b. Sept. 23, 1943, Madrid, Spain
Vocals / Latin Pop, Adult Contemporary, Soft Rock, Club-Dance
Julio Iglesias was the most popular Latin singer of the '70s and '80s, selling over 100 million albums around the world. Iglesias was a smooth, romantic crooner and his appeal translated to many different countries in many different languages.

Initially, Iglesias planned to be a lawyer. As he studied, he was a goalkeeper for the Real Madrid football team. His career as an athlete was ended after an automobile accident in the mid-'60s. While he was recovering, Iglesias started playing guitar and writing songs. Before he began a musical career, he finished his law studies at Cambridge University. In 1968, he was a contestant at the 1968 Spanish Song Festival at Benidorm, singing his original song "La Vida Sigue Igual." Iglesias won the

first prize at the contest, which led to a record contract with Discos Columbia, an independent record label.

During the '70s, he toured Europe and Latin America, gaining a large fan base with hits like 1975's "Manuela." By the end of the decade, he was extremely popular—so popular, CBS International sought out a contract with him. He signed with the label in 1978. Iglesias began to record not only in Spanish, but in Italian and French as well.

At the turn of the decade, Julio Iglesias began to pursue the American and British markets by concentrating on his English recordings. His efforts began to pay off in 1981, when his cover of "Begin the Beguine" became a No. 1 hit. It was quickly followed by the compilation record *Julio*, which became a big success in England and America. However, his major crossover success was 1984's *1100 Bel Air Place*, a collection of duets. Featuring the Top Ten hit duet with Willie Nelson, "To All the Girls I've Loved Before," the album sold over three million copies in America and peaked at No. 5 on the pop charts; it also spawned "All of You," a hit duet with Diana Ross. Iglesias' popularity continued to grow throughout the '80s, although he only had one more pop crossover hit, 1988's "My Love," a duet with Stevie Wonder.

By the 1990s, he had stopped courting the English pop market and concentrated on recording mainly in Spanish, as well as a handful of other languages. His popularity did not diminish at all in his third decade of recordings—he was still capable of selling millions of records and selling out concerts around the world. *—Stephen Thomas Erlewine*

● **Julio** / 1983 / Columbia ♦♦♦♦

1100 Bel Air Place / 1984 / Columbia ♦♦♦

The Ink Spots

R&B, Pop
The Ink Spots played a large role in pioneering the Black vocal group-harmony genre, helping to pave the way for the doo wop explosion of the '50s. The quavering high tenor of Bill Kenny presaged hundreds of street-corner leads to come, and the sweet harmonies of Carlie Fuqua, Deek Watson, and bass Hoppy Jones (who died in 1944) backed him flawlessly.

Kenny's impeccable diction and Jones' deep drawl were both prominent on the Ink Spots' first smash on Decca in 1939, the sentimental "If I Didn't Care." From there through 1951, the group was seldom absent from the pop charts, topping the lists with "We Three (My Echo, My Shadow, and Me)" (1940), "I'm Making Believe" and "Into Each Life Some Rain Must Fall" (both in 1944), and "The Gypsy" and "To Each His Own" (both in 1946).

Watson eventually split to form his own group, the Brown Dots, and appeared in numerous low-budget film musicals, while Kenny attempted a solo career, notching a solo hit in 1951 with the uplifting "It Is No Secret." Countless groups masquerading as the Ink Spots have thrived across the nation since the '50s. *—Bill Dahl*

★ **The Greatest Hits 1939-46** / 196 / MCA ♦♦♦♦♦
The authentic Decca recordings showcase this seminal doo wop vocal unit. *—Ron Wynn*

Al Jolson (Asa Yoelson)

b. 1888, **d.** Oct. 23, 1950
Vocals, Dancer / Dancing / Nostalgia, Easy Listening, Ballads
An entertainment dynamo who quickly established himself as Broadway's leading star by the dawn of the 20th century, Jolson was America's first superstar, years before the phrase was ever coined. A truly competitive and high-energy performer, Jolson left most of the competition in the dust with his impassioned singing, dancing, and jokes (borrowing much from Black ragtime music and early jazz and performing in the then-popular minstrel blackface style). His place in popular history was assured when he starred in the first successful talking picture, *The Jazz Singer*, in 1927. His tireless efforts performing for American troops during World War II (he almost single-handedly started the USO) won him a whole new audience who had never seen him perform in his halcyon days. When the film biography of his life became a major hit 20 years later, Jolson's popularity leapt to legendary status, making no one doubt his title of "The World's Greatest Entertainer." *—Cub Koda*

● **You Ain't Heard Nothin' Yet** / 1975 / ASV/Living Era ♦♦♦♦

The Best of the Decca Years / 1992 / Decca ♦♦♦

Early Years / Pearl Flapper ♦♦♦♦
Great single-disc compilation of the earliest Jolson material, which made him a sensation on Broadway. Essential sides and a fascinating glimpse into vaudeville's heyday. *—Cub Koda*

The Legendary Al Jolson / CBS ♦♦♦
A three-disc set of Jolson's early Columbia recordings (1914-1923), with a sixth side devoted to early-'30s Brunswick recordings from his movie days. Some duplication with the above-mentioned *Early Years* compilation, but worth having nonetheless. *—Cub Koda*

Etta Jones

b. Nov. 25, 1928, Aiken, SC
Vocals / Standards
An excellent singer who is always worth hearing, Etta Jones grew up in New York and at 16 toured with Buddy Johnson. She debuted on record with Barney Bigard's pickup band (1944) for Black & White, singing four Leonard Feather songs, three of which (including "Evil Gal Blues") were hits for Dinah Washington. She recorded other songs during 1946-47 for RCA and worked with Earl Hines (1949-52). Jones' version of "Don't Go to Strangers" (1960) was a hit and she made many albums for Prestige during 1960-65. Jones toured Japan with Art Blakey (1970) but was largely off record during 1966-75. However, starting in 1976, Etta Jones began recording regularly for Muse, often with her husband, the fine tenor saxophonist Houston Person. —*Scott Yanow*

● **Don't Go to Strangers** / Jun. 21, 1960 / Original Jazz Classics ✦✦✦✦

Something Nice / Sep. 16, 1960-Mar. 30, 1961 / Original Jazz Classics ✦✦✦✦
An excellent reissue of some prime cuts with Oliver Nelson (reeds) and Roy Haynes (drums) from 1960 and 1961. —*Ron Wynn*

Etta Jones and Strings / Jun. 9, 1961-Jul. 28, 1961 / Original Jazz Classics ✦✦

Lonely and Blue / Apr. 6, 1962-May 4, 1962 / Original Jazz Classics ✦✦✦

Fine and Mellow / 1987 / Muse ✦✦✦✦
With fine sax from Houston Person. —*Ron Wynn*

I'll Be Seeing You / Sep. 23, 1987 / Muse ✦✦✦✦
With good Houston Person tenor sax cuts. Originally recorded on September 23, 1987. —*Ron Wynn*

Sugar / Oct. 18, 1989 / Muse ✦✦✦✦
Nice (though limited) soul-jazz and light-swing cuts. Recorded in October 1989. —*Ron Wynn*

Sammy Kaye

b. Mar. 31, 1910, d. Jun. 2, 1987
Reeds (Multiple) / Big Band
Kaye's band was a textbook example of "sweet" dance bands: large groups whose arrangements seldom swung in the true sense, but were very popular among those who enjoyed overly sentimental light pop and novelty tunes. Kaye began building his reputation in college, then became a hit on radio in Cincinnati. He moved to Pittsburgh and eventually became a national staple. His radio show "Sunday Serenade" was a huge hit in the '40s and '50s. Kaye had many pop hits, some of them adapted for Broadway shows. His gimmick of having fans volunteer to lead his band was highly popular and was transferred to television in the '50s. Perry Como and Nat King Cole had hits with Kaye material. This was far from being a jazz band in the real sense, but made enjoyable material of its kind and is a big favorite to this day. —*Ron Wynn*

● **The Best of Sammy Kaye** / 1974 / MCA ✦✦✦✦
Decent collection of his Decca dates. —*Ron Wynn*

Gene Kelly

b. 1912, Pittsburgh, PA
Vocals
Showing an early aptitude in both gymnastics and dance, Eugene Curran Kelly had devoured, by his early teens, everything he could about dance in general and ballet in particular. He was already a successful dance teacher in his hometown when he began his ascent in the original Broadway production of Rodgers and Hart's *Pal Joey*. This led to a film contract with David O. Selznick, which was sold to MGM before Kelly even reported to Hollywood. The allegiance with MGM proved a godsend for both the studio and Kelly, who (with the help of producer Arthur Freed) came to energize the film company's musical output for the next 15 years. Kelly quickly revealed himself to be a quintuple threat: dancer, actor, singer, choreographer, and director. Beginning with his first film, *For Me and My Gal*, he showed an engaging personality on screen, and his voice, while never strong, was equally pleasing. As his influence at the studio grew, Kelly began proposing more ambitious projects as a director as well as a choreographer and performer. Kelly was never a popular singer, despite the fact that he acquitted himself onscreen alongside even the likes of Frank Sinatra in several films, but his on-screen geniality and overall popularity—as a younger, more masculine, and more conventionally handsome rival to Fred Astaire (who was at MGM at exactly the same time)—allowed him to effectively repopularize many songs by George Gershwin, Arthur Freed, Nacio Herb Brown, and others through his performances of them in films such as *An American in Paris* and *Singin' in the Rain*. His most popular and influential work as a singer can be found on the soundtracks for those films, plus *Brigadoon*,

It's Always Fair Weather, Summer Stock, and the compilation soundtrack *That's Entertainment Part 2*.

As the '50s wore on and the public's taste for musicals waned, Kelly turned increasingly toward directing (*Gigot, Hello Dolly!*) and producing, allowing his acting—which he had never entirely forsaken but had never built into great prominence before, either—to become the focus of his film work in movies such as *Marjorie Morningstar* and *Inherit the Wind*. He proved to be as adept at drama as he had been at dance. In the '70s, spurred on by the growing interest in America's cinematic past that coalesced around MGM's compilation feature *That's Entertainment*, Kelly directed the equally fine follow-up, *That's Entertainment Part 2*. —*Bruce Eder*

★ **'S Wonderful** / Jun. 1996 / Rhino ✦✦✦✦✦
The majority of Gene Kelly's best-known songs are collected on *'S Wonderful*, including his duets with Judy Garland and Fred Astaire. Since Kelly was a better dancer than singer, this collection functions as the definitive retrospective of his musical career. —*AMG*

Jerome Kern

b. 1885, d. 1945
Nostalgia, Show Tunes
Jerome Kern is arguably the father of modern American musical theater. Born in New York of German heritage, he attended the New York College of Music and began to break into Broadway theater during the first decade of the century by having songs of his interpolated into shows. An Anglophile and friend of P.G. Wodehouse, Kern scored his first success with songs inserted into *The Girl from Utah*, a British import, in 1914, including the ballad "They Didn't Believe Me." Breaking away from the European model of waltz music, Kern proved adept at adapting contemporary dance music into his songs as well as producing subtle, inventive ballads. He collaborated with Guy Bolton and, later, Wodehouse on a series of shows presented at the Princess Theater in the middle of the decade, notably *Very Good Eddie*, and continued to score successes into the '20s.

But Kern really entered the history books with *Show Boat* (1927), the first truly modern American musical, with an integrated story and such memorable songs as "Ol' Man River" and "Can't Help Lovin' Dat Man." Like many of his contemporaries, Kern divided his time between Broadway and Hollywood in the '30s, after sound came into the movies, and his movie hits included the Fred Astaire-Ginger Rogers film *Swing Time*, with such songs as "A Fine Romance" and "The Way You Look Tonight" (with lyrics by Dorothy Fields). Kern worked steadily—he wrote or contributed to 37 shows during his career—and was beginning work on *Annie Get Your Gun* when he died suddenly in 1945. He left behind one of the richest catalogs of show music in history. —*William Ruhlmann*

Jerome Kern Showcase / Pearl Flapper ✦✦✦

Swing Time / Angel ✦✦

● **Columbia Album** / CBS ✦✦✦✦

Morgana King (Morgana Messina)

b. Jun. 4, 1930, Pleasantville, NY
Vocals / Standards
An accomplished actress, King has also made some albums in the jazz vein. She worked in several New York clubs during the late '50s and early '60s. Her 1964 album, *A Taste of Honey*, made some impact, although King didn't display strong jazz technique. Her late-'70s albums for Muse had better material and more convincing performances but didn't match her appearances in the films *The Godfather* and *The Godfather Part II* for wide-ranging impact. King makes nice, occasionally arresting albums, and is a very good vocalist. —*Ron Wynn*

A Taste of Honey / 1964 / Mainstream ✦✦✦✦
Nice cuts; clean vocals. —*Ron Wynn*

Everything Must Change / Aug. 8, 1978 / Muse ✦✦✦
Good interpretations and arrangements from King. —*Ron Wynn*

Portraits / Oct. 19, 1983 Jan. 2, -1984 / Muse ✦✦✦
Competent set presenting actress/vocalist Morgana King doing jazz-oriented pop, standards, and ballads backed by a tight combo. She has good technique, delivery, and style; there is nothing innovative or particularly original about either the material or the performances, but they are thoroughly professional and often enjoyable. —*Ron Wynn*

● **Simply Eloquent** / 1986 / Muse ✦✦✦✦
Smooth and tasteful. Recorded on February 24, 1986. —*Ron Wynn*

This Is Always / 1992 / Muse ✦✦✦

Eartha Kitt

Vocals / Vocal
This alluring vocalist enjoyed a series of pop hits in 1953 and 1954, including the seductive Yuletide perennial "Santa Baby." Kitt's exotic style

was first showcased in the Broadway production of *New Faces of 1952* (a film version was made in 1954), and she waxed the enticing "Cest Si Bon" in 1953 for RCA Victor. "Santa Baby" arrived in time for the 1953 holidays, and her 1954 output included "Somebody Bad Stole De Wedding Bell (Who's Got De Ding Dong)." Kitt has remained active as an actress and singer; she was a convincing Catwoman on the campy mid-'60s TV series "Batman," and she co-starred in the movies *Pink Chiquitas* and *Erik the Viking*. —*Bill Dahl*

● **The Best of Eartha Kitt** / 1975 / MCA ✦✦✦✦
Decent overview that concentrates on her pop-oriented material. —*Ron Wynn*

Frankie Laine (Lo Vecchio, Frank Paul)

b. Mar. 30, 1913, Chicago, IL
Vocals / Vocal
Laine, one of the biggest recording stars of the late '40s and early '50s, is famous for his robust baritone. After working radio shows, dance marathons, and a brief stint replacing Perry Como in Freddy Carlone's band, Laine broke into the national spotlight in 1947 with his million-selling "That's My Desire." Nearly seventy Top 100 hits followed, with "Jezebel" and "I Believe" among the finest. (Note: Frankie Laine has re-recorded his Columbia hits numerous times; thus most Laine compilations contain later material with little warning. Check the label and select CBS if possible.) —*Stephen Thomas Erlewine & Bil Carpenter & Hank Davis*

The Frankie Laine Collection: The Mercury Years / 1991 / PolyGram ✦✦✦✦
This starts with studio chatter and runs through 22 tracks, dated 1946-1950. It's far more bluesy-jazzy than his later Columbia material. —*Hank Davis*

★ **Greatest Hits** / Columbia ✦✦✦✦✦
The essential collection is wild and energetic, with "Jezebel" and others. —*Hank Davis*

16 Most Requested Songs / Columbia ✦✦✦✦

Peggy Lee

b. May 26, 1920
Vocals / Swing, Pop
Peggy Lee only had a small voice and she never improvised much, but her singing often crossed over into jazz and she always swung. She came to fame with Benny Goodman (1941-43) although she was so scared at her first recording session ("Elmer's Tune") that John Hammond urged Goodman to fire her. BG knew better and she had a big hit within a year with "Why Don't You Do Right." After marrying Dave Barbour in 1943, Lee retired briefly but was soon a major recording artist for Capitol, and during the 1940s and '50s she had quite a few popular recordings including "It's a Good Day," "Black Coffee," "Mañana," and "Fever"; she also proved to be a talented songwriter. Lee appeared in the Dixieland movie *Pete Kelly's Blues* and recorded *Beauty and the Beat* (1959) with the George Shearing Quintet but then moved farther away from jazz in the 1960s. Peggy Lee's often atmospheric records from her prime years can be easily enjoyed by jazz fans. —*Scott Yanow*

Black Coffee / Apr. 3, 1952-Jun. 8, 1956 / MCA/Decca ✦✦✦✦

● **Beauty and the Beat** / Apr. 28, 1959 / Capitol ✦✦✦✦

☆ **Capitol Collectors Series, Vol. 1: The Early Years** / May 21, 1990 / Capitol ✦✦✦✦✦
Capitol Collectors Series, Vol. 1: The Early Years is the best collection of Lee's jazz and blues hits. —*Ron Wynn*

The Lettermen

Pop
Though styles changed drastically and frequently throughout the '60s, the Lettermen held still (for the most part), producing light pop songs full of easy harmonies. Tony Butala (b. Nov. 20, 1940), Jim Pike (b. Nov. 6, 1938), and Bob Engemann (b. Feb. 19, 1936) formed the trio in Los Angeles in 1960, cutting their first record a year later. The Lettermen charted 20 times on the Hot 100 from 1961 to 1971. —*Stephen Thomas Erlewine*

● **Capitol Collectors Series** / 1992 / Capitol ✦✦✦✦
All six of the Lettermen's Top 40 hits are here, along with a generous selection of lesser-known singles and album tracks. Informative liner notes and excellent sound help make this the definitive Lettermen collection. —*Stephen Thomas Erlewine*

Limeliters

Folk
A folk group formed in 1959 by Louis Gottlieb (bass), Alex Hassilev (baritone, guitar, banjo), and Glenn Yarbrough (tenor, guitar). They played in concert and at folk houses like San Francisco's Hungry I and appeared on

TV and radio nationwide. They disbanded in the mid-'60s. —*Michael Erlewine*

The Slightly Fabulous Limeliters / 1961 / RCA ✦✦✦
This album reached No. 8 on the charts in 1961. —*Michael Erlewine*

● **Tonight in Person** / 1961 / RCA ✦✦✦✦
Live concert at the Ash Grove. One of their bestsellers. —*Michael Erlewine*

Julie London

b. Sep. 26, 1926, Santa Rosa, CA
Vocals / Vocal, Pop
Not only was Julie London absolutely gorgeous, she possessed one of the sultriest vocal deliveries around (perhaps best spotlighted on her smoky 1955 pop smash "Cry Me a River"). Born in Santa Rosa, CA, London landed roles in several films during the '40s and married tight-jawed "Dragnet" cop Jack Webb. London's singing ability was encouraged by her next hubby, Bobby Troup (the composer of "Route 66"). She signed with Liberty and hit big with "Cry Me a River," performing it in a memorable scene in the 1956 rock flick *The Girl Can't Help It*. Although that was her only pop hit, London's many Liberty albums were perfect mood music for late-night makeout sessions, and her acting resume includes a long stint during the '70s as a nurse on the Webb-produced TV hospital drama "Emergency." —*Bill Dahl*

The Best of Julie / 1957-1960 / Liberty ✦✦✦✦
This English Liberty LP from the 1980s has one selection apiece from 13 of Julie London's earlier albums. Although she never thought of herself as a singer, London had a sensuous and surprisingly flexible voice that sounded at its best in intimate jazz settings. Highlights of this set (in addition to the miniature reproductions of London's famed album covers) are her hit "Cry Me a River," "They Can't Take That Away from Me," "Mad About the Boy," "Invitation to the Blues," "The Nearness of You," and "Daddy." This hard-to-find LP serves as a perfect introduction to the magic of Julie London's music. —*Scott Yanow*

★ **Time for Love: Best of Julie London** / 1991 / Rhino ✦✦✦✦✦
Often over-orchestrated but still effective, these are her best-known songs. —*Dan Heilman*

Julie London Sings Cole Porter / 1991 / EMI America ✦✦✦

Julie Is Her Name, Vols. 1 & 2 / 1992 / Liberty ✦✦✦✦
A '50s album accompanied by bass and by Barney Kessel's guitar with hip chord voicings. This made a big splash in its day, with many guitarists working to decipher Kessel's work. —*Richard Lieberson*

Trini Lopez

b. May 15, 1937
Vocals / Vocal, Pop
Trini Lopez recorded a series of upbeat tunes for Reprise during the mid-'60s, including a smash rendering of the folk standard "If I Had a Hammer" in 1963. The Dallas native cut some Ritchie Valens-influenced rockers for the King label prior to his discovery by producer Don Costa. Lopez's hits capture the excitement of his live performances, and his driving renditions of "Kansas City" (1963), "Lemon Tree" (1965), and "I'm Comin' Home, Cindy" (1966) were substantial sellers. Reportedly one of Dean Martin's favorite performers, Lopez hosted his own network TV variety program and co-starred as one of *The Dirty Dozen* in the popular 1967 movie. —*Bill Dahl*

Trini Lopez / Bella Musica ✦✦✦
Original Reprise hits and some remakes fill this hard-to-find import. —*Jeff Tamarkin*

● **From the Original Master Tapes** / Reprise ✦✦✦✦
This Japanese import is an exquisite-sounding 20-song collection of the Mexican-American folk-rocker's '60s hits. It serves as evidence that the nearly forgotten Lopez deserves more credit as an interpretive artist. —*Jeff Tamarkin*

Jon Lucien

b. 1942
Bass, Guitar, Vocals / Ballads
During the '70s, Jon Lucien became a popular figure as a jazz-tinged romantic song specialist. Lucien's deep, prominent baritone, his penchant for sentimental fare, and his suave, commanding personality and presence made him enormously popular on the cabaret/supper-club circuit as well as among fans of love ballads and similar material. After a long absence, Lucien returned in 1991 with a release that was very much what he'd done in his peak '70s years. Unfortunately, the response wasn't anywhere near what it had been before. —*Ron Wynn*

Listen Love / Apr. 24, 1991 / Mercury ✦✦✦
The comeback/return project for '70s romantic sensation Jon Lucien. Lucien, who had once been among the top vocalists making orches-

trated, jazz-tinged R&B, tried to equal his past success by doing essentially the same material with updated production touches (more synthesized support). He also had heavy promotional backup from his record label. But he was unable to recapture his position at the top of the heap, although the release was just as solid as his past efforts. —*Ron Wynn*

● **The Best of Jon Lucien** / RCA ✦✦✦✦
Anthology featuring top hits by a romantic crooner who was dominant in the '70s. Lucien had a deep, lush voice and specialized in doing romantic material with a light Caribbean touch. He also sometimes added a quasi-jazz feel with moderate scat singing. —*Ron Wynn*

Dean Martin

b. Jun. 17, 1917, **d.** Dec. 25, 1995
Vocals / Pop
Martin's boozy, easygoing vocal style doesn't feature Sinatra's dazzle or Bennett's kitsch, but it remains one of the friendliest in pop. He made his debut in 1948 with "That Certain Party," a duet with his then-partner Jerry Lewis, but Martin's best work came in the early '50s, when he had scores of singles in the pop Top 40. His nonchalant way of twisting syllables and slurring notes played a major role in the development of Elvis Presley's ballad style; compare Martin's "I'd Cry Like a Baby" with Presley's "Love Me." He recorded a slew of albums, but his chart run was exhausted by the '60s. Throughout the '70s, he was a fixture in Las Vegas, where he rubbed stage elbows with the likes of Frank Sinatra and Liza Minnelli. During the late '80s, Martin effectively retired from performing, retreating into private seclusion. The vocalist died on Christmas Day, 1995. —*John Floyd*

★ **Capitol Collectors Series** / Oct. 25, 1989 / Capitol ✦✦✦✦✦
A terrific 20-song overview of the Capitol years, it includes everything you need, from "That's Amore" and "Volare" to "Ain't That a Kick in the Head." —*John Floyd*

The Best of Dean Martin / 1996 / Capitol ✦✦✦✦
Like *Capitol Collectors Series,* this offers a 20-song overview of his Capitol years (the 1950s and early '60s), with a different track selection and an unfortunate absence of liner notes. It does have his biggest hits from the era, including "That's Amore," "Memories Are Made of This," "Innumerato," and "Volare." —*Richie Unterberger*

★ **The Best of Dean Martin 1962-1968** / 1996 / Charly ✦✦✦✦✦
Dean Martin had 22 singles chart entries on Reprise Records between 1962 and 1969, and all of them are on this 66-minute, 25-track import compilation, along with covers of "Gentle on My Mind," "By the Time I Get to Phoenix," and "King of the Road." What makes this foolproof collection, highlighted by the Top Ten hits "Everybody Loves Somebody" (a chart-topping million-seller), "The Door Is Still Open to My Heart," and "I Will," particularly notable is that these recordings, owned by the singer (and now his estate), have been out of print for years and, at this writing (May 1996), remain so in the US. It is arguable that Martin's Capitol recordings of the 1950s are superior to these Jimmy Bowen-produced tracks, the earlier ones paced by rock 'n' roll rhythms, the later ones country-tinged, and all featuring prominent backup vocal groups. But as usual, Martin's nonchalance allows him to be comfortable in any context, and the arrangements are undeniably catchy, especially Billy May's punchy chart for "You're Nobody Till Somebody Loves You." And if the Capitols always evoke the straight man of the Martin & Lewis comedies, the Reprises call to mind the tuxedo-clad swinger on the fireman's pole and the suave star of the Matt Helm spy spoofs—boozy, bawdy, and brilliant. (Though the selection of material earns this album landmark status, its sound quality could be better.) —*William Ruhlmann*

☆ **Capitol Years** / 1996 / Capitol ✦✦✦✦✦
Spanning two discs and 40 songs, *The Capitol Years* is the most thorough retrospective of Dean Martin's Capitol recordings. From "Memories Are Made of This" to "Return to Me" and "Volare," all his major hits for the label are included, as are several album tracks, lesser-known singles, and a handful of rarities. The collection may have too many songs for casual fans, but it's the only album that presents the important Capitol tracks with care, thought, and first-class sound. —*Stephen Thomas Erlewine*

Al Martino (Alfred Cini)

b. Oct. 7, 1927, Philadelphia, PA
Vocals
Italian singer Al Martino had four hits from 1952 to 1953 and then vanished until the end of the decade—the result of being too young to handle his success and having various disreputable elements vying for control of his career. Martino tried to continue recording in England, to no avail, and returned to America in 1958. After re-signing with Capitol Records the following year, he launched a string of 34 Hot 100 singles that would last until 1977. During the '60s Martino blended country elements with pop songs, blurring the lines between the two genres. In 1972 he appeared in Francis Ford Coppola's masterpiece, *The Godfather,* as

singer Johnny Fontaine, a role that strongly resembled Frank Sinatra's life. —*Stephen Thomas Erlewine*

● **Capitol Collectors Series** / 1992 / Capitol ✦✦✦✦
All of Martino's major hits—"Here in My Heart," "Take My Heart," "I Love You Because," "I Love You More and More Every Day," and "Speak Softly Love" (the love theme from *The Godfather)*—are included on this comprehensive 25-track compilation, along with informative, lively liner notes and sparkling fidelity. The best Martino collection available. —*Stephen Thomas Erlewine*

Johnny Mathis

b. 1935
Guitar, Vocals / Pop
Mathis (born James Royce Mathis) made the smoothest makeout music ever recorded, and his rise to stardom in the mid-'50s flew in the face of rock 'n' roll's early domination. Staying almost exclusively with lushly orchestrated ballad material, Mathis racked up hit after hit and now has had albums in the charts for 30 years, an achievement few will better. —*Cub Koda*

Open Fire, Two Guitars / 1959 / Columbia ✦✦✦✦
A warm and intimate setting, with stellar guitar work from Al Caiola and Tony Mottola. —*Cub Koda*

★ **Johnny's Greatest Hits** / 1962 / Columbia ✦✦✦✦✦
The original greatest-hits package, which stayed on the charts for ten years; includes "Chances Are," "It's Not for Me to Say," "Wonderful! Wonderful!" and "The Twelfth of Never." It seldom gets more romantic than this. —*Cub Koda*

Amanda McBroom

Vocals
This Los Angeles-based songwriter and cabaret singer is probably best known for her song "The Rose," a hit in 1979 for Bette Midler. McBroom has also appeared on stage in *Jacques Brel Is Alive and Well* and *See Saw,* and also tours regularly. Her debut album, *Growing Up in Hollywood* with Lincoln Mayorga, was a bestseller for the prestigious Sheffield Labs label, as was her follow-up, *West of Oz.* —*AMG*

Growing Up in Hollywood Town / 1980 / Sheffield Lab ✦✦✦

● **Dreaming** / 1986 / Gecko ✦✦✦✦
Amanda McBroom remains best known for her composition "The Rose," the hit that served as the title song for the Bette Midler movie. McBroom's version of the song is included here, along with a collection of equally moving love songs. —*William Ruhlmann*

Maureen McGovern

b. 1949
Vocals
Maureen McGovern was a secretary when she was hired by Russ Regan to sing the theme from the movie *The Poseidon Adventure* in 1973. It was a No. 1 hit. The next year, McGovern sang the theme from *The Towering Inferno,* "We May Never Love Like This Again," which was not a hit, though it did win an Academy Award. McGovern went on to other movie themes, then distanced herself from such work, appearing on Broadway in *The Pirates of Penzance.* She built a reputation as a sophisticated pop singer to the point that she was able to headline at Carnegie Hall by the '90s, singing show music and standards by George Gershwin and other songwriters. —*William Ruhlmann*

The Morning After / 1973 / 20th Century ✦✦✦
Contains that big ballad, of course, though there is no album compiling all of McGovern's movie themes. —*William Ruhlmann*

Naughty Baby / 1989 / CBS ✦✦✦✦
McGovern as sophisticated pop singer, effectively handling an album of Gershwin material. Includes "Of Thee I Sing," the theme from a show in which she starred in 1987. —*William Ruhlmann*

● **Greatest Hits** / 1990 / Curb ✦✦✦✦
The best of her movie work and other hits, including "Different Worlds." —*Cub Koda*

Johnny Mercer

b. Nov. 18, 1909, Savannah, GA, **d.** Jun. 25, 1976, Los Angeles, CA
Vocals / Vocal, Standards
A marvelous lyricist and multifaceted composer, talent scout, and recording artist, Johnny Mercer truly did it all. He wrote or co-wrote more than 1,000 songs, and his compositions have been played and sung by numerous jazz greats and many pop stars. Mercer as a vocalist, despite lacking great technique or tools, had many hits from the late '30s into the early '50s, done in a relaxed, easygoing style. He teamed with Bing Crosby on Decca from 1938 to 1940, then had 25 hits on Capitol over a 10-year period, including chart toppers "Candy" with Jo Stafford, "Ac-cent-tchu-

ate the Positive" and "On the Atchinson, Topeka and the Santa Fe." Mercer won multiple Oscars, co-founded Capitol Records, and signed Nat King Cole and Peggy Lee, was a co-founder and president of the Songwriters Hall of Fame and a director of ASCAP in 1940 and 1941. His lyrics were unfailing upbeat and optimistic; by today's cynical standards he'd be deemed not just a hopeless romantic, but a foolish one. Mercer gems include "I'm an Old Cowhand," "Dream (When You're Feelin' Blue)," "That Old Black Magic," "One for My Baby," "Lazy Bones," and numerous others. He collaborated on masterpieces with Henry Mancini, Harold Arlen, Hoagy Carmichael, Harry Warren, Billy Strayhorn, and Duke Ellington, Ralph Burns, Jerome Kern, Gordon Jenkins, and Rube Bloom, among others. Mercer sang with Benny Goodman on radio, hosted his own shows with Paul Whiteman serving as music director, contributed to films and plays, and recorded duets with Bobby Darin. There's almost no facet of American popular entertainment Mercer didn't affect positively. Compilations of various singers doing his compositions have recently been issued on Rhino and are available on other labels like RCA. Mercer's vocals are featured on CD compilations by Capitol, Hindsight, and other labels. —*Ron Wynn and Kenneth M. Cassidy*

The Uncollected Johnny Mercer (1944) / 1944 / Hindsight ✦✦✦✦
A collection of radio transcripts, they were recorded in 1944 with the Paul Weston Orchestra. —*Kenneth M. Cassidy*

● **Capitol Collectors Series** / Jul. 26, 1989 / Capitol ✦✦✦✦
This is a collection of his best recordings from the '40s. —*Kenneth M. Cassidy*

Mabel Mercer

b. 1900, d. 1984
Vocals / Vocal, Cabaret
Mercer was popular in cabaret work, both in Paris and the US, for years. Her strong interpretive skills as a chanteuse and her penchant for popularizing obscure tunes such as "Fly Me to the Moon" brought her a loyal cult following. Admirers of her work included Lena Horne, Nat King Cole, and Frank Sinatra. —*Cub Koda*

● **Art of Mabel Mercer** / May 21, 1952 / Atlantic ✦✦✦✦
Good two-record anthology that features outstanding cabaret vocalist Mabel Mercer. Her approach was brilliant, but not for everyone; it was stiff by jazz phrasing standards and put far more emphasis on technique than feeling. Yet, few have been better at doing highly stylized material. This has not yet been reissued on disc. —*Ron Wynn*

Sings Cole Porter / 1994 / Atlantic ✦✦✦✦
A great song stylist working in a perfect lyric setting. —*Ron Wynn*

Ethel Merman (Ethel Agnes Zimmerman)

b. 1908, New York City, NY, d. 1984
Vocals / Nostalgia
Merman developed her booming vocal style on her own. She attracted attention in Gershwin's *Girl Crazy* (1930), capping the show with her rendition of "I Got Rhythm." Dubbed the "Queen of Broadway," Merman starred in Cole Porter's *Anything Goes* (1934), Irving Berlin's *Annie Get Your Gun* (1946), and *Call Me Madam* (1950). She also appeared in 14 movie musicals, including *There's No Business Like Show Business*. —*David Szatmary*

● **Musical Autobiography** / 1963 / Decca ✦✦✦✦
This two-album set provides a solid introduction to Merman's distinctive style. —*David Szatmary*

Bette Midler

b. Dec. 1, 1945, Patterson, NJ
Vocals / Nostalgia, Adult Contemporary, Pop, Soft Rock
Bette Midler counts singing as only one of her talents; at times, since 1972, when she first came to national recognition, it has seemed to be the least of her talents. Still, she has managed to score a number of major hits in a roller-coaster career as a recording artist. Born in Patterson, NJ, and raised in Hawaii, Midler early on showed an interest in singing and acting, and by the '60s she had moved to New York and gotten a role in the long-running Broadway hit *Fiddler on the Roof*. Midler developed a nightclub act that included comedy and singing of a variety of material, including show tunes, pop hits, and even a takeoff on the Andrews Sisters, and appeared with increasing frequency in New York with her accompanist, Barry Manilow. She was signed to Atlantic Records and released *The Divine Miss M* (1972), which went gold and included a Top Ten single cover of the Andrews Sisters' "Boogie Woogie Bugle Boy." *Bette Midler* (1973) was similarly successful.

Midler's album sales fell off during the rest of the '70s, though her records always reached the Top 100 in the album chart. But in 1979 she starred in the film *The Rose*, a fictional account of the life of Janis Joplin, and the title track became a Top Ten hit. 1980 saw the release of Midler's concert film, *Divine Madness*, and her bestselling book, *A View from a*

Broad. Her next film, *Jinxed* (1982), however, was a flop, and subsequent records didn't fare well. Midler made a comeback with *Down and Out in Beverly Hills* (1986), but it wasn't until 1989 that she had another pop hit, when her version of "Wind Beneath My Wings" from her film *Beaches* became a No. 1 hit. This rejuvenated her singing career, and 1990's *Some People's Lives* became a Top Ten, million-selling album, with the song "From a Distance" hitting No. 2. Midler's soundtrack album to her 1991 film *For the Boys* was also a gold-selling hit. —*William Ruhlmann*

The Divine Miss M / 1972 / Atlantic ✦✦✦✦
Midler's early camp style is captured in this debut album, which features her torchy version of "Do You Want to Dance?," the bubbly remake of "Boogie Woogie Bugle Boy," and Buzzy Linhart's "Friends," all Top 40 hits. —*William Ruhlmann*

Bette Midler / 1973 / Atlantic ✦✦✦
This is an earthy mix of blues, R&B, and '40s boogie-woogie. —*Bil Carpenter*

Songs for the New Depression / 1976 / Atlantic ✦✦✦✦
Notable for a duet with Bob Dylan on "Buckets of Rain" and an excellent version of Tom Waits' "Shiver Me Timbers." —*William Ruhlmann*

The Rose / 1979 / Atlantic ✦✦✦✦
The soundtrack to Midler's successful film, with the title track written by Amanda McBroom. —*William Ruhlmann*

Divine Madness / 1980 / Atlantic ✦✦✦✦
This record showcases Midler at her liveliest, during a concert at Pasadena Civic Auditorium. —*Larry Lapka*

No Frills / 1983 / Atlantic ✦✦✦
Top 40 pop and light rock. —*Bil Carpenter*

Beaches / 1989 / Atlantic ✦✦✦
The soundtrack to Midler's musical comeback film, featuring her version of "Wind beneath My Wings." —*William Ruhlmann*

For the Boys / 1991 / Atlantic ✦✦✦
A film placing Midler in the Andrews Sisters' milieu of WWII was an inspired choice, and the soundtrack shows her abilities on period material as well as giving her a chance to sing a touching version of the Beatles' "In My Life." —*William Ruhlmann*

● **Divine Collection** / Jun. 22, 1993 / Atlantic ✦✦✦✦
Bette Midler's first compilation features most of her hits, including "Wind Beneath My Wings," "The Rose," "Boogie Woogie Bugle Boy," "From a Distance," and her version of "One More for My Baby (And One More for the Road)," recorded on one of the final episodes of "The Tonight Show" starring Johnny Carson. *Divine Collection* is the greatest-hits collection that Midler has needed for quite some time. —*AMG*

Mills Brothers

Group / Vocal, Swing, Pop, Classic Jazz
The Mills Brothers became so popular as a middle-of-the-road pop vocal group that one forgets just how innovative they were in the 1930s. Billed as "Four Boys and a Guitar," they were experts at imitating instruments including trumpet, trombone, tuba, and string bass. With the backing of just a guitar, they simulated a full band and amazed listeners. The Mills Brothers (Herbert, Harry, Donald, and John Jr.) started out singing in vaudeville and tent shows, were featured on a radio show for ten months in Cincinnati, arrived in New York, and by the end of 1931 were an instant hit. They recorded frequently throughout the decade, made appearances in many films (including 1932's *Big Broadcast*) and recorded with Bing Crosby, the Boswell Sisters, and Duke Ellington. John Jr.'s death in 1935 was a tragic loss, although John Sr. effectively took his place. However by 1942 with their hit "Paper Doll," the old sound gave way to a more conventional pop setting. Fortunately the English JSP label has reissued on six CDs all of the Mills Brothers' early recordings (1931-39) and these feature the group at the peak of their creativity. —*Scott Yanow*

★ **Mills Brothers: The Anthology (1931-1968)** / Aug. 1, 1995 / MCA ✦✦✦✦✦
The Mills Brothers: The Anthology is a comprehensive 48-song overview of the vocal group's career, spanning their entire career and featuring 32 of their biggest hits. Most of their most famous songs—including "Paper Doll," "Glow-Worm," "Lazy River," and "Rockin' Chair"—are included on this double-disc set, and the sound is the best it has ever been. In short, it is the definitive retrospective of this groundbreaking vocal quartet. —*Stephen Thomas Erlewine*

Liza Minnelli

b. 1946
Vocals / Pop
The daughter of Judy Garland and movie director Vincente Minnelli, Liza started in show business early on, guest-dueting as a youngster with her mother, from whom she inherited much of her energetic singing and performing abilities. She scored on Broadway at age 20 with the original

cast of *Cabaret*, later winning an Oscar for the movie version. Hollywood beckoned, as Minnelli is a fine actress, but her musical show and cabaret roots hold fast to this day. —*Cub Koda*

● **Liza with a "Z"** / 1972 / Columbia ✦✦✦✦
This was an Emmy-winning TV concert performance. —*Larry Lapka*

Liza Minnelli at Carnegie Hall / 1981 / Telarc ✦✦✦
Concert performances from 1979. —*Larry Lapka*

Vaughn Monroe

b. 1911, **d.** May 21, 1973
Trombone, Vocals / Vocal
Big-voiced baritone Vaughn Monroe caught on at the tail end of the big-band era with "Racing with the Moon" and followed with over 20 Top Ten hits through the early '50s, among them "There! I've Said It Again," "The Trolley Song," "Cool Water," "Ghost Riders in the Sky," and "Red Roses for a Blue Lady." His pleasing delivery and deep voice worked well for him when he became pitchman for parent company RCA in 1955, doing commercials to introduce America to color TV. —*Cub Koda*

● **The Best of Vaughn Monroe** / 1987 / MCA ✦✦✦✦
The big-band leader's original hits are here, including "Ghost Riders in the Sky," "Racing with the Moon," and "Ballerina." Until RCA reissues its collection, these versions will suffice. —*Hank Davis*

1950-1951 Live / Collector's Choice Music ✦✦
1950-1951 Live compiles selections from radio broadcasts recorded at the Camel Caravan and the Waldorf-Astoria, adding a handful of bonus tracks from a 1966 concert. Though it is primarily for collectors, the album does contain several first-rate performances which will interest fans. —*Stephen Thomas Erlewine*

Ella Mae Morse

b. Sep. 12, 1924, Mansfield, TX
Vocals / Vocal, Pop
One of the most talented and overlooked vocalists of the '40s, Ella Mae Morse blended jazz, country, pop, and R&B; at times she came remarkably close to what would be known as rock 'n' roll. When she wasn't yet 14, Morse had her first taste of the big time, when Jimmy Dorsey's band came to Dallas for a stay at the Adolphus Hotel and she called for an audition. Unbeknownst to her, the band needed a new female vocalist. Believing that Morse was around 19, as she and her mother claimed, Dorsey hired her. When he received a letter from the school board declaring that he was responsible for Morse's care, Dorsey fired her. Morse joined former Dorsey pianist Freddie Slack's band in 1942; she was only 17 when they cut "Cow Cow Boogie," which became Capitol Records' first gold single. The following year, Morse began recording solo. Although her recordings were consistently solid and sold fairly well (frequently charting better on the Black charts than on the pop charts), Morse never obtained a huge following. She retired from recording in 1957. —*Stephen Thomas Erlewine*

★ **Capitol Collectors Series** / 1992 / Capitol ✦✦✦✦✦
After being out of print for many years, a well-chosen sampling of Morse's groundbreaking recordings are now available on this splendid compilation. Her ten charting solo singles are here, along with sides recorded with Freddie Slack and some obscure tracks. Morse blazes through every song, particularly "House of Blue Lights," "Milkman, Keep Those Bottles Quiet," "Pig Foot Pete," "The Blacksmith Blues," and her first recording, "Cow Cow Boogie." The album has terrific liners and superlative sound. —*Stephen Thomas Erlewine*

Nana Mouskouri

b. Oct. 13, 1936, Athens, Greece
Vocals / Vocal
Mouskouri grew up on American jazz and Black gospel. She attended a classical music conservatory, but was thrown out when it was learned that she was playing jazz on the side. She later worked with Harry Belafonte and Quincy Jones. She's an articulate, resonant soprano. The bestselling female artist of all time with 800 million in sales under her belt, she is to Europe what Streisand is to America. —*Bil Carpenter*

Tu M'Oublies / 1986 / Polydor ✦✦✦
Of these French pop songs, "Parle-t-il de moi?" and "L'amour, qu'est-ce que c'est?" are the best cuts. —*Bil Carpenter*

Oh Happy Day / 1990 / Philips ✦✦✦

● **Only Love: The Best of Nana** / 1991 / Philips ✦✦✦✦
Includes Nana's English covers of '80s hits like Cyndi Lauper's "Time After Time." —*Bil Carpenter*

Wayne Newton

b. 1942
Guitar, Vocals
Though best known for his long-standing love affair with Las Vegas-style

entertainment, Newton started in a country & western/rockabilly act with his brother Jerry, recording as the Newton Rascals. Newton came to national prominence early in the '60s with regular appearances on "The Jackie Gleason Show." Though most effective with ballad material and a Vegas-glitz style of performing, he is actually a fine guitarist whose voice packs more wallop than critics generally give him credit for. —*Cub Koda*

★ **Capitol Collectors Series** / 1989 / Capitol ✦✦✦✦✦
Thorough overview of his best sides for that label, with great fidelity and comprehensive notes. —*Cub Koda*

Ray Noble

b. Dec. 17, 1903, Brighton, England, **d.** Apr. 2, 1978, London, England
Swing, Pop
An arranging and compositional mainstay as well as a good pianist and top bandleader, England's Ray Noble enjoyed great popularity both in America and Europe. He cleverly infused his songs with jazz, swing, and pop influences, creating numbers that were popular and artistic successes. Noble was HMV's music director in the late '20s and early '30s, and wrote such early '30s hits as "Love Is the Sweetest Thing," "The Very Thought of You," "The Touch of Your Lips" and the instrumental anthem "Cherokee." Charlie Barnet had a hit with it in 1938, and Charlie Parker was quoted as saying it was improvising on the song that let him play the music he'd been hearing in his mind. Noble scored four No. 1 hits in 1933 and 1934, among them "Isle of Capri" and "The Old Spinning Wheel." Noble came to America in 1934 with Al Bowlly and drummer/manager Bill Harty. Glenn Miller assembled a band for him that included Bud Freeman, Claude Thornhill, and Will Bradley. The results were such songs as "Paris in the Spring" and "Let's Swing It" in 1935. Noble backed Fred Astaire on the hit songs "Nice Work If You Can Get It," "A Foggy Day," and "Change Partners" in the late '30s on Brunswick. He signed to the label as an artist, then moved to Columbia in 1940. The song "By the Light of the Silvery Moon" was on the charts in 1941 and 1944. Noble's last No. 1 hit was "Linda" in 1947. He recorded on Victor in America and for Sunbeam, Aircheck, and Monmouth Evergreen, among others. Import and jazz specialty stores are the place to consult for Noble CDs. —*Ron Wynn*

● **1935-1936** / 1935-1936 / Jazz Band ✦✦✦✦

The Nylons

Vocals/Pop
The Nylons signed with Attic Records in 1981, just two years after forming in Toronto. Though the original members were Denis Simpson, Paul Cooper, Marc Connors, and Claude Morrison, Simpson soon left. Ralph Cole replaced him for a year, but Arnold Robinson replaced Cole in 1980. The a cappella group's self-titled debut appeared in 1982, as did *One Size Fits All*. After 1984's *Seamless*, the Nylons hit the Top 30 with a remake of Steam's "Na Na Hey Hey Kiss Him Goodbye." The album it appeared on, *Happy Together*, also did well. Paul Cooper left the quartet after 1989's *Rockapella* and was replaced by Micah Barnes. *Four on the Floor* was released in 1991, but Mark Connors died the same year. New addition Billy Newton-Davis had been a successful solo artist (*Love Is a Contact Sport*, *Spellbound*) before joining the Nylons for 1992's *Live to Love*. *Run for Cover* was released in 1996. —*John Bush*

The Nylons / 1982 / Attic ✦✦

One Size Fits All / 1982 / Open Air ✦✦✦

Seamless / 1986 / Open Air ✦✦✦✦

Happy Together / 1987 / Open Air ✦✦✦✦

Rockapella / Oct. 1989 / Windham Hill ✦✦✦
In addition to an exultant a cappella-with-percussion version of the Parachute Club's paean to liberation, "Rise Up," this 1989 release includes originals like "Another Night like This" and covers of great tunes such as "Drift Away," "Poison Ivy," "Wildfire," and "(All I Have to Do Is) Dream." It is one of their best recordings to date. —*Ladyslipper*

Four on the Floor / 1991 / Scotti Bros. ✦✦✦
Marc Connor died in 1991, and this 1990 in-concert recording is a wonderful commemoration of his contribution to this fantastic quartet. Included are Connor's lead vocals on his original *Amazon*, as well as on *Up on the Roof* and *Wildfire*. It also contains "Good Old Acappella," "Dream," "Heavenly Bodies," and "Kiss Him Goodbye." —*Ladyslipper*

Live to Love / Sep. 29, 1992 / Scotti Bros. ✦✦✦

● **The Best of the Nylons** / 1993 / Windham Hill ✦✦✦✦

Because / 1994 / Scotti Bros. ✦✦✦

Another Fine Mesh / Apr. 26, 1994 / Scotti Bros. ✦✦✦

Run for Cover / Mar. 12, 1996 / Scotti Bros. ✦✦✦✦

Patti Page (Clara Ann Fowler)

b. Nov. 8, 1927, Claremore, OK
Vocals / Pop
Patti Page was one of pop music's leading singers during the early '50s.

Her double-tracked vocals, highly innovative at the time, translated into gigantic commercial success. By the age of 19, Page was working as a singer at a Tulsa radio station, and she signed with Mercury in 1948. Page's use of multi-tracked vocals gave her a unique, full sound, and in 1950 her renditions of "All My Love" and "Tennessee Waltz" were both pop chart-toppers, the latter for a good three months. "Mockin' Bird Hill" (1951), "I Went to Your Wedding" (1952), and "Doggie in the Window" (1953) were only a few of her gold records for Mercury, and she persevered through the early rock era with "Allegheny Moon" in 1956 and "Old Cape Cod" the next year. Her last major pop smash in 1965, "Hush, Hush, Sweet Charlotte," was the theme song to a popular movie. — *Bill Dahl*

★ **The Mercury Years, Vol. 1** / Jan. 1991 / Mercury ✦✦✦✦✦
These original hits from 1948-1952 include "Tennessee Waltz" in an excellent package. — *Hank Davis*

The Mercury Years, Vol. 2 / Feb. 1991 / Mercury ✦✦✦✦
Twenty hits from 1952-1962 include "Old Cape Cod" and "Allegheny Moon." Informative packaging. — *Hank Davis*

Mandy Patinkin

b. Nov. 20, 1947
Vocals / Vocal
A versatile stage and screen actor and singer, Mandy Patinkin first gained notice in the Broadway musical *Evita*. He has since made his mark in films (*Ragtime, The Princess Bride*), television ("Chicago Hope"), and on Broadway (*Sunday in the Park with George, The Secret Garden*). He launched a recording career in 1989; in 1990 he had a one-man show on Broadway, *Dress Casual*. — *William Ruhlmann*

● **Mandy Patinkin** / 1989 / Columbia ✦✦✦✦
Patinkin has reserves of emotion that seem boundless on this tour de force collection mainly given over to show songs. Employing a vocal range that begins in a clear high tenor and plunges to a gruff baritone, Patinkin is able to act and sing duets with himself or sing beautifully alone. But feeling—sometimes overflowing feeling—is the core of his sense of interpretation. As a result, some very old songs sound newly written in his hands. — *William Ruhlmann*

Dress Casual / 1990 / Columbia ✦✦✦✦
An enormously ambitious collection of show and film music dominated by suites and medleys taken from Stephen Sondheim's obscure *Evening Primrose* (with guest Bernadette Peters) and *Pal Joey*. — *William Ruhlmann*

Experiment / May 17, 1994 / Nonesuch ✦✦✦

Oscar and Steve / Oct. 24, 1995 / Nonesuch ✦✦✦

The Pied Pipers

Vocal
Originally consisting of eight members, the Pied Pipers had their greatest success after nearly half of the members left the group. The remaining Pipers (Billy Wilson, Chuck Lowry, Jo Stafford, and her then-husband John Huddleston) joined the Tommy Dorsey Band in 1939, backing Sinatra on many classic recordings. In 1942 the Pied Pipers broke away from Dorsey, and Huddleston joined the Army, to be replaced by Hal Hopper, one of the original eight members. The group backed Johnny Mercer on several tracks during the early '40s, including "Candy" and "Blues in the Night." Their first single ("Deacon Jones"/"Pistol Packin' Mama") was released in 1943. Stafford had become quite busy with her solo career and left the group in 1944, to be replaced by June Hutton. Throughout the rest of the decade the Pied Pipers charted frequently, yet their popularity waned in the '50s. A group bearing the Pied Pipers' name still tours today. — *Stephen Thomas Erlewine*

★ **Capitol Collectors Series** / 1992 / Capitol ✦✦✦✦✦
A terrific 20-track overview of this early vocal group featuring all of their best-known songs, including "The Trolley Song," "Dream," "Open the Door, Richard," "Mam'selle," and "My Happiness." The remastering is top-notch, and the liner notes contain many anecdotes and a great deal of information. — *Stephen Thomas Erlewine*

Cole Porter

b. 1891, d. Oct. 15, 1964
Piano / Standards
Many arguments could be generated over whether Cole Porter or Irving Berlin should be considered America's greatest tunesmith. Both wrote music and lyrics; it's clearly a pick-'em situation. Porter had violin and piano lessons as a child, and studied law and music at Harvard, courtesy of a rich grandfather. His grandfather was appalled Porter would consider music as a career and never forgave him. Porter was in the French army during World War I and spent the '20s in Paris as the husband of a wealthy woman. He began scoring hits in that decade, but "I'm in Love Again" didn't click until 1929, though Porter wrote it in 1924. The list of Porter shows and films is immense; his lyrics were literate, sophisticated,

yet could be charming, suggestive, even naughty. His first show was *Paris* in 1928; it included "Let's Do It." That was followed by *Frenchmen* in 1929 containing "You Do Something to Me." Porter returned to New York in 1930, but was a lifelong Parisian in his heart. *Wake Up and Dream, The New Yorkers, The Gay Divorcée, Jubilee, Leave It to Me*, and *Kiss Me Kate* are only a few of his marvelous shows. The song list is just as impressive: "What Is This Thing Called Love," "Love for Sale," "Anything Goes," "You're the Top," "Begin the Beguine," and "Count Your Blessings" for starters. There were also such films as *Silk Stockings, Born to Dance, Broadway Melody of 1940, High Society*, and *Night and Day*. Porter's legs were crushed by a horse in 1937, and he endured numerous operations the rest of his life, as well as being a semi-invalid. He finally lost his right leg in 1958, only four years after his wife died. But his songs live on; numerous anthologies and songbooks devoted to his music have been issued and are available on CD, including the Smithsonian four-disc set issued in 1993. — *Ron Wynn*

● **Cole Porter Collection** / 1926-1941 / Jass ✦✦✦
This is a delightful 25-song anthology of vintage (1928-1941) recordings of obscure but equally arch-Porter songs. Performers include Ethel Waters, the Dorsey Brothers, the Paul Whiteman Orchestra, and others. — *Mark A. Humphrey*

Louis Prima

b. Dec. 1911, New Orleans, LA, d. Aug. 24, 1978, New Orleans, LA
Trumpet, Vocals / Dixieland, Vocal, Swing, Early R&B
Louis Prima became very famous in the 1950s with an infectious Las Vegas act co-starring his wife (singer Keely Smith) that mixed R&B (particularly the honking tenor of Sam Butera), early rock 'n' roll, comedy, and Dixieland. Always a colorful personality, Prima was leading a band in New Orleans when he was just 11. In 1934 he began recording as a leader with a Dixieland-oriented unit and soon he was a major attraction on 52nd Street. His early records often featured George Brunies and Eddie Miller, and Pee Wee Russell was a regular member of his groups during 1935-36. Prima, who composed "Sing, Sing, Sing" (which for a period was his theme song), recorded steadily through the swing era, had a big band in the 1940s, and achieved hits in "Angelina" and "Robin Hood." In 1954 he began having great success in his latter-day group (their recordings on Capitol were big sellers and still sound joyous today), emphasizing vocals and Butera's tenor, but he still took spirited trumpet solos. Although he eventually broke up with Keely Smith, Louis Prima (who played a character in Walt Disney's animated film *The Jungle Book* in 1966) remained a popular attraction into the 1970s. — *Scott Yanow*

Play Pretty for the People / 1940 / Savoy ✦✦✦✦

Capitol Collectors Series / Apr. 19, 1956-Feb. 23, 1962 / Capitol ✦✦✦✦
This is the best single CD available of Louis Prima's exuberant Capitol recordings of the 1950s. Prima's music during the era was a successful mixture of rhythm & blues (propelled by Sam Butera's passionate tenor), New Orleans jazz, pop, and showbiz. Prima's occasional trumpet solos were joyful, but it was his vocal interplay with the mock-serious Keely Smith that really made these spirited performances memorable. The 26 selections are drawn from six LPs plus a few rare singles. Highlights include a medley of "Just a Gigolo" and "I Ain't Got Nobody," another medley of "Basin Street Blues" and "When It's Sleepy Time Down South," "Baby Won't You Please Come Home, "Sing, Sing, Sing," and a classic rendition of "That Old Black Magic." — *Scott Yanow*

★ **Zooma Zooma: the Best of Louis Prima** / Rhino ✦✦✦✦✦
This is the best retrospective. — *Myles Boisen*

Johnnie Ray

b. Jan. 10, 1927, Dallas, OR, d. Feb. 25, 1990, Los Angeles, CA
Vocals / Vocal
Although practically deaf, Johnnie Ray's tear-inflected delivery tabbed him as an early-'50s sensation. Leaving Oregon for Detroit, Ray found a gig at the Flame Club, an R&B and jazz institution. In 1951, Ray signed with Columbia's R&B subsidiary Okeh Records, although "Cry," his histrionic million-seller that year, was a pop entry all the way, with background vocals by the Four Lads. Produced by Mitch Miller, "Cry" remained perched atop the pop charts for nearly three months. Ray encored with "The Little White Cloud That Cried" before moving to the parent Columbia logo and enjoying a steady stream of pop hits, including "Walkin' My Baby Back Home" in 1952 and a cover of the Prisonaires' "Just Walking in the Rain" in 1956. Ray's frenzied antics set off riots among female admirers during his heyday, but the advent of rock soon dulled his hitmaking powers. By 1959, the hits were through. Guidelines: Stick with original Columbia recordings and select the most generous sample, such as *16 Most Requested Songs*. — *Bill Dahl*

★ **16 Most Requested Songs** / 1991 / Columbia/Legacy ✦✦✦✦✦
These are the original '50s recordings of Ray's best, including "Cry" and "Just Walking in the Rain." — *Hank Davis*

Helen Reddy

b. Oct. 25, 1942, Melbourne, Australia
Vocals / Vocal, Pop, Soft Rock
Reddy began performing at the age of four in her native Australia; by the early '60s she had her own television series. Between 1971 and 1978, Reddy hit the Top 40 14 times with her smooth, airy light-pop singles, including No. 1s "Delta Dawn," "Angie Baby," and "I Am Woman." As her hits petered out toward the end of the '70s, her acting work increased, including roles in *Pete's Dragon, Sgt. Pepper's Lonely Hearts Club Band,* and *Airport 1975. — Stephen Thomas Erlewine*

I Am Woman / 1972 / Capitol ✦✦✦
● **Greatest Hits** / 1975 / Capitol ✦✦✦
This set includes Reddy's biggest light-pop hits. *— Bil Carpenter*
● **When I Dream** / Apr. 1996 / Varese Vintage ✦✦✦✦

Paul Robeson

b. Apr. 9, 1898, **d.** Jan. 23, 1976
Vocals
Paul Robeson's commanding voice was capable of many wonders—he powerfully sang spirituals and acted in Shakespearean plays and numerous movies (including *Emperor Jones* in 1933 and *King Solomon's Mines* in 1937). Robeson recorded for Victor in 1925, the same year he began collaborating with pianist Lawrence Brown, and his immortal "Ol' Man River" was immensely popular in 1928. As the decades passed, Robeson proved an eloquent spokesman for equality and freedom. *— Bill Dahl*

The Golden Classics, Vol. 3 / 1977 / Collectables ✦✦✦
This erratic collection ranges from decent to marvelous. *— Ron Wynn*
The Power and the Glory / 1991 / Columbia/Legacy ✦✦✦✦
This is a retrospective of Robeson's best-known spirituals and folk music. *— Bil Carpenter*
Golden Classics, Vol. 1 / Collectables ✦✦✦
Golden Classics—Vol. 1 (American Balladeer). A great singer tries hard on established standards. *— Ron Wynn*
☆ **Ballad for Americans** / Vanguard ✦✦✦✦✦
Superb songs, Americana, and more. *— Ron Wynn*
★ **Essential** / Vanguard ✦✦✦✦✦
Some of his strongest and most defiant vocals. *— Ron Wynn*
A Man and His Beliefs: Golden Classics, Vol. 2 / Collectables ✦✦✦
Political/topical material. *— Ron Wynn*

Richard Rodgers and Oscar Hammerstein

Show Tunes
Composer Richard Rodgers (1902-1979) and lyricist Oscar Hammerstein, II (1895-1960) both had extensive careers in Broadway theater music before they scored their first hit together with *Oklahoma!* in 1943. Rodgers first teamed with Lorenz Hart (1895-1943), with whom he scored a series of Broadway successes that began when the team's song "Manhattan" was interpolated into *The Garrick Gaities of 1925.* Rodgers and Hart's shows included *Present Arms* (1928), *On Your Toes* (1936), *Babes in Arms* (1937), and *Pal Joey* (1940), and they are responsible for a slew of song standards including "You Took Advantage of Me," "Dancing on the Ceiling," "There's a Small Hotel," "Where or When," "The Lady Is a Tramp," "My Funny Valentine," "I Wish I Were in Love Again," "Isn't It Romantic," and "Bewitched, Bothered and Bewildered." But Hart's health declined, and Rodgers had sought out Hammerstein before his partner's death from pneumonia.

Hammerstein, scion of a theatrical family (his grandfather owned several theaters and wrote shows, and his father and brother were also involved in the theater), attended Columbia University, where he wrote college shows with Rodgers. He was a considerable success in the 1920s, collaborating with Jerome Kern on *Show Boat* (1927) and also working with Sigmund Romberg, but he went for a long stretch in the '30s without having a hit.

The Rodgers and Hammerstein team returned to the plot-oriented, socially conscious style of *Show Boat* for a series of landmark musicals in the '40s and '50s, notably *Carousel* (1945), *South Pacific* (1949), *The King and I* (1951), and *The Sound of Music* (1959).

Rodgers, who had the luck to work with two of the most gifted lyricists of the century, continued after Hammerstein's death, though without lucking into a third major partner. He wrote music and lyrics to *No Strings* in 1962, and tried working with Stephen Sondheim on *Do I Hear a Waltz?* (1956), but his later work was less successful. *— William Ruhlmann*

The Rodgers and Hammerstein 50th Anniversary Collection (Oklahoma!/Carousel/The King & I) / 1993 / MCA ✦✦✦✦
This is a four-CD box set released to commemorate the 50th anniversary of the opening of Richard Rodgers and Oscar Hammerstein, II's first Broadway show, *Oklahoma!* It contains the original cast albums of *Okla-*

homa!, Carousel, and *The King and I,* as well as an album called *The Rodgers and Hammerstein Collection,* featuring various artists, ranging from Rosemary Clooney to Sylvia Sims, singing Rodgers and Hammerstein favorites. The last is dispensable, but the three cast albums are landmarks of the music business of the '40s and '50s, as well as the Broadway theater. (All four discs are available separately.) *— William Ruhlmann*

● **Rodgers and Hammerstein** / ✦✦✦✦
Columbia Album / CBS ✦✦✦

Dinah Shore

b. Mar. 1, 1917, Winchester, TN, **d.** Feb. 24, 1994
Vocals
Shore's public debut came at the age of four in Nashville. She sang at WSM there before moving in 1937 to New York, where she did radio shows with Eddie Cantor. Later she starred in Hollywood musicals and her own TV talk show. During the '50s Shore was one of the top singers in the country. *— Bil Carpenter*

Bouquet of Blues / 1942 / RCA ✦✦✦
This is a superb album of blues cuts in pop style. It includes "St. Louis Blues," among others. *— Bil Carpenter*
★ **Greatest Hits [Cema]** / CEMA ✦✦✦✦✦
16 Most Requested Songs / Columbia ✦✦✦✦
Her best hits, including the peppy "Buttons and Bows." *— Bil Carpenter*

Nina Simone

b. Feb. 21, 1933, Tryon, NC
Piano, Vocals / Vocal, Jazz, Pop, R&B
Of all the major singers of the late 20th century, Nina Simone is one of the hardest to classify. She's recorded extensively in the soul, jazz, and pop idioms, often over the course of the same album; she's also comfortable with blues, gospel, and Broadway. It's perhaps most accurate to label her as a "soul" singer in terms of emotion, rather than form. Like, say, Aretha Franklin, or Dusty Springfield, Simone is an eclectic, who brings soulful qualities to whatever material she interprets. These qualities are among her strongest virtues; paradoxically, they also may have kept her from attaining a truly mass audience. The same could be said of her stage persona; admired for her forthright honesty and individualism, she's also known for feisty feuding with audiences and promoters alike.

If Simone has a chip on her shoulder, it probably arose from the formidable obstacles she had to overcome to establish herself as a popular singer. Raised in a family of eight children, she originally harbored hopes of becoming a classical pianist, studying at New York's prestigious Juilliard School of Music—a rare position for an African-American woman in the 1950s. Needing to support herself while she studied, she generated income by working as an accompanist and giving piano lessons. Auditioning for a job as a pianist in an Atlantic City nightclub, she was told she had the spot if she would sing as well as play. Almost by accident, she began to carve a reputation as a singer of secular material, though her skills at the piano would serve her well throughout her career.

In the late '50s, Simone began recording for the small Bethlehem label (a subsidiary of the vastly important early R&B/rock 'n' roll King label). In 1959, her version of George Gershwin's "I Loves You Porgy" gave her a Top 20 hit—which would, amazingly, prove to be the only Top 40 entry of her career. Nina wouldn't need hit singles for survival, however, establishing herself not with the rock 'n' roll/R&B crowd, but with the adult/nightclub/album market. In the early '60s, she recorded no less than nine albums for the Candix label, about half of them live. These unveiled her as a performer of nearly unsurpassed eclecticism, encompassing everything from Ellingtonian jazz and Israeli folk songs to spirituals and movie themes.

Simone's best recorded work was issued on Philips during the mid-'60s. Here, as on Candix, she was arguably over-exposed, issuing seven albums within a three-year period. These records can be breathtakingly erratic, moving from warm ballad interpretations of Jacques Brel and Billie Holiday and instrumental piano workouts to brassy pop and angry political statements in a heartbeat. There's a great deal of fine music to be found on these, however. Simone's moody-yet-elegant vocals are like no one else's, presenting a fiercely independent soul who harbors enormous (if somewhat hard-bitten) tenderness.

Like many African-American entertainers of the mid-'60s, Simone was deeply affected by the civil-rights movement and burgeoning Black pride. Some (though by no means most) of her best material from this time addressed these concerns in a fashion more forthright than almost any other singer. "Old Jim Crow" and, more particularly, the classic "Mississippi Goddamn" were especially notable self-penned efforts in this vein, making one wish that Simone had written more of her own material instead of turning to outside sources for most of her repertoire.

Not that this repertoire wasn't well chosen. Several of her covers from the mid-'60s, indeed, were classics: her revision of Weill-Brecht's "Pirate

Jenny" to reflect the bitter elements of African-American experience, for instance, or her mournful interpretation of Brel's "Ne Me Quitte Pas." Other highlights were her versions of "Don't Let Me Be Misunderstood," covered by the Animals for a rock hit; "I Put a Spell on You," which influenced the vocal line on the Beatles' "Michelle"; and the buzzing, jazzy "See Line Woman."

Simone was not as well served by her tenure with RCA in the late '60s and early '70s, another prolific period which saw the release of nine albums. These explored a less eclectic range, with a considerably heavier pop-soul base to both the material and arrangements. One bonafide classic did come out of this period: "Young, Gifted & Black," written by Simone and Weldon Irvine, Jr., would be successfully covered by both Aretha Franklin and Donny Hathaway. She did have a couple of Top Five British hits in the late '60s with "Ain't Got No" (from the musical *Hair*) and a cover of the Bee Gees' "To Love Somebody," neither of which rank among her career highlights.

Simone fell on turbulent times in the 1970s, divorcing her husband/manager Andy Stroud, encountering serious financial problems, and becoming something of a nomad, settling at various points in Switzerland, Liberia, Barbados, France, and Britain. After leaving RCA, she recorded rarely, although she did make the critically well-received *Baltimore* in 1978 for the small CTI label. She had an unpredictable resurgence in 1987, when an early track, "My Baby Just Cares for Me," became a big British hit after being used in a Chanel perfume television commercial. 1993's *A Single Woman* marked her return to an American major label, and her profile was also boosted when several of her songs were featured in the film *Point of No Return*. She published her biography, *I Put a Spell on You*, in 1991. —*Richie Unterberger*

☆ **Nina at Town Hall** / 1959 / Colpix ♦♦♦♦♦

Nina Simone at Newport / 1960 / Colpix ♦♦♦♦

Nina Simone at the Village Gate / 1961 / Roulette ♦♦♦♦
1991 reissue of a killer concert. —*Ron Wynn*

Nina Simone in Concert / 1964 / Philips ♦♦♦♦
This is probably the most personal album that Simone issued during her stay on Philips in the mid-'60s. On most of her studio sessions, she worked with orchestration that either enhanced her material tastefully or smothered her, and she tackled an astonishingly wide range of material that, while admirably eclectic, made for uneven listening. Here, the singer and pianist is backed by a spare, jazzy quartet, and some of the songs rank among her most socially conscious declarations of African-American pride: "Old Jim Crow," "Pirate Jenny," "Go Limp," and especially "Mississippi Goddam" were some of the most forthright musical reflections of the civil rights movement to be found at the time. In a more traditional vein, she also reprises her hit "I Loves You, Porgy," and the jazz ballad "Don't Smoke in Bed." This LP was combined with the 1965 album *I Put a Spell on You* on a CD reissue. —*Richie Unterberger*

Pastel Blues / May 19, 1965-May 20, 1965 / Mercury ♦♦♦

Nina Simone Sings the Blues / Dec. 19, 1966-Jan. 5, 1967 / RCA ♦♦♦♦

Live at Ronnie Scott's / Nov. 17, 1984 / DRG ♦♦♦♦

★ **Best of the Colpix Years** / 1992 / Roulette ♦♦♦♦♦
Nineteen tracks from her Colpix label recordings. Dating from 1959 to 1963, this mix of studio and live material is considerably more weighted toward jazz and standards by the likes of Ellington, Cole Porter, Rodgers/Hammerstein, and Irving Berlin than the more eclectic albums she would later cut in the '60s and '70s for Philips and RCA. The highlights are when she steps out of the soulful supper club style into more earthier settings, as on "House of the Rising Sun," "Forbidden Fruit," "Gin House Blues," "Work Song," and her own "Children Go Where I Send You" (all of which she would considerably rework over the years). Includes three previously unreleased tracks in a traditional jazz style with minimal arrangements. Note: the version of "(I Loves You) Porgy," her sole Top 20 entry, is not her 1959 hit single, but a live 1960 version. —*Richie Unterberger*

A Single Woman / 1993 / Asylum ♦♦♦
Vocalist, composer, and pianist Nina Simone returned from a lengthy self-imposed exile in 1993 with an autobiography and outstanding CD highlighting her still impressive singing and interpretative skills in ån intriguing context, surrounded by strings and guitars. While the backdrops were lush and occasionally corny, Simone's deep, penetrating voice, careful pacing, and dramatic delivery kept the songs from becoming sappy. While she's always been a great protest and political singer, Simone is also a superb romantic/love song stylist. Simone remains among America's premier performers, and this CD was a welcome addition to her sparkling legacy. —*Ron Wynn*

The Essential Nina Simone / Sep. 1993 / RCA ♦♦
Nina Simone has penned unforgettable protest material, covered jazz, folk, rock, and pop with equal flair, and created a body of work that's kept her popularity high. While this title is hardly accurate, since it only covers RCA material from 1967-1972, there's plenty of anthemic fare

among the CD's 16 selections. These include "Mr. Bojangles," "To Be Young, Gifted, and Black," "Seems I'm Never Tired Lovin' You," and "Since I Fell for You." While the absence of "Baltimore," "I Wish I Knew How It Feels to Be Free," and "Here Comes the Sun" (to name only three) is sizable, and the weighting of this compilation toward well-known rock types (Bob Dylan, Randy Newman, Jimmy Webb, George Harrison, two Bee Gees cuts) debatable, there's still no way it can be dismissed. —*Ron Wynn*

Essential, Vol. 2 / 1994 / RCA ♦♦

Frank Sinatra

b. Dec. 12, 1915, Hoboken, NJ
Vocals / Swing, Soft Rock
A certified American music legend, Francis Albert Sinatra represents the ultimate male romantic vocalist to many people. A huge argument starter as the 20th century ends is who's America's premier singer: Armstrong, Holiday, Sinatra, or Presley. Aside from the fact several others could legitimately be named, a serious case can be made for Sinatra. As a relaxed, yet swinging stylist, he was magnificent in his prime, and this quality has slipped more dramatically than anything else in his arsenal. Though not a good scatter nor great vocal improviser, Sinatra helped expand Crosby's breakthroughs with microphone singing, achieving a wide range of dynamics and displaying a delivery and crystal-clear enunciation that projected any and every possible nuance or emotional shade in a lyric. Until age turned his act into a parody, Sinatra was among the most convincing singers ever; the sincerity he expressed frequently fooled people into thinking his offstage character was as innocent and good-natured as the onstage persona. Indeed, Sinatra's rocky personal life, while not plagued with public drug incidents outside of alcohol, nevertheless makes many jazz and popular music bad boys (and girls) look like candidates for sainthood. Still, Sinatra had enormous impact on pre-rock era vocalists, and has never hesitated to say how much Billie Holiday influenced his style.

Sinatra's parents were Italian immigrants, and he quit school at age 16 to sing anywhere he could get an audience. He was in the Hoboken Four singing group when they won the Major Bowes Amateur Hour talent show on the radio in 1935. This quartet toured with Bowes and had the dubious distinction of being caught on film performing as blackface minstrels. They sang from 1937 to 1939 at the Rustic Cabin roadhouse in New Jersey, with Sinatra doubling as head waiter. He started singing sans fee on a WNEW radio program "Dance Parade" in 1939. Harry James was starting a band after leaving Benny Goodman and quickly contacted Sinatra. A song that Sinatra recorded with James in the summer of 1939, "All or Nothing at All," sold 8,000 copies when initally issued with Sinatra uncredited; it topped the charts when Columbia reissued it in 1943. On the recommendation of a Columbia executive, Tommy Dorsey went to hear Sinatra sing. James let Sinatra leave to join Dorsey and his ascension to icon status began. He recorded with Dorsey in 1940, backed by a vocal quartet with Jo Stafford and Connie Hines called the Pied Pipers. Sinatra made his first film appearance in 1940 with the band; *Las Vegas Nights* didn't win anyone any Oscars. But Sinatra soon became a commercial juggernaut; "I'll Never Smile Again," "Delores," "There Are Such Things," and "In the Blue of the Evening" all topped the charts between 1940 and 1943.

Sinatra bought out his contract with Dorsey in 1942. He appeared for a month at the Paramount Theatre in 1942 with Benny Goodman, and the screams and yells from girls (some rumored to be paid for their trouble) are considered the beginning of modern pop idolatry and groupies. A Sinatra return engagement in 1944 resulted in 25,000 teenagers blocking the streets. He cut his first solo dates for Columbia in 1943 and had 86 hit records for them from 1943-1952, 33 in the Top Ten. Sinatra began to appear frequently in films and in gossip columns after he left his wife Nancy to marry actress Ava Gardner in 1951. He was even targeted for accusations of communism. His support of Franklin D. Roosevelt and winning of a special Oscar in 1946 for his efforts on behalf of religious and racial tolerance established Sinatra's reputation as a liberal, progressive-minded individual (at least in public). He held it well into the '60s, before switching party allegiances to the Republicans.

Sinatra rebounded from a slump in the mid-'50s, winning an Oscar for his film role in *From Here to Eternity* in 1954. He cut several tremendous records for Capitol with arrangements from top arrangers like Billy May and Nelson Riddle. He was successfully remarketed as a seasoned vocalist singing adult love songs for older audiences. He made 13 enormously profitable albums for Capitol from 1954 to 1961. Some, like *Songs for Swinging Lovers* in 1956, creatively used big-band arrangements and support; others such as *In the Wee Small Hours* in 1955 featured him doing songs around a singular concept or developing themes and moods with related tunes throughout an album.

Sinatra reaffirmed his jazz credentials in the '60s, with albums that had arrangements from Don Costa and Neal Hefti, plus collaborations with Count Basie and albums featuring Quincy Jones arrangements. He even tackled the bossa nova. But decline and exhaustion began to set in, and there were unfortunate flirtations with dubious material like Rod McKuen poetry. Sinatra did land another No. 1 hit in 1966, "Strangers in the Night," but the '60s established the fact that he now needed the right material, producers, and arrangers. No longer could he survive just by being Sinatra, at least not in the creative arena. The '70s would clearly prove that. He retired for a while, but the 1973 comeback album *Ol' Blue Eyes Is Back* reached the No. 15 spot on the charts. He remained in the Top 40 with the next album, *Sinatra—The Main Event*, even though the two-record set was littered with painful material.

Sinatra returned to the charts in 1980 with *Trilogy: Past, Present, Future*, thanks to arrangements from May, Riddle, and others. Jones arranged and released on his own label *L.A. Is My Lady* in 1984. Sinatra kept touring and performing into the '90s, issuing an album of duets featuring collaborations with U2's Bono, Tony Bennett, and Aretha Franklin, among others, in the fall of 1993. It also topped the charts and closed out 1993 among the Top Ten sellers among pop releases. The list of horrendous Sinatra marriages; ugly affairs; hotel and nightclub incidents; rumors of reprisals against club owners, performers, critics, and managers; and supposed gangster links filled several magazines long before Kitty Kelley's infamous biography. But none of that deserves equal billing with Frank Sinatra's achievements. Even if you feel some Sinatra boosters think he invented music, there's no denying he earned his spurs many years ago. —*Ron Wynn and John Floyd*

☆ **The Song Is You** / Feb. 1, 1940-Jul. 2, 1942 / RCA ✦✦✦✦✦
This very attractive five-CD box set has every studio recording that Frank Sinatra recorded with Tommy Dorsey's Orchestra plus a full disc of mostly unreleased radio broadcasts. Since Sinatra has never really been a jazz singer and most of the selections are ballads, jazz listeners may not consider this box essential, but Frank Sinatra fans will not need to be told of its existence twice. Sinatra's first session as a leader (from early 1942) is also included (along with a large and colorful booklet), giving listeners a very definitive look into his early days. —*Scott Yanow*

☆ **Songs for Young Lovers/Swing Easy** / 1955 / Capitol ✦✦✦✦✦
Combining Frank Sinatra's first two 10-inch albums for Capitol, the compact disc *Songs for Young Lovers/Swing Easy* not only contains some of the best music Sinatra recorded, it captures a turning point in popular music. *Songs for Young Lovers* was the first album Frank Sinatra recorded for Capitol, as well as his first collaboration with Nelson Riddle. It was also one of the first—arguably the very first—concept albums. Sinatra, Riddle, and producer Voyle Gilmore decided that the new album format should be a special event, featuring a number of songs that are arranged around a specific theme; in addition, the new format was capable of producing a more detailed sound, which gave Riddle more freedom in his arrangements and orchestrations. *Songs for Young Lovers* is a perfect example of this. Supported by a small orchestra, Sinatra and Riddle create an intimate, romantic atmosphere on the record, breathing new life into standards like "My Funny Valentine," "They Can't Take That Away from Me," "I Get a Kick Out of You," and "A Foggy Day." Sinatra sounds revived. No longer does he have to sing the lightweight pop drivel that was forced on him during his latter days at Columbia—he is given weighty songs, and he tears into them. There is a breezy confidence to his singing, as he inhabits each song as if he were living the emotions. Riddle's arrangements are light but jazzy and are more complex than they intially appear. Sinatra and Riddle expanded this approach on his second Capitol album, *Swing Easy!* As the title implies, the record concentrates on uptempo swingers. Again, the songs were all standards—"Just One of Those Things," "Wrap Your Troubles in Dreams," "All of Me"—that benefited from the new thematic setting, the new arrangements, and, of course, Sinatra's increasingly playful and textured vocals. Sinatra plays around with the melodies without leaving them behind, delivering each line with precision. It ranks as one of his most jazzy performances, as well as one of his most fun and carefree records. —*Stephen Thomas Erlewine*

☆ **In the Wee Small Hours** / Mar. 1, 1954-Mar. 4, 1955 / Capitol ✦✦✦✦✦
Expanding on the concept of *Songs for Young Lovers*, *In the Wee Small Hours* was a collection of ballads arranged by Nelson Riddle. The first 12-inch album recorded by Sinatra, *Wee Small Hours* was more focused and concentrated than his two earlier concept records. It's a blue, melancholy album, built around a spare rhythm section featuring a rhythm guitar, celesta, and Bill Miller's piano, with gently aching strings added every once and a while. Within that melancholy mood is one of Sinatra's most jazz-oriented performances; he restructures the melody, and Miller's playing is bold throughout the record. Where *Songs for Young Lovers* emphasized the romantic aspects of the songs, Sinatra sounds like a lonely, broken man on *In the Wee Small Hours*. Beginning with the newly written title song, the singer goes through a series of standards that are lonely and desolate. In many ways the album is a personal reflection of the heartbreak of his doomed love affair with actress Ava Gardner, and the standards that he sings form their own story. Sinatra's voice had deepened and worn to the point that his delivery seems rav-

ished and heartfelt, as if he were living the songs. —*Stephen Thomas Erlewine*

★ **Songs for Swingin' Lovers!** / Oct. 17, 1955-Jan. 16, 1956 / Capitol ✦✦✦✦✦
After the ballad-heavy *In the Wee Small Hours*, Frank Sinatra and Nelson Riddle returned to uptempo, swing material with *Songs for Swingin' Lovers*, arguably the vocalist's greatest swing set. Like Sinatra's previous Capitol albums, *Songs for Swingin' Lovers* consists of reinterpreted pop standards, ranging from the ten-year old "You Make Me Feel So Young" to the 20-year-old "Pennies from Heaven" and "I've Got You Under My Skin." Sinatra is supremely confident throughout the album, singing with authority and joy. That joy is replicated in Riddle's arrangements, which manage to rethink these standards in fresh yet reverent ways. Working with a core rhythm section and a full string orchestra, Riddle writes scores that are surprisingly subtle. "I've Got You Under My Skin," with its breathtaking middle section, is a perfect example of how Sinatra works with the band. Both swing hard, stretching out the rhythms and melodies but never losing sight of the original song. *Songs for Swingin' Lovers* never loses momentum. The great songs keep coming and the performances are all stellar, resulting in one of Sinatra's true classics. —*Stephen Thomas Erlewine*

☆ **A Swingin' Affair!** / 1957 / Capitol ✦✦✦✦
In some ways, *A Swingin' Affair* is *Songs for Swingin' Lovers!, Pt. 2*, following the same formula as Sinatra's hit album of the previous year. Beneath the surface, there are enough variations on *A Swingin' Affair* to make it a distinctive and equally enjoyable listen. The most noticeable difference between the two records is their basic approach. Where *Songs for Swingin' Lovers!* swung hard but managed to stay rather light, *A Swingin' Affair* is a forceful, brassy album—it exudes a self-assured, confident aura. It is a hard, jazzy album. However, the attack is more brash. —*Stephen Thomas Erlewine*

☆ **Where Are You** / 1957 / Capitol ✦✦✦✦✦
Following the hard-driving *A Swingin' Affair*, Frank Sinatra released another all-ballads record, *Where Are You?* The album was the first he recorded at Capitol without Nelson Riddle, as well as the first he recorded in stereo. Where Nelson Riddle's downbeat albums are stately and sullen, Jenkins favors lush, melancholy arrangements played by large, string-dominated orchestras. Jenkins' arrangements suggested classical textures, although the tempos alluded to Billie Holiday's ballad style. *Where Are You?* primarily consists of torch songs, including "The Night We Called It a Day," "I Cover the Waterfront," and "Lonely Town." Throughout the record, Sinatra blends with Jenkins' sumptuous strings, making his voice sound rich, relaxed, and regretful. It doesn't have the stark despair of *In the Wee Small Hours*, but its luxurious sadness makes *Where Are You?* a majestic experience of its own. —*Stephen Thomas Erlewine*

Close to You / 1957 / Capitol ✦✦✦✦

☆ **Come Fly with Me** / Oct. 1, 1957-Oct. 8, 1957 / Capitol ✦✦✦✦✦
Constructed around a lighthearted travel theme, *Come Fly with Me*, Frank Sinatra' first project with arranger Billy May, was a breezy change of pace from the somber *Where Are You*. From the first swinging notes of Sammy Cahn and Jimmy Van Heusen's "Come Fly with Me"—which is written at Sinatra's request—it's clear that the music on the collection is intended to be fun. Over the course of the album, Sinatra and May travel around the world in song, performing standards like "Moonlight in Vermont" and "April in Paris," as well as humorous tunes like "Isle of Capri" and "On the Road to Mandalay." May's signature bold, brassy arrangements give these songs a playful, carefree, nearly sarcastic feel, but never is the approach less than affectionate. In fact, *Come Fly with Me* is filled with varying moods and textures, as it moves from boisterous swing numbers to romantic ballads, and hitting any number of emotions in between. There may be greater albums in Sinatra's catalog, but few are quite as fun as *Come Fly with Me*. —*Stephen Thomas Erlewine*

☆ **Only the Lonely** / 1958 / Capitol ✦✦✦✦✦
Originally, Frank Sinatra had planned to record *Only the Lonely* with Gordon Jenkins, who had arranged his previous all-ballads album, *Where Are You?* Jenkins was unavailable at the time of the sessions, which led Sinatra back to his original arranger at Capitol, Nelson Riddle. The result is arguably his greatest ballads album. *Only the Lonely* follows the same formula as his previous down albums, but the tone is considerably bleaker and more desperate. Riddle used a larger orchestra for the album than he had in the past, which lent the album a stately, nearly classical atmosphere. At its core, however, the album is a set of brooding saloon songs, highlighted by two of Sinatra's tour de forces—"Angel Eyes" and "One for My Baby." Sinatra never forces emotion out of the lyric, he lets everything flow naturally, with grace. It's a heartbreaking record, the ideal late-night album. —*Stephen Thomas Erlewine*

☆ **Come Dance with Me!** / Dec. 9, 1958-Dec. 23, 1958 / Capitol ✦✦✦✦✦
Working with Billy May again, Frank Sinatra recorded his hardest swing album ever with *Come Dance with Me!* Driven by an intensely swinging

horn section, the album has a fair share of slower numbers, but the songs that make the biggest impression are the uptempo cuts. With May's charts wildly careening all over the place, Sinatra relies on his macho swagger; as a result, *Come Dance with Me!* is an intoxicating rush of invigorating dance songs. —*Stephen Thomas Erlewine*

No One Cares / 1959 / Capitol ✦✦✦✦
Frank Sinatra's second set of torch songs recorded with Gordon Jenkins, *No One Cares* was nearly as good as its predecessor, *Where Are You?* Expanding the melancholy tone of the previous collaboration, *No One Cares* consists of brooding, lonely songs. Jenkins gives the songs a subtly tragic treatment, and Sinatra responds with a wrenching performance. It lacks the grandiose melancholy of *Only the Lonely*, nor is it as lush as *Where Are You?*, but in its slow, bluesy tempos and heartbreaking little flourishes, it is every bit as moving. —*Stephen Thomas Erlewine*

☆ **Nice 'n' Easy** / 1960 / Capitol ✦✦✦✦✦
Breaking slightly from his pattern of a swing album following the release of a ballads set, Frank Sinatra followed *No One Cares* with *Nice 'n' Easy*, a breezy collection of midtempo numbers arranged by Nelson Riddle. Not only is it the lightest set that he recorded for Capitol, it is the one with the loosest theme. Sinatra selected a collection of songs he had sung early in his career, having Riddle rearrange the tunes with warm, cheery textures. Unlike his previous ballads albums, *Nice 'n' Easy* doesn't have a touch of brooding sorrow—it rolls along steadily, charming everyone in its path. —*Stephen Thomas Erlewine*

I Remember Tommy / 1961 / Warner Brothers ✦✦✦
As the title suggests, *I Remember Tommy* is an affectionate tribute to Tommy Dorsey, the legendary bandleader that helped elevate Frank Sinatra to stardom. Arranged by Sy Oliver, who also gained attention through Dorsey, the album contains a number of songs that were part of the Sinatra/Dorsey repertoire, given slightly new readings. Though the intentions were good, the new versions pale in comparison to the originals. Nevertheless, there are a handful of gems included on the record, making it worthwhile for dedicated Sinatra aficionados. —*Stephen Thomas Erlewine*

Sinatra's Swingin' Session!!! / 1961 / Capitol ✦✦✦✦
Sinatra' Swingin' Session is a fast, driving album, the speediest and hardest swing collection Frank Sinatra ever recorded. The majority of the album is a re-recording of six of the eight songs from his first LP, *Sing and Dance with Frank Sinatra*, as rearranged by Nelson Riddle. Sinatra performed the songs twice as fast as was expected; consequently, it's one of his jazziest swing sets, with the musicians spitting out energetic, forceful solos and providing tough, gutsy support. Not only do the uptempo numbers speed by, the ballads are sprightly. It doesn't have the brassy verver of *A Swingin' Affair*, but *Sinatra's Swingin' Session* does have a confident, swaggering flavor of its own that makes it nearly as enjoyable. —*Stephen Thomas Erlewine*

Come Swing with Me / 1961 / Capitol ✦✦✦
Arranged by Billy May, *Come Swing with Me* was Frank Sinatra's final swing session for Capitol Records. The album falls somewhere between the carefree *Come Fly with Me* and the hard-swinging *Come Dance with Me*, borrowing elements of the humor of *Fly* and the intense, driving rhythms of *Dance*. Recorded without strings or saxes, the brass-heavy sound of the album was noticeable, but it wasn't nearly as distinctive as the ping-ponging, stereo effects of the album. With its extreme stereo separation, *Come Swing with Me* has a bizarre, off-kilter feel that is accentuated by Sinatra's restless vocals. At the time of recording the album, Sinatra was also recording *I Remember Tommy* for Reprise and his affections were with his new label. That doesn't mean he sounds careless on *Come Swing with Me*—in fact, his intense, speedy energy gives the album an edge that distinguishes the record. The album might not be as special as his two previous May collaborations, but it does have enough genuine gems to make it necessary. —*Stephen Thomas Erlewine*

All the Way / 1961 / Capitol ✦✦✦
All the Way was an entertaining collection of Sinatra singles that have since been collected as bonus tracks on compact disc editions of the singer's original albums. —*Stephen Thomas Erlewine*

Ring a Ding Ding / 1961 / Reprise ✦✦✦
Ring a Ding Ding, Frank Sinatra's first album for his own record label, broke somewhat from the strict concepts of his Capitol records; in the process, it set a kind of template for the rest of his '60s Reprise albums. Instead of following a theme, the record captures the atmosphere of Sinatra in 1961—a time when he was running the Rat Pack, so it's no coincidence that the album is named after one of his favorite phrases of the era. The title track was written especially for Sinatra by Sammy Cahn and Jimmy Van Heusen. And that song reflects the brassy, swaggering feeling of the record—even the ballads are arrogant and self-confident. —*Stephen Thomas Erlewine*

Sinatra Swings [Swing Along with Me] / 1961 / Reprise ✦✦✦
Recorded with Billy May, *Sinatra Swings* was Frank Sinatra's first straight swing album for Reprise Records. In terms of content and approach, the

record is remarkably similar to his final Capitol swing effort, *Come Swing with Me*. In fact, Capitol thought the album, originally titled *Swing Along with Me*, was so close in its sound and title that they sued Sinatra. The record label won the suit and the singer had to change the name of his Reprise album to *Sinatra Swings*. Of course, that didn't change the actual content of the record. Even though the tone was similar, there were some differences from *Come Swing with Me*—the ballads have strings, there are saxophones on the record, and the material is more lighthearted on *Sinatra Swings*, much like the songs on *Come Fly with Me*. The restored sense of humor makes *Sinatra Swings* preferable to *Come Swing with Me*, even if it doesn't have the concentrated precision of the first two Sinatra/May sets. —*Stephen Thomas Erlewine*

Point of No Return / Nov. 11, 1961 / Capitol ✦✦✦

Sinatra Sings Great Songs from Great Britain / 1962 / Warner Brothers ✦✦

Sinatra/Basie / 1962 / Reprise ✦✦✦✦
The pairing of Frank Sinatra and Count Basie always promised more rewards than it actually yielded. *Sinatra/Basie* was the first of their three collaborations and it is the most successful studio album they recorded as a pair. Sinatra isn't in particularly fine voice, nor does Basie shine, but the two come up with enough fine moments to make it worthwhile for devoted listeners. —*Stephen Thomas Erlewine*

Sinatra and Strings / Jan. 1962 / Reprise ✦✦✦
Sinatra and Strings, Frank Sinatra's first album with arranger Don Costa, is an exquisite, romantic collection of ballads and is one of his most sensual records. Costa has given the songs—which consist entirely of standards (the CD version added two newer songs)—exceedingly lush, heavily orchestrated arrangements that sound like updated, contemporary versions of Axel Stordahl's ornate charts. Sinatra responds with smooth, nuanced yet powerful vocals that make these traditional songs sound fresh. The pair take some chances with their arrangements—"Stardust" never reaches the chorus, for instance—but *Sinatra and Strings* remains a definitive ballads album, complete with impassioned readings and endlessly rich, detailed arrangements. —*Stephen Thomas Erlewine*

Sinatra and Swingin' Brass / 1962 / Reprise ✦✦✦
Sinatra and Swingin' Brass, a collection of brash, bold uptempo numbers, followed the all-ballads effort, *Sinatra & Strings*. Again working with Billy May, Sinatra turned in a robust, energetic performance, which was infectious even when his voice was showing signs of wear—he was suffering from a cold during the sessions. The record captures the spirit of the Rat Pack era nearly as well as *Ring a Ding Ding*. —*Stephen Thomas Erlewine*

All Alone / Jan. 1962 / Reprise ✦✦✦

The Concert Sinatra / 1963 / Reprise ✦✦✦

Sinatra's Sinatra / Apr. 1963 / Reprise ✦✦✦
In the early '60s, Columbia and Capitol were issuing collections of Frank Sinatra's biggest hits, which tended to sell quite well. *Sinatra's Sinatra* was the singer's attempt to get a piece of that action for his new record label, Reprise. Arranged and conducted by Nelson Riddle, the album is a collection of re-recorded versions of 12 of his favorite songs, including two new charts ("Nancy" and "Oh What It Seemed to Be"). Some of his biggest hits and most famous songs are included in his picks, including "I've Got You Under My Skin" and "Young at Heart," and while many of the performances are quite enjoyable, they tend to pale in direct comparison to the originals. Nevertheless, *Sinatra's Sinatra* is successful on its own terms—it's entertaining, if inconsequential. —*Stephen Thomas Erlewine*

Sings Days of Wine and Roses, Moon River and Other Academy Award Winners / 1964 / Reprise ✦✦✦
Featuring a selection of Oscar-winning standards, ranging from 1934's "The Continental" to 1962's "Days of Wine and Roses," *Academy Award Winners* is a professional and stylish album, but it only yields a handful of true gems. That isn't the fault of either Frank Sinatra or arranger/conductor Nelson Riddle. Although their performances aren't quite as distinguished as their past collaborations, they are nevertheless highly enjoyable. Sinatra is charming and lively, even if he doesn't demonstrate the full range of his technique on each track, while Riddle's charts are light and entertaining. The main problem with the record is how it plays as a series of individual moments, not as a cohesive collection. Granted, some of the moments are first-rate—"The Way You Look Tonight" is one of Sinatra's classic performances, and "Three Coins in the Fountain" and "All the Way" are nearly as good—but the moments never form a whole, which makes the album an occasionally frustrating listen. —*Stephen Thomas Erlewine*

Softly, As I Leave You / Feb. 14, 1964 / Reprise ✦✦✦
Softly, As I Leave You was Frank Sinatra's first tentative attempt to come to terms with the rock 'n' roll revolution, even if it was hardly a rock 'n' roll album. In fact, it wasn't much of an album to begin with. The high-

light of the record was the hit title song, which featured a subdued but forceful steady backbeat. The rhythm itself was indicative of Sinatra's effort to accept the new popular music. Arranged by Ernie Freeman, "Softly, As I Leave You," "Then Suddenly Love," and "Available" are definitely stabs at incorporating rock 'n' roll into Sinatra's middle-of-the-road pop, featuring drum kits, backing vocals, and keyboards. As pop singles, they were well constructed and deservedly successful. The rest of the album is pieced together from leftovers from various early '60s sessions, giving the record a decidedly uneven tone. Some of the songs work well as individual moments, particularly the Nelson Riddle-arranged "Emily," but the varying tone is too distracting to make the album a satisfying listen. — *Stephen Thomas Erlewine*

It Might As Well Be Swing / Dec. 1964 / Reprise ✦✦✦
Frank Sinatra and Count Basie's second collaboration, *It Might As Well Be Swing*, was a more structured, swing-oriented set than *Sinatra/Basie* and in many ways the superior album. The album consists of recently written songs, arranged as if they were swing numbers. The results work splendidly, not just because arranger/conductor Quincy Jones found the core of each of the songs, but because Basie and his band were flexible. Adding a string section to their core band, Basie plays a more standard swing than he did on *Sinatra/Basie*, but that doesn't mean *It Might As Well Be Swing* is devoid of jazz. Both Basie and Sinatra manage to play with the melodies and the beat, even though the album never loses sight of its purpose as a swing album. However, what makes *It Might As Well Be Swing* more successful is the consistently high level of the performances. On their previous collaboration, both Sinatra and Basie sounded a bit worn out, but throughout this record they play with energy and vigor. — *Stephen Thomas Erlewine*

My Kind of Broadway / 1965 / Reprise ✦✦✦
Pieced together from a variety of sessions and soundtracks, *My Kind of Broadway* is an uneven record, featuring a handful of gems among a bunch of competent, but undistinguished, peformances. Most of the songs—from "Luck Be a Lady" and "Hello, Dolly!" to "I'll Only Miss Her When I Think of Her," "They Can't Take That Away from Me," "Yesterdays," and "Nice Work If You Can Get It"—are classics, but the arrangements and performances frequently are nothing more than competent. When Sinatra delivers, as he does on the showstopper "Luck Be a Lady," the results are pretty spectacular, but the majority of the album is merely pleasant. — *Stephen Thomas Erlewine*

☆ **September of My Years** / Apr. 13, 1965-May 27, 1965 / Reprise ✦✦✦✦✦
September of My Years is one of Frank Sinatra's triumphs of the '60s, an album that consolidated his strengths while moving him into new territory, primarily in terms of tone. More than the double-disc set *A Man and His Music*—which was released a year after this album—*September of My Years* captures how Sinatra was at the time of his 50th birthday. Gordon Jenkins' rich, stately, and melancholy arrangements give the album an appropriate reflective atmosphere. Most of the songs are new or relatively recent numbers; every cut fits into a loose theme of aging, reflection, and regret. Sinatra, however, doesn't seem stuck in his ways—though the songs are rooted in traditional pop, they touch on folk and contemporary pop. As such, the album offered a perfect summary, as well as suggesting future routes for the singer. — *Stephen Thomas Erlewine*

Moonlight Sinatra / Nov. 1965 / Reprise ✦✦✦

A Man and His Music / Dec. 1965 / Reprise ✦✦✦
Released around his 50th birthday, *A Man and His Music* is an ambitious double-album set that provides a brief history of Frank Sinatra's career. Though the concept sounds quite promising in theory, the execution is somewhat lacking. Instead of using the original recordings—which were made for RCA, Columbia, and Capitol, not his then-current label, Reprise—Sinatra re-recorded the majority of the album's songs. That in itself isn't bad. Many of the new versions are quite enjoyable, with lively, inspired vocals. However, there is also an intrusive narration from Sinatra that runs throughout the album. Although it does offer some amusing anecdotes and gives a sense of his long, complex history, the narration prevents the album from being a consistently engaging listen. — *Stephen Thomas Erlewine*

Strangers in the Night / 1966 / Reprise ✦✦✦
Strangers in the Night marked Frank Sinatra's return to the top of the pop charts in the mid-'60s, and it consolidated the comeback he started in 1965. Although he later claimed he disliked the title track, the album was an inventive, rich effort from Sinatra, one that established him as a still-viable star to a wide, mainstream audience without losing the core of his sound. Combining pop hits—"Downtown," "On a Clear Day (You Can See Forever)," "Call Me"—with show tunes and standards, the album creates a delicate but comfortable balance between big-band and pop instrumentation. Using strings, horns, and organ, Riddle constructed an easy, deceptively swinging sound that appealed to both Sinatra's dedicated fans and pop radio. And Sinatra's singing is relaxed, confident, and surprisingly jazzy, as he plays with the melody "The Most Beautiful Girl in the World" and delivers a knockout punch with the assured, breathtak-

ing "Summer Wind." Although he would not record another album with Riddle, Sinatra would expand the approach of *Strangers in the Night* for the rest of the decade. — *Stephen Thomas Erlewine*

That's Life / 1966 / Reprise ✦✦✦

Sinatra at the Sands / Jan. 1966-Feb. 1966 / Reprise ✦✦✦✦
In many ways, *Sinatra at the Sands* is the definitive portrait of Frank Sinatra in the '60s. Recorded in April of 1966, *At the Sands* is the first commercially released live Frank Sinatra album, recorded at a relaxed Las Vegas club show. For these dates at the Sands, Sinatra worked with Count Basie and His Orchestra, which was conducted by Quincy Jones. Like any of his concerts, the material was fairly predictable, with his standard show numbers punctuated by some nice surprises. Throughout the show, Sinatra is in fine voice, turning in a particularly affecting version of "Angel Eyes." He is also in fine humor, constantly joking with the audience and the band, as well as delivering an entertaining, if rambling, monologue halfway through the album. Some of the humor has dated poorly, appearing insensitive, but that sentiment cannot be applied to the music. Basie and the orchestra are swinging and dynamic, inspiring a textured, dramatic, and thoroughly enjoyable performance from Sinatra. — *Stephen Thomas Erlewine*

Frank Sinatra and the World We Knew / 1967 / Reprise ✦✦

Francis Albert Sinatra and Antonio Carlos Jobim / 1967 / Reprise ✦✦✦✦

Francis A. Sinatra and Edward K. Ellington / 1968 / Reprise ✦✦✦✦

Frank Sinatra's Greatest Hits! / 1968 / Reprise ✦✦✦✦
Frank Sinatra's Greatest Hits concentrates on the Chairman of the Board's pop hits from the mid and late-'60s, several of which were single-only releases or only available on movie soundtracks. Appropriately, it begins with his biggest solo hit of the '60s, "Strangers in the Night," and then vacillates between adult contemporary pop songs and ballads. Much of the production has dated, with its guitars, reverb, and arrangements bearing all the hallmarks of '60s pop. While some of the songs rank among Sinatra's finest moments, particularly "Summer Wind" and "It Was a Very Good Year," most of these songs are guilty pleasures. They might not have the emotional resonance of his finest ballad and swing albums, but fluff like the Nancy Sinatra duet "Somethin' Stupid," the fuzz guitar-tinged "The World We Knew (Over and Over)," and the bluesy "This Town" are enjoyable as pop singles. As such, *Frank Sinatra's Greatest Hits* isn't a good introduction to his music, as it isn't even a representative chronicle of his '60s Reprise recordings. Instead, it's a fun and effective portrait of Sinatra as he was in the late '60s, illustrating how he was struggling to come to terms with contemporary pop music. — *Stephen Thomas Erlewine*

Cycles / 1968 / Reprise ✦✦

My Way / 1969 / Reprise ✦✦✦

A Man Alone and Other Songs of Rod McKuen / 1969 / Reprise ✦✦

Watertown / 1970 / Reprise ✦✦✦
Watertown is Frank Sinatra's most ambitious concept album, as well as his most difficult record. Not only does it tell a full-fledged story, it is his most explicit attempt at rock-oriented pop. Since the main composer of *Watertown* is Bob Gaudio, the author of the Four Seasons' hits "Can't Take My Eyes Off of You," "Walk like a Man," and "Big Girls Don't Cry," that doesn't come as a surprise. With Jake Holmes, Gaudio created a song cycle concerning a middle-aged, small-town man whose wife had left him with the kids. Constructed as a series of brief lyrical snapshots that read like letters or soliloquies, the culminating effect of the songs is an atmosphere of loneliness, but it is a loneliness without much hope or romance—it is the sound of a broken man. Producer Charles Calello arranged musical backdrops that conveyed the despair of the lyrics. Weaving together prominent electric guitars, keyboards, drum kits, and light strings, Calello uses pop-rock instrumentations and production techniques, but that doesn't prevent Sinatra from warming to the material. In fact, he turns in a wonderful performance, drawing out every emotion from the lyrics, giving the album's character depth. — *Stephen Thomas Erlewine*

Sinatra and Company / 1971 / Warner Brothers ✦✦✦

Greatest Hits, Vol. 2 / 1972 / Reprise ✦✦✦
Much like its predecessor, *Frank Sinatra's Greatest Hits, Vol. 2* is more effective as a portrait of Sinatra at a particular stage in his career than as a comprehensive collection. Like *Greatest Hits*, the album mainly consists of pop hits and songs pulled from movie soundtracks, adding in a pair of pop-rock hits for good measure. Although "My Way" became Sinatra's signature song of the '70s and '80s—primarily because his spectacular performance rescues the cliched song—none of these tracks were particularly big hit; several of the cuts are album tracks, while the highest-charting single was "Cycles," which peaked at No. 23. While the 11 tracks might not all be hits, they are fairly representative of the sound of Sinatra's music in the late '60s. There's a couple of forgotten gems, particularly the wonderfully moving "What's Now Is Now" and a gorgeous

arrangement of George Harrison's "Something," but there is also more dross than the previous *Greatest Hits* collection. Even with a handful of mediocre tracks, *Greatest Hits, Vol. 2* remains an enjoyable sampler, containing several classic Sinatra performances ("My Way," "The September of My Years"). *—Stephen Thomas Erlewine*

Ol' Blue Eyes Is Back / 1973 / Reprise ✦✦

Some Nice Things I've Missed / 1974 / Reprise ✦✦

Trilogy / Jul. 1980 / Reprise ✦✦

She Shot Me Down / 1981 / Reprise ✦✦✦

L.A. Is My Lady / Dec. 1984 / Qwest ✦✦

The Capitol Years: The Best of Frank Sinatra / 1990 / Capitol ✦✦✦✦
Released to coincide with Frank Sinatra's 75th birthday, the three-disc set *The Capitol Years* has an abundance of classic Sinatra performances—however, it isn't the best place to hear most of these cuts. Sinatra's Capitol albums were designed as cohesive works and it is disconcerting to hear all of the different moods jammed together on one collection, with a handful of singles used as breathers. There is certainly plenty of wonderful music here, and the box is somewhat of an effective sampler, but to really appreciate what the singer achieved during the '50s, it is necessary to listen to the original albums. *—Stephen Thomas Erlewine*

The Reprise Collection / 1990 / Reprise ✦✦✦✦
Like *The Capitol Years*, the four-disc box set *The Reprise Collection* was released to celebrate Frank Sinatra's 75th anniversary. However, it works as a better sampler than the Capitol set, partially because Sinatra released so many albums on Reprise that it is necessary to have an introduction to such a large body of work. Also, his Reprise records, while still being concept albums, were more inconsistent and therefore easier to anthologize. Many highlights, as well as most of his biggest hits from the era, are included on *The Reprise Collection*, along with a handful of rarities that are nearly as enjoyable. It's a dynamite collection and proves that the '60s and '70s were a surprisingly diverse, rewarding time for Sinatra. *—Stephen Thomas Erlewine*

The Capitol Collectors Series / 1990 / Capitol ✦✦✦✦
Capitol Collectors Series collects a selection of Frank Sinatra's biggest hit singles from the '50s, making for a scattershot but entertaining sampler, even if it is in no way a definitive retrospective of the era. *—Stephen Thomas Erlewine*

★ **Sinatra Reprise: The Very Good Years** / Mar. 26, 1991 / Warner Brothers ✦✦✦✦✦
Sinatra Reprise: The Very Good Years is an excellent single-disc retrospective of his career at Reprise, including most of his signature songs from the '60s, '70s, and '80s. Hits like "My Way," "That's Life," "Summer Wind," "Strangers in the Night," "It Was a Very Good Year," and "New York, New York" are present, as are songs that were never singles but were extremely popular, like "Luck Be a Lady," "Fly Me to the Moon," "Love and Marriage," and "The Way You Look Tonight." For many casual fans, this disc captures the essence of Sinatra as an icon and provides a perfect introduction to the singer. *—Stephen Thomas Erlewine*

★ **Sinatra** / 1992 / Reprise ✦✦✦✦✦
This is the two-disc soundtrack to a 1992 television mini-series about the life of Frank Sinatra. There is no musical scoring, and there are no re-recordings. Rather, this is a collection of 30 songs recorded between 1931 and 1979, most by Sinatra, although Bing Crosby, Benny Goodman, and Billie Holiday also make appearances. What is notable about the set is that it is the only album to combine tracks from Sinatra's recordings on Columbia, RCA Victor, Capitol, and Reprise, and thus the only one offering the breadth of his work over a period of 40 years. Of course, it remains a sampler, and there's far more great Sinatra material, but the unique circumstances make this an excellent compilation for the beginner. *—William Ruhlmann*

The Best of the Capitol Years: Selections from "The Capitol Years" Box Set / Oct. 26, 1992 / Capitol ✦✦✦✦
The Best of the Capitol Years is an effective distillation of the three-disc set, *The Capitol Years*. Featuring singles and album tracks, the disc contains a fair number of highlights from one of Sinatra's most creative periods. Although the albums really are more effective as individual works—and, therefore, straight singles compilations would be ideal—*The Best of the Capitol Years* gives a good introduction to this pivotal phase of Sinatra's career. *—Stephen Thomas Erlewine*

The Columbia Years (1943-1952): The Complete Recordings / 1993 / Columbia ✦✦✦✦
For serious students of popular singing, this 12-disc box set is indispensable. During his early years at Columbia, Sinatra defined what popular singing was, and these 285 songs show why he was so revolutionary. For many, 12 discs is too much music, but for collectors, the set is essential. *—Stephen Thomas Erlewine*

Sinatra and Sextet: Live in Paris / 1994 / Reprise ✦✦✦✦
If you've cringed at the quality of recent Sinatra projects, this 1962 session will remind you of his glorious past. The 26 cuts include many Sinatra signature pieces ("I've Got You Under My Skin," "The Second Time Around," "Night and Day," "Moonlight in Vermont") with backing from an intimate, small band that provides lush, supportive frameworks around which Sinatra can build and create his inimitable charm. The session also shows Sinatra at his most loutish, with some crude (even for the time) commentary during the beginning of "One for My Baby," and borderline racist cracks at the end of "Ol' Man River" and start of "The Lady Is a Tramp." But Sinatra's vocal excellence often overcame his idiocy and bad manners, and it does on this fine set. *—Ron Wynn*

The V-discs: Columbia Years: 1943-45 / 1994 / Sony ✦✦✦
Sinatra's earliest wartime recordings are finally collected on this lovingly assembled two-disc set, which is essential for his serious fans. Sinatra's style isn't as smooth as on his recordings with Tommy Dorsey or his Capitol records, but his developing style is very exciting in its own right. *—Stephen Thomas Erlewine*

★ **I'll Be Seeing You** / Aug. 30, 1994 / RCA Bluebird ✦✦✦✦✦
Containing many seminal Sinatra performances, *I'll Be Seeing You* distills the highlights from the extensive five-disc *The Song Is You* box set, giving listeners an effective portrait of Sinatra at the beginning of his career. *—Stephen Thomas Erlewine*

The Complete Reprise Studio Recordings / Oct. 17, 1995 / Warner Brothers ✦✦✦✦

★ **The Best of the Columbia Years: 1943-1952** / Oct. 31, 1995 / Sony ✦✦✦✦✦
A four-disc distillation of the mammoth 12-disc box *The Columbia Years (1943-1952): The Complete Recordings*, *The Best of the Columbia Years 1943-52* provides everything most listeners need to know about Frank Sinatra's early career. Nearly all of his classic performances of the era are included in these 100 tracks, which are sequenced chronologically. Completists will need the 12-disc set, but *The Best of the Columbia Years* will satisfy the needs of most fans. *—Stephen Thomas Erlewine*

Sinatra 80th—All the Best / Nov. 1995 / Capitol ✦✦✦✦
Released to coincide with Frank Sinatra's 80th birthday, *Sinatra 80th*—All the Best is a double-disc set that draws from his classic Capitol concept albums as well as singles from the '50s and a couple of rarities, which aren't particularly compelling. The main strength of the package is as an introduction, since it recaps most of his essential recordings of the '50s and gives a sense of his accomplishments. Nevertheless, the set is only a teaser, since most of Sinatra's Capitol records—both the original albums and single compilations—are better sequenced and more rewarding. *—Stephen Thomas Erlewine*

Complete Capitol Singles Collection / Sep. 3, 1996 / Capitol ✦✦✦✦

Stephen Sondheim

b. 1930
Show Tunes

According to most critics and theater historians, Stephen Sondheim stands among Broadway show composers and lyricists not only as the greatest of his generation, but as the only great one of his generation. There may be many reasons why Broadway has failed to produce consistently great writers to follow the Rodgers and Hammersteins and Lerner and Loewes of the '40s and '50s, but the fact remains that though he operates without serious competition, Sondheim clearly ranks with such masters, as well as with the Jerome Kerns and Irving Berlins of an even earlier generation.

Sondheim became a mentor of Hammerstein's after befriending the lyricist's son in school, but he got his first big break when he was hired to write lyrics to Leonard Bernstein's score for *West Side Story* (1957), which turned out to be one of the biggest hits and most memorable works of its time. This led to a lot of lyric-writing work, though Sondheim always wanted to write music as well. Nevertheless, he worked with Jule Styne on *Gypsy* (1959), another enormous hit, and would later agree to do the same with Richard Rodgers for the unsuccessful *Do I Hear a Waltz?* (1965).

Before that, however, Sondheim scored his first success as composer and lyricist with *A Funny Thing Happened on the Way to the Forum* (1962). It was his last hit until *Company* (1970), a show about contemporary life and mores that did much to revolutionize the Broadway musical and, as Hammerstein's 50 shows had, move it more toward serious and exotic subjects. Since that time, Sondheim's shows have been amazingly daring in terms of subject matter, with unusual musical ideas and stunningly original lyrics. But they have not always been big hits and have marked a time in theater when Broadway show music became a marginalized art form in terms of popular culture.

Nevertheless, Sondheim's shows of the '70s and '80s are benchmarks of the genre: *Follies* (1971) brought together aging follies girls for a look at middle-aged American life; *A Little Night Music* (1973) is based on

Ingmar Bergman's film *Smiles of a Summer Night* and contains Sondheim's sole hit song, "Send in the Clowns"; *Pacific Overtures* (1976) ambitiously took on the subject of Japanese-American relations; *Sweeney Todd* (1979) was an operetta based on the British grand guignol tale of a murderous barber; *Sunday in the Park with George* (1984) was a biography of impressionist painter Georges Seurat; and *Into the Woods* (1987) wove together children's fairy tales with the theories of psychologist Bruno Bettelheim. At this writing, Sondheim's latest show is *Assassins* (1991), a short piece about presidential killers. In recent years, he has turned more to the films (he wrote a score for Stravinsky in the '70s, writing songs for Madonna in *Dick Tracy* in 1990, and reportedly working on an original movie musical. — *William Ruhlmann*

★ **Sondheim: A Musical Tribute** / 1973 / RCA ◆◆◆◆◆
A two-disc recording of a special benefit show held March 11, 1973, featuring many of the original performers from Stephen Sondheim musicals, reprising their performances of his songs. Thus, the album is a kind of "Sondheim's Greatest Hits," with the added excitement of being a one-time event. Originally issued as a two-LP set by Warner in 1973, it was reissued by RCA on CD/cassette with previously unreleased tracks. — *William Ruhlmann*

☆ **Side by Side by Sondheim** [Orig. London Cast] / 1976 / RCA ◆◆◆◆◆
A two-disc London cast recording of a revue culled from songs written by Stephen Sondheim for such musicals as *A Funny Thing Happened on the Way to the Forum, Company, A Little Night Music, Follies, Anyone Can Whistle, Pacific Overtures, Do I Hear a Waltz?, West Side Story,* and *Gypsy,* and more obscure works such as "Evening Primrose" (a TV show), *The 7% Solution,* and *The Mad Show.* In anthology and presented starkly, the songs are (if possible) even more impressive than when heard in the shows for which they were written. If there was any doubt that Stephen Sondheim is the greatest talent writing contemporary musicals, this show erased it. — *William Ruhlmann*

A Collector's Sondheim / 1985 / RCA ◆◆◆◆
A four-LP box-set compilation that gathers material from a variety of Stephen Sondheim scores over the 30 years 1954-1984 (those for which he only provided lyrics are excluded). This is an outstanding, if pricey, sampler that features many rarities and is a must for Sondheim fans. — *William Ruhlmann*

Sondheim / 1985 / Book of the Month Club ◆◆◆
A three-LP box set of newly recorded Sondheim songs, featuring such singers as Cris Groenendaal, Bob Gunton, and Debbie Shapiro and conducted by frequent Sondheim orchestrator Paul Gemignani. The album presents Sondheim's songs outside a theatrical context, in renditions by great singers. A welcome addendum to the Sondheim library. — *William Ruhlmann*

Barbra Streisand

b. Apr. 24, 1942
Vocals / Show Tunes, Adult Contemporary, Pop, Soft Rock
Barbra Streisand's status as one of the most successful singers of her generation is all the more remarkable not only because her popularity has been achieved in the face of a dominant musical trend—rock 'n' roll—that she did not follow, but also because, despite an amazing singing voice that has enthralled practically anyone who has heard it, she has always used singing as a mere stepping stone to other careers, as a stage and film actress and as a film director.

Streisand struggled briefly as an actress and nightclub singer in New York in the early 1960s before landing her first part in a Broadway show, *I Can Get It for You Wholesale,* in 1962. The cast album for that show and a subsequent appearance on a studio revival of *Pins and Needles* were her first recordings. Signed to Columbia Records, she released her first album, *The Barbra Streisand Album,* in 1963. It became a Top Ten, gold-selling record, turning Streisand into one of the bestselling recording artists of the early 1960s. But despite three successful albums by early 1964, Streisand turned her back on potentially lucrative concert bookings in favor of a starring role in the Broadway show *Funny Girl,* in which she appeared for more than two years. "People" from that show became her first Top Ten single, and the *People* album her first chart-topping LP. She turned to television in 1965 with "My Name Is Barbra," the first of five network specials. In 1967, Streisand went to Hollywood to film *Funny Girl,* for which she would win an Academy Award. But by 1970, with her second and third films flops and her recording career flagging in the face of rock, she seemed consigned to Las Vegas before turning 30. Instead, she returned to hit-making with a Top Ten cover of Laura Nyro's "Stoney End" and a successful non-singing performance in the comedy *The Owl and the Pussycat.*

In the 1970s Streisand successfully married her musical and film acting interests, first in *The Way We Were,* a hit film with a theme song that became her first No. 1 single, and then with *A Star Is Born,* which featured her second No. 1 single, "Evergreen," a song she co-wrote. From that point on, every album she released sold at least a million copies. In the late '70s she found recording success in collaboration: her duet with

Neil Diamond, "You Don't Bring Me Flowers," hit No. 1, as did "No More Tears (Enough Is Enough)," a dance record sung with Donna Summer. She had her biggest-selling album in 1980 with *Guilty,* which was written and produced by Barry Gibb of the Bee Gees and which contained the No. 1 hit "Woman In Love." In 1983 Streisand's first directorial effort, *Yentl,* became a successful film with a Top Ten soundtrack album. In 1985 *The Broadway Album* returned her to the top of the charts. In 1991 *Just for the Record ...,* a box set retrospective, was released, as was her second film as a director, *The Prince of Tides.* Streisand returned to the concert stage in 1994, resulting in the Top Ten, million-selling album *The Concert.* In 1996, she directed her third film, *The Mirror Has Two Faces.* — *William Ruhlmann*

Pins and Needles [O.S.T.] / 1962 / Columbia ◆◆◆

☆ **The Barbra Streisand Album** / Feb. 25, 1963 / Columbia ◆◆◆◆◆
Of course, the first thing that strikes you listening to the first Barbra Streisand album, recorded and released before the singer's 21st birthday, is *that great voice.* And it isn't just the sheer quality of the voice, its purity and its strength throughout its register, it's also the mastery of vocal effects that produce dramatic readings of the lyrics—each song is like a one-act musical. Streisand opens with Julie London's signature torch song, "Cry Me a River," and not only does she surpass London, she sets off a thermonuclear explosion. From there, versatility and novelty are emphasized—a breakneck version of "Who's Afraid of the Big Bad Wolf?," a slow, emotion-drenched performance of "Happy Days Are Here Again." But Streisand's debut, inventively arranged and conducted by Peter Matz, is notable as much for the surprising omissions as the surprising selections. Arriving in 1963, ten years into the revival of sophisticated interwar theater songs led by Frank Sinatra and followed by all other adult pop singers, Streisand virtually ignores the modern masters like Gershwin and Berlin. When she does do Rodgers and Hart or Cole Porter, she picks obscure songs; her idea of a good 1930s number is Fats Waller and Andy Razaf's "Keepin' Out of Mischief Now." She is much more comfortable with recent theater material, choosing two songs from *The Fantasticks* (1960) and the title song from the stage play *A Taste of Honey* (1962). *The Barbra Streisand Album* is an essential recording in the field of pop vocals because it redefines that genre in contemporary terms. (*The Barbra Streisand Album* won Grammy Awards for Album of the Year, Best Female Vocal Performance, and Best Album Cover.) — *William Ruhlmann*

The Second Album / 1963 / Columbia ◆◆◆
Barbra Streisand's second album might have been subtitled "The Harold Arlen Album," since Arlen is the composer of five of the 11 selections, including four of five on the first side. Streisand had demonstrated an affinity for Arlen's work on her first album, singing "A Sleepin' Bee." Here, she is most impressive on "Down with Love," the 1937 song with a lyric by E.Y. Harburg that lampoons the love songs of other writers of the period. Never given to singing the Gershwins and other classic pop writers, Streisand relishes the chance to condemn them, and she sings with a vengeance. But in general, Arlen's bluesy music, combined with the second-rate contemporary material on the second side, makes Streisand's second album less accomplished than her first. In fact, where the first album, with its surprising arrangements, surprising song choices, humor, and emotionalism, reconceived pop singing for a new singer, the second album, with its sameness of tone, surrenders to the old mold. On an already unlikely piece of material like Sigmund Romberg and Oscar Hammerstein, II's "Lover, Come Back to Me," arranger/conductor Peter Matz uses an updated, uptempo Billy May-style arrangement (with bongos). Streisand gives it a bravura reading, but she is competing against the arrangement rather than riding over it. *The Second Barbra Streisand Album* was typically well-sung, but instead of continuing the innovations of her debut, Streisand seemed to be trying simply to consolidate her triumph, and it was a bit too early for that. — *William Ruhlmann*

The Third Album / Feb. 1964 / Columbia ◆◆◆
On her first album, Barbra Streisand established herself as a singer who discovered or created new standards instead of one who revived or recreated old ones. She wavered from this commitment on her second album, and on her third gave in to convention completely. There was nothing wrong with her interpretations of such old favorites as "My Melancholy Baby," "Taking a Chance on Love," "As Time Goes By," or "It Had to Be You," except perhaps that they seemed overly tame for a performer of such demonstrated individuality. And Streisand was far less successful on "Bewitched (Bothered and Bewildered)," betraying little understanding of Lorenz Hart's nuanced lyric, or on Jerome Kern and Oscar Hammerstein, II's "Make Believe," which had none of the playfulness the song needed, and of which Streisand certainly was capable. She did seem assured going back to Harold Arlen's *St. Louis Woman* for "I Had Myself a True Love," using its bluesy tone for some emotional fireworks. But *The Third Album,* while it was another demonstration of the beauty of Barbra Streisand's voice, also suggested that her interpretive abilities remained limited. — *William Ruhlmann*

People / 1964 / Columbia ✦✦✦✦
After two less successful albums, Barbra Streisand returned to form on her fourth album with a selection of songs that showed some of the imagination of her debut album. Much of the material was new: The album opened and closed with songs by Jule Styne and Bob Merrill, first "Absent Minded Me," and then the Top Ten title song that was the hit from Streisand's triumphant Broadway show, *Funny Girl.* Streisand introduced Cy Coleman and Carolyn Leigh's "When in Rome (I Do As the Romans Do)," a lively song that allowed her to display some of the spirit and humor that had been missing on her last two outings. And when picking from older songs, she again found obscure or atypical tunes from prominent composers or lost gems she could make her own. In the former category were Irving Berlin's "Supper Time," a blues song unlike any the composer had ever done, and "My Lord and Master," from Rodgers and Hammerstein's *The King and I.* In the latter was the delightful "Fine and Dandy," from the 1930 show of the same name, with a lyric by Kay Swift. Add in some obvious choices like James Van Heusen and Sammy Cahn's "Love Is a Bore" (a companion to the previously recorded "Down with Love") and "Don't Like Goodbyes," another selection from Harold Arlen and Truman Capote's *House of Flowers,* from which Streisand had earlier picked "A Sleepin' Bee," and you have an album fashioned to play to the singer's strengths and musical tastes instead of trying to fit her into existing ones. That wasn't quite enough to match the quality of the debut album, but it was a definite improvement over the second and third albums. (*People* won Grammy Awards for Best Vocal Performance and Best Album Cover.) — *William Ruhlmann*

My Name Is Barbra / 1965 / Columbia ✦✦✦✦
An album containing many of the songs used in Barbra Streisand's TV special of the same name, *My Name Is Barbra* followed the general outline of two of the three sections of the show. The first side was a concept set of songs about childhood and growing up that allowed Streisand, in the songs "I'm Five" and "Sweet Zoo," to take a comic approach for the first time in several albums. The second side was a set of adult songs performed in Streisand's big, dramatic style. "I Can See It," her third borrowing from *The Fantasticks,* was the best yet, and Streisand's first attempt at a Gershwin tune, "Someone to Watch over Me," was at least a qualified success. "I've Got No Strings," from the movie *Pinocchio,* was no "Who's Afraid of the Big Bad Wolf" (one of the highlights of her debut album), but it wasn't bad. And best of all was Streisand's reading of "My Man," Fanny Brice's signature song, though it had not been used in *Funny Girl,* the Broadway show about her life, in which Streisand had starred. After this demonstration, however, it would be interpolated into the movie version. (*My Name Is Barbra* won a Grammy Award for Best Female Vocal Performance.) — *William Ruhlmann*

My Name Is Barbra Two / Oct. 1965 / Columbia ✦✦✦
This is not exactly a sequel to *My Name Is Barbra,* though it contains a medley of songs about poverty that was performed as one of the three sections of the TV special. For the most part, this is just the next Barbra Streisand album, containing the usual mixture of recent songs ("He Touched Me," "The Shadow of Your Smile," "No More Songs for Me") and lesser-known songs by classic pop writers (Rodgers and Hart's "Quiet Night" and "Where's That Rainbow?"), filled out by full-length versions of songs from the medley ("Second Hand Rose," a song associated with Fanny Brice that became Streisand's second Top 40 hit, and "I Got Plenty o' Nothin' " from *Porgy and Bess*). The medley lacks the TV show's visual complement of Streisand cavorting in a department store, but the arrangement and her performance still camp up songs like "Brother Can You Spare a Dime?" and "Nobody Knows You When You're Down and Out" a dubious choice of interpretation. — *William Ruhlmann*

Color Me Barbra / 1966 / Columbia ✦✦✦
All of the songs on *Color Me Barbra* were featured on Barbara Streisand's second TV special of the same name. (There were some more songs as well, but they had appeared on earlier albums.) It was a strong collection on which Streisand successfully tackled such standards as Jerome Kern and Otto Harbach's "Yesterdays" and Rodgers and Hart's "Where or When," as well as introducing some good new show material in "Where Am I Going?" from *Sweet Charity* and Maltby and Shire's "Starting Here, Starting Now," and displaying her comedic skills on "The Minute Waltz." The long medley of "face" songs ("Funny Face," "I've Grown Accustomed to Her Face," etc.) made more sense on TV, when Streisand sang it to a studio zoo full of animals, but was still enjoyable. The material wasn't all great, with a retread of "Gotta Move" by Streisand's arranger/conductor Peter Matz and a couple of French songs looking forward to *Je M'Appelle Barbra* among the filler. — *William Ruhlmann*

Je M'Appelle Barbra / Nov. 1966 / Columbia ✦✦✦
Je M'Appelle Barbra is an album of songs with a French orientation, either because they are actually sung, at least in part, in French, or because they originated in France before having English lyrics added. Streisand does not embarrass herself in French, but the album is more an experiment than a triumph, and is notable primarily for marking her

first collaboration with Michel Legrand, who arranged and conducted. — *William Ruhlmann*

Simply Streisand / Oct. 1967 / Columbia ✦✦✦
After three albums related to television specials and one of French songs, *Simply Streisand* was Barbra Streisand's first "regular" new album since *People* three years earlier and her first new release of any kind in a year. (Before, her albums came regularly every six months.) By now, the singer was spending her time in Hollywood shooting movies, and the music scene had moved heavily into rock, developments that made this a perfunctory set and one released into an indifferent climate; unlike her previous eight albums, *Simply Streisand* missed the Top Ten. But it isn't *that* bad. Streisand is not an accomplished performer of classic pop standards like "My Funny Valentine" and "More Than You Know," largely because she seems too intimidated by the material to put an individual stamp on it, but she is a great singer, and if arranger Ray Ellis' charts lack the invention of Peter Matz, they are conventionally competent. If this were the only Streisand album you ever heard, you'd still think she was good. It's only in comparison to what went before that it seems mediocre. — *William Ruhlmann*

A Happening in Central Park / 1968 / Columbia ✦✦✦
Recorded at a concert in front of 135,000 people in New York's Central Park in June 1967, Barbra Streisand's first live album was something of a throwback to her early days, and not only because it waited in the can 15 months before release. (Also filmed, the performance was used as a TV special.) Songs like "Happy Days Are Here Again" and "Cry Me a River" dated from Streisand's 1963 debut album, while the comic "Value" was a previously unrecorded song from her first off-Broadway show, *Another Evening with Harry Stoones,* which ran for one night in October 1961. Streisand was dangerously close to being a musical anachronism in the pop music scene of 1968, even as her Hollywood stardom was confirmed by the release of the *Funny Girl* movie. This album did nothing to change that, though Streisand proved a charming and funny live performer and, as ever, a great singer. It was amazing that she could pull off what remained essentially a nightclub act in front of such a large audience. — *William Ruhlmann*

What About Today? / 1969 / Columbia ✦✦

The Owl and the Pussycat / 1970 / Columbia ✦

● **Greatest Hits** / 1970 / Columbia ✦✦✦✦
At a time when Barbra Streisand's career was in decline, what turned out to be only her first greatest-hits album seemed to serve as both a summing up and a kiss-off of her 1960s recordings. Streisand was not primarily a singles artist; between 1964 and 1969, she enjoyed nine chart singles, of which only one, "People," made the Top Ten, with only one other, "Second Hand Rose," reaching the Top 40. But in that time, she scored seven gold-selling, Top Ten albums. If this collection contained seven of her chart singles, plus her noncharting early single, "My Coloring Book," "Happy Days Are Here Again," which was one of the highlights of her debut album (heard here in the live version from *A Happening in Central Park*), and "Don't Rain on My Parade" from the *Funny Girl* soundtrack. For casual fans, that made for a good sampling of Streisand's most prominent '60s work, and if at the time it seemed likely that this was all the hits there would be, instead the '60s proved to be only the first chapter in Streisand's career. — *William Ruhlmann*

On a Clear Day You Can See Forever / Jul. 1970 / Sony ✦✦✦
The film version of the Broadway musical *On a Clear Day You Can See Forever* was something of a disaster, but the soundtrack album is better because the focus is on the Burton Lane/Alan Jay Lerner songs and on the primary singer, Barbra Streisand, who has six vocals out of ten selections. Far less impressive is co-star Yves Montand, whose singing voice is as suspect as his English, such that the album is a mixed success. — *William Ruhlmann*

Stoney End / Feb. 1971 / Columbia ✦✦✦✦
Barbra Streisand scored her second Top Ten hit in early 1971 by treating Laura Nyro's recording of her song "Stoney End" as a demo and copying it practically note for note. "Mama, let me start all over," she sang, and her wish was granted. The follow-up album of the same title was in its way as surprising as Streisand's debut album eight years earlier. Where that record had redefined the role of the traditional pop singer in contemporary terms for the early '60s, *Stoney End* redefined Streisand as an effective pop-rock singer, which her last outing, *What About Today?,* had failed to do. Maybe she listened as closely to Nyro and Joni Mitchell as she had to Ethel Merman and Judy Garland a decade earlier, but somehow she reoriented her approach to music, adapting herself to vocal demands that were very different in terms of dynamics, expressiveness, and especially rhythm from the traditional pop and theater music she had sung previously. Producer Richard Perry may have eased the transition by using sessionmen like Randy Newman, who played piano on two of his own compositions, and who bridged the worlds of show music and rock. But Streisand herself found something to identify with in songs like Gordon Lightfoot's "If You Could Read My Mind" (maybe that pas-

sage about the movie queen) and Mitchell's "I Don't Know Where I Stand." *Stoney End* was not a perfect album—the reliance on minor Brill Building material and two more Nyro copies kept it from classic status—but it was so far removed from what Streisand's fans and her detractors thought her capable of that it stands as one of her major triumphs. It was also her biggest seller in four years and launched the comeback that saw her through the '70s. *— William Ruhlmann*

Barbra Joan Streisand / 1971 / Columbia ✦✦✦✦
On her follow-up to the comeback album *Stoney End*, Barbra Streisand tried to do for (or to) Carole King what she had done the last time around with Laura Nyro, that is, redo her material in a similar manner and essentially hijack it (while providing a big jump in songwriter royalties, of course). This was not so easy to do in the case of "Beautiful," "Where You Lead," and "You've Got a Friend," however, since, unlike the Nyro songs, by the time Streisand got to these tunes, they were already on King's own chart-topping album, *Tapestry*. Nevertheless, Steisand, who after all is a much more powerful singer than King, did them well and even eked out a Top 40 single on "Where You Lead." And the album contained other gems, such as a delicate reading of John Lennon's "Love" (a take on his "Mother" was far less successful) and the only recording of "I Mean to Shine," written by Donald Fagen and Walter Becker, soon to launch Steely Dan. Streisand was not able to make the final transition into the pop-rock realm for the simple reason that she wasn't a writer, but she had spent a career making other people's songs her own, and she was as effective doing that here as she had been on very different material in the '60s. *— William Ruhlmann*

Live Concert at the Forum / Oct. 1972 / Columbia ✦✦✦

Barbra Streisand . . . and Other Musical Instruments / Nov. 1973 / Columbia ✦✦

The Way We Were / Jan. 1974 / Columbia ✦✦✦

ButterFly / Oct. 1974 / Columbia ✦✦✦
Barbra Streisand's first album of newly recorded, nonsoundtrack studio material in three years, *ButterFly* was ridiculed at the time of its release because it credited producer was her boyfriend, Jon Peters, whose musical credentials were nonexistent. In retrospect, the real power on the album was arranger Tom Scott, a reed player who had perfected a light jazz-pop style in his work on Joni Mitchell's *Court and Spark* earlier in the year. *ButterFly* backed off from the pop-rock style of its predecessors, *Stoney End* and *Barbra Joan Streisand*, but it still found Streisand essaying contemporary material by such writers as Bob Marley, Graham Nash, and David Bowie. Unlike Richard Perry, who had produced those albums, Scott adapted the songs to Streisand's powerful and individual vocal style rather than having her ape existing versions of the songs. The result was more of a compromise with contemporary pop that, while it sold only to Streisand's existing fan base, nevertheless had its charms. *— William Ruhlmann*

Lazy Afternoon / 1975 / Columbia ✦✦✦
Lazy Afternoon was Barbra Streisand's Rupert Holmes album. Holmes, later known for his No. 1 hit "Escape (The Pina Colada Song)," arranged, conducted, and co-produced the album and wrote or co-wrote four songs. He helped Streisand to continue her evolution into a kind of post-rock contemporary pop artist. This was achieved largely through the sympathetic ballad arrangements, which surrounded Streisand's voice with delicately played individual instruments while focusing on her calm vocals. The exception was a cover of the Four Tops' "Shake Me, Wake Me," which was given a disco treatment. For the most part, *Lazy Afternoon* was true to its title, a collection of relaxed performances that was pleasant without being particularly impressive. *— William Ruhlmann*

Classical Barbra / Feb. 1976 / Columbia ✦✦✦
One of Barbra Streisand's more esoteric projects, *Classical Barbra* is an album of European art songs composed by Debussy, Handel, Schumann, and others and sung in French, German, Latin, Italian, and English. Streisand is in typically good voice, and while the album must have been a stretch for her usual audience and a surprise to the classical audience, she carries the performances off. *— William Ruhlmann*

Streisand Superman / 1977 / Columbia ✦✦✦
Appearing only seven months after *A Star Is Born*, *Streisand Superman* seemed to continue much of its rock-oriented feel, even including several songs that had been intended for the film. It was unusual in featuring all recently written songs, many first recorded here. Streisand co-wrote the rockish "Don't Believe What You Read," an attack on her negative press coverage, while Alan Gordon contributed both the discoish "I Found You Love" and the album's Top Ten single ballad "My Heart Belongs to Me." *Streisand Superman* seemed to be an unusually personal album for the singer, reflecting her feelings and viewpoints. That did not make it one of her best, however. *— William Ruhlmann*

★ **Barbra Streisand's Greatest Hits, Vol. 2** / 1978 / Columbia ✦✦✦✦✦
Between the release of Barbra Streisand's first hits collection in 1970 and her second in 1978, she essentially became a different kind of recording artist. In the 1960s, she made a series of consistent albums devoted

largely to show music material, but she scored precious few singles hits, with only one, "People," reaching the Top Ten. But in the 1970s, she shifted to contemporary soft rock and released a series of highly successful ballad singles, while her albums became largely inconsistent. For that reason, the hit quotient of her second hits album was much higher—"The Way We Were," "Love Theme from 'A Star Is Born' (Evergreen)," and the duet version of "You Don't Bring Me Flowers," sung with songwriter Neil Diamond and released on album here for the first time, all were No. 1 hits, while "Stoney End" and "My Heart Belongs to Me" were Top Tens, and "Sweet Inspiration/Where You Lead," "Songbird," and "Love Theme from 'Laura Mars' (Prisoner)" reached the Top 40. That was enough material to make *Vol. 2* Streisand's definitive hits collection, so much so that later compilations like *Memories* and *A Collection/Greatest Hits . . . and More* would be forced to cannibalize it. It was also a genre-defining album in terms of the emergence of a post-'60s contemporary pop music that drew upon the rock revolution to redefine classic pop for a new generation. *— William Ruhlmann*

Songbird / 1978 / Columbia ✦✦✦
Songbird was a competent, professional effort from Barbra Streisand, typical of the soft-rock style of her '70s work, but unexceptional. Gary Klein, who had produced *Streisand Superman*, guided a middle course between bombast and balladry, resulting in, for example, perhaps the least objectionable version possible of the frankly awful "Tomorrow" from the Broadway musical *Annie* and a good reading of Neil Diamond's "You Don't Bring Me Flowers" that would help inspire the hit duet version a year later. But though Streisand now seemed to have access to the efforts of a raft of good songwriters, most of the material here was not memorable. The intended hit, obviously, was the title song, which was patterned after Streisand's recent string of hit ballads. But it was not as effective as its predecessors and didn't perform as well as they had in the charts, only breaking into the Top 40. *— William Ruhlmann*

Wet / 1979 / Columbia ✦✦✦

Guilty / 1980 / Columbia ✦✦✦✦
The biggest selling album of Barbra Streisand's career is also one of her least characteristic. The album was written and produced by Barry Gibb in association with his brothers and the producers of the Bee Gees, and in essence it sounds like a post-*Saturday Night Fever* Bee Gees album with vocals by Streisand. Gibb adapted his usual style somewhat, especially in slowing the tempos and leaving more room for the vocal, but his melodic style and the backup vocals, even when they are not sung by the Bee Gees, are typical of them. Still, the record was more hybrid than compromise, and the chart-topping single "Woman in Love" has a sinuous feel that is both right for Streisand and new for her. Other hits were the title song and "What Kind of Fool," both duets with Gibb. (The song "Guilty" won a Grammy Award for Best Pop Vocal by Duo or Group.) *— William Ruhlmann*

Memories / Nov. 1981 / Columbia ✦✦✦

Yentl / 1983 / Columbia ✦✦✦

Emotion / Oct. 1984 / Columbia ✦✦✦
Barbra Streisand's first album of contemporary material in four years was a typical '80s adult contemporary superstar release, each track written and produced as a potential "power ballad" single by an extensive team of other performers, in this case including Richard Perry, Kim Carnes, Maurice White (of Earth, Wind and Fire), Jim Steinman, Albhy Galuten (the Bee Gees' producer), Richard Baskin, Diane Warren, John Mellencamp, and Streisand herself. Streisand proved capable of handling everything from White's space-age R&B to Steinman's melodramatic overproduction. (He was the man who brought you Meat Loaf.) But as usually happens with such big-budget efforts, the album lacked consistency; and as Columbia tried to pull several singles off it without notable success, it sold only to Streisand's million-member base audience. *— William Ruhlmann*

☆ **The Broadway Album** / 1985 / Columbia ✦✦✦✦✦
Barbra Streisand's abandonment of Broadway was the worst thing that happened to the theater in the '60s. Her retreat from theater music on record was less of a loss, if only because she had tended to focus on second-rank composers and obscure songs by first-rate ones, while practically ignoring, for example, Stephen Sondheim, who, as of the early '70s, became the pre-eminent Broadway songwriter. When she returned to show songs in 1985, she reversed these failings. Now, the singer who had never done much with Rodgers and Hammerstein, Frank Loesser, George Gershwin, or Jerome Kern finally felt confident enough to take on "If I Loved You" from *Carousel*, "Adelaide's Lament" from *Guys and Dolls*, "Can't Help Lovin' That Man" from *Showboat*, and a medley from *Porgy and Bess*, and she did them well. Even better, on seven tracks with Sondheim's name on them, she proved the perfect interpreter of the most contemporary and intellectual of Broadway's writers, whether singing his lyrics over the music of Leonard Bernstein (another composer she'd largely neglected) from *West Side Story* or making the most of material drawn from shows like *Company*, *A Little Night Music*, *Sweeney Todd*, and *Sun-*

day in the Park with George. Sondheim collaborated with Streisand, penning special lyrics for songs like "Putting It Together" and even his standard, "Send in the Clowns." Also on board was Streisand's arranger from the early and mid-'60s, Peter Matz. The result was an album that repositioned some of Broadway's best in a pop context (doubtless many people heard these great songs for the first time) and showed that Streisand was still at her best when presenting the dramatically satisfying story-songs of the theater. Apparently, many longtime fans agreed: At sales over three million, *The Broadway Album* was Streisand's most commercially successful album in five years. (*The Broadway Album* won a Grammy Award for Best Female Pop Vocal.) —*William Ruhlmann*

One Voice / Apr. 1987 / Columbia ✦✦✦

Till I Loved You / Oct. 1988 / Columbia ✦✦✦
Barbra Streisand's first album of new studio material in four years, *Till I Loved You* was led by its title song, a duet with Streisand's current paramour, actor Don Johnson, on a tune from a Columbia Records pet project, a studio musical called *Goya*, written by Maury Yeston (composer of the Broadway show *Nine*), that the label was encouraging its artists to promote. That embarrassing recording made the album as a whole seem worse than it was. But *Till I Loved You*, which was given over to newly written romantic ballads by people like Burt Bacharach and Carole Bayer Sager, still wasn't very good. Eighteen songwriters, six producers, nine recording studios: like *Emotion*, *Till I Loved You* was a big-budget effort. But it was like a movie with a great star, great production values, and a mediocre script, so how much you liked it depended on how much you liked Barbra Streisand, and it sold to her fans only. —*William Ruhlmann*

Greatest Hits . . . and More / 1989 / Columbia ✦✦✦
Like *Memories, A Collection/Greatest Hits . . . and More* was an odd compilation, not quite a hits set, though it gathered up the big hits not heard on the earlier record—"The Main Event/Fight," "Woman in Love," "Guilty," "What Kind of Fool"—since it also seemed to be a grab-bag, including a few stray album tracks, recycling the two new songs from *Memories(!)*, "Comin' In and Out of Your Life" and "Memory," and adding a couple of new recordings, "We're Not Makin' Love Anymore" (by Diane Warren and Michael Bolton) and "Someone That I Used to Love." The selection made no apparent sense, but then neither had *Memories*, and that album sold several million copies. This one wasn't as fortunate, though many Streisand fans must have received it as a present for Christmas in 1989, which probably was the idea. —*William Ruhlmann*

Prince of Tides / 1991 / Columbia ✦✦✦

Just for the Record . . . / Sep. 24, 1991 / Columbia ✦✦✦✦

Back to Broadway / Jun. 29, 1993 / Columbia ✦✦✦

Barbra: The Concert / 1994 / Sony ✦✦✦✦

The Concert—Highlights / 1995 / Columbia ✦✦✦✦

Rudy Vallee

b. Jul. 28, 1901, d. Jul. 3, 1986
Vocals / Nostalgia
Rudy Vallee was an immensely popular vocalist in the late '20s and '30s. Singing into a megaphone became his vocal trademark. At the height of his popularity, he had his own national radio show. As his singing career faded with the arrival of Bing Crosby, he switched to a career on the stage and screen. The 1966 novelty hit "Winchester Cathedral" was inspired by Vallee. He attempted a brief, unsuccessful comeback, recording an album that included his own version of "Winchester Cathedral." —*Kenneth M. Cassidy*

★ **Vagabond Lover** / Pro Arte ✦✦✦✦✦
These are the best of Vallee's recordings from the '20s and '30s. —*Kenneth M. Cassidy*

Bobby Vinton

b. Apr. 16, 1941, Canonsburg, PA
Clarinet, Vocals / Pop, Vocal
Every era needs its crooner, and in the early '60s, it was Bobby Vinton. Vinton's sentimental balladeering and orchestral, middle-of-the-road arrangements were a throwback to a decade earlier, before rock 'n' roll had found its mass market. If Vinton is sometimes identified with a rock 'n' roll audience, it's only because his music was bought by young listeners for a time, and because he still catches some airplay on oldies stations. What he sang was vocal pop, landing some of the biggest hits of the early '60s with "Roses Are Red (My Love)," "Blue on Blue," "There! I've Said It Again," "Mr. Lonely," and "Blue Velvet," the last of which has become his signature song in the wake of its notorious prominence in David Lynch's film, *Blue Velvet.*

Vinton originally aspired to lead a big band, and made big-band versions of contemporary hits on his first recordings in the early '60s. When he began singing, however, he was quickly successful, reaching No. 1 with "Roses Are Red (My Love)" in mid-1962. The syrupy, saccharine

arrangements set the mold for his plaintive, occasionally mournful hits throughout the early '60s. His banner year was 1963, as he hit No. 3 with "Blue on Blue" and then topped the charts with "Blue Velvet" and "There! I've Said It Again."

"There! I've Said It Again" was knocked out of the number one spot by the Beatles' "I Want to Hold Your Hand." But the British Invasion, surprisingly, didn't spell commercial death for Vinton, as it did for so many other balladeers and teen idols. Indeed, he had one of his biggest hits (and his final No. 1), the sobbing "Mr. Lonely," in late 1964. Although he didn't maintain quite the same superstar ranking, he was consistently popular throughout the next decade; between 1962 and 1972, in fact, he had an astonishing 28 Top 40 entries. Often he updated quaint 1960-era pop tunes such as "Halfway to Paradise," "Take Good Care of My Baby," and "Sealed with a Kiss." A couple of these, "Please Love Me Forever" and "I Love How You Love Me," made the Top Ten, which was quite an anachronism in 1967 and 1968. Vinton seemed to have launched a major comeback in 1974 with "Melody of Love," which made No. 3 and enjoys the distinction of being the only major American hit single sung partially in Polish. Only one more Top 40 hit was in the offing, though. This probably didn't particularly bother Vinton, who had his own TV series for a few years in the late '70s and can always count on lucrative gigs on the cabaret circuit. —*Richie Unterberger*

● **The Essence of Bobby Vinton** / Dec. 1, 1995 / Epic/Legacy ✦✦✦✦
Only ten tracks here, but they include his most famous '60s hits—"Blue Velvet," "Blue on Blue," "Mr. Lonely," and "Roses Are Red, My Love." There are more extensive Vinton compilations, but this will be enough to satisfy a lot of listeners. —*Richie Unterberger*

Roger Whittaker

b. 1936, Kenya, Africa
Vocals
British singer and whistler Roger Whittaker was born in Kenya. His first break came in 1970 with "Durham Town", a No. 12 hit on the UK charts. This was soon followed by a string of hits that became an avalanche of hit albums. *The Very Best of Roger Whittaker* reached No. 5 on the UK charts and logged an incredible 42 weeks on the British charts. With almost 100 albums in print, Whittaker has become one of the most popular of the easy-listening singers. —*Michael Erlewine*

The Best of Roger Whittaker / 1984 / RCA ✦✦✦
Best of Roger Whittaker is a budget-priced collection of re-recordings of the singer's greatest hits that aren't as strong as his original versions. —*Stephen Thomas Erlewine*

● **Greatest Hits** / RCA ✦✦✦✦

Andy Williams

b. Dec. 3, 1928
Vocals / Pop, Standards
Andy Williams parlayed his relaxed vocal delivery into massive pop success and TV stardom during the '60s. After starting out singing with his brothers over various Midwestern radio stations as a youth, the Wall Lake, IA, native went solo in 1952 and became a regular on Steve Allen's "Tonight Show" through 1955. He signed with Archie Bleyer's Cadence Records the next year and hit with "Canadian Sunset," topping the charts with a cover of Charlie Gracie's rock-tinged "Butterfly" in 1957. "Are You Sincere" (1958) and "Lonely Street" (1959) preceded a move to Columbia in 1961 and the huge seller "Can't Get Used to Losing You" in 1963. Williams has long been one of America's top middle-of-the-road entertainers, hosting his own TV variety series throughout the '60s, and he remains popular. —*Bill Dahl*

★ **Andy Williams' Best** / 1962 / Cadence ✦✦✦✦✦
A nice retrospective of Williams' early sides. —*Cub Koda*

Moon River and Other Great Movie Themes / 1962 / Columbia ✦✦✦
The hit title song and lush interpretations of movie-theme classics. —*Cub Koda*

Greatest Hits, Vol. 2 / 1981 / Columbia ✦✦✦
Picks up where the Cadence compilation left off, including "Can't Get Used to Losing You," "Days of Wine and Roses," "Dear Heart," and others. —*Cub Koda*

★ **I Like Your Kind Of Love: The Best of the Cadence Years** / Mar. 26, 1996 / Varese Sarabande ✦✦✦✦✦
This 20-track CD collection of Cadence material from the late '50s and early '60s is the best retrospective of his early work. A couple of the early tracks ("Butterfly," "I Like Your Kind of Love") betray a slight, watered-down rockabilly-pop influence, but mostly this is straight adult pop, less ornately produced than his subsequent major-label material. Includes the huge hits "Lonely Street," "The Hawaiian Wedding Song," "Canadian Sunset," and "The Village of St. Bernadette," as well as a couple of singles ("Wake Me When It's Over," "Promise Me, Love") that were previously unavailable on album. —*Richie Unterberger*

Various Artists

Art Deco: The Crooners / Sep. 1926-Oct. 6, 1941 / Columbia/Legacy
✦✦✦✦✦
A wide span of styles is represented on this two-CD salute to the male singers of the 1930s, the "crooners." Some of the vocalists are quite enjoyable to hear, while a few are very dated, but overall the 49 performances contain more than their share of highlights. There are selections featuring Willard Robison, Gene Austin, Seger Ellis, Smith Ballew, the completely forgotten Lew Bray, Bing Crosby, Harlan Lattimore, Russ Columbo, Red McKenzie, Cliff Edwards (who is heard on eight songs), Pinky Tomlin, Chick Bullock, Jack Teagarden, Harold Arlen ("You're a Builder-Upper"), Buddy Clark, Eddy Howard (a rare jazz session with an all-star group that includes trumpeter Bill Coleman, pianist Teddy Wilson, and guitarist Charlie Christian), Frank Sinatra (with Harry James), and Dick Haymes. This set acts as a perfect introduction to these mostly very talented singers. — *Scott Yanow*

The Best of the Great Girl Singers / Oct. 1995 / Ranwood ✦✦✦
It should be called best of the great adult women singers: This is a 20-song collection of female pop artists from the late '40s and '50s, singing the kind of material that dominated the hit parade in the days just before the rise of rock 'n' roll. Contains two songs each by ten of the heavyweight contenders of the genre (Patti Page, Jo Stafford, Doris Day, Kay Starr, Teresa Brewer, Rosemary Clooney, the Andrews Sisters, Margaret Whiting, Peggy Lee). The songs are both classic ("You Belong to Me," "Fever") and horrid (Kay Starr's "The Rock and Roll Waltz," a contradiction in terms if there ever was one). Since you get only a sliver of each performer, it's best designed for someone with a mild interest in this period who wants only a sampler, rather than those who are passionate about this stuff. — *Richie Unterberger*

Bob Hope's Christmas Party / 1945 / Vintage Jazz Classics ✦✦✦
"Command Performances" were half-hour radio programs recorded for the Armed Forces Radio Service, shipped to World War II troops as 16-inch platters. On this collection there is a humorous sketch from Mel Blanc as "P-P-Private Sad Sack," using the Porky Pig voice; banter with Hope, Bing Crosby, Judy Garland, and other celebrities; and musical performances from Dinah Shore, Harry James, Johnny Mercer, and others. Carols performed by Garland, Shore, Crosby, and more conclude the CD. —*Decibel Dennis MacDonald*

● **Celebrate Broadway, Vol. 1: Sing Happy** / 1994 / RCA Victor ✦✦✦✦✦
The first in a series of compilations of songs from Broadway shows recorded by RCA Victor, this album puts together an hour's worth of what used to be called "eleven o'clock numbers." These were the show stoppers that woke you up shortly before the end of the show and got you ready to hit the street with a smile on your face. (Although, to tell the truth, some of these are first-act finales meant to send you into the lobby anticipating the rest of the evening.) "Blow, Gabriel, Blow," from *Anything Goes*, "I've Gotta Crow," from *Peter Pan*, "Oklahoma!" from *Oklahoma*, these are the big, bright Broadway songs audiences have hummed to themselves for generations. The RCA catalog is mixed—not all of these performances are taken from the original casts, and the notes don't make that clear—but this is a good sampler for the casual fan who likes Broadway's stirring songs. — *William Ruhlmann*

Celebrate Broadway, Vol. 2: You Gotta Have a Gimmick / 1994 / RCA Victor ✦✦✦
For this collection, RCA has scoured its vaults for Broadway novelty songs, comic numbers frequently performed by the supporting players in shows that provide a change of pace and some laughs. Songs like "I Cain't Say No," from *Oklahoma!*, and "Arthur in the Afternoon," from *The Act*, show that being risqué is not a problem, but just as often these songs are just odd: what else to say about the celebratory "Lizzie Borden," from *New Faces of 1952?* That song, from a revue, had no real context in a show, and some of these songs are actually ringers, such as Fats Waller's "Your Feet's Too Big" from *Ain't Misbehavin'* and the "Caribbean Plaid" medley from *Forever Plaid*, material not actually written for Broadway. This is an episodic album, to be sure, but you won't get through it without laughing a few times. —*William Ruhlmann*

Celebrate Broadway, Vol. 3: Lullaby of Broadway / 1994 / RCA Victor ✦✦✦✦✦
Broadway has always had a great ability to celebrate itself, actually, and that ability is showcased on the third volume of RCA's anthology series in songs about show business, starting with the title track (actually written for the movie musical *Forty-Second Street*, which then became a Broadway musical) and ending, inevitably, with "There's No Business like Show Business." In between are songs by Sondheim, Coleman, Styne, Herman, Kern, Yeston, and Kander, all exploring aspects of the biz. As with the other volumes in this series, the caveat is that these songs come from various sources including but not limited to original Broadway cast albums—concert versions, revivals, revues, etc.—but there isn't a performance here that isn't good, and the selection makes a powerful case for Broadway. — *William Ruhlmann*

Celebrate Broadway, Vol. 4: Overtures! / 1994 / RCA Victor ✦✦✦
Overtures introduce Broadway audiences to the music they're going to hear during the course of the evening. Played one after another, they can take on the quality of Muzak, not unpleasant but not compelling. This collection of 12 overtures taken from shows that played on Broadway between the 1940s and 1980s displays the consistency of style in Broadway music. Much of it is appealing, but then, that's the problem: it's like trying to make a dinner out of appetizers. — *William Ruhlmann*

Ertegun's New York—New York Cabaret Music / 1987 / Atlantic ✦✦✦✦✦
Once upon a time (roughly the early '50s), in a faraway land (Manhattan), there lived a group of singers, piano players, and other musicians and a fascinated audience that crowded into dozens of little clubs to hear them sing and play some of the best songs ever written. Most of them are gone now, but the music lives on in this six-record boxd set that gathers the work of Mel Torme, Bobby Short, Mabel Mercer, Sylvia Sims, Billy Taylor, and many other great nightclub performers. — *William Ruhlmann*

☆ **Front Row Center: The Broadway Gold Box** / Mar. 12, 1996 / MCA ✦✦✦✦✦
The first thing to note about *Front Row Center*—The Broadway Gold Box 1935-1988, a four-CD, 93-track, five-hour boxed set retrospective, is that it gathers original cast recordings of Broadway shows exclusively from the MCA catalog, most of them originally released on Decca. Decca was the first major American record label to release cast albums, starting with *Oklahoma!* in 1943 (though it brought Broadway stars into the studio to record isolated tracks as early as 1935), and, as annotator Max O. Preeo notes, it had the field to itself, not joined by Columbia until 1946 or RCA Victor until 1947. From then until the 1970s, when the majors stopped recording musicals on a regular basis, the three labels competed for shows, Decca frequently losing out. Therefore, compilation producer Ron O'Brien necessarily weights the set heavily toward the period of Decca's dominance—15 tracks come from before *Oklahoma!*, and more than half the album dates from the '40s. (In fact, the focus on early material is even greater than the recording dates suggest, since many of the later selections come from revivals.) Even so, this is a rich collection. The shows include *Pins And Needles, Porgy and Bess, This Is the Army, Oklahoma!, One Touch of Venus, On the Town, Carousel, Annie Get Your Gun, Anything Goes, Where's Charley?, Lost in the Stars, Call Me Madam, Guys & Dolls, Lady in the Dark, The King and I, Wonderful Town, On Your Toes, Man Of La Mancha, Applause, Jesus Christ Superstar, The Best Little Whorehouse In Texas, Evita, Big River*, and *Me and My Girl*. All of which is to say that, despite its limitations, *Front Row Center* presents a large chunk of the best-remembered show music of more than 50 years. — *William Ruhlmann*

The George and Ira Gershwin Songbook / RCA ✦✦✦
The Gershwins' continuing appeal is demonstrated on this 20-track collection of recordings from the '50s and '60s, which features Benny Goodman, Julie Andrews, Perry Como, the Ames Brothers, and other stars of the era. — *William Ruhlmann*

☆ **I Got Rhythm: The Music of George Gershwin** / Sep. 9, 1924-Mar. 10, 1992 / Smithsonian ✦✦✦✦✦
This wide-ranging four-CD set has performances of George Gershwin's music divided into four categories: Popular Song, Stage and Screen, Concert Hall, and Jazz. The 71 recordings range from fairly straight Broadway singers to classical music, jazz, and several piano solos from Gershwin himself. Although not all of the music is of equal interest, there are enough rarities included to interest even veteran collectors, and the 64-page booklet is quite appealing. A well-conceived and successful reissue of valuable music. — *Scott Yanow*

★ **Irving Berlin: A Hundred Years** / 1988 / Columbia ✦✦✦✦✦
Issued to commemorate Berlin's 100th birthday, this 21-track compilation of his songs is culled from recordings made primarily in the '30s, though there are also a few from the '40s and '50s. The artists include Connee Boswell, Bing Crosby, Eddie Cantor, Fred Astaire, Benny Goodman, Dinah Shore, Tony Bennett, and Johnny Mathis. — *William Ruhlmann*

Nipper's Greatest Hits: 1902-1920 / 1991 / RCA ✦✦✦✦
Al Jolson, George M. Cohan, Enrico Caruso: RCA Victor was there at the beginning, and this 20-song volume captures the times nicely. —*Jeff Tamarkin*

Nipper's Greatest Hits: The 30's, Vol. 1 / RCA ✦✦✦✦✦
A wonderful collection starring Duke Ellington, Bing Crosby, Benny Goodman, Glenn Miller—all giants. —*Jeff Tamarkin*

Nipper's Greatest Hits: The 30's, Vol. 2 / Apr. 19, 1991 / RCA ✦✦✦✦✦
As strong as the first volume. Louis Armstrong, Artie Shaw, Gene Krupa—the big-band era begins here. —*Jeff Tamarkin*

Nipper's Greatest Hits: The 40's, Vol. 1 / 1940-1949 / RCA ✦✦✦✦✦
With the likes of Frank Sinatra, Tommy Dorsey, Glenn Miller, and Spike Jones, this is a solid set. —*Jeff Tamarkin*

Nipper's Greatest Hits: The 40's, Vol. 2 / RCA ✦✦✦✦✦
A bit weaker than the early-'40s collection, but you still can't go wrong with Count Basie, Dizzy Gillespie, and even Desi Arnaz. —*Jeff Tamarkin*

Nipper's Greatest Hits: The 50's, Vol. 1 / RCA ✦✦✦
Some truly lightweight fluff here, and a weird mix—Elvis, meet Mario Lanza—but it's an accurate reflection of the early '50s. —*Jeff Tamarkin*

Pop Memories: 1955-1959 / 1994 / Rhino ✦✦✦
The final disc in Rhino's pre-rock pop series moves through the middle and end of the 1950s, with mainstream pop still mostly avoiding the emerging rock revolution. The lush sound of Dean Martin and the Four Aces remained prominent, although Tommy Edwards did break the embargo somewhat with "It's All in tThe Game." Perez Prado capitalized on the mambo craze with "Cherry Pink and Apple Blossom White," while orchestral background music reaped dividends. A couple of songs outlined the industry's basic strategy to deal with early rock; Pat Boone's "Love Letters in the Sand" was a teen pop attempt at presenting an alternative to such feared artists as Little Richard, and the McGuire Sisters' saccharine remake of "Sincerely" was one of many R&B hits reworked by White groups because they were deemed too harsh (i.e., Black) for the mainstream market. —*Ron Wynn*

Pop Memories: 1940-1944 / 1994 / Rhino ✦✦✦✦
The early '40s were an interesting time in American pop music annals, as shown by this third CD in this Rhino pre-rock series. The big bands were still dominant, with selections featuring the Harry James, Artie Shaw, Tommy Dorsey, Glenn Miller, and Jimmy Dorsey orchestras. Bing Crosby continued to assert himself, both as a lead act and teaming with the Andrews Sisters. Other spotlight performers are the Mills Brothers, with some early and influential scatting/jive work, and Dick Haymes & the Song Spinners. —*Ron Wynn*

Pop Memories: 1945-1949 / 1994 / Rhino ✦✦✦✦
As the 1940s wore on, the end of the big-band/swing era resulted in changes on the pop music horizon. This fourth disc in Rhino's latest pre-rock series shows how sophisticated, jazzy fare declined, and forgettable, novelty/humorous numbers reigned. Peggy Lee's "Manana," with its phony Afro-Latin vocal and exaggerated rhythms, Dinah Shore's "Buttons and Bows," and Frankie Carle's "Rumors Are Flying" were symptomatic of the lightweight lyrical fare that dominated the era's popular music. The CD also features breezy, pleasant but ultimately trivial material from Ted Weems, Les Brown, Russ Morgan, and Vaughn Monroe. —*Ron Wynn*

Pop Memories: 1950-1954 / 1994 / Rhino ✦✦✦✦✦
Rock 'n' roll seemed the farthest thing from anyone's mind during the early '50s. Highly arranged songs such as Tony Bennett's "Rags to Riches," Rosemary Clooney's "Come on-a My House," and Kay Starr's "Wheel of Fortune" were the norm, plus the overwrought and frenzied vocals of Eddie Fisher and Johnny Ray with the Four Lads. There were also sentimental tunes by Patti Page, Jo Stafford, and folk from Gordon Jenkins and His Orchestra with the Weavers. Only "How High the Moon" by Les Paul and Mary Ford provide any inkling of what's on the horizon—songs with a more pronounced rhythm and emotional vocal style. —*Ron Wynn*

Pop Memories: The 1920s / 1994 / Rhino ✦✦✦✦
Another in Rhino's continuing line of pre-rock popular music anthologies featuring ten hits from the 1920s. This six-disc slate accents tunes that were hits as determined by *Billboard*. The first disc contains seminal country from Vernon Dalhart alongside light fluff from Guy Lombardo and Selvin's Novelty Orchestra. The dominant acts are Paul Whiteman & His Orchestra, Al Jolson, and Gene Austin, who have six of the ten selections, including "Valencia," "Sonny Boy," and "My Blue Heaven." The mastering is superb. —*Ron Wynn*

Pop Memories: The 1930s / 1994 / Rhino/RCA ✦✦✦✦
The second Rhino pre-rock hits CD covers the 1930s, showcasing the rise of big bands and the phasing out of novelty/comic types such as Rudy Vallee. Bing Crosby's majestic sound, as well as the orchestras of Artie Shaw, Duke Ellington, Benny Goodman, and Glenn Miller are featured. Two of the least musically interesting tracks were huge hits, Vallee's "Stein Song" and "Deep Purple" by Larry Clinton and His Orchestra. They're more than balanced by Crosby's wondrous "Pennies from Heaven," with George Stoll and His Orchestra, and "Night and Day," with Fred Astaire's stately lead vocal and Leo Reisman and His Orchestra. —*Ron Wynn*

☆ **The Rodgers & Hart Songbook** / RCA ✦✦✦✦✦
A 20-track album of show songs by Richard Rodgers and Lorenz Hart, recorded by a variety of pop singers in the '50s and '60s, among them Perry Como, Jack Jones, and Ann-Margret. —*William Ruhlmann*

☆ **Sentimental Journey, Vol. 1** / Jun. 15, 1993 / Rhino ✦✦✦✦✦
The first volume of Rhino's pop vocal collection, *Sentimental Journey* covers the years 1942-1946 and includes such vocalists as Bing Crosby, Doris Day, Judy Garland, Jo Stafford, Vaughn Monroe, and Frank Sinatra (with "Swinging on a Star," "Sentimental Journey," "The Trolly Song," "Candy," "There! I've Said It Again," and "Night and Day," respectively).

Not only does the music sound great, but the liner notes are extensive, with complete musician credits. —*AMG*

☆ **Sentimental Journey, Vol. 2** / Jun. 15, 1993 / Rhino ✦✦✦✦✦
Sentimental Journey: Pop Vocal Classics, Vol. 2 (1947-1950) includes Dinah Shore's "Buttons and Bows," Patti Page's "The Tennessee Waltz," "Again" by Mel Torme, Eileen Barton's "If I Knew You Were Comin' I'd've Baked a Cake," and (on CD) "Goodnight Irene" by the Weavers and "Music! Music! Music!" by Teresa Brewer among its 18 tracks. —*AMG*

☆ **Sentimental Journey, Vol. 3** / Jun. 15, 1993 / Rhino ✦✦✦✦✦
Sentimental Journey: Pop Vocal Classics, Vol. 3 (1950-1954) includes Johnny Ray's "Cry," Tony Bennett's "Because of You," "Come on-a My House" by Rosemary Clooney, Jo Stafford's "You Belong to Me," Kay Starr's "Wheel of Fortune," Dean Martin's "That's Amore," and "How High the Moon" by Les Paul and Mary Ford. It's another good installment in the Rhino pop vocal series. —*AMG*

☆ **Sentimental Journey, Vol. 4** / Jun. 15, 1993 / Rhino ✦✦✦✦✦
Arguably the best, most consistent entry in Rhino's pop vocal series, *Sentimental Journey: Vol. 4 (1954-1959)* includes "Mack the Knife" by Bobby Darin, Peggy Lee's "Fever," Dinah Washington's "What a Diff'rence a Day Makes," Guy Mitchell's "Singing the Blues," Doris Day's "Whatever Will Be, Will Be (Que Sera, Sera)," Dean Martin's "Memories Are Made of This," and "Chances Are" by Johnny Mathis. —*AMG*

Sondheim: A Celebration at Carnegie Hall / 1993 / RCA Victor ✦✦✦
This two-CD set is the recording of a benefit concert for Carnegie Hall performed at the hall on June 10, 1992, and featuring the American Theatre Orchestra, conducted by Paul Gemignani, supporting a variety of soloists doing songs written by Stephen Sondheim for Broadway musicals and films. As several anthologies of Sondheim's work and tributes to him have been recorded in the past, the organizers weren't able to find much new in the composer's catalog, and they have settled for sometimes gimmicky arrangements of his familiar songs. Nevertheless, many of the performances are strong, and the stars are many: Glenn Close ("Send in the Clowns"), Madeline Kahn ("I'm Not Getting Married Today"), Patti Lupone ("Being Alive"), Liza Minnelli (the sole new song, "Water Under the Bridge"), and Bernadette Peters ("Not a Day Goes By") are standouts, but the cream of Broadway is represented. Also, it's worth noting that, while the album may be a disappointment to diehard Sondheim fans, newcomers not familiar with this material may well be bowled over by its quality. Sondheim is Broadway's top contemporary composer, and this album demonstrates that as well as any. (Also available as a video, which actually works better, given that some of the numbers have strong visual elements.) —*William Ruhlmann*

★ **Sondheim: A Musical Tribute** / 1973 / RCA ✦✦✦✦✦
A two-disc recording of a special benefit show held Mar 11, 1973, featuring many of the original performers from Stephen Sondheim musicals, reprising their performances of his songs. Thus, the album is a kind of "Sondheim's Greatest Hits," with the added excitement of being a one-time event. Originally issued as a two-LP set by Warner in 1973, it was reissued by RCA on CD/cassette with previously unreleased tracks. —*William Ruhlmann*

Songs That Got Us Through WW2 / Rhino ✦✦✦✦✦
This excellent collection of songs from the "War Years" includes The Andrews Sisters, Frank Sinatra, the Dorsey Brothers, and Harry James, among others. It's great for the novice. —*Kenneth M. Cassidy*

☆ **The Sullivan Years: Best of Broadway [Original Cast]** / 1992 / TVT ✦✦✦✦✦
This two-disc set collects TV performances of some of Broadway's biggest hits as they were done with original cast members on Broadway. Among the priceless material from shows like *Camelot*, *West Side Story*, and *My Fair Lady* is a bonus interview with Richard Rodgers and Oscar Hammerstein, II (not on the cassette version). —*William Ruhlmann*

● **Teen Idols for a Moment** / 1995 / Collector's Choice Music ✦✦✦✦✦
For every Paul Anka and Frankie Avalon, there was another teen idol with only one or two hits to his credit in the late '50s and early '60s, doing his best to dilute rock 'n' roll for the masses. This 24-song compilation represents a lot of the one- and two-shot artists from the genre, including Mark Dinning, Carl Dobkins, Jr., George Hamilton, IV, Sal Mineo, Eddie Hodges, Tony Orlando (yes, the Dawn guy), Tommy Sands, Dickey Lee, and even more obscure names like Buzz Clifford, Donnie Brooks, and Johnny Ferguson. No, it's not exhibit A in the case to demonstrate rock 'n' roll's vitality during the era; in fact, it's quite the opposite. But there are some cool goofy novelties (Edd Byrnes' "Kookie, Kookie" and Tommy Facenda's "High School, USA."), and the better tunes have a catchy, idiotic cheerfulness that provide guilty pleasure despite themselves (though it's hard to imagine anyone pining to find such dreadfully sappy hits as Mike Clifford's "Close to Cathy" or Dale Ward's "A Letter from Sherry," even for nostalgic purposes). A lot of these tunes are hard to find on CD compilations, and it fills in many gaps missed by Rhino's *The Best of the Teen Idols* compilation, which focuses on the biggest stars of the style. —*Richie Unterberger*

EASY LISTENING

Listening to music can have either a primary or a secondary focus. The musical genre we call easy listening clearly falls into the latter category. Its main function is usually as background music; for example, it can provide a pleasant backdrop for dinner, a romantic evening, or just relaxing. While one can't deny the musical contributions of artists such as Miles Davis, Jimi Hendrix, or Bob Dylan, they are not most people's idea of dinner music. In short, there is a time and a place for everything. Not all music is meant to challenge or stimulate.

Easy listening is comprised of two elements: 1) soft string-laden arrangements of old familiar standards, plus some newer pop tunes, and 2) the vocal stylings of such perennial favorites as Perry Como or Andy Williams, and the lighter fare of artists such as Frank Sinatra, Tony Bennett, and Elvis Presley. Ironically, according to Joel Whitburn's *Top Easy-Listening Records 1961-1974*—which was compiled from *Billboard*'s Easy Listening charts—the No. 1 artist on the chart during this period was Elvis Presley; however, you will not find Elvis listed in the Easy Listening section of this book, as his main musical contributions lie elsewhere. Also, for the sake of conformity, vocalists will be found in the Vocal section. Basically, this section consists of albums that are primarily instrumental, with some including an occasional vocal. Some of the most famous artists here are Liberace, Percy Faith, Lawrence Welk, and Mantovani, whose name is almost synonymous with the term easy listening. If there is one common denominator for most of the artists in this section, it is that they have not created a body of work readily identified with them but have relied mostly on interpreting songs that were proven hits. Two notable exceptions to this are Henry Mancini and Leroy Anderson.

Newer artists in this field, such as Zamfir and Richard Clayderman, have relied heavily on TV advertising and mail-orders to sell their records and establish an identity. The two most likely reasons for this are: 1) most easy listening stations do not announce what they play, and 2) many fans of this music feel uncomfortable walking into the average record store, which clearly caters to the youth market.

The audience for easy listening can perhaps best be described as the parents of the baby-boomers, for they were the main buyers of the music when it was a much more dominant force in the marketplace, and they continue to support it today. But the times are changing. In 1979, *Billboard* changed the name of its Easy Listening Chart to Adult-Contemporary, acknowledging the shift in musical tastes of the baby-boomers themselves. Adult-contemporary, or soft-rock as it is sometimes called, features the familiar soft-rock hits of the last 30 years, and some stations sprinkle new-age instrumentals into the mix. It's a different name but the same concept for a younger generation. The more things change, the more they stay the same. —*Ken Cassidy*

Eden Ahbez

b. Brooklyn, NY, **d.** 1995
Exotica
One of the genuinely strange characters of pre-rock American popular music, Eden Ahbez's main claim to fame was as the composer of "Nature Boy." The melodically and lyrically beguiling song was a huge pop hit for Nat King Cole; it would be covered by many other reputable performers, including Frank Sinatra, John Coltrane, Sarah Vaughan, and the Great Society (Grace Slick's pre-Jefferson Airplane band). But Ahbez's current stature rests on a 1960 album that mixed exotica album and beatnik poetry. It rates as one of the goofiest efforts in the goofy exotica genre—and brother, that's saying something, given the stiff competition. Ahbez boasted a resume as colorful and mysterious as his music. Born Alexander Aberle in Brooklyn in the early 20th century, he changed his name in the '40s shortly after moving to (where else?) California. A hippie a good 20 years before his time, he cultivated a Christ-like appearance with his shoulder-length hair and beard. He claimed to live on three dollars a week, sleeping outdoors with his family, eating vegetables, fruits, and nuts.

Ahbez's big success was getting Nat King Cole to record "Nature Boy," after diligently pestering some of Cole's associates at the Million Dollar Theater in Los Angeles, where Cole was performing. Some of the luster was taken off that triumph when a publishing company claimed that Ahbez had taken some of the lyrics from "Nature Boy" from one of their copyrights, the Yiddish song "Schweig Mein Hertz" (the parties reached an out-of-court settlement). Ahbez did manage to place another tune with Cole, "Land of Love (Come My Love and Live with Me)." In the mid-'50s, he did some recording with jazz musician Herb Jeffries; he also did some occasional composing and singing, sometimes for rock 'n' roll novelty records. His most comprehensive statement as a recording artist, however, was the 1960 LP *The Music of an Enchanted Isle*, which wedded Martin Denny-style exotica to Ahbez's near-stereotypical beatnik poetry. Nat King Cole, for one, claimed that Ahbez's hippie-mystical image was no act. That doesn't mean that his desert-island paradise trip doesn't sound darned silly today. It was ripe for revival by space-age pop aficionados in the '90s, however, and reissued on CD in 1995. Ahbez was photographed with Brian Wilson in the studio in 1966, lending further credence to the theory that the head Beach Boy was influenced by exotica during the *Pet Sounds* and *Smile* sessions. Ahbez died in 1995 after an auto accident. —*Richie Unterberger*

● Eden's Island / 1960 / Del-Fi ✦✦✦

Steve Allen (Stephen Valentine Patrick William Allen)

b. Dec. 21, 1921, New York City, NY
Piano / Easy Listening
Steve Allen is most famous as a comedian and talk show personality (he hosted the original incarnation of "The Tonight Show"), but he was also a piano player and composer. Indeed, he wrote prolifically, and contributed to songs that were performed by Bing Crosby, Nat King Cole, Margaret Whiting, and Louis Armstrong. He also recorded fairly frequently on his own, favoring a sort of cocktail jazz, with occasional journeys into bossa nova and soundtrack-type music. Innocuous if fairly accomplished stuff with debts to jazz pianists like Erroll Garner, it found a new audience in the '90s, when it qualified (fairly loosely) for reassessment as part of the space-age pop/cocktail/lounge revival. —*Richie Unterberger*

● Plays Hi-Fi Music for Influentials / Feb. 27, 1996 / Varese Sarabande ✦✦✦✦
Sixteen tracks selected from albums released between 1957 and 1966. Allen distributes the material fairly evenly between his own compositions and interpretations of standards by the likes of Cole Porter, Johnny Mercer, and Irving Berlin. As cocktail jazz goes, it's very straightahead (though some cuts take a bossa nova approach), and perhaps not eccentric enough to appeal to the lounge revival crowd. —*Richie Unterberger*

Herb Alpert

b. Mar. 31, 1935, Los Angeles, CA
Trumpet / Pop, Jazz, Instrumental Pop
Trumpeter Herb Alpert started in rock 'n' roll, working with Jan & Dean and others. He took a $200 demo of the instrumental "Twinkle Star," overdubbed bullfight crowd noises, and retitled it "The Lonely Bull." It became

his first hit record. Shortly thereafter Alpert formed A&M Records with Jerry Moss as well as a studio group named the Tijuana Brass. The TJB scored consistently on both the single and album charts over the next ten years, with five albums going to No. 1. Alpert's laidback vocal style later found mega-success with the smash "This Guy's in Love with You," trading his original Latin-flavored style for straight MOR. — *Cub Koda*

The Lonely Bull / Dec. 1962 / A&M ✦✦✦
The early breakthrough sound of the TJB featuring the title track and the cream of Los Angeles session players. — *Cub Koda*

Whipped Cream & Other Delights / Apr. 1965 / A&M ✦✦✦✦
Whipped Cream & Other Delights is usually celebrated for its cover, but the music here shouldn't be ignored. It's the first time that Alpert recorded an album full of tunes with crossover potential; it makes perfect sense that it topped the album charts for eight weeks. — *Stephen Thomas Erlewine*

Greatest Hits / Mar. 1970 / A&M ✦✦✦
Herb Alpert & the Tijuana Brass' well-timed *Greatest Hits* album appeared at the start of the '70s, just as the group's star was fading. It may be that Alpert already had in mind a second volume, since several of the album's tracks were not among its successful singles and several of those singles were missing. But the LP did include the Top Ten hits "The Lonely Bull" and "A Taste of Honey," the Top 40 hits "Spanish Flea," "Tijuana Taxi," and "Zorba the Greek," and the chart singles "Mexican Shuffle" and "Whipped Cream," providing a good sampler of what made the Brass such fun in the '60s. — *William Ruhlmann*

Four Sider / Nov. 1973 / A&M ✦✦
When Herb Alpert wound down activity with the Tijuana Brass at the end of the '60s and the beginning of the '70s, his record label, A&M, began releasing hits collections and compilations culled from the group's catalog. First came *Greatest Hits*, then *Solid Brass*, then *Greatest Hits, Vol. 2*, and then this 21-track album, originally released as a double LP (hence the title). Twelve of Alpert's 27 pop chart hits up to this point were included (which was twice as many as you would find on *Greatest Hits*), among them the Top Tens "The Lonely Bull" and "A Taste of Honey," and the chart-topping "This Guy's in Love with You." But most of these songs had turned up on one of the earlier compilations already, not to mention the original albums on which they were featured. The major exception was Alpert's most recent hit at the time, a minor chart entry from Gato Barbieri's theme from the movie *Last Tango in Paris*, which was making its first LP appearance. The music was, as always, pleasant, but the repeated cannibalization of Alpert's catalog was beginning to become a consumer concern. — *William Ruhlmann*

Rise / Sep. 1979 / A&M ✦✦✦✦
On *Rise*, Alpert experimented with a jazz-funk fusion, which resulted in one of his finest albums. On the strength of the hit title track, the album sold over a million copies, making it his most popular record. — *Stephen Thomas Erlewine*

● **Classics, Vol. 1** / Jan. 1987 / A&M ✦✦✦✦
All the high points from the ten-year dominance of Alpert and the Tijuana Brass; includes "A Taste of Honey," "Spanish Flea," and others. — *Cub Koda*

● **Classics, Vol. 2** / Feb. 1987 / A&M ✦✦✦✦
This set features Alpert's solo hits from "This Guy's in Love with You" to "Rise." — *Cub Koda*

Leroy Anderson

b. Jun. 29, 1908, Cambridge, MA, **d.** May 18, 1975
Easy Listening, Orchestral Pop
Leroy Anderson was a light-classical pop composer, most popular in the '40s and '50s. Anderson studied at both the New England Conservatory of Music and Harvard University. At Harvard, he was the orchestral director, choirmaster, and organist for six years, between 1929-1935. Anderson began his musical career in 1935, writing and arranging for the Boston Pops Orchestra and Arthur Fiedler. In 1942, he entered the US Army; four years later, he returned to writing music. The sound effects Anderson incorporated into many of his compositions became his musical signature. Among his most popular songs are the Christmas classic "Sleigh Ride," "The Syncopated Clock" (the old "Late Show" theme), "Blue Tango," and "Forgotten Dreams." Anderson's witty, melodic compositions gained wide acceptance in both pop and classical circles. — *Kenneth M. Cassidy*

★ **Leroy Anderson Collection** / MCA ✦✦✦✦✦
Anderson's best songs appear on this double-disc set, including "Sleigh Ride," "Blue Tango," "Syncopated Clock," and "Forgotten Dreams." — *Kenneth M. Cassidy*

Les Baxter

b. Mar. 14, 1922, Detroit, MI, **d.** 1996
Saxophone / Salsa, Exotica
Les Baxter is a pianist who composed and arranged for the top swing

bands of the '40s and '50s, but he is better known as the founder of exotica, a variation of easy listening that glorified the sounds and styles of Polynesia, Africa, and South America, even as they retained the traditional string-and-horn arrangements of instrumental pop. Exotica became a massively popular trend in the '50s, with thousands of record buyers listening to Baxter, Martin Denny, and their imitators. Baxter also pioneered the use of the electronic instrument the theremin, which has a haunting, howling sound.

Les Baxter studied piano at the Detroit Conservatory and Pepperdine College in Los Angeles. After he completed school, he abandoned the piano and became a vocalist. When he was 23, he joined Mel Torme's Mel-Tones. The group sang on Artie Shaw records, including the hit "What Is This Thing Called Love."

In 1950, he became an arranger and conductor for Capitol Records, working on hits by Nat King Cole, including "Mona Lisa." Around the same time, Baxter began recording his own albums. In 1948, he released a triple-78 album called *Music Out of the Moon*, which ushered in space-age pop with its use of the theremin. Four years later, he began recording exotica albums with *Le Sacre du Sauvage*.

On his early '50s singles Baxter was relatively straightforward, performing versions of standards like the No. 1 hits "Unchained Melody" and "The Poor People of Paris," but on his albums he experimented with all sorts of world musics, adapting them for his orchestra. As he was recording his exotica albums, Baxter was also the musical director for the radio show "Halls of Ivy," plus Abbott & Costello radio shows; he also composed over 100 film scores, concentrating on horror movies and teenage musicals and comedies, though he also did dramas like *Giant*.

Baxter's heyday was in the '50s and '60s. Although he continued to compose and record in the '70s, his output was sporadic. Nevertheless, a cult following formed around his exotica recordings that persisted into the '90s. — *Stephen Thomas Erlewine*

The Lost Episode / 1995 / Dionysus ✦✦✦
Taken from the soundtrack to a 1961 television broadcast, this is a marginal item of Baxter's discography, given more weight by the space-age pop revival of the '90s, and the fact that little of his work is available on CD. At a mere 18 minutes, and with fidelity (from a video transfer) on par with listenable bootlegs, its appeal is mostly limited to Baxter aficionados. Within those parameters, though, it's not bad, including a version of "Quiet Village." Future Bill Evans drummer Larry Bunker handles vibes, blocks, timpani, bongos, and tambourine; singer Beverly Ford closely mimics the sound of the theremin with her astonishing high-pitch frequencies on "Ruby" and "Lover." — *Richie Unterberger*

● **Baxter's Best** / Jun. 25, 1996 / Capitol ✦✦✦✦
This may not be his "best" if you favor his more adventurous and weirder outings; these are the kind of Baxter productions that became building blocks of the easy listening genre. However, these 16 tracks from 1951-1961 are among his most popular successes, including the hits "The Poor People of Paris," "Blue Tango," "Wake the Town and Tell the People," and "Unchained Melody." — *Richie Unterberger*

Exotic Moods of Les Baxter / Jul. 1996 / Capitol ✦✦✦✦
Over the course of two compact discs, *The Exotic Moods of Les Baxter* collects most of Baxter's biggest hits, plus a selection of rare and previously unreleased material. For casual fans, the collection is fine, if a little long—two discs is a lot of Baxter for listeners with a passing interest in exotica. For the more dedicated easy listening/exotica collector, this compilation is useful, if a little frustrating, since much of this material is available on other collections. Still, this gives a good overview of the scope and variety of his music and it emphasizes his wilder, unpredictable side more effectively than *Baxter's Best*. — *Stephen Thomas Erlewine*

Frank Chacksfield

b. May 9, 1914, Battle, Sussex, England, **d.** Jun. 9, 1995
Organ, Piano / Easy Listening, Orchestral Pop
Frank Chacksfield is a pianist and organist who had a series of hit singles in the '50s, most notably with "Ebb Tide."

Chacksfield learned how to play piano as a child. While he was a boy, he was the deputy organist for the local church. Though his parents discouraged him to pursue music as a career, he persevered. In the late '30s, when he was in his mid-20s, he was leading small musical bands in Britain. In 1940, he enlisted in the British army. During the war, he had his first radio broadcast, "Original Songs at the Piano," which originated from Glasgow. Shortly after this broadcast, Chacksfield landed a job as the arranger for Stars in Battledress, a World War II entertainment troupe.

After the war, Chacksfield supported Charlie Chester's comedy group, Stand Easy. The connection with Chester led to Chacksfield's first recording, as the accompanist for Frederick Ferrari, one of Chester's lead singers. During this time, he formed his own group, the Tunesmiths, and conducted orchestras for Henry Hall and Geraldo.

Frank Chacksfield signed with Decca and made his recorded solo debut in the early '50s. Soon, he scored a novelty hit single with "Little

Red Monkey," which climbed to No. 3 on the British charts in the spring of 1953. That summer, he had a Top Ten hit on both sides of the Atlantic with the "Theme from Limelight," which featured a lush, sweeping orchestra. The next year, Chacksfield followed with "Ebb Tide," which replicated the arrangement for "Limelight" and was equally successful. It was his first US hit single, peaking at No. 2.

For the rest of the '50s, Chacksfield released a series of popular instrumental singles, as well as accompanying albums. In the '60s, he had a weekly program on British radio; as he got older, he made the occasional appearance on UK radio shows.

Frank Chacksfield continued to record into the '90s; his last album was *Thanks for the Memories (Academy Award Winners 1934-55)*, which was 1991. —*Stephen Thomas Erlewine*

Ebb Tide / 1960 / Richmond ++++

The New Ebb Tide / 1964 / London +++

● **First Hits of 1965** / 1965 / London ++++

Unmistakable Frank Chacksfield / RIN +++

Richard Clayderman

b. 1954, Paris, France
Piano / Easy Listening
Pianist Richard Clayderman is France's most internationally successful recording star. His grand style has earned him more than 114 gold albums. He offers a mix of classical standards and originals played in soft piano stylings and bathed in soothing strings. —*Michael Erlewine*

A Little Romance / Mar. 29, 1994 / Quality ++++

Unchained Melody / Apr. 12, 1995 / Sony Music Special Prod +++

● **Romance of Richard Clayderman** / Dec. 1, 1995 / Sony Special Products ++++

Ray Conniff

b. Jun. 11, 1916, Attelboro, MA
Trombone / Easy Listening, Orchestral Pop
Conniff came up through the big-band ranks of the late '30s, eventually landing staff work on network TV by the early '50s. Arranging slick pop studio hits for singers Johnnie Ray, Don Cherry, Johnny Mathis, and others, he became most successful with a long series of chorus-laden easy-listening albums for the non-rock 'n' roll market. —*Cub Koda*

Somewhere My Love / 1966 / Columbia +++
The lushest of all Conniff albums, this one features the theme from *Dr. Zhivago*. —*Cub Koda*

Conniff Meets Butterfield / 1978 / Columbia ++++
Showing off a jazzier side to Conniff that recalls his big-band work, this is a nice album with great trumpet work from Billy Butterfield. In and out of print. —*Cub Koda*

★ **16 Most Requested Songs** / 1986 / Columbia +++++
Featuring most of his biggest hits, including "Somewhere, My Love" and "Love Is a Many Splendored Thing," *16 Most Requested Songs* offers a good overview of Ray Conniff's career. Though it isn't as comprehensive as some other discs, it is easy to find and has a representative track selection, making it a good introduction to Conniff. —*Stephen Thomas Erlewine*

☆ **Ray Conniff** / Time Life +++++
Time-Life's *Ray Conniff* disc offers a slightly more comprehensive overview of his career than Columbia's *16 Most Requested Songs*, making it a preferable alternative for those that can track it down. —*Stephen Thomas Erlewine*

Jesse Crawford

b. Dec. 2, 1895, Woodland, CA, d. May 28, 1962, Sherman Oaks, CA
Organ, Piano
Jesse Crawford was one of the most popular organists of the first half of the 20th century. Originally, he was a pianist in a dance band, but he changed his instrument in 1911, choosing to play organ instead. That year, he played a concert at the Spokane Gem Theater, which set him on a circuit of concerts in theaters. In 1918, he became the first organist to play Los Angeles' Grauman's Theater. Crawford continued to perform throughout the '20s, landing a regular job at New York's Paramount Theater in 1926, where he would occasionally perform organ duets with his wife Helen.

In 1925, Jesse Crawford signed a contract with RCA/Victor, which resulted in several hit records—including "Rose Marie," "Russian Lullaby," "At Dawning," "Valencia," and "Roses of Picardy"—between 1925-27. For the rest of the '20s, he performed a series of popular concerts and played background music for radio plays. During the '30s, he led a dance orchestra, in addition to playing his regular concerts.

Crawford continued to record and perform throughout the '40s and '50s. —*Stephen Thomas Erlewine*

● **Wedding Music** / 1980 / MCA ++++

Lenny Dee

Organ / Exotica
Lenny Dee was a versatile organist who enjoyed a Top 20 hit with "Plantation Boogie" in 1955 and recorded a series of albums. He is best known for being able to make his organ sound like a wide variety of other musical instruments.

Dee was born in Illinois, but raised in Florida, where he learned to play piano when he was seven years old. After he began playing the piano, he also learned how to play accordion and banjo. In his late teens, he studied music in Chicago. While he was studying, he began performing concerts on organ; during this time, he perfected his distinctive style.

Dee began touring the US after completing his studies. At a Nashville concert, Red Foley was impressed with his style and brought the organist to Decca Records. Dee signed a contract in the mid-'50s, releasing his first single, "Plantation Boogie," in 1955. The single became a hit, peaking at No. 19. He followed it with his first album, *Dee-lightful!*, which peaked at No. 11. The hits dried up for Dee quickly, though he continued to release records and tour. He returned to the charts in 1968, with his *Gentle on My Mind* album. Two other hit albums followed—*Turn Around*, *Look at Me* (1969), *Spinning Wheel* (1970)—which peaked in the lower reaches of the charts. Dee stopped recording in the mid-'70s. —*Stephen Thomas Erlewine & Kenneth M. Cassidy*

● **Best of Lenny Dee** / MCA ++++

Best of Lenny Dee, Vol. 2 / MCA ++++

Martin Denny

b. 1911
Piano / Easy Listening, Exotica
In the mid-'50s, composer/pianist Denny combined lounge jazz, Hawaiian music, Latin rhythms, bird calls, and then-exotic ethnic instruments like koto, gamelans, and Burmese temple bells into the sound known as exotica. The short-lived craze saw Denny record several popular instrumental albums and hit No. 4 with "Quiet Village," one of the most unusual Top Ten singles of all time, in 1959. Born on the mainland, Denny drew upon his worldwide experiences as a touring musician to conjure a sound that evoked the tranquility and mystery of the South Pacific. Puerto Rican bongo player Augie Colon (who also contributed the bird calls) and vibesman Arthur Lyman (who went on to a successful solo exotica career of his own) were also key elements of Denny's melange. Virtually forgotten for decades, Denny (and exotica itself) has experienced a resurgence of popularity since the mid-'80s, and been cited as an inspiration by a surprising array of alternative musicians. Debates continue to rage as to whether Denny's exotica was inspired genius or ethnic Muzak. —*Richie Unterberger*

★ **Exotica: The Best of Martin Denny** / 1990 / Rhino +++++
Drawing from eight of his late-'50s albums, this 20-track compilation includes everything that all but the truly hard-bitten will need to hear by the "King of Exotica," complete with informative liner notes. Includes "Quiet Village," of course, as well as Denny's only other Top 40 hit, "The Enchanted Sea." —*Richie Unterberger*

Afro-Desia / 1995 / Scamp +++
Nominally, this represents Denny's attempt to evoke the ambience of the African continent, after having done the same for the South Pacific via a series of early albums. Denny does use marimba, vibes, bongos, congas, and timbales—not to mention sound effects of a buzzing tsetse fly and the rainforest. But the result is even less genuinely African (to the nth degree) than, say, Paul Simon's *Graceland*. Not to mention that the Randy Van Horne Singers, who contribute backing vocals (as they did for the Flintstones and Jetsons cartoons), were probably about as authentically African as a Disneyland voodoo doll. Denny never pretended to offer a genuinely ethnic experience, though. This is, despite any impressions generated by the title, more exotica music, pure and simple. There isn't much Denny on CD, but almost everyone will be content to pick up the Rhino best-of (which admittedly only duplicates a few cuts from *Afro-Desia*) and leave it at that. —*Richie Unterberger*

Bachelor in Paradise / 1996 / Pair +++
Misleading, this is subtitled "The Best of Martin Denny"; Rhino's *Best of Martin Denny* is a much more accurate representation of his most notable work. If you do want more Denny after you've finished digesting the Rhino set, this 20-track disc is a good collection to have. It duplicates little from the Rhino set (though "Quiet Village," of course, is here), going a bit heavier on Denny's interpretations of standards like "A Taste of Honey," "Ebb Tide," and "Cast Your Fate to the Wind." —*Richie Unterberger*

Robert Drasnin

Clarinet, Flute, Sax (Alto)
Drasnin has a host of television composition under his belt, including

work for "Lost in Space," "Playhouse 90," "The Man from U.N.C.L.E.," "Mission Impossible," and "The Twilight Zone." From 1977 until the early '90s, he was the Director of Music for CBS Entertainment. Before all of that, he played alto, clarinet, and flute in the jazz bands of such leaders as Tommy Dorsey and Red Norvo. His current status as an *artiste*, however, rests upon an album that he might have considered a trifle at the time. *Voodoo*, issued around the late '50s on the tiny Tops label, closely approximated the exotica sound of Martin Denny—under, apparently, instructions from the Tops A&R chief himself. Drasnin devised a satisfying approximation of Denny's tropical-Latin-lounge jazz hybrid, in somewhat of a more low-key fashion than Denny himself. Indeed, Drasnin later arranged Denny's *Latin Village* album. The rare *Voodoo* LP was reissued on CD in 1996. — *Richie Unterberger*

Voodoo / Feb. 13, 1996 / Dionysus ◆◆◆
Exotica fans will treat the reissue of this super-rare album as a Holy Grail of sorts, akin to, say, the re-release of a highly rated, locally pressed '60s rock LP by garage band collectors. The rest of you are probably better off sticking with the Martin Denny best-of, if you get that far. In other words, if you swoon over Martin Denny, you're not going to be disappointed with this somewhat more sedate and dignified effort; otherwise, you'll find it competent but superfluous. — *Richie Unterberger*

Esquivel

b. Jan. 20, 1918, Tampico, Mexico
Piano / Exotica, Space-Age Pop
In the mid-'90s, Juan Garcia Esquivel enjoyed one of the most unexpected resurgences of popularity—and hipness—in the annals of 20th-century pop. The composer and arranger skirted the lines between lounge music, eccentric experimentalism, and stereo sound pioneer in the late '50s and early '60s on a series of albums aimed at the easy-listening market. Both cheesy and goofily unpredictable, these records were forgotten by all but thrift-store habitues for decades. With the space-age pop/exotica revival of the mid-'90s, however, Esquivel was not just being rediscovered, but was being championed as a cutting-edge innovator by certain segments of the hipper-than-thou alternative crowd.

Esquivel (in the manner of Dion or Melanie, he billed himself with a single name) actually enjoyed a long and varied career, of which his space-age pop recordings were only a portion. Born in a small Mexican village, the pianist became a popular performer on a Mexican radio station, and studied briefly at Julliard in New York. The radio (and later television and film) work actually gave him valuable experience in the art of quickly devising varied background music and orchestral arrangements, which he'd put to good use when he began recording for RCA in the late '50s.

This was the era in which stereo albums were first starting to be marketed. Esquivel—along with several other of "space-age pop's" leading lights—took advantage of this development to use his albums as laboratories of sorts to explore the spectrum of recorded sound, as reflected in LP titles like *Other Worlds, Other Sounds*, and *Four Corners of the World*. He employed then-exotic instruments such as the theremin, the ondioline, early Fender-Rhodes keyboards, Chinese bells, bass accordion, and boo-bams (a 24-bongo kit tuned to F) to get what he wanted.

What kept Esquivel from serious critical appreciation at the time are, perhaps, the same factors that exert a strange fascination upon listeners of the '90s. In its form and content, Esquivel's material was lightweight martini-mixing fare, more geared toward suburban easy listening than challenging innovation. He threw in just enough sly, oddball quirks, however, to make one wonder whether he was in fact deftly satirizing the form, or at least using it as a forum to slip in some unbridled zaniness. Chipper whitebread background chorus singers will slip into strange nonsense syllables like "boink, boink." Weird instrumental flourishes add unpredictable tension to bathetic easy-listening instrumentals, sometimes almost jarring the listener from the state of bland relaxation for which the records were purportedly designed. The strains of cha-chas and mambos (then in vogue among much of mainstream America) run through much of his work, though in a much more loungish vein than what you would find in sweaty Havana ballrooms. Tempos and arrangements change with unnerving frequency and charge forward with unsettling manic energy, though never so often that the music sounds more experimental than pop.

So when post-moderns tired of punk, grunge, and industrial music, and needed some suitably different (but still ironic) music to chill out to in their dank clubs and cafes, they turned to forgotten artists such as Esquivel. The man himself had passed his heyday as a recording artist after the early '60s. He remained active for years with his live act (Frank Sinatra was a fan of Esquivel's Las Vegas sets) and television and film scores. By the '90s, he was confined to a wheelchair in his brother's home in Mexico, the victim of numerous back injuries. He wasn't so ill that he couldn't be interviewed, however. His lengthy profile in the first volume of the *Incredibly Strange Music* book kicked off the Esquivel revival in earnest. 1995 suddenly saw Esquivel reissues flooding the market (at

least three appeared that year, with more apparently on the way). Respected alternative figureheads like John Zorn and R.E.M. sang his praises. Esquivel was no longer gathering mold in the attic—he was the epitome of hip.

As is the case with other space-age pop heroes such as Martin Denny, some listeners will be dumbfounded, or even angered, by the current appeal enjoyed by Esquivel. His work will never be treated with respect by the "serious" music community; his music is too consciously geared toward light entertainment for that. And just as one wonders whether Esquivel was mixing irony and entertainment in his recordings, one wonders whether some current Esquivel fans are championing his cause out of a desire to be more jaded-than-thou. Do they groove to his sounds precisely *because* Esquivel's records sound so ridiculously outdated, or simply because they want to become hip by attaching themselves to the most unfashionable music possible? Easy answers are not forthcoming, but Esquivel isn't complaining. In fact, he's become something of the spokesperson emeritus for the whole space-age pop craze, conducting regular interviews for national publications from his Mexico bed, and hoping to eventually recover some of his mobility. — *Richie Unterberger*

More of Other Worlds, Other Sounds / 1962 / Reprise ◆◆
More of Other Worlds, Other Sounds isn't as space age as the title suggests. It is one of Esquivel's more serious works, featuring subdued orchestration and few of the effects and affectations that made him a cult figure. There are some good moments on the album, but it is a record designed for contemplative listening—in other words, it's not much fun. — *Stephen Thomas Erlewine*

★ **Space Age Bachelor Pad Music** / 1994 / Bar/None ◆◆◆◆◆
Esquivel was one of the most interesting easy-listening composers of the '50s and '60s, creating open, futuristic sonic landscapes. Part of his music's appeal is its pure campiness; "Mucha Muchacha," with its bad puns and exaggerated Latin rhythms and vocals, is hilarious. *Space Age Bachelor Pad Music*, a collection of his "greatest hits," makes it apparent that the humor is at least partially intentional. Using dissonance and aural humor, along with intricately structured arrangements, Esquivel created records that were indeed "space-age bachelor pad music"—they sounded out of this world and they swung. The music may sound dated, but it also sounds peculiarly fresh; no one made music like this then, and no one makes music like this now. — *Stephen Thomas Erlewine*

Music from a Sparkling Planet / 1995 / Bar/None ◆◆◆◆
Bar/None's second collection of Esquivel tracks from the '60s, *Music from a Sparkling Planet* isn't quite as infectiously listenable as *Space Age Bachelor Pad Music*, containing nothing quite as mind-bending as the best moments of the first compilation. Nevertheless, there is plenty of wonderful music found on the album, even though most of it sounds like pleasant soundtrack or elevator music, devoid of much of the quirkiness that fueled *Space Age*. — *Stephen Thomas Erlewine*

Cabaret Manana / Nov. 1995 / RCA ◆◆◆◆
Esquivel's output is pretty diverse, yet it's hard to rate one compilation against another. They're of such a similar qualitative standard that none can be singled out as definitive, or even recommended above the others. *Cabaret Manana* is as good as any a place to start (and no worse or better than the compilations on Bar/None). The 20 tracks are drawn from RCA releases spanning 1958 to 1967, including both original compositions and oddball versions of standards like "Harlem Nocturne," "Night and Day," "Malaguena," and "Take the 'A' Train." Whether this rings your chimes or not, it's certainly different, unpredictable, and full of idiosyncratic touches like whistlers, berserk organ solos, choruses of "zu-zu" vocals, Bugs Bunny cartoon slide guitar, and sassy horn sections that blow with an energy more savage than anything else you'll hear on "easy" listening recordings. — *Richie Unterberger*

Percy Faith

b. 1908, d. 1976
Piano / Easy Listening
Percy Faith was one of the most popular film composers and easy-listening recording artists of the '50s and '60s. Not only did he have a number of hit albums and singles under his own name, but Faith was responsible for arranging hits by Tony Bennett, Doris Day, Johnny Mathis, and Burl Ives, among others as the musical director for Columbia Records in the '50s.

Born and raised in Toronto, Canada, Faith was a child piano prodigy, giving his first recital at Massey Hall at the age of 15 and playing various movie theaters, providing the soundtrack to silent films. His career as a concert pianist was cut short when he injured his hands in a fire when he was 18. Faith moved into arranging, beginning with local hotel orchestras but quickly moving to radio. It was here where he developed his lush pop-instrumental style. For most of the '30s, he worked for Canadian Broadcast Company. At the end of the decade his radio show, "Music by Faith," was also being aired within the US.

Upset with CBC slashing the budget of his program, Faith moved to Chicago in 1940. Shortly afterward, he relocated to New York; by 1945, he had become an official US citizen. Working for NBC in New York, he arranged and conducted for a number of shows and singers, including Coca-Cola's radio show and Buddy Clark. During the late '40s, he recorded for both Decca and RCA Victor.

Faith joined Columbia Records as musical director and a recording artist in 1950. While he arranged traditional pop songs, as well as show tunes and folk songs for the label's vocalists, Faith became a pioneer of easy-listening "mood music" with his own albums. In addition to popularizing the light, orchestrated pop, he was the first to record albums solely consisting of songs from Broadway shows; he also was one of the first mainstream composers/arrangers to experiment with Latin rhythms.

Percy Faith had his first No. 1 single, "Song from the Moulin Rouge (Where Is Your Heart)," in 1953. In the mid-'50s, he began composing film scores, beginning with the Oscar-nominated collaboration with Georgie Stoll, *Love Me or Leave Me*. His most successful score was for the 1960 film *A Summer Place*. The "Theme to *A Summer Place*"became a No. 1 hit and earned him his first Grammy.

As rock 'n' roll took over popular music in the early '60s and his work became more schlocky in format (easy-listening arrangements of Beatles and pop-rock songs, etc.), the musical quotient remained high, thanks in large part to Faith's arranging skills and penchant for picking good material. Faith slowly withdrew from a professional career in the late '60s, releasing his last album in 1970. —*Stephen Thomas Erlewine & Cub Koda*

★ **16 Most Requested Songs** / 1978 / Columbia ✦✦✦✦✦
Featuring hits like "Theme from a Summer Place," *16 Most Requested Songs* is an excellent sampler of Percy Faith's biggest hits and an effective introduction to his career. —*Stephen Thomas Erlewine*

Percy Faith / Time Life ✦✦✦✦
Time-Life's *Percy Faith* collection offers a slightly more comprehensive overview of Faith's career than *16 Most Requested Songs*, but it is a bit more difficult to track down. For those who can find it, it is a preferable alternative. —*Stephen Thomas Erlewine*

Ferrante & Teicher

Easy Listening
A piano duo, Arthur Ferrante and Louis Teicher met while both were studying at Juilliard in the late '40s. After years of being guests in front of large orchestras and cutting several cleverly arranged duo albums, they hit their stride in the early '60s with a string of lush orchestrated hit singles and albums based around their interlocking piano style. —*Cub Koda*

★ **Greatest Hits** / 1965 / Curb ✦✦✦✦✦
Curb's *Greatest Hits* is a budget-line collection that contains Ferrante & Teicher's greatest hits, including "Theme from the Apartment," "Exodus," "Tonight," "Lisa," and "Midnight Cowboy," as well as five other tracks. It's a brief collection, but it gives a good sense of what their easy listening was all about. —*Stephen Thomas Erlewine*

West Side Story & Other Motion Picture & Broadway Hits / United Artists ✦✦✦✦
Despite the unwieldy title, some of their best work. —*Cub Koda*

● **10th Anniversary: Golden Piano Hits** / United Artists ✦✦✦✦
Theme from "The Apartment" / United Artists ✦✦✦✦
Their breakthrough album, both in chart success and the establishment of the orchestrated formula that would carry them through the '60s. —*Cub Koda*

Arthur Fiedler

b. Dec. 17, 1894, Boston, MA, **d.** Jul. 10, 1979, Brookline, MA
Arthur Fiedler, the conductor of the internationally known Boston Pops Orchestra, has introduced much of America to classical music, if only on the lighter side. He has recorded dozens of albums over the years; most of them make excellent easy-listening music. —*Michael Erlewine*

● **Fiedler's Greatest Hits** / RCA Victor ✦✦✦✦

James Galway

Flute / Easy Listening
James Galway gained fame as one of Ireland's most popular flautists in the late '70s. Over the next two decades, Galway's smooth, lightly Celtic instrumental stylings were internationally popular, selling numerous records and earning him several awards.

Galway began playing music with penny whistles and mouth organs as a child, soon moving to flute. At the age of ten, he was the winner of all three classes of the Irish Flute Championships, which earned him a BBC radio session, as well as a spot in the Belfast Youth Orchestra. Galway earned scholarships first at London's Guildhall School of Music, then the

Paris Conservatoire; he would occasionally busk on the subways to earn extra money.

After spending some time at Sadlers Wells, Galway became the Berlin Philharmonic's principal flautist in 1969. His time with the orchestra was popular, which led his manager, Michael Emerson, to persuade the flautist to go solo in 1975. Galway was instantly successful as a solo artist, both as a live performer and a recording artist. He was soon playing 120 concerts a year, as well as recording both classical and popular albums. In 1978, his version of John Denver's "Annie's Song" became an international hit. While his pop recordings were commercially successful, his classical albums were warmly received by critics and peers alike, as his records of Mozart and Vivaldi compositions won awards.

Though he wasn't able to replicate the success of "Annie's Song" in the '80s, he continued to sell out concerts around the world well into the '90s and his infrequent records have proven nearly as successful. —*Stephen Thomas Erlewine*

Celtic Minstrel / Jan. 30, 1996 / RCA ✦✦✦
James Galway's collection of Irish songs is a pleasant album, but it will appeal more to fans of his smooth style than Celtic aficionados. —*Sara Sytsma*

● **Greatest Hits** / RCA ✦✦✦✦
Although there are a couple of tracks missing, *Greatest Hits* has the majority of James Galway's best-loved numbers and offers a good introduction to the popular flautist. —*Sara Sytsma*

Jackie Gleason (Herbert John Gleason)

b. Feb. 26, 1916, **d.** Jun. 24, 1987
Vocals / Easy Listening
Not only was he one of the finest comedians America has ever produced, Jackie Gleason applied his prodigious talents to music as well. With a strong jazz roots background (leaning to mesmerized idolatry when dealing with good trumpet players), Gleason developed a chart-topping series of mood music albums in the '50s, citing his reason for their existence: "Every time I ever watched Clark Gable do a love scene in the movies, I'd hear pretty, really pretty music, real romantic, come up behind him and help set the mood. So I'm figuring that if Clark Gable needs that kinda help, then a guy in Canarsie has gotta be dyin' for somethin' like this!"

Gleason began making films in the '40s, but he rose to stardom in the early '50s, thanks to the late '40s/early '50s television series "The Life of Riley" and "Cavalcade of Stars." His television stardom led to a contract with Capitol Records, who released his first album, *Music for Lovers Only*, in 1953. As a musician, Gleason favored lush, dramatically orchestrated instrumentals, patterned after the mood music of Paul Weston. Gleason wasn't a trained musician, but he was responsible for the musical direction of his records; when he did write a piece, he would dictate to someone who could read and write music.

Music for Lovers Only was a surprise hit, selling over 500,000 copies. Every subsequent Gleason album was a major hit, reaching the Top Ten and selling a large number of copies. Gleason continued to release albums into the '60s, but his popularity dipped dramatically after 1957. After that year, he no longer was able to make it into the Top 15, even though his records continued to appear in the lower regions of the charts.

Gleason's records have continued to be popular cult items and they have come to be regarded as definitive mood music albums. —*Cub Koda & Stephen Thomas Erlewine*

Night Winds/Music to Make You / 1953 / Capitol ✦✦✦✦
Gleason's late-night-and-lonely album, lush and emotional, all the right feelings in place. Excellent, though out of print. —*Cub Koda*

● **Best of Jackie Gleason** / 1993 / Capitol/Curb ✦✦✦✦
Although the track selection is skimpy and there are no liner notes to speak of, *The Best of Jackie Gleason* is an effective, inexpensive introduction to his lush, romantic music, featuring a good cross-section of his Capitol hits. —*Stephen Thomas Erlewine*

And Awaaay We Go! / 1996 / Scamp ✦✦✦
Divided about equally between easy-listening orchestral works and comedy routines, with the latter decidedly outshining the former. On the musical side, "Melancholy Serenade" is here, as well as some familiar themes from "The Honeymooners," one of which is built around Gleason's famous "One of These Days—Pow!" schticks. Highlights of the comedy routines include Gleason's recitation of "Casey at the Bat" and his "Reggie Van Gleason III" character. The music means virtually nothing to anyone except "Honeymooners" fanatics, and as for the comedy, it's a lot funnier to see Gleason's characters than only hear the dialog. —*Richie Unterberger*

Champagne, Candlelight and Kisses / Capitol ✦✦✦
Not enough Os in smooth to describe this one; everything the title implies and more. —*Cub Koda*

Movie Themes: For Lovers Only / Capitol ✦✦✦
Gleason conducting double string orchestra with jazz soloists Charlie Ventura and Pee Wee Irwin, interpreting a dozen film-score melodies with typically lush Gleason results. Uniformly excellent. —*Cub Koda*

For Lovers Only / CEMA/GSC ✦✦✦✦
A three-disc set that draws from his mood music albums of the late '50s, *For Lovers Only* features 40 of Jackie Gleason's finest romantic pieces. Although the running time of the three discs is relatively short, all the music is first rate and this mail-order-only package is the most comprehensive Gleason package currently available. —*Stephen Thomas Erlewine*

Bert Kaempfert

d. Jun. 21, 1980
Easy Listening, Orchestral Pop
A band whose sound and selections put them much more in the arena of middle-of-the-road music than in jazz, though they're loved by many of the same people who enjoy Lawrence Welk and Glenn Miller. They have absolutely no influence or importance from an innovative standpoint, but have managed to retain a sizable following and are heard religiously on Music of Your Life stations and Muzak outlets. —*Ron Wynn*

● **Very Best of Bert Kaempfert** / TAR ✦✦✦✦
The Very Best of Bert Kaempfert collects 16 of the easy-listening composer's biggest hits, including "Red Roses for a Blue Lady," "Spanish Eyes (Moon over Naples)," and "Three O'Clock in the Morning." Not all of his hits are included, but it is the best American CD collection available of Kaempfert's singles. —*Stephen Thomas Erlewine*

Andre Kostelanetz

b. Dec. 23, 1901, St. Petersburg, Russia, **d.** 1980, US
Easy Listening, Orchestral Pop
Andre Kostelanetz arranged classical pieces as easy-listening numbers, bringing the music to a broad, middle-brow audience that wouldn't normally have listened to the music. In the process, he inadvertently invented easy-listening music. Kostelanetz grasped the power of radio and he adapted his arrangements to fit the conventions of mass communications.

Kostelanetz began performing music in his childhood as a member of the Petrograd choir. He would eventually become leader of the choir. In 1922, he moved to the US. Initially, he didn't find jobs as a conductor/arranger, so he had to perform as an accompanist. In 1924, Kostelanetz made his radio debut, conducting an orchestra.

In the '30s, he assembled a 65-piece orchestra, which happened to be the largest orchestra broadcast on radio, for the national show "Andre Kostelanetz Presents." By the mid-'30s, he was one of the most popular radio stars in the US, as evidenced by the sheer number of awards he won and polls he topped. In 1943, a poll of US and Canadian audiences commended him for his support for popular and serious music.

Not only was he popular, he was quite innovative as well. Kostelanetz understood the potential of recording as a way to expose mass audiences to music. Consequently, he also grasped the technological necessities of recording, and helped promote the value of recording engineers. But his most noteworthy technological advance was his invention of a mechanical tuning instrument, which told musicians whether they were in pitch or not. The device was adapted by the military and used as a way to track submarines.

Kostelanetz never lost his popularity, even as musical styles shifted dramatically over the next four decades. Over the course of his career, he sold over 52 million records. The arranger continued to interpret classical pieces, as well as show tunes and popular songs, until his death in 1980. —*Stephen Thomas Erlewine*

● **16 Most Requested Songs** / 1972 / Columbia ✦✦✦✦
Meet Andre Kostelanetz / Columbia ✦✦✦✦
Early-'50s compilation of material, showcasing Kostelanetz's best arrangements of material by Gershwin, Porter, Jerome Kern, and Vincent Youmans. —*Cub Koda*

The Beautiful Music of Tchaikovsky / Columbia ✦✦✦
The classical side of Kostelanetz, and at the time of its 23-song production the most comprehensive Tchaikovsky album ever done. —*Cub Koda*

Erich Kunzel

Easy Listening
Classically trained conductor who has also worked extensively in the jazz and pop fields. He has collaborated with Dave Brubeck, Duke Ellington, Ella Fitzgerald, and many others. In 1977, he founded the Cincinnati Pops Orchestra and has since made many pop recordings with them. —*Kenneth M. Cassidy*

● **Big Band Hit Parade** / 1988 / Telarc ✦✦✦✦
Fiesta! / 1990 / Telarc ✦✦✦

The Magical Music Of Disney / 1995 / Telarc ✦✦✦
Andrew Lloyd Webber / Jan. 30, 1996 / Telarc ✦✦✦
Featuring a selection of Andrew Lloyd Webber's most popular songs—including numbers from *Cats, Evita, Sunset Boulevard*, and *Phantom of the Opera*—this recording of Erich Kunzel conducting the Cincinnati Pops is a pleasant disc, though it isn't as compelling or rewarding as the original cast recordings of the shows. —*Sara Sytsma*

Chiller / Telarc ✦✦✦✦

James Last

Bass / Easy Listening
James Last is a German big-band leader with a large fan base in Europe, although he has never had a comparable following in the US. Last's trademark is arranging pop hits in a big-band style; his series of "party albums" is equally well known. Over the course of his career, he has sold well over 50 million albums.

Last learned how to play piano as a child, switching to bass as a teenager. He joined Hans-Gunther Oesterreich's Radio Bremen Dance Orchestra in 1946, when he was 17 years old. In 1948, he became the leader of the Becker-Last Ensemble, which performed for seven years. During that time, he was voted the best bassist in the country by a German jazz poll for three consecutive years, from 1950-1952. After the disbandment of the Becker-Last Ensemble, he became the in-house arranger for Polydor Records, as well as for a number of European radio stations. For the next decade, he helped arrange hits for artists like Helmut Zacharias and Caterina Valente.

Last released his first album, *Non-Stop Dancing*, in 1965. The record consisted of brief renditions of popular songs, all tied together by an insistent dance beat and joyous crowd noises. It was a hit and helped make him a major European star. Over the next two decades, Last released over 50 records, including several more volumes of *Non-Stop Dancing*. On these records, he varied his formula by adding different songs from different countries and genres, as well as guest performers like Richard Clayderman and Astrud Gilberto.

Though his concerts and albums were consistently successful—especially in England, where he had 52 hit albums between 1967-86, which made him second to Elvis Presley in terms of number of charting records—he only had one hit single with "The Seduction," the theme from *American Gigolo* (1980). —*Stephen Thomas Erlewine*

● **Romantic Dreams** / Polydor ✦✦✦✦

Liberace (Wladziu Valentino Liberace)

b. 1919, **d.** Feb. 4, 1987
Piano / Easy Listening
Liberace (born Wladziu Valentino Liberace) was the most flamboyant, popular easy-listening pianist of the '60s and '70s by a wide margin. His campy, theatrical appearance and performances often disguised his prodigious talent.

Liberace was a child prodigy born to a musical family. His father, Salvatore, played French horn in John Philip Sousa's Concert Band, as well as the Milwaukee Symphony Orchestra. Instead of following in his father's footsteps and playing horn, Liberace decided to play piano instead. Liberace was exceptionally gifted at piano, earning strong words of praise from Ignace Paderewski, which helped him land a scholarship at the Wisconsin College of Music at the age of seven; he retained his scholarship for 17 years, the longest period of time in the history of the academy. When he was 11, he debuted as a concert soloist. When he was in his teens, he was performing with symphony orchestras.

Instead of following the accepted path of classical recitals and university courses, Liberace chose to be a showman. At encores at his concerts, he began playing novelty songs like "Mairzy Doats." To ensure that he had widespread appeal as an entertainer, he took elocution lessons in order to mask his Polish accent.

During World War II, Liberace performed in a variety of overseas entertainment units. When he came back to America, he began performing in clubs, playing and singing with dance bands. While he was on the club circuit, he began performing under the sole name of Liberace.

In 1940, he moved to New York City, where he became a fixture on the club circuits. However, his stint in New York wasn't particularly successful, as the Musicians Union banned the pianist after he began playing counterpoints to certain records played over the club's sound system. Undaunted, Liberace moved to California. While he was playing at a local hotel, he was spotted by Decca Record executives who offered him a contract. Decca attempted to make Liberace into a big-band leader, but it was unsuccessful. In the late '40s, he signed with Columbia Records and, under the direction of producer Mitch Miller, recorded an over-the-top rendition of "September Song." Along with a live concert album, the single helped bring Liberace to a national audience.

Liberace became a star in the '50s, both through his records and assorted television and film appearances. His appearance and repertoire were becoming increasingly campy, as he dressed himself in rhinestone, gold lamé, furs, and sequins while playing everything from Gershwin and show tunes to lounge jazz and light classical pieces, with a candelabra placed on his piano. Liberace's star rose rapidly in the early '50s, as he had his own television show, appropriately titled "The Liberace Show." His celebrity reached a peak in the mid-'50s. Not only did he star in the 1955 film *Sincerely Yours,* a movie about a deaf concert pianist, but he was mentioned in "Mr. Sandman" by the Chordettes and he published his own cookbook. In 1956, Liberace celebrated his 25 years in show business with an extravagant concert at the Hollywood Bowl. That same year, he made some headway in the UK market, playing three Royal Command Performances.

Though it was a heady time for the pianist, 1956 was also the year that his star began to dim somewhat. Cassandra, a columnist for the English tabloid *The Daily Mirror,* inferred that Liberace was homosexual. He sued the paper and won, yet he still made an effort to tone down his appearance. However, the public didn't want a subdued Liberace and he reverted to his kitschy showmanship in the early '60s.

Liberace didn't have any more pop hits in the '60s, '70s, and '80s, yet he continued to sell out concerts around the world and sell a number of records, even though he never earned the favor of the critics. In 1982, a former chauffeur and bodyguard sued the pianist for palimony; the case was settled out of court. Liberace remained a celebrity and a popular performer until his death in 1987. *—Stephen Thomas Erlewine*

● **The Best of Liberace** / 1972 / MCA ✦✦✦✦
This is an excellent sampler that showcases the flamboyant, semiclassical style of the pianist, including "Schubert's Serenade." *—David Szatmary*

16 Most Requested Songs / 1990 / Columbia ✦✦✦

Enoch Light

Exotica
Enoch Light was a popular bandleader of the '40s and '50s, who is best known for his *Persuasive Percussion* and *Provocative Percussion* albums of the mid-'50s, which were some of the first albums to exploit the capabilities of stereo recording and 35mm film as a recording device.

During the '30s, he headed the Enoch Light and the Light Brigade big band. The Light Brigade primarily played in theaters and on the radio, although they also toured Europe. The band also managed a hit in 1937 with "Summer Night," which was sung by Johnny Muldowney.

After the Light Brigade disbanded, Light became a session musician, playing on various records and radio broadcasts, including "Hit Parade." During the '40s, he recorded versions of popular hits for budget labels, for sale in discount stores.

Enoch Light's career bounced back in the late '60s, when the Charleston City All-Stars, under his direction, had a series of hit albums entitled *Roaring Twenties.* After their success, he founded the Command record label, which gave him an outlet for his sonically adventurous records. Light happened to begin the label around the time stereo became widely available, and he exploited the new technology to its fullest, creating albums that used the full sonic spectrum of stereo. The first of these albums were *Persuasive Percussion* and *Provocative Percussion,* and they were wildly popular, charting in the American Top Ten. One of the most notable features of these albums was their "ping-pong stereo," which featured the music jumping from the left speaker to the right, and vice versa. During this time, Light and Command also pioneered the use of 35mm film as a recording method instead of tape.

Light remained the managing director of Command until 1965. While he was the head of the label, he recorded classical albums, big-band records, and collections of film themes. After 1965, Command was bought out by ABC Records who, in turn, was quickly bought out by MCA Records. MCA made Command into a budget label, pressing the albums on poor vinyl and putting them into discount stores. By 1970, the label was no longer profitable and MCA shut it down. Light continued working, both as an arranger/conductor and the head of Project 3 Records. His activity slowed in the '70s, though he did continue to record. Enoch Light died on July 31, 1978. *—Stephen Thomas Erlewine*

★ **Persuasive Percussion, Vol. 1** / 195_ / Command ✦✦✦✦✦
Persuasive Percussion, Vol. 1, collects a number of tracks featuring layers of exotic percussion. Primarily, this record—like its companion, *Provocative Percussion*—was designed to showcase hi-fi equipment, but its weird, inventive polyrhythms made it a cult favorite. *—Stephen Thomas Erlewine*

☆ **Provocative Percussion** / 195_ / Varese Sarabande ✦✦✦✦✦
Like *Persuasive Percussion, Provocative Percussion* essentially consists of layers of percussion—though these are actual songs, they are performed on xylophones and marimbas. Over the years, the album became a kitsch classic, but the polyrhythms on *Provocative Percussion* are actually quite inventive. On the whole, *Provocative* is the more listenable album, but both records are high-water marks of '50s space-age pop. *—Stephen Thomas Erlewine*

Guy Lombardo

b. Jun. 19, 1902, **d.** Nov. 5, 1977
Vocals / Easy Listening
"The Sweetest Music This Side of Heaven" was the logo of Guy Lombardo and His Royal Canadians, who by 1930 had established themselves as America's top dance band. Unfairly lumped in with unswinging "mickey mouse" bands of the era, the music of Lombardo's outfit was actually top-notch, and they were constantly cited by Louis Armstrong as his favorite band for their purity of intonation. A cache of early sides for Gennett reveals that the band was capable of playing "hot" any time they wanted to, but sweet music and singing novelties featuring brother Carmen is what the public wanted, and Lombardo failed to disappoint. He became a national institution hosting televised New Year's Eve broadcasts from New York, making his rendition of "Auld Lang Syne" part of our national memory chest and his lasting legacy.

Guy Lombardo began his musical career in 1924, when he and his brothers Lebert, Carmen, and Victor—who joined slightly later—formed a big dance band. Originally, Guy was a violinist for the band, but he soon became its leader and conductor. The band received a moderate amount of success in Canada and soon went to the US, where they landed a regular gig in Cleveland, OH. While they were performing in Cleveland, they began using the name Guy Lombardo and His Royal Canadians. After their Cleveland engagement, they moved to Chicago and then New York City, which became their home base after a successful stay at the Roosevelt Grill.

Lombardo and His Royal Canadians played numerous radio broadcasts from New York and they began a long string of hits in 1927 that ran all the way to 1954. By the early '30s, Lombardo was an international celebrity, having hit records and appearing in films like *Many Happy Returns.* During this time, not only Lombardo's records were massively popular, but so were his radio broadcasts; it was his annual New Year's Eve show that made "Auld Lang Syne" a national standard. Lombardo also became a well-known speedboat racer during the '40s and, in fact, won many awards for his skills, including a National Championship in the late '40s.

Between 1927 and 1954, Lombardo and His Royal Canadians sold well over 100 milllion records on a variety of labels, including Columbia, Brunswick, Decca, and RCA/Victor; it's estimated that his total worldwide record sales ranged between 100 and 300 million copies. In 1954, Lombardo assumed the operation of the Marine Theatre, located at New York's Jones Beach. At the Marine Theatre, he staged a number of musical revues that were very popular. Lombardo continued to lead these musical productions until his death in 1977. *—Cub Koda & Stephen Thomas Erlewine*

Legendary Performer / RCA ✦✦✦
A nice selection of middle-period material in straightahead mono. *—Cub Koda*

Guy Lombardo Medleys / Capitol ✦✦✦
The first volume in a continuing series, featuring nice bandstand medleys done in the typical Lombardo fashion with nice fidelity. *—Cub Koda*

★ **The Best of Guy Lombardo** / Capitol/Curb ✦✦✦✦✦
All the hits, including the legendary "Boo Hoo." *—Cub Koda*

Arthur Lyman

Guitar, Piano, Bongos, Conga, Vibes
As the vibraphonist for Martin Denny's group, Lyman was instrumental in crafting the sound of exotica. Lyman didn't stay with Denny for long, however, leaving the ensemble in 1957 to start a solo career that was nearly as successful as Denny's. To no one's surprise, Lyman's albums sounded very much like Denny's, with even more of a somnambulant feel. Much of the public wanted to relax, though, and they sent his debut, *Taboo,* to No. 6 in the album charts in 1958. In addition to playing vibes on his group's recordings, Lyman also played some guitar, piano, and drums, as well as paying careful attention to using stereophonic sound.

Lyman also had a few hit singles, with "Taboo" and "Love for Sale" reaching the middle of the charts, and "Yellow Bird" (the only big exotica hit besides Denny's "Quiet Village") making No. 4 in 1961. Like Denny (though to a lesser extent), Lyman experienced a resurgence in popularity in the '90s, when the space-age pop revival made it acceptable to drag out his old LPs and sit in tiki bars again. *—Richie Unterberger*

Exotic Sound of Arthur Lyman Group / 1979 / DCC ✦✦✦✦

The Best of the Arthur Lyman Group / 1996 / DCC ✦✦✦
For those that are hooked on Martin Denny and want something similar—or, for those who find Martin Denny just a tad too upbeat and extroverted. This has 18 of Lyman's vintage tracks, including the modest hits "Taboo" and "Love for Sale." Oddly, his Top Ten single "Yellow Bird" is missing, although it's on DCC's *More of the Best of the Arthur Lyman Group. —Richie Unterberger*

● **More of the Best of the Arthur Lyman Group** / 1996 / DCC ♦♦♦♦
When you choose between vintage Arthur Lyman compilations, there's really no specific criteria to use. You're about as well off with this one as DCC's *The Best Of*—if you like Lyman a lot, you'll want both, and if you're lukewarm about his brand of exotica, you shouldn't get either. The only reason this gets a slight edge is for the inclusion of "Yellow Bird," his 1961 Top Ten hit. It also has Lyman's version of "Quiet Village," a Top Ten hit for his former employer, Martin Denny. —*Richie Unterberger*

Taboo/Yellow Bird / DCC ♦♦♦

Magic Organ

Easy Listening
No easy-listening collection would be complete without at least one Magic Organ album. And there are dozens of theater-organ album masterpieces to choose from: old standards, carousel music, waltzes, and, most of all, polkas. —*Michael Erlewine*

★ **22 All Time Organ Favorites** / 1984 / Vanguard ♦♦♦♦♦
22 All Time Organ Favorites contains 22 of the Magic Organ's best-known songs, making it both a definitive retrospective and excellent introduction to the sound of the Magic Organ. —*Stephen Thomas Erlewine*

22 Great Organ Favorites / Ranwood ♦♦♦♦

Henry Mancini

b. 1924, d. Jun. 14, 1994
Piano / Easy Listening
If the recognition of one's peers is the true measure of success, then few men are as successful as composer, arranger, and conductor Henry Mancini. In a career that spanned 40 years, writing for film and television, Mancini won four Oscars and 20 Grammies, the all-time record for a pop artist. For 1961's *Breakfast at Tiffany's* alone, Mancini won five Grammies and two Oscars. *Breakfast at Tiffany's* includes the classic "Moon River" (lyrics by Johnny Mercer), arguably one of the finest pop songs of the last 50 years. At last count, there were over 1000 recordings of it. His other notable songs include "Dear Heart," "Days of Wine and Roses" (one Oscar, two Grammies), and "Charade," the last two with lyrics by Mercer. He also had a No. 1 record and won a Grammy for Nino Rota's "Love Theme from *Romeo and Juliet*." Among his other notable film scores are *The Pink Panther* (three Grammies), *Hatari!* (one Grammy), *Victor/Victoria* (an Oscar), *Two for the Road, Wait Until Dark,* and *10*. His television themes include "Peter Gunn" (two Grammies, recorded by many rock artists), "Mr. Lucky" (two Grammies), "Newhart," "Remington Steele," and the "Thorn Birds" television mini-series.

As a child, Mancini learned how to play a variety of musical instruments, and as a teenager, he became enamored with jazz and big bands. He began to write arrangements and sent a few to Benny Goodman, who wrote the teenager back, encouraging him to pursue a career in music. Mancini enrolled in the Julliard School of Music in 1942, but his studies were cut short when he served in the military during World War II. After the war, he was hired by Tex Beneke, the leader of the Glenn Miller Orchestra, as a pianist and arranger. In the late '40s, he began writing scores for record and film studios, first for a recording session by the Mel-Tones, which featured his wife Ginny O'Connor, and then the Abbott and Costello film *Lost in Alaska*, the first movie he scored.

Lost in Alaska led to more film scores, in particular 1954's *The Glenn Miller Story* and 1956's *The Benny Goodman Story*, which both showcased his big-band roots. Soon, he was working on a large number of films and television, including Orson Welles' *Touch of Evil* and the TV show "Peter Gunn." Mancini's scores frequently straddled the line between jazz and Hollywood dramatics, making his music both distinctive and influential.

Mancini's heyday was the early '60s, when his score for *Breakfast at Tiffany's* (1961) yielded the Oscar-winning hit single "Moon River," which instantly became a pop standard. The following year, he wrote the music for *Days of Wine and Roses*, which also won an Oscar for its title song. Throughout the next three decades, he continued to be one of the most successful film composers in the world, as well as a popular concert conductor. He continued working until his death in 1994; just prior to his demise, he was writing the score for the musical adaption of *Victor/Victoria*.

What kept Mancini's work fresh was his ability to write in almost any style imaginable and his successful experimentations with unusual sounds and instruments. In his 1989 memoir *Did They Mention the Music?*, Mancini's co-author Gene Lees wrote that "more than any other person, he Americanized film scoring, and in time even European film composers followed in his path," and that Mancini wrote scores that "contained almost as many fully developed song melodies as a Broadway musical." Had he not remained true to his first love, film scoring, Mancini would have more than likely made as large an impact on the

Broadway stage as he made on the silver screen. —*Kenneth M. Cassidy & Stephen Thomas Erlewine*

The Music from "Peter Gunn" / 1959 / RCA ♦♦♦
Soundtrack and incidental music from Mancini's early "Hollywood jazz" period. Great listening. —*Cub Koda*

★ **The Best of Mancini** / 1987 / RCA ♦♦♦♦♦
Mancini's most memorable scores, including "The Pink Panther," "Moon River," and others. The best overview of his voluminous work. —*Cub Koda*

Blues and the Beat / 1995 / RCA Victor ♦♦♦
With *The Blues and the Beat*, Henry Mancini delivered one of his bluesiest, jazziest records. Though it isn't an entirely successful experiement, it has its share of delightful moments, as proved by "Mood Indigo" and "Sing, Sing, Sing." Mancini could never deliver straight jazz, but his easy, orchestrated approximations are enjoyable as their own entity. The CD reissue includes four bonus tracks. —*Stephen Thomas Erlewine*

☆ **Days of Wine and Roses** / Oct. 10, 1995 / RCA ♦♦♦♦♦
Days of Wine and Roses is a comprehensive three-disc box set featuring all of Henry Mancini's most popular and best-known works in their original versions. For some, the sheer extensiveness of the set may be a bit intimidating—after all, three discs is a lot for casual fans—but for serious fans of the composer, it's an essential purchase. —*Stephen Thomas Erlewine*

In the Pink: The Ultimate Collection / Feb. 1996 / RCA ♦♦♦♦

Mr. Lucky [TV Soundtrack] / RCA ♦♦♦
Henry Mancini tried for something similar to "Peter Gunn" in his music for this Blake Edwards-produced series, but didn't quite succeed. This music is moody and occasionally interesting, but nowhere near as driving as the other. —*Bruce Eder*

Mantovani

b. Nov. 15, 1905, Venice, Italy, d. Mar. 30, 1980, England
Violin / Easy Listening, Orchestral
Violinist, composer, and conductor Annunzio Paolo Mantovani was born in Venice, Italy. He started working in London at 16 and was conducting the Hotel Metropal Orchestra by 1925. Mantovani was a major pioneer in the heavy use of strings and one of the first to be almost exclusively interested in recorded rather than live music. He also was one of the first popular artists to concentrate on producing albums rather than singles. He had seven million-selling albums, including *Immortal Classics* (1954) and *Exodus and Other Great Themes* (1960). In 1935-1936 Mantovani had hits in the US with "Red Sails in the Sunset" and "Serenade to the Night." He was soon recognized as the undisputed king of easy listening, or mood music, as it was called then. He had 51 hit albums in the US alone. —*Michael Erlewine*

● **Mantovani's Golden Hits** / 1967 / London ♦♦♦♦

Mantovani's Italia / 1987 / Bainbridge ♦♦♦

Paul Mauriat

French composer/conductor Paul Mauriat is a classically trained musician who decided to pursue a career in popular music. His first major success came in 1962, as a co-writer of the European hit, "Chariot." In 1963, the song was given English lyrics, renamed "I Will Follow Him," and became a No. 1 American hit for Little Peggy March. Mauriat is best remembered for his 1968 worldwide smash, "Love Is Blue."

Mauriat's ancestors were all classical musicians and he originally planned to follow in their footsteps, studying the music as a child and enrolling in the Conservatoire in Paris when he was ten years old. As a teenager, he became infatuated with jazz and popular music, which made him stray from his initial career path. At the age of 17, he formed an orchestra and began touring concert halls throughout Europe. These concerts earned him the attention of vocalist/songwriter Charles Aznavour, who hired Mauriat as an arranger and conductor. Through Aznavour, he began working with a variety of other French artists. For the remainder of the '40s and the '50s, he worked primarily as an arranger for other musicians.

Mauriat began a solo career in the early '60s, recording a series of instrumental albums that were distinguished by their sweeping, melodic strings and gently insistent contemporary rhythms. Using the pseudonym Del Roma, he co-wrote "Chariot" which became a hit for Petula Clark in 1962. The following year, the song was given a new, English lyric by Arthur Altman and Norman Gimbel and recorded by Little Peggy March as "I Will Follow Him"; it became a No. 1 hit in the US.

Throughout the '60s, Mauriat continued to record his pop instrumental albums, which became more popular as the decade progressed. His popularity peaked in 1968, when his version of "L'Amour Est Bleu" ("Love Is Blue"), which was Luxembourg's submission to the 1963 Eurovision Song contest, became an international hit, reaching No. 1 on a number of charts, including America. The single was supported by

Blooming Hits, an album that featured a selection of '60s pop hits; the album was massively popular and it is estimated that it sold in excess of two million copies worldwide. Mauriat became an international recording star, touring North and Latin America, Europe, and Japan, and making television appearances in several countries.

Although Mauriat's popularity dipped in the early '70s—he only had two other US hit singles, "Love in Every Room" and "Chitty Chitty Bang Bang," which were both minor—he continued to sell respectably throughout the world, particularly in Europe. He continued recording into the '80s. —*Stephen Thomas Erlewine and Kenneth M. Cassidy*

● **Love Is Blue** / 1967 / Mercury ◆◆◆◆

George Melachrino

b. May 1, 1909, **d.** Jun. 18, 1965

British composer/arranger George Melachrino is famous for his *Moods in Music* series, which attempted to provide a soundtrack for everyday events like dining, working, and romance. Melachrino's records were distinctive for his lush, rich strings with gave his music a luxurious, romantic quality. In addition to his *Moods in Music* albums, he had a string of hit singles and recording albums consisting of movie themes, popular songs, and show tunes.

Melachrino began playing music as a child. His Greek parents gave him a violin at the age of five and he immediately wrote his first composition. When he was 14 years old, he enrolled at the Trinity College of Music, where he studied strings and chamber music. Two years later, while he was still a student, he wrote a piece for a string sextet which he performed throughout London. Before he completed school, he decided to learn every orchestral instrument; by the time he graduated, he had fulfilled his goal, learning every instrument besides piano and harp.

Melachrino began a performing career in 1927 with a British Broadcasting Company session. As he continued to play, he began to expand his tastes from classical music, experimenting with jazz and pop music. He joined dance bands, including groups led by Ambrose, Harry Hudson, Carroll Gibbons, and Bert Firman. Melachrino formed a dance band in 1939, which played at the respected London theatre the Cafe de Paris; it disbanded in 1940.

When World War II began, Melachrino joined the British service as a military policeman. He would later earn the ranking of a regimental sergeant-major, after which he joined the *Stars of Battledress* troupe. During the War, he was also the leader of the British Band of the Allied Expeditionary Forces, as well as the leader of the British Orchestra in Khaki, which consisted entirely of serving soldiers, and the musical director of the Army Radio Unit. Melachrino also sang with the American and Canadian Allied Expeditionary Forces bands. With each of his wartime bands, he was working with bands that had large string sections, which would prove to be crucial to the music he made after the war.

Once the war was over, Melachrino led two separate outfits—the George Melachrino Orchestra and the Melachrino Strings—which were quite similar in sound. Both units featured sentimental, string-laden arrangements, with light brass and woodwind touches. In addition to leading these bands, he founded the Melachrino Music Organization, which provided music for films, radio, and records. In the late '40s, he wrote scores for films, including *Woman to Woman, No Orchids for Miss Blandish, Code of Scotland Yard, Story of Shirley Yorke,* and *Dark Secret;* he also wrote the music for the musical *Starlight Roof.*

Melachrino began recording for RCA, making over 100 78s and over 50 LPs. Out of all of his albums—which were frequently hits—the most notable were his *Music for Moods* series, which included such records as *Music for Dining, Music to Help You Sleep, Music for Two People Alone, Music for Faith and Inner Calm, Music for Daydreaming,* and *Music for Relaxation,* among many others. All of the *Music for Moods* albums were produced by Ethel Gabriel, who helped mastermind their sound and direction.

Melachrino's career was going strong into the '60s, as he began recording for ABC Paramount. In 1965, he suffered a fatal accident at his home. He was still successful at the time of his death, and the Melachrino Strings and Orchestra continued without him under the direction of Robert Mandell. —*Stephen Thomas Erlewine*

● **Under Western Skies** / RCA ◆◆◆◆

Sergio Mendes

b. 1941
Piano / Easy Listening

An early proponent of his native Brazil's bossa-nova style, he formed the group, Brasil '65 (which later became Brasil '66 and was updated in semiyearly increments) and scored hits with soothing, Latin-tinged pop throughout the '60s. —*Cub Koda*

Four Sider / 1966 / A&M ◆◆◆◆

Sergio Mendes & Brasil 66 / 1966 / A&M ◆◆◆◆

Classics / 1966-1986 / A&M ◆◆◆◆

★ **Greatest Hits of Brasil '66** / A&M ◆◆◆◆◆
Smooth-as-silk arrangements. His best sides and major hits such as "Fool on the Hill" and "The Look of Love." —*Cub Koda*

Frank Mills

Piano

Canadian-born composer/pianist Frank Mills scored a minor US hit in 1972 with "Love Me, Love Me Love." It wasn't until the release of "Music Box Dancer" and its subsequent success in 1979 that Mills became more of a household name. Success was to be short-lived however, and it wasn't long before Mills was back to performing in his native Canada.

After studying music in Montreal, Mills joined the Bells in the late '60s. Although the Bells did perform some of his songs, Mills left for a solo career in 1972. Released in the same year he left the group, "Love Me, Love Me Love" was his first solo record. The single was a hit in Canada and made some headway in the US, reaching No. 46. Although he followed the single with several minor hits in Canada, his audience continued to shrink and he was left without a record contract by 1974.

Undaunted, Mills recorded and released *Music Box Dancer* with his own money in the mid-'70s. In 1979, an executive at Polydor Records heard the record and believed that the title track had hit potential, so he persuaded the company to release the song as a single. "Music Box Dancer" was a surprise hit, climbing to No. 3 on the American charts. Following the success of the single, the album was also re-released. Like the single, the album was also a hit, reaching No. 21.

Mills released another album, *Prelude to Romance,* in the US in 1981 and it was a minor hit. Nevertheless, the album wasn't a big enough hit for him to keep his US record contract, and after its release, he was only left with a Canadian contract. Mills continued to record into the '90s. In the course of his career, he has released over ten albums. —*Stephen Thomas Erlewine*

Best Of / 1994 / Macola ◆◆◆◆

● **Music Box Dancer** / Polydor ◆◆◆◆

Hugo Montenegro

d. Feb. 6, 1981

Hugo Montenegro was a composer, arranger, and conductor, who is primarily known for his movie work in the '60s, as well as his adaptations of film scores like *The Good, the Bad, and the Ugly.* Montenegro began his musical career in the US Navy, where he arranged scores for various military bands. After he left the Navy, he completed school at Manhattan College, then he began a professional music career.

Initially, Montenegro was the staff manager to Andre Kostelanetz at Columbia Records in New York, which eventually led to a job as a conductor/arranger for several of the label's artists, most notably Harry Belafonte. By the mid-'50s, Montenegro was making his own albums of easy-listening orchestral music.

Montenegro moved to California in the mid-'60s and began to write film scores, starting with Otto Preminger's *Hurry Sundown* in 1967. That same year, he recorded a version of the theme to *The Good, the Bad and the Ugly,* which was written by Ennio Morricone. Featuring an arrangement that relied on a chorus, electric instruments, and special effects, the single was a major hit, reaching No. 1 in the UK and No. 2 in the US; internationally, it sold over a million copies. An album titled *Music from "A Fistful of Dollars" & "For a Few Dollars More" & "The Good, the Bad and the Ugly"* appeared shortly after the single's release, and it reached the Top Ten in the spring of 1968. Later in the year, Montenegro released a single of the theme from *Hang 'Em High,* which was a lesser hit, as was the album of the same name.

Montenegro began to branch out after the *Hang 'Em High* album, recording a diverse array of albums, ranging from show tunes to electronic experiments. Throughout the late '60s and '70s, he continued to score films, including *Lady in Cement, The Undefeated, The Wrecking Crew, Tomorrow,* and *The Ambushers,* among many others. He continued composing and recording until his death in 1981. —*Stephen Thomas Erlewine*

★ **The Good, the Bad & the Ugly** / 1992 / RCA ◆◆◆◆◆
Certainly purists will prefer the versions of these classic Ennio Morricone spaghetti Western soundtracks that were conducted by Morricone himself to the ones on this compilation, which were arranged and conducted by Hugo Montenegro. Still, anyone who likes premier Morricone from that era will probably enjoy this CD quite a bit. Containing pieces from three of the most famous Morricone-scored films, all of the material was released in 1967, and it must be said that Montenegro didn't miss a trick, employing the low twangy guitars, weeping horns, and ghostly whistles that are usually identified as Morricone trademarks. Perhaps these are a tad more bombastic, orchestrated, and pop-slanted than Morricone's own versions, but if anything, Montenegro's touches enhance the grandiose sadness of the melodies. Contains the massive hit

version of the theme from "The Good, the Bad and the Ugly," which went to No. 2 in 1968. —*Richie Unterberger*

Peter Nero (Bernard Nierow)

b. May 22, 1934, Brooklyn, NY
Piano / Easy Listening, Swing
Peter Nero (born Bernard Nierow) is a pianist and New York native who started with Paul Whiteman, then moved up to symphony until the early '60s, when RCA Victor signed him and successfully promoted him into a pop music interpreter. He won the 1961 Grammy for Best New Artist. His lush orchestrated albums continued through the early '70s, when he returned to a harder jazz format, recording with a trio.

Nierow began playing piano as a child, learning the instrument quite rapidly; by the age of 11, he was playing Haydn concertos. However, he was restless and quickly grew tired of classical music, becoming infatuated with jazz as a teenager. In fact, after Nierow finished studying music at Brooklyn College, he became a jazz pianist. However, instead of playing straight jazz, he created a swinging hybrid of jazz and classical music.

Nierow didn't have much success as a performer, which meant he had to take a gig as a saloon pianist in a New York club called the Hickory House. Unsatisfied with the compromises he was making at the club, he headed out to Las Vegas, where he didn't find much success. He returned to New York, taking a lesser job at the Hickory House. For several years, he played New York's club circuit before he came to the attention of Stan Greeson, an executive at RCA Records. Convinced that Nierow had star potential, Greeson signed the pianist and had him change his name to Peter Nero; he also persuaded Nero to add pop songs like "Over the Rainbow" to his repertoire.

Piano Forte, Peter Nero's first album, was released in 1961 and he began touring the country. That same year, he won the Grammy for Best New Artist. Nero's popularity continued to rise throughout the early '60s; his jazzy hybrid of pop, classical, swing, and bop became one of the most popular mainstream sounds of the era. Eventually, he became the musical director of the Philadelphia Pops Orchestra, where he frequently performed classical arrangements of pop songs. In the '70s, he returned to playing jazz in trios, though he still made orchestral records occasionally. —*Cub Koda*

Nero Goes "Pops" / RCA ✦✦✦
An interesting, largely successful album with Arthur Fiedler and the Boston Pops Orchestra. —*Cub Koda*

● **Peter Nero's Greatest Hits** / Columbia ✦✦✦✦

Now / Concord Jazz ✦✦✦
This is a smartly played set of standards interpreted in a trio setting. —*Cub Koda*

Hail the Conquering Nero / RCA ✦✦✦✦
The biggest of his early-'60s successes. —*Cub Koda*

101 Strings Orchestra

Easy Listening
Published by Alshire International Inc., there are over 200 albums in this series of lush string-laden instrumentals designed for easy listening. —*Michael Erlewine*

● **Best of the 101 Strings** / Alshire ✦✦✦✦

Frank Pourcel

Violin
French violinist Frank Pourcel is best known for his jazzy string arrangements of pop hits, as well as his lush easy-listening arrangements and film scores.

Initially, Pourcel studied classical violin at the Paris Conservatoire, but he found the allure of jazz irresistible. In particular, he was an idol of Stephane Grappelli. Following his studies, he joined a number of jazz combos, which led him to his role as the leader of the French Fiddlers, who he joined in the late '40s. The French Fiddlers were a group of violinists that performed jazzy versions of classical numbers or classical arrangements of pop and jazz tunes. They signed to Pathe-Marconi and continued to refine their sound so they could reach a broader audience. The group earned their first hit in 1952 with a version of "Blue Tango."

In 1959, the French Fiddlers had a hit with an easy-listening version of the Platters' "Only You" that featured a prominent beat; appropriately, it was credited to Pourcel and His Rockin' Strings. It was a sound that became quite popular during the '60s, though frequently other musicians were more successful with it than Pourcel. Indeed, "Only You" was his only US Top Ten hit. Nevertheless, he and the Fiddlers—who recorded under a variety of names—sold over 15 million records internationally by the early '70s. Pourcel continued to record easy-listening albums and compose film scores throughout the '70s and into the '80s. —*Stephen Thomas Erlewine*

In a Nostalgic Mood / 1984 / EMI America ✦✦✦

● **Somewhere, My Love** / Imperial ✦✦✦✦
The romantic strings of *Somewhere, My Love* offers a good portrait of Frank Pourcel's style, making the record a fine introduction to the violinist. —*David Jehnzen*

Nelson Riddle

b. Jun. 1, 1921, Oradell, NJ, **d.** Oct. 6, 1985, Los Angeles, CA
Trombone / Easy Listening, Orchestral Pop
While Nelson Riddle had experience as a trombonist and arranger for Charlie Spivak, Jerry Wald, and Tommy Dorsey in the '40s and was a staff arranger for NBC Radio later in that era, he achieved his greatest success and notoriety during the '50s. Riddle was the arranger and conductor for Judy Garland, Jimmy Wakely, Betty Hutton, Ella Mae Morse, and many others in the early '50s, including Nat King Cole, but became the top arranger in Hollywood through his collaborations with Frank Sinatra during 1953. Riddle's orchestrations and careful, intelligent use of first-class jazz musicians accented Sinatra's voice perfectly, without obscuring, challenging, or threatening. No one was better at knowing when to increase the brass section's volume, how to support a singer, and what soloist to spotlight and for how long.

Riddle enjoyed some success on his own during the '50s, including a Grammy award in 1958 and a No. 1 pop hit in 1955. He later expanded his activities to work with Ella Fitzgerald, Oscar Peterson, Rosemary Clooney, and Johnny Mathis and became a busy film soundtrack arranger, composer, and conductor as well. He contributed to hit movies such as *The St. Louis Blues* and *Pajama Game* and did the theme music for the TV shows "Route 66" and "The Untouchables." He was musical director for the Julie Andrews variety show in the '70s and came back from health problems to arrange and conduct Grammy-winning albums for Linda Ronstadt in the '80s. His last work was a 1985 arrangement for opera singer Kiri Te Kanawa. —*Ron Wynn*

★ **Best of Nelson Riddle** / Capitol ✦✦✦✦✦
The Best of Nelson Riddle doesn't offer a comprehensive overview of the composer/arranger's career, but it does have enough highlights to make it an effective introduction. —*Stephen Thomas Erlewine*

David Rose

d. Aug. 23, 1990
Piano
David Rose was one of the most popular and distinctive mainstream instrumental pop composers of the '40s, '50s, and '60s, writing a number of pieces that became part of the nation's collective memory. From "Holiday for Strings" to "The Stripper," his music was usually distinguished by a loose, humorous approach, where the strings mimicked voices and the horns and percussion were alternately swinging and supportive. In addition to those two signature songs, Rose composed scores for many films and television programs, including "Bonanza" and "Little House on the Prairie."

Born in London, Rose and his family moved to the US when he was four years old. As a teenager, he studied at the Chicago College of Music; after he graduated at the age of 16, he joined a dance band led by Ted Fio Rito. He stayed with Rito for three years, then he began working as a standby pianist for NBC Radio. Rose was employed by NBC for most of the '30s as an arranger, conductor, and pianist, though he also did work outside of the network. Most notably, he arranged Benny Goodman's hit "It's Been So Long" in 1936.

Rose left New York in 1938 for Hollywood. Shortly after arriving in California, he assembled the David Rose Orchestra for the Mutual Broadcast System, where he also conducted a program called "California Melodies." That same year, he met and married Martha Raye, whom he accompanied on her hit single "Melancholy Mood." However, their union lasted less than a year and he soon began a relationship with Judy Garland which led to marriage in 1941; the couple divorced in 1945.

In 1941, MGM Studios hired Rose as a musical director. At MGM, he wrote scores for films starring Doris Day, Don Ameche, Esther Williams, Dorothy Lamour, and Martha Raye. "Holiday for Strings," which became one of his trademark tunes, became a major hit in 1943. It was a hit while Rose was performing military service in World War II. During the war, he was a composer and conductor for the US Army and Air Force's musical *Winged Victory*, which was turned into a movie in 1944. That same year, "So in Love"—a song he wrote with lyricist Leo Robin—was nominated for an Oscar after appearing in the Danny Kaye film *Wonder Man*.

Once the war was finished, Rose became a regular on Red Skelton's radio program, which frequently featured "Holiday for Strings." Rose also appeared on Skelton's television show, which began in the early '50s.

Television became the next medium Rose conquered, as he provided theme music to over 20 TV series during the '50s, '60s, and early '70s. Most notably, he composed the music for "Bonanza" for 14 years, which earned him several Emmy awards. In the late '50s and early '60s, he provided the music for three critically acclaimed and popular Fred Astaire television specials.

In the late '50s, Rose began releasing albums, which alternated between collections of show tunes, film themes, and mood music. He also dabbled with Calypso, which resulted in a minor hit single, "Calypso Melody," in 1957. Rose also arranged and provided accompaniment for pop hits, most notably Connie Francis' 1959 single "My Happiness." However, his biggest pop chart success was with one of his own records in 1962. Taken from the television program "Burlesque," Rose's jaunty, comical "The Stripper" became a smash single, climbing to number one on the US charts. The accompanying album, *The Stripper and Other Fun Songs for the Family*, was also a hit, peaking at No. 1. Though he released over 50 albums throughout his career, no other LP of his reached the charts.

During the '70s, he composed the music for "Little House on Prairie," which was nearly as well received as his scores for "Bonanza." Rose also conducted a number of symphony concerts during the decade, as well as recording the occasional album. Though his activity slowed considerably in the '80s, he still released a handful of albums and performed a couple of concerts. David Rose died in 1990. *—Stephen Thomas Erlewine*

The Stripper and Other Fun Songs for the Family / 1962 / MGM ✦✦✦✦

Though it doesn't have the sparkling arpeggios that distinguished his '50s recordings, *The Stripper and Other Fun Songs for the Family* is a swinging, pseudo-burlesque collection that showcases his flair for parody. *—Stephen Thomas Erlewine*

● **Very Best of David Rose** / 1996 / MGM ✦✦✦✦
The Very Best of David Rose offers a good cross-section of his light easy-listening pop instrumentals of the '50s and functions as an excellent introduction to his career. *—Stephen Thomas Erlewine*

Sandpipers

The Sandpipers were a male vocal trio that recorded a handful of easy-listening pop hits in the mid-'60s. The group was distinguished by their light, breezy harmonies, which floated over delicate, breezy string arrangements, as well as the occasional appearance of a wordless female backing vocalist who drifted in and out of the music. Though they didn't manage to have a long, sustained career, the group did have one Top Ten hit with "Guantanamera" in 1966.

Originally, the Sandpipers were known as the Four Seasons. The three members—Jim Brady, Mike Piano, and Richard Shoff—were part of the Californian Mitchell Boys Choir before they formed their own group. Shortly after their formation, they learned that there was a New York group using the name the Four Seasons, so they changed their name to the Grads. As the Grads, they cut a handful of singles, which helped the group secure a residency at a Lake Tahoe nightclub.

After the Grads had been performing in Lake Tahoe for a while, a friend of the group introduced them to trumpeter Herb Alpert, who ran his own record label, A&M. Impressed, he signed the group to a record contract. A&M released a handful of singles by the Grads before the trio changed their name to the Sandpipers. None of the singles the group released were successful until their producer, Tommy LiPuma, recommended that they record a South American folk song called "Guantanamera." Once "Guantanamera" was released in 1966, it became a major hit, reaching the Top Ten in both the US and Britain.

The Sandpipers managed to follow "Guantanamera" with several minor hits, including versions of "Louie Louie" and "Kumbaya." During this time, the group had taken to recording and performing with a supporting female vocalist named Pamela Ramcier. Ramcier contributed ethereal, wordless vocals to the group. Her vocals never acted as harmonies to the group's singing; they functioned in a supporting role, much like the strings that comprised the band's instrumental backing. Although Ramcier was never credited on the albums and was always shrouded in shadows during concerts—though her hip, mod outfits complete with miniskirts and go-go boots often made her more noticeable than the actual Sandpipers—her voice was one of the most distinctive elements of the group's music.

In 1970, they contributed songs to *The Sterile Cuckoo* ("Come Saturday Morning") and Russ Meyer's *Beyond the Valley of the Dolls*.

Though the Sandpipers continued to record into the '70s, their audience diminished with each successive year. After spending five years without any chart success, the group disbanded in the mid-'70s. *—Stephen Thomas Erlewine*

Guantanamera / 1966 / A&M ✦✦✦✦
Guantanamera, the Sandpipers' one big hit album and single, is their strongest collection of songs, featuring the hit title track and their subdued cover of "Louie Louie." *—Stephen Thomas Erlewine*

Come Saturday Morning / 1970 / A&M ✦✦✦✦
Come Saturday Morning was the Sandpipers' last hit album, featuring the hit title track, plus the minor hits "Free to Carry On" and the theme from *Beyond the Valley of the Dolls*. The sound on *Come Saturday*

Morning is more vaguely psychedelic and rock-influenced than their past records, but the light vocals still dominate the proceedings. *—Stephen Thomas Erlewine*

● **Greatest Hits** / A&M ✦✦✦✦
Though *Greatest Hits* doesn't quite live up to its title—only one of the Sandpipers' four Top 100 singles appear on the collection—it offers a good sampling of the band's sound and does include their big hit, "Guantanamera." *—Stephen Thomas Erlewine*

John Schroeder

Arranger/conductor/producer Schroeder does have a few pop-rock credentials: he wrote a No. 1 UK hit for British singer Helen Shapiro ("Walkin' Back to Happiness") in the early '60s, made the first licensing deal for a Motown product on British shores, and formed Sounds Orchestral, which had a Top Ten hit on both sides of the Atlantic in 1965 with "Cast Your Fate to the Wind." To the current space-age pop crowd, however, he's known as one of the chief exponents of what the British call "easy"—recordings, mostly instrumental, which welded easy-listening pop arrangements to soul, rock, and psychedelic source material. At the time, naturally, it was critically ignored, as his work was really aimed at creating background music for those who found the original versions way too intense to handle. In the mid-'90s, of course, it's all the rage in London clubs, where his blaring horn charts and pumping Hammond organs provide—um—suitable background music for those looking for the cutting edge in retro sounds. Placed in the home CD unit rather than the dance floor, it tends to sound rather trivial, if occasionally possessed of an inspired oddball charm. The demand is there, though (maybe for the first time), which paved the way for the reissue of some of his recordings decades after they made a beeline for the cutout bin. *—Richie Unterberger*

Working in the Soul Mine / 1966 / Pye ✦✦✦
All but two of these 14 tracks were covers of mid-'60s American soul favorites like "You've Lost That Lovin' Feelin'," "Sunny," and "Rescue Me," in which Schroeder bled most of the funk (and vocals) from the originals to craft instrumentals that were at once more tolerable to elderly ears than the originals, but still mildly rhythmic and danceable. It sounds silly now—it sounded silly *then*. *—Richie Unterberger*

● **Space Age Soul** / 1996 / Sequel ✦✦✦✦
Twenty-one-track compilation of '60s material includes the entirety of his 1966 *Working in the Soul Mine* LP (which consisted mostly of covers of American soul hits), as well as some other tracks from the '60s, some credited to Sounds Orchestral, and a couple previously unreleased (!). As much hip appeal as this may have in certain quarters, it's hard to fathom why you'd want to hear an easy-listening-cum-go-go instrumental arrangement of "Papa's Got a Brand New Bag" or "You Can't Hurry Love," except for a laugh (once). Occasionally soulful female vocals wander in for a phrase or two, as if they've accidentally stumbled on the session without realizing that it's supposed to be instrumental. The relatively few originals (mostly found on the non-*Working in the Soul Mine* cuts) have the advantage of more, well, originality, as the arranger's working in a vein more akin to his experience. "Soul Coaxing," for instance, has some gorgeous strings and spectral moaning female vocals worthy of Ennio Morricone, and "Lovin' You Girl" weds some jelly-thick Hammond organ grooves to suitably mournful brass. *—Richie Unterberger*

Yma Sumac (Sumac del Castillo Zoila Imperatriz Charrari)

b. 1928
Vocals / Vocal, Exotica
A singer with an amazing four-octave range, Yma Sumac was said to have been a descendant of Inca kings, an Incan princess that was one of the Golden Virgins. Her offbeat stylings became a phenomenon of early-'50s pop music. While her album covers took advantage of her strange costumes and voluptuous figure, rumors abounded that she was, in actuality, a housewife named Amy Camus. It mattered little, since there has been no one like her before or since in the annals of popular music.

According to the Yma Sumac legend, she was the sixth child of an Indian mother and an Indian/Spanish father, who raised her as a Quechuan. She began performing in local festivals, before her family moved to Lima, Peru. Once she was in Lima, she became a member of the Compania Peruana de Arte, which was a collective of nearly 50 Indian singers, musicians, and dancers. Sumac married Moises Vivanco, the leader of the Compania, in 1942. Four years later, Vivanco, Sumac, and her cousin Colita Rivero formed the Inca Taqui Trio and moved to New York. By the end of the decade, they were performing in nightclubs throughout New York and playing radio and television programs, most notably Arthur Godfrey's TV show. The Trio also became a fixture on the Borscht Belt circuit and the Catskills.

Yma Sumac was signed as a solo artist to Capitol Records in 1950, releasing her first album, the 10-inch *Voice of Xtabay*, the same year.

Voice of Xtabay was released without much publicity, but it slowly became a hit, and Capitol began pushing Sumac with a massive marketing campaign. In 1951, she made her Broadway debut in the musical *Flahooley*, which featured three songs written by Vivanco; the musical's lifespan was quite brief, and it completed its run by the end of the year. Nevertheless, Sumac's career was ascending at a rapid rate, as she continued to release hit records and played sellout concerts across the country, including one at the Hollywood Bowl and another at Carnegie Hall. She also toured Europe and South America, as well as Las Vegas nightclubs. In 1954, she appeared in a movie called *Secret of the Incas*, which starred Charlton Heston.

By the end of the '50s, Sumac's audience had begun to decline and she was no longer as hip as she was in the first half of the decade. Sensing the erosion of her popularity, Sumac retired in the early '60s, without leaving any word of her location. She performed a handful of unannounced concerts in the mid-'70s, and in 1987, she played New York's Ballroom nightclub for a total of three weeks; she also had a stint in a Los Angeles club that same year. She followed these shows with occasional concert dates around the world.

Though Yma Sumac did not perform frequently in the '90s, she experienced a popular revival, as a cult of alternative music fans discovered the exotica records of the '50s. The ongoing interest in exotica and Sumac led to the CD release of her catalog in 1996. —*Stephen Thomas Erlewine and Cub Koda*

Inca Taqui / 1953 / Capitol ◆◆◆◆

Legend of the Sun Virgin / 1954 / Capitol ◆◆◆
One of Sumac's most operatic and melodramatic outings, incantationally performed to approximate an Incan ritual. The cinematic string arrangements, though, are pure Hollywood. —*Richie Unterberger*

Mambo / 1954 / Capitol ◆◆◆◆
Capitol got on top of two '50s fads at once by issuing an album of Sumac tackling mambo. Yma (characteristically) held nothing back, and the result was one of her more enjoyable LPs, with respectably swinging mambo grooves crafted by Billy May. "Five Bottles Mambo" is one of her most astonishing vocal workouts, dropping into guttural growls that are downright bestial, and making one wonder how exactly they got away with that in the conservative milieu of the '50s. —*Richie Unterberger*

Legend of the Jivaro / 1957 / The Right Stuff ◆◆
According to the liner notes, Sumac and her composer-husband, Moises Vivanco, went into the headhunting territory of the Jivaros, tape recorder in hand, to accumulate source material for this album. Whether you believe that or not, what they came up with once it had been run through the studio was one of her chintzier products. If it's folk music, it's been heavily modified for North American audiences, with period '50s pop production, mainstream Latin pop influences, and occasional spurts of quasi-rock 'n' roll guitar. —*Richie Unterberger*

Fuego del Ande / 1959 / Capitol ◆◆◆
Even those who find Sumac unbearable would have to admit that she was nothing if not adaptable. *Fuego del Ande* has her interpreting South American folk songs with characteristic panache, although it's not one of her better '50s albums. —*Richie Unterberger*

● **Voice of Xtabay** / Mar. 5, 1996 / The Right Stuff ◆◆◆◆

● **Exotic Sampler** / Apr. 1996 / The Right Stuff ◆◆◆◆
Yma Sumac's albums are intriguing but uneven, which is what makes *Exotic Sampler* a welcome addition to her catalog. Culled from her original albums, the compilation offers a good cross-section of her material, giving the curious enough of a taste to know whether they want to dig deeper or not. —*Stephen Thomas Erlewine*

Enchantress / Pair ◆◆◆◆
Early-'50s recordings by a self-proclaimed Incan princess are exotic music with a multioctave vocal range. —*Hank Davis*

Billy Vaughn

b. Apr. 12, 1919, Glasgow, KY, **d.** Sep. 14, 1991
Vocals / Orchestral Pop
Billy Vaughn was one of the most popular orchestra leaders and pop music arrangers of the '50s and early '60s. In fact, he had more pop hits than any other orchestra leader during the rock 'n' roll era. Vaughn was also the musical director for many of the hitmakers on Dot Records, including Pat Boone, the Fontane Sisters, and Gale Storm. As a pop music arranger, his most distinctive feature was his clean, nonoffensive mainstream adaptations of rock 'n' roll and R&B hits. Vaughn was also a recording artist, and he cut a number of albums of easy-listening, instrumental music that were very popular throughout the '60s.

Vaughn began his professional music career in 1952, forming the vocal quartet the Hilltoppers with Don McGuire, Jimmy Sacca, and Seymour Speigelman. From 1952 to 1957, the Hilltoppers had numerous hit singles, beginning with Vaughn's song "Trying." He left the group in 1955 to join Dot Records as a musical director. Vaughn was responsible for most of Dot's biggest hits of the '50s, as he rearranged popular rock 'n'

roll and R&B songs for White, mainstream groups. His first success was with the Fontane Sisters, who sang with his orchestra on all their singles, including their 1954 breakthrough hit "Hearts of Stone." However, Dot's biggest success was Pat Boone, who had a series of hits with Vaughn's cleaned-up arrangements of rock 'n' roll songs.

At the same time he was leading the pop vocal division of Dot, Billy Vaughn was recording his own instrumental records, which frequently were also covers of R&B and country songs. Beginning with 1954's "Melody of Love," Vaughn had a string of easy-listening US hit singles that ran for over a decade. He also recorded numerous hit albums, with 36 of his records entering the US album charts between 1958 and 1970.

Though he was the most successful orchestra leader of the rock 'n' roll era, he wasn't able to sustain an audience in the late '60s. Vaughn released his last album in 1970 and quietly retired. —*Stephen Thomas Erlewine*

★ **Melody of Love: The Best of Billy Vaughn** / 1995 / Ranwood ◆◆◆◆◆
Melody of Love: The Best of Billy Vaughn is a definitive 18-track collection that contains the great majority of Billy Vaughn's biggest hits, including "Melody of Love," "The Shifting Whispering Sands (Parts 1 & 2)," "Sail Along Silvery Moon," and "Blue Hawaii." —*Stephen Thomas Erlewine*

Lawrence Welk

b. 1903, **d.** May 17, 1992
Accordion / Easy Listening
Long a butt of comedians and music fans, Lawrence Welk survived into the '90s as America's most successful bandleader. From dirt-poor beginnings in rural North Dakota, the relatively uneducated and heavily accented Welk seemed an unlikely candidate to carve out a successful, 60-plus-year career in the music business, but through sheer dogged persistence and belief in himself, that's exactly what transpired. His "Champagne music" style (lighter and less rhythmic than Guy Lombardo's) remained remarkably unchanged over the years. Changes in music have been constant—the end of the big-band era, rock 'n' roll, country & western, the Beatles, disco—with Welk seemingly impervious to it all, and a built-in audience that felt the same way. While jazz legends like Coleman Hawkins were lucky to land a Timex jazz special once a year, Welk was on ABC-TV twice a week! After being dropped by that network, he was one of the first to successfully move into television syndication, ending up more visible than he had been on ABC at his peak. Expanding his musical family to include tap dancers, jazz musicians (notably Pete Fountain), and multitudes of singers (the Lennon Sisters, etc.), Welk made no pretense of being remotely hip, merely delivering simple, well-played music and solid, family-oriented entertainment year after year. —*Cub Koda*

Lawrence Welk Plays Dixieland / 1956 / Ranwood ◆◆◆
Although Lawrence Welk gets top billing and his picture is on the back cover of the LP, this is actually a fairly strong Dixieland date by Welk's sidemen with many solos from its new star, clarinetist Pete Fountain. The music is not quite as strong as Fountain's first albums as a leader but there are good moments to be heard on such standards as "China Boy," "Barnyard Blues," and "'S Wonderful." —*Scott Yanow*

★ **16 Most Requested Songs** / Columbia ◆◆◆◆◆
Though it's far from a comprehensive collection, Lawrence Welk's *16 Most Requested Songs* contains most of the bandleader's best-known songs, presented in top-notch versions. It's a good way to get acquainted with his laidback style. —*Stephen Thomas Erlewine*

Calcutta! / Dot ◆◆◆
Welk's early-'60s stab at pop-rock instrumentals. Out of print. —*Cub Koda*

In Concert / Ranwood ◆◆◆◆
A two-record set. A nice sampling from the '70s version of Welk's burgeoning organization. —*Cub Koda*

Favorites / Coral ◆◆◆
A nice 12-song overview of Lawrence's '50s television band. No big hits, just nicely played and sequenced. Out of print. —*Cub Koda*

Paul Weston (Paul Weststein)

b. Mar. 12, 1912, Springfield, MA
Easy Listening
Paul Weston was one of the most diverse and talented arrangers and conductors of the '40s and '50s, moving from mainstream swing and jazz to instrumental easy-listening pop in the course of his career. Though he began his career playing hard swing, Weston is the father of mood music—lush, relaxing instrumental orchestral pop designed to provide a soundtrack to everyday events like romance and dining. Originally, Weston was an economics major at Dartmouth. While he was a student, he became fascinated with jazz, particularly swing, and began playing in various college bands. Soon, he decided to pursue a career in music. Weston became known as a vocal arranger. His work with Rudy Vallee brought him to national attention. After arranging for Vallee, he

attempted to work with Bing Crosby, but the results were unsuccessful. Following the failed Crosby venture, Weston became an arranger for Tommy Dorsey, which is where he made his reputation. While with Dorsey, he wrote jumping, swinging charts for the band and vocalists like Dinah Shore and Jo Stafford, whom he would marry in the mid-'40s.

Paul Weston became the A&R director for Capitol Records in 1944, when the label was just beginning. Though he continued to write fast swing charts for a time, Weston noticed that the tastes of the public were beginning to move toward gentler material, so he adjusted his music accordingly. Weston released his first album of mood music, *Music for Dreaming*, in 1945. *Music for Dreaming* was decidedly calmer than his previous work, though there was a subtle swing driving the subdued music. The album was a major success, and Weston continued to record albums of smooth, string-laden music for the next five years. By 1950, the term "mood music" had been adopted by the press to describe this style of instrumental pop.

Weston left Capitol Records in 1950 for Columbia Records, where he continued to record albums of instrumental mood music. He also continued to write arrangements and conduct sessions for artists like Sarah Vaughan, Ella Fitzgerald, Dinah Shore, and Doris Day. By the end of the decade, he had returned to Capitol Records, where he stayed throughout the '60s.

During this time, he and Jo Stafford recorded a handful of albums as Jonathan and Darlene Edwards. The Jonathan and Darlene albums were comedy records that parodied nightclub acts; on each record Stafford sang off-key and Weston horribly played out of time and out of key.

In the early '70s, Weston and Stafford both retired. The couple began a reissue label, Corinthian Records, in the early '90s which has released CD versions of their music. — *Stephen Thomas Erlewine*

★ **Music for Memories/Music for Dreaming** / Jan. 20, 1992 / Capitol ◆◆◆◆◆
Music for Memories/Music for Dreaming combines Paul Weston's two groundbreaking 10-inch albums of lush, romantic mood music. It offers a perfect introduction to Weston, as well as the entire genre of mood music. — *Stephen Thomas Erlewine*

Columbia Album of Jerome Kern / CBS ◆◆◆
Currently, the *Columbia Album of Jerome Kern* is the only Paul Weston record available. While it doesn't offer an accurate portrait of why Weston was important, it is a pleasant collection of some of Kern's best-known songs, done in the lush style that made Weston influential. — *Stephen Thomas Erlewine*

Roger Williams (Louis Weertz)

b. 1925
Piano / Easy Listening
Pianist Roger Williams' (born Louis Weertz) sweeping, sparkling arpeggios, showy technique, and gentle, easy-listening arrangements made him one of the most popular pop instrumentalists of the late '50s and '60s. Like many other easy-listening musicians, he blurred the boundaries between pop, jazz, and classical, creating a smooth, relaxing hybrid. Between 1955 and 1972, he had 38 hit albums and 22 hit singles, including the No. 1 hit, "Falling Leaves."

Williams began playing piano as a child, but he was lured into boxing while he was a high school student. After suffering several injuries—including breaking his nose a number of times—he decided to turn his full attention to music, enrolling as a piano major at Drake University. As a student, he began playing hybrids of jazz, classical, and pop. A school official heard him playing "Smoke Gets in Your Eyes" in one of the university's practice rooms and expelled the young musician.

Following his expulsion, Williams joined the Navy, where he earned a B.A. in engineering. When his tenure in the Navy was finished, he went back to Drake and re-enrolled in the university. After a couple of years, he moved to Juilliard, where he studied under jazz pianists Lenny Tristano and Teddy Wilson.

Williams' first big break arrived when he was scheduled to provide accompaniment for a Juilliard vocalist on "Arthur Godfrey's Talent Scouts." The vocalist didn't appear at the show, leaving the pianist to play a solo spot. Dave Kapp, the head of Kapp Records, heard Williams on the show and was impressed. Kapp signed the pianist to a contract, and changed his name from Louis Weertz to Roger Williams; the name derived from the founder of Rhode Island.

After releasing a few singles, Roger Williams had his first hit with the arpeggio-laden "Autumn Leaves" in 1955. The single reached No. 1 on the US charts and began a streak of 22 hit singles that ran through 1969; he had two other Top Ten hits, "Near You" in 1958 and "Born Free" in 1966. Williams was equally successful on the album charts, racking up a total of 38 hit records between 1956 and 1972, including the Top Ten albums *Songs of the Fabulous Fifties* (1957), *Till* (1958), *Maria* (1962), and *Born Free* (1966).

Roger Williams' audience faded away in the early '70s, but he continued to record into the '80s. Williams remains one of the most popular

pianists of the postwar era. He was the first pianist to receive a star on the Hollywood Walk of Fame, and he played for every President of the US between Harry Truman and Bill Clinton. — *Stephen Thomas Erlewine*

☆ **The Artist's Choice** / 1992 / MCA ◆◆◆◆◆
The Artist's Choice is a splendid double-disc set featuring all of Roger Williams's biggest hits, as well as a select amount of the pianist's favorite tracks. Devoted Williams fans will find this compilation a treasure, but those that want just a taste of his easy listening should stick with MCA's single-disc *Greatest Hits* collection. — *Stephen Thomas Erlewine*

★ **Roger Williams' Greatest Hits** / MCA ◆◆◆◆◆
Roger Williams' Greatest Hits is a good single-disc sampling of the pianist's biggest hits and should satisfy most of his casual fans. Listeners that want to dig deeper should pick up the double-disc set, *The Artist's Choice*. — *Stephen Thomas Erlewine*

Frankie Yankovic

Accordion
Frankie Yankovic was one of the most popular polka band leaders of the '40s and '50s. Yankovic taught himself how to play the accordion when he was a child. At the age of 15, he began playing professionally. Soon, he was leading one of the most popular polka bands in the country. He was at the peak of his popularity at the end of the '40s, when his version of the Czechoslovakian song "Blue Skirt Waltz" was a hit single. Although they never sold many records, Yankovic and his band continued to perform into the '70s, selling out concerts across the US. — *Stephen Thomas Erlewine*

● **Greatest Hits** / CBS ◆◆◆◆
Featuring all of his best-known numbers, *Greatest Hits* offers a solid introduction to the master of the accordion, Frankie Yankovic. — *Stephen Thomas Erlewine*

Gheorghe Zamfir

Flute, Nai, Pan Flute/Panpipes / Easy Listening
Romanian panpipe player Gheorghe Zamfir first reached No. 4 on the UK charts in 1976 with an ethereal hit called "Doina De Jale"—a traditional Eastern funeral piece. He has gone on to make dozens of albums and entrance millions of buyers with the otherworldly sound of the panpipes. His repertoire includes Romanian folk music and classical melodies, but most of all popular film themes. — *Michael Erlewine*

● **Best of Zamfir** / Philips ◆◆◆◆
The Best of Zamfir offers a good cross-section of the pan flautist's best material, making it an effective introduction. Then again, all of Zamfir's albums are remarkably similar, so any of them are a good starting point. — *David Jehnzen*

Romance of the Pan Flute / Philips ◆◆◆
Romance of the Pan Flute offers a good introduction to the ethereal yet lovely sound of Zamfir, showcasing his mastery of tone and his light, romantic phrasing. Nearly all of Zamfir's albums are of equal quality—if you enjoy this, you should enjoy his other records. — *David Jehnzen*

Various Artists

Bachelor Pad Royale / Feb. 1996 / Capitol ◆◆◆
As the title implies, the songs on this 18-song compilation were intended for bachelors who wanted to create a suitably suave atmosphere between the mid-'50s and mid-'60s. So although the music draws from jazz (both big-band and cool), lounge pop, and film/TV soundtracks, it's primarily designed to set a mood or background. That means that when it's pushed to the foreground, it really doesn't sound all that entertaining, even as it evokes archetypical (and oft-silly) vibes of a certain era. Martin Denny, Julie London, Nelson Riddle, and a host of no-names from the Capitol vaults bring you that sound here. When an occasional element of excitement, even danger, creeps in (Riddle's "Theme from Route 66," Elliott Fisher's "Theme from Our Man Flint," Jimmie Haskell's "A Shot in the Dark"), the interest level rises, as it does for any slice of good soundtrack music. Otherwise, these days it makes the ambience stuffier, not cooler. — *Richie Unterberger*

Cocktail Mix, Vol. 1 / Jan. 23, 1996 / Rhino ◆◆◆
This 18-track compilation is largely devoted to lounge/cocktail/easy listening outings of the late '50s and early '60s that were aimed at exploiting the new dimensions of stereo sound. The actual musical content was often trifling; what was more interesting were the somewhat unusual arrangements and utilization of sonic textures. Shimmering percussion, often with a Latin rhythm, was a big element, as were blaring horns and unexpected swoops on the keyboards, along with some embellishments of sound effects and weird (by the era's standards) instruments. It was daring, in a very limited sense, for the time, and charmingly dated several years later. But the slight nature of the material is often tiring, as is its tendency to wander into novelty territory. — *Richie Unterberger*

Cocktail Mix, Vol. 2 / Jan. 23, 1996 / Rhino ✦✦✦✦✦
Certainly the best of Rhino's *Cocktail Mix* series, focusing on the most dance-oriented aspects of "space-age pop." This 18-song compilation could be said to stretch the boundaries of that newly coined genre a bit. After all, Mose Allison, Cal Tjader, Brother Jack McDuff, and Pucho & the Latin Soul Brothers were not so much cocktail musicians as respected jazzmen who drew liberally from Latin music, blues, and pop. Mel Torme (represented by the classic "Comin' Home Baby") and Nancy Wilson were respected "straight" pop vocalists; Quincy Jones and Connie Francis wandered into the playing field with their bossa nova novelties. Ann-Margaret, Sergio Mendes, and Walter Wanderley are more the kind of chintzy good-bad acts you'd expect, but it's silly to get bogged down in classification. The bottom line is that this is infectious suave vintage dance music. It may be suitable for cocktail lounges, but only raucous ones—which is a compliment. —*Richie Unterberger*

Cocktail Mix, Vol. 3 / Jan. 23, 1996 / Rhino ✦✦✦✦✦
A look at the roster of cuts assembled for this 18-cut compilation may have you anticipating a staid set of pre-rock pop, with the likes of Rosemary Clooney, Sammy Davis, Jr., Tony Bennett, Dean Martin, Mel Torme, Bobby Darin, and Peggy Lee. Actually, this is lounge music at its most hepped-up, even getting a bit raucous in spots, and often deploying Latin rhythms to raise the energy level. As for the Rat Packers and Vegas habitues, this is about as hard as they ever swang; from the other direction, we get some of the more dance-conscious sides from performers with higher critical credentials, like Della Reese, Sarah Vaughan, Ella Fitzgerald, and Stan Kenton. Robert Mitchum (singing calypso), Henry Mancini (with one of his best instrumentals, "Something for Cat"), and Latin bandleader Xavier Cugat add variety and novelty to a set that may appeal even to those who disdain adult pop, lounge or otherwise. —*Richie Unterberger*

Easy Rhythms for Your Cocktail Hour / 1995 / DCC ✦✦✦✦✦
As space-age bachelor pad music goes, this is among the goofiest and edgiest. This 14-song survey is heavy on two aspects of the cocktail kitsch genre: then-futuristic, now-primitive synthesizer squawks (Richard Hayman, Dick Hyman, Perrey-Kingsley) and double-entendre sexual innuedos. Sometimes that double entendre was vocal, as in Julie London's "Hot Toddy," or Mel Henke's ridiculous "The Lively Ones" (some of whose dialogue is delivered by Herschel Bernardi). Sometimes the titles of the instrumentals sufficed by themselves (Les Baxter's "Lust," Jerry Murad's "Music to Watch Girls By," Hyman's "The Topless Dancers of Corfu"). And there are old space-age pop standbys like Latin rhythms, stereophonic experimentation, exotica, and mutation of time-honored pop standards worked in. This compilation may not be long on consistency, but on the other hand the track selection is very good, assembling some of the most amusing, fun, and adventurous cocktail music available. —*Richie Unterberger*

● **The History of Space Age Pop, Vol. 1: Melodies and Mischief** / 1995 / RCA ✦✦✦✦✦
"Space-age pop" wasn't called by that name during its heyday; it's the label that's been dreamed up in the '90s, when this sort of experimental easy-listening music, which was in vogue in the '50s and early '60s, had a mini-revival among collectors and pop culture historians. These 16 tracks, all taken from the vaults of RCA, date from the early days of the LP format, when many easy listening albums were aimed at the market of adults who had recently bought their first hi-fi equipment. Accordingly, the records often featured innovative (for the time) stereophonic effects, organ timbres, elaborate orchestration, and ersatz big-band/cool jazz/lounge music designed both to soothe and to utilize the full range of recorded sound. The hybrids that resulted were not just imaginative in the kitschiest fashion, but sometimes downright bizarre, as cornball melodies and vocals collided head on with idiot savant-like quirkiness. There are actually a few big artists here (Henry Mancini, Perez Prado, Esquivel), but the bulk of these names are long forgotten. Is it fun? Certainly. Is it important? Not really. Does it stand up to repeated listenings? I would say not, except if you're a nut for this stuff, in which case it's one of the top (and few) compilations available. Highlight: Sir Juilan's zany, bouncing arrangement of "Caravan" for organ, featuring some of densest, most explosive clusters of tones that could be squeezed from the instrument. —*Richie Unterberger*

● **The History of Space Age Pop, Vol. 2: Mallets in Wonderland** / 1995 / RCA ✦✦✦✦✦
The focus of this volume of *Space Age Pop*, as the title implies, is on percussion instruments. Within the space-age pop rubric, this didn't just mean drums, but all sorts of exotic (by the standards of the '50s and early '60s) touches on vibes, xylophones, bongos, steel drums, and even some instruments more associated with ethnomusicology studies, such as the Burmese gong. The music itself, though, isn't much different from what's found on other *Space Age Pop* volumes: imaginative easy listening, sometimes goofy, sometimes bizarre. In fact, some of the same artists on other volumes reappear here (the Three Suns, Henry Mancini, Esquivel, Perez Prado). Fun, if hardly profound, stuff with some cheesy quasi-eth-

nic flourishes of Latin and South Pacific rhythms. Martin Denny fans will enjoy the exotica-like outings of the wonderfully named Markko Polo Adventurers, particularly on "Rain in Rangoon." —*Richie Unterberger*

● **The History of Space Age Pop, Vol. 3: The Stereo Action Dimensio** / 1995 / RCA ✦✦✦✦✦
RCA's *Stereo Action* series of the early '60s was designed to showcase the possibilities of the then-new medium, particularly the separation of instruments and the "panning" effects that could be created with more than one speaker. This collection concentrates on the kinds of arrangements that highlighted these characteristics: rapid up-and-down scales and glissandos, chimes of bells and glockenspiels for decorative flavor, vibrant organs that run the gamut of high and low timbres, nifty sound effects, and pieces which seem to have been recorded specifically to simultaneously highlight different ends of the sonic spectrum. It still, however, doesn't sound all that much different than the other *Space Age Pop* volumes. That's not a criticism: what you, the modern-day jaded listener, want from this stuff is good clean kitschy fun, not a demonstration of stereo technology, which you've been familiar with for decades. And on that count, this delivers, with cuts from RCA space-age pop faves Esquivel, the Three Suns, and Henry Rene, and similar easy-listening-with-a-strange-twist from several other names that are more obscure. —*Richie Unterberger*

★ **Instrumental Gems of the '60s** / 1995 / Collector's Choice Music ✦✦✦✦✦
A good concept for a collection, one that will appeal to many rock listeners, although this is mostly not rock. Two CDs and 40 tracks, covering most of the biggest nonrock instrumental hits of the '60s, songs which got played on the AM dial right next to the Beatles and Motown. Think of the biggest songs of the type from the era, and they're likely to be here: "Love Is Blue" (Paul Mariat), "Theme from a Summer Place" (Percy Faith), "Calcutta" (Lawrence Welk), "Classical Gas" (Mason Williams), "Washington Square" (the Village Stompers), "Bonanza" (Al Caiola), and so on, including some more obscure numbers and some nearly forgotten one-shot hits by the likes of Arthur Lyman and Bill Purcell (whose "Our Winter Love" has some of the most overmodulated electric bass ever captured on record). A few rock instrumentals do pop up by the String-A-Longs, the T-Bones, and Bill Black, but by and large this doesn't have much to do with rock, encompassing movie themes, pseudo-classical, bossa nova jazz, cocktail jazz, novelties, and more. Sure, some of this is sappy, but many of the tunes are enduring, and sometimes imaginative (or even innovative) in a way found in few easy listening/popular instrumental recordings from subsequent decades. —*Richie Unterberger*

Music for a Bachelor's Den / 1995 / DCC ✦✦✦
As space-age bachelor pad music goes, these were among the most widely heard examples of the genre. Over half of these 15 cuts, in fact, were hit singles, including such smashes as "Quiet Village" (Martin Denny), "So Rare" (Jimmy Dorsey), "Moritat" (Dick Hyman, and later to be changed into "Mack the Knife" by Bobby Darin), "Yellow Bird" (Arthur Lyman), "Theme from Route 66" (Nelson Riddle), and "Moonglow and Love Theme from Picnic" (Morris Stoloff). This means that experts might sniff and deride this collection as too "mainstream." Popular lounge music, however, was no less interesting than collectible lounge music, and perhaps more so. This is a good sampler of the style that was a subordinate but notable part of American popular music in the late '50s and early '60s, especially if you weren't around when these hits were played on AM radio. —*Richie Unterberger*

Music for a Bachelor's Den, Vol. 2: Exotica / 1995 / DCC ✦✦✦✦✦
This 14-track survey isn't the most extensive exotica compilation and lacks the single-minded depth of those Martin Denny and Arthur Lyman anthologies. What it lacks in depth, however, it more than compensates for in breadth, especially as it's not limited to the back catalog of a single specific label. Cuts by some of the standard-bearers of the genre are here (Arthur Lyman, Les Baxter, Yma Sumac, the South Sea Serenaders), as well as more unexpected contributions from Duke Ellington and Percy Faith. The absence of Martin Denny excludes this from the top of the field, but it's one of the better introductions to the strange world of exotica, with the expected more-or-less-equal doses of kitsch and off-the-wall goofiness. —*Richie Unterberger*

RE/SEARCH: Incredibly Strange Music, Vol. 1 / 1994 / Plan 9/Caroline ✦✦✦
RE/SEARCH's two *Incredibly Strange Music* books are fascinating interviews with collectors and musicians, exploring the limits of weird and unclassifiable records, mostly from the '50s and '60s. If this compilation of excerpts from 13 of the LPs discussed in those books is an indication, though, this stuff is a lot more fun to read about than listen to. Most of these, essentially, are novelty records: bad psychedelic sitar, normal enough sounding songs with weirdly awful lyrics, mood music enlivened by off-the-wall sound effects, the "William Tell Overture" performed by a whistler, an interminable "Cosmic Telephone Call," and the like. In other words, the kind of things that are fun to hear once, and maybe later to

pull out and play for friends—once—but not music to stand up to repeated listening. —*Richie Unterberger*

Sound Gallery / Mar. 26, 1996 / Scamp ✦✦✦

Ultra-Lounge, Vol. 10: A Bachelor in Paris / 1996 / Capitol ✦✦✦
Songs with a Parisian motif were a natural for bachelor pad music, the whole genre putting a premium on the sort of suave grace for which French culture is noted. *Bien sur*, when it's refracted through Hollywood easy-listening musicians, you're getting a sound which is about as authentically French as french fries. But no matter—bachelor pad music isn't about authenticity, and this compilation presents some enjoyably cheesy attempts at evoking the city of lights, recorded for Capitol in the '50s and '60s. Whether instrumental or vocal, English or French, giants of the idiom like Les Baxter, Nelson Riddle, and the immortal Dicky Doo & the Don'ts offer their homages, filled with B-movie soundtrack orchestration and blindingly White vocal choruses. There are some surprisingly hot, uptempo jazzy lounge takes on the theme, though, by Sam Butera, Elmer Bernstein, Jack Costanzo, and the Double Six of Paris, featuring a faster-than-light French scat vocal from Mimi Perrin. —*Richie Unterberger*

Ultra-Lounge, Vol. 11: Organs in Orbit / 1996 / Capitol ✦✦✦
The organ has a respected slot in the space-age pop/lounge lineup, and *Organs in Orbit* gives the Hammond its due by featuring 18 cuts in the style, originally recorded for Capitol in the '50s and '60s. It's a long way from here to Jimmy Smith, and you should check any hopes for funkiness at the door. If you've got a yen for the inimitable vibrant qualities of the instrument in some of its less critically respected contexts, however, it's a solid sampling of vintage recordings, even if it sometimes sounds like organs in search of a roller rink. Often these artists revamped standards like "Patricia," "The Third Man Theme," "Perfidia," and "Fever," but the Forbidden Five's "Enchanted Farm" (a "Quiet Village" satire?) pushes the envelope by inserting sound effects of roosters crowing. Besides organ outings by well-known space-age popsters Martin Denny, Ernie Freeman, John Buzon, Billy May, and Walter Wanderley, you also hear it put to weirder use by unknowns like Sir Julian, who gave the instrument a shaky quality with frequencies that could probably burst martini glasses. Another bonus is the inclusion of two instrumentals by none other than Denny McLain, the notorious '60s star baseball pitcher who played organ on the side. —*Richie Unterberger*

Ultra-Lounge, Vol. 12: Saxophobia / 1996 / Capitol ✦✦✦
The lounge sounds of the '50s and '60s on this compilation are very much of a piece with the other volumes of the *Ultra-Lounge* series. But as you'd expect from the title, the emphasis is on vintage lounge at its jazziest, with the saxophone to the fore. This isn't the kind of jazz you're going to read about in *Down Beat*, despite the presence of some bona fide jazzers, like Count Basie (doing the "Goldfinger" theme) and Bill Perkins; the influence of soundtrack music, pre-'50s pop standards, Latin rhythms, and bongo percussion is too strong. When you want some light lounge-jazz hybrids to unwind to after your jazz scholar friends have gone home, though, this isn't bad. Les Baxter, Nelson Riddle, and Gordon Jenkins make their expected appearances on this compilation; more surprising is the inclusion of top R&B saxophonist King Curtis, who does a pop-friendly version of Herbie Hancock's "Watermelon Man," and teams up with ace rock session drummer Earl Palmer on "One Mint Julep." Also worth noting are Vegas-jump blues kings Louis Prima and Sam Butera, who do a smoky version of "Harlem Nocturne." —*Richie Unterberger*

Ultra-Lounge, Vol. 1: Mondo Exotica / Feb. 1996 / Capitol ✦✦✦
An 18-song exhumation of the Capitol exotica back catalog, placing old standbys like Martin Denny, Les Baxter, and Yma Sumac alongside lesser-knowns like Webley Edwards, Bas Sheva, and the wonderfully named 80 Drums Around the World. This favors easy-listening-friendly exotica, rather than the style at its most outrageous. It may be too narcoticizing for some, but connoisseurs will appreciate the inclusion of the rarer material; a couple of the cuts were even previously unreleased. —*Richie Unterberger*

Ultra-Lounge, Vol. 2: Mambo Fever / Feb. 1996 / Capitol ✦✦✦
When Latin bandleaders popularized mambo in the early '50s, this set many pop and big-band acts scrambling to get in on the action. *Mambo Fever*, part two of Capitol's *Ultra-Lounge* series, takes 18 such examples from the vaults, spanning the mid-'50s to the early '60s. Yma Sumac and Billy May are the only readily recognizable names on this compilation, which is akin to hearing competent, somewhat Whited-out derivations of Perez Prado. There are odd touches like Sumac's high-frequency warbles, John Buzon's roller-rink organ runs, and the sheer silliness of Chuy Reyes' "Oink, Oink Mambo." But the results are oddly similar, on one level, to hearing some White bands try to play the blues—in comparison to the most genuine article, it's somewhat sanitized for broader consumption. That's not to deny its considerable fun (if lightweight) qualities; this usually works up respectable heat, in addition to evoking the slightly kitschy '50s mentality that is a necessary ingredient of the space-age pop revival. —*Richie Unterberger*

Ultra-Lounge, Vol. 3: Space Capades / Feb. 1996 / Capitol ✦✦✦
In the late '50s and early '60s, this was the easy-listening music that tried to anticipate the space age. Utilizing theremin or spooky organ figures helped, as did then-novel tricks like stereo separation and then-exotic instruments and hi-fi effects. It wasn't just novelty artists that got in on the act; bandleaders Les Baxter and David Rose, who perform some of the 18 tracks assembled here, also tried their hands. This compilation still falls closer to novelty than either innovation or period kitsch (although there's plenty of the latter). Some will complain that I'm not getting into the spirit of the thing, but there's more banality than entertainment here. As amusing as some of these gimmicky records sound upon first or second hearing, it lends itself even less to repeated plays than most of the space-age bachelor pad reissues. —*Richie Unterberger*

Ultra-Lounge, Vol. 5: Wild Cool & Swingin / Feb. 20, 1996 / Capitol ✦✦✦
This 18-song compilation is the showbiz-encased, Vegasized school of late '50s and early '60s pop vocals. The emphasis is certainly more on the "cool" than the wild and swinging; if it ever breaks out a sweat, there will be a martini-dipped silk handkerchief on hand to wipe it away. You get selections from Rat Packers (Dean Martin, Sammy Davis, Jr.), African-American mainstream pop (Nat King Cole, Lou Rawls), adult pop stars (Bobby Darin, Peggy Lee, Julie London), adult pop with a dash of vaudevillian slapstick (Louis Prima & Keely Smith), and those for whom Vegas was always the prize (a teenaged Wayne Newton). Targeted toward the nuevo cocktail crowd (five of Capitol's *Ultra Lounge* series), it's not the most satisfying survey of the form. Serious fans of pop vocals will find it too scattershot, and its packaging too flippant; space-age poppers will find it too old-school cornball for their tastes, even if they're told it's part of some sort of cutting edge. —*Richie Unterberger*

Ultra-Lounge, Vol. 6: Rhapsodesia / Feb. 20, 1996 / Capitol ✦✦✦
The sixth volume of Capitol's *Ultra Lounge* series, this focuses on the most sedate face of space-age bachelor pad music: the sounds designed for dimming the lights, unwinding with martinis, and (stated implicitly: this was the '50s, remember) seduction. It might not have worked for those purposes then, and it certainly won't now, since prospective partners will be giggling too much at the cheesiness of it all to get it on. As far as sheer listening value, this, even more than other reissues of this sort, needs to be taken lightly or not at all. Julie London, Les Baxter, April Stevens, and a host of nonentities from the Capitol vaults may produce relaxing sounds, but not very involving ones. Those creepy organ lines that form the undercurrent of some of the selections provide the most fascination. At its worst, though, it's barely any better than the music you'll hear after you're put on hold by the airlines or the phone company. —*Richie Unterberger*

Ultra-Lounge, Vol. 7: Crime Scene / Jul. 1996 / Capitol ✦✦✦
One of the kitschier installments in the *Ultra Lounge* series, *Vol. 7, Crime Scene* features a cross-section of easy-listening and movie music culled primarily from Capitol Records' vaults. All of the songs are allegedly "about" or inspired by detective and crime novels and films, so you have movie and television themes (Nelson Riddle's "The Untouchables," "Peter Gunn Suite" as performed by Ray Anthony), as well as songs whose titles imply a crime connection of some sort. It's an enjoyable collection, but it's too incoherent and campy to really be consistently entertaining. —*Stephen Thomas Erlewine*

Ultra-Lounge, Vol. 8: Cocktail Capers / 1996 / Capitol ✦✦✦✦✦
If you've been following the *Ultra-Lounge* series this far, you know what to expect: a mixture of stars (Les Baxter, Nelson Riddle) and no-names from the Capitol vaults, playing space-age pop/cocktail music of all hues in the '50s and '60s. Yet this has an edge over most of the previous titles in the series: there's more of a sense of swing, groove, even (dare we say) *danger* on much of this, albeit danger of a very safe sort. Hints of rock 'n' roll and spy music even creep in from time to time, with James Bond-type reverb guitar decorating cuts like Al Caiola's "Underwater Chase," and top rock 'n' roll session drummer Earl Palmer getting into the bongo/lounge vibe on "Binga Banga Bongo/Percolator." Another highlight is the highly sought-after theme song to Stanley Kubrick's 1962 film *Lolita*, performed as a tongue-in-cheek rock 'n' roll satire by Nelson Riddle (with surfish twangy guitar, orchestration, and a chipper chorus of young girls adding wordless "ya-ya" vocals throughout). —*Richie Unterberger*

Ultra-Lounge, Vol. 9: Cha-Cha De Amor / 1996 / Capitol ✦✦✦
Cha-cha music at its Whitest and most easy-listening-friendly, recorded for Capitol in the '50s and '60s by Dean Martin, Julie London, Billy May, Martin Denny, Les Baxter, Walter Wanderley, and a number of other performers who are only coming to light in the lounge revival. Yma Sumac, Perez Prado, and Tito Rodriguez add a little (a very little) raunch and guts on their tracks, and there are also hints of bossa nova at times. But overall it's cha-cha at its ch-cheesiest. —*Richie Unterberger*

NEW AGE

As the Beatles took the US by storm, jazz artist Tony Scott took a deep breath and played the first notes of *Music for Zen Meditation*. Back then, no one really knew what to do with an exotic set of interactions between clarinet, Japanese koto, and shakuhachi flute. Released on Verve in 1964, *Music for Zen Meditation* remained an anomaly in the jazz label's bebop and swing catalog until this subtle cross-cultural venture was hailed as the first "new age" album some 20 years later. If Scott had come up with the same American-Japanese collaboration in the '90s, he might just have easily found himself under the "world music" banner.

Scott's story is not unusual among contemporary instrumental artists. If these musicians have anything in common at all, it's their ability and intention to defy categorization. Of course, this sort of attitude tends to confound everyone else: from record labels, distributors, critics, and retailers to listeners trying to find the music in stores.

After a few frustrating decades trying to force innovative, instrumental releases into jazz and classical markets, some members of the record industry thought they had come across a handy new term. In the mid-'80s, new age music became the catchall designation for recordings that didn't seem to fit anywhere else. This phrase arose from the music's success in alternative outlets like health food stores, bookstores, and occult-oriented stores, as well as massage and meditation centers associated with the new age movement. However,

while a small number of artists openly supported new age lifestyles and concepts through their music, most instrumentalists resented the association. As the '80s came to a close, cynical members of the media were having a field day allying the new age music-marketing category with crystal gazers and trance channelers, in the process ignoring the merits of serious artists with highly original ideas. The whole thing left a bad taste in everyone's mouth, and much effort was made in the early '90s to wipe out the stigma of this unfortunate development.

Back when the phrase "new age" was being thrown around as a musical designation, some people lobbied for the more general designation "contemporary instrumental." It wasn't short or catchy enough for most marketing executives, but increasing numbers of artists, record companies, critics, and radio producers have been using it. Contemporary instrumental (or CI for short, if you wish) is one of the few terms broad enough to encompass the myriad approaches and innovations taking place daily in this field. We've also come up with a list of subgenres to distinguish certain trends that have arisen in recent years; however, most artists regularly cross, combine, and recombine these tendencies as well. It's just the nature of CI musicians to create new fusions based on fusions of fusions. *—Linda Kohanov*

Philip Aaberg

Keyboards, Vocals / Solo Instrumental, Adult Alternative, Chamber Jazz
This Montana-born keyboardist and composer studied music at Harvard on a Leonard Bernstein scholarship before paying his dues on the San Francisco blues scene. Aaberg's wide range of abilities led to guest appearances on over 80 albums. He also toured with artists as varied as Peter Gabriel, John Hiatt, Kenny Rogers, and the Doobie Brothers. Upon signing with Windham Hill in 1985, Aaberg made his eclectic background pay off through a series of solo albums that show off his rigorous keyboard technique, diverse influences, and colorful compositional style. *—Linda Kohanov*

High Plains / Windham Hill ◆◆◆
Aaberg's Windham Hill debut features solo piano pieces with folk and impressionistic elements that evoke the wide-open spaces of the American West. *—Linda Kohanov*

● **Out of the Frame** / 1979 / Windham Hill ◆◆◆◆
These lush, yet pensive, instrumental pieces masterfully combine acoustic and electronic sounds. *—Linda Kohanov*

Upright / 1980 / Windham Hill ◆◆◆
Aaberg calls this the first Windham Hill dance record. Upbeat toe-tappers are complemented by graceful slow numbers. *—Linda Kohanov*

William Ackerman

b. Nov. 1949, Germany
Guitar / New Age, Solo Instrumental, Adult Alternative, Chamber Jazz
William Ackerman has gained prominence both as a musician and a businessman, and at least one of those occupations seems to have been unintentional. Though Ackerman has played guitar since the age of 12, when he dropped out of college it was to become a carpenter, and his first company was called Windham Hill Builders. But Ackerman composed guitar music for Stanford University theater productions, and the encouragement of friends led him to record an album of his tunes, *The Search for the Turtle's Navel*, in 1976. The album was surprisingly successful, and Ackerman found himself in the music business. Since then, Ackerman has continued to record his own albums, to produce Windham Hill

albums for such other artists as George Winston, Alex de Grassi, and Liz Story, and to serve in various capacities in the record company. (He stepped down as CEO in 1986; his function now is primarily A&R, the liaison between a record company and its artists.) Though Ackerman has long since sickened of the new age tag, threatening physical violence against anyone categorizing Windham Hill's music with the term, he has had more to do with the rise of acoustic-based instrumental music as a popular form in the '70s and '80s than anyone else. *— William Ruhlmann*

In Search of the Turtle's Navel / 1976 / Windham Hill ◆◆◆

Passage / 1981 / Windham Hill ◆◆◆◆
These four pieces are arranged for solo guitar along with four duets, featuring cello, English horn, piano by George Winston, and violin by Darol Anger. Four new Ackerman compositions and four digitally recorded versions of previously recorded works. *—MusD*

Past Light / 1983 / Windham Hill ◆◆◆

Imaginary Roads / 1990 / Windham Hill ◆◆◆◆
William Ackerman plays guitar and owns his own record label in California. *Imaginary Roads* finds Will Ackerman playing mostly in an ensemble context, with nice textures and melodies. *—MusD*

The Opening of Doors / 1992 / Windham Hill ◆◆◆

★ **Windham Hill Retrospective** / 1993 / Windham Hill ◆◆◆◆◆
Reflecting a body of work spanning eight albums, Will Ackerman's guitar music has become synonymous with the Windham Hill sound of excellence. This retrospective features guest artists Shadowfax, George Winston, Michael Hedges, and others. It's an hour's worth of great Ackerman. Whether the dialogue is between Ackerman and piano, or Ackerman and violin, or Ackerman and clarinet, the conversation scintillates, rings true, and leaves us wanting to spend more time listening. *—MusD*

Ancient Future

Adult Alternative, Ethnic Fusion
Ancient Future was formed in 1978 by guitarist Matthew Montfort, who was interested in combining ancient musical traditions with modern technology. The band's inviting melodies, exotic instruments, and ethnic textures helped popularize world music fusion. *—Linda Kohanov*

Quiet Fire / 1986 / Sona Gaia ✦✦✦
A more subtle approach to the mix of new age lyricism and world music rhythms. —*Linda Kohanov*

Dreamchaser / 1988 / Narada ✦✦✦
Dreamchaser presents world music at its best, with a sampling of influences ranging from the Andes to India to Bali and beyond. Great dynamics and a sense of drama. —*MusD*

● **World Without Walls** / 1990 / Sona Gaia ✦✦✦✦
This squeaky-clean acoustic romp by the San Francisco quartet through African and Asian rhythms has a dose of jazz and a dollop of Zakir Hussain sitting in on Indian percussion. —*Bob Tarte*

Asian Fusion / 1993 / Narada ✦✦✦
Jim Hurley and Matthew Montfort's shared violin-and-guitar-line leads catch hold of a strong melody and bite down hard. But despite Zhao Hui's Chinese *gu sheng* board zither, Bui Hui Nhut's *dan bao* Vietnamese one-stringed lute, and assorted ethnic percussion, vernacular instruments don't share equal weight with the band's folk-classical thrust, and the cuts that are carved from indigenous music—"The Dusk Song of the Fisherman" or the lovely Indonesian *degung* of "Sunda Strait"—tilt somewhat toward the generic. Still, the disc's got plenty of fire, and its loveliness often surprises. —*Bob Tarte*

Natural Rhythms / 1994 / Arista ✦✦✦✦
While the Bay Area ensemble's duets with Balinese and Pacific frogs don't live up to the hype of "interspecies recordings," the blend of bamboo percussion instruments, zither, and peeps from the pond is enchanting, far better realized than shared billings with wolves, whales, lemurs, or porcupines encountered elsewhere. Among the evocative instrumental pieces that owe no debts to any specific genre is "Hummingbird," a showcase for Future cofounder Mindia Klein's *bansuri* flute in a performance so breathtakingly lovely I'm grateful for the puffs of breath between phrasings as proof this isn't interspecies jamming with an ethereal lifeform. —*Bob Tarte*

Tuck Andress

Guitar / New Age, Instrumental Pop, Solo Instrumental, New Acoustic
Probably best known as half of the guitar/vocal duo Tuck And Patti, Andress' music is a blend of jazz, funk, R&B, and blues. His incredible technique enables him to sound like three guitarists playing simultaneously. —*Paul Kohler*

● **Reckless Precision** / 1990 / Windham Hill ✦✦✦✦
Tuck Andress is the instrumental half of the successful Windham Hill guitar and vocal duo Tuck and Patti. On his first solo album Andress' extraordinary technical skills and musical range are given center stage. For sheer virtuosity, few guitarists can match his pyrotechnical wizardry. He has developed a unique style that allows him to play lead, rhythm, and bass parts simultaneously, often at dizzying speed, but never sacrificing warmth and sensitivity. Recorded live in the studio, without overdubs, the material ranges from Michael Jackson's "Man in the Mirror" and the garage rock classic "Louie Louie" to the jazz standards "Body and Soul" and "Begin the Beguine" to a Wizard of Oz medley, "Over the Rainbow/If I Only Had a Brain." Three originals are included: "Sweet P," dedicated to his wife and musical partner Patti Cathcart; "Manonash," written at the tomb of his spiritual teacher, Meher Baba; and the extended collage "Grooves of Joy." Though it was never in doubt, the aptly titled *Reckless Precision* should solidify Andress' reputation as one of the most brilliant guitar players alive today. —*Backroads Music/Heartbeats*

David Arkenstone

Guitar, Keyboards / Adult Alternative, Progressive Electronic
Southern California-based Arkenstone honed his chops as a guitarist and keyboardist in various local bands and touring groups before the music of Kitaro inspired him to create a lavish synthesizer-based sound of his own. Most of his albums have enjoyed lengthy runs on new age sales charts due to a combination of accessible melodies, pop sensibilities, and cinematic textures. —*Linda Kohanov*

★ **Valley in the Clouds** / 1987 / Narada ✦✦✦✦✦
Arkenstone's finest album of electronic soundscapes is also his least commercial effort. Nicely designed atmospheres and warm, flowing melodies characterize Arkenstone's first album for Narada. —*Linda Kohanov*

Island / 1989 / Narada ✦✦
Citizen of Time / 1990 / Narada ✦✦✦
This sonic odyssey tells the story of a traveler who visits earth's past and present civilizations. The album has some nice moments, but generally the concept is more ambitious than the music. —*Linda Kohanov*

In the Wake of the Wind / 1991 / Narada ✦✦
The Spirit of Olympia / 1992 / Narada ✦✦✦
David Arkenstone, David Lanz, and Kostia of the Soviet Union teamed up to create an album in the spirit of the Olympic games, celebrating the

beauty, energy, camaraderie, and ideals of athletic competition. They have taken traditional orchestral arrangements and added their own personal style and vision to a modern uptempo rendering via synthesizer, electric guitar, and percussion. Broad in scope and far-reaching in its collective musical vision. Arkenstone and his comrades provide varied, adventurous listening. —*Backroads Music/Heartbeats*

Chronicles / 1993 / Narada Artist ✦✦✦✦
With his collection titled *Chronicles*, it is possible to hear Arkenstone's most influential and successful compositions in one carefully packaged effort. Along with Richard Burmer, Peter Buffet, and Patrick O'Hearn, Arkenstone has been one of the most enduring artists of the more active side of the genre. —*Backroads Music/Heartbeats*

Ashra

Adult Alternative, Progressive Electronic, Ambient, Minimalism
Formed in the late '60s by guitarist and synthesist Manuel Gottsching, this German group was highly influential in contemporary electronic music. Ashra's album *New Age of Earth* (1977) is a classic in that it foreshadows the serene atmospherics used by subsequent "space-music" composers. Gottsching continues to record, though the results have been uneven. His rock-based albums are generally uninspiring, while his more recent work, which tends toward a form of trance-inducing electronic minimalism, is interesting, though not particularly original. —*Linda Kohanov*

● **New Age of Earth** / 1977 / Blue Plate ✦✦✦✦
The last great Ashra disc—all spacey, floating guitars and synthesizers. —*Michael P. Dawson*

William Aura

Synthesizer / New Age, Adult Alternative
Before signing with Higher Octave Records in the late '80s, Aura composed music for the healing arts based on research into psycho-acoustic audio production. He mixed zithers and other acoustic instruments with synthesizers to create a warm, relaxing bath of sounds. Aura has picked up the tempo on his latest albums with pleasant results. —*Linda Kohanov*

Half Moon Bay / 1987 / Higher Octave ✦✦✦✦
Aura's first recording for Higher Octave was recorded at a seaside studio in Half Moon Bay, CA. It has lots of ocean ambience and silky synthesizer washes. —*Linda Kohanov*

● **Timepiece** / 1988 / Higher Octave ✦✦✦✦
Timepiece (A Ten Year Perspective) is a good introduction to Aura's style and appeal. The album is a compilation of selected works from the first ten years of his career. —*Linda Kohanov*

Paradise / 1991 / Higher Octave ✦✦✦
Some remixes of Aura's early music for healing come complete with 3-D nature sounds. —*Linda Kohanov*

Every Act of Love / 1992 / Higher Octave ✦✦✦
Though the album is billed as "global fusion for the contemporary mainstream," it really has more to do with pop and light jazz than anything ethnic. Aura's characteristic synthesizer timbres are enhanced by saxophone, piano, drums, and flute. —*Linda Kohanov*

The World Keeps Turning / Jan. 15, 1992 / Higher Octave ✦✦

Paul Avgerinos

Progressive Electronic, Ethnic Fusion, Ambient, Space
Avgerinos is a classically trained composer who served as principal bassist with the Hong Kong Philharmonic and performed with numerous other orchestras. He has also toured with popular music and jazz acts and has done some scoring for films and television commercials. His true calling, however, seems to be as an electronic-music composer. The three albums he has released so far are gems. —*Linda Kohanov*

Balancing Spheres / 1988 / World Room ✦✦✦
Softly unfolding sequencer patterns, whispered synthesizer harmonies, and evocative electronic effects that shimmer and melt characterize this two-part journey through "Day Dreams" and "Night Illusions." —*Linda Kohanov*

Maya: The Great Katun / 1988 / World Room ✦✦✦
A powerful portrayal of an ancient Mayan ritual, this deliciously cryptic music consists of sacred words chanted over ceremonial percussion and atmospheric electronic sounds that draw forth shadows from other realms. —*Linda Kohanov*

● **Muse of the Round Sky** / 1992 / Hearts of Space ✦✦✦✦
These richly impressionistic soundscapes were inspired by Avgerinos' ancestral homeland of Greece. Guest artists include guitarist Brian Keane and Omar Faruk Tekbilek, who plays Middle Eastern flutes. The composer's dense synthesizer textures and dreamy electronic effects make the album feel like one long, luscious mirage. —*Linda Kohanov*

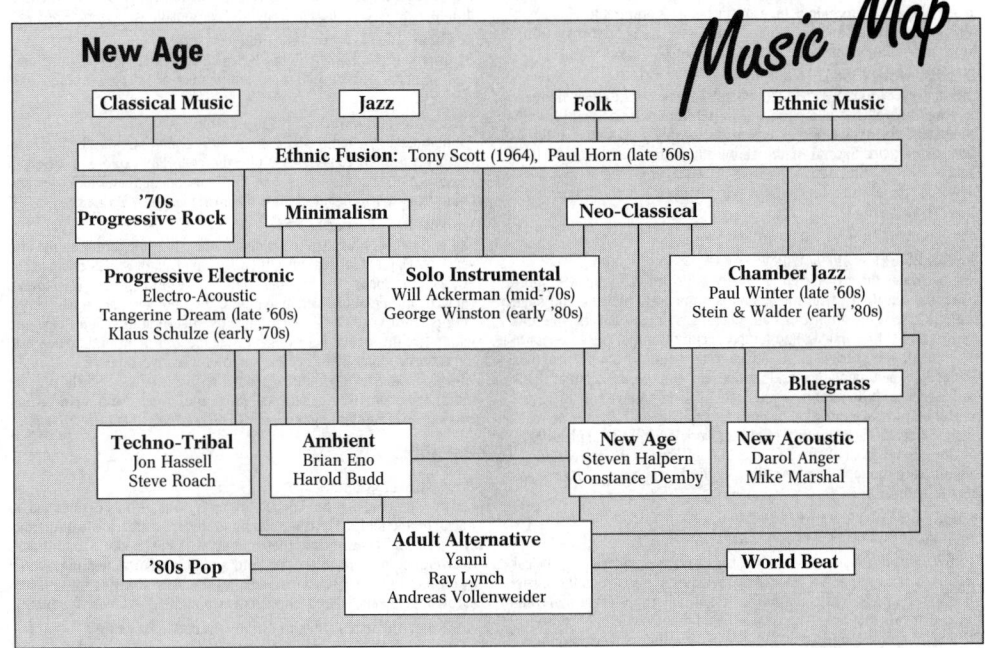

New Age — Music Map

Classical Music | Jazz | Folk | Ethnic Music

Ethnic Fusion: Tony Scott (1964), Paul Horn (late '60s)

'70s Progressive Rock | Minimalism | Neo-Classical

Progressive Electronic
Electro-Acoustic
Tangerine Dream (late '60s)
Klaus Schulze (early '70s)

Solo Instrumental
Will Ackerman (mid-'70s)
George Winston (early '80s)

Chamber Jazz
Paul Winter (late '60s)
Stein & Walder (early '80s)

Bluegrass

Techno-Tribal
Jon Hassell
Steve Roach

Ambient
Brian Eno
Harold Budd

New Age
Steven Halpern
Constance Demby

New Acoustic
Darol Anger
Mike Marshal

'80s Pop

Adult Alternative
Yanni
Ray Lynch
Andreas Vollenweider

World Beat

Wally Badarou

b. 1955
Synthesizer / Adult Alternative, Ethnic Fusion, Ambient, Electro Acoustic
Badarou was born in Paris, where his physician parents were educated and his father later served as ambassador from their West African homeland of Cotonon Benin (formerly Dahomey). Although he planned a career as a pilot, he was seduced by synthesizers and rock 'n' roll, eventually becoming a well-known session keyboardist in England and his own Nassau, Bahamas, studio. Badarou's early career included work with M (on the hit "Pop Musik"), Joe Cocker, Herbie Hancock, and Island Records artists like Grace Jones, Black Uhuru, and the British funk band Level 42. In addition to his production and keyboard work for Level 42, he has done several film scores, most notably *Kiss of the Spider Woman*. You can hear both the rhythmic sensitivity of his African heritage and the harmonic sensibility of his classical training in his music. His expressive and sophisticated synthesizer textures are full of life, especially on his more dance-oriented *Echoes* album. —*Scott Bultman*

● **Echoes** / 1985 / Island ✦✦✦✦
You can actually feel Caribbean sunshine with this music. Badarou breathes real life into his synthesizers on this album of happy, upbeat, and danceable instrumentals. —*Scott Bultman*

Words of a Mountain / 1989 / Island ✦✦✦
This album has a more contemplative mood than his last and a classical feel, although the atmospheres are no less vivid. —*Scott Bultman*

Patrick Ball

Harp / Irish, Solo Instrumental
With a vast knowledge of folklore and music from the British Isles, Celtic harp player Patrick Ball calls forth the music of a simpler, more magical time. His scintillating performances on the traditional wire-strung harp are by far the best-selling titles on the Fortuna label. —*Linda Kohanov*

● **Celtic Harp 1: Music of Turlough O'Carolan** / Jan. 1983 / Fortuna ✦✦✦✦
Lovers of folk, classical, and new age music have described this album as enchanting. It features the bell-like tones and spacious resonance of the traditional wirestrung Celtic harp. Patrick Ball plays 17 instrumental pieces, of which all but two were composed by Turlough O'Carolan. O'Carolan's music blends the richness of Italian Baroque influences with the lilting charm of the music of his native Ireland. —*MusD*

Celtic Harp 2: From a Distant Time / Feb. 1983 / Fortuna ✦✦✦
The crystal clear sounds of the Celtic harp make this a lovely sequel to Patrick Ball's first album. In this recording, he plays 18 pieces from the rich and timeless folk traditions of the British Isles, as well as one contemporary American piece written in the traditional form. With the release of

his first album, Ball established himself as one of the leading talents in the current renaissance of the wirestrung Celtic folk harp. —*MusD*

Fiona / 1993 / Celestial Harmonies ✦✦✦
Internationally acclaimed harpist Patrick Ball presents selections from the legacy of historic Gaelic music. The brass-strung Celtic harp, with its deep resonance and crystalline, bell-like voice, is dear to the hearts of the Gaelic people. It was how they celebrated their feasts and sang their legends. Ball addresses this renowned instrument with grace and strength made even more impressive with the addition of uillean bagpipes, fiddle, and tin whistle. Cuts include "Castle Kelly," "Morrison's Jig," and "Brian Boru's March." —*MusD*

Pete Bardens

Keyboards / Adult Alternative, Progressive Electronic
Best known for his work with the '70s progressive rock band Camel, Bardens has played with a number of rock legends over the years. His solo instrumental music is catchy and well-produced, yet rarely ventures beyond the tenets of pop music and suffers as a result. —*Linda Kohanov*

● **Seen One Earth** / 1987 / Capitol ✦✦✦✦
This concept album was based on the space exploration and astronaut book *The Right Stuff*. —*Linda Kohanov*

Speed of Light / 1988 / Cinema ✦✦✦
This half-instrumental/half-vocal project was released as a follow-up to the popular *Seen One Earth*. —*Linda Kohanov*

Water Colors / 1991 / Miramar ✦✦✦✦
During Pete Bardens' successful musical career he has been a member of many bands and has played with such respected musicians as Ray Davies, Mick Fleetwood, and Pete Green (who went on to form Fleetwood Mac), Rod Stewart, and Van Morrison. Today, Bardens is a successful solo artist, and this release proves that. *Water Colors* is based visually and musically on a water theme and is crafted with rich textures and beautiful melodies. The album is inspired by a video of the same name that was filmed in Yellowstone National Park and Alaska. —*MusD*

Further Than You Know / 1993 / Miramar ✦✦✦
Bardens was leader of the group Camel and has several solo albums since the demise of the group. *Further Than You Know* continues his journey into contemporary vocal compositions, while he remains true to his roots with three exciting instrumentals that showcase his unique, sophisticated, and rhythmic blend of jazz and rock styles. —*Backroads Music/Heartbeats*

Bruce BecVar

Synthesizer, Guitar / Adult Alternative
This California guitarist and synthesist writes highly melodic, commer-

cially accessible ensemble music. Though he plays most of the instruments himself, his technique on acoustic guitar is admirable. He's also a well-known luthier; one of his hand-crafted guitars is on display at the New York Metropolitan Museum of Art. —*Linda Kohanov*

Take It to Heart / 1986 / Willow ✦✦✦✦
Each and every song fits together and falls into place like a warm breeze fanning the branches of a palm tree in the tropics. If you want to fully understand the appeal of new age music, simply give a good listen to *Take It to Heart*. Several of the compositions on this debut, such as "Jenna's Song," "Blue Ridge," "Tropic of Daydream," and "Hymn for a New Age" are now classics in this wonderful musical genre. —*Backroads Music/Heartbeats*

The Nature of Things / 1988 / Willow ✦✦✦
★ **Forever Blue Sky** / 1989 / Willow ✦✦✦✦✦
No one relates the acoustic guitar to electronic orchestration with more grace and sensitivity, with music that is immensely melodic and open hearted. Like a breath of fresh air, BecVar's stylings span the rainbow spectrum of colors, moods, and tempos, gently transporting listeners to the tranquil and spacious destinations conjured up by the album's title. The endless panorama of sparkling hues pouring from his guitar floats the listener on billows of new music that is ever so inviting, offering a masterful musical expression by one of today's top new age artists. Without question, this is Bruce BecVar's finest work yet and a total pleasure in all ways. To top it all off, the sound quality of *Forever Blue Sky* is totally superb, each nuance and transition perfectly captured. —*Backroads Music/Heartbeats*

Arriba / 1993 / Willow ✦✦✦
Rhythms of Life / Higher Octave ✦✦✦
On *Rhythms of Life,* Bruce BecVar reaches a new pinnacle of musical heights with the expansive, cascading melodies of his rich guitar music. He is joined on his fourth album by a cast of stellar musicians, and combines elements that travel across and blend many contemporary styles. His music sounds immediately familiar in a number of ways, as innovative musical progressions come to life in his recognizable style, consummately expressed with synthesizer, percussion, and melodic vocal tones. His success is a result of his heartfelt and sensitive acoustic melodies and lead lines combined with dynamic, multi-instrumental arrangements. —*Backroads Music/Heartbeats*

Pierre Bensusan

Guitar / Solo Instrumental, Chamber Jazz, Ethnic Fusion
This French guitarist was actually born in Algeria and has long been fascinated with his North African roots as well as the Celtic folk traditions of western Europe. After making a name for himself as a folk musician in the late '70s, Bensusan began to incorporate jazz and classical elements into his music, creating a virtuosic, highly original style on the acoustic guitar. —*Linda Kohanov*

Solilai / 1982 / CBS ✦✦✦✦
Pierre Bensusan did long, spirited numbers on this session, which was issued in America in 1993 by Dadgad. He played both acoustic and electro-acoustic guitar, as well as adding his own bass and percussive accompaniment at times. Bensusan stretched out on "Bamboule," "Suite Flamande aux Pommes" and the title cut, doing more than slight melodic variations. He demonstrated a craft and ability indicating that he could be a fine improviser if so inclined. Those who have shied away from other Bensusan albums due to the lack of ambitiousness might try this one; it's the closest he's come on any CD to displaying significant jazz skills. —*Ron Wynn*

Spices / 1987 / Rounder ✦✦✦
Pres de Paris / 1991 / Rounder ✦✦✦
Pres de Paris/P.B. 2 / 1992 / Rounder ✦✦✦
● **Musiques** / 1993 / Lost Lake Arts ✦✦✦✦
Pierre Bensusan is a marvelous technical guitarist; he has speed, flair, touch, and expressiveness. While he doesn't play with either fire or improvisational elan, he demonstrates tremendous skills throughout the 13 pieces on this anthology of late-'70s singles. With the exception of "Perles de Cristal" and "Si Bhig, Si Mnor/The Rakish Paddy," these are short, ethereal, atmospheric pieces played nicely by Bensusan. The melodies and voicings are stylish, done in a dreamy, catchy manner. There are bits of flamenco and Spanish guitar, and it's all brilliantly executed. If you're seeking tough, harsh, or gritty material, look elsewhere. —*Ron Wynn*

Daniel Blanchet

Guitar / Neo-Classical, Progressive Electronic, Ambient
A classically trained guitarist, Montreal-based Blanchet is part of a growing electronic music contingent in Canada. He began experimenting with synthesizers in 1985, intrigued by their endless possibilities of sound color and spatial enhancement. Blanchet's early fascination with

Bach's oratorios is reflected in his use of electronic reverb to create cathedral-like dimensions for his thoughtful compositions. —*Linda Kohanov*

Le Chemin de l'Ermite / 1987 / Rubicon ✦✦✦
Blanchet's first album features lyrical pieces that suggest imaginary environments with an innocence reminiscent of Kitaro. —*Linda Kohanov*

● **L'Harmonie des Mondes** / 1991 / Rubicon ✦✦✦✦
An homage to the famous *Harmony of the Spheres* treatise by the 16th-century astronomer Johannes Kepler, this collection explores a variety of musical moods and settings with the same poetic theme of order and beauty that Kepler believed ruled the universe. —*Linda Kohanov*

Les Voilers de l'Espace / ✦✦✦
Old and new are blended to create a fantasy journey through time and space by Daniel Blanchet on *Les Voilers de l'Espace*, which means "The Voyagers of Space." His previous titles, *Le Chemin* and *Les Harmonies*, showed considerable diversity within contemporary space music styles. On his latest venture, Blanchet takes us in several directions. Opening with a five-movement suite of gentle synthesizer orchestration supporting acoustic guitar, Blanchet leads into provocative, modern landscapes with sweeping textures and sensuous harp melodies. Stylistically, the music falls somewhere between Jarre and Lynch, with planetarium atmospherics similar to Jonn Serrie's. —*Backroads Music/Heartbeats*

Botanica

Progressive Electronic
Led by synthesist Sanford Ponder, this group creates music generated by fractal mathematics. The computer programs are connected to numerous synthesizers. The musicians then interact with the resulting soundtracks by overdubbing percussion, sax, flute, and piano. For something created by the seemingly impartial mathematics of "chaos" theories, this music is surprisingly beautiful and emotionally stimulating. —*Linda Kohanov*

● **A Garden of Earthly Delights** / 1989 / Deep Music ✦✦✦✦
Though both Botanica releases are well worth owning, the band's first fractal effort is more serene and melodious, thus more accessible. —*Linda Kohanov*

Strange Attractor / 1991 / Deep Music ✦✦✦
The album's title is probably the best description of this music. Sometimes mysterious and floating, other times aggressively beat-oriented, *Strange Attractor* sounds like something you might encounter in outer space. —*Linda Kohanov*

Kevin Braheny

Synthesizer / New Age, Progressive Electronic, Ambient
This Los Angeles-based synthesist builds much of his own equipment, including the 3-D binaural recording technology he uses on his *Secret Rooms* album. His sounds and special effects are sophisticated and highly evocative, but Braheny's music is not all technique. His graceful improvisations on electronic wind instruments bring a lyrical dimension to his music. —*Linda Kohanov*

● **The Way Home** / 1978 / Hearts of Space ✦✦✦✦
Expressive, tender music for synthesizer and electronic woodwinds, this sound-space of profound serenity is a true space music classic. —*Backroads Music/Heartbeats*

Galaxies / 1988 / Hearts of Space ✦✦✦✦
Braheny's score for a planetarium soundtrack is filled with slowly evolving, synthesized atmospheres that are appropriately spacey. —*Linda Kohanov*

Secret Rooms / 1991 / Hearts of Space ✦✦✦
A varied album, it has a few uneven tracks. Overall, the album showcases Braheny's meticulous production standards and virtuosity on the electronic wind instrument. —*Linda Kohanov*

Lullaby for the Hearts of Space / Hearts of Space ✦✦✦
This album is a lively improvisation on the mighty Serge synthesizer. It is a musical passage of day into night . . . into dreamtime. The second side, "After I Said Goodnight," a live improvisation, begins in dream-time. —*MusD*

Spencer Brewer

Piano / Adult Alternative
This Northern California-based pianist has released a half-dozen records on the Narada label. His pleasant, pop-flavored style and strong melodic sense make for nice easy-listening music that often suffers under the scrutiny of concentrated listening. His collaborations with other artists on the Narada label are stronger. —*Linda Kohanov*

● **Shadow Dancer** / 1984 / Narada ✦✦✦✦
Where Angels Dance / 1985 / Narada ✦✦✦
Solo piano music containing beautiful melodic compositions ranging in style from light contemporary jazz to richly textured lyrical expressions

New Age Music Styles

SOLO INSTRUMENTAL — Solo instrumental recordings launched successful labels like Windham Hill and Narada, ushering in a whole movement oriented toward impressionistic, often folk-inspired originals for piano, guitar, celtic harp, even hammered dulcimer. Though some of these releases offer innovative, emotionally moving performances, enough second-rate opportunists have jumped on the bandwagon to give the genre its "aural wallpaper" reputation. Still, some fine musicians continue to battle this stigma.

ADULT ALTERNATIVE — This genre attracts a wide cross-section of listeners who are looking for something a little different without straying too far from the mainstream. It's actually hard to say whether new adult contemporary radio formats were created to play this music or whether the music was created for radio airplay. Adult alternative styles—whether acoustic, electronic, or electro-acoustic—are heavily influenced by pop, rock, and jazz fusion elements. (Some albums feature a few vocal selections with lyrics, although the main orientation remains instrumental.) The best artists have a flair for melodic invention, colorful instrumentation, and rhythmic vitality while retaining a strong level of accessibility. At worst, adult alternative releases sound like trite pop songs without words.

PROGRESSIVE ELECTRONIC & ELECTRO-ACOUSTIC — This music thrives in more unfamiliar territory. The styles that emerge are often dictated by the technology itself. Rather than sampling or synthesizing acoustic sounds to electronically replicate them, these composers tend to mutate the original timbres, sometimes to an unrecognizable state. True artists in the genre also create their own sounds (as opposed to using the preset sounds that come with modern synthesizers). In progressive electro-acoustic music, the electronics play an equal if not greater part in the overall concept. Acoustic instruments performed in real time are usually processed through reverb, harmonizing, etc., which adds an entirely new dimension to the player's technique. At best, this music opens up new worlds of listening, thinking, and feeling. At worst, progressive electronic artists worship technology for its own sake, relinquishing the heart and soul of true artistic expression.

NEW AGE — Born from an aesthetic that aims to induce a sense of inner calm, new age music emerged from the meditational and holistic fields. Generally these are harmonious and nonthreatening albums that are allied with new age philosophies encouraging spiritual transcendence and physical healing. Some of these albums are artistically satisfying as well as therapeutic. Lesser musicians, however, often make ridiculous claims in the liner notes as to their ability to catapult listeners into advanced spiritual states through specially designed sonic vibrations and "immaculately conceived" musical ideas.

AMBIENT — A term popularized by Brian Eno but used here in a broader sense. Ambient composers use echo, electronic reverb, and other spatial techniques as important musical elements in creating atmospheric pieces and sonic environments. The best artists have developed the ability to manipulate the listener's sense of space and time in highly sophisticated ways. Many ambient recordings involve

extended compositions that change subtly in content and timbre over a long period of time. Though some musicians use ambient techniques for their meditative benefits (and can thus be allied with the new age movement), other ambient composers create ethereal, alien environments that are more mysterious and confrontational than comforting.

NEO-CLASSICAL — Many contemporary instrumentalists are conservatory trained, yet don't subscribe to the modern classical world's emphasis on intellectual, atonal forms of composition. As these artists follow their own vision, however, classical music may continue to be an important inspiration. In the context of contemporary instrumental music, the neoclassical distinction refers to any style influenced by classical music, whether the performer is offering updated arrangements of actual works by an established composer (Bach, Pachelbel, and Debussy seem to be popular in this respect) or weaving elements from the baroque, classical, romantic, impressionistic, and/or more challenging 20th-century styles into a more original approach.

NEW-ACOUSTIC — An exhilarating mix of bluegrass and jazz. Folk instruments like the mandolin, fiddle, banjo, and acoustic guitar play lead roles on new-acoustic albums. Virtuosity is the name of the game as the musicians stretch the boundaries of their traditional roles with heated improvisations and complex jazz harmonies.

ETHNIC FUSION — One of the major trends among all contemporary instrumental subgenres is the fusion of ethnic instruments, modes, and rhythms with Western styles. The possibilities are as wide-ranging as the world's vast musical cultures.

TECHNO-TRIBAl — A more specific variation on the ethnic fusion theme, techno-tribal music is becoming more prominent among progressive electro-acoustic artists who are fascinated by the idea of combining man's most primeval musical expressions with his most technologically advanced inventions. Tribal rhythms and instruments from the aboriginal cultures of Africa, Australia, and North and South America are mixed with sophisticated electronics. Though successful efforts are immensely powerful, it takes great skill and sensitivity to keep the music from sounding like cheap parodies of the cultures from which these artists are borrowing.

CHAMBER JAZZ — This style is distinguished by small, acoustic-based ensembles in which improvisation is a major factor. Though some groups are more jazz-based than others, they all tend to employ neo-classical aesthetics, particularly from the Impressionistic period and later 20th-century movements. Ethnic elements are also an important factor. These world-music leanings, however, are usually oriented toward the classical traditions of other cultures (Indian, Middle Eastern, and Oriental), although South American styles also figure prominently in a lot of these recordings.

MINIMALISM — One of the main innovations in the contemporary classical field, minimalism has also influenced many contemporary instrumental composers, particularly in progressive electronic styles where sequencers play an important role. Generally this music is characterized by a strong and relentless pulse, the insistent repetition of short melodic fragments, and harmonies that change over long periods of time. —*Linda Kohanov*

---

of visual imagery. This is a passionate album of deeply felt, subtle music. A truly distinctive album enhanced by the exceptional quality of its production. —*MusD*

Emerald / 1986 / Narada ✦✦✦
A collaboration with guitarist Eric Tingstad and wind player Nancy Rumble, it puts Brewer in a more substantial musical setting than on his own albums. —*Linda Kohanov*

Dorian's Legacy / 1989 / Narada ✦✦✦✦
This is an optimistic jaunt through contemporary instrumental textures. —*Linda Kohanov*

The Piper's Rhythm / 1991 / Narada ✦✦✦
Featured is more of Brewer's light, yet technically proficient, style. —*Linda Kohanov*

Romantic Interludes / 1993 / Narada ✦✦✦
Spencer Brewer's album glows with his trademark melodic charm. Brewer's romanticism breathes life into each of his new, primarily acoustic compostions. His all-star lineup of guest musicians includes Paul McCandless on reeds, Steve Kindler on violin, and Teja Bell (the album's co-producer) on guitar. —*MusD*

Jim Brickman

Piano
Though classically trained, pianist Jim Brickman prefers to play more pop-flavored, gently lyrical new age music. His unique compositions are emotional and structured, but not rigidly so. Brickman enrolled in the

Cleveland Institute of Music in his late teens. The focus was on classical music, but Brickman could not escape the lure of mainstream music and at age 19 began writing commercial jingles. This led him to compose music for such major outfits as the Gap, Isuzu, Sprint, and Kellogg as well as with Jim Henson and Henson Associates. During his association with Henson, he composed for the Muppets and for projects on *Sesame Street*. He also assisted on some of Henson's Disney projects. Brickman recorded his debut album *No Words* on Windham Hill in 1994. The next year he released *By Heart* on the same label. —*Sandra Brennan*

No Words / Mar. 15, 1994 / Windham Hill ✦✦✦✦
The first piano solo artist to sign with the record label in seven years. Brickman is no mere repeat; he throws his own spin on the traditional Windham Hill sound of expressive, moody piano pieces. His music tends toward a pop sound without the words. It is upbeat and romantic. Cuts such as "Open Doors" are as fine an adagio as one may hear anywhere in the genre. "Old Times" is imbued with feeling for the past. —*MusD*

● **By Heart/Piano Solos** / Apr. 11, 1995 / Windham Hill ✦✦✦✦
Brickman delivers an album filled with peaceful melodies that evoke romantic images and intimate feelings. He considers himself a pop songwriter, using piano-based instrumentals as a canvas, allowing him to connect with mainstream listeners on his sonic paintings of romantic longings. The song "On the Edge" features a duet with cellist Martin Tillman, while other selected tracks include strings and percussion. The album closes with the title track "By Heart," highlighted by Laura Creamer, an exciting vocalist known for her work with Bruce Hornsby and Michael Bolton. —*MusD*

Michael Brook

Guitar / Progressive Bluegrass, Electronic, Techno-Tribal
This innovative guitarist and producer received early recognition as an engineer and performer on projects with Brian Eno, Daniel Lanois, and Jon Hassell. Brook went on to produce albums on Peter Gabriel's Real World label by African artist Youssou N'Dour and Pakistani singer Nusrat Fateh Ali Khan. Brook also did some fine guitar work on the latter release. His style as a composer is characterized by a unique "infinite guitar" sound (created through heavy signal processing), mixed with Eno-style ambience and Hassell-influenced "fourth-world" rhythms. —*Linda Kohanov*

Hybrid / 1985 / EG ✦✦✦✦
An album by which all world music fusions should be judged, this has incredible musicianship, production, compositional ideas, and voodoo percussion. —*Linda Kohanov*

● **Cobalt Blue** / Jul. 1987 / 4AD ✦✦✦✦
Michael Brook has a decided talent for subtlety. Taking a musical or rhythmic theme, he stretches it, lays out variations, and, when finished, offers us a musical environment that we can climb into. Joining Brook on this album are luminaries Brian Eno, Roger Eno, and Daniel Lanois, all of whom Brook has collaborated with in the past. Using such instruments as guitar, infinite guitar, synthesizers, and various percussion, Brook and friends lead us into the dreamlike imagery of "Ten," but only after we have experienced the more upbeat "Ultramarine" and "Slipstream." Middle Eastern influences run throughout "Shona Bridge," and "Breakdown" brings us into territory we might call "funky Cajun." "Red Shift" must be that perfect minor-key theme for the gunfighter all dressed in black. This album is a must for those who like to walk a little closer to the edge. —*Backroads Music/Heartbeats*

Harold Budd

b. May 24, 1936, Los Angeles, CA
Synthesizer, Piano / Neo-Classical, Ambient, Avant-Garde
Budd is America's sovereign slow-motion composer. You could practically drive a truck through the spaces between each note on many of his compositions—that is, if you weren't so tempted to ease on the brakes and linger in the expansiveness of the sound.

A principal figure in the California avant-garde of the '60s, Budd developed a talent for composing lyrical, liquid music that unfolded at rarefied speeds. His solo albums and collaborations with Brian Eno have since become classics for their depth of expression and masterful execution. With every tone reverberating into a translucent silence, Budd always manages to sustain a keen sense of emotional intensity and anticipation. The effect is that of romantic yearnings and perilous undercurrents turned loose among wide-open spaces. —*Linda Kohanov*

Pavillion of Dreams / 1978 / EG ✦✦✦
Pavilion of Dreams is a cycle of works composed and recorded by Harold Budd from 1972-1975, each unique in form and inspiration. Strong in electric piano, harp, and voice, this album provides a look at Budd's formative years. —*Backroads Music/Heartbeats*

Ambient 2: The Plateaux of Mirror A / 1980 / EG ✦✦✦✦
This meditative solo piano work was a collaboration with Brian Eno, an installment of the *Ambient* series. —*Scott Bultman*

● **The Pearl** / 1984 / EG ✦✦✦✦
A collaboration with Brian Eno, this is one of the finest ambient albums of all time, a beautiful, highly emotional work of art. —*Linda Kohanov*

The White Arcades / 1988 / Opal ✦✦✦
On *The White Arcades*, Budd offers his most varied work yet, due in part to various collaborators such as the Cocteau Twins. For the most part, the music offers a revealing depth and spatial approach, and a readily apparent maturity. A track co-composed with Brian Eno called "Totems of the Red-Sleeved Warrior" soars and drifts from that place explored in *The Pearl*. —*Backroads Music/Heartbeats*

By the Dawn's Early Light / 1991 / Opal ✦✦✦
Contemporary chamber music in slow motion, it's filled with a delicious sense of yearning. —*Linda Kohanov*

Peter Buffett

Piano / Adult Alternative, Ethnic Fusion
Buffett's full-bodied electronic sound and rock-influenced accessibility make his music a congenial transition between the lighter pop instrumentals that have flooded the market and artists who are pushing the boundaries of modern electronic music with more challenging fare. The Nebraska-born pianist went to Stanford University, where he converted his Bay Area apartment into an efficient recording studio that provides soundtracks for numerous advertising, television, and film companies. Upon hearing of Kevin Costner's plans to create the movie *Dances with Wolves*, Buffett sent the actor a copy of his album *One by One*, which featured several cuts inspired by the plight of Native Americans. Costner

was impressed enough to use some of Buffett's music in the film. Buffett's four Narada recordings combine a flair for drama and cinematic-style electronic orchestrations with his interest in Native American cultures. His later albums feature a progressively more prominent use of acoustic timbres, both sampled and authentic. —*Linda Kohanov*

The Waiting / 1987 / Narada ✦✦✦✦
Buffett's first album is characterized by grand sweeps of sound and dramatic themes that are a bit on the trite side at times. —*Linda Kohanov*

One by One / 1989 / Narada ✦✦✦
The composer's interest in orchestral grandeur is further refined as he routes various acoustic sources—cellos and guitars to owls and basketball sounds—through his samplers and keyboards to create thick timbral tapestries. His Native American interests emerge on several cuts. —*Linda Kohanov*

● **Lost Frontier** / 1991 / Narada ✦✦✦✦
A collection of sonic essays inspired by the American West and its original inhabitants. Buffett's keyboards are enhanced by an ensemble of strings, woodwinds, and guitar. —*Linda Kohanov*

Yonnondio / 1992 / Narada ✦✦✦
Buffett's most recent effort is breezy and lighthearted while maintaining a certain level of instrumental intricacy and imaginative sound construction. —*Linda Kohanov*

Richard Burmer

Synthesizer, Piano, Sitar / Electronic, Adult Alternative, Progressive Electronic, Ambient
Burmer is a gifted melodist and a meticulous electronic craftsman. His style grew out of a love for East Indian and European folk music, as well as an interest in the progressive rock of the '70s à la Moody Blues and Pink Floyd. Adept in sophisticated studio techniques, Burmer honed his craft in the Southern California electronic scene of the mid-'80s before returning to his Michigan homeland at the end of the decade. —*Linda Kohanov*

Mosaic / 1984 / American Gramaphone ✦✦✦
An early collection of electronic vignettes, it showcases an already original style. —*Linda Kohanov*

★ **Bhakti Point** / 1987 / Fortuna ✦✦✦✦✦
A well-balanced collection of Burmer's styles, it consists of imaginative, often luxurious, electronic textures and themes. —*Linda Kohanov*

On the Third Extreme / 1990 / American Gramaphone ✦✦✦✦
Burmer in a more commercial setting. Well constructed and interesting, yet lacking the soul of his earlier works. —*Linda Kohanov*

Invention / 1992 / American Gramaphone ✦✦✦✦

Doug Cameron

Violin / Adult Alternative, Ethnic Fusion
The Ohio-born, classically trained violinist developed an interest in jazz early on. He later toured with Gregg Allman, moved to Southern California, and became a popular session man. His albums as a leader subsist on urban beats and spicy Latin rhythms that provide exhilarating settings for his violin improvisations; yet the compositions themselves often lack the substance to support repeated listening. —*Linda Kohanov*

● **Mil Amore** / Aug. 1989 / Narada ✦✦✦✦
Mil Amores combines the energy of jazz, the rhythms of Latin America, and the heart of new age. The other musicians on the record are the cream of the crop in the jazz world and include Lee Ritenour, who plays on five selections. —*MusD*

Journey to You / 1991 / Narada ✦✦✦
A few insubstantial compositions grow tiresome after a while, but Cameron's jazz-tinged improvisations show that he has talent. —*Linda Kohanov*

Jim Chappell

Piano / Solo Instrumental, Adult Alternative, Chamber Jazz
While trying to make it as a country/pop star in Nashville, Chappell accidentally hit upon a formula for success. At night, he'd noodle around on the piano to help himself unwind from the frustrations of the music business. A friend suggested he should release some of these piano vignettes instead of struggling in the pop world. Chappell followed the advice, and his first two albums (*Tender Ritual* and *Dusk*) were enthusiastically received by fans of solo piano music. On later albums, he composed and arranged works for various ensemble settings, gaining considerable exposure on the new adult contemporary charts. Chappell's strength lies in his ability to create memorable themes with lyrical, impressionistic accompaniments. Though his large-ensemble music leans toward a contemporary easy-listening style, its moodiness saves it from banality. He remains most expressive in the solo piano and small-ensemble realms. —*Linda Kohanov*

Tender Ritual / 1979 / Real Music ◆◆◆◆
This impressionistic solo piano music comes from a sensitive composer and performer. —*Linda Kohanov*

Dusk / 1987 / Real Music ◆◆◆
More piano vignettes are featured. —*Linda Kohanov*

Living the Northern Summer / 1989 / Real Music ◆◆◆
Chappell's first ensemble efforts show his promise as an arranger. —*Linda Kohanov*

Saturday's Rhapsody / 1990 / Real Music ◆◆

Nightsongs and Lullabies / 1991 / Real Music ◆◆◆◆
Although his solo piano efforts are arguably his best, this album (which offers a cross-section of solo piano pieces and works for small ensemble) is a good all-around introduction to Chappell's style. —*Linda Kohanov*

In Search of the Magic / 1992 / Real Music ◆◆◆
In Search of the Magic is Chappell's most rhythmic work to date. Recorded live in the studio, the music features piano, sax, bass, acoustic and electric guitars, and percussion. Truly emotional music. —*MusD*

Craig Chaquico

Vocals / Adult Alternative, Electro Acoustic
During the '70s and '80s guitarist/songwriter Craig Chaquico played lead guitar with the popular rock band Jefferson Starship (which later became Starship). In 1995, he released his first adult/contemporary acoustic effort, *Acoustic Highway*. Chaquico, a musician since childhood, started professionally in nightclubs at age 14. He began his association with Jefferson Starship when he was 16. At first he began recording with a few of the members and then was formally asked to join them on tour as a lead guitarist. Simultaneously, Chaquico helmed his own band, Steelwind. He toured with both until joining Starship permanently. Soon afterward he developed into one of their main songwriters. Among the songs he has penned or co-penned are "Jane," "Find Your Way Back," and "Layin' It on the Line." Since the early '90s Chaquico has worked on diversifying his music and branching out more into new age or world music, as can be heard in his song "Just One World," his blend of guitar playing and recordings of African and Native American music. The song became part of NASA's Space Ark project and is now in permanent orbit around the Earth. When not playing music, Chaquico enjoys auto racing and riding his Harley in benefits for the Muscular Dystrophy Association. He is also a graphic artist and amateur astronomer. —*Sandra Brennan*

Acoustic Highway / 1993 / Higher Octave ◆◆◆◆
After years as lead guitarist for Jefferson Starship, Craig Chaquico makes his solo instrumental debut with *Acoustic Highway*. The album is filled with uniquely memorable harmonies and emotional guitar melodies which rotate and shine, turning on its own diverse axis through passionate rhythms on "Return of the Eagle," romantic sensual moods of "Summer's End" or the irresistible opening riffs on the first cut, "Mountains in the Mist." Keyboards and percussion are ably handled by co-writer and co-producer Ozzie Ahlers, with all the guitars and stereo guitar sound effects provided by Chaquico. *Acoustic Highway* features songs that sparkle like finely faceted gems mined from the depths of his musical experience and considerable finesse. —*Backroads Music/Heartbeats*

Acoustic Planet / 1994 / Higher Octave ◆◆◆◆

A Thousand Pictures / Feb. 27, 1996 / Higher Octave ◆◆◆

Checkfield

Instrumental Pop, Adult Alternative
A new age group that uses mostly synthesizers and acoustic guitars, they are better than most new age music due to the arrangements of the songs. —*Paul Kohler*

Through the Lens / 1972 / American Gramophone ◆◆

A View from the Edge / 1990 / American Gramophone ◆◆◆
Marks a shift in direction in that it contains three vocals. The musical elements remain consistent. This is upbeat music aimed more at a pop than a pure new age market. —*MusD*

Water, Wind, and Stone / American Gramophone ◆◆◆◆

Distant Thunder / American Gramophone ◆◆◆

Spirit / PA/USA ◆◆

Chi

Adult Alternative, Ethnic Fusion
Taking its name from the Chinese word for energy, this instrumental duo composes the kinds of animated, well-performed, yet sometimes frivolous tunes that new adult contemporary radio tends to eat up. With its heavy pop/jazz orientation, this is fun music for listeners interested in taking an upbeat aural vacation from the pressures of everyday life. —*Linda Kohanov*

Pacific Rim / 1990 / Sonic Atmospheres ◆◆◆
This is Chi's debut. —*Linda Kohanov*

Jet Stream / 1990 / Sonic Atmospheres ◆◆◆◆
Chi core members Tom Chase on guitars and Steve Rucker on keyboards are joined by consummate percussionist Luis Conte and other guest artists, including the West African Goun ensemble. This is a colorful, multicultural romp. —*Linda Kohanov*

Sun Lake / 1991 / Sonic Atmospheres ◆◆◆
This is a little more upbeat and acoustically oriented than the *Jet Stream* album. —*Linda Kohanov*

Colin Chin

Guitar / Adult Alternative
This San Francisco native got his start hanging out and eventually touring with the members of Group 87, a late-'70s instrumental ensemble that featured Mark Isham and Patrick O'Hearn. With Isham, Chin attended a seminar conducted by Brian Eno on applying advanced technology to music. The event was a revelation for the young guitarist, who was motivated to expand his horizons into the field of electronic music. —*Linda Kohanov*

Intruding on a Silence / 1988 / Narada ◆◆◆◆
Chin's debut as a leader, though not particularly adventurous, features some well-designed electronic atmospheres with rock influences. Isham and O'Hearn add some characteristic solos as guest artists, giving the entire album a Group 87 reunion feel without the band's original edge. Overall, however, it's a promising beginning for Chin. —*Linda Kohanov*

Suzanne Ciani

Synthesizer / Adult Alternative, Progressive Electronic
One of the first and finest woman artists to make a name in the electronic music world, Ciani earned a master's degree in composition from the University of California at Berkeley, where she studied with electronic pioneers Max Matthews, John Chowning, and Don Buchla. In 1975 she moved to New York, where she got involved in the Soho art scene, and also worked with minimalist Philip Glass. She began to hit the big time with the establishment of Ciani Musica, Inc., one of the foremost commercial production companies in the country. Ciani later expanded into film scoring and gained recognition for her work on Lily Tomlin's *The Incredible Shrinking Woman* as well as the award-winning feature documentary *Mother Teresa*. Ciani's career as a recording artist, however, took a more indirect route. Her 1982 Japanese release *Seven Waves* became an underground hit, prompting its American release in 1984. Then *Velocity of Love* came along, which, with its intriguing synthesizer work balanced by strong melodies and pop sensibilities, helped define various contemporary instrumental radio formats, including the Wave. —*Linda Kohanov*

★ **The Velocity of Love** / 198_ / Private Music ◆◆◆◆◆
State of the Heart is technically masterful and emotionally warm. The overall feeling is floating in warm, clear water while soaring to the heights of the heart's imagination. —*Backroads Music/Heartbeats*

Hotel Luna / 1986 / Private Music ◆◆◆
Suzanne Ciani finds a new maturity that does not take away from or dramatically alter her signature style of heartfelt warmth. Her musical flights of fantasy are vividly portrayed through her new compositions, and the depth of sound has expanded due to the increase in supporting players, notably violinist Steve Kindler, Isham O'Hearn, Kurt Wortman on percussion, and flutist Peter Gordon. —*Backroads Music/Heartbeats*

Neverland / 1988 / Private Music ◆◆◆◆
Ciani is a master at constructing complex compositions using electronic keyboard instruments that nevertheless retain the ability to speak to listeners emotionally. On her most accomplished work, Ciani explores a broad musical range, from majestic landscapes to humorous percussive patterns, always retaining a strong sense of melody and overall structure. —*William Ruhlmann*

History of My Heart / 1989 / Private Music ◆◆◆

Seven Waves / 1989 / Private Music ◆◆◆
Seven Waves is Suzanne Ciani's first release. It was out of print, but has now been re-released on the Private Music label. —*MusD*

Album of Solo Piano Music / 1990 / Private Music ◆◆◆
After 20 years of perfecting her abilities with electronic music, Ciani turned back to the acoustic piano for this live recording of material taken largely from *Neverland* and its excellent follow-up, *History of My Heart*. Demonstrates that Ciani is not dependent on electricity to produce vital music. —*William Ruhlmann*

The Private Music of Suzanne Ciani / 1992 / Private Music ◆◆◆◆

Tim Clark

Synthesizer, Vocals / Progressive Electronic, Ethnic Fusion, Ambient
You'd expect high-quality electronics from a musician who has clocked in

a good 20,000 hours composing soundtracks for Toronto's McLaughlin Planetarium and writing scores for numerous other planetarium programs, award-winning radio dramas, films, and theater productions. Clark's graduate studies in composition also seem to come in handy. Though he has only one solo album out so far, *Tales of the Sun People* is impressive because he refuses to settle for the exciting sounds and few engaging melodies many electronic players work hard to attain. Clark's engaging music is filled with unexpected turns and inventive new twists on old ideas. —*Linda Kohanov*

● **Tales of the Sun People** / 1990 / Hearts of Space ✦✦✦✦
A clever, richly evocative album of electronic music, it deserved more attention when it was first released. —*Linda Kohanov*

Tim Clement

Synthesizer, Guitar, Vocals / Progressive Electronic, Ethnic Fusion, Ambient
Best known for the electronic environments he created as half of the Canadian duo Danna and Clement, this Toronto-based composer has also written music for theater, dance, and film. His early work with Danna explored ways of translating the serenity of Canada's Ontario wilderness into music through ambient compositions that combine synthesizers with recordings of natural sounds. Clement's first major album as a leader, however, is more tuneful and rhythmic as it successfully incorporates ethnic influences into an engaging electro-acoustic context. —*Linda Kohanov*

★ **Waterstation** / 1990 / Solitudes ✦✦✦✦✦
One of the most creative and eclectic contemporary instrumental albums of 1990, *Waterstation* features everything from an atmospheric take on country music with liquid pedal-steel guitar musings by Kim Deschamps (of Cowboy Junkies fame) to extended pieces fueled by relentless, yet almost translucent, ethnic rhythms. Other compositions involve highland bagpipes, Egyptian reed flute, and zither. One selection even features a bizarre union of electronics, glassy trance rhythms, and spoken-word tracks. —*Linda Kohanov*

Wolfsong Night / 1994 / Chacra Alternative Music ✦✦✦
There is a wonderful country air to *Wolfsong Night* generated by the liberal use of steel and lap-top guitars and the occasional buzz of nature sounds. The reflective, impressionistic music invites an exploration of both the human condition and the vast wild landscapes of the mind. The themes are similar. For instance, there is the nature experience that pervades the title cut, "Wolfsong Night," and the introspective, Edward Hopper-like loneliness of "Lantern Sky." Tim Clement proves a master in background percussion and keyboards, while Kim Deschamps exhibits soulful, sometimes searing, guitar work. —*MusD*

Scott Cossu

Piano, Cello, Harp / Neo-Classical, Adult Alternative, Chamber Jazz
Scott Cossu's ensemble works have the heart, soul, and skill that come from an artist motivated by personal vision rather than industry trends. His 1980 debut album *Still Moments* featured harp, cello, and vibes as foils for his own pianistic improvisations, at a time when solo instrumentals were the rage. His style has evolved and become more sophisticated over the years. Yet because each stage in his development was carried out with the utmost sincerity and expressive intent, each album he has recorded continues to have a life of its own. —*Linda Kohanov*

Still Moments / 1980 / Lost Lake Arts ✦✦✦
His debut, originally released on a small independent label, was later remastered and reissued through Windham Hill. —*Linda Kohanov*

Spirals / Jun. 1983 / Music Is Medicine ✦✦✦

Islands / 1984 / Windham Hill ✦✦✦
Cossu began to expand his musical vocabulary with larger arrangements featuring horns, bass, and drums. The more impressionistic leanings of his previous releases are also expanded upon through the album's fusion of blues, jazz, Latin, and classical elements. *Islands* features some major contemporary jazz names like flutist Dave Valentin, bassist Mark Egan, drummer Danny Gottlieb, and violinist Michael Urbaniak. —*Linda Kohanov*

● **Wind Dance** / 1984 / Windham Hill ✦✦✦✦
The pianist's first original release for Windham Hill features duets with Alex de Grassi and Dan Reiter. —*Linda Kohanov*

Reunion / 1986 / Windham Hill ✦✦✦✦
A return to his roots in small ensemble music, this album centers around performances with cellist Eugene Friesen with additional appearances by de Grassi, Shadowfax violinist Charles Bisharat, and English-horn player Bob Hubbard. —*Linda Kohanov*

Switchback / 1989 / Windham Hill ✦✦✦
Cossu's forays into rock and blues were co-produced with jazz flutist Dave Valentin. —*Linda Kohanov*

Retrospective / 1992 / Windham Hill ✦✦✦✦

She Describes Infinity / Feb. 14, 1992 / Windham Hill ✦✦✦
An artistically satisfying summation of Cossu's previous styles, this album includes lyrical duet and trio performances as well as arrangements for an expanded rhythm section. It's a thoughtful and mature collection of pieces. —*Linda Kohanov*

Stained Glass Memories / 1992 / Windham Hill ✦✦

Coyote Oldman

Ethnic Fusion, Ambient
This duo creates highly reverberant soundscapes featuring Native American flutes. Michael Graham Allen began visiting museums to research ancient musical instruments over 20 years ago. He went on to construct and play many kinds of flutes and panpipes, later naming his own flute-building company Coyote Oldman. In 1986 Allen was selling his hand-crafted instruments at an Oklahoma arts fair when he met Barry Stramp, an accomplished studio engineer who played flute, keyboards, and guitar. Using synthesizers and other digital processors to manipulate the "physics of echoes," Stramp helped define the Coyote Oldman sound by electronically enhancing and multi-tracking Allen's haunting flute melodies. —*Linda Kohanov*

● **Tear of the Moon** / 1987 / Coyote Oldman ✦✦✦✦
Though there is an earlier Coyote Oldman release available on cassette only, *Tear of the Moon* is really the first in which Stramp's special engineering techniques are as important to the music as the flutes themselves. A sophisticated use of reverb augments the effects of primal flute sounds to create an otherworldly, almost aquatic atmosphere. —*Linda Kohanov*

Landscape / 1988 / Coyote Oldman ✦✦✦
Native American flutes with Incan, Peruvian, and bass panpipes as well as Aztec log drum, bells, and Chapman stick are used in original compositions with plaintive melodies that echo through meditative atmospheres. —*Linda Kohanov*

Thunder Chord / 1990 / Hearts of Space ✦✦✦✦
Allen and Stramp's most masterful execution of the sound that had begun to mature on previous albums. It took 18 months of patient work to record these timeless flute melodies, elegantly enveloped in a lush, 3-D digital ambience. —*Linda Kohanov*

In Medicine River / 1992 / Coyote Oldman ✦✦✦
The duo known as Coyote Oldman use native flutes, Aztec log drums, congas, bass Incan pan pipes, and 1000-year-old clay flutes from Central America in their gentle and haunting soundscapes. Audiences will be receptive to Michael Graham Allen's hand-made Native American flutes and the rhythmic accompaniment of Michael Fitzsimmons. The blend of ancient flute voices is both stirring and peaceful. —*Heartbeats*

Rusty Crutcher

Saxophone / Progressive Electronic, Ambient
A former Los Angeles studio musician, saxophonist Crutcher performed with pop stars like Lionel Richie and the Commodores before moving to Santa Fe, NM, and developing his own introspective style of music. Crutcher's main body of work falls under his *Sacred Sites* series, a set of concept albums that convey his musical impressions of historic locations. As part of the compositional process, Crutcher visits these ancient areas to record environmental sounds that he weaves into his synthesized soundscapes. Crutcher is producing a new *Sacred Sites* project dealing with the Serpent Mound built by Ohio's prehistoric Hopewell Indian culture. —*Linda Kohanov*

Amazon Song / 1980 / Emerald Green ✦✦

● **Machu Picchu Impressions** / 1988 / Plan 9/Caroline ✦✦✦✦
One of Crutcher's earliest *Sacred Sites* projects, this album features synthesized atmospheres and subtle melodies with sounds recorded at Machu Picchu. —*Linda Kohanov*

Love Dance / 1989 / Plan 9/Caroline ✦✦✦
A set of spontaneous improvisations paired Crutcher's alto saxophone with Jim Oliver's subtle, yet highly melodic keyboard work. Tuneful and relaxing, it's still not as compelling as Crutcher's *Sacred Sites* releases. —*Linda Kohanov*

Chaco Canyon / 1990 / Emerald Green ✦✦✦✦
Crutcher went to New Mexico's Chaco Canyon to record environmental sounds primarily during solstices and equinoxes. This prehistoric archeological site is thought to have been the trading and spiritual center for the Anasazi, one of the earliest-known Native American cultures in the Southwest. Crutcher's music, often performed on wind synthesizer, is reminiscent of Native American styles. —*Linda Kohanov*

Ocean Eclipse / 1992 / Plan 9/Caroline ✦✦✦✦
Based on Crutcher's experience of a total solar eclipse in Baja California, *Ocean Eclipse* lays evocative music over the sounds of the tidal-quieted ocean at Las Cruces, near La Paz, Baja, Mexico. The tracks move from the morning sunrise to the approaching darkness, the actual total eclipse, and the first rays of the sun as it reappears. This living tapestry of life

portrayed in sound includes flutes, keyboards, and soprano sax, with acoustic guitar by Bruce Dunlap and percussion by Jeff Sussman. —*Backroads Music/Heartbeats*

Cusco

Adult Alternative, Ethnic Fusion

Two German keyboardists lead this band: Michael Holm had a long string of Top Ten vocal records in Germany during the '60s and '70s; Kristian Schultze is one of Europe's busiest studio musicians. They share an interest in South America's prehistoric musical heritage; yet their albums are far from traditional. Cusco combines catchy melodies and steady rock/funk beats with enough ethnic percussion and electronically generated panpipe sounds to give a South American flavor. —*Linda Kohanov*

● Apurimac / 1988 / Higher Octave ✦✦✦✦
Cusco's first US release is the band's celebration of the Amazon River, with plenty of Peruvian rhythms and panpipe sounds to set the mood. Their subsequent albums are variations on this theme. —*Linda Kohanov*

Mystic Island / 1989 / Higher Octave ✦✦✦

Water Stories / 1990 / Higher Octave ✦✦✦
The third US release by the German keyboard-based group Cusco is a tribute to some of the world's great lakes and seas. The joyful sound of synthesized panpipes and flutes that first endeared Cusco to American audiences on *Apurimac* appears on several cuts, notably on the opening track, "Waters of Cesme." Their catchy melodies and playful spirit of celebration have earned Cusco a place among the best-loved of the more pop-oriented new age artists. —*Backroads Music/Heartbeats*

Cusco 2000 / 1992 / Higher Octave ✦✦✦✦
Cusco's philosophy is that human beings must understand, respect, and rejoice in the natural world. The music on this recording was created especially for the 20-part TV series "Sielmann 2000," which focuses on changes in our natural environment over the past 30 years. *Cusco 2000* features ten themes from the series. Listeners will experience a likable sound that blends classical styles, euphoric melodies, and rhythms of Old Europe with surprisingly compatible Peruvian pan flutes. This release brings the group's unique style to a new height with a mix of natural instrumentation, including majestic horns, articulate strings, and rich woodwinds. —*MusD*

Apurimac 2 / 1994 / Higher Octave ✦✦✦
Cusco, under the watchful direction of Michael Holm, has adapted traditional world music melodies and instrumentation into a Western Euro-jazz sound with *Apurimac II*. Taking the music of the Andes, with its strong rhythms and ethereal flute sound, Holm has added the music of modern technology. The result is a near-full orchestra of wonderful music with new depth and complexity that does not betray its native roots, where Holm had found his inspiration. —*MusD*

Malcolm Dalglish

Dulcimer, Vocals / Ethnic Fusion, New Acoustic

This American hammer dulcimer virtuoso managed to liberate the instrument from its folk roots through his masterful solo recording for Windham Hill. At the same time, he enjoys playing Celtic and northern European traditional music as a member of the group Metamora (see listings under Metamora). —*Linda Kohanov*

● Jogging the Memory / Windham Hill ✦✦✦✦
This contemporary, highly inventive music for hammer dulcimer is intriguing and entrancing. —*Linda Kohanov*

Danna and Clement

Electronic, Ambient

Though both artists have released satisfying solo albums (see the separate listings), these Canadian electronic musicians first became widely known as a team. Their music together is an organic synthesis of sounds from nature and softly unfolding electronic ambiences. —*Linda Kohanov*

A Gradual Awakening / 1982 / Fortuna ✦✦✦
The duo's first release is a haunting collection of tone poems inspired by Canada's untamed landscapes. Synthesizers, guitars, harps, and flutes are enhanced by natural sounds like rushing water and the cries of timber wolves. —*Linda Kohanov*

● Summerland / 1984 / Chacra ✦✦✦✦
This gentle collection of pieces evoking the essence of the summer season combines lush electronics with sounds of surf, gulls, songbirds, and cathedral bells. —*Linda Kohanov*

Mychael Danna

Synthesizer, Piano, Keyboards / Neo-Classical, Ambient, Progressive Alternative, Space

Danna is one of Canada's busiest composers. With a degree in composition from the University of Toronto, he has won numerous prizes for his

music, including the Glenn Gould Award. In addition to his classically oriented work, Danna has long had an interest in electronic music. Since the '80s, he has released several albums of synthesized soundscapes in collaboration with Tim Clement (see Danna & Clement). He also serves as composer-in-residence at Toronto's McLaughlin Planetarium, where his electronic music skills are widely appreciated. —*Linda Kohanov*

★ Sirens / 1991 / Hearts of Space ✦✦✦✦✦
Danna's first widely available album as a leader is sensual and spacey, with episodes of melting pedal-steel guitar solos and sighing female vocals that symbolize his fascination with the mysteriously compelling qualities of feminine archetypes. —*Linda Kohanov*

Skys / 1992 / Hearts of Space ✦✦✦

Adjuster: Music From the Films of Atom Egoyan / Jan. 30, 1996 / Varese ✦✦
Mychael Danna, the director and composer of the haunting *Exotica*, compiled *The Adjuster: Music From the Films of Atom Egoyan*, which draws from the scores of *Speaking Parts*, *The Adjuster*, and *Family Viewing*. Not all of the music is compelling when separated from the visuals, but enough of the disc is affecting, particularly at its most atmospheric and moody. —*Stephen Thomas Erlewine*

Mars: The Journey Begins, Planets, Stars and Galaxies / ✦✦✦
This release features music from the McLaughlin Planetarium Star Theatre Production of *Mars: The Journey Begins*. This outstanding space music sequel to his *Planets, Stars, and Galaxies* album is part of the "Night Music" series. —*MusD*

Alex de Grassi

Guitar / New Age, Solo Instrumental, Adult Alternative, Chamber Jazz, Ethnic Fusion

Music has long been a family affair for de Grassi. Though he's primarily self-taught as a guitarist, his grandfather played violin with the San Francisco Symphony and his father was a classical pianist. Even more significant are de Grassi's ties to one of contemporary instrumental music's most influential labels: Windham Hill. In addition to his status as one of the company's finest and most consistently intriguing artists, de Grassi is literally a member of the Windham Hill clan. After earning a degree in urban geography from U. C. Berkeley and performing as a street musician in London, he made ends meet by learning the carpentry trade from his cousin, Will Ackerman, who was just starting a small instrumental record label. De Grassi was encouraged to record his first album, *Turning: Turning Back*, for the fledgling Windham Hill company. As it turns out, he had more going for him than good connections. Over the years, de Grassi has proven to be an innovative guitarist and composer whose mastery of acoustic finger-picking styles has grown to include a variety of other techniques and ethnic influences. Though he left briefly to record on RCA Novus, de Grassi has since returned to the Windham Hill fold. In the mid-'80s, his travels to Bolivia became a major inspiration. He made numerous field recordings during his visits and first incorporated indigenous influences from the culture on his 1987 RCA Novus release *Altiplano*. His contacts with Bolivia's Contemporary Orchestra of Native Instruments also set in motion the ensemble's first American release, *Arawl*, on the New Albion label. —*Linda Kohanov*

● Turning: Turning Back / 1978 / Windham Hill ✦✦✦✦
An excellent technician, de Grassi is able to vary his effects on the acoustic guitar from textured chording to involved picking, evoking folk and madrigal styles and alternating his approaches at will. He somehow seems to have absorbed all the important guitar styles of the previous 20 years and can mix and recreate them at will. —*William Ruhlmann*

Slow Circle / 1979 / Windham Hill ✦✦✦
De Grassi is a celebrated guitarist whose technique and style have made him a hit on the contemporary instrumental (new age) circuit. He's not really known as a jazz or fusion player; all albums, this one included, are more suites designed to showcase different moods rather than sessions to present any musical style or message. —*Ron Wynn*

Southern Exposure / 1980 / Windham Hill ✦✦✦✦

Deep at Night / 1983 / Windham Hill ✦✦✦
Alex de Grassi's reunion with Windham Hill is cause for celebration with this collection of original, lyrical pieces in a wide range of styles and moods. *Deep at Night* is an immediately accessible return to form by one of the most important finger-style guitarists recording today. Nine solo guitar compositions are complemented by "Hidden Voices," the album's closing track, which features the debut of the sympitar, an Eastern-influenced guitar variant of intriguing sitar-like character. —*Backroads Music/Heartbeats*

Altiplano / 1987 / Jive/Novus ✦✦✦
He branched out from his solo guitar albums on Windham Hill to this ambitious effort, which finds him in a variety of band settings that underscore his acoustic flights, bringing out previously unheard aspects of his music. —*William Ruhlmann*

A Windham Hill Retrospective / 1992 / Windham Hill ✦✦✦✦
The World's Getting Loud / 1993 / Windham Hill ✦✦✦
Beyond the Night Sky / Sep. 3, 1996 / Rhino ✦✦✦

Constance Demby

Synthesizer, Piano, Vocals / New Age, Neo-Classical, Progressive Electronic, Ambient

Demby is one of the few representatives of the new age movement (in both her music and her personal philosophies) who consistently creates artistic, highly expressive compositions. She was a member of an East Coast experimental group in the early '70s and began releasing her own music on cassette in 1978, shortly after moving to California. Her early recordings consist primarily of extended pieces for hammer dulcimer, atmospheric compositions featuring instruments of her own design, and (increasingly) original works based on her love of sacred classical music from the Baroque period. She really came into her own, however, when digital sampling synthesizers arrived on the scene. Recording in her own 16-track studio, Demby integrated electronically sampled sounds of orchestral instruments into her ambitious, two-part masterpiece *Novus Magnificat*, released in 1986. It has since been acknowledged as a classic in the realms of new age and progressive electronic music. Though subsequent recordings have not matched the scope and emotional power of this work, Demby continues to evolve as an artist in some promising new directions. —*Linda Kohanov*

★ Novus Magnificat: Thru the Stargate / 1986 / Hearts of Space ✦✦✦✦✦
Novus Magnificat (Through the Stargate) is an electronic masterpiece. Demby's extended, classically influenced composition is also a deeply moving work. —*Linda Kohanov*

Sacred Space Music / 1988 / Hearts of Space ✦✦✦
An early precursor to *Novus*, this classically influenced, yet meditative album was rereleased on CD in 1988. —*Linda Kohanov*

Set Free / 1989 / Hearts of Space ✦✦✦
Demby's first release since her landmark recording *Novus Magnificat* features selections reminiscent of that work, as well as shorter pieces heading in new directions, including some influenced by Balinese music and other tunes more on the pop side. —*Linda Kohanov*

Sunborne / Ladyslipper ✦✦✦
Subtitled *Fire Series*, part one of *The Elements*, this symphonic poem includes the following movements: "The Dawning," "Darkness of Space," "Lift Thine Eyes," "Sunborne," and "One with the Light," and does feel like a journey. Instrumentation includes bowed gamelon, space bass, and whale sail. —*Ladyslipper*

Constance Demby at Alaron: Live Concert Recording / Potentials Unlimited ✦✦
The delightful title cut represents a true departure for the artist: a pop-rock/gospel song, on which she's joined by backup vocalists from the Edwin Hawkins Singers. A rousing new age-gospel statement of joy and oneness. The remainder is a best-of, with selections from her first five albums; it's a good overview of her work. —*Ladyslipper*

Light of This World / Ladyslipper ✦✦✦
The delightful title cut represents a true departure for the artist: a pop-rock/gospel song, on which she's joined by backup vocalists from the Edwin Hawkins Singers. A rousing new age-gospel statement of joy and oneness. The remainder is a best-of, with selections from her first five albums; it's a good overview of her work. —*Ladyslipper*

Skies Above Skies / Potentials Unlimited ✦✦✦
Ethereal, mythical, mystical, and beautiful music for meditation and sheer listening pleasure. This multitalented woman composed, performed (on hammer dulcimer, cheng, tamboura, synthesizer, cello, piano, organ, and vocal tones), and produced this recording with an East-West spiritual theme. —*Ladyslipper*

Deuter

Flute, Guitar, Vocals / New Age, Ethnic Fusion, Ambient

Like many artists in the contemporary instrumental realm, Deuter mixes acoustic and electronic instruments, ethnic influences, and sounds from nature—only he's been doing it since the early '70s. Born in the German village of Falkenhagen, Deuter learned flute and taught himself to play guitar but was discouraged from pursuing music as a career. The trauma of a nearly fatal auto accident in 1970, however, motivated him to pursue his dreams. His first recording, *D*, was released on Kuckuck in 1971. (He still records for this label.) Over the years, Deuter's spiritual search has taken him around the world, most notably to India, where he lived in an ashram, studied Indian music, and recorded several albums. In the mid-'80s he moved to the US, eventually settling in Santa Fe, NM. Deuter's style is characterized by gentle melodies and joyful rhythms that render his music accessible even as he presents an intriguing blend of Eastern and Western styles. —*Linda Kohanov*

Haleakala / 1978 / Kuckuck ✦✦✦
Haleakala is as deep, mysterious, and awe-inspiring as its namesake, the majestic and legendary mountain crater on the island of Maui. —*Backroads Music/Heartbeats*

● Land of Enchantment / 1978 / Kuckuck ✦✦✦✦
Land of Enchantment is an album of celebration, of jubilant light-hearted tunes that perfectly capture the feeling of springtime. The dominant instruments are bright steel-string acoustic guitar and dancing flutes, supported by light touches of percussion and tasteful synthesizer that sounds at times like a chiming music box. —*Backroads Music/Heartbeats*

Ecstasy / 1981 / Kuckuck ✦✦✦✦
Ecstasy is quintessential Deuter circa 1979. This classic release offers many flavors of joyous sounds, from resonant guitars to waves of synthesizers and oceanic space music, as heard in the title piece. For deep tuning and expanded listening, *Ecstasy* remains an essential tape. —*Backroads Music/Heartbeats*

Silence Is the Answer / 1981 / Kuckuck ✦✦✦✦
Actually two releases in one, this double set combines the best elements of Deuter's two main styles. "Silence Is the Answer," the first half, offers some of the purest meditative music we know, combining bells and gongs with the lightest of synthesizers, recorders, and guitar parts. The second half of this recording, "Buddham Sharnam Gachchami," moves to the other end of the spectrum with the finest of Deuter's "celebration music," strumming guitars and joyous recorders mixed with a bubbly synth sound and rhythmic undertones. —*Backroads Music/Heartbeats*

Cicada / 1982 / Kuckuck ✦✦✦
This 1982 album, recorded in the south of France, is characterized by some of the most exquisite melodies Deuter has ever composed. Primarily using recorders, bubbling synthesizers, and acoustic guitars, *Cicada* has an idyllic pastoral feel, underscored by judicious use of nature sounds. A subtle renaissance feel adds an elegant touch to the simple but enchanting tunes. —*Backroads Music/Heartbeats*

Nirvana Road / 1984 / Kuckuck ✦✦✦
Recorded in northern California, where this peripatetic musician temporarily settled in 1984, *Nirvana Road* combines neo-classical, medieval, and Indian elements to produce one of Deuter's most consistently popular albums. Sitar, tabla, hammer dulcimer, and harp build upon Deuter's standard guitar, synth, and recorder arrangements, resulting in a multi-faceted work that happily alternates between the lively and the meditative. —*Backroads Music/Heartbeats*

Call of the Unknown 1972-86 / 1986 / Kuckuck ✦✦✦✦
This compilation features selections from eight releases as well as two works recorded especially for the project. —*Linda Kohanov*

Aum / 1989 / Kuckuck ✦✦
Celebration / 1989 / Kuckuck ✦✦✦
Deuter's synthesizer replicates everything on *Celebration*, from the flutter of birds to lapping water. Although some segments are quiet and meditative, a feeling of rejoicing and serenity permeates the album. —*MusD*

Sands of Time / 1991 / Kuckuck ✦✦✦
Henon / 1992 / Kuckuck ✦✦✦✦
Deuter's latest album is consistent with the style he established 20 years ago. The music here, while taking advantage of the latest in recording technology, hasn't evolved much over the last decade, yet it retains its expressive integrity and uplifting, celebratory qualities. —*Linda Kohanov*

San / Kuckuck ✦✦✦
San is generally a quiet album, full of light, sparkling, bell-like tones, ocean waves, liquid rhythms, and dreamy wordless vocals. Even Deuter's uptempo pieces are so smooth that the percussiveness seems derivative of rain drops. Recorded in 1986 in Northern California and the Cote d'Azur, France, *San* has a gentle, impressionistic quality and represents Deuter at his purest. —*Backroads Music/Heartbeats*

Do'ah

Adult Alternative, Ethnic Fusion

Two New Hampshire residents, Randy Armstrong and Ken LaRoche, are the ringleaders of this long-standing ensemble founded in 1974. The name, which was spelled "Do'a" on the band's first few recordings, comes from an Arabic word signifying a call to prayer and meditation; but the music is often upbeat and festive. The members of Do'ah play somewhere in the neighborhood of 75 instruments from various ethnic persuasions; yet the overall feeling owes much to Western music. Some of their compositions seem a little too good-natured and naive at times; however, you have to admire their virtuosic playing and vision, especially since Do'ah was creating world-music fusions a good ten or 15 years before the idea hit the mainstream. —*Linda Kohanov*

● Light upon Light / 1979 / Philo ✦✦✦✦
Do'ah's first album was recorded when Armstrong and LaRoche were working as a duo. —*Linda Kohanov*

Ornament of Hope / 1986 / Philo ✦✦✦
Do'ah's second album is significant in that Armstrong and LaRoche were beginning to hear larger orchestrations in their compositions. On this

release, they brought in other musicians to perform on various pieces. —*Linda Kohanov*

Companions of the Crimson Coloured Ark / 1987 / Philo ♦♦♦
Do'ah finally decided on a quintet instrumentation, and that's how the band has operated since. —*Linda Kohanov*

The Early Years / 1988 / Rounder ♦♦♦♦
This is a collection of tunes from the band's first two albums and, as such, is a document of Do'ah's early development. —*Linda Kohanov*

John Doan

Guitar, Harp, Lute / Neo-Classical, Chamber Jazz
Though Doan is a master of renaissance lute as well as classical and contemporary guitar styles, he's one of the few artists around who has explored the possibilities of the harp guitar. The instrument was popular in America around the turn of the century, yet today has been all but forgotten. The way Doan plays it, you have to wonder how this intriguing medium could ever have slipped into obscurity. In addition to the standard six strings of regular guitars, the harp guitar features five bass strings that add a special warmth and richness, as well as several treble strings that create a translucent sense of delicacy. —*Linda Kohanov*

● **Departures** / 1988 / Narada ♦♦♦♦
Doan's ensemble settings for harp guitar take full advantage of the instrument's expressive range and rich timbral palette. This is contemporary instrumental music at its finest; however, its thoughtful, often sublime lyricism and subtle classical music influences didn't add up to commercial success when the album was first released. It's still available and is definitely worth going out of your way to find. —*Linda Kohanov*

Remembrance / 1993 / Tapestry Productions ♦♦♦
Remember colorful traditions, old dusty instruments, and simple, yet inspired, melodies? *Remembrance* was inspired by John Doan's own musical traditions in folk tunes of the American West, the elegance and introspection of classical music, and the charm of parlor songs. Doan performs on harp, guitar, classical banjo, banjuerine, and harp mandolin, with guest performers Billy Oskay on harmonium, violin, and keyboards, and Michael Harrison on piano. —*MusD*

Wrapped in White / 1994 / Tapestry ♦♦♦

Bill Douglas

Bassoon / Neo-Classical, Chamber Jazz, Ethnic Fusion, Space
This Canadian-born artist couldn't have a much more varied musical background. His first band did Elvis covers in the '50s; yet Douglas gained a music degree and spent several years as a classical bassoonist with the Toronto Symphony. He has also worked as a jazz improviser, an avant-garde composer, and a college professor. He finally settled in Boulder, CO, where he remains music director at the Naropa Institute. For the last seven years, he has toured and recorded with classical clarinetist Richard Stoltzman, as well as writing much of the material for Stoltzman's popular crossover albums *Begin Sweet World* and *New York Counterpoint*. Those who've enjoyed these recordings will find Douglas' own releases for the Hearts of Space label similar in conception. There's no mistaking his sweet, lyrical melodies; his combination of Western, folk, and classical styles; his virtuosity on several instruments; and the poignant sense of innocence in much of his music. —*Linda Kohanov*

★ **Jewel Lake** / 1988 / Hearts of Space ♦♦♦♦♦
Douglas' debut as a leader was a surprise hit in Spain, of all places. The composer's style on this release, however, may be a little too sweet for some tastes. —*Linda Kohanov*

Cantilena / 1990 / Hearts of Space ♦♦♦
This is his most masterful and well-balanced effort so far. Most of the selections are smooth, melodious songs-without-words, inspired by everything from spirited-yet-flowing Celtic dances and modal folk songs to some deeply emotional music that conveys a near religious profundity. —*Linda Kohanov*

William Eaton

Koto / Chamber Jazz, Ethnic Fusion, Ambient
Eaton designs and builds many of the stringed instruments he plays, and he's come up with some unique hybrids like the "koto harp guitar," the "o'ele 'n strings" (a double-necked instrument), and even a 26-string guitar. The Phoenix-based artist performs and records most often with Native American flutist R. Carlos Nakai. Together they create haunting, highly resonant, original pieces inspired by places and cultures of the Southwest. (See also albums listed under Nakai.) —*Linda Kohanov*

● **Tracks We Leave** / 1989 / Canyon ♦♦♦♦
This is an evocative collection of highly impressionistic compositions. Eaton plays some of his most intriguing instruments (including the lyre and the koto harp guitar) in sparse ensemble settings that feature special guests like Nakai on Native American flutes, Rich Rogers on the Japa-

nese shakuhachi flute and percussion, and Udi Arouh on guitar and tablas. —*Linda Kohanov*

William Ellwood

Guitar / Neo-Classical, Solo Instrumental, Chamber Jazz
As the story goes, Ellwood cajoled his parents into buying him a cheap, nearly unplayable guitar when he was 12 years old. The instrument was too warped to play chords, so he came up with the right-handed picking style he uses to this day. The Canadian-born artist later developed an interest in renaissance and baroque music, taught himself to play the lute, and eventually designed a seven-string guitar so he could transcribe lute pieces without sacrificing any voicings. Ellwood's classical music leanings are apparent on his Narada recordings, although his music has a gentle, contemporary feel. —*Linda Kohanov*

Openings / 1986 / Narada ♦♦♦
Like many contemporary instrumentalists, Ellwood began his recording career as a solo artist. His debut for Narada is a collection of pieces for guitar. —*Linda Kohanov*

● **Renaissance** / 1987 / Narada ♦♦♦♦
Ellwood expands his scope a bit on this album, with subtle ensemble works that elegantly express his love for renaissance and baroque music in an updated context. Keyboards, percussion, flute, and bassoon are used sparingly and effectively in arrangements that feature several guest artists (including fellow Canadian Bill Douglas). This is a delicate, well-balanced effort. —*Linda Kohanov*

Vista / 1989 / Narada ♦♦♦
Ellwood dives further into ensemble music on his third Narada release. Violinist Billy Oskay of Nightnoise, keyboardist Robert O'Hearn (Patrick O'Hearn's brother), and keyboardist George Mitchell (who performs with Diana Ross) are among the musicians who thicken the sound and provide some nice moments, at the cost of the intimacy of Ellwood's previous albums. —*Linda Kohanov*

Touchstone / 1993 / Narada ♦♦

Emerald Web

Progressive Electronic, Ambient
In addition to releasing a dozen albums on various independent labels, husband-and-wife team Bob Stohl and Kat Epple have scored and produced music for numerous film and TV projects at the state-of-the-art recording studio in their Florida home. These projects have gained them numerous awards, including several Emmy and Addy awards and a 1986 Grammy nomination. In 1990 their close creative partnership ended when Stohl tragically drowned. *Manatee Dreams of Neptune*, one of the finest albums Emerald Web ever made, was recorded shortly before his death. Though many of their releases are difficult to find, the evocative, mood-altering compositions on the releases listed here exemplify the Emerald Web sound. —*Linda Kohanov*

Nocturne/Lights of Ivory Plain / 1989 / Fortuna ♦♦♦
This CD-only release brings together selections from two albums recorded in 1983 and 1984. Haunting bass flute and Celtic harp melodies flow into the rhythmic permutations of digital synthesizers and the colorful sounds of the Lyricon wind synthesizer. —*Linda Kohanov*

● **Manatee Dreams of Neptune** / 1990 / Scarlet ♦♦♦♦
Emerald Web's last album is arguably the duo's best. The inspiration comes from an unusual juxtaposition of experiences. Several of the selections were inspired by Voyager's photographs of Neptune and its moons. (Emerald Web provided music for television programs on the space probe's rendezvous with Neptune.) At the time this album was made, the composers were also spending a lot of time watching manatees swim in the waterways near their home, enjoying the graceful movements of these endangered marine mammals. The resulting music is mysterious and otherworldly, while conveying a deep appreciation for life on this planet. —*Linda Kohanov*

Roger Eno

Piano / Progressive Electronic, Ethnic Fusion, Ambient, Avant-Garde
Brian Eno's brother plays romantic, heavily processed piano music that sounds like a cross between Harold Budd's poignant minimal phrasing and the miniatures of French composer Erik Satie. —*Linda Kohanov*

● **Voices** / 1985 / EG ♦♦♦♦
This is lilting, atmospheric piano music in slow motion. —*Linda Kohanov*

Between Tides / 1988 / Opal ♦♦♦

Enya

b. Donegal, Ireland
Keyboards, Vocals / Alternative Pop-Rock
Enya (Eithne Ni Bhraonain) is from Gweedore, County Donegal, Ireland,

which she left in 1980 to join the Irish band Clannad, the group that already featured her older brothers and sisters. She stayed with Clannad for two years, then left, hooking up with producer Nicky Ryan and lyricist Roma Ryan, with whom she recorded film and television scores. The result was a successful album of TV music for the BBC. Enya then recorded *Watermark* (1988), which featured her distinctive, flowing music and multi-overdubbed trancelike singing; the album sold four million copies worldwide. It was followed by *Shepherd Moons* (1991), which confirmed Enya's status as a new age superstar. —*William Ruhlmann*

Enya / 1987 / Atlantic ✦✦✦
Enya's debut album is truly glorious: multi-layered harmonies, chords like a church choir, and the magic of ancient Celtic culture. Enya's definitely charting some new musical territory, in her blending of classical, medieval, traditional, new age idioms with totally new, original, and experimental ones. Enya composed and co-arranged the music, performs all the vocal and keyboard parts, and veritably makes a new instrument of her voice, complemented by uillean pipes, violin, and electric guitar. —*Ladyslipper*

● **Watermark** / 1988 / Reprise ✦✦✦✦
Singing in Gaelic, Latin, and English, Enya draws on her twin Celtic and Catholic heritages to conjure up achingly beautiful songs that poignantly express the yearnings of the soul. Her piano and synthesizers, along with occasional additional instrumentation, provide graceful orchestrations that give wings to her songs, drawing the listener into her musical vision of mystery and redemption. —*Backroads Music/Heartbeats*

Shepherd Moons / Nov. 1991 / Reprise ✦✦✦✦
While it follows the same basic formula as the multi-million-seller *Watermark*, *Shepherd Moons* isn't quite as captivating, but that's only a relative term. Most of the album captures the same mystical, trance-inducing mood that made *Watermark* a success. —*Stephen Thomas Erlewine*

Oiche Chiun (Silent Night) [maxi-single] / 1992 / Reprise ✦✦✦
This is a ten-minute, three-track, seasonal maxi-single on which Enya sings "Silent Night" in Gaelic. "Oriel Window" is a piano instrumental, and "'S Fagaim Mo Bhaile" is another Gaelic selection performed in Enya's characteristic, ethereal style. —*William Ruhlmann*

Celts / Nov. 1992 / Reprise ✦✦✦

Memory of Trees / Dec. 5, 1995 / Reprise ✦✦✦
Memory of Trees took Enya four years to complete, but most fans will find the wait worthwhile. Enya doesn't depart from her trademark sound—there are still layers of atmospheric synthesizers and ethereal vocals—yet it doesn't repeat *Watermark* and *Shepherd Moons*, it builds on them. *Memory of Trees* may lack the original spark that made its predecessors so fascinating, but it remains an endlessly intriguing listen. —*Sara Sytsma*

Esteban (Stephen Paul)

Guitar / Neo-Classical, Solo Instrumental, Ethnic Fusion
Guitarist Stephen Paul was affectionately called "Esteban" by his teacher, the legendary classical virtuoso Andres Segovia. He shows much promise as both a composer and a performer. —*Linda Kohanov*

● **Duende** / 1991 / Sound Designs of Arizona ✦✦✦✦
Esteban calls his style "new-world guitar music," an accurate moniker for *Duende*'s combination of classical, flamenco, and ethnic influences from various cultures. Esteban's touch is expressive and his technique impressive; the album was recorded without editing or overdubbing. —*Linda Kohanov*

Runaway / 1993 / Sound Designs Of Arizona ✦✦✦

Dean Evenson

Flute / New Age, Ambient
In the '70s, Evenson and his wife Dudley traveled across the country with early portable video equipment to document "the awakening consciousness as it was manifesting in people's lives." The couple eventually settled in Tucson, AZ, and built a small empire with their Soundings of the Planet record company. Their stated purpose was to help people "experience the healing energies of music and natural sounds and get in touch with a more peaceful place inside themselves." Soundings of the Planet has had amazing success in creating and distributing recordings that communicate this goal. Evenson produces many of the label's artists. He also has several albums of his own that combine natural sounds with his softly flowing flute melodies and various other acoustic and electronic instruments. —*Linda Kohanov*

Peaceful Pond / 1986 / Soundings of the Planet ✦✦✦

Ocean Dreams / 1989 / Soundings of the Planet ✦✦✦✦
Ocean waves and whale sounds weave in and out of music that is highly atmospheric and melodic. Though the motivation is sincere, it's all been done better before, most notably by Paul Winter. —*Linda Kohanov*

Desert Dawn Song / 1991 / Soundings of the Planet ✦✦✦✦
An environmentally inspired thematic album, it's more accomplished than *Ocean Dreams*. —*Linda Kohanov*

Wind Dancer / 1992 / Soundings of the Planet ✦✦✦
Wind Dancer takes as its inspiration the grandeur of the Pacific Northwest. With themes built from nature sounds heard intermittently in the background, these seaside soundtracks reflect a watery world of misty isles, as the piano and synth of Tom Barabas blend with the sensuous synthesizers and silver flutes of Dean Evenson. Add saxophone, percussion, and guitar, and these majestic, circular melodies allow you to enter a world of mystery and wonder. *Wind Dancer* is less ambient and nature-oriented than prior releases, —*Backroads Music/Heartbeats*

Lifestreams / Soundings of the Planet ✦✦

Whistling Woodhearts / Soundings of the Planet ✦✦

Forrest Fang

Violin
Chinese-American multi-instrumentalist Forrest Fang's first instrument was the violin. In 1980-81 he studied electronic music, composition, and jazz improvisation at Washington University in St. Louis, MO. At the same time, he learned fiddling at regional fiddling festivals and gained an appreciation for stringed instruments such as the mandolin and mandola.

Fang's first records were rooted in electronic music and progressive rock. His study of Chinese classical music, with zheng (Chinese zither) player Zhang Yan from mainland China, led to a stylistic shift that was evident in his fourth release, *The Wolf at the Ruins* (1989).

Since 1991, Fang has studied gagku (ancient Japanese court music) with imperial court musician Suenobu Togi and gamelan with Balinese composer I Wayan Sujana. In 1993 Fang composed music for a Balinese shadow theater production of *In Zanadu*, which was awarded a Citation of Excellence from the International Puppetry Association. Some of this material was rearranged and adapted for his sixth release, *Folklore*. —*Jim Dorsch*

World Diary / Ominous Thud ✦✦✦
Forrest Fang previously released *The Wolf at the Ruins*, an intriguing mixture of styles, from eerie Eno-esque terrain to multifaceted ethnic colorings. Now Fang has created the fascinating *World Diary*, a further exploration of non-Western influences, drawing on his Chinese heritage. He is joined on a couple of tracks by musicians from Tibet and China, while using instruments from Bali, Kenya, Syria, Bolivia, and the Far East. From ominous rumbles to rich drones, Fang builds fertile backdrops for his conveyance of the dark beauty and focused intensity at the heart of his intriguing compositions. —*Backroads Music/Heartbeats*

● **The Wolf at the Ruins** / 1989 / ✦✦✦✦
Forrest Fang is a Chinese-American musician with a strong interest in non-Western music, primarily the music of his Chinese ancestors, but he mixes and matches different ethnic styles and instruments with gay abandon. Even the most traditionally Chinese track, "The Windmill," mixes the Chinese zither with the Japanese palm harp, African balafon, and the Western mandola and synthesizer. The Chinese zither, or gu-zheng (also known as the cheng) is the more complex forerunner of the better-known Japanese koto, and its elegant tones also grace the multi-layered "The Luminous Crowd." Also featured is the bandurria, a large South American guitar-like instrument that Fang plays in an unorthodox way with hammers, producing a resonant dulcimer sound. He is not afraid to use dramatic tension in his music and, as befits his marvelously named Ominous Thud record label, there is an eerie quality to much of his music, especially on the 24-minute "An Amulet and a Travelogue." Other tracks—notably "Amelia," with its layered electric guitar, and the all-electronic "Silent Fields"—move into more familiar Eno-esque terrain. *The Wolf at the Ruins* is an intriguing album that freely mixes space music with multifaceted ethnic colorings in a way that is sure to appeal to connoisseurs of experimental global music. —*Backroads Music/Heartbeats*

Christopher Franke

Keyboards / Adult Alternative, Progressive Electronic, Minimalism
After nearly two decades as one of the main pillars of the legendary electronic group Tangerine Dream, this German keyboardist struck out on his own in the late '80s. Before he left, his mastery of sequencer-driven synthesizer techniques defined much of the trademark TD sound with its pulsing, multi-layered mosaics of precise yet exhilarating note patterns. —*Linda Kohanov*

● **Pacific Coast Highway** / 1991 / Private Music ✦✦✦✦
Franke's first solo album is surprisingly melodic, highly accessible, and immaculately produced. As the title suggests, this music would make the perfect soundtrack for a drive up the California coast. The innovative sequencer work of his Tangerine Dream years has given way on this

album to more predictable pop electronic orchestrations that would easily fit into new adult-contemporary radio formats. —*Linda Kohanov*

The London Concert / 1993 / Varese Sarabande ✦✦✦✦
While three tracks are versions of pieces from *Pacific Coast Highway*, the material is mostly new, starting with "Empire of Light," with its powerful, hypnotic entrance into Franke's spellbinding world of sonic images, combining dramatic electronic and calming acoustic sounds. "Purple Waves," at 16-plus minutes, stretches to a lofty stature of melodic orchestration. The remaining pieces fuse Franke's skilled dynamics into a forceful blend of classical electronic and contemporary sound. —*Heartbeats*

New Music for Films, Vol. 1 / 1993 / Varese Sarabande ✦✦✦
Franke has released his second and third solo efforts simultaneously, following last year's successful *Pacific Coast Highway*.... [His third album] is *New Music for Films— Vol. 1*, compiling three soundtrack ventures into a rich album of surprising textures and motifs that reach beyond the hard-driving style popularized by Tangerine Dream. Shorter pieces make up many of the 24 selections, from "Eye of the Storm," "McBain," and "She Woke Up." —*Heartbeats*

Celestine Prophecy / 1996 / Priority ✦✦✦
Christopher Franke's adaptation of James Redfield's best-selling book *The Celestine Prophecy* is layered with worldbeat flourishes, drawing from all manner of Eastern and ancient musics. Franke layers rhythms and sonic textures, from African percussion to sampled pianos and high falsetto vocals. By and large, the soundscapes are evocative, even if they aren't necessarily evocative of the book itself. Nevertheless, *The Celstine Prophecy* is yet another impressive work from a gifted and adventurous new age composer. —*Rodney Batdorf*

Friedemann

Guitar / Solo Instrumental, Adult Alternative, Ethnic Fusion
West German guitarist Friedemann Witecka is a popular arranger, producer, and studio musician in his homeland. His US releases for Narada prove he's also one of the most imaginative composers of instrumental music influenced by rock and jazz fusion styles. This catchy, spirited music gracefully sidesteps most pop clichés. —*Linda Kohanov*

● **Indian Summer** / 1987 / Narada ✦✦✦✦
The guitarist's North American debut is an engaging mix of styles and instrumental colors. Standard guitars and keyboards are enhanced by Chinese hammer dulcimer, harp, vibes, marimba, and lots of percussion. —*Linda Kohanov*

Aquamarine / 1990 / Narada ✦✦✦
Friedemann is working with an even larger palette of colors here (12 guest musicians). —*Linda Kohanov*

Eugene Friesen

Cello / Neo-Classical, Chamber Jazz
Best known for his work with the Paul Winter Consort, this classically trained cellist was inspired by equal parts sacred orchestral music and mid-'60s pop styles. (The innovative use of the cello by the Beatles in some of their arrangements was a strong influence on young Friesen.) His work with a diverse roster of artists over the years has further expanded his scope. He has recorded and performed with everyone from Dave Brubeck and Anthony Davis to Scott Cossu and Steven Halpern. —*Linda Kohanov*

● **New Friend** / 1986 / Living Music ✦✦✦✦
New Friend, highlighting Eugene Friesen on cello, with Paul Halley on piano and pipe organ, comes alive in a tapestry of spellbinding excellence. The musicians blossom on this haunting, acoustic showcase of interplay. —*MusD*

Arms Around You / 1989 / Living Music ✦✦✦
Friesen's lyrical cello solos are the highlight of this romantic, contemporary, instrumental album. —*Linda Kohanov*

Edgar Froese

Guitar, Mellotron / Electronic, Adult Alternative, Progressive Electronic, Ambient
A founding member of the pioneering German synthesizer group Tangerine Dream, Froese proved to be the most ambitious in releasing solo albums alongside the voluminous output of the band. He was also considered a master of the Mellotron, an early keyboard device (made famous by the rock group Moody Blues) that produced its sound through key-activated tape loops of actual recordings of orchestras, choirs, and other acoustic sounds. Froese's individual style has a more direct and personal quality, while still drawing from TD's trademark sequencer sound. These albums also feature his penchant for rock-style guitar work. —*Linda Kohanov*

Aqua / 1974 / Blue Plate ✦✦✦
This is the debut from Tangerine Dream's leader. —*Michael P. Dawson*

● **Epsilon in Malaysian Pale** / 1975 / Blue Plate ✦✦✦✦
Lush, entrancing electronic pieces. —*Michael P. Dawson*

Stuntman / 1979 / Blue Plate ✦✦✦
It's a less otherworldly version of Froese's sound. —*Michael P. Dawson*

Kamikaze [1989 Soundtrack] / 1982 / Blue Plate ✦✦✦
A patchy soundtrack effort. —*Michael P. Dawson*

Gandalf (Hein Strobl)

b. Austria
Synthesizer / New Age, Adult Alternative, Progressive Electronic, Ambient
Austrian musician Hein Strobl took his stage name from the magician in J. R. Tolkien's trilogy *Lord of the Rings*. As such, the composer's goal is to create music that magically inspires positive thoughts and feelings in his listeners as an antidote to the negative forces of modern life. From his early spatial electronic and guitar soundscapes to his more recent symphonic compositions, Gandalf's work conveys his love of nature and commitment to preserving the environment. —*Linda Kohanov*

More Than Just a Seagull / 1988 / Eurock ✦✦✦
Gandalf's US debut was originally composed as the soundtrack for a multimedia performance of Richard Bach's book *Jonathan Livingston Seagull*. Sounds of the sea mix with bird calls, bells, guitars, synthesizers, mellotron, and grand piano to create wistful music that floats and soars. —*Linda Kohanov*

Labyrinth / 1990 / Eurock ✦✦✦✦
This music was composed as the soundtrack to an Austrian experimental film screened at the Berlin and Cannes Film Festivals in 1989. A refreshing departure from Gandalf's eternally optimistic style, *Labyrinth* explores the deeper psychological realms of sound through dense, darkly evocative melodies, minimalist rhythmic patterns, and contemplative soundscapes. —*Linda Kohanov*

● **Reflection** / 1991 / Eurock ✦✦✦✦
This collection of essential pieces recorded between 1986 and 1990 was chosen by Gandalf himself to represent various aspects of his style. Influences range from classical and symphonic music to rock, pop, new age, and oriental. —*Linda Kohanov*

Gallery of Dreams / 1993 / Eurock ✦✦✦✦
Gandalf's latest features the talented Steve Hackett, formerly with the popular group Genesis in their heyday. From biting electric leads to serene classical guitars, Hackett adds a new dimension. Gandalf has his own multifaceted approach. Flute and oboe expand the sound even further, and Gandalf's versatility is heard on guitars, keyboards, mandolin, and percussion. Stately melodies and symphonic flair tie the selections together, while Hackett, who appears on more than half the tracks, shows his lyrical side. To top it off, the CD booklet and packaging are perfectly eloquent, adding just the right touch to a powerful and enjoyable release. —*Backroads Music/Heartbeats*

On Wings / Eurock ✦✦✦
This compilation features five different Austrian artists, with all tracks produced by Gandalf except for three by Robert Julian Horkey. Both Sandy de Larny and Mako contribute two or three pieces, and Gandalf's electric guitar is heard here and there. Over 67 minutes, this album will have extensive appeal to space music fans. —*Backroads Music/Heartbeats*

T.K. Gardner

Guitar / Adult Alternative
New age? Light jazz? Adult-contemporary? The eight-string guitar work of T.K. Gardner may be hard to classify, but it makes for great listening. Too much of so-called space music is just that—vacuous. Although Gardner's music has that new spacious sound, it also has definition and real substance—integrity. This is how new age music should sound. —*Michael Erlewine*

● **8 X 10** / 1990 / Wildcard ✦✦✦✦
You may have trouble finding his one album, *8 X 10*, in stores, so here is the address: Wildcard Records, P.O. Box 4565, Anaheim, CA 92803. —*Michael Erlewine*

Michael Garrison

Synthesizer, Keyboards, Vocals / Progressive Electronic, Minimalism
A longstanding American exponent of sequencer-based music, Garrison has released over a half-dozen albums of high-energy electronics. Strongly influenced by European innovators like Klaus Schulze and Tangerine Dream, this Oregon-based artist enjoys propelling listeners into rhythmic travels along the space-time continuum. —*Linda Kohanov*

Eclipse / 1983 / Winspell ✦✦✦✦
One of Garrison's finest sequencer scorchers is featured, with some quiet, impressionistic moments to balance things out. —*Linda Kohanov*

Earth-Star Trilogy / 1988 / Windspell ✦✦✦
This isn't quite as frenetic and hard-edged as many of Garrison's previous releases. —*Linda Kohanov*

The Rhythm of Life / 1991 / Windspell ✦✦✦✦
This recent release accelerates into the breathless sequencer work Garrison is known for, though his style is rather predictable at this point. —*Linda Kohanov*

● **Collection #1: A Positive Reflecting Glow and Collection #2: Tranquility Cove** / ✦✦✦✦
Two long-awaited collections from Oregon synthesist Michael Garrison offer his broad body of music, broken down into his two predominant styles. *A Positive Reflecting Glow* covers the more uptempo, sequencer-driven tracks from his eight releases, plus one new track, "Upon Blue Heaven." "Tranquility Cove" gathers slower tracks from four of his albums, and adds an unreleased piece, "Invisible Sun." —*Heartbeats*

Robert Gass

Synthesizer, Piano, Vocals / New Age, Neo-Classical, Choral, Ambient, Chant
A nationally known lecturer, Gass holds a doctorate in clinical psychology from Harvard and has received classical training in music at the New England Conservatory and Tanglewood. As director of the 30-person performing group On Wings of Song, he has produced a number of recordings under his *Extended Chant* series that feature uplifting, updated versions of sacred choral traditions from around the world. Though many of these works are based on authentic spiritual texts and melodies, Gass' primary goal seems to be making the music as comforting and as accessible as possible to modern audiences. However, listeners who enjoy Middle Eastern chanting, American Indian music, and medieval plain-chant singing in their purest, most traditional forms will likely find Gass' interpretations a little too sweet and Westernized. —*Linda Kohanov*

Heart of Perfect Wisdom / 1990 / Spring Hill ✦✦✦✦
This fine recording is Gass' adaptation of the Buddhist heart sutra. Striking a delicate balance between Eastern and Western sensibilities, the album features full chorus, Tibetan bells, Nepalese wooden flutes, and some overtone singing, with a subtle use of acoustic guitar and Celtic harp. The presentation retains a sense of mystery and reverence for Eastern tradition that is lost to various degrees on some of Gass' other recordings, which lean toward the sentimental at the expense of the mystical. —*Linda Kohanov*

Kalama / 1990 / Spring Hill ✦✦✦
On *Kalama: A Sufi Song of Love*, the members of On Wings of Song sing ancient Sufi lyrics in Arabic to contemporary melodies and arrangements featuring guitars, violin, tabla, and sarod. —*Linda Kohanov*

Gloria / 1991 / Spring Hill ✦✦✦
Gass' arrangement of the *Gloria* from the Catholic mass mixes some elements of Gregorian chant with classical guitar accompaniments. —*Linda Kohanov*

Shri Ram / 1991 / Shm ✦✦✦

Om Namaha Shivaya/Hara Hara / 1992 / Shm ✦✦✦
Om Namaha Shivaya, the best-selling title in the *Chants of the World* series by Robert Gass and On Wings of Song, is now available on CD, along with "Hara Hara," another beautiful Sanskrit mantra, sung to simple backing. —*Backroads Music/Heartbeats*

● **Alleluia to Pachelbel Canon in D A** / Shm ✦✦✦✦
This popular year-round favorite has a special appeal during the holidays. Recorded at Christmas time with the 30 voices of On Wings of Song, *Alleluia* creates an environment for relaxation, movement, and healing. —*MusD*

Pilgrimage / Shm ✦✦✦
A musical outpouring by Robert Gass of a different nature than his usual *Extended Chant* series, these nine instrumental journeys are open-hearted expressions of a personal nature that seem to combine 19th-century romantic music with the more pop style within new age music. The strings of the Denver Symphony weave a lyrical counterpoint to the soaring melodies of Gass' piano, which are imbued with a sense of joy throughout. — *Backroads Music/Heartbeats*

Opening the Heart / ✦✦✦
The first guided imagery and music tape by Robert Gass offers a simple but powerful process for opening the heart and experiencing the healing power of love. Side Two of *Opening the Heart* has heart-filled songs by the 30-voice choir on Wings of Song. —*Backroads Music/Heartbeats*

● **Medicine Wheel** / Shm ✦✦✦✦
Medicine Wheel blends the uplifting sounds of On Wings of Song with traditional Native American music. The first half has several meditative chants woven with the sounds of Indian flutes, crickets, cicadas, and birds. The second half uses the words of Chief Seattle as a starting point,

set to music by Robert Gass in a passionate call to honor and care for the Earth. —*Backroads Music/Heartbeats*

Michael Gettel

Synthesizer / Solo Instrumental, Adult Alternative
This Seattle-based composer and music teacher writes contemporary piano-based ensemble works inspired by family, friends, and the beauty of the Pacific Northwest. Though his uptempo pieces are on the trite side, he is at his best when he creates flowing, impressionistic music involving acoustic piano and melodic instruments like oboe, French horn, and fluegelhorn. —*Linda Kohanov*

● **San Juan Suite** / 1988 / Sounding ✦✦✦✦
Michael Gettel has an instantly appealing piano style reminiscent of George Winston. On his first album, Gettel's only accompaniment are the sounds of the ocean, whales and other marine mammals, along with natural ambient sounds. Otherwise, *San Juan Suite* is solo piano only, with each piece a personal portrait. This music really flows, like the waters of Puget Sound around the San Juan Islands that inspired this album. —*Backroads Music/Heartbeats*

Return / 1990 / Narada ✦✦✦
Michael Gettel's covers show a different place in time, more remote and still, yet full of wind and nature, while his music expresses the same feelings, filled with survival and beauty. Besides Gettel's piano, instruments include oboe, classical guitar, fiddle, soprano sax, synthesizer, percussion, accordion, and even a chromatic harmonica. The music and each of Gettel's compositions, all between five and seven minutes, stand up well for the most part. —*Backroads Music/Heartbeats*

Places in Time / 1992 / Narada ✦✦✦
A finely produced album, *Places in Time* features a wide variety of guest artists including violinist Billy Oskay, oboists Nancy Rumbel and Russel Walder, and synthesist David Arkenstone, among others. —*Linda Kohanov*

Skywatching / 1993 / Narada ✦✦

The Key / Oct. 1993 / Narada ✦✦✦
Already well established as a skilled musician on piano and synthesizers, Gettel coordinates the efforts of guest performers, including Paul Speer, Nancy Rumbel, and Randy Sherwood, to help mold an extraordinary instrumental sound. "Breaking Silence" treats the subject of silence with respect, but breaks it with verve and daring. "When Hearts Collide," composed with the help of Sherwood, treats one to an unexpected happy ending. And "The Search," motivated by an ambitious beat, leads naturally "Through the Doorway." —*MusD*

Jerry Goodman

Violin / Adult Alternative, Progressive Electronic
As a member of John McLaughlin's influential jazz/rock fusion band Mahavishnu Orchestra in the early '70s, Goodman used his violin to create phrasings and sonorities previously associated with the electric guitar. His subsequent albums as a leader for Private Music expand on these experiences to create a dynamic and aggressive style that fuses rock textures with classical dynamics through tightly arranged compositions. —*Linda Kohanov*

Ariel / 1985 / Private Music ✦✦✦
Featured are vivid fusion textures and combustible fiddle playing. —*Linda Kohanov*

● **On the Future of Aviation** / 1989 / Private Music ✦✦✦✦
Goodman's debut as a leader features his abilities on guitar, mandolin, synthesizers, and percussion, in addition to violin solos that subsist on his characteristic screaming, electronically distorted sound. —*Linda Kohanov*

Govi

Guitar, Mandolin, Cello / New Age, Ethnic Fusion
This California-based artist was born in Germany. His inspiration and style are similar to that of another German immigrant, Deuter, who co-produced and performed on Govi's debut album *Sky High*. Like Deuter, Govi spent a number of years living and studying in India, where he added sitar to his vocabulary of acoustic and electric guitars, mandola, and cello. His music is a gentle, melodious combination of influences from around the world. —*Linda Kohanov*

Sky High / 1986 / Real Music ✦✦✦
Sky High includes Deuter on every cut, and these two complement each other wonderfully. Govi retains his own unique expression throughout, and the second half, in particular, plays beautifully as a whole. For breezy guitar stylings with enough depth and strength to entice guitar aficionados while still retaining the light, airy feel of a balmy summer day, *Sky High* may become an often-played favorite in your collection. —*Backroads Music/Heartbeats*

● **Heart of a Gypsy** / 1987 / Real Music ◆◆◆◆

On Govi's latest recording, he heads south of the border and lands squarely in the heart of the Andes. But in true Gypsy form, he manages to invoke the flavors of other cultures and lands as he travels through the musical spaces on this breezy tour-de-force. The strong South American influence is, however, less in the Inti-Illimani vein than in the style that fellow-countryman Deuter has previously explored on a few cuts, and similarities between these two artists are apparent on at least two or three of the tracks on *Heart of a Gypsy*. —*Backroads Music/Heartbeats*

Cuchama / Jun. 1993 / Real Music ◆◆◆

Govi is a spirited guitarist with a recognizable style that incorporates elements from flamenco, Caribbean, and jazz influences to create his musical statements. With no shortage of passion or virtuosity, Govi has a memorable sound that ranges from airy, tropical tempos to slower pieces to lively south-of-the-border rhythms. Other musicians such as Anugama, Karunesh, and tabla player Daniel Paul make solid contributions to this fine effort from a superb instrumentalist with an obvious flair for the guitar. —*Backroads Music/Heartbeats*

Wayne Gratz

Piano, Keyboards / Solo Instrumental, Adult Alternative, Chamber Jazz
Gratz spent over a decade playing keyboards in a Florida-based pop band before he sent a tape of some of his more reflective solo piano pieces to Narada. The label was immediately intrigued by his songwriting skills and signed him up. Though he's primarily self-taught, Gratz possesses a natural talent for creating lush, impressionistic music that somehow sidesteps the cliches many of his labelmates lapse into. Though he's not as well known as David Lanz or Spencer Brewer, Gratz is in many ways more successful at creating subtle, artistically satisfying compositions. —*Linda Kohanov*

● **Reminiscence** / 1989 / Narada ◆◆◆◆

Gratz' debut for Narada is devoted primarily to solo piano music, with a few guest performances by Scottish fiddler Alasdair Fraser and oboist Nancy Rumbel. This is evocative, understated music with an innate sense of elegance. —*Linda Kohanov*

Panorama / 1990 / Narada ◆◆◆

Gratz plays keyboards and guitar as well as piano on this collection of ensemble pieces produced by violinist Billy Oskay. Though the composer has managed to keep the subtleties of his own style intact for the most part, the Gratz sound occasionally gets mired in thick arrangements that threaten to obscure his delicate insights. —*Linda Kohanov*

Follow Me Home / 1993 / Narada ◆◆◆

Blue Ridge / 1995 / Narada ◆◆◆◆

Wayne Gratz musically recreates the beauty of Appalachia's Blue Ridge Mountains in an alluring new dimension with his fourth career release, *Blue Ridge*. Gratz' skill as a composer has reached new summits, and the result is an exquisitely crafted, stylish hybrid of accessible pop with warm classical impressions. Lending a hand to Gratz' lyrical piano and synthesizer mastery are guest performers Forest Rogers on mandolin and guitar, Doug Mathews on six-string fretless bass, Joseph Ruback on dulcimer, and Paul "Slim" Fleury and Peter Lund on cello and violin, respectively. A fantastic percussion section comprised of Lloyd Hansen, Carlos Fernandez, and Trevor Sadler adds to the instrumental blend. —*MusD*

Green Isac

Progressive Electronic, Ethnic Fusion
Green Isac is a Norwegian-based duo featuring Morten Lund on keyboards, guitar, and flute. His partner, Andreas Eriksen, is an imaginative percussionist well versed in African and Arabic styles. —*Linda Kohanov*

● **Strings and Pottery** / 1991 / Eurock ◆◆◆◆

From the intricate minimalist patterns of Steve Reich, the techno-tribal mystery of Jon Hassell, and the tango seductions of Astor Piazzolla to the rhythmic vitality of rock and the percussive ecstasy of third-world traditions, Green Isac seems to have summed up the major innovations of the late 20th century in a single well-crafted album. —*Linda Kohanov*

Happy Endings / 1992 / Eurock ◆◆◆

Chuck Greenberg

d. May 29, 1995
Flute, Keyboards, Saxophone / Adult Alternative, Progressive Electronic, Ethnic Fusion
One of the founding members of the influential world-music/fusion band Shadowfax, Greenberg played flute, saxophone, and keyboards. The California-based artist was also well known for his use of the lyricon, an electronic wind instrument he helped develop. The lyricon added an ethereal dimension to his masterful melodic improvisations. As a composer, Greenberg combined rock, pop, and jazz elements in his music

while retaining a progressive edge. Greenberg died as the result of a heart attack in mid-1995. —*Linda Kohanov*

From a Blue Planet / 1991 / Capitol ◆◆◆◆

Greenberg's first album as a leader allows him to shine as a soloist, though he is accompanied by some first-class artists like guitarist Alex de Grassi, as well as fellow Shadowfax bandmates Charles Bisharat on violin and Phil Maggini on bass. This is an impressive album. —*Linda Kohanov*

Sylvan Grey

Kantele / Neo-Classical, Solo Instrumental, Ethnic Fusion
Grey works wonders with the 36-string Finnish folk zither known as the kantele, which she discovered during a trip to England and studied briefly with Finland's highly regarded teacher Ulla Katajavuori. Back in the US, Grey devoted herself to composing music for the kantele and honed her chops performing in coffeehouses. She recorded her first album, *Ice Flowers Melting*, for Fortuna Records in 1981. (It was re-released in 1988.) Her finest effort, however, is her rhapsodic follow-up recording *Recurring Dream*. —*Linda Kohanov*

● **Ice Flowers Melting** / 1981 / Fortuna ◆◆◆◆

Recurring Dream / 1989 / Fortuna ◆◆◆

Without the use of electronic processing of any kind, Grey produces a lush, scintillating sound from the kantele through her skillful use of bell-like accents, ringing harmonics, arpeggios, and delicate ostinatos. The music is both stirring and intimate. —*Linda Kohanov*

Paul Halley

Piano, Harpsichord, Keyboards / Neo-Classical, Solo Instrumental, Chamber Jazz
Though he's best known as a member of the Paul Winter Consort, this English-born pianist has an impressive career of his own. After receiving a master's degree from Cambridge, with prizes in composition and harpsichord playing, Halley was named musical director at New York's Cathedral of St. John the Divine. There he expanded its music program to include a rich combination of contemporary as well as classical styles. He also wrote choral works and Broadway scores. Winter, whom Halley met in 1980, was the first to recognize the keyboardist's talent for improvisation and invited him to join the Paul Winter Consort. Halley has since been a featured performer on many of the Consort's finest albums. —*Linda Kohanov*

New Friend / 1988 / Living Music ◆◆◆

This is an imaginative collection of improvisations for cello and piano with Eugene Friesen, featuring two of the Paul Winter Consort's long-standing members. —*Linda Kohanov*

● **Pianosong** / 1989 / Living Music ◆◆◆◆

Halley's first solo album for Winter's Living Music label consists of rich and varied solo piano improvisations, augmented on three cuts by the sonorous sounds of the Cathedral of St. John the Divine's pipe organ. —*Linda Kohanov*

Angel on a Stone Wall / 1991 / Living Music ◆◆◆

Steven Halpern

Synthesizer, Piano, Vocals / New Age, Ethnic Fusion, Ambient
Halpern is the original new age artist, in the most accurate sense of the term. In 1975 he released *Spectrum Suite*, his first album of music specifically designed for relaxation and healing. Before that, Halpern had been immersed in the New York City jazz scene as a trumpeter and guitarist. His disgust at the adverse effects of life in the fast lane were accentuated by a move to California, where he perfected his idea of "anti-frantic alternative" music. Based partly on his metaphysical beliefs and partly on more solid scientific research into the effects of sound on the human body, he came to the conclusion that the Western foundation of tension and release in music couldn't by nature provide listeners with relief from stress. He decided the answer was to create music that "didn't go anywhere" in the traditional sense but instead immersed the listener in a positive atmosphere conducive to recuperative and transcendental experiences. Halpern created music that was centered largely around cascades of major-key arpeggios improvised at the electric piano, and he added generous helpings of reverb to create a spacey, other-worldly feeling. He took a certain amount of inspiration from oriental classical music and looked into the ceremonial, magical, and healing aspects of sound used by ancient cultures. While some of his ideas take on the pseudo-science pallor of new age mysticism, Halpern's importance as one of the true fathers of modern meditational and healing forms of music cannot be overemphasized. He has released over 50 instrumental and guided meditation recordings, some of which are better than others. He has also written two books on his theories: *Tuning the Human Instrument* and *Sound Health*. —*Linda Kohanov*

★ **Spectrum Suite** / 1975 / Atlantic ✦✦✦✦✦
Halpern's first release is a cornerstone of the new age genre and one of
the best examples of the comforting electric-piano reverberations that
have continued to dominate his style over the years. —*Linda Kohanov*

Connections / 1984 / Atlantic ✦✦✦✦
This collaboration with flutist Paul Horn is appropriately soothing, yet
delightful on a purely musical level as well. —*Linda Kohanov*

● **Crystal Suite** / 1988 / Sound Rx ✦✦✦✦
More music for relaxation in the typical Halpern mode, it is couched in
the composer's more eccentric new age theories involving the healing
powers of crystals. —*Linda Kohanov*

Higher Ground / 1991 / Sound Rx ✦✦✦✦
Arguably Halpern's most artistically accomplished album, *Higher
Ground* mixes his trademark sounds of the past with some new directions, particularly a more skillful use of synthesizers. For those interested
in Halpern's latest therapeutic developments, there's an added benefit:
the composer has included what he calls "binaural beat phrasing" to the
music, which he says "sonically entrains your brain to an immediate 8-
cycles per second response" that locks you "into phase with the natural
harmonics of the Earth." —*Linda Kohanov*

Key of Healing / Jul. 1996 / Relaxation ✦✦✦
Throughout his body of work, Steven Halpern has developed a distinctly
spiritual and healing sound. On *Key of Healing*, he uses an approach that
is quite similar to his other works, creating a tapestry of synthesizers,
lush keyboards, and horns. *Key of Healing* isn't a particularly distinctive
effort from Halpern, but it remains an enriching, nurturing listen all the
same. —*Sara Sytsma*

Peter Michael Hamel

b. 1947
Organ, Piano, Keyboards / Neo-Classical, Ethnic Fusion, Minimalism
As a young man Hamel studied music, psychology, and sociology in his
native Germany. He then spent three extensive periods in Asia, where
his studies of Eastern musical traditions (particularly Tibetan and
Indian) had a profound effect not only on his compositional style but on
his views concerning Western music as a whole. Hamel shared his
unconventional insights on music and its place in society in his influential book *Through Music to the Self*. First published in 1976, the treatise
discusses the transformational effects of music through the ages and
calls for a more spiritual approach to composition in 20th-century Western music. While many of his concepts fueled the American new age
movement, Hamel's music is a far cry from the good-natured doodling
often associated with that genre. Though some of his works are more
successful than others, they all exhibit the grace and intelligence of classical music, the spontaneity of jazz, the hypnotic qualities of Far Eastern
styles, and (quite often) the relentless drive of American minimalist techniques. —*Linda Kohanov*

☆ **Transition** / 1983 / Kuckuck ✦✦✦✦✦
All of Hamel's albums have their moments, but *Transition* presents
some of the composer's most beautiful and most emotionally arresting
music. Hamel performs several extended works on piano that combine
rhapsodic melodies with rich harmonic flourishes. There's also an ambitious essay for pipe organ, PPG wave computer, and synthesizer that
takes listeners out of the realm of everyday experience. The real gem,
however, is a 25-minute masterpiece for prepared piano that transforms
the standard 88 keys into a sort of miniature percussion ensemble. The
music on this clever, yet highly expressive work sounds like everything
from an Indonesian gamelan to an African bamboo orchestra. —*Linda
Kohanov*

● **Let It Play** / 1984 / Kuckuck ✦✦✦✦
This fine introduction to Hamel's varied style presents him in various
moods from 1979 to 1983. Samples are taken from *Transition, Colours
of Time, Bardo,* and a few previously unreleased selections. —*Linda
Kohanov*

Organum / 1986 / Kuckuck ✦✦✦
Hamel's contemporary interpretation of the medieval musical concept
known as "organum" involved an intricate interplay of modal melodies.
These four extended works on pipe organ culminate in acutely intense
barrages of sound and sensation. This is a challenging album. —*Linda
Kohanov*

Michael Harrison

Piano / Solo Instrumental, Ethnic Fusion, Minimalism
A protégé of minimalist godfather La Monte Young, this conservatory-
trained pianist and composer successfully mixes classical, jazz, and ethnic influences in his music. Harrison also works extensively with alternate tuning systems and invented what he calls the "harmonic piano."
This instrument is capable of playing 24 notes per octave (as opposed to

the standard 12). The strings are also designed to resonate sympathetically, like those of a sitar. —*Linda Kohanov*

● **In Flight** / 1987 / Fortuna ✦✦✦✦
A most unusual album of piano solos, it combines lyrical melodies and
impressionistic harmonies with some Indian and Oriental influences. A
couple of the pieces were also performed in "just intonation." Unfortunately, the passionate and sublime flights of fancy featured on this
recording never got the attention they deserved. —*Linda Kohanov*

Don Harriss

Keyboards / Electronic, Adult Alternative
This keyboardist and computer whiz has derived his unique sound from
a diverse background that includes classical training, '60s Haight-Ashbury psychedelia, stints of touring and recording with rock idol Pat
Travers, and jobs composing corporate film soundtracks. Though he
lapses into glitzy pop triteness on occasion, he is light years ahead of
most adult contemporary synthesists in his sophisticated use of texture
and sound. He has several albums on the market that did well on new
adult contemporary radio, including *Shell Game, Vanishing Point,* and
Elevations, but his best release by far is *Abacus Moon*. —*Linda Kohanov*

★ **Abacus Moon** / 1989 / Sonic Atmospheres ✦✦✦✦✦
This is a brilliant combination of pop sensibilities and playful, imaginative sound designs. —*Linda Kohanov*

Shell Game / 1990 / Sonic Atmospheres ✦✦✦
Keyboard extraordinaire Don Harriss discovers paradise and takes us on
an exotic musical excursion with *Shell Game*. Additional instrumentation is provided by acoustic and electric guitarist Peter Maunu and percussionist Luis Conte. —*MusD*

Mysterium / 1992 / Sonic Atmospheres ✦✦✦
Don Harriss' handcrafted compositions on *Mysterium* polish his pop
sculptures to a terraced beauty. Smooth, yet dramatic, Harriss fits in well
with the music of Yanni, O'Hearn, or Ciani, offering memorable compositions with a lot of backbone. His use of texture and sound makes brilliant, playful, and imaginative sound designs. —*Heartbeats*

Jon Hassell

b. Mar. 22, 1937
Trumpet / Ethnic Fusion, Minimalism, Techno-Tribal, Avant-Garde
When the album *Earthquake Island* was released in 1978, Jon Hassell
appeared to be a gifted trumpeter working at the edges of jazz with Caribbean and Latin American rhythms. Subsequent releases confounded
expectation, however, as it became clear that Hassell's improvisational
approach was related less to jazz than it was directly inspired by classical
Indian music. Most of his compositions can be thought of as ragas, where
fierce African and Asian rhythms lead into coolly detached trumpet soloing influenced by Karnatic vocal techniques. Inseparable from Hassell's
flowing, breathy style of playing is the distinctive timbre of his electronically processed horn, which sounds halfway between an African wood
trumpet and a digital synthesizer. Hassell's association with Brian Eno
brought the Canadian musician into contact with the world of pop. He
worked with Talking Heads on *Remain in Light* and contributed to Peter
Gabriel's soundtrack for Alan Parker's film *Birdy*.
   As if in atonement for his brush with pop, Hassell released a succession of decidedly noncommercial if not abstract releases guided as much
by the philosophy as the music of foreign cultures. More recently, his
brilliance has shone closer to the mainstream. In 1989 he recorded an
album with the west African percussion group Farafina, and his latest
release, *City: Works of Fiction,* chooses hip-hop rather than worldbeat as
the point of departure. —*Bob Tarte*

Earthquake Island / 1979 / Tomato ✦✦✦
Hassell's first album with Miroslav Vitous, Nana, Dom Um Romao, and
Badal Roy. Stunning music and cover art. —*Michael G. Nastos*

★ **Fourth World, Vol. 1: Possible Musics** / 1980 / EG ✦✦✦✦✦
Brian Eno's most satisfying and captivating set of mood music came
through this collaboration with Jon Hassell. Evocative, eerie, and druggy,
jungle music on Venus is an apt description of *Fourth World—Vol. 1: Possible Musics*. Recorded with percussionists Nana Vasconcelos and Ayibe
Dieng, and bassists Percy Jones and Jerome Harris, this album is essential. —*John Floyd and Michael G. Nastos*

Fourth World, Vol. 2: Dream Theory in Malaya / 1981 / EG ✦✦✦
An academic feel proceeds from the subject matter, a meditation on the
inspirational seed of artistic composition. It takes its lead from the
dream-telling of Malaysian aborigines, the Senoi, whose environment,
beliefs, and music shape Hassell's approach. —*Bob Tarte*

Aka Darbari Java / 1983 / EG ✦✦✦
This is a wild combination of Pygmy voices, Indian ragas, Senegalese
drumming, Javanese gamelan styles, and computer-enhanced trumpet
choruses. —*Linda Kohanov*

Power Spot / 1986 / ECM ✦✦✦
An unexpectedly hot raga approach and rock sensibility contribute to the most accessible of Hassell's solo recordings, which proves he can manipulate Asian and African rhythms in the service of the body as well as the mind. —*Bob Tarte*

Flash of the Spirit / 1988 / Intuition ✦✦
City: Works of Fiction / 1990 / Opal ✦✦✦
Hassell's *Fourth World* explorations move into a futuristic metropolis. Tribal sensibilities combine with hip-hop rhythms to create a *Blade Runner* atmosphere. —*Linda Kohanov*

Steve Haun

Keyboards / Adult Alternative, Contemporary Instrumental
With his gift for catchy melodies and vibrant keyboard textures, this Colorado-based artist has consistently placed well on both *Billboard* and major NAC/adult-alternative radio charts. Tight musicianship is an important feature of Haun's contemporary jazz- and pop-based ensemble recordings, although his compositional style is not particularly original. —*Linda Kohanov*

● **Midnight Echoes** / 1989 / Silver Wave ✦✦✦
Inside the Sky was a surprise success, reaching the heart of radio audiences. This sensational follow-up is a work of epic proportion, involving a more jazzy sound (swingin' sax from Nelson Rangell), in addition to the full, lush sound provided by a live string section featuring members of the Denver Symphony Orchestra. —*Backroads Music/Heartbeats*

Collage / 1991 / Silver Wave ✦✦✦✦
This is a nice fusion-flavored mixture of acoustic and electronic sounds. —*Linda Kohanov*

Michael Hedges

Guitar / Solo Instrumental, New Acoustic
A virtuoso acoustic guitarist, Hedges records for the Windham Hill label. On his first two albums, *Breakfast in the Field* and *Aerial Boundaries*, his playing style combined two-handed tapping ostinatos with percussive slides and slaps to produce rhythmic intensity and hypnotic melodies. This is compositional guitar, with Hedges coaxing a full ensemble of sounds from his guitar. His acoustic sound is treated with reverb and delays, producing a spacious atmosphere that is warm and inviting. His third album, *Watching My Life Go By*, is a change of pace, on which Hedges adds his voice to the music and interprets Bob Dylan's "All Along the Watchtower." Following a double live album, he returned with *Taproot*, on which he again did vocals and, for the first time, included other musicians. —*Scott Bultman*

Breakfast in the Field / 1981 / Windham Hill ✦✦✦
This debut album featured extraordinary guitar work with alternate tunings and his two-handed tapping technique. —*Paul Kohler*

★ **Aerial Boundaries** / 1985 / Windham Hill ✦✦✦✦✦
Hedges shines on his second album, producing an amazing variety of sounds with just his acoustic guitar and ample reverberation. One track from this melodic and musical work features extensive electronic processing. —*Scott Bultman*

Watching My Life Go By / 1987 / Open Air ✦✦
Live on the Double Planet / 1987 / Windham Hill ✦✦✦✦
This exceptional live release features both vocal and instrumental pieces. —*Paul Kohler*

Taproot / 198 / Windham Hill ✦✦✦
Acoustic guitar with a small group, it includes two tracks of Hedges on electric guitar! —*Paul Kohler*

Danny Heines

Guitar / Solo Instrumental, Adult Alternative, Chamber Jazz, Contemporary Instrumental
The Colorado-based guitarist seems inspired by jazz, rock, and contemporary acoustic guitar styles exemplified by Windham Hill artists like Alex de Grassi and Michael Hedges. Heines, however, has transcended his influences to create a spirited style of his own. —*Linda Kohanov*

● **Aqua Touch** / 1986 / Silver Wave ✦✦✦✦
This debut features solo and ensemble pieces, with guest appearances by woodwind player Paul McCandless and cellist Eugene Friesen. —*Linda Kohanov*

One Heart Wild / 1987 / Silver Wave ✦✦✦
This is another finely crafted collection of Heines' work. —*Linda Kohanov*

★ **Every Island** / 1988 / Silver Wave ✦✦✦✦✦
The richly hued guitar stylings of Heines are enhanced by the lyricism of soprano saxophonist and oboist Paul McCandless and the spicy Latin rhythms of Brazilian percussionist Cafe. —*Linda Kohanov*

Vanishing Borders / Oct. 1995 / Silverwave ✦✦✦

Max Highstein

Keyboards / New Age, Adult Alternative
With a B.A. in music, a masters degree in psychotherapy, and a license to practice massage therapy, this keyboardist began his recording career creating guided relaxation tapes. His later instrumental albums combine gentle pop rhythms with optimistic melodies designed for the new age lifestyle market already familiar with his narrated work. —*Linda Kohanov*

Touch the Sky / 1987 / Serenity ✦✦✦
This is music that soars, for piano, winds, cello, bass, and percussion. The first cut, "Full Circle," was a radio hit, and the whole album plays very cohesively with lots of appeal. One piece after another leads the listener through joyous and positive spaces, ranging from "Ferris Wheel" to "Mars in Scorpio" and "Back at the Castle." —*Backroads Music/Heartbeats*

★ **Stars** / 1988 / Serenity ✦✦✦✦✦
This new age pop music features Highstein on acoustic piano and synthesizers, accompanied by some top studio musicians on flute, oboe, violin, cello, trumpet, electric bass, and drums. —*Linda Kohanov*

Daydreams / 1992 / Serenity ✦✦✦✦
Max Highstein's *Daydreams* is a compilation from his previous albums, bringing us nearly an hour's worth of quiet musical reflections. The music, composed and produced by Highstein, features his sure touch on piano and synthesizers, with added accompaniment of Jon Clarke on oboe, English horn and flutes; Ed Willett on cello,;Sid Page on violin; and Carl Sealove and Bob Bowman on bass. The upbeat, light jazz style maintains a sense of gentleness and relaxation throughout. —*MusD*

The Healing Waterfall / ✦✦✦✦
This popular guided journey and imagery tape uses the lush synthesizer sound and cascading piano music of Max Highstein. Jill Andre's voice facilitates deep relaxation and self-healing. —*Backroads Music/Heartbeats*

The Healing Waterfall II Tropical Paradise / Serenity ✦✦✦
On *Healing Waterfall II*, a soothing body relaxation prepares the way for an enchanting journey to a tropical island paradise. The natural beauty of the Healing Waterfall warmly invites you to experience deep inner healing and peace. Inspiring music by Max Highstein sets the tone for your journey, as Jill Andre's caring narration gently guides you along the way. This recording has been a long awaited expansion of one of the best selling relaxation programs of all time. —*MusD*

12 Cosmic Healers / ✦✦✦
Journey through the 12 signs of the zodiac and meet the 12 cosmic healers. Real or imaginary, each one has a celestial melody for its special area of the body. Leigh Taylor-Young narrates this guided meditation with the transformation music of Max Highstein on side one; side two contains the music by itself. A valuable healing tool; a unique listening pleasure. —*MusD*

Lightbeing / ✦✦✦✦
The same team that created the popular *Healing Waterfall* has put together another guided healing journey, this time to another planet. This wondrous voyage was written by Highstein, narrated by Andre, and has music that was composed and performed by Highstein as well. Side two is music only. —*Backroads Music/Heartbeats*

Himekami

Synthesizer / Adult Alternative, Ethnic Fusion
This Japanese synthesist creates lush, pop-influenced music that's almost symphonic in conception. A composer of film and television scores in his native country, Himekami is also well known for his multimedia events at historic shrines and temples throughout Japan. His recorded music, however, is inconsistent in quality. Even his "best of" collections released in the US feature sweet, easy-listening fluff alongside his more masterful musical journeys. —*Linda Kohanov*

● **Moonwater** / 1989 / Higher Octave ✦✦✦✦
Himekami's first release in the US is actually a collection of some of the better selections from his numerous Japanese recordings. Oriental influences are couched in thick synthetic textures and Western harmonies. —*Linda Kohanov*

Snow Goddess / 1991 / Higher Octave ✦✦✦
This is a follow-up to his successful US debut release, *Moonwater*. —*Linda Kohanov*

Journey to Zipangu / 1993 / Higher Octave ✦✦✦
Like Kitaro, Himekami belongs to an elite handful of Japanese synthesizer artists. The group's music captures the pristine beauty of Japan, as the ancient myths come alive in their contemporary musical interpretations that use the most advanced technologies. Keyboard synthesizers are enhanced with violin, slide guitar, bouzouki, and percussion. These musical poems range from expansive and majestic to upbeat and even, at times, playful. —*MusD*

Michael Hoenig

Synthesizer, Keyboards / Progressive Electronic, Minimalism
Hoenig was one of many German composers to emerge from the innovative, electronic underground scene thriving in that country during the '60s and '70s. He first came to recognition in the progressive rock group Agitation Free in the '70s. After a short stint with Tangerine Dream, Hoenig went on to produce what is considered by many to be one of the most important albums to come out of the German electronic school. He has since moved to Los Angeles, where he currently pursues a career as a film composer. — *Linda Kohanov*

★ **Departure from the Northern Wasteland** / 1978 / Kuckuck ✦✦✦✦✦
Departure from the Northern Wasteland, a classic of the progressive electronic genre, contains four pieces that are almost perfect in their realization of the sequencer as a compositional tool. Hoenig took the concept of repetitive music further than most anyone in his homeland and claimed his inspiration was drawn from American minimalist composers Philip Glass, Steve Reich, and Terry Riley. The title track is a sublime 20-minute journey through ever-changing melodic and rhythmic phase relationships, creating the vivid sensation of a train ride through misty Northern European landscapes. — *Linda Kohanov*

Walter Holland

Synthesizer, Guitar / Adult Alternative, Progressive Electronic
This California-based synthesist and guitarist honed his chops in the progressive rock band Amber Route. His solo albums firmly state his love of powerful, rock-anthem-style electronic pieces inspired in part by Tangerine Dream and Pink Floyd. Holland has also been instrumental in supporting the vital underground electronic scene that continues to develop outside the mainstream music industry. Toward this end, he established his independent Coriolis record label and distribution company, which released the critically acclaimed, multi-artist concept album *Dali: the Endless Enigma* (see entry under the collections and compilations of various artists at the end of this chapter). — *Linda Kohanov*

● **Relativity** / 1986 / Coriolis ✦✦✦✦
Urgent sequencer-driven pieces are mixed with searing electric guitar solos and rock-influenced acoustic drums. — *Linda Kohanov*

Transcience of Love / 1989 / Coriolis ✦✦✦
This is an ambitious but inconsistent example. — *Linda Kohanov*

Robert Julian Horky

Flute, Percussion, Keyboards / New Age, Neo-Classical, Ethnic Fusion, Ambient, Minimalism
Horky received both classical and modern music training in some of the best music schools in Vienna, Austria. Though he plays keyboards and percussion, his main instrument is the flute. This includes bass, alto, soprano, bamboo, and glass flutes, as well as others of exotic origin. His style is characterized by traces of minimalist, ambient, ethnic, and ritual music. Horky is also closely allied with the new age movement in his desire to create deeply spiritual, uplifting music. — *Linda Kohanov*

★ **Voyager** / 1986 / Eurock ✦✦✦✦✦
Horky's first US release ranges from free-flowing meditative pieces to a 30-minute new age symphony. One of the most intriguing sections, however, is based on ancient Greek scales played on instruments from that period. This is a good cross-section of Horky's varied approaches, with some uneven moments. — *Linda Kohanov*

Ios / 1987 / Eurock ✦✦✦
This flute concert was recorded live on the Greek island. — *Linda Kohanov*

Apolys / 1988 / Eurock ✦✦✦
This is an intriguing collection of music for clavichord tuned to an ancient Greek scale. — *Linda Kohanov*

Narayama / ✦✦✦✦
Narayama is a concept album inspired by a Japanese novel and the mountain after which it was named. Austrian artist Robert Julian Horky's main instrument is flute or, more accurately, a whole array of flutes—European alto, soprano, and bass; Indian bamboo; and even a high-pitched glass flute. To these he adds instruments such as musical glasses, which produce soft bell-like tones and drones; the hypnotic, resonant strings of a polychord; and the mysterious aerophone, along with touches of keyboards, mandolin, cymbals, and gongs, to paint a portrait of the quiet power and mystical aura of the great mountain. *Narayama* is a subtle but powerful work that takes the listener on a magic carpet ride where flights of fancy become indistinguishable from deep states of meditation. — *Backroads Music/Heartbeats*

Paul Horn

b. Mar. 17, 1930, New York, NY
Clarinet, Flute, Sax (Alto) / New Age, World Fusion, Hard Bop
When one evaluates Paul Horn's career, it is as if he were two people, pre-

and post-1967. In his early days Horn was an excellent cool-toned altoist and flutist, while in more recent times he has been a new age flutist whose mood music is often best used as background music for meditation. Horn started on piano when he was four and switched to alto at the age of 12. After a stint with the Sauter-Finegan Orchestra on tenor, Horn was Buddy Collette's replacement with the popular Chico Hamilton Quintet (1956-58), playing alto, flute and clarinet. He became a studio musician in Los Angeles but also found time during 1957-66 to record cool jazz albums for Dot (later reissued on Impulse), World Pacific, Hi Fi Jazz, Columbia, and RCA, and he participated in a memorable live session with Cal Tjader in 1959. In 1964 Horn recorded one of the first *Jazz Masses*, utilizing an orchestra arranged by Lalo Schifrin. In 1967 Horn studied transcendental meditation in India and became a teacher. The following year he recorded unaccompanied flute solos at the Taj Mahal (where he enjoyed interacting with the echoes) and in the future would record in the Great Pyramid, tour China (1979) and the Soviet Union, record using the sounds of killer whales as "accompaniment" and found his own label, Golden Flute. — *Scott Yanow*

● **Something Blue** / Mar. 1960 / Original Jazz Classics ✦✦✦✦
Years before Paul Horn became famous for his pioneering new age and mood music albums, he was an adventurous bop-based improviser trying to create an alternative to the hard bop music of the era. On this CD reissue of a set cut for Hi Fi, Horn plays alto, flute, and clarinet on six complex originals (four are by the leader) in a quintet with vibraphonist Emil Richards, pianist Paul Moer, bassist Jimmy Bond, and drummer Billy Higgins. All of the music is pretty episodic, with tricky frameworks and some unusual time signatures. The results are generally stimulating, if rarely all that relaxed; Richards is actually the most impressive soloist on the interesting, if often dry, release. — *Scott Yanow*

The Sound of Paul Horn / Mar. 30, 1961 / Columbia ✦✦✦✦

Inside / 1967 / Rykodisc ✦✦✦

Inside the Great Pyramid / 1976 / Kuckuck ✦✦✦

China / 1983 / Kuckuck ✦✦✦

Traveler / 1985 / Kuckuck ✦✦✦

The Peace Album / 1988 / Kuckuck ✦✦✦✦
This holiday release from 1988 is by one of the greatest flutists of our time. The exquisite elegance of the music comes partly from the uniquely conceived "multi-flute orchestra," in which Horn is the only musician, adding unusual depth and dimension to the performances of these pieces, ranging from "Silent Night" to "We Three Kings" to "Ave Maria." This Celestial Harmonies release is dedicated to the peace inside each one of us and offers sterling performances throughout. — *Backroads Music/Heartbeats*

Brazilian Images / Oct. 1989 / Black Sun ✦✦

● **Nomad** / 1990 / Kuckuck ✦✦✦✦
This is a collection of pieces from eight of his albums: *Inside the Cathedral, The Peace Album, In Concert, China,* and *Traveler,* among others. — *Linda Kohanov*

Inside the Taj Mahal 2 / 1991 / Kuckuck ✦✦✦

Africa / 1994 / Gema ✦✦✦✦
West African tradition is upheld in Paul Horn's *Africa.* Horn delicately adds color to the texture of the original compositions by Guinean musician Sekou Camara Cobra. The music falls squarely within the realm of griots—hereditary West African storytellers and minstrels. The jazzy overtones of Horn's flute and saxophone blend well with the syncopated rhythms of Sekou's percussion and guitar work. The songs are sung in the traditional languages of Malinke and Susa. — *MusD*

Music / Kuckuck ✦✦✦✦
On this release, flutist Paul Horn steps into the timeless beauty of baroque music's most quietly appealing composers. Pachelbel, Bach, and Palestrina are all represented, with Horn's focus on the extravagant beauty of the flute family, including the low, low sounds of the contrabass flute and combinations of c flute, alto flute, and bass flute. Simple purity gives way to massive sonorities created by the three choirs of flutes used in one of Palestrina's motets. Paul Horn's music has been heard in virtually every corner of the globe—a partial list of his recordings takes up no less than 13 pages in his fine autobiography, *Inside Paul Horn.* — *Backroads Music/Heartbeats*

Lucia Hwong

Lute, Vocals / Progressive Electronic, Ethnic Fusion, Ambient
Hwong has a degree in ethnomusicology, experience in writing for New York dance companies and multimedia artists, and a stamp of approval from minimalist innovator Philip Glass, who has acted as her mentor to a certain extent. Her masterfully produced, electro-acoustic albums on the Private Music label are filled with ethereal, yet sensual, dreamscapes and breathless, rhythmic journeys through fantastic worlds. Unfortu-

nately, Hwong disappeared from the recording scene after the release of her second album, *Secret Luminescence*. —*Linda Kohanov*

★ **House of Sleeping Beauties** / 1985 / Private Music ✦✦✦✦✦
Though both of her Private Music releases are excellent, this particular collection of colorful, Oriental-inspired music is stunning. —*Linda Kohanov*

Secret Luminescence / 1987 / Private Music ✦✦✦
More ethereal and moody than her first release, this is also downright erotic at times. —*Linda Kohanov*

Iasos

Synthesizer / New Age, Electronic, Minimalism
One of the original new age musicians, this California synthesist creates expansive, uplifting music that floats and shimmers. Iasos has always been sincere in his desire to induce higher states of consciousness through his music. Sometimes his lofty aims get bogged down in an overly sweet presentation, but at other times he succeeds in creating transcendent and artistically satisfying music. —*Linda Kohanov*

★ **Angelic Music** / 1978 / Inter-Dimensional Music ✦✦✦✦✦
Iasos' truly classic 1978 release shows this California sound magician at his best. At once calming and uplifting, meditative and joyous, *Angelic Music* is composed of two extended tracks (about half an hour each). "Angels of Comfort," perhaps Iasos' best-known work, is completely non-rhythmic, washing wave after floating wave of shimmering synthesizer music over the listener. "Angel Play," the second track, is similar in feel and effect but slightly different in sound. The two pieces form a beautiful, melodious whole, leaving the listener refreshed. —*Backroads Music/ Heartbeats*

● **Elixir** / 1983 / Sound Rx ✦✦✦✦
This is the quintessential Iasos recording. Whether the album has the potential to carry people to Nirvana on wings of song is up to the personal experience of each listener. In any case, the music is beautiful and deeply inspired. —*Linda Kohanov*

Bora Bora 2000 / 1991 / Global Pacific ✦✦✦

Essence of Spring / 1993 / ✦✦✦
Essence of Spring captures the buoyant enthusiasm and bubbling optimism of spring. Side one contains five musical selections with nature sounds interspersed, while side two is an environmental tape, with a continuous half-hour of brooks and birds. Iasos was 1993's recipient of the Crystal Award in the new age artist category. —*Backroads Music/Heartbeats*

Timeless Sound / 1994 / ✦✦✦
This cassette-only release contains two long tracks designed for deep meditation. Side one, "Cloud Prayer," is an extended half-hour version of a track from his release *Wave No.1 (Interdimensional Music)*, with deep, slow drones, soaring highs that advance and recede, and fluttering tones like birds or butterflies occasionally passing through. The second side, "Throne Realms," is a new work in Iasos' trademark flowing, celestial style, with shimmering synthesizers floating gently throughout. Each is lovely, and, at 30 uninterrupted minutes per side, offers an extended space for meditation. —*Backroads Music/Heartbeats*

Liquid Crystal Love / ✦✦✦
A curving spiral above the changes that seesaw back and forth beneath the fabric of life. Many instruments (synthesizer, recorders, guitars) layered into a dense weave. —*MusD*

Ralf Illenberger

Guitar / Adult Alternative
Inspired by the Beatles and the Rolling Stones, this German guitarist essentially taught himself to play from records, later adding Leo Kottke, J.S. Bach, and Keith Jarrett to his list of influences. Honing his chops in local dance bands, Illenberger graduated to concert dates and eventually released seven albums in Europe before signing with Narada Records in the US. His style is an intelligent mix of pop and jazz, making him one of the better adult-alternative instrumentalists on the market. —*Linda Kohanov*

● **Circle** / 1988 / Narada ✦✦✦✦
Illenberger's American debut mixes colorful instrumentals with warm introspective moods. —*Linda Kohanov*

Heart and Beat / 1990 / Narada ✦✦✦
This more energetic and lighthearted album features a number of prominent European sidemen. —*Linda Kohanov*

Soleil / 1993 / Narada ✦✦✦
On *Soleil* (so-LAY, French for "sun"), Ralf Illenberger lights up your listening experience by providing his own unique blend of soft jazz and new age music. Guest musicians include Peter and Walter Keiser, who have both worked with Andreas Vollenweider, and a vocal track with Susan Osborn. —*MusD*

Inkuyo

Ethnic Fusion
Inkuyo is comprised of four musicians who bring the ancient instruments and songs of their South American Incan heritage firmly into the 20th century. Their name and inspiration are taken from a remote mountain village high in the heart of the Andes, where the people retain many of the customs their ancestors followed centuries ago. In addition to performing their own arrangements of traditional tunes, the members of Inkuyo present modern compositions inspired by the Chilean "new-song" movement, as well as a number of spirited folk-inspired originals. —*Linda Kohanov*

★ **Land of the Incas** / 1988 / Fortuna ✦✦✦✦✦
Although both of Inkuyo's albums are equal in artistic merit, this is perhaps the best place to start. This festive collage of tradition and innovation features a wide variety of intriguing South American instruments: cane flutes, panpipes of all sizes, and traditional drums and percussion, as well as acoustic guitar, violin, and harp. —*Linda Kohanov*

Temple of the Sun / 1992 / Fortuna ✦✦✦
Featured are more crisp, evocative performances from these masterful performers. This time the music is inspired by the legends surrounding Coricancha, the famous fallen temple of the sun located in the Incan capital city of Cusco. With its exterior walls covered in gold, the building was mercilessly plundered by the Spanish in the 1500s. Inkuyo succeeds in capturing the mystery, majesty, and tragedy of this historical wonder. —*Linda Kohanov*

The Double-Headed Serpent / 1993 / Celestial Harmonies ✦✦✦✦
Inkuyo brings us traditional Andean folk songs and dances, some dating back to the Incan Empire. Styles ranging from festive to melancholic are realized by an astounding array of rare and traditional instruments: wooden and bone flutes, various pan pipes, and more familiar stringed instruments and drums. The cold, timeless winds of the altiplano whistle and pre-Columbian music are heard on this album from Inkuyo. —*MusD*

Art from Sacred Landscapes / 1994 / Celestial Harmonies ✦✦✦✦
Inkuyo's fourth release combines traditional Andean music with original Incan-influenced material, featuring traditional flutes, whistles, pipes, percussion, and strings. The album's two vocal tracks are sung in Quechua, the language of the Incas. —*MusD*

Mark Isham

Synthesizer, Trumpet / Chamber Jazz, Progressive Electronic, Ambient
Born in New York but now based in San Francisco, this multi-instrumentalist and composer made his reputation early in the '70s while playing with progressive rock bands and jazz groups like Art Lande's Rubisa Patrol. He has performed or recorded with such artists as Van Morrison, Was (Not Was), and David Sylvian. His trumpet sound is reminiscent of Miles Davis with his use of a mute and his sparse phrasing, but his great talent as a composer lies in his ability to combine synthesizer and acoustic instruments into an effective whole; as a result, he is in demand for film scores. Isham's stately and often dreamy music reveals his classical training while inventively exploring the sonic possibilities of electronic instruments. —*Scott Bultman*

★ **Vapor Drawings** / 1983 / Windham Hill ✦✦✦✦✦
Crystalline synthesizer textures form the perfect atmosphere for Isham's melodic trumpet solos (with percussion from his Group 87 bandmate Peter Van Hooke). His talent for blending electronic and acoustic sounds produces beautiful and organic music, and this first album for Windham Hill cemented his reputation. —*Scott Bultman*

Film Music / 1987 / Windham Hill ✦✦✦✦
His scores for *Never Cry Wolf*, the Academy Award-winning documentary *The Times of Harvey Milk*, and the Mel Gibson/Diane Keaton film *Mrs. Soffel* showcase his musical depth and dreamy style. On the *Mrs. Soffel* score, Isham's blend of acoustic and synthesizer textures is haunting and deeply moving. —*Scott Bultman*

Castalia / 1988 / Virgin ✦✦✦
More jazz-oriented music is featured on this ensemble recording including Isham's muted trumpet over a dense and percussive backdrop from longtime Isham sidemen David Torn, Peter Maunu, and Patrick O'Hearn, plus Paul McCandless, Terry Bozzio, and Mick Karn. The sweeping strings and classical guitar on "My Wife with Champagne Shoulders" and the evocative "A Dream of Three Acrobats" are highlights. —*Scott Bultman*

Tibet / 1989 / Windham Hill ✦✦✦✦
This is the soundtrack to a video on Tibet, and features Isham's distinctive trumpet and synthesizer work. Also prominent in the mix is the electric and acoustic guitar work of Peter Maunu. —*MusD*

Emperor's New Clothes / 1990 / Windham Hill ✦✦✦

Mark Isham / 1991 / Virgin ✦✦✦
Isham continues his ensemble-style collaborations with guests Tanita

Tikaram, Chick Corea, John Patitucci, and John Novello, and the contributions of sidemen David Torn, Peter Maunu, and Peter Van Hooke. The pleasing group work provides a nice complement to the two vocal tracks. If you like these, try Isham's soundtrack recording for *Trouble in Mind* with Marianne Faithfull. — *Scott Bultman*

Songs My Children Taught Me / 1991 / Windham Hill ✦✦✦
More than 70 minutes of Isham's musical accompaniment to the Windham Hill children's story series, minus their voice-over. It works quite nicely as background music. — *Scott Bultman*

The Net / 1995 / Varese ✦✦✦
Mark Isham's score to *The Net* is comprised of electronics, disembodied voices, and orchestras, resulting in an eerie, disquieting feeling. — *Daevid Jehnzen*

Jean Michel Jarre

Synthesizer, Vocals / Electronic, Adult Alternative, Progressive Electronic
Son of film composer Maurice Jarre, Jean Michel became France's most famous electronic musician in the '70s, when two of his finest albums, *Oxygene* and *Equinoxe*, were released. He has since had an interesting, if uneven, career. His later rock-oriented work seems a bit heavy on the testosterone as well as the ego, a development no doubt influenced by the impact of playing for hundreds of thousands of people in settings such as his giant outdoor concert in Houston during the mid-'80s. — *Linda Kohanov*

★ **Oxygene** / 1977 / Dreyfus ✦✦✦✦✦
This album conveys the excitement and freshness you'd expect from a talented young man embarking on a career in what was still a relatively unknown and unjaded electronic music scene. Sometimes innocent and introspective, other times ambitious and even a little spooky, this is a must for anyone interested in electronic music. — *Linda Kohanov*

Equinoxe / 1978 / Dreyfus ✦✦✦
Progressive, multilayered electronic music, it features glistening sequencer patterns, flowing melodies, and futuristic special effects that sound as if you're blasting off into outer space. After all these years, most of it holds up. — *Linda Kohanov*

The Essential / 1983 / Pacific ✦✦✦✦
Interesting at times, it's certainly not essential. — *Linda Kohanov*

Zoolook / 1984 / Dreyfus ✦✦✦✦
Jarre went off in an unexpected and intriguing direction on this album. Taped voices in a number of languages are juiced up through electronic processing and then combined with synthesizers and live musicians. Guitarist Adrian Belew and vocal wizard Laurie Anderson add some interesting angles of their own. For adventurous listeners. — *Linda Kohanov*

Rendez-Vous / 1986 / Dreyfus ✦✦✦
Jarre explores more conventional rock ground, much of it already hoed by other artists. — *Linda Kohanov*

Revolutions / 1988 / A&M ✦✦✦
This work isn't particularly revolutionary. — *Linda Kohanov*

Waiting for Cousteau / 1990 / American Gramaphone ✦✦✦✦

Chronologie / 1993 / Disques Dreyfus ✦✦✦✦
For fans of Jean-Michel Jarre, *Chronologie* contains more of Jarre's proven ability to blend familiar sounds in the new music tradition into unusual, inventive compositions. The uninitiated will find *Chronologie's* blend of 19th century classical musical themes with pop, rave, and rap sounds downright danceable. Many of the pieces begin with a classical sound—in one song it's deeply resonating pipe organ—and almost invariably pick up the tempo quickly and slide right into a Gloria Estefan beat. — *MusD*

● **Images** / American Gramaphone ✦✦✦✦

Eddie Jobson

Violin, Keyboards / Adult Alternative, Progressive Electronic
This dynamic rock violinist has played with everyone from UK, Roxy Music, and Frank Zappa to Jethro Tull. Jobson's recordings as a leader showed much promise in their use of keyboards, computer-generated sounds, and wailing electric-violin solos. Too bad he hasn't released more of his own music. — *Linda Kohanov*

Zinc / 1983 / CBS ✦✦✦
Jobson's solo debut is mostly instrumental, with a few vocals. — *Paul Kohler*

★ **Theme of Secrets** / 1985 / Private Music ✦✦✦✦✦
This masterpiece of soundscapes was created using the synclavier and is a brilliant album from start to finish. — *Paul Kohler*

Marnie Jones

Guitar, Vocals / New Age, Neo-Classical
Jones came to a professional recording career late in life—after 15 years of working in industrial design. Though she had sung and played guitar as an avocation since childhood, Jones later taught herself to play the harp and began releasing albums of improvised music for that instrument. Her more recent recordings show a steady growth in her abilities as a performer and composer of tender, contemplative music that Jones herself says is great for meditation, relaxation, or massage. — *Linda Kohanov*

● **Journeys** / 1988 / Thrival ✦✦✦✦
Jones' harp music is enhanced by guest artists playing flute, clarinet, bells, percussion, synthesizers, and Indian drum. — *Linda Kohanov*

Golden Wave / 1989 / Thrival ✦✦✦
This is another album of tender ensemble settings. — *Linda Kohanov*

Divine Blush / 1991 / Thrival ✦✦
Grace / 1994 / Thrival Productions ✦✦✦✦
This gentle and lovely album blends whale and dolphin sounds with Marnie Jones' harp and angelic vocal harmonies. *Grace* flows in the combining of her harp and psaltery with woodwinds and percussion touches. Half of the pieces lead off with the sounds of whales or dolphins, recorded in Hawaii, Florida, and the Caribbean. *Grace* provides peaceful, inspiring listening as the creatures of the deep move the musicians to create music from their deeper selves. — *Backroads Music/Heartbeats*

Michael Jones

Piano / Neo-Classical, Solo Instrumental
A native of Ontario, Canada, Jones studied classical piano and kept up his chops throughout his college courses in psychology. During seminars he conducted as part of his own business-management consulting practice, he began including interludes of piano improvisations. Finally, after years of encouragement from friends and clients, he released *Pianoscapes* in 1983. It was the first album ever released on the Narada record label. Over the years, Jones has recorded a number of solo piano and small-ensemble albums. Especially nice is his 1987 duo with cellist David Darling. — *Linda Kohanov*

Seascapes / 1984 / Narada ✦✦✦
This release is filled with soulful piano solo improvisations from a special place in the heart. "Mexican Memories" is a gentle prelude to the dynamic technique displayed in "Improvisation" and "Romance" on side one. Arpeggios flow effortlessly from within improvised harmonies, creating thematic transcendences and joyous recapitulations. Side two features "Nostalgia" and "Beyond the Dream," a 20-minute composition that completes this wholly satisfying continuum of music. — *MusD*

Pianoscapes / 1985 / Narada ✦✦✦
A double album of original piano compositions for reflection, created and produced by Michael Jones. The music is heart-centered and clear, ranging from the very quiet and still to the joyful and expansive. The style of this acoustic piano double release is flowing; the mood deeply personal and loving. — *MusD*

Solstice / 1985 / Narada ✦✦✦
These seasonal piano pieces come from two of Narada's best-selling artists, Michael Jones and David Lanz. — *Linda Kohanov*

★ **Amber** / 1987 / Narada ✦✦✦✦✦
Jones teams up with cellist David Darling for a delicate set of improvisational pieces. — *Linda Kohanov*

After the Rain / 1988 / Narada ✦✦✦
These are impressionistic pieces in small ensemble settings. — *Linda Kohanov*

Magical Child / 1989 / Narada ✦✦✦
Magical Child has proven to be one of Michael Jones' most successful recordings. For the first time, he has recorded an entire ensemble album digitally. This gave him the opportunity to record the piano over a long period of time, at his own pace and in his own home. Thanks to his DAT recorder, the piano pieces were then transferred to state-of-the-art multitrack. Nancy Rumbel, David Darling, and Karen Doe each added their own magic. — *MusD*

Michael's Music / Jul. 21, 1990 / Narada ✦✦✦✦
This is a retrospective of Jones' subtle solo piano and ensemble pieces. — *Linda Kohanov*

Morning in Medonte / 1992 / Narada ✦✦
Touch / Aug. 27, 1996 / Narada ✦✦✦
Touch is a solo piano album from Michael Jones. Since it was recorded directly to two-track, the album has an immediate, lively feel but the music remains peaceful and graceful. With *Touch*, Jones remains at the forefront of new age keyboardists—very few musicians can create music this lucid and lovely. — *Rodney Batdorf*

Peter Kater

Piano / Solo Instrumental, Ethnic Fusion, Contemporary Instrumental, Bluegrass

This German-born pianist and composer lives in rural Virginia. Since 1983 he has released over a dozen albums spanning solo piano music to contemporary jazz ensemble projects. Though some of his music comes from more predictable light-jazz molds, his finest work in recent years is featured on two inspired collaborations with Native American flutist R. Carlos Nakai. —*Linda Kohanov*

For Christmas / 1987 / Silver Wave ✦✦✦✦
Supper-club piano stylings of familiar holiday songs. Very fine pianist. It works. —*Michael Erlewine*

★ **Natives** / 1990 / Silver Wave ✦✦✦✦✦
Kater and R. Carlos Nakai's first collaboration got excellent reviews for good reason. —*Linda Kohanov*

● **Collection 1983-1990** / 1991 / Silver Wave ✦✦✦✦
Here's a full platter of 16 pieces from the extensive catalog of pianist Peter Kater. Throughout the 75 minutes, we revisit his debut, *Spirit*, from 1983, move along with his emergence as an ensemble player on *The Fool and the Hummingbird* (1987) and other subsequent releases, drop in on full-blown jazz-based compositions such as "Emergence" (1985), and hear the "Shaman's Call," composed by Native American flutist R. Carlos Nakai (1988). Through it all Kater's captivating and stellar musicianship and uncompromising lightheartedness lead the way. —*Backroads Music/Heartbeats*

Rooftops / 1991 / Silver Wave ✦✦

Homage / Jan. 29, 1991 / Gaia ✦✦✦
Homage is a tribute to the American Southwest and a return to a more melodic and new age approach. —*MusD*

Coming Home / 1992 / Silver Wave ✦✦✦
Coming Home is Peter Kater's first ensemble recording. The album embodies the familiar Kater sound and is one of the first musical projects to successfully create a fusion of new age and jazz. This blend includes the sterling performances of saxman Bob Rebholz, bassist Kim Stone, and Brandon Fields. *Coming Home* is fresh, exciting, and beautifully melodic. —*MusD*

Migration / 1992 / Silver Wave ✦✦✦✦
Peter Kater and R. Carlos Nakai took the musical world by surprise with their first collaboration, the best-selling *Natives*, in 1990. An unlikely combination at first, their creative spirits merged with a warmth and beauty that touched the heart in many ways, and the recording was given a perfect 10/10 by *CD Review*. *Migration* takes the journey another step along the path of creating and experiencing ritual in one's life. Kater's wonderful piano playing and Nakai's sonorous Native American flute are at the heart of the compositions, beginning with "Wandering" and "Initiation," passing through such places as "Surrender" and "Transformation," and completing the journey with "Service." Other featured musicians include David Darling on cello, Mark Miller on soprano sax and flute, and Chris White leading various vocal embellishments along with Nakai's chanting and a live vocal ensemble arranged by Kater. These outstanding talents blend to create an experience not to be missed. —*Backroads Music/Heartbeats*

Spirit / 1993 / Optimism ✦✦✦
The *Spirit* album, one of the first solo piano recordings of its kind, was originally recorded and released in 1983. Ten years later, Peter has recorded three new improvisations, plus a current version of his classic "Spirit" composition. Bringing them all together, resequencing and remastering entirely in the digital domain, brings new life and clarity to an already timeless solo piano album. —*MusD*

How the West Was Lost / Mar. 1993 / Silver Wave ✦✦✦✦
This popular pianist records in both solo and ensemble format, and has recently collaborated on two releases with acclaimed flutist R. Carlos Nakai. Here in full ensemble setting Kater provides the evocative music for the current PBS-TV show, *How the West Was Lost*, stories of the frontier days told from Native American perspective. Solos and duets, with and without Nakai, plus several powerful and complex tracks, combine for a work of depth and poignancy. —*Backroads Music/Heartbeats*

Two Hearts / 1994 / Optimism ✦✦

Honorable Sky / 1994 / Silver Wave ✦✦✦
Honorable Sky by Peter Kater and R. Carlos Nakai is a continuation of their acclaimed acoustic music accomplishments. Piano, flute, and alto sax flow together seamlessly in sound so subtle—sometimes just barely a whisper—it begs your attention. Named the best new age recording in 1992 by NAIRD. Composers of the soundtrack for the Discovery Channel series "How the West Was Lost," Kater and Nakai continue to produce music that is stirring and enlivening. —*MusD*

Migration / Silver Wave ✦✦✦✦
Kater's piano and R. Carlos Nakais' Native American flute are at the

heart of the compositions. Other featured musicians include David Darling on cello, Mark Miller on soprano saxophone and flute, and Chris White with vocals. —*MusD*

Brian Keane

Guitar / Progressive Electronic, Ethnic Fusion, Electro Acoustic

This virtuoso guitarist and sought-after producer has performed with some of the biggest names in jazz, including Bobby McFerrin, Larry Coryell, and Paco de Lucia. In addition to his own contemporary jazz albums, Keane is an accomplished composer and arranger who has written soundtracks for award-winning films. His score to the documentary *Suleyman the Magnificent* caught the ear of Celestial Harmonies owner Eckart Rahn, who eventually released the soundtrack. The label has since commissioned several other albums of Middle East-inspired instrumentals from Keane, with Turkish multi-instrumentalist Omar Faruk Tekbilek. These exotic recordings are among Keane's finest work. —*Linda Kohanov*

Suleyman . . . / 1988 / Flying Fish ✦✦✦
Suleyman the Magnificent, Keane's imaginative soundtrack to the documentary and traveling art exhibit on the Ottoman Empire, also features Tekbilek and several other Middle Eastern musical experts. —*Linda Kohanov*

Fire Dance / 1990 / Celestial Harmonies ✦✦✦
This masterful collection of music mixes traditional Turkish, Egyptian, and North African folk melodies and dances with synthesized atmospheres that sound like hot desert winds blowing over the Sahara. It is an artful union of Eastern and Western sensibilities, with Omar Faruk Tekbilek. —*Linda Kohanov*

★ **Beyond the Sky** / 1992 / Celestial Harmonies ✦✦✦✦✦
Reuniting the innovative duo of Brian Keane and Omar Faruk Tekbilek, *Beyond the Sky* is an even more adventurous excursion than their two earlier recordings. The listener is transported to exotic regions of the Mediterranean, including Turkey, the Middle East, and North Africa. Amidst the Middle Eastern harmonies, the listener catches whiffs of Moroccan and even Afro-Cuban or South American styles, in a unique marriage of musical cultures. —*Backroads Music/Heartbeats*

Georgia Kelly

Harp / New Age, Neo-Classical, Solo Instrumental, Ethnic Fusion

Kelly was a major force in popularizing the harp in contemporary instrumental music. Years before American audiences had heard of Andreas Vollenweider, Kelly was gaining attention for her albums of solo harp performances, which she initially released through her own recording and distribution company. The relaxing and inspirational qualities of her music attracted the attention of hospitals, cancer clinics, and drug abuse programs, which regularly use her recordings for therapeutic purposes. A sensitive and skillful musician, Kelly has made several noteworthy recordings for Global Pacific, some of which are highly recommended collaborations with other artists. —*Linda Kohanov*

★ **Seapeace** / 1970 / Global Pacific ✦✦✦✦✦
Originally released in the '70s, Kelly's influential recording of solo harp music is now considered classic. —*Linda Kohanov*

Harp and Soul / 1983 / Global Pacific ✦✦✦
Kelly mixes her own originals with arrangements of works by Barbra Streisand and Satie. Wind player Richard Hardy joins the harpist on several cuts. —*Linda Kohanov*

Fresh Impressions / 1987 / Global Pacific ✦✦✦✦
This set of classical duos with violinist Steven Kindler offers arrangements of some of the most famous impressionist pieces by Gabriel Fauré, Erik Satie, and Claude Debussy, plus two originals in the French style by Kelly and Kindler. —*Linda Kohanov*

Winter Classics / 1989 / Global Pacific ✦✦✦✦
Winter Classics is a beautiful and sophisticated album that more than lives up to the promise of its title. —*Backroads Music/Heartbeats*

A Journey Home / 1989 / Global Pacific ✦✦✦
This elegant, heartfelt collaboration with Yugoslavian guitarist Dusan Bogdanovich was inspired by Kelly's quest to connect with her own Yugoslavian roots. Traditional folk songs from the region come to life in contemporary arrangements. Sprinkled between are original compositions inspired by the beauty and spirit of the duo's shared heritage. —*Linda Kohanov*

Birds of Paradise / 1990 / Global Pacific ✦✦✦✦
Birds of Paradise uniquely captures the romantic at its most transcendental. The first side begins with a burst of thunder in "Rainbow Showers." "Primavera" is a natural resolution in that it deals musically with the essence of spring growth after the storm. —*MusD*

Gardens of the Sun / 1994 / Global Pacific ✦✦✦✦
On *Gardens of the Sun*, Kelly brings an utter sensitivity to her work, inspired partly by her recent visits to Dubrovnik and Zagreb and

her efforts to bring about renewed diplomacy and peace in these deeply troubled times. Her music exposes the soulful relationship with the homeland of her relatives, and this poignancy can be heard in the music, along with a hopeful joy and the beauty of nature's creations. Of the eight songs heard, five are harp solos and show why Georgia Kelly has often been referred to as "the first lady of the harp." The others are duets—one with former collaborator and guitarist Dusan Bogdanovic on their jointly composed "Requiem," one with flutist Stephen Schultz, and the third adding tambourine by recording and mixing engineer Warren Dennis. —*Backroads Music/ Heartbeats*

Al Gromer Khan

Keyboards, Sitar / Electronic, Ethnic Fusion, Ambient
German composer Alois Gromer decided to dedicate himself to playing the sitar after he attended a 1969 recital in London given by Indian classical music master Vilayat Khan. During a 1975 ceremony conducted by respected teacher Imrat Khan, Gromer became the first European to be inducted into the legendary Khan dynasty of sitar players, which dates back to Moghul India. Adding the Khan surname to his professional identity, he created a number of albums that skillfully combined his adopted Eastern heritage with his Western classical birthright. —*Linda Kohanov*

Divan I Khas / 1970 / Beyond/Allegiance ✦✦✦
Khan's pop instrumentals with Middle Eastern and Indian influences are interesting but not entirely successful. —*Linda Kohanov*

★ **Mahogany Nights** / 1990 / Hearts of Space ✦✦✦✦✦
This album of "night music" is a collection of exotic, highly atmospheric soundscapes with subdued sitar occasionally wafting out of Khan's lush synthesizer tapestries like a fine incense. Although the composer's sitar talents are better represented on other albums, this is a good, all-around introduction to his style, especially for those who normally shy away from Indian music. —*Linda Kohanov*

Monsoon Point / Oct. 10, 1995 / New Earth ✦✦✦
This CD has one cut on it. The music is a meandering, meditative piece on a soothing synthesizer with Indian Dhrupad singing over some parts. Crank this one up, chant, get the massage oil, and light the incense. —*Richard Meyer*

Bob Kindler

Cello / Neo-Classical, Chamber Jazz, Ethnic Fusion
This classically trained cellist performed with the Honolulu Symphony for 14 years, played jazz with Dave Brubeck's son Darius, and formed a guild that organized cross-cultural events involving dancers, poets, artists, and musicians from around the world. All of these influences and experiences are apparent in his contemporary instrumental albums, which are eclectic to say the least. —*Linda Kohanov*

Tiger's Paw / 1990 / Global Pacific ✦✦✦
This is an exceptional album of contemporary, ethnic-inspired instrumentals. In addition to cello, autoharp, and flutes, the album features an extended range of tablas (an Indian drum) used in creative settings. —*Linda Kohanov*

● **Waters of Life: Music from the Matrix 3** / Nov. 4, 1991 / Global Pacific ✦✦✦✦
Beautifully striking music from Hawaii's Bob Kindler, this is the culmination of his *Music from the Matrix* series (this being *Vol. III*). Playing cello, guitar, and autoharp, he is joined by Steve Kindler on violin, Benjy on tablas, and Richard Garneau on sitar. The melody of "Grace" is especially gorgeous. —*Backroads Music/Heartbeats*

Steve Kindler

Violin / Neo-Classical, Chamber Jazz, Ethnic Fusion
Like his brother Bob, violinist Steve Kindler played in the Honolulu Symphony, but he cut his jazz chops as a member of John McLaughlin's fusion band, Mahavishnu Orchestra. Kindler has also toured and recorded with Jan Hammer, Jeff Beck, and Kitaro. Kindler's smooth, yet impassioned, violin improvisations are the perfect vehicle for his own highly melodic compositions, combining classical, jazz, rock, and ethnic influences. In addition, Kindler is a member of Barefoot, a co-op world-music dance group. —*Linda Kohanov*

Across a Rainbow Sea / 1970 / Global Pacific ✦✦✦
Kindler's melodic gifts are topped off by some sophisticated keyboard work and lively Latin grooves. —*Linda Kohanov*

★ **Dolphin Smiles** / 1987 / Global Pacific ✦✦✦✦✦
A series of duets with synthesist Teja Bell features lush, fluid textures and flowing melodies. —*Linda Kohanov*

Paradise Lost / 1993 / Mesa/Global ✦✦✦

Ben Tavera King

Guitar / Chamber Jazz, Ethnic Fusion
A Texas-born master of the nylon-string guitar, King likes to call his music "Southwestern Hispanic jazz." Not only does he combine flamenco with jazz and Native American styles, he throws in influences from Mexico and the Caribbean as well. Acknowledged as a leader in the renaissance of Hispanic music, King has been the subject of a PBS television special and has performed at Lincoln Center. —*Linda Kohanov*

Desert Dreams / 1984 / Global Pacific ✦✦✦
Though not as well produced as *Coyote Moon,* King's debut for Global Pacific is a gem, with lively, more straightforward pieces for guitar, sax, bass, and percussion. —*Linda Kohanov*

Visions and Encounters / 1992 / Talking Taco ✦✦✦
During the past several years, Ben Tavera King has carved a niche for himself as one of the leading composers of Southwestern music. King enjoys combining elements of Hispanic guitar with melodies and rhythms native to the Southwest. On his newest release, the Native American flute and nylon-string guitar blend in a series of compositions reflecting the culture, myths, and ceremonies of the American Southwest. Additional instrumentation includes synthesizer and percussion. —*MusD*

● **Coyote Moon** / Jan. 20, 1992 / Global Pacific ✦✦✦✦
This is an infectious mix of impassioned flamenco guitar stylings with all kinds of Hispanic references—everything from Tex-Mex grooves to mariachi rhythms with a jazz twist. —*Linda Kohanov*

Kitaro

Guitar / New Age, Progressive Electronic, Ethnic Fusion
Kitaro's style is the epitome of the contemplative, highly melodic synthesizer music often associated with the new age movement. Interestingly enough, this famous Japanese composer taught himself to play electric guitar in high school—inspired by the R&B music of Otis Redding. In the early '70s, Kitaro formed the Far East Family Band, which released two albums of progressive rock. In 1972, however, he met the innovative German synthesist Klaus Schulze during a trip to Europe. Kitaro was hooked. He built his first synthesizer and began experimenting with all kinds of unusual sounds. His first solo album, *Astral Voyage,* appeared in 1978 and quickly gained a cult following. Two years later, he produced the first of several soundtracks for *Silk Road,* a Japanese television documentary series that ran for five years. Several albums of music from *Silk Road* were released to a growing international contingent of fans who admired his combination of lush, majestic textures and gentle, almost naive, melodies. Kitaro, however, was still considered an underground artist in America until he signed with Geffen Records in 1986, which re-released seven of his earlier albums and gave him the support to expand his scope in many ways. For instance, after years of creating albums in the privacy of his home studio near Japan's Mt. Fuji, Kitaro produced his 1987 release, *The Light of the Spirit,* with the help of Mickey Hart. The album featured an array of American musicians and was nominated for a Grammy Award in the Best New Age Performance category. That same year, Kitaro made his first live tour of North America and sold two million albums in the US alone. Kitaro's style had changed as well, becoming more theatrical and assertive while retaining a certain level of innocence and purity. His more recent recordings show a renewed interest in the rock and pop elements that originally attracted him to music in the late '60s. —*Linda Kohanov*

Oasis / 1979 / Gramavision ✦✦✦✦
On *Oasis,* Kitaro's masterful command of the synthesizer creates abstract, ethereal impressions. Aided by occasional acoustic guitar and percussion, the arrangements glide from sparse segments through dense, deeply textured movements. This is contemplative, introspective music. —*MusD*

Silk Road Suite / Oct. 1980 / Gramavision ✦✦✦
This double album, produced in Germany, features orchestral passages from the Japanese television documentary *Silk Road.* All of the compositions were written by Kitaro and performed by the London Symphony Orchestra. —*MusD*

● **Ki** / 1981 / Gramavision ✦✦✦✦
Sensitively woven, tranquil textures of sound wash through the mind of the listener on this album from sound master Kitaro. The instrumentation includes synthesizers, slide guitar, mellotron, percussion, tabla, and Irish harp. —*MusD*

Silver Cloud / 1986 / Geffen ✦✦✦✦
This album takes the listener beyond the clouds and into a finely crafted space journey. Kitaro's creative use of synthesizer is well-known, and the introduction of 12-string guitar, tambura, harp, and sitar in his arrangements gives the crisp harmonic sound a softer glow. A peaceful and relaxing journey. —*MusD*

Tunhuang / 1986 / Gramavision ✦✦✦
Another impressive performance from the master synthesist from Japan. This is the closing chapter to the epic *Silk Road* trilogy. Recommended and guaranteed to move your mind and soul. —*MusD*

● **My Best** / 1986 / Gramavision ✦✦✦✦
Kitaro's synthesizer-based compositions are extended aural landscapes full of dramatic peaks of intensity and valleys of emotional calm. He is fond of loud, tympani-like drums, sweeps of sound that approximate electronic winds, and majestic melodies played in singing, upper-register tones. And his music is quite consistent. If you like this, you'll probably like every record he's made. —*William Ruhlmann*

☆ **Silk Road, Vols. 1 & 2** / 1986 / Gramavision ✦✦✦✦✦
Kitaro's masterwork remains this two-record score for a Japanese TV series. His most ambitious themes and involved playing are found here. —*William Ruhlmann*

● **The Light of the Spirit** / 1987 / Geffen ✦✦✦✦
With the help of Grateful Dead drummer Mickey Hart, Kitaro made this album using American musicians, which gives it slightly more of an ensemble feeling than his usual productions. — *William Ruhlmann*

Ten Years [anthology] / Apr. 1988 / Geffen ✦✦✦✦
Here is a ten-year Kitaro retrospective covering the releases on the Geffen label (double album). —*MusD*

Kojiki / 1990 / Geffen ✦✦✦
This new album is classic Kitaro, with many layers of synthesizer and orchestral textures stating the themes. There are more classical elements on this record, and a more "composed" feel to the songwriting. —*MusD*

Live in America / 1991 / Geffen ✦✦✦
Kitaro's already dramatic music is given even greater force when played before a live audience, as this 1990 show from Atlanta's Fox Theatre demonstrates. — *William Ruhlmann*

Dream / 1992 / Geffen ✦✦✦✦
Two giants in contemporary music have joined forces to create one of the most awe-inspiring albums of the '90s. Kitaro has taken his signature style into a new dimension of orchestral drama with three tracks featuring the breathtaking vocals of Jon Anderson, from Yes. Anderson, a long-time Kitaro fan, showed up on Kitaro's Japanese mountaintop and hung out for a month. Their ensuing "marriage" of vocals and music is the result. Kitaro composed the music, while Anderson wrote the lyrics. The songs revolve around the eternal theme of love, as in the transcendental romanticism of "Lady of Dreams" and the ecstasy of spiritual liberation in "Agreement." This is a special album full of soaring emotion. —*Backroads Music/Heartbeats*

★ **Silk Road** / Kuckuck ✦✦✦✦✦
Kitaro carves shimmering visual images of real and imagined landscapes on the double album *Silk Road*. His delicate, sometimes medieval melodies whirl within modulating rhythms and a web of orchestrated electronic and natural sounds, including drums, acoustic guitar, percussion, and chanting bell. —*MusD*

Gary Lamb

Piano, Drums / Solo Instrumental, Adult Alternative
Lamb, a Northern California native, grew up listening to R&B and was playing drums in Bay Area rock bands before the age of 20. Along the way, he dabbled in piano and actually took some time off from the club scene to concentrate on building his chops on that instrument. He recorded a couple of solo piano albums in the mid-'80s, eventually adding electronic keyboards to the mix on his 1989 release *Watching the Night Fall*, his first album to get national radio airplay. His subsequent recordings mix his love of catchy, generally cheerful, pop melodies with his penchant for rock 'n' roll backbeats. —*Linda Kohanov*

Walk in the Garden / 1987 / Golden Gate ✦✦✦
This is an early album of piano vignettes. —*Linda Kohanov*

Watching the Night Fall / 1989 / Petrale Soul Music ✦✦✦
Lamb's first blend of acoustic piano with synthesizers and percussion was inspired by California's Big Sur coastline. —*Linda Kohanov*

● **Distant Fields** / 1990 / Golden Gate ✦✦✦✦
Lamb's all-electronic album retains the sounds of acoustic piano and percussion through the use of sophisticated sampling programs. Though he expands his palette with a few unusual tone colors here and there, the sounds remain fairly conventional. Generally, these are lively tunes with a subtle use of backbeats. —*Linda Kohanov*

Love Themes / 1992 / Golden Gate ✦✦✦

Imaginations / 1993 / Golden Gate ✦✦✦
This adventurous release by keyboardist Gary Lamb is fun, light, warm, sensitive, energetic, and refreshing. *Imaginations* has the power of going straight to listeners' hearts. Lamb plays all of the instrumentation on this album, including concert grand piano, synthesizer, and drums. From the

opening chord to the closing phrase, *Imaginations* offers a harmonic and melodic journey. —*MusD*

David Lanz

Piano / Solo Instrumental, Adult Alternative
One of the most popular artists in the solo instrumental and adult-alternative spheres, Lanz played in several rock bands during his teens, then began developing his style as a solo pianist in a small Seattle nightclub. He introduced some of his originals into the bar's required mix of standards and pop tunes, receiving such a positive response from patrons that before long he was playing his own material almost exclusively. His early albums of solo piano works are still among the Narada label's bestsellers. His two collaborative efforts with guitarist Paul Speer also hit the *Billboard* Top 200 Albums chart; yet as Lanz's national popularity grew, he began to experiment with works for larger and larger ensembles, culminating in full orchestral accompaniments on *Skyline Firedance* (1990). His most recent album is a refreshing return to his solo piano roots. —*Linda Kohanov*

Heartsounds / 1983 / Narada ✦✦✦
Heartsounds is a unique and exciting collection of new acoustic piano music. The album combines a virtuoso performance with inventive melodies that evoke exuberant, vibrant musical expressions. Lanz has a very personal style in the impressionistic mode, with each composition creating a breathtakingly beautiful statement. —*MusD*

Solstice / 1985 / Narada ✦✦✦
Solstice presents music of a seasonal nature as interpreted by two of Narada's most renowned pianists, David Lanz and Michael Jones. Each selection on this release bears the distinctive personal imprints of these two gifted musicians with songs such as "Good King Wenceslas," and "Carol of the Bells." —*MusD*

★ **Cristofori's Dream** / 1988 / Narada ✦✦✦✦✦
Among the most popular new age recordings ever made, this is an album of instrumental piano music (with other instruments, especially strings and string-like synthesizers, added). Its selections have a calm elegance, as Lanz spends most of his time in the upper register of the piano, delivering precise, articulated melodies, culminating in a re-creation of Procol Harum's "A Whiter Shade of Pale" that features original organist Matthew Fisher. — *William Ruhlmann*

Skyline Firedance / 1990 / Narada ✦✦✦
On his popular follow-up to *Cristofori's Dream*, Lanz turns in two discs of the same music, one scored for orchestra and the other played solo on the piano. The alternate approaches to the music bring out Lanz' talents as a composer. —*William Ruhlmann*

Return to the Heart / 1991 / Narada ✦✦✦✦
Return to the Heart is a return to Lanz' roots as a solo pianist. His new compositions for this medium show a remarkable sense of maturity, elegance, and taste. —*Linda Kohanov*

Bridge of Dreams / 1993 / Narada Productions ✦✦✦
Spanning the full spectrum of emotions in sound, Lanz and Speer reunite for another spectacular release. Acclaimed Gold Record Winner (*Cristofori's Dream*), Lanz makes his debut here as vocalist on two outstanding cuts bearing his unmistakably lyrical signature. As David romances the piano, Speer adds the verve and bravura of pop-rock fusion, nicely balancing the piano music with his incisive guitar drive. Guest appearances of Queensryche drummer Scott Rockenfield, the Seattle Symphony Orchestra and Brass Ensemble, and Steve Reid give added dimension to this outstanding collaboration between two bestsellers. —*MusD*

Max Lasser

Guitar / Adult Alternative, Chamber Jazz, Ethnic Fusion
The Swiss guitarist was best known for his association with boyhood chum Andreas Vollenweider. Lasser's tours and recordings with the harpist culminated in Vollenweider's Grammy-winning album *Down to the Moon*. A year later, the guitarist formed Max Lasser's Ark and made several colorful, versatile albums. —*Linda Kohanov*

● **Earthwalk** / 1988 / CBS ✦✦✦✦
Max Lasser's Ark combines a wide variety of influences on this release—everything from classical, jazz, and folk to touches of ethnic styles. It's a thoroughly enjoyable romp though a variety of moods and textures. —*Linda Kohanov*

Timejump / 1990 / Narada ✦✦✦
Lasser's release is slickly produced, with some intriguing approaches to the guitar, from sparkling classical miniatures and powerful electric solos to Indian raga-style melodies played on slide guitar, among other things. The album also features Lasser's abilities on keyboards. —*Linda Kohanov*

A Different Kind of Blue / Oct. 1992 / Real Music ✦✦✦

Adrian Legg

Guitar / Solo Instrumental, Chamber Jazz, New Acoustic
Grounded in folk and classical harmonies during his childhood in London, guitarist Adrian Legg has released three albums on Relativity Records: 1991's *Guitars And Other Cathedrals*, *Guitar For Mortals* the following year, and *Mrs. Crowe's Blue Waltz* in 1993. —*John Bush*

Requiem for a Hick / 1977 / Westwood ✦✦

Techno Picker / 1983 / Spindrift ✦✦✦
If you enjoy great acoustic guitarists, do yourself a favor and check out his debut album. —*Paul Kohler*

Fretmelt / 1984 / Spindrift ✦✦✦
This brilliant release features Legg (sounding like three guitarists playing at once) with a small group. —*Paul Kohler*

Lost for Words / 1986 / Making Waves ✦✦✦
This album from the British acoustic guitar wizard features jaw-dropping playing. —*Paul Kohler*

● **Guitars and Other Cathedrals** / 1990 / Relativity ✦✦✦✦
Using an acoustic guitar modified with banjo tuners, Legg takes his guitar where no one has gone before. —*Paul Kohler*

Guitar for Mortals / 1992 / Relativity ✦✦✦✦
British string-bender Adrian Legg plays on *Guitar For Mortals*. Still, the songs retain structure and muscle without dissolving into ambient noodling. Legg's expressive but never excessive performances range from the moving "A Candle in Notre Dame" and wistful "Mrs. Jack's Last Stand" to the witty "Chicken Licken's Last Ride" and playful "Walking With Jesus." Instrumental music for those who are prepared to listen and think. —*Roch Parisien*

Mrs. Crowe's Blue Waltz / 1993 / Relativity ✦✦✦✦
Mrs. Crowe's Blue Waltz strays from Legg's usual all-acoustic format, perhaps in hopes of reaching a wider audience with electric guitar, string, and vocal arrangements. Unique melding of folk, blues, country, jazz, and new age styles, all played with dazzling dexterity and a truly unusual style. —*Backroads Music/Heartbeats*

Wine, Women and Waltz / Nov. 9, 1993 / Relativity ✦✦✦

Andreas Leifeld

Adult Alternative, Progressive Electronic, Ethnic Fusion
This brilliant, yet little-known, German artist has a flair for combining refined ambiences with driving funk bass lines and rock beats. His well-constructed melodies and improvisations are often quite catchy, and his song titles and symbolic sonic imagery are lined with social commentary. Classically trained, Leifeld makes a living as a music teacher in Paderborn, Germany, and his modest apartment is overrun with all manner of electronic gadgetry. He is truly a living, breathing example of the cyberpunk mentality—you get the feeling he would gladly leave earthly concerns behind if he could download the essence of his mind, body, and soul onto a hard disk. —*Linda Kohanov*

Mysterious Messages / 1990 / Musique Intemporelle ✦✦✦
Though not as polished as *Discoveries*, this album is another fine example of Leifeld's style. Most of the pieces are upbeat with ethereal underpinnings and some disco grooves. On "Tokio" he also hints at the Japanese mentality of technological supremacy by mutating oriental melodies through heavy-handed electronics. —*Linda Kohanov*

● **Discoveries** / 1991 / Musique Intemporelle ✦✦✦✦
Futuristic in conception and execution, this album still harkens back to the sequencer-driven sound of the German electronic school. Yet unlike Tangerine Dream, Leifeld has managed to add rock and pop influences without losing his progressive edge. His two-part suite "African Dreams" delves into the techno-tribal realm. He also adds some amusing political cynicism on the final selection, "Same Old Game," by layering recorded voice fragments of George Bush's most banal catchphrases over combat sounds and a brooding, almost sinister electronic score. —*Linda Kohanov*

Ottmar Liebert

Guitar, Percussion / Adult Alternative, Ethnic Fusion
Liebert has said that "flamenco is a music both romantic and dangerous; it is an attitude as much as it is a musical genre." Therein lies the philosophy that catapulted him to fame at the end of the '80s with an engaging mix of subdued flamenco guitar and South American percussion, rock, jazz, and pop influences. Liebert's "attitude" actually suppresses the more challenging and "dangerous" aspects of flamenco in favor of the romantic—and the stylish. He's not a technical wizard on the guitar, but he has a feel for the music's innate sensuality and a gift for creating memorable melodies. Born in Cologne, Germany, to a Chinese-German father and a Hungarian mother, Liebert traveled throughout Russia and Asia before moving to Boston and eventually settling in Santa Fe, NM. After years of trying to hit the big time in various jazz-funk bands, he began playing

acoustic guitar in Santa Fe restaurants. His first (self-produced) cassette, *Nouveau Flamenco*, was basically recorded for friends, but the album received heavy radio airplay on WAVE in Los Angeles. Higher Octave Records re-released it nationally in 1990. After his subsequent album *Borrasca* quickly climbed the charts, Liebert was picked up by a major label, Epic. With his exotic good looks and enigmatic stage presence, Liebert has brought flamenco to mainstream America with a certain level of class and accessibility. His prowess as a composer and instrumentalist has steadily improved over the years. —*Linda Kohanov*

★ **Nouveau Flamenco** / 1990 / Higher Octave ✦✦✦✦✦
Originally released in 1988, this independently produced album topped *Billboard*'s new age chart and sold a half-million copies. The music, however, lacks the craftsmanship of later releases. In fact, almost all of the short selections end in mediocre fadeouts. —*Linda Kohanov*

Borrasca / 1991 / Higher Octave ✦✦✦
Borrasca means tempest or storm, and that's exactly what Ottmar Liebert has created in the music world. His latest effort has been eagerly anticipated, and the reception has been nothing short of phenomenal. This third release augments the "power-trio" approach of Ottmar and his mates Jon Gagan (bass and keyboards) and Dave Bryant (hot percussion and drums) with special horn arrangements that lend an almost mariachi flavor and strong Latin appeal. —*Backroads Music/Heartbeats*

Solo Para Ti / 1992 / Epic ✦✦✦✦
Liebert's first recording for Epic is his finest effort to date. Along with his group Luna Negra (bassist Jon Gagan and percussionist Dave Bryant), the album also features a guest appearance by rock guitarist Carlos Santana on a couple of cuts and some subtle vocals by Santa Fe artist Joe Bradley. A few of Liebert's originals also add strings, horns, and piano, although acoustic guitar remains the prominent voice throughout. —*Linda Kohanov*

The Hours Between Night and Day / 1993 / Epic ✦✦✦
Fresh from opening up for Natalie Cole on her tour last year, Ottmar Liebert will begin his own tour with the spectacular new release *The Hours Between Night and Day*. Breaking new stylistic ground, Liebert combines the intimacy of acoustic guitar with electric musicianship mixed with light touches of computer-added harmonies. Spanish flamenco, the signature sound so strongly associated with Liebert and Luna Negra, is still easily heard on this new title, perhaps nowhere so apparent as on the Spanish language Marvin Gaye classic "Mercy Mercy Me." —*MusD*

Ray Lynch

Lute / New Age, Neo-Classical, Adult Alternative
Though he's one of the most influential artists in "new age pop" and adult-alternative circles, Lynch has extensive formal music training. Inspired by Andres Segovia's classical guitar recordings, Lynch studied the instrument in Barcelona, Spain, in the early '60s. He later attended the University of Texas as a composition student. Toward the end of the decade, Lynch moved to New York and became a fixture in the city's "early music" scene as a lutenist with the Renaissance Quartet. A period of personal and spiritual crisis, however, led him to retreat from his career in conventional classical music. He moved to California, spent some time investigating various spiritual traditions and philosophies, and started experimenting with electronic music. His 1983 debut album, *The Sky of Mind*, artfully meshed his early classical music leanings with spatial, synthesized orchestrations and became an underground success with virtually no promotional support. Two years later, he released his most famous album, *Deep Breakfast*. While much of the album continued in a neo-classical vein (with some lyrical duets for viola and keyboards, among other things), Lynch's catchy tune "Celestial Soda Pop" became a hit in the newly emerging WAVE radio formats. The album was one of the first new age releases to sell over 500,000 copies. While Lynch's later albums have their moments, his increasingly pop-oriented style seems to have lost the expressive intensity of his earlier work. Still, growing numbers of listeners seem attracted to his vibrant electronic textures and heartrending melodies. —*Linda Kohanov*

The Sky of the Mind / 1983 / Windham Hill ✦✦✦
The Sky of Mind was his debut from 1983. The current version features new arrangement of the six pieces, which are classically inspired and heartfelt, performed on both acoustic and electronic instruments. The radiant compositions also make for ideal morning listening, with Tibetan bells connecting the pieces, and its emotional nature paving the way for a true musical journey—a classic example of the genius of Ray Lynch. —*Backroads Music/Heartbeats*

★ **Deep Breakfast** / 1986 / Windham Hill ✦✦✦✦✦
Ray Lynch's synthesizer playing sometimes approximates keyboard instruments and sometimes sounds like individually plucked strings on electrified string instruments, but always has a deeply textured melodic structure and a buoyant rhythmic underpinning. Isolated notes in series and patterns make a pointillistic mosaic of sound that alternately

soothes and stimulates. No wonder this is one of the best-selling new age albums of all time. — *William Ruhlmann*

No Blue Thing / 1989 / Windham Hill ✦✦✦
Ray Lynch continues to explore the interface between acoustic and electronic instrumentation, as well as between popular and classical elements, with an obvious debt to the pastoral works of Ralph Vaughan Williams. The synthesizers—with their characteristic plucked, harp-like, and harpsichord tones—are beautifully complemented on almost every piece by oboe, flute, English horn, cello, violin, viola, or classical guitar, with the acoustic instruments much more prominent than on *Deep Breakfast*. Once again this meticulous artist has produced a sublime album of sensitive and deep compositions and sophisticated yet uncluttered arrangements. — *Backroads Music/Heartbeats*

The Music of Ray Lynch / 1990 / Music West ✦✦✦
This set of Ray Lynch's three albums comes with a handsome slip case, making it ideal either for your own collection or as a gift. — *Backroads Music/Heartbeats*

● **Nothing Above My Shoulders But the Evening** / Sep. 28, 1993 / Windham Hill ✦✦✦✦
Nothing Above My Shoulders But the Evening refers to the inexplicable freedom of headlessness. Keyboards and guitar by Lynch, with guest musician Daniel Kobialka on violin, and others on flute, viola, French horn, piano, oboe, English horn, and trumpet. — *MusD*

Mannheim Steamroller

Neo-Classical, Adult Alternative, Progressive Electronic
This Omaha-based group has sold a lot of albums over the years with its high production standards and accessible pop orchestral sound. Best known for their extensive *Fresh Aire* series of albums, the members of Mannheim Steamroller mix a certain level of classical inspiration with piano, synthesizers, guitar, bass, drums, and sometimes full symphony orchestra. The resulting music is sometimes fascinating, yet often no better than muzak on amphetamines. In fact, it's extremely difficult to recommend one album over the next: they all offer a few arresting moments next to forgettable music that, at its worst, can be downright embarrassing. (Some of the albums are even accompanied by pretentious liner notes analyzing the music's form and inspiration, yet the compositions inside don't begin to live up to these classical references.) — *Linda Kohanov*

Fresh Aire 1 / 1975 / American Gramaphone ✦✦✦
Composer Chip Davis' instrumental new age album is, as the album cover says, "a collection of original music set in a hybrid musical style, combining the long-lived forms of the classics, performed on both old-world and contemporary instruments," to which we might add that Davis mixes in the sounds of nature, especially rain, on an album meant to evoke spring. — *William Ruhlmann*

Fresh Aire 2 / 1977 / American Gramaphone ✦✦✦
Davis' "fall" collection is also a recasting of madrigal and Renaissance musical styles—harpsichord and flute sounds in stately cadences. With typical eclecticism he mixes in drums and rhythms that would not be out of place on a rock stage. — *William Ruhlmann*

Fresh Aire 3 / 1979 / American Gramaphone ✦✦✦
The "summer" album is dominated by a version of a 16th-century toccata, played rapidly and evoking the energy and life of the season. — *William Ruhlmann*

Fresh Aire 4 / 1981 / American Gramaphone ✦✦✦
Bach is the touchstone for this 18th-century tribute that constitutes the "winter" selection in the *Fresh Aire* series, appropriately filled with organ-like sounds. — *William Ruhlmann*

★ **Fresh Aire 5** / 1983 / American Gramaphone ✦✦✦✦✦
Accompanied by the London Symphony and the Cambridge Singers, Mannheim Steamroller journeys back in time to 1609, then takes off for the moon. It's all a dream, but it makes for some of the liveliest music of the series. — *William Ruhlmann*

Fresh Aire 6 / 1986 / American Gramaphone ✦✦✦
Siren-like sounds and stately melodies dominate on an album whose theme is "impressions of Greek mythology." — *William Ruhlmann*

Fresh Aire 7 / 1982 / American Gramaphone ✦✦✦✦
As meticulous in detail as it is epic in scope, *Fresh Aire VII* is a truly grand statement, fusing the past with the present, creating music of the future. It is a powerful album and was awarded the Grammy in the new age category. — *Backroads Music/Heartbeats*

● **Christmas 1984** / 1984 / American Gramaphone ✦✦✦✦
This classical Christmas music was so well produced that many hi-fi shops used the album to demonstrate high-end equipment and speakers. — *David A. Milberg*

Video Sampler I / 1986 / Atlantic ✦✦✦

Video Sampler II / 1986 / Atlantic ✦✦✦

Saving the Wildlife / 1986 / American Gramaphone ✦✦✦✦
This 1986 release is the soundtrack from a PBS special about endangered species. Each cut is devoted to a particular country and species. Tributes to seals, pandas, grizzlies, penguins, and whales are done in uniquely playful ways that are cross-cultural and delightfully typical of the dynamic "Mannheim style." — *Backroads Music/Heartbeats*

Classical Gas / 1987 / American Gramaphone ✦✦✦
Guitarist Mason Williams teams up with the Steamroller for an orchestrated, synthesized version of his 1968 instrumental hit, plus more in the same vein. — *William Ruhlmann*

● **Yellowstone: The Music of Nature** / 1989 / American Gramaphone ✦✦✦✦
Growing out of an attempt to bring positive awareness to the natural cycles and outstanding beauty of Yellowstone National Park, Chip Davis' inspiration for this album began with a visit there. Four classical compositions, by Respighi, Grofe, Debussy, and Vivaldi, are given full orchestral treatment. Mixed with several classic Steamroller pieces and assorted nature sounds, this release has a Fantasia-like dramatic presence of symphonic grandeur. This is also a fund-raising effort, the first of its kind endorsed by the National Park Service. — *Backroads Music/Heartbeats*

To Russia With Love / 1994 / American Gramaphone ✦✦✦

Fresh Aire Interludes / American Gramaphone ✦✦✦✦
Interludes consists of the softer, mellow pieces from the *Four Seasons* series of *Fresh Aire I-IV*. Consistent, resonant keyboard-centered pieces provide a pleasing backdrop, with environmental sounds mixed in, showing a more sensitive Steamroller side. — *Backroads Music/Heartbeats*

Michael Manring

Adult Alternative, Chamber Jazz
Inspired by his teacher Jaco Pastorius, Manring has taken the electric bass into new territory. A native of the Washington DC area, he played classical bass in high school chamber groups and orchestra while working in local Top 40 bands. From 1979 to 1982 he honed his chops in the DC fusion group Natural Bridge and started performing with guitarist Michael Hedges. Manring played on Hedges' Windham Hill debut *Breakfast in the Fields*. Since then the bassist has become *the* Windham Hill session man, recording on albums by Will Ackerman, Ira Stein, and Russel Walder in addition to his frequent tours with Hedges. Manring is also a key member in the label's all-star band, Montreux. — *Linda Kohanov*

● **Unusual Weather** / 1986 / Windham Hill ✦✦✦✦
Manring's debut as a leader is a striking combination of ethereal atmospheres and stormy solos. — *Linda Kohanov*

Toward the Center of the Night / 1989 / Windham Hill ✦✦✦
This is another finely crafted bass exploration. — *Linda Kohanov*

Drastic Measures / 1991 / Windham Hill ✦✦✦✦
Manring takes drastic measures in his continuing crusade to push the bass out of the rhythm section and into the spotlight. Lyrical solos, bass overdubs, some virtuosic arpeggios, and breathless passage work illuminate ensemble-oriented originals as well as updated versions of Jimi Hendrix' "Purple Haze" and Chick Corea's "500 Miles High." — *Linda Kohanov*

Jon Mark

Guitar, Vocals / Progressive Electronic, Ambient
A top English session musician in the '60s, Mark played with everyone from the Rolling Stones and Marianne Faithfull to blues sensation John Mayall. As the decade came to a close, the vocalist, composer, and guitarist began exploring the potential of jazz/rock fusion as co-leader of the highly influential Mark-Almond Band. After the group dispersed in the late '70s, Mark moved to New Zealand, where he has so far produced two albums of impressionistic synthesizer pieces. — *Linda Kohanov*

★ **The Standing Stones of Callanish** / 1988 / Kuckuck ✦✦✦✦✦
Standing Stones of Callanish, Mark's tribute to his Celtic roots, is a set of elegant synthesizer sketches that capture the mystery and the simple beauty of the British Isles. — *Linda Kohanov*

● **The Best of Mark-Almond [Rhino]** / 1991 / Rhino ✦✦✦✦
A smartly compiled sampler of this English group's blend of light jazz, folk, and a hint of rock, it contains most of their first two albums. Highlights include "The City" and "One Way Sunday." — *Rick Clark*

Land of Merlin / 1992 / Kuckuck ✦✦✦✦
Mark's most recent album is almost a seamless continuation of the softly melodic synthesizer style he established on *Standing Stones. Land of Merlin* was inspired by Mark's childhood experiences traveling through the enchanted landscapes of Cornwall, the legendary birthplace of King Arthur and home to his fabled Knights of the Round Table. — *Linda Kohanov*

Gerald Jay Markoe

Synthesizer / New Age, Electronic, Ambient
Since the early '60s, this composer and astrologer has been fascinated by the relationships among music, meditation, sacred geometry, and spiritual teachings. Boasting bachelor's and master's degrees from Juilliard and the Manhattan School of Music, respectively, Markoe has also received ASCAP awards for his scores for theatrical productions. Though he's obviously a knowledgeable musician, his potential as an electronic composer is inhibited by his blatantly new age ideas. —*Linda Kohanov*

● **Music from the Pleiades** / 1989 / AstroMusic ✦✦✦✦
These 11 synthesizer pieces were designed to create the sensation of an otherworldly voyage to the Pleiades, a star cluster in the constellation of Taurus often cited as the origin of extraterrestrial visitors to Earth. Markoe recorded the album in a studio filled with crystals, which he says gives the music a very special vibration. One reviewer called *Music from the Pleiades* "a good tape for out-of-body projection." However, the spacey, orchestra-inspired compositions themselves don't necessarily stand up to concentrated listening. —*Linda Kohanov*

Pleiadian Danses / 1990 / AstroMusic ✦✦
This is a concept album with an inappropriate concept. Markoe billed this as world music from other worlds, but since these floating synthesizer pieces have little or no rhythmic content, you don't really get the feeling he's creating world or dance music at all. —*Linda Kohanov*

Sacred Music from Seven Stars / 1991 / AstroMusic ✦✦✦
This album is more on the neo-classical side, with thick layers of synthesized sound suggesting celestial orchestras. —*Linda Kohanov*

Music of the Angels / 1994 / AstroMusic ✦✦✦

Melodies from the Pleiades / Audio & Video ✦✦✦
Gerald Markoe was inspired by the Pleiades, that extraordinarily beautiful cluster of seven stars in the constellation Taurus, to write his ethereal score for cosmic travelogue. His electronically synthesized harmonies blend with orchestral dimensions, pipes, chimes, harp, angelic voices, and flute. He invites the listener to embark on astral ventures soundly enveloped in glorious harmonies, melodic mysteries, and celestial wonders of space music. This uplifting and soothing music is appropriate for meditation, relaxation, and massage. —*MusD*

Peter Maunu

Guitar / Adult Alternative, Progressive Electronic
Though he's not publicly well known, this veteran guitarist is highly respected in the inner music circles of Los Angeles for session work ranging from Claus Ogermann, Jean-Luc Ponty, and Mark Isham to Bobby McFerrin, the Commodores, and the Pointer Sisters. Together with Isham and Patrick O'Hearn, Maunu performed in the short-lived but still-talked-about Group 87, an early '80s progressive band. Maunu's single release as a leader is one of the finest albums on the Narada label. —*Linda Kohanov*

★ **Warm Sound in a Gray Field** / 1990 / Narada ✦✦✦✦✦
This is an exceptional album of electronically based ensemble music. From atmospheric country-blues numbers to inventive reworkings of Gregorian chants and Sufi whirling-dervish influences, Maunu's music is filled with well-designed synthetic textures, compelling melodies, and absorbing solos. Guest appearances by O'Hearn and Isham also give the album a Group 87 reunion feel. —*Linda Kohanov*

Wim Mertens

Synthesizer, Piano / Neo-Classical, Progressive Electronic, Minimalism
This Belgian composer is not well known among US audiences, although he has made several highly regarded appearances at the New Music America festivals. In Spain, however, where he was the subject of a major television special, he is a new-music celebrity. Mertens' style employs mesmerizing minimalist techniques with a sense of the romantic that appeals to both serious music aficionados and more mainstream listeners. The keyboardist uses a certain amount of electronics along with some acoustic instruments like violin, flute, and saxophone. —*Linda Kohanov*

● **Close Cover** / 1991 / Windham Hill ✦✦✦✦
Compiled from Mertens' solo and group projects recorded during the early to mid-'80s, this Windham Hill collection offers an overview of his textural, multilayered style of minimalist composition. —*Linda Kohanov*

Metamora

Chamber Jazz, Ethnic Fusion, New Acoustic
This trio excels at instrumentals that combine traditional Northern European folksongs, jigs, hornpipes, and reels with modern improvisational techniques. Malcolm Dalglish, Grey Larsen, and Pete Sutherland are all multi-instrumentalists who tackle a virtual bandstand of acoustic and electric sounds. All of their albums provide fresh perspectives on folk music played with grace, humor, and a sense of adventure. —*Linda Kohanov*

● **Morning Walk** / Windham Hill ✦✦✦✦
Though it's difficult to choose among the group's albums based on musical reasons, this Windham Hill release holds the highest production standards. —*Linda Kohanov*

David Michael

Harp
These two multi-instrumentalists met in 1973 and founded various ensembles together over the years. Harpist David Michael is also skilled on zithers, guitars, bowed psaltery, cello, and bouzouki. Flutist Randy Mead, who has toured and recorded with Ancient Future, is an expert on ancient tunings. He also built the zith-harp played by Michael on the engaging duo project *Petals in the Stream*. —*Linda Kohanov*

★ **Petals in the Stream** / 1987 / Fortuna ✦✦✦✦✦
This is a kaleidoscopic jaunt through Renaissance, Baroque, Impressionistic, Oriental, and Irish traditions. —*Linda Kohanov*

Keystone Passage / 1994 / ✦✦✦✦
This album makes perfect listening on a warm, breezy afternoon, with its pastoral beauty and acoustic gentleness. Both David Michael and Randy Mead are skilled players, and *Keystone Passage* is in many ways a culmination of a musical relationship that has spanned 20 years and a variety of creative explorations. Soothing and romantic themes sweep the listener through centuries and around the globe, visiting the Andes, British Isles, Norway, and Washington's Olympic Peninsula. —*Backroads Music/ Heartbeats*

Edge of the Sky / ✦✦✦

Spirit Rising / ✦✦✦
This release from Michael and Mead serves up some beautiful melodies and scintillating textures. David Michael's Celtic harp and Randy Mead's flute provide a firm foothold in folk and Celtic traditions, while exploring a bit of jazz terrain here and there. Violin and oboe add a heartfelt touch to the compositions, and the vocalese of Stacey Richman invokes an angelic feeling of peace and harmony. A couple of tracks feature tasteful tabla and percussion, enhancing the overall mood. This is excellent music for morning tea or sitting in front of a late-night fire. —*Backroads Music/Heartbeats*

Stephan Micus

Shakuhachi, Vocals, Zither, Dulcimer (Hammer) / Neo-Classical, Ethnic Fusion, Minimalism
This respected German composer and multi-instrumentalist made his first journey to the Orient at the age of 16. He has since traveled around the world. He spent extensive periods studying ancient musical techniques in India and Japan and collected a number of ethnic instruments previously unknown in the West. His recordings for the ECM label are essentially solo efforts in which the illusion of an ensemble is created by the composer's extensive overdubs. Micus' intention is not to play these instruments according to tradition, but to combine modes of expression from around the world in exciting new ways. Though he sometimes creates sounds you'd swear were the result of electronic keyboards, Micus is an acoustic purist who often develops unconventional performance techniques on ethnic instruments. —*Linda Kohanov*

Implosions / Mar. 1977 / ECM ✦✦✦✦
These pieces for various ethnic instruments are all played by Micus. —*Michael P. Dawson*

Til the End of Time / Jun. 1978 / ECM ✦✦✦

Listen to the Rain / Jun. 1980+Jul. 1983 / Japo ✦✦✦
It's hard to tell whether to consider Micus a jazz, fusion, or new age performer and composer. He's a versatile musician who has used Bavarian, Japanese, Afghan, Irish, Spanish, North African, Indian, and Southeastern Asian instruments on different projects. There's some stunning music on this session, and it's certainly worth hearing; it's also probably not jazz. —*Ron Wynn*

East of the Night / Jan. 1985 / ECM ✦✦✦
Included are two long fantasias for guitars and Japanese flutes. —*Michael P. Dawson*

Ocean / 1986 / ECM ✦✦✦
A four-part suite, it's similar to *Implosions* but recorded nine years later. —*Michael P. Dawson*

Twilight Fields / 1987 / ECM ✦✦✦
The always innovative Stephan Micus has consistently produced superb work. For world music aficionados, this one's a treat, as Micus plays up to 56 ordinary clay flowerpots tuned with water—for that "organic" percussion sound. Hammered dulcimers, zither, shakuhachi, and nay flutes

round out an affecting set with strong Middle Eastern and Asian overtones. —*Backroads Music/Heartbeats*

★ **The Music of Stones** / 1989 / ECM ✦✦✦✦✦
Micus is joined by three other musicians playing sculpted, resonant stone blocks. —*Michael P. Dawson*

Wings over Water / Aug. 24, 1990 / ECM ✦✦✦
He even coaxes beautiful music from ordinary items like tuned flowerpots! —*Michael P. Dawson*

Darkness and Light / Dec. 31, 1990 / ECM ✦✦✦

● **To the Evening Child** / 1992 / ECM ✦✦✦✦

Radhika Miller

Flute, Piano, Cello, Harp / Neo-Classical, Ethnic Fusion
Though she studied classical piano as a child, Miller took up the flute in college after reading some passages about the instrument in a yoga book. It turned out to be more than a whim. By the end of her first year, she was studying in France with famed classical virtuoso Jean-Pierre Rampal. Three years later, Miller graduated from San Francisco State University with a degree in music. Inspired by her love of sacred vocal music, she developed a style she calls "the singing flute." Over the years, Miller has arranged and transcribed sacred classical scores, choral works, and spirituals for her own performances, involving flute, harp, piano, and cello to create prayerful, uplifting works. In 1983 she launched the independent record label Radhika Miller Music (RRM) and has since released high-quality albums that include soulful interpretations of Gregorian chant, Palestrina, Bach, Debussy, Telemann, Vaughan Williams, American spirituals, and Irish folk music in addition to her own compositions and improvisations. —*Linda Kohanov*

★ **Gems of Grace** / Real Music ✦✦✦✦✦
Though all of Miller's recordings could be considered gems, this collection of lullaby-like serenades is particularly satisfying in conception and execution. It helps that she has some top-notch musicians with her: cellist David Darling, pianist Allaudin Mathieu, harpist Michelle Sell, and French horn player Alicia Telford. —*Linda Kohanov*

The Lark's Bride / Real Music ✦✦✦
An exquisitely woven tapestry of dance-like chamber duets improvised in a classical style, this features cellist Eugene Friesen (of the Paul Winter Consort), combined with Radhika's gorgeous arrangements for flute and harp (Michelle Sell) or piano (Rob Ramos) of some of the most majestic renaissance and traditional melodies—from the 13th century on. —*Ladyslipper*

Lotus Love Call / Real Music ✦✦✦
Peaceful meditation for solo flute accompanied by keyboards, temple bells, flute, and sounds of nature. Selections of classical and original compositions by Miller are performed with an open heart and an inner focus. Featured classical pieces are "Duet" by Telemann, "New World" by Dvorak, "Vivace"—a solo sonata by W.F. Bach—and "Adoremus Te Devote" by St. Thomas Aquinas. —*MusD*

The Modern Mandolin Quartet

New Age, Neo-Classical, Chamber Jazz, New Acoustic
This ensemble was formed in the mid-'80s as the brainchild of Mike Marshall, an internationally acclaimed mandolin player best known for his work with David Grisman and Montreux. Marshall was looking for a way to bring respectability to an instrument primarily known for bluegrass and quaint folk tunes. Toward this end, he established a string-quartet-style group featuring the extended family of mandolin instruments. Marshall and Dana Rath play standard mandolins (which take the place of violins), John Imholz plays mandocello (with a range similar to the cello), and Paul Binkley holds up the middle with his mandola (the alto counterpart to the viola). Together they interpret well known classical works and premiere newly commissioned compositions of "serious mandolin music." —*Linda Kohanov*

Modern Mandolin Quartet / 1988 / Lost Lake Arts ✦✦✦✦
A fine debut for Windham Hill, it's not quite as sophisticated as *Intermezzo*. —*Linda Kohanov*

● **Intermezzo** / 1990 / Windham Hill ✦✦✦✦
Selections by Haydn, Ravel, Debussy, Copland, Brahms, and Shostakovich take on new levels of scintillating intensity and charm at the hands of the Modern Mandolin Quartet. —*Linda Kohanov*

The Nutcracker Suite / Sep. 10, 1991 / Windham Hill ✦✦✦
This version of Tchaikovsky's "The Nutcracker Suite" performed by the Modern Mandolin Quartet is magnificently orchestrated. It also features music from Vivaldi's "Four Seasons," Mozart's "Magic Flute," and guest appearances by Ransom Wilson on flute and Edgar Meyer on bass. —*MusD*

Pan American Journeys / 1993 / Windham Hill ✦✦✦

Montreux

Chamber Jazz, New Acoustic
This Windham Hill "all-star" band features Mike Marshall, Darol Anger, Barbara Higbie, and Michael Manring. All of the musicians involved come from eclectic musical backgrounds. Their work in this band mixes folk, bluegrass, and new-acoustic elements with more subtle traces of jazz improvisation. —*Linda Kohanov*

Sign Language / 1987 / Windham Hill ✦✦✦✦
Montreux's debut adds selected percussion and some vocal harmonies to an uplifting, shape-shifting conglomeration of acoustic-oriented styles. —*Linda Kohanov*

Let Them Say / 1989 / Windham Hill ✦✦✦
The quartet expands to a quintet with drummer Tom Miller. —*Linda Kohanov*

● **Windham Hill Retrospective** / 1993 / Windham Hill ✦✦✦✦
Featuring some of the most recognizable Windham Hill radio tracks, Montreux combines the collected work of Barbara Highie, Darol Anger, Mike Marshall, and Michael Manring. Vibrant violin, cutting edge guitar work, sterling synth backup, some progressive piano—this music offers something for everyone with ears attuned to the exciting, groundbreaking sounds of ensemble jazz. —*MusD*

R. Carlos Nakai

Synthesizer, Flute, Guitar, Piano, Trumpet, Harp / New Age, Neo-Classical, Chamber Jazz, Ethnic Fusion, Contemporary Instrumental, Native American, Traditional
Tucson-based multi-instrumentalist R. Carlos Nakai is a Native American musician and cultural anthropologist of Navajo-Ute descent. Though he received classical training on the trumpet, his numerous recordings consist primarily of resonant solo performances of Native American flute improvisations with a judicious use of synthesizers, chanting, and nature sounds. Nakai only occasionally features arrangements of traditional melodies from various tribes; instead, he is primarily concerned with creating original compositions that capture the essence of his heritage in highly personalized ways. In addition to his solo recordings, Nakai has had the opportunity to create new avenues of expression for the Native American flute through collaborations with various artists over the years, including the ethnic jazz band Jackalope, keyboardist Peter Kater, contemporary classical composer James DeMars, and multi-instrumentalist William Eaton. —*Linda Kohanov*

Cycles / 1985 / Canyon ✦✦

★ **Earth Spirit** / 1987 / Canyon ✦✦✦✦✦
At times criticized for modernizing the spirit of Native Americans, Nakai crystallizes these melodies and rhythms into an accessible and enjoyable palette of wonderful meditational music. All his work is very worthwhile, but this is his best. He plays North American flute and is an expert visual artist as well. Go see him if he's in town. —*Michael G. Nastos*

Sundance Season / 1987 / Celestial Harmonies ✦✦✦✦
Native American themes combined with contemporary and classical motifs. Nakai's use of Tibetan bells is intriguing. —*Michael G. Nastos*

Desert Dance / Aug. 1989 / Celestial Harmonies ✦✦✦
Desert Dance is a musical meditation on the spirits of the desert and forces of nature that shape it. Using flutes, drums, rattles, and voice, Nakai sketches poignant sound pictures. —*Backroads Music/Heartbeats*

Winter Dreams / 1990 / Canyon ✦✦✦

Ancestral Voices / Canyon ✦✦✦
In a cross-cultural vein is *Ancestral Voices*, Nakai's third collaboration with guitarist/luthier William Eaton. In addition to the flute/stringed instrument duets, whistles, rattles, and drums, there are two tracks that feature the renowned Black Lodge Singers. —*Backroads Music/Heartbeats*

Spirit Horses (Concerto for Native American Flute and Chamber Orchestra) / Canyon ✦✦

Emergence: Songs of the Rainbow World / Canyon ✦✦✦✦
Nakai's album features Indian flute music and includes a haunting version of "Amazing Grace." —*Janet Schnol*

Feather, Stone and Light / Canyon ✦✦✦
R. Carlos Nakai's collaboration with William Eaton is also a venture with percussionist Will Clipman. *Feather, Stone & Light* consists of material composed by these three artists, blending Nakai's cedar flute with Eaton's lyraharp and spiral clef guitars and Clipman's indigenous percussion, including cymbal, udu, djembe, lyre, congas, and tom toms. Three bonus CD tracks include the beautiful "Midnight in the Sacred Grove," "River Dawn," and "Three Worlds." —*MusD*

Winter Dreams for Christmas / Canyon ✦✦✦
The Native American flute playing of R. Carlos Nakai blended with the string artistry of William Eaton gives this release a unique sound for

Christmas. Listeners will hear the world's most loved Christmas songs that can be played and enjoyed throughout the year. Selections include "What Child Is This?," "Lo, How A Rose E'er Blooming," and "Silent Night." —*MusD*

Emergence / Canyon ✦✦✦
Emergence mixes traditional Plains Indian pieces with nature improvisations, rattles, chanting, digital delay, and synthesizers. —*Backroads Music/Heartbeats*

● **Canyon Trilogy** / Canyon ✦✦✦✦
Canyon Trilogy represents a return to the simplicity of Carlos Nakai's earlier albums such as *Changes* and *Journeys*. There are no additional instruments here, no rattles, and no chanting, just his haunting flutes, either solo or multi-tracked. The "trilogy" in the title refers to the three sections of the tape–"Dawn's Mirage," "Dreamscapes," and "Resonance." —*Backroads Music/Heartbeats*

Changes / Canyon ✦✦✦
The beautiful and haunting sounds of the Native American flute are captured in this album of original compositions and arrangements of traditional tunes from the Zuni, Blood and Lakota tribes. Original compositions include "Whippoorwill" and "Solstice." Fourteen memorable compositions for solo flute. —*MusD*

Journeys / Canyon ✦✦✦
Nakai performs on several different handmade wood flutes. Eight selections are for solo flute, and five have a background of synthesizer-generated sounds of nature. This recording runs 55 minutes. —*MusD*

Carry the Gift / Canyon ✦✦✦✦
Nakai is joined by guitarist William Eaton in 13 selections for Native American flute. The flute is accompanied by guitar, lyre, harp-guitar, and synthesizer guitar, plus two selections for solo guitar. The panoramic harmonies of Eaton's guitars and haunting melodies of Nakai's flute conjure visions of the mesas, canyons, and plains of the American West. —*MusD*

Nightnoise

Neo-Classical, Chamber Jazz, Ethnic Fusion
The brainchild of American violinist Billy Oskay and Irish guitarist Michael O'Domhnill, Nightnoise has evolved from a studio-oriented duo to a high-energy performing band. The music has been described as "classical Celtic pop" and "Irish-flavored, jazzy chamber music." Whatever you call it, the band's style is infectious, fun, and technically impressive. —*Linda Kohanov*

★ **The Parting Tide** / 1990 / Windham Hill ✦✦✦✦✦
The band's most sophisticated album to date uses computer-triggered synthesizers to expand the palette of colors beyond the already impressive acoustic talents of the quartet. The album also includes originals by O'Domhnill's sister, Triona, whose abilities on keyboards, whistle, and accordion are second only to her expressive vocals. —*Linda Kohanov*

A Windham Hill Retrospective: Nightnoise / 1992 / Windham Hill ✦✦✦✦

Patrick O'Hearn

Synthesizer, Bass, Flute, Violin, Cello / Adult Alternative, Progressive Electronic
In the early '80s, this bassist and synthesist was mired in the glitz and grind of pop music as a member of the group Missing Persons. Then friend Peter Baumann, best known for his work with Tangerine Dream, made O'Hearn an offer he couldn't refuse. Baumann had visions of starting a record label catering to his first love, contemporary electronic music, and he wanted O'Hearn to become a charter member of the new company. Nearly a decade and a half-dozen albums later, O'Hearn is still amazed at the success of *Ancient Dreams*, the richly hued debut release that established his career as a solo artist and helped launch the Private Music label. Born in Los Angeles and raised in Oregon, O'Hearn was exposed to a wide variety of music by his parents, who were both working musicians. Though he studied cello, violin, and flute, he gained early experience playing bass with his parents' lounge act. As his musicianship began to excel, he found himself accompanying jazz greats like Joe Henderson, Joe Pass, Tony Williams, and Charles Lloyd. While living in San Francisco in the mid-'70s, he played with Frank Zappa and cofounded the visionary progressive band Group 87 with Mark Isham and Peter Maunu before joining Missing Persons. O'Hearn's style reflects all of these experiences within the context of a highly personal electronic sound. During the late-'80s, however, his innovative vision seemed to blur under the strain of the commercialism infiltrating the new age and contemporary instrumental realms. Urged on by increasingly conservative, pop-oriented executives at Private Music, O'Hearn conformed to more conventional song forms on albums like *Between Two Worlds* and *Rivers Gonna Rise*. His music suffered from excessive predictability as a result. The record label even released some crass disco mixes of the composer's most tuneful selections on the embarrassing *Mix Up*. Fortunately,

O'Hearn's good musical sense prevailed in the long run. His more recent releases *Eldorado* and *Indigo* are both admirable, highly satisfying albums. He is, however, the last remnant of the Private Music label's original roster of innovative, electronic-based instrumentalists. —*Linda Kohanov*

★ **Ancient Dreams** / 1985 / Private Music ✦✦✦✦✦
Though *Eldorado* and *Indigo* are certainly among O'Hearn's finest albums, his startling debut, *Ancient Dreams*, remains the purest example of his innovative style. The keyboardist creates a sense of understated drama through a starkly elegant interplay of synthesized melodies and pseudo-pop rhythms. This unpredictable manipulation of the composer's rock and jazz roots suggests the wide open spaces of surreal landscapes. It is an all-time classic in the contemporary electronic field. —*Linda Kohanov*

● **Between Two Worlds** / 1987 / Private Music ✦✦✦✦

Rivers Gonna Rise / 1988 / Private Music ✦✦✦
These are watered-down, yet technically proficient, examples of O'Hearn's sound. —*Linda Kohanov*

El Dorado / 1989 / Private Music ✦✦✦✦
This is a marvelous experiment in contemporary, Middle-Eastern-flavored electro-acoustic music. O'Hearn seemed to be embarking on a new direction in his musical career with this thoughtful yet sensuous blending of ancient and modern modes of expression. The album features two prominent Iranian artists—singer Shahla Sarshar and violinist Farid Farjad—though the music was obviously ahead of its time in the notoriously conservative world of adult alternative music. Hopefully, O'Hearn will someday be able to return to the exotic world he touched on in *Eldorado* and create more music from the Fertile Crescent. —*Linda Kohanov*

Indigo / 1991 / Private Music ✦✦✦
O'Hearn's most recent release is an unabashed return to the style he pioneered on *Ancient Dreams*. His characteristically expansive textures are anchored by booming bass drums that feel simultaneously primeval and futuristic. Featured are lush electronics with a hefty dose of rhythmic testosterone. —*Linda Kohanov*

● **The Private Music of Patrick O'Hearn** / 1992 / Private Music ✦✦✦✦

Mike Oldfield

b. May 15, 1953, Reading, Berkshire, England
Bass, Guitar, Percussion, Keyboards / Progressive Electronic, Art Rock/ Progressive Rock
Had he come along 15 years later, composer Mike Oldfield might have invented new age music, which is where he is often lumped today anyway. In 1973, however, he successfully approached youthful entrpeneur Richard Branson with an idea for an experimental album-length instrumental composition, and the result was *Tubular Bells*, whose success—spurred by the music's use as the theme from *The Exorcist*—became the foundation of Virgin Records, Virgin Atlantic Airways, et al. (Branson's corporate ventures). Since then, Oldfield—who had previously recorded in a progressive English folk vein with his sister Sally—has never had so massive a hit, but has delved into spacious (some would say aimless) long-form instrumentals. —*Michael G. Nastos*

★ **Tubular Bells** / 1973 / Reprise ✦✦✦✦✦
Virgin Records allowed Oldfield a year to complete this 49-minute conceptual effort, which required him to record 80 tracks of himself playing 28 different instruments. *Tubular Bells* achieved Top Ten chart success in the US when it was used in the soundtrack for *The Exorcist*, selling more than ten million copies. —*Scott Bultman*

Hergest Ridge / 1974 / Virgin ✦✦✦
A well-made follow-up, with a strange, otherworldly quality in evidence. —*Bruce Eder*

The Orchestral Tubular Bells / 1975 / Virgin ✦✦✦
A nice idea that comes out rather silly—the original record was livelier and fresher, although this version of *Tubular Bells* does offer some distinct timbral differences for those who care enough. —*Bruce Eder*

Ommadawn / 1975 / Virgin ✦✦✦
New age meanderings begin to dominate, but the textures change just enough to hold interest. —*Bruce Eder*

Tubular Bells II / 1992 / Warner Bros. ✦✦✦
The composer plays virtually all the instruments, including guitars, mandolin, banjo, piano, organ, synthesizers, percussion, and—of course—tubular bells. The album opens with quiet passages that echo the original and use it as a launch pad without merely reproducing what has come before. The 70-minute composition flows nicely from ambient movements to those featuring Oldfield's fluid electric guitar work. Oldfield incorporates passages that are downright playful and irreverent. —*Roch Parisien*

Elements: Mike Oldfield 1973-1991 / Nov. 16, 1993 / Virgin America ✦✦✦✦

● **The Best of Mike Oldfield** / Feb. 8, 1994 / Virgin America ✦✦✦✦
The Songs of Distant Earth / Jan. 30, 1996 / Warner Bros. ✦✦

David Parsons

Synthesizer, Drums / Progressive Electronic, Ethnic Fusion, Ambient
Since 1975 this New Zealand artist has made numerous trips to India to absorb the culture, study the music, and record performances by indigenous artists. In addition to producing two albums of traditional Tibetan ritual music by the monks of the Dip Tse Chok Ling Monastery (for the Fortuna Records *Sacred Ceremonies* series), Parsons has translated the essence of his Oriental journeys through the lush, yet profound, soundscapes he has created for a number of highly regarded solo albums. Originally a jazz-rock drummer, he became interested in the music of India when he heard a performance by sitar master Ravi Shankar. Parsons bought a sitar and explored the instrument on his own for several years before studying with Krishna Chakravarty, one of Shankar's most accomplished disciples. After several trips to the East, Parsons composed almost exclusively for Indian instruments until 1979, when he purchased his first synthesizer. He now owns one of the largest electronic recording studios in New Zealand, where he composes for radio, TV, and film. His devotion to both Western technology and Eastern music has made for a potent, highly imaginative style of composition. —*Linda Kohanov*

Himalaya / 1989 / Fortuna ✦✦✦
This is an artfully austere sonic ascent of the legendary mountain range. —*Linda Kohanov*

★ **Yatra** / 1990 / Fortuna ✦✦✦✦✦
Though all of the albums recorded by Parsons are highly recommended, this double CD (which includes 35 minutes of material not featured on the cassette versions) offers a balance of shorter, more uptempo pieces and longer, more contemplative works. *Yatra* (which means "journey" in Sanskrit) is a musical travelog through the Indian countryside, with its busy open-air markets and joyful folk melodies. Gradually, the composer moves into the ethereal realm of Tibet, a landscape imbued with secret ceremonies and hidden knowledge. —*Linda Kohanov*

Sounds of the Mothership / 1991 / Fortuna ✦✦✦
This music is played on electronic synthesizers and classical Indian instruments. It is intended to be listened to in a relaxed frame of mind. —*MusD*

Tibetan Plateau/sounds of The Mothership / 1991 / Fortuna ✦✦✦
Tibetan Plateau/Sounds of the Mothership is a CD collection from the first two Fortuna releases recorded by Parsons in 1980-1982; it features deep spatial compositions for synthesizer, enhanced by classical Indian instruments. —*Linda Kohanov*

● **Dorje Ling** / 1992 / Fortuna ✦✦✦✦
Parsons' release was inspired by his return to Dharamsala, India, the seat of Tibetan Buddhism in exile. Samples of traditional Tibetan music (taken from his recordings for the *Sacred Ceremonies* series) are mixed into these gently evolving electronic compositions. —*Linda Kohanov*

Penguin Cafe Orchestra

New Age, Neo-Classical, Ambient
The Penguin Cafe Orchestra creates dreamlike music. It is beautiful, yet illogical, unpredictable, and often bizarre. Lush violins swirl between classical melodies and country hoedowns. Is that Beethoven or "Walk, Don't Run" they're playing? Is that a touch-tone telephone playing the melody? Yes to all the above, and much more. And don't forget the repetition. Things go on just a little longer than you think they should. Remember Supersax, the jazz group that fully orchestrated Charlie Parker's sax solos and gave them a fuller and richer sound? Well, it's almost as if the Pengies have taken the two-note picking of Luther Perkins (Johnny Cash's guitarist) and taught his repetitive, minimalist picking to a string quartet. The incredible thing is that these are beautiful, compelling records. You may feel as if you dreamed the whole thing, but it is not a nightmare. Probably because no one knows how to classify their music, Penguin Cafe Orchestra is often described as new age. Until a better label comes along, don't let that put you off. Instead, find a copy of the album called *Penguin Cafe Orchestra*—great cover!—and see what the subconscious mind sounds like when it's given some stringed instruments to play. —*Hank Davis*

Music from the Penguin Cafe Orchestra / 1976 / EG ✦✦✦
In many ways, this release is virtually interchangeable with *Broadcasting from Home*. Haunting melodies are played over hypnotically repeated string patterns. —*Hank Davis*

● **Penguin Cafe Orchestra** / 1981 / EG ✦✦✦✦
This is stunning and inventive string music. —*Hank Davis*

Signs of Life / 1991 / EG ✦✦✦
"Southern Jukebox Music" is beautiful. This is a superb collection. —*Hank Davis*

Frank Perry

Percussion / New Age, Ethnic Fusion, Ambient
Frank Perry is a modern musical mystic who takes his inspiration from ancient ideas concerning the power of sound to transform consciousness. Buddhist traditions, the writings of Plato, and Pythagoras' famous treatise *Music of the Spheres* are all seriously taken into consideration by this percussionist. Perry has rejected the rhythmic qualities of drums, woodblocks, etc., in favor of instruments like Chinese Buddha gongs and Tibetan bells, producing ethereal, elongated resonances. His albums feature extended compositions that are quiet and delicate, yet abstract in nature, and his liner notes are filled with lengthy discussions of the philosophies behind the music. His work is likely to be fascinating to many listeners, especially those who also enjoy the Celestial Harmonies *Tibetan Bells* series of releases by Henry Wolff and Nancy Hennings. However, people with more conventional musical and religious tastes may find Perry's style and ideas disturbing. —*Linda Kohanov*

★ **Deep Peace/New Atlantis** / 1983 / Celestial Harmonies ✦✦✦✦✦
Deep Peace/New Atlantis, a double-CD collection, features two albums originally recorded in 1980 and 1983. The four extended works featured are exemplary of Perry's mystical, meditative style. They also illustrate his skill in composing for a variety of ancient instruments that are by nature extremely difficult to manipulate artistically. —*Linda Kohanov*

☆ **New Atlantis** / Sep. 1983 / Celestial Harmonies ✦✦✦✦✦

Zodiac / 1986 / Celestial Harmonies ✦✦✦
As the title suggests, this album offers a suite of pieces symbolizing the 12 zodiac signs. Due to the appeal of this programmatic element and the shorter selections involved, you would expect this album to be the most accessible introduction to Perry's style. However, with music as abstract and unfamiliar as this, it doesn't really matter. Perry's vision just seems most effective in the long-form mode. —*Linda Kohanov*

Richard Pinhas

Synthesizer, Guitar / New Age
French guitarist Richard Pinhas led the group Heldon from 1974-8, releasing seven albums with that group and six solo LPs, often featuring members of Heldon. Born in 1951, Pinhas earned a Ph.D. in philosophy at the Sorbonne and taught at that school. In 1972 he became a part of Schizo, a group whose music contained a great deal of electronics. After Schizo's demise, Pinhas formed Heldon, whose only constant was himself.

Pinhas' solo work covered a lot of ground. His first solo LP, *Rhizosphere*, was performed entirely on synthesizers, except for drums on the side-long title track. *Chronolyse* ranges from simple sequencer pieces to *Paul Atreides*, a 30-minute piece performed by Heldon. The *Iceland* LP successfully captures the feel of an ancient, frozen land. *East-West* was Pinhas' most commercial work. *L'Ethique*, was a varied work with a more structured feel than some of his previous efforts. Pinhas retired from music until releasing *DWW*, which contained work from the period 1983-91. Pinhas released *Cyborg Sally* with John Livengood in 1994. —*Jim Dorsch*

● **East/West** / 1980 / Cuneiform ✦✦✦

Michael Pluznick

Percussion, Drums / Adult Alternative, Ethnic Fusion, Electro Acoustic
This New Jersey native has been fascinated with percussion since childhood. Like Mickey Hart, Pluznick has gone beyond Western traditions in his lifelong pursuit of the magic of rhythm. His music weaves electronic drums and synthesized melodies with a vast collection of ethnic instruments and rhythms hailing primarily from Africa, South America, and the Caribbean. —*Linda Kohanov*

Where the Rain Is Born / 1989 / Sona Gaia ✦✦✦
Here is a dynamic worldbeat release from this Bay Area percussionist working in partnership with synthesist Peter Scaturro. From evocative, impressionistic dreamscapes to bass-heavy polyrhythmic stomps, this album surprises and engages the listener throughout with its grand-scale synthesizer coloring and dense layers of percussive sounds. The album ends with the superb title track, a neo-African chant in honor of the rain, where his raindrop percussion masterfully builds over the hypnotic lilt of the male and female voices. —*Backroads Music/Heartbeats*

Cradle of the Sun / 1990 / Sona Gaia ✦✦✦
There are 17 artists and what seems to be nearly 100 different instruments scattered throughout this album, but the effect is never overpowering. In fact, there's a strong emphasis on Western pop beats and fusion-style synthesizer melodies, with some jazzy trumpet solos. The ethnic influences are primarily rhythmic and often quite subtle, making this music accessible to a wide variety of listeners. Some nice keyboard textures add to the appeal of these familiar-sounding yet well-crafted originals. —*Linda Kohanov*

● **Rhythm Harvest** / 1992 / Narada ✦✦✦✦
On his third release, percussionist-extraordinaire Michael Pluznick finds all the pieces meshing perfectly in a dynamite brew of Haitian, Caribbean, and West African influences. This animated release features male and female vocals, guitar, trumpet, keyboards and, above all, Pluznick on over 20 rhythm instruments. Lindheimer plays guitar and charango, Robert Powell pedal steel guitar, and Kim Atkinson adds extra touches of percussion on several tracks. Highlights include the swaying "Mozambique," based on a Cuban dance craze in the '60s; the catchy "Rumbacito"; and "Giant Step," from traditional music that pays homage to the mountain spirit of the Yoruba people of western Nigeria. While the band is undeniably hot, it's Pluznick who holds the reins, leading his group through complex, dynamic polyrhythms in this fruitful *Rhythm Harvest*. —*Backroads Music/Heartbeats*

Drummers Journey / 1994 / ✦✦✦

Sanford Ponder

Synthesizer / Progressive Electronic, Minimalism
This California-based synthesist recorded two albums in the early '80s during the initial years of the Private Music label. He dropped out of sight for a while, then went on to establish the group Botanica, which has so far released two fascinating albums of music created by fractal mathematics programs. —*Linda Kohanov*

● **Etosha** / 1985 / Private Music ✦✦✦✦
Serene, unpretentious synthesizer music with minimalist underpinnings characterize Ponder's debut album. —*Linda Kohanov*

Tigers Are Brave / 1986 / Private Music ✦✦✦
Ponder's second release is more varied in conception and instrumentation, with traces of violin and other acoustic instruments. —*Linda Kohanov*

Popol Vuh

Neo-Classical, Progressive Electronic, Ethnic Fusion
One of Germany's premiere progressive electronic bands, Popol Vuh was founded in 1969 by keyboardist Florian Fricke. The band took its name from the Mayan Indian bible, and, in fact, the group's first album *Affenstunde* (*The Time of the Monkey King*) was a strong reflection of Fricke's interest in Mayan lore. Over the course of nearly 20 albums, Popol Vuh combined sacred musical traditions and instruments from around the world with classical, jazz, and rock elements. It also created quite a stir as one of the first bands to use the Moog synthesizer in the early '70s. As such, the band influenced several generations of electronic and contemplative artists. Popol Vuh also gained considerable attention for its scores to films by the celebrated German director Werner Herzog, including *Nosferatu* and *Aguirre, the Wrath of God.* —*Linda Kohanov*

In Den Garten Pharads / 1972 / Pilz ✦✦✦✦
"In Pharoah's Garden" was the first true work of "Sacred Music" by Florian Fricke, guiding light of the mythical group Popol Vuh. Consisting of two extended works, his mixture of electronics and church organ with assorted winds and percussives, conjures up visions of the celestial light. Deeply emotional and filled with mysticism, this album marked the dawning of new age music, and still today is a wonder. —*Archie Patterson*

● **Tantric Songs** / 1991 / Celestial Harmonies ✦✦✦✦
Tantric Songs/Hosianna Mantra is new age devotional-rock chamber music that is spacey and spacious on this pairing of two early albums (from 1973 and 1978) on one CD. —*Michael P. Dawson*

● **For You and Me** / Jan. 1991 / Milan ✦✦✦✦
Mixing elements of world music with breathless guitars and inspired vocals, *For You and Me* re-establishes the German group Popol Vuh as a band to be reckoned with. Group-founder Florian Fricke holds down the center of creativity, with Daniel Fichelscher on guitar and the stirring vocals of Renate Knaup-Aschauer as they freely mix styles from India, Africa, Tibet, and South America among soaring passages and lilting reggae beats. This surprisingly melodic music tends to stay right with you in the manner of classic pop innovation. —*Backroads Music/Heartbeats*

Giles Reaves

Percussion, Keyboards / Progressive Electronic, Ambient, Space
Though his music is of the progressive electronic variety, this keyboardist and percussionist got his start through country music channels. While living in Nashville in the '80s, Reaves hooked up with producer Marshall Montgomery and ended up working as his assistant engineer. Eventually Reaves' own music caught the ear of MCA producer Tony Brown, who signed the synthesist up to the company's Master Series label. Reaves recorded two solo albums and one collaboration with Jon Goin before a tightening in the music market forced MCA to let go of artists on its instrumental sub-label. Reaves' latest album for Hearts of Space is a finely produced, technically accomplished evolution of his textural electronic style. —*Linda Kohanov*

★ **Wunjo** / 1986 / MCA ✦✦✦✦✦
Reaves' debut is arguably his best effort for MCA in its subtle, yet refined, use of space and electronics. —*Linda Kohanov*

Sea of Glass / 1992 / Hearts of Space ✦✦✦✦
Subdued drums and percussion, liquid soundscapes, and slowly shifting layers of melting electric guitars are among the evocative sounds Reaves uses on this sensitively designed electro-acoustic album. —*Linda Kohanov*

Jorge Reyes

Flute, Percussion / Progressive Electronic, Ethnic Fusion, Techno-Tribal
This enigmatic multi-instrumentalist draws from the diverse culture and history of his Mexican homeland, as well as his early experiences playing in progressive rock bands south of the border. Currently based in Mexico City, Reyes combines flute, pre-Columbian instruments, and percussion with synthesizers and voice to cast a spell of ritualistic intensity. Like shadows from Mexico's sultry and savage past, his music has a dark quality to it that sometimes scares off the unprepared, but adventurous listeners will find plenty to admire in his evocation of jungles, jaguars, and Aztec rites. Though his albums are often difficult to find, most of his imported releases are well worth the extra effort and expense involved. —*Linda Kohanov*

Comala / 1989 / Mundo ✦✦✦
If the Aztecs and Mayans had been able to play synthesizers and electric guitars along with their flutes and drums, it might have sounded something like this. —*Linda Kohanov*

● **Bajo el Sol Jaguar** / 1991 / Paraiso ✦✦✦✦
This is techno-tribal music to raise the dead, rip the hearts out of your sacrifices, or dance to under the full moon. Reyes' album also features the innovative sounds of Spanish electric guitarist Suso Saiz. Some booming Peter Gabriel-style beats can be found among mysterious atmospheres and virtuosic percussion. —*Linda Kohanov*

Nierika / Silent ✦✦✦✦
A must for lovers of powerful trance music, *Nierika* is tribal primal at its core while seeking to discover the transpersonal, the collective unconscious behind the self. —*Backroads Music/Heartbeats*

Robert Rich

Flute, Guitar, Percussion / Progressive Electronic, Ethnic Fusion, Ambient, Techno-Tribal, Space
Building his first synthesizers at the age of 13, Rich spent his teen years hiding out in his unique sound environments. While gaining a degree in psychology from Stanford University, he became more adept at translating his interests in dreams and trance states into music. (After graduation, he remained a part of the lucid-dream-research team headed by pioneer Stephen LaBerge.) Rich's all-night Sleep Concerts and all-evening Trance Concerts introduced his style to audiences in the San Francisco Bay Area. At the same time, he was developing his chops by diligently practicing baroque keyboard music, experimenting with ethnic influences, and delving into alternate tuning systems and sacred geometry. Rich's music has been appreciated throughout the new-music underground in Europe and North America for years, though his three *Hearts of Space* albums have since brought his music to wider audiences. Besides a wide array of synthesizers, Rich plays flutes, steel guitar, and acoustic percussion, which not only add depth to his music, but allow him to explore his obsession with microtonality and tunings based on non-Western scales. Ranging from latticelike polyrhythms and pieces with a strong Indonesian feel, to deep, time-suspended studies of stasis and slow motion, his compositions are meticulous in detail and subtlety. In 1990 Rich also teamed up with longtime friend Steve Roach to create the critically acclaimed *Strata*, which successfully merged their individual sounds into a shared musical vision. Rich and Roach released their second collaboration, *Soma*, in the fall of 1992. —*Linda Kohanov*

Rainforest / 1989 / Hearts of Space ✦✦✦
Robert's debut for Hearts of Space is a finely wrought collection of lush, textural pieces and engaging uptempo works inspired by the intricacies of baroque counterpoint exemplified by Bach and the fluid melodies of Indonesian gamelan music. —*Linda Kohanov*

● **Strata** / 1990 / Hearts of Space ✦✦✦✦
This highly regarded collaboration between Rich and Steve Roach uses layers of the earth as a metaphor for exploring layers of the psyche. With a wide variety of acoustic and electronic instruments, the two create surreal landscapes of throbbing world music rhythms, broad synthesizer washes, and ethereal sounds. —*Linda Kohanov*

Gaudi / 1991 / Hearts of Space ✦✦✦
Like the melting, three-dimensional visions of the album's namesake—early-20th-century Spanish architect Antonin Gaudi—Rich's musi-

cal structures are geometrical, yet organic. Throughout the recording, his offbeat timbres flow in swirls of mutating patterns, their subtle sense of strangeness resulting from Rich's extensive use of just intonation. —*Linda Kohanov*

Geometry / 1991 / LDN ✦✦✦
Originally recorded in 1986-87, *Geometry* is an early example of the delicate, synthesized latticework Rich creates by mapping various mathematical relationships directly into shimmering, intertwining musical structures. —*Linda Kohanov*

Numena / 1993 / Badlands ✦✦✦

Steve Roach

Synthesizer, Flute, Percussion, Vocals / Electronic, Progressive Electronic, Ambient, Techno-Tribal, Space

Roach's major longstanding influences are not necessarily musical; rather he draws inspiration from empowered geological places, particularly the Mojave and Sonoran deserts and the aboriginal rock-art sites of the Australian outback. In the early years of his career, however, this former adrenaline addict and motocross racer cited the European electronic scene of the '70s as an important impetus in his fascination with sequencer-based music. Yet by the release of his 1983 album, *Structures from Silence*, it was clear Roach was developing his own style. His thick, breathing waves of sound were initially embraced by listeners, meditators, and therapists in the holistic fields; however, Roach's music was far from angelic or superficially comforting. His inspiration grew from the expansive landscapes of the Southwest, complete with the feelings of danger and mystery he associated with these places. A chance to score music for a PBS documentary on the rock art of the Dreamtime (a system of aboriginal mythology) gave Roach the opportunity to visit a number of sites deep in the Australian outback. He also met up with aboriginal didgeridoo master David Hudson, who taught Roach how to play the ancient wind instrument and helped him build his own didgeridoo. These experiences fueled his landmark double album *Dreamtime Return*. Now considered a classic in the progressive electronic field, it marked the synthesis of Roach's earlier sequencer-based sound with his expansive, chordal atmospheres and his growing infusion of tribal aesthetics. In the late '80s, Roach moved from his base in Los Angeles to the Sonoran desert outside of Tucson, AZ. There he has produced a number of projects that continue to blur the lines between ancient ritual and modern technology. His numerous collaborations include albums with Michael Stearns, Kevin Braheny, Robert Rich, and Michael Shrieve. In addition, he has recently worked with Mexican multi-instrumentalist Jorge Reyes and Spanish guitarist Suso Saiz (*Suspended Memories*, *Forgotten Gods*). —*Linda Kohanov*

Traveler / 1977 / Fortuna ✦✦

Structures from Silence / 1984 / Fortuna ✦✦✦✦
This influential album of extended works marked the emergence of his serene, yet haunting synthesizer breaths. —*Linda Kohanov*

● **Quiet Music** / 1986 / Fortuna ✦✦✦✦

★ **Dreamtime Return** / 1988 / Fortuna ✦✦✦✦✦
Roach's sojourn into the mythological mind of the Australian aborigines demonstrates that electronic music's greatest potential may lie in bringing our most elusive dreams and ancient memories into focus through potent, highly imaginative soundscapes. Altered chords that breathe ever so slowly, floating textures, digitally sampled aboriginal instruments, primitive trance rhythms, and arresting abstract sounds lead you through an unfolding maze of sonic dimensions that depict a sense of mystery and confrontation with the unknown. The double CD has 38 minutes of music not in the cassette version. —*Linda Kohanov*

Quiet Music / 1988 / Fortuna ✦✦✦
A subtle collection of ambient pieces with subdued melodies, *Quiet Music* evokes images of shimmering desert mirages. —*Linda Kohanov*

Desert Solitaire / 1989 / Fortuna ✦✦✦
The second of two collaborations with Kevin Braheny inspired by the desert, this album pays homage to the Edward Abbey book of the same title. It inadvertently became a memorial to that Southwestern nature writer when Abbey died shortly after the music was recorded. Featuring some powerful work by Michael Stearns, this album taps into the psychological depths of stark Southwestern landscapes through a subtle set of soundscapes depicting the hidden dangers, unseen gifts, and intoxication that the desert promises. —*Linda Kohanov*

Western Spaces / 1990 / Chameleon ✦✦✦
This reissue of Roach and Kevin Braheny's first evocation of the American Southwest features several selections not included on the original 1987 version. This album is considered by many to be a classic in the progressive electronic and ambient genres. —*Linda Kohanov*

Australia: Sound of the Earth / 1990 / Fortuna ✦✦✦
After the success of *Dreamtime Return*, which was inspired by Australian aboriginal mythology, Roach returned to Australia. He traveled the

continent with a tape recorder collecting natural sounds and capturing performances by native musicians, which he then wove into a sonic journey through the outback. The album is significant in that it features high-quality recordings of aboriginal didgeridoo master David Hudson, who does some startling things with this ancient wind instrument. There are also some powerful performances by a group of five didgeridoo players, as well as some intriguing contemporary compositions by Australian composer Sarah Hopkins. —*Linda Kohanov*

World's Edge / 1992 / Fortuna ✦✦✦✦
Roach's first solo release since *Dreamtime Return* is another double CD. With shorter pieces on the first disc and a single 67-minute work on the second, *World's Edge* explores the paradoxical relationships between sound and silence, space and rhythm, ancient ritual and modern technology. It is an accomplished album. —*Linda Kohanov*

Now/Traveler / 1992 / Fortuna ✦✦✦
This CD reissue features music from Roach's first two albums, originally recorded in the early '80s. A good example of his early, high-energy, sequencer-based style, with some hints at his developing ambient and tribal leanings. —*Linda Kohanov*

Gabrielle Roth

Vocals / Minimalism, Techno-Tribal

Roth doesn't actually play the ritualistic, heavily percussive music featured on her recordings. Instead, the style emerged from her dance performances and movement workshops in which she strives to unite spiritual and sexual energies into what is often referred to as the "dance of ecstasy." Her book, *Maps to Ecstasy: Teachings of an Urban Shaman*, explains the philosophy behind the music she requisitions for her performances and ultimately her albums. She has her own New York-based label, Raven Recording, which has expanded its scope in recent years to release other artists as well. Listed as "musical director" in the liner notes to her five albums, Roth often "composes" by dancing along with a musician's improvisations to communicate her vision, relying on her husband, percussionist Robert Ansell, to lead their ensemble, the Mirrors. —*Linda Kohanov*

Initiation / 1984 / Raven ✦✦✦
The albums *Initiation*, *Bones*, *Ritual*, and *Waves* feature techno-tribal trance music of various tempos and moods, designed for everything from meditation and massage to ecstatic dancing. —*Linda Kohanov*

Bones / 1989 / Raven ✦✦✦
Her latest, the first available on CD, is a musical lament for the past and a prayer for the future. With more synth and production emphasis than before, we still find an amazing mix of swirling and engrossing percussion sounds, with some flute and violin added to the basic tracks. *Bones* is a calling to the inner dance, the dance around your bones. —*Backroads Music/Heartbeats*

Ritual / 1990 / Raven ✦✦✦

★ **Waves** / 1991 / Raven ✦✦✦✦✦
Roth's most aggressive and accomplished recording features some respected percussionists, including Mino Cinelu. Driving tribal rhythms are the basis for six compositions, several of which also make effective use of wailing female vocals. Some synthesizers and electronic guitars add to the sense of mystery Roth craves in her music. —*Linda Kohanov*

Trance / 1993 / Raven ✦✦✦✦
Trance is the latest in Roth's cutting-edge musical series exploring primeval dance rhythms and ecstatic trance. Since her earlier drum-based efforts, her music has become more worldbeat in orientation, propelled by a powerful percussion section. At times funky and danceable, there are other portions that are airy and melodic, with trilling flutes and smoky sax. Jai Uttal adds to half the cuts, and Daniel Lauter and bandleader Robert Ansell join in. Rhythmic but restrained, earthy but ethereal, *Trance* is a strong pancultural statement about the hypnotic power of rhythm. —*Backroads Music/Heartbeats*

Totem / Raven ✦✦✦✦
Totem is urban dance music featuring trap drums, assorted percussion, and occasional synthesizers, guitar, flute, and voice. —*Backroads Music/Heartbeats*

Dancing Toward the One / Raven ✦✦

Teachings of an Urban Shaman / Raven ✦✦

Trance (Music Only) / Raven ✦✦✦✦
This is the music-only version (as distinguished from the workout version) of *Trance*, a trance-dance album centered around percussion. Extremely high-energy, of course. —*Ladyslipper*

Bernardo Rubaja

Piano / Adult Alternative, Ethnic Fusion

Raised in Argentina, Rubaja studied piano formally as a child, performed in local pop groups during his teens, and advanced to Argentina's

National Academy of Fine Arts. Several years spent studying music in the multicultural climate of Paris added to his skills as a performer and composer. Rubaja, who now lives in Southern California, released his first album as a leader on the Narada label. —*Linda Kohanov*

● **High Plateaux** / 1987 / Windham Hill ✦✦✦✦
High Plateaux, a collaboration with Cesar Hernandez, was Rubaja's recording debut. The album was produced in 1987 by Mark Isham. —*Linda Kohanov*

New Land / 1990 / Narada ✦✦✦
Amidst his rich synthesized sounds, pop textures, and spicy Latin rhythms, Rubaja also performs on such exotic South American instruments as the charango (a guitarlike instrument made from an armadillo shell) and the bandoneon (a button accordion made famous by fellow Argentinian Astor Piazzolla). Guest artists include trumpeter Mark Isham and percussionist Alex Acuna. —*Linda Kohanov*

Ryuichi Sakamoto

Keyboards / Progressive Electronic, Ethnic Fusion
An electronic keyboard whiz, Sakamoto received his training at the University of Tokyo. He released his first solo effort in 1978 and shortly thereafter formed the techno-pop band Yellow Magic Orchestra. Sakamoto has successfully combined electronics and world music. He has written the scores for several soundtracks, including half of *The Last Emperor* soundtrack, which won an Oscar. —*David Szatmary*

● **Beauty** / 1990 / Virgin ✦✦✦✦
A world-music tapestry featuring a mixture of Eastern, Western, and African elements, it includes such musicians as Robbie Robertson, Sly Dunbar, and even Brian Wilson. —*David Szatmary*

Neo Geo / Nov. 14, 1991 / Epic ✦✦✦
An interesting combination of Japanese and funk rhythms, it features jazz drummer Tony Williams, reggae star Sly Dunbar, and Iggy Pop. —*David Szatmary*

Eberhard Schoener

Synthesizer, Keyboards / Progressive Electronic, Ambient
German composer Schoener is a sonic explorer who has not only stepped outside European traditions for inspiration, but has created breathtaking music from the most unlikely sources, both natural and electronic. After an extended journey through the Far East, in which he studied religious as well as musical practices, he came to the conclusion that artists need to come to terms with their own cultural heritages to be truly effective. His 1973 release *Meditation*, for instance, expressed the ideal of spiritual contemplation often associated with the East, through synthesized music rooted in Western experience. —*Linda Kohanov*

Meditation/Sky Music . . . / 1973 / Kuckuck ✦✦✦✦
This double-CD reissue features music originally on two albums of extended pieces recorded in 1973 and 1983, respectively. *Meditation* consists of two reflective works for synthesizers. On *Sky Music—Mountain Music*, however, Schoener creates delicate, transparent soundscapes from more natural sources, though it was actually created by attaching tuned whistles to carrier pigeons and allowing the birds to fly through air currents generated by BMW's wind tunnel. —*Linda Kohanov*

● **Trance-formation** / 1977 / Innovative ✦✦✦✦
Recorded in 1977, this classic work is an expression of Schoener's personal and subjective experiences from frequent trips to southeast Asia. Joined by Andy Summers (of the Police) on guitar and the other members of the band, the Secret Society, Schoener's moog, mellotron, and keyboards lay a unique foundation for Gregorian vocals. —*Backroads Music/Heartbeats*

Schonherz and Scott

Adult Alternative, Progressive Electronic, Ambient
This duo features Vienna-born keyboardist Richard Schonherz, who has written music for full orchestra as well as soundtracks for Austrian films and television projects. A native of San Francisco, Peter Scott studied guitar privately, then enrolled in the Musicians Institute of Technology, where he concentrated on composing and arranging. Both artists have played a wide variety of styles over the years, from classical and jazz to rock and blues.

Shortly after the two musicians met, they began producing a series of pop demos as well as a series of instrumental selections. The latter became the basis for the duo's 1987 Windham Hill debut, *One Night in Vienna*. Their pop demos provided the impetus for a second release, *Under a Big Sky*, which includes vocal tunes as well as more pop-oriented instrumentals. —*Linda Kohanov*

● **One Night in Vienna** / 1987 / Windham Hill ✦✦✦✦
Dazzling electronic-based music with romantic underpinnings, these warm, atmospheric pieces are best listened to by candlelight. —*Linda Kohanov*

Under a Big Sky / 1991 / Windham Hill ✦✦✦
While the duo has a flair for sensual, yet subdued, instrumentals, the vocal selections that tend to dominate this album are completely pedestrian. —*Linda Kohanov*

Klaus Schulze

Synthesizer / Electronic
One of the cornerstone figures in the German electronic scene, this pioneering synthesist has recorded nearly two dozen solo albums over the past 20 years. His music has grown and changed with the evolution of technology, but his concept of long-form, highly rhythmic sequencer music pulsing under soaring melodies has remained constant. Though he established his own identity years ago, Schulze was briefly a member of Tangerine Dream, appearing on one album, *Electronic Meditation*, in 1970. He did not, however, cave in to convention or engage in cheap pop-electronic exploits, as did his former TD colleagues in the mid-'80s and beyond. Still, Schulze's collaborations with former Santana drummer Michael Shrieve brought a new level of percussive intensity to his music, as well as a wider audience from the progressive rock world. The availability of Schulze's music has always been inconsistent in the US, and many Americans have no idea how strong his influence has been on electronic music worldwide. (He was, for instance, the inspiration behind Kitaro's initial investigations of synthesizer music.) Schulze continues to perform throughout Europe and is tireless in releasing new recordings, some of which are better than others. When Schulze does hit the nail on the head, his music is immensely powerful. —*Linda Kohanov*

Cyborg / 1973 / A&M ✦✦✦✦
Cyborg was Schulze's second solo album. From the early days of electronic experimentation in the pop field, it stands as one of the most powerful examples of ambient pulse music ever conceived. The dense layers of rhythm and synthetic tone colors melt into a seamless, flowing soundscape of melody, motion, and spatial effects. It's a monumental double album of "cosmic music." —*Archie Patterson*

Timewind / 1975 / Blue Plate ✦✦✦✦
Two masterful sequencer essays make effective use of minimalistic patterns to suspend and ultimately erase all sense of objective "clock-time" experience. —*Linda Kohanov*

Mirage / 1977 / Island ✦✦✦
Mirage gives the listener impressionistic sequencer work depicting winter landscapes. —*Linda Kohanov*

X / 1978 / Gramavision ✦✦✦
Schulze's tenth solo release marks the peak of his most influential period of work. Presented with a classic sense of German drama, this double CD artfully combines the composer's synthesizers and sequencer patterns with live drums and full orchestra. Intense, driving, long-form pieces frame surreal, abstract sounds. Each of six pieces is named for a historical figure Schulze admires, beginning with a 24-minute selection titled "Friedrich Nietzsche." —*Linda Kohanov*

● **Beyond Recall** / 1991 / Venture ✦✦✦✦
Schulze is in a more sedate and reflective mood here, with acoustic guitar samples creating lyrical melodies. —*Linda Kohanov*

Dresden Performance / Jul. 12, 1991 / Venture ✦✦✦✦
In 1989, Klaus Schulze, the pioneer of Euro-electronic space music, accepted an invitation to perform at an outdoor concert in the then East German city of Dresden. This double-CD package contains two long compositions that were captured live, plus studio versions of material Schulze had prepared for the concert. *The Dresden Performance* uses an immensely expanded emotional and musical palette to encompass what has previously been ignored or swept under the carpet by many new age composers. Here, in all of its humanness, is a powerful depiction of "The Dark Night of the Soul," expressing the spiritual warrior's initiation of endurance while crossing frontiers of alien landscapes. The pulsing rhythmic foundations of each piece create a timeless reflection on the process of the hero's journey. Along the way we are confronted by apocalyptic subsonic demons that symbolically represent our primal impulses, darkest fears, and disowned grief. And yet, amid this trial by fire, the angelic voices of the feminine send out soothing waves of comfort, compassion, forgiveness, and hope. This is challenging music that accurately portrays the awesome power of the archetypal unconscious with its metallic nightmares and glittering celestial cities. Through repeated listenings Schulze's message becomes even more clear—in order for true healing and love to become real, we must learn to value and accept the shadow with the same willingness and enthusiasm we employ to covet the light. —*Backroads Music/Heartbeats*

☆ **Royal Festival Hall, Vol. 1, and Royal Festival Hall, Vol. 2** / ✦✦✦✦✦
With around 25 albums to date, this pioneer of electronic music continues to stay topical and current with his singular vision and unique performances. Two new releases are from London concerts in September 1991, and include lengthy studio tracks as well. Sequencer percussion and complex, driving electronics form the basis of Klaus Schulze's free-

form compositions. Each 70-minute CD is filled with a widespread tapestry of sound collages, found percussion, and distant voices, which mix in compelling, dense ways to enhance the intricate textures. —*Heartbeats*

● **Dome Event** / Plan 9/Caroline ◆◆◆◆

John Serrie

Synthesizer / Adult Alternative, Progressive Electronic, Ambient
Leading planetarium composer Serrie has been looking to the heavens for inspiration for over a decade. Coming from a family ensconced in the aviation field, Serrie now soars and glides with his hands on the controls of analog and digital synthesizers. His rhythmic outings often have an understated heroic feel, although he has also done some more pop-oriented instrumentals on his 1990 release *Tingri*. However, he seems most at home in the longer-form space-music journeys for which he initially became known. —*Linda Kohanov*

Flight Path / 1989 / Miramar ◆◆◆◆
This album offers the best of both worlds in terms of Serrie's style, from sequencer patterns that sail through hyperspace to enigmatic, ambient textures that sparkle like star clusters or float with shrouded density through black holes and other cosmic wonders. —*Linda Kohanov*

Tingri / 1990 / Miramar ◆◆◆
The first few cuts have more of a superficial, adult-alternative feel to them. The latter part of the album opens up into beautifully produced spaces that drift and hover. —*Linda Kohanov*

★ **And the Stars Go with You** / Dec. 5, 1990 / Miramar ◆◆◆◆◆
Serrie's debut release on CD captures the development of ten years of planetarium work. Lush romantic pieces with episodes of subtle sequencer patterns maintain a consistently peaceful, yet wondrous, mood, perfect for stargazing. —*Linda Kohanov*

Planetary Chronicles, Vol. 1 / 1992 / Miramar ◆◆◆◆
Serrie's most recent effort is a continuation of the liquid stargazing music pioneered on his 1988 debut *And the Stars Go with You.* —*Linda Kohanov*

Michael Shrieve

Percussion, Drums / Avant-Garde
Shrieve has had a long and interesting career as a rock drummer, percussionist, and progressive electronic composer. Gaining early recognition as the powerhouse drummer for Santana, the teenage Shrieve was launched into the popular culture maelstrom when he performed an extended drum solo during Santana's appearance at the legendary Woodstock festival. Over the years, Shrieve has continued to strive for innovative approaches to percussion-based music. His numerous collaborations include work with Stomu Yamash'ta, Klaus Schulze, Steve Roach, David Beal, David Torn, and Andy Summers. —*Linda Kohanov*

● **Transfer Station Blue** / 1986 / Fortuna ◆◆◆◆
Transfer Station Blue combines the talents of one of America's great rock percussionists with electronic music's most influential masters. Michael Shrieve, former percussionist with Santana and numerous other groups, and Klaus Schulze, Germany's great synthesizer genius, combine their talents to create a new and powerfully distinctive music. Space rhythms that will get your heart and body moving. Instrumentation includes electronic drums, synthesizers, and electric guitar. —*MusD*

The Leaving Time / 1988 / RCA ◆◆◆
Virtuoso percussionist Shrieve teams with synthesist Roach to create some highly atmospheric soundscapes, replete with unusual sounds, and stray melodies. —*William Ruhlmann*

● **The Big Picture** / 1989 / Fortuna ◆◆◆◆
This collaboration between Shrieve and the talented young drummer David Beal is an electronic percussion tour-de-force with epic rhythms, powerful melodies, and broad textural brushstrokes. Amazingly enough, this innovative album fell through the cracks when it was first released and didn't get nearly the attention or distribution it deserved. —*Linda Kohanov*

Stiletto / Aug. 1989 / Jive/Novus ◆◆◆
Always a team player (witness his long stint in Santana), Shrieve puts together an unusual ensemble for his first "solo" album, including trumpeter Mark Isham and former Police guitarist Andy Summers. The tracks (combining elements of rock, jazz, and industrial noise) are dominated by percussion elements, and even the guitar and trumpet playing are more rhythmically than melodically handled. But this extraordinarily inventive album yields subtle pleasures. —*William Ruhlmann*

Software

Adult Alternative, Progressive Electronic
Formed in 1983, this German electronic duo of Peter Mergener and Michael Weisser owes much to electronic pioneer Klaus Schulze. Software's music usually builds on sequencer patterns and simple melodies,

creating a lighter version of the Schulze style. Their later work is woven into concept albums, yet the music rarely lives up to their poetic aspirations. Software's earlier recordings with Peter Mergener are generally more satisfying. —*Linda Kohanov*

★ **Past, Present, Future, Vol. 2** / 1987 / Innovative ◆◆◆◆◆
This is an efficient collection of music from five of the group's mid-'80s recordings. Vol. 1 (IC 7/10.060) is also nice. —*Linda Kohanov*

● **Chip Meditation** / Jan. 1987 / Innovative ◆◆◆

Chip Meditation, Pt. 2 / Sep. 1989 / Innovative ◆◆◆

Fragrances / Oct. 1990 / Innovative ◆◆◆

● **Modesty Blaze** / Jan. 1992 / Innovative ◆◆◆
The sole creative constant in Software is German artist Michael Weisser, who also writes science-fiction novels. He draws on science fiction, high-tech poetry, computer graphics, holograms, and thoroughly entertaining ideas in the "electronic multi-media event" that each new Software becomes. *Modesty Blaze* heads for modern terrain, R-rated in parts (along with the erotic packaging layout), and occasionally captures the dance-mix style of the group Enigma (on last year's *MCMXC A.D.*). There are typically spacey portions that Software specializes in. With song titles like "Erotic Desire," "Naked Skin," "Slippery Dune," and "Masculine Magic," as well as three versions of the title track, you get the idea that the dance crowd and rave party scene are prime targets. Subtitled *The Erotic Message*, there is little that is soft about the latest from Software. —*Backroads Music/Heartbeats*

Solitaire

Progressive Electronic, Ambient, Techno-Tribal
The brainchild of German keyboardist Elmar Schulte, this recording entity is based in the small town of Paderborn, yet draws inspiration from foreign landscapes, particularly the wide open spaces of the American Southwest, Scotland, and Norway. Schulte named the group, in fact, after his admiration for the music on *Desert Solitaire*, an album by American synthesists Steve Roach, Kevin Braheny, and Michael Stearns (see listing under Roach). Solitaire's dark, textural pieces and occasional ethnic rhythms are a marked contrast to the sequencer-dominated heritage of the '70s German electronic school popularized by Tangerine Dream and Klaus Schulze. —*Linda Kohanov*

Altered States / 1990 / Musique Intemporelle ◆◆◆
On this commendable debut, "Heart of the Desert," a long, hypnotic dirge, is particularly well done. —*Linda Kohanov*

● **Plains and Skies** / 1992 / Musique Intemporelle ◆◆◆◆
Schulte's slowly emerging compositional voice is urged along by the obvious influences of his favorite artists, particularly Steve Roach, Jon Hassell, and Michael Brook. —*Linda Kohanov*

Richard Souther

Keyboards / Adult Alternative, Ethnic Fusion
As a promising session keyboardist in Los Angeles, Souther began landing work in recording studios while still in his teens, eventually performing with such artists as Barry McGuire, Debby Boone, the Mothers of Invention, and Phil Keaggy. In 1980, however, a near-fatal bout with food poisoning suspended Souther's career for several years. After his recovery, he began to focus on developing a solo career that would involve more personal themes, including his Christian perspective on life. Strong, hopeful melodies are his trademark; yet his albums for the Narada label also reflect his pop background as well as his early classical training, his feeling for contemporary jazz, and his subsequent interests in ethnic music. —*Linda Kohanov*

Cross Currents / 1989 / Narada ◆◆◆
Featured are optimistic melodies in a pop-jazz ensemble setting. —*Linda Kohanov*

● **Twelve Tribes** / 1990 / Narada ◆◆◆◆
Souther's second release shows a marked evolution in style from his first album, recorded just a year earlier. Not only are his keyboard parts based on more original timbres, Souther also abandons customary drum sounds for a stronger emphasis on live and sampled percussion. Rather than a standard kick drum, for instance, he uses an African log drum. In place of cymbals, he uses samples of someone breathing. The emphasis is still on catchy melodies and contemporary jazz textures; yet Souther's creative use of ethnic rhythms and instruments adds a new level of sophistication to his accessibility. —*Linda Kohanov*

Hilary Stagg

Harp / Adult Alternative
Stagg was working as an electrician when he heard Swiss harp sensation Andreas Vollenweider in concert. At that moment, the Northern California native was inspired to learn all he could about the electro-acoustic harp. A few years later, he was releasing his own albums, using his

knowledge as an electrician to amplify his instrument to suit the soft, dreamy music he was developing. Stagg also credits the sweet melodic stylings of Loggins and Messina, the Doobie Brothers, and the Moody Blues as influences. Over the course of three recordings, Stagg has grown increasingly accomplished as a performer and composer. —*Linda Kohanov*

Beyond the Horizon / 1987 / Real Music ✦✦✦
This is Stagg's debut release. —*Linda Kohanov*

Feather Light / 1989 / Real Music ✦✦✦
Using his customized acoustic-electric harp, Stagg's *Feather Light* style is complemented by judicious use of additional instruments, from bluesy slide guitar to violin, dobro, and synthesizer. For the most part these instruments appear separately, but the final track, "No Pressure," brings several of them together in an upbeat ensemble celebration. He plays with his trademark light touch to produce this gentle but upbeat album. —*Backroads Music/Heartbeats*

★ **Dream Spiral** / 1991 / Real Music ✦✦✦✦✦
Though Stagg is backed by an ensemble featuring synthesizer, electric bass, percussion, acoustic guitar, and violin, his custom-electrified Troubadour harp remains the focus of eight originals that take on a silky, dreamlike quality through the composer's resonant techniques. —*Linda Kohanov*

The Edge of Forever / Jul. 1, 1993 / Real Music ✦✦✦✦
With *The Edge of Forever*, Stagg takes his playing to new heights of inspiration. While his instrument has a naturally attractive sound, it is his sensitive and gently spirited playing that makes this album come together in such a cohesive manner. Additional flute and keyboards add to the sound on the seven tracks, culminating in the 11-minute closer, simply titled "Forever." Cover art by environmental artist George Sumner tops it off perfectly. —*Backroads Music/Heartbeats*

Bruce Stark

Piano / Neo-Classical, Solo Instrumental
As a physics major in college, Stark found himself spending more time in the dormitory lounge playing piano than doing his homework. Inspired by Keith Jarrett's extended improvisations, the self-taught musician abandoned his scientific studies and just barely managed to get accepted into the music department of California State University at the age of 22. He gained a master's degree in composition from Juilliard, studying with heavies like Roger Sessions and Vincent Persichetti. Yet along the way, Stark never lost his interest in the tonal, highly improvisational styles that attracted him to music in the first place. Unlike the George Winston clones who gave solo piano music a bad name in the '80s, this Tokyo-based artist starts out with strong compositional ideas and actually develops them in intelligent and emotionally charged ways. —*Linda Kohanov*

● **Song of Hope** / 1991 / Hearts of Space ✦✦✦✦
One of the finest solo piano releases in recent years, *Song of Hope* strikes a rare balance between musical literacy and pure emotion. —*Linda Kohanov*

Michael Stearns

Synthesizer, Flute, Vocals / Progressive Electronic, Ambient
An accomplished sound sculptor, Stearns developed an appetite for psychedelic music from listening to Jimi Hendrix and Cream in the '60s while playing in his own rock bands. In 1974 a fortuitous meeting with dance/movement icon Emilie Conrad provided Stearns with the impetus to move to Los Angeles from his hometown of Tucson, AZ, leaving behind plans to become a Sufi mystic in the process. During the next dozen years, Stearns worked in close association with Conrad's Continuum dance collective, creating spontaneous live accompaniment for the group's explorations of movement and sound. In the process, he developed an electronic-based style that mixed environmental recordings with synthesizers and exotic instruments including "the beam," a 12-foot aluminum shaft strung with piano wire that produced extremely low tones. In 1983 Stearns was selected to score the IMAX film *Chronos*, an opportunity that allowed the composer to further develop his interests in sophisticated multi-channel techniques and mind-expanding soundscapes. Over the last decade, Stearns has scored numerous IMAX and OMNIMAX films and has been able to build and refine a state-of-the-art studio to continue his search for new sounds. —*Linda Kohanov*

★ **Planetary Unfolding** / 1985 / Sonic Atmospheres ✦✦✦✦✦
A masterful electronic symphony, it is based on the idea that the universe is made of sound rather than solid matter (a notion that has its roots in oriental philosophy as well as in some modern theoretical physics circles). Stearns' performances on the Serge synthesizer actually give the feeling that atoms, cells, planets, and other celestial bodies are creating a complex orchestration that is unfolding on itself and expanding into deep space. —*Linda Kohanov*

Chronos / 1985 / Sonic Atmospheres ✦✦✦
This soundtrack for the IMAX film by Ron Fricke stands on its own. Stearns' interests in sound design and innovative recording techniques take an equal seat with the music, which captures the drama of large-format film and inspires majestic visuals in the mind of the listener. —*Linda Kohanov*

● **Encounter** / 1988 / Hearts of Space ✦✦✦✦
A musical science-fiction fantasy, *Encounter* is "space music" in the most obvious sense of the word. Stearns' ten-piece suite depicts contact with a UFO, culminating in a journey to the stars. The imagery is so effective that it's probably not advisable to listen to this album alone in the desert. —*Linda Kohanov*

● **Sacred Site** / 1993 / Hearts of Space ✦✦✦✦
Since his 1988*Encounter*, Michael Stearns has been turning out spectacular multichannel music for IMAX and 70mm widescreen features and exhibition rides. A decade (1983-1993) of soundtracks, scores, and related music inspired by world travels is collected here, including the spine-tingling theme for director Ron Fricke's 70mm release *Baraka*. —*MusD*

Stein and Walder

Neo-Classical, Chamber Jazz
Keyboardist Ira Stein and oboist Russel Walder met in 1981 at a series of master classes taught at the Naropa Institute by two of their major influences, Ralph Towner and Paul McCandless. Shortly thereafter, Stein and Walder produced a demo and were signed to Windham Hill. Their sound has expanded from the acoustic duets of their 1982 debut, *Elements*, to a satisfying blend of electronic keyboards, drums, bass, and intricate studio enhancements. —*Linda Kohanov*

Transit / 1978 / Windham Hill ✦✦✦
Produced by Mark Isham, this album added lush electronics and a number of talented sidemen to the mix, including bassist Michael Manring. —*Linda Kohanov*

● **Under the Eye** / 1990 / Narada ✦✦✦✦
An invigorating display of the duo's diversity, maturity, and inventiveness, *Under the Eye* features ensemble settings with guitarist Tom Vatlin, bassist Shido, drummers Robbie Bean and Gene Refkin, and percussionist Marc Anderson. —*Linda Kohanov*

Liz Story

Piano / Neo-Classical, Solo Instrumental, Adult Alternative
Story studied classical piano while growing up in Southern California and even thought about becoming a music librarian or theorist for a while. Then she heard jazz pianist Bill Evans at a New York club, and the experience changed her perspective on music overnight. Story, who had studied at Juilliard and was enrolled at Hunter College at the time, abandoned her academic program in favor of jazz lessons with Sanford Gold, a teacher Evans had recommended. Back in Los Angeles, she continued her musical education at UCLA and the Dick Grove Music Workshops, but it was a job playing piano at a French restaurant that sparked her major breakthrough as a composer. Since the front casing of the piano was missing, Story had no place to put her sheet music and was forced to improvise freely. Eventually she put some of her spontaneous compositions on tape and sent them to Windham Hill. Within four days Will Ackerman had called her back and the contract was signed for her first release, *Solid Colors*, an album of impressionistic piano miniatures. Over the course of five recordings, including a two-album stint with RCA Novus, Story's style has expanded to include electronic duets with Mark Isham and works for various types of ensembles; yet the piano remains the prominent voice in her finely crafted compositions. —*Linda Kohanov*

● **Solid Colors** / 1983 / Windham Hill ✦✦✦✦
With remarkable technical facility, tremendous feel, and a playful sense of musical progression, Liz Story proves a moving and fascinating pianist on her debut album. Intuitive, yet intellectual, Story has a strong sense of structure, and her quick, light playing keeps things moving. —*William Ruhlmann*

Unaccountable Effect / 1985 / Windham Hill ✦✦✦
This is a particularly striking album of rhapsodic piano solos and gorgeous collaborations with synthesist Mark Isham. —*Linda Kohanov*

Part of Fortune / 1988 / Jive/Novus ✦✦✦
On several tracks of this label debut, Story experiments with added instrumentation—percussion, a cello, strings, a choir—giving her music a more formal cast that does not reduce its attraction. —*William Ruhlmann*

Speechless / 1989 / Jive/Novus ✦✦✦
Story's second and final recording for RCA Novus is a return to the solo piano realm after her forays into arrangements involving other instruments. —*Linda Kohanov*

● **Escape of the Circus Ponies** / 1991 / Windham Hill ✦✦✦✦
It's actually difficult to recommend one of Story's albums over all the rest, because they all offer different sides of her musical personality, complete with brilliant moments and less successful ideas. Her 1990 return to Windham Hill, however, shows a level of maturity in her ability to compose for solo piano, especially in her creative use of altered harmonies and her mastery of the thoughtful lyricism associated with her greatest inspiration, Bill Evans. —*Linda Kohanov*

Tim Story

Piano / Neo-Classical, Progressive Electronic, Ambient, Space
Though he also recorded for Windham Hill at one time, this Ohio-based keyboardist is not related to Liz Story. His intimate style thrives on cavernous spaces, an element that eventually caught the attention of Hearts of Space Records, which released *Beguiled*. Other than some early guitar lessons, Tim Story is self-taught. With experience as a recording engineer and a studio musician under his belt, he turned his attention to composing and released his first albums on a tiny Norwegian label called Uniton in 1982. His music attracted the attention of Windham Hill's Will Ackerman, who released two of his albums in the late '80s and included several of Story's pieces on some of the label's samplers. Though his melodic voice is often expressed with uncommon delicacy on grand piano, Story sets the contours of his pieces with broad synthesized brushstrokes in hazy, enigmatic veils of color. Like Harold Budd, he also injects a profound sense of ambiguity into his compositions, suggesting emotions for which there are no words. —*Linda Kohanov*

Glass Green / 1987 / Windham Hill ✦✦✦
More upbeat selections are included in the midst of Story's characteristically elegant, open-ended lyricism. —*Linda Kohanov*

★ **Beguiled** / 1991 / Hearts of Space ✦✦✦✦✦
Story's most subtle and masterful work to date can best be described as graceful, visceral chamber music for 21st-century romantics. His miniatures for Steinway grand piano and synthesizers, sometimes enhanced by the velvet richness of Martha Reikow's cello, embody passion at a whisper. —*Linda Kohanov*

Wheat and Rust / ✦✦✦
His stately synthesizer and introspective piano evoke images of wintery landscapes—perfect music to listen to while curled up in front of the fire or on a lazy, rainy day. Story has a gift for creating charming little melodic poems full of lightness, grace, and whimsy—delicate, unpretentious, and skillfully concocted combinations of acoustic piano and synthesizer voicings. —*Backroads Music/Heartbeats*

Strunz and Farah

Guitar (Classical), Guitar / World Fusion
Combining elements of Latin and Middle Eastern music (Strunz is Costa Rican, while Farah is Iranian), this acoustic guitar duo's world-jazz fusion style offers an interesting blend of music. Interesting percussion and rhythms from traditional instruments, plus the occasional guest (like India's L. Subramaniam), add to the blend. —*AMG*

Guitarras / 1961 / Milestone ✦✦

Frontera / 1976 / Milestone ✦✦

Mosaico / May 1984 / Mesa Blue Moon ✦✦✦
The first and still best record for this team of Iranian guitarist Andeshir Farah and guitarist Jorge Strunz. It includes seven originals with a multi-ethnicity that is truly global. Latin, African, and jazz influences most prominent. —*Michael G. Nastos*

● **Primal Magic** / 1991 / Mesa Blue Moon ✦✦✦✦
Struntz and Farah are both masters of flamenco-influenced guitar. This album has some very hot guitar work, with ensemble accompaniment. —*MusD*

● **Americas** / May 12, 1992 / Mesa Blue Moon ✦✦✦✦
The latest from this dazzling and astonishing guitar duo surpasses 1990's award-winning *Primal Magic* with blazing intensity and passion. Their uptempo flamenco sound really vaults way beyond standard fare. Jorge Strunz occupies the left channel, while Ardeshir Farah holds down the right. Visual images abound, conjuring up remote, romantic islands, tropical rainforests and warm, moonlit waters. *Americas* melds the flair, dexterity, and cultural roots of their combined Latin American and Middle Eastern heritages with the surrounding septet of tremendous musicians. —*Backroads Music/Heartbeats*

Tangerine Dream

Electronic, Avant-Garde, Art Rock/Progressive Rock
Formed as a rock group in 1967 by Edgar Froese, Tangerine Dream is one of the most important entities to shape contemporary instrumental music. The turbulent '60s, Froese's association with surrealist painter Salvador Dali, and the arrival of the Moog synthesizer were just a few of the forces that helped to fuel this German electronic group through a bar-

rage of constant change in style and personnel. Core members over the years have included Froese and Chris Franke as well as Peter Baumann, who went on to start the Private Music label. Curiously enough, the band's most recent addition is Jerome Froese, Edgar's son, whose baby photos can be found in the artworkf or TD's early albums. The TD sound has moved from the droning nightmares of *Zeit* to the mesmerizing sequencer-based masterpieces of *Rubycon* and *Ricochet* in the '70s to the sparkling high-tech rock of the '80s. A cult phenomenon for decades, Tangerine Dream gained wider recognition when the group's highly evocative music attracted the interest of William Friedkin. This resulted in the score to the film *Sorcerer* and the beginning of a large number of soundtracks. (TD's music for the Tom Cruise scorcher *Risky Business* probably attracted the most attention.) In recent years Tangerine Dream has moved toward shorter, song-based pieces that seem superficial and predictable compared to the group's pioneering work. —*Linda Kohanov*

Zeit / 1972 / Relativity ✦✦✦
TD's purest expression of "space music," this double album ebbs and flows effortlessly from one tone cluster to another. Almost classical in construction, the music is structured so as to evolve in sections as one theme literally melts into the next. Florian Fricke (of Popol Vuh) played the big moog on this album and the overall texture of the electronics is warm and shimmering. —*Archie Patterson*

Rubycon / 1975 / Virgin ✦✦✦
Classic, uncompromising Tangerine Dream, it is a must for any serious collector of electronic music. —*Linda Kohanov*

Logos / 1982 / Virgin ✦✦✦✦
This live recording captures the Dream at a high point that occurred midway through the band's career. Longer, more intricate, pieces are present; yet the action takes place at a brisk pace, moving through many of the trademark TD motifs and soundscapes. The recording's studio quality and engrossing performances are clearly inspired. —*Linda Kohanov*

Le Parc / 1985 / Relativity ✦✦✦✦
A selection of different moods, all of a consistently high quality, each track takes its name and inspiration from a different park in the world, like Central, or Yellowstone for example. —*Vladimir Bogdanov*

Legend / 1986 / MCA ✦✦

Tyger / 1987 / Relativity ✦✦✦

Canyon Dreams / 1987 / Miramar ✦✦✦✦
TD received its first Grammy nomination with this album. The music was originally composed for a scenic video on the Grand Canyon, released under the same title. The style is a rather ingenious combination of the group's progressive style and current commercial leanings, and, as such, is Tangerine Dream's finest album of recent years. —*Linda Kohanov*

Miracle Mile / 1989 / Private Music ✦✦✦

Lily on the Beach / 1989 / Private Music ✦✦✦

The Best of / 1989 / Jive ✦✦✦

Destination Berlin / 1989 / American Gramaphone ✦✦✦

Melrose / 1990 / Private Music ✦✦✦
Quite a contrast from *Logos Live*, this album is one of the better examples of the band's recent immersion in adult-alternative electronic pop. —*Linda Kohanov*

Rockoon / 1992 / Miramar ✦✦✦
Though the music has its moments, TD's most recent album is listed mostly as a reference. —*Linda Kohanov*

220 Volt Live / 1993 / Miramar ✦✦✦

Turn of the Tide / 1994 / Miramar ✦✦

● **Tangents: 1973-83** / 1994 / Capitol ✦✦✦✦

Dead Solid Perfect / Silva Screen ✦✦

L'Affaire Wallraff (The Man Inside) / EMI France ✦✦

John Tesh

Synthesizer, Piano / New Age, Progressive Electronic
New age composer and instrumentalist John Tesh has become a popular figure on the adult contemporary music front. He was born on Long Island, NY. Though a talented musician, he is perhaps best known as the cohost of the TV show "Entertainment Tonight." —*Sandra Brennan*

Tour de France . . . .the Early Years / 1970 / Private Music ✦✦✦

The Games / 1992 / GTS ✦✦✦
Entertainment Tonight host John Tesh has released an instrumental album featuring music that was played on NBC's telecast of the Olympic Games in Barcelona. *The Games* features a blend of straight-ahead rock instrumentation and acoustic treatment, with piano and electric violin as the centerpieces. From the lush orchestrations on the ballad "April Song" to the driving unison piano/violin melodies of "Exit Mulholland" and

"Barcelona," this release takes the listener inside the power and passion of the world's greatest athletic event, the Olympics. —*MusD*

Monterey Nights / 1993 / GTS ✦✦✦
Giving us another look at some of his best on this recent compilation from *Garden City,The Games*, and others, Tesh incorporates his piano and synthesizer music with violin, bass guitar, and percussion. Lush melodies pour forth for our delight with cuts like the romantic "Goodnight Moon," the samba sound of "Concetta," and the synthesized splendor of "Rhapsody in Love," with its lyrical violin. Also included are stronger, bolder tunes that found their inspiration in the '92 Barcelona Games and Tesh's composing for the grueling Tour de France. It's a polished selection of winners. —*MusD*

Winter Song / 1994 / GTS ✦✦✦
Winter Song is the first in the series of instrumental albums designed to evoke the moods of the seasons. This collection of classic and modern compositions features grand piano, acoustic guitar, and full orchestra arrangements. Although *Winter Song* was conceived and recorded as a seasonal tribute, it will no doubt provide listeners year-round enjoyment . . . —*MusD*

● **Sax by the Fire** / 1994 / GTS ✦✦✦✦
The John Tesh Project has taken some of contemporary music's most popular songs and performed them in a decidedly sophisticated and romantic way. Alto, tenor, and soprano saxes are played by some of the best. Each saxophonist puts his own musical signature on each track, creating an alluring, new version of each song. Included are "Desperado," "Tears in Heaven," "End of Innocence," and "Field Of Gold." —*MusD*

Live at Red Rocks / 1995 / GTS ✦✦✦✦
Sax on the Beach / 1995 / GTS ✦✦✦

Tingstad and Rumbel

Neo-Classical, Chamber Jazz
Guitarist Eric Tingstad and oboist Nancy Rumbel create music directly inspired by the chamber-jazz styles of Oregon and the Paul Winter Consort. After studying at Northwestern University, San Antonio-born Rumbel moved to New York. There she met oboist Paul McCandless, (who played with the Winter Consort before helping to establish Oregon with guitarist Ralph Towner). McCandless put her in contact with Winter, and before she knew it, Rumbel herself was touring and recording with the Paul Winter Consort. After a five-year stint with the group, Rumbel dropped out to start a family. She met Eric Tingstad at an outdoor festival. The Seattle-based guitarist had been influenced by Oregon's Ralph Towner. Tingstad studied classical guitar in college and spent the better part of the '70s playing lead guitar in a Seattle progressive rock band. In the '80s, however, he returned to the acoustic guitar and released two solo albums that established his popularity as a regional musician known for creating "Northwest Impressionism." When Rumbel moved to Washington, she and Tingstad agreed to collaborate. They have since recorded a number of contemporary chamber music-style albums for the Narada label. The musicians, who have a long history of environmental activism, often create albums with outdoor themes and have been known to give away tree seedlings at their live performances. —*Linda Kohanov*

Woodlands / 1987 / Narada ✦✦✦
This is an early collaboration with pianist David Lanz. —*Linda Kohanov*

Legends / May 1988 / Narada ✦✦✦
This release builds on the foundation of Tingstad and Rumbel's previous releases and explores some exciting new directions. Tingstad's distinctive use of the mandolin is especially effective, and the cover photo is striking. —*MusD*

● **Homeland** / 1990 / Narada ✦✦✦✦
Tingstad and Rumbel's pastoral sound is a bit more aggressive on this album, due to a stronger rhythmic emphasis and the appearance of more than a dozen guest artists. The overall effect, however, remains subtle, with snatches of Oriental and South American influences mixed with the duo's usual fusion of classical and North American folk influences. —*Linda Kohanov*

In the Garden / 1991 / Narada ✦✦✦
The duo created this album based on their mutual interests in gardening and to promote responsible land stewardship concepts. Some of the proceeds were donated to national gardening organizations. —*Linda Kohanov*

Give and Take / 1993 / Narada ✦✦✦
With *Give and Take*, Eric Tingstad and Nancy Rumbel present their seventh collaborative album. These two fast friends share a commonality of interests beyond their finely-crafted compositions: a personal involvement in humanitarian and environmental issues, a passion for reading, and a wry sense of humor. Here Tingstad's classical guitar and Rumbel's work on oboe, English horn, and ocarinas meld to make music that is

warm, personal, and inviting. Understated percussion gently flavors this outstanding album. —*MusD*

Renewal / 1994 / ✦✦✦

Tri Atma

Adult Alternative, Ethnic Fusion
Founded in 1977 by German guitarist Jens Fischer and Indian tabla player Asim Saha, Tri Atma specializes in fusing Eastern musical elements with Western electronic pop. In 1982 the duo met Klaus Netzle, a veteran German record and television producer who brought the space-age sounds of the fairlight and synclavier computer synthesizers to their music. —*Linda Kohanov*

★ **Yearning and Harmony** / 1982 / Fortuna ✦✦✦✦✦
Buoyant Eastern rhythms and Western grooves support some intricate acoustic guitar work and compelling electronic keyboard solos. —*Linda Kohanov*

Essential Tri Atma / 1990 / Higher Octave ✦✦✦✦
This is a collection of digitally remastered pieces from three of Tri Atma's previous recordings, with an emphasis on their more pop-oriented fusions. —*Linda Kohanov*

Nik Tyndall

Progressive Electronic, Ambient
As a designer of sound units and amplifiers in the '70s, this German artist made a natural progression into composing for electronic instruments at the end of the decade when he formed the avant-garde duo Tycoon with Rudolf Lager. In the mid-'80s, he struck out on his own and released a number of recordings on the German Sky label, in addition to composing soundtracks for film and television. His style combines primarily lush environmental soundscapes with the delicate percussive textures of bamboo, gongs, and windchimes. —*Linda Kohanov*

● **Lagoon** / 1990 / Hearts of Space ✦✦✦✦
Tyndall's first American release concentrates on shorter pieces, with each selection exploring a single mood through finely crafted, primarily computer-generated sounds. —*Linda Kohanov*

Vangelis (Evangelos Papathanassiou)

Keyboards / Neo-Classical, Progressive Electronic, Ambient
With his lush synthesizer textures, sweeping romantic melodies, and undeniable flair for the dramatic, Vangelis has been called "the electronic Tchaikovsky." This self-taught artist grew up in Athens, Greece, where he shunned piano lessons at an early age in favor of conducting his own musical experiments by playing with radio interference and stuffing the family piano with nails and other foreign objects. After achieving considerable success in Greece with his early-'60s rock group, Vangelis moved to Paris at the age of 25 and formed the progressive band Aphrodite's Child. He was even invited to replace Rick Wakeman in Yes, but turned the position down as his interests floated away from rock and into soundtrack work. His early scores to Frederic Roussif's *Apocalypse des Animaux* and *Opera Sauvage* were released as albums. Nearly 20 years later, this music stands on its own as some of Vangelis' finest work. In the mid-'70s, the composer moved to London where he set up an extensive electronic music studio. There he recorded some of his most popular solo albums while continuing to create masterful soundtracks for film and television projects, including the theme to Carl Sagan's *Cosmos* and the ethereal, futuristic music for *Blade Runner*. He is best known, however, for his Academy Award-winning score to *Chariots of Fire*. Though many electronic composers have fallen in and out of fashion over the years, Vangelis' music possesses the kind of originality and quality that makes it seem timeless. His sophisticated use of texture and atmosphere is balanced by highly expressive melodies and swells of emotional intensity. It's hard not to be moved by this music. —*Linda Kohanov*

China / 1979 / Polydor ✦✦✦✦
One of the composer's least-known albums is also one of his best. Exalted invocations of oriental majesty frame playful, folk-like melodies and mystical rites of passage. —*Linda Kohanov*

● **Odes** / 1979 / Polydor ✦✦✦✦

Opera Sauvage / 1981 / Polydor ✦✦✦✦
This warm, lyrical album was derived from Vangelis' music for a French television series. Rich, electronic orchestrations range from grandly symphonic to simple and serene. The title has experienced a major revival since the opening cut, "Hymne," was used for a Gallo wine commercial. An excellent introduction to his music. —*Backroads Music/Heartbeats*

☆ **Chariots of Fire** / 1982 / Polydor ✦✦✦✦✦
Vangelis' Academy Award-winning score to the movie continues to be his most famous album, probably because the theme is immediately recognizable, yet quickly lures listeners into a musical world that stands on its own. —*Linda Kohanov*

Soil Festivities / 1984 / Polydor ✦✦✦
A five-movement suite, it emerges from a thunderstorm into a celebration of nature's savage beauty. —*Linda Kohanov*

The Mask / 1985 / Polydor ✦✦✦
Primal rituals in a futuristic setting. —*Linda Kohanov*

Direct / 1988 / Arista ✦✦✦
Vangelis released *Direct* in 1988, at the time a major new work that covered all aspects of his previous career. The results were quite exciting, from his familiar dynamic pieces and rhythmic approaches to more reflective passages, and a wonderful "Glorianna" with superb female operatic vocals closing out the first half. —*Backroads Music/Heartbeats*

★ **Antarctica** / 1988 / Polydor ✦✦✦✦✦
Originally composed for a forgettable Japanese film on the South Pole, this album is a masterpiece of sonic sensations depicting vast plains of ice, sunlight glittering across the snow, and the sting of Antarctic winds. Expansive melodies are punctuated by the lashing sounds of whips urging dog sleds into mysterious and forbidden landscapes. —*Linda Kohanov*

Themes / 1989 / Polydor ✦✦✦✦
These are selections from his most famous soundtracks, including many themes never before available on a recording (such as those from *Blade Runner*, *The Bounty*, and *Missing*). —*Linda Kohanov*

The City / 1990 / Atlantic ✦✦✦
Vangelis has created another masterwork of truth, sensitivity, and grace. —*Backroads Music/Heartbeats*

1492: Conquest of Paradise [O.S.T.] / 1994 / East West ✦✦✦✦
Suitably grand in scale and far-reaching in scope, this soundtrack stands up well next to Vangelis' classic *Chariots of Fire*. He succeeds in capturing the 15th-century mood, mixing rich choral portions with modern elements, and portraying the larger than life character of Columbus. —*Backroads Music/Heartbeats*

Blade Runner / 1994 / Atlantic ✦✦✦✦

David Van Tieghem

b. Apr. 21, 1955
Percussion, Drums / Progressive Electronic, Techno-Tribal
New York-based percussionist David Van Tieghem has shown a remarkably broad sense of what constitutes a percussion instrument, "playing" everything from kitchen items to a theater itself. Sometimes coming under the heading "performance art," his work as a soloist with several albums under his own name and as an accompanist to Laurie Anderson and others is wildly imaginative. —*William Ruhlmann*

These Things Happen / 1984 / Warner Bros. ✦✦✦
David Van Tieghem is a percussionist, nominally speaking, but as far as he's concerned, everything on earth is a percussion instrument. On this album, which features a variety of found sounds (including radio transmissions) mixed in with more conventional instruments, Van Tieghem plays a wine bottle, a hair comb, metal ashtrays, and balloons, among other things. But this musically arranged junk heap is often amazingly musical. If you like it, try Van Tieghem's three albums on Private Music, especially *Strange Cargo*. —*William Ruhlmann*

Safety in Numbers / 1987 / Private Music ✦✦✦
Not comfortably labeled new age, or percussion music, or pop, or electronic music, Van Tieghem's music has that "downtown" mix of all these and yet is distinctly his own, from the lush "Crystals" to the droll and rhythm steady "Night of the Cold Noses." This is twisted "easy listening." —*Blue* Gene Tyranny

● **Strange Cargo** / 1989 / Private Music ✦✦✦✦
This New York artist has built himself a reputation both as an innovative percussionist and sometime performance artist. On his latest album he further explores the quirky fusion of funk, rock, jazz, Asian, and progressive electronic elements that characterize his music. We are taken on a journey through wildly diverse terrains—from tight structured melodies to impressionistic pastiches of weird and wonderful sounds, all multi-layered and full of interesting background effects best captured on headphones. —*Backroads Music/Heartbeats*

Andreas Vollenweider

Harp / Adult Alternative, Ethnic Fusion
Vollenweider was one of the few musicians to gain superstar status as a "new age artist" when the term was first used as a marketing category in the mid-'80s. The Swiss harpist, however, quickly transcended the need for alternative record sales when his albums simultaneously broached *Billboard*'s pop, jazz, and classical charts in 1986. Born in Zurich in 1953, Vollenweider was ensconced in the city's fine art scene, courtesy of his father, one of Europe's leading organists. After becoming proficient on guitar, flute, and other instruments, the young Vollenweider developed a passion for the harp, which he modified to suit his needs. Not only did he construct a damper to expedite more rhythmic playing, he broadened the

harp's tonal range by electrifying it. His buoyant funk beats, exotic pan-cultural influences, and colorful harp improvisations began to sweep Europe in the early '80s as Vollenweider signed with CBS Records to release *Behind the Gardens . . . Behind the Wall*. Three albums later, he won his first Grammy for 1987's *Down to the Moon*. Over the years, Vollenweider has managed to maintain his artistic integrity and vision despite increasing commercial success. The harpist's 1991 album *Book of Roses* is a testament to his ability to expand his scope as a composer while keeping his trademark sound intact. —*Linda Kohanov*

Behind the Gardens (Behind the Wall—Under the Tree) / 1982 / Columbia ✦✦✦
Vollenweider performs on a mechanically altered concert harp. His instrument enables him to counteract the meditative properties of the harp with a strong rhythmic pulse. The results are very low-frequency bass tones in the harp, coupled with an almost orchestral sense of harmony. This album is upbeat, centering, and a real delight. —*MusD*

★ **Caverna Magica** / 1983 / Columbia ✦✦✦✦✦
Caverna Magica put Andreas Vollenweider on the space music map. The music is lightly jazzy, performed on modified harp, "rhythmanatomic acousticolors and UFO," and drums, with vocal colorings. From the delightful title track through the sublime "La Paix Verde," this work is current and enjoyable. —*Backroads Music/Heartbeats*

White Winds / 1985 / Columbia ✦✦✦
This is a fantastic album of intricate compositions and moods. —*Paul Kohler*

Down to the Moon / 1986 / Columbia ✦✦✦✦
This is a masterpiece of beautiful melodies and rhythms from Vollenweider's electric harp. —*Paul Kohler*

Dancing with the Lion / 1989 / Columbia ✦✦✦
A recent release of Vollenweider's new age/jazz harp music is in a large-group setting. —*Paul Kohler*

The Trilogy / 1991 / CBS ✦✦✦
This excellent double-disc compilation contains the first three albums plus *Pace Verde* and half of *Eine Art Suite in 13 Teilen*. —*Paul Kohler*

Book of Roses / 1992 / CBS ✦✦✦
A multicultural tapestry, it combines symphonic, flamenco, African, and Eastern European elements with Vollenweider's characteristic "otherworldly" atmospheres and spirited pop rhythms. —*Linda Kohanov*

Eolian Minstrel / 1993 / ERG ✦✦

Eine Art Suite in 13 Teilen / Audion ✦✦✦
A rare import-CD from Switzerland, it features early material not found on any other release and is worth looking for. —*Paul Kohler*

Kit Watkins

Keyboards / Adult Alternative, Progressive Electronic, Ethnic Fusion
The Virginia-based keyboardist creates finely crafted music that always seems to straddle a handful of genres with ease. He was a founding member of the short-lived, yet highly original, progressive '70s band, Happy the Man. In the early '80s, Watkins began building his own home studio and produced consistently inviting music that draws on his first-rate keyboard skills and his keen ear for sonic detail. He has recently been exploring a darker, more ambient side with the release of his two *Thought Tones* albums, both of which are highly recommended. —*Linda Kohanov*

Thought Tones, Vol. 1 / 1990 / Linden Music ✦✦✦

Azure / 1990 / East Side Digital ✦✦✦
This truly eclectic brew includes progressive rock, classical, jazz, world, and ambient music. —*Michael P. Dawson*

● **Sunstruck** / 1990 / East Side Digital ✦✦✦✦
Kit Watkins has been at the forefront of keyboard-oriented music for a very long time. In the mid-'70s, he fronted the progressive rock band Happy the Man. With this release, Watkins again emerges as one of the most talented of keyboard maestros. *SunStruck* is really two releases in one. The first half is uptempo, driving, with stellar rhythms and accessible melodies, evoking Watkins' sense of his past. The second half is remarkably different, not merely dabbling, but rather mastering the genre of space music. What has always separated Watkins from his contemporaries is his unique synthesizer voicings. Besides using keyboards to mimic acoustic instruments, he creates electronic sounds full of breath and life, showing the grace of imperfection, reflecting the fragility of humanity, rather than striving for the absolute consistency available from electronic instruments. —*Backroads Music/Heartbeats*

Thought Tones, Vol. 2 / 1991 / Linden Music ✦✦✦✦
The second volume in Kit Watkins' *Thought Tones* series continues the exploration of mysterious, abstract soundscapes intended to assist "creative thinking, contemplation, imagination, and other forms of direct and indirect perception." While the first volume eschewed the use of synthesizers, *Volume 2* happily employs them, along with interactive soft-

ware and samplers that draw on the sounds of cars, hummingbirds, cats, sawblades, and wine glasses, as well as conventional instruments. —*Backroads Music/Heartbeats*

Sampler / Aug. 1991 / Linden Music ✦✦✦✦

☆ **Circle** / 1993 / Linden ✦✦✦✦✦

An hour of continuous environmental sound and quiet music, *Circle* was inspired by the surroundings of Watkin's home in Virginia's Blue Ridge mountains. A variety of natural sounds interlaced with subtle music. —*Backroads Music/Heartbeats*

Wind Machine

Adult Alternative, Chamber Jazz, New Acoustic, Contemporary Instrumental

Since its inception in 1986, Wind Machine has excelled at creating guitar-based music that dabbles in styles ranging from blues and bluegrass to jazz, rock, and new age atmospherics. Core members Steve Mesple, Joe Scott, and Blake Eberhard utilize a vast arsenal of instruments ranging from mandolin, dobro, banjo, and some of their own guitar-hybrid inventions to trombone, harmonica, and fretless bass. —*Linda Kohanov*

● **Rain Maiden** / 1985 / Silver Wave ✦✦✦✦

Wind Machine is a guitar-dominated band from Colorado consisting of Steve Mesple on acoustic guitars, Joe Scott on acoustic guitars and guitjos (a six- or seven-string Wind Machine permutation of the guitar), and Blake Eberhard on bass. Additional keyboards and percussion help produce a light, breezy, often shimmering sound, full of amazing guitar virtuosity and bouncy melodies. —*Backroads Music/Heartbeats*

Voices in the Wind / 1991 / Silver Wave ✦✦✦

These breezy instrumentals have an emphasis on contemporary jazz and folk influences. The production is crystal clear and as smooth as silk, which gives the group's upbeat originals a soothing quality. —*Linda Kohanov*

Change of Face / 1993 / Blue Meteor ✦✦

Sketches Of Christmas / 1993 / Blue Meteor ✦✦✦

This release combines beautiful original compositions with traditional songs, including Spanish, French, and Jewish pieces. In addition to zither, guitars, keyboards, bass, and percussion, many of the selections feature the music of the guitjo, a Wind Machine invention that has the bass strings of the guitar replaced with higher-pitched treble strings, giving the instrument a unique, harp-like sound. Two of the cuts are culled from the classical repertoire: Pachelbel's Canon and the Adagio, —*MusD*

Show of Hands / 1994 / Blue Meteor ✦✦✦

Pick a favorite guitar style: flatpicking, fingerpicking, jazz, swing, classical. *A Show of Hands* can offer a taste of each. Steve Mesple and Joe Scott are guitarists and co-founders of the group Wind Machine and instrumentalists par excellence. *A Show of Hands* is a collection of duets and solo pieces that exhibit their remarkable skill and dexterity, as well as their ear for the subtleties and intricacies in the sound of various guitar styles. It is amazing how much music two guitars, and two guitar masters, can make. —*MusD*

Road to Freedom / Silver Wave ✦✦✦

The twelve tunes range from sweet, serene songs of love to blistering acoustic frenzies. Several are tributes to various freedom fighters, both near and far, and the fervent feelings of the universal struggle for peace and justice are translated well through the music. —*Backroads Music/Heartbeats*

George Winston

Piano / Neo-Classical, Solo Instrumental

Though George Winston is one of the most popular solo pianists in the history of contemporary instrumental music, he didn't start playing until after high school. Inspired by blues, rock, and R&B styles, he initially gravitated toward the organ and electric piano. Then in 1971 he heard the records of legendary stride pianist Fats Waller, which motivated him to concentrate on the acoustic piano and develop his own style. After recording his first solo album, *Ballads and Blues*, in 1972, he stopped playing for several years. He eventually was encouraged to delve into the instrument again when he discovered the music of New Orleans R&B pianist Professor Longhair. In 1980 he released the first of four solo piano albums for the Windham Hill label. These became amazingly successful and helped create industry support for more pastoral forms of the instrumental music subsequently referred to as "new age." Winston's recording style combines his gift for impressionistic melodies with American folk influences; yet his live performances continue to reflect his longstanding interests in stride and blues piano styles as well. —*Linda Kohanov*

Ballads and Blues: 1972 / 1972 / Windham Hill ✦✦

☆ **Autumn** / 1980 / Windham Hill ✦✦✦✦✦

Winston's impressions of the fall season are full of slow chording and sudden melodic runs on his acoustic piano. He captures the mixed feel-

ings of the season, both its final flaring of life and its gradual retreat. —*William Ruhlmann*

★ **December** / 1982 / Windham Hill ✦✦✦✦✦

The mother of all solo instrumental albums, and with good reason. Mixing traditional carols with Pachelbel's Canon and a few originals, Winston produces a solo piano album of unparalleled—and undeniable—beauty. How can music be simultaneously stirring and soothing, relaxed yet exalted? Millions have found the answer here, and an industry has spent more than a decade trying to duplicate it. —*William Ruhlmann*

Winter into Spring / 1982 / Windham Hill ✦✦✦

In a sense, this second seasonal album follows an opposite direction from *Autumn*, its hard, isolated notes and stop-and-start style gradually giving way from the stasis of winter to the growth and movement of spring. It's a good album for beginning your day. —*William Ruhlmann*

Summer / 1991 / Windham Hill ✦✦✦

Forest / 1994 / Windham Hill ✦✦✦

Paul Winter (Paul Theodore Winter, Jr.)

b. Aug. 31, 1939, Altoona, PA
Sax (Alto), Sax (Soprano) / New Age, World Fusion

Environmental causes have been Paul Winter's concern as much, if not more than, music since the '70s. He's joined Greenpeace expeditions, recorded accompanying whales and wolves, and formed an organization linking environmental issues with musical concerns. Winter's music has never been among the more soulful, hard-edged, funky or bluesy; he's utilized improvisation but also incorporated elements from ethnic, European folk, symphonic/classical and other sounds that gradually became known as "new age" (now contemporary instrumental in some circles.) His alto and soprano sax playing is melodically enticing but seldom harmonically or rhythmically challenging. Winter founded the Paul Winter Sextet while a Northwestern University student. This group was a winner at the 1961 Intercollegiate Jazz Festival held at Notre Dame, where judges included John Hammond and Dizzy Gillespie. The group proved quite popular, and the State Department sponsored a Latin American tour for them in 1962. But five years later, Winter broke from a strict jazz sound with the Winter Consort, a band blending ethnic influences from Africa and Latin America, as well as Europe and America. Ralph Towner, Glen Moore, Collin Walcott, Paul McCandless, and David Darling at one time were all members, and the instrumentation included acoustic guitar, sitar, bass, cello, and oboe. But the Consort eventually disbanded, with its core members forming a similiar, even more successful band, Oregon. Winter has blended music and environmental politics throughout the '80s and '90s. He's recorded as a leader for Columbia, A&M, Epic, and Living Music. Winter has several sessions available on CD. —*Ron Wynn and Linda Kohanov*

★ **Icarus** / 1970 / Epic ✦✦✦✦✦

Classic, early new age ensemble music featuring vocals and a wide variety of instruments from around the world. Members of this consort eventually formed the highly acclaimed group Oregon. Brilliant musicianship and delightfully inventive composing. —*MusD*

★ **Common Ground** / 1977 / A&M ✦✦✦✦✦

This is a good example of Winter's nature-conscious music, as he has incorporated the sounds of birds, wolves, and humpback whales into his ensemble. It's surprising how close such wild animals come to playing pop music. —*William Ruhlmann*

Wintersong / 1979 / Living Music ✦✦✦

Dedicated to the spirit of giving and forgiving, this fine instrumental work includes traditional songs from Sweden, Italy, England, France, Germany, and the Appalachians as well as Bach's "Joy," and "Beautiful Star" by Odetta. —*Backroads Music/Heartbeats*

Callings / 1980 / Living Music ✦✦✦✦

Callings is a two-album set of the songs and compositions of Paul Winter's three-year expedition to Newfoundland, the Hebrides, Baja, the Bahamas, and California. The musicians on this digital recording are otters, beluga whales, and dolphins in harmony with oboe, soprano sax, cello, and pipe organ. This is truly radiant work. —*MusD*

Sun Singer / 1983 / Living Music ✦✦✦✦

On this striking example of Winter's lyricism, Paul Halley is on keyboards and Glen Velez plays frame drum and percussion. —*Linda Kohanov*

Concert for the Earth / 1985 / Living Music ✦✦✦

Celebrating the UN's 40th anniversary and recorded on World Environment Day, this album features the Consort, soprano vocalist Susan Osborn, seven guest artists, and the 80-voice Back Bay Chorale. —*Ladyslipper*

Canyon / 1985 / Living Music ✦✦✦✦

Half of the compositions for *Canyon* were recorded in the Grand Canyon, while the rest were recorded in St. John's Cathedral in New York.

The musicians are Paul McCandless, David Darling, Eugene Friesen, Glen Velez, Paul Halley, John Clark, and Oscar Castro-Neves. —*Backroads Music/Heartbeats*

Whales Alive! / 1987 / Living Music ✦✦✦
Whales Alive! is a deep, dynamic, and dramatic listening experience. Artist royalties from *Whales Alive!* are donated to the World Wildlife Fund for its efforts to preserve whales. —*Backroads Music/Heartbeats*

● **Wolf Eyes** / 1988 / Living Music ✦✦✦✦
This is a retrospective of Paul Winter's work from 1980-1988, featuring cuts from most of his albums of this period (not his two more specialized Whales Alive and *Wintersong*). Five of the tracks were recorded in the Cathedral of St. John the Divine in New York City, and three were recorded live in the General Assembly of the United Nations on World Environment Day in 1984, including a fine version of "Icarus," the longtime favorite from his repertoire. Winter's soprano sax is supported by his Consort and augmented by the voices of dolphins, birds, and wolves. —*Backroads Music/Heartbeats*

Earthbeat / 1988 / Living Music ✦✦✦
Billed as the album of original music created by Americans and Russians together, this album features Halley, Velez, guitarist Oscar Castro-Neves, and cellist Eugene Friesen collaborating on some selections with the Dmitri Pokrovsky Singers, a vocal ensemble rooted in the tradition of Russian village music. Traditional music from throughout Russia is mixed with Winter's Brazilian-influenced sound. There are also some beautiful instrumentals and, true to Winter's style, some natural sounds, most notably the calls of the Alaskan tundra wolf and Russian loon. —*Linda Kohanov*

Earth: Voices of a Planet / 1990 / Living Music ✦✦✦
Winter regulars and some special guest artists have put together a musical journey that starts in North America and travels through Africa, Antarctica, South America, Australia, Asia, and Europe. Selections feature indigenous nature sounds and traditional influences from various regions. —*Linda Kohanov*

Anthems / 1992 / Living Music ✦✦✦✦
Featuring Paul Halley, Eugene Friesen, and Winter himself, this anthology amply displays the tradition of interweaving diverse instruments and voices from different parts of the world. Mid-tempo and jazzy in parts, but consistently melodic, *Anthems* celebrates the people, places, creatures, and cultures of the Earth. With 17 tracks, the disc lasts 72 minutes. in all. —*Backroads Music/Heartbeats*

Paul Winter Consort

Sax (Alto), Sax (Soprano) / New Age, Hard Bop
For the past 30 years, Paul Winter has been following a steady path toward his ideal of creating what he calls "earth music," a vital celebration of the creatures and cultures of the planet. Much of that time has been spent touring the world with his influential Paul Winter Consort, which combines jazz, classical, Brazilian, and other ethnic influences with sounds from nature. Best known for his attempts to weave humpback whale songs and wolf cries into his music, Winter's desire to awaken listeners to the plight of endangered species has won him the World Wildlife Fund Award and the United Nations Global 500 Award, among other distinctions. *Earthbeat*, his collaboration with Moscow's Dmitri Pokrovsky Singers, became the first album to feature original music by Russians and Americans together. This project brought Winter international attention as a musical peacemaker and gained him the 1991 Peace Abbey "Courage of Conscience" Award. Musically, Winter's most admirable features include his soaring lyricism as a soprano saxophone soloist, his ability to surround himself with top-notch musicians, and his gift for weaving natural sounds and atmospheres into his music while retaining the spontaneous spirit associated with jazz. —*Linda Kohanov*

● **Winter Consort's Road** / 1969-1970 / A&M ✦✦✦✦

Icarus / Mar. 1973 / Epic ✦✦✦

Missa Gaia / Earth Mass / 1982 / Living Music ✦✦
On this two-album set, Paul Winter and the Paul Winter Consort with the chorus, choristers and pipe organ of the largest Gothic cathedral in the world, along with the voices of wolf, whale and loon, create a rhythmic, joyous, and contemporary celebration. —*MusD*

Wolff and Hennings

Ethnic Fusion, Ambient
The mystical sounds of Tibetan bells and singing bowls have been used for centuries in Buddhist meditation and religious rites. Henry Wolff and Nancy Hennings first encountered these instruments during a 1969 trip to India and Nepal where they studied with the Kagyu branch of Tibetan Buddhism. Since 1971 the duo has been releasing a subtle, haunting series of recordings featuring Tibetan bells, including a collaboration with Grateful Dead percussionist Mickey Hart called *Yamantaka*. Wolff

and Hennings also contributed their skills to the Philip Glass soundtrack for the film *Koyaanisqatsi*, which brought the transcendent sound of the bells to wider audiences. The uncanny resonances of these acoustic instruments produce music that often sounds electronically generated. —*Linda Kohanov*

● **Tibetan Bells 2** / 1978 / Celestial Harmonies ✦✦✦✦
While the duo creates its own compositions, this early album is closer in concept to the way these instruments are traditionally used. —*Linda Kohanov*

Tibetan Bells 3: The Empty Mirror / 1988 / Celestial Harmonies ✦✦✦
Tibetan Bells III: The Empty Mirror is another compelling album of purely acoustic Tibetan bell music. —*Linda Kohanov*

Yamantaka / Celestial Harmonies ✦✦✦
Grateful Dead drummer and world musicologist Mickey Hart's most ethereal work is on this collaboration with Wolff and Hennings. —*Linda Kohanov*

Eric Wollo

Guitar / Progressive Electronic, Ethnic Fusion, Ambient
Norwegian composer Erik Wollo started out as a jazz guitarist and dabbled in jazz-rock fusion on his early recordings. In 1984, however, he came out with *Traces*, an electronic album of startling originality. His most recent release is equally impressive. While there's always a sense of warmth to his atmospheric pieces, his music resounds with the stark beauty of Norway's wintry landscapes. Through his subtle minimalist patterns and nebulous breaths of sound, you can easily imagine the composer staring through windows splayed with ice crystals as Arctic winds whisper across the snow fields and ethereal northern lights pulse steadily in the distance. —*Linda Kohanov*

● **Traces** / 1984 / Badland ✦✦✦✦
Expansive synthesizer textures float over the slowly churning, hypnotic drives of sequencer patterns and primal rhythms on this collection of richly hued electronic dreamscapes. —*Linda Kohanov*

Images of Light / 1990 / Eurock ✦✦✦
This is another sublime set of Northern visions with a few darker, more experimental pieces. On "Urban Space," for instance, some gritty sampled saxophone undulations and long melodic lines successfully romanticize the cold, hard imagery of mechanized life. —*Linda Kohanov*

Danny Wright

Piano
The many recordings of keyboardist/composer Danny Wright are difficult to classify. He specializes in three distinct music styles: adult contemporary compositions, Broadway show tunes and movie themes, and classical music. His original compositions tend to be in the adult contemporary mode and are frequently inspired by classical composers such as Beethoven, Pachelbel, and Debussy as well as by such Broadway greats as Gershwin, Andrew Lloyd Webber, Jerome Kern, and Stephen Sondheim.

Wright was born and raised in Fort Worth, TX. He began playing piano at age four. He then studied classical piano under Dr. Harris Cavender for ten years. While studying, Wright demonstrated a gift for improvising in the exact style he was playing and he has used this talent for making each piece uniquely his. Later he won a full scholarship to Christian University, where he studied music education. He dropped out of school at 22 to begin his professional career. Wright began composing his own music in 1985. With Dori and Bob Nichols, he founded the label Nichols-Wright Records (later Moulin d'Or Recordings) to release his own albums.

He made his recording debut with *Black and White* (1986), which was first marketed to a select group of friends, relatives, and restaurant patrons. It took two years, but eventually the Nichols got local Dallas/Fort Worth radio stations to play Wright's songs. His second album, *Time Windows* (1987), was a showcase of Wright's compositions. This and the first were sold via mail order. By 1987 his albums were being distributed throughout North America. His third album, *Phantasys* (1988), became one of his most popular and also features Wright's own compositions. His 1992 album, *Autumn Dreams*, made it to the Top Ten on *Billboard's* Top Adult Alternative sales chart and stayed there for over six months, becoming one of the top new age albums of the year. As of the mid-'90s, Wright plays concerts all over the US, including benefits for such charitable organizations as the Children's Foundation and the Humane Society. —*Sandra Brennan*

● **Black and White** / 1986 / Moulin D'or ✦✦✦✦
This is Danny Wright's first release and features solo piano versions of a number of pop tunes. —*MusD*

Black and White 2 / 1989 / Nichols-Wright ✦✦✦✦
This is the sequel to *Black and White*, his very successful solo piano tape of popular show tunes. *Volume 2* continues in the same vein, with a couple of modern classical pieces by Debussy and Rachmaninoff mixed in with favorite tunes from Broadway musicals and movie soundtracks. Selections from *Porgy and Bess*, *Out of Africa*, *Phantom of the Opera*, and others, plus a fine version of "Moon River," are given his trademark romantic treatment. —*Backroads Music/Heartbeats*

Remembering Christmas / 1989 / Moulin D'or ✦✦✦
Danny Wright captures the feeling of the season with his flowing, patient piano style, while the use of synclavier broadens the musical capabilities, adding a classical, orchestrated sound to several of the pieces. The familiar tunes pour forth from this inspiring musician with sensitivity and warmth. —*Backroads Music/Heartbeats*

Shadows / 1990 / Moulin D'or ✦✦✦

Autumn Dreams / 1991 / Moulin D'or ✦✦✦
This album by the prolific Danny Wright is a meditation on the "dreams of changes . . . as well as warm memories of times past." Performing on a Steinway concert piano, Wright plays original compositions, all tender ballads glowing with warm introspection. There is no synthesizer backup here, but several of the pieces are graced by wistful violin, gentle oboe, and English horn. *Autumn Dreams* once again shows Wright to be a sensitive pianist and a master of sweet sentiment and nostalgic expressiveness. —*Backroads Music/Heartbeats*

Black and White Encore / 1991 / Nichols-Wright ✦✦✦✦
The third release in Danny Wright's extremely popular *Black and White* series once again offers a selection of tunes from Broadway musicals, movie soundtracks, and popular culture. —*Backroads Music/Heartbeats*

Just Wright for Christmas / 1992 / Moulin D'or ✦✦✦
Warm piano renditions of holiday songs, including "Silver Bells," "White Christmas," "Away in a Manger," and "O Little Town of Bethlehem." —*MusD*

Black and White Encore / Sep. 16, 1992 / Moulin D'or ✦✦✦
. . . This is a new release featuring sensational hits such as "On My Own" (*Les Miserables*), "Papa, Can You Hear Me?" (*Yentl*), "What I Did For Love" (*A Chorus Line*), the theme from *The Thorn Birds*, "Brian's Song," and many more. The song "Salute to Freedom" is a medley dedicated to the service men and women of our country, both past and present. —*MusD*

Day In The Life . . . / 1993 / Moulin D'or ✦✦✦✦
Neither a flamboyant improvisational exercise nor a rigidly structured presentation, it combines nice piano melodies, elaborate but not pompous or bombastic arrangements, and a modicum of synthesizer/electronic backing and orchestration. The 11 songs are short enough and arranged in such a manner that the suite feeling Wright seeks is maintained. The most interesting numbers are "Peace" and "Gabriel's Oboe," longer compositions with more musical variety and thematic contrast than the disc's shorter tunes. —*Ron Wynn*

Applause / Jan. 17, 1995 / Moulin D'or ✦✦

Yanni

Piano / Adult Alternative, Progressive Electronic
Yanni's grandiose keyboard style is both accessible and exciting, two elements that have led to his success in the realm of adult-alternative radio. His explosive, pop-influenced instrumentals and romantic pianistic ballads have also made him a popular touring and recording artist for the Private Music label. In addition to his original television, commercial, and film scores, Yanni's music has been used extensively on programs like *Wide World of Sports* and coverage of the Olympic Games. This aspect of his career seems especially appropriate when you consider that he achieved early success not as a musician, but as a member of the Greek National Swimming Team. (He broke the national freestyle record at age 14.) Born in Kalamata, Greece, Yanni arrived in the US after high school and obtained a degree in psychology from the University of Minnesota before diving headfirst into music. It didn't take long for the self-taught keyboardist and composer to establish himself as a studio musician, jingles composer and producer. After gaining an impressive cult following for his first independently released album, Yanni was picked up by Private Music and has become one of the label's best-selling artists. One of the most visible artists in the contemporary instrumental realm, Yanni's rise to fame was expedited in the early '90s by his romantic relationship with actress Linda Evans, which gained him coverage on mainstream programs like *Lifestyles of the Rich and Famous* as well as appearances on the daytime talk-show circuit. —*Linda Kohanov*

★ **Keys to Imagination** / 1986 / Private Music ✦✦✦✦✦
A masterpiece of dramatic synthesizer music. Yanni's music is lusty and brilliant, richly melodious and memorable, full of passion and life. One of the ultimate car-stereo albums. Yanni's flamboyant, superb style of composition makes *Keys to Imagination* some of the most extravagant, hyperspace music we know. —*Backroads Music/Heartbeats*

Out of Silence / 1987 / Private Music ✦✦✦
Recorded entirely on synthesizers at his home studio. The composer/performer makes extensive use of the orchestral possibilities of electronics, creating big themes to play across elaborate, echoing rhythm tracks. Unlike much adult alternative music, it's constantly stimulating foreground music with an extremely modern sound. —*William Ruhlmann*

Chameleon Days / 1988 / Private Music ✦✦✦
With *Chameleon Days*, Yanni again explores new and fascinating rhythms, while maintaining the same balance between high-energy space-cruisers and gorgeous, evocative ballad-like slower pieces. —*Backroads Music/Heartbeats*

Optimystique / 1989 / Private Music ✦✦

Niki Nana / 1989 / Private Music ✦✦✦
Yanni takes a more overtly pop approach here, adding other musicians and vocalists (on the title track) and even playing in dance rhythms, so what was always an engaging style of music becomes more accessible to a wider audience. —*William Ruhlmann*

● **Reflections of Passion** / May 15, 1990 / Private Music ✦✦✦✦
Here are 15 romantic songs from Yanni's five earlier releases, plus three new songs recorded especially for this album. Much of *Reflections of Passion* is from *Niki Nana* and *Chameleon Days*, while his two earliest are represented by only one cut each, and the tempos vary from the slower, dramatic pieces to his unique "rocket-fuel" style, full of dazzling cross-rhythms and intricate development. —*Backroads Music/Heartbeats*

In Celebration of Life / 1991 / Private Music ✦✦✦✦
A strong collection of pieces from four of Yanni's earlier albums, plus "Song for Antarctica," composed for the *Polar Shift* compilation. The focus is on drama, power, and passion, common elements throughout his music. —*Backroads Music/Heartbeats*

Dare to Dream / 1992 / Private Music ✦✦✦
Dare to Dream was his first new music in three years. He seems to have slowed down and become less extravagant in his intricate development and rhythms. Beyond the overall beauty of the new pieces, special attention is likely to go to "Aria," an inspired vocal piece co-conceived by Yanni and Malcolm McLaren. —*Backroads Music/Heartbeats*

In My Time / 1993 / Private Music ✦✦✦
Yanni's latest is another extension of his creative spirit and stirring passion for life. Focusing on piano as his primary instrument, Yanni infuses his "signature" style with timeless, eloquent themes and plenty of romantic energy. No longer are rhythm and dynamic currents as vital to his sound, since he seems to have stopped fueling his music with "rocket power." His romantic outpourings lend a personal nature to *In My Time*, and this new effort should be received with enthusiasm far and wide. Yanni is uniquely expressive, and this new music is deeply touching on many levels. —*Backroads Music/Heartbeats*

Yanni Live at the Acropolis / Sep. 1993 / Private Music ✦✦✦✦
Live at the Acropolis is Yanni at his broadest, fullest sound ever. This much-awaited live album is a collection of his now-classic compositions that have redefined the traditional symphony experience. The collection includes "Santorini," "Keys to the Imagination," and "Reflections of Passion." Yanni's own passionate sound is counterpoint to the refined fullness of the Royal Philharmonic Concert Orchestra. This is a recording of his first homeland concert. All the energy and all the passion of a live concert are here. —*MusD*

Yas-Kaz

Percussion / Progressive Electronic, Ethnic Fusion
A university-trained percussionist, Japanese artist Yasukazu Sato gained attention for his international tours as composer for the innovative dance group Sankaijuku. His unusual combination of ancient Oriental forms, spacious musical atmospheres, and ceremonial percussion provided perfect accompaniment to the ritualistic movements and slowly unfolding acrobatic feats of this modern Japanese dance company. He has also scored several award-winning Japanese films, performed with American jazz saxophonist Wayne Shorter and Japanese synthesist Himekami, and recorded a number of imaginative solo albums. —*Linda Kohanov*

★ **Darkness in Dreams** / 1991 / Kuckuck ✦✦✦✦✦
Compiled from six of his finest recordings, these selections illustrate the composer's gift for translating fantasy into sonic reality. Each cut is a world in itself, in which luminous zither cascades and tribal percussion tracks alternate with joyous folk dances and oriental melodies for full string orchestra that soar over waves of synthesized sequencer patterns. A good introduction to the varied moods of Yas-Kaz (most of his recordings are rare Japanese imports). —*Linda Kohanov*

Various Artists

American Gramophone Sampler #1 / 1987 / American Gramophone ✦✦✦

American Gramaphone Samplers No.1 & No.2 feature a number of selections from Mannheim Steamroller's *Fresh Aire* series as well as pieces by other American Gramaphone mainstays like Eric Hansen, Ron Cooley, and Checkfield. —*Linda Kohanov*

Anthems / 1992 / Living Music ✦✦✦✦✦

In celebration of the label's tenth anniversary, Living Music has brought together music from 18 of the 22 albums in its catalog, featuring Eugene Friesen, Oscar Castro Neves, Glen Velez, Paul Halley, Russia's Dmitri Pokrovsky Singers, and of course, the label's founder, Paul Winter. Though Living Music has two other samplers on the market, *Anthems: Ten Years of Living Music* is by far the most comprehensive. —*Linda Kohanov*

Au-Del Du Rubicon (Beyond Rubicon) / 1994 / ✦✦✦

A host of fine space music artists from Canada, plus the prolific Steve Roach, make up the 77 minutes of this excellent anthology. Spacey and melodic pieces offer a veritable treasure of sounds, from the acoustic touch of Daniel Blanchet to upbeat cruisers by Serge Laporte and the space drift of Francois Kiraly. The ten-minute track by Steve Roach, "Full Moon Prophesy," is not on any of his releases. Stately, visceral, occasionally solemn, and always intelligent, this sampler is a superb intro to this style of music. —*Backroads Music/Heartbeats*

Changing Woman / Changing Woman ✦✦✦

This 1992 collection of women's spirituality songs and chants is performed by three women, Lou Montgomery, Adele Getty, and Rebecca Hyde-Skeele (some will recognize Getty from her work with Acoustic Medicine), with drumming accompaniment. Their material includes originals by Montgomery and Getty, as well as Starhawk, Brooke Medicine Eagle, and others. It includes "Power of a Woman," "Woman of Radiance," "Dance of the Moon and Sun," and "Our Magic Is Our Giveaway." There are 13 in all, and lyrics are included, making this an excellent source of material for circles. —*Ladyslipper*

A Childhood Remembered / 1991 / Narada ✦✦✦

Nancy Rumbel, Trapezoid, Carol Nethan, David Arkenstone, David Lanz, Eric Tingstad, and other Narada artists created original compositions specially for this tribute to the wonder of childhood. This magical collection of refined music for adults evokes images and memories, and calls to the child within each of us. All selections are based on renowned works of children's literature . . . and the CD comes with a beautiful 32-page booklet with illustrations from the 12 books that inspired the music, making it an especially good buy. It includes "Maria Morevna" and "The Dragon's Daughter." —*Ladyslipper*

● **A Door in the Air** / 1991 / Echodiscs ✦✦✦✦

Like the Hearts of Space record label, Echodiscs is the offshoot of a widely syndicated contemporary instrumental radio program—in this case, "Echoes" (Box 224, Eagle, PA 19480). The company's first release is a collection of noteworthy recordings made especially for broadcast. These "Living Room Concerts" are captured in the homes of the artists by "Echoes" producer and host John Diliberto. *A Door in the Air* offers a sampling of his favorites by Robert Rich, Stein & Walder, Arco Iris, Michael Brook, David Torn, and Steve Roach. —*Linda Kohanov*

● **Erdenklang Music Sampler, Vol. 2** / 1992 / Erdenklang ✦✦✦✦

This German label has an extensive roster of European contemporary instrumental artists with an emphasis on electronic music (both pop-oriented and progressive). *Magic Age II* is the second in a series that features evocative pieces of a more ambient nature, including some previously unreleased material from Peeter Vahi, Hector Zazou, Blue Chip Orchestra, and Lightwave, among others. —*Linda Kohanov*

● **Fruits of Our Labor: Global Pacific Sampler** / 1986 / Rhino ✦✦✦✦

The Global Pacific label's first sampler, *Global Pacific—The Fruits of Our Labor*, features the early work of artists like Steve Kindler, Ben Tavera King, Paul Greaver, and Bob Kindler, among others. —*Linda Kohanov*

Global Pacific: Global Voyage / 1988 / Rhino ✦✦✦✦

These selections from popular Global Pacific recordings include Paul Horn, David Friesen, Georgia Kelly, Bob Kindler, Do'ah, Steve Kindler, and Teje Bell. —*Linda Kohanov*

Gramavision 10th Anniversary Sampler / 1990 / Gramavision ✦✦✦

An occasionally interesting cross-section of label cuts assembled to show diversity over a decade of Gramavision titles. —*Ron Wynn*

Guitar Fingerstyle / Jun. 18, 1996 / Narada ✦✦✦✦

Narada's *Guitar Fingerstyle* presents a collection of the label's progressive new age, bluegrass, folk, and country guitarists who all believe they are exploring new avenues of guitar playing. Some of the musicians do come up with distinctive, fresh textures but just as many recycle old ideas professionally. Nevertheless, fans of mellow guitar music should

seek this out—there are some genuinely talented artists buried on the collection. —*Thom Owens*

Harvest Moon / 1994 / ✦✦✦

Harvest Moon features three gifted yet very different proponents of the harp. Kim Robertson, Michelle Sell, and Carlos Reyes play, in turn, Celtic harp, classical and folk harp, and Paraguayan harp. Each has five tracks, all solo; they flow perfectly one into the next, from O'Carolan to Debussy, with Reyes' original compositions providing several highlights. For harp fans of any background this is a winner, right down to the catchy Sugo artwork. —*Backroads Music/Heartbeats*

● **Hearts of Space: Cruisers 1.0** / 1988 / Hearts of Space ✦✦✦✦

Produced in the tradition of the "Music from the Hearts of Space" syndicated radio show, *Cruisers 1.0* is a tightly programmed musical journey in which selections by various artists flow in and out of each other almost seamlessly over the course of an hour—an effect more akin to a "soundtrack for the mind" than a label sampler. Don Harriss, Gershon Kingsley, Klaus Schonning, Michael Stearns, and Ken Stover are featured on these gently rhythmic pieces. —*Linda Kohanov*

Hearts of Space: Sampler '90 / 1990 / Hearts of Space ✦✦✦✦

While the previous *Hearts of Space* collections featured music from other labels, the *Universe Sampler '90* is the first compilation of artists signed to the Hearts of Space record company (which grew out of the radio program). Music is by Kevin Braheny, Bill Douglas, Constance Demby, Raphael, and others. —*Linda Kohanov*

● **Hearts of Space: Starflight 1** / 1986 / Hearts of Space ✦✦✦✦

Also originally produced for the popular weekly radio show, the overall feeling of this album is quite different than *Cruisers 1.0*. The ten lush, ambient pieces featured are taken from albums by Michael Amerlan, Tim Clark, and Steve Roach. —*Linda Kohanov*

☆ **Imaginary Landscapes: New Electronic Music** / Elektra/Nonesuch ✦✦✦✦

Contains Ron Kuivila, "Loose Canons" (excerpt); Shelly Hirsch and David Weinstein, "On the Swing" (an excerpt from "Pomp and Circumstances") ; Neil B. Rolnick, "Balkanization" (excerpt); Mark Trayle, "Simple Degradation (Border)"; Gordon Monahan, "Speaker Swinging" (excerpt); Laetitia deCompiegne Sonami, "What Happened"; Maryanne Amacher, "Stain –The Music Rooms" (excerpt); Alvin Lucier, "Music for Alpha Waves, Assorted Percussion and Automated Code Relays"; David Tudor, "Dialects" (excerpt) / Nicolas Collins, "Real Electronic Music" ; Voice Crack, "A Spoonful of Tea in a Barrel Full of Honey" (excerpt); Christian Marclay, "Black Stucco"; "Blue" Gene Tyranny, "Somewhere in Arizona 1970," for baritone and electronics. Seventy minutes of some of the best and most innovative of new electronic music of varied idiosyncratic approaches. —*"Blue" Gene Tyranny*

Inner Landscapes / 1991 / Clear Productions ✦✦✦✦

The best and most recent Clear Productions venture includes selections by Kit Watkins, John Serrie, Laraaji, and Steve Roach, among others. —*Linda Kohanov*

Kalama: A Sufi Song of Love / Spring Hill ✦✦✦

This 1990 release carries the extended chant to a new level of complexity, with 48 tracks and 32 separate lines of choral music, while maintaining the stunning simplicity which creates wholeness and peace in the listener. Sides one and two are mixed differently; the first side, "Remembrance," is gentler, more ambient; side two's "Celebration" features more variation, faster transitions and some intense male chanting. Sufism is a native Middle Eastern mysticism which stresses the underlying unity of all traditions. —*Ladyslipper*

● **Looking East: Hungary** / 1991 / Erdenklang ✦✦✦✦

The unexpected opening of the Iron Curtain has recently given birth to Erdenklang's collections of synthesizer music from Eastern European countries. This album offers an evocative cross-section of pop, cross-cultural, and avant-garde electronic composers who have never before been heard in the West. It is a noteworthy achievement. —*Linda Kohanov*

The Narada Wilderness Collection / 1990 / Narada ✦✦✦

Although Narada has released numerous samplers over the years, this Wisconsin-based label has become the leader in producing engaging thematic albums. The *Narada Wilderness Collection* features impressionistic works by company staples like David Arkenstone, Spencer Brewer, Tingstad and Rumbel, Peter Buffett, David Lanz, and others. The extensive CD booklet includes a statement from each artist about the specific landscape that inspired his or her piece, as well as stunning nature photography to go along with it. —*Linda Kohanov*

● **Narada: Alma Del Sur** / 1992 / Narada ✦✦✦✦

One of Narada's classiest packages yet, *Alma Del Sur* is a showcase for contemporary South American music by Argentinian multi-instrumentalist Bernardo Rubaja, Brazilian flutist and percussionist Junior Homrich, Bolivian panpipe virtuoso Gonzalo Vargas (accompanied by the North American band Ancient Future), Paraguayan harpist Roberto Perera, and the Bolivian ensemble Rumillajta, among others. Liner notes include exquisite photos of traditional artwork and overviews of South American history and music, as well as biographies of the artists. Don't be misled into thinking this is a collection of traditional music, however. It is instead a survey of modern styles palatable to a wide variety of listeners. —*Linda Kohanov*

Narada: A Childhood Remembered / 1991 / Narada ✦✦✦
Twelve Narada artists were commissioned to compose pieces inspired by favorite works of children's literature, each colorfully illustrated in storybook fashion in the CD booklet. —*Linda Kohanov*

● **Polar Shift** / 1991 / Earth Sea ✦✦✦✦✦
This benefit for Antarctica includes songs from Enya, Yanni, John Tesh, Paul Sutin, Vangelis, Chris Spheeris, Jim Chappeil, Paul Voudouris, Steve Howe, Constance Demby, Kitaro, and Suzanne Ciani. —*AMG*

The Private Music Sampler 1988 / Private Music ✦✦✦
As Private Music moves more and more towards the mainstream, it is gratifying to see that they haven't lost their competitive cutting edge. This latest version of their periodic label samplers includes just five artists or groups, each with the ability to stretch musical boundaries and incorporate a myriad of elements into their expression. Yanni has two cuts from *Reflections of Passion*, while the accomplished German trio Tangerine Dream has a pair from *Melrose*. Interspersed are two each from *Charming Snakes* by Andy Summers, formerly guitarist with the Police, and Patrick O'Hearn's wild and crazy *Mix Up*, plus one scintillating tune from *The Odd Get Even* by Shadowfax. Though the label's popularity and recognition grows by leaps and bounds, their mainstream success has not diverted their mission of offering a roster of artists who strive for consistently unusual and memorable sounds culled from a wonderful range of styles and backgrounds. —*Backroads Music/Heartbeats*

The Private Music Sampler, Vol. 5 / 1990 / Private Music ✦✦✦
A more recent sampler, it features selections by artists like Yanni, Tangerine Dream, Andy Summers, and Patrick O'Hearn. —*Linda Kohanov*

● **Raven: A Sampler** / 1991 / Raven ✦✦✦✦✦
This is an eclectic sampling of the recordings released on the small New Jersey-based company, Raven Recording, including music by the label's founder and main artist Gabrielle Roth as well as pieces by Matt Balitsaris, Nicholas, and Raphael. —*Linda Kohanov*

Songs of Pagan Folk / Circle ✦✦✦
Thirteen songs and chants are here, including "Isis Invocation," "Healer Song," "Circle Round," and other songs about neo-paganism, Wicca, goddess cultures, feminist spirituality, etc. —*Ladyslipper*

● **Surreality Sampler** / ✦✦✦✦✦
Here is an ear-opening tour by the U's top electronic synthesists, conceived and compiled by Surreal to Real label. The cast includes Mark Shreeve, Ian Boddy, and John Dyson, formerly of Wavestar, as well as many upcoming prospects such as Tranceport, Stephan Whitlan, Waveform, and six others. Most of the tracks are previously unreleased. Boddy's power-packed "Drive" gets things going. Then "The Journeyman (Long Walk)," a bluesy, mind-bending excursion by Tranceport, winds into a snake like rhythm. The popular Glyn Lloyd-Jones offers the dreamiest and most serene piece, "Xiological Sky," which leads to the closing "Time-Node," the epic live anthem by John Dyson and friends. You'll hear awesome synth-rock with varying degrees of reward and staying power. —*Backroads Music/Heartbeats*

Universe Sampler 90 / 1990 / Hearts of Space ✦✦✦✦✦
A beautifully conceived release with high grades for packaging, sequence, song selection, and price, this is the first sampler from Hearts of Space—with over 70 minutes of 1989-90 highlights and recent cuts

from Rich/Roach and Al Gromer Khan, as well as Tyndall, Demby, Douglas and the whole gang. The Geoffrey Chandler cover painting becomes, for CD buyers, a mini-poster of epic proportions. —*Backroads Music/Heartbeats*

Visionaries / 1989 / Clear Productions ✦✦✦✦✦
Clear Productions (1489 Coddington Rd., Brooktondale, NY 14817) occasionally puts out admirable collections of work by independent artists. Often these pieces are commissioned especially for the project rather than taken from previously released albums. This particular recording features new age synthesist Iasos, hammered-dulcimer virtuoso Dan Duggan, and pianist Richard Shulman, among others. —*Linda Kohanov*

Windham Hill Sampler '89 / 1985 / Windham Hill ✦✦✦
Sampler '92 is the newest release of Windham Hill's successful sampler series, another inspired testimony to the development of this pioneering label. From Michael Manring, Michael Hedges, and Mark Isham, to Liz Story, Philip Aaberg, Nightnoise and label founder Will Ackerman, the 12 cuts showcase a variety of contemporary musical expressions from the label's most popular artists. —*Backroads Music/Heartbeats*

Windham Hill Sampler '92 / Sep. 10, 1991 / Windham Hill ✦✦✦
This is a taste of the most recent work from label mainstays like Michael Manring, Alex de Grassi, Nightnoise, Michael Hedges, Mark Isham, Montreux, David Torn, Liz Story, Modern Mandolin Quartet, Phil Aaberg, and Will Ackerman. —*Linda Kohanov*

Windham Hill Sampler '94 / 1994 / Windham Hill ✦✦✦
Featuring several of the label's biggest stars, *Windham Hill Sampler '94* is a good portrait of the new age label's mid-'90s roster and has very few weak moments. —*Stephen Thomas Erlewine*

● **Windham Hill: First Ten Years** / 1990 / Windham Hill ✦✦✦✦✦
Windham Hill has put out so many samplers that it can be confounding to choose one over another. This double CD, however, features a selection or two from just about everyone who has ever recorded for the *main* label (not the Windham Hill jazz or singer-songwriter divisions). This is a comprehensive overview of the contemporary instrumental sound for which the company is most famous. —*Linda Kohanov*

Windham Hill: Soul of . . . / 1987 / Windham Hill ✦✦✦✦✦
Windham Hill's *Soul of the Machine* collection of contemporary electronic and electro-acoustic music primarily features little-known artists, many of whom are not signed to the label: Michael Foreman, Fred Simon, Michael Whiteley, Schoenherz and Scott, Colin Chin, Philippe Saisse, Mark Darnell, Tim Story, Roy Finch, Ted Greenwald, Scott Hiltzik. —*Linda Kohanov*

● **Yi-ching Music for Health: Regimen** / ✦✦✦✦✦
Do not let the prosaic album title fool you; contained within is 50 minutes of truly lovely Chinese orchestral music, designed to harmonize the body, emotions, and mind. For millennia the Chinese have been aware of the healing properties of music, but in recent years research has thrown new light on the relationship between music and the medical and philosophical model of the Five Element system. *Regimen* is the outcome of this study, a collaboration between medical researchers and leading Chinese composers. Two long tracks offer sweeping melodies performed by the Shanghai Racial Music Troupe, featuring shimmering strings, soaring flute, piping reeds, massed lutes, tuned bells, and assorted percussion. Designed to balance all five of the elements within the listener, *Regimen* is an uplifting album that does indeed have a calming and inspiring effect. Besides *Regimen*, there are five other titles in the series, each addressing one of the five elements. The entire series may also be purchased in a box set. —*Backroads Music/Heartbeats*

AVANT GARDE

Categories are at best relative, and this is especially true in avant garde music. In this section, you'll find music made with stones and symphony orchestras, home-built computers and the unadorned human voice. The subjects are diverse—from personal political concerns to meditations on natural phenomena. Of course there are innovations in all genres of music. What these pieces have in common are composers who pursued unique visions intertwined with their lives—composers whose works have a deep conceptual component. This may be born in the quiet of the night, in sudden insights, in desires to go beyond prescribed behavior and the usual outcomes of circumscribed fate, in surprising social interactions, in contact with ancient cultural and religious traditions, and in many other life experiences. The works that result go beyond any recognized categories, and help enchance our sensitivity to both physical and imaginary worlds (both of which are "real" because, after all, we do the imagining).

The wide range of musical invention includes:

(1) pattern music, that gradually evolves over a steady pulse into complex and changing forms (incidentally mimicking natural processes such as the "divine proportion" patterns of the chambered nautilus, or the splitting of an amoeba (for example, the pieces of Terry Riley, Steve Reich, Tom Johnson, John Adams, Philip Glass, Jon Gibson);

(2) music which takes single sounds and other elements from pop music's song forms and formally expands on them to make music of universal vision (Glenn Branca, the Residents, Rhys Chatham);

(3) music employing chance procedures (sometimes called "aleatory" which is actually a limited special case of chance operations) that produce the unexpected at every moment for performer, listener and even composer—compositions are often described as indeterminate of their "realization" (a one-time performance like sand paintings erased after a particular ceremony, with the basic tradition or score remaining until the next realization); this music gives the performer both greater responsibility and freedom, and encourages us to fully experience the myriad events of every moment outside and inside ourselves, a sort of "ecology of the mind" (John Cage, Earle Brown, Christian Wolff, Morton Feldman, Marcel Duchamp); in a very real sense, this music is not "about" something, but is that "thing" itself;

(4) music based on psychoacoustic illusions and natural phenomena—brainwaves, sonic blasts from sand dunes, chaotic vibrations, a plant's apparent response to emotional even telepathic stimuli (the Backster Effect used in Tom Zahuranec's) unrecorded *Plant Music* of 1972), a bat's echolocation sense, whistling "sferics" from outer space, analogues of brain systems, shadowing and intense amplification of environmental sound, and much more (Alvin Lucier, Maryanne Amacher, Paul De Marinis, David Tudor, Maggi Payne, Annea Lockwood, "Blue" Gene Tyranny, Hildegard Westerkamp);

(5) compositions for home-built and composer-built instruments (Harry Partch, David Behrman, Fast Forward, Ellen Fullman);

(6) sound-installations and other pieces designed to happen in places other than the usual concert halls (Ron Kuivila, Bill Fontana, Gordon Monahan);

(7) music in alternate tunings that creates new sensations of hearing (Ben Johnston, Ivan Wyschnegradsky, LaMonte Young) and music that explores new ways of playing traditional instruments (Malcolm Goldstein, Guy Klucevsek, Joseph Celli, Jin Hi Kim);

(8) unique approaches to melody, harmony and rhythm, and to traditional music (Alan Hovhaness, Virgil Thomson, Peter Garland, Toshio Hosokawa, Toru Takemitsu, Moondog), including what could be called "the downtown sound" where pop/world/techno/folk/concert sounds have all become part of the general vocabulary, not "collaged" in some artificial way but a result of the musicians having grown up hearing and playing these musics (Lenny Pickett, Peter Gordon, John Zorn);

(9) New Narrative opera with its political, humanitarian and spiritual concerns, text-sound pieces, and other unusual uses of language and the voice (Robert Ashley, Kenneth Atchley, Beth Anderson, Ben Neill, Mikel Rouse, Lars Gunnar-Bodin, Joan LaBarbara, Christopher Butterfield, Gregory Whitehead, Carlos Santos);

(10) deeply meditative music of an altered and expanded time sense (Lois Vierk, Phill Niblock, Eliane Radique, Pauline Oliveros, Jerry Hunt);

(11) unique "crossover" pieces from jazz, rock, etc. (Ornette Coleman's} "Skies of America," Lou Reed's} "The Amino Ring"),

(12) super-formalist pieces, even by academics who are even seen by their fellows as somewhat out of the fold (Stefan Wolpe, Jean Barraqui, Milton Babbitt, Elliott Carter, Iannis Xenakis);

(13) the whole array of electronic and tape music—generated by digital computers (John Chowning, Joel Chadabe, James Tenney, Larry Polansky, Joel Ryan, David Rosenboom) by analog synthesizers (Sun Ra, Walter Carlos, Morton Subotnick), "musique concrite" made with manipulation of tape speed and editing (also sound accumulation by covering the erase head, delay by multiple tape loops, etc., pioneers like Pierre Henry, Vladimir Ussachevsky), "live electronic" performance and interactive performance with acoustic instruments and voices (the Bifurcators, John Cage, David Tudor, Max Neuhaus, Gordon Mumma, Karlheinz Stockhausen, Rochard Teitelbaum), sampling of acoustic and electronic sounds and modulating them with waveshaping synthesis etc.—including the outrageous "plunderphonics" cultural commentaries of John Oswald} and others—computer-controlled installations and acoustic instruments, electronically-amplified instruments and environmental sounds, live computer music (Jim Horton, John Bischoff, the Hub) and much more;

(14) collective improvisation and group "process"/"procedural" work (the Deep Listening Band, Machine for Making Sense, Cornelius Cardew} and the Scratch Orchestra, Yankees, Jacques Bekaert); and, of course,

(15) composer/performers and their pieces that can be described as employing several of the techniques, aesthetics and influences mentioned above.—*"Blue" Gene Tyranny*

John Adams

An American minimalist composer who is known for *Nixon in China.* —*AMG*

Shaker Loops (1978) / In LCO 8 (London Chamber Orchestra) "Minimalist" / 1990 / New Albion ♦♦♦
An exceptionally good performance: rushing, trembling sounds represent the practices of the utopian religious sect the Shakers and also the musical "shake." The two lovely inner movements, "Hymning Slews" and "Loops and Verses," are Adams' best harmonic writing—a lot of activity for so-called "minimal" music. —*"Blue" Gene Tyranny*

Harmonielehre / 1993 / EMI Classics ♦♦♦
City of Birmingham Symphony Orchestra, conducted by S. Rattle. A bright, spirited performance of this intriguing work by Adams, a thrill-

ing study in new harmonies and orchestral textures. One of Adams' finest scores. —*"Blue" Gene Tyranny*

Maryanne Amacher

Composer / Psychoacoustic Experimental

Stain—The Music Rooms/ In "Imaginary Landscapes" / 1989 / Elektra/ Nonesuch ✦✦✦✦
Amacher has created some of the finest pieces and sound-installations based on psychoacoustic illusions. Until the advent of CDs, most of her work was unrecordable, partly because of the extreme ranges of pitch and dynamics, the duration of the piece necessary to create some illusions, and the stability of the medium. The "music rooms" are literally that—installed on floors of a house or in adjacent rooms that the audience walks through to create their own mix from enormously amplified environmental and electronic sounds. —*"Blue" Gene Tyranny*

Beth Anderson

b. 1950
Composer / Modern Song, Political
Very original composer in a variety of forms and musical styles, including textsound and tape pieces. —*"Blue" Gene Tyranny*

● **Torero Piece (1973) / In "10 + 2 — 12 American Text Sound Pieces"** / 1974 / 1750 Arch Street Records ✦✦✦✦
This unfortunately not-yet-reissued disc contains this duet for the composer and her mother in which the mother describes her relationship to her daughter while the daughter makes unrelated phonemic sounds decoded from a paint-by-number picture she found in a junk antique store. An imaginative and drolly humorous piece by this very original composer who is also known for her opera about Queen Christina. —*"Blue" Gene Tyranny*

Revel (1981/1984) / 1984 / Opus One ✦✦✦
Performed by the Richmond Symphony, conducted by Jacques Houtman. New romantic music that combines rock harmony and an interest in world music. —*"Blue" Gene Tyranny*

Jorge Antunes

b. 1942
Composer / Electronic, Political
Musica Electronica / Joias Musicais ✦✦✦
This is the first electronic music made in Brazil. Antunes is a wonderful composer who constructed the Center for Chomo-Musical Research in Rio de Janeiro and thereby became the first composer of electronic music in his country. "Valso Sideral" (1962) and "Contrapunctus Contra Contrapunctus" (1965) are early uses of patterning in "rhythmic cells" where the rhythms are gradually distorted. In "Cintra Cita" (1969) the composer has a "bande rendezvous" (tape meeting) with himself over materials and chance rhythms and thoughts used throughout his work. The fascinating "Auto-Retrato sonre Paisaje Porteno" (1969) used a scratch in an old 78 rpm record played on a wind-up phonograph as the basic rhythmic element for the construction of an electronically modified samba where the words are inflected by the composer's voice and lose all actual meaning. "Historia de un Pueblo" (1970) is a dramatic work alternating between sweet persuasion and aggression, a not explicitly narrrative story that can nevertheless be understood by anyone. —*"Blue" Gene Tyranny*

Robert Ashley

b. Mar. 28, 1930, Ann Arbor, MI
Composer / New Narrative Opera, Electronic
In the past 15 years, Robert Ashley, influential for several decades as both a composer and writer, has created a series of operas-for-TV that speak on many levels of the lives of the people that constitute present-day America. —*"Blue" Gene Tyranny*

She Was a Visitor / In "Extended Voices" / 1968 / Odyssey ✦✦✦
The Brandeis University Chamber Chorus, conducted by Alvin Lucier. Describes musically how "rumor" is spread among people, with leaders of a group selecting phonemes of the chanted line "She was a visitor" and the group sustaining each individual sound. The amassed sound, a "surface" of normalized little disturbances, in which an audience could also participate, begins to resemble airplanes, cars, trains—or perhaps the subatomic world. —*"Blue" Gene Tyranny*

Music with Roots in the Aether / 1980 / Lovely Music ✦✦✦
The legendary 14-hour videotape series (seven two-hour programs) with interviews and performances by post-serial, post-Cage composers David Behrman, Philip Glass, Alvin Lucier, Gordon Mumma, Pauline Oliveros, Terry Riley and Robert Ashley. Not mere MTV or PBS, the series is actually a "music-theater piece in color video" that finds new ways to show music being performed in highly unusual, visually exciting and continuous-shot (uncut) approaches. —*"Blue" Gene Tyranny*

Music Word Fire and I Would Do It Again: The Lessons / 1981 / Lovely Music ✦✦✦
Available now in its full videotape form. Robert Ashley, Jill Kroesen, and David Van Tieghem (vocals), with prepared piano solos improvised by "Blue" Gene Tyranny, and instrumental and vocal percussion by Van Tieghem. "This may be the first—dazzling—use of variation form in rock and roll" (Gregory Sandow, *The Village Voice*). —*"Blue" Gene Tyranny*

Atalanta (Acts of God) / 1985 / Lovely Music ✦✦✦
The three-LP vinyl set from the Italian performance of this innovative opera. Atalanta, the princess who was discarded by her family and raised by animals to become the fastest-running human, is later reclaimed by her father in order to marry her off for dynastic purposes. She is approached by three characters from the 20th century whose personalities are presented in stories and anecdotes as they are considered for the role of the "successful suitor." These are Max Ernst, the surrealist painter, William Reynolds, shaman storyteller (and, incidentally, a relative of Ashley's), and Bud Powell, the famed composer-pianist. These men also represent three aspects of the opera: image, narrative, and music. Each approaches Atalanta with specific arias: the Odalisque arias remind her of her excellence, the Character Reference arias recommend to her characteristics of excellence in men, and the Anecdotes are sung for her amusement. A brilliant work full of subtle insights and humor. —*"Blue" Gene Tyranny*

Yellow Man with Heart with Wings (1978) / 1990 / Lovely Music ✦✦✦
An inspired prose-poem in Spanish and English about agriculture and other perspectives and feelings that occur to people in cities and to those who live outside cities. Heart-lifting. —*"Blue" Gene Tyranny*

★ **Perfect Lives** / 1991 / Lovely Music ✦✦✦✦✦
Available in CD and videotape, *Perfect Lives* is part of a trilogy of operas-for-TV including *Atalanta (Acts of God)* and *Now Eleanor's Idea* (a total of 39 half-hour episodes). *Perfect Lives* was realized for Channel Four of British Television. In this epic work set in the American Midwest, the rhythms of the music, the geometry of the scenes, the relations of the characters all seem to be from the same cloth, as if being described by the martyred first natural scientist Giordano Bruno, who is a "background" character never appearing in this work. For the characters who do appear, this is the basic plot: Raoul de Noget (No-zhay), a singer, and his friend Buddy, "The World's Greatest Piano Player," have come to a small town in the Midwest to entertain at the Perfect Lives Lounge. For some unexplained reason, they have fallen in with two people from the town, Isolde ("nearing 30 and not yet spoken for") and her brother, "D," just out of high school and known as "The Captain of the Football Team" (his parents call him Donnie), to commit the perfect crime (a metaphor for something philosophical): in this case, to remove a sizable amount of money from the bank for one day (one day only) and "let the whole world know it was missing." The seven episodes are "The Park (Privacy Rules)," "The Supermarket (Famous People)," "The Bank (Victimless Crime)," "The Bar (Differences)," "The Living Room (The Solutions)," "The Church (After the Fact)," and "The Backyard (T'Be Continued)." "*Perfect Lives* is nothing less than the first American opera" (Allan Evans, *Fanfare*). —*"Blue" Gene Tyranny*

● **In Sara Mencken Christ and Beethoven There Were Men and Women** / 1991 / Cramps ✦✦✦✦
The text by the legendary John Barton Walgamot traces a hidden story of social progress underneath the gradual repetition, addition, and subtraction of names and organized variation of syntactical parts. The reading voice activates beautiful and humorous electronic sounds designed by composer Paul DeMarinis for this piece. —*"Blue" Gene Tyranny*

☆ **Don Leaves Linda (Improvement)** / 1992 / Elektra/Nonesuch ✦✦✦✦✦
Don Leaves Linda, in a completely new sound for voices and an electronic orchestra, recalls the Spanish influence in America. By touching and genuinely humorous metaphorical incidents and characters, and a music that is equally intimate and dramatically universal, we are presented with a driving sense of the "eternal present." A masterpiece. —*"Blue" Gene Tyranny*

El / Aficionado / 1994 / Lovely Music ✦✦✦
Described in the catalog as "incidences in the life and career of a person who has reason to believe himself to be an 'agent of the department,' featuring Thomas Buckner as The Agent and Jacqueline Humbert, Sam Ashley, and Robert Ashley as his interrogators," this new opera is a grand metaphor of the interior life of most of us who question our actions and thoughts at different times in our lives. Beautiful and mysterious electronic orchestrations by Ashley, working with composer Tom Hamilton. —*"Blue" Gene Tyranny*

Superior Seven: Concerto for Flute and Orchestra/Tract for Orchestra and Voice / 1995 / New World ✦✦✦
Superior Seven is for a flute soloist and a computer-controlled electronic orchestra that presents seven independent ensembles of various numbers and kinds of instruments. The tones, their octave displacements, the event occurrences (say of the sustain vocal chord), etc. were originally

generated from the word composition of various newspaper ads for "superior" houses. The music is built from overlapping long cycles which generate a sustained "aura" of great beauty. *Tract*, performed here by famed new music baritone Tom Buckner with electronic orchestra, is an orchestration of a work from 1955, and is a serial composition with a feeling for shifting, actually illusionary, harmonic centers. The music seems to float in your mind. (See also Ashley's wonderful ensemble piece for flute and chamber orchestra *Outcome Inevitable* in the collection *Relache: Outcome Inevitable*.) — *"Blue" Gene Tyranny*

Automatic Writing and Other Works / 1996 / Lovely Music ✦✦✦
Re-release of three new music landmarks: *Automatic Writing* (1979) in which the composer explores spontaneous speech unfiltered (as much as is possible) by his normal language behavior ("My mind is censoring my own mind"); *Purposeful Lady Slow Afternoon* (1968) from the *Wolfman Motor City Review*, a sensual and captivating study of random vocal reactions (sung by the vocal trio of Mary Ashley, Mary Lucier and Barbara Lloyd) with a personal story (by Cynthia Liddell) about the sense of touch, which with smell is repressed in Western society; and *She Was a Visitor* (1967) from the opera *That Morning Thing*, performed by the Brandeis University Chamber Chorus, conducted by Alvin Lucier—this wonderful piece describes musically how "rumor" is spread, with leaders of a chorus group selecting phonemes of the chanted line "she was a visitor" and the group sustaining each individual sound. The amassed sound, a "surface" of normalized little disturbances, in which an audience could also participate, begins to resemble airplanes, cars, trains . . . or perhaps the subatomic world. — *"Blue" Gene Tyranny*

Kenneth Atchley

b. Nov. 7, 1954, Lebanon, Tennessee
Composer / New Narrative Opera, Electronic
Atchley studied at Mills College with Robert Ashley and David Behrman. He describes himself as "listening to news & noise" and as "a dilettante Buddhist." A comprehensive article on his work, *An Introduction to the Operatic Works of K. Atchley Including an In-Depth Discussion of an Original Opera Titled 'Don Giovanni*,' is published in the *Leonardo Music Journal* (Jan. 1991). His writings and scores also appear in *The Guests Go in to Supper* (Burning Books). Other works: *Light of Hand (LumiÈre de Main)* (1982) for voices and computer, *Cabinet (Enclosed Spaces)* from the opera *Edison's Last Projection* (1985), *Wasserglocken mit Electronics* (1985), and *Marconi*—The Last Seven Words (1986). — *"Blue" Gene Tyranny*

Don Giovanni, Act I, Scenes 1-4 / In "Anthology of Music for the 21st Century" / 1991 / Leonardo Music Journal, Vol. 1 No. 1 ✦✦✦✦
A musical conversation with the characters of Da Ponte's libretto for Mozart's opera about the cultural myth of Don Juan and the history of our attitudes about sexuality (and "going to hell" for sharing sensual feeling). A subtle, surreal evocation for voices and electronics with a highly poetic and intelligent text by the composer. — *"Blue" Gene Tyranny*

6 House / In the collection "Views from the Imaginary City" / 1995 / Inial ✦✦✦
The text is extracted from a much longer libretto about Nikola Tesla. The composer writes, "The inventor believed that human behavior could be described in scientific expressions, explained, and eventually predicted. This excerpt portrays a specific human relationship—a crush—in terms of phase relations. The work also provides a view of the relationship through the filter of Duchamp's "Nude Descending a Staircase." With K. Atchley (vocal and electronics) and Mark Trayle (electric guitar solo). — *"Blue" Gene Tyranny*

Larry Austin

Austin received his education at North Texas State University and taught at University of California-Davis, and later at University of South Florida and at the Center of the Creative and Performing Arts of SUNY in Buffalo, NY. He was a principal founder and editor of *Source*, a journal of avant garde music. He achieved his first success with his composition *Improvisations for Orchestra and Jazz Soloists* in 1961, performed by the New York Philharmonic and commercially recorded. He experimented with an open style in which sections of the composition are designated for free improvisation by the performers and the work's overall form is controlled by analog notation. He also uses electronic and theatrical devices in his composition. — *Lynn Vought*

Hybrid Music: Four Compositions: Quadrants (Event/Complex No. 1/ Second Fantasy on Ives' Universe Symphony—The Heavens/ Catalogo Voce/ Maroon Bells for Voice and Tape / 1980 / Irida ✦✦✦
A prolific composer of acoustic and electronic music, Austin's early music combined elements of jazz improvisation with advanced compositional techniques such as in his cantata for soprano and jazz at the University of California at Davis in 1963. Works composed in his "open style" include "Catharsis: Open Style for Two Improvisational Ensembles, Tape and Conductor" (1967) and the theater piece "The Maze"

(1966) for percussionists, dancer, tape, and films. He later developed combinatorial pieces, the "event/complexes" of the '70s, wrote fantasies for voice and the legendary *Source* magazine anthology of new music, and composed many other electro-acoustic works. His recent work with computers on the CDs above continues to combine electronics and acoustical instruments/voices by transforming with a sense of humor recognized historical material into "mini opera-buffas." — *"Blue" Gene Tyranny*

Milton Babbitt

b. May 10, 1916, Philadelphia, PA
Composer / Serialist, Electronic
Studied with Marion Bauer, Roger Sessions. Teacher at Huilliard and Princeton. Co-director Columbia-Princeton Electronic Music Center, consultant in creation of Mark II RCA Synthesizer. Early use of serialist techniques in America. *Generatrix* for orchestra (1935), *Composition for Four Instruments* (1948), *Vision and Prayer* for soprano and synthesized tape (1961), *String Quartet No. 4* (1970). — *"Blue" Gene Tyranny*

All Set, for Jazz Ensemble (1957) / 1990 / Elektra/Nonesuch ✦✦✦
Formal writing for a jazz group, like experiments for other "progressive jazz" ensembles of the late '40s and '50s—the Sauter-Finegan Ensemble, the Stan Kenton Orchestra, and so forth. This is a piece of its decade, but still interesting. Other works on this CD are by other well-known formalist composers: George Rochberg (1918-), Lalo Schifrin (1932-), Richard Wernick (1934-), and Stefan Wolpe. — *"Blue" Gene Tyranny*

Correspondences for String Orchestra and Synthesizer Tape (1967) / In "Cage/Carter/Babbitt/Schuller" / 1994 / Deutsche Grammaphon ✦✦✦
A fascinating classic of electro-acoustic illusions within a formalist style. — *"Blue" Gene Tyranny*

Ensembles for Synthesizer / Columbia ✦✦✦
One of the first composers in America to employ Arnold Schönberg's method of composition with twelve-tones, Babbitt also extended this method, before the young European school of Boulez/Stockhausen/Nono/Berio, into the even more highly organized system of serial composition in the mid-'40s, with his pieces *Three Compositions for Piano* (1947) and the *Composition for Four Instruments* (1948). This electronic composition from 1964 was realized at the Columbia-Princeton Electronic Music Center, and demonstrates Babbitt's methods applied to this medium. His primary musical material employs the 12 tones of the even-tempered scale, and a vast array of pitch, rhythmic, registral, textural and timbral degrees which are contained within interrelating collections or ensembles. Babbitt uses the synthesizer primarily for this ability to move very quickly and accurately between this delineated parameters. The result is a kaleidoscope of electronic timbres. — *"Blue" Gene Tyranny*

Tadeusz Baird

Composer / Atonal, Chromatic

Psychodrama for Orchestra / Concert for Oboe and Orchestra / Scenes for Cello, Harp, and Orchestra / Canzona for Orchestra / Concer / 1993 / Koch ✦✦✦
An interesting blend of dramatic Schoenbergian romanticism, serial pointillism, and original orchestral colors written by a composer who went from a rather bland style of what was then imagined to be "people's music" to a radical change in the '60s. — *"Blue" Gene Tyranny*

Llorenç Barber

Concierto de Campanas Sacra Lucus (The "Sacra Lucus" Concerto for Church Bells) / 1992 / Unio Musics ✦✦✦
Written for more than one hundred musicians located in 14 bell towers in Lugo, this astonishing piece, similar to many that Barber has presented in Spanish cities, was presented on June 8, 1991. All traffic ceased during the performance, and suddenly Lugo was transported back in time, as the persistent rhythm of the "Hymn of the Ancient Kingdom of Galicia," with the "Alabado sea el Santisimo" played simultaneously on a cathedral carrillon, began to ring from the outermost bell towers toward the center of the city, the queen tower of the cathedral. The sound is stunning, floating over the area like a sonorous "decibel net" or mystical blanket, or the humming of UFOs. The performers were given chronometers and a precise time score for their various parts, which required preexercising for and strenuous playing during the 40-minute performance. Barber has recently gotten the Spanish navy to cooperate in a piece that uses modern battle cruisers, ancient frigates, cannon, and cathedrals on shore and again the involvement of an entire city for a performance. — *"Blue" Gene Tyranny*

Jean Barraqué

b. 1928, d. 1973
A French composer of chamber music; a contemporary of Messiaen; one

of the first serialists. His unique style combined a rich impressionism with extremely formal pointillism. The use of jazz instrumentalists in classical ensembles playing his serial music led to social stigmatization in the late '50s. The pieces . . . *au delà du hasard* and *Chant après Chant* (1966) for six percussionists, voice, and piano were inspired by *The Death of Virgil*, by Hermann Broch. These pieces do not merely set the text but reflect upon it, as shown in "Unable to evolve or regress," "Before the quotation," and "On a thought without night." —*"Blue" Gene Tyranny*

. . . **au delà du hasard** (. . . **beyond mere luck**) (**1959**) **for Four Instrumental Formations and a Vocal Formation** / 1981 / Astree ✦✦✦

Barraqué was one of the first serialists with a unique style that combined a rich impressionism and extremely formal pointillism. His beautiful "Sonate pour Piano" (1950-1952) (recorded by Claude Helffer on Astre AS 36, out-of-print disc) was praised by jazz critic Andre Hodeir in an early book. This praise and Barraqué's use of jazz instrumentalists (playing his serial music) sitting together with classic ensembles led to Barraqué being stigmatized socially. This was the late '50s. ". . . au dela du hasard," like "Chant apres Chant" (1966) for six percussionists, voice, and piano, was inspired by Hermann Broch's poem "The Death of Virgil," not merely setting the text, but reflecting upon it. The titles of the movements will give some idea of this impulse—"The light without rays," "Unable to evolve or regress," "Which ephemeral signs?" "Abusive exaggerations," "In the wandering multitude," "For the unknown edge of chance," "Before the quotation," "Blinded by the dream (quotation)," "Beyond the direct line of sight," "On a thought without night." —*"Blue" Gene Tyranny*

Le Temps Restitu (1968), excerpt from "La Mort de Virgile" (The Death of Virgil) by Hermann Broch / 1987 / Harmonia Mundi
A work similar in many aspects to ". . . au delà du hasard," although more in the pointillistic serial style. Beautiful performance by mezzo-soprano Anne Bartelloni. On the same CD is the virtuosic "Concerto" (1962-1968) for alternating trios of instruments (violin-bassoon-trumpet, violoncello-flute-tenor saxophone, and others). —*"Blue" Gene Tyranny*

Louis and Bebe Barron

Composers / Early electronic, Instrument builders
Wrote electronic music for film. The Barrons also assisted John Cage in making "Williams Mix." —*"Blue" Gene Tyranny*

Forbidden Planet (1954) / 1988 / Planet Records ✦✦✦
The first Hollywood film score to use electronic music (the first all-electronic soundtrack was for Anaïs Nin's *The Bells of Atlantis* in 1952). The sound results from cybernetic (controlled feedback) circuitry, especially designed by the Barrons, producing Krells and monsters from the Id. —*"Blue" Gene Tyranny*

Martin Bartlett

b. 1939
Composer / Electronic

Pythagoras' Ghost / 1993 / Front ✦✦✦
The title piece on this CD is for four electronic wind instruments and contains sections that are lighthearted, even goofy in their sense of humor ("Akousmata—ear whisperings," "Xenomelophilia—love of strange melodies"), one movement of elegant transparency ("Chromopneuma—breath colours"), and a tiny pedantic march ("Gymnosophia—naked philosophies or nude philosophers"). My favorite work is "The Arrival of Sir John Franklin in Paradise" (1988) for a wonderful variety of synthesized sounds surrounding and supporting Bartlett's chanting and sometimes electronically modified voice on texts from Dante. A composer with a definitely original manner. —*"Blue" Gene Tyranny*

David Behrman

b. Aug. 16, 1937, Salzburg, Austria
Composer / Interactive Electro-Acoustic, Computer, Software Design
Behrman holds degrees from Harvard and Columbia. He produced the *Music of Our Time* series for Columbia Records in the 1960s. A co-founder of the Sonic Arts Union, Behrman toured with the Merce Cunningham Dance Company in the 1970s and 1990s. From 1975-1980 he was co-director of the Center for Contemporary Music, Mills College. He also taught at Ohio State University and CAL Arts, and designed children's computer games at Children's Television Workshop. Behrman toured under friendship grants from the Japan-United States Friendship Commission and the DAAD (Berlin). He has created many sound installations, which can be played by nonprofessionals at the Whitney Museum, the Museum of Contemporary Art in Chicago, Für Augen und Ohren (For Eye and Ear) in Berlin, the DeCordova Museum in Lincoln, MA, and La Villette in Paris. —*"Blue" Gene Tyranny*

On the Other Ocean / Figure in a Clearing / 1977 / Lovely Music ✦✦✦✦
Subtle, sustained, serene. Electronics with flute, bassoon, cello soloists. Innovative interactive performance setup and a beautiful listening experience. —*"Blue" Gene Tyranny*

Leapday Night / 1990 / Lovely Music ✦✦✦
Several pieces with computer-aided interactive electronics and improvising musicians on mutatrumpet, trumpets, keyboards, violin. With Takehisa Kosugi, Ben Neill, Rhys Chatham. Warm, beautiful, and gently humorous. —*"Blue" Gene Tyranny*

☆ **Unforeseen Events** / 1992 / Experimental Intermedia ✦✦✦✦✦
Beautiful interactive computer music with Ben Neill, mutatrumpet. Contains: *Unforeseen Events* with four sections: "View Finder," a canon with gradually more ornate response to what the trumpeter is playing; "Fishing for Complements," a trio for computer, mutatrumpet, and a listener to the interchange who enters changes into the computer on a silent keyboard as the music progresses from simple repeating figures to hundreds of rapidly cascading sounds; "Witch Grass," more complex figures with sustained computer chords gradually slipping away from their tonal centers; and "Canyon," a cerebral canyon with shadowy trains of pitch-shifted chords. "Refractive Light," in which tonal changes occur as "deflections" at the on-and-off edges of overlapping events, has three sections: "Harbinger," "Crisscrossed Eights," and "Ein Glaesele Warems." —*"Blue" Gene Tyranny*

Navigation and Astronomy / 1992 / Classic Masters ✦✦✦
In the collection *Music from Japan, Vol. I: Acoustic Instruments with Computer Music Systems*, Kazue Sawai, koto, David Behrman, electronics. In this fascinating and beautiful composition from 1990, 16 of the 21 strings of a Japanese koto are tuned to a set of pitches that the computer software is waiting to "hear." As the performer plays, elements of the music made by the computer—in a form akin to a three-voiced canon—are altered in various ways. "Voices halt and restart, speed up and slow down, and change in pitch . . . this is a piece in which the composer does not tell the performer what to do. The music made by the system has a personality of its own which permits—but does not insist upon—a broad style of playing . . . the [performer] using [his] own imagination and resources will be free to explore within an environment created by the system" (Behrman). —*"Blue" Gene Tyranny*

Jacques Bekaert

b. May 11, 1940, Belgium
Composer / Verbal scores, Open Scoring for Ensembles
Well-known as an adventurous political news reporter for *Le Monde* (Paris) and English-language papers in Thailand, as a counsellor at the Embassy of the Sovereign Military Order of Malta (Cambodia), and the author of *Nixon's the One* and several important commentaries on world politics, Bekaert has also helped art and music organizations in Southeast Asia. His scores combine instructions and poetic imagery toward interactive and spontaneous creation. — *"Blue" Gene Tyranny*

Summer Music 1970 / 1977 / Lovely Music ✦✦✦
Twelve musical portraits, vignettes in sound with various instrumentalists performing verbal-instruction scores. Varied and charming. At the time of this recording, Bekaert was the voice of the legendary "King Kong" new*music radio show for Radio Belgium.* —*"Blue" Gene Tyranny*

Luciano Berio

b. 1925
An avant-garde composer, Berio feels that music is derived from "the integration of any sound phenomenon—from speech to instrument, from 'noise' to 'sound'— into a generalized harmonic continuum." [*The International Encyclopedia of Music and Musicians*, p. 200] To this end, he employs such techniques as integrating language sounds and quotations from established symphonies to redefine the musical language. Initially a serial composer, Berio moved beyond to explore the use of exotic sounds to tap into the archetypes of musical communication. —*Lynn Vought*

Coro for 40 Voices and 40 Instruments (1976) / 1991 / Deutsche Grammaphon ✦✦✦
Performed by the Cologne Symphony Orchestra and Chorus conducted by the composer. Probably Berio's masterpiece in his romantic-pointillism style. —*"Blue" Gene Tyranny*

Johanna Magdelena Beyer

b. 1888, d. 1984
Composer / Innovative Scoring and Performance Techniques

IV for Percussion (1935) / 1991 / Aerial ✦✦✦
Performed by Essential Music. Percussion music for nine unspecified (!) instruments, completely unique but appeals to a fundamental feeling. Beyer was involved in much new-music activity but her personal life

remains a mystery, and her music is still largely unperformed. (See *New Music for Electronic and Recorded Media* in 20th-Century Collections in this section.) —*"Blue" Gene Tyranny*

The Bifurcators

Gang of Two / 1995 / Artifact
A new great group with composers Philip Perkins (bowed bass, electronic noisemakers, computers) and Scott Fraser (electric guitar) plus, for this CD, performers Bonnie Barnett (vocals), Tim Perkis (computer), and Doug Carroll (electric cello). Includes: "The Rose Window," inspired by the stained-glass windows of Notre Dame (Paris), for guitar, computers, sampler, and other sound-makers; "White Eagles," a sparse, elegiac work in memory of the Bosnian war dead; "A New Work," a live performance over phone lines to the group improvisation about slowness and inexorability where electronics "shadow" the players like the optical illusion of a steady shadow appearing to move. The performers may or may not "go along with it." —*"Blue" Gene Tyranny*

John Bischoff

b. Dec. 7, 1949, San Francisco
Composer / Electronic, Computer Network Bands
Studied at CA Institute of the Arts, Mills College. Composed with Robert Moran, James Tenney, Robert Ashley. Founding member of League of Automatic Music Composers, the first computer network band, and the Hub, a computer performance collective. Published writings on computer music. Currently on faculty and staff of Center for Contemporary Music, Mills College. *Outdoor Memory* constructed in 1970 is a computer-implemented listening system that responds to tuning in environmental sounds. — *"Blue" Gene Tyranny*

Next Tone Please / Frog Peak Music ◆◆◆
Six subtle and mysterious electronic compositions by this legendary Bay Area composer. See also his "Rendezvous" in *Just for the Record.* —*"Blue" Gene Tyranny*

Rendezvous (1978) / In "Just for the Record" / 1981 / ◆◆◆
Melodic phrases that "sometimes go their own separate ways, sometimes drifting apart and at other times coordinating together." Multi-timbral synthesizer sounds suggest an underlying surreal story. —*"Blue" Gene Tyranny*

Artificial Horizon (with Tim Perkis) (1951) / 1989 / Artifact ◆◆◆◆
Wonderful collaborative and individual compositions for personal computer systems. Includes: "Touch Typing," "Next Tone, Please," "Engagement," "Dovetail," "Artificial Horizon," "Clicks," "Clavitron 6000," "Audio Wave," "Happy Trails." See also The Hub. —*"Blue" Gene Tyranny*

The Glass Hand/ In CDCM Computer Music, Vol. 17 / 1994 / Centaur ◆◆◆
An electronically generated live performance piece where "unwanted artifacts," or "low-level synthesizer behaviors" are highlighted, revealing "in a poetic way the often hidden nature of electronic instruments." Mysterious and fascinating. —*"Blue" Gene Tyranny*

Bob and Bob

Across America (1981) / M.I.T.B. Records ◆◆◆
A wonderful record as well as a "document" of a performance art piece: poetry and comments and stories from a crosscountry journey. You may also want to follow up with their band record *We Know You're Alone* backed with *We've Been Seeing Things* on Polygram/Polydor Records (New York, 12-inch EP disc, 1983). And one of them, The Dark Bob, has also made *One Bob Job* (includes "Outside of Moab", "The List," "Interstate") (1982, one-sided 12-inch LP) and *Kabbalamobile* (cassette, from soundtrack of theater work), all available from M.I.T.B. Records. —*"Blue" Gene Tyranny*

Lars-Gunnar Bodin

b. 1935
Composer / Electro-acoustic, Computer
For Jon (Fragments of a Time to Come) (1977) / 1978 / Folkways ◆◆◆
An out-of-print disc well worth searching for. A "surrealistic science fiction," even cyberpunk (the term wasn't in wide usage at the time) cantata for narrator, chamber choir, and electronics with the text processed through and triggering the electronics. Reflects Bodin's continuing concern with concepts connected with modern science and technology, and the role of art in a post-revolutionary (Marcusean sense) society. —*"Blue" Gene Tyranny*

Anima (1984) / In "Computer Music Currents 7" / 1990 / Wergo ◆◆◆◆
A brief work perfectly depicting a profound psychic process—the unification of consciousness with the higher self. The human voice (soprano) hears its counterpart in the computer voice, and gradually the two

merge throughout the course of the piece. Beautiful. —*"Blue" Gene Tyranny*

David Borden/Mother Mallard

David Borden has long been on the forefront of live electronic and minimalist music. Borden first surfaced as the force behind Mother Mallard, the world's first all-synthesizer ensemble. Mother Mallard released two LPs between 1973-76, *Mother Mallard's Portable Masterpiece Company* and *Like a Duck to Water.* After the breakup of Mother Mallard in the late 1970s, Borden refined his compositional skills, releasing his first solo LP, *Music for Amplified Keyboard Instruments*, in 1981. He released *Anatidae* in 1986 and *Migration* in 1988. His three-hour, 12-part composition, *The Continuing Story of Counterpoint*, was released on three separate CDs over the period 1988-91. *Cayuga Night Music* displayed a more introspective Borden, while *Places, Times & People* featured a range, from piano duets to soundscapes to dense, interlocking keyboard pieces. —*Jim Dorsch*

Double Portrait (1987) / In Double Edge "U.S. Choice" / 1992 / ◆◆◆
Influenced by pattern music, Borden's music nevertheless has its own character made from rich layers of free-wheeling solos over the patterns with some very lovely textures. The structure of the music is built on composer and performer names and birthdates in an elevated soap-opera structure. Performed by Mother Mallard's Portable Masterpiece Co., a well-known 1970s East Coast synthesizer group with Borden, Linda Fisher, and Steve Drews. The group used many modern techniques in its pieces from chance procedures to pattern music and various forms of improvisation. —*"Blue" Gene Tyranny*

Linda Bouchard

Black Burned Wood / In Dora Ohrenstein's "Urban Diva" / 1993 / CRI ◆◆◆
An accomplished composer of more than 50 works in various genres from opera to chamber works, Bouchard has created an intense song concerning a mysterious girl, Sara, running through woods, obsessed, who may have murdered her parents. See also Bouchard's "Lung Ta" for string quartet in *Bang on a Can, Vol. 3.* —*"Blue" Gene Tyranny*

Andre Boucourechliev

Boucourechliev started his musical career as a pianist, studying at the Sofia Conservatory and the Ecole Normale de Musique in Paris. In 1951 he earned his "licence de concert" and pursued a career as a concert pianist and a teacher. He began to compose in 1954 and since then has been active in that area as well as music criticism and musicology. Boucourechliev has composed with tape and indeterminate elements. The series *Archipels* (1967-72) gained him a respected reputation as a composer. The score for this work resembles a large navigational chart that contains an "archipelago" of musical structures that are designed as possibilities for the performer to employ. Although the structure is determined by the course of the performance, the players must listen and communicate in order for the work to be successful. —*Lynn Vought*

Ombres (Shades) (Hommage à Beethoven) / EMI ◆◆◆
Performed by the National Chamber Orchestra of Toulouse, directed by Louis Auriacombe. Recordings of Boucourechliev's music are difficult to find but well worth the effort. This is an "hommage" to the Father of Modern Music. Beethoven's Third Symphony *Eroica* and sometimes other works are often credited with being the first modernist compositions, partly because they were built from small "kernels" of ideas rather than as variations on full melodies, and also because the music did not need outside references to justify it. Instead of falling for the rather obvious idea of collaging Beethoven's works, Boucourechliev creates an impression of the "interior" nature of Beethoven's democratic and universal pieces. This is difficult to put in words, but is something like the "feeling" you have left after the music has ended. This is a transcendental and sustained piece, unique in character. —*"Blue" Gene Tyranny*

Pierre Boulez

b. 1925, Montbrison, Loire, France
Composer / Serialist, Electronic
After initially studying mathematics, Boulez entered the Paris Conservatoire as a student in theory and harmony (he failed the pianists' entrance examination). His principal teacher was Messiaen, and he also studied counterpoint privately with Andrée Vaurabourg. According to Boulez, composition is a form of aesthetic research and should be pursued logically. He viewed personal stylistic development as having no importance and deemed atonality as necessary. He adopted 12-tone serialism after being exposed to it by Liebowitz, a student of Schoenberg. In *Structures* for two pianos (1952), Boulez utilized a serial control of rhythm, dynamics, and tone. These works brought him initial public recognition, but it was his *Le marteau sans maître* (1954) that was to become a landmark of 20th century music. Scored for small ensemble, it is rhythmically

monotonous with sudden tempo changes and large sections of improvisatory melodies. The success of these pieces led to an invitation to teach at Darmstadt, as a professor of composition. It was here that he gave a series of lectures that was to become the book *Musikdenken heute*, an outline of his ideas concerning total serialization. At this time Boulez was expanding his serial techniques to include open form, or "organized delirium." He also developed techniques that allowed performer and conductor to make many more creative choices in form and tonal duration. Boulez is also an active conductor, his performances marked by analytical clarity. He has served as head conductor for the BBC Symphony in London and the New York Philharmonic. —*Lynn Vought*

Improvisations sur Mallarma (Improvisations on Mallarma) I & II (1957) for Soprano and Instrumental Ensemble / Hungaroton
This composition, together with "Le Marteau sans Maitre (The Hammer without a Master)," established the particular sound of Boulez's approach to serialist composition, a poetic pointillism with a Debussyian sense of timbres that has characterized most of his works and is more interesting than most of the later, rather arid pieces that followed it. This CD also contains two lovely classics of 12-tone music (upon which serialism is based), Arnold Schoenberg's *Pierrot Lunaire, op. 21* (1912) and Anton Webern's *5 Canons on Latin Texts, for Soprano and Instrumental Ensemble, op. 16 (1923-1924)*, plus two of his songs. —*"Blue" Gene Tyranny*

Structures pour Deux Pianos (Livre I, 1952; Livre II, 1961) / 1992 / Wergo ✦✦✦
A reissue of the marvelously accurate and colorful performances by the great Alfons and Aloys Kontarsky. —*"Blue" Gene Tyranny*

Paul Bowles

b. 1910
Bowles studied with Copland, Thomson, and Boulanger during the 1920s and early '30s, while living in Europe and north Africa. For the next three decades he wrote music for the New York theater. In 1941 he received a Guggenheim Fellowship to compose the opera *The Wind Remains*. He returned to Tangier in 1948 to write his second opera, *Yerma*, for blues singer Libby Holman. He conducted ethno-musicological research in Tangier under a Rockefeller grant during the 1960s. Most of his compositions were written before 1949. In that year his novel about travelers, *The Sheltering Sky*, was published. As a composer, Bowles wrote in short forms. Even his operas are constructions of suites of songs. They draw heavily upon American jazz, Moroccan rhythm and Mexican dance for inspiration. His fiction is generally dark in character and centers around insights of psychological perception. —*Lynn Vought*

The Voices of Paul Bowles / Tellus #23 ✦✦✦✦
Audio portrait on cassette of the author/composer with stories, selected works, early compositions (*Music for a Farce, Interlude and Prelude No. 2,* long unavailable), and environmental recordings made near his Moroccan home. In a library you may still find his wonderful pieces *A Picnic Cantata* (1955) for four women's voices, two pianos, and percussion (including a milk bottle and cigar box) (Columbia LP with pianists Gold and Fizdale) and *The Wind Remains* (1943) (an opera based on an abstraction of the third act of Garcia Lorca's "Asi que pasen cinco anos") (MGM Records disc E3549; also contains composer Peggy Glanville-Hick's "Letters from Morocco," which are settings of texts by Bowles). —*"Blue" Gene Tyranny*

Black Star at the Point of Darkness / 1992 / Psalmodia Sub Rosa ✦✦✦
A wonderful sound and soul journey featuring the voice of Paul Bowles reading narrations and poems, his recordings of ritual Moroccan music, and the six preludes for piano. —*"Blue" Gene Tyranny*

Glenn Branca

b. Oct. 6, 1948, Harrisburg, PA
Composer / Experimental, Minimalist
Formed the late-'70s bands Theoretical Girls and the Static. Influenced by Dane Rudyhar's harmonic theories, dense rock guitar music, minimalist-style cyclic organization, and tone cluster music. —*"Blue" Gene Tyranny*

The Ascension / 1981 / 99 ✦✦✦
A reissue on CD of the original 1981 vinyl LP that, along with works by a few other composer-performers equally at home in rock and conceptual music, marked the birth of an alliance between these genres. With four electric guitars, bass and drums. Powerful sound and convincing music. —*"Blue" Gene Tyranny*

Symphony No. 1 (Tonal Plexus) / 1983 / Roir ✦✦✦✦

Music for Peter Greenaway's Film "The Belly of an Architect" (1987) / 1987 / Les Disques Du Crepuscule ✦✦✦
A different light-music for string orchestra with the gradually sliding tone-densities of the guitar music transferred to orchestral strings for some of the best moments in the score. —*"Blue" Gene Tyranny*

Symphony No. 6 (Devil Choirs at the Gates of Heaven) for 10 guitars, keyboard, bass, drums / 1989 / Blast First ✦✦✦✦
Studies in gradually denser sonorities ("resultant masses") with a rock-steady pulse, this music digs deep into the mind/feeling to elicit bardo-like sensations often approached by the profoundest Buddhist chant. (Cage and Branca once had a disagreement about Branca's music being "fascist." Cage argued that densities creating a "sustained climax" restrict the mind from opening up. I doubt that fascists would like these symphonies.) —*"Blue" Gene Tyranny*

Symphony #2 (The Peak of the Sacred) / 1992 / Atavistic

The World Upside Down / 1992 / Les Disques du Crepuscule ✦✦✦

Symphony Nos. 8 & 10 / 1994 / Atavistic ✦✦✦
Subtitled "The Mystery" and "The Mystery Pt. 2" these two symphonies concern themselves with the two big questions: Life and Death. They are both scored for eight guitars, two basses, keyboard, drums, vocal, and two conductors. *Symphony No. 8* has two movements: "The Passion" and "Spiritual Anarchy," which both build upon sustained tones that create a counterpoint by means of delays in scale and other patterns and microtunings. The effect is tremendously intense and beautiful. There are also two movements in *Symphony No. 10:* "The Final Problem" and "The Horror." These are built in a similar manner to the techniques in *No. 8,* but the tuning and scales employed are different, creating another sensation, yet still as intense and continuous in rhythm as *No. 8.* Especially successful is the final movement, "The Horror," which employs masses of moving clusters that are very close in tuning and thoroughly convincing in the image they portray. It is a gigantic chant of worlds never before imagined. Incidentally, the CD comes with a nifty holographic cover that visually simulates Branca's dense textures. —*"Blue" Gene Tyranny*

Symphony No. 9 / 1995 / Point ✦✦✦
This is a very unique work and highly recommended. —*"Blue" Gene Tyranny*

Indeterminate Activity of Resultant Masses / 1996 / Newtone ✦✦✦
A most welcome issue of the live performance of this important and stirring work from 1982. In conception, its title incorporates a tribute to and commentary on some of the fundamental concepts of John Cage's work, as well as describes a sonic and musically spiritual phenomena that occurs over the course of a performance of this hypnotic, important piece. —*"Blue" Gene Tyranny*

Henry Brant

b. Sep. 15, 1913, Montreal, Quebec, Canada
Composer / Antiphonal "Spatial," Polytonal
Brant studied with George Antheil, Aaron Copland, Wallingford Riegger, and Rubin Goldmark. A scorer and arranger of radio broadcasts and films, he taught at Columbia, Juilliard, and Bennington. *Variations for Any Four Instruments* was composed using his original concept of "oblique harmony." His *Music for a 5 and 10¢ Store* (1932) was written for violin, piano, kitchen utensils, and alarm clocks; *Angels and Devils* (1931, 1956, 1979) for three piccolos, five flutes, and two alto flutes. Brant's other works include *Encephalograms II* (1955), *Spatial Concerto (Questions from Genesis)* (1976), and Ives/Brant *The Concord Symphony* (30 years of composition, premiered in 1996). —*"Blue" Gene Tyranny*

Orbits (1979), A Spatial Symphonic Ritual for 80 Trombones, Organ, and Sopranino Voice / CRI ✦✦✦
Played by the Bay Bones Trombone Choir with Brant (organ), Amy Snyder (vocal), and conducted by Gerhard Samuel. One of Brant's most ambitious spatial pieces: sounds accelerate in a circular motion ascending the cupola of St. Mary's Cathedral in San Francisco. His enormous multispatial work *Meteor Farm* (1982), which requires a symphony, two choruses, jazz band, Javanese gamelan, West African drummers and singers, Western percussion groups and two sopranos, has not yet been recorded. —*"Blue" Gene Tyranny*

☆ **Angels and Devils for Flute and Flute Orchestra (1932, revised 1947)** / 1991 / Centaur ✦✦✦✦✦
Played by the Eastman Wind Ensemble. Brant is the composer who reintroduced spatial distribution as a parameter of musical expression, such as it was in Gabrieli's time. This is Brant's classic work of "spatial music" for 14 flutes with performers standing on ladders or on different levels. —*"Blue" Gene Tyranny*

Ghost Nets (1988) / 1992 / AmCam ✦✦✦
Spatial narratives for double bass solo and two separated instrumental groups. Lewis Paar, double bass. This CD also includes Gordin Cyr's "String Quartet No. 2" (1983). —*"Blue" Gene Tyranny*

Anthony Braxton

b. Jun. 4, 1945, Chicago, IL
Composer / Wind Instrumentalist, Multi-orchestral, Closed-and-open Form Composition
See the Jazz section for his biography.

Four Compositions 1982-1988 / 1990 / Hat Art ✦✦✦

☆ **Composition No. 107 (excerpt, 1982)** / **In CDCM Computer Music Series, Vol. 10** / 1991 / Centaur ✦✦✦✦✦
A "dry and glass-like sound universe" punctuated with high-energy improvisation. Excellent performances. Braxton has taken the "graph score" to a new level for his compositions, which involve a combination of spontaneous and charted playing, and has extended his imagination into the future—like Charles Ives in his "Universe Symphony" to be played from mountaintops—to pieces to be played from planet to planet. —*"Blue" Gene Tyranny*

Composition 98 / 1991 / Hat Art ✦✦✦

Composition No. 165 for 18 Instruments / 1992 / Hat Art
Excellent solo and ensemble pieces. —*"Blue" Gene Tyranny*

Two Lines / 1995 / Lovely Music ✦✦✦
Rosenboom on MIDI Grand Piano, his invention the HFG (Hierarchical Form Generator), and Responding Sampled Piano, with Anthony Braxton on sopranino, soprano and alto saxophones, clarinet and flute. Two legendary composer-performers join forces to unite composition and improvisation. A rich and continuously creative flow toward achieving the experience of "a composition that is immediately heard" (Rosenboom). —*"Blue" Gene Tyranny*

Chris Brown

b. Sep. 9, 1953, Mendota, IL
Composer / Electronic, Computer

Snakecharmer / 1989 / Artifact
Five pieces for solo performer and live electronics: in each piece a different acoustic instrument is played through an electronic system that responds automatically to the sounds and actions of the performer. Performed by the composer on piano, keyboards, voice and electronics with William Winant, percussion. —*"Blue" Gene Tyranny*

LAVA / 1995 / Tzadik ✦✦✦
Composed in 1992, this dramatic and gritty electro-acoustical work is scored for brass quartet, four percussionists and live electronics. "Aspects of the physical structure of a volcano are applied to control musical elements. The change from a solid (earth) to a liquid (lava) is modeled by the transformation of the acoustic sounds into electronic sounds . . . a primordial state of flux." The electronics create fascinating "3D imaging" illusions. —*"Blue" Gene Tyranny*

Earle Brown

b. Dec. 26, 1926
Composer / Indeterminate, Graphic Notation
Brown is known for his innovative graphic notational methods influenced by Schillinger and Calder. He collaborated with John Cage on the *Project for Music for Magnetic Tape* (1952-55). His other compositions include: *Music for "Tender Buttons"* for speaker, flute, horn, and harp (1953), *Indices* for chamber orchestra (1954), *Calder Piece* for four percussion and mobile (1967), *Modules I-II* for orchestra (1966), *Event: Synergy II* for 11 woodwinds and eight strings (1968), *Time Spans* for orchestra (1972), *Tracer* for ensemble and tape (1984), and *Tracking Pierrot* for ensemble (1992). —*"Blue" Gene Tyranny*

Times Five (1963) / **Octet 1 (1953)** / **December (1952)** / **Novara (1962)** / CRI ✦✦✦✦
Elegant kaleidoscopic mobiles for various instrumental combinations and electronics read from various original graphic scores. Brown is one of the composers of The New York School (along with Cage, Feldman, and Wolff) who radically altered our concepts of the freedom possible in music. —*"Blue" Gene Tyranny*

Available Forms II/ In "New Music" / 1968 / RCA Victrola ✦✦✦
Ethereally beautiful performance, conducted by Bruno Maderna. The score is constructed in blocks of music ('available forms') that the conductor cues and guides with various signals, like an engineer with tracks of recorded material to mix. A combination of spontaneous music making and precomposed intentions that works well. Enthusiasts may also want to check out his "Four Systems for Four Amplified Cymbals" (1964) in *Electronics and Percussion*, with Max Neuhaus on percussion (Columbia MS 7139 disc, currently out of print). —*"Blue" Gene Tyranny*

Folio (1952/1953) / **Music for Cello and Piano (1954)** / **In "The New York School"** / 1993 / Hat Hut ✦✦✦
Two classic works by Brown, including four realizations of the famous multidimensional graph score "Folio." —*"Blue" Gene Tyranny*

Music for Piano(s), 1951-1995 / 1996 / New Albion ✦✦✦
Solo works and multi-tracked pieces. "Corroboree" for three pianos, composed during the winter of 1964, refers to "a nocturnal festivity with songs and symbolic dances by which the Australian aborigines celebrate events of importance; a noisy festival, tumult" (*Webster's Dictionary*). Toward this effect, Brown used five kinds of piano sounds—single notes, chords, hand and forearm clusters, pizzicato and hand-muted sounds on

the interior strings—to make "a kind of sonic-spatial conversation." "Folio" (1952-53) is a set of three pieces for piano containing early and remarkable experiments in music notation and the performance process. They grew out of Brown's enjoyment of group and solo jazz improvisation, a desire to find a way out of metric music and his fascination with sculptor Alexander Calder's mobiles—how they were "variable but always the same." "25 Pages, for any number of pianists up to 25" (1953) is made of "fully described material, of pitch, dynamic and duration, in a relative sense." Since the pitch is determined and the duration is relative—notated in stemless black notes with extended lines of varying lengths, each note with a specific dynamic marking—the composer considers this work a true realization of his notion of the "open form" (as compared to the "open content" of the "Folio" pieces). There are five additional works also on this fascinating and long overdue CD. —*"Blue" Gene Tyranny*

Leif Brush

Composer / Original Acoustic ("Terrain") Instruments, Electronic Transducers
Teaches at University of Minnesota. —*"Blue" Gene Tyranny*

Terrain Instruments Are Activated (1990) / 1992 / The Aerial #4 ✦✦✦
Since 1968, Leif Brush has made sound installations and performances in galleries and public places around the world using his Terrain instruments: Minnesota Permanent Forest Terrain, Signal Disc, Whistler, Wind Ribbons, Rainpattern Tree Filters, Treeharps Networking, Modified Treeways—and an array of transducers (solar-powered sensor amplifiers connected to microprocessors controlled and updated by telephone) and speaker-environments that amplify and articulate natural phenomena. Mysterious and beautiful. —*"Blue" Gene Tyranny*

Gavin Bryars

b. 1943
Bryars studied philosophy at Sheffield University as well as music on a private basis. He played in jazz groups during the 1960s and has lectured at Leicester Polytechnic since 1970. Bryars is an experimental composer, influenced by Satie and Cage and also modern literature. He often writes for unusual forces and locations. These works are published by Experimental Music Catalogue. —*Lynn Vought*

First Viennese Dance (M.H.) (1985-1986) / **In "Three Viennese Dancers"** / 1986 / ✦✦✦
Scored for French horn and percussion, this ethereal, slowly unfolding music is different from Bryars' other "sound" of jauntily repeating, minimally changing chords that he shares with Michael Nyman. —*"Blue" Gene Tyranny*

Jesus' Blood Never Failed Me Yet / 1993 / Point ✦✦✦
Six realizations for orchestra and the gravelly old man's voice of Tim Waits (who sounds very much like the original tape-recorded voice of a street singer used in the earlier Obscure Records recording of this piece). Each realization shows Bryars' gift for invention and variation and simple, appealing emotionality. A very touching and beautiful recording of nearly 75 minutes' duration. Highly recommended. —*"Blue" Gene Tyranny*

Warren Burt

b. 1949, Baltimore, MD
Composer / Electronic, Experimental Mixed-media
Studied at State University of NY and University of California at San Diego. Moved to Melbourne, Australia in 1975 to teach at La Trobe University, Sydney Conservatorium and Victoria College of the Arts. —*"Blue" Gene Tyranny*

Of Course / **Anyway You Can Always Put Language Down to Experience (with Chris Mann)** / ✦✦✦
This 77-minute piece comes on a cassette accompanied by a plastic glove and a red rock from Australia, but no liner notes. Needless to say, a strange electronic piece with the natural voice as a "trigger." —*"Blue" Gene Tyranny*

Sylvano Bussotti

b. 1931
Bussotti was a gifted child musician. He entered the Florence Conservatory in 1940 and left four years later to pursue independent study in composition. He was influenced by Deutsch, Metzger, Boulez, and Cage, among others. His music participates in and also criticizes the decadence of modernism. He uses graphic notation in a flamboyant style that is often difficult to perform, in works that are erotic and artificial and often refer to his personal life, which is seemingly colorful. *La passion selon Sade* (1969) and *Lorenzaccio* (1972) are his main works for theater. In addition to music he has worked in the fields of painting, graphic art, and journalism. —*Lynn Vought*

Rara Requiem / Bergkristall / The Lorenzaccio Symphony / 1992 / Deutsche Grammaphon ✦✦✦

As a talented graphic artist, Bussotti has made some of the most amazing looking graph scores, like the famous "Five Pieces for David Tudor," a score made in 1959 from a drawing made in 1949. Lines run in every direction, there are wild squiggles and vortices, small icons of imaginary characters, laconic word phrases of equal import as the other symbols, and formless dark areas. Likewise, the score for "Coeur pour Batteur" in Max Neuhaus' out-of-print Columbia 7139 disc *Electronics and Percussion* is as defined as it is open (synesthetically) to subjective readings by the performer. In this recording, Neuhaus divides the score into spatial directions for unusual body movements that result in sounds, together with inadvertent body movements, and instruments set up to sympathetically vibrate out of the control of the performer. In Bussotti's later works heard in this two CD re-issue of recordings from 1976 and 1978, his approach is more traditional in procedure but not in sound: "Bergkristall" is a ballet in one act and seven scenes based on a tale by Adalbert Stifter of a young boy and girl who get lost in a snowstorm on Christmas Day while returning home from the valley where their grandparents live in the dyeworks. Following the spirit of a long-lost baker's boy, they wander off toward the "regions of eternal ice." Nature takes on supernatural forms—snow spirits, comets—which dance with the children to keep them awake (together with their mouthfuls of coffee), and in the morning the children are rescued as the sun "burns like fire over the vast expanses of snow and glittering quartz as though a mass of roses were shining." The music is presented often in brief "illustrations," as dense (in a good sense) as multicolored drawings in a children's book—the Christmas tree decorations, the dancing spirits, the icy dissonance. If Charles Ives had decided to write with serialistic gestures and sounds, the result would probably be close to this unusual and exciting score. —*"Blue" Gene Tyranny*

Christopher Butterfield

b. 1952, Vancouver, British Columbia
Composer / Acoustic Experimental
Butterfield was co-founder of the rock group Klo. He collaborated with writer John Bentley Mays on the music drama *Project for an Opera of the Twentieth Century G.S.: Something that happened once and it is very interesting.* Now a teacher of composition at the University of Victoria, Butterfield has composed for many of Canada's principal ensembles. —*"Blue" Gene Tyranny*

Music for Klein and Beuys (1987) / Pillar of Snails (1984-1987) / 1993 / Not for Sale (Musicworks) ✦✦✦

Highly original chamber music ("Music for Klein and Beuys") by this Canadian composer with snatches of delightful tunelike passages that are somewhat more like melodic gestures, brief responses, bon mots to the accompaniment of percussion that often sounds like amplified crumpled bags. But it's not "joke music". It's something else. "Pillar of Snails" is a piano piece that begins with single unharmonized melodic line statements separated by an appropriate silence, and gradually glorious chords are added but only briefly as a shading. The title refers to a tower or pillar, a massive black basalt cube that once sat on a pedestal but has now fallen and is half-submerged in a marsh in a mausoleum on a hill (The Spindles) in the once ancient Phoenician port of Amrit in what is now Syria. This CD is literally not for sale but came included in a package from the Canadian Musicworks magazine, which may still have some. Butterfield also excellently performs Kurt Schwitters's "Ursonate" (Sonate in Urlauten) on this CD. —*"Blue" Gene Tyranny*

Empress of Russia / 1993 / Artifact ✦✦✦

In the collection *Arraymusic: New World.* A charming ensemble composition built on waves of motoric pulses and tones which rise and fall back into a center in a kind of cresting motion. "The title is . . . that of a passenger ship, one of Canadian Pacific's 'White Empresses' which served on that line's Vancouver-Yokohama-Shanghai run until 1939." (See also Butterfield's *Flamingo Limo* in the collection *Strange Companions*). —*"Blue" Gene Tyranny*

Michael Byron

b. Sep. 7, 1953
Composer / Minimalist Harmonic and Pattern Works for Orchestra and Ensembles
Influential as a writer and commentator on new music, and an editor of new music anthologies. —*"Blue" Gene Tyranny*

Marimbas in the Dorian Mode/ In "Cold Blue Anthology" / 1990 / Cold Blue Records ✦✦✦✦

Unusual fluttering sounds from four marimbas played in a sustained and very quiet manner—absolutely peaceful. If you run across one, grab a copy of the lovely orchestral pieces on *Tidal* on the defunct Neutral Records. —*"Blue" Gene Tyranny*

George Cacioppo

☆ **Time on Time in Miracles / In "Music from the ONCE Festival"** / 1966 / Advance ✦✦✦✦✦

Cacioppo produced some remarkably original ensemble music—the graph score based directly on the form of the constellation "Cassiopeia"; "Two Worlds" (1962), which contrasts the worlds of instrumental and vocal sounds; "Advance of the Fungii," based on ideas in the book by E. C. Large, which describes various plagues that overwhelm plants and animals from time to time; and "Bestiary 1 Eingang." Several works generated pitches and overall form based on Markov chains. —*"Blue" Gene Tyranny*

John Cage

b. Sep. 5, 1912, Los Angeles, CA, d. Aug. 12, 1992, New York, NY
Composer / Indeterminate, Prepared Piano, Live Electronic Music, Philosophy, Percussion
Cage studied with Richard Buhlig, Adolph Weiss, Henry Cowell, and Arnold Schoenberg. He taught at various schools and universities, and was music director for the Merce Cunningham Dance Company from 1944-66. His early work was serial and cyclic and was influenced by world-music, e.g., *Sonatas and Interludes for Prepared Piano* (1948), and *Imaginary Landscape No. 1* (1939). Cage is known as the inventor of "prepared piano." He created a live electronic music performance with pianist-composer David Tudor in the late '50s, and developed conceptual pieces with graphic scoring on transparencies, notably in the *Variations* series. Cage extended some of these techniques to visual arts (silkscreens, etc.) in later years. —*"Blue" Gene Tyranny*

Four Walls / Tomato
This beautiful piece for piano solo, with a scene for unaccompanied solo voice in the middle, is approximately an hour long. It was originally written as music for a "dance play" psychodrama by the dancer Merce Cunningham, which had only one performance. The music is played entirely on the white keys of the piano, which gives the work natural modal qualities, and the music is not complex; it was designed to be easily played as Cage could not attend rehearsals with the pianist. All of these circumstances resulted in a work of direct, evocative, and mesmerizing musical gestures, some set off by silences of varying length, some of insistent rhythm with simple variation. There are 14 Scenes, plus two sections for dance alone, each with a different dynamic—the text they were to accompany, now lost, can only be imagined by the listener. Written at a time when Cage was considering ceasing to write music in order to devote time to being psychoanalyzed, the title (as in the expression "staring at four walls" for intense, cabin-fever boredom) must have taken on poignant personal significance for the composer. He resolved to keep on with music, which led to the radical and highly influential solutions of his post-1950 work. —*"Blue" Gene Tyranny*

Etudes Boreales (1978) / Ryoanji (1983) / 1985 / Mode ✦✦✦

One of the most beautiful albums of Cage's music: wonderful silences, no sense of pulse, perfectly played gestures on piano, cello with mezzo-soprano vocal, peaceful, eternal. Highly recommended. —*"Blue" Gene Tyranny*

☆ **Empty Words (Part III, Live Teatro Lyrico Di Milano 2 Dec. 1977)** / 1991 / Cramps ✦✦✦✦✦

Cage reading a gradually fragmenting text based on Thoreau's "Walden Pond," this heartwarming piece shows how Cage's chance procedures serve to enhance, rather than distance, human feeling and attention. The entire *Empty Words* (Parts I-IV) on 8 CDs will be issued in the near future by Lovely Music. —*"Blue" Gene Tyranny*

"John Cage": Music for Marcel Duchamp (1947) / Music for Amplified Toy Pianos (1960) / Radio Music (1956) / 4'33" in Three Parts / 1991 / Cramps ✦✦✦

Wonderful performances by composer/performers Hidalgo, Marchetti, Simonetti, and Stratos of these well-known pieces, including the famous "silent piece" (4'33") in three parts. —*"Blue" Gene Tyranny*

☆ **Singing Through / Vocal Compositions by John Cage** / 1991 / New Albion ✦✦✦✦✦

Beautifully performed pieces from 1942-1985 by vocalist Joan LaBarbara with piano and percussion. Contains: "A Flower" (1950), "Mirakus" (1984), "Eight Whiskus" (1984), "The Wonderful Widow of 18 Springs" (1942) for voice and closed piano, "Nowth upon Nacht" (1984), "Sonnekus" (1985), "Forever and Sunsmell" (1942), "Solos for Voice (from the Songbooks) No.'s 49, 52, 67" (1970), "Music for Two (by One)" (1984). —*"Blue" Gene Tyranny*

Music for Merce Cunningham: Five Stone Wind (Collaboration with David Tudor and Takehisa Kosugi) / Cartridge Music (1960) Realizat / 1991 / Mode ✦✦✦

Amplified violin, bamboo flute, nine clay pots, tapes, and live electronics. The spirit of gentle indeterminacy. "Cartridge Music" is a classic of graph music for phonograph cartridges and amplified small objects. —*"Blue" Gene Tyranny*

Cheap Imitation / 1991 / Cramps ♦♦♦
With the composer at the piano. A lovely performance of melodies that are fragments and transformations of melodies for Erik Satie's opera *Socrate* on the death of Socrates. Cage had to produce "cheap imitations" of these melodies for a performance when the rights for the Satie score could not be obtained. —*"Blue" Gene Tyranny*

Diary: How to Improve the World (You Will Only Make Matters Worse) / 1992 / Wergo ♦♦♦
An eight-CD set of brilliant observations, from the humorous to the speculative to the heart-filling. Cage speaks of lives and notions of the well-known—B. Fuller, Thoreau, the Vietnam War, Meister Eckhart, Schoenberg; being crammed in a subway car and odd confrontations with airplane employees; of unique and everyday events—unemployment, free worldwide communications, dads and moms, electric clothing, workable anarchy. The typography determines the stereo distribution and level of Cage's voice, the effect of someone talking inside your head, disembodied. (The printed texts additionally used color changes to parallel this effect.) Some of the text, pictures of Cage reading and the clean water supply, and chronologies accompany the discs. —*"Blue" Gene Tyranny*

Fontana Mix and Solo for Voice 2 / 1993 / Hat Hut ♦♦♦
Three parts of the classic tape music piece "Fontana Mix" are superimposed while the "Solo for Voice 2" is performed simultaneously with them. When pieces employed the same chance operations or other similar methods in their composition, Cage would often specify in the score that they could be played at the same time. —*"Blue" Gene Tyranny*

Indeterminancy, New Aspect of Form in Instrumental and Electronic Music / 1993 / Smithsonian/Folkways ♦♦♦
A CD reissue of the legendary early '60s discs in which Cage relates enlightening and entertaining stories from his life, from ancient texts, from secondhand sources and spontaneous insight, while pieces composed using indeterminant procedures are performed on piano and live electronics by David Tudor. Essential for an understanding of Cage at the root level. (It's OK that the voice is obscured at times.) —*"Blue" Gene Tyranny*

Concert for Piano and Orchestra / Atlas Eclipticalis / 1993 / Wergo ♦♦♦
This has got to be one of the finest recordings of Cage's music ever. The careful consideration given to musical and sonic details by the Orchestra of the S.E.M. Ensemble with conductor Petr Kotik and the wonderful performance of piano soloist Joseph Kubera finally makes understandable in sound Cage's philosophical and poetical insights. In the performance of "Atlas Eclipticalis," for example, we finally hear the ongoing universe of stars, planets, solar winds, and asteroids (etc.) much as Cage may have imagined a performance of his work. These musicians play the music with respect, accuracy, and a more than ordinary sense of what is beautiful. —*"Blue" Gene Tyranny*

Europera, Vol. 5 / 1994 / Mode ♦♦♦
The challenge of Cage's "4'33," the renowned "silent piece," is how to unintentionally divide or distinguish something (silence) in three parts (I. Tacet, II. Tacet, III. Tacet) that is by its very nature indivisible and without distinctions. The challenge of *Europeras 1 & 2* (1986-87) can be seen as the opposite task: to take the mythologized, linear, dramatic, pre-composed and culturally inherited material of the European opera, and then "distinguish all the elements of theater . . . [in order to] ventilate people's heads." In Cage's solution, each element is treated as a center, and the piece as a whole becomes a system of interpenetration and nonobstruction. All of the independent elements—arias (one to six at any time, each chosen by the singers themselves), orchestral music (one to sixteen measures from 70 operas from Gluck to Puccini), tape music (Truckera, 101 operatic fragments in sweeping stereo), stage action and blocking (singers are lifted and carried by assistants, flown into the air with harnesses attached), sets (36 different flats entering from stage left, right and above, images of 19th-century composers, singers, sets and animals), props (including a giant bubble machine, a coffin, a garbage can, an igloo that unzips, a jeep, a mynah bird, a radio-controlled Zeppelin, etc.), lighting, costumes (they have nothing to do with "roles") and even program notes (random permutations from various opera synopses, audience members receiving differing notes)—are modified by chance operations utilizing a computer program called IC which simulates the coin tosses of the *I Ching*. Although fantastic in the true sense, this piece is not a parody of opera, but introduces new moods, states of awareness and an almost Cubist overview of freely interrelating culturally charged material. *Europeras 3, 4 & 5* are a continuation of the idea guiding the *Europeras 1 & 2* (1987). —*"Blue" Gene Tyranny*

Orchestral Works, Vol. 1: 101 for Large Orchestra / Apartment House 1776 / Ryoanji / 1994 / Mode ♦♦♦
Three major works performed by the New England Conservatory Phil-

harmonia. Composed in 1989, *101,* as the title suggests, is for 101 instrumentalists all playing from individual parts and not coordinated by a "score"—the instrumental parts contain a note from Cage quoting Thoreau—"The best form of government is no form of government at all and that is the form we'll have when we are ready for it"—and comparing the orchestra to a society. *Apartment House 1776* for four voices and chamber orchestra, written for a Bicentennial commission, simultaneously presents four performers of unaltered, traditional songs of Protestant, Sephardic, Native-American and African-American origins, with a chamber orchestra playing chance-operation transformations of music from the American landscape of that year: There are 44 variants of hymn settings, called Harmonies, with notes selectively removed as if lost in time, revealing the presence of silence in the writers' lives. There are also two Imitations for clarinet and cello based on Moravian church music, four Marches for solo drums, and 14 Tunes for melody instruments. Any combination of this material can be arranged into a performance. The total effect is likewise a mixed mood of echoes from long ago, religious feeling, the contemporaneity of fleeting images, of a hopeful future. In this version of *Ryoanji* (1983-1985), the four soloists play sliding pitches, shapes traced from the outlines of 15 stones that comprise the famous Zen Buddhist rock garden in Kyoto. The orchestra of 20 performers play steady, widely spaced pulses, slightly before, slightly after, and on a beat. Employing these two basic ingredients—the sliding tones for the soloists and the "Korean unison" beats for the orchestra—Cage created a work of gentle suspense and plaintive beauty. This feeling, or sensibility, also occurs in performances of the original version of this piece for one or more soloists and a percussionist. —*"Blue" Gene Tyranny*

The Number Pieces, Vol. 1: Four / One / Two / 1995 / Mode ♦♦♦
Four (1991) was composed for Merce Cunningham's dance *Beach Birds* and offers four "activities," including silence, which are realized on this recording by four performers on two pianos, violin and 12 rainsticks. Simple amelodic tones and gentle washings comprise these lovely 30 minutes. In *One* (1990) for piano, tones are retrieved from 21 conceptual sound "tanks" and sustained just on the verge of being perceived as harmony or melody; a very subtle task. In *Two* (1992) for violin and piano, "time brackets" are filled from "data banks," and the decisions search for an "acausal harmony," comparable to not needing to ask "why" a rose, for example, exists. —*"Blue" Gene Tyranny*

Music of Changes, Books I-IV / 1996 / Lovely Music ♦♦♦
An exquisitely played and beautiful recording of Cage's masterpiece, one of the most technically difficult pieces in all of piano repertoire. After studying the details of the work with David Tudor, who premiered it, and refining his interpretation in live performance over several years, pianist Kubera has applied his amazing range of touch and inflection to this accurate and highly musical recording. Because of advanced recording techniques, we are able to hear the fine harmonic and resonant combinations that were scored by Cage, and that form the interior life of the piece. One unique and surprising sound follows the next over wide dynamic (pppp to ffff applied to each individual event), durational (blazingly fast grace note figures to events or silence held for a page), and pitch ranges (the entire tessitura of the piano is employed). This is one of the first compositions to use organized parameters and chance-operations (using the Chinese *Book of Changes* or *I-Ching*) in its composition. It provides a continually fascinating listening experience. —*"Blue" Gene Tyranny*

Alison Cameron

b. Jul. 12, 1963, Edmonton, Alberta, Canada

Alison Cameron / 1995 / Experimental Intermedia ♦♦♦
A premiere CD of compositions for chamber ensemble by this innovative Canadian composer. Includes: "Runa" for viola, bassoon, sax, piano, electric piano, and percussion; "Raw Sangudo" for alto sax, C trumpet, and tuba; "Blank Sheet of Metal" for three electric guitars, keyboards, bass, piano, organ, tuba, and percussionists; "Gibbous Moon" for baroque quartet; and "Chamber of Statues" for violin, bass clarinet, French horn, bass, piano, and percussion. —*"Blue" Gene Tyranny*

Unknown Leaves / 1995 / Musicworks ♦♦♦
In the collection *Musicworks No. 63.* Performed by the Arcana Ensemble. Lovely descending scalar lines and shifting harmonies sustain a delicate landscape that changes its overall timbre from a bright springtime texture to a sadder, more resigned mood with silences gradually being introduced. A marimba coda concludes the work—first we hear tremolo chords, then a single note "dripping" sound imitated by the other instruments, and very briefly a repeat of the descending scale, as the music (leaf?) just drops away. —*"Blue" Gene Tyranny*

Cornelius Cardew

b. May 7, 1936, d. Dec. 13, 1981
Cardew was a chorister at Canterbury Cathedral for eight years, and he

later studied at the RAM. He received a scholarship from the RAM in 1957 to study electronic music in Köln. He served as an assistant to Stockhausen from 1958-60 and collaborated with him on the composition *Carré*. After a period as a graphic designer, Cardew became professor of composition at the RAM in 1967. Influenced by Cage and Tudor, Cardew was interested in the idea of performer participation in the creation of a work. He composed music that could be realized in several ways with notation that is a suggestion of the possible interpretations of the score. His most important work with this method is his graphic score *Treatise* (1963-67). In it, the performers must interpret the work as a sound version of how they see the score. This score can also be read as an abstract visual artwork. Cardew was also a frequent performer of the work of Stockhausen, Cage, Feldman, and Wolff. Together with pianist John Tilbury, Cardew became known as a leading interpreter of experimental and indeterminate music in England. —*Lynn Vought*

☆ **Memorial Concert 16th May 1982: First Movement for String Quartet / Octet '71 / Treatise / The Great Learning No. 1 and Other Pieces** / Gelbe Musik ✦✦✦✦✦
A retrospective of this musically and morally influential British composer's work played by his composer-friends Bryars, Nyman, Dave Smith, John White, John Tilbury, Rzewski, Tom Philips, Christopher Hobbs, Balanescu, Janos Negyesy, and members of the "Scratch Orchestra," a collective performing group for musicians and non-musicians that Cardew cofounded in 1969. In their constitution draft they stated that "the word music is here not understood to refer exclusively to sound (but) is flexible and depends entirely on the members." —*"Blue" Gene Tyranny*

Wendy (Walter) Carlos

Carlos stirred popular interest in synthesizer music with her *Switched-On Bach* recordings, and continues to explore the possibilities of electronic music. —*AMG*

Secrets of Synthesis / CBS ✦✦✦
More than just a demonstration disc on electronic music, the examples are original creations from her own works, from the best-selling "Switched-On Bach" to "Digital Moonscapes," and contain extremely interesting theories and a new procedure for harmonic synthesis that results in sounds never heard before. (There's an interesting article on this with a floppy disc demo in *Keyboard*, November, 1986.) —*"Blue" Gene Tyranny*

Elliott Carter

Composer / Atonal-chromaticism, Neo-classical
American composer influenced by Hindemith, Stravinsky, and VarSse. His compositions include ballets, chamber pieces (*First Quartet*, 1951), and symphonic works (*A Symphony of Three Orchestras*, 1976). —*AMG*

String Quartet no. 3 (1971) / Elegy (1943) / In "The Music for String Quartet, Vol. II" / 1988 / Etcetera ✦✦✦✦
Amazing performances by the renowned Arditti String Quartet. Pieces that illustrate the best of his early and later styles. Particularly noteworthy is the dense "abstract expressionist" complexity of the third quartet—instrumental conversations—and the unpredictable but warm, advanced-Coplandesque harmonies of the "Elegy." —*"Blue" Gene Tyranny*

Holiday Overture (1944, Revised 1961) / Suite from Pocahontas / Syringa / 1991 / CRI ✦✦✦
Reissues of Carter in his early style. Sweeping energetic performance of the "Holiday Overture." —*"Blue" Gene Tyranny*

Variations for Orchestra (1954-1955) / In "Cage/Carter/Babbitt/Schuller" / 1994 / Deutsche Grammaphon ✦✦✦
The shocking classic that was a signal of Carter's change to a radically new American serialist style. —*"Blue" Gene Tyranny*

Joseph Celli

b. Mar. 19, 1944, Bridgeport, CT
Composer / Experimental Acoustic, Electronic (incl. satellite), Installations
Developed new performing techniques for oboe and English horn, plays many double reed instruments including Korean p'iri, tae'ponso, Indian Mukha Veena, Japanese hickiricki, and employs electronics in his performances. Celli created the first American satellite performance piece with Jerry Hunt entitled, *PHALBA*. He has produced over 1500 contemporary concerts and art activities, and commissioned works from many composers, including Ornette Coleman, Pauline Oliveros, and Roberta Friedman. Celli has premiered over 35 inter-media works by various artists. —*"Blue" Gene Tyranny*

No World Improvisations / 1992 / ✦✦✦
Virtuoso solo and duo improvisations with Jin Hi Kim (b. 1956) (Korean komungo, changgo, and electric komungo) and Celli (Indian Mukha

Veena, English horn without reeds, and Yamaha WX-7 MIDI-breath controller). Wonderful. —*"Blue" Gene Tyranny*

No World (Trio) Improvisations / 1992 / O.O. Discs ✦✦✦
Imaginative group improvs by Joseph Celli (double reeds), and Jin Hi Kim (komungo and electric komungo), in trio format with different guest soloists, including Alvin Curran (electronics), Shelley Hirsch (voice), and Malcolm Goldstein (violin). —*"Blue" Gene Tyranny*

Sky: S for J (1976) for Five English Horns Without Reeds / In "Organic Oboe" / 1992 / O.O. Discs ✦✦✦
New and startling techniques for the English horn. —*"Blue" Gene Tyranny*

Music Eyes Video Ears / 1995 / O.O. Discs ✦✦✦
A collection of five works of music written to accompany multi-channel video presentations. *36 Strings* (1992) is for the Korean komungo, played here with much expression and feeling by Jin Hi Kim, and five channels of video. It is dedicated to the reconciliation of North and South Korean families. *8 Mallets Four Brian* (1986) is for marimba, vibraphone, xylophone and orchestra bells and three channels of video. It is an evocative work with dense, sustained textures. *Andes* (1990) was realized by seven Peruvian musicians, and is set amongst a "Mountain of Televisions." It is played here by the Grupo de Musica Folklorica del Peru on cajon, mama cuena, cuena, zampoona, cahita, and charango, and was recorded at Peruvian National Television in Lima with submachine gun-toting guards standing around while the musicians obliged with simultaneous rhythms of African 4/4 and Spanish 3/4. *Video Sax* (1993) is for various saxes and five channels of video. It begins with slow, dissonantly meshing scale patterns, and then begins to accelerate and "get stuck" in repeating rhythmic nodes; the slow process is started again and winds its way to a free-for-all wailing jam for a coda. *Violin & Video* (1988) for multitracked solo violin and three channels of video, is a triple counterpoint of stereo pulsing chops, a descending sustained tone track and a wild central improvised solo track. This entire CD is a richly rewarding listening experience. —*"Blue" Gene Tyranny*

Joel Chadabe

b. 1938
Chadabe studied with Elliott Carter and composes mainly electronic music. He founded the electronic studio at SUNY Albany and later served as president of the Composer's Forum in New York. —*Lynn Vought*

Settings for Spirituals / 1985 / Lovely Music ✦✦✦
Available on vinyl LP only. A computer program follows the nuances of a soprano's voice and generates "settings" to expand the musical quality of the vocal sound. In the second composition, "Solo," Chadabe controls a computer generating melodies and accompaniments by moving his hands in relation to two proximity-sensitive antennas. —*"Blue" Gene Tyranny*

Modalities/ In CDCM Computer Music Series, Vol. 7 / 1990 / Centaur ✦✦✦
Gamelan-like, peaceful. —*"Blue" Gene Tyranny*

Rhys Chatham

Composer / Minimalism, Rock-influenced
Die Donnergoetter (The Thundergods) (1984-1986) for 6 Electric Guitars, Bass, and Drums / Waterloo, no. 2 (1986) for Solo Percussion / Homestead Records ✦✦✦
Rhys merges both pattern rock-influenced riffs (like Peter Gordon) and dense sonorities (like Glenn Branca) to produce music of an extended time sense—with imagery of thundergods. Waterloo is complete with the requisite drums and massed trumpets, and the '60s rock trio. —*"Blue" Gene Tyranny*

Mary Ellen Childs

Kilter / 1996 / Experimental Intermedia ✦✦✦
A collection of six compositions by this composer who prefers to work using her intuition and sense of musical balance, rather than employ specific compositional systems to create her lyrical compositions, which delight in rhythmic variation and subtlety of mood. *Four of One of Another* (1988) for accordion and string quartet, modulates from an initially peaceful state to some energetic propulsions, with occasional sighing passages. *Parterre* (1988) is a bright work with multiple pulsings and lovely melodic patterns, for accordion, saxes, winds, and vocal. *The Capacity of Calm Endurance* (1990), for piano, is built from a cyclic reiteration of the same body of notes that is played for the most part in an extremely quiet dynamic, but every once in a while the pianist steps forth in either an aggressive flurry of notes or a comparatively florid romantic style. *Whistling in the Dark* (1993), for solo accordion, is similar to the previous work in its use of a set body of tones that are reiterated in shifting rhythmic cycles, at times almost, but not quite, lapsing into dance pat-

terns. *Kilter* (1992) is a wonderful study of rhythmic counterpoint for two pianists employing delicately restrained energy and approaches used in the previous two works. *Night* (1992) for soprano and piano is a plaintive song, an echo of a wandering soul. *—"Blue" Gene Tyranny*

John Chowning

b. Aug. 22, 1934

Chowning studied with Boulanger and at Stanford University. He teaches computer-synthesized music at Stanford. His compositions include the work *Stria* (1977). *—Lynn Vought*

☆ **Phone (1980-1981) / Turenas (1972) / Stria (1977) / Sabelithe (1971) / 1988 / Wergo ♦♦♦♦♦**
Lyrical and sophisticated FM synthesis computer music with mysterious and surprising psychoacoustic illusions (especially found in "Turenas," the first piece to create the impression of sound sources moving in a 360-degree space). *—"Blue" Gene Tyranny*

Henning Christiansen

A composer who uses normal instruments and noises and who also makes art objects in the Fluxus tradition: e.g., his "Betrayal, op. 144," a carton filled with various small objects and an EP, signed and numbered (available from Gelbe Musik). *—"Blue" Gene Tyranny*

Abschiedssymphonie (Farewell Symphony) (1985) / 1985 / Edition Block ♦♦♦
The Farewell Symphony was composed for the opening of the Friedensbiennale (Freedom Biennale) in Hamburg, 1985, and is played by Joseph Beuys, Nam June Paik, and Christiansen. For further listening try the LPs *Fluxid: Hoehlenmonat* ("A Month in a Hole"); *Concerto for Flute and Noises; Fressmonat* ("A Month of Devouring"); *Concerto for Sax, Cello, and Noises; Fluxyl: Koenig Frost* ("King Frost"); *Concerto for Oboe and Noises; Maskenmonat* ("A Month of Disguises"); *Concerto for Trumpet, Tuba, and Noises* (available from Gelbe Musik). *—"Blue" Gene Tyranny*

Jay Cloidt

b. Oct. 5, 1949, Omaha, NE
Composer / Electronic, Computer
Cloidt has collaborated and performed with the Paul Dresher Ensemble, Margaret Jenkins Dance Company, ODC San Francisco and Kronos String Quartet. *Exploded View* is a live performance work with digital sampling electronics. Cloidt worked with Paul Dresher's *Looking West to the East* as composer, sound engineer, and performer. His other works include: *Light Fall* (1989) for Margaret Jenkins Dance Co., *Meteorology* (1988) and *Love It to Death* (1989) for the G. Palmer Dance Co. *—"Blue" Gene Tyranny*

Light Fall / 1995 / Inial ♦♦♦
In the collection *Views from the Perfect City.* Exquisite and mysterious electronic sound from many sources: modified bell-tones, city environments, a sampled housefly, "singing" frequencies of a chainsaw at varying speeds, disembodied and indistinct public-information voices, etc. And somehow the composer has made them all combine beautifully. *—"Blue" Gene Tyranny*

Ornette Coleman

b. Mar. 9, 1930
See the Jazz section for his biography.

Forms and Sounds / Bluebird ♦♦
Legendary as the performer/composer who freed jazz from the harmony and songforms of Tin Pan Alley ballads, these pieces show more of Coleman's path since his densely chromatic orchestral piece "Skies of America" (some movements are entitled "Holiday for Heroes," "Place in Space," "Foreigner in a Free Land," "Sunday in America"). This CD includes "Forms and Sounds" (played by the Philadelphia Woodwind Quartet): densities of melodies alternately freely floating or played to an automaton pulse with commentary-like to bluesy to celebratory trumpet interludes played by Coleman—calls to reconsider life; "Saints and Soldiers": repression by the religious and political contrasted with saintly discernment; "Space Flight": flashes of unidentified fluttering things that suddenly disappear (performed by the Chamber Symphony of Philadelphia String Quartet). *—"Blue" Gene Tyranny*

Trinity/ In Malcolm Goldstein's "Sounding the New Violin" / What Next? ♦♦♦
Fragments of melodies—joyous to contemplative to spontaneous exploring. *—"Blue" Gene Tyranny*

Nicolas Collins

b. 1954

100 of the World's Most Beautiful Melodies / 1989 / Trace Elements ♦♦♦
Played by an all-star "downtown" group: Nicolas Collins, Pippin Bar-

nett, Anthony Coleman, Tom Cora, Peter Cusack, Shelley Hirsch, George Lewis, Christian Marclay, Ben Neill, Zeena Parkins, Robert Poss, Ned Rothenberg, Elliott Sharp, Davey Williams, John Zorn, and Peter Zummo. A tongue-in-cheek title, perhaps, depending on your idea of "beautiful melody." Ranges from electronically and physically modified instruments with a definite "edge" to the barely perceptible, and awakes the ear. Collins is also part of the Impossible Music group (with David Weinstein, David Shea, Ted Greenwald, and Tim Spelios) who, performing live, manipulate CD players in the spirit of Plunderphonics and rap-scratch style to create a new style of electronic ensemble with works like the spatial and surreal "Simulcatastrophy"; a performance of Collins' "In CD" (a title pun on Riley's "In C," of course) often humorously rethinking Beethoven's and Mozart's cadences and form (he has made some recent work with Ben Neill along this same line); and the dense work "Salvador Dali's Digital Cinema." *—"Blue" Gene Tyranny*

It Was a Dark and Stormy Night / 1992 / Trace Elements ♦♦♦
More ensemble work with a sound like *100 Melodies* but with a more through-composed style. *—"Blue" Gene Tyranny*

Philip Corner

b. Apr. 10, 1933
Composer / Meditative, Early Graph Scores
Many of Corner's scores from the early '60s were partly verbal instruction and partly graphic fragments for open improvisation ensembles—for example, *Passionate Expanse of the Law, This Is It This Time* (scores hung on string throughout orchestra), etc. His later work involves more meditative concerns. *—"Blue" Gene Tyranny*

(Gamelan) The Gold Stone (1985) / In Malcolm Goldstein's "Sounding the New Violin" / What Next? ♦♦♦
Sighing, sliding tones of rough to sweet texture like a "folk" violinist, restrained to pleading. *—"Blue" Gene Tyranny*

Pictures of Pictures, from "Pictures of Pictures" / Frog Peak Music ♦♦♦
Ten fascinating movements for piano solo. *—"Blue" Gene Tyranny*

Gong / Ear / 1993 / Aerial #5 ♦♦♦
A brief piece for gongs of all nationalities, sizes, and tunings. From slightly mysterious gestural sounds (objects tumbling on the rims, rubbings, etc.) to long, sustained resonances. *—"Blue" Gene Tyranny*

Henry Cowell

Quartet Euphometric (1916-1919) / 1977 / New World ♦♦♦♦♦
Like the "Quartet Romantic" (1915-1917) and the "Concerto for Rhythmicon and Orchestra," this brief, two-minute work, played here by the Emerson String Quartet, is built on yet another of Cowell's groundbreaking "resources." Converting pitch intervals into rhythms (all tones vibrate in rhythmic cycles but you can hear the separate beats only on very low notes). Although these works were too difficult for players of that decade, they are quite playable now. Cowell was the prime mover of the "ultramodernist" (the term used then) music scene in the early part of the century, who established the vitally important New Music editions (publishing some modern classics) and who produced many concerts of new music. He invented many technical musical devices (see his 1930 book *New Music Resources*), such as playing inside the piano (in his famous work "Banshee")and producing artificial harmonics on the piano. Like Charles Ives, he was writing "atonally" before the similar technique reached America from Europe (Schoenberg, Berg, Webern, Hauer). His interest in the musical techniques of other cultures led to attempts at synthesizing a "world music" and greatly influenced his later, more conservative works (his writing seemed to change after the sad episode of his undeserved imprisonment). A recording of his piano works is essential to any new music collection, but at the moment of this writing there are (amazingly) none available. *—"Blue" Gene Tyranny*

Persian Set / 1993 / Koch ♦♦♦
This is a collection of Cowell's more conservative but still original later works that reflect a fascination with "world music" and redefining traditional harmony and counterpoint. Performed beautifully by the Manhattan Chamber Orchestra, conducted by Richard Aulden Clark, this CD contains: "Persian Set," "Old American Country Set," "American Melting Pot," "Hymn and Fuguing Tune," "Air," and "Adagio" from "Ensemble." *—"Blue" Gene Tyranny*

Piano Music / 1994 / Smithsonian/Folkways ♦♦♦
At last, a reissue of the 1963 recording of Cowell playing several of his piano works in his casual style, so that the listener regards the unusual sounds and techniques as completely natural within the context of each piece's imagery. A recording of the complete piano works is definitely needed, but this CD, with Cowell's spoken commentary at the end, is a precious thing to have at the moment. *—"Blue" Gene Tyranny*

Ruth Crawford (Seeger)

Quartet 1931 / In "Arditti String Quartet" / Gramavision ✦✦✦✦✦
A highly expressive piece and an innovative breakthrough in its use of harmonics and extended tones. Crawford invented structural techniques that have had great influence on avant-garde music. —*"Blue" Gene Tyranny*

Sonata for Violin and Piano / Study in Mixed Accents for Piano (1930) / 9 Preludes for Piano / Diaphonic Suite #1 for Solo Oboe / 1993 / CRI
A CD reissue of mostly earlier pieces by Crawford showing her innovations and originality. —*"Blue" Gene Tyranny*

Alvin Curran

Composer / New age, electronic
American composer and student of Elliott Carter who has written small- and large-scale pieces that make use of environmental sounds. —*AMG*

Electric Rags II / 1990 / New Albion ✦✦✦✦✦
Rova Saxophone Quartet with Curran (electronics) and Scot Gresham-Lancaster (Oberheim expander) playing lots of tuneful and rhythmic material ("Z Train," "Corny Island," "Scusami, I Walk Alone," "Continental Shelf-Dance," etc.). The computer spontaneously structures the concert while the sax players control synthesizers, and all is constantly transformed in real time. —*"Blue" Gene Tyranny*

Songs and Views of the Magnetic Ocean / 1994 / Catalyst ✦✦✦
Sounding a bit like Terry Riley plus sound effects, this CD is a lovely, almost New Age mix of environmental, vocal, and synthesized sounds. Sections include "At Harmony Ranch" and "Crystal Aires." —*"Blue" Gene Tyranny*

Schtyx (1991) / VSTO (1993) / 1994 / CRI ✦✦✦
Schtyx is scored for three dog whistles, piano, prepared piano, harmonica, bass drum, two violins, and percussion. *VSTO* is for string quartet. —*"Blue" Gene Tyranny*

Anthony Davis

b. Feb. 20, 1951

Lost Moon Sisters / In Dora Ohrenstein's "Urban Diva" / 1993 / CRI ✦✦✦
Best known for his dramatic 12-tone style as in the opera *X, The Life and Times of Malcolm X* (1986) and his incidental music for the award-winning Broadway play *Angels in America*, Davis has written here a lovely, modest, blues-influenced (with some echoes of Dave Brubeck) chamber work to a mythically ranging, brilliant text by Diane DiPrima. —*"Blue" Gene Tyranny*

Bob Davis

b. Jul. 17, 1947, Philadelphia, PA
Composer / Theater, Environmental Sounds, Modern Song

Ecomania / 1991 / Earwax ✦✦✦
Cassette of a wonderful production for radio containing opinions, musical fantasies, natural sound, etc., showing all aspects and attitudes concerning the idea of "ecology." —*"Blue" Gene Tyranny*

Planetary Diversions / 1991 / Emergency Records ✦✦✦
Weird and wonderful settings of texts by G.P. Skratz—"The Mass of the Scattered Animals" (live performance at Life on the Water, San Francisco), "I Can't Stand My Body," "Song of the Fang," "Advert," "The Fall of Polyphemus," and "Mating Song of the Planets." (Also his new album *Definitely Not a Band* has become available on cassette from Earwax.) —*"Blue" Gene Tyranny*

Deep Listening Band

Troglodyte's Delight (1989) / 1990 / What Next? ✦✦✦✦✦
This group of renowned improvisors (Stuart Dempster on trombone and didjeridu, Pauline Oliveros on accordion with voice and whistles, the vocals of Panaiotis and Julie Lyon Balliett, and the percussion of Fritz Hauser) explore the sound properties of the Tarpaper Cave in Rosendale, New York. Satisfying natural and meditative beauty with two cuts featuring just cave water ("Cave Water"). My favorite cut is "After Dinner with the Trogs." —*"Blue" Gene Tyranny*

The Ready Made Boomerang / 1991 / New Albion
This time our intrepid new music crew are found mucking around underground in the Cistern Chapel, Fort Worden Cistern, Olympic Peninsula, Washington, exploding a balloon ("Balloon Payment") to demonstrate the natural reverberation time of the space, making suspended vocal ("CCCC" or Cistern Chapel Chance Chants) and unusual instrumental sounds, and dropping percussive stuff. Lovely and mysterious. —*"Blue" Gene Tyranny*

Aurelio de la Vega

b. Nov. 28, 1925, La Habana, Cuba
De la Vega studied with Fritz Kramer in Havana (1943-46) and with Ernst Toch in Los Angeles (1947-48). A lecturer and essayist on contemporary music, his early works include *The Infinite Foundation* (post-impressionist), *Elegy for String Orchestra* (1954) (freely chromatic), and *String Quartet* (serialist). His graph scores of the '70s include *Olep ed Arudamot, The Infinite Square, Astralis,* and *The Magic Labyrinth.* De la Vega's other works include: *Undici Colori* (1981) for solo bassoon and projections of abstract drawings, *Inflorescencia* (1976) for soprano, bass clarinet and tape, and *Magias e Invenciones* (1986), a song cycle for soprano and piano. —*"Blue" Gene Tyranny*

Tropimapal / Opus One ✦✦✦
In the collection *Latin American Composers in the US* Scored (1983) for flute, clarinet, bassoon, trombone, percussion (one player), violin, viola, cello, and double bass. It is written in a free, post-serialist style, with indeterminate sections and textures that wander between a dreamy mysteriousness and intense, explosive, and multi-rhythmic sound events. Although not programmatic, these are sounds of a wild, untamed landscape. —*"Blue" Gene Tyranny*

Paul DeMarinis

b. 1948
Composer / Electronic, Mixed-media Installation Pieces
DeMarinistudied at the Center for Contemporary Music, Mills College, and collaborated with composer Robert Ashley on the music for *In Sara, Mencken, Christ and Beethoven, There Were Men and Women.* He has made many innovative uses of modern technology to make audio installations, for example, the movements of fish in a tank to generate electronic cues, and tapping the lasers found in CD players to read grooves and textures of natural surfaces and ancient ceramics as "Sound Archaeology." —*"Blue" Gene Tyranny*

I Want You / Kokole / In "Another Coast" / 1988 / Music and Arts ✦✦✦
Inventive and charming interactive vocals with electronics. —*"Blue" Gene Tyranny*

☆ **Music as a Second Language / 1991 / Lovely Language ✦✦✦✦✦**
Interactive electronics outlining voices with computer shadowing melodies, beautiful sustains, gentle humor, and humanity. Contains: "Fonetica Francese," a take-off on language lessons; "Odd Evening," about a Chinese radio play; "An Appeal," "a fit of legal dictation plagued by spurious vocal melodies"; "The Sand Clock"; "Cincinnati 1830-1850"; "The Power of Suggestion," based on the voices of hypnotists, evangelists, and salesmen; and "Beneath the Numbered Sky," based on an Indonesian folksong. Marvelously imaginative. —*"Blue" Gene Tyranny*

Stuart Dempster

In the Great Abbey of Clement VI / 1987 / Arch ✦✦✦✦✦
Mellow solo trombone calls, earth energy drones, and cries of a didjeridu invoke the resonate standing waves built into the harmonic geometry of the architecture. —*"Blue" Gene Tyranny*

Robert Dick

Venturi Shadows / 1992 / O.O. Discs ✦✦✦
Music of this flute revolutionary/composer in performances by Neil Rolnick, Steve Gorn, Ned Rothenberg, and Mary Kay Fink. —*"Blue" Gene Tyranny*

Die Toedliche Doris (Deadly Doris)

Naturkatastrophen (Natural Catastrophes) (1985) / Gelbe Musik ✦✦✦
Seven-inch disc with booklet in German and English. Instructions on how to produce do-it-yourself disasters—a way of dealing with "the dread generated by State, society, and nature," as kids do by means of fairy tales, and others do by forms of resistance. Toedliche Doris, "Deadly Doris," is three visual artists, centered in Berlin, who manifest a good sense of humor, a very raw and raucous approach to music, and a lot of well-placed angst, and who refer to their group as "she." This record is one of their milder productions, but be warned: playing this album will definitely not endear you to the neighbors. —*"Blue" Gene Tyranny*

Jaques Diennet

Aubracs: Wuevres pur Batterie, Synclavier et Bande Magnetique (Works for Percussion, Synclavier, and Tape) / 1987 / GMEM ✦✦✦
One of the most interesting composers in the lively scene at the Groupe de la Musique Experimentale de Marseilles. This CD contains two atmospheric works: "Aubracs-sur-Maguelonne" (1982) and "Aubracs-les-Canaux" (1984) for percussion sounds and Synclavier synthesizers;

many of the percussive type sounds are in fact generated by the electronics, and an illusion is created in which the listener cannot tell who is playing what. "This is an imaginary place tinkering about the scenery. I may mix limestone (Les Quatre-Maguelonne) with granite (Aubrac) and so hasten the continental drift. The drawing out of sound is also the principle of confrontation: the blunt, almost harsh tone of the percussion instruments and those most sophisticated instruments of digital technology." —*"Blue" Gene Tyranny*

Herbert Distel

Die Reise (The Journey) / 1990 / ✦✦✦
A dazzling four-part work designed for radio broadcast. —*"Blue" Gene Tyranny*

Lucia Dlugoszewski

b. Jun. 16, 1934, Detroit, MI
Composer / Acoustic Music, Radical Rhythmic/Timbre Techniques, Instrument Builder
Dlugoszewski studied with Edgard Varèse and Grete Sultan. She devised "timbre piano," and scores for Living Theater and Erick Hawkins dances. She has created over 100 percussion instruments. A teacher at NYU, the New School for Social Research, and the Foundation for Modern Dance, Dlugoszewski has received many awards and orchestral commissions. —*"Blue" Gene Tyranny*

Tender Theatre Flight Nageire (1971 / 1978) / CRI ✦✦✦
A "series of musical rituals involved with the poetic roots of erotic experience, *Nageire* is an oriental aesthetic principle of nondevelopment, of nonlinear leap. It uses constant and extreme surprise . . . leaping into unknown material . . . for the flexibility of the mind. One drop of water can unhinge my throat into miracles of swallowing. The sudden shiver of a delicate paper rattle or an unusually sensitive tonguing on a brass instrument becomes transparency utterly alive" (from notes by the composer). For brass ensemble with the composer playing on many of her 100 percussion instruments: lovely silence, surprising sounds. —*"Blue" Gene Tyranny*

Angels of the Inmost Heaven / 1975 / Folkways ✦✦✦✦✦
Performed by a brass ensemble, conducted by Gerard Schwarz. Music for a dance by Erick Hawkins, these "Angels" are described by transformations called Nova (bursts of energy), Corona (transparent densities), and Clear Core (tiny distinctions in static walls, a nervous surface of extremely quick pulses). Extraordinary variations of glissandos, fast lip and finger trills, and constant shifting of mutes are the ingredient techniques of a very unique style that flows with high energy and also the eloquence of a Debussy orchestral brass section. —*"Blue" Gene Tyranny*

Fire Fragile Flight / 1979 / Candide ✦✦✦
This gorgeous piece, performed by the Orchestra of our Time, is totally unique in sound and conception. A chamber orchestra with an unusual percussion section (four players on slide whistles, hanging bells, playing inside the piano, etc.) recreates the physical phenomena of falling leaves in early March in the Great Lakes country. The music has 65 freely chosen, musically dangerous "leap-points," which trigger whirling "startle-juxtapositions" of varying speed, like the reflected light on turning and falling leaves will sometimes appear to set them on fire. —*"Blue" Gene Tyranny*

Charles Dodge

b. Jun. 5, 1942, Ames, IA
Composer / Electronic, Computer Speech Synthesis, Instrumental
Charles Dodge studied with Richard Hervig, Gunther Schuller, Jack Beeson, Chou Wen-chung, and Otto Luening; electronic music with Ussachevsky, and computer music with Godfrey Winham. A researcher at IBM Thomas J. Watson Research Center, Bell Telephone Labs, and the University of CA at San Diego, Dodge also taught at Columbia, Princeton, and Brooklyn College. His well-known oieces include *Rota* for orchestra (1966), *Changes* for computer-synthesized sound (1970), *Earth's Magnetic Field* for computer-synthesized sound (1970), and *Any Resemblance Is Purely Coincidental* (1980) for piano and synthesized voice on tape. —*"Blue" Gene Tyranny*

Earth's Magnetic Field (1970) / 1971 / Nonesuch ✦✦✦
Realized at the Columbia University Computer Center, this piece is built from directly translating a record of the magnetic changes (Kp indices) for planet Earth in 1961. Eight values a day are read from graphic charts that look so much like music they are popularly known as Julius Bartel's "musical diagrams." An interesting experiment. —*"Blue" Gene Tyranny*

In Celebration / Speech Songs / The Story of Our Lives / 1990 / CRI ✦✦✦
Reissue of a 1978 disc in which poetry readings are digitized and restructured in the computer to modify vocal and other sounds. —*"Blue" Gene Tyranny*

Any Resemblance Is Purely Coincidental / 1992 / New Albion ✦✦✦
A new collection of Dodge's compositional modifications of preexisting material. Includes: "Any Resemblance Is Purely Coincidental" for voice (Enrico Caruso) and piano (Alan Feinberg); "Speech Songs" (see above); "The Waves"; and "Viola Elegy." —*"Blue" Gene Tyranny*

Paul Dolden

b. Canada
Composer / Acoustic with Tape, "Morphological" Layering
Solo concerts with violin, guitar, and cello wih tape, and improvisation. *The Threshhold of Deafening Silence* has up to 400 tracks or parts occurring simultaneously (70-80 parts are traditional Western instruments and the rest are gamelan, hand percussion, drum kits, electric guitar, and voice). Dolden has won 18 Canadian and international awards for composition, including Canada's Jean A. Chalmers Award for "L'Ivresse de la Vitesse." —*"Blue" Gene Tyranny*

The Threshold of Deafening Silence / 1992 / Tronia ✦✦✦
Wonderfully uninhibited and compact densities of amassed acoustic sounds, like the 400 tracks of "Below the Walls of Jericho," or the modulated galactic racket of "In the Natural Doorway I Crouch" for alternately tuned balalaikas. Highly recommended. —*"Blue" Gene Tyranny*

Paul Dresher

b. 1951, Los Angeles, CA
Composer / Minimalist, Pattern Music, Experimental Opera and Theater
Dresher studied with Robert Erickson, Roger Reynolds, Pauline Oliveros, and Bernard Rands. His works include Ghanaian drumming with C.K. and Kobla Ladzekpo, Hindustani classical music with Nikhil Banerjee, and Balinese and Javanese music. Known for his live delay systems on guitar, Dresher's collaborations about American culture include *Slow Fire* (1985-88), *Power Failure* (1988-89), and *Pioneer* (1990). *The Gates* (1993) was composed for dancer Margaret Jenkins. Dresher has won many awards, orchestral and opera commissions. —*"Blue" Gene Tyranny*

Other Fire (1984) In "Another Coast" / 1988 / Music and Arts ✦✦✦
A rich mix of naturally occurring rhythmic and cycling environmental sounds (birds, temple bells, and more) from tape recordings made during Asian and Southeast Asian travels that nonetheless gives the illusion of electronic synthesis. —*"Blue" Gene Tyranny*

Liquid and Stellar Music / This Same Temple / 1994 / Lovely Music ✦✦✦
A CD reissue of these lovely phase music pieces, in which repetitive processes gradually change melodic figures. —*"Blue" Gene Tyranny*

James Drew

b. Feb. 9, 1929, St. Paul, MN
Composer / Innovative Theater, Contemporary Tonal, Collective Group Improvisation, Open Scoring
This very original composer studied with Wallingford Riegger and Edgard Varése. He has taught at Northwestern University, Yale University, UCLA, Cal State, and other institutions, and also teaches privately. He has performed with and co-founded several musical groups: the Crossfire Mission Orchestra in the late '60s in New Haven (radical performances often behind barbed wire), the Mysterious Traveling Cabaret, the American Music Theater in CA, and the Blast Opera Theater, and has undertaken concerts and arts education work with the Grey Wolf Project. His works include: *Survivors in Pale Light*, a theater piece recently taped for PBS-TV with the Blast Opera players both singing and acting (he refers to the form as an opera "ostrannie," a Russian word meaning "laid bare," or "everything exposed"; for example, the actors are acting and at the same time not "acting"); *Hypothetical Structures, Books I and II; Cantalobosolo* (1995) a monodrama for contrabassist/singer/actor; *Dances of the Tunnel Saints* (1995), for two pianos and percussion; and *Powder Songs of the Lady Magicians* (1996), staged in a ritualistic circle for singer-actor, percussion, and droning strings. —*"Blue" Gene Tyranny*

The Celestial Cabaret, A Concerto for Pianist and Chamber Orchestra Symphony No. 3 / 1991 / Artistry Production ✦✦✦
Called by Nicolas Slonimsky "an authentic American original," Drew has received many awards for composition. He taught at Yale University and UCLA in the '70s, but is also an illusive figure, a legendary underground jazz pianist who has played with Elvin Jones, Clark Terry, Donald Byrd, and Earl Turbinton. He has created a style entirely his own, each piece beautifully conceived. "Symphony No. 3" is one movement of long, slow melodies that create a mysterious yet hopeful feeling with very brief percussion punctuations and chordal brass writing, none of these elements suggesting anything we have heard before yet we somehow understand the meaning. The remarkable "Celestial Cabaret" is built featuring the unaccompanied piano soloist in a lyrical, flowing style that is not romantic but like a commentary, free-flowing thought suddenly surrounded by brief, strange versions of cabaret music of a

very refined type, not satirical and not immediately recognizable. You really must hear his music to get the idea. —*"Blue" Gene Tyranny*

Marcel Duchamp

Visual artist / Conceptual Art, Chance Procedures

Erratum Musical (for Three Voices) (1913) / "Sculpture Musicale" (Realized as Mesostic by John Cage) and a Version for Music-boxes / 1990 / Edition Block ✦✦✦✦✦
The S.E.M. Ensemble, directed by Petr Kotik, realizes these early pieces using chance operations for "any instrument in which the virtuoso intermediary is suppressed." Another interesting realization is by percussionist Donald Knaack, who used a large funnel, five open-connected wagons, and numbered balls (Finnadar Records SR-9017, disc, issued 1977, out of print). —*"Blue" Gene Tyranny*

William E. Duckworth

b. 1943
Composer / Minimalism, New Compositional Procedures
Professor at Bucknell University. —*"Blue" Gene Tyranny*

Thirty-One Days (1987) for Alto Saxophone / 1990 / Lovely Music ✦✦✦✦✦
Singing and wailing sax, solo and multitracked in ensemble, great playing by Michael Swartz, who uses movement in the stereo space to change presence and "throw" sounds. —*"Blue" Gene Tyranny*

The Time Curve Preludes (1982): Books I and II, Preludes I-XXIV / 1990 / Lovely Music ✦✦✦
Described quite accurately by a reviewer as a "new-age *Well-Tempered Clavier,*" the *Time Curve Preludes* are played elegantly by pianist Neely Bruce. —*"Blue" Gene Tyranny*

☆ **Southern Harmony (1980-1981)** / 1994 / Lovely Music ✦✦✦✦✦
The Gregg Smith Singers, assisted by the Rooke Chapel Choir of Bucknell University, conducted by Gregg Smith, create the first complete recording of this exceptionally fascinating and moving choral work by concentrating and sampling only certain aspects—such as rhythm and a single gesture—of shaped-note ("sacred harp") singing (a style of the rural South). The interior nature of these hymns is brought to the surface—a very different idea from merely "setting" the hymns with new harmonies. —*"Blue" Gene Tyranny*

David Dunn

b. May 22, 1953, San Diego, CA
Composer / Alternate Tuning Systems, Tape, Environment-wildlife Sounds
Dunn studied with David Ernst, Norman Lowrey, Pauline Oliveros, and Kenneth Gaburo. From 1970-74 he was an assistant to Harry Partch and performed in the Harry Partch ensemble for over a decade. Dunn cofounded the Independent Media Labs in Santa Fe, NM and was a featured artist at the international sound festival SoundCulture in Tokyo, Japan. The author of *Music, Language, and Environment* and *Skydrift,* a large environmental sound project, Dunn's many theoretical writings include *Harry Partch: An Anthology of Critical Perspectives.* —*"Blue" Gene Tyranny*

Chaos and the Emergent Mind of the Pond / 1990 / ✦✦✦
An assembly of bio-acoustical underwater recordings that lets us listen to a burgeoning level of life we do not normally hear. —*"Blue" Gene Tyranny*

Angels and Insects / 1992 / What Next ✦✦✦
"Tabula Angelorum Onorum 49" is based on alchemist John Dee's psychic communications (see also Jerry Hunt's work along these lines). Computer-fractal voices, disembodied informants. Includes an extended re-mix of "Chaos and the Emergent Mind of the Pond," an assembly of micro bio-acoustical underwater events—insect dronings, buzzings, clickings—recorded very (macro-) closely—that lets us listen to a burgeoning level of life we normally do not hear. Dunn has also edited a splendid book, "Pioneers of Electronic Art," available from Nonsequitur. See also his " . . . With Zitterings of Flight Released (in Memoriam Kenneth Gaburo)" in the collection *Views from the Perfect City.* —*"Blue" Gene Tyranny*

With Zitterings of Flight Released, in Memoriam Kenneth Gaburo / 1995 / Inial ✦✦✦
In the collection *Views from the Perfect City.* Created with the use of a hybrid analog synthesizer, originally intended as a "hyper Lissajous pattern generator" control for a video display. The real-time processing of small audio fragments results in sonic imagery that evokes visions of otherworldly birds in flight, and perhaps interplanetary communications. —*"Blue" Gene Tyranny*

Tim Labor Crosses the Bay of Fundy with a Smile on His Face and a Song in His Heart / 1995 / Inial ✦✦✦
In the collection *Views from the Perfect City.* An absolutely delightful

and lighthearted, enormously fast, multitracked patchwork of old-time movie and cartoon-like music on a synthesizer, with a song from Stephen Foster thrown in for good measure. —*"Blue" Gene Tyranny*

Hanns Eisler

b. Jul. 6, 1898, Leipzig, Germany, **d.** Sep. 6, 1962, Berlin, Germany
Composer / 12-tone, Chromatic, Political, Vocal and Instrumental Works, Film Scores
Eisler studied with Schoenberg, collaborated with Bertold Brecht, and attended the Vienna Conservatory. He was in the Hungarian regiment in World War I and wrote *Gegen den Krieg* (Against War) the following year. In 1933 he escaped from Germany and was trailed by the Gestapo. In 1935 he lectured in the US, and became President of the International Music Bureau. In 1937 he traveled to Spain, Paris, Denmark, and Prague, worked with Ernst Bloch on political art, and composed *Lenin Requiem.* He moved to the US in 1938, and taught at the New School for Social Research, composing a 12-tone string quartet. In 1942, he moved to Hollywood, where he wrote *Composing for the Films* with T. Adorno. He was expelled by HUAC from the US in 1948. In 1949 he composed the national anthem for the GDR and became a professor at the Musikhochschule in Berlin. He composed the film score for Alain Resnais' *Nuit et brouilliard* (Night and Fog)in 1956. Eisler later became president of the Music Advisory Committee of the GDR. —*"Blue" Gene Tyranny*

Deutsche Sinfonie, Op. 50 (German Symphony) / 1995 / London ✦✦✦
Performed by various vocal soloists with the Ernst Senff Chor Berlin and the Gewandhausorchester Leipzig, conducted by Lothar Zagrosek. Part of London's *Entartete Musik [Degenerate Music,* music suppressed by the Third Reich] series. At various times dubbed an "anti-fascist cantata," a "concentration camp symphony" and an "anti-Hitler symphony," this soul-moving, humanist, provocative, and important work for chorus, soloists and orchestra is in 11 sections, written for the most part from 1935 through 1957. Eight of its movements have words by Bertold Brecht, with the eighth movement also containing portions from Ignazio Silone's novel *Bread and Wine* (1936), who was called a "renegade" by the USSR after he condemned the show trials as a "slaughtering of the opposition." The Symphony's history can also be viewed as a biography of the composer's tumultuous life: the final movement is an "Epilogue," a plea to save children from the literal cold as well as the coldness of man's previous acts. —*"Blue" Gene Tyranny*

Duke Ellington (Edward Kennedy Ellington)

See the Jazz section for his biography.

The Clothed Woman/ In "Mirage: Avant-Garde and Third Stream Jazz" / 1977 / New World ✦✦✦✦✦
Much is written about the magnificent compositions and career of Duke Ellington in the Jazz section of this guide, but this piece, recorded on December 30, 1947 (originally issued on Columbia 38236), deserves special attention as a precursor of the pointillistic style in both advanced Afro-American and Eurocentric music. The opening and closing statements of this short work are in free or open time (no pulse or rhythm) and are made from chordal forms abstracted from Ellington's piano "punctuation" accompaniment style (developed over 20 years at the time of this recording). The resulting sound is several years in advance of a similar sound in serialist music and "free jazz." Avoiding the usual idea of the "bridge" of a song, the midsection of this composition has a steady pulse that he built by placing these gestures over a chromatic boogie-bass figure that serves as a nonmodulating, suspended-in-time nervous drone. —*"Blue" Gene Tyranny*

Suite from "The River" / 1993 / Chandos ✦✦✦
A wonderful orchestration by Ron Collier of one of Ellington's many "suites" (Examples: "The Queen's Suite," "The Goutelas Suite," "The Uwis Suite," "Suite Thursday," "Far East Suite") played by the Detroit Symphony Orchestra, conducted by Neeme JSrvi. Several of Ellington's own orchestrations can be heard on the MCA Classics CD (1989) of *Ellington: Orchestral Works* with the pieces "New World A'Coming," "Harlem," and "The Golden Broom and the Green Apple." —*"Blue" Gene Tyranny*

Brian Eno

See the Rock section for his biography.

Discreet Music / 1975 / Obscure Records ✦✦✦✦✦
Taking a cue from Satie's idea of "musique d'ameublement" (furniture music), music that just exists, like furnishings in an apartment, played so as not to draw attention to itself (not really Muzak, a company which seeks to produce a more intentional work-product effect), Eno created several albums of what he termed "ambient music," which combined a softer style of pattern music (influenced by Bryars, Nyman, Harold Budd) with environmental noises. *Discreet Music* is from probably the best of these, using an Oliveros-style tape delay arrangement to slowly change patterns of repeating sounds. —*"Blue" Gene Tyranny*

Robert Erickson

Robert Erickson: Ricercar ˆ 3 (1967) for Contrabass Solo / Sierra (1984) for Baritone and Ensemble / 1991 / CRI ✦✦✦
The "Ricercar" is a bass solo with an improvised quality played sensitively by Bertram Turetzky. "Sierra," with text by Erickson and sung here by Philip Larson with the SONOR Ensemble, is a very peculiar recitative with instrumental colors about the California environs, interspersed with greetings to friends. Erickson's writing is built from "academic" elements but is always personal, unique, and lively. —"Blue" Gene Tyranny

John Fahey

The Singing Bridge of Memphis, Tennessee / March! for Martin Luther King in "The Yellow Princess" / 1992 / Vanguard ✦✦✦✦✦
In this CD reissue, we hear how Fahey, like Moondog, has often used environmental sound, not as background, but as integral to his improvised, modern folk-style guitar music, like the mournful train sounds in the distance for his "Raga for Pat" (Takoma Records, out of print). —"Blue" Gene Tyranny

Morton Feldman

b. Jan. 12, 1926, New York, NY, **d.** 1987, Buffalo, NY
Composer / Indeterminate, Large Scale Time Works, Graphic Notation
Feldman studied piano with Madame Maurina-Press, and composition with Wallingford Riegger and Stefan Wolpe. He was Edgard VarÈse's professor at the State University of New York at Buffalo. Feldman began his graphic works, with open pitch and rhythm, and music "free from a compositional rhetoric" in the early '50s, e.g., *Structures* for string quartet (1951). He later explored music with freedom of rhythm, e.g., *The Swallows of Salagan* (1960). His fully notated works are mostly quiet (in order to perceive timbre and overtone material) with non-dramatic gestures, e.g., *Piano and Orchestra* (1975). Feldman's last works were of long durations, up to six hours, e.g., *String Quartet No. 2* (1983). — *"Blue" Gene Tyranny*

Pieces for More than Two Pianos / Sub Rosa ✦✦✦
Sublime, slowly evolving chordal textures. Contains "Four Pianos," in which the four players all read from the same material but play at their own speed, gradually creating a landscape of indeterminate delays. Sensitively performed by Le Bureau des Pianistes. —"Blue" Gene Tyranny

☆ **Rothko Chapel (1971) for Chorus, Viola, and Percussion/ Why Patterns? (1978)** / 1991 / New Albion ✦✦✦✦✦
After inventing graph notation in the early '50s ("Projection I" for solo cello in 1950), Feldman began to write works that used long tones and wordless singing and were played very quietly (allowing sounds that could not be otherwise heard), creating a changing but unbroken "surface." In the '70s, he began to work with gently pulsing mobile-like rhythmic figures of which "Why Patterns?" is a good example. —"Blue" Gene Tyranny

For Samuel Beckett / 1991 / Newport Classic ✦✦✦
San Francisco Contemporary Players, directed by Stephen Mosko. Mobiles for chamber orchestra, similar to his last orchestral work, "Coptic Light." Unfortunately, recording was made with instruments at normal volume, which affects the delicate transparency of sound intended by Feldman, and so, even though the producers wish you to "play this CD very quietly," the sound is much fuller and harsher than it would be if they had played quietly from the outset. —"Blue" Gene Tyranny

Piano and Orchestra / 1991 / Col Legnio ✦✦✦
In the collection *20 Ans de Musique Contemporaine á Metz*, with Roger Woodward, pianist, and the Rundfunk-Sinfonieorchester Saarbrücken (Radio Orchestra of Saarbrücken) conducted by Hans Zender. Completed in 1975, this work is part of a series of compositions—*Cello and Orchestra, Chorus and Orchestra, String Quartet and Orchestra*—that Feldman referred to as "still-lives." "The desire here is to arouse attention to the color of the work (orchestration) rather than to the compositional method used." Specific and striking combinations of timbres are introduced, at first isolated from each other. Patterns are varied and overlap; after a while, the listener hears these patterns as characters. There is no specific program for the piece, but the surprising lushness of some chords, the plaintive simplicity of the piano writing, the highly inventive orchestral timbres, and the feeling of character surrounded by stillness all evoke deep spirituality (approached by but beyond the emotional). Upon reaching the conclusion of the piece, the listener feels transformed in some unnamed way. —"Blue" Gene Tyranny

The Viola in My Life (1970) / False Relationships and the Extended Ending (1968) / Why Patterns? (1978) / 1992 / CRI ✦✦✦✦
Reissues of some wonderful pieces: *False Relationships and the Extended Ending* alternates between exact proportions and "free time" in the vertical style (slowly changing chords, common-tone suspensions) in pieces such as "Atlantis" (1958) and "The Swallows of Salangan," which came after the counterpoint style of the early '50s graph pieces.

The Viola in My Life was the next development, adding melody-like gestures. Ethereal, heartfelt. —"Blue" Gene Tyranny

String Quartet (1979) / 1994 / Koch ✦✦✦
Astonishingly well played by the Group for Contemporary Music, this piece is a masterwork. Continually new inventions of harmonic colors, mobile-like patterns, and crystalline to shockingly rich timbres occur in an unpredictable but ultimately aesthetically satisfying time placement, and the whole performance of 78 minutes and 27 seconds takes the listener through a wide range of transcendental mental spaces. —"Blue" Gene Tyranny

Luc Ferrari

b. 1929
Composer / Electronic, Musique Concrète

Brise-glace (et Si Toute Entiere Maintenant . . .)("Icebreaker, Supposing Now I Were To . . .") / 1991 / Adda ✦✦✦✦
Winner of the Prix Italia 1987. Surreal, poetic interior monologue of passenger on shipboard near the Arctic Circle. Beautiful and original blend of orchestral writing, natural and electronic sounds. French text by Colette Fellous. —"Blue" Gene Tyranny

David First

b. Aug. 20, 1953, Philadelphia, PA
Rock & Jazz-Influenced/New Narrative Opera

The Good Book's (Accurate) Jail of Escape Dust Coordinates Part 2 / 1995 / O.O. Discs ✦✦✦
A continuous work in four sections—"Drift," "Contact," "Gallop," "Assemblage"—for winds, synthesizers, many types of guitars and percussion. "Drift" is a lovely, meditative piece with slowly changing drones on a synthesizer that are added to by other instruments playing sustained tones or soft percussion, while a muted bass guitar plays a quasi-random staccato line. The second section, "Contact," a kind of interlude, features solo synthesizer with slow de-tuning beats and additional waveforms. This evolves into "Gallop," which adds Indo-Arabian drum beats and guitar stereo rhythms to the synth drone. A center channel guitar, and winds and trumpet play a rhythmic descending modal pattern. The music then gradually settles, after eight minutes, segueing into the fourth section, "Assemblage," which slowly grows into a multi-rhythmic, gloriously dense combination of material from the previous sections. This section ends in a sustained, settled unison. Probably First's best and most successful integration of his conceptual and rhythmic music interests. (Also recommended is First's CD *Resolver* on O.O. Discs). —"Blue" Gene Tyranny

Fluxus

☆ **FluxTellus** / Tellus Audio Cassette Magazine #24 ✦✦✦✦
Soundworks by the legendary East Coast artists group who, together with other 60's performers like The ONCE Group in Michigan, radically accepted all activity of art and life in their work. Contributions from George Brecht (organizer of the New Jersey-based Yamday Festivals), Dick Higgins (writer and publisher of the famous Something Else Press), Alison Knowles, George Maciunas, Emmet Williams, LaMonte Young, Takaka Saito, Jackson Mac Low, Joe Jones, Tomas Schmit, James Tenney, Robert Watts, and Larry Miller. —"Blue" Gene Tyranny

Bill Fontana

Australian Sound Sculptures / Edition Block ✦✦✦
Fascinating sounds by one of the pioneers of sound installation pieces. This work was made while Fontana was a producer for the Australian Broadcasting Commission (1975-1978). Based on eight-channel field recordings he made for a tape archive of Australian environmental sounds, which were presented as an exhibition called "Sound Sculpture" at the National Gallery of Victoria in Melbourne. —"Blue" Gene Tyranny

Landscape Sculpture with Fog Horns (Installation Version, 1981; Live Radio Version, 1982) / 1982 / KQED-FM ✦✦✦✦✦
The installation version on this unfortunately out-of-print disc, created for the San Francisco New Music America '81 Festival, involved eight loudspeakers each playing a broadcast of ambient sound from distant locations in the Bay Area, as listeners walked along the 600 foot pier (East Wall of Pier 2, Fort Mason Center) on a trajectory toward Angel Island three miles away. A changing and drifting configuration of echo and delay patterns was created by the uncoordinated pulses of the horns and the wide spatial placement of the microphones at Point Blunt, West Garrison, Treasure Island, the Yacht Harbor, Fort Point, China Beach, the Legion of Honor, and the Cliff House. Four locations were used for the live radio version. The sound of a fog horn can travel about 5 miles. Under certain atmospheric conditions, the fog will mask certain pitches (on the radio version, the horns form a mysteriously beckoning major chord with a flat second added, plus seagulls and some brief unintelligi-

ble conversation by passersby). Certain horns are louder at a distance than at close proximity. These variations make for a beautiful listening experience. —*"Blue" Gene Tyranny*

Fast Forward

Composer / Percussion, Theater

Fast Forward studied with Stuart Marshall in Newcastle, and Robert Ashley and David Behrman at the Center for Contemporary Music at Mills College from 1976-78. The owner and operater of Pink Noise Studios, a research center for experimental audio and video techniques, Forward is known for *The Accident* (1993), nine evenings of performance music with the Wooster Group. He has received numerous grants and commissions. — *"Blue" Gene Tyranny*

Same Same / Experimental Intermedia ✦✦✦
Great new pieces featuring Fast's improvisation group. —*"Blue" Gene Tyranny*

Panhandling / 1990 / Lovely Music ✦✦✦✦
Not your usual percussion music. Sometimes studies of a single sound . . . a bullroarer (Africa, Australia) in "Bullroarer" and a metal ball rolled about a water-filled tuned oil drum, producing beautiful harmonics, in "Waterball." Also assemblies of metals from life . . . a bathtub, metal snake and two temple bells in "Precious Metals" to the bright emotion of steel pan solos in "Red Dance"; "The Big Wind" and "Stix" exploring closely placed tones moving on a steady rhythm figure, like some guitar picking, Bach prelude or African marimba music. —*"Blue" Gene Tyranny*

Fred Frith

Brilliant British avant-garde electric guitarist and multi-instrumentalist specializing in improvisation, incorporating trace-elements of free jazz and progressive rock with lots of noise and "treated" guitars à la John Cage's "treated" pianos. Solo, duo, and group (see Henry Cow) recordings range from flat-out noise (*Guitar Solos, With Enemies Like These, Who Needs Friends?*), to lovely, airy, almost lullaby-like compositions (parts of *Gravity*), to industrial dance music (side two of *Speechless*). Even the prettiest tunes have an edge, and the others (the majority) may make you re-evaluate what you consider music. Challenging and complex. It is hard to be halfway about Frith's music; you either love it or hate it. Definitely not for the weak-hearted, weak-minded, or weak-spirited. —*Niles J. Frantz*

Guitar Solos (1974) / ESD ✦✦✦
Made in four days; improvised, some to a roughly preconceived idea. "Glass c/w Steel": "four layers of sound in an eerie face out of which bounds a rubbery, animal-like line" (Cole Gagne, *Sonic Transports*); "Ghosts": distorted chords appearing and disappearing; "Out of Their Heads (on Locoweed)": "like being harangued by an automobile accident" (Gagne); "Hello Music," a cheery welcome; "No Birds": a tour through imaginary landscapes. A remarkable album that predated so much radical guitar playing of the next decades, and still has a lot of originality to offer. —*"Blue" Gene Tyranny*

☆ **The Technology of Tears (1987) and Other Music for Dance and Theatre** / 1988 / SST Records ✦✦✦✦✦
"Sadness, Its Bleached Bones Behind Us" and "You Are What You Eat" are unrelenting slices of hard-edged sounds over a pulse. "The Palace of Laughter, The Technology of Tears" is an imaginative, intense, varied suite comparing music that represents the past "frozen tears" of sadness—displayed by the media as images before us—with the "hot tears" of the moment that cannot be absorbed by technology. "Jigsaw" and "Jigsaw Coda" (1986) create patterns with constantly shifting accents and subdivisions—uneven pieces to be fit together. "Propaganda" (1987), music for a theater production, is a series of brilliantly evocative soundpieces with electronics, guitar, and sound effects: feedback and explosions in the distance, tantric harmonizing in the desert: "A Deeper Understanding of Conflict," "The Relentless Landscape," "The Excellent Hyena," "The Wolf Demon." With John Zorn (alto sax), Tenko (voice), Christian Marclay (turntables), Jim Staley (trombone). —*"Blue" Gene Tyranny*

James Fulkerson

b. 1945, Texas
Composer / Electro-acoustic, experimental

James Fulkerson: Co-ordinative Systems No. 10 for Trombone and Tape Delay (1976) / Music for Brass Instruments II (1975) / 1980 / Irida ✦✦✦
A talented composer/trombonist who uses alternate mouthpieces to create electronic-like tones, which are fed into a delay network in "Co-ordinative Systems No. 10." In "Music for Brass Instruments II," the bass trombone player follows an "aural score" of two other trombones on tape and attempts to follow and blend with them. "We play and think differently when we follow only our ears." —*"Blue" Gene Tyranny*

Force Fields and Spaces / 1994 / Etcetera ✦✦✦
Imaginative, experimental, mysterious works for solo trombone with tape-delay systems, with the fourth part being a tape collage composition. — *"Blue" Gene Tyranny*

Ellen Fullman

b. 1957, Memphis, Tennessee
Composer, sculptor / Original sound sculptures, collective improvisation

Staggered Stasis / The Aerial
Rich acoustic waves of sound from Fullman's original invention, the Long String Instrument. Floating harmonics and ancient Pythagorean intervals. —*"Blue" Gene Tyranny*

Body Music / 1993 / Experimantal Intermedia
Five more astonishing compositions on long string sculpture-instruments, including the marvelously flowing "Work for 4," performed on a 145-foot-long string installation, already a modern classic. "Space Between" surprisingly produces some sounds normally associated with electronic music, and "Body Music" suggests a kind of celestial Delta-blues with its bar chording technique. A CD that will appeal to many listeners. —*"Blue" Gene Tyranny*

Diamanda Galas

Harsh, assaultive art-punk with quasi-operatic delivery. Not for the faint-hearted. —*John Dougan*

Masque of the Red Death / 1989 / Mute ✦✦✦
Contains: "The Divine Punishment," "Saint of the Pit," and "You Must Be Certain of the Devil (A Plague Mass in 3 Parts)." A two-CD set with pieces similar in intensity to the "Plague Mass." —*"Blue" Gene Tyranny*

☆ **Plague Mass (1984**—End of the Epidemic) / 1991 / Mute ✦✦✦✦✦
Galas, who has been known for both her own work and as a singer of extremely demanding modern scores, has created this heart-wrenching cry about the physical suffering caused by AIDS, compounded by the shameful arrogance of self-appointed moralists. Maintaining an incredible intensity and depth for over an hour's solo vocal (recorded live at the Cathedral of St. John the Divine, NYC, with suitably minimal band and electronics backup), Galas proceeds through Mahalia Jackson-influenced spiritual singing, breaking at points into high saxophone-like wails, to dramatic dialogs in many dialects and languages ("There are no more tickets to the funeral") to engrossing Portugese "fado" singing to taking on the attributes of Satan (in "Sono L'Antichristo," I Am the Anti-Christ) in order to challenge the concept of a vengeful, instead of compassionate deity (and society), much as Nina Simone did in her controversial song "God Is a Killer" in the '60s. The Mass ends with the heartfelt lyrics "I go to sleep each evening now dreaming of the grave and see the friends I used to know calling out my name. O Lord Jesus, do you think I've served my time?" At times, the singing is "self-indulgent", but, well. . . . —*"Blue" Gene Tyranny*

Singer / 1992 / Mute ✦✦✦
Contains a mix of original, traditional gospel and Chicago blues tunes such as "Balm in Gilead" / "Swing Low Sweet Chariot" and "I Put a Spell on You" with Galas' personal "twist." —*"Blue" Gene Tyranny*

Ge Gan-Ru

Yi Feng (Ancient Wind) / In "New Music China" / Tellus #19 ✦✦✦✦✦
Gu Yue/ In "Sonic Encounters" / 1990 / Mode ✦✦✦
China's first avant-garde composer. After receiving degrees in violin and composition from the Shanghai Conservatory of Music, he was forbidden to play anything but scales during the Cultural Revolution and was later incarcerated and tortured. In 1983 he was awarded a fellowship to Columbia University, where he studied with Chou Wen-chung and Mario Davidovsky and received his Doctor of Musical Arts degree. He has composed concert music, as well as music for dance, theater, and several film scores: "Tang Dynasty," "Who Killed Vincent Chin?" (1988 Oscar nominee for Best Documentary Film), and "A Great Wall," the first Chinese-American feature film collaboration. His dramatic and effective music combines "contemporary Western compositional techniques with my Chinese feeling and experience along with Chinese musical characteristics inherited from thousands of years ago, so as to set up a universal music world expressing natural and primitive beauty." Watch for a future recording of his composition "Wu" (Rising to Height) (1986) for piano and chamber orchestra. —*"Blue" Gene Tyranny*

Orlando Jacinto Garcia

b. 1954, Havana, Cuba

La Belleza del Silencio (The Beauty of Silence) / 1992 / O.O. Discs ✦✦✦✦✦
Beautiful groups of sounds and soft, sharp, sustained dissonances in con-

stantly varying permutations characterize the music by this Cuban-born, Miami-based composer, who studied with Morton Feldman. Perfect performances by Joan LaBarbara (voice), the Gregg Smith Singers, Jan Williams, percussion, and other musicians. —*"Blue" Gene Tyranny*

Colores Ultraviolados / In "Bang on a Can, Vol. 3" / 1994 / CRI ♦♦♦
A lovely rhythmic mobile of sensual sounds from voice, flute, violin, and bass. —*"Blue" Gene Tyranny*

Spheres / Opus One ♦♦♦
In the collection *Latin American Composers in the US* This work for small orchestra was inspired by the sculptures of artist Rafael Jesus Soto—patterns and forms suspended in space and time. The gradual pacing and transformation of the melodic and rhythmic fragments, the isolation of steel-like and contrasting lyrical motifs echo the construction of these sculptures as creatures in a mysterious, timeless (without clock time) universe. —*"Blue" Gene Tyranny*

Peter Garland

Border Music / 1992 / What Next ♦♦♦
Early percussion pieces and works for solo harp, as well as a newer piece for harp, violin, and percussion influenced by Yaqui Indian pascola dances. Peter Garland is the publisher of *Soundings Press*, which for years has been an invaluable source for scores and information about new music. —*"Blue" Gene Tyranny*

Walk in Beauty / 1992 / New Albion ♦♦♦
Two piano pieces and an ensemble work with Aki Takahashi (piano), and the Abel-Steinberg-Winant trio. The title piece "Walk in Beauty," named after the Beauty Way chant of Navajo curing and peyote ceremonies, is a bit stiff and uninflected in performance and composition, but the final piano work "Jornada del Muerto (in memoriam Lew Welch)" (Journey of the Dead One—the name of a place in southern New Mexico where travelers have perished in its desert and where the first atomic bomb was exploded) has much interesting and beautiful patterning especially in the final section "The View from Vulture Peak." The eight-section ensemble piece "Sones de Flor" (Flower Songs), based structurally on the Japanese poetic form renga, a chain of linked couplets, played on violin, piano, vibraphone, and tom-tom, is beautiful, clear, and a full realization of Garland's folk music-minimalist-formal aesthetic and also makes for good listening. Listeners may also enjoy checking out Garland's *Nana + Victorio* (1993) on the new AVAN label. —*"Blue" Gene Tyranny*

Peter Gena

Mother Jones/ In Thomas Buckner's "Full Spectrum Voice" / 1991 / Lovely Music ♦♦♦
A new approach to political song, a complex vocalise gradually gains momentum, breaking into a ballad, "The Death of Mother Jones," and then, returning to the vocalise, brings the music into another dimension. —*"Blue" Gene Tyranny*

Jon Gibson

b. Apr. 27, 1940
Composer / Instrumental, pattern music, improvisation
Saxophonist, flutist, and employs many world-music instruments in his ensembles, and uses delay systems in his solo performances. For many years performer with the Philip Glass Ensemble, and also performed in the world premieres of Terry Riley's *In C* and Steve Reich's *Drumming*. —*"Blue" Gene Tyranny*

"Two Solo Pieces": Cycles (1973) / Untitled (1974) / 1977 / Chatham Square ♦♦♦
With the composer performing on organ and alto flute. Using seven notes in very slow four-part harmony, Gibson builds an organ texture of exquisite presence; improvising on a simple long melody with dedicated sweetness, Gibson constantly varies with innate musicianship the piece "Untitled," which closes this album of two classics of music truly built on "minimal" means. —*"Blue" Gene Tyranny*

Jon Gibson / Two Solo Pieces / 1996 / New Tone ♦♦♦
Re-releases of two music classics too long out of print, together with three shorter works released for the first time. Gibson's lyrical minimalism and performance skills shine in the hypnotic *Cycles* (1973) for pipe organ, and *Untitled* (1974) for alto flute, both works that represent the composer's work in combining formal structures with improvisation. In *Cycles* some of the sound capabilities of the pipe organ are explored "by using sustained tones in various groupings, clusters, and stop-settings to allow the instrument to 'sound itself.'" *Untitled* "is essentially a long melody that repeats and expands upon itself." Articulation, feeling, rhythmic changes, etc. are spontaneously determined by the performer. Gibson's *Melody IV Part I* (1975) is played here by the SEM Ensemble, with the parameters of pitch, duration and placement determined by overlapping compositional systems. *Melody III* (1975) played here on the Yamaha organ by the composer, again uses the same basic long melody "played 36 times at nine

different lengths simultaneously." *Song I* (1972) performed on this CD with soprano sax, violin and two cellos "is built on an expanding four-pitch melodic fragment." Music of pure beauty. —*"Blue" Gene Tyranny*

Visitations I & II + Thirties (30's) / 1996 / New Tone ♦♦♦
One welcome re-release and a new release of two legendary pattern music classics. The hypnotic and exotic *Visitations* (1973), subtitled "a 16-Track Multi-Textured Environmental Soundscape," originally on Chatham Square Records, features slowly changing wind instrument (saxes, wood flutes, etc.) sweeps and sighs with a dense and gradually evolving timbre of rolling cymbals, bells, shakers and rattles, environmental sounds (water, etc.). The newly released live concert performance of *Thirties* (1970) at the London ICES Festival (August 19, 1972) features nine percussionists (on tuned and un-tuned instruments), two keyboardists, and electric violin. The structure is built around subdivisions of the number 30 (1,2,3,5,6,10,15,30) contained within the 32-beat cycle played on just two alternating notes or ranges (C, A, or a high sound and a low sound). Marvellous and unpredictable beat patterns and timbres result as the performers freely move among the notations coordinated only by a set of four 16ths played in unison by the whole ensemble. This London performance evolves spontaneously through sensations and textures of machine rock, Gamelan, progressive jazz, etc., never losing its distinctive, hypnotic pulse and character: a feeling of eternal heartbeat and thought. (See also Gibson's deeply evocative sax solo *Ballade* in the collection *A Confederacy of Dances, Vol. 2*). —*"Blue" Gene Tyranny*

Michael William Gilbert

Moving Pictures (1978) / 1978 / Gibex ♦♦♦♦♦
An out-of-print disc featuring heavenly electronic music from this Massachusetts composer. Echoes of Far East folk musics combined with synthesizers, flutes, voice, and percussion. —*"Blue" Gene Tyranny*

Janice Giteck

Home (Revisited) / 1992 / New Albion ♦♦♦
An album of pieces dedicated to people living with AIDS, this is music of hope and humanity rather than overt raging. Giteck's music is influenced by the gamelan and cyclic music traditions, especially in the lovely "Om Shanti." "Home (Revisited)" is a heart-filling piece for choir (mostly singing the word "home") and instruments, sung here by the Philandros of the Seattle Men's Choir. There is also the touching "Tapasya" for viola and percussion. See also Giteck's "Breathing Songs from a Turning Sky (excerpt)" in the collection "Music from Mills." —*"Blue" Gene Tyranny*

Philip Glass

b. Jan. 31, 1937, Baltimore, Maryland
Composer / Minimalism, Opera
American composer primarily of minimalist music for film, ballet, and opera using an ensemble of electronic and amplified acoustic instruments. Glass also has a body of instrumental works for acoustic instruments. —*AMG*

Einstein on the Beach / 1979 / Atlantic
This opera, composed in 1975 and premiered in 1976, is scored for four principal actors, 12 singers doubling as dancers and actors, a solo violinist, and an amplified ensemble of keyboards, winds and voices. It is imbued with the postmodern spirit both in its non-linear, poetic, mystic narrative and the floating, eternal world created by the shifting, mathematically precise patterns of Glass' modal music. There are three primary visual sets linked to three musical themes that recur within the work: trains (recalling the metaphors Einstein used to illustrate the theory of relativity, and with which he played as a child), a trial setting (modern life and modern science examined), and a spaceship (a metaphor for transcendence, and/or an escape from nuclear disaster). Also Einstein himself appears midway between the orchestra and the stage as a violinist (his hobby) and observer/witness. There are also additional spoken texts written by Christopher Knowles, Samuel M. Johnson and Lucinda Childs, which appear in various arrangements for single and multiple voices. This work locates itself as a midpoint between the composer's early-'70s work linking rhythmic and harmonic structures and his later series of operas and vocal works and film scores employing expanded narrative and/or timbral experiments. —*"Blue" Gene Tyranny*

☆ **Music in 12 Parts** / 1990 / Virgin ♦♦♦♦♦
Glass is renowned for his pattern music style, presented in its most developed form in this early work, and still one of his best. He has developed a method of writing that retains the sense of the timeless "present," while bringing a new possibility to rethink melody and harmony in a nonvirtuosic sense. At times this is very elegant and profound as in this CD, and the opera *Akhnaten* (on CBS-2-M2K-42457), and at times verges on the direct appeal of a movie-music sensibility, as in *1000 Airplanes on the Roof* (on Virgin 91065-2); for having this range he remains a very controversial composer. —*"Blue" Gene Tyranny*

Glassworks / 1993 / Columbia ✦✦✦
With a richer sound and variation of timbres than in the usual Glass keyboard renditions, Donald Joyce plays, with great attention and feeling, various solo works by Glass on a large church organ. Appealing. —*"Blue" Gene Tyranny*

Music with Changing Parts / 1994 / Elektra/Nonesuch ✦✦✦
A reissue of the 1971 recording. Glass at his most fundamental and best. —*"Blue" Gene Tyranny*

Vinko Globokar

Les Emigras (The Emigrants) (1982-1986) / 1991 / Harmonia Mundi ✦✦✦
Performed by the Ensemble Musique Vivante. A music-theater work by this Yugoslavian composer/jazz trombonist, who lives in Paris and whose works are nearly impossible to classify. "Any model of organisation existing in nature or in culture can become music." Five narrators singing, shouting, and speaking in many languages "give the impression of sitting in a court that is in the process of judging the public," with the listener also placed in a similar situation. We are dealing with people who left their countries in order to survive or improve their way of life. The first part, "Miserere," is an historical allegory: letters from Italians who had emigrated to Brazil and also from Turkish emigrants, interviews with women who follow their husbands, and so on. The second part, "Realities/Augenblicke" (Realities/Flashes), contrasts hope accompanied by dance music against projected images of potential misery. The third part, "Sternbild der Grenze" (Border Constellation), with a text by Peter Handke, is a series of nine tableaux performed by giant puppets contriving to cross "a hermetically sealed border" in a clandestine way. At various points, the singers cross the "border" of the stage and go into the audience. There are also parts for an orchestra, a small choir, two vocal soloists, and a jazz trio. —*"Blue" Gene Tyranny*

Anthony Gnazzo

Asparagas/ In "Music from Mills" / Music from Mills ✦✦✦
A gradual "process piece" using drum-set outtakes from a recording session re-edited to emphasize the rhythmic irregularities into a wild cluster of drum beats. —*"Blue" Gene Tyranny*

Malcolm Goldstein

Soweto Stomp (1985) / 1991 / Musicworks #46 ✦✦✦
Performed by the Malcolm Goldstein Workshop Ensemble in Montreal. Freely accessed sax and wind riff patterns with African 6/4 rhythms gradually mutating dense to simple textures suggest some incredible celebration of simultaneous emotions. —*"Blue" Gene Tyranny*

Summoning of Focus (1977) / In Joseph Celli's "Organic Oboe," A / 1992 / O.O. Discs ✦✦✦
A framework for improvisation, a ritual of sorts. A richness of sound textures and depth of intensity and presence sustained to the end. —*"Blue" Gene Tyranny*

Tongues of My Mother's Teaching (1988) / 1992 / Musicworks ✦✦✦
A touching piece with Goldstein softly playing violin, picking out strains from collages of old recordings of many types of violin and fiddle folk music. —*"Blue" Gene Tyranny*

Luis Gonzalez/Yomo Toro

b. San Juan, Argentina
Graduated from the Universidad Nacional de Cuyo in piano and theory. Studied privately with Erwin Leuchter in Buenos Aires. Degree from Peabody Conservatory, studied composition with Earle Brown and Robert Hall. Compositions for orchestra, chamber ensembles and solo instruments. —*"Blue" Gene Tyranny*

Voces II / Opus One ✦✦✦
In the collection *Latin American Composers in the US* This work for chamber orchestra is the musical equivalent of the literary style known as "magical realism." "In these compositions 'things' have voices with spaces to be discovered and explored, and those voices, as if they were sorcerers, perform magic." (Mercedes Otero). There are two movements in *Voces II*—the first, "Por los espacios de la voz (Through the spaces of the voice)", opens with a sustained chord, which is then expanded by fleeting, gently rhythmic, free serialist-style scoring, and the second, "Tu voz de fuego blanco(Your voice of white fire)," like its title implies, is energetic, with splendid timbral coloration and with Varése-like bursts and multiple calls somewhere between birds and trumpets. —*"Blue" Gene Tyranny*

Daniel Goode

Clarinet Songs / 1993 / Experimental Intermedia ✦✦✦
A fascinating collection of short pieces for solo clarinet skillfully played by the composer. Each piece features a different playing technique. My personal favorites are "Clarinet Drum," the odd tunings of "Six New

Fractal Fingers," the almost-Tibetan "Clarinet Trumpet," and the lovely double stop harmonies of "Long Distance." Daniel Goode is one of the founders of the well-known Downtown Ensemble in New York City and has created many other larger works such as the mixed-media piece "Manaqua-Matagalpa-Music," about the Nicaraguan revolution, and "Three Talking Sculptures for Election Day" (1992), about guns, pornography, and sexual expression. —*"Blue" Gene Tyranny*

Michael Gordon

Big Noise from Nicaragua / 1992 / CRI ✦✦✦
Complex works from the '80s by this dynamic composer: "Thou shalt not! Thou shalt not!" (1983), with passages of triple-meter rhythms in strings and winds, countering to quarter notes in the percussion; "The Low Quartet" (1985/1986), for four bass clarinets; "Four Kings Fight Give" (1988), for chamber strings and winds, which has a passage in seven tempi at once, performed by the Michael Gordon Philharmonic, conducted by Linda Bouchard; and "Acid Rain" (1986), played by the Spectrum Ensemble, conducted by Guy Proteroe. —*"Blue" Gene Tyranny*

Peter Gordon

b. Jun. 20, 1951, New York City
Composer / Art-rock, pattern music, electronics, tape music, opera

Leningrad-Xpress / 1990 / Newtone Records ✦✦✦✦✦
Music from dance and theater productions in a musical language equally informed by world music, tough New York City rock, pattern music, Albert Ayler jazz, and electronic music. Gordon makes it all work in these highly original tone poems, from the almost Weillian "Leningrad Express" and "Warsaw" to the disco-Italian folk music of "Toscana," the electronic and dissonant "In the Fields," "Trinity Site," and "Inside the Nuclear Power Plant" (text by Kathy Acker), the sublime atonal chamber music of "Inside Marie," the Chopinesque-Tibetan "Woyzeck's Dream," the 1920's Berlin-style "Der Kindertotentanz," and the unabashedly pretty "Pastis" acoustic guitar solo. —*"Blue" Gene Tyranny*

Geneva / Extended Niceties / 1992 / New Tone ✦✦✦
Imaginative polytonal rock songs and instrumentals reissued from the post-art-rock period of the early '80s. Bold and beautiful genuine lyricism and humor with various combinations of the Love of Life Orchestra. —*"Blue" Gene Tyranny*

Still Life and the Deadman / 1993 / Newtone ✦✦✦
From the lush string orchestra of the first piece, "Awareness," to the excellent performances of the Balanescu and Parsley Club string quartets (respectively in "De Dode [The Dead Man]" music for a Bataille drama and in "Rembrandt Suite"), this melodic, evocative album fulfills the promise of the thorny rose on its cover—romantic harmonies with strange melodic turns, the sweet with the dissonant, the humorous with the plaintive, and the traditional with the "downtown." This CD, with additional winds and percussion, presents a turning point and a maturing of style in Gordon's work. —*"Blue" Gene Tyranny*

Peter Gordon & The Love of Life Orchestra Quartet / 1995 / New Tone ✦✦✦
A terrific overview of this cross-genre composer's music that lies somewhere between new music tone poems and pop styles. Contains: "Nannies and Chauffeurs"; a three-part political suite, "Nightmare in Tobaccoland" (1. Misadventures of President Limp, 2. Reflective Moment, 3. The March of Morality); two pieces influenced by Gordon's study of Korean music, "Chejudo" and "Sorak San"; a rock commentary, "Gnarly Youth"; a lovely ballad, "My Bed," from Gordon's recent opera *The Strange Life of Ivan Osokin*, "The Khazars," "Ivan's Rag," and a live performance recording, "Raw Chihuahua," featuring the quartet playing at breakneck speed for a wildly enthusiastic audience. With P. Gordon, saxes and Farfisa organ; Jeffrey Berman, percussion; Paul Nowinski, bass; and "Blue" Gene Tyranny, piano. —*"Blue" Gene Tyranny*

The Yellow Box / 1996 / Piano Records (Voiceprint) ✦✦✦
Fabulous new CD of an ongoing collaborative project in England from 1981-1983, and just released now, by these two talented composer-performer-producers. Basically, 17 selections were created by a live and loop processing/extraction method resulting in a kind of "sample record" made just before samplers were invented. The selections include: "Are You a Fish?," "Russians," "Out in the Yard," "The Unpopular Statement," "The Non-Loop," "Unlooped," "Eighth," "Sixth," "Seventh," and "God." With John Greaves, bass; Anton Fier, drums; David Van Tieghem, percussion triggers; Peter Gordon, sax, piano, keyboards, percussion, and guitar; and David Cunningham, guitars, loops and treatments, prepared piano, percussion, and keyboards. There are also found spoken voices including some of famous people who, for legal reasons, can't be identified (but undoubtedly you can). —*"Blue" Gene Tyranny*

Henryk Mikolaj Gorecki

b. Dec. 6, 1933, Czernica, Silesia
Composer / Experimental, tonal, religious vocal works

The Essential Gorecki / Olympia ✦✦✦
A collection of the earlier more radical and interesting works by this Polish composer, whose current tonal style is a kind of syrupy sentimentalism that has a certain popularity. Included are excellent performances of "Epitafium (Epitaph)," for mixed choir and instrumental group (1958); "Zderzenia-Scontri (Collisions)" (1960); "Genesis II: Canti Strumentali per 15 Esecutori (Genesis II: Instrumental Songs for 15 Performers)" (1962); "Refren (Refrain)" (1965); and "Muzyka Staropolska (Old Polish Music)" (1969). Performances by the Polish National Orchestra and the National Philharmonic Choir. —*"Blue" Gene Tyranny*

Gerard Grisey

b. 1946, France
Composer / Spectralism

Partiels for 16 or 18 Musicians/ Derives for Two Orchestral Groups / Erato ✦✦✦
Ensemble Ars Nova, directed by Boris de Vinogradov; Orchestre National de France, directed by Jacques Mercier. Extremely quiet washes of harmonic colors over the orchestral surface with other unusual timbres. —*"Blue" Gene Tyranny*

Gerard Grisey / 1995 / Accord ✦✦✦
Beautiful chamber works in the "spectralism" style. Includes *Talea for ensemble* (1986), *Prologue* for alto and resonators (1976), *Anubis* for sax (1983), *Nout* for sax (1983), and *Jour Contre Jour* for ensemble (1979). —*"Blue" Gene Tyranny*

Tom Hamilton

b. Aug. 15, 1946, Appleton, Wisconsin
Composer / Electronic

Pieces for Kohn / 1976 / ✦✦✦
Four electronic pieces that are musical responses to four paintings by artist Bill Kohn, large geometrics of mythical cities. —*"Blue" Gene Tyranny*

Formal and Informal Music / 1981 / Somnath ✦✦✦✦✦
Complex and rich live electronic music improvisations. Contains "Formal and Informal Music" (1980) and "Crimson Sterling" (1973), for electronics, winds, and percussion. J. D. Parran (woodwinds and saxes), Rich O'Donnell (percussion). Watch for a 1995 issue of Hamilton's music on the Experimental Intermedia labels. —*"Blue" Gene Tyranny*

Off-Hour Wait State / 1996 / O.O. Discs ✦✦✦
Employing analog synthesizers that emulate various sounds and their placement design in the New York City subway system, a sound environment is created for improvising musicians who use that electronic sound as an "aural score...I am...privileged to ride the same train with them." The excellent musicians for this ride are Thomas Buckner, baritone vocal, Roscoe Mitchell, alto sax, Ralph Samuelson, shakuhachi, Peter Zummo, trombone, and Jonathan Haas, percussion. Often delicate and mysterious, at times gently humorous and just plain odd, the sounds unfold inner, emotional experience among the subterranean. Fascinating and original. —*"Blue" Gene Tyranny*

Moondog (Louis Hardin)

b. May 26, 1916, Marysville, KS
Composer / Early Minimalist, Jazz and Modal-music Influenced
An instrument inventor and builder and poet, Moondog studied with Burnet Tuthill, and at the Iowa School for the Blind. Also self-taught in Native American music. Championed by Artur Rodzinski, a conductor of the New York Philharmonic in the '40s, he lived for three decades on the streets of New York City. He currently lives in Germany, where his music and recordings are published. —*"Blue" Gene Tyranny*

☆ **The Music of Moondog** / 1990 / CBS ✦✦✦✦✦
A reissue of two LPs recorded in 1969 and 1972. Rounds, canons, and other pieces that are the precursor of much pattern music. Incidentally, John Fahey has made a wonderful arrangement of Moondog's "Theme and Variations" (1952) for guitars, percussion and synthesizer on *John Fahey: Rain Forests, Oceans, and Other Themes* (Varrick CD 019). —*"Blue" Gene Tyranny*

More Moondog / The Story of Moondog / 1990 / Prestige ✦✦✦
CD reissues of two LPs on the Prestige label from 1956 and 1957. Moondog on the street and everywhere else. The sources in everyday life with music and life blending as a whole. A soundtrack to spur the imagination. Contains: "Softshoe and Hardshoe" (7/4), "A Duet with the Queen Elizabeth Whistle and Bamboo Pipe," "Ostrich Feathers Played on Drums," "All Is Loneliness," "5/8 in Two Shades," "Violetta's Barefoot

Dance," "A Portrait of Ninon-A Cocker Spaniel," and others. —*"Blue" Gene Tyranny*

Elpmas / 1991 / KOPF ✦✦✦✦✦
Contains: "Wind River Powwow," "Westward Ho!," "Suite Equestria," "Marimba Mondo 1—The Rain Forest," "Fujiyama 1," "Marimba Mondo 2—Seascape of the Whales," "Fujiyama 2," "Bird of Paradise," "The Message," "Introduction and Overtone Continuum," and "Cosmic Meditation"—environmental sounds, gently rocking marimbas, lovely counterpoint for winds, sweetly sung wisdom, "a protest against our treatment of aboriginal people...and nature, plants, and animals...." —*"Blue" Gene Tyranny*

Lou Harrison

b. May 14, 1917, Portland, Oregon
Composer / World Music-influenced
American composer whose style has been influenced by Asian music, including the Javanese gamelan. His ensembles rely on Asian folk instruments, especially the percussion. —*AMG*

☆ **Music for Guitar and Percussion** / 1990 / Etcetera ✦✦✦✦✦
With John Schneider, well-tempered guitar, and the Cal Arts Percussion Ensemble, conducted by John Bergamo. A good overview of Harrison's work, especially the alternately pastoral and crashingly celebratory "Canticle No. 3, for ocarina, guitar and percussion" (1941). The ocarina suggests Native American and Japanese folk melodies; the guitar is used as a percussion instrument along with gamelan-like suspended brake drums and shaker. Also contains the more melodic "Suite no. 1" (1976), (though it's still in unusual Pythagorean, just-tuning, Babylonian/Arabic, and artificial scales); "Plaint and Variations on Song of Palestine"; "Serenado por Gitaro" (1952), with the strange chromatic "Infinite Canon" and Usul movements; "Serenade for Guitar with a Percussion Player" (1978); and "Waltz for Evelyn Hinrichsen" (1977). Excellent performances. —*"Blue" Gene Tyranny*

Double Music (1941), Collaboration with John Cage, for 4 Percussionists/ In The New Music Consort's "Pulse" / 1990 / New World ✦✦✦
A wild and wacky, by-now classic percussion piece, using a small range of pitches, that begins as a modest melody and winds up like a heated and joyous village celebration for many unusual instruments. Excellent example of a successful collaboration in composition. This CD is especially recommended as a good collection of percussion music. —*"Blue" Gene Tyranny*

Gamelan Music / 1992 / Music Masters ✦✦✦
Beautiful and meditative pieces that reflect Harrison's abiding affection for the gamelan, which has dominated his musical thought in the last few decades. —*"Blue" Gene Tyranny*

Pierre Henry

French composer of electronic musique concrète pieces for ballet and on religious themes. —*AMG*

Futuriste / 1980 / ✦✦✦
All hauntingly beautiful albums from this composer's over 40 years of work in electronic music and "musique concrète" and his collaborations with Pierre Schaeffer. Watch for a future reissue of a collection of these currently out-of-print discs. —*"Blue" Gene Tyranny*

Bernard Herrmann

b. Jun. 29, 1911, New York City, **d.** Dec. 24, 1975, Hollywood, CA
Composer / Opera, filmscores, pattern music techniques
The dean of film composers, Bernard Herrmann was probably the most gifted musician ever to work in movies, with barely a note of music to his credit that is not worthwhile. A classically trained composer, Herrmann worked for Orson Welles' Mercury Theatre and the CBS radio network before going to Hollywood with Welles in 1940. His first two film scores, *Citizen Kane* and *The Devil and Daniel Webster*, were both nominated for Oscars in the same year (Webster won), and he was established from then on. Herrmann worked principally for 20th Century-Fox from the mid '40s until the end of the '50s, and did brilliant work on such movies as *The Ghost and Mrs. Muir, The Day the Earth Stood Still, Beneath the 12-Mile Reef*, and *Journey to the Center of the Earth;* in the '50s and '60s, Herrmann also contributed notably to the success of Alfred Hitchcock's films, and wrote inspired scores for early films by Brian De Palma and Martin Scorsese. He died the night he finished work on *Taxi Driver*. —*William Ruhlmann*

North by Northwest / Unicorn - Kachana ✦✦✦
Bernard Herrmann completely changed the idea of the film score from heavily operatic and kitschy "incidental music" to the use of bare melody-like gestures or patterns in pure theme-and-variations form, which was to prove an influence on later avant-gardists. This procedure is fully demonstrated in his score for Hitchcock's *Vertigo* (1958) with its shock-

ing polytonal harmonies (Mercury 1986), and in his last score, for Martin Scorsese's *Taxi Driver* (1976) (Varese Sarabande 1986), where the patterns over jazz harmonies are as totally symmetrical as in the work of John Coltrane (esp. *Naima* and *Giant Steps*). The orchestrations, with signature extended harp arpeggios, for the two films above recall his music for Nicholas Ray's *On Dangerous Ground* (1951) (videodisc, Image Entertainment 1989) and Robert Wise's *The Day the Earth Stood Still* (1951) (videodisc, CBS Fox), which sounds remarkably like a Phil Glass score—in interviews, Glass has stated his early interest in Herrmann's music. —*"Blue" Gene Tyranny* ✦✦✦

Torn Curtain / 1978 / Warner Brothers ✦✦✦
This film music (on the out-of-print vinyl WB BSK 3185 or FMC-10) was to be the last that Herrmann wrote for an Alfred Hitchcock movie; they had collaborated from 1955 through 1965, and viewing the films without their soundtracks, one can tell that the dramatic and suspenseful impacts were due as much to the music as to the actors and scenarios. The studios in the mid-'60s had begun to ask for scores which would conceivably contain a hit tune or hummable theme song, and wanted composers to provide scores reflecting some of the pop music styles. Herrmann refused to do this and instead wrote a bold symphonic score for a large and unusual ensemble: 12 flutes (alternating with piccolos), 16 horns, nine trombones, two tubas, two sets of tympani, eight cellos and eight basses—a perfect sound for the coldly objective, paranoid, Orwellian film noir spy thriller, and almost the opposite timbre of the string orchestra employed for *Psycho*, which depicts a frightening and enclosed, internal world. A momentous argument at the recording session ensued between Hitchcock and Herrmann, and marked the end of their work together. Another, milder score and lots of silence was eventually used for the movie, which in turn suffered from having no underpinning for its dramatic acting. It is possible now to view the film with some of the initially recorded parts of Herrmann's score in synchronization and realize what the work could have been. — *"Blue" Gene Tyranny*

Psycho (Complete Music For The Hitchcock Film) (1960) / 1989 / Unicorn - Kanchana ✦✦✦
Performed by The National Philharmonic Orchestra, conducted by the composer. An early champion of new music, conducting premieres of several Charles Ives scores in the '30s, Herrmann completely changed the idea of the film score from heavily operatic and kitschy "incidental music" to using only the barest of melody-like gestures or patterns in pure theme-and-variations form. Herrmann's concert music is more traditional but still remarkable for its clarity of line (especially recommended is the *Souvenirs de Voyage* for clarinet and string quartet [1967] issued in 1991 on Delos DE 3088). —*"Blue" Gene Tyranny*

Vertigo / 1990 / Mercury ✦✦✦
Composed for the Alfred Hitchcock film in 1958, *Vertigo* is one of Herrmann's best film scores. He develops longer melodies than usual in this score but employs many of the same variation and motif-mixing techniques that he has previously used. The score opens in high energy drama with a propulsive polytonal arpeggio (E flat minor over D minor) in triplets that is one of the central motifs throughout the score (this also recalls the opening of *The Day the Earth Stood Still*). As an amusing touch, when the credit "Directed by Alfred Hitchcock" appears on the screen, we hear a low, rotund D note on the tuba. — *"Blue" Gene Tyranny*

Symphony #1 / 1992 / Koch ✦✦✦
Herrmann's own concert music is somewhat more traditional—the "Currier and Ives Suite" is like Shoshtakovich with "wrong notes," and the lovely "Silent Noon" recalls Delius, whom Herrmann admired—but the music is still remarkable for its clarity of line; especially recommended are "For the Fallen" on this CD, and the "Souvenirs de Voyage" for clarinet and string quartet (1967) on "American Chamber Music from Chamber Music Northwest," issued in 1991 on Delos. The bold, solid brass writing in "The Devil and Daniel Webster Suite," from the 1942 film, is similar to that in his sweeping "Symphony No. 1" played by the Phoenix Symphony and conducted by James Sedares. —*"Blue" Gene Tyranny*

Wuthering Heights / 1992 / Unicorn-Kanchana ✦✦✦

Echoes String Quartet (1966) / Clarinet Quintet "Souvenirs de Voyage" (1967) / 1994 / Unicorn-Kanchana ✦✦✦
Performed by the Amici Quartet, and Robert Hill (clarinet) with the Ariel Quartet. The elegiac "Echoes" was originally for a ballet in black-and-white decor, and recalls the mystery and foreboding of Herrmann's "black-and-white" string scoring for Hitchcock's *Psycho*. It also contains Herrmanesque reinterpretations of traditional forms like the "Habañera," "Valse Lente (Slow Waltz)" and a "Scherzo Macabre." The composer re-explores his technique of gradually varied repeated fragments and patterns. Somber, with overtones of the gothic but warmer in tone than the "Echoes" Quartet, the first movement of the "Clarinet Quintet" was inspired by a poem in A.E. Housman's "A Shropshire Lad," and the second movement was inspired by impressions of the Aran Islands off the cost of Ireland. The third movement is by contrast a sentimental journey through twilight Venice. —*"Blue" Gene Tyranny*

Juan Hidalgo

Around the year 1631 Hidalgo was a player of the harp and harpsichord in the royal chapel in Madrid after receiving musical instruction from, no doubt, members of his family. He kept the position in the royal chapel for the rest of his life, did not leave Madrid, and was honored as a familiar after the Inquisition investigated him. Several famous musicians were in the court at Madrid (Galan, del Vado, Marin) but none were as favored as Hidalgo. The majority of Hidalgo's compositions were secular forms of opera or villancicos but he also composed masses and motets (very few). He would rarely write for more than four voices and composed numerous duets and quartets. From 1650 on, his compositions were very much in the vein of the Italian operatic style particularly regarding his use of recitative, aria and arioso. This was his primary contribution to Spanish music: the popularization of the Italian opera styles within the court of Spain. Two of his operas were "La purpura de la rosa," and "Los celos hacen estrellas." The music for the former has been lost but the latter was composed for the Queen mother's birthday and is the earliest zarzuela that has survived with most of its music. —*Keith Johnson*

☆ **Tamaran: Gocce di Sperma per Dodici Pianoforti** / 1990 / Cramps ✦✦✦✦✦
A brilliant conceptual work for 12 pianos by a leading figure in Spanish avant-garde music. —*"Blue" Gene Tyranny*

Lejaren Hiller

b. Feb. 23, 1924, New York, NY
Composer / Computer, Electronic, Instrumental
Hiller studied with Harvey Officer, composition with Milton Babbitt, Roger Sessions, and oboe with Joseph Marx. He received his Ph.D. in Chemistry from Princeton. Hiller founded the Experimental Music Studio at the University of Illinois in the late '50s, and was a Professor of Composition at the State University of NY at Buffalo. He collaborated on the first significant computer music composition, *Illiac Suite*, in1957 with Leonard Issacson. Later he employed the techniques of indeterminancy, serialism, and tonality. Hiller collaborated with John Cage on *HPSCHD* for one to seven harpsichords and 51 tapes (1968). Also *Computer Cantata* for soprano, tape and chamber ensemble (1963), *Midnight Carnival* (1976) for principal tape, and a number of subsidiary tapes and other events. — *"Blue" Gene Tyranny*

Illiac Suite (excerpt) / In "The Voice of the IBM 7090 Computer" / 1960 / Bell Telephone Labs ✦✦✦
You'll find this disc only in libraries at the moment. The "Illiac Suite," composed with engineer L. M. Issacson, was the first computer music piece. It demonstrated possibilities for complex rhythms and transpositions of melody, and it suggested a spectrum of controlled to quasi-random systems for composition. The IBM 7090 computer, with the computing ability now possessed by a modest personal computer, occupied two rooms. Included on this disc are brief experiments by Drs. J. R. Pierce, M. V. Mathews, Newman Guttman, David Slepian, David Lewin, and M. E. Shannon. —*"Blue" Gene Tyranny*

Algorithms, Versions I and IV (1968) / 1969 / Deutsche Grammaphon ✦✦✦
An interesting ensemble piece for acoustic instruments and magnetic tape, composed using the IBM 7094 computer. Titles of the three sections reflect some of the mathematical constructs represented—"The Decay of Information," "Icosahedron," and "The Incorporation of Constraints." This currently out-of-print disc is to be reissued on CD. —*"Blue" Gene Tyranny*

Metaphors/ In the Buffalo Guitar Quartet's "New Music for Guitars" / 1990 / New World ✦✦✦
Interesting work with new guitar techniques. —*"Blue" Gene Tyranny*

Jim Horton

b. Sep. 6, 1944, Minnesota
Composer / Computer, Electronic
Horton studied with Robert Ashley at the Center for Contemporary Music, Mills College. The co-founder of the League of Automatic Music Composers, Horton is also a member of RotaLeague, and a founding member of Just Intonation Network and the Cactus Needle Project. Horton is currently compiling texts toward a history of experimental music in northern California. Since 1976 he has created interactive real-time computer music. — *"Blue" Gene Tyranny*

Simulated Winds and Cries / 1996 / Artifact ✦✦✦
Finally (!) an album of real-time, performer-manipulated computer works in various alternative tunings by one of the Bay Area's most delightfully creative composer-philosopher-visionaries. Selections include: "I Heard a Thousand Blended Notes" (title from a 1794 poem by William Wordsworth), "Simulated Winds and Cries" (1992) made from justly intoned sliding intervals selected by 1/f fractal patterns, "Some Pointillism" (1990), "Rebirth," (1990) in which "the computer, empty of

suffering (running the language Formula), simulates high-speed attainment of Nirvana by playing [a] medieval Tibetan Buddhist game," and "Rave Patterns" (1992), created for a rave dance party that the police shut down before it got going. ("Thus was the underground confirmed in its oppositions.") The composer has this to say about the various pieces: "I like to imagine that they are precursors to uplifting, slightly alien musical A.I.s of the 21st century. Oh, how I hope and wish that contemporary cyber-culture will lead to a beautiful utopian compassionate world of Good!" — *"Blue" Gene Tyranny*

Toshio Hosokawa

b. 1955, Hiroshima, Japan
Ancient Japanese Music and Contemporary European Music-influenced/Alternate Tunings
Hosokawa studied piano and music theory in Tokyo, composition with Isang Yun, Klaus Huber, and Brian Ferneyhough; theory with Witold Szaloneck at Hochschule der Künste in Berlin. In 1980, he won first prize in the Valentino Bucchi competition in Rome; in 1982 he won the Irino prize in Japan, and first prize at the 100th anniversary competition of the Berlin Philharmonic Orchestra. Hosokawa was the guest composer at the 1988 International Davos Music Festival. — *"Blue" Gene Tyranny*

Seeds of Contemplation (Mandara) for Shomyo and Gagaku Ensemble (1986) / Fragmente I for Shakuhachi, Koto, and Sangen (1988) / 1990 / Fontec ◆◆◆
Two exquisitely spare compositions combining ancient court-music gestures with matrix-combinatory European compositional techniques. Beautifully paced performances in the "breath" tempo of traditional Gagaku ensembles. Hosokawa studied with Isang Yun and Witold Szaloneck in (West) Berlin and has received commissions and prizes in Japan, Europe, and the United States. His "pure" use of the Gagaku ensemble is different from Takemitsu's somewhat more romantic approach. For comparison with the tradition, listen to the still excellent *Gagaku: The Imperial Court Music of Japan* by the Kyoto Imperial Court Music Orchestra, reissued on CD on Lyrichord. — *"Blue" Gene Tyranny*

Alan Hovhaness (Chakmakjian)

b. Mar. 8, 1911, Somerville, MA
Composer / Armenian (7th century) and Eastern Music-influenced
Though Hovhaness is primarily known as a classical composer, he is revered as one of the fathers of the new-age and world-music movements. He is without a doubt one of the earliest artists in any genre to make significant use of ethnic music elements, spiritual concepts from other cultures, and sounds from nature in his compositions. In the '30s, he refused to conform to the atonal intellectualism of his colleagues and began combining influences from his Armenian heritage with the great musical traditions of the Far East. A series of fellowships allowed him to travel to India, Japan, and Korea to study and compose during the '50s and '60s. During that time, his eclectic, mystical compositions began to strike a chord with American audiences. Continually ahead of his time, Hovhaness was actually the first to mix the recorded songs of humpback whales in an orchestral context. Carl Sagan even used some of Hovhaness' music in the "Cosmos" television series. Though most of the composer's music is available through classical music outlets, several contemporary instrumental labels have released collections of his piano pieces, bringing his expressive and sophisticated style to wider audiences. — *Linda Kohanov*

Wind Music of Alan Hovhaness: Return and Rebuild the Desolate Places (Concerto for Trumpet) / Symphony no. 7 (Nanga Parvat) (1959) / Mace ◆◆◆
An out-of-print disc that can still be found in used record bins. With the North Jersey Wind Symphony and percussion, Keith Brion conducting. Another side of Hovhaness: dissonant clusters, fury and devastation, wild improvised village marches, a mountain frozen forever in treeless snow, the fierceness of volcanic earthquakes, rocks sculptured by tornados. Visions from Armenia. Hovhaness in the church of nature. — *"Blue" Gene Tyranny*

And God Created Great Whales (1970) for Orchestra and Whale Songs / Concerto no. 8 for Orchestra (1953) / Elibris (Dawn God of the Urardu) / 1989 / Crystal ◆◆◆
Magnificently beautiful recording of an orchestra in an old abbey and a good overview of the composer's work. — *"Blue" Gene Tyranny*

☆ **Lousadek (Dawn of Light), op. 48 (1945) for Piano and Orchestra / Symphony no. 2, op. 132 "Mysterious Mountain"** / 1990 / Musicmasters ◆◆◆◆◆
Performed by the American Composers Orchestra, Dennis Russell Davies conducting, with Keith Jarrett as piano soloist. Informed by the highly mellismatic, floating melodic sense of Armenian song together with simple, refined orchestration, "Lousadek" is a lovely work that nearly caused a riot at its New York premiere as it innocently stepped on the mental toes of the academic chromaticists and the American nation-

alists in the audience. The symphony "Mysterious Mountain" combines many of the elements of Hovhaness' later style: parallel chordal passages of universal religious feeling (similar to Eastern Orthodox Church chanting), the treatment of canon and fugue in an entirely original manner (more of a variation form), quasi-random pizzicati and strange transparent bells on odd harmonics that suggest landscapes at long distances from civilization. Hovhaness is a prolific composer of nearly 500 compositions to date, but these two pieces will give the listener a good idea of his general instrumental approach. — *"Blue" Gene Tyranny*

Lady of Light, op. 227 (1968) / 1991 / Crystal ◆◆◆
With Patricia Clark (soprano), Leslie Fyson (baritone), the Ambrosian Singers and the Royal Philharmonic Orchestra, conducted by Hovhaness. Simple elegiac chant and solo song with and without text mixed with sudden random rushings of voices, harmonizations on non-European scales, and a protest against war based on the Swiss "Chalabala" legend: "Dancing to the Stars over Bridges of Thread," "I Am Dancing in Heaven," "No More Serve Your Brutal War Lords." — *"Blue" Gene Tyranny*

Mount St. Helen's Symphony (sym. no. 50) / City of Light Symphony (sym. no. 22) / 1993 / Delos ◆◆◆
Performances by the Seattle Symphony, conducted by Gerrard Schwartz (sym. no. 50) and composer Alan Hovhaness (sym. no. 22). Soaring, magnificent works. — *"Blue" Gene Tyranny*

Hub

The Hub / Computer Network Music / 1989 / Capitol ◆◆◆◆◆
A totally new idea in live electronic music, the six composers of The Hub play computer music live by interacting with musically sensitive responses to each other's programs, the computers often physically connected through complex networks that make many aspects of their performances spontaneous. Contains: John Bischoff's terrific "Perry Mason in East Germany," Tim Perkis' "Farabi," Chris Brown's "Rol'Em," Phil Stone's "Borrowing and Stealing," Scot Gresham-Lancaster's "Whackers," Perkis/Brown/Stone's "Hot Pig," Bischoff/Perkis/Trayle's "Dovetail," Perkis' "The Minister of Pitch," and Mark Trayle's "Simple Degradation." — *"Blue" Gene Tyranny*

Wreckin' Ball / 1994 / ART ◆◆◆
More live computer music by this seminal ensemble in collaborations with others. Contains: "Hub Renga," a live radio broadcast with poets using The Well computer network and with Ramon Sender Barayon; "VEX," with the Rova Saxophone Quartet, and based on Erik Satie's famous *Vexations;* "Electric Rags III," a collaboration with composer-pianist Alvin Curran. Also "The Glass Hand," "Crybaby," "Wheelies," and "Waxlips." — *"Blue" Gene Tyranny*

Jerry Hunt

One of the most original composers of our time, Hunt, often creating scores of complex physical moves in space, made a concert into an occasion that re-creates music's role in divination of all countries and ages—for example, his "Sur John Dee" (1966) in John Cage's thought-provoking compilation "Notations" (1969, Something Else Press). Hunt was also an innovative computer systems designer and created mysterious alliances of computers and primal energy in his installation pieces (one a voodoo hut with computerized proximity detectors triggering electronic sounds for the New Music America Festival in Houston). — *"Blue" Gene Tyranny*

Transform (Stream) (1977) / Cantegral Segment 18, 17 (1977-1976) / Transphalba (1978) / Volta (Kernel) (1977) / 1979 / IRIDA ◆◆◆
An out-of-print disc but well worth searching for. Using various mechanical and electronic instruments and systems, Hunt investigates the relation of nerve bonding in the human body and its descriptive, analogous patterning in electronic systems. IRIDA vinyl discs are still available (see addresses section) and the CRI label will be issuing a new CD soon of 70 minutes of Hunt's music, all of the music that appeared on IRIDA and an early piano work. — *"Blue" Gene Tyranny*

☆ **Fluud for Dual Synclaviers/ In CDCM Computer Music Series, Vol. 1** / 1988 / Centaur ◆◆◆◆◆
Ceremonial moves based on Robert Fluud's *monochordum mundi syphiphoniacum* (1622). Otherworldly. — *"Blue" Gene Tyranny*

Babalon (string) / In "The Aerial #1" / 1990 / Aerial ◆◆◆
Mysterious hermetic evocations with shamanic rattles and bells, and an interactive computer system for sound retrieval. — *"Blue" Gene Tyranny*

Ground / Five Mechanic Convention Streams / 1992 / O.O. Discs ◆◆◆
In five compositions, Hunt investigates "nonconventional intention" and how it is transformed into gestures, much of this activity based on a system of translation gestures using the angelic tables produced by the mystic John Dee through the skrying of Edward Kelley (1582-1589). Pieces include "Chimanazzi (Olun): Core" for violins, keyed violin, and

(electronic) device arrays, "Lattice (Stream): Ordinal" for piano and auxiliary device arrays, and "Bitom (Stream): Link" for cow horns, pianos, and device arrays. Hunt is assisted by composer Rod Stasick and vioinist Jane Henry. — *"Blue" Gene Tyranny*

Haramand Plane / 1994 / What Next? ✦✦✦
A fabulous Jerry Hunt recording featuring three "links" of his electronic relays and processes with simultaneous tracks of acoustic percussion in an evocative (literally) ceremonial performance. — *"Blue" Gene Tyranny*

Four Video Translations / 1995 / O.O. Discs ✦✦✦
A 55-minute 15-second videotape collection of four magical and mystic performances—perhaps shamanic conjuring sessions is more apt. In "Birome [zone]: plane (fixture)" Hunt, dressed like a "central Texas meat inspector" (Michael Schell), performs arcane shaking moves holding and manipulating surreal devices toward some unknown end. In "Talk (slice): duplex" two spontaneous talkers are attenuated in their lines of thought by a percussive claves-like sound off camera, which appears to be keeping some type of time schedule. At times they seem to be holding a conversation in the normal sense, but for the most part they perform spontaneous free-association solos within proximity of each other. It is actually mildly shocking when they seem to connect. The subjects of their off-the-cuff speech are fascinating. In "Bitom (fixture): topogram," Hunt is The Agent and Michael Galbreth is The Patient, holding a metal grounding plate, as Hunt works a shamanic sort of healing/examination upon Galbreth, while blowing a tin whistle and wielding a probe that measures the skin's galvanic response and converts that information to control the intense electronic sound in the background (talk about your alien abductions!). For "Transform (stream): core" Hunt wears an Elizabethan collar, suggesting the time of mystic philosopher John Dee, whose work served as a constant inspiration to Hunt. We hear the shaking of rattles and bells and gourds punctuated by poltergeist-like thumps. Hunt seems to be calling up angels (à la Dee) with odd breath sounds, whistling, guttural throat noises, etc., which are echoed by some unseen presence. A brilliant example of the use of music to express philosophical concerns and to update spiritual ceremonies for a contemporary audience. — *"Blue" Gene Tyranny*

Lattice / 1996 / CRI ✦✦✦
A welcome reissue on CD of the original vinyls on Hunt's Irida label (from *Texas Music* and Irida No. 32). Contains: "Lattice" (1979), "Transform (Stream)" (1977), "Cantegral Segment 18.17" (1977, 1976), "Transphalba" (1978), and "Volta (Kernel)" (1977). — *"Blue" Gene Tyranny*

Song Drape 2 / Song Drape 1 / Song Drape 11 / 1996 / Musicworks ✦✦✦
In the collection *Musicworks No. 65*. In *Song Drape 2* (1992), the voice of former president Lyndon Johnson and a respondent with a Texas accent are heard taped in a remarkable private phone conversation, with an interlude in which we hear a man coughing and a baby crying. Strange, nebulous music with a steady, slow rhythm accompanies the taped material. Very, very odd. For *Song Drape 1* (1992), Hunt created a texture of thick, propulsive music with a triplet pulse, surrounded by percussive shakers and popping and banging sounds, that speaks of magic and wonder. In the massive pounding clusters of *Song Drape 11* (1992), we hear gradually changing pitches; the effect is of an irresistible, ceremonial pulse evoking spirit. More treasures left by this truly gifted and original composer. (See also Hunt's "Lattice" in the collection *Gay American Composers*). — *"Blue" Gene Tyranny*

David Hykes

Hearing Solar Winds / 1983 / Ocora ✦✦✦
An extended choral work made from Hoomi singing of western Mongolia and the overtone chanting of Tantric Buddhism. Spectacular shimmering surfaces (overtones from clusters of fundamentals beating against each other) and other effects. Contains "Multiplying Voices at the Heart of the Body of Sound," "Gravity Waves," and "Rainbow Voice." — *"Blue" Gene Tyranny*

Harmonic Meetings / 1990 / New Albion ✦✦✦
A reissue of the two-disc set on CD. Lovely as always. — *"Blue" Gene Tyranny*

Current Circulation / 1992 / Celestial Harmonies ✦✦✦
A reissue of the well-known 1984 album. More like single studies of the singing techniques. Includes "Free Ascents," "Subject to Change," "Ascending Mount Summation." — *"Blue" Gene Tyranny*

True to the Times / How to Be? / 1993 / New Albion ✦✦✦
Includes: "Worldwind Psalm" and "Prayer Songs for the Sorrow / Pythagoras over Persia." — *"Blue" Gene Tyranny*

Toshi Ichiyanagi

b. 1933

7 Life Music / 1978 / Varèse Sarabande ✦✦✦
In the collection *Orchestral Space* performed by the Yomiuri Nippon

Symphony Orchestra conducted by Seiji Ozawa. Composed in 1966, this work is scored for various electronic modulators, magnetic tape, and orchestra. The tape sounds are played from behind the orchestra, which reacts to and performs with them. The acoustic instruments of the orchestra also have contact microphones attached to them, and this sound is sent to the electronic modulators to be processed and reintroduced into the loudspeakers. The score for the orchestra was arrived at by chance means, similar to the work of John Cage, the composition indeterminate of its performance (realization). The sonic effect is of many varied, independent, and surprising sounds separated by silences that seem "intense" because of the nature of the sounds they set off, like negative space in Japanese painting. There is an overall pacing of the orchestral densities which gives a non-specific narrative quality to its form. Stage lighting changes, also determined by chance, add to the dramatic quality. It is the music of life, before things are named. — *"Blue" Gene Tyranny*

Solo Compositions / 1991 / Camerata ✦✦✦
Includes "Cloud Figures for Solo Oboe," "Hoshi-No-Wa" for sho; "Scenes III for Solo Violin," "Time Sequence for Piano." Lovely pieces by the composer who introduced much of new music to Japan by organizing concerts and exhibitions of graph music, and whose early pieces such as "Kaiki" (1960), for sho, organ, koto, harmonica, and saxophone, and early theater music works such as "Sapporo" (1963) are classics. See also his work "Extended Voices" in the collection *Extended Voices*. — *"Blue" Gene Tyranny*

Violin Concerto "Junkansuru Fukei" (Circulating Scenery) / 1994 / Camerata ✦✦✦
Performed at the Min-On Contemporary Music Festival with Paul Zukofsky, violin, Tokyo Philharmonic Orchestra, Tadaaki Otaka, conductor.
This dramatic concerto in three movements, described by the composer as a "violin solo with an orchestra attached," was composed in 1983. The descriptive title "Circulating Scenery" applies to the evocative, mysteriously rotating patterns of "memory . . . linked with a scene" stated by the orchestra. These sometimes impressionistically cloudy, sometimes rhythmically propulsive patterns continuously segue into new and unexpected territories. The complex and virtuoso solo violin writing provides lyrical and at times impassioned commentaries on the memory evoked. The orchestration is a rich palette with the depth of an Alban Berg score and the transparencies of the best contemporary composers, like Takemitsu. But the composer's voice is unique and convincing. This concerto and the five pieces for violin and piano from the years 1976 through 1982 form a new departure into narrative music for a composer involved with more Cage-ian influences in his earlier music. These earlier works, such as "Kaiki" (1960) for sho, organ, koto, harmonica and saxophone, the theater music pieces "Sapporo" (1963) and "Distance" (1979) for Noh-dance and chamber ensemble, and the remarkable "Extended Voices" for chorus with Moog and Buchla synthesizers (1967), still, however, always possessed an internal dramaticism externalized by this new concerto. Ichiyanagi was also responsible for bringing much European and American new music to Japan in the 1960s by organizing concerts and exhibitions of graph music. His other recent solo works—for example, "Cloud Figures" for solo oboe, "Hoshi-No-Wa" for sho, "Scenes III for Solo Violin," the "Time Sequence" and "Kumo no Hyojo (Cloud Atlas)" (1987) for piano solo—as well as larger pieces, for example, the "Zoku-gaku Symphony/Yami o Tokashite Otozureru Kage (Visit of a Shade Melting the Darkness)" (1987) for antique instruments, gagaku orchestra, shomyo and dance—also provide engaging listening. — *"Blue" Gene Tyranny*

Cosmos of Toshi Ichiyanagi / 1995 / Camerata ✦✦✦
A wonderful overview of the composer's chamber instrumental work ranging from his lyrical to his conceptual compositions. Includes: "Paganini Personal" for marimba and piano, "Flowers Blooming in Summer" for harp and piano, "Two Existences" for 2 pianos, "Scenes II" for violin and piano, and the splendid "Cloud Atlas" for piano. In the series *New Aspect of Japanese Music–5*. — *"Blue" Gene Tyranny*

Charles Ives

Highly original American composer of orchestral, chamber, and solo vocal and piano music who used and anticipated polytonality, atonality, and polymeter/polytone clusters. A unique quality of his music is the combination of well-known hymns and popular tunes with a complex dissonant accompaniment. Notable works include *Three Places in New England* (1914) and the *Sonata for Piano no. 2, "Concord, Mass"* (1920). — *Mary K. Scanlan*

☆ **Unanswered Question (1908) / Central Park in the Dark (1898-1907) / The Holidays Symphony (1904-1913)** / CBS ✦✦✦✦✦
This recording by the Chicago Symphony is particularly interesting because both the original and revised versions of *The Unanswered Question* are performed. The dissonant flute clusters and trumpet theme are played completely free of the consonant, serene chords of the strings

in the original version, another innovation by Charles Ives. —*"Blue" Gene Tyranny*

Ives Plays Ives / Record No. 4/ In "Charles Ives, The 100th Anniversary" / Columbia ♦♦♦

This out-of-print five-disc set is a treasure of music and memorabilia, Ives playing spontaneously (improvising) on published and unpublished material/ideas. Reveals the creative process in its searching mode (apart from the necessary structural work), with Ives enthusiastically letting his hands discover what cannot be preconceived. Especially remarkable are the so-called "X, Y, Z Improvisations." —*"Blue" Gene Tyranny*

Three Quarter-Tone Pieces/ In "New Music in Quarter-Tones" / Odyssey ♦♦♦♦♦

Three beautiful pieces—"Largo," "Allegro," and "Chorale"—for two pianos tuned quarter-tones apart from each other. This is a fine recording and performance, but these pieces should really be heard live. As with much of Ives, additional transparent "ghost" sounds occur in the performance space, caused by the strange combinations of harmonics and tunings, which can be heard by listeners but not recorded. This is especially true for these pieces. As a child, Ives sang tunes, in quarter-tones, along with other children in the family inspired by their bandleader father, George E. Ives, who also staged such experimental spectacles as bands playing different tunes marching from opposite ends of town and crossing in the middle. That event is re-created in "Three Places in New England." —*"Blue" Gene Tyranny*

The Orchestral Music of Charles Ives / 1990 / Koch ♦♦♦

With the Orchestra New England, conducted by J. Sinclair. Includes "Calcium Night Light," "Country Band March," "Postlude in F," "Set for Theater Orchestra," "Set of Four Ragtime Dances," "Three Places in New England," and "The Yale-Princeton Football Game." Great performances. The collection does not include other orchestral works such as the *Orchestral Set No. 2* (probably the best performance of this was Stokowski conducting the London Symphony Orchestra on the out-of-print disc London Records SPC 21060), or the visionary "Tone Roads," a 12-tone piece written many years before that technique found its way from Europe to the States. —*"Blue" Gene Tyranny*

● **Symphony No. 4 (1910-1916) / Robert Browning Overture (1908-1912), Songs: An Election; Lincoln, The Great Commoner / 1991 / Sony Classical Masterworks ♦♦♦♦♦**

With Leopold Stokowski conducting the American Symphony Orchestra, and the Gregg Smith Singers. A magnificent transcendental vision of life performed with full spirit by Stokowski's orchestra with attention to the polyrhythms, transparent "memory" textures, and harmonic layerings of this completely innovative writing. The songs (especially "Lincoln, the Great Commoner," with its amazing tone-cluster glissandos for voices and strings) are perfect complements to the symphony. —*"Blue" Gene Tyranny*

The Complete Piano Music of Charles Ives / Voxbox ♦♦♦

A welcome reissue on CD of the marvelous performances by pianist Alan Mandel. Includes the two sonatas, masterpieces of 20th-century music, and the shorter works "The Three-Page Sonata," "Song Without (Good) Words," "Baseball Take-off," "The Seen and Unseen," many of the "Studies," and other works. —*"Blue" Gene Tyranny*

Leroy Jenkins

b. Mar. 11, 1932

Leroy Jenkins Live! (featuring Computer Minds) / 1993 / Black Saint ♦♦♦

Two CDs that give an overview of Jenkins' earlier tune-oriented and later free playing. Muhal Richard Abrams is a composer who has served as an important musical, spiritual, and social influence as president of the AACM (Association for the Advancement of Creative Musicians), founded in Chicago in 1965 by members of his earlier group The Experimental Band. His own work may be heard on *Blu Nlu Blu* (Black Saint, 1991) and *Family Talk* (Black Saint, 1993) in excellent performances that reach out to the listener. Abrams' recent and daring work, the masterpiece "Duet for Pianos No. 1" has yet to be recorded. —*"Blue" Gene Tyranny*

Santa Fe / 1994 / Lovely Music ♦♦♦

A magnificent CD of violin and viola solos showing the dynamic "pure music" side of this great composer/performer who worked with the AACM in Chicago in the '60s, then moved to New York City and founded The Revolutionary Ensemble (they recorded five albums). Jenkins has composed many large works played by the Brooklyn Philharmonic, the Cleveland Chamber Symphony, the Albany Symphony, and Kronos Quartet and he was included in the Kennedy Center's American Composer series; he recently premiered his opera-for-dance *The Mother of Three Sons*, commissioned by the Munich Biennale, and his *Off-Duty Dryad* (1990) was played by the Soldier String Quartet with dancers. He is currently at work on a new opera that includes three rappers as characters and a piece about the recently uncovered Negro Graveyard in

Manhattan. He is a totally engaging performer who keeps the listener on the edge of their seat, waiting for the next surprising variation and invention. —*"Blue" Gene Tyranny*

Terry Jennings

☆ **Terry's G Dorian 12-Bar Blues (9 X 5) + 3 (1962) / In "Jon Gibson" / 1992 / Point ♦♦♦♦♦**

Gibson on sax with two synthesizers and percussion. Terry Jennings was one of the first players on any wind instrument to play multi-phonic chords, which are produced by a combination of unusual fingering and overblowing. Classics of extended time-sense music, his ethereally beautiful piano music, and especially the remarkable "String Quartet" (September 1960) (see score in La Monte Young's *An Anthology*) have yet to be recorded. —*"Blue" Gene Tyranny*

Scott Johnson

John Somebody / No Memory for Electric Guitar, Woodwinds, Percussion, and Electronics (1981-1983) / 1986 / Elektra/Nonesuch ♦♦♦♦♦

"Remember that guy . . . John Somebody? He was a . . . sort of a b . . . " asks a woman's voice on the repeating master tape loop, as other smaller loops join in, and then pop-jazz instrumental figures imitate the rhythm and add funky melodies and cross-rhythms (built on the smaller samples of the loop) in accumulating levels, which suddenly break and start again with interpretations of the loops. We find ourselves tapping our feet and wanting to dance. An original and appealing album, in which Johnson clearly demonstrates for his listeners the relation between ordinary speech and musical rhythms. Speech in this case also includes the laughter of "Involuntary Songs." *No Memory* is also built on this speech sampling idea but is more complex in its modulation of both the loop sounds and the layering of the more chromatic instrumental phrases. —*"Blue" Gene Tyranny*

Confetti of Flesh/ In Dora Ohrenstein "Urban Diva" / 1993 / CRI ♦♦♦

A sensual rhapsody about New York City living with text by Jayne Cortez ("I am new york city of blood police and fried pies"), this chamber piece shows Johnson in a more melodious and somewhat more "uptown" mode than in his previous compositions, the whole texture grown from a three-note motive, but still with an underlying hip beat. Beautifully performed. —*"Blue" Gene Tyranny*

Tom Johnson

b. Nov. 18, 1939

Composer / Minimalist, Conceptual Systems

For many years Johnson was the music critic for *The Village Voice* newspaper. —*"Blue" Gene Tyranny*

An Hour for Piano / 1985 / Lovely Music ♦♦♦

Available on vinyl LP only. A terrific and intense performance by composer-performer Frederic Rzewski on piano of this trance music piece made up of repeating 4/4 cells in which an absolutely steady eight-note motion predominates, resulting in large-scale shifts in density and tonality over the time span. —*"Blue" Gene Tyranny*

Music for 88 / 1993 / Experimental Intermedia ♦♦♦

Just the disc to give to those people who remark inquisitively about the relationship of music and mathematics. Johnson actually explains out front before, and at times during, each piece about the math being used, and also how musicians and mathematicians differ in their views. Many charming and lovely minimalist pieces for voice and very well-recorded piano with sometimes unintentionally (?) droll humor. A very original piece (as in "Why didn't I think of that?"). (See also his piece "Failing: A Very Difficult Piece for Solo Bass" in *Bang on a Can Live, Vol. 1*. —*"Blue" Gene Tyranny*

Rational Melodies (1982) (21 Pieces for Any Instrument) / 1993 / Hat Art ♦♦♦

Lovely conceptual pieces performed by Eberhard Blum on piccolo, flute, alto flute, and bass flute. —*"Blue" Gene Tyranny*

Ben Johnston

b. Mar. 15, 1926, Macon, GA

Composer / Microtonality, Chance Operations, Serialist, Tonal

Johnston studied with Darius Milhaud, Harry Partch, Burrill Phillips, Robert Palmer, and John Cage. A professor of theory and composition at the University of Illinois, his selected works include: "Somewhere i have never traveled" (1949) for tenor and piano, "Knocking Piece Collage" (1969) for tape, "In Memory, Harry Partch, 1975" (1975) for soprano, computer tape, tape, string quartet, eight percussionists, and slide show, "Suite for Microtonal Piano" (1978), and "Twelve Partials" (1980) for flute and microtonal piano. —*"Blue" Gene Tyranny*

☆ **Amazing Grace (String Quartet no. 4) (1973)** / 1991 / Elektra/None-such ✦✦✦✦✦
Heartrendingly beautiful microtonal setting with variations on this traditional melody played by the Kronos Quartet. It is also called the "String Quartet no. 4" on out-of-print vinyl Gasparo GS-205, where it is played in more accurate tuning by the Fine Arts Quartet. —*"Blue" Gene Tyranny*

Calamity Jane to Her Daughter / In Dora Ohrenstein "Urban Diva" / 1993 / CRI ✦✦✦
With a text based on a section from a disputed diary (which includes a recipe for a "20-year cake") that may or may not be the authentic account of the historical Calamity Jane's secret marriage to James Butler (Wild Bill) Hickok, Johnston spins a wonderfully melodious vocal line in just intonation with beautiful consonances and dissonances amongst the accompanying instruments. —*"Blue" Gene Tyranny*

Ponder Nothing: Chamber Music of Ben Johnston / 1993 / New World ✦✦✦
Compelling works in just intonation played by Music Amici: "Septet," "Three Chinese Lyrics," "Gambit," "Five Fragments," "Trio," and "Ponder Nothing" for solo clarinet . —*"Blue" Gene Tyranny*

Victoria Jordanova

Requiem for Bosnia (An Improvisation for Broken Piano, Harp, and Child's Voice)/Four Preludes for Harp (On a Sunday, A L'Espagnol, By the Seashore, Harp Wind)/Once Upon a Time/Variations / 1994 / CRI ✦✦✦
Strong, neo-romantic/modernist works for harp. —*"Blue" Gene Tyranny*

Mauricio Kagel

b. 1931, Buenos Aires, Argentina
Composer / Political Theater, Innovative Notation, New Instrument Techniques, Electronic

Staats Theater (1967-1970) / Deutsche Grammaphon ✦✦✦
Kagel takes apart the apparatus of the State Theater of operas, plays, and other spectacles and examines in detail the images and sounds we are presented with apart from plot, libretto, and subject matter. Not a satire but a surreal concentration. Many of Kagel's original instruments and sound-making devices (listen to "Akustica" (1968-1970), a two-disc set on Deutsche Grammaphon, if you can find a copy) are used, both for the sound they make and because of their symbolic value. A steel strip partially strapped to the player's feet (he is part of the circuit) is in the form of a Mobius strip, which is associated with getting from one side, the "real," to the other side, "the figurative," without going over the edge. Likewise, tape music, choral and operatic ensembles, stage sets (Wagnerian to pop-art large soda bottles), stock characters (the Barber, the Imaginary Invalid, Amor, and the Troubadour Knight), and stock themes (Concern, Virginity, Iron Curtain, Investigation, Nighttime), movement (Contradance), the players in the pit, calisthenics done by the performers to keep in shape, and even the resultant waste paper of programs and notices are all presented in their physical and imaginary contexts. —*"Blue" Gene Tyranny*

☆ **String Quartet I (1965-1967) / Pan (1985) for Piccolo and String Quartet / String Quartet II (1965-1967) / String Quartet III (1986-1988)** / 1991 / Disques Montaigne ✦✦✦✦✦
Played with great sensitivity by the Arditti String Quartet. The marvelous first and second quartets take some late Bartok string techniques to new levels: snap string, tremolos of bow wood (col legno) rebounding off strings, non-vibrato glassy textures, maximum bow "crunch," random pizzicato, playing on the wood of the instrument. The quartet is treated compositionally like electronic music—at turns mysterious, dramatic, and lyrical. With scale-like fragments and operatic "bird" figures, *Pan* seems to reset *The Magic Flute*. The third quartet, like *Pan*, contains elements of past musical gestures treated for their sound value (not as quotes or satire), combined with techniques from the first quartets. All this makes for very original music. —*"Blue" Gene Tyranny*

Les Idees Fixes (Rondo for Orchestra), Musik fur Tasteninstrumente und Orchester (Music for Keyboards and Orchestra), op. 1991 (Concerpiece for Orchestra) / 1993 / Col Legno ✦✦✦
Fascinating new pieces played by the Rundfunk Sinfonieorchester (Radio Symphony Orchestra) of Saarbrucken, conducted by the composer, with four pianists. —*"Blue" Gene Tyranny*

Der Tribun (The Tribune) /...Nach Einer Lektüre von Orwell (...After a Lecture by Orwell) / 1996 / Wergo ✦✦✦
Two brilliant and insightful satiric political works. *The Tribune* (1979) is scored "für einer politischen Redner, Marschklänge und Lautsprecher" (for a political orator, march sounds and loudspeaker). .... *After a lecture by Orwell* was composed later in 1984. —*"Blue" Gene Tyranny*

Franz Kamin

Rugugmool / 1980 / Station Hill ✦✦✦
This work involves an unusual combination: linear, poetic texts com-

bined with instrumental music that has structured openness (indeterminancy of well-defined events) and a surface level that suggests narrative atmospheres. "Rugugmool" has an impressionist description of a boatsman piloting a woman to meet lovers and friends, with words and phrases recurring magically, a "one-to-one code language" with everything becoming one, followed by instrumental "dances" based on charts defined in a *Book of Animal Models*. In "Behavioral Drift II," elements of a complex of sounds are traded from instrument to instrument, the whole always being present, and the performers are guided by a light panel controller. The text here is from the composer's book *Ann Margaret Loves You and Other Psychotopological Diversions.*" Kamin's earlier works include "7 Dog W" for seven supra-audible dog whistles, and "A Concert of Doors," a composition for doors in the woods. —*"Blue" Gene Tyranny*

The Kanary Grand Band

The KGB Adapted to Human Ears and Human Speed / 1994 / Musicworks ✦✦✦
In the collection *Musicworks No. 59: Beyond Boundaries, Sound Ecology 2.* In this very odd, intriguing work based in Eindhoven, the Netherlands, the sounds of pond creatures are manipulated, mostly by speed and pitch change, to produce sounds like the secret "messages" heard on shortwave radios. —*"Blue" Gene Tyranny*

Udo Kasemets

b. 1919, Estonia
Composer / Indeterminate, Theater, Philosophy
A music reviewer for the *Toronto Daily Star* (63), an organizer of multimedia and new music performances at Issacs Gallery (1965-67), and director of the "Sightsoundsystems" festival (1968), a branch of Experiments in Art and Technology (E.A.T., New York), Kasemets taught sound studies at Ontario College of Art (1970-87). He was influenced by the ideas of John Cage, Marshall McLuhan, and Buckminster Fuller. —*"Blue" Gene Tyranny*

Timetrip to Big Bang, Big Bang and Back / 1993 / Artifact Music ✦✦✦
Subtitled "A sonic celestial voyage from here and now to the end of the universe and from the beginning of time: a sonic cosmological journey to here and now," this music attempts, quite literally, to describe in electro-acoustic sound the ultimate trip (at least as far as science can conceive). "Part One: Astronomics" "is based on the premise that when we look at the night sky, we see TIME ... in Part One we travel from EARTH and NOW ... at ever-accelerating speed until we arrive at the limit of the universe where there is NOTHING ON THE OTHER SIDE: NO SPACE, NO TIME." (Kasemets, his emphasis). In "Part Two: Big Band or Turning the TimeGlove Inside Out," in order to return "we take our imaginary glove of time—the five fingers ... pointed ... to the five phases of our trip (via the moon, the planets, the comets, the stars and the galaxies)—and turn it inside out ... [to] follow time's forward motion through five phases of cosmological evolution." The concluding "Part Three: Chaosmosis" ... charts the course of the emergence of cosmic life from the beginnings of nuclear evolution through the pivotal fusions of the chemical evolution to the structuring of the DNA double-helix and the formation of the protein chain." Quite a program (!) but it is achieved through a thoroughgoing structural miniaturization of the stages of the journey, and by use of deceptively simple musical means. This is a piece to study in detail. —*"Blue" Gene Tyranny*

Carson Kievman

b. 1949, California
Composer / Orchestral, Opera, Ensemble, Theater and Multimedia
Kievman studied with Earle Brown, Olivier Messiaen, and James Tenney. He received his MFA from CAL Arts, and earned fellowships at Tanglewood, the MacDowell Colony, Eugene O'Neill Music Theater, and in Darmstadt, Germany. A lecturer at Darmstadt and at universities in South Florida and New York, Kievman composed the music for the NY Shakespeare Festival from 1978-79 and 1987-91. —*"Blue" Gene Tyranny*

Symphony No. 2 (42) / 1996 / New Albion ✦✦✦
Performed by the Polish Radio National Symphony Orchestra and the Polish Radio Choir of Kraków, conducted by Delta David Gier. An original and brilliantly expansive work by this Florida-based composer. Using the historical and spiritually internal life of Mozart as a framework, this incredible piece depicts "a metaphorical journey from youth through death, and beyond." The entry of Mozart's *Requiem* at the finale is developed by Kievman into universal realms, truly inspired and elegantly composed. —*"Blue" Gene Tyranny*

Jin Hi Kim

b. 1957, Seoul, Korea
Composer / Korean-influenced, Group Instrumental Improvisation
Kim studied the komungo, a zither of six silk strings most often used in meditation of male Confucian scholars, at an early age, breaking tradition

as most girls study kayagum, a brighter, more popular zither. Kim studied at Seoul National University, and electronic music and composition at Mills College. She has worked with Derek Bailey, Bill Frisell, Oliver Lake, Elliott Sharp, and Eugene Chadbourne. A co-founder of the No World Improvisations quartet, Kim designed an electric version of the komungo, and a MIDI-version of the changgo, a Korean percussion instrument, in collaboration with Danny Ferrington. — *"Blue" Gene Tyranny*

Komungo Permutations / 1990 / What Next ✦✦✦
Electronic exploration of this ancient Korean instrument, bamboo on silk. — *"Blue" Gene Tyranny*

Living Tones / 1995 / O.O. Discs ✦✦✦
Four elegantly composed and expressively played compositions influenced by Korean music and conceptual music. "Nong Rock" (1992), for komungo and string quartet, employs many shaken, sliding, multiple vibratos to move the tones, giving the sense of each sound being a living being. Midway through, the music employs a more steady, rock 'n' roll influenced texture, almost as an interlude. Then the tonalities become cosmic. A thoroughly engaging, deeply felt work. "Tchong" (1995), for daegum and flutes, is built from a haunting series of calls. "Yoeum" (1995), for kagok singer and baritone, is a moving duet with incidental harmonies, subtle overtones, and contrasting vocal styles. The ancient and eternal are expressed in the nobility of the music. "Piri Quartet" (1993), for three piri (reed flutes) and oboe/English horn, is simply intense and wonderful, with the combined piri suggesting the Japanese sho of courtly Gagaku music, and the Western reeds providing an almost electronic artificial harmonic texture. At times, the winds flit like birds among the trees, and sometimes they wail (with joy? with hurt?) definitely from the heart. A great CD. — *"Blue" Gene Tyranny*

Guy Klucevsek

Flying Vegetables of the Apocalypse / 1991 / Experimental Intermedia ✦✦✦✦✦
Dance music for accordion solo with top-notch combos of winds, strings, saxes, percussion. Unique transitions between the new-music, downtown style, tango, blues, polka, and more—poetic, even hum-along. My favorite cuts: "Waltzing Above Ground," "Fez Up." See also his *Manhattan Cascade* CD. — *"Blue" Gene Tyranny*

Manhattan Cascade / Apr. 1991 / Composers ✦✦✦
A marvelous, uplifting concert of twisted tunes and new uses for the "free bass accordion" containing Mary Ellen Childs' charming Pygmy music-like "Oa Poa Polka," Anthony Coleman's plaintive "Below 14th Street, Above 125th Street," Rolf Groesbeck's tone cluster and conjuring "Polka 1," Aaron Kernis' cinematic joke "Phantom Polka" (Kernis is also a composer of some brilliant orchestral music, watch for future recordings), John King's hymn-based "All Together Now," Guy Klucevsek's "Samba D Hiccup" and the lovely "An Air of Gathering Pipers," Christian Marclay's "Ping Pong Polka" with wildly modulated record collage, Lois Vierk's "Manhattan Cascade" (see review under composers) and John Zorn's humorous "Road Runner." — *"Blue" Gene Tyranny*

Alison Knowles

Frijoles Canyon / 1992 / What Next ✦✦✦
An extended work weaving together text and field recordings of the New Mexico landscape by this former member of the Fluxus group. Mixed sounds of rocks, sticks, trees, cacti, and of course beans. — *"Blue" Gene Tyranny*

Gottfried Michael Koenig

Klangfiguren II (Soundfigures II) (1955-1956) / Essay (1957-1958) / **Terminus 1** (1962) / **Terminus 2** (1966-1967) / **Output** (1979) / **Funktionen** / 1990 / Bvhaast ("Acousmatrix I/II") ✦✦✦✦✦
Classic pointillistic electronic music. — *"Blue" Gene Tyranny*

Takehisa Kosugi

Violin Improvisations New York, September 1989 / 1992 / Lovely Music ✦✦✦
Warm melodic phrases, sometimes almost romantic, sometimes slipping away like a bird heavenward. Always unpredictable and unanalyzable. — *"Blue" Gene Tyranny*

Petr Kotik

Petr Kotik's S.E.M. Ensemble / 1991 / Ear-Rational ✦✦✦
Petr Kotik's music is a very personal blend of austere and often strange rhythmic feelings and a Gregorian-chant simple melodic sensibility, with sudden startling chromatic and other tonal shifts, hypnotic and compelling music ranging from his now-legendary setting of Gertrude Stein's "Many Many Women" (out-of-print disc set) to the recent magnificent "Explorations in the Geometry of Thinking," a four-hour-long setting of the "Numerology" section of F. Buckminster Fuller's brilliant

"Synergetics," scored for three drummers, woodwinds and trombones, and vocal soloists, and partially excerpted on this Ear-Rational CD. Included also is the melodic "Solos and Incidental Harmonies" for flute, brass, and tambourine. — *"Blue" Gene Tyranny*

Jill Kroesen

Stop Vicious Cycles / 1982 / Lovely Music ✦✦✦
Like the albums of Ned Sublette and Laurie Anderson, this disc presents only the songs that make up part of the material for her extended and inventive performance pieces. Jill Kroesen, a performer as intense as Diamanda Galas and Lydia Lunch but more flexible, has made stage works, including a ballet *The Lou and Walter Story*, that reduce historical and social icons, like Alexander the Great and even the History of the World (as an icon in itself), to the personal and emotional, thereby stripping away much of the pomposity and abstraction that often accompanies the cant of the historical imperative. One European fan said to her, "You try to make everything so simple, whereas we try to make everything complex." These songs with a beat also make use of electronic and acoustic noise, free-style brass playing, bizarre percussion and mixing, and a totally new approach to the idea of pitched/non-pitched singing. Some of the pieces include "I'm Sorry I'm Such a Weenie," "I Am Not Seeing That You Are Here," "I'm Just A Human Being" ("I'm just a human being who can hardly keep her own house clean. And I lie in bed and think how the president is just a human being and it scares me to think about the life he leads."), "Alexander The Great" (". . . I want to travel all around and get lost conquering everybody's ground. And send plunder to my mother and kill my threatening brother. I'm Alexander and I'm pretty and I ain't in no hurry to get home."), and the legendary "Fay Shism Blues." — *"Blue" Gene Tyranny*

Philip Krumm

b. Apr. 7, 1941, Baltimore, MD
Composer / Electronic, Indeterminate
Krumm studied with Raymond Moses and Frank Sturchio at St. Mary's University, and at Rackham Graduate School at the University of Michigan with Ross Lee Finney. He also composed with Karlheinz Stockhausen at UC Davis, CA. Krumm presented new music festivals at McNay Art Institute with "Blue" Gene Tyranny in the late '50s and early '60s. He traveled with the ONCE Group, and appeared with Yoko Ono, George Brecht, and Terry Jennings at Carnegie Hall. He has toured with Jerry Hunt, including Roger Shattuck's Pataphysics Festival in Austin, TX. For ten years Krumm has been the host of the radio show *Musica Nova* on Texas Public Radio. — *"Blue" Gene Tyranny*

Sound Machine (1966) / In "Texas Music" / 1979 / IRIDA ✦✦✦
An electronic but somehow also a living being with a gently insistent pulse (or is it a purr?) that sometimes emits quasi-random tiny beeps and sighs. A lovely short piece from the composer of much innovative music: *Music for Clocks* (for multiple clock/metronomes and orchestra, composed several years before Ligeti's *Poeme Symphonique* (1965) for 100 metronomes and before Ichiyanagi's *Music for Electronic Metronome* (1961) was published); the "Piano Variations" (all on one C chord; the "variations" consist of fingering changes affecting the pressure and consequently the timbre of the chord); the outer space *Formations* (*Score of Heavenly Lattices*), and much more. — *"Blue" Gene Tyranny*

Concerto for Bass Clarinet / Opus One ✦✦✦
In the collection *The Orchestra According to the Seven*. Performed by soloist Scott Vance, with the University of Redlands Chamber Ensemble, conducted by Barney Childs.

Composed in 1964, this unique conceptual work has received many performances since that time. Each of the instrumental parts, written in innovative notation, are in large formats, about four feet by six feet, and are placed on the floor, so that all the players except for the soloist and the pianist move about while playing the piece. Surreal artificial harmonics and many other unusual playing techniques are employed. The resulting textures, although not intentionally programmatic, can evoke an untamed landscape, a protean world of delicate and primal sounds and unfettered expression. — *"Blue" Gene Tyranny*

Henry Kucharzyk

b. 1953, Toronto, Canada.
Composer / Acoustic, Multimedia, Theater
The Artistic Director of ARRAYMUSIC, this pianist studied composition at the University of Toronto with John Beckwith and John Weinzweig, and at Yale School of Music with Jacob Druckman, Earle Brown, and Morton Subotnick. Kucharzyk's work includes *Personal History* (1986), a multimedia work, *Collisions* (1986), a ballet score performed at Expo '86, and *Targeting* (1982). — *"Blue" Gene Tyranny*

Beating / 1988 / Artifact Music ✦✦✦
In the collection *Arraymusic: Strange City*. A composition in two parts, the first built on lush and beautiful vibraphone tones which beat against

each other, and the second a rhythmic study built with MIDI-controlled percussion and amplified heartbeats, with hybrid tones that are part sampled vocal and part white noise "chaff" attacks. Fascinating sonic poetry. —*"Blue" Gene Tyranny*

Ron Kuivila

Blurred Genres / Slowscan #6
Electronic music by a composer renowned for his evocative and beautiful sound-installation pieces based on subtle concepts and realized with self-designed and built electronics, this latest work is a high-voltage arcing sound sculpture entitled *Dolci Mura* (Sweet Walls). —*"Blue" Gene Tyranny*

Loose Canons / 1995 / Inial ✦✦✦
In the collection *Views from the Perfect City*. Creating fascinating timbres, this piece is made using "homemade" computer-driven electronic sound equipment that constantly throws up permutations, which the performer attempts to "steer to moments of self-parody and subversion" (the composer calls this playing "through" the system, rather than "on" or "with" it). —*"Blue" Gene Tyranny*

Joan La Barbara

Sound Paintings / 1990 / Lovely Music ✦✦✦✦✦
Extended vocal techniques (circular breathing, multiphonics like that in Buddhist chant, imitation of environmental sounds, speech just on the edge of comprehensibility) multitracked into some beautiful pieces. I especially like "Erin" on a photograph of an Irish child with his father's coffin, and "Klee Alee," inspired by the imagery of Paul Klee's paintings and the squiggles and brushstrokes when viewed up close. —*"Blue" Gene Tyranny*

73 Poems (Texts by Kenneth Goldsmith) / 1994 / Lovely Music ✦✦✦
A beautiful collaboration with both the musical setting and the poems created for the most part at the same time. La Barbara's voice is multitracked and her composition and vocal techniques are responsive to both the meaningful content and the physical character of the words; for example, a tone cluster for a towering wall. —*"Blue" Gene Tyranny*

Mary Jane Leach

Composer Mary Jane Leach grew out of a strong grounding in the arts, singing at church as a child, playing bass clarinet in high school, writing theater pieces in college, and finally getting into New York City's performance art scene in the late '70s while studying music at Columbia. Leach decided in the early '80s that she wanted to make her name as a composer and began to experiment with slow-paced pieces and layered tapes, as well as compositions for voices. She has worked with the New York Treble Singers and the Western Wind, and has released several albums, including *Celestial Fires.* —*Steve Huey*

Celestial Fires / 1993 / Experimental Intermedia ✦✦✦
Beginning from simple means—close harmonies with phasing rhythms, each of the six compositions on this CD gradually blossoms in the intricacy of its exquisite movement and sound. Each uses an ensemble of instruments or voices of a similar family, which emphasizes the textural binding—"Bruchstuck," "Green Mountain Madrigal," "Mountain Echoes," and "Ariel's Song" for eight treble voices; "Feu de Joie" for solo bassoon and six taped bassoons; and the illusionary "Trio for Duo" for live and taped alto flute and voice. Truly beautiful. —*"Blue" Gene Tyranny*

Anne LeBaron

b. May 30, 1953, Baton Rouge, Louisiana
Composer / Electronic, Blues-influenced, Orchestra & Chamber Works
LeBaron studied with Frederick Goosen, Bulent Arel, Daria Semegen, Mauricio Kagel, György Ligeti, Chour Wen-chung, Jack Beeson, and Mario Davidovsky. A harpist, and improvisor with many groups, including the LeBaron/Smith/Dixon trio and the LeBaron Quintet, she taught at SUNY Stony Brook, the University of Alabama, and Columbia University. He work includes *Concerto for Active Frogs* (1975) and *Strange Attractors* for large orchestra (1987). —*"Blue" Gene Tyranny*

Dish / In Dora Ohrenstein's "Urban Diva" / 1993 / CRI ✦✦✦
A sensual and humorous chamber work based on the texts "Seeing You Again Makes Me Wanna Wash the Dishes," "On Being Irresponsible About Lovers and Those Who Swoop on You," and "The Swooper and the Swoopee." LeBaron is an accomplished composer with chamber music recorded on the Mode label. The German Ear-Rational label features her jazz group The Anne LeBaron Quintet with the Phantom Orchestra. The voice in *Dish*, especially at the beginning of the piece, is amplified and echoed to create tactile effects. See also LeBaron's "Blue Harp Study 1" and "Blue Harp Study 2" in the collection *Jewel Box*. Listeners may also enjoy checking out her new album with several ensemble works on Mode Records (1993). —*"Blue" Gene Tyranny*

Richard Lerman

Within Earreach / 1994 / Artifact ✦✦✦
Sounds from the composer's site-specific sound installations using self-made microphones and transducers, and also composed "soundscapes." The recordings are from all around the world—Australia, Newfoundland, Hong Kong, Bali, Argentina, Jerusalem—with the devices attached to trees, metal objects, strings, leaves etc. Fascinating and mind-expanding. —*"Blue" Gene Tyranny*

George Lewis

b. 1952

★ **Homage to Charles Parker** / Black Saint ✦✦✦✦✦
Both of Lewis' compositions on this album are for an ensemble with Anthony Davis (piano), Douglas Ewart (bass clarinet), George Lewis (tenor trombone and electronics), and Richard Teitelbaum (Polymoog, Multimoog, and Micromoog synthesizers). "Blues" (1977) is a "collective orchestration" that builds in a fragmentary style of changing timbres, with a spirit that ranges from happy to that of Tibetan meditation, taken from material arranged in four basically diatonic choruses, using the essential harmonic sequence of the classic blues form as a starting point—but don't expect to hear a traditional "blues" because this music goes to the spirit behind the tune, rather than playing the tune. In the "Homage to Charles Parker" (1978), "the iconography [of the first section]... represents the life of Charles Parker—what is known, what is thought to be known, what is dreamed, heard, and said—and his 'reality,' i.e., birth and death." The second part is based on the traditional solo with chordal accompaniment form that Charles Parker "brought to a rare level of perfection" and making "loving inferences as to Parker's afterlife," pointing "to a new appraisal of world music after his life—one in which Afro-American creative music decisively affirms its place as a living, growing, vital part of world culture." —*"Blue" Gene Tyranny*

Changing With The Times / 1993 / New World ✦✦
Innovative pieces, each with a speaker, poet, or singer reflecting on modern living. Titles include "Chicago Dadagram," "So You Say," "The View from Skates in Berkeley," "Airplane," "Epilogue." Listeners may also enjoy checking out Lewis' CD *George Lewis* (1993) on the Avan label. —*"Blue" Gene Tyranny*

György Ligeti

b. 1923, Dicsöszentmarton, Transylvania, Romania
Composer / Electronic, Vocal Ensemble, Atonal-chromatic
Austrian composer of keyboard, electronic, orchestral, chamber, opera, and choral works. —*AMG*

Lux Aeterna, for 16-Voice Mixed Chorus (1966) / Deutsche Grammaphon ✦✦✦✦✦
Performed by the North German Radio Chorus, conducted by H. Franz. The famed "sound of the monolith" in Stanley Kubrick's film *2001* was lifted from *Lux Aeterna*, in a lovely performance. There's a surface of sustained and overlapping clusters of multitimbral quality that suggests universality without bigness. —*"Blue" Gene Tyranny*

☆ **Atmospheres (1961) for Large Orchestra/ Lontano (1967) for Large Orchestra/ In "Wien Modern"** / 1990 / Deutsche Grammaphone ✦✦✦✦✦
Performed by the Vienna Philharmonic, conducted by Claudio Abbado. Transparent washes of neo-impressionistic colors; inter-dimensional landscapes. Perfect companion pieces; beautiful. —*"Blue" Gene Tyranny*

Annea Lockwood

b. 1939, Christchurch, New Zealand
Composer / Electronic, Experimental Instrumental, Psychoacoustic
Lockwood teaches electronic music and composition at Vassar College. Trained in classical piano, she spent her childhood in the rugged New Zealand wilderness, hiking and climbing, and later based much of her work on recording and processing natural sounds. Her works include sound sculptures, environmental installations, and mixed-media. "Glass Concert" (1966) was written for two performers and an environment of glass objects; "World Rhythms" (1975), is a live mix of sounds transmitted by earthquake, fire, quasar, volcano, mudpool, tides and birds to which a beaten gong responds; "Nautilus" was written for didjeridu, conch and percussion. —*"Blue" Gene Tyranny*

A Sound Map of the Hudson River / 1990 / Lovely Music ✦✦✦
This is listening to natural sound in heightened detail, beautiful for the ear and mind. —*"Blue" Gene Tyranny*

Thousand Year Dreaming / 1992 / What Next ✦✦✦
An evocation perfectly described by the title. Use of native instruments and percussion sounds from natural objects. Meditative. See also her song "Night and Fog" in Thomas Buckner's vocal CD *Full Spectrum Voice.* —*"Blue" Gene Tyranny*

Red Mesa / Opus One ✦✦✦
In the collection *Loretta Goldberg: Soundbridge.* Composed in 1989, this piano piece vividly evokes the arid beauties and small life of the vast tablelands both through an original composition technique (patterns emerging from tonal material expanded vertically and horizontally) and the use of unusual percussive materials that, upon striking various internal piano parts, create creature-like sounds. However, the means and the structural integrity are never emphasized above the poetry and lyricism of this intriguing work. —*"Blue" Gene Tyranny*

Alvin Lucier

Composer / Electronic, Minimalism, Psychoacoustics, Acoustic Phenomena

Music for Solo Performer (1964-1965) for Enormously Amplified Brain Waves and Percussion / 1982 / Lovely Music ✦✦✦✦✦
The first music to use brain waves to generate sound. World instruments, as well as a cardboard box and a trash can, are vibrated by loudspeakers placed near and under them, as bursts and trains of the amplified alpha waves disturb the cones of the speakers. —*"Blue" Gene Tyranny*

☆ **I Am Sitting in a Room** / 1990 / Lovely Music ✦✦✦✦✦
A new music classic. Thirty-two repetitions of a simple line of text over 40 minutes, constantly broadcast and re-recorded in a room until the nodal tones of the room and the voices undergo a magical transformation of a sense of person and place into a sense of universal presence. Lucier is the dean of psychoacoustic music. —*"Blue" Gene Tyranny*

Crossings / 1991 / Lovely Music ✦✦✦
Pure, profound, and classic. Complex ideas realized simply. This CD includes the pieces "In Memoriam Jon Higgins" (1984), "Septet for Three Winds, Four Strings, and Pure Wave Oscillator" (1985), "Crossings" (1982) for small orchestra with slow-sweep, pure wave oscillator. —*"Blue" Gene Tyranny*

Music on a Long Thin Wire / 1992 / Lovely Music ✦✦✦
Recording of an installation made on May 10, 1979, in the rotunda of the US Customs House, Bowling Green, New York City. The wire was extended 80 feet through the oval of the rotunda and was driven by one pure wave oscillator. The wire played itself, registering all changes in volume, timbre, harmonic structure, rhythmic and cyclic patterning, and other sonic phenomena. —*"Blue" Gene Tyranny*

Clocker / 1994 / Lovely Music ✦✦✦
For amplified clock, performer with galvanic response sensor, and digital delay system. —*"Blue" Gene Tyranny*

Panorama / 1996 / Lovely Music ✦✦✦
Four innovative and intriguing works based on the poetry of physical phenomena. "Wind Shadows" (1994), written for two pure wave oscillators and a trombonist, employs exacting tuning modulations (three cycles above and three cycles below given pitches) to produce spinning wave illusions. In "Music for Piano with One or More Snare Drums" (1990), overlapping patterns of piano tones cause snare drums to resonate, defining a geography of the performance space. In "Music for Piano with Amplified Sonorous Vessels" (1990), the interior resonances of small vessels—such as wine glasses, sea shells, clay pots, bamboo cups etc.—placed near the piano are amplified over loudspeakers, their sound in turn creating interference patterns. "Panorama" (1993) employs a photograph of the Swiss and Austrian Alps as a score for a trombonist who "draws" the mountains by sliding tones, punctuated at peaks by a pianist's single tones and intervals. —*"Blue" Gene Tyranny*

Ralph Lundsten

Fagel Bla (Blue Bird) (1969) / Tellus (1968) / 1970 / Telestar ✦✦✦
Two wonderful enviromental pieces by these two Swedish composers. *Blue Bird,* commissioned by the Foundations for Nationwide Concerts as inauguration music for the Expo-Norr festival in 1969 at Ostersund, is a two-channel composition performed from giant balloons that floated over the city. The strange effect is that the sounds do not dissipate when over a listener, so that the height of the balloons made no difference; *Tellus,* commissioned by the Swedish Institute, was a sight/sound performance for the 1968 Triennal in Milan. The theme was "global welfare in social, technical, and emotional light." —*"Blue" Gene Tyranny*

Witold Lutoslawski

Pianist and composer of orchestral, chamber, and piano music. —*AMG*

Preludes and Fugue (1972) for 13 Solo Strings/ Mi-parti for Orchestra (1976) / Novelette (1979) / 1989 / Polskie Nagrania ✦✦✦
Performed by the National Chamber Orchestra in Warsaw and the Polish Radio National Symphony Orchestra, conducted by Lutoslawski and Hollinger. Totally redefines "preludes" as mysterious sound-pieces with a "fugue" of brilliant, aleatoric, sliding, perpendicular lines. Both *Mi-Parti* (French for a whole with two parts not the same) and the *Novelette* imply nonspecified narratives. —*"Blue" Gene Tyranny*

Postlude I for Orchestra (1958) / Paroles Tissees (Weaving Songs) (1965) for Tenor, Strings, Harp, Piano, and Percussion / Livre Pour Orchestre / 1990 / Polskie Nagrania ✦✦✦
Although his pre-1960 works are almost 19th-century in their gestures and development, the pieces on this CD are strikingly different in their tone-colors and organization, especially the beautiful *Livre pour orchestre* and the highly original *Cello Concerto.* —*"Blue" Gene Tyranny*

Les Espaces du Sommeil (The Spaces of Sleep) / 1990 / Philips ✦✦✦
Some lovely timbral effects for a setting of this poem by Robert Desnos about the discovery of one's soul or others' presence ("There is you undoubtedly whom I do not know . . .") during the internal wanderings of sleep. The singing of Dietrich Fischer-Dieskau is of course superb. CD also includes the "Symphony No. 3." Both works performed by the Berlin Philharmonic, conducted by the composer. —*"Blue" Gene Tyranny*

The Machine for Making Sense

On Second Thoughts / 1994 / O.O. Discs (Tall Poppies) ✦✦✦
A . . . well . . . bizarre concept music group of Sydney (Australian)- based composer-performers. The tracks (26, A-Z) take the kind of (mostly vocal) inflections associated with "making sense" in all its forms, and explore these in a musical manner that is at turns humorous, mysterious, lyrical, and rambunctious, the music of a hereto unsuspected culture, the birth noises of a new species. Wonderfully, barely readable and appropriately dense notes accompany the disc. Performers are Jim Denley, flutes, sax and voice; Chris Mann, voice and text; Rik Rue, digital and analog samples and tape manipulation; Amanda Stewart, voice and text; Stevie Wishart, violin, live electronics, hurdy-gurdy and voice. (See also their great short piece in the collection *Aerial No. 5*). —*"Blue" Gene Tyranny*

Angus Maclise

Angus Maclise (Various Works) / 1992 / Mela Foundation ✦✦✦
A cassette collection of various works by the marvelous poet, mystic, composer, drummer, and cembalum player who wrote music for independent films (Ron Rice's *Chumlum,* Warhol's *EPI (Exploding Plastic Inevitable)* and combined American forms with music of expanded time sense; for example, "12 I 64 AM NYC the first twelve; Sunday Morning Blues" (1964) for bowed gong, hand drums, sopranino saxophone, bowed guitar, plucked mandola, and viola. —*"Blue" Gene Tyranny*

Jackson Mac Low

b. 1922

Poet / Performance Systems, Computer-generated Poetry/Music

Open Secrets / 1994 / Experimental Intermedia ✦✦✦
MacLow began writing music and poetry when he was 15, and later he developed his "simultaneities" after 1953 for speakers, vocalists, instrumentalists, and/or projectionists. His poetry, published to date in 25 volumes, is written following the many indeterminate/nonintentional procedures that he has invented. This CD provides a good overview of MacLow's creativity: the "1st Milarepa Gatha" (1976), "Thanks" (1960), the "38th and 39th Merzgedichte in Memoriam Kurt Schwitters" (1989), "Phoneme Dance in Memoriam John Cage" (by MacLow and Anne Tardos) (1993). "Free Gatha 1" (1978), and "Free Gatha 2" (1981) are works for massed, multitracked voices speaking/singing at the same time with complex compositional procedures described in the notes. The "Milarepa Quartet for Four Like Instruments" (1982) employs a letter-to-pitch-class code that translates text into music in the manner of procedures used by Messiaen, Ashley, Cage, and others. "Winds/Instruments" (1980) is for voices and instrumentalists who sometimes speak, and "Lucas 1 to 29: for One or More Instrumentalists (In Memoriam Morton Feldman and for the Musicians of Germany)" (1990) is based on the Lucas sequence. —*"Blue" Gene Tyranny*

Bruno Maderna

b. 1920, Venice Italy, d. 1973, Darmstadt, Germany
Composer, Conductor / Serialism

☆ **Quadrivium (Crossroads) (1969) for Four Percussionists and Four Orchestral Groups / Aura (1972) for Orchestra / Biogramma (1972) for Lar** / 1990 / Deutsche Grammaphon ✦✦✦✦✦
A reissue on CD of the 1980 discs. Performances by the North German Radio Symphonie Orchester, conducted by Giuseppe Sinopoli. The expressive, shimmering neo-impressionism of "Aura" and "Biogramma," and the ever-changing landscape (guided by the conductor's choices, different for each performance) of "Quadrivium," by the poet of the serialist composers. —*"Blue" Gene Tyranny*

Giardino Religioso (The Religious Garden) / 1991 / Col Legno ✦✦✦
In the collection *20 Ans de Musique Contemporaine á Metz,* Netherlands Radio Chamber Orchestra, conducted by Hans Zender. Completed in 1972, this piece is scored for percussion, two pianos and two harps,

which are seated in the center of the stage surrounded symmetrically by ten string players, with trumpet and horn players on either side. This seating also reflects the structure of the piece—the center players work toward and fall away from a grand climax, the strings play at the beginning and at the end, the brass enter quietly, play in the chorus in the middle and play fragments at the end. There are also three choral sections, which start together; then the conductor abandons the players, leaving the music to disintegrate. There is a wonderful balance of completely scored material, lush in timbre, and excitingly rich, complex, and spontaneous interplay among the players. —*"Blue" Gene Tyranny*

Bruno Maderna Dirige Maderna / 1993 / Arkadia ✦✦✦
Wonderful performances of Maderna, an accomplished conductor as well as composer, conducting his own music. Contains the "Concerto for Violin and Orchestra" (1970 version), "Grande Aulodia" for flute and oboe soloists and orchestra, and the magnificient "Aura." —*"Blue" Gene Tyranny*

David Mahler

The King of Angels / Frog Peak Music ✦✦✦
Two tributes to Elvis Presley: the song "Every Song You Sang" and the tape piece "The King of Angels." Also the word piece "Cup of Coffee." Surprising works by this important Seattle-based composer. —*"Blue" Gene Tyranny*

Chris Mann

La-de-da / Talking About Healesville / 38'37" A Machine for Making Sense / Frog Peak Music ✦✦✦
Three cassettes by this influential Australian composer, poet, text sound and visual artist. "La-de-da" is the classic "truly stereo" test piece; "Talking about Healesville" was banned in Healesville; and "38'37" A Machine for Making Sense" is the improvisational group of which Mann is a member. —*"Blue" Gene Tyranny*

The Birth of Peace / NMA ✦✦✦
Cassette tape with book of Mann's multimedia piece for goldfish-controlled computers and poets. Includes plastic goldfish. —*"Blue" Gene Tyranny*

Frankie Mann

b. 1955, Charlotte, NC
Composer / Computer, Electronic, Songs
Mann studied at Oberlin Conservatory of Music and the Center for Contemporary Music, Mills College. A pianist and flutist, her weekly radio program *Blank Spot Punch*, aired on KPFA-FM, Berkeley, CA, from 1975-79. Innovative computer programming in visual arts, CD-ROM design, and industrial communications. —*"Blue" Gene Tyranny*

I Was a Hero (From The Mayan Debutante Revue) / How to Be Very, Very Popular / 1980 / Lovely Music ✦✦✦
In the collection *Lovely Little Records*. Two wonderfully droll songs, the first a "reinterpretation of religious history" (one of her several songs in a peculiarly Southern humorous vein), and the second about "one of the preoccupations of Americans . . . worrying about one's intelligence. Many of my friends and I feel as if we were much more intelligent when we were children than we are now, and this leads us to believe that we are becoming stupider every day." —*"Blue" Gene Tyranny*

Walter Marchetti

Vandalia / 1991 / Cramps ✦✦✦

Per la Sete Dell'Orecchio (For the Thirst of the Ear) / 1991 / Cramps ✦✦✦
The legendary, conceptually surreal piano recordings finally reissued. —*"Blue" Gene Tyranny*

Christian Marclay

Black Stucco/ In "Imaginary Landscapes" / 1989 / Elektra/Nonesuch ✦✦✦✦✦
Marclay plays turntables—using the clicks of vinyl discs, by "scratching," back-and-forward manual rotation, mixing, varispeed—using recordings as "artifacts" of our society. He has also created art objects with the same records—"Footsteps" is a one-sided record containing the sounds of footsteps. 3500 copies were spread on the floor of the Shedhalle galleries in Zurich and people were invited to walk on them over the course of six weeks, and 1000 of the records with dirt and scratches are available from Gelbe Musik. He has also made a "Record without grooves" with a gold label housed in a black velour cover with golden writing, signed and numbered. —*"Blue" Gene Tyranny*

Maria Callas / 1994 / Musicworks ✦✦✦
In the collection *Musicworks No. 60: Plunderphonics & Vox*. An excerpt from Marclay's German album *More Encores* (published by Review

Records and Recommended No Man's Land). An outrageous, humorous, yet perhaps loving portrait of the diva utilizing her recordings and very subtle versions of "plunderphonics" techniques; Marclay's musical ear is finely tuned to shifts in harmonic content (nothing is ever resolved in this piece, but just sort of slides, or as the case may be, drips into another sonic zone) and his mind attuned to just the right moment to make a change. —*"Blue" Gene Tyranny*

Ingram Marshall

Three Penitential Visions / Hidden Voices / 1993 / Elektra/Nonesuch ✦✦✦
Atmospheric, subtle, with almost new-age transparency but more ideas: one of Marshall's best albums. —*"Blue" Gene Tyranny*

Richard Maxfield

Composer / Electronic, Tape Collage

Night Music in "New Sounds in Electronic Music" / Odyssey ✦✦✦✦✦
This exquisite pre-synthesizer electronic music is made like his pieces *Sine Music* (1959) and *Trinity Piece* (1960), with only the supersonic bias signal of a tape recorder and a supersonic sawtooth waveform from an oscilloscope producing audio-range difference-tone "ghosts." Identical in feeling to a response to the sound of birds and insects on a summer night in a city park. —*"Blue" Gene Tyranny*

☆ **Richard Maxfield: Electronic Music** / 1992 / Mela Foundation ✦✦✦✦✦
A cassette reissue of the original out-of-print Advance Recordings disc (1969), this collection contains some of the most beautiful and imaginative electronic and "live electronic" music ever made (I'm serious) using only pre-synthesizer Army-surplus store electronics. *Pastoral Symphony* (1960) for three channels—one behind the audience—is a lovely work, as is *Night Music* on Odyssey records (see above) and his *A Swarm of Butterflies Encountered on the Ocean* (unissued). "Bacchanale" (1963) is made from a noise-improv-collage ensemble with poetry by Edward Fields, folk music recordings (many from Henry Cowell), jazz hang-outs, scraping violin noises, underwater clarinet, drum, typewriter, and parts of Maxfield's *African Symphony* and the poetic "Wind." The latter is made of events separated from each other by beautifully timed silences. The sounds are composed of wind and the sounds of things that wind moves, like squeaking rusty gates. Maxfield turns it all into an intriguing piece. Other pieces on this recording include "Piano Concert for David Tudor" (1961), for piano and tapes made from the performer's improvisations; "Amazing Grace" (1960), a mass of tape loops cut to a score (like Maxfield's "Cough Music" [1959-1961] and "Italian Folk Music"), humorous samples from a religious revival; and part of the sketches for Maxfield's opera *Stacked Deck*. "Composers, Performance, and Publication," a very interesting essay, appears in *An Anthology* by La Monte Young. —*"Blue" Gene Tyranny*

Toshiro Mayuzumi

Mandala Symphony (1960) / Odyssey
Performed by the NHK Symphony Orchestra, conducted by Hiroyuki Iwaka. Although bordering on a large contemporary romantic work, this symphony attempts to express a Japanese "Buddhist view of the omnipotent universe," and uses only collections of sounds to achieve this aim. The two parts of the mandala are expressed in the two parts of the symphony: "Kongokai-Mandala" symbolizes spiritual awakening through contemplation and oneness with eternity; "Taizokai-Mandala" represents the world of Sokushin Jyobutsu, which is made up of the phases of life, such as Gakido (a place of hunger and thirst where sinners go in the afterlife) and Shurado (a passage of pandemonium, the world of the immature until they attain spiritual awakening). (See also *String Quartet* by LaSalle in 20th-Century Collections in this section.) —*"Blue" Gene Tyranny*

Barton McLean

A Little Night Music / Demons of the Night/ In CDCM Computer Music Series, vol. 7, A / 1990 / Centaur ✦✦✦
Nocturnal tone poems, beautifully formed computer sounds expressing different night sensations. —*"Blue" Gene Tyranny*

Olivier Messiaen

b. 1908, d. Apr. 28, 1992
A French composer and organist, one of the most influential teachers of this century. Messiaen was the organist at the Sainte Trinite cathedral and composed a large body of organ music. His harmonic idiom is always highly colorful, and rhythmically ingenious. He was able to unify the rhythmic intensity of Stravinsky with the dodecaphonic technique of Schoenberg, being one of the first instructors to carefully analyze their music and pave the way for such students as Boulez and Stockhausen.

Messiaen was also one of the first composers to apply serial principles to rhythmic organization, though serial techniques are used only as one means among many in his arsenal. He had a predilection for cyclic forms, often using juxtaposed blocks of differing sonority in his larger works. His thematic material is drawn primarily from two sources: Catholic religious themes, and birdsong. To this is added an advanced feeling for modality, building on the work of Charles Tournemire. Messiaen composed in every form of the time, though his concertos and symphonic works are not titled as such. His music revels in naturalistic evocations and spiritual meditation. His *Quartet for the End of Time*, composed in a German prison camp, is one of the signature pieces of the mid-20th century. — *Todd McComb*

L'Ascension (Four Symphonic Meditations for Orchestra) (1933) / Koch Schwann ✦✦✦
Performed by the Bavarian Radio Orchestra, directed by Karl Anton Rickenbacher. Compassionate, sacramental, similar to *Les Offrandes Oubliees* (1930); unlike the severe religious works of his later style. CD includes "Chronochromie" (1959/1960). — *"Blue" Gene Tyranny*

Trois Petites Liturgies (Three Brief Liturgies) (1943-1944) for Women's Chorus, Chamber Orchestra with Ondes Martenot / Erato ✦✦✦
A curious, Byzantine work with a poetic and controversial text by the composer; the poetry of gems and colors mixed with reflections on the presence of the Creator, in us, in others, in things. — *"Blue" Gene Tyranny*

☆ **Des Canyons Aux Etoiles (From the Canyons to the Stars) (1971-1974) / Oiseaux Exotiques (Exotic Birds) (1956) / Couleurs de la Cite** / 1991 / CBS ✦✦✦✦✦
London Sinfonetta, directed by Esa-Pekka Salonen. A terrific collection of the best of Messiaen's later style. Pointillistic tone paintings and good performances, but I prefer the out-of-print Erato discs with Marius Constant conducting. — *"Blue" Gene Tyranny*

O Sacrum Convivium/ In "Of Eternal Light" / 1993 / Catalyst ✦✦✦
A warm, hopeful religious work in Messiaen's early style in a beautifully subtle performance by Musica Sacra, conducted by Richard Westenburg. This CD also contains the enchanting and energetic "Return to Earth" by Meredith Monk, and pieces by Moran and Ligeti. — *"Blue" Gene Tyranny*

Eclairs sur L'Au-Dela (1992) / 1994 / Jade ✦✦✦
The generally agreed-upon translation for this title, "Illuminations from the Beyond," is a little tame compared to the equally appropriate and somewhat more apt "Lightning-Flashes from the Beyond." The full-brass unisons with whipcracks and deep rolls from bass drum and gong in the section "Seven Angels with Seven Trumpets" elicit the most chilling, majestic feelings from a pre-modern sense of the eternal mystery. "The Way to the Invisible" likewise opens gates of the subconscious with beautifully bizarre harmonic sweeps in the strings, full chordal annunciations in the brass, and "total chromatic" backdrops for the song of the pied butcherbird to wander through. As in several other Messiaen works, the birds are seen as intermediaries between the heavenly and the earthly: there is a gorgeous menagerie of 25 bird songs played freely and simultaneously in the section "Several Birds from the Trees of Life," and birds appear throughout the piece. Lovely, unique melodic strains appear in several sections: "God Will Wipe Every Tear from Their Eyes"; the very moving, yet not sensual in the usual manner, "Dwelling in Love"; and the final "Christ, Light of Paradise." This piece is a testament to faith in the natural revelation of the Great Mystery expressed in clear, beautiful musical images, neither overemotional nor overaustere. Recorded in a live performance by the National Polish Radio Orchestra of Katowice, conducted by Antoni Wit. — *"Blue" Gene Tyranny*

Roscoe Mitchell

b. Aug. 3, 1940, Chicago, Illinois
Composer / Early Free Jazz, Post- Coltrane Avant-garde, Composed Open Forms
See the Jazz section for his biography.

☆ **Four Compositions** / 1992 / Lovely Music ✦✦✦✦✦
Fleeting chromatic gestures; bizarre multiphonic acoustics; unusual instruments (triple contrabass, viol, and contrabass sarrusophone); touching, brief melodies; and humor combine to create unique music. Selections include "NONAAH," "Duet for Wind and String," "Cutouts," and "Prelude." Excellent performances. Recommended. — *"Blue" Gene Tyranny*

Pilgrimage / 1994 / Lovely Music ✦✦✦
Fabulous new pieces featuring the Roscoe Mitchell New Chamber Ensemble: Mitchell, Thomas Buckner (vocal), Joseph Kubera (piano), and Vartan Manoogian (violin). — *"Blue" Gene Tyranny*

Dary John Mizelle

b. Jun. 14, 1940
Composer / Electronic, Acoustic
Mizelle received his Ph.D. from the University of CA, San Diego; studied

with Austin, Erickson, Gaburo, and Stockhausen; and taught at Oberlin and the Sonavera Studio for Sonic Arts. — *"Blue" Gene Tyranny*

Polyphonies (1975) for Shakuhachi and Electronic Sounds / Spectra (1975-1979) for Bass and Computer Tape / Primavera-Heterophony, for 24 Celli / 1981 / Irida ✦✦✦
Polyphonies of earth, air, fire, and water sounds; dualities of musical gesture (such as slow/fast); and varieties of musical organization (drone, pointillistic, gestural, polyphonic, stochastic, and cyclic) in a strange duet. Unique dramatic sounds from massed strings. — *"Blue" Gene Tyranny*

Gordon Monahan

The Long Aeolian Piano / 1990 / Musicworks #45 ✦✦✦✦✦
A lovely "aeolian harp," sculpted with Thaddeus Holownia, made from strings attached to an upright piano, stretched down a hill, and set in resonance by the wind. (Incidentally, another lovely "aeolian harp" with metal resonators built by Doug Hollis lives as a permanent installation atop the Exploratorium in San Francisco. See *Soundviews* in 20th-Century Collections in this section.) See also Canadian composer Monahan's piece "Speaker Swinging" (excerpt) in the collections *Imaginary Landscapes* and *Soundviews*. — *"Blue" Gene Tyranny*

This Piano Thing / 1992 / Swerve Editions ✦✦✦
Studies in producing unusual sounds from both an unaltered acoustic piano in "Piano Mechanics" and a prepared piano in "This Piano Thing." Monahan has invented several original playing techniques ("Fingers and Arms Becoming Four Hands," "High Trills Becoming Difference Tones," "Voices Emerging along High Tension Wires") that also require an ear sensitive to the momentary buildups of rushing waveforms and overtone changes. Fascinating and original work. — *"Blue" Gene Tyranny*

Music for Mechanical Metal / 1995 / Musicworks ✦✦✦
In the collection *Musicworks No. 63*. This is the sound from the recent sound installation (installed in galleries and music spaces worldwide, and recorded here from a performance at the Kitchen, NYC) with the collective title "Sounds and the Machines That Make Them." Another part of this piece includes "Spinner." Always interesting both for their socially philosophical as well as acoustical bases (and the composer's infective sense of humor), this part of Monahan's highly experimental work is produced on mechanical machines called Flaphos, which consist of oscillating sheets of metal, the movements of which are controlled by computer. A related work is Monahan's 1991-present installation piece *Music from Nowhere* characterized by the use of raw materials used to make loudspeakers and other sound-transducing and -creating devices. — *"Blue" Gene Tyranny*

Meredith Monk

Key / 1993 / Lovely Music ✦✦✦
Rerelease on CD of the 1973 classic. Monk's modern folk music from her beautiful and noble performance-ceremonies that recall former times and a lineage of human understanding beyond the present state of things. Songs include "Porch," "Under Street," "What Does it Mean?," "Vision," "Fat Stream," "Do You Be?" "Vision" (reprise), "Change," and "Dungeon" with Meredith Monk (voice, organ, jew's harp) and Daniel Ira Sverdlik, Dick Higgins, Colin Walcott, Lanny Harrison, and Mark Monstermaker (voices). See also her beautiful "Phantom Waltz" in the collection *US Choices* by the piano duet Double Edge. — *"Blue" Gene Tyranny*

Steve Montague

b. Mar. 10, 1943

Slow Dance on a Burial Ground / 1985 / Lovely Music ✦✦✦
Three works on a vinyl LP of a different approach to pattern, or "minimalist" music, called "paramell" by the composer, an invented word indicating a series of works in which the instrumentalists play fast, mostly unison lines. The title piece is a musique concrète tape made from manipulated studio recordings of log drums and folk flutes. — *"Blue" Gene Tyranny*

Robert Moran

b. 1937
Studied with Apostel, Berio, Milhaud. Co-founder of the San Francisco New Music Ensemble at the San Francisco Conservatory of Music in the '60s. Composed the large-scale event "Pachelbel Promenade" for the city of Graz, Austria, in the '70s. Composer-in-residence at Northwestern University. Operas *From the Towers of the Moon* (1992) for the Minnesota Opera, *The Dracula Diary*, and *Night Passage* (1995) for the 180 male voices of the Seattle Men's Chorus, about the Oscar Wilde trial and sentence. — *"Blue" Gene Tyranny*

Arias, Interlude, and Inventions from "Desert of Roses" / Ten Miles High over Albania for Eight Harps / Open Veins for Orchestra / 1993 / Argo ✦✦✦
A very original composer whose orchestral sound has touches of exotic

color, phase music, and tuneful invention, Moran collaborated with Philip Glass on the opera *The Juniper Tree*. Highly recommended. —*"Blue" Gene Tyranny*

Rocky Road to Kansas / Requiem: Chant du Cygne (Requiem: Swan Song) / 32 Cryptograms / 1995 / Argo ✦✦✦
The title of the title work comes from the name given to a Pennsylvania quilt pattern, circa 1865, that reminded the composer of the multitracked quartet design (thick layers, repeated patterns, etc.) for this charming percussion piece, featuring a variety of African, Israeli, and Moroccan drums. Premiered in 1990, the *Requiem: Swan Song* is an inspired piece for four choruses and four chamber orchestras dispersed throughout a cathedral. The text is based on the last words of Mozart as recorded by his wife and sister ("I compose this Requiem for my self . . . I can smell death . . . And now I must leave my art behind"). The rhythmic units of the words closely match those of the instrumental parts—for example, short words occur with pizzicato string notes, choral swells with complementary brass and string sustains. Moran views the work as a "gigantic sound-tapestry . . . the sounds of some unearthly musical Ping-Pong game," no doubt an image that would have delighted Mozart, who loved dice and billiards and created compositional methods using them. *32 Cryptograms for Derek Jarman* is a delightful, highly rhythmic work from 1995, painted in bright timbres for chamber orchestra. Borrowing the bassline of a well-known aria from Henry Purcell's *Dido and Aeneas,* Moran builds cryptograms from pitch aggregates pitches, consulting the *I-Ching* (John Cage's well-known procedure) to determine the "sound-thickness." Dynamics and repetitions may be altered by performers and conductor. Derek Jarman was the brilliant British filmmaker who was once chosen by Moran to direct his opera *Desert of Roses*. —*"Blue" Gene Tyranny*

Charles Morrow

BP for BP / Musicworks ✦✦✦
Unique works by a composer who has an abiding interest in world music and has produced some fine compositions with minimalist instrumentation. —*"Blue" Gene Tyranny*

David Moss

Language Linkage (1988) / 1990 / Aerial ✦✦✦
Energetic setting of Italo Calvino text for many processed voices, electronic sounds, and percussion. Like a parallel universe. A very different sound. —*"Blue" Gene Tyranny*

Raphael Mostel

Nightsongs / 1991 / Scarlet/Infinity ✦✦✦
Not a "new age" group, this ensemble is described on their first CD cover as creating "new music for old instruments," and that's what they do. Raphael Mostel resonates Tibetan brass meditation bowls, gradually introducing sharp and startling sounds that will awaken the chakras. "Jacob's Ladder" combines didjeridus, water, and breaking sounds with wailing thighbone trumpets. John Charles Thomas produces a solo on the ancient lyzarden with jazz-line inflections in "Nightsong." The brilliant singer and instrumentalist Mieczyslaw Litwinski is also featured throughout. —*"Blue" Gene Tyranny*

Blood on the Moon / 1992 / Digital Fossils ✦✦✦
Original music of a transparent, eternal quality that also suggests many Asian and Middle Eastern traditions, primarily because of the acoustic instruments used to play it: singing bowls, shakuhachi, Tibetan thighbone trumpets, ram's horn, and others. Highly meditative and sustained, with moments of restrained intense emotion. —*"Blue" Gene Tyranny*

Gordon Mumma

b. Mar. 30, 1935, Framingham, MA
Composer / Electronic, Tape Collage, Instrument Builder and Designer
Gordon Mumma is a cofounder, with Robert Ashley, of the Cooperative Studio for Electronic Music in Ann Arbor, MI, which has been in existence since the early '60s. —*AMG*

☆ **Mesa/Pontpoint/Fwyyn** / Lovely Music ✦✦✦✦✦
Performed by the composer, with Pauline Oliveros and David Tudor (bandoneons). "Fwyyn" is a lament to bring back to life a dancing princess who had been enchanted—beautiful, slowly evolving textures. "Mesa" describes expansive, eroded mesa landscapes, and "Pontpoint" interprets a bridge in a rural French village through an analogous bridging movement in the acoustical space. Pure electronic music. —*"Blue" Gene Tyranny*

Dresden Interleaf 13 February 1945/ Music from the Venezia Space Theatre/ The Megaton for William Burroughs / Lovely Music ✦✦✦✦✦
Live electronic music created for multimedia theaters. Performances by the ONCE Group on tour. Fascinating and mysterious. —*"Blue" Gene Tyranny*

Hornpipe (1967) / In "The Sonic Arts Union" / 1970 / Mainstream ✦✦✦
A piece for French horn played with unusual reed mouthpieces, cybersonic circuits, and other devices. We hear the sound of the processing circuits balancing and unbalancing themselves, as the horn player's chosen responses gradually build an "orchestra" of accumulated decisions. A mysterious live performance. —*"Blue" Gene Tyranny*

Conlon Nancarrow

b. Oct. 27, 1912, Texarkana, TX
Composer / Player Piano, Chamber and Orchestral
An American composer residing in Mexico since 1940, Nancarrow's works involve manipulation of the workings of player pianos, producing sounds and gestures not possible for human performers. —*AMG*

☆ **Studies for Player Piano, vols. I-V** / 1990 / Wergo ✦✦✦✦✦
Secluded in a quiet suburban district of Mexico City, Conlon Nancarrow spent three decades composing these incomparable pieces, punching the player piano rolls himself. Of unparalleled rhythmic complexity and fascinating energy, with boogie woogie in some studies like you've never heard before. —*"Blue" Gene Tyranny*

Studies / 1991 / RCA Victor Red Seal ✦✦✦
Performed by the Ensemble Modern, conducted by Ingo Metzmacher.
Several brightly rhythmic and sensitively played arrangements for chamber orchestra of Nancarrow's player piano *Studies*, as well as a "Tango" and a "Toccata." There are the original instrumentations of "Piece No. 2 for Small Orchestra," a "Trio" and the "Sarabande & Scherzo." Highly recommended. —*"Blue" Gene Tyranny*

Study no. 15 (1950s), Transcribed for Piano Four-Hands by Yvar Mikhashoff/ In "Continuum Performs Nancarrow" / 1992 / Musicmasters ✦✦✦
The same surprising rhythmic complexities and drive as the piano rolls. Played here by live performers. —*"Blue" Gene Tyranny*

Ben Neill

Mainspring / 1992 / Ear-Rational ✦✦✦✦✦
Pieces featuring Neill's invention, the mutatrumpet, a combination of three trumpets plus slide, which makes rapid change between a variety of sonorities possible. An electronic processing system by Robert Moog and a computer program by David Behrman have both been designed to work with the mutatrumpet. This CD exemplifies the idea of "unified multisidedness" in the sounds and the compositional style. For example, "Mainspring" (1985), after a fanfare-type introduction, goes into a riff-steady march tune over a half-stepping accompaniment with steel guitar country music slides and, later, a solo for the bridge—really delightful and peculiar. "Dis-solution 2" (1986) is for mutatrumpet, percussion, and pitch-sensing electronics (David Behrman) providing a lovely treble shadow. "No More People" (1988), with text by Stevie Smith for soprano and band, is a classic aria over constantly intense telegraphic figures. Wow . . . —*"Blue" Gene Tyranny*

Itsofomo (In the Shadow of Forward Motion) (Complete Work) / 1993 / New Tone ✦✦✦
The raw truth of a personal experience of anti-gay violence: the energetically telegraphing style of the music is excellently imagined and perfectly complements the impassioned text and delivery by the late Wojnarowicz. Extraordinarily moving. —*"Blue" Gene Tyranny*

Phill Niblock

Four Full Flutes / 1991 / Experimental Intermedia ✦✦✦✦✦
Meditative, sustained, divine; slowly changing clusters. —*"Blue" Gene Tyranny*

Music by Phill Niblock / 1993 / Experimental Intermedia ✦✦✦
This CD contains two compositions—"Five More String Quartets" and "Early Winter"—both of which are long, sustained sound universes that slowly change in pitch and timbre, redefining the form of the sonic space they simultaneously create and occupy. For example, in "Early Winter" for string quartet, multitracked bass flute, sampled and synthesizer voices, and flute, harmonics slowly appear and vanish like the slow onset of winter weather. "Five More String Quartets" creates ghostly different tones by the detuning/retuning of pitches from multitracked strings. —*"Blue" Gene Tyranny*

Luigi Nono

b. 1924, Venice, Italy, **d.** 1990, Venice
Composer / 12-tone, Opera, Political Works, Electronic
An Italian composer in the 12-tone or atonal style, whose work encompasses many forms, including opera and electronic music. Many fundamental pieces by Nono are out of print: "Y Su Sangre Ya Viene Cantando (And Even Your Blood Comes Singing)," for flute, strings, and percussion, from *Epitaffio per Garcia Lorca* ("Epitaph for Garcia Lorca," RCA Vic-

trola VICS 1313, 1968); the choral settings of texts by Cesare Pavese; and the operas *Intolleranze* ("Intolerance," 1960, which attacks segregation, the bomb, and Nazism); *Al Gran Sole Carico d'Amore* ("To the Great Sun Charged with Love," 1975, about the Paris Commune of 1871). —*"Blue" Gene Tyranny*

Floresta e Jovem e Cheja de Vida (1965-1966) for Soprano, Voices, Clarinet, Copper Plate, and Tape / 1979 / Deutsche Grammaphon ♦♦♦

A good example of Nono's pieces (like "Non Consumiamo Marx" and "La Fabricca Illuminata," both for voices and tape) that calls for attention to immediate situations, in this case, the escalation of the Vietnam War by American forces. Nono uses tapes that mix multiphonics played on the clarinet with various electronic sounds produced at the national radio RAI studios, as well as texts from pro- and anti-war groups and individuals, a Vietnamese partisan, American workers and students, vocalized by the legendary New York-based group The Living Theater. In live performance with this tape, a soprano and other live voices sing a lament and deliver other texts, accompanied by five suspended copper metal plates of various thicknesses (ancient sounds of the call to war). —*"Blue" Gene Tyranny*

☆ **Das Atmende Klarsein (fragment) for Bass Flute and Magnetic Tape/ In Roberto Fabbriciani's "Flute XX"** / 1991 / Koch ♦♦♦♦♦
Breath and the clarity of being—"pneuma moving through metal": mysterious, dramatic, and beautiful. —*"Blue" Gene Tyranny*

Pierre/ Dell' Azzuro Silenzio/ Inquietum for Voices, Winds, and Live Electronics (1985) / Quando Stanno Morendo, Diario Polacco 2 / 1991 / Dischi Ricordi ♦♦♦
Excellent set of three works combining acoustical instruments and voices with live electronics (i.e., not on tape). —*"Blue" Gene Tyranny*

A Carlo Scarpa Architetto Ai Suoi Infiniti Possibili (To Carlo Scarpa Architect, To His I / 1991 / Col Legno ♦♦♦
In the collection *20 Ans de Musique Contemporaine á Metz*, SWF Sinfonieorchester Baden-Baden, conducted by Michael Gielen.

Composed in 1984, this orchestral work of approximately 12 minutes' duration, is a funeral chant for a deceased friend. The feeling is created of a very primitive, sparse environment and ceremony—fluttering and tremolo sounds, extremely soft mysterious sustains, "reedy" winds with drum accents like Japanese Gagaku music, low brass bent tones like Tibetan horns. Dynamics range from fff to ppppp. This piece continues the inward search of Nono's later years, following his earlier, externalized social-reality works. —*"Blue" Gene Tyranny*

La Lontananza Nostalgica Utopica Futura ("Nostalgia for a Far-Away Future Utopia") for Violin and Taped Electronics / 1992 / Disques Montaigne ♦♦♦♦♦
With Irvine Arditti (violin). The electronically modulated sound of the violin is distributed among eight loudspeakers according to various structural and dynamical processes. Mysterious and beautiful. —*"Blue" Gene Tyranny*

Fragmente—Stille, An Diotima (1980) ("Fragments—Stillness, to Diotima") / 1992 / Disques Montaigne ♦♦♦
Performed by the Arditti String Quartet. Seeking to "externalize as fully as possible that which has been internalized . . . that is what matters today." Nono is guided by lines from Holderlin's famous poem (Diotima was Socrates's teacher and is associated with the concept "Time"), which are present only as an unspoken meditation and guidepost written into the score in 52 places. Nono poses the fundamental question "Where am I, and who am I?" by examining old music and memories from the distant past as producers of both pain and hope. Written for the Beethoven Festival in Bonn, Nono uses Beethoven's piano sonata instruction "mit innigster Empfindung" (roughly, "with innermost searching of the heart") to imply a readiness to break out of the habitual "into the open air." This quartet produces a positive sensation that has been used as an instruction in several of John Cage's works—"play until you feel the presence of silence." (There is also a lovely 1986 performance by the LaSalle Quartet on Deutsche Grammaphon 415 513-2.) —*"Blue" Gene Tyranny*

Il Canto Sospeso (1956) / 1994 / Sony Classical ♦♦♦
This piece, based on letters of World War II resistance fighters, introduced new choral writing techniques of word fragmentation and suspension. Nono was one of the leading serialist composers who developed the 12-tone techniques of pre-World War II composers, primarily those of Anton Webern. Excellent performance by the Rundfunkchor Berlin (Berlin Radio Choir) and the Berlin Philharmonic, conducted by Claudio Abbado. Mahler's "Kindertotenieder" (Songs on the Deaths of Children) is also included. —*"Blue" Gene Tyranny*

Prometeo: Tragedia Dell'Ascolto (Prometheus: a Tragedy About Listening) / 1995 / EMI Classics (Ricordi) ♦♦♦
The Soloistenchor Freiburg and the Ensemble Modern conducted by Ingo Metzmacher, with live electronic realizations by the Experimentalstudio der Heinrich-Strobel-Stiftung des Südwestfunks Freiburg. Composed in 1984-85, this most unusual dramatic and philosophical work of

some 2 hours' duration is written for recorded and live singing and speaking voices, chorus (at times acapella), four orchestral groups, and many solo instruments including musical glasses. It is intended as a "dramma in musica" (a drama in music) and uses electronic sound (projection techniques, amplification, distribution, reverberation, echo, etc.) to enhance the acoustic space. Nono pointed out that his previous "azione scenica" (scenic action) entitled *Al gran sole carico d'amore*, a lavish stage spectacle about failed revolutions of the 20th century, was " . . . unbelieveably limited." With *Prometeo*, he went the other direction and avoided all historical references and theatricality. "We must learn to live with . . . multiplicities and with differences" (Massimo Cacciari, librettist for *Prometeo* and philosopher). Prometheus is thus a wanderer in this world. The text of *Prometeo* contains fragments from Greek, Italian, and German classics, modern philosophy, poetry and mythology, which are further dissolved into sound per se, no longer recognizable as words. Instrumental doublings of vocal pitches also give the illusion of the voices as textures. An unremitting atmosphere of mystery and spiritual transparency pervades the continuously evolving invention of the work. —*"Blue" Gene Tyranny*

Michael Nyman

A Zed and Two Noughts / 1990 / Virgin Records ♦♦♦
Score for the film by Peter Greenway. Nyman's film scores make effective use of baroque harmonies (Pergolesi, Vivaldi, Purcell—often in a traditional "chain of suspensions" technique) and Phil Glass-like harmonies (Wagnerian thirds mixed with modal scales), combined with obsessive patterns in the British "minimalist" style to make a sound of his own. Excellent production by composer David Cunningham. —*"Blue" Gene Tyranny*

The Piano Concerto / 1994 / Pauline Oliveros ♦♦♦
Notwithstanding the rather droll British joke of the title, and barely skirting a style of Romantic period kitsch, this piece still features surprising harmonic changes and lovely melodies à la Nyman, and retains the post-modern "edge" of his earlier film music. The concerto is of course based on Nyman's music for Jane Compton's award-winning movie *The Piano*.
—*"Blue" Gene Tyranny*

Pauline Oliveros

b. May 30, 1932, Houston, TX
Composer / Electronic, Group-oriented Process and Ritual Music, Improvisation, Meditation
Oliveros studied with Paul Koepke and Robert Erickson, and electronic music with Hugh LeCaine. Her first free improvisation was in 1958 (!) An accordionist and a member of the San Francisco Tape Music Center in the '60s, Oliveros has taught at the University of California at San Diego, York University, and Stanford University. Her work includes "Sonic Meditations" (1971), "Deep Listening Pieces" (1970-90), "Software for People" (1984), and "To Valerie Solanas and Marilyn Monroe in Recognition of Their Despair" (1970). —*"Blue" Gene Tyranny*

I of IV (1966) / In "New Sounds in Electronic Music" / 1968 / Odyssey ♦♦♦♦♦
This is a good example of Oliveros' earlier electronic music, using a configuration of tape recorders patched into each other with magnetic tape spliced in loops so that a form of "automatic generation" system was created by feedback. Similar to Richard Maxfield, Oliveros used bias frequencies of tape recorders and lower "ghost tones" produced by the interference of very high frequencies. —*"Blue" Gene Tyranny*

Lullaby for Daisy Pauline/ In "Sleepers" / 1985 / Finnadar ♦♦♦
A lovely choral work. —*"Blue" Gene Tyranny*

☆ **The Roots of the Moment** / 1988 / Hat Hut ♦♦♦♦♦
Oliveros with accordion in just intonation within an interactive electronic environment created by Peter Ward. An amazing hour-long live creation (improvisation). Images of valleys, other universes, whatever comes to mind—an exercise in true "deep listening" as she refers to the concerts her Foundation presents in upstate New York. —*"Blue" Gene Tyranny*

Crone / 1992 / Lovely Music ♦♦♦
Oliveros on accordion, with electronics creating various illusionary movements in space. Beautiful. —*"Blue" Gene Tyranny*

Bob Ostertag

Sooner or Later (Tarde o Temprano) / 1991 / Recrec ♦♦♦♦♦
Known for his technique of live performance sampling before there were samplers (by recording a performance, cutting the tape, making a loop, and then playing it back on a tape recorder with the tape guards held up by balloons), Ostertag has created a stark and moving work based on the recorded voice of a young Salvadoran boy burying his father, who had been killed by El Salvador's National Guard. "There is

the sound of the boy's voice, a fly buzzing nearby, and the shovel digging the grave. In Part Two, there are additional sounds from a 20-second sample of the guitar playing of Fred Frith." Ostertag spent the last 10 years working in or around El Salvador. "I saw a lot of death. In that culture, which is both Catholic and highly politicized, death gets surrounded with all kinds of trappings that are intended to make it heroic and purposeful, God's will, or else it is irrelevant, since the victims "live on in the struggle." It's all glorious and heroic . . . but some 70,000 people have died there . . . most . . . because they were in the wrong place at the wrong time. They didn't want to. There was no plan. There was no glory. Even for the heroes there is a starker, more immediate side to their death . . . sooner or later. No angels sang and no one was better. If there is a beauty, we must find it in what is really there . . . the boy, the shovel, the fly. If we look closely, despite the unbearable sadness, we will discover it." — "Blue" Gene Tyranny

All the Rage (1992) / 1993 / Elektra/Nonesuch ✦✦✦
This moving, 17-minute CD performed by the Kronos Quartet concerns responses to the AIDS epidemic. Part of the purchase price is donated to AIDS relief agencies. — "Blue" Gene Tyranny

John Oswald

b. May 30, 1953
Composer / Electronic, Plunderphonics Technique
Director of Research at the Mystery Laboratory, Toronto, Canada. Founding member of the CEC. — "Blue" Gene Tyranny

Rubiyat Plunderphonics / 1991 / Elektra ✦✦✦
This promo-CD (PRCD 8247-2) uses copyrighted material lifted from Elektra's own 40th anniversary Rubiyat collection and other issues: imaginative and probing recombinations of musical gestures from the Doors, Carly Simon, Metallica, Tim Buckley, Faster Pussycat, MC5. — "Blue" Gene Tyranny

Discosphere / 1991 / ReR Jocd ✦✦✦
This is a wonderful compilation of short, effective, single-themed pieces written for dance, or that had dances made to them or with them. From very delicate studies like "Skindling Shades" made from incendiary sounds, and the wild rhythmic rock of "Angle" to the thousandfold overdubbing of a tiny bell sound in "Amina" and the hilarious fractured mystery-tale "The Case of Death," Oswald points out the bones and flesh of our illusions with a funny kind of love. — "Blue" Gene Tyranny

Nine Examples of Plunderphonic Techniques / 1992 / Musicworks #47 ✦✦✦✦✦
These are the techniques used to make the legendary, not-for-sale, but nevertheless illegal-to-possess "Plunderphonics" (1989). Copies were destroyed by the Canadian Recording Industry Association, even though the quoted recordings were so distorted by creative sampling that no one would mistake them for the "real" thing. Canadian composer Oswald comments hilariously and surrealistically on sound material that has become the archtypical if not the downright kitsch-geck detritus of civilization. A procedure and attitude reminiscent of presamplers James Tenney ("Collage No. 1: Blue Suede," 1961), Richard Maxfield ("Amazing Grace" and "Cough Music" from the early '60s), and Gordon Mumma ("Epoxy"). — "Blue" Gene Tyranny

Plexure / 1993 / Avan ✦✦✦
This nonstop, high-energy mind bender contains brief detailed and formal studies of passion/pleasure textures in pop culture from the musical equivalent of the involuntary entoptic visions ever-present when we close our eyes. Structural numerics guide precise collaging of gestures lifted from many well-known singers, and we as listeners begin to understand the underlying nature of their emotional expressions/manipulations. Some sections are: "Urge (Marianne Faith No Morrissey)," "Blur (Bolton Chili Overdire: Moment, Wow, Nest)," and "Temperature (Beastie Shop Beach: Tempus Amore/Hyper Love Theme, Tempo Pact)." If this were a painting, it would be Abstract Expressionist Pop/Op Art—for those who can listen with their minds as well as their nerves. — "Blue" Gene Tyranny

Power / 1994 / Musicworks ✦✦✦
In the collection *Musicworks No. 60: Plunderphonia & Vox.* This piece, composed in 1975, combines a raving sermon with great instrumental rock music, cued by the reiterated vocal beat of "Power!," revealing through humor the real intent of the so-called Religious Right. Other equally outrageous and inspired pieces by this composer utilizing the technique of sample-manipulation, or "plunderphonics" on this same CD include "7th" (1988), a cosmic reinterpretation of Beethoven's *Seventh Symphony,* the fractured radio mystery "More from the Case of Death by Agatha Smith" (1991), a deconstruction that will leave you in stitches, and "Urge/Manifold" (1992-1993), with the submovements entitled "slow, slice, blink, philosophy, phase and phase 2" from *Plexure.* — "Blue" Gene Tyranny

Grayfolded: Transitive Axis / 1995 / Swell/Artifact ✦✦✦
In 1994, Oswald was invited to "plunderphonicize" the music of the legendary rock band the Grateful Dead, and he went through over a hundred performances from 1969 upward (onward) to accumulate over 40 hours of tape. The music he chose was the unnamed song, sometimes simply referred to as "It," a open, simple modal improvisation that suggests a kind of celestial yearning or universal understanding. He has a soloist "harmonizing with himself over the years," interrelates and studies details of isolated gestures, and creates multiple overlays of the band that add a depth and texture perhaps more in the mind of the group than was actually realized, or realizable, in live performance. After analyzing and organizing the original material over several years, two separate CDs were made (the last shortly before Jerry Garcia's death) from this compositional process: *Grayfolded: Transitive Axis* (utilizing 51 of the original performances) and *Grayfolded: Mirror Ashes.* These are now available as a two-CD set. (See also his "Bell Speeds" in the collection *Électro Clips*). — "Blue" Gene Tyranny

Grayfolded: Mirror Ashes / 1996 / Swell/Artifact ✦✦✦
In 1994, Oswald was invited to "plunderphonicize" the music of the legendary rock band the Grateful Dead, and he went through over a hundred performances from 1969 upward (onward) to accumulate over 40 hours of tape. The music he chose was the unnamed song, sometimes simply referred to as "It," a open, simple modal improvisation that suggests a kind of celestial yearning or universal understanding. He has a soloist "harmonizing with himself over the years," interrelates and studies details of isolated gestures, and creates multiple overlays of the band that add a depth and texture perhaps more in the mind of the group than was actually realized, or realizable, in live performance. After analyzing and organizing the original material over several years, two separate CDs were made (the last shortly before Jerry Garcia's death) from this compositional process: *Grayfolded: Transitive Axis* (utilizing 51 of the original performances) and *Grayfolded: Mirror Ashes* These are now available as a two-CD set. (See also his "Bell Speeds" in the collection *Électro Clips*). — "Blue" Gene Tyranny

Charlemange Palestine

Strumming Music / 1991 / Newtone ✦✦✦
Reissue on CD of the classic Shandar label LP. A powerful solo piano performance by this somewhat lesser-known "minimalist" composer and often iconoclastic creator. — "Blue" Gene Tyranny

Stephen Parkinson

b. Canada
Composer / Acoustic Experimental
Studied with Michael Longton and Rudolf Kumorous at the University of Victoria. Music Director of Open Space Gallery. Cofounder and performer in Drystone Orchestra. — "Blue" Gene Tyranny

Catch the Bonner / 1995 / Musicworks ✦✦✦
In the collection *Musicworks No. 63.* Composed in 1994, this piece presents a beautiful and gentle sonic mystery. From a tape, we hear faint shadows of blues-like wailing, gradually overlapped in the background. Gentle tapping and staccato sounds of neutral pitch are heard slightly more in the foreground, like something blown by the wind striking a piece of lumber late at night. The pace of this ghostly scene never falters or varies much, and at the end the music just fades away. Totally captivating. — "Blue" Gene Tyranny

Harry Partch

b. Jun. 24, 1901, Oakland, California, **d.** 1974
Composer / Alternative Tunings, World Music-influenced, Opera, Speech-song
A self-taught composer of music featuring microtonality using self-made instruments, Harry Partch was the most original thinker on tuning theory in centuries (see his *Genesis of a Music,* Da Capo Press), as well as an instrument designer and builder extraordinaire. His songs were often open as to vocal pitch, pre-cursors of the New Narrative Opera. He has written several innovative film scores. — "Blue" Gene Tyranny

And on the Seventh Day, Petals Fell on Petaluma (1964) / The Bewitched: Final Scene and Epilogue (1952-1955) / Castor and Pollux / CRI ✦✦✦
Instrument designer/builder extraordinaire of the Chromelodeon (1945-1949), the Blo-Boy (1958), the Cloud-Chamber Bowls (1950-1951), the Boo (1955-1957), the Spoils of War (1950-1955), the Marimba Eroica (1951-1955), the Crychord (1960-1961), the Eucal Blossom (1964-1967), the Xymo-Xyl (1963), the Mazda Marimba (1963), the Quadrangularis Reversum (1965), and the Harmonic Canon III (Blue Rainbow, 1965), just for starters. Partch had a wonderful sense of humor even while he was discussing serious philosophical questions of life and death. "The Letter" is from a fellow hobo traveling the rails in the 1930s: lots of sliding and suggestive sounds of the "if you know what I mean" type and

naturally a kind of world-weariness; there is sophisticated canonic writing in "Petals . . ." and a sublime mystery in the Cloud Chamber Music. —*"Blue" Gene Tyranny*

Delusion of the Fury / Columbia ✦✦✦
A ritual of voices, mime, original instruments, dance, lighting, and staging in which instrumentalists sometimes sing and act—complete theater as ancient as it is new. Titles of some scenes: "A Son in Search of His Father's Face," "The Quiet Hobo Meal," "Pray for Me Again." —*"Blue" Gene Tyranny*

Bewitched, A Dance Satire (1955), The / 1990 / CRI ✦✦✦
A total theater experience like "Delusion of the Fury" above. Titles of some sections are: "The Lost Musicians Mix Magic," "Three Undergrads Become Transfigured in a Hong Kong Music Hall," "Exercises in Harmony and Counterpoint Are Tried in a Court of Ancient Ritual," "The Romancing of a Pathological Liar Comes to an Inspired End," and "Two Detectives on the Trail of a Tricky Culprit Turn in Their Badges." —*"Blue" Gene Tyranny*

Enclosure Two: Harry Partch / 1995 / Innova ✦✦✦
A four-CD set of historic speech-music recordings from the Partch archives. A captivating assemblage of Partch's vocal works (outside of the operas) played on his original instruments and tunings, recorded near the times of their composition. Includes several pithy, humorous and pointed commentaries by Partch, such as "A Wagnerian Wrestling Match," "The Use of English in Serious Music," "Life Is Too Precious to Spend It with Important People," "You Are Charged with Being Guilty. Are You Drunk or Not Drunk?" recorded mostly in his later years, and the pieces "By the Waters of Babylon," the lovely "Ten Li Po Lyrics," "Barstow—Eight Hitch-hiker's Inscriptions from a Highway Railing at Barstow, California," "San Francisco—Newsboy Cries," "US Highball—A Musical Account of Slim's Transcontinental Hobo Trip," "While My Heart Keeps Beating Time," "Two Settings from Joyce's *Finnegan's Wake*," "*Dark Brother*," "*A Quarter-Saw Section of Motivations and Intonations*," "*36 Extracts from Bitter Music*, a hobo journal," "Y.D. Fantasy—On the Words of an Early American Tune," "O Frabjous Day!," "Ring Around the Moon," and "Bless This Home." —*"Blue" Gene Tyranny*

Maggi Payne

b. Dec. 23, 1945, Temple, Texas
Composer / Electronic, Flute, Multimedia
Payne composed music for two of dancer Carolyn Brown's works, *Synergy II* and *House Party*. A recording engineer and music instructor, and currently co-director at the Center for Contemporary Music, Mills College, Payne's multimedia performances often involve the use of video, film, abstract slides, and/or dance. —*"Blue" Gene Tyranny*

Airwaves (Realities) (1987) / In "Another Coast" / 1988 / Centaur ✦✦✦
A comparison of consensual reality in desert and urban cultures by slow sound-imaging. One step beyond the idea of the tone poem into a kind of reality-based illusionism. —*"Blue" Gene Tyranny*

Crystal / 1991 / Lovely Music ✦✦✦
Some of the most beautiful and well-crafted electronic music ever, suggesting vast interior and exterior dimensions. Some titles are: "Subterranean Network," "White Night" (a French expression for a sleepless night of repeating thoughts), and "Solar Wind" (based on shockwave interactions of Saturn and Venus with the solar wind). —*"Blue" Gene Tyranny*

Krzysztof Penderecki

A Polish composer of choral and orchestral music, opera, and chamber music in a modern harmonic setting. —*AMG*

"K. Penderecki, Vol. 1": Threnody for the Victims of Hiroshima for 52 Strings (1959) / Polymorphy for 48 Strings (1961) / 1989 / Polskie Nagrania ✦✦✦
This collection, performed by the LaSalle Quartet and the Warsaw and Cracow Philharmoni Orechestras and Choirs, is a good overview of the dramatic and original orchestral timbres of Penderecki's early work with, for example, the famous "Threnody" for massed solo strings making sounds never heard before, like thousands of objects randomly falling, sirens, searing fire, rushing storms, and wind. The conceptual and emotional spaces of the "Dimensions of Time and Silence" are everything the title promises. Sensitive performances and great pieces. —*"Blue" Gene Tyranny*

Jutrznia/Utrenya (The Entombment and Resurrection of Christ) (1969-1970) for Two Mixed Choirs, Solo Voices, and Symphony Orchestra / 1989 / Polskie Nagrania ✦✦✦
Performed by the Warsaw National Philharmonic Orchestra and Choir. Although there are references to sections of the orthodox mass in the program notes, this is rarely heard in this deeply felt music that speaks to the naked soul—before the churches appeared—and could be Bud-

dhist just as well as Christian. The elegant choral and orchestral material is made of tone clusters, chants, and percussive punctuation, taking us into intradimensional and at times hair-raising boundless interior and exterior worlds. —*"Blue" Gene Tyranny*

Matrix 5: Penderecki / 1994 / EMI Classics ✦✦✦
A splendid collection of Penderecki's orchestral music, performed by the Polish Radio National Symphony Orchestra. Includes: "Anaklasis" (1959), "Threnody for the Victims of Hiroshima" (see comments above), "Fonogrammi" (1961), "De Natura Sonoris no. 1" (1966), "Capriccio" (1967), "De Natura Sonoris no. 2" (1971), "The Dream of Jacob" (1974), and the "Canticum Canticorum Salmonis" (1970). —*"Blue" Gene Tyranny*

Philip Perkins

b. Aug. 24, 1951, Coatsville, PA
Composer / Electronic, Environmental Sounds, Tape Collage, New Song
Neighborhood with a Sky / 1982 / Fun Music ✦✦✦
A beautiful album of compositions where the electronic and "natural" sounds are barely distinguishable; significantly, Perkins does not try to simulate the "natural sounds" but lets their dynamic form and movement influence his electronic sounds (somewhat in the way that Cage, using chance methods, tries to imitate nature, not in its appearance but in its manner of working). The "neighborhood" for Perkins is that of the disc itself, where the natural and the artificial coexist successfully. Contains: "Bird Variations," "The Black and White Cat," "Este's Request," "The Fountain," Equinox Weather," "Rico in the Birdhouse" for trombone solo in an environment, and "Retreat." —*"Blue" Gene Tyranny*

The Flame of Ambition / 1986 / Fun Music ✦✦✦
A collection of pieces about people "burning literally with ambition . . . the root of both mankind's greatest triumphs and worst self-made calamities," with scenes from a corporate skyscraper, the company fort: "Taking the Stairs," "Worrisome Fanfare/Weekend with the Kids," "At the Bar," "Talk/Exit (for Corazon Aquino)." A good blend of Perkins' electronic, natural sound, and tuneful mixes. —*"Blue" Gene Tyranny*

☆ **The Remotes (I) (1990)** / 1990 / Fun Music ✦✦✦✦✦
A mix on cassette tape of nine live radio broadcasts of "The Remotes," a live performance work for an interactive electronic system and various guest musicians, where spontaneous playing and processing allows for all sorts of interesting, communal, and intuitive music making. —*"Blue" Gene Tyranny*

Virgo Ramayana and Other Works for Radio / 1992 / Fun Music ✦✦✦
An excellent set on cassette tape of four works, each rich in content and original in concept. "Virgo Ramayana" (Perkins was born under the sign of Virgo) is a 23-minute journey of mysterious ambience and soulfulness with sounds recorded in Indonesia—beautifully mixed with aural textures, blending seamlessly as in a dream, and at other times modulating each other with hidden messages. A great performance realization of John Cage's "Radio Music" (1956) follows. The six-minute edit called "Remotitude" comes next, a live electronic work realized at the Berkeley KPFA studios, with sounds difficult to describe in words—like you've tuned in on a broadcast from an alien world. Side B contains the 45-minute piece "Say Again," a live radio work with a vocalist (Bonnie Barnett), computer synthesist (Tim Perkis), percussionist/guitarist (Scott Fraser), and Perkins mixing radios, signal and MIDI processes, sampler, and tapes and playing electric bass. Beginning with an odd story about a woman from California offering US herbal tea to some Swiss farmers, the piece moves, modulates, and carries you along in the moment-to-moment mental flow of this ensemble. Highly recommended for its healthy avant-gardism. —*"Blue" Gene Tyranny*

Emanuel Dimas De Melo Pimenta

Rings (1989) / Rozart (1989) / Structures II (1988) / Short Waves (1985) / 1990 / Mode ✦✦✦
An emerging composer who works in a "pure" style influenced by American and European aesthetics, "Rozart" incorporates the voice of Enrico Caruso. "Short Waves" was written for the dance "Fabrications" by the Merce Cunningham Dance Company. —*"Blue" Gene Tyranny*

Larry Polansky

Movement for Andrea Smith (My Funny Valentine for Just String Quartet) / In "Just Intonation" / Tellus #14 ✦✦✦
An extremely slowed-down angularized ballad. How can I possibly describe the pleading feeling? —*"Blue" Gene Tyranny*

The Theory of Impossible Melody / 1989 / Artifact ✦✦✦✦✦
Fascinating formal (transformational) logic programs generating electronic and acoustic pieces, using the HMSL (Hierarchical Music Specification Language, designed by Phil Burk, Polansky, and David Rosenboom). A feeling of the Cabalistic mysteries. Contains: "B'rey'sheet (In the Beginning)," computer-aided melodic transformations of traditional

Hebrew tropes and melodies used for singing the Torah; "Cantillation Study no. 1 for Jody Diamond," for voice and electronics; "Four Voice Canons nos. 3-6 (No. 3 for computer, No. 4 for marimbas, No. 5 for percussion, No. 6 for computer); "Simple Actions—Rules of Compossibility for Voice and Live Computer"; "Psaltery for Lou Harrison." —*"Blue" Gene Tyranny*

Simple Harmonic Motion / 1994 / Artifact ✦✦✦
A collection of four works for instruments in experimental intonation from the '70s to the late '80s, with a recent work entitled "Horn" for French horn and live interactive electronics. The other three compositions are "Another You" 17 variations for harp in just intonation, "Movement for Andrea Smith" for string quartet in just intonation, and "Movement for Lou Harrison" for bass quartet in just intonation. — *"Blue" Gene Tyranny*

Henri Pousseur

Scambi (Exchanges) (1954) / **Trois Visages de Liege (Three Faces of Liege) (1961)** / **Paraboles-Mix (1972)** / 1990 / BV Haast ("Acousmatrix 4") ✦✦✦✦
The pure evolving electronic masses of "Scambi," a portrait of the city of the composer's youth (and commissioned by the city of Liege), and a semi-improvised live electro-acoustic mixture changed every evening of the performance (containing a "love duet," "Viva Cuba," "Hymn to the Ornithological Zeus," "Aerial View of Haiphong, Massachusetts") by this wonderfully poetic composer. —*"Blue" Gene Tyranny*

Traverser La Foret (1987) / 1993 / Adda ✦✦✦
Although it can be a bit coy at times, this odd, mythological cantata for narrator, two solo voices, choir, and 12 instruments has its charms and probably a hidden meaning that I'm not getting. The vocal writing and harmonies are exquisite and transparent in texture. —*"Blue" Gene Tyranny*

Eliane Radique

☆ **Kyema, Intermediate States** / 1992 / Experimental Intermedia ✦✦✦✦✦
Profound and serenely meditative electronic music inspired by the *Bardo Thodol* (*Tibetan Book of the Dead*). Six states: Kyene (Birth), Milam (Dream), Samten (Contemplation), Chikai (Death), Chonye (Clear Light), Sippai (Becoming). This is the real thing. —*"Blue" Gene Tyranny*

Mila's Journey Inspired by a Dream / 1992 / Lovely Music ✦✦✦
With Tibetan singing by Lama Kunga Rinpoche, and English singing by Robert Ashley. Wonderful images and stories from the "100,000 Songs of Milarepa," the musical setting of which is Radique's lifelong project. —*"Blue" Gene Tyranny*

Songs of Milarepa / 1996 / Lovely Music ✦✦✦
Deeply meditative and compassionate, these are settings (realized 1981-1983 in Paris) of the Milarepa songs, some of the most famous works of Tibetan culture, for voices (on this recording Lama Kunga, Tibetan language, and Robert Ashley, English language) and electronics. The four songs here are "Mila's Song in the Rain," "Song of the Path Guides," "The Elimination of Desires" and "Symbol for Yogic Experiences." —*"Blue" Gene Tyranny*

Jetsun Mila / Lovely Music ✦✦✦
Available on cassette only. The marvelous 84-minute musical evocation of Milarepa's life in nine sections with prelude, corresponding to major periods of the life of this famous yogi. — *"Blue" Gene Tyranny*

Lou Reed (Louis Firbank)

See the Rock section for his biography.

The Amine Ring in "Metal Machine Music" / Great Expectations ✦✦✦
On this CD reissue of the original 1975 RCA Records disc, we hear an unrelenting, searingly beautiful electro-acoustic composition for electric guitar and an array of "consumer-priced" sound-processing devices and amplifiers used by most bands of the mid-'70s. Inspired by La Monte Young's Dream Music installations, this one-time spontaneous production of Reed's predated a great deal of rock-sound inspired new music (Branca, Chatham, and others). Feedback and a lot of the Keith Richards-effect (maximum volume through small speakers) lends a feeling of infinite universal and atomic surface compression permeating everything. "Passion-realism was the key" is the significant line from the otherwise rather posed liner notes. Sudden silences leave the listener floating. —*"Blue" Gene Tyranny*

Steve Reich

Composer / Minimalist, Phas Music, World-Music Influenced

Steve Reich deserves attention as an improviser and percussionist not really fitting into either a traditional jazz or a classical vein. Reich studied both music at Juilliard and philosophy at Cornell and later was a student of Darius Milhaud and Luciano Berio at Mills College in California. He formed his own ensemble in 1966, and immersed himself in African

drumming in 1970 by living in Ghana. In 1973, he studied Balinese gamelan music. Recognized as a major figure in the minimalist school, his compositions emphasize repetition, with chords changing one note at a time and arrangements that include ethnic and ancient rhythmic elements. Reich released acclaimed albums in the '70s and '80s featuring multiple drums, marimbas, voices, and unusual instruments. —*Ron Wynn*

Different Trains (1988) for String Quartet and Tape / 1989 / Elektra/Nonesuch ✦✦✦✦✦
In an acoustic equivalent to interactive electronics, Reich creates a rhythmic tape of train whistles of the '30s and '40s and of speakers recalling train rides of the past in the US and occupied lands. The natural pitch inflections of the voices are then transferred to pitches for the instruments. A rich emotional experience akin to his earlier pieces—"It's Gonna Rain" (1965) and the shocking "Come Out" (1966) (both on Elektra/Nonesuch 79169-2)—a more interesting use of the rather mechanistic edge of his pattern music. —*"Blue" Gene Tyranny*

Brian Reinbolt

It's Not That Simple / 1990 / Artifact ✦✦✦
Interesting microcomputer music, especially the three-dance set "Simple Dance" ("Simple—dance on the plain of a dream," "IV—the patron saint of lawyers," "Cones—made of ever-increasing and decreasing circles") and "Black Noise." —*"Blue" Gene Tyranny*

Bathtub Curve / 1996 / Artifact ✦✦✦
Humorous and touching synthesizer compositions based on the composer's adventures with the Roland D-550. The various patches, used to develop installations, were labeled "Moronscapes" which occur amongst the 14 selections on the CD: "Spores" (the image of the theory of DNA spread through the universe "like powdered yeast launched by a sneeze"), "Snort" ("A dance for a neo-primitive pierced robot"). Also "Men and Boys," "Tinnitus," "Ululate," "Hatchet," "Still Not Answered," "Knocks," "Fingernail," "Chuckle," "Wedding March," "Diva," "Pass," and "Termination." —*"Blue" Gene Tyranny*

The Residents

The Residents are one of rock's oddest and most mysterious groups. Their identity has been a closely guarded secret for two decades. In rare public appearances, they are typically disguised as giant eyeballs decked out in tuxes and top hats. But behind all the weirdness is . . . more weirdness—primitive mutations of popular songs by the likes of Elvis, James Brown, and Hank Williams; frightening nursery rhymes; elaborate mythological epics that span several albums; and pure sonic explorations. Like the most adventurous modern composers, the Residents understand the emotive power of sound; early pieces like "Eskimo" are unforgettably evocative. Their later projects contain subtle social commentary. Even when the parody verges on self-parody, the music retains shock value and sophistication. —*Myles Boisen*

The **Commercial Album (1980)** / East Side Digital ✦✦✦
Forty brief stories, homilies, instrumentals, slices of life, each exactly 60 seconds long: "The Coming of the Crow," "Nice Old Man," "My Work Is So Behind," "Die in Terror," "Floyd," "Act of Being Polite,"—each unique in vocals and instrumentation, and each weirdly humorous and momentarily stunning. —*"Blue" Gene Tyranny*

★ **God in Three Persons** / 1988 / Ryko ✦✦✦✦✦
Employing the same stress-scheme as Poe's "The Raven" throughout its 62 minutes, *God in Three Persons* is an extended work in "talking-blues" style for narrator, electronic instruments, and a chorus providing comments not to be found in the libretto—they sing production credits at the beginning, and lines like "something's coming, but not real soon," and "this is a sad part, oh, such a sad part." This surreal and yet directly delivered work is as lovingly human as it is comic, with profound experience simply expressed—in short, an original masterpiece of American music, directly in the tradition of the Thomson-Stein and Robert Ashley operas. As in all Residents pieces, the voices are modified electronically and the musical elements are deceptively minimal—most of its 14 episodes have only two chords which, however, still manage to instantly produce the correct atmosphere (Phil Glass-like Wagnerian thirds for mythic import, tonic-dominant in triplets for '50s teenage love story, and more). There are only passing riffs, more like comments, and the only melody in the whole piece is a wheezy organ quote of the standard doxology hymn "Holy, Holy, Holy (God in Three Persons)." The subject matter is, in part, the derivation of religious and other symbolic images from the naturally erotic, but that's only part of it. Please give this one a listen. —*"Blue" Gene Tyranny*

Eskimo (1979) / 1990 / ESD ✦✦✦✦✦
A CD reissue of the 1979 record. A wild vision of what original polar Eskimo life was like before government housing came along in the late '60s. Contains "The Walrus Hunt," "Birth," "Artic Hysteria," "The Angry Angakok," "A Spirit Steals a Child," "The Festival of Death." A totally

engaging tone-poem, filled with humor, pathos, shamanism, and all the other great things, with skillful electronic sound-painting and always the right touch. —*"Blue" Gene Tyranny*

Roger Reynolds

b. Jul. 18, 1934, Detroit, MI
Composer / Electronic, Vocal, Music Theater
Reynolds studied with Ross Lee Finney and Roberto Gerhard. A founding member of the ONCE Group and teacher at the University of California at San Diego, Reynolds founded the Center for Music Experiment and Related Research in 1979 and was composer-in-residence at IRCAM, Paris, France. His works include "The Emperor of Ice Cream" (1962), "Blind Men" (1966) for 24 voices and chamber ensemble, "I/O: A Ritual for 23 Performers" (1970), and "Fiery Wind" for orchestra (1978). —*"Blue" Gene Tyranny*

Distant Images / 1985 / Lovely Music ✦✦✦
A delicate and mysterious vinyl LP release of two works for chamber ensemble in which Reymolds addresses the dualistic nature of aural perception, approaching the elusive territory between the polarized pair and the unified whole. — *"Blue" Gene Tyranny*

Whispers out of Time / Transfigured Wind II / 1990 / New World ✦✦✦
Lovely and mysterious works for flute and computer-generated tape. —*"Blue" Gene Tyranny*

Voicespace: Still (1975) / A Merciful Coincidence (1976) / Eclipse (1979) / The Palace (1980) / 1992 / Lovely Music ✦✦✦✦✦
A reissue of the two-record set. Four pieces for computer electronics and voices that amplify to an extreme degree the components and expressive qualities of the voice. "Still," with a text from Samuel Coleridge's *The Wanderings of Cain* (1798), moves extremely slowly in a "vocal fry" across the aspirate clicks and wind of the performer; "A Merciful Coincidence," on a text from Samuel Beckett's *Watt* (1953), uses the aggressive-passive inflections of the frog-performers croaking, which seems to have intent, if not syntactical, "meaning"; "Eclipse," with a combined text from Borges, Gabriel Marquez, Issa, James Joyce, Melville, and Wallace Stevens, eclipses strains of modulated texts into one another; "The Palace," on a translated text by Jorge Luis Borges (1976), is a dramatic monodrama about how the Self imagines its confines within the space of the Mind, and a prerecorded, modified voice is added to the singer onstage, yielding an enormous, supra-human quality. —*"Blue" Gene Tyranny*

Electroacoustic Music / 1993 / New World ✦✦✦
Dramatic new pieces for instruments and electronics: "Versions/Stages" (1988-1991) and "The Ivanov Suite" (1991) created for Tadashi Suzuki's version of Chekhov's play. —*"Blue" Gene Tyranny*

Terry Riley

b. Jun. 24, 1935, Colfax, CA
Composer / Minimalist, Indian- and Jazz-influenced, Just Intonation
An American composer of minimalist electronic keyboard music, Riley studied with Wendall Otey, Seymour Shifrin, William Denny, and Robert Erockson, ragtime piano with Wally Rose, Indian drumming with Phil Ford, Kanai Dutt, Narayan Rao, and North Indian classical vocal music with the late Pandit Pran Nath. A saxophonist and keyboardist, Riley has taught at Mills College, the Royal Academy of Music in Stockholm, NYU, Cleveland Institute, the Danish Academy of Music, and California College of Performing Arts. —*"Blue" Gene Tyranny*

In C / 1989 / Celestial Harmonies ✦✦✦✦✦
Performed by the Shanghai Film Orchestra, conducted by Wang Yongji. Truly celestial, with a different feeling from American/European performances of this famous piece. This CD also contains David Mingyue Lang's gorgeous "Music of a Thousand Springs" and his "Zen (Ch'an) of Water." Highly recommended. —*"Blue" Gene Tyranny*

☆ **Rainbow in Curved Air/Poppy Nogood and the Phantom Band** / 1990 / CBS ✦✦✦✦✦
A CD reissue of the classic 1969 recording. After several graph compositions and early pattern-pieces with jazz ensembles in the late '50s and early '60s (see "Concert for Two Pianists and Tape Recorders" and "Ear Piece" in La Monte Young's book *An Anthology*), Riley invented a whole new music, which has since gone under many names (minimal music—a category often applied to sustained pieces as well, pattern music, phase music, and others). This music is set forth in its purest form in the famous "In C" (1964) (for saxophone and ensemble, CBS MK 7178). "Rainbow in Curved Air" demonstrates the straightforward pattern technique, but also has Riley improvising with the patterns, making gorgeous timbre changes on the synthesizers and organs, and presenting crescenting sections that have become the basic structuring of his current works: "Candenza on the Night Plain" and other pieces, Kronos Quartet, Gramavision R22Z-79444, two CDs; "Salome Dances for Peace" (1989), Kronos Quartet, Elektra/Nonesuch 79217-2, two CDs; and the

recently premiered and as-yet-unrecorded "The Jade Palace" (1991), commissioned and played by the St. Louis Symphony. Scored for large orchestra with extra percussion and electronics, some of this work's seven movements are: "Star Night," "Blue Lotus," "The Earth Below," and "Island of the Rhumba King." —*"Blue" Gene Tyranny*

Tread on the Trail (1964-1965) for Sax and Synthesizer/ In "Jon Gibson" / 1992 / ✦✦✦
Gibson's exquisite tone shines. —*"Blue" Gene Tyranny*

June Buddhas from "Mexico City Blues" / 1992 / Musicmasters ✦✦✦
Another side of Riley. CD also includes Lou Harrison's "Seven Pastorales" and Peggy Granville-Hicks' "Etruscan Concerto." —*"Blue" Gene Tyranny*

Persian Surgery Dervishes / 1993 / Newtone ✦✦✦
Reissue of Riley's masterpiece from the '70s. —*"Blue" Gene Tyranny*

Cactus Rosary (A Semi-Secular Song for Bruce Conner) / 1993 / Artifact Music ✦✦✦
As the pun on "semi-circular" in the title implies, this music emphasizes the side-to-side as well as foreground-to-background musical dimensions—for example, gradual tuning changes generate beats that move tones in the space, a shaker sweeps from left to right, and repeated words of the text (e. 6., "I was born, born, born, born . . . in India, India, India, India") gradually disappear into deep silence. A mesmerizing and original piece. — *"Blue" Gene Tyranny*

Terry Riley: Zeitgeist-Intuitive Leaps / 1994 / Work Music London ✦✦✦
This CD by the group Zeitgeist contains two works by Riley which he personally supervised and created in close cooperation with the group. These performances are perhaps the best ones recorded of Riley's music played by others. *The Room of Remembrance* (1987) is built around five melodic phrases, each of which serves as a "door" . . . when the musicians go out they are in the realm of improvisation and must construct ways to re-enter the room. The internal story of the piece is built around the image of a "medicine man," having expired in the wintry north of future America, being carried slowly up an icy incline as "snow clams" chant the Om Mane Padme Hum. A beautiful hymn in steady jazz-voiced chords opens the first section, and is interrupted at times by jolly phrases that recall gamelan music; snowflake patterns and windy tremolos are added, making the aural landscape wintry. Rushing patterns follow. The piece concludes with a subdued but fuller textured repeat of the initial hymn in steady chords. *Salome's Excellent Extension* (1989) is in four sections for quartet (piano, marimba, sax, vibraphone/steel drum) and part a series of works with a similar title: the string quartets called *Salome Dances for Peace*. This work offers a unique combination of the rich harmonic and gestural field of American West Coast jazz with Riley's pattern and Indian music sensibilities, with occasionally themes of a 1920s French "Les Six" turn. —*"Blue" Gene Tyranny*

Jean-Claude Risset

Songs (Dreams) (1979) / Passages (1982) for Flute and Tape / Computer Suite from Little Boy (1968) / Sud (South) (1985) / 1988 / Wergo ✦✦✦
One of the early developers of computer music, with Max Matthews at Bell Laboratories and at IRCAM in Paris. Exquisite textures in an aural space that constantly changes its dimensions—soft velvet to digital glacier edges to the ringing of huge bells after they are struck. "Sud" is filled with electronic tropical sounds and washes like extended raindrops and wind chimes. A delight to the ear. —*"Blue" Gene Tyranny*

Neil B. Rolnick

Macedonian Air Drumming / 1992 / Bridge ✦✦✦
Contains "Sanctus," a computer-generated tape; the complete "Balkanization" (see also *Imaginary Landscapes in 20th-Century Collections* in this section); "ReRebong," for the gamelon Son of Lion; and "Macedonian Air Drumming," for MIDI-controlled instruments. —*"Blue" Gene Tyranny*

Electricity / 1992 / O.O. Discs ✦✦✦
Great performances of Rolnick's music by George Lewis (trombone), the New York Contemporary Music Ensemble, and Robert Dick (flute). —*"Blue" Gene Tyranny*

Requiem Songs: For the Victims of Nationalism (1993) / Screen Scenes (1995) / 1996 / Albany ✦✦✦
Moving and poignant *Requiem Songs* with lyrics by Ed Sanders, Rolnick, and from traditional songs, scored for vocals, violin, percussion, and sampling electronics. Selections include: "Bosnia's Mountains," "Ethnic Cleansing," and "Home Is a Ghost." The second composition *Screen Scenes* is divided into Playlists 1-4 and is scored for flute and tenor sax, violin, bass, percussion, synthesizer, and prepared piano. — *"Blue" Gene Tyranny*

David Rosenboom

b. 1947

A pianist and violinist, Rosenboom studied at the University of Illinois with Salvatore Martirano. His early work utilized brainwaves and the nervous system, cross-cultural collaborations, and compositional algorithms. Dean of the School of Music and Co-Director of the Center for Experiments in Art, Information and Technology at CAL Arts since 1990, Rosenboom was a music professor at Mills College from 1979-1990, where he also was head of the Music Department and director of the Center for Contemporary Music, and held the Darius Milhaud Chair from 1987 to 1990. Rosenboom worked and taught at the Center for Creative and Performing Arts at SUNY Buffalo, the Electric Circus, and York University in Toronto, among numerous other teaching posts, including NYU, San Francisco Art Institute, and California College of Arts and Crafts. — *"Blue" Gene Tyranny*

Systems of Judgment (1987) / 1990 / Centaur
A many-timbred computer music composition, sweeping in scope: dynamic sonic illusions of natural sound—mythical and philosophical worlds meeting. — *"Blue" Gene Tyranny*

Precipice in Time (1966) / In CDCM Computer Music Series, Vol. 10 / 1991 / ✦✦✦✦✦
A unique blend of "free jazz," live "phantom doubles" (computer re-synthesis of acoustic instruments), and graphed structure. From high energy to quiet anticipations with interior tension. Terrific playing. — *"Blue" Gene Tyranny*

Rotodoti

Tarzan Speaks / 1991 / Artifact ✦✦✦
An ensemble devoted to improvised music with Doug Carroll on cello expanded with electronics and acoustic preparations, Ron Heglin playing trombone with extended techniques and a vocalist of "fictitious spoken and sung languages," Tom Nunn on original musical instruments and sound sculptures, and Tim Perkis on computer-based hardware and software instruments. Selections include: "Bambi's Dilemma," "Lava Bird," "Gravity Ruins," "Tarzan Speaks," and "Slicker on the Sphinx." — *"Blue" Gene Tyranny*

Mikel Rouse

b. 1957, St. Louis, MO

Composer / New Narrative Opera, Pop-influenced
Rouse studied at Kansas City Art Institute and the Conservatory of Music at the University of Missouri. Employs African and world musics, Schillinger Method of Composition. He formed the Mikel Rouse Broken Consort, which recorded many pop music CDs. Electronic works: "Colorado Suite" (1984), "Quorum," (1984). Music for Alvin Ailey Dance Co. "Autorequiem" (1994) for strings, percussion and voices, "Book One" for string quartet, "Two Paradoxes Resolved," a piano suite. — *"Blue" Gene Tyranny*

Living Inside Design / 1994 / New Tone ✦✦✦
In "Soul Menu" there is some excellent, positive, spirited pattern music combined with rock and soul music instrumentation and rhythmic support, material developed for one of Rouse's groups, Broken Consort, which plays his more concert-oriented music; Tirez Tirez is his pop group. Simultaneous Gamelan-like phrases of seven and eight beats occur in "Hope Chest," a tongue-in-cheek jazz riff in the lively "Ranger"; group rhythm studies in "Copperhead" and "Leading the Machine." The CD *Living Inside Design* continues many of these sounds and techniques but applies them to an excellently produced sequence of songs that goes from the almost-pop "Forever Tonight" to the heartfelt "Kiss Him Goodbye" ("Mouth congress: a kiss, a second parade. An orgy of logic, a romance replayed, and up to the minute, a best out of three"), in which multiple voices occur in an overlay and deconstruction technique Rouse calls "counterpoetry," backed up with vocal and instrumental drones over a beat. Like Arthur Russell, Rouse at times creates that peculiar cosmically "airy" sound associated in pop music with Julee Cruise, the Cocteau Twins, early Fleetwood Mac, and even the Tuff Records version of "Sally Go Round the Roses." — *"Blue" Gene Tyranny*

Failing Kansas / 1995 / Newtone ✦✦✦
A "postmodern," surreal work for voices, electronics and acoustic instruments. An example of New Narrative Opera, utilizing a technique the composer calls Counterpoetry: "the use of multiple unpitched voices in strict metric counterpoint." The text is based on the Clutter family murder in Holcomb, KS (the basis for Truman Capote's *In Cold Blood*). The work is organized in a prelude, four scenes—"The Last to See Them Alive," "Persons Unknown," "Answer," "The Corner"—connected by three interludes or "traveling scenes"—"Like My Dream," "A Brief History of My Boy's Life," "The Private Diary of Parry Edward Smith"—and a postlude. Touches of Americana, such as the sound of the lonely harmonica accompanied by acoustic guitar, quotes from the hymn "In the Garden," and primary chord progressions in unusual rhythmic cycles and harmoniza-

tions. Keenly wrought, expressionistic lyrics: obsessions with religious imagery ("Nuns nuns, Priests crossing a road, nuns nuns, Snakes appearing in a dream"), morbid examination of the details of the crime ("There's blood on the walls, you didn't really look"), childhood memories of a suicide mixed with claims of extramental powers, grammatical and factual obsessiveness ("CLUES ARE FEW IN SLAYING OF 4, You don't have to read it fifty times . . . For this killer or killers . . . That's incorrect . . . The grammar is . . . It ought to be 'For this killer or these killers' . . . Aw, come on, baby, get the bubbles out of your blood, we scored, it was perfect"). One is left with an impression of images and language floating around in the culture ready to feed and/or manipulate dangerous impulses. A remarkably original work. — *"Blue" Gene Tyranny*

Dane Rudhyar (Daniel Chenneviere)

Syntony / Pentagram III for Piano / Orion ✦✦✦
Rudhyar was somewhat like the poet Ezra Pound (who also wrote music), a "Renaissance man"—painter, poet, author of texts on astropsychology and mystic philosophy, a pianist, and a composer. In the 1920s, his discords and polytonal and polyrhythmic writing made him a young avant-gardist, and he was to be guided by metaphysical and theosophical concepts and "spontaneous exteriorizations of peak experiences" throughout his life. His composition was influenced directly by Debussy (whom he met and wrote a book about, *Debussy and the Cycle of Musical Civilization*), late Liszt and Scriabin, and early Stravinsky in his neoprimitive stage. Rudhyar's sense of large, cyclic phases of life and civilization and individuation led him to write the brilliant classic *The Astrology of Personality* in 1936, but his compositional style remained noncyclic, linear, asymmetrical, and highly emotional. "Five Stanzas" is almost unremittingly tense in sweeping writing reminiscent of Carl Ruggles, but contains an otherworldly Andante expressivo mid-movement pianoworks "Epic Poem" played by Robert Black. "Syntony," "Pentagram III" played by Michael Sellers, and "Transformation," played brilliantly by Marcia Mikulak, alternate dissonant counterpoint melodies with massive chords (reminding one of Ives' "First Sonata"), and the two string quartets "Advent" and "Crisis and Overcoming" move through constant statement-like passages to describe psychic processes —in "Advent" with its movements Visitation, Tumult in the Soul, Tragic Vision, Summons and Response, and Acceptance (referring to Christ's mother Mary), and in "Crisis and Overcoming" from a troubled minor key to a calm major key "realization" at the end. A unique voice. —*"Blue" Gene Tyranny*

Advent for String Quartet (1976) / Crisis and Overcoming for String Quartet (1978) / Transmutation for Piano (1976) / 1992 / CRI ✦✦✦

Carl Spaque Ruggles

Ruggles' eclectic education included private lessons in theory and composition from professors at Harvard. While supporting himself as an engraver, Ruggles honed his compositional craft and gave lectures on modern music. The year 1907 marked the beginning of an active musical period during which Ruggles taught at the Mar d'Mar School of Music in Minnesota, founded the Winona Symphony Orchestra, and began work on the opera *The Sunken Bell*. A move to New York in 1917 brought Ruggles private patronage and acquaintances with Varese and Ives, relationships that opened many professional doors for Ruggles. Ruggles' largest work, *Sun Treader*, for orchestra, was performed in Paris and Berlin in 1932. In addition to a professorship at the University of Miami as director of composition (1938-1943), Ruggles continued composing and revising his scores. Though he received many honors for his musical work, in later years he began to shift his creative emphasis to painting. Although not a serial composer, Ruggles wrote melodies so that no note was repeated until a set number had been played. His music is atonal with an emphasis on the chromatic. His love for American and English literature is evident in his use of the works of Whitman and Browning as settings for his work. —*Lynn Vought*

Vox Clamans in Deserto (A Voice Crying in the Wilderness) (1923) / In "The Complete Works of Carl Ruggles" / CBS Masterworks ✦✦✦✦✦
A magnificent work with texts by Robert Browning, Walt Whitman, and C. 6. Meltzer, years ahead of its time. Sweeping performance. Performed by Beverly Morgan (mezzo-soprano), with the Speculum Musicae, conducted by M. Tilson Thomas. —*"Blue" Gene Tyranny*

☆ **Sun-Treader (1926-1931)** / 1990 / Deutsche Grammaphon ✦✦✦✦✦
Dramatic and soaring peformance by the Boston Symphony Orchestra, conducted by Michael Tilson Thomas. Ruggles, like Ives, shared the same Emersonian transcendentalist vision of society and the soul's possibilities, and this work is his most eloquent expression of that insight. Ruggles would work by placing enormous scores on the floor and craft every note and passage in detail. An earlier recording of the orchestral "Lilacs" and "Portals," played by the Juillard String Orchestra, conducted by Frederick Prausnitz, is also recommended. —*"Blue" Gene Tyranny*

Arthur Russell

b. 1951, **d.** 1992

Tower of Meaning / 1983 / Chatham Square ✦✦✦✦✦
Julius Eastman conducted an almost medievally pure music in which tone combinations of two or three notes tuned to modal/raga scales are played by various instrumental groups. There is a love of listening to the pure combinations per se, as they are delivered at a regular, moderate pace—then, unpredictibly, rich or dissonant chords will be held that open your mind's ear and take your breath away. The sudden ceasing of the music at certain points also has a similar effect. — *"Blue" Gene Tyranny*

World of Echo / 1986 / Upside ✦✦✦
An incredible assemblage of solo versions of this influential and unique downtown musician. Contains the songs and instrumentals written from 1980-1986: "Soon-To-Be Innocent Fun/Let's See," "Tower of Meaning / Rabbit's Ear / Home Away from Home," "Tone Bone Kone," "Answers Me," "Being It," "Place I Know/ Kid Like You," "She's the Star/I Take This Time," "Treehouse," "See-Through," "Hiding Your Present from You," "Wax the Van," "All-Boy All-Girl," "Lucky Cloud," and "Let's Go Swimming." Subtle, transcendental with gentle rock beats and new music influences in patternings and textures. — *"Blue" Gene Tyranny*

William Russell

Made in America / The Complete Works of William Russell / 1993 / Mode ✦✦✦
At last! The complete works of composer and ragtime violinist Russell, who during the 1930s composed some of the most cantankerous and original percussion music ever heard. This CD includes such works as his six-minute "Trumpet Concerto"; his lively "Four Dance Movements"; "Three Cuban Pieces"; "March Suite" with the movements School March, Wedding March, Military March, Hunger March, and Funeral March; the "Chicago Sketches," with each movement named after an address (3525 S. Dearborn, 5507 S. Michigan, 4726 S. State); the music for the ballet "Ogou Badagri" (1933), based on the voodoo rites of Haiti; and of course "Made in America" (1936). Another true American original. — *"Blue" Gene Tyranny*

Bill Ruyle

No. 3 / Tall Poppies ✦✦✦
In the CD *Synergy Percussion* (Tall Poppies TP030). The composer is a well-known downtown NYC marimba virtuoso and percussionist who has composed a multitude of exquisite and award-winning dance and theater scores. *No. 3* (1989) is played by Dave Samuels on solo vibraphone backed up by the ensemble. It is a percussion ensemble arrangement of a section of a dance score composed for Joanne Fragellete-Jansen's dance *Aromas and Infidels.* — *"Blue" Gene Tyranny*

Joel Ryan

b. Jan. 1, 1945, Connecticut
Composer / Electronic, Computer
Ryan studied with Jose Barroso (Mexican film composer and guitarist), Ravi and Lakshmi Shankar, Robert Ashley, and David Behrman, and was influenced by the live concerts of John Coltrane. He collaborated with composers and artists including George E. Lewis, Malcolm Goldstein, Evan Parker, Steina and Woody Vasulka, and "Blue" Gene Tyranny. He has been creating digital sound processing instruments for live electronic music since 1979. Currently Director of Research at STEIM in Amsterdam, and Docent at the Institute of Sonology at the Royal Conservatory in The Hague. — *"Blue" Gene Tyranny*

☆ **The Number Readers** / OR Ltd (London) ✦✦✦✦✦
One of our most original writers on the aesthetics of new music, Ryan also has been associated as an original software designer with the STEIM studios in Amsterdam. This elegant work for live computer-driven electronics, video, and spoken text is based on shortwave radio transmissions heard in the evenings, of women's voices reading numbers, with great precision, in German and sometimes Spanish and Czech, sometimes preceded by electronic chime patterns. "No nation or agency has claimed authorship of these broadcasts." Joel observed a middle-aged woman in Amsterdam sitting at the front window of a well-kept old house with pad and pencil in semi-darkness by an old style model radio; he soon began to realize that there was a "synchrony of the number readers' broadcasts with the woman's vigils." Ryan weaves a variety of musical imagery using this central "coding" idea as a steppingstone: "Codes to protect property," "Julius Caesar's code to confuse the Gauls," "Code as reason contradicting itself," "The Language of Flowers," "Codes You Can Eat," and many others. Fascinating, innovative work. — *"Blue" Gene Tyranny*

Enfolded Strings Inial Mix / 1994 / Inial ✦✦✦
In the collection *Views from the Perfect City.* A collaboration between violinist Malcolm Goldstein and composer Joel Ryan, the piece is completely interactive with the violin tuning the internal net program (in the form of a musical instrument) of the computer which in turn digitally processes the sound of the violin. This is all achieved live, and results in evocative, mysterious and curious and subtle sounds. — *"Blue" Gene Tyranny*

Frederic Rzewski

☆ **Winnsboro Cotton Mill Blues (1980) / In Double Edge "US Choice"** / 1992 / CRI ✦✦✦✦✦
The whirring and clanging of the factory mixed with the rhythmic blues of the workers. Thrilling music played with a lot of heart by this astonishingly talented duo. — *"Blue" Gene Tyranny*

The People United Will Never Be Defeated / 1994 / New Albion ✦✦✦
The thrilling, virtuoso, political classic for piano: 36 variations on "El Pueblo Unido Jamas Sera Vencido!" played brilliantly by Stephen Drury, with excerpts from a live performance in Buenos Aires of the tune by Quillapayun. — *"Blue" Gene Tyranny*

De Profoundis (1992) for Speaking Pianist / Sonata (1991) for Piano / 1994 / Hat Hut ✦✦✦
Two moving examples of how political concerns can be expressed with rich human emotions. — *"Blue" Gene Tyranny*

A Decade: Zeitgeist Plays Rzewski / 1994 / O.O. Discs ✦✦✦
Four chamber works—"Wails" (1984), "Spots" (1986), "The Lost Melody" (1989), and "Crusoe" (1993)—beautifully and energetically played by the Zeitgeist chamber ensemble. Highly tuneful, often playful, riff-like melodies over colorful harmonies equally reminiscent of the '20s "Les Six" composers and the voicings of Duke Ellington. — *"Blue" Gene Tyranny*

Carlos Santos

Voicetracks / P.A. Taylor ✦✦✦
A self-described "romantic structuralist." Outrageous humor, vocal virtuosity, sharply contrasting emotions. — *"Blue" Gene Tyranny*

Erik Satie

Satie's music, in sound and aesthetics, was fundamentally different from the prevailing 19th-century German school that prized ideals of continuity and development. It is music as sound per se (*Musique d'ameublement,* that is, "Furniture Music" or "Music for Furnishing," 1920). Satie invented many musical techniques—the use of whole-tone scales, chords built in fourths, pattern melodies, unresolved "dissonances" used for their value as sounds, "open" large forms without contrasting or developing sections, and others. Perhaps more important, he was the first conceptual composer. — *"Blue" Gene Tyranny*

Piano Works, Vol. 1 "First and Last Works" / Piano Works, Vol. 2 "Mystical Works" / Piano Works, Vol. 3 "Etudes" / Piano Works, Vol. 4 / 1989 / Angel ✦✦✦
Pianist Aldo Ciccolini produced the first complete recordings of all of Satie's piano works, and his playing of them is still the best. He treats them with clarity, lightness, and the appropriate humor but never with the rubato sweetness that some performers slip into. In these piano works, Satie can probably be most clearly seen creating a music that in both its sound and aesthetics is fundamentally different from that produced under the ideals of continuity and development prized by the 19th-century Germanic school (which until about the 1950s still held the most influence in the US). With originality from the root of the soul and some amazing titles, Satie focuses on music as "sound" per se, especially in "Musique d'ameublement" ("Furniture Music" or "Music for Furnishing") (1920), for piano, three clarinets, and a bassoon. He seems to regard any music as a direct result of the interests of that music's creator regardless of whatever poetic, religious, or other description "out there" has been attributed to the music—he has fun with this in the lovely "Descriptions Automatiques." With Buddhist-like attention and perhaps the first true attempt to describe the "conceptual" nature of human mental activity, he requires the performer(s) to simultaneously experience and examine in detail the exact moments of shifting psychological states, in such works as "Musiques intimes et secrétes" ("Intimate and Secret Musics": I. Nostalgia, II. Cold Reverie, III. Unfortunate Example), and in his famous "Vexations" from the "Pages mystiques" (1892-1895), a piece that attracted John Cage's attention and was discussed widely by him, making the piece famous: the music is a short musical passage of neutral feeling (or, perhaps, ennui—composed of augmented and diminished chords) to be repeated 840 times very slowly, for a total duration of around 18 hours, 40 minutes, usually requiring 10 pianists. His beautiful "Messe des Pauvres" (Mass for the Poor) (1893-1895) speaks for compassion, in modern harmonies moving in 10th-century parallel monastic singing (organum). Other pieces emphasize natural and spontaneous mentation apart from "ideas": "The Dreaming Fish," "Heures seculaires et instantanées" ("Ordinary and Snapshot Times"), and "Véritables préludes flasques—pour un chien" ("Authentic Flabby Preludes—for a Dog": I. Severe Reprimand, II. Alone at Home, III. We Play). He uses

ironic titles and written commentaries in his scores to poke fun at pomposity and officialism: "Le duc de Connaught et le Président aux maneuvres" (The Duke of Connaught and the President on Maneuvers), "En habit de cheval" (In a Riding Outfit," with movements titled I. Chorale, II. Latin Fugue, III. Another Chorale, IV. A Fugue on Paper); "Sonatine bureaucratique" ("Bureaucratic Sonatina"); and the piano suite "Enfantines" ("Infantile Pieces") (1913), with titles like "The Bean-King's War Chant" and "Importune Peccadillos"—I. Being Jealous of His Comrade with the Big Head, II. Him Eat His Cookie, III. Taking Advantage of His Corns to Steal His Hoop." Satie's religious feeling was of a mystical, precleric kind expressed in works like "Première pensée rose + croix" (1891) ("First Rose Thought + Cross," French word play on "Rosicrucians"), the first and second "Prélude du Nazaréen" ("Prelude of the Nazarene"), and in his moving work "Socrate" (1918) on the death of Socrates based on texts by Plato. —*"Blue" Gene Tyranny*

The Complete Ballets / 1990 / Vanguard Classics ✦✦✦
Wonderful performances by the Utah Symphony Orchestra, conducted by Maurice Abravanel. Contains "Parade" (1917, realist ballet after Jean Cocteau), "Mercure" (Mercury, 1924, plastic poses in 13 scenes, designed by Pablo Picasso), "Relache" (Respite, 1924, instantaneous ballet in two acts, a cinematic intermission, and a dog's tail, designed by Francis Picabia, film by Rene Clair), "Jack in the Box" (1899, pantomime, orchestrated by Milhaud, 1925), "Gymnopedies" 1 and 3 (1888, orchestrated by Debussy—music for ancient Greek gymnastic exercises written in old modal scales), "Trois morceaux en forme de poire" (1903, three pieces in the form of a pear, orchestrated by Desormiere), "Cinq Grimaces pour 'Le Songe d'une nuit d'ete'" ("Five Grimaces for a Planned Cocteau Production of "A Mid-Summer Night's Dream," 1914), and "The Grand Ritournelle" from "La belle excentrique" ("The Beautiful Eccentric Lady") (1920). —*"Blue" Gene Tyranny*

Giacinto Scelsi

Pfhat (1974) for Chorus and Orchestra / 1988 / Accord ✦✦✦
Unlike the heaviness with which Scelsi at times depicts mythologies of Buddhist, Egyptian, Latin, and other ancient cultures (in a ponderous style sometimes called "the new religiosity"), *Pfhat* employs a concentrated pallette of sounds and compositional ideas—breathing sounds from the chorus, imitation of a single giant ringing bell, and a lovely finale for two flutes holding a dissonance surrounded by (about) a hundred small, tinkling bells. For comparison, this CD also contains "Aion" (1961) and "Konx-om-pax" (1969). —*"Blue" Gene Tyranny*

Botba / 1992 / Hat Art ✦✦✦
Marianne Schroeder (piano). More conservative but more concentrated early works beautifully played. Includes "Un Adieu," the "Sonata no. 2," and the interesting "Suite no. 8" (1952), an evocation of Tibet with its monasteries, rituals, prayers, and dances. —*"Blue" Gene Tyranny*

Pierre Schaeffer

b. 1910
Composer / Musique concrète, sound sculptures

Erotica "Symphonie Pour un Homme Seul" (Collaboration with Pierre Henry) / In "Concert Imaginaire" / 1984 / INA.GRM - INA ✦✦✦
A short and sweetly humorous feuilleton (or bob-bon, as the case may be) by the composer who led early French work on composing with environmental, extra-musical sounds or "musique concrète"—resulting in his "Concert de Bruits" (Concert of Noises) broadcast in 1948 and the establishment in 1951 of the Groupe de Recherches de Musique Concrète and in 1958 of the Group for Musical Research of the Office of French Radio-Television (O.R.T.F.). "Musique concrète" now also includes electronic and world music. —*"Blue" Gene Tyranny*

Ramon Sender

Audition (excerpt) / 1986 / Music from Mills ✦✦✦
One of my favorite composers ever since I heard, at a ONCE Festival in the mid-'60s, both his electronic tape "Kore" (1962) and "Information": the score was a huge roll of transparent material, for performer(s) giving improvised "information," a few receiving instructions on headphones while performing on accordion with his wonderful electronic tape, "Desert Ambulance." —*"Blue" Gene Tyranny*

Elliott Sharp

b. 1951
Perhaps next to John Zorn as the most eclectic and outrageous member of the '90s "downtown" group, Elliot Sharp does free, ethnic, and rock music and a wild mixture of everything else in the musical spectrum. The composer/performer plays electric and steel guitar, electric bass, soprano sax, bass clarinet, and many other things and with his band Carbon brings to his dates a spirit of adventure, bizarre antics, and rampag-

ing musical experimentation that makes it difficult to assess much of his material. It may be improvisational, but it's also deliberately chaotic, sometimes horrendous, other times quite insightful. He's recorded for the Enemy label, and has been featured on Knitting Factory sessions. Sharp's one musician who's truly not for all or even most tastes. —*Ron Wynn*

Twistmap / Ear-Rational ✦✦✦✦✦
Four works performed by the Soldier String Quartet, Carbon, and Sharp. Like the first Kagel quartets, these pieces introduce new playing techniques and sounds, some stimulating the ear and mind with the aural equivalent of painting with gravel. Raw and beautiful, especially the second cut "Shapeshifter." —*"Blue" Gene Tyranny*

● **Hammer, Anvil, Stirrup** / 1989 / SST Records ✦✦✦✦✦
An excellent rendering by the Soldier String Quartet of some of Sharp's best music. Visceral patterns with searing harmonic content and new string techniques. The unique title piece, presented in two takes interesting to contrast, seems to be partly a gritty and humorous take-off on hoedown/cowboy horseback-riding music (as depicted in movies) and partly a wandering into some strange slithery tuning zones traversed by squiggly melodies, using the Fibonacci series to generate tunings, rhythms, and forms. The next selection, "Tessalation Row," delivers an electrifyingly gorgeous image as geometric and scintillating as the Zapotec design from Oaxaca, Mexico, on the CD's cover. "Digital" is a toe-tapping rhythmic study that uses a strip of spring steel woven into the strings near the bridge as a preparation; the instruments are then all played with a two-handed hammering technique. "Diurnal" and "Ringtoss" study massed and unison melodic gestures using looping and deconstruction techniques. "Re/Iterations" is for string orchestra (made here by overdubbing the Quartet), with contact microphones attached to the instruments to pick up the subtle difference or "ghost" tones produced by the combinations of high harmonics—dense masses of swirling frequency/rhythm patterns lovely in their rawness. —*"Blue" Gene Tyranny*

Sleepers

Sleepers / Finnadar ✦✦✦
Available from Deep Listening Publications. Eight takes on the lullaby. Contains: Doris Hays' "Hush," Annea Lockwood's "Malolo," Ilhan Mimaroglu's "Sleepsong for Sleepers," Daniel Goode's "The Red and White Cows," Tom Johnson's "Lullaby," Pauline Oliveros' "Lullaby for Daisy Pauline," a choral piece, Alison Knowles' "Mantra for Jessie (Some Help in Sleeping)" for speaker with shaker, and Ann Silsbee's "Go Gentle" for three flutes. —*"Blue" Gene Tyranny*

Stuart Saunders Smith

Crux / 1992 / O.O. Discs ✦✦✦
"The most important part of music . . . is music's autobiography . . . the dead other—our made-up selves—a mourning of the missed other." This CD is a meeting point of four compositions: "Tunnels" (1982), for musician/actor; "Notebook" (1980), for trumpet, piano, contrabass, flute; "Family Portraits" (1992) (Sylvia, Ivy, Earle), for piano; and "Here and There" (1971), for flute, shortwave radio, and piano interior. A fascinating composer. —*"Blue" Gene Tyranny*

Laetitia Sonami

Pie Jesu—Sounds from Empty Spaces No. 3/ In "Another Coast" / 1988 / Music and Art ✦✦✦✦✦
We hear Moslem song, sweet synthesizer tones, CB radio, the beginnings of an anxious explanation, a dog bark, and other environmental sounds that depict an imaginary world built from the drama of "unforeseen change." See also her compositions "What Happened" in the collection *Imaginary Landscapes* (1989), and "Story Road" in the collection *Jewel Box* (1992). —*"Blue" Gene Tyranny*

Bernadette Speach

b. Jan. 1, 1948, Syracuse, NY
Speach studied composition with Nicolas Roussakis, Jacques-Louis Monod, Morton Feldman, and Lejaren Hiller. She is president of Buffalo New Music Ensemble, on the board of directors of the Musicians of Brooklyn Initiative (MOBI), and executive director of the Composers' Forum, Inc. in NYC. —*"Blue" Gene Tyranny*

Dualities / 1991 / Mode ✦✦✦
A duo CD with Jeffrey Schanzer, electric and classical guitars, and Bernadette Speach on piano. Sensitive pieces that successfully combine advanced harmonies and compositional techniques with some gestures suggesting folk music and jazz/pop genres: "Two in the Morning" has a nocturnal mysterious ballad feel with a hint of Spanish guitar, works its way through more aggressive fast pointillism, and returns to a moody, introspective time to close up the bar coda; "3 1/2" is a fascinating pattern piece that gradually shifts phase and accents in this complex time

signature, becoming splendidly aggressive with guitar string snaps and massive piano clusters; "It's Your Turn" has a lovely, pensive balladic feel; "Tracings," for solo guitar, is likewise a lyrical piece with an introspective, at times even eerie, nature; "a page upon which . . ." for piano solo is a lyric piece in an improvisatory style with a romantic yet clear texture in which patterns are re-examined and constantly varied along a fascinatingly rich path of their gradual unfolding, sensitively and beautifully performed by the composer; "Blue," for guitar and piano, is a joyous, pointillistic, pattern blues with complex rhythms and harmonies; "Ajiaco," by composer/conductor Tania León, is the last piece, and, like the Speach/Schanzer duo's pieces, also combines advanced writing with a variety of American rhythmic styles. — "Blue" Gene Tyranny

Without Borders / Mode ✦✦✦
A collection of some of the composer's finest work, beautifully performed. The pieces are each gems of instrumental color, of original combinations of pop and folk musics with advanced compositional techniques: "Moto" (1982), performed by the Bowery Ensemble is a study of momentum with lovely patterns and figures somewhere between pointillism and American minimalism; "Pensées" (Thoughts) (1983), for solo guitar, is a portrait of the composer's husband, each movement representing aspects of his personality, and it again achieves that wonderful blending of a folk music emotionality with an advanced compositional technique; "Trajet" (1983), for percussion and trombone, is a charmingly humorous, and at times rhythmically dance-like and tongue-in-cheek journey through interactive "colors, patterns and designs . . . inspired by the motions and movements of our tropical fish"; the "Sonata" (1986), for piano, is a 12-minute "sonata" in the older sense of the term, signifying "soundpiece," and it moves between serialist statements, gently rocking loops that create a suspended-in-the-air sensation, and extended, suspenseful melody; "Shattered Glass" (1987), for percussion, presents distinct motives of multirhythmic character and gesture, playful, aggressive, and extremely gentle, which are fragmented and "enhanced, recalled, accelerated, slowed down and sometimes almost entirely eliminated until they resolve into a singular sound"; "Telepathy: Poetry/Music Suite" (1987), for reciter and bass, trombone, alto sax, piano and guitar, is a collaboration with poet Thulani Davis and is in three parts: the first,"Contessas and Cardsharks," is a portrait of Malcom X's early life, the second, "Telepathy," is a kind of love poem about people separated by a great distance, and its motifs suggest Coltrane's "Naima" and the descending chords of his "Giant Steps"; the third section, "Boppin' Is Safer Than Grindin'," recalls dancin' and romancin' and is a mix of blues, rock steady bass, and advanced harmonic 'comping. — "Blue" Gene Tyranny

Laurie Spiegel

b. Sep. 20, 1945, Chicago, IL
Composer / Electronic, Computer Music
Spiegel studied at Oxford, composition with J.W. Duarte, Vincent Persichetti, Hall Overton, Jacob Druckman, and Emmanuel Ghent. A guitarist and lute player, she worked at Bell Labs from 1973-74 and in computer graphics. Spiegel created the computer music program Music Mouse, which eliminates reliance on keyboards, sampled or acoustic sounds. She has composed for numerous soundtracks, and collaborated on video projects with Nam June Paik and others; her realization of Kepler's *Music of the Spheres* was sent into space by NASA. — "Blue" Gene Tyranny

Unseen Worlds / 1991 / Scarlet Records/Infinity ✦✦✦✦✦
This album gives a good overview of her approaches to digital synthesis, from folk music-like steady sequences of single sounds to the stately, galactic "Sound Zones," a beautiful and original piece using sweeps of clusters, sounds-within-sounds, images-within-images, tunings never before experienced. A truly moving experience. A similar mix can be heard in her currently out-of-print CD *The Expanding Universe* on Philo PH 9003. — "Blue" Gene Tyranny

Cavis Muris (1986) / In CDCM Computer Music Series, Vol. 13 / 1993 / Centaur ✦✦✦
A charming piece in five parts. Computer-generated using Spiegel's self-designed computer program "Music Mouse—An Intelligent Instrument." The title, meaning "mouse hole" or "the mouse's cave," was a result of her imaging what it would be like for mice to experience our ordinary human spaces: "such a vast and foreign world from their tiny perspectives." — "Blue" Gene Tyranny

Jim Staley

Don Giovanni / 1992 / Einstein ✦✦✦
A reconstructed montage of improvisations: pointillistic pop, primal nonverbal vocals, lyric synchronicity, "A hyper-suite of Mozartean dogfights [by] master virtuosos of the proto-form [who] stir up the red soup." Produced by Fred Frith, this is a terrific "downtown" album with Ikue Mori (drums and electric drums), Zeena Parkins (electric and acoustic

harps), Jim Staley (the "kinesthetic trombonist" and on didjeridu), Tenko Ueno (the Tokyo vocalist), and Davy Williams (the Birmingham-based power guitarist). A great "world" mix. — "Blue" Gene Tyranny

Mumbo Jumbo / 1994 / Einstein ✦✦✦
Reissue of some wonderful improvisational trios with vocalist Shelley Hirsch, Sam Bennett, keyboardist Wayne Horowitz, Elliott Sharp, Bill Grisell, Ikue Mori, John Zorn, and Fred Frith. — "Blue" Gene Tyranny

Karlheinz Stockhausen

b. 1928
Composer / Serialism, Live Electronic, Acoustic, Meditation
A German composer in electronic and acoustic media who is concerned with abstract processes in composition, Stockhausen composed for many forms, including opera, orchestral, chamber, and vocal works. —AMG

☆ **Konkrete und Elektronische Musik**—Etude/ Studie I U. II/ Gesang Der Junglinge (Song of the Youths) / Kontakte / Stockhausen Gesamtausgabe CD #3 ✦✦✦✦✦
Classic and well-developed electronic music—some pieces with specific images, like the "Song of the Youths" in the fiery Biblical furnace—and others without extra-musical images. — "Blue" Gene Tyranny

Kurzwellen (Shortwaves) / Stockhausen Gesamtausgabe (Complete Edition) ✦✦✦
This piece, probably largely influenced by John Cage's early works using "extra-musical" sounds including radios etc., was composed in 1968 for Stockhausen's touring group of six performers—on piano, electronium, large tam-tam with microphone, viola with contact microphone, two filters with four potentiometers, and four shortwave receivers (some substitute instruments are possible). Their task is to react on the spur of the moment to the unpredictable sounds received on shortwave radios. What is pre-composed is how they react: imitate, modulate, transpose, change their rhythmic articulation, higher or lower in pitch, softer or louder, when and how often they play in combinations, how they call out to each other in order to share a single event among them, condensing that event, embellishing it, losing it, and so forth. The primary aim of each performance is to bring out the human spirit within a sense of nowness, "everything is the whole" (Stockhausen), thus bypassing dichotomies. — "Blue" Gene Tyranny

Spiral for Solo Performer (1968) / 1993 / Hat Hut ✦✦✦
A strange, mysterious composition performed by Eberhard Blum on flute, voice, and shortwave receiver. — "Blue" Gene Tyranny

Klavierstucke (Piano Pieces) / David Tudor, Piano / 1994 / Hat Hut ✦✦✦
A reissue of the incredible performances of the Piano Pieces in their first recording made on Sept. 19, 1958, and Sept. 27, 1959, at the WDR Radio in Cologne, Germany. Tudor at that time was the renowned pianist of avant-garde music, having played Boulez's monumentally complex "First Piano Sonata" from memory, for instance, and the exponent of the new "indeterministic" music of Cage. At some point after these performances, Tudor swore that he would never play a piece of Stockhausen's again, probably for political reasons. Anyhow, these are astonishing concerts of the Klavierstucke I-VIII, and four versions of Klavierstucke XI. Highly recommended. — "Blue" Gene Tyranny

Carré für Vier Orchester u. Vier Chöre (Carré [Square] for Four Orchestras and Four Cho / Deutsche Grammaphon ✦✦✦

Inori / Anbetungen für Einen der Zwei Soloisten und Orchester (Inori / Adorations for O / Deutsche Grammaphon ✦✦✦

Gruppen für Drei Orchester (Groups for Three Orchestras) / Deutsche Grammaphon ✦✦✦
Composed between 1955 and 1957, this work is a brilliant example of the post-World War II school of serialist composition. Initiated by the composer's fascination with the spatial distribution of sound as a musical element, the score positions three orchestras, each with its own conductor, around a concert hall, ideally in a semi-circle. The orchestras sometimes perform independently at their own specified tempi, but at other times they will begin to interchange musical information by calls and responses to each other, echoing material, or coordinating in a mutually shared tempo and pulse. At times musical material may move from one orchestra to another, one orchestra furthering or completing the task of another—"They fall apart or cling together . . . one receives the other into itself, and plays with it, extinguishes it . . . they become transformed." The composer's aim is to create for the listener a "common time-world" among all the sound, where the music is not contrapuntal points of sound, but groups of combined sounds and noises. But the ensembles can never entirely coalesce, and hence the music is always in flux, moving and dividing. A marvelous palette of timbral combinations and exciting, as well as at times internally lyrical, orchestral images await the listener. — "Blue" Gene Tyranny

Hymnen (Anthems) / Deutsche Grammaphon ✦✦✦
Realized in 1967 in the electronic composition studios of the WDR (Western German Radio), this piece for magnetic tape, in versions with and without solo instrumentalists, is made from electronically modulated national anthems of many countries, modulated shortwave broadcasts and musique concrète "sound effects" like human yelling and animal noises. There are four movements called Regions: the first is built from the "Internationale" and the "Marsellaise," the second from the hymn of the German Federal Republic, several African national anthems, and the beginning of the Russian anthem. The third Region is made from the American and Russian anthems, and the fourth from the Swiss anthem and a theme associated with what the composer calls the "Utopia of Hymunion in Harmondie unter Pluramon (hymn-union within the harmony of the world—harmonium mundi—under plurality and monism)." This uniquely original composition gives the impression both of international contemporaneity and also of our part in a great universal mystery. —*"Blue" Gene Tyranny*

Kontra-Punkte (Counter-Points) for 10 Instruments / RCA Victrola ✦✦✦

Mikrophonie I and II (Microphony I and II) / CBS ✦✦✦

Momente (Moments) for Soprano Solo, 4 Choral Groups and 13 Instrumentalists / Wergo ✦✦✦

Zyklus (Cycle) for Solo Percussionist / Columbia ✦✦✦

Carl Stone

b. Feb. 10, 1953

Woo Lae Oak (1981) / 1983 / Wizard Records ✦✦✦✦✦
Lovely, sustained, and slowly changing music made by classic "musique concrète" means—a rubbed string, blowing in a bottle, and other sounds are made into tape loops and changed by means of precise tape speed change, layering, and other techniques. —*"Blue" Gene Tyranny*

Kamiya Bar / 1991 / Newtone ✦✦✦
The composer samples the sounds of Tokyo—street noises, voices, TV programs—to create a journey through the daily life of the city. Varied and mysterious ambient environment sound. —*"Blue" Gene Tyranny*

Mom's / 1992 / New Albion ✦✦✦
Captivating in its simplicity. Stone has an underlying feeling for modality and rhythm from American folk music without ever imitating it. "Banteay Srey," for example, has a simple two-note pulse to which is gradually added a walking bass line and harmonies, transparent in their textures in a West Coast way, creating an engaging romantic and also otherworldly feeling. "Mom's" has a guitar riff that goes on simply for a while; then suddenly a whole slew of salsa-sampling musicians step in—a sheer delight. Other selections are beautiful character studies. An original and widely listenable composer. —*"Blue" Gene Tyranny*

Ned Sublette

Western Classics with the Southwesterners / 1980 / Lovely Music ✦✦✦
Sublette's music is a good example of someone working with known styles whose attitude, not toward the music but toward life in general, is just a bit "off" from the normative, and this makes the music just different enough to be "avant." This CD, recorded in Albuquerque, NM, is the traditional straight roots music from which Sublette created a unique and eccentric cowboy/downtown music with great words (the infamous cattle mutilation song, and many others) that appeal equally to both C&W and new-music fans. Recently the music has been evolving through Texas-Mexican Border music and Cuban influences. Sublette traveled to Cuba to study the remaining authentic bands and musicians outside the cities. In the late '70s and early '80s, he produced many unusual new-music programs of other composers' music, especially commissioned for National Public Radio in the Southwest (single compositions lasting most of the day). He recently produced a score for Chinese instruments, written both in European and in Chinese notations, for an opera, with text by Lawrence Weiner. Sublette currently runs a distributing company primarily for discs of real Cuban music. —*"Blue" Gene Tyranny*

Cowboys Are Frequently Secretly/ In "Life Is a Killer" / 1982 / ✦✦✦✦✦
The famous gay cowboy song. —*"Blue" Gene Tyranny*

Ships at Sea, Sailors and Shoes / 1993 / Excellent ✦✦✦
To unbelievably great texts by Lawrence Weiner, Ned Sublette sings, in his decidedly cowboy accent, with the Persuasions (yes, those Persuasions!) in this entertaining CD of fractured doo-wop art songs/pieces with an underlying philosophical earnestness ("There Is No Light at the End of the Tunnel," "Ever Widening Circles of Remorse") and reflecting ecological concerns, as in "Big Bang/New Flora" ("Row, row, row, your boat as the shit flows gently down the stream . . . what we don't flush away we'll blow away another day"), and transcendent situations ("Postcards from Heaven," like the title of Cage's piece for harps) with a collage of Spanish dialog, seashore sounds, and choir from somewhere. There

are also poetry readings, and the pieces never "develop" in any ordinary song fashion. Deserves to be in both the pop and avant-garde bins in the record outlets. Highly recommended. —*"Blue" Gene Tyranny*

Morton Subotnick

b. Apr. 14, 1933, Los Angeles, CA
Composer / Electronic, Acoustic
Subotnick studied with Leon Kirchner and Darius Milhaud. Co-founder of the San Francisco Tape Music Center, Music Director of the Repertory Theater at Lincoln Center, artist-in-residence at NYU School of the Arts. Created the live electronic performance "ghost score" method in the 1970s for *Liquid Strata* (1977) and *The Wild Beasts* (1978). Scores for CD-ROM include *Five Scenes for an Imaginary Ballet* (1992) and a recent method designed for children to spontaneously compose music. Taught at Mills College, University of Maryland, University of Pittsburgh, Yale, and CA Institute of the Arts. Co-director of the Center for Experiments in Art, Information, and Technology. —*"Blue" Gene Tyranny*

Key to Songs (1985) / **Return (1985-1986), The** / 1986 / New Albion ✦✦✦✦✦
Subotnick's music from the electronic music classics "Silver Apples of the Moon" and "The Wild Bull" has always contained poetic, lyrical imagery. Similarly, "The Key to Songs" is based on Max Ernst's collage novel *Une Semaine de Bonte* ("A Week of Kindness or the Seven Deadly Elements"). *Return*—A Triumph of Reason refers to the change from dread and foreboding to reason that was accomplished by Edmond Halley upon explaining the circuit of his well-known comet. A good example of modern "tone poem" electronic music. —*"Blue" Gene Tyranny*

Sun Ra (Herman "Sonny" Blount)

Composer / Jazz-influenced, Pianist, Synthesist, Philosopher, Collective Improvisations, Visionary
See the Jazz section for his biography.

☆ **The Heliocentric Worlds of Sun Ra, Vol. 1** / Base Record ✦✦✦✦✦
The ESP-Disk 1014, issued 1965, re-pressed. The first of the series by Sun Ra and the Solar Arkestra. —*"Blue" Gene Tyranny*

Voice of the Eternal Tomorrow / The Rose Hue Mansions of the Sun / Saturn 80 ✦✦✦
This unfortunately out-of-print album has all the spectacular excitement of a live Sun Ra event. "Voice of the Eternal Tomorrow" is a sequence of astonishing solos by members of the Arkestra, and the end solo by Sun Ra is so "out there" that the audience sits in stunned silence before applauding respectfully. "The Rose Hue Mansions of the Sun" begins with a high-energy, loose-chordal hymn by the group and then launches into another incredible 20-minute solo by Sun Ra, punctuated by the band. Sun Ra demonstrates a mastery of electronic modulation. The alternation between solo and the various Arkestra entrances leads unceasingly into the most unpredictable zones. —*"Blue" Gene Tyranny*

The Cosmic Explorer (1970) / **In "Nuits de la Fondation Maeght"** / 1981 / Recommended Records ✦✦✦
Sun Ra was one of the first instrumentalists to use a Moog synthesizer in live performance. This 20-minute solo improvisation (with minimal extra sounds from the ensemble), ranging between high energy clusters and the lyrical, shows his ability to create an astonishing range of sound and emotion, inspiring a truly "cosmic" conclusion from the Arkestra. —*"Blue" Gene Tyranny*

John Cage Meets Sun Ra (June 8, 1986 at "Sideshows by the Seashore," Coney Island, NY) / 1981 / Meltdown Records ✦✦✦
Two on the surface apparently different aesthetic approaches on the same stage. It worked as everyone became "attuned to the next moment, the next sound." —*"Blue" Gene Tyranny*

☆ **Cosmic Equation** / 1990 / Magic Music ✦✦✦✦✦
A retitled reissue of "The Heliocentric Worlds of Sun Ra, Vol. 2," ESP-Disc 1017, issued in 1966. The astonishing sessions that went lightyears beyond "free jazz" improvisation to create a music of deeply felt explosive and gentle gesture made from sound itself without reference to previous notions of melody or harmony. —*"Blue" Gene Tyranny*

Akio Suzuki

Soundsphere / 1990 / Het Apollohuis Publications ✦✦✦
This CD, with a 36-page booet in English and Japanese, features two instruments—an echo instrument created by Suzuki in 1970 called the "Analapos" and his version of a Glass Harmonica used in the installation piece "Space in the Sun." —*"Blue" Gene Tyranny*

Toru Takemitsu

b. 1930, Tokyo, Japan, **d.** 1996
Composer / Experimental Orchestral, Eastern-Western Fusion, Electronic, Film Scores
Largely self-taught, Takemitsu worked with the Experimental Work-

shop in Tokyo in the early '50s. A guitarist and pianist, he received the Italia Prize in 1958. Influenced by John Cage, jazz, serialism, Debussy, ancient Japanese music, and many world cultures. He employed unique polyrhythmic and open scoring methods combined with traditional Western notation. Takemitsu created one of the first combinations of Western orchestra with traditional Japanese instruments and Gagaku ensembles. His film scores include *Woman in the Dunes* (1964), *Kwaidan* (1964), *Dode'skaden* (1970), *Under the Cherry Blossoms* (1975), *Empire of Passion* (1978), and *Ran* (1985). *—"Blue" Gene Tyranny*

☆ **Works of Toru Takemitsu IV, Includes Music of Tree (1961) / Coral Island for Soprano and Orchestra (1962) / Kaidan (1966) for Magnetic Tape** / 1988 / JVC ✦✦✦✦✦
Stunningly beautiful tone poems that combine pointillistic writing with a Debussyian harmonic sense. The tape composition "Vocalism A-I" ("Ai" means love in Japanese) is already a classic. *—"Blue" Gene Tyranny*

Dreamtime/Nostalghia/Vers, L'Arc-En-Ciel, Palma (Verse, Rainbow, Palma) /Far Calls, Comi / 1990 / ABC Classics ✦✦✦
Incredible performances by the Melbourne Symphony Orchestra, directed by Hiroyuki Iwaki. The title *Dreamtime* (1982) comes from the Australian Aboriginal expression to indicate a state more "real" than physical reality. Rich fanning motions of shimmering impressionist color sweep over the orchestra. Rays of light seem to shine out of a gloomier atmosphere, shapes arise and disappear. A vast timbral space that is guided by a masterfully delicate touch. One of this composer's finest scores. *Nostalgia*, for solo violin (originally for Yehudi Menuhin) and string orchestra (1987), received its Italian title from one of Russian director Andrei Tarkovskij's films. The piece is not descriptive of the film's narrative but of a quiet, elegiac mood with images of mist and rain. The music seems to achieve a sort of peaceful equilibrium, with its final sustained chord leaving the solo violin on a high plateau. *Vers, L'Arc-En-Ciel, Palma* (1984), for guitar and oboe d'amore soloists with orchestra, is an homage to the painter Joan Miró. The lovely, nostalgic music rises with orchestral imitations of rising guitar arpeggios, constantly adding more rich harmonies to the texture. *Far Calls, Coming, Far!* (1980) is scored for solo violin and orchestra. The title, a quote from James Joyce's *Finnegan's Wake*, is what Anna Livia sings out upon sighting the River Liffy meeting the sea. The music, likewise, attempts to depict a flowing river, taking winding routes, rushing or barely in motion, until it finally reaches a great C-major tonal sea. *A Flock Descends into the Pentagonal Garden* (1977), for orchestra, was inspired by a dream of the composer's where he saw a flock of birds swirling around and then descending into a pentagonal garden; the garden, however, was the star on the back of Marcel Duchamp's head in the famous photograph. Lushly harmonized, lyrical melodies float like clouds. Silvery glissandi whistle by. Booming bass tones create a surreal storm. The flight of the birds is depicted by sensuous melodies surrounded by trilling figures and cries from the winds. Steely non-vibrato chords suggest a metallic garden. *— "Blue" Gene Tyranny*

Riverrun for Piano and Orchestra (1984) / Waterways (1977) / Rain Coming for Chamber Orchestra (1982) / Rain Spell (1982) / Tree Line (1982) / 1991 / Virgin ✦✦✦
Pointillistic, colorful tone poems for various instrumental ensembles. with many new orchestral techniques, especially in the elegant "Rain Coming." Played by the London Sinfonetta, conducted by Paul Crossley. *—"Blue" Gene Tyranny*

Visions / 1992 / Denon ✦✦✦
The Tokyo Metropolitan Symphony Orchestra, conducted by Hiroshi Horigome, presents Takemitsu classics: the richly harmonic Debussylike "Requiem for Strings"; "November Steps"; the newer, thinner-in-texture but abundant in orchestral color pieces "Far Calls, Coming, Far" (1980) for violin and orchestra; and the new "Visions" (1989) with its section "Mystere" and an orchestration of his piano work "Les yeux clos" for the second section. *— "Blue" Gene Tyranny*

A Flock Descends into the Pentagonal Garden (1977) for Orchestra / Dreamtime (1981) for O / 1996 / Bis ✦✦✦

Cecil Taylor (Cecil Percival Taylor)

See the Jazz section for his biography.

Alms/Tiergarten (Spree) (1988) / In "Cecil Taylor in Berlin '88" / 1989 / Free Music Production ✦✦✦
Two CDs from a large set, with an extensive booklet describing the pieces in detail with analyses, and the workshop sessions that led to the final concert, with pictures galore. This set is interesting primarily to hear European musicians interpret Taylor's kinesthetic directing—mostly an intense density of "free playing" (actually following specific internalized instructions and images), with almost everyone going off in different gestures at once. Slow unison melodies emerging from

the environment. The most interesting series is "Weight/Breath/Sounding Trees." *—"Blue" Gene Tyranny*

Richard Teitelbaum (Richard Lowe Teitelbaum)

Blends (1977) / 1985 / Lumina ✦✦✦✦✦
As the title promises, one of the most perfect blends of world music, with Katsuya Yokoyama on shakuhachi, Trilok Gurtu on tabla and other percussion, and Teitelbaum on synthesizer. The score is written in different notations based on Japanese, Indian, and American practices. *—"Blue" Gene Tyranny*

James Tenney

b. Aug. 10, 1934, Silver City, NM
Composer and Theorist / Electronic, Acoustic, Computer
Tenney studied piano with Eduard Steuermann, composition with Chou Wen-chung, Lionel Nowak, Paul Boepple, Henry Brant, Carl Ruggles, Kenneth Gaburo, Lejaren Hiller, and Edgard Varése. Associate Member of the Technical Staff at Bell Telephone Labs from 1961-64. Developed computer systems at Yale and the Polytechnic Institute of Brooklyn. Co-founder of the Tone Roads Chamber Ensemble (1963-70), and performer with many ensembles including those of Steve Reich, Philip Glass, Harry Partch, John Cage, and Fluxus. Lecturer at New School for Social Research. Also teacher at University of South Florida, University of California at Santa Barbara, and Stanford University. A respected theorist, he has written *META + HODOS* (1961), *John Cage and the Theory of Harmony* (1984), and *A History of Consonance and Dissonance* (1988). *—"Blue" Gene Tyranny*

★ **Music of James Tenney: Selected Works 1963-1984** / Musicworks ✦✦✦✦✦
Includes: "Three Indigenous Songs No. 3 (Hey, when I sing these songs; Hey, look what happens" (1979) with words based on Iroquois chant coded into instrumental music; "Phases" (1963), a computer-generated tape composition; "Quiet Fan for Erik Satie" (1970-1971), for an ensemble of 13 instruments—lyrical, hypnotically phase-modulated, Satie-like pastoral melodies; "For Ann (Rising)" (1969), a tape composition; "Spectral CANON for CONLON Nancarrow" (1974), for harmonic player piano; "Bridge" (excerpt) (1982-1984), for two pianos, eight-hands; "Voice(s)" (1982-1984), for instrumental ensemble, voice(s), tape, and tape delay—like a field of supernatural rainbows. See also his "Septet for Electric Guitars" in *Tellus No. 4* (collections), "Koan" in Malcolm Goldstein's "Sounding the New Violin," and "Critical Band" played by the Relache ensemble on Mode. *—"Blue" Gene Tyranny*

Harmonium #5 / 1988 / Artifact ✦✦✦
In the collection *Arraymusic: Strange City*. In *Harmonium No. 9* (1978) for string trio "pure tones become crossed strands of sonorities, much like the cat's cradle, transformed by a finger's twist" (Tenney). Exquisite and surprising harmonies in overlapping rhythmic arpeggios. *—"Blue" Gene Tyranny*

Critical Band / 1990 / Mode ✦✦✦
In the collection *Relache: On Edge*. Tenney's *Critical Band* (1988) for chamber music ensemble involves slow micro-intervallic tuning expansions within the range (band) of a major second above and below a central pitch (440Hz), exploring the perceptual borders of what we consider "consonance." The combinations evoke images (unintended by the composer) of oncoming trains, street accordions, etc. *— "Blue" Gene Tyranny*

Selected Works: 1961-1969 / 1992 / Artifact ✦✦✦
Some of the earliest and most imaginative electronic and computer-generated music. Tenney was one of the first composers to use Max Mathew's computer music synthesis system at Bell Labs, and this CD includes some works created there: "Ergodos II (for John Cage)" and "Analog No. 1: Noise Study." Also included is his humorous study of Elvis Presley's voice in "Collage No. 1 (Blue Suede)," the terrifying "Fabric for Che," and the illusionary "For Ann (Rising)," an audio version of the persistence-of-motion visual illusion (for example, when a stopped train still seems to a passenger to be moving): tones rise but get nowhere—until the final ascension. Also included is a Nancarrow-like player piano piece but with stochastically generated notes. *—"Blue" Gene Tyranny*

Collage No. 2, Viet Flakes (1967) / 1992 / Musicworks ✦✦✦
A tape collage with silences utilizing snatches of pop music urging love and sensibility ("think about it") contrasted with ominous classical phrases and folk music. Very subtle way to make political/humanist music. *—"Blue" Gene Tyranny*

Three New Seeds / 1993 / Artifact ✦✦✦
In the collection *Arraymusic: New World*. Composed in 1991 for clarinet/bass clarinet, trumpet, contrabass, piano and two percussionists, this piece treats a similar dramatic gesture to three different pointillistic orchestrations. The title is based on a set of very short and early pieces (1956-1957) entitled *Seeds*, which was inspired by the music of Webern, Varése and Cage. *—"Blue" Gene Tyranny*

Virgil Thomson

b. 1896, d. 1989

Thomson is one of the few true modernists in America. Thomson's music is almost disconcertingly spare and direct. In the consciously American pieces especially, there is a kind of aural equivalent to Cubist collage, as ragtime, waltzes, tangos, two-steps, fiddle tunes, and hymns get pasted onto the texture. Unlike Ives, there's an unsentimental distance and clarity to it all, like someone without illusions able to state exactly what's on his mind. Thomson gets this effect in his prose, too. Although overshadowed by Copland (who, by the way, always acknowledged his debts to Thomson), Thomson achieved far more in the realm of opera and vocal music, in which almost everyone acknowledges him a master. Try the powerful (and, to my ear, deeply American) "5 Songs from William Blake," the incredibly beautiful "Feast of Love" for baritone and chamber ensemble (a real lesson in how to vary orchestral texture and how to continue a musical line), "4 Southern Hymns"(a choral classic), the sinewy cello concerto, the "Symphony on a Hymn Tune," "Acadian Songs and Dances" (which deserves the recognition given to the sister suite "Louisiana Story"), "Praises and Prayers," the delicate "4 Songs to Poems of Thomas Campion" for voice and chamber group, and the heartbreaking "Stabat Mater" for mezzo and string quartet. — *Steven Schwartz*

★ **Four Saints in Three Acts (1934)** / Elektra/Nonesuch ◆◆◆◆◆
A setting of the magnificent text by Gertrude Stein (1874-1946). For this opera, Thomson employed her writing technique of having characters and images just appear on the landscape of the stage—no linear plotline, only a real/historical/imaginary connection to a specified subject. This frees the creative process to attempt great character and language combinations that hopefully will provide insights, making for a completely modern opera where melodies, moods, and other elements follow in surprising sequences but with a sense of the whole being always present, what Stein called "the eternal present." There are humorous choruses about "pigeons on the grass, alas," "Lucy Lily"; subtle lines about perception: "the garden inside and outside of the wall"; St. Ignatius predicting the Last Judgment; St. Teresa painting flowers on very large eggs. An all African-American cast gave the first productions of this opera because Thomson wanted clear American speech. Thomson had set three songs on Stein's texts before attempting this opera. — *"Blue" Gene Tyranny*

The Mother of Us All (1947) / 1990 / New World ◆◆◆◆◆
Performed by the Santa Fe Opera. The text for this opera is again by Stein but the organization is somewhat more narrative, with even semblances of a plot. The theme is the life and struggles of suffragette Susan B. Anthony—the weariness of leading a totally public life, and the seemingly endless fight for rights—deep reflections about the meaning of "family" and humanity versus laws. Beautiful atmospheric musical writing. Much of Thomson's other writing is very lyrical, always with a sound of his own, but conventional in structure; however, if you love these operas, try the "Sonata da Chiesa" (Church Sonata) (1926); the award-winning film scores for "The River" (1937), "The Plow That Broke the Plains" (1936), and the "Louisiana Story" (1948); and "A Portrait Album" (Elektra/Nonesuch D4-79024), which contains selections from Thomson's 147 musical portraits of friends—a task similar to Stein's many portraits in writing. — *"Blue" Gene Tyranny*

Helen Thorington

Building a Universe: Rifts, Absences, and Omissions (1987) / 1992 / Musicworks ◆◆◆
An eerie radio piece about modern medicine's total insensitivity toward women's bodies. See also her piece "In the Dark" in the collection *Aerial No. 5*. — *"Blue" Gene Tyranny*

Yasunao Tone

Composer / Electronic, Computer

Musica Iconologos / 1994 / Lovely Music ◆◆◆
In this beautiful CD, Tone continues his refined, elegant work in the transformation of one sense sphere into another (for example, flute tones into computer haiku in "Lyrictron" on Barbara Held's CD in 20th-Century Collections in this section): here, the sound is an encoded description, via a video-to-sound transformation array (bringing to mind David Behrman's '70s installation piece, "Clouds") that scans Chinese character "poems" describing photographic images into an optical music recognition computer program, a very direct process bypassing the electronic-ness of the devices. Intriguing. — *"Blue" Gene Tyranny*

Mark Trayle

b. 1955, California

Composer / Electronic, Computer

Studied at University of Oregon and at Mills College with Robert Ashley, David Behrman and David Rosenboom. Artist-in-residence at STEIM (Amsterdam) and at the Lab. Collaborated with Maryanne Amacher at

the Capp Street Project in SF (1985). Created soundtrack for *Menagerie*, a virtual-reality installation shown at Centre Pompidou in Paris. Article "Nature, Networks, Chamber Music" published in the *Leonardo Music Journal*. — *"Blue" Gene Tyranny*

Etudes and Bagatelles / 1994 / ART ◆◆◆
Found sounds, found processes, and homebrew gear, "the flotsam and jetsam of popular culture." Trayle used a data-glove to manipulate sounds stored in the "virtual shelves" before him in live performance. Terrific. — *"Blue" Gene Tyranny*

Megabitchin' / 1994 / Inial ◆◆◆
In the collection *Views from the Perfect City*. Composed in 1989-92, this live electronic piece uses surf-guitar and cymbal samples, with modifying electronics triggered by a performer wearing a "dataglove." The result is a surreally beautiful "homage to '60s surf music and Gordon Mumma's *Megaton for William Burroughs* (a live electronics classic from the early '60s). — *"Blue" Gene Tyranny*

David Tudor

b. Jan. 20, 1926, Philadelphia, PA, d. Aug. 13, 1996, Tomkins Cove, NY
Composer, pianist / Live Electronic, Neural Systems

Tudor studied organ with William Hawke, composition with Stefan Wolpe, and piano with Irma Wolpe. He premiered many new works of Cage, Boulez, Stockhausen, etc. Tudor pioneered a "live electronic music" performance with John Cage. He began working with the Merce Cunningham Dance Company in 1953, and composing in the late '60s. Tudor taught at the University of California at Davis and at Mills College. He was Artistic Director of Experiments in Art and Technology (E.A.T.) at the Pepsi Pavilion for the Expo '70 in Osaka, Japan. — *"Blue" Gene Tyranny*

★ **Microphone (1975)** / 1991 / Cramps ◆◆◆◆◆
A reissue on CD of this classic. One of the great and wild "live electronic" pieces with sounds that Tudor once described as sounding to him like dinosaur howls echoing in prehistoric caves to timid, sweet calls of unidentifiable creatures. The original circuitry was designed by Tudor and Gordon Mumma. — *"Blue" Gene Tyranny*

Neural Network Plus / 1994 / Lovely Music ◆◆◆
Composed incorporating a synthesizer designed around an analog neural network chip by Intel Corporation, this work was a commission from Merce Cunningham and the Paris Opera to accompany the hour-long dance, "Enter." Well known as both a composer and a brilliant pianist, Tudor continues his pioneering electronic work ("Rainforest IV" on Block Records, "Pulsers" and "Untitled" on Lovely Music, and others) with this piece. — *"Blue" Gene Tyranny*

Neural Synthesis, Nos. 6-8 / 1995 / Lovely Music ◆◆◆
Derived from the score *Neural Synthesis Plus* used to accompany Merce Cunningham's dance "Enter." The primary electronic instrument employed in the piece is a synthesizer with 64 non-linear amplifiers (metaphorical neurons) with 10,240 programmable interconnections, that emulates neuron cells in our brains and can process many analog signals in parallel. Sixteen of the 64 "neurons" are connected in feedback circuits to create sound oscillators, with tank circuits to control their frequencies. During a performance, Tudor chooses up to 14 channels of output, further modifying them with other electronic devices . . . while he also listens, learns patterns (heuristically) and responds and modifies his actions. In this recording, Tudor uses a new binaural technique for translating sound into out-of-head localizations, seeming to surround the listener. For all this technology, the sound results still reflect Tudor's love of simple, characterful sounds that are often drolly humorous even if not identifiable in any ordinary context. — *"Blue" Gene Tyranny*

Three Works for Live Electronics: Pulsers / Untitled / Phonemes / 1996 / Lovely Music ◆◆◆
A CD reissue of the original vinyl release. *Pulsers* (1976), a delightful study of "the world of rhythms created electronically by analog circuitry" using "home-brewed" electronics, incorporating an improvised tape on electronic violin by Takehisa Kosugi. *Untitled* (1972) is an experiment in multiple feedback loops in real spaces, recorded, mixed and played back to loops in other spaces—electronic music without oscillators or recorded natural sound materials. *Phonemes* (1981) is an additional piece to the original vinyl release, which uses a percussion generator and a vocoder with small discrete bands to take short sounds and lengthen them, or long sounds and shorten them in a unique live interplay. — *"Blue" Gene Tyranny*

Simon Fisher Turner

Blue (Music for the Film by Derek Jarman) / 1994 / Mute/Elektra Nonesuch ◆◆◆
To write music to underscore a political message, to protest war, to promote human rights, or, in this case, to respond to the current AIDS plague are difficult enough assignments. To also be sensitive to a brilliant and moving text, that contains an artist's deepest feelings in the form of ironic personal stories ("With yellow infection bubbling at the corner I

said this looks like a planet. The doctor says 'Oh, I think it looks like a pizza' ") and transcendent poetic expression, is a more challenging task. On the screen, and on the CD booklet and disc label, we see only the color blue, no images. In the soundtrack, with some additional music—Brian Eno, Szymanowski ("Scheherazade" from "The Masques") "Disco Hospital," Satie etc.—and several excellent surreal environment ambience segues, Turner succeeds in inventing a dramatic score of great variety. It works best when the sound avoids directly illustrating one-for-one the images in the text; otherwise, at times the effect is like Orson Welles delivering a mythological radio play, which overwhelms the humanity and directness of the text. "From the bottom of your heart, pray to be released from image," Jarman exhorts us, "Blue is the universal love in which man bathes—it is the terrestial paradise." *—"Blue" Gene Tyranny*

"Blue" Gene Tyranny (Robert Sheff)

Robert Sheff, aka *Blue* Gene Tyranny, has composed and performed avant-garde music for 30 years, writing over 60 works for various ensembles of electronic and acoustic instruments and voices. He has produced and recorded many albums of music by other composers, published articles on contemporary music, and composed over 30 soundtracks for film and video productions. He writes for *Music with Roots in the Ether* and *Music Beyond the Boundaries*, and his compositions have been reviewed in *Sonic Transports, Soundpieces 2: Interviews with American Composers*, and *Talking Music: Conversations with Five Generations of American Experimental Composers*. He has received a New York Foundation for the Arts Fellowship in Composition. *—AMG*

Real Life and the Movies / 1981 / Fun Music ✦✦✦

Intermediary, The / 1982 / Lovely Music ✦✦✦✦✦
This spontaneously performed piano piece is shadowed interactively by computer voicings designed by Joel Ryan. An illusion is created—the inspirational "message" seems to occur sometimes before and sometimes after the performer plays material of similar shape: time linear and all-at-once. "A genuine delight."*—Recordings of Experimental Music.—AMG*

Free Delivery / 1990 / Lovely Music ✦✦✦✦✦
Live keyboard performances from 1983-1989. Includes: "Five Takes on the Nocturne with and without Memory" (1989) for solo piano, "The Country Boy Country Dog Intro" (1984) for piano and tape, "The Intermediary Following Traces of the Song" (1988) for acoustic piano and live sampling keyboard, "The Intermediary with a Rendition of Stardust" (1983) for solo piano and electronics, and "Sunrise or Sunset in Texas" (1983) from a film soundtrack." "Blue" Gene Tyranny: Cecil Taylor's keyboard energy, Morton Feldman's ear—the most original aspect of [his] works is the way they create continuity: they're tonal, yet rigorously asymmetrical. They satisfy the ear without letting it take anything for granted. They evolve, with the labyrinthine irreversibility of deep psychic forces." Kyle Gann (*The Village Voice*). *—AMG*

Nocturne with and without Memory / In Lois Svard's "With and without Memory" / 1994 / Lovely Music ✦✦✦

Country Boy Country Dog / How to Discover Music in the Sounds of Your Daily Life / 1994 / Lovely Music ✦✦✦
In a small Midwestern town, a natural mystery that's always been there is revealed. Using the procedural score "How to Discover Music in the Sounds of Your Daily Life" (1967), a variety of orchestral, electronic, and natural sounds describe the interaction between mental events and the daily environment: the "inside"—intuitive decision, spontaneous mental activity, feeling—and the "outside" that makes up reality. The score sets up an ecological chain in which natural sounds and voices are recorded and analyzed electronically (for hidden rhythmic codes, continuous melodic streams, harmonic attractions), and then electro-acoustical pieces are made from these analyses and played back into the environment. The five parts form an "audio-storyboard" (a movie soundtrack independent of a film): "A Dream without Images" (before dawn, inside); "The CBCD Intro" (sunrise, outside); "Country Boy Country Dog" (midday, inside and out); "X Marks the Spot (Daydream)" (afternoon, inside); and "The CBCD Variations for Soloist and Orchestra" (twilight, outside). *—AMG*

Vladimir Ussachevsky

Suite from "No Exit" (1962) / Line of Apogee (1967) / 1990 / New World ✦✦✦✦✦
Two lyrical, eerie, and innovative film scores for the film of Sartre's play and Lloyd William's avant-garde film by the master of the Columbia-Princeton electronic music sound. Also employs vocal, animal, and environmental sounds. (See also "Pioneers of Electronic Music" in 20th-Century Collections in this section.) *—"Blue" Gene Tyranny*

Galina Ustvolskaya

b. Jun. 17, 1919, Petrograd, Russia
Composer / Experimental Instrumental and Vocal, Neo-primitive, Religious Works
Ustvolskaya studied with Dimitri Shoshtakovitch until 1947 and at the

Conservatory of Petrograd from 1937-1939. Often criticized for her modernism, she was defended by Shoshtakovitch. Also an instrument builder of unique instruments for her pieces. *—"Blue" Gene Tyranny*

Composition I / Composition II / Composition III / 1995 / Philips ✦✦✦
Performed by the Schönberg Ensemble, conducted by Reinbert De Leeuw. A pupil of Shostakovich, Ustvolskaya remained for many years both in isolation from musical styles in the West, and rejected any kowtowing to the official musical circles in Russia, which often attacked her for her "modernism." She thus maintained a freshness in her music that is imbued in its aesthetic and sound with an almost prehistoric love of directness. The cycle of works, *Composition I / Composition II / Composition III*, is intended to be played in a church, and forms a kind of instrumental version of the mass. *Composition I*—Dona nobis pacem (1970-71) is scored for the odd combination of piccolo, tuba, and piano and is a plea for peace on earth. The subtle shiftings and rhythmic variations are subtly complex, so that the listener is always kept aware of the raw, bracing directness of expression. Composed in 1972-73, the second part, *Composition II*—Dies irae, is evocative of ancient Coptic Christian music, and is scored for eight double basses, a 43 x 43 centimeter cubical drum, and piano. Some of the orchestral combinations are almost brutal, with prehistoric vigor and highly evocative, gut feeling. Part X alternates between very peaceful, quiet notes, an insistent chant pattern, and loud (Judgement?) knocks on the drum. The effect is deeply shocking. The third section of the composer's religious triptych, *Composition III*—Benedictus qui venit, composed in 1974-75, is scored for another unusual ensemble combination: four flutes, four bassoons, and piano, and is perhaps the purest of the pure, utilizing only two primary elements: a steady beat chant harmonized in clusters distributed amongst the ensemble, alternating with more sustained cluster groups out of which a single note steadily emerges, like a plea. Its effect is again that of people discovering music for the first time—directly connecting an instrument to their range of feeling-thought (to borrow Buckminster Fuller's expression), not barbarically, but with little distance between the particular emotion and an expressive medium. *—"Blue" Gene Tyranny*

Peter Van Riper

Sound to Movement / VRBLU ✦✦✦
Beautiful sax music sometimes played while spinning, sometimes mixed with natural sounds. Similar work can be heard in "Room Space" (VRBLU 13) and "Indian Circle" (VRBLU 16). *—AMG*

Heart (from Acoustic Metal Music) / 1992 / Aerial #4 ✦✦✦
Playing on a twirling metal strip about eight feet long which a sculptor-friend used to make interlocking heart constructions, Van Riper makes a transparently beautiful and almost electronic effect. *—"Blue" Gene Tyranny*

Windows to the Sky / Van Riper Editions ✦✦✦
Subtly mixed and modified pieces based on mysterious environmental and pre-verbal human sounds, "Windows to the Sky" is a vocal duo, with high sliding tones and low drones; "Synchronies" features wood, glass, and mechanical sounds in some mysterious place; in "Nook and Cranny," suspended bells and tuned bowls underscore delicate vocal intoning; "Sustainable Music: Acoustic Cups" is a mix of strange breathing sounds (like blowing up a balloon) with light chimes and rain and the sounds of moving, unidentifiable objects; "Susmusic I" is a set of variations on bells with water sounds (and in the background a family pet is being called by name); "Susmusic II—in memory of John Cage," is made from environmental sounds, children's voices with sustained bell resonances, bird squawks, various drier percussion rattles, and a "Coda" of light bell sounds; for "Limits," a highly reverberated rainstick is the primary sound, with mysterious low rolling and clicking sounds gradually added into the mix; the pertinently titled "What's Going On" is composed of rain, birdsong, footsteps walking around, and sustained bell sounds; the final "d'Accord" contrasts electronic pulsing and reverberated clicking which is interrupted at times by duet drone singing. *—"Blue" Gene Tyranny*

David Van Tieghem

New York-based percussionist David Van Tieghem has shown a remarkably broad sense of what constitutes a percussion instrument, "playing" everything from kitchen items to a theater itself. Sometimes coming under the heading "performance art," his work as a soloist with several albums under his own name and as an accompanist to Laurie Anderson and others is wildly imaginative. *— William Ruhlmann*

Safety in Numbers / 1987 / Private Music ✦✦✦
Not comfortably labeled new-age, or percussion music, or pop, or electronic music, Van Tieghem's music has that "downtown" mix of all these and yet is distinctly his own: from the lush "Crystals" to the droll and rhythm-steady "Night of the Cold Noses." This is twisted "easy listening." *—"Blue" Gene Tyranny*

Edgard Varése

b. 1883, d. 1965

Composer / Innovative Orchestral Textures, Electronic, Timbre Clusters
French-American composer of music for orchestra, percussion ensemble,
and electronic music, using theremin, Ondes Martenot, tape, and early
electronic devices; his works emphasize dissonance, intricate rhythms,
and the exploration of sound. —*AMG*

★ **Offrandes (1921) / Integrales (1925) / Octandre (1923) / Ecuatorial
(1934) / 1990 / Elektra/Nonesuch ◆◆◆◆◆**
The Contemporary Chamber Ensemble, conducted by Arthur Weisberg.
The best performances available of Varése's acoustic and vocal works.
"Ancient Forests," "Queen of the Polar Dawns," the sacred Mayan
texts—musical and verbal imagery par excellence. —*"Blue" Gene Tyranny*

☆ **Poeme Electronique (1958) / In "Electroacoustic Music: Classics" /
1990 / Neuma ◆◆◆◆◆**
A visionary piece: "opacities and rarefactions," the jungle, outer space,
the Golden Section, strange ceremonies. The booklet that comes with
the CD includes a spectrogram score of the music. —*"Blue" Gene Tyranny*

**Integrales for 11 Winds and Percussionists (1924-1925) / Ameriques (1918-1922) / Arcana (1927) for 120 Musicians / Density
21.5 / 1990 / Sony Classical ◆◆◆**
The wonderful orchestral music conducted by Pierre Boulez—not the
best performances but passable, and the only one of "Arcana" currently
available. "Ameriques" is played beautifully on Vanguard Classics OVC
4031 by the Utah Orchestra, conducted by Maurice Abravanel. Watch for
future recordings of "Deserts" with the original tape interpolations (once
available on the out-of-print disc *The Varese Record* on Finnadar SR
9018, issued 1977, with notes by Frank Zappa). —*"Blue" Gene Tyranny*

Lois Vierk

Simoom / 1992 / Experimental Intermedia ◆◆◆◆◆
Cuts include "Go Guitars," for five electric guitars; "Cirrus," for six trumpets; "Simoom," for eight cellos. Sighing, sliding tones, rhythmic pulse,
strange harmonics. Reaches an indescribable state, like music from an
unknown culture. Influenced by Japanese Buddhist chant. Seriously
meditative. —*"Blue" Gene Tyranny*

**Manhattan Cascade / In Guy Klucevsek's "Manhattan Cascade" /
1992 / CRI ◆◆◆**
A beautiful work that gradually develops from repeating single tones to
masses of swirling clusters. More of a horizontal "cascade" between harmonic dimensions than a vertical "waterfall." —*"Blue" Gene Tyranny*

Timberline / 1995 / O.O. Discs ◆◆◆
In the collection *Relache: Outcome Inevitable*. In *Timberline* (1991),
written for ensemble, sliding mournful wind and string tones, a simple
piano arpeggio, pentatonic scales, and woodblock tones (imitating the
piano arpeggios) are gradually added together and then endlessly varied. A lovely outdoors sense is created. At the five-minute mark, a cymbal crash begins the process again, very slowly, with new material:
pitches slightly varied, pulsations in the winds and strings (like an imitation of electronically decaying echoes), slow and low sliding tones, lyrical and pulsing material in the piano part, flutters in the winds, cymbal
crashes, high drum rhythms. Gradually the ensemble becomes more
mechanistically rhythmical, with descending glissandi added to the
piano part. This seems to depict the chopping and felling of trees.
—*"Blue" Gene Tyranny*

Claude Vivier

b. 1948, Montreal, Canada, d. 1983, Paris, France

Composer / Acoustic, World-music Influenced, Pattern Music
Studied with Gilles Tremblay and Irving Heller, Stockhausen, Koenig
and Paul Mefano. Named Composer of the Year by Canadian Music
Council (1982). Influenced by travels in Bali and Thailand. —*"Blue" Gene
Tyranny*

Et Je Reverrai Cette Ville Étrange / 1988 / Artifact ◆◆◆
In the collection *Arraymusic: Strange City*. A very odd suite of six movements with very strange and unique timbres—something like wheezing
winds, Chinese opera orchestra textures, Harry Partch pieces; but really
different from all of those—and lots of noble, melodic, moving, colorful
unisons. Truly a strange city! "As the title suggests, this piece is a comeback to a certain spot in my life, certain melodies. Melancholia derives
from my taste for past stories, my own stories, few melodies embedded
into silence, into the time continuum. This piece is an act of despair insofar as creation is always trying to link past and future, melancholia and
hope, to recreate the time continuum that human life has disrupted"
(Vivier). —*"Blue" Gene Tyranny*

Larry Wendt

Bring Your Mom Too / WEN 04 (Frog Peak Music) ◆◆◆
"Sadness Without Brains" is a sound-assembly cassette of small hand
tools, amplified auto parts, shortwave radios, stories, junk, and an assortment of other sounds. The tape is packaged in a metal case opened with
a Phillips-head screwdriver. Other Wendt cassettes are available from
the same distributor: "Guided Missile Favorites," "Slowscan vol. 3" with
Nicolas Collins, "Upper and Lower California," "Live from Bakersfield."
—*"Blue" Gene Tyranny*

Kenneth Werner (aka Phil Harmonic)

Composer / Tape, Theater, Alternate Sound Spaces & Installations
A fascinating pianist/electronic keyboardist who is bound by few restrictions. An absolutely astounding trio pianist, he can back singers (notably
Roseanna Vitro) with perfect empathy and has done some interesting
synthesizer programming. —*Michael G. Nastos*

**Timing (1978) / In "Blue" Gene Tyranny's "Just for the Record" /
1979 / Lovely Music ◆◆◆◆◆**
Improvised, sustained synthesizer chords are changed on a spontaneous
verbal cue from the composer. A simple but surprisingly engaging experience for the listener: the externalization of a musical sense that the
public normally never hears. Werner also created many art installations
in the form of walk-in store fronts called "Art While You Wait." (See also
Lovely Little Records in 20th-Century Collections in this section.)
—*"Blue" Gene Tyranny*

Hildegard Westerkamp

Composer / Acoustic Ecology, Tape, Environmental Sounds
Teaches courses in acoustic communication at SFU. —*"Blue" Gene Tyranny*

Cricket Voice (1987) / 1990 / The Aerial ◆◆◆
Score from electronically modified environmental sounds made by
"playing" the desert (plucking on cactus spikes, dried roots, and palm
leaves; resonance of an old water reservoir). Beautifully assembled.
—*"Blue" Gene Tyranny*

Gregory Whitehead

**William S. Burroughs Tape Worm Mutation (1991), The / 1992 /
Musicworks ◆◆◆**
A hilarious piece for speaker and audience response, in which the
degenerative re-recording of a voice leads one through human aging
and the gradual complete breakdown of spoken language. The phrase
chosen to be treated to 327 degenerations is aptly, "I am a degenerate."
—*"Blue" Gene Tyranny*

Christian Wolff

b. Mar. 8, 1934, Nice, France

Composer / Indeterminate, Political, Graphic Notations
Wolff studied a few weeks with John Cage, but otherwise self-taught. The
pianist and guitarist received his Ph.D. in Comparative Literature from
Harvard. Pioneered scores in open instrumentation, open cueing systems, scores for non-musicians and, along with others, scores in verbal
instructions only. Teacher, Classics Department at Harvard (1962-70), lecturer Darmstadt 1972 and '74, Classics/Comparative Lit. & Music at Dartmouth. Wolff's works include: "Changing the System" (1973), "Peace
Marches 1, 2 & 3" (1984), "Black Song Organ Preludes" (1987), "Play"
(1968), "For Five or Ten Players" (1962). —*"Blue" Gene Tyranny*

**Summer (1961) for String Quartet / In "The Avant-Garde String
Quartet in the U.S.A." / Vox Box ◆◆◆**
A sensitive performance of this graph score in the composer's "early"
style. —*"Blue" Gene Tyranny*

**"For 1, 2, or 3 People" (1964) / In "A Second Wind for Organ" / 1968
/ Odyssey ◆◆◆**
A sensitive, imaginative realization by David Tudor using the baroque
organ like a synthesizer. Sounds never to be expected from a baroque
organ. Great recording in wide stereo adds to the effect. Tudor has a
refined sense of timing. —*"Blue" Gene Tyranny*

☆ **Mayday Materials/ In CDCM Computer Music Series, Vol. 6 / 1990 /
Centaur ◆◆◆◆◆**
A "mix of abstraction, lightheartedness, and perhaps political suggestiveness," an interesting combination of Wolff's earlier new-music sensibilities and his later use of folk songs as guiding lines (rather than directly
quoted). Nine out of 20 pieces made for a dance by Lucinda Childs.
—*"Blue" Gene Tyranny*

**Malvina (1989) for Koto / In Kazue Sawai's "Three Pieces" / 1992 /
Jasrac ◆◆◆**
A tribute to Malvina Reynolds, a singer and songwriter who championed the causes of oppressed people. The composer scored variable tun-

ing changes on Reynolds' "On the Rim of the World" and Walter Robinson's song "Harriet Tubman"—six sections of running or sustained sounds, and a certain range of freedom is indicated on how the performer may play. A delicate combination of tune and contemporary procedures. —*"Blue" Gene Tyranny*

For Prepared Piano (1951) / For 1, 2, or 3 People (1964) / In "The New York School" / 1993 / Hat Hut ✦✦✦

Two classic turning points in contemporary music. Concerning "For Prepared Piano," Wolff was once asked to close the window while he was playing (I believe it was) this piece. But he declined, saying that all the sounds happening at that moment constituted the music. Excellent performances and realizations of the score. —*"Blue" Gene Tyranny*

Stefan Wolpe

String Quartet (1968-1969) / 1991 / CRI ✦✦✦✦✦

Performed by the Juilliard String Quartet. Although writing in a strict atonal style, Wolpe wrote clear, angular music that wove gestures directly appealing to the body senses, sometimes with a sense of humor; a nonabstract academic composer (not always recognized as one by contemporary academics). This Quartet is one of his finest works and stands out among the other two works on this CD by Roger Sessions and Milton Babbitt. Also recommended are "Enactments for Three Pianos" (1950-1953) on Elektra/Nonesuch 78024-4 (cassette tape) and the "Passacaglia" from *Four Studies of Basic Rows* (1936) on New World NW-344-2. —*"Blue" Gene Tyranny*

Quartet for Trumpet, Tenor Saxophone, Percussion and Piano / Nonesuch ✦✦✦

Performed by the Contemporary Chamber Ensemble, Arthur Weisberg, conductor. Written in 1950 and revised in 1954, this piece marked the beginning of a new phase of complex work of Wolpe's in the mid-'50s. However, it is highly "accessible" music with gestures and melodic arcs clearly defined, original and emotionally appealing. Wolpe was always influenced by the socially conscious Gebrauchsmusik (music for everyday use) movement in the '20s and '30s in Europe. In the first movement, a central rising and falling, somewhat wistful melodic gesture is shared and reinterpreted by each player. In the second movement, the influence of American jazz can be clearly felt among the almost-Dixieland complexity of counterpoint; it is still a European idea of jazz however, recalling textures of Darius Milhaud's *La Création du Monde* of 1923. New methods of non-linear continuity (partial canonic imitation, for example) are explored by Wolpe in this work as in others appearing at this time, so the music has fluidity and a captivating modern tunefulness throughout. —*"Blue" Gene Tyranny*

Ivan Wyschnegradsky

Compositions for String Quartet and String Trio / 1990 / Edition Block ✦✦✦

Performed by the Arditti String Quartet. Includes the three microintervallic string quartets, a Composition (op. 43), and a Trio (op. 53). A pioneer (with Willy Moellendorf, Joerg Mager, Alois Haba, and Fredrich Trautwein) in quarter-tone and "ultrachromatic" music. The "Trio," with its tone leaps that collapse into each other, and the first quartet are probably the most unique discoveries. —*"Blue" Gene Tyranny*

Iannis Xenakis

Composer / Electronic, Orchestral Architectonics, Math Theory
Greek-born French composer whose mathematical compositional techniques and electronic media in orchestral, chamber, choral, vocal, ballet, and acoustic works have considerably influenced the development of composition in Europe and America. —*Mary K. Scanlan*

Medea for Male Choir, Hand-held Stones, and Orchestra / 1969 / Erato ✦✦✦✦✦

Performed by the Orchestra and Choir of the French Radio-Televisio, directed by Marius Constant. A good combination of Xenakis' more spare abstract music combined with ancient Greek chant: more involving than the often-violent themes or forced humor of his music based on stochastic procedures, transformation groups, Poisson's law of probabilities, etc., where structure is the only content. But some people like that sort of thing. This record also includes "Syrmos," for 18 strings, and "Polytope," for four orchestras disseminated in the audience." —*"Blue" Gene Tyranny*

Mycenae-Alpha (1978) / In "Electroacoustic Music: Classics" / 1990 / Neuma ✦✦✦

Images of natural phenomena digitized directly into dense and intense computer music. —*"Blue" Gene Tyranny*

Jonchaies / 1991 / Col Legno ✦✦✦

In the collection *20 Ans de Musique Contemporaine á Metz*, performed by the Nouvel Orchestre Philharmonique, conducted by Gilbert Amy. Premiered in 1981, this orchestral piece is both similar and very differ-

ent from the usual Xenakis "sound." It begins with a giantic glissando for the entire orchestra, and there are the sound-masses that characterize much of Xenakis' orchestra writing. But then he creates wonderful harmonies around a simple Phrygian (Japanese) mode melody, and celebratory, steadily phasing rhythms undulating between two tone clusters. A massive and crazed dance develops from simple beats to ragtime syncopation. Great masses of sliding brass sound like great beasts and sawing strings create a marvelous new texture unheard before in orchestra writing. A uniquely different and attractive manner of writing for this composer. —*"Blue" Gene Tyranny*

Gayle Young

Amaranth / Musicworks ✦✦✦

A fascinating work by this important Canadian composer, instrument builder, author, and editor of *Musicworks* magazine. —*"Blue" Gene Tyranny*

La Monte Young

b. 1935, Berne, ID
Composer / Alternative Tuning, Meditation, Minimalist, Jazz-influenced
The founder of the Theater of Eternal Music, Young studied sax and clarinet with William Green at the L.A. Conservatory of Music, composition with Leonard Stein and Seymour Shifrin. He composed electronic music with Richard Maxfield at the New School for Social Research, North Indian classical vocal music with Pandit Pran Nath. His early work involved verbal instruction pieces, later pieces utilizing just intonation and large time scales. He was awarded a Guggenheim Fellowship and DAAD residency in Berlin. Young's pieces include "The Four Dreams of China" (1962), "The Lower Map of the Eleven's Division in the Romantic Symmetry" (over a 60-Cycle Base) in Prime Time form from 144 to 112 with 119 (1989-90), "Chronos Kristalla" for string quartet (1990). —*"Blue" Gene Tyranny*

89 VI 8 C. 1:42-1:52 AM Paris Encore from "Poem for Chairs, Tables, Benches, Etc." (1960) / In "Fluxtellus" / Tellus ✦✦✦

A piece with a verbal instruction score (what we used to call "music without notes," "procedural music," or "events," etc.—see the FluxTellus collection) that uses the floor sounds of precisely moved furniture in a resonate space. Young's "early style." —*"Blue" Gene Tyranny*

☆ **90 XII 9C. 9:35-10:52 PM NYC, The Melodic Version (1984) of the Second Dream of the High-Tension Line Stepdown Transformer from the Four / 1991 / Gramavision ✦✦✦✦✦**

Eight trumpets with Harmon mutes slowly develop, over a 60-plus minute duration, an image, in just intonation tuning, of the gradual accumulation of harmonics one might hear in a high-tension line as voltages change and intermodulate each other. In the liner notes, Young recalls two such listening experiences in his life: one next to a telephone pole in Bern, ID, and the other near 20 transformers outside of Montpelier where his grandfather ran a gas station. Mysterious and meditative. Tuning as a function of events compared over time. —*"Blue" Gene Tyranny*

The Well Tuned Piano / Gramavision ✦✦✦

The legendary just intonation work in a set of five CDs. The booklet goes on a bit much justifying Young's place in history, so just listen to the music which is non-virtuosic in the usual sense, and pleasant. —*"Blue" Gene Tyranny*

Isang Yun

b. Sep. 17, 1917, Korea
Composer / Orchestral, Vocal, Atonal-chromatic, Korean Folk Song-influenced
The soaring, impassioned *Symphonies Nos. 1 & 3* of Isang Yun come from the heart of a man persecuted by the paranoia of the state "authorities"—works written after he was twice imprisoned by South Korean police on suspicion of espionage, once even being kidnapped by them from Europe and forced back to South Korea. (He is, of course, innocent of these "crimes.") Yun is one of our fine new symphonists. —*"Blue" Gene Tyranny*

Fanfare and Memorial / Distanzen (Distances) / Etudes for Flute Solo / 1992 / Arcadia ✦✦✦

Fanfare and Memorial is a highly original work for large orchestra composed in 1979. The composer manages to balance directness and emotional tension with grace and clarity even in the richer orchestral writing. In this work, the listener can immediately sense the depth of emotional understanding possessed by this often honored composer, whose life has been filled with turmoil—he studied in Japan (during the 35-year occupation of Korea), was arrested and imprisoned by the Japanese for underground activities, escaped to Seoul, was active in Korean culture and studied in Paris and Germany, was kidnapped with his wife from Berlin in 1967 by agents of the South Korean Secret Service, imprisoned for life but released after worldwide protests, including a petition from 180 composers, including Stravinsky, and he is now a German citizen. In *Distanzen* (1988) for woodwind quintet and string quintet, the performers surround the audience, or in a standard concert hall proscenium sit with the strings in front and the woodwinds behind. As in other works by Yun, there is a semi-narrative contrast and intermixing between moments of high dramatic tension, gentle beauty and compassion, and a serene transcendence. — *"Blue" Gene Tyranny*

Frank Zappa (Francis Vincent Zappa)

See the Rock section for his biography.

Freak Out! (1966) / 1966 / Verve ✦✦✦
An early "art rock" album with a unified program throughout the whole ("concept album"): characterized by unusual rhythmic meters and a wide use of sound-processing techniques available at that time (speed changes, tape delay, multitracking, echo, and flanging). The final piece, "The Return of the Son of Monster Magnet," is pure musique concrète. The albums *Lumpy Gravy* Verve V6-8741, 1967) and *Uncle Meat* (Bizarre 2Ms-2024, 1969), are also recommended for these techniques, as well as the use of orchestral sections mostly written in a Varése-wannabe style. —*"Blue" Gene Tyranny*

Black Page (1977), The / 1987 / Keyboard Magazine ✦✦✦✦✦
A floppy vinyl disc insert of an extremely interesting one-line solo programmed on a Synclavier. The solo is notated in complex polyrhythmic ratios (à la Stockhausen), but has the effect of the "stretch-rhythm" used in the most sensitive jazz solos. A score is included in the text of the magazine. —*"Blue" Gene Tyranny*

John Zorn

Composer / Jazz- and World Music-influenced, Group Improvisation
See the Jazz section for his biography.

Yankees / 1983 / Celluloid Cell ✦✦✦✦
A collective improvisation by Derek Bailey (acoustic and electric guitars), George Lewis (trombone), John Zorn (alto and soprano saxes, clarinets, game calls). Subtle, droll, hilarious takes on the trivia of baseball sounds—Lewis speaks through the trombone, "ball one, ball one"; there are snippets of a slipping and sliding version of "Take Me Out to the Ball Game"; and so on. Sections are titled "City City City"; "The Legend of Enos Slaughter"; "Who's on First"; followed by "On Golden Pond," a tongue-in-cheek tone poem of the flora and fauna, mosquitos, etc.; and "The Warning Track," about a very tiny railroad system. —*"Blue" Gene Tyranny*

Classic Guide to Strategy, The / 1985 / Lumina ✦✦✦
Solo woodwind improvisations with gamecalls, parts of saxes and clarinets. Eccentric, pure Zorn. —*"Blue" Gene Tyranny*

Classic Guide to Strategy, Vol. 2, The / 1986 / Lumina ✦✦✦
More beautifully intense solo pieces with inflections like ancient Japanese music. Sections are named after various Japanese artists: Aoyama Michi, Enoken, Kazumi Shigeru, Kondo Toshinori, Yano Akiko, Togawa Jun, and Mori Ikue. Cover art is calligraphy of the character for "water." —*"Blue" Gene Tyranny*

Cobra / 1990 / Hat Art ✦✦✦
A studio and live performance recording with many of NYC's "downtown" improvisors: Anthony Coleman, Bill Frisell, Wayne Horwitz, Bob James, Guy Klucesvek, Arto Lindsay, Christian Marclay, Zeena Parkins, Bobby Previte, Elliott Sharp, Jim Staley, David Weinstein, J. A. Deane, and Carol Emanuel. —*"Blue" Gene Tyranny*

More News for Lulu / 1992 / Hat Hut ✦✦✦✦✦
Another CD of wonderful trio improvisations with John Zorn, George Lewis, and, this time, Bill Frisell. Odd, humorous, melodic, dramatic. —*"Blue" Gene Tyranny*

Elegy / Oct. 1995 / Tzadik ✦✦✦
A mysterious, elegant, exotic tone poem built around Jean Genet's image relating flowers and prisoners. There are four parts, entitled *Blue, Yellow, Pink* and *Black.* A constantly changing soundscape of images—sweet, tortured, folk ceremony, hellishly cosmic, dungeon sounds of chains and locks, breathing and much more—highlighted by silences. Brilliantly evocative. With Barbara Chaffe, alto and bass flutes, David Abel, viola, Scummy, guitar, David Shea, turntables, David Slusser, sound effects, William Winant, percussion, and Mike Patton, voice. — *"Blue" Gene Tyranny*

Peter Zummo

b. 1948, East Cleveland, OH
Composer / Group Improvisation, Extended Wind Instrument Techniques, Open Scoring
Zummo received instrument training on trombone and other winds with the legendary Carmine Caruso. Also studied with Roswell Rudd and Jim Fulkerson, didjeridu with Stuart Dempster, electronic music with Alvin Lucier, and was in the World Music program at Wesleyan University.

Zummo's many compositions for ensemble (including Zummo Labs, the Environmental Combo, etc.) build on original melody and melodic fragments, generating interactive situations for musicians. "Radical Filtering" premiered at the BAM Next Wave Festival, "Semiotic Handgun" premiered at Lincoln Center Out-Of-Doors, "Fast Dream" at Boston Opera House. Zummo composed music for dancer Trisha Brown's *Newark* and *Lateral Pass*, and several other dance and theater works. —*"Blue" Gene Tyranny*

Zummo with an X—Contains: Instruments (1980) / Song IV from the Suite Six Songs (Commissioned for Trisha Brown's Dance "Lateral" / 1985 / Loris Bend Foundation ✦✦✦✦✦
"Instruments" is a pure, spare study of musical intervals with a gently humorous quality, using phase (mobile) techniques to produce variations. The "Six Songs" are all played over the same peacefully persuasive tabla pulse from Bill Ruyle; Arthur Russell's singing and cello playing (harmonics, counter-rhythms) together creating one warm voice; and Peter Zummo's open and muted trombone statements (simple riffs, sweet pleas, and sometimes snores)—all combine to make an irresistible mental dance. Highly recommended. —*"Blue" Gene Tyranny*

Experimenting with Household Chemicals / 1995 / Experimental Intermedia ✦✦✦
Another great CD, like a suite but continuous: "Fresh Batteries," "Includes Free Information," "Sung, Played, Heard," "Rocket Scientist," "In Three Movements," and "Peaceful Transportation." With many of the same qualities as the album above, obviously including the gentle humor. Highly recommended. —*"Blue" Gene Tyranny*

Various Artists

20 Ans de Musique Contemporaine á Metz (20 Years of Contemporary Music at Metz) / 1991 / Col Legno ✦✦✦
A five-CD set with booklet containing premieres of important contemporary works, mostly orchestral. Contains: Rolf Gehlhaar's "Phase" (1972), Yoshihisa Taïra's "Radiance" (1973), Morton Feldman's "Piano and Orchestra" (1975), Pierre Boulez's "Rituel in memoriam Bruno Maderna" (1976), Kazimierz Serocki's "Pianophonie" (1978), Iannis Xenakis' "Jonchaies" (1981), Michaël Levinas' "Les rires du Gilles [The Laughter of Gilles]" (1981), Bernd Alois Zimmermann's "Musique pour les soupers du Ubu Roi [Music for the Suppers of King Ubu]" (1982) , György Ligeti's "Magyar Etüdök [Hungarian Etudes for 16-voice a capella choir]" (1983), Paul Méfano's "La Scéne III" (1984), Klaus Huber's "2. Streichquartett erster Satz [2nd String Quartet, First Movement]" (1985), Younghi Pagh-Paan's "Nim" (1987), John Cage's "ASLSP Organ 2" (1987), Luigi Nono's "A Carlo Scarpa Architetto Ai Suoi Infiniti Possibili [To Carlo Scarpa, Architect, to His Infinite Possibilities]" (1987), Mauricio Kagel's "Quodlibet" (1988), Carlos Roqué Alsina's "Suite indirecte" (1989), Bruno Maderna's "Giardino Religioso [The Religious Garden]" (1989), and Hans Zender's "Furin No Kyo" [literal translation: "Wind Bell Stillness Mute"], based on a Zen text sung in four languages (1989). —*"Blue" Gene Tyranny*

Act of Finding / 1995 / O.O. Discs ✦✦✦
A collection of pieces by members of the group Act of Finding, "a collective quartet dedicated to group improvisation." Includes: Ratso B. Harris' *To Dick Dickson*—a humorous narrative from comic books, e-mail, and other periodicals found while the composer was moving, delivered rhythmically over bass patterns from a thesaurus of scales and patterns; Tom Hamilton's "Another Family Resemblance"—a charming song with reminiscences; Bruce Arnold's "Quiet Is the Movement of the Moon"—a pointillistic-like and often funny-sweet study in rhythms derived from the title; Ratso B. Harris' "Solos"—a timbrally rich and wonderfully odd redefinition of the idea of soloist with accompaniment; Bruce Arnold's "Silent Travels"—a delicate etude in silent moments and touches of inspired sound combinations that gradually replace the silence; a collective work, *New Territory (Spring Collection)*, with individual movements entitled "Fast Fast Fast Fast Fast Slow" (Harris)—a robust rhythmic gem with textures from free-jazz and free-rock and that special Act of Finding mania; "Textural Threads" (Arnold), with some incredible electronic work; "Can't See the Figure for the Ground" (Tom Buckner), in which soloist and accompanist roles are quickly switched; and "Destination A" (Harris), in which the group improvises over an unresolved drone; and the concluding work by Bruce Arnold, "Now and Then," for which the group creates a spontaneous, time-stretching and beautifully rich environment about a repeated lyrical melody. —*"Blue" Gene Tyranny*

Aerial #1—A Journal in Sound, The / Aerial ✦✦✦
Contains: David Moss "Language Linkage" / Terry Setter "Aphorism III; Like a Coat or Mask" / Christine Baczewska "Day of the Dead" / Richard Kostelanetz "Murdoch and the Sufi from Invocations" / Rich Jensen "Folly" / Loren Mazzacane and Suzanne Langille "Haunted House" / Lost Souls "Idumea" / Malcolm Goldstein "Qerneraq; Our Breath As Bones" / Floating Concrete Octopus "Burial Song" / Jerry Hunt "Babalon (String)" / Stuart Sherman "Four Sound Pieces: Doors, Water, Click, Pin-Ball" / Bern Porter "The Last Acts of St. Fuckyou." —*"Blue" Gene Tyranny*

Aerial #2—A Journal in Sound, The / Aerial ✦✦✦✦✦
Contains: Bob Davis and Jon Raskin "Poison Hotel" / David Dunn "Chaos and the Emergent Mind of the Pond" / Jin Hi Kim "Komungo Permutations" / Jeff Greinke "Road to Solo" / Christopher Shultis "Motion/less" / Chris Cochrane "Santiago Penando Estas" / Sue Ann Harkey "In This Year of the Snake" / Annea Lockwood "Nautilus" / LaDonna Smith and Davey Williams "Green Song" / Hildegard Westerkamp "Cricket Voice." —*"Blue" Gene Tyranny*

The Aerial # 3 / 1991 / Aerial ✦✦✦
Another wonderful compilation covering a variety of styles. Contains: Ellen Fullman "Staggered Stasis," Mark Barreca "Messier Crosses the Blue Line," Nicolas Collins "Tobabo Fonio," Peter Cusack "Dandelion Clock," Tom Guralnick "Over Time," Johanna Beyer/Essential Music "IV for Percussion," Zae Munn "Interface," Myra Melord/Marion Brandis Duo "Three Interludes," William Hooker "The Dream: Red," and Lesli Dalaba "Core Sample (Sylvan)." —*"Blue" Gene Tyranny*

Aerial# 4, The / Aerial ✦✦✦
Another terrific anthology of the latest. Contains: Brenda Hutchinson "Eeeyah!" / Peter Van Riper "Heart" / Erik Belgum "Dick Tracy All Over His Body" / Leif Brush "Terrain Instruments Are Activated" / Elodie Lauten "Music for the Trine, Part IV" / Elise Kermani "Spiral" / Anna Homler and Steve Mosher "Sirens" / Joseph Weber "Transformation of the Brothers into the Sun and Moon" / Patsy Rahn "Trojan Horse"/ and N. Sean William "Come Window Golds Coming." —*"Blue" Gene Tyranny*

The Aerial # 5 / 1992 / Aerial ✦✦✦
A compilation of great spoken and radiophonic works. Contains: Willem De Ridder & Hafler Trio "Report," Helen Thorington "In the Dark," Gustavo Matamoros "Portrait: Bob Gregory," Sarah Peebles "Excerpts from Kai," Sydney Davis "Star Axis" Philip Corner "Gong/Ear" Richard Klein & Mark Hosler "Wildman" The Machine for Making Sense "Changing the Subject" and Derek Bailey "In My Studio." — *"Blue" Gene Tyranny*

The Aerial # 6 / 1994 / Aerial ✦✦✦
A wonderful collection with plenty of variety. Contains: Carter Scholz "Talus," Ricardo del Ferra "Xastock," Hal Rammel "Afterthought (sonance in limbo)," Larry Polansky "Study: Anna the Long and Short of It," John Duesenberry "Wave Break," Robert Carl, "Levitation," Mary Jane Leach "Xantippe's Rebuke," Steven Dressler "Woonsocket," Yat-Kha "Tundra's Ghosts/Wanderer's Charm," Frances White "Walk Through Resonant Landscape No.2," and Ellen Band "Railroad Gamelan." — *"Blue" Gene Tyranny*

All Guitars / Tellus ✦✦✦
All the weirdest guitarists on the New York scene. Includes contributions from Lee Ranaldo, Bob Mould, Arto Lindsay, the Butthole Surfers, Blixa Bargeld, Tim Schellenbaum, Elliott Sharp, David Linton, and others. —*"Blue" Gene Tyranny*

☆ **Another Coast (New Works from the West)** / Music and Arts ✦✦✦✦✦
Contains: Carl Stone "Wall Me Do" and "Hop Ken" / Paul Dresher "Other Fire and Water Dreams" / Maggi Payne "Airwaves (Realities)" / Paul DeMarinis "I Want You" and "Kokole" / Laetitia Sonami "Pie Jesu—Sounds from Empty Places no. 3." —*"Blue" Gene Tyranny*

Anthology of Music for the 21st Century Leonardo Music Journal Vol.1 No.1 / ✦✦✦
Contains music by Marc Battier, Sarah Hopkins, Larry Austin, Ed Osborn, Daniel Goode, I. Wayan Sadra (Gamelan), Craig Harris, Amnon Wolman, Graeme Gerrard, Steven Paxton with Paula Claire, David Rothenberg, Simon Running, Erling Wood, and Kenneth Atchley (see review under composers). —*"Blue" Gene Tyranny*

Arraymusic: New World / 1993 / Artifact ✦✦✦
Another excellent compilation of acoustic works by this Canadian ensemble. Contains: Michael J. Baker "Columbus," Stephen Parkinson "Desires Are Already Memories," James Tenney "Three New Seeds," Rudolf Komorous "Dame's Rocket," Christopher Butterfield "Empress of Russia," and Terry Riley "Cactus Rosary." —*"Blue" Gene Tyranny*

Arraymusic: Strange City (Ville Étrange) / 1988 / Artifact ✦✦✦
Four innovative acoustic works played by the excellent Canadian ensemble Arraymusic. Contains: Claude Vivier "Et je reverrai cette ville étrange," James Tenney "Harmonium No.5," Henry Kucharzyk "Beating," Michael J. Baker "Unfinished Business." —*"Blue" Gene Tyranny*

Audio Works by Visual Artists / Tellus ✦✦✦
Visual artists from the Futurists to the present. Includes pieces by Joseph Beuys, A. Russolo, Kurt Schwitters, Lawrence Weiner, Richard Huelsenbeck, Joan Jonas, Terry Allen, Marcel Duchamp, Y Pants, Magdalena Abakanowicz, and many others. —*"Blue" Gene Tyranny*

Avant-Garde String Quartet in the U.S.A., The / Vox Box ✦✦✦
Marvelous performances by the Concord String Quartet with quartets by Earle Brown, John Cage, George Crumb, Jacob Druckman, Morton Feldman, Lejaren Hiller, Leon Kirchner, Christian Wolff, Stefan Wolpe. Hopefully it will be reissued. —*"Blue" Gene Tyranny*

CDCM Computer Music Series Vol. 1, CEMI: Center for Experimental Music and Intermedia at the University of North Texas, Denton, The / Centaur ✦✦✦
Contains music by Larry Austin "Sinfonia Concertante: A Mozartean Episode" (1988), Thomas Clark "Peninsula" (1988) for piano and computer, Jerry Hunt "Fluud" (1988) (see comments in "composers") for dual synthesizers, and Phil Winsor "Dulcimer Dream" (1988) for amplified piano. —*"Blue" Gene Tyranny*

CDCM Computer Music Series Vol. 2, EAR Studios at Rensselear Polytechnic Institute, The / Centaur ✦✦✦
Contains music by Richard Teitelbaum "Golem 1" (1987), Martin Bresnick "Lady Neil's Dumpe" (1987), Neil B. Rolnick "What Is the Use?" (1985), Rick Baitz "Kaleidocycles" (1985), Scott Lindroth "Syntax" (1985). —*"Blue" Gene Tyranny*

CDCM Computer Music Series Vol. 3, Experimental Music Studios and Computer Music Project at the University of Illinois at Urbana-Champaign, The / Centaur ✦✦✦
Music by Salvatore Martirano "Everything Goes When the Whistle Blows" for Zeta violin and YahaSalmaMAC MIDI Orchestra (1985), John Melby "Chor der Waisen" (Chorus of the Orphans) for computer-generated tape (1985), Sever Tipei "Cunculi" (1986) for five tubas—mostly quietly played clusters with complex beat patterns—pleasant to hear, Scott A. Wyatt "Still Hidden Laughs" (1988) for Synclavier and Yahama systems, Herbert Bruen "Project SAWDUST No. 6: I Told You So!" (1981)—speechlike gestures made from filtered spectrum noise sources for computer-generated tape, and Carla Scaletti "SunSurgeAutomata" (1987)—a mysterious short work built from clicks that are collected to resemble pitch and rhythm. "This is expressive of Lewis Thomas' proposal that the development of life on Earth may have been 'thermodynamically inevitable,' given the steady stream of energy from the sun to the unfillable sink of space by way of the Earth. Thomas suggests that the 'urge to make music' may be a desire to recapitulate this transformation of inanimate, random matter in chaos into the improbable ordered dance of living forms" realized using the Platypus Digital Processor. —*"Blue" Gene Tyranny*

CDCM Computer Music Series Vol. 6, Bregman Electronic Music Studio at Dartmouth College, Hanover, NH, The / Centaur ✦✦✦
Music by Jon Appleton "Brush Canyon" (1983)—a wonderful short tone-poem using the Synclavier / Paul Moravec "Devices and Desires" for Synclavier—a "musique concrète" work about certain social reins / David Evan Jones "Still Life in Wood and Metal" for percussion ensemble and tape / Jon Appleton "Degitaru Ongaku" (1983) for Synclavier / Christian Wolff "Mayday Materials" (see comments in "composers") / and David Evan Jones "Still Life Dancing" for percussion ensemble and tape. —*"Blue" Gene Tyranny*

CDCM Computer Music Series Vol. 7, Ear Studios at Rensselaer Polytechnic Institute, Troy, NY, The / Centaur ✦✦✦
Music by Neil B. Rolnick "Vocal Chords" (1988) for voice and digital processors and "A Robert Sampler" (1987) / Pauline Oliveros "Lion's Tale" (1989) for digital sampler / Julie Kabat "Child and the Moon-Tree" (1989) for vocalist and electronics / Barton McLean "Visions of a Summer Night" (1989) for MIDI-based computer system (see comments in "composers") / and Joel Chadabe "Modalities" (1989) for interactive computer music system. —*"Blue" Gene Tyranny*

CDCM Computer Music Series Vol. 10, The Virtuoso in the Computer Age—I, The / Centaur ✦✦✦✦✦
Music by Paul Lansky "As If" for string trio and computer-synthesized sound / Larry Austin "Montage: Themes and Variations for Violin and Computer Music on Tape" (1985) / John Melby "Concerto no. 1 for Flute and Computer-Synthesized Tape" (1984) / David Rosenboom "A Precipice in Time" (1966) (see comments in "composers") and Anthony Braxton "Composition no. 107" (excerpt, 1982) . —*"Blue" Gene Tyranny*

CDCM Computer Music Series Vol. 17—Music From The Center for Contemporary Music (CCM) / 1994 / Centaur ✦✦✦
A great collection of unique compositional interests that somehow add up to a West Coast sound. Contains: John Bischoff "The Glass Hand" (1992); Chris Brown "Chain Reaction" (1991), performed by ROOM with Chris Brown piano and MIDI-piano, William Winant Airdrums MIDI-controller, Larry Ochs tenor sax, Scot Gresham-Lancaster computer and electronics; Tom Erbe "After a Day" (1991); Maggi Payne "Resonant Places" (1992); Alvin Curran "Animal Behavior" (1992); and a collaborative composition "CCM Flotsam" (1993) that consists of short segments that can be ordered any way the listener desires on their programmable CD. Highly recommended. (See further descriptions under the composer's listing). —*"Blue" Gene Tyranny*

Cassette Mythos Audio Alchemy CD/K7, The / What Next? Records ✦✦✦
So much of the newest music is just in cassettes and computer discs freely exchanged through the mail, contact made by word-of-mouth and small publications soliciting contributions. (I'm reminded of Frankie

Mann's remark that some of the best music in the country is made by "12 year olds in their attics with cassettes.") This is a collection with some of the most inspired, sometimes gawd-awful but always unique, samplings of the cassette culture—maybe more in-the-air than underground. 21 selections: Heather Perkins "What You Think Will Happen Will"/ Ric E. Braden "Columbus Ave. 10 PM"/ Jim Steele "Splatter Experience of the Green Gods"/ Daniel Johnston "Grievances"/ John Wiggins "TimbreMelody"/ Yximalloo "China-Pong"/ Qubais Ghazala "The Delphian Oracle"/ Frederick Lonberg-Holm "The Second Minuet"/ Costes "Oh Fortuna"/ Kitchen Table Ensemble "Exploded Views"/ Solomonoff and Von Hoffmanstahl "Banzai Noir"/ Vosch "Tunnel at Dawn"/ Philip Perkins "Remoting (excerpt from Berkeley Remote)"/ Min¨y "Sspress"/ Triptic of a Pastel Fern "Shiny Things"/ Gregory Whitehead "It Makes Me Blush"/ Mystery Laboratory "Excerpt from V.T."/ Bat Lenny "Delphi"/ Collapse/Relapse "Webs"/ Hope Organ "Sneaky"/ (no composer given) "Tentatively, a convenience drying clothes made entirely from zippers (partial cycle)." —*"Blue" Gene Tyranny*

Cathy Berberian, Voice / Mainstream ✦✦✦
Astonishing performances by one of new-music's first vocal sound experimenters: Berberian (1925-1983) had many pieces written especially for her. Includes Luciano Berio "Circles" (text by e.e. cummings), Bussotti "Frammento," and an especially noteworthy presentation of the John Cage "Aria with Fontana Mix." You may also wish to hear her "Stripsody for Solo Voice" (1966) on Wergo WER 60054-50. —*"Blue" Gene Tyranny*

Century XXI–UK I / 1996 / Newtone ✦✦✦
New composers from the British Isles. Contains works by Laurence Crane, David Cunningham, Graham Fitkin, John Godfrey, Orlando Gouch, Jeremy Peyton Jones and Steve Martland. —*"Blue" Gene Tyranny*

Century XXI–UK II / 1996 / Newtone ✦✦✦
New and rare recordings by Andrew Poppy, Michael Nyman, Howard Skempton, Nicholas Wilson and others (not yet announced). —*"Blue" Gene Tyranny*

Century XXI–USA I–Electronics / 1995 / Newtone ✦✦✦
A fascinating survey of several post-minimalist composers in the USA. Contains: Carl Stone "Kamiya Bar," Ben Neill "678 Streams," Mikel Rouse "Autorequiem," Kyle Gann "Ghost Town" and Nicolas Collins "Devil's Music." —*"Blue" Gene Tyranny*

Century XXI–USA II–Electroacoustics / 1995 / Newtone ✦✦✦
Unissued and rare tracks by Rhys Chatham "An Angel Moves Too Fast to See (5th Movement)," Evan Ziporyn "Be In," Dave Soldier "Utah Dances," Michael Gordon "Strange Quiet," Glenn Branca "Les Honneurs du Pica (Parts 1 & 2)," and Lois V. Vierk "Go Guitars." —*"Blue" Gene Tyranny*

Chicago 82–A Dip in the Lake / Les Disques Du Crepescule ✦✦✦
Music from New Music America '82. A terrific overview. —*"Blue" Gene Tyranny*

Cinq Quartuors Espagnols (Five Spanish String Quartets) Arditti Quartet / Disques Montaigne Ref. ✦✦✦
Great performances of quartets by Luis de Pablo, Mira Fornes, Ramon Ramos, Tomas Marco, and Cristobal Halffter. —*"Blue" Gene Tyranny*

Cold Blue Anthology / Cold Blue Records ✦✦✦✦✦
When you listen to the pieces in their order on the record, an unnameable, evocative narrative seems to underlie the whole. Includes: Chas Smith "Beatrix"/ Ingram Marshall "Gradual Siciliano (for Gus)"/ Peter Garland "The Three Strange Angels (1972-1973)" for piano, drum, and bullroarer / Daniel Lentz "You Can't See the Forest . . . Music, 1971"/ Michael Byron "Marimbas in the Dorian Mode" (May Day, 1976) / Jim Fox "Appearance of Red"/ Read Miller "Weddings, Funerals, and Children Who Cannot Sleep"/ John Kuhlmann "In This Light"/ Rick Cox "Necessity"/ Michael Jon Fink "Celesta Solo" (1981) / Eugene Bowen and Harold Budd "Wonder's Edge"/ James Tenney "Spectral CANON for CONLON Nancarrow" for player piano. —*"Blue" Gene Tyranny*

Compositoras Madrileñas (Women Composers of Madrid) / RTVE ✦✦✦
Contains: Alicia Santos "Sonata para flauta y piano" (1958) / Marisa Manchado "Obertura" (1956) / Consuelo Diez "Naggareth" for percussion ensemble (1958) / Zulema de la Cruz "Pulsares" for piano and taped electronics (1958) / Maria Escribano "Jondo" for sax ensemble, piano, and percussion (1954) . —*"Blue" Gene Tyranny*

Computer Music Currents 7 / Wergo ✦✦✦
Contains: Richard Karpen (1957) "Il Nome" (1987) / Jean-Claude Risset "L'autre face"/ Lars-Gunnar Bodin "Anima" (1984) / Tracy L. Petersen "Digital Tantra I" (1978) / Frances White "Ogni Pensiero Vola" (1985) / and Joji Yuasa "A Study in White" (1987). —*"Blue" Gene Tyranny*

Concert Imaginaire, GRM (Imaginary Concert) / INA ✦✦✦
A good collection of "musique concrète" pieces by the GRM (Groupe de Recherches Musicales, "Group for Musical Research"): J. Schwarz "And

Around"/ Bernard Parmegiani "La Roue Ferris"/ Pierre Schaeffer-Pierre Henry "Erotica –symphonie pour un homme seul"/ Michel Chion "La Ronde"/ Jacques Lejeune "L'invitation au départ"/ Ivo Malec "Reflets"/ Jean Schwarz "Suite N"/ Christian Zanesi "D'un jardin l'autre"/ Denis Dufour "Bocalises"/ Philippe Mion "Puzzlasept"/ Francois Bayle "Erosphére." —*"Blue" Gene Tyranny*

Confederacy of Dances, Vol. 1 / Einstein Records ✦✦✦
Concert recordings from the Roulette Experimental Music Series. Comes with a 32-page booklet containing essays by Mark Dery, Tim Page, Kevin Whitehead, and David Weinstein on Roulette and the "downtown scene." CD selections are: Bill Frisell "April 16, 1988"/ Christian Marclay "Untitled"/ Tohban Djan (Ikue Mori and Luli Shioi) "Blue Seed"/ Zeena Parkins "Scruples"/ Billy Bang "One for Albert"/ Anthony Coleman "Acid Jazz Burnout"/ David Weinstein "Icetralia"/ Chris Cochrane "To Dis-enfranchise (Repatriation)"/ Ron Kuivila "Canon Y"/ John Zorn "Sebastopol"/ Guy Klusevik "Sylvan Steps"/ Davbid Weinstein "Poland"/ Hirsch-Mori-Shea-Staley Quartet "Ulula Zone"/ and Jeanne Lee and Wadada Leo Smith "Beauty Is a Rarity." —*"Blue" Gene Tyranny*

A Confederacy of Dances, Vol. 2 / 1994 / Einstein ✦✦✦
Another fabulous collection of live performances from the famed Roulette downtown New York space. Contains: Jerome Cooper "They Told Me This—But They Did That," Earl Howard & Denman Maroney "Elijah," Iréne Schweitzer "Unexpected Demand," Jon Gibson's lovely and compelling sax solo with electronic delays "Ballade," Davey Williams & La Donna Smith "Dance of the Poppies," Robert Ashley "Love Is a Good Example," and J.A. Deane & Martin Schütz "Sounds from the Third Stone." —*"Blue" Gene Tyranny*

Contemporary Contrabass; Bertram Turetzky, Contrabass, The / Nonesuch Records ✦✦✦
Great playing. Contains: John Cage "26' 1.1499" for a String Player" (1955) / Pauline Oliveros "Outline" for flute, percussion, and string bass (an improvisation chart) (1963) / Ben Johnston "Casta Bertram" (1969) for live recording, playback loops, and chance processes. —*"Blue" Gene Tyranny*

Cultures Electroniques / 6: Les Magisteres du 19e Concours International de Musique Electroacoustique (Magisterium of the 19th Electroacoustic Competition) / Harmonia Mundi ✦✦✦
An excellent compilation of elegant, subtle, and poetic electronic works including Bernard Parmegiani (1927-) "Exercisme 3" (Exercise/Exorcism 3) (1986) / Barry Truax (1947-) "Riverrun" (1986) / Wilhelm Zobl (1950-) "Andere die Welt, Sie Brauchtes" (Change the World, It Needs Changing) (1973) / and James Dashow (1944-) "Whispers Out of Time" (1976). —*"Blue" Gene Tyranny*

Cultures Electroniques / 6: Prix Quadrivium / Bourges 1991 / Harmonia Mundi ✦✦✦
Another interesting collection of prize-winning electro-acoustic pieces, although sometimes their "tastefulness" makes them seem somewhat similar. Especially unique are Andrew Lewis (from Great Britain, born 1963) "Time and Fire"/ Mike Vaughan (from Great Britain, born 1954) "Ensphered" for soprano sax and tape / Ake Parmerud (from Sweden, born 1953) "Alias"/ Justice Olsson (from France, born in Johannesburg in 1949) "Up!"/ and Alicyn Warren (US, 1955) "Longing for the Light." Other compositions are by Cort Lippe (US, 1953) "Music for Harp and Tape"/ David Arzouman (US, 1955) "Precipitation"/ Jon Appleton (US, 1939) "Stereopticon"/ Roderik De Man (Pays Bas, born in Indonesia, 1941) "Chordis Canam"/ and Georg Katzer (West Germany, 1935) "Rondo." —*"Blue" Gene Tyranny*

Double Edge / ✦✦✦
Contains: Frederic Rzewski "Winnsboro Cotton Mill Blues" (1980) / David Borden "Double Portrait" (1987) / "Blue" Gene Tyranny "The Decertified Highway of Dreams" (1991) / James Tenney "Chromatic Canon" (1983) / Paul Bowles "Night Waltz" (1949) / "Duke" Ellington and Billy Strayhorn "Tonk" (1940) / Meredith Monk "Phantom Waltz" (1989) and "Ellis Island" (1981) / Mel Powell "A Setting for Two Pianos" (1987) / Morton Feldman "Two Pianos" (1957). —*"Blue" Gene Tyranny*

Electro Clips (25 Instantanés Électroacoustiques / 25 Électroacoustic Snaps / 1990 / Empreintes Digitales ✦✦✦
Twenty-five brief and highly individual, insightful works by as many composers from Quebec, Canada, the US, and Mexico assembled for the New Music America Festival in Montréal, November, 1990. Contains: Michel Smith "Style de bougalou [Boogaloo-like]", Craig Harris "Somewhere between," Jean-François Denis "Point-virgule [Semicolon]", John Oswald "Bell Speeds," Yves Daoust "Mi bémol [E-flat]", Claude Schryer "Les oiseaux de Bullion [de Bullion's Birds]", Martin Gotfrit "The Machine's Four Humours," John Oliver "Marimba Disremembered," Zack Settel "Skweeit-Chupp," Stéphane Roy "Résonances d'arabesques," Daniel Scheidt "What If," Bruno Degazio "Humoresque 901534," Richard Truhlar "Simulant [a neologism made from assimilate and simulate]", Gilles Gobeil "Associations libres [Free Associations]", Robert Nor-

mandeau "Bédé" [a pun on bande dessinée—comic book], Laurie Radford "Landlocked," C. Calon / C. Schryer "Prochaine Station [Next Station]", Hildegard Westerkamp "Breathing Room," Amnon Wolman "Man-Bridge," Francis Dhomont "Qui est la? [Who's there?]", Roxanne Turcotte "Minisérie [Mini-series]", Christian Calon "Temps incertains [Unsettled Times]", Dan Lander "I'm looking at my hand," Javier Alvarez "Mambo a la Braque," Charles Amirkhanian "Bajanoom." —"Blue" Gene Tyranny

☆ **Electro-Acoustic Music: Classics** / Neuma Records ✦✦✦✦✦
Contains: Varese "Poeme Electronique" / Milton Babbitt "Phenomena" and "Philomel," both with soprano Judith Bettina / Roger Reynolds "Transfigured Wind IV" with Harvey Sollberger (flute) / Iannis Xenakis "Mycenae-Alpha." Some of the best of the European-academic style. —"Blue" Gene Tyranny

Electronic Music / Vox Turnabout ✦✦✦
Contains: Ilhan Mimaroglu "Agony" (1965), John Cage "Fontana Mix" (1958), and Luciano Berio "Visage" (1961), based on the fabulous vocal sounds of Cathy Berberian. —"Blue" Gene Tyranny

Electronic Music / Folkways ✦✦✦
Early works from independent composers in Canada, the US, and Australia. Victor Grauer "Inferno" / Jean Ivey "Pinball" / John Robb "Collage" / Hugh Le Caine "Dripsody," one of the first Canadian tape pieces / Walter Olnick-Schaeffer "Summer Idyl Noesis" / Myron Schaeffer "Dance R 43" / Val Stephen "Fireworks" and "Orgasmic Opus." —"Blue" Gene Tyranny

Electronics and Percussion: Five Realizations by Max Neuhaus / 1965 / Columbia ✦✦✦
One of the great performances and collections of new music. Composer-performer Max Neuhaus, also renowned for his permanent electronic installations in many cities, creates five realizations of open-ended, graphed, or performance-indeterminate pieces by five composers. Includes: Earle Brown "Four Systems" for four amplified cymbals, Morton Feldman "The King of Denmark," Sylvano Bussotti "Coeur pour Batteur—Positively Yes," Karlheinz Stockhausen "No. 9, Zyklus," for one percussionist, and John Cage "Fontana Mix" for contact microphones on various percussion instruments. —"Blue" Gene Tyranny

Elektroakustische Musik aus Finnland (Electro-Acoustic Music from Finland) / Edition ✦✦✦
Music by Patrick Kosk, Petri Hiidenkari, Harri Nouri, Tapio Nevanlinna. —"Blue" Gene Tyranny

Experimental Theater / Tellus ✦✦✦
Sound from "performance art" presentations: Spaulding Gray "Sex and Death to the Age 14 (excerpt)"/ Vulcan Death Grip with Ann Magnuson "Get It Up or Get Out" (1986), vocals with band/ Mike Kelley with Sonic Youth "Plato's Cave, Rothko's Chapel, Lincoln's Profile" (1986) / Jerri Allyn "Queer Revolution" (1984)/ Ann Magnuson "Arachnae X. Pudenda" (1987) / Lydia Lunch "The Cancer Has Finally Become Contagious" (1987). —"Blue" Gene Tyranny

Explosions, The Bob James Trio / ESP-Disk ✦✦✦
Probably the first recording of improvised jazz combined with electronic music, as well as playing inside the piano and other new-music techniques. Contains lively and often humorous compositions by Bob James and Gordon Mumma "Peasant Boy" / Bob Ashley and Bob James "Untitled Mixes" / Bob James "Explosions" / Barre Phillips "An On" / and a version (not the full one for voice and electronics found in Source magazine) of "Wolfman" by Bob Ashley and Bob James. With Bob James (piano), Barre Phillips (bass), and Robert Pozar (percussion). —"Blue" Gene Tyranny

Exquisite Corpses from P.S. 122 / What Next ? Recordings ✦✦✦
Not actually a collection, but a collective improvisation by 30 performer/composers, in which each participant was given only a hint of the contributions of other participants, the whole of the improvisations then collected together, unedited and without overdubbing or retakes. A panorama of approaches to the meaning of improvisation. —"Blue" Gene Tyranny

☆ **Extended Voices; The Brandeis University Chamber Chorus, Directed by Alvin Lucier** / Odyssey ✦✦✦✦✦
New pieces for chorus and voices altered electronically. Contains Pauline Oliveros "Sound Patterns" / Alvin Lucier "North American Time Capsule 1967," for voices and Sylvania Electronic Systems Vocoder / John Cage "Solos for Voice 2" electronic realization / Robert Ashley "She Was a Visitor" / Toshi Ichiyanagi "Extended Voices" / Morton Feldman "Chorus and Instruments (II)" and Christian Wolff "Cambridge." Some of the best performances and recording of new music ever. —"Blue" Gene Tyranny

False Phonemes / Tellus ✦✦✦
A wonderful anthology of works for computer-generated voice. Contains Remko Scha "katadeedo daynatadoh (restored to youth according to beauty I walk)" from Impressions of Africa, and French Recitatif/ Larry Wendt "Galaxy Love" / Brian Reinbolt "Brain Monkey"/ Mark Rudolph

"Beautiful but Marred by the Blemish of a Perpetual Dissatisfaction"/ Alice Shields "Mass for the Dead"/ Paul DeMarinis "Mind Power"/ Paul Lansky "Not Just More Idle Chatter"/ Jon English and Jim Pomeroy "The Hartford Address"/ Ron Kuivila "Linear Predictive Zoo"/ John Cage "Writings through the Essay: On the Duty of Civil Disobedience "(excerpt). —"Blue" Gene Tyranny

Full Spectrum Voice; Thomas Buckner (vocals) / Lovely Music ✦✦✦
An edition of premiere inspirations beautifully sung for voice, instruments, and electronics. Includes Robert Ashley "Odalisque" / Jon Gibson "Rainforest/Brazil (He Was Not Disappointed)" / Nils Vigeland "March, Hymn, and Waltz" / Peter Gena "Mother Jones" / Annea Lockwood "Night and Fog" / and Roscoe Mitchell "because it's," "this," and "dim"—three songs on poems of e.e. cummings. Highly recommended. —"Blue" Gene Tyranny

Funnel Zone / Dossier ✦✦✦
Music by Vivante Tableaux, Setrakian, Slap, TVD, Marilyn Manson, Quayle, Rivet Ecks, Vociferous Mutes, Happiness Boys, Chameleon Circus, King Felix. Wonderful grass roots new music and some industrial rock mostly from the Miami, FL, area. I especially like "Second Nature" and "Haides" by King Felix. —"Blue" Gene Tyranny

Futura 1-5 (Soundtext Poetry) / Cramps Records ✦✦✦
A great series of poetry, utilizing vocal sounds as well as words, called "soundtext" in the US. It isn't necessary to know the base language in which the poem-performances are given. Futura 1: "La declamazione futurista (The futurist declamation)" and "Lo Zaum', linguaggio trasmentale (Zaum', the transmental language)"; Futura 2: "Simultaneismo francese (French simultaneism)" and "Precursori e dadaisti in Germania (Forerunners and dadists in Germany)"; Futura 3: "L'urlo: Antonin Artaud (The howl: ultralettristes)" and "La poesia sonora oggi (Sound poetry today)"; Futura 4 and 5: "La poesia sonora oggi (Sound poetry today)". —"Blue" Gene Tyranny

Gay American Composers / 1996 / CRI ✦✦✦
An incredible overview of contemporary music from academic to eclectic styles, wonderfully performed by various groups including the Kronos Quartet. The CD was assembled to present the question "Is there a gay sensibility to American classical music?" Contains: Robert Helps "Homage á Rachmaninoff," Lee Hoiby "I Was There," Lou Harrison from String Quartet Set: Variations; "Estampe," Chester Biscardi "Invitation to Desire: Tango," Ned Rorem from The Nantucket Songs, David Del Tredici "Fantasy Pieces," Robert Maggio "Desire Movement," Conrad Cummings "In the Department of Love," William Hibbard "Bass Trombone, Bass Clarinet, Harp," Jerry Hunt "Lattice," Lou Harrison "Serenade for Betty Freeman & Franco Assetto," Chris DeBlasio "Walt Whitman in 1989," and Robert Helps "Homage á Fauré." —"Blue" Gene Tyranny

Gerd Zacher, Organ / Deutsche Grammophon ✦✦✦
Great realizations of Giuseppe Giorgio Englert "Vagans animula" (1969), Morton Feldman "Intersection 3" (1953), Gerd Zacher "Re" for organ and intoner (1969) , and John Cage "Variations III" (1963), realized for three organs, percussion, and winds. —"Blue" Gene Tyranny

Historical CD of Digital Sound Synthesis, The / Computer Music Currents # 13 / 1995 / Wergo ✦✦✦
An excellent and well chosen overview of the birth of computer-generated music in the late '50s and early '60s. Contains: Newmann Guttman: "The Silver Scale" (1957), "Pitch Variations" (1957), John R. Pierce "Stochatta" (1959), "Variations in Timbre and Attack" (1961), "Sea Sounds" (1963), "Eight-Tone Canon" (1966), Max V. Matthews "Numerology" (1960), "The Second Law" (1961), "Bicycle Built for Two" (1961), "Masquerades" (1963), "International Lullaby" (1966), David Lewin "Study No. 1," "Study No. 2" (1961), James Tenney "Dialogue" (1963), Ercolino Ferretti "Pipe and Drum" (1963), "Trio" (1965), James Randall "Mudgett, Monologues for a Mass Murderer" (1965). There are also copious and interesting articles by each of the composers. —"Blue" Gene Tyranny

Images Fantastiques / Mercury Limelight ✦✦✦
A great collection of musique concrète pieces. Contains: Luciano Berio "Momenti" and "Omaggio a Joyce" / Bruno Maderna "Continuo" / Luc Ferrari "Visage V" / Iannis Xenakis "Orient-Occident" / Jean Baronnet and Francois Dufrene "U 47." —"Blue" Gene Tyranny

☆ **Imaginary Landscapes** / Elektra/Nonesuch ✦✦✦✦✦
Contains: Ron Kuivila "Loose Canons" (excerpt) / Shelly Hirsch and David Weinstein "On the Swing" (an excerpt from Pomp and Circumstances) / Neil B. Rolnick "Balkanization" (excerpt) / Mark Trayle "Simple Degradation (Border)" / Gordon Monahan "Speaker Swinging" (excerpt) / Laetitia deCompiegne Sonami "What Happened" / Maryanne Amacher "Stain—The Music Rooms" (excerpt) / Alvin Lucier "Music for Alpha Waves, Assorted Percussion, and Automated Code Relays" / David Tudor "Dialects" (excerpt) / Nicolas Collins "Real Electronic Music" / Voice Crack "A Spoonful of Tea in a Barrel Full of Honey" (excerpt) / Christian Marclay "Black Stucco" / "Blue" Gene Tyranny "Somewhere in Arizona 1970" for baritone and electronics. 70 minutes of some of the

best and most innovative of new electronic music of varied idiosyncratic approaches. —*"Blue" Gene Tyranny*

Island of Sanity: New Music from New York City / Review Records ✦✦✦✦✦

Contains: David Linton "Lumbago" / Mofungo "Slimeball Necktie" / Christian Marclay "1930" / Fish and Roses "Checkered Past" / Details at Eleven "Music for Secretaries" / Skeleton Crew "The Sparrow Song" (Frith) / Mark Dery "Banging Khruschev's Shoe" / Charles K. Noyes "Mouse and Ermine" / Locus Solus "Wrap Backwards and the Usual Snowflakes" and "Beda Fomm" / David Fulton "Border Patrol" / David Garland "The Golden Years" / Bump "Spies in Space / Beer in My Bed" / Chris Vine "Alignment" / Carbon "Cormorant" / Bosho "Boy Yaca" / The Scene Is Now "Lullaby Stomp/Cool Pool" / H/M/D "Runner" / Robert Previte "Requiem for Vincent." Edited by Elliott Sharp, this collection clearly shows the spillover of people and styles from New Music to new-music and art-rock and no-wave bands and other styles, in what may be called the "downtown style." Composer/performers who play gigs at bars and also at new-music festivals in academia. This has been happening with the American avant-garde since Ives played ragtime in East Village bars, or for any composer, familiar with dance and song, who also wants to express the conceptual/meditative flashes that occur in life. —*"Blue" Gene Tyranny*

Jewel Box / Tellus 26 / 1992 / Tellus ✦✦✦

An excellent collection of works by women composers in avant-garde styles. Contains: Anne LeBaron "Blue Harp Study 1," Laetitia Sonami "Story Road," Sussan Deiham "Navai," Bun Ching Lam "EO-9066," Catherine Jauniaux & Ikue Mori "Smell," Sapphire "Boys Love Baseball," Mary Ellen Childs "Ruler Etude: A Work in Progress," Michelle Kinney "Coordinated Universal Time" and Anne LeBaron "Blue Harp Study 2." —*"Blue" Gene Tyranny*

John Cage Tribute / KOCH ✦✦✦

A collection of instrumental and vocal pieces and memories honoring the memory of John Cage: Excerpt from Cage's "Thirty Pieces for String Quartet" played by the Kronos Quartet / "Three Dances for Two Prepared Pianos, Dance No.1" played by Patrick Moraz and Jackson MacLow / Anne Tardos "First Four Language Word Event" / Christian Wolff's "Six Melodies Variation" for solo violin (variations on Cage's "Six Melodies") / Ken Nordine's "A Cage Went in Search of a Bird" / composer Earle Brown playing Cage's "Three Solos for Trumpet" from the "Concert for Piano and Orchestra" / Laurie Anderson's "Cunningham Stories: at the age of twelve . . . , Merce Cunningham phoned his mother . . . , Every morning . . . , The Cunningham Company . . . "/ Ryuichi Sakamoto's "Haiku FM"/ Larry Austin's "art is self-alternation is Cage is . . . "/ David Tudor's "Webwork" music for the Cunningham dance "Shards" / Yoko Ono's "Georgia Stone" / Oregon's "Chance/Choice" / David van Tieghem playing Cage's "Living Room Music" / James Tenney's "Ergodos 1 for John Cage" / Robert Ashley's "Factory Preset" / Frank Zappa performing Cage's "4'33" / John Cale's "In Memoriam John Cage—Call Waiting" / Meredith Monk singing Cage's "Aria" / and selection marker No.82 is simply "New York City." —*"Blue" Gene Tyranny*

Jon Gibson / Point Music ✦✦✦

The essential collection for understanding the variety of expressions possible in pattern or phase music (sometimes rather misleadingly called "minimal" music). Amazingly gorgeous saxophone playing by Jon Gibson. Includes: Terry Riley "Tread the Trail (1964-1965) / Steve Reich "Reed Phase" (1967) / Philip Glass "Bed from Einstein on the Beach (Act IV/2)" (1976) / John Adams "Pat's Aria from Nixon in China (Act II/I)" (1987) / Philip Glass "Gradus for Jon Gibson" (1968) / Jon Gibson "Waltz" (1981), "Song Three (1976) , and "Extensions II" (1981/1982) for sound environment and saxophone / Terry Jennings "Terry's G Dorian 12-Bar Blues (9 X 5) + 3" (ca. June 1962) / LaMonte Young "Any Integer (to Henry Flynt)" (April 1960). —*"Blue" Gene Tyranny*

Just for the Record / Lovely Music ✦✦✦✦✦

"Blue" Gene Tyranny plays multikeyboard works by Robert Ashley "Sonata" with "Trio: Christopher Columbus Crosses to the New World in the Nina, the Pinta, and the Santa Maria Using Only Dead Reckoning and a Crude Astrolabe" / John Bischoff "Rendezvous" / Phil Harmonic "Timing" / and Paul DeMarinis "Great Masters of Melody." —*"Blue" Gene Tyranny*

Just Intonation / Tellus ✦✦✦✦✦

"Just intonation" is any tuning system in which all of the intervals can be represented by whole-number ratios, with a strong preference for simple ratios. Contains pieces radically different from each other but all aiming for this "maximum clarity" tuning. —*"Blue" Gene Tyranny*

LCO 8 (London Chamber Orchestra) "Minimalist" / Virgin ✦✦✦

A very well played and good overview of some of the better-known pattern ("minimalist") composers. Contains: John Adams "Shaker Loops" / Philip Glass "Facades" / Steve Reich "Eight Lines" / Philip Glass "Company" / and Dave Heath (1956) "The Frontier." —*"Blue" Gene Tyranny*

Les Ondes Martenots (50th Anniversary of the Ondes Martenot Electronic Keyboard) / Productions Disques Ades ✦✦✦

Classic and newer works for 1 to 6 Ondes Martenots, sometimes with piano. Somewhat patterned after the Russian Theremin, the Ondes Martenot (the "Martenot Waves") was another early electronic music instrument that was first presented publicly in May 1928 at the Parisian Opera House by its inventor Maurice Martenot. This collection contains: "Fete des belles eaux" (1937), "Suite for Ondes Martenot and Piano" (1933) by Darius Milhaud, "3 Poemes" (1935) by Andre Jolivet, and "Hexade" (1973) by Roger Tessier. —*"Blue" Gene Tyranny*

Life Is a Killer / Giorno Poetry Systems ✦✦✦✦✦

A Dial-A-Poem Poets life-centering collection of different ensembles of speakers with and without instrumental music. Works by Amiri Baraka, William S. Burroughs, Jim Carroll, Jayne Cortez, The Four Horsemen (b.p. Nichol, Steve McCaffery, Paul Dutton, Rafael Barreto Rivera), John Giorno, Brion Gysin, Rose Lesniak, Ned Sublette. —*"Blue" Gene Tyranny*

Logos Works / Moniek Darge, Godfried-Willem Raes / 1995 / Experimental Intermedia ✦✦✦

A retrospective of aural works over the last 25 years by the Ghent-based Logos Duo based on their search for spiritual locations around the planet: "Shifts" is a wonderful computer-generated rhythmic study, like a gamelan playing Western pop music, "Man-Mo" is a collage of temple bells, running water and other location sounds, "Jonas" is a strange chromatic piece for church organ, "ShSh" collages cricket noises (the shsh-sound), chanting with bells and other location sounds; "Fuga Momento" is an odd chromatic piece where tuned instruments keep losing their tuning; "AlviCeba" is a strongly dramatic piece for strings; "Fuga Otto Nove" is a complex, giddy canon for synthesized acoustic instruments; the computer in "Spring '94" generates both global instructions and specific events which the composers liken to elements struggling during springtime. —*"Blue" Gene Tyranny*

Lois Svard: With and Without Memory / 1994 / Lovely Music ✦✦✦

Three premieres for solo piano brilliantly played by this tasteful, lyrical, and adventurous pianist. Includes "Blue" Gene Tyranny "Nocturne With and Without Memory," William Duckworth "Imaginary Dances," and Robert Ashley "Van Cao's Meditation." —*"Blue" Gene Tyranny*

Loretta Goldberg: Soundbridge / Opus One ✦✦✦

Six premieres of works by contemporary women composers brilliantly and sensitively performed on piano, MIDI grand piano, and quartertone piano. Contains: Sorrel Hays "Past Present," (1978), and "90's—A Calendar Bracelet" for MIDI-piano (1990), Tui St. George Tucker's classic "Second Piano Sonata (The Peyote)" (1956), Daria Semegen "Rhapsody" for MIDI-piano (1990), Annea Lockwood "Red Mesa" (1989), and Tui St. George Tucker "My Melancholy Baby—Fantasy on Ernie Burnett's Famous Theme" for quartertone piano (1984). —*"Blue" Gene Tyranny*

Lovely Little Records / Lovely Music ✦✦✦✦✦

Box of six 7-inch discs with booklet. Contains: John Bischoff "Silhouette" (1979) and "The League of Automatic Music Composers: Recording, December 17, 1978" / Paul DeMarinis "If God Were Alive (and He Is) You Could Reach Him by Telephone" and "Forest Booties" / Phil Harmonic "Phil Harmonic's Greatest Hits" and "WPA/Composite Mix: John Bischoff and Phil Harmonic" / Frankie Mann "I Was a Hero (from The Mayan Debutante Revue" and "How to Be Very Very Popular" / Maggi Payne "Lunar Disk" and "Lunar Earthrise"/ "Blue" Gene Tyranny "Harvey Milk (Portrait) Part I: The Action, Part II: The Feeling." —*"Blue" Gene Tyranny*

Mallets, Hands, Sticks, and Drums / O.O. Discs ✦✦✦

With Brian Johnson, Jan Williams, and drummers from Africa, Cuba, and Brazil. "Channeled violence . . . perceptual minimalism full of uncontrollable variations" (*Village Voice*). Features the cut "Snare for Camus." Recorded in Studio B (the Toscanni studio) at Radio City Music Hall. Wild. —*"Blue" Gene Tyranny*

Mosaic / 1996 / Erato ✦✦✦

Four brilliant compositions for piano solo and orchestra. Includes: Galina Ustvolskaya's dramatic and inspirational "Concerto for piano, string orchestra and timpani" moving from an oppressive (Soviet) atmosphere to hopeful future images, Sofia Gubaidulina "Introitus Concerto for piano and chamber orchestra," Henryk Górecki "Concerto for piano and string orchestra Op. 40," Georgs Pelécis "Concertino bianco for piano and chamber orchestra in C major," a charming work written all in natural "white key" modes (an idea also explored earlier by Cage's "String Quartet," Philip Krumm's "Piano Variations," Jon Gibson's "R.C. Chorales," etc). Played by the Deutsche Kammerphilharmonie Bremen (German Chamber Philharmonic of Bremen), conducted by Heinrich Schiff. —*"Blue" Gene Tyranny*

Music from Japan, Vol. 1: Acoustic Instruments with Computer Music Systems / 1992 / Classic Masters ✦✦✦

Fascinating collection with subtle interplay of acoustic and electronic sounds. Includes: Yuji Takahashi "Tree" (1991) for MIDI piano, played by

Haruna Miyake; trombone, played by composer-performer George E. Lewis; and Takahashi on electronics; originator of interactive music, composer David Behrman's "Navigation and Astronomy" (1990) for 21-string koto and pitch-sensing system; and Takahashi's "Iki to Ishi" (1990) for voice and computer performance system. — *"Blue" Gene Tyranny*

Music from Mills / Mills College ✦✦✦
A centennial anthology produced and compiled at The Center for Contemporary Music at Mills College. Contains: Lou Harrison "Sonata No. 2" for cembalo / Terry Riley "The Ethereal Time Shadow (excerpt)" / Luciano Berio "Chamber Music" / Dave Brubeck "Summer Song" / David Rosenboom "In the Beginning: Etude 1 (Trombones)" / Robert Ashley "Flying Saucer Dialogue from the Opera *Atalanta (Acts of God)*" / Anthony Braxton "Composition No. 62 (+30 +96)" / David Behrman "Interspecies Smalltalk, Part 2" (Excerpt) / Elinor Armer "Thaw" / Steve Reich "Melodica" / Maggi Payne "Subterranean Network" (excerpt)/ Darius Milhaud "Segoviana" / Pauline Oliveros "Alien Bog" (excerpt) / Anthony Gnazzo "Asparagas" / Katrina Krimsky "Apparitions" / Larry Polansky "Four Voice Cannon No.3" / Pandit Pran Nath "Dira Dira Ta Na in Raga Bhairavi" (excerpt) / Janice Giteck "Breathing Songs from a Turning Sky" (excerpt) / "Blue" Gene Tyranny "Remembering" / Ramon Sender "Audition" (excerpt) / and Morton Subotnick "The Key to Songs" (excerpt). — *"Blue" Gene Tyranny*

Music from the ONCE Festival / Advance ✦✦✦✦✦
The only recording of compositions from this legendary festival that presented the newest in avant-garde music, film, and dance from 1961-1968. Contains: Gordon Mumma "Music from the Venezia Space Theatre" / Robert Ashley "Crazy Horse Symphony" / George Cacioppo "Time on Time in Miracles" / Donald Scarvarda "Landscape Journey." — *"Blue" Gene Tyranny*

Music with Memory / Tellus ✦✦✦✦✦
A collection of works by composers who use microcomputers as their instruments. Includes Nicolas Collins "Devil's Music" (1985) / John Driscoll "Stall" (excerpt) with Phil Edelstein and Peter Labiak's rotating robotic loudspeaker system (1981) / Brenda Hutchison "Interlude from Voices of Reason" (1984) / Ron Kuivila "Parodicals" and "Cannon Y for C.N." (1985) / Paul DeMarinis "Eenie Meenie Chillie Beenie" (1983) and "Yellow Yankee" (1983). — *"Blue" Gene Tyranny*

Musica Futurista / Cramps ✦✦✦
A terrific collection of early soundtext, piano, radio, and noise pieces from the Italian futurists 1913-1933 with Italian and English liner notes. Works by Luigi Russolo, Filippo Marinetti, A. Casella, Virgilio Mortari, Franco Casavola, Francesco Pratella, Daniele Napoletano. — *"Blue" Gene Tyranny*

Musik um den Futurismus / Akademie der Kuenste ✦✦✦
More futurist music 1915-1925 including also Russian, French and German composers influenced by this movement. "Formes en l'air—a Pablo Picasso" (1915) by Arthur V. Lourie / "Le temple est mesure—l'esprit est incarne" ("The temple is measured—the spirit is incarnate") , "Je t'attendrai" ("I will wait for you") (1913) , "Le Sang!" ("The Blood!") (1918) by Nicholas Obouchov / "Musik fuer Klavier, op. 1" (1916), "Ich hatt' einen Kameraden—Groteske" (I had a comrade—a grotesque) (1919), "Musik fuer Klarinette, Klavier und freihangendes Blechsieb" ("Music for clarinet, piano, and free-hanging perforated sheet metal") (1919) by Hans-Juergen von der Wense / "Streichquartett op. 13 in Vierteltoenen" ("String Quartet op. 13 in Quarter-tones") (1925) by Ivan Wyschnegradsky / "Fragmente aus der Oper 'L'aviatore Dro'" ("Fragment from the opera 'Dro the aviator'") (1914) by Francesco Balilla Pratella / and "La Pioggia" ("The Rain") by Antonio Russolo. — *"Blue" Gene Tyranny*

Musique Expérimentale Groupe de Recherches Musicales de la R.T.F. (Musical Research Group of French Radio-Television) / Disques ✦✦✦✦✦
An exquisite collection of musique concrète pieces. "Volumes" (1960) by Francois-Bernard Mache for 12-track tape and a chamber orchestra consisting of seven trombones, two pianos, and two percussionists—cosmic sounds of great import on the distant horizon slowly approaching and suddenly disappearing, great rattlings and small ones like crickets, breaking, impacting percussion; "Crucifixion" (excerpts) by Romuald Vandelle, based on a poem by Poe spoken by a fragmented voice, gloomy and terrifying; the surreal, elegant "Ambiance II (Toast FunÄbre)" by Michel Philippot for woman's spoken voice and tape based on a Mallarme text; one of the best musique concrète compositions, "Tautologos II" by Luc Ferrari—masses of speech-inflected, tape-manipulated sounds like conversations amongst alien beings, bizarre glasslike drones (rotating metal resonators on piano strings), humorous mobiles of sounds combining and recombining: a soundtrack to stimulate the imagination; "Texte II" (1953) by André Boucourechliev, described as "a form in movement" employing "controlled chance", recorded on two tapes to be played simultaneously on two tape recorders so that coincidences of the mono tracks are always variable from performance to performance—an astonishingly rich palette of sounds for such an early piece. — *"Blue" Gene Tyranny*

Neue Chormusik (New Music for Chorus), Vol. 3 Schola Cantorum Stuttgart, Clytus Gottwal / Wergo ✦✦✦
This volume contains the Brian Ferneyhough (1943) "Time and Motion Study III" (1974-75) for 16 voices, percussion and electronics, and also excellent performances of compositions by Mahler, Aribert Reimann (1936), Messiaen, Ligeti, Alban Berg, and Maurice Ravel. Vol. I in this series contains works by Dieter Schnebel (composer of "Für Stimmen . . . Missa Est" (For Voices . . . Missa Est) (1956-58, 1964-68) with movements entitled "dt 31", "AMN" and "! (madrasha II)" and "Atemzüge" (Respirations) for voices), Hans Otte, Bussotti, Ligeti, Pousseur, Webern, Nono; and Vol. II has works by Hans Holliger, Schnebel, Penderecki, and Cerha. — *"Blue" Gene Tyranny*

New American Music, Vol. 4 / Folkways ✦✦✦
An interesting collection of compositions using a variety of compositional techniques and sound sources. Contains: Gordon Mumma "Cybersonic Cantilevers," a live electro-acoustic performance / Joel Chadabe "Echoes," interactive computer music with percussionist / V. Ussachevsky "Conflict," voice plus electronics / Noa Ain "Used to Call Me Sadness," a text-sound piece with violin accompaniment / and Ann McMillan "Whale," modified whale sounds and "Carrefours." — *"Blue" Gene Tyranny*

New Music Articles Magazine Cassettes / Frog Peak Music ✦✦✦
The NMA is a primary source of new and experimental music in Australia; each issue is accompanied by a tape. NMA Tape 1: computer music, improvised work and computer-controlled piano pieces by Warren Burt, Brian Parish, David Hurst, Graeme Gerrard, John Jenkins, Jon Rose, Alistair Riddell, and Essendon Airport / Tape 2: vocal, electronic, and chamber music by Chris Mann, Ron Nagorcka, Anti Music, Mark Pollard, John Gillies, Ernie Althoff, Les Gilbert, and Rainer Linz / Tape 3: Jon Rose and Martin Wesley-Smith, Richard Vella, Rik Rue, John Oswald, Makers of the Dead, Travel Fast, Japanese Coke Ads, and the Australian Bicentennial Authority / Tape 4: music by women composers, including solo and chamber compositions, electronic and computer music, installations and improvised works by Jennifer Fowler, Ros Bandt, Sarah Hopkins, Annea Lockwood, Caroline Wilkins, Vineta Lagazdina, and others / Tape 5: vocal, instrumental, and electronic work by Chris Mann, Rainer Light, SWSW THRGHT, Syd Clayton, Amanda Stewart, Ernie Althoff, Daniel Kahans, Caroline Wilkins, John Gillies and Greg Hooper, and Densil Cabrera / Tape 6: recent computer and computer-assisted music by Greg Schiemer, David Hurst, Alistair Riddell, Warren Burt, Mark Randolph, Cindy John, Amanda Baker, and Graeme Gerrard / Tape 7: music accompanying the "history" issue: performance and radio pieces, environmental composition, and music theater by Greg Schiemer, Jon Rose, Ron Nagorcka, Helen Gifford, Ernie Gallagher, Percy Grainger. — *"Blue" Gene Tyranny*

New Music China / Tellus ✦✦✦
Contains both new popular and folk music as well as new music: Fred Houn "I Wor Kuen (The Boxers)" from Bamboo That Snaps Back/ Chen Yi "Xie Zi" / Ge Gan-Ru "Yi Feng (Ancient Wind)" for solo cello / Zhou Long "Kong Gu Liu Shui (Valley Stream)" for traditional ensemble / Wu Wen Guang "Liu Shui (Flowing Water)" for guqin (ancient seven-string zither) / Tan Dun "Plucking Instruments Suite" (excerpt) / R.I.P. Hayman "Nightsongs" score from film about immigrant life in Chinatown / Jing Luo "Monologue Part 1": she also writes for large orchestra and traditional Chinese ensembles. — *"Blue" Gene Tyranny*

New Music for Electronic and Recorded Media / 1750 Arch Street Records ✦✦✦
A great collection of music by contemporary women composers writing from 1938-1977. Contains a realization of Johanna Beyer's "Music of the Spheres" (1938) / Annea Lockwood "World Rhythms" / Pauline Oliveros "Bye Bye Butterfly" (1965) / Laurie Spiegel "Appalachian Grove I" / Megan Roberts "I Could Sit Here All Day" / Ruth Anderson "Points" / Laurie Anderson "New York Social Life," "Time to Go," and "For Diego." — *"Blue" Gene Tyranny*

New Music for Guitars, Buffalo Guitar Quartet / New World Records ✦✦✦
Interesting, mostly melodious music with many new techniques of guitar playing, including having the guitars sound like other string instruments: harps, sitars, ancient kithara. Contains Lejaren Hiller "Metaphors" / Stephen Funk Pearson "Mummychogs (Le Monde)" / Walter Hartley "Quartet for Guitars" / James Piorkowski "The Struggle of Jacob" / William Ortiz "Abrazo" / and Loris Chobanian "Sonics." — *"Blue" Gene Tyranny*

New Music for Piano, Yuji Takahashi (Piano) / Mainstream Records ✦✦✦
Excellent performances of Xenakis "Herma"/ Reynolds "Fantasy for Pianist" / Takahashi "Metatheses" / and especially Earle Brown's "Corroboree." — *"Blue" Gene Tyranny*

New Music from Poland 1956-1961 / Philips ✦✦✦
Beautifully recorded orchestral compositions: Penderecki "To The Victims of Hiroshima" (1956) / Grazyna Bacewicz (b. 1913) "Music for Strings, Trumpets, and Percussion" (1958) / Tadeusz Baird "Erotica, Six

Lovesongs for Soprano and Orchestra" (1960-1961) / and Kazimierz Serocki (b. 1922) "Sinfonietta for Two String Orchestras" (1956). —*"Blue" Gene Tyranny*

☆ **New Sounds in Electronic Music** / Columbia Odyssey ✦✦✦✦✦
One of the most beautifully pressed vinyls of electronic music, with three important works: Steve Reich "Come Out" / Richard Maxfield "Night Music" / and Pauline Oliveros "I of IV" . —*"Blue" Gene Tyranny*

The Orchestra According to the Seven / Opus One ✦✦✦
Six well-played and composed traditional, tonal and romantic works—Stefania de Kenessey's "Wintersong, Opus 44," John Sichel's "Three Places in New Jersey," Newton Strandberg "The Legend of Emmeline Labiche—an interlude for string orchestra," Michael Dellaira "Three Rivers" and F. di Arta Angeli's "Intermezzo" and "Pantokrator"—and two adventurous, original voices—Philip Krumm's "Concerto for Bass Clarinet" and Mary Jeanne van Appledorn's "Cycles of Moons and Tides." —*"Blue" Gene Tyranny*

Organ Music From The U.S.A. / 1992 / Bis ✦✦✦
A fascinating collection offering a wide range of innovative techniques and compositional possibilities, with excellent and sensitive performances by Swedish organist Hans-Ola Ericsson. Contains: Charles Ives *Variations on America* (1891), *Adeste Fidelis in an Organ Prelude* (1897), Aaron Copland *Preamble (For a Solemn Occasion)*, *Episode*, Morton Feldman *Principal Sound*, and John Cage *Some of 'The Harmony of Maine' (Supply Belcher)*. —*"Blue" Gene Tyranny*

Organic Oboe / O.O. Discs ✦✦✦
Wonderful performances by Joseph Celli in this historic recording rereleased on CD. Contains: the only American release of Stickhausen's "Spiral" (1968) for soloist on shortwave radio and other instruments / Celli "Sky: S for J" (1976) (see comments in "composers") / Elliott Schwartz "Extended Oboe" (1973-1974) for oboe and electronic tape / and Malcolm Goldstein "A Summoning of Focus" (1977) for wind instrument (see comments in "composers"). —*"Blue" Gene Tyranny*

Panorama Électronique / Mercury Limelight ✦✦✦✦✦
Classic pure electronic and musique concrète compositions from studios in Paris and Cologne. Includes: Pierre Henry "Entite" / György Ligeti "Artikulation" / Herbert Eimert "Selection I" / Mauricio Kagel "Transition I" / André Boucourechliev "Texte I" / and Henri Pousseur "Scambi." —*"Blue" Gene Tyranny*

Paul Zukofsky, Violin / CP 2 Recordings ✦✦✦
Works by three composers beautifully played: Giacinto Scelsi "Anahit," Iannis Xenakis "Mikka" (1972) and "Mikka 'S'" (1975), Philip Glass "Strung Out" (1967). —*"Blue" Gene Tyranny*

Pioneers of Electronic Music / CRI ✦✦✦
The Columbia-Princeton sound from 1952 to 1971. Compositions by Ussachevsky, Otto Luening (b. 1900), Pril Smiley, Bulent Arel, Mario Davidovsky, Alice Shields. Recommended: "Incantation" by Luening and Ussachevsky, "Stereo Electronic Music" by Arel. —*"Blue" Gene Tyranny*

Portraits / New Albion ✦✦✦
A good sampler . . . excerpts from Ingram Marshall's "Fog Tropes," Somei Satoh's "Birds in Warped Time," Paul Dresher's "Channels Passing, Stephen Scott's "Rainbows," Daniel Lentz's "O-KE-WA," and John Adams "Light Over Water." —*"Blue" Gene Tyranny*

Pulse, The New Music Consort / New World Records ✦✦✦
A great collection with some classic percussion music. Contains: John Cage and Lou Harrison "Double Music" (1941), John Cage's rhythmically sophisticated "Second Construction" (1940) and jazzy "Third Construction" (1941), Henry Cowell "Pulse" (1939) for six percussionists, Harvey Sollberger "The Two and the One" (1972), and Lukas Foss "Percussion Quartet" (1983). —*"Blue" Gene Tyranny*

Radius #1: Transmissions from Broadcast Artists / 1993 / What Next? ✦✦✦
Imaginative, entertaining and definitely different sound creations for radio on strange subjects performed by even stranger subjects. Contains: Sheila Davies "What Is the Matter in Amy Glennon?," Helen Thorington "Partial Perceptions," and Terry Allen "Bleeder." —*"Blue" Gene Tyranny*

Radius #2: Transmissions from Broadcast Artists / 1993 / What Next? ✦✦✦
More wonderful combinations of altered voices and odd sounds creating new atmospheres in the collective electronic mind that is radio. Contains: Jackie Apple "Voices in the Dark," Donald Swearingen, and Gregory Whitehead "Pressures of the Unspeakable." —*"Blue" Gene Tyranny*

Relache: On Edge / 1990 / Mode ✦✦✦
Chamber music by three composers written especially for the group. Contains: Paul A. Epstein (b. 1938) "Chamber Music: Three Songs from Home" (1986), Thomas Albert (b. 1948) "A Maze (With Grace)" (1975), and "Devil's Rain" (1977, revised 1986) and James Tenney's important work "Critical Band" (1988). —*"Blue" Gene Tyranny*

Relache: Outcome Inevitable / 1995 / O.O. Discs ✦✦✦
A fine program of four compositions written especially for this Philadelphia-based ensemble. Contains: Robert Ashley "Outcome Inevitable," Lois V. Vierk "Timberline," Eleanor Hovda "Borealis Music," and Fred Wei-han Ho "Contradiction, Please! The Revenge of Charlie Chan." —*"Blue" Gene Tyranny*

Response: Electronic Music from Norway / Mercury Limelight ✦✦✦
A mid-1960s collection. Contains: Arne Nordheim "Epitaffio for Orchestra and Tape" and "Response I" / Alfred Janson "Canon for Chamber Orchestra and Tape" / and the outstanding Bjorn Fongaard "Galaxy for Three Electric Guitars in Quarter-Tones." —*"Blue" Gene Tyranny*

Severino Gazzelloni, Flute with Aloys Kontarsky (Piano) / Time Records ✦✦✦
Lovely performances of flute solo pieces by Franco Evangelisti "Proporzioni," Luciano Berio "Sequenza," and Yoritsune Matsudaira "Somaksah"; and for flute and piano by Niccolo Castiglioni "Gymel," Olivier Messian "Merles Noir," and Bruno Maderna "Honeyreves." —*"Blue" Gene Tyranny*

Site-Less Sounds / Tellus ✦✦✦✦✦
Powerful personal and political visions by Shelley Hirsch "No.39" / Gregory Whitehead "How to Pronounce 'Prothesis,'" "M is for the Million Things," and "This Is Not a Test" / David Moss "Conjure" / Jacki Apple, Keith Antar Mason, Linda Albertano, Akilah Nayo Oliver "Redefining Democracy in America: Episodes in Black and White" / David Wojnarowicz and Ben Neill "The Collapse of the Illusory One-Tribe Nation from ITSOFOMO (In the Shadow of Forward Motion)" / Constance DeJong with Brenda Hutchinson "Vanishing Act." Highly recommended. —*"Blue" Gene Tyranny*

Sonic Arts Union, The / Mainstream ✦✦✦
The famous American new music group. Contains Alvin Lucier "Vespers" (1968) for echolocation devices / Robert Ashley "Purposeful Lady Slow Afternoon" / David Behrman "Runthrough" / Gordon Mumma "Hornpipe" (1967). —*"Blue" Gene Tyranny*

Sound Forms for Piano / 1995 / New World ✦✦✦
A welcome re-release on CD of great performances of works by four composers. Contains: Henry Cowell "The Banshee," "Aeolian Harp," and "Piano Piece (Paris 1924)," John Cage from "Sonatas and Interludes," Ben Johnston "Sonata for Microtonal Piano," and Conlon Nancarrow "Studies for Player Piano: No. 1, No. 27, No. 36." —*"Blue" Gene Tyranny*

Soundviews, Vol. One: Sources / What Next? ✦✦✦✦✦
An audio magazine with cassette and booklet. Contains excerpts from dozens of different pieces—almost an entire new music festival on one cassette. A very well-organized collection, especially interesting for the many "sound installation" pieces, which are usually never issued on recordings. —*"Blue" Gene Tyranny*

State of the Union / 1966 / Atavistic ✦✦✦
Produced by composer-performer Elliott Sharp, this is an incredible two-CD collection of one-minute pieces by 146 artists (poets, musicians, writers, visual artists) with proceeds from the sale going to benefit the National Coalition Against Censorship. This has been an ongoing project since a similar release in 1982 on zOaR records. "Changing political, cultural and technical climate plus inspired response yields biting satire, bracing sound, sly observations." —*"Blue" Gene Tyranny*

Strange Companions / Elissa Poole, Baroque Flute. Rick Sacks, percussion / 1991 / Artifact ✦✦✦
Six compositions by six composers for this rather unusual, very talented and musical duet. Contains: Claudio Pompili "Lo Spécchio del Fiore (The Flower Looking-Glass)" (1988), a lovely, florid baroque flute solo; Christopher Butterfield "Flamingo Limo" (1988), a sweetly humorous duet for flute and vibraphone; John Abram's gentle and odd urban music "Aeneid Music V" (1988) for Baroque flute, log drum, prepared guitar, and a tape of rainfall on a "ghetto blaster" portable disc player; Owen Underhill "Partita" (1983) for marimba; Michael J. Baker's charming "Bird in Hand" (1990) for Baroque flute, vibraphone and tape; and Rudolf Komorous "The Necklace of Clear Understanding" (1986), a plaintive and lyrical work for Baroque flute solo. —*"Blue" Gene Tyranny*

String Quartets; The LaSalle Quartet / Deutsche Grammaphon ✦✦✦✦✦
Fundamental statements of new ideas about the string quartet form by composers Cage, Lutoslawski, Penderecki, and Mayuzumi. Sensitive performances. —*"Blue" Gene Tyranny*

Tango / Tellus ✦✦✦✦✦
Retakes on the idea and spirit of the tango. Includes works by Carlos Gardel, David Garland with Cinnie Cole and Zeena Parkins, Chris DeBlasio, Keith Keeler, B. Hutchinson with Gerry Lindahl, A. Tomlinson, Elodie Lauten, Jo Basile and Orchestra, "Blue" Gene Tyranny, Molly Elder, Mathew Nash, Christopher Berg, Fast Forward, and Mader. —*"Blue" Gene Tyranny*

Upper Air Observation, Barbara Held (Flute) / Lovely Music ✦✦✦
Selections: Nils Vigeland "Vara" (1979) / Alvin Lucier "Self Portrait"

(1979/1990) / Yasunao Tone "Trio for Flute Player" and "Lyrictron" / Barbara Held "Upper Air Observation." Remarkable musicality on originally commissioned works producing new possibilities for flute and electronics: Lucier's "Self-Portrait" uses a wind anemometer, activated by streams of air from the flutist's lips, that causes a light beamed through its blades to gradually reveal parts of the player's body; haiku poems are generated by a computer that detects the pitches of the flute in Yasunao Tone's beautiful "Lyrictron"; Held's "Upper Air Observation" uses recordings of a radio sound weather balloon launching and other sounds. —*"Blue" Gene Tyranny*

Utopia Americana / New Tone Records ✦✦✦✦✦
A wonderful view of what is "American" in contemporary American Music from an Italian producer's perspective. Containing primarily rhythmic-based music and soundtext rhythms from ordinary speech (Ginsberg's works) with some dreamy electronic music by Oliveros and solo jazz by Steve Lacy, this is an interesting collection of new recordings and reissues of tracks from out-of-print or hard-to-get vinyls. Nice cover photo of Joey's Navajo Cafe and Dining Room framed by the grills of several pickup trucks parked outside. Contains: Allen Ginsberg "Hum Bomb" (1992) / Steve Reich "Music for 18 Musicians" (live, 1976) / Michael Galasso "Baroque" (live, 1992) / Ben Neill "Bal" / John Cage "Third Construction" (from a 1983 Italian studio recording) / David Behrman "A Traveller's Dream Journal (EWR-LAX)" (1992) / Pauline Oliveros "A Woman Sees How the World Goes with No Eyes" (from the Lovely Music LCD 1903 "Crone Music") / Steve Lacy "Pannonica" / John Zorn/Andrea Centazzo "First Environment for Sextet" (recorded in New York WKCR Radio 1978 from "Environment for Sextet" Ictus Records 0017) / Allen Ginsberg "Father Death Blues." —*"Blue" Gene Tyranny*

Views from the Perfect City / 1995 / Inial ✦✦✦
Highly innovative short electronic works of North American composers. Contains: Ron Kuivila's "Loose Canons," Jay Cloidt "Light Fall" (1989), Mark Trayle "Megabitchin'" (1989-92), David Dunn " . . . with zitterings of flight released, in memoriam Kenneth Gaburo" (1993), "Song" (1994), "Tim Labor Crosses the Bay of Fundy with a Smile on His Face and a Song in His Heart" (1992), Joel Ryan "Enfolded Strings Inial Mix" (1994), Kenneth Atchley "6 House" (from the opera on Tesla), and Tim Labor "Clutch" (1990). —*"Blue" Gene Tyranny*

Voice of the Computer / Decca ✦✦✦
Bell Labs computer music from the '60s. Contains James Tenney "Stochastic Quartet" / Max Mathews "Masquerades," "Slider," and "Swan Song" / J. C. Risset "Computer Suite from Little Boy" / J. R. Pierce "Eight-Tone Canon." —*"Blue" Gene Tyranny*

Wai-te-ata Press Music Editions / Frog Peak Music ✦✦✦
Independent publisher of new music by New Zealand composers. —*"Blue" Gene Tyranny*

Wergo Collection: Music of Our Century / Wergo ✦✦✦✦✦
An excellent sampler of 15 works giving a quick "taste" of many composers: Herbert Henck, Cage, Ligeti, Penderecki, Henze, Stockhausen, and others. —*"Blue" Gene Tyranny*

Word / Tellus ✦✦✦
Spoken works with music, processed voices, and many other combinations by novelists and poets. —*"Blue" Gene Tyranny*

JAZZ

Jazz is a music with a history and a heart. Born around the turn of the century in the rich melting pot of the New Orleans area, the East Coast, and the South West, jazz has grown into a vast and deep current of American musical culture. Although it is undoubtedly Black America's gift to the world, it is culturally a profound integration of musical factors: African rhythms and tonalities, the sensibilities of blues and gospel expression, European styles and instrumentation, and the creative energy of America's expansive and tumultuous early 20th century. Important battles against racism were won in the jazz era as bands and audiences began to integrate by virtue of sharing the music. Thus, jazz is both historically and musically a very deep expression of American culture. We achieved in this music what we couldn't—and have yet to—achieve in our social environment: a true and harmonious integration of the diverse streams of human culture that converge in America. Even more than R&B or rock 'n' roll, jazz has become a melting pot, absorbing and integrating the musical styles of the whole world, which is in fact our cultural legacy. Although its originators (and greatest performers) have been African Americans, today jazz knows no racial or geographical barriers.

And chances are that you may already be somewhat of a jazz expert. Although most Americans claim they know little about jazz, the fact is that most of us (whether we recognize it or not) listen to it all the time. The majority of movie and TV background music is jazz, either straight up or in the form of one of its many fusions. Whether it's a Woody Woodpecker cartoon, an old Laurel & Hardy bit, or the latest full-length movie, jazz is the predominant music behind the video that we watch. Although not first in CD sales (jazz recordings make up some 12% of music sales), jazz is probably (indirectly) the most listened to of all musics. Of the many characteristics of jazz, at least in its early forms, two seem to be essential by almost all accounts. Jazz is above all an improvisational music. Players compose on the spot, often around agreed upon or standard themes. In fact, jazz is synonymous with the spontaneous and unrehearsed expression of musical ideas. Once common in classical European music (Bach and Mozart were awesome, among others), improvisation was gradually eliminated from music education. Jazz brought it

back to us in full force. Its improvisational nature has remained to this day an indispensable element of all jazz.

A second component of all early jazz is that it swings (it is danceable) and has a groove. Early jazz was almost always danceable. If it was jazz, then you were moving either onto the dance floor or just marching down the street. There was always the "groove." However, this swing or danceable component has not fared so well over time. With the advent of bop, West Coast cool, free, and the other forms of progressive jazz, a portion of jazz has become listener's music, a kind of American classical chamber music. In other words, jazz became a cultural event—art. The dance floors in many venues were filled in with table and chairs for listeners and the jazz concert was born. The danceable element was lost. However, while many styles of jazz became an art form (the music of the cultured elite), the more danceable forms remained very popular with the masses, particularly with African Americans and, in recent years, have emerged with a renewed life of their own. Reissues of soul-jazz, funk, and the more energetic hard bop styles are heard everywhere these days. In addition, many of these "groovier" jazz forms are being sampled by rappers and acid jazz enthusiasts. Jazz as a danceable improvisational music is on the comeback. Aside from the various forms of soul-jazz and funk, Latin jazz (with its very danceable rhythms) is also a fast growing market. People are dancing to jazz again.

And the types of jazz are many, ranging from blues-based styles drenched in feeling to the more airy styles of jazz that are almost indistinguishable from modern classical music. For all this cultural significance, jazz is remarkably easy to listen to, with an unpretentious, spontaneous feeling and a wide emotional range. It has tremendous diversity in its styles and historical eras, and the richness of recorded jazz (recorded music started about the same time as jazz itself) makes it a wonderful project for long-term enjoyment and learning. Most of us who listen to jazz have found one or two favorite types of jazz that we can really get into. We work outward from there. Your own favorite kind of jazz is in there somewhere; you just have to find it. What is important is to hear the different styles of jazz and find ones that work for you. —*Michael Erlewine, Michael G. Nastos, David Nelson McCarthy*

John Abercrombie

b. Dec. 16, 1944, Port Chester, NY
Guitar / Post-Bop
Perhaps the most skilled of the contemporary jazz guitarists who've embraced and utilized rock techniques and electronic devices in an improvising framework, John Abercrombie has made many superb recordings since the early '70s. He's used phase shifters, volume pedals, and guitar synthesizers on a regular basis, as well as the electric mandolin. Abercrombie is cited (or blamed) in many circles for helping create the "ECM sound," a patchwork of acoustic and electric sounds made by eclectic musicians who combine jazz, European, and Asian/Indian sources, elements, and influences. But Abercrombie can also swing, play in the distorted, jagged rock style, execute bebop changes, improvise in 12-bar blues patterns, or engage in free dialogues. He began playing guitar at 14, taking lessons from a local teacher. He attended Berklee in the mid-'60s, while also playing in rock bands. Abercrombie studied guitar with Jack Petersen, and in 1967 and 1968 toured with Johnny "Hammond" Smith. He moved to New York in 1969, working briefly with the group Dreams, then playing with Chico Hamilton, in whose band he made his first visit to Europe. Abercrombie later played with Jeremy Steig, Gil Evans, and Gato Barbieri, while recording with Dave Liebman and playing in Billy Cobham's Spectrum. He recorded with them and attracted extensive critical attention.

Abercrombie began recording with Jack DeJohnette and also as a leader in the mid-'70s, working mainly for ECM. Since that time, he's done duo albums with Ralph Towner, played in various DeJohnette bands, and headed various groups. Abercrombie's recorded with Jan Hammer, Dave Holland, Mike Brecker, Richie Beirach, George Mraz, Peter Donald, Marc Johnson, Adam Nussbaum, Peter Erskine, Vince Mendoza, and Jon Christensen among others. He has many titles currently available on CD. Recently John Abercrombie had a reunion of his early '70s trio Timeless with Dave Holland and Jack DeJohnette. —*Ron Wynn and David Nelson McCarthy*

● **Timeless** / Jun. 21, 1974-Jun. 22, 1974 / ECM ◆◆◆◆
Guitarist John Abercrombie debuted on ECM in 1974 working in a format that would become familiar, a trio setting. Jan Hammer, on synthesizer, organ, and piano, and drummer Jack DeJohnette accompanied him on a date that included crisp, taut riffs and solos from Abercrombie, sparse and tasty fills and licks by DeJohnette, and a bonus in long stretches of first-rate organ work by Hammer, minus the rock gimmicks that eventually plagued his keyboard work. —*AMG*

Gateway / Mar. 1975 / ECM ◆◆◆

Gateway 2 / Jul. 1977 / ECM ◆◆◆

Arcade / Dec. 1978 / ECM ◆◆◆

M / Nov. 1980 / ECM ✦✦✦
Five Years Later / Mar. 1981 / ECM ✦✦✦
Witchcraft / Jun. 24, 1986-Jun. 25, 1986 / Justin Time ✦✦✦
John Abercrombie, Marc Johnson, & Peter Erskine / Aug. 14, 1991 / ECM ✦✦✦
While We're Young / Jun. 1992 / ECM ✦✦✦
November / Nov. 1992 / ECM ✦✦✦
Gateway: Homecoming / Dec. 1994 / ECM ✦✦✦✦

Muhal Richard Abrams

b. Sep. 19, 1930, Chicago, IL
Piano / Avant-Garde
Although somewhat underrated through the years due to his behind-the-scenes work, Muhal Richard Abrams was one of the most important figures to emerge from the Association for the Advancement of Creative Musicians (AACM), an organization whose successes would have been much fewer without his participation. Influential as an avant-garde pianist who bridged the gap between hard bop, free jazz, and (to a certain extent) contemporary classical music, Abrams' additional significance as a composer, arranger, and bandleader has long put him near the top of the avant-garde field. Although he went to music college when he was 17, Muhal Richard Abrams was essentially self-taught, learning his craft on the job and through his own explorations. Influenced early on by pianist Bud Powell, Abrams performed at a wide variety of jobs during the '50s, gained some early attention for his playing on the MJT+3's album *Branching Out*, and through the years gigged and/or recorded with such musicians as Max Roach, Sonny Stitt, Dexter Gordon, Eddie Harris, Ruth Brown, and Woody Shaw. In 1961 Abrams formed a short-lived orchestra (the Experimental Band) and then on May 8, 1965, he was a major force in the founding of the AACM, a still-active Chicago-based organization that emphasizes self-reliance by performing original compositions, organizing one's own concerts, and educating the community (including younger musicians) about the new music. The innovators who emerged from the AACM (including the Art Ensemble of Chicago, Anthony Braxton, and Henry Threadgill) invigorated the avant-garde, taking the music out of the potential dead end of consistently intense improvisations into an appreciation of the value of space and silence and a logical mix of compositions with individual expression. As the AACM's first president, Abrams established the organization as a vital force on the Chicago jazz scene. Fortunately he did not neglect his own playing, and through the years, most notably on Delmark (starting with the groundbreaking *Levels and Degrees of Light* in 1967) and continuing on India Navigation, Arista/Freedom, and Black Saint, Abrams (who moved to New York in 1977) has recorded in a wide variety of settings, from solo piano to leader of his own innovative big band. He has stuck consistently to his principles (which became the philosophy of the AACM) and forged his own singular path in jazz. —*Scott Yanow*

Levels and Degrees of Light / Jun. 7, 1967-Dec. 21, 1967 / Delmark ✦✦✦✦
This was one of Muhal Richard Abrams' early gems, a 1967 session that included him playing both piano and synthesizer and heading a quartet with Anthony Braxton on clarinet, Thurman Barker on drums, and Gordon Emmanuel on vibes. Abrams' superbly interspersed free, hard bop, and blues elements, while Braxton's solos and the intriguing front line and contrasts provided by vibes and drums rather than bass resulted in some unusual and striking compositions. This has been reissued on CD. —*AMG*

Young at Heart, Wise in Time / Jul. 2, 1969-Aug. 2, 1969 / Delmark ✦✦✦
Sightsong / Oct. 13, 1975-Oct. 14, 1975 / Black Saint ✦✦✦
Mama and Daddy / Jun. 16, 1980-Jun. 19, 1980 / Black Saint ✦✦✦
Blues Forever / Jul. 20, 1981-Jul. 27, 1981 / Black Saint ✦✦✦✦
Tremendous large orchestra session, with Abrams heading a crew that includes the cream of '70s and '80s improvisers, plus some '60s survivors. Although every arrangement doesn't click, the band successfully romps and stomps through enough cuts to show that the big band sound doesn't just mean "ghost" groups recreating dusty numbers from the '30s and '40s. —*Ron Wynn*

● **Rejoicing with the Light** / Jan. 8, 1983-Jan. 25, 1983 / Black Saint ✦✦✦✦
Muhal Richard Abrams blended vintage and progressive sensibilities on this outstanding session. It was a large band, and Abrams assembled many of the finest active improvisers. His orchestra did not include just saxophones and trumpets but also French horns, bass clarinets, cello, guitar, vibes, and timpani. This assured Abrams a varied, rich sound. He led the orchestra through pieces that were sometimes introspective and other times jubilant and swinging, but never simple or predictable. This session was a challenging, instructive, and entertaining lesson in modern big-band writing, arranging, and performing. —*Ron Wynn*

The Hearinga Suite / Jan. 17, 1989-Jan. 18, 1989 / Black Saint ✦✦✦✦
Pianist Muhal Richard Abrams leads an 18-piece orchestra on his seven originals that make up the *Hearinga Suite*. Much of the music is quite

Abbreviations

The following abbreviations are used in some reviews following the musicians' names to indicate instruments played on a particular recording or session.

as	alto saxophone	k	keyboards
b	bass	org	organ
bcl	bass clarinet	p	piano
bj	banjo	per	percussion
bs	baritone saxophone	pkt-t	pocket-trumpet
cnt	cornet	sno	sopranino saxophone
cl	clarinet	ss	soprano saxophone
clo	cello	syn	synthesizer
d	drums	tpt	trumpet
euph	euphonium	tb	trombone
f	flute	tba	tuba
flhn	flugelhorn	ts	tenor saxophone
frhn	french horn	vib	vibraphone
g	guitar	vn	violin

adventurous, although "Oldfotalk" is fairly conventional. Although the personnel includes such fine players as trumpeters Jack Walrath and Cecil Bridgewater and saxophonists John Purcell and Marty Ehrlich, the emphasis is on group interplay and the colorful arrangements. Throughout this very interesting set, Abrams shows how a big band can logically be utilized in freer forms of jazz. —*Scott Yanow*

Blu Blu Blu / Nov. 9, 1990-Nov. 10, 1990 / Black Saint ✦✦✦
Family Talk / 1993 / Black Saint ✦✦✦

George Adams

b. Apr. 29, 1940, Covington, GA, **d.** Nov. 14, 1992, New York, NY
Flute, Sax (Tenor) / Avant-Garde, Post-Bop
A passionate tenor and flute player who was not shy to break up chordal improvising with an unexpected scream or roar, George Adams was an original voice who (like his friend Don Pullen) crossed over several stylistic boundaries. He started on piano, but by the time he was in high school he was playing tenor in funk bands. In 1961 he toured with Sam Cooke, and in 1963 Adams moved to Ohio, where he played with organ groups for the next few years. In 1968 he relocated to New York, where he played with Roy Haynes, Gil Evans, and Art Blakey among others. However it was his association with Charles Mingus (1973-76) that gave him his initial fame. After playing a bit with McCoy Tyner, Adams co-led a stimulating quartet with Don Pullen that made many records. Late in life Adams (who enjoyed taking an occasional raspy blues vocal) teamed up with James "Blood" Ulmer in the group Phalanx and occasionally played with Mingus Dynasty. —*Scott Yanow*

Don't Lose Control / Nov. 2, 1979-Nov. 3, 1979 / Soul Note ✦✦✦
● **America** / May 24, 1989-Jul. 18, 1989 / Blue Note ✦✦✦✦
Saxophonist George Adams was nearing the end of his creative road on 1989's *America*, so it was appropriate for him to go back to his roots and play some blues. He alternates between terse, rippling solos and impassioned, almost serene ones, something that puzzled many critics when this was released. Pianist Hugh Lawson, bassist Cecil McBee, and drummer Marc Johnson took their cues from Adams, mostly playing it straight in their roles and when in the spotlight keeping things simple and restrained, except when Adams himself turned up the intensity. —*Ron Wynn*

Old Feeling / Mar. 11, 1991-Mar. 12, 1991 / Blue Note ✦✦✦✦
Old Feeling ranks as one of George Adams' most exciting and happily eccentric sessions. Unlike some other avant-gardists who seem to lose their personality and purpose when they play standard material, Adams turns even overplayed songs into his own inventive devices; three standards get the "Adams treatment" on this CD. —*Scott Yanow*

Pepper Adams (Pepper Park Adams, III)

b. Oct. 8, 1930, Highland Park, MI, **d.** Sep. 10, 1986, New York, NY
Sax (Baritone) / Hard Bop
Pepper Adams was one of the all-time great baritonists, ranking at the top with Harry Carney, Serge Chaloff, and Gerry Mulligan. But Mulligan overshadowed Adams throughout virtually his entire career, which is a little strange because Pepper had a much different sound (heavier and more intense) than the light-toned and playful Mulligan.

Adams grew up in Rochester, NY, and when he was 16 he moved to Detroit, where he became an important part of the very fertile local jazz scene. Other than a period in the military (1951-53), Adams was a major fixture in Detroit, playing with such up-and-coming musicians as Donald

JAZZ STYLES

Because jazz in its 100 years has consistently inspired musicians to develop their own individual approaches to self-expression, there are almost as many different styles as there are innovators. The 19 categories listed in this section are a simplification that makes it possible to give readers a hint as to what particular musicians sound like. It should be assumed that the most original players do not fit neatly into any one style and that the boundaries between these terms are not absolute or uncrossable.

RAGTIME — Although not really jazz (ragtime does not have improvisation or the feeling of the blues), this style, at its prime during 1899-1915, was a strong influence on the earlier forms of jazz. Best-known as a piano music, ragtime (which is totally written-out) was also performed by orchestras. Its syncopations and structure, blending together aspects of classical music and marches, hint strongly at jazz and some of its melodies were played in later years by dixieland musicians.

NEW ORLEANS JAZZ — The first style of jazz, the music played in New Orleans from the time that Buddy Bolden formed his first band in 1895 until Storyville was closed in 1917 went totally unrecorded. However with the success of the Original Dixieland Jazz Band in 1917 and the many performances documented in the '20s, that situation changed. Ensemble oriented with fairly strict roles for each instrument, New Orleans jazz generally features a trumpet or cornet providing a melodic lead, harmonies from the trombone, countermelodies by the clarinet and a steady rhythm stated by the rhythm section (which usually consists of piano, banjo or guitar, tuba or bass and drums). This music is a direct descendant of marching brass bands and, although overlapping with dixieland, tends to de-emphasize solos in favor of ensembles. Due to its fairly basic harmonies and the pure joy of the ensembles, it is consistently the happiest and most accessible style of jazz.

CLASSIC JAZZ — The '20s were a rich decade with jazz-influenced dance bands and a gradual emphasis on solo (as opposed to collective) improvisations. Whether it be the stride pianists, the increasingly adventurous horn soloists or arranged music that predates swing, much of the jazz from this decade can be given the umbrella title of "Classic Jazz." Some of the modern-day revivalists who look beyond the dixieland repertoire to the music of Fletcher Henderson, Clarence Williams and Bix Beiderbecke (to name three examples) can be said to be playing in this open-ended style.

DIXIELAND — A style that overlaps with New Orleans jazz and classic jazz, dixieland has also been called "Chicago jazz" because it developed to an extent in Chicago in the '20s. Most typically the framework involves collective improvisation during the first chorus, individual solos with some riffing by the other horns, and a closing ensemble or two with a four bar tag by the drummer being answered by the full group. Although nearly any song can be turned into dixieland, there is a consistent repertoire of forty or so songs that have proven to be consistently reliable. This music has had a fairly large audience since its revival in the '40s.

SWING — Due to the utilization of more than three or four horns in big bands, it became necessary for ensembles to be written out. Swing caught on in the mid-'30s as dance music of the era and the saxophone grew in importance as did the role of the arranger. Swing differs from New Orleans jazz and dixieland in that the ensembles (even for small groups) are simpler and generally filled with repetitious riffs while in contrast the solos are more sophisticated. Individual improvisations still pay close attention to the melody but, due to the advance in musicianship, the solo flights are more adventurous while staying accessible.

BEBOP — Also known as bop, bebop was a radical new music that developed gradually in the early '40s and seemed to explode in 1945 with the emergence of Charlie Parker and Dizzy Gillespie. The main difference between bop and swing is that in the former the soloists engage in chordal (rather than melodic) improvisation, often discarding the melody altogether after the first chorus and using the chords as the basis for the solo. The virtuosic pacesetters of the style divorced themselves from the pop music world yet their once-futuristic style became a conservative alternative by the '60s to the avant-garde.

COOL (OR WEST COAST) — Cool jazz is a mixture of bop with certain aspects of swing that had been overlooked or temporarily discarded. Dissonances were smoothed out, tones were softened, arrangements became important again and the rhythm section's accents were less jarring. Many of the style's leaders were based near the studios of Los Angeles, some of the recordings were experimental in nature (hinting at classical music) and for a period in the '50s this was a very popular style.

MAINSTREAM — The term "mainstream" was coined by critic Stanley Dance to describe the style that veterans of the swing era) were playing in the '50s, music between dixieland and bop. Although this idiom was overshadowed for quite awhile, with the rise of tenor saxophonist Scott Hamilton and trumpeter Warren Vache in the '70s and the beginning of the Concord label (which emphasized the music), mainstream (which is essentially small group swing) has become a potent force.

THIRD STREAM — "Third stream" (a term invented by composer Gunther Schuller in 1957) means a mixture of jazz and classical music. During the mid-to-late '50s, serious experiments took place although most attempts at fusing the two very different idioms have been at best mixed successes with non-improvising string sections tending to weigh down jazz soloists. Overshadowed by the avant-garde in the '60s, the idea of the third stream lives on and more recent projects sometimes shown great promise.

LATIN (OR AFRO-CUBAN) JAZZ — Of the post-swing styles, Latin jazz has been the most consistently popular and it is easy to see why. The emphasis on percussion and Cuban rhythms make the style (essentially a mixture of loop-oriented jazz with Latin percussion) quite danceable and accessible. Among the pioneers in mixing together the two styles in the '40s were the big bands of Dizzy Gillespie and Machito and the music (which has never gone out of style) has remained a viable force through the '90s.

Byrd, Kenny Burrell, Tommy Flanagan, Barry Harris, and Elvin Jones. Adams had opportunities to tour with Stan Kenton, Maynard Ferguson, and Chet Baker, and he moved to New York in 1958. In addition to recording both as a leader and a sideman, Adams played with Benny Goodman (1958-59) and Charles Mingus (off and on between 1959-63) and co-led a quintet with Donald Byrd (1958-62). He was a longtime member of the Thad Jones-Mel Lewis band (1965-78) and a major stylist up until his death. —*Scott Yanow*

Jazzmen: Detroit / Apr. 28, 1956 / Savoy ♦♦♦

Pepper Adams Quintet / Jul. 10, 1957 / VSOP ♦♦♦

● **10 to 4 at the 5-Spot** / Apr. 5, 1958 / Original Jazz Classics ♦♦♦♦
The best example of the bebop baritone saxophonist from Detroit includes a young Donald Byrd (tpt) and pianist Bobby Timmons. —*David Szatmary*

● **Conjuration: Fat Tuesday's Session** / Aug. 19, 1983-Aug. 20, 1983 / Reservoir ♦♦♦♦
The great baritonist Pepper Adams is teamed up with the adventurous trumpeter Kenny Wheeler and veteran pianist Hank Jones for this live quintet date. Wheeler, although often associated with the avant-garde, has never had any difficulty playing changes and his strong style clearly inspired Adams. Together they perform three of the baritonist's originals, Thad Jones' "Tis," Wheeler's "Old Ballad," and the standard "Alone Together." —*Scott Yanow*

Cannonball Adderley (Julian Edwin Adderley)

b. Sep. 15, 1928, Tampa, FL, **d.** Aug. 8, 1975, Gary, IN
Sax (Alto) / Soul-Jazz, Hard Bop, Groove

One of the great alto saxophonists, Cannonball Adderley had an exuberant and happy sound (as opposed to many of the more serious stylists of his generation) that communicated immediately to listeners. His intelligent presentation of his music (often explaining what he and his musicians were going to play) helped make him one of the most popular of all jazzmen. Adderley already had an established career as a high school band director in Florida when during a 1955 visit to New York he was persuaded to sit in with Oscar Pettiford's group at the Cafe Bohemia. His playing created such a sensation that he was soon signed to Savoy and persuaded to play jazz full-time in New York. With his younger brother cornetist Nat, Cannonball formed a quintet that struggled until its breakup in 1957. Adderley then joined Miles Davis, forming part of his super sextet with John Coltrane and participating on such classic recordings as *Milestones* and *Kind of Blue*. Adderley's second attempt to form a quintet with his brother was much more successful, for in 1959 with pianist Bobby Timmons he had a hit recording of "This Here." From then on, Cannonball was always able to work steadily with his band.

During its Riverside years (1959-63), the Adderley Quintet primarily played soulful renditions of hard bop, and Cannonball really excelled in the straightahead settings. During 1962-63 Yusef Lateef made the group a sextet, and pianist Joe Zawinul was an important new member. The

HARD BOP — An extension of bop that started in the early-to mid '50s and has been the dominant mainstream of jazz since the '60s, hard bop differs from classic bop in that the melodies tend to be simpler and often more "soulful," the rhythm section is usually looser with the bassist not as tightly confined to playing a metronomic four-beats-to-the-bar and quite often the saxophonists and pianists show the influence of both gospel and rhythm and blues. Art Blakey's Jazz Messengers and Horace Silver were among the early pacesetters and the style was greatly revived by the "Young Lions" in the '80s.

BOSSA-NOVA — The Brazilian version of cool jazz, bossa-nova emphasizes an attractive subtle rhythm and soft tones (particularly in its vocals, acoustic guitars and occasional tenor). Antonio Carlos Jobim's compositions defined the idiom which was a major fad in the early '60s but survived that period to become an element in jazz'smainstream and a significant part of Brazil's musical legacy.

FREE JAZZ — Free jazz was a radical departure from past styles for, typically after playing a quick theme, the soloist does not have to follow any set chord progression or structure and can go in any unpredictable direction. Free jazz, which overlaps with the avant-garde, remains a controversial and mostly underground style. Having dispensed with many of the rules as far as pitch, rhythm and development are concerned, the success of a free jazz performance can be measured by the musicianship and imagination of the performers, how colorful the music is and whether it seems logical or merely random. Ornette Coleman was a major force in pioneering free jazz in the late '50s and for a period in the '60s (when it was sometimes called "The New Thing") the music was a source of constant debate.

AVANT-GARDE — Avant-garde jazz differs from free jazz in that it tends to have some pre-planned structure in the ensembles (more of a "game plan") although the individual improvisations can be just as free of conventional rules. In the best avant-garde performances it is difficult to tell where compositions end and improvisations begin; the goal is to have the solos be an outgrowth of the arrangement. As with free jazz, the avant-garde came of age in the '60s and has continued almost unnoticed as a menacing force in the jazz underground, scorned by the mainstream that it influences.

FUSION — The word "fusion" has been used so liberally during the past quarter-century as to become almost meaningless. Its original definition is best: a mixture of jazz improvisation with the power and rhythms of rock. After some early experiments, by the early '70s fusion had its own separate identity as a creative jazz style (although sneered upon by many purists). Unfortunately as it became a moneymaker and as rock declined artistically from the mid-'70s on, much of what was labelled fusion was actually a combination of jazz with easy-listening pop music and lightweight r&b. The promise of fusion to an extent went unfulfilled although it continues to exist creatively in the '90s in groups such as Tribal Tech and Chick Corea's Elektric Band.

FREE FUNK — A mixture of funk rhythms with avant-garde jazz solos, this somewhat eccentric idiom was introduced by Ornette Coleman's Prime Time in the '70s and became the backbone of Steve Coleman's M-Base movement of the '80s and '90s. Despite using the power of rock and funky rhythms, there is nothing predictable about the performances!

CROSSOVER — Often called "contemporary jazz" or "fusion" (terms that really do not fit), crossover is an accessible and very melodic mixture of jazz with elements of pop, R&B and World music; Grover Washington Jr. and David Sanborn are two of the best players in this idiom although their imitators tend to be much less interesting. Crossover has sometimes been valuable in increasing the jazz audience (some of whom end up exploring other styles). In some cases the music is quite worthwhile while in other instances the jazz co tent is a relatively small part of the ingredients. When the style is actually pop music with only an insignificant amount of improvis tion for flavor, the term "Instrumental Pop" applies best.

POST BOP (OR MODERN MAINSTREAM) — It has become increasingly difficult to categorize modern jazz. A large segment of the music does not fit into any historical style, is not as rock-oriented as fusion or as free as the avant-garde. Starting with the rise of Wynton Marsalis in 1979, a whole generation of younger players (called "the Young Lions") chose to play an updated variety of hard bop that was also influenced by the mid-'60s Miles Davis Quintet and aspects of free jazz. Since this music (which often features complex chordal improvisation) has become the norm for jazz in the '90s, the term "Modern Mainstream" or "Post Bop" symbolizes the eclectic scene as jazz enters its second century.

SOUL-JAZZ — Soul-jazz, also called funky jazz, original funk, or just plain funk, is a form of jazz that originated in the mid-'50s. It is often played by small groups—trios led by a tenor or alto sax, pianist, or Hammond organ. Funk music is very physical, usually down and dirty. The funk style emerged as a reaction to the cool jazz prevalent at the time. Funky music is everything that cool jazz is not: hot, sweaty, and never straying far from its blues roots. Fast-paced funk pieces have a bright melodic phrasing set against a hard, percussive dance rhythm. Funk ballads are never more than a few steps from the blues. Above all, this is dynamic, relaxin' music that is easy to listen to. Those of you who like blues and R&B, but find some jazz just a touch remote, will like funk. There is no better music to kick back to than this. Soul Jazz artists include the later work of Gene Ammons, Jimmy Smith, Grant Green, Stanley Turrentine, Charles Earland, Eddie Harris, Groove Holmes, Willis "Gator" Jackson, Les McCann, Brother Jack McDuff, Jimmy McGriff, Houston Person, Shirley Scott, Horace Silver, Johnny Hammond, Howard Roberts, and Bobby Timmons. —*JME*

—Scott Yanow

---

collapse of Riverside resulted in Adderley signing with Capitol, and his recordings became gradually more commercial. Charles Lloyd was in Lateef's place for a year (with less success), and then with his departure the group went back to being a quintet. Zawinul's 1966 composition "Mercy, Mercy, Mercy" was a huge hit for the group, Adderley started doubling on soprano, and the Quintet's later recordings emphasized long melody statements, funky rhythms, and electronics. However, during his last year, Cannonball Adderley was revisiting the past a bit, and on *Phenix* he recorded new versions of many of his earlier numbers. But before he could evolve his music any further, Cannonball Adderley died suddenly from a stroke. —*Scott Yanow*

Sophisticated Swing: The EmArcy Small Group Sessions / Jul. 12, 1956-Mar. 6, 1958 / EmArcy ◆◆◆◆

Cannonball's Sharpshooters / Mar. 4, 1958-Mar. 6, 1958 / EmArcy ◆◆◆

★ **Somethin' Else** / Mar. 9, 1958 / Blue Note ◆◆◆◆◆
Shortly after Adderley broke up his original quintet and joined Miles Davis' sextet, he recorded this LP with Davis in the rare role of a sideman. Actually, Davis dominates several of the selections (including "Autumn Leaves," "Love for Sale" and "One for Daddy-o") but both hornmen (backed by pianist Hank Jones, bassist Sam Jones, and drummer Art Blakey) sound quite inspired by each other's presence. —*Scott Yanow*

Portrait of Cannonball / Jul. 1, 1958 / Original Jazz Classics ◆◆◆
Adderley's first album for Riverside, recorded while he was working as a sideman in Miles Davis' classic sextet. With Blue Mitchell (tpt), Bill Evans (p), Sam Jones (b), and Philly Joe Jones (d). —*Michael Erlewine*

● **Cannonball Adderley Quintet in San Francisco** / Oct. 18, 1959-Oct. 20, 1959 / Original Jazz Classics ◆◆◆◆
This live date with Bobby Timmons (p), Nat Adderley (cnt), Sam Jones (b), and Louis Hayes (d) contains the classic and soulful "This Here." This is an exciting session. —*Hank Davis*

What Is This Thing Called Soul? / Nov. 1960 / Pablo ◆◆◆

Know What I Mean? / Jan. 27, 1961-Feb. 21, 1961 / Riverside ◆◆◆
Great album. With Bill Evans (p), Percy Heath (b), and Connie Kay (d). —*Michael Erlewine*

Nancy Wilson/Cannonball Adderley / Jun. 27, 1961-Aug. 24, 1961 / Capitol ◆◆◆◆
Adderley's abilities as a talent scout have long been overlooked. He helped discover Nancy Wilson early in her career, and by 1961 she was already on her way to becoming a popular middle-of-the-road singer. This CD (which adds a previously unissued "Little Unhappy Boy" to the original LP), instead of alternating instrumental performances by his quintet with Wilson's vocals as on the LP, sounds like two separate sets due to the placement of the seven vocals at the beginning of the program. Nancy Wilson, who was never really a jazz singer, sounds more influenced by jazz on these numbers (particularly on "Never Will I Marry," "The Masquerade Is Over," and "A Sleepin' Bee") than she would

later on. The instrumentals include fine versions of "I Can't Get Started" and "Unit 7." —*Scott Yanow*

In New York / Jan. 12, 1962-Jan. 14, 1962 / Original Jazz Classics ◆◆◆
Live date at the Village Vanguard in NYC. With Nat Adderley (cnt), Yusef Lateef (ts, fl), Joe Zawinul (p), Sam Jones (b), and Louis Hayes (d). —*Michael Erlewine*

Lugano, 1963 / Mar. 24, 1963 / TCB ◆◆◆◆
This Italian concert (broadcast by Swiss radio) features the 1963 Cannonball Adderley Sextet, which was arguably the altoist's finest band. In addition to the leader, the performance features cornetist Nat Adderley, the versatile Yusef Lateef on tenor, flute, and oboe, pianist Joe Zawinul, bassist Sam Jones, and drummer Louis Hayes. Highlights include "Jive Samba," "Dizzy's Business," a lengthy "Trouble in Mind," and "Work Song," but all seven selections are quite rewarding. Cannonball Adderley fans can consider every recording by this classic unit to be essential! —*Scott Yanow*

Nippon Soul / Jul. 9, 1963-Jul. 15, 1963 / Riverside ◆◆◆
First live jazz album. Recorded in Tokyo by Cannonball Adderley, with Yusef Lateef (ts). —*Michael G. Nastos*

Mercy, Mercy, Mercy / Oct. 20, 1966 / Capitol ◆◆◆◆
This set (reissued on CD) is one of Cannonball Adderley's finest albums of his last decade. "Mercy, Mercy, Mercy," a soulful Joe Zawinul melody that is repeated several times without any real improvisation, became a surprise hit, but the other selections on this live date ("Fun," "Games," "Sticks," "Hippodelphia," and "Sack O'Woe") all have plenty of fiery solos from the quintet (which is comprised of the leader on alto, cornetist Nat Adderley, pianist Joe Zawinul, bassist Victor Gaskin, and drummer Roy McCurdy). Cannonball sounds quite inspired (his expressive powers had expanded due to the unacknowledged influence of the avant-garde), and Nat shows just how exciting a player he was back in his prime. "Sack O'Woe" is particularly memorable. This CD, which is far superior to most of Cannonball's later Capitol recordings, is highly recommended. —*Scott Yanow*

Radio Nights / 1967-1968 / Night ◆◆◆

Phenix / Feb. 1975-Apr. 1975 / Fantasy ◆◆◆

Nat Adderley

b. Nov. 25, 1931, Tampa, FL
Cornet / Soul-Jazz, Hard Bop, Groove
Nat Adderley's cornet (which in its early days was strongly influenced by Miles Davis) was always a complementary voice to his brother Cannonball in their popular quintet. His career ran parallel to his older brother for quite some time. Nat took up trumpet in 1946, switched to cornet in 1950, and spent time in the military, playing in an Army band during 1951-53. After a period with Lionel Hampton (1954-55), Nat made his recording debut in 1955, joined Cannonball's unsuccessful quintet of 1956-57, and then spent periods with the groups of J.J. Johnson and Woody Herman before hooking up with Cannonball again in Oct. 1959. This time the group became a major success, and Nat remained in the quintet until Cannonball's death in 1975, contributing such originals as "Work Song," "Jive Samba," and "The Old Country" along with many exciting hard-bop solos. Nat Adderley, who was at the peak of his powers in the early to mid-'60s and became adept at playing solos that dipped into the subtone register of his horn, has led his own quintets since Cannonball's death; his most notable sidemen were altoists Sonny Fortune (in the early '80s) and Vincent Herring. Although his own playing has declined somewhat (Adderley's chops no longer have the endurance of his earlier days), he has continued recording worthwhile sessions. Many of his recordings through the years (for such labels as Savoy, EmArcy, Riverside, Jazzland, Atlantic, Milestone, A&M, Capitol, Prestige, SteepleChase, Galaxy, Theresa, In + Out, and Landmark) are currently available. —*Scott Yanow*

Branching Out / Sep. 1958 / Original Jazz Classics ◆◆◆◆
This 1958 date had some of his hottest playing as a leader. Adderley concentrates on cornet, and there haven't been many on that instrument to take it into more abrupt and challenging harmonic contexts. Johnny Griffin's bluesy, taut tenor keeps things moving, while using pianist Gene Harris, bassist Andy Simpkins, and drummer Bill Dowdy (better known as the Three Sounds) for a rhythm section was inspiring. —*Ron Wynn*

● **Work Songs** / Jan. 25, 1960-Sep. 15, 1960 / Original Jazz Classics ◆◆◆◆
Guitarist Wes Montgomery was also aboard for *Work Song,* a Nat Adderley date with Bobby Timmons (p), Louis Hayes (d), Sam Jones, and Ketter Betts or Percy Heath (clo, b). This was, of course, Nat Adderley's date, and Montgomery's role was not so much that of guitarist extraordinaire, but as one of the plucked strings that give this date its ambience . . . . A thoughtful and varied date with a multidimensional personality, this has been previously issued as part of a two-fer. —*Bob Rusch, Cadence*

That's Right!: Nat Adderley & the Big Sax Section / Aug. 9, 1960-Sep. 15, 1960 / Original Jazz Classics ◆◆◆◆
Nat Adderley has seldom played with more fire, verve, and distinction than he did on *That's Right!* It placed him in the company of an expanded sax section that included his brother Cannonball on alto, Yusef Lateef on tenor,

flute, and oboe, Jimmy Heath and Charlie Rouse on tenor, and baritone saxophonist Tate Houston. Solos crackled, the backing was tasty and stimulating, and the eight songs ranged from brisk standards to delightful originals. This CD reissue, despite lacking any new or alternate material, is most welcome due to the full, striking sound that the big reed section provided. —*Ron Wynn*

Natural Soul / Sep. 23, 1963 / Milestone ◆◆◆
With Kenny Burrell (g) and Junior Mance (p). —*Michael Erlewine*

The Old Country / Dec. 5, 1990-Dec. 6, 1990 / Enja ◆◆◆
Adderley has evidently found a soul mate in alto saxophonist Vince Herring, with whom he works once more on this 1990 date. Herring's voice has grown more impressive with each release, and he now offers more than just dazzling lines and phrases; he's constructing and completing confident statements. Pianist Rob Bargad, another regular, is on board, with bassist James Genus and drummer Billy Drummond. —*Ron Wynn*

Air

Group / Modern Creative, Avant-Garde, Free Jazz
Comprised originally of Henry Threadgill on reeds, bassist Fred Hopkins, and drummer Steve McCall, Air emphasized equality of roles by the instruments (without any clear-cut leader) and a smooth mixture of advanced arrangements and free improvisations. In 1971 Threadgill was asked to arrange some of Scott Joplin's songs for a production at Columbia College in Chicago. He teamed up with Hopkins and McCall as the trio Reflection. A few years later in 1975 the musicians came together again as Air, touring Europe, Japan, and America and recording 11 records for such labels as Nessa, India Navigation, Black Saint, Novus, and Antilles. By far their most popular release was 1979's *Air Lore,* which found the group performing abstract versions of tunes by Joplin and Jelly Roll Morton. In 1982 when McCall returned to Chicago and was replaced by Pheeroan AkLaff, the group changed its name to New Air. A year before their breakup in 1986, Andrew Cyrille took over the drum slot. Since then all of the musicians (other than McCall who passed away in 1989) have had very productive careers. —*Scott Yanow*

Air Song / Sep. 10, 1975 / India Navigation ◆◆◆

Open Air Suite / Feb. 21, 1978-Feb. 22, 1978 / Novus ◆◆◆

● **Air Lore** / May 11, 1979-May 12, 1979 / RCA/Bluebird ◆◆◆◆
This was the most unusual and accessible recording ever made by Air. Instead of performing their complex originals as usual, this group (in addition to Threadgill's brief "Paille Street") stretches out on two songs apiece by Jelly Roll Morton and Scott Joplin. Most memorable is their investigation of Joplin's "The Ragtime Dance." Threadgill's solos in particular really fit the mood of these classic pieces. —*Scott Yanow*

Air Mail / Dec. 28, 1980 / Black Saint ◆◆◆◆
The Chicago trio Air was at a high point on this 1980 date, thanks in part to remarkable percussive foundations provided by the late Steve McCall and his interaction with bassist Fred Hopkins, plus the amazing solos and versatility of nominal leader Henry Threadgill. Besides alto and tenor sax, flute, and bass flute, Threadgill plays his own unique instrument called the hubkaphone and makes it just as memorable a weapon as the other horns. —*Ron Wynn*

80 Degrees Below '82 / Jan. 23, 1982-Jan. 24, 1982 / Antilles ◆◆◆

Air Show No. 1 / Jun. 2, 1986-Jun. 3, 1986 / Black Saint ◆◆◆

Toshiko Akiyoshi

b. Dec. 12, 1929, Dairen, China
Piano / Bop, Hard Bop
As an arranger Toshiko Akiyoshi (influenced originally by Gil Evans and Thad Jones) has been particularly notable for incorporating elements of traditional Japanese music into her otherwise boppish charts. A strong (and underrated) pianist in the Bud Powell tradition, Akiyoshi was born in China but moved to Japan in 1946. She played locally (Sadao Watanabe was among her sidemen) and, after being noticed and encouraged by Oscar Peterson, studied at Berklee during 1956-59. Married for a time to altoist Charlie Mariano, she co-led the Toshiko-Mariano quartet in the early '60s. After working with Charles Mingus for a period in 1962 (including Town Hall Concert), she returned to Japan for three years. Back in New York by 1965, she did a radio series and formed a quartet with her second husband, Lew Tabackin, in 1970. After moving to Los Angeles in 1972, Akiyoshi put together her very impressive big band which featured such fine soloists as Bobby Shew, Gary Foster, and Tabackin. They recorded several notable albums before Akiyoshi decided in 1981 to move to New York. Since their relocation, Akiyoshi and Tabackin have both been quite active, although her reformed big band has actually received less publicity than it did in Los Angeles. She ranks as one of the top jazz arrangers of the past 25 years. —*Scott Yanow*

Road Time / Jan. 30, 1976-Feb. 8, 1976 / RCA ◆◆◆◆
This two-LP set, which, like most of the Toshiko Akiyoshi Orchestra's recordings, is out of print, gives one a definitive look at her '70s orchestra. Akiyoshi's arrangements are colorful and swinging; the best charts on this

two-fer are "Tuning Up," the nearly 23-minute "Henpecked Old Man," "Kogun" (which pays tribute to her Japanese heritage), and "Road Time Shuffle." This edition of the orchestra includes such major players as trumpeter Steve Huffstetter and Bobby Shew, trombonist Jimmy Knepper, altoists Dick Spencer and Gary Foster, and Lew Tabackin on tenor and flute. It's highly recommended, if it can be found. —*Scott Yanow*

Interlude / Feb. 1987 / Concord Jazz ✦✦✦

Remembering Bud: Cleopatra's Dream / Jul. 31, 1990-Aug. 1, 1990 / Evidence ✦✦✦

● **Carnegie Hall Concert** / Sep. 20, 1991 / Columbia ✦✦✦✦

Desert Lady-Fantasy / Dec. 1, 1993-Dec. 3, 1993 / Columbia ✦✦✦

Toshiko Akiyoshi at Maybeck / Jul. 10, 1994 / Concord Jazz ✦✦✦

Gerald Albright

b. 1957
Sax (Tenor) / Instrumental Pop, Crossover
Gerald Albright has occasionally shown the ability to play jazz (most notably on his Atlantic set *Live at Birdland West*) but has chosen to make his career as an R&B saxophonist. Originally he studied piano before switching to tenor, and in college he began doubling on electric bass. Through the years Albright has performed in a variety of R&Bish settings (with Patrice Rushen, Anita Baker, Quincy Jones, the Temptations, etc.), content to play simplistic music and disappointingly little jazz. —*Scott Yanow*

Dream Come True / Nov. 6, 1990 / Atlantic ✦✦✦

● **Live at Birdland West** / 1991 / Atlantic ✦✦✦✦
Virtually all of saxophonist Gerald Albright's previous recordings were in the pop/R&B field, making this mostly straightahead session a major surprise. Albright, alternating between alto and tenor, plays quite well throughout this set, which is highlighted by versions of "Impressions," "Georgia on My Mind," and "Limehouse Blues." Tenorman Kirk Whalum helps out on three tracks, and Eddie Harris makes a guest appearance on "Bubblehead McDaddy." This is easily Gerald Albright's most rewarding session to date. —*Scott Yanow*

Smooth / Feb. 22, 1994 / Atlantic ✦✦

Monty Alexander (Montgomery Bernard)

b. Jun. 6, 1944, Kingston, Jamaica
Piano / Bop, Hard Bop, Trinidad, Caribbean
Monty Alexander long ago combined together the influence of Oscar Peterson with the soul of Gene Harris and Nat King Cole to form his own appealing and personable style. Long a bit underrated (due to the shadow of Peterson), Alexander has recorded more than a score of excellent albums. Monty Alexander began piano lessons when he was six, and he played professionally in Jamaica clubs while still a teenager; his band, Monty and the Cyclones, was quite popular locally during 1958-60. He first played in the US when he appeared in Las Vegas with Art Mooney's Orchestra. Soon he was accompanying a variety of top singers, formed a friendship with vibraphonist Milt Jackson, and began gigging with bassist Ray Brown. With the recording of a pair of Pacific Jazz albums in 1965, an RCA date in 1967, and a Verve session in 1969, Alexander began to gain a strong reputation. His series of exciting albums for MPS during 1971-77 found him in prime form, and later recordings (most notably on Pablo and Concord) found him building on his original style. Alexander has occasionally paid tribute to his Jamaican heritage but most of the time performs with his trio and swings hard in his own voice. —*Scott Yanow*

Live! Montreux Alexander / Jun. 10, 1976 / Verve ✦✦✦

● **Triple Treat 1** / Mar. 1982 / Concord Jazz ✦✦✦✦
One can excuse pianist Monty Alexander if his playing on this Concord set recalls Oscar Peterson, for his sidemen in the trio are O.P.-alumni guitarist Herb Ellis and bassist Ray Brown. The combination lives up to its potential with the group romping on such songs as "The Flintstones," Blue Mitchell's "Fungi Mama," and an uptempo "Small Fry." —*Scott Yanow*

Triple Treat 2 / Jun. 1987 / Concord Jazz ✦✦✦✦
Five years after the original *Triple Treat*, pianist Monty Alexander has a reunion with guitarist Herb Ellis and bassist Ray Brown in a program that is in the tradition of both Oscar Peterson and Nat King Cole. A special bonus is violinist John Frigo, who sits in on four of the eight songs. High points include Ray Brown's "Lined with a Groove," "Straighten up and Fly Right," "Seven Come Eleven," and "Lester Leaps In." —*Scott Yanow*

Steamin' / Sep. 14, 1994-1994 / Concord Jazz ✦✦✦

Maybeck Recital Hall Series, Vol. 40 / Sep. 26, 1994 / Concord Jazz ✦✦✦✦

Geri Allen

b. Jun. 12, 1957, Pontiac, MI
Piano / Post-Bop
A shining light among '80s pianists, Geri Allen has achieved a synthesis of

bebop, free, hard bop, and funk/R&B influences, melding them into an individualistic, exciting style. Her touch, phrasing, melodic, and rhythmic abilities are superb, and she's been both a busy session player with numerous credits and recording dates and a featured artist on the Soul Note, DIW, JMT/Polygram, and Blue Note labels. Allen cites the unpredictability of Thelonious Monk and Herbie Nichols, and virtuosity of Eric Dolphy, as sources that have had strong impact on her style. She's noted for her ability to solo in a quiet, yet intense fashion, and this skill has been illuminated on some remarkable trio dates with Charlie Haden and Paul Motian. Allen once backed the Supremes during her early days in Detroit. After studying music at Howard University and the University of Pittsburgh with Nathan Davis, she studied privately with Roscoe Mitchell. Allen moved to New York in the early '80s, working with James Newton and Lester Bowie before recording her debut for Minor. She's also played with Marcus Belgrave, Kenny Garrett, Robert Hurst, Jeff Watts, Oliver Lake, Andrew Cyrille, and Robin Eubanks. Allen has worked closely with both Coleman's M-Base and the Black Rock Coalition, an organization of musicians, artists, and cultural activists working to improve conditions and opportunities for African-Americans in every area of American music. She's also played with Betty Carter. Recently she has played in several settings with Wallace Roney, and in 1994 she toured with Ornette Coleman's acoustic quartet. —*Ron Wynn*

Twylight / 1989 / Verve ✦✦✦

In the Year of the Dragon / Mar. 1989 / Verve ✦✦✦✦
Throughout *In the Year of the Dragon*, whether the music is classic bop or very free, this trio is creative, colorful, and right on the mark. The musical communication between the three musicians seems telepathic; each of them obviously possesses large ears. —*Scott Yanow, Cadence*

● **Maroons** / 1992 / Blue Note ✦✦✦✦
Allen has developed into one of the major voices of the modern jazz piano. On *Maroons* she brings out the best in trumpeter Wallace Roney, welcomes her mentor, trumpeter Marcus Belgrave, on a few tracks, and performs 15 fresh compositions, 13 of them her originals. The music is unpredictable and explorative but still tied enough to the tradition to make the results quite coherent. This is a strong example of Allen's playing and compositional talents. —*Scott Yanow*

Twenty One / 1994 / Blue Note ✦✦✦

Henry "Red" Allen

b. Jan. 7, 1908, New Orleans, LA, d. Apr. 17, 1967, New York, NY
Trumpet / Dixieland, Swing, New Orleans Jazz
One of the last great New Orleans trumpeters to emerge during the post-Louis Armstrong era, Henry "Red" Allen has long been overshadowed by Satch and his successors but actually had a fresh new approach of his own to offer. Allen sounded modern no matter what the setting, and the rhythmic freedom he achieved made his solos consistently unpredictable and exciting. The son of Henry Allen, Sr. (a famous New Orleans brass band leader), he learned trumpet early on and played in his father's parade band along with other local groups. After working on the riverboats with Fate Marable and with Fats Pichon the following year, Allen joined King Oliver in Chicago. He returned to New Orleans with Oliver and Clarence Williams, and then Red Allen joined Luis Russell's superb orchestra and began his own solo recording career. Signed by Victor as an alternative to Okeh's Louis Armstrong, Allen's solos were original and brilliant from the start (particularly "It Should Be You"); throughout the '30s his trumpet and gruff vocals would be heard on dozens of recordings and, even when the material was indifferent, Allen was usually able to uplift the music. After notable stints with Luis Russell (1929-32), Fletcher Henderson (1933-34), and the Mills Blue Rhythm Band (1934-37), Allen became part of Louis Armstrong's backup band for three years, secure but somewhat anonymous work. However, starting in 1940 Red Allen led a series of impressive combos that were Dixieland-based but also open to certain aspects of rhythm & blues. Trombonist J.C. Higginbotham (a lifelong friend) and altoist Dan Stovall were on many of his recordings. From 1954-65 Allen's frequently riotous group played regularly at New York's Metropole (Coleman Hawkins was occasionally among his sidemen), he visited Europe several times (including in 1959 with Kid Ory's band) and was one of the most memorable participants in the CBS TV special "The Sound of Jazz." Red Allen remained very active up until his death and was proclaimed in the '60s by Don Ellis as "the most creative and avant-garde trumpeter in New York." The European Classics label documents his recordings of the '30s, and many (but not all) of his later performances are also available on CD. —*Scott Yanow*

● **Henry "Red" Allen 1929-1933** / Jul. 16, 1929-Nov. 9, 1933 / Classics ✦✦✦✦
The first of a five-volume CD series released by the European Classics label that reissues all of the recordings led by trumpeter Red Allen during 1929-41 is one of the best. The great trumpeter is first heard fronting the Luis Russell Orchestra for such classics as "It Should Be You" and "Biff'ly Blues," he interacts with blues singer Victoria Spivey, and on the selections

from 1933 (two were previously unreleased) he co-leads a group with tenor saxophonist Coleman Hawkins. Not all of the performances are gems, but there are many memorable selections including "How Do They Do It That Way," "Pleasin' Paul," "Sugar Hill Function," and "Patrol Wagon Blues." Other soloists include trombonists J.C. Higginbotham and Dicky Wells, clarinetist Albert Nicholas, and altoist Charlie Holmes. —*Scott Yanow*

★ **World on a String** / Mar. 21, 1957-Apr. 10, 1957 / Bluebird ♦♦♦♦♦
This CD is a true classic. Trumpeter Red Allen is heard at the peak of his creative powers with a remarkable octet also featuring trombonist J.C. Higginbotham, clarinetist Buster Bailey, and the great tenor Coleman Hawkins. "I Cover the Waterfront" has a wonderfully abstract statement from Allen, "Love Is Just Around the Corner" is joyous Dixieland, "Let Me Miss You, Baby" is a particularly strong blues (featuring Allen's vocal), and the simple blues line that serves as a melody on "Algiers Bounce" is quite catchy. The other seven selections from the classic veterans are also quite enjoyable. Although the music has its basis in Dixieland and swing, the solos of Allen and Hawkins in particular look ahead towards the future. There is nothing dated about these essential performances; highly recommended. —*Scott Yanow*

Mose Allison

b. Nov. 11, 1927, Tippo, MS
Piano, Vocals / Hard Bop, Folk-Jazz, Jazz Blues
Not unlike his namesake, Luther Allison, pianist Mose Allison has suffered from "categorization problem," given his equally brilliant career. Although his boogie-woogie and bebop-laden piano style is innovative and fresh sounding when it comes to blues and jazz, it is as a songwriter that Allison really shines. Allison's songs have been recorded by the Who ("Young Man Blues"), Leon Russell ("I'm Smashed"), and Bonnie Raitt ("Everybody's Cryin' Mercy"). Other admirers include Tom Waits, John Mayall, Georgie Fame, the Rolling Stones, and Van Morrison. But because he's always played both blues and jazz, and not one to the exclusion of the other, his career has suffered. As he himself admits, he has a "category" problem that lingers to this day. "There's a lot of places I don't work because they're confused about what I do," he explained in a 1990 interview in *Goldmine* magazine. Despite the lingering confusion, Allison remains one of the finest songwriters in 20th century blues.
Born in Tippo, MS, on November 11, 1927, Allison's first exposure to blues on record was through Louis Jordan recordings, including "Outskirts of Town" and "Pinetop Blues." Allison credits Jordan as being a major influence on him, and also credits Nat "King" Cole, Louis Armstrong, and Fats Waller. He started out on trumpet but later switched to piano. In his youth, he had easy access, via the radio, to the music of Pete Johnson, Albert Ammons, and Meade Lux Lewis. Allison also credits the songwriter Percy Mayfield, "The Poet Laureate of the Blues," as being a major inspiration on his songwriting. After a stint in college and the Army, Allison's first professional gig was in Lake Charles, LA, in 1950. He returned to college to finish up at Louisiana State University in Baton Rouge, where he studied English and philosophy, a far cry from his initial path as a chemical engineering major.
Allison began his recording career with the Prestige label in 1956, shortly after he moved to New York. He recorded an album with Al Cohn and Bobby Brookmeyer, and then in 1957 got his own record contract. A big break was the opportunity to play with Cohn and Zoot Sims shortly after his arrival in New York, but he later became more well known after playing with saxophonist Stan Getz. After leaving Prestige Records, where he recorded now classic albums like *Back Country Suite* (1957), *Young Man Mose* (1958), and *Seventh Son* (1958-59), he moved to Columbia for two years before meeting up with Neshui Ertegun of Atlantic Records. He recalled that he signed his contract with Atlantic after about ten minutes in Neshui's office. Allison spent a big part of his recording career at Atlantic Records, where he became most friendly with Ertegun. After the company saw substantial growth and Allison was no longer working directly with him, he became discouraged and left. Allison has also recorded for Columbia (before he began his long relationship with Atlantic) and the Epic and Prestige labels.
Allison's discography is a lengthy one, and there are gems to be found on all of his albums, many of which can be found in vinyl shops. His output since 1957 has averaged at least one album a year until 1976, when he finished up at Atlantic with the classic *Your Mind Is on Vacation*. There was a gap of six years before he recorded again, this time for Elektra's Musician subsidiary in 1982, when he recorded *Middle Class White Boy*. Since 1987, he's been with Bluenote/Capitol. His debut for that label was *Ever Since the World Ended*. Allison has recorded some of the most creative material of his career with the Bluenote subsidiary of Capitol Records, including *My Backyard* (1992) and *The Earth Wants You* (1994), both produced by Ben Sidran. Also in 1994, Rhino Records released a boxed set, *Allison Wonderland*. —*Richard Skelly*

The Seventh Son / Mar. 7, 1957-Mar. 19, 1959 / Prestige ♦♦♦♦
This is a compilation of cuts from Allison's albums from 1957 to 1959: *Back Country Suite, Local Color, Young Man Mose, Ramblin' with Mose, Creek Bank*, and *Autumn Song.* —*AMG*

Mose Allison / Mar. 7, 1957-Nov. 8, 1957 / Prestige ♦♦♦
Reissue of two fine Allison albums, *Back Country Suite* (1957) and *Local Color* (1957). —*Michael Erlewine*

Mose Allison Plays for Lovers / Mar. 7, 1957-Feb. 13, 1959 / Prestige ♦♦♦
Selections from five albums ranging from 1957 to 1959. —*Michael Erlewine*

● **Allison Wonderland: Anthology** / Mar. 7, 1957-Dec. 7, 1989 / Rhino/Atlantic ♦♦♦♦
Only Dave Frishberg and possibly Mark Murphy can rival Mose Allison when it comes to creative use of irony in lyric writing and neither compares as an instrumentalist. He's a fine bop pianist able to play challenging instrumentals and eclectic enough to integrate country blues and gospel elements into his style. Allison's unique mix of down-home and uptown styles has made him a standout since the '50s. He's one of the few jazz musicians on Atlantic's roster ideally suited for Rhino's two-disc anthology format. Allison recorded so many different kinds of songs and was always as much, if not more, a singles than an album artist. In addition, Rhino thankfully sequenced the selected songs—which span over 40 years, from 1957 to 1989, and include all of his best-known songs—chronologically. Allison does reflective duo and trio pieces, moves into uptempo combo numbers with a jump beat, then returns to the intimate small group sound. His ability to highlight key lyrics, delivery, timing, and packing is superb. The set includes such classics as "Back Country Blues," "Parchman Farm," "Western Man," and "Ever Since the World Ended," plus definitive covers of Willie Dixon's "The Seventh Son" and Sonny Boy Williamson, II's "Eyesight to the Blind." It's an essential introduction to Allison's catalog. —*Ron Wynn*

● **Greatest Hits** / Nov. 8, 1957-Feb. 13, 1959 / Original Jazz Classics ♦♦♦♦
Basic, no-frills anthology of 13 of his better late-'50s Prestige sides, all of which feature his vocals. It has most of his most famous songs, particularly to listeners from a rock background, including his versions of "The Seventh Son," "Eyesight to the Blind" (covered by the Who on *Tommy*, though Sonny Boy Williamson did it before Allison), "Parchman Farm" (done by John Mayall), and "Young Man's Blues" (also covered by the Who). Were it not for the significant omission of "I'm Not Talking" (retooled by the Yardbirds), this would qualify as the basic collection for most listeners, although more thorough retrospectives are available (particularly Rhino's *Anthology*). *Greatest Hits* does include liner notes by Pete Townshend, originally penned for a 1972 collection. —*Richie Unterberger*

Creek Bank / Jan. 24, 1958-Aug. 15, 1958 / Prestige ♦♦♦♦
When Mose Allison recorded his six early albums for Prestige, he was best known as a bop-based pianist who occasionally sang. This single CD (which reissues in full *Young Man Mose* and *Creek Bank*) has 15 instrumentals including a rare appearance by Allison on trumpet ("Stroll"), but it is his five typically ironic vocals that are most memorable, particularly Allison's classic "The Seventh Son" and "If You Live." His piano playing, even with the Bud Powell influence, was beginning to become original, and he successfully performs both revived swing songs and moody originals. —*Scott Yanow*

Mose Allison Trilogy: High Jinks! / Dec. 21, 1959-May 23, 1961 / Columbia/Legacy ♦♦♦♦
Trilogy compiles the three original albums Mose Allison cut for Columbia and Epic Records during the early '60s *(Transfiguration of Hiram Brown, I Love the Life I Live, V-8 Ford Blues)*, adding all the unreleased tracks and alternate takes from the sessions that comprised the three albums. In other words, it's the complete Mose Allison on Columbia. Although this material isn't as well known as the Prestige albums that preceded it or the Atlantic albums that followed, that doesn't mean it's not as good—in fact the best moments on these discs rival anything he's ever recorded. —*Thom Owens*

I Don't Worry About a Thing / Mar. 15, 1962 / Rhino/Atlantic ♦♦♦♦

Middle Class White Boy / Feb. 2, 1982 / Elektra ♦♦♦

Earth Wants You / Sep. 8, 1993-Sep. 9, 1993 / Blue Note ♦♦♦

Laurindo Almeida

b. Sep. 2, 1917, Sao Paulo, Brazil, d. Jul. 26, 1995, Los Angeles, CA
Guitar / Brazil, Latin Continuum, Brazilian Jazz
Laurindo Almeida helped introduce the Brazilian guitar to jazz, and in his 1953 recordings with Bud Shank was essentially playing bossa nova seven years before Stan Getz! After spending time as a staff guitarist in Brazil, Almeida moved to Los Angeles and was a member of Stan Kenton's Orchestra (1947-48). A studio guitarist in Los Angeles from 1950 on, Almeida also continued playing jazz along with classical music. A decade after the Shank sessions, Almeida recorded some bestselling bossa nova dates for Capitol. He co-founded the L.A. Four in the mid-'70s (which reunited him with Bud Shank), collaborated on recordings with Charlie Byrd, and made several worthwhile sessions for Concord. —*Scott Yanow*

Brazilliance, Vols. 1 & 2 / Apr. 15, 1953-Apr. 22, 1953 / World Pacific ♦♦♦♦
With Bud Shank (as, fl) on both albums. With Gary Peacock (b) and Chuck

Flores (d) on the second album. It is almost possible to hear the birth of bossa nova in these albums. —*Michael Erlewine*

● **Artistry in Rhythm** / Apr. 1983 / Concord Jazz ✦✦✦✦
With Bob Magnusson (b) and Milt Holland (per). This is lovely easy-listening music, in the best sense of the term. —*Michael Erlewine*

Tango: Laurindo Almeida and Charlie Byrd / Aug. 1985 / Concord Jazz ✦✦✦

Albert Ammons

b. Sep. 23, 1907, Chicago, IL, d. Dec. 2, 1949, Chicago, IL
Piano / Boogie-Woogie, Swing
Albert Ammons was one of the big three of late-'30s boogie-woogie along with Pete Johnson and Meade Lux Lewis. Arguably the most powerful of the three, Ammons was also flexible enough to play swing music. Ammons played in Chicago clubs from the '20s on, although he also worked as a cab driver for a time. Starting in 1934 he led his own band in Chicago, and he made his first records in 1936. In 1938 Ammons appeared at Carnegie Hall with Pete Johnson and Meade Lux Lewis, an event that really helped launch the boogie-woogie craze. Ammons recorded with the other pianists in duets and trios, fit right in with the Port of Harlem Jazzmen on their Blue Note session, appeared regularly at Cafe Society, recorded as a sideman with Sippie Wallace in the '40s, and he even cut a session with his son, the great tenorman Gene Ammons. Albert Ammons worked steadily throughout the '40s, playing at President Harry Truman's inauguration in 1949; he died later that year. Many of his recordings are currently available on CD. —*Scott Yanow*

☆ **Complete Blue Note Albert Ammons** / Jan. 6, 1939 / Mosaic ✦✦✦✦✦
This is everything you thought you knew about the Albert Ammons-Meade Lux Lewis Blue Note recordings plus eight previously unissued sides. This was a three-record set, on which producers Mike Cuscuna and Charlie Lourie had a limited run of 5,000 copies.... Ammons played his music, poised with excitement, but paced by a rich blues as swampy as it was concrete, while Lux Lewis, with frumpy deliberateness, was pounding out poetry on the piano. —*Bob Rusch*

● **The First Day** / Jan. 6, 1939 / Blue Note ✦✦✦✦
King of Boogie Woogie (1939-1949) / 1939-1949 / Blues Classics ✦✦✦

Gene Ammons

b. Apr. 14, 1925, Chicago, IL, d. Aug. 6, 1974, Chicago, IL
Sax (Tenor) / Bop, Soul-Jazz, Hard Bop, Groove
Gene Ammons, who had a huge and immediately recognizable tone on tenor, was a very flexible player who could play bebop with the best (always battling his friend Sonny Stitt to a tie) yet was an influence on the R&B world. Some of his ballad renditions became hits and, despite two unfortunate interruptions in his career, Ammons remained a popular attraction for 25 years.

Son of the great boogie-woogie pianist Albert Ammons, Gene Ammons (who was nicknamed "Jug") left Chicago at age 18 to work with King Kolax's band. He originally came to fame as a key soloist with Billy Eckstine's orchestra during 1944-47, trading off with Dexter Gordon on the famous Eckstine record *Blowing the Blues Away*. Other than a notable stint with Woody Herman's Third Herd in 1949 and an attempt at co-leading a two-tenor group in the early '50s with Sonny Stitt, Ammons worked as a single throughout his career, recording frequently (most notably for Prestige) in settings ranging from quartets and organ combos to all-star jam sessions. Drug problems kept him in prison during much of 1958-60 and, due to a particularly stiff sentence, 1962-69. When Ammons returned to the scene in 1969 he opened up his style a bit, including some of the emotional cries of the avant-garde while utilizing funky rhythm sections, but he was still able to battle Sonny Stitt on his own terms. Ironically the last song that he ever recorded (just a short time before he was diagnosed with terminal cancer) was "Goodbye." —*Scott Yanow*

Young Jug / Oct. 12, 1948-Mar. 24, 1952 / Chess ✦✦

All Star Sessions / Mar. 5, 1950-Jun. 16, 1955 / Original Jazz Classics ✦✦✦✦
This enjoyable and frequently exciting CD contains a variety of performances mostly featuring the tenors of Gene Ammons and Sonny Stitt. The two combative saxophonists battle it out on "Blues Up and Down" (heard in three takes), the superior "New Blues Up and Down," and two versions of "You Can Depend on Me." In addition Ammons has a few ballad features, and there are a pair of extended jams from 1955 matching him in a sextet with trumpeter Art Farmer, altoist Lou Donaldson, pianist Freddie Redd, bassist Addison Farmer, and drummer Kenny Clarke. The music is perhaps not essential but has enough exciting moments to fully satisfy bebop collectors. —*Scott Yanow*

The Gene Ammons Story: The 78 Era / Mar. 5, 1950-Nov. 4, 1955 / Prestige ✦✦✦✦
This CD contains 26 of the 30 selections included on the two-LP set of the same name (and catalog number). Although mostly cut during an era

when Ammons co-led a two-tenor group with Sonny Stitt, the focus is almost entirely on Ammons. All but the final five titles are from the 1950-51 period, and these concise performances were originally on 78s. Even at this early stage, Ammons tone was quite distinctive, and he was able to combine the innovations of bop with the simplicity of R&B in his forceful and direct solos; also, few could play ballads with the passion he possessed. This CD is recommended to listeners who do not already own the two-fer. —*Scott Yanow*

● **The Happy Blues** / Apr. 23, 1956 / Original Jazz Classics ✦✦✦✦
This is one of the great studio jam sessions. Tenor saxophonist Gene Ammons is teamed up with trumpeter Art Farmer, altoist Jackie McLean, pianst Duke Jordan, bassist Addison Farmer, drummer Art Taylor, and the congas of Candido for four lengthy selections. Best is "The Happy Blues," which has memorable solos and spontaneous but perfectly fitting riffing by the horns behind each other's playing. The other numbers ("The Great Lie," "Can't We Be Friends," and "Madhouse") are also quite enjoyable, making this a highly recommended set. —*Scott Yanow*

Jammin' with Gene / Jul. 13, 1956 / Original Jazz Classics ✦✦✦✦
The tenor saxophonist led a series of excellent all-star jam sessions for the Prestige label during the mid-'50s that took advantage of the extra time available on LPs (as opposed to the three-minute 78). This CD is a straight reissue of the original LP and features versions of "Jammin' with Gene" (a blues), "We'll Be Together Again" (which evolves from being an Ammons ballad feature into a group jam and then back again), and "Not Really the Blues" that clocks in between ten and over 16 minutes. With such sidemen as trumpeters Art Farmer and Donald Byrd, altoist Jackie McLean, pianist Mal Waldron, bassist Doug Watkins, and drummer Art Taylor, this is an excellent (and rather spontaneous) straightahead session. —*Scott Yanow*

Funky / Jan. 11, 1957 / Original Jazz Classics ✦✦✦
A blues-oriented bop album that is funky jazz but not "funky" in the soul-jazz sense of that word. An exception is the title cut, a bluesy tune with Kenny Burrell (g). With Jackie McLean (as), Art Farmer (tpt), and Mal Waldron (p). Recorded in NYC. —*Michael Erlewine*

Jammin' in Hi Fi with Gene Ammons / Apr. 12, 1957 / Original Jazz Classics ✦✦✦

Groove Blues / Jan. 3, 1958 / Original Jazz Classics ✦✦✦
On Jan. 3, 1958, Gene Ammons led one of his last all-star jam sessions for Prestige. The most notable aspect to this date (which resulted in two albums of material) is that it featured among its soloists John Coltrane, on alto. This CD, a straight reissue of one of the original LPs, includes baritonist Pepper Adams, the tenor of Paul Quinichette and Coltrane on two of the four selections, and Jerome Richardson's flute during three of the songs in addition to a fine rhythm section (pianist Mal Waldron, bassist George Joyner, and drummer Art Taylor). This set consists of three of Waldron's originals in addition to the standard ballad "It Might As Well Be Spring," and it (along with the CD *The Big Sound*) fully documents the productive day. —*Scott Yanow*

Big Sound / Jan. 3, 1958 / Original Jazz Classics ✦✦✦
Along with its fellow CD *Groove Blues*, this reissue fully documents all of the music recorded by tenor saxophonist Gene Ammons on the busy day of Jan. 3, 1958. Although there were many guest soloists, only one of the four songs on this half of the set (Mal Waldron's "The Real McCoy") has appearances by John Coltrane (on alto) and the tenor of Paul Quinichette. However, baritonist Pepper Adams is aboard for two of the performances, and flutist Jerome Richardson (along with pianist Mal Waldron, bassist George Joyner, and drummer Art Taylor) are on all four. Ammons is easily the main star (he really excelled in this setting), and he is in generally fine form on the two standards ("That's All" and "Cheek to Cheek") and his own "Blue Hymn" and the Waldron original. —*Scott Yanow*

Blue Gene / May 3, 1958 / Original Jazz Classics ✦✦✦

Boss Tenor / Jun. 16, 1960 / Original Jazz Classics ✦✦✦✦
There are many Gene Ammons recordings currently available on CD in Fantasy's Original Jazz Classics since the versatile tenorman was a long-time Prestige recording artist. Unlike his earlier jam sessions, this particular outing finds Ammons as the only horn, fronting a talented rhythm section (pianist Tommy Flanagan, bassist Doug Watkins, drummer Art Taylor, and Ray Barretto on congas). Jug explores standards (including a near-classic version of "Canadian Sunset"), blues, and ballads in his usual warm, soulful, and swinging fashion. This is a fine outing by one of the true "bosses" of the tenor. —*Scott Yanow*

The Gene Ammons Story: Organ Combos / Jun. 17, 1960-Nov. 28, 1961 / Prestige ✦✦✦
Gene Ammons recorded frequently for Prestige during the '50s and early '60s, and virtually all of the tenor's dates were quite rewarding. This two-LP set reissues *Twistin' the Jug* plus part of *Angel Eyes* and *Velvet Soul*. Ammons, a bop-based but very versatile soloist, sounds quite comfortable playing a variety of standards and lesser-known material in groups featuring Jack McDuff or Johnny "Hammond" Smith on organ and either trumpeter Joe Newman or Frank Wess on tenor and flute. This version of "Angel Eyes" became a surprise hit. —*Scott Yanow*

Soul Summit / Jun. 13, 1961-Apr. 13, 1962 / Prestige ✦✦✦

We'll Be Together Again / Aug. 26, 1961 / Original Jazz Classics ✦✦✦

Live! in Chicago / Aug. 29, 1961 / Original Jazz Classics ✦✦✦

● **Prime Cuts** / Aug. 1961-Feb. 1962 / Verve ✦✦✦✦
Gene Ammons and Sonny Stitt always made for a perfect team, and it is a real pity that the music on this double LP has not yet surfaced on CD. The two tenors (with Stitt doubling on alto) are heard at their most combative during these consistently exciting performances; one session is with a piano trio led by John Houston, while the other features organist Donald Patterson. High points include "John Brown's Body," "Bye, Bye Blackbird," "Blues Up and Down," and "There Is No Greater Love." —*Scott Yanow*

Up Tight / Oct. 17, 1961-Oct. 18, 1961 / Prestige ✦✦✦✦

Jug and Dodo / May 1962 / Prestige ✦✦✦

The Boss Is Back / Nov. 10, 1969-Nov. 11, 1969 / Prestige ✦✦✦

Cat Anderson (William Alonzo Anderson)

b. Sep. 12, 1916, Greenville, SC, **d.** Apr. 29, 1981, Norwalk, CA
Trumpet / Swing
Cat Anderson was arguably the greatest high-note trumpeter of all time. His solo on "Satin Doll" from Duke Ellington's *70th Birthday Concert* is a perfectly coherent chorus consisting of notes that are so high that it is doubtful if another trumpeter from all of jazz history could hit more than one or two! He first learned trumpet while at the Jenkins Orphanage in Charleston and toured with the Carolina Cotton Pickers, a group in which he made his recording debut. During 1935-44 Anderson played with many groups including those of Claude Hopkins, Lucky Millinder, Erskine Hawkins, and Lionel Hampton. Anderson took his high-note mastery, although Hawkins reportedly fired Cat out of jealousy. In 1944 Cat Anderson was first hired by Duke Ellington, and it ended up being the perfect setting for him. Duke enjoyed writing impossible parts for Cat to play, and Anderson received publicity and a steady income. He was more than just a high-note player, being a master with mutes and having a fine tone in lower registers, but no one could really challenge him in the stratosphere (although Maynard Ferguson, Jon Faddis, and Arturo Sandoval have come close!). Anderson was with Ellington during 1944-47, 1950-59, and off and on during 1961-71. Occasionally he would go out on his own to lead his own bands but he always came back. After Ellington's death, Cat Anderson settled on the West Coast, where he often played with local big bands including an exciting one led by Bill Berry. —*Scott Yanow*

Cat Anderson & the Ellington All Stars in Paris / Oct. 30, 1958-Mar. 21, 1964 / Disques Swing ✦✦✦

● **Plays W.C. Handy** / Jun. 1977-May 1978 / Black & Blue ✦✦✦✦

Ernestine Anderson

b. Nov. 11, 1928, Houston, TX
Vocals / Standards
A fine vocalist equally gifted at singing upbeat, spirited blues, big-band/swing numbers, and jazzy pop standards, Anderson began her career in the early '40s, singing with the bands of Russell Jacquet, Eddie Heywood, Shifty Henry, and Johnny Otis. Her version of "K.C. Loving" in 1947 with Henry was a mild hit. These orchestras modified swing arrangements, added shouting vocalists, and divided their musical menus between their vocals, jump blues, and fast-paced instrumentals. This formula was eventually labeled rhythm & blues or R&B. But Anderson moved away from that style in the '50s, and became a prominent jazz stylist. She worked with Lionel Hampton in 1952 and 1953, and also sang in New York clubs. While in Hampton's band she met saxophonist Gigi Gryce. Anderson recorded with Quincy Jones in 1953, and Gryce in 1955, then toured Sweden in 1956 with Rolf Ericson's band that included Duke Jordan and Cecil Payne. While there she recorded *Hot Cargo* with Harry Arnold's orchestra, which was well received when it was issued in America on Mercury. Her 1958 album *Ernestine Anderson* with Pete Rugolo was also praised, and Anderson won the New Star award from Down Beat's critics in 1959. She did more recording for Mercury, but encountered difficult times in the early '60s, moving to England in 1965. Anderson recorded "He Says He Loves Me" for the soundtrack of Sidney Poitier's film "The Lost Man" in 1969. The song attracted some attention. Ray Brown heard her singing at Turnwater Conservatory in 1975 during a weekend festival in Canada. He became her manager, and helped her get a contract with Concord Records. The 1976 album *Hello Like Before* generated great response throughout the jazz community. Anderson was suddenly an in-demand singer. There were recordings with Hank Jones, Ray Brown, and Monty Alexander, and by the mid-'80s Anderson was cutting sessions with her own quartet. Her 1981 album *Never Make Your Move Too Soon* received a Grammy nomination, and she continued making strong sessions with Benny Carter in 1984 and the Capp-Pierce big band in 1987. She's more visible today than ever, and has become an established star. Her roots weren't fully in bebop, but she's firmly in the jazz camp, though she does include pop and blues material on her albums. —*Ron Wynn*

Ernestine Anderson / 1958 / PolyGram ✦✦✦

Hello Like Before / Oct. 8, 1976-Oct. 10, 1976 / Concord Jazz ✦✦✦

● **Never Make Your Move Too Soon** / Aug. 1980 / Concord Jazz ✦✦✦✦
A great mix of old and new. —*Ron Wynn*

Be Mine Tonight / Dec. 1986 / Concord Jazz ✦✦✦

Now & Then / Sep. 24, 1992-Feb. 12, 1993 / Qwest ✦✦✦

Lil Armstrong

b. Feb. 3, 1898, Memphis, TN, **d.** Aug. 27, 1971, Chicago, IL
Piano, Vocals / Swing, New Orleans Jazz
Lil Harden Armstrong will always be best known for her influence in shaping Louis Armstrong's career (persuading him to leave King Oliver's band and accept Fletcher Henderson's offer in New York) and for her work with Louis' Hot Five and Seven, but she actually had an interesting career after she parted with Armstrong. Early on she worked in Chicago demonstrating new songs at a music store. She worked with Sugar Johnny's Creole Orchestra and then Freddie Keppard's Original Creole Orchestra before becoming a member of King Oliver's Creole Jazz Band. Lil's rhythmic piano helped keep the ensembles solid, and she made her recording debut with Oliver in 1923. She met Louis Armstrong while in the band, and their marriage lasted from 1924 to 1938 although they separated in 1931. Lil played piano and occasionally sang on Louis' famous Hot Five and Seven recordings, and she composed "Struttin' with Some Barbecue." During the latter half of the '30s she was house pianist at Decca, recording 26 titles as a leader (mostly as a vocalist) during 1936-40 including her "Just for a Thrill." Although she rarely recorded during the remainder of her career (12 titles during 1945-47, six songs in 1953-54, two selections in 1959 and an album in 1961), Lil remained active during her last 30 years in Chicago. She recorded a talking record in 1959 on which she reminisced about her days with Louis Armstrong, and ironically she died of a heart attack while playing "St. Louis Blues" at an Armstrong tribute concert less than two months after Louis himself had passed away. —*Scott Yanow*

● **1936-1940** / Oct. 27, 1936-Mar. 18, 1940 / Classics ✦✦✦✦

Chicago: The Living Legends / Sep. 1961 / Original Jazz Classics ✦✦✦

Louis Armstrong

b. Aug. 4, 1901, New Orleans, LA, **d.** Jul. 6, 1971, New York, NY
Trumpet, Vocals / Dixieland, Swing, New Orleans Jazz
Louis Armstrong was the most important and influential musician in jazz history. Although he is often thought of by the general public as a lovable, clowning personality, a gravel-voiced singer who played simple but dramatic trumpet in a New Orleans-styled Dixieland setting, Armstrong was much, much more.

One of the first soloists on record (although he was preceded by Sidney Bechet), Louis was more responsible than anyone else for jazz changing from an ensemble-oriented folk music into an art form that emphasized inventive solo improvisations. His relaxed phrasing was a major change from the staccato style of the early '20s (helping set the stage for the swing era), and Armstrong demonstrated that it was possible to have both impressive technique and a strong feeling for the blues. One of jazz's first true virtuosos, his influence over his contemporaries was so powerful that nearly every trumpeter to record between 1927 and 1940 sounded to an extent like one of his followers!

Louis Armstrong's unique singing voice was imitated by a countless number of listeners through the years, he popularized scat singing (using nonsense syllables rhythmically rather than words), and his phrasing (carried over from his horn playing) affected virtually every singer to emerge after 1930, including Bing Crosby, Billie Holiday, and Frank Sinatra. In addition, Louis Armstrong's accessible humor and sunny stage personality were major assets in popularizing jazz with larger audiences. Many youngsters were inspired to take up the trumpet after hearing or seeing him and millions more were introduced to jazz through Armstrong; in later years Louis Armstrong's worldwide tours resulted in him being widely known as "America's goodwill ambassador."

Few would have predicted greatness for Louis Armstrong based on his humble beginnings. Born in New Orleans on Aug. 4, 1901 (until his birth certificate was discovered in the late '80s, Armstrong's birth date was believed to have been July 4, 1900), Louis grew up in the poorest part of the city, sometimes singing in a vocal quartet on the street for pennies. On New Year's Eve of 1912 he got his hands on a pistol, shot it in the air in celebration, and was quickly arrested and sent to live in a waif's home that functioned as a type of juvenile hall. This would be the turning point of his life, for it was at the waif's home that he learned to play the cornet. Released after two years, Armstrong began playing with jazz groups and brass bands in New Orleans, developing quickly. When King Oliver, who had befriended Louis, left New Orleans in 1918, he recommended the young player as his replacement in a popular band led by trombonist Kid Ory. Four years later, Oliver sent for his protégé to join his Creole Jazz Band in Chicago as second cornetist. During 1922-24 King Oliver led the top classic jazz orchestra of the era, an octet which, although emphasizing group improvisation, also left room for short solos. While Oliver was a fine cornetist (more an inspiration than a direct influence on Armstrong's playing), it soon became obvious that Armstrong was surpassing him. Fortunately this very significant band recorded 41 tracks in 1923 for four labels, for by the following year pianist Lil Harden (who became Louis' second of four wives) talked him into leaving Oliver and joining Fletcher Henderson's big band in New York. Although considered the top jazz orchestra of the time, Henderson's band had not yet learned how to swing, really improvise, or play the blues; at the time New York musicians were generally behind those from Chicago. However, Armstrong's playing soon inspired the musicians, and it was at this point that his impact was first really felt. Armstrong also began to record as an accompanist to blues singers (including Bessie Smith and Ma Rainey), teamed up with Sidney Bechet in Clarence Williams' Blue Five, and in 1925 (after he left Henderson and moved back to Chicago) he began his remarkable series of Hot Five and Hot Seven recordings.

With clarinetist Johnny Dodds, trombonist Kid Ory, pianist Lil Armstrong, and banjoist Johnny St. Cyr, Armstrong recorded one classic after another during 1925-27, music that can be thought of as both the height of New Orleans jazz and the death of it due to the increasing emphasis on Armstrong's virtuosity. "Cornet Chop Suey" amazed fellow trumpeters (Louis switched from cornet to the similar-sounding trumpet in 1927), "Heebies Jeebies" was a hit that greatly popularized scat singing, and both "Potato Head Blues" and "Struttin' with Some Barbecue" had perfectly constructed and thrilling solos. In 1928 Armstrong led a completely different group in the studio, the Savoy Ballroom Five, that used the trombone and clarinet more as color than as competing voices and put the emphasis on the interplay between the trumpeter and the remarkable pianist Earl Hines. "West End Blues," with its remarkable opening trumpet cadenza, was considered by many (including Louis himself) to be his greatest recording, while "Weather Bird" is a duet between Armstrong and Hines that found the two taking many chances with time; Armstrong's classic versions of "St. James Infirmary" and "Basin Street Blues" (which helped to introduce the two future standards) are almost afterthoughts next to these other remarkable records.

The odd part is that, with the exception of one appearance, the Hot Five and Seven never played in public. Louis Armstrong was featured in Chicago with big bands led by Erskine Tate and Carrol Dickerson and was developing his talents as a showman. Starting in 1929 he began recording almost exclusively as the head of a variety of big bands, emphasizing superior pop standards of the era (such as "I Can't Give You Anything But Love"). During the next decade he became a household name, making two acclaimed visits to Europe during 1932-34, appearing in small but memorable roles in movies, and leading a swing-oriented big band that mostly functioned as a backdrop for his vocals and trumpet solos. Although the most advanced playing of his career took place with Earl Hines in 1928 and his Decca recordings of 1935-44 often involved novelties and commercial material, Armstrong provided some musical magic to nearly all of the records and his singing voice was at its peak in the early '40s.

Still, by the mid-'40s, Louis Armstrong was considered out of style. His orchestra had declined, and his own solos and clowning sounded at odds with his younger more bop-oriented sidemen. But after appearing with a variety of veteran players in the interesting if flawed Hollywood film *New Orleans* and having success playing with a small group at an acclaimed Town Hall concert in 1947, Armstrong broke up his big band and formed the All-Stars. His sextet (which originally included trombonist Jack Teagarden and clarinetist Barney Bigard and soon had Earl Hines) was an immediate success playing Dixieland and swing standards along with some comedy numbers, and Armstrong began a schedule of nearly nonstop travelling that lasted until his death. After a few years the routines became fairly predictable and critics tired of them, while some in the civil rights community thought of Armstrong as an Uncle Tom. However, they all missed the point. While Armstrong was quick to make fun of himself and his nickname of "Satchmo" (short for "Satchelmouth") could be considered objectionable, Armstrong always stood up for his race (most notably during the struggle to integrate schools in the South) and spread more goodwill than anyone; his brilliant trumpet-playing set an example that busted stereotypes. Audiences the world over loved the joy of Louis Armstrong's music and his inspiring trumpet and vocals; his main concern was always to please the people who paid to see him. And although Armstrong's music did not evolve much after the '40s, neither did the playing of Johnny Hodges and Thelonious Monk!

In the '50s Hines left the All-Stars, and Teagarden and Bigard were replaced by Trummy Young and Edmond Hall, but the basic sound of the group did not change. Armstrong, who also occasionally recorded with larger orchestras and with Ella Fitzgerald, found his celebrity status continuing to grow. He had major hits in "Blueberry Hill," "Mack the Knife," and "Hello Dolly," and when he died on July 6, 1971, there was no jazz musician who could approach him in popularity. With all of the reissues

and continued acclaim (including a postage stamp), there is little chance that Louis Armstrong will ever be forgotten! — *Scott Yanow*

Louis Armstrong and King Oliver / Apr. 6, 1923-Dec. 22, 1924 / Milestone ✦✦✦

Portrait of the Artist As a Young Man / Apr. 6, 1923-Oct. 1934 / Columbia ✦✦✦
This very attractive four-CD box set has definitive liner notes from Dan Morgenstern and draws its 81 selections from Louis Armstrong's prime period. Why then does it not receive the highest rating? Armstrong's immortal Hot Five and Hot Seven recordings, along with his early big-band sides, had already been reissued complete and in chronological order on seven Columbia CDs, and his less interesting performances as an accompanist to various blues singers (some of which are on this set) have also been reissued in similar fashion. Therefore this box is of no real interest to veteran collectors and, although a good introduction to beginners just starting to explore Satch's classic music, they too will eventually be moved to duplicate many of these recordings by getting the more complete series. As for the music, this set has literally dozens of influential classics and 19 performances that actually predate the Hot Fives but, since everything is available elsewhere, this box is recommended only for the informative booklet. — *Scott Yanow*

Highlights from His Decca Years / Oct. 10, 1924-Feb. 4, 1958 / Decca ✦✦

☆ **Hot Fives, Vol. 1** / Nov. 12, 1925-Jun. 23, 1926 / Columbia ✦✦✦✦✦
With these first 16 recordings by Louis Armstrong's Hot Five, the trumpeter revolutionized jazz, changing it from an ensemble-oriented folk music into an art form dominated by virtuoso soloists. Among the historic gems on this CD (which also features classic solos by the great clarinetist Johnny Dodds and trombone stylist Kid Ory) are "Come Back, Sweet Papa," Armstrong's highly influential scat chorus on "Heebies Jeebies," and his dazzling solo on "Cornet Chop Suey," which made many of his contemporaries re-evaluate how they played. — *Scott Yanow*

☆ **Hot Fives and Sevens, Vol. 2** / Jun. 23, 1926-May 13, 1927 / Columbia ✦✦✦✦✦
Eight apiece from Louis Armstrong's Hot Five and Seven with some stunning trumpet on "Willie the Weeper" and "Potato Head Blues" and Johnny Dodds' very distinctive clarinet at its best during "Weary Blues." Classic and very influential New Orleans jazz. — *Scott Yanow*

★ **Hot Fives and Sevens, Vol. 3** / May 13, 1927-Jun. 28, 1927 / Columbia ✦✦✦✦✦
The last (and some of the best) of the Hot Sevens and Fives with Armstrong in brilliant form and followed closely by clarinetist Johnny Dodds and guest guitarist Lonnie Johnson. Armstrong is stunning on "Struttin' with Some Barbecue," "Hotter than That," and (with his new pianist Earl Hines) "A Monday Date." — *Scott Yanow*

★ **The Louis Armstrong Collection, Vol. 4: Louis Armstrong and Earl Hines** / May 9, 1928-Dec. 12, 1928 / Columbia ✦✦✦✦✦
Louis Armstrong was at his most advanced at these timeless recordings with pianist Earl Hines. Hines challenged Satch to stretch himself. Their duet "Weather Bird" is futuristic for 1928, their version of "Basin Street Blues" was that standard's earliest recording, and the stunning "West End Blues" was Armstrong's personal favorite recording ever. — *Scott Yanow*

Plays and Sings the Standards, Vol. 1 (1928-1932) / 1928-1932 / Black & Blue ✦✦✦

Louis Armstrong Collection, Vol. 5: Louis in New York / Mar. 5, 1929-Nov. 26, 1929 / Columbia/Legacy ✦✦✦✦
By 1929, Louis Armstrong had switched from New Orleans jazz to fronting a variety of larger orchestras, widening his repertoire to include pop tunes but always leaving room for closing trumpet solos. This set includes all known versions (including a few new alternates) of his recordings of this era, including appearances by backing singers Seger Ellis and Victoria Spivey. High points include "Mahogany Hall Stomp" and "Ain't Misbehavin'." — *Scott Yanow*

Louis Armstrong Collection, Vol. 6: St. Louis Blues / Dec. 10, 1929-Oct. 9, 1930 / Columbia/Legacy ✦✦✦✦
Using different big bands purely as a backdrop by 1930, Louis Armstrong was free to stretch out with flashy virtuosic trumpet solos and often scat-filled vocal choruses. "St. Louis Blues," "Body and Soul," and "Tiger Rag" are classics, but his rendition of "I'm a Ding Dong Daddy" (which has a solo that gradually builds to a tremendous finish) is a true gem. — *Scott Yanow*

From the Big Band to the All Stars (1946-56) / Aug. 12, 1932-Jan. 8, 1956 / RCA ✦✦✦✦

Rhythm Saved the World / Oct. 3, 1935-Feb. 4, 1936 / GRP ✦✦✦

Pocketful of Dreams, Vol. 3 / Oct. 3, 1935-Jun. 21, 1938 / GRP ✦✦✦✦

1940-42 / May 1, 1940-Apr. 17, 1942 / Classics ✦✦✦

Pops: 1940's Small Band Sides / Sep. 6, 1946-Oct. 16, 1947 / RCA/Bluebird ✦✦✦✦
Recorded at the time Armstrong was in the film *New Orleans*, broke up

his orchestra, and formed his very popular "All-Stars," these 20 tracks feature Satch in prime form, whether playing relaxed standards, New Orleans gems, or duetting with trombonist/vocalist Jack Teagarden. High points include a reunion with his old boss, trombonist Kid Ory, five selections from his classic 1947 Town Hall concert (including definitive versions of "Ain't Misbehavin'," "Rockin' Chair," and "Back o' Town Blues"), sharing the spotlight with Jack T. on "A Song Was Born" and "Please Stop Playing Those Blues, Boy," and taking one of his greatest-ever solos on "Jack-Armstrong Blues." An outstanding set. *— Scott Yanow*

The Complete Town Hall Concert / May 17, 1947 / RCA ✦✦✦

Satchmo at Symphony Hall / Nov. 30, 1947 / Decca ✦✦✦

The Complete Decca Studio Louis Armstrong All Stars / Apr. 26, 1950-Oct. 8, 1958 / Mosaic ✦✦✦✦

Porgy and Bess / Aug. 18, 1957 / Verve ✦✦✦

Armstrong/Ellington: Together for the First Time/The Great Reunion / Apr. 3, 1961-Apr. 4, 1961 / Mobile Fidelity ✦✦✦✦
Formerly available as a two-LP set and also released on CD by Roulette, these 17 selections are the entire results of the only meeting in the studio by Louis Armstrong and Duke Ellington. Although it might have been preferable to have Armstrong perform with Duke Ellington's orchestra, Ellington's performance as pianist with Satch's All-Stars is quite satisfying. The all-Ellington program gave Armstrong a rest from his usual repertoire and permitted him an opportunity to work his magic on fresh material. Lots of surprises, some sensitive vocalizing, and fine supporting work from trombonist Trummy Young and clarinetist Barney Bigard make this a gem. *— Scott Yanow*

The Essential Louis Armstrong / Jun. 4, 1965 / Vanguard ✦✦✦

Art Ensemble of Chicago

Group / Avant-Garde, Free Jazz
The Art Ensemble of Chicago has long been one of the most significant avant-garde jazz groups and the most famous band to come out of the AACM. At a time when most musicians involved with the free-jazz movement were playing at a consistently intense level, the Art Ensemble showed how to use space and dynamics creatively and to mix together free-form passages with arranged sections. Not shy to hint at earlier styles while playing originals, the Art Ensemble also helped introduce the concept of "little instruments" (such as bicycle horns, gongs, sirens, and unusual percussive devices) to jazz. The group began as saxophonist Roscoe Mitchell's band. After trumpeter Lester Bowie, saxophonist Joseph Jarman, and bassist Malachi Favors joined, it became a co-op. Its original drummer was Phillip Wilson but, when he departed to tour with the Butterfield Blues Band, the Art Ensemble continued for a time as a drumless quartet. During the early part of a two-year period spent in Paris (1969-71), Don Moye permanently took over the drum slot. The Art Ensemble was in its prime during the '70s, but by the '80s individual projects began to result in fewer performances. The group has continued on a part-time basis into the mid-'90s and has remained influential. *— Scott Yanow*

Art Ensemble: 1967/68 / May 18, 1967-Mar. 11, 1968 / Nessa ✦✦✦

Tutankhamun / Jun. 26, 1969 / Black Lion ✦✦✦

Certain Blacks / Feb. 10, 1970 / Inner City ✦✦✦

● **Live** / 1972 / Delmark ✦✦✦✦
The Art Ensemble of Chicago fuse theatrical fireworks, improvisational elan, and rhythmic flexibility in their concerts, and they successfully displayed all these elements and more on this date, which was previously available on vinyl. The Mandel Hall concert included lengthy, sprawling sax and brass dialogues, verbal thrusts, and multiple African, Afro-Latin, and funk beats and textures. They were all performed in a nonstop fashion with the volume and pace building, exploding, easing, and rebuilding, and the music presented in various movements. It could be joyful, furious, comical, cohesive, and chaotic, and sounds even more thrilling in digital. *—Ron Wynn*

Fanfare for the Warriors / Sep. 6, 1973 / Atlantic ✦✦✦✦
The Art Ensemble of Chicago's first (and arguably most significant) period concluded with this high-quality studio session. The quintet (trumpeter Lester Bowie, Roscoe Mitchell and Joseph Jarman on reeds, bassist Malachi Favors, and drummer Don Moye) provides concise but adventurous performances. High points include Mitchell's "Nonnaah," Bowie's humorous "Barnyard Scuffel Shuffle," and "Thoona," but all of the selections have their own musical personality. It's a fine showcase for this important avant-garde unit. *— Scott Yanow*

Nice Guys / May 1978 / ECM ✦✦✦

Dreaming of the Masters Suite / 1991 / DIW ✦✦✦

Roy Ayers

b. Sep. 10, 1940, Los Angeles, CA
Vibes / Instrumental Pop, Soul-Jazz
A very talented vibist, Ayers was among the top jazz players of the '60s. He

had speed, technique, and the good fortune to appear on some high-profile albums with Herbie Mann. He turned more and more to R&B and funk in the '70s. His group Ubiquity began with prototype jazz-based R&B, then moved more into straight R&B/funk through the '70s. By the late '70s and early '80s, Ayers was essentially an R&B bandleader, with eight albums making the *Billboard* charts in 1976-1979.

During the '80s and '90s, Roy Ayers has divided his time between bandleading, performing, writing, and producing. He issued *Love Fantasy* in 1980, then toured Africa the next year, performing with Nigerian Afrobeat king Fela Anikulapo-Kuti. Kuti appeared on Ayers' 1981 LP *Africa, Center of the World.* He departed Polydor after 1982's *Feeling Good,* which contained the single "Turn Me Loose." Ayers formed the company Uno Melodic Records and worked with Bobby Humphrey, Eighties Ladies, and Sylvia Striplin. He co-wrote "Turned On to You" with Edwin Birdsong for Eighties Ladies and produced "Give Me Your Love" for Striplin, as well as recording and issuing his own *Lots of Love* LP for Uno Melodic. Ayers signed with Columbia in 1984 and landed one Top 20 R&B single in 1986, "Hot," while cutting a number of LPs. He began recording with Ichiban in 1989. Ayers has also returned to jazz: he recorded a live LP at Ronnie Scott's in 1991 and did a guest stint on the hip-hop/jazz release *Jazzamatazz* in 1993. The session was produced by Gang Starr's Guru, and Ayers has also made club appearances with Guru and Donald Byrd in New York. His LPs with Ubiquity are being reissued. *—Ron Wynn*

★ **Mystic Voyage** / 1975 / Polydor ✦✦✦✦✦
Nice outing, although there's minimal jazz content. Ayers, once a Downbeat New Star winner, decided at the end of the '60s to forego the rigors of straight jazz life and investigate the world of funk and R&B. He would (and still does) dabble back into light soul-jazz, but has become far more known for his funk and R&B releases like this one. *—Ron Wynn*

Evolution: The Polydor Anthology / Polydor Chronicles ✦✦✦

Live at the Montreux Jazz Festival / Polygram ✦✦✦
Generally disregarded by jazz purists, Roy Ayers' *Live at the Montreux Jazz Festival* is nevertheless a thoroughly engaging set of funky jazz fusion. In fact, the album is one of the most sampled jazz records in hip-hop. Loops of this performance of "Everybody Loves the Sunshine" have appeared on tracks by A Tribe Called Quest, Brand Nubian, and several others. The original grooves on this album are just as funky as those the hip-hop artists have derived from it. In fact, Ayers is probably funkier and looser than the musicians who borrowed from him several years later. *Live at the Montreux Jazz Festival* is one of the core recordings of acid jazz, "rare grooves," and jazz hip-jazz; it's a record that sounds better 20 years after its release than it did when it first appeared. *—Stephen Thomas Erlewine*

Albert Ayler

b. Jul. 13, 1936, Cleveland, OH, **d.** Nov. 5, 1970, New York, NY
Sax (Alto), Sax (Tenor) / Free Jazz
One of the giants of free jazz, Albert Ayler was also one of the most controversial. His huge tone and wide vibrato were difficult to ignore, and his 1966 group sounded like a runaway New Orleans brass band from 1910. It could be said of Ayler's music that he was so far advanced that he came in at jazz's beginning!

Unlike John Coltrane or Eric Dolphy, Albert Ayler was not a virtuoso who had come up through the bebop ranks. His first musical jobs were in R&B bands including one led by Little Walter, although oddly enough he was nicknamed "Little Bird" in his early days because of a similarity in sound on alto to Charlie Parker! During his period in the army (1958-61) he played in a service band and switched to tenor. Unable to find work in the US after his discharge due to his uncompromising style, Ayler spent time in Sweden and Denmark during 1962-63, making his first recordings (which reveal a tone with roots in Sonny Rollins) and working a bit with Cecil Taylor. Ayler's prime period was during 1964-67. In 1964 he toured Europe with a quartet that included Don Cherry and was generally quite free and emotional. The following year he had a new band with his brother Donald Ayler on trumpet and Charles Tyler, and the emphasis in his music began to change. Folk melodies (which had been utilized a bit with Cherry) had a more dominant role as did collective improvisation, and yet, despite the use of spaced-out marches, Irish jigs, and brass-band fanfares, tonally Ayler remained quite free. His ESP recordings from this era and his first couple of Impulses find Ayler at his peak and were influential; John Coltrane's post-1964 playing was definitely affected by Ayler's innovations. However, during his last couple of years Albert Ayler's career seemed to become a bit aimless, and his final Impulse sessions, although experimental (with the use of vocals, rock guitar, and R&Bish tunes), were at best mixed successes. A 1970 live concert that was documented features him back in top form, but in November 1970 Ayler was found drowned in New York's East River under mysterious circumstances. *—Scott Yanow*

Witches and Devils / Feb. 24, 1964 / Freedom ✦✦✦

Prophecy / Jun. 14, 1964 / ESP ✦✦✦

Spiritual Unity / Jul. 10, 1964 / ESP ✦✦✦

Vibrations / Sep. 14, 1964 / Freedom ✦✦✦✦
1964 was a busy year for Albert Ayler, who recorded at least seven albums worth of material. This particular session, a quartet date with trumpeter Don Cherry, bassist Gary Peacock, and drummer Sunny Murray, was probably his most significant of the period. Switching between tenor and alto, Ayler is often ferocious on the six performances, jumping from simple melodies (of which "Ghosts" is the most memorable) to intense sound explorations overflowing with emotion; he even makes Cherry seem conservative. It helps greatly to have open ears to appreciate this music, although Ayler's jams would become a bit more accessible the following year. Recommended. — *Scott Yanow*

● **Spirits Rejoice** / Sep. 1965 / ESP ✦✦✦✦
Tenor saxophonist Albert Ayler's 1965 group (with trumpeter Donald Ayler, altoist Charles Tyler, both Henry Grimes and Gary Peacock on basses, drummer Sunny Murray, and an appearance by Call Cobbs on harpsichord) is a fairly strong and sometimes riotous effort. As is often true of the ESP releases, the playing time is brief (32 minutes), but the quality of the free-form improvisations is high and the music is somewhat groundbreaking while always being stimulating. — *Scott Yanow*

Live at Lorrach: Paris, 1966 / Nov. 7, 1966-Nov. 13, 1966 / Hat Art ✦✦✦✦
Originally released as a double LP (with the second half being a 45), this single CD finds tenor saxophonist Albert Ayler in top form in 1966. At the time, his music could be considered to have been so advanced that it came in at the beginning of jazz. The folk melodies and some of the ensembles sound very much like an out-of-control New Orleans brass band circa 1900, yet the individual improvisations are as explorative as any heard in free jazz. Ayler heads a quintet with his brother Donald on trumpet, violinist Michel Sampson (whose sawing often sets a drone effect), bassist William Folwell, and drummer Beaver Harris. Together they perform two versions of "Ghosts" and such group originals as "Bells," "Jesus," "Our Prayer," "Spirits," "Holy Ghost," and "Holy Family." Due to the accessible nature of some of the melodies, this is the perfect place for open-eared listeners unfamiliar with Albert Ayler's unique music to start. — *Scott Yanow*

Love Cry / Aug. 31, 1967 / Impulse ✦✦✦

Fondation Maeght Nights, Vol. 1 / Jul. 25, 1970-Jul. 27, 1970 / Jazz View ✦✦✦✦
A little over three months before he was found drowned, Ayler was caught performing in concert at the height of his powers. Unlike his Impulse releases which often featured him trying to incorporate commercial elements into his music, the release from the European label Jazz View (the first of two CDs) allows Ayler to stretch out and "preach" in his emotional and unique style with just sparse backing (pianist Call Cobbs, bassist Steve Tintweiss, and drummer Allen Blairman). This and the second volume would be Albert Ayler's final recordings and are quite memorable. — *Scott Yanow*

Benny Bailey (Ernest Harold Bailey)

b. Aug. 13, 1925, Cleveland, OH
Trumpet / Bop, Hard Bop
A tremendous hard bop soloist and exciting trumpeter, Benny Bailey has resided in Europe since the '60s. His extensive range, dynamic sound and tone, and often striking high-note solos have been heard on many albums with European orchestras, all star groups and combos. Bailey learned piano and flute as well as trumpet, studying at the Cleveland Conservatory of Music, and privately with George Russell. He worked in the early '40s with Bull Moose Jackson and Scatman Crothers, then toured with Jay McShann and played with Teddy Edwards. Bailey joined Dizzy Gillespie's big band in the late '40s, touring Europe with them. He was one of the principal soloists in Lionel Hampton's orchestra from 1948 to the mid-'50s, before he settled in Europe. Bailey played with Harry Arnold's band and recorded with Stan Getz in Sweden during the late '50s. He joined Quincy Jones' orchestra in 1959. Bailey returned to America briefly in 1960, then moved to Germany. He recorded with Eric Dolphy in 1961, and contributed many splendid solos to the huge hit album *Swiss Movement* with Eddie Harris and Les McCann in 1969. Bailey was a soloist with the Kenny Clarke-Francy Boland big band from the early '60s until 1973. He played with George Gruntz in the '70s, as well as various radio bands, before joining the Paris Reunion Band in 1986. They've frequently toured both America and Europe. Bailey has recorded for Candid, Enja, Ego, and Jazzcraft among others. Some of his session mates have included Mal Waldron, Kenny Clarke, Sal Nistico, Charlie Rouse, Billy Hart, Richard Wyands, Sam Jones, Albert Dailey, Buster Williams, and Keith Copeland. — *Ron Wynn and Michael Erlewine*

● **Big Brass** / Nov. 25, 1960 / Candid ✦✦✦✦
Trumpeter Benny Bailey has had an on-and-off recording career and due to his longtime residency in Europe has been underrated through the years. This CD reissue of his Candid date is one of the high points of his career. Bailey is joined by an all-star septet including altoist Phil Woods, Julius Watkins on French horn, and pianist Tommy Flanagan, and the

high-quality arrangements (some by Quincy Jones) give a lot of variety to this highly recommended set. — *Scott Yanow*

Grand Slam / Oct. 14, 1978 / Jazzcraft ✦✦✦✦
Trumpeter Benny Bailey was teamed with veteran tenor saxophonist Charlie Rouse on this hard-blowing quintet date. The fresh material (two songs by Fritz Pauer, who arranged the date, a pair from Bailey, and one by Pepper Adams) inspires the soloists to play near their peak. With a fine rhythm section (pianist Richard Wyands, bassist Sam Jones, and drummer Billy Hart) pushing the horns, this set is even better than expected. — *Scott Yanow*

Buster Bailey (William C. Bailey)

b. Jul. 19, 1902, Memphis, TN, **d.** Apr. 12, 1967, New York, NY
Clarinet, Saxophone / Big Band, Swing
Buster Bailey was a brilliant clarinetist who, although known for his smooth and quiet playing with John Kirby's Sextet, occasionally really cut loose with some wild solos (including on a recording called "Man with a Horn Goes Berserk!"). Expertly trained by the classical teacher Franz Schoepp (who also taught Benny Goodman), Bailey worked with W.C. Handy's band in 1917. He moved to Chicago in 1919 and was soon working with Erskine Tate and King Oliver's Creole Jazz Band. He gained some fame in 1924 when he joined Fletcher Henderson's Orchestra in New York. Bailey was with Henderson off and on during 1924-34 and 1936-37, also playing with Noble Sissle and the Mills Blue Rhythm Band (1934-35). Next up was the cool-toned swing of John Kirby's Sextet (1937-46), a role he fit perfectly. With the end of the Kirby band, Bailey was mostly employed in Dixieland settings with Wilbur DeParis (1947-49), Big Chief Russell Moore (1952-53), Henry "Red" Allen (1950-51 and 1954-60), Wild Bill Davison (1961-63), and the Saints and Sinners (1963-65), finishing up with the Louis Armstrong All-Stars (1965-67). One of the most technically skilled of the clarinetists to emerge during the '20s, Buster Bailey never modenized his style or became a leader, but he contributed his talents and occasional wit to a countless number of rewarding and important recordings. — *Scott Yanow*

All About Memphis / Feb. 13, 1958 / Felsted ✦✦✦✦
Buster Bailey was one of the top clarinetists to emerge during the '20s, but he led relatively few sessions throughout his long career. This LP features Bailey with a quartet (along with pianist Red Richards, bassist Gene Ramey, and drummer Jimmie Crawford) and, with the horns of trumpeter Herman Autrey, trombonist Vic Dickenson, and altoist Hilton Jefferson added, a septet. In addition to W.C. Handy tunes, the other five songs are Bailey originals that mix together swing and the flavor of New Orleans jazz. It's a fine outing for the classic clarinetist. — *Scott Yanow*

Mildred Bailey

b. Feb. 27, 1907, Tekoa, WA, **d.** Dec. 12, 1951, Pougakeepsie, WA
Vocals / Swing, Standards
Although her high-pitched childlike voice (which contrasted with her plump body) takes a bit of getting used to for some, Mildred Bailey was one of the finest jazz singers to emerge during the '30s. She learned from her predecessors, Ethel Waters, Bessie Smith, and Connie Boswell, and had her own lightly swinging style. After singing locally, Bailey sent a demonstration record to Paul Whiteman in 1929; he immediately added her to his band. During her four years with Whiteman, Bailey mostly sang ballads and became identified with "Rockin' Chair" and "Georgia on My Mind." In 1933 she married Red Norvo and they eventually were known as "Mr. and Mrs. Swing." Mildred Bailey was famous and well paid throughout the '30s, appearing regularly on radio, recording some superb small-group jazz dates, and featured with Red Norvo's Orchestra during 1936-39. Unfortunately her insecurities about her appearance made her an erratic personality. Bailey's marriage ended in divorce in 1943, although she worked with Norvo on and off in the '40s. After 1945 her health faded, and the singer died in 1951 when she was 44. Many of Mildred Bailey's records are currently available, and she would probably be shocked to know that she is on a postage stamp! — *Scott Yanow*

Volume 1 / Oct. 5, 1929-Mar. 2, 1932 / TOM ✦✦✦
The first of two Mildred Bailey CDs from the TOM label contains 21 of the vocalist's first 23 recordings; the two bypassed selections are included on the second volume. The superior swing singer is mostly heard on ballads (some of which are a bit dated) with orchestras led by Eddie Lang ("What Kind o' Man Is You?"), Frankie Trumbauer ("I Like to Do Things for You"), Jimmie Noone, Glen Gray, and Paul Whiteman in addition to her initial sessions as a leader; this release is accurately subtitled "Sweet Beginnings," and the jazz content is generally not all that high. Although there are fairly long liner notes (the same ones are used on both volumes), the personnel for these early recordings are not included. Despite that inexcusable omission, fans of Mildred Bailey should be delighted to have these interesting sides reissued; highlights include "Concentratin' on You," "Home," "All of Me," and her original version of "Georgia on My Mind." — *Scott Yanow*

● **Her Greatest Performances (1929-1946)** / Oct. 5, 1929-Oct. 1946 / Columbia ✦✦✦✦
This three-LP box set (which deserves to be reissued on CD) lives up to its name. Bailey was one of the top singers of the '30s, and this package, which features highlights from her career (mostly dating from 1933-39), shows why. She holds her own with a variety of all-star groups which include such classic players as trumpeters Bunny Berigan, Buck Clayton, Charlie Shavers, and Roy Eldridge (the latter is great on "I'm Nobody's Baby"), trombonist Tommy Dorsey, clarinetist Benny Goodman, altoist Johnny Hodges, tenors Coleman Hawkins and Chu Berry, pianists Teddy Wilson and Mary Lou Williams, and her husband, xylophonist Red Norvo. There are lots of gems on this definitive set. —*Scott Yanow*

The Rockin' Chair Lady / Sep. 15, 1931-Apr. 25, 1950 / Decca ✦✦✦

Volume 2 / Dec. 1, 1931-Feb. 2, 1934 / TOM ✦✦✦
The second of two CDs from the TOM ("The Old Masters") label finishes the documentation of singer Mildred Bailey's earliest recordings. Bailey is featured with Paul Whiteman, the Dorsey Brothers Big Band, the Casa Loma Orchestra ("Heat Wave"), an all-star group with Benny Goodman (and tenor-great Coleman Hawkins), and on a few of her own sessions. Although the emphasis is on ballads, the program generally holds on to one's interest (despite a few songs with racist lyrics, notably "Snowball"), and the Goodman session (which is rounded off with an instrumental version of "Georgia Jubilee") is a near-classic. Other highlights include "I'll Never Be the Same," "Love Me Tonight," a touching "There's a Cabin in the Pines," and Bailey's earliest version of her future theme song, "Rockin' Chair." —*Scott Yanow*

Legendary V-Disc Series / 1940-1951 / Vintage Jazz Classics ✦✦✦✦
Mildred Bailey fans will find this to be a very interesting CD, for the talented swing singer is heard on some previously unavailable V-Disc sessions from the war years (including a few false starts) along with some radio appearances. There is a complete radio show with her guests the Delta Rhythm Boys, four duets with pianist Teddy Wilson, three selections with vibraphonist Red Norvo's quintet, a few songs with either Paul Baron's studio orchestra or the Ellis Larkins Trio, one number ("There'll Be a Jubilee") with Benny Goodman's big band, and two selections ("Lover, Come Back to Me" and "It's So Peaceful in the Country") from a 1951 radio aircheck that ended up being her last recordings. Any listener who wonders why Mildred Bailey was awarded her own postage stamp should be required to get this CD. —*Scott Yanow*

Chet Baker (Chesney Henry Baker)
....

b. Dec. 23, 1929, Yale, OK, d. May 13, 1988, Amsterdam, Netherlands
Trumpet, Vocals / Cool
What a strange life Chet Baker had! A popular cool-toned trumpeter and a fragile singer whose charisma made up for his limited voice, with his good looks Baker probably could have been a movie star. Instead he became a drug addict in the mid-'50s and had an extremely erratic lifestyle with horrific episodes alternating with some wonderful musical moments.

Chet Baker certainly started out on top. After getting out of the Army, he gigged with Charlie Parker on the West Coast in 1952 and then joined the Gerry Mulligan Quartet, a pianoless unit that soon became among the most popular in jazz. After Mulligan was jailed for his own drug problems, Baker (who had helped make "My Funny Valentine" into a hit) formed a quartet with pianist Russ Freeman. He began to win polls on both trumpet and vocals, toured Europe in 1955, and seemed on his way to a lucrative career. But by 1960 Baker was in an Italian jail and, although he made a few worthy recordings in the '60s, by the end of the decade his teeth had been knocked out after a botched drug deal and he was out of music.

Against all odds Chet Baker made a gradual comeback in the '70s. Although Baker recorded far too much during his final 15 years, his nomadic lifestyle (never kicking drugs and essentially wandering all over Europe) was unstable, and his occasional vocals (always an acquired taste) were generally poor, his trumpet playing improved as the decade progressed. In fact, despite everything, Chet Baker was still in his musical prime when he fell out of a second-story window (pushed or slipped?) to his death in 1988. He remains one of the great cult figures of jazz. —*Scott Yanow*

Pacific Jazz Years / Oct. 15, 1952-Dec. 9, 1957 / Pacific Jazz ✦✦✦

★ **Complete Pacific Jazz Studio Recordings of the Chet Baker Quartet with Ross Freeman** / Jul. 24, 1953-Nov. 6, 1956 / Mosaic ✦✦✦✦✦
This essential four-LP box set features trumpeter Chet Baker leading his own group during the 1953-56 period (shortly after the breakup of the Gerry Mulligan Quartet) with pianist Russ Freeman; either Bob Whitlock, Carson Smith, Joe Mondragon, Jimmy Bond, or Leroy Vinnegar on bass; and Bobby White, Larry Bunker, Shelly Manne, Bob Neel, Peter Littman, or Lawrence Marable on drums. Baker is heard at his coolest (mostly before he became influenced by Miles Davis); some of the later selections also fea-

ture his first recorded vocals. Because the Mosaic box sets are limited editions, they should be acquired as soon as possible. —*Scott Yanow*

Grey December / Dec. 22, 1953-Feb. 28, 1955 / Pacific Jazz ✦✦✦

Chet Baker with Strings / Dec. 30, 1953-Feb. 20, 1954 / Columbia ✦✦✦

Boston / Mar. 16, 1954-Oct. 19, 1954 / Uptown ✦✦✦

● **Complete Pacific Jazz Live Recordings** / May 9, 1954-Oct. 1954 / Mosaic ✦✦✦✦
Chet Baker and his popular quartet (pianist Russ Freeman, bassist Carson Smith, and drummer Bob Neel) recorded live for Pacific Jazz on three different occasions in 1954. While their appearance at Ann Arbor was released, less than half of the music recorded in Los Angeles and none of the five selections cut in Santa Cruz, CA, were issued until this limited-edition four-LP box set was put out by Mosaic. Throughout this instrumental set Baker and Freeman are in their early peak form, showing that their variations of bop were not as cool as the stereotype of West Coast jazz might lead one to expect. Get this gem while you can. —*Scott Yanow*

Chet Baker Big Band / Sep. 9, 1954-Oct. 26, 1954 / Pacific Jazz ✦✦✦

Chet in Paris, Vol. 1 / Oct. 11, 1955-Oct. 25, 1955 / EmArcy ✦✦✦✦
The first of four CDs documenting Baker's first visit to Europe has nine selections on which the trumpeter is heard in a quartet with the ill-fated pianist Dick Twardzik and four other numbers with a fine French sextet. Baker shows that his "cool" style actually had plenty of fire. All of the sets in this valuable series contain rewarding music. —*Scott Yanow*

Chet in Paris, Vol. 2: Everything Happens to Me / Oct. 24, 1955-Nov. 28, 1955 / EmArcy ✦✦✦✦
The second in a four-CD series that documents his first trip to Europe has the studio sides from two separate sessions in which the trumpeter was teamed with French rhythm sections. The music (all but one are standards) finds Baker in top early form, making this cool-toned bop music well worth hearing. —*Scott Yanow*

Chet in Paris, Vol. 3: Cheryl / Dec. 26, 1955-Mar. 15, 1956 / EmArcy ✦✦✦✦
The third of four CDs in this valuable series continues the documentation of Baker's first trip to Europe with three interesting sessions. Baker is teamed with tenor saxophonist Bobby Jaspar and pianist Rene Urtreger for four selections, interacts with the tenor of Jean-Louis Chautemps and pianist Francy Boland on the next four songs, and is finally heard with a fine French octet. Throughout this entire series, the trumpeter is in fine form. —*Scott Yanow*

Chet in Paris, Vol. 4: Alternate Takes / Oct. 25, 1955-Feb. 10, 1956 / EmArcy ✦✦✦

Chet Baker & Crew / 1956 / Pacific Jazz ✦✦✦

The Route / Jul. 26, 1956 / Pacific Jazz ✦✦✦

Playboys / Oct. 31, 1956 / Pacific Jazz ✦✦✦

Reunion / Dec. 3, 1957-Dec. 17, 1957 / EMI-Manhattan ✦✦✦✦
The Gerry Mulligan Quartet of 1952-53 was one of the best-loved jazz groups of the decade, and it made stars out of both the leader and trumpeter Chet Baker. Mulligan and Baker had very few reunions after 1953, but this particular CD from 1957 is an exception. Although not quite possessing the magic of the earlier group, the music is quite enjoyable and the interplay between the two horns is still special. With expert backup by bassist Henry Grimes and drummer Dave Bailey, these 13 selections (plus two new alternate takes) should please fans of both Mulligan and Baker. —*Scott Yanow*

Chet Baker in New York / Sep. 1958 / Original Jazz Classics ✦✦✦

Chet (The Lyrical Trumpet of Chet Baker) / Dec. 30, 1958-Jan. 19, 1959 / Original Jazz Classics ✦✦✦

Chet Baker Plays the Best of Lerner and Loewe / Jul. 21, 1959-Jul. 22, 1959 / Original Jazz Classics ✦✦✦

● **The Italian Sessions** / 1962 / RCA/Bluebird ✦✦✦✦
Throughout the '50s Chet Baker gained fame as a quiet low-register trumpeter with a cool tone and a relaxed style. This CD therefore should be a major surprise to listeners who believe he was incapable of playing heated material or of utilizing the upper register of his horn. Assisted by a fine European sextet (including Bobby Jaspar on tenor and flute and guitarist Rene Thomas), Baker is heard in peak form throughout this memorable and frequently exciting bop date. —*Scott Yanow*

Baker's Holiday: Plays & Sings Billie Holiday / May 1965 / EmArcy ✦✦✦

Smokin' / Aug. 23, 1965-Aug. 29, 1965 / Prestige ✦✦✦

The Best Thing for You / Feb. 16, 1977-May 13, 1977 / A&M ✦✦✦
This CD features previously unissued material from the same sessions that resulted in *You Can't Go Home Again* and, if anything, the music is a touch better. While an alternate take of Don Sebesky's "El Morro" uses a larger group, the other five performances find Baker accompanied just by a rhythm section (pianist Kenny Barron, bassist Ron Carter, drummer Tony Williams, and, on one song, guitarist Gene Bertoncini). As a special bonus,

altoist Paul Desmond makes memorable appearances on three songs during what would be his final recording session. Throughout, Chet Baker shows that his playing during his much documented final period would be equal if not superior to his more acclaimed recordings of the '50s. —*Scott Yanow*

Live at Nick's / Nov. 1978 / Criss Cross ✦✦✦✦
Considering his erratic lifestyle, it is surprising how many good records Chet Baker made during his final 15 years. This quartet outing with pianist Phil Markowitz, bassist Scott Lee, and drummer Jeff Brillinger has been greatly expanded in its CD reissue. Four songs (including a 17-minute version of Wayne Shorter's obscure "Beautiful Black Eyes") are joined by previously unreleased and fairly long versions of "I Remember You" and "Love for Sale." The quiet but swinging music is quite enjoyable and finds Baker in fine form. —*Scott Yanow*

Blues for a Reason / Sep. 30, 1984 / Criss Cross ✦✦✦✦
This combination works quite well. For what might have been the only time in their careers, trumpeter Chet Baker and tenor saxophonist Warne Marsh were teamed together in a quintet (which also includes pianist Hod O'Brien, bassist Cecil McBee, and drummer Eddie Gladden) for this Criss Cross session. The CD reissue adds two alternate takes to the original six songs, which consist of "If You Could See Me Now," "Imagination," Marsh's "Well Spoken," and three Baker originals. Recommended. —*Scott Yanow*

Chet's Choice / Jun. 6, 1985-Jun. 25, 1985 / Criss Cross ✦✦✦✦
One of the best settings for trumpeter Chet Baker was when he was accompanied by a guitar-bass duo. On this excellent Criss Cross CD, Baker is joined by guitarist Philip Catherine and bassist Jean-Louis Rassinfosse on a variety of high-quality standards that include such songs as "If I Should Lose You," Horace Silver's "Doodlin'," "Conception," and "Love for Sale." A special treat is hearing the talented but forgotten Bob Zieff's "Sad Walk." This is one of Baker's better albums from his later period. —*Scott Yanow*

My Favourite Songs, Vols. 1 and 2: The Last Great Concert / Apr. 28, 1988 / Enja ✦✦✦✦
Despite a rough up-and-down life, Baker remained an excellent trumpeter to the end of his career. This concert, performed two weeks before his mysterious fall out of an Amsterdam hotel window (and his last known recording), is a near-perfect summation of his career. The emphasis is on his trumpet playing, and Baker, whether backed by a symphony orchestra, a big band, or playing in a small group with altoist Herb Geller, is in inspired form. This double-CD set is also available as two separate CDs and, in one form or another, is highly recommended. —*Scott Yanow*

My Favourite Songs, Vol. 2: Straight from the Heart / Apr. 28, 1988 / Enja ✦✦✦✦
This CD is the second half of Baker's final recording, a rather impressive concert in which the trumpeter was joined (in separate sections) by a symphony orchestra, a big band, and a small group with Herb Geller. Highlights include "Look for the Silver Lining," "Sippin' at Bells," and a touching rendition of "My Funny Valentine." Both parts of this memorable performance are highly recommended. —*Scott Yanow*

The Best of Chet Baker Sings: Let's Get Lost / Capitol/Pacific Jazz ✦✦✦

Young Chet / Blue Note ✦✦✦
This CD brings together some leftover tracks from trumpeter Chet Baker's Pacific Jazz sessions. The first five songs originally featured Baker's overdubbed vocals, but Richard Bock had a change of heart and also had "alternate" versions made with either tenor saxophonist Bill Perkins or (on one song) clarinetist Jimmy Giuffre overdubbed where Baker's vocals had been! It is those renditions that form the first half of this CD. The remainder is from a 1956 session by Baker with his quintet when it included tenor saxophonist Phil Urso and pianist Bobby Timmons. Baker plays well on five songs from this set but is actually not present on "It's Only a Paper Moon" (an Urso feature) and "Autumn in New York" (which is played by the trio). Although there is some good music on the CD, this release is mostly for Baker completists since there are many more essential Chet Baker albums currently available. —*Scott Yanow*

Billy Bang

b. Sep. 20, 1947, Mobile, AL
Violin / Avant-Garde
One of the most stimulating, bluish, and accessible violinists in the avant-garde, Billy Bang had a false start on his instrument as a youth and then became serious in 1968. Along the way he studied with Leroy Jenkins and by 1972 he was gigging. In 1977 Bang helped form the co-op group the String Trio of New York with guitarist James Emery and bassist John Lindberg, leaving in 1986. Bang, who has played with Ronald Shannon Jackson's Decoding Society and Material, has recorded frequently as a leader (including an intriguing Stuff Smith tribute set with Sun Ra in a quartet). —*Scott Yanow*

Rainbow Gladiator / Jun. 10, 1981 / Soul Note ✦✦✦✦
Ever since his emergence in the late '70s, Billy Bang has been one of the top violinists in the jazz avant-garde (along with his predecessor Leroy Jen-

kins), a musician not shy to play either melodies or sound explorations. This set, his first as a leader, finds Bang holding his own with a strong cast of players including Charles Tyler on alto and baritone and pianist Michele Rosewoman. All six compositions are Bang's, making this a good introduction to his music for those who have an open mind towards adventurous jazz. —*Scott Yanow*

The Fire from Within / Sep. 19, 1984-Sep. 29, 1984 / Soul Note ✦✦✦
● **Live at Carlos 1** / Nov. 23, 1986 / Soul Note ✦✦✦✦
Violinist Billy Bang uses the same instrumentation on this set as on his previous *The Fire from Within* although his sextet had two new members: trumpeter Roy Campbell and drummer Zen Matsuura. A more rhythmic album, this melodic avant-garde set rewards repeated listenings and has an impressive amount of variety. —*Scott Yanow*

Valve, No. 10 / Mar. 8, 1988-Mar. 9, 1988 / Soul Note ✦✦✦

Paul Barbarin (Adolphe Paul Barbarin)

b. May 5, 1899, New Orleans, LA, d. Feb. 17, 1969, New Orleans, LA
Drums / New Orleans Jazz
A member of one of New Orleans' most renowned drumming dynasties, Paul Barbarin developed his drumming style on the streets of the Crescent City playing with bands like Buddy Petit's Young Olympians while still a teenager. In 1917 he left home to find work in the stockyards of Chicago but soon found more conducive employment playing with transplanted homeboys like King Oliver and Jimmie Noone, as well as a number of Chicago outfits. Over the course of his career he maintained a strong association with New Orleans artists, working with Oliver's Dixie Syncopators in the mid-'20s before joining Luis Russell's Orchestra in 1928, a move which afforded opportunities to play with Jelly Roll Morton and Louis Armstrong in the '30s. By 1939 Barbarin was back in New Orleans, but he returned to Chicago in 1942-1943 to join Henry "Red" Allen's Sextet and in the following year Sidney Bechet. After World War II he stayed in his hometown, performing with a variety of small combos and brass bands, including the Onward Brass Band (formed in 1960 and named after the original Onward which his father Isidore had led at the turn of the century). In the last decade of his life he became affiliated with many of the musicians who worked at Preservation Hall, such as Sweet Emma Barrett, with whom he recorded. During this period he also made several recordings under his own leadership, for Atlantic, Nobility, and Southland. His death in 1969 occurred while he was leading the Onward for a street parade, ending his career as he first began it.

As a drummer, Paul Barbarin excelled in the simple, straightforward approach which is associated with New Orleans, reflecting the parade beats which pervade the city's festival traditions. His forte was the press roll, and he required no more than a basic kit of snare, bass drum, tom tom, and wood block to get his message across. Cymbals were used primarily to accent the upbeat on "out choruses," and he almost never engaged in extended drum solos. His approach, like that of Warren "Baby" Dodds, was to play for the band, to provide just enough swing and lift to hold the band together and inspire the frontline soloists. For players like Barbarin, less was always more. In addition to his contributions as a "rhythm man," he was also known for several of his musical compositions, particularly "Bourbon Street Parade" and "The Second Line," which have become standards among New Orleans jazz bands, both on the street and in the dance halls. —*Bruce Boyd Raeburn*

Paul Barbarin and Percy Humphrey / 1951 / Storyville ✦✦✦
● **And His New Orleans Jazz** / Jan. 7, 1955 / Atlantic ✦✦✦✦
Drummer Paul Barbarin (a fine composer whose "Bourbon Street Parade" is included on this set) always had New Orleans bands that played in tune, knew how to solo, and could jam coherent and often exciting ensembles. This Atlantic release features his 1955 septet (with trumpeter John Brunious, clarinetist Willie Humphreys, trombonist Bob Thomas, pianist Lester Santiago, Danny Barker on banjo, and guest bassist Milt Hinton) playing a variety of traditional and ancient themes. These performances, ranging from three to nine minutes, find the band really stretching out and creating memorable and easily enjoyable music. —*Scott Yanow*

Chris Barber

b. Apr. 17, 1930, Welwyn Garden City, Hertfordshire
Trombone / Dixieland
One of the leaders of England's early-'60s Trad Jazz movement, Chris Barber (a solid trombonist) has been leading his own bands since 1948. In 1954 trumpeter Pat Halcox joined Barber, and with the later additions of clarinetist Monty Sunshine, banjoist/singer Lonnie Donegan, and blues singer Ottilie Patterson, Barber had an all-star crew. Sunshine's hit version of "Petite Fleur" made both Barber and the clarinetist into big names. Although his group was based in Dixieland, Barber has long been open-minded towards ragtime, swing, mainstream, blues, R&B, and rock. He has collaborated with many artists including Louis Jordan, Russell Procope, Wild Bill Davis, and Dr. John and has toured the US several times since 1959. —*Scott Yanow*

Petite Fleur / Apr. 12, 1953-Sep. 12, 1957 / Hallmark ✦✦✦
This long out-of-print LP gives one a good overview of trombonist Chris Barber's recordings of the mid-'50s. His English trad band had an unexpected hit with their version of Sidney Bechet's "Petite Fleur," a feature for clarinetist Monty Sunshine. That recording is included on this LP along with hot versions of a variety of well known (such as "The Saints" and "Sweet Georgia Brown") and obscure (including "Olga" and "Thriller Rag") tunes from the '20s. Pat Halcox's trumpet solos and Ottilie Patterson's vocals are major assets. — *Scott Yanow*

In Budapest / Jul. 7, 1962 / Storyville ✦✦✦
Live in East Berlin / Nov. 26, 1968 / Black Lion ✦✦✦✦
This CD features the 1968 Chris Barber band playing music that ranges from English trad to early Duke Ellington and even some gospel numbers. The trombonist/leader, his longtime trumpeter Pat Halcox, and John Crocker (on clarinet and alto) form a potent front line for spirited renditions of such numbers as "Royal Garden Blues," "Saratoga Swing," "Wild Cat Blues," and Johnny Hodges' "Sweet as Bear Meat." — *Scott Yanow*

● **Copulatin Jazz** / 1993 / Great Southern ✦✦✦✦
The repertoire performed by Chris Barber's band on this CD may be full of warhorses, but the hot Dixieland performances are full of such enthusiasm and high musicianship that this set is highly recommended. With trumpeter Pat Halcox and the reeds of John Crocker and Ian Wheeler joining trombonist Barber on the front line, this band infuses such songs as "Down by the Riverside," "Swanee River," "My Old Kentucky Home," and even "The Saints" with new life. Dixieland fans should consider this CD to be essential for their collections. — *Scott Yanow*

Gato Barbieri (Leandro J. Barbieri)

b. Nov. 28, 1934, Rosario, Argentina
Sax (Tenor) / Avant-Garde, Pop, Latin Jazz
Gato Barbieri's enjoyed success in several contexts from the late '60s through the '90s. He's played free, jazz-rock, traditional South American, film, and light pop material, and scored crossover hits in the '70s and '80s. His early work was heavily influenced by late '60s John Coltrane and Pharoah Sanders sessions; his tenor sax solos echoed their voicelike effects, with screams, overblowing and false fingering, honks and bleats, plus their accompaniments which were based on long stretches of simple, repeating two-chord sequences in minor keys to support soaring, sustained-tone solo lines. He used a wide vibrato and would sometimes hum and blow at the same time, producing a high-pitched, wailing tone. Later Barbieri began playing in a more mellow, sentimental fashion on ballads while retaining the energy focus on uptempo dates. He still sometimes utilizes the rising, upper register approach, but has exchanged his once fiery method for a more restrained approach on pop and fusion dates. A native of Argentina, Barbieri's family included several musicians, and he studied clarinet as a child. He moved to Buenos Aires in 1947, where he learned alto sax and made an early impact in Lalo Schfrin's band in 1953. Barbieri switched to tenor and formed his own quartet. He moved to Rome in the early '60s, and joined Don Cherry's group in Paris during 1963. He appeared on such fierce dates as *Complete Communion* on Blue Note in 1966 and recorded with Steve Lacy and Abdullah Ibrahim (then Dollar Brand). Barbieri combined free jazz and traditional South American rhythms. His late '60s album *The Third World* for Flying Dutchman won him his first widespread recognition, though earlier ESP dates introduced the formula. Barbieri's early '70s Flying Dutchman LPs included contributions from Stanley Clarke, John Abercrombie, Nana Vasconcelos, and one live date pairing him with Oliver Nelson and Eddie "Cleanhead" Vinson. But the album that made Barbieri a genuine star was his Grammy-winning soundtrack for the film *Last Tango in Paris* in 1972. He changed directions in 1973, forming a band of South American musicians and recording several traditional Latin albums. *Chapter One: Latin America* inaugurated the series, and Barbieri's band was a popular college attraction in the early '70s. Barbieri appeared at various festivals through the '70s, among them Newport, Montreux, and Bologna. During the '80s he had another smash with the LP *Caliente*. Barbieri essentially played pop and fusion while recording for A&M in the '80s. But in 1989 he returned to the traditional South American vein with *Gato... Para Los Amigos* for Bob Thiele's Signature label. He's continued working in the '90s, but hadn't enjoyed similiar exposure or popularity through '93. — *Ron Wynn*

In Search of Mystery / Mar. 15, 1967 / ESP ✦✦✦
★ **Fenix** / Apr. 27, 1971-Apr. 28, 1971 / Flying Dutchman ✦✦✦✦✦
The manic album that won him fame on college campuses in the early '70s. — *Ron Wynn*

El Pampero / Jun. 18, 1971 / RCA ✦✦✦
Chapter 1: Latin America / 1973 / Impulse ✦✦✦✦
The four "Chapters" in this series found Gato Barbieri rediscovering his South American roots and displaying his intense tone in melodic settings where his energy would be better focused than it had been on his earlier avant-garde albums. Joined by a large group of Argentinian musicians, Barbieri is in top form throughout this heated set, particularly on "Encune-

tros" and "India." Each of the "Chapters" is recommended, although *Chapter Three* is the only one currently available on CD. — *Scott Yanow*

Chapter 2: Two Hasta Siempre / Apr. 18, 1973 / Impulse ✦✦✦✦
As with *Chapter One*, this follow-up album features Gato Barbieri's fiery tenor playing strong melodies while joined by top Latin American musicians with an emphasis on percussionists. Barbieri was at his peak in the mid-'70s, and this "Chapter" (along with the three others) is easily recommended as examples of him at his best. — *Scott Yanow*

The Third World Revisited / 1974 / Bluebird ✦✦✦
● **Chapter 3: Viva Emiliano Zapata** / Jun. 25, 1974 / Impulse ✦✦✦✦
On the third of four "Chapters," the intense tenor saxophonist Gato Barbieri is accompanied by a big band playing Chico O'Farrill arrangements. The charts really showcase Barbieri at his peak, performing four of his melodic originals, "Milonga Triste," and "What a Difference a Day Makes." This CD (a straight reissue of the original LP) is highly recommended. — *Scott Yanow*

Chapter 4: Alive in New York / Feb. 20, 1975-Feb. 23, 1975 / ABC/ Impulse ✦✦✦
Apasionado / Jan. 1983 / Doctor Jazz ✦✦✦

Danny Barker

b. Jan. 13, 1909, New Orleans, LA, d. Mar. 13, 1994, New Orleans, LA
Banjo, Guitar, Vocals / Swing, New Orleans Jazz
A humorous personality as important for his storytelling and teaching as for his playing, Danny Barker had a long and colorful career. He played with the Boozan Kings early on in New Orleans and toured Mississippi with Little Brother Montgomery. In 1930 he moved to New York, switching from banjo to guitar and working with Dave Nelson, Sidney Bechet, Fess Williams, Albert Nicholas, James P. Johnson, Lucky Millinder (1937-38), Benny Carter (1938), and Cab Calloway (1939-46). He wrote "Don't You Feel My Leg" for his wife Blue Lu Barker (with whom he recorded frequently) and also had a hit with "Save the Bones for Henry Jones" (recorded by Nat King Cole). By 1947 Barker was fully involved in the Dixieland revival (he never cared for bebop), appearing on the "This Is Jazz" radio series, recording with Bunk Johnson, and returning to the banjo. He performed at Ryan's throughout the '50s (often with Conrad Janis or Wilbur DePairs) and then returned to New Orleans in 1965, where he worked as the assistant curator of the New Orleans Jazz Museum (1965-75), led the Onward Brass Band, encouraged younger players, and wrote about his experiences. Danny Barker, who appeared at the 1993 Monterey Jazz Festival with Milt Hinton, penned his memoirs (*A Life in Jazz*) in 1986 and was active in keeping New Orleans jazz alive up until to the end. His definitive recording is a solo set for Orleans; Barker can also be heard late in life on records by Wynton Marsalis and the Dirty Dozen Brass Band. — *Scott Yanow*

● **Save the Bones** / 1988 / Orleans ✦✦✦✦
Veteran guitarist Danny Barker made a countless number of sessions through a five-decade period as a sideman but only two full-length dates as a leader. This CD is quite definitive, for Barker is heard singing and playing guitar unaccompanied on a variety of ancient standards and obscurities. Barker's version of "St. James Infirmary" (which contains many of his own lyrics and asides) is classic. — *Scott Yanow*

Charlie Barnet

b. Oct. 26, 1913, New York, NY, d. Sep. 4, 1991
Sax (Tenor) / Swing
Charlie Barnet was unusual in several ways. One of the few jazzmen to be born a millionaire, Barnet was a bit of a playboy throughout his life, ending up with a countless number of ex-wives and anecdotes. He was one of the few White big-band leaders of the swing era to openly embrace the music of Duke Ellington (he also greatly admired Count Basie). Barnet was a pioneer in leading integrated bands (as early as 1935) and, although chiefly a tenor saxophonist (where he developed an original sound out of the style of Coleman Hawkins), Barnet was an effective emulator of Johnny Hodges on alto in addition to being virtually the only soprano player (other than Sidney Bechet) in the '30s and '40s.

And yet Charlie Barnet was only significant in jazz for about a decade (1939-49). Although his family wanted him to be a lawyer, he was a professional musician by the time he was 16 and ironically in his career made more money than he would have in business! Barnet arrived in New York in 1932 and started leading bands on records the following year, but his career was quite erratic until 1939. Many of Barnet's early records are worthy, but some are quite commercial as he attempted to find a niche. Best is a sideman appearance on a 1934 Red Norvo date that also includes Artie Shaw and Teddy Wilson.

In 1939, with the hit recording of his theme "Cherokee" and a very successful run at the Famous Door in New York, Charlie Barnet soon became a household name. In addition to the fine trumpeter Bobby Burnet (who soloed on many of Barnet's Bluebird records), such sidemen as guitarist Bus Etri, drummer Cliff Leeman, singers Lena Horne, Francis Wayne, and Kay Starr, pianist Dodo Marmarosa, clarinetist Buddy DeFranco, guitarist Barney Kessel, and even trumpeter Roy Eldridge spent time with Barnet's bands. Although at the height of his popularity during 1939-42 (when his orchestra could often play a close imitation of Ellington's), Barnet's recordings for Decca during 1942-46 were also of great interest, with "Skyliner" being a bestseller.

By 1947 Barnet was starting to look towards bop. Clark Terry was his star trumpeter that year, and in 1949 his screaming trumpet section included Maynard Ferguson, Doc Severinsen, Rolf Ericson, and Ray Wetzel. Barnet, however, soon lost interest, and near the end of 1949 he broke up his band. Semiretired throughout the remainder of his life, Charlie Barnet occasionally led swing-oriented big bands during short tours and appearances, making his last recording in 1966. —Scott Yanow

Clap Hands, Here Comes Charlie / Aug. 3, 1936-Jan. 7, 1941 / Bluebird ✦✦✦

● **Drop Me Off in Harlem** / Apr. 30, 1942-Jun. 16, 1946 / Decca ✦✦✦✦
Charlie Barnet reached his greatest popularity during his years with Bluebird (1939-42), but the orchestra he led during his period with Decca (1942-46) was even more powerful. This CD contains 20 of their best recordings and, even if "Skyliner" was their only commercial hit, such top soloists as trumpeters Peanuts Holland, Al Killian, and Roy Eldridge, clarinetist Buddy DeFranco, pianists Dodo Marmarosa and Al Haig, guitarist Barney Kessel, and singer Kay Starr (not to mention Barnet himself) make strong appearances on this well conceived and hard-swinging set. —Scott Yanow

Ray Barretto

b. Apr. 29, 1929, Brooklyn, NY
Percussion / Latin-Jazz, Cuba, Latin Continuum
A legend among Latin jazz musicians and fans, Ray Barretto helped popularize the conga in jazz, salsa, and other Latin styles, as well as R&B and rock. He's arguably the most recorded Latin musician of all time, with numerous recordings either as a leader or session player from the '50s through the '90s. While not quite a polyrhythmic dynamo like Mongo Santamaria or rhythmic innovator like Chano Pozo, Barretto has displayed remarkable flexibility, foresight, and tremendous accompaniment skills, while also being a superb soloist and first-class talent scout. He began on conga while in the Army, stationed in Germany. Upon his return to America, Barretto began working with New York jazz musicians. His first major job was with Eddie Bonnemere's Latin Jazz Combo. After working with Jose Curbelo, Barretto joined Tito Puente, replacing Mongo Santamaria. While staying in Puente's band four years, he also did R&B and jazz session work, playing on singles and working with Red Garland, Gene Ammons, and Lou Donaldson in the late '50s. Barretto made his recording debut as a leader in the early '60s on a Riverside session. *Pachanga with Barretto* featured arrangements by Hector Rivera. Barretto later took many of the same musicians and established his own band. He recorded with Kenny Burrell, Freddie Hubbard, and Cal Tjader during the '60s, while cutting albums for Riverside and on Tico for the Latin market. Barretto scored a crossover hit with the single "El Watusi." He helped modernize the charanga style by incorporating brass into his band. Barretto's Tico LPs blended traditional Latin sounds, jazz improvisation, and even pop and rock covers such as his version of "If I Had a Hammer." He subsequently recorded for United Artists before joining Fania in 1967. Barretto eventually became music director of the all-star lineup known as the Fania All Stars. They became quite controversial during their heyday, with proponents praising them for introducing pop and rock audiences to Latin jazz and pop, while detractors labelled them Latin muzak. The group at one point featured Barretto, Willie Colon, bandleader Johnny Pacheco, and vocalists Celia Cruz, Cheo Feliciano, Hector Lavoe, and Ismael Rivera. Barretto remained with them into the '80s. They sold out shows at Madison Square Garden in the '70s, teamed with jazz-fusion stars like Jan Hammer and Billy Cobham, Afropop instrumentalist Manu Dibango, and performed with such special guests as Kris Kristofferson, Rita Coolidge, Stephen Stills, Weather Report, and Steel Pulse. They were even on Columbia as a group, while the members retained separate pacts with other labels. Barretto's '60s albums included everything from film soundtracks to soul-flavored cuts and two-trumpet conjuntos as well as straight bebop and Latin jazz. Barretto worked with George Benson, the Average White Band, and the Rolling Stones in the '70s, as well as the Fania All Stars, continuing to update and expand his Latin base. He experimented with a three-trumpet front line and brought emerging, fresh performers such as vocalists Ruben Blades and Tito Allen and bassists Andy Gonzalez and Dave Perez into his band. He was nominated for a Grammy for his '75 album *Barretto*, and other '70s LPs *The Other Road* and *Indestructible* were heavily praised. Barretto headed a large jazz-rock, instrumental pop, and Latin aggregation while recording for Atlantic. He made albums with two trumpets and saxophonists, Blades' vocals, and a trombonist. The Crusaders produced one Barretto album, and Joe Sample and Wilton Felder also played on it. Such Barretto albums as *Rican! Struction* featured

adventurous arrangements and blazing, freewheeling solos and rhythms. Barretto won many honors during the '70s. He was voted top conga player by Latin New York magazine in 1975, 1976, and 1980, and Musician of the Year in 1977 and 1980. Barretto remained in the spotlight during the '80s. His CTI LP *La Cuna* with Tito Puente, Charlie Palmieri, and Joe Farrell among others was hailed as a Latin jazz masterpiece and was also a good seller (despite the fact it had been withheld nearly two years). He received another Grammy nomination and continued introducing fresh faces, among them vocalists Willie Torres, Cali Aleman, and Ray Babu. Barretto was music director of the "Bravisimo" television show and got some high-profile rock exposure when he appeared in the anti-apartheid video and on the album *Sun City.* He hasn't slowed down in the '90s, with recent albums issued by Messidor and Concord Picante, as well as others on Latin labels. His contributions to Latin-jazz, jazz, and popular music are immeasurable. Barretto currently has a few titles available on American jazz labels on CD; many more can be obtained through Latin specialty stores. —*Ron Wynn*

Carnaval / 1962 / Fantasy ✦✦✦

● **Handprints** / Mar. 1991 / Concord Picante ✦✦✦✦
Percussionist Ray Barretto, best-known as a sideman, had a rare chance to lead a session in 1991, and his Concord Picante debut is quite impressive. With saxophonist Steve Slagle, trumpeter Tim Ouimette, and trombonist Barry Olson leading the front line of this septet, Barretto mostly sticks to group originals for an infectious Latin jazz session. —*Scott Yanow*

Taboo / 1994 / Concord Picante ✦✦✦✦
Ray Barretto's group New World Spirit quickly became one of the top Latin jazz bands of the mid-'90s. Trumpeter Ray Vega, saxophonist Adam Kolker, and pianist Hector Martignon create some worthy solos, Barretto takes some strong improvisations on congas, and the band's repertoire finds the middle ground between salsa and jazz. —*Scott Yanow*

Kenny Barron

b. Jun. 9, 1943, Philadelphia, PA
Piano / Post-Bop, Hard Bop
In recent years Kenny Barron has been recognized as one of the giants of modern mainstream piano. The younger brother of the late saxophonist Bill Barron (who was 16 years older), he started on piano when he was 12 and played with Mel Melvin's R&B band in 1957. Barron moved to New York in 1961, where he worked briefly with James Moody, Lee Morgan, Roy Haynes, and Lou Donaldson. Most significant were his four years (1962-66) playing and recording with Dizzy Gillespie. Barron followed that important association with periods in the groups of Freddie Hubbard (1966-70), Yusef Lateef (1970-75), and Ron Carter's two-bass quartet (1976-80). Barron was a co-leader of the group Sphere in the '80s and since then has generally been the leader of his own trios. The pianist was on Stan Getz's final session (a series of brilliant duets) and has recorded many dates as a leader. In the '90s Barron received long overdue recognition for his talents. —*Scott Yanow*

Golden Lotus / Apr. 4, 1980 / Muse ✦✦✦

Scratch / Mar. 11, 1985 / Enja ✦✦✦✦
Kenny Barron, one of those talented pianists who always seems to be underrated, breaks away from playing standards and conventional bebop on this frequently exciting trio date. Matched up with bassist Dave Holland and drummer Daniel Humair, Barron explores five of his originals and Carmen Lundy's "Quiet Times." The fresh material and close interplay between the musicians make this set one of Barron's best trio recordings to date. —*Scott Yanow*

● **Live at Maybeck Recital Hall, Vol. 10** / Dec. 3, 1990 / Concord Jazz ✦✦✦✦
Wonderful Kenny Barron solo set. Bonus cuts in disc. —*Ron Wynn*

Invitation / Dec. 20, 1990 / Criss Cross ✦✦✦

Gary Bartz

b. Sep. 26, 1940, Baltimore, MD
Sax (Alto), Sax (Soprano) / Post-Bop
When Gary Bartz burst upon the scene in the late '60s and particularly when he led his Ntu Troop in the early '70s, he showed the potential of becoming one of the important leaders of jazz. Although he spent an aimless period in commercialism and never quite fulfilled the initial potential, by the late '80s Bartz was in prime form. He had started on alto at age 11 and, after studying at Juilliard and the Peabody Conservatory, Bartz worked with the Max Roach-Abbey Lincoln group in 1964. He followed that up by stints with Art Blakey's Jazz Messengers (1965-66), McCoy Tyner, and Blue Mitchell. Bartz made a strong impression with Miles Davis' 1970-71 fusion group, emerging as perhaps the strongest soloist on the recording *Live/Evil.* The altoist, who had recorded as a leader for Milestone and Prestige fairly regularly since 1967, did some of his finest work at the 1973 Montreux Jazz Festival (released on Prestige as *I've Known Rivers and Other Bodies*). From that point on, his recordings

became funkier and more commercial; 1978's *Love Affair* on Capitol (which featured a discofied version of "Giant Steps") was an obvious low point. However, by 1987 Bartz started recording stronger albums for Mapleshade, SteepleChase, and Candid. Now, instead of being a potential giant, Gary Bartz is an underrated (and often totally overlooked) jazz great. —*Scott Yanow*

I've Known Rivers and Other Bodies / Jul. 7, 1974 / Prestige ✦✦✦✦
At the time of this Montreux Festival concert (which has been released almost complete), altoist Gary Bartz was one of the most promising players in jazz. Already a veteran of the Miles Davis and McCoy Tyner bands, Bartz's future appeared limitless. Although he has not quite lived up to his potential and maintained a rather low profile since the '70s, Bartz is still playing well over 20 years after this impressive effort. His 1974 quartet (which consisted of pianist Hubert Eaves, bassist Stafford James, and drummer Howard King) is in top form on this lengthy two-LP set of original music, creating a new modern mainstream of fresh material that never really caught on. —*Scott Yanow*

● **West 42nd Street** / Mar. 31, 1990 / Candid ✦✦✦✦
Another fine recent release by Gary Bartz, who seems determined not to let his reputation slip in the '90s. From burning hard bop to convincing blues with a touch of funk, this is someone with something to say, rather than another instrumentalist confused and plugging into the latest trends. —*Ron Wynn*

Episode One Children of Harlem / Jan. 20, 1994 / Jazz Challenge ✦✦
Red & Orange Poems / Sep. 24, 1994-Sep. 25, 1994 / Atlantic Jazz ✦✦✦

Count Basie (William Basie)
....
b. Aug. 21, 1904, Red Bank, NJ, **d.** Apr. 26, 1984, Hollywood, CA
Piano / Swing
Throughout his career the name of Count Basie was synonymous with swing. Basie, whose influence remains huge over a decade after his death, not only led two of the finest jazz orchestras ever but he redefined the role of the piano in the rhythm section. Originally a stride pianist in the vein of his idol Fats Waller, Basie had such a strong rhythm section in the mid-'30s that he pared down his style drastically, eliminating the oom-pah timekeeping function of his left hand. With bassist Walter Page, rhythm guitarist Freddie Green and drummer Jo Jones filling in the spaces, Count stuck to simple phrases that were strategically placed to add momentum to the ensembles and he unwittingly acted as a transitional figure towards the bop of Bud Powell.

But Count Basie was really an institution by himself. Born as William Basie, he played for silent movies (under the tutelage of Waller), learned from the great stride pianists of New York and played the vaudeville circuit. Stranded in Kansas City in 1927 he soon joined Walter Page's Blue Devils (the best small group in the city) and eventually when Bennie Moten (himself a pianist) made Basie a better offer, he became the main pianist with Moten's Kansas City Orchestra, recording with Moten during 1929-32. The final session of Moten's band sound very much like a predecessor of Count Basie's Orchestra. After Moten's premature death in 1935, Basie formed his own band (known originally as The Barons Of Rhythm) and was based in Kansas City's Reno Club. The nine-piece band had a regular radio program and in 1936 producer John Hammond happened to hear them on his car radio. He was so impressed that he quickly travelled to Kansas City in hopes of singing up Basie to Columbia. However his articles (which raved about the great unknown band) alerted Decca and scouts from the rival label beat Hammond to it (although Basie would switch to Columbia in 1939).

After a period of struggle in which the orchestra (which was immediately expanded) had some rough moments, by late 1937 the Count Basie band had caught on. With such important soloists as the cool-toned tenor Lester Young (whose sound was an alternative to Coleman Hawkins), trumpeters Buck Clayton and Harry "Sweets" Edison, trombonist Dickie Wells, vocalist Jimmy Rushing (and for a period Billie Holiday) and the classic rhythm section, Basie's orchestra could hold its own against any other swing band. Its theme "One O'Clock Jump" soon became widely recorded (almost serving as an anthem for the era) and "Jumpin' at the Woodside" became a standard. In the '40s the band's arrangements (many of which were originally thought up by sidemen while on the bandstand) became more formalized. While Lester Young's departure in late 1940 left a hole, such other fine soloists as tenors Don Byas, Illinois Jacquet, Lucky Thompson and Paul Gonsalves, altoist Tab Smith, trumpeters Joe Newman and Clark Terry, and trombonist Vic Dickenson kept the band's music swinging. Bad money management and the change in the public's musical taste led Basie to reluctantly break up his orchestra at the end of 1949 and use a small group (ranging from a sextet to a nonet) for the next two years; it often featured Terry, Wardell Gray on tenor and clarinetist Buddy DeFranco.

In 1952, during a period when very few jazz orchestras were being formed, Count Basie put together what became known as his "New Testament" (as opposed to the earlier "Old Testament") band. Against all odds, Basie's orchestra caught on, especially after recording "April in

Paris" and after singer Joe Williams signed on the following year. Although it featured more than its share of top soloists including trumpeters Joe Newman and Thad Jones, and tenors Frank Wess (who helped introduce the flute to jazz) and Frank Foster, it was the arrangements (particularly those of Neal Hefti, Ernie Wilkins, Wess, Foster, Thad Jones and later on Sammy Nistico) and the sound of the swinging ensembles (along with the distinctive rhythm section) that were emphasized.

Although there was a lot of turnover in the '60s, the Basie sound never changed and the orchestra did not decline nor stop travelling. A series of indifferent commercial records in the mid-to-late '60s (which often found famous singers using the Basie band as a prop) were far inferior to the band's live performances, but when Basie renewed ties with producer Norman Granz in the '70s and signed with Pablo Records, his recordings (which by then often featured Jimmy Forrest on tenor and trombonist Al Grey) were greatly improved. Count Basie's health gradually failed in the '80s and his death was greatly mourned. However his orchestra (under the direction first of Thad Jones then Frank Foster and most recently Grover Mitchell) became the only viable ghost band in jazz history. —*Scott Yanow*

Basie's Basement / Oct. 23, 1929-Dec. 13, 1932 / Bluebird ✦✦✦✦
The genesis of the Count Basie band can be heard in these recordings by Bennie Moten's Kansas City Orchestra. With Basie on piano, trumpeter Hot Lips Page, tenor saxophonist Ben Webster, and such future Basieites as trombonist/guitarist Eddie Durham, baritonist Jack Washington, bassist Walter Page, and the great singer Jimmy Rushing, there are times when Moten's orchestra almost sounds like Basie's. Eight selections from the 1929-30 period are followed by eight numbers recorded at Moten's last and greatest sesssion (from Dec. 13, 1932). Such tunes as "Moten's Swing," "Lafayette," and "Blue Room" are prime examples of early swing. —*Scott Yanow*

☆ **The Complete Decca Recordings (1937-1939)** / GRP ✦✦✦✦✦
This magnificent three-disc set has the first 63 recordings by Count Basie's Orchestra, all of his Deccas. The consistency is remarkable (with not more than two or three turkeys) and the music is the epitome of swing. With such soloists as Lester Young and Herschel Evans on tenors, trumpeters Buck Clayton and Harry "Sweets" Edison, the great blues singer Jimmy Rushing, and that brilliant rhythm section of Basie, guitarist Freddie Green, bassist Walter Page, and drummer Jo Jones, the music is timeless. It's all here: "One O'Clock Jump," "Sent for You Yesterday," "Blue and Sentimental," "Jumpin' at the Woodside," "Jive at Five," and many others. This is the first Count Basie collection to acquire and should be in every jazz collection. —*Scott Yanow*

Rock-a-Bye Basie, Vol. 2 / Aug. 9, 1938-Mar. 7, 1940 / Vintage Jazz Classics ✦✦✦

Count Basie, Vol. 1 (1939) / Jan. 1939-Apr. 1939 / Classics ✦✦✦

Count Basie, Vol. 2 (1939) / May 1939-Nov. 1939 / Classics ✦✦✦

Old Manuscripts, Broadcast Transcriptions (1944-45) / Jul. 1943-1945 / Music & Arts ✦✦✦✦
This CD contains 25 selections featuring the Count Basie Orchestra taken from radio broadcasts. Ten numbers are from an April 1944 session in which tenor great Lester Young (who had rejoined the band the following year) is well featured. In addition there is one number ("G.I. Stomp") from 1943 while the remainder are from several sessions during 1944-45. In addition to Young, the main soloists include trumpeter Harry "Sweets" Edison, trombonist Dickie Wells, Buddy Tate on tenor, clarinetist Rudy Rutherford, and the pianist/leader; plus there are occasional vocals from Jimmy Rushing, Thelma Carpenter, Maxine Johnson, and Earl Warren. This underrated version of Basie's big band was one of his best, and the 76 minutes on this CD contain many high points. —*Scott Yanow*

Beaver Junction (1944-1946) / May 27, 1944-Nov. 12, 1947 / Vintage Jazz Classics ✦✦✦✦
A worthy CD full of Basie rarities, it includes unissued and alternate versions of V Discs and two radio broadcasts; the one from 1944 features drummer Buddy Rich filling in for the recently drafted Jo Jones. Rich had so much fun being part of the swing machine that when Basie handed him a blank check for his services, he tore it up! The music throughout this CD will be equally fun for the listener. —*Scott Yanow*

Brand New Wagon: Count Basie 1947 / Jan. 3, 1947-Dec. 12, 1947 / Bluebird ✦✦✦

Class of '54 / Sep. 2, 1954-Sep. 7, 1954 / Black Lion ✦✦✦
This fine CD consists of two radio airchecks from 1954, featuring Count Basie with a nonet and his full orchestra. The smaller group also has trumpeter Joe Newman, trombonist Henry Coker, and the tenors of Frank Wess and Frank Foster well featured, while the big-band tracks (which mostly sport Neal Hefti arrangements) find the orchestra on the brink of great success. —*Scott Yanow*

Count Basie, Lester Young & the Stars of Birdland / Feb. 1955 / Jass ✦✦✦✦
This live CD documents a tour by top performers who appeared regularly at Birdland. Count Basie's orchestra backs Basie alumnus Lester Young on

three tracks, welcomes Stan Getz to sit in for four numbers (including an exciting version of "Little Pony"), accompanies Sarah Vaughan during eight songs, and performs seven tunes by itself, four of which feature Joe Williams (who had just recently joined the band). This historic set will be prized by collectors. —*Scott Yanow*

★ **Count Basie Swings, Joe Williams Sings** / Jul. 17, 1955-Jul. 26, 1955 / Verve ◆◆◆◆◆

Joe Williams' debut on records with the Basie orchestra was so successful in every way that the band's future was secure for the next few decades. Included on this essential set are the classic versions of "Every Day I Have the Blues," "The Comeback," "Alright Okay, You Win," "In the Evening," and "Teach Me Tonight," hits that Williams and Basie would have to perform nightly for the remainder of the '50s. Highly recommended. —*Scott Yanow*

☆ **April in Paris** / Jul. 26, 1955-Jan. 5, 1956 / Verve ◆◆◆◆◆

A true classic, this studio album includes Count Basie's hit versions of "April in Paris," "Shiny Stockings," and "Corner Pocket"; these three tunes have remained in the Basie band's repertoire ever since. Actually all ten selections are very enjoyable, and this exciting and of course swinging record is definitive of '50s Count Basie. —*Scott Yanow*

Count Basie in London / Sep. 7, 1956 / Verve ◆◆◆

● **Count Basie at Newport** / Sep. 7, 1957 / Verve ◆◆◆◆

At the 1957 Newport Jazz Festival the music was consistently inspired and often historic. Count Basie welcomed back tenor great Lester Young and singer Jimmy Rushing for part of a very memorable set highlighted by "Boogie Woogie" and "Evenin'"; Young plays beautifully throughout and Rushing is in prime form. An exciting full-length version of "One O'Clock Jump" features Young, Illinois Jacquet, and trumpeter Roy Eldridge; the Basie band stretches out on "Swingin' at Newport"; and five previously unreleased selections (put out for the first time on this CD) include four Joe Williams vocals. It's a great set of music. —*Scott Yanow*

Atomic Mr. Basie / Oct. 21, 1957-Oct. 22, 1957 / Roulette ◆◆◆◆

Known as the "Atomic" album due to the cover picture of an A-bomb exploding, this is one of the great Count Basie records, ranking with *April in Paris*. The 1957 edition of the Basie orchestra romps through "The Kid from Red Bank" (a superlative feature for its leader), "Whirly Bird," and "Lil' Darlin'" among others; everything works on this essential album. —*Scott Yanow*

The Complete Roulette Studio Count Basie / Oct. 21, 1957-Jul. 26, 1962 / Mosaic ◆◆◆◆

Some of Count Basie's finest recordings were cut for the Roulette label during 1957-62, and all of his studio performances are included on this massive Mosaic ten-CD box set. Among the classic former LPs that are reissued here are *The Atomic Mr. Basie, Basie Plays Hefti, Chairman of the Board, Everyday I Have the Blues*, and *Kansas City Suite*. With such soloists as trumpeters Thad Jones and Joe Newman, the tenors of Frank Foster and Eddie Lockjaw Davis, and Frank Wess on alto and flute, vocals by Joe Williams, and the timeless arrangements of Neal Hefti, Thad Jones, Frank Foster, Ernie Wilkins, and Frank Wess among others, this essential (but unfortunately limited-edition) set features the second Count Basie Orchestra at its very best. —*Scott Yanow*

The Complete Roulette Live Recordings of Count Basie and His Orchestra (1958-1962) / May 31, 1959-Aug. 1, 1962 / Mosaic ◆◆◆◆

This consistently exciting eight-CD set features the Count Basie Orchestra at three different locations and time periods: at a convention in Florida in 1959, at Birdland on two nights in 1961, and in Stockholm during a four-day period. Of the 133 selections, only 28 were released before, making these hard-swinging performances (which would be essential for Basie fans on the basis of the music alone) of even greater interest. During this era Basie had such top soloists as Frank Wess on alto and flute, the tenors of Frank Foster and Billy Mitchell, trumpeters Thad Jones and Joe Newman, and trombonists Al Grey and Quentin Jackson. In addition, drummer Louis Bellson is featured throughout the Stockholm engagement, and such guests as trumpeter Harry "Sweets" Edison and singers Joe Williams, Sarah Vaughan, and Jon Hendricks are heard from. But it is the swinging Basie rhythm section and the enthusiasm of the ensembles that make this a truly classic and somewhat historic set. —*Scott Yanow*

First Time! The Count Meets the Duke / Jul. 6, 1961 / Columbia ◆◆◆◆

This session was an impossible dream come true, the teaming of the entire Count Basie and Duke Ellington orchestras, including the principals on joint pianos. Whether it be "Take the 'A' Train," "Jumpin' at the Woodside," or "Until I Met You," everything works on this album and somehow the ensembles avoid sounding overcrowded. This version of "Segue in C" is the outstanding performance of a unique and highly enjoyable set. —*Scott Yanow*

Ella and Basie! / Jul. 15, 1963-Jul. 16, 1963 / Verve ◆◆◆

☆ **Basie's Beat** / Oct. 7, 1965-Feb. 15, 1967 / Verve ◆◆◆◆◆

During an era when the Count Basie Orchestra was often being used as a mere prop behind other singers, this album was quite refreshing. With the

exception of trombonist Richard Boone's two eccentric vocals, this is an instrumental date with arrangements provided by band members past and present, and concise solos contributed by quite a few talented players. —*Scott Yanow*

Jazz Fest Masters: Count Basie / Jun. 1969 / Scotti Bros. ◆◆◆

Afrique / Dec. 22, 1970-Dec. 23, 1970 / Doctor Jazz ◆◆◆

For the First Time / May 22, 1974 / Pablo ◆◆◆

Satch and Josh / Dec. 2, 1974 / Pablo ◆◆◆

● **Basie and Zoot** / Apr. 9, 1975 / Original Jazz Classics ◆◆◆◆

Pianist/bandleader Count Basie and tenor saxophonist Zoot Sims were beautiful and this was a fine pairing—Sims being at an age when he had caught up to the Count and the Count was hip enough to pass the baton and keep right up with him. There were no musical cliches here; the music sustained itself. John Heard's bass was a pleasure, sensitively walking itself throughout the album. Drummer Louis Bellson was near perfect, keeping the music Kansas City light and rolling, only pushing and prodding Sims and Basie with a delicate tension on "I Surrender Dear." The mark of Norman Granz's productions for Pablo was a give and response relationship between producer, artist, and listener, and the level remained incredibly high on the album; inventive, timeless, and classic. —*Bob Rusch, Cadence*

Fun Time: Count Basie Big Band at Montreux '75 / Jul. 19, 1975 / Pablo ◆◆◆

Prime Time / Jan. 18, 1977-Jan. 20, 1977 / Pablo ◆◆◆◆

One of arranger Sammy Nestico's most enjoyable sessions for Count Basie, these eight selections (six composed by Nestico, including the title cut and "Ya Gotta Try") are performed by an inspired Basie orchestra. Tenor saxophonist Jimmy Forrest and trombonist Al Grey star among the soloists. —*Scott Yanow*

Farmers Market Barbecue / May 1982 / Original Jazz Classics ◆◆◆

88 Basie Street / May 11, 1983-May 12, 1983 / Original Jazz Classics ◆◆◆◆

One of Basie's final albums, the very appealing title cut seems to sum up his career, a lightly swinging groove with a strong melody. Two small-group performances with guest Joe Pass on guitar and the tenor of Kenny Hing add variety to a particularly strong set. —*Scott Yanow*

Basie's Bag / Nov. 1992 / Telarc ◆◆◆

Mario Bauza

b. Apr. 28, 1911, Havana, Cuba, **d.** Jul. 11, 1993, New York, NY
Trumpet / Latin Continuum, Afro-Cuban Jazz

A talented section player who rarely soloed, Mario Bauza's main importance to music was behind the scenes as one of the main instigators of Afro-Cuban jazz, the potent mixture of Latin rhythms with jazz improvisation. A multi-instrumentalist, Bauza played clarinet and oboe with the Havana Philharmonic before moving to New York in 1930. During a stint with Noble Sissle in 1932 he switched to trumpet. As musical director with Chick Webb (1933-38), Bauza helped convince the drummer of the potential greatness of Ella Fitzgerald. He was with Don Redman during 1938-39 and then Cab Calloway (1939-41). Bauza was largely responsible for Calloway hiring Dizzy Gillespie, and in 1947 he would introduce Dizzy to Chano Pozo. Bauza became the longtime musical director of his brother-in-law Machito's orchestra (1941-76), encouraging Machito to add jazz solos to his music. In the '80s and early '90s as the head of his own Afro-Cuban Orchestra, Mario Bauza (who had long since given up playing trumpet) recorded three excellent albums of his arrangements and finally received some recognition for his important contributions to music. —*Scott Yanow*

● **The Tanga Suite** / Jul. 29, 1992 / Messidor ◆◆◆◆

Mario Bauza's place as one of the key founders of Latin-jazz was overlooked for decades until he formed the exciting orchestra found on this Messidor CD. This 23-piece big band, along with a variety of singers, performs a full set of Bauza's originals including the five movements of his Afro-Cuban jazz suite "Tanga." Victor Paz's lead trumpet drives the ensembles, and Paquito D'Rivera has a strong appearance sitting in on alto. —*Scott Yanow*

944 Columbus / May 27, 1993-May 28, 1993 / Messidor ◆◆◆

Sidney Bechet

b. May 14, 1897, New Orleans, LA, **d.** May 14, 1959, Paris, France
Clarinet, Sax (Soprano) / Dixieland, New Orleans Jazz

Sidney Bechet was the first important jazz soloist on records in history (beating Louis Armstrong by a few months). A brilliant soprano saxophonist and clarinetist with a wide vibrato that listeners either loved or hated, Bechet's style did not evolve much through the years, but he never lost his enthusiasm or creativity. A master at both individual and collective improvisation within the genre of New Orleans jazz, Bechet was such a dominant player that trumpeters found it very difficult to play with him. Bechet wanted to play lead, and it was up to the other horns to stay out of his way!

Sidney Bechet studied clarinet in New Orleans with Lorenzo Tio, Big Eye Louis Nelson, and George Baquet, and he developed so quickly that as a child he was playing with some of the top bands in the city. He even taught clarinet, and one of his students (Jimmie Noone) was actually two years older than him! In 1917 he travelled to Chicago, and in 1919 he joined Will Marion Cook's Orchestra, touring Europe with Cook and receiving a remarkably perceptive review from Ernst Ansermet. While overseas he found a soprano sax in a store, and from then on it was his main instrument. Back in the US, Bechet made his recording debut in 1923 with Clarence Williams, and during the next two years he appeared on records backing blues singers, interacting with Louis Armstrong, and playing some stunning solos. He was with Duke Ellington's early orchestra for a period and at one point hired a young Johnny Hodges for his own band. However, from 1925-29 Bechet was overseas, travelling as far as Russia but getting in trouble (and spending jail time) in France before being deported.

Most of the '30s were comparatively lean times for Bechet. He worked with Noble Sissle on and off and had a brilliant session with his New Orleans Feetwarmers in 1932 (featuring trumpeter Tommy Ladnier). But he also ran a tailor's shop which was more notable for its jam sessions than for any money it might make. However, in 1938 he had a hit recording of "Summertime," Hugues Panassie featured Bechet on some records, and soon he was signed to Bluebird, where he recorded quite a few classics during the next three years. Bechet worked regularly in New York, appeared on some Eddie Condon Town Hall concerts, and in 1945 he tried unsuccessfully to have a band with the veteran trumpeter Bunk Johnson (whose constant drinking killed the project). Jobs began to dry up about this time, and Bechet opened up what he hoped would be a music school. He only had one main pupil, but Bob Wilber became his protégé.

Sidney Bechet's fortunes changed drastically in 1949. He was invited to the Salle Pleyel Jazz Festival in Paris, caused a sensation, and decided to move permanently overseas. Within a couple years he was a major celebrity and a national hero in France even though the general public in the US never did know who he was! Bechet's last decade was filled with exciting concerts, many recordings, and infrequent visits back to the US before his death from cancer. His colorful (if sometimes fanciful) memoirs, *Treat It Gentle*, and John Chilton's magnificent Bechet biography, *The Wizard of Jazz* (which traces his life week by week), are both highly recommended. Many of Sidney Bechet's recordings are currently available on CD. —*Scott Yanow*

The Chronological Sidney Bechet, 1923-1936 / Oct. 1923-Mar. 1936 / Classics ✦✦✦✦
The first in a series of Classics CDs focusing on the recordings of Sidney Bechet, this disc features the clarinetist/soprano saxophonist on two early titles with blues singer Rosetta Crawford, his torrid 1932 session with the New Orleans Feetwarmers (which also features trumpeter Tommy Ladnier and is highlighted by "Shag" and "Maple Leaf Rag"), and sides from Noble Sissle's somewhat commercial orchestra. Fortunately Sissle was wise enough to give Bechet plenty of solo space on some of his selections, most notably "Polka Dot Rag." Even with a few indifferent vocals, this CD is recommended to those not already owning this music. —*Scott Yanow*

● **Master Takes: Victor Sessions (1932-1943)** / 1932-1943 / Bluebird ✦✦✦✦
A three-disc set containing the bulk of Bechet's recordings made in the US, it covers 17 different combinations of musicians (including the renowned one-man-band session in which Bechet accompanied himself in 1941). This is the epitome of passion by one of New Orleans' greatest clarinet/soprano masters. —*Bruce Raeburn*

The Chronological Sidney Bechet, 1937-1938 / Apr. 1937-Nov. 1938 / Classics ✦✦✦

1938-1940 / Nov. 28, 1938-Feb. 5, 1940 / Classics ✦✦✦

★ **Complete Blue Note Recordings** / 1939-1953 / Mosaic ✦✦✦✦✦
Mosaic, a mail-order company, has compiled a series of remarkable box sets that feature the complete recordings of various immortal musicians at the peak of their careers. This limited-edition six-LP set (get it while you can) has all of Sidney Bechet's recordings for Blue Note including three songs with the Port of Harlem Seven (climaxed by his hit version of "Summertime"), two blues with guitarist Josh White, and Bechet's sessions from 1940, 1944, 1945, 1946, 1949, 1950, 1951, and 1953, in which he shares the front line with such trumpeters as Sidney DeParis, Max Kaminsky, Bunk Johnson, Wild Bill Davison, and Jonah Jones. The music ranges from hot swing to exuberant Dixieland, and Bechet somehow always sounds inspired. —*Scott Yanow*

1940 / Mar. 7, 1940-Jun. 4, 1940 / Classics ✦✦✦✦
Classics' chronological reissue of Bechet's recordings (at least the regular takes) continues with a pair of songs made with blues singer Josh White; eight very enjoyable performances cut with a quartet consisting of cornetist Muggsy Spanier, guitarist Carmen Mastren, and bassist Wellman

Braud; and a pair of Bechet's Victor sessions. This is one of the strongest entries in this valuable series. —*Scott Yanow*

1940-1941 / Sep. 6, 1940-Oct. 14, 1941 / Classics ✦✦✦✦
Classics' Sidney Bechet series continues with this CD, a generous set full of the soprano's prime Victor recordings, including appearances by cornetist Rex Stewart and pianist Earl Hines, Bechet's guest shot with the Chamber Music Society of Lower Basin Street, and his innovative "one-man-band" recordings of "The Sheik of Araby" and "Blues of Bechet." —*Scott Yanow*

Masters of Jazz, Vol. 4 / Aug. 29, 1945-Dec. 20, 1947 / Storyville ✦✦✦

La Legende de Sidney Bechet / Oct. 14, 1949-Jul. 4, 1958 / Vogue ✦✦✦

Live in New York, 1950-51 / Apr. 1, 1950-Oct. 19, 1951 / Storyville ✦✦✦
Neglected in his homeland, the great soprano saxophonist Sidney Bechet first moved to France (where he quickly became known as a national hero) in 1949 but made a couple of trips back to the US during the next few years. His Storyville CD features Bechet in the US during two occasions, leading a quartet/quintet with only a trombone joining him in the front line; at least he was not compelled to battle for the lead with a trumpeter. There are eight selections with trombonist Vic Dickenson, pianist Ken Kersey, bassist Herb Ward, and drummer Cliff Leeman that include individual features for Dickenson and Kersey along with spirited renditions of "Muskrat Ramble," "High Society," and "Royal Garden Blues"; in addition Bechet caresses the melody of "Laura" and romps through "Just One of Those Things." However, it is the other 11 numbers (which were only previously released on LP by Pumpkin) that are most notable, for these are probably the finest recordings of the underrated trombonist Big Chief Russell Moore. With pianist Red Richards and drummer Art Trappier functioning quite well as the entire rhythm section (without a bassist), the trombonist stays out of Bechet's way and adds some robust and humorous solos of his own. During memorable versions of "I Found a New Baby," "Bugle Call Rag," "Panama," and even "Casey Jones," Bechet never runs out of infectious riffs and is in consistently exciting form. —*Scott Yanow*

Olympia Concert, October 19, 1955 / Oct. 19, 1955 / Vogue ✦✦✦

Bix Beiderbecke

b. Mar. 10, 1903, Davenport, IA, **d.** Aug. 6, 1931, New York, NY
Cornet / Classic Jazz
Bix Beiderbecke was one of the greatest jazz musicians of the '20s. His colorful life, quick rise and fall, and eventual status as a martyr made him a legend even before he died, and he has long stood as proof that not all the innovators in jazz history were Black. Possessor of a beautiful distinctive tone and a strikingly original improvising style, Bix's only competitor among cornetists in the '20s was Louis Armstrong, and (due to their different sounds and styles) one really could not compare them.

Beiderbecke was a bit of a child prodigy, picking out tunes on the piano when he was three. While he had conventional training on the piano, he taught himself the cornet. Influenced by the original Dixieland Jazz Band, Beiderbecke craved the freedom of jazz, but his straight-laced parents felt he was being frivolous. He was sent to Lake Forest Military Academy in 1921, but by coincidence it was located fairly close to Chicago, the center of jazz at the time. Beiderbecke was eventually expelled he missed so many classes! After a brief period at home he became a full-time musician. In 1923 Beiderbecke became the star cornetist of the Wolverines, and a year later this spirited group made some classic recordings.

In late 1924 Beiderbecke left the Wolverines to join Jean Goldkette's Orchestra, but his inability to read music resulted in him losing the job. In 1925 he spent time in Chicago and worked on his reading abilities. The following year he spent time with Frankie Trumbauer's Orchestra in St. Louis. Although already an alcoholic, 1927 would be Beiderbecke's greatest year. He worked with Jean Goldkette's Orchestra (most of their records are unfortunately quite commercial), recorded his piano masterpiece "In a Mist" (one of his four Debussy-inspired originals), cut many classic sides with a small group headed by Trumbauer (including his greatest solos: "Singin' the Blues," "I'm Comin' Virginia," and "Way Down Yonder in New Orleans"), and then signed up with Paul Whiteman's huge and prosperous orchestra. Although revisionist historians would later claim that Whiteman's wide mixture of repertoire (much of it outside of jazz) drove Bix to drink, he actually enjoyed the prestige of being with the most popular band of the decade. Beiderbecke's favorite personal solo was his written-out part on George Gershwin's "Concerto in F."

With Whiteman, Bix's solos tended to be short moments of magic, sometimes in odd settings; his brilliant chorus on "Sweet Sue" is a perfect example. He was productive throughout 1928, but by the following year his drinking really began to catch up with him. Beiderbecke had a breakdown, made a comeback, and then in September 1929 was reluctantly sent back to Davenport to recover. Unfortunately, Bix made a few sad records in 1930 before his death at age 28. The bad liquor of the Prohibition era did him in.

For the full story, *Bix: Man & Legend* is a remarkably detailed book. Beiderbecke's recordings (even the obscure ones) are continually in print, for his followers believe that every note he played was special. This writer agrees. —*Scott Yanow*

The Indispensable / Nov. 24, 1924-Sep. 15, 1930 / RCA ✦✦✦
This double-CD from French RCA in their Jazz Tribune series (a reissue of an earlier double LP) gives one a good overview of cornetist Bix Beiderbecke's Victor recordings. More serious collectors will want to acquire this music as part of a more complete series (since all of his solos are significant), while beginning collectors are advised to pick up his Columbia reissue CDs (which feature Beiderbecke in smaller groups) first. The 36 performances on this two-fer mostly focus on his sideman appearances with the large dance orchestras of Jean Goldkette and Paul Whiteman during 1926-28, although there is one 1924 track ("I Didn't Know") with Goldkette and a few later sessions from 1930. Highlights include "Clementine," "San," "There Ain't No Sweet Man," "From Monday On," and "You Took Advantage of Me." —*Scott Yanow*

★ **Bix Beiderbecke, Vol. 1: Singin' the Blues** / Feb. 4, 1927-Sep. 30, 1927 / Columbia ✦✦✦✦✦
With Frankie Trumbauer (sax), Eddie Lang (g), and others. —*Richard Lieberson*

At the Jazz Band Ball, Vol. 2 / Oct. 1927-Apr. 3, 1928 / Columbia ✦✦✦✦
1990 reissue, follow-up to material on *Singin' the Blues*. —*Ron Wynn*

Bix Lives / 1927-1930 / RCA ✦✦✦✦
This album includes Jean Goldkette and Whiteman material. It's a nice complement to the Columbia Records compilations (*Vols. 1 & 2*). —*Richard Lieberson*

Louie Bellson (Luigi Paulino Alfredo Francesco Antonion Balassoni)

b. Jul. 26, 1924, Rock Falls, IL
Drums / Bop, Swing
One of the great drummers of all time (and one of the few whose name can be said in the same sentence with Buddy Rich), Louie Bellson has the rare ability to continually hold one's interest throughout a 15-minute solo. He became famous in the '50s for using two bass drums simultaneously, but Bellson was never a gimmicky or overly bombastic player. In addition to being able to drive a big band to exciting effect, Bellson can play very quietly with a trio and sound quite satisfied.
Winner of a Gene Krupa talent contest while a teenager, Bellson was with the big bands of Benny Goodman (1943 and 1946), Tommy Dorsey (1947-49), and Harry James (1950-51) before replacing Sonny Greer with the Duke Ellington Orchestra. A talented writer, Bellson contributed "Skin Deep" and "The Hawk Talks" to Duke's permanent repertoire. He married Pearl Bailey in 1952 and the following year left Ellington to be her musical director. Bellson toured with Jazz at the Philharmonic (1954-55), recorded many dates in the '50s for Verve, and was with the Dorsey Brothers (1955-56), Count Basie (1962), Duke Ellington (1965-66), and Harry James (1966). He has been continually active up to the present day, leading big bands (different ones on the East and West Coasts), putting together combos for record dates, giving clinics for younger drummers, and writing new music. Bellson has recorded extensively for Roulette (early '60s), Concord, Pablo, and most recently Music Masters. —*Scott Yanow*

150 M.P.H. / May 25, 1974 / Concord Jazz ✦✦✦

Black Brown & Beige / Oct. 20, 1992-Oct. 22, 1992 / Music Masters ✦✦✦
Rather than try to recreate Duke Ellington's famous "Black, Brown & Beige," Louie Bellson's big band does a reinterpretation of the 50-minute work on this CD that takes a lot of liberties with the composition. A little more space is allocated to solos, Johnny Hodges' famous "Come Sunday" melody statement is given to Clark Terry, Joe Williams sings "The Blues," and such players as trumpeter Barrie Lee Hall, Art Baron on plunger trombone, pianist Harold Danko, and baritonist Joe Temperley are heard from. This version does give some new life to the classic suite. In addition, Bellson's band plays five of the drummer's originals including the boppish "Hawk Talks" and "Skin Deep." The shorter orchestral pieces fit into the general mood of the respectful but fairly creative tribute. —*Scott Yanow*

● **Live from New York** / Jan. 20, 1994 / Telarc ✦✦✦✦
At 71 Louie Bellson on this CD displays more energy than most drummers half his age. Bellson not only takes solos on more than half the selections (including a lengthy workout on "Santos"), but he composed all seven originals; the only surprise is that Bellson decided to let some of his musical friends (including Matt Catingub, Tommy Newsom, and Bob Florence) arrange the charts instead of writing them himself. With concise solos from such sidemen as trumpeters Marvin Stamm and Glenn Drewes, tenorman Ted Nash, altoists Joe Roccisano and Steve Wilson, and trombonist Keith O'Quinn, Bellson's music is given perfectly suitable interpretations. But just in case, the equally ageless fluegelhornist Clark Terry (at 75) stars on two songs including the exquisite ballad "Blow Your Horn." With Louie Bellson constantly driving the ensembles, this is a big-band disc well worth acquiring. —*Scott Yanow*

David Benoit

b. 1953, Bakersfield, CA
Piano / Crossover
One of the more popular performers in the idiom somewhat inaccurately called "contemporary jazz," David Benoit has mostly performed light melodic background music, what critic Alex Henderson has dubbed "New Age with a beat." Benoit has done a few fine jazz projects (including a tribute to Bill Evans and a collaboration with Emily Remler), but most of his output for GRP has been aimed clearly at the charts. He studied composition and piano at El Camino College and in 1975 played on the soundtrack of the film *Nashville*. After recording with Alphonse Mouzon and accompanying singer Gloria Lynne, he was signed to the AVI label when he was 24, recording sets that paved the way towards his later output. Benoit has been a solo artist for GRP since 1986. —*Scott Yanow*

Christmastime / 1983 / Blue Moon ✦✦✦✦
Recorded several years before David Benoit hit it big commercially, this set of Christmas songs (originally recorded for AVI and reissued on CD by Bluemoon) is surprisingly jazz-oriented. Pianist Benoit performs ten traditional songs in a quartet with guitarist Jimmy Fox, bassist Wade Short, and drummer Tony Morales and really digs into some of the familiar themes, particularly "Christmastime Is Here," "Santa Claus Is Coming to Town," and "Greensleeves." Much better than expected. —*Scott Yanow*

Freedom at Midnight / 1987 / GRP ✦✦✦

● **Waiting for Spring** / Feb. 5, 1989-May 25, 1989 / GRP ✦✦✦✦
David Benoit strives for a more acoustic and introspective feel on his newest release. While the jazz playing that he is known for is still present, there is also a more impressionist side to some of the tracks. —*MusD*

Shaken Not Stirred / 1994 / GRP ✦✦

George Benson

b. Mar. 22, 1943, Pittsburgh, PA
Guitar, Vocals / Pop, Hard Bop, Crossover
George Benson has emulated two of his strongest influences in career path and direction: Wes Montgomery and Nat "King" Cole. As with Montgomery and Cole, Benson is a supremely talented individual whose highly marketable skills have often required him to compromise his musical talents. Benson's guitar playing has a swinging flexibility and bluesy, soulful grit. His solos are deftly played and nicely executed, performed in a manner that makes him the equal of any contemporary stylist. He can accompany a vocalist or band, work with, off, or against the beat, play tasteful ballads or torrid solos, do wailing soul-jazz or slow, steamy blues. His singing has the sentimental, lush touches of Cole but recalls the gospel-tinged delivery of Donny Hathaway. Benson rode to fame in the '70s on the strength of songs just a cut above easy listening; he became an urban-contemporary celebrity with a blend of mellow vocals and light instrumental filler and has sought to keep record labels and urban radio outlets happy with hit fodder while retaining his integrity doing occasional jazz projects. Benson sang in clubs as a youngster, and formed a rock band at 17. He played with Jack McDuff's quartet twice in the '60s, appearing at the Antibes-Juan-les-Pins Jazz Festival in 1964 and playing on a Swedish television broadcast with Jean Luc Ponty. He briefly had his own trio in Pittsburgh before reteaming with McDuff. Benson later led and recorded with groups that included Ronnie Cuber and Jimmy Smith. He recorded with Billy Cobham, Miles Davis (who sought in vain to get Benson to join his group), Herbie Hancock, Freddie Hubbard, Ron Carter, and Lee Morgan in the '60s. When Creed Taylor, formerly Wes Montgomery's producer, sought a replacement for his departed star, he signed Benson to A&M, cutting with him the same string-laden, lightweight pop and rock filler that made Montgomery a star. When Taylor began a new label, CTI, Benson was one of his first signees. Benson continued making pleasant, at times interesting, records through the early and mid-'70s until he switched to Warner Bros. His cover of a Leon Russell tune "This Masquerade" took Benson to the next level, crossover success. The single was a Top Ten pop hit, and the subsequent *Breezin'* album eventually topped the pop charts and won Grammy awards. Not only did both Columbia and A&M promptly reissue his earlier albums, Benson began a run of hit records that continued into the early '80s. He had seven Top 40 singles between 1976 and 1983, and four more Top Ten albums. But even Benson expressed displeasure at the content of these albums after awhile, and in the '80s began to try and expand without losing his urban-contemporary base. He did make a command appearance at the White House in 1979, showing everyone he hadn't lost his jazz chops. Benson recorded with fellow guitarist Earl Klugh in the late '80s, and in 1990 did a nice album with the Count Basie Orchestra. Almost every album Benson's done over the '60s, '70s, '80s, and '90s has been reissued on CD, while Columbia has reissued anthologies collecting his soul-jazz and blues cuts, and Prestige has reissued an anthology of his work with McDuff. —*Ron Wynn*

The New Boss Guitar / May 1, 1964 / Original Jazz Classics ✦✦✦✦
A definitive early album, it features Brother Jack McDuff (organ). —*Michael G. Nastos*

George Benson/Jack Mc Duff / May 1, 1964-Oct. 19, 1965 / Prestige ♦♦♦♦

Guitarist George Benson spent an important period early in his career as a sideman with organist Jack McDuff. This two-LP set brings back two albums that they recorded together; one was originally under Benson's name, while the other was led by McDuff. With tenor saxophonist Red Holloway adding his distinctive solo voice, this quartet/quintet (depending on whether they use a bassist) was an exciting blues-oriented unit that was rightfully popular in the mid-'60s. The two-fer gives one a valuable look at George Benson in his early years. —*Scott Yanow*

Benson Burner / 1965-1966 / Columbia ♦♦♦

Hot, soulful mid-'60s organ combo material from a period when George Benson was playing with bluesy abandon and reflecting the considerable influence of Grant Green. Anyone hearing these songs shouldn't be surprised at his eventual crossover success, but these weren't as overproduced and orchestrated as his A&M or Warner Bros. recordings. —*Ron Wynn*

The Cookbook / Aug. 1, 1966-Oct. 19, 1966 / Columbia ♦♦♦

Simmering interplay, fueled by guitarist Benson and baritone saxophonist Ronnie Cuber, make this early-'60s effort one to savor. Six Benson originals and four standards are included. It was produced by John Hammond. Lonnie Smith (organ), Bennie Green (tb). —*Michael G. Nastos*

The Other Side of Abbey Road / Oct. 22, 1969-Nov. 1969 / A&M ♦♦

Beyond the Blue Horizon / Feb. 2, 1971-Feb. 3, 1971 / Columbia ♦♦♦♦

Essentially a glorified guitar-organ date, this was topnotch in its field. Clarence Palmer's organ was economical and workmanlike; George Benson's guitar was an honest effort and dug in with ideas, though I still think the best George Benson is found in sidemen roles. —*Bob Rusch, Cadence*

● White Rabbit / Nov. 1971 / Columbia ♦♦♦♦

This is the best collaboration between Benson and guitarist Earl Klugh. —*Ron Wynn*

The Best of George Benson [CBS] / 1971-1976 / Columbia ♦♦♦♦

This 1989 compilation covers Benson's tenure at CTI Records, 1971-1975, and presents his best as a pure jazz guitarist, prior to his move to singing and the pop-jazz approach found on "Breezin'" and later albums. —*William Ruhlmann*

Good King Bad / Jul. 1975 / Columbia ♦♦♦

This is a good place to hear Benson playing at his jazz best, rather than his commercial best. —*Michael Erlewine*

Breezin' / Jan. 6, 1976-Jan. 9, 1976 / Warner Bros. ♦♦♦

This was the definitive Benson album commercially; counterpart to Wes Montgomery's pop works of the '60s. —*Ron Wynn*

The George Benson Collection / 1976-1981 / Warner Bros. ♦♦♦

Anthology featuring big hits from his years on Warner Bros., plus some new material. It included another Top Ten hit in the single "Turn Your Love Around" and represented the peak for Benson on the label in terms of commercial potency, although he did do some other records that sold rather well later in the '80s. —*Ron Wynn*

Weekend in LA / Feb. 1, 1977 / Warner Bros. ♦♦

Tenderly / 1989 / Warner Bros. ♦♦♦

Big Boss Band / 1990 / Warner Bros. ♦♦♦

Bunny Berigan (Rowland Bernart Berrigan)

b. Nov. 2, 1908, Hilbert, WI, d. Jun. 2, 1942, New York, NY
Trumpet, Vocals / Swing

Bunny Berigan during 1935-39 was arguably the top trumpeter in jazz (with his main competition being Louis Armstrong and Roy Eldridge). Blessed with a beautiful tone and a wide range (Berigan's low notes could be as memorable as his upper register shouts), Bunny brought excitement to every session he appeared on. He was not afraid to take chances during his solos and could be a bit reckless, but Berigan's successes and occasional failures were always colorful to hear, at least until he drank it all away.

Bunny Berigan played in local bands and then college groups in the Midwest. He tried out for Hal Kemp's Orchestra unsuccessfully in 1928 (rejected because of his thin tone!) but showed tremendous improvement by 1930 when he was hired. After a few recordings and a trip to Europe, Bunny joined Fred Rich's CBS studio band in 1931, where (except for a few months with Paul Whiteman) he would remain up to 1935. Berigan soon gained a strong reputation as a hot jazz soloist, and he appeared on quite a few records with studio bands, the Boswell Sisters, and the Dorsey Brothers. In 1935 he spent a few months with Benny Goodman's Orchestra, but that was enough to launch the swing era. Berigan had classic solos on Goodman's first two hit records ("King Porter Stomp" and "Sometimes I'm Happy") and was with BG as he went on his historic tour out West, climaxing in the near-riot at the Palomar Ballroom in Los Angeles.

Berigan soon returned to the more lucrative studio scene, making his only film appearance in 1936 with Fred Rich. In 1937 he joined Tommy

Dorsey's band and was once again largely responsible for two hits: "Marie" and "Song of India." Bunny's solos on these tunes became so famous that in future years Dorsey had them written out and orchestrated for the full trumpet section! After leaving Dorsey, Bunny Berigan finally put together his own orchestra. He scored early on with his biggest hit "I Can't Get Started." With Georgie Auld on tenor and Buddy Rich on drums, Berigan had a potentially strong band. Unfortunately he was already an alcoholic and a reluctant businessman. By 1939 there had been many lost opportunities, and the following year Bunny (who was bankrupt) was forced to break up his band. He rejoined Tommy Dorsey for a few months but never stopped drinking and was not happy being a sideman again. Soon Berigan formed a new orchestra, but his health began declining, and on June 2, 1942, he died when he was just 33. What would this brilliant swing trumpeter have done in the bop era?

Bunny Berigan's life is definitively profiled in Robert Dupuis' book *Elusive Legend of Jazz. —Scott Yanow*

● The Pied Piper / Jul. 1, 1935-Aug. 3, 1940 / Bluebird ♦♦♦♦

This is the best single-CD compilation of Bunny Berigan recordings issued to date. Although all of the trumpeter's big-band sides for Bluebird have come out on three double LPs, this set gives more general collectors a better overview of his talents. One of the top trumpeters to be active during the 1935-39 period (only Louis Armstrong and the up-and-coming Roy Eldridge were on his level), Berigan was largely responsible for the success of important hit records for Benny Goodman ("King Porter Stomp" and "Sometimes I'm Happy") and Tommy Dorsey ("Marie" and "Song of India") in addition to having a bestseller of his own ("I Can't Get Started"). Unfortunately Berigan's alcoholism eventually did him in, but this CD has all of the hits plus appearances with Gene Gifford's Orchestra (a majestic solo on "Nothin' But the Blues"), Frankie Trumbauer, Fats Waller in a jam session, and with the Metronome All-Stars in addition to more titles as a leader, with BG, and with Dorsey (including a radio broadcast version of "I've Found a New Baby" from 1940). This is a well conceived reissue of important and often-exciting swing by one of the greats. —*Scott Yanow*

Sing! Sing! Sing!, Vol. 1: 1936-1938 / Jul. 20, 1936-Jun. 27, 1938 / Jass ♦♦♦

Devil's Holiday, Vol. 2: 1938 / Jun. 27, 1938-Aug. 9, 1938 / Jass ♦♦♦

Tim Berne

b. 1954, Syracuse, NY
Sax (Alto) / Avant-Garde

One of the top avant-garde saxophonists of the '80s and '90s, Tim Berne was even able to keep his noncompromising music intact during a short association with Columbia Records. After moving to New York in 1974 and studying with Julius Hemphill, Berne recorded a few records for his own Empire label. He later recorded for Soul Note, Columbia, and JMT. Although he participated in John Zorn's Ornette Coleman tribute (*Spy vs. Spy*), Berne has mostly played as a leader, carving out his own unique path in improvised music. —*Scott Yanow*

Fulton Street Maul / 1986 / Columbia ♦♦♦♦

How did avant-gardist Tim Berne get signed to Columbia? During his relatively brief alliance with that media giant, the passionate altoist was somehow able to continue recording his uncompromising music with apparently no real interference. On this set, he teams up with the amazing guitarist Bill Frisell, cellist Hank Roberts, and percussionist Alex Cline for five explorative pieces that one can safely bet did not receive much airplay. —*Scott Yanow*

Sanctified Dreams / Jun. 1988 / Columbia ♦♦♦

Alto saxophonist Tim Berne ranks among the more progressive players around, someone who keeps looking ahead rather than behind. This 1988 set was no different; it contains odd passages, moments of indecision, and segments where Berne and associates blazed away. —*Ron Wynn*

● Diminutive Mysteries / Sep. 1992 / JMT ♦♦♦♦

This is certainly the most unusual David Sanborn recording to date. Avant-gardist Tim Berne (heard here on alto and baritone) and the popular R&B star Sanborn (mostly leaving his trademark alto behind to play soprano) share a great respect for altoist Julius Hemphill and the St. Louis free-jazz movement. Along with guitarist Marc Ducret, cellist Hank Roberts, and drummer Joey Baron, they perform seven often-emotional Hemphill pieces plus Berne's "The Maze." Sanborn is to be congratulated for successfully stretching himself, although this is very much Berne's date. —*Scott Yanow*

Bill Berry (William R. Berry)

b. Sep. 14, 1930, Benton Harbor, MI
Trumpet / Swing

Bill Berry has been leading big bands in the Los Angeles area since the early '70s, still inspired by his years with Duke Ellington. After being discharged from the Air Force in 1955, he studied at both the Cincinnati College of Music and Berklee. Berry worked in the big bands of Woody Herman and Maynard Ferguson before joining Ellington (1961-64). After leaving Duke he was with the Thad Jones-Mel Lewis Orchestra (1966-68), led his own New York Big Band, and did studio work. After he moved to Los Angeles in 1971, Berry formed the L.A. Big Band, which he has continued leading on a part-time basis up to the present time. He has also toured with Louie Bellson and been involved in the jazz education program run by the Monterey Jazz Festival. Bill Berry is an excellent veteran mainstream trumpet player who has recorded several sets (with both small groups and his big band) for Concord. — *Scott Yanow*

● **Hello Rev** / Nov. 1977 / Concord Jazz ◆◆◆◆
Bill Berry L.A. Big Band. Stylized big-band cuts, good production. — *Ron Wynn*

For Duke / Jan. 11, 1978-Jan. 12, 1978 / Real Time ◆◆◆

The Ellington All-Stars / Jan. 11, 1978-Jan. 12, 1978 / Drive Archive ◆◆◆

Chu Berry (Leon Brown Berry)

b. Sep. 13, 1910, Wheeling, WV, **d.** Oct. 30, 1941, Conneaut, OH
Sax (Tenor) / Swing
Chu Berry was considered a top tenor saxophonist of the '30s, just below Coleman Hawkins (his main influence), Lester Young, and Ben Webster. Particularly strong on uptempo numbers (although his ballad statements could be overly sentimental), Berry might have become an influential force if he had not died prematurely. After playing alto in college, he switched to tenor in 1929 when he joined Sammy Stewart's band. In 1930 he moved to New York, playing with Benny Carter's band and Charlie Johnson's Orchestra. He was prominently featured in Spike Hughes 1933 recording sessions, was a star with the bands of Teddy Hill (1933-35) and Fletcher Henderson (1936) (to whom he contributed his song "Christopher Columbus"), and then found a permanent home with Cab Calloway in 1937. Berry was used on many sessions including with his friend Roy Eldridge, Lionel Hampton (a classic version of "Sweethearts on Parade"), Teddy Wilson, and Calloway (his version of "Ghost of a Chance" became well known); in addition he led a couple of his own fine dates. Chu Berry died from the effects of a car crash when he was just 33. — *Scott Yanow*

Chu Berry Story / 1937-1938 / Zeta ◆◆◆

● **A Giant of Tenor Sax** / Nov. 1938-Aug. 1941 / Commodore ◆◆◆◆

Barney Bigard (Albany Leon Bigard)

b. Mar. 3, 1906, New Orleans, LA, **d.** Jun. 27, 1980, Culver City, CA
Clarinet / Swing, New Orleans Jazz
Barney Bigard was one of the most distinctive clarinetists in jazz and a longtime asset to Duke Ellington's Orchestra. Although he took clarinet lessons with Lorenzo Tio, Bigard's initial reputation was made as a tenor saxophonist; in fact, based on a few of his recordings (particularly those with Luis Russell), Bigard was No. 2 behind Coleman Hawkins in the mid-'20s. After working with several groups in New Orleans, Bigard moved to Chicago in 1924, where he played with King Oliver during 1925-27. He would also record with Jelly Roll Morton, Johnny Dodds, and future boss Louis Armstrong in the '20s but, after short stints with Charles Elgar and Luis Russell, Bigard found his true home with Duke Ellington's Orchestra, with whom he almost exclusively played clarinet. Between 1927 and 1942 he was well featured on a countless number of recordings with Ellington, who understood Bigard's musical strengths and wrote to showcase him at his best. From "Mood Indigo" (which he co-composed) to "Harlem Air Shaft," Bigard was an important fixture of the Ellington Orchestra.

When he quit the band in 1942 (due to tiring of the road), Bigard played with Freddie Slack's big band, Kid Ory's New Orleans group, and appeared in the 1946 film *New Orleans*. Bigard then joined the Louis Armstrong All-Stars, constantly travelling the world during 1947-55 and 1960-61; he spent 1958-59 with Cozy Cole's band. Bigard became largely semi-retired after 1962 but still played now and then, recording with Art Hodes, Earl Hines, and as a leader. However, Barney Bigard, whose swing style was sometimes out-of-place with Armstrong, really sounded at his best during his Duke Ellington years. — *Scott Yanow*

Paris: December 14-15, 1960 / Dec. 14, 1960-Dec. 15, 1960 / Vogue ◆◆◆◆

● **Bucket's Got a Hole in It** / Jan. 1968 / Delmark ◆◆◆◆
This is one of clarinetist Barney Bigard's best recordings of his later period. On four of the eight selections he is well featured on swing standards with a quartet that also includes the great pianist Art Hodes. The other four tracks are more in the Dixieland vein, with trumpeter Nappy Trottier and the veteran trombonist George Brunis making the band a sextet. Throughout, Bigard (whose tone was instantly recognizable) is the main star and in splendid form. — *Scott Yanow*

Walter Bishop, Jr.

b. Apr. 10, 1927, New York, NY
Piano / Bop
A fine bop and hard-bop pianist and the son of songwriter Walter Bishop,

Walter Bishop, Jr., has been an effective bandleader, composer, and educator. He played with Art Blakey in the late '40s, played with Charlie Parker, Miles Davis, and Oscar Pettiford in the '50s, and with Curtis Fuller in 1960 before forming his own trio with Jimmy Garrison and G.T. Hogan. Bishop toured with Terry Gibbs in the mid-'60s and studied with Hall Overton at Juilliard. He combined studies and recording after moving to the West Coast in 1969, cutting dates with Supersax and Blue Mitchell. Bishop became an instructor before he moved back to New York in the '70s. He wrote a book on jazz theory in 1976, was in Clark Terry's big band in the late '70s, and toured Switzerland while leading various bands. He taught at the University of Hartford in the early '80s and had a solo Carnegie Hall concert in 1983. Bishop recorded for DIW, Prestige, Black Lion, Seabreeze, Muse, Red, and Black Jazz among others. — *Ron Wynn*

Milestones / Mar. 14, 1961 / Black Lion ◆◆◆

Valley Land / Dec. 30, 1974 / Muse ◆◆◆

Soul Village / Jun. 1977 / Muse ◆◆◆

● **What's New** / Oct. 25, 1990 / DIW ◆◆◆◆
Pianist Walter Bishop, Jr., displayed his bop proficiency on this 1991 release, one of his finest. His solos are electric, nicely constructed, and often brilliantly executed. He seldom got much recognition except from musicians, but Bishop was certainly among the finest bop and mainstream pianists of his era. — *Ron Wynn*

Midnight Blue / Dec. 1991 / Red ◆◆◆

Eubie Blake (James Hubert Blake)

b. Feb. 7, 1883, Baltimore, MD, **d.** Feb. 12, 1983, New York, NY
Piano / Ragtime
Eubie Blake had a rather unique career. Although his main importance was as a songwriter for Broadway shows in the '20s, late in life he became known as the last living link to ragtime. Blake always had a colorful life. He wrote his first rag, "The Charleston Rag," in 1899, spent years playing with medicine shows and in sporting houses, and by 1915 was teaming up with singer Noble Sissle in vaudeville. Sissle and Blake wrote for the 1921 hit show *Shuffle Along* (the first all-Black musical), and it was followed by *Revue Negre, Plantation Review, Rhapsody in Black*, and *Bamville Review*. The team of Sissle and Blake, in addition to making recordings, was filmed for some early experimental sound shorts. Among Blake's hit songs of the '20s were "I'm Just Crazy About Harry," "You're Lucky to Me," and "Memories of You."

Although he made some recordings in 1931, Eubie Blake generally had a lower profile for the next three decades. He worked with Sissle now and then and earned a degree from New York University but was largely forgotten until 1969. That year he recorded a double LP for Columbia (*The Eighty-Six Years of Eubie Blake*) that amazed listeners who had never heard of him. During his remaining 14 years, Eubie Blake was a very popular performer, playing and singing ragtime-era pieces, charming audiences, making new records, appearing on Broadway in the 1978 show *Eubie* (he was 95 at the time), and running his own label, Eubie Blake Music. He continued performing until he was 98, and Eubie Blake made it to his 100th birthday with five days to spare. — *Scott Yanow*

Memories of You: From Rare Piano Rolls / 1915-1973 / Biograph ◆◆◆

● **Blues and Ragtime (1917-1921)** / 1917-1921 / Biograph ◆◆◆◆
Collection featuring vintage tunes done by ragtime and early jazz great Eubie Blake. The feeling and energy he generates is tremendous, and even when the solos aren't impressive, Blake's attitude and personality keep things moving. — *Ron Wynn*

Blues & Spirituals (1921) / Mar. 1921-Dec. 1921 / Biograph ◆◆◆◆
More classic songs from pianist Eubie Blake, whose 100-year lifespan kept him in the public eye through much of the 20th century. He reflected that experience through his playing, which rocks, sways, and rips at times, and then is appropriately mournful or reverent. — *Ron Wynn*

● **The 86 Years of Eubie Blake** / Dec. 26, 1969 / Columbia ◆◆◆◆
This solo piano recording was produced by John Hammond. It also includes sessions done on Feb 6, 1969, and Mar 12, 1969. — *AMG*

Live Concert / May 22, 1973 / Eubie Blake Music ◆◆◆
Pianist/singer/composer Eubie Blake (who was 90 years old at the time) is in pretty good shape on this LP, telling stories and playing piano continuously for 37 minutes before an enthusiastic audience. Some of his stories (and playing) might be a bit fanciful, but it is all quite enjoyable. In addition to performing some of his own tunes (including "Tricky Fingers" and "Memories of You"), Blake sounds fine on a James P. Johnson medley. — *Scott Yanow*

Ran Blake

b. Apr. 20, 1935, Springfield, MA
Piano / Avant-Garde
A champion of "Third Stream" music (mixing together aspects of jazz and classical music), Ran Blake has long had a very individual and unusual piano style. His solos are generally very dramatic, making inventive use of

explosive outbursts and silence. When performing standards he often keeps the melody intact but drops the chord structure, creating fresh new music. Blake graduated from Bard College, attended the Lenox School of Jazz during several summers, and starting in 1957 had an association with singer Jeanne Lee; they toured Europe in 1963 and performed some fairly free piano-vocal duets. Blake, who recorded for ESP in 1965, became very involved in jazz education at the New England Conservatory of Music, where he has worked since 1967. He has recorded on an infrequent basis throughout his career, including solo dates on several labels and collaborations with Ricky Ford, Anthony Braxton, Houston Person, and Jeanne Lee. —Scott Yanow

The Newest Sound Around / Nov. 15, 1961-Dec. 7, 1961 / Bluebird ✦✦✦

● **Duke Dreams** / May 29, 1981-Jun. 2, 1981 / Soul Note ✦✦✦✦
Ran Blake's tribute to Billy Strayhorn and Duke Ellington, *Duke Dreams*, was recorded May 29, 1981-June 2, 1981. Now, a tribute to these men might appear to be an "in-the-tradition" gambit, but Blake's realization of his own tribute (the title cut), Dave Brubeck's "The Duke," and the other material was a glance backward actually looking toward the present/future. Some of the very familiar tunes were given a most creative reworking. None of the original intent/feeling was destroyed . . . but instead developed and distilled through this unique artist, whose quirky voicings, rhythms, and lines make everything he does unmistakably Blake. —*Bob Rusch, Cadence*

Painted Rhythms: The Compleat Ran Blake, Vol. 1 / Dec. 1985 / GM ✦✦✦✦
First in a projected series dedicated to the work of pianist/composer Ran Blake, a genuine iconoclast. His songs can be moving, muddled, dense, or aggressive, but they're never dull. His playing is the same way; always changing, seldom flashy, and usually rewarding for listeners with open ears. —*Ron Wynn*

Painted Rhythms: The Compleat Ran Blake, Vol. 2 / Dec. 1985 / GM ✦✦✦

You Stepped Out of a Cloud / Aug. 11, 1989 / Owl ✦✦✦✦
This is pianist Blake and vocalist Jeanne Lee's first record since the mid-'60s. —*Michael G. Nastos*

Epistrophy / 1991 / Soul Note ✦✦✦

Round About / Dec. 19, 1992-Sep. 29, 1993 / Music & Arts ✦✦✦✦
Ran Blake has long been a very emotional pianist whose use of space and sometimes-thunderous outbursts are always stimulating if unpredictable. For this set he performs solos and duets with the straightforward but very effective vocalist Christine Correa, alternating stirring versions of standards with five of his songs. Among the more memorable selections are "Angel Eyes," "Drop Me Off in Harlem," "The Short Life of Barbara Monk," "Long as You're Living," and "I Get a Kick Out of You." Thought-provoking music. —*Scott Yanow*

Art Blakey

b. Oct. 11, 1919, Pittsburgh, PA, d. Oct. 16, 1990
Drums / Hard Bop
Art Blakey was hard-bop's guru, the percussive anchor of countless brilliant bands, and its ultimate talent scout. Blakey's technique was famous, with his frequent, high-volume snare and bass drum accents. Though he sometimes dismissed the idea of an African/jazz rhythm connection, Blakey incorporated some African devices after visiting in the '40s. These included the habit of rapping on the side of the drum and using his elbow on the tom-tom to alter the pitch. He was also known for the dramatic closing of the hi-hat on every second and fourth beat. Blakey played with such force and fury he eventually lost much of his hearing, and at the end was often playing strictly on instinct. But he maintained the Jazz Messengers as the idiom's foremost repertory band from its beginnings in the late '40s and mid-'50s into the '90s. The roster of greats whose careers Blakey nurtured include Donald Byrd, Hank Mobley, Jackie McLean, Johnny Griffin, Bobby Timmons, Benny Golson, Lee Morgan, Wayne Shorter, Curtis Fuller, Cedar Walton, Freddie Hubbard, Billy Harper, Joanne Brackeen, Valery Ponomarev, Bill Pierce, Bobby Watson, Wynton Marsalis, Branford Marsalis, James Williams, Terence Blanchard, Donald Harrison, Wallace Roney, Javon Jackson, and Brian Lynch among others, even Keith Jarrett and Chuck Mangione! Blakey had a few piano lessons in his childhood and was playing full-time by the seventh grade, heading a band. He switched to drums, essentially teaching himself through listening to such players as Chick Webb and Sid Catlett. He joined Mary Lou Williams in 1942, then played with the Fletcher Henderson Orchestra in 1943 and 1944, touring the south. He briefly led a big band in Boston, then joined Billy Eckstine's new band. During his years with Eckstine, Blakey met many bebop pioneers, including Miles Davis, Fats Navarro, and Dexter Gordon. Blakey organized a rehearsal band he called the 17 Messengers upon leaving Eckstine. He later recorded with an octet called the Jazz Messengers. Blakey traveled to Africa in the late '40s, living there more than a year and learning about African music and Islam (he eventually converted to Islam and took the name Buhaina.) He performed and did radio broadcasts in the

'50s with Charlie Parker, Clifford Brown, and Miles Davis, as well as Horace Silver. Blakey was in the Buddy DeFranco quartet from 1951 to 1953. He and Silver formed a co-operative group with Hank Mobley and Kenny Dorham in 1955, using the familiar name Jazz Messengers. When Silver departed in 1956, Blakey became the band's leader and held that position the remainder of its existence. They became the prototype hard-bop ensemble, playing aggressive, exciting bebop material with a vivid blues foundation. Blakey took pride in holding onto musicians just long enough to develop them, seeing them move on and fresh ones arrive. The coveted position of Messengers' music director belonged to a host of superb players, from Wayne Shorter to Bobby Watson. At the same time, Blakey never confined his duties to the Messengers. He found time to record with Monk, the Modern Jazz Quartet, John Coltrane, various African, jazz, and Latin drummers on a summit session, do a film soundtrack with Benny Golson, tour with the Giants of Jazz (Gillespie, Monk, Sonny Stitt, and Al McKibbon), often appear as a soloist at the Newport Jazz Festival, and keep abreast of changes and fresh faces. The Messengers recorded from the '50s until the '90s primarily on Blue Note, but also on Impulse, Timeless, Concord, and Bethlehem, plus some foreign labels. Though it seemed he would live forever, Blakey finally passed in 1992. His spirit and presence are celebrated in the music of the '80s and '90s hard-bop revivalists. Mosaic issued a tremendous box set featuring the complete 1960 recordings of his group in 1993. Blue Note issued a three-disc greatest hits collection, and there are also many single-disc reissues from the different Messengers periods. —*Ron Wynn*

New Sounds / Dec. 22, 1947-1948 / Blue Note ✦✦✦

A Night at Birdland, Vol. 1 / Feb. 21, 1954 / Blue Note ✦✦✦✦
Just prior to forming the first edition of the Jazz Messengers, drummer Art Blakey led a superb quintet at Birdland for a brief gig in 1954. The band featured the great trumpeter Clifford Brown, altoist Lou Donaldson, pianist Horace Silver, and bassist Curly Russell in addition to the leader/drummer. All of the music has since been reissued as part of a Clifford Brown box set for Mosaic, but this is the original LP. The first volume is highlighted by "A Night in Tunisia," "Quicksilver," and "Once in a While" and finds all of the participants in inspired form. Classic bop. —*Scott Yanow*

A Night at Birdland, Vol. 2 / Feb. 21, 1954 / Blue Note ✦✦✦✦
The second volume taken from Art Blakey's pre-Jazz Messengers gig at Birdland features the immortal trumpeter Clifford Brown, altoist Lou Donaldson, pianist Horace Silver, bassist Curly Russell, and the leader/drummer romping through the blues "Wee-Dot," two Charlie Parker tunes, an alternate version of "Quicksilver," and a Donaldson ballad feature on "If I Had You." All of the musicians are inspired, none more than Blakey, who would soon form the Jazz Messengers as a permanent outlet for his hard-swinging drums. —*Scott Yanow*

A Night at Birdland, Vol. 3 / Feb. 21, 1954 / Blue Note ✦✦✦✦

At the Cafe Bohemia, Vol. 1 / Nov. 11, 1955 / Blue Note ✦✦✦

The Jazz Messengers at the Cafe Bohemia, Vol. 2 / Nov. 23, 1955 / Blue Note ✦✦✦

Hard Bop / Dec. 12, 1956-Dec. 13, 1956 / Columbia ✦✦✦

Theory of Art / Apr. 2, 1957 / Bluebird ✦✦✦
This CD contains two unique sessions in the history of Art Blakey's Jazz Messengers. Five numbers feature a sextet that includes both altoist Jackie McLean, who had recently left the band, and his replacement, tenor saxophonist Johnny Griffin, along with trumpeter Bill Hardman; "A Night in Tunisia" best shows off this short-lived group. The remaining two numbers were unissued until this CD came out and feature Blakey heading a nonet that included future Messenger Lee Morgan, trombonist Melba Liston, and Griffin. The music is consistently excellent and also succeeds as a historical curiosity that should greatly interest Blakey collectors. —*Scott Yanow*

★ **Moanin': Art Blakey and the Jazz Messengers** / Oct. 30, 1958 / Blue Note ✦✦✦✦✦
The third version of Art Blakey's Jazz Messengers debuted with this stunning LP which has since been reissued (along with an alternate version of "Moanin'") on CD. Tenor saxophonist Benny Golson helped give the quintet its own personality with his compositions and arrangements (contributing "Blues March," "Along Came Betty," "Are You Real," and "The Drum Thunder Suite" to this set), 20-year old trumpeter Lee Morgan quickly emerged as a powerful soloist, and the funky pianist Bobby Timmons' "Moanin'" became the Messengers' first real hit. This classic album, a major influence on hard bop, is highly recommended. —*Scott Yanow*

And the Jazz Messengers / Apr. 15, 1959 / Blue Note ✦✦✦✦

Live in Stockholm (1959) / Nov. 23, 1959 / Dragon ✦✦✦✦
The version of Art Blakey's Jazz Messengers heard on this CD differs from most from the period because pianist Bobby Timmons had just departed to join Cannonball Adderley, so Walter Davis, Jr., is in the piano chair. Otherwise the lineup (with trumpeter Lee Morgan, tenor saxophonist Wayne Shorter, bassist Jymie Merritt, and drummer Blakey) is familiar. Performing three standards (including "Night in Tunisia") and two group originals (best known is one of the earliest versions of Shorter's "Lester Left Town"),

the Jazz Messengers are up to their usual high standards; both Morgan and Shorter are in particularly strong form while Davis fits in quite well. —*Scott Yanow*

The Big Beat / Mar. 6, 1960 / Blue Note ✦✦✦✦
In 1960, Art Blakey led one of the greatest versions of his Jazz Messengers. The particular edition heard on this CD features three distinctive soloists (trumpeter Lee Morgan, tenor saxophonist Wayne Shorter, and pianist Bobby Timmons). Highlights of *The Big Beat* include Timmons' "Dat Dere" and Shorter's "Lester Left Town" in addition to a colorful arrangement of "It's Only a Paper Moon," heard in two versions. A gem. —*Scott Yanow*

★ **The Complete Blue Note Recordings of Art Blakey's 1960 Messengers** / Mar. 6, 1960-May 27, 1961 / Mosaic ✦✦✦✦✦
This six-CD limited-edition box set from Mosaic is quite remarkable. It includes all of the music from the Jazz Messenger albums *The Big Beat, A Night in Tunisia,* the two volumes of *Meet You at the Jazz Corner of the World, The Freedom Rider, Like Someone in Love, The Witch Doctor, Roots and Herbs,* and *Pisces* (the latter was originally issued only in Japan) along with two previously unissued alternate takes. More importantly, the music is consistently brilliant, featuring one of the great editions of Art Blakey's band, the group with trumpeter Lee Morgan, tenor saxophonist Wayne Shorter, pianist Bobby Timmons, and bassist Jymie Merritt. But one will have to act fast to get this essential music before it goes out of print and starts showing up on auction lists! —*Scott Yanow*

Like Someone in Love / Aug. 7, 1960 / Blue Note ✦✦✦

Night in Tunisia / Aug. 14, 1960 / Blue Note ✦✦✦✦
The lengthy title track on this CD easily overshadows the rest of the program, for it is one of the most exciting versions ever recorded of Dizzy Gillespie's "A Night in Tunisia." Trumpeter Lee Morgan (then only in his early 20s), tenor saxophonist Wayne Shorter, pianist Bobby Timmons, and bassist Jymie Merritt formed one of the strongest of the many versions of Art Blakey's Jazz Messengers and are actually in fine form during the remainder of the satisfying (if anticlimatic) set. The CD augments the LP by adding a version of "When Your Lover Has Gone" and an alternate take of "Sincerely Diana" to the original program. —*Scott Yanow*

Meet You at the Jazz Corner of the World, Vol. 1 / Sep. 14, 1960 / Blue Note ✦✦✦

Meet You at the Jazz Corner of the World, Vol. 2 / Sep. 14, 1960 / Blue Note ✦✦✦

The Witch Doctor / Mar. 14, 1961 / Blue Note ✦✦✦

The Freedom Rider / May 27, 1961 / Blue Note ✦✦✦✦
The final recording by this edition of the Jazz Messengers (featuring trumpeter Lee Morgan, tenor saxophonist Wayne Shorter, pianist Bobby Timmons, bassist Jymie Merritt, and drummer/leader Art Blakey) finds the group consolidating their year-and-a-half of experience into yet another exciting document. Blakey's unaccompanied drum feature on "The Freedom Rider" is full of drama, while the rest of the program (two compositions apiece by Morgan and Shorter) makes this last chapter for this particular band quite memorable. —*Scott Yanow*

Mosaic / Oct. 2, 1961 / Blue Note ✦✦✦

Three Blind Mice, Vol. 1 / Mar. 1962 / Blue Note ✦✦✦

Three Blind Mice, Vol. 2 / Mar. 9, 1962-Mar. 18, 1962 / Blue Note ✦✦✦

Live Messengers / Mar. 9, 1962-Mar. 18, 1962 / Blue Note ✦✦✦✦
This two-LP set contains live performances from the 1961-62 Jazz Messengers (the all-star sextet that included trumpeter Freddie Hubbard, trombonist Curtis Fuller, and Wayne Shorter on tenor) in addition to three additional selections from the 1954 Birdland quintet; the latter features the great trumpeter Clifford Brown, altoist Lou Donaldson, and pianist Horace Silver. Happily, all of the music is up to the level of the originally released recordings and finds Blakey really pushing the two ensembles. While the earlier group jams on "Wee-Dot," "The Way You Look Tonight," and a blues, the early-'60s Messengers mostly play fresh versions of their originals, including "The Promised Land," "Ping Pong," and "Up Jumped Spring." This hard-to-find two-fer is recommended. —*Scott Yanow*

Free for All / Feb. 10, 1964 / Blue Note ✦✦✦
During most of 1961-64 Art Blakey's Jazz Messengers (except for bassist Reggie Workman replacing Spanky DeBrest) managed to keep the same personnel, a remarkable feat when one considers the strong talent (which included trumpeter Freddie Hubbard, trombonist Curtis Fuller, Wayne Shorter on tenor,, and pianist Cedar Walton). *Free for All* was this particular group's last recording before Freddie Hubbard went out on his own, and it includes lengthy versions of two Shorter tunes, Hubbard's "The Core," and the standard "Pensativa." Fine music. —*Scott Yanow*

Indestructible / Apr. 24, 1964-May 15, 1964 / Blue Note ✦✦✦
In 1964, trumpeter Lee Morgan rejoined the Jazz Messengers, replacing his original replacement, Freddie Hubbard. The hard-swinging style of this influential unit remained unchanged, with drummer/leader Art Blakey still insisting on distinctive solos and constant new material. Typically, the

music on this fine LP consists of five then-recent compositions by band members, one apiece from Morgan, pianist Cedar Walton ("When Love Is New"), and tenor saxophonist Wayne Shorter, and two from trombonist Curtis Fuller. Enjoyable music. —*Scott Yanow*

Buttercorn Lady / Jan. 1, 1966-Jan. 9, 1966 / Limelight ✦✦✦

Child's Dance, Vol. 1 / May 23, 1972-Mar. 27, 1973 / Prestige ✦✦✦✦
Art Blakey's three albums for Prestige from 1972-73 have been reissued with additional material on two CDs. For this volume the four songs that originally comprised *Child's Dance* are joined by a previously unissued "Kaku Aka" and two tunes from *Anthenagin.* The different instrumentation featured on some of these numbers was a real change of pace for Blakey; on "Song for the Lonely Woman" and "Kaku Aka" he utilizes several percussionists, a flute-soprano front line, and electric piano. The great trumpeter Woody Shaw is in typically fine form and is showcased on a memorable version of "I Can't Get Started"; other sidemen include Carter Jefferson on tenor, keyboardists Cedar Walton and George Cables, and bassist Stanley Clarke (20 at the time). Even with some funky and electrified moments, the music definitely holds onto one's interest throughout. —*Scott Yanow*

Mission Eternal, Vol. 2 / May 26, 1973-May 29, 1973 / Prestige ✦✦✦✦
The second of two CDs that reissue the music from three Art Blakey LPs plus additional material (reshuffling the order to make it more logical), this set features trumpeter Woody Shaw, Carter Jefferson on tenor and soprano, Cedar Walton on keyboards, bassist Mickey Bass, Tony Waters on congas, and the drummer/leader plus three guests: guitarist Michael Howell, trombonist Steve Turre, and (on "Moanin'" and "Along Came Betty"), singer Jon Hendricks. Shaw is in excellent form and Blakey propels and inspires his sidemen as usual. In addition to the two vocals, the nine instrumentals (which had originally been divided between the LPs *Buhaina* and *Athenagin*) are consistently swinging and well worth hearing. —*Scott Yanow*

And the Jazz Messengers Big Band / Jul. 13, 1980-Jul. 17, 1980 / Timeless ✦✦✦

In Sweden / Mar. 9, 1981 / Evidence ✦✦✦

Album of the Year / Apr. 12, 1981 / Timeless ✦✦✦✦
The 1981 edition of the Jazz Messengers featured more than its share of young greats (trumpeter Wynton Marsalis, altoist Bobby Watson, tenor saxophonist Billy Pierce, pianist James Williams, and bassist Charles Fambrough), reinforcing drummer Art Blakey's recognition as jazz's greatest talent scout. This high-quality set, recorded in Paris, includes new material (highlighted by James Williams' "Soulful Mister Timmons"), Wayne Shorter's "Witch Hunt," and the Charlie Parker blues "Cheryl." —*Scott Yanow*

Straight Ahead / Jun. 1981 / Concord Jazz ✦✦✦✦
One of the best recordings by Art Blakey's 1981 Jazz Messengers, this set features Wynton Marsalis (then 19) on "How Deep Is the Ocean" and other illustrious sidemen (including altoist Bobby Watson, tenor saxophonist Bill Pierce, and pianist James Williams) playing such group pieces as "Falling in Love with Love," "My Romance," and Watson's "E.T.A." Highly recommended. —*Scott Yanow*

Keystone 3 / Jan. 1982 / Concord Jazz ✦✦✦✦
Wynton Marsalis' final recording as a member of Art Blakey's Jazz Messengers finds his brother Branford taking Bobby Watson's place on alto. The remainder of this superb sextet includes tenor saxophonist Bill Pierce, pianist Donald Brown, bassist Charles Fambrough, and the veteran drummer/leader. All concerned sound in top form on both new (Wynton's "Waterfalls" and Watson's "Fuller Love") and old ("In Walked Bud" and "In a Sentimental Mood") material alike. Mostly high-powered hard bop in the best tradition of the Jazz Messengers. —*Scott Yanow*

Oh, by the Way / May 20, 1982 / Timeless ✦✦✦

New York Scene / May 1984 / Concord Jazz ✦✦✦

Live at Sweet Basil: Art Blakey and the Jazz Messengers / Mar. 24, 1985 / GNP ✦✦✦
This excellent all-around session showcases the 1985 edition of Art Blakey's Jazz Messengers, a band that boasted such fine young soloists as trumpeter Terence Blanchard, altoist Donald Harrison, tenor saxophonist Jean Toussaint, and pianist Mulgrew Miller. In addition to Harrison's "Mr. Babe" and Walter Davis' "Jodi," the ensemble successfully updates two Jazz Messenger classics: "Blues March" and "Moanin'." —*Scott Yanow*

Not Yet: Art Blakey and His Jazz Messengers / Mar. 19, 1988 / Soul Note ✦✦✦

I Get a Kick out of Bu / Nov. 11, 1988 / Soul Note ✦✦✦

Chippin' In: Art Blakey and His Jazz Messengers / Feb. 1, 1990-Feb. 2, 1990 / Timeless ✦✦✦
Thirty-five years after first officially forming the Jazz Messengers, drummer Art Blakey entered his final year still at it. Due to the many promising young players around at the time, Blakey expanded the Messengers from its usual quintet or sextet into a septet for this fine recording session. In

addition to trumpeter Brian Lynch, pianist Geoff Keezer, and bassist Essiet Okon Essiet, this version of the Messengers had two tenors (Javon Jackson and Dale Barlow) and a pair of alternating trombonists (Frank Lacy and Steve Davis). Quite typically, other than Wayne Shorter's obscure "Hammerhead" and two standards, all of the material on this CD was new and composed by Blakey's sidemen. Because Blakey constantly persuaded his musicians to write music, the Jazz Messengers stayed young in spirit, just like its leader. A fine effort. — *Scott Yanow*

One for All / Apr. 10, 1990-Apr. 11, 1990 / A&M ✦✦✦

Terence Blanchard

b. Mar. 13, 1962, New Orleans, LA
Trumpet / Post-Bop, Hard Bop
Although he originally rose to prominence in the shadow of Wynton Marsalis, Terence Blanchard was one of the first Young Lions to develop his own sound, mixing in elements of Freddie Hubbard and Marsalis. He studied piano from the age of five and took up trumpet in 1976. Blanchard was with Lionel Hampton during 1980-82 and then replaced Marsalis with Art Blakey's Jazz Messengers. He found fame while with Blakey during 1982-86 and then co-led a group with Donald Harrison. After taking time off to work on his embouchure (and returning with a greatly increased range), Blanchard became active writing film scores for Spike Lee. He played in the films *Do the Right Thing* and *Mo' Better Blues* and then wrote for *Jungle Fever* and *Malcolm X*, launching a potentially lucrative second career. Fortunately Blanchard has not neglected his own playing, and in the '90s he has recorded several superior sets of advanced hard-bop music. — *Scott Yanow*

New York Second Line / Oct. 15, 1983-Oct. 16, 1983 / George Wein Collection ✦✦✦

Fire Waltz: Eric Dolphy and Booker Little Remembered / Oct. 3, 1986-Oct. 4, 1986 / Projazz ✦✦✦

Crystal Stair / Apr. 1, 1987-Apr. 3, 1987 / Columbia ✦✦✦

Black Pearl / 1988 / Columbia ✦✦✦✦
Blanchard-Harrison. This is the best by trumpeter Blanchard and saxophonist Donald Harrison, especially the title track. — *Michael G. Nastos*

Terence Blanchard / 1991 / Columbia ✦✦✦

Simply Stated / 1992 / Columbia ✦✦✦

● **Malcolm X Jazz Suite** / Dec. 10, 1992-Dec. 14, 1992 / Columbia ✦✦✦✦
Trumpeter Terence Blanchard continues to grow and develop with each year. He wrote the score for *Malcolm X*, and this set finds him exploring 11 of his themes from the movie with his quintet (which also includes Sam Newsome on tenor, pianist Bruce Bath, bassist Tarus Matten, and drummer Troy Davis). Many moods are explored and the fresh material really invigorates the quintet. Newsome's Trane-isms blend well with Blanchard (whose range has become quite impressive), and the performances (which easily stand apart from the film) are quite memorable. It's one of Terence Blanchard's finest recordings. — *Scott Yanow*

The Billie Holiday Songbook / 1995 / Columbia ✦✦

Carla Bley

b. May 11, 1938, Oakland, CA
Piano / Post-Bop
A wonderful composer whose madcap personality and humor carries over into her songwriting, Carla Bley has been at the forefront of many music co-operatives and bands since the '60s. While her piano playing has the unpredictability of Thelonious Monk's, her compositions reflect multiple music genres. She includes early jazz references, improvisational and symphonic elements, and snippets of any and everything from bebop to rock. Bley's father, a church musician, taught her a few fundamentals, but she otherwise trained herself. She moved to New York from Oakland at 17 and divided her time between playing piano and writing songs for such musicians as George Russell, her husband Paul Bley, and Jimmy Giuffre. Bley worked with Pharoah Sanders and Charles Moffett in 1964, then became a full-time musician. She and Michael Mantler co-formed the Jazz Composers Guild Orchestra in the mid-'60s; he'd become her second husband. The Orchestra gave a concert at Town Hall in 1964, and Bley went to Europe with a quintet in 1965, recording and appearing on radio and television. Bley also co-founded the Jazz Composer's Orchestra Association (JCOA), in 1966, a nonprofit organization that commissioned, produced, and distributed a wide range of material ignored by the major labels. The JCOA distributed many labels into the '70s before money woes forced them to close shop. They recorded a two-record (now disc) album on their own label that year. Bley's 1967 work "A Genuine Tong Funeral," recorded by Gary Burton's Quartet, brought her widespread public and critical attention, as did several compositons and arrangements for Charlie Haden's Liberation Music Orchestra album on Impulse in 1969. Her most acclaimed composition was 1971's "Escalator over the Hill." The album was hailed by both the national and international jazz press, and Bley received many composing grants. She's divided her time in the '70s, '80s, and '90s between recording,

leading various large bands, and composing. She and Mantler began their own company, Watt Records, which is now distributed by ECM. Bley and Mantler have issued many records on Watt, and Bley's worked with Roswell Rudd and others in the '80s. She provided the soundtrack for a 1985 film *Mortelle randonnée*. Bley contributed new compositions to another Haden Liberation Music Orchestra session in 1983, a Monk tribute album in 1984, and a Kurt Weill tribute in 1986. She played organ on a Steve Swallow album in 1986 and did her own session in 1988. She continued recording with a nine- and ten-piece band into the '90s, and in 1993 did another album with Swallow. There's a good amount of Bley material on CD, though none of the JCOA sessions are currently in print. — *Ron Wynn*

● **European Tour (1977)** / Sep. 1977 / Watt ✦✦✦✦
One of Carla Bley's most rewarding recordings, this set features her tentet playing such numbers as "Wrong Key Donkey," "Drinking Music," and the 19-minute "Spangled Banner Minor and Other Patriotic Songs." Bley's wry humor is often felt, and she utilizes such colorful players as trumpeter Michael Mantler, Gary Windo on tenor, trombonist Roswell Rudd, and Bob Stewart on tuba in this unusual, somewhat innovative, and always fun music. — *Scott Yanow*

Musique Mecanique / Aug. 1978-Nov. 1978 / Watt ✦✦✦✦
Carla Bley's tentet performs some of her most colorful themes on this often-humorous and generally stimulating set. "Jesus Maria and Other Spanish Strains" and the three-part "Musique Mecanique" are particularly memorable. This is the perfect setting for Bley's music, with such musicians as trumpeter Michael Mantler, Gary Windo on tenor and bass clarinet, trombonist Roswell Rudd, and Bob Stewart on tuba making their presence felt. — *Scott Yanow*

Duets: Carla Bley and Steve Swallow / 1988 / Watt ✦✦✦✦

Hamiet Bluiett

b. 1940, Lovejoy, IL
Sax (Baritone) / Avant-Garde
The finest baritone saxophonist of the '70s and beyond, Hamiet Bluiett has demonstrated a huge, impressive sound, superb technique, and mastery of his horn in every register, plus the ability to provide an array of tonal colors and harmonic options in his solos. A first-rate free player who's just as proficient on standards and bebop, Bluiett has played in many excellent groups, led his own bands, and been featured on numerous magnificent recordings. He began taking music lessons from his aunt, who was a choral director. Bluiett started on clarinet at nine. He attended Southern University, where he studied flute and baritone. Following a stint in the Navy, Bluiett moved to St. Louis in the mid-'60s. He played with Lester and Joseph Bowie, Charles "Bobo" Shaw, Julius Hemphill, and Oliver Lake and worked with the Black Artists Group (BAG), that city's equivalent of Chicago's Association for the Advancement of Creative Musicians (AACM). He moved to New York in 1969, joining Sam Rivers' large ensemble. Bluiett worked with various bands before joining Charles Mingus's quintet in 1972, remaining until 1975. A pair of mid-'70s Bluiett concerts were later issued as albums on India Navigation. Bluiett, Hemphill, Lake, and David Murray formed a quartet in 1976 for a New Orleans concert. They decided to remain intact as a working unit and named themselves the World Saxophone Quartet. They've continued performing and performing into the '90s, though Arthur Blythe replaced Hemphill. Bluiett has also worked with other bands; he was a co-leader of the Clarinet Family group that featured seven clarinetists. It recorded with Black Saint in the '80s. Bluiett recorded on his own for Black Saint, Soul Note, Chiaroscuro, Enja, and Tutu among others in the '70s, '80s, and '90s. He played with Lester Bowie, Hemphill, Abdullah Ibrahim, Phillip Wilson, Marcello Melis, Famadou Don Moye, Don Pullen, Fred Hopkins, Billy Hart, Irene Datcher, Buddy Collette, and Ronnie Burrage during the '70s and '80s. — *Ron Wynn*

Birthright / Jun. 1978 / India Navigation ✦✦✦✦
This concert performance is quite unusual: an unaccompanied recital by the great baritonist Hamiet Bluiett. Although its subtitle is "A Solo Blues Concert," the "blues" refers to the feeling that Bluiett puts into his music rather than the structure of his originals itself. "In Tribute to Harry Carney" is a high point. Bluiett is in top form during this adventurous but fairly melodic performance. — *Scott Yanow*

The Clarinet Family / Nov. 1984 / Black Saint ✦✦✦

● **Young Warrior, Old Warrior** / Dec. 1995 / Mapleshade ✦✦✦✦

Arthur Blythe

b. Jul. 5, 1940, Los Angeles, CA
Sax (Alto) / Avant-Garde, Post-Bop
Alto saxophonist Arthur Blythe is a gifted soloist with a wide vibrato, pungent style that reflects several artists from Charlie Parker to Cannonball Adderley, and an interest in unusual configurations and harmonic/melodic possibilities that's seen him lead bands with tuba, guitar, and cello; Blythe excels playing traditional bebop, hard bop, or free music and has also worked effectively in funk, blues, and R&B situations. His solos are taste-

ful, swinging, and superbly played. But from his days as "Black Arthur" on the West Coast (which made some think he was a reincarnated Malcom X on alto) to his ill-fated Columbia era when they marketed him as "the greatest saxophonist in the world," Blythe has suffered exaggerated expectations and false impressions. These haven't affected his output as much as they've created a climate making it seem he's underachieving when he's actually accomplished as much, if not more, than virtually any other player of his generation. Blythe played in school bands as a youngster, then studied with Kirtland Bradford, a one-time member of Jimmie Lunceford's orchestra, as a teen. He worked with Horace Tapscott during his '60s and early '70s in Los Angeles; both were founding members of the Union of God's Musicians and Artists Ascension. Blythe was part of the West Coast exodus to New York in the '70s that also saw David Murray, James Newton, and Stanley Crouch move east. He played with Chico Hamilton in the mid-'70s and Gil Evans in the late '70s and early '80s, as well as being in the "loft jazz" movement of the '70s. Blythe recorded and played with Lester Bowie and Jack DeJohnette's Special Edition in the late '70s and early '80s. He signed with Columbia in the late '70s and led two groups in the early '80s. One was known as In the Tradition, and was a bebop and swing-oriented ensemble with Fred Hopkins, Steve McCall, and either Stanley Cowell or John Hicks. The other was an unnamed quintet with Abdul Wadud, Bob Stewart, Bobby Battle, and sometimes James "Blood" Ulmer and Kelvyn Bell. They did more challenging, nontraditional material as well as some hard bop and even some pop, R&B, and funk. Blythe joined the Leaders in the mid-'80s, replaced Julius Hemphill in the World Saxophone Quartet, and did more sessions with Stewart, Bell, and Battle. He began recording with Crouch in the late '60s and early '70s. His own albums started with sessions in the mid-'70s for India Navigation and Adelphi. The Columbia dates began in the late '70s and continued until the mid-'80s. Blythe also recorded for Blackhawk and has recently done sessions for Enja. *—Ron Wynn*

The Grip / Feb. 26, 1977 / India Navigation ✦✦✦✦
The debut album as a leader by altoist Arthur Blythe is quite impressive. Even at this early stage, Blythe's tone is instantly recognizable. His band (playing five of his originals plus "Spirits in the Field") includes trumpeter Ahmed Abdullah, cellist Abdul Wadud, tuba player Bob Stewart, drummer Steve Reid, and percussionist Muhamad Abdullah, and together they live up to their potential. *—Scott Yanow*

Lenox Avenue Breakdown / 1978 / Columbia ✦✦✦✦
The signing of Arthur Blythe to Columbia in 1978 received a great deal of attention. Fortunately, the adventurous altoist was able to record for that giant label for a few years without being pressured to water down his sound or his music. This set matchs Blythe with such talents as flutist James Newton, guitarist James "Blood" Ulmer, bassist Cecil McBee, drummer Jack DeJohnette, tuba player Bob Stewart, and percussionist Guillermo Franco; no weak spots to this group. The band performs four of Blythe's diverse originals with creativity and a strong bluesy feeling. *—Scott Yanow*

In the Tradition / Oct. 1978 / Columbia ✦✦✦✦
Sometimes the easiest way to get "in" to someone's music is to see how they handle standards. Altoist Arthur Blythe, who—although he has been associated somewhat with the avant-garde—does not fit easily into any category, is heard on this 1978 studio session exploring four veteran songs plus two of his originals. The instrumentation of his quartet is conventional, but the musicianship is exceptionally high (pianist Stanley Cowell, bassist Fred Hopkins, and drummer Steve McCall), and it is quite interesting to hear how they stretch such songs as "In a Sentimental Mood," "Jitterbug Waltz," and "Caravan," making them sound fresh and original. *—Scott Yanow*

Light Blue: Arthur Blythe Plays Thelonious Monk / Jan. 27, 1983 / Columbia ✦✦✦

● **Retroflection** / Jun. 25, 1993-Jun. 26, 1993 / Enja ✦✦✦✦
Arthur Blythe, whose alto tone has been quite original ever since the start of his career, is joined by pianist John Hicks, bassist Cecil McBee, and drummer Bobby Battle on this superior quartet date from Enja. Blythe really stretches out at this "Live at the Village Vanguard" set, with six of the seven songs being over nine minutes long. "Jana's Delight" (which is based on a five-note pattern), "JB Blues," a remake of Blythe's "Lenox Avenue Breakdown," and one of the best versions ever of Thelonious Monk's "Light Blue" are the high points of the explorative program. Arthur Blythe fans are strongly advised to pick up this particularly strong effort. *—Scott Yanow*

Willie Bobo (William Correa)

b. Feb. 28, 1934, New York, NY, **d.** Sep. 15, 1983, Los Angeles, CA
Percussion / Latin Jazz
Willie Bobo was a superb percussionist who made major inroads in jazz, Latin-jazz, R&B, and pop. Bobo's father was a musician, and he began on bongos at 14, then played congas, timbales, and trap drums. Bobo was a band boy for Machito's Afro-Cubans, then studied with Mongo Santamaria

in the late '40s. Santamaria taught him percussion, and Bobo served as Santamaria's translator. He recorded with Mary Lou Williams in the early '50s, who gave him his nickname. Bobo replaced Manny Oquendo in Tito Puente's band in 1954. He would double on timbales when Puente took vibes solos. Bobo later played in Shearing's group on drums and timbales with Armando Peraza, Cal Tjader, and Santamaria. He appeared on radio in the '50s as Willie Boborosa. Bobo worked in the late '50s with Cal Tjader and also played with a short-lived Puente splinter group, Orquesta Manhattan. He and Santamaria co-formed La Saborsa, a charanga (flute & violin) band in the early '60s; their recording of "Afro-Blue" became both a hit and a standard. Bobo also played on Santamaria's *Our Man In Havana* before starting his own band with Victor Panoja on congas. Bobo recorded for Tico and Roulette in the mid-'60s. Bobo participated in Cal Tjader's hit album *Soul Sauce* for Verve in the mid-'60s. He issued his own albums in the mid-'60s, combining soul and funk with Latin beats. The single "Spanish Grease" became an R&B hit. Bobo worked with Miles Davis, Stan Getz, Cannonball Adderley, Sonny Stitt, Herbie Mann, Terry Gibbs, and Herbie Hancock on various '60s sessions. He worked on the West Coast in the late '60s, and made weekly appearances on Bill Cosby's television show. Bobo recorded for Sussex, Blue Note, and Columbia through the '70s. All his classic albums must be obtained from Latin music stores; there are presently no listings for Bobo in most record catalogs. *—Ron Wynn*

● **Spanish Grease** / Aug. 20, 1965-Sep. 8, 1965 / Verve ✦✦✦✦
One pass through the title cut, and you know that Carlos Santana was listening. The easy R&B-Latin-jazz shuffle on this Bobo original, with its mix of Spanish and English vocals, is an obvious touchstone of cuts like "Evil Ways" on Santana's first two albums. What a shame, then, that the rest of the record is primarily comprised of covers of pop hits of the day like "It's Not Unusual" (a vocal AND an instrumental version!) and "Our Day Will Come." The timbales player and his band lay down respectable grooves, but "Spanish Grease" is the only original on the album, and by far the most rewarding number. *Spanish Grease* has been combined with the 1966 LP *Uno Dos Tres 1-2-3* on one CD reissue. *—Richie Unterberger*

Uno, Dos, Tres / Jan. 1966 / Verve ✦✦✦

Lester Bowie

b. Oct. 11, 1941, Frederick, MD
Trumpet / Avant-Garde
While he's well known as a member of the Art Ensemble of Chicago, Lester Bowie's amassed almost as many credentials as a leader. His remarkable bag of trumpet and fluegelhorn tricks includes half-valve effects, growls, slurs, smears, bent notes, and a wide vibrato punctuating one of the most humorous, yet striking solo styles among modern brass players. His eclecticism has led Bowie to issue harsh denunciations of contemporary artists he feels revere only the bebop and hard-bop jazz tradition, and he's led such groups as Brass Fantasy and the New York Organ Ensemble through wild versions of Michael Jackson and James Brown compositions. He's also ventured to the furthest reaches during extended free dialogues, blowing frenetic upper-register solos. Bowie played in many blues and R&B bands growing up in St. Louis, among them Albert King and Little Milton. He moved to Chicago in 1965 to become music director for R&B/soul singer Fontella Bass, who was his wife at the time. Bowie met Joseph Jarman, Roscoe Mitchell, Malachi Favors, and Don Moye through the Association for the Advancement of Creative Musicians (AACM), which was just getting organized. Bowie eventually became its second president (Muhal Richard Abrams was the first). The album *Numbers 1&2* was issued as a Lester Bowie LP on Nessa in 1967 but was actually the first Art Ensemble release, though the group hadn't yet begun calling themselves by that name. That occured in Paris during 1969, where he, Jarma, Mitchell, and Favors officially formed the Art Ensemble of Chicago. Moye joined the next year. While the Art Ensemble has been a steady proposition since 1969, Bowie's never rested on his laurels. He worked in the early '70s with the 50-piece Baden Baden Free Jazz Orchestra along with Jarman and Roscoe Mitchell. He co-led the group From the Root to the Source, which blended jazz, rock, soul, and gospel and included both Bass and Martha Peaston in the '70s. He later founded and still heads both Brass Fantasy and the New York Organ Ensemble. Bowie recorded albums as a leader in the '70s for Muse, Black Saint, and IAI. He played in Jack DeJohnette's New Directions band in the late '70s and did guest spots on other albums. During the '80s he recorded for ECM, Muse, and Venture, as well as DIW. He's recorded with the New York Organ Ensemble for DIW in the '90s. *—Ron Wynn*

● **The Great Pretender** / Jun. 1981 / ECM ✦✦✦✦
This is one of trumpeter Lester Bowie's most accessible albums; certainly his brief versions of "It's Howdy Doody Time" and "When the Moon Comes over the Mountain" are not difficult to understand. But actually the bulk of this album is taken up with the 16-minute title cut and a variety of Bowie's colorful originals. The highly expressive trumpeter is mostly heard with a quartet (although "The Great Pretender" also adds two vocalists and baritonist Hamiet Bluiett), and this set offers many fine examples of his origi-

nal approach to making music, technically avant-garde but also borrowing aspects of earlier styles in unusual combinations. — *Scott Yanow*

All the Magic! / Jun. 1982 / ECM ✦✦✦

Twilight Dreams / Apr. 1987 / Venture ✦✦✦

Charles Brackeen

b. 1940, White's Chapel, OK

Sax (Tenor) / Avant-Garde, Free Jazz

An excellent avant-garde tenor who has always been a bit underrated, Charles Brackeen originally studied violin and piano. Settling on tenor, he worked in both New York and Los Angeles, meeting and marrying pianist Joanne Brackeen. In New York he was associated with "the new thing" and in 1968 recorded an interesting set for Strata-East with three of the members of the Ornette Coleman Quartet (Don Cherry, Charlie Haden, and Ed Blackwell). After a long period of obscurity he began playing with Paul Motian (with whom he recorded for ECM), and in 1987 he started making records for Silkheart. An explorative high-energy player, Charles Brackeen's performances are always stimulating. — *Scott Yanow*

Bannar / Feb. 13, 1987 / Silkheart ✦✦✦✦

Charles Brackeen Quartet. Outward bound. —*Michael G. Nastos*

● **Worshippers Come Nigh** / Nov. 29, 1987 / Silkheart ✦✦✦✦

Rousing, declarative session from a grossly underrecorded tenor and soprano saxophonist. Charles Brackeen was persuaded to return to the recording scene in 1986 by the Silkheart label's managing director, and this was one of three great albums he made in 1986 and 1987. The pithy, crisp cornet solos supplied by Olu Dara are almost as striking as Brackeen's sax lines, and there aren't any better bassists and drummers in this style than Fred Hopkins and Andrew Cyrille. — *Ron Wynn*

Joanne Brackeen

b. Jul. 26, 1938, Ventura, CA

Piano / Post-Bop

A brilliant pianist flexible enough to play free, modal music and standards, Joanne Brackeen has been a major player for 25 years. She taught herself to play jazz piano. During 1958-59 Brackeen worked in Los Angeles with Teddy Edwards, Harold Land, Dexter Gordon, and Charles Lloyd. After marrying Charles Brackeen (they later divorced) she took time off to bring up their four children. Brackeen moved to New York in 1965, worked with Woody Shaw and David Liebman, and became the first female member of Art Blakey's Jazz Messengers (1969-72). After working regularly with Joe Henderson (1972-75) and Stan Getz (1975-77), Brackeen (an original stylist) has mostly performed as a leader of her own trios, making numerous records for Choice, Timeless, Tappan Zee, and Concord. — *Scott Yanow*

Aft / Sep. 1979 / Timeless ✦✦✦

Havin' Fun / Jun. 1985 / Concord Jazz ✦✦✦✦

Good trio session by the underrated pianist Joanne Brackeen. She's complemented by bassist Cecil McBee and drummer Al Foster, and shows rhythmic verve, harmonic strength, and good solo technique throughout the album. This has been reissued on CD. —*Ron Wynn*

● **Fi-Fi Goes to Heaven** / 1986 / Concord Jazz ✦✦✦✦

CD version features this energized, capable pianist at her best, with some sharp assistance from Branford Marsalis (ts) and Terence Blanchard (tpt). —*Ron Wynn*

Live at Maybeck Recital Hall / Jun. 1989 / Concord Jazz ✦✦✦✦

She shows her mettle in live solo context. —*Ron Wynn*

Turnaround / Feb. 27, 1992-Feb. 28, 1992 / Evidence ✦✦✦✦

The talented and highly original pianist Joanne Brackeen leads an all-star quartet (with altoist Donald Harrison, bassist Cecil McBee, and drummer Marvin "Smitty" Smith) at Sweet Basil for this 1992 live session. Brackeen is in top form digging into two standards, Ornette Coleman's "Turnaround" (which is taken as a conventional blues), and three of her originals including a 16-minute "Picasso." The explorative music holds one's interest throughout. —*Scott Yanow*

After Dark / Jan. 5, 1993 / Criss Cross ✦✦✦

Take A Chance / Jun. 15, 1993-Jun. 16, 1993 / Concord Jazz ✦✦

Bobby Bradford

b. Jul. 19, 1934, Cleveland, MS

Cornet / Avant-Garde, Post-Bop

One of the best trumpeters to emerge from the avant-garde, Bobby Bradford largely fulfilled the potential of Don Cherry (whose chops declined through the years due to the amount of time allocated to performing on flute and other instruments). Bradford grew up in Dallas, playing trumpet with such local players as Cedar Walton and David Newman. In 1953 he moved to Los Angeles, where he met and played with Ornette Coleman and Eric Dolphy. Bradford spent time in the military and in school before becoming Don Cherry's replacement with the Ornette Coleman Quartet in 1961-63, a period when the group unfortunately rarely worked. After mov-

ing to Los Angeles, Bradford became a school teacher and also began a longtime association with clarinetist John Carter; his mellow trumpet blended in well with Carter's dissonant flights. He recorded with Ornette Coleman in 1971 but otherwise is best-known for his playing and recordings with Carter. Since the clarinetist's death, Bradford has frequently led a quintet (the Mo'tet) featuring Vinny Golia and occasionally Marty Ehrlich. He has also performed since the early '90s with John Stevens' Freebop, the David Murray Octet, and Charlie Haden's Liberation Music Orchestra. —*Scott Yanow*

Lost in L.A. / Jun. 1983 / Soul Note ✦✦✦

● **One Night Stand** / Nov. 1986 / Soul Note ✦✦✦✦

A melodic player with a healthy sense of humor who has become more expressive through the years, Bobby Bradford really got a chance to stretch out on this fine session. Although pianist Frank Sullivan is essentially a bop player, he did a good job of keeping up during the more adventurous performances. Bassist Scott Walton (who has learned from the innovations of Charlie Haden) and drummer Billy Bowker were excellent in support. "Ashes" (a calypso version of "I Got Rhythm") and the mysterious "Woman" were the high points of this highly recommended disc. — *Scott Yanow, Cadence*

Ruby Braff

b. Mar. 16, 1927, Boston, MA

Cornet / Swing, New Orleans Jazz

One of the great swing/Dixieland cornetists, Ruby Braff went through long periods of his career unable to find work because his music was considered out of fashion, but his fortunes improved by the '70s. A very expressive player who in later years liked to build his solos up to a low note, Braff's playing is instantly recognizable within seconds.

Braff mostly worked around Boston in the late '40s. He teamed up with Pee Wee Russell when the clarinetist was making a comeback (they recorded live for Savoy), and after moving to New York in 1953 he fit easily into a variety of Dixieland and mainstream settings. Braff recorded for Vanguard as a leader and with Vic Dickenson, Buck Clayton, and Urbie Green. He was one of the stars of Buck Clayton's Columbia jam sessions and in the mid-'50s worked with Benny Goodman. But despite good reviews and occasional recordings, work was hard for Braff to come by at times. In the '60s he was able to get jobs by being with George Wein's Newport All-Stars and at jazz festivals, but it was not until the cornetist formed a quartet with guitarist George Barnes in 1973 that he became more secure. Since that time Braff has been heard in many small-group settings including duets with Dick Hyman and Ellis Larkins (he had first met up with the latter in the '50s), quintets with Scott Hamilton, and matching wits with Howard Alden. He remains one of the greats of mainstream jazz. —*Scott Yanow*

Hustlin' and Bustlin' / 1951-Jun. 9, 1954 / Black Lion ✦✦✦✦

● **Two by Two: Ruby and Ellis Play Rodgers and Hart** / Oct. 14, 1955 / Vanguard ✦✦✦✦

In 1955 trumpeter Ruby Braff recorded two duet album, with the sensitive pianist Ellis Larkins and both projects were very well received. This CD reissue brings back the second session, in which they perform a dozen songs written by Rodgers and Hart. The passionate Braff and Larkins (a masterful accompanist) work quite well together. Although the emphasis is on ballads, there are a few hotter pieces that find Braff pushing Larkins a bit. Highlights include "Mountain Greenery," "Blue Moon," "My Romance," and "You Took Advantage of Me." —*Scott Yanow*

This Is My Lucky Day / Aug. 19, 1957-Dec. 26, 1957 / Bluebird ✦✦✦

With the Newport All Stars / Oct. 28, 1967 / Black Lion ✦✦✦✦

Cornetist Ruby Braff and tenor saxophonist Buddy Tate make for a very complementary team on this fine CD reissue which also includes pianist George Wein, bassist Jack Lesberg, and drummer Don Lamond. Several alternate takes and a previously unreleased "Lullaby of the Leaves" expand this fine session, which has among its highlights enjoyable versions of "Mean to Me," "My Monday Date," "Take the 'A' Train," and "The Sheik of Araby," among others. This is high-quality small-group swing by some of the best, which was recorded at a time when the idiom was considered very much out of style by the modernists. —*Scott Yanow*

Hear Me Talkin' / Nov. 8, 1967 / Black Lion ✦✦✦✦

This is a fun Dixieland/swing date featuring cornetist Ruby Braff with an octet led by the fine English trumpeter Alex Welsh. In addition to the two leads, trombonist Roy Williams, tenor saxophonist Al Gay, and baritonist Johnny Barnes get some solo space on the mixture of standards, '20s obscurities (including Don Redman's "No One Else but You"), and basic originals. Everyone sounds in a good mood and is heard swinging in prime form throughout this recommended CD reissue. —*Scott Yanow*

● **Plays Rodgers & Hart** / Oct. 1974 / Concord Jazz ✦✦✦✦

For the fourth of five recordings made by the classic Ruby Braff-George Barnes Quartet, ten songs by Rodgers and Hart are given melodic, swinging, and creative treatment. Cornetist Braff and guitarist Barnes worked very well together (feeding off of each other), while rhythm guitarist

Wayne Wright and bassist Michael Moore always gave them impeccable support. Highlights of this easily enjoyable set include "Isn't It Romantic," "Blue Room," "You Took Advantage of Me," and "The Lady Is a Tramp." —*Scott Yanow*

● **A Sailboat in the Moonlight** / Feb. 1985 / Concord Jazz ✦✦✦✦
Taken from the same sessions as *A First*, this collaboration between veteran cornetist Ruby Braff and the relatively young tenor great Scott Hamilton lives up to its potential. With strong assistance from pianist John Bunch, guitarist Chris Flory, bassist Phil Flanigan, and drummer Chuck Riggs, Braff and Hamilton are a perfect team on such joyful swing tunes as "A Sailboat in the Moonlight," "Deed I Do," "Jeepers Creepers," and "Sweethearts on Parade." All eight selections (even the obscure "Milkman's Matinee") are well worth hearing, making this a highly recommended set. —*Scott Yanow*

A First / Feb. 1985 / Concord Jazz ✦✦✦✦
Although it is implied with its title that this was the first collaboration between cornetist Ruby Braff and tenor saxophonist Scott Hamilton, they had recorded a date back in December 1983 for the Swedish Phontastic label. Accompanied by Hamilton's regular quartet of the period (pianist John Bunch, guitarist Chris Flory, bassist Phil Flanigan, and drummer Chuck Riggs), Braff and Hamilton inspire each other and play some explosive and consistently passionate solos. Highlights include a surprisingly hard-swinging "Rockin' Chair," "Dinah," "All My Life," and "Bugle Blues." Recommended. —*Scott Yanow*

Music from My Fair Lady / Jul. 1989 / Concord Jazz ✦✦✦✦
The many Lerner and Loewe songs written for the play *My Fair Lady* have long been rightfully acclaimed. Even with several decades of fine recordings, this duet set by cornetist Ruby Braff and pianist Dick Hyman is one of the finest interpretations of the famous music. Braff and Hyman come up with new ideas during melodic versions of such songs as "Wouldn't It Be Lovely," "I Could Have Danced All Night," "On the Street Where You Live," and "Get Me to the Church on Time," among others. Every Braff-Hyman collaboration is well worth getting and this set is no exception. —*Scott Yanow*

● **Music from "South Pacific"** / Jun. 12, 1990-Jun. 13, 1990 / Concord Jazz ✦✦✦✦
This CD is much better than it looks. Cornetist Ruby Braff and pianist Dick Hyman can always be relied upon to create exciting music, but the songs from *South Pacific* (best known are "Some Enchanted Evening" and "Younger than Springtime") would not seem to have much potential. However, through witty frameworks and creativity, Braff and Hyman greatly uplift the music, particularly their two versions of "Bali Ha'i." This consistently surprising CD is well worth checking out. —*Scott Yanow*

Ruby Braff & His New England Songhounds, Vol. 1 / Apr. 29, 1991 / Concord Jazz ✦✦✦✦
Cornetist Ruby Braff and tenor saxophonist Scott Hamilton have teamed up on several memorable occasions. On the first of two CD volumes, Braff and Hamilton are joined by a fine quartet ("The New England Songhounds") which is comprised of guitarist Howard Alden, pianist Dave McKenna, bassist Frank Tate, and drummer Alan Dawson. Alternating stomps with warm ballads, the horns sound at their best on such numbers as "I'm Crazy 'Bout My Baby," "This Can't Be Love," "My Shining Hour," "Down in Honky Tonk Town," and "More than You Know." Highly recommended to mainstream and straightahead jazz fans. —*Scott Yanow*

Live at the Regattabar / Nov. 22, 1993 / Arbors ✦✦✦✦
The Ruby Braff Quartet heard on this fine session is reminiscent of the group he had with George Barnes in the '70s. The instrumentation is the same (with guitarists Gray Sargent and Jon Wheatley and bassist Marshall Wood), but in this case both guitarists get a chance to solo. Braff had recorded nearly all of the selections previously; however, he comes up with plenty of fresh statements on such songs as "It's Wonderful," "Louisiana," "Crazy Rhythm," and "Give My Regards to Broadway," among others. Throughout this easily enjoyable date, Braff often displays his ability to build up his solos to a low note! —*Scott Yanow*

Controlled Nonchalance, Vol. 1 / Nov. 26, 1993-Nov. 27, 1993 / Arbors ✦✦✦✦
Cornetist Ruby Braff has teamed up with tenor saxophonist Scott Hamilton on several occasions, and the combination always proves to be exciting. This live sextet session, which also features the great swing pianist Dave McKenna and guitarist Gray Sargent, finds the classic players bringing new life to eight veteran standards including "Rosetta," "Struttin' with Some Barbecue," and "The Lady Is a Tramp." Braff in particular is full of subtle surprises and sly humor, spontaneously concluding a slower-than-usual version of "Sunday" with a quick tribute to Louis Armstrong. Dixieland and swing fans should go out of their way to get this one. —*Scott Yanow*

Calling Berlin, Vol. 1 / Jun. 28, 1994-Jul. 1, 1994 / Arbors ✦✦✦✦
Cornetist Ruby Braff and pianist Ellis Larkins recorded a classic album of duets in 1955 and had a reunion in 1972. They waited another 22 years before cutting their third set but, despite the passing of time, the magic

heard on their earlier recordings is still very much present on their Arbors release. Both Braff and Larkins love melodies and rarely leave the themes behind in their improvisations. They perform 15 Irving Berlin tunes, ranging from the famous ("Alexander's Ragtime Band," "Easter Parade," and "How Deep Is the Ocean") to the more obscure ("My Walking Stick," "You're Laughing at Me," and "Steppin' Out with My Baby"). In all cases the interpretations are loving, personal, and uplifting. Guitarist Bucky Pizzarelli makes the group a trio on two numbers, and his mellow playing fits right into the intimate setting. Because Braff (who has always had his own sound) has long been a jazz giant, and Larkins is rightfully considered an extraordinary accompanist and perfect on melodic ballads, their most recent matchup is quite successful and delightful. —*Scott Yanow*

Anthony Braxton

b. Jun. 4, 1945, Chicago, IL
Clarinet, Piano, Reeds, Clarinet (Contrabass), Sax (Alto) / Avant-Garde
Of all the current leaders of the avant-garde, Anthony Braxton's music has possibly the least chance of ever being accepted by the bebop establishment. His complex lines, staccato attack, and enormous quantity of compositions have a logic all their own. Some detractors (like Wynton Marsalis) may deny that Braxton's music is even jazz, but because it does contain a large amount of improvisation and the feeling of the blues, it is unquestionably jazz. And for what it is worth, this writer regards him as an obvious genius, although the huge quantity of his work can be rather daunting.

Braxton began studying music when he was 17, and after serving in the military he became involved in Chicago's AACM in 1966. He made his recording debut in 1968, and from the start Braxton's approach was unusual; he used diagrams as song titles and wrote difficult-to-understand liner notes. Although alto has always been his main ax (and his second recording as a leader was an unprecedented double LP of unaccompanied alto explorations), Braxton eventually mastered virtually every reed instrument from the clarinet and sopranino to the contrabass clarinet and bass sax. He went to France for a period in 1969 and the following year teamed up with Chick Corea, Dave Holland, and Barry Altschul in the mostly free-form unit Circle. When Corea decided to quit the group so as to play more accessible music, Braxton kept Holland and Altschul and added trumpeter Kenny Wheeler to his quartet; in 1976 trombonist George Lewis took his place. From this point forward Braxton's chronology is difficult to follow because each of his recordings seemed to use a different combination of musicians, and a large number of his projects were documented. Luckily Braxton had a good relationship with Arista in the '70s; since that time he has recorded extensively for many European labels (including Hat Art and Black Saint) and recently the American company Music and Arts. Braxton has cut duet albums with Joseph Jarman, Muhal Richard Abrams, Evan Parker, Derek Bailey, and Max Roach, utilized a big band (the Creative Music Orchestra), performed standards with a trio headed by Tete Montoliu (with very advanced improvisations from the altoist), come out with a three-LP set of wholly written-out orchestral works, paid tribute (in an abstract way) to the music of Charlie Parker, Thelonious Monk, and Warne Marsh, and recorded more unaccompanied alto solos. Since 1984 Braxton has often toured with a quartet comprised of the brilliant pianist Marilyn Crispell, either John Lindberg or Mark Dresser on bass, and drummer Gerry Hemingway. In addition, Braxton has been a teacher at Mills College and Wesleyan College.

Anthony Braxton's accomplishments and contributions to jazz will take decades to fully assess. —*Scott Yanow*

The Complete Braxton / Feb. 4, 1971-Feb. 5, 1971 / Arista ✦✦✦
This two-LP set features the innovative multi-reedist in a variety of settings. Recorded while he was a member of the group Circle, Braxton is heard in two duets with pianist Chick Corea; three fairly exciting quartet tracks with trumpeter Kenny Wheeler, bassist Dave Holland, and drummer Barry Altschul; an unaccompanied solo on contrabass clarinet; a piece (which Braxton wrote but does not play on) for five tubas; and a selection in which he overdubbed four sopranino saxes. Lots of very interesting performances come from a master of the avant-garde who has always followed his own musical path. —*Scott Yanow*

Saxophone Improvisations, Series F / Feb. 25, 1972 / America ✦✦✦

New York (Fall 1974) / Sep. 27, 1974 / Arista ✦✦✦✦

★ **The Montreux / Berlin Concerts** / Jul. 20, 1975 / Arista ✦✦✦✦✦
Anthony Braxton has recorded so extensively during the past two decades that it is potentially foolhardy to call any of his recordings "definitive," but this two-LP set comes close. Braxton (mostly on alto and clarinet but also playing contrabass clarinet, flute, and sopranino) is heard with two of his best quartets on these live performances. Featured are either trumpeter Kenny Wheeler or trombonist George Lewis along with bassist Dave Holland and drummer Barry Altschul in exciting group improvisations based on six of Braxton's difficult compositions. There is a surprising amount of humor on one of these selections, and the interplay between these masterful musicians (making expert use of space and dynamics) sometimes bor-

ders on miraculous. The fourth side of this two-fer contains a lengthy performance of Braxton and Lewis playing with the Berlin New Music Group that is of slightly lesser interest; the CD reissue leaves out that selection. In either form, this music is highly recommended and by itself demonstrates the greatness and uniqueness of Anthony Braxton's music. This imprtant set (other than side four) has been reissued on CD. —*Scott Yanow*

Creative Orchestra Music (1976) / Feb. 1976 / Arista ✦✦✦
This is one of Braxton's most interesting recordings. Six of his compositions are performed by groups ranging from 15-20 pieces and featuring such soloists as trumpeters Cecil Bridgewater, Leo Smith, Kenny Wheeler, and Jon Faddis, baritonist Bruce Johnstone, trombonist George Lewis, reed player Roscoe Mitchell, bassist Dave Holland, pianist Muhal Richard Abrams, and Braxton himself. There is a lot of variety on this set. One of the pieces finds Braxton combining free elements with a Sousa-type march, while another one looks towards Ellington. There are quite a few memorable moments on this program. —*Scott Yanow*

Donaueschingen (Duo) 1976 / Oct. 23, 1976 / Hat Art ✦✦✦✦
A live set featuring duets by trombonist George Lewis and the reeds of Anthony Braxton might seem as if it would be a bit tedious, but the instant communication between the two keep, the music continually fascinating. Braxton (who is heard on alto, soprano, clarinet, contrabass clarinet, flute, and contrabass saxophone) and Lewis engage in some colorful sound explorations on their compositions on a continuous basis for 41 minutes, showing off not only their technique but their very sharp imagination. As an encore they surprised everyone by playing an effective 3-minute version of Charlie Parker's "Donna Lee"! Listeners with open ears will enjoy this colorful set. —*Scott Yanow*

★ **Dortmund (Quartet-1976)** / Oct. 31, 1976 / Hat Art ✦✦✦✦✦
This is the perfect Anthony Braxton recording for listeners to start with. The innovative multi-reedist (heard here on alto, clarinet, soprano, flute, and the remarkable contrabass sax) led a particularly strong group during part of 1976, a quartet with trombonist George Lewis, bassist Dave Holland, and drummer Barry Altschul. This CD releases for the first time the often-stunning music they performed at their final concert. Braxton's complex but exciting compositions are among his most accessible (one of them is based on a circus march and another is a hard-swinging original dedicated to Lou Donaldson), both Braxton and Lewis take consistently emotional solos, Holland really drives the group, Altschul contributes his colorful percussion, and the ensembles are very spirited. Give this recording to a bebopper who claims that what Anthony Braxton plays is not jazz. —*Scott Yanow*

Creative Orchestra (Koln) 1978 / May 12, 1978 / Hat Art ✦✦✦✦
Although Anthony Braxton does not play on this double CD (whose contents were released for the first time in 1995), his presence is certainly felt. He conducts the band through a fairly free improvisation and five of his compositions. Braxton showed a great deal of insight in originally picking the personnel, for nearly every one of the 21 musicians has had an important, career in advanced jazz, particularly Marty Ehrlich, Vinny Golia, Michael Mossman, Leo Smith, Kenny Wheeler, Ray Anderson, George Lewis, Marilyn Crispell, and John Lindberg. The music is often dense and atonal but never dull, and the closing composition is a superb piece that displays Braxton's love of marching band music! Although one wishes that Anthony Braxton himself had played, there is a set easily recommended to his fans. —*Scott Yanow*

Five Compositions (1986) / Jul. 2, 1986-Jul. 3, 1986 / Black Saint ✦✦✦

Six Monk's Compositions (1987) / Jun. 30, 1987-Jul. 1, 1987 / Black Saint ✦✦✦
This may be Braxton's finest straight jazz release, and among his best in any style. Bassist Mal Waldron and bassist Buell Neidlinger are fully equipped to handle Monk's tricky passages, chord structures, and movements, while Braxton displays an affinity for Monk's work that his detractors would find astonishing. Drummer Bill Osborne isn't intimidated by Neidlinger or Waldron and drives the session effectively. —*Ron Wynn*

Eugene (1989) / Jan. 31, 1989 / Black Saint ✦✦✦

Seven Compositions (Trio) 1989 / Mar. 21, 1989 / Hat Art ✦✦✦✦
The great avant-garde reed player Anthony Braxton (who on this set switches between alto, C-melody sax, clarinet, flute, soprano, and sopranino), bassist Adelhard Roidinger, and drummer Tony Oxley play five of Braxton's complex originals, Oxley's "The Angular Apron," and the standard "All the Things You Are." As usual, Braxton's improvising is quite advanced and original but is colorful and fiery enough to always hold on to open-eared listeners' attention. This is one of literally dozens of stimulating Anthony Braxton sessions currently available. —*Scott Yanow*

● **Tristano Compositions (1989)** / Dec. 10, 1989-Dec. 11, 1989 / Hat Art ✦✦✦✦
This is a particularly interesting and somewhat accessible Anthony Braxton set. The avant-garde reed master (who sticks here to alto, soprano, and flute), performs eight Lennie Tristano compositions (including two versions of "Victory Ball") plus a pair of standards and Warne Marsh's "Sax of a Kind." With baritonist John Raskin, pianist Dred Scott, bassist Cecil

McBee, and drummer Andrew Cyrille swinging in an advanced way, Braxton pays close attention to performing the complex melody lines correctly before going off on his free flights. This music might cause some beboppers to reassess their opinion of Anthony Braxton. —*Scott Yanow*

Willisau (Quartet) / Jun. 2, 1991-Jun. 5, 1991 / Hat Art ✦✦✦✦
This four-CD set features Anthony Braxton's longtime quartet (with pianist Marilyn Crispell, bassist Marc Dresser, and drummer Gerry Hemingway) performing the leader's complex compositions both live and in the studio (two CDs apiece). On this occasion Braxton switches between alto (his main ax), clarinet, contrabass clarinet, flute, and sopranino. Since Braxton sometimes had his players perform two or three of his compositions simultaneously (!) and the music was difficult to begin with, it may take a few listens to appreciate the performances, but the results are of a consistently high caliber. This release will not convert any detractors but should be of great interest to Braxton's followers, for he plays at the top of his form. —*Scott Yanow*

Twelve Compositions / Jul. 13, 1993-Jul. 16, 1993 / Music & Arts ✦✦✦✦
Of all of the avant-garde players of the past 30 years, Anthony Braxton has been perhaps the most diligent at documenting his work. The brilliant multi-reedist has been very fortunate to have a stable quartet for the past nine years with the frequently astounding pianist Marilyn Crispell, bassist Mark Dresser, and drummer Gerry Hemingway doing justice to his very complex originals. This double-CD set features Braxton and his group on two continuous and complete live performances. Not only do the musicians tackle a dozen of Braxton's complicated originals, but during part of four of them individual members are assigned the task of playing a different composition than the rest of the group! Obviously this is not music to be taken lightly or merely played in the background. However, listeners with the time and interest will find much to enjoy in the very lively explorations from these masterful musicians. —*Scott Yanow*

Knitting Factory (Piano/Quartet) 1994, Vol. 1 / 1995 / Leo ✦✦✦✦

Joshua Breakstone
....
b. Jul. 22, 1955, Elizabeth, NJ
Guitar / Cool
A fine bop-based guitarist, Joshua Breakstone discovered jazz when he was 14. He studied for several years with Sal Salvador yet at the time was gigging regularly with a rock group. He attended Berklee and in 1977 toured Canada with the reed player Glen Hall, making his recording debut on Hall's Sonora release. During and after teaching guitar at the Rhode Island Conservatory of Music (1979-81), Breakstone worked in New York with Warne Marsh, Emily Remler, Dave Schnitter, and Vic Juris. In 1983 he recorded his first album (*Wonderful!*) for Sonora. While that date had Barry Harris on piano, his follow-up featured Kenny Barron. Breakstone has since recorded for Contemporary (including a quartet date featuring Pepper Adams), Capri, and Evidence, helping keep the legacy of quiet bop guitar alive. —*Scott Yanow*

4/4 " 1 / Jun. 1984 / Mobile Fidelity ✦✦✦

Echoes / Feb. 19, 1986 / Contemporary ✦✦✦✦

Self-Portrait in Swing / Feb. 1990 / Contemporary ✦✦✦

9 by 3 / Oct. 30, 1990 / Contemporary ✦✦✦

Walk Don't Run / Aug. 1991 / Evidence ✦✦✦

● **Evening Star** / Jan. 14, 1992 / Contemporary ✦✦✦✦

Sittin' on the Thing with Ming / Jan. 29, 1993 / Capri ✦✦✦

Michael Brecker
....
b. Mar. 29, 1949, Philadelphia, PA
Sax (Tenor) / Post-Bop, Crossover
A remarkable technician and an influential tenor saxophonist (the biggest influence on other tenors since Wayne Shorter), Michael Brecker took a long time before getting around to recording his first solo album. He has spent much of his career as a top-notch studio player who often appeared backing pop singers, leading some jazz listeners to overlook his very strong improvising skills. Michael Brecker originally started on clarinet and alto before switching to tenor in high school. Early on he played with rock and R&B-oriented bands. In 1969 he moved to New York and soon joined Dreams, an early fusion group. Brecker was with Horace Silver during 1973-74, gigged with Billy Cobham, and then co-led the Brecker Brothers (a commercially successful funk group) with his brother-trumpeter Randy Brecker for most of the '70s. He was with Steps (later Steps Ahead) in the early '80s, doubled on an EWI (electronic wind instrument), and made a number of studio sessions during the '70s and '80s, popping up practically everywhere (including with James Taylor, Yoko Ono, and Paul Simon). With the release of his first album as a leader in 1987 (when he was already 38), Brecker appeared more often in challenging jazz settings. He recorded additional sets as a leader (in 1988 and 1990), teamed up with McCoy Tyner on one of 1995's most rewarding jazz recordings, and toured with a reunited Brecker Brothers band. —*Scott Yanow*

● **Michael Brecker** / Dec. 1986-1987 / Impulse ♦♦♦♦
The highlight of this very good album is "Nothing Personal." With Pat Metheny (g), Charlie Haden (b), and Jack DeJohnette (d). —*Michael G. Nastos*

Don't Try This at Home / 1988 / Impulse ♦♦♦

Now You See It . . . Now You Don't / 1990 / Impulse ♦♦♦

Randy Brecker

b. Nov. 29, 1945, Philadelphia, PA
Trumpet / Bop, Crossover
Randy Brecker is a fine hard-bop trumpet soloist but one versatile enough to fit into nearly any setting including in the pop world, funk bands, and electronic fusion. He studied classical trumpet and attended Indiana University. Brecker was with Blood, Sweat & Tears in 1967 and spent 1968-69 playing with Horace Silver's Quintet. He also appeared with the big bands of Clark Terry, Duke Pearson, Frank Foster, and the Thad Jones-Mel Lewis Orchestra. After playing with the early fusion group Dreams in 1969, he worked with Larry Coryell's Eleventh House and Billy Cobham in addition to keeping very busy with studio work. He teamed up with Michael Brecker in the popular funk-oriented Brecker Brothers (1974-79), in the '80s often collaborated with his wife, pianist/vocalist Eliane Elias, and in the '90s toured with the reunited Brecker Brothers. But Randy Brecker still sounds best when in a freewheeling bebop combo, and fortunately he occasionally records in that type of spontaneous setting. —*Scott Yanow*

Score / Jan. 24, 1969-Feb. 3, 1969 / Blue Note ♦♦♦

● **Live at Sweet Basil: Randy Brecker Quintet** / Jan. 11, 1992 / GNP ♦♦♦♦

Dee Dee Bridgewater (née Dee Dee Garrett)

b. May 27, 1950, Memphis, TN
Vocals / Standards
One of the best jazz singers of her generation, Dee Dee Bridgewater (who was married to trumpeter Cecil Bridgewater in the early '70s) had to move to France to find herself. She performed in Michigan during the '60s and toured the Soviet Union in 1969 with the University of Illinois big band. She sang with the Thad Jones-Mel Lewis Orchestra (1972-74) and appeared in the Broadway musical *The Wiz* (1974-76). Due to erratic records and a lack of direction, Dee Dee Bridgewater was largely overlooked in the jazz world by the time she moved to France in the '80s. She appeared in the show *Lady Day* and at European jazz festivals, and eventually formed her own backup group. By the late '80s Bridgewater's Verve recordings were starting to alert American listeners to her singing talents. Her 1995 Horace Silver tribute disc (*Love and Peace*) is a gem and resulted in the singer extensively touring the US. —*Scott Yanow*

In Montreux / Jul. 18, 1990 / Verve ♦♦♦♦
Dee Dee Bridgewater's move to France awhile back has resulted in her having a relatively low profile in jazz. This excellent live set should help restore her reputation. Whether it be a three-song Horace Silver medley, the warhorse "All of Me," Jobim's "How Insensitive," "Night in Tunisia," or the rarely performed "Strange Fruit," Bridgewater (who is backed by a French rhythm section) is in top form, singing with swing and sensitivity. —*Scott Yanow*

Keeping Tradition / Dec. 1992 / Verve ♦♦♦

★ **Love and Peace: A Tribute to Horace Silver** / 1994 / Verve ♦♦♦♦♦
Dee Dee Bridgewater performs 13 of Horace Silver's songs on her very well conceived release. On most selections she is accompanied by her French quintet, but there are also two guest appearances apiece for organist Jimmy Smith and pianist Silver ("Nice's Dream" and "Song for My Father"). Bridgewater uplifts Silver's lyrics, proves to be in prime form, and swings up a storm. Other high points include "Filthy McNasty," "Doodlin'," and "Blowin' the Blues Away." A gem. —*Scott Yanow*

Nick Brignola

b. Jul. 17, 1936, Troy, NY
Sax (Baritone), Sax (Soprano) / Hard Bop
A strong baritone soloist in the tradition of Pepper Adams, Nick Brignola has long been overshadowed by Adams and Gerry Mulligan but actually ranks near the top. He occasionally doubles on other instruments (soprano, alto, and flute). After studying at Ithaca College and Berklee he played and recorded with Reese Markewich in the late '50s, Herb Pomeroy, Cal Tjader, and the Mastersounds. Brignola worked with Woody Herman's Orchestra (1963), Sal Salvador, and Ted Curson (1967) but has generally been a leader of his own small groups. For a time he played fusion in the early '70s but since then has mostly performed hard bop. Among the many labels Nick Brignola has recorded for are Priam (his own company), Beehive, Interplay, SeaBreeze, Discovery, and Reservoir. —*Scott Yanow*

Raincheck / Sep. 12, 1988-Sep. 13, 1988 / Reservoir ♦♦♦♦
The fine baritonist Nick Brignola (who here also plays a bit of soprano, tenor, and clarinet) is well featured on a wide range of superior standards

and obscurities. With the strong assistance of pianist Kenny Barron, bassist George Mraz, and drummer Billy Hart, Brignola is heard at his best playing everything from bop and swing to Ralph Towner's ballad "North Star." —*Scott Yanow*

On a Different Level / Sep. 25, 1989 / Reservoir ♦♦♦

What It Takes / Oct. 9, 1990 / Reservoir ♦♦♦

It's Time / Dec. 2, 1991 / Reservoir ♦♦♦

● **Like Old Times** / May 19, 1994 / Reservoir ♦♦♦♦
Some jazz recordings take pages to explain and analyze. Such is not the case with Nick Brignola's Reservoir release, for the baritonist (who ranks with Gerry Mulligan, Hamiet Bluiett, and Ronnie Cuber as pacesetters on his instrument in the mid-'90s) jams four standards and three straighta-head originals with an all-star quintet, also featuring trumpeter Claudio Roditi and pianist John Hicks. In addition to his robust baritone solos, Brignola has excellent outings on clarinet ("More Than You Know") and soprano. With bassist George Mraz and drummer Dick Berk ably supporting the group, and both Roditi and Hicks heard at the peak of their powers, Brignola's album is a strong set of bop-oriented music. —*Scott Yanow*

Bob Brookmeyer

b. Dec. 19, 1929, Kansas City, MO
Piano, Trombone (Valve) / Cool, Post-Bop
Bob Brookmeyer has long been the top valve trombonist in jazz and a very advanced arranger whose writing is influenced by modern classical music. He started out as a pianist in dance bands but was on valve trombone with Stan Getz (1953). He gained fame as a member of the Gerry Mulligan quartet (1954-57), was part of the unusual Jimmy Giuffre Three of 1957-58 (which consisted of Giuffre's reeds, Brookmeyer's valve trombone, and Jim Hall's guitar) and then rejoined Mulligan as arranger and occasional player with his Concert Jazz Band. Brookmeyer, who was a strong enough pianist to hold his own on a two-piano date with Bill Evans, occasionally switched to piano with Mulligan. He co-led a part-time quintet with Clark Terry (1961-66), was an original member of the Thad Jones-Mel Lewis orchestra (1965-67), and became a busy studio musician. Brookmeyer was fairly inactive during much of the '70s but made a comeback in the late '70s with some very advanced arrangements for the Mel Lewis band (of which he became musical director for a time). Brookmeyer has since moved to Europe where he continually writes and occasionally records on his distinctive valve trombone. —*Scott Yanow*

The Dual Role of Bob Brookmeyer / Jun. 30, 1955 / Original Jazz Classics ♦♦♦

The Ivory Hunters / May 12, 1959 / United Artists ♦♦♦

● **Paris Suite** / Oct. 15, 1993-Jan. 5, 1994 / Challenge ♦♦♦♦
Veteran valve trombonist/composer Bob Brookmeyer has not recorded many small group dates during the '80s and '90s, making this Challenge CD with a young European rhythm section (pianist Kris Goessens, bassist Riccardo Del Fra, and drummer Dre Pallemaerts) a bit special. Brookmeyer plays eight obscurities (four by him and three by his pianist) that are complex, harmonically advanced, and yet still able to be swung. Well worth searching for. —*Scott Yanow*

Tina Brooks (Harold Floyd Brooks)

b. Jun. 7, 1932, Fayetteville, NC, d. Aug. 13, 1974, New York, NY
Sax (Tenor) / Hard Bop
A fine hard-bop tenor player who after a burst of activity largely faded out of jazz in 1962 (due to continual drug problems), Tina Brooks never reached his potential but did record some rewarding music. He made his recording debut in 1951 on four titles with Sonny Thompson's R&B band. After time spent touring with Amos Milburn and Lionel Hampton and freelancing in New York, Brooks began to record for Blue Note in 1958. In addition to four sessions as a leader cut between 1958-61, he appeared on Blue Note dates as a sideman with Jimmy Smith, Kenny Burrell, Freddie Hubbard, Freddie Redd, Jackie McLean, and with Howard McGhee on Felsted. But his last session was on June 17, 1961, and, although he continued playing (mostly Latin and R&B jobs in New York), Brooks let his drug habit ruin his life. He died of kidney failure when he was 42. Ironically Tina Brooks is probably better known now (due to the release of a definitive Mosaic four-LP box set) than he was in his lifetime. —*Scott Yanow*

● **Blue Note Recordings** / 1958-1961 / Mosaic ♦♦♦♦
Tenor saxophonist with four different bands, including Lee Morgan, Freddie Hubbard, Blue Mitchell, and Johnny Coles (trumpets). Also Jackie McLean. Trios led by pianists Sonny Clark, Duke Jordan, and Kenny Drew. Fifteen Brooks originals, seven standards. Brooks was an unsung hero. His work deserves your investigation. —*Michael G. Nastos*

● **True Blue** / Jun. 25, 1960 / Capitol ♦♦♦♦

Clifford Brown

b. Oct. 30, 1930, Wilmington, DE, d. Jun. 26, 1956, Pennsylvania
Trumpet / Hard Bop
Clifford Brown's death in a car accident at the age of 25 was one of the

great tragedies in jazz history. Already ranking with Dizzy Gillespie and Miles Davis as one of the top trumpeters in jazz, Brownie was still improving in 1956. Plus he was a clean liver and was not even driving; the up-and-coming pianist Richie Powell and his wife (who was driving) also perished in the crash.

Clifford Brown accomplished a great deal in the short time he had. He started on trumpet when he was 15 and by 1948 was playing regularly in Philadelphia. Fats Navarro, who was his main influence, encouraged Brown, as did Charlie Parker and Dizzy Gillespie. After a year at Maryland State University he was in a serious car accident in June 1950 that put him out of action for a year. In 1952 Brown made his recording debut with Chris Powell's Blue Flames (an R&B group). The following year he spent some time with Tadd Dameron and from August to December was with Lionel Hampton's band, touring Europe and leading some recording sessions. In early 1954 he recorded some brilliant solos at Birdland with Art Blakey's quintet (a band that directly preceded the Jazz Messengers) and by mid-year had formed a quintet with Max Roach. Considered one of the premiere hard-bop bands, the group lasted until Brown's death, featuring Harold Land (and later Sonny Rollins) on tenor and recording several superb sets for EmArcy. Just hours before his death, Brownie appeared at a Philadelphia jam session that was miraculously recorded and played some of the finest music of his short life.

Clifford Brown had a fat warm tone, a boppish style quite reminiscent of the equally ill-fated Fats Navarro, and a mature improvising approach; he was as inventive on melodic ballads as he was on rapid jams. Amazingly enough, a filmed appearance of him playing two songs in 1955 on a Soupy Sales variety show has recently turned up after being lost for 40 years, the only known footage of the great trumpeter. Fortunately, virtually all of his recordings are currently available, including his Prestige dates (in the OJC series), his work for Blue Note and Pacific Jazz (on a four-CD set), and his many EmArcy sessions (reissued on a magnificent ten-disc set). But the one to pick up first is Columbia's *The Beginning and the End*, which has Brown's first and last recordings. —*Scott Yanow*

★ **The Beginning and the End** / Mar. 21, 1952+Jun. 25, 1956 / Columbia ◆◆◆◆◆

This CD, a straight reissue of the original LP, has some incredible music. Trumpeter Clifford Brown is heard at the beginning of his tragically brief career, taking solos on a pair of R&B sides by Chris Powell's Blue Flames. The remainder of the package features Brown on the last night of his life, just a few hours before his death in a car accident. Performing in his hometown of Philadelphia before a loving crowd, the 25-year-old is heard playing at his absolute peak. He performs "Walkin" with a local sextet that includes Billy Root on tenor and pianist Sam Dockery (a future member of Art Blakey's Jazz Messengers), "A Night in Tunisia" with a quintet, and concludes both his night and his career with a quartet rendition of "Donna Lee" that is simply brilliant. Brownie's death was one of the great tragedies of jazz history, and his "goodbyes" to the audience are ironic and in retrospect quite sad; don't listen to it twice! But Clifford Brown's playing on this date is so memorable that the CD is essential for all jazz collections. —*Scott Yanow*

● **Clifford Brown Quartet in Paris** / 1953 / Original Jazz Classics ◆◆◆◆

This straight CD reissue of a Clifford Brown LP features the great trumpeter with a quiet rhythm section consisting of pianist Henri Renaud, bassist Pierre Michelot, and drummer Benny Bennett. There are six songs and six alternate takes (including three versions apiece of "I Can Dream, Can't I" and "You're a Lucky Guy"), but each of Brownie's solos are different, and his tone is so warm that every performance is well worth hearing. Ironically the finest solo, a classic version of "It Might As Well Be Spring," was improvised in one take. Highly recommended. —*Scott Yanow*

Brownie Eyes / Jun. 9, 1953-Aug. 28, 1953 / Blue Note ◆◆◆◆

The great trumpeter Clifford Brown is heard in several settings on this LP (all of the titles have since been reissued on a box set by Mosaic). The songs find Brownie with a quintet featuring altoist Lou Donaldson and pianist Elmo Hope ("De-Dah" and "Brownie Speaks" are most memorable), there is an alternate take of "Get Happy" with a sextet headed by trombonist J.J. Johnson, and the remaining five titles have Brown teamed in a sextet with altoist Gigi Gryce and tenor saxophonist Charlie Rouse. Of the latter, "Easy Living" and "Cherokee" are classics. Although superceded by later reissues, this set has more than its share of superb music. —*Scott Yanow*

● **Complete Blue Note-Pacific Jazz** / Jun. 9, 1953-Aug. 13, 1954 / Pacific Jazz ◆◆◆◆

This four-CD set has the exact same music as an earlier Mosaic five-LP box, but is highly recommended to those listeners not already possessing the limited-edition set. Trumpeter Clifford Brown is heard on the most significant recordings from the first half of his tragically brief career. Whether co-leading a date with altoist Lou Donaldson, playing as a sideman with trombonist J.J. Johnson, interacting with an all-star group of West Coast players, or jamming with the first (although unofficial) edition of Art Blakey's Jazz Messengers (a two-disc live performance with a quintet that also includes the drummer/leader, Donaldson, and pianist Horace Silver), Brownie is the main star. Highlights are many, including versions of

"Brownie Speaks," Elmo Hope's "De-Dah," "Cherokee," "Get Happy," "Daahoud," and "Joy Spring." The attractive packaging, with its 40 pages of text and many rare pictures, is an added bonus. —*Scott Yanow*

Memorial / Jun. 11, 1953+Sep. 15, 1953 / Original Jazz Classics ◆◆◆◆

This CD reissues a Prestige LP plus a "new" alternate take of "Choose Now." Trumpeter Clifford Brown is heard in two unusual and unrelated sessions. On four selections, Brown is featured with arranger/pianist Tadd Dameron's Orchestra; other soloists include Benny Golson on tenor and altoist Gigi Gryce. The other date was recorded in Sweden while Brown was touring with Lionel Hampton's Orchestra. Clifford Brown and fellow trumpeter Art Farmer play four Quincy Jones arrangements with a Swedish group that includes altoist Arne Domnerus, baritonist Lars Gullin, and pianist Bengt Hallberg. "Lover Come Back to Me" really cooks, and Brownie and Farmer get to trade off in exciting fashion during "'Scuse These Blues." —*Scott Yanow*

Clifford Brown Big Band in Paris / Sep. 28, 1953-Oct. 11, 1953 / Original Jazz Classics ◆◆◆◆

The Clifford Brown Sextet in Paris / Sep. 29, 1953-Oct. 8, 1953 / Original Jazz Classics ◆◆◆◆

While in Paris with Lionel Hampton's Orchestra, trumpeter Clifford Brown teamed up with altoist Gigi Gryce and a top-notch rhythm section (which includes pianist Henri Renaud, guitarist Jimmy Gourley, bassist Pierre Michelot, and drummer Jean-Louis Viale) for two fine sessions that are reissued in full (other than a couple of rare alternate takes) on this enjoyable CD. Although Gryce was not a major soloist, he held his own with the trumpeter and was a talented composer. Most of the songs on this date are his, including "Minority" (Gryce's most famous original). But it is for Brownie's brilliant playing on such tunes as "All the Things You Are," "I Cover the Waterfront," and "Minority" that this CD is most significant. —*Scott Yanow*

Clifford Brown Quartet / Oct. 15, 1953 / Blue Note ◆◆◆◆

Simply brilliant playing by Brown and his comrades, notably Max Roach. The Brown/Roach unit had everything; they played as a cohesive group, yet everyone could also spin out majestic solos, and in pianist Richie Powell, Clifford's brother, there was a third fantastic soloist. This is essential, as are most Brown recordings. —*Ron Wynn*

The Best of Max Roach and Clifford Brown in Concert / Apr. 1954-Aug. 30, 1954 / GNP ◆◆◆◆

This set has the earliest documented performances of the Clifford Brown/Max Roach Quintet. Trumpeter Brown and drummer Roach, along with tenor saxophonist Teddy Edwards, pianist Carl Perkins, and bassist George Bledsoe, perform four numbers, including hot versions of "All God's Chillun Got Rhythm" and Edwards' "Sunset Eyes." In addition there is a later set with the permanent lineup of the Quintet: Brown, Roach, tenorman Harold Land, pianist Richie Powell, and bassist George Morrow. Together they play "Jordu," Brown's feature on "I Can't Get Started," and versions of "I Get a Kick Out of You" and "Parisian Thoroughfare" that are both heated and colorful. This is a very rewarding and somewhat historic release of high-quality straightahead jazz from one of the great hard-bop bands. —*Scott Yanow*

★ **Brownie: The Complete EmArcy Recordings of** / Aug. 2, 1954-Feb. 16, 1956 / EmArcy ◆◆◆◆◆

Although undoubtedly an expensive acquisition, this ten-CD set is perfectly done and contains dozens of gems. The remarkable but short-lived trumpeter Clifford Brown has the second half of his career fully documented (other than his final performance) and he is showcased in a wide variety of settings. The bulk of the numbers are of Brownie's Quintet with co-leader and drummer Max Roach, either Harold Land or Sonny Rollins on tenor, pianist Richie Powell, and bassist George Morrow (including some previously unheard alternate takes), but there is also much more. Brown stars at several jam sessions (including a meeting with fellow trumpeters Clark Terry and Maynard Ferguson), accompanies such singers as Dinah Washington, Helen Merrill, and Sarah Vaughan, and is backed by strings on one date. Everything is here, including classic versions of "Parisian Thoroughfare," "Joy Spring," "Daahoud," "Coronado," a ridiculously fast "Move," "Portrait of Jenny," "Cherokee," "Sandu," "I'll Remember April," and "What Is This Thing Called Love." Get this set while it stays in print! —*Scott Yanow*

★ **Brownie** / Aug. 1954-Feb. 1956 / PolyGram ◆◆◆◆◆

The complete EmArcy recordings. The definitive record for a one-of-a-kind band. A must-own with Max Roach (d). —*Michael G. Nastos*

Clifford Brown with Strings / Jan. 18, 1955-Jan. 20, 1955 / EmArcy ◆◆◆

A Study in Brown / Feb. 23, 1955-Feb. 25, 1955 / EmArcy ◆◆◆◆

This CD reissue features the 1955 version of the Clifford Brown/Max Roach Quintet, a group also including tenor saxophonist Harold Land, pianist Richie Powell, and bassist George Morrow. One of the premiere early hard-bop units, this band had unlimited potential. Highlights of this set are "Cherokee" (during which trumpeter Brownie is brilliant), "Swingin'," and "Sandu." All of the group's recordings (which have been included in the Clifford Brown ten-CD box set) are well worth acquiring. —*Scott Yanow*

● **At Basin Street** / Jan. 4, 1956-Feb. 17, 1956 / EmArcy ✦✦✦✦
The last official album by the Clifford Brown/Max Roach Quintet is the only one that featured the great Sonny Rollins on tenor. With pianist Richie Powell and bassist George Morrow completing the group, this CD reissue is a hard-bop classic. Brownie and Rollins fit together perfectly on memorable versions of "What Is This Thing Called Love," "I'll Remember April," and a witty arrangement of "Love Is a Many Splendored Thing." Highly recommended. —*Scott Yanow*

Marion Brown

b. Sep. 8, 1935, Atlanta, GA
Flute, Sax (Alto) / Avant-Garde, Free Jazz
One of the brightest and most lyrical voices of the '60s avant-garde, Marion Brown participated in many stimulating recordings during the '60s and '70s while never really becoming an influential force. He played alto in high school and in Army bands and attended Clark College. In 1965 Brown moved to New York and recorded the monumental *Ascension* with John Coltrane and *Fire Music* with Archie Shepp. Soon Brown was leading his own dates for ESP and Impulse. He worked with Sun Ra, lived in Europe during 1968-70, and in the early '70s in the US played with Leo Smith. Since recording with Gunter Hampel in 1983 and making an unaccompanied solo date in 1985, ill health has limited Marion Brown's musical activities. —*Scott Yanow*

Why Not? / Oct. 23, 1966 / ESP ✦✦✦

Marion Brown Quartet / Dec. 1, 1966 / ESP ✦✦✦✦

● **Three for Shepp** / Dec. 1, 1966 / Impulse ✦✦✦✦

Afternoon of a Georgia Faun / Aug. 10, 1970 / ECM ✦✦✦

Ray Brown

b. Oct. 13, 1926, Pittsburgh, PA
Bass / Bop
The huge and comfortable sound of Ray Brown's bass has been a welcome feature on loop-oriented sessions for a half-century. He played locally in his native Pittsburgh in his early days.

Arriving in New York in 1945, on his first day in town Brown met and played with Dizzy Gillespie, Charlie Parker, and Bud Powell! He was hired by Gillespie for his small groups and his big band; "One Bass Hit" and "Two Bass Hit" were early features, and he can be seen with Dizzy in the 1947 film *Jiving in Bebop*. Although not a soloist on the level of an Oscar Pettiford, Brown's quick reflexes and ability to accompany soloists in a swinging fashion put him near the top of his field. After playing with Jazz at the Philharmonic, he married Ella Fitzgerald (their marriage only lasted during 1948-52) and for a time led his own trio to back the singer. Brown recorded with an early version of the Modern Jazz Quartet (under Milt Jackson's leadership) and then became a permanent member of the Oscar Peterson Trio (1951-66).

With Peterson the bassist travelled the world, guested with other top jazz artists, was featured on JATP tours, became famous, and recorded constantly. He began playing cello in the late '50s and used it on a few of his own dates. After leaving Peterson, Brown settled in Los Angeles, worked in the studios, continued recording jazz, and worked as a manager of several artists (including the Modern Jazz Quartet and Quincy Jones). He played with the L.A. Four starting in 1974, did a great deal to revive the careers of Ernestine Anderson and Gene Harris, and recorded extensively for Pablo and Concord. The Ray Brown Trio of the '90s features pianist Benny Green and drummer Greg Hutchison and has recorded for Telarc. —*Scott Yanow*

This One's for Blanton / Dec. 5, 1972 / Original Jazz Classics ✦✦✦

The Giants / Dec. 7, 1974 / Pablo ✦✦✦

Something for Lester / Jun. 22, 1979-Jun. 24, 1979 / Original Jazz Classics ✦✦✦

Ray Brown Three / Feb. 1982 / Concord Jazz ✦✦✦

Super Bass / 1986 / Capri ✦✦✦

Black Orpheus / 1989 / Evidence ✦✦✦✦

Moore Makes 4 / May 22, 1990 / Concord Jazz ✦✦✦

Two Bass Hits / Apr. 29, 1991 / Capri ✦✦✦

Bass Face / Apr. 1993 / Telarc ✦✦✦

● **Don't Get Sassy** / Apr. 21, 1994-Apr. 22, 1994 / Telarc ✦✦✦✦

Some of My Best Friends Are . . . the Piano Players / Nov. 18, 1994-Nov. 21, 1994 / Telarc ✦✦✦

Seven Steps to Heaven / May 22, 1995-May 23, 1995 / Telarc ✦✦✦✦
The Ray Brown Trio in 1995 featured pianist Benny Green and drummer Gregory Hutchinson along with the leader/bassist. In the tradition of the mid-'50s Oscar Peterson Trio, the group featured tight arrangements with concise but consistently brilliant solos. For this Telarc session, guitarist Ulf Wakenius (a little reminiscent of Herb Ellis) fits in perfectly. Highlights include "Seven Steps to Heaven" and "Cotton Tail." —*Scott Yanow*

Dave Brubeck

b. Dec. 6, 1920, Concord, CA
Piano / Cool
Dave Brubeck has long served as proof that creative jazz and popular success can go together. Although critics who had championed him when he was unknown seemed to scorn him when the Dave Brubeck Quartet became a surprise success, in reality Brubeck never watered down or altered his music in order to gain a wide audience. Creative booking (being one of the first groups to play regularly on college campuses) and a bit of luck resulted in great popularity, and Dave Brubeck today remains as one of the few household names in jazz.

From nearly the start Brubeck enjoyed utilizing polyrhythms and polytonality (playing in two keys at once). He had classical training from his mother but fooled her for a long period by memorizing his lessons and not learning to read music. He studied music at the College of the Pacific during 1938-42. Brubeck led a service band in General Patton's Army during World War II and then in 1946 he started studying at Mills College with the classical composer Darius Milhaud, who encouraged his students to play jazz. During 1946-49 Brubeck led a group mostly consisting of fellow classmates, and they recorded as the Dave Brubeck Octet; their music (released on Fantasy in 1951) still sounds advanced today with complex time signatures and some polytonality. The octet was too radical to get much work, so Brubeck formed a trio with drummer Cal Tjader (who doubled on vibes) and bassist Ron Crotty. The trio's Fantasy recordings of 1949-51 were quite popular in the Bay Area, but the group came to an end when Brubeck hurt his back during a serious swimming accident and was put out of action for months.

Upon his return in 1951, Brubeck was persuaded by altoist Paul Desmond to make the group a quartet. Within two years the band had become surprisingly popular. Desmond's cool-toned alto and quick wit fit in well with Brubeck's often heavy chording and experimental playing; both Brubeck and Desmond had original sounds and styles that owed little to their predecessors. Joe Dodge was the band's early drummer, but after he tired of the road the virtuosic Joe Morello took his place in 1956, while the revolving bass chair finally settled on Eugene Wright in 1958. By then Brubeck had followed his popular series of Fantasy recordings with some big sellers on Columbia and had appeared on the cover of *Time* (1954). The huge success of Paul Desmond's "Take Five" (1960) was followed by many songs played in "odd" time signatures such as 7/4 and 9/8; the high-quality soloing of the musicians kept these experiments from sounding like gimmicks. Dave and Iola Brubeck (his wife and lyricist) put together an anti-racism show featuring Louis Armstrong (*The Real Ambassadors*), which was recorded, but its only public appearance was at the Monterey Jazz Festival in the early '60s.

The Dave Brubeck Quartet constantly travelled around the world until its breakup in 1967. After some time off during which he wrote religious works, Brubeck came back the following year with a new quartet featuring Gerry Mulligan, although he would have several reunions with Desmond before the altoist's death in 1977. Brubeck joined with his sons Darius (keyboards), Chris (electric bass and bass trombone), and Danny (drums) in Two Generations of Brubeck in the '70s. In the early '80s tenor saxophonist Jerry Bergonzi was in the Brubeck Quartet, and since the mid-'80s clarinetist Bill Smith (who was in the original Octet) has alternated with altoist Bobby Militello.

There is no shortage of Dave Brubeck records currently available; practically everything he has cut for Fantasy, Columbia, Concord, and Telarc (his most recent label) are easy to locate. Brubeck, whose compositions "In Your Own Sweet Way," "The Duke," and "Blue Rondo à la Turk" have become standards, has remained very busy (despite some bouts of bad health) into the mid-'90s. —*Scott Yanow*

The Dave Brubeck Octet / 1946-Jul. 1950 / Original Jazz Classics ✦✦✦✦
On infrequent occasions during 1946-50, pianist Dave Brubeck led an octet that was dominated by students of the composer Darius Milhaud. This pioneering West Coast outfit combined bop with modern classical music to form an interesting new blend of styles, but since they only recorded one LP's worth of material (which has remained obscure through the decades), the octet's life and general influence were limited. With such players as trumpeter Dick Collins, altoist Paul Desmond, Bill Smith on clarinet and baritone, tenor saxophonist Dave Van Kreidt, and a rhythm section comprised of Brubeck, bassist Ron Crotty, and Cal Tjader on drums, this fascinating group performs highly original music throughout this CD reissue. —*Scott Yanow*

● **Time Signatures: A Career Retrospective** / 1946-May 7, 1991 / Columbia ✦✦✦✦
This four-CD box set does a near-perfect job of summing up Dave Brubeck's extensive recorded legacy. Drawing its recordings from not only Columbia but Fantasy, Atlantic, and Music Masters, the attractive package also includes an extensive booklet written by Doug Ramsey that can serve as a mini-biography. The focus is naturally on Brubeck's quartet with altoist Paul Desmond, but there is also music from before and after their association, even including one otherwise unissued performance, a

remarkable polytonal polyrhythmic version of "Tritonis." Although completists will prefer to acquire Dave Brubeck's individual releases, this set is perfect for those just beginning to explore the magic of his music. — *Scott Yanow*

24 Classic Original Recordings / Sep. 1949-Nov. 1950 / Fantasy ✦✦✦✦
During 1949-51 pianist Dave Brubeck led a San Francisco-based trio with bassist Ron Crotty and Cal Tjader doubling on drums and vibes. This double LP has all 24 of this group's recordings, interpretations of standards that are full of surprising moments. Even at this early stage, Brubeck had his own style and sounds nothing at all like Bud Powell, the dominant influence of the era. — *Scott Yanow*

Jazz Collection / Mar. 9, 1954-1970 / Columbia ✦✦✦

● **Jazz Goes to College** / Mar. 1954 / Columbia ✦✦✦✦
A true classic, this CD reissues the original LP. Altoist Paul Desmond's lengthy solo on the blues "Balcony Rock" was one of the greatest of his career, with one fresh idea leading (through repetition and gradual development) logically into another; pianist Brubeck's improvisation on this piece almost reaches the heights of Desmond's. Bassist Bob Bates and drummer Joe Dodge give a solid and quiet accompaniment to Desmond and the unpredictable pianist/leader with other highlights, including "Out of Nowhere," "The Song Is You," and "Don't Worry 'Bout Me." This is the Brubeck Quartet at its best. — *Scott Yanow*

Interchanges '54: Featuring Paul Desmond / Oct. 1954-Nov. 1954 / Columbia ✦✦✦✦
This excellent CD reissues the LP *Brubeck Time* plus half of *Red Hot and Cool.* One of the few early studio (as opposed to club) recordings by the early Dave Brubeck Quartet (this version has bassist Bob Bates and drummer Joe Dodge in addition to pianist Brubeck and altoist Paul Desmond), the fine unit performs nine standards plus three new compositions: "Stompin' for Mili," "Audrey" (dedicated to Audrey Hepburn), and Brubeck's classic, "The Duke." — *Scott Yanow*

Dave Digs Disney / Jun. 29, 1957-Aug. 3, 1957 / Columbia/Legacy ✦✦✦

★ **Time Out** / Jun. 25, 1959-Aug. 18, 1959 / Columbia ✦✦✦✦✦
This is one of the most popular jazz recordings of all time. Altoist Paul Desmond's memorable "Take Five" became a huge hit, showing that it is possible for creative jazz to sell. In addition to "Take Five" (which is still a standard), other high points of this album include "Blue Rondo à la Turk" and "Three to Get Ready." It's essential for all jazz collections. — *Scott Yanow*

Real Ambassadors / Sep. 1961-Dec. 1961 / Columbia ✦✦✦✦
In 1961 Dave Brubeck put together a remarkable musical show. Using the talents of Louis Armstrong and his All-Stars, Carmen McRae, the innovative bop vocal group Lambert, Hendricks, and Ross, and his own rhythm section, Brubeck and his wife, lyricist Iola, wrote a largely upbeat play full of anti-racism songs and tunes that celebrated human understanding. Although it had only one live performance (at the 1962 Monterey Jazz Festival), *The Real Ambassadors* was recorded for posterity and now, with its reissue on CD, the original 15 selections have been augmented by five more. It is important to listen to this music without prior expectations because Paul Desmond is nowhere to be found, Louis Armstrong does not play that much trumpet here, and Lambert, Hendricks, and Ross essentially function as background singers. However, Satch and Carmen McRae make for a very potent team, and there are many touching and surprising moments. — *Scott Yanow*

● **Live at the Berlin Philharmonie** / Nov. 7, 1970 / Columbia/Legacy ✦✦✦✦
Out of the 13 selections included on this double CD, six were originally released just in Europe, two ("Out of Nowhere" and "Mexican Jumping Bean") were never out before, and only five songs were on the American LP. Considering how inspired the Dave Brubeck Quartet sounds, it is surprising that the music has been so obscure for so long. Baritonist Gerry Mulligan is particularly heated on the opening two numbers (the unreleased tracks!), pianist Dave Brubeck really stretches himself (check him out on "Things Ain't What They Used to Be," where he progresses from stride to free), and bassist Jack Six and drummer Alan Dawson, in addition to their solo space, are quite alert and constantly pushing the lead voices. Not only are the musicians in top form, but the audience is very enthusiastic, demanding three encores. The extensive liner notes by Geoffrey Smith are also a major plus. Highly recommended. — *Scott Yanow*

Marian McPartland's Piano Jazz with Guest Dave Brubeck / Mar. 1984 / Jazz Alliance ✦✦✦

Blue Rondo / Nov. 1986 / Concord Jazz ✦✦✦✦
The 1987 edition of the Brubeck Quartet featured pianist Brubeck, his son Chris on electric bass and bass trombone, clarinetist Bill Smith, and drummer Randy Jones. In addition to remakes of "Blue Rondo a la Turk," "Strange Meadowlark," and "Swing Bells," the leader contributed six new originals, including "I See, Satie" and a tribute to Dizzy Gillespie and Stan Getz called "Dizzy's Dream." Bill Smith, who uses electronics with taste on his clarinet during a few songs, has long been a major asset to the later Brubeck Quartets. This is one of their better Concord CDs. — *Scott Yanow*

Moscow Nights / Mar. 1987 / Concord Jazz ✦✦✦✦
Nightshift / Oct. 5, 1993-Oct. 10, 1993 / Telarc ✦✦✦✦
Just You Just Me / 1994 / Telarc ✦✦✦

Ray Bryant (Raphael Bryant)

b. Dec. 24, 1931, Philadelphia, PA
Piano / Bop, Swing, Soul-Jazz, Groove
Although he could always play bop, Ray Bryant's playing combines together older elements (including blues, boogie-woogie, gospel, and even stride) into a distinctive, soulful, and swinging style; no one plays "After Hours" quite like him. The younger brother of bassist Tommy Bryant and the uncle of Kevin and Robin Eubanks (his sister is their mother), Bryant started his career playing with Tiny Grimes in the late '40s. He became the house pianist at the Blue Note in Philadelphia in 1953, where he backed classic jazz greats (including Charlie Parker, Miles Davis, and Lester Young) and made important contacts. He accompanied Carmen McRae (1956-57), recorded with Coleman Hawkins and Roy Eldridge at the 1957 Newport Jazz Festival (taking a brilliant solo on an exciting version of "I Can't Believe That You're in Love with Me"), and played with Jo Jones' trio (1958). Bryant settled in New York in 1959, played with Sonny Rollins, Charlie Shavers, and Curtis Fuller, and soon had his own trio. He had a few funky commercial hits (including "Little Susie" and "Cubano Chant") which kept him working for decades. Bryant has recorded often throughout his career (most notably for Epic, Prestige, Columbia, Sue, Cadet, Atlantic, Pablo, and EmArcy), and even his dates on electric piano in the '70s are generally rewarding. However, Ray Bryant is heard at his best when playing the blues on unaccompanied acoustic piano. — *Scott Yanow*

Ray Bryant Trio / 1957 / Original Jazz Classics ✦✦✦
Con Alma / Nov. 25, 1960-Jan. 26, 1961 / Columbia ✦✦✦
Alone at Montreux / Jul. 1972 / Atlantic ✦✦✦✦
Ray Bryant has long been a well rounded and versatile yet distinctive pianist. His style, modern compared to the swing and stride players but traditional when matched against the boppers, is flexible enough to fit into many settings. This solo outing finds Bryant playing swing standards, blues, soulful versions of a couple of current pop tunes and even a bit of boogie. This LP's only fault is that it is out of print. — *Scott Yanow*

Here's Ray Bryant / Jan. 10-12, 1976 / Original Jazz Classics ✦✦✦
● **Montreux '77** / Jul. 13, 1977 / Original Jazz Classics ✦✦✦✦
Plays Basie and Ellington / Feb. 15, 1987-Feb. 16, 1987 / EmArcy ✦✦✦
Golden Earrings / Jan. 23, 1988-Jun. 26, 1988 / EmArcy ✦✦✦
All Mine . . . and Yours / Oct. 19, 1989-Oct. 20, 1989 / EmArcy ✦✦✦

Rusty Bryant

b. Nov. 29, 1929, Huntington, WV, **d.** Mar. 91, 1991
Sax (Tenor) / Soul-Jazz, Post-Bop, Groove
Among the finest funky and soul-jazz tenors of the '70s, Bryant is noted for his thick tone, robust sound, and jam-session-style albums. Rusty Bryant was one of the original bar-walking sax players. Royal G. "Rusty " Bryant was born on November 25, 1929, in Huntington, WV, but was raised in Columbus, OH. He credits Gene Ammons and Sonny Stitt as his main influences. He played with and learned from Tiny Grimes and Stomp Gordon, and was leading his own groups by 1951. Bryant toured with Hammond organist Mike Marr during the '60s. He settled in Columbus, OH. — *Michael Erlewine & Ron Wynn*

Rusty Bryant Returns / Feb. 17, 1969 / Original Jazz Classics ✦✦✦
★ **Soul Liberation** / Aug. 1970 / Prestige ✦✦✦✦✦
Soul-jazz classic. His most popular composition. — *Ron Wynn*

Milt Buckner

b. Jul. 10, 1915, St. Louis, MO, **d.** Jul. 27, 1977, Chicago, IL
Organ, Piano / Swing, Groove
Milt Buckner had a dual career. As a pianist he largely invented the "locked hands" style (parallel chords) that was adopted by many other players including George Shearing and Oscar Peterson. And as an organist he was one of the top pre-Jimmy Smith stylists, helping to popularize the instrument. The younger brother of altoist Ted Buckner (who played with Jimmie Lunceford), Milt Buckner grew up in Detroit and gigged locally in addition to arranging for McKinney's Cotton Pickers in 1934. He came to fame as pianist and arranger with Lionel Hampton (1941-48, 1950-52, and occasionally in later years), where he was a crowd pleaser. During 1948-50 Buckner led his own bands, and after 1952 he generally played organ with trios or quartets. In later years he sometimes teamed up with Illinois Jacquet or Jo Jones. Buckner recorded many dates as a leader, particularly for Black & Blue in the '70s. — *Scott Yanow*

★ **Rockin' Hammond** / Feb. 22, 1956-Mar. 15, 1956 / Capitol ✦✦✦✦✦
Classic organ combo with a master. From blues to ballads. A fine representation of Buckner's brilliance. — *Michael G. Nastos*

Midnight Slows, Vol. 3 / Aug. 1, 1973 / Black & Blue ✦✦✦

● **Green Onions** / Feb. 21, 1975 / Inner City ✦✦✦✦
With French rhythm section, guitarist Roy Gaines, drummer Panama Francis. Funky and groove-laden. —*Michael G. Nastos*

Jane Bunnett

b. 1955, Toronto, Canada
Flute, Sax (Soprano) / Post-Bop
One of the finest soprano saxophonists in jazz of the '90s, Jane Bunnett originally studied classical piano, but tendonitis cut short that career. After seeing the Charles Mingus group in San Francisco, Bunnett was inspired to play advanced jazz. On soprano she recalls Steve Lacy a bit (whom she has studied with), while her flute playing is quite distinctive. Bunnett has always had major players on her records; in addition to her husband, trumpeter Larry Cramer, the late pianist Don Pullen had been a fixture on her records, her 1988 debut for Dark Light also featured Dewey Redman, and she has utilized Sheila Jordan and Jeanne Lee.
Bunnett has recorded for Dark Light, Music & Arts (a series of duets with Pullen), and Denon. Her most adventurous work thus far is 1991's *Spirits of Havana*, which matches her playing with many of Cuba's top jazz musicians in Cuba. In recent years Jane Bunnett has been living in Paris. —*Scott Yanow*

In Dew Time / Feb. 1988 / Dark Light ✦✦✦✦

New York Duets / 1989 / Music & Arts ✦✦✦

Live at Sweet Basil / 1990 / Denon ✦✦✦

★ **Spirits of Havana** / Sep. 27, 1991-Oct. 4, 1991 / Denon ✦✦✦✦✦
Bunnett, a Canadian musician, went to Havana in 1991 and recorded there with a wealth of Cuban talent. (Canada has full relations with Cuba so, unlike US musicians, she can do this.) Singer Mercedita Valdes appears, as does her husband, percussionist Guillermo Barretto (who died a few months after this album was recorded). You certainly couldn't hire a better crew of pianists—Gonzalo Rubalcaba, Hilario Duran (of Perspectiva), and 72-year-old Frank Emilio. —*Ned Sublette*

Water Is Wide / Aug. 18, 1993-Aug. 19, 1993 / Evidence ✦✦✦✦
This intriguing set has more than its share of variety. Jane Bunnett pays tribute to Rahsaan Roland Kirk with some speechlike flute on "Serenade to a Cuckoo," recalls Steve Lacy a bit with her soprano on two Thelonious Monk pieces ("Pannonica" and "Brake's Sake"), and her originals (along with those of trumpeter Larry Cramer) range from advanced bop to fairly free improvising. Vocalists Sheila Jordan (wonderful on "You Must Believe in Spring") and Jeanne Lee have individual features and are both major parts of the ancient hymn "The Water Is Wide" while the rhythm section (pianist Don Pullen, bassist Kieran Overs, and drummer Billy Hart) consistently displays flexibility and creative reactions to the directions of the lead voices. —*Scott Yanow*

Rendez-Vous / 1995 / Justin Time ✦✦✦

Dave Burrell (Herman Davis Burrell)

b. Sep. 10, 1940, Middletown, OH
Piano / Avant-Garde
A heavily percussive, rhythmic pianist, Dave Burrell has adeptly merged African and Caribbean influences into his compositions and playing style. His solos are often aggressive, sparse and animated, though he's also effective on ballads and standards, and is a steady accompanist and bandleader. Burrell's mother was a vocalist, and helped generate an early interest in jazz. He attended the University of Hawaii in the late '50s and early '60s, and graduated from Berklee in the mid-'60s. Burrell worked in Boston with Tony Williams and Sam Rivers, then moved to New York. He played with Grachan Moncur, III, and Marion Brown, before forming the Untraditional Jazz Improvisational Team with Byard Lancaster. This group included Sirone and Bobby Kapp. In addition, Burrell helped initate the 360 Degree Music Experience with Moncur and Beaver Harris in 1968. He served as a music instructor for Harlem's Community Thing Organization and appeared at the 1969 Pan African Festival in Algiers. Burrell worked and recorded with Pharoah Sanders, Alan Silva, Sunny Murray, Harris and particularly Archie Shepp. Burrell wrote a jazz opera, "Windward Passages," in the late '70s. He continued recording and playing both solo dates and with such musicians as David Murray, Hamiet Bluiett, and Cecil McBee. Burrell has recorded for Black Saint, Victor, Denon, Hat Hut, Douglas, Gazell, and BYG. He has a few sessions available on CD. —*Ron Wynn*

● **Windward Passages** / Sep. 13, 1979 / Hat Hut ✦✦✦✦

Daybreak / Mar. 30, 1989 / Gazell ✦✦✦

Kenny Burrell (Kenneth Earl Burrell)

b. Jul. 31, 1931, Detroit, MI
Guitar / Bop, Groove
Kenny Burrell has been a very consistent guitarist throughout his career. Cool-toned and playing in an unchanging style based in bop, Burrell has

always been the epitome of good taste and solid swing. Duke Ellington's favorite guitarist (though he never actually recorded with him), Burrell started playing guitar when he was 12, and he debuted on records with Dizzy Gillespie in 1951. Part of the fertile Detroit jazz scene of the early '50s, Burrell moved to New York in 1956. Highly in demand from the start, Burrell has appeared on a countless number of records during the past 40 years as a leader and as a sideman. Among his more notable associations have been dates with Stan Getz, Billie Holiday, Milt Jackson, John Coltrane, Gil Evans, Sonny Rollins, Quincy Jones, Stanley Turrentine, and Jimmy Smith. Starting in the early '70s Burrell began leading seminars and teaching, often focusing on Duke Ellington's music. He toured with the Phillip Morris Superband during 1985-86 and has led three-guitar quintets, but generally Kenny Burrell plays at the head of a trio/quartet. —*Scott Yanow*

Introducing Kenny Burrell / May 29, 1956 / Blue Note ✦✦✦

For Charlie Christian & Benny Goodman / Dec. 15, 1956-Mar. 28, 1967 / Verve ✦✦✦

Monday Stroll / Dec. 17, 1956+Jan. 5, 1957 / Savoy ✦✦✦

All Night Long / Dec. 28, 1956 / Original Jazz Classics ✦✦✦✦
Two of guitarist Kenny Burrell's best sessions from the '50s were this release (reissued on CD in the OJC series) and its companion *All Day Long*. Burrell is teamed with an impressive group of young all-stars, including trumpeter Donald Byrd, tenor saxophonist Hank Mobley, Jerome Richardson on flute and tenor, pianist Mal Waldron, bassist Doug Watkins, and drummer Art Taylor. In addition to the lengthy "All Night Long" and three group originals (two by Mobley and one from Waldron), the LP program has been augmented by a medley of "Body and Soul" and "Tune Up" from the same session. Jam sessions such as this one are only as good as the solos; fortunately, all of the musicians sound quite inspired, making this an easily recommended set. —*Scott Yanow*

All Day Long / Dec. 28, 1956+Jan. 4, 1957 / Original Jazz Classics ✦✦✦✦
For this CD reissue, "C.P.W." has been added to the original LP program. Guitarist Kenny Burrell and the young all-stars (trumpeter Donald Byrd, Frank Foster on tenor, pianist Tommy Flanagan, bassist Doug Watkins, and drummer Art Taylor) sound fine on the four group compositions, but the 18-minute blues "All Day Long" is easily the most memorable selection. Well worth picking up, as is *All Night Long*, which was recorded a week earlier. —*Scott Yanow*

Blue Moods / Feb. 1, 1957 / Prestige ✦✦✦✦
Smooth, cool, yet musically impressive late-'50s date that has both blowing session fervor and soulful undergirding. Burrell's fluid guitar voicings and Cecil Payne's robust baritone make nice partners, while Tommy Flanagan adds his usual sparkling piano riffs and solos, and bassist Doug Watkins teams with Elvin Jones, who shows he can drive a date without dominating things on drums. —*Ron Wynn*

Kenny Burrell / Feb. 1, 1957 / Prestige ✦✦✦
His first Prestige recording (in NYC) with an all-Detroit crew (plus baritone sax) in New York. Burrell as we love him—clear, bluesy, with a touch of funk. —*Michael Erlewine*

Kenny Burrell, Vol. 2 / Feb. 1, 1957 / Original Jazz Classics ✦✦✦
Guitarist Kenny Burrell, 25 at the time, is heard during one of his earlier sessions playing in his already recognizable straightahead style with a quintet that also features the underrated baritonist Cecil Payne, pianist Tommy Flanagan, bassist Doug Watkins, and drummer Elvin Jones. This CD reissue of the original LP is a bit brief in time (just over 36 minutes) but contains plenty of fine swinging on tunes such as "Don't Cry Baby," "Drum Boogie," "All of You" and Bud Powell's "Strictly Confidential." It's easily enjoyable music. —*Scott Yanow*

K.B. Blues / Feb. 10, 1957 / Blue Note ✦✦✦
Worth searching for. Burrell with funky pianist Horace Silver and Hank Mobley on tenor sax. As you might guess, the tunes are mostly blues. —*Michael Erlewine*

Two Guitars / Mar. 5, 1957 / Original Jazz Classics ✦✦✦

Kenny Burrell & John Coltrane / Mar. 7, 1958 / Prestige ✦✦✦✦
John Coltrane recorded many interesting jam-session-type dates in the '50s. This matchup with guitarist Kenny Burrell (in a quintet with pianist Tommy Flanagan, bassist Paul Chambers, and drummer Jimmy Cobb) finds the group stretching out on two Flanagan compositions: Burrell's "Lyresto" and the standard "I Never Knew." In addition, Coltrane and Burrell play a short duet on "Why Was I Born." Overall the music is excellent for the time period, with Coltrane displaying some of his "sheets of sound" and Burrell sounding happy with 'Trane's presence. It was formerly available as the first half of a two-LP set, *Kenny Burrell/John Coltrane*. —*Scott Yanow*

Blue Lights, Vol. 1 / May 14, 1958 / Blue Note ✦✦✦✦
On the first of two CD reissues, guitarist Kenny Burrell leads a strong jam session that features the talented but very underrated trumpeter Louis Smith (who sounds a bit like Lee Morgan), the similar but contrasting tenors of Junior Cook and Tina Brooks, pianist Duke Jordan, bassist Sam Jones, and drummer Art Blakey. Jordan's tongue-in-cheek "Scotch Blues"

and "I Never Knew" (the latter was not on the original LP) are among the high points of this easily enjoyable straightahead session. —*Scott Yanow*

Blue Lights, Vol. 2 / May 14, 1958 / Blue Note ✦✦✦✦
The second of two CD reissues of a jam session led by guitarist Kenny Burrell features the talented if forgotten trumpeter Louis Smith, both Junior Cook and Tina Brooks on tenors, pianist Bobby Timmons (Duke Jordan was on the first volume), bassist Sam Jones, and drummer Art Blakey. The all-star group performs two standards ("Caravan" and the guitarist's feature on "Autumn in New York"), Sam Jones' "Chuckin'," and Burrell's "Rock Salt." This is excellent music that easily fits into the bop mainstream of the period. —*Scott Yanow*

Moonglow / Nov. 7, 1958-Sep. 14, 1962 / Prestige ✦✦

On View at the Five Spot Cafe / Aug. 26, 1959 / Blue Note ✦✦✦

A Night at the Vanguard / Sep. 16, 1959-Sep. 17, 1959 / Chess ✦✦✦

Bluesy Burrell / Sep. 14, 1962 / Prestige ✦✦✦

● **Midnight Blue** / Jan. 6, 1963 / Blue Note ✦✦✦✦
This album was one of guitarist Kenny Burrell's best-known sessions for the Blue Note label, although it has yet to be reissued on CD. Burrell is matched with tenor saxophonist Stanley Turrentine, bassist Major Holley, drummer Bill English, and Ray Barretto on conga for a blues-oriented date highlighted by "Chitlins con Carne," "Midnight Blue," "Saturday Night Blues," and the lone standard "Gee Baby Ain't I Good to You." —*Scott Yanow*

Crash! / Feb. 26, 1963 / Prestige ✦✦✦

Freedom / Mar. 27, 1963 / Blue Note ✦✦✦✦
A date with the Kenny Burrell Sextet that includes Stanley Turrentine (sax), Herbie Hancock (p), Ben Tucker (b), Bill English (d), and Ray Barrett (cga). A funky blues set. —*Michael Erlewine*

Blue Bash / Jul. 16, 1963 / Verve ✦✦✦
Groove great Kenny Burrell and Jimmy Smith (Hammond organ) together on the same album. Includes a rendition of "Fever." —*Michael Erlewine*

Soul Call / Apr. 7, 1964 / Original Jazz Classics ✦✦✦

Guitar Forms / Dec. 4, 1964-Apr. 12, 1965 / Verve ✦✦✦✦
This LP is a near-classic, matching guitarist Kenny Burrell (who is heard at his most versatile) with the Gil Evans Orchestra. Actually, three numbers are performed by a quintet (with pianist Roger Kellaway), and Gershwin's "Prelude No.2" is taken solo, but the five numbers, which range from bossa novas to classical and ballads, feature Burrell matched by a 13-piece band playing Gil Evans arrangements. Although Burrell is the only soloist throughout the set, there is plenty of variety. This is considered one of Kenny Burrell's finest recordings of the '60s. —*Scott Yanow*

Sylvia Is! / 1965 / Fantasy ✦✦✦

A Generation Ago Today / Dec. 15, 1966-Mar. 28, 1967 / Verve ✦✦✦

★ **Ellington Is Forever, Vol. 1** / Feb. 4, 1975-Feb. 5, 1975 / Fantasy ✦✦✦✦✦
This two-CD set is a splendid and well conceived tribute to Duke Ellington by guitarist Kenny Burrell. In a variety of settings, he utilizes such special players as trumpeters Thad Jones, Snooky Young, and Jon Faddis, tenors Joe Henderson and Jerome Richardson, organist Jimmy Smith, and a fine rhythm section headed by pianist Jimmy Jones. Ernie Andrews has two vocals, all of the horn players get their chances to solo, and 15 Ellington and Strayhorn songs receive tasteful yet inventive treatments. It's recommended along with the second volume. —*Scott Yanow*

★ **Ellington Is Forever, Vol. 2** / 1977 / Fantasy ✦✦✦✦✦
The second two-CD set to result from guitarist Kenny Burrell's marathon tribute to Duke Ellington is even wider ranging than the first. In addition to such stars as guitarist Burrell, trumpeters Snooky Young and Thad Jones, tenors Joe Henderson and Jerome Richardson, organist Jimmy Smith, pianist Jimmy Jones, and singer Ernie Andrews, this release has solo space for cornetist Nat Adderley, trombonist Quentin Jackson, altoist Gary Bartz, and pianist Roland Hanna. By varying the personnel and instrumentation from track to track, Kenny Burrell pays homage in a memorable fashion to 15 classic songs by Ellington and Strayhorn. It comes recommended, as does the first volume. —*Scott Yanow*

Live at the Village Vanguard / Dec. 15, 1978 / Muse ✦✦✦
Trio date at the famed Village Vanguard, with Burrell backed by bassist Larry Gales and drummer Sherman Ferguson. The location and live context combine to make this a more exuberant session than many Burrell cut in the '70s. His playing has more fire, and he takes longer solos and puts more fervor behind them. —*Ron Wynn*

Listen to the Dawn / Dec. 9, 1980-Dec. 12, 1980 / Muse ✦✦✦

Togethering / Apr. 5, 1984-Apr. 23, 1984 / Blue Note ✦✦

Pieces of Blue and the Blues / Oct. 24, 1986-Oct. 25, 1986 / Blue Note ✦✦✦

Guiding Spirit / Aug. 4, 1989-Aug. 5, 1989 / Contemporary ✦✦✦✦
This "live at the Village Vanguard" CD has a combination that works: guitarist Kenny Burrell, vibist Jay Hoggard, bassist Marcus McLaurine, and drummer Yoron Israel. Burrell and Hoggard blend together quite well, and

the superior tunes they picked for this date (including two from Duke Ellington, Mal Waldron's "Soul Eyes," John Coltrane's "Moment's Notice," and Hoggard's title cut) challenge the soloists. This strong straightahead outing is one of Kenny Burrell's better sets from the past decade. —*Scott Yanow*

Sunup to Sundown / Jun. 10, 1991-Jun. 12, 1991 / Contemporary ✦✦✦
Guitarist Kenny Burrell has a strong all-around showcase on this release from Contemporary. Assisted by pianist Cedar Walton, bassist Rufus Reid, drummer Lewis Nash, and percussionist Ray Mantilla, Burrell swings harder than he usually does when paying tribute to the past, coming up with fresh statements on the varied material. Although there are a few standards in the program (such as "I'm Old Fashioned," "Autumn Leaves," and "Speak Low"), there are also such obscurities as "Out There" (a medium-uptempo blues), "Sunup to Sundown," and "Love Dance." This set serves as an excellent introduction to Kenny Burrell's enjoyable brand of straightahead playing. —*Scott Yanow*

Gary Burton

b. Jan. 23, 1943, Anderson, IN
Vibes / Post-Bop, Early Fusion
One of the two great vibraphonists to emerge in the '60s (along with Bobby Hutcherson), Gary Burton's remarkable four-mallet technique (best displayed on an unaccompanied version of "No More Blues" from 1971) can make him sound like two or three players at once. He has recorded in a wide variety of settings and always sounds distinctive. Self-taught on vibes, Burton made his recording debut with country guitarist Hank Garland when he was 17, started recording regularly for RCA in 1961 and toured with George Shearing's Quintet in 1963. He gained some fame while with Stan Getz's pianoless quartet during 1964-66 and then put together his own groups. In 1967 with guitarist Larry Coryell, he led one of the early "fusion" bands; Coryell would later be succeeded by Sam Brown, Mick Goodrick, John Scofield, Jerry Hahn, and Pat Metheny. Burton recorded duet sets with Chick Corea (they also toured extensively), Ralph Towner, Steve Swallow, and Paul Bley and collaborated on an album apiece with Stephane Grappelli and Keith Jarrett. Among his sidemen in the late '70s/'80s were Makoto Ozone, Tiger Okoshi, and Tommy Smith. Very active as an educator at Berklee since joining its faculty in 1971, Burton (who teamed up with Eddie Daniels in the early '90s for an interesting Benny Goodman/Lionel Hampton tribute tour and recording) has remained a prominent stylist up until the present time. He recorded during different periods of his career for RCA, Atlantic, ECM, and GRP. —*Scott Yanow*

3 in Jazz / Feb. 14, 1963 / RCA ✦✦✦✦

● **Artist's Choice** / Aug. 15, 1963-Aug. 16, 1967 / Bluebird ✦✦✦✦
This session traces vibist Gary Burton's musical evolution with selections taken from eight of Burton's 13 RCA LPs. Burton was among the very first to incorporate elements of rock, pop, and freer forms of jazz into his own music without trivializing any of the styles. *Artist's Choice* is a fine retrospective of the early Gary Burton, although one wishes these sessions were available in full rather than piecemeal. —*Scott Yanow*

Throb / Jun. 2, 1969+Jun. 3, 1969 / Atlantic ✦✦✦

★ **Gary Burton & Keith Jarrett/Throb** / Jun. 2, 1969-Jul. 23, 1970 / Atlantic ✦✦✦✦✦
Two of vibraphonist Gary Burton's albums from 1969-70 and reissued in full on this single CD. Burton teams up with pianist Keith Jarrett for five numbers (including four of Jarrett's originals) in 1970, using a quintet that also features guitarist Sam Brown, bassist Steve Swallow, and drummer Bill Goodwin. The other session has more of an avant-country flavor, with Burton, Swallow, and Goodwin joined by guitarist Jerry Hahn and violinist Richard Greene; Michael Gibbs and Steve Swallow contributed most of the obscurities. Burton was at his most explorative during this period, which is why he can be considered one of the pioneers of fusion (although his music never really fit into a tight category). This is excellent music that mostly still sounds fresh. —*Scott Yanow*

Crystal Silence / Nov. 6, 1972 / ECM ✦✦✦✦
Debut on ECM with Corea (k). The first of many successful pairings of the two. —*Ron Wynn*

Gary Burton and the Berklee All Stars / Jul. 28, 1985 / JVC ✦✦✦✦
This set (reissued in 1995 on CD) was a change of pace for vibraphonist Gary Burton after so many relatively introspective sets for ECM. Burton is featured with an octet that also includes Bill Pierce on tenor, altoist Larry Monroe, and trumpeter Jeff Stout. The music is generally modern hard bop with some real cookers (such as Cedar Walton's "Firm Roots") alternating with solid ballads. Among the highlights are James Williams' jazz waltz "Soulful Bill," John Scofield's playful "Why'd You Do It," and Burton's unaccompanied workout on the thoughtful "Crystal Silence." This mostly straightahead set is not all that essential but does adds to the strong musical legacy of Gary Burton. —*Scott Yanow*

Reunion [with Pat Metheny] / May 6, 1989-May 10, 1989 / GRP ✦✦✦
The leader reunites with his prize student. —*Ron Wynn*

Face to Face / Oct. 31, 1994-Nov. 1, 1994 / GRP ✦✦✦✦

Jaki Byard (John A. Byard, Jr.)

b. Jun. 15, 1922, Worcester, MA
Piano / Bop, Stride, Free Jazz
Possessor of a very eclectic style, Jaki Byard has long been able to play stride, swing, bop, completely free, and funky in addition to being able to imitate closely both Erroll Garner and Dave Brubeck. His playing fit perfectly with Charles Mingus' band in 1964 during their famous European tour with Eric Dolphy, but otherwise he has never been given the recognition he deserved.

As a youth he played piano and trumpet, switched to trombone while in the Army and then (back on piano) gigged with Earl Bostic (1949-50). Byard (also a fine tenor saxophonist) played with the big bands of Herb Pomeroy and Maynard Ferguson (1959-61) and then gigged and recorded with Dolphy, Don Ellis, Booker Ervin, Charlie Mariano, and Mingus (1962-65 and 1970); he also recorded as a leader frequently in the '60s and collaborated with Rahsaan Roland Kirk. Although he has recorded fairly often through the years (including duet albums with Earl Hines and Ran Blake) and headed a big band (the Apollo Stompers), Byard has been mostly active as an educator since the late '60s. *—Scott Yanow*

● **Blues for Smoke** / Dec. 16, 1960 / Candid ✦✦✦✦
An early Byard solo set in which he displays an array of influences, ranging from ragtime and stride to bop and free. *—Ron Wynn*

Here's Jaki / Mar. 14, 1961 / Original Jazz Classics ✦✦✦

Out Front! / Mar. 14, 1961-May 28, 1964 / Original Jazz Classics ✦✦✦

Live! / Apr. 15, 1965 / Prestige ✦✦✦

● **The Jaki Byard Experience** / Sep. 17, 1968 / Prestige ✦✦✦✦
Pianist Jaki Byard and the wondrous Roland Kirk (here switching between tenor, clarinet, and manzello) were two of the few jazz musicians who could play in literally every jazz style, from New Orleans to bop and free form. If only they had recorded a history-of-jazz album. Fortunately, they did meet up on a few occasions, including this brilliant quartet session with bassist Richard Davis and drummer Alan Dawson. They romp on Bud Powell's "Parisian Thoroughfare," Thelonious Monk's "Evidence," "Shine on Me," and "Teach Me Tonight." Byard duets with Davis on his own "Hazy Eve," but best of all is the pianist's duet with Kirk on "Memories of You." This set was also reissued as half of the Roland Kirk two-LP set *Pre-Rahsaan. —Scott Yanow*

Live at Maybeck Recital Hall, Vol. 17 / Sep. 8, 1991 / Concord Jazz ✦✦✦✦
A dynamic, topflight piano soloist and bandleader gets a chance to present his complete package in another superb Maybeck set. Byard employs stride, shuffle, and hard-bop rhythms, playing with a density and controlled force that makes each selection a treasure. *—Ron Wynn*

Don Byas

b. Oct. 21, 1912, Muskogee, OK, **d.** Aug. 24, 1972, Amsterdam, Netherlands
Sax (Tenor) / Bop, Swing
One of the greatest of all tenor players, Don Byas' decision to move permanently to Europe in 1946 has resulted in him being vastly underrated in jazz history books. His knowledge of chords rivalled Coleman Hawkins, and due to their similarity in tones, Byas can be considered an extension of the elder tenor. He played with many top swing bands including those of Lionel Hampton (1935), Buck Clayton (1936), Don Redman, Lucky Millinder, Andy Kirk (1939-40), and most importantly, Count Basie (1941-43). An advanced swing stylist, Byas' playing looked towards bop. He jammed at Minton's Playhouse in the early '40s, appeared on 52nd Street with Dizzy Gillespie and performed a pair of stunning duets with bassist Slam Stewart at a 1944 Town Hall concert. After recording extensively during 1945-46 (often as a leader), Byas went to Europe with Don Redman's band and (with the exception of a 1970 appearance at the Newport Jazz Festival) never came back to the US. He lived in France, the Netherlands, and Denmark, often appeared at festivals, and worked steadily. Whenever American players were touring, they would ask for Byas, who had opportunities to perform with Duke Ellington, Bud Powell, Kenny Clarke, Dizzy Gillespie, Jazz at the Philharmonic (including a recorded tenor battle with Hawkins and Stan Getz), Art Blakey, and (on a 1968 recording) Ben Webster. Byas also recorded often in the '50s but was largely forgotten in the US by the time of his death. *—Scott Yanow*

Don Byas in Paris / Oct. 18, 1946-Jan. 5, 1949 / Prestige ✦✦✦✦
Often explosive blues, ballads, and standards cut in Paris by the great swing tenor saxophonist Don Byas. His huge tone, expressive phrasing, and hard blowing were ideal for this collection that's heavy on standards and includes a sterling rendition of "Body and Soul." The backing band proves capable, if unexciting, keyed by pianist Billy Taylor. *—Ron Wynn*

● **On Blue Star** / 1950-1952 / Verve ✦✦✦✦
Don Byas on Blue Star is a collection of 23 sides cut in Paris between January 1, 1997, and March 1952. The material on this CD is gracious and gen-

erally mellow, and fans of the mainstream tenor of Byas will have good reason to acquire the material. *—Bob Rusch, Cadence*

Anthropology / Jan. 13, 1963 / Black Lion ✦✦✦✦
Don Byas was one of the great tenor saxophonists in jazz history, but due to his decision to move permanently to Europe in 1946, he remains very underrated in the jazz history books. This superlative set (in which he is backed by pianist Bent Axen, bassist Niels Pedersen, and drummer William Schiopffe) finds Byas stretching out in a club on five jazz standards; listen to him tear into "Anthropology" and "Billies' Bounce." It is hard to believe, listening to this heated music, that Byas (who would live until 1972) only would be recorded twice more as a leader. *—Scott Yanow*

A Night in Tunisia / Jan. 13, 1963-Jan. 14, 1963 / Black Lion ✦✦✦✦
Consistent mid-'60s quartet date with Byas' sweeping, majestic tenor again sparkling in standards, ballads, and blues format. He's supported by mostly journeyman pros, with the exception of gifted bassist Niels Henning Orsted-Pedersen, who anchors the rhythm section. *—Ron Wynn*

Walkin' / Jan. 13, 1963-Jan. 14, 1963 / Black Lion ✦✦✦✦
More from a series of mid-'60s sessions done at the Montmarte in Copenhagen. Byas was at his most evocative, playing shopworn anthems and ancient ballads with vigor and conviction. He often soars over the competent but limited rhythm section, although bassist Niels Henning Orsted-Pedersen keeps them from being savaged. *—Ron Wynn*

Charlie Byrd

b. Sep. 16, 1925, Chuckatuck, VA
Guitar / Bop, Brazilian Jazz
Guitarist Charlie Byrd perfected the application of classical guitar techniques to a jazz setting and helped introduce American audiences to Latin American sounds in the early '60s, particularly samba and bossa nova. His style is delightful, attractive, and impressive, reflecting training he received in the '50s from Sophocles Papas and Andres Segovia. Byrd was born into a musical family, and his brother Joe (Gene) studied at the Peabody Conservatory and has worked in his groups since the mid-'60s. Byrd played with Django Reinhardt while in France during World War II. Following his discharge, he worked with Sol Yaged, Joe Marsala, and Freddie Slack. Byrd for a while decided to change fields and become a concert guitarist. He spent half the '50s studying with Papas and Segovia. But he began playing regularly around Washington, DC, and eventually returned to jazz, working and recording with Woody Herman. He began recording as a leader for Savoy in 1957 and did sessions for Riverside, Prestige, Offbeat, Columbia, and Milestone in the '60s. Visits to South America on State Department-sponsored tours led to an interest in Latin sounds. Byrd and Stan Getz made the chart-topping album *Jazz Samba* in 1962. It was Byrd's suggestion that they do some compositions by Antonio Carlos Jobim. Byrd did other Latin dates, working with Keter Betts, Cal Tjader, and Charlie Terry, among others. Along with Barney Kessell and Herb Ellis, Byrd formed the Great Guitars group in the '70s. They made several Concord albums, and Byrd also recorded with Nat Adderley and cut his own sessions on Fantasy. He wrote an instruction manual in 1973 that's become widely used. Byrd made other trio dates, as well as quartet and sextet sessions for Concord in the '70s and '80s, working with Laurindo Almeida and Bud Shank. He recorded with the Washington Guitar Quintet in 1990 for the Concord Concerto label. *—Ron Wynn*

Midnight Guitar / Aug. 4, 1957 / Savoy ✦✦✦

● **Byrd at the Gate** / May 9, 1963+May 10, 1963 / Original Jazz Classics ✦✦✦✦
Byrd at the Gate presented the unique jazz guitar approach of Charlie Byrd and his trio (Keter Betts, bass; Bill Reichenbach, drums) live at the Gate. The program was also joined by the guesting of Clark Terry (trumpet) and/or Sheldon Powell (tenor sax) on five of the tracks. *—Bob Rusch, Cadence*

Great Guitars / Jul. 28, 1974 / Concord Jazz ✦✦✦✦
Charlie Byrd was teamed up with Barney Kessell and Herb Ellis (along with bassist Joe Byrd and drummer John Rae) for this rather exciting concert. While Ellis and Kessel have three unaccompanied duets, the inclusion of Byrd (thought of as a Brazilian specialist rather than a bopper) is the wild card that makes this set a major success. While Byrd is excellent on his features "Charlie's Blues" and "O Barquinho," it is the three stomps featuring all the guitarists ("Undecided," "Topsy," and "Benny's Bugle") that are most memorable. *—Scott Yanow*

The Bossa Nova Years / Apr. 16, 1991-Apr. 17, 1991 / Concord Jazz ✦✦✦✦

The Washington Guitar Quartet / 1992 / Concord Jazz ✦✦✦

Moments like This / Aug. 9, 1994-Aug. 10, 1994 / Concord Jazz ✦✦✦

Donald Byrd (Donaldson Toussaint L'Ouverture Byrd II)

b. Dec. 9, 1932, Detroit, MI
Trumpet / R&B, Hard Bop, Crossover
Donald Byrd has been hailed as a visionary and condemned as a traitor. He's played vigorous hard bop, displayed technical skills that put him at

the top of his generation, and presided over inspirational, superb record sessions. He's also been responsible for hideous, commercially successful, artistically barren releases that by even the most minimal standards didn't qualify as either good jazz or good pop. He's among the most educated musicians around, has worked tirelessly on behalf of music education and African-American culture, yet also been quoted making highly inflammatory, debatable statements. Byrd may be jazz's ultimate loose cannon now that Miles Davis has departed. His '50s solos, with their ringing, assertive lines and wonderfully full tone, can stand with anyone's. What he played on many of his '70s dates qualifies as immediately forgettable. Byrd began his music studies at Wayne State University in the early '50s, but they were halted by military service. He played in an Air Force band, then attended the Manhattan School of Music, where he earned his M.A. in music education. Byrd served as Prestige's main studio trumpeter in the late '50s, while cutting dates for Transition, Savoy, Columbia, Discovery, Blue Note, and Prestige. He co-led a group with Pepper Adams from the late '50s into the early '60s. Byrd remained an active bandleader in the '60s, recording for Bethlehem, then cutting a string of Blue Note dates, mostly combos in vintage hard-bop fashion. At times he'd experiment, as with the mid-'60s *Christo Redentor*, a hymn written and arranged by Duke Pearson. The album included the Coleridge Perkinson Choir. Byrd also studied composition in Europe in 1962 and 1963, and later became an active instructor. He taught at Rutgers, Hampton Institute, Howard, and North Carolina Central. Byrd began changing direction in the '70s. He worked with a 12-member group on *Electric Byrd*, then turned more and more toward fusion, urban contemporary, and instrumental pop. These albums were big sellers; *Black Byrd* was Blue Note's single biggest hit album in 1973. But the barrage of electronics, funk and urban-contemporary arrangements, rigid backbeats, and background vocalists generated enormous controversy. Byrd denounced his critics as "jazz snobs." He earned a law degree from Howard and received his doctorate in 1982 from Columbia. He served as chairman of Black music at Howard and helped turn an unknown student ensemble into a hugely successful pop fusion act called the Blackbyrds. His late '70s and early '80s albums continued in the fusion/urban-contemporary/instrumental-pop vein. Then in the late '80s Byrd returned to the music he'd once championed. He played on a Sonny Rollins session and did an album with Mulgrew Miller and Kenny Garrett. During the '90s he's hedged his bets, cutting jazz material for Landmark and recording with hip-hopper Guru on his rap-jazz project. —*Ron Wynn*

First Flight / Aug. 23, 1955 / Delmark ✦✦✦

Long Green / Sep. 29, 1955 / Savoy ✦✦✦

House of Byrd / Aug. 3, 1956+Nov. 2, 1956 / Prestige ✦✦✦

Byrd in Paris, Vols. 1 & 2 / Oct. 22, 1958 / Polydor ✦✦✦

Byrd in Paris, Vol. 2: Parisian Thoroughfare / Oct. 22, 1958 / Polydor ✦✦✦

Byrd in Hand / May 31, 1959 / Blue Note ✦✦✦

Fuego / Oct. 4, 1959 / Blue Note ✦✦✦
This CD reissue brings back a typically excellent Donald Byrd Blue Note session; virtually all of the trumpeter's most rewarding dates were for that label. Teamed with altoist Jackie McLean, pianist Duke Pearson, bassist Doug Watkins, and drummer Lex Humphries, Byrd plays six of his originals, with the most memorable ones being "Fuego," "Funky Mama," and "Amen." An above-average hard-bop set that still sounds fresh nearly 40 years later. —*Scott Yanow*

Byrd in Flight / Jul. 10, 1960 / Blue Note ✦✦✦✦
Two separate dates are combined on this Blue Note album. Trumpeter Donald Byrd, pianist Duke Pearson, and drummer Lex Humphries are heard in both quintets with either tenorman Hank Mobley or altoist Jackie McLean, and Doug Watkins or Reggie Workman on bass. The consistently strong originals by Pearson and Byrd ("Little Boy Blue" is the lone standard) give this set its own personality and purpose. An excellent example of early '60s hard bop. —*Scott Yanow*

Donald Byrd at the Half Note Cafe, Vol. 1 / Nov. 11, 1960 / Blue Note ✦✦✦✦

Donald Byrd at the Half Note Cafe, Vol. 2 / Nov. 11, 1960 / Blue Note ✦✦✦✦

Has two bonus cuts; good though rather standard early-60s hard bop with Pepper Adams (bar sax) and Duke Pearson (p). —*Ron Wynn*

Chant / Apr. 17, 1961 / Blue Note ✦✦✦✦
Not released until 1979, this excellent quintet session features the always formidable team of trumpeter Donald Byrd and baritonist Pepper Adams. The accompanying rhythm section includes pianist Herbie Hancock shortly before he joined Miles Davis. The repertoire consists of six likable tunes including an uptempo "I'm an Old Cowhand," "That's All," "Sophisticated Lady," two Byrd originals, and Duke Pearson's "Chant." This is superior hard bop from the early '60s. —*Scott Yanow*

The Cat Walk / May 2, 1961 / Blue Note ✦✦✦
Of the many albums shared by trumpeter Donald Byrd and baritonist Pepper Adams, this Blue Note LP is one of the most rewarding. The composi-

tions (three by pianist Duke Pearson, Byrd's "The Cat Walk," and a collaboration by the pair on "Each Time I Think of You" along with Neal Hefti's "Cute") are superior, and the musicians (who also include Pearson, bassist Laymon Jackson, and drummer Philly Joe Jones) sound consistently inspired. High points of this easily enjoyable hard-bop date include Pearson's "Duke's Mixture," his happy "Hello Bright Sunflower," and the complex title cut. —*Scott Yanow*

Free Form / Dec. 11, 1961 / Blue Note ✦✦✦

● **A New Perspective** / Jan. 12, 1963 / Blue Note ✦✦✦✦
This unusual set (reissued on CD by Blue Note) was one of the most successful uses of a gospel choir in a jazz context. Trumpeter Donald Byrd and a septet that also includes tenor saxophonist Hank Mobley, guitarist Kenny Burrell, and pianist Herbie Hancock are joined by an eight-voice choir directed by Coleridge Perkinson. The arrangements by Duke Pearson are masterful, and one song, "Cristo Redentor," became a bit of a hit. This is a memorable effort that is innovative in its own way, a milestone in Donald Byrd's career. —*Scott Yanow*

Up with Donald Byrd / Nov. 3, 1964-Nov. 4, 1964 / Verve ✦✦✦

I'm Tryin' to Get Home / Dec. 17, 1964-Dec. 18, 1964 / Blue Note ✦✦

Mustang! / Jun. 24, 1966 / Blue Note ✦✦✦

Blackjack / Jan. 9, 1967 / Blue Note ✦✦✦

Slow Drag / May 12, 1967 / Blue Note ✦✦✦

The Creeper / Oct. 5, 1967 / Blue Note ✦✦✦

Fancy Free / May 9, 1969-Jun. 6, 1969 / Blue Note ✦✦✦

Kofi / 1969 / Blue Note ✦✦✦

Electric Byrd / May 15, 1970 / Blue Note ✦✦
Pivotal release with Byrd using 12-piece group. Duke Pearson on electric piano. The arrangements and mood are harbingers of Byrd's shift into pop, funk, and R&B. —*Ron Wynn*

Ethiopian Knights / Aug. 25, 1971-Aug. 26, 1971 / Blue Note ✦✦

Black Byrd / Apr. 3, 1972-Apr. 4, 1972 / Blue Note ✦✦✦

Harlem Blues / Sep. 1987 / Landmark ✦✦✦

Getting Down to Business / Oct. 10, 1989-Oct. 12, 1989 / Landmark ✦✦✦

A City Called Heaven / Jan. 17, 1991-Jan. 19, 1991 / Landmark ✦✦✦

George Cables

b. Nov. 14, 1944, New York, NY
Piano / Post-Bop, Hard Bop
Equally skilled as a leader or as a sideman, George Cables has helped to define modern mainstream jazz piano of the '80s and '90s. When he was 18 and at Mannes College, he formed the Jazz Samaritans with Steve Grossman and Billy Cobham. Cables gained recognition during his stints with Art Blakey's Jazz Messengers, Sonny Rollins (both in 1969), Joe Henderson (1969-71), and Freddie Hubbard (1971-76). He was with Dexter Gordon (1976-78) during the tenor's successful return to the US and became known as Art Pepper's favorite pianist (1979-82). In addition to his occasional work with Bebop and Beyond (starting in 1984), Cables has appeared in a countless number of situations through the years and has recorded frequently as a leader, most notably for Contemporary (including the 1979 classic *Cables Vision*), Concord, and SteepleChase. —*Scott Yanow*

● **Cables' Vision** / Dec. 17, 1979-Dec. 19, 1979 / Original Jazz Classics ✦✦✦✦
Strong late '70s release with Cables leading a larger-than-usual group boasting a strong lineup. Freddie Hubbard, Bobby Hutcherson, and Ernie Watts all prove to be fiery, dynamic soloists, while Cables shows the phrasing and pianistic magic that made him Art Pepper's favorite, and the Tony Dumas/Peter Erskine bass and drums duo sparkle behind and underneath the front line. —*Ron Wynn*

Phantom of the City / May 14, 1985-May 15, 1985 / Contemporary ✦✦✦

By George / Feb. 27, 1987 / Contemporary ✦✦✦

At Maybeck / Jan. 9, 1994 / Concord Jazz ✦✦✦

Cab Calloway (Cabell Calloway)

b. Dec. 25, 1907, Rochester, NY, d. Nov. 18, 1994, Delaware
Vocals / Swing
One of the great entertainers, Cab Calloway was a household name by 1932 and never really declined in fame. A talented jazz singer and a superior scatter, Calloway's gyrations and showmanship on stage at the Cotton Club sometimes overshadowed the quality of his always-excellent bands. The younger brother of singer Blanche Calloway (who made some fine records before retiring in the mid-'30s), Cab grew up in Baltimore, attended law school briefly, and then quit to try to make it as a singer and a dancer. For a time he headed the Alabamians, but the band was not strong enough to make it in New York. The Missourians, an excellent group that had previously recorded heated instrumentals but had fallen upon hard

times, worked out much better. Calloway worked in the 1929 revue "Hot Chocolates," started recording in 1930, and in 1931 hit it big with both "Minnie the Moocher" and his regular engagement at the Cotton Club. Calloway was soon (along with Bill Robinson, Ethel Waters, Louis Armstrong, and Duke Ellington) the best-known Black entertainer of the era. He appeared in quite a few movies (including 1943's *Stormy Weather*), and "Minnie the Moocher" was followed by such recordings as "Kicking the Gong Around," "Reefer Man," "Minnie the Moocher's Wedding Day," "You Gotta Hi-De-Ho," "The Hi-De-Ho Miracle Man," and even "Mister Paganini, Swing for Minnie." Among Calloway's sidemen through the years (who received among the highest salaries in the business) were Walter "Foots" Thomas, Bennie Payne, Doc Cheatham, Eddie Barefield, Shad Collins, Cozy Cole, Danny Barker, Milt Hinton, Mario Bauza, Chu Berry, Dizzy Gillespie, Jonah Jones, Tyree Glenn, Panama Francis, and Ike Quebec. His 1942 recording of "Blues in the Night" was a big hit.

With the end of the big-band era, Calloway had to reluctantly break up his orchestra in 1948, although he continued to perform with his Cab Jivers. Since George Gershwin had originally modelled the character "Sportin' Life" in *Porgy and Bess* after Calloway, it was fitting that Cab got to play him in a '50s version. Throughout the rest of his career Calloway made special appearances for fans who never tired of hearing him sing "Minnie the Moocher." —*Scott Yanow*

● **Cab Calloway (1930-1931)** / Jul. 24, 1930-Jun. 17, 1931 / Classics ✦✦✦✦
Calloway is long overdue for a reappraisal. Long put down by some writers as a mere entertainer, he was actually a superior jazz-influenced singer whose vocal abilities were often overshadowed by his showmanship. The ideal way to acquire his best recordings is to get the 11 CDs in Classics' *Complete* series. Not only do these reissues include his hits but some jazz instrumentals and enjoyable obscurities that give one a more well rounded picture of the "Hi-De-Ho Man." This particular Classics CD has his first 24 recordings; from the start his colorful style was already fully formed. It is particularly interesting to hear Calloway performing some material associated with others, especially "Happy Feet" (Paul Whiteman), "The Viper's Drag," and "I'm Crazy 'Bout My Baby" (the latter two with Fats Waller), along with several Duke Ellington hits. Calloway's band in the early days (one of the better Harlem orchestras) had been formerly known as the Missourians and included several fine soloists, particularly trumpeter Lammar Wright and Walter Thomas on tenor and baritone. Highlights include "St. Louis Blues," "Some of These Days," a classic rendition of "St. James Infirmary," "Nobody's Sweetheart," and the original version of "Minnie the Moocher." —*Scott Yanow*

Cab Calloway (1931-1932) / Jul. 9, 1931-Jun. 7, 1932 / Classics ✦✦✦✦
Cab Calloway (1932) / Jun. 7, 1932-Dec. 7, 1932 / Classics ✦✦✦✦
The third of 11 Cab Calloway CDs put out by Classics (which on a whole reissues the master takes of all of the popular singer's recordings from 1930-42) covers a busy six-month period. His big band (which tended to be greatly overshadowed) was actually quite excellent, with good soloists in trumpeter Lammar Wright, clarinetist Eddie Barefield, Walter Thomas on tenor, and pianist Bennie Payne, but of course Calloway was the main star. Highlights of this very enjoyable set include "Old Yazoo," "Reefer Man," "Old Man of the Mountain," "You Gotta Ho-De-Ho," "I've Got the World on a String," the bizarre "Dixie Doorway," "Beale Street Mama," and "The Man from Harlem." Many of the titles on this rewarding release had never been reissued before, making the Classics series a collection worth picking up in a hurry before they disappear. —*Scott Yanow*

Cab Calloway (1932-1934) / Dec. 7, 1932-Sep. 4, 1934 / Classics ✦✦✦✦
Cab Calloway (1934-1937) / Sep. 4, 1934-Mar. 3, 1937 / Classics ✦✦✦✦
Cab Calloway, who first became popular in 1930, retained his popularity (despite a lot of competition) throughout the swing era. On this excellent CD (the fifth of 11 in the European label Classics' *Complete* Calloway series), highlights include "Keep That Hi-De-Hi in Your Soul," "Nagasaki," "Copper Colored Gal," "Frisco Flo," and a crazy "That Man Is Here Again." With fine soloists in trumpeters Lammar Wright and Shad Collins, trombonist Claude Jones, and (by 1936) the great tenor Ben Webster (along with a top-notch rhythm section that includes bassist Milt Hinton), this was a much better swing orchestra than it is generally rated in jazz history books. —*Scott Yanow*

Cab Calloway (1939-1940) / Mar. 28, 1939-Mar. 8, 1940 / Classics ✦✦✦✦
Cab Calloway (1940) / Mar. 8, 1940-Aug. 28, 1940 / Classics ✦✦✦✦
With such soloists as trumpeter Dizzy Gillespie, Chu Berry on tenor, and trombonist Tyree Glenn, along with a rhythm section that includes bassist Milt Hinton and drummer Cozy Cole, this was a particularly strong edition of the Cab Calloway Orchestra. There are six instrumentals among the 22 selections on this Classics CD (the ninth of 11 Calloway *Complete* sets), including Berry's famous version of "Ghost of a Chance" and a spot for Gillespie on "Bye Bye Blues," but nearly every performance has its interesting solos; most of the ones with short spots for Gillespie have rarely been reissued. Cab Calloway, who as usual is the main star, is in spirited form. The other highlights include "Hi-De-Ho Serenade," "Fifteen Minute Intermission," "Papa's in Bed with His Britches On," and "Are You Hep to

the Jive?" It's recommended, as are all of the CDs in this important series. —*Scott Yanow*

1940-41 / Aug. 28, 1940-Jul. 24, 1941 / Classics ✦✦✦✦
Cab Calloway is in superior form throughout this CD (the tenth of 11 Calloway releases from the European Classics label), but it is often the short solos by his sidemen that hold onto one's interest, particularly those of trumpeter Dizzy Gillespie and tenor Chu Berry. By the last ten numbers (including his feature "Jonah Joins the Cab"), trumpeter Jonah Jones had become a member of the powerful band which could rank at the top echelon of swing orchestras. Calloway is also heard near the peak of his powers, and the highlights of this fine set include Benny Carter's "Lonesome Nights" (one of six instrumentals among the 22 numbers), "A Chicken Ain't Nothin' but a Bird," "Ebony Silhouette," "Hep Cat's Love Song," and two versions of "St. James Infirmary." —*Scott Yanow*

Cab Calloway (1941-1942) / Jul. 24, 1941-Jul. 27, 1942 / Classics ✦✦✦✦
★ **Kicking the Gong Around** / ASV/Living Era ✦✦✦✦✦
Cab's naughtier side, with the virtues of substance use imbuing the lyrical text of several tunes included here. If you thought drug songs didn't start until the late '60s in rock music, be prepared for a shock. —*Cub Koda*

Michel Camilo

b. Apr. 4, 1954, Santo Domingo, Dominican Republic
Piano / Latin-Jazz, Hard Bop
An exciting and high-powered virtuoso pianist, Michel Camilo came from a very musical family (with all nine of his uncles being musicians). Originally playing accordion, he switched to piano when he was 16. After moving to New York in 1979, his song "Why Not?" became a hit for the Manhattan Transfer and caught on as a standard, and "Caribe" entered the repertoire of Dizzy Gillespie. Camilo, who worked with Paquito D'Rivera's band for three years (cutting an album with "Why Not" as the title cut), has recorded for Electric Bird (sessions reissued by Evidence) and Columbia and worked as a leader for the past decade. —*Scott Yanow*

Why Not / Feb. 25, 1985-Feb. 27, 1985 / Evidence ✦✦✦
Suntan / Jun. 29, 1986-Jun. 30, 1986 / Evidence ✦✦✦
● **On Fire** / Jun. 20, 1989-Jun. 25, 1989 / Epic ✦✦✦✦
Burning Latin-jazz piano trio. Recommended. —*Michael G. Nastos*
Rendezvous / Jan. 18, 1993-Jan. 20, 1993 / Columbia ✦✦✦
One More Once / May 20, 1994-May 26, 1994 / Sony ✦✦✦✦

Conte and Pete Candoli

b. Jul. 12, 1927, Mishawaka, IN
Trumpet / Bop
Conte and Pete Candoli are both solid players in the cool bop vein, each a trumpeter. Pete Candoli (1927) is the older, and both are good ballad soloists, fine interpreters, and technically accomplished trumpeters with reputations for polished playing with a steady, swinging quality. Pete Candoli played with several swing bands in the '40s, among them Sonny Dunham, Will Bradley, Ray McKinley, Tommy Dorsey, Teddy Powell, Woody Herman, and Boyd Raeburn. He moved to the West Coast in the '50s, and worked with Les Brown and Stan Kenton. He and his brother worked together in the late '50s and early '60s, then Pete Candoli led his own band. He started a nightclub act with his wife, Edie Adams, in the early '70s, with Candoli singing, dancing, playing, and directing the band. The Candoli Brothers played the 1973 Monterey Jazz Festival and appeared and recorded at the 1981 Aurex Festival in Japan with Lionel Hampton. They continued playing together through the '80s.

Besides the band with his brother, Conte Candoli played in the '40s with Woody Herman, Chubby Jackson, Stan Kenton, and Charlie Ventura. He worked in the '50s with Charlie Barnet and Kenton again, before moving to Chicago to head his own group. But he came back to California later in 1954 and played with both his brother's band and Howard Rumsey's Lighthouse All Stars through the end of the '50s. Candoli recorded and played with Terry Gibbs from 1959 to 1962, and recorded with Gerry Mulligan and Sonny Criss during the '60s. He played with Woody Herman at the Monterey Festival and with Kenton's Los Angeles Neophonic Orchestra. Candoli also played regularly with Shelly Manne, worked in the studios on film and television projects, and was in the "Tonight Show" band. During the '70s, he recorded with Frank Strazzeri and Teddy Edwards. Candoli was a member of Supersax in the '70s.

The brothers have worked together into the '90s and have recorded for Dot, Mercury, Crown, and Somerset, among others, as a joint band. Conte Candoli has recorded solo sessions for Bethlehem, Atlantic, and Andex. —*Ron Wynn and Michael Erlewine*

● **Conte Candoli Quartet** / Jun. 1957 / VSOP ✦✦✦✦
Reissued by the V.S.O.P. label, this session features the excellent bop trumpeter Conte Candoli in a quartet with pianist Vince Guaraldi, bassist Monty Budwig, and drummer Stan Levey. In addition to the joy of hearing Candoli so well showcased, this set is recommended because of the interesting repertoire. In addition to "Flamingo," "Diane," and "No Moon at All," one

gets to hear rare selections penned by the likes of Al Cohn, Osie Johnson, Conte's brother Pete Candoli, and the leader himself. *— Scott Yanow*

Judy Carmichael

b. 1952, Lynwood, CA
Piano / Swing, Stride

Judy Carmichael is a real rarity, a pianist that came up since 1950 who specializes in the pre-World War II piano style called stride. Carmichael, who was not even born in 1950, started on piano when her grandfather offered $50 to the first grandchild who could play "Maple Leaf Rag." She played music for the first time professionally when she was 19 and was a ragtime pianist at Disneyland when she discovered stride piano. In 1980 she made her recording debut on Progressive, utilizing four veteran players (including Marshall Royal and Freddie Greene). The following year Carmichael moved to New York and has worked steadily ever since. She recorded more sets for Progressive/Statiras and most recently for her own C&D label. Judy Carmichael plays at the same level as the classic masters. *—Scott Yanow*

Two Handed Stride / Apr. 4, 1980+Apr. 29, 1980 / Statiras ✦✦✦

Jazz Piano / Jun. 11, 1983 / Statiras ✦✦✦✦
Solo piano from a lady who knows this music well. Interprets music from Earl Hines, Fats Waller, James P. Johnson, and the like. She is one of a kind and is a very good player. *—Michael G. Nastos*

Trio / Jan. 6, 1989-Jan. 7, 1989 / C&D ✦✦✦✦
With Michael Hashim (sax), Chris Flory (g). There are 11 cuts without a bass, but based in early piano swing. Fats Waller, James P. Johnson, Ellington, and Basie repertoire featured. *—Michael G. Nastos*

● **Judy** / Sep. 18, 1994-Sep. 19, 1994 / C&D ✦✦✦✦
Although she could certainly recreate the recordings of James P. Johnson and Fats Waller if she wanted to, when the talented pianist Judy Carmichael plays stride it is not as a precious museum piece but rather as a natural part of her musical vocabulary. On this excellent release, she is teamed successfully with electric guitarist Chris Flory, whose solos greatly recall Charlie Christian. Carmichael is in particularly wonderful form on the slower pieces (such as "Gee Baby, Ain't I Good to You?" and "Lazy River"), but she also includes several stomps for variety, making this an easily recommended CD. *— Scott Yanow*

Chops / Oct. 8, 1994 / C&D ✦✦✦✦

Harry Carney

b. Apr. 1, 1910, Boston, MA, d. Oct. 8, 1974, New York, NY
Sax (Baritone) / Swing

Although he was not the first jazz baritone saxophonist, Harry Carney achieved his goal of making the instrument "necessary" in a big band. His tone was huge and definitive, and his style mixed together Coleman Hawkins and Adrian Rollini; he was also one of the first jazz musicians to master circular breathing (which he generally used to hold an endless long note). Early on he played piano, clarinet, and alto before deciding on baritone. Carney joined Duke Ellington's Orchestra when he was 17 in 1927 and remained for over 46 years, passing away in 1974 a few months after Ellington. Although he originally doubled on alto for Duke, added bass clarinet in later years, and traditionally took the clarinet solo on "Rockin' in Rhythm," he otherwise stuck exclusively to baritone. Other than two obscure record dates as a leader, Harry Carney can only be heard on Duke Ellington-associated recordings, but he has many short solos and his presence was always felt in the ensembles. *—Scott Yanow*

● **Moods for Girl and Boy** / Dec. 14, 1954 / Verve ✦✦✦

Benny Carter (Bennett Lester Carter)

b. Aug. 8, 1907, New York, NY
Trumpet, Sax (Alto) / Swing

To say that Benny Carter has had a remarkable and productive career would be an extreme understatement. As an altoist, arranger, composer, bandleader, and occasional trumpeter, Carter has been at the top of his field since at least 1928, and in 1996 Carter is as strong an altoist at the age of 88 as he was in 1936 (when he was merely 28)! His gradually evolving style has not changed much through the decades but neither has it become at all stale or predictable except in its excellence. Although preceded on record by Doc Cheatham and Benny Waters (who are both still active at this writing), Carter has been a major figure in every decade since the '20s, and his consistency and longevity are unprecedented.

Essentially self-taught, Benny Carter started on the trumpet and, after a period on C-melody sax, switched to alto. In 1927 he made his recording debut with Charlie Johnson's Paradise Ten. The following year he had his first big band (working at New York's Arcadia Ballroom) and was contributing arrangements to Fletcher Henderson and even Duke Ellington. Carter was with Henderson during 1930-31, briefly took over McKinney's Cotton Pickers, and then went back to leading his own big band (1932-34). Already at this stage he was considered one of the two

top altoists in jazz (along with Johnny Hodges), a skilled arranger and composer ("Blues in My Heart" was an early hit and would be followed by "When Lights Are Low"), and his trumpet playing was excellent; Carter would also record on tenor, clarinet (an instrument he should have played more), and piano, although his rare vocals show that even he was human!

In 1935 Benny Carter moved to Europe, where in London he was a staff arranger for the BBC dance orchestra (1936-38); he also recorded in several European countries. Carter's "Waltzing the Blues" was one of the very first jazz waltzes. He returned to the US in 1938, led a classy but commercially unsuccessful big band (1939-41), and then headed a sextet. In 1943 he relocated permanently to Los Angeles, appearing in the film *Stormy Weather* (as a trumpeter with Fats Waller) and getting lucrative work writing for the movie studios. He would lead a big band off and on during the next three years (among his sidemen were J.J. Johnson, Miles Davis, and Max Roach) before giving up on that effort. Carter has written for the studios for over 50 years, but he continued recording as an altoist (and all-too-rare trumpeter) during the '40s and '50s, making a few tours with Jazz at the Philharmonic and participating on some of Norman Granz's jam session albums. By the mid-'60s his writing chores led him to hardly playing alto at all, but he made a full "comeback" by the mid-'70s and has maintained a very busy playing and writing schedule even at his advanced age. Even after the rise of such stylists as Charlie Parker, Cannonball Adderley, Eric Dolphy, Ornette Coleman, and David Sanborn (in addition to their many followers), Benny Carter still ranks near the top of active altoists! *—Scott Yanow*

The Chronological Benny Carter (1929-1933) / Sep. 18, 1929-May 19, 1933 / Classics ✦✦✦✦
The European Classics series has been reissuing on CD the complete output of many top jazz artists of the '20s and '30s. Benny Carter's music at last receives the treatment it deserves in this program. His first volume features the great altoist with a pickup group (the Chocolate Dandies) from 1929-30 that showcases sidemen from Fletcher Henderson's Orchestra, with his own orchestra in 1932-33 (three of the five numbers have rare vocals from Carter), and on 11 sides with Spikes Hughes' all-star band, an orchestra that also features trumpeter Red Allen, trombonist Dicky Wells, Wayman Carver on flute, and the tenors of Coleman Hawkins and Chu Berry. This is wonderful and, in many cases, formerly rare music. *—Scott Yanow*

The Chronological Benny Carter (1933-1936) / May 19, 1933-Apr. 1936 / Classics ✦✦✦✦
The second volume of the complete early Benny Carter from the European Classics label features Carter on alto, trumpet, clarinet, and as arranger (in addition to contributing a bit of piano and even a vocal) on three numbers with Spike Hughes' all-star orchestra, as part of the 1933 edition of the Chocolate Dandies (an interracial outfit put together by Mezz Mezzrow), and with his own big band in 1933-34 and in England two years later. Highlights include "Symphony in Riffs," "Blue Lou," and "Everybody Shuffle." *—Scott Yanow*

● **All of Me** / May 7, 1934-Mar. 1959 / Bluebird ✦✦✦✦
A strong sampling of Benny Carter's music is heard in this hodgepodge CD reissue. Twelve of the altoist's 16 Bluebird big-band recordings of 1940-41 (including a previously unissued version of "Ill Wind") precede nine titles gathered from a wide variety of sessions, with one song apiece taken from dates led by Mezz Mezzrow, Willie Bryant, Ethel Waters, Artie Shaw, and Lucky Thompson and four performances reissued from Carter's soundtrack album of his score for the *M Squad* in 1959. Obviously not a set recommended to completists (the European Classics series is much preferred), the high quality of the music ("All of Me" has a classic Carter arrangement) makes this a worthwhile purchase for more casual collectors. *—Scott Yanow*

Cosmopolite: The Oscar Peterson Verve Sessions / Sep. 18, 1952-Nov. 12, 1954 / Verve ✦✦✦✦
These timeless Benny Carter performances match the great altoist with pianist Oscar Peterson, bassist Ray Brown, either Barney Kessel or Herb Ellis on guitar, Buddy Rich, J.C. Heard or Bobby White on drums, and, on four numbers, trombonist Bill Harris. The 17 standards (four of which are also heard in alternate versions) are treated with respect, taste, and swing. Carter always sounds flawless and is in excellent form throughout this easily enjoyable set. *—Scott Yanow*

3, 4, 5: The Verve Small Group Sessions / Mar. 1955 / Verve ✦✦✦✦
Has there ever been a more consistent performer in jazz history over a longer period of time than Benny Carter? The classic altoist, who had fully formed his sound by the early '30s (he first recorded in 1927), has not altered his style much in the past 65 (and counting) years. The music on this Verve reissue CD features Carter in three settings: in a trio with pianist Teddy Wilson and drummer Jo Jones (those performances were only previously out in Japan); heading a quartet with pianist Don Abney, bassist George Duvivier, and drummer Louis Bellson; and showcased on three previously unissued tracks with the Oscar Peterson trio plus drummer Bobby White. Carter knew most of these standards extremely well, and he

glides effortlessly over the chord changes, infusing the music with swing and subtle creativity. —*Scott Yanow*

Jazz Giant / Jul. 22, 1957-Apr. 21, 1958 / Original Jazz Classics ✦✦✦✦
Benny Carter had already been a major jazz musician for nearly 30 years when he recorded this particularly strong septet session for Contemporary. With notable contributions from tenor saxophonist Ben Webster, trombonist Frank Rosolino, and guitarist Barney Kessel, Carter (who plays a bit of trumpet on "How Can You Lose") is in superb form on a set of five standards and two of his originals. This timeless music is beyond the simple categories of "swing" or "bop" and should just be called "classic." —*Scott Yanow*

☆ **Further Definitions** / Nov. 13, 1961-Nov. 15, 1961 / Impulse ✦✦✦✦✦
One of the truly classic sessions and a high point in Benny Carter's career, this set of eight tunes (all arranged by him) boasts quite a lineup of players: Carter and Phil Woods on altos, Coleman Hawkins and Charlie Rouse on tenors, and a strong four-piece rhythm section. These versions of "Honeysuckle Rose" and "Crazy Rhythm" look back to the 1937 recordings of Carter and Hawk with Django Reinhardt and actually hold their own; both renditions are quite exciting. In addition to a wonderful remake of "Body and Soul" (that lets Coleman Hawkins revisit his famous recording), the other ballads ("The Midnight Sun Will Never Set," "Blue Star," and "Cherry") and stomps ("Cotton Tail" and "Doozy") are all memorable in their own way. No serious jazz collection is complete without this very enjoyable recording. —*Scott Yanow*

B.B.B. & Co. / 1962 / Original Jazz Classics ✦✦✦

Live and Well in Japan / Apr. 29, 1977 / Original Jazz Classics ✦✦✦✦

My Man Benny, My Man Phil / Nov. 21, 1989-Nov. 22, 1989 / Music Masters ✦✦✦✦
It is extremely difficult to believe that Benny Carter was 82 years old at the time of this recording, for his strong sound (nothing feeble about his playing) and fertile ideas on alto make him sound as if he were a contemporary of Phil Woods, who was born 24 years later. Together Carter and Woods form a mutual-admiration society which can be heard on "My Man Phil." The repertoire on this CD is particularly inspired (highlighted by "Sultry Serenade," "I'm Just Wild About Harry," and two versions of the atmospheric "Just a Mood"). Carter takes two trumpet solos while, on "We Were in Love," Woods contributes some tasteful clarinet. A special and relaxed but occasionally hard-swinging date, this Music Masters CD is quite enjoyable. —*Scott Yanow*

Harlem Renaissance / Feb. 7, 1992-Feb. 9, 1992 / Music Masters ✦✦✦✦

Legends / Jun. 16, 1992-Jun. 17, 1992 / Music Masters ✦✦✦✦
For once the term "legend" is not being misused. The great altoist Benny Carter (at age 85) is in typically remarkable form with a quartet, on five duets with pianist Hank Jones, and on three selections with the truly remarkable trumpeter Doc Cheatham (who was 87 years old at the time). Whether it be happy jams on "Honeysuckle Rose" and "There Is No Greater Love" or original ballads, there is not a weak track on this classic disc. This set would be recommended even if Carter were 55 rather than 85; the music is timeless and often glorious. —*Scott Yanow*

Songbook / Jun. 26, 1995-Aug. 26, 1995 / Music Masters ✦✦✦✦

Betty Carter (Lorraine Carter)

b. May 16, 1930, Flint, MI
Vocals / Avant-Garde, Bop
A long period of struggling and near-complete obscurity preceded Betty Carter's surprising rise to fame; through it all she never compromised her musical vision. Although she has never cared much for avant-garde jazz, her own interpretations of standards and originals are still as radical (with tonal distortions, a very wide range of tempos, and many unexpected changes of direction) that there is simply no other term to describe her unique music. Carter studied piano and worked as a singer in Detroit in 1946. During 1948-51 she toured with Lionel Hampton (where she was nicknamed Betty "Bebop" Carter). After that association ended she settled in New York, gradually developed her style, and recorded with Gigi Gryce in 1958. Although she recorded a 1961 duet album with Ray Charles that received some attention, it would be quite awhile before she gained much recognition. After doing some records for Roulette, Carter retired for a few years to raise a family. In 1969 she formed a trio and in 1971 organized her own record label Bet-Car. Gradually Betty Carter's innovative singing began to be recognized, and after she signed with Verve in the early '80s, she finally became a household name (and a consistent poll winner) in the jazz world. Carter's singing is not to everyone's taste, but her willingness to take chances is quite admirable, and her ability as a talent scout (her pianists have included John Hicks, Mulgrew Miller, Benny Green, Stephen Scott, and Cyrus Chestnut) is beyond criticism. —*Scott Yanow*

Round Midnight / Aug. 10, 1962-Jan. 15, 1963 / Atco ✦✦✦

At the Village Vanguard / May 1970 / Verve ✦✦✦✦
Betty Carter's remarkable early-'70s LPs were initially available only on her own poorly distributed label. This live date captured Carter when her

voice was its most pliable, her delivery in full bloom, and her range and power at their peak. She could scat with a fury and rhythmic intensity that were almost magical, then turn a slow tune like "The Sun Died" or "Body and Soul" into a showcase by emphasizing key lyrics, subtly changing each stanza, or increasing the pace at an unexpected moment. This deserves full attention, as it represents Betty Carter still evolving and perfecting her matchless technique. —*Ron Wynn*

● **The Audience with Betty Carter** / Dec. 6, 1979-Dec. 8, 1979 / Verve ✦✦✦✦
Definitive two-fer live set with John Hicks Trio. A must-buy. —*Michael G. Nastos*

Look What I Got / 1988 / Verve ✦✦✦✦
This well rounded set gives listeners a good look at the adventurous music of Betty Carter. For this CD, she is joined by one of two rhythm sections (with either Benny Green or Stephen Scott on piano) and, on four of the nine songs, tenor saxophonist Don Braden. Carter twists and turns some familiar songs (such as "The Man I Love," "Imagination," and "The Good Life") along with a variety of lesser-known material, including two songs of her own. Consistently unpredictable (whether scatting or stretching out ballads), Betty Carter's recordings are always quite stimulating. —*Scott Yanow*

It's Not About the Melody / 1992 / Verve ✦✦✦

Feed the Fire / Oct. 30, 1993 / Verve ✦✦✦

John Carter

b. Sep. 24, 1929, Fort Worth, TX, d. Mar. 31, 1991, Inglewood, CA
Clarinet / Avant-Garde
John Carter was a major clarinet innovator, turning the swing-associated instrument into a device for very advanced explorations. His upper-register screeches could be grating, but his solos had a logic all their own, and his five-part suite depicting the history of Blacks in America (released on Black Saint and Gramavision) displayed his compositional talents. Carter taught in the Fort Worth public school system during 1949-61 before switching to Los Angeles (1961-82). He played with Ornette Coleman and Charles Moffett as early as the late '40s, and in LA of the '60s he became one of the leaders of the local scene's avant-garde, originally doubling on clarinet and alto. In 1964 he formed the New Art Jazz Ensemble with cornetist Bobby Bradford, who would be his longtime musical partner. Carter (who by 1974 was playing clarinet exclusively) played with Bradford on a fairly regular basis during the remainder of his life in settings ranging from duets to a larger orchestra. By the '80s with his suite, participation in Clarinet Summit, and formation of the Wind College with James Newton, Red Callender, and Charles Owens, John Carter finally received some long overdue recognition. —*Scott Yanow*

● **West Coast Hot** / Jan. 3, 1969-Apr. 1, 1969 / Novus ✦✦✦✦
This very valuable release documents two important but underrated avant-garde units that were based in Los Angeles. Clarinetist John Carter (here also heard on tenor and alto) and trumpeter Bobby Bradford co-led bands for many years in virtual obscurity. With bassist Tom Williamson and drummer Buzz Freeman, they are both abstract and logical on four originals, with Carter's passionate sounds contrasting, as usual, with Bradford's lyricism. The second half of this disc features Los Angeles' great undiscovered legend, pianist Horace Tapscott. He is heard in superlative form on four tracks (including the 17-minute "The Giant Is Awakened") in a two-bass quintet also co-starring the young altoist Arthur Blythe. Tapscott is still quite active in Los Angeles. When will an enterprising label finally record his working band? —*Scott Yanow*

Dauwhe / Feb. 25, 1982-Mar. 8, 1982 / Black Saint ✦✦✦✦
This recording brought together some of the best of the West (cornetist Bobby Bradford; flutist James Newton; soprano saxophonist, clarinetist, and oboe player Charles Owens; bassist Roberto Miranda; drummer Williams Jeffrey; percussionist/waterphone player Luis Peralta) for a set of five John Carter compositions. The title track was brilliant both in its open construction and in solos executed by the leader, Bradford, and Newton. In fact, this was arguably Newton's most inspired work. —*Bob Rusch*

Castles of Ghana / Feb. 1985 / Gramavision ✦✦✦

Suite of Early American Folk Pieces for Solo Clarinet / Apr. 1985 / Moers ✦✦✦

Fields / Mar. 1988 / Gramavision ✦✦✦

Ron Carter

b. May 4, 1937, Ferndale, MI
Bass, Cello, Piccolo Bass / Post-Bop, Hard Bop
The epitome of class and elegance, though not stuffy, Ron Carter has been a world class bassist and cellist since the '60s. He's among the greatest accompanists of all time but has also done many albums exhibiting his prodigious technique. He's a brilliant rhythmic and melodic player, who uses everything in the bass and cello arsenal: walking lines; thick, full, prominent notes and tones; drones and strumming effects; and melody

snippets. His bowed solos are almost as impressive as those done with his fingers. Carter has been featured in clothing, instrument, and pipe advertisements; he's close to being the bass equivalent of a Duke Ellington in his mix of musical and extra-musical interests. Carter's nearly as accomplished in classical music as jazz and has performed with symphony orchestras all over the world. He's almost exclusively an acoustic player; he did play electric for a short time in the late '60s and early '70s, but hasn't used it in many, many years. Carter began playing cello at 10. But when his family moved from Ferndale, MI, to Detroit, Carter ran into problems with racial stereotypes regarding the cello and switched to bass. He played in the Eastman School's Philharmonic Orchestra and gained his degree in 1959. He moved to New York and played in Chico Hamilton's quintet with Eric Dolphy, while also enrolling at the Manhattan School of Music. Carter earned his master's degree in 1961. After Hamiliton returned to the West Coast in 1960, Carter stayed in New York and played with Dolphy and Don Ellis, cutting his first records with them. He worked with Randy Weston and Thelonious Monk, while playing and recording with Jaki Byard in the early '60s. Carter also toured and recorded with Bobby Timmons' trio, and played with Cannonball Adderley. He joined Art Farmer's group for a short time in 1963, before he was tapped to become a member of Miles Davis' band. Carter remained with Davis until 1968, appearing on every crucial mid-'60s recording and teaming with Herbie Hancock and Tony Williams to craft a new, freer rhythm section sound. The high-profile job led to the reputation that's seen Carter become possibly the most recorded bassist in jazz history. He's been heard on an unprecedented number of recordings; some sources claim 500, others have estimated it to be as many as 1,000. The list of people he's played with is simply too great to be accurately and completely cited. Carter's been a member of the New York Jazz Sextet and New York Jazz Quartet, V.S.O.P. tour, Milestone Jazzstars, and was in one of the groups featured in the film *Round Midnight* in 1986. He's led his own bands at various intervals since 1972, using a second bassist to keep time and establish harmony so he's free to provide solos. Carter even invented his own instrument, a piccolo bass. Carter's also contributed many arrangements and compositions to both his groups and other bands. He's done duo recordings with either Cedar Walton or Jim Hall. Carter's recorded for Embryo/Atlantic, CTI, Milestone, Timeless, EmArcy, Galaxy, Elektra, and Concord. —*Ron Wynn*

● **Where?** / Jun. 20, 1961 / Original Jazz Classics ✦✦✦✦
Essential session with Carter on both bass and cello. Awesome solos by Eric Dolphy (sax)—stunning pieces. With Mal Waldron. —*Ron Wynn*

Uptown Conversation / Oct. 6, 1969 / Atlantic ✦✦✦✦
Arguably his best release. A 1989 reissue of Embryo album that featured some rangy, vibrant Carter solos. —*Ron Wynn*

Blues Farm / Jan. 10, 1973 / Columbia ✦✦✦
One of his best dates as a leader. A good set with Bob James (k), Richard Tee (k), and Hubert Laws (fl)—revealing jazz chops they've seldom shown otherwise. —*Ron Wynn*

All Blues / Oct. 24, 1973 / CTI ✦✦✦✦
One of bassist Ron Carter's better albums as a leader, this CTI LP features a very compact quartet comprised of tenor saxophonist Joe Henderson, pianist Roland Hanna (keyboardist Richard Tee sits in on one number), drummer Billy Cobham, and Carter. All of the music (even the ballad "Will You Still Be Mine?") has a blues feeling, although several are not really blues. However, the quality of the solos is high, and this date lives up to one's expectations. —*Scott Yanow*

Spanish Blue / Nov. 1974 / Columbia ✦✦✦

Pastels / Oct. 18, 1976+Oct. 19, 1976 / Original Jazz Classics ✦✦✦

Piccolo / Mar. 25, 1977-Mar. 26, 1977 / Milestone ✦✦✦✦
This double LP is mostly recommended to lovers of bass solos. With Ron Carter functioning as the main soloist on piccolo bass, only the solos of pianist Kenny Barron offer a bit of contrast. Bassist Buster Williams and drummer Ben Riley, who complete the quartet, are mostly featured in support. These performances, which are well played, are almost all quite long, so listeners who prefer more variety in their music are advised to look elsewhere. —*Scott Yanow*

Third Plane / Jul. 13, 1977 / Original Jazz Classics ✦✦✦

A Song for You / Jun. 1978 / Milestone ✦✦✦
A change of pace session for Carter. He pairs his formidable bass lines and playing against a backdrop of four cellists, outstanding drummer Jack DeJohnette, and at various times pianists Kenny Barron or Leon Pendarvis, guitarist Jay Berliner, and percussionist Ralph McDonald. Things generally work, although sometimes the low energy level and lack of tension threaten to turn this into easy-listening material. —*Ron Wynn*

1 + 3 / Jul. 29, 1978 / Fantasy ✦✦✦
Exactly the kind of impressive, high-level playing and interaction you'd expect from this trio. Pianist Herbie Hancock, bassist Ron Carter, and drummer Tony Williams comprised the rhythm section on many '60s Miles Davis classics; nearly three decades later, they're still in sync with

each other. While it's Carter's session, there's really no leader or followers, just three wonderful musicians fully attuned to each other. —*Ron Wynn*

Parade / Mar. 1979 / Milestone ✦✦✦✦
Bassist Carter heads a sterling mid-sized band with three trumpeters and saxophonists and two trombones, but no bass or drums. He handles the job of being both the primary and secondary rhythm support, while guests Joe Henderson, Jon Faddis, and Frank Wess, among others, provide some standout solos. The ensemble interaction clicks as well. —*Ron Wynn*

Live at Village West / Nov. 1982 / Concord Jazz ✦✦✦
The CD reissue of these duets by bassist Ron Carter and guitarist Jim Hall adds two new selections (one original apiece) to the LP program (which was comprised of eight standards). Hall's harmonically advanced style always brings out the best in Carter, and their quiet but passionate interplay is full of subtle surprises. —*Scott Yanow*

☆ **Telephone** / Aug. 1984 / Concord Jazz ✦✦✦✦✦
A live performance—a concert. Lots of space, and a slow pace. Music to listen to, perhaps a tad too intellectual. Still . . . lovely. —*Michael Erlewine*

Meets Bach / Dec. 15, 1991-Dec. 16, 1991 / Blue Note ✦✦✦

Friends / Dec. 27, 1992-Dec. 29, 1992 / Blue Note ✦✦✦✦

Jazz, My Romance / Jan. 4, 1994-Jan. 5, 1994 / Blue Note ✦✦

Mr. Bow Tie / 1995 / Blue Note ✦✦✦✦
Bassist Ron Carter varies the personnel often enough to keep one's interest throughout this CD. Carter, who contributed six of the ten compositions (which alternate with four familiar standards) takes his share of bass solos but also showcases pianist Gonzalo Rubalcaba (who is pretty restrained throughout) on the opening "Mr. Bow-Tie" and allocates a generous amount of solo space on some selections to trumpeter Edwin Russell (inspired by Miles Davis but possessing his own fire) and Javon Jackson, who often sounds like a close relative of Joe Henderson. Rubalcaba sits out on four of Carter's originals, making the group occasionally a pianoless quartet/quintet (depending on whether percussionist Steve Kroon is present). All of the music is straightahead and the playing is consistently colorful. This is an impressive effort that is easily recommended. —*Scott Yanow*

Serge Chaloff

b. Nov. 24, 1923, Boston, MA, **d.** Jul. 16, 1957, Boston, MA
Sax (Baritone) / Bop
One of the great baritone saxophonists and the first major soloist on that instrument to emerge since Harry Carney (he preceded Gerry Mulligan), Serge Chaloff was a drug addict during his prime years, resulting in broken friendships and lost opportunities. After playing with the orchestras of Boyd Raeburn (1944-45), Georgie Auld (1945-46), and Jimmy Dorsey (1946-47), he found fame as one of the "Four Brothers" with Woody Herman's Second Herd (1947-49). After a stint with Count Basie's octet (1950), Chaloff returned to his native Boston, where he eventually worked on kicking his dangerous habit. Ironically, when he finally got off drugs, Chaloff contracted spinal paralysis, and he played his final recording session (a reunion of the Four Brothers in 1957) seated in a wheelchair. Mosaic's 1993 limited-edition four-CD Serge Chaloff box set has all of his sessions as a leader, and his exciting solos still put him near the top of his field. —*Scott Yanow*

● **The Complete Serge Chaloff Sessions** / Sep. 21, 1946-Mar. 14, 1956 / Mosaic ✦✦✦✦
This is the type of project the Mosaic label does best: releasing the complete output as a leader of a classic jazz musician including obscurities and a couple of fairly well known sessions. Serge Chaloff, one of the top baritone saxophonists in jazz history, is featured as the leader of bop-based small groups on sessions originally out on Dial, Savoy, Futurama, Motif, Storyville, and Capitol. Such sidemen as trumpeters Red Rodney and Herb Pomeroy, tenorman Al Cohn, altoist Charlie Mariano and Boots Mussuli, vibraphonist Terry Gibbs, and pianists Ralph Burns, George Wallington, Dick Twardzik, Russ Freeman, Barbara Carroll, and Sonny Clark have solo space, but it is the somewhat forgotten Chaloff who rightfully is the main focus. A definitive booklet rounds out this essential package. —*Scott Yanow*

Boston 1950 / 1946 / Uptown ✦✦✦✦
The previously unreleased material included on this 1994 CD features the great baritonist Serge Chaloff performing on radio broadcasts from Boston. Most intriguing are four concise duets from 1946 (before Chaloff became famous) with pianist Rollins Griffith. Otherwise Chaloff is heard in 1950 with quartets and quintets which often include pianist Nat Pierce and sometimes trombonists Sonny Truitt or Milt Gold. The recording quality is decent for the period and Chaloff (who at one point is briefly interviewed by a disc jockey) is in excellent form on the boppish material. Highlights include "The Goof and I," "Four Brothers," "Body and Soul," two versions of "Pennies from Heaven," and "Keen and Peachy." —*Scott Yanow*

The Fable of Mable / Jun. 9, 1954+Sep. 3, 1954 / Black Lion ✦✦✦

Joe Chambers

b. Jun. 25, 1942, Stoneacre, VA
Piano, Drums / Avant-Garde, Post-Bop

A steady, reliable player who's worked in hard-bop, big-band, and free groups, Joe Chambers has never attained stardom but enjoys healthy respect within the jazz community, among musicians and critics. He's not flashy or bombastic, but can provide anything from consistent timekeeping to excellent solos, varied rhythms, multiple accents and colors, plus precise interaction within the rhythm section. Chambers worked in the Washington, DC, area for a few years in the late '50s and early '60s before moving to New York in 1963. He worked with Eric Dolphy, Freddie Hubbard, Jimmy Giuffre, Lou Donaldson, and Andrew Hill, then in the mid-'60s and early '70s performed and recorded with Bobby Hutcherson. Chambers also played with Donald Byrd's quintet, Duke Pearson's big band, and Joe Henderson's group, and recorded with Sam Rivers, Chick Corea, Wayne Shorter, and Miroslav Vitous. He was among the originals in M'Boom Re', the percussion ensemble founded by Max Roach in 1970. He played in the '70s with Sonny Rollins, Tommy Flanagan, and Art Farmer, while recording and performing with Charles Mingus and Joe Zawinul. Chambers was in the Super Jazz Trio with Reggie Workman and Flanagan in the late '70s, recorded with Chet Baker in the early '80s, and played with Ray Mantilla's Space Station. Hubbard, Hutcherson, and M'Boom Re have performed Chambers' compositions. They've also been featured on his infrequent albums. Chambers co-led a group with Larry Young in the late '70s, and did albums for Muse and a solo date for Denon. He recorded for Candid in 1992 with Philip Harper, Bob Berg, George Cables, and Santi Debriano. *—Ron Wynn*

The Almoravid / Oct. 8, 1973-Nov. 1, 1973 / Muse ✦✦✦✦
1971 and 1973 recordings for pianist/percussionist. A great album. *—Michael G. Nastos*

Double Exposure / Nov. 16, 1977 / Muse ✦✦✦

● **Phantom of the City** / Mar. 8, 1991-Mar. 9, 1991 / Candid ✦✦✦✦
Drummer Joe Chambers works with an intriguing lineup on this '91 quintet set. Young lion trumpeter Phillip Harper teams with journeyman Bob Berg, who holds his own with the lyrical, energetic Harper. Chambers never hurries or crowds the soloists, and he interacts easily and fully with pianist George Cables and bassist Santi Debriano. *—Ron Wynn*

Paul Chambers

b. Apr. 22, 1935, Pittsburgh, PA, **d.** Jan. 4, 1969, New York, NY
Bass / Hard Bop

One of the top bassists of 1955-65, Paul Chambers was among the first in jazz to take creative bowed solos (other than Slam Stewart who hummed along with his bowing). He grew up in Detroit, where he was part of the fertile local jazz scene. After touring with Paul Quinichette, Chambers went to New York, where he played with the J.J. Johnson-Kai Winding quintet and George Wallington. He spent the bulk of his prime years (1955-63) as a member of the Miles Davis Quintet, participating in virtually all of Davis' classic recordings of the era. When he left, "Mr. P.C." (as John Coltrane called him in one of his originals) worked with the Wynton Kelly Trio (1963-66) and freelanced until his death. Chambers, a consistently inspired accompanist who was an excellent soloist, made many recordings during his brief period, including some with Sonny Rollins, Coltrane, Cannonball Adderley, Donald Byrd, Bud Powell, and Freddie Hubbard in addition to a few as a leader *—Scott Yanow*

● **High Step** / Apr. 20, 1955+Nov. 1955 / Blue Note ✦✦✦✦
Complete all-star sessions from mid-'50s that include John Coltrane contributions. Rare two-record set that was part of mid-'70s Blue Note reissue line. *—Ron Wynn*

Chambers' Music / Apr. 20, 1955-Mar. 1956 / Blue Note ✦✦✦

Whims of Chambers / Sep. 21, 1956 / Blue Note ✦✦✦

★ **Bass on Top** / Jul. 14, 1957 / Blue Note ✦✦✦✦✦
Extraordinary bassist. Highly recommended. A definition for modal-jazz expression. *—Michael G. Nastos*

Go / Feb. 2, 1959-Feb. 3, 1959 / Vee-Jay ✦✦✦

1st Bassman / May 12, 1960 / Vee-Jay ✦✦✦

Teddy Charles (Theodore Charles Cohen)

b. Apr. 13, 1928, Chicopee Falls, MA
Vibes / Cool

Teddy Charles' conception and approach have changed considerably from his early days of working with big bands led by Benny Goodman, Chubby Jackson, Artie Shaw, and Buddy DeFranco. In the '50s, both in his own groups and playing with others, Charles began to play aggressively and try newer things, especially as a producer. He created groups for recordings with three trumpets and a rhythm section or a tenor and two baritones; his '50s solos on vibes were far-reaching and a precursor to the things being done currently by Jay Hoggard or Steve Nelson. Charles was both a dedi-

cated and advanced improviser and a superior composer. He was a regular participant in Charles Mingus' Jazz Composers Workshop in 1954 and 1955, and he wrote such compositions as "Variations on a Theme by Bud" and others featuring unusual arrangements, modality, and polytonality. His 1956 tenet LP has been reissued on CD by Atlantic, as has a 1953 duo effort on Prestige with Shorty Rogers. Charles also has a more recent session on Soul Note and an earlier date on Bethlehem with Zoot Sims (now on Fresh Sound) available on CD. *—Ron Wynn*

Collaboration: West / Aug. 21, 1953+Aug. 31, 1953 / Original Jazz Classics ✦✦✦

Evolution / Aug. 31, 1953+Jan. 6, 1955 / Original Jazz Classics ✦✦✦

Coolin' / Apr. 14, 1957 / Original Jazz Classics ✦✦✦

● **Live at the Verona Jazz Festival (1988)** / Jun. 25, 1988 / Soul Note ✦✦✦✦
Concert date with Harold Danko trio. Highlight is the Mingus composition "Nostalgia in Times Square." *—Michael G. Nastos*

Doc Cheatham (Adolphus Anthony Cheatham)

b. Jun. 13, 1905, Nashville, TN
Trumpet, Vocals / Dixieland, Swing

Doc Cheatham is without question the greatest 90-year-old trumpeter of all time; in fact no brass player over the age of 80 has ever played with his power, range, confidence, and melodic creativity. Most trumpeters fade while in their 60s due to the physical difficulty of their instrument, but Cheatham did not truly find himself as a soloist until he was nearly 70!

Doc Cheatham's career reaches back to the early '20s, when he played in vaudeville theatres backing such travelling singers as Bessie Smith and Clara Smith. He moved to Chicago, recorded with Ma Rainey (on soprano sax!), played with Albert Wynn, subbed for Louis Armstrong (his main idol), and had his own group in 1926. After stints with Wilbur DeParis and Chick Webb, he toured Europe with Sam Wooding. Due to his wide range and pretty tone, Cheatham worked as a nonsoloing first trumpeter with McKinney's Cotton Pickers and Cab Calloway throughout the '30s. He spent time with Teddy Wilson's big band and was with the commercially successful Eddie Heywood Sextet (backing Billie Holiday on some recordings). In the '50s Cheatham alternated between Dixieland (Wilbur DeParis, guest spots with Eddie Condon) and Latin (Perez Prado, Herbie Mann) bands. He was with Benny Goodman during 1966-67, but it was not until the mid-'70s that Cheatham felt truly comfortable as a soloist. Duet sets with pianist Sammy Price launched his new career, and since then he has recorded fairly prolifically, including dates for Sackville, New York Jazz, Parkwood, Stash, GHB, Columbia, and several European labels. Cheatham is also a charming singer whose half-spoken half-sung vocals take nothing away from his chance-taking trumpet flights. *—Scott Yanow*

It's a Good Life / Dec. 6, 1982-Dec. 7, 1982 / Parkwood ✦✦✦✦
The 77-year-old trumpeter proves to be very much in his prime during this excellent session. In fact Cheatham, who is backed by a fine rhythm section led by pianist Chuck Folds, dominates this set, taking melodic but passionate trumpet solos and contributing charming vocals. His versions of "Struttin' with Some Barbecue" and "You're Lucky to Me" are particularly memorable. *—Scott Yanow*

● **The Fabulous** / Nov. 16, 1983-Nov. 17, 1983 / Parkwood ✦✦✦✦
The ageless trumpeter Doc Cheatham (who was 78 years old at the time of this studio session) is remarkable. Most trumpeters fade when they hit their 60s, but he continues to gain in strength, hitting reasonably high notes with confidence and power; his melodic invention also continues to develop. This quartet session with the late pianist Dick Wellstood is one of his finest recordings. Cheatham is in particularly top form on "Deed I Do," "Swing That Music," and "I Double Dare You," but all nine selections (which also feature his charming whispered vocals) are quite enjoyable. *—Scott Yanow*

Dear Doc / Aug. 30, 1988-Aug. 31, 1988 / Orange Blue ✦✦✦✦
An excellent outing, this little-known French CD features the ageless Doc Cheatham when he was a mere 83. Assisted by pianist Kenny Drew, bassist Jimmy Woode, and drummer Idris Muhammad, Cheatham is the main star throughout, displaying a strong range, plenty of power, and ideas that are both creative and melodic, in addition to taking some charming vocals. Highlights include "I Only Have Eyes for You," "Dinah," "I Double Dare You," "Rump Steak Serenade," and "New Orleans." Worth searching for. *—Scott Yanow*

The Eighty-Seven Years of Doc Cheatham / 1993 / Columbia ✦✦✦✦
There has never been a trumpeter in recorded history over the age of 80 on Doc Cheatham's level. Age 87 at the time of this CD, he plays with power, creativity, and confidence on this quartet set of swing standards. He dominates the music with his trumpet solos and quiet but charming vocals, and even with the participation of a strong rhythm section led by pianist Chuck Folds, Cheatham is the obvious star. This historic set is a real gem on several levels and is highly recommended. *—Scott Yanow*

Don Cherry

b. Nov. 18, 1936, Oklahoma City, OK, **d.** Oct. 19, 1995, Malaga, Spain
Flute, Trumpet / Avant-Garde, World, Free Jazz

Don Cherry has been a pivotal free-jazz player/composer/theorist and invigorating, experimental world-music improviser. He's learned several non-Western instruments while studying and incorporating aspects of Asian, traditional Indian, and African sounds into his work. Cherry's trumpet approach reflects the influences of traditional beboppers like Miles Davis, hard-bop greats Fats Navarro and Clifford Brown, and swing veteran Harry Edison. His technique isn't always the most efficient; frequently his rapid-fire solos contain numerous missed or muffed notes. But he's a master at exploring the trumpet and cornet's expressive, voicelike properties; he bends notes, adds slurs and smears, and his twisting solos are tightly constructed and executed regardless of flaws. He can play on the beat, against it, or totally ignore it, and in recent years has tended to bypass preset song forms and bebop chord changes in favor of mantras or extended vamps. Cherry currently plays bamboo flutes, berimbau, and various percussive devices along with his unusual pocket cornet (he calls it a "pocket trumpet"), trumpet, fluegelhorn, and bugle. He played piano in an R&B band with Billy Higgins as a teen, then attracted attention in the late '50s playing with Ornette Coleman, where his "pocket trumpet" and pithy, brittle sound drew almost as much reaction as Coleman's surging solos and concepts. He was featured on Coleman's first seven albums, and accompanied him to New York in 1959. Cherry and Coleman spent the summer of 1959 at the Lenox School of Music, and the Coleman quartet with Charlie Haden and Billy Higgins made a controversial New York debut that autumn. Then Cherry played with Steve Lacy, Sonny Rollins, and John Coltrane in the early '60s, recording with Coltrane. He was in the New York Contemporary Five in 1963 and 1964 with Archie Shepp and John Tchicai, and played in Europe with Albert Ayler. Cherry co-led a quintet with Gato Barbieri in the mid-'60s and did sessions in Europe and America, some of them later released on Blue Note. He did other dates with Pharoah Sanders and in 1969 recorded in Berlin with an octet that included European musicians Albert Mangelsdorff and Arild Andersen, plus Sonny Sharrock. Cherry recorded duets with Edward Blackwell for the BYG label. He taught at Dartmouth in 1970, then was based in Sweden for four years. Cherry traveled through Europe and the Middle East extensively, playing informally while rigorously studying non-Western music styles. He continued a busy recording schedule for mostly European and Japanese labels in the early '70s. Cherry recorded in 1973 with the Jazz Composers Orchestra of America, then in Sweden, before finally doing some dates for a major American company. He cut albums in the mid-'70s for A&M, Atlantic, and Chiaroscuoro, playing with Frank Lowe, Charlie Haden, Billy Higgins, Hamiet Bluiett, and Abdullah Ibrahim, among others. He, Haden, Blackwell, and Dewey Redman recorded in the late '70s for ECM as the quartet Old and New Dreams, and Cherry also recorded with Indian musician Latif Khan. He had a highly publicized collaboration with rock guitarist and vocalist Lou Reed. During the '80s Cherry recorded in the trio Codona with percussionists Colin Walcott and Nana Vasconcelos. He also did another duo session with Blackwell. After Codona disbanded, Cherry formed a new group, Nu, that included Vasconcelos and Carlos Ward. He worked with the more traditional jazz group the Leaders in the mid-'80s. Cherry appeared at the Berlin Jazzfest with Jabbo Smith in 1986, and toured England with Nu in 1987. Mosaic in 1993 issued a fine box set covering Cherry's Blue Note recordings. *—Ron Wynn*

● **The Avant-Garde** / Nov. 29, 1961 / Atlantic ◆◆◆◆
Misleading title, but substantial session that was really Cherry's, though John Coltrane (ts) plays with fire.*—Ron Wynn*

Complete Communion / Dec. 24, 1965 / Blue Note ◆◆◆

The Complete Blue Note Recordings of Don Cherry / Dec. 24, 1965-Nov. 11, 1966 / Mosaic ◆◆◆◆
This limited-edition two-CD set reissues trumpeter Don Cherry's three Blue Note albums: *Complete Communion, Symphony for Improvisers,* and *Where Is Brooklyn.* The avant-garde cornetist is teamed with the tenors of Gato Barbieri and Pharoah Sanders on one album apiece and with both of them on the explosive *Symphony.* All of the music (much of which is performed as continuous medleys) is quite fiery and free and displays Cherry's musical direction during his post-Ornette Coleman and pre-world-music phase. These sessions are not essential but they make for stimulating listening. *—Scott Yanow*

Symphony for Improvisers / Sep. 19, 1966 / Blue Note ◆◆◆

Brooklyn Is Now / Nov. 11, 1966 / Blue Note ◆◆◆

Where Is Brooklyn / Nov. 11, 1966 / Blue Note ◆◆◆

● **Art Deco** / Aug. 27, 1988-Aug. 30, 1988 / A&M ◆◆◆◆

Charlie Christian

b. Jul. 29, 1916, Dallas, TX, **d.** Mar. 2, 1942, New York, NY
Guitar / Bop, Swing
It can be said without exaggeration that virtually every jazz guitarist that

emerged during 1940-65 sounded like a relative of Charlie Christian! The first important electric guitarist, Christian played his instrument with the fluidity, confidence and swing of a saxophonist. Although technically a swing stylist, his musical vocabulary was studied and emulated by the bop players, and when one listens to players ranging from Tiny Grimes, Barney Kessel, and Herb Ellis to Wes Montgomery and George Benson, the dominant influence of Christian is obvious.

Charlie Christian's time in the spotlight was terribly brief. He played locally in Oklahoma and began to utilize an amplified guitar in 1937. John Hammond, the masterful talent scout and producer, heard about Christian (possibly from Mary Lou Williams), was impressed by what he saw, and arranged for the guitarist to travel to Los Angeles in August 1939 and try out with Benny Goodman. Although the clarinetist was initally put off by Christian's primitive wardrobe, as soon as they started jamming on "Rose Room," Christian's talents were obvious. For the next two years he would be well featured with Benny Goodman's Sextet, there were two solos (including the showcase "Solo Flight") with the full orchestra, and the guitarist had the opportunity to jam at Minton's Playhouse with such up-and-coming players as Thelonious Monk, Kenny Clarke, and Dizzy Gillespie. All of the guitarist's recordings (including guest spots and radio broadcasts) are currently available on CD. Tragically he contracted tuberculosis in 1941 and died at the age of 25 on March 2, 1942. It would be 25 years before jazz guitarists finally moved beyond Charlie Christian. *—Scott Yanow*

Solo Flight (1939-1941) / Aug. 19, 1939-Jun. 1941 / Vintage Jazz Classics ◆◆◆◆
Charlie Christian, who died in 1942 at the age of 25, was the first important electric guitarist, and his solos would be the basis of jazz guitar for the next 25 years. This CD is filled with live performances (mostly from radio shows) of the Benny Goodman Sextet featuring Christian solos on every track. With such sidemen as vibraphonist Lionel Hampton and later tenor saxophonist Georgie Auld and trumpeter Cootie Williams, this unit was a perfect outlet for both Christian and Benny Goodman. And, in addition to a big-band performance of "Solo Flight" (virtually a tour de force for the guitarist), there are five selections from a remarkable all-star group comprised of Goodman, Christian, trumpeter Buck Clayton, Lester Young on tenor, and Count Basie along with his rhythm section. This CD is highly recommended as an example of some of the very best in small-group swing and as a tribute to Charlie Christian's highly influential style. *—Scott Yanow*

★ **The Genius of the Electric Guitar** / Oct. 2, 1939-Mar. 13, 1941 / Columbia ◆◆◆◆◆
This set contains some of guitarist Charlie Christian's greatest recordings (although he did not live long enough to record any bad ones). Christian is heard with the Benny Goodman Sextet on famous versions of "Seven Come Eleven," "Benny's Bugle," and "Air Mail Special"; is showcased with Goodman's orchestra on "Solo Flight"; and jams with the members of the Sextet (minus their leader) on "Blues in B" and a fascinating ad-lib, "Waitin' for Benny." This important release belongs in every jazz collection and contains a great deal of essential music. *—Scott Yanow*

Pete Christlieb

b. Feb. 16, 1945, Los Angeles, CA
Sax (Tenor) / Bop
Though identified with the West Coast where he lives and thus assumed to be a cool, detached player, Pete Christlieb has always been one of the more powerful soloists in any style. His blistering lines, especially on uptempo numbers, are often red hot, while he can also play effective blues and stirring ballads. Christlieb initially studied violin before starting sax at 13. He played with Si Zentner, Chet Baker, and Woody Herman in the '60s, then began working with Louis Bellson. They've maintained a musical relationship through the '80s and into the '90s. Christlieb has worked extensively in the studios doing film and television projects since the late '60s, and was a regular member of the "Tonight Show" orchestra. He played in the backing bands of Della Reese and Sarah Vaughan among other vocalists, and has also done sessions with Count Basie, Quincy Jones, Mel Lewis, Shelly Manne, Gene Ammons, Frank Rosolino, and Carl Fontna. Christlieb headed his own quartet in 1980 and began a record label in 1981. Bosco has issued albums by Bellson, Bob Florence, and Christlieb. He's recorded for RAHMP, Capri, and Warner Bros. A duet album with Warne Marsh in the late '70s was critically praised. *—Ron Wynn and Michael G. Nastos*

● **Conversations with Warne, Vol. 1** / Sep. 15, 1978 / Criss Cross ◆◆◆◆

Conversations with Warne, Vol. 2 / Sep. 15, 1978 / Criss Cross ◆◆◆◆
This matchup works quite well. With alert contributions made by bassist Jim Hughart and drummer Nick Ceroli, tenors Pete Christlieb and Warne Marsh match wits, swing, and ideas throughout nine runthroughs on "originals" based on common chord changes. This second of two CDs has four alternate takes of songs included on the earlier CD plus five other numbers. With titles such as "Woody and You," "Bess You Is My Man," and "So What's Old," experts should have little difficulty in most cases figuring out which standards the "new" pieces are based on. Because Marsh and Chris-

tlieb had very different sounds but competitive natures, plenty of sparks flew during this date. — *Scott Yanow*

Mosaic / Feb. 16, 1990 / Capri ✦✦✦

Sonny Clark (Conrad Yeatis Clark)

b. Jul. 21, 1931, Herminie, PA, **d.** Jan. 13, 1963, New York, NY

Piano / Bop, Hard Bop

Before drugs drastically shortened his life, Sonny Clark was one of the top Bud Powell inspired bop pianists. He worked in San Francisco with Vido Musso and Oscar Pettiford in the early '50s, settled in Los Angeles, made his first recordings with Teddy Charles, and then worked with Buddy DeFranco's quartet (1953-56); all of his records with DeFranco have been reissued by Mosaic on a deluxe limited-edition box set. During the same period he worked with Sonny Criss, Frank Rosolino, and the Lighthouse All-Stars. Moving to New York in 1957, Clark became a fixture on Blue Note, recording several classics as a leader (*Dial S for Sonny, Cool Struttin',* and *Sonny's Crib,* to name three from 1957 alone) and appearing as a sideman with Sonny Rollins, Hank Mobley, and Curtis Fuller, among many others. Sonny Clark's premature death (at age 31) was a major loss to jazz. — *Scott Yanow*

Oakland, 1955 / Jan. 13, 1955 / Uptown ✦✦✦

● **Sonny's Crib** / Oct. 9, 1957 / Blue Note ✦✦✦✦
Striking sextet performances. Memorable efforts from John Coltrane (ts), Curtis Fuller (tb), and Donald Byrd (tpt). 1987 CD reissue has three fine bonus cuts. — *Ron Wynn*

Sonny Clark Trio / Oct. 13, 1957 / Bainbridge ✦✦✦

Sonny Clark Trio / Nov. 13, 1957 / Blue Note ✦✦✦✦
Captivating trio date. With Paul Chambers (b) and Philly Joe Jones (d). — *Ron Wynn*

Cool Struttin', Vols. 1 & 2 / Dec. 8, 1957 / Blue Note ✦✦✦

Leapin' and Lopin' / Nov. 13, 1961 / Blue Note ✦✦✦✦
Mainstream, mostly uptempo jazz with a slight taste of funk. One of Clark's best albums as a leader. The CD has two extra tracks. — *Michael Erlewine*

Kenny Clarke

b. Jan. 9, 1914, Pittsburgh, PA, **d.** Jan. 26, 1985, Paris, France

Drums / Bop

Kenny Clarke was a highly influential if subtle drummer who helped to define bebop drumming. He was the first to shift the timekeeping rhythm from the bass drum to the ride cymbal, an innovation that has been copied and utilized by a countless number of drummers since the early '40s. Clarke played vibes, piano, and trombone in addition to drums while in school. After stints with Roy Eldridge (1935) and the Jeter-Pillars band, Clarke joined Edgar Hayes' Big Band (1937-38). He made his recording debut with Hayes (which is available on a Classics CD) and showed that he was one of the most swinging drummers of the era. A European tour with Hayes gave Clarke an opportunity to lead his own session, but doubling on vibes was a definite mistake! Stints with the orchestras of Claude Hopkins (1939) and Teddy Hill (1940-41) followed, and then Clarke led the house band at Minton's Playhouse (which also included Thelonious Monk). The legendary after-hours sessions led to the formation of bop, and it was during this time that Clarke modernized his style and received the nickname "Klook-Mop" (later shortened to "Klook") due to the irregular "bombs" he would play behind soloists. A flexible drummer, Clarke was still able to uplift the more traditional orchestras of Louis Armstrong and Ella Fitzgerald (1941) and the combos of Benny Carter (1941-42), Red Allen, and Coleman Hawkins; he also recorded with Sidney Bechet. However, after spending time in the military, Clarke stayed in the bop field, working with Dizzy Gillespie's big band and leading his own modern sessions; he co-wrote "Epistrophy" with Monk and "Salt Peanuts" with Gillespie. Clarke spent the late '40s in Europe, was with Billy Eckstine in the US in 1951, and became an original member of the Modern Jazz Quartet (1951-55). However he felt confined by the music and quit the MJQ, freelance performing on an enormous amount of records during 1955-56. In 1956 Clarke moved to France, where he did studio work, was hired by touring American all-stars, and played with Bud Powell and Oscar Pettiford in a trio called the Three Bosses (1959-60). Clarke was co-leader with Francy Boland of a legendary all-star big band (1961-72), one that had Kenny Clarke playing second drums! Other than a few short visits home, Kenny Clarke worked in France for the remainder of his life and was a major figure on the European jazz scene. — *Scott Yanow*

The Paris Bebop Sessions / Oct. 9, 1950 / Prestige ✦✦✦

● **Bohemia After Dark** / Jun. 26, 1955-Jul. 26, 1955 / Savoy ✦✦✦✦
The June 26, 1955 session is most notable for being the recorded debut of the recently discovered altoist Cannonball Adderley and his brother, cornetist Nat (who is also featured on the lone number from July 26, a quartet version of "We'll Be Together Again"). Although drummer Kenny Clarke is

the nominal leader and the other sidemen include trumpeter Donald Byrd, Jerome Richardson on tenor and flute, pianist Horace Silver, and bassist Paul Chambers, the impressive performance by the young Adderleys makes this a historic session that has often been reissued under Cannonball's name. — *Scott Yanow*

Klook's Clique / Feb. 6, 1956 / Savoy ✦✦✦

Kenny Clarke Meets the Detroit Jazzmen / Apr. 30, 1956+May 9, 1956 / Savoy ✦✦✦

Pieces of Time / 1983 / Soul Note ✦✦✦

Stanley Clarke (Stanley M. Clarke)

b. Jun. 30, 1951, Philadelphia, PA

Bass / R&B, Fusion, Post-Bop

A brilliant player on both acoustic and electric basses, Stanley Clarke has spent much of his career outside of jazz, although he has the ability to play jazz with the very best. He played accordion as a youth, switching to violin and cello before settling on bass. He worked with R&B and rock bands in high school, but after moving to New York he worked with Pharoah Sanders in the early '70s. Other early gigs were with Gil Evans, Mel Lewis, Horace Silver, Stan Getz, Dexter Gordon, and Art Blakey; everyone was impressed by his talents. However Clarke really hit the big time when he started teaming up with Chick Corea in Return to Forever. When the group became a rock-oriented fusion quartet, Clarke mostly emphasized electric bass and became an influential force, preceding Jaco Pastorius. But starting with his *School Days* album (1976) and continuing through his funk group with George Duke (the Clarke/Duke Project) up to his current projects writing movie scores, Clarke has largely moved beyond the jazz world into commercial music; his 1988 Portrait album *If This Bass Could Only Talk* and his 1995 collaboration with Jean Luc Ponty and Al DiMeola on the acoustic *The Rite of Strings* are two of his few jazz recordings of the past decade. — *Scott Yanow*

Children of Forever / Dec. 26, 1972+Dec. 27, 1972 / Polydor ✦✦✦

Stanley Clarke / 1974 / Epic ✦✦✦✦
Definitive early-period funk/fusion. Clarke's finger-pop bass is up front. — *Michael G. Nastos*

Journey to Love / 1975 / Epic ✦✦✦

I Wanna Play for You / Nov. 1979 / Epic ✦✦✦

● **If This Bass Could Only Talk** / 1988 / Portrait ✦✦✦✦
One of a few of his contemporary releases with some good music and an indication of his prodigious talent. — *Ron Wynn*

Live at the Greek / 1993 / Epic ✦✦✦

Rite of Strings / 1995 / Gai Saber ✦✦✦

Buck Clayton (Wilbur Dorsey Clayton)

b. Nov. 12, 1911, Parsons, KS, **d.** Dec. 8, 1991, New York, NY

Trumpet / Swing

An excellent bandleader and accompanist for many vocalists including Billie Holiday, Buck Clayton was a valued soloist with the Count Basie orchestra during the '30s and '40s, and later was a celebrated studio and jam session player, writer, and arranger. His tart, striking tone and melodic dexterity were his trademark, and Clayton provided several charts for Basie's orchestra and many other groups. Clayton began his career in California, where he organized a big band that had a residency in China in 1934. When he returned, Clayton led a group and played with other local bands. During a 1936 visit to Kansas City, he was invited to join Basie's orchestra as a replacement for Hot Lips Page. Clayton was also featured on sessions with Lester Young, Teddy Wilson, and Holiday in the late '30s. He remained in the Basie band until 1943, when he left for Army service. After leaving the Army, Clayton did arrangements for Basie, Benny Goodman, and Harry James before forming a sextet in the late '40s. He toured Europe with this group in 1949 and 1950. Clayton continued heading a combo during the '50s and worked with Joe Bushkin, Tony Parenti, and Jimmy Rushing, among others. He organized a series of outstanding recordings for Columbia in the mid-'50s under the title *Jam Session* (compiled and reissued by Mosaic in 1993). There were sessions with Rushing, Ruby Braff, and Nat Pierce. Clayton led a combo with Coleman Hawkins and J.J. Johnson at the 1956 Newport Jazz Festival, then reunited with Goodman in 1957 at the Waldorf Astoria. There was another European tour, this time with Mezz Mezzrow. He appeared in the 1956 film *The Benny Goodman Story* and played the 1958 Brussels World Fair with Sidney Bechet. Clayton later made another European visit with a Newport Jazz Festival tour. He joined Eddie Condon's band in 1959, a year after appearing in the film *Jazz on a Summer's Day*. Clayton toured Japan and Australia with Condon's group in 1964 and continued to revisit Europe throughout the '60s, often with Humphrey Lyttelton's band, while playing festivals across the country. But lip and health problems virtually ended his playing career in the late '60s. After a period outside of music, Clayton once again became active in music, this time as a nonplaying arranger, touring Africa as part of a State Department series in 1977. He provided arrangements and compositions for a 1974 Lyttleton and Buddy Tate album, and did more jam session albums for Chiaroscuro in 1974 and 1975. He also became an educator, teaching at Hunter College in the early '80s. Clayton led a group of Basie sidemen on a European tour in 1983, then headed his own big band in 1987 that played almost exclusively his compositions and arrangements. That same year Clayton's extensive autobiography *Buck Clayton's Jazz World* with Nancy Miller-Elliot was published. —*Ron Wynn*

The Classic Swing of Buck Clayton / 1946 / Original Jazz Classics ✦✦✦

Buck Clayton in Paris / Oct. 10, 1949-Oct. 21, 1953 / Vogue ✦✦✦✦
There are lots of rare and swinging performances on this valuable reissue CD from Vogue. The great swing trumpeter Buck Clayton (for whom critic Stanley Dance coined the phrase "mainstream") is heard in a sextet that co-stars tenor saxophonist Don Byas, heading a nonet that also features fellow trumpeter Bill Coleman (who gets almost as much solo space as Buck) and tenor saxophonist Alix Combelle, and guesting with Combelle's 14-piece orchestra in 1953; the latter group performs eight of its leader's originals, all arranged in swinging fashion by Clayton. This disc is easily recommended to straightahead jazz fans. —*Scott Yanow*

Dr. Jazz Series, Vol. 3 / Dec. 13, 1951-Jan. 24, 1952 / Storyville ✦✦✦

★ **Complete CBS Buck Clayton Jam Sessions** / Dec. 14, 1953-Mar. 5, 1956 / Mosaic ✦✦✦✦✦
Trumpeter Buck Clayton led a series of exciting studio jam sessions during the mid-'50s. All of the performances are on this superlative three-CD box set, including a few "new" alternate takes and several that have been restored to their full length. Among the many soloists (most of them swing-oriented stylists) are Clayton, Joe Newman, Joe Thomas, Billy Butterfield, and Ruby Braff on trumpets; trombonists Urbie Green, Benny Powell, Henderson Chambers, Trummy Young, Bennie Green, Dicky Harris, J.C. Higginbotham, and Tyree Glenn; altoist Lem Davis; tenors Coleman Hawkins, Al Cohn, and Buddy Tate; Julian Dash doubling on tenor and alto; baritonist Charlie Fowlkes; several rhythm sections with pianists Sir Charles Thompson, Jimmy Jones, Billy Kyle, Ken Kersey, and the forgotten Al Waslohn; and a guest appearance by Woody Herman on clarinet. These generally lengthy performances contain plenty of spontaneous riffing behind soloists and lots of special moments; "How Ili the Fi" is quite memorable. —*Scott Yanow*

The Essential Buck Clayton / Dec. 30, 1953-Mar. 14, 1957 / Vanguard ✦✦✦

Copenhagen Concert / Sep. 17, 1959 / SteepleChase ✦✦✦

Buck and Buddy / 1960 / Original Jazz Classics ✦✦✦

Goin' to Kansas City / Oct. 5, 1960-Oct. 6, 1960 / Original Jazz Classics ✦✦✦

★ **Olympia Concert (22 April 61)** / Apr. 22, 1961 / Vogue ✦✦✦✦✦
A splendid set with vintage sensibility and a jam session atmosphere. Buddy Tate (ts) and Sir Charles Thompson (p) are on the money. —*Ron Wynn*

Baden, Switzerland 1966 / Feb. 6, 1966 / Sackville ✦✦✦✦
For this Swiss concert, the great swing trumpeter Buck Clayton is joined by three Swiss players (Michel Pilet on tenor, pianist Henri Chaix, and bassist Isla Eckinger) in addition to the veteran swing drummer Wallace Bishop. Clayton is in particularly inspired form even though he had played the songs in this repertoire (seven swing standards plus a blues) a countless number of times. His range was at its peak during this period, and Clayton comes up with consistently creative ideas on such warhorses as "All of Me," "Stompin' at the Savoy," "You Can Depend on Me," and "One O'Clock Jump." Highly recommended to swing collectors. —*Scott Yanow*

Clayton-Hamilton Orchestra

Big Band / Bop, Swing
The Clayton-Hamilton Jazz Orchestra is unusual in that it has three leaders: drummer Jeff Hamilton, altoist Jeff Clayton, and bassist John Clayton. While Hamilton (who has played regularly with Oscar Peterson, Ray Brown, Monty Alexander, Gene Harris, and the L.A. Four) really drives the band, and Jeff Clayton (whose sound is inspired by Cannonball Adderley) is one of the orchestra's top soloists, it is John Clayton's colorful and unpredictable arrangements that really give this big band its own personality. In addition Clayton (who was formerly with Count Basie) is a very talented soloist, particularly when bowing. The swinging orchestra, filled with top Los Angeles players (including such soloists as Rickey Woodard, Charlie Owens, Bobby Bryant, Snooky Young, Oscar Brasheer, George Bohannon, Thurman Green, and Bill Cunliffe) can hold its own with any other big band of the '90s, as shown on its two Capri sets (*Groove Shop* and *Heart and Soul*) and its Lake Street release *Absolutely*. —*Scott Yanow*

● **Groove Shop** / Apr. 18, 1989-Apr. 19, 1989 / Capri ✦✦✦✦
The 1989 debut by the orchestra co-led by drummer Jeff Hamilton and bassist John Clayton. They stay in the background, anchoring and fueling the big band that includes several seasoned pros, exciting youngster Ricky Woodard on tenor sax and clarinet, and longtime session trumpeter Snooky Young. —*Ron Wynn*

Heart and Soul / Feb. 1991 / Capri ✦✦✦✦
Nineteen-piece big band plays five standards, four compositions by bassist John Clayton. Great solos from younger and older musicians. Jeff Hamilton (co-leader), Ricky Woodward (ts), Shooley Young, Oscar Brasheer, George Bohannon on brass, and Bill Cunliffe (p). —*Michael G. Nastos*

Arnett Cobb

b. Aug. 10, 1918, Houston, TX, **d.** Mar. 24, 1989, Houston, TX
Sax (Tenor) / Swing, Early R&B, Groove
A stomping Texas tenor player in the tradition of Illinois Jacquet, Arnett Cobb's accessible playing was between swing and early rhythm & blues. After playing in Texas with Chester Boone (1934-36) and Milt Larkin (1936-42), Cobb emerged in the big leagues by succeeding Illinois Jacquet with Lionel Hampton's Orchestra (1942-47). His version of "Flying Home No. 2" became a hit, and he was a very popular soloist with Hampton. After leaving the band, Cobb formed his own group, but his initial success was interrupted in 1948 when he had to undergo an operation on his spine. After recovering he resumed touring. But a major car accident in 1956 crushed Cobb's legs, and he was reduced to using crutches for the rest of his life. However, by 1959 he returned to active playing and recording. Cobb spent most of the '60s leading bands back in Texas, but starting in 1973 he toured and recorded more extensively, playing a tenor summit with Jimmy Heath and Joe Henderson in Europe as late as 1988. Arnett Cobb made many fine records through the years for such labels as Apollo, Columbia/Okeh, Prestige (many of the latter are available on the OJC series), Black & Blue, Progressive, Muse, and Bee Hive. —*Scott Yanow*

● **Blows for 1300** / May 1947-Aug. 1947 / Delmark ✦✦✦✦
This Delmark CD reissues all 15 of Arnett Cobb's recordings for Apollo. The spirited tenor (who straddled the boundaries between swing and early R&B) is in prime early form with his sextet on a variety of basic material, much of it blues-oriented. Milt Larkins takes vocals on three of the tracks, and there are short solos by either Booty Wood or Al King on trombone, but otherwise the main focus is on Cobb's tough tenor. This very accessible music is both danceable and full of exciting performances that were formerly rare. —*Scott Yanow*

Blow, Arnett, Blow / Jan. 9, 1959 / Original Jazz Classics ✦✦✦✦
Seldom has there been any album that could more accurately be termed a blowing session than this 1959 date. It matched a pair of frenetic, furious tenor saxophonists in Arnett Cobb and Eddie "Lockjaw" Davis, and also boasted a propulsive organist in Strethen Davis, a resourceful bassist in George Duvivier, and an ideal drummer in Arthur Edgehill. Edgehill kept the rhythms tight and crashing, while Cobb and Davis exchanged blistering solos, honks, grunts, and bluesy dialogues. Duvivier's heavy backbeat and lines, along with Davis' stomping riffs, added vital supporting ingredients and helped make this a soul-jazz and jam session classic. The six cuts here are a delight for fans of steamy, joyous jazz with a soul-blues sensibility. —*Ron Wynn*

Blue and Sentimental / Oct. 31, 1960-Nov. 13, 1960 / Prestige ✦✦✦

Tenor Tribute, Vol. 1 / Apr. 30, 1988 / Soul Note ✦✦✦

Al Cohn

b. Nov. 24, 1925, New York, NY, **d.** Feb. 15, 1988, Stroudsburg, PA
Sax (Tenor) / Bop
An excellent tenor saxophonist and a superior arranger/composer, Al Cohn was greatly admired by his fellow musicians. Early gigs included associations with Joe Marsala (1943), Georgie Auld, Boyd Raeburn (1946), Alvino Rey, and Buddy Rich (1947). But it was when he replaced Herbie Steward as one of the "Four Brothers" with Woody Herman's Second Herd (1948-49) that Cohn began to make a strong impression. He was actually overshadowed by Stan Getz and Zoot Sims during this period, but unlike the other two tenors, he also contributed arrangements, including "The Goof and I." He was with Artie Shaw's short-lived bop orchestra (1949) and then spent the '50s quite busy as a recording artist (making his first dates as a leader in 1950), arranger for both jazz and nonjazz settings, and a performer. Starting in 1956 and continuing on an irregular basis for decades, Cohn co-led a quintet with Zoot Sims. The two tenors were so complementary that it was often difficult to tell them apart! Al Cohn continued in this fashion in the '60s (although playing less), in the '70s he recorded many gems for Xanadu, and during his last few years when his tone became darker and more distinctive, Cohn largely gave up writing to concentrate on playing. He made many excellent loop-based records throughout his career for such labels as Prestige, Victor, Xanadu, and Concord; his son Joe Cohn is a talented cool-toned guitarist. —*Scott Yanow*

Broadway / Jul. 29, 1954 / Fantasy ✦✦✦

From A to Z / Jan. 23, 1956-Jan. 24, 1956 / Bluebird ✦✦✦

Al and Zoot / Mar. 26, 1957-Mar. 27, 1957 / MCA/Decca ✦✦✦

Body and Soul / Mar. 23, 1973 / Muse ✦✦✦✦
With Zoot Sims. Immortal tenor pair with Jaki Byard (p), plus George Duvivier (b) and Mel Lewis (d). Can't miss. —*Michael G. Nastos*

Tour de Force / Aug. 11, 1981 / Concord Jazz ✦✦✦✦
A wonderful meeting between Hamilton, Buddy Tate, and Al Cohn. —*Ron Wynn*

Overtones / Apr. 1982 / Concord Jazz ✦✦✦

● **Standards of Excellence** / Nov. 1983 / Concord Jazz ✦✦✦✦
Accurate title. Confident veterans going through their paces with a minimum of flash and a maximum of talent. Herb Ellis (g) shines. —*Ron Wynn*

Al Cohn Meets Al Porcino / Mar. 30, 1987 / Red Baron ✦✦✦

Rifftide / Jun. 1987 / Timeless ✦✦✦✦
This was tenor saxophonist Al Cohn's final recording. His tone had deepened quite a bit during his last few years (he no longer sounded like Zoot Sims), but Cohn showed no signs of decline on this fine quartet date. Joined by pianist Rein de Graaff, bassist Koos Serierse, and drummer Eric Ineke, Cohn plays a fine tune called "The Thing" and seven jazz standards, including two ("Secret Love" and "Do Nothing Till You're True," which is really "Do Nothing Till You Hear from Me") that mistakenly list him as composer! This is fine bop-based music which features Al Cohn exiting on top. —*Scott Yanow*

Cozy Cole

b. Oct. 17, 1909, East Orange, NJ, **d.** Jan. 29, 1981, Columbus, OH
Drums / Swing
A popular performer throughout much of his career, Cozy Cole was one of the top drummers to emerge during the '30s. He recorded with Jelly Roll Morton in 1930 (including a song titled "Load of Cole") and played with the big bands of Blanche Calloway (1931-33), Benny Carter (1933-34), and Willie Bryant (1935-36). His stint with Stuff Smith at the Onyx Club (1936-38) gave him some recognition. Cole was well featured with Cab Calloway's Orchestra (1938-42), playing in a strong rhythm section with Bennie Payne, Danny Barker, and Milt Hinton; his showcases included "Crescendo in Drums" and "Paradiddle." Cole popped up in many different types of jazz and studio settings throughout the '40s and headed several record sessions with swing all-stars. He was with Louis Armstrong's All-Stars (1949-53), opened a drum school with Gene Krupa, and in 1957 toured Europe with Jack Teagarden and Earl Hines. A 1958 recording of "Topsy" became a surprise hit, allowing Cole to lead his own band throughout much of the '60s; he also played with Jonah Jones' quintet later in the decade. —*Scott Yanow*

● **1944-1945** / Nov. 14, 1944-Apr. 1945 / Classics ✦✦✦✦
This Classics CD reissues drummer Cozy Cole's sessions for Continental, Keynote, and Guild, most of which have been out of print for years. The two Continental dates feature overlapping all-star groups (with trumpeter Charlie Shavers, clarinetist Hank D'Amico, Coleman Hawkins, Walter "Foots" Thomas, and/or Don Byas on tenors, Clyde Hart or Johnny Guarnieri on piano, guitarist Tiny Grimes, bassist Slam Stewart, and the drummer/leader) but are sometimes a bit frustrating. Since every player is a potential soloist and the performances are limited to around three minutes apiece, the solos are almost cameos, generally eight or sixteen bars apiece. The most memorable spot, Hawkins' exploration of "When Day Is Done," finds the great tenor doing what he can with his half-chorus. The Keynote session is most notable for Don Byas' solos and for the recording debut of 20-year-old trumpeter Shorty Rogers. The Guild sides have Don Byas well showcased in a quintet, two extensive drum features ("Stompin" and "Strictly Drums"), and three dramatic vocals from June Hawkins. Overall this is an interesting and enjoyable CD, swing music with slight touches of bop. —*Scott Yanow*

Nat King Cole (Nathaniel Adams Cole)

b. Mar. 17, 1917, Montgomery, AL, **d.** Feb. 15, 1965, Santa Monica, CA
Piano, Vocals / Swing, Pop
Nat King Cole had two overlapping careers. He was one of the truly great swing pianists, inspired by Earl Hines and a big influence on Oscar Peterson. And he was a superb pop ballad singer whose great commercial success in that field unfortunately resulted in him greatly de-emphasizing his piano after 1949. Perhaps if his talents had been divided between two different people!

Nat Cole grew up in Chicago, and by the time he was 12 he was playing organ and singing in church; his three brothers (Eddie, Fred, and Isaac) would become jazz musicians. After making his recording debut with Eddie Cole's Solid Swingers in 1936, he left Chicago to lead the band for the revival of the revue *Shuffle Along* and settled in Los Angeles when the show ended. Cole struggled a bit, put together a trio with guitarist Oscar Moore and bassist Wesley Prince, and eventually settled in for a long residency in Hollywood. In the early days (documented on radio transcriptions), most of the group's repertoire was comprised of instrumentals, although the Trio often sang jivey novelty vocals together. However, by the time the Trio had its first opportunity to record for Decca in December 1940, Nat King Cole had gained more confidence in his own singing. "Sweet Lorraine" resulted from that session, and the Trio soon became

quite popular. In future years Art Tatum, Oscar Peterson, and Ahmad Jamal would all form piano/guitar/bass combos inspired by Cole's group.

Nat Cole recorded a great deal of exciting jazz during the '40s, including dates featuring Lester Young and Illinois Jacquet, the first Jazz at the Philharmonic concert (1944), and a countless number of selections for Capitol with his trio; all of the latter are included on a gigantic Mosaic limited-edition box set. Although his singing began to become quite popular by the mid-'40s (and particularly after "The Christmas Song" and "Nature Boy"), Cole mostly performed with his Trio during this era; Johnny Miller took over on bass, and in 1947 Irving Ashby became the guitarist. Nat Cole was open to the influence of bop and in 1949 started utilizing Jack Costanzo on bongo and conga for some songs. However, his career changed permanently in early 1950 with the recording of "Mona Lisa," which became a No. 1 hit. Suddenly Nat King Cole became famous to the nonjazz public as a singer, and many new fans never realized that he also played piano! During the '50s and '60s he mostly recorded pop ballads, although there were a few exceptions (including 1956's *After Midnight* album), and he never lost his ability to play stimulating jazz. Cole had a regular television show during 1956-57 (some of which has been released on video), but due to the racism of the period he could never find a sponsor. However, the popularity of his records and public appearances remained at a remarkable level, and the world mourned Nat King Cole's death from lung cancer in early 1965 at age 47. —*Scott Yanow*

☆ **Complete Early Transcriptions** / Oct. 1938-Feb. 1941 / Vintage Jazz Classics ✦✦✦✦✦
This four-CD set contains 112 performances by the Trio from 1938-41, radio transcriptions made especially to be played on the air. The early trio is instantly recognizable, and although there is a greater reliance on group vocals and guest singers (including Bonnie Lake, Juanelda Carter, Pauline and Her Perils, and the Dreamers) rather than on Cole's solo vocals, the music is not all that different from what the King Cole Trio would be playing a few years later when they became much better known. —*Scott Yanow*

● **Hit That Jive Jack: The Earliest Recordings** / Dec. 1940-Oct. 1941 / Decca ✦✦✦✦
These early '40s Decca sides have a hip, swinging '40s trio sound. —*Hank Davis*

The Trio Recordings / 1940-1956 / Laserlight ✦✦✦✦
This five-CD set, despite the lack of definitive liner notes, is highly recommended. The bulk of this package (most of four discs) features the Trio on radio transcriptions during 1944-45, and these renditions are easily the equal of their more famous studio recordings. The fifth disc is a hodgepodge that reaches back to 1940 for six numbers and forward to 1956 for a few songs performed on the Dorsey Brothers TV show and on Nat Cole's own program. Although the music could actually have fit on three discs (averaging around 40 minutes apiece), this set is usually available at a budget price and contains many exciting performances. —*Scott Yanow*

WWII Transcriptions / 1941-1944 / Music & Arts ✦✦✦✦
With the exception of a couple of Anita Boyer vocals from 1941, this CD (which contains 30 broadcast transcriptions by Nat King Cole's Trio) dates from 1944. Two numbers apiece feature vocals from a young Anita O'Day and Ida James, but otherwise Cole and his Trio only sing four other songs. The emphasis is on instrumentals (including two interesting medleys) and the leader's talents as a great swing pianist. Most of this material does not duplicate the Laserlight CDs, making this a recommended set for Nat King Cole's jazz fans. —*Scott Yanow*

☆ **Complete Capitol Trio Recordings** / Oct. 11, 1942-Mar. 2, 1961 / Mosaic ✦✦✦✦✦
This 18-CD box set lives up to its title, containing not only all of the Nat King Cole Trio's recordings for Capitol during 1943-49 but a remarkable amount of previously unavailable radio transcriptions owned by Capitol. Also, all of Cole's post-1949 recordings that at least have the presence of the trio are here, including the entire *After Midnight* sessions of 1956 and various odds and ends that feature Cole's piano—349 selections in all with a countless number of formerly unissued tracks. Since this is a limited-edition set that will sell out, get this remarkable box as soon as possible. —*Scott Yanow*

Straighten Up and Fly Right / Dec. 19, 1942-Jan. 28, 1948 / Pro Arte ✦✦✦✦
This CD consists of some of the Nat King Cole Trio's radio appearances, including guest shots on shows hosted by Bing Crosby, Perry Como, and Frank Sinatra; Ol' Blue Eyes sits in with the trio on "I've Found a New Baby" and "Exactly like You." Considering that 12 of these 25 songs were never recorded commercially by the Trio, this set is quite valuable for fans of swing and Nat Cole's piano. The colorful music is easily recommended. —*Scott Yanow*

Jumpin' at Capitol / Nov. 30, 1943-Jan. 5, 1950 / Rhino ✦✦✦✦
For those who cannot afford or get a hold of the magnificent Mosaic 18-CD box set, this single CD offers a fine sampling of Nat King Cole's talents as a pianist and jazz singer with his popular trio in the '40s. These 16 selections

(highlighted by "Straighten Up and Fly Right," "Sweet Lorraine," and "Route 66") are still quite enjoyable a half-century later. —*Scott Yanow*

★ **Nat King Cole** / Nov. 30, 1943-Jun. 3, 1964 / Capitol ✦✦✦✦✦
For an overview of Nat King Cole's years as a remarkably popular singer, this four-CD box would be difficult to top. Containing 100 songs spanning a 20-year period, this box has virtually all of Cole's hits, some of his best jazz sides, and more than its share of variety, including a humorous previously unreleased version of "Mr. Cole Won't Rock & Roll." Recommended to beginners and veteran collectors alike, its attractive booklet is also a major asset. —*Scott Yanow*

   The Capitol Collector's Series / Nov. 30, 1943-Jun. 3, 1964 / Capitol ✦✦✦✦
This 20-song single CD gives one an excellent introduction to the very popular singing of Nat King Cole. Concentrating on his hits, it contains virtually all of the biggest, including "Route 66," "The Christmas Song," "Nature Boy," "Mona Lisa," and even "Those Lazy-Hazy-Crazy Days of Summer." It has since been succeeded by the more ambitious four-CD box set *Nat King Cole* but is recommended to those with a tight budget. —*Scott Yanow*

★ **Jazz Encounters** / Mar. 30, 1945-Jan. 5, 1950 / Blue Note ✦✦✦✦✦
This CD has many of Cole's most interesting Capitol dates away from his trio. The great jazz pianist is heard with the 1947 Metronome All-Stars, jamming with the all-star Capitol International Jazzmen, backing the straight vocals of Jo Stafford, and collaborating with Nellie Lutcher, Woody Herman (on a remarkable version of "Mule Train"), and Johnny Mercer (highlighted by the joyful "Save the Bones for Henry Jones"). This colorful set is highly recommended. —*Scott Yanow*

   The King Cole Trios Live: 1947-1948 / Mar. 1, 1947-Mar. 13, 1948 / Vintage Jazz Classics ✦✦✦✦
This excellent CD contains five of the Trio's radio shows for NBC during 1947-48. There are some guests (singer Clark Dennis, the Dinning Sisters, Pearl Bailey, Woody Herman, and Duke Ellington) for a song apiece, but the focus is on the Trio with occasional vocals from trio. This historical music is enjoyable, although the performances (many around the two-minute mark) are sometimes frustratingly brief. It's still worth acquiring. —*Scott Yanow*

   Lush Life / Mar. 29, 1949-Jan. 11, 1952 / Capitol ✦✦✦✦
This is a very interesting transitional collection featuring Nat King Cole when he was gradually emphasizing his vocals over his jazz piano playing and phasing out his Trio. All 25 of the selections on this generous set feature the arrangements of Pete Rugolo; highlights include "Lush Life," "Time Out for Tears," "That's My Girl," "Red Sails in the Sunset," "It's Crazy," and "You Stepped Out of a Dream." There is enough jazz content and popular appeal on this CD to satisfy both of Cole's audiences. —*Scott Yanow*

   Big Band Cole / Aug. 16, 1950-Sep. 6, 1961 / Blue Note ✦✦✦✦
Cole's collaborations with the Count Basie and Stan Kenton Orchestras (all of which are included on this CD) found him mostly sticking to singing but enjoying the jazz-oriented backgrounds. He first met up with Kenton in 1950, recording the memorable "Orange Colored Sky" and starring on piano during the instrumental "Jam-Bo." They had a reunion in 1960-61, cutting a remake of "Orange Colored Sky" and two more poppish songs. The matchup with Basie showcased Cole purely as a singer in 1958; Gerald Wiggins took Basie's place at the keyboards. One of Cole's better vocal sessions, he is in top form on a variety of standards (particularly on "The Late Late Show" and "Welcome to the Club"); pity he did not sit in with the band on piano. This CD is recommended for its rare examples of Nat King Cole as a big-band singer. —*Scott Yanow*

   The Billy May Sessions / Sep. 4, 1951-Nov. 22, 1961 / Capitol ✦✦✦✦
Nat King Cole recorded with arranger/bandleader Billy May on several occasions, and all of their collaborations are on this excellent double CD. Dating from 1951, 1953, 1954, 1957, and 1961, some of the more memorable numbers include "Walkin' My Baby Back Home," "Angel Eyes," "Papa Loves Mambo," "Send for Me," "Who's Sorry Now," "The Party's Over," and "When My Sugar Walks Down the Street" (Cole also takes organ solos on three of the selections from 1961 (the only time he ever recorded on that instrument), though he plays no piano on this set. It's recommended for his superior middle-of-the-road singing. —*Scott Yanow*

   Sings for Two in Love / 1954 / Capitol ✦✦✦✦
Nat King Cole Sings for Two in Love was Nat King Cole's first album to be specifically for the new 12-inch LP format. Like Frank Sinatra, with whom he shared a record company and a conductor, Cole made a thematic album, in this case a set of 12 romantic ballads. But they aren't actually all for "two in love." There are songs for two who think "This Can't Be Love" or that it's "Almost Like Being in Love" or who tell each other "Let's Fall in Love." And then there are post-love songs: "Autumn Leaves," "Dinner for One Please, James." If Cole really wants to sing for two in love, he's telling them good news and bad. Of course, his plaintive, undisturbed singing makes the happy and sad sentiments seem equally content, and Nelson Riddle's orchestrations consistently support the singer without challenging

him or getting in his way. (Originally released in 1954, *Nat King Cole Sings for Two in Love* was reissued on CD in March 1987 under the title *Nat King Cole Sings for Two in Love (and More)*. The reissue contained three bonus tracks culled from the 1959 album *To Whom It May Concern*.) —*William Ruhlmann*

Piano Stylings / Jun. 7, 1955-Aug. 27, 1955 / Capitol ✦✦✦✦
One of Cole's most obscure albums, these 16 selections from 1955 feature his piano backed by an orchestra arranged by Nelson Riddle; no vocals. Different in style than the earlier recordings by the Trio, these performances put the focus purely on his lyrical and swinging playing, and his improvisations are often quite inspired. This CD deserves to be much better known. —*Scott Yanow*

Complete After Midnight Sessions / Aug. 15, 1956-Sep. 2, 1956 / Capitol ✦✦✦✦
After several years of hearing criticism from the jazz press about his decision to break up his Trio and become a pop singer, Nat King Cole was persuaded to record this jazz set. Joined by a strong rhythm section (including guitarist John Collins), Cole welcomed four guests for several selections apiece: altoist Willie Smith, trumpeter Harry "Sweets" Edison, violinist Stuff Smith, and valve trombonist Juan Tizol. The performances on this CD (which include five selections released for the first time) are quite enjoyable, highlighted by "Just You, Just Me," "Sweet Lorraine," "It's Only a Paper Moon," and "Route 66." Cole did hedge his bet a bit by not recording any instrumentals or having any performances feature his trio without a guest. Despite that, this is a great set, and the last time that Nat King Cole would perform an album's worth of jazz material. —*Scott Yanow*

Just One of Those Things / Nov. 1957 / Capitol ✦✦✦

To Whom It May Concern / Jun. 1959 / Capitol ✦✦✦

Nat King Cole Story / 1960 / Capitol ✦✦✦✦
This double CD finds him revisiting his earlier hits with new versions. The 36 selections mostly focus on his pop successes of the '50s, although there are a few wistful looks back at his trio days. Not as essential as the original renditions of these popular recordings, these remakes nevertheless find Cole in peak form and form a highly enjoyable retrospective of his vocal career. —*Scott Yanow*

Sings, George Shearing Plays / Dec. 1961 / Capitol ✦✦✦✦
Although it would have been interesting to hear Nat Cole play piano behind George Shearing's vocals, this session was a big success. Cole is in prime form on such songs as "September Song," "Pick Yourself Up," and "Serenata." Shearing's accompaniment is tasteful and lightly swinging, and the string arrangements help to accentuate the romantic moods. This CD adds three "new" selections from the same sessions to the original program. —*Scott Yanow*

Ramblin' Rose / Aug. 1962 / Capitol ✦✦✦

● **The Greatest Hits** / Capitol ✦✦✦✦

Spotlight on Nat King Cole / Capitol ✦✦✦✦
Part of a Capitol reissue series called "Great Ladies and Gentlemen of Song," *Spotlight on . . . Nat King Cole* is a 18-track compilation that, for once, eschews the over-familiar Cole hits in favor of pop standards originally strewn across several of his late '50s and early '60s albums, plus a couple of previously unreleased Cole Trio recordings. Here, Cole sings Rodgers and Hart, Gershwin, Berlin, Mercer, and Ellington, among others, with arrangements by Nelson Riddle, among others, and backed in some cases by the Count Basie Band. It's classy stuff, and Cole handles it all effortlessly. Longtime fans may find this set largely redundant, but it makes a good introduction to the breadth of the singer's work for those who know him only for "Nature Boy," "Mona Lisa," and "Unforgettable." —*William Ruhlmann*

George Coleman

b. Mar. 8, 1935, Memphis, TN
Sax (Tenor) / Hard Bop
George Coleman's highest visibility occured when he was a member of the Miles Davis Quintet (1963-64), playing alongside Miles, Herbie Hancock, Ron Carter, and Tony Williams. His decision to leave the group after several notable recordings cut short his potential fame (his eventual replacement was Wayne Shorter), but Coleman has created a great deal of rewarding music since. Part of the rich Memphis jazz scene of the early '50s, he started playing in blues bands in the South (including with B.B. King in 1952 and 1955-56). He moved to Chicago in 1957 (where he played with the MJT+3) and to New York the following year. Coleman was with the Max Roach Quintet (1958-59), Slide Hampton's Octet (1959-61), and Wild Bill Davis (1962) before joining Miles Davis. Following that association he was with Lionel Hampton, Elvin Jones, and Charles McPherson. Since the mid-'70s George Coleman has mostly led his own groups and has recorded both as a leader (for Timeless, Theresa, and Verve) and as a sideman quite frequently; one of his more notable appearances from earlier years was on Herbie Hancock's 1964 classic *Maiden Voyage*. —*Scott Yanow*

Amsterdam After Dark / Nov. 2, 1977-Nov. 3, 1977 / Timeless ✦✦✦✦
Legendary tenor saxophonist blows up a storm with the Hilton Ruiz Trio.
This has been reissued on CD. Best cut is "New Arrival." —*Michael G. Nastos*

Manhattan Panorama / 1984 / Evidence ✦✦✦

● **At Yoshi's** / Aug. 1987 / Evidence ✦✦✦✦
George Coleman's animated, anguished tenor sax solos are the hook on
this seven-track live set done at Yoshi's in Tokyo during 1989. Coleman
offered some lush, sensitive playing, but much of the time ripped through
chord changes, expanding through the upper register. Drummer Alvin
Queen and bassist Ray Drummond wisely gave Coleman extensive space,
spreading and splitting the beat while he roared above. Pianist Harold
Mabern added contrasting elements with bluesy, passionate solos or sensitive, subtle understatements that followed and reaffirmed Coleman's
emphatic lines. —*Ron Wynn*

My Horns of Plenty / Mar. 4, 1991-Mar. 5, 1991 / Verve ✦✦✦✦
A recent date by Coleman, stepping into the '90s in style. He displays his
versatility by playing alto and soprano along with his usual tenor, and scor-
ing on each one. The rhythm trio this time includes his favorite pianist,
Harold Mabern, plus bassist Ray Drummond and drummer Billy Higgins.
—*Ron Wynn*

Ornette Coleman

b. Mar. 9, 1930, Fort Worth, TX
Trumpet, Violin, Sax (Alto) / Free Jazz, Free Funk
One of the most important (and controversial) innovators of the jazz
avant-garde, Ornette Coleman gained both loyal followers and lifelong
detractors when he seemed to burst on the scene in 1959 fully formed.
Although he and Don Cherry in his original quartet played opening and
closing melodies together, their solos dispensed altogether with chordal
improvisation and harmony, instead playing quite freely off of the mood
of the theme. Coleman's tone (which purposely wavered in pitch) rattled
some listeners, and his solos were emotional and followed their own
logic. In time his approach would be quite influential and the quartet's
early records still sound advanced over 35 years later.

Unfortunately Ornette Coleman's early development was not documented. Originally inspired by Charlie Parker, he started playing alto at
14 and tenor two years later. His early experiences were in R&B bands in
Texas, including those of Red Connors and Pee Wee Crayton, but his
attempts to play in an original style were consistently met with hostility
both by audiences and fellow musicians. Coleman moved to Los Angeles
in the early '50s, where he worked as an elevator operator while studying
music books. He met kindred spirits along the way in Don Cherry, Charlie Haden, Ed Blackwell, Bobby Bradford, Charles Moffett, and Billy Higgins, but it was not until 1958 (after many unsuccessful attempts to sit in
with top Los Angeles musicians) that Coleman had a nucleus of musicians who could play his music. He appeared as part of Paul Bley's Quintet for a short time at the Hillcrest Club (which is documented on live
records) and recorded two very interesting albums for Contemporary.
With the assistance of John Lewis, Coleman and Cherry attended the
Lenox School of Jazz in 1959 and had an extended stay at the Five Spot
in New York. This engagement alerted the jazz world towards the radical
new music, and each night the audience was filled with curious musicians who alternately labelled Coleman a genius or a fraud.

During 1959-61 Ornette Coleman recorded a series of classic and somewhat startling quartet albums for Atlantic (all of which have been reissued
on a six-CD set by Rhino). With Don Cherry, Charlie Haden, Scott LaFaro,
or Jimmy Garrison on bass and Billy Higgins or Ed Blackwell on drums,
Coleman created music that would greatly affect most of the other
advanced improvisers of the '60s, including John Coltrane, Eric Dolphy,
and the free-jazz players of the mid-'60s. One set, a nearly 40-minute jam
called *Free Jazz* (which other than a few brief themes was basically a pulse-
driven group free improvisation) had Coleman, Cherry, Haden, LaFaro,
Higgins, Blackwell, Dolphy, and Freddie Hubbard forming a double quartet.

In 1962 Ornette Coleman, feeling that he was worth much more
money than the clubs and his label were paying him, surprised the jazz
world by retiring for a period. He took up trumpet and violin (playing the
latter as if it were a drum!) and in 1965 he recorded a few brilliant sets on
all his instruments with a particularly strong trio featuring bassist David
Izenzon and drummer Charles Moffett. Later in the decade Coleman had
a quartet with the very complementary tenor Dewey Redman, Haden,
and either Blackwell or his young son Denardo Coleman on drums. In
addition Coleman wrote some atonal and wholly composed classical
works for chamber groups and had a few reunions with Don Cherry.

In the early '70s Ornette Coleman entered the second half of his
career. He formed a "double quartet" comprised of two guitars, two electric bassists, two drummers, and his own alto. The group, called "Prime
Time," featured dense, noisy, and often-witty ensembles in which all of
the musicians are supposed to have an equal role but the leader's alto
always ended up standing out. He now calls his music "Harmolodics"

(symbolizing the equal importance of harmony, melody, and rhythm),
although "free funk" (combining together loose funk rhythms and free
improvising) probably fits better; among his sidemen in Prime Time
have been drummer Ronald Shannon Jackson and bassist Jamaaladeen
Tacuma in addition to his son Denardo.

Prime Time was a major (if somewhat unacknowledged) influence on
the M-Base music of Steve Coleman and Greg Osby. Pat Metheny (a lifelong Ornette admirer) collaborated with Coleman on the intense *Song X*,
Jerry Garcia played third guitar on one recording, and Ornette had irregular reunions with his original quartet members in the '80s.

Ornette Coleman, who currently records for Verve, has remained true to
his highly original vision throughout his career and, although not technically a virtuoso and still considered controversial, is an obvious giant of
jazz. —*Scott Yanow*

The Music of Ornette Coleman: Something Else!!! / Feb. 10, 1958-Mar.
24, 1958 / Original Jazz Classics ✦✦✦

Tomorrow Is the Question! / Jan. 16, 1959-Mar. 10, 1959 / Original Jazz
Classics ✦✦✦

The Shape of Jazz to Come / May 22, 1959 / Atlantic ✦✦✦✦
Altoist Ornette Coleman's first Atlantic recording was his first with his
somewhat revolutionary quartet, which included cornetist Don Cherry,
bassist Charlie Haden, and drummer Billy Higgins. Because the solos did
not follow any set chord pattern, this music became known as "free jazz."
This CD reissue, which has also been included in Rhino's six-CD Ornette
Coleman box set, is highlighted by the original version of Coleman's most
famous composition, "Lonely Woman," plus "Peace" and "Congeniality."
This music would greatly influence jazz of the mid-'60s and still sounds
quite advanced. —*Scott Yanow*

Twins / May 22, 1959 / Atlantic ✦✦✦

The Art of Improvisers / May 22, 1959-Mar. 27, 1961 / Atlantic ✦✦✦

☆ **Beauty Is a Rare Thing: Complete Atlantic Recordings** / May 22,
1959-Mar. 27, 1961 / Rhino/Atlantic ✦✦✦✦✦
This six-CD box set (which includes a very informative and colorful 70-
page booklet) has all of altoist Ornette Coleman's recordings for the Atlantic label. These performances, considered quite revolutionary at the time
since Coleman did not use any chord changes, still sound futuristic today.
Not only is all the music included from the albums *The Shape of Jazz to
Come*, *This Is Our Music*, *Free Jazz*, *Ornette* and *Ornette on Tenor* along
with the two later sets of unissued material (*The Art of the Improvisers*
and *Twins*) but a record only previously out in Japan (*To Whom Who
Keeps a Record*), two songs that feature Coleman on a Gunther Schuller
album, and six cuts never out before. Although more general listeners may
be content with one or two of Ornette Coleman's albums, serious collectors
will want to get this very valuable set while it is still around, for it contains
some of the most important jazz recordings of the early '60s. —*Scott
Yanow*

Change of the Century / Oct. 8, 1959-Oct. 9, 1959 / Atlantic ✦✦✦✦
Altoist Ornette Coleman originally recorded six albums for Atlantic (not
counting later releases of temporarily discarded tracks), and this particular
one was his second. With Don Cherry (on pocket trumpet), bassist Charlie
Haden, and drummer Billy Higgins, Coleman introduces such interesting
and unpredictable "free" pieces as the rhythmic "Una Muy Bonita," "Ramblin'," and "Bird Food." This is important (and still advanced) music that
deserves to be heard either in this set or as part of the comprehensive
Rhino six-CD box of Coleman's Atlantic recordings. —*Scott Yanow*

This Is Our Music / Jul. 19, 1960-Aug. 2, 1960 / Atlantic ✦✦✦✦

Free Jazz (A Collective Improvisation) / Dec. 21, 1960 / Atlantic ✦✦✦✦
This was one of the most controversial jazz recordings of the period,
although when compared to John Coltrane's *Ascension* of five years later,
Free Jazz sounds quite melodic and even slightly conservative. Altoist
Ornette Coleman gathered together a "double quartet" comprised of bass
clarinetist Eric Dolphy, Don Cherry and Freddie Hubbard on trumpets,
Scott LaFaro and Charlie Haden on basses, and both Billy Higgins and Ed
Blackwell on drums. Although there is an opening melody, a steady pulse
and loose but organized parts between the solos, otherwise this music
(which is continuous for around 36.5 minutes) is completely free. While
one player improvises, the other musicians are free to "comment" behind
the solo. The ten-minute stretch when Ornette Coleman is the lead voice
and the other three horns come up with free "riffs" is the high point of this
very interesting recording (which has also been reissued in Rhino's six-CD
Coleman box set). —*Scott Yanow*

Jazzlore: Ornette Coleman, Vol. 29 / Jan. 31, 1961 / Atlantic ✦✦✦

Ornette on Tenor / Mar. 22, 1961-Mar. 27, 1961 / Atlantic ✦✦✦

Town Hall Concert 1962 / Dec. 21, 1962 / ESP ✦✦✦

● **At the "Golden Circle" in Stockholm, Vol. 1** / Dec. 3, 1965-Dec. 4, 1965
/ Blue Note ✦✦✦✦
Ornette Coleman was at the peak of his powers by 1965. His alto playing
had become quite a bit stronger than in his early days, and Coleman's trio
with bassist David Izenson and drummer Charles Moffett was as exciting

as his earlier quartet. On this CD reissue of a Blue Note LP, he stretches out on four of his originals ("Faces and Places," "European Echoes," "Dee Dee," and "Dawn") and plays consistently innovative and surprising solos that probably confused the majority of his audience while delighting others. This set is recommended, as is the second volume. — *Scott Yanow*

At the "Golden Circle" in Stockholm, Vol. 2 / Dec. 3, 1965-Dec. 4, 1965 / Blue Note ✦✦✦✦
The second of two volumes (reissued on CD) documenting a series of concerts in Stockholm, Sweden, by the 1965 Ornette Coleman Trio is almost the equal of the first. Coleman plays his primitive violin and trumpet on "Snowflakes and Sunshine" but sticks to alto (at its prime during this period) during his other three originals ("Morning Song," "The Riddle," and "Antiques"). The interplay between brilliant bassist David Izenson and drummer Charles Moffett is also quite impressive on this recommended set of free jazz. — *Scott Yanow*

Empty Foxhole / Sep. 9, 1966 / Blue Note ✦✦✦

Love Call / Apr. 29, 1968+May 7, 1968 / Blue Note ✦✦✦✦
Ornette Coleman's 1968 quartet featured the explorative tenor of Dewey Redman (who blended in very well with Coleman's alto), bassist Jimmy Garrison, and drummer Elvin Jones. For this CD reissue, which was recorded at the same sessions that resulted in *New York Is Now*, the original four songs are augmented by two "new" alternate takes and "Just for You," which was previously available only in Japan. The interplay between Coleman and Redman on these free-jazz jams and the similarity of their approaches, even though they had different sounds, make this unit a particularly strong group. This CD is about as accessible as Ornette Coleman ever became. — *Scott Yanow*

New York Is Now / Apr. 29, 1968+May 7, 1968 / Blue Note ✦✦✦✦
Altoist Ornette Coleman had a particularly strong group at the time of his 1968 Blue Note recordings, which resulted in the music heard on this CD and its companion, *Love Call*. Dewey Redman was the equivalent of Coleman on tenor, while bassist Jimmy Garrison and drummer Elvin Jones were alumni of John Coltrane's Quartet. For the CD version, a "new" alternate take of "Broad Way Blues" was added to the original program, and although none of the melodies caught on, the complementary playing by Coleman and Redman in particular is quite impressive, making this free-jazz set highly recommended. — *Scott Yanow*

Science Fiction / Sep. 9, 1971-Sep. 13, 1971 / Columbia ✦✦✦

Broken Shadows / Sep. 1971-Sep. 1972 / Columbia ✦✦✦

Virgin Beauty / 1988 / Portrait ✦✦✦

Tone Dialing / Oct. 1995 / Harmolodic/Verve ✦✦✦✦
Ornette Coleman's first album in several years and first recording for a major label in quite some time features his 1995 version of Prime Time with two guitars, two bassists, son Denardo Coleman on drums, and Badal Roy on tables and percussion. In addition the band includes Dave Bryant, Coleman's first keyboardist in decades (although his part is actually fairly minor). The ensembles are funky and quite dense, Coleman really wails on alto (also playing a bit of violin and trumpet), and despite the inclusion of one obnoxious rap, this free-funk set is well worth picking up by openminded listeners. — *Scott Yanow*

Steve Coleman

b. Sep. 20, 1956, Chicago, IL
Sax (Alto) / Post-Bop, Free Funk
The leader of what he termed "M-Base" (short for macro-basic array of structured extemporization), Steve Coleman has a strikingly original alto style (very different from bebop), and his groups through the years have utilized funk rhythms and some nonjazz elements in an unpredictable and creative fashion. Coleman started on alto when he was 15 and played R&B in his early days. After moving to New York in 1978, Coleman played with the Thad Jones-Mel Lewis Orchestra, Cecil Taylor, and Sam Rivers. After the mid-'80s he has usually been heard either with his group Five Elements or with such M-Base players as Greg Osby, Gary Thomas, Graham Haynes, Robin Eubanks, Geri Allen, and Cassandra Wilson. Coleman has recorded sessions as a leader for JMT and Novus and been a sideman with David Murray, Dave Holland, and Branford Marsalis. He is one of the most potentially significant saxophonists of the '90s. — *Scott Yanow*

Motherland Pulse / Mar. 1985 / JMT ✦✦✦

On the Edge of Tomorrow / Jan. 1986+Feb. 1986 / JMT ✦✦✦✦
Modern soul music. This is real contemporary funk, most of it danceable. With Geri Allen (synth) and Cassandra Wilson (v). — *Michael Erlewine*

World Expansion / Nov. 1986 / JMT ✦✦✦
With Geri Allen (k) and Robin Eubanks (tb). Not his jazziest release, but a lot of good clean funk. — *Michael Erlewine*

Rhythm People (The Resurrection of Creative Black Civilization) / 1990 / Novus ✦✦✦
Steve Coleman & the Five Elements. Funky, creative improvisations along the lines of Ornette Coleman's harmolodic music. With Dave Holland (b) and Robin Eubanks (tbn). — *Michael Erlewine*

● **Black Science** / 1991 / Novus ✦✦✦✦
Rhythm in Mind (The Carnegie Project) / Apr. 29, 1991 / Novus ✦✦✦

Buddy Collette (William Marcell Collette)

b. Aug. 6, 1921, Los Angeles, CA
Clarinet, Flute, Sax (Tenor) / Cool
An important force in the Los Angeles jazz community, Buddy Collette was an early pioneer at playing jazz on the flute. Collette started on piano as a child and then gradually learned all of the woodwinds. He played with Les Hite in 1942, led a dance band while in the Navy during World War II, and then freelanced in the Los Angeles area with such bands as the Stars of Swing (1946), Edgar Hayes, Louis Jordan, Benny Carter, and Gerald Wilson (1949-50). An early teacher of Charles Mingus, Collette became the first African-American musician to get a permanent spot in a West Coast studio band (1951-55). He gained his greatest recognition as an important member of the Chico Hamilton Quintet (1955-56), and he recorded several albums as a leader in the mid-to-late '50s for Contemporary. Otherwise he mostly stuck to the Los Angeles area, freelancing, working in the studios, playing in clubs, teaching and inspiring younger musicians. Although a fine tenor player and a good clarinetist, Collette's most distinctive voice is on flute; he recorded an album with one of his former students, the great James Newton (1989). In addition Collette participated in a reunion of the Chico Hamilton Quintet and recorded a two-disc "talking record" for the Issues label in 1994, in which he discussed some of what he had seen and experienced through the years. — *Scott Yanow*

Tanganyika / 1954 / VSOP ✦✦✦

● **Man of Many Parts** / Feb. 13, 1956-Apr. 17, 1956 / Original Jazz Classics ✦✦✦✦
Compiled from three 1956 recording sessions—his first as a leader. — *Michael Erlewine*

Nice Day with Buddy Collette / Nov. 6, 1956-Feb. 18, 1957 / Original Jazz Classics ✦✦✦✦

Jazz Loves Paris / Jan. 24, 1958 / Original Jazz Classics ✦✦✦

Alice Coltrane

b. Aug. 27, 1937, Detroit, MI
Organ, Piano, Harp / Avant-Garde, Free Jazz
Alice Coltrane was a good hard-bop pianist with Terry Gibbs who subsequently altered her style and became a McCoy Tyner follower when she joined John Coltrane's band in the late '60s. She replaced Tyner in 1966, a move of epic proportions. She added colors and textures to the expansive, constantly shifting wave of sound generated by Coltrane, Pharoah Sanders, and Rashied Ali. Alice Coltrane has harp playing, with its rippling, ethereal impact, and her swirling organ solos heard on later albums were often more striking than her piano solos. She studied classical music and jazz as a child, playing in church groups. Coltrane worked in the bands of Kenny Burrell, Johnny Griffin, Lucky Thompson, and Yusef Lateef. During the early '60s, while working and recording with Terry Gibbs, she met John Coltrane. They married in 1965, and a year later she was in the group. After his death, Alice Coltrane led various bands, playing with Sanders, Archie Shepp, Joe Henderson, Frank Lowe, and Carlos Ward, as well as Cecil McBee, Jimmy Garrison, Ben Riley, and Roy Haynes. Her early '70s albums blended strings, Asian, and Eastern melodies, rhythms, instrumentation, and influences, plus free-jazz elements. Alice Coltrane moved to California in the early '70s. She formed the Vedantic Center in 1975, a retreat for the study of Eastern/Asian religions. Since the 1978 album *Transfiguration* Coltrane's seldom performed, although she did play with a quartet including her sons in a 1987 tribute to John Coltrane at the Cathedral of St. John the Divine in New York. Alice Coltrane has only a couple of selections available on CD but can also be heard on many late-period John Coltrane reissues. — *Ron Wynn*

● **Ptah the El Daoud** / Jan. 26, 1970 / Impulse ✦✦✦✦
After John Coltrane's death in 1967, his widow Alice Coltrane recorded a few albums and then dropped out of the jazz scene to raise a family and become much more involved in her religious life. This album was arguably her finest post-1967 recording. Playing piano and harp in a quintet with the tenors of Pharoah Sanders and Joe Henderson, bassist Ron Carter, and drummer Ben Riley, Coltrane stretches out on four of her compositions, sounding both soulful and spiritual. She had grown as a pianist during the past three years, and it is a pity that she did not continue after this session on a full-time basis. — *Scott Yanow*

Journey in Satchidananda / Jul. 4, 1970+Nov. 8, 1970 / MCA ✦✦✦
Harp and strings with jazz and Indian influences. Extraordinarily beautiful. — *Michael G. Nastos*

John Coltrane

b. Sep. 23, 1926, Hamlet, NC, d. Jul. 17, 1967, New York, NY
Sax (Soprano), Sax (Tenor) / Avant-Garde, Hard Bop, Free Jazz, Groove
The most influential jazz musician of the past 35 years (only Miles Davis

comes close), one of the greatest saxophonists of all time, and a remarkable innovator, John Coltrane certainly made his impact on jazz! Unlike most musicians, Coltrane's style changed gradually but steadily over time. His career can be divided into at least five periods: Early days (1947-54), searching stylist (1955-56), sheets of sound (1957-59), the classic quartet (1960-64), and avant-garde (1965-67). Originally an altoist, he played in a Navy band during his period in the military, recording four privately issued songs in 1946. He settled in Philadelphia and then toured with King Kolax (1946-47), switched to tenor when he played with Eddie "Cleanhead" Vinson (1947-48), joined the Dizzy Gillespie big band (1948-49), and was with Dizzy's sextet (1950-51). Radio broadcasts from the latter association find Coltrane sounding heavily influenced by Dexter Gordon and hinting slightly at his future sound. He followed that gig with periods spent with the groups of Gay Crosse (1952), Earl Bostic (1952), Johnny Hodges (1953-54), and in Philadelphia for a few weeks with Jimmy Smith (1955).

The John Coltrane story really starts with his joining the Miles Davis Quintet in 1955. At first some observers wondered what Miles saw in the 28-year-old tenor who had an unusual sound and whose ideas sometimes stretched beyond his technique. However, Davis was a masterful talent scout who could always hear potential greatness. Coltrane improved month by month and by 1956 was competing with Sonny Rollins as the top young tenor; he even battled him to a draw on their recording of "Tenor Madness." Coltrane (along with Red Garland, Paul Chambers, and Philly Joe Jones) formed an important part of the classic Miles Davis Quintet, recording with Miles for Prestige and Columbia during 1955-56. In addition, 'Trane was starting to be featured on many of Prestige's jam-session-oriented albums.

1957 was the key year in John Coltrane's career. Fired by Miles Davis due to his heroin addiction, Coltrane permanently kicked the habit. He spent several months playing with Thelonious Monk's Quartet, a mutually beneficial association that gave Monk long-overdue acclaim and greatly accelerated the tenor's growth. His playing became even more adventurous than it had been, he recorded *Blue Train* (his first great album as a leader), and when he rejoined Miles Davis in early 1958, Coltrane was unquestionably the most important tenor in jazz. During his next two years with Davis, 'Trane (whose style had been accurately dubbed "sheets of sound" by critic Ira Gitler) really took the chordal improvisation of bop to the breaking point, playing groups of notes with extreme speed and really tearing into the music. In addition to being one of the stars of Davis' recordings (including *Milestones* and *Kind of Blue*), Coltrane signed a contract with Atlantic and began to record classics of his own; "Giant Steps" (with its very complex chord structure) and "Naima" were among the many highlights.

By 1960 John Coltrane was long overdue to be a leader, and Miles Davis reluctantly let him go. 'Trane's direction was changing from utilizing as many chords as possible (it would be difficult to get any more extreme in that direction) to playing passionately over one- or two-chord vamps. He hired pianist McCoy Tyner, drummer Elvin Jones, and went through several bassists (Steve Davis, Art Davis, Reggie Workman) before settling on Jimmy Garrison in late 1961. The first artist signed to the new Impulse label, Coltrane was given complete freedom to record what he wanted. He had recently begun doubling on soprano, bringing an entirely new sound and approach to an instrument previously associated with the Dixieland of Sidney Bechet (although Steve Lacy had already started specializing on it) and Coltrane's 1960 Atlantic recording of "My Favorite Things" became a sort of theme song that he revisited on a nightly basis.

John Coltrane continued to evolve during 1961-64. He added Eric Dolphy as part of his group for a period and recorded extensively at the Village Vanguard in late 1961; the lengthy explorations were branded by conservative critics as "anti-jazz." Partly to counter their stereotyping (and short memories), 'Trane recorded with Duke Ellington in a quartet, a ballad program, and a collaboration with singer Johnny Hartman; his playing throughout was quite beautiful. But live in concert his solos (which could be 45 minutes in length) were always intense and continually searching. He utilized such songs as "Impressions" (which used the same two-chord framework as Miles Davis' "So What") and "Afro Blue" for long workouts and took stunning cadenzas on the ballad "I Want to Talk About You." In addition to the Impulse recordings, European radio broadcasts have since been released that show Coltrane's progress and consistency. And in December 1964 he displayed his vast interest in Eastern religion by recording the very popular *A Love Supreme*.

In 1965 it all began to change. Influenced and inspired by the intense and atonal flights of Albert Ayler, Archie Shepp, and Pharoah Sanders, Coltrane's music dropped most of the melodies and essentially became passionate sound explorations. *Ascension* from mid-year featured six additional horns (plus a second bassist) added to the quartet for almost totally free improvisations. Fast themes (such as "One Down, One Up" and "Sun Ship") were quickly disposed of on the way to waves of sound. Coltrane began to use Pharoah Sanders in his group to raise the intensity level even more, and when he hired Rashied Ali as second drummer, it eventually

caused McCoy Tyner (who said he could no longer hear himself) and Elvin Jones to depart.

In 1966 Coltrane had a quintet consisting of his wife Alice on piano, Sanders, Ali, and the lone holdover Jimmy Garrison. After a triumphant visit to Japan, Coltrane's health began to fail. Although the cause of his death on July 17, 1967, was listed as liver cancer, in reality it was probably overwork. Coltrane used to practice ten to twelve hours a day, and when he had a job (which featured marathon solos), he would often spend his breaks practicing in his dressing room! It was only through such single-mindedness that he could reach such a phenomenal technical level, but the net result was his premature death.

Virtually every recording that John Coltrane made throughout his career is currently available on CD, quite a few books about him have been written, and a video (*The Coltrane Legacy*) gives today's jazz followers an opportunity to see him performing on a pair of half-hour television shows. Since Coltrane's passing no other giant has dominated jazz on the same level. In fact many other saxophonists have built their entire careers on exploring music from just one of John Coltrane's periods! —*Scott Yanow*

The Last Giant: Anthology / 1946 / Rhino ♦♦

This deluxe two-CD set is a major disappointment. It contains a few revelations (a brief 1946 recording of "Hot House" featuring a 20-year-old Coltrane, an aircheck with Dizzy Gillespie, and a rare side by Gay Crosse's Good Humor Six in 1952) but mostly repackages familiar material and includes nothing from Coltrane's very important years with Impulse. Why weren't all four of the 1946 sides included and why are only the first 90 seconds heard from Coltrane's final performance before it fades out? The accompanying booklet is quite attractive, but this set (which will greatly frustrate completists) only gives an incomplete picture of the great saxophonist. —*Scott Yanow*

☆ John Coltrane: The Prestige Recordings / May 7, 1956-Dec. 26, 1958 / Prestige ♦♦♦♦♦

During 1956-58 Coltrane participated in 27 recording sessions for the Prestige label (not counting his three dates with the Miles Davis Quintet), both as a leader and as a sideman. Although these recordings are not as significant on a whole as Coltrane's later Impulse albums, there are many gems among the jam sessions, and all of the music (except the Davis sessions) have been released in their entirety on this somewhat remarkable 16-CD set. Coltrane and a constantly changing all-star cast perform such classics as "Tenor Madness" (his one-time meeting on records with Sonny Rollins), "On a Misty Night," "While My Lady Sleeps," "Like Someone in Love," "Black Pearls," and "Stardust," among many others. This expensive box may not be for all jazz collections, but any true fan of John Coltrane will have to acquire it. —*Scott Yanow*

Dakar / Mar. 22, 1957-Apr. 20, 1957 / Prestige ♦♦♦

Wheelin' / Apr. 19, 1957-Sep. 20, 1957 / Prestige ♦♦♦

Cattin' with Coltrane and Quinichette / May 17, 1957 / DCC Jazz ♦♦♦♦

Although John Coltrane gets top billing, this CD reissue from DCC Jazz is really an excellent set by tenor Paul Quinichette, who was always most notable for the similarity of his sound and style to Lester Young in the '50s. There are the five selections from the original album which, in addition to Quinichette (who has "Exactly like You" as his feature) and Coltrane, includes pianist Mal Waldron, bassist Julian Euell, and drummer Ed Thigpen, plus an unreleased version of "Tea for Two" without Coltrane and three previously unknown numbers from a 1952 Quinichette session with a four-piece rhythm section. The sound quality on this CD is superb, and the swing-bop music has plenty of strong moments. There were not that many recordings made by Paul Quinichette and most are out of print, making this rare release fairly significant. —*Scott Yanow*

Bahia / May 17, 1957-Dec. 26, 1958 / Prestige ♦♦♦

More Lasting than Bronze / May 31, 1957 / Prestige ♦♦♦♦

Lush Life / Aug. 16, 1957 / Original Jazz Classics ♦♦♦♦

Fine session in which Coltrane stripped away his usual surrounding sound and recorded in a trio format. He's backed only by bassist Earl May and drummer Art Taylor, working in a pianoless format championed by Sonny Rollins. The extra space seems to benefit him, as his solos on these cuts are emphatic and exuberant. —*Ron Wynn*

Rain or Shine / Aug. 16, 1957 / Prestige ♦♦♦

The Last Trane / Aug. 16, 1957-Mar. 26, 1958 / Original Jazz Classics ♦♦♦

Traning In / Aug. 23, 1957 / Original Jazz Classics ♦♦♦

★ Blue Train / Sep. 15, 1957 / Blue Note ♦♦♦♦♦

A landmark album—stunning. This is Coltrane's only Blue Note recording as a leader, and he never made a better album in this particular hard-bop style. A must-hear for all jazz fans, Blue Train includes Coltrane's most impressive early composition, "Moment's Notice." With outstanding performances from sidemen Lee Morgan (tpt), Curtis Fuller (tb), and Kenny Drew (p). —*Michael Erlewine*

Black Pearls / Jan. 10, 1958-May 23, 1958 / Prestige ♦♦♦♦

Soultrane / Feb. 7, 1958 / Prestige ✦✦✦✦
Coltrane works with the Red Garland trio, a busy unit during this period. He tackles these standards with a quiet confidence, sometimes extending his solos, other times merely expanding the original melody. Garland was an excellent soloist on standards and ballads, while Paul Chambers on bass and drummer Art Taylor provided their own sterling counterpoint. —*Ron Wynn*

Coltrane Time / Oct. 13, 1958 / Blue Note ✦✦✦✦
This is a most unusual CD due to the inclusion of Cecil Taylor on piano. Although Taylor and John Coltrane got along well, trumpeter Kenny Dorham (who is also on this quintet date) hated the avant-garde pianist's playing and was clearly bothered by Taylor's dissonant comping behind his solos. With bassist Chuck Israels and drummer Louis Hayes doing their best to ignore the discord, the group manages to perform two blues and two standards with Dorham playing strictly bop, Taylor coming up with fairly free abstractions, and Coltrane sounding somewhere in between. The results are unintentionally fascinating. —*Scott Yanow*

★ **Heavyweight Champion: The Complete Atlantic Recordings** / Jan. 15, 1959-May 25, 1961 / Rhino/Atlantic ✦✦✦✦✦
John Coltrane's two years with Atlantic can be thought of as his "middle period" during which he evolved from his sheets of sound approach to intense explorations over two-chord vamps. It is difficult to see how Rhino could have done a better job with this reissue, for they have come out with every scrap that could be found from Coltrane's Atlantic period. On the seven-CD box set is reissued the complete contents of the albums *Bags & Trane, Giant Steps, Coltrane Jazz, My Favorite Things, Coltrane Plays the Blues, Ole Coltrane, The Avant-Garde,* and *Coltrane's Sound,* the selections originally issued on *Alternate Takes* and three "new" alternate takes, plus (for the final CD) many previously unheard versions of five numbers including nine takes of "Giant Steps!" With such supporting players as vibraphonist Milt Jackson (who was actually the co-leader of *Bags and Trane*); pianists Hank Jones, Cedar Walton, Tommy Flanagan, Wynton Kelly, and McCoy Tyner; bassists Paul Chambers, Charlie Haden, Percy Heath, Steve Davis, Art Davis, and Reggie Workman; drummers Connie Kay, Lex Humphries, Art Taylor, Jimmy Cobb, Ed Blackwell, and Elvin Jones; trumpeters Don Cherry and Freddie Hubbard; and Eric Dolphy on alto and flute, it is not too surprising that the music is both innovative and classic. This perfectly done box (which also has a fine booklet) is essential for all serious jazz collections. —*Scott Yanow*

★ **Giant Steps** / Apr. 1, 1959 / Atlantic ✦✦✦✦✦
This is one of John Coltrane's classic sets; in fact this CD reissue (which adds alternate takes to five of the seven original recordings) almost doubles one's pleasure. In "Giant Steps" Coltrane built a tongue-twister of chord changes (stretching bop to its logical breaking point), which he would soon abandon in favor of long drones on simpler patterns. Not only does this CD give one the two earliest versions of "Giant Steps" but also "Naima," "Cousin Mary," "Spiral," "Syeeda's Song Flute," the underrated but remarkable "Countdown," and "Mr. P.C." Recorded while Coltrane was still with Miles Davis' group, this CD (which mostly features pianist Tommy Flanagan, bassist Paul Chambers, and drummer Art Taylor) made it obvious that Coltrane had something very important of his own to say and that he would need his own band in the future to fully express himself. —*Scott Yanow*

Coltrane Jazz / Nov. 24, 1959-Dec. 2, 1959 / Atlantic ✦✦✦
This CD contains the original LP program plus alternate takes of "Like Sonny" and "I'll Wait and Pray." With the exception of "Village Blues" (which features Coltrane's 1960 quartet) and the earlier alternate of "Like Sonny," this set features Coltrane in 1959 with the Miles Davis rhythm section of the time: pianist Wynton Kelly, bassist Paul Chambers, and drummer Jimmy Cobb. "My Shining Hour" and "Harmonique" are among the highlights of this excellent release. —*Scott Yanow*

Avant Garde / Jun. 20, 1960-Jul. 8, 1960 / Atlantic ✦✦✦

Coltrane Plays the Blues / Oct. 24, 1960 / Atlantic ✦✦✦✦
Recorded during the same week as his original version of "My Favorite Things," this LP by John Coltrane features six blues-oriented originals (five by Trane) including "Blues to Bechet" and "Mr. Syms." The music is more melodic than usual, with Coltrane playing soprano on two of the six tracks; "Blues to You" is the best showcase for his intense tenor. —*Scott Yanow*

Coltrane's Sound / Oct. 24, 1960 / Atlantic ✦✦✦✦
Although one may not think of *Coltrane's Sound* as being one of John Coltrane's most famous recordings, when one looks at its contents it quickly becomes obvious that this set ranks near the top. This CD reissue contains such classic material as "Central Park West," "Equinox," a reharmonized (and influential) version of "Body and Soul," the underrated "Satellite," "Liberia," and an intense rendition of "The Night Has a Thousand Eyes." Also included on this reissue is an alternate version of "Body and Soul" and the lesser-known "262." Co-starring pianist McCoy Tyner, bassist Steve Davis, and drummer Elvin Jones, this set is highly recommended. —*Scott Yanow*

★ **My Favorite Things** / Oct. 24, 1960-Oct. 26, 1960 / Atlantic ✦✦✦✦✦
This LP was very influential when it came out and remains a classic. The first full album by the classic John Coltrane Quartet (with pianist McCoy Tyner, drummer Elvin Jones, and their bassist of the time Steve Davis) consists of a fiery "Summertime," the lyrical "But Not for Me," a nice ballad for Trane's soprano on "Everytime We Say Goodbye," and most importantly, the lengthy "My Favorite Things." On the latter, Coltrane, who had used a seemingly endless number of chords on the prior year's "Giant Steps," reduces the chords to a minimum and plays passionately over a repetitious vamp, creating startlingly new music. This set has since been reissued on CD, and in one form or another, is essential. —*Scott Yanow*

Complete Africa/Brass Sessions / May 23, 1961+Jun. 4, 1961 / Impulse ✦✦✦✦
John Coltrane's first recordings for Impulse are different than any of his later ones for they feature the saxophonist accompanied by large brass-heavy 14- to 17-piece groups. This two-CD set has all of the music which was originally released on *Africa/Brass,* the later *Africa/Brass Sessions—Volume Two,* and *Trane's Modes.* In general the arrangements are essentially an expansion of the style and sound of the John Coltrane Quartet with much of the improvising ("Blues Minor" excepted) taking place over two-chord vamps. Eric Dolphy wrote all but a pair of the charts (there are one apiece from McCoy Tyner and Calvin Massey), and he based his orchestrations on the piano voicings of Tyner. The only soloists are Coltrane (on both tenor and soprano) and his regular quartet members; it is disappointing that Dolphy, Freddie Hubbard, and Booker Little are not really heard from. While Massey's "The Damned Don't Cry" falters and sounds underrehearsed, the three renditions of "Africa" are quite colorful. But since over half of the performance time is taken up by "Africa," this two-CD set is not for everyone! —*Scott Yanow*

Ole Coltrane / May 25, 1961 / Atlantic ✦✦✦✦
One of John Coltrane's most interesting sessions for Atlantic was also his last before exclusively switching to Impulse. This CD, which contains the original three selections from the LP ("Ole," "Dahomey Dance," and "Aisha") in addition to one item from the same date that was not released until decades later ("To Her Ladyship"), features the great saxophonist leading an all-star group (Eric Dolphy on alto and flute, trumpeter Freddie Hubbard, pianist McCoy Tyner, bassists Reggie Workman and Art Davis, and drummer Elvin Jones) on a variety of very interesting material. "Ole" is quite haunting and "Dahomey Dance" became a minor standard. The solos are more concise than is usual on a Coltrane session, and this set is quite accessible even to listeners who prefer his earlier "sheets of sound" recordings. —*Scott Yanow*

Live at the Village Vanguard / Nov. 2, 1961-Nov. 3, 1961 / Impulse ✦✦✦✦
It is surprising, considering how much additional material from John Coltrane's week at the Village Vanguard in Nov. 1961 has surfaced, that this CD reissue only includes the original LP program. However, the music is consistently excellent, with the moody "Spiritual" (which features Coltrane's soprano and Eric Dolphy's bass clarinet) living up to its title, Trane jamming happily on a bebopbish "Softly as in a Morning Sunrise" and roaring on a marathon tenor solo during "Chasin' the Trane." This classic music hopefully will be released someday along with all of the other surviving performances in a larger set. —*Scott Yanow*

Newport '63 / Nov. 2, 1961-Jul. 7, 1963 / Impulse ✦✦✦✦
Three of the four lengthy performances on this CD are taken from one of the John Coltrane Quartet's greatest performances: the 1963 Newport Jazz Festival. With pianist McCoy Tyner, bassist Jimmy Garrison, and drummer Roy Haynes (filling in for an absent Elvin Jones), Coltrane performs what is arguably his greatest version of "My Favorite Things" along with memorable renditions of "Impressions" and "I Want to Talk About You." Two of those selections originally appeared on the LP *Selflessness,* while "Impression" was included in a later collection. This set is rounded out by "Chasin' Another Trane," the only recording from Trane's famous Nov. 1961 engagement at the Village Vanguard that had Roy Haynes sitting in for Elvin Jones; altoist Eric Dolphy is also heard from on that heated selection. —*Scott Yanow*

Ballads / Dec. 21, 1961 / Impulse ✦✦✦
Stung by criticism from conservative jazz critics, Coltrane decided to show his detractors that he had not forgotten how to embrace a melody; the problem is that on this brief set (reissued on CD by GRP in an attractive fold-out package) he never really gets away from the themes. While Trane (who sticks to tenor) plays quite pretty, pianist McCoy Tyner actually has the more interesting solos. Coltrane shows the tunes an excess of respect, making this outing with his classic quartet enjoyable as background music but lacking much passion. —*Scott Yanow*

Coltrane / Apr. 11, 1962-Jun. 29, 1962 / Impulse ✦✦✦✦
John Coltrane and his classic Quartet (pianist McCoy Tyner, bassist Jimmy Garrison, and drummer Elvin Jones) are in fine form for this 1962 studio LP. High points include a passionate "Out of This World" (what did Johnny Mercer think of this version?) and a classic version of Mal Waldron's "Soul Eyes." The remainder of the program includes "The Inch Worm" and the

two Coltrane compositions "Tunji" and "Miles' Mode." Not as intense as many of 'Trane's other albums, this is still a recommended and easily enjoyable set. —*Scott Yanow*

☆ **John Coltrane and Johnny Hartman** / Mar. 7, 1963 / Impulse ✦✦✦✦✦
John Coltrane's matchup with singer Johnny Hartman, although quite unexpected, works extremely well. Hartman, who had not recorded since 1956, was in prime form on the six ballads, and his versions of "Lush Life" and "My One and Only Love" have never been topped. Coltrane's playing throughout the session is beautiful, sympathetic, and still explorative; he sticks exclusively to tenor on the date. At only a half-hour one wishes there were twice as much music, but what is here is classic, essential for all jazz collections. —*Scott Yanow*

Dear Old Stockholm / Apr. 29, 1963 / Impulse ✦✦✦

★ **Live at Birdland** / Oct. 8, 1963 / Impulse ✦✦✦✦✦
Arguably John Coltrane's finest all-around album, this LP (which has since been reissued on CD) has brilliant versions of "AfroBlue" and "I Want to Talk About You"; the second half of the latter features Coltrane on unaccompanied tenor tearing into the piece but never losing sight of the fact that it is a beautiful ballad. The remainder of this album ("Alabama," "The Promise," and "Your Lady") is almost at the same high level. It is highly recommended, either on LP or CD. —*Scott Yanow*

Crescent / Apr. 27, 1964+Jun. 1, 1964 / Impulse ✦✦✦
One of only two studio albums cut by the John Coltrane Quartet during 1964, *Crescent* is most notable for including five Coltrane compositions including the title cut, "Lonnie's Lament," and the swinging "Bessie's Blues." The music is excellent although not as fiery as the Quartet's live performances of the period. —*Scott Yanow*

★ **A Love Supreme** / Dec. 9, 1964 / Impulse ✦✦✦✦
John Coltrane recorded more exciting albums than this one (which has been reissued on CD by GRP) but the highly influential *A Love Supreme* is the project that meant the most to him, his gift to God. In addition to the famous chanting of the title, Coltrane performs a couple of particularly memorable themes (it is surprising that "Resolution" did not become a standard), and the soloing is on a consistently high level. This recording (which also features pianist McCoy Tyner, bassist Jimmy Garrison, and drummer Elvin Jones) closed the book on what could be considered 'Trane's most significant period, for he would begin to more fully explore atonality with the coming of 1965. —*Scott Yanow*

John Coltrane Quartet Plays . . . / Feb. 18, 1965 / Impulse ✦✦✦✦
1965 was one of the turning points in the career of John Coltrane. The great saxophonist, whose playing was always very explorative and searching, crossed the line into atonality during that year, playing very free improvisations (after stating quick throwaway themes) that were full of passion and fury. This particular studio album (the CD is a straight reissue of the original LP) has two standards (a stirring "Chim Chim Cheree" and "Nature Boy") along with two recent Coltrane originals ("Brazilia" and "Song of Praise"). Art Davis plays the second bass on "Nature Boy," but otherwise this set (a perfect introduction for listeners to Coltrane's last period) features the classic Quartet comprised of the leader, pianist McCoy Tyner, bassist Jimmy Garrison, and drummer Elvin Jones. —*Scott Yanow*

Transition / May 26, 1965-Jun. 10, 1965 / Impulse ✦✦✦✦
The title of this CD (a straight reissue of the LP) fits perfectly, for Coltrane was at an important transitional point in his career at the time. Although he was still utilizing the same Quartet that he had had for over three years (pianist McCoy Tyner, bassist Jimmy Garrison, and drummer Elvin Jones) and his music had always been explorative, now he was taking his solos one step beyond into passionate atonality, usually over simple but explosive vamps. Other than the tender ballad "Welcome," most of this set is uncompromisingly intense; in fact the closing 9-minute "Vigil" is a fiery tenor-drums duet. The 21-minute "Suite," even with sections titled "Prayer and Meditation: Day" and "Affirmation," is not overly peaceful. It must have seemed clear, even at this early point, that McCoy Tyner and perhaps Elvin Jones would not be with the band much longer. —*Scott Yanow*

Ascension / Jun. 28, 1965 / Impulse ✦✦✦✦
Coltrane's first album considered tonally "free." —*Michael Erlewine*

The Major Works of John Coltrane / Jun. 1965-Oct. 1965 / Impulse ✦✦✦✦

New Thing at Newport / Jul. 2, 1965 / Impulse ✦✦✦

Sun Ship / Aug. 26, 1965 / Impulse ✦✦✦

Live in Seattle / Sep. 30, 1965 / Impulse ✦✦✦✦

Om / Oct. 1, 1965 / Impulse ✦✦✦
Perhaps Coltrane's only major release of questionable quality, this was reportedly recorded on his first (and only) LSD trip. Featuring screechy playing and moaning vocals, this is for true believers and historical interest only. —*David Nelson McCarthy*

Meditations / Nov. 23, 1965 / Impulse ✦✦✦✦
A perfect companion to *A Love Supreme*. As powerful and pure in spiritual content and intent. Long, extended, embellished passages in hymnlike

prayer session. With Pharoah Sanders (ts), Elvin Jones (d), Rashied Ali (d), McCoy Tyner (p), Jimmy Garrison (b). —*Michael G. Nastos*

Live in Japan / Jul. 1966 / Impulse ✦✦✦

Stellar Regions / Feb. 15, 1967 / Impulse ✦✦✦✦
This is a major set, "new" music from John Coltrane that was recorded February 15, 1967 (five months before his death) but not released for the first time until 1995. One of several "lost" sessions that were stored by Alice Coltrane for decades, only one selection ("Offering," which was on *Expression*) among the eight numbers and three alternates was ever out before. The music, although well worth releasing, offers no real hints as to what Coltrane might have been playing had he lived into the '70s. The performances by the quartet (with pianist Alice Coltrane, bassist Jimmy Garrison, and drummer Rashied Ali) are briefer (2:48-8:54) than Coltrane's recordings of the previous year, but that might have been due to the fact that this music was played in the studio (as opposed to the marathon live blowouts with Pharoah Sanders) or to Coltrane's worsening health. Actually 'Trane (who sticks here exclusively to tenor) is as powerful as usual, showing no compromise in his intense flights and indulging in sound explorations that are as free (but with purpose) as any he had ever done. Coltrane's true fans will want to go out of their way to acquire this intriguing CD. —*Scott Yanow*

Expression / Feb. 15, 1967-Mar. 1967 / Impulse ✦✦✦✦

Interstellar Space / Feb. 22, 1967 / Impulse ✦✦✦✦
Posthumously released, freewheeling date by Coltrane with drummer Rashied Ali in a series of slashing, complementary, and explosive duets. Coltrane was now playing more rhythms than anything else, having leaped beyond notions of chord changes, structure, and melody. Ali sometimes supported him, sometimes challenged him, and held things together as best he could. —*Ron Wynn*

The Best of John Coltrane / Atlantic ✦✦✦✦
I can't imagine not owning lots of Coltrane, but here is an excellent one-disc selection of some of the best of the Coltrane material (on Atlantic) with the accent on the slower tunes. The disc is very easy to listen to. Favorites on the slow side include "Naima" and the much-loved "My Favorite Things." The only more uptempo pieces are the classic "Giant Steps" and "Cousin Mary." The disc was produced by Neshui Ertegun. —*Michael Erlewine*

Eddie Condon (Albert Edwin Condon)

b. Nov. 16, 1905, Goodland, IN, **d.** Aug. 4, 1973, New York, NY
Guitar / Dixieland
A major propagandist for freewheeling Chicago jazz, an underrated rhythm guitarist, and a talented wisecracker, Eddie Condon's main importance to jazz was not so much through his own playing as in his ability to gather together large groups of all-stars and produce exciting, spontaneous, and very coherent music.

Condon started out playing banjo with Hollis Peavey's Jazz Bandits when he was 17, he worked with members of the famed Austin High School Gang in the '20s, and in 1927 he co-led (with Red McKenzie) the McKenzie-Condon Chicagoans on a record date that helped define Chicago jazz (and featured Jimmy McPartland, Jimmy Teschemacher, Joe Sullivan, and Gene Krupa). After organizing some other record sessions, Condon switched to guitar, moved to New York in 1929, worked with Red Nichols' Five Pennies and Red McKenzie's Blue Blowers, and recorded in several settings, including with Louis Armstrong (1929) and the Rhythm Makers (1932). During 1936-37 he co-led a band with Joe Marsala.

Although Condon had to an extent laid low since the beginning of the Depression, in 1938, with the opportunity to lead some sessions for the new Commodore label, he became a major name. Playing nightly at Nick's (1937-44), Condon utilized top musicians in racially mixed groups. He started a long series of exciting recordings (which really continued on several labels up until his death), and his Town Hall concerts of 1944-45 (which were broadcast weekly on the radio) were consistently brilliant and gave him an opportunity to show his verbal acid wit; the GHB label has been at last reissuing them complete and in chronological order. Condon opened his own club in 1945, recorded for Columbia in the '50s (all of those records have been made available by Mosaic on a limited-edition box set), and wrote three colorful books, including his 1948 memoirs, *We Called It Music.* A partial list of the classic musicians who performed and recorded often with Condon include trumpeters/ cornetists Wild Bill Davison, Max Kaminsky, Billy Butterfield, Bobby Hackett, Rex Stewart, and Hot Lips Page; trombonists Jack Teagarden, Lou McGarity, Cutty Cutshall, George Brunies, and Vic Dickenson; clarinetists Pee Wee Russell, Edmond Hall, Joe Marsala, Peanuts Hucko, and Bob Wilbur; Bud Freeman on tenor; baritonist Ernie Caceres; pianists Gene Schroeder, Joe Sullivan, Jess Stacy, and Ralph Sutton; drummers George Wettling, Dave Tough, and Gene Krupa; a string of bassists; and singer Lee Wiley. Many Eddie Condon records are currently available, and no jazz collection is complete without at least a healthy sampling. —*Scott Yanow*

Dixieland All Stars / Aug. 11, 1939-Mar. 27, 1946 / GRP/Decca ✦✦✦✦
Some but not all of Eddie Condon's studio recordings for Decca are included on this single CD. Since five of the 20 selections are actually previously unissued alternate takes and several songs are bypassed altogether, this release will probably drive some collectors mad, but the music is consistently enjoyable. The rhythm guitarist heads an impressive outfit (with trumpeter Max Kaminsky, valve trombonist Brad Gowans, clarinetist Pee Wee Russell, Bud Freeman on tenor, and pianist Joe Sullivan) on four titles from 1939, along with a variety of groups from 1944-46 that feature other top stylists, including trumpeters Billy Butterfield, Bobby Hackett, Yank Lawson, Max Kaminsky, and Wild Bill Davison; trombonists Jack Teagarden and Lou McGarity; baritonist Ernie Caceres; clarinetist Edmond Hall; Tony Parenti; and Joe Dixon; the latter bands perform a variety of standards including eight George Gershwin songs. Dixieland and small-group swing fans will enjoy this set, which serves as a strong example of Eddie Condon's music, at least until a more complete reissue of the valuable recordings takes place. — *Scott Yanow*

Live at Town Hall (1944) / May 11, 1944 / Jass ✦✦✦✦
This consistently exciting CD predates all of the Eddie Condon Town Hall concerts released by Jazzology by a couple of months. Rhythm guitarist Condon, as usual, put together a spontaneous but logical show featuring quite a few top Dixieland all-stars. Trumpeter/vocalist Hot Lips Page takes honors with his "Uncle Sam Blues," but there are also two well received features apiece for pianists Cliff Jackson and Joe Bushkin and plenty of solo space for trumpeters Billy Butterfield and Max Kaminsky, cornetist Bobby Hackett (whose chops are just a little off), trombonist Miff Mole, and clarinetists Edmond Hall and Pee Wee Russell; bassists Bob Casey and Pops Foster and drummers Kansas Fields and George Wettling also make notable contributions. With Condon as the wisecracking M.C. and such highlights as "Muskrat Ramble," "Ja Da," and the lengthy "Impromptu Ensemble," this CD is highly recommended to Eddie Condon and Dixieland fans. — *Scott Yanow*

Town Hall Concerts, Vol. 1 / May 20, 1944-Jun. 10, 1944 / Jazzology ✦✦✦✦
Eddie Condon's *Town Hall Concerts* were historic in several ways. These weekly half-hour radio shows were very uncommercial (in fact they could not attract a sponsor), featured interracial bands, and gave Condon an opportunity to put together well paced programs. He would gather together a core band of Condonites who would have ensemble jams and individual features, and there were always a couple of numbers set aside for guest artists, who would also join in on the show's concluding jam (titled "Impromptu Ensemble") with the regulars. Plus Condon, despite making a few too many jokes at the expense of Pee Wee Russell, proved to be a perfect host. After decades of only being available as incomplete excerpts, these programs have finally been issued complete and in chronological order on a series of two-CD sets by George Buck of Jazzology. The first volume, which has four complete shows, features such classic players as trumpeters Billy Butterfield, Bobby Hackett, Max Kaminsky, Hot Lips Page, and Rex Stewart; clarinetists Pee Wee Russell and Edmond Hall; trombonists Bill Harris, Miff Mole, and Benny Morton; the greatly underrated baritonist Ernie Caceres; and pianists James P. Johnson and Gene Schroeder. Although the recording quality of the very first show is subpar (the only one in the series that is less than flawless technically), all of the volumes in this wonderful series (which find the participants at the peak of their powers) are highly recommended. — *Scott Yanow*

Town Hall Concerts, Vol. 2 / Jun. 17, 1944-Jul. 8, 1944 / Jazzology ✦✦✦✦
This two-CD set has four complete radio shows featuring Eddie Condon's all-star groups during their legendary series of Town Hall concerts. Despite having large ensembles of classic players, Condon was able to feature virtually everyone on every show, still leaving room for ensemble pieces and interplay between the unique musicians. In addition, the verbal commentary of Condon and announcer Fred Robbins is informative and witty (even if they picked on Pee Wee Russell a bit too much). Among the musicians heard on the well recorded set (which like the other volumes in this extensive series is highly recommended to fans of Chicago jazz) include trumpeters Bobby Hackett, Hot Lips Page, Max Kaminsky, Jonah Jones, and Billy Butterfield; trombonists Bill Harris and Benny Morton; clarinetists Pee Wee Russell, Joe Marsala, and Edmond Hall; baritonist Ernie Caceres; and pianists James P. Johnson, Willie "The Lion" Smith, and Gene Schroeder. — *Scott Yanow*

Town Hall Concerts, Vol. 3 / Jul. 15, 1944-Aug. 5, 1944 / Jazzology ✦✦✦✦
The third volume in this very valuable series of two-CD sets contains four half-hour weekly radio shows featuring Eddie Condon's all-star ensembles at Town Hall concerts. Condon (who supplies verbal commentary along with annnouncer Fred Robbins) programmed each show quite skillfully, featuring the large groups of all-stars in logical fashion. This set (which is highly recommended along with the other volumes in the series to followers of traditional jazz) features quite a roster: trumpeters Bobby Hackett, Jonah Jones, Max Kaminsky, and Sterling Bose; trombonist Benny Morton; baritonist Ernie Caceres (who is really in peak form throughout the Condon programs); clarinetists Edmond Hall and Pee Wee Russell; guitarists

Carl Kress and Tony Mottola; pianists Harry "The Hipster" Gibson (taking a couple of rare solos), Willie "The Lion" Smith, Jess Stacy, and Gene Schroeder; bassist Bob Haggart; drummers Gene Krupa, Joe Grauso, and George Wettling; and singer Lee Wiley. — *Scott Yanow*

Town Hall Concerts, Vol. 4 / Aug. 12, 1944-Sep. 2, 1944 / Jazzology ✦✦✦✦
Although they were never able to get a paying sponsor, the "Eddie Condon Town Hall Concerts" (a weekly half-hour radio show) was quite popular at the time and became legendary. For *Volume 4* of this colorful series of well recorded two-CD sets (which is highly recommended to all followers of Chicago jazz), there are four complete programs featuring a remarkable ensemble of top musicians (virtually all of whom are showcased individually and collectively in logical fashion): trumpeters Billy Butterfield, Bobby Hackett, Jonah Jones, Max Kaminsky, and Muggsy Spanier; trombonists Bill Harris, Miff Mole, and Benny Morton; baritonist Ernie Caceres; clarinetists Edmond Hall, Joe Marsala, and Pee Wee Russell; and pianists James P. Johnson, Willie "The Lion" Smith, and Gene Schroeder, in addition to guest drummer Gene Krupa and singer Lee Wiley. — *Scott Yanow*

Town Hall Concerts, Vol. 5 / Sep. 9, 1944-Sep. 30, 1944 / Jazzology ✦✦✦✦

The Town Hall Concerts, Vol. 6 / Oct. 7, 1944-Oct. 28, 1944 / Jazzology ✦✦✦✦

The Town Hall Concerts, Vol. 7 / Nov. 4, 1944-Dec. 2, 1944 / Jazzology ✦✦✦✦

The Town Hall Concerts, Vol. 8 / Dec. 16, 1944-Jan. 6, 1945 / Jazzology ✦✦✦✦

The Town Hall Concerts, Vol. 9 / Jan. 13, 1945-Feb. 3, 1945 / Jazzology ✦✦✦✦

The Dr. Jazz Series, Vol. 5 / Dec. 24, 1951-Mar. 31, 1952 / Storyville ✦✦✦

★ **The Complete CBS Eddie Condon All Stars** / Nov. 24, 1953-Sep. 4, 1962 / Mosaic ✦✦✦✦✦
Chicago jazz and Dixieland fans should go out of their way to pick up this limited-edition five-CD box set. The first four discs date from 1953-57 and feature freewheeling performances (originally out on seven LPs) with such classic soloists as cornetists Wild Bill Davison and Bobby Hackett; trumpeter Billy Butterfield; trombonists Cutty Cutshall, Lou McGarity, and Vic Dickenson; clarinetists Edmond Hall, Peanuts Hucko, Bob Wilber, and Pee Wee Russell; and tenorman Bud Freeman, among others. Eddie Condon's comments during his band's waterlogged performance at the 1957 Newport Jazz Festival alone are worth the price. The final disc of material (all from 1962) is somewhat commercial but still has its moments of interest. — *Scott Yanow*

In Japan / Mar. 1964-Apr. 1964 / Chiaroscuro ✦✦✦
Relaxed and often brilliant soloing from Condonites Buck Clayton, Vic Dickenson, and Pee Wee Russell, with three vocals by Jimmy Rushing. "Stompin' at the Savoy," "Three Little Words," "Rose Room," and more are included. — *Bruce Raeburn*

● **Live at the New School 1972** / Apr. 1972 / Chiaroscuro ✦✦✦✦
This CD reissue (which adds two previously unreleased and rather loose selections to the original program) is historic because it has the final recordings of both rhythm guitarist Eddie Condon and drummer Gene Krupa (who ironically back in 1927 made their recording debut together). More importantly the spirited music made by this quintet (which also features cornetist Wild Bill Davison, Kenny Davern on soprano, and pianist Dick Wellstood) is quite enjoyable and creative within the boundaries of Dixieland and swing. Wellstood in particular is in excellent form, making up for the absence of a bass, and it is very rewarding to hear Krupa in such a spontaneous setting on what may have been the best recording of his final decade. — *Scott Yanow*

Junior Cook (Herman Cook)

b. Jul. 22, 1934, Pensacola, FL, d. Feb. 4, 1992, New York, NY
Sax (Tenor) / *Hard Bop*
An expert hard bop tenor who tended to be overshadowed by more innovative contemporaries, Junior Cook was always a solid improviser. After playing with Dizzy Gillespie in 1958, Cook gained some fame for his long-time membership in the Horace Silver Quintet (1958-64); when he and Blue Mitchell left the popular band, Cook played in Mitchell's quintet (1964-69). Later associations included Freddie Hubbard, Elvin Jones, George Coleman, Louis Hayes (1975-76), Bill Hardman (1979-81), and the McCoy Tyner big band. In addition to many appearances as a sideman, Junior Cook recorded as a leader for Jazzland (1961), Catalyst (1977), Muse, and SteepleChase. — *Scott Yanow*

● **Somethin's Cookin'** / Jun. 12, 1981 / Muse ✦✦✦✦
Junior Cook, who was best known for playing tenor with the Horace Silver Quintet during the period that Blue Mitchell was the group's trumpeter, recorded relatively few sessions as a leader during his career. The muscular but smooth saxophonist is heard at his best on this Muse quartet release, which really showcases his playing (with fine support from pianist

Cedar Walton, bassist Buster Williams, and drummer Billy Higgins). The original program (which includes originals by Walton and Larry Willis) is augmented by four alternate takes for the CD reissue. —*Scott Yanow*

The Place to Be / Nov. 1988 / SteepleChase ✦✦✦

On a Misty Night / Jun. 1989 / SteepleChase ✦✦✦✦

Bob Cooper

b. Dec. 6, 1925, Pittsburgh, PA, **d.** Aug. 5, 1993, Hollywood, CA
Sax (Tenor) / Cool, Hard Bop
One of the great West Coast tenors, Bob Cooper made even the most complex solos sound swinging and accessible. Coop joined Stan Kenton's big band in 1945, and he was a fixture with several of the editions (including the Innovations Orchestra) through 1951; in 1947 he married Kenton's singer, June Christy. After leaving Kenton, Cooper settled in Los Angeles, where he was a busy studio musician for the next four decades. He was a regular member of the Lighthouse All-Stars from 1952-62, sometimes playing oboe and English horn (being the first strong jazz soloist on both of those instruments). The cool-toned tenor (whose sound fit into the "Four Brothers" style) was on many records in the '50s (including those of Shorty Rogers, Pete Rugolo, and June Christy) and continued working steadily in Los Angeles-area clubs up until his death. He appears on records with the big bands of Frank Capp/Nat Pierce, Bob Florence, and the '80s version of the Lighthouse All-Stars and participated in the 1991 Stan Kenton 50th-anniversary celebration. As a leader Coop recorded for Capitol in the '50s, Contemporary, Trend, Discovery, and Fresh Sound. —*Scott Yanow*

● **Coop! The Music of Bob Cooper** / Aug. 26, 1958-Aug. 27, 1958 / Original Jazz Classics ✦✦✦✦
Excellent aggregation with delightful work from Cooper and friends. —*Ron Wynn*

In a Mellotone / Oct. 27, 1985 / Contemporary ✦✦✦✦
Enchanting mid-'80s collaboration. Snooky Young (tpt) sounds energized. —*Ron Wynn*

For All We Know / Aug. 15, 1990-Aug. 16, 1990 / Fresh Sound ✦✦✦✦

Chick Corea (Armando Anthony Corea)

b. Jun. 12, 1941, Chelsea, MA
Piano, Keyboards / Fusion, Post-Bop, Free Jazz
Chick Corea has been one of the most significant jazzmen of the past 30 years. Not content at any time to rest on his laurels, Corea has been involved in quite a few important musical projects, and his musical curiosity has never dimmed. A masterful pianist who along with Herbie Hancock and Keith Jarrett was one of the top stylists to emerge after Bill Evans and McCoy Tyner, Corea is also one of the few selective keyboardists to be quite individual and recognizable on synthesizers. In addition he has composed several jazz standards, including "Spain," "La Fiesta," and "Windows."

Corea began playing piano when he was four, and early on Horace Silver and Bud Powell were influences. He picked up important experience playing with the bands of Mongo Santamaria and Willie Bobo (1962-63), Blue Mitchell (1964-66), Herbie Mann, and Stan Getz. He made his recording debut as a leader in 1966's *Tones for Joan's Bones*, and his 1968 trio set (with Miroslav Vitous and Roy Haynes) *Now He Sings, Now He Sobs* is considered a classic. After a short stint with Sarah Vaughan, Corea joined Miles Davis as Herbie Hancock's gradual replacement, staying with Miles during a very important transitional period (1968-70). He was persuaded by the trumpeter to start playing electric piano and was on such significant albums as *Filles de Kilimanjaro, In a Silent Way, Bitches Brew*, and *Miles Davis at the Fillmore*. When he left Davis, Corea at first chose to play avant-garde acoustic jazz in Circle, a quartet with Anthony Braxton, Dave Holland, and Barry Altschul. But at the end of 1971 he changed directions again.

Leaving Circle, Corea played briefly with Stan Getz and then formed Return to Forever, which started out as a melodic Brazilian group with Stanley Clarke, Joe Farrell, Airto, and Flora Purim. Within a year Corea (with Clarke, Bill Connors, and Lenny White) had changed Return to Forever into a pacesetting and high-powered fusion band; Al DiMeola took Connors' place in 1974. While the music was rock-oriented, it still retained the improvisations of jazz, and Corea remained quite recognizable, even under the barrage of electronics. When RTF broke up in the late '70s, Corea retained the name for some big-band dates with Clarke. During the next few years he generally emphasized his acoustic playing and appeared in a wide variety of contexts, including separate duet tours with Gary Burton and Herbie Hancock, a quartet with Michael Brecker, trios with Miroslav Vitous and Roy Haynes, tributes to Thelonious Monk, and even some classical music.

In 1985 Chick Corea formed a new fusion group, the Elektric Band, which eventually featured bassist John Patitucci, guitarist Frank Gambale, saxophonist Eric Marienthal, and drummer Dave Weckl. To balance out his music, a few years later he formed his Akoustic Trio with Patitucci and Weckl. When Patitucci went out on his own in the early '90s, the personnel

changed, but Corea has continued leading stimulating groups (including a recent quartet with Patitucci and Bob Berg) up until the present time. He remains an important force in modern jazz, and every phase of his development has been well documented on records. —*Scott Yanow*

☆ **Inner Space** / 1966 / Atlantic ✦✦✦✦✦

Jazz for a Sunday Afternoon / Oct. 1, 1967 / Blue Note ✦✦✦

☆ **Now He Sings, Now He Sobs** / Feb. 26, 1968 / Blue Note ✦✦✦✦✦
The original LP (using the same title) only had five selections, but this CD contains 13, with the added eight (from the same sessions) having first been released on the double LP *Circling In*. Age 26 at the time, and on the brink of gaining major recognition in the jazz world, pianist Chick Corea is featured with a very strong trio that also includes bassist Miroslav Vitous and drummer Roy Haynes. The music includes 11 of Corea's originals, including "Matrix," "Windows," and "Samba Yantra," Thelonious Monk's "Pannonica," and the standard "My One and Only Love" and is essentially advanced hard bop with an open-minded attitude towards free jazz. Listen to how part of "Steps What Was" has hints of Corea's future composition "Spain." —*Scott Yanow*

Early Circle / Apr. 3, 1970 / Blue Note ✦✦✦✦
Chick Corea's most esoteric music of his career was performed when he was a member of Circle, an avant-garde quartet that during 1970-71 featured pianist Corea, the reeds of Anthony Braxton, bassist Dave Holland, and drummer Barry Altschul. This CD contains some of their briefer performances, including bass/piano and clarinet/piano duets, two versions of "Chimes," "Percussion Piece," a free ballad, and Braxton's "73 Degrees—A Kelvin." These free explorations are worth listening to closely, but one has to put away any preconceptions that they have about Corea. The title of this CD is a bit silly though, for Circle broke up only a few months after these recordings! —*Scott Yanow*

Song of Singing / Apr. 7, 1970-Apr. 8, 1970 / Blue Note ✦✦✦

Circulus / Aug. 21, 1970 / Blue Note ✦✦✦✦

A.R.C. / Jan. 1971 / ECM ✦✦✦✦
This LP features pianist Chick Corea, bassist Dave Holland, and drummer Barry Altschul during the brief period that, along with Anthony Braxton, they were members of the fine avant-garde quartet Circle. The music heard on this set is not quite as free as Circle's but often very explorative. Four of the six songs are Corea originals, which, in addition to Holland's "Vedana" and Wayne Shorter's "Nefertiti," form a very viable set of adventurous jazz, recorded just a few months before Corea changed direction. —*Scott Yanow*

★ **Paris Concert** / Feb. 21, 1971 / ECM ✦✦✦✦✦
Chick Corea (the pure improviser) with Dave Holland (b), Anthony Braxton (sax), and Barry Altschul (d). Definitive improvisational music. For special tastes only. —*Michael G. Nastos*

Piano Improvisations, Vol. 1 / Apr. 21, 1971-Apr. 22, 1971 / ECM ✦✦✦

Piano Improvisations, Vol. 2 / Apr. 21, 1971-Apr. 22, 1971 / ECM ✦✦✦

Return to Forever / Feb. 2, 1972-Feb. 3, 1972 / ECM ✦✦✦✦
Chick Corea's original version of Return to Forever (featuring Joe Farrell on flute and soprano, bassist Stanley Clarke, Airto on drums and percussion, and singer Flora Purim along with the pianist/leader) only was in existence long enough to record two albums. This self-titled set is highlighted by a sidelong medley of "Sometime Ago" and "La Fiesta" and demonstrates that it is possible to create music that is both strong jazz and popular. —*Scott Yanow*

● **Light as a Feather** / Sep. 1972 / Polydor ✦✦✦✦
Of the three versions of Return to Forever, the initial version is of the greatest interest from the jazz standpoint. With Joe Farrell on reeds, bassist Stanley Clarke, Airto on drums and percussion, and Flora Purim contributing vocals, this contingent was one of the finest groups of the 1972-73 period even if they only actually cut two records. This particular set includes the original version of Chick Corea's greatest composition ("Spain") along with versions of "500 Miles High" and "Captain Marvel." This music crosses many boundaries and still sounds fresh two decades later. —*Scott Yanow*

Crystal Silence / Nov. 6, 1972 / ECM ✦✦✦

Hymn of the Seventh Galaxy / Aug. 1973 / Polydor ✦✦✦✦
The second (and most popular) version of Return to Forever debuted with this strong fusion effort. This was guitarist Bill Connors' only recording with the group, and he is particularly fiery on "Captain Senor Mouse" and "Hymn of the Seventh Galaxy." With Chick Corea on keyboards, Stanley Clarke on electric bass, and drummer Lenny White, this was one of the top fusion bands, mixing together the power and sound of rock with the sophisticated improvisations of jazz. Fans of late-'60s rock were able to enter the world of jazz through albums such as this near-classic. —*Scott Yanow*

Where Have I Known You Before / Jul. 1974-Aug. 1974 / Polydor ✦✦✦✦
Crackling electric Return to Forever. Includes one killer composition, but marks the beginning of the end if you are looking for a jazz influence. —*Ron Wynn*

Romantic Warrior / Feb. 1976 / Columbia ✦✦✦

● **My Spanish Heart** / Oct. 1976 / Polydor ✦✦✦✦
Chick Corea has long been one of the most distinctive of all electric keyboardists, being able to transfer his mastery of the acoustic piano successfully to synthesizers. This double LP, a classic of its genre, is full of delightful new melodies (particularly the last section of "El Bozo") and masterful
keyboard playing along with a few guest appearances by a string quartet, a
small brass section, singer Gayle Moran, bassist Stanley Clarke, and drummer Steve Gadd. — *Scott Yanow*

Music Magic / Jan. 1977-Feb. 1977 / Columbia ✦✦

Chick Corea and Gary Burton in Concert / Oct. 23, 1978+Oct. 25, 1978
/ ECM ✦✦✦

Friends / 1978 / Polydor ✦✦✦✦
Although this set contains eight lesser-known Chick Corea compositions, it
is in reality a fine blowing date. Corea, on both acoustic and electric pianos,
is joined by his old friend Joe Farrell on reeds, bassist Eddie Gomez, and
drummer Steve Gadd for some fine straightahead jazz. — *Scott Yanow*

Secret Agent / 1978 / Polydor ✦✦✦

Three Quartets / Jan. 1981-Feb. 1981 / Stretch ✦✦✦✦
This encounter between Chick Corea (sticking to acoustic piano), tenor saxophonist Michael Brecker, bassist Eddie Gomez, and drummer Steve Gadd
lives up to one's expectations. The original program featured three lengthy
"Quartet" pieces, including sections dedicated to Duke Ellington and John
Coltrane. The CD reissue adds four briefer pieces that were previously
unissued, including an unaccompanied Brecker workout on "Confirmation" that would be perfect for "blindfold" tests. This blowing date is highly
recommended for all true jazz fans. — *Scott Yanow*

The Meeting / Jun. 27, 1982 / Philips ✦✦✦

Trio Music: Live in Europe / Sep. 1984 / ECM ✦✦✦

The Elektric Band / 1986 / GRP ✦✦✦

Light Years / 1987 / GRP ✦✦✦✦
The second recording by Chick Corea's Elektric Band was the first to feature altoist Eric Marienthal and guitarist Frank Gambale in addition to
bassist John Patitucci, drummer Dave Weckl, and the leader/keyboardist.
Unlike most other fusion groups, these musicians displayed original musical personalitites and Corea's compositions tended to be memorable. This
is one of the Elektric Band's better releases. — *Scott Yanow*

Eye of the Beholder / 1988 / GRP ✦✦✦✦

Akoustic Band / 1989 / GRP ✦✦✦✦
As a contrast to his Elektric Band, Chick Corea formed the Akoustic Band
with bassist John Patitucci and drummer Dave Weckl. This trio gave him a
chance to stretch out acoustically in a straightahead setting on a variety of
standards and originals. Their debut release is highlighted by "Bessie's
Blues," "My One and Only Love," "Someday My Prince Will Come," and
Corea's "Spain." — *Scott Yanow*

Inside Out / 1990 / GRP ✦✦✦✦
Chick Corea's Elektric Band was always a well integrated unit, featuring
passionate solos from the rockish guitarist Frank Gambale and the
R&Bish saxophonist Eric Marienthal in addition to major statements from
the distinctive leader who utilized a battery of keyboards yet remained
quite recognizable. With John Patitucci (arguably jazz's top electric bassist)
and drummer Dave Weckl pushing the ensemble, this pacesetting fusion
unit is heard at its peak on these Corea originals. — *Scott Yanow*

Alive / 1991 / GRP ✦✦✦

Beneath the Mask / Aug. 22, 1991 / GRP ✦✦✦

Paint the World / 1993 / GRP ✦✦✦✦

Expressions / 1993 / GRP ✦✦✦✦
Although Chick Corea has recorded quite a few releases throughout his
career, solo albums are rare, particularly ones in which he explores standards. This acoustic set (which he dedicated to Art Tatum) finds Corea performing such songs as "Lush Life," "My Ship," Bud Powell's "Oblivion," and
even the veteran warhorse "I Want to Be Happy" with individuality,
respect, and creativity. — *Scott Yanow*

Time Warp / 1995 / GRP ✦✦✦

Larry Coryell

b. Apr. 2, 1943, Galveston, TX
Guitar / Fusion, Post-Bop
Larry Coryell has been a splendid guitar stylist in jazz-rock, bebop, Latin,
and classical contexts. His only negative attributes have been inconsistency
in material selection and supporting musicians for his bands and recording projects. Coryell has marvelous skills; he can play entrancing melodies,
lighting fast phrases, spectacular solos, or soothing statements. He's equally
masterful on electric or acoustic, and has creatively used wah-wah pedals,
attachments, distortion, dissonance, and feedback. He's played 12-string,
hollow-bodied, double neck, and guitar synthesizers, as well as conventional acoustic. Coryell has few discernible musical weaknesses besides

occasional inconsistency, and his ratio of topflight recorded output to junk
has been quite high. Coryell worked in a band with Mike Mandel as a teenager. He moved to New York from Texas in the mid-'60s, where he initially
worked with Chico Hamilton and the early jazz-rock band Free Spirits. He
played with Gary Burton in 1967 and 1968, doing an intriguing blend of
jazz-rock and jazz/country/western swing. Coryell and Mandel formed
Foreplay in 1969, and with Steve Marcus continued the group until 1973.
Coryell also played in Herbie Mann's band on such crossover hits as *Memphis Underground* and *Memphis Two-Step* during this period. He formed
another jazz-rock band with Mandel and Marcus, Eleventh House, in 1973.
The group also included Randy Brecker and Alphonse Mouzon, but it
degenerated from a promising beginning into an overly loud unit playing
second-rate arena rock by its end. Coryell periodically worked with Miroslav Vitous and John McLaughlin; he and McLaughlin later recorded some
superb duets. Coryell has worked with many duos and small combos,
recording and playing with John Scofield, Michael Urbaniak, Steve Khan,
Emily Remler, Brian Keane, and Philip Catherine. He's also recorded with
Charles Mingus, Stephane Grappelli, and Sonny Rollins. Coryell began
cutting his own albums for Vanguard in the late '60s. He continued in the
'70s, '80s, and '90s, recording for Vanguard, Flying Dutchman, Arista, Elektra, Atlantic, Mood, Keystone, Flying Fish, Concord, and Shanachie, among
others. Coryell's worked with a host of great musicians besides guitarists;
these include Jimmy Garrison, Ron Carter, Roy Haynes, Joachim Kuhn,
Ray Mantilla, Eddie Gomez, Albert Dailey, and vocalists Urszula Dudziak
and his wife Julie. Recent Coryell projects have included a Brazilian session for CTI and some acoustic guitar workouts for Shanachie. He has an
ample supply of sessions available on CD, though unfortunately none of
his best jazz-rock dates from either his time with Gary Burton or on Flying
Dutchman are currently available. — *Ron Wynn*

★ **Barefoot Boy** / 1971 / Philips ✦✦✦✦✦
Tremendous interaction between Steve Marcus (tenor/soprano sax) and
Coryell. Roy Haynes stars on drums. — *Ron Wynn*

Introducing Larry Coryell & the 11th House / 1972 / Vanguard ✦✦✦

Bolero / Apr. 18, 1981-Nov. 1983 / Evidence ✦✦✦✦

Comin' Home / Feb. 7, 1984 / Muse ✦✦✦

☆ **Just Like Being Born** / 1984 / Flying Fish ✦✦✦✦✦
With Brian Keane (g), it features soothing acoustic guitar duets by two
excellent players. — *Paul Kohler*

● **Together** / Aug. 1985 / Concord Jazz ✦✦✦✦
Coryell works easily and decisively with the late Emily Remler. — *Ron
Wynn*

Shining Hour / Oct. 20, 1989 / Muse ✦✦✦

Twelve Frets to One Octave / 1991 / Shanachie ✦✦✦

Live from Bahia / 1992 / CTI ✦✦✦

Curtis Counce

b. Jan. 23, 1926, Kansas City, MO, **d.** Jul. 31, 1963, Los Angeles, CA
Bass / Hard Bop
A first-rate accompanist and session bassist, Curtis Counce played on
numerous recording dates in the '50s. He was a solid, swinging player with
a great tone, one of the finest "walking" bassists. Counce studied violin,
bass, and tuba as a teen, then played in the early '40s with Nat Towles'
orchestra. He settled in Los Angeles and worked with Edgar Hayes from
1945 to 1948, followed by stints with Billy Eckstine, Bud Powell, Buddy
DeFranco, Wardell Gray, and Hampton Hawes. Counce later played in a
group co-led by Benny Carter and Ben Webster, while recording with
Lester Young. He studied composition and arranging with Spud Murphy.
During the '50s, there were recording sessions with Teddy Charles, Shorty
Rogers, Buddy Collette, Claude Williamson, Herb Geller, Bob Cooper, Clifford Brown, and Milt Bernhart. Counce later played with DeFranco again,
then toured Europe with Stan Kenton's orchestra. He formed a quintet in
the mid-'50s that at various times included Jack Sheldon, Harold Land,
Carl Perkins, and Frank Butler. Some of Counce's recordings were *Land-
slide, Carl's Blues,* and *Counciliation* (also known as *You Get More
Bounce*). He was also a bass teacher and did some film work. Most of
Counce's albums have been reissued on CD. — *Ron Wynn*

Sonority / Jan. 1956 / Contemporary ✦✦✦

● **Landslide** / Oct. 8, 1956+Oct. 15, 1956 / Original Jazz Classics ✦✦✦✦
Curtis Counce Group. This is the same lineup as *Sonority*, and the music
swings just as hard. — *Ron Wynn*

Counceltation, Vol. 1 & 2 / Oct. 8, 1956-Sep. 3, 1957 / Contemporary
✦✦✦✦
Bassist Curtis Counce led one of the finer West Coast-based groups of the
'50s, a quintet that was greatly underrated. With trumpeter Jack Sheldon,
tenor saxophonist Harold Land, pianist Carl Perkins, and drummer Frank
Butler completing the group, this was a band with plenty of solo strength.
Their second Contemporary recording features five standards (including

"Stranger in Paradise") and two numbers by the leader. This excellent music falls somewhere between hard bop and cool jazz. —*Scott Yanow*

You Get More Bounce with Curtis Counce / Apr. 15, 1957-Sep. 3, 1957 / Contemporary ✦✦✦✦
Excellent bassist from the West Coast. Slightly naughty artwork. Worth looking for. —*Michael G. Nastos*

Carl's Blues / Aug. 29, 1957-Jan. 6, 1968 / Contemporary ✦✦✦✦
The Curtis Counce (bass) group was a working group when they recorded *Carl's Blues*. This album, with its cool-hot late night ambiance was a sleeper when it was first released and remains so years later. —*Bob Rusch*

Stanley Cowell

b. May 5, 1941, Toledo, OH
Piano / Post-Bop, Hard Bop
An excellent modern mainstream pianist who is adaptable to many acoustic jazz settings, Stanley Cowell has long been underrated except among knowing musicians. He studied the piano from the time he was four, and Art Tatum made an early impact. After attending Oberlin College Conservatory and the University of Michigan, Cowell (who had played with Rahsaan Roland Kirk while at Oberlin) moved to New York in 1966. He played regularly with Marion Brown (1966-67), Max Roach (1967-70), and the Bobby Hutcherson-Harold Land Quintet (1968-71). In the early '70s Cowell worked in Music Inc. with Charles Tolliver, and they co-founded the label Strata-East. He played regularly with the Heath Brothers during 1974-83 and since 1981 has been a busy jazz educator. Cowell has recorded as a leader for Arista-Freedom (1969), ECM (1972), Strata East, Galaxy, Unisson, DIW, Concord, and SteepleChase. —*Scott Yanow*

Blues for the Viet Cong / Jun. 5, 1969 / Freedom ✦✦✦✦
Stanley Cowell's debut as a leader features his piano (and on two selections rare outings on electric keyboards) with a trio also including bassist Steve Novosel and drummer Jimmy Hopps. Cowell's style at the time was often modal and already quite powerful. After hearing seven of his often-somber pieces, Cowell's stride version of "You Took Advantage of Me" (inspired by Art Tatum) is a welcome change of pace. —*Scott Yanow*

Back to the Beautiful / Jul. 1989 / Concord Jazz ✦✦✦✦
A good session, with Steve Coleman (reeds) in an unusual mainstream role. —*Ron Wynn*

● **Live at Maybeck Recital Hall, Vol. 5** / Jun. 1990 / Concord Jazz ✦✦✦✦
This is part of an outstanding solo piano series. Cowell displays impressive technique and holds his own in the solo setting. —*Ron Wynn*

Close to You Alone / Aug. 2, 1990 / DIW ✦✦✦

Hank Crawford (Bennie Ross Crawford, Jr.)

b. Dec. 21, 1934, Memphis, TN
Piano, Sax (Alto) / R&B, Soul-Jazz, Hard Bop, Groove
Hank Crawford's greatest contribution to music has been his soulful sound, one that is immediately identifiable and flexible enough to fit into several types of settings. Early on he played with B.B. King, Bobby Bland, and Ike Turner in Memphis before moving to Nashville to study at Tennessee State College. He gained fame with Ray Charles (1958-63), at first playing baritone before switching to alto and becoming the music director. During 1959-69 Crawford recorded a popular series of soul-jazz albums for Atlantic that made his reputation. His '70s sets for Kudu were more commercial and streakier, but in 1982 Crawford started recording regularly for Milestone, often matched up with organist Jimmy McGriff or pianist Dr. John. An influence on David Sanborn, Crawford's very appealing sound can still be heard in prime form in the mid-'90s. —*Scott Yanow*

Heart And Soul / Jul. 5, 1958-Aug. 27, 1992 / Rhino/Atlantic ✦✦✦

After Hours / Oct. 19, 1965-Jan. 19, 1966 / Atlantic ✦✦✦

Soul Survivors / Jan. 29, 1986-Jan. 30, 1986 / Milestone ✦✦✦✦
With Jimmy McGriff (organ), George Benson (g), Mel Lewis (d). Soul-jazz the way they did it in the '60s (almost). —*Ron Wynn*

Mr. Chips / Nov. 1986 / Milestone ✦✦✦

Soul Brothers / Jun. 15, 1987+Jun. 16, 1987 / Milestone ✦✦✦
Hank Crawford with Jimmy McGriff on the Hammond B-3 and George Benson (or Jimmy Ponder) on guitar. Worth seeking out. —*Michael Erlewine*

Steppin' Up / Jun. 15, 1987-Jun. 16, 1987 / Milestone ✦✦✦✦
With Jimmy McGriff (organ), Jimmy Ponder (g). Solid, exuberant soul-jazz. —*Ron Wynn*

● **On the Blue Side** / Apr. 4, 1989+Aug. 9, 1989 / Milestone ✦✦✦✦
With Jimmy McGriff on Hammond organ and Jimmy Ponder on guitar. Funky, mellow, and gritty. —*Ron Wynn*

Portrait / Mar. 19, 1991-Mar. 20, 1991 / Milestone ✦✦✦

South Central / Aug. 11, 1992+Aug. 27, 1992 / Milestone ✦✦✦

Marilyn Crispell

b. Mar. 30, 1947, Philadelphia, PA
Piano / Avant-Garde
One of the finest pianists of the avant-garde, Marilyn Crispell has been greatly inspired by Cecil Taylor and can be nearly as powerful but also is not shy to use space or occasionally play a spiritual standard. She studied piano at the Peabody Music School in Baltimore from age seven and later went to the New England Conservatory. Crispell was outside of music during 1969-75 but then became very interested in advanced jazz. She met Anthony Braxton, toured Europe with his Creative Music Orchestra in 1978, and has been in his regular quartet since the early '80s. Marilyn Crispell has also led her own groups (both live and on records) since then, recording several notable sets for Leo, Cadence, and Music & Arts. She is near the top of her field. —*Scott Yanow*

● **Spirit Music** / May 15, 1981+Jan. 13, 1982 / Cadence ✦✦✦✦
Marilyn Crispell is one of the most significant piano voices of the avant-garde. A powerful player influenced by Cecil Taylor but who has her own way of using space, Crispell has been closely associated with Anthony Braxton's group during the past decade. This Cadence release, however, finds her leading her own trio, an unusual group which also includes violinist Billy Bang and drummer John Betsch. On one of the four lengthy improvisations heard on this set, guitarist Wes Brown makes the band a quartet. These stirring performances serve as a fine introduction to the passionate music of Marilyn Crispell. —*Scott Yanow*

Live in Zurich / Apr. 1989 / Leo ✦✦✦✦
Crispell keeps cranking out furious, aggressive free dates for the European market. They're devoid of any devices now in vogue on the jazz circuit: no standards, no electronics, no hard bop, adult contemporary, strings, or fusion. If you enjoy hearing spirited dialogues between Crispell, bassist Reggie Workman, and drummer Paul Motian, this one's for you. —*Ron Wynn*

Live in San Francisco / Oct. 20, 1989 / Music & Arts ✦✦✦✦
Free music has almost disappeared from the American landscape, and certainly isn't coming from the major labels. So it's no surprise that this 1989 collaboration between multi-instrumentalist Anthony Braxton and pianist Marilyn Crispell, which is almost wholly spontaneous improvisations, has been relegated to an English company. In addition, the music is so fierce and uncompromising that there's absolutely no chance that anyone except avant-garde fans will like it. —*Ron Wynn*

Images / Aug. 1991 / Music & Arts ✦✦✦✦
The current piano favorite among the new generation of outside players, Crispell doesn't tone down the intensity until she concludes the session. Her approach, attack, tone, and phrasing have often been compared to her mentor Cecil Taylor, but she's not quite as percussive (no one is). However, this is as close as any living being can get to duplicating his energy and power. —*Ron Wynn*

Inference / Jun. 25, 1992 / Music & Arts ✦✦✦

Band on the Wall / May 26, 1994 / Matchless ✦✦✦✦

Sonny Criss (William Criss)

b. Oct. 23, 1927, Memphis, TN, d. Nov. 19, 1977, Los Angeles, CA
Sax (Alto) / Hard Bop
A talented bop altoist, Sonny Criss was influenced by Charlie Parker but had his own heavier sound. He spent most of his life in the Los Angeles area starting in 1942. In 1946 he worked in Howard McGhee's band with Charlie Parker and Teddy Edwards and can be heard on several jam sessions on Savoy in 1947. Criss spent periods playing with Johnny Otis, Gerald Wilson, and Billy Eckstine (1950-51) and was with Stan Kenton in 1955. He also worked with Howard Rumsey's Lighthouse All-Stars and Buddy Rich's quartet (1958) in addition to leading his own groups, recording three albums for Imperial in 1956. Criss lived in Europe during 1962-65, recorded some excellent sets for Prestige during 1966-69, and in the '70s headed sessions for Fresh Sound, Xanadu, Muse, and a couple of commercial efforts for Impulse. After European tours in 1973 and 1974, Sonny Criss' career seemed on an upswing. But due to the pain of cancer, he chose to commit suicide in 1977. —*Scott Yanow*

Sonny's Dream / May 8, 1968 / Original Jazz Classics ✦✦✦✦
For Sonny Criss this was an unusual date. The altoist is backed for the set by a nonet arranged by the great Los Angeles legend Horace Tapscott. The arrangements are challenging but complementary to Criss' style, and he is in top form on the six Tapscott originals. The CD reissue includes two additional alternate takes and is highly recommended for both Criss' playing and Tapscott's writing. —*Scott Yanow*

I'll Catch the Sun / Jan. 20, 1969 / Original Jazz Classics ✦✦✦✦
Altoist Sonny Criss made some of his finest recordings for Prestige during the mid-to-late '60s; *I'll Catch the Sun* was the seventh and final. Since this CD reissue is only 35 minutes long, it is overly brief, but the straightahead music (featuring Criss with pianist Hampton Hawes, bassist Monty Budwig, and drummer Shelly Manne) is often excellent as the altoist performs

two blues, two standards (including a passionate "Cry Me a River"), and two forgotten pop tunes from the era. —Scott Yanow

★ **Crisscraft** / Feb. 24, 1975 / Muse ✦✦✦✦✦
This is one of the very best Sonny Criss albums. The distinctive altoist, who is here joined by guitarist Ray Crawford, pianist Dolo Coker, bassist Larry Gales and drummer Jimmy Smith, is in prime form on a lengthy "The Isle of Celia," Benny Carter's "Blues in My Heart," the boppish blues "Crisscraft," and two shorter pieces. Criss, who had not recorded as a leader in six years, was really ready for this session, making this his definitive set to get. —Scott Yanow

Crusaders

Group / Soul-Jazz, Hard Bop, Crossover
Back in 1954 Houston pianist Joe Sample teamed up with high-school friends tenor saxophonist Wilton Felder and drummer Stix Hooper to form the Swingsters. Within a short time they were joined by trombonist Wayne Henderson, flutist Hubert Laws, and bassist Henry Wilson, and the group became the Modern Jazz Sextet. With the move of Sample, Felder, Hooper, and Henderson to Los Angeles in 1960, the band (a quintet with the bass spot constantly changing) took on the name the Jazz Crusaders. The following year they made their first recordings for Pacific Jazz, and throughout the '60s the group was a popular attraction, mixing together R&B and Memphis soul elements with hard bop; its trombone/tenor front line became a trademark. By 1971, when all of the musicians were also busy with their own projects, it was decided to call the group simply the Crusaders so it would not be restricted to only playing jazz. After a few excellent albums during the early part of the decade (with guitarist Larry Carlton a strong asset), the group began to decline in quality. In 1975 the band's sound radically changed when Henderson departed to become a full-time producer. 1979's "Street Life" was a hit but also a last hurrah. With Hooper's decision to leave in 1983, the group no longer sounded like the Crusaders, and gradually disbanded. In the mid-'90s Henderson and Felder had a reunion as the Crusaders, but in reality only Joe Sample has had a strong solo career. —Scott Yanow

★ **I** / 1970 / Chisa ✦✦✦✦✦
Their finest modern soul-jazz date. Wilton Felder burns on tenor, and the arrangements meld funk beats and jazz licks to maximum success. —Ron Wynn

Crusaders, Vol. 1 / 1971 / MCA ✦✦✦

Second Crusade / 1972 / Chisa ✦✦✦✦
Another fine two-record set. Prototype of their "Gulf Coast" sound. —Ron Wynn

Scratch / 1975 / MCA ✦✦✦

Street Life / 1979 / MCA ✦✦✦
This album contains their single biggest hit with the title cut. —Ron Wynn

Live in Japan / Jan. 1981 / GRP ✦✦✦

Ronnie Cuber

b. Dec. 25, 1941, New York, NY
Sax (Baritone) / Hard Bop
A powerful baritonist in the tradition of Pepper Adams, Ronnie Cuber has been making excellent records for over 20 years. He was in Marshall Brown's Newport Youth Band at the 1959 Newport Jazz Festival and was featured with the groups of Slide Hampton (1962), Maynard Ferguson (1963-65), and George Benson (1966-67). After stints with Lionel Hampton (1968), Woody Herman's Orchestra (1969), and as a freelancer, he recorded a series of fine albums (both as a leader and as a sideman) for Xanadu and performed with Lee Konitz's nonet (1977-79). In the mid-'80s Cuber recorded for Projazz (in both straightahead and R&Bish settings), in the early '90s he headed dates for Fresh Sound and SteepleChase, and Cuber performed regularly with the Mingus Big Band. —Scott Yanow

● **Cuber Libre** / Aug. 20, 1976 / Xanadu ✦✦✦✦
This quartet session was a perfect setting for baritonist Ronnie Cuber, who was 34 years old at the time. Joined by the impeccable pianist Barry Harris, bassist Sam Jones, and drummer Albert "Tootie" Heath, Cuber gets to swing hard on such standards as "Star Eyes," "Rifftide," and "Tin Tin Deo." Throughout this bop-oriented date, Cuber shows why he has been considered one of the top masters of the baritone during the past 20 years. —Scott Yanow

The Scene Is Clean / Dec. 1993 / Milestone ✦✦✦

Ted Curson

b. Jun. 3, 1935, Philadelphia, PA
Trumpet / Avant-Garde, Post-Bop, Hard Bop
An excellent and flexible trumpeter, Ted Curson will always be best known for his work with Charles Mingus' 1960 quartet (which also included Eric Dolphy and Dannie Richmond). He studied at Granoff Musical Conservatory, moved to New York in 1986, and played in New York

with Mal Waldron, Red Garland, and Philly Joe Jones and recorded with Cecil Taylor (1961). After the 1959-60 Mingus association (which resulted in some classic recordings), Curson co-led a quintet with Bill Barron (1960-65), played with Max Roach, and led his own groups. He spent time from the late '60s on in Europe (particularly Denmark) but has had a lower profile than one would expect since his return to the US in 1976. Ted Curson has led sessions for Old Town (1961), Prestige, Fontana, Atlantic, Arista, Inner City, Interplay, Chiaroscuro, and several European labels but has been barely on records at all since 1980. —Scott Yanow

● **Fire Down Below** / Dec. 10, 1962 / Original Jazz Classics ✦✦✦✦
Good 1990 reissue by Prestige of a dashing session. —Ron Wynn

Tears for Dolphy / Aug. 1, 1964 / Freedom ✦✦✦✦
Trumpeter Ted Curson, a distinctive player who is still best known for his association with Charles Mingus in 1960, is heard here in a pianoless quartet with tenor saxophonist Bill Barron, bassist Herb Bushler, and drummer Dick Berk. Recorded shortly after Eric Dolphy's premature death, this date is highlighted by Curson's tribute to Eric, but the other eight pieces (all originals by either Curson or Barron) are also worthy, ranging from early free bop to conventional swinging with occasional hints of the trumpeter's avant-garde past. —Scott Yanow

Tadd Dameron

b. Feb. 21, 1917, Cleveland, OH, **d.** Mar. 8, 1965, New York, NY
Piano / Bop
The definitive arranger/composer of the bop era, Tadd Dameron wrote such standards as "Good Bait," "Our Delight," "Hot House," "Lady Bird," and "If You Could See Me Now." Not only did he write melody lines but also full arrangements, and he was an influential force from the mid-'40s on, even though he never financially prospered. Dameron started out in the swing era touring with the Zack Whyte and Blance Calloway bands, he wrote for Vido Musso in New York and most importantly contributed arrangements for Harlan Leonard's Kansas City Orchestra, some of which were recorded. Soon Dameron was writing charts for such bands as Jimmie Lunceford, Count Basie, Billy Eckstine, and Dizzy Gillespie (1945-47) in addition to Sarah Vaughan. Dameron was always very modest about his own piano playing, but he did gig with Babs Gonzales' Three Bips and a Bop in 1947 and led a sextet featuring Fats Navarro (and later Miles Davis) at the Royal Roost during 1948-49. Dameron co-led a group with Davis at the 1949 Paris Jazz Festival, stayed in Europe for a few months (writing for Ted Heath), and then returned to New York. He wrote for Artie Shaw's last orchestra that year, played and arranged R&B for Bull Moose Jackson (1951-52), and in 1953 led a nonet featuring Clifford Brown and Philly Joe Jones. However drug problems started to get in the way of his music. After recording a couple of albums (including 1958's *Mating Call* with John Coltrane), he spent much of 1959-61 in jail. After he was released, Dameron wrote for Sonny Stitt, Blue Mitchell, Milt Jackson, Benny Goodman, and his last record but was less active in the years before his death from cancer. Tadd Dameron's classic Blue Note recordings of 1947-48, his 1949 Capitol sides, and Prestige/Riverside sets of 1953, 1956, 1958, and 1962 are all currently in print on CD. —Scott Yanow

Anthropology / Aug. 1949 / Spotlite ✦✦✦

Fontainebleau / Mar. 9, 1956 / Original Jazz Classics ✦✦✦

Mating Call / Nov. 30, 1956 / Original Jazz Classics ✦✦✦✦
Super quartet session with John Coltrane (ts). —Ron Wynn

● **The Magic Touch of Tadd Dameron** / Feb. 27, 1962 / Original Jazz Classics ✦✦✦✦
Some wonderful arrangements, plus Bill Evans (p). —Ron Wynn

Eddie Daniels

b. Oct. 19, 1941, New York, NY
Clarinet, Sax (Tenor) / Post-Bop, Hard Bop
One of the truly great jazz clarinetists (ranking at the top with Benny Goodman, Artie Shaw, and Buddy DeFranco), Daniels makes the impossible look effortless. On his first GRP release *Breakthrough* in 1984, Daniels switched back and forth on a second's notice between jazz and classical, and he has since explored Charlie Parker, Roger Kellaway tunes, crossover, and even swing with consistent brilliance. He is also a dazzling (if underrated) tenor player. Daniels appeared at the 1957 Newport Jazz Festival in Marshall Brown's Youth band (playing alto) and after graduating from Juilliard in 1966 he played tenor with the Thad Jones-Mel Lewis Orchestra for six years. Daniels recorded *First Prize* as a leader (1966) and made albums with Freddie Hubbard (1969), Richard Davis, Don Patterson, and duets with Bucky Pizzarelli (1973). Although he recorded as a leader for Muse and Columbia during 1977-78, Eddie Daniels did not make it big until he started specializing on clarinet and recording regularly for GRP in 1984. In 1992 he started doubling on tenor again now that his reputation on clarinet was secure. —Scott Yanow

First Prize / Sep. 8, 1966+Sep. 12, 1966 / Original Jazz Classics ✦✦✦✦
When one hears this early Eddie Daniels CD (a straight reissue of the orig-

inal LP), it is surprising to realize that he would remain in relative obscurity for almost another 20 years. As shown on the three of the eight selections on which he plays clarinet, Daniels (even at this early stage) ranked near the top, while his tenor playing on the remaining numbers was already personal and virtuosic. With the assistance of the Thad Jones/Mel Lewis rhythm section of the time (pianist Roland Hanna, bassist Richard Davis, and drummer Mel Lewis), Daniels is in top form on three standards, four originals, and the pop tune "Spanish Flea." —*Scott Yanow*

★ **Breakthrough** / 1986 / GRP ✦✦✦✦✦
Better compositions, but material is still not up to the talent of the leader. —*Ron Wynn*

To Bird with Love / 1987 / GRP ✦✦✦✦
This clarinetist's best solid and swinging studio date, with Fred Hirsch (p) and Al Foster (d). —*Michael G. Nastos*

Benny Rides Again / Jan. 14, 1992-Jan. 15, 1992 / GRP ✦✦✦

Under the Influence / 1993 / GRP ✦✦✦✦
After a decade of exclusively playing clarinet (and establishing himself as one of the greats), Eddie Daniels began doubling on tenor again on this recording. Switching between his two axes, Daniels sounds in top form on some diverse but consistently rewarding originals and a few standards ("I Hear a Rhapsody," "Weaver of Dreams," "I Fall in Love Too Easily," and an exciting version of Bill Evans' "Five"). Joined by pianist Alan Pasqua, bassist Mike Formanek, and drummer Peter Erskine, Eddie Daniels really digs into these tunes, and both his virtuosity and his inventive improvisations are quite impressive. —*Scott Yanow*

Eddie Daniels Collection / GRP ✦✦✦

Kenny Davern (John Kenneth Davern)

b. Jan. 7, 1935, Huntington, NY
Clarinet / Dixieland, Swing
One of the finest clarinetists in traditional jazz of the past 20 years (and able to hit notes far above the normal register), Davern has been an excellent player since the '50s. He started playing professionally when he was 16 and in 1954 made his recording debut with Jack Teagarden. He picked up experience playing with Phil Napoleon's Memphis Five (1955), Pee Wee Erwin, Wild Bill Davison, Red Allen, Buck Clayton, and Jo Jones. Davern led a band at Nick's in the early '60s and was with the Dukes of Dixieland during 1962-63. After associations with Eddie Condon, Herman Autrey, and Ruby Braff, Davern co-led Soprano Summit during 1974-79 with Bob Wilber. Up until that point Davern had doubled on clarinet and soprano, but after the group's breakup he decided to specialize exclusively on clarinet. He formed the Blue Three (with Dick Wellstood and Bobby Rosengarden) in the early '80s, recorded several fine sets for Music Masters in the '80s and '90s, and in recent times has had several matchups with Bob Wilber in a new Soprano Summit, retitled Soprano Reunion. —*Scott Yanow*

★ **Soprano Summit** / Mar. 1976 / Concord Jazz ✦✦✦✦✦
Live at the Concord Festival with Bob Wilber and quintet. Two Wilber originals, one by guitarist Marty Grosz. A fine representation of two artists in Dixie-early-swing mode with blues and a touch of Ellington. —*Michael G. Nastos*

Kenny Davern and Dick Wellstood / Jan. 15, 1984 / Challenge ✦✦✦✦
Clarinetist Kenny Davern and pianist Dick Wellstood make for a potent duo on this live session. Two of the top trad jazz musicians to emerge during the '40s (thereby making them a bit out of place in their generation), both Davern and Wellstood developed their own individual voices. Their strong performance of stomps and ballads also has a bit of storytelling as Wellstood talks about how he got started and the challenges of playing stride piano while Davern recalls his reaction when he first heard fellow clarinetist Pee Wee Russell. But more importantly the music is very enjoyable and often surprisingly wistful. This CD release from the Dutch label Challenge is fortunately readily available in the US. —*Scott Yanow*

I'll See You in My Dreams / Jan. 1988 / Music Masters ✦✦✦✦
Outstanding, musically conservative date, with fine playing from Davern and Howard Alden (g). —*Ron Wynn*

One Hour Tonight / Jan. 1988 / Music Masters ✦✦✦✦
A warm, traditional-sounding session. —*Ron Wynn*

My Inspiration / Sep. 11, 1991 / Music Masters ✦✦✦

East Side, West Side / Jun. 24, 1994 / Arbors ✦✦✦

Eddie "Lockjaw" Davis

b. Mar. 2, 1922, New York, NY, d. Nov. 3, 1986, Culver City, CA
Sax (Tenor) / Bop, Swing, Hard Bop, Groove
Possessor of a cutting and immediately identifiable tough tenor tone, Eddie "Lockjaw" Davis could hold his own in a saxophone battle with anyone. Early on he picked up experience playing with the bands of Cootie Williams (1942-44), Lucky Millinder, Andy Kirk (1945-46), and Louis Armstrong. He began heading his own groups from 1946, and Davis' earliest recordings as a leader tended to be explosive R&B affairs with plenty of

screaming from his horn; he matched wits successfully with Fats Navarro on one session. Davis was with Count Basie's Orchestra on several occasions (including 1952-53, 1957, and 1964-73) and teamed up with Shirley Scott's trio during 1955-60. During 1960-62 he collaborated in some exciting performances and recordings with Johnny Griffin, a fellow tenor who was just as combative as Davis. After temporarily retiring to become a booking agent (1963-64), Davis rejoined Basie. In his later years Lockjaw often recorded with Harry "Sweets" Edison, and he remained a busy soloist up until his death. Through the decades he recorded as a leader for many labels including Savoy, Apollo, Roost, King, Roulette, Prestige/Jazzland/Moodsville, RCA, Storyville, MPS, Black & Blue, Spotlite, SteepleChase, Pablo, Muse, and Enja. —*Scott Yanow*

Jaws / Sep. 12, 1958 / Original Jazz Classics ✦✦✦

Smokin' / Sep. 12, 1958+Dec. 5, 1958 / Original Jazz Classics ✦✦✦✦
Tenor saxophonist Eddie "Lockjaw" Davis recorded many albums with organist Shirley Scott during 1956-60, cutting enough material on two dates to fill up four records. The seven selections included on this brief 36-minute CD (a straight reissue of an LP recorded during the same period as Davis' better-known *Cookbook* albums) also include Jerome Richardson (switching between flute, tenor, and baritone) on three of the numbers, bassist George Duvivier, and drummer Arthur Edgehill. Together the group swings hard on basic originals, blues, and an occasional ballad, showing why this type of accessible band was so popular during the era. —*Scott Yanow*

The Eddie Lockjaw Davis Cookbook, Vol. 2 / Dec. 1958 / Original Jazz Classics ✦✦✦✦
Eddie "Lockjaw" Davis' "cookbook" series helped make the group that the tenorman had in the late '50s with organist Shirley Scott famous. The quintet (which also includes flutist Jerome Richardson, bassist George Duvivier, and drummer Arthur Edgehill) is heard on this CD reissue performing three Davis-Scott originals, "Stardust," "I Surrender Dear," and a version of "Willow Weep for Me" that was originally part of a sampler. The straightahead music is interpreted quite colorfully by Davis and his group, one of the first popular organ combos. —*Scott Yanow*

The Eddie Lockjaw Davis Cookbook, Vol. 3 / Dec. 15, 1958 / Prestige ✦✦✦✦
Tenorman Eddie "Lockjaw" Davis made quite a few records with organist Shirley Scott during the late '50s. The basic originals in their *Cookbook* series tended to have titles that dealt with cooking; in this case "Heat 'n Serve," "The Goose Hangs High," and "Simmerin'" apply as does the standard "My Old Flame." Jerome Richardson's flute, baritone, and tenor give this CD reissue some variety, bassist George Duvivier and drummer Arthur Edgehill are fine in support, and Shirley Scott shows that she was one of the top organists to emerge after the rise of Jimmy Smith. But Davis is the main star, and his instantly recognizable sound is the most memorable aspect of this swinging session. —*Scott Yanow*

Very Saxy / Apr. 29, 1959 / Prestige ✦✦✦
With Buddy Tate, Coleman Hawkins, and Arnett Cobb. Red-hot jam session. Summit meeting of mainstream veterans. —*Ron Wynn*

Jaws in Orbit / May 1, 1959 / Original Jazz Classics ✦✦✦
Includes Shirley Scott on the Hammond organ. This is early Scott, not yet all that funky. Traditional swinging, uptempo music. —*Michael Erlewine*

Gentle Jaws / Dec. 11, 1959_Jan. 31, 1960 / Prestige ✦✦✦

I Only Have Eyes for You / Nov. 15, 1962 / Prestige ✦✦✦
A five piece with Don Patterson on the Hammond B-3 and Paul Weeden on guitar. —*Michael Erlewine*

Trackin' / Nov. 15, 1962 / Prestige ✦✦✦
A five piece with Don Patterson on the Hammond B-3 and Paul Weeden on guitar. —*Michael Erlewine*

Streetlights / Nov. 15, 1962 / Prestige ✦✦✦✦
This CD combines together the music from two complete LPs (*I Only Have Eyes for You* and *Trackin'*) that were recorded the same day with the identical personnel. Eddie "Lockjaw" Davis' tough tenor is well featured with his regular group of the time, a combo consisting of the powerful organist Don Patterson (who dominates many of the ensembles), guitarist Paul Weeden (talented but quite obscure), drummer Billy James, and guest bassist George Duvivier. The emphasis is on standards and intense blowing (even on the ballads), with the set being a good example of a strong tenor organ band. —*Scott Yanow*

Montreux '77 / Jul. 1977 / Original Jazz Classics ✦✦✦

★ **All of Me** / Aug. 23, 1983 / SteepleChase ✦✦✦✦✦
Tenorman Eddie "Lockjaw" Davis had already been a potent force in jazz for 35 years when he recorded this set, but as it turned out his Steeple-Chase date (his next-to-last session) was one of the strongest of his career. Accompanied by a trio led by pianist Kenny Drew, Lockjaw really tears into these standards, which are highlighted by "I Only Have Eyes for You," two versions of "There Is No Greater Love" (the alternate version was released for the first time on this CD reissue), "Four," and the title cut.

Davis was at the peak of his powers during this recording, making his lone SteepleChase outing one of his very best. —*Scott Yanow*

Miles Davis

b. May 25, 1926, Alton, IL, **d.** Sep. 28, 1991, Santa Monica, CA
Trumpet / Avant-Garde, Bop, Cool, Fusion, Hard Bop, Groove
Miles Davis had quite a career, one with so many innovations that his name is one of the few that can be spoken in the same sentence with Duke Ellington. As a trumpeter, Davis was never a virtuoso on the level of his idol Dizzy Gillespie, but by 1947 he possessed a distinctive cool-toned sound of his own. His ballad renditions (utilizing a Harmon mute) were exquisite yet never predictable, he mastered and then stripped down the bebop vocabulary to its essentials, and he generally made every note count; as with Thelonious Monk, less was more in Miles' music.

But Miles Davis was much more than just a trumpeter. As a bandleader he was a brilliant talent scout, able to recognize potential in its formative stage and bring out the best in his sidemen. Among the musicians who greatly benefitted from their association with Davis were Gerry Mulligan (virtually unknown when he played with Miles' Birth of the Cool nonet), Gil Evans, John Coltrane, Red Garland, Paul Chambers, Philly Joe Jones, Cannonball Adderley, Bill Evans, Jimmy Cobb, Wynton Kelly, George Coleman, Wayne Shorter, Herbie Hancock, Ron Carter, Tony Williams, Chick Corea, Jack DeJohnette, Dave Holland, John McLaughlin, Joe Zawinul, Keith Jarrett, Steve Grossman, Gary Bartz, Dave Liebman, Al Foster, Sonny Fortune, Bill Evans (the saxophonist), Kenny Garrett, Marcus Miller, Mike Stern, and John Scofield. This partial list forms a who's who of modern jazz.

In addition to his playing and nurturing of young talent, Miles Davis was quite remarkable in his rare ability to continually evolve. Most jazz musicians (with the exceptions of John Coltrane and Duke Ellington) generally form their style early on and spend the rest of their careers refining their sound. In contrast Miles Davis every five years or so would forge ahead, and due to his restless nature he not only played bop but helped found cool jazz, hard bop, modal music, his own unusual brand of the avant-garde, and fusion. Jazz history would be much different if Davis had not existed.

Born in Alton, IL, Miles Davis grew up in a middle-class family in East St. Louis. He started on trumpet when he was nine or ten, played in his high-school band, and picked up early experience gigging with Eddie Randall's Blue Devils. Miles Davis has said that the greatest musical experience of his life was hearing the Billy Eckstine Orchestra (with Dizzy Gillespie and Charlie Parker) when it passed through St. Louis.

In September 1944 Davis went to New York to study at Juilliard but spent much more time hanging out on 52nd Street and eventually dropped out of school. He played with Coleman Hawkins, made his recording debut in early 1945 (an impressive and nervous session with Rubberlegs Williams), and by late 1945 was playing regularly with Charlie Parker. Davis made an impression with his playing on Bird's recordings of "Now's the Time" and "Billie's Bounce." Although influenced by Dizzy Gillespie, even at this early stage the 19-year-old had something of his own to contribute.

When Charlie Parker went with Gillespie out to California, Miles followed him a few months later by travelling cross-country with Benny Carter's Orchestra. He recorded with Parker in California, and when Bird formed a quintet in New York the following year, Davis was a key member. By late 1948 when he went out on his own, Miles Davis had formed a nonet that, with arrangements by Gerry Mulligan, Gil Evans, and John Lewis, helped usher in "cool jazz." Although the group only had one paying job (two weeks in September 1948 as an intermission band for Count Basie at the Royal Roost), its dozen recordings for Capitol were highly influential in the West Coast jazz movement.

Typically, by the time his nonet dates were renamed "Birth of the Cool," Miles Davis had moved on. He played at the Paris Jazz Festival in 1949 with Tadd Dameron and during 1951-54 was recording music with such sidemen as J.J. Johnson, Jimmy Heath, Horace Silver, Art Blakey, and Sonny Rollins that directly led to hard bop. However this was very much an off period for Miles because he was a heroin addict who was only working on an irregular basis. In 1954 he used all of his willpower to permanently kick heroin, and his recording that year of "Walkin'," although overlooked at the time, is a classic.

1955 was Miles Davis' breakthrough year. His performance of "'Round Midnight" at the Newport Jazz Festival alerted the critics that he was "back." Davis formed his classic quintet with John Coltrane, Red Garland, Paul Chambers, and Philly Joe Jones, and during 1955-56 they recorded four well received albums for Prestige and *'Round Midnight* for Columbia. Davis' muted ballads were very popular, and he became a celebrity. Even the breakup of the quintet in early 1957 did not slow up the momentum. Miles recorded the first of his full-length collaborations with arranger Gil Evans (*Miles Ahead*) which would be followed by *Porgy and Bess* (1958) and *Sketches of Spain* (1960); on these recordings Davis became one of the first trumpeters to stretch out on fluegelhorn. In 1957 he went to France

to record the soundtrack for *Lift to the Scaffold*, and then in 1958 he formed his greatest band, a super sextet with Coltrane, Cannonball Adderley, Bill Evans, Paul Chambers, and Philly Joe Jones. Although Evans and Jones were eventually succeeded by Wynton Kelly and Jimmy Cobb, all of the recordings by this remarkable group somehow live up to their potential, with *Milestones* and *Kind of Blue* being all-time classics that helped to introduce modal (or scalar) improvising to jazz.

If Miles Davis had retired in 1960, he would still be famous in jazz history, but he had many accomplishments still to come. The sextet gradually changed, with Adderley departing and Coltrane's spot being taken first by Sonny Stitt, then Hank Mobley. Although 1960-63 is thought of as a sort of resting period for Davis, his trumpet chops were in prime form and he was playing at the peak of his powers. With the departure of the rhythm section in 1963, it was time for Miles to form another group. By 1964 he had a brilliant young rhythm section (Herbie Hancock, Ron Carter, and Tony Williams) who were open to the innovations of Ornette Coleman in addition to funky soul-jazz. With George Coleman on tenor, the sidemen really inspired Davis, and although he was sticking to his standard repertoire, the renditions were full of surprises and adventurous playing. By late 1964 Coleman had departed, and after Sam Rivers filled in for a European tour, Wayne Shorter was the new tenor. During 1965-68 Miles Davis' second classic quintet bridged the gap between hard bop and free jazz, playing inside/outside music that was quite unique. Although at the time the quintet was overshadowed by the avant-garde players, in the '80s the music of this group would finally become very influential, particularly on Wynton and Branford Marsalis.

During 1968-69 Miles Davis' music continued to change. He persuaded Hancock to use electric keyboards, Shorter started doubling on soprano, the influence of rock began to be felt, and after the rhythm section changed (to Chick Corea, Dave Holland, and Jack DeJohnette), Davis headed one of the earliest fusion bands. Rock and funk rhythms combined with jazz improvisations to form a new hybrid music, and Miles' recordings of *In a Silent Way* and *Bitches Brew* (both of which used additional instruments) essentially launched the fusion era.

Many of Miles Davis' fans essentially write off his post-1968 music, not realizing that not all of the recordings sound the same and that some were more successful than others. If Miles Davis had sold out so as to gain a larger audience, then why did he record so many 20-minute jams that could not possibly be played on the radio? During 1970-75 the ensembles of his group (which sometimes utilized two or three guitars and a couple of keyboardists) became quite dense, the rhythms were often intense, and Davis unfortunately often used electronics that distorted the sound of his horn. Actually the only album from this era that is a complete failure is *On the Corner* (Davis is largely absent from that fiasco), and *Live/Evil, Jack Johnson*, and 1975's *Panagea* all have memorable sections.

And then suddenly in 1975 Miles Davis retired. He was in bad health and, as he frankly discusses in his autobiography *Miles*, very much into recreational drugs. The jazz world speculated about what would happen if and when he returned. In 1981 Davis came back with a new band that was similar to his '70s group except that the ensembles were quite a bit sparser. The rock influence was soon replaced by funk and pop elements, and as he became stronger, Miles Davis' trumpet playing proved to still be in excellent form. He toured constantly during his last decade, and his personality seemed to have mellowed a bit. Where once he had been quite forbidding and reluctant to be friendly to nonmusicians, Davis was at times eager to grant interviews and talk about his past. Although he had never looked back musically, in the summer of 1991 he shocked everyone by letting Quincy Jones talk him into performing Gil Evans arrangements from the past at the Montreux Jazz Festival. Even if he had Wallace Roney and Kenny Garrett take some of the solos, Davis was in stronger-than-expected form playing the old classics. And then two months later he passed away at the age of 65.

There are currently over 120 valuable Miles Davis recordings in print, including many live sets issued on European labels. Taken as a whole, these form quite a legacy. —*Scott Yanow*

★ **Birth of the Cool** / Jan. 21, 1949-Mar. 9, 1950 / Capitol ✦✦✦✦✦
This CD contains all 12 of the recordings by Miles Davis' highly influential *Birth of the Cool* nonet. Emphasizing arrangements and softer tones than bebop, this music led the way for West Coast jazz of the '50s. With arrangements by Gil Evans, Gerry Mulligan, John Lewis, Johnny Carisi, and Davis, and concise solos from Davis, altoist Lee Konitz, baritonist Mulligan, and either J.J. Johnson or Kai Winding on trombones, this music still sounds fresh and exciting today. —*Scott Yanow*

☆ **Blue Note and Capitol Recordings** / Jan. 21, 1949-1958 / Capitol ✦✦✦✦✦
This four-CD set is actually just a repackaging of four CDs that are available separately: the classic *Birth of the Cool* sessions, Cannonball Adderley's 1958 date with Miles Davis as a sideman *(Somethin' Else) Volume One* and *Volume Two*. The latter two sets feature three often-overlooked sessions from 1952-54 that actually are among the earliest hard-bop recordings, starring Davis, trombonist J.J. Johnson, tenorman Jimmy Heath, altoist Jackie McLean, pianist Horace Silver, and drummer Art

Blakey, among others. All of this music was quite influential and is essential (in one form or another) to all jazz libraries. —*Scott Yanow*

And Horns / Jan. 17, 1951+Jan. 19, 1951 / Prestige ✦✦✦

Dig / Jan. 17, 1951-Feb. 19, 1953 / Prestige ✦✦✦

Collector's Items / Oct. 5, 1951-Mar. 16, 1956 / Prestige ✦✦✦✦
This two-LP set lives up to its title by including such interesting sessions as the 1953 date on which Miles Davis welcomed the two tenors of Sonny Rollins and Charlie Parker, other meetings with Rollins in 1951 and 1956, and a moody 1955 date with bassist Charles Mingus, trombone, vibes, and drums (a young Elvin Jones). Highlights include "No Line," "Vierd Blues," "In Your Own Sweet Way," "Nature Boy," and "There's No You." It's classic if often overlooked music from a variety of immortal jazzmen. —*Scott Yanow*

☆ **Miles Davis: Chronicle—The Complete Prestige Recordings (1951-1956)** / 1951-1956 / Prestige ✦✦✦✦✦
The complete Prestige recordings. This is an unbelievable eight-disc set of 93 performances containing everything on the Prestige label. —*Ron Wynn*

Miles Davis / May 9, 1952-Mar. 6, 1954 / Prestige ✦✦✦✦

Miles Davis, Vol. 1 / May 9, 1952-Mar. 6, 1954 / Blue Note ✦✦✦✦
Miles Davis' recordings of 1951-54 tend to be overlooked because of his erratic lifestyle of the period and because they predated his first classic quintet. Although he rarely recorded during this era, what he did document was often classic. The two sessions included on this CD (which includes three alternate takes) are among the earliest hard-bop recordings and would indirectly influence the modern mainstream music of the '60s. The first session features Davis in a sextet with trombonist J.J. Johnson, altoist Jackie McLean, pianist Gil Coggins, bassist Oscar Pettiford, and drummer Kenny Clarke; highlights include "Dear Old Stockholm," "Woody 'n' You" and interpretations of "Yesterdays" and "How Deep Is the Ocean." The remaining six numbers showcase Davis in a quartet with pianist Horace Silver, bassist Percy Heath, and drummer Art Blakey, stretching out on such numbers as "Take Off" and "Well You Needn't." On "It Never Entered My Mind," Davis' muted statement (his only one on this set) looks towards his treatments of ballads later in the decade. —*Scott Yanow*

Miles Davis All-Stars, Vols. 1 & 2 / Dec. 24, 1952 / Prestige ✦✦✦

Miles Davis, Vol. 2 / Apr. 20, 1953 / Blue Note ✦✦✦✦
This CD contains all of the music recorded by a particularly strong sextet in 1953, six selections and five alternate takes. With trumpeter Miles Davis, trombonist J.J. Johnson, tenor saxophonist Jimmy Heath, pianist Gil Coggins, bassist Percy Heath, and drummer Art Blakey all in fine form, "Tempus Fugit" and "C.T.A." receive definitive treatment along with two Johnson compositions. —*Scott Yanow*

Ballads and Blues / Apr. 20, 1953-Mar. 9, 1958 / Blue Note ✦✦✦✦
What a treat! An incredible compilation for those Davis fans who love his cooler bluesy/modal material. The brilliant producer Michael Cuscuna has combed through the early Davis "Birth of the Cool" sessions (1950), several Blue Note sessions in 1952 and 1954, plus one cut from the classic Adderley/Davis album *Somethin' Else* to create a cool blues compilation of Davis' stuff stripped of all the bop uptempo elements. The result is a precursor to *Kind of Blue*, an album that shows all of the bluesy cool Miles Davis that many of us are so very fond of. Don't miss it. —*Michael Erlewine*

Tallest Trees / May 19, 1953-Oct. 26, 1956 / Prestige ✦✦✦

Blue Haze / 1953 / Prestige ✦✦✦

☆ **Bags Groove** / 1954 / Prestige ✦✦✦✦✦
Sterling sessions with Miles and Monk (p), Milt Jackson (vib), Sonny Rollins (ts), and Horace Silver (p). —*Ron Wynn*

Walkin' / Apr. 3, 1954-Apr. 29, 1954 / Prestige ✦✦✦✦
In 1954 Miles Davis was on the verge of making a comeback. Somewhat obscure during 1951-53 due to his erratic lifestyle and low-profile gigs, Davis at 28 was entering his creative prime. On April 3 of that year he recorded three fine numbers (including his "Solar") in a quintet with the forgotten altoist Dave Schildkraut and pianist Horace Silver, but the real reasons to acquire this set are for the exciting versions of "Walkin'" and "Blue 'n' Boogie" performed by Davis, Silver, trombonist J.J. Johnson, and tenor saxophonist Lucky Thompson. —*Scott Yanow*

★ **Miles Davis & the Modern Jazz Giants** / Dec. 24, 1954 / Prestige ✦✦✦✦✦
This CD (which contains almost 58 minutes of music) has the complete session of Dec. 24, 1954, the classic date that matched together trumpeter Miles Davis, vibraphonist Milt Jackson, pianist Thelonious Monk, bassist Percy Heath, and drummer Kenny Clarke. Davis and Monk did not get along all that well, and the trumpeter did not want Monk playing behind his solos, but a great deal of brilliant music occurred on the day of their encounter. There are two very different versions apiece of "Bags' Groove" (Monk's solo on the first take was one of his best) and "The Man I Love" along with single performances of "Bemsha Swing" and "Swing Spring";

the shortest selection is eight minutes long. Timeless music that defies easy classification, this set belongs in every jazz collection. —*Scott Yanow*

Odyssey / 1955 / Prestige ✦✦✦

Green Haze / 1955 / Prestige ✦✦✦

☆ **Miscellaneous Miles Davis 1955-1957** / Jul. 17, 1955-Dec. 18, 1957 / Jazz Unlimited ✦✦✦✦✦
One of the great legendary moments took place during the 1955 Newport Jazz Festival when (the very first) when Miles Davis unexpectedly sat in on a jam session and (with Thelonious Monk playing behind him) constructed a brilliant solo on "Round Midnight." Davis had been in danger of being forgotten, but that moment, which took place before many of the top jazz critics, was a minor sensation and gave momentum to his career. Now for the first time the performance (which also includes versions of "Hackensack" and "Now's the Time" with a sextet featuring baritonist Gerry Mulligan and Zoot Sims on tenor) has been made available, and it lives up to its legendary status. Also on this essential CD are three numbers on which Miles plays with the Rene Urtreger Trio (the great Lester Young sits in on "Lady Be Good"), two songs with his 1957 quintet with Bobby Jaspar on tenor, and three tunes in which Davis is backed by a European orchestra. This Danish import is highly recommended. —*Scott Yanow*

★ **Round About Midnight** / Oct. 27, 1955-Sep. 10, 1956 / Columbia ✦✦✦✦✦
Davis' first Columbia album is a classic. His quintet (with tenor saxophonist John Coltrane, pianist Red Garland, bassist Paul Chambers, and drummer Philly Joe Jones) was quickly becoming one of the pacesetters in jazz, and each of these six performances are memorable. In addition to the definitive non-Monk rendition of "Round Midnight," one hears the quintet making such diverse songs as "Ah-Leu-Cha," Cole Porter's "All of You," "Tadd's Delight," and "Dear Old Stockholm" sound as if they were all written for the group. Their version of "Bye Bye Blackbird" is the ultimate in cool sophistication. —*Scott Yanow*

☆ **Miles & Coltrane** / Oct. 27, 1955-Jul. 4, 1958 / Columbia ✦✦✦✦✦
In addition to two selections ("Little Melonae" and "Budo") from his first session for Columbia, this CD contains his complete performance at the 1958 Newport Jazz Festival. When one considers that Davis' sextet at the time included such giants as tenor saxophonist John Coltrane, altoist Cannonball Adderley, pianist Bill Evans, bassist Paul Chambers, and drummer Jimmy Cobb, it is not surprising that fireworks resulted. Still, the power and drive of this intense version of "Ah-Leu-Cha" is a revelation, and the band really swings and stretches out on "Straight, No Chaser," "Fran Dance," "Two Bass Hit," and "Bye Bye Blackbird." —*Scott Yanow*

Circle in the Round / Oct. 27, 1955-Jan. 27, 1970 / Columbia ✦✦✦

☆ **Cookin'** / Nov. 16, 1955-Oct. 26, 1956 / Prestige ✦✦✦✦✦
Trumpeter Davis (along with tenor saxophonist John Coltrane, pianist Red Garland, bassist Paul Chambers, and drummer Philly Joe Jones) are heard on such tunes as "My Funny Valentine" (Davis' earliest version of this standard), "Blues by Five," "Airegin," and a medley of "Tune Up" and "When Lights Are Low." This classic music has great sound. —*Scott Yanow*

☆ **Relaxin' with the Miles Davis Quintet** / May 11, 1956-Oct. 26, 1956 / Prestige ✦✦✦✦✦
Miles Davis Quintet. His great early-'50s group. —*Michael G. Nastos*

☆ **Workin'** / May 11, 1956-Oct. 26, 1956 / Prestige ✦✦✦✦✦
Miles Davis' 1956 quintet was one of his classic groups, featuring tenor saxophonist John Coltrane, pianist Red Garland, bassist Paul Chambers, and drummer Philly Joe Jones. They recorded four albums for Prestige in two marathon sessions. Among the highlights are "It Never Entered My Mind," "Four," "In Your Own Sweet Way," and two versions of "The Theme." The music is essential in one form or another. —*Scott Yanow*

☆ **Steamin'** / May 11, 1956-Oct. 26, 1956 / Prestige ✦✦✦✦✦
This classic Prestige session (one of four) has been reissued many times. The release from the audiophile label DCC Jazz is a gold compact disc. Davis is heard with his classic quintet of 1956 (which featured tenor saxophonist John Coltrane, pianist Red Garland, bassist Paul Chambers, and drummer Philly Joe Jones) performing six numbers, all of which are somewhat memorable. High points are "Surrey with the Fringe on Top," "Diane," and "When I Fall in Love." Davis' muted tone rarely sounded more beautiful. —*Scott Yanow*

★ **Miles Ahead** / May 6, 1957-May 27, 1957 / Columbia ✦✦✦✦✦
Miles Davis' first collaboration with arranger Gil Evans since *The Birth of the Cool* recordings of 1949-50 resulted in this classic album. The advantage that this CD reissue has over the LP is that since the music was recorded as a continuous suite, this way there is no break between the fifth and sixth songs. Davis' trumpet (backed by Evans' 19-piece orchestra) is heard at its best on such selections as "The Duke," "My Ship," "Miles Ahead," "Blues for Pablo," and "I Don't Wanna Be Kissed." Although a bit brief (just 36 minutes), this set is highly recommended. —*Scott Yanow*

★ **Milestones** / Feb. 4, 1958-Mar. 4, 1958 / Columbia ✦✦✦✦✦
Kind of Blue might have received most of the acclaim, but *Milestones*, the recorded debut of the Miles Davis Sextet, is in the same league. This remarkable super group (featuring Davis' trumpet, tenor saxophonist John

Coltrane, altoist Cannonball Adderley, pianist Red Garland, bassist Paul Chambers, and drummer Philly Joe Jones) was arguably the greatest one Miles Davis ever led. "Two Bass Hit" features the two saxes trading off with fire, and "Billy Boy" showcases the Red Garland trio (showing what they learned from Ahmad Jamal), but "Straight No Chaser" really demonstrates what a powerhouse band this was. —*Scott Yanow*

58 Sessions Feat. Stella by Starlight / May 26, 1958-Jul. 28, 1958 / Columbia ✦✦✦✦

Miles Davis had quite an all-star group in 1958: Tenor saxophonist John Coltrane, altoist Cannonball Adderley, pianist Bill Evans, bassist Paul Chambers, and drummer Jimmy Cobb (who had recently replaced Philly Joe Jones). This frequently exciting CD has three of the four performances originally on an LP titled *Jazz at the Plaza* ("Straight No Chaser," "My Funny Valentine," and "Oleo"), a lengthy "Love for Sale" was unreleased until the '70s, and three other songs ("On Green Dolphin Street," "Fran Dance," and "Stella by Starlight") most notable for the lyricism of Davis and Evans. —*Scott Yanow*

At Newport / May 26, 1958-Apr. 15, 1961 / Columbia ✦✦✦✦

☆ **Porgy & Bess** / Jul. 22, 1958-Aug. 18, 1958 / Columbia ✦✦✦✦✦
The second of the three great Miles Davis-Gil Evans collaborations features the trumpeter backed by Evans' 18-piece orchestra on 13 selections from George Gershwin's *Porgy and Bess*. This version of "Summertime" (with Evans' countermelody) is definitive, and the entire suite should be savored in one sitting. —*Scott Yanow*

★ **Kind of Blue** / Mar. 2, 1959-Apr. 22, 1959 / Columbia ✦✦✦✦✦
Miles Davis' most famous recording remains his most influential. It is not just that this album helped popularize modal jazz (improvising based on modes or scales rather than running chord changes) or that it introduced two future standards ("So What" and "All Blues") and three other gems ("Freddie Freeloader," "Blue in Green," and "Flamenco Sketches"). Most impressive is how the solos of Miles Davis, John Coltrane, and Cannonball Adderley (what a lineup), despite their differing styles, fit the songs perfectly. —*Scott Yanow*

☆ **Sketches of Spain** / Nov. 10, 1959-Mar. 11, 1960 / Columbia ✦✦✦✦
The third and final of the great Miles Davis-Gil Evans collaborations of 1957-59 was also their most ambitious. This set finds Davis in the forefront improvising on two numbers associated with Spanish music and three Evans compositions in that idiom. Much of the music is quite dramatic and emotional (notably "Saeta"), and Davis plays at his best throughout, really stretching the boundaries of jazz. —*Scott Yanow*

Someday My Prince Will Come / 1961 / Columbia ✦✦✦✦
Miles Davis' 1961 quintet was more relaxed and less adventurous than his earlier groups with John Coltrane. The trumpeter was at the peak of his powers in the early '60s and comfortable with his own playing. This CD, a straight reissue of the earlier LP, features Davis, tenor saxophonist Hank Mobley, pianist Wynton Kelly, bassist Paul Chambers, either Jimmy Cobb or Philly Joe Jones on drums, and, as a special bonus, guest appearances by John Coltrane (the last time he would record with Miles) on "Teo" and the title cut. —*Scott Yanow*

In Person: Friday Night at the Blackhawk / Apr. 21, 1961 / Columbia ✦✦✦✦
The first of two sets recorded during a weekend in 1961 features the Miles Davis Quintet at a period of time when Hank Mobley was on tenor and the rhythm section was comprised of pianist Wynton Kelly, bassist Paul Chambers, and drummer Jimmy Cobb. Davis is in particularly strong form on "Walkin'," "Bye Bye Blackbird," and "No Blues," and Kelly proved to be the perfect pianist for this hard-driving and swinging set. —*Scott Yanow*

Saturday Night at the Blackhawk / Apr. 22, 1961 / Columbia ✦✦✦

Live Miles: More Music from the Legendary Carnegie Hall Concert / May 19, 1961 / Columbia ✦✦✦

At Carnegie Hall / May 19, 1961 / Columbia ✦✦✦✦
For this concert, the Quintet (with tenor saxophonist Hank Mobley and pianist Wynton Kelly) are featured along with the Gil Evans Orchestra. The small group plays "So What," "Spring Is Here," "Oleo," and "Someday My Prince Will Come" before the 21-piece big band backs the trumpeter on three numbers originally recorded for the *Miles Ahead* album. Although nothing all that new occurs in these remakes, this retrospective of Davis' previous four years has fresh solos and enthusiastic performances. —*Scott Yanow*

Quiet Nights / Jul. 27, 1962-Nov. 6, 1962 / Columbia ✦✦✦

Sorcerer / Aug. 23, 1962-May 24, 1967 / Columbia ✦✦✦✦
Six of the seven selections on this CD (a straight reissue of the earlier LP with newer liner notes) showcase Miles Davis' second classic quintet, the band with such young talents as tenor saxophonist Wayne Shorter, pianist Herbie Hancock, bassist Ron Carter, and drummer Tony Williams. Shorter contributed four of the six group originals (including "Masquelero" and "Limbo"), while Hancock's "The Sorceror" and Williams' "Pee Wee" rounded out the advanced set of complex music. An oddity, a 1962 Bob

Dorough vocal ("Nothing like You") with Davis and Shorter as sideman, is also on this generally rewarding CD. —*Scott Yanow*

Seven Steps to Heaven / Apr. 16, 1963-May 14, 1963 / Columbia ✦✦✦✦
In 1963 Miles Davis was at a transitional point in his career, without a regular group and wondering what his future musical direction would be. At the time he recorded the music heard on this CD (a straight reissue of the earlier LP given newer liner notes), he was in the process of forming a new band, as can be seen from the personnel: tenor saxophonist George Coleman, Victor Feldman (who turned down the job) and Herbie Hancock on pianos, bassist Ron Carter, and Frank Butler and Tony Williams on drums. Recorded at two separate sessions, this set is highlighted by the classic "Seven Steps to Heaven," "Joshua," and slow passionate versions of "Basin Street Blues" and "Baby Won't You Please Come Home." —*Scott Yanow*

☆ **The Complete Concert: 1964 (My Funny Valentine & Four and More** / Feb. 12, 1964 / Columbia ✦✦✦✦✦
This two-CD set, which completely reissues the two lengthy LPs *My Funny Valentine* (a set of lyrical ballads) and *Four & More* (which is filled with very rapid versions of Davis' standard repertoire), features the 1963-64 Quintet at its best. This particular unit consisted of the greatly underrated tenor saxophonist George Coleman and the young rhythm section of pianist Herbie Hancock, bassist Ron Carter, and drummer Tony Williams. Since Davis' future studio albums with this group (after Wayne Shorter replaced Coleman) would be sticking exclusively to group originals, this exciting set gives one the opportunity to hear this band really stretching out on older tunes, showing off the influence of the avant-garde along with the players' own individual styles. It's highly recommended transitional music. —*Scott Yanow*

My Funny Valentine / Feb. 12, 1964 / Columbia ✦✦✦✦
Miles Davis' concert of Feb. 12, 1964, which has since been reissued on a two-CD set, was originally divided into two LPs, with all of the ballads put on *My Funny Valentine*. These five lengthy tracks (which include "All of You," "Stella by Starlight," "All Blues," "I Thought About You," and the title cut) put the emphasis on the lyricism of Miles Davis along with some strong statements from tenor saxophonist George Coleman and freer moments from the young rhythm section of pianist Herbie Hancock, bassist Ron Carter, and drummer Tony Williams. This hour-long LP complements the uptempo romps of *Four & More*. —*Scott Yanow*

☆ **Four & More** / Feb. 12, 1964 / Columbia ✦✦✦✦✦
In an odd bit of programming, Columbia placed the ballads from Miles Davis' Feb. 12, 1964 concert on *My Funny Valentine* and the uptempo romps on this LP; all of the music has since been reissued on CD. Davis, probably a bit bored by some of his repertoire and energized by the teenage Tony Williams' drumming, performed many of his standards at an increasingly faster pace as time went on. These versions of "So What," "Walkin'," "Four," "Joshua," "Seven Steps to Heaven," and even "There Is No Greater Love" are remarkably rapid, with the themes quickly thrown out before Davis, George Coleman, and Herbie Hancock take their solos. Highly recommended and rather exciting music, it's one of the last times Davis would be documented playing a full set of standards. —*Scott Yanow*

E.S.P. / Jan. 20, 1965-Jan. 22, 1965 / Columbia ✦✦✦✦
The first of six studio albums by Miles Davis' second classic quintet features seven originals by band members including "Eighty-One," "Agitation," "Iris," and "E.S.P." This music was quite original although somewhat overshadowed at the time by John Coltrane and some of the avant-garde players. Influenced by Ornette Coleman, the soloing by Davis, Wayne Shorter, and Herbie Hancock was quite advanced by this time, and this band's music would later be a major influence on Wynton and Branford Marsalis. —*Scott Yanow*

☆ **Complete Live at the Plugged Nickel** / Dec. 22, 1965-Dec. 23, 1965 / Columbia ✦✦✦✦✦
All of the music that trumpeter Miles Davis and his second classic quintet (with tenor saxophonist Wayne Shorter, pianist Herbie Hancock, bassist Ron Carter, and drummer Tony Williams) played at the Plugged Nickel in Chicago on two nights in 1965 have been released on this eight-CD box. The packaging is a bit confusing because Davis' group actually performed seven full sets, but, since their second one on the 22nd ran over, it has been issued on two CDs but placed inside the same package! In any case, the music during these two nights, primarily explorative versions of standards (as opposed to Miles' all-original studio albums of the period), is continually fascinating. A few titles are repeated, but the interpretations differ greatly from each other. The trumpeter's chops are actually not quite in peak form (although his creativity is), but Wayne Shorter (who often takes solo honors) is consistently brilliant and the rhythm section (propelled by Tony Williams) was one of the best of the period. Although some of this music had been issued earlier on three LPs, most of it had been out previously only in Japan. This was a very significant group (even if it were somewhat overshadowed by John Coltrane's Quartet at the time), and their advanced versions of such Miles Davis standards as "Walkin'," "My Funny Valentine," "I Fall in Love Too Easily," "If I Were a Bell," "Stella by Starlight," and "So What" are among the many highlights. One of the top releases of 1995. —*Scott Yanow*

★ **Miles Smiles** / 1966 / Columbia ✦✦✦✦✦
Of the six studio albums recorded by Miles Davis' second classic quintet, *Miles Smiles* is their definitive set. This CD reissue of the original LP (which has been given new liner notes) features the trumpeter/leader, tenor saxophonist Wayne Shorter, pianist Herbie Hancock, bassist Ron Carter and drummer Tony Williams in superb form on adventurous versions of "Freedom Jazz Dance," "Gingerbread Boy," Wayne Shorter's "Footprints," and three lesser-known pieces ("Orbits," "Circle," and "Dolores"). The music is challenging but quite rewarding. — *Scott Yanow*

Nefertiti / 1967 / Columbia ✦✦✦✦
The fourth of the six studio albums by the Miles Davis Quintet of the '60s was their last all-acoustic session. Wayne Shorter, Herbie Hancock, and Tony Williams contributed all of the music to this adventurous set, including such classics as "Nefertiti," "Riot," and "Pinocchio." This CD reissue of the original LP (which has new liner notes) is brief at under 40 minutes, but the music is consistently stimulating and unpredictable. It's funny that this group's playing had little influence on the music of 1967 for by 1987 it was becoming the mainstream of jazz. — *Scott Yanow*

Miles in the Sky / Jan. 16, 1968-May 17, 1968 / Columbia ✦✦✦✦
The fifth of the six studio albums by the second classic quintet found Davis continuing to move ahead. For the first time Herbie Hancock is heard a bit on electric piano, guitarist George Benson guests on "Paraphernalia," and the extended performances were just beginning to open themselves to the influences of pop and rock music. This CD reissues the original LP but has new liner notes. This important set of music can be seen as either early fusion, the beginning of the end of the Miles Davis Quintet, or both. — *Scott Yanow*

Filles de Kilimanjaro / Jun. 19, 1968-Sep. 24, 1968 / Columbia ✦✦✦✦
The sixth and final studio album by Miles Davis' second classic quintet finds the group looking towards early fusion. Herbie Hancock (who doubles on electric piano) and bassist Ron Carter are replaced by Chick Corea and Dave Holland on the two selections from Sept. 24, 1968, although Wayne Shorter and drummer Tony Williams are still key members of Davis' band. The music is less esoteric than his music of a year or two earlier, with funky rhythms and hints at pop and rock music becoming more prevalent although not dominant yet. To many of the jazz purists, this was Miles Davis' final jazz album, but to those with open ears towards electronics and danceable rhythms, this set was the predecessor of his next great innovation. This CD reissue of the original LP is well worth checking out. — *Scott Yanow*

☆ **In a Silent Way** / Feb. 18, 1969 / Columbia ✦✦✦✦✦
The beginning of fusion (although other groups such as Gary Burton's Quartet with Larry Coryell had hinted strongly at it), this set found Miles Davis for the first time really combining jazz improvising with the rhythms and power of rock. On this LP, Davis jams with an octet (which includes the magical names of tenor saxophonist Wayne Shorter, keyboardists Herbie Hancock, Chick Corea, and Joe Zawinul, guitarist John McLaughlin, bassist Dave Holland, and drummer Tony Williams; all future bandleaders) on two lengthy side-long medleys. Those jazz purists with their minds closed towards electronics of any kind are advised to check out this fairly accessible date before tackling *Bitches Brew*. The strong solos on this early fusion classic might very well win them over. — *Scott Yanow*

★ **Bitches Brew** / Aug. 19, 1969-Aug. 21, 1969 / Columbia ✦✦✦✦✦
No jazz collection is complete without this double CD. This very influential set was one of the first successful attempts to form a new music (soon termed fusion) by combining jazz solos with rock rhythms. "Miles Runs the Voodoo Down" is the most memorable of the six lengthy selections, featuring a fascinating ensemble with Wayne Shorter's soprano, Bennie Maupin's bass clarinet, guitarist John McLaughlin, the keyboards of Chick Corea and Larry Young (Joe Zawinul is on some of the other selections), Dave Holland and Harvey Brooks on basses, drummers Jack DeJohnette, Charles Alias, and Lenny White, and percussionist Jim Riley. Not for the close-minded, this music brought many rock listeners into jazz and gave jazz musicians new possibilities to explore. — *Scott Yanow*

Big Fun / Nov. 19, 1969-Jun. 12, 1972 / Columbia ✦✦
This double LP features Davis on four side-long jams taken from different sessions during 1969-72. "Great Expectations" features most of the players from *Bitches Brew* along with two sitarists, and "Ife" has the trumpeter's 1972 band (with saxophonists Carlos Garnett and Sonny Fortune), but the two best tracks ("Lonely Fire" and "Go Ahead John") are from 1970; the latter features the quintet of Davis, Steve Grossman on soprano, guitarist John McLaughlin, bassist Dave Holland, and drummer Jack DeJohnette. Very interesting if erratic music, it's not essential but fans of Davis' fusion years will enjoy much of it. — *Scott Yanow*

Live: Evil / Feb. 6, 1970 / Columbia ✦✦✦✦
Forget the inexcusably ugly (and somewhat racist) artwork and a few of the weaker tracks. At its best this double LP has some of Davis' finest playing of the '70s, and the solos by altoist Gary Bartz, guitarist John

McLaughlin, and keyboardist Keith Jarrett are not that far behind on such lengthy pieces as "What I Say" and "Funky Tonk." This is fusion at its most adventurous (and sometimes most riotous), before the record labels and radio stations turned it into meaningless "smooth jazz." — *Scott Yanow*

A Tribute to Jack Johnson / Apr. 7, 1970 / Columbia ✦✦✦✦
Davis' odd soundtrack for a documentary on the boxer Jack Johnson did not really fit the movie (it was far too modern) but stands alone very well as a strong piece of music. On this straight reissue of the original LP, the two lengthy jams (25-minute-plus versions of "Right Off" and "Yesternow") feature fine playing by a sextet comprised of Davis' trumpet, Steve Grossman's soprano sax, keyboardist Herbie Hancock, guitarist John McLaughlin, electric bassist Michael Henderson, and drummer Billy Cobham. Even listeners who write off the fusion years will find moments of interest on this set. — *Scott Yanow*

At the Fillmore / Jun. 17, 1970 / Columbia ✦✦✦
The four side-long excursions on this double LP are full of self-indulgent moments, particularly when Chick Corea and Keith Jarrett almost literally battle each other on their arsenal of electric keyboards, but there are also hot solos from Miles Davis and occasionally saxophonist Steve Grossman. This occasionally out-of-control set will not win any converts to Davis' fusion years, but it does have its enjoyable and humorous moments. — *Scott Yanow*

On the Corner / Jun. 1, 1972-Jun. 6, 1972 / Columbia ✦✦✦
On the Corner is Miles Davis' most controversial album. Jazz purists detest the album, dismissing it out of hand for the very reason that its fans celebrate it—there are no fully formed songs on the record, just funky rhythmic vamps. Davis assembled a large group of musicians, who aren't credited on the record, and had them play one groove, which demonstrated a heavy debt to Sly Stone. Miles rarely plays trumpet on the record and when he does, it is distorted and processed. Instead, he plays organ, blending into the dense, electric funk. None of the players take extended solos and all of the songs are brief, but improvisation isn't the point of the record. *On the Corner* is about funk and rhythm, not about jazz. With this record, Davis laid the foundation of the genre-blurring hip-hop and acid-jazz revolutions in popular music in the '80s and '90s. — *Stephen Thomas Erlewine*

Get Up with It / 1974 / Columbia ✦✦✦

Pangaea / Feb. 1, 1975 / Columbia ✦✦✦✦
Although Davis' health was shaky at the time of this two-CD set (recorded the same day as the weaker *Agharta*), he has a few strong trumpet solos on these two very lengthy pieces ("Zimbabwe" and "Gondwana"); Davis would drift into retirement for six years shortly after this concert. The music is actually quite rewarding (at least it will be for listeners with open ears), with the dense ensembles and heated solos (Sonny Fortune on soprano, alto, and flute and the guitars of Pete Cosey and Reggie Lucas) being quite dangerous, as opposed to the safe fusion of the '90s. *Pangaea* is the finest recording from the least-understood period of Davis' career (1971-75). — *Scott Yanow*

Agharta / Feb. 1, 1975 / Columbia ✦✦✦

The Man with Horn / 1981 / Columbia ✦✦✦

We Want Miles / 1982 / Columbia ✦✦✦✦
Davis' second recording since ending his six-year retirement was one of his best of the '80s. Unlike his bands from the '70s, this particular unit leaves plenty of space and plays much more melodically. Guitarist Mike Stern lets loose some fury, but electric bassist Marcus Miller is not reluctant to walk now and then in a straightahead fashion, drummer Al Foster and percussionist Mino Cinelu are tasteful, and Bill Evans gets in a few good spots on soprano. As for Davis, he was gradually regaining his earlier form. This double LP is highlighted by "Back Seat Betty," a side-long investigation of "My Man's Gone Now," and two versions of Davis' childlike "Jean Pierre." — *Scott Yanow*

Star People / 1983 / Columbia ✦✦✦✦
On this 1983 release, Miles Davis rediscovers the blues. He really stretches out on "Star People," making dramatic use of silence and placing each note carefully. "Come Get It" is also memorable, although "U 'n' I" (which had the potential to catch on) is only heard in a truncated version. In general Davis is in fine form on this set, and although saxophonist Bill Evans is barely heard from (many of his solos were edited out), the contrasting guitars of Mike Stern and John Scofield hold one's interest. — *Scott Yanow*

Decoy / 1984 / Columbia ✦✦

You're under Arrest / 1985 / Columbia ✦✦

Aura / 1985 / Columbia ✦✦✦
Miles Davis' final Columbia release was this two-LP set, an unusual effort from his fusion years. Palle Mikkelborg composed a challenging nine-part suite that finds the trumpeter in fairly inspired form, joined by a colorful big band. Guitarist John McLaughlin and bassists Niels Pedersen and Bo Stief have some solos, but otherwise the spotlight is entirely on Davis, who mostly rises to the occasion. — *Scott Yanow*

Tutu / 1986 / Warner Bros. ✦✦✦

Music from Siesta / 1988 / Warner Bros. ✦✦✦

Amandla / 1989 / Warner Bros. ✦✦✦✦
A particularly strong set by late-period Miles Davis, this set is highlighted by a surprisingly straightahead performance titled "Mr. Pastorius." In addition to Davis and his new altoist Kenny Garrett, various guests (including Marcus Miller, guitarist Jean Paul Boureiiy, Joey DeFrancesco on keyboards, Rick Margitza on tenor, pianist Joe Sample, and bassist Foley) get their chances to play next to the great legend who is in top form. An excellent effort, it was really his last studio recording with his regular band. —*Scott Yanow*

Live at Montreux / Jul. 8, 1991 / Warner Bros. ✦✦✦

Doo-Bop / 1991 / Warner Bros. ✦✦
If *On the Corner* suggested hip-hop beats as far back as two decades ago, then consider *Doo-Bop* as offspring. Miles' teaming with producer Easy Mo Bee is a natural—more in league with England's acid-jazz scene than anything in the trumpeter's recent canon. Those who've howled over the post-*Bitches' Brew* work will find no solace here; instead, chalk this up as one of Miles' most entertaining efforts. —*Steve Aldrich*

Highlights from the Plugged Nickel / 1995 / Columbia ✦✦✦

Walter Davis, Jr.

b. Sep. 2, 1932, Richmond, VA, **d.** Jun. 2, 1990, New York, NY
Piano / Bop, Hard Bop
In 1959 Walter Davis, Jr., led one of the great Blue Note sessions, a quintet set with Donald Byrd and Jackie McLean called *Davis Cup*. It seems strange that not only did he not have an opportunity for an encore, but his next session as a leader was for Denon, in 1977! An excellent bop-based pianist, Walter Davis picked up early experience in the late '40s working with Babs Gonzales' Three Bips and a Bop before playing and recording with Charlie Parker in 1952. Following were associations with Max Roach (1952-53), Dizzy Gillespie's big band (1956), Donald Byrd (1959), and Art Blakey's Jazz Messengers (1959). After a long period outside of music Davis came back to play with Sonny Rollins (1973-74), the Jazz Messengers (1975-77), and then as leader of his own group. He was on the soundtrack of the film *Bird* and recorded extensively as a leader during 1977-79 (for Denon, Bee Hive, Red, and Owl) and in 1987-89 (for Jazz Heritage, Jazz City, Mapleshade, and SteepleChase). —*Scott Yanow*

★ **Davis Cup** / Aug. 2, 1959 / Blue Note ✦✦✦✦✦
Propulsive hard bop, it features Donald Byrd (tpt) and Jackie McLean (as).—*David Szatmary*

☆ **In Walked Thelonious** / Apr. 1987 / Mapleshade ✦✦✦✦✦
Some spectacular solo playing by Walter Davis, Jr., a severely underrated pianist. He did 15 Monk classics, among them complex works like "Tinkle, Tinkle" and "Panonica," and made them his own. All the songs were complete first takes, and there was no overdubbing or multitracking—just Davis displaying his brilliance on each cut. —*Ron Wynn*

Wild Bill Davis

b. Nov. 24, 1918, Glasgow, MO, **d.** 1995
Organ / Swing, Groove
Prior to the rise of Jimmy Smith in 1956, Wild Bill Davis was the pacesetter among organists. He actually played guitar and wrote arrangements for Milt Larkin's legendary band during 1939-42. Davis played piano with Louis Jordan's Tympany Five (1945-49) before switching to organ in 1950 and heading his own influential organ/guitar/drums trios. Davis was originally supposed to record "April in Paris" with Count Basie's Orchestra in 1955, but when he could not make the session, Basie used his arrangement for the full band and had a major hit. In addition to working with his own groups in the '60s, Davis made several albums with his friend Johnny Hodges, leading to tours during 1969-71 with Duke Ellington. In the '70s he recorded for Black & Blue with a variety of swing all-stars and played with Lionel Hampton, appearing at festivals through the early '90s. —*Scott Yanow*

★ **In Atlantic City** / Aug. 10, 1966+Aug. 11, 1966 / RCA ✦✦✦✦✦

Impulsions / May 9, 1972+May 10, 1972 / Black & Blue ✦✦✦

Wild Bill Davison

b. Jan. 5, 1906, Defiance, OH, **d.** Nov. 14, 1989, Santa Barbara, CA
Cornet / Dixieland
One of the great Dixieland trumpeters, Wild Bill Davison had a colorful and emotional style that ranged from sarcasm to sentimentality with plenty of growls and shakes. His unexpected placement of high notes was a highlight of his solos, and his strong personality put him far ahead of the competition. In the '20s he played with the Ohio Lucky Seven, the Chubb-Steinberg Orchestra (with whom he made his recording debut), the Seattle Harmony Kings, and Benny Meroff. After he was involved in a fatal car accident that ended the life of Frankie Teschemacher in 1932 (his auto was

blindsided by a taxi), Davison spent the remainder of the '30s in exile in Milwaukee. By 1941 he was in New York and in 1943 made some brilliant recordings for Commodore (including a classic version of "That's a Plenty") that solidified his reputation. After a period in the Army, Davison became a fixture with Eddie Condon's bands starting in 1945, playing nightly at Condon's. In the '50s he was quite effective on a pair of albums with string orchestras, but most of his career was spent fronting Dixieland bands either as a leader or with Condon. Wild Bill toured Europe often from the '60s, recorded constantly, had a colorful life filled with remarkable episodes, and was active up until his death. —*Scott Yanow*

And His Jazz Band, 1943 / Dec. 3, 1944 + Oct. 13, 1955 / Jazzology ✦✦✦✦

★ **Showcase** / Dec. 27, 1947-Oct. 19, 1976 / Jazzology ✦✦✦✦✦
Two unrelated but rewarding sessions by the great Dixieland cornetist Wild Bill Davison are combined on this delightful CD. The first session, a six-song ballad-oriented date that also includes trombonist Jimmy Archey, Garvin Bushell on clarinet and (on "Yesterdays") bassoon, pianist Ralph Sutton, bassist Sid Weiss, and drummer Morey Feld, has some particularly ferocious playing from Davison (who takes his first recorded vocal on "Ghost of a Chance"). The remaining dozen tunes come from a very successful matchup in 1976 between Davison and the Classic Jazz Collegium Orchestra, a talented ten-member Czechoslovakian group. Some of the numbers (most notably a classic rendition of "Sunday") have inventive arrangements that make the band sound like a unit from the '20s. Wild Bill is quite inspired throughout, making this one of his most rewarding sets of the '70s. Highly recommended. —*Scott Yanow*

Rompin' 'n' Stompin' / Oct. 30, 1964 / Jazzology ✦✦✦

After Hours / Apr. 6, 1966-Apr. 10, 1966 / Jazzology ✦✦✦✦
The fiery cornetist Wild Bill Davison is heard in a rather sparse setting on this CD reissue, jamming 13 standards in a quartet with clarinetist Kenny Davern, pianist Charlie Queener, and drummer George Wettling. Actually the live set finds Davison sitting in with the Wettling Trio, and the results are generally quite exciting. Highlights include "I Never Knew," "Big Butter and Egg Man," "Song of the Wanderer," "Wolverine Blues," and "You're Lucky to Me." Easily enjoyable and spirited Dixieland. —*Scott Yanow*

"Wild" Bill Davison/Papa Bue's Viking Jazz Band / Feb. 1974 / Storyville ✦✦✦✦

Joey DeFrancesco

b. 1971, Springfield, PA
Organ / Bop, Soul-Jazz, Hard Bop, Groove
The comeback of the organ in jazz during the late '80s was partly due to the rise of Joey DeFrancesco, a brilliant and energetic player whose style is heavily influenced by Jimmy Smith.
Joey DeFrancesco was born April 10, 1971, in Springfield, PA and was raised in the Philadelphia area. The son of Papa John DeFrancesco, a fierce Hammond organ player himself, Joey got an early start on piano when he was five and within a year had switched to his father's instrument, the organ.
He won all kinds of major awards in high school including the Philadelphia Jazz Society's McCoy Tyner Scholarship. In the first Thelonious Monk International Jazz Piano Competition in 1987 he was a finalist at the age of 16. He is a decent player, too.
He had a record contract with Columbia, was playing with Miles Davis (1988) by the time he left high school, and has led his own groups ever since. DeFrancesco is the most important new organist to emerge during the past decade. He has recorded for Columbia and Muse. —*Scott Yanow & Michael Erlewine*

Part III / 1991 / Columbia ✦✦✦

● **Where Were You?** / 1991 / Columbia ✦✦✦✦
Nice mix-and-match quartet sessions. The lineup is split between esteemed veterans like Illinois Jacquet (sax) and Milt Hinton (b) and the younger Wallace Roney (tpt) and Kirk Whalum (ts). —*Ron Wynn*

Live at the 5 Spot / 1993 / Columbia ✦✦✦

All About My Girl / 1994 / Muse ✦✦✦✦

The Street of Dreams / 1995 / Big Mo ✦✦✦

Buddy DeFranco (Boniface Ferdinand Leonardo DeFranco)

b. Feb. 17, 1923, Camden, NJ
Clarinet / Bop
Buddy DeFranco is one of the great clarinetists of all time, and until the rise of Eddie Daniels, he was indisputably the top clarinetist to emerge since 1940. It was DeFranco's misfortune to be the best on an instrument that after the swing era dropped drastically in popularity, and unlike Benny Goodman and Artie Shaw, he has never been a household name for the general public.
When he was 14 DeFranco won an amateur swing contest sponsored by Tommy Dorsey. After working with the big bands of Gene Krupa (1941-42) and Charlie Barnet (1943-44), he was with TD on and off during 1944-48.

DeFranco, other than spending part of 1950 with Count Basie's septet, was mostly a bandleader from then on. Among the few clarinetists to transfer the language of Charlie Parker onto his instrument, DeFranco has won a countless number of polls and appeared with the Metronome All-Stars in the late '40s. He recorded frequently in the '50s (among his sidemen were Art Blakey, Kenny Drew, and Sonny Clark) and participated in some of Norman Granz's Verve jam sessions. During 1960-63 DeFranco led a quartet that also featured the accordion of Tommy Gumina, and he recorded an album with Art Blakey's Jazz Messengers on which he played bass clarinet. However, work was difficult to find in the '60s, leading DeFranco to accept the assignment of leading the Glenn Miller ghost band (1966-74). He has found more artistic success co-leading a quintet with Terry Gibbs off and on since the early '80s and has recorded through the decades for many labels. —*Scott Yanow*

★ **Complete Verve Recordings of Buddy De Franco with Sonny Clark** / Apr. 7, 1954-Aug. 26, 1955 / Mosaic ◆◆◆◆◆

Blues Bag / 1964 / Affinity ◆◆◆

The Girl from Ipanema / 1964 / Mercury ◆◆◆◆
During 1960-64 clarinetist Buddy DeFranco co-led a quartet/quintet with accordionist Tommy Gumina. They recorded five albums that have been long out of print, including this session which was their last before the group broke up. Actually DeFranco plays a fairly minor role on the date. In the ensembles he blends in with the accordion so closely as to be almost inaudible! Gumina takes the lion's share of the solo space on the standards and ballads and is well showcased on the rapid and somewhat bizarre "Lunar Lunacy." Other highlights include the title tune, "Satin Doll," and "It Could Happen to You." This LP will be difficult to find, but it is better than it looks! —*Scott Yanow*

Free Sail / Jul. 1974 / Choice ◆◆◆

★ **Like Someone in Love** / Mar. 11, 1977 / Mosaic ◆◆◆◆◆
Simply incredible in every way! Sonny Clark offers moving, heated piano, and this is some of DeFranco's most sumptuous, engaging, and accomplished playing. With majestic Tal Farlow guitar work. —*Ron Wynn*

Mr. Lucky / 1982 / Pablo ◆◆◆

Born to Swing! / 1988 / Hindsight ◆◆◆

Holiday for Swing / Aug. 22, 1988-Aug. 23, 1988 / Contemporary ◆◆◆◆
An often intriguing teamup with Terry Gibbs (vib). —*Ron Wynn*

Chip off the Old Bop / 1992 / Concord Jazz ◆◆◆

Jack DeJohnette

b. Aug. 9, 1942, Chicago, IL
Drums, Keyboards / Avant-Garde, Post-Bop
A premier percussionist and drummer, as well as fine pianist, composer, electric keyboards, and melodica soloist, Jack DeJohnette has been a familiar face on the jazz scene since the '60s. He's often considered the finest modern jazz drummer of the '70s after Elvin Jones and Tony Williams, and has worked in and/or led jazz-rock, free, pop, rock, reggae, bebop, and hard-bop groups, distinguishing himself no matter the context. DeJohnette can provide a steady, sustained pulse indefinitely, or break up the beat and redirect it. He's a marvelous percussionist, can be an equally remarkable timekeeper, uses brushes expertly, and can either provide booming volume or soft underpinning. DeJohnette was an eclectic drummer and artist long before the term became a defining virtue. He's led numerous bands and done even more recording sessions.

DeJohnette played drums in a high-school concert band in Chicago and took classical piano lessons for 10 years. He graduated from the American Conservatory of Music and spent his early days working in all types of bands in Chicago from R&B and soul to free jazz, while maintaining a busy practice schedule on drums and piano. He moved to New York in 1966 and worked with Big John Patton. DeJohnette later played with Jackie McLean, Betty Carter, and Abbey Lincoln. His first job that won him major recognition outside jazz circles came in Charles Lloyd's late '60s quartet. They were the first jazz band to visit the Soviet Union and also play several rock halls. Lloyd's band toured Europe six times, the Far East once, and enjoyed crossover attention via Lloyd's "Forest Flower" cut. DeJohnette kept busy in New York, working with John Coltrane, Thelonious Monk, Freddie Hubbard, Bill Evans, his Lloyd bandmate Keith Jarrett, Chick Corea, and Stan Getz. DeJohnette also worked with Miles Davis, playing on the *Bitches Brew* album and joining the band full-time in 1970. He remained with them until 1971. DeJohnette's first band was a jazz-rock group called Compost. He was almost ECM's house drummer in the '70s, appearing on sessions with Kenny Wheeler, Jarrett, John Abercrombie, Jan Garbarek, and George Adams. He had a separate deal as a bandleader, and recorded with his groups New Directions in the '70s and Jack DeJohnette's Special Edition in the '80s. New Directions debut album won the Prix du Jazz Contemporain de l'Academie Charles Cros in 1979. DeJohnette continued recording for ECM in the '80s. He's also recorded for Milestone, Columbia, Landmark, MCA/Impulse, and Prestige. He's played with Bennie Maupin, David Murray, Lester Bowie, Arthur Blythe, Slex Foster, Chico

Freeman, Ornette Coleman, Pat Metheny, and Nana Vasconcelos, among others. During the '90s, DeJohnette has been responsible for some original blends of Native American music and jazz. There are currently several DeJohnette titles available on CD, including a recent trio session with Metheny and Herbie Hancock.

During the '70s DeJohnette appeared as a sideman on many ECM recordings under the leadership of such players as Kenny Wheeler, John Abercrombie, and Jan Garbarek. He led two groups of his own: New Directions (which also included Lester Bowie and Abercrombie) and Jack DeJohnette's Special Edition. The latter band was quite successful, featuring such sidemen at various times as David Murray, Arthur Blythe, Chico Freeman, John Purcell, Peter Warren, Rufus Reid, and later on Greg Osby, Gary Thomas, and Mick Goodrick; DeJohnette not only played drums with Special Edition but keyboards. In 1985 he recorded a full trio album on piano and did not sound like he was playing his "second" instrument. In the '90s DeJohnette has teamed up with Abercrombie and Dave Holland in Gateway and with Keith Jarrett and Gary Peacock in their Standards Trio. He remains one of the most consistently interesting drummers on the modern jazz scene. —*Ron Wynn and Scott Yanow*

New Rags / May 1977 / ECM ◆◆◆

★ **Special Edition** / Mar. 1979 / ECM ◆◆◆◆◆
Arguably his finest small combo. David Murray and Arthur Blythe light up the sky. —*Ron Wynn*

Tin Can Alley / Sep. 1980 / ECM ◆◆◆◆
Special Edition has long been the best vehicle for Jack DeJohnette's drumming, occasional keyboard work, and writing. The 1980 version of this quartet featured Chico Freeman on tenor and bass clarinet, John Purcell's work on baritone and alto, and bassist Peter Warren. The wide-ranging music on this fine set ranges from African rhythms and colors reminiscent of Duke Ellington to some boppish moments and a bit of light funk. Although not the most powerful version of Special Edition, this set is recommended. —*Scott Yanow*

Album, Album / Jun. 1984 / ECM ◆◆◆◆
Most of Special Edition's recordings are quite rewarding and this set is no exception. Drummer/keyboardist Jack DeJohnette contributed five of the six compositions (all but "Monk's Mood"), and they cover a wide range of styles and moods, from "New Orleans Suite" and "Festival" to the ambitious "Third World Anthem" and a revisit to his "Zoot Suite." This was one of the most stimulating jazz groups of the '80s, and this particular lineup (with John Purcell on alto and soprano, tenor saxophonist David Murray, Howard Johnson doubling on tuba and baritone, and bassist Rufus Reid) was one of DeJohnette's strongest. —*Scott Yanow*

Parallel Realities / 1990 / MCA ◆◆◆
An overlooked session with Pat Metheny (g) in definite jazz phase. Herbie Hancock shows his steadfast piano form. —*Ron Wynn*

Extra Special Edition / 1994 / Blue Note ◆◆

Barbara Dennerlein

b. Sep. 25, 1964, Munich, Germany
Organ / Post-Bop, Hard Bop
Barbara Dennerlein differs from most organists by not sounding all that much like Jimmy Smith. She utilizes MIDI with her organ in order to get a different sound, and her baselines (which she operates through her foot pedals) really do sound like a bass. Dennerlein began playing organ at 11 and four years later was already gigging in local clubs. She recorded on her own Bebap label and since 1988 has also made albums for Enja that have created a bit of a stir in the US, using such sidemen as Ray Anderson and Mitch Watkins. —*Scott Yanow*

★ **Straight Ahead** / Jul. 18, 1988-Jul. 20, 1988 / Enja ◆◆◆◆
Organ-fired and guitar-laced modern jazz from this up-and-coming keyboardist. A solid album throughout. —*Michael G. Nastos*

Hot Stuff / Jun. 6, 1990-Jun. 8, 1990 / Enja ◆◆◆
Emerging organ star comes out with adventurous session. —*Ron Wynn*

● **That's Me** / Mar. 3, 1992-Mar. 10, 1992 / Blue Moon ◆◆◆◆
This CD reissues German organist Barbara Dennerlein's initial Enja release, which was her first to make a strong impression in the US. By adding synthesizers and MIDI to her sound, Dennerlein has largely escaped from the dominant Jimmy Smith influence that buries most organists' potential musical personalities. With the exception of the somewhat overblown "Love Affair—The Ballad," she excels on the swinging set, holding her own with such extroverted soloists as trombonist Ray Anderson, tenor saxophonist Bob Berg, and guitarist Mitch Watkins; drummer Dennis Chambers completes the quintet. Dennerlein's expert foot pedal work often makes it sound as if there is an independent bassist on the colorful date. She contributed all of the originals except Anderson's "One for Miss D.," and the mixture of blues, ballads, a jazz waltz, and more complex pieces works quite well. This set is a very good example of Barbara Dennerlein's appealing talents. —*Scott Yanow*

Paul Desmond

b. Nov. 25, 1924, New York, NY, **d.** May 30, 1977, New York, NY
Sax (Alto) / Cool
The definitive "cool" alto saxophonist, Paul Desmond (who had a beautiful floating tone that owed little to Charlie Parker) took his time in his solos (rarely double-timing) but his melody ideas were full of surprising twists and turns. He played his first and his last gigs with Dave Brubeck and spent his prime years (1951-67) with Brubeck's popular quartet. Early on he studied clarinet in school and then during 1948-50 recorded and gigged on alto with the Dave Brubeck octet. During the years with the quartet, Desmond was a key part of the sound, indulging in counterpoint with the pianist/leader, writing "Take Five" (in his will he left the huge royalties of this hit to the Red Cross), and taking witty and logical solos that inspired Brubeck. Away from the group, Desmond occasionally recorded as a leader (usually in pianoless settings) including a couple of encounters with Gerry Mulligan and a series of records with Jim Hall. After the quartet broke up, Desmond was mostly semiretired, although a concert with the Modern Jazz Quartet (1971) was recorded and he teamed up with guitarist Ed Bickert on a few live albums. The altoist also had reunions with Brubeck during 1972-75 before his death from cancer. His Jim Hall sets have been reissued in a Mosaic box set, most of the Brubeck albums are currently in print, and Desmond also recorded as a leader for Fantasy, A&M, Finesse, CTI, Telarc, and Artists House. *—Scott Yanow*

Paul Desmond/Gerry Mulligan Quartet / Sep. 2, 1952 / Fantasy ✦✦✦✦
Lovely. Four dates, from 1952 to 1954. *—Michael Erlewine*

Blues in Time / 1957 / Fantasy ✦✦✦
An evocative, effective set with Gerry Mulligan (bar sax). *—Ron Wynn*

East of the Sun / Sep. 5, 1959-Sep. 7, 1959 / Discovery ✦✦✦✦
First-rate quartet session. Jim Hall (g), Percy Heath (b), and Connie Kay (d) are super. *—Ron Wynn*

★ **Paul Desmond: Jim Hall Recordings** / Sep. 5, 1959-Jun. 1, 1965 / Mosaic ✦✦✦✦✦
Incredible music! A six-disc boxed set of recordings from 1959-1965 featuring Desmond with Jim Hall. Desmond plays flawless sax, and Jim Hall likewise on guitar. In brief, these are classic cuts, the best. Whether a beginning listener or a jazz expert, this is satisfying music. Mosaic does it again. *—Michael Erlewine*

Two of a Mind / Jun. 26, 1962-Aug. 13, 1962 / Bluebird ✦✦✦✦
Old pros of one mind. It's hardly challenging, yet quite attractive. Another Desmond/ Gerry Mulligan (bar sax) winner. *—Ron Wynn*

Take Ten / Jun. 5, 1963-Jun. 25, 1963 / RCA/Bluebird ✦✦✦

Easy Living / Sep. 9, 1964-Jun. 1, 1965 / Bluebird ✦✦✦
A wonderful reissue of a timeless, captivating set with Jim Hall (g), Percy Heath (b), and Connie Kay (d). *—Ron Wynn*

Summertime / Oct. 10, 1968-Dec. 20, 1968 / A&M ✦✦✦

In Concert at Town Hall / Dec. 25, 1971 / DRG ✦✦✦✦
This delightful collaboration with MJQ has been reissued several times. *—Ron Wynn*

Like Someone in Love / 1975 / Telarc ✦✦✦

Vic Dickenson (Victor Dickenson)

b. Aug. 6, 1906, Xenia, OH, **d.** Nov. 16, 1984, New York, NY
Trombone / Dixieland, Swing
A distinctive trombonist with a sly wit and the ability to sound as if he were playing underwater (!), Vic Dickenson was an asset to any session in which he appeared. He started out in the '20s and '30s playing in the Midwest. Associations with Blanche Calloway (1933-36), Claude Hopkins (1936-39), Benny Carter (1939), Count Basie (1940), Carter again (1941), and Frankie Newton (1941-43) preceded a high-profile gig with Eddie Heywood's popular sextet (1943-46); Dickenson also played and recorded with Sidney Bechet. From then on he was a freelancing soloist who spent time on the West Coast, Boston, and New York, appearing on many recordings (including some notable dates for Vanguard) and on the legendary "Sound of Jazz" telecast (1957). In the '60s Dickenson co-led the Saints and Sinners, toured with George Wein's Newport All-Stars and worked with Wild Bill Davison and Eddie Condon. During 1968-70 he was in a quintet with Bobby Hackett; in the '70s he sometimes played with the World's Greatest Jazz Band Vic Dickenson was active up until his death. *—Scott Yanow*

★ **The Essential Vic Dickenson** / Dec. 29, 1953-Nov. 29, 1954 / Vanguard ✦✦✦✦✦
This single CD reissues ten of the dozen songs originally on a double LP of the same name. Trombonist Vic Dickenson did not get to lead that many sessions, and he is generous in allocating solo space on these mainstream sessions. Trumpeters Ruby Braff and/or Shad Collins along with the distinctive clarinetist Edmond Hall and pianist Sir Charles Thompson (who often sounds here like Count Basie) are well featured, and the music is easily enjoyable; highlights include "Russian Lullaby," a 12-minute rendition

of "Jeepers Creepers," "Old Fashioned Love," and "Everybody Loves My Baby." *—Scott Yanow*

Plays Bessie Smith: "Trombone Cholly" / Mar. 21, 1976 / Gazell ✦✦✦✦
This set is unusual, for although it is a tribute to Bessie Smith, there are no vocals. Trombonist Vic Dickenson takes the place of Smith's favorite trombonist Charlie Green, and his witty sound and expressive slides are well showcased in a sextet with trumpeter Joe Newman and tenor saxophonist Frank Wess; Milt Hinton was the natural choice for the bass spot. Bessie Smith, though known as the "Empress of the Blues," actually recorded a lot of other material throughout her career, so there is more variety on this enjoyable set (which is not recommended to '20s purists) than one might expect. *—Scott Yanow*

Just Friends / Oct. 1981-Mar. 1985 / Sackville ✦✦✦✦

Al DiMeola

b. Jul. 22, 1954, Jersey City, NJ
Guitar / World, Fusion
Al DiMeola has had a dual career as a blazing fusion electric guitarist and as an acoustic player eager to explore music from other cultures. DiMeola burst upon the scene by replacing Bill Connors with Return to Forever in 1974 before he turned 20. He had been attending Berklee but essentially started out on top, immediately becoming an influential fusion guitarist. Criticized for playing an excess of notes and not showing enough feeling in his playing (faults he has since overcome), DiMeola has matured through the years. After Return to Forever broke up, he went on several tours with John McLaughlin and Paco DeLucia in an acoustic guitar trio (1980-83). Since that time DiMeola has led his own groups, alternating between electric and acoustic guitars and changing musical direction a few times. DiMeola, who toured with the Rite of Strings in 1995 (a trio with Jean Luc Ponty and Stanley Clarke), has recorded sets as a leader since 1976 including dates for Columbia, Manhattan, and Tomato. *—Scott Yanow*

Elegant Gypsy / 1976 / Columbia ✦✦✦

Land of the Midnight Sun / 1976 / Columbia ✦✦✦✦
One of the guitar heroes of fusion, Al DiMeola was just 22 years old at the time of his debut as a leader but already a veteran of Chick Corea's *Return to Forever*. The complex pieces (which include the three-part "Suite-Golden Dawn," an acoustic duet with Corea on "Short Tales of the Black Forest," and a brief Bach violin sonata) show DiMeola's range even at this early stage. With assistance from such top players as bassists Jaco Pastorius and Stanley Clarke, keyboardist Barry Miles, and drummers Lenny White and Steve Gadd, this was a very impressive beginning to DiMeola's solo career. *—Scott Yanow*

Casino / 1977 / Columbia ✦✦✦

★ **Splendido Hotel** / 1980 / Columbia ✦✦✦✦✦
Talk about ambitious, this two-LP set finds guitarist Al DiMeola performing with his quintet of the time (featuring keyboardist Philippe Saisse), with studio musicians, solo, in a reunion with pianist Chick Corea, singing a love song, and welcoming veteran Les Paul for a version of "Spanish Eyes"! Most of the music works quite well, and it shows that DiMeola (best known for his speedy rock-oriented solos) is a surprisingly well rounded and versatile musician. *—Scott Yanow*

Friday Night in San Francisco / Dec. 5, 1980 / Columbia ✦✦✦✦
With John McLaughlin (g), Paco De Lucia (g). *—Ron Wynn*

Tour de Force: Live / Feb. 4, 1982 / Columbia ✦✦✦

Soaring Through a Dream / 1985 / EMI ✦✦✦

Kiss My Axe / Sep. 24, 1988-May 1991 / Tomato ✦✦✦✦

World Sinfonia / Oct. 1990 / Tomato ✦✦✦✦
This is an outstanding venture into the international/Latin arena. *—Ron Wynn*

Heart of the Immigrants / 1993 / Mesa ✦✦✦✦
Guitarist Al DiMeola has been alternating electric and acoustic projects for the past few years. For this acoustic affair, he teams up with Dino Saluzzi on bandoneon to pay tribute to the tango master Astor Piazzolla. The music (even a duet version of "Someday My Prince Will Come") has the flavor of Argentina and uses a wide variety of instrumentations, including an occasional string section and the voice of Hernan Romero. It's recommended to lovers of world music, the modern tango, and those who think of DiMeola's guitar playing as being one-dimensional and purely based on speed. *—Scott Yanow*

The Dirty Dozen Brass Band

Group / New Orleans R&B
The Dirty Dozen Brass Band in its prime mixed together R&B with the instrumentation of a New Orleans brass band. Featuring Kirk Joseph on sousaphone playing with the agility of an electric bassist, the group revitalized the brass band tradition, opening up the repertoire and inspiring younger groups to imitate their boldness. Generally featuring five horns (two trumpets, one trombone, and two saxes) along with the sousaphone, a

snare drummer, and a bass drummer, the DDBB was innovative in its own way, making fine recordings for Rounder, Columbia, and the George Wein Collection (the latter released through Concord); guest artists included Dr. John, Dizzy Gillespie, and Danny Barker. Unfortunately in recent years the group has become more conventional, still using R&B riffs but now with a standard (and less distinctive) rhythm section. — *Scott Yanow*

★ **My Feet Can't Fail Me Now** / 1984 / Concord Jazz ✦✦✦✦
Lots of rock and R&B influence, big-name guests, and striving, robust cuts. — *Ron Wynn*

Live: Mardi Gras in Montreux / Jul. 1985 / Rounder ✦✦✦

Voodoo / Aug. 1987-Sep. 1987 / Columbia ✦✦✦

New Orleans Album / Aug. 1989-Dec. 1989 / Columbia ✦✦✦
This time, veteran Orleanians Danny Barker, Eddie Bo, and Dave Bartholomew join in, plus Elvis Costello—the fun quotient runs off the meter with plenty of solos and absolutely infectious rhythms. — *Bruce Raeburn*

Open Up: Whatcha Gonna Do for the Rest of Your Life? / Jan. 1991-Apr. 1991 / Columbia ✦✦✦✦

Jelly / Aug. 1992-Jan. 1993 / Columbia ✦✦✦

Johnny Dodds

b. Apr. 12, 1892, New Orleans, LA, d. Aug. 8, 1940, Chicago, IL
Clarinet / Classic New Orleans Jazz
One of the all-time great clarinetists and arguably the most significant of the '20s, Johnny Dodds (whose younger brother Baby Dodds was among the first important drummers) had a memorable tone in both the lower and upper registers, was a superb blues player, and held his own with Louis Armstrong (no mean feat) on his classic Hot Five and Hot Seven recordings. He did not start on clarinet until he was 17 but caught on fast, being mostly self-taught. Dodds was with Kid Ory's band during most of 1912-19, played on riverboats with Fate Marable in 1917, and joined King Oliver in Chicago in 1921. During the next decade he recorded with Oliver's Creole Jazz Band, Jelly Roll Morton, Louis Armstrong, and on his own heated sessions, often utilizing trumpeter Natty Dominique. He worked regularly at Kelly's Stables during 1924-30. Although Dodds continued playing in Chicago during the '30s, part of the time was spent running a cab company. The clarinetist led recording sessions in 1938 and 1940 but died just before the New Orleans revival movement began. — *Scott Yanow*

★ **1926** / May 19, 1926 / Classics ✦✦✦✦
Dodds was one of the very finest New Orleans clarinetists, and the only non-Creole among them. The peak experiences here, and some of the finest small-group recordings ever made, are the New Orleans Wanderers sessions—Armstrong's Hot Five with George Mitchell instead of Armstrong. Also present are Freddie Keppard's only two recordings and a bunch of marginally lesser cuts that Dodds transmutes into gold. — *John Storm Roberts*

Blue Clarinet Stomp / Dec. 11, 1926-Feb. 7, 1929 / Bluebird ✦✦✦✦
This is classic jazz (1927-29) at its best—Dodds with Jelly Roll Morton's Trio, with his own orchestra, his Washboard Band, and the Dixieland Jug Blowers. Alternate takes show improvisational character of Dodd's approach. The CD has four bonus cuts. — *Bruce Raeburn*

☆ **1927** / Jan. 19, 1927-Aug. 10, 1927 / Classics ✦✦✦✦✦

Eric Dolphy

b. Jun. 20, 1928, Los Angeles, CA, d. Jun. 29, 1964, Berlin, Germany
Flute, Clarinet (Bass), Sax (Alto) / Avant-Garde, Post-Bop
Eric Dolphy was a true original with his own distinctive styles on alto, flute, and bass clarinet. His music fell into the "avant-garde" category, yet he did not discard chordal improvisation altogether (although the relationship of his notes to the chords were often pretty abstract). While most of the other "free jazz" players sounded very serious in their playing, Dolphy's solos often came across as ecstatic and exuberant. His improvisations utilized very wide intervals, a variety of nonmusical speechlike sounds, and its own logic. Although alto was his main ax, Dolphy was the first flutist to move beyond bop (influencing James Newton), and he largely introduced the bass clarinet to jazz as a solo instrument. He was also one of the first (after Coleman Hawkins) to record unaccompanied horn solos, preceding Anthony Braxton by five years.

Eric Dolphy first recorded while with Roy Porter's Orchestra (1948-50) in Los Angeles; he was in the Army for two years and then played in obscurity in Los Angeles until he joined Chico Hamilton's Quintet in 1958. In 1959 he settled in New York and was soon a member of Charles Mingus' Quartet. By 1960 Dolphy was recording regularly as a leader for Prestige and gaining attention for his work with Mingus, but throughout his short career he had difficulty gaining steady work due to his very advanced style. Dolphy recorded quite a bit during 1960-61 including three albums cut at the Five Spot while with trumpeter Booker Little, *Free Jazz* with Ornette Coleman, sessions with Max Roach, and some European dates. Late in 1961 Dolphy was part of the John Coltrane Quintet; their engagement at

the Village Vanguard caused conservative critics to try to smear them as playing "anti-jazz" due to the lengthy and very free solos. During 1962-63 Dolphy played Third Stream music with Gunther Schuller and Orchestra USA. and gigged all too rarely with his own group. In 1964 he recorded his classic *Out to Lunch* for Blue Note and travelled to Europe with Charles Mingus' Sextet (which was arguably the bassist's most exciting band as shown on *The Great Concert of Charles Mingus*). After he chose to stay in Europe, Dolphy had a few gigs but then died suddenly from a diabetic coma at the age of 36, a major loss.

Virtually all of Eric Dolphy's recordings are in print, including a nine-CD box set of all of his Prestige sessions. In addition Dolphy can be seen on film with John Coltrane (included on *The Coltrane Legacy*) and with Mingus from 1964 on a video released by Shanachie. — *Scott Yanow*

☆ **Eric Dolphy** / 1960 / Prestige ✦✦✦✦✦
Eric Dolphy was not only a very original stylist (no one has ever sounded like him, before or after) but a talented instrumentalist, as well, who was able to develop his own styles on alto, bass clarinet, and flute. This two-LP set contains a pair of his best sessions from the busy year of 1960. Dolphy is teamed in a relatively conventional quintet with the young trumpeter Freddie Hubbard, pianist Jaki Byard, bassist George Tucker, and drummer Roy Haynes for half of the two-fer. Highlights of this date include Dolphy's "G.W." (named for bandleader/arranger Gerald Wilson), "Glad to Be Unhappy," and the exuberant "Miss Toni." The other session is more unusual, with Dolphy (who takes a rare solo on clarinet) in a quartet with cellist Ron Carter, bassist George Duvivier, and drummer Roy Haynes. His ferocious bass clarinet solo on the well titled "Out There" sounds very conversational (almost like a verbal argument), and the cello of Carter is often quite eerie on these atmospheric pieces. Highly recommended music. — *Scott Yanow*

Dash One / Apr. 1, 1960-Jul. 16, 1961 / Prestige ✦✦✦

Status / Apr. 1, 1960-Sep. 8, 1961 / Prestige ✦✦✦

☆ **The Complete Prestige Recordings** / Apr. 1, 1960-Sep. 8, 1961 / Prestige ✦✦✦✦✦

Other Aspects / Jul. 8, 1960-1962 / Blue Note ✦✦✦✦
This CD contains some unusual music by Eric Dolphy that was released for the first time more than two decades after his death. The lengthy "Jim Crow" matches the multi-instrumentalist with a classical singer and a rhythm section for a stirring performance, while "Improvisations and Tukras" finds Dolphy on flute backed by two Indian percussionists. These two selections are unlike anything else in Dolphy's discography. In addition, this album has a duet with bassist Ron Carter and two brief unaccompanied flute solos. Consistently fascinating music. — *Scott Yanow*

☆ **Out There** / Aug. 15, 1960 / Original Jazz Classics ✦✦✦✦✦
Dolphy at his evocative best, with wonderful support from Ron Carter and Roy Haynes. — *Ron Wynn*

Candid Dolphy / Oct. 20, 1960-Apr. 4, 1961 / Candid ✦✦✦✦
The great Eric Dolphy recorded several albums for the Candid label as a sideman including dates with bassist Charles Mingus, trumpeter Booker Little, singer Abbey Lincoln, and the Newport Rebels. This CD features eight alternate takes from these sessions, six of which were previously unissued. "Reincarnation of a Love Bird" and "Stormy Weather" are with Mingus in a group also featuring trumpeter Ted Curson, two numbers have vocals by Abbey Lincoln (Coleman Hawkins is heard from on "African Lady"), Dolphy is matched wtih trombonist Jimmy Knepper and the veteran trumpeter Roy Eldridge on "Body and Soul," and he proves to be a perfect partner of Booker Little in a sextet. Even the "complete" box sets that have been issued of these sessions do not include all of this music, which in general is up to the level of the originally issued versions. — *Scott Yanow*

The Great Concert of Eric Dolphy / Jul. 16, 1961 / Prestige ✦✦✦✦
For two weeks, the multi-instrumentalist (alto, flute, and bass clarinet) Eric Dolphy appeared at the Five Spot in New York with a quintet comprised of trumpeter Booker Little (who would pass away before the year ended), pianist Mal Waldron, bassist Richard Davis, and drummer Ed Blackwell. One night, July 16, 1961, was fully recorded and the results released on three LPs. This three-LP box set contains all of the music and, despite an out-of-tune piano, the results are consistently brilliant. The seven selections (all over 12 minutes long, with "The Prophet" going on for over 21) give the principals plenty of space in which to stretch out, and the long improvisations consistently hold one's interest. All of the material (except the standard "Like Someone in Love") was composed by Dolphy, Little, or Waldron. Classic and adventurous music. — *Scott Yanow*

The Complete Uppsala Concert / Sep. 4, 1961 / Jazz Door ✦✦✦

Copenhagen Concert / Sep. 8, 1961 / Prestige ✦✦✦

Stockholm Sessions / Sep. 25, 1961-Nov. 1, 1961 / Enja ✦✦✦

Vintage Dolphy / Mar. 10, 1962-Apr. 18, 1963 / GM ✦✦✦✦
This posthumous collection features the remarkable Eric Dolphy in prime form. On three songs, Dolphy (switching between alto, bass clarinet, and flute) performs two originals and Jaki Byard's "Ode to Charlie Parker" with

a quartet that includes trumpeter Edward Armour, bassist Richard Davis, and J.C. Moses. In addition, Dolphy is heard on three third stream avant-garde classical pieces by Gunther Schuller (taking a rare clarinet solo on "Densities") and jamming on a wild version of "Donna Lee" with an all-star group including such players as trumpeter Don Ellis, trombonist Jimmy Knepper, Benny Golson on tenor, and guitarist Jim Hall; the ensembles are rather uproarious. Highly recommended. — *Scott Yanow*

★ **Out to Lunch** / Feb. 25, 1964 / Blue Note ✦✦✦✦✦
Eric Dolphy's debut as a leader on Blue Note was also his last American recording before his unexpected death four months later. On this brilliant set, Dolphy performs five of his colorful originals with quite an all-star group (even though at the time none of these young players were all that well known): trumpeter Freddie Hubbard, vibraphonist Bobby Hutcherson, bassist Richard Davis, and drummer Tony Williams. Whether playing alto, flute, or bass clarinet, Dolphy had a highly original style, and this set remains one of his finest statements. — *Scott Yanow*

☆ **Last Date** / Jun. 2, 1964 / Verve ✦✦✦✦✦
Although one slighty later session has since been discovered, *Last Date* remains a near-classic, with the great Eric Dolphy (heard on alto, flute, and bass clarinet) backed by a top European rhythm section—pianist Misha Mengelberg, bassist Jacques Schols, and drummer Han Bennink—performing exciting versions of "Epistrophy," "You Don't Know What Love Is," and four of his originals. The innovative music points out what a giant loss Dolphy's premature death was; he passed away just 27 days after this memorable performance. — *Scott Yanow*

Lou Donaldson

b. Nov. 1, 1926, Badin, NC
Sax (Alto) / Bop, Soul-Jazz
A truly great bebop player, alto saxophonist Lou Donaldson strayed from the path in the early '70s, making some decent soul-jazz and funk records, and a couple of mediocore fusion dates. But he returned in the late '70s to the style that's his best; hard-edged, searing bop, played with as much vigor as any living performer. Like Frank Morgan and Phil Woods, Donaldson at his best exemplifies the Charlie Parker spirit without being a slavish imitator. He can insert clever quotes, make dazzling harmonic maneuvers at fast or slow tempos, and play beautiful, compelling blues and ballads. Donaldson began clarinet studies at 15, and later joined the Navy, continuing his education. He played in a Navy band with Willie Smith, Clark Terry, and Ernie Wilkins, having switched to alto sax. In 1952, Donaldson made his recording debut with Milt Jackson and Thelonious Monk. He began leading various combos, playing with Charlie Parker, Sonny Stitt, Blue Mitchell, Horace Silver, Art Blakey, Clifford Brown, and Philly Joe Jones before joining Blakey's Jazz Messengers with Brown in 1954. Since leaving the Messengers, Donaldson has been a busy leader and session contributor, recording numerous albums and touring frequently nationally and overseas. He initially recorded for Blue Note from 1952 to 1962, cutting albums with Silver, Brown, Horace Parlan, Baby Face Willette, and Big John Patton, among others. He started including soul-jazz material on his Blue Note dates, but began to switch more to funk in 1963, when he moved to Argo (later Cadet). Donaldson recorded again with Patton and made a nine-piece session with Oliver Nelson before returning to Blue Note in 1967. There was another nine-piece group date, and Donaldson also recorded with George Benson, Charles Earland, and Lonnie Smith. These were mostly soul-jazz and funk, but they were earthy and enjoyable. Donaldson's solos still reflected his bebop heritage. During the early '70s Blue Note joined other labels in the jazz-rock/fusion/instrumental pop phase (or craze). Donaldson made albums with overdubbed female vocals, strings, and heavy electronic backgrounds. He defended albums like *Cosmos* and *Sweet Lou* in magazine and newspaper interviews at the time, but by the late '70s he returned to the music he knew and played best. His '80s sessions for Timeless, Muse, and Blue Note reaffirmed those values: tart, sizzling bop and animated blues and ballads. He has continued recording in the '90s for Milestone. Donaldson's formative Blue Note dates, both as a leader and with the Jazz Messengers, have been periodically reissued, while the bulk of his other material, except the Argo/Cadet records, is still in print. — *Ron Wynn and Bob Porter*

The Lou Donaldson Quartet/Quintet/Sextet / Jun. 10, 1952-Aug. 22, 1954 / Blue Note ✦✦✦✦
Both soul-jazz and more mainstream/hard-pop sessions. Elmo Hope (p), Horace Silver (p), Blue Mitchell (tpt), Kenny Dorham (tpt), and cast of all-stars. — *Ron Wynn*

★ **Blues Walk** / Jul. 28, 1958 / Blue Note ✦✦✦✦✦
This early session from Lou Donaldson is pure bebop with the altoist romping on such pieces as "Blues Walk," "Move," "Play Ray," and "Callin' All Cats." The rhythm section (pianist Herman Foster, bassist Peck Morrison, drummer Dave Bailey) is supportive if not particularly distinctive, although the congas of Ray Barretto add some color to the accompaniment. No matter, Lou Donaldson is the main star of this swinging and easily enjoyable set. — *Scott Yanow*

Here 'tis / Jan. 23, 1961 / Blue Note ✦✦✦
Robust, earthy soul-jazz and blues with overlooked organist Baby Face Willette. — *Ron Wynn*

Natural Soul / May 9, 1962 / Blue Note ✦✦✦✦
Pure soul-jazz. — *Ron Wynn*

Good Gracious / Jan. 24, 1963 / Blue Note ✦✦✦
Look out for smoking Big John Patton on organ. — *Ron Wynn*

Rough House Blues / Dec. 1964 / Cadet ✦✦✦

Lush Life / Jan. 20, 1967 / Blue Note ✦✦✦✦
Smooth, moody, suggestive, and enlightening. — *Ron Wynn*

Alligator Bogaloo / Apr. 17, 1967 / Blue Note ✦✦✦✦
Altoist Lou Donaldson had a big hit at the time with the catchy title cut. This CD reissue (a straight reproduction of the original LP) features Donaldson in a quintet with cornetist Melvin Lastie, Sr., guitarist George Benson, organist Lonnie Smith, and drummer Leo Morris. The material (originals by Donaldson, Smith, and Freddie McCoy along with the standard "I Want a Little Girl") is pretty basic (generally bluesy and funky), but there are fine solos on this session from Donaldson, Benson, and Smith. — *Scott Yanow*

Hot Dog / Apr. 25, 1969 / Blue Note ✦✦

Everything I Play Is Funky / Aug. 22, 1969+Jan. 9, 1970 / Blue Note ✦✦

Pretty Things / Jan. 9, 1970-Jun. 12, 1970 / Blue Note ✦✦
Lou Donaldson has recorded many strong sessions throughout his career, but this CD reissue brings back one of the less-significant ones. Organist Leon Spencer dominates the ensembles, the material is a bit trivial, and the altoist/leader uses a baritone sax on some of the selections, which makes him sound much less individual than usual. Trumpeter Blue Mitchell's solos and a fine closing jam on "Love" help upgrade the music a bit, but there are many better Donaldson recordings to acquire first. — *Scott Yanow*

The Scorpion: Live at the Cadillac Club / Nov. 7, 1970 / Blue Note ✦✦

Forgotten Man / Jul. 2, 1981 / Timeless ✦✦✦

Play the Right Thing / Dec. 19, 1990-Dec. 20, 1990 / Milestone ✦✦✦

Birdseed / Apr. 28, 1992-Apr. 29, 1992 / Milestone ✦✦✦✦
Recent album with Donaldson and small organ group. Nice music. Nothing exceptional. Bop and ballads, with one blues (Donaldson sings on this one) and a bossa nova. — *Michael Erlewine*

Sentimental Journey / Aug. 14, 1994-Aug. 15, 1994 / Columbia ✦✦✦✦
This Lou Donaldson Quintet set (which also features organist Lonnie Smith, guitarist Peter Bernstein, drummer Fukushi Tainaka, and the percussion of Ray Mantilla) offers few surprises but no real disappointments either. Altoist Donaldson plays his usual mixture of blues, ballads, and standards with a fine organ trio, and the results are predictably swinging. The music could have been performed in 1965, but strangely enough the familiar style heard on this CD has not dated and still communicates. The enthusiasm of the musicians (who sound perfectly at home) has kept this popular idiom alive and sounding reasonably fresh. — *Scott Yanow*

Kenny Dorham

b. Aug. 30, 1924, Fairfield, TX, d. Dec. 5, 1972, New York, NY
Trumpet / Hard Bop, Latin Continuum
Throughout his career Kenny Dorham was almost famous for being underrated since he was consistently overshadowed by Dizzy Gillespie, Fats Navarro, Miles Davis, Clifford Brown, and Lee Morgan. Dorham was never an influential force himself but a talented bop-oriented trumpeter and an excellent composer who played in some very significant bands. In 1945 he was in the orchestras of Dizzy Gillespie and Billy Eckstine, recorded with the Be Bop Boys in 1946, and spent short periods with Lionel Hampton and Mercer Ellington. During 1948-49 Dorham was the trumpeter in the Charlie Parker Quintet. After some freelancing in New York in 1954 he became a member of the first version of Art Blakey's Jazz Messengers and for a short time led a group called the Jazz Prophets, which recorded on Blue Note. After Clifford Brown's death, Dorham became his replacement in the Max Roach Quintet (1956-58), and then he led several groups of his own. He recorded several fine dates for Riverside (including a vocal album in 1958), New Jazz, and Time, but it is his Blue Note sessions of 1961-64 that are among his finest. Dorham was an early booster of Joe Henderson (who played with his group in 1963-64). After the mid-'60s Kenny Dorham (who wrote some interesting reviews for *Downbeat*) began to fade, and he died in 1972 of kidney disease. Among his many originals is one that became a standard, "Blue Bossa." — *Scott Yanow*

Kenny Dorham Quintet / Dec. 15, 1953 / Original Jazz Classics ✦✦✦✦

★ **Afro-Cuban** / Jan. 30, 1955+Mar. 29, 1955 / Blue Note ✦✦✦✦✦
This is a particularly strong set from trumpeter Kenny Dorham, for it has the debut versions of "Lotus Flower," "Minor Holiday," and "La Villa," three of his most rewarding compositions. The first half of the set is Afro-Cuban in nature due to the inclusion of Carlos "Potato" Valdes's conga; also on the

four songs (plus a previously unreleased alternate take of "Minor's Holiday") are trombonist J.J. Johnson, pianist Hank Mobley on tenor, baritonist Cecil Payne, pianist Horace Silver, bassist Oscar Pettiford, and drummer Art Blakey. The final four numbers (including a "new" song added to the CD reissue, "K.D.'s Cab Ride") are more straightahead in nature and drop out Valdes and Johnson while substituting Percy Heath for Pettiford. In both cases, Dorham has an all-star group of young hard boppers eager to play his challenging and memorable originals. —*Scott Yanow*

'Round About Midnight at the Cafe Bohemia / May 31, 1956 / Blue Note ✦✦✦✦

This is a double-CD reissue of two prior single-CD reissues, which expand the original Kenny Dorham LP from 42 minutes to over two hours. Although not necessarily trumpeter Dorham's finest hour, this surprisingly consistent set features the trumpeter and his sextet (with J.R. Monterose on tenor, guitarist Kenny Burrell, pianist Bobby Timmons, bassist Sam Jones, and drummer Arthur Edgehill) performing 17 selections, ten (counting alternate takes) are the trumpeter's hard-bop originals, although one also gets fine versions of such standards as "'Round Midnight," "A Night in Tunisia," and "My Heart Stood Still." Considering how extensive this recording is (virtually the whole evening's performance), it is fortunate that Kenny Dorham's group (which was a short-lived venture called the Jazz Prophets) was in top form that night. —*Scott Yanow*

Jazz Contrasts / May 21, 1957+May 27, 1957 / Original Jazz Classics ✦✦✦✦

Some of trumpeter Kenny Dorham's finest recordings were his sessions as a leader for Riverside in the '50s, and fortunately all of that music has been reissued on CD. This straight reissue of an original LP is a bit brief in time (41 minutes) but contains many memorable selections. Three of the songs ("Falling in Love with Love," a 12-minute version of "I'll Remember April," and the trumpeter's "La Villa") match Dorham in an all-star quintet with the great tenor Sonny Rollins, pianist Hank Jones, bassist Oscar Pettiford, and drummer Max Roach. The other three numbers (of which only "My Old Flame" includes Rollins) add a fine harp player (Betty Glamman) and focus on Dorham's lyricism. —*Scott Yanow*

2 Horns, 2 Rhythms / Nov. 13, 1957+Dec. 1957 / Original Jazz Classics ✦✦✦✦

Trumpeter Kenny Dorham was one of the most underrated talents of the bop and hard-bop eras. Although he did not hit high notes or influence a lot of players, Dorham's appealing sound and consistently creative ideas should have made him a star in the jazz world instead of just a journeyman. On this CD reissue (which adds an alternate take of "Sposin'" to the original eight-song LP program), Dorham and altoist Ernie Henry (on his final session) are heard in a pianoless quartet (with either Eddie Mathias or Wilbur Ware on bass and drummer G.T. Hogan) playing three of the trumpeter's originals (including "Lotus Blossom") and four standards. Highlights include "I'll Be Seeing You" and a rare revival of "Is It True What They Say About Dixie?" The sparse setting (unusual for a Dorham session) works quite well. —*Scott Yanow*

Blue Spring / Feb. 18, 1959 / Original Jazz Classics ✦✦✦✦

This is one of trumpeter Kenny Dorham's most intriguing sessions. His arrangements of five songs that have "Spring" in their title plus the tune "Poetic" are colorful, making use of altoist Cannonball Adderley, baritonist Cecil Payne, the French horn of Dave Amram, and a fine rhythm section. Plus, Dorham's melodic solos (he was never just a bop stylist) are often memorable. —*Scott Yanow*

Quiet Kenny / Nov. 13, 1959 / Original Jazz Classics ✦✦✦

Jazz Contemporary / Feb. 11, 1960 / Bainbridge ✦✦✦

Showboat / Dec. 9, 1960 / Bainbridge ✦✦✦✦

This CD reissue of a Kenny Dorham session that was originally on the Time label features the talented trumpeter and an all-star quintet (with Jimmy Heath on tenor, pianist Kenny Drew, bassist Jimmy Garrison, and drummer Art Taylor) playing six famous themes from the Jerome Kern play *Showboat*. All of the melodies ("Why Do I Love You?," "Nobody Else but Me," "Can't Help Lovin' Dat Man," "Make Believe," "Ol' Man River," and "Bill") are heard in likable and swinging versions. This is one of Dorham's better sessions from the era and is easily recommended to his fans and collectors of hard bop. —*Scott Yanow*

Whistle Stop / Jan. 15, 1961 / Blue Note ✦✦✦✦

Kenny Dorham was always underrated throughout his career, not only as a trumpeter but as a composer. This CD reissue features seven of his compositions, none of which have been picked up by any of the "Young Lions" of the '90s despite their high quality and the many fresh melodies. Dorham teams up with tenor saxophonist Hank Mobley (whom he had recorded with previously with Art Blakey and Max Roach), pianist Kenny Drew, bassist Paul Chambers, and drummer Philly Joe Jones for a set of lively, fresh, and consistently swinging music. This is a generally overlooked near-classic set. —*Scott Yanow*

West 42nd Street / Mar. 13, 1961 / Black Lion ✦✦✦

Osmosis / Oct. 4, 1961 / Black Lion ✦✦✦

Matador / Inta Somethin' / Nov. 1961-Apr. 15, 1962 / Blue Note ✦✦✦✦

Two full LPs are combined on this single CD. Both dates feature trumpeter Kenny Dorham and altoist Jackie McLean (two very compatible players), although the rhythm sections (pianist Bobby Timmons or Walter Bishop, bassist Teddy Smith or Leroy Vinnegar, and drummer J.C. Moses or Art Taylor) differ between the two sessions. McLean was beginning to look forward and be influenced by the avant-garde; the passion he puts into his tone on such tunes as "Smile," "Beautiful Love," "It Could Happen to You," and "Lover Man" is memorable. Dorham was able to keep up with the times during this era, and his three compositions (particularly "El Matador" and "Una Mas") add a lot to the music. This generous CD is worth picking up as an example of veteran players stretching the boundaries of hard bop. —*Scott Yanow*

Una Mas / Apr. 1, 1963 / Blue Note ✦✦✦✦

When one thinks of great talent scouts in jazz, the name of Kenny Dorham is often overlooked. However, many top young players benefitted from playing in his groups, and for proof one need look no further than the lineup on this 1963 CD reissue: tenor saxophonist Joe Henderson, bassist Butch Warren, and (before either player joined Miles Davis) pianist Herbie Hancock and drummer Tony Williams. Together the quintet performs three of the trumpeter's originals ("Una Mas" is the most famous) along with the standard ballad "If Ever I Would Leave You." Even if the playing time (under 37 minutes) is a bit brief, the explorative yet swinging music lives up to its potential. —*Scott Yanow*

Short Story / Dec. 19, 1963 / SteepleChase ✦✦✦

Trompeta Toccata / Sep. 4, 1964 / Blue Note ✦✦✦✦

It seems strange and somewhat tragic that this was trumpeter Kenny Dorham's last full album as a leader for he was only 40 at the time and still in his prime. Dorham contributed three of the four selections to the session (Joe Henderson's catchy "Mamacita" also receives its debut), and his very underrated abilities as a writer, trumpeter, and talent scout are very much in evidence. This modern hard-bop quintet set with Henderson on tenor, pianist Tommy Flanagan, bassist Richard Davis, and drummer Albert "Tootie" Heath served as a strong (if premature) ending to Dorham's impressive career as a solo artist. —*Scott Yanow*

Jimmy Dorsey

b. Feb. 29, 1904, Shenandoah, PA, **d.** Jun. 12, 1957, New York, NY

Clarinet, Sax (Alto) / Swing

The older of the two Dorsey Brothers, Jimmy was the superior jazz player. An excellent clarinetist and one of the finest altoists to emerge during the '20s, JD's jazz playing was overshadowed during the swing era by the commercial hits of his orchestra. Trumpet was actually his first instrument, and Jimmy recorded on it a couple of times in the '20s, but by the time he was a teenager he was specializing on reeds. He started out playing with his brother Tommy in Dorsey's Novelty Six, the Scranton Sirens, and the California Ramblers, and his solos with Red Nichols' Five Pennies made a strong impression. Dorsey recorded with Frankie Trumbauer (including Bix Beiderbecke's "Singin' the Blues"), Jean Goldkette, and Paul Whiteman and became a busy studio musician during the Depression. In addition, starting in 1928 he co-led the Dorsey Brothers Orchestra with Tommy. Strictly a studio group at first, the Dorseys put together a full-time big band in 1934, only to break up in late 1935. Jimmy took over the nucleus of the band, and after a period of struggle, the orchestra hit it big in the early '40s with a series of vocal records featuring Bob Eberle and Helen O'Connell. By late in the decade Dorsey was alternating between some boppish big-band performances (Maynard Ferguson was among his sidemen) and Dixieland jams with his Dorseyland Band. In 1953 he broke up the band to join Tommy in a new Dorsey Brothers Orchestra that emphasized dance music. After Tommy's sudden death in late 1956, Jimmy took over the orchestra and had a surprise hit in "So Rare" before passing away from cancer. —*Scott Yanow*

★ **Contrasts** / Jul. 7, 1936-Oct. 7, 1943 / GRP ✦✦✦✦✦

This CD, virtually the only example of Jimmy Dorsey's orchestra currently available on CD, puts the emphasis on his jazz sides rather than the vocal bestsellers. Popular singer Helen O'Connell does make three appearances (including the hit "Tangerine") but most of these selections are instrumentals with Dorsey's alto and clarinet in outstanding form (it was easy to forget how talented an instrumentalist he was during these commercial years). Most of the other fine soloists are lesser names, although they include future-bandleaders Ray McKinley (on drums) and pianist Freddie Slack. Highlights are "Parade of the Milk Bottle Caps," "I Got Rhythm," "John Silver," "Ducks in Upper Sandusky," Dorsey's theme "Contrasts," and "King Porter Stomp," although there isn't a weak track on this release. Recommended, this is Dorsey's definitive set. —*Scott Yanow*

Tommy Dorsey

b. Nov. 19, 1905, Shenandoah, PA, **d.** Nov. 26, 1956, Greenwich, CT

Trombone / Swing

Tommy Dorsey was the definitive ballad player of the swing era, possessing a beautiful tone and very impressive breath control. A better jazz player than he thought, Dorsey enjoyed playing Dixieland now and then but preferred later in life to stick to ballads. In his early days he played with older brother Jimmy in Dorsey's Novelty Six and the Scranton Sirens before moving to New York and appearing on records with Jean Goldkette, Paul Whiteman, and Red Nichols. TD occasionally doubled on trumpet in the '20s, playing in a style as rough and primitive as his trombone was smooth. He was a busy studio player during the Depression until agreeing to co-lead the Dorsey Brothers Orchestra in 1934. Late in 1935 a blowup on stage led to Tommy leaving and forming his own big band, taking over the Joe Haymes Orchestra. After a short struggle, major hits in 1937 ("Marie" and "Song of India," both highlighted by classic Bunny Berigan trumpet solos) made the Tommy Dorsey Orchestra into a major attraction. TD, who learned from Paul Whiteman how to mix together a diverse repertoire, alternated swing romps, ballads (often featuring the vocals of his girlfriend Edythe Wright), novelties, and features from his Clambake Seven (which at times included Yank Lawson and Bud Freeman). In the early '40s with the hiring of Sy Oliver as chief arranger, drummer Buddy Rich, and a vocal group featuring Frank Sinatra and Jo Stafford, the orchestra evolved and continued to have hits including "I'll Never Smile Again" and "Opus One." In 1942 Dorsey was able to hire the string section of the Artie Shaw Orchestra, greatly expanding his band. By the end of World War II and the collapse of the swing era, TD had to drop the strings and cut back a bit, even breaking up his band for a period after 1946. He appeared in the unfortunate fictional movie *The Fabulous Dorseys* with Jimmy in 1947, reformed his orchestra, and did his best to ignore bop (which he detested). Charlie Shavers was the key soloist in Tommy Dorsey's band from the mid-'40s on. In 1953 Jimmy Dorsey agreed to join forces with his brothers. Tommy Dorsey's band was renamed the Dorsey Brothers Orchestra, emphasizing dance music. The nostalgia formula worked well until Tommy's sudden death in November 1956. — *Scott Yanow*

● **Music Goes Round and Round** / Dec. 9, 1935-Feb. 25, 1947 / Bluebird ✦✦✦✦

In 1935, Tommy Dorsey first jammed with musicians from his big band in a Dixieland format, calling the little band the Clambake Seven. He recorded frequently with the unit up until 1939 and then on a rare basis up until 1950. This particular CD has 21 of the Clambake's better performances, and although it would have been preferable to reissue all of the group's recordings, this serves as a strong introduction to their music. With such soloists as trumpeters Yank Lawson, Max Kaminsky, and Pee Wee Erwin, clarinetists Johnny Mince and Joe Dixon, tenorman Bud Freeman, and TD himself, this music was quite joyous and spirited. Edythe Wright ably sings on many of the songs, which are highlighted by the title cut, "At the Codfish Ball," two versions of "The Sheik of Araby," and "When the Midnight Choo-Choo Leaves for Alabama." These are Dixieland recordings that predated the New Orleans revival of 1940. — *Scott Yanow*

Seventeen Number Ones / 1935-1942 / Bluebird ✦✦✦

★ **Yes, Indeed!** / Jun. 15, 1939-Sep. 20, 1945 / Bluebird ✦✦✦✦✦

This CD includes many of Tommy Dorsey's very best recordings from 1939-42 along with four selections dating from 1944-45. During this period the sound of his orchestra had changed from the earlier days, thanks in large part to Sy Oliver's arrangements and the hard-driving drums of Buddy Rich. With such soloists as trumpeter Ziggy Elman, tenor saxophonist Don Lodice, and clarinetist Johnny Mince (in addition to Dorsey's trombone), this orchestra could play jazz with the best of their contemporaries, although many of their other recordings (not included here) actually showcased vocals and dance music. Highlights of this recommended disc include "Well, All Right," "Stomp It Off," "Quiet Please," "Swing High," "Swanee River," "Deep River," and "Well, Git It!," while the later tracks include "Opus One," the Charlie Shavers feature "At the Fat Man's," and a guest appearance by Duke Ellington on "The Minor Goes Muggin'." — *Scott Yanow*

The Post-War Era / Jan. 31, 1946-Jun. 13, 1950 / Bluebird ✦✦✦

Having a Wonderful Time / RCA ✦✦✦

Kenny Drew

b. Aug. 28, 1928, New York, NY, d. Aug. 4, 1993, Copenhagen, Denmark
Piano / Hard Bop
A talented bop-based pianist (whose son has been one of the brightest pianists of the '90s), Kenny Drew was somewhat underrated due to his decision to move permanently to Copenhagen in 1964. He made his recording debut in 1949 with Howard McGhee and in the '50s was featured on sessions with the who's who of jazz including Charlie Parker, Coleman Hawkins, Lester Young, Milt Jackson, Buddy DeFranco's quartet, Dinah Washington, and Buddy Rich (1958). Drew led sessions for Blue Note, Norgran, Pacific Jazz, Riverside, and the obscure Judson label during 1953-60; most of the sessions are currently available on CD. He moved to Paris in 1961 and relocated to Copenhagen in 1964, where he was co-owner of the Matrix label. He formed a duo with Niels-Henning Orsted Pederson and

worked regularly at the Montmartre. Drew recorded many dates for SteepleChase in the '70s and remained active up until his death. — *Scott Yanow*

The Kenny Drew Trio / Sep. 20, 1956+Sep. 26, 1956 / Original Jazz Classics ✦✦✦✦

Kenny Drew, with the assistance of bassist Paul Chambers (whose bowed solos are always welcome) and drummer Philly Joe Jones, explores six standards and two of his originals. Although Drew would have to move to Europe in the early '60s in order to get the recognition he deserved, it is obvious (in hindsight) from this enjoyable date that he was already a major improviser. — *Scott Yanow*

Plays the Music of Harry Warren and Harold Arlen / Feb. 1957 / Milestone ✦✦✦✦

This CD reissue combines together the complete contents of two similar sessions by pianist Kenny Drew. With the assistance of bassist Wilbur Ware, Drew performs a dozen songs apiece from the Harry Warren and Harold Arlen songbooks. The interpretations, originally released on the Judson label, are quite melodic, tasteful, and lightly swinging. Drew does not come out with any new revelations while playing songs such as "Lullaby of Broadway," "I Only Have Eyes for You," "That Old Black Magic," and "It's Only a Paper Moon," but neither do these versions sound overly nostalgic or tired. This is a nice set if not all that essential. — *Scott Yanow*

★ **Pal Joey: Stage and Screen Classic** / Oct. 15, 1957 / Original Jazz Classics ✦✦✦✦✦

It seems strange that (with the exception of a 1960 session for Blue Note) this would be pianist Kenny Drew's last session as a leader until 1973. With bassist Wilbur Ware and drummer Philly Joe Jones, Drew interprets eight Rodgers and Hart tunes, five written for the play *Pal Joey* and three of their earlier hits that were included in the film version. Drew contributes swing and subtle bop-based improvising to these superior melodies (which are highlighted by "Bewitched, Bothered and Bewildered," "I Could Write a Book," and "The Lady Is a Tramp"), and the results are quite memorable. — *Scott Yanow*

It Might As Well Be Spring / Nov. 23, 1981 / Soul Note ✦✦✦

Your Soft Eyes / Nov. 1981 / Soul Note ✦✦✦

And Far Away / Feb. 21, 1983 / Soul Note ✦✦✦

Paquito D'Rivera

b. Jun. 4, 1948, Havana, Cuba
Clarinet, Sax (Alto) / Bop, Latin Continuum, Afro-Cuban Jazz
One of Cuba's finest exports, Paquito D'Rivera is a distinctive altoist with an impressive upper register and a skilled clarinetist. He studied at the Havana Conservatory from 1960 and played professionally starting when he was 14. After playing in an army band, D'Rivera joined the Orquesta Cubana de Musica Moderna and Irakere (1973-80); the latter was Cuba's top band. After defecting to the US in 1980, D'Rivera moved to New York and worked with Dizzy Gillespie and McCoy Tyner before starting his own band. He has directed Dizzy Gillespie's last group, the United Nation Orchestra, since Dizzy's death. D'Rivera has recorded an impressive string of albums for Columbia, Chesky, Messidor, and Candid. — *Scott Yanow*

Blowin' / 1981 / CBS ✦✦✦✦

Altoist Paquito D'Rivera's first American recording after defecting from Cuba is an often-jubilant affair. D'Rivera, who also plays some soprano and flute on this album, is heard in groups ranging from a duet with pianist Jorge Dalto to a septet. The impressive lineup also includes pianist Hilton Ruiz, bassist Eddie Gomez, and drummer Ignacio Berroa, among others. The music is high-quality modern bebop with a strong dose of Latin rhythms—a fine example of D'Rivera's talents. — *Scott Yanow*

Mariel / 1982 / Columbia ✦✦✦✦

With pianists Hilton Ruiz and Jorge Dalto. Becoming more funky. Also includes "Moment's Notice." Funk and jazz from Cuban fire-spitter. — *Michael G. Nastos*

Why Not / Jun. 19, 1984-Jun. 21, 1984 / Columbia ✦✦✦✦

With a backup crew that includes trumpeter Claudio Roditi, pianist Michel Camilo, guest Toots Thielemans on harmonica and guitar, and several fiery percussionists, it is not surprising that this is a very successful date. Paquito D'Rivera, heard here on alto and clarinet, has long had a very distinctive bop-oriented style, and his technique (which includes a wide range) and creativity are fully displayed on this well rounded set. High points include "Manteca" and Camilo's "Why Not." — *Scott Yanow*

Tico! Tico! / Jul. 1989-Aug. 1989 / Chesky ✦✦✦

★ **Who's Smoking?!** / May 21, 1991-May 22, 1991 / Candid ✦✦✦✦✦

Hot, surging Afro-Latin set by alto saxophonist Paquito D'Rivera, matching him with both celebrated veterans and established session stars. D'Rivera doesn't falter through any of these pieces and gets strong assistance from special guest James Moody and super trumpet solos by Claudio Roditi. The percussive backgrounds supplied by Danilo Perez and Al Foster are varied and constantly shifting and changing. — *Ron Wynn*

Havana Cafe / Aug. 28, 1991-Aug. 29, 1991 / Chesky ✦✦✦✦
His latest, some sterling solos, fine Latin arrangements. —*Ron Wynn*

Reunion / 1991 / Messidor ✦✦✦✦
Excellent session done for German label, distributed domestically by Rounder. D'Rivera at top of his game. —*Ron Wynn*

40 Years of Cuban Jam Session / 1993 / Messidor ✦✦✦✦
Despite its title, this CD does not offer one a sampler of Cuban jams of the past 40 years, but it does contain a recent session featuring 25 of the top Cuban expatriates. Organized to a large extent by altoist Paquito D'Rivera (who is only actually on six of the 11 selections), these performances utilize a wide variety of instrumentations. Carlos Gomez has a vocal, there is a laidback feature for Jose Silva's tenor, Juan Pablo Torres takes a couple of impressive trombone solos, and on "Descarga para Banda y Combo," there is a humorous blending of circus music, Dixieland, and a boppish blues. With D'Rivera in fine form on alto and clarinet during his appearances, this is a continually interesting and stimulating set. —*Scott Yanow*

A Night in Englewood / Jul. 1993 / Messidor ✦✦✦✦

Charles Earland

b. May 24, 1941, Philadelphia, PA
Organ / Soul-Jazz, Hard Bop, Groove
Charles Earland has played organ and other keyboards plus soprano sax. His style has been influenced by Jimmy Smith and Jimmy McGriff, and combines elements of soul-jazz with blues, funk, and pop. He doesn't have as heavy a sound as Groove Holmes or Jack McDuff but has done some solid dates for Prestige, Muse, and other labels. He became one of the most popular organists in the '70s using walking and rolling bass pedal lines in either soul-jazz or jazz-rock and funk contexts. Earland actually began his career as a saxophonist working with McGriff. He began heading his own band in the '60s and, unable to either attract or keep organists in his bands, switched to the instrument in 1963. Earland played organ with Lou Donaldson in the late '60s, then issued his own albums on Choice and Prestige. His *Black Talk* album in 1969 featured his own compositions. The LP's success won Earland a long-term deal with Prestige. He started mixing soprano sax, synthesizer, electric piano, and organ in his bands. During the '70s Earland appeared at the Montreux and Newport jazz festivals and played on the soundtrack for the film *The Dynamite Brothers*. His '70s Prestige albums alternated between combos, large groups, and some sessions with vocalists. His 1973 date *Leaving This Planet* included guest appearances from Freddie Hubbard, Eddie Henderson, and Joe Henderson. After a live session recorded in Montreux in 1974, Earland switched labels to Mercury, cutting one studio date, then Muse for four albums. The first three reunited Earland with guitarist Jimmy Ponder, who'd played on his first album as a leader. He then recorded with Columbia on sessions ranging from large bands to dates with the Brecker Brothers and female vocalists. During the '80s and '90s, Earland returned to Muse for quartet/combo dates, including one co-led by George Coleman. —*Ron Wynn and Michael Erlewine*

★ **Black Talk** / Dec. 15, 1969 / Original Jazz Classics ✦✦✦✦✦
This CD reissue of a Prestige date is one of the few successful examples of jazz musicians from the late '60s taking a few rock and pop songs and turning them into creative jazz. Organist Charles Earland and his sextet, which includes trumpeter Virgil Jones, Houston Person, on tenor and guitarist Melvin Sparks, perform a variation of "Eleanor Rigby" titled "Black Talk," two originals, a surprisingly effective rendition of "Aquarius," and a classic rendition of "More Today than Yesterday." Fans of organ combos are advised to pick up this interesting set. —*Scott Yanow*

Soul Crib / 1969 / Choice ✦✦✦✦
Earland with George Coleman on tenor sax, Jimmy Ponder on guitar, and Walter Perkins on drums. —*Michael Erlewine*

Black Drops / Jun. 1, 1970 / Prestige ✦✦✦

Living Black / Sep. 17, 1970 / Prestige ✦✦✦

Charles 3 / Feb. 16, 1972+Feb. 17, 1972 / Prestige ✦✦✦
Sparkling vocals by Joe Lee Wilson. —*Ron Wynn*

Leaving This Planet / Dec. 11, 1973-Dec. 13, 1973 / Prestige ✦✦✦✦
Great stints by Joe Henderson (sax), Eddie Henderson (tpt), and Freddie Hubbard (tpt). His most ambitious album. —*Ron Wynn*

Front Burner / Jun. 27, 1988-Jun. 28, 1988 / Milestone ✦✦✦

Third Degree Burn / May 15, 1989-May 16, 1989 / Milestone ✦✦✦✦
Sparkling funky tenor from David "Fathead" Newman and solid organ from Earland. Also: Grover Washington, Jr. —*Ron Wynn*

Whip Appeal / May 23, 1990 / Muse ✦✦✦

Unforgettable / Dec. 1991 / Muse ✦✦✦

Billy Eckstine

b. Jul. 8, 1914, Pittsburgh, PA, **d.** Mar. 8, 1993, Pittsburgh, PA
Trumpet, Trombone (Valve), Vocals / Bop, Pop, United States, Standards
An influential ballad singer with a very appealing baritone voice, Billy Eck-

stine made a very important contribution to jazz early on, leading one of the first bebop big bands and keeping it together (while turning down lucrative offers to work as a single) as long as possible. He worked in Chicago starting in 1937 and was with the Earl Hines Orchestra during 1939-43, having a few hit records including the blues "Jelly, Jelly." Near the end of his stay with Hines, the big band had become bop-oriented with such sidemen as Dizzy Gillespie, Charlie Parker, and the young Sarah Vaughan. After leaving Hines, Eckstine hired those three as part of his very modern orchestra, and other members of his band during parts of 1944-47 included Gene Ammons, Dexter Gordon, Frank Wess, Miles Davis, Kenny Dorham, Fats Navarro, Sonny Stitt, Leo Parker, and Art Blakey; virtually all of the musicians were fairly unknown at the time. Unfortunately they did not make many recordings in 1944 (and by then Charlie Parker was gone) but they did have a minor hit with "Blowin' the Blues Away" and recorded more frequently during 1945-47; the latter performances have been reissued by Savoy. Eckstine, who occasionally took decent solos on valve trombone and trumpet, alternated ballads with bop instrumentals and made a short film in 1945 but by 1947 was forced financially to give up the band. Switching to middle-of-the-road pop ballads, Mr. B. became a very popular attraction (in a later era he would have been a romantic movie star), recording many string-filled arrangements for MGM that were best-sellers. But he never lost his feeling for jazz and a 1959 collaboration with Count Basie finds Eckstine swinging with the best. —*Scott Yanow*

● **I Want to Talk About You** / Feb. 13, 1940-Mar. 4, 1945 / Xanadu ✦✦✦✦
The warm baritone voice of Billy Eckstine made him one of the most popular vocalists of the '40s and '50s. Although not a jazz singer himself, Eckstine always had a strong sympathy for the music and his championing of a bebop big band during 1944-47 (when he could have made a lucrative living as a single) was quite heroic. This Xanadu LP features Eckstine's earliest recordings, 13 selections taken from his 1940-41 Victor sides with Earl Hines' Orchestra. Ballads naturally dominate, but "Jelly, Jelly" (Eckstine's first hit), "The Jitney Man" and "Stormy Monday Blues" are among the more memorable performances. This set is rounded out by three ballads taken from a 1945 broadcast with his own big band. Bop collectors will prefer to get a full set of orchestral sides by Eckstine's pioneering big band, but fans of his warm vocals should pick up this appealing album. —*Scott Yanow*

Airmail Special / Feb. 1945-Mar. 1945 / Drive Archive ✦✦✦✦
This Drive Archive budget CD reissues an Alamac LP, material that has also appeared on the English Spotlite label. Singer Billy Eckstine led one of the first bebop big bands and this set of 1945 broadcasts features such important modernists as trumpeter Fats Navarro, the tenors of Gene Ammons and Budd Johnson, drummer Art Blakey, and singer Sarah Vaughan. The arrangements of the instrumentals (particularly "Airmail Special" and "Opus X") are a bit futuristic, Eckstine takes four fine vocals and Sarah Vaughan's two features ("Mean to Me" and "Don't Blame Me") are among her earliest appearances on record. The recording quality overall is just decent but the fire of the music makes these performances worth acquiring (in one form or another) by bop collectors. —*Scott Yanow*

★ **Mister B and the Band** / May 2, 1945-Apr. 21, 1947 / Savoy ✦✦✦✦✦
Generally excellent and sometimes great music but very dumb packaging. This Savoy CD, put out by the Japanese Denon label, reissues a former double-LP, shrinking the liner notes to the point where they are completely unreadable. Due to time limitations, the last five numbers of the 32 songs are dropped out, yet they appear in the liners! The music by singer Billy Eckstine's bop big band of 1946-47 alternates between hard-swinging instrumentals and smooth vocal ballads. There is a bit of solo space for some of the notable modernists (including trumpeters Fats Navarro and Miles Davis and tenorman Dexter Gordon) and the performances (highlighted by "I Love the Rhythm in a Riff," "The Jitney Man," "Second Balcony Jump," and the two versions of "Oo Bop Sh'bam") are often exciting. But owners of the two-LP set are advised to keep it (and their eyesight!) and skip this one. —*Scott Yanow*

MGM Years / May 20, 1947-Apr. 26, 1957 / PolyGram ✦✦✦✦
Two-fer with a ton of great songs and great singing. —*Michael G. Nastos*

Basie and Eckstine, Inc. / 1959 / Roulette ✦✦✦✦

No Cover, No Minimum / Aug. 1960 / Roulette ✦✦✦✦
An outstanding '60 live set, with Eckstine backed by a good combo doing classics like "Lush Life" and "Moonlight In Vermont." The intimate nightclub setting, coupled with Bobby Tucker's simple yet effective arrangements, make this perhaps Eckstine's best album outside his prime '40s and early '50s dates. It has been reissued on CD with 12 previously unissued cuts. —*Ron Wynn*

★ **Everything I Have Is Yours** / Metro ✦✦✦✦✦
This two-CD set improves upon the original two-LP package by adding 14 more songs. The pop side of Billy Eckstine was emphasized during his period with MGM and many of these selections (including hit versions of "Everything I Have Is Yours," "Blue Moon," "Caravan," "My Foolish Heart," and "I Apologize") feature his warm baritone backed by string sections. There are some exceptions including "Mr. B's Blues" (which gives Eckstine

a chance to solo on valve trombone), dates with Woody Herman and George Shearing, eight numbers on which the singer is accompanied by the Bobby Tucker Quartet, and a pair of wonderful performances with the Metronome All-Stars in 1953 (a group that includes trumpeter Roy Eldridge, both Lester Young and Warne Marsh on tenors and vibraphonist Terry Gibbs). Although not as essential from the jazz standpoint as Billy Eckstine's earlier big-band dates, this two-fer features the singer at the peak of his powers; five ballad duets with Sarah Vaughan are a highlight. *—Scott Yanow*

Harry "Sweets" Edison

b. Oct. 10, 1915, Columbus, OH
Trumpet / Swing
Harry "Sweets" Edison gets the most mileage out of a single note, like his former boss Count Basie. Edison, who is immediately recognizable within a note or two, has long used repetition and simplicity to his advantage while always swinging. He played in local bands in Columbus and then in 1933 joined the Jeter-Pillars Orchestra. After a couple of years in St. Louis, MO, Edison moved to New York where he joined Lucky Millinder and then in June 1938 Count Basie, remaining with that classic orchestra until it broke up in 1950. During that period he was featured on many records, appeared in the 1944 short *Jammin' the Blues*, and gained his nickname "Sweets" (due to his tone) from Lester Young. In the '50s Edison toured with Jazz at the Philharmonic, settled in Los Angeles and was well featured both as a studio musician (most noticeably on Frank Sinatra records) and on jazz dates. He had several reunions with Count Basie in the '60s and by the '70s was often teamed with Eddie "Lockjaw" Davis; Edison also recorded an excellent duet album for Pablo with Oscar Peterson. One of the few swing trumpeters to be influenced by Dizzy Gillespie, Sweets has led sessions through the years for Pacific Jazz, Verve, Roulette, Riverside, Vee-Jay, Liberty, Sue, Black & Blue, Pablo, Storyville, and Candid among others. Although his playing faded during the '80s and '90s, Edison can still say more with one note than nearly anyone. *— Scott Yanow*

Jawbreakers / Apr. 18, 1962 / Original Jazz Classics ✦✦✦✦
Solid, inviting duo work, matching Edison with Eddie "Lockjaw" Davis (ts). *—Ron Wynn*

Ben Webster and Sweets Edison / Jun. 6, 1962-Jun. 7, 1962 / Columbia ✦✦✦✦

Oscar Peterson and Harry Edison / 1974 / Original Jazz Classics ✦✦✦✦
★ **Edison's Lights** / May 5, 1976 / Original Jazz Classics ✦✦✦✦✦
Simply Sweets / Sep. 22, 1977 / Pablo ✦✦✦
Swing Summit / Apr. 27, 1990-Apr. 28, 1990 / Candid ✦✦✦

Teddy Edwards

b. Apr. 26, 1924, Jackson, MS
Sax (Tenor) / Bop, Hard Bop
Teddy Edwards was, with Dexter Gordon and Wardell Gray, the top young tenor of the late '40s. Unlike the other two, he chose to remain in Los Angeles and has been underrated through the years, but even in his early '70s, Edwards remains in prime form. Early on he toured with Ernie Fields' Orchestra, moving to Los Angeles in 1945 to work with Roy Milton as an altoist. Edwards switched to tenor when he joined Howard McGhee's band and was featured in many jam sessions during the era, recording "The Duel" with Dexter Gordon in 1947. A natural-born leader, Edwards did work briefly with Max Roach and Clifford Brown (1954), Benny Carter (1955), and Benny Goodman (1964) and he recorded in the '60s with Milt Jackson and Jimmy Smith. But it is his own records from Onyx (1947-48), Pacific Jazz, Contemporary (1960-62), Prestige, Xanadu, Muse, Steeple-Chase, Timeless, and Antilles that best show off his playing and writing; "Sunset Eyes" is Edwards' best-known original. *— Scott Yanow*

★ **Teddy's Ready** / Aug. 17, 1960 / Original Jazz Classics ✦✦✦✦✦
Many feel this album is this West Coast group's finest hour. W/Joe Castro (p), Leroy Vinnegar (b), and Billy Higgins (d). *—Michael Erlewine*

Back to Avalon / Dec. 7, 1960-Dec. 13, 1960 / Original Jazz Classics ✦✦✦

Together Again! / May 15, 1961+May 17, 1961 / Contemporary ✦✦✦✦
Dynamite pairing with Howard McGhee (tpt). Incredible piano by Phineas Newborn Jr. (p) *—Ron Wynn*

Good Gravy! / Aug. 23, 1961-Aug. 25, 1961 / Original Jazz Classics ✦✦✦✦
Teddy Edwards has long been one of the most underrated of the bop tenors, due in large part to his decision to settle in Los Angeles. Edwards is in typically swinging form on this quartet date with either Phineas Newborn, Jr., or Danny Horton on piano, bassist Leroy Vinnegar, and drummer Milt Turner. The tenor contributed four originals and also performs the obscure "A Little Later" and four standards with warmth and creativity within the hard bop genre. *— Scott Yanow*

Mississippi Lad / Mar. 13, 1991-Mar. 14, 1991 / Antilles ✦✦✦
☆ **Blue Saxophone** / Jun. 8, 1992-Jun. 10, 1992 / Antilles ✦✦✦✦✦
One of the major tenor saxophonists in jazz since his emergence in the

mid-'40s, Teddy Edwards has not led enough sessions throughout his career considering his great talent. In the '90s, he has been making up for some lost time by putting a great deal of planning into his releases. For this ambitious effort he is joined by five brass, five strings, a harp, a four-piece rhythm section, and on two songs the fine young singer Lisa Nobumoto. As if that were not enough, Edwards wrote ten of the 12 songs, arranged all of them, takes "Prelude" unaccompanied, and plays a bit of clarinet on "Serenade in Blue." It's an impressive effort. *—Scott Yanow*

● **Horn to Horn** / Dec. 27, 1994 / Muse ✦✦✦✦
This is a logical and very successful collaboration featuring the East Coast tenor Houston Person and Los Angeles' legendary Teddy Edwards. Although one can generally tell the two veterans apart (Person has a heavier sound than the comparatively light-toned Edwards), the co-leaders are quite complementary and work together well in the tradition of Sonny Stitt and Gene Ammons. With fine backup from pianist Richard Wyands, bassist Peter Washington, and drummer Kenny Washington, Edwards and Person pay tribute to eight great tenors of the past (John Coltrane, Ben Webster, Lester Young, Stan Getz, Coleman Hawkins, Gene Ammons, Dexter Gordon, and Eddie "Lockjaw" Davis) through their renditions of eight standards. Highlights include a romp on "Lester Leaps In," a surprisingly successful version of "The Girl from Ipanema," and a spirited "Red Top." Recommended. *— Scott Yanow*

Marty Ehrlich

b. 1955, St. Louis, MO
Clarinet, Flute, Clarinet (Bass), Sax (Alto), Sax (Soprano) / Avant-Garde
A versatile player, Marty Ehrlich has led stimulating sessions and been a valuable sideman in several different situations. He first recorded with the Human Arts Ensemble in 1972, studied at the New England Conservatory of Music, and in 1978 moved to New York. Since then he has worked with many top musicians including Muhal Richard Abrams, Anthony Braxton, Julius Hemphill, and Bobby Bradford (where he fills in for the late John Carter). Ehrlich has also duetted with Anthony Cox, led his Dark Woods Ensemble and recorded as a leader for Cecma, Sound Aspects, Muse, New World, and most often Enja. *—Scott Yanow*

Pliant Plaint / Apr. 1987 / Enja ✦✦✦✦
The Traveller's Tale / May 30, 1989-Jun. 1, 1989 / Enja ✦✦✦✦
Solid, energized solos by Marty Ehrlich on a variety of saxophones and flute, plus equally animated playing from co-saxophonist Stan Strickland on tenor, soprano, and flute. The two-sax frontline, plus tasteful, probing bass/drum help from Lindsey Horner and Robert Previte, not only fills the spaces open due to the absence of a pianist, but periodically shift the mood, focus, and tempo. *—Ron Wynn*

Emergency Peace / Dec. 14, 1990-Dec. 16, 1990 / New World ✦✦✦✦
It's a fascinating blend of improvisation and original structures. *—Myles Boisen*

Side by Side / Jan. 1991 / Enja ✦✦✦✦
★ **Can You Hear A Motion?** / Sep. 22, 1993-Sep. 23, 1993 / Enja ✦✦✦✦✦
This quartet release matches the cool-toned reeds of Marty Ehrlich (heard on clarinet, alto, and soprano) and Stan Strickland (doubling on flute and tenor) with bassist Michael Formanek (who operates as an active partner) and the quietly supportive drummer Bobby Previte. Their unpredictable music ranges from free bop à la Ornette Coleman (including a tenor-alto duet rendition of Coleman's "Comme Il Faut") and a pair of John Carter tributes to Jaki Byard's "Ode to Charlie Parker" (which includes transcriptions of part of trumpeter Booker Little's solo from its original recording) and the modern classical harmonies of "Pictures in a Glass House." Throughout the improvisations are a logical outgrowth of the written sections and vice versa. The musicians constantly react to each other, making this stimulating and passionate but quiet music well worth acquiring. *—Scott Yanow*

Roy Eldridge (David Roy Eldridge)

b. Jan. 30, 1911, Pittsburgh, PA, **d.** Feb. 26, 1989, Valley Stream, NY
Trumpet / Swing
One of the most exciting trumpeters to emerge during the swing era, Roy Eldridge's combative approach, chance-taking style and strong musicianship were an inspiration (and an influence) to the next musical generation, most notably Dizzy Gillespie. Although he sometimes pushed himself farther than he could go, Eldridge never played a dull solo!

Roy Eldridge started out playing trumpet and drums in carnival and circus bands. With the Nighthawk Syncopators he received a bit of attention by playing a note-for-note recreation of Coleman Hawkins' tenor solo on "The Stampede." Inspired by the dynamic playing of Jabbo Smith (Eldridge would not discover Louis Armstrong for a few years), Roy played with some territory bands including Zack Whyte and Speed Webb and in New York (where he arrive in 1931) he worked with Elmer Snowden (who nicknamed him "Little Jazz"), McKinney's Cotton Pickers and most importantly Teddy Hill (1935). Eldridge's recorded solos with Hill, backing Billie Holiday, and with Fletcher Henderson (including his

1936 hit "Christopher Columbus") gained a great deal of attention. In 1937 he appeared with his octet (which included brother Joe on alto) at the Three Deuces Club in Chicago and recorded some outstanding selections as a leader including "Heckler's Hop" and "Wabash Stomp." By 1939 Roy had a larger group playing at the Arcadia Ballroom in New York. With the decline of Bunny Berigan and the increasing predictability of Louis Armstrong, Eldridge was arguably the top trumpeter in jazz during this era.

During 1941-42 Eldridge sparked Gene Krupa's Orchestra, recording classic versions of "Rockin' Chair" and "After You've Gone" and interacting with Anita O'Day on "Let Me Off Uptown." The difficulties of travelling with a White band during a racist period hurt him, as did some of the incidents that occurred during his stay with Artie Shaw (1944-45), but the music during both stints was quite memorable. Eldridge had a short-lived big band of his own, toured with Jazz at the Philharmonic and then had a bit of an identity crisis when he realized that his playing was not as modern as the beboppers.

A successful stay in France during 1950-51 restored his confidence when he realized that being original was more important than being up-to-date. Eldridge recorded steadily for Norman Granz in the '50s, was one of the stars of JATP (where he battled Charlie Shavers and Dizzy Gillespie) and by 1956 was often teamed with Coleman Hawkins in a quintet; their 1957 appearance at Newport was quite memorable. The '60s were tougher as recording opportunities and work became rarer. Eldridge had brief and unhappy stints with Count Basie's Orchestra and Ella Fitzgerald (feeling unnecessary in both contexts) but was leading his own group by the end of the decade. He spent much of the '70s playing regularly at Ryan's and recording for Pablo and, although his range had shrunk a bit, Eldridge's competitive spirit was still very much intact. Only a serious stroke in 1980 was able to halt his horn. Roy Eldridge recorded throughout his career for virtually every label. —*Scott Yanow*

★ **Little Jazz** / Feb. 26, 1935-Apr. 2, 1940 / Columbia ✦✦✦✦✦
This CD contains the best recordings from the early years of the fiery trumpeter Roy Eldridge. Eldridge, one of the great swing trumpeters and a powerful player into the '70s, is heard with Teddy Hill's Orchestra, backing singer Putney Dandridge, on four titles with Fletcher Henderson (including the hit "Christopher Columbus"), starring on a four-song session with Teddy Wilson, joining Billie Holiday on "Falling in Love Again," soloing on two numbers with Mildred Bailey (his "I'm Nobody's Baby" solo is years ahead of its time) and, best of all, leading a small group through six songs (plus an alternate) from his own explosive sessions of Jan. 1937. This brilliant music is essential for all serious jazz collections. —*Scott Yanow*

After You've Gone / Feb. 5, 1936-Sep. 24, 1946 / GRP ✦✦✦✦
This excellent CD features the great swing trumpeter Roy Eldridge shortly after the breakup of the Gene Krupa Orchestra. Eldridge is heard leading his own recording groups (mostly big bands) and, although his own orchestra never really caught on, the trumpet solos are always quite exciting. This CD skips over five of Eldridge's Decca sides (it should have been a "complete" set) but does include three previously unissued performances plus a recently discovered jam on "Christopher Columbus" from 1936. —*Scott Yanow*

● **Uptown** / May 8, 1941-May 9, 1949 / Columbia ✦✦✦✦
1941-1942. An outstanding compilation of some prime Eldridge cuts with Anita O'Day (v) and Krupa (d). Nice for those who only want a limited amount of his material. —*Ron Wynn*

Roy Eldridge In Paris / Jun. 9, 1950 & Jun. 14, 1950 / Vogue ✦✦✦✦

Just You Just Me, Live in 1959 / 1959 / Stash ✦✦✦✦
In the late '50s trumpeter Roy Eldridge and tenor saxophonist Coleman Hawkins teamed up on a fairly regular basis. Since they always brought out the best in each other (their solos could be quite competitive and fiery), all of their joint recordings are recommended. Two LPs from their gig at Washington D.C.'s Bayou Club in 1959 were previously released on the Honeysuckle Rose label. Five of those selections plus four previously unissued cuts are included on this Stash CD. Most of the tunes are medium-tempo jams such as "Just You, Just Me," "Rifftide," and "How High the Moon," but there is also an excellent ballad medley. Backed by a local rhythm section, Eldridge and Hawk are both in superior form, making this a highly recommended disc even for those listeners who already have the earlier LPs. —*Scott Yanow*

Nifty Cat / Nov. 24, 1970 / New World ✦✦✦✦
One of only two Eldridge-led studio sessions from the 1961-74 period, this CD reissue of a set originally recorded for Master Jazz matches the great swing trumpeter with Budd Johnson (who doubles on tenor and soprano), trombonist Benny Morton, pianist Nat Pierce, bassist Tommy Bryant, and drummer Oliver Jackson. All six of the jump tunes are by Eldridge with "5400 North" and "Ball of Fire" being best-known. For this album the veteran trumpeter had a very rare opportunity to call his own shots on a recording date and the generally inspired playing makes this CD a fine example of small-group swing from the early '70s. —*Scott Yanow*

★ **Mexican Bandit Meets Pittsburg Pirate** / Aug. 24, 1973 / Fantasy ✦✦✦✦✦
Interesting title for this wonderful collaboration between Eldridge and Paul Gonsalves (ts); a delightful date. —*Ron Wynn*

Happy Time / Jun. 4, 1975 / Original Jazz Classics ✦✦✦

★ **Montreux 1977** / Jul. 13, 1977 / Original Jazz Classics ✦✦✦✦✦
Eldridge's final recording as a leader is a real gem. Although his chops were no longer in prime form, he was still pushing himself to the limit. With a brilliant rhythm section egging him on (pianist Oscar Peterson, bassist Niels Pedersen and drummer Bobby Durham), Eldridge still went for the high notes (and generally hit them) during this exciting set from the 1977 Montreux Jazz Festival. Although the musicians did not know it at the time, the last two songs ("Perdido" and "Bye Bye Blackbird") were a perfect ending to a brilliant career. This dramatic CD reissue is highly recommended. —*Scott Yanow*

Duke Ellington (Edward Kennedy Ellington)

b. Apr. 29, 1899, Washington, DC, **d.** May 24, 1974, New York, NY
Piano / Big Band, Swing
Duke Ellington's contributions to jazz and American music were simply enormous. As a bandleader, his orchestra during 1926-74 was always among the top five, whether it be 1929 or 1969. As a composer, Ellington ranked with George Gershwin, Cole Porter, Irving Berlin and their contemporaries. He wrote literally thousands of songs (the exact number is not known) of which hundereds became standards. As an arranger Ellington was particularly innovative, writing for his very individual players rather than for an anonymous horn section and, not being content to play his songs the same way every time, he constantly rearranged them; "Mood Indigo" sounded different in 1933 than it did in 1953 or 1973. As a pianist Duke Ellington was originally an excellent stride player who gained the respect of such giants as James P. Johnson, Fats Waller and his main influence Willie "The Lion" Smith. Unlike virtually all of his contemporaries (other than Mary Lou Williams), Duke was able to modernize his style through the years, keeping the percussive approach of the stride players but leaving more space and using more complex chords; his playing was an influence on Thelonious Monk and (in a more abstract fashion) Cecil Taylor.

Duke Ellington always considered his orchestra to be his main instrument and with it he recorded constantly from 1926 on. In the early days he recorded for many labels, sometimes under pseudonyms, and by the '50s he often seemed to live in the studios when not performing before audiences, trying out new material and fresh versions of older songs. The result is that there are currently a countless number of Ellington albums available (way over 200) with "new" (previously unissued) ones coming out nearly every month as if he were still alive. What is more remarkable than the quantity is the consistently high quality; there are few if any throwaways in Ellington's entire discography!

There is simply no explanation for Edward Kennedy Ellington's musical genius. Although he started studying piano when he was seven, for a time it seemed that Duke (who picked up his lifelong nickname early) was going to be an artist. However he so enjoyed hearing the ragtime and barrelhouse piano players of the era that he soon chose music. Ellington started playing music in Washington, D.C. in 1917 and, after wisely taking out the biggest ad in the telephone yellow pages, was soon leading several bands despite the fact that his repertoire was very limited. Ellington, whose first composition "Soda Fountain Rag" was written during this era, worked on building up his technique by slowing down James P. Johnson piano rolls and analyzing the fingering. A brief visit to New York in 1922 (playing with Wilbur Sweatman) was unsuccessful but Ellington returned the following year and was determined to stick it out. He and such hometown friends as Sonny Greer, Otto Hardwicke and Arthur Whetsol worked for a period under banjoist Elmer Snowden's leadership and then, after an argument over missing money, Ellington became the leader. His early group was called the Washingtonians.

Duke Ellington soon gained a job at the Hollywood Club (later renamed the Kentucky Club) for his band. For a brief time Sidney Bechet starred on soprano but more important to Duke's development was the playing of trumpeter Bubber Miley, a brilliant plunger specialist who largely founded the "jungle sound" that made Ellington's group sound different than anyone else. Duke recorded two titles with his group in November 1924 ("Choo Choo" and "Rainy Nights") that found his band already sounding recognizable despite only having three horns (with altoist Otto Hardwicke and trombonist Charles Irvis). Oddly enough the eight other selections that he recorded during 1925-26 are primitive and disappointing; Miley is absent and the band sounds as if it were struggling. However with the debut of Ellington's early theme song "East St. Louis Toodleoo" along with "Birmingham Breakdown" on the session of November 29, 1926, the Duke Ellington Orchestra was essentially born. The band was up to 11 pieces including the wonderful wa-wa trombonist Tricky Sam Nanton, who made for a perfect team with Miley. 1927 was the breakthrough year for Duke Ellington. In addition to recording more versions of "East St.Louis Toodle-oo," he debuted "Black and Tan Fantasy" and "Creole Love Call"; the latter used Adelaide Hall's voice as an instrument. Baritonist Harry Carney (who would remain with Duke nonstop through 1974!) became a key member of the ensemble. And Ellington's band (through the help of manager Irving Mills) gained a permanent spot at the Cotton Club. Not only would its radio broadcasts soon make Ellington famous throughout the country but he had the opportunity to write for the floor shows and the experience led to him growing rapidly as a composer/arranger.

Duke Ellington's life would never be a good topic for a Hollywood movie because from 1927 on it was one success after another. In 1928 clarinetist Barney Bigard and altoist Johnny Hodges became long-time members and Arthur Whetsol (whose lyrical trumpet offered a contrast to the speech-like playing of Miley) gained a more prominent role. In early 1929 Bubber Miley, whose alcoholism led to him becoming increasingly unreliable, was reluctantly let go but his replacement Cootie Williams would eventually be a more flexible soloist. Ellington appeared in his first film (*Black and Tan*) that year, and unlike most other Black celebrities of the '20s and '30s, his performance did not find him acting as a clown or inferior to White people. Ellington always appeared as a classy and charming genius (just as he did in real life) and, despite the "inconvenience" of being Black in a racist society, Duke Ellington was able to survive (and eventually prosper) due to his brilliance without compromising himself.

While most big bands might have three or four notable soloists, Ellington's Orchestra in the '30s featured eight: trumpeters Cootie Williams and Rex Stewart (the latter joined on cornet in 1935), trombonists Tricky Sam Nanton and Lawrence Brown, clarinetist Barney Bigard, altoist Hodges, baritonist Carney and the leader on piano; in addition Ivie Anderson was their fine singer. After leaving the Cotton Club in 1931 (although he would return on an occasional basis throughout the rest of the decade), the Ellington Orchestra became a road band, touring Europe and Sweden in 1933 and 1939 and becoming a major attraction in every key city in the US Ellington, who had recorded a two-sided six-minute version of "Tiger Rag" in 1929 began to compose longer works including "Creole Rhapsody" (1931), and "Reminiscing in Tempo" (1935), and his three-minute masterpiece "Daybreak Express" found the orchestra doing an uncanny imitation of a train's journey. Although there was a lot more competition from big bands with the rise of the swing era in 1935, Ellington remained a major name. Such compositions as "Mood Indigo," "Rockin' in Rhythm," "It Don't Mean a Thing If It Ain't Got That Swing," "Sophisticated Lady," "Drop Me Off at Harlem," "In a Sentimental Mood," "Caravan" (written by valve trombonist Juan Tizol), "I Let a Song Go Out of My Heart," "Prelude to a Kiss," "Solitude," and "Boy Meets Horn" became standards.

By 1940 Duke Ellington's Orchestra had become, if anything, even stronger. Ben Webster joined as their first major voice on tenor, the innovative bassist Jimmy Blanton became the first important soloist on his instrument in jazz history and Billy Strayhorn, as arranger and composer, became Ellington's musical partner up until his death in 1967. When Cootie Williams departed in late 1940, Ray Nance (a fine trumpeter, violinist and vocalist) easily fit into the spot. Many critics consider Duke's 1940-42 big band to be his greatest. Certainly there was an explosion of activity with such new pieces as "Concerto for Cootie," "Cotton Tail," "Harlem Air Shaft," "All Too Soon," "Warm Valley," "Take the 'A' Train," "Just A-Settin' and A-Rockin'," "I Got It Bad," "Jump for Joy," "Chelsea Bridge," "Perdido," "The 'C' Jam Blues," "Johnny Come Lately" forming only a partial list of the orchestra's accomplishments.

In 1943 Duke Ellington gave his first Carnegie Hall concert (it would be an annual series lasting until 1950) and debuted his 50-minute work "Black, Brown and Beige" which, although it received mixed reviews, can now be heard and evaluated as a major success. The turnover in his orchestra increased during the latter half of the '40s but the quality remained consistently high and, despite the collapse of the big-band era and the rise of bebop (a music that Ellington accepted and borrowed from), Duke's orchestra never did break up; his royalty payments from his hits helped keep the big band together. Such new players as trumpeters Taft Jordan, Shorty Baker and the remarkable high-note player Cat Anderson (who had several long stints with Duke), Tyree Glenn (on trombone and vibes), Al Sears on tenor and bassist Oscar Pettiford passed through the band and clarinetist Jimmy Hamilton stayed into the late '60s. "Don't Get Around Much Anymore" was a hit and Ellington also wrote such lengthy works as "The Perfume Suite," "The Deep South Suite" and "The Liberia Suite"; the last theme of "Happy Go Lucky Local" was "borrowed" by Jimmy Forrest and retitled "Night Train."

By the early '50s, Duke Ellington was in the only slump of his career but it was more a commercial slip than artistic. Johnny Hodges, Lawrence Brown and Sonny Greer suddenly left to form a small group under Hodges' leadership. In what was called "The Great James Robbery," Duke persuaded three members of Harry James' Orchestra to join him: drummer Louie Bellson, altoist Willie Smith and Juan Tizol (who had left Ellington in the '40s). But by 1953-54 the orchestra was struggling a bit during an era when few big bands survived. However in 1955

Hodges returned to the fold and at the 1956 Newport Jazz Festival tenor saxophonist Paul Gonsalves took an exciting marathon solo on "Diminuendo and Crescendo in Blue" that caused a sensation. Ellington was big again and the momentum would continue through the remainder of his life.

With such fine soloists as trumpeters Clark Terry, Ray Nance, Cat Anderson and Willie Cook, trombonists Buster Cooper and Britt Woodman and a reed section that was together for over a decade (Hodges, Carney, Hamilton, Gonsalves and Russell Procope on clarinet and alto), Ellington's late-'50s orchestra could hold its own with any of his groups. Although "Satin Doll" in the early '50s was his last pop hit, Duke continued working major works with Strayhorn. In the '60s he turned towards religion, writing music for three sacred concerts and also composing "The Far East Suite," a very impressive and modern work. Duke also recorded albums on which he played piano in a trio with Charles Mingus and Max Roach, sat in with both the Louis Armstrong All-Stars and the John Coltrane Quartet and he had a double big-band date with Count Basie and a combo session with Coleman Hawkins. Constantly traveling the world and receiving long overdue honors (although not a Pulitzer Prize), Duke Ellington was finally recognized as a remarkable national treasure.

By the latter half of the '60s, Ellington's associates were starting to die off. Billy Strayhorn's loss in 1967 was major as was Johnny Hodges' passing in 1970. There were important new members in Harold Ashby on tenor, altoist Norris Turney and (in 1973) trumpeter Barry Lee Hall. But in 1974 Duke Ellington was stricken with cancer and spent his 75th birthday in a hospital. His death four weeks later has left a huge hole that will never be filled. — *Scott Yanow*

☆ **Early Ellington (1926-1931)** / Nov. 29, 1926-Jan. 20, 1931 / Decca ✦✦✦✦✦

This three-CD set, which has all of Duke Ellington's recordings for the Brunswick and Vocalion labels, dwarfs all of the earlier reissues that Decca and MCA have put out of this important material. Starting with the first session in which the Ellington Orchestra sounds distinctive ("East St. Louis Toodle-oo" and "Birmingham Breakdown" from Nov. 29, 1926) and progressing through the Cotton Club years, this essential release (which contains 67 performances) adds a few "new" alternate takes and rare items ("Soliloquy" and a few titles by the "Six Jolly Jesters") to make this collection truly complete, at least for MCA's holdings (since Ellington also recorded for Columbia and Victor-owned labels during the same period). With such major soloists as trumpeters Bubber Miley (and his replacement Cootie Williams), Freddy Jenkins, and Arthur Whetsol, trombonist Tricky Sam Nanton, clarinetist Barney Bigard, altoist Johnny Hodges, baritonist Harry Carney, and the pianist/leader, along with the classic arrangements/compositions, this set is essential for all serious jazz collections. — *Scott Yanow*

The Brunswick Recordings, Vol. 1 (1926-1929) / Dec. 29, 1926-Jan. 8, 1929 / MCA ✦✦✦

Okeh Ellington / Mar. 22, 1927-Nov. 8, 1930 / Columbia ✦✦✦✦
Although generally not as celebrated as his Victor recordings of the same period, Duke Ellington's performances for OKeh (late acquired by Columbia) are among the best of the period, featuring distinctive solos by the likes of trumpeter Bubber Miley (and later his replacement Cootie Williams), trombonist Tricky Sam Nanton (who, like Miley, was an expert with wa-wa mutes), clarinetist Barney Bigard and altoist Johnny Hodges, among others. These 50 performances (which bypass Ellington's alternate takes) contain many classics including his original theme "East St. Louis Toodle-oo," "Black and Tan Fantasy," "The Mooche," "Mood Indigo," and his two earliest solo piano sides. This is one of the best sets of early Ellington currently available. — *Scott Yanow*

Early Ellington (1927-1934) / Oct. 26, 1927-Jan. 10, 1934 / Bluebird ✦✦✦

Jungle Nights in Harlem / Dec. 19, 1927-Jan. 9, 1932 / Bluebird ✦✦✦

Jubilee Stomp / Mar. 26, 1928-May 9, 1934 / Bluebird ✦✦✦

Brunswick Era, Vol. 2 / Jan. 8, 1929-Jan. 20, 1931 / Decca ✦✦✦

Solos, Duets and Trios / Feb. 9, 1932-Aug. 30, 1967 / Bluebird ✦✦✦✦
This CD puts the focus on Duke Ellington the piano player, featuring the genius in several different settings. He is heard playing two duets with Billy Strayhorn, taking rare piano solos in 1932, 1941, and 1967, meeting up with Earl Hines in 1965, and leading a trio in 1945. However, the real reason to acquire this set are the four duets (plus five alternate takes) with Jimmy Blanton, the first important bass soloist in jazz history. From 1940, those recordings find Blanton sounding like the Charles Mingus of 20 years later and Ellington unselfishly but masterfully playing the role of an accompanist. — *Scott Yanow*

★ **The Duke's Men: Small Groups, Vol. 1** / Dec. 12, 1934-Jan. 19, 1938 / Columbia ✦✦✦✦✦
In the '30s Ellington started recording prolifically with small groups taken from his big band. It gave him an opportunity both to debut new works and to let his sidemen stretch out and act as leaders once in awhile (under his direction). This two-disc set contains 45 recordings, almost all of them

brilliant, including sessions ostensibly under the leadership of cornetist Rex Stewart (including two selections cut before he joined Ellington), clarinetist Barney Bigard, trumpeter Cootie Williams, and altoist Johnny Hodges. In addition to early versions of such future standards as "Caravan," "Stompy Jones," and "Echoes of Harlem," there are many hot stomps performed that feature strong solos from these very distinctive stylists. Brilliant music, highly recommended. — *Scott Yanow*

Duke's Men, Vol. 2 / Mar. 28, 1938-Mar. 20, 1939 / Columbia/Legacy ✦✦✦✦
This second two-disc set, like the first, includes all of the master takes (no alternates) from the small-group sessions led by Duke Ellington's sidemen. During the year covered on this volume, Johnny Hodges, Cootie Williams, and Rex Stewart all had opportunities to head sessions and the results included early versions of "Jeep's Blues," "Pyramid," "Prelude to a Kiss," "The Jeep's Jumping," and "Hodge Podge" along with many hot obscurities. There are few duds and many memorable performances during these 43 recordings. — *Scott Yanow*

Small Groups, Vol. 2 / 1938 / Columbia/Legacy ✦✦✦

The Webster: Blanton Years / 1939-1942 / RCA/Bluebird ✦✦✦✦
Fine three-disc anthology of late '30s/early '40s Ellington material covering contributions by pioneer bassist Jimmy Blanton. It includes full orchestra selections, plus bass/piano duets and small combo sessions. While much of this material is also available on more costly packages, this is a good domestic package. — *Ron Wynn*

In a Mellotone / May 28, 1940-Jun. 26, 1942 / RCA ✦✦✦

The Great Ellington Units / Nov. 2, 1940-Sep. 29, 1941 / RCA ✦✦✦

★ **Fargo ND, November 7, 1940** / Nov. 7, 1940 / Vintage Jazz Classics ✦✦✦✦✦

Take the "A" Train: The Legendary Blanton-Webster / Jan. 15, 1941-Dec. 3, 1941 / Vintage Jazz Classics ✦✦✦✦
During 1941, one of Ellington's peak years, not only did he record frequently in the studios but also made this CD's worth of transcriptions for radio. Of the 26 selections on this generous set, eight of the songs were never recorded commercially, and six others are heard here in their earliest versions, including his theme "Take the 'A' Train" and "Perdido." The all-star orchestra is propelled by the great bassist Jimmy Blanton. Highly recommended. — *Scott Yanow*

★ **The Carnegie Hall Concerts (January 1943)** / Jan. 23, 1943-Jan. 28, 1943 / Prestige ✦✦✦✦✦
This two-CD set captures one of the milestones in Duke Ellington's long and extremely productive career, highlighted by his monumental suite "Black, Brown and Beige" in the only full-length version ever recorded by his orchestra; soon it was only performed as excerpts. In addition, Ellington's all-star orchestra (including such stylists as trumpeters Rex Stewart, Ray Nance, and Shorty Baker, trombonists Tricky Sam Nanton and Lawrence Brown, and a saxophone section boasting Johnny Hodges, Ben Webster, and Harry Carney) excels on the shorter pieces, a mixture of older and recent compositions. Every serious jazz library should contain this set. — *Scott Yanow*

The Carnegie Hall Concerts (December 1944) / Dec. 19, 1944 / Prestige ✦✦✦✦
The Ellington orchestra was undergoing some personnel (and personality) changes during this era, none of it unexciting. This Carnegie Hall concert (available on two CDs) introduced Ellington's "Perfume Suite," and includes a half-hour series of selections from "Black, Brown and Beige," but also in the shorter pieces shows the impact of tenorman Al Sears and high-note wizard Cat Anderson on the band's sound, making it a more potentially boisterous and extroverted ensemble. Lots of great moments from this brilliant orchestra occurred during this concert. — *Scott Yanow*

The Carnegie Hall Concerts (January 1946) / Jan. 4, 1946 / Prestige ✦✦✦

The Great Chicago Concerts / Jan. 20, 1946 & Nov. 10, 1946 / Music Masters ✦✦✦✦

The Carnegie Hall Concerts (December 1947) / Dec. 27, 1947 / Prestige ✦✦✦✦
One of Duke Ellington's most enjoyable Carnegie Hall concerts, this two-CD set contains among its high points a superior live version of "Liberian Suite," a Johnny Hodges medley, the beautiful "On a Turquoise Cloud," a roaring version of "Cotton Tail" (featuring Al Sears' tenor), the nearly atonal "Clothed Woman," and a trumpet battle on "Blue Skies." Well worth acquiring. — *Scott Yanow*

Carnegie Hall Concerts (November 1948) / Nov. 13, 1948 / Vintage Jazz Classics ✦✦✦✦
The sixth and final of Duke Ellington's acclaimed Carnegie Hall concerts, this two-CD set allows one to hear the largely undocumented 1948 orchestra, which was kept off record because of a musicians' union strike. With Ben Webster temporarily back in the band and such solo stylists as altoist Johnny Hodges, Al Sears on tenor, clarinetist Jimmy Hamilton, and trumpeters Ray Nance and Shorty Baker, the Ellington orchestra performs both

newer material (such as "The Tattooed Bride" and several obscurities) and some surprising older compositions including a revival of "Reminiscence in Tempo" and a "hits medley." An oddity is one of the very few Ellington performances of Billy Strayhorn's classic "Lush Life." — *Scott Yanow*

☆ **Uptown** / Dec. 7, 1951-Dec. 8, 1952 / Columbia ✦✦✦✦✦
Although some historians have characterized the early '50s as Duke Ellington's "off period" (due to the defection of alto-star Johnny Hodges), in reality his 1951-52 orchestra could hold its own against his best. This set has many classic moments, including Betty Roche's famous bebop vocal on "Take the 'A' Train," a version of "The Mooche" that contrasts the different clarinet styles of Russell Procope and Jimmy Hamilton, a hot "Perdido" that is highlighted by some great Clark Terry trumpet, Louie Bellson's drum solo on "Skin Deep," a definitive version of "The Harlem Suite," and the two-part "Controversial Suite" which contrasts New Orleans jazz with futuristic music worthy of Stan Kenton. One of the great Duke Ellington sets. — *Scott Yanow*

☆ **The Complete Capitol Recordings Of Duke Ellington** / Apr. 6, 1953-May 19, 1955 / Mosaic ✦✦✦✦✦
This five-CD box set from Mosaic documents Duke Ellington's least-known period, his two years on Capitol. Although thought of by some as his off-years due to the absence of Johnny Hodges, the set serves as evidence that a great deal of viable music was created. During this period the orchestra had 11 distinctive soloists including four very different trumpeters (Clark Terry, Cat Anderson, Willie Cook, and Ray Nance). In addition to a well known trio set that showcases Ellington's underrated piano playing, there are quite a few unissued selections highlighted by four numbers from 1955 that find Ellington playing electric piano. Even vocalist Jimmy Grissom (best on "Balling the Blues") sounds better than usual and one should not miss Ray Nance's humorous singing and playing on "Basin Street Blues." Toss in the original version of "Satin Doll," the unusual *Ellington '55* album (which found the band playing their versions of swing hits associated with other orchestras) and an oddity such as "Twelfth Street Rag Mambo," and one has a highly enjoyable reissue that Duke Ellington fans should pick up immediately. — *Scott Yanow*

Piano Reflections / Apr. 13, 1953-Dec. 3, 1953 / Capitol ✦✦✦✦
At the time of its release this was a true rarity, a full album of Duke Ellington featured with a trio sans his orchestra. Although his talents at the piano sometimes have been overshadowed by his many accomplishments as a composer, arranger, and bandleader, Ellington was actually one of the very few stride pianists (along with Mary Lou Williams) to effectively make the transition into more modern styles of jazz without losing his own musical personality; in fact Duke was an early influence on both Thelonious Monk and Cecil Taylor. Throughout this CD (which contains one previously unissued track), Ellington sounds modern (especially rhythmically and in his chord voicings) and shows that he could have had a viable career out of just being a pianist. — *Scott Yanow*

Ellington at Newport / Jul. 7, 1956 / Columbia ✦✦✦✦
After several years of struggle, Duke Ellington made a spectacular commercial comeback, launched by this memorable appearance at the Newport Jazz Festival. Following an inventive but somewhat overlooked "Newport Jazz Festival Suite" and a routine version of Johnny Hodges' feature "Jeep's Blues," the orchestra launched into "Diminuendo and Crescendo in Blue" with great intensity. The passion really grew during a marathon 27-chorus blues solo by tenor saxophonist Paul Gonsalves that inspired some wild dancing and a near-riot in the audience; the crowd's reaction can easily be heard on this recording. Following Gonsalves, the full ensemble built to a tremendous climax with trumpeter Cat Anderson screaming on top. This performance made headlines all around the world and Ellington's "off period" was finally over. It can all be heard on this classic recording. — *Scott Yanow*

Black, Brown and Beige / Mar. 4, 1958-Mar. 5, 1958 / Columbia ✦✦

Live at The Blue Note / Aug. 9, 1959 / Roulette ✦✦✦✦
This two-CD set is a good example of how Duke Ellington's Orchestra sounded in 1959. Greatly expanded from the original single LP, the release essentially brings back a full night by the Ellington band, three nearly complete sets. The music ranges from old favorites to some newer material and highlights include Billy Strayhorn sitting in on his "Take the 'A' Train," several selections from the recent *Anatomy of a Murder* soundtrack, versions of "Drawing Room Blues" and "Tonk" that have both Ellington and Shearing on piano, an 11-minute rendition of "Mood Indigo," and quite a few features for altoist Johnny Hodges. — *Scott Yanow*

The Duke Ellington: Louis Armstrong Years / Apr. 3, 1961-Apr. 4, 1961 / Roulette ✦✦✦✦
Although Duke Ellington and Louis Armstrong were jazz music's most famous and acclaimed musicians, their only meeting on record (other than a couple of isolated selections in the '40s) is the music contained on this two-CD set. Rather than have Armstrong sit in with the orchestra, Ellington temporarily became a member of Satch's All-Stars. For this all-Ellington program, Armstrong is inspired by the fresh repertoire and his vocals are often jubilant. With strong assistance from trombonist Trummy Young

and clarinetist Barney Bigard (a former Ellington bandmember then travelling with Armstrong), Pops and Ellington created a very memorable and quite unique program of classic music. — *Scott Yanow*

☆ **First Time! Count Meets Duke** / Jul. 6, 1961 / Columbia ✦✦✦✦✦
At first glance this collaboration should not have worked. The Duke Ellington and Count Basie Orchestras had already been competitors for 25 years but the leaders' mutual admiration (Ellington was one of Basie's main idols) and some brilliant planning made this a very successful and surprisingly uncrowded encounter. On most selections Ellington and Basie both play piano (their interaction with each other is wonderful) and the arrangements allowed the stars from both bands to take turns soloing. "Segue in C" is the high point, but versions of "Until I Met You," "Battle Royal," and "Jumpin' at the Woodside" are not far behind. — *Scott Yanow*

Duke Ellington Meets Coleman Hawkins / Aug. 18, 1962 / Impulse ✦✦✦✦
Reissued on CD by GRP in 1995, this classic set is made even more attractive than usual by the inclusion of fresh pictures from the session along with the original colorful liner notes. In 1962 Coleman Hawkins, after nearly four decades at the top, finally had an opportunity to record with Duke Ellington. The great tenor does not actually play with Duke's full orchestra but jams with an all star octet that includes Ellington on piano, Ray Nance (doubling on cornet and violin), trombonist Lawrence Brown, altoist Johnny Hodges, baritonist Harry Carney, bassist Aaron Bell, and drummer Sam Woodyard. Hawkins fits right in and the highlights include "Mood Indigo," "Self Portrait Of The Bean," "Solitude" (a bonus track from the date that was not on the original LP), and a memorable version of "The Jeep Is Jumpin." — *Scott Yanow*

Money Jungle / Sep. 17, 1962 / Blue Note ✦✦✦✦
In 1962 Duke Ellington was teamed on record with a trio consisting of bassist Charles Mingus and drummer Max Roach. The setting may have seemed "modern" for a pianist from his generation, but one should realize that he was a major influence on both Thelonious Monk and Cecil Taylor. Ellington, one of the few veterans of the '20s to make a smooth transition to the relatively modern era, is in superlative form on this date, even when challenged on "Money Jungle" by the potentially combative Mingus. This LP version includes four selections not on the original release; the later CD also added a couple of "new" alternate takes. Well worth acquiring. — *Scott Yanow*

☆ **Duke Ellington and John Coltrane** / Sep. 26, 1962 / MCA ✦✦✦✦✦
For this classic encounter, Duke Ellington "sat in" with the John Coltrane Quartet for a set dominated by Ellington's songs; some performances have his usual sidemen (bassist Aaron Bell and drummer Sam Woodyard) replacing Jimmy Garrison and Elvin Jones in the group. Although it would have been preferable to hear Coltrane play in the Duke Ellington Orchestra instead of the other way around, the results are quite rewarding. Their version of "In a Sentimental Mood" is a high point, and such numbers as "Take the Coltrane," "Big Nick," and "My Little Brown Book" are quite memorable. Ellington always recognized talent and Coltrane seemed quite happy to be recording with a fellow genius. — *Scott Yanow*

The Great Paris Concert / Feb. 1, 1963-Feb. 23, 1963 / Atlantic ✦✦✦✦
A definitive look at the early-'60s edition of the Duke Ellington Orchestra, this live two-LP set contains many highlights: fresh versions of "Rockin' in Rhythm," "Concerto for Cootie" (featuring Cootie Williams), and "Jam with Sam," extended renditions of "Suite Thursday" and the "Harlem Suite," and a few newer selections. Eleven soloists (without counting the pianist/leader) are heard from in memorable settings, including both Cootie Williams and Ray Nance. Highly recommended music, either as a two-fer or on CD. — *Scott Yanow*

The Far East Suite (Special Mix) / Dec. 19, 1966-Dec. 21, 1966 / Bluebird ✦✦✦✦
This CD differs from the previous release of "The Far East Suite" by the inclusion of four "new" alternate takes. This particular nine-part suite was arguably Duke Ellington's finest major work of the '60s. The haunting ballad "Isfahan" (a showcase for altoist Johnny Hodges) is the best-known section but several other pieces (particularly "Bluebird of Delhi," "Mount Harissa," and "Ad Lib on Nippon") are also quite memorable. Clarinetist Jimmy Hamilton and tenor saxophonist Paul Gonsalves co-star with Hodges but it is the creative writing of Ellington and Billy Strayhorn that makes this CD quite essential. — *Scott Yanow*

★ **His Mother Called Him Bill** / Aug. 28, 1967-Sep. 1, 1967 / RCA ✦✦✦✦✦
Shortly after Billy Strayhorn's early death in 1967, the Duke Ellington Orchestra recorded a dozen of his compositions during a series of emotional and passionate sessions. The results are consistently inspired with such selections as "Blood Count" (Strayhorn's final composition), "Rain Check," "Lotus Blossom," and "The Intimacy of the Blues" receiving definitive versions. In addition, this CD reissue also contains an alternate take of "Lotus Blossom" and remakes of three more Strayhorn classics that were previously unissued. This was one of Duke Ellington's finest sessions and, considering his huge recorded legacy, that is saying a lot. — *Scott Yanow*

★ **Seventieth Birthday Concert** / Nov. 25, 1969-Nov. 26, 1969 / Blue Note ✦✦✦✦✦

Mercer Ellington

b. Mar. 11, 1919, Washington, DC, **d.** 1996
Trumpet / Swing
Mercer Ellington had the impossible task of trying to escape from his father Duke Ellington's shadow and he never really succeeded, perhaps not trying hard enough. He studied music early on and made several attempts to lead his own band (1939, 1946-49, and 1959) that were all ultimately unsuccessful. During the ASCAP strike of the early '40s when Duke was desperate for new material, Mercer wrote several notable songs including "Things Ain't What They Used to Be," "Jumpin' Punkins," "Moon Mist," and "Blue Serge" but nothing he composed since then approached their stature. Among his many other jobs were working as road manager for Cootie Williams' Orchestra, musical director for Della Reese, and as a salesman, a record-company executive, and a disc jockey. Finally in 1965 he gave up trying to be independent and became Duke Ellington's road manager and a nonsoloing section trumpeter. After Duke's death in 1974, Mercer took over the band but within a couple years it had greatly declined. Mercer wrote a biography in 1978 *Duke Ellington in Person*, directed the so-so musical *Sophisticated Ladies* (1981-83), supervised the release of many previously unavailable Ellington recordings, and led the inaccurately titled "Duke Ellington Orchestra" on an occasional basis, recording a few dates that often had all-stars as ringers. — *Scott Yanow*

Continuum / Jul. 14, 1974-May 12, 1975 / Fantasy ✦✦✦✦

● **Digital Duke** / 1987 / GRP ✦✦✦✦
The Duke Ellington Orchestra pretty much fell apart after its leader's death in 1974, but his son, Mercer, on an occasional basis has put together pickup bands to perform Duke's music. This particular CD uses quite an all-star group, mixing together such Ellington alumni as fluegelhornist Clark Terry, trumpeter Barry Lee Hall, altoist Norris Turney, trombonist Britt Woodman, and on four cuts, drummer Louie Bellson with such other major players as trumpeter Lew Soloff, clarinetist Eddie Daniels, tenorman Branford Marsalis (on two songs), trombonist Al Grey, and pianist Roland Hanna. The big band does a fine job of performing a dozen songs associated with Duke, making this one of the best of Mercer Ellington's efforts. — *Scott Yanow*

Take the Holiday Train / Nov. 18, 1992 / Special Music ✦✦

Don Ellis

b. Jul. 25, 1934, Los Angeles, CA, **d.** Dec. 17, 1978, Hollywood, CA
Trumpet / Avant-Garde, Post-Bop
A talented trumpeter with a vivid musical imagination and the willingness to try new things, Don Ellis led some of the most colorful big bands of the 1965-75 period. After graduating from Boston Unversity, Ellis played in the big bands of Ray McKinley, Charlie Barnet, and Maynard Ferguson (he was featured with the latter on "Three More Foxes"), recorded with Charles Mingus and played with George Russell's sextet (at the same time as Eric Dolphy). Ellis led four quartet and trio sessions during 1960-62 for Candid, New Jazz, and Pacific Jazz, mixing together bop, free jazz, and his interest in modern classical music. However it was in 1965 when he put together his first orchestra that he really started to make an impression in jazz. Ellis' big bands were distinguished by their unusual instrumentation (which in its early days had up to three bassists and three drummers including Ellis himself), the leader's desire to investigate unusual time changes (including 7/8, 9/8 and even 15/16), their occasionally wacky humor (highlighted by an excess of false endings), and an openness towards using rock rhythms and (in later years) electronics. Ellis invented the four-valve trumpet and utilized a ring modulator and all types of wild electronic devices by the late '60s. By 1971 his band consisted of an eight-piece brass section (including French horn and tuba), a four-piece woodwind section, a string quartet, and a two-drum rhythm section. A later unrecorded edition even added a vocal quartet.

Among Don Ellis' sidemen were Glenn Ferris, Tom Scott, John Klemmer, Sam Falzone, Frank Strozier, Dave MacKay, and the brilliant pianist (straight from Bulgaria) Milcho Leviev. The orchestra's most memorable recordings (none are out on CD yet) were *Autumn, Live at the Fillmore*, and *Tears of Joy* (all for Columbia). After suffering a mid-'70s heart attack, Ellis returned to live performing, playing the "superbone" and a later edition of his big band featured Art Pepper. Ellis' last recording was at the 1977 Montreux Jazz Festival, a year before his heart finally gave out. — *Scott Yanow*

Out of Nowhere / Apr. 21, 1961 / Candid ✦✦✦

New Ideas / May 11, 1961 / Original Jazz Classics ✦✦✦✦
The original thinking-jazz-lover's music. Quintet with unsung vibist Al Francis, and the Jaki Byard Trio. All originals by Ellis, who has a lot to say with combos like this. Variations, nay mutations of familiar themes crop

up, along with staggered and fractured time signatures. Very innovative musician. —*Michael G. Nastos*

● **Don Ellis at Fillmore** / 1970 / Columbia ✦✦✦✦
The release that helped break him into a mass audience. It is live, daring, loud, annoying, and distinctive all at once. —*Ron Wynn*

Live at Montreux / Jul. 24, 1977 / Atlantic ✦✦✦

Herb Ellis (Mitchel Herbert Ellis)

b. Aug. 4, 1921, Farmersville, TX
Guitar / Bop, Swing
An excellent bop-based guitarist with a slight country twang to his sound, Herb Ellis became famous playing with the Oscar Peterson Trio during 1953-58. Prior to that he had attended North Texas State Unversity and played with the Casa Loma Orchestra, Jimmy Dorsey (1945-47), and the sadly under-recorded trio Soft Winds. While with Peterson, Ellis was on some Jazz at the Philharmonic tours and had a few opportunities to lead his own dates for Verve including his personal favorite, *Nothing but the Blues* (1957). After leaving Peterson, Ellis toured a bit with Ella Fitzgerald, became a studio musician on the West Coast, made sessions with the Dukes of Dixieland, Stuff Smith, and Charlie Byrd, and in the '70s became much more active in the jazz world. He is on the first three Concord releases (interacting with Joe Pass on the initial two) and toured with the Great Guitars (along with Byrd and Barney Kessel) through much of the '70s and into the '80s. After a long series of Concord albums, Herb Ellis cut a couple of excellent sessions in the '90s for Justice. —*Scott Yanow*

☆ **Nothing But the Blues** / Oct. 11, 1957-May 1, 1958 / Verve ✦✦✦✦✦
Guitarist Herb Ellis considers this is his favorite personal album, and it is easy to see why. With trumpeter Roy Eldridge and tenor saxophonist Stan Getz contributing contrasting but equally rewarding solos and lots of inspired riffing while bassist Ray Brown and drummer Stan Levey join Ellis in the pianoless rhythm section, these performances have plenty of color and drive. Ellis does indeed stick to the blues during the original eight selections, yet there is also a surprising amount of variety. This CD reissue has been augmented by four numbers from 1958 originally recorded for a European soundtrack. Getz, Eldridge, and Coleman Hawkins all have their features but Dizzy Gillespie fares best. —*Scott Yanow*

Jazz at Concord / Jul. 29, 1973 / Concord Jazz ✦✦✦

Seven Come Eleven / Jul. 29, 1973 / Concord Jazz ✦✦✦✦
With Joe Pass. Concord's second record. Titans clash. Great music. Good on CD. First-rate band doing prototype arrangements. —*Ron Wynn*

★ **Roll Call** / 1991 / Justice ✦✦✦✦✦
well done recent release with Ellis backed by a solid lineup of session and studio pros, among them trumpeter Jay Thomas and violinist Johnny Frigo. They play a mix of blues, traditional jazz stomps, and standards, with organist Mel Rhyne adding soulful support alongside drummer Jake Hanna. —*Ron Wynn*

Texas Swings / 1992 / Justice ✦✦✦✦
Texas-born guitarist Herb Ellis teams up with a variety of country musicians on this Justice CD for a set of Western swing-oriented jazz. Essentially an instrumental country date with Ellis as one of the lead voices, the enjoyable set also has Willie Nelson's guitar added on some of the tracks along with steel guitar, two violinists, and a standard rhythm section. The twangy sound of the steel guitar may not appeal to everyone but the fairly basic music (mostly swing standards) is played with plenty of spirit. This recording gives Ellis a fresh setting after years in trios and quartets. —*Scott Yanow*

Peter Erskine

b. Jun. 5, 1954, Somers Point, NJ
Drums / Fusion, Post-Bop
A very versatile drummer, Peter Erskine has excelled in several types of jazz settings. He was with Stan Kenton's Orchestra (1972-75) and Maynard Ferguson's big band (1976-78) before gaining fame with Weather Report (1978-82) where he made a perfect team with Jaco Pastorius. Since that time he has been a member of Steps Ahead (which he had originally joined when they were Steps in 1979), John Abercrombie's band, Bass Desires, and groups headed by Kenny Wheeler in addition to leading his own units. Peter Erskine has led sessions for Contemporary (1982), Denon, Ah-Um, Novus, and most recently ECM. —*Scott Yanow*

● **Peter Erskine** / Jun. 22, 1982-Jun. 23, 1982 / Contemporary ✦✦✦✦
First release by a first-rate drummer and lots of New York friends. "All's Well that Ends" is a winning track, as is "Leroy St." —*Michael G. Nastos*

Sweet Soul / Mar. 4, 1991-Mar. 5, 1991 / Novus ✦✦✦✦
A terrific date, it features John Scofield (g), Joe Lovano (s), Bob Mintzer (s), Kenny Werner (p). Erskine's abilities as a composer are quite evident on this recording. —*Paul Kohler*

You Never Know / Jul. 1992 / ECM ✦✦✦

Time Being / Nov. 1993 / ECM ✦✦✦

Booker Ervin

b. Oct. 31, 1930, Denson, TX, d. Jul. 31, 1970, New York, NY
Sax (Tenor) / Avant-Garde, Post-Bop, Hard Bop
A very distinctive tenor with a hard passionate tone and an emotional style that was still tied to chordal improvisation, Booker Ervin was a true original. He was originally a trombonist but taught himself tenor while in the Air Force (1950-53). After studying music in Boston for two years, he made his recording debut with Ernie Fields' R&B band (1956). Ervin gained fame while playing with Charles Mingus (off and on during 1956-62), holding his own with the volatile bassist, and Eric Dolphy. He also led his own quartet, worked with Randy Weston on a few occasions in the '60s, and spent much of 1964-66 in Europe before dying much too young from kidney disease. Ervin, who is on several notable Charles Mingus records, made dates of his own for Bethlehem, Savoy, and Candid during 1960-61, along with later sets for Pacific Jazz and Blue Note, but it is his nine Prestige sessions of 1963-66 (including *The Freedom Book*, *The Song Book*, *The Blues Book*, and *The Space Book*) that are among the high points of his career. —*Scott Yanow*

Exultation! / Jun. 19, 1963 / Original Jazz Classics ✦✦✦✦
Booker Ervin's debut for Prestige (which has been reissued on CD with two shorter alternate takes added) matches the intense tenor with altoist Frank Strozier, pianist Horace Parlan, bassist Butch Warren, and drummer Walter Perkins for some bop-based music that is actually quite adventurous. Highlights include "Mour" (based on "Four"), "Black and Blue," and Ervin's "Mooche Mooche." Ervin and Strozier made a mutually inspiring team; pity that this was their only recording together. —*Scott Yanow*

Freedom Book / Dec. 3, 1963 / Original Jazz Classics ✦✦✦✦

The Song Book / Feb. 27, 1964 / Original Jazz Classics ✦✦✦✦
Another in a series of exceptional quartet dates led by tenor saxophonist Booker Ervin in the mid-'60s. This time, Tommy Flanagan replaced Jaki Byard on piano, with absolutely no dip in the quartet's execution. Ervin's solos were once more robust and well played, while the Davis/Dawson bass-and-drum duo did their customary excellent job. This has been issued on vinyl as part of the two-record set *The Blues Book/The Song Book* and on both vinyl and CD as a single session. —*Scott Yanow*

★ **The Blues Book** / Jun. 30, 1964 / Original Jazz Classics ✦✦✦✦✦
For this CD reissue in his series of *Books*, Ervin and his quintet (with trumpeter Carmell Jones, pianist Gildo Mahones, bassist Richard Davis, and drummer Alan Dawson) perform four very different blues: the speedy "One for Mort," a lowdown "No Booze Blooze," the modal "True Blue," and the minor-toned "Eerie Dearie." The consistently passionate Ervin makes each of the fairly basic originals sound fresh, and the performances are frequently exciting inside/outside music. —*Scott Yanow*

Space Book / Oct. 2, 1964 / Prestige ✦✦✦✦
The fourth and final Booker Ervin "book" release, each done in 1964. Ervin does two exceptional ballads here, stunning versions of "I Can't Get Started" and "There Is No Greater Love," plus his usual arresting uptempo and blues numbers. Jaki Byard is back on piano, and again Richard Davis and Alan Dawson are paired on bass and drums. This has been issued on vinyl as part of the two-record set *The Freedom and Space Sessions*, and as a single release under the title *Groovin' High*. —*Ron Wynn*

Kevin Eubanks

b. Nov. 15, 1957, Philadelphia, PA
Guitar / Post-Bop
During the past couple of years Kevin Eubanks has been seen by millions of viewers nightly as the leader of Jay Leno's Tonight Show Band where his main purpose is to assist the comedian/host rather than play creative jazz. Eubanks comes from a musical family that included Ray and Tommy Bryant as uncles and older brother/trombonist Robin Eubanks. After studying at Berklee, he was with the Art Blakey big band (1980-81), had stints with Roy Haynes, Slide Hampton, and Sam Rivers and then in 1983 started leading his own groups. Starting in 1985, after debuting on Elektra, Eubanks began recording regularly for GRP. Some of the sets were a bit commercial while others were fairly explorative. Switching to Blue Note in the '90s, Eubanks has been emphasizing acoustic guitar in more recent years. —*Scott Yanow*

● **Turning Point** / Dec. 16, 1991-Jan. 9, 1992 / Blue Note ✦✦✦✦
In this Blue Note session, Eubanks disproves those who have questioned his jazz and improvising credentials. There are only four cuts, and they're designed for intense solos and exacting ensemble interaction. Besides Eubanks on electric and acoustic guitar, the cast features alto flutist Kent Jordan, bassist Dave Holland, and drummer Marvin "Smitty" Smith. —*Ron Wynn*

Spirit Talk / 1993 / Blue Note ✦✦✦✦

Spiritalk 2 / Jun. 25, 1994-Jun. 28, 1994 / Blue Note ✦✦✦
The most notable aspect to this CD from Kevin Eubanks is the instrumental blend between his acoustic guitar, trombonist Robin Eubanks, and the alto flute of Kent Jordan; bassist Dave Holland and either Marvin "Smitty"

Smith or Gene Jackson on drums completes the quintet. Eubanks' originals are moody and thoughtful (even in the more heated moments) but do little more than set introspective moods; none of the themes are particularly memorable. The playing is of a consistent high quality on this set but the music is much easier to respect than to love. —*Scott Yanow*

Bill Evans

b. Aug. 16, 1929, Plainfield, NJ, **d.** Sep. 15, 1980
Piano / Cool, Post-Bop
Bill Evans was (along with McCoy Tyner) the most influential pianist in jazz during the '60s and '70s, and since his death in 1980 his influence has exceeded Tyner's. Evans, who was the next step beyond Bud Powell, had a sophisticated way of voicing chords that has been adopted by a countless number of pianists. Very popular even among nonjazz audiences to his sensitive interpretations of ballads, Evans could always swing as hard as anyone when he was inspired.

After attending Southwestern Louisiana University, working with Mundell Lowe and Red Mitchell, and serving in the Army, Evans first emerged on the New York scene playing with Tony Scott in 1956, and that year he made his first trio album, *New Jazz Conceptions*. After working with George Russell and recording with Charles Mingus, Evans was part of the 1958 Miles Davis Sextet with John Coltrane and Cannonball Adderley. Other than a few live dates and "So What" from the 1959 classic *Kind of Blue*, Evans did not record all that much during his months with Davis but he made a strong impact and contributed one future standard, "Blue in Green," which ranks with "Waltz for Debby" as his most famous original.

By 1959 Bill Evans was leading his own trio which soon utilized the great bassist Scott LaFaro and drummer Paul Motian. The interplay between the three musicians (with an almost equal role by each of the players) was highly influential and nearly telepathic. Tragically, shortly after they recorded extensively at the Village Vanguard in June 1961, LaFaro was killed in a car accident. Evans went into isolation for the remainder of the year. In 1962 he re-emerged with Chuck Israels as his new bassist and recorded the first of two classic albums in duet with guitarist Jim Hall. In future years Evans would continue touring and recording with his trio, which included such sidemen as bassists Israels (1962-65), Gary Peacock (1963), Eddie Gomez (1966-77), and Marc Johnson (1978-80) and drummers Motian (1959-62), Larry Bunker (1963-5), Philly Joe Jones (1967), Jack DeJohnette (1968), Marty Morell (1969-75), Eliot Zigmund (1975-78), and Joe LaBarbera (1979-80). Drug addiction cut short Bill Evans' life prematurely but he fortunately had recorded extensively from 1956 on, most notably for Riverside, Verve, Fantasy, and Warner Bros. Several videos are also available of this major force in modern jazz, whose innovations helped form the styles of Herbie Hancock and Keith Jarrett. —*Scott Yanow*

New Jazz Conceptions / Sep. 18, 1956-Sep. 27, 1956 / Original Jazz Classics ✦✦✦✦
This was pianist Bill Evans debut as a leader. He had backing from bassist Teddy Kotick and drummer Paul Motian. The album swings hard but really did not develop the grace and cutting execution that would be found on *Explorations*. —*Bob Rusch, Cadence*

☆ **The Complete Riverside Recordings (1956-63) [box]** / 1956-1963 / Riverside ✦✦✦✦✦
All the marvelous Evans one could ever want is on this incredible 18-disc box set. It is a wonderful, comprehensive collection of superb performances, with some of his most majestic trio and solo dates. —*Ron Wynn*

Undercurrent / May 15, 1959 / Blue Note ✦✦✦✦
A must-have reissue of brilliant date with Jim Hall (g). —*Ron Wynn*

Portrait in Jazz / Dec. 28, 1959 / Original Jazz Classics ✦✦✦✦
Here is an excellent reissue of a solid concert, with some typically stunning Scott LaFaro bass. —*Ron Wynn*

★ **Sunday at the Village Vanguard** / Jun. 25, 1961 / Original Jazz Classics ✦✦✦✦✦
This represents one of the best known sessions from the Village Vanguard and most of the material from this date was on a previous two-fer. Simply put, it sounds like pianist Bill Evans, bassist Scott LaFaro, and drummer Paul Motian, and it sounds like Sunday. —*Bob Rusch, Cadence*

More from the Vanguard / Jun. 25, 1961 / Milestone ✦✦✦✦
Material recorded live at the Village Vanguard during several sessions with arguably the finest Bill Evans trio: pianist Evans, bassist Scott LaFaro, and drummer Paul Motian. They did enough tracks to fill several albums; these were sessions not included on the original *Live At The Village Vanguard* dates. —*Ron Wynn*

★ **Waltz for Debby** / Jun. 25, 1961 / Original Jazz Classics ✦✦✦✦✦
This second issue of the Bill Evans trio (Scott Lafaro, bass; Paul Motian, drums) had a good run on Riverside, as one of the first Milestone two-fers and also as part of the 19-LP Bill Evans box. The material here has, because of its lasting popularity and the influence of Evans, become somewhat its own cliché, which of course is really an ironic distortion of time and place.

For this date, time, place, artists were right, and for two decades this, for many, continues to be a stimulating comfort. —*Bob Rusch, Cadence*

How My Heart Sings! / May 17, 1962-Jun. 5, 1962 / Original Jazz Classics ✦✦✦✦
Bill Evans Trio. More from the Evans-Chuck Israels-Paul Motian lineup. —*Ron Wynn*

Moonbeams / May 17, 1962-Jun. 5, 1962 / Original Jazz Classics ✦✦✦✦
Bill Evans Trio. Top trio again features Evans, Israels (b), and Motian (d). —*Ron Wynn*

Interplay / Jul. 16, 1962 / Original Jazz Classics ✦✦✦✦
Quintet. A dazzling small-group date with top-flight Freddie Hubbard (tpt). 1987 reissue. —*Ron Wynn*

Conversations with Myself / Jan. 1963-Feb. 1963 / Verve ✦✦✦✦
Stunning multiple-tracked piano solos. Great playing and admirable use of multitrack technology. —*Ron Wynn*

Bill Evans Trio at Shelly's Manne-Hole / May 30, 1963 & May 31, 1963 / Original Jazz Classics ✦✦✦

Trio 1964 / Dec. 18, 1963 / Verve ✦✦✦✦
This is among his most captivating trio dates. —*Ron Wynn*

Bill Evans Trio with Symphony Orchestra / Oct. 1965-Dec. 1965 / Verve ✦✦

Bill Evans at Town Hall / Feb. 21, 1966 / Verve ✦✦✦✦
Excellent and appealing, a wonderful live set. —*Ron Wynn*

Intermodulation / Apr. 7, 1966-May 10, 1966 / Verve ✦✦✦✦
A beautiful return engagement with Jim Hall (g). —*Ron Wynn*

At the Montreux Jazz Festival / Jun. 15, 1968 / Verve ✦✦✦✦
A superb trio date. Eddie Gomez (b) and Jack DeJohnette (d) are brilliant in accompanying roles. —*Ron Wynn*

☆ **The Complete Fantasy Recordings** / Nov. 1973-May 13, 1979 / Fantasy ✦✦✦✦✦
This gorgeous box set is a collection of his '70s selections. It covers everything in all contexts and is a must-have for piano fans. —*Ron Wynn*

But Beautiful / Aug. 9, 1974 & Aug. 16, 1974 / Milestone ✦✦✦✦
Pianist Bill Evans and tenor saxophonist Stan Getz only recorded in the studio together on one occasion, making these previously unreleased concert performances (issued for the first time in 1996) quite valuable. Evans (due to a misunderstanding) sits out on much of "Stan's Blues," and there are two trio features without the tenor, but otherwise the other seven numbers match Getz with Evans, bassist Eddie Gomez, and drummer Marty Morell. Although released under the pianist's name, this CD is very much Stan Getz's show, and his beautiful tone sounds quite exquisite on "But Beautiful," "Emily," "The Peacocks," and the swinging "You and the Night and the Music." This historic and somewhat unique release has many enjoyable moments. —*Scott Yanow*

Intuition / Nov. 7, 1974-Nov. 8, 1974 / Original Jazz Classics ✦✦✦

The Tony Bennett/Bill Evans Album / Jun. 10, 1975-Jun. 13, 1975 / Original Jazz Classics ✦✦✦✦
Exquisite collaboration between a great romantic vocalist and a tremendous melodic interpreter. Bennett and Evans mesh as though they had been working together for years, never having any problems with tempo, pacing, or mood. This has been reissued on CD. —*Ron Wynn*

Montreaux, Vol. 3 / Jul. 20, 1975 / Original Jazz Classics ✦✦✦✦
For this duet set from the 1975 Montreux Jazz Festival (a Fantasy date that has been reissued on CD in the OJC series), Bill Evans alternates between acoustic and electric pianos while Eddie Gomez offers alert support and some near-miraculous bass solos. The audience is attentive and appreciative as they should be, for the communication between the two masterful players (on such songs as "Milano," "Django," "I Love You," and their encore "The Summer Knows") is quite special. —*Scott Yanow*

Alone (Again) / Dec. 16, 1975 / Original Jazz Classics ✦✦✦

Eloquence / Dec. 16, 1975 & Dec. 18, 1975 / Original Jazz Classics ✦✦✦

Quintessence / May 1976 / Original Jazz Classics ✦✦✦

Cross-Currents / Feb. 28, 1977-Mar. 2, 1977 / Original Jazz Classics ✦✦✦✦
A change of pace for the Bill Evans trio, with the usual threesome paired with saxophonists Warne Marsh and Lee Konitz on some numbers. There's one excellent duet by Evans and Konitz on "When I Fall In Love," and one quartet number without Konitz, but otherwise Evans shows that he could head a quintet, play solos, and interact with a combo as effectively as he did his trio. Konitz and Marsh are superb, while bassist Eddie Gomez and drummer Eliot Zigmund work effectively in different format. —*Ron Wynn*

You Must Believe in Spring / Aug. 23, 1977-Aug. 25, 1977 / Warner Bros. ✦✦✦

★ **Marian Mc Partland's Piano Jazz with Guest Bill Evans** / Nov. 6, 1978 / Jazz Alliance ✦✦✦✦✦

I Will Say Goodbye [OJC] / May 11, 1979-May 13, 1979 / Original Jazz Classics ✦✦✦

We Will Meet Again / Aug. 6, 1979-Aug. 9, 1979 / Warner Bros. ✦✦✦
Paris Concert, Edition One / Nov. 26, 1979 / Elektra ✦✦✦✦
The two LPs recorded at this Paris concert are the last examples of Bill Evans' playing that have been released to date although there are other concert performances from 1980 that are expected to come out eventually. With bassist Marc Johnson and drummer Joe LaBarbera, Evans had one of the strongest trios of his career, as can be heard on such pieces as "My Romance," "I Loves You Porgy," and "Beautiful Love." The close communication between the players is reminiscent of Evans' 1961 unit with Scott LaFaro and Paul Motian. —*Scott Yanow*

Paris Concert, Edition Two / Nov. 26, 1979 / Elektra ✦✦✦✦
Bill Evans' death in 1980 ended the career of the most influential (along with McCoy Tyner) acoustic pianist in jazz of the past 20 years. This second of two LPs features Evans, bassist Marc Johnson, and drummer Paul Motian closely interacting on four of the pianist's originals, Gary McFarland's "Gary's Theme," and Miles Davis' "Nardis." The music is sensitive and subtly exciting. Until some later live sessions from 1980 are released, this can be considered Bill Evans' final recording and serves as evidence that, rather than declining, he was showing a renewed vitality and enthusiasm in his last year. —*Scott Yanow*

Gil Evans (Ian Ernest Gilmore Green)

b. May 13, 1912, Toronto, Canada, d. Mar. 20, 1988, Cuernavaca, Mexico
Piano / Cool, Fusion, Post-Bop
One of the most significant arrangers in jazz history, Gil Evans' three album-length collaborations with Miles Davis (*Miles Ahead*, *Porgy and Bess*, and *Sketches of Spain*) are all considered classics. Evans had a lengthy and wide-ranging career that sometimes ran parallel to the trumpeter. Like Davis, Gil became involved in utilizing electronics in the '70s and preferred not to look back and recreate the past. He led his own band in California (1933-38) that eventually became the backup group for Skinnay Ennis; Evans stayed on for a time as arranger. He gained recognition for his somewhat futuristic charts for Claude Thornhill's Orchestra (1941-42 and 1946-48), which took advantage of the ensemble's cool tones, utilized French horns and a tuba as frontline instruments and by 1946 incorporated the influence of bop. He met Miles Davis (who admired his work with Thornhill) during this time and contributed arrangements of "Moon Dreams" and "Boplicity" to Davis' "Birth of the Cool" nonet. After a period in obscurity, Evans wrote for a Helen Merrill session and then collaborated with Davis on *Miles Ahead*. In addition to his work with Miles (which also included a 1961 recorded Carnegie Hall concert and the half-album *Quiet Nights*), Evans recorded several superb and highly original sets as a leader (including *Gil Evans and Ten*, *New Bottle Old Wine*, and *Great Jazz Standards*) during the era. In the '60s among the albums he worked on for other artists were notable efforts with Kenny Burrell and Astrud Gilberto. After his own sessions for Verve during 1963-64, Evans waited until 1969 to record. That year's *Blues in Orbit* was his first successful effort at combining acoustic and electric instruments; it would be followed by dates for Artists House, Atlantic (*Svengali*), and a notable tribute to Jimi Hendrix in 1974. After 1975's *There Comes a Time* (which features among its sidemen David Sanborn), most of Evans' recordings were taken from live performances. Starting in 1970 he began playing with his large ensemble on a weekly basis in New York clubs. Filled with such all-star players as George Adams, Lew Soloff, Marvin "Hannibal" Peterson, Chris Hunter, Howard Johnson, Pete Levin, Hiram Bullock, Hamiet Bluiett, and Arthur Blythe, among others, Evans' later bands were top-heavy in talent but tended to ramble on too long. Gil Evans, other than sketching out a framework and contributing his keyboard, seemed to let the orchestra largely run itself, inspiring rather than closely directing the music. There were some worthwhile recordings from the '80s (when the band had a long string of Monday night gigs at Sweet Basil in New York), but in general they do not often live up to their potential. Prior to his death, Gil Evans recorded with his "arranger's piano" on duets with Lee Konitz and Steve Lacy, and his body of work on a whole ranks with the top jazz arrangers. —*Scott Yanow*

★ **Gil Evans and Ten** / Sep. 6, 1957-Oct. 10, 1957 / Original Jazz Classics ✦✦✦✦✦
Although arranger Gil Evans had been active in the major leagues of jazz ever since the mid-'40s and had participated in Miles Davis' famous *Birth of the Cool* recordings, this set was his first opportunity to record as a leader. The CD reissue features a typically unusual 11-piece unit consisting of two trumpets, trombonist Jimmy Cleveland, Bert Varsalona on bass trombone, French horn player Willie Ruff, Steve Lacy on soprano, altoist Lee Konitz, Dave Kurtzer on bassoon, bassist Paul Chambers, and either Nick Stabulas or Jo Jones on drums, plus the leader's sparse piano. As good an introduction to his work as any, this program includes diverse works ranging from Leadbelly to Leonard Bernstein, plus Evans' own "Jambangle." The arranger's inventive use of the voices of his rather unique sidemen make this a memorable set. —*Scott Yanow*

New Bottle, Old Wine / Apr. 9, 1958-May 26, 1958 / Blue Note ✦✦✦✦
Early, intriguing Gil Evans orchestra material, one of the sessions that established his reputation as an arranger and bandleader. The band, which

included Johnny Coles, Cannonball Adderley, Paul Chambers, and Art Blakey, did rousing, fresh versions of vintage songs like "St. Louis Blues" and "King Porter Stomp." This material has also been issued as a vinyl album and CD under the title *Pacific Standard Time*. —*Ron Wynn*

Great Jazz Standards / Feb. 5, 1959 / Blue Note ✦✦✦✦
1988 reissue of a brilliant album. —*Ron Wynn*

Out of the Cool / Nov. 18, 1960-Dec. 15, 1960 / MCA ✦✦✦✦
Gil Evans recordings (particularly those without Miles Davis) were not a common occurrence in the pre-1970 era, making this set a special treat. Evans' 14-piece band (which includes trumpeter Johnny Coles, trombonist Jimmy Knepper, Budd Johnson on tenor, and soprano and guitarist Ray Crawford, among others) investigates a wide variety of complex material including the leader's "La Nevada" and "Sunken Treasure," John Benson Brooks' obscure "Where Flamingos Fly," George Russell's "Stratusphunk," and Kurt Weill's "Biobao"; some reissues of this album also add Horace Silver's "Sister Sadie." The orchestrations are both thoughtful and colorful, the main reason to acquire this music. —*Scott Yanow*

The Individualism of Gil Evans / Sep. 1963-Oct. 29, 1964 / Verve ✦✦✦
Blues in Orbit / 1969 / Enja ✦✦✦✦
Arranger Gil Evans' first recording as a leader in five years found him leading an orchestra that could be considered a transition between his '50s groups and his somewhat electric band of the '70s. Several of these charts, particularly his reworking of George Russell's "Blues in Orbit," are quite memorable, and Evans utilizes his many interesting sidemen, including the distinctive voices of trombonist Jimmy Cleveland, Howard Johnson on tuba and baritone, tenor saxophonist Billy Harper, and guitarist Joe Beck in unexpected and unpredictable ways. A near-classic release that has been made available on CD by Enja. —*Scott Yanow*

Gil Evans' Orchestra Plays the Music of Jimi Hendrix / Jun. 11, 1974-Jun. 13, 1974 / Bluebird ✦✦✦✦
This CD reissue (which adds additional material to the original LP program) is much more successful than one might have expected. Jimi Hendrix was scheduled to record with Gil Evans' orchestra but died before the session could take place. A few years later, Evans explored ten of Hendrix's compositions with his unique 19-piece unit, an orchestra that included two French horns, the tuba of Howard Johnson, three guitars, two basses, two percussionists, and such soloists as altoist David Sanborn, trumpeter Hannibal Marvin Peterson, Billy Harper on tenor, and guitarists Ryo Kawasaki and John Abercrombie. Evans' arrangements uplift many of Hendrix's more blues-oriented compositions and create a memorable set that is rock-oriented but retains the improvisation and personality of jazz. Recommended. —*Scott Yanow*

There Comes a Time / Mar. 6, 1975-Jun. 12, 1975 / Bluebird ✦✦✦✦
This CD reissue differs greatly from the original LP of the same name. Not only are there three previously unreleased performances ("Joy Spring," "So Long," and "Buzzard Variation") but also "The Meaning of the Blues" has been expanded from six minutes to 20(!). Two numbers ("Little Wing" and "Aftermath the Fourth Movement Children of the Fire") have been dropped (the former was reissued on Evans' Jimi Hendrix tribute), and the remaining four tracks were re-edited and remixed under Evans' direction. So in reality, this 1987 CD was really a "new" record when it came out. The remake of "King Porter Stomp" (with altoist David Sanborn in Cannonball Adderley's spot) is a classic, the "new" version of "The Meaning of the Blues" is memorable, and overall the music (which also has solos by Billy Harper and George Adams on tenors along with trumpeter Lew Soloff) is quite rewarding, creative big-band fusion that expertly mixes together acoustic and electric instruments. This was one of Gil Evans' last truly great sets. —*Scott Yanow*

Bud & Bird / Dec. 1, 1986 / Evidence ✦✦✦
Rhythm-A-Ning / Nov. 2, 1987-Nov. 26, 1987 / EmArcy ✦✦✦

Jon Faddis

b. Jul. 24, 1953, Oakland, CA
Trumpet / Bop
When Jon Faddis burst on the jazz scene as a teenager, observers were amazed by his technique and his ability to sound like an identical twin of Dizzy Gillespie (whose complex style had never been successfully duplicated before). After a period he was typecast as a Dizzy imitator, but Faddis' remarkable range (hitting higher notes than Gillespie ever could) and the gradual development of his individual sound have helped him to overcome the early fault. In fact, Faddis can now also imitate Roy Eldridge and Louis Armstrong quite well too. Dizzy was always Jon Faddis' idol, from the time he started playing trumpet at age eight. After moving to New York in the early '70s, Faddis played with Lionel Hampton and Charles Mingus (guesting on a recorded concert with the bassist when Roy Eldridge became ill) and then recorded two notable albums for Pablo, including a duet session with Oscar Peterson. After playing a bit with Dizzy Gillespie (their best encounters in the mid-'70s were unfortunately not recorded), Faddis seemed to disappear, sticking to studio work and playing first trumpet with the Thad Jones-Mel Lewis Orchestra. After re-emerging in the

mid-'80s, Jon Faddis recorded for Concord and Epic and in 1993 became the musical director of the Carnegie Hall Jazz Orchestra. — *Scott Yanow*

Youngblood / Jan. 8, 1976-Jan. 9, 1976 / Pablo ✦✦✦✦
This date with Kenny Barron Trio is an ode to Dizzy Gillespie. — *Michael G. Nastos*

★ **Legacy** / Aug. 1985 / Concord Jazz ✦✦✦✦✦
A tremendous mainstream session to which Harold Land (ts) and Kenny Barron (p) make excellent contributions. — *Ron Wynn*

Into the Faddisphere / May 2, 1989-May 8, 1989 / Epic ✦✦✦

Charles Fambrough

b. Aug. 25, 1950, Philadelphia, PA
Bass / Post-Bop, Hard Bop
Best-known for his stint with Art Blakey's Jazz Messengers, bassist Charles Fambrough has led three very effective all-star dates for CTI that were filled with his stimulating originals. He first studied classical piano but switched to bass when he was 13. In 1968 Fambrough began playing with local pit bands for musicals, and after some freelancing in 1970 he joined Grover Washington, Jr.'s band, staying with the popular saxophonist until 1974. Fambrough was with Airto (1975-77), McCoy Tyner (1978-80), and then Art Blakey (1980-82). Since that time he has freelanced in many different situations. Fambrough's sidemen on his CTI recordings have thus far included both Wynton and Branford Marsalis, Roy Hargrove, Kenny Kirkland, Jerry Gonzalez, Steve Turre, Donald Harrison, Kenny Garrett, Abdullah Ibrahim, and Grover Washington, Jr.! — *Scott Yanow*

The Proper Angle / May 29, 1991-May 31, 1991 / CTI ✦✦✦✦
Excellent bassist Charles Fambrough steps into the spotlight with his debut album as a leader. While his compositions are straightforward hard bop, he's recruited an impressive guest list. The lineup includes both Wynton and Branford Marsalis, Roy Hargrove, Kenny Kirkland, Jeff Watts, Jerry Gonzalez, and Steve Berrios. — *Ron Wynn*

The Charmer / 1992 / CTI ✦✦✦✦

● **Blues at Bradley's** / 1993 / CTI ✦✦✦✦
Charles Fambrough, who first gained recognition as a bassist with Art Blakey's Jazz Messengers, has proven with his releases thus far that he is also a talented composer and bandleader. Four of the five diverse pieces on this CD are his and Fambrough's octet (which includes altoist Donald Harrison, trombonist Steve Turre, and Joe Ford on soprano), does a splendid job of interpreting the often-challenging but swinging repertoire. This is high-quality modern mainstream music. — *Scott Yanow*

Tal Farlow

b. Jun. 7, 1921, Greensboro, NC
Guitar / Bop, Cool
Nearly as famous for his reluctance to play as for his outstanding abilities, guitarist Tal Farlow has been semiretired since 1958, although whenever he gets around to playing, he sounds in peak form. He did not take up the guitar until he was 21 years old but within a year was playing professionally and in 1948, played with Marjorie Hyams' band. While with the Red Norvo Trio (which originally included Charles Mingus) from 1949-53, Farlow became famous in the jazz world. His huge hands and ability to play rapid yet light lines made him one of the top guitarists of the era. After six months with Artie Shaw's Gramercy Five in 1953, Farlow put together his own group which for a time included pianist Eddie Costa. Late in 1958 Farlow settled in New England, became a sign painter, and just played locally. He only made one record as a leader during 1960-75 but emerged a bit more often during 1976-84, recording for Concord fairly regularly before largely disappearing again. Profiled in the definitive documentary *Talmage Farlow*, the guitarist can be heard on his own records for Blue Note (1954), Verve, Prestige (1969), and Concord. — *Scott Yanow*

Tal Farlow Returns / Sep. 23, 1969 / Original Jazz Classics ✦✦✦✦
This exceptional release spotlights an often stunning guitar master. — *Ron Wynn*

Chromatic Palette / Jan. 1981 / Concord Jazz ✦✦✦✦
Superior interaction with Tommy Flanagan (p). — *Ron Wynn*

● **Cookin' on All Burners** / Aug. 1982 / Concord Jazz ✦✦✦✦
Excellent piano from James Williams, plus outstanding guitar by Farlow. — *Ron Wynn*

The Legendary / Sep. 1984 / Concord Jazz ✦✦✦✦
A good set. — *Ron Wynn*

Art Farmer

b. Aug. 21, 1928, Council Bluffs, IA
Trumpet, Fluegelhorn / Cool, Hard Bop
Largely overlooked during his formative years, Art Farmer's consistently inventive playing has been more greatly appreciated as he continues to develop. Along with Clark Terry, Farmer helped to popularize the fluegelhorn among brass players. His lyricism gives his bop-oriented style its own

personality. Farmer studied piano, violin, and tuba before settling on trumpet. He worked in Los Angeles from 1945 on, performing regularly on Central Avenue and spending time in the bands of Johnny Otis, Jay McShann, Roy Porter, Benny Carter, and Gerald Wilson among others; some of the groups also included his twin brother bassist Addison Farmer (1928-63). After playing with Wardell Gray (1951-52) and touring Europe with Lionel Hampton's big band (1953), Farmer moved to New York and worked with Gigi Gryce (1954-56), Horace Silver's Quintet (1956-58), and the Gerry Mulligan Quartet (1958-9). Farmer, who made many recordings in the latter half of the '50s (including with Quincy Jones and George Russell and on some jam-session dates for Prestige) co-led the Jazztet with Benny Golson (1959-62) and then had a group with Jim Hall (1962-64). He moved to Vienna in 1968, where he joined the Austrian Radio Orchestra, worked with the Kenny Clarke-Francy Boland Big Band, and toured with his own units. Since the '80s Farmer has visited the US more often and has remained greatly in demand up to the present day. Art Farmer has recorded many sessions as a leader through the years including for Prestige, Contemporary, United Artists, Argo, Mercury, Atlantic, Columbia, CTI, Soul Note, Optimism, Concord, Enja, and Sweet Basil. — *Scott Yanow*

The Art Farmer Septet / Jul. 1953-Jun. 1954 / Original Jazz Classics ✦✦✦✦
This CD reissue features the mellow-toned but hard-swinging trumpeter Art Farmer on a pair of four-song sessions from 1953 and 1954. Among Farmer's sidemen are trombonist Jimmy Cleveland, either Clifford Solomon or Charlie Rouse on tenor, and Horace Silver or Quincy Jones on piano. In addition Farmer is showcased on a version of "When Your Lover Has Gone" that is taken from a 1956 album titled *Two Trumpets*. Highlights overall include "Mau Mau," "Up in Quincy's Room," "Evening in Paris," and "Elephant Walk." An excellent early hard bop set. — *Scott Yanow*

Early Art / Jan. 20, 1954 & Nov. 9, 1954 / Original Jazz Classics ✦✦✦
Two of trumpeter Art Farmer's earlier sessions as a leader are reissued on this CD in the OJC series. Farmer teams up with an all-star quintet (which includes tenorsaxophonist Sonny Rollins, pianist Horace Silver, bassist Percy Heath, and drummer Kenny Clarke) for four songs and dominates a quartet (with pianist Wynton Kelly, bassist Addison Farmer, and drummer Herbie Lovelle) on six other tunes. Farmer's sound is lyrical even on the uptempo pieces, and he is heard throughout his early prime. Highlights include "Soft Shoe," "I'll Take Romance," "Autumn Nocturne," and an uptempo "Gone with the Wind." One should note that the programming differs from what is listed, with "Soft Shoe" (which should have been the opener) actually appearing fifth and the songs listed as appearing second through fifth moving up to first through fourth! Despite that flaw, the music is quite enjoyable and a must for '50s bop collectors. — *Scott Yanow*

When Farmer Met Gryce / May 19, 1954 & May 26, 1955 / Original Jazz Classics ✦✦✦✦
This CD reissue brings back a former LP featuring trumpeter Art Farmer, altoist Gigi Gryce, and two rhythm sections with either Horace Silver or Freddie Redd on piano, Percy Heath or Addison Farmer on bass, and Kenny Clarke or Art Taylor on drums. The early hard bop music is highlighted by "Social Call" (one of Gryce's best-known compositions), "Capri," "A Night at Tony's," and "Blue Concept" but all eight numbers will easily be enjoyed by straightahead jazz fans. — *Scott Yanow*

The Art Farmer Quintet / Oct. 21, 1955 / Original Jazz Classics ✦✦✦✦
During 1955 trumpeter Art Farmer had a short-lived quintet with altoist Gigi Gryce, but because neither of the co-leaders were big names at the time, the band did not last long. Fortunately they did record two records of material, of which this CD reissue (originally known as *Evening in Casablanca*) was the second. In addition to Farmer and Gryce, the unit includes pianist Duke Jordan, bassist Addison Farmer, and drummer Philly Joe Jones. With the exception of Duke Jordan's "Forecast," the cool-toned hardbop date consists entirely of Gigi Gryce compositions, of which "Evening in Casablanca" and "Nice's Tempo" are best-known. Excellent music well deserving a close listen. — *Scott Yanow*

● **Portrait of Art Farmer** / Apr. 19, 1958 & May 1, 1958 / Original Jazz Classics ✦✦✦✦
This CD reissue (which adds a version of "The Folks Who Live on the Hill" to the original LP program) is an excellent showcase for trumpeter Art Farmer in the '50s. Farmer is showcased with a quartet that also includes pianist Hank Jones, bassist Addison Farmer, and drummer Roy Haynes. The repertoire alternates veteran standards with lesser-known material, including three of Farmer's originals and George Russell's "Nita" along with a particularly strong version of Benny Golson's "Stablemates." An excellent outing. — *Scott Yanow*

Modern Art / Sep. 10, 1958-Sep. 14, 1958 / Blue Note ✦✦✦✦
For this CD reissue from over a year before the Jazztet was formed, trumpeter Art Farmer teams up with his future co-leader tenor saxophonist Benny Golson. With a strong rhythm section consisting of pianist Bill Evans, bassist Addison Farmer, and drummer Dave Bailey, Farmer and Golson perform two of their originals and such songs as "Darn That Dream," "Like Someone in Love," and "Cool Breeze." The straightahead

hard-bop music (originally out on United Artists) is as successful as one would expect; Farmer and Golson always brought out the best in each other. — *Scott Yanow*

★ **Meet the Jazztet** / Feb. 6, 1960-Feb. 10, 1960 / MCA/Chess ◆◆◆◆◆
Although this CD has the same program as the original LP, it gets the highest rating because it is a hard-bop classic. Not only does it include superior solos from trumpeter Art Farmer, trombonist Curtis Fuller, tenor saxophonist Benny Golson, and pianist McCoy Tyner (who was making his recording debut) along with fine backup from bassist Addison Farmer and drummer Lex Humphries, but it also features the writing of Golson. Highlights include the original version of "Killer Joe" along with early renditions of "I Remember Clifford" and "Blues March." This was Fuller and Tyner's only recording with the original Jazztet, and all ten selections (which also include "Serenata," "It Ain't Necessarily So," "It's All Right with Me," and "Easy Living") are quite memorable. — *Scott Yanow*

Blues On Down / Sep. 16, 1960-May 15, 1961 / Chess ◆◆◆◆

On the Road / Jul. 26, 1976-Aug. 16, 1976 / Original Jazz Classics ◆◆◆◆
This CD reissue of a Contemporary set from 1976 features a logical but only one-time collaboration between fluegelhornist Art Farmer and altoist Art Pepper. With pianist Hampton Hawes, bassist Ray Brown, and either Steve Ellington or Shelly Manne on drums completing the quintet, the five standards and Hawes' original "Downwind" were certainly in good hands! A special highlight is a duet version of "My Funny Valentine" featuring Farmer and Hawes. Everyone plays up to par on this spirited straightahead set. — *Scott Yanow*

Work of Art / Sep. 1981 / Concord Jazz ◆◆◆◆
Fluegelhornist Art Farmer is in top form on this quartet set with pianist Fred Hersch, bassist Bob Bodley, and drummer Billy Hart. Farmer had, if anything, grown through the years and although he had lived in Europe for 13 years at the time of this album, he was still getting better! Farmer is heard in peak form on such numbers as Charlie Parker's "Red Cross," "She's Funny That Way," "Change Partners," and "Love Walked In." A fine example of his artistry. — *Scott Yanow*

● **Warm Valley** / Sep. 1982 / Concord Jazz ◆◆◆◆
The second of fluegelhornist Art Farmer's two Concord albums is the equal of his first. For this Concord outing, the mellow-toned brassman performs four standards (including "Moose the Mooche," "Three Little Words," and the title cut), along with selections from Fred Hersch (who plays piano on this quartet outing), Tommy Flanagan, and Benny Golson. With fine support from bassist Ray Drummond and drummer Akira Tana, Art Farmer is heard in prime form, playing in his appealing lyrical bop style. — *Scott Yanow*

● **Real Time** / Feb. 21, 1986-Feb. 22, 1986 / Contemporary ◆◆◆◆
This CD features the reunited Jazztet with fine playing from fluegelhornist Art Farmer, tenor saxophonist Benny Golson, and trombonist Curtis Fuller (who was actually only on the very first Jazztet record). Quite happily all three of the veterans are heard in prime form. With the assistance of a supportive rhythm section (pianist Mickey Tucker, bassist Ray Drummond, and drummer Marvin "Smitty" Smith), the group performs "Autumn Leaves" and four Golson compositions including "Whisper Not" and "Along Came Benny." This highly recommended disc is a near-classic that was recorded at the same sessions that resulted in *Back to the City*. — *Scott Yanow*

Back to the City / Feb. 21, 1986-Feb. 22, 1986 / Original Jazz Classics ◆◆◆◆

★ **Something to Live for: the Music of Billy Strayhorn** / Jan. 14, 1987-Jan. 15, 1987 / Contemporary ◆◆◆◆◆
This very logical set is a real gem. The lyrical fluegelhornist Art Farmer and his quintet (which consists of tenor saxophonist Clifford Jordan, pianist James Williams, bassist Rufus Reid, and drummer Marvin "Smitty" Smith) interpret seven of Billy Strayhorn's compositions. Highlights include "Isfahan," "Johnny Come Lately," "Raincheck," and the title cut. Farmer brings the right combination of sensitivity, swing, respect for the melody, and creativity to these renditions, and the results are quite memorable. — *Scott Yanow*

Central Avenue Reunion / May 26, 1989-May 27, 1989 / Contemporary ◆◆◆◆
Three of the five musicians on this quintet date (fluegelhornist Art Farmer, altoist Frank Morgan, and pianist Lou Levy) had played on Central Avenue in Los Angeles of the late '40s. Not all of the eight songs that they perform with bassist Eric Von Essen and drummer Albert "Tootie" Heath are from the era ("Blue Minor" and "Cool Struttin'" were written by Sonny Clark several years later) but the outing is very much in the bop style of the period. Their live set is highlighted by spirited versions of "Star Eyes," "Farmer's Market," "I Remember You," and "Donna Lee." This CD is filled with high-quality bebop that is easily recommended to straightahead jazz fans. — *Scott Yanow*

Soul Eyes / Jun. 23, 1992 / Enja ◆◆◆

Company I Keep / 1994 / Arabesque ◆◆◆◆
The two fluegelhornists Art Farmer and Tom Harrell meet up on this 1994 Arabesque CD, and although few fireworks occur (the two brassmen mostly sound complementary and mellow), the music is easily enjoyable advanced hard bop. With Ron Blake (doubling on tenor and soprano), pianist Geoff Keezer, bassist Kenny Davis, and drummer Carl Allen completing the group, Farmer and Harrell explore group originals, a song by Fritz Pauer, Duke Ellington's "TGTT," and Bill Evans' "Turn Out the Stars." Tasteful music. — *Scott Yanow*

Victor Feldman

b. Apr. 7, 1934, London, England, **d.** May 12, 1987, Los Angeles, CA
Percussion, Piano, Drums, Vibes / Cool, Post-Bop, Crossover
Victor Feldman was a child prodigy who was a professional from the age of seven and sat in on drums with Glenn Miller's Army Air Force Band in 1944 when he was ten. He was active in his native England through the bebop years (mostly on drums), debuting as a leader in 1948. By 1952 Feldman was getting better known for his vibes playing and he recorded extensively during the '50s. After touring with Woody Herman (1956-57), he decided to move to the US in 1957, where he worked at the Lighthouse with Howard Rumsey. Feldman recorded (on vibes and piano) for Mode, Contemporary, and Riverside during 1957-61, a period in which he became a busy studio musician. Feldman played with Cannonball Adderley's Quintet (mostly as a pianist) for six months in 1960-61 and recorded with Miles Davis in 1963 (who offered him a job with his new quintet and recorded his original "Seven Steps to Heaven"), but remained in Los Angeles and the studios. He cut jazz dates for Choice, Contemporary, Palo Alto, and TBA, and in the '80s up until his death he led a soulful crossover group (The Generation Band) that often featured his son Trevor Feldman on drums. — *Scott Yanow*

★ **Suite Sixteen** / Aug. 19, 1955-Sep. 21, 1955 / Original Jazz Classics ◆◆◆◆◆
This interesting set (a CD reissue of the original LP) features Victor Feldman shortly before he left England for the US. Feldman, mostly heard on vibes but also making strong appearances on piano and drums, heads several groups filled with English all-stars including such notable musicians as trumpeters Jimmy Deuchar and Dizzy Reece, tenors Ronnie Scott and Tubby Hayes, and pianist Tommy Pollard. The music is boppish with some surprises in the consistently swinging arrangements, giving one a definitive look at Victor Feldman near the beginning of his career. — *Scott Yanow*

With Mallets a Fore Thought / Sep. 1957 / VSOP ◆◆◆◆
This CD reissue of a set from the long-defunct Interlude label brings back an outing by vibraphonist Vic Feldman. Feldman is showcased in a quartet with pianist Carl Perkins, bassist Leroy Vinnegar, and drummer Stan Levey on half of the selections, while the remaining tracks add trombonist Frank Rosolino and tenor saxophonist Harold Land. An obscurity ("Chart of My Heart"), two standards, and four Feldman originals comprise this easily enjoyable and relaxed bop date. — *Scott Yanow*

Latinsville / Mar. 2, 1959-Mar. 20, 1959 / Contemporary ◆◆◆

The Artful Dodger / Jan. 26, 1977 / Concord Jazz ◆◆◆

Maynard Ferguson

b. May 4, 1928, Montreal, Canada
Trumpet / Bop, Hard Bop, Crossover
When he debuted with Stan Kenton's orchestra in 1950, Maynard Ferguson could play higher than any other trumpeter up to that point in jazz history, and he was accurate. Somehow he has kept most of that range through the decades and since the '70s has been one of the most famous musicians in jazz. Never known for his exquisite taste (some of his more commercial efforts are unlistenable), Maynard Ferguson has nevertheless led some important bands and definitely made an impact with his trumpet playing.

After heading his own big band in Montreal, Ferguson came to the US in 1949 with hopes of joining Kenton's orchestra, but that ensemble had just recently broken up. So instead, Ferguson gained experience playing with the big bands of Boyd Raeburn, Jimmy Dorsey, and Charlie Garnet. In 1950 with the formation of Kenton's Innovations Orchestra, Ferguson became a star, playing ridiculous high notes with ease. In 1953 he left Kenton to work in the studios of Los Angeles and three years later led the all-star "Birdland Dreamband." In 1957 he put together a regular big band that lasted until 1965, recorded regularly for Roulette (all of its recordings with that label are on a massive Mosaic box set), and performed some of the finest music of Ferguson's career. Such players as Slide Hampton, Don Ellis, Don Sebesky, Willie Maiden, John Bunch, Joe Zawinul, Joe Farrell, Jaki Byard, Lanny Morgan, Rufus Jones, Bill Berry, and Don Menza were among the more notable sidemen.

After economics forced him to give up the impressive band, Ferguson had a few years in which he was only semiactive in music, spending time in India and eventually forming a new band in England. After moving back to the US, Ferguson in 1974 drifted quickly into commercialism. Young trumpeters in high school and colleges were amazed by his high notes but jazz fans were dismayed by the tasteless recordings which resulted in hit versions of such songs as the themes from *Star Wars* and *Rocky* and much worse. After cutting back on his huge orchestra in the early '80s, Ferguson recorded some bop in a 1983 session, led a funk band called High Voltage during 1987-88, and then returned to jazz with his "Big Bop Nouveau Band," a medium-size outfit with which he still tours the world. Although Ferguson's range finally started to shrink a little in the '90s, he is still an enthusiastic and exciting player —*Scott Yanow*

The Birdland Dream Band / Sep. 7, 1956-Sep. 25, 1956 / Bluebird ✦✦✦✦

★ **The Complete Roulette Maynard Ferguson** / May 6, 1958-Mar. 1962 / Mosaic ✦✦✦✦✦

Trumpeter Maynard Ferguson led his greatest big band during the years that he was signed to Roulette, and all of the music from his 13 Roulette LPs (plus 11 previously unissued selections) are included on this deluxe limited-edition ten-CD box set. Although three of the LPs were originally recorded as dance records (and stick close to the melodies), this box as a whole finds Maynard at his peak and with an orchestra that includes such talented soloists as trombonists Slide Hampton and Don Sebesky (both of whom contributed arrangements), altoist Lanny Morgan, the tenors of Carmen Leggio, Willie Maiden, Joe Farrell and Don Menza, pianists Jaki Byard and Joe Zawinul, and drummer Rufus Jones in addition to the leader. The music is very jazz-oriented and contains more than its share of classic moments, particularly the sessions that resulted in *A Message from Newport* and *Newport Suite*. It's highly recommended. —*Scott Yanow*

Si! Si!: M.F. / 1962 / Roulette ✦✦✦✦

This single CD reissues the contents of two former LPs by the Maynard Ferguson Orchestra: *Si! Si!* and *Maynard '64*. These 16 performances have been reissued by Mosaic in a ten-CD box set, but those listeners who do not have that set should get this one. In addition to the high-note trumpet master, the boppish performances feature such soloists as altoist Lanny Morgan, the tenors of Willie Maiden and Don Menza, and pianist Mike Abene. The arrangements (by Ernie Wilkins, Marty Paich, Don Sebesky, Don Rader, Maiden, Abene, and Menza) took advantage of the band's many strengths and the result is a solid set (actually two) of swinging music. —*Scott Yanow*

Orchestra 1967 / Jun. 8, 1967 / Just a Memory ✦✦✦✦

M.F. Horn / Feb. 1970 / Columbia ✦✦✦

M.F. Horn 2 / Jan. 1972 / Columbia ✦✦

M.F. Horn 3 / Apr. 18, 1973 / Columbia ✦✦

Chameleon / Apr. 1, 1974 & Apr. 4, 1974 / Columbia ✦✦

Live from London / 1993 / Avenue Jazz ✦✦✦✦

Utilizing a 13-piece band that includes ten horns, Maynard Ferguson performs bebop with his Big Bop Nouveau on this CD. All of the music is fairly basic, using common chord changes and charts that leave plenty of room for solos. Ferguson shows at age 65 that he still has most of his outstanding range, and assisted by a trumpet section full of screamers, the performances are boisterous and sometimes a bit bombastic. Chip McNeill takes a passionate soprano solo on "A Night in Tunisia," Matt Wallace has a couple of rewarding spots on tenor, and trumpeter Walter White fares well on "Fox Hunt," but it is the leader who gives this music its main personality. —*Scott Yanow*

Verve Jazz Masters / Verve ✦✦✦

Clare Fischer

b. Oct. 22, 1928, Durand, MI
Piano, Keyboards / Latin Jazz, Hard Bop
Clare Fischer has had a varied career as keyboardist, composer, arranger, and bandleader. The composer of two standards, "Pensativa" and "Morning," Fischer has long had an interest in Latin rhythms. After graduating from Michigan State University he moved to Los Angeles in 1957, working as accompanist and arranger for the Hi-Lo's. He wrote for a 1960 Dizzy Gillespie album (*A Portrait of Duke Ellington*) and recorded bossa nova as early as 1962; that same year he recorded two trio sets, and the following year he led his first big-band date. Fischer, who has alternated between the two formats through the years, has recorded in a wide variety of settings from solo piano to heading a vocal-dominated Latin group Salsa Picante. Based in Los Angeles, Fischer (who is also an effective organist and a strong electric keyboardist) has recorded extensively through the years for such labels as Pacific Jazz/World Pacific, Revelation, Discovery, MPS, and Concord. —*Scott Yanow*

'Twas Only Yesterday / Oct. 1968 / Discovery ✦✦✦

Machacha / May 16, 1979-May 17, 1979 / Discovery ✦✦✦✦

Salsa Picante at its instrumental best. Latin-jazz hots with Rick Zunigar (g), Gary Foster on saxophone and flute, and Alex Acuna and Poncho Sanchez on percussion. —*Michael G. Nastos*

● **Starbright** / Nov. 23, 1982 / Discovery ✦✦✦✦

Memento / 1992 / Discovery ✦✦✦

Just Me: Solo Piano Excursions / Mar. 31, 1995-Apr. 7, 1995 / Concord Jazz ✦✦✦✦

Ella Fitzgerald

b. Apr. 25, 1917, Newport News, VA, d. Jun. 14, 1996
Vocals / Bop, Swing
"The First Lady of Song," Ella Fitzgerald was arguably the finest female jazz singer of all time (although some may vote for Sarah Vaughan or Billie Holiday). Blessed with a beautiful voice and a wide range, Fitzgerald could outswing anyone, was a brilliant scat singer, and had near-perfect elocution; one could always understand the words she sang. The one fault was that since she always sounded so happy to be singing, Fitzgerald did not always dig below the surface of the lyrics she interpreted, and she even made a downbeat song such as "Love for Sale" sound joyous. However, when one evaluates her career on a whole, there is simply no one else in her class.

One could never guess from her singing that Fitzgerald's early days were as grim as Billie Holiday's. Growing up in poverty, Fitzgerald was literally homeless for the year before she got her big break. In 1934 she appeared at the Apollo Theater in Harlem, winning an amateur contest by singing "Judy" in the style of her idol, Connee Boswell. After a short stint with Tiny Bradshaw, Fitzgerald was brought to the attention of Chick Webb by Benny Carter (who was in the audience at the Apollo). Webb, who was not impressed by the 17-year-old's appearance, was reluctantly persuaded to let her sing with his orchestra on a one-nighter. She went over well and soon the drummer recognized her commercial potential. Starting in 1935, Fitzgerald began recording with Webb's Orchestra and by 1937 over half of the band's selections featured her voice. "A-Tisket, A-Tasket" became a huge hit in 1938, and "Undecided" soon followed. During this era Fitzgerald was essentially a pop/swing singer who was best on ballads, while her medium-tempo performances were generally juvenile novelties. She already had a beautiful voice, but did not improvise or scat much; that would develop later. On June 16, 1939 Chick Webb died. It was decided that Fitzgerald would front the orchestra even though she had little to do with the repertoire or hiring or firing the musicians. She retained her popularity, and when she broke up the band in 1941 and went solo, it was not long before her Decca recordings contained more than their share of hits. She was teamed with the Ink Spots, Louis Jordan, and the Delta Rhythm Boys for some bestsellers and in 1946 began working regularly for Norman Granz's Jazz at the Philharmonic. Granz became her manager, although it would be nearly a decade before he could get her on his label. A major change occured in Fitzgerald's singing around this period. She toured with Dizzy Gillespie's big band, adopted bop as part of her style, and started including exciting, scat-filled romps in her set. Her recordings of "Lady Be Good," "How High the Moon," and "Flying Home" during 1945-47 became popular and her stature as a major jazz singer rose as a result. For a time (1948-52) she was married to bassist Ray Brown and used his trio as a backup group. Fitzgerald's series of duets with pianist Ellis Larkins in 1950 (a 1954 encore with Larkins was a successful follow-up) found her interpreting George Gershwin songs, predating her upcoming *Songbook* series.

After appearing in the film *Pete Kelly's Blues* in 1955, Fitzgerald signed with Norman Granz's Verve label, and over the next few years she would record extensive "Songbooks" of the music of Cole Porter, the Gershwins, Rodgers and Hart, Duke Ellington, Harold Arlen, Jerome Kern, and Johnny Mercer. Although (with the exception of the Ellington sets) those were not her most jazz-oriented projects (Fitzgerald stuck mostly to the melody and was generally accompanied by string orchestras), the prestigious projects did a great deal to uplift her stature. At the peak of her powers around 1960, Fitzgerald's hilarious live version of "Mack the Knife" (in which she forgot the words and made up her own) from *Ella in Berlin* is a classic and virtually all of her Verve recordings are worth getting.

Fitzgerald's Capitol and Reprise recordings of 1967-70 are not on the same level as she attempted to "update" her singing by including pop songs such as "Sunny" and "I Heard It Through the Grapevine," sounding quite silly in the process. But Fitzgerald's later years were saved by Norman Granz's decision to form a new label, Pablo. Starting with a Santa Monica Civic concert in 1972 that climaxes with her incredible version of "C Jam Blues" (in which she trades off with and "battles" five classic jazzmen), Fitzgerald was showcased in jazz settings throughout the '70s with the likes of Count Basie, Oscar Peterson, and Joe Pass, among others. Her voice began to fade during this era, and by the '80s her decline due to age was quite noticeable. Troubles with her eyes and heart knocked her out of action for periods of time, although her increasingly rare appearances found Fitzgerald still retaining her sense of swing and joyful style. By 1994 Fitzgerald was in retirement but she remained a household name and dozens of her recordings were easily available on CD. Fitzgerald died in the spring of 1996. —*Scott Yanow*

The Early Years, Pt. 1 / Jun. 12, 1935-Oct. 6, 1938 / GRP ✦✦✦

☆ **75th Birthday Celebration** / May 2, 1938-Aug. 5, 1955 / GRP ✦✦✦✦✦
This attractive two-CD set, released to celebrate Fitzgerald's 75th birthday, is a perfect greatest-hits collection spanning the first half of her very productive career. All 39 songs are winners, highlighted by "A-Tisket, A-Tasket," "Undecided," "Flying Home," "Lady Be Good," "How High the Moon," "Smooth Sailing," "Airmail Special," "Lullaby of Birdland," and "Hard Hearted Hannah." During the period covered by this package, she developed from a fine big-band pop vocalist into the definitive jazz singer, one who could scat and swing with the best musicians. This set is a perfect introduction to her magic. —*Scott Yanow*

Ella: The Legendary Decca Recordings / May 2, 1938-Aug. 5, 1955 / GRP ✦✦✦✦

Ella Fitzgerald 1939 / Feb. 17, 1939-Jun. 29, 1939 / Classics ✦✦✦✦
Unlike GRP, which has merely reissued the "best" of early Ella Fitzgerald domestically, the European Classics label has released all of the great singer's early recordings (from the 1935-41 period) on six CDs. This, the fourth volume, has her final recordings with Chick Webb's orchestra (before the legendary drummer's premature death) and her first after she took control of his big band. Fitzgerald is best on "'Tain't What You Do" and the ballads (particularly "Don't Worry About Me," "Little White Lies," "Stairway to the Stars," and "Out of Nowhere") although she is less memorable on such uptempo novelties as "Chew-Chew-Chew Your Bubble Gum" and "I Want the Waiter with the Water." This CD is well worth acquiring along with the other entries in this definitive series. —*Scott Yanow*

The Early Years, Pt. 2 / Feb. 17, 1939-Jul. 31, 1941 / GRP ✦✦✦✦
GRP on this two-CD set reissues 42 of the 69 recordings that Ella Fitzgerald cut during a two-and-one-half-year period. Not as valuable as the European Classics "complete" series, this set does give one a good introduction to the classic singer's music during a time when she led Chick Webb's orchestra after the drummer's death. Highlights include "Undecided," "Don't Worry About Me," "Stairway to the Stars," "Taking a Chance on Love," "The One I Love," and "Can't Help Lovin' Dat Man"; the medium-tempo novelties are less significant. It is recommended to the more casual collector. —*Scott Yanow*

The War Years / Oct. 6, 1941-Dec. 20, 1947 / GRP/Decca ✦✦✦✦
Covering an important six-year period in Ella Fitzgerald's career, this two-CD set contains some of the highlights of the period as she develops from a top big-band singer into a masterful jazz improviser. Although one wishes that this survey were complete, the 43 selections do feature Fitzgerald in a wide variety of settings, including with small groups, collaborating with the Ink Spots, the Delta Rhythm Boys, Louis Jordan, Louis Armstrong, and fronting various studio groups. Most of her hits from the period are here along with previously unissued alternate takes of "It's Only a Paper Moon," "Flying Home," and two of "How High the Moon," making this a strong introduction to her early years. —*Scott Yanow*

The First Lady of Song / Sep. 18, 1949-Jul. 29, 1966 / Verve ✦✦✦✦
This attractive three-CD set gives listeners an overview of Ella Fitzgerald's Verve recordings, although the inclusion of seven previously unissued cuts (in addition to 44 that are mostly available in more complete form elsewhere) will frustrate some completists. However, the careful selection of representative performances along with the informative and lengthy text makes this highly enjoyable reissue (which captures her in prime form) recommended even to collectors who have most of the singer's albums. —*Scott Yanow*

Pure Ella / Sep. 11, 1950-Mar. 30, 1954 / GRP/Decca ✦✦✦✦
In 1950, six years before her acclaimed *Songbook* series for Verve, Fitzgerald recorded eight George and Ira Gershwin classics in intimate duets with the sensitive and lightly swinging pianist Ellis Larkins. Four years later she recorded a dozen more songs (this time by a variety of composers) with Larkins, and all 20 performances are included on this wonderful CD. Although the emphasis is on ballads and fairly straightforward treatment of the high-quality melodies, she does improvise with subtlety and gives great meaning to the lyrics. The exquisite and very memorable set is highlighted by "But Not for Me," "How Long Has This Been Going On?," "People Will Say We're in Love," "Stardust," and "My Heart Belongs to Daddy." It is highly recommended. —*Scott Yanow*

The Concert Years / Nov. 18, 1953-1983 / Pablo ✦✦✦✦
This four-CD set features highlights from ten concert appearances by Ella Fitzgerald. All of the music (which is taken from a Japanese concert in 1953, collaborations with Duke Ellington in 1966 and 1967, a French concert in 1971, her famous Santa Monica Civic performance of 1972, a gig at Ronnie Scott's in 1974, concerts at the Montreux Jazz Festival in 1975, 1977, and 1979, and a Japanese concert from 1983) has been out previously on Pablo. There are some remarkable moments (particularly 1972's "C Jam Blues" on which she trades off in very humorous fashion with Al Grey, Stan Getz, Harry "Sweets" Edison, Eddie "Lockjaw" Davis, and Roy Eldridge) even if she was starting to decline a bit by the later concerts. Completists will want to get the original sets (all of which are still available) but,

for those wanting a sampler of live Fitzgerald, this attractive set will fit the bill. —*Scott Yanow*

☆ **The Complete Ella Fitzgerald Song Books** / Feb. 7, 1956-Oct. 21, 1964 / Verve ✦✦✦✦✦
With her signing to Verve in 1956, Ella Fitzgerald (under producer Norman Granz's guidance) began a series of *Songbook* projects in which the singer (backed by orchestras) performed the works of various major composers. Her *Cole Porter Song Book* was so well received that it was followed by ones featuring the music of Rodgers And Hart, Duke Ellington (half of which featured his band), Irving Berlin, a massive salute to George and Ira Gershwin, Harold Arlen, Jerome Kern, and Johnny Mercer. This 16-CD box set is not for everyone (due to its cost) and is not the most jazz-oriented of Ella Fitzgerald's recordings (she does not scat and some of the string arrangements weigh the music down a little), but her voice is in peak form, and this was a very classy (and extensive) project. The reissue (which uses miniature reproductions of the original LPs along with a definitive book, all placed in a red box) is a gem, perfectly done. —*Scott Yanow*

For the Love of Ella / Feb. 7, 1956-Jul. 20, 1966 / Verve ✦✦✦

Ella and Louis / Aug. 16, 1956 / Verve ✦✦✦
Ella Fitzgerald and Louis Armstrong make for a charming team on this CD. Accompanied by pianist Oscar Peterson, guitarist Herb Ellis, bassist Ray Brown, and drummer Buddy Rich, Fitzgerald and Armstrong perform 11 standards with joy and swing. There are touches of Satch's trumpet but this is primarily a vocal set with the emphasis on tasteful renditions of ballads. Its follow-up *Ella & Louis Again* is also worth getting. —*Scott Yanow*

Sings the Rodgers & Hart Songbook / Aug. 21, 1956-Aug. 31, 1956 / Verve ✦✦✦

Like Someone in Love / 1957 / Verve ✦✦✦

Ella & Louis Again / Aug. 13, 1957 & Aug. 23, 1957 / Verve ✦✦✦
As with their first full-length meeting on records, *Ella and Louis*, this CD features Ella Fitzgerald and Louis Armstrong swinging their way through a dozen standards. Armstrong plays a bit of trumpet (best on "Stompin' at the Savoy") but the emphasis is on their vocals (which are accompanied by pianist Oscar Peterson, guitarist Herb Ellis, bassist Ray Brown, and drummer Louie Bellson). The results are quite delightful and charming. —*Scott Yanow*

Duke Ellington Songbook, Vol. 2 / Sep. 4, 1957-Oct. 17, 1957 / Verve ✦✦✦

At the Opera House / Sep. 29, 1957 & Oct. 7, 1957 / Verve ✦✦✦

Ella in Rome: The Birthday Concert / Apr. 25, 1958 / Verve ✦✦✦✦
This concert performance finds Ella Fitzgerald celebrating her 40th birthday. A top singer for 23 years at that point, she was at the peak of her powers. Backed by her regular rhythm section (with pianist Lou Levy, bassist Max Bennett, and drummer Gus Johnson), she puts on her usual show of the period, uplifting the ballads and swinging the faster material. Highlights include "St. Louis Blues," "Caravan," "It's All Right with Me," and "I Can't Give You Anything but Love," during which she imitates both Louis Armstrong and Rose Murphy. This set concludes with a jam version of "Stompin' at the Savoy" with the Oscar Peterson Trio and drummer Gus Johnson. —*Scott Yanow*

Ella Swings Lightly / Nov. 22, 1958-Nov. 23, 1958 / Verve ✦✦✦
CD reissue featuring Ella Fitzgerald's flowing vocals and Marty Paich's Dek-tette band backing her. This was among several hit albums that Fitzgerald enjoyed in the '50s, when she was reaching the mass audience cutting pre-rock standards. —*Ron Wynn*

Ella Swings Brightly with Nelson / Jan. 5, 1959-Dec. 27, 1961 / Verve ✦✦✦✦
Nelson Riddle, whose arrangements were an asset on some of Ella Fitzgerald's *Songbook* projects, also made two albums with her during 1961: this one plus *Ella Swings Gently with Nelson*. The singer has rarely sounded better than during this period. For the *Swings Brightly* set (which gets a slight edge over the other one) Fitzgerald sticks mostly to familiar standards and is particularly memorable on "Don't Be That Way," "What Am I Here For," "I'm Gonna Go Fishin'," and "I Won't Dance." Three slightly earlier "bonus" tracks round out this enjoyable big-band effort. —*Scott Yanow*

The Intimate Ella / 1960 / Verve ✦✦✦✦
This is a most unusual Ella Fitzgerald recording, reissued on CD by Verve. Recorded around the time when she performed some of these songs for the film *Let No Man Write My Epitaph*, the masterful singer is heard in duets with pianist Paul Smith interpreting 13 songs (even "I Cried for You," "I Can't Give You Anything but Love," and "Who's Sorry Now") at slow, expressive tempos. Listeners who feel that Ella Fitzgerald was mostly a scat singer who had trouble giving the proper emotional intensity to lyrics will be surprised by this sensitive and often haunting set. —*Scott Yanow*

☆ **The Complete Ella In Berlin** / Feb. 13, 1960 / Verve ✦✦✦✦✦
Ella Fitzgerald was at the peak of her form during her 1960 tour of Europe. Her Berlin concert is most remembered for her hilariously inventive version of "Mack the Knife" during which she forgot the words and substituted ones of her own that somehow fit, amazing herself in the process. In

addition to the original LP program, this CD has two previously unissued titles and a pair of others only briefly released on a very rare LP. With fine support from her quartet (pianist Paul Smith, guitarist Jim Hall, bassist Wilfred Middlebrooks, and drummer Gus Johnson), Fitzgerald is brilliant throughout the well rounded set with highlights including "Misty" (a version very different from Sarah Vaughan's), "The Lady Is a Tramp," "Too Darn Hot," and a scat-filled "How High the Moon." This is essential music. *—Scott Yanow*

The Sings the Harold Arlen Songbook / Aug. 1, 1960-Jan. 16, 1961 / Verve ✦✦✦✦
Of all of her *Songbooks* (which are now available on the remarkable 16-CD set *The Complete Ella Song Books*), the Harold Arlen and Duke Ellington sets are the most jazz-oriented. With perfectly suitable arrangements by Billy May for the big band and occasional strings, she really digs into the 26 Arlen songs, giving her own sympathetic interpretations to such classics as "Blues in the Night," "Stormy Weather," "My Shining Hour," "That Old Black Magic," "Come Rain or Come Shine" "It's Only a Paper Moon," and even "Ding-Dong! The Witch Is Dead." *—Scott Yanow*

Ella Swings Gently with Nelson / Nov. 13, 1961-Apr. 10, 1962 / Verve ✦✦✦

★ **Sings the Jerome Kern Songbook** / Jan. 5, 1963-Jan. 7, 1963 / Verve ✦✦✦✦✦
By 1963, Ella Fitzgerald's *Songbook* series had almost run its course and was becoming much less ambitious in scope. Her Jerome Kern set features her interpretations of 14 songs while backed by an orchestra arranged by Nelson Riddle. Treatments of such classics as "A Fine Romance," "All the Things You Are," and "Yesterdays" are pretty straightforward and would have pleased the composer. All of her songbooks are now included in the massive 16-CD box set *The Complete Ella Fitzgerald Song Books*. *—Scott Yanow*

These Are the Blues / Oct. 28, 1963 / Verve ✦✦✦

Dream Dancing / Jun. 12, 1972 & Feb. 13, 1978 / Pablo ✦✦✦✦
Originally released on Atlantic as *Ella Loves Cole* and then reissued on Pablo with two extra cuts from 1978, this set features the great Ella Fitzgerald (still in excellent form) backed by an orchestra arranged by Nelson Riddle performing an extensive set of Cole Porter songs. Fifteen years earlier Fitzgerald had had great success with her *Cole Porter Songbook* and this date, even with a few hokey arrangements, almost reaches the same level. Trumpeter Harry "Sweets" Edison and pianist Tommy Flanagan are among the supporting cast. Highlights include "I Get a Kick out of You," "I've Got You Under My Skin," "All of You," "My Heart Belongs to Daddy," and "Just One of Those Things." *—Scott Yanow*

Take Love Easy / 1973 / Pablo ✦✦✦

★ **Ella in London** / Apr. 11, 1974 / Pablo ✦✦✦✦✦
This is one of Fitzgerald's most enjoyable recordings from her later years. With pianist Tommy Flanagan, guitarist Joe Pass, bassist Keter Betts, and drummer Bobby Durham serving as a backup group (not a bad band), she swings everything from "Sweet Georgia Brown" and "It Don't Mean a Thing" to "Lemon Drop" and even Carole King's "You've Got a Friend." Her ballad interpretations are only topped by her scatting talents. This set serves as a perfect introduction to the mature Ella Fitzgerald. *—Scott Yanow*

Ella and Oscar Peterson / May 19, 1974 / Pablo ✦✦✦✦
For this Pablo set (reissued on CD), Ella Fitzgerald is heard on half of the program in duets with pianist Oscar Peterson and for the remainder in trios with Peterson and bassist Ray Brown. In general the performances are memorable (particularly "How Long Has This Been Going On," "More than You Know," "Midnight Sun," and "April in Paris") with the emphasis on ballads. Although her voice had slipped a little by this time, the results are still rewarding and swinging. *—Scott Yanow*

At the Montreux Festival / 1975 / Original Jazz Classics ✦✦✦✦
This CD from the 1975 Montreux Jazz Festival has a typical late-period set from Ella Fitzgerald. Backed by the Tommy Flanagan Trio (with bassist Keter Betts and drummer Bobby Durham), she is in fine form on such songs as "Teach Me Tonight," "It's All Right with Me," "How High the Moon," and even "The Girl from Ipanema." This is a good example of Fitzgerald singing in the '70s with some scatting, a few ballads, and lots of swinging. *—Scott Yanow*

Montreux '77 / Jul. 14, 1977 / Original Jazz Classics ✦✦✦

Lady Time / Jun. 19, 1978-Jun. 20, 1978 / Original Jazz Classics ✦✦✦

Love Songs: Best Of Verve Songbooks / Verve ✦✦✦

Tommy Flanagan

b. Mar. 16, 1930, Detroit, MI
Piano / Bop, Hard Bop
Known for his flawless and tasteful playing, Tommy Flanagan long overdue recognition for his talents in the '80s. He played clarinet when he was six and switched to piano five years later. Flanagan was an

important part of the fertile Detroit jazz scene (other than 1951-53 when he was in the Army) until he moved to New York in 1956. He was used for many recordings after his arrival during that era, cut sessions as a leader for New Jazz, Prestige, Savoy, and Moodsville and worked regularly with Oscar Pettiford, J.J. Johnson (1956-58), Harry "Sweets" Edison (1959-60), and Coleman Hawkins (1961). Flanagan was Ella Fitzgerald's regular accompanist during 1963-65 and 1968-78 which resulted in him being underrated as a soloist. However, starting in 1975 he began leading a series of superior record sessions and since leaving Fitzgerald, Flanagan has been in demand as the head of his own trio, consistently admired for his swinging and creative bop-based style. Among the many labels that he has recorded for since 1975 have been Pablo, Enja, Denon, Galaxy, Progressive, Uptown, Timeless, and several European and Japanese companies. *—Scott Yanow*

The Cats, with John Coltrane and Kenny Burrell / Apr. 18, 1957 / Original Jazz Classics ✦✦✦

Jazz . . . Its Magic / Sep. 5, 1957 / Savoy ✦✦✦

In Stockholm 1957 / 1957 / Dragon ✦✦✦✦

The Tommy Flanagan Trio / May 18, 1960 / Prestige ✦✦✦

Montreux 1977 / Jul. 13, 1977 / Original Jazz Classics ✦✦✦✦
This Pablo recording was cut at a time when pianist Tommy Flanagan, due to his long stint with Ella Fitzgerald's backup band, was almost forgotten. The fine trio outing (with bassist Keter Betts and drummer Bobby Durham) has been reissued on CD in the *Original Jazz Classics* series with one track ("Heat Wave") added to the original program. The two ballad medleys are enjoyable, but it is on "Barbados," "Woody'n You," and "Blue Bossa" that Flanagan shows how hard-swinging a pianist he can be. Happily, his solo career really started to take off a few years after this concert appearance. *—Scott Yanow*

● **Thelonica** / Nov. 30, 1982-Dec. 1, 1982 / Enja ✦✦✦✦
Recorded just ten months after Thelonious Monk's death, pianist Tommy Flanagan's tribute features eight of Monk's compositions plus Flanagan's own "Thelonica." Assisted by bassist George Mraz and drummer Art Taylor, Flanagan does not sound at all like Monk but he recaptures his spirit and hints strongly now and then at his style on this fine (and often introspective) outing. *—Scott Yanow*

Jazz Poet / Jan. 17, 1989-Jan. 19, 1989 / Timeless ✦✦✦✦

☆ **Beyond the Blue Bird** / Apr. 29, 1990 & Apr. 30, 1990 / Timeless ✦✦✦✦✦
Veteran pianist Tommy Flanagan, in a quartet with guitarist Kenny Burrell, bassist George Mraz, and drummer Lewis Nash, performs blues, ballads, and some obscurities during one of his most rewarding recordings. Flanagan has never recorded an indifferent album, but this set seems more inspired than most, making it a perfect introduction to this tasteful, swinging, and creative (within the bop mainstream) pianist. *—Scott Yanow*

Let's Play the Music of Thad Jones / Apr. 4, 1993 / Enja ✦✦✦✦
This relatively little-known trio set by pianist Tommy Flanagan (with bassist Jesper Lundgaard and drummer Lewis Nash) is a minor classic. Flanagan performs 11 of cornetist Thad Jones' compositions, the majority of which had never been played by a piano trio before. Easily the best-known selection is "A Child Is Born" with "Mean What You Say," "Three in One," and "Quietude" being the closest of the other songs to being standards. But despite their relative obscurity, this body of work is quite diverse and flexible enough to be covered by other jazz musicians. Congratulations are due to Tommy Flanagan for putting together a consistently swinging and tasteful salute to Thad Jones, a very talented composer. *—Scott Yanow*

Lady Be Good . . . For Ella / Jul. 30, 1993-Jul. 31, 1993 / Verve ✦✦✦✦

Bela Fleck & the Flecktones

b. 1958, New York, NY
Banjo / Bluegrass, Fusion, Post-Bop
Bela Fleck, as leader of the Flecktones, has certainly carved out his own place in the music world. Virtually the only banjoist playing modern music (which includes fusion, advanced jazz, and bluegrass all mixed together), Fleck began playing banjo when he was 15. In 1978 he moved to Boston to play with the Tasty Licks, and in 1979 he recorded his first solo album, *Crossing the Tracks*. During the next few years he co-founded the group Spectrum and played with the New Grass Revival, recording frequently. Then in 1989 Fleck moved away from bluegrass and new acoustic music into jazz with the formation of the Flecktones, which has thus far recorded four sets for Warner Bros. Originally the often-humorous group was a quartet with Howard Levy on harmonica and piano, but Levy's decision to go out on his own made the band a trio with Fleck's powerful banjo interacting with bassist Victor Wooten and the electronic percussion of Roy "Future Man" Wooten. *—Scott Yanow*

Bela Fleck & The Flecktones / 1990 / Warner Bros. ✦✦✦✦
After disbanding New Grass Revival, Bela Fleck began re-creating the role of the banjo in the same way Charlie Parker redefined the role of the saxophone. But Fleck may be the least innovative member of this quartet: Howard Levy gets chromatics from his blues harp, Victor Wooten picks

banjo rolls on his bass, and Roy "Future Man" Wooten plays a Franken-stein-monster drum-machine/guitar synthesizer. For all the flash, there's little pretense; the group's astonishing musicianship keeps an "aw-shucks" accessibility that lets everybody follow the melody while they marvel. —*Brian Mansfield*

★ **Flight of the Cosmic Hippo** / 1991 / Warner Bros. ✦✦✦✦
The Flecktones owe more to bebop than bluegrass, and here the group finally names its style "blu-bop." That's why *Cosmic Hippo* topped the jazz, not the country, chart. The Flecktones continue to make it look easy, adding banjo power chords to "Turtle Rock" and reworking Lennon/McCartney's "Michelle." —*Brian Mansfield*

Three Flew over the Cuckoo's Nest / 1993 / Warner Bros. ✦✦✦

Tales From The Acoustic Planet / 1994 / Warner Bros. ✦✦✦✦

Bob Florence (Robert C. Florence)

b. May 20, 1932, Los Angeles, CA
Piano / Post-Bop
A top arranger influenced by Bill Holman, Bob Florence regularly leads a big band in the Los Angeles area. He worked as a pianist and arranger for Si Zentner's band during 1959-64; his chart on "Up a Lazy River" was a hit in 1960. Florence has worked extensively in the studio and in commercial music (he is the longtime musical director for Julie Andrews) and played with the '80s version of the Dave Pell Octet, but has also led his own orchestra off and on since 1958. That year he recorded an obscure trio date and a couple of big-band albums. His orchestra backed Big Miller in 1961, and there were recordings in 1965 and 1968, but Florence hit his stride in 1979 with a big-band set for Trend. Since then he has recorded fairly regularly for Trend/Discovery, Bosco, USA, and most recently the MAMA Foundation. Florence's arrangements are among the most colorful (and challenging) in jazz. —*Scott Yanow*

State of the Art / 1988 / USA Music Group ✦✦✦✦
Bob Florence Limited Edition. Five standards, four Florence originals. —*Michael G. Nastos*

Treasure Chest / 1990 / USA Music Group ✦✦✦✦

Funupsmanship / 1992 / Mama Foundation ✦✦✦✦
Bob Florence has long been one of the most stimulating arrangers in jazz, and this live set from his big band features some of his most interesting charts. With such soloists as trumpeters Steve Huffsteter and Warren Luening, trombonists Alex Iles, Charlie Loper, and Rick Culver, altoist Lanny Morgan, and the reeds of Kim Richmond, Don Shelton, and Bob Efford (along with the pianist/leader), Florence's dense and often witty ensembles alternate with fine improvisations. Highlights of this consistently exciting set include "Slimehouse" (based on "Limehouse Blues"), "Funupsmanship," "Lester Left Town," and "All Blues." —*Scott Yanow*

★ **With All The Bells And Whistles** / Feb. 20, 1995-Feb. 21, 1995 / MAMA Foundation ✦✦✦✦✦
Arranger/pianist Bob Florence's release for the MAMA Foundation may very well be his finest; it certainly offers a strong sampling of his talents. Four of the ten songs are standards and "Oceanography" is based closely on "How Deep Is the Ocean," but Florence's complex yet logical arrangements make each piece sound like it was written for the band. To name a few examples, "In a Mellow Tone" at times appears to be in two keys at once, "Laura" (normally an emotional ballad) really cooks, and "Teach Me Tonight" is so intense as to be purposely humorous in spots. Among the other highlights of this well conceived release are Don Shelton's clarinet feature on "Shimmer," the competitive interplay between Dick Mitchell and Terry Harrington throughout "Tenors, Anyone?," and the fluency of trombonist Bob McChesney on "In a Mellow Tone." The ensembles are consistently clean, exciting, and remarkably relaxed considering how tricky some of the charts must be. This CD offers modern big-band jazz at its best. —*Scott Yanow*

Ricky Ford

b. Mar. 4, 1954, Boston, MA
Sax (Tenor) / Post-Bop, Hard Bop
An excellent veteran tenor inspired by Dexter Gordon and Sonny Rollins, Ricky Ford was playing creative hard bop several years before Wynton Marsalis, and his talent has been often overlooked. After studying at the New England Conservatory, he recorded in 1974 with Gunther Schuller. After touring with the Duke Ellington Orchestra (under Mercer Ellington's leadership during 1974-76), Ford was with Charles Mingus (1976-77), Dannie Richmond's Quintet (1978-81), Lionel Hampton and Mingus Dynasty (1982); he also played in 1985 with Abdullah Ibrahim. Ricky Ford has recorded as a leader for New World, an excellent string of dates for Muse (1978-89), and more recently for Candid. —*Scott Yanow*

★ **Shorter Ideas** / Aug. 28, 1984 / Muse ✦✦✦✦✦
An inspired idea that works, Ford, who has usually recorded with small groups, here heads an all-star sextet with altoist James Spaulding and trombonist Jimmy Knepper. They perform four Wayne Shorter numbers, a

couple of Ford's originals, and Duke Ellington's "Happy Reunion." Ford takes the lion's share of the solo space and is clearly up to the task, making these sometimes complex compositions seem accessible and logical. Ford has long been underrated (too old to be a Young Lion and too young to be an elder statesman), but based on the evidence of this recording alone, he clearly deserves much greater acclaim. —*Scott Yanow*

Looking Ahead / Feb. 14, 1986-Oct. 9, 1986 / Muse ✦✦✦✦
An outstanding session, with a first-rate supporting cast. —*Ron Wynn*

Saxotic Stomp / Sep. 4, 1987 / Muse ✦✦✦✦
Nice multi-sax outing. CD bonus track. —*Ron Wynn*

Hard Groovin' / Feb. 24, 1989 / Muse ✦✦✦

Manhattan Blues / Mar. 4, 1989 / Candid ✦✦✦✦

Ebony Rhapsody / Jun. 2, 1990 / Candid ✦✦✦✦
A high-level date with Jaki Byard immense on piano. —*Ron Wynn*

Hot Brass / Apr. 30, 1991 / Candid ✦✦✦✦
Nice session matching tenor saxophone standout Ricky Ford with crew of fiery trumpet and trombone players, plus bassist Christian McBride, drummer Carl Allen, and percussionist Danilo Perez. Ford was a young lion back in the '70s, when there was no hype. He's now an experienced, skilled veteran, and teams superbly with trumpeters Lew Soloff and Claudio Roditi and trombonist Steve Turre. —*Ron Wynn*

Jimmy Forrest

b. Jan. 24, 1920, St. Louis, MO, **d.** Aug. 26, 1980, Grand Rapids, MI
Sax (Tenor) / Swing, Early R&B, Groove
A fine all-around tenor player, Jimmy Forrest is best known for recording "Night Train," a song that he "borrowed" from the last part of Duke Ellington's "Happy Go Lucky Local." While in high school in St. Louis, Forrest worked with pianist Eddie Johnson, the legendary Fate Marable, and the Jeter-Pillars Orchestra. In 1938 he went on the road with Don Albert and then was with Jay McShann's Orchestra (1940-42). In New York Forrest played with Andy Kirk (1942-48) and Duke Ellington (1949) before returning to St. Louis. After recording "Night Train," Forrest became a popular attraction and recorded a series of jazz-oriented R&B singles. Among his most important later associations were with Harry "Sweets" Edison (1958-63), Count Basie's Orchestra (1972-77), and Al Grey, with whom he co-led a quintet until his death. Forrest recorded for United (reissued by Delmark), Prestige/New Jazz (1960-62), and Palo Alto (1978). —*Scott Yanow*

★ **Night Train** / Nov. 27, 1951-Sep. 7, 1953 / Delmark ✦✦✦✦✦
This is tremendous early '50s material from Forrest's days on the pioneering United label. The title cut was a huge jukebox and R&B hit. —*Ron Wynn*

Out of the Forrest / Apr. 18, 1961 / Original Jazz Classics ✦✦✦✦
With Joe Zawinul (piano), Tommy Potter (bass), and Clarence Johnston (drums) backing Jimmy Forrest on eight tracks. An honest and rewarding big tenor date with a touch of Lester Young. This was excellent smokey soulful tenor playing probably been overlooked by many. —*Bob Rusch*

Sonny Fortune (Cornelius Fortune)

b. May 19, 1939, Philadelphia, PA
Flute, Sax (Alto), Sax (Tenor) / Post-Bop
Sonny Fortune has continued to grow with time, and in the mid-'90s he is in prime form. Fortune started his career playing in R&B groups in Philadelphia. He moved to New York in 1967 where he worked with Elvin Jones, Mongo Santamaria (1967-70), and McCoy Tyner (1971-73 and occasionally since). After a stint with Buddy Rich, Fortune played quite effectively with Miles Davis (1974-75). His solo albums during the '70s for Horizon and Atlantic were generally unsuccesful mixtures of advanced jazz with funk and pop elements. However, he has cut excellent dates for Konnex (1984, 1991, and 1993) including a well received Monk set, and Fortune has toured in recent times with Nat Adderley (on tenor, an instrument he should play more often) with Elvin Jones' Jazz Machine. —*Scott Yanow*

Long Before Our Mothers Cried / Sep. 8, 1974 & Sep. 15, 1974 / Strata East ✦✦✦

Serengeti Minstrel / Apr. 6, 1977-Apr. 8, 1977 / Atlantic ✦✦✦

★ **Four In One** / Jan. 25, 1993-Jan. 26, 1993 / Blue Note ✦✦✦✦✦

A Better Understanding / Feb. 19, 1995 / Blue Note ✦✦✦✦

Frank Foster

b. Sep. 23, 1928, Cincinnati, OH
Sax (Tenor) / Swing, Hard Bop, Groove
A very talented tenor saxophonist and arranger, Frank Foster has been associated with the Count Basie Orchestra off and on since 1953. Early on he played in Detroit with many talented local players and, after a period in the Army (1951-53), he joined Basie's big band. Well featured on tenor during his Basie years (1953-64), Foster also contributed plenty of arrangements and such originals as "Down for the Count," "Blues Backstage," and

the standard "Shiny Stockings." In the latter half of the '60s Foster was a freelance writer. In addition to playing with Elvin Jones (1970-72) and occasionally with the Thad Jones-Mel Lewis Orchestra, he led his Loud Minority big band. In 1983 Foster co-led a quintet with Frank Wess, and he toured Europe with Jimmy Smith in 1985. Although influenced by John Coltrane in his playing, Foster was able to modify his style when he took over the Count Basie ghost band in 1986, revitalizing it and staying at the helm until 1995. Outside of his Basie dates, Foster has led sessions for Vogue, Blue Note (1954 and 1968), Savoy, Argo, Prestige, Mainstream, Denon, Catalyst, Bee Hive, SteepleChase, Pablo, and Concord. —*Scott Yanow*

Two for the Blues / Oct. 11, 1983 & Oct. 12, 1983 / Original Jazz Classics ✦✦✦✦
Excellent duo set. —*Ron Wynn*

● **Frankly Speaking** / Dec. 1984 / Concord Jazz ✦✦✦✦
One of Foster's many sparkling collaborations with his longtime friend, fellow Basie bandmate Frank Wess. Outstanding rhythm section as well. —*Ron Wynn*

Pete Fountain

b. Jul. 3, 1930, New Orleans, LA
Clarinet / Dixieland
One of the most famous of all New Orleans jazz clarinetists, Pete Fountain has the ability to play songs that he has performed a countless number of times (such as "Basin Street Blues") with so much enthusiasm that one would swear he had just discovered them! His style and most of his repertoire have remained unchanged since the late '50s, yet he never sounds bored. In 1948 Fountain (who is heavily influenced by Benny Goodman and Irving Fazola) was a member of the Junior Dixieland Band, and this was followed by a stint with Phil Zito and an important association with the Basin Street Six (1950-54) with whom the clarinetist made his first recordings. In 1955 Fountain was a member of the Dukes of Dixieland, but his big breakthrough came when he was featured playing a Dixieland number or two on each episode of *The Lawrence Welk Show* during 1957-59. After he left, he moved back to New Orleans, opened his own club, and has played there regularly since. Fountain's finest recordings were a lengthy string for Coral during 1959-65 (they turned commercial for a period after that) although he has made relatively few CDs considering his continuing popularity. —*Scott Yanow*

● **Standing Room Only** / 1965 / Coral ✦✦✦✦
This is one of the best Pete Fountain records, for the clarinetist (who recorded so often with just a rhythm section or very subservient horns) is challenged by the presence of trumpeter Charlie Teagarden, trombonist Bob Havens, and the great tenor Eddie Miller. With drummer Nick Fatool pushing the rhythm section, the band romps through eight standards (highlighted by "Muskrat Ramble," "Struttin' with Some Barbecue," and "You Are My Sunshine") and a memorable four-song "Ramblin' Medley." This LP, as with all of Pete Fountain's valuable output for Coral, has yet to be reissued on CD. —*Scott Yanow*

Live At The Ryman / 1992 / Sacramento ✦✦✦

Cheek to Cheek / May 1993 / Ranwood ✦✦

★ **The Best of Pete Fountain, Vols. 1 & 2** / MCA ✦✦✦✦✦
Good overview of recent cuts. —*Ron Wynn*

Fourplay

Group / Instrumental Pop, Crossover
This all-star group (comprised of keyboardist Bob James, guitarist Lee Ritenour, bassist Nathan East, and drummer Harvey Mason) was formed in 1991 after the quartet all came together on part of James' *Grand Piano Canyon* album. They have since recorded three CDs for Warner Brothers that have all been big-sellers, not surprising considering the popularity of James and Ritenour. The group's music borders on jazz with some strong improvisations mixed with large doses of pop and R&B, about what one would expect from these studio musicians. —*Scott Yanow*

Fourplay / 1991 / Warner Bros. ✦✦
A pleasant fusion effort, it never really lives up to potential possibilities. —*Steve Aldrich*

Between the Sheets / Aug. 17, 1993 / Warner Bros. ✦✦✦

● **Elixir** / 1995 / Warner Bros. ✦✦✦

Panama Francis (David Albert Francis)

b. Dec. 21, 1918, Miami, FL
Drums / Swing, Early R&B
Panama Francis has had a long and versatile career, equally at home in swing and R&B sessions. Playing for church revival meetings were among his earliest gigs, and he also gigged with George Kelly's group the Cavaliers in Florida (1934-38) before moving to New York. The following year he worked with Roy Eldridge (making his recording debut), and this was

followed by a long period at the Savoy with the Lucky Millinder big band (1940-46) and an association with Cab Calloway (1947-52). Francis then became a busy studio drummer, performing anonymously on many pop and rock 'n' roll records. In 1979 when he was in danger of being forgotten, Francis formed the Savoy Sultans, a group based on the small unit that used to play opposite Millinder at the Savoy. The Sultans recorded a steady stream of exciting hot swing records for Black & Blue and Stash during 1979-83. Since that time Panama Francis has continued freelancing, including recording and touring with the Statesmen of Jazz (1994-95). —*Scott Yanow*

Francis & The Savoy Sultans / Jan. 31, 1979 / Classic Jazz ✦✦✦

● **Savoy Sultans** / Jan. 31, 1979-Feb. 11, 1979 / Classic Jazz ✦✦✦✦
Although their recordings do not always show it, the Savoy Sultans in the late '30s were considered one of the hottest small swing groups in existence. Decades later, drummer Panama Francis decided to revive the group's concept by putting together a new *Savoy Sultans*, using occasional alumni but mostly utilizing other surviving veteran players. This classic jazz LP finds the group at its best, cooking on such numbers as "Song of the Islands," "Frenzy," "Little John Special," and "Clap Hands, Here Comes Charlie." With George Kelly contributing the arrangements as well as his tenor, and such other fine soloists as trumpeters Francis Williams and Irv Stokes, altoists Norris Turney and Howard Johnson, and pianist Red Richards, this is a hot band that could outswing the original group. This LP deserves to be reissued on CD. —*Scott Yanow*

Bud Freeman (Lawrence Freeman)

b. Apr. 13, 1906, Chicago, IL, d. Mar. 15, 1991, Chicago, IL
Sax (Tenor) / Dixieland, Swing
When Bud Freeman first matured, his was the only strong alternative approach on the tenor to the harder-toned style of Coleman Hawkins, and he was an inspiration for Lester Young. Freeman, one of the top tenors of the '30s, was also one of the few saxophonists (along with the slightly later Eddie Miller) to be accepted in the Dixieland world and his oddly angular but consistently swinging solos were an asset to a countless number of hot sessions. Freeman, excited (as were the other members of the Austin High School Gang in Chicago) by the music of the New Orleans Rhythm Kings, took up the C-melody sax in 1923, switching to tenor two years later. It took him time to develop his playing, which was still pretty primitive in 1927 when he made his recording debut with the McKenzie-Condon Chicagoans. Freeman moved to New York later that year and worked with Red Nichols' Five Pennies, Roger Wolfe Kahn, Ben Pollack, Joe Venuti, Gene Kardos, and others. He starred on Eddie Condon's memorable 1933 recording "The Eel." After stints with Joe Haymes and Ray Noble, Freeman was a star with Tommy Dorsey's orchestra and Clambake Seven (1936-38) before having a short unhappy stint with Benny Goodman (1938). He led his short-lived but legendary Summe Cum Laude Orchestra (1939-40) which was actually an octet, spent two years in the military, and then from 1945 on alternated between being a bandleader and working with Eddie Condon's freewheeling Chicago jazz groups. Freeman travelled the world, made scores of fine recordings, and stuck to the same basic style that he had developed by the mid-'30s (untouched by a brief period spent studying with Lennie Tristano). Bud Freeman was with the World's Greatest Jazz Band (1968-71), lived in London in the late '70s, and ended up back where he started, in Chicago. He was active into his 80s and a strong sampling of his recordings are currently available on CD. —*Scott Yanow*

● **The Commodore Years (1938-1939)** / Jan. 17, 1938-Jun. 13, 1939 / Commodore ✦✦✦

The All Stars with Shorty Baker / May 13, 1960 / Original Jazz Classics ✦✦✦✦
Tenor sax great Bud Freeman, who is often associated with the Eddie Condon school of Nicksieland, is heard heading an excellent swing quintet for this 1960 studio session. Trumpeter Harold "Shorty" Baker (best known for his periods with Duke Ellington) made too few small-group recordings throughout his life, so this is one of his best. With the often overlooked but virtuosic stride pianist Claude Hopkins heard in the rhythm section along with bassist George Duvivier and drummer J.C. Heard, the group plays superior standards and a couple of originals on this fine swing date. —*Scott Yanow*

● **Something to Remember You By** / Jan. 15, 1962 / Black Lion ✦✦✦✦

Chico Freeman (Earl Lavon Freeman, Jr.)

b. Jul. 17, 1949, Chicago, IL
Sax (Soprano), Sax (Tenor) / Post-Bop
An excellent tenor saxophonist and the son of Von Freeman, Chico Freeman has had a busy and diverse career, with many recordings ranging from advanced hard bop to nearly free avant-garde jazz. He originally played trumpet, not taking up the tenor until he was a junior in college. Freeman graduated from Northwestern University in 1972, played with R&B groups, and joined the AACM. In 1977 he moved to New York where

he worked with Elvin Jones, Sun Ra, Sam Rivers' big band, Jack DeJohnette's Special Edition, and Don Pullen in addition to leading his own groups. He recorded a dozen albums as a leader during 1975-82. Starting in 1984 Freeman has played on a part-time basis with the Leaders, he has recorded on a few occasions with his father, and in 1989 he put together an electric band called Brainstorm. Chico Freeman has recorded through the years as a leader for Dharma, India Navigation, Contemporary, Black Saint, Elektra/Musician, Black Hawk, Palo Alto, Jazz House, and In + Out. —*Scott Yanow*

Beyond the Rain / Jun. 21, 1977-Jun. 23, 1977 / Original Jazz Classics ✦✦✦✦
With the Hilton Ruiz Trio, featuring the compositions of M.R. Abrams and Freeman's hard-charging playing. —*Michael G. Nastos*

● **The Outside Within** / 1978 / India Navigation ✦✦✦✦
A sterling quartet session. —*Ron Wynn*

Peaceful Heart, Gentle Spirit / Mar. 6, 1980-Mar. 7, 1980 / Contemporary ✦✦✦✦
Chico Freeman (a tenor saxophonist who on this date also plays soprano, flute, alto flute, clarinet, and bass clarinet) recorded many sessions in the late '70s and early '80s but this is one of his very best. Utilizing an unusual instrumentation (flutist James Newton, pianist Kenny Kirkland, vibraphonist Jay Hoggard, cello, bass, drums, and two percussionists), Freeman infuses his five challenging—but generally logical—compositions with rich colors and shades. This music is stimulating and represents one of the high points of Freeman's rather streaky career. —*Scott Yanow*

Destiny's Dance / Oct. 29, 1981 / Original Jazz Classics ✦✦✦✦
Chico Freeman established himself in the '70s as one of that decade's finest, most ambitious and exciting saxophone stylists. He continued his impressive playing on this 1981 date, which was recently reissued on CD (no bonus cuts). While it was a short (37 minutes) session, it was distinguished both by superb tenor sax solos and bass clarinet playing from Freeman, and equally distinctive contributions from a great cast. This lineup included trumpeter Wynton Marsalis, then known solely within the jazz world, vibist Bobby Hutcherson, pianist Dennis Moorman, and a rhythm section sparked by bassist Cecil McBee and anchored by drummer Ronnie Burrage and percussionist Paulinho Da Costa. —*Ron Wynn*

Tangents / 1984 / Elektra ✦✦✦
You'll Know When You Get There / Aug. 1988 / Black Saint ✦✦✦
Up and Down / Apr. 26, 1989-Apr. 27, 1989 / Black Saint ✦✦✦
In The Moment / Oct. 15, 1992-Oct. 16, 1992 / Edgetone ✦✦✦

Russ Freeman

b. May 28, 1926
Piano / Cool
Not to be confused with the leader of the Rippingtons, this Russ Freeman is best-known for his work in the West Coast scene of the '50s, most noticeably with the first Chet Baker Quartet. He moved to Los Angeles in the mid-'40s and worked with Howard McGhee, sat in with Charlie Parker, and recorded with Dexter Gordon (1947), Art Pepper, Wardell Gray, the Lighthouse All-Stars, Shorty Rogers, and Baker (1954). Freeman was with Shelly Manne's Men for a long period (1955-66) and toured with Benny Goodman in 1959. After the mid-'60s he appeared less often in jazz settings, (other than a 1978 recording with Art Pepper and a 1982 duet set for Atlas with Shelly Manne), mostly working in the studio; by the mid-'80s he was largely retired. Freeman made records as a leader for Pacific Jazz and Jazz West Coast during 1953-59. His song "The Wind" has been recorded by several other artists including Keith Jarrett. —*Scott Yanow*

● **Trio with Richard Twardzik** / Oct. 27, 1953-Aug. 12, 1957 / Pacific Jazz ✦✦✦✦
This single CD contains 12 performances by pianist Russ Freeman (with either Joe Mondragon or Monty Budwig on bass and drummer Shelly Manne) plus the one regular studio session (eight songs) that the ill-fated pianist Richard Twardzik led (in a trio with bassist Carson Smith and drummer Peter Littman). Due to its rarity, the Twardzik date is more important historically but actually Freeman generally takes solo honors. Fine straightahead music from two of the mid-'50s more promising pianists. —*Scott Yanow*

Von Freeman (Earl Lavon Freeman, Sr.)

b. Oct. 3, 1922, Chicago, IL
Sax (Tenor) / Post-Bop
Veteran tenor Von Freeman is essentially a bop-oriented improviser whose unusual tone (admired by some, disliked by others) is an acquired taste. The father of tenor Chico Freeman and the brother of guitarist George Freeman and drummer Bruz Freeman, Von worked early on with Horace Henderson's orchestra (l940-41), with a Navy band while in the military (1941-45), and with Sun Ra (1948-49). He was in the house band at the Pershing Hotel in Chicago (1946-50) with his brothers Bruz and George, accompanying the many top bop stars who passed through town. Free-

man, who did not record as a leader until 1972 and only three times until 1989, became a local legend, playing with many types of groups in Chicago. He had a quartet with his brothers in the '50s that used Ahmad Jamal and later Andrew Hill as their pianist. Freeman also worked with many AACM musicians (including Muhal Richard Abrams), played with blues bands in the '60s and from the early '70s on has generally led his own groups. Von Freeman has recorded as a leader for Atlantic (1972), Nessa, Daybreak, Columbia (a set with his son Chico in 1981), Southport, and SteepleChase. —*Scott Yanow*

● **Serenade and Blues** / Jun. 11, 1975 / Nessa ✦✦✦✦
It is surprising that Von Freeman's supporters never seem to grasp why the veteran tenor saxophonist has never become all that popular. Freeman has one of the odder tones of any saxophonist and it takes some getting used to. This Nessa release, which finds Freeman joined by pianist John Young, bassist Dave Shipp, and drummer Wilbur Campbell, is as accessible as any of his recordings. Von Freeman performs lengthy versions of two ballads, an original blues, and his theme song "After Dark." —*Scott Yanow*

Walkin' Tuff / Jan. 1991 / Southport ✦✦✦

Bill Frisell

b. Mar. 18, 1951, Baltimore, MD
Guitar / Modern Creative, Early Jazz-Rock
One of the most remarkable guitarists of the '80s and '90s, Bill Frisell gets bizarre (and sometimes humorous) sounds out of his instrument that have not been heard before. Immediately recognizable, Frisell has the ability to sound like a Nashville country session guitarist, a heavy metal specialist, a Jim Hall devotee, and an unusual avant-gardist. After growing up in Denver, he went to Berklee in the mid-'70s, toured England with Mike Gibbs' orchestra (1978), and recorded with Eberhard Weber (1979).
Frisell soon began appearing on many recordings for ECM including dates led by Jan Garbarek and Paul Motian. He had two ECM albums of his own during 1982-84 before forming a quartet with cellist Hank Roberts, bassist Kermit Driscoll, and drummer Joey Baron. Frisell, who has recorded in several piano- bass-less groups with Motian and has been a guest on many other artists' albums, is heard at his best on his own sessions. 1992's *Have a Little Faith* (which ranges from Sousa to Madonna with stops for Aaron Copland, Stephen Foster, and Muddy Waters) is a good place to start! —*Scott Yanow*

Rambler / Aug. 1984 / ECM ✦✦✦✦
This relatively early set from Bill Frisell is a fine showcase for the utterly unique guitarist. Frisell has the ability to play nearly any extroverted style of music and his humor (check out the date's "Music I Heard") is rarely far below the surface. This particular quintet (with trumpeter Kenny Wheeler, tuba player Bob Stewart, electric bassist Jerome Harris, and drummer Paul Motian) is not exactly short of original personalities, and their outing (featuring seven Frisell compositions) is one of the most lively of all the ones in the ECM catalog. —*Scott Yanow*

● **Smash & Scatteration** / Dec. 1984 / Rykodisc ✦✦✦✦
With Vernon Reid (g). This is one of the best '80s guitar duo dates. It has everything from far-out to far-in, and lots in the middle-jazz, rock, blues, and pop. —*Ron Wynn*

Lookout for Hope / Mar. 1987 / ECM ✦✦✦✦
"Country and Eastern" music with Frisell's distinct guitar sound. Constantly challenging listening. —*Michael G. Nastos*

Works / 1989 / ECM ✦✦✦
Smash & Scatteration / 1989 / Rykodisc ✦✦✦
Before We Were Born / Aug. 1989-Sep. 1988 / Elektra ✦✦✦
Where in the World? / 1991 / Elektra ✦✦✦

★ **Have a Little Faith** / Mar. 1992 / Elektra/Nonesuch ✦✦✦✦✦
Bill Frisell has long been one of the most unique guitarists around. Able to switch on a moment's notice from sounding like a Nashville studio player to heavy metal, several styles of jazz, and just pure noise, Frisell can get a remarkable variety of sounds and tones out of his instrument. This set features Frisell in a quintet with Don Byron (on clarinet and bass clarinet), Guy Klucevsek on accordion, bassist Kermit Driscoll, and drummer Joey Baron. To call the repertoire wide-ranging would be an understatement. In addition to eight melodies from Aaron Copland's *Billy the Kid*, Frisell and company explore (and often re-invent) pieces written by Charles Ives, Bob Dylan, Muddy Waters, Madonna, Sonny Rollins, Stephen Foster, and John Philip Sousa. This is one of the most inventive recordings of the '90s and should delight most listeners from any genre. —*Scott Yanow*

This Land / 1994 / Elektra ✦✦✦

David Frishberg

b. Mar. 23, 1933, St. Paul, MN
Piano, Vocals / Bop, Swing
Arguably the top living lyricist, Dave Frishberg has written more than his

share of witty (yet insightful) classics including "I'm Hip," "Peel Me a Grape," "Dear Bix," "The Underdog," "Saratoga Hunch," "Slappin' the Cakes on Me," "Z's," "My Attorney Bernie," "Blizzard of Lies," "Another Song About Paris," "You Are There," "El Cajon," "Can't Take You Nowhere," and "Let's Eat Home." A fine swing pianist and a world-weary sounding vocalist, the multi-talented Dave Frishberg moved to New York in 1957. He worked early on as a pianist with Carmen McRae, Kai Winding, Gene Krupa (1960-63), Wild Bill Davison, Bud Freeman, Ben Webster, the Al Cohn-Zoot Sims Quintet, and Bobby Hackett, among others and cut an album with Jimmy Rushing. He recorded a commercial record for CTI (1968) that generated a surprise hit in "Van Lingle Mungo." However, it was not until Frishberg moved to the West Coast (1971) and started recording for the Concord label (1977) as a vocalist/pianist that he began to make a big impression. Dave Frishberg has since cut albums for Omnisound, Fantasy, Bloomdido, and a purely instrumental duet set with Dixieland trumpeter Jim Goodwin (1992) for Arbors. Many of his originals have been recorded by other vocalists. —*Scott Yanow*

★ **Getting Some Fun out of Life** / Jan. 25, 1977-Jan. 26, 1977 / Concord Jazz ◆◆◆◆◆

Dave Frishberg Classics / Apr. 29, 1981-Dec. 1982 / Concord Jazz ◆◆◆◆
This hits collection reissued almost all of his most well known tunes. A must-buy. —*Michael G. Nastos*

☆ **Live at Vine Street** / Jan. 1984 / Original Jazz Classics ◆◆◆◆◆
Arguably the greatest living lyricist, Dave Frishberg sings and plays piano on this very enjoyable solo disc. His nine originals include such memorable (and humorous) tunes as "El Cajon" (a Johnny Mandel melody), "The Dear Departed Past," and "Blizzard of Lies." In addition, Frishberg plays a lengthy medley of Johnny Hodges-associated songs. This witty set is easily recommended. —*Scott Yanow*

Can't Take You Nowhere / Sep. 21, 1986 / Fantasy ◆◆◆◆
A good live set, with some humor. —*Ron Wynn*

Let's Eat Home / Aug. 1989 / Concord Jazz ◆◆◆◆
Good rhythm section and material, plus acceptable vocals. CD bonus cut. —*Ron Wynn*

Where You At? / Mar. 4, 1991 / Bloomdido ◆◆◆

Double Play / Oct. 3, 1992-Oct. 4, 1992 / Arbors ◆◆◆◆
Dave Frishberg, best known for his impressive abilities as a lyricist and vocalist, sticks exclusively to instrumentals on this enjoyable disc. Frishberg the pianist is teamed with cornetist Jim Goodwin on a duet set comprised of 17 trad and swing classics that mostly date from the '20s and '30s. To their credit the duo constantly walk a musical tightrope, taking chances within the idiom and not being afraid to make mistakes; neither musician felt that the music should be edited afterward. The result is colorful classic jazz interpreted by two strong stylists who, while paying tribute to their predecessors, infuse the music with their own personalities. —*Scott Yanow*

Tony Fruscella

b. Feb. 4, 1927, Orangeburg, NY, **d.** Aug. 14, 1969, New York, NY
Trumpet / Cool
A promising trumpeter whose career never had a chance to flourish due to a drug problem, Tony Fruscella had a style close to that of Chet Baker's, though he developed it independently. He played in an Army band in the '50s, then worked with Lester Young and Gerry Mulligan, and performed and recorded with Stan Getz in 1955. He did some recordings heading his own group that same year, then was basically finished as a prime musician due to his habit. Fruscella did occasional dates with fellow trumpeter Don Joseph but was dead in 1969 at the age of 42. His 1955 album *I'll Be Seeing You* on Atlantic was an example of his potential. A Fruscella session is available on CD released by Cool N' Blue, *Tony's Blues*, issued in 1992. Fruscella's also featured on a Getz Verve anthology. —*Ron Wynn and Michael Erlewine*

Debut / Dec. 10, 1948-1953 / Spotlite ◆◆◆

Fru 'n Brew / 1953 / Spotlite ◆◆◆

● **Tony Fruscella [Jazzlore # 25]** / 1955 / Atlantic ◆◆◆◆

Curtis Fuller

b. Dec. 15, 1934, Detroit, MI
Trombone / Hard Bop
Curtis Fuller belongs in the select circle with J.J. Johnson, Kai Winding, and a few others who make the trombone sound fluid and inviting rather than awkward. His ability to make wide octave leaps and play whiplash phrases in a relaxed, casual manner is a testament to his skill. Fuller's solos and phrases are often ambitious and creative, and he's worked in several fine bands and participated in numerous great sessions. Fuller studied music in high school, then began developing his skills in an Army band, where he played with Cannonball Adderley. He worked in Detroit with Kenny Burrell and Yusef Lateef, then moved to New York. Fuller made his recording debut as a leader on Transition in 1955 and recorded in the late '50s for

Blue Note, Prestige, United Artists, and Savoy. He was a charter member of the Jazztet with Benny Golson and Art Farmer in 1959, then played in Art Blakey's Jazz Messengers from 1961 to 1965. There were additional recording dates for Warwick, Smash/Trip, Epic, and Impulse in the '60s. Fuller toured Europe with Dizzy Gillespie's big band in 1968, then did several sessions in New York. During the '70s, he experimented for a time playing hard-bop arrangements in a band featuring electronic instruments, heading a group with guitarist Bill Washer and Stanley Clarke. He concluded that phase with the 1973 album *Crankin'.* Fuller toured with the Count Basie Band from 1975 to 1977, and did dates for Mainstream, Timeless, and Bee Hive. He co-led the quintet Giant Bones with Winding in 1979 and 1980, and played with Art Blakey, Cedar Walton, and Benny Golson in the late '70s and early '80s. During the '80s, Fuller toured Europe regularly with the Timeless All-Stars, and performed and recorded with the revamped Jazztet. There are a few Fuller sessions available on CD, mostly early dates. —*Ron Wynn*

New Trombone / May 11, 1957 / Original Jazz Classics ◆◆◆

Curtis Fuller with Red Garland / May 14, 1957 / Original Jazz Classics ◆◆◆◆
This CD reissue features trombonist Curtis Fuller in a quintet with altoist Sonny Red, pianist Red Garland, bassist Paul Chambers, and drummer Louis Hayes performing a pair of originals, two blues, and a couple of ballad features. Red is outstanding on "Moonlight Becomes You" (one of his finest recordings), while Fuller does a fine job on "Stormy Weather." Even with the new material, this set has a feel of a jam session; the blend between the trombone and the alto is particularly appealing. Despite the overly critical liner notes (written in 1962), this is an excellent hard-bop oriented date. —*Scott Yanow*

Blues-Ette / May 21, 1959 / Savoy Jazz ◆◆◆◆
A powerhouse session with Fuller leading a stalwart group. Benny Golson (ts) and Tommy Flanagan (p) are sublime. —*Ron Wynn*

● **All-Star Sextets** / Aug. 25, 1959 & Dec. 17, 1959 / Savoy ◆◆◆◆
Combos led by trombonist Fuller, members of the Jazztet and Coltrane ensembles. Essential jazz/post-bop. Seminal material from a brilliant trombonist. Features Lee Morgan (tpt), Wynton Kelly (p), McCoy Tyner (p), and others. —*Ron Wynn*

★ **Crankin' and Smokin'** / 1973 & 1974 / Mainstream ◆◆◆◆◆
At the time, this was his most adventurous playing in quite a while. —*Ron Wynn*

Jazz . . . It's Magic / Nov. 12, 1992 / Savoy Jazz ◆◆◆

Kenny G. (Kenneth Gorelick)

b. 1959, Seattle, WA
Sax (Soprano) / Instrumental Pop, Crossover
During the '80s, Kenny G. became the biggest-selling saxophonist of all time. While he did have several pop hits, he carved out a niche in adult contemporary and lite radio stations with his light jazz/pop-fusion instrumentals. Kenny G.'s soprano sax style is smooth and fluid, spinning out airy melodic tunes like the Top Five hit "Songbird." Such polished confections have made the saxophonist a commercial heavy-hitter.

Born Kenneth Gorelick, Kenny G. began playing saxophone professionally with Barry White's Love Unlimited Orchestra in 1976 when he was 17. Shortly afterward, he left the group to study accounting at the University of Washington. However, he didn't give up music—he recorded with the Seattle funk band Cold, Bold & Together and frequently played in supporting bands for major artists. Once he graduated from college, he became part of the Jeff Lorber Fusion, recording an album with the combo. That appearance led to a solo deal with Arista; he released his self-titled debut album in 1982.

Kenny G.'s first few records find him experimenting with both jazz and R&B, without developing a real feel for either genre. With 1986's *Duotones* he landed on the formula that would make him an international multimillion seller. Propelled by the No. 4 hit single "Songbird," the record sold over three million copies. In addition to establishing his stardom, the album led to work with Aretha Franklin, Whitney Houston, and Natalie Cole, among others.

Every subsequent Kenny G. album has sold at least two million copies in the US, while shifting impressive numbers in other countries as well; 1992's *Breathless* has sold over eight million copies in the US alone. Although he has been an unqualified commercial success, Kenny G. has suffered at the hands of critics, who have called his music both lightweight and worthless. However, Kenny G.'s music is not jazz, nor does he claim that it is jazz. There are elements of jazz in his music, as well as R&B, funk, and pop. In the end, it is smooth, polished pop music and it rarely has pretensions of being anything more than that. —*Stephen Thomas Erlewine*

Kenny G. / 1982 / Arista ◆◆
Although he hadn't perfected his stylish amalgam of pop melodies and jazz improvisation, Kenny G.'s first album is worthwhile to his fans, simply as a document of his formative era. Parts of *Kenny G.* may be rough, but it is sporadically enjoyable. —*Stephen Thomas Erlewine*

G Force / 1983 / Arista ◆◆

Gravity / 1985 / Arista ◆◆

● **Duotones** / 1986 / Arista ◆◆◆◆
Kenny G's breakthrough effort featured the hit "Songbird," which is the definitive example of the saxophonist's smooth, lyrical playing; the rest of the album is nearly as good, highlighting his melodic, jazzy pop. —*Stephen Thomas Erlewine*

Silhouette / 1988 / Arista ◆◆◆◆
Kenny G was at the top of his form with *Silhouette*, the follow-up to his breakthrough *Duotones*, turning in a set of smooth, melodic sax that cemented his position as America's favorite pop instrumentalist. —*Stephen Thomas Erlewine*

Breathless / Oct. 20, 1992 / Arista ◆◆◆

Miracles / 1994 / Arista ◆◆◆◆
Kenny G. chills out on nine holiday standards plus two originals of easy listening soprano saxophone instrumentals. —*Roch Parisien*

Hal Galper

b. Apr. 18, 1938, Salem, MA
Piano / Post-Bop
An excellent if generally overlooked advanced hard-bop pianist, Hal Galper studied at Berklee (1955-58) and worked in many groups including Chet Baker's, Stan Getz's, the Brecker Brothers, Bobby Hutcherson's, and with such singers as Joe Williams, Chris Connor, and Anita O'Day. He played electric piano (an instrument he has since dropped) with the Cannonball Adderley Quintet during its last years (1973-75) and spent time playing with Lee Konitz and John Scofield. Galper, who has recorded as a leader for Mainstream, SteepleChase, Enja, Concord (including a solo set at Maybeck Recital Hall), and Blackhawk, gained his greatest notoriety for being pianist with Phil Woods' quartet/quintet from 1981 to 1990. —*Scott Yanow*

★ **Speak with a Single Voice** / Feb. 1978 / Enja ◆◆◆◆◆
First quintet recording with the Brecker Brothers, at Rosie's in New Orleans. Essential. —*Michael G. Nastos*

Live at Maybeck Recital Hall, Vol. 6 / Jul. 1990 / Concord Jazz ◆◆◆◆
First-rate, stately solo piano. —*Ron Wynn*

Invitation to a Concert / Nov. 18, 1990 / Concord Jazz ◆◆◆◆
Hal Galper Trio. This is one of his most recent. The pianist dominates the session. —*Ron Wynn*

Hal Galper Quartet / Jun. 23, 1992 / Enja ◆◆◆◆

Tippin' / Nov. 16, 1992 / Concord Jazz ◆◆◆

Just Us / Sep. 20, 1993 / Enja ◆◆◆

Rebop / 1995 / Enja ◆◆◆

Jan Garbarek

b. Mar. 4, 1947, Mysen, Norway
Sax (Soprano), Sax (Tenor) / New Age, Post-Bop
The Norwegian saxophonist Jan Garbarek's icy tone, liberal use of space, and long tones has long been perfect for the ECM sound, and as a result he is on many recordings for that label, both as a leader and as a sideman. He had won a competition for amateur jazz players in 1962, leading to his first gigs. Garbarek worked steadily in Norway throughout the remainder of the '60s, usually as a leader, but also for four years with George Russell (who was in Scandinavia for a long stretch). Garbarek began recording for ECM in the early '70s, and although he had opportunities to play with Chick Corea and Don Cherry, his association with Keith Jarrett's European quartet in the mid-'70s made him famous, resulting in the classic recordings *My Song* and *Belonging*. In the '80s Garbarek's groups included bassist Eberhard Weber and at various times guitarists Bill Frisell and David Torn. Garbarek, whose sound is virtually unchanged since the '70s, collaborated with the Hilliard Ensemble in 1993 (a vocal quartet singing Renaissance music) and the result was surprisingly popular. —*Scott Yanow*

The Esoteric Circle / 1969 / Freedom ◆◆◆◆
The 1969 album that introduced the stark, careening soprano sax of Norway's Jan Garbarek to American audiences. Composer and theorist George Russell helped get Garbarek entry to American recording studios, and the rest is history. —*Ron Wynn*

Afric Pepperbird / Sep. 22, 1970-Sep. 23, 1970 / ECM ◆◆◆◆
Jan Garbarek Group. His best, most exciting date from 1970. —*Ron Wynn*

Triptykon / Nov. 8, 1972 / ECM ◆◆◆

● **Witchi-Tai-To** / Nov. 27, 1973-Nov. 28, 1973 / ECM ◆◆◆◆
An album that defined the ECM Records sound. —*Michael G. Nastos*

Folk Songs / Nov. 1979 / ECM ◆◆◆

Paths, Prints / Dec. 1981 / ECM ◆◆◆

I Took up the Runes / Aug. 1990 / ECM ◆◆◆

Star / Jan. 1991 / ECM ◆◆◆◆

Places / Feb. 4, 1991 / ECM ◆◆◆

Madar / Aug. 1992 / ECM ◆◆◆

Twelve Moons / Sep. 1992 / ECM ◆◆

Officium / Sep. 1993 / ECM ◆◆

Red Garland (William M. Garland)

b. May 13, 1923, Dallas, TX, **d.** Apr. 23, 1984, Dallas, TX
Piano / Hard Bop
Red Garland mixed together the usual influences of his generation (Nat Cole, Bud Powell, and Ahmad Jamal) into his own distinctive approach; Garland's block chords themselves became influential on the players of the '60s. He started out playing clarinet and alto, switching to piano when he was 18. During 1946-55 he worked steadily in New York and Philadelphia, backing such major players as Charlie Parker, Coleman Hawkins, Lester Young, and Roy Eldridge but still remaining fairly obscure. That changed when he became a member of the classic Miles Davis Quintet (1955-58), heading a rhythm section that also included Paul Chambers and Philly Joe Jones. After leaving Davis, Garland had his own popular trio and recorded very frequently for Prestige, Jazzland, and Moodsville from 1956 to 1962 (the majority of which are currently available in the Original Jazz Classics series). The pianist eventually returned to Texas and was in semiretirement but came back gradually in the '70s, recording for MPS (1971) and Galaxy (1977-79) before retiring again. —*Scott Yanow*

Garland of Red / Aug. 17, 1956 / Original Jazz Classics ◆◆◆◆
Thirty-three years old at the time of his first recording as a leader, pianist Red Garland already had his distinctive style fully formed and had been with the Miles Davis Quintet for a year. With the assistance of bassist Paul Chambers (also in Davis' group) and drummer Art Taylor, Garland is in superior form on six standards, Charlie Parker's "Constellation" (during which he shows that he could sound relaxed at the fastest tempos), and his own "Blue Red." Red Garland recorded frequently during the 1956-62 period and virtually all of his trio recordings are consistently enjoyable, this one being no exception. —*Scott Yanow*

Red Garland's Piano / Dec. 14, 1956 & Mar. 22, 1957 / Original Jazz Classics ◆◆◆

Groovy / May 24, 1957 / Original Jazz Classics ◆◆◆◆
As the liner notes properly state, this CD (Red Garland's fourth as a leader for the Prestige label) has "jazz standards, ballad standards, blues ballads, and just plain blues." The pianist's trio (with bassist Paul Chambers and drummer Art Taylor) swings such numbers as "C Jam Blues," "Will You Still Be Mine" (the latter from the Ahmad Jamal songbook), and "What Can I Say After I Say I'm Sorry" with spirit and subtle invention. All of Red Garland's Prestige recordings are worth getting. —*Scott Yanow*

All Mornin' Long / Nov. 15, 1957 / Original Jazz Classics ◆◆◆
Loose, with elements of funk and soul-jazz, plus the usual excellence from Donald Byrd (tpt), Coltrane (ts), and Garland. —*Ron Wynn*

Soul Junction / Nov. 15, 1957 / Original Jazz Classics ◆◆◆◆
Quintet. More Donald Byrd (tpt), John Coltrane (ts), Red Garland. Solos from Coltrane and Byrd are better than on *High Pressure*. —*Ron Wynn*

Dig It! / Dec. 13, 1957-Feb. 7, 1958 / Original Jazz Classics ◆◆◆

Rojo / Aug. 22, 1958 / Original Jazz Classics ◆◆◆◆
Pianist Red Garland recorded frequently with trios for Prestige during the second half of the '50s. For this set (reissued on CD), Garland, bassist George Joyner, and drummer Charlie Persip are joined by Ray Barretto on congas, and the emphasis is on forceful swinging. Garland takes such ballads as "We Kiss in a Shadow" and "You Better Go Now" at faster than expected tempos. "Ralph J. Gleason Blues" and the Latin feel of "Rojo" are among the highlights of this enjoyable disc. —*Scott Yanow*

All Kinds Of Weather / Nov. 27, 1958 / Original Jazz Classics ◆◆◆

★ **Red Garland at the Prelude, Vol. 1** / Oct. 1959 / Prestige ◆◆◆◆◆
Originally released as two LPs (*Red Garland at the Prelude* and *Red Garland/Live!*), this single CD (which has around 77 minutes of music) features a particularly strong trio set by the pianist, bassist Jimmy Rowser, and drummer Specs Wright. Garland mostly sticks to standards, and the highlights include "Perdido," "Bye Bye Blackbird" (which is reminiscent of the famous Miles Davis version), and two versions of "One O'Clock Jump." Straightahead jazz fans should get this one. —*Scott Yanow*

Bright and Breezy / Jul. 19, 1961 / Original Jazz Classics ◆◆◆

When There Are Grey Skies / Oct. 9, 1962 / Original Jazz Classics ◆◆◆◆

Red Alert / Dec. 2, 1977 / Original Jazz Classics ◆◆◆◆
A 1991 issue of an excellent album date with superb Garland piano and top contributions by Nat Adderley (cnt), Harold Land (ts), and Ira Sullivan (tpt). —*Ron Wynn*

Crossings / Dec. 1977 / Original Jazz Classics ◆◆◆

Erroll Garner

b. Jun. 15, 1921, Pittsburgh, PA, **d.** Jan. 2, 1977, Los Angeles, CA
Piano / Bop, Swing
One of the most distinctive of all pianists, Erroll Garner proved that it

was possible to be a sophisticated player without knowing how to read music, that a creative jazz musician can be very popular without watering down his music, and that it is possible to remain an enthusiastic player without changing one's style once it is formed. A brilliant virtuoso who sounded unlike anyone else, Erroll Garner on medium-tempo pieces often stated the beat with his left hand like a rhythm guitar while his right played chords slightly behind the beat, creating a memorable effect. His playful free-form introductions (which forced his sidemen to really listen), his ability to play stunning runs without once glancing at the keyboard, his grunting, and the pure joy that he displayed while performing were also part of the Erroll Garner magic. Garner, whose older brother Linton is also a fine pianist, appeared on the radio with the Kan-D-Kids at the age of ten. After working locally in Pittsburgh, he moved to New York in 1944 and worked with Slam Stewart's trio from 1944 to 1945 before going out on his own. By 1946 Garner had his sound together, and when he backed Charlie Parker on his famous "Cool Blues" session of 1947, the pianist was already an obvious giant. His unclassifiable style had an orchestral approach straight from the swing era but was open to the innovations of bop. From the early '50s Garner's accessible style became very popular, and he never seemed to have an off day up until his forced retirement (due to illness) in early 1975. His composition "Misty" became a standard. Garner, who had the ability to sit at the piano without prior planning and record three albums in one day (all colorful first takes), made many records throughout his career for such companies as Savoy, Mercury, RCA, Dial, Columbia, EmArcy, ABC-Paramount, MGM, Reprise, and his own Octave label. —*Scott Yanow*

The Elf / Sep. 25, 1945-Mar. 29, 1949 / Savoy ✦✦✦

Long Ago and Far Away / Jun. 28, 1950-Jan. 11, 1951 / Columbia ✦✦✦
This is great Garner. Unfortunately, the remastering is not as great. —*Michael Erlewine*

Too Marvelous for Words, Vol. 3 / May 26, 1954 / EmArcy ✦✦✦✦
The third in the Polygram series of overviews. Plenty of majestic performances. —*Ron Wynn*

Mambo Moves Garner / Jul. 27, 1954 / Mercury ✦✦✦✦
For this lengthy session, pianist Erroll Garner added a conga player (Candido) to his trio (which includes bassist Wyatt Ruther and drummer Eugene Heard) for the first time. Throughout the remainder of his career he would occasionally play in the Latin idiom. This CD reissue (which adds two songs from the same session to the original LP program) finds the pianist in typically enthusiastic form and the highlights include "Mambo Garner," "Night and Day," "Cherokee," and "Sweet Sue." —*Scott Yanow*

The Original Misty / Jul. 27, 1954-Mar. 14, 1955 / EmArcy ✦✦✦✦
This is a reissue of the first Garner version of Misty made in the early '50s. —*Ron Wynn*

Solitaire / Mar. 14, 1955 / Mercury ✦✦✦

★ **Concert by the Sea** / Sep. 19, 1955 / Columbia ✦✦✦✦✦
Concert by the Sea was arguably the finest record pianist Erroll Garner ever made, and he made many—a few outstanding—good recordings. But this live recording with his trio (Eddie Calhoun, bass; Denzil Best, drums) presented a typical Garner program; it was a mixture of originals, show biz, and pop standards infused with his unique delivery and enthusiasm. The rhythms and brilliant use of tension and release was perfectly captured. And while for many jazz listeners Garner's deliberate structures were too orchestrated, there was an equal spontaneity in the propulsion of these orchestrations that swung as well as anything. —*Bob Rusch, Cadence*

Dancing on the Ceiling / Jun. 1, 1961-Aug. 19, 1965 / EmArcy ✦✦✦✦
The great pianist Erroll Garner is heard on these 11 selections, happily jamming standards with bassist Eddie Calhoun and drummer Kelly Martin. One number is from 1964 and another from a year later, but the remainder was performed in 1961; all of the selections were previously unreleased. The music is marvelous and sometimes miraculous, with Garner's distinctive style heard at its best throughout. —*Scott Yanow*

Dreamstreet & One World Concert / 1961 & 1963 / Telarc ✦✦✦✦

Magician & Gershwin And Kern / 1974-1976 / Telac ✦✦✦

Kenny Garrett

b. Oct. 9, 1960, Detroit, MI
Sax (Alto) / Post-Bop
Kenny Garrett was one of the last significant graduates of Miles Davis' groups and is one of the potential greats in jazz. He started early on playing in Detroit with Marcus Belgrave and toured with the Mercer Ellington Orchestra before moving to New York in 1980. He made his debut recording for Criss Cross (1984) and was part of the group Out of the Blue before joining Davis for the trumpeter's last few years. Garrett recorded an obscure session for Paddlewheel (1988) and the weak *Prisoner of Love* (1989) and the recommended *African Exchange Student* (1990) as a leader for Atlantic. Since Miles Davis' death, Garrett has led his own

groups and recorded for Warner Bros., justifying Davis' faith in him. —*Scott Yanow*

Black Hope / 1992 / Warner Bros. ✦✦✦✦
Alto saxophonist Kenny Garrett hasn't been as heavily publicized as his fellow young lions, but he can play with as much authority, conviction, and sheer energy as anyone. Only some uneven material keeps his 1992 album from being exceptional, and even on the weak songs, Garrett's playing forces you to pay attention. —*Ron Wynn*

★ **Triology** / 1995 / Warner Bros. ✦✦✦✦✦

Charles Gayle

b. 1939, Buffalo, NY
Sax (Tenor) / Free Jazz
The logical successor to Albert Ayler (circa 1965), Charles Gayle is a high-energy player whose improvisations are filled with extreme emotions and speechlike screams. He did not emerge in the avant-garde scene until the mid-'80s, making his recording debut with three albums for Silkheart in 1988 that were cut within a five-day period (April 10-14). Gayle, who recorded frequently for the Knitting Factory label starting in 1992 (he has also made CDs for Black Saint and Victor), is a ferocious tenor player who in recent times has also been playing bass clarinet and fairly basic piano in addition to taking some eccentric vocals full of strange right-wing preaching. Charles Gayle is certainly a talent not to be taken lightly! —*Scott Yanow*

★ **Repent** / 1992 / Knitting Factory ✦✦✦✦
There is absolutely no one currently playing tenor (or any other saxophone) coming close to making the kind of music created by Charles Gayle. While it's reminiscent of Albert Ayler's energetic, twisting '60s free dates, Gayle's saxophone acrobatics and stamina are astonishing. This two-song CD was recorded live and features one number that runs 23 minutes; it's the short tune. "Jesus Christ and Scripture," the second piece, proceeds for over 50 minutes, much of that featuring Gayle's honks, bleats, turnarounds, moans, and anguished cries on tenor. After listening closely to this disc, its lack of repetition and gimmickry is commendable. It's certainly not for all (or even most tastes), but those who listen fairly and intently to Charles Gayle will be rewarded. —*Ron Wynn*

More Live / 1993 / Knitting Factory ✦✦✦✦
Tenor saxophonist Charles Gayle plays with such fury and intensity that it seems he won't make it through the performances featured on these two discs. They spotlight his quartet during concerts. Hearing Gayle's overtones, screams, and blistering solos, backed by equally spirited playing from bassists Vattel Cherry and William Parker, and either Michael Wimberly or Marc Edwards on drums, it's easy to forget you're hearing it as they played it, with little pacing or variance in volume. It's impossible not to remember the '60s and '70s free and loft jazz schools, but it's also appropriate to emphasize that Gayle doesn't sound like anyone else currently active and deserves significant attention beyond tiny jazz publications and sympathetic, but small, audiences. —*Ron Wynn*

Translation / Jan. 21, 1993-Jan. 22, 1993 / Silkheart ✦✦✦✦

Raining Fire / Jan. 21, 1993-Jan. 22, 1993 / Silkheart ✦✦✦✦

Consecration / Apr. 17, 1993-Apr. 18, 1993 / Black Saint ✦✦✦

Kingdom Come / 1994 / Knitting Factory ✦✦✦

Herb Geller

b. Nov. 2, 1928, Los Angeles, CA
Sax (Alto), Sax (Soprano) / Bop, Hard Bop
Herb Geller is a survivor of the Los Angeles jazz scene of the '50s who is playing better than ever in the mid-'90s. Geller played in 1946 with Joe Venuti's Orchestra and in 1949 he traveled to New York to play with Claude Thornhill. In 1951 he moved back to Los Angeles and married the excellent bop pianist Lorraine Walsh. Geller was a fixture in Los Angeles, playing with Billy May (1952), Maynard Ferguson, Shorty Rogers, Bill Holman, and Chet Baker, among others, jamming with Clifford Brown and Max Roach (1954) and leading a quartet that included his wife (1954-55). Lorraine Geller's sudden death in 1958 eventually resulted in the altoist deciding to leave the country to escape his grief. He played with Benny Goodman off and on between 1958 and 1961, spent time in Brazil, and in 1962 moved to Berlin. Geller worked in German radio orchestras for 30 years, played in European big bands, and continued to grow as a musician, although he was pretty much forgotten in the US. From the early '90s on, Herb Geller has begun returning to the States on a more regular basis, and he recently recorded a tribute to Al Cohn for Hep. Geller also recorded as a leader in the '50s for EmArcy, Jubilee, and Atco and in the '80s and '90s for Enja, Fresh Sound, and V.S.O.P. —*Scott Yanow*

Stax of Sax / 1958 / Jubilee ✦✦✦✦
This somewhat obscure recording by the bop-oriented altoist Herb Geller features him in a 1958 quintet with vibraphonist Victor Feldman, pianist Walter Norris, bassist Leroy Vinnegar, and drummer Anthony Vazley. Other than a session for Atco, this was Geller's last American album until

1993; it would be 1975 before he recorded as a leader again. Geller is in fine form on three of his originals and two standards ("Change Partners" and "It Might as Well Be Spring"). Originally cut for Jubilee, this Fresh Sound CD is part of an extensive series that has brought back many forgotten dates from the '50s. Bop collectors will enjoy this one. —*Scott Yanow*

★ **Herb Geller Quartet** / Aug. 5, 1993-Aug. 6, 1993 / VSOP ✦✦✦✦✦
This quartet outing with pianist Tom Ranier, bassist John Leitham, and drummer Louis Bellson is one of altoist Herb Geller's finest recordings. Geller, whose long period in Europe has resulted in him being somewhat forgotten in the US, has actually improved through the years and was even stronger in the mid-'90s than in the mid-'50s. For this date he contributes five originals (including a tribute to Lenny Bruce, "Stand-Up Comic," in which Geller sings) and performs six mostly lesser-known standards, highlighted by "The Peacocks," which has its composer Jimmy Rowles sitting in on piano. This CD is easily recommended to bop collectors for it finds Herb Geller at the peak of his powers. —*Scott Yanow*

Stan Getz

b. Feb. 2, 1927, Philadelphia, PA, **d.** Jun. 6, 1991, Malibu, CA
Sax (Tenor) / Cool, Bossa Nova, Post-Bop
One of the all-time great tenor saxophonists, Stan Getz was known as "The Sound" because he had one of the most beautiful tones ever heard. Getz, whose main early influence was Lester Young, grew to be a major influence himself and to his credit he never stopped evolving.

Stan Getz had the opportunity to play in a variety of major swing big bands while a teenager due to the World War II draft. He played with Jack Teagarden (1943) when he was just 16, and this was followed by stints with Stan Kenton (1944-45), Jimmy Dorsey (1945), and Benny Goodman (1945-46); he soloed on a few records with Goodman. Getz (who had his recording debut as a leader in July 1946 with four titles) became famous during his period with Woody Herman's Second Herd (1947-49), soloing (along with Zoot Sims, Herbie Steward, and Serge Chaloff) on the original version of "Four Brothers," and having his sound well featured on the ballad "Early Autumn." After leaving Herman, Getz was (with the exception of some tours with Jazz at the Philharmonic) a leader for the rest of his life.

During the early '50s Getz broke away from the Lester Young style to form his own musical identity and was soon among the most popular of all jazzmen. He discovered Horace Silver in 1950 and used him in his quartet for several months. After touring Sweden in 1951 he formed an exciting quintet that co-featured guitarist Jimmy Raney; their interplay on uptempo tunes and tonal blend on ballads was quite memorable. Getz's playing helped Johnny Smith have a hit in "Moonlight in Vermont," from 1953 to 1954 Bob Brookmeyer made his group a quintet, and despite some drug problems during the decade, Getz was a constant pollwinner. After spending 1958-60 in Europe, the tenorman returned to the US and recorded his personal favorite album, *Focus*, with arranger Eddie Sauter's orchestra. Then in February 1962 Getz helped usher in the bossa nova era by recording *Jazz Samba* with Charlie Byrd; their rendition of "Desafinado" was a big hit. During the next year Getz made bossa nova-flavored albums with Gary McFarland's big band, Luiz Bonfa, and Laurindo Almeida, but it was *Getz/Gilberto* (a collaboration with Antonio Carlos Jobim and João Gilberto) that was his biggest seller, thanks in large part to "The Girl from Ipanema" (featuring the vocals of Astrud and Joao Gilberto).

Stan Getz could have spent the next decade sticking to bossa nova but instead he de-emphasized the music and chose to play more challenging jazz. His regular group during this era was a pianoless quartet with vibraphonist Gary Burton; he recorded with Bill Evans (1964), played throughout the 1965 Eddie Sauter soundtrack for *Mickey One*, and made the classic album *Sweet Rain* (1967) with Chick Corea. Although not all of Getz's recordings from the 1966-80 period are essential, he proved that he was not shy to take chances. *Dynasty* with organist Eddie Louiss (1971), *Captain Marvel* with Chick Corea (1972), and *The Peacocks* with Jimmy Rowles (1975) are high points. After utilizing pianist Joanne Brackeen in his 1977 quartet, Getz explored some aspects of fusion with his next unit, which featured keyboardist Andy Laverne. Getz even used an echoplex on a couple of songs but despite some misfires, most of his dates with this unit are worthwhile. However, purists were relieved when he signed with Concord in 1981 and started using a purely acoustic backup trio on most dates. Getz's sidemen in later years included pianists Lou Levy, Mitchell Forman, Jim McNeely, and Kenny Barron. His final recording, 1991's *People Time*, (despite some shortness in the tenor's breath) is a brilliant duet set with Barron.

Throughout his career Stan Getz recorded as a leader for Savoy, Spotlite, Prestige, Roost, Verve, MGM, Victor, Columbia, SteepleChase, Concord, Sonet, Black Hawk, A&M, and EmArcy, among other labels (not to mention sessions with Lionel Hampton, Dizzy Gillespie, and Gerry Mulligan), and there are dozens of worthy records by the tenor currently available on CD. —*Scott Yanow*

Early Stan / Mar. 14, 1949-Apr. 23, 1953 / Original Jazz Classics ✦✦✦✦
This two-LP set includes seven sessions from 1949-50 and one from 1953 that feature the great tenor saxophonist Stan Getz. Getz is heard with a Terry Gibbs septet, in quartets with either pianist Al Haig or Tony Aless, with Haig in a sextet that features vocals from Blossom Dearie, on a couple of collaborations with guitarist Jimmy Raney, and in a classic if odd date with four other tenors (Al Cohn, Allen Eager, Brew Moore, and Zoot Sims), all of whom sounded identical at the time. This two-fer (which contains several alternate takes) gives one a fine overview into the early days of Stan Getz. —*Scott Yanow*

Five Brothers / Apr. 8, 1949 / Original Jazz Classics ✦✦✦

Roost Quartets / May 17, 1950-Mar. 1, 1951 / Roulette ✦✦✦✦
After leaving Woody Herman's Orchestra, tenor saxophonist Stan Getz became one of the leaders of the "cool school" due to his attractive light tone and his strong jazz abilities. This CD features his 1950-51 quartets. On the first seven selections, Getz is accompanied by pianist Al Haig, bassist Tommy Potter, and drummer Roy Haynes; they play such numbers as "On the Alamo," "Yesterdays," and the appealing "Hershey Bar." By late 1950 Getz had a new band, a rhythm section that he had discovered and immediately hired in Connecticut. Although bassist Joe Calloway and drummer Walt Bolden are obscure, pianist Horace Silver later became a major star. On his recording debut (15 performances including three alternate takes), Silver displays a style that was already recognizable and fit in perfectly with Getz. —*Scott Yanow*

★ **The Complete Recordings of the Stan Getz Quintet with Jimmy Raney** / Aug. 15, 1951-Apr. 23, 1953 / Mosaic ✦✦✦✦✦
This limited-edition three-CD set will be hard to acquire but it is a gem. Tenor saxophonist Stan Getz and guitarist Jimmy Raney had very complementary cool-toned but hard-swinging styles. Their gig at Storyville in Boston resulted in some classic music that, along with five studio sessions, is included in this box. The supporting cast includes pianists Al Haig, Horace Silver, Duke Jordan, and Hall Overton; the music was originally recorded for Roost, Clef, Norgran, and Prestige. This essential set is filled with exciting performances from Stan Getz when he was first becoming a highly influential force in jazz. —*Scott Yanow*

Plays / Dec. 12, 1952-Jan. 14, 1954 / Verve ✦✦✦✦
Tenor saxophonist Stan Getz is in excellent form playing with one of his finest groups, a quintet with guitarist Jimmy Raney and pianist Duke Jordan. Although the music does not quite reach the excitement level of the Getz-Raney Storyville session, this music (particularly the ballads) shows off the tenor's appealing tone. This CD is rounded out by four titles that Getz cut with a quartet in 1954 that co-starred pianist Jimmy Rowles. —*Scott Yanow*

★ **Diz and Getz** / Dec. 9, 1953 / Verve ✦✦✦✦✦
This is prime material with two giants playing bop and old-time standards with characteristic verve and wit. John Lewis (p) and the Oscar Peterson quartet join the masters. —*Michael G. Nastos*

At the Shrine Auditorium / Nov. 8, 1954 / Verve ✦✦✦

Stan Getz at the Shrine / Nov. 8, 1954 / Verve ✦✦✦✦
Tenor Stan Getz and valve trombonist Bob Brookmeyer made a mutually beneficial team. Although they had not played together all that much in 1954 (Brookmeyer had left Getz's band earlier in the year to join the Gerry Mulligan Quartet), the strong musical communication between the two horns during this CD reissue is obvious. Eight of the ten selections are from a live concert (with pianist John Williams, bassist Bill Anthony, and drummer Art Mardigan), while the final two numbers (on what was originally a pair of LPs) were cut in the studio the following day with the same personnel except that Frank Isola is on drums. Highlights of this cool-toned bop music (which, in addition to the solos, has many exciting ensembles) include "Lover Man," "Pernod," "Tasty Pudding," and "It Don't Mean a Thing." —*Scott Yanow*

Hamp and Getz / Aug. 1, 1955 / Verve ✦✦✦✦
The cool tenor of Stan Getz and the extroverted vibraphonist Lionel Hampton might have seemed like an unlikely matchup but once again producer Norman Granz showed his deftness at combining complementary talents. Hampton and Getz really battle hard on "Cherokee" and "Jumpin' at the Woodside," and other than a ballad medley, the other selections on this CD (which include two previously unreleased performances) are also heated. Classic music from two of the best. —*Scott Yanow*

☆ **Stan Getz and J.J. Johnson at the Opera House** / Sep. 29, 1957-Oct. 7, 1957 / Verve ✦✦✦✦✦
On two Jazz at the Philharmonic concerts, tenor saxophonist Stan Getz and trombonist J.J. Johnson (backed by the Oscar Peterson Trio plus drummer Connie Kay) performed an identical repertoire during the two sets of music, one recorded in mono and the other in stereo. All of the music from those dates (with the exception of one number left out due to lack of space) is included on this very exciting release: two versions apiece of "Billie's Bounce," "My Funny Valentine," "Crazy Rhythm," and "Blues in the Closet" plus tries at "Yesterdays" and "It Never Entered My Mind." Surprisingly Oscar Peterson and guitarist Herb Ellis do not solo at all, but Getz and

Johnson make a perfect combination and are in peak form. Bebop at its best, it has plenty of uptempo jamming and no shortage of ideas. — *Scott Yanow*

Stan Getz and the Oscar Peterson Trio / Oct. 10, 1957 / Verve ✦✦✦✦
This very enjoyable CD for the first time gathers together all of the music recorded at this timeless session. Tenor saxophonist Stan Getz is joined by pianist Oscar Peterson, guitarist Herb Ellis, and bassist Ray Brown for a well rounded set filled with appealing standards, three Getz originals (two of which are blues), and a fine ballad medley. Everyone is in top form, and Getz clearly enjoyed playing with Peterson. — *Scott Yanow*

Stan Getz at Large: Vol. 1 / Jan. 14, 1960-Jan. 15, 1960 / Jazz Unlimited ✦✦✦✦
This music on this CD and the second volume was originally only available as a pair of limited-edition LPs overseas. What makes the first volume of these quartet sessions (with pianist Jan Johansson) special is that much of the material (including "Pammie's Tune," "I Like to Recognize the Tune," and the previously unissued "A New Town Is a Blue Town") is fresh and some of it is quite obscure. Even on "Night and Day" and Dave Brubeck's "In Your Own Sweet Way," Getz's playing is enthusiastic and full of surprising twists. — *Scott Yanow*

Stan Getz at Large: Vol. 2 / Jan. 14, 1960-Jan. 15, 1960 / Jazz Unlimited ✦✦✦✦
The second of two CDs recorded by Stan Getz while in Copenhagen finds the great tenor performing such fresh material as Johnny Mandel's "Just a Child," Harold Land's "Land's End" and "He Was Good to Me," in addition to two previously unreleased selections with a fine quartet featuring pianist Jan Johansson. These very obscure performances are well recorded and should delight all Stan Getz fans. — *Scott Yanow*

☆ **Focus** / Jul. 1961-Oct. 1961 / Verve ✦✦✦✦✦
Stan Getz's personal favorite recording, this challenging session found the great tenor improvising over a big band, performing seven songs composed and arranged by Eddie Sauter. Nothing was written out for Getz but he was up to the challenge, creating beautiful and logical statements, and interacting closely with the orchestra. Music worth hearing several times. — *Scott Yanow*

Stan Getz and Bob Brookmeyer / Sep. 12, 1961-Sep. 13, 1961 / Verve ✦✦✦✦
Shortly after returning to the US (following three years in Copenhagen) Stan Getz had a musical reunion with Bob Brookmeyer. As usual, the cool-toned tenor blends in very well with the valve trombonist and, backed by a fine rhythm section (pianist Steve Kuhn, bassist John Neves, and drummer Roy Haynes), they perform three Brookmeyer pieces (including one titled "Minuet Circa '61"), two standards, and Buck Clayton's "Love Jumped Out." This little-known session is often quite memorable. — *Scott Yanow*

Jazz Samba / Feb. 13, 1962 / Verve ✦✦✦✦
This classic session which launched the bossa nova craze in the early '60s was originally recorded for Verve. The reissue from DCC Compact Classics improves the sound a bit and adds the shortened 45 version of "Desafinado" to the original program. The music, which matches Stan Getz's cool tenor with guitarist Charlie Byrd and his lightly swinging group, helped introduce Antonio Carlos Jobim's music to the US through the hit recordings of "Desafinado" and "One Note Samba." It's essential music, no matter in what format one acquires it. — *Scott Yanow*

★ **The Bossa Nova Years (Girl from Ipanema)** / Feb. 13, 1962-Oct. 9, 1964 / Verve ✦✦✦✦✦
This five-LP box set (which has been reissued on CD) contains nearly all of Stan Getz's classic bossa nova sessions, five wonderful yet diverse LPs (*Jazz Samba*, *Big Band Bossa Nova*, *Jazz Samba Encore*, *Stan Getz/Laurindo Almeida*, and *Getz/Gilberto*). The cool-toned tenor is heard on his groundbreaking collaboration with guitarist Charlie Byrd (which resulted in the bestselling "Desafinado"), is showcased with a big band arranged by Gary McFarland (introducing "No More Blues" and "One Note Samba"), stars in recordings with guitarists Laurindo Almeida and Luiz Bonfa, and is heard at the famous meeting with composer/pianist Antonio Carlos Jobim, guitarist João Gilberto and singer Astrud Gilberto, which resulted in the major hit "The Girl from Ipanema." This essential set finishes off with three previously unissued performances from a 1964 Carnegie Hall concert, concluding with a remake of "The Girl from Ipanema." These recordings stand as proof that it is possible for good music to sell. — *Scott Yanow*

★ **Getz/Gilberto** / Mar. 18, 1963-Mar. 19, 1963 / Mobile Fidelity ✦✦✦✦✦
This straight CD reissue of Verve's famous *Getz/Gilberto* album was released as part of Mobile Fidelity's Ultradisc II series. The music is timeless with the surprise hit "The Girl from Ipanema" (during which Astrud Gilberto made her debut not only on records but as a singer), "Corcovado," "So Danco Samba," and "Desafinado" among the high points. Stan Getz's tenor fit in perfectly with Antonio Carlos Jobim's music (six of the eight songs are Jobim's) and Joao Gilberto's vocals. — *Scott Yanow*

Getz Au Go Go Featuring Astrud Gilberto / Aug. 19, 1964 / Verve ✦✦✦

Getz and Gilberto, Vol. 2 / Oct. 9, 1964 / Verve ✦✦✦

Chick Corea / Bill Evans Sessions / 1964-Mar. 1967 / Verve ✦✦✦✦
This double LP, whose contents have since been reissued on two separate CDs, combines together two of tenor saxophonist Stan Getz's finest albums of his post-bossa nova period. Getz and pianist Bill Evans (along with drummer Elvin Jones and either Ron Carter or Richard Davis on bass) perform lyrical versions of five standards (including "But Beautiful" and "My Heart Stood Still") along with Evans' "Funkallero." The second half of this set has Getz in a quartet with pianist Chick Corea, bassist Ron Carter, and drummer Grady Tate. The music is quite a bit more modern, particularly Corea's two originals "Litha" and "Windows." In both cases the cool-toned tenor is in inspired form, making this music highly recommended in one form or another. — *Scott Yanow*

Dynasty / Jan. 11, 1971-Mar. 17, 1971 / Polydor ✦✦✦

The Peacocks / Jul. 1975 / Columbia ✦✦✦✦
Although listed under Stan Getz's name, this CD is a showcase for pianist Jimmie Rowles, an underrated stylist loved by singers and musicians alike. Rowles is heard in exquisite duets with Getz, solo, in a quartet with Getz, bassist Buster Williams, and drummer Elvin Jones, and on "The Chess Players," during which the quartet is joined by four vocalists including three from Jon Hendricks' family. Most memorable are the haunting title cut, "Lester Left Town" and several of Rowles' touching vocals. — *Scott Yanow*

★ **Gold** / Jan. 1977-Feb. 1977 / SteepleChase ✦✦✦✦✦
This double CD has been reissued on two CDs by SteepleChase for it finds tenor saxophonist Stan Getz in superb form. His modern quartet (featuring pianist Joanne Brackeen, bassist Niels Pedersen, and drummer Billy Hart) is heard live at Copenhagen's Montmartre, celebrating Getz's 50th birthday with some brilliant playing. The emphasis is mostly on standards, but there have been few versions of such songs as "Lady Sings the Blues," "Lush Life," "Lester Left Town," and "Eiderdown" that could compare with the lyricism and creativity of these renditions. This is essential music featuring a master at his best. — *Scott Yanow*

The Dolphin / May 1981 / Concord Jazz ✦✦✦

Spring Is Here / May 1981 / Concord Jazz ✦✦✦

● **People Time** / Mar. 3, 1991-Mar. 6, 1991 / Verve ✦✦✦✦
Stan Getz's final recording, a two-CD live set of duets with pianist Kenny Barron that was cut just three months before his death, finds the great tenor in surprisingly creative form despite an occasional shortness of breath. Getz's tone is as beautiful as ever and he does not spare himself on this often exquisite set. His version of Charlie Haden's "First Song" is a highlight, but none of the 14 performances are less than great. A brilliant farewell recording by a masterful jazzman. — *Scott Yanow*

Best Of the Verve Years, Vol. 1 / Verve ✦✦✦✦
This two-CD sampler is most highly recommended for listeners not familiar with Stan Getz's recordings of the '50s and '60s. Starting with a version of "Stella by Starlight" that co-stars guitarist Jimmy Raney, this set matches Getz's cool tenor with such artists as trumpeters Dizzy Gillespie and Conte Candoli, trombonist J.J. Johnson, baritonist Gerry Mulligan, pianists Oscar Peterson, Bill Evans and Chick Corea, valve trombonist Bob Brookmeyer, and vibraphonist Gary Burton. Also included are his two main bossa nova hits "Desafinado" and "The Girl from Ipanema," along with a couple of tracks from Getz's highly rated *Focus* album. It's a fine overview of the great tenor's middle years. — *Scott Yanow*

Terry Gibbs (Julius Gubenko)

b. Oct. 13, 1924, New York, NY
Vibes / Bop
One of the most hyper of all jazzmen (even his ballads are taken mostly doubletime), Terry Gibbs is a consistently exciting and competitive vibraphonist. As a xylophonist he won an amateur contest when he was 12. After spending three years in the military during World War II, Gibbs played on 52nd Street, gigged with Tommy Dorsey (1946 and 1948), Chubby Jackson (touring Scandinavia during 1947-48), Buddy Rich (1948), Woody Herman's Second Herd (1948-49), and Benny Goodman (1950-52). Gibbs settled in Los Angeles in 1957, worked in the studios, led jazz orchestras (his late-'50s version was callled the Terry Gibbs Dream Band), was the musical director of *The Steve Allen Show* during the '60s and in the '80s and '90s has often teamed up in a quintet with Buddy DeFranco. Terry Gibbs, who recorded as a leader for Prestige, Savoy, Brunswick, EmArcy, Mercury, Verve, Time, Impulse, Dot, Xanadu, Jazz à La Carte, and Contemporary (among others), had such fine pianists as his sidemen through the years as Terry Pollard, Pete Jolly (on accordion in 1957), Alice McLeod (in 1963 before she became Alice Coltrane), and John Campbell. — *Scott Yanow*

● **Dream Band, Vol. 1** / Mar. 17, 1959-Mar. 19, 1959 / Contemporary ✦✦✦✦
Reissue of a session with Gibbs leading a fine big band. — *Ron Wynn*

Dream Band, Vol. 2: Sundown Sessions / Nov. 1959 / Contemporary ✦✦✦✦
Terry Gibbs Dream Band. A 1987 reissue of big-band dates. Nicely played, with excellent arrangements but a low energy level. — *Ron Wynn*

● **Air Mail Special** / Oct. 4, 1981-Oct. 5, 1981 / Contemporary ✦✦✦✦
Another Gibbs/DeFranco pairing that has some sparks but not enough
fire. —*Ron Wynn*

Holiday for Swing / Jul. 1987-Aug. 1988 / Contemporary ✦✦✦✦

Memories of You / Apr. 13, 1991-Apr. 15, 1991 / Contemporary ✦✦✦✦

Kings of Swing / Apr. 13, 1991-Apr. 15, 1991 / Contemporary ✦✦✦✦
Recorded at Kimball's East, Emmeryville, CA, with the Terry Gibbs, Buddy
DeFranco, and the Herb Ellis Sextet. A late and very nice album of cuts like
"Body and Soul" and "Stompin' at the Savoy" that features these kings of
swing as fresh today as ever. The CD is 68 minutes. —*Michael Erlewine*

Astrud Gilberto

b. 1940, Bahia, Brazil
Vocals / Bossa Nova
Astrud Gilberto is a limited but strangely memorable singer known
mostly for her very first recording. At the famous 1963 collaboration
between Stan Getz, Antonio Carlos Jobim and her then-husband João Gilberto, Astrud was spontaneously asked to sing the English lyrics to "The
Girl from Ipanema" even though she was a housewife and not a professional singer. Her cool-toned voice fit the song perfectly and, after it
became a giant hit, she unwittingly became a celebrity. Gilberto recorded
with Stan Getz again in 1964 and made a series of albums for Verve during 1965-69. Although lightning did not strike again, the easy-listening
encounters with string orchestras sold well. Astrud Gilberto has continued
singing on a part-time basis, and it is doubtful if she has performed anywhere in the past 33 years without having to sing "The Girl from Ipanema."
—*Scott Yanow*

The Shadow of Your Smile / Oct. 21, 1964 / Verve ✦✦✦

The Astrud Gilberto Album / Jan. 27, 1965 & Jan. 28, 1965 / Verve ✦✦✦
Demure Brazilian vocalist Astrud Gilberto became a hit artist in 1963 with
the song "The Girl from Ipanema." She recorded it with her husband João
Gilberto, plus tenor saxophonist Stan Getz and Antonio Carlos Jobim. The
resulting furor eventually got her a solo album, this 1965 work. It's got
some charming moments, and she was ideal for the light bossa nova
sound. But the jazz content is minimal. —*Ron Wynn*

● **Look at the Rainbow** / 1966 / Verve ✦✦✦✦
For this CD reissue the music on singer Astrud Gilberto's LP *Look at the
Rainbow* is combined with half of the songs from her following album *A
Certain Smile*. The former session was one of the bossa nova singer's best
(11 perfectly suitable songs on which her soft voice is accompanied by an
orchestra arranged by Gil Evans and Al Cohn) while on the latter she inter-
acts successfully with a trio led by organist Walter Wanderley. —*Scott
Yanow*

A Certain Smile, a Certain Sadness / Sep. 20, 1966-Sep. 23, 1966 / Verve
✦✦✦

Astrud Gilberto with Stanley Turrentine / 1971 / Columbia ✦✦

Dizzy Gillespie (John Birks Gillespie)

b. Oct. 21, 1917, Cheraw, SC, **d.** Jan. 7, 1993
Trumpet / Bop
Dizzy Gillespie's contributions to jazz were huge. One of the greatest jazz
trumpeters of all time (some would say the best), Gillespie was such a
complex player that his contemporaries ended up copying Miles Davis
and Fats Navarro instead, and it was not until Jon Faddis's emergence in
the '70s that Gillespie's style was successfully recreated. Somehow
Gillespie could make any "wrong" note fit, and harmonically he was
ahead of everyone in the '40s, including Charlie "Bird" Parker. Unlike
Bird, Gillespie was an enthusiastic teacher who wrote down his musical
innovations and was eager to explain them to the next generation,
thereby insuring that bebop would eventually become the foundation of
jazz.

Gillespie was also one of the key founders of Afro-Cuban (or Latin)
jazz, adding Chano Pozo's conga to his orchestra in 1947 and utilizing
complex polyrhythms early on. The leader of two of the finest big bands
in jazz history, Gillespie differed from many in the bop generation by
being a masterful showman who could make his music seem both accessible and fun to the audience. With his puffed-out cheeks, bent trumpet
(which occurred by accident in the early '50s when a dancer tripped over
his horn), and quick wit, Dizzy was a colorful figure to watch. A natural
comedian, Gillespie was also a superb scat singer and occasionally
played Latin percussion for the fun of it, but it was his trumpet playing
and leadership abilities that made him into a jazz giant.

The youngest of nine children, Dizzy Gillespie (born John Birks
Gillespie) taught himself trombone and then switched to trumpet when
he was 12. He grew up in poverty, won a scholarship to an agricultural
school (Laurinburg Institute in North Carolina) and then in 1935
dropped out of school to look for work as a musician. Inspired and initially greatly influenced by Roy Eldridge, Gillespie (who soon gained the
nickname of Dizzy) joined Frankie Fairfax's band in Philadelphia. In

1937 he became a member of Teddy Hill's orchestra in a spot formerly
filled by Eldridge. Dizzy made his recording debut on Hill's rendition of
"King Porter Stomp" and during his short period toured Europe with the
band. After freelancing for a year, Gillespie joined Cab Calloway's
orchestra (1939-41), recording frequently with the popular bandleader
and taking many short solos that trace his development; "Pickin' the
Cabbage" finds Dizzy starting to emerge from Eldridge's shadow. However, Calloway did not care for Gillespie's constant chance-taking, calling
his solos "Chinese music." After an incident in 1941 when a spitball was
mischievously thrown at Calloway (he accused Gillespie but the culprit
was actually Jonah Jones), Dizzy was fired. By then Gillespie had already
met Charlie Parker, who confirmed the validity of his musical search.
During 1941-43 Dizzy passed through many bands including those led
by Ella Fitzgerald, Coleman Hawkins, Benny Carter, Charlie Barnet, Fess
Williams, Les Hite, Claude Hopkins, Lucky Millinder (with whom he
recorded in 1942), and even Duke Ellington (for four weeks). Gillespie
also contributed several advanced arrangements to such bands as Benny
Carter's, Jimmy Dorsey's, and Woody Herman's; Herman advised him to
give up his trumpet playing and stick to full-time arranging!

Dizzy ignored the advice, jammed at Minton's Playhouse and Monroe's Uptown House, where he tried out his new ideas, and in late 1942
joined Earl Hines's big band. Charlie Parker was hired on tenor, and the
sadly unrecorded orchestra was the first orchestra to explore early
bebop. By then Gillespie had his style together and wrote his most
famous composition "A Night in Tunisia." When Hines' singer Billy Eckstine went on his own and formed a new bop big band, Gillespie and Bird
(along with Sarah Vaughan) were among the members. Gillespie stayed
long enough to record a few numbers with Eckstine in 1944 (most
noticeably "Opus X" and "Blowing the Blues Away"). That year he also
participated in a pair of Coleman Hawkins-led sessions that are often
thought of as the first full-fledged bebop dates, highlighted by Gillespie's
composition "Woody'n You."

1945 was the breakthrough year. Gillespie, who had led earlier bands
on 52nd Street, finally teamed up with Charlie Parker on records. Their
recordings of such numbers as "Salt Peanuts," "Shaw Nuff," "Groovin'
High," and "Hot House" confused swing fans who had never heard the
advanced music as it was evolving, and Dizzy's rendition of "I Can't Get
Started" completely reworked the former Bunny Berigan hit. It would
take two years for the often frantic but ultimately logical new style to
start catching on as the mainstream of jazz. Gillespie led an unsuccessful
big band in 1945 (a Southern tour finished it), and late in the year he
travelled with Parker to the West Coast to play a lengthy gig at Billy
Berg's club in Los Angeles. Unfortunately the audiences were not enthusiastic (other than local musicians), and Dizzy (without Parker) soon
returned to New York. The following year Gillespie put together a successful and influential orchestra that survived for nearly four memorable
years. "Manteca" became a standard, the exciting "Things to Come" was
futuristic, and "Cubana Be/Cubana Bop" featured Chano Pozo. With such
sidemen as the future original members of the Modern Jazz Quartet
(Milt Jackson, John Lewis, Ray Brown, and Kenny Clarke), James Moody,
J.J. Johnson, Yusef Lateef, and even a young John Coltrane, Gillespie's big
band was a breeding ground for the new music. Gillespie's beret, goatee,
and "bop glasses" helped make him a symbol of the music and its most
popular figure. During 1948-49 nearly every former swing band was trying to play bop and for a brief period the major record companies tried
very hard to turn the music into a fad.

By 1950 the fad had ended, and Gillespie was forced due to economic
pressures to break up his groundbreaking orchestra. He had occasional
(and always exciting) reunions with Charlie Parker (including a fabled
Massey Hall concert in 1953) up until Bird's death in 1955, toured with
Jazz at the Philharmonic (where he had opportunities to "battle" the
combative Roy Eldridge), headed all-star recording sessions (using Stan
Getz, Sonny Rollins, and Sonny Stitt on some dates), and led combos that
for a time in 1951 also featured Coltrane and Milt Jackson. In 1956
Gillespie was authorized to form a big band and play a tour overseas
sponsored by the State Department. It was so successful that more travel-
ing followed, including extensive tours to the Near East, Europe, and
South America, and the band survived up to 1958. Among the young
sidemen were Lee Morgan, Joe Gordon, Melba Liston, Al Grey, Billy
Mitchell, Benny Golson, Ernie Henry, and Wynton Kelly; Quincy Jones
(along with Golson and Liston) contributed some of the arrangements.
After the orchestra broke up, Gillespie went back to leading small
groups, featuring such sidemen in the '60s as Junior Mance, Leo Wright,
Lalo Schifrin, James Moody, and Kenny Barron. He retained his popularity, occasionally headed specially assembled big bands, and was a fixture
at jazz festivals. In the early '70s, Gillespie toured with the Giants of Jazz;
around that time his trumpet playing began to fade, a gradual decline
that would make most of his '80s work quite erratic. However Gillespie
remained a world traveler, an inspiration and teacher to younger players,
and during his last couple of years he was the leader of the United
Nation's Orchestra (featuring Paquito D'Rivera and Arturo Sandoval). He
was active up until early 1992. Gillespie's career was very well docu-

mented from 1945 on, particularly on Musicraft, Dial, and RCA in the '40s, Verve in the '50s, Philips and Limelight in the '60s, and Pablo in later years. —*Scott Yanow*

★ **Complete RCA Victor Recordings 1937-1949** / May 17, 1937-Jul. 6, 1949 / Bluebird ✦✦✦✦✦

This two-CD set dwarfs all previous reissues of the trumpeter's Victor output. Gillespie's pioneering bebop big band made many of their greatest recordings for that label, and they are all here, including the original version of "Manteca," "Two Bass Hit," "Cubana Be/Cubana Bop," "Good Bait," "Hey Pete! Le's Eat Mo' Meat," and "Jumpin' with Symphony Sid"; among the soloists are tenors James Moody and Yusef Lateef, trombonist J.J. Johnson, and Chano Pozo on congas. In addition this essential reissue has Gillespie's three earliest recorded solos (with Teddy Hill's Orchestra in 1937), "Hot Mallets" with Lionel Hampton's all-star group in 1939, a combo session (four songs and three alternate takes) with Don Byas and Milt Jackson in 1946, and the two versions of "Overtime" and "Victory Ball" he made with the 1949 Metronome All-Stars; "Overtime" has a trade-off between Gillespie, Fats Navarro, and Miles Davis. No jazz collection is complete without this innovative and exciting music. —*Scott Yanow*

Shaw Nuff / Feb. 9, 1945-Nov. 12, 1946 / Musicraft ✦✦✦✦

This CD has Dizzy Gillespie's classic Musicraft sides (all except "A Handfulla Gimme"), some of the most famous recordings of his long career. These influential performances (which set the standard for bebop) include "Blue 'N' Boogie" (with tenor saxophonist Dexter Gordon), seven gems with Charlie Parker (highlighted by "Groovin' High," "Hot House," and "Salt Peanuts"), a few numbers with Sonny Stitt and nine big-band recordings including "Our Delight," "Ray's Idea," and the futuristic "Things to Come." If Gillespie's career had ended after these recordings, he would still be famous in the jazz world. —*Scott Yanow*

Dizzy Gillespie And Max Roach In Paris / Feb. 28, 1948 & May 15, 1949 / Vogue ✦✦✦✦

Dizzy Gillespie and His Big Band / Jul. 26, 1948 / GNP ✦✦✦✦

The Dizzy Gillespie Big Band was the most innovative jazz orchestra of 1946-49, proof that bebop was not exclusively a small group music. All of its recordings are well worth acquiring and this particular CD gives a well rounded picture of the orchestra at a concert before an enthusiastic crowd. With prominence given James Moody's tenor, Cecil Payne on baritone, and Chano Pozo on congas (he was killed a short time after this performance) in addition to the remarkable leader/trumpeter, the band is heard at its absolute prime. Versions of "Good Bait," "One Bass Hit," and "Manteca" are among the highlights of this recommended CD. —*Scott Yanow*

Dizzy's Diamonds: The Best of Verve Years [box] / Jun. 6, 1950-Nov. 6, 1964 / Verve ✦✦✦

Dee Gee Days: Savoy Sessions / Mar. 1, 1951-Jul. 18, 1952 / Savoy ✦✦✦

Dizzy Gillespie in Paris, Vol. 1 / Feb. 9, 1953 / Vogue ✦✦✦

Dizzy Gillespie in Paris, Vol. 2 / Mar. 27, 1952-Feb. 22, 1953 / Vogue ✦✦✦✦

The second of two CD volumes of Dizzy Gillespie performances put out by Vogue has the full contents from three of his Paris studio sessions. The great trumpeter heads a quintet that includes tenor saxophonist Don Byas and pianist Arnold Ross on four songs (plus three alternate takes); highlights include Gillespie's playing on "I Cover the Waterfront" and his vocal on the two versions of "Say Eh." The most rewarding of the sets finds him leading a septet on such numbers as "Cripple Crapple Crutch" (which has his classic blues vocal), "Somebody Loves Me," and two versions of "Wrap Your Troubles in Dreams." The final eight selections feature Gillespie's regular band of 1953 (with trombonist Nat Peck in baritonist Bill Graham's place). Vocalist Joe Carroll helps out on a couple of the numbers and Gillespie is in particularly memorable form on "My Man" and "'S Wonderful." This highly enjoyable music is easily recommended. —*Scott Yanow*

★ **Greatest Jazz Concert Ever** / May 15, 1953 / Prestige ✦✦✦✦✦

With Charlies Mingus, Charlie Parker, and Bud Powell. Despite a debatable title, this was a summit meeting of jazz legends at Massey Hall in the early '50s. Gillespie and Charlie Parker are transcendent, while Bud Powell makes some slashing statements on piano. Mingus (b) and Max Roach (d) complete the brilliant lineup. —*Ron Wynn*

Diz and Getz / Dec. 9, 1953-Oct. 16, 1956 / Verve ✦✦✦✦

★ **Dizzy Gillespie with Roy Eldridge** / Oct. 29, 1954 / Verve ✦✦✦✦✦

To call this music "classic" would be a great understatement. Producer Norman Granz loved to team together combative musicians in jam sessions, both live and in the studios. Since Roy Eldridge was one of the most competitive of trumpeters and Dizzy Gillespie considered him his original idol, they made a perfect matchup. This two-CD includes a ballad medley and a few slower pieces, but to hear Gillespie and Eldridge battling on "I've Found a New Baby" and "Limehouse Blues" is to hear two of the very best trying to cut each other. Highly recommended for all jazz collections. —*Scott Yanow*

★ **Birks Works: Verve Big Band Sessions** / May 18, 1956-Jul. 8, 1957 / Verve ✦✦✦✦

Dizzy Gillespie's globetrotting big band of 1956-57 was one of his finest groups, a very exciting orchestra that at various times had such players as trumpeters Gillespie, Joe Gordon, and Lee Morgan, trombonists Melba Liston and Al Grey, altoists Phil Woods and Ernie Henry, the tenors of Billy Mitchell, Ernie Wilkins, and Benny Golson, and pianists Walter Davis, Jr. and Wynton Kelly. With arrangements contributed by Quincy Jones (who was in the trumpet section), Wilkins, Liston, and Golson, this was a classic orchestra. Its three studio albums plus a few numbers only previously out on samplers and nine previously unreleased performances (mostly alternate takes) are on this wonderful two-CD set. The high points are many including "Dizzy's Business," "Jessica's Day," "The Champ," "Cool Breeze," "Birks Works," "Whisper Not," "Stablemates," and "I Remember Clifford." Essential music. —*Scott Yanow*

★ **At Newport** / Jul. 6, 1957 / Verve ✦✦✦✦

This CD features Dizzy Gillespie's second great big band at the peak of its powers. On the rapid "Dizzy's Blues" and a truly blazing "Cool Breeze," the orchestra really roars; the latter performance features extraordinary solos by Gillespie, trombonist Al Grey, and tenor saxophonist Billy Mitchell. In addition to fine renditions of "Manteca" and Benny Golson's then-recent composition "I Remember Clifford," the humorous "Doodlin'," is given a definitive treatment, there is a fresh version of "A Night in Tunisia," and pianist Mary Lou Williams sits in for a lengthy medley of selections from her "Zodiac Suite." This brilliant CD captures one of the high points of Dizzy Gillespie's remarkable career and is highly recommended. —*Scott Yanow*

Sonny Rollins / Sonny Stitt Sessions / Dec. 11, 1957-Dec. 19, 1957 / Verve ✦✦✦✦

This two-LP set (of which the contents have since been reissued on CD) contains a couple of the very best Norman Granz studio sessions. Dizzy Gillespie is matched with the great tenor Sonny Rollins on two selections, Sonny Stitt (sticking to tenor) takes Rollins' place for a couple of other songs, and then the two Sonnys team up with Gillespie for four remarkable selections. Gillespie sings "On the Sunny Side of the Street" with good humor, and "After Hours" is given a fine treatment, but it is Rollins' ferocious stoptime solo on "I Know That You Know" and the pure fire that is felt on a rapid "The Eternal Triangle" that makes this set truly memorable. —*Scott Yanow*

Gillespiana/Carnegie Hall Concert / Nov. 14, 1960-Mar. 4, 1961 / Verve ✦✦✦✦

This CD combines two complete and related LPs. When Lalo Schifrin joined Dizzy Gillespie's Quintet in 1960, he was encouraged by Gillespie to write an extended work for him. "Gillespiana" was the result, an impressive five-movement suite that showcased the trumpeter's talents with a large orchestra. The latter half of this CD was recorded at Carnegie Hall the same day that "Gillespiana" debuted live, but those five pieces are more conventional, highlighted by remakes of "Manteca" and "Night in Tunisia" (the latter as the more involved "Tunisian Fantasy"). Only an overly silly version of "Ool Ya Koo" with Joe Carroll detracts from this otherwise superb release. —*Scott Yanow*

The Cool World/Dizzy Goes Hollywood / Sep. 11, 1963-Apr. 23, 1964 / Verve ✦✦✦✦

Live at the Village Vanguard / Oct. 1, 1967 / Blue Note ✦✦✦✦

This double CD reissues material formerly on LPs, restoring several of the selections that were originally issued in edited form. A pair of unusual jam sessions, on the first date (and more eccentric of the two) trumpeter Dizzy Gillespie is paired with baritonist Pepper Adams, pianist Chick Corea, bassist Richard Davis, either Mel Lewis or Elvin Jones on drums, and violinist Ray Nance (who is in particularly adventurous form). The second date substitutes Garnett Brown for Nance and is a bit more conventional. These lengthy performances (all but one of the seven songs are over 11 minutes) contain some loose and rambling moments but also plenty of creative playing by this unusual group of all-stars. —*Scott Yanow*

Dizzy Gillespie's Big Four / Sep. 19, 1974 / Original Jazz Classics ✦✦✦✦

Arguably Dizzy Gillespie's most rewarding recording of the '70s, this quartet date (with guitarist Joe Pass, bassist Ray Brown, and drummer Mickey Roker) finds the 57-year-old trumpeter near peak form on three of his compositions and four standards. These versions of "Tanga" and "Be Bop" are brilliant. —*Scott Yanow*

Trumpet Summit Meets Oscar Peterson Big Four / Mar. 1980 / Original Jazz Classics ✦✦✦

To a Finland Station / Sep. 9, 1982 / Original Jazz Classics ✦✦✦✦

This unique set finds Dizzy Gillespie (who was nearly age 65) sharing the front line with the great Cuban trumpeter Arturo Sandoval. Backed by a fine Finnish rhythm section, Sandoval and the great trumpeter are both in good spirits playing five of Gillespie's originals including "Wheatleigh Hall" and "And Then She Stopped." Considering that it would be another decade before Sandoval was able to defect from Cuba (and finally play the music he wanted), this recording is of great historic value. —*Scott Yanow*

Live at Royal Festival Hall / Jun. 10, 1989 / Enja ✦✦✦✦
Dizzy Gillespie, who was nearing 72 years old at the time of this concert, headed one of his finest big bands during his later years, The United Nation Orchestra. With such stellar sidemen as trumpeters Arturo Sandoval and Claudio Roditi, trombonists Slide Hampton and Steve Turre, altoist Paquito D'Rivera, James Moody on tenor and alto, pianist Danilo Perez, and singer Flora Purim, Gillespie was relieved from having to carry this concert by himself and could concentrate on taking short solos and enjoying listening to the band play. Whether it is "Tanga," "And Then She Stopped," or an 18-minute version of "A Night in Tunisia," every selection on this excellent CD works. — *Scott Yanow*

To Diz with Love: Diamond Jubilee Recordings / Jan. 29, 1992-Feb. 1, 1992 / Telarc ✦✦✦

Egberto Gismonti

b. Dec. 5, 1947, Carmo, Brazil
Guitar, Piano / World Fusion, Brazil, Latin Continuum
A marvelous Brazilian guitarist, Egberto Gismonti has blended classical, traditional ethnic and jazz influences into a distinctive, very personal, and alternately lyrical and aggressive style. A self-taught guitarist, Gismonti began on six-string in the '70s, later switched to an eight-string instrument, and finally settled on a 10-string with an extended bass range in the early '80s. Gismonti began studying piano at six and continued until he journeyed to Paris to study orchestration and composition many years later. His teachers were Nadia Boulanger and Jean Barraque. Gismonti became interested in the choro, a Brazilian variation on African-American funk, when he returned home in 1966. While learning guitar, Gismonti closely examined the music of Baden Powell and flutist Pixinguinha. He toured America with Airto and Flora Purim in the mid-'70s and also with Nana Vasconcelos. Gismonti spent extensive time studying the music of the Xingu Indians in 1977, and later included their compositions on a pair of albums. In addition to his many recordings for ECM and EMI, Gismonti has recorded with Paul Horn, Charlie Haden, Jan Garbarek, and Nana Vasconcelos. — *Ron Wynn and Terri Hinte*

Danca Das Cabecas / Nov. 1976 / ECM ✦✦✦✦
The initial American release features extended pieces for guitarist and percussionist Nana Vasconcelos. A tour de force, with the pieces segueing together beautifully. — *Michael G. Nastos*

Sanfona / Nov. 1980 & Apr. 1981 / ECM ✦✦✦

Solo / 1985 / ECM ✦✦✦✦

★ **Danca Dos Escravos** / 1989 / ECM ✦✦✦✦✦

Infancia / Nov. 1990 / ECM ✦✦✦✦
This is a stunning effort by Egberto and his current (1991) working group: guitarist/synthesist Nando Carneiro, bassist Zeca Assumpao, and cellist Jacques Morelen-Baum. — *Terri Hinte*

Musica De Sobrevivencia / Apr. 1993 / ECM ✦✦✦

Academia De Dancas / EMI ✦✦✦
An ensemble with strings enhances the beauty of Gismonti's improvisations. — *Michael G. Nastos*

Jimmy Giuffre

b. Apr. 26, 1921, Dallas, TX
Flute, Sax (Baritone), Sax (Soprano), Sax (Tenor) / Avant-Garde, Cool
Jimmy Giuffre has had many accomplishments in a long career that has never been predictable. Giuffre graduated from North Texas State Teachers College (1942), played in an Army band during his period in the service, and then had stints with the orchestras of Boyd Raeburn, Jimmy Dorsey, and Buddy Rich. His composition "Four Brothers" became a hit for Woody Herman, an orchestra that Giuffre eventually joined in 1949.

Settling on the West Coast, the cool-toned tenor started also playing clarinet and occasional baritone. He was with Howard Rumsey's Lighthouse All-Stars (1951-52) and Shorty Rogers' Giants (1952-56), recording with many top West Coast jazz players. In 1956 he went out on his own, forming the Jimmy Giuffre 3 with guitarist Jim Hall and bassist Ralph Pena (later Jim Atlas). Giuffre had a minor hit with his recording of "The Train and the River," a song that he played during his notable appearance on the 1957 television special *The Sound of Jazz*. In 1958 Giuffre had a most unusual trio with valve trombonist Bob Brookmeyer and guitarist Hall (no piano, bass, or drums!), appearing in the movie *Jazz on a Summer's Day*. After a couple of years of reverting back to the reeds-guitar-bass format, in 1961 the new Jimmy Giuffre 3 featured pianist Paul Bley and bassist Steve Swallow and was involved in exploring the more introspective side of free jazz. From 1963 on, Giuffre maintained a lower profile working as an educator, although Don Friedman and Barre Phillips were in his unrecorded 1964-65 group. He popped up on records now and then in the '70s with diverse trios (including a session with Bley and Bill Connors), and his '80s unit often utilized the synthesizer of Pete Levin. Giuffre, who started late in life playing flute and soprano and seems to have made a career out of playing surprising music, reunited with Bley and Swallow in 1992. He has

recorded as a leader through the years for Capitol, Atlantic, Columbia, Verve, Hat Art, Choice, Improvising Artists, Soul Note, and Owl. — *Scott Yanow*

The Jazzlore: the Jimmy Giuffre Three, Vol. 46 / Dec. 3, 1956-Dec. 2, 1957 / Atlantic ✦✦✦

Lee Konitz Meets Jimmy Giuffre / May 12, 1959-May 13, 1959 / Verve ✦✦✦✦
A simply amazing collaboration. Extra spice comes from Hal McKusick (as), Warne Marsh (ts), and Bill Evans (p). — *Ron Wynn*

The Easy Way / Aug. 6, 1959-Aug. 7, 1959 / Verve ✦✦✦✦
A compelling trio date with Jim Hall (g). — *Ron Wynn*

● **1961** / Mar. 3, 1961 & Aug. 4, 1961 / ECM ✦✦✦✦
This is an excellent 1992 reissue of a pivotal set featuring multi-instrumentalist Jimmy Giuffre with bassist Steve Swallow and pianist Paul Bley. It's actually two separate, compelling albums, *Fusion* and *Thesis*, issued as one CD. The three interacted so completely that there was more emphasis on mood, sound, and texture than individual voices. — *Ron Wynn*

Quiet Song / Nov. 1974 / Improvising Artists ✦✦✦

Diary of a Trio: Saturday / Dec. 1989 / Owl ✦✦✦

Diary of a Trio: Sunday / Dec. 1989 / Owl ✦✦✦

Larry Goldings

b. 1968, Boston
Organ, Piano / Post-Bop
One of the top organists to emerge since Joey DeFrancesco, Larry Goldings began piano lessons when he was nine. Goldings, who graduated from the New School for Social Research in the late '80s, was Jon Hendricks' accompanist during 1987-89, worked with Jim Hall for three years, and (inspired by Jimmy Smith) led a trio that gave him an opportunity to play organ. He worked on the Hammond B-3 with Maceo Parker and in 1990 recorded his first set for Minor Music. Since then Goldings has toured and recorded with John Scofield and signed with Warner Bros. — *Scott Yanow*

Light Blue / Sep. 1992 / Minor Music ✦✦✦✦

Caminhos Cruzados / Dec. 19, 1993-Dec. 20, 1993 / Novus ✦✦✦✦
Listening to this CD, it is surprising to note that few bossa nova records up to now have featured organs. Larry Goldings' subtle style (a laidback Jimmy Smith) perfectly fits the idiom, and some of the selections performed on his set are given straightahead sections for variety. The music is mostly easy listening with an appealing ensemble sound, consistently excellent concise solos from Goldings and guitarist Peter Bernstein, and tasteful backup from drummer Bill Stewart and percussionist Guilherme Franco. The three guest appearances by Joshua Redman make one wish that he were on more tracks, for his tenor fits very comfortably into this setting. — *Scott Yanow*

● **Whatever It Takes** / Oct. 1995 / Warner Bros. ✦✦✦✦

Vinny Golia

b. 1956, Bronx, NY
Reeds / Avant-Garde
One of the unsung heroes of avant-garde jazz, Vinny Golia has been recording prolifically in Los Angeles (on his Nine Winds label) and staging concerts (ranging from solo improvisations and trios to his Large Ensemble) since 1977. He started out as a visual artist and even designed a Chick Corea album cover (*The Song of Singing*), not taking up the saxophone until he was 21 years old. Within a short time Golia was playing gigs in settings ranging from blues bands to a folk-rock group and Indian music. He started on the soprano and soon added flute, tenor, piccolo, clarinet, bass clarinet, baritone, bass sax, and more, currently playing 19 reeds! In 1973 he moved to Los Angeles, played regularly with John Carter and Bobby Bradford, and was becoming a force in the underground new music scene. In 1977 Golia founded Nine Winds, and although the first few records were of his music, the label has since broadened its scope and put out over 70 releases to date documenting the Los Angeles avant-garde jazz scene. Vinny Golia has played in recent times with the saxophone octet Figure 8 (recording for Black Saint), William Parker's big band in New York, Bradford's quartet, and his own many diverse groups. — *Scott Yanow*

Spirits in Fellowship / Oct. 1977 / Nine Winds ✦✦✦✦
His first album, quartet recordings with John Carter (cl). "Haiku" is Balinese- or Tibetan-like. "The Human Beings" for Louis Armstrong and "Duke Ellington & the American Indian" show Golia's passion and compass for freedom. Boldly inventive. — *Michael G. Nastos*

★ **Goin' Ahead** / Mar. 23, 1985-Mar. 24, 1985 / Nine Winds ✦✦✦✦✦

Pilgrimage to Obscurity / Jul. 1991 / Nine Winds ✦✦✦

Decennium Dans Axlan / Apr. 11, 1992 / Nine Winds ✦✦✦✦

Against the Grain / 1993 / Nine Winds ✦✦✦✦

Tutto Contare / Nov. 20, 1995 / Nine Winds ✦✦✦✦

Benny Golson

b. Jan. 25, 1929, Philadelphia, PA
Sax (Tenor) / Hard Bop
Benny Golson is a talented composer/arranger whose tenor playing has continued to evolve with time. After attending Howard University (1947-50) he worked in Philadelphia with Bull Moose Jackson's R&B band (1951) at a time when it included one of his writing influences, Tadd Dameron on piano. Golson played with Dameron for a period in 1953, and this was followed by stints with Lionel Hampton (1953-54), Johnny Hodges, and Earl Bostic (1954-56). He came to prominence while with Dizzy Gillespie's globetrotting big band (1956-58), as much for his writing as for his tenor playing (the latter was most influenced by Don Byas and Lucky Thompson). Golson wrote such standards as "I Remember Clifford" (for the late Clifford Brown), "Killer Joe," "Stablemates," "Whisper Not," "Along Came Betty," and "Blues March" during 1956-60. His stay with Art Blakey's Jazz Messengers (1958-59) was significant, and during 1959-62 he co-led the Jazztet with Art Farmer. From that point on Golson gradually drifted away from jazz and concentrated more on working in the studio and with orchestras including a couple of years (1964-66) in Europe. When Benny Golson returned to active playing in 1977, his tone had hardened and sounded much closer to Archie Shepp than Don Byas. Other than an unfortunate commercial effort for Columbia (1977), Golson has recorded consistently rewarding albums (many for Japanese labels) since that time, including a reunion with Art Farmer and Curtis Fuller in a new Jazztet. Through the years he has recorded as a leader for Contemporary, Riverside, United Artists, New Jazz, Argo, Mercury, and Dreyfus, among others. *—Scott Yanow*

★ **Benny Golson's New York Scene** / Oct. 14, 1957 & Oct. 17, 1957 / Original Jazz Classics ✦✦✦✦✦
This was one of the first albums to establish Golson's reputation as a soloist and composer. *—Ron Wynn*

The Other Side of Benny Golson / Nov. 12, 1958 / Original Jazz Classics ✦✦✦✦
Tenor saxophonist Benny Golson's third recording as a leader was significant in two ways. It was his first opportunity to work with trombonist Curtis Fuller (the two would be members of The Jazztet by 1960), and it was one of his first chances to really stretch out on record as a soloist; up to this point Golson was possibly better known as a composer. Three of the six originals on this CD reissue of a Riverside date are Golson's ("Are You Real" was the closest one to catching on), but the emphasis is on the solos of the leader, Fuller, and pianist Barry Harris; bassist Jymie Merritt and drummer Philly Joe Jones are excellent in support. *—Scott Yanow*

Gone with Golson / Jun. 20, 1959 / Original Jazz Classics ✦✦✦✦
Shortly before the formation of The Jazztet, tenor saxophonist Benny Golson and trombonist Curtis Fuller teamed up for this quintet set with pianist Ray Bryant, bassist Tommy Bryant, and drummer Al Harewood. Although Golson contributed three of the six songs ("Blues After Dark" is the best-known one), the emphasis is on his playing; the tenor is quite heated on the uptempo blues "Jam for Bobbie." The CD reissue adds "A Bit of Heaven" (originally on a sampler but part of the same session) to the original program, a fine example of hard bop of the late '50s. *—Scott Yanow*

Groovin' with Golson / Aug. 28, 1959 / Original Jazz Classics ✦✦✦
A mainstream date with traces of soul-jazz. Golson is solidly in the pocket on tenor. *—Ron Wynn*

Gettin' with It / Dec. 23, 1959 / Original Jazz Classics ✦✦✦

Moment to Moment / 1983 / Soul Note ✦✦✦

● **Live** / 1991 / Dreyfus ✦✦✦✦

I Remember Miles / Oct. 5, 1992-Oct. 6, 1992 / Evidence ✦✦✦✦
There are a few remarkable recreations on tenor saxophonist Benny Golson's tribute to Miles Davis, particularly "'Round Midnight" and parts of "So What" and "Bye Bye Blackbird." Trumpeter Eddie Henderson (especially when muted) comes very close to duplicating not only the sound but the spirit of Davis, while Golson sometimes discards his own strong musical personality to do close impressions of John Coltrane. Trombonist Curtis Fuller, pianist Mulgrew Miller, bassist Ray Drummond, and drummer Tony Reedus are also in fine form on a program that not only has five songs associated with '50s Miles Davis but three Golson originals including "One Day, Forever (I Remember Miles)," which (although worthy) is not in the same league as his earlier classic "I Remember Clifford." This heartfelt tribute album has enough unique moments to make it easily recommended. *—Scott Yanow*

Eddie Gomez

b. Oct. 4, 1944, San Juan, Puerto Rico
Bass / Post-Bop
Eddie Gomez is a brilliant bassist whose flexibility and quick reflexes make him an ideal accompanist (although his own albums tend to be a bit erratic jazzwise). He grew up in New York and was with the Newport Festival Youth Band during 1959-61. After studying at Juilliard, Gomez played with Rufus Jones' sextet, Marian McPartland (1964), Paul Bley (1964-65),

Giuseppe Logan, Gerry Mulligan, and Gary McFarland, among others. Gomez came to fame during his long period with the Bill Evans Trio (1966-77). He has since worked in a countless number of settings including filling in for Charles Mingus (1978) and with Steps Ahead (1979-84), Benny Wallace, Joanne Brackeen, Jack DeJohnette, Chick Corea, and in commercial settings as a studio musician. Eddie Gomez has recorded as a leader for Columbia, ProJazz, and Stretch. *—Scott Yanow*

Gomez / Jan. 1984-Feb. 1984 / Denon ✦✦✦

Discovery / Nov. 1985 / Columbia ✦✦✦✦
A powerful recording, it features Michael Brecker on sax and E.W.I., an electronic wind instrument. Musically this album covers jazz and classical and a little avant-garde. *—Paul Kohler*

Street Smart / 1990 / Columbia ✦✦

● **Next Future** / 1993 / Stretch ✦✦✦✦
Bassist Eddie Gomez is better as a sideman than as a leader on recording dates, but this is one of his stronger efforts in the latter category (even if one has to get used to him taking or sharing virtually all of the melodies). Chick Corea sticks exclusively to an atmospheric synthesizer, but otherwise this is a fairly straightahead quintet session featuring Gomez with the Coltranish tenor of Rick Margitza, pianist James Williams, drummer Lenny White, and a guest appearance from flutist Jeremy Steig. *—Scott Yanow*

Paul Gonsalves

b. Jul. 12, 1920, Boston, MA, d. May 14, 1974, London, England
Sax (Tenor) / Bop, Swing
The greatest moment of Paul Gonsalves' musical career occurred at the 1956 Newport Jazz Festival when, to bridge the gap between "Diminuendo in Blue" and "Crescendo in Blue," Duke Ellington urged him to take a long solo, egging him on through 27 exciting choruses that almost caused a riot. That well publicized episode resulted in Ellington having a major "comeback," and Gonsalves forever earning Duke's gratitude.
　Gonsalves had already earned a strong reputation during his stints with Count Basie (1946-49) and the Dizzy Gillespie Orchestra (1949-50). Joining Ellington in 1950, Gonsalves' warm, breathy tone and harmonically advanced solos were a constant fixture for 24 years (except for a brief time in 1953 when he was with Tommy Dorsey), and he was well featured up until his death, just ten days before Ellington passed on. In addition to his countless number of recorded performances with Ellington, Gonsalves led dates of his own on an occasional basis including ones for Argo, Jazzland, Impulse (highlighted by a combative meeting with Sonny Stitt), Storyville, Black Lion, and Fantasy. *—Scott Yanow*

★ **Cookin'** / Aug. 6, 1957 / Argo ✦✦✦✦✦
With Clark Terry on trumpet. *—Michael G. Nastos*

Gettin' Together! / Dec. 20, 1960 / Original Jazz Classics ✦✦✦✦
With Nat Adderley (cnt). *—Ron Wynn*

Just A-Sittin' and A-Rockin' / Aug. 28, 1970 & Sep. 3, 1970 / Black Lion ✦✦✦

Paul Gonsalves Meets Earl Hines / Dec. 15, 1970 & Nov. 29, 1972 / Black Lion ✦✦✦

Mexican Bandit Meets Pittsburgh Pirate / Aug. 24, 1973 / Original Jazz Classics ✦✦✦

Jerry Gonzalez

b. Jun. 5, 1949, New York, NY
Percussion, Trumpet / Post-Bop, Latin Continuum, Afro-Cuban Jazz
A multitalented musician, Jerry Gonzalez plays trumpet in the tradition of Miles Davis and Dizzy Gillespie and is also one of the top Latin percussionists. He played in salsa bands as a teenager and freelanced in the '70s and '80s with (among others) Dizzy Gillespie, Tony Williams, Eddie Palmieri, Tito Puente, and McCoy Tyner. In 1980 Gonzales formed the Fort Apache Band, a group that has creatively Latinized all types of challenging jazz compositions, including a full set of Thelonious Monk tunes. Gonzalez and his important group have recorded for Enja and Sunnyside. *—Scott Yanow*

Rhumba Para Monk / Oct. 27, 1988-Oct. 28, 1988 / Sunnyside ✦✦✦✦
With the Fort Apache Band. Great production by Jim Anderson on eight Monk standards. Stripped to quintet with Carter Jefferson, the tenor sax foil. Very intriguing concept, melding Latin rhythms to Monk's off minorisms. *—Michael G. Nastos*

★ **Obatala** / Nov. 6, 1988 / Enja ✦✦✦✦✦
The Fort Apache Band is typical—a largely Latino group including several heavy New York salsa percussionists, with a couple of excellent Anglos on sax and drums. The numbers range from Shorter, Davis, and Monk to the lucumi-inflected title cut. *—John Storm Roberts*

Crossroads / 1994 / Milestone ✦✦✦✦

Pensativo / 1995 / Milestone ✦✦✦✦

Benny Goodman

b. May 30, 1909, **d.** Jun. 13, 1986
Clarinet / Swing

The greatest jazz clarinetist of all time, Benny Goodman deserved his title as "The King of Swing." Although not the actual founder of swing, Goodman's phenomenal success in 1935 launched the swing era, and without watering down his music or displaying an extroverted show-biz personality, he became a major pop star. His eccentricities (like being very self-possessed) resulted in some odd incidents and a great deal of misunderstanding through the years, but they were consistent with the fact that Goodman's main interest in life was playing clarinet and that everything else was secondary.

Benny Goodman began on clarinet when he was 11 and had two years of study with the classically trained Franz Schoepp (whose other students included Jimmy Noone and Buster Bailey). Goodman, who first played in public doing an imitation of Ted Lewis when he was 12, developed fast. By 1923 he was a member of the Musicians Union and playing regularly in Chicago. In August 1925, when he was 16, Goodman joined Ben Pollack's orchestra, and in December 1926 he made his recording debut with Pollack. Technically gifted from the start, Goodman was a major soloist with Pollack (along with Jimmy McPartland, Glenn Miller, and later Jack Teagarden) and had his first opportunities to lead his own recording sessions in 1928 including two songs with a trio. After leaving Pollack in 1929, Goodman worked with Red Nichols' Five Pennies and then became a very busy studio musician, recording a countless number of performances (often in anonymous settings) during 1929-33. He even doubled during this era on alto, baritone, and (on one session) trumpet. His own dates in 1933-4 featured Teagarden, Billie Holiday (in her recording debut), Mildred Bailey, Coleman Hawkins, and the up-and-coming Gene Krupa. In 1934 Goodman put together his first orchestra, started recording for Columbia, and appeared as one of three big bands on the *Let's Dance* radio series; the show's trademark melody would permanently become his own opening theme. Using Fletcher Henderson arrangements, Goodman's well rehearsed ensemble showed that it was possible to play both jazz and dance music simultaneously.

But when the radio show ended in May 1935, Benny Goodman's future as a bandleader was far from secure. With Bunny Berigan on trumpet, the band made popular records for Victor of "King Porter Stomp" and "Sometimes I'm Happy." The clarinetist also teamed up with Teddy Wilson and Gene Krupa for the first recordings of the Benny Goodman Trio and then agreed to go on a cross-country tour with the orchestra. After some minor successes and major disasters, the group was well received in Oakland, and then on August 21, 1935 they nearly caused a riot at the Palomar Ballroom in Los Angeles as teenagers went crazy over the band; unknown to Goodman, his national broadcasts on the *Let's Dance* series had been very popular in California. From that point on, he went from success to success, causing sensations in Chicago and then New York. Although Berigan did not stay long with the band, his successors (Ziggy Elman, Harry James, and Chris Griffin) formed one of the great trumpet sections, Gene Krupa became the pacesetter among drummers, and pianist Jess Stacy and singer Helen Ward (later Martha Tilton) were major assets. Goodman, by using Teddy Wilson and Lionel Hampton regularly in his quartet, broke boundaries in race relations. He had the most popular band in the world during 1935-38.

The high point to Benny Goodman's success was his historic January 16, 1938 Carnegie Hall concert, which was miraculously recorded and released for the first time in the early '50s. "Sing, Sing, Sing" made Krupa such a star that that fact (plus a personality conflict with Goodman) resulted in him being the first of Goodman's stars to depart. Although Goodman's popularity was soon matched and then exceeded during the swing era by Artie Shaw and Glenn Miller, his orchestra (even with its turnover) remained a major force. By 1940 James, Wilson, and Stacy were gone, but Goodman had the pioneering electric guitarist Charlie Christian playing in his new sextet, he had signed with Columbia, the clarinetist was starting to record challenging arrangements by Eddie Sauter, and he was using such fine sidemen as Cootie Williams, Georgie Auld, and Johnny Guarnieri. As the '40s advanced, other top players (such as Mel Powell, Lou McGarity, Red Norvo, and even a young Stan Getz) and singers (Helen Forrest and Peggy Lee) made contributions, and Goodman remained "King of Swing." He even took some time to show the classical music world that he could play their music too.

By 1945 and the rise of bebop, Goodman's music started to be thought of as old-fashioned. Goodman's own playing rarely changed from that point forward but he remained enthusiastic about performing the old repertoire, and no one played it better. He broke up his band in 1946 and then opened his music temporarily to bebop. Goodman had a 1948 septet with fellow clarinetists Stan Hasselgard and Wardell Gray, used Fats Navarro on one recording, and his 1949 orchestra had some very advanced arrangements by Chico O'Farrill in its book. But by the following year, Goodman returned permanently to swing. He led small groups and occasional big bands throughout the remainder of his career. While the orchestras tended

to be nostalgic affairs (revisiting the Henderson charts), the combos allowed Goodman to stretch out and display his brilliant style. He had some reunions with his Trio and Quartet, participated in the rather fictional 1956 movie *The Benny Goodman Story* (playing the clarinet solos), and toured the USSR in 1962. Among Goodman's sidemen in the '50s were Terry Gibbs, Buck Clayton, Ruby Braff, Paul Quinichette, Roland Hanna, Jack Sheldon, Bill Harris, Flip Phillips, and Andre Previn. During his last three decades Goodman often used alumni and even such youngsters as Herbie Hancock and George Benson. Goodman was less active in the '60s and made no records during 1973-77. He came back in 1978 to play at his 40th-anniversary Carnegie Hall concert before drifting back into retirement again. However, in the early '80s Goodman began to show a strong interest in performing and put together his final big band (which was really founded by Loren Schoenberg), playing on a public television show just a short time before his death.

Due to his continuing popularity, Goodman (still a household name) is represented on more records than any jazz leader other than Duke Ellington. Most of his radio broadcasts and lesser-known recordings from the '30s and '40s were released on Sunbeam LPs, his output for Victor during the swing era has been fully reissued, his Columbia performances have come out in more piecemeal fashion, and there are a countless number of later combo sessions that are available; Music Masters, possessor of Goodman's private tapes, has thus far come out with ten CDs of previously unreleased material. — *Scott Yanow*

B.G. & Big Tea in NYC / Apr. 1929-Oct. 1934 / GRP ✦✦✦✦
CD reissue of some early '30s material that doesn't feature clarinetist Benny Goodman in a leadership role. Instead, he's in bands under the direction of Red Nichols, Arthur Rollini, and Irving Mills. Yet, he's the star soloist, along with trombonist Jack Teagarden. — *Ron Wynn*

★ **The Birth of Swing** / Apr. 4, 1935-Nov. 5, 1936 / Bluebird ✦✦✦✦✦
This three-CD set includes all of Benny Goodman's big band's recordings from April 1935 through November 1936, a period when the orchestra became the most popular and influential in the world, making both swing and Goodman into household words. Augmented by some alternate takes, this set shows just how solid and musical a unit Goodman had from the start. Key soloists include trumpeters Bunny Berigan and Ziggy Elman, pianist Jess Stacy, and the band's excellent singer Helen Ward, but Goodman usually emerges as the main star with the tight and swinging ensembles being a close second. In addition to the hits ("King Porter Stomp," "Sometimes I'm Happy," "When Buddha Smiles," "Stompin' at the Savoy," and "Goody-Goody") even the lesser-known numbers and pop tunes have their strong moments. This music is essential to any serious jazz collection. — *Scott Yanow*

Sing, Sing, Sing / Apr. 4, 1935-Apr. 11, 1939 / Bluebird ✦✦✦

Original Benny Goodman Trio and Quartet Sessions, Vol. 1: After You've Gone / Jul. 11, 1935-Feb. 3, 1937 / Bluebird ✦✦✦✦
Although Benny Goodman came to fame as leader of a big swinging orchestra, from nearly the beginning he always allocated some time to playing with smaller groups. On July 13, 1935 the Benny Goodman Trio debuted (featuring drummer Gene Krupa and pianist Teddy Wilson) and 13 months later vibraphonist Lionel Hampton made the unit a quartet. The first interracial group to appear regularly in public, this outlet gave Goodman an opportunity to stretch out and interact with his peers. The CD *After You've Gone* contains the first ten Trio recordings and the initial 12 studio performances by the Quartet. Helen Ward contributes two fine vocals but the emphasis is on the close interplay between these brilliant players. — *Scott Yanow*

● **The Complete Small Combinations, Vols. 1-2** / Jul. 11, 1935-Jul. 30, 1937 / RCA ✦✦✦✦
This two-CD set from the French RCA Jazz Tribune series (a straight reissue of a two-LP set) has the first 30 recordings by the Benny Goodman Trio and Quartets, groups featuring the leader-clarinetist, pianist Teddy Wilson, drummer Gene Krupa, and sometimes vibraphonist Lionel Hampton. A special bonus of this historic set is the inclusion of five formerly rare alternate takes (including "After You've Gone" and "Body and Soul" from the first trio session). Although used by Goodman as a brief departure from his big band, his trio and quartet became famous in their own right, and their recordings are essential to any serious jazz collection. This two-fer was followed by a second one tracing Goodman's small groups into 1939. — *Scott Yanow*

★ **On the Air 1937-1938** / Mar. 3, 1937-Sep. 20, 1938 / Columbia/Legacy ✦✦✦✦✦
In the early '50s, after the unexpectedly large sales of Benny Goodman's 1938 Carnegie Hall concert, Columbia came out with a two-LP set of broadcasts from 1937-39 that also sold well. This recent double-CD set not only includes the music on the original LPs but adds 14 additional tracks only previously put out on collector's labels. *On the Air* really captures the Benny Goodman Big Band (along with some examples of the Trio and Quartet) at its peak and shows why the original swing orchestras (as opposed to the weak nostalgia bands that are currently around) were so

popular with younger people in the '30s and '40s. These performances are still exciting. —*Scott Yanow*

Avalon: the Small Bands, Vol. 2 (1937–1939) / Jul. 30, 1937-Apr. 6, 1939 / Bluebird ✦✦✦✦

This second of two CDs reissuing all of Benny Goodman's trio and quartet recordings for Victor starts out with eight performances co-starring the magical team of vibraphonist Lionel Hampton, pianist Teddy Wilson, and drummer Gene Krupa (including their famous version of "Avalon"), and then finishes off with 14 recordings from the post-Krupa era. The latter have either Dave Tough or Buddy Schutz in the drummer's spot, and three cuts (including a classic version of "I Cried for You") add bassist John Kirby. No matter what the personnel, Benny Goodman is in top form on these highly enjoyable classics from his early prime. —*Scott Yanow*

★ **Benny Goodman Carnegie Hall Jazz Concert** / Jan. 16, 1938 / Columbia ✦✦✦✦✦

One of the greatest concerts ever captured on record is in itself a turning point in the way jazz is judged by outsiders. Never before had a full jazz concert been held at Carnegie Hall; it is hard to believe that tapes of this momentous event were kept in a closet, forgotten until rediscovered by accident in 1950. There are many many high points, including exciting versions of "Don't Be That Way" and "One O'Clock Jump," a tribute to the 20 years of jazz that were then on record, a jam-session version of "Honeysuckle Rose," which found sidemen of the orchestras of Duke Ellington and Count Basie interacting with Goodman's stars, exciting performances by Goodman's trio and quartet, and of course "Sing, Sing, Sing" with Gene Krupa's creative (if not too subtle) drumming and Jess Stacy's remarkable ad-lib piano solo. Fortunately this program has been reissued in full on CD and it belongs in every serious music library, capturing Benny Goodman and the swing era in general at its height. —*Scott Yanow*

Wrappin' It Up: the Harry James Years, Part II / Mar. 9, 1938-May 4, 1939 / Bluebird ✦✦✦

★ **Featuring Charlie Christian** / Oct. 2, 1939-Mar. 13, 1941 / Columbia ✦✦✦✦✦

Charlie Christian was not the first electric guitarist but he was its first giant. He elevated the guitar from a member of the rhythm section (where it was often inaudible) to the front line, taking solos that could challenge any saxophonist. His playing was so appealing to his contemporaries that it was not until the emergence of rock in the mid-to-late '60s that more advanced guitarists emerged. By then it was over a quarter-century since Christian's premature death from tuberculosis. He spent his only two high-profile years as a member of the Benny Goodman Sextet and 18 of their best recordings are on this CD. Christian and Goodman are joined by Lionel Hampton on the first dozen performances while the final six boast the explosive combination of trumpeter Cootie Williams and Georgie Auld's tenor. The riffing inspires heated yet melodic solos, resulting in classic music that is impossible to dislike. —*Scott Yanow*

Featuring Helen Forrest / Mar. 1, 1940-Jun. 4, 1941 / Columbia ✦✦✦

Featuring Peggy Lee / Aug. 15, 1941-Dec. 10, 1941 / Columbia ✦✦✦

Small Groups: 1941-1945 / Oct. 28, 1941-Feb. 4, 1945 / Columbia ✦✦✦✦

When one thinks of Benny Goodman's small groups, it is generally his original trio and quartet (with Lionel Hampton, Teddy Wilson, and Gene Krupa) or his sextet with Charlie Christian that comes immediately to mind. This superior set dates from a slightly later period and features a sextet with trombonist Lou McGarity and pianist Mel Powell (the clarinet-trombone blend works very well) and his 1944-45 quintet/sextet with vibraphonist Red Norvo. Vocalists Peggy Lee, Jane Harvey, and Peggy Mann give this set some variety. The music (and the clarinet playing) is consistently brilliant. —*Scott Yanow*

Way Down Yonder (1943-1944) / Dec. 9, 1943-Jan. 1946 / Vintage Jazz Classics ✦✦✦✦

This valuable CD contains performances from 1943-46 originally recorded for World War II servicemen. VJC has fleshed out the original recordings with alternate takes and breakdowns, which due to the high quality of the music, makes this CD even more interesting. Gene Krupa is heard with Goodman's 1943 big band and in a trio with pianist Jess Stacy while the bulk of this set features the Benny Goodman Quintet with vibraphonist Red Norvo during 1944, including an early version of the classic "Slipped Disc." —*Scott Yanow*

Complete Capitol Small Group Recordings / Jun. 12, 1944-Dec. 14, 1955 / Mosaic ✦✦✦✦

Swing Sessions / Oct. 17, 1945-Jan. 11, 1946 / Hindsight ✦✦✦

Undercurrent Blues / Jan. 28, 1947-Oct. 15, 1949 / Blue Note ✦✦✦✦

During 1947-49 on an irregular basis, clarinetist Benny Goodman's band recorded bebop for Capitol before he permanently switched back to swing in 1950. All of Goodman's small group recordings from this period have been reissued on a Mosaic set, and five are duplicated on this single CD, but there are also four previously unissued big-band performances along with six others on this recommended reissue. Goodman and his band

interpret a pair of Mary Lou Williams originals, and other highlights include "Stealin' Apples" (a septet track with trumpeter Fats Navarro), "Bop-Hop," "Dreazag," "Bedlam," and "Blue Lou." Key soloists include trumpeter Doug Mettome, Wardell Gray on tenor, and pianist Buddy Greco while Chico O'Farrill provided most of the big-band charts. It is very interesting to hear the great swing clarinetist adapting to the new music. —*Scott Yanow*

Sextet / Nov. 24, 1950-Oct. 22, 1952 / Columbia ✦✦✦✦

In 1950 Benny Goodman formed a new sextet, and although he used a big band for some recordings, the small group was his main outlet for the next couple of years. This CD features this somewhat forgotten unit, a hot swing combo featuring vibraphonist Terry Gibbs and usually pianist Teddy Wilson. Rather than repeat his older hits, the clarinetist clearly enoyed playing other standards not generally associated with him. Excellent and easily enjoyable music. —*Scott Yanow*

B.G. In Hi-Fi / Nov. 8, 1954-Nov. 16, 1954 / Capitol ✦✦✦

On this all-around excellent CD, Benny Goodman performs a dozen selections (mostly Fletcher Henderson arrangements) with a big band filled with sympathetic players in 1954 and eight other numbers with a pair of smaller units that also feature pianist Mel Powell and either Charlie Shavers or Ruby Braff on trumpets. Although the big-band era had been gone for almost a decade, Benny Goodman (then 46) plays these swing classics with enthusiasm and creativity and shows that there was never any reason for anyone to write him off as "behind the times." —*Scott Yanow*

Yale Recordings, Vols. 1-5 / Mar. 26, 1955-Jun. 28, 1967 / Music Masters ✦✦✦✦

In his will, Benny Goodman gave to Yale not only all of his band arrangements (over 1,500) but 400 ten-inch master tapes of unreleased studio and concert recordings. Some of the more rewarding sessions have now been issued by Music Masters, and this particular box set includes the first five volumes (and a 40-page booklet), six CDs in all (since *Vol. 5* had two CDs by itself), which are also available separately. The music dates from 1955-84 (the second half of Benny Goodman's career) and is taken from quite a few sessions, including a full CD of material by his excellent septet of 1955 (featuring trumpeter Ruby Braff and Paul Quinichette on tenor), big-band performances from 1958 with several vocals by Jimmy Rushing, and many selections from a 1959 engagement with a nonet featuring trumpeter Jack Sheldon, trombonist Bill Harris, and tenorman Flip Phillips. Although no longer a pacesetter, Goodman remained one of the jazz world's most brilliant performers, making this set well worth acquiring. —*Scott Yanow*

Together Again! (1963 Reunion with Lionel Hampton, Teddy Wilson & Gene Krupa / Feb. 13, 1963-Aug. 27, 1963 / Bluebird ✦✦✦✦

In 1963, almost exactly 25 years after Gene Krupa left Benny Goodman's orchestra, the Benny Goodman Quartet recorded together for the first time in a quarter-century. This CD, a straight reissue of the original LP, finds Goodman, Lionel Hampton, Teddy Wilson, and Gene Krupa clearly happy to be back together, not so much revisiting their older "hits" as having a good time playing songs that they missed the first time around. One can feel the absence of a bass (the more primitive recording quality of the '30s helped cover it up originally) but the music is so joyful and swinging that one does not mind. —*Scott Yanow*

Dexter Gordon

b. Feb. 27, 1923, Los Angeles, CA, **d.** Mar. 25, 1990, Philadelphia, PA
Sax (Tenor) / Bop, Hard Bop

Dexter Gordon led such a colorful and eventful life (with three separate comebacks) that his story would make a great Hollywood movie. The top tenor saxophonist to emerge during the bop era and possessor of his own distinctive sound, Gordon sometimes was long-winded and quoted excessively from other songs, but he created a large body of superior work and could battle nearly anyone successfully at a jam session. His first important gig was with Lionel Hampton (1940-43), although due to Illinois Jacquet also being in the sax section, Gordon did not get any solos. In 1943 he did get to stretch out on a recording session with Nat King Cole. Short stints with Lee Young, the Fletcher Henderson Orchestra, and Louis Armstrong's big band preceded his move to New York in December 1944 and becoming part of Billy Eckstine's orchestra, trading off with Gene Ammons on Eckstine's recording of "Blowin' the Blues Away." Dexter recorded with Dizzy Gillespie ("Blue 'N' Boogie") and as a leader for Savoy before returning to Los Angeles in the summer of 1946. He was a major part of the Central Avenue scene, trading off with Wardell Gray and Teddy Edwards in many legendary tenor battles; studio recordings of "The Chase" and "The Duel" helped to document the atmosphere of the period.

After 1952, drug problems resulted in some jail time and periods of inactivity during the '50s (although Gordon did record two albums in 1955). By 1960 he recovered and was soon recording a consistently rewarding series of dates for Blue Note. Just when he was regaining his former popularity, Gordon moved to Europe in 1962 where he would stay until 1976. While on the continent, he was in peak form, and Dexter's many SteepleChase recordings rank with the finest work of his career. Gordon did return to the US on an occasional basis, recording in 1965, 1969-70, and 1972, but he was to an extent forgotten in his native land. It was therefore a major surprise that his return in 1976 was treated as a major media event. A great deal of interest was suddenly shown in the living legend with long lines of people waiting at clubs in order to see him. Gordon was signed to Columbia and remained a popular figure until his gradually worsening health made him semiactive by the early '80s. His third comeback occurred when he was picked to star in the motion picture *'Round Midnight* and even if his playing by then was past its prime, Gordon's acting was quite realistic and touching. He was nominated for an Academy Award four years before his death after a very full life. Most of Dexter Gordon's recordings for Savoy, Dial, Bethlehem, Dootone, Jazzland, Blue Note, SteepleChase, Black Lion, Prestige, Columbia, Who's Who, Chiaroscuro, and Elektra Musician are currently available. —*Scott Yanow*

Long Tall Dexter / Oct. 30, 1945-Dec. 22, 1946 / Savoy ◆◆◆◆
In the mid-to-late '40s, there were three great young tenor saxophonists: Dexter Gordon, Wardell Gray, and Teddy Edwards. Of the trio, Dexter Gordon had the greatest influence on upcoming players and was the most bop-oriented. This superb two-LP set contains all 17 selections Gordon cut for Savoy during 1945-47 plus eight alternate takes and a jam session performance (with trumpeter Howard McGhee and altoist Sonny Criss) titled "After Hours Bop." Gordon is heard in a quartet, with several quintets (featuring such major players as pianist Bud Powell, drummers Max Roach and Art Blakey, baritonist Leo Parker, and trumpeter Fats Navarro) and in a septet with trumpeter Joe Newman and trombonist J.J. Johnson. Throughout, Gordon holds his own with the slightly older players and gets his career off to a brilliant start. —*Scott Yanow*

Master Takes: The Savoy Recordings / Oct. 30, 1945-Dec. 22, 1947 / Savoy ◆◆◆◆

★ **The Chase!** / Jun. 5, 1947-Dec. 4, 1947 / Stash ◆◆◆◆◆
During the mid-to-late '40s Dexter Gordon, one of the top young tenors to emerge during the bop era, had nightly tenor "battles" in Los Angeles clubs with his two top competitors, Wardell Gray and Teddy Edwards. Fortunately Gordon also had opportunities to meet up with his fellow tenors on record; "The Chase" (featuring Gray and Gordon) is a classic, and "The Duel" (which was recorded twice with Edwards) is close behind. Although issued as part of Stash's budget series, the vintage music on this CD (which has all of Dexter Gordon's recordings for Dial in 1947) is often quite memorable. In addition to the battles, Gordon teams up with trombonist Melba Liston in a quintet, leads a couple of his own quartets, and "Blues in Teddy's Flat" features Edwards. Since all of the alternate takes are also included, this highly recommended release is quite definitive and recaptures some of the excitement of the period. —*Scott Yanow*

Daddy Plays the Horn / Sep. 18, 1955 / Bethlehem ◆◆◆

Doin' Alright / May 6, 1961 / Blue Note ◆◆◆◆
The title of this Blue Note set perfectly fit at the time, for tenor saxophonist Dexter Gordon was making the first of three successful comebacks. Largely neglected during the '50s, Gordon's Blue Note recordings (of which this was the first) led to his rediscovery. The tenor is teamed with the young trumpeter Freddie Hubbard, pianist Horace Parlan, bassist George Tucker, and drummer Al Harewood for a strong set of music that is highlighted by "You've Changed" (which would become a permanent part of Dexter's repertoire), "Society Red" (a blues later used in the film *'Round Midnight*), and "It's You or No One." —*Scott Yanow*

Dexter Calling . . . . / May 9, 1961 / Blue Note ◆◆◆◆
Tenor saxophonist Dexter Gordon recorded seven Blue Note albums during 1960-64, and all are easily recommended. The power and creativity he showed during those performances led to his first successful comeback and display him in prime form. This particular CD (the reissue adds a version of "Landslide" not released at the time) showcases the distinctive tenor with a quartet that also includes pianist Kenny Drew, bassist Paul Chambers, and drummer Philly Joe Jones. Gordon and Drew contributed six originals to the date, but it is the leader's interpretations of the two standards ("End of a Love Affair" and particularly "Smile") that are most memorable. —*Scott Yanow*

Landslide / May 9, 1961-Jun. 25, 1962 / Blue Note ◆◆◆

Go! / Aug. 27, 1962 / Blue Note ◆◆◆◆
Dexter Gordon is in hard-swinging yet lyrical form throughout this particularly strong release. Accompanied by pianist Sonny Clark, bassist Butch Warren, and drummer Billy Higgins, Gordon is heard at his best on "I Guess I'll Hang My Tears out to Dry," "Where Are You," and "Three O'Clock in the Morning," three rarely performed standards. All of Dexter Gordon's Blue Note recordings (and in reality 90% of his releases) are recommended to lovers of bop and straightahead jazz. —*Scott Yanow*

A Swingin' Affair / Aug. 29, 1962 / Blue Note ◆◆◆◆
Recorded just two days after his popular album *Go* and using the same personnel (pianist Sonny Clark, bassist Butch Warren and drummer Billy Higgins), tenor great Dexter Gordon stretches out on two of his originals, Warren's "The Backbone" and (best of all) three standards: "You Stepped

out of a Dream," "Until the Real Thing Comes Along," and the high point "Don't Explain." This CD is well worth getting. —*Scott Yanow*

Cry Me a River / Nov. 28, 1962 / SteepleChase ◆◆◆

Our Man in Paris / May 23, 1963 / Blue Note ◆◆◆◆
Tenor saxophonist Dexter Gordon, who had recently moved to Europe, is featured on this set with the all-star rhythm section sometimes called "the Three Bosses": pianist Bud Powell, bassist Pierre Michelot, and drummer Kenny Clarke. The repertoire is strictly bop standards and Powell in particular is in excellent form. Gordon sounds fine too on such songs as "Scrapple from The Apple," "Stairway to the Stars," and "A Night in Tunisia." —*Scott Yanow*

Cheesecake / Jun. 11, 1964 / SteepleChase ◆◆◆◆
Dexter Gordon's long stint at the Club Montmartre in Copenhagen during the summer of 1964 included weekly radio broadcasts. Happily, these live performances have been preserved and released by SteepleChase on a series of albums. This particular LP features the great tenor with a rhythm section comprised of Europe's best (pianist Tete Montoliu, bassist Niels Pedersen, and drummer Alex Riel) performing Dexter's "Cheese Cake," "Manha De Carnival," and "Second Balcony Jump." Gordon takes long solos that never seem to run out of ideas, making this set a valuable addition to his lengthy discography. —*Scott Yanow*

Body and Soul / Jul. 20, 1967 / Black Lion ◆◆◆◆
Tenor saxophonist Dexter Gordon recorded three CD's worth of material during a two-day period at Copenhagen's legendary Montmartre Club; *Take the 'A' Train* and *Both Sides of Midnight* have also been released by Black Lion on CD. Gordon and his impressive quartet (pianist Kenny Drew, bassist Neils Henning Orsted Pedersen, and drummer Albert "Tootie" Heath) play versions of "Like Someone in Love," "Come Rain or Come Shine," "There Will Never Be Another You," "Body and Soul," and "Blues Walk" that clock in between nine and 14 minutes. Ironically, Dexter, who was in peak form during his years in Europe, was somewhat forgotten in the US at the time. This set is recommended along with the two other CDs from this well documented engagement. —*Scott Yanow*

Both Sides of Midnight / Jul. 20, 1967 / Black Lion ◆◆◆◆
Tenor saxophonist Dexter Gordon is accompanied by an all-star rhythm section (pianist Kenny Drew, bassist Niels Pedersen, and drummer Albert "Tootie" Heath) on this easily enjoyable club recording from Copenhagen's Montmartre. In addition to Ben Tucker's modal "Divlette," Gordon explores four jazz standards, really digging into the material. Bop fans are advised to pick up this excellent CD. —*Scott Yanow*

Take the "A" Train / Jul. 21, 1967 / Black Lion ◆◆◆◆
During a two-day period (July 20-21, 1967) tenor saxophonist Dexter Gordon and his quartet (pianist Kenny Drew, bassist Niels Pedersen, and drummer Albert "Tootie" Heath) recorded enough music to fill up three CDs, all of which have been released by the English Black Lion label. Four of the six standards on this hard-swinging set ("But Not for Me," "Take the 'A' Train," "Blues Walk," and "Love for Sale") are over ten minutes long while the other two ("For All We Know" and "I Guess I'll Have to Hang My Tears out to Dry") are a little more concise. Throughout, Dexter Gordon is in consistently creative form, making this CD well worth getting by his fans. —*Scott Yanow*

The Tower of Power / Apr. 2, 1969 & Apr. 4, 1969 / Original Jazz Classics ◆◆◆

More Power / Apr. 2, 1969 & Apr. 4, 1969 / Original Jazz Classics ◆◆◆

Power / Apr. 2, 1969 & Apr. 4, 1969 / Prestige ◆◆◆

The Panther / Jul. 7, 1970 / Original Jazz Classics ◆◆◆◆
Although Dexter Gordon contributed three originals to this American session, it is his rendition of the three standards that are most memorable. The great tenor romps on the familiar line "The Blues Walk," digs into "Body and Soul" (giving this warhorse a fresh new interpretation), and makes a classic statement on "The Christmas Song." With the assistance of pianist Tommy Flanagan, bassist Larry Ridley, and drummer Alan Dawson, Gordon is in typically spirited form for this happy set. —*Scott Yanow*

Generation / Jul. 22, 1972 / Original Jazz Classics ◆◆◆◆
Veteran tenor saxophonist Dexter Gordon welcomed trumpeter Freddie Hubbard to his recording group several times during his career, and each collaboration was quite rewarding. For this Prestige studio set the two horns (who are joined by pianist Cedar Walton, bassist Buster Williams, and drummer Billy Higgins) work together quite well on "Milestones" (a second version is included as a bonus track), "Scared to Be Alone," Thelonious Monk's "We See," and Gordon's "The Group." This CD should please collectors. —*Scott Yanow*

More Than You Know / Feb. 21, 1975-Mar. 27, 1975 / SteepleChase ◆◆◆◆
Dexter Gordon's SteepleChase recordings of the early to mid-'70s are among the most rewarding of his career. This particular session (which finds Gordon backed by a string orchestra arranged by Palle Mikkelborg) is one of the lesser items from this fertile period. Dexter is in memorable form on "Naima" and "More than You Know" but the backup orchestra has little interplay with Gordon, and the lush charts offer few surprises. This set

does not quite live up to its potential although Gordon fans will still find moments to enjoy. —*Scott Yanow*

★ **Stable Mable** / Mar. 10, 1975 / Inner City ◆◆◆◆
Dexter Gordon is in frequently exuberant form on this quartet session with pianist Horace Parlan, bassist Niels Pedersen, and drummer Tony Inzalaco. The material, which includes "Just Friends," "Misty," "Stablemates," and "Red Cross," is familiar, but the veteran tenor sounds quite inspired throughout the joyous outing. —*Scott Yanow*

Swiss Nights, Vol. 1 / Aug. 23, 1975 / Inner City ◆◆◆◆
The first of three volumes taken from the 1975 Zurich Jazz Festival features tenor saxophonist Dexter Gordon (with his reliable sidemen pianist Kenny Drew, bassist Niels Pedersen, and drummer Alex Riel) stretching out on "Tenor Madness," "Wave," "You've Changed," and "Days of Wine and Roses." All of the performances are at least ten minutes long and there are some rambling moments, but in general, the music is quite rewarding. This was one of Gordon's prime periods. —*Scott Yanow*

Swiss Nights, Vol. 2 / Aug. 23, 1975-Aug. 24, 1975 / SteepleChase ◆◆◆◆
The second of three CDs taken from Gordon's appearances at the 1975 Montreux Jazz Festival showcases the veteran tenor in peak form. With strong support from the talented rhythm section (pianist Kenny Drew, bassist Niels Henning Orsted Pedersen, and drummer Alex Riel), Gordon is particularly exciting on a nearly 15-minute version of "There Is No Greater Love," "Wave," and Thelonious Monk's "Rhythm-A-Ning"; the latter two songs were issued for the initial time on this six-song CD reissue. Gordon is heard throughout at his best. —*Scott Yanow*

Swiss Nights, Vol. 3 / Aug. 23, 1975-Aug. 24, 1975 / SteepleChase ◆◆◆◆
The third of three CDs taken from tenor saxophonist Dexter Gordon's appearances at the 1975 Zurich Jazz Festival has more variety than his other two. There are previously unissued versions of "Tenor Madness" and "Days of Wine and Roses" (the latter has a guest appearance by trumpeter Joe Newman), tender ballad renditions of "Didn't We" and "Sophisticated Lady," an effective vocal by Gordon on "Jelly Jelly," and a rollicking rendition of "Rhythm-A-Ning." With pianist Kenny Drew, bassist Niels Pedersen, and drummer Alex Riel offering strong support, Gordon is heard in happy and hard-swinging form. —*Scott Yanow*

★ **Bouncin' with Dex** / Sep. 14, 1975 / SteepleChase ◆◆◆◆◆
Dexter Gordon recorded nine albums for SteepleChase during 1975-76 (seven in 1975 alone) and was at the peak of his powers. This particular release finds Gordon joined by pianist Tete Montoliu, bassist Niels Pedersen, and drummer Billy Higgins for two of his originals and three jazz standards. Gordon is in superlative form, jamming with enthusiasm and melodic creativity on these familiar chord changes. —*Scott Yanow*

Lullaby for a Monster / Jun. 15, 1976 / SteepleChase ◆◆◆◆
Recorded shortly before his triumphant return to the US after 12 years overseas, this Dexter Gordon album features him in a surprisingly sparse setting, accompanied only by bassist Niels Pedersen and drummer Alex Riel. Whether it be the humorous melody "Nursery Blues," Pedersen's title cut, or the four jazz standards (of which "Good Bait" was first released on this CD reissue), he is up to the challenge and his lengthy solos never lose one's interest. —*Scott Yanow*

Biting the Apple / Nov. 9, 1976 / SteepleChase ◆◆◆◆
Many of Dexter Gordon's finest recordings were cut in Europe just prior to his triumphant return to the US. This album was recorded just weeks before and is one of the veteran tenor's best. With strong assistance from pianist Barry Harris, bassist Sam Jones, and drummer Al Foster, Gordon plays exciting solos on "I'll Remember April," a warm version of "Skylark," and his two originals "Apple Jump" and "A La Modal." It is highly recommended, as are all of Dexter Gordon's SteepleChase recordings from this period. —*Scott Yanow*

Homecoming: Live at the Village Vanguard / Dec. 11, 1976-Dec. 12, 1976 / Columbia ◆◆◆◆
The acclaim that met Dexter Gordon when he returned to the US after his years in Europe was completely unexpected. Not only did the jazz critics praise the great tenor, but there were literally lines of young fans waiting to see his performances. This double CD, recorded during his historic first American tour, improved on the original double LP with the inclusion of previously unreleased versions of "Fried Bananas" and "Body and Soul." Gordon in a quintet with trumpeter Woody Shaw, pianist Ronnie Mathews, bassist Stafford James, and drummer Louis Hayes frequently sounds exuberant on these lengthy performances; all ten songs are at least 11 minutes long. The excitement of the period can definitely be felt in this excellent music. —*Scott Yanow*

Nights at the Keystone, Vols. 1-3 / May 13, 1978-Mar. 24, 1979 / Blue Note ◆◆◆◆
Nights at the Keystone dates from a couple of years after Dexter Gordon had returned triumphantly to America (1978-79). He took strong solos on several lengthy performances. One can fault the occasional excess of song quotes (especially "Laura," which seemed to pop up in every solo) but Gordon's authoritative sound, fresh ideas, and confident explorations easily compensated. Pianist George Cables was often in dazzling form (check out

"Tangerine") and was continually inventive. Bassist Rufus Reid and drummer Eddie Gladden were perfect in support. In addition, the ambience of the late, lamented Keystone Korner, San Francisco's top jazz club and possessor of one of the most knowledgeable jazz audiences anywhere, can be felt. —*Scott Yanow, Cadence*

Stephane Grappelli (Stephane Grappelly)
....

b. Jan. 26, 1908, Paris, France
Violin / Swing

One of the all-time great jazz violinists (ranking with Joe Venuti and Stuff Smith as one of the big three of pre-bop), Stephane Grappelli's longevity and consistently enthusiastic playing has done a great deal to establish the violin as a jazz instrument. He was originally self-taught as both a violinist and a pianist, although during 1924-28 he studied at the Paris Conservatoire. Grappelli played in movie theaters and dance bands before meeting guitarist Django Reinhardt in 1933. They hit it off musically from the start even though their lifestyles (Grappelli was sophisticated while Django was a gypsy) were very different. Together as the Quintet of the Hot Club of France (comprised of violin, three acoustic guitars, and bass) during 1933-39 they produced a sensational series of recordings and performances. During a London engagement in 1939, World War II broke out. Reinhardt rashly decided to return to France but Grappelli stayed in England, effectively ending the group. The violinist soon teamed up with the young pianist George Shearing in a new band that worked steadily through the war. In 1946 Grappelli and Reinhardt had the first of several reunions although they never worked together again on a regular basis (despite many new recordings). Grappelli performed throughout the '50s and '60s in clubs throughout Europe and other than recordings with Duke Ellington (*Violin Summit*) and Joe Venuti, he remained somewhat obscure in the US until he began regularly touring the world in the early '70s. Since then Grappelli has been a constant traveller and a consistent pollwinner, remaining very open-minded without altering his swing style; he has recorded with David Grisman, Earl Hines, Bill Coleman, Larry Coryell, Oscar Peterson, Jean Luc Ponty, and McCoy Tyner, among many others. Even at the age of 88, Stephane Grappelli remains at the top of his field. His early recordings are all available on Classics CDs and he has recorded quite extensively since the '70s. —*Scott Yanow*

★ **Stephane Grappelli 1935-1940** / Sep. 30, 1935-Jul. 30, 1940 / Classics ◆◆◆◆◆
This Classics CD has all of the recordings made under violinist Stephane Grappelli's name during the 1935-40 period. The earlier selections (with his Hot Four) match his violin with Django Reinhardt's guitar in what was essentially the Quintet of the Hot Club of France. There are also nine duets with Reinhardt; a couple find Grappelli switching to piano. The set concludes in 1940 with Grappelli (in London) leading an octet on two numbers that also feature the young pianist George Shearing. —*Scott Yanow*

Stephane Grappelli 1941-1943 / Feb. 28, 1941-Dec. 8, 1943 / Classics ◆◆◆◆
This Classics CD reissues some very rare recordings made by violinist Stephane Grappelli: all of his performances as a leader during a difficult three-year period. The violinist had decided to stay in England during World War II (when Django Reinhardt returned to France) and soon had a new group featuring the young pianist George Shearing. This CD has seven sessions with quartets and quintets, along with one featuring a larger group that includes other strings and a harp. Although there are vocals on eight of the numbers (by Beryl Davis and Dave Fullerton), the swinging performances and the rarity of the recordings easily compensate. —*Scott Yanow*

Limehouse Blues / Jun. 23, 1969-Jun. 24, 1969 / Black Lion ◆◆◆◆
In 1969 violinist Stephane Grappelli and guitarist Barney Kessel teamed up for a few albums. This CD, in addition to five hot performances that originally came out on LP, has five previously unreleased performances from the same sessions. Throughout, the two principals (backed by rhythm guitarist Nini Rosso, bassist Michel Gaudry, and drummer Jean-Louis Viale) are in top form, consistently inspiring each other. —*Scott Yanow*

Meets Barney Kessel / Jun. 23, 1969-Jun. 24, 1969 / Black Lion ◆◆◆◆
This excellent set features a logical combination. Violinist Stephane Grappelli originally came to fame through his recordings with guitarist Django Reinhardt. Barney Kessel, although more influenced by Charlie Christian than by Django, was one of the top jazz guitarists of the '50s and '60s, and his style was quite complementary to Grappelli's. The two teamed up for several albums' worth of material in 1969. This CD reissues the former LP *I Remember Django*, adding four additional selections and serving as a perfect introduction to the brilliant playing of Stephane Grappelli. —*Scott Yanow*

Venupelli Blues / Oct. 22, 1969 / Charly ◆◆◆◆
Stephane Grappelli and Joe Venuti, arguably the two top violinists in jazz history, only made one recording together, this heated 1969 studio session. With pianist George Wein and guitarist Barney Kessel helping out as part of the supporting four-piece rhythm section, Grappelli and Venuti often

romp during the title cut and the six standards that comprise this memorable session. This violin "battle" ends up as a dead heat, a joyous and historic occasion for all concerned. —*Scott Yanow*

★ **Live in London** / Nov. 5, 1973 / Black Lion ✦✦✦✦
One of the best groups that violinist Stephane Grappelli collaborated with during the second half of his long career has been the Hot Club of London, a unit led by guitarist Diz Disley and usually including a second rhythm guitarist and a bassist. This Black Lion CD reissues the entire contents of a former two-LP set (*I Got Rhythm*) and even has room for a previously unreleased version of "Them There Eyes." Grappelli sounds particularly inspired playing with this group, very comfortable with the drumless setting, and free to dominate the proceedings. —*Scott Yanow*

Young Django / Jan. 19, 1979-Jan. 21, 1979 / Verve ✦✦✦✦
This CD finds veteran violinist Stephane Grappelli joined by bassist Niels Pedersen and guitarists Philip Catherine and Larry Coryell for a memorable tribute to Django Reinhardt. Grappelli has recorded many Reinhardt memorial albums through the years but this one is particularly special, for both Coryell and Catherine go out of their way to display the unexpected influence that Reinhardt has had on their styles. The guitarists contribute a song apiece and also enjoy playing seven compositions cowritten by Django and Grappelli. —*Scott Yanow*

★ **Stephane Grappelli and David Grisman Live** / Sep. 7, 1979-Sep. 20, 1979 / Warner Bros. ✦✦✦✦✦
One of the most exciting of the many Stephane Grappelli recordings, this live session (a straight CD reissue of the original LP) teams the veteran violinist with mandolist David Grisman's band, an ensemble that (in addition to its leader) boasts hot solos from Mike Marshall on violin, guitarist Mark O'Connor (who switches to violin to battle Grappelli on a memorable "Tiger Rag"), and bassist Rob Wasserman. The first two songs ("Shine" and "Pent-Up House") are taken at breakneck tempos and then, after the group tries to cool off on "Misty," they really burn on "Sweet Georgia Brown" and "Tiger Rag." Essential music with more than its share of great solos. —*Scott Yanow*

Olympia 1988 / Jan. 24, 1988 / Atlantic ✦✦✦
One on One, with McCoy Tyner / Apr. 18, 1990 / Milestone ✦✦✦✦
Violinist Stephane Grappelli, although a veteran of the swing era, has always kept an open mind towards newer styles even while he has retained his own sound and veteran repertoire. This duet set with pianist McCoy Tyner might seem unlikely at first glance, but it works quite well. The duo sticks to standards (including two that are associated with John Coltrane) and find plenty of common ground. The mutual respect they have for each other is obvious and they both sound a bit inspired. —*Scott Yanow*

Wardell Gray

b. Feb. 13, 1921, Oklahoma City, OK, **d.** May 25, 1955, Las Vegas, NV
Sax (Tenor) / Bop, Swing
Wardell Gray was one of the top tenors to emerge during the bop era (along with Dexter Gordon and Teddy Edwards). His Lester Young-influenced tone made his playing attractive to swing musicians as well as younger modernists. He grew up in Detroit, playing in local bands as a teenager. Gray was with Earl Hines during 1943-45, recording with him in 1945. That same year he moved to Los Angeles and became a major part of the Central Avenue scene, having nightly tenor battles with Dexter Gordon; their recording of "The Chase" was popular. Gray recorded with Charlie Parker in 1947, and yet his style appealed to Benny Goodman with whom he played the following year. Among his own sessions, his solos on "Twisted" (1949) and "Farmer's Market" (1952) were turned into memorable vocals by Annie Ross a few years later. Back in New York, Gray played and recorded with Tadd Dameron and the Count Basie Septet and Big Band (1950-51); "Little Pony," his showcase with the Basie orchestra, is a classic. Gray was featured on some Norman Granz jam sessions ("Apple Jam" has a particularly heated solo) and recorded with Louie Bellson (1952-53). Ironically Gray, who in the late '40s was an inspiration to some younger musicians due to his opposition to drug use, himself became involved in drugs and died mysteriously in Las Vegas on May 25, 1955, when he was just 34. —*Scott Yanow*

One for Prez / Nov. 23, 1946 / Black Lion ✦✦✦✦
★ **Wardell Gray Memorial, Vol. 1** / 1949-1953 / Original Jazz Classics ✦✦✦✦✦
The legendary tenor is in sympathetic quartets and larger combos where he can duel at big. 1949, 1950, 1952, and 1953 sessions in Detroit, Los Angeles (live at the Hula Hut), and New York City. There are lots of bonus tracks on CD. Participants include Dexter Gordon, Art Mardigan, Art Farmer, Hampton Hawes, Al Haig, Frank Morgan, and Teddy Charles. A must-buy for veteran listeners and newcomers alike. —*Michael G. Nastos*

Wardell Gray Memorial, Vol. 2 / Nov. 11, 1949-Dec. 1951 / Original Jazz Classics ✦✦✦✦
Both this and the first volume were originally paired together in the '60s as one of the first two-fers initiated by Prestige. It was a terrific bargain then, a

great bargain again almost 10 years later, when it was included in another two-fer, and now in single album incarnation the music remains fine. The material here contained almost all of Gray's (tenor sax) Prestige material and some classics. —*Bob Rusch, Cadence*

☆ **Central Ave.** / Nov. 11, 1949-Feb. 20, 1953 / Prestige ✦✦✦✦✦
These are landmark West Coast jazz recordings from a neglected figure who was definitely not part of the dominant cool school. Wardell Gray was a superb soloist, particularly when involved in combative jam sessions with fellow players such as Dexter Gordon. These late '40s and early '50s recordings were among the finest done by Black jazz musicians playing bop in hostile territory. They were re-released as part of the Prestige two-record reissue line in the '70s and are now available on compact disc. —*Ron Wynn*

Benny Green

b. Apr. 4, 1963, New York, NY
Piano / Hard Bop
Although not yet an innovator himself, Benny Green has managed to combine the styles of Bobby Timmons, Wynton Kelly, Gene Harris, and especially Oscar Peterson in his playing; his fast octave runs are often wondrous. He grew up in Berkeley and played as a teenager with Joe Henderson and Woody Shaw. After moving to New York, he spent important periods with Betty Carter (1983-87) and Art Blakey's Jazz Messengers (1987-89), becoming quite well known during the latter association. In addition to working with Freddie Hubbard, Green popped up in many bop-oriented settings for a few years before joining Ray Brown's Trio in 1992. At the same time he has worked with his own trio, which originally included Christian McBride and Carl Allen. When Oscar Peterson in 1992 was asked to name his protégé for a concert, Green was his choice. Benny Green has recorded for Criss Cross and Blue Note in addition to his work with Ray Brown on Telarc and his earlier Blakey dates. —*Scott Yanow*

★ **Testifyin'!: Live at the Village Vanguard** / Nov. 1992 / Blue Note ✦✦✦✦
A former member of Betty Carter's band, Green shows on this set that the word on him was correct; he's both an aggressive and sensitive stylist, able to rip through songs and make quick yet correct chord changes. Yet he can also play a passionate ballad and not rush through it, instead developing and then completing his solos impressively. —*Ron Wynn*

That's Right! / Dec. 21, 1992-Dec. 23, 1992 / Blue Note ✦✦✦✦
At the time of this 1992 recording, Benny Green had developed into a masterful pianist who thought fast, swung hard, and played with soul, mixing together Oscar Peterson, Gene Harris, and Bobby Timmons. The only problem was that his music had become somewhat predictable, sticking closely to the boundaries of hard bop circa 1962. In his trio with bassist Christian McBride and drummer Carl Allen, Green is heard in top form for the period (his version of Bud Powell's "Celia" is particularly memorable) and performs a program that is easily recommended to lovers of bop. Benny Green plays with such enthusiasm and joy that it almost sounds as if he had invented the style. —*Scott Yanow*

Bunky Green

b. 1935
Sax (Alto) / Post-Bop, Hard Bop
Bunky Green has long had his own sound, but unfortunately most of his recordings have gone long out of print as he has conducted a career as an educator (including a term as the president of the International Association of Jazz Educators). In 1960 Green had a stint with Charles Mingus, and later that year moved to Chicago, where he played with Ira Sullivan, Andrew Hill, Louie Bellson, Yusef Lateef, and Sonny Stitt, among others. Originally strongly influenced by Charlie Parker, Green spent a period reassessing his style and studying, emerging with a much more distinctive sound. He recorded for Exodus (1960) and Argo (1964-66), but his best work was his mid-to-late-'70s recordings for Vanguard and a 1989 session for Delos. A self-described "inside/outside" player, Bunky Green has had an influence on the styles of Steve Coleman and Greg Osby. —*Scott Yanow*

Places We've Never Been / Feb. 21, 1979 & Feb. 22, 1979 / Vanguard ✦✦✦✦
With Randy Brecker (tpt), Al Dailey Trio. Modal "East & West" shows alto saxophonist at his improvisational best. —*Michael G. Nastos*

In Love Again / 1987 / Mark ✦✦✦✦
Quintet with trumpeter Willie Thomas. Three by saxophonist Green, one by Thomas, one cowritten by the pair, and one standard ("You Stepped out of a Dream"). —*Michael G. Nastos*

● **Healing the Pain** / Dec. 13, 1989-Dec. 14, 1989 / Delos ✦✦✦✦
With Billy Childs Trio, sharp drummer Ralph Penland, and the great bassist Art Davis. All standards save two are Bucky's originals. A bright alto voice shines through. —*Michael G. Nastos*

Freddie Green

b. Mar. 31, 1911, Charleston, SC, **d.** Mar. 1, 1987, Las Vegas, NV
Guitar / Swing

Freddie Green was known throughout his long career as the definitive rhythm guitarist. He rarely soloed (briefly on a few records early on), stuck to acoustic guitar, and was often more felt than heard. Although he had originally played banjo, Green was playing guitar in New York in early 1937 when producer John Hammond heard him and immediately recommended him to Count Basie. A quick audition and Green had the job, forming a classic rhythm section with Basie, Walter Page, and Jo Jones. After 13 years with the orchestra, Green was not originally included in Basie's small group in 1950 but one night sat down uninvited on the bandstand and never left! He stayed with the band even after its leader's death, making a recording with Dianne Schuur and the Frank Foster-led orchestra in 1987 shortly before he passed on after nearly 50 years of service. Freddie Green also composed "Corner Pocket" (later renamed "Until I Met You" for the vocal version) and "Down for Double." — *Scott Yanow*

● **Natural Rhythm** / Feb. 3, 1955 & Dec. 18, 1955 / Bluebird ✦✦✦✦
Green's *Mr. Rhythm* & Al Cohn's *Natural Seven* albums combined. A wonderful collaboration between Freddie Green (away from the Basie band) and Al Cohn (ts). — *Ron Wynn*

Grant Green

b. Jun. 6, 1931, St. Louis, MO, **d.** Jan. 31, 1979, New York, NY
Guitar / Soul-Jazz, Hard Bop, Groove

Grant Green was born in St. Louis on July 6, 1931, learned his instrument in grade school from his guitar-playing father, and was playing professionally by the age of 13 with a gospel group. He worked gigs in his home town and in East St. Louis, IL, until he moved to New York in 1960 at the suggestion of Lou Donaldson. Green told Dan Morgenstern in a *Down Beat* interview "The first thing I learned to play was boogie woogie. Then I had to do a lot of rock 'n' roll. It's all blues, anyhow."

His extensive foundation in R&B combined with a mastery of bebop and simplicity that put expressiveness ahead of technical expertise. Green was a superb blues interpreter, and his later material was predominantly blues and R&B, though he was also a wondrous ballad and standards soloist. He was a particular admirer of Charlie Parker, and his phrasing often reflected it. Green played in the '50s with Jimmy Forrest, Harry Edison, and Lou Donaldson.

He also collaborated with many organists, among them Brother Jack McDuff, Sam Lazar, Baby Face Willette, Gloria Coleman, Big John Patton, and Larry Young. During the early '60s, both his fluid, tasteful playing in organ/guitar/drum combos and his other dates for Blue Note established Green as a star, though he seldom got the critical respect given other players. He was off the scene for a bit in the mid-'60s, but came back strong in the late '60s and '70s. Green played with Stanley Turrentine, Dave Bailey, Yusef Lateef, Joe Henderson, Hank Mobley, Herbie Hancock, McCoy Tyner, and Elvin Jones.

Sadly, drug problems interrupted his career in the '60s and undoubtedly contributed to the illness he suffered in the late '70s. Green was hospitalized in 1978 and died a year later. Despite some rather uneven LPs near the end of his career, the great body of his work represents marvelous soul-jazz, bebop and blues.

A severely underrated player during his lifetime, Grant Green is one of the great unsung heroes of jazz guitar. Like Stanley Turrentine, he tends to be left out of the books. Although he mentions Charlie Christian and Jimmy Raney as influences, Green always claimed he listened to horn players (Charlie Parker and Miles Davis) and not other guitar players, and it shows. No other player has this kind of single-note linearity (he avoids chordal playing). There is very little of the intellectual element in Green's playing, and his technique is always at the service of his music. And it is music, plain and simple, that makes Green unique.

Green's playing is immediately recognizable—perhaps more than any other guitarist. Green has been almost systematically ignored by jazz buffs with a bent to the cool side, and he has only recently begun to be appreciated for his incredible musicality. Perhaps no guitarist has ever handled standards and ballads with the brilliance of Grant Green. Mosaic, the nation's premier jazz reissue label, issued a wonderful collection *The Complete Blue Note Recordings with Sonny Clark*, featuring prime early '60s Green albums plus unissued tracks. Some of the finest examples of Green's work can be found there. — *Michael Erlewine and Ron Wynn*

Grant's First Stand / Jan. 28, 1961 / Blue Note ✦✦✦
His first album, with Baby Face Willette on Hammond organ and Ben Dixon on drums. Hard to find. Some of this material was released in Japan. — *Michael Erlewine*

Green Blues / Mar. 15, 1961 / Black Lion ✦✦✦
With Frank Haynes on tenor sax, Billy Gardner on piano, Ben Tucker on bass, and Dave Bailer on drums. Originally issued on *Jazztime* under Dave Bailey's name and now reissued in this format. This is early Green, his second session, and the music is straightahead mainstream jazz with a bluesy

flavor. This material is available on *Reaching Out*, a release on the Black Lion label. — *Michael Erlewine*

Reaching Out / Mar. 15, 1961 / Black Lion ✦✦✦
Green is in fine form as is pianist Gardner (better known as an organist), but the album is perhaps most valuable for the contributions of the obscure tenorman Frank Haynes, who died in 1965; his sound will remind some a little of Stanley Turrentine. — *Scott Yanow, Cadence*

Green Street / Apr. 1, 1961 / Blue Note ✦✦✦✦
Most of guitarist Grant Green's recordings of the '60s feature him in larger groups, making this trio outing with bassist Ben Tucker and drummer Dave Bailey (a CD reissue of the original LP plus two added alternate takes) a strong showcase for his playing. Green, whose main competitor on guitar at the time was Wes Montgomery, already had his own singing sound and a highly individual hornlike approach. He stretches out on a full set of attractive originals plus "'Round Midnight" and "Alone Together," so this reissue is an excellent introduction to his appealing and hard-swinging style. — *Scott Yanow*

Sunday Mornin' / Jun. 4, 1961 / Blue Note ✦✦✦
Sunday Mornin' is Green's fourth album with Blue Note and his first quartet with a piano rather than a Hammond organ. Sidemen include Kenny Drew (piano), Ben Dixon (drums), and Ben Tucker (bass). The result is a sound that is spacious and crisp—a solid setting for Green's single-note leads. This early Grant Green is straightahead jazz with a bluesy tone, similar to what you will find on his album *Matador*. Tunes include the blues "Freedom March," the gospel-influenced "Sunday Mornin'," the lovely theme from "Exodus," a delicate rendition of Billie Holiday's "God Bless the Child," and a great version of the Miles Davis classic "So What." — *Michael Erlewine*

Grantstand / Aug. 1, 1961 / Blue Note ✦✦✦✦
A quartet session with Yusef Lateef (ts, fl) and vintage Jack McDuff on the Hammond organ. Al Harewood is on drums, the organ taking up the bass chores. The 15-minute "Blues in Maude's Flat" is very nice indeed, and "My Funny Valentine" (with Lateef on flute) is just plain lovely. No one does standards like Green. — *Michael Erlewine*

Born to Be Blue / Dec. 11, 1961 & Mar. 1, 1962 / Blue Note ✦✦✦✦
This is the one to get, a taste of what is in the (now out of print) Mosaic box set *The Complete Blue Note Recordings of Grant Green with Sonny Clark*. This is vintage Green with Sonny Clark on piano and Ike Quebeck on tenor sax. The combination is mesmerizing. This is the stuff groove addicts dream of—a desert island classic pick. Green is the master of standards and the set includes "Someday My Prince Will Come," "Count Every Star," and "Back in Your Own Back Yard." Aside from being just the best jazz, it makes for great easy-listening music. Grandma will love it too. — *Michael Erlewine*

Gooden's Corner / Dec. 23, 1961 / Blue Note ✦✦✦✦
This is an album of real beauty and synergy between Green and pianist Sonny Clark, who along with Sam Jones on bass and Louis Hayes on drums rounds out the quartet. Green, an expert with standards, offers "Moon River," "On Green Dolphin Street," and "Count Every Star." This album was also released on *The Complete Blue Note Recordings of Grant Green and Sonny Clark*. — *Michael Erlewine*

★ **Complete Blue Note with Sonny Clark** / Dec. 23, 1961-Sep. 7, 1962 / Mosaic ✦✦✦✦✦
Guitarist Grant Green and pianist Sonny Clark recorded together on five separate occasions during the 1961-62 period but virtually none of the music was released domestically until decades later. These performances were clearly lost in the shuffle, for the solos are of a consistent high quality and the programs were well paced and swinging. Now on this Mosaic limited-edition four-CD box set, the long-lost music (much of which had been previously available only in Japan) is saved for posterity. Green and Clark blend together well, tenor saxophonist Ike Quebec joins their quartet for one session, and the final two numbers add Latin percussion. All of this music should be easily enjoyed by hard-bop fans. Includes Blue Note albums *Gooden's Corner, Nigeria, Oleo, Born to Be Blue* (w/ Ike Quebec), plus unissued tracks. — *Scott Yanow*

Nigeria / Jan. 13, 1962 / Blue Note ✦✦✦✦
This is a great album with the classic synergy of Green and pianist Sonny Clark, who along with Sam Jones on bass and Art Blakey complete the quartet. This album was also released on *The Complete Blue Note Recordings of Grant Green and Sonny Clark*. Just classic Green. — *Michael Erlewine*

Oleo / Jan. 31, 1962 / Blue Note ✦✦✦✦
This is an another excellent album with Green and pianist Sonny Clark, who along with Sam Jones on bass and Louis Hayes on drums make the foursome. The entire album is fine with "My Favorite Things," an old favorite of Green. This album was also released on *The Complete Blue Note Recordings of Grant Green and Sonny Clark*. If you can find this album, or the Mosaic set anywhere, you will be very satisfied. The best. — *Michael Erlewine*

The Latin Bit / Apr. 26, 1962 / Blue Note ✦✦✦
A good title, these are Latin standards with Grant Green in Latin mode and performing standards like "Tico Tico," "Brazil," "Grenada," "Besame Mucho," and "Hey There." The group includes Johnny Acea (p), Wendell Marshall (b), Willie Bobo (d), and added percussion from Carlos "Potato" Valdez on conga and Carvin Masseaux on chekere. As an added bonus, Ike Quebec plays on two of the standards. One wonders whether these standards were often played by Green. The brightness of the Latin tunes replaces the more substantial soul-jazz feel Grant fans expect. Still, Green in his prime. —*Michael Erlewine*

Goin' West / Nov. 30, 1962 / Blue Note ✦✦✦
Another Blue Note album yet to be reissued, this one (like *Feelin' the Spirit*) includes Herbie Hancock on piano, Reggie Workman on bass, and Billy Higgins on drums. It includes tunes like (can you believe?) "On Top of Old Smokey" and "Tumbling Tumbleweeds." Only Green could carry this off, but he is "the man" when it comes to standards. —*Michael Erlewine*

Feelin' the Spirit / Dec. 21, 1962 / Blue Note ✦✦✦✦
An entire album of spirituals—all jazz instrumentals. Green, already a bluesy guitarist, lets himself out in the gospel format. The result is an album that remains true to both the soul-jazz and gospel genres. With Green on this date is Herbie Hancock on piano. Every Grant Green fan loves this unique gospel-toned album. It includes standards like "Just a Closer Walk with Thee," "Nobody Knows the Trouble I've Seen," and "Sometimes I Feel Like a Motherless Child." A Grant Green classic. —*Michael Erlewine*

Am I Blue? / May 16, 1963 / Blue Note ✦✦✦✦
A date for Blue Note with Joe Henderson (tenor sax), John Patton (Hammond organ), Johnny Coles (tpt), and Ben Dixon (d). —*Michael Erlewine*

★ **Idle Moments** / Nov. 4, 1963 & Nov. 11, 1963 / Blue Note ✦✦✦✦✦
Excellent mid-size group album, with Green in good form. Bobby Hutcherson (vibes) in the group produces a somewhat different sound than the usual Green album, so make a note of it. Duke Pearson is there on piano along with Joe Henderson (ts), who is hot. All things considered, the groove is there and this is worth having. —*Michael Erlewine*

☆ **Matador** / May 20, 1964 / Blue Note ✦✦✦✦✦
This is an exceptional Grant Green album for several reasons. For one, it (along with *Solid*) is one of very few Green outings that are straightahead jazz, rather than out-and-out soul-jazz. Second, this is one of Coltrane's finest bands with Green as the featured soloist rather than Coltrane—McCoy Tyner (p), Bob Cranshaw (b), and Elvin Jones (d). Coltrane had just finished recording his classic album *Crescent*, and the band is hot. Green shows a lot of guts to lead this band, not to mention tackling the Coltrane hit "My Favorite Things" and pulls it off. Green's soul-jazz fans need not fear that this is too dry. This is a great album and classic Grant Green. —*Michael Erlewine*

Solid / Jun. 12, 1964 / Blue Note ✦✦✦✦
Not released until 1979, this set contains more challenging material than many of guitarist Grant Green's other Blue Note sessions. In a state-of-the-art sextet with tenor saxophonist Joe Henderson, altoist James Spaulding, pianist McCoy Tyner, bassist Bob Cranshaw, and drummer Elvin Jones, Green performs tunes by Duke Pearson, George Russell ("Ezz-thetic"), Sonny Rollins, Henderson ("The Kicker"), and his own "Grant's Tune." Perhaps this music was considered too uncommercial initially, or maybe it was simply lost in the shuffle. In any case, this is one of Green's finer recordings. —*Scott Yanow*

Talkin' About! / Sep. 11, 1964 / Blue Note ✦✦✦
A rare trio date for Grant Green with Larry Young (organ), and Elvin Jones (d). Although Green was the leader for this date, it is now available on the Mosaic label as part of *The Complete Blue Note Recordings of Larry Young*. One of the first albums by Larry Young. This is classic Green. —*Michael Erlewine*

Street of Dreams / Nov. 16, 1964 / Blue Note ✦✦✦
Vibist Bobby Hutcherson joins Green, Larry Young (organ), and Elvin Jones (d) for this fine release, which is now available on the Mosaic label as part of *The Complete Blue Note Recordings of Larry Young*. This is great soul-jazz. Larry Young and Green are, as usual, just excellent. Contains "Somewhere in the Night" and "Street of Dreams." —*Michael Erlewine*

I Want to Hold Your Hand / Mar. 31, 1965 / Blue Note ✦✦✦✦
Tenor saxophonist Hank Mobley joins Green, Larry Young (organ), and Elvin Jones (d) for this very excellent album, which is now available on the Mosaic label as part of *The Complete Blue Note Recordings of Larry Young* (worth getting while it is still available!) Unlike some of Young's later work, this music is in the soul-jazz vein and under Green's lead. It has groove and great playing from Green and Young. —*Michael Erlewine*

His Majesty, King Funk / May 26, 1965 / Verve ✦✦✦
Don't be scared off by the title of this album; this is not Green's later commercial stuff. This is excellent Grant Green with Larry Young on organ, Harold Vick on sax, Ben Dixon on drums, and Candido Camero on conga—essentially a classic four piece. And this is soul-jazz with a deep

groove. This is the last of five albums Green recorded with Larry Young. Produced by Creed Taylor, this is the only album Green did for Verve and perhaps his last real jazz album before several years of inactivity, after which he became somewhat more commercial in his approach. Includes the standard "That Lucky Old Sun." —*Michael Erlewine*

Iron City / 1967 / Muse ✦✦✦

Carryin' On / Oct. 3, 1969 / Blue Note ✦✦
Grant Green's recording career was just starting to slip at the time of this release, although the talented guitarist always played as well as he could under the circumstances. He manages to uplift the dated R&Bish and pop material a bit, but his backup band (which includes tenor saxophonist Claude Bartee and either Clarence Palmer or Earl Neal Creque on electric piano) seems content to repeat the same grooves endlessly and play it safe, making this CD reissue of rather limited interest. —*Scott Yanow*

Green Is Beautiful / 1970 / Blue Note ✦✦✦
Of the five songs included on this CD reissue, the first three are one-chord vamps; not one of these renditions were destined to be remembered as a classic. "Ain't It Funky Now" makes the set worthwhile, for it has tenor saxophonist Claude Bartee doing a close imitation of Eddie Harris, and trumpeter Blue Mitchell taking an exciting solo. But the unimaginative material in general does not really inspire guitarist Green and keeps this CD from being too essential. —*Scott Yanow*

Alive! / Aug. 15, 1970 / Blue Note ✦✦

Shades of Green / Nov. 23, 1971 / Blue Note ✦✦
A Blue Note date with a large group including horns, reeds, woodwinds, vibes, et al. Consists of standards and even a medley. This is not the old Grant Green. —*Michael Erlewine*

The Final Come Down / Dec. 13, 1971 / Blue Note ✦✦✦
A soundtrack for Blue Note with a very large group, including Harold Vick (sax), Cornell Dupree (g), and Grady Tate (d). —*Michael Erlewine*

Visions / 1971 / Blue Note ✦✦✦

Live at the Lighthouse / Apr. 21, 1972 / Blue Note ✦✦✦

The Main Attraction / Mar. 1976 / Kudu ✦✦✦
On the Kudo label, a larger group (many horns) with Hubert Laws (fl), Steve Khan (g), John Faddis (tp), and Michael Brecker (sax). —*Michael Erlewine*

The Best of Grant Green, Vol. 1 / Oct. 19, 1993 / Blue Note ✦✦✦
While the "best-of" format often leaves quite a bit to be desired in a jazz setting, this set contains good Green material from his most productive period, the early and mid-'60s. There's a nice mix between uptempo and slower numbers, standards, and his own compositions, as well as soul-jazz and straight mainstream and bop material. Although this isn't as far-reaching or comprehensive as Green's Mosaic set, this set will satisfy the needs of those unfamiliar with his work or listeners who just want a good cross section of his cuts. —*Ron Wynn*

Al Grey

b. Jun. 6, 1925, Aldie, VA
Trombone / Bop, Swing
Al Grey's trademark phrases and often humorous use of the plunger mute have long made him quite distinctive. After getting out of the service, he played with the orchestras of Benny Carter (1945-46), Jimmie Lunceford (1946-47), Lucky Millinder, and Lionel Hampton (off and on during 1948-53). Grey was a well featured soloist with the classic Dizzy Gillespie globetrotting orchestra during 1956-57 (taking an exciting solo at the 1957 Newport Jazz Festival on a blazing version of "Cool Breeze"). He was with Count Basie's orchestra on three separate occasions (1957-61, 1964-66, and 1971-77), led a band with Billy Mitchell in the early '60s, and had a group with Jimmy Forrest after leaving Basie in 1977. In recent years Grey has performed and recorded often with Clark Terry, made a CD with the Statesmen of Jazz, and for a time led a quintet that featured his son Mike Grey on second trombone. Al Grey recorded as a leader for Argo (1959-64), Tangerine, Black & Blue, Stash, Chiaroscuro, and Capri and co-led an excellent Pablo date in 1983 with J.J. Johnson. —*Scott Yanow*

★ **Things Are Getting Better All the Time** / 1983 / Original Jazz Classics ✦✦✦✦✦

Fab / Feb. 4, 1990 & Feb. 7, 1990 / Capri ✦✦✦✦

Live at the Floating Jazz Festival / Oct. 22, 1990-Oct. 25, 1990 / Chiaroscuro ✦✦✦

Center Piece, Live at the Blue Note / Mar. 23, 1995-Mar. 26, 1995 / Telarc Jazz ✦✦✦

Johnny Griffin

b. Apr. 24, 1928, Chicago, IL
Sax (Tenor) / Bop, Hard Bop, Groove
Once accurately billed as "the world's fastest saxophonist," Johnny Griffin (an influence tonewise on Rahsaan Roland Kirk) has been one of the top

bop-oriented tenors since the mid-'50s. He gained early experience playing with the bands of Lionel Hampton (1945-47) and Joe Morris (1947-50) and also jammed regularly with Thelonious Monk and Bud Powell. After serving in the Army (1951-53), Griffin spent a few years in Chicago (recording his first full album for Argo) and then moved to New York in 1956. He held his own against fellow tenors John Coltrane and Hank Mobley in a classic Blue Note album, was with Art Blakey's Jazz Messengers in 1957, and proved to be perfect with the Thelonious Monk Quartet in 1958 where he really ripped through the complex chord changes with ease. During 1960-62 Griffin co-led a "tough tenor" group with Eddie "Lockjaw" Davis. He emigrated to Europe in 1963 and became a fixture on the Paris jazz scene both as a bandleader and a major soloist with the Kenny Clarke—Francy Boland Big Band. In 1973 Johnny Griffin moved to the Netherlands but has remained a constant world traveller, visiting the US often and recording for many labels including Blue Note, Riverside, Atlantic, SteepleChase, Black Lion, Antilles, Verve, and some European companies. —*Scott Yanow*

Introducing Johnny Griffin / Apr. 17, 1956 / Blue Note ✦✦✦✦
A date that shows Griffin's speed, technique, and power. —*Ron Wynn*

☆ **A Blowing Session** / Apr. 6, 1957 / Blue Note ✦✦✦✦✦
More than just a mere "blowing session," these four jams (on a pair of standards and two Johnny Griffin compositions) match together three very different tenor stylists: Griffin, Hank Mobley, and John Coltrane. Although the solos and trade-offs are often quite combative, the result is a three-way dead heat, for each of these tenor greats has a different approach and a distinctive sound. Of all of the '50s jam sessions, this is one of the most successful and exciting. —*Scott Yanow*

★ **The Congregation** / Oct. 13, 1957 / Blue Note ✦✦✦✦✦
The great tenor saxophonist Johnny Griffin is heard in top form on this near-classic quartet set. Assisted by pianist Sonny Clark, bassist Paul Chambers, and drummer Kenny Dennis, Griffin is exuberant on "The Congregation" (which is reminiscent of Horace Silver's "The Preacher"), thoughtful on the ballads, and swinging throughout. It's recommended for bop collectors. —*Scott Yanow*

Johnny Griffin Sextet / Feb. 25, 1958 / Original Jazz Classics ✦✦✦✦
The great tenor Johnny Griffin made his debut on Riverside with this sextet set which has been reissued on CD in the OJC series. Griffin is teamed with trumpeter Donald Byrd, baritonist Pepper Adams, pianist Kenny Drew, bassist Wilbur Ware, and drummer Philly Joe Jones for three obscure tunes, the ballad "What's New," and a cooking version of "Woody'N You." High-quality hard bop from some of the best. —*Scott Yanow*

Way Out! / Feb. 26, 1958-Feb. 27, 1958 / Original Jazz Classics ✦✦✦✦
This formerly obscure quartet set by tenor saxophonist Johnny Griffin (reissued on CD in the OJC series) features the soloist on five little-known originals written by Chicagoans plus a burning version of "Cherokee." Virtually all of Griffin's recordings are worth getting and, with the assistance of pianist Kenny Drew, bassist Wilbur Ware, and drummer Philly Joe Jones, the tenor is in superior form for this spirited date. —*Scott Yanow*

The Little Giant / Aug. 4, 1959-Aug. 5, 1959 / Original Jazz Classics ✦✦✦

The Big Soul Band / May 24, 1960-Jun. 3, 1960 / Original Jazz Classics ✦✦✦

Griff and Lock / Nov. 4, 1960 & Nov. 10, 1960 / Original Jazz Classics ✦✦✦✦
For a couple years in the early '60s, tenors Johnny Griffin and Eddie "Lockjaw" Davis co-led a popular quintet, jamming bop standards and occasional originals. Although their sounds were very different (one never had trouble telling them apart), their styles were quite complementary and their combative approaches constantly inspired each other to some heated playing. This former Jazzland LP finds the tough tenors at their best. —*Scott Yanow*

White Gardenia / Jul. 13, 1961-Jul. 17, 1961 / Original Jazz Classics ✦✦✦

Tough Tenor Favorites / Feb. 5, 1962 / Original Jazz Classics ✦✦✦✦
Johnny Griffin and Eddie "Lockjaw" Davis, the two "tough tenors" in question, always made for an exciting team. With pianist Horace Parlan, bassist Buddy Catlett, and drummer Ben Riley completing the quintet for this CD reissue of a Jazzland date from 1962, Griff and Lockjaw are in top form and quite competitive on a variety of standards. Highlights include "Blue Lou," "Ow," "I Wished on the Moon," and "From This Moment On." The main winner in these fiery tenor "battles" is the listener! —*Scott Yanow*

The Jams Are Coming / Dec. 1975-Oct. 1977 / Timeless ✦✦✦

☆ **Bush Dance** / Oct. 18, 1978-Oct. 19, 1978 / Galaxy ✦✦✦✦✦
Johnny Griffin has (at least since the mid-'50s) been one of the masters of the tenor sax although consistently underrated. This studio session is one of his great achievements, particularly a fascinating (and cleverly constructed) 17-minute version of "A Night in Tunisia." Whether it be his own "The Jams Are Coming" or a lyrical version of the veteran ballad "Since I Fell for You," Griffin (joined here by guitarist George Freeman, bassist Sam Jones, drummer Albert Heath, and percussionist Kenneth Nash) is inspired and quite creative throughout this highly recommended gem. —*Scott Yanow*

Call It Whachawana / Jul. 25, 1983-Jul. 26, 1983 / Galaxy ✦✦✦✦
The emphasis is on ballads and slower tempos on this often exquisite outing by tenor saxophonist Johnny Griffin. With strong support from the young rhythm section (pianist Mulgrew Miller, bassist Curtis Lundy, and drummer Kenny Washington), Griffin is heard at his best on a definitive version of "Lover Man," recalls his days (25 years earlier) with Thelonious Monk on "I Mean You" and introduces two recent originals. Superlative music by a masterful player. —*Scott Yanow*

The Cat / Oct. 26, 1990-Oct. 29, 1990 / Antilles ✦✦✦✦
Griffin's latest—a tasty, often impressive, outing. —*Ron Wynn*

3 Dances of Passion / Apr. 29, 1992-Apr. 30, 1992 / Antilles ✦✦✦

Chicago, New York, Paris / 1995 / Verve ✦✦✦✦

Tiny Grimes (Lloyd Grimes)

b. Jul. 7, 1916, Newport News, VA, d. Mar. 4, 1989
Guitar / Bop, Early R&B
Tiny Grimes was one of the earliest jazz electric guitarists to be influenced by Charlie Christian and he developed his own bluish swinging style. Early on he was a drummer and worked as a pianist in Washington. In 1938 he started playing electric guitar and two years later he was playing in a jive group, the Cats and a Fiddle. During 1943-44 Grimes was part of a classic Art Tatum Trio which included Slam Stewart. In September 1944 he led his first record date, using Charlie Parker; highlights include the instrumental "Red Cross" and Grimes' vocal on "Romance Without Finance (Is a Nuisance)." He also recorded for Blue Note in 1946 and put together an R&B-oriented group, the Rockin' Highlanders, that featured the tenor of Red Prysock during 1948-52. Although maintaining a low profile, Tiny Grimes was active up until his death, playing in an unchanged swing/bop transitional style and recording as a leader for such labels as Prestige/Swingville, Black & Blue, Muse, and Sonet. —*Scott Yanow*

● **Tiny in Swingsville** / Aug. 13, 1959 / Original Jazz Classics ✦✦✦✦
Guitarist Tiny Grimes was a bit obscure when he had the opportunity to first record for Prestige in 1958. This particular CD (a reissue of the original LP) was the final of his three Prestige albums and it really puts the focus on Grimes' bluish but swinging guitar playing. With the strong assistance of Jerome Richardson (who is in top form on flute, tenor, and baritone), pianist Ray Bryant, bassist Wendell Marshall, and drummer Art Taylor, Grimes is heard in excellent form on "Annie Laurie," his "Durn Tootin'," "Ain't Misbehavin'," "Frankie and Johnnie," and a couple of original blues. —*Scott Yanow*

Profoundly Blue / Mar. 6, 1973 / Muse ✦✦✦

Steve Grossman

b. Jan. 18, 1951, New York, NY
Sax (Soprano), Sax (Tenor) / Hard Bop
Although he started out playing in fusion-oriented settings, Steve Grossman has developed into an excellent hard bop tenor in the tradition of Sonny Rollins (although he has developed his own sound). Grossman originally started on alto when he was eight years old, added soprano at age 15, and tenor at age 16. He started at the top as Wayne Shorter's replacement with Miles Davis, playing in his fusion group from late 1969 until September 1970. Grossman was with Lonnie Liston Smith in 1971, spent a valuable period (1971-73) as part of Elvin Jones' group, and in the mid-'70s was with Gene Perla's Stone Alliance. Steve Grossman has mostly led his own bands ever since, recording as a leader for P.M., Owl, Red, and Dreyfus. —*Scott Yanow*

My Second Prime / Dec. 17, 1990 / Red ✦✦✦✦

Do It / Apr. 1991 / Dreyfus ✦✦✦✦

★ **In New York** / Sep. 13, 1991-Sep. 14, 1991 / Dreyfus ✦✦✦✦✦

Time to Smile / Feb. 12, 1993 / Dreyfus ✦✦✦✦
This outing is one of tenor saxophonist Steve Grossman's finest recordings to date. He has mixed together the almost equal influences of John Coltrane and Sonny Rollins to achieve his own style and sound. The program is quite strong with its superior yet generally underplayed standards joined by two of the leader's originals, Elvin Jones' "E.J.'s Blues" and Freddie Redd's "Time to Smile"; also, the lineup of musicians would be difficult to top. Pianist Willie Pickens shows a lot of versatility on the hard bop-oriented music, trumpeter Tom Harrell (who is on around half of the tracks) is fiery and alert as usual, bassist Cecil McBee has a strong musical personality that comes across even when restricted to accompanying the soloists, and drummer Elvin Jones remains in prime form. The main focus however, is mostly on Grossman and he continues to grow as an improviser year by year. Highly recommended. —*Scott Yanow*

Dave Grusin

b. Jun. 26, 1934, Denver, CO
Piano / Bop, Crossover
Dave Grusin has been a highly successful performer, producer, composer,

record label executive, arranger, and bandleader. His piano playing ranges from mildly challenging to competent to routine, but he's an accomplished film and television soundtrack composer. Grusin played with Terry Gibbs and Johnny Smith while studying at the University of Colorado. He was assistant music director and pianist with Andy Williams from 1959 to 1966, and then started his television composing career. Grusin recorded with Benny Goodman in 1960 and with a hard-bop trio that included Milt Hinton and Don Lamond in the early '60s. He also played a session with a quintet including Thad Jones and Frank Foster. Grusin did arrangements and recorded with Sarah Vaughan, Quincy Jones, and Carmen McRae in the early '70s. He played electric keyboards with Gerry Mulligan and Lee Ritenour in the mid-'70s, then helped establish GRP Records out of a production company. GRP developed into one of the top contemporary jazz and fusion companies; they were later taken over by Arista, and then by MCA. Grusin continued recording through the '80s and '90s, doing numerous projects from fusion and pop to working with symphony orchestras. He's also conducted the GRP big band, continued scoring such films as The Fabulous Baker Boys, and doing duet sessions with his brother Don and Ritenour. Besides his numerous GRP releases, Grusin has also recorded for Columbia, Sheffield Lab and Polygram. —Ron Wynn

● **Sticks and Stones** / 1988 / GRP ✦✦✦✦

Zephyr / 1988 / GRP ✦✦✦

Migration / 1989 / GRP ✦✦✦

The Gershwin Collection / 1991 / GRP ✦✦✦✦
In one of his most creative efforts, Dave Grusin has fashioned an album that expresses the music of George Gershwin for the '90s. While eclectic, marked by virtuoso performances and improvisation, it is filled with the authenticity of Gershwin's original musical premise. Grusin, at the piano, is supported by a full orchestra, including his friends Chick Corea, Lee Ritenour, Don Grusin, and many more. Selections include "Prelude II," "S'Wonderful," "Bess You Is My Woman/I Loves You Porgy," and others. —MusD

● **Homage to Duke** / 1993 / GRP ✦✦✦✦
Although Dave Grusin is best known as a soundtrack composer and for his jazz-pop recordings, he has always had a great admiration for jazz. This CD (released in a fairly deluxe package) gave Grusin an opportunity to pay tribute to Duke Ellington. He performs ten mostly familiar songs associated with Ellington and wisely features fluegelhornist Clark Terry on five of the selections. Other prominent soloists include tenor saxophonist Pete Christlieb, trombonist George Bohanon, tenor saxophonist Tom Scott (returning to his roots), clarinetist Eddie Daniels (on an orchestrated version of "Mood Indigo"), and pianist Grusin himself. This is a respectful and well conceived tribute. —Scott Yanow

The Orchestral Album / 1994 / GRP ✦✦

Gigi Gryce (Basheer Quism)

b. Nov. 28, 1927, Pensacola, FL, d. Mar. 17, 1983, Pensacola, FL
Sax (Alto) / Hard Bop
Gigi Gryce was a fine altoist in the '50s, but it was his writing skills (including composing the standard "Minority") that were considered most notable. After growing up in Hartford, CT, and studying at the Boston Conservatory and in Paris, Gryce worked in New York with Max Roach, Tadd Dameron, and Clifford Brown. He toured Europe in 1953 with Lionel Hampton and led several sessions in France. After freelancing in 1954 (including recording with Thelonious Monk), Gryce worked with Oscar Pettiford's groups (1955-57) and led the Jazz Lab Quintet (1955-58), a band featuring Donald Byrd. He had a quintet with Richard Williams during 1959-61 but then stopped playing altogether to become a teacher. During his short career Gigi Gryce recorded as a leader for Vogue (many of the releases have been issued domestically on Prestige), Savoy, Metrojazz, New Jazz, and Mercury. —Scott Yanow

And the Jazz Lab Quintet / Feb. 27, 1957 / Riverside ✦✦✦✦

● **Gigi Gryce & The Jazz Lab Quintet** / Feb. 27, 1957 & Mar. 7, 1957 / Original Jazz Classics ✦✦✦✦
During 1957 altoist Gigi Gryce and trumpeter Donald Byrd co-led a quintet that sought to extend and come up with new variations to bebop. Unfortunately the group did not survive the year but Gryce and Byrd did combine for several memorable recordings, including an excellent Prestige LP reissued on this CD. Their quintet (with pianist Wade Legge, bassist Wendell Marshall, and drummer Art Taylor) turn "Love for Sale" into a jazz waltz (an innovation for 1957), introduce Gryce's best-known composition "Minority," swing "Zing Went the Strings of My Heart," and perform a tricky but memorable blues line "Straight Ahead." This is exciting and still fresh-sounding bebop. —Scott Yanow

Sayin' Somethin'! / Mar. 11, 1960 / Original Jazz Classics ✦✦✦✦
Altoist Gigi Gryce's last regular group before moving to Africa and largely retiring from music was the quintet featured on this CD, two other Prestige/New Jazz sessions, and an album for Trip. Gryce's alto matched well with Richard Williams' impressive trumpet, and with fine support from

pianist Richard Wyands, bassist Reggie Workman, and drummer Mickey Roker, the two horns explore mostly blues-based originals by Gryce, Curtis Fuller, and Hank Jones. There is more variety than expected, and the contrast between Gryce's lyricism and the extroverted nature of Williams' solos make this set fairly memorable. —Scott Yanow

The Hap'nin's / May 3, 1960 / Original Jazz Classics ✦✦✦✦
Altoist Gigi Gryce, who would retire from playing altogether within a few years, leads his promising 1960 quintet on this CD reissue. Trumpeter Richard Williams and pianist Richard Wyands take fine solos on the six jazz standards (two of which, "Minority" and "Nice's Tempo" were Gryce's best-known tunes) while bassist Julian Euell and drummer Mickey Roker are fine in support. The hard bop set has its strong moments even though this group was largely forgotten after Gryce's retirement. Worth investigating. —Scott Yanow

Vince Guaraldi (Vincant Anthony Guaraldi)

b. Jul. 17, 1928, San Francisco, CA, d. Feb. 6, 1976, Menlo Park, CA
Piano / Cool, Latin Jazz
Vince Guaraldi occupies an unusual place in jazz history. Although not a major pianist, his playing in the late '50s on ballads influenced the new age pacesetter George Winston two decades later. He was an Italian whose work in Latin-jazz impressed many and he became best known for writing the scores for the *Peanuts* television cartoons. Guaraldi played with Cal Tjader's first trio in 1951, gigged with the Bill Harris/Chubby Jackson Band (1953), Georgie Auld (1953) and Sonny Criss (1955), toured with Woody Herman's orchestra (1956-57), gained fame playing with Tjader again (1957-59), and returned to Herman for part of 1959. Guaraldi, who recorded two albums for Fantasy during 1956-57, led his own groups from 1960 on and made seven more records for Fantasy during 1962-66 including a recording of his hit original "Cast Your Fate to the Wind" and his 1965 jazz mass. —Scott Yanow

Vince Guaraldi Trio / Apr. 1956 / Original Jazz Classics ✦✦✦
This CD reissue in the OJC series brings back the first full session led by pianist Vince Guaraldi. Teamed up with the fine guitarist Eddie Duran and bassist Dean Reilly, Guaraldi swings lightly and with subtle creativity on two group originals and eight standards including "Django," "Chelsea Bridge," "Fascinatin' Rhythm," and "The Lady's in Love with You." Tasteful music. —Scott Yanow

A Flower Is a Lovesome Thing / Apr. 16, 1957 / Original Jazz Classics ✦✦✦✦
This is one of pianist Vince Guaraldi's better sets. Showcased in a San Francisco-based trio with guitarist Eddie Duran and bassist Dean Reilly, Guaraldi plays seven standards plus his own "Like a Mighty Rose" tastefully and with light swing, making this a program that is equally successful as both cool jazz and background music. —Scott Yanow

● **Jazz Impressions of "Black Orpheus"** / Apr. 18, 1962 / Original Jazz Classics ✦✦✦✦
Guaraldi blends jazz improvisation with Afro-Latin and bossa-nova stylings. —Ron Wynn

A Boy Named Charlie Brown / 1964 / Fantasy ✦✦✦✦
A most delightful album. —Michael G. Nastos

The Latin Side of Vince Guaraldi / 1964 / Fantasy ✦✦

Bobby Hackett

b. Jan. 31, 1915, Providence, RI, d. Jun. 7, 1976, Chatham, MA
Cornet / Dixieland, Swing
Bobby Hackett's mellow tone and melodic style offered a contrast to the brasher Dixieland-oriented trumpeters. Emphasizing his middle register and lyricism, Hackett was a flexible soloist who actually sounded little like his main inspiration, Louis Armstrong.

When Hackett first came up he was briefly known as "the new Bix" because of the similarity in his appproach to that of Bix Beiderbecke, but very soon he developed his own distinctive sound. Originally a guitarist (which he doubled on until the mid-'40s), Hackett performed in local bands and by 1936 was leading his own group. He moved to New York in 1937, played with Joe Marsala, appeared at Benny Goodman's 1938 Carnegie Hall concert (recreating Beiderbecke's solo on "I'm Coming Virginia"), recorded with Eddie Condon, and by 1939 had a short-lived big band. Hackett played briefly with Horace Heidt and during 1941-42 was with Glenn Miller's orchestra, taking a famous solo on "String of Pearls." Next up was a stint with the Casa Loma Orchestra; then he became a studio musician while still appearing with jazz groups. Hackett was a major asset at Louis Armstrong's 1947 Town Hall Concert, in the '50s he was a star on Jackie Gleason's commercial but jazz-flavored mood music albums, and he recorded several times with Eddie Condon and Jack Teagarden. During 1956-57 Hackett led an unusual group that sought to modernize Dixieland (using Dick Cary's arrangements and an unusual instrumentation) but that band did not catch on. Hackett recorded some commercial dates during 1959-60 (including one set of Hawaiian songs and another in which he was backed by pipe organ), he worked with Benny Goodman (1962-63), backed

Tony Bennett in the mid-'60s, co-led a well recorded quintet with Vic Dickenson (1968-70), and made sessions with Jim Cullum, the World's Greatest Jazz Band and even Dizzy Gillespie and Mary Lou Williams, remaining active up until his death. Among the many labels Bobby Hackett recorded for as a leader were Okeh (reissued by Epic), Commodore, Columbia, Epic, Capitol, Sesac, Verve, Project 3, Chiaroscuro, Flying Dutchman, and Honey Dew. — *Scott Yanow*

The Hackett Horn / Feb. 16, 1938-Jan. 25, 1940 / Epic ✦✦✦✦
This set of 16 songs has been reissued intact several times. It includes 12 of the first 16 songs cut at dates led by cornetist Bobby Hackett, featuring a pair of hot combos and a larger big band (why are the other four rewarding sides always left out?) along with two Bix-associated songs recorded under the sponsorship of bandleader Horace Heidt and a pair of jams from a set led by critic Leonard Feather. Throughout, Hackett (then barely in his mid-20s) shows why his original reputation as "the new Bix" never quite fit. Even this early in his career his pretty tone was distinctive. Among the other stars of these swing/trad performances are trombonists George Brunies and Brad Gowans, and clarinetists Pee Wee Russell and Joe Marsala. — *Scott Yanow*

Jazz in New York / Apr. 15, 1944-Sep. 23, 1944 / Commodore ✦✦✦✦
This CD has plenty of hot traditional jazz as played by a variety of top Condonites who were in their prime in the mid-'40s. The three seperate bands feature overlapping personnel with cornetist Bobby Hackett's octet including trombonist Lou McGarity and the great baritonist Ernie Caceres, trombonist Miff Mole's Nicksielanders also showcasing Hackett and Caceres, and cornetist Muggsy Spanier's Ragtimers featuring Mole; clarinetist Pee Wee Russell is also heard with all three groups. But even if the individual bands are pick-up affairs, a few classic performances resulted, most notably Mole's version of "Peg of My Heart," Spanier's "Angry" and "Alice Blue Gown," and Bobby Hackett's "At Sundown" and "Soon." Fun Dixieland from some of the best. — *Scott Yanow*

Dr. Jazz Series, Vol. 2 / Feb. 11, 1952-Apr. 17, 1952 / Storyville ✦✦✦

Coast Concert / Oct. 18, 1955 & Oct. 19, 1955 / Capitol ✦✦✦✦
In the '50s, Hackett's pretty tone was often utilized on mood music albums, most notably by Jackie Gleason, but he never lost his ability to play hot jazz. *Coast Concert* finds him leading a particularly strong octet that also featured clarinetist Matty Matlock and both Jack Teagarden and Abe Lincoln on trombones. On nine familiar standards (including tunes such as "I Want a Big Butter and Egg Man," "Basin Street Blues," and "Struttin' with Some Barbecue"), the top-notch players really inspire each other with some heated ensembles and creative solo work. This is one of Hackett's best sessions of the decade. — *Scott Yanow*

★ **Live at the Roosevelt Grill with Vic Dickenson** / Apr. 19, 1970-May 1970 / Chiaroscuro ✦✦✦✦✦
For a period of time during 1969-71, Bobby Hackett co-led a memorable reedless quintet with trombonist Vic Dickenson that also featured pianist Dave McKenna. This superb swing combo gave fresh interpretations to a wide variety of tunes (mostly from the '30s) and featured colorful interplay between the two highly distinctive horns. Of the many live recordings that resulted, this Chiaroscuro CD was the first and best. — *Scott Yanow*

Charlie Haden

b. Aug. 6, 1937, Shenandoah, IL
Bass / Hard Bop, Free Jazz
What would Ornette Coleman have done in 1959 if Charlie Haden were not around? There was probably not another jazz bassist who fully understood Coleman's radical music that early. Haden's large and distinctive tone, his unhurried approach, and his ability to state a pulse without handcuffing the lead voices to a repeated chord structure were unprecedented at the time. He played country music on a regular radio show with his family as a child, arrived in Los Angeles in the mid-'50s and gigged with Art Pepper, Hampton Hawes, and Paul Bley during 1957-59. It was with Bley at the Hillcrest Club that Haden first performed with Ornette Coleman and Don Cherry and he soon became an important member of their quartet. Haden traveled with Coleman to New York in 1959 and was with him through 1961, including making some innovative records for Atlantic. He worked with Denny Zeitlin during 1964-66, had several reunions with Ornette through the years (including some later recordings), was part of the Jazz Composers' Orchestra Association in the late '60s, and in 1969 formed the Liberation Music Orchestra. Always outspoken against injustice and political repression, Haden's avant-garde orchestra was quite political. He also played often with Keith Jarrett (1967-75) including his excellent quintet that featured Dewey Redman, recorded with Alice Coltrane (1968-72), led a pair of diverse duet albums (1975-76), and played with Old and New Dreams in the mid-to-late '70s. A perennial pollwinner, Haden (who teaches at Cal Arts) had a trio during 1982-83 with Jan Garbarek and Egberto Gismonti and since 1986 has led the comparatively conservative Quartet West (which also includes Ernie Watts, Alan Broadbent, and Larance Marable) in addition to occasionally putting together a new version of the Liberation Music Orchestra. Haden, composer of the standard

"First Song," has recorded as a leader for Impulse, Artists House, Horizon, ECM, Verve, Blue Note, Soul Note, and Antilles. — *Scott Yanow*

☆ **Liberation Music Orchestra** / 1969 / Impulse ✦✦✦✦✦
One of the few message/protest jazz vehicles that works on every level. It has brilliant compositions, arrangements, playing, and lineup, plus passionate material. — *Ron Wynn*

As Long As There's Music / Jan. 25, 1976 / Artists House ✦✦✦✦
Although one would not immediately associate bassist Charlie Haden with pianist Hampton Hawes, they had performed together on an occasional basis since first meeting in 1957. This Artists House LP, a set of five duets, was their last opportunity to play together because Hawes would pass away the following year. The music includes a fairly free improvisation on "Hello/Goodbye," the duo's intepretation of the title cut, a collaboration on "This Is Called Love," and two originals from the pianist. This quiet and often lyrical set contains a great deal of thoughtful and subtle music by two masters. — *Scott Yanow*

Closeness / Jan. 26, 1976-Mar. 21, 1976 / A&M ✦✦✦✦
This one is absolutely essential. One duet apiece with Ornette Coleman (sax), Alice Coltrane (p), Keith Jarrett (p), Paul Motian (d). — *Michael G. Nastos*

Golden Number / Jun. 7, 1976-Dec. 20, 1976 / A&M ✦✦✦✦
Superb album featuring bassist Charlie Haden in various duet situations, each one a gem. The guest list included Ornette Coleman, Hampton Hawes, and Don Cherry. It was issued on John Synder's Artist House, a treasured label that went defunct, and thus far few of its CD's have been reissued. — *Ron Wynn*

● **Old and New Dreams** / 1976 / Black Saint ✦✦✦✦

Magico / Jun. 1979 / ECM ✦✦✦✦
With Gismonti and Garbarek. Outstanding trio work on this reunion of the group that made the superb "Folk Songs" in 1979. — *Ron Wynn*

The Ballad of the Fallen / Nov. 1982 / ECM ✦✦✦

☆ **Quartet West** / Dec. 22, 1986-Dec. 23, 1986 / Verve ✦✦✦✦✦
Fine quartet material, with Ernie Watts (d) far more aggressive and animated than usual. — *Ron Wynn*

Etudes / Sep. 14, 1987-Sep. 15, 1987 / Soul Note ✦✦✦

In Angel City / May 30, 1988-Jun. 1, 1988 / Verve ✦✦✦✦
Charlie Haden Quartet West. This is a solid session, with the undervalued Lawrence Marable on drums. Ernie Watts (reeds) does his best playing with Haden. — *Ron Wynn*

Montreal Tapes / Jul. 2, 1989 / Verve ✦✦✦

Dialogues / Jan. 28, 1990-Jan. 29, 1990 / Antilles ✦✦✦

★ **Dream Keeper** / 1991 / Blue Note ✦✦✦✦✦
Consensus Album of the Year, with the Liberation Music Orchestra. — *Ron Wynn*

Haunted Heart / Oct. 27, 1991-Oct. 28, 1991 / Verve ✦✦✦✦
Charlie Haden loves film as much as music, combining both loves on the critically acclaimed *Haunted Heart*. Haden led his tremendous group Quartet West through 12 numbers, several, like Cole Porter's "Every Time We Say Goodbye," Alan Broadbent's "Lady In The Lake," Arthur Schwartz and Howard Dietz's "Haunted Heart," and even the short introduction, with film ties and/or links. Haden transferred vocals on some numbers from Jeri Southern, Billie Holiday, and Jo Stafford into the mix without disrupting or disturbing the group framework. Quartet West has emerged as a premier small combo, and Haden nicely paid tribute to the past without being held hostage to it. — *Ron Wynn*

Always Say Goodbye / Jul. 30, 1993-Aug. 1, 1993 / Verve ✦✦✦✦

Steal Away / Jun. 29, 1994-Jun. 30, 1994 / Verve ✦✦✦

Al Haig

b. Jul. 22, 1924, Newark, NJ, d. Nov. 16, 1982, New York, NY
Piano / Bop
One of the finest pianists of the bop era (and one who learned from Bud Powell's innovations quite early), Al Haig was quite busy during two periods of his career but unfortunately was pretty obscure in the years between. After serving in the Coast Guard (playing in bands during 1942-44) and freelancing around Boston, Haig worked steadily with Dizzy Gillespie (1945-46), Charlie Parker (1948-50), and Stan Getz (1949-51) and was on many recordings, mostly as a sideman (including some classic Diz and Bird sessions) but also as a leader for Spotlite, Dawn, and Prestige. However (other than little-known dates in 1954 for Esoteric, Swing, and Period), Haig did not lead any more albums until 1974. He played fairly often during the 1951-73 period but was generally overlooked. That changed during his last decade when he was finally recognized as a bop giant and recorded for Spotlite, Choice, SeaBreeze, Interplay, and several Japanese and European labels. — *Scott Yanow*

Al Haig Quartet / Sep. 1954 / Fresh Sound ✦✦✦

Al Haig Today / 1965 / Fresh Sound ✦✦✦

● **Strings Attached** / Mar. 27, 1975 / Choice ✦✦✦✦
A stalwart early bopper, pianist Al Haig returned to the recording spotlight briefly in the mid-'70s with this set, which could just as easily been made in the '40s. Haig's fluidity and ability to navigate blistering passages and make the appropriate chord changes enabled him to survive the turbulent bop era; those skills are now second nature, as he shows with crisp, rippling solos throughout the album. —*Ron Wynn*

Al Haig Plays (Music of Jerome Kern) / 1978 / Inner City ✦✦✦
Bebop Live / May 27, 1982 / Spotlite ✦✦✦

Edmond Hall

b. May 15, 1901, New Orleans, LA, **d.** Feb. 11, 1967, Boston, MA
Clarinet / Swing, New Orleans Jazz
It took Edmond Hall a long period to develop his own musical individuality but by the early '40s he had a very distinctive and dirty sound on the clarinet that was immediately recognizable within one note. One of four clarinet playing brothers (including Herbie Hall) that were the sons of an early clarinetist Edward Hall, Edmond worked in many bands in New Orleans (including Buddy Petit during 1921-23) before going to New York in 1928 with Alonzo Ross. He was with Claude Hopkins' orchestra (1929-35), doubling on baritone and only occasionally sounding like his future self on clarinet. Hall played with Lucky Millinder, Zutty Singleton, and Joe Sullivan and had his style together by the time he joined Red Allen in 1940. He was with Teddy Wilson's sextet (1941-44) and turned down an opportunity to be Barney Bigard's successor with Duke Ellington's orchestra in 1942. In 1944 Hall began working with Eddie Condon (including appearances on his *Town Hall Concert* radio series), led his own group at Cafe Society, spent a few years based in Boston, and then during 1950-55 was in the house band at Condon's club. Edmond Hall toured the world as a member of Louis Armstrong's All-Stars (1955-58), worked in the '60s now and then with Condon, and made his final recording (before his death from a heart attack) at John Hammond's 1967 *Spirituals to Swing* concert. He recorded as a leader for Blue Note (1941-44), Commodore, Savoy, Storyville, United Artists, and some smaller labels. —*Scott Yanow*

● **Edmond Hall: 1937-1944** / 1937 / Classics ✦✦✦✦
Edmond Hall in Copenhagen / Dec. 2, 1966-Dec. 7, 1966 / Storyville ✦✦✦✦

Jim Hall (James Stanley Hall)

b. Dec. 4, 1930, Buffalo, NY
Guitar / Cool, Post-Bop
A harmonically advanced cool-toned and subtle guitarist, Jim Hall has been an inspiration to many current guitarists including some (such as Bill Frisell) who sound nothing like him. Hall attended the Cleveland Institute of Music and studied classical guitar in Los Angeles with Vincente Gomez. He was an original member of the Chico Hamilton Quintet (1955-56) and during 1956-59 was with the Jimmy Giuffre Three. After touring with Ella Fitzgerald (1960-61) and sometimes forming duos with Lee Konitz, Hall was with Sonny Rollins' dynamic quartet in 1961-62, recording *The Bridge*. He co-led a quartet with Art Farmer (1962-64), recorded on an occasional basis with Paul Desmond during 1959-65 (all of their quartet performances are collected on a Mosaic box set), and then became a New York studio musician. He has mostly been a leader ever since, and in addition to his own projects for World Pacific/Pacific Jazz, MPS, Milestone, CTI, Horizon, Artists House, Concord, Music Masters, and Telarc, Hall recorded two classic duet albums with Bill Evans. —*Scott Yanow*

Where Would I Be? / Jul. 1971 / Original Jazz Classics ✦✦✦
★ **Alone Together** / Aug. 4, 1972 / Original Jazz Classics ✦✦✦✦✦
With Ron Carter. Best bass/guitar duets. A must-buy. —*Michael G. Nastos*
Jim Hall's Three / Jan. 1986 / Concord Jazz ✦✦✦
Live at Town Hall, Vol. 2 / Jun. 26, 1990 / Music Masters ✦✦✦✦
Live at Town Hall, Vol. 1 / Jun. 26, 1990 / Music Masters ✦✦✦
Jim Hall and friends. A recent live date with outstanding personnel. —*Ron Wynn*
● **Something Special** / Mar. 6, 1993-Jun. 8, 1993 / Music Masters ✦✦✦✦

Chico Hamilton (Forestorn Hamilton)

b. Sep. 21, 1921, Los Angeles, CA
Drums / Cool, Post-Bop, Hard Bop, Crossover
Chico Hamilton, a subtle and creative drummer, will probably always be better known for the series of quintets that he led during 1955-65 and for his ability as a talent scout than for his fine drumming. Hamilton first played drums while in high school with the many fine young players (including Dexter Gordon, Illinois Jacquet, and Charles Mingus) who were in Los Angeles at the time. He made his recording debut with Slim Gaillard, was house drummer at Billy Berg's, toured with Lionel Hampton, and served in the military (1942-46). In 1946 Hamilton worked briefly with Jimmy Mundy, Count Basie, and Lester Young (recording with Young). He

toured as Lena Horne's drummer (on and off during 1948-55) and gained recognition for his work with the original Gerry Mulligan pianoless quartet (1952-53). In 1955 Hamilton put together his first quintet, a chamber jazz group with the reeds of Buddy Collette, guitarist Jim Hall, bassist Carson Smith, and cellist Fred Katz. One of the last important West Coast jazz bands, the Chico Hamilton Quintet, was immediately popular and appeared in a memorable sequence in 1958's *Jazz on a Summmer's Day* and the Hollywood film *The Sweet Smell of Success*. The personnel changed over the next few years (with Paul Horn and Eric Dolphy heard on reeds, cellist Nate Gersham, guitarists John Pisano and Dennis Budimir, and several bassists passing through the group) but it retained its unusual sound. By 1961 Charles Lloyd was on tenor and flute, Gabor Szabo was the new guitarist, and soon the cello was dropped in favor of trombone (Garnett Brown and later George Bohanon), giving the group an advanced hard bop style.

In 1966 Chico Hamilton started composing for commercials and the studios and broke up his quintet. However, he continued leading various groups, playing music that ranged from the avant-garde to erratic fusion and advanced hard bop. Such up-and-coming musicians as Larry Coryell (1966), Steve Potts (1967), Arthur Blythe, Steve Turre (on bass!), and Eric Person (who played in Hamilton's '90s group Euphoria) were among the younger players he helped discover. In 1989 Chico Hamilton had a recorded reunion with the original members of his 1955 Quintet (with Pisano in Hall's place) and in recent times he has been making records for Soul Note. —*Scott Yanow*

Transfusion / 1962 / Studio West ✦✦✦
● **Passin' Thru** / Sep. 18, 1962 & Sep. 20, 1962 / Impulse ✦✦✦✦
One of Hamilton's best groups, with Charles Lloyd (reeds) and Gabor Szabo (g). —*Ron Wynn*

Man from Two Worlds / Sep. 18, 1962 & Dec. 11, 1963 / GRP ✦✦✦✦
Although it tended to get overlooked at the time, one of drummer Chico Hamilton's finest groups was his 1962-63 quartet/quintet. With Charles Lloyd at his most fiery on tenor and flute and the colorful solos of the up-and-coming Hungarian guitarist Gabor Szabo, this band placed a stronger emphasis on melody and softer sounds than the more avant-garde groups of the time but still pushed away at musical boundaries. Trombonist George Bohanon is also on the final four numbers of this CD reissue which brings back all of the music from Hamilton's *Man from Two Worlds* LP and four of the six numbers originally on *Passin' Thru*. Highlights include the original version of Lloyd's most famous song, "Forest Flower." —*Scott Yanow*

The Dealer / Sep. 1966 / Impulse ✦✦✦
Reunion / Jun. 28, 1989 & Jun. 29, 1989 / Soul Note ✦✦✦✦
In 1989, 34 years after the formation of the somewhat unique Chico Hamilton Quintet, the original members (with one exception) reunited for a tour and this Soul Note recording. In addition to drummer Hamilton, Buddy Collette (heard on flute, clarinet and alto), cellist Fred Katz, bassist Carson Smith, and guitarist John Pisano (who was Jim Hall's first replacement) complete the group. This studio session only includes one standard remake of "I Want to Be Happy," and is comprised of then-recent originals by bandmembers with two selections ("Brushing with B" and "Conversation") being freely improvised duets by Collette and Hamilton. So, rather than merely being an exercise in nostalgia, this excellent set features the Quintet members as they sounded in the late '80s, creating new music for their classic sound. —*Scott Yanow*

Trio! / May 1, 1992-May 17, 1992 / Soul Note ✦✦✦✦
★ **My Panamanian Friend** / Aug. 21, 1992-Aug. 28, 1992 / Soul Note ✦✦✦✦✦

Scott Hamilton

b. Sep. 12, 1954, Providence, RI
Sax (Tenor) / Swing
When Scott Hamilton appeared in the mid-'70s fully formed with an appealing swing style on tenor (mixing together Zoot Sims and Ben Webster) he caused a minor sensation, for few other young players during the fusion era were exploring pre-bop jazz at his high level. He began playing when he was 16 years old and developed quickly, moving to New York in 1976. Hamilton played with Benny Goodman in the late '70s but has mostly performed as a leader, sometimes sharing the spotlight with Warren Vache, Ruby Braff, Rosemary Clooney, the Concord Jazz All-Stars, or George Wein's Newport Jazz Festival All-Stars. Scott Hamilton, other than a session each for Famous Door and Progressive, has recorded a long string of dates for Concord that are notable for their consistency and solid swing. —*Scott Yanow*

Good Wind Who Is Blowing Us No Ill / Mar. 1, 1977 / Concord Jazz ✦✦✦✦
Tenor saxophonist Scott Hamilton's 1977 debut as a leader astounded the jazz world at the time. Unlike the '80s and '90s generation, whose muses are '50s hard boppers, Hamilton took his inspiration from the lusty swing

sound of the '30s; Coleman Hawkins particularly, but also Ben Webster and Lester Young. —*Ron Wynn*

● **Scott's Buddy** / Aug. 1980 / Concord Jazz ✦✦✦✦
This was the second recorded encounter between tenors Buddy Tate and Scott Hamilton and, despite their vast age difference (41 years), it is difficult to tell from their playing who is the older musician. Hamilton is one of the few hornmen from his generation to make the grade as a major swing stylist and his respect for the elder Tate (who returns the feeling) is obvious. With guitarist Cal Collins, pianist Nat Pierce, bassist Bob Maize, and drummer Jake Hanna, the two tenors are in spirited form on these standards and riff-filled originals; this combination works well. —*Scott Yanow*

Major League / May 1986 / Concord Jazz ✦✦✦✦
Dave McKenna (p) and Jake Hanna (d) share the spotlight with Hamilton. —*Ron Wynn*

Scott Hamilton Plays Ballads / Mar. 1989 / Concord Jazz ✦✦✦
Its title accurately describes the music on this CD. The warm tenor of Scott Hamilton (accompanied by pianist John Bunch, guitarist Chris Flory, bassist Phil Flanigan, and drummer Chuck Riggs) brings out a great deal of beauty on 11 ballads including his own "Two Eighteen" and a variety of veteran melodies. This romantic disc is easy to enjoy. —*Scott Yanow*

Radio City / Feb. 1990 / Concord Jazz ✦✦✦✦
With fine contributions from Dennis Irwin (b). The CD version has two bonus tracks. —*Ron Wynn*

At Last / Jan. 1991 / Concord Jazz ✦✦✦

East of the Sun / Aug. 1993 / Concord Jazz ✦✦✦

Organic Duke / May 18, 1994-May 19, 1994 / Concord Jazz ✦✦✦

Live At The Brecon Jazz Festival / Aug. 13, 1994 / Concord Jazz ✦✦✦

Lionel Hampton

b. Apr. 12, 1909, Louisville, KY
Piano, Drums, Vibes / Swing
Lionel Hampton was the first jazz vibraphonist and has been one of the jazz giants since the mid-'30s. He has achieved the difficult feat of being musically open-minded (even recording "Giant Steps") without changing his basic swing style. Hampton started out as a drummer, playing with the Chicago Defender Newsboys' Band as a youth. His original idol was Jimmy Bertrand, a '20s drummer who occasionally played xylophone. Hampton played on the West Coast with such groups as Curtis Mosby's Blue Blowers, Reb Spikes, and Paul Howard's Quality Serenaders (with whom he made his recording debut in 1929) before joining Les Hite's band, which for a period accompanied Louis Armstrong. At a recording session in 1930, a vibraphone happened to be in the studio, Armstrong asked Hampton (who had practiced on one previously) if he could play a little bit behind him and on "Memories of You" and "Shine" Hampton became the first jazz improviser to record on vibes.

It would be another six years before he found fame. Hampton, after leaving Hite, had his own band in Los Angeles' Paradise Cafe until one night in 1936 when Benny Goodman came into the club and discovered him. Soon Hampton recorded with Benny Goodman, Teddy Wilson, and Gene Krupa as the Benny Goodman Quartet and six weeks later he officially joined Goodman. An exciting soloist whose enthusiasm even caused Goodman to smile, Hampton became one of the stars of his organization, appearing in films with Goodman, at the famous 1938 Carnegie Hall Concert, and nightly on the radio. In 1937 he started recording regularly as a leader for Victor with specially assembled all-star groups that formed a who's who of swing; all of these timeless performances (1937-41) were reissued by Bluebird on a six-LP set, although thus far in piecemeal fashion on CD.

Hampton stayed with Goodman until 1940, sometimes substituting on drums and taking vocals. In 1940 Lionel Hampton formed his first big band and in 1942 had a huge hit with "Flying Home" featuring a classic Illinois Jacquet tenor spot (one of the first R&B solos). During the remainder of the decade, Hampton's extroverted orchestra was a big favorite, leaning towards R&B, showing the influence of bebop after 1944, and sometimes getting pretty exhibitionistic. Among his sidemen in addition to Jacquet were Arnett Cobb, Dinah Washington (who Hampton helped discover), Cat Anderson, Marshall Royal, Dexter Gordon, Milt Buckner, Earl Bostic, Snooky Young, Johnny Griffin, Joe Wilder, Benny Bailey, Charles Mingus, Fats Navarro, Al Gray, and even Wes Montgomery and Betty Carter. Hampton's popularity allowed him to continue leading big bands off and on into the mid-'90s, and the 1953 edition that visited Paris (with Clifford Brown, Art Farmer, Quincy Jones, Jimmy Cleveland, Gigi Gryce, George Wallington, and Annie Ross) would be difficult to top, although fights over money and the right of the sidemen to record led to its breakup. Hampton appeared and recorded with many all-star groups in the '50s including reunions with Benny Goodman, meetings with the Oscar Peterson Trio, Stan Getz, Buddy DeFranco, and as part of a trio with Art Tatum and Buddy Rich. He also was featured in *The Benny Goodman Story* (1956). Since the '50s, Lionel Hampton has mostly repeated past triumphs, always playing "Hamp's Boogie Woogie" (which features his very rapid

two-finger piano playing), "Hey Ba-Ba-Re-Bop," and "Flying Home." However his enthusiasm still causes excitement and he remains a household name. Hampton has recorded through the years for nearly every label including two of his own (Glad Hamp and Who's Who) and most recently Mojazz. Despite strokes and the ravages of age, Lionel Hampton as of this writing is still a vital force. —*Scott Yanow*

Lionel Hampton (1937-1938) / Feb. 8, 1937-Jan. 18, 1938 / Classics ✦✦✦✦

Lionel Hampton's Jumpin' Jive, Vol. 2 / Feb. 8, 1937-Oct. 12, 1939 / Bluebird ✦✦✦

Hot Mallets, Vol. 1 / Apr. 14, 1937-Sep. 11, 1939 / Bluebird ✦✦✦

Lionel Hampton (1938-1939) / Jan. 18, 1938-Jun. 13, 1939 / Classics ✦✦✦✦

Lionel Hampton (1939-1940) / Jun. 13, 1939-May 10, 1940 / Classics ✦✦✦✦

Tempo and Swing / Oct. 30, 1939-Aug. 21, 1940 / Bluebird ✦✦✦

● **Midnight Sun** / Jan. 29, 1946-Nov. 10, 1947 / GRP/Decca ✦✦✦✦
Although firmly identified with Benny Goodman and the swing era, vibraphonist Lionel Hampton led one of the most bop-oriented and forward-looking big bands of the mid-to-late '40s; for proof check out "Mingus Fingers" (by Charles Mingus) on this CD. This set reissues some of Hampton's most boppish sides from 1946-47 along with the original version of "Midnight Sun" and is full of extroverted solos and exciting ensembles. Although tenorman Arnett Cobb (heard in the earlier selections) and pianist Milt Buckner are the best-known sidemen; such musicians as the screaming trumpeters Jimmy Nottingham and Leo "the Whistler" Sheppard and tenors Morris Lane, John Sparrow, and the young Johnny Griffin provide their own strong moments. Until Decca gets around to reissuing all of Hampton's big band sides in chronological order, this is one of the sets to get. —*Scott Yanow*

Lionel Hampton in Paris / Sep. 28, 1953 / Vogue ✦✦✦

★ **Hamp and Getz** / Aug. 1, 1955 / Verve ✦✦✦✦✦
If one were to believe the clichés and stereotypes common in some jazz history books, this matchup should not have worked. By 1955 Lionel Hampton was a veteran swing vibraphonist while Stan Getz was the leader of the "cool school" of young tenors. But what these two masters had in common (in addition to a healthy respect for each other's talents) was the ability to swing as hard as possible. Joined by a fine trio, the duo really rip into "Cherokee" and "Jumpin' at the Woodside" (listen to their blistering trade-offs) and even with a fine ballad medley, it is these torrid jams that make this a highly recommended disc. —*Scott Yanow*

Reunion at Newport 1967 / Jun. 30, 1956-Jul. 3, 1967 / RCA/Bluebird ✦✦✦✦
Most of this CD is taken up by a special Newport Jazz Festival concert featuring a big band full of Lionel Hampton's alumni. With trombonist Al Grey, Frank Foster on tenor, and a screaming trumpet section that boasted Snooky Young, Jimmy Nottingham, Joe Newman, and Wallace Davenport, the explosive nature of the music is not too surprising; the climax is provided by guest Illinois Jacquet on "Flying Home." The remainder of this disc contains half of a very effective 1956 session cut in Spain in which the medium-size group includes a castanet player, and two songs match Hampton with the great Spanish pianist Tete Monteliu. —*Scott Yanow*

Newport Uproar / Jul. 3, 1967 / RCA ✦✦✦✦
This LP, since reissued on CD, has Lionel Hampton's first concert at the Newport Jazz Festival and overall is quite exciting. Hampton gathered together an all-star alumni band that, in addition to trombonist Al Grey, Frank Foster on tenor, and a couple of appearances by pianist Milt Buckner, boasts the extraordinary trumpet section of Snooky Young, Jimmy Nottingham, Joe Newman, and Wallace Davenport. The climax is provided on Hamp's perennial "Flying Home" which finds Illinois Jacquet reprising and then extending his famous solo. —*Scott Yanow*

Mostly Blues / Mar. 10, 1988-Apr. 8, 1988 / Music Masters ✦✦✦

Live at the Blue Note / Jun. 11, 1991-Jun. 13, 1991 / Telarc ✦✦✦

For The Love Of Music / 1994-1995 / Mojazz ✦✦

Slide Hampton (Locksley Wellington Hampton)

b. Apr. 21, 1932, Jeannette, PA
Trombone / Bop, Hard Bop
Slide Hampton has been a fine trombonist and arranger since the mid-'50s, helping to keep the tradition of bop alive in both his playing and his writing. After working with Buddy Johnson (1955-56) and Lionel Hampton, he became an important force in Maynard Ferguson's excellent big band of 1957-59. He led octets in the '60s with such sidemen as Freddie Hubbard and George Coleman. After traveling with Woody Herman to Europe in 1968, Hampton settled overseas where he stayed very active. Since returning to the US in 1977, he has led his World of Trombones (which features nine trombonists), played in a co-op quintet called Con-

tinuum and been involved in several Dizzy Gillespie tribute projects, recording in the '90s for Telarc. —*Scott Yanow*

World of Trombones / Jan. 8, 1979-Jan. 9, 1979 / Black Lion ◆◆◆◆
Ambitious project with nine trombonists merging their skills under the leadership of Slide Hampton. The list includes both established veterans like Curtis Fuller and Steve Turre and emerging newcomers Janice Robinson and Afro-Latin star Papo Vasquez. Hampton's arrangements are excellent, but there's more emphasis on performance style than real solo development. Pianist Albert Dailey and bassist Ray Drummond were also outstanding. —*Ron Wynn*

● **Roots** / Apr. 1985 / Criss Cross ◆◆◆◆
Tremendous 1985 quintet session with trombonist Slide Hampton heading a distinguished group and nicely teaming with tenor saxophonist Clifford Jordan in a first-rate hard-bop front line. The rhythm section's quality isn't far behind, especially pianist Cedar Walton and drummer Billy Higgins. —*Ron Wynn*

Herbie Hancock

b. Apr. 12, 1940, Chicago, IL
Piano, Keyboards / Fusion, Post-Bop

If not for the amazing reign of Miles Davis, pianist Herbie Hancock might qualify as jazz's most well known, popular performer since the '60s. Hancock had 11 albums chart during the '70s and 17 between 1973 and 1984, including three in 1974, figures that put him well ahead of any other jazz musician in the '70s and beyond. He's also among jazz's finest eclectics, having played everything from bebop to free, jazz-rock, fusion, funk, instrumental pop, dance, hip-hop, and world fusion. Hancock's style, greatly influenced by Bill Evans, mixes introspective and energetic elements, and fuses blues and gospel influences with bebop and classical elements. He is both a great accompanist and excellent soloist whose voicings, phrasing, melodic and interpretative skills, and harmonic facility were impressive early in his career and remain sharp no matter what style or idiom he is working. Hancock began studying piano at seven and performed the first movement of a Mozart concerto with the Chicago Symphony Orchestra in a young people's concert at age 11. He formed his own jazz ensemble while attending Hyde Park High School. He was influenced harmonically by the arrangements Clare Fischer provided for the Hi-Los and Robert Farnon's orchestrations of pop songs. Hancock had begun working in Chicago jazz clubs with Donald Byrd and Coleman Hawkins when he left Grinnel College in 1960. Byrd invited him to join his group and Hancock moved to New York. After he recorded with Byrd's band, Blue Note offered Hancock his own pact. Hancock's debut *Takin' Off* was issued in 1962 and yielded a hit with "Watermelon Man." He joined Miles Davis in 1963. Hancock's solo style became an integral part of Davis' evolving '60s approach. His interaction with Ron Carter and Tony Williams was at the core of songs that increasingly became more flexible and less fixed, while Hancock also cut important albums as a leader for Blue Note and gained status as a composer. Some major compositions during the '60s included "Maiden Voyage," "Dolphin Dance," "Speak Like A Child," and "I Have A Dream" dedicated to Dr. Martin Luther King, Jr. During the '70s Hancock led a sextet that merged jazz, rock, African, and Indian musical references and was mostly electric. This band was one of the great jazz-rock groups, though Hancock finally disbanded it due to the group having limited market appeal and financial success. The Sextant group sometimes performed in African garb, and Hancock even issued the album *Mwandishi* with the musicians' African names given along with their English ones. He was playing many electronic instruments, adding the Hohner Clavinet, various synthesizers, and Mellotron to his Fender Rhodes. Hancock disbanded the Sextant in 1973 and formed the Headhunters, a funk, rock, and instrumental pop band that scored a huge crossover hit with the album *Headhunters*. Hancock's records were now being played by the emerging upper- and middle-class Black professionals, who for the most part had little or no knowledge of his past sound. The single "Chameleon," which reflected the influence of accompanists in Sly Stone's band, was a club and radio smash in edited fashion. Hancock turned more to strict pop music, though he also did an acoustic V.S.O.P. tour in the late '70s and a series of duo concerts with Chick Corea. He repeatedly defended his right to make any and all kinds of music, and often labeled criticism of his commercial projects "elitist," an extension of the charge that some Black nationalists leveled against the '60s free players. During the '80s, Hancock alternated between acoustic and electric material. He had another big hit in 1983 with "Rockit," a song that utilized the scratching technique and predated its popularity in hip-hop production with a multitextured, heavily edited snippet/rhythm framework. The video and single gained Hancock MTV coverage and exposure, and triggered a fresh round of debate over whether he was selling out. Hancock spent the next two years doing mostly conventional jazz dates, even winning an Oscar for his score of the film *Round Midnight*. Hancock collaborated with African musician Foday Musa Suso for a fine duet album that made the charts as well. He toured Europe in 1987 with Buster Williams and Al Foster and did a series of American and Japanese dates with a quartet that included Mike Brecker, Ron Carter, and Tony Wil-

liams. Hancock also hosted a variety show on the Showtime cable television network and did lecture/performances on public television. He has done numerous albums for Blue Note, Columbia, and Warner Bros. The lengthy list of musicians Hancock has played with reads like a jazz who's who; it includes Joe Henderson, Freddie Hubbard, Wynton Marsalis, George Coleman, Johnny Coles, Bobby Hutcherson, George Benson, and Paul Desmond, among many others. His versatility and track record ensure Hancock will never have difficulty getting recording opportunities. It would be silly to insist everything he's done was great, but much of it, even his most commercial, trendy dates, has retained a high level of musicianship and attention to stylistic detail. —*Ron Wynn and William Ruhlmann*

● **Takin' Off** / May 28, 1962 / Blue Note ◆◆◆◆
This CD reissues pianist Herbie Hancock's first album as a leader, a set best known for introducing his catchy song "Watermelon Man." The release not only brings back the original hard bop-oriented program but adds three previously unissued alternate takes, including one of "Watermelon Man." The all-star quintet (which includes trumpeter Freddie Hubbard, tenor saxophonist Dexter Gordon, bassist Butch Warren, and drummer Billy Higgins) sounds consistently inspired with Gordon just starting to be influenced by John Coltrane and Hubbard full of youthful fire. Even at this early stage, Hancock had his own original voice. —*Scott Yanow*

My Point of View / Mar. 19, 1963 / Blue Note ◆◆◆◆
Tremendous compositions and playing in an all-star date that helped make Hancock a star. —*Ron Wynn*

Inventions and Dimensions / Aug. 30, 1963 / Blue Note ◆◆◆◆
First-rate early work. Willie Bobo makes a scintillating percussive contribution. —*Ron Wynn*

Empyrean Isles / Jun. 17, 1964 / Blue Note ◆◆◆◆
1985 reissue of one of Hancock's seminal releases. Freddie Hubbard (tpt) is daring and aggressive. —*Ron Wynn*

★ **Maiden Voyage** / Mar. 17, 1965 / Blue Note ◆◆◆◆◆
The definitive Blue Note Herbie with an ensemble. You can't go wrong with this one. —*Michael G. Nastos*

Speak Like a Child / Mar. 9, 1968 / Blue Note ◆◆◆◆
A simply beautiful title cut, plus wondrous arrangements and playing throughout. —*Ron Wynn*

The Prisoner / Apr. 18, 1969-Apr. 23, 1969 / Blue Note ◆◆◆
A poignant tribute to Dr. Martin Luther King, Jr. from pianist Herbie Hancock, whose 1969 album featured Hancock's compositions for large orchestra and was sparked by superb playing from the leader and Joe Henderson on tenor sax. —*Ron Wynn*

★ **Mwandishi: The Complete Warner Bros. Recordings** / Oct. 4, 1969-Feb. 17, 1972 / Warner Archives ◆◆◆◆◆
This two-CD set reissues the complete contents of three LPs: *Fat Albert Rotunda*, *Mwandishi*, and *Crossings*. The earliest session (extensions of generally memorable funk themes used in a Bill Cosby cartoon) features the keyboardist in a sextet on most selections with tenor saxophonist Joe Henderson, trumpeter Johnny Coles, and trombonist Garnett Brown; two songs use a 15-piece group. However, the bulk of this set showcases Hancock's regular sextet of the era (which was comprised of trumpeter Eddie Henderson, Benny Maupin on bass clarinet, alto flute, and soprano, trombonist Julian Priester, bassist Buster Williams, and drummer Billy Hart); the later session also adds Patrick Gleeson's moog synthesizer. The somewhat unique music is both explorative and loosely funky, avant-garde yet influenced by rock and funk. The results are often quite fascinating but this group (which only recorded one further album for Columbia) was a commercial flop that Hancock would eventually break up in favor of The Headhunters. —*Scott Yanow*

☆ **Headhunters** / 1973 / Columbia ◆◆◆◆◆

Evening with Chick Corea and Herbie Hancock / Feb. 1978 / Columbia ◆◆◆◆
In 1978, Chick Corea and Herbie Hancock teamed up for a tour, playing duets exclusively on acoustic pianos. One double LP was issued under each of their names. The *Corea* set has lengthy versions of three of Chick's tunes ("Homecoming," "Bouquet," and "La Fiesta"), Hancock's "Maiden Voyage," and their joint work, "The Hook," in addition to a short piece by Bela Bartok. This collaboration brought out the best in both pianists and restored a bit of credibility to two players who had had great success playing more commercial electronic music. —*Scott Yanow*

An Evening With / Feb. 1978 / Columbia ◆◆◆◆
Since Chick Corea and Herbie Hancock had by 1978 spent several years mostly playing electric keyboards, their acoustic duet tour surprised many listeners who thought that they would always specialize in fusion. This double LP contains many fine performances including lengthy versions of "Maiden Voyage" and "La Fiesta," but it is the striding by Corea and Hancock on "Liza" that is most unique. —*Scott Yanow*

Live under the Sky / Jul. 26, 1979 / Columbia ◆◆◆

Quartet / Jul. 25, 1981 / Columbia ✦✦✦✦
A fine mainstream set that showed detractors Hancock hadn't lost his jazz chops. Wynton Marsalis (tpt) (then reaping a wave of prodigy/discovery headlines) is in the group. —*Ron Wynn*

Future Shock / 1983 / Columbia ✦✦
Dis Is Da Drum / 1994 / Mercury ✦✦
New Standard / 1995 / Verve ✦✦✦✦
On first glance this record would not seem to have much promise from a jazz standpoint. Herbie Hancock performs a set of tunes which include numbers from the likes of Peter Gabriel, Stevie Wonder, Sade, Paul Simon, Prince, the Beatles ("Norwegian Wood"), and Kurt Cobain! However by adding vamps, reharmonizing the chord structures, sometimes quickly discarding the melodies, and utilizing an all-star band, Hancock was able to transform the potentially unrewarding music into creative jazz. Hancock, who sticks to acoustic piano, shows that he is still in prime form, taking quite a few fiery solos. With Michael Brecker on tenor and surprisingly effective soprano, guitarist John Scofield, bassist Dave Holland, drummer Jack DeJohnette, and percussionist Don Alias (along with an occasional horn or string section that was dubbed in later), the results are often quite hard swinging and certainly never predictable. Although it is doubtful that any of these songs will ever become a jazz standard, Herbie Hancock has successfully created a memorable set of "new" music. Well worth investigating. —*Scott Yanow*

John Handy

b. Feb. 3, 1933, Dallas, TX
Sax (Alto), Sax (Tenor) / Post-Bop, Crossover
A talented and adventurous altoist whose career has gone through several phases, John Handy started playing alto in 1949. After moving to New York in 1958, he had a fiery period with Charles Mingus (1958-59) that resulted in several passionate recordings that show off his originality; he also recorded several dates as a leader for Roulette. Handy led his own bands during 1959-64 and played with Mingus at the 1964 Monterey Jazz Festival, but it was at the following year's festival that he was a major hit, stretching out with his quintet (which included violinist Michael White and guitarist Jerry Hahn) on two long originals. Soon Handy was signed to Columbia where he recorded his finest work (three excellent albums) during 1966-68. Since that time he has performed world music with Ali Akbar Khan, recorded the R&B hit "Hard Work" for Impulse in 1976, gigged and recorded with Mingus Dynasty, and in the late '80s led a group (called Class) featuring three female violinists who sing. John Handy (no relation to the Dixieland altoist Capt. John Handy) remains a strong soloist who can hit high notes way above his horn's normal register with ease, but he has mostly maintained a low profile, teaching in the San Francisco Bay Area. —*Scott Yanow*

★ **Live at Monterey** / Sep. 18, 1965 / Koch ✦✦✦✦✦
An album of red hot, animated work from Handy—some of his best. —*Ron Wynn*

Centerpiece / Jan. 2, 1992 / Milestone ✦✦✦

Sir Roland Hanna

b. Feb. 10, 1932, Detroit, MI
Piano / Swing, Hard Bop
A talented pianist with a style diverse enough to fit into swing, bop, and more adventurous settings, Roland Hanna was one of the last in an impressive line of great pianists who emerged in Detroit after World War II (including Hank Jones, Barry Harris, and Tommy Flanagan). After serving in the Army and studying music at Eastman and Juilliard, Hanna made a strong impression playing with Benny Goodman (1958). He worked with Charles Mingus for a period in 1959 and since then has generally led his own trios. Hanna was an integral part of the Thad Jones-Mel Lewis Orchestra (1967-74) and in 1974 helped found the New York Jazz Quartet (with Frank Wess). He was given knighthood (thus the "Sir") from the President of Liberia in 1970. Sir Roland Hanna has led sessions for many labels including Atco (1959), MPS, Choice, Freedom, Inner City, and Music Masters. —*Scott Yanow*

★ **Perugia** / Jul. 2, 1974 / Freedom ✦✦✦✦✦
Excellent piano solos—some of Hanna's sharpest. —*Ron Wynn*

Live at Montreux / Jul. 2, 1974 / Freedom ✦✦✦

Duke Ellington Piano Solos / Mar. 22, 1990-Mar. 23, 1990 / Music Masters ✦✦✦✦
Includes some exquisite solo work—a moving tribute to Duke Ellington. —*Ron Wynn*

● **Maybeck Recital Hall, Vol. 32** / Aug. 15, 1993 / Concord Jazz ✦✦✦✦
Elegance and artistry are the two qualities that best define both Sir Roland Hanna's piano style and this superb CD, the 32nd in Concord's continuing Maybeck solo series. Hanna devotes half of the eight selections to Gershwin compositions, and his interpretations of "Love Walked In," "The Man I Love," "How Long Has This Been Going On," and others are sublime, mar-

velously crafted, and magnificent in their ideas and execution. Seldom will you hear a solo date less self-indulgent and more satisfying. —*Ron Wynn*

Bill Hardman

b. Apr. 6, 1933, Cleveland, OH, **d.** Dec. 1990
Trumpet, Fluegelhorn / Hard Bop
A reliable hard bop-oriented trumpeter, Bill Hardman never became famous but he helped out on many sessions. While a teenager Hardman gigged with Tadd Dameron and after graduating high school played with Tiny Bradshaw (1953-55). He debuted on record with Jackie McLean (1955), played with Charles Mingus (1956), and gained recognition for his work with Art Blakey's Jazz Messengers (1956-58). Hardman worked with Horace Silver (1958), Lou Donaldson (on and off during 1959-66), rejoined Blakey twice (1966-69 and in the late '70s), was with Mingus again during parts of 1969-72, and led a group with Junior Cook (1979-81). Bill Hardman had an appealing style in the Clifford Brown tradition and recorded as a leader for Savoy (1961) and Muse. —*Scott Yanow*

Home / Jan. 10, 1978 / Muse ✦✦✦

● **Politely** / Jul. 7, 1981 / Muse ✦✦✦✦

Roy Hargrove

b. 1970
Trumpet / Hard Bop
Roy Hargrove is a hard bop-oriented Young Lion who has a great deal of potential. A fine straightahead player who does not sound overly influenced by any of his predecessors, Hargrove's fiery solos resulted in him winning the *Downbeat* Readers' Poll in 1995. He met Wynton Marsalis in 1987 when the trumpeter visited his high school and impressed Marsalis, who let him sit in with his band. With the help of Marsalis, Hargrove was soon playing with major players including Bobby Watson, Ricky Ford, Carl Allen, and in the group Superblue. Hargrove attended Berklee (1988-89) and in 1990 released his first of four recordings for Novus; he was 20 at the time. He has been touring ever since with his own group which for several years included Antonio Hart. In addition to Novus, Hargrove has recorded for Verve and as a sideman with quite a few notables, including Sonny Rollins, James Clay, Frank Morgan, and Jackie McLean plus the group Jazz Futures. —*Scott Yanow*

Beauty & The Beast / Nov. 20, 1992-Nov. 21, 1992 / Novus ✦✦✦✦

Of Kindred Souls / May 1993 / Novus ✦✦✦✦
Of all the "Young Lions" to emerge in jazz after the rise of Wynton Marsalis, trumpeter Roy Hargrove is among the most impressive, filling in the major gap left by the early departure of Lee Morgan. On his fifth session as a leader, Hargrove is heard live with his quintet (which also features pianist Marc Cary and Ron Blake on tenor and soprano) with cameo appearances on a selection each by altoist Gary Bartz and trombonist Andre Hayward. Hargrove is in excellent form on a set of group originals, a brief ballad medley and the standard "My Shining Hour." All of the trumpeter's releases thus far are worth picking up. —*Scott Yanow*

● **With the Tenors of Our Time** / Dec. 18, 1993-Jan. 17, 1994 / Verve ✦✦✦✦
Trumpeter Roy Hargrove has the opportunity of a lifetime on this recording, sharing separate songs with five great tenors: Johnny Griffin, Joe Henderson, Branford Marsalis, Joshua Redman, and Stanley Turrentine. Everyone fares well, including Hargrove's group (Ron Blake on tenor and soprano, pianist Cyrus Chestnut, bassist Rodney Whitaker, and drummer Gregory Hutchinson). The young trumpeter (who is vying for Lee Morgan's unoccupied chair) keeps up with the saxophonists on this generally relaxed affair; recommended for hard bop fans. —*Scott Yanow*

Family / Jan. 26, 1995-Jan. 29, 1995 / Verve ✦✦✦✦

Parker's Mood / Apr. 12, 1995-Apr. 14, 1995 / Verve ✦✦✦✦
Sixteen songs associated with (and in 12 cases composed by) Charlie Parker are jammed by a drumless trio consisting of trumpeter Roy Hargrove, pianist Stephen Scott, and bassist Christian McBride. To add variety to the set, there are three duets (using all of the possible combinations) and one unaccompanied solo each including a Hargrove workout on "Dewey Square." Other highlights include "Klactoveesedstene," "Laura," "Yardbird Suite," McBride's spot on "Red Cross," "Cardboard," and "Star Eyes," but all 16 performances are enjoyable. —*Scott Yanow*

The Harper Brothers

Group / Hard Bop
One of the most hyped jazz groups of the late '80s, the Harper Brothers (co-led by drummer Winard Harper and trumpeter Phillip Harper) symbolized what was right and wrong about the Young Lions movement. The musicianship in this hard bop unit was excellent and the young players respected their elders, but strong originality was lacking (they were largely revisiting the past) and the Harper Brothers received an excess of publicity at the expense of more innovative players. Still, during its five years, the group produced four enjoyable bop albums for Verve and its sidemen (altoist Justin Robinson, tenors Javon Jackson and Walter Blanding, pianists

Stephen Scott and Kevin Hays, and bassists Michael Bowie and Nedra Wheeler among them) all had strong starts to their career. Both Winard and Phillip Harper have grown musically since the band's breakup. —*Scott Yanow*

● **Harper Brothers** / Jun. 21, 1988 / Verve ◆◆◆◆
The introductory album for the jazz-playing brothers who became staples among mainstream fans in the late '80s and early '90s. Winard and Phillip Harper's music reflected the influence of Art Blakey and Horace Silver, but was played with a youthful zest and individualistic flair. This late '80s release was reissued in '92 on CD with a bonus cut. —*Ron Wynn*

Remembrance / Sep. 8, 1989-Sep. 9, 1989 / Verve ◆◆◆◆
A solid live album from young cats. —*Michael G. Nastos*

Artistry / 1991 / Verve ◆◆◆

You Can Hide Inside the Music / Oct. 15, 1991-Oct. 16, 1991 / Verve ◆◆◆◆

Billy Harper

b. Jan. 17, 1943
Sax (Tenor) / Post-Bop, Hard Bop
An intense tenor saxophonist whose music has stretched the boundaries of hard bop and modal music, Billy Harper graduated from North Texas State College and in 1966 moved to New York. He worked on and off with Gil Evans for the next ten years, was with Art Blakey's Jazz Messengers (1968-70), played with Elvin Jones (1970), Max Roach, the Thad Jones-Mel Lewis Orchestra (recording a notable solo on "Fingers"), and Lee Morgan. Harper has recorded as a leader for Strata-East, Black Saint, Denon, and Soul Note and has maintained a low profile during the past decade, but he did record a set for Evidence in 1993. —*Scott Yanow*

● **Somalia** / Oct. 18, 1993 & Oct. 21, 1993 / Evidence ◆◆◆◆
The passionate tenor saxophonist Billy Harper had not been heard on record as a leader in quite a few years when this superlative Evidence CD was released in 1995. Harper (who is joined by trumpeter Eddie Henderson, pianist Francesca Tanksley, bassist Louie Spears, and both Newman Taylor Baker and Horacee Arnold on drums) brings back the spirit of John Coltrane, performing a very spiritual and generally intense set of music. The five originals are highlighted by the title cut, "Quest" and the nearly 22-minute "Thy Will Be Done." This CD contains some of Billy Harper's finest playing in years. —*Scott Yanow*

Tom Harrell

b. Jun. 16, 1946, Urbana, IL
Trumpet, Fluegelhorn / Hard Bop
Tom Harrell has managed to fight courageously (and thus far successfully) against schizophrenia to become one of jazz's top trumpeters of the '80s and '90s. On stage he is totally focused on his playing and seems to only come alive when he is improvising. Harrell grew up in Northern California and toured with Stan Kenton (1969), Woody Herman (1970-71), and Horace Silver (1973-77). He moved to New York in the mid-'70s and played during this period with Cecil Payne, Bill Evans (1979), Lee Konitz's Nonet (1979-81), and George Russell (1982). Harrell traveled the world with the Phil Woods Quintet (1983-89) and has since then generally led his own bands, recording for Contemporary and Chesky. His style mixes together the power of Clifford Brown with the lyricism of Chet Baker. —*Scott Yanow*

★ **Sail Away** / Mar. 22, 1989-Mar. 23, 1989 / Contemporary ◆◆◆◆◆
Spirited originals and his best effort to date. Featuring Dave Liebman (sop sax) and Joe Levano (ts). —*Michael G. Nastos*

Form / Apr. 8, 1990-Apr. 9, 1990 / Contemporary ◆◆◆◆
On this top quintet session, Joe Lovano (ts) enhances his sizable reputation. —*Ron Wynn*

Passages / Oct. 10, 1991-Oct. 11, 1991 / Chesky ◆◆◆◆

Upswing / Jun. 11, 1993-Jun. 12, 1993 / Chesky ◆◆◆◆

Barry Harris

b. Dec. 15, 1929, Detroit, MI
Piano / Bop
One of the major bop pianists of the past 40 years, Barry Harris has long had the ability to sound very close to Bud Powell, yet he can also do convincing impressions of Thelonious Monk and has his own style within the bop idiom. He was an important part of the Detroit jazz scene of the '50s and has been a jazz educator since that era. Harris recorded his first set as a leader while in 1958 and moved to New York in 1960 where he spent a short period with Cannonball Adderley's Quintet. He also recorded with Dexter Gordon, Illinois Jacquet, Yusef Lateef, and Hank Mobley and was with Coleman Hawkins off and on throughout the decade (including Hawk's declining years). In the '70s Harris was on two of Sonny Stitt's finest records (*Tune Up* and *Constellation*) and made many recordings in a variety of settings for Xanadu. Barry Harris has mostly been working with his

trio during the past 20 years and he has recorded as a leader for Argo (1958), Riverside, Prestige, MPS, Xanadu, and Red. —*Scott Yanow*

Barry Harris at the Jazz Workshop / May 15, 1960-May 16, 1960 / Original Jazz Classics ◆◆◆◆
Barry Harris has been remarkably consistent over the years. *At the Jazz Workshop* captured him live in 1960 with Sam Jones (bass) and Louis Hayes (drums). Adding to the expected pleasures of Harris was the slick work of Sam Jones' active bass and the powerful (as in accomplished) drumming of Louis Hayes. —*Bob Rusch, Cadence*

Preminado / Dec. 21, 1960 & Jan. 19, 1961 / Original Jazz Classics ◆◆◆◆
A fine 1991 reissue of high-quality trio performances. —*Ron Wynn*

Chasin' the Bird / May 31, 1962 & Aug. 23, 1962 / Original Jazz Classics ◆◆◆◆
Barry Harris has long been one of the top interpreters of the piano styles of Bud Powell and Thelonious Monk. This CD reissue of a trio session with bassist Bob Cranshaw and drummer Clifford Jarvis finds him performing near the top of his form. Highlights include "Chasin' the Bird" (during the theme, Harris plays both countermelodies simultaneously), "'Round Midnight," "The Way You Look Tonight," and three fine originals. This is excellent music that should please bop collectors. —*Scott Yanow*

★ **Live in Tokyo** / Apr. 12, 1976 & Apr. 14, 1976 / Xanadu ◆◆◆◆◆
Barry Harris has been a major force on piano in keeping the pure styles of Bud Powell and Thelonious Monk alive. This trio outing with bassist Sam Jones and drummer LeRoy Williams is quite successful and frequently exciting. Harris is heard at his best on such numbers as "Tea for Two," "Dance of the Infidels," and "Un Poco Loco." —*Scott Yanow*

Live at Maybeck Recital Hall, Vol. 12 / Mar. 1990 / Concord Jazz ◆◆◆◆
Barry Harris has long been the perfect bebop pianist. This solo recital finds Harris paying tribute to Bud Powell and Thelonious Monk as well as Art Tatum, not so much in their compositions (although he does perform Bud's "I'll Keep Loving You") but in aspects of their styles that he has enveloped into his own musical personality. Harris is even able to make bebop sense out of a medley consisting of "It Never Entered My Mind" and the themes from *The Flintstones* and *I Love Lucy!* —*Scott Yanow*

Confirmation / Sep. 1, 1991 / Candid ◆◆◆

Craig Harris

b. Sep. 10, 1954, Hempstead, NY
Trombone / Avant-Garde
One of the more esoteric trombonists of the avant-garde, Craig Harris has been an original stylist throughout his career. He played in R&B bands early on, graduated from college in 1976 and had stints with Sun Ra (1976-78) and Abdullah Ibrahim (1979-81). During the '80s and '90s he has worked with the who's who of the avant-garde including David Murray's octet and big band, Henry Threadgill, Lester Bowie's Brass Fantasy, Olu Dara, Cecil Taylor, Sam Rivers, Muhal Richard Abrams, and Charlie Haden's Liberation Orchestra. Harris has also led a few of his own groups (best-known are Tailgater's Tales and the R&Bish Cold Sweat) and has recorded as a leader for several labels including India Navigation, Soul Note, and JMT. —*Scott Yanow*

★ **Blackout in the Square Root of Soul** / Nov. 1987 / JMT ◆◆◆◆◆
A first-rate example of a fresh direction in jazz that blends improvisatory zeal, funk, and R&B references. —*Ron Wynn*

Cold Sweat Plays J.B. / Nov. 1988 / JMT ◆◆◆

Four Play / Aug. 1990 / JMT ◆◆◆

F Stops / Jun. 24, 1993-Jun. 25, 1993 / Soul Note ◆◆◆

Eddie Harris

b. Oct. 20, 1934, Chicago, IL
Sax (Tenor) / Soul-Jazz, Hard Bop, Groove
Eddie Harris has had a diverse and erratic recording career, leading to many observers greatly underrating his jazz talents. Harris has had his own sound on tenor since at least 1960, his improvisations range from bop to free, he was a pioneer with utilizing the electric sax (and was much more creative on it than most who followed), he introduced the reed trumpet, he is a fine pianist (one of his first professional jobs was playing piano with Gene Ammons), he composed the standard "Freedom Jazz Dance," and, although his vocals are definitely an acquired taste, he is a skilled comedian.

After getting out of the military, Harris' very first recording resulted in a hit version of "Exodus." His high-note tenor playing (which managed to sound comfortable in the range of an alto or even soprano) was well featured on a series of strong selling Vee-Jay releases (1961-63). After two outings for Columbia (1964), he switched to Atlantic for a decade. In 1966 Harris started utilizing an electric sax and debuted the popular "Listen Here" (although the 1967 recording is better known). At the 1969 Montreux Jazz Festival Harris and Les McCann made for a very appealing combination, recording such songs as "Compared to What" and "Cold Duck Time." Harris' later output for Atlantic was streaky, sometimes rock-oriented and occasionally pure comedy. He has since generally recorded strong jazz sets for such labels as Impulse, Enja, and SteepleChase and has remained a unique musical personality. —*Scott Yanow*

★ **Exodus to Jazz** / Jan. 17, 1961 / Vee-Jay ✦✦✦✦✦
Eddie Harris managed to have a hit ("Exodus") on his very first record. This CD reissue brings back the eight songs of the original LP (including "A.T.C.," "Little Girl Blue," and "Velocity") and adds the edited single versions of "Exodus" and "Alicia." From the start the young tenor had his own sound and he amazed some listeners by playing high notes (almost in the soprano range) with ease, always sounding quite relaxed. For this classic session, Harris is joined by an excellent Chicago-based quintet that includes pianist Willie Pickens and guitarist Joe Diorio. Highly recommended. —*Scott Yanow*

The Artist's Choice: the Eddie Harris Anthology / Jan. 1961-Feb. 20, 1977 / Rhino ✦✦✦

Mighty Like a Rose / Apr. 14, 1961 / Vee-Jay ✦✦✦✦
Tenor saxophonist Eddie Harris' second album, following on the heels of his surprise hit "Exodus," did not have any big sellers but the eight performances are rewarding. This long out-of-print LP features the same quintet as the earlier date (with guitarist Joe Diorio and pianist Willie Pickens also getting solo space). The highlights include "My Buddy," the theme from *Spartacus*, a couple of originals, and a brief version of the title cut. Harris' distinctive sound has always been well worth hearing; hopefully the revitalized Vee-Jay label will get around to bringing this date back one day. —*Scott Yanow*

The Lost Album Plus the Better Half / 1962-1963 / Vee-Jay ✦✦✦✦
This CD contains an LP's worth of unissued material plus half of an album that was released. With a supporting cast on different tracks includes Ira Sullivan on trumpet, altoist Bunky Green, organist Mel Rhyne, and guitarist Joe Diorio among others, the underrated but very distinctive tenor is in consistently spirited form. Harris stretches out on the rhythm changes of "Cuttin' Out" and the blues "Shakey Jake" (both of which are over 15 minutes long) and is heard on a variety of much shorter performances. A few of the briefer pieces are throwaways, but all of Eddie Harris' Vee-Jay recordings are enjoyable and this one is no exception. —*Scott Yanow*

The In Sound/Mean Greens / Aug. 9, 1965-Jun. 7, 1966 / Rhino/Atlantic ✦✦✦✦

☆ **The "In" Sound** / Aug. 30, 1965 / Atlantic ✦✦✦✦✦
This is one of Eddie Harris' great records and fortunately all of the music from the LP has returned as part of a reissue in the Rhino/Atlantic CD series (combined with Harris' *Mean Greens* date). The underrated but popular tenor saxophonist introduces his standard "Freedom Jazz Dance," plays one of the earlier versions of "The Shadow of Your Smile," romps on "Love for Sale" and "'S Wonderful," and also performs "Born to Be Blue" and his own "Cryin' Blues." Harris is heard in prime form in a quartet/ quintet with pianist Cedar Walton, bassist Ron Carter, drummer Billy Higgins, and sometimes trumpeter Ray Codrington. A gem. —*Scott Yanow*

The Electrifying Eddie Harris/Plug Me In / 1967 / Rhino/Atlantic ✦✦✦✦
This CD combines two fine Harris dates from 1967 and 1968. *The Electrifying Eddie Harris* had bluesy, soulful examples of Harris on baritone sax. "Listen Here" ranked second only to "Freedom Jazz Dance" among his most popular compositions, while he stretched out on "Spanish Bull." "Theme In Search Of A Movie," "Sham Time," and "Judie's Theme" were goodtime concessions to pop and jazz-soul audiences, yet still retained some fiber and spark. Once more, Harris found a good compromise between artistic and commercial concerns, although this date was more weighted toward funk and pop. —*Ron Wynn*

★ **Swiss Movement** / Jun. 1969 / Atlantic ✦✦✦✦✦
With Les McCann. Contains the monster hit "Compared to What." A must-buy. —*Michael G. Nastos*

Second Movement / 1971 / Atlantic ✦✦✦

Eddie Who? / Feb. 27, 1986 / Timeless ✦✦✦✦
Eddie Harris plays tenor, reed trumpet, piano, and takes a few vocals on this well rounded CD. The trio outing with bassist Ralphe Armstrong and drummer Sherman Ferguson starts out with the humorous "Eddie Who?" and has among its highlights "Daahoud," "Softly as in a Morning Sunrise," and "There Was a Time." In general this is a straightahead outing that shows off Eddie Harris' mastery of the bebop vocabulary. Well worth picking up. —*Scott Yanow*

There Was a Time (Echo of Harlem) / May 9, 1990 / Enja ✦✦✦✦
Eddie Harris, famous as the master of the electrified sax and for his brand of funky jazz, sticks exclusively to acoustic straightahead music on this rewarding Enja CD. With assistance from pianist Kenny Barron, bassist Cecil McBee, and drummer Ben Riley, Harris is heard in peak form on such songs as "Love Letters," "Autumn in New York," "The Song Is You," and a lengthy "Harlem Nocturne." Although Harris has maintained a fairly low profile during the past decade, he is still playing in his prime as this highly recommended CD demonstrates. —*Scott Yanow*

Gene Harris

b. Sep. 1, 1933, Benton Harbor, MI
Piano / Soul-Jazz, Hard Bop, Groove
One of the most accessible of all jazz pianists, Gene Harris' soulful style (influenced by Oscar Peterson and containing the bluesiness of a Junior Mance) is immediately likable and predictably excellent. After playing in an Army band (1951-54) he formed a trio with bassist Andy Simpkins and drummer Bill Dowdy that was by 1956 known as the Three Sounds. The group was quite popular and recorded regularly during 1956-70 for Blue Note and Verve. Although the personnel changed and the music became more R&B-oriented in the early '70s, Harris retained the Three Sounds name for his later Blue Note sets. He retired to Boise, ID, in 1977 and was largely forgotten when Ray Brown persuaded him to return to the spotlight in the early '80s. Harris worked for a time with the Ray Brown Trio and has led his own quartets ever since, recording regularly for Concord and heading the Phillip Morris Superband on a few tours. —*Scott Yanow*

Feelin' Good / Jun. 28, 1960 / Blue Note ✦✦✦✦
Prototypical Three Sounds release. Elements of funk, soul-jazz, and blues merge into a workable jazz concept. —*Ron Wynn*

Anita O'Day and the Three Sounds / Oct. 12, 1962-Oct. 15, 1962 / Verve ✦✦✦

Live at the It Club / Mar. 6, 1970 / Blue Note ✦✦✦

Live at Otter Crest / Apr. 24, 1981 / Bosco ✦✦✦

The Plus One / Nov. 19, 1985-Dec. 1985 / Concord Jazz ✦✦✦

Tribute to Count Basie / Mar. 1987-Jun. 1987 / Concord Jazz ✦✦✦

Live at Town Hall / Sep. 23, 1989 / Concord Jazz ✦✦✦✦
A fine, traditional big-band outing. The song selection is predictably conservative, but there is enough boldness in the arrangements and playing to even things out and make this an above-average entry in a domain screaming for fresh blood. —*Ron Wynn*

● **At Last** / May 1990 / Concord Jazz ✦✦✦✦
A wonderful teamup of Gene Harris with Scott Hamilton. —*Ron Wynn*

Black and Blue / Jun. 29, 1991 / Concord Jazz ✦✦✦✦
Although there are few actual blues on this CD, pianist Gene Harris gives all of the songs (whether complex standards, ballads, or near-blues) a bluesy feel, adding soul and a church feeling to each of the melodies. With the assistance of guitarist Ron Eschete, bassist Luther Hughes, and drummer Harold Jones, Harris is in typically fine form. —*Scott Yanow*

Ste. Chapelle Winery / 1993 / Concord Jazz ✦✦✦

Donald Harrison

b. Jun. 23, 1960, New Orleans, LA
Sax (Alto), Sax (Soprano) / Post-Bop
A talented post-bop altoist with a personal angular style, Donald Harrison came to fame with Art Blakey's Jazz Messengers, but has not become a major name in jazz yet despite his talent. He studied at the New Orleans Center for the Creative Arts with Ellis Marsalis, went to Berklee (1979-80), worked with Roy Haynes and Jack McDuff, and was with Blakey during 1982-84, sharing the front line with Terence Blanchard. Harrison and Blanchard co-led a group for a few years, recording frequently before they broke up their band. Donald Harrison returned to the Jazz Messengers on a few brief occasions, led his own groups, and recorded as a leader for Candid, making guest appearances on CTI sessions. —*Scott Yanow*

● **Crystal Stair** / 1987 / CBS ✦✦✦✦

For Art's Sake / Nov. 9, 1990-Nov. 10, 1990 / Candid ✦✦✦✦
A tribute album to great drummer Art Blakey from onetime Jazz Messenger alto saxophonist Donald Harrison. This was one of the first sessions after Harrison and longtime partner Terence Blanchard (trumpet) went their separate ways, and Harrison was working with new trumpeter Marlon Jordan and other young lions, such as pianist Cyrus Chestnut, bassist Christian McBride, and drummer Carl Allen. The results would have made Blakey smile. —*Ron Wynn*

Indian Blues / May 22, 1991-May 23, 1991 / Candid ✦✦✦

Johnny Hartman

b. Jul. 3, 1923, Chicago, IL, d. Sep. 15, 1983, New York, NY
Vocals / Ballads, Standards
A superior ballad singer with a warm baritone voice, Johnny Hartman was rediscovered to an extent posthumously when some of his recordings were used on the soundtrack of the 1995 Clint Eastwood film *Bridges of Madison County*, but jazz fans had never forgotten him for his classic date with John Coltrane. After military service, Hartman sang with Earl Hines (1947), the Dizzy Gillespie Big Band (1948-49), and Erroll Garner. Although he recorded two Bethlehem albums in 1956, Hartman was generally overlooked during the '50s. However his three Impulse albums (1963-64) were well received, particularly the Coltrane collaboration which was highlighted by the definitive version of "Lush Life" and a memorable "My One

and Only Love." But it would be 1977 before he recorded again, and despite some fine later sessions (including for Bee Hive), Johnny Hartman was underrated throughout his lifetime. — *Scott Yanow*

All of Me / Nov. 1956 / Bethlehem ✦✦✦✦
Reissued on CD by Evidence, the original 12-song program has been augmented by four "new" alternate takes, but the CD lists the wrong personnel! The warm baritone singer Johnny Hartman is actually accompanied by the Ralph Sharon Trio and trumpeter Howard McGhee on four songs and the Frank Hunter String Orchestra on the remainder of the set. The emphasis is on ballads (always Hartman's strong point) with the highlights including "Blue Skies," "Tenderly," "The Lamp Is Low," and "I Concentrate on You." — *Scott Yanow*

Sittin' In With / 1961 / VGM ✦✦✦

★ **John Coltrane and Johnny Hartman** / Mar. 7, 1963 / Impulse ✦✦✦✦✦
Marvelous love songs, superior playing. — *Ron Wynn*

I Just Dropped by to Say Hello / Oct. 9, 1963 & Oct. 17, 1963 / Impulse ✦✦✦✦
This 1995 GRP CD reissue brings back ballad singer Johnny Hartman's second Impulse session, following his classic collaboration with John Coltrane. Hartman is heard in peak form throughout these 11 pieces which include "In The Wee Small Hours Of The Morning," "Sleepin' Bee," "Stairway To The Stars," and even "Charade." Tenor saxophonist Illinois Jacquet is on five of the songs, guitarists Kenny Burrell and Jim Hall help out on a few tunes, and Hartman is consistently accompanied by pianist Hank Jones, bassist Milt Hinton, and drummer Elvin Jones. This is one of his finest recordings. — *Scott Yanow*

The Voice That Is / Sep. 22, 1964-Sep. 24, 1964 / Impulse ✦✦✦

For Trane / Nov. 29, 1972 & Dec. 1, 1972 / Blue Note ✦✦✦

Hampton Hawes

b. Nov. 13, 1928, Los Angeles, CA, **d.** May 22, 1977, Los Angeles, CA
Piano, Keyboards / Bop, Hard Bop, Crossover
Hampton Hawes was one of the finest jazz pianists of the '50s, a fixture on the Los Angeles scene who brought his own interpretations to the dominant Bud Powell style. In the mid-to-late '40s he played with Dexter Gordon, and Wardell Gray, among others on Central Avenue. He was with Howard McGhee's band (1950-51), played with Shorty Rogers and the Lighthouse All-Stars, served in the Army (1952-54), and then led trios in the Los Angeles area, recording many albums for Contemporary. Arrested for heroin possession in 1958, Hawes spent five years in prison until he was pardoned by President Kennedy. He led trios for the remainder of his life, using electric piano (which disturbed his longtime fans) for a period in the early-to-mid-'70s but returning to acoustic piano before dying from a stroke in 1977. Hampton Hawes' memoirs *Raise Up off Me* (1974) are both frank and memorable, and most of his records (for Xanadu, Prestige, Savoy, Contemporary, Black Lion, and Freedom) are currently available. — *Scott Yanow*

Piano: East/West / Dec. 1952 / Original Jazz Classics ✦✦✦
Hawes and Freddie Redd (p) split an album, revealing their differing, yet mutually appealing, stylistic tendencies. — *Ron Wynn*

Everybody Likes Hampton Hawes, Vol. 1 / Jun. 28, 1955 / Original Jazz Classics ✦✦✦
An essential set of powerhouse mid-50s trio works with Hawes, Red Mitchell (b), and Chuck Thompson (d). — *Ron Wynn*

Everybody Likes Hampton Hawes, Vol. 2 / Dec. 3, 1955-Jan. 25, 1956 / Original Jazz Classics ✦✦✦✦
The second volume of mid-'50s trio sessions featuring pianist Hampton Hawes. He does moving ballads, reinterprets standards with elan, and pens originals that show his blues and gospel influence, while also exhibiting his voicings and fluidity. — *Ron Wynn*

Everybody Likes Hampton Hawes, Vol. 3: The Trio / Jan. 25, 1956 / Contemporary ✦✦✦
The trio. The powerhouse conclusion to this series. — *Ron Wynn*

★ **Four! Hampton Hawes!!!!** / Jan. 27, 1958 / Original Jazz Classics ✦✦✦✦
This is an outstanding date, with excellent Barney Kessel guitar. — *Ron Wynn*

For Real! / Mar. 17, 1958 / Original Jazz Classics ✦✦✦✦

The Sermon / 1958 / Contemporary ✦✦✦✦
A 1988 reissue of a tight, tough trio work. — *Ron Wynn*

The Green Leaves of Summer / Feb. 17, 1964 / Original Jazz Classics ✦✦✦✦
Frequently amazing piano work from Hawes. — *Ron Wynn*

Here and Now / May 12, 1965 / Original Jazz Classics ✦✦✦

Trio At Montreux / Jun. 1971 / Fresh Sound ✦✦✦✦
This CD consists of a continuous 57-minute set performed by pianist Hampton Hawes' Trio with bassist Henry Franklin and drummer Mike Carvin. Two songs (Bert Bacharach's "This Guy's in Love with You" and

Hawes' "High in the Sky") are fully explored, and despite the extreme length and some wandering sections, the performance holds one's interest throughout. — *Scott Yanow*

Recorded Live at the Great American Music Hall / Jun. 10, 1975 / Concord Jazz ✦✦✦✦
This album, one of pianist Hampton Hawes' last recordings, is a surprise success. First Hawes, in duets with bassist Mario Suraci, really digs into two rather unpromising pop tunes ("Fly Me to the Moon" and "Sunny") in extended versions ("Sunny" is given over 14 minutes) and brings out surprising beauty in those overdone songs. For the second side of this LP, Hawes performs his own suite for solo piano, an impressive three-movement work that he titled "The Status of Maceo" that has enough variety in its 20-plus minutes to keep one's interest throughout. — *Scott Yanow*

Coleman Hawkins

b. Nov. 21, 1904, St. Joseph, MO, **d.** May 19, 1969, New York, NY
Sax (Tenor) / Bop, Swing, Classic Jazz
Coleman Hawkins was the first important tenor saxophonist and he remains one of the greatest of all time. A consistently modern improviser whose knowledge of chords and harmonies was encyclopediac, Hawkins had a 40-year prime (1925-65) during which he could hold his own with any competitor.

Coleman Hawkins started piano lessons when he was five, switched to cello at age seven and two years later began on tenor. At a time when the saxophone was considered a novelty instrument, used in vaudeville and as a poor substitute for the trombone in marching bands, Hawkins sought to develop his own sound. A professional when he was 12, Hawkins was playing in a Kansas City theater pit band in 1921 when Mamie Smith hired him to play with her Jazz Hounds. Hawkins was with the blues singer until June 1923, making many records in a background role and he was occasionally heard on instrumentals. After leaving Smith he freelanced around New York, played briefly with Wilbur Sweatman and in August 1923 made his first recordings with Fletcher Henderson. When Henderson formed a permanent orchestra in January 1924, Hawkins was his star tenor.

Although (due largely to lack of competition) Coleman Hawkins was the top tenor in jazz in 1924, his staccato runs and use of slap-tonguing sound quite dated today. However after Louis Armstrong joined Henderson later in the year, Hawkins learned from the cornetist's relaxed legato style and advanced quickly. By 1925 Hawkins was truly a major soloist and the following year his solo on "Stampede" became influential. Hawk (who doubled in early years on clarinet and bass sax) would be with Fletcher Henderson's Orchestra up to 1934 and during this time he was the obvious pacesetter among tenors; Bud Freeman was about the only tenor who did not sound like a close relative of the hard-toned Hawkins! In addition to his solos with Henderson, Hawkins backed some blues singers, recorded with McKinney's Cotton Pickers, and with Red McKenzie in 1929 he cut his first classic ballad statement on "One Hour."

By 1934 Coleman Hawkins had tired of the struggling Fletcher Henderson Orchestra and he moved to Europe, spending five years (1934-39) overseas. He played at first with Jack Hylton's Orchestra in England and then freelanced throughout the continent. His most famous recording from this period was a 1937 date with Benny Carter, Alix Combille, Andre Ekyan, Django Reinhardt and Stephane Grappelli that resulted in classic renditions of "Crazy Rhythm" and "Honeysuckle Rose." With World War II coming close, Hawkins returned to the US in 1939. Although Lester Young had emerged with a totally new style on tenor, Hawkins showed that he was still a dominant force by winning a few heated jam sessions. His recording of "Body and Soul" that year became his most famous record. In 1940 he led a big band that failed to catch on so Hawkins broke it up and became a fixture on 52nd Street. Some of his finest recordings were cut during the first half of the '40s including a stunning quartet version of "The Man I Love." Although he was already a 20-year veteran, Hawkins encouraged the younger bop-oriented musicians and did not need to adjust his harmonically-advanced style in order to play with them. He used Thelonious Monk in his 1944 quartet, led the first official bop record session (which included Dizzy Gillespie and Don Byas), had Oscar Pettiford, Miles Davis and Max Roach as sidemen early in their careers, toured in California with a sextet featuring Howard McGhee and in 1946 utilized J.J. Johnson and Fats Navarro on record dates. Hawkins toured with Jazz at the Philharmonic several times during 1946-50, visited Europe on a few occasions and in 1948 recorded the first unaccompanied saxophone solo, "Picasso."

By the early '50s the Lester Young-influenced Four Brothers sound had become a much greater influence on young tenors than Hawkins' style and he was considered by some to be out-of-fashion. However Hawkins kept on working and occasionally recording and by the mid-'50s was experiencing a renaissance. The up-and-coming Sonny Rollins considered Hawkins his main influence, Hawk started teaming up regularly with Roy Eldridge in an exciting quintet (their appearance at the 1957 Newport Jazz Festival was notable) and he proved to still be in his prime. Coleman Hawkins appeared in a wide variety of settings, from Red Allen's heated Dixieland band at the Metropole and leading a bop date featuring Idrees Sulieman and J.J. Johnson to guest appearances on records that included Thelonious Monk, John Coltrane and (in the early '60s) Max Roach and Eric Dolphy. During the first half of the '60s Coleman Hawkins had an opportunity to record with Duke Ellington, collaborated on one somewhat eccentric session with Sonny Rollins and even did a bossa nova album. By 1965 Hawkins was even showing the influence of John Coltrane in his explorative flights and seemed ageless.

Unfortunately 1965 was Coleman Hawkins' last good year. Whether it was senility or frustration, Hawkins began to lose interest in life. He practically quit eating, increased his drinking, and quickly wasted away. Other than a surprisingly effective appearance with Jazz at the Philharmonic in early 1969, very little of Hawkins' work during his final 3 1/2 years (a period during which he largely stopped recording) is up to the level one would expect from the great master. However there are dozens of superb Coleman Hawkins recordings currently available and, as Eddie Jefferson said in his vocalese version of "Body and Soul," "He was the king of the saxophone." —*Scott Yanow*

Three Great Swing Saxophones / Nov. 14, 1929-Aug. 23, 1946 / Bluebird ✦✦✦

☆ **In Europe 1934/39** / Nov. 18, 1934-May 26, 1939 / Jazz Up ✦✦✦✦✦
In 1934 Hawkins, after 11 years as the star soloist with Fletcher Henderson's pioneering jazz big band, was looking for other worlds to conquer. To satisfy his curiosity he travelled to Europe and for the next five years was a major celebrity overseas, only returning to the US when World War II was about ready to start. This magnificent three-CD set contains every recording that the great tenor saxophonist made in Europe, 71 in all (including alternate takes). Whether featured in London, Switzerland, Paris, or Holland, Hawkins dominates these recordings, which find him in a variety of settings, from duets with pianist Freddie Johnson to medium-size bands. Benny Carter and Django Reinhardt also make a few notable appearances. This perfectly done set is highly recommended. —*Scott Yanow*

★ **Body and Soul** / Oct. 11, 1939-Jan. 20, 1956 / RCA/Bluebird ✦✦✦✦✦
Much of the material on this two-LP set has been since reissued on CD but one way or the other, this music (particularly the first 16 tracks) belongs in every serious jazz collection. In 1939 Hawkins returned to the US after five years in Europe and it took him very little time to reassert his prior dominance as king of the tenors. This set starts off with the session that resulted in Hawkins' classic version of "Body and Soul," teams him with Benny Carter (on trumpet) for some hot swing (including a memorable rendition of "My Blue Heaven"), and then finds Hawkins using younger musicians (including trumpeter Fats Navarro and trombonist J.J. Johnson) on some advanced bop originals highlighted by "Half Step Down Please." The remainder of this set is also good but less historic with Hawkins being well showcased with three larger groups in 1956, culminating in a remake of "Body and Soul." —*Scott Yanow*

★ **Rainbow Mist** / Feb. 16, 1944-May 22, 1944 / Delmark ✦✦✦✦✦
Hawkins was always an open-minded musician. A very advanced player even when he first emerged with Fletcher Henderson's orchestra in the '20s, by the '40s he may have been technically middle aged but remained a young thinker. For his recording session of February 16, 1944, the great tenor invited some of the most promising younger players (including trumpeter Dizzy Gillespie, bassist Oscar Pettiford, and drummer Max Roach), and the result was the very first bebop on records. During these two sessions, the large ensemble recorded six selections including Gillespie's "Woody'n You," Hawkins' "Disorder at the Border," and a new treatment of "Body and Soul" by the tenorman which he retitled "Rainbow Mist." Also on this highly recommended CD are four titles matching together the tenors of Hawkins, Ben Webster, and Georgie Auld (with trumpeter Charlie Shavers included as a bonus) and a session from Auld's big band, highlighted by Sonny Berman's trumpet solo on "Taps Miller." —*Scott Yanow*

● **Hollywood Stampede** / Feb. 23, 1945-Mar. 9, 1945 / Capitol ✦✦✦✦
Hawkins led one of his finest bands in 1945, a sextet with the fiery trumpeter Howard McGhee that fell somewhere between small-group swing and bebop. This CD contains all of that group's 12 recordings, including memorable versions of "Rifftide" and "Stuffy"; trombonist Vic Dickenson guests on four tracks. This CD concludes with one of Hawkins' rarest sessions, an Aladdin date from 1947 that finds the veteran tenor leading a septet that includes 20-year-old trumpeter Miles Davis. —*Scott Yanow*

Coleman Hawkins And Johnny Hodges In Paris / Dec. 21, 1949-Jun. 20, 1950 / Vogue ✦✦✦✦

Body and Soul Revisited / Oct. 19, 1951-Oct. 13, 1958 / Decca ✦✦✦

The Hawk Returns / May 27, 1954 / Savoy ✦✦

Cool Groove / May 10, 1955 / Drive Archive ✦✦✦✦

Hawk in Paris / Jul. 9, 1956-Jul. 13, 1956 / VIK ✦✦✦✦
This CD is a major surprise. Hawkins had always wanted to record with a large string section and he received his wish on the majority of these 12

romantic melodies, all of which have some association with Paris. The surprise is that he plays with a great deal of fire (his doubletiming on "My Man" is wondrous), and that Manny Albam's arrangements mostly avoid being muzaky and quite often are creative and witty. What could have been a novelty or an insipid affair is actually one of Coleman Hawkins' more memorable albums. —*Scott Yanow*

The Gilded Hawk / Oct. 17, 1956-Feb. 8, 1957 / Capitol ✦✦✦

● **Hawk Flies High** / Mar. 12, 1957-Mar. 15, 1957 / Original Jazz Classics ✦✦✦✦
1957 was one of the great years for the veteran tenor saxophonist (who was then 51); he suddenly became rediscovered, even though he had never suffered a period of decline. *The Hawk Flies High* found him playing mostly with bop-oriented musicians a couple decades his junior (including trombonist J.J. Johnson and trumpeter Idrees Sulieman) and more than holding his own. The memorable "Sanctity" has a particularly classic Hawkins solo but each of the six tracks are quite enjoyable. —*Scott Yanow*

Think Deep / Mar. 12, 1957-Mar. 15, 1957 / Riverside ✦✦✦✦
This LP has been reissued on CD as *The Hawk Flies High*. Hawkins, 35 years after his recording debut, was indeed flying high in 1957, a year when he seemed to be rediscovered by the jazz world. He has no difficulty keeping up with the younger players he picked for this date (including trombonist J.J. Johnson and trumpeter Idrees Sulieman) and comes up with a new classic solo on "Sanctity." —*Scott Yanow*

The Genius of Coleman Hawkins / Oct. 16, 1957 / Verve ✦✦✦✦
Genius may not be the right word, but "brilliance" certainly fits. At the age of 51 in 1957 Hawkins had already been on records for 35 years and had been one of the leading tenors for nearly that long. This CD matches him with the Oscar Peterson Trio (plus drummer Alvin Stoller) for a fine runthrough on standards. Hawk plays quite well, although the excitement level does not reach the heights of his sessions with trumpeter Roy Eldridge. —*Scott Yanow*

Coleman Hawkins and Roy Eldridge at the Opera House / Oct. 19, 1957 / Verve ✦✦✦

Soul / Nov. 7, 1958 / Original Jazz Classics ✦✦

Hawk Eyes / Apr. 3, 1959 / Original Jazz Classics ✦✦✦✦
Tenor-great Coleman Hawkins tended to be at his best when challenged by another horn player. On this highly enjoyable CD, Hawkins is joined by the superb trumpeter Charlie Shavers and a strong rhythm section that includes guitarist Tiny Grimes and pianist Ray Bryant. With such superior songs as "Through for the Night," "I Never Knew," and "La Rosita," in addition to long jams, plenty of fireworks occur during this frequently exciting session. —*Scott Yanow*

Dali / 1959-May 1962 / Stash ✦✦✦✦
This Stash CD, despite some silly graphics on the liners, has quite a bit of rewarding music. There are three examples of the fireworks that generally occured when tenor saxophonist Coleman Hawkins and trumpeter Roy Eldridge met up (taken from a live session in 1959), while the remainder of this disc finds Hawkins playing in Brussels in 1962. The veteran tenor is particularly strong on "Disorder at the Border" and "Rifftide," but the high point is a rare unaccompanied solo on "Dali," the fourth and final time that Hawkins recorded an improvisation by himself. It is a pity he never recorded an entire album like that. —*Scott Yanow*

Bean Stalkin' / Oct. 1960-Nov. 1960 / Pablo ✦✦✦✦
In contrast to Hawkins' sometimes sleepy studio albums from this era, his live performances were generally quite exciting. This set features the great tenor at two European concerts in 1960, performing three fairly heated numbers with a four-piece rhythm section, matching wits with trumpeter Roy Eldridge on "Crazy Rhythm" and leading two all-star jams with Eldridge, fellow tenor Don Byas, and altoist Benny Carter. Some of the music is quite fiery, making this a recommended disc. —*Scott Yanow*

★ **In a Mellow Tone** / Dec. 30, 1960 / Prestige ✦✦✦✦✦
A superior session with Hawkins, Eddie "Lockjaw" Davis (ts), and others. —*Ron Wynn*

Night Hawk / Dec. 30, 1960 / Original Jazz Classics ✦✦✦✦
Hawkins was one of the main inspirations of his fellow tenor Eddie "Lockjaw" Davis, so it was logical that they would one day meet up in the recording studio. This CD has many fine moments from these two highly competitive jazzmen, particularly the lengthy title cut and a heated trade-off on "In a Mellow Tone," on which Davis goes higher but Hawkins wins on ideas. —*Scott Yanow*

Hawkins! Alive! at the Village Gate / Aug. 13, 1962-Aug. 15, 1962 / Verve ✦✦✦✦
The great Hawkins (who debuted on records 40 years earlier) gets to stretch out on this live outing by his 1962 quartet (which also features pianist Tommy Flanagan). This CD, which as a former LP had lengthy versions of "All the Things You Are," "Joshua Fit the Battle of Jericho," "Mack the Knife," and "Talk of the Town," is augmented by previously unreleased versions of "Bean and the Boys" and "If I Had You," all of which show that Coleman Hawkins in his late 50s was still a powerful force. —*Scott Yanow*

Alive! / Aug. 15, 1962 / Verve ✦✦✦✦
From the mid-'50s until Coleman Hawkins' death in 1969, the tenor saxophonist frequently teamed up with trumpeter Roy Eldridge to form a potent team. However, Hawkins rarely met altoist Johnny Hodges on the bandstand, making this encounter a special event. Long versions of "Satin Doll," "Perdido," and "The Rabbit in Jazz" give these three classic jazzmen (who are ably assisted by the Tommy Flanagan Trio) chances to stretch out and inspire each other. The remainder of this CD has Eldridge and Hodges absent while Coleman Hawkins (on "new" versions of "Mack the Knife," "It's the Talk of the Town," "Bean and the Boys," and "Caravan") heads the quartet for some excellent playing. Timeless music played by some of the top veteran stylists of the swing era. — *Scott Yanow*

Duke Ellington Meets Coleman Hawkins / Aug. 18, 1962 / Impulse ✦✦✦✦
This CD documents a historic occasion. Although Coleman Hawkins had been an admirer of Duke Ellington's music for at least 35 years at this point, and Ellington had suggested they record together at least 20 years prior to their actual meeting in 1962, this was their first (and only) meeting on record. Although it would have been preferable to hear the great tenor performing with the full orchestra, his meeting with Ellington and an all-star group taken out of the big band does feature such greats as Ray Nance (on cornet and violin), trombonist Lawrence Brown, altoist Johnny Hodges, and baritonist Harry Carney. High points include an exuberant "The Jeep Is Jumpin'," an interesting remake of "Mood Indigo," and a few new Ellington pieces. This delightful music is recommended in one form or another. — *Scott Yanow*

Desafinado / Sep. 12, 1962-Sep. 16, 1962 / Impulse ✦✦✦✦
In the '60s Hawkins led three sessions for Impulse, a label best known for its recordings of John Coltrane. This particular LP (which has since been reissued on CD) was a real surprise for, at first glance, the concept should not have worked that well. The hard-blowing tenor is backed by two guitars, bass, and three percussionists in an attempt to cash in on the bossa nova fad of the early '60s but even when the ensemble performs such potentially unsuitable material as "I'm Looking over a Four Leaf Clover" and "I Remember You" (in addition to "Desafinado" and a classic rendition of "O Pato"), the music is delightful. — *Scott Yanow*

Wrapped Tight / Feb. 22, 1965-Mar. 1, 1965 / Impulse ✦✦✦✦
Hawkins' last strong recording finds the veteran, 43 years after his recording debut with Mamie Smith's Jazz Hounds, improvising creatively on a wide variety of material on this CD, ranging from "Intermezzo" and "Here's That Rainy Day" to "Red Roses for a Blue Lady" and "Indian Summer." Best is an adventurous version of "Out of Nowhere" that shows that the tenor saxophonist was still coming up with new ideas in 1965. — *Scott Yanow*

Erskine Hawkins

b. Jul. 26, 1914, Birmingham, AL, **d.** Nov. 1993
Trumpet / Swing, Early R&B
A talented high-note trumpeter and a popular bandleader, Erskine Hawkins was nicknamed "The 20th Century Gabriel." He learned drums and trombone before switching to trumpet when he was 13. While attending the Alabama State Teachers College, he became the leader of the college band the 'Bama Street Collegians. They went to New York in 1934, became the Erskine Hawkins Orchestra, started making records in 1936, and by 1938 were quite successful. With Hawkins and Dud Bascomb sharing the trumpet solos, Paul Bascomb or Julian Dash heard on tenors, Haywood Henry on baritone, and pianist Avery Parrish, this was a solidly swinging band that delighted dancers and jazz fans alike. Hawkins had three major hits ("Tuxedo Junction," "After Hours," and "Tippin' In") and was able to keep the big band together all the way until 1953; some of their later sessions were more R&B-oriented yet never without jazz interest. Hawkins led a smaller unit during his last few decades (the survivors of the big band had a recorded reunion in 1971) and the trumpeter kept on working into the '80s. — *Scott Yanow*

★ **The Original Tuxedo Junction** / Sep. 12, 1938-Jan. 10, 1945 / Bluebird ✦✦✦✦✦
These sessions for 14-piece band include pianist Avery Parrish on his immortal "After Hours" and teaming up with the leader for "Swing Out." The sessions feature tenor Julian Dash, baritonist and clarinetist Haywood Henry, and Buscomb and Hawkins on trumpet. — *Michael G. Nastos*

Erskine Hawkins 1940-1941 / Nov. 6, 1940-Dec. 22, 1941 / Classics ✦✦✦✦

1941-1945 / Dec. 22, 1941-Nov. 21, 1945 / Classics ✦✦✦✦
All of the recordings cut by the always-underrated Erskine Hawkins Orchestra during a four-year period are reissued on this Classics CD. Actually there is only one cut from 1941 and seven songs from 1942, so the bulk of the set deals with the 1945 edition of the orchestra. In general the instrumentals are much more rewarding than the vocals, featuring solos by the trumpeter/leader, altoist Bobby Smith (who stars on the hit record of "Tippin' In"), and tenor saxophonist Julian Dash. The vocals by James

Mitchelle, Ida James, Carol Tucker, and Dolores Brown are harmless if forgettable; pianist Ace Harris fares best singing "Caldonia." In addition to "Tippin' In," highlights include "Lucky Seven," "Bear Mash Blues" (a near-classic by Sammy Lowe), "Caldonia," "Good Dip," and "Holiday for Swing." This is the fifth Erskine Hawkins CD from Classics and due to the consistency of the band, all are recommended. — *Scott Yanow*

Louis Hayes

b. May 31, 1937, Detroit, MI
Drums / Hard Bop
A superior hard-bop drummer best known for supporting soloists rather than taking the spotlight himself, Louis Hayes led a band in Detroit as a teenager and was with Yusef Lateef during 1955-56. He had three notable associations: Horace Silver's Quintet (1956-59), the Cannonball Adderley Quintet (1959-65), and the Oscar Peterson Trio (1965-67). Hayes often teamed up with Sam Jones, both with Adderley and Peterson and in freelance settings. He led a variety of groups during the '70s including quintets co-led by Junior Cook and Woody Shaw. Louis Hayes has appeared on many records through the years with everyone from John Coltrane and Cecil Taylor to McCoy Tyner, Freddie Hubbard, and Dexter Gordon and has led sessions for Vee-Jay (1960), Timeless (1976), Muse (1977), and Candid (1989). — *Scott Yanow*

Louis Hayes (Featuring Yusef Lateef & Nat Adderley) / Apr. 26, 1960 / Vee-Jay ✦✦✦✦
The 1960 Cannonball Adderley Quintet (with drummer Louis Hayes, cornetist Nat Adderley, pianist Barry Harris, and bassist Sam Jones) performs on this Vee-Jay CD reissue with tenor saxophonist Yusef Lateef in Cannonball's place. Although one misses the fiery altoist, the contrast between Adderley's exciting (if sometimes erratic) cornet and Lateef's dignified yet soulful tenor make this an above-average session of swinging bop. The high-quality originals are augmented by five "new" alternate takes. — *Scott Yanow*

Ichi-Ban / May 5, 1976 / Timeless ✦✦✦
Tight, tough duo work with Junior Cook (ts). — *Ron Wynn*

★ **The Real Thing** / May 20, 1977-May 21, 1977 / Muse ✦✦✦✦✦
His best band, with Woody Shaw (tpt), Rene McLean (sax), and Slide Hampton (tb). All originals, all excellent. — *Michael G. Nastos*

Light and Lively / Apr. 21, 1989 / SteepleChase ✦✦✦✦
Another good one, with Charles Tolliver (tpt) and Bobby Watson (as). — *Michael G. Nastos*

The Crawl / Oct. 14, 1989 / Candid ✦✦✦✦
Live at Birdland, with Charles Tolliver (tpt) and Gary Bartz (sax). Very good. — *Michael G. Nastos*

Una Max / Dec. 1989 / SteepleChase ✦✦✦✦

Tubby Hayes (Edward Brian Hayes)

b. Jan. 30, 1935, London, England, **d.** Jun. 8, 1973, London, England
Flute, Sax (Tenor), Vibes / Bop, Hard Bop
One of England's top jazz musicians of the '50s and '60s, Tubby Hayes was a fine hard bop stylist on tenor and occasionally vibes and flute. A professional at 15, Hayes played with Kenny Baker and in the big bands of Ambrose, Vic Lewis, and Jack Parnell during 1951-55. He led his own group after that and started doubling on vibes in 1956. Hayes co-led the Jazz Couriers with Ronnie Scott (1957-59) and appeared in the US a few times during 1961-65. He headed his own big band in London, sat in with Duke Ellington's Orchestra in 1964, and was featured at many European festivals. Heart trouble forced him out of action during 1969-71 and caused his premature death. Tubby Hayes led sessions for Tempo (1955-59), London, Jazzland (1959), Fontana, Epic (a 1961 date with Clark Terry and Horace Parlan), Smash (a 1962 album which matched him with James Moody and Roland Kirk), 77, Spotlite, and Mole. — *Scott Yanow*

● **New York Sessions** / Oct. 3, 1961-Oct. 4, 1961 / Columbia ✦✦✦✦
Tubby Hayes (UK tenor man) blows strong with Clark Terry (tpt). A sleeper. — *Michael G. Nastos*

Roy Haynes

b. Mar. 13, 1926, Roxbury, MA
Drums / Bop, Hard Bop
A veteran drummer long overshadowed by others but finally in the '90s recognized for his talents and versatility, Roy Haynes has been a major player for 45 years. He worked early on with the Sabby Lewis big band, Frankie Newton, Luis Russell (1947-49), and Lester Young (1947-49). After some engagements with Kai Winding, Haynes was a member of the Charlie Parker quintet (1949-52); he also recorded during this era with Bud Powell, Wardell Gray, and Stan Getz. Haynes toured with Sarah Vaughan (1953-58), played with Thelonious Monk in 1958, led his own group, and gigged with George Shearing, Lennie Tristano, Eric Dolphy, and Getz (1961). He was Elvin Jones' occasional substitute with John Coltrane's classic quartet during 1961-65, toured with Getz (1965-67), and

played with Gary Burton (1967-68). In addition to touring with Chick Corea (1981 and 1984) and Pat Metheny (1989-90), Haynes has led his own Hip Ensemble on and off during the past 28 years. When one considers that he has also gigged with Miles Davis, Art Pepper, Horace Tapscott, and Dizzy Gillespie, it is fair to say that Haynes has played with about everyone! He led dates for EmArcy and Swing (both in 1954), New Jazz (1958 and 1960), Impulse (a 1962 quartet album with Roland Kirk), New Jazz, Pacific Jazz, Mainstream, Galaxy, and more recently Dreyfus, Evidence, and Storyville. In 1994 Roy Haynes was awarded the Danish Jazzpar prize. His son Graham Haynes is an excellent cornetist. —*Scott Yanow*

★ **We Three** / Nov. 14, 1958 / New Jazz ✦✦✦✦✦
A wonderful session, with spectacular piano by Phineas Newborn and great bass from Paul Chambers. —*Ron Wynn*

Just Us / Jul. 5, 1960 / Original Jazz Classics ✦✦✦

Out of the Afternoon / May 16, 1962 & May 23, 1962 / Original Jazz Classics ✦✦✦✦
Definitive creative music with Roland Kirk (reeds) and Tommy Flanagan (p). —*Michael G. Nastos*

Cracklin' / Apr. 10, 1963 / Original Jazz Classics ✦✦✦✦
A fine date, with Booker Ervin center stage on tenor sax. —*Ron Wynn*

★ **Te Vou!** / 1994 / Dreyfus ✦✦✦✦✦
Veteran drummer Roy Haynes only has a single short solo on this CD but one suspects that his presence helped solidify and inspire the illustrious sidemen (altoist Donald Harrison, guitarist Pat Metheny, pianist David Kikoski, and bassist Christian McBride). Harrison and Metheny are the lead solo voices on a program that ranges from compositions by Chick Corea, Thelonious Monk (the difficult "Trinkle Twinkle"), and Ornette Coleman to three by Metheny. Strong as the other musicians are, Christian McBride often comes close to stealing the show (as can be heard during his solo on Charlie Haden's "Blues M45"). This all-star matchup works quite well. —*Scott Yanow*

My Shining Hour / 1995 / Storyville ✦✦✦✦

Jimmy Heath

b. Oct. 25, 1926
Flute, Sax (Soprano), Sax (Tenor) / Hard Bop
The middle of the three Heath Brothers, Jimmy Heath has a distinctive sound on tenor, is a fluid player on soprano and flute, and a very talented arranger/composer whose originals include "C.T.A." and "Gingerbread Boy." He was originally an altoist, playing with Howard McGhee during 1947-48 and the Dizzy Gillespie big band (1949-50). Called "Little Bird" because of the similarity in his playing to Charlie Parker, Heath switched to tenor in the early '50s. Although out of action for a few years due to personal problems, Heath wrote for Chet Baker and Art Blakey during 1956-57. Back in action in 1959, he worked with Miles Davis briefly that year in addition to Kenny Dorham and Gil Evans and started a string of impressive recordings for Riverside. In the '60s Heath frequently teamed up with Milt Jackson and Art Farmer and also worked as an educator and a freelance arranger. During 1975-82 Jimmy Heath teamed up with Percy and Tootie in the Heath Brothers and since then has remained active as a saxophonist and writer. In addition to his earlier Riverside dates, Jimmy Heath has recorded as a leader for Cobblestone, Muse, Xanadu, Landmark, and Verve. —*Scott Yanow*

The Thumper / Sep. 1959 / Original Jazz Classics ✦✦✦✦
Jimmy Heath at age 33 made his recording debut as a leader on this Riverside session which has been reissued on CD in the OJC series. The hard-bop tenor saxophonist is in superior form, contributing five originals (of which "For Minors Only" is best known), jamming with an all-star sextet (including cornetist Nat Adderley, trombonist Curtis Fuller, pianist Wynton Kelly, bassist Paul Chambers, and drummer Albert "Tootie" Heath) and taking two standards as ballad features. The excellent session of late '50s straightahead jazz is uplifted above the normal level by Heath's writing. —*Scott Yanow*

Really Big / Jun. 24, 1960-Jun. 28, 1960 / Original Jazz Classics ✦✦✦✦
This is one of Heath's earliest as a leader and showcases his savvy as both a leader and a player. —*Ron Wynn*

The Quota / Apr. 14, 1961 & Apr. 20, 1961 / Original Jazz Classics ✦✦✦✦

★ **On the Trail** / 1964 / Original Jazz Classics ✦✦✦✦✦
Unlike some of his other Riverside recordings, the accent on this Jimmy Heath CD reissue is very much on his tenor playing (rather than his arrangements). Heath is in excellent form with a quintet that also includes pianist Wynton Kelly, guitarist Kenny Burrell, bassist Paul Chambers, and drummer Albert "Tootie" Heath. The instantly recognizable hard-bop saxophonist performs four standards and three of his own compositions, including the original versions of "Gingerbread Boy" and "Project S." It's a good example of his playing talents. —*Scott Yanow*

Little Man, Big Band / Jan. 30, 1992-Mar. 3, 1992 / Verve ✦✦✦✦

Julius Hemphill

b. 1940, Fort Worth, TX
Sax (Alto), Sax (Soprano) / Avant-Garde, Free Jazz
One of the giants of the jazz avant-garde, Julius Hemphill had a distinctive sound, a bluish yet dissonant style, and was also a talented arranger/composer. An influence on many forward-thinking young players including Tim Berne and (more indirectly) David Sanborn, Hemphill took lessons in Ft. Worth on clarinet from John Carter, studied music at North Texas State and played locally in Texas in addition to serving in the military. After moving to St. Louis in 1968, Hemphill became a major force in the city, forming the Black Artists Group, founding his own label Mbari, and recording two albums later reissued on Freedom. He moved to New York in the mid-'70s, recorded with Anthony Braxton and Lester Bowie in 1974 and was part of the loft jazz scene. Hemphill was a founding member of the World Saxophone Quartet (1976) and became the main writer for the group. He was also closely involved in multimedia events and his own individual projects. After being forced out of the WSQ in 1990 (the group has declined ever since), Hemphill had his own saxophone sextet before his health failed. He recorded as a leader for several labels including Freedom, Sackville, Elektra/Musician, and Black Saint. —*Scott Yanow*

★ **Dogon A.D.** / Feb. 1972 / Freedom ✦✦✦✦✦
This historic album features four then-unknowns on three lengthy avant-garde explorations that were quite influential not only in St. Louis (where they were recorded) but eventually on such diverse players as altoists Tim Berne and David Sanborn. Julius Hemphill (on alto and flute), trumpeter Baikida Carroll, cellist Abdul Wadud, and drummer Philip Wilson are in superb form, both as soloists and in ensembles where they react instantly to each other. This important music is better to be heard than described. —*Scott Yanow*

☆ **Fat Man and the Hard Blues** / Jul. 15, 1991 & Jul. 16, 1991 / Black Saint ✦✦✦✦✦
After leaving The World Saxophone Quartet, the innovative altoist/composer Julius Hemphill recorded with an unaccompanied sax sextet. This CD features such great players as Marty Ehrlich, Carl Grubbs, the young James Carter, Andrew White, and baritonist Sam Furnace along with the leader on 14 of Hemphill's compositions. These miniatures (all under seven minutes) are most notable for their fresh melodies, logical arrangements, and spirited ensembles. —*Scott Yanow*

Live from the New Music Cafe / Sep. 27, 1991 / Music & Arts ✦✦✦✦

Oakland Duets / Nov. 13, 1992-Nov. 14, 1992 / Music & Arts ✦✦✦

Five Chord Stud / Nov. 18, 1993-Nov. 19, 1993 / Black Saint ✦✦✦✦
Although altoist Julius Hemphill gets top billing on this CD, his heart surgery in 1993 forced him to stop playing. However, this saxophone sextet was his regular group; he contributed six of the eight compositions (the other two are free improvisations) and the chance-taking heard throughout this adventurous music definitely makes most of the performances sound like they came from a Julius Hemphill recording, even if his alto is missed. The sextet has a very strong lineup (altoists Tim Berne, Marty Ehrlich, and Sam Furnace, tenors James Carter and Andrew White, and baritonist Fred Ho) and the resulting CD contains more than its share of variety. The music ranges from the soulful "Spiritual Chairs" and a boppish "Band Theme" to introspective ballads and wild passionate interplay. Other than Fred Ho (who is not heard from enough), each of the players has their chance to star. The generally fascinating music rewards repeated listenings, but one has to have an open mind before putting it on. —*Scott Yanow*

Fletcher Henderson

b. Dec. 18, 1897, Cuthbert, GA, **d.** Dec. 29, 1952, New York, NY
Piano / Swing, Classic Jazz
Fletcher Henderson was very important to early jazz as leader of the first great jazz big band, as an arranger and composer in the '30s, and as a masterful talent scout. Between 1923-39 quite an all-star cast of top young Black jazz musicians passed through his orchestra including trumpeters Louis Armstrong, Joe Smith, Tommy Ladnier, Rex Stewart, Bobby Stark, Cootie Williams, Red Allen, and Roy Eldridge, trombonists Charlie Green, Benny Morton, Jimmy Harrison, Sandy Williams, J.C. Higginbotham, and Dickie Wells, clarinetist Buster Bailey, tenors Coleman Hawkins (1924-34), Ben Webster, Lester Young (whose brief stint was not recorded), and Chu Berry, altoists Benny Carter, Russell Procope, and Hilton Jefferson, bassists John Kirby and Israel Crosby, drummers Kaiser Marshall, Walter Johnson, and Sid Catlett, guest pianist Fats Waller and such arrangers as Don Redman, Benny Carter, Edgar Sampson, and Fletcher's younger brother Horace Henderson. And yet at the height of the swing era, Henderson's band was little known.

Fletcher Henderson had a degree in chemistry and mathematics, but when he came to New York in 1920 with hopes of becoming a chemist, the only job he could find (due to the racism of the times) was as a song demonstrator with the Pace-Handy music company. Harry Pace soon founded the Black Swan label and Henderson, a versatile but fairly basic pianist, became an important contributor behind the scenes, organizing bands and backing blues vocalists. Although he started recording as a leader in 1921, it was not until January 1924 that he put together his first permanent big band. Using Don Redman's innovative arrangements, he was soon at the top of his field. His early recordings (Henderson made many records during 1923-24) tend to be both futuristic and awkward with strong musicianship but staccato phrasing. However, after Louis Armstrong joined in late 1924 and Don Redman started contributing more swinging arrangements, the Fletcher Henderson Orchestra had no close competitors artistically until the rise of Duke Ellington in 1927. By then Henderson's band (after a period at the Club Alabam) was playing regularly at the Roseland Ballroom but, due to the bandleader being a very indifferent businessman, the all-star outfit recorded relatively little during its peak (1927-30).

With the departure of Redman in 1927 and the end of interim periods when Benny Carter and Horace Henderson wrote the bulk of the arrangements, Fletcher himself developed into a top arranger by the early '30s. However, the Depression took its toll on the band, and the increased competition from other orchestras (along with some bad business decisions and the loss of Coleman Hawkins) resulted in Henderson breaking up the big band in early 1935. Starting in 1934 he began contributing versions of his better arrangements to Benny Goodman's new orchestra (including "King Porter Stomp," "Sometimes I'm Happy," and "Down South Camp Meeting") and ironically Goodman's recordings were huge hits at a time when Fletcher Henderson's name was not known to the general public. In 1936 he put together a new orchestra and immediately had a hit in "Christopher Columbus," but after three years he had to disband again in 1939. Henderson worked as a staff arranger for Goodman and even played in Goodman's Sextet for a few months (although his skills on the piano never did develop much). He struggled through the '40s, leading occasional bands (including one in the mid-'40s that utilized some arrangements by the young Sun Ra). In 1950 Henderson had a fine sextet with Lucky Thompson, but a stroke ended his career and led to his death in 1952. Virtually all of Fletcher Henderson's recordings as a leader (and many are quite exciting) are currently available on the Classics label and in more piecemeal fashion domestically. —Scott Yanow

1921-1923 / Jun. 1921-Jun. 11, 1923 / Classics ✦✦✦

★ **A Study In Frustration** / Aug. 9, 1923-May 28, 1938 / Columbia ✦✦✦✦✦
Formerly a four-LP set, this three-CD box contains some of the finest recordings of the '20s and '30s. Fletcher Henderson's big band during this period featured many of the top Black jazz soloists including trumpeters Louis Armstrong, Joe Smith, Rex Stewart, Tommy Ladnier, Bobby Stark, Cootie Williams, Red Allen, and Roy Eldridge, trombonists Charlie Green, Jimmy Harrison, and J.C. Higginbotham, tenors Coleman Hawkins, Ben Webster, and Chu Berry, clarinetist Buster Bailey and altoist Benny Carter, and guest pianist Fats Waller, among others. With Don Redman and later Benny Carter and Henderson himself contributing advanced arrangements, Henderson had the leading big band of 1923-27 and one of the best jazz orchestras of the next few years. This is an essential acquisition for all serious jazz collections. —Scott Yanow

Fletcher Henderson and Louis Armstrong / Oct. 10, 1924-Oct. 21, 1925 / Timeless ✦✦✦

Fletcher Henderson (1925-1926) / Nov. 23, 1925-Apr. 14, 1926 / Classics ✦✦✦✦
The Classics series has undergone the admirable task of reissuing on CD in chronological order every selection (although no alternate takes) of Fletcher Henderson's orchestra. This set finds the post-Armstrong edition of this pacesetting big band swinging hard on a variety of standards and obscurities. With cornetist Joe Smith, trombonist Charlie Green, clarinetist Buster Bailey and tenor great Coleman Hawkins contributing many fine solos and Don Redman's often-innovative arrangements inspiring the musicians, at this period Fletcher Henderson's orchestra had no close competitors among jazz-oriented big bands. Even the weaker pop tunes (like "I Want to See a Little More of What I Saw in Arkansas") have their strong moments. —Scott Yanow

● **Fletcher Henderson (1926-1927)** / Apr. 14, 1926-Jan. 22, 1927 / Classics ✦✦✦✦
This CD, in Classics' chronological series that captures the Fletcher Henderson Orchestra at its peak, is overloaded with classics: "Jackass Blues," "The Stampede" (which has a very influential tenor solo by Coleman Hawkins), "Clarinet Marmalade," "Snag It," and "Tozo" among others. In addition to Coleman Hawkins, Tommy Ladnier emerges as a major trumpeter and Fats Waller drops by for his "Henderson Stomp." Eight years before the official beginning of the swing era, Fletcher Henderson's orchestra was outswinging everyone. —Scott Yanow

● **Fletcher Henderson (1927)** / Mar. 11, 1927-Oct. 24, 1927 / Classics ✦✦✦✦
Fletcher Henderson's orchestra was at the peak of its powers during this period, as can be heard on such torrid recordings as "Fidgety Feet," "Sensation," "St. Louis Shuffle," and "Hop Off"; even the overly complex Don Redman arrangement "Whiteman Stomp" (which Paul Whiteman's musicians apparently had trouble learning) is no problem for this brilliant orchestra.

Classics' chronological reissue of Henderson's valuable recordings on this CD covers the many high points of the peak year of 1927; only Duke Ellington's orchestra was on the level of this pacesetting big band. —Scott Yanow

The Complete Fletcher Henderson (1927-1936) / Mar. 11, 1927-Aug. 4, 1936 / RCA/Bluebird ✦✦✦✦
"Complete" is in this case a relative term, meaning every recording by Fletcher Henderson's orchestra owned by RCA/Bluebird rather than every record he made during this period. A perfectly done two-LP set, these 34 songs include three from 1927 (featuring trumpeters Tommy Ladnier and Joe Smith at their best), 12 varying sides from 1931-32 (during which tenor saxophonist Coleman Hawkins and trumpeters Rex Stewart and Bobby Stark make even the most commercial material into worthwhile music), a session from 1934 with trumpeter Red Allen, and 15 numbers from 1936 that co-star trumpeter Roy Eldridge and Chu Berry on tenor. Throughout, the consistent high quality of the solos and the musicianship (even with some off moments) makes one regret that this classic orchestra was not more commercially successful. —Scott Yanow

Hocus Pocus / Apr. 27, 1927-Aug. 4, 1936 / Bluebird ✦✦✦

Fletcher Henderson (1934-1937) / Sep. 25, 1934-Mar. 2, 1937 / Classics ✦✦✦✦
In early 1935 Fletcher Henderson broke up his classic orchestra but a year later, with the success of so many other big bands, he formed a new ensemble. This Classics CD includes four songs from 1934, Henderson's entire output from 1936 and his first recording of 1937. The main difference between the two units is that the later one boasted the trumpet of Roy Eldridge and tenor solos from Coleman Hawkins' potential successor, Chu Berry. "Christopher Columbus" became a hit as did the band's new theme song ("Stealin' Apples") but the brief bit of glory would not last. However, Henderson's brand of swing music still sounds fresh today, and this CD is easily recommended. —Scott Yanow

Indispensable / RCA ✦✦✦✦
This double-CD from RCA's *Jazz Tribune* series (a straight reissue of an earlier two-LP set) has highlights from bandleader Fletcher Henderson's Victor recordings. Dating from 1927, 1931-32, 1934, and 1936, several editions of Henderson's orchestra are represented with such soloists as trumpeters Tommy Ladnier, Bobby Stark, Rex Stewart, Red Allen, and Roy Eldridge, trombonists Jimmy Harrison, Benny Morton, Sandy Williams, and J.C. Higginbotham, clarinetist Buster Bailey, altoist Edgar Sampson, and tenors Coleman Hawkins, Ben Webster, and Chu Berry being among the key soloists; Henderson always used the best! Although not as complete as some series, there are many high points on this two-fer including two takes each of "St. Louis Shuffle" and "Variety Stomp," "Sugar Foot Stomp," "Roll On, Mississippi, Roll On," "Singing the Blues," "Poor Old Joe," "Hocus Pocus," "Jangled Nerves," "Riffin'," and "You Can Depend on Me." An excellent set filled with classics. —Scott Yanow

Joe Henderson

b. Apr. 24, 1937, Lima, Ohio
Sax (Tenor) / Post-Bop, Hard Bop
Joe Henderson is proof that jazz can sell without watering down the music; it just takes creative marketing! Although his sound and style are virtually unchanged from the mid-'60s, Joe Henderson's signing with Verve in 1992 was treated as a major news event by the label (even though he had already recorded many memorable sessions for other companies); his Verve recordings had easy-to-market themes (tributes to Billy Strayhorn, Miles Davis, and Antonio Carlos Jobim), and as a result he became a national celebrity and a constant pollwinner while still sounding the same as when he was in obscurity in the '70s!

The general feeling is that it couldn't happen to a more deserving jazz musician. After studying at Kentucky State College and Wayne University, Joe Henderson played locally in Detroit before spending time in the military (1960-62). He played briefly with Jack McDuff and then gained recognition for his work with Kenny Dorham (1962-63), a veteran bop trumpeter who championed him and helped Henderson get signed to Blue Note. Henderson appeared on many Blue Note sessions both as a leader and as a sideman, spent 1964-66 with Horace Silver's Quintet, and during 1969-70 was in Herbie Hancock's band. From the start he had a very distinctive sound and style which, although influenced a bit by both Sonny Rollins and John Coltrane, also contained a lot of brand new phrases and ideas. Henderson has long been able to improvise in both inside and outside settings, from hard bop to free form. In the '70s he recorded frequently for Milestone and lived in San Francisco but was somewhat taken for granted. The second half of the '80s found him continuing his freelancing and teaching while recording for Blue Note, but it was when he hooked up with Verve that he suddenly became famous. Virtually all of his recordings are currently in print on CD including a massive collection of his neglected (but generally rewarding) Milestone dates. —Scott Yanow

The Blue Note Years / Apr. 1, 1963-Feb. 15, 1990 / Blue Note ✦✦✦

★ **Page One** / Jun. 3, 1963 / Blue Note ✦✦✦✦✦
Tenor saxophonist Joe Henderson's debut as a leader is a particularly
strong and historic effort. With major contributions made by trumpeter
Kenny Dorham, pianist McCoy Tyner, bassist Butch Warren, and drummer
Pete La Roca, Henderson (who already had a strikingly original sound and
a viable inside/outside style) performs six generally memorable compositions on this CD reissue. Highlights include the original versions of
Dorham's "Blue Bossa" and Henderson's "Recorda Me." It's highly recommended. —*Scott Yanow*

Our Thing / Sep. 9, 1963 / Blue Note ✦✦✦✦
Joe Henderson's second recording as a leader features a very strong supporting cast: trumpeter Kenny Dorham (one of Henderson's earliest supporters), pianist Andrew Hill, bassist Eddie Khan, and drummer Pete La
Roca. Together they perform three Dorham and two Henderson originals,
advanced music that was open to the influence of the avant-garde while
remaining in the hard-bop idiom. The uptempo blues "Teeter Totter" contrasts with the four minor-toned pieces and, even if none of these songs
became standards, the playing is consistently brilliant and unpredictable.
Even at this relatively early stage, Joe Henderson was a potentially great
tenorman. —*Scott Yanow*

In 'n Out / Apr. 10, 1964 / Blue Note ✦✦✦✦
Joe Henderson's third Blue Note release (which is here reissued on CD with
the addition of a previously unissued version of the title cut) matches the
very distinctive tenor with the veteran trumpeter Kenny Dorham and an
unbeatable rhythm section: pianist McCoy Tyner, bassist Richard Davis,
and drummer Elvin Jones. Henderson, who has always had the ability to
make a routine bop piece sound complex and the most complicated free
improvisation seem logical, and Dorham provided all of the material, and
the music still sounds fresh over three decades later. —*Scott Yanow*

Inner Urge / Nov. 30, 1964 / Blue Note ✦✦✦✦
The fourth of Joe Henderson's early Blue Note recordings is his first in a
quartet setting without trumpeter Kenny Dorham. Henderson (who is
accompanied by pianist McCoy Tyner, bassist Bob Cranshaw, and drummer Elvin Jones) is in explorative form on three of his originals (including
"Inner Urge" and the original version of "Isotope"), Duke Pearson's "You
Know I Care," and the standard "Night and Day." The music straddles the
boundaries between hard bop and the avant-garde, and while Henderson's
improvisations are chordal-based, they are also quite unpredictable and
prone to emotional outbursts. This colorful music is highly recommended.
—*Scott Yanow*

Mode for Joe / Jan. 27, 1966 / Blue Note ✦✦✦✦
Tenor saxophonist Joe Henderson's fifth and final early Blue Note album is
his only one with a group larger than a quintet. Henderson welcomes quite
an all-star band (trumpeter Lee Morgan, trombonist Curtis Fuller, vibraphonist Bobby Hutcherson, pianist Cedar Walton, bassist Ron Carter, and
drummer Joe Chambers) and together they perform originals by Henderson (including "A Shade of Jade"), Walton, and Morgan ("Free Wheelin'").
The advanced music has plenty of exciting moments and all of the young
talents play up to the level one would hope. —*Scott Yanow*

● **The Kicker** / Aug. 10, 1967 / Original Jazz Classics ✦✦✦✦
Joe Henderson's first recording for Milestone was very much a continuation of the adventurous acoustic music he had recorded previously for Blue
Note. For those listeners who do not wish to invest in the tenor saxophonist's "complete" eight-CD Milestone box set, this single-CD is a good place
to start in investigating his "middle period" music. Henderson is featured
in a sextet with trumpeter Mike Lawrence, trombonist Grachan Moncur,
III, pianist Kenny Barron, bassist Ron Carter, and drummer Louis Hayes on
a well rounded set highlighted by "Mamacita," "Chelsea Bridge," "If,"
"Without a Song," and "Nardis." —*Scott Yanow*

☆ **The Milestone Years** / Aug. 10, 1967-Sep. 26, 1976 / Milestone ✦✦✦✦✦
Tenor saxophonist Joe Henderson's most famous recordings are his early
Blue Notes and his more recent Verves, but in between he recorded exclusively for Milestone, and although he was in consistently fine form in the
diverse settings, Henderson was somewhat neglected during his middle
years. This massive eight-CD set contains all of the music from Henderson's dozen Milestone LPs plus a duet with altoist Lee Konitz and his guest
appearances with singer Flora Purim and cornetist Nat Adderley. The
music ranges from Blue Note-style hard bop and modal explorations to
fusion and '70s funk with important contributions made by trumpeters
Mike Lawrence, Woody Shaw, and Luis Gasca, trombonist Grachan Moncur and keyboardists Kenny Barron, Don Friedman, Joe Zawinul, Herbie
Hancock, George Cables, Alice Coltrane, Mark Levine, and George Duke,
among others. Not all of the music is classic (some of the later sets are
unabashedly commercial) but none of the 82 selections are dull and the
very distinctive Joe Henderson always gives his best. It's highly recommended. —*Scott Yanow*

Four / Apr. 21, 1968 / Verve ✦✦✦✦
Released for the first time on this CD in 1994, the previously unknown live
session from 1968 features the great tenor Joe Henderson (who was then
just a few days short of turning 31) playing for the first and possibly only

time with the Wynton Kelly Trio. Henderson, pianist Kelly, bassist Paul
Chambers, and drummer Jimmy Cobb really stretch out on six standards
(including a two-song medley), all of which clock in between 11:47 and
16:05 (except for a three-minute "Theme"). Henderson really pushes the
rhythm section (which although they had not played with the tenor previously, had been together for a decade) and he is certainly inspired by their
presence. This is a frequently exciting performance by some of the modern
bop greats of the era. —*Scott Yanow*

Relaxin' at Camarillo / Aug. 20, 1979 & Dec. 29, 1979 / Original Jazz Classics ✦✦✦

★ **The State of the Tenor (Live at The Village Vanguard)** / Nov. 1985 /
Blue Note ✦✦✦✦✦
The very distinctive tenor saxophonist is heard at his best on this two-CD
set recorded live at the Village Vanguard. Accompanied only by bassist Ron
Carter and drummer Al Foster, Henderson at times recalls Sonny Rollins
but none of his searching improvisations are predictable. Of the 14 selections, 12 were originally released on two Blue Note LPs while the renditions of "Stella by Starlight" and "All the Things You Are" were previously
unissued. Highlights of this particularly strong set (recorded over a three-
day period) include "Beatrice," several Thelonious Monk tunes (particularly "Friday the Thirteenth" and "Ask Me Now"), "Soulville," and "Isotope."
—*Scott Yanow*

★ **Lush Life** / Sep. 3, 1991-Sep. 8, 1991 / Verve ✦✦✦✦✦
With the release of this CD, the executives at Verve and their marketing
staff proved that, yes indeed, jazz can sell. The veteran tenor Joe Henderson
has had a distinctive sound and style of his own ever since he first entered
the jazz major leagues, yet he has spent long periods in relative obscurity
before reaching his current status as a jazz superstar. As for the music on
his "comeback" disc, it does deserve all of the hype. Henderson performs
ten of Billy Strayhorn's most enduring compositions in a variety of settings
ranging from a full quintet with trumpeter Wynton Marsalis and duets
with pianist Stephen Scott, bassist Christian McBride, and drummer Gregory Hutchinson to an unaccompanied solo exploration of "Lush Life." This
memorable outing succeeded both artistically and commercially and is
highly recommended. —*Scott Yanow*

☆ **So Near, So Far (Musings for Miles)** / Oct. 12, 1992-Oct. 14, 1992 / Verve
✦✦✦✦
Joe Henderson's follow-up to his hugely successful *Lush Life* disc is
another concept album, this time involving ten songs (including many
lesser-known ones) associated with Miles Davis. Henderson only actually
played with Davis for a few weekends around 1967 but he shows a great
deal of understanding for this potentially difficult music. With particularly
strong assistance from guitarist John Scofield, bassist Dave Holland, and
drummer Al Foster, Henderson revives such forgotten songs as "Teo,"
"Swing Spring," and "Side Car" in addition to coming up with fresh interpretations of "Miles Ahead," "Milestones," and "No Blues." He is to be congratulated for not taking the easy way out and sticking to the simpler
material of Davis' earlier years. —*Scott Yanow*

Double Rainbow / Sep. 19, 1994-Nov. 6, 1994 / Verve ✦✦✦✦
The third of tenor saxophonist Joe Henderson's tribute CDs on Verve was
originally supposed to be a collaboration with the great bossa nova composer Antonio Carlos Jobim, but Jobim's unexpected death turned this
project into a memorial. Henderson performs a dozen of the composer's
works with one of two separate groups: a Brazilian quartet starring pianist
Eliane Elias and a jazz trio with pianist Herbie Hancock, bassist Christian
McBride, and drummer Jack DeJohnette. In general Henderson avoids
Jobim's best-known songs in favor of some of his more obscure (but
equally rewarding) melodies and in some cases (such as a very straightea-
head "No More Blues"), the treatments are surprising. Highlights of this
very accessible set include "Felicidade," "Triste," "Zin-
garo," and a duet with guitarist Oscar Castro-Neves on "Once I Loved"
although all of the performances are quite enjoyable. Highly recommended. —*Scott Yanow*

Scott Henderson

Guitar / Fusion
One of the finest fusion (as opposed to crossover) guitarists of the '80s and
'90s, Scott Henderson's explosive playing is often teamed up with electric
bassist Gary Willis in their group Tribal Tech. Originally most influenced
by rock, Henderson (who grew up in West Palm Beach, FL) played in local
funk and rock bands. In 1980 he moved to Los Angeles to attend the Guitar Institute of Technology, studying with Joe Diorio. After graduating he
became a teacher himself at GIT. Henderson played with Jeff Berlin and
Jean Luc Ponty and in 1985 toured with the original version of Chick
Corea's Elektric Band. During 1987-89 he worked on and off with Joe
Zawinul's Syndicate, and since then Tribal Tech has been his main band.
As a leader Scott Henderson has recorded for Passport, Relativity, and
Bluemoon. —*Scott Yanow*

Spears / Jun. 1985 / Passport ✦✦✦

Dr. Hee / May 19, 1987 / Relativity ◆◆◆◆
Recorded with Tribal Tech, this exceptional album of jazz, rock, and fusion compositions is a must for guitarists. —*Paul Kohler*

Tribal Tech with Gary Willis / Nov. 19, 1990 / Relativity ◆◆◆◆
An interesting, sometimes enchanting, blend of technology, aggressive rhythms, and improvisatory zeal. —*Ron Wynn*

Nomad / 1990 / Relativity ◆◆◆◆
Recorded with Tribal Tech, this jazz-fusion is similar to Weather Report at times. —*Paul Kohler*

Tribal Tech / 1991 / Combat ◆◆◆◆
Guitarist Henderson once again displays his talents as a composer in the jazz-fusion idiom. Unlike his earlier releases, this album reveals a bluesier side to his playing. The interplay amongst the band members is superb and extremely satisfying! —*Paul Kohler*

★ **Illicit** / Apr. 1992 / Blue Moon ◆◆◆◆◆

Face First / Apr. 1993-May 1993 / Blue Moon ◆◆◆◆

Dog Party / 1994 / Blue Moon ◆◆◆

Jon Hendricks

b. Sep. 16, 1921, Newark, OH
Vocals / Bop, Vocalese
The genius of vocalese, Jon Hendricks' ability to write coherent lyrics to the most complex recorded improvisations is quite notable as were his contributions to the classic jazz vocal group Lambert, Hendricks, and Ross. Hendricks grew up in Toledo, OH, singing on local radio. After a period in the military (1942-46), he studied law but eventually switched to jazz. He spent a period of time playing drums before becoming active as a lyricist and vocalist. In 1952 his "I Want You to Be My Baby" was recorded by Louis Jordan. In 1957 Hendricks made his recording debut (cutting "Four Brothers" and "Cloudburst" while backed by the Dave Lambert Singers). Soon he teamed up with fellow singers Dave Lambert and Annie Ross to form their vocal trio, starting off with a recreation (through overdubbing) of some of Count Basie's recordings. Lambert, Hendricks, and Ross (after 1962 Yolande Bavan took Ross' place) stayed together until 1964, and they have yet to be topped as a jazz vocal group, influencing those that would follow (including the Manhattan Transfer). In 1960 Hendricks wrote and directed the show *Evolution of the Blues* for the Monterey Jazz Festival; he would revive it several times during the next 20 years. During 1968-73 he lived and worked in Europe. After returning to San Francisco, Hendricks wrote about jazz for the *San Francisco Chronicle*, taught jazz, and formed a group with his wife Judith, children Michelle and Eric, and other singers (including for a time Bobby McFerrin) called the Hendricks Family that is, active on a part-time basis. Although he never recorded often enough, Hendricks did cut a classic Denon album featuring McFerrin, George Benson, Al Jarreau, and himself recreating all the solos in the original version of "Freddie the Freeloader." He also recorded through the years as a leader for World Pacific, Columbia, Smash, Reprise, Arista, and most recently Telarc. —*Scott Yanow*

Evolution of the Blues / Sep. 21, 1960 / Columbia ◆◆◆◆
Jazz vocalist and lyricist Jon Hendricks conceived a musical presentation on jazz history for the 1960 Monterey Jazz Festival and called it "Evolution of the Blues." Columbia subsequently issued this similarly titled album, which features Hendricks' stylized vocals and other presentations linked to the theme. This presentation was revived and presented again in 1975. —*Ron Wynn*

★ **Freddie Freeloader** / 1990 / Denon ◆◆◆◆◆
Tour-de-force recording with Bobby McFerrin (v), George Benson (v), Al Jarreau (v), and Manhattan Transfer (v). —*Michael G. Nastos*

● **Boppin' At The Blue Note** / Dec. 23, 1993-Dec. 26, 1993 / Telarc ◆◆◆◆

Woody Herman (Woodrow Charles Herman)

b. May 16, 1913, Milwaukee, WI, d. Oct. 29, 1987
Clarinet, Sax (Alto), Sax (Soprano) / Bop, Swing
A fine swing clarinetist, an altoist whose sound was influenced by Johnny Hodges, a good soprano saxophonist, and a spirited blues vocalist, Woody Herman's greatest significance to jazz was as the leader of a long line of big bands. He always encouraged young talent and more than practically any bandleader from the swing era kept his repertoire quite modern. Although Herman was always stuck performing a few of his older hits (he played "Four Brothers" and "Early Autumn" nightly for nearly 40 years), he much preferred to play and create new music.

Woody Herman began performing as a child, singing in vaudeville. He started playing saxophone when he was 11 and four years later he was a professional musician. He picked up early experience playing with the big bands of Tom Gerun, Harry Sosnik, and Gus Arnheim and then in 1934 he joined the Isham Jones orchestra. He recorded often with Jones and when the veteran bandleader decided to break up his orchestra in 1936, Herman formed one of his own out of the remaining nucleus. The great majority of the early Herman recordings feature the bandleader as

a ballad vocalist, but it was the instrumentals that caught on, leading to his group being known as "The Band That Plays the Blues." Woody Herman's theme "At the Woodchopper's Ball" became his first hit (1939). Herman's early group was actually a minor outfit with a Dixieland feel to many of the looser pieces and fine vocals contributed by Mary Ann McCall in addition to Herman. They recorded very frequently for Decca and for a period had the female trumpeter/singer Billie Rogers as one of their main attractions.

By 1943 the Woody Herman Orchestra was beginning to take its first steps into becoming the Herd (later renamed the First Herd). Herman had recorded an advanced Dizzy Gillespie arrangement ("Down Under") the year before and during 1943 Herman's band became influenced by Duke Ellington; in fact Johnny Hodges and Ben Webster made guest appearances on some recordings. It was a gradual process, but by the end of 1944 Woody Herman had what was essentially a brand new orchestra. It was a wild good-time band with screaming ensembles (propelled by first trumpeter Pete Candoli), major soloists in trombonist Bill Harris and tenorman Flip Phillips, and a rhythm section pushed by bassist/ cheerleader Chubby Jackson and drummer Dave Tough. In 1945 (with new trumpeters in Sonny Berman and Conte Candoli), the First Herd was considered the most exciting new big band in jazz. Several of the arrangements of Ralph Burns and Neal Hefti are considered classics and such Herman favorites entered the book as "Apple Honey," "Caldonia," "Northwest Passage," "Bijou" (Harris' memorable if eccentric feature), and the nutty "Your Father's Mustache." Even Igor Stravinsky was impressed and he wrote "Ebony Concerto" for the orchestra to perform in 1946. Unfortunately family troubles caused Woody Herman to break up the big band at the height of its success in late 1946; it was the only one of his orchestras to really make much money. Herman recorded a bit in the interim and then by mid-1947 had a new orchestra, the Second Herd, which was also soon known as the Four Brothers band. With the three cool-toned tenors of Stan Getz, Zoot Sims, and Herbie Steward (who a year later was replaced by Al Cohn) and baritonist Serge Chaloff forming the nucelus, this orchestra had a different sound than its more extro-verted predecessor but it could also generate excitement of its own. Trumpeter/arranger Shorty Rogers and eventually Bill Harris returned from the earlier outfit and with Mary Ann McCall back as a vocalist, the group had a great deal of potential. But despite such popular numbers as Jimmy Giuffre's "Four Brothers," "The Goof and I," and "Early Autumn" (the latter ballad made Getz into a star), the band struggled financially. Before its collapse in 1949 such other musicians as Gene Ammons, Lou Levy, Oscar Pettiford, Terry Gibbs, and Shelly Manne made important contributions.

Next up for Woody Herman was the Third Herd, which was similar to the Second except that it generally played at danceable tempos and was a bit more conservative. Herman kept that band together during much of 1950-56, even having his own Mars label for a period; Conte Candoli, Al Cohn, Dave McKenna, Phil Urso, Don Fagerquist, Carl Fontana, Dick Hafer, Bill Perkins, Nat Pierce, Dick Collins, and Richie Kamuca were among the many sidemen. After some short-lived small groups (including a sextet with Nat Adderley and Charlie Byrd), Herman's New Thundering Herd was a hit at the 1959 Monterey Jazz Festival. He was able to lead a big band successfully throughout the '60s, featuring such soloists as high-note trum-peter Bill Chase, trombonist Phil Wilson, the reliable Nat Pierce, and the exciting tenor of Sal Nistico. Always open to newer styles, Woody Herman's boppish unit gradually became more rock-oriented as he utilized his young sidemen's arrangements, often of current pop tunes (starting in 1968 with an album titled *Light My Fire*). Not all of his albums from this era worked but one always admired Herman's open-minded attitude. As one of only four surviving jazz-oriented bandleaders from the swing era (along with Duke Ellington, Count Basie and Stan Kenton) who was still touring the world with a big band, Herman welcomed such new talent in the '70s as Greg Herbert, Andy Laverne, Joe Beck, Alan Broadbent, and Frank Tiberi; he also recorded with Chick Corea, had a reunion with Flip Phillips and celebrated his 40th anniversary as a leader with a notable 1976 Carnegie Hall Concert.

Woody Herman returned to emphasizing straightahead jazz by the late '70s. By then he was being hounded by the IRS due to an incompetent manager from the '60s who did not pay thousands of dollars of taxes out of the sidemen's salaries. Herman, who might very well have taken it easy, was forced to keep on touring and working constantly into his old age. He managed to put on a cheerful face to the public, celebrating his 50th anni-versary as a bandleader in 1986. However his health was starting to fail and he gradually delegated most of his duties to Frank Tiberi before his death in 1987. Tiberi still leads a Woody Herman Orchestra on a part-time basis, but it has never had the opportunity to record. Fortunately Herman was well documented throughout all phases of his career and his major contributions are still greatly appreciated. —*Scott Yanow*

★ **Blues on Parade** / Apr. 26, 1937-Jul. 24, 1942 / GRP ◆◆◆◆
This single CD gives a definitive look at Woody Herman's first orchestra, the Decca ensemble he led during 1936-42 billed "the Band That Plays the Blues." Although he also recorded many vocal ballads during this era, the

emphasis here is on hot swing with such highlights as the original version of "Woodchopper's Ball," "Blue Prelude," "Blue Flame," the humorous "Fan It," and two takes of "Blues on Parade." Also heard are performances by Herman's early small combos (the Woodchoppers and the Four Chips) along with a Dizzy Gillespie composition/arrangement ("Down Under") that hints at Woody Herman's future. — *Scott Yanow*

Woodchopper's Ball, Vol. 1 / Aug. 2, 1944-Oct. 18, 1944 / Jass ✦✦✦✦
1944 was a pivotal year in Herman's career, the year his orchestra gradually evolved into The First Herd, his most exciting band. This CD features music from two radio shows in August (actually rehearsals for the broadcasts) plus performances from two prestigious engagements at the Hotel Pennsylvania in August and the Hollywood Palladium that October. With Flip Phillips' jump tenor and Bill Harris' expressive trombone already emerging as the band's top soloists and Francis Wayne contributing a few fine vocals, Ralph Burns and Neal Hefti were hurriedly putting together colorful arrangements to challenge the young sidemen. The music on this set, which precedes The Herd's first commercial recordings, could be titled *The Birth of the Herd*. Recommended, particularly to serious Woody Herman fans. — *Scott Yanow*

Northwest Passage, Vol. 2 / Feb. 18, 1945-Aug. 22, 1945 / Jass ✦✦✦
Unlike the first volume in this CD series, *Vol. 2* does not find the First Herd in transition but instead in its early prime. Taken from five separate radio broadcasts, these live performances are generally colorful and sometimes quite exciting, although there are more vocals than normal. More for First Herd fanatics and completists than for general collectors. — *Scott Yanow*

☆ **Thundering Herds 1945-1947** / Feb. 19, 1945-Dec. 27, 1947 / Columbia ✦✦✦✦✦
Since the definitive three-LP box set *Thundering Herds* is out-of-print, this single CD is the best place for listeners to go first when starting to explore the music of Woody Herman. There are 14 selections from what was arguably his best band, his First Herd, and two numbers (including the original version of "Four Brothers") by the Second Herd. A few rarities (such as "A Jug of Wine" and "The Blues Are Brewing") are mixed in with such classics as "Apple Honey," "Northwest Passage," "Your Father's Mustache," and a new version of "Woodchopper's Ball," but there is unavoidably a lot missing from this single disc, a set which will have to suffice until a more complete reissue series comes along. — *Scott Yanow*

Best of the Big Bands / Feb. 26, 1945-Dec. 22, 1947 / Columbia ✦✦

★ **Keeper of the Flame: Complete Capitol Recordings** / Dec. 29, 1948-Jul. 21, 1949 / Capitol ✦✦✦✦✦
Subtitled *The Complete Capitol Recordings of the Four Brothers Band*, this CD contains 19 selections from Herman's Second Herd, including three songs never before released. Top-heavy with major soloists (including trumpeters Red Rodney and Shorty Rogers, trombonist Bill Harris, tenors Al Cohn, Zoot Sims, Stan Getz, and Gene Ammons, and vibraphonist Terry Gibbs, not to mention Herman himself) this boppish band may have cost the leader a small fortune but they created timeless music. Highlights include "Early Autumn" (a ballad performance that made Stan Getz a star), the riotous "Lemon Drop," and Gene Ammons' strong solo on "More Moon." — *Scott Yanow*

The Raven Speaks / Aug. 28, 1972-Aug. 30, 1972 / Original Jazz Classics ✦✦✦✦
The best of his Fantasy releases of the '70s, this well rounded CD is highlighted by a great jam on "Reunion at Newport" and strong soloing from Herman (on soprano and clarinet), pianist Harold Danko, trumpeter Bill Stapleton, and the tenors of Gregory Herbert and Frank Tiberi. The Herman orchestra performs a couple of modern ballads ("Alone Again Naturally" and "Summer of '42"), some blues, and a few swinging numbers, showing off their versatility with expertise and spirit. — *Scott Yanow*

Giant Steps / Apr. 9, 1973-Apr. 12, 1973 / Original Jazz Classics ✦✦✦✦
Woody Herman always went out of his way during his long career to encourage younger players, often persuading them to write arrangements of recent tunes for his orchestra. On this LP one gets to hear his band interpret such selections as Chick Corea's "La Fiesta," Leon Russell's "A Song for You," "Freedom Jazz Dance," "A Child Is Born," and "Giant Steps"; what other bandleader from the '30s would have performed such modern material? With strong solo work from tenors Gregory Herbert and Frank Tiberi, trumpeter Bill Stapleton, and Herman himself, this is an impressive effort. — *Scott Yanow*

Thundering Herd / Jan. 2, 1974-Jan. 4, 1974 / Original Jazz Classics ✦✦✦

40th Anniversary Carnegie Hall Concert / Nov. 20, 1976 / Bluebird ✦✦✦✦

The Live at Concord Jazz Festival (1981) / Aug. 15, 1981 / Concord Jazz ✦✦✦

Fiftieth Anniversary Tour / Mar. 1986 / Concord Jazz ✦✦✦✦
This set, which is the best of the Woody Herman Orchestra's Concord recordings, celebrates his 50th year as a bandleader, quite an accomplishment. No guest stars are needed for this set, which shows just how strong a big band he still had. With tenor saxophonist Frank Tiberi gradually taking

over leadership duties (today he leads the ghost Woody Herman Orchestra) and trombonist John Fedchock contributing the arrangements, the band was in fine shape even if the leader was aging. Whether it be "It Don't Mean a Thing," John Coltrane's "Central Park West" (a great arrangement), or Don Grolnick's "Pools," every selection is excellent. — *Scott Yanow*

John Hicks

b. 1941, Atlanta, GA
Piano / Post-Bop, Hard Bop
A versatile pianist who is able to retain his own personality whether playing hard bop, free, or anything in between, John Hicks has recorded many records throughout his career, both as a leader and as a sideman. After studying music at Lincoln University in Missouri, Hicks attended Berklee and started working as a freelance musician. He moved to New York in 1963 and was a member of Art Blakey's Jazz Messengers (1964-66) and the groups of Betty Carter (1966-68) and Woody Herman (1968-70). He later worked again with Blakey (1973) and Carter (1975-80) in addition to recording with Oliver Lake, Lester Bowie, Charles Tolliver, and Chico Freeman (1978-79). From the early '80s on, Hicks has led his own trio and worked regularly with David Murray, Arthur Blythe, Pharoah Sanders, and others. As a leader John Hicks has recorded for Strata-East, Theresa, Limetree, DIW, Timeless, Red Baron, Concord, Evidence, Novus, Reservoir, Mapleshade, and Landmark among others. — *Scott Yanow*

● **Live at Maybeck Recital Hall, Vol. 7** / Aug. 1990 / Concord Jazz ✦✦✦✦
Rollicking, thoughtful, unpredictable, and eclectic solo piano. — *Ron Wynn*

Friends Old and New / Jan. 14, 1992 / Novus ✦✦✦✦
1992 session with pianist John Hicks playing in various combo settings with some excellent musical associates. Bassist Ron Carter, tenor saxophone dynamo Joshua Redman, trumpeter Clark Terry, trombonist Al Grey, and drummer/vocalist Grady Tate are among the friends who join Hicks for some powerhouse numbers. — *Ron Wynn*

Lover Man: Tribute to Billie Holiday / 1993 / Red Baron ✦✦✦

Beyond Expectations / Sep. 1, 1993 / Reservoir ✦✦✦✦

Single Petal Of A Rose / 1994 / Mapleshade ✦✦✦✦

In the Mix / Nov. 13, 1994 / Landmark ✦✦✦✦

Billy Higgins

b. Oct. 11, 1936, Los Angeles, CA
Drums / Hard Bop, Free Jazz
A very adaptable drummer, Billy Higgins came to fame playing with Ornette Coleman's Quartet, but proved to be an expert bop player too. He started his career playing R&B and rock in the Los Angeles area, then teamed up with Don Cherry and James Clay in an unrecorded group called the Jazz Messiahs. In the mid-'50s Higgins started rehearsing with Ornette Coleman. He was on Ornette's first records (starting in 1958), came to New York, and played with Coleman during 1959-60 before Ed Blackwell (who was actually his predecessor) replaced him. Higgins and Blackwell were both on Coleman's monumental *Free Jazz* album and Higgins would participate in occasional reunions with Ornette through the years. He kept busy during the '60s, '70s, and '80s, freelancing with a countless number of major players including recordings with Thelonious Monk, Steve Lacy, Sonny Rollins, Lee Morgan, Donald Byrd, Dexter Gordon, Jackie McLean, Hank Mobley, Mal Waldron, Milt Jackson, Art Pepper, Joe Henderson, Pat Metheny, and David Murray's big band. From 1966 on Higgins also often played with Cedar Walton's trio and later with the Timeless All-Stars. Based in Los Angeles during most of the '80s and '90s, Higgins became an inspiration to younger musicians (including the members of the B Sharp Quartet and Black/Note), opening the World Stage as a performance venue and recording label. — *Scott Yanow*

Soweto / Jan. 21, 1979 / Red ✦✦✦✦

Bridgework / Jan. 4, 1980-Apr. 23, 1986 / Contemporary ✦✦✦✦
A rare Higgins album, with conservative arrangements and compositions, plus outstanding technique and percussive foundations. — *Ron Wynn*

● **Mr. Billy Higgins** / Apr. 12, 1984-May 29, 1984 / RIZA ✦✦✦✦
One of jazz's greatest session drummers got a rare date as a leader on this set, but it was tough to tell that it was Billy Higgins' album. He was in his usual place, driving and pacing the session on drums, while soprano and tenor saxophonist Gary Bias took the spotlight on such songs as "Morning Awakening" and "Humility." — *Ron Wynn*

Once More / May 25, 1990 / Red ✦✦✦

Andrew Hill

b. Jun. 30, 1937, Port Au Prince, Haiti
Piano / Avant-Garde, Post-Bop
Andrew Hill has long been a highly original pianist and composer. Never quite free form but too advanced to be accepted by bop fans, Hill's complex music has never really caught on although he is widely respected as an innovative jazz musician. He started on piano when he was 13, studied

with the composer Paul Hindemith, and throughout the '50s freelanced in jazz and R&B settings in Chicago. In 1961 Hill moved to New York and became Dinah Washington's accompanist. After a stint with Rahsaan Roland Kirk in 1962, he has mostly worked as a leader. Hill's series of explorative and advanced Blue Note albums (1963-1966) have been reissued in a Mosaic box set; *Point of Departure* (1964) has such sidemen as Kenny Dorham, Eric Dolphy, and Joe Henderson and other dates feature John Gilmore, Freddie Hubbard, Sam Rivers, and Henderson. Hill also recorded for Blue Note during 1968-70, became an educator, and by the mid-'70s was teaching in public schools in California. He has recorded less frequently during the past couple of decades for labels such as Steeple-Chase, Freedom, East Wind, Soul Note, and Blue Note, but he remains a very viable performer who has stuck to his own singular musical vision. —*Scott Yanow*

★ **Black Fire** / Nov. 8, 1963 / Blue Note ✦✦✦✦✦
Haiti's gift to jazz piano of the '50s and now. For adventurous listeners. —*Michael G. Nastos*

Smoke Stack / Dec. 13, 1963 / Blue Note ✦✦✦
This is an early example of Hill's percussive, Afro-Caribbean sound. —*Ron Wynn*

Judgment! / Jan. 8, 1964 / Blue Note ✦✦✦✦

★ **Point of Departure** / Mar. 31, 1964 / Blue Note ✦✦✦✦✦
A 1989 reissue of a remarkable session that still has avant-garde quality today. Eric Dolphy (sax) and Joe Henderson (sax) break barriers with their splendid solos. —*Ron Wynn*

Compulsion / Oct. 8, 1965 / Blue Note ✦✦✦✦
Exacting, dynamic compositions, with intense playing. —*Ron Wynn*

Involution / Mar. 7, 1966 / Blue Note ✦✦✦
Hill splits this two-record set with Sam Rivers (sax). Both are incredible. —*Ron Wynn*

Lift Every Voice / May 16, 1969 / Blue Note ✦✦✦

One for One / Aug. 1, 1969-Jan. 23, 1970 / Blue Note ✦✦✦✦
These are previously unreleased sessions from 1969 & 1970. Group efforts, at times with a string quartet. Hefty solos from B. Maupin, P. Patrick, J. Henderson, F. Hubbard, and C. Tolliver. —*Michael G. Nastos*

Invitation / Oct. 17, 1974 / SteepleChase ✦✦✦

Spiral / Dec. 20, 1974 & Jan. 20, 1975 / Freedom ✦✦✦✦
This is a wonderful quintet with Ted Curson (tpt), Lee Konitz (sax). —*Ron Wynn*

Live at Montreux / Jul. 1975 / Freedom ✦✦✦✦
Beautiful, authoritative solo playing. —*Ron Wynn*

Nefertiti / Jan. 25, 1976 / Inner City ✦✦✦✦
Powerful, outstanding trio session cut in 1976 for the East Wind label. Hill was at one time Dinah Washington's pianist, then moved from that to writing adventurous outside pieces and playing fiery, experimental music. These songs are not very outside, but they are certainly done in an aggressive, captivating manner. —*Ron Wynn*

From California with Love / Oct. 12, 1978 / Artists House ✦✦✦

Faces of Hope / Jun. 13, 1980-Jun. 14, 1980 / Soul Note ✦✦✦✦
Sometimes loping, sometimes soaring solo piano from Andrew Hill, one of several impressive releases he made in the '80s. Hill often used rhythms from his native Haiti in his compositions. This time, however, it is neither the arrangements nor the songs that score, but Hill's emphatic execution of them. —*Ron Wynn*

Verona Rag / Jul. 5, 1986 / Soul Note ✦✦✦✦
Although Andrew Hill in this solo recital does wonders with the standards "Darn That Dream" and "Afternoon in Paris" and contributes two other superior originals, it is his breakdown of his striding "Verona Rag" that is most fascinating, transforming the piece from a spiritual-type rag into a very advanced improvisation. Hill, a true individualist, embodies the best in creative jazz. —*Scott Yanow*

But Not Farewell / Jul. 12, 1990-Sep. 1990 / Blue Note ✦✦✦✦
A latter-day set with the smoldering Greg Osby on alto sax. Hill updates his sound. —*Ron Wynn*

Earl Hines

b. Dec. 28, 1903, Dusquesne, PA, **d.** Apr. 22, 1983, Oakland, CA
Piano / Swing, Classic Jazz
Once called "the first modern jazz pianist," Earl Hines differed from the stride pianists of the '20s by breaking up the stride rhythms with unusual accents from his left hand. While his right hand often played octaves so as to ring clearly over ensembles, Hines had the trickiest left hand in the business, often suspending time recklessly but without ever losing the beat. One of the all-time great pianists, Hines was a major influence on Teddy Wilson, Jess Stacy, Joe Sullivan, Nat King Cole, and even to an extent on Art Tatum. He was also an underrated composer

responsible for "Rosetta," "My Monday Date," and "You Can Depend on Me" among others.

Earl Hines played trumpet briefly as a youth before switching to piano. His first major job was accompanying vocalist Lois Deppe, and he made his first recordings with Deppe and his orchestra in 1922. The following year Hines moved to Chicago where he worked with Sammy Stewart and Erskine Tate's Vendome Theatre Orchestra. He started teaming up with Louis Armstrong in 1926 and the two masterful musicians consistently inspired each other. Hines worked briefly in Armstrong's big band (formerly headed by Carroll Dickerson) and they unsuccessfully tried to manage their own club. 1928 was one of Hines' most significant years. He recorded his first ten piano solos including versions of "A Monday Date," "Blues in Thirds," and "57 Varieties." Hines worked much of the year with Jimmy Noone's Apex Club Orchestra and their recordings are also considered classic. Hines cut brilliant (and futuristic) sides with Louis Armstrong's Hot Five, resulting in such timeless gems as "West End Blues," "Fireworks," "Basin Street Blues," and their remarkable trumpet-piano duet "Fireworks." And on his birthday on December 28, Hines debuted with his big band at Chicago's Grand Terrace.

A brilliant ensemble player as well as soloist, Earl Hines would lead big bands for the next 20 years. Among the key players in his band through the '30s would be trumpeter/vocalist Walter Fuller, Ray Nance on trumpet and violin (prior to joining Duke Ellington), trombonist Trummy Young, tenor saxophonist Budd Johnson, Omer Simeon and Darnell Howard on reeds, and arranger Jimmy Mundy. In 1940 Billy Eckstine became the band's popular singer and in 1943 (unfortunately during the musicians' recording strike), Hines welcomed such modernists as Charlie Parker (on tenor), trumpeter Dizzy Gillespie, and singer Sarah Vaughan in what was the first bebop orchestra. By the time the strike ended Eckstine, Parker, Gillespie, and Vaughan were gone, but tenor Wardell Gray was still around to star with the group during 1945-46.

In 1948 the economic situation forced Hines to break up his orchestra. He joined the Louis Armstrong All-Stars but three years of playing second fiddle to his old friend were difficult to take. After leaving Armstrong in 1951, Hines moved to Los Angeles and later San Francisco, heading a Dixieland band. Although his style was much more modern, Hines kept the group working throughout the '50s, at times featuring Muggsy Spanier, Jimmy Archey, and Darnell Howard. Hines did record on a few occasions but was largely forgotten in the jazz world by the early '60s. Then in 1964 jazz writer Stanley Dance arranged for him to play three concerts at New York's Little Theater, both solo and in a quartet with Budd Johnson. The New York critics were amazed by Hines' continuing creativity and vitality, and he had a major comeback that lasted through the rest of his career. Hines travelled the world with his quartet, recorded dozens of albums, and remained famous and renowned up until his death at the age of 79. Most of the many recordings from his career are currently available on CD. —*Scott Yanow*

☆ **Earl Hines (1928-1932)** / Dec. 1928-Jun. 1932 / Classics ✦✦✦✦✦

Earl Hines (1932-1934) / Jul. 1932-Mar. 1934 / Classics ✦✦✦✦

Earl Hines (1934-1937) / Sep. 1934-Feb. 1937 / Classics ✦✦✦✦

● **Earl Hines (1937-1939)** / Feb. 10, 1937-Oct. 6, 1939 / Classics ✦✦✦✦

● **Piano Man** / Jul. 12, 1939-Mar. 19, 1942 / Bluebird ✦✦✦✦
This sampler of Earl Hines' Bluebird recordings features five brilliant piano solos from the often breathtaking pianist, "Blues in Thirds" by Sidney Bechet's Trio with Hines, and 16 of the better performances from his big band of 1939-42. An excellent purchase for those not familiar with Hines' big-band days, this CD includes such classics as "Piano Man," "Boogie Woogie on St. Louis Blues," and "Jelly, Jelly" along with many hot swinging performances from this very underrated orchestra. —*Scott Yanow*

Earl Hines (1939-1940) / Oct. 6, 1939-Dec. 2, 1940 / Classics ✦✦✦✦

And the Duke's Men / May 16, 1944-May 14, 1947 / Delmark ✦✦✦

Another Monday Date / Nov. 1955-Dec. 1956 / Prestige ✦✦✦✦
Two of pianist Earl Hines' finest recordings sessions of the '50s are included on this CD. One is a 'tribute to Fats Waller on which Hines (with guitarist Eddie Duran, bassist Dean Reilly and drummer Earl Watkins) explores songs associated with Waller. The other date is Hines' only solo session of the decade and features him playing his own compositions (including "Everything Depends on You," "You Can Depend on Me," "Piano Man," and "My Monday Date") along with "Am I Too Late?" During the '50s, Hines was somewhat forgotten in jazz, reduced to playing Dixieland dates, so this two-fer is far superior to his other sessions prior to his comeback of 1964. —*Scott Yanow*

Spontaneous Explorations / Mar. 7, 1964-Jan. 17, 1966 / Red Baron ✦✦✦✦
This two-CD set contains a pair of very exciting sessions by the great pianist Earl Hines. The earlier set, recorded the same day as his historic comeback concert at the Little Theater, was Hines' first solo session since 1956 and is full of stunning performances. The later session finds Hines, a veteran of the '20s, sounding quite comfortable in a trio with two young mod-

ernists: bassist Richard Davis and drummer Elvin Jones. The pianist, in fact, sounds quite youthful throughout these classic recordings, taking wild chances and constantly pushing himself. — *Scott Yanow*

Grand Reunion / Mar. 14, 1965 / Verve ✦✦✦✦
For a session at the Village Vanguard, pianist Earl Hines and his trio were joined part of the time by the great tenor Coleman Hawkins and trumpeter Roy Eldridge. But on this LP, the three giants only actually play together on a fine version of "Take the 'A' Train." Eldridge has "The Man I Love" and "Undecided" as his features (Hines is absent on the latter), Hawkins gets to roar on "Sweet Georgia Brown," and Hines and his trio play a lengthy "Grand Terrace Medley." The music is excellent but not as explosive as one might expect from these competitive players. — *Scott Yanow*

At the Village Vanguard / Jun. 29, 1965-Jun. 30, 1965 / Columbia ✦✦✦

It Don't Mean A Thing If It Ain't Got That Swing! / Dec. 15, 1970-Nov. 29, 1972 / Black Lion ✦✦✦✦
This recommended set teams the great pianist Earl Hines with Duke Ellington's longtime tenor saxophonist Paul Gonsalves in a quartet. Since Hines mostly recorded in trios and unaccompanied during his last decade, it is particularly enjoyable to hear him interacting with a horn player. The repertoire includes three Duke Ellington songs, "Over the Rainbow," "Moten Swing," and, from 1972, a piano solo version of "Blue Sands." — *Scott Yanow*

Earl Hines Plays Duke Ellington / Jun. 1, 1971-Dec. 10, 1971 / New World ✦✦✦✦
During a four-year period, pianist Earl Hines recorded enough of Duke Ellington's compositions to fill up four LPs. This double CD contains 20 of his better performances including both Ellington's better-known standards and a few obscurities (most notably lengthy versions of "The Shepherd" and "Black Butterfly"). The music is satisfying, although one wishes that New World had reissued all of the music from this extensive project on three CDs. — *Scott Yanow*

★ **Tour de Force** / Nov. 22, 1972-Nov. 29, 1972 / Black Lion ✦✦✦✦✦
Pianist Earl Hines is in top form on this brilliant set of solo piano. This CD (which has three previously unreleased performances along with five of the six numbers from its counterpart LP) and *Tour de Force Encore* greatly expand upon the original set. Whether it be "Mack the Knife," "Indian Summer," or "I Never Knew," Hines is near the peak of his creativity on this CD, taking wild chances with time and coming up with fresh new variations on these veteran standards. — *Scott Yanow*

Piano Solos / Jan. 29, 1974 / Laserlight ✦✦✦✦

Honor Thy Fatha / 1978 / Drive Archive ✦✦✦

Milt Hinton

b. Jun. 23, 1910, Vicksburg, MS
Bass / Swing

Bassist Milt Hinton has probably appeared on more records than any other musician in the world and remains a vital figure in jazz even at the age of 86. He grew up in Chicago and worked with many legendary figures from the late '20s to the mid-'30s including Freddie Keppard, Jabbo Smith, Tiny Parham (with whom he made his recording debut in 1930), Eddie South, Fate Marable, and Zutty Singleton. He played with Cab Calloway's orchestra and his later small group during 1936-51. Considered the best bassist before the rise of Jimmy Blanton in 1939, Hinton was featured on "Pluckin' the Bass" (1939) and was an ally of Dizzy Gillespie in modernizing Calloway's music.

After leaving Cab, Hinton worked in clubs with Joe Bushkin, had brief stints with Count Basie and Louis Armstrong's All-Stars, and in 1954 became a staff musician at CBS, appearing on a countless number of recordings (jazz and otherwise) during the next 15 years; everything from Jackie Gleason mood music and polka bands to commercials and Buck Clayton jam sessions. By the '70s Hinton was appearing regularly at jazz parties and festivals and his activities have not slowed down during the past two decades; in 1995 he toured with the Statesmen of Jazz. Although a modern soloist, Hinton has also kept the art of slap bass alive. A very skilled photographer, Hinton has released two books of his candid shots of jazz musicians including one (*Bass Line*) and his fascinating memoirs. Milt Hinton has recorded as a leader for Bethlehem, Victor (both in 1955), Famous Door, Black & Blue, and Chiaroscuro and as a sideman for virtually every label! — *Scott Yanow*

★ **Old Man Time** / Oct. 3, 1989-Mar. 2, 1989 / Chiaroscuro ✦✦✦✦✦

Laughing At Life / 1994 / Columbia ✦✦✦✦
Milt Hinton's major label debut as a leader (at age 85!), other than a 1955 date for Victor, finds the great bassist utilizing two separate rhythm sections on a variety of standards. In addition to fine solos from pianists Richard Wyands and Derek Smith, there are guest appearances by trumpeter Jon Faddis (who defies his stereotype by sounding closer here to Roy Eldridge than to Dizzy Gillespie) and veteran Harold Ashby whose warm tenor recalls Ben Webster. Even if Hinton's three vocals are one too many, his singing has its charm. The finale "The Judge and the Jury" adds four

other bassists for a very musical tribute to one of the few veterans of the '20s still to be heard in his prime in the mid-'90s. — *Scott Yanow*

Al Hirt (Alois Maxwell Hirt)

b. Nov. 7, 1922, New Orleans, LA
Trumpet / Dixieland
A virtuoso on the trumpet, Al Hirt is often "overqualified" for the Dixieland and pop music that he performs. He studied classical trumpet at the Cincinnati Conservatory (1940-43) and was influenced by the playing of Harry James. He freelanced in swing bands (including both Tommy and Jimmy Dorsey and Ray McKinley) before returning to New Orleans in the late '40s and becoming involved in the Dixieland movement. He teamed up with clarinetist Pete Fountain on an occasional basis from 1955 on and became famous by the end of the decade. An outstanding technician with a wide range along with a propensity for playing far too many notes, Hirt had some instrumental pop hits in the '60s and also recorded swing and country music but mostly stuck to Dixieland in his live performances. He remains a household name today, although one often feels that he could have done so much more with his talent. Hirt's early Audiofidelity recordings (1958-60) and collaborations with Fountain are the most rewarding of his career. — *Scott Yanow*

● **That's a Plenty** / Mar. 29, 1988-Mar. 31, 1988 / Pro Arte ✦✦✦✦
Jumbo appears with Peanuts Hocko, Bobby Breaux, Dalton Hagler, and others pouncing on New Orleans favorites like "Royal Garden Blues," "Bourbon Street Parade," and "Saints." — *Bruce Raeburn*

Art Hodes

b. Nov. 14, 1904, Nikoliev, Russia, d. Mar. 4, 1993
Piano / Blues, Dixieland
Throughout his long career, Art Hodes was a fighter for traditional jazz, whether through his distinctive piano playing, his writings (which included many articles and liner notes), or his work on radio and educational television. Renowned for the feeling he put into blues, Hodes was particularly effective on uptempo tunes where his on-the-beat chordings from his left hand could be quite exciting. Born in Russia, he came to America with his family when he was six months old and grew up in Chicago. Hodes witnessed Chicago jazz during its prime years in the '20s and he learned from other pianists. In 1928 he made his recording debut with Wingy Manone but spent most of the '30s in obscurity in Chicago until he moved to New York in 1938. He played with Joe Marsala and Mezz Mezzrow before forming his own band in 1941. Hodes recorded for Solo Art, his Jazz Record label, Signature, Decca, and Black & White during 1939-42, but he made more of an impression with his heated Dixieland recordings for Blue Note during 1944-45 (all of which have been reissued on a Mosaic box set). During 1943-47 Hodes edited the important magazine *The Jazz Record*, had a radio show, and became involved in the moldy fig vs. bebop wars with Leonard Feather and Barry Ulanov; jazz on a whole lost from the latter. In 1950 he returned to Chicago where he remained active locally and made occasional records. Hodes hosted a television series *Jazz Alley* for a time in the '60s, wrote for *Downbeat* and was a jazz educator. Art Hodes recorded frequently during the '70s and '80s and was widely recognized as one of the last survivors of Chicago jazz. His later recordings were for such labels as Audiophile, Jazzology, Delmark, Storyville, Euphonic, Muse, Parkwood, Candid, and Music & Arts. — *Scott Yanow*

★ **Complete Blue Note Art Hodes Sessions** / Mar. 18, 1944-Dec. 16, 1945 / Mosaic ✦✦✦✦✦

Hodes' Art / Oct. 22, 1968 / Delmark ✦✦✦

South Side Memories / Nov. 29, 1983 / Sackville ✦✦✦

Blues in the Night / Jun. 16, 1985 / Sackville ✦✦✦

Solos, Vol. 1 / Apr. 20, 1987-Jul. 10, 1989 / Parkwood ✦✦✦✦
Pianist Art Hodes is heard on two different solo albums on this single CD. First he performs eight Christmas songs, infusing the familiar melodies with a strong dose of blues and rhythm (although the emphasis is on relaxed tempos). The later set has eight of Hodes' blues-oriented originals. Hodes was one of the top pianists in classic jazz with a distinctive voice of his own. This set from his later years is a fine example of his talents. — *Scott Yanow*

Live from Toronto's Cafe Des Copains / 1988 / Music & Arts ✦✦✦✦

Keepin' Out of Mischief Now / Nov. 3, 1988-Nov. 4, 1988 / Candid ✦✦✦✦
For this Candid CD, an 84-year old Art Hodes performs an effective set of solo piano. Renowned for his blues playing, Hodes is actually at his best on more uptempo romps where his left hand is used to state and push the beat. He plays a wide variety of material during the program, ranging from "See See Rider" and "Struttin' with Some Barbecue" to Duke Ellington's "Saturday Night Function," Horace Silver's "The Preacher," and even "Tennessee Waltz." This is an excellent outing from a veteran great near the end of his career. — *Scott Yanow*

★ **Pagin' Mr. Jelly** / Nov. 14, 1988 / Candid ✦✦✦✦✦

Final Sessions / Jul. 30, 1990-Aug. 19, 1990 / Music & Arts ✦✦✦✦

Johnny Hodges

b. Jul. 25, 1907, Cambridge, MA, d. May 11, 1970
Sax (Alto), Sax (Soprano) / Swing

Possessor of the most beautiful tone ever heard in jazz, altoist Johnny Hodges formed his style early on and had little reason to change it through the decades. Although he could stomp with the best swing players and was masterful on the blues, Hodges' luscious playing on ballads has never been topped. He played drums and piano early on before switching to soprano sax when he was 14. Hodges was taught and inspired by Sidney Bechet although he soon used alto as his main ax; he would regretfully drop soprano altogether after 1940. His early experiences included playing with Lloyd Scott, Chick Webb, Luckey Roberts, and Willie "The Lion" Smith (1924) and he also had the opportunity to work with Bechet. However Johnny Hodges' real career began in 1928 when he joined Duke Ellington's orchestra. He quickly became one of the most important solo stars in the band and a real pacesetter on alto; Benny Carter was his only close competition in the '30s. Hodges was featured on a countless number of performances with Ellington and also had many chances to lead recording dates with Duke's sidemen. Whether it was "Things Ain't What They Used to Be," "Come Sunday," or "Passion Flower," Hodges was an indispensable member of Ellington's orchestra in the '30s and '40s. It was therefore a shock in 1951 when he decided to leave Duke and lead a band of his own. Hodges had a quick hit in "Castle Rock" (which ironically showcased Al Sears' tenor and had no real contribution by the altoist), but his combo ended up struggling and breaking up in 1955. Hodges' return to Duke Ellington was a joyous occasion, and he never really left again. In the '60s Hodges teamed up with organist Wild Bill Davis on some sessions, leading to Davis joining Ellington for a time in 1969. Hodges, whose unchanging style always managed to sound fresh, was still with Duke Ellington when he suddenly died in 1970. — *Scott Yanow*

Hodge Podge / Mar. 28, 1938-Oct. 14, 1939 / Epic/Legacy ◆◆◆

● **Passion Flower** / Nov. 2, 1940-Jun. 9, 1946 / Bluebird ◆◆◆◆
For 42 years (with a four-year interruption), altoist Johnny Hodges was the top soloist in Duke Ellington's all-star orchestra. This excellent CD reissue has the eight selections (plus an alternate take) from Hodges' two Bluebird sessions of 1940-41; among the sidemen on such classics as "Day Dream," "Good Queen Bess," "Passion Flower," and "Things Ain't What They Used to Be" are either Cootie Williams or Ray Nance on trumpet, trombonist Lawrence Brown, and Ellington himself. In addition there are 13 selections by the Duke Ellington Orchestra of 1940-46 that feature Hodges, including "Don't Get Around Anymore," "In a Mellotone," "Warm Valley," "I Got It Bad," and "Come Sunday." This is classic music that has been intelligently repackaged. — *Scott Yanow*

Caravan / Jun. 1947-Jun. 19, 1951 / Prestige ◆◆◆◆
This single CD, which reissues all of the music from a double-LP, has a variety of formerly rare sessions from 1947-51. Although the great altoist Johnny Hodges gets top billing, and he leads three sessions from 1947 (featuring such top Ellington stars as trombonist Lawrence Brown, tenorman Al Sears, baritonist Harry Carney, and either Taft Jordan or Harold Baker on trumpet), he is actually absent on the second half of the release. With Billy Strayhorn and/or Duke Ellington as leader and Willie Smith on alto, these enthusiastic swing performances range in personnel from a three-trombone septet to a version of "Caravan" with Ellington on piano and Strayhorn making a rare appearance on organ. Although the music falls just short of classic, Ellington collectors will love these rarities. — *Scott Yanow*

☆ **Complete Johnny Hodges Sessions (1951-1955)** / Jan. 15, 1951-Sep. 8, 1955 / Mosaic ◆◆◆◆◆
As is true of most Mosaic box sets, it would be very difficult to improve upon this reissue. Altoist Johnny Hodges left Duke Ellington's Orchestra in 1950 after 22 years to try to make it on his own as a bandleader. Five years later, he returned to Ellington for the final 15 years of his life after having recorded the music heard on this six-LP set. Hodges' small group, a unit that emphasized blues, ballads, and riff-filled romps, was an extension of the Ellington band. Hodges had a big hit with "Castle Rock" (ironically a feature for tenor saxophonist Al Sears), but otherwise he eventually had trouble making ends meet. Other notable sidemen on these easily enjoyable performances include trumpeters Emmett Berry and Harold "Shorty" Baker, trombonist Lawrence Brown, and tenors Flip Phillips, Ben Webster, and John Coltrane on one session (during which he unfortunately does not solo; the final session, from Sept. 8, 1955 (after Hodges had already returned to Ellington), also has trumpeter Clark Terry and pianist Billy Strayhorn. Most of this music had been long out of print at the time this 1989 box was released. A highly recommended gem of swinging jazz. — *Scott Yanow*

Used to Be Duke / Jul. 2, 1954 & Aug. 5, 1954 / Verve ◆◆◆◆
Recorded during his five year "vacation" from Duke Ellington's orchestra, this Johnny Hodges set (reissued on CD) features his band sticking mostly to standards. With trumpeter Harold "Shorty" Baker, trombonist Lawrence Brown, baritonist Harry Carney, pianist Call Cobbs or Richie Powell, bass-

ist John Williams, drummer Louis Bellson, and either Jimmy Hamilton or John Coltrane (who unfortunately does not solo) on tenor, Hodges had a particularly strong group. High points include "On the Sunny Side of the Street," the title track, and a seven-song ballad medley. This session was also included in Mosaic's six-LP Johnny Hodges set. — *Scott Yanow*

Masters of Jazz, Vol. 9 / Nov. 22, 1960-Mar. 14, 1961 / Storyville ◆◆◆◆
Here is a CD that is highly recommended for swing collectors. Altoist Johnny Hodges and tenor saxophonist Ben Webster team up for a sextet set from 1960, a club appearance that was released for the first time on this set. Their six performances (all are basic Hodges originals) find the pair of veteran swing stylists in prime form. The remainder of the program (three standards plus Hodges' "Good Queen Bess") is played by a septet dominated by Ellington musicians including the leader/altoist, baritonist Harry Carney, trumpeter Ray Nance, and trombonist Lawrence Brown. Excellent music that still has not been dated. — *Scott Yanow*

At the Berlin Sportpalast / Mar. 1961 / Pablo ◆◆◆◆
This double-CD, a straight reissue of a Pablo double-LP, documents a fun set. Altoist Johnny Hodges and some fellow members of Duke Ellington's Orchestra (Ray Nance on cornet, violin, and vocals, trombonist Lawrence Brown, baritonist Harry Carney, bassist Aaron Bell, drummer Sam Woodyard, and guest pianist Al Williams) jam through a mostly typical set of standards and Ellington tunes. Everyone gets featured and, even if there are no real surprises, the musicians are consistently heard in top form. Superior small-group swing by some of the best. — *Scott Yanow*

● **Everybody Knows** / Feb. 6, 1964 & Mar. 8, 1965 / Impulse ◆◆◆◆
This excellent single CD has the complete contents of two Impulse LPs: *Everybody Knows Johnny Hodges* and *Inspired Abandon*, which was actually a Lawrence Brown album featuring Hodges. The two similar and equally rewarding swing-oriented albums find Hodges joined by a variety of top Ellington stars, including trumpeters Cat Anderson and Ray Nance, either Harold Ashby or Paul Gonsalves on tenor, and trombonist Brown, among others. The renditions of "310 Blues," "The Jeep Is Jumpin'," "Stompy Jones," and "Mood Indigo" in particular, sound quite fresh and inventive. Recommended. — *Scott Yanow*

Johnny Hodges/Wild Bill Davis, Vols. 1 & 2 / Jan. 7, 1965-Sep. 11, 1966 / RCA Jazz Tribune ◆◆◆◆
This enjoyable double-CD from the RCA's Jazz Tribune series combines a pair of sessions from altoist Johnny Hodges and organist Wild Bill Davis. While the earlier set has the pair joined by two guitarists (Mundell Lowe and Dickie Thompson), bassist Milt Hinton, and drummer Osie Johnson, the second session has trombonist Lawrence Brown, Bob Brown on tenor and flute, Thompson returning on guitar, and drummer Bobby Durham. Another difference between the two dates is that the later album (which has been reissued on CD in the Bluebird series) was recorded in concert. The music generally sticks to standards (many written by Duke Ellington), ballads, and an occasional blues. Hodges and Davis were a surprisingly complementary team (their collaborations were a brief vacation from their usual settings) and they seem to inspire each other. Fine swing-based music. — *Scott Yanow*

In a Mellotone / Sep. 10, 1966-Sep. 11, 1966 / Bluebird ◆◆◆◆
Altoist Johnny Hodges and organist Wild Bill Davis teamed up successfully on quite a few albums in the '60s. This set, reissued on CD, was their final and quite possibly their most rewarding. With solo work provided not only by the co-leaders, but trombonist Lawrence Brown, obscure tenor Bob Brown, and guitarist Dickie Thompson (drummer Bobby Durham helps out in support), this is a particularly interesting unit. Unlike most of their other collaborations, this outing by Hodges and Davis sticks mostly to better-known material, including a previously unissued version of Duke Ellington's "Squeeze Me But Please Don't Tease Me" and four Hodges originals. Highlights include "It's Only a Paper Moon," "Taffy," "Good Queen Bess," and "In a Mellotone." This release is recommended as a strong (and swinging) example of Johnny Hodges outside of the Duke Ellington Orchestra. — *Scott Yanow*

Triple Play / Jan. 9, 1967-Jan. 10, 1967 / Bluebird ◆◆◆◆
Altoist Johnny Hodges is heard in three different settings on this reissue CD. Such top swing stars as trumpeters Ray Nance, Cat Anderson, and Roy Eldridge, trombonists Buster Cooper, Lawrence Brown, and Benny Powell, tenors Paul Gonsalves and Jimmy Hamilton, baritonist Harry Carney, pianists Hank Jones and Jimmy Jones (the latter two sometimes together), guitarists Tiny Grimes, Les Spann, and Billy Butler, bassists Milt Hinton, Aaron Bell, and Joe Benjamin and drummers Gus Johnson, Rufus Jones and Oliver Jackson are heard in nonets with the great altoist. Despite the many changes in personnel, the music is pretty consistent, with basic swinging originals, blues, and ballads all heard in equal proportion. As usual, Johnny Hodges ends up as the main star. — *Scott Yanow*

Jay Hoggard

b. Sep. 24, 1954, New York, NY
Vibes / Avant-Garde, Post-Bop

Jay Hoggard has had a wide-ranging career. One of the top vibraphonists to emerge during the '70s, Hoggard originally started on piano and saxophone before switching to vibes. By the early '70s he was working in New England with such top avant-garde players as Anthony Davis and Leo Smith. Hoggard moved to New York in 1977 where he played with Chico Freeman and Anthony Davis. In 1978 he recorded a solo avant-garde vibes performance, but he followed it up with a more commercial date. Hoggard has worked with such greats as Sam Rivers, Cecil Taylor, James Newton, and Kenny Burrell in addition to leading his own group; he has recorded hard bop-oriented dates as a leader for Contemporary, India Navigation, and several for Muse. — *Scott Yanow*

Solo Vibraphone / Nov. 18, 1978 / India Navigation ✦✦✦✦
The finest, most complete record released thus far by vibist Jay Hoggard. This solo date put him alone in the spotlight, and he used the vehicle to display his total skills, from delicate melodies to aggressive harmonies and expressive solos. — *Ron Wynn*

Mystic Winds, Tropical Breezes / 1982 / India Navigation ✦✦✦✦
Strong, free-wheeling date by vibist Jay Hoggard. He was working with a topflight group, which featured pianist Anthony Davis, bassist Cecil McBee, drummers Billy Hart and Don Moye, and Dwight Andrews on various saxophones. The compositions were loosely structured and extended, and solos were fierce. — *Ron Wynn*

Overview / Jun. 22, 1989 / Muse ✦✦✦✦
Very good, with Geri Allen (p). — *Michael G. Nastos*

The Little Tiger / Jun. 10, 1990 / Muse ✦✦✦✦
An album with the vibist at his best. The title track is worth the price alone. With Benny Green. — *Michael G. Nastos*

★ **The Fountain** / Jul. 10, 1991 / Muse ✦✦✦✦✦
Vibraphonist Jay Hoggard has had a diverse recording career, playing everything from very free jazz to a couple of commercial efforts. In the '90s he seemed to discover straightahead jazz and this quintet session (with guitarist Kenny Burrell and pianist James Weidman) is mostly very much in that idiom. Hoggard is fine on standards such as "Stompin' at the Savoy" (a tribute to Lionel Hampton) and Monk's "Epistrophy," but it is on his originals (the soulful "Sweet Potato" and a fairly free "The Fountain") that Hoggard sounds most individual. — *Scott Yanow*

In the Spirit / May 4, 1992 / Muse ✦✦✦✦

Love Is The Answer / Jan. 9, 1994-Feb. 27, 1994 / Muse ✦✦✦✦

Billie Holiday (Eleanora Fagan)

b. Apr. 7, 1915, Baltimore, MD, d. Jul. 17, 1959, New York, NY
Vocals / Swing
Billie Holiday remains (37 years after her death) the most famous of all jazz singers. "Lady Day" (as she was named by Lester Young) had a small voice and did not scat but her innovative behind-the-beat phrasing made her quite influential. The emotional intensity that she put into the words she sang (particularly in later years) was very memorable and sometimes almost scary; she often really did live the words she sang.

Her original name and birthplace have been wrong for years, but are listed correctly above thanks to Donald Clarke's definitive Billie Holiday biography *Wishing on the Moon*. Holiday's early years are shrouded in legend and rumors due to her fanciful ghostwritten autobiography *Lady Sings the Blues* but it is fair to say that she did not have a stable life. Her father Clarence Holiday (who never did marry her mother) played guitar with Fletcher Henderson and abandoned his family early on, while her mother was not a very good role model. Holiday essentially grew up alone, feeling unloved and gaining a lifelong inferiority complex that led to her taking great risks with her personal life and becoming self-destructive.

Holiday's life becomes clearer after she was discovered singing in Harlem clubs by John Hammond. He arranged for her to record a couple of titles with Benny Goodman in 1933, and although those were not all that successful, it was the start of her career. Two years later she was teamed with a pickup band led by Teddy Wilson and the combination clicked. During 1935-42 she would make some of the finest recordings of her career, jazz-oriented performances in which she was joined by the who's who of swing. Holiday sought to combine together Louis Armstrong's swing and Bessie Smith's sound; the result was her own fresh approach. In 1937 Lester Young and Buck Clayton began recording with Holiday and the interplay between the three of them was timeless.

Holiday was with Count Basie's orchestra during much of 1937, but because they were signed to different labels, all that exists of the collaboration are three songs from a radio broadcast. She worked with Artie Shaw's Orchestra for a time in 1938 but the same problem existed (only one song was recorded), and she had to deal with racism, not only during a Southern tour but in New York too. She had better luck as a star attraction at Cafe Society in 1939. Holiday made history that year by recording the horribly picturesque "Strange Fruit," a strong antiracism statement that became a permanent part of her repertoire. Her records of 1940-42 found her sidemen playing a much more supportive role than in the past, rarely sharing solo space with her. Although the settings were less jazz-oriented than before (with occasional strings and even a background vocal

group on a few numbers) Holiday's voice was actually at its strongest during her period with Decca (1944-49). She had already introduced "Fine and Mellow" (1939) and "God Bless the Child" (1941), but it was while with Decca that she first recorded "Lover Man" (her biggest hit), "Don't Explain," "Good Morning Heartache," and her renditions of "Ain't Nobody's Business If I Do," "Them There Eyes," and "Crazy He Calls Me." Unfortunately it was just before this period that she became a heroin addict and she spent much of 1947 in jail. Due to the publicity she became a notorious celebrity and her audience greatly increased. Holiday did get a chance to make one Hollywood movie (*New Orleans*) in 1946, and although she was disgusted by the fact that she was stuck playing a maid, she did get to perform with her early idol Louis Armstrong.

Holiday's story from 1950 on is a gradual downhill slide. Although her recordings for Norman Granz (which started in 1952) placed her once again with all-star jazz veterans (including Charlie Shavers, Buddy DeFranco, Harry "Sweets" Edison, and Ben Webster), her voice was slipping fast. Her unhappy relationships distracted her, the heroin use and excessive drinking continued and by 1956 she was way past her prime. Holiday had one final burst of glory in late 1957 when she sang "Fine and Mellow" on *The Sound of Jazz* telecast while joined by Lester Young (who stole the show with an emotional chorus), Ben Webster, Coleman Hawkins, Gerry Mulligan, and Roy Eldridge, but the end was near. Holiday's 1958 album *Lady in Satin* found the 43-year old singer sounding 73 (barely croaking out the words) and the following year she collapsed; in the sad final chapter of her life she was placed under arrest for heroin possession while on her deathbed!

Fortunately Holiday's recordings have been better treated than she was during her life and virtually all of her studio sides are currently available on CD. — *Scott Yanow*

★ **The Quintessential Billie Holiday, Vol. 1 (1933-1935)** / Nov. 27, 1933-Dec. 3, 1935 / Columbia ✦✦✦✦✦
After years of reissuing her recordings in piecemeal fashion, Columbia finally got it right with this nine-CD *Quintessential* series. All of Holiday's 1933-42 studio recordings (although without the alternate takes) receive the treatment they deserve in this program. *Vol. 1* has Holiday's first two tentative performances from 1933 along with her initial recordings with Teddy Wilson's all-star bands. High points include "I Wished On the Moon," "What a Little Moonlight Can Do," "Miss Brown to You," and "Twenty-Four Hours a Day." — *Scott Yanow*

Billie Holiday: The Legacy Box 1933-1958 / Nov. 27, 1933-Feb. 19, 1958 / Columbia ✦✦✦
The logic behind this sampler is puzzling. Rather than reissue the very best of Billie Holiday's Columbia recordings on a three-CD box set or a package of her rare alternate takes, CBS tries it both ways by including 60 common selections already available in the *Quintessential* series along with 10 rarities that were either unissued or alternates. This otherwise attractive box (which includes a colorful booklet) will drive completists and veteran collectors crazy. The music (mostly from 1933-42 with three weaker performances from 1957-58) is often classic but duplicates more coherent reissues. — *Scott Yanow*

★ **The Quintessential Billie Holiday, Vol. 2 (1936)** / Jan. 30, 1936-Oct. 21, 1936 / Columbia ✦✦✦✦
The second of nine volumes in this essential series (all are highly recommended) continues the complete reissue of Billie Holiday's early recordings (although the alternate takes are bypassed). This set is highlighted by "I Cried for You" (which has a classic alto solo from Johnny Hodges), "Billie's Blues" (from Holiday's first session as a leader), "A Fine Romance," and "Easy to Love." Holiday's backup crew includes such greats as pianist Teddy Wilson, baritonist Harry Carney, trumpeters Jonah Jones and Bunny Berigan, and clarinetist Artie Shaw. There's lots of great small-group swing. — *Scott Yanow*

★ **The Quintessential Billie Holiday, Vol. 3 (1936-1937)** / Oct. 28, 1936-Feb. 18, 1937 / Columbia ✦✦✦✦
The third of nine CDs that document all of Billie Holiday's studio recordings of 1933-42 for Columbia has classic versions of "Pennies from Heaven," "I Can't Give You Anything but Love" (on which she shows the influence of Louis Armstrong), and "My Last Affair," along with Lady Day's first meeting on record with tenor saxophonist Lester Young. Their initial encounter resulted in four songs including "This Year's Kisses" and "I Must Have That Man." All nine volumes in this admirable series (if only the alternate takes had been included!) are highly recommended. — *Scott Yanow*

☆ **The Quintessential Billie Holiday, Vol. 4 (1937)** / Mar. 31, 1937-Jun. 15, 1937 / Columbia ✦✦✦✦
The fourth of nine CDs in this essential series of Billie Holiday's studio recordings of 1933-42 features the great tenor Lester Young on eight of the 16 performances. Young and Holiday make a perfect match on "I'll Get By" (although altoist Johnny Hodges steals the honors on that song), "Mean to Me," "Easy Living," "Me Myself and I," and "A Sailboat in the Moonlight." Other strong selections without Young include "Moanin' Low," "Let's Call the Whole Thing Off," and "Where Is the Sun." It's highly recommended

along with all of the other CDs in this perfectly done Billie Holiday reissue program. — *Scott Yanow*

★ **The Quintessential Billie Holiday, Vol. 5 (1937-1938)** / Jun. 15, 1937-Jan. 27, 1938 / Columbia ✦✦✦✦✦
The fifth of nine CDs in the complete reissue of Billie Holiday's early recordings (sans alternate takes), this great set has 18 selections, all but four featuring tenor saxophonist Lester Young and trumpeter Buck Clayton. Among the classics are "Getting Some Fun out of Life," "Trav'lin' All Alone," "He's Funny That Way," "My Man," "When You're Smiling" (on which Young takes a perfect solo), "If Dreams Come True," and "Now They Call It Swing." All nine volumes in this series are highly recommended, but if one can only acquire a single entry, this is the one. — *Scott Yanow*

☆ **Quintessential Billie Holiday, Vol. 6 (1938)** / May 11, 1938-Nov. 9, 1938 / Columbia ✦✦✦✦✦
The sixth of nine CDs in this very worthy series traces Billie Holiday's recording career throughout most of 1938. Although not containing as many true classics as *Vol. 5*, most of these 18 selections are quite enjoyable, particularly "You Go to My Head," "Having Myself a Time," "The Very Thought of You," and "They Say." All of the sets in this reissue program are recommended, featuring Holiday when she was youthful and still optimistic about life. — *Scott Yanow*

The Quintessential Billie Holiday, Vol. 7 (1938-1939) / Nov. 28, 1938-Jul. 5, 1939 / Columbia ✦✦✦✦
By 1939 when the bulk of these 17 selections were recorded, Billie Holiday was dominating her own recordings, allocating less space for her sidemen to solo. This was not really a bad thing since Holiday's voice was getting stronger each year. On the seventh of nine CD volumes that reissue all of Holiday's 1933-42 Columbia recordings (other than the alternate takes which have been bypassed), Holiday sounds at her best on "More than You Know, Sugar" (featuring a superb Benny Carter alto solo), "Long Gone Blues," and "Some Other Spring." It's recommended along with all of the other entries in the *Quintessential* series. — *Scott Yanow*

Billie Holiday / Apr. 20, 1939-Apr. 8, 1944 / Commodore ✦✦✦✦
This CD includes all of Billie Holiday's Commodore recordings (the master takes but no alternates): four titles from 1939 (including the still haunting "Strange Fruit" and "Fine and Mellow") and the remainder dating from 1944 when Holiday's voice was at its peak. The latter sessions are highlighted by "I'll Get By," "Billie's Blues," "He's Funny That Way," and "I'm Yours." Pianist Eddie Heywood has many sparkling solos on the 1944 selections. This definitive single CD contains music essential for every jazz collection. — *Scott Yanow*

☆ **Quintessential Billie Holiday, Vol. 8 (1939-1940)** / Jul. 5, 1939-Sep. 12, 1940 / Columbia ✦✦✦✦✦
The eighth of nine volumes that feature all of the master takes from Billie Holiday's Columbia recordings of 1933-42 is one of the better sets although all nine CDs are recommended. High points include "Them There Eyes," "Swing, Brother, Swing," "The Man I Love," "Ghost of Yesterday," "Body Arid Soul," "Falling in Love Again," and "I Hear Music." Among the variety of all-stars backing her, tenor saxophonist Lester Young makes his presence known on eight of the 18 numbers. — *Scott Yanow*

I'll Be Seeing You / 1939 / Commodore ✦✦✦
Quintessential Billie Holiday, Vol. 9 (1940-1942) / Oct. 15, 1940-Feb. 10, 1942 / Columbia ✦✦✦✦
The final volume in this nine-CD series contains all of Billie Holiday's recordings from her final 16 months with the label. Highlights include "St. Louis Blues," "Loveless Love," "Let's Do It," "All of Me" (arguably the greatest version ever of this veteran standard), "Am I Blue," "Gloomy Sunday," and "God Bless the Child." All 153 of Holiday's Columbia recordings (even the occasional weak item) are well worth hearing and savoring. — *Scott Yanow*

Billie's Blues / Jun. 12, 1942-Jan. 5, 1954 / Blue Note ✦✦✦✦
Most of this excellent CD features one of Billie Holiday's finest concert recordings of the '50s. Recorded in Europe before an admiring audience, this enjoyable set finds Holiday performing seven of her standards with her trio and joining in for jam session versions of "Billie's Blues" and "Lover Come Back to Me" with an all-star group starring clarinetist Buddy DeFranco, vibraphonist Red Norvo, and guitarist Jimmy Raney. These performances (which find Holiday in stronger voice than on her studio recordings of the period) have also been included in Verve's massive CD box set. This program concludes with Holiday's four rare sides for Aladdin in 1951 (between her Decca and Verve periods) which are highlighted by two blues and "Detour Ahead," and her 1942 studio recording of "Trav'lin' Light" with Paul Whiteman's Orchestra. — *Scott Yanow*

★ **The Complete Decca Recordings** / Oct. 4, 1944-Mar. 8, 1950 / Decca ✦✦✦✦✦
Billie Holiday is heard at her absolute best on this attractive two-CD set. During her period on Decca, Holiday was accompanied by strings (for the first time), large studio orchestras, and even background vocalists, so jazz solos from her sidemen are few. But her voice was at its strongest during the '40s (even with her personal problems) and to hear all 50 of her Decca

performances (including alternate takes and even some studio chatter) is a real joy. Among the high points of this essential set are her original versions of "Lover Man" (Holiday's biggest selling record), "Don't Explain," "Good Morning Heartache," "Tain't Nobody's Business if I Do," "Now or Never," "Crazy He Calls Me," and remakes of "Them There Eyes" and "God Bless the Child." — *Scott Yanow*

☆ **The Complete Billie Holiday on Verve 1945-1959** / Feb. 12, 1945-Mar. 1, 1959 / Verve ✦✦✦✦✦
This is a rather incredible collection, ten CDs enclosed in a tight black box that includes every one of the recordings that Verve owns of Billie Holiday, not only the many studio recordings of 1952-57 (which feature Holiday joined by such jazz all-stars as trumpeters Charlie Shavers and Harry "Sweets" Edison, altoist Benny Carter and the tenors of Flip Phillips, Paul Quinichette and Ben Webster) but prime performances at Jazz at the Philharmonic concerts in 1945-47, an enjoyable European gig from 1954, her "comeback" Carnegie Hall concert of 1956, Holiday's rather sad final studio album from 1959 and even lengthy tapes from two informal rehearsals. It's a perfect purchase for the true Billie Holiday fanatic. — *Scott Yanow*

Billie Holiday at Storyville / Oct. 29, 1951-1953 / Black Lion ✦✦✦
Lady in Satin / Feb. 18, 1958-Feb. 20, 1958 / Columbia ✦✦✦✦
This is the most controversial of all Billie Holiday records. Holiday herself said that this session (which finds her accompanied by Ray Ellis' string orchestra) was her personal favorite, and many listeners have found her emotional versions of such songs as "I'm a Fool to Want You," "You Don't Know What Love Is," "Glad to Be Unhappy," and particularly "You've Changed" to be quite touching. But Holiday's voice was essentially totally gone by 1958, and although not yet 43 years old, she could have passed for 73. Ellis' muzaky arrangements do not help; most of this record is very difficult to listen to. Late in life, Holiday expressed the pain of life so effectively that her croaking voice had become almost unbearable to hear. — *Scott Yanow*

Dave Holland

b. Oct. 1, 1946, Wolverhampton, England
Bass / Avant-Garde, Post-Bop
One of the top bassists of free bop and the avant-garde, Dave Holland has long been quite flexible. He started on bass in 1963 and studied extensively in England, playing with many of the British players including Humphrey Lyttelton, John Surman, Evan Parker, Tubby Hayes, Ronnie Scott, and Kenny Wheeler (which is quite a variety!). After playing with the Spontaneous Music Ensemble, he worked with Miles Davis during 1968-70 as Ron Carter's replacement, recording several albums including most noticeably *Bitches Brew*. He next teamed up with Chick Corea, Anthony Braxton, and Barry Altschul in Circle (1970-71) and after Corea's decision to play more accessible music, Holland became a member of Braxton's quartet up until 1976. He also played with Paul Bley (1972-73) and Stan Getz during the period (1973-75). Holland was in Gateway with John Abercrombie and Jack DeJohnette (1975-77), a group that in the mid-'90s had a reunion. The bassist played regularly with Sam Rivers during 1976-80 and in 1982 formed his own group which through the years have included Kenny Wheeler, Steve Coleman, and Robin Eubanks among others. He has been active as an educator, worked with the M-Base collective, toured with Pat Metheny, Herbie Hancock, and DeJohnette in a quartet and has recorded as a leader since 1971 for ECM. — *Scott Yanow*

★ **Jumpin' In** / Oct. 1983 / ECM ✦✦✦✦✦
Bassist Dave Holland leads one of his most stimulating groups on this superlative quintet date. With the young Steve Coleman on alto and flute, trumpet great Kenny Wheeler, trombonist Julian Priester, and drummer Steve Ellington in the band, Holland had a particularly creative group of musicians in which to interpret and stretch out his six originals; Coleman also contributed one composition. This set, which has plenty of variety in moods, tone, colors, and styles, is one of Holland's better recordings. — *Scott Yanow*

The Razor's Edge / Feb. 1987 / ECM ✦✦✦✦
Brisk, edgy work with some top young-lion types, notably Steve Coleman. — *Ron Wynn*

Triplicate / Mar. 1988 / ECM ✦✦✦✦
This is the best setting for hearing Holland's bass mastery and compositional logic at work. — *Myles Boisen*

Extensions / Sep. 1989 / ECM ✦✦✦✦
Dave Holland Quartet. With Kevin Eubanks (g). This was the 1990 *Down Beat* Critic's Album of the Year. Very good band/album music. Percussionist Smitty Smith is unreal. Recommended. — *Michael G. Nastos*

Red Holloway

b. 1927
Sax (Alto), Sax (Tenor) / Bop, Swing, Soul-Jazz, Groove
An exuberant player with attractive tones on both tenor and alto, Red Holloway is also a humorous blues singer. Whether it be bop, blues, or R&B,

Holloway can hold his own with anyone. Holloway played in Chicago with Gene Wright's big band (1943-46), served in the Army, and then played with Roosevelt Sykes (1948) and Nat Towles (1949-50) before leading his own quartet (1952-61) during an era when he also recorded with many blues and R&B acts. Holloway came to fame in 1963 while touring with Jack McDuff, making his first dates as a leader for Prestige (1963-65). Although he has cut many records in R&B settings, Red Holloway is a strong bop soloist at heart as he proved in the '70s when he battled Sonny Stitt to a tie on their recorded collaboration. He has mostly worked as a leader since then but has also guested with Juggernaut and the Cheathams and played with Clark Terry on an occasional basis. — *Scott Yanow*

Burner / Oct. 10, 1963 / Prestige ✦✦✦
Early date with Holloway and John Patton (or George Butcher) on Hammond organ. — *Michael Erlewine*

Cookin' Together / Feb. 2, 1964 / Original Jazz Classics ✦✦✦✦
With the Jack McDuff Quartet (includes George Benson on guitar). A 1988 reissue of a textbook soul-jazz date. — *Ron Wynn*

Brother Red / Feb. 6, 1964-Feb. 7, 1964 / Prestige ✦✦✦✦
The 11 selections included on this CD reissue include seven songs from a session headed by tenor saxophonist Red Holloway that used the members of the Jack McDuff Quintet (with the organist, guitarist George Benson, bassist Wilfred Middlebrooks, and drummer Joe Dukes), three pieces from a McDuff date in which the lead voices are backed by an orchestra arranged by Benny Golson, and a selection from a sampler. The material varies a bit ("Wives and Lovers" and Holloway's soul ballad "No Tears" are forgettable) but the blues and the uptempo pieces (highlighted by "This Can't Be Love") are quite enjoyable and the underrated saxophonist is in excellent form. — *Scott Yanow*

Red Soul / Dec. 1965 / Prestige ✦✦✦
Good to get, if you can find it. Holloway with Lonnie Smith on organ and George Benson on guitar. Tunes like "Big Fat Lady" and "Good and Groovy." — *Michael Erlewine*

Nica's Dream / Jul. 7, 1984 / SteepleChase ✦✦✦✦

Red Holloway and Company / Jan. 1987 / Concord Jazz ✦✦✦✦
A fine session that juggles blues, swing feeling, and soul-jazz sensibility. —*Ron Wynn*

● **Locksmith Blues** / Jun. 1989 / Concord Jazz ✦✦✦✦
Raucous jazz and blues from trumpeter Clark Terry and saxophonist Red Holloway. —*Michael G. Nastos*

Christopher Hollyday

b. 1970
Sax (Alto) / Hard Bop
One of the "Young Lions" of the late '80s, altoist Christopher Hollyday created a big stir when he appeared on the scene but has maintained a surprisingly low profile during the past couple of years. He started playing alto when he was nine, developed quickly and was playing in clubs when he was 14, the same year he recorded his first album on his own Jazzbeat label. Back then he was heavily influenced by Charlie Parker, but a few years later Hollyday almost sounded like a clone of Jackie McLean. In 1988 he took a group into the Village Vanguard and the following year he toured with Maynard Ferguson's big band. During 1989-92, Hollyday recorded four CDs for Novus and was starting to develop his own voice when he was dropped from the label. — *Scott Yanow*

● **Christopher Hollyday** / Jan. 25, 1989-Jan. 26, 1989 / Novus ✦✦✦✦
Teen wizard Hollyday, the newest young lion to find his way onto a major label Cedar Walton is around to lend some keyboard seasoning while fabled drummer Billy Higgins and bassist David Williams complete the cast in a session blending McLean, Parker, and Gillespie songs with the occasional Gershwin standard. — *Ron Wynn*

On Course / Jan. 16, 1990-Jan. 17, 1990 / Novus ✦✦✦✦
Some rough spots, but also many fine moments. — *Ron Wynn*

The Natural Moment / Jan. 21, 1991-Jan. 22, 1991 / Novus ✦✦✦✦
The progress on this album is evident. —*Michael G. Nastos*

And I'll Sing Once More / 1992 / Novus ✦✦✦✦
Rlease by youthful saxophonist Christopher Hollyday, this time recording with a large group including several contemporaries. These include Kenny Werney, Scott Robinson, Eric Charry, John Mosca, and Ed Neumeister. He's also experimenting with more ambitious compositions and displaying other aspects of his playing style. —*Ron Wynn*

Bill Holman (Willis Leonard Holman)

b. May 21, 1927, Olive, CA
Sax (Tenor) / Post-Bop, Hard Bop
One of the great arrangers, Bill Holman's dense but hard-swinging charts often have so much of value going on that they reward repeated listenings. After a stint with Charlie Barnet (1950-51), Holman became well known for his arrangements for Stan Kenton (1952-56) which helped advance the

Kenton sound. Although a fine tenor saxophonist, Holman's writing has always overshadowed his playing. He concentrated on studio work by the '60s but also wrote through the years for Woody Herman, Maynard Ferguson, Gerry Mulligan, Count Basie, and Buddy Rich among others. Holman wrote the charts for Natalie Cole's bestselling *Unforgettable* album (1991) and has led his own part-time big band in the Los Angeles area since 1975. Bill Holman recorded as a leader for Capitol, Coral (reissued on Sackville), Andex, and Hi Fi during 1954-60 and more recently his Los Angeles band has been documented by JVC. — *Scott Yanow*

In a Jazz Orbit / Feb. 11, 1958-Feb. 13, 1958 / VSOP ✦✦✦✦
Considering his talents, arranger Bill Holman has led relatively few recording sessions through the years. This formerly rare big-band set from 1958 (originally on the Andex label and reissued on CD by V.S.O.P.) features a 15-piece band filled with West Coast all-stars. Among the soloists on these five standards and four originals are trombonists Frank Rosolino, Carl Fontana, and Ray Sims, altoists Charles Mariano and Herb Geller, trumpeter Jack Sheldon, Richie Kamuca on tenor, pianist Victor Feldman, and Holman himself on tenor. The leader's arrangements were quite distinctive (although not as complex as they would become) at this fairly early stage and the results are a big band album that still sounds fresh nearly four decades later. — *Scott Yanow*

Jive for Five / May 29, 1958-Jun. 6, 1958 / VSOP ✦✦✦✦
For a brief time, tenor saxophonist Bill Holman and drummer Mel Lewis led a hard-swinging quintet based in Los Angeles. Trumpeter Lee Katzman, pianist Jimmy Rowles, and bassist Wilford Middlebrook complete the group, a band that benefits greatly from the arrangements of Holman. Rowles contributed "502 Blues Theme," Holman brought in two songs, and the unit also performs the obscure "Mah Lindy Lou" and two originals. This LP (originally on the Andex label) serves as proof that not all jazz recordings from Los Angeles in the '50s are quiet and cool. — *Scott Yanow*

★ **A View from the Side** / Apr. 24, 1995-Apr. 25, 1995 / JVC ✦✦✦✦✦
Although he never seems to win any popularity polls, Bill Holman is among the most respected and unique arrangers of the past 40 years. This CD features his band of the mid-'90s, an outfit that includes many of the top Los Angeles-based musicians. Holman's writing is often colorfully overcrowded (rewarding repeated listenings) yet logical with the charts progressing and developing from beginning to end rather than repeating the same basic ideas continuously. Whether it be the many complex themes of "No Joy in Mudville," the showcases for tenor saxophonist Pete Christlieb ("But Beautiful") and Bob Efford's bass clarinet ("The Peacocks"), the very advanced "Make My Day," or the rebuilding of "Tennessee Waltz," this JVC release is a consistently memorable set from a masterful arranger who deserves much greater recognition in the jazz world. — *Scott Yanow*

Richard "Groove" Holmes (Richard Arnold Holmes)

b. May 2, 1931, Camden, NJ, d. Jun. 29, 1991
Organ / Soul-Jazz, Hard Bop, Groove
A great jazz organist, "Groove" Holmes taught himself organ and developed a strongly swinging style with powerful bass lines and a superb harmonic and melodic edge, something that reflects Holmes's ability to play acoustic bass and the influence of saxophonists on his approach. He worked in local New Jersey clubs for a number of years. Holmes had successful albums with such guests as Les McCann, Ben Webster, Gene Ammons, and Clifford Scott (using the alias Joe Splink) in the early '60s. Though Holmes played well, these sessions got more exposure due to their illustrious guests. He did more trio settings in the mid-'60s, and also got better quality recordings. Holmes scored a huge pop hit with his version of "Misty." His late '60s releases yielded neither hits nor memorable efforts, while his early '70s sessions, particularly those with Jimmy McGriff in a pair of organ battles, were good. Holmes turned in several fine efforts from the late '70s on through the late '80s, often working with Houston Person. But Holmes also experimented with various electronic keyboards during the '70s on dates that are short of his best work. —*Ron Wynn and Bob Porter*

Groove / Mar. 1961 / Pacific Jazz ✦✦✦✦
A 1990 reissue of an interesting meeting between Groove Holmes and Ben Webster (ts). Webster shows he's capable of adapting his robust soul into a soul-jazz context. —*Ron Wynn*

Groovin' with Jug / Aug. 15, 1961 / Pacific Jazz ✦✦✦✦
Recorded live at the Black Orchid and at the Pacific Jazz Studio earlier that afternoon. Gene Ammons was at his peak of popularity, and Holmes was just about to become well known on the only date they ever played together. Both players are on. Holmes, also a bassist and famous for his organ bass lines, can be heard to good advantage on "Morris the Minor." —*Michael Erlewine*

After Hours / 1961 / Pacific Jazz ✦✦✦✦
The original *After Hours* album had Joe Pass on guitar and Lawrence Marable on drums. This combines most of another album (*Tell It Like It Is*) with Gene Edwards on guitar. This is early Groove Holmes, 13 tracks in all.

This is fine soul-jazz and it is clear why many feel that Holmes is the man of the groove, when it comes to the Hammond B-3. —*Michael Erlewine*

Tell It Like It Is / 1961 / Pacific Jazz ✦✦✦
Very fine Hammond B-3 with Holmes, Gene Edwards on guitar, and Leroy Henderson on drums. Near the start of his career, this is classy soul-jazz. —*Michael Erlewine*

Soul Message / Aug. 3, 1965 / Original Jazz Classics ✦✦✦✦
Organist Richard "Groove" Holmes hit upon a successful formula on this Prestige session (reissued on CD in the OJC series), mixing together boogaloo rhythms with emotional solos. His doubletime version of "Misty" became a big hit, and the other selections, including Horace Silver's "Song for My Father" and a pair of soulful originals, are in a similar vein. The lone ballad of the set ("The Things We Did Last Summer") is a fine change of pace. With the assistance of guitarist Gene Edwards and drummer Jimmie Smith, Groove Holmes shows that it is possible to create music that is both worthwhile and commercially successful. —*Scott Yanow*

Misty / Aug. 3, 1965-Aug. 12, 1966 / Original Jazz Classics ✦✦✦✦
Organist Richard "Groove" Holmes in the mid-'60s had a hit with his medium-tempo rendition of "Misty." This CD reissue has the original short version (which was cut as a 45) plus other medium-tempo ballads performed in similar fashion. Holmes and his trio (featuring guitarist Gene Edwards and drummer George Randall) play enjoyable if not overly substantial versions of such songs as "The More I See You," "The Shadow of Your Smile," "What Now My Love," and "Strangers in the Night," trying unsuccessfully for another pop hit; the organist's sound is more appealing than some of the tunes. —*Scott Yanow*

★ **Blue Groove** / Mar. 15, 1966-May 29, 1967 / Prestige ✦✦✦✦✦
This CD, which reissues two former LPs by Richard "Groove" Holmes (*Get Up & Get It* and *Soul Mist*), showcases the organist in a quintet featuring the tenor of Teddy Edwards and guitarist Pat Martino, with his trio, and (on two standards) with trumpeter Blue Mitchell and tenor saxophonist Harold Vick. Overall, this 73-minute set has many fine solos, spirited ensembles and two well rounded programs. —*Scott Yanow*

☆ **That Healin' Feelin'** / Aug. 26, 1968 / Prestige ✦✦✦✦✦
Rusty Bryant smokes on tenor, as does Richard "Groove" Holmes on organ. —*Ron Wynn*

Double Exposure / 1973 / Lester Recording Catalog ✦✦
This album contains two albums, one by Groove Holmes and the other by Jimmy McGriff. They do not play together here. Holmes is with Kwasi Jay Ourba on bongo/congas, Garald Hubbard on guitar, Jerry Jemmott on bass, and Larry Willis on piano, and drums. Six cuts by McGriff and five by Groove Holmes. The tunes "Catherine" and "Rainy Day" are very nice. —*Michael Erlewine*

Comin' on Home / 1974 / Blue Note ✦✦✦

Shippin' Out / Jun. 1977 / Muse ✦✦✦✦
There is a lot of fine music here—all of it funky, spacious, clear. This album feels good. It has some of that soul-jazz magic. —*Michael Erlewine*

Good Vibrations / Dec. 19, 1977 / Muse ✦✦✦✦
An album of uptempo cookers from his middle period. With Houston Person (ts). —*Michael Erlewine*

Broadway / Dec. 2, 1980 / Muse ✦✦✦
With Houston Person (ts). Tight band. Later, uptempo but slick. It lacks the space that his early small-combo funk albums have. —*Michael Erlewine*

Blues All Day Long / Feb. 24, 1988 / Muse ✦✦✦✦
With Houston Person (ts) and Jimmy Ponder (g). Respectable, and enjoyable later effort by Holmes. Slightly uptempo, but funky. Very nice album. —*Michael Erlewine*

Hot Tat / Sep. 5, 1989 / Muse ✦✦✦
One of the last recordings of "Groove" Holmes. With Houston Person (ts), Cecil Bridgewater (tpt), and Jimmy Ponder (g). The album is bit uneven, but its good to know that someone is still playing this old-style funk. There is some good guitar by Jimmy Ponder. —*Michael Erlewine*

Elmo Hope ((St.) Elmo Sylvester Hope)

b. Jun. 27, 1923, New York, NY, **d.** May 19, 1967, New York, NY
Piano / Bop, Hard Bop
Overshadowed throughout his life by his friends Bud Powell and Thelonious Monk, Elmo Hope was a talented pianist and composer whose life was cut short by drugs. His first important gig was with Joe Morris' R&B band (1948-51). He recorded in New York as a leader (starting in 1953) and with Sonny Rollins, Lou Donaldson, Clifford Brown, and Jackie McLean, but the loss of his cabaret card (due to his drug use) made it very difficult for him to make a living in New York. After touring with Chet Baker in 1957, Hope relocated to Los Angeles. He performed with Lionel Hampton in 1959, recorded with Harold Land and Curtis Counce, and returned to New York in 1961. A short prison sentence did little to help his drug problem and, although he sounds fine on his trio performances of 1966, he died less than a year later. Elmo Hope's sessions as a leader were cut for Blue Note, Pres-

tige, Pacific Jazz, Hi Fi Jazz, Riverside, Celebrity, Beacon, and Audio Fidelity; his last albums were initially released on Inner City. Hope was also a fine composer although none of his songs became standards. —*Scott Yanow*

★ **Trio and Quintet** / Jun. 1953-Oct. 1957 / Blue Note ✦✦✦✦✦
Three early sessions: 1953, 1954, & 1957. —*Michael Erlewine*

Meditations / Jul. 28, 1955 / Original Jazz Classics ✦✦✦✦
Although Elmo Hope was one of the more interesting jazz composers of the '50s, the emphasis on his trio set with bassist John Ore and drummer Willie Jones is on Hope's piano playing. Influenced greatly by Bud Powell (his contemporary), Hope performs standards (such as "All the Things You Are" and "Falling in Love with Love") along with some originals, most of which are based on the chord changes of earlier songs. Fans of bop piano and Bud Powell will want this enjoyable CD reissue. —*Scott Yanow*

The All Star Sessions / May 7, 1956-Nov. 14, 1961 / Original Jazz Classics ✦✦✦✦
Includes two sessions, in 1956 and 1961. A gathering of greats, supervised and sparked by Hope on piano. The list includes Coltrane (ts), Donald Byrd (tpt), and Jimmy Heath (sax). —*Ron Wynn*

Hope Full / Nov. 9, 1961 & Nov. 14, 1961 / Original Jazz Classics ✦✦✦✦
During the early years of the bop revolution, few of its younger pianists recorded unaccompanied solos. Even by 1961, solo albums by the bop musicians were considered a bit unusual, but Elmo Hope (an underrated composer and pianist) fares quite well during this Riverside set, which has been reissued on CD. Hope is joined by his wife Bertha on second piano during three of the eight numbers, most notably on a swinging "Blues Left and Right." Of the solo pieces, Elmo Hope is at his best on "When Johnny Comes Marching Home" and a cocktailish, but appealing, version of "Liza." —*Scott Yanow*

Claude Hopkins

b. Aug. 24, 1903, Alexandria, VA, **d.** Feb. 19, 1984, New York, NY
Piano / Swing, Stride
A talented stride pianist, Claude Hopkins never became as famous as he deserved. He was a bandleader early on and toured Europe in the mid-'20s as the musical director for Josephine Baker. Hopkins returned to the US in 1926, led his own groups, and in 1930 took over Charlie Skeete's band. Between 1932-35 he recorded steadily with his big band (all of the music has been reissued on three Classics CDs) which featured Jimmy Mundy arrangements and such fine soloists as trumpeter/vocalist Ovie Alston, trombonist Fernando Arbello, a young Edmond Hall on clarinet and baritone, and tenorman Bobby Sands along with the popular high-note vocals of Orlando Roberson. The orchestra's recordings are a bit erratic with more than their share of mistakes from the ensembles and a difficulty in integrating Hopkins' powerhouse piano with the full group, but they are generally quite enjoyable. Mundy's eccentric "Mush Mouth" is a classic and Hopkins introduced his best-known original "I Would Do Anything for You." Although they played regularly at Roseland (1931-35) and the Cotton Club (1935-36) and there were further sessions in 1937 and 1940, the Claude Hopkins Big Band never really caught on and ended up breaking up at the height of the swing era. Hopkins did lead a later unrecorded big band (1944-47) but mostly worked with small groups for the remainder of his career. He played with Red Allen's group during the second half of the '50s, led his own band during 1960-66, and in 1968 was in the Jazz Giants with Wild Bill Davison. Claude Hopkins led an obscure record for 20th Century Fox (1958) and three Swingville albums (1960-63) but his best later work were solo stride dates for Chiaroscuro and Sackville (both in 1972) and a trio session for Black and Blue in 1974; it is surprising that his piano skills were not more extensively documented. —*Scott Yanow*

● **Claude Hopkins 1932-1934** / May 24, 1932-Jan. 1, 1932 / Classics ✦✦✦✦
Claude Hopkins 1934-1935 / Jan. 11, 1934-Feb. 1934 / Classics ✦✦✦✦
And His Orchestra / 1935 / Jazz Panorama ✦✦✦

Shirley Horn

b. May 1, 1934, Washington, DC
Piano, Vocals / Ballads
A superior ballad singer and a talented pianist, Shirley Horn put off potential success until finally becoming a major attraction while in her 50s. She studied piano from the age of four. After attending Howard University, Horn put together her first trio in 1954 and was encouraged in the early '60s by Miles Davis and Quincy Jones. She recorded three albums during 1963-65 for Mercury and ABC-Paramount but chose to stick around Washington, DC, and raise a family instead of pursuing her career. In the early '80s she began recording for SteepleChase but Horn really had her breakthrough in 1987 when she started making records for Verve, an association that continues to the present day. —*Scott Yanow*

Travelin' Light / 1965 / ABC/Paramount ✦✦✦
A Lazy Afternoon / Jul. 9, 1978 / SteepleChase ✦✦✦
Afternoon / Aug. 9, 1978 / SteepleChase ✦✦✦

Violets for Your Furs / Jul. 10, 1981-Jul. 12, 1981 / SteepleChase ✦✦✦✦

★ **Close Enough for Love** / Nov. 1988 / Verve ✦✦✦✦✦
Shirley Horn's second Verve recording consolidated the success that she had had with her previous release, *I Thought About You*, and resulted in her gaining a large audience for her ballad vocals and solid jazz piano playing. Performing with her usual trio (which includes bassist Charles Ables and drummer Steve Williams) and guest tenor Buck Hill on five of the 13 tracks, Horn is heard in definitive form throughout these studio sessions. Highlights include "Beautiful Friendship," "Baby, Baby All the Time," "This Can't Be Love," "I Wanna Be Loved," "But Beautiful," "Get out of Town," and "It Could Happen to You." —*Scott Yanow*

You Won't Forget Me / Jun. 12, 1990-Aug. 1990 / Verve ✦✦✦✦
Miles Davis (tpt) and Wynton (tpt) and Branford Marsalis (ts) are part of the guest cast. Great piano and delightful vocals. —*Ron Wynn*

Here's to Life / 1991 / Verve ✦✦✦

I Love You Paris / Mar. 7, 1992 / Verve ✦✦✦

Light out of Darkness (A Tribute to Ray Charles) / Apr. 30, 1993-May 3, 1993 / Verve ✦✦✦✦

Main Ingredient / May 15, 1995-May 18, 1995 / Verve ✦✦✦✦

Joe Houston
....

b. Austin, TX
Guitar, Vocals / Rock & Roll, Blues, Groove
Joe Houston is a honking R&B saxman of wallpaper-peeling potency who recorded for virtually every major independent R&B label in Los Angeles during the '50s. When the jump blues tradition faded, he segued right into rock 'n' roll, even cutting budget "twist" and "surf" albums for Crown that didn't sound very different from what he was doing a decade before. Houston played around Houston, TX, with the bands of Amos Milburn and Joe Turner during the late '40s. It was Turner who got the young saxist his first deal with Freedom Records in 1949. Houston found his way to the West Coast in 1952 and commenced recording for labels big and small: Modern, RPM, Lucky, Imperial, Dootone, Recorded in Hollywood, Cash, and Money (as well as the considerably better-financed Mercury, where he scored his only national R&B hit, "Worry, Worry, Worry," in 1952). Houston's formula was simple and savagely direct—he would honk and wail as hard as he could, from any conceivable position: on his knees, lying on his back, walking the bar, etc. His output for the Bihari brothers' Crown label (where he was billed "Wild Man of the Tenor Sax") is positively exhilarating: "All Nite Long," "Blow Joe Blow," and "Joe's Gone" are herculean examples of single-minded sax blasting. Houston remains active musically, emphasizing his blues vocal talent more than he used to. —*Bill Dahl*

● **Cornbread and Cabbage Greens** / 1952 / Specialty ✦✦✦✦
Los Angeles was a mecca for honking, wailing R&B tenor saxmen during the '50s, and Joe Houston was one of the wildest in town. Twenty-six blasting workouts from the early-to-mid-'50s mark this CD as the best digital indication of Houston's sax-sational wailing now available (pretty much the only vintage one on the shelves, in fact). "All Night Long," "Celebrity Club Drag," and "Rockin' and Boppin'" are among the highlights, taken from the archives of John Dolphin's Recorded in Hollywood and Cash labels. —*Bill Dahl*

Rockin' at the Drive in / 1984 / Ace ✦✦✦✦
Fourteen characteristic sax-driven R&B tunes, most instrumental, from the '50s. There's no duplication with the Specialty *Cornbread and Cabbage Greens* CD, except for the well known "All Night Long," so it's worth finding if you want more than one Houston collection. —*Richie Unterberger*

George Howard
....

Sax (Soprano) / R&B, Instrumental Pop
Heavily influenced by Grover Washington, Jr.'s sound (with whom he toured in 1979) but not his improvising style, George Howard's recordings are essentially R&B/funk with an emphasis on backbeats, lightweight vocals and melody statements with very little spontaneity. From the jazz standpoint his dates for Palo Alto/TBA, GRP, and MCA have very little to offer. —*Scott Yanow*

● **Do I Ever Cross Your Mind?** / 1992 / GRP ✦✦✦✦
Unlike most of the soprano blowers out there in the pop-jazz market, Howard avoids the "Fuzak" plague, and keeps a stronghold on his R&B roots. At the same time, Howard's latest stays away from the vocal-dominated tracks, which pop up all the more frequently in this genre. A solid, masterful set of funk/fusion. —*Steve Aldrich*

Attitude Adjustment / 1995 / GRP ✦✦✦

Freddie Hubbard (Frederick Dewayne Hubbard)
....

b. Apr. 7, 1938, Indianapolis, IN
Trumpet, Fluegelhorn / Post-Bop, Hard Bop
One of the great jazz trumpeters of all time, Freddie Hubbard formed his

sound out of the Clifford Brown/Lee Morgan tradition and by the early '70s was immediately distinctive and the pacesetter in jazz. However, a string of blatantly commercial albums later in the decade damaged his reputation and, just when Hubbard in the early '90s (with the deaths of Dizzy Gillespie and Miles Davis) seemed perfectly suited for the role of veteran master, his chops started causing him serious troubles.

Born and raised in Indianapolis, Hubbard played early on with Wes and Monk Montgomery. He moved to New York in 1958, roomed with Eric Dolphy (with whom he recorded in 1960), and was in the groups of Philly Joe Jones (1958-59), Sonny Rollins, Slide Hampton, and J.J. Johnson before touring Europe with Quincy Jones (1960-61). He recorded with John Coltrane, participated in Ornette Coleman's *Free Jazz* (1960), was on Oliver Nelson's classic *Blues and the Abstract Truth* album (highlighted by "Stolen Moments"), and started recording as a leader for Blue Note that same year. Hubbard gained fame playing with Art Blakey's Jazz Messengers (1961-64) next to Wayne Shorter and Curtis Fuller. He recorded *Ascension* with Coltrane (1965), *One Step Beyond* (1964) with Eric Dolphy, and *Maiden Voyage* with Herbie Hancock and after a period with Max Roach (1965-66), he led his own quintet which at the time usually featured altoist James Spaulding. A blazing trumpeter with a beautiful tone on fluegelhorn, Hubbard fared well in freer settings but was always essentially a hard bop stylist.

In 1970 Freddie Hubbard recorded two of his finest albums (*Red Clay* and *Straight Life*) for CTI. The follow-up, *First Light* (1971), was actually his most popular date, featuring Don Sebesky arrangements. But after the glory of the CTI years (during which producer Creed Taylor did an expert job of balancing the artistic with the accessible), Hubbard made the mistake of signing with Columbia and recording one dud after another; *Windjammer* (1976) and *Splash* (a slightly later effort for Fantasy) are low points. However, in 1977 he toured with Herbie Hancock's acoustic V.S.O.P. Quintet and in the '80s on recordings for Pablo, Blue Note, and Atlantic he showed that he could reach his former heights (even if much of the jazz world had given up on him). But by the late '80s Hubbard's personal problems and increasing unreliability (not showing up for gigs) started to really hurt him and a few years later his once-mighty technique started to seriously falter. Whether Freddie Hubbard will ever make a serious comeback is open to question, but his fans can certainly enjoy his many recordings for Blue Note, Impulse, Atlantic, CTI, Pablo, and his first Music Masters sets. —*Scott Yanow*

Open Sesame / Jun. 19, 1960 / Blue Note ✦✦✦✦
Freddie Hubbard's first recording as a leader, *Open Sesame* features the 22-year old trumpeter in a quintet with tenor saxophonist Tina Brooks, the up-and-coming pianist McCoy Tyner, bassist Sam Jones, and drummer Clifford Jarvis. The CD reissue adds two alternate takes to the original six-song program and shows that even at this early stage Hubbard had the potential to be one of the greats. On the ballad "But Beautiful" he shows maturity, and other highlights include "Open Sesame," a driving "All or Nothing at All," and "One Mint Julep." It's an impressive start to what would be a very interesting career. —*Scott Yanow*

Goin' Up / Nov. 6, 1960 / Blue Note ✦✦✦✦
For his second recording as a leader, trumpeter Freddie Hubbard (22 at the time) performs two compositions apiece by Kenny Dorham and Hank Mobley, the obscure "I Wished I Knew" and his own "Blues for Brenda." Hubbard (featured in a quintet with tenor saxophonist Mobley, pianist McCoy Tyner, bassist Paul Chambers, and drummer Philly Joe Jones) takes quite a few outstanding solos, playing lyrically on the ballads and building his own sound out of the Clifford Brown/Lee Morgan tradition. It's an excellent set of advanced hard bop. —*Scott Yanow*

Here to Stay / Apr. 9, 1961-Dec. 27, 1962 / Blue Note ✦✦✦✦

★ **Ready for Freddie** / Aug. 21, 1961 / Blue Note ✦✦✦✦
Trumpeter Freddie Hubbard really came into his own during this Blue Note session. He is matched with quite an all-star group (tenor saxophonist Wayne Shorter, pianist McCoy Tyner, bassist Art Davis, and drummer Elvin Jones in addition to Bernard McKinney on euphonium), introduces two of his finest compositions ("Birdlike" and "Crisis") and is quite lyrical on his ballad feature "Weaver of Dreams." Hubbard's sidemen all play up to par and this memorable session is highly recommended; it's one of the trumpeter's most rewarding Blue Note albums. —*Scott Yanow*

Caravan / Jul. 2, 1962 / Impulse ✦✦✦✦

Hub-Tones / Oct. 10, 1962 / Blue Note ✦✦✦✦
Trumpeter Freddie Hubbard teams up on record with James Spaulding (who doubles on alto and flute) for the first time on this excellent set. With the assistance of pianist Herbie Hancock, bassist Reggie Workman, and drummer Clifford Jarvis, the quintet performs four of the trumpeter's originals (including "Lament for Booker" and the title cut) plus an advanced version of the standard "You're My Everything." John Coltrane's modal music was starting to influence Hubbard's conception, and his own playing was pushing ahead the modern mainstream without really entering the avant-garde. —*Scott Yanow*

The Body and Soul / Mar. 8, 1963-May 2, 1963 / Impulse ✦✦✦✦
The second of trumpeter Freddie Hubbard's two Impulse albums features the 25-year-old in three separate settings. He is heard along with tenor saxophonist backed by with strings ("Skylark," "I Got It Bad," and "Chocolate Shake" are all given beautiful treatments), with a 16-piece band and in a septet with Eric Dolphy and Wayne Shorter. This well rounded and highly recommended showcase demonstrates why Freddie Hubbard was considered the top trumpeter to emerge during the early '60s. —*Scott Yanow*

Breaking Point / May 7, 1964 / Blue Note ✦✦✦✦
This CD reissue (which augments the original five-song program with alternate takes originally issued on 45s of "Blue Frenzy" and "Mirrors") brings back the first recording Hubbard cut with his own working band (as opposed to an all-star studio group). On these selections (particularly the memorable "Breaking Point"), Hubbard and his quintet (James Spaulding on alto and flute, pianist Ronnie Matthews, bassist Eddie Khan, and drummer Joe Chambers) play music that falls in between hard bop and the avant-garde, stretching the boundaries of the jazz modern mainstream. Their explorative flights are still quite interesting more than three decades later and Hubbard, having broken away from his earlier Clifford Brown and Lee Morgan influences, really sounds very much like himself. —*Scott Yanow*

Blue Spirits / Feb. 19, 1965-Mar. 5, 1966 / Blue Note ✦✦✦✦
This CD, Freddie Hubbard's last Blue Note release of the '60s (with the exception of the blowing session *The Night of the Cookers*), adds two numbers to the original LP program and features the great trumpeter in three challenging settings ranging from a sextet to an octet. Hubbard uses such sidemen as altoist James Spaulding, tenors Joe Henderson and Hank Mobley, the euphonium of Kiane Zawadi, pianists Harold Mabern, McCoy Tyner, and Herbie Hancock, bassists Larry Ridley, Bob Cranshaw, and Reggie Workman, drummers Clifford Jarvis, Pete La Roca, and Elvin Jones, the congas of Big Black, and on one song bassoonist Hosea Taylor. The set is comprised of seven diverse Hubbard originals and even though none of the songs caught on to become standards, the music is quite challenging and fairly memorable. —*Scott Yanow*

The Night of the Cookers: Live at Club La Marchal, Vols. 1 & 2 / Apr. 9, 1965-Apr. 10, 1965 / Blue Note ✦✦
Backlash / Oct. 19, 1966 & Oct. 24, 1966 / Atlantic ✦✦✦✦
Trumpeter Freddie Hubbard led a particularly fine quintet in the mid-'60s that has long been underrated. The edition heard on this Atlantic LP features James Spaulding on alto and flute, pianist Albert Dailey, bassist Bob Cunningham, and drummer Otis Ray Appleton. This studio recording is most notable for debuting Hubbard's "Little Sunflower" and also has a good remake of "Up Jumped Spring" along with four other obscure pieces. The music straddles the boundaries between hard bop, soul and the avant-garde and has plenty of unpredictable moments. This is the strongest of Freddie Hubbard's three Atlantic records of the period. —*Scott Yanow*

☆ **Red Clay** / Jan. 27, 1970-Jan. 29, 1970 / CTI ✦✦✦✦✦
Freddie Hubbard has long considered this recording to be his best, and with good reason. The trumpeter is heard at the peak of his powers performing five originals (one, "Cold Turkey," was released for the first time on this CD reissue) in a quintet with tenor saxophonist Joe Henderson, keyboardist Herbie Hancock, bassist Ron Carter, and drummer Lenny White. "Red Clay" is a classic and the other selections ("The Intrepid Fox," "Suite Sioux," and "Delphia") all feature Hubbard taking colorful solos in a style that blends together hard bop with subtle funky rhythms. Classic music of the early '70s. —*Scott Yanow*

★ **Straight Life** / Nov. 16, 1970 / CTI ✦✦✦✦✦
Recorded between trumpeter Freddie Hubbard's better-known classics *Red Clay* and *First Light*, *Straight Life* is actually arguably Hubbard's greatest recording, and it hasn't been reissued on CD yet. Hubbard, joined by an all-star group that includes tenor saxophonist Joe Henderson, keyboardist Herbie Hancock, guitarist George Benson, bassist Ron Carter, and drummer Jack DeJohnette, is frequently astounding on "Straight Life" (check out that introduction!) and "Mr. Clean," constructing classic solos. The very memorable set is rounded off by the trumpeter's duet with Benson on a lyrical version of the ballad "Here's That Rainy Day." This exciting LP is essential for all serious jazz collections. —*Scott Yanow*

First Light / Sep. 1971 / CTI ✦✦✦✦
The third of Freddie Hubbard's "big three" recordings for CTI (it was preceded by *Red Clay* and *Straight Life*), *First Light* was probably the trumpeter's most popular album. The first of his recordings to utilize the string and woodwind arrangements of Don Sebesky, Hubbard sounds quite inspired by his accompaniment and plays at his best throughout, particularly on "First Light" and "Uncle Albert/Admiral Halsey." The CD reissue by Columbia adds one previously unissued selection ("Fantasy in D") to the original program. —*Scott Yanow*

Outpost / Mar. 16, 1981-Mar. 17, 1981 / Enja ✦✦✦✦
This little-known CD is actually a special outing for Freddie Hubbard. Pianist Kenny Barron, bassist Buster Williams, and drummer Al Foster are quite complementary on the diverse material, which includes "You Don't

Know What Love Is," two Hubbard originals, Williams' "Dual Force," and Eric Dolphy's "Loss." Throughout, Hubbard is heard in prime form. —*Scott Yanow*

Keystone Bop / Nov. 27, 1981 & Nov. 29, 1981 / Fantasy ✦✦✦
Keystone Bop: Sunday Night / Nov. 29, 1981 / Prestige ✦✦✦
Born to Be Blue / Dec. 14, 1981 / Original Jazz Classics ✦✦✦✦
Trumpeter Freddie Hubbard teams up with veteran tenor saxophonist Harold Land and Hubbard's regular rhythm section of the period (keyboardist Billy Childs, bassist Larry Klein, drummer Steve Houghton, and percussionist Buck Clark) on this fine modern hard bop CD, a straight reissue of the original Pablo LP. Hubbard had hurt his reputation with his very commercial Columbia recordings of the mid-to-late '70s, so in 1981 he was doing his best to return to his brand of straightahead jazz. This date is highlighted by "Gibraltar," Clifford Brown's "Joy Spring," and a revisit to Hubbard's "Up Jumped Spring." —*Scott Yanow*

Born to Be Blue / Aug. 1982 / Pablo ✦✦✦
Sweet Return / Jun. 13, 1983-Jun. 14, 1983 / Atlantic ✦✦✦✦
One of Freddie Hubbard's best albums since the early '70s, this quintet date finds him joined by quite an all-star lineup: Lew Tabackin on tenor and flute, pianist Joanne Brackeen (who has many fine solos throughout the album), bassist Eddie Gomez, and drummer Roy Haynes. High points include Hubbard's tender version of "Misty" (at the time he had a particularly lovely tone on fluegelhorn), Brackeen's "Heidi-B," and the quintet's rendition of the standard "The Night Has a Thousand Eyes." —*Scott Yanow*

★ **Double Take** / Nov. 21, 1985 / Blue Note ✦✦✦✦✦
Other than their joint appearance as sidemen on Benny Golson's *Time Speaks* in 1983, Freddie Hubbard and Woody Shaw had never recorded together before *Double Take*. At this point in their evolution, Hubbard still gets the edge (his range is wider and he cannot be surpassed technically). Although Shaw tended to play more harmonically sophisticated lines and is remarkably inventive, they are both trumpet masters. Their meeting on *Double Take* was more of a collaboration than a trumpet battle; in fact, the brass giants only trade off briefly on "Lotus Blossom." —*Scott Yanow, Cadence*

Life Flight / Jan. 23, 1987-Jan. 24, 1987 / Blue Note ✦✦✦✦
This CD captures the great trumpeter Freddie Hubbard at the age of 48 just before he began to decline. Hubbard is heard in excellent shape on two selections each with two separate bands. One group, a sextet with tenor saxophonist Stanley Turrentine and guitarist George Benson, recalls the trumpeter's glory days on CTI although the material ("Battlescar Galorica" and "A Saint's Homecoming Song") was of recent vintage. The other band, a quintet with tenor saxophonist Ralph Moore, looks back towards his earlier Blue Note and Atlantic days; they perform two Hubbard originals ("The Melting Pot" and "Life Flight"). Overall this set (from an era when the veteran trumpeter was being overshadowed by Wynton Marsalis) gives listeners one of the last opportunities to hear Freddie Hubbard in peak form. —*Scott Yanow*

Eternal Triangle with Woody Shaw / Jun. 11, 1987-Jun. 12, 1987 / Blue Note ✦✦✦
Live at Fat Tuesday / Dec. 6, 1991-Dec. 7, 1991 / Music Masters ✦✦

Helen Humes

b. Jun. 23, 1913, Louisville, KY, **d.** Sep. 9, 1981, Santa Monica, CA
Vocals / Blues, Swing
Helen Humes was a versatile singer equally skilled in blues, swing standards, and ballads. Her cheerful style was always a joy to hear. As a child she played piano and organ in church and made her first recordings (ten blues in 1927) when she was only 13 and 14 years old. In the '30s she worked with Stuff Smith and Al Sears, recording with Harry James in 1937-38. In 1938 Humes joined Count Basie's Orchestra for three years. Since Jimmy Rushing specialized in blues, Humes mostly got stuck singing pop ballads, but she did a fine job. After freelancing in New York (1941-43) and touring with Clarence Love (1943-44), Humes moved to Los Angeles. She began to record as a leader and had a hit in "Be-ba-ba-le-ba"; her 1950 original "Million Dollar Secret" was a classic. Humes sometimes performed with Jazz at the Philharmonic but was mostly a single in the '50s. She recorded three superb albums for Contemporary during 1959-61 and had tours with Red Norvo. She moved to Australia in 1964, returning to the US in 1967 to take care of her ailing mother. Humes was out of the music business for several years, but made a full comeback in 1973 and stayed busy up until her death. Throughout her career Humes recorded for such labels as Savoy, Aladdin, Decca, Dootone, Contemporary, Classic Jazz, Black & Blue, Black Lion, Jazzology, Columbia, and Muse. —*Scott Yanow*

Tain't Nobody's Biz-Ness If I Do / Jan. 5, 1959-Feb. 10, 1959 / Original Jazz Classics ✦✦✦✦
This Helen Humes date will lock in one's mind—because she was one of the immediately identifiable jazz stylists and because it was an excellent example, perhaps one of the best post-Count Basie days examples, of her

work. Emotion, open, warm and swinging, is what you've got here. —*Bob Rusch*

★ **Songs I Like to Sing** / Sep. 6, 1960-Sep. 8, 1960 / Original Jazz Classics ✦✦✦✦

Nice, classy set from vocalist Helen Humes, who enjoyed success throughout her career singing everything from classic blues to jazz and gospel to rock. She sticks to jazz on this 1960 date, doing both scat and sophisticated ballads. —*Ron Wynn*

Swingin' with Humes / Jul. 27, 1961-Jul. 29, 1961 / Original Jazz Classics ✦✦✦✦

A solid early '60s set by vocalist Helen Humes, doing a program of standards with a fine combo sparked by tenor saxophonist Teddy Edwards and trumpeter Joe Gordon. The four-member rhythm section includes pianist Wynton Kelly, guitarist Al Viola, bassist Leroy Vinnegar, and drummer Frank Butler. —*Ron Wynn*

On the Sunny Side of The Street / Jul. 2, 1974 / Black Lion ✦✦✦✦

Several major jazz personalities are heard on this Black Lion reissue CD, recorded live at the 1974 Montreux Jazz Festival. The fine singer Helen Humes sticks to standards and blues while accompanied by either Earl Hines or Jay McShann on piano, tenor saxophonist Buddy Tate, bassist Jimmy Woode, and drummer Ed Thigpen. Although Hines and McShann are not the ideal accompanists, Humes fares quite well, winning the audience over with her enthusiasm and sincerity. —*Scott Yanow*

Helen / Jun. 17, 1980 & Jun. 19, 1980 / Muse ✦✦✦✦

Helen Humes was one of the most appealing jazz singers of the late '30s, and of the late '70s. Her comeback in her last few years was a happy event and all of her recordings for Muse are recommended. This one finds her backed by a veteran sextet including tenorman Buddy Tate, trumpeter Joe Wilder, and pianist Norman Simmons. Her versions of "There'll Be Some Changes Made," "Easy Living" and "Draggin' My Heart Around" are particularly memorable. —*Scott Yanow*

Bobby Hutcherson

b. Jan. 27, 1941, Los Angeles, CA
Marimbas, Vibes / Post-Bop, Hard Bop

Although when he first came up vibraphonist Bobby Hutcherson was associated with the avant-garde, he has since settled down into being "merely" a brilliant stylist whose playing falls between hard bop and post bop rather than an innovator. Hutcherson originally studied piano and then started concentrating on vibes as a teenager. He worked in the Los Angeles area with Curtis Amy and Charles Lloyd before joining the Al Grey-Billy Mitchell Quintet. Hutcherson moved to New York in 1961, made a big impression with his playing on Eric Dolphy's *Out to Lunch* (1964), and worked with everyone from Jackie McLean, Hank Mobley, and Grachan Moncur, III, to Hank Mobley, Herbie Hancock, Andrew Hill, McCoy Tyner, and Grant Green. Whenever an advanced vibraphonist was needed for a recording, Hutcherson got the call. He recorded a long series of albums as a leader for Blue Note (1965-77), co-led a quintet with Harold Land (1967-71), and has headed his own groups ever since other than his dates with the Timeless All Stars in the '80s. In addition to Blue Note, Bobby Hutcherson has recorded as a leader for Cadet, Columbia, Timeless, Evidence, Contemporary, and Landmark. —*Scott Yanow*

☆ **Dialogue** / Apr. 3, 1965 / Blue Note ✦✦✦✦✦

An album that was a landmark work in its time, this still has an edgy, avant-garde feeling, thanks to Sam Rivers (ts) and Andrew Hill (p). —*Ron Wynn*

● **Components** / Jun. 14, 1965 / Blue Note ✦✦✦✦

This CD reissue spans a wide variety of styles, from hard bop (Bobby Hutcherson's attractive "Little B's Poem") to mostly atonal sound explorations ("Air"). There are four compositions apiece by the vibraphonist/leader and drummer Joe Chambers with Chambers tending to be freer and more avant-garde. The talented young musicians (trumpeter Freddie Hubbard, James Spaulding on alto and flute, pianist Herbie Hancock, bassist Ron Carter, Chambers, and Hutcherson) are up to the challenge and the results are always stimulating. Open-eared listeners are advised to pick up this CD, taken from a period when the versatile Bobby Hutcherson was considered one of the brightest new voices of what was called "the New Thing." —*Scott Yanow*

Happenings / Feb. 8, 1966 / Blue Note ✦✦✦✦

This is an excellent showcase for Bobby Hutcherson who plays vibes and marimba in a quartet with pianist Herbie Hancock, bassist Bob Cranshaw, and drummer Joe Chambers. On the straight CD reissue of the original LP, Hutcherson performs six of his diverse originals (which range from advanced hard bop to the nearly free form "The Omen") plus Hancock's "Maiden Voyage." Hutcherson's outings on marimba are particularly interesting since they show the influence of modern classical music. His own style would become more conservative and predictable through the years, making Bobby Hutcherson's earlier records the ones to get for adventurous listeners. —*Scott Yanow*

Total Eclipse / Jul. 12, 1967 / Blue Note ✦✦✦✦

Although thought of as an avant-garde vibraphonist when he first emerged, Bobby Hutcherson eventually became an important part of the modern mainstream. This set, with its modal originals, is somewhere in between where Hutcherson had been and where he was going. Joined by tenor saxophonist Harold Land (with whom he had just started co-leading a quintet) and the up-and-coming pianist Chick Corea, Hutcherson is in excellent form on four of his originals and Corea's "Matrix." —*Scott Yanow*

Oblique / Jul. 21, 1967 / Blue Note ✦✦✦✦

A Blue Note date reissued. Interesting dialogs with Herbie Hancock (k). —*Ron Wynn*

Patterns / Mar. 14, 1968 / Blue Note ✦✦✦

Bobby Hutcherson was one of the last viable jazz artists to be associated with the original Blue Note label. His *Patterns* from 1968 has concise but searching solos from the leader, James Spaulding (a major but underrated talent) on alto and flute, and pianist Stanley Cowell; drummer Joe Chambers contributed four of the six tunes. The music is complex but coherent and surprisingly accessible due to the lightly funky rhythms and some long melody statements. —*Scott Yanow*

Medina / Aug. 11, 1969 / Blue Note ✦✦✦✦

The Bobby Hutcherson-Harold Land Quintet was one of the main unsung groups of this era. Not avant-garde enough to be grouped with the free jazz innovators and owing nothing to fusion, vibraphonist Hutcherson and tenor saxophonist Land seemed to fall between the cracks, as bandleaders if not as solo musicians. This 1969 recording, not released until 1980, teams the co-leaders with pianist Stanley Cowell, bassist Reggie Johnson, and drummer Joe Chambers for a variety of complex originals; two apiece by Hutcherson, Cowell, and Chambers. The modal music is between hard bop and the avant-garde but can simply be called explorative and unpredictable. —*Scott Yanow*

Blow Up / 1969 / Jazz Music Yesterday ✦✦✦

This wonderful concert recording of the Hutcherson/Land group never surfaced until now. —*Ron Wynn*

Now / 1969 / Blue Note ✦✦✦

San Francisco / Jul. 15, 1970 / Blue Note ✦✦✦✦

This CD reissue is an exact duplicate of the original LP. Vibraphonist Bobby Hutcherson and tenor saxophonist Harold Land co-led a quintet on the West Coast for quite a few years. The remainder of the personnel was often open to change and on this particular release the duo is augmented by keyboardist Joe Sample (normally with The Jazz Crusaders at the time), bassist John Williams, and drummer Mickey Roker. The music is often quite advanced, yet more accessible than one would expect. There are hints of rock rhythms on a few tracks along with modal melodies influenced by John Coltrane and plenty of rewarding solos from the co-leaders. —*Scott Yanow*

Head on / 1971 / Cadet ✦✦✦

Another super work, among the last for the Hutcherson/Land unit. —*Ron Wynn*

In San Francisco / 1971 / Blue Note ✦✦✦✦

This studio date with saxophonist Harold Land and Joe Sample (p) is one in a series of excellent records from this premier jazz quintet. —*Michael G. Nastos*

Natural Illusions / Mar. 2, 1972 & Mar. 3, 1972 / Blue Note ✦✦

Live at Montreux / Jul. 5, 1973 / Blue Note ✦✦✦✦

By 1973 Blue Note was pretty well a dead label and this often-brilliant advanced hard bop set was only released at the time in Europe and Japan. Now with the CD reissue, Americans can finally hear the mutually inspiring performance of vibraphonist Bobby Hutcherson and trumpeter Woody Shaw. Joined by a fine rhythm section, they create fiery solos on modal originals with Shaw in particular in prime form. Highly recommended. —*Scott Yanow*

Solo / Quartet / Sep. 28, 1981-Mar. 1, 1982 / Original Jazz Classics ✦✦✦✦

This is one of vibraphonist Bobby Hutcherson's most unusual and interesting releases. The first half of the set features Hutcherson all by himself although, by utilizing overdubbing, he almost sounds like Max Roach's M'Boom ensemble. Hutcherson is heard on vibes, marimbas, bass marimba, chimes, xylophone, and bells and these three selections are quite fun and energetic. The second half is more conventional, with Hutcherson welcoming pianist McCoy Tyner (in his first sideman appearance in a decade), bassist Herbie Lewis, and drummer Billy Higgins for two standards and a pair of the vibist's originals. The quartet set is excellent but it is Bobby Hutcherson's solo performances that are most memorable and unique. —*Scott Yanow*

Farewell to Keystone / Jul. 10, 1982-Jul. 11, 1982 / Evidence ✦✦✦✦

Vibist Bobby Hutcherson paid the storied Keystone Korner a wonderful tribute by cutting one of the last live dates done there in July of 1982; the club closed almost exactly a year later. Hutcherson's swinging, joyous phrases and bluesy riffs were nicely buttressed by the hard-driving tenor sax of Harold Land, plus excellent rhythm section assistance and textures from pianist Cedar Walton, bassist Buster Williams, and drummer Billy Higgins. Trumpeter Oscar Brashear added competent solos and meshed smoothly in the ensembles. —*Ron Wynn*

● **In the Vanguard** / Dec. 5, 1986 & Dec. 6, 1986 / Landmark ✦✦✦✦
Vibraphonist Bobby Hutcherson was once associated with the avant-garde to a certain extent but by the '70s it was clear he had found his voice in the modern mainstream of jazz. This live set from the Village Vanguard features him on both vibes and marimbas with stellar sidemen: pianist Kenny Barron, bassist Buster Williams, and drummer Al Foster. Their repertoire (in addition to Hutcherson's "I Wanna Stand over There") is comprised of five standards and the results are high-quality modern bebop. The communication between the players is quite impressive. —*Scott Yanow*

Cruisin' the Bird / Apr. 15, 1988 & Apr. 16, 1988 / Landmark ✦✦✦✦
Both reverential and intense. —*Ron Wynn*

Mirage / Feb. 15, 1991 & Feb. 18, 1991 / Landmark ✦✦✦

Landmarks / Feb. 12, 1992 / Landmark ✦✦✦

Acoustic Masters II / Mar. 1993 / Atlantic ✦✦✦✦

Dick Hyman

b. Mar. 8, 1927, New York, NY
Piano / Swing, Stride, Classic Jazz
A very versatile virtuoso, Dick Hyman once recorded an album on which he played "A Child Is Born" in the styles of 11 different pianists from Scott Joplin to Cecil Taylor. Hyman can clearly play anything he wants and during the past two decades he has mostly concentrated on pre-bop swing and stride styles. Hyman worked with Red Norvo (1949-50) and Benny Goodman (1950) and then spent much of the '50s and '60s as a studio musician. He appears on the one known sound film of Charlie Parker (*Hot House* from 1952), recorded honky tonk under pseudonyms, played organ and early synthesizers in addition to piano, was Arthur Godfrey's music director (1959-62), collaborated with Leonard Feather on some History of Jazz concerts (doubling on clarinet), and even performed rock and free jazz, but all of this was a prelude to his present-day work. In the '70s Hyman played with the New York Jazz Repertory Company, formed the Perfect Jazz Repertory Quintet (1976), and started writing soundtracks for Woody Allen films. He has recorded frequently during the past 20 years (sometimes in duets with Ruby Braff) for Concord, Music Masters, and Reference and ranks at the top of the classic jazz field. —*Scott Yanow*

Charleston / Apr. 29, 1975-May 29, 1975 / Columbia ✦✦✦✦

Themes and Variations on "A Child Is Born" / Oct. 11, 1977-Oct. 12, 1977 / Chiaroscuro ✦✦✦✦
Dick Hyman took "A Child Is Born" and beat it to death by playing it not only in his style, but also in the style of 11 other pianists (Scott Joplin, Jelly Roll Morton, James P. Johnson, Fats Waller, Earl Hines, Teddy Wilson, Erroll Garner, George Shearing, Cecil Taylor, Art Tatum, and Bill Evans). —*Bob Rusch, Cadence*

☆ **Music of Jelly Roll Morton** / Feb. 26, 1978 / Smithsonian ✦✦✦✦✦
Of all the Jelly Roll Morton tribute albums that have been recorded through the years, Dick Hyman's is one of the most rewarding. He uses a suitable septet (with clarinetist Bob Wilber, trumpeter Warren Vache, trombonist Jack Gale, Marty Grosz on guitar and banjo, Major Holley doubling on bass and tuba, and Morton alumnus Tommy Benford on drums) on nine of Morton's best tunes, including two ("King Porter Stomp" and "Wolverine Blues") not recorded by Morton in this format. In addition, there is a close recreation of the quartet piece "Mournful Serenade," a couple of trios with Wilber and Benford, and two piano solos ("Fingerbreaker" and "The Pearls") that give Hyman an opportunity to do his Jelly Roll Morton impressions. This LP should satisfy all traditional jazz fans. —*Scott Yanow*

Live At Michael's Pub / Jul. 24, 1981-Jul. 25, 1981 / JazzMania ✦✦✦✦

Manhattan Jazz / 1987 / Music Masters ✦✦✦✦
With Ruby Braff. A wonderful, if very dated, example of vintage swing-era material. It's not traditional, simply a classic approach. —*Ron Wynn*

Face the Music: A Century of Irving Berlin / Dec. 8, 1987-Dec. 9, 1987 / Music Masters ✦✦✦✦
A tribute to Irving Berlin, done by various artists. Interesting, but nothing fresh. —*Ron Wynn*

● **Plays Fats Waller** / Dec. 1988 / Reference ✦✦✦✦
Pianist Dick Hyman has mastered reproducing classic songs by jazz masters without losing his identity. That was the case on this Fats Waller tribute done directly to disc. Hyman neatly, respectfully, and flawlessly plays such songs as "Honeysuckle Rose" and "Ain't Misbehavin'," captures and reproduces the rhythms and spirit, and injects enough personal twists and phrases to show he understands that he's not Fats Waller, just someone who loves his music and wants to convey its importance to the listener. —*Ron Wynn*

Plays Duke Ellington / Aug. 23, 1992 / Reference ✦✦✦✦

The Gershwin Songbook: Jazz Variations / Sep. 15, 1992-Sep. 16, 1992 / Music Masters ✦✦✦

● **Dick Hyman/Ralph Sutton** / 1993 / Concord Jazz ✦✦✦✦
The two top living stride pianists, Dick Hyman and Ralph Sutton, are teamed up for an exciting live duo session recorded at Maybeck Recital Hall. Hearing the two masters explore jazz standards (mostly from the pre-1940 era) is analogous to seeing Fats Waller and James P. Johnson sharing the same stage in the '30s. Somehow Hyman and Sutton leave just enough room for the other one to slip in and the ensembles, although sometimes bursting at the seams, are never overcrowded. Sutton has "Everything Happens to Me" as his ballad feature while Hyman tears into "Old Man River" by himself, but it is the stomps by the duo (such as "Sunday," "Dinah," "The World Is Waiting for the Sunrise," and "I'm Sorry I Made You Cry") that make the session so memorable. This historic encounter is a gem. —*Scott Yanow*

Abdullah (Dollar Brand) Ibrahim
(Adolph Johannes Brand)

b. Oct. 9, 1934, Cape Town, South Africa
Piano / Africa, Post-Bop
A highly individual pianist/composer whose music is influenced by Duke Ellington, Thelonious Monk, and especially his own South African heritage, Abdullah Ibrahim (who until the '70s was known as Dollar Brand) performs explorative originals that are full of strong melodies and spirituality. He started on piano when he was seven and was a member of the Jazz Epistles, recording South Africa's first jazz album in 1960. Ibrahim and his future wife, singer Sathima Bea Benjamin, went into self-imposed exile from the apartheid system in 1962, going to Zurich. Duke Ellington heard them perform and arranged for recording sessions. Ibrahim was also sponsored by Ellington at the 1965 Newport Jazz Festival and even got to sub for him with his orchestra during a tour. In 1966 Ibrahim worked with Elvin Jones but otherwise he has generally been a bandleader. He has recorded for many labels in settings ranging from being a piano soloist and head of a large band to his septet Ekaya including numerous sessions for Enja. Ibrahim, who visited South Africa in 1976, has returned home several times since its liberation from apartheid. —*Scott Yanow*

★ **Anatomy of a South African Village** / Jan. 30, 1965 / Black Lion ✦✦✦✦✦
A sublime, transcendent date. Trio live at Cafe Montmartre in Copenhagen. Rare. —*Michael G. Nastos*

Sangoma / Feb. 18, 1973 / Sackville ✦✦✦✦
The great South African musician Abdullah Ibrahim (then going by his original name of Dollar Brand) performs a six-song suite dedicated to his main influences "Fats, Duke, and the Monk," along with a couple of three-part originals: "The Aloe and the Wild Rose" and "Ancient Africa." Ibrahim's distinctive percussive style with its emphasis on folk melodies was very much in evidence at this relatively early stage. —*Scott Yanow*

African Space Program / Nov. 7, 1973 / Enja ✦✦✦
Poorly recorded, but a great 12-piece group date. —*Ron Wynn*

The Banyana: Children of Africa / Jan. 27, 1976 / Enja ✦✦✦

Africa: Tears and Laughter / Mar. 11, 1979 / Enja ✦✦✦

Echoes from Africa / Sep. 7, 1979 / Enja ✦✦✦

Mantra Mode / 1991 / Enja ✦✦✦✦
This was a very special recording for pianist/composer Abdullah Ibrahim because, after nearly 30 years of exile, he was back in Cape Town, South Africa performing with local musicians. The musicianship is surprisingly high and the African septet does a fine job of interpreting eight of Ibrahim's newer folk melodies. —*Scott Yanow*

Irakere

Group / Cuba, Latin Continuum, Afro-Cuban Jazz
Many of the top Cuban jazz musicians have played in Irakere during the past 23 years including altoist Paquito D'Rivera and trumpeter Arturo Sandoval (before both individually defected). Pianist Chucho Valdes has been the orchestra's longtime leader and its music ranges from Latin-jazz and bop to Cuban folk melodies with an emphasis on infectious rhythms and advanced improvisations. Several of Irakere's records have been made available domestically (including sets for Columbia and more recently Jazz House) but the exciting band has never been allowed to visit the US —*Scott Yanow*

★ **Live at Ronnie Scott's** / Sep. 1991 / World Pacific ✦✦✦✦✦
In Irakere's earlier days, this premiere Cuban group often had to disguise the fact that they were playing imperalistic music from the West (i.e., jazz). Maybe now the masquerade is no longer necessary, for the music on this definitive CD would never be mistaken for anything else. Heavily influenced both by Dizzy Gillespie and the rhythms of Cuba and South America, the 11-piece group is in top form interpreting the compositions of its pianist/leader Chuco Valdes (who has a memorable workout on "Mr. Bruce"). Five of the six selections are primaily features for individual players. Throughout this memorable set, the ensemble work is clean and loose,

the percussionists keep the proceedings fiery and the soloists are excellent. —*Scott Yanow*

Milt Jackson

b. Jan. 1, 1923, Detroit, MI
Vibes / Bop, Hard Bop
Before Milt Jackson there were only two major vibraphonists: Lionel Hampton and Red Norvo. Jackson soon surpassed both of them in significance and, despite the rise of other players (including Bobby Hutcherson and Gary Burton), still wins the popularity polls. Jackson (or Bags as he has long been called) has been at the top of his field for 50 years, playing bop, blues, and ballads with equal skill and sensitivity.

Milt Jackson started on guitar when he was seven and piano at 11; a few years later he switched to vibes. He actually made his professional debut singing in a touring gospel quartet. After Dizzy Gillespie discovered him playing in Detroit, he offered him a job with his sextet and (shortly after) his innovative big band (1946). Jackson recorded with Dizzy and was soon in great demand. During 1948-49 he worked with Charlie Parker, Thelonious Monk, Howard McGhee, and the Woody Herman Orchestra. After playing with Gillespie's sextet (1950-52), which at one point included John Coltrane, Jackson recorded with a quartet comprised of John Lewis, Percy Heath, and Kenny Clarke (1952), which soon became a regular group called the Modern Jazz Quartet. Although he recorded regularly as a leader (including dates in the '50s with Miles Davis and/or Thelonious Monk, Coleman Hawkins, John Coltrane, and Ray Charles), Jackson stayed with the MJQ through 1974, becoming an indispensable part of their sound. By the mid-'50s Lewis became the musical director and some felt that Jackson was restricted by the format but it actually served him well, giving him some challenging settings. And he always had an opportunity to jam on some blues, including his "Bags' Groove." However in 1974 Jackson felt frustrated by the MJQ (particularly financially) and broke up the group. He recorded frequently for Pablo in many all-star settings in the '70s and after a seven-year vacation the MJQ came back in 1981. In addition to the MJQ recordings, Jackson cut records as a leader throughout his career for many labels including Savoy, Blue Note (1952), Prestige, Atlantic, United Artists, Impulse, Riverside, Limelight, Verve, CTI, Pablo, Music Masters, and Qwest. —*Scott Yanow*

In the Beginning / Apr. 1948 / Original Jazz Classics ✦✦✦
This is a very interesting CD, particularly for bop collectors, since it contains very rare early performances by altoist Sonny Stitt and vibraphonist Milt Jackson; some of the titles were originally under trumpeter Russell Jacquet's name. There are eight songs by a quintet with Stitt, Jacquet, and pianist Sir Charles Thompson, what could be considered the first Modern Jazz Quartet records (actually a quintet with Milt Jackson, pianist John Lewis, drummer Kenny Clarke, bassist Al Jackson, and Chano Pozo on congas) and five songs from a septet with Jacquet, Stitt, trombonist J.J. Johnson, and baritonist Leo Parker. Recorded in Detroit for the tiny Galaxy label, these performances are not essential but they do give listeners an early glimpse at the future stars. —*Scott Yanow*

Milt Jackson Quartet / May 20, 1955 / Original Jazz Classics ✦✦✦

Opus De Jazz / Oct. 28, 1955 / Savoy ✦✦✦

● **Plenty, Plenty Soul** / Jan. 5, 1957 / Atlantic ✦✦✦✦
This superior reissue combines together two sessions led by vibraphonist Milt Jackson. Actually, although Jackson is in fine form (and contributed four of the seven selections), he is often overshadowed by rather inspired solos from his sidemen. The first side of this LP, which features a nine-piece group, is highlighted by the contributions of the exuberant altoist Cannonball Adderley, while the flip side has a sextet that is not hurt by the solos of tenor saxophonist Lucky Thompson. With pianist Horace Silver helping out on both dates, these all-star dates still sound fresh and enthusiastic decades later. —*Scott Yanow*

Bags' Opus / Dec. 28, 1958-Dec. 29, 1958 / Blue Note ✦✦✦✦
Vibraphonist Milt Jackson welcomes the two future co-leaders of The Jazztet (trumpeter Art Farmer and tenor saxophonist Benny Golson) along with a fine rhythm section (pianist Tommy Flanagan, bassist Paul Chambers, and drummer Connie Kay) on this CD reissue. The repertoire (which includes early versions of Golson's "Whisper Not" and "I Remember Clifford" in addition to two standards, a Milt Jackson blues and John Lewis' "Afternoon in Paris") is very much in the Jazztet hard bop vein and Jackson fits in very well with the two lyrical horn soloists. A successful outing by some of the greats. —*Scott Yanow*

☆ **Bags and Trane** / Jan. 15, 1959 / Atlantic ✦✦✦✦✦
Vibraphonist Milt Jackson and tenor saxophonist John Coltrane make for a surprisingly complementary team on this 1959 studio session, their only joint recording. With fine backup by pianist Hank Jones, bassist Paul Chambers, and drummer Connie Kay, Jackson and Coltrane stretch out on two of Jackson's originals (including "The Late Late Blues") and three standards: a romping "Three Little Words," "The Night We Called It a Day," and the rapid "Be-Bop." This enjoyable music has been included as part of Rhino's *Complete Coltrane on Atlantic* box. —*Scott Yanow*

Bags Meets Wes / Dec. 18, 1961 & Dec. 19, 1961 / Original Jazz Classics ✦✦✦✦
His Riverside debut album was a stunner. Wonderful Wes Montgomery guitar. —*Ron Wynn*

Big Bags / Jun. 19, 1962-Jul. 1962 / Original Jazz Classics ✦✦✦✦
Vibraphonist Milt Jackson is backed by a big band for this change-of-pace release, reissued on CD along with two alternate takes. The Ernie Wilkins and Tadd Dameron arrangements fit the high-quality standards well and Jackson (who contributed two originals) is in top form. There were short solos for cornetist Nat Adderley, trombonist Jimmy Cleveland, and the tenors of James Moody and Jimmy Heath, but Milt Jackson is the main voice throughout this melodic and always-swinging set. —*Scott Yanow*

Invitation / Aug. 30, 1962-Nov. 7, 1962 / Original Jazz Classics ✦✦✦

For Someone I Love / Mar. 19, 1963 / Original Jazz Classics ✦✦✦✦
The main reason for this CD reissue's success is Melba Liston's inventive and unpredictable arrangements for the brass orchestra. Vibraphonist Milt Jackson has nearly all the solos (although trumpeter Clark Terry, trombonist Quentin Jackson, Julius Watkins on French horn, and Major Holley on tuba do make their presence known) and seems understandably inspired by the backup orchestra which consists of four or five trumpets, three trombones, three or four French horns, Holley's tuba, and a rhythm section. The well conceived set (which includes such songs as "Days of Wine and Roses," "Save Your Love for Me," some Duke Ellington ballads, and "Bossa Bags") is consistently excellent, making this a highly recommended set. —*Scott Yanow*

Live at the Village Gate / Dec. 9, 1963 / Original Jazz Classics ✦✦✦✦
Vibraphonist Milt Jackson's own sessions outside of the Modern Jazz Quartet tend to be hard-swinging jams through attractive chord changes, a mixture of boppish romps, and thoughtful ballad statements. Jackson has frequently worked with tenors and Jimmy Heath, who is well featured throughout this set (a CD reissue that brings back an earlier LP plus two "new" selections) became an occasional associate. With fine work by pianist Hank Jones, bassist Bob Cranshaw, and drummer Al "Tootie" Heath, Jackson is in typically swinging form on some blues, standards, ballads, and Jimmy Heath's "Gemini." —*Scott Yanow*

Olinga / Jan. 1974 / Columbia ✦✦✦

★ **The Big 3** / Aug. 25, 1975 / Pablo ✦✦✦✦✦
This CD (a straight reissue of the original LP) features a rather notable pianoless combo: vibraphonist Milt Jackson, guitarist Joe Pass, and bassist Ray Brown. During the Pablo years these three masterful players recorded together in many settings but only this once as a trio. The colorful repertoire (which ranges from "The Pink Panther" and "Blue Bossa" to "Nuages" and "Come Sunday") acts as a device for the musicians to construct some brilliant bop-based solos. —*Scott Yanow*

Night Mist / Apr. 14, 1980 / Original Jazz Classics ✦✦✦✦
Most of vibraphonist Milt Jackson's recordings as a leader have been at the head of a quartet or quintet. This spirited set has a variety of "near blues" material being interpreted by an all-star septet featuring such unique voices as trumpeter Harry "Sweets" Edison, the tenor of Eddie "Lockjaw" Davis, and altoist Eddie "Cleanhead" Vinson in addition to Jackson, pianist Art Hillery, bassist Ray Brown, and drummer Larance Marable. There are plenty of magical moments created on this set by these classic jazzmen. —*Scott Yanow*

★ **Mostly Duke** / Apr. 23, 1982-Apr. 24, 1982 / Pablo ✦✦✦✦✦
The third of three sets released by Pablo from Milt Jackson's engagement at Ronnie Scott's Club in London in 1982 (this CD first came out in 1991) lives up to its title. The great vibraphonist, pianist Monty Alexander, bassist Ray Brown, and drummer Mickey Roker play two standards, the leader's "Used to Be Jackson" and six songs associated with Duke Ellington. The music swings hard, Alexander competes with Bags for solo honors, and the music should please all straightahead jazz fans. —*Scott Yanow*

Bebop / 1988 / East West ✦✦✦

The Prophet Speaks / 1994 / Qwest ✦✦✦✦
Forty-eight years after he first made a major impression on a Dizzy Gillespie recording date, vibraphonist Milt Jackson proved that he was still at the top of his form on this CD. The happy straightahead date finds his quartet (with pianist Cedar Walton, bassist John Clayton, and drummer Billy Higgins) welcoming guests Joshua Redman (whose tenor is on six of the dozen selections) and singer Joe Williams who helps out on three songs. Redman easily fits into the role that other tenors (such as Teddy Edwards and Jimmy Heath) have had with Jackson, taking concise solos while allowing the great vibist to be the lead in most of the ensembles. Joe Williams is fine during his three spots, but it is the apparently ageless Milt Jackson who is the main star during this enjoyable set. —*Scott Yanow*

Ronald Shannon Jackson

b. Jan. 12, 1940, Fort Worth, TX
Guitar / Hard Bop
Drummer Ronald Shannon Jackson and his Decoding Society of the '80s

learned from the example of Ornette Coleman's Prime Time and are a logical extension of the group. They featured colorful and noisy ensembles, were not afraid of the influence of rock, and their rhythms were funky, loud and unpredictable. Jackson played professionally in Texas with James Clay when he was 15. He moved to New York in 1966 where he worked with Byard Lancaster, Charles Mingus, Betty Carter, Stanley Turrentine, Jackie McLean, McCoy Tyner, Kenny Dorham, and most significantly Albert Ayler (1966-67) among others. He took time off the scene and then joined Ornette Coleman's Prime Time (1975-79). Jackson also worked with Cecil Taylor (1978-79) and James "Blood" Ulmer (1979-80). The Decoding Society (formed in 1979) through the years featured many talented and advanced improvisers with the best-known ones being Vernon Reid, Zane Massey, Billy Bang, and Byard Lancaster. Jackson also played with the explosive group Last Exit (starting in 1986) and in the early '90s with Power Tools. Ronald Shannon Jackson's music is not for easy-to-offend ears! —*Scott Yanow*

★ **Eye on You** / 1980 / About Time ✦✦✦✦✦
Drummer Roland Shannon Jackson's Decoding Society on this LP is comprised of quite an all-star lineup: violinist Billy Bang, altoist Byard Lancaster, tenor saxophonist Charles Brackeen, Vernon Reid and Bern Nix on guitars, bassist Melvin Gibbs, and percussionist Erasto Vasconcelos. The Decoding Society plays what could be called "free funk," a combination of loud funky rhythms with free jazz and the melodics pioneered by Ornette Coleman's Prime Time. Everyone solos together constantly, leading to dense and exciting ensembles that are overflowing with passion. Although this style of jazz (a forerunner of Steve Coleman's groups) never really caught on, the music is quite stimulating and a logical extension of '70s fusion. —*Scott Yanow*

Mandance / Jun. 1982 / Antilles ✦✦✦✦
The ensemble-oriented "free funk" music of drummer Roland Shannon Jackson's Decoding Society never can be accused of being overly mellow or lacking in excitement. The 1982 version of his band features trumpeter Henry Scott, Zane Massey on reeds, guitarist Vernon Reid, and both Melvin Gibbs and Bruce Johnson on electric basses. The frenetic and intense ensembles (essentially everyone solos at once) would not be classified as relaxing background music. —*Scott Yanow*

Barbeque Dog / Mar. 1983 / Antilles ✦✦✦✦
Erratic, powerful, and explosive. —*Ron Wynn*

Pulse / Jan. 1984 / Celluloid ✦✦✦✦
Furious, classic jazz-rock in the absolute sense of the term, plus some free and R&B influences filtered through the compositions as well. Drummer Ronald Shannon Jackson has played with Ornette Coleman and Cecil Taylor and led his own Decoding Society band. His music rips and roars, while seamlessly moving through multiple idioms, sometimes blurring and combining them as he goes along. —*Ron Wynn*

Red Warrior / 1990 / Axiom ✦✦✦

Taboo / 1990 / Venture ✦✦✦
Some dynamic adventures with Vernon Reid (g) venturing outside Living Colour arena. —*Ron Wynn*

Willis "Gator" Jackson

b. Apr. 25, 1932, Miami, FL, **d.** Oct. 25, 1987, New York, NY
Sax (Tenor) / Soul-Jazz, Hard Bop, Early R&B, Groove
An exciting tenor saxophonist whose honking and squeals (although influenced by Illinois Jacquet) were quite distinctive, Willis Jackson was also a strong improviser who sounded perfectly at home with organ groups. He played locally in Florida early on until joining Cootie Williams (on and off during 1948-55). His two-sided honking feature "Gator Tail" with Williams (which earned him a lifelong nickname) was a hit in 1948 and he started recording as a leader in 1950. Jackson was married to singer Ruth Brown for eight years and often appeared on her recordings during this era. His extensive series of Prestige recordings (1959-64) made him a big attraction on the organ circuit. Although generally overlooked by critics, Willis Jackson continued working steadily in the '70s and '80s. In 1977 he recorded one of the finest albums of his career for Muse, *Bar Wars*. —*Scott Yanow*

★ **Call of the Gators** / Dec. 21, 1949-May 2, 1949 / Delmark ✦✦✦✦✦

On My Own / 1950 / Whiskey Women And... ✦✦✦
1950-1955. Frenetic soul-jazz, with torrid organ from Charles Earland. —*Ron Wynn*

Please Mr. Jackson / May 25, 1959 / Original Jazz Classics ✦✦✦✦
Quintet. 1988 reissue of fine soul-jazz date. —*Ron Wynn*

★ **Together Again** / May 25, 1959-Aug. 16, 1960 / Prestige ✦✦✦✦✦
Jackson with Jack McDuff on the Hammond B-3 and Bill Jennings on guitar. —*Michael Erlewine*

Together Again, Again / May 25, 1959-Dec. 31, 1961 / Prestige ✦✦✦
Jackson with Jack McDuff on the Hammond B-3 and Bill Jennings on guitar. Tunes like "Snake Crawl" and "Backtrack" should give you a clue as to the music on this album. —*Michael Erlewine*

Gentle Gator / Jan. 10, 1961-Oct. 30, 1962 / Prestige ✦✦

Thunderbird / Mar. 31, 1962 / Prestige ✦✦✦✦
Great Jackson, robust Freddy Roach organ. —*Ron Wynn*

★ **Shuckin'** / Oct. 30, 1962 / Prestige ✦✦✦✦✦
His second great album that year. All-star lineup included Kenny Burrell (g), Tommy Flanagan (p). —*Ron Wynn*

Loose / Mar. 26, 1963 / Prestige ✦✦✦
Willis Jackson with Carl Wilson on Hammond organ. —*Michael Erlewine*

Grease N' Gravy / May 23, 1963 / Prestige ✦✦✦
Willis Jackson with Carl Wilson on organ. —*Michael Erlewine*

The Good Life / May 23, 1963 / Prestige ✦✦✦
With Carl Wilson on Hammond organ. —*AMG*

More Gravy / Oct. 24, 1963 / Prestige ✦✦✦
Still more. Jackson with Carl Wilson on Hammond organ. —*Michael Erlewine*

Boss Shoutin' / Jan. 9, 1964 / Prestige ✦✦✦
Willis Jackson with Carl Wilson on Hammond organ. —*Michael Erlewine*

With Pat Martino / Mar. 21, 1964 / Prestige ✦✦✦✦
Although guitarist Pat Martino (19 at the time) gets second billing on this CD reissue, tenor saxophonist Willis Jackson is the main star throughout. Recorded live at the Allegro in New York, this CD releases the complete contents of two Jackson LPs (*Action* and *Live Action*). "Gator Tail" puts on his usual exuberant show with screams and honks being a logical part of his colorful style. The music, fairly basic material with a few standards and blues tossed in, gives listeners a good example of Jackson's music of the '60s; the quintet also includes trumpeter Frank Robinson, organist Carl Wilson, and drummer Joe Hadrick. An enjoyable crowd-pleasing set. —*Scott Yanow*

Smokin' with Willis / Nov. 15, 1965 / Cadet ✦✦✦

Star Bag / Mar. 22, 1968 / Prestige ✦✦✦
Willis Jackson with Trudy Pitts on the Hammond B-3. —*Michael Erlewine*

West Africa / Oct. 22, 1973 / Muse ✦✦✦

Headed and Gutted / May 16, 1974 / Muse ✦✦✦✦
Brilliant soul-jazz date. —*Ron Wynn*

In the Alley / 1976 / Muse ✦✦✦

☆ **Bar Wars** / Dec. 21, 1977 / Muse ✦✦✦✦✦
Willis Jackson, a veteran of the jazz-oriented R&B music of the late '40s, was a powerful tenor in the tradition of Gene Ammons. This is a particularly exciting release with Charles Earland pumping away at the organ, guitarist Pat Martino offering a contrasting solo voice, and Jackson in top form, wailing away on the uptempo pieces. The CD reissue of the original LP adds two alternate takes to the program. The chord changes might be fairly basic but Jackson plays with such enthusiasm and exuberance that it almost sounds as if he had discovered the joy of playing music. —*Scott Yanow*

Single Action / Apr. 26, 1978 / Muse ✦✦✦✦

Illinois Jacquet (Jean Baptiste Illinois Jacquet)

b. Oct. 31, 1922, Boussard, LA
Sax (Alto), Sax (Tenor) / Bop, Swing, Early R&B, Groove
One of the great tenors, Illinois Jacquet's 1942 "Flying Home" solo is considered the first R&B sax solo and spawned a full generation of younger tenors (including Joe Houston and Big Jay McNeely) who built their careers from his style practically from that one song!

Jacquet, whose older brother Russell (1917-1990) was a trumpeter who sometimes played in his bands, grew up in Houston and his tough-toned and emotional sound defined the Texas tenor school. After playing locally, he moved to Los Angeles where in 1941 he played with Floyd Ray. He was the star of Lionel Hampton's 1942 big band ("Flying Home" became a signature song for Jacquet, Hampton and even Jacquet's successor Arnett Cobb), and also was with Cab Calloway (1943-44) and well featured with Count Basie (1945-46). Jacquet's playing at the first Jazz at the Philharmonic concert (1944) included a screaming solo on "Blues" that found him biting on his reed to achieve high register effects; the crowd went wild. He repeated this idea during his appearance in the 1944 film short *Jammin' the Blues*. In 1945 Jacquet put together his own band and both his recordings and live performances were quite exciting. He appeared with JATP on several tours in the '50s, recorded steadily and never really lost his popularity. In the '60s he sometimes doubled on bassoon (usually for a slow number such as "'Round Midnight") and it was an effective contrast to his stomping tenor. In the late '80s Jacquet started leading an exciting part-time big band that thus far has only recorded one album, an Atlantic date from 1988. Through the years Illinois Jacquet (whose occasional features on alto are quite influenced by Charlie Parker) has recorded as a leader for such labels as Apollo, Savoy, Aladdin, RCA, Verve, Mercury, Roulette, Epic, Argo, Prestige, Black Lion, Black & Blue, JRC, and Atlantic. —*Scott Yanow*

★ **The Black Velvet Band** / Dec. 18, 1947-Jul. 1967 / Bluebird ✦✦✦✦✦
Prime 8- & 10-piece group cuts from 1947-50, plus one cut from 1967 New-port festival. —*Ron Wynn*

Swing's the Thing / Jul. 1957 / Verve ✦✦✦

Flies Again / Aug. 11, 1959 / Roulette ✦✦✦✦
1991 reissue. Incendiary set. Explosive Jacquet. —*Ron Wynn*

Illinois Jacquet / Feb. 5, 1962-May 21, 1962 / Epic/Legacy ✦✦✦

The Message / May 7, 1963-May 8, 1963 / Argo ✦✦✦

Go Power / Mar. 15, 1966-Mar. 17, 1966 / Cadet ✦✦✦
A rare trio date with Milt Buckner on organ and Alan Dawson on drums.
—*Michael Erlewine*

Bottoms Up / Mar. 26, 1968 / Original Jazz Classics ✦✦✦✦
Even in 1968 when the jazz avant-garde was becoming quite influential, tenor saxophonist Illinois Jacquet played in his own timeless style, per-forming in an idiom little changed during the past 20 years. With the assis-tance of pianist Barry Harris, bassist Ben Tucker, and drummer Alan Daw-son, Jacquet is heard throughout this CD reissue (which adds a previously unissued "Don't Blame Me" to the original program) swinging hard and generally expressing himself in a typically extroverted fashion. "Bottoms Up" (a relative of "Flying Home"), "Jivin' with Jack the Bellboy," and Jac-quet's excellent original ballad "You Left Me All Alone" are most memora-ble. —*Scott Yanow*

The King / Aug. 20, 1968 / Original Jazz Classics ✦✦✦

The Soul Explosion / Mar. 25, 1969 / Original Jazz Classics ✦✦✦✦
The great tenor Illinois Jacquet is joined by a ten-piece group that includes trumpeter Joe Newman and Milt Buckner on piano and organ for this 1969 Prestige studio session which has been reissued on CD by the OJC series. Jacquet is in prime form, particularly on "The Soul Explosion" (which benefits from a Jimmy Mundy arrangement), a definitive "After Hours," and a previously unissued version of "Still King." This blues-based set is full of soul but often swings quite hard with the focus on Jacquet's exciting tenor throughout. —*Scott Yanow*

★ **The Blues: That's Me!** / Sep. 16, 1969 / Original Jazz Classics ✦✦✦✦✦
Tenor saxophonist Illinois Jacquet is heard in top form throughout this quintet set with pianist Wynton Kelly, guitarist Tiny Grimes, bassist Buster Williams, and drummer Oliver Jackson. The music, which falls between swing, bop, and early rhythm & blues, is generally quite exciting, especially "Still King," "Everyday I Have the Blues," and the lengthy title cut. A partic-ular surprise is a moody version of "'Round Midnight" which features some surprisingly effective Illinois Jacquet on bassoon. This CD reissue is highly recommended. —*Scott Yanow*

Genius at Work / Apr. 13, 1971-Apr. 14, 1971 / Jzm ✦✦✦

Illinois Jacquet with Wild Bill Davis / Jan. 15, 1973-Jan. 16, 1973 / Clas-sic Jazz ✦✦✦

Ahmad Jamal

b. Jul. 2, 1930, Pittsburgh, PA
Piano / Cool, Post-Bop
One of the few pianists in the '50s who did not sound like a close copy of Bud Powell, Ahmad Jamal's use of space, ability to gradually increase or decrease the volume with his trio, and brilliant use of tension and release were quite original. He greatly impressed Miles Davis (who borrowed from his repertoire and insisted that Red Garland try to sound like him), and Jamal also cut some very popular records without altering his style.

Jamal began playing professionally in Pittsbrugh when he was 11 years old. In the late '40s he joined George Hudson's Orchestra. In 1951 he formed his first trio, the Three Strings, a group with guitarist Ray Crawford and bassist Eddie Calhoun. Israel Crosby took Calhoun's place in 1955. One of Jamal's recordings from that year was a version of "Pavanne" that at one point states the melody from John Coltrane's "Impressions," five years before 'Trane "wrote" the song! In 1956 Jamal switched to a piano-bass-drums trio with Walter Perkins replacing Crawford. With Vernell Fournier on drums by 1958, Jamal recorded his most popular album, *Ahmad Jamal at the Pershing,* and his version of "Poinciana" is still famous. The trio broke up in 1962 but Jamal continued growing as a pianist (sometimes doubling on electric piano in the '70s), and he remains one of the most dis-tinctive (and indirectly influential) pianists in jazz. Ahmad Jamal recorded through the years for Epic, Argo/Cadet, Impulse, Catalyst, 20th Century, Atlantic, and Telarc. —*Scott Yanow*

★ **At the Pershing/But Not for Me** / Jan. 16, 1958 / Chess ✦✦✦✦✦
Recorded at Pershing Club, Chicago, IL. A two-fer. Third album (includes hit "Poinciana") was the turning point in his career. His liberal use of silence influenced many jazz musicians, including Miles Davis. —*Michael Erlewine*

★ **But Not for Me** / Jan. 16, 1958-Jan. 17, 1958 / Affinity ✦✦✦✦✦
Arguably his greatest album, a smash hit. —*Ron Wynn*

Ahmad Jamal Trio, Vol. 4 / Sep. 5, 1958-Sep. 6, 1958 / Argo ✦✦✦✦
One of his most popular albums ever in its original issue. —*Ron Wynn*

Ahmad's Blues / Sep. 6, 1958 / Chess ✦✦✦✦
This CD reissues most of the music recorded on one night by the 1958 Ahmad Jamal Trio (which consisted of the pianist/leader, bassist Israel Crosby, and drummer Vernel Fournier) during a live performance in Washington D.C. Originally released as the LP *Ahmad Jamal* plus part of *Portfolio of Ahmad Jamal,* these 16 selections display the uniqueness and tightness of this memorable unit. With great attention paid to dynamics and the use of space yet always swinging (at least lightly), the Ahmad Jamal Trio is heard at its best on such numbers as "It Could Happen to You," "Stompin' at the Savoy," "Squatly Roo," "A Gal in Calico," and "Let's Fall in Love." —*Scott Yanow*

The Awakening / Feb. 3, 1970 / MCA ✦✦✦

Freeflight / Jul. 1971 / GRP ✦✦✦✦
This CD reissue from the 1971 Montreux Jazz Festival has one of pianist Ahmad Jamal's finest recordings of the early '70s. Performing with bassist Jamil Sulieman Nasser and drummer Frank Gant, Jamal shows that his basic style has evolved since the '50s but is still quite recognizable. He uses the electric piano as a double for color and stretches out on three numbers (including a remake of his hit "Poinciana") in addition to playing a five-minute version of Herbie Hancock's "Dolphin Dance." An excellent effort. —*Scott Yanow*

Chicago Revisited: Live at Joe / Nov. 13, 1992-Nov. 14, 1992 / Telarc ✦✦✦✦

I Remember Duke, Hoagy & Strayhorn / Jun. 2, 1994-Jun. 3, 1994 / Telarc ✦✦✦✦

Bob James

b. Dec. 25, 1939, Marshall, MO
Keyboards / Instrumental Pop, Crossover
Bob James' recordings have practically defined pop-jazz and crossover dur-ing the past two decades. Very influenced by pop and movie music, James has often featured R&Bish soloists (most notably Grover Washington, Jr.) who add a jazz touch to what is essentially an instrumental pop set. He actually started out in a much different direction. In 1962 Bob James recorded a boppish trio set for Mercury and three years later his album for ESP was quite avant-garde, with electronic tapes used for effects. After a period with Sarah Vaughan (1965-68), he became a studio musician and by 1973 was arranging and working as a producer for CTI. In 1974 James recorded his first purely commercial effort as a leader; he later made big-selling albums for his own Tappan Zee label, Columbia, and Warner Bros., including collaborations with Earl Klugh and David Sanborn. Listeners who prefer challenging jazz to background dance music will be consis-tently disappointed by Bob James' post-1965 albums. —*Scott Yanow*

Explosions / May 10, 1965 / ESP ✦✦✦

One / Apr. 1974 / Warner Bros./Tappan Zee ✦✦✦

Lucky Seven / 1979 / Warner Bros./Tappan Zee ✦✦✦✦
Successful fusion album by a superstar in the genre. James made an art form of short solos, pop-tinged instrumentals, multi-tracked vocals by guest stars, and unchallenging tracks. This album utilized all those ele-ments. —*Ron Wynn*

Sign of the Times / 1979 / Warner Bros./Tappan Zee ✦✦✦

● **Grand Piano Canyon** / 1990 / Warner Bros. ✦✦✦✦
James displays his forgotten jazz roots. —*Ron Wynn*

● **Straight Up** / Dec. 20, 1995-Dec. 21, 1995 / Warner Bros. ✦✦✦✦
This record is an unexpected treat. Bob James has had a lucrative career writing and playing crossover pop-jazz. Although he had actually started his career with a straightahead trio date for Mercury in 1962 and also led a bizarre avant-garde session for ESP in 1965, his career since 1974 has offered very little of interest to consumers who prefer to hear inventive jazz as opposed to pleasant background music. But for this session Bob James returned to the roots few knew he had. Playing in an acoustic trio with bassist Christian McBride and drummer Brian Blade, James contrib-utes five straightforward originals in addition to the standard "Lost April" and interprets tunes by Pat Metheny/Lyle Mays, Horace Silver ("The Jody Grind"), and Denny Zeitlin. James plays quite well, takes plenty of chances and sounds influenced a bit by Bill Evans while not hinting at all at his usual pop material. With McBride and Blade contributing consistently stimulating interplay, James has recorded what is certainly the finest jazz album of his career. —*Scott Yanow*

Harry James

b. Mar. 15, 1916, Albany, GA, **d.** Jul. 5, 1983, Las Vegas, NV
Trumpet / Swing
Harry James was the most famous trumpeter of the swing era, and his big band was the most popular in the world during 1942-46 (after Glenn Miller went in the Army). A household name even today, James was a talented player with a wide range and impressive technique whose heart

was always in jazz even when playing schmaltzy versions of pop melodies or flashy versions of classical themes.

James gained early experience working with his father's circus band, building up his endurance and technique. After playing locally, he made his recording debut while with Ben Pollack's big band (1935-36). Harry James was a star from the time he first joined Benny Goodman's Orchestra (1937-39), and he greatly overshadowed the band's former soloist, Ziggy Elman. He had a few record sessions of his own while still with Goodman, and when he formed his own big band in 1939 it was with Goodman's blessing.

The Harry James Orchestra struggled for a time but in 1941 they had their first huge hit with an instrumental version of "You Made Me Love You." Other big sellers followed including "Strictly Instrumental," "Sleepy Lagoon," "I'll Get By," "I Had the Craziest Dream" (one of many Helen Forrest vocals), and the classic "It's Been a Long Long Time"; James' repertoire also always included his theme "Ciribiribin" and "Two O'Clock Jump." A celebrity who had speaking parts in several movies, James married Betty Grable, added a string section to his band for a few years, and was flying high. Even with the end of the big-band era, James was able to keep his orchestra together (although he dropped the strings after 1947). With altoist Willie Smith and tenor saxophonist Corky Corcoran as key soloists, James' postwar bands played a large share of jazz, and there was even a period in the late '40s when James sounded open to bop; his solo on "Tuxedo Junction" in 1947 shows that he was well aware of Dizzy Gillespie.

Despite such drummers as Louis Bellson and Buddy Rich, by the '50s Harry James seemed happy to have his band sound like Count Basie's (helped out by Ernie Wilkins' arrangements) and to often revisit the past. He remained a popular attraction into the early '80s but failed to advance any further. Perhaps he did not really need to, for no one played Harry James' music better than Harry James! Far too few of his prime Columbia recordings (1941-55) have been reissued on CD. —*Scott Yanow*

And His Great Vocalists / Jan. 5, 1938-May 12, 1952 / Columbia/Legacy ✦✦✦✦

This CD puts the emphasis on Harry James' vocal hits. Such fine singers as Dick Haymes, Helen Forrest, Helen Humes, Kitty Kallen, Art Lund, Rosemary Clooney, and even Willie Smith and Betty Grable (among others) are heard from. Among the more famous recordings are "I'll Get By," "I Don't Want to Walk Without You," "I Had the Craziest Dream," "I've Heard That Song Before," and "It's Been a Long, Long Time." There are some spots for James' trumpet on these popular numbers, but the jazz content is not that strong. When is Columbia going to do a much more complete reissue of Harry James' valuable recordings? —*Scott Yanow*

● **Bandstand Memories 1938 to 1948** / Apr. 2, 1938-Nov. 30, 1948 / Hindsight ✦✦✦✦

This very interesting three-CD set features trumpeter Harry James' Orchestra on a variety of previously unreleased radio broadcast performances. While there are many vocals from Frank Sinatra (in his pre-Tommy Dorsey days), Helen Forrest and Kitty Kallen, it is the instrumentals that are of greatest interest, particularly the earliest tracks that date from the period before James really hit it big. Many of these songs were not recorded commercially by the trumpeter, and this strong jazz-oriented set is highly recommended to swing fans. —*Scott Yanow*

Best of Big Bands / Feb. 20, 1939-Nov. 13, 1946 / Columbia ✦✦✦

All or Nothing at All / Mar. 28, 1939-Nov. 9, 1939 / Hindsight ✦✦✦

★ **Snooty Fruity** / Nov. 21, 1944-Feb. 15, 1955 / Columbia ✦✦✦✦✦

Although altoist Willie Smith is strangely enough given top billing, all 18 selections in this CD actually feature the great swing trumpeter Harry James and his popular bands (of which Smith was a key sideman). Many of James' most exciting jazz performances are on this set, including the extended "Tuxedo Junction," "Moten Swing," the "New Two O'Clock Jump," "The Great Lie," and "Stompin' at the Savoy." This essential CD is especially recommended to detractors who think that Harry James was overrated! —*Scott Yanow*

Wild About Harry / May 1957 / Capitol ✦✦✦

Joseph Jarman

b. Sep. 14, 1937, Pine Bluff, AR
Reeds / Avant-Garde, Free Jazz

A longtime member of the Art Ensemble of Chicago, Joseph Jarman's playing has always been adventurous and utterly unpredictable. He grew up in Chicago, played drums in high school, and started on saxophones and clarinet while in the Army. He was in Muhal Richard Abrams' Experimental Band, and in 1965 he joined the AACM. Jarman's first album as a leader, 1966's *Song For*, was a very radical statement with an unusual utilization of sound and silence. Although he would record occasional records as a leader for Delmark, India Navigation, and Black Saint (including *The Magic Triangle* with Don Pullen and Don Moye), Jarman's main vehicle has been the Art Ensemble of Chicago, where his theatrical performances

keep the music from ever getting too conservative or comfortable. —*Scott Yanow*

● **Song For** / Oct. 20, 1966-Dec. 1, 1966 / Delmark ✦✦✦✦

This was one of the early classics of the AACM. Altoist Joseph Jarman, who would become a permanent member of the Art Ensemble of Chicago shortly after this recording, is heard in a sextet with trumpeter William Brimfield, the legendary tenor Fred Anderson, pianist Christopher Gaddy, bassist Charles Clark, and either Steve McCall or Thurman Barker on drums. The four very diverse improvisations include one that showcases a Jarman recitation, a dirge, the intense "Little Fox Run," and the title cut, which contrasts sounds and a creative use of silence. Overall this music was the next step in jazz after the high-energy passions of the earlier wave of the avant-garde started to run out of fresh ideas. It's recommended for open-eared listeners. —*Scott Yanow*

As If It Were the Seasons / 1967-1968 / Delmark ✦✦✦✦

A textbook '60s Chicago free jazz album from a founding member of the AACA, multi-instrumentalist Joseph Jarman. He employs his full array of horns, and is joined by several mainstays, among them pianist Muhal Richard Abrams, bassist Charles Clark, drummer Thurman Barker, and tenor saxophonist John Stubblefield. This is not compromising material; the songs are long, and everything from bells to whistles to shakers to energized sax screaming comprises the music. —*Ron Wynn*

☆ **Magic Triangle** / Jul. 24, 1979-Jul. 26, 1979 / Black Saint ✦✦✦✦✦

Black Paladins / Dec. 1979 / Black Saint ✦✦✦✦

Earth Passage Density / Feb. 16, 1981-Feb. 17, 1981 / Black Saint ✦✦✦✦

Keith Jarrett

b. May 8, 1945, Allentown, PA
Piano / Post-Bop

One of the most significant pianists to emerge since the '60s, Keith Jarrett's career has gone through several phases. He gained international fame for his solo concerts, which found him spontaneously improvising all of the music without any prior planning, but he has also led a couple of dynamic quartets/quintets, performed classical music, and recently been playing explorative versions of standards with his longtime trio. Although his tendency to "sing along" with his piano now and then is distracting, Jarrett continues to grow as a powerful improviser after 30 years of important accomplishments.

Keith Jarrett started on the piano when he was three years old, and age seven he had already played a recital. A child prodigy, Jarrett was a professional while still in grade school. In 1962 he studied at Berklee and then started working in the Boston area with his trio. He moved to New York in 1965 and spent four months with Art Blakey's Jazz Messengers. As a member of the very popular Charles Lloyd Quartet (1966-69), Jarrett traveled the world and became well known; he also began doubling occasionally on soprano (which he would utilize through the '70s). During 1969-71 he was with Miles Davis' fusion group, playing organ and electric keyboards; Chick Corea was also in the band for the first year. Jarrett can be heard "battling" Corea throughout Davis' *Live at the Fillmore* but is in more creative form on *Live/Evil*.

Upon leaving Miles Davis, Jarrett permanently swore off electric keyboards. He had cut sessions as a leader for Vortex (1967-69) and Atlantic (1971), but starting in November 1971 he recorded extensively for ECM (in addition to some sessions in the '70s for ABC/Impulse), an association that continues to the present day. In the '70s Jarrett led two groups, an exciting unit with Dewey Redman, Charlie Haden, Paul Motian, and occasional percussionists (often Guilherme Franco) and a European band with Jan Garbarek, Palle Danielsson, and Jon Christensen, who recorded the popular "My Song." In addition, starting in 1972 Jarrett began his famous series of improvised concerts that resulted in such popular recordings as *Solo Concerts, Koln Concert*, and the mammoth *Sun Bear Concerts*. By the '80s Jarrett was performing classical music as much as jazz but in the '90s he has recorded extensively (including a six-CD live set) with his "standards trio," which includes Gary Peacock and Jack DeJohnette. Although initially influenced by Bill Evans, Keith Jarrett has had an original and influential style of his own since the early '70s and remains a vital force in jazz. —*Scott Yanow*

Somewhere Before / Oct. 30, 1968-Oct. 31, 1968 / Atlantic ✦✦✦✦

A 1968 live trio recording with Charlie Haden's Manne Hole in Hollywood, with Charlie Haden (b) and Paul Motian (d). Rare and excellent. —*Michael G. Nastos*

Foundations / 1968 / Rhino/Atlantic ✦✦✦✦

The Mourning of a Star / Jul. 9, 1971 / Atlantic ✦✦✦

Birth / Jul. 15, 1971-Jul. 16, 1971 / Atlantic ✦✦✦

● **Facing You** / Nov. 10, 1971 / ECM ✦✦✦✦

Keith Jarrett's first solo acoustic piano recording remains one of his best. At this point in late 1971, Jarrett had just started improvising completely freely. That does not mean that his solos were necessarily atonal, but simply that they were not planned in any way in advance. The music on these eight improvisations are often quite melodic, very rhythmic, and bluesy.

This set makes for a perfect introduction to Jarrett's many solo piano recordings. —*Scott Yanow*

Fort Yawuh / Feb. 24, 1973 / MCA ✦✦✦✦
This live set features pianist Keith Jarrett's finest regular band; all of their recordings are heartily recommended. Jarrett, joined by tenor saxophonist Dewey Redman, bassist Charlie Haden, drummer Paul Motian, and percussionist Danny Johnson, performs four diverse originals. The two ballads in particular work well (this group from the start had its own sound), although Redman's playing on Chinese musette might take a bit of getting used to. —*Scott Yanow*

★ **Solo Concerts: Bremen and Lausanne** / Mar. 20, 1973+Jul. 1, 1973 / ECM ✦✦✦✦✦
These are the recordings that made Keith Jarrett famous. Originally released as a three-LP set, the two solo piano recitals feature Jarrett freely improvising and never seeming to run out of ideas. A simple figure often develops through repetition and subtle variations into a rather complex sequence and eventually evolves into a new figure. One of the improvisations lasts for three LP sides (64 minutes), while the second concert has two long solos for 30 and 35 minutes, respectively. Despite the length, the music never loses one's interest, making this an essential recording for all jazz collections. —*Scott Yanow*

Treasure Island / Feb. 27, 1974-Feb. 28, 1974 / Impulse ✦✦✦✦
Originally an Impulse LP that surfaced on MCA as a straight reissue on CD, this fine recording features pianist Keith Jarrett's best regular group. Dewey Redman is heard from on tenor, bassist Charlie Haden, drummer Paul Motian, and percussionists Guilherme Franco and Danny Johnson are superb in ensembles and Jarrett's rich melodies; he contributed eight originals to this enjoyable modern set. —*Scott Yanow*

Death and the Flower / Oct. 1974 / GRP ✦✦✦

Backhand / Oct. 9, 1974-Oct. 10, 1974 / Impulse ✦✦✦✦
Landmark quintet with Dewey Redman (ts), Charlie Haden (b), Paul Motian (d), Guilherme Franco (per). Any recording by this band is worthwhile. —*Michael G. Nastos*

Shades / 1975 / Impulse ✦✦✦✦
Pianist Keith Jarrett's mid-'70s quintet was the strongest regular group that he ever led, and all of its recordings (even some that ramble a bit) are worth picking up. Thanks to its strong start, *Shades* is one of this unit's most rewarding recordings. "Shades of Jazz" has a memorable melody and logical (if unpredictable) improvisations by Jarrett and tenor saxophonist Dewey Redman. The momentum slows down a bit with the gospel-inspired "Southern Smiles" and "Rose Petals" but picks up again with the final number, the rather intense "Diatribe," an excellent vehicle for this classic group. Throughout, bassist Charlie Haden, drummer Paul Motian, and percussionist Guilherme Franco keep the band's juices flowing. —*Scott Yanow*

★ **The Koln Concert** / Jan. 24, 1975 / ECM ✦✦✦✦✦
Many critics consider this to be Keith Jarrett's most rewarding solo recording, although *Solo Concerts* from the previous year is on the same level. Originally released as a two-LP set, this music is best suited for CD because, while the first 26-minute improvisation fits on one LP side, the second of the two solos (which totals 41 minutes) was programmed over the remaining 11 LPs, with side four being only seven minutes long. Logistics aside, the music is quite brilliant, with Jarrett (who was improvising freely without any prior planning) developing the most interesting and occasionally startling ideas. The strong, fresh melodies and his bluesy feel make this a very enjoyable outing. —*Scott Yanow*

Death and the Flower / May 1975 / ABC/Impulse ✦✦✦

☆ **The Survivor's Suite** / Apr. 1976 / ECM ✦✦✦✦✦
This is one of the finest recordings by pianist Keith Jarrett's mid-'70s group. Jarrett (on piano, soprano, and bass recorder), tenor saxophonist Dewey Redman, bassist Charlie Haden, and drummer Paul Motian (no percussionist this time) by 1976 were thinking alike during the ensemble's improvisations. "The Survivor's Suite," a 49-minute two-part work, finds the group continually building up and then releasing tension together. There are strong individual solos, but it is the interplay between the band members that makes this a particularly memorable outing. —*Scott Yanow*

Silence / Sep. 9, 1977 / ECM ✦✦✦✦
Tremendous mid-'70s quartet session headed by pianist Keith Jarrett. Jarrett was in the midst of an impressive recording and touring string with this group, which included tenor saxophonist Dewey Redman, bassist Charlie Haden, and drummer Paul Motian. Almost every release they issued was superb; this one was no different. It has been reissued on CD. —*Ron Wynn*

Bop-Be / Nov. 1, 1977 / Impulse ✦✦✦✦

My Song / Nov. 1977 / ECM ✦✦✦✦
In addition to his solo piano concerts and the American group he led that featured tenor saxophonist Dewey Redman, Keith Jarrett was also busy in the mid-'70s with his European band, a quartet comprising Jan Garbarek

on tenor and soprano, bassist Palle Danielsson, and drummer Jon Christensen. Due to the popularity of the haunting "My Song," this album is the best-known of the Jarrett-Garbarek collaborations and it actually is their most rewarding meeting on records. Jarrett contributed all six compositions, and the results are relaxed and introspective yet full of inner tension. —*Scott Yanow*

Changes / Jan. 1983 / ECM ✦✦✦✦
Unlike the other two Keith Jarrett trio recordings from January 1983, this collaboration with bassist Gary Peacock and drummer Jack DeJohnette does not feature standards. The trio performs the 30-minute "Flying" and a 6-minute "Prism," both of them Jarrett originals. "Flying," which has several sections, keeps one's interest throughout, while the more concise "Prism" has a beautiful melody. It is a nice change to hear Jarrett (who normally plays unaccompanied) interacting with a trio of superb players. —*Scott Yanow*

Standards, Vol. 1 / Jan. 1983 / ECM ✦✦✦✦
In January of 1983, Keith Jarrett returned to the trio format, and his collaboration with bassist Gary Peacock and drummer Jack DeJohnette resulted in three albums. The first release finds the trio digging into five standards with "God Bless the Child" being dragged out (although not unmercifully) for 15 minutes. The performances, which usually do not swing in a conventional sense, do have a momentum of their own. Jarrett is generous in allocating solo space to Peacock, and it is obvious that the three musicians were listening very closely to each other. —*Scott Yanow*

Standards, Vol. 2 / Jan. 1983 / ECM ✦✦✦✦
One of three trio albums that pianist Keith Jarrett recorded with bassist Gary Peacock and drummer Jack DeJohnette during the same month, this second volume of *Standards* gets the edge over the first due to its slightly more challenging material. Jarrett, who has often taken himself a bit too seriously, is surprisingly playful at times in this format. In addition to Jarrett's "So Tender," there are such superior songs explored on this date as Alec Wilder's "Moon and Sand," "If I Should Lose You," and "I Fall in Love Too Easily." Bassist Gary Peacock and drummer Jack DeJohnette listen closely to Jarrett, and no matter what direction the pianist turns, they are already there waiting for him. —*Scott Yanow*

Standards Live / Jul. 2, 1985 / ECM ✦✦✦✦
Standards Live, from 1987, continued at the same high level of previous *Standards Vol. 1 & 2* with pianist Keith Jarrett often recalling his early influence, Bill Evans. The well integrated trio (Gary Peacock, bass; Jack DeJohnette, drums) plays three frequently performed tunes and three obscurities. The interplay between the players was constantly impressive. —*Scott Yanow*

Standards In Norway / Oct. 7, 1989 / ECM ✦✦✦

Bye Bye Blackbird / Oct. 1991 / ECM ✦✦✦✦

At the Deer Head Inn / Sep. 1992 / ECM ✦✦✦✦
Keith Jarrett returns to his roots, both musically and physically, on this CD. His first significant jazz gig was at the Deer Head Inn in Allentown, PA (his hometown), and 30 years later Jarrett agreed to perform at the venue again. With the assistance of bassist Gary Peacock and drummer Paul Motian, Jarrett plays six jazz standards (several of which were associated with Miles Davis) plus Jaki Byard's medium-tempo blues, "Chandra." The inventive interpretations give listeners plenty of surprises and variety, making this a very enjoyable outing. —*Scott Yanow*

☆ **Keith Jarrett at the Blue Note: The Complete Recordings** / Jun. 3, 1994-Jun. 8, 1994 / ECM ✦✦✦✦✦
The six-CD box set *Keith Jarrett at the Blue Note* fully documents three nights (six complete sets from June 3-5, 1994) by his trio with bassist Gary Peacock and drummer Jack DeJohnette. Never mind that this same group has already had ten separate releases since 1983; this box is still well worth getting! The repertoire emphasizes (but is not exclusively) standards with such songs as "In Your Own Sweet Way," "Now's the Time," "Oleo," "Days of Wine and Roses," and "My Romance" given colorful and at times surprising explorations. Some of the selections are quite lengthy (including a 26 1/2 minute version of "Autumn Leaves"), and Jarrett's occasional originals are quite welcome; his 28 1/2 minute "Desert Sun" reminds one of the pianist's fully improvised "Solo Concerts" of the '70s. Throughout the three nights at the Blue Note, the interplay between the musicians is consistently outstanding. Those listeners concerned about Jarrett's tendency to "sing along" with his piano have little to fear, for other than occasional shouts and sighs, he wisely lets his piano do the talking. —*Scott Yanow*

Bobby Jaspar

b. Feb. 20, 1926, Liège, Belgium, d. Feb. 28, 1963, New York, NY
Flute, Sax (Tenor) / Cool, Hard Bop
A fine, bop-oriented soloist equally skilled on his cool-toned tenor and flute, Bobby Jaspar's early death from a heart ailment was a tragic loss. As a teenager he played tenor in a Dixieland group with Toots Thielemans in Belgium. He recorded with Henri Renaud (1951 and 1953) and played with touring Americans including Jimmy Raney, Chet Baker (1955), and his future wife, Blossom Dearie. In 1956 Jaspar moved to New York where he

worked with J.J. Johnson and was briefly with Miles Davis (1957) and Donald Byrd. He mostly freelanced during the remainder of his career. Jaspar recorded for Swing, Vogue, and Barclay while in Paris and led dates for Prestige and Riverside in the US during 1957. —*Scott Yanow*

● **Bobby Jaspar in Paris** / Dec. 1955 / Disques Swing ◆◆◆◆
Wonderful 1986 reissue of prime Jaspar small-combo dates from mid-'50s. Tommy Flanagan (p), Elvin Jones (d), Milt Hinton (b) among the crew. —*Ron Wynn*

Memory of Dick / Dec. 27, 1955 & Dec. 29, 1955 / EmArcy ◆◆◆◆
Nice session from under-recorded Belgian musician. —*Ron Wynn*

With George Wallington, Idrees Sulieman / May 23, 1957 & May 28, 1957 / Original Jazz Classics ◆◆◆◆
Bobby Jaspar was one of Europe's top jazzmen of the '50s. This CD reissue (which adds one track to the original six-song LP program) features him on tenor and flute in a quintet with trumpeter Idrees Sulieman, pianist George Wallington, bassist Wilbur Little, and drummer Elvin Jones. The music is straightahead bop/cool jazz with many fine solos from Jaspar, Sulieman, and Wallington. Nothing all that surprising occurs as the quintet jams on a variety of attractive chord changes, but this set serves as a fine example of the somewhat forgotten Bobby Jaspar's talents. —*Scott Yanow*

Phenil Isopropil Amine / Dec. 19, 1958 / Verve ◆◆◆
Ungainly title, excellent date fueled by Kenny Clarke (d). —*Ron Wynn*

Eddie Jefferson (Edgar Jefferson)

b. Aug. 3, 1918, Pittsburgh, PA, **d.** May 9, 1979, Detroit, MI
Vocals / Bop, Vocalese
The founder of vocalese (putting recorded solos to words), Eddie Jefferson did not have a great voice, but he was one of the top jazz singers, getting the maximum out of what he had. He started out working as a tap dancer, but by the late '40s he was singing and writing lyrics. A live session from 1949 (released on Spotlite) finds him pioneering vocalese by singing his lyrics to "Parker's Mood" and Lester Young's solo on "I Cover the Waterfront." However, his classic lyrics to "Moody's Mood for Love" was recorded first by King Pleasure (1952), who also had a big hit with his version of "Parker's Mood." Jefferson had his first studio recording that year (which included Coleman Hawkins' solo on "Body and Soul") before working with James Moody (1953-57). Although he recorded on an occasional basis in the '50s and '60s, his contributions to the idiom seemed to be mostly overlooked until the '70s. Jefferson worked with Moody again (1968-73) and during his last few years often performed with Richie Cole. He was shot to death outside of a Detroit club in 1979. Eddie Jefferson, who also wrote memorable lyrics to "Jeannine," "Lady Be Good," "So What," "Freedom Jazz Dance," and even "Bitches' Brew," recorded for Savoy, Prestige, a single for Checker, Inner City, and Muse. —*Scott Yanow*

★ **Letter from Home** / Dec. 18, 1961-Feb. 8, 1962 / Original Jazz Classics ◆◆◆◆◆
This CD (which augments the original LP program with two alternate takes) is a fine showcase for the vocalese master Eddie Jefferson. Backed by either a tentet or a quintet, which gives solo space to altoist James Moody and the tenor of Johnny Griffin, Jefferson sings his lyrics to such numbers as "Take the 'A' Train," "Billie's Bounce," "I Cover the Waterfront," "Parker's Mood" (the latter differs from the famous lines immortalized by King Pleasure), "A Night in Tunisia," and "Body and Soul" among others. Jefferson is in prime form, and these boppish renditions as a whole form a near-classic. —*Scott Yanow*

Body and Soul / 1968 / Original Jazz Classics ◆◆◆◆
Eddie Jefferson had not been on record in quite a few years when he recorded this set (reissued on CD) for Prestige. A few of the songs ("Mercy, Mercy, Mercy," "Psychedelic Sally," and "See if You Can Git to That") were attempts to update the singer's style in the mod idiom of the late '60s, but the most memorable selections are "So What" (on which Jefferson re-creates Miles Davis' famous solo), "Body and Soul," "Now's the Time," "Oh Gee," and "Filthy McNasty"; the latter has very effective lyrics by writer Ira Gitler. Tenorman James Moody, trumpeter Dave Burns, and pianist Barry Harris are in the supporting cast of this excellent set. —*Scott Yanow*

Come Along with Me / Aug. 12, 1969 / Original Jazz Classics ◆◆◆◆
Vocalist Eddie Jefferson (the founder of vocalese) is in top form throughout this outstanding set, a CD reissue of the original LP. There is a liberal amount of solo space for trumpeter Bill Hardman, altoist Charles McPherson, and pianist Barry Harris, but it is Jefferson's singing and his witty lyrics to such songs as Horace Silver's "The Preacher," "Yardbird Suite," "Dexter Digs In," "Baby Girl" (based on "These Foolish Things"), and even "When You're Smiling" that are the main reasons to acquire this very enjoyable disc. —*Scott Yanow*

Budd Johnson (Albert J. Johnson)

b. Dec. 14, 1910, Dallas, TX, **d.** Oct. 20, 1984, Kansas City, MO
Sax (Soprano), Sax (Tenor) / Bop, Swing
Budd Johnson was a talented and valuable jazz musician for many

decades, a behind-the-scenes player and writer who uplifted a countless number of sessions from the '30s into the '80s. Johnson started off playing in Kansas City in the late '20s with the bands of Terrence Holder, Jesse Stone, and George E. Lee. He made his recording debut while with Louis Armstrong's big band (1932-33) and gained attention for his work as tenor soloist and arranger during three stints with the Earl Hines Orchestra (1932-42). One of the first tenor saxophonists to be influenced by Lester Young (although by the '40s he had a distinctive tone of his own), Johnson had brief stints with Gus Arnheim (1937) and the bands of Fletcher and Horace Henderson (1938) between his periods with Hines. He contributed arrangements to several big bands including those of Woody Herman, Buddy Rich, Boyd Raeburn, and Billy Eckstine and was partly responsible for Hines hiring young modernists during 1942-43. He recorded with Coleman Hawkins on the first bebop session (1944), worked with Dizzy Gillespie and Sy Oliver (1947), and in the '50s led his own groups in addition to touring with Snub Mosley (1952) and Benny Goodman (1957). Johnson was with the big bands of Quincy Jones (1960) and Count Basie (1961-62) before renewing ties with Earl Hines, with whom he played on and off again starting in 1964. He formed the JPJ Quartet, which worked on an occasional basis during 1969-75, held his own at the 1971 Newport in New York jam sessions, became a jazz educator, and recorded an excellent album with Phil Woods eight months before his death. Budd Johnson led some obscure sessions during 1947-56 in addition to notable albums for Felsted (1958), Riverside, Swingville, Argo, Black & Blue, Master Jazz, Dragon, and Uptown. —*Scott Yanow*

And the Four Brass Giants / Sep. 6, 1960 & Sep. 22, 1960 / Original Jazz Classics ◆◆◆◆
This was one of Budd Johnson's finest leadership moments; he not only wrote charts that did a marvelous job of setting up his gems, but he also made particularly clever use of four distinctive trumpeters. Cannonball Adderley produced this date. —*Bob Rusch, Cadence*

★ **Let's Swing** / Dec. 2, 1960 / Original Jazz Classics ◆◆◆◆
Stout, robust vehicle with standard Johnson solos. —*Ron Wynn*

The JPJ Quartet / 1969-Jun. 20, 1971 / Storyville ◆◆◆◆
The short-lived (1969-75) JPJ Quartet consisted of Budd Johnson on tenor and soprano, pianist Dill Jones, bassist Bill Pemberton, and drummer Oliver Jackson. This valuable CD has six previously unreleased studio performances plus the music from a former Master Jazz LP recorded at the 1971 Montreux Jazz Festival. The quartet plays small-group swing (or mainstream) with melodic creativity. Highlights include Johnson's "Tag Along" (one of six originals by group members), Dill Jones' feature on "Honeysuckle Rose," "Lester Leaps In," and a roaring "The Best Things in Life Are Free." —*Scott Yanow*

The Ole Dude and the Fundance Kid / Feb. 4, 1984 / Uptown ◆◆◆◆
The veteran tenor saxophonist Budd Johnson (who first emerged 50 years before this recording) was still in fine form when he met up with altoist Phil Woods for this frequently heated quintet session. During what would be his final recording date (he died later in 1984), Johnson is excellent on the ballads but even better on the faster material where his interplay and trade-offs with Woods are a constant joy. There is a lot of spirit on this happy set; the mutual love and respect felt by the saxophonists is obvious. —*Scott Yanow*

Bunk Johnson (William Geary Johnson)

b. Dec. 27, 1889, New Orleans, LA, **d.** Jul. 7, 1949
Trumpet / New Orleans Jazz
Due to the difference of opinion between his followers (who claimed he was a brilliant stylist) and his detractors (who felt that his playing was worthless), Bunk Johnson was a controversial figure in the mid-'40s when he made a most unlikely comeback. The truth is somewhere in between.

Johnson, who tended to exaggerate, claimed that he was born in 1879 and that he played with Buddy Bolden in New Orleans, but it was discovered that he was actually a decade younger. He did have a pretty tone and, although not an influence on Louis Armstrong (as he often stated), he was a major player in New Orleans starting around 1910 when he joined the Eagle Band. Johnson was active in the South but during the early '30s but did not record during that era. Discovered in the latter part of the decade by Bill Russell and Fred Ramsey, he was profiled in the 1939 book *Jazzmen*. A collection was taken up to get Bunk new teeth and a horn. In 1942 he privately recorded in New Orleans and the next year he was in San Francisco playing with the wartime edition of the Yerba Buena Jazz Band. An alcoholic, Johnson's playing tended to be erratic and when Sidney Bechet recruited him for a band in 1945, he essentially drank himself out of the group. In 1946 Bunk led a group that included the nucleus of the ensemble George Lewis would make famous a few years later, but Johnson disliked the playing of the primitive New Orleans musicians. He was more comfortable the following year heading a unit filled with skilled swing players, and his final album (Columbia's *Last Testament of a Great Jazzman*) was one of his best recordings. In 1948 the trumpeter (who was only 59 but seemed much older) returned to Louisiana and retired. Many of Johnson's better recordings have been reissued on CD by Good Time Jazz and American Music. — *Scott Yanow*

Bunk Johnson and His Superior Jazz Band / Jun. 11, 1942 / Good Time Jazz ✦✦✦

'91 reissue of magnificent early '40s traditional jazz album with the great New Orleans trumpeter Bunk Johnson. Johnson didn't make many records, and this was among his greatest. The supporting lineup included two other Crescent City greats, Jim Robinson and George Lewis. — *Ron Wynn*

Bunk Johnson in San Francisco / Sep. 1943-Jan. 1944 / American Music ✦✦✦

1944 [2nd Masters] / Jul. 29, 1944-Aug. 1944 / American Music ✦✦✦✦

★ **Last Testament of a Great Jazzman** / Dec. 23, 1947-Dec. 26, 1947 / Columbia ✦✦✦✦✦

Venerable New Orleans jazz legend Bunk Johnson teamed with a group of mostly swing-era veterans in the mid- and late '40s for several controversial albums. Rather than cutting strictly traditional material, Johnson's band blended rags, spirituals, blues, swing, and some traditional numbers. The music was largely successful, but the band didn't attract a wide enough audience to make it fiscally worthwhile. The 14 cuts on this CD reissue were done in 1947, the band's final year, and originally released on Columbia. Johnson, clarinetist Garvin Bushnell, trombonist Eddie Cuffee, guitarist Danny Barker, bassist Wellman Braud and drummer Alphonse Steele meshed and played with fire, precision, and fervor. — *Ron Wynn*

J.J. Johnson (James Louis Johnson)

b. Jan. 22, 1924, Indianapolis, IN
Trombone / Bop, Hard Bop
Considered by many to be the finest jazz trombonist of all time, J.J. Johnson somehow transferred the innovations of Charlie Parker and Dizzy Gillespie to his more awkward instrument, playing with such speed and deceptive ease that at one time some listeners assumed he was playing valve (rather than slide) trombone! Johnson toured with the territory bands of Clarence Love and Snookum Russell during 1941-42 and then spent 1942-45 with Benny Carter's big band. He made his recording debut with Carter (taking a solo on "Love for Sale" in 1943) and played at the first JATP concert (1944). Johnson also had plenty of solo space during his stay with Count Basie's Orchestra (1945-46). During 1946-50 he played with all of the top bop musicians including Charlie Parker (with whom he recorded in 1947), the Dizzy Gillespie big band, Illinois Jacquet (1947-49), and the Miles Davis Birth of the Cool Nonet. His own recordings from the era included such sidemen as Bud Powell and a young Sonny Rollins. Johnson, who also recorded with the Metronome All-Stars, played with Oscar Pettiford (1951) and Miles Davis (1952) but then was outside of music, working as a blueprint inspector for two years (1952-54). His fortunes changed when in August 1954 he formed a two-trombone quintet with Kai Winding that became known as Jay and Kai and was quite popular during its two years.

After Johnson and Kai went their separate ways (they would later have a few reunions), Johnson led a quintet that often included Bobby Jaspar. He began to compose ambitious works starting with 1956's "Poem for Brass" and including "El Camino Real" and a feature for Dizzy Gillespie, "Perceptions"; his "Lament" became a standard. Johnson worked with Miles Davis during part of 1961-62, led some more small groups of his own, and by the late '60s was kept busy writing television and film scores. Johnson was so famous in the jazz world that he kept on winning *Downbeat* polls in the '70s even though he was not playing at all! However, starting with a Japanese tour in 1977, Johnson gradually returned to a busy performance schedule, leading a quintet in the '80s that often featured Ralph Moore. In the mid-'90s he remains at the top of his field. Johnson has recorded as a leader for Savoy, Prestige, Blue Note, RCA, Bethlehem, Columbia, Impulse, Verve, A&M, Pablo, Milestone, Concord, and Antilles. — *Scott Yanow*

Jay and Kai / Dec. 24, 1947-Aug. 26, 1954 / Savoy Jazz ✦✦✦

Trombone by Three / May 26, 1949-Oct. 5, 1951 / Original Jazz Classics ✦✦✦✦

The Eminent Jay Jay Johnson, Vol. 1 / Jun. 22, 1953 / Blue Note ✦✦✦✦
The CD reissue of the two volumes titled *The Eminent Jay Jay Johnson* straighten out his three Blue Note sessions of 1953-55 and add alternate takes. This particular CD concentrates exclusively on the trombonist's 1953 sextet date with the great trumpeter Clifford Brown, Jimmy Heath (who doubles on tenor and baritone), pianist John Lewis, bassist Percy Heath, and drummer Kenny Clarke. The six titles (plus three alternates) are highlighted by "It Could Happen to You," "Turnpike," and a classic rendition of "Get Happy." Although Johnson has a couple of features, Clifford Brown largely steals the show. This CD is well worth getting by listeners who do not have the music on Brownie's own *Complete* Blue Note set. — *Scott Yanow*

The Eminent Jay Jay Johnson, Vol. 2 / Sep. 24, 1954+Jun. 6, 1955 / Blue Note ✦✦✦✦
The second of two Blue Note CDs (which differ in their content from the

similarly titled LPs) contains two complete sessions that showcase trombonist J.J. Johnson. The first six titles (highlighted by "Old Devil Moon" and "Too Marvelous for Words") feature Johnson in a quintet with pianist Wynton Kelly, bassist Charles Mingus, drummer Kenny Clarke, and the congas of Sabu. For the latter session, there are also six titles (including "Pennies from Heaven" and "Portrait of Jennie") plus three alternate takes; Johnson is joined by Hank Mobley on tenor, pianist Horace Silver, bassist Paul Chambers, and drummer Kenny Clarke. Both of these dates offer listeners excellent examples of the talents of the great trombonist who always played his instrument with the fluidity of a trumpet. Recommended. — *Scott Yanow*

Trombone Master / Apr. 26, 1957-Dec. 22, 1960 / Columbia ✦✦✦

The Great Kai and J.J. / Nov. 4, 1960-Nov. 9, 1960 / Impulse ✦✦✦✦
This Impulse set (which was given the catalog number of A-1 when it first came out) was the first recorded reunion of trombonists J.J. Johnson and Kai Winding. Given a straight reissue on CD (the original liner notes are reproduced so small as to be largely unreadable), the music still sounds fresh and lively. With pianist Bill Evans, either Paul Chambers or Tommy Williams on bass, and Roy Haynes or Art Taylor on drums, the two trombonists are in melodic and witty form on such tunes as "This Could Be the Start of Something Big," "Blue Monk," "Side by Side" and the "Theme from Picnic." Recommended. — *Scott Yanow*

Proof Positive / May 1, 1964 / Impulse ✦✦✦✦
This CD reissue finds trombonist J.J. Johnson in prime form. In fact, his melancholy minor-toned explorations often recall Miles Davis, whose group he had played with the year before. Backed on six of the seven tracks by pianist Harold Mabern, who at the time was heavily influenced by McCoy Tyner, bassist Arthur Harper, and drummer Frank Gant, Johnson gets to really stretch out on "Neo," "Minor Blues," and "Blues Waltz"; "Gloria" was previously available only on an Impulse sampler. Manny Albam's "Lullaby of Jazzland," on which Johnson is joined by guitarist Toots Thielemans, pianist McCoy Tyner, bassist Richard Davis, and drummer Elvin Jones, rounds out the excellent set. — *Scott Yanow*

Say When / Dec. 7, 1964-Dec. 5, 1966 / Bluebird ✦✦✦✦
Most of two of trombonist J.J. Johnson's Victor big-band dates (seven of nine numbers from a 1964 album and eight of the nine selections on Johnson's *The Total* LP from 1966) are included on this Bluebird single CD from 1987. In addition to his typically brilliant trombone playing, Johnson did virtually all of the arranging, except for Oliver Nelson's work on his own "Stolen Moments," and contributed nine of the compositions. The emphasis is on the writing, with J.J. Johnson and pianist Hank Jones generally being the main soloists; Johnson's reworkings of George Russell's challenging "Stratusphunk" and Miles Davis' "Swing Spring" are among the highlights. — *Scott Yanow*

★ **Things Are Getting Better All the Time** / Nov. 28, 1983-Nov. 29, 1983 / Original Jazz Classics ✦✦✦✦✦
J.J. Johnson teams up with fellow trombonist Al Grey for a variety of superior standards and obscurities in a quintet with pianist Kenny Barron, bassist Ray Brown, and drummer Mickey Roker. Reissued on CD, this session has many joyful moments, and the interaction between the two very different-sounding trombonists (Grey is hot, while Johnson is cool) on such tunes as "Soft Winds," "It's Only a Paper Moon," "Boy Meets Horn," and the title cut is consistently memorable and enjoyable. Recommended. — *Scott Yanow*

● **Quintergy: Live** / Jul. 1988 / Antilles ✦✦✦✦
Trombonist J.J. Johnson, 64 at the time, is heard in top form on this "Live at the Village Vanguard" set. His quintet, which includes Ralph Moore on tenor and soprano, pianist Stanley Cowell, bassist Rufus Reid, and drummer Victor Lewis, is perfectly suited to interpret the spirited set of advanced bop. Highlights include Johson's feature on "You've Changed," "Coppin' the Bop," "Lament," and his unaccompanied playing on "It's All Right with Me." Excellent music. Another Antilles CD, *Standards*, comes from the same sessions. — *Scott Yanow*

● **Standards: Live at the Village** / Jul. 1988 / Antilles ✦✦✦✦
The second of two CDs coming from the same engagement at the Village Vanguard (the first was *Quintergy*), this set features trombonist J.J. Johnson's quintet with Ralph Moore on tenor and soprano, pianist Stanley Cowell, bassist Rufus Reid, and drummer Victor Lewis jamming on nine standards, plus the leader's "Shortcake." Johnson is in top form, particularly on "My Funny Valentine," "Just Friends," "Misterioso," and "Autumn Leaves." A good example of the ageless trombonist's talents. — *Scott Yanow*

● **Let's Hang Out** / Dec. 1992 / Verve ✦✦✦✦
Forty-nine years after his recording debut, trombonist J.J. Johnson still sounds in peak form. Most of the numbers on his Verve CD find him accompanied by either Stanley Cowell or Renee Roenes on piano, bassist Rutus Reid, and Victor Lewis or Lewis Nash on drums with occasional contributions from trumpeter Terence Blanchard (whose chops sound a little off) and Ralph Moore on tenor and soprano. In addition tenor saxophonist Jimmy Heath makes a couple of guest appearances, and "Beautiful Love"

is taken by Johnson as an unaccompanied solo. Despite the strong supporting cast, the great trombonist is the star throughout, particularly on "It Never Entered My Mind," his "Kenya," "It's You or No One," and a tasteful quartet rendition of "I Got It Bad." Excellent music. — *Scott Yanow*

Tangence / Jul. 13, 1994-Jul. 15, 1994 / Gitanes ✦✦✦✦
Trombonist J.J. Johnson is joined by a string orchestra arranged by Robert Farnon for most of the performances on this CD. Farnon's sweeping scores can sometimes come closer to movie music and Muzak than jazz, but the high quality of the songs and a few surprising departures make this CD recommended. Wynton Marsalis has three guest appearances (including a spirited unaccompanied duet with Johnson on the old Jimmy Lunceford hit "For Dancers Only"), Johnson takes his blues "Opus De Focus" as a duet with bassist Chris Laurence, and the trombonist is in particularly fine form on such numbers as "The Meaning of the Blues," "Dinner for One, Please, James," "The Very Thought of You," and his own "Lament." — *Scott Yanow*

James P. Johnson

b. Feb. 1, 1894, New Brunswick, NJ, d. Nov. 17, 1955, New York, NY
Piano / Stride, Classic Jazz
One of the great jazz pianists of all time, James P. Johnson was the king of stride pianists in the '20s. He began working in New York clubs as early as 1913 and was quickly recognized as the pacesetter. In 1917 Johnson began making piano rolls. Duke Ellington learned from these (by slowing them down to half-speed), and a few years later Johnson became Fats Waller's teacher and inspiration. During the '20s (starting in 1921), James P. Johnson began to record; he was the nightly star at Harlem rent parties (accompanied by Waller and Willie "The Lion" Smith); and he wrote some of his most famous compositions. For the 1923 Broadway show *Running Wild* (one of his dozen scores), James P. composed "The Charleston" and "Old Fashioned Love," his earlier piano feature "Carolina Shout" became the test piece for other pianists, and some of his other songs included "If I Could Be with You One Hour Tonight" and "A Porter's Love Song to a Chambermaid."

Ironically, James P. Johnson, the most sophisticated pianist of the '20s, was also an expert accompanist for blues singers, and he starred on several memorable Bessie Smith and Ethel Waters recordings. In addition to his solo recordings, Johnson led some hot combos on records and guested with Perry Bradford and Clarence Williams; he also shared the spotlight with Fats Waller on a few occasions. Because he was very interested in writing longer works, Johnson (who had composed "Yamekraw" in 1927) spent much of the '30s working on such pieces as "Harlem Symphony," "Symphony in Brown," and a blues opera. Unfortunately, much of this music has been lost through the years. Johnson, who was only semiactive as a pianist throughout much of the '30s, started recording again in 1939, often sat in with Eddie Condon, and was active in the '40s despite some minor strokes. A major stroke in 1951 finished off his career. Most of his recordings have been reissued on CD. — *Scott Yanow*

Carolina Shout / May 1917-Jun. 1925 / Biograph ✦✦✦
★ **Harlem Stride Piano** / Aug. 1921-Nov. 18, 1929 / Hot 'N Sweet ✦✦✦✦✦
This European import consists of the first 24 recordings led by the great stride pianist James P. Johnson plus the piano roll version of his hit "The Charleston." Many of these performances have been formerly issued in haphazard or incomplete fashion, but this exciting CD has all of Johnson's dates up until his 1930 solos. There are three early band sides from 1921 (including Johnson's "Carolina Shout"), 13 piano solos ("Snowy Morning Blues," "Riffs," and "Feeling Blue" are particularly memorable) and hot combos that feature such sidemen as cornetists/trumpeters Louis Metcalfe, Cootie Williams, and King Oliver and (on two songs) fellow pianist Fats Waller. The somewhat obscure CD is the perfect way to accumulate these historic performances. — *Scott Yanow*

★ **Snowy Morning Blues** / Jan. 21, 1930-Sep. 22, 194 / GRP ✦✦✦✦✦
James P. Johnson was one of the greatest jazz pianists of all time and in the '20s was considered the "king of the stride piano." This Decca reissue CD contains a great deal of valuable music. Johnson is first heard on four classic piano solos from 1930 ("You've Got to Be Modernistic" and "Jingles" are particularly memorable) and then on eight Fats Waller-associated tunes in duets with drummer Eddie Dougherty from 1944; the latter performances differ from the eight identical Waller songs that Johnson had recorded earlier in the same year as solos. Since Waller (who had passed away in 1943) was his close friend and former student, there is a lot of emotion in the tributes but also much joy. This highly recommended CD concludes with James P. Johnson romping on eight of his own timeless compositions including "Carolina Shout," "Old Fashioned Love," and "If I Could Be with You." — *Scott Yanow*

Victory Stride / Feb. 1992 & Jan. 1994 / Music Masters ✦✦✦

Pete Johnson

b. Mar. 25, 1904, Kansas City, MO, d. Mar. 23, 1967, Buffalo, NY
Piano / Blues, Boogie-Woogie
Pete Johnson was one of the three great boogie-woogie pianists (along with

Albert Ammons and Meade Lux Lewis) whose sudden prominence in the late '30s helped make the style very popular. Originally a drummer, Johnson switched to piano in 1922. He was part of the Kansas City scene in the '20s and '30s, often accompanying singer Big Joe Turner. Producer John Hammond discovered him in 1936 and got him to play at the Famous Door in New York. After taking part at Hammond's 1938 *Spirituals to Swing* Carnegie Hall concert in 1938, Johnson started recording regularly and appeared on an occasional basis with Ammons and Lewis as the Boogie Woogie Trio. He also backed Turner on some classic records. Johnson recorded often in the '40s and spent much of 1947-49 based in Los Angeles. He moved to Buffalo in 1950 and, other than an appearance at the 1958 Newport Jazz Festival, he was in obscurity for much of the decade. A stroke later in 1958 left him partly paralyzed. Johnson made one final appearance at John Hammond's January 1967 *Spirituals to Swing* concert, playing the right hand on a version of "Roll 'Em Pete" two months before his death. — *Scott Yanow*

● **Pete Johnson 1938-1939** / Dec. 30, 1938-Dec. 1938 / Classics ✦✦✦✦
Central Avenue Boogie / Apr. 18, 1947-Nov. 29, 1947 / Delmark ✦✦✦

Pete Jolly (Peter A. Ceragioli)

b. Jun. 5, 1932, New Haven, CT
Piano / Bop, Cool
A powerful pianist who came to fame on the West Coast in the '50s, Pete Jolly has been a fixture in Los Angeles for over 40 years. He started on accordion when he was three and began piano when he was eight. He played his first jobs when he was 12. In 1946 his family moved to Phoenix, and the following year he joined the Musicians Union and started working extensively in clubs. During a visit to Los Angeles in 1954, Jolly sat in the Lighthouse, which led to his joining Shorty Rogers' Giants (1954-56). He recorded three albums as a leader for Victor in 1956 (taking rare jazz accordion solos on a few tracks), worked with Buddy DeFranco, Terry Gibbs, Richie Kamuca, Chet Baker, and Art Pepper among others, in the late '50s and had a surprise hit with "Little Bird" in 1963. Jolly became a busy studio musician in the '60s but has led his trio with bassist Chuck Berghofer and drummer Nick Martinis regularly in local clubs for over 30 years. In addition to RCA, Pete Jolly has recorded for Metrojazz, MGM, Ava, Charlie Parker Records, Columbia, A&M, Atlas, Holt, and V.S.O.P. as a leader. — *Scott Yanow*

Pete Jolly Trio and Friends / Nov. 1962-Aug. 1964 / VSOP ✦✦✦✦
● **Yours Truly** / 1993 / Bainbridge ✦✦✦✦
Pete Jolly and his longtime sidemen (Chuck Berghofer has been his regular bassist since the late '50s while drummer Nick Martinis joined up in 1964) perform 11 standards plus his old hit "Little Bird" on this fine outing. The virtuosic pianist dominates the ensembles, but the contributions of Berghofer and Martinis (who have to think fast to keep up with him) should not be overlooked. Jolly's total command of the piano and infectious enthusiasm, which can result in some explosive outbursts, do not overshadow his good taste and the self-restraint that he shows on the ballads. — *Scott Yanow*

Elvin Jones

b. Sep. 9, 1927, Pontiac, MI
Drums / Avant-Garde, Post-Bop, Hard Bop
Elvin Jones will always be best known for his association with the classic John Coltrane Quartet (1960-65), but he has also had a notable career as a bandleader and has continued being a major influence during the past 30 years. One of the all-time great drummers (bridging the gap between advanced hard bop and the avant-garde), Elvin is the younger brother of a remarkable musical family that also includes Hank and Thad Jones. After spending time in the Army (1946-49), he was a part of the very fertile Detroit jazz scene of the early '50s. He moved to New York in 1955, worked with Teddy Charles and the Bud Powell Trio, and recorded with Miles Davis and Sonny Rollins (the latter at his famous Village Vanguard session). After stints with J.J. Johnson (1956-57), Donald Byrd (1958), Tyree Glenn, and Harry "Sweets" Edison, Jones became an important member of John Coltrane's Quartet, pushing the innovative saxophonist to remarkable heights and appearing on most of his best recordings. When Coltrane added Rashied Ali to his band in late 1965 as second drummer, Jones was not pleased and he soon departed. He went on a European tour with the Duke Ellington Orchestra and then started leading his own groups, which in the '90s became known as Elvin Jones' Jazz Machine. Among his sidemen have been saxophonists Frank Foster, Joe Farrell, George Coleman, Pepper Adams, Dave Liebman, Pat LaBarbera, Steve Grossman, Andrew White, Ravi Coltrane, and Sonny Fortune, trumpeter Nicholas Payton, pianists Dollar Brand and Willie Pickens, keyboardist Jan Hammer, and bassists Richard Davis, Jimmy Garrison, Wilbur Little and Gene Perla, among others. Elvin Jones has recorded as a leader for many labels, including Atlantic, Riverside, Impulse, Blue Note, Enja, PM, Vanguard, Honey Dew, Denon, Storyville, Evidence, and Landmark. — *Scott Yanow*

Elvin Jones and Company / Jul. 11, 1961-Jan. 3, 1962 / Riverside ✦✦✦

Elvin! / Jul. 11, 1961-Jan. 3, 1962 / Original Jazz Classics ✦✦✦✦
Drummer Elvin Jones' first full-length album as a leader (reissued on CD in the OJC series) is different than one would expect when it is taken into consideration that he was a member of the fiery John Coltrane Quartet at the time. This sextet session, which also includes his brothers Thad and Hank on cornet and piano in addition to flutist Frank Wess, Frank Foster on tenor and bassist Art Davis, is straightahead with a strong Count Basie feel. Elvin is still recognizable on the fairly obscure material (only "You Are Too Beautiful" qualifies as a standard) and shows that he can cook in the fairly conventional setting. All of the musicians are in fine form, and two selections feature the rhythm section as a trio. —*Scott Yanow*

Dear John C. / Feb. 23, 1965+Feb. 25, 1965 / Impulse ✦✦✦

Midnight Walk / Mar. 24, 1966 / Atlantic ✦✦✦

Heavy Sounds / 1968 / Impulse ✦✦✦

Puttin' It Together / Apr. 8, 1968 / Blue Note ✦✦✦✦
Solid pianoless trio date, Joe Farrell handles heavy reed load. Jimmy Garrison on bass. —*Ron Wynn*

★ **Live at the Lighthouse, Vol. 1** / Sep. 9, 1972 / Blue Note ✦✦✦✦✦
Originally solid twin-record set reissued in separate versions. Strong quartet with saxmen Steve Grossman and Dave Liebman. CD has two bonus cuts. —*Ron Wynn*

☆ **Live at the Lighthouse, Vol. 2** / Sep. 9, 1972 / Blue Note ✦✦✦✦✦
Second volume of dynamic Lighthouse set. CD has three bonus cuts. —*Ron Wynn*

★ **It Don't Mean a Thing** / Oct. 18, 1993-Oct. 19, 1993 / Enja ✦✦✦✦✦
Elvin Jones has participated in many recording sessions through the years, but this CD is one of the most well rounded sets he has ever led. The lineup of musicians is very impressive: trumpeter Nicholas Payton, Sonny Fortune on tenor and flute, trombonist Delfeayo Marsalis, pianist Willie Pickens, bassist Cecil McBee, and vocalist Kevin Mahogany. Everyone plays up to their potential, and the material has plenty of variety, ranging from Monk, Ellington, and Strayhorn to a traditional Japanese folk song arranged by Elvin's wife, Keiko ("A Lullaby of Itsugo Village"), two features for Mahogany (a touching version of "Lush Life" and his scat-filled "Bopsy"), and some authentic-sounding R&B (Sam Cooke's "A Change Is Gonna Come"). Payton, Marsalis, and Fortune are not on every selection, but each has a chance to shine while pianist Willie Pickens is showcased with the trio on a medley of "A Flower Is a Lovesome Thing" and "Ask Me Now." And as for the drummer, there is still no one around who has captured the sound and spirit of Elvin Jones. —*Scott Yanow*

Hank Jones

b. Jul. 31, 1918, Vicksburg, MS
Piano / Bop, Swing
The oldest of the three illustrious Jones brothers (which include Thad and Elvin), Hank Jones was also the first of the great Detroit pianists (including Tommy Flanagan, Barry Harris, and Roland Hanna) to emerge after World War II, although by then he had long since left town. Jones played in territory bands while a teenager, and in 1944 he moved to New York to play with Hot Lips Page. He had stints with John Kirby, Howard McGhee, Coleman Hawkins, Andy Kirk, and Billy Eckstine. Influenced by Teddy Wilson and Art Tatum, Jones' style was also open to bebop, and his accessible playing was flexible enough to fit into many genres. He was on several Jazz at the Philharmonic tours (starting in 1947), worked as accompanist for Ella Fitzgerald (1948-53), and recorded with Charlie Parker. In the '50s Jones performed with Artie Shaw, Benny Goodman, Lester Young, Cannonball Adderley, and many others. He was on the staff of CBS during 1959-1976 but always remained active in jazz. In the late '70s Jones was the pianist in the Broadway musical *Ain't Misbehavin'*, and he recorded with a pickup unit dubbed the Great Jazz Trio at various times includes Ron Carter, Buster Williams, or Eddie Gomez on bass, and Tony Williams, Al Foster or Jimmy Cobb on drums. Among the many labels that Hank Jones has recorded as a leader are Verve, Savoy, Epic, Golden Crest, Capitol, Argo, ABC-Paramount, Impulse, Concord, East Wind, Muse, Galaxy, Black & Blue, MPS, Inner City, and Chiaroscuro. —*Scott Yanow*

● **Trio** / Aug. 4, 1955 / Savoy ✦✦✦✦
Seminal stuff from Hank Jones, with Kenny Clarke (d), Wendell Marshall (b). —*Ron Wynn*

Bluebird / Aug. 1955-Nov. 1955 / Savoy ✦✦✦✦
These relaxed cool jazz performances feature pianist Hank Jones in a variety of settings. In addition to drummer Kenny Clarke and either Eddie Jones or Wendell Marshall on bass, "Hank's Pranks" has both Donald Byrd and Manny Dice on trumpets, trumpeter Joe Wilder and flutist Herbie Mann are on a song each, and Jerome Richardson (doubling on flute and tenor) drops by for two. It's a tasteful set of melodic bop. —*Scott Yanow*

Hanky Panky / Jul. 14, 1975-Jul. 15, 1975 / Inner City ✦✦✦

● **Solo Piano** / Jan. 24, 1976 / All Art Jazz ✦✦✦✦
One of Hank Jones' finest solo sessions, this date (recorded in Tokyo but recently reissued on CD through an association with the Jazz Alliance

label) finds the veteran pianist performing seven Duke Ellington ballads and seven other fairly well known standards. The music is melodic, sometimes exquisite and full of subtle twists and turns. It is worth picking up as an example of Hank Jones' tasteful and very musical style. —*Scott Yanow*

Bop Redux / Jan. 18, 1977-Jan. 19, 1977 / Muse ✦✦✦✦
Veteran pianist Hank Jones teams up with bassist George Duvivier and drummer Ben Riley for a set of high-quality explorations of eight bop standards; four apiece by Charlie Parker and Thelonious Monk. Jones is sensitive on the ballads and lightly but firmly swinging on the more uptempo material. Typically tasteful performances come from one of the greats. —*Scott Yanow*

Just for Fun / Jun. 27, 1977-Jun. 28, 1977 / Original Jazz Classics ✦✦✦✦
Includes some good working by this always-insightful, creative soloist. —*Michael G. Nastos*

Tiptoe Tapdance / Jun. 29, 1977-Jan. 21, 1978 / Original Jazz Classics ✦✦✦

● **Live at Maybeck Recital Hall, Vol. 16** / Nov. 11, 1991 / Concord Jazz ✦✦✦✦
A high point in the career of distinguished pianist Hank Jones was being among the artists tabbed for a solo release in the Maybeck series. While he's always been known as a great accompanist and good trio contributor, his solo skills have sometimes been undervalued. But after hearing him work in this unaccompanied setting, there should be no doubt that Hank Jones is a superb soloist, along with all of his other talents. —*Ron Wynn*

Handful of Keys / Apr. 28, 1992-Apr. 29, 1992 / Verve ✦✦✦✦

Jo Jones (Jonathan Jones)

b. Oct. 7, 1911, Chicago, IL, d. Sep. 3, 1985, New York, NY
Drums / Swing
Jo Jones shifted the timekeeping role of the drums from the bass drum to the hi-hat cymbal, influencing all swing and bop drummers. Buddy Rich and Louie Bellson were two who learned from his light but forceful playing, as Jones swung the Count Basie Orchestra with just the right accents and sounds. After growing up in Alabama, Jones worked as a drummer and tap dancer with carnival shows. He joined Walter Page's Blue Devils in Oklahoma City in the late '20s. After a period with Lloyd Hunter's band in Nebraska, Jones moved to Kansas City in 1933, joining Count Basie's band the following year. He went with Basie to New York in 1936 and with Count, Freddie Green, and Walter Page he formed one of the great rhythm sections. Jones was with the Basie band (other than 1944-46 when he was in the military) until 1948, and in later years he participated in many reunions with Basie alumni. He was on some Jazz at the Philharmonic tours and recorded in the '50s with Illinois Jacquet, Billie Holiday, Teddy Wilson, Lester Young, Art Tatum, and Duke Ellington, among others; Jones appeared at the 1957 Newport Jazz Festival with both Basie and the Coleman Hawkins-Roy Eldridge Sextet. Jo Jones led sessions for Vanguard (1955 and 1959) and Everest (1959-60), a date for Jazz Odyssey on which he reminisced and played drum solos (1970) and mid-'70s sessions for Pablo and Denon. In later years he was known as "Papa" Jo Jones and thought of as a wise if brutally frank elder statesman. —*Scott Yanow*

The Main Man / Nov. 29, 1976-Nov. 30, 1976 / Original Jazz Classics ✦✦✦✦
This date with Harry Edison (tpt), Roy Eldridge (tpt), Vic Dickerson (tb) and others is sterling silver. —*Michael G. Nastos*

Our Man Papa Jo! / Dec. 12, 1977 / Denon ✦✦✦✦
The final session for a jazz legend. Drummer Jo Jones was nearing the end when he got together with his old friends, pianist Hank Jones and bassist Major Holley, for this 1982 session. He still managed to play with some degree of authority and anchor the rhythm section, while saxophonist Jimmy Oliver and Jones took care of solo responsibilities. This has been reissued on CD. —*Ron Wynn*

★ **The Essential Jo Jones** / Vanguard ✦✦✦✦✦
Jo Jones, one of the most influential drummers of the swing era, did not lead that many record sessions of his own during his career. Producer John Hammond gave him his first two dates when he was working for Vanguard and, with the exception of a second take of "Shoe Shine Boy," all of the music from the two LPs is on this single-CD reissue. The first session is very much in the spirit of Count Basie's band; in fact, Basie himself makes a guest appearance on "Shoe Shine Boy." The other swing-oriented players include trumpeter Emmett Berry, trombonist Freddie Green, tenor saxophonist Lucky Thompson, and (on one song apiece) trombonist Lawrence Brown and clarinetist Rudy Powell. The later date is quite a bit different, a trio session with pianist Ray Bryant and bassist Tommy Bryant. There are a liberal amount of drum solos, but of greatest interest are the early versions of Ray Bryant's "Cubano Chant" and "Little Susie." —*Scott Yanow*

Philly Joe Jones (Joseph Rudolph Jones)

b. Jul. 15, 1923, Philadelphia, PA, d. Aug. 30, 1985, Philadelphia, PA
Drums / Hard Bop
A fiery drummer and a masterful accompanist, Philly Joe Jones came to

fame as a key member with the first classic Miles Davis Quintet. After serving in the Army, he moved to New York in 1947, became the house drummer at Cafe Society, and played with the who's who of bop (including Charlie Parker, Dizzy Gillespie, and Fats Navarro). He worked regularly with Ben Webster, Joe Morris, Tiny Grimes, Lionel Hampton, and Tadd Dameron (19530. Jones was with Miles Davis during 1955-58 including the quintet years (1955-56) with John Coltrane, Red Garland, and Paul Chambers and the beginnings of the super sextet that also included Cannonball Adderley (recording the classic *Milestones* album). In 1958 he started leading his own groups, recording for Riverside (1958-59) and Atlantic (1960). Jones lived in London and Paris during 1967-72 (performing and recording with some avant-garde players including Archie Shepp). He eventually returned to Philadelphia where he led the fusion group Le Grand Prix, toured with Bill Evans during 1976, recorded for Galaxy in 1977 and 1979, and worked with Red Garland. Starting in 1981 he led the group Dameronia, which revived Tadd Dameron's music. But in reality everything that Philly Joe Jones did after Miles Davis was anticlimactic. —*Scott Yanow*

Drums Around the World / May 28, 1959-May 29, 1959 / Original Jazz Classics ✦✦✦

Showcase / Nov. 17, 1959 / Original Jazz Classics ✦✦✦✦
Fine sextet and septet material. —*Ron Wynn*

Drum Song / Oct. 10, 1978-Oct. 12, 1978 / Galaxy ✦✦✦✦
Hard bop is spoken here on this straight-ahead set. Drummer Philly Joe Jones is the leader, but the main emphasis is on such soloists as trumpeter Blue Mitchell (heard in one of his last recordings), the tenors of Harold Land and Charles Bowen, pianist Cedar Walton, and trombonist Slide Hampton, who arranged the four full-band numbers. Hampton (who also contributed two originals) gets "I Wait for You" as his feature, while Bowen is showcased on "High Fly." In addition, these versions of "Our Delight" and "Two Bass Hit" have their heated moments. —*Scott Yanow*

● **To Tadd with Love** / Jun. 28, 1982 / Uptown ✦✦✦✦
Drummer Philly Joe Jones during his last years led the group Dameronia, a band dedicated to performing the music of the great composer Tadd Dameron. Their debut disc for Uptown has Donald Sickler's transcriptions of six Dameron originals (including "Philly J.J.," "Soultrane," and "On a Misty Night"). The nonet comprises many fine veteran players: trumpeters Sickler and Johnny Coles, trombonist Britt Woodman, altoist Frank Wess, Charles Davis on tenor, baritonist Cecil Payne, pianist Walter Davis, Jr., bassist Larry Ridley, and Jones himself. This loving tribute (which perfectly balances the arrangements with concise solo space) is highly recommended. —*Scott Yanow*

Look Stop and Listen / Jul. 11, 1983 / Uptown ✦✦✦✦
Tadd Dameron was arguably the top composer/arranger of the early bebop years. Drummer Philly Joe Jones put together the group Dameronia specifically to perform Dameron's music, and this was their second and final album before Jones' death. The lineup of this band was very impressive (trumpeters Don Sickler and Virgil Jones, trombonist Benny Powell, altoist Frank Wess, Charles Davis on tenor, baritonist Cecil Payne, pianist Walter Davis Jr, bassist Larry Ridley, and Jones on drums) and, when one adds in guest soloist Johnny Griffin on tenor and Sickler's accurate transcriptions of the seven Dameron compositions (plus Benny Golson's "Killer Joe"), the result is an album that is significant both historically and musically. In other words, get this one. —*Scott Yanow*

Quincy Jones

b. Mar. 14, 1933
Piano, Trumpet / Bop, Swing, Pop, Crossover
Quincy Jones has had several very successful careers, largely leaving jazz altogether by the early '70s to make his money producing pop, R&B, and even rap records. His earlier years were much more significant to improvised music. He grew up in Seattle and his first important job was playing trumpet and arranging for Lionel Hampton's Orchestra (1951-53), sitting in a trumpet section with Clifford Brown and Art Farmer. During the '50s he started freelancing as an arranger, writing memorable charts for sessions led by Oscar Pettiford, Brown, Farmer, Gigi Gryce, Count Basie, Tommy Dorsey, Cannonball Adderley and Dinah Washington, amomng others. He toured with Dizzy Gillespie's big band (1956), started recording as a leader for ABC-Paramount in 1956 and worked in Paris (1957-58) for the Barclay label as an arranger and producer. In 1959 Jones toured Europe with his all-star big band, which was originally put together to play for Harold Arlen's show *Free and Easy*. He kept the orchestra together through 1960, recording for Mercury. In 1961 Jones returned to New York and became the head of Mercury's A&R department, becoming a vice president in 1964. Although he kept on recording throughout the '60s, Jones' focus shifted to writing for films and television. During 1969-81 he worked for A&M, founding Qwest Records in 1980, a label that has become both active in the '90s. Among his best jazz compositions have been "Stockholm Sweetnin'," "For Lena and Lennie," "Quintessence," "Jessica's Day," and "The Midnight Sun Never Sets." Although he deserves credit for talking

Miles Davis into performing Gil Evans' arrangements at the 1991 Montreux Jazz Festival and for signing such artists as Milt Jackson and Sonny Simmons to his Qwest label in the '90s, very little that Quincy Jones has accomplished during the past 25 years is of any real relevance to jazz. —*Scott Yanow*

Sweden-American All Stars / Nov. 10, 1953 / Prestige ✦✦✦

★ **This Is How I Feel About Jazz** / 1956 / GRP ✦✦✦✦✦
Arranger Quincy Jones made many excellent straight jazz records in the '50s and '60s before he began gravitating towards pop and R&B. He assembled a strong cast and made his arrangements the focal point for *This Is How I Feel About Jazz*, which serves as a yardstick for directions that the music was heading at the time. —*Ron Wynn*

Swiss Radio Days Jazz Series, Vol. 1 / Jun. 27, 1960 / TCB ✦✦✦
Quincy Jones led one of his finest orchestras in 1960. This spirited CD is taken from a live concert (and radio broadcast) from Switzerland. With such soloists as trumpeter Benny Bailey, trombonist Jimmy Cleveland, altoist Phil Woods, Jerome Richardson on tenor, and baritonist Sahib Shihab (among others), the repertoire mostly sticks to bebop. Surprisingly enough not all of the arrangements heard on the CD are Jones'; there are also swinging charts from Ernie Wilkins, Billy Byers, Melba Liston, Phil Woods, and Al Cohn. This well recorded and previously unissued performance (which came out for the first time in 1994) makes one wish that Quincy Jones would return to jazz someday. —*Scott Yanow*

The Best of Quincy Jones, Vol. 2 / 1967-1981 / A&M ✦✦✦

The Best / 1967-1981 / A&M ✦✦✦

Walking in Space / Jun. 1969 / A&M ✦✦✦✦
A Grammy-winning work that marked the beginning of Jones' shift into R&B and pop. —*Ron Wynn*

Gula Matari / Mar. 25, 1970-May 1, 1970 / A&M ✦✦✦✦
A superb follow-up that might have been better than *Walkin' in Space* overall. —*Ron Wynn*

Smackwater Jack / 1971 / Mobile Fidelity ✦✦

Roots / 1974 / A&M ✦✦✦

25th Anniversary Series, Vol. 3 / 1978 / A&M ✦✦✦✦
A good overview and compilation from an R&B/pop perspective. —*Ron Wynn*

The Dude / 1981 / A&M ✦✦✦
A wonderful production that leans more toward soul pop than jazz. —*Ron Wynn*

Classics, Vol. 3 / 1987 / A&M ✦✦

Strike up the Band / 1988 / Verve ✦✦

Q's Jook Joint / Nov. 7, 1995 / Qwest ✦✦
The multi-talented Quincy Jones has excelled at idiomatic combinations in his albums since the '60s, when his mix-and-match soundtracks for television and films alerted everyone he'd switched from a pure jazz mode to a populist bent. *Q's Juke Joint* blends the latest in hip-hop flavored productions with sleek urban ballads, vintage standards, and derivative pieces; everything's superbly crafted, though few songs are as exciting in their performance or daring in their conception as such past Jones epics like *Gula Matari* or the score from *Roots*. Still, you can't fault Jones for his choice of musical collaborators; everyone from newcomer Tamia to longtime stars like Ray Charles, rappers, instrumentalists, male and female vocalists, percussionists, and toasters. The CD really conveys the seamless quality one gets from attending a juke joint, though it lacks the dirt-floor grit or blues fervor of traditional Southern and chitlin' circuit hangouts. But no one's more knowledgeable about the spectrum of African-American music, or better able to communicate it via disc than Quincy Jones. —*Ron Wynn*

Sam Jones (Samuel Jones)

b. Nov. 12, 1924, Jacksonville, FL, d. Dec. 15, 1981, New York, NY
Bass, Cello / Hard Bop
Sam Jones, a greatly in-demand bassist who often teamed up with drummer Louis Hayes, was also a talented jazz cello soloist. He always took advantage of the fairly rare opportunities he had to lead sessions to create memorable music. He played with Tiny Bradshaw (1953-55), moved to New York in 1955, and worked with the groups of Kenny Dorham, Cannonball Adderley (1957), Dizzy Gillespie (1958-59), and Thelonious Monk, among others. While a member of Cannonball Adderley's very successful quintet (1959-65), Jones wrote such originals as "Unit 7" and "Del Sasser" and led three highly recommended albums for Riverside during 1960-62 (all have been reissued in the OJC series) that featured some of his finest cello playing. Sam Jones was with the Oscar Peterson Trio (as Ray Brown's first replacement) during 1966-70 and then freelanced for the remainder of his life, making many recordings including albums of his own for East Wind (1974), Xanadu, Muse, Inner City, SteepleChase, Interplay, and SeaBreeze. —*Scott Yanow*

★ **The Soul Society** / Mar. 8, 1960+Mar. 10, 1960 / Original Jazz Classics ✦✦✦✦✦
Bassist Sam Jones' debut as a leader resulted in one of his finest recordings. On four of the eight selections on the CD reissue of his Riverside set, Jones is well featured on bass while the other four numbers find him playing very effective cello. The uncredited arrangements for the groups are uniformly excellent and there is solo space for cornetist Nat Adderley, trumpeter Blue Mitchell, Jimmy Heath on tenor, baritonist Charles Davis, and pianist Bobby Timmons. The repertoire is superior, with highlights including the debut of Adderley's "The Old Country," a fine jam on "Just Friends," Keter Betts' "Some Kinda Mean," Jones' bowing on "Home," and Bobby Timmons' "So Tired." Actually, all eight selections are memorable on this highly recommended disc. —*Scott Yanow*

The Chant / Jan. 13, 1961+Jan. 26, 1961 / Original Jazz Classics ✦✦✦✦
Bassist Sam Jones' Riverside recordings have long been underrated. This CD reissue features Jones on bass and cello for four songs apiece with a particularly strong supporting cast including cornetist Nat Adderley, trumpeter Blue Mitchell, trombonist Melba Liston, altoist Cannonball Adderley (who only takes one solo), and Jimmy Heath on tenor; Victor Feldman and Heath provided the colorful arrangments. Highlights include "Four," "Sonny Boy," Jones' "In Walked Ray," and "Over the Rainbow" but all eight selections in this straightahead set are rewarding. —*Scott Yanow*

Down Home / Aug. 15, 1962-Aug. 16, 1962 / Original Jazz Classics ✦✦✦✦
Bassist Sam Jones, always best known for being a sideman (most notably with Cannonball Adderley's Quintet), recorded three superior Riverside albums as a leader during 1960-62 that have all been reissued on CD in the OJC series. This particular one, the third, features Jones on bass and cello in several settings. Four selections (including Horace Silver's "Strollin'" and "Unit Seven") are with an all-star nonet/tentet, while four others showcase Jones' cello in quintets with either Les Spann or Frank Strozier on flute and Israel Crosby or Ron Carter on bass. This is excellent hard bop-based music, but it would be another 12 years before Jones had his next opportunity to be a leader! —*Scott Yanow*

Thad Jones (Thaddeus Joseph Jones)

b. Mar. 28, 1923, Pontiac, MI, **d.** Aug. 20, 1986, Copenhagen, Denmark
Trumpet, Cornet / Bop, Hard Bop
A harmonically advanced trumpeter/cornetist with a distinctive sound and a talented arranger/composer, Thad Jones (the younger brother of Hank and older brother of Elvin) had a very productive career. Self-taught on trumpet, he started playing professionally when he was 16 with Hank Jones and Sonny Stitt. After serving in the military (1943-46), Jones worked in territory bands in the Midwest. During 1950-53 he performed regularly with Billy Mitchell's quintet in Detroit, and he made a few recordings with Charles Mingus (1954-55). Jones became well known during his long period (1954-63) with Count Basie's Orchestra, taking a "Pop Goes the Weasel" chorus on "April in Paris" and sharing solo duties with Joe Newman. While with Basie, Jones had the opportunity to write some arrangements, and he became a busy freelance writer after 1963. He joined the staff of CBS, co-led a quintet with Pepper Adams, and near the end of 1965 organized a big band with drummer Mel Lewis that from February 1966 on played Monday nights at the Village Vanguard. During the next decade the orchestra (although always a part-time affair) became famous and gave Jones an outlet for his writing. He composed one standard ("A Child Is Born") along with many fine pieces including "Fingers," "Little Pixie," and "Tiptoe." Among the sidemen in the Thad Jones-Mel Lewis Orchestra (which started out as an all-star group and later on featured younger players) were trumpeters Bill Berry, Danny Stiles, Richard Williams, Marvin Stamm, Snooky Young, and Jon Faddis, trombonists Bob Brookmeyer, Jimmy Knepper, and Quentin Jackson, the reeds of Jerome Richardson, Jerry Dodgion, Eddie Daniels, Joe Farrell, Pepper Adams and Billy Harper, pianists Hank Jones and Roland Hanna, and bassists Richard Davis and George Mraz. In 1978 Jones surprised Lewis by suddenly leaving the band and moving to Denmark, an action he never explained. He wrote for a radio orchestra and led his own group called Eclipse. In late 1984 Jones took over the leadership of the Count Basie Orchestra, but within a year bad health forced him to retire. Thad Jones recorded as a leader for Debut (1954-55), Blue Note, Period, United Artists, Roulette, Milestone, Artists House, and Metronome and many of the Thad Jones-Mel Lewis Orchestra's best recordings have been reissued on a five-CD Mosaic box set. —*Scott Yanow*

Lust for Life / Mar. 7, 1954-Nov. 4, 1957 / Drive Archive ✦✦✦

Fabulous Thad Jones / Aug. 11, 1954-Mar. 10, 1955 / Original Jazz Classics ✦✦✦✦
A 1991 reissue of super cuts from Debut label. —*Ron Wynn*

★ **Magnificent Thad Jones** / Jul. 14, 1956 / Blue Note ✦✦✦✦✦
An excellent reissue. Subtle, harmonic ensemble jazz. —*Michael G. Nastos*

☆ **The Complete Solid State Recordings of the Thad Jones/Mel L** / May 4, 1966-May 25, 1970 / Mosaic ✦✦✦✦✦

★ **Thad Jones and the Mel Lewis Quartet** / Sep. 24, 1977 / A&M ✦✦✦✦✦
This is one of the finest small-group sessions of cornetist Thad Jones' career. With strong and very alert assistance from drummer Mel Lewis (his co-leader in their celebrated big band), pianist Harold Danko, and bassist Rufus Reid, Jones plays at his peak on six standards, two of which were issued for the initial time on this CD reissue. Four of the songs are at least nine minutes long (two are over 15 minutes), yet Thad never loses his momentum. The musicians constantly surprise each other, and there are many spontaneous moments during this often-brilliant outing. —*Scott Yanow*

Scott Joplin

b. Nov. 24, 1868, **d.** Apr. 1, 1917
Piano / Ragtime
Ragtime was jazz's direct predecessor (differing from jazz in the absence of blues and improvisation), and Scott Joplin was ragtime's greatest composer. Joplin lived in St. Louis during 1885-93, playing in local bars and clubs. In 1894 he led a band at the Chicago World's Fair and formed the Texas Medley Quartet, which played in vaudeville shows. Relocating to Sedalia, MO, Joplin began having pieces published as early as 1895 and in 1899 his "Maple Leaf Rag" (published by his supporter John Stark) became ragtime's most popular number, selling over 75,000 copies of sheet music during its first year. Joplin soon had many other rags published that helped to make ragtime the pop music of its day, but the tragedy of his life was that his goals were beyond ragtime. He staged a ballet (*The Ragtime Dance*) and two ragtime operas (*The Guest of Honor* and *Treemonisha*) but none were successful, a fact that continually frustrated him. By 1910 Joplin was becoming ill with syphilis and at his death in 1917, ragtime was in the process of being replaced by jazz. Ironically, 57 years after his death, Scott Joplin finally became a household name because his music (most notably "The Entertainer") was used by Marvin Hamlisch in his score for the popular film *The Sting*. Although he never recorded, Scott Joplin's music has been fully documented with "Maple Leaf Rag" becoming a Dixieland jazz standard and pianist Richard Zimmerman (on an excellent five-LP set for Murray Hill) recording everything that Joplin ever wrote. —*Scott Yanow*

Ragtime, Vol. 3 (Early 1900's) / Mar. 15, 1899-May 11, 1909 / Biograph ✦✦✦✦
The third volume of digitally remastered classic piano rags by Scott Joplin from the early 1900s. If you're a die-hard ragtime lover or piano student, you'll be enthralled by hearing this much ragtime. Others may find it a bit wearing, especially since there's almost no variation in arrangements, pacing, or voicings, only in the player's intensity. —*Ron Wynn*

Ragtime, Vol. 2 (1900-1910) / 1900-1911 / Biograph ✦✦✦✦
Classic Scott Joplin ragtime compositions ranging from early in his career to near the end. Despite the restrictive form (which Joplin rigidly followed), he managed to find ways to creatively rework themes and vary his sound a bit. —*Ron Wynn*

Joplin, Scott: 1916 (Classic Solos from Piano Rolls) / Apr. 16, 1916-May 1917 / Biograph ✦✦✦
More vintage ragtime taken from piano rolls. Scott Joplin was incensed whenever he heard someone playing his rags too fast, so he tried to put them down on piano rolls himself to keep them from being speeded up. These were transferred digitally from rolls. —*Ron Wynn*

● **The Elite Syncopations: Classic Ragtime from Rare** / Biograph ✦✦✦✦
If you want to hear exactly how ragtime should be played, here's the real thing from a founding father. These vintage Scott Joplin rags were transferred to digital from piano rolls and are the way he wanted his rags to sound. —*Ron Wynn*

Clifford Jordan

b. Sep. 2, 1931, Chicago, IL, **d.** 1993
Sax (Tenor) / Post-Bop, Hard Bop
Clifford Jordan was a fine inside/outside player who somehow held his own with Eric Dolphy in the 1964 Charles Mingus Sextet. Jordan had his own sound on tenor almost from the start. He gigged around Chicago with Max Roach, Sonny Stitt, and some R&B groups before moving to New York in 1957. Jordan immediately made a strong impression, leading three albums for Blue Note (including a meeting with fellow tenor John Gilmore) and touring with Horace Silver (1957-58), J.J. Johnson (1959-60), Kenny Dorham (1961-62), and Max Roach (1962-64). After performing in Europe with Mingus and Dolphy, Jordan worked mostly as a leader but tended to be overlooked since he was not overly influential or a pacesetter in the avant-garde. A reliable player, Clifford Jordan toured Europe several times, was in a quartet headed by Cedar Walton in 1974-75, and during his last years led a big band. He recorded as a leader for Blue Note, Riverside, Jazzland, Atlantic (a little-known album of Leadbelly tunes), Vortex, Strata-East, Muse, SteepleChase, Criss Cross, Bee Hive, DIW, Milestone, and Mapleshade. —*Scott Yanow*

★ **Blowing in from Chicago** / Mar. 3, 1957 / Blue Note ✦✦✦✦✦

Spellbound / Aug. 10, 1960 / Original Jazz Classics ✦✦✦✦

Tenor saxophonist Clifford Jordan was sponsored by Cannonball Adderley on this set for Riverside, which has been reissued on CD in the OJC series. Jordan did not at this point quite have the distinctive sound that he would develop by his period with Charles Mingus, but he was already a strong hard bop stylist. Assisted by pianist Cedar Walton, bassist Spanky DeBrest, and drummer Albert "Tootie" Heath, Jordan performs four originals ("Toy" is best known), an unusual waltz version of "Lush Life," the ballad "Last Night When We Were Young," and the romping Charlie Parker blues "Au Privave." It's an excellent straightahead outing. — *Scott Yanow*

Starting Time / Jun. 14, 1961 / Original Jazz Classics ✦✦✦

Bearcat / Oct. 1961-1962 / Original Jazz Classics ✦✦✦

The Highest Mountain / Apr. 18, 1975 / Muse ✦✦✦✦

Although not an innovator himself, tenor-saxophonist Clifford Jordan almost from the start of his career had a distinctive tone and an adventurous style. Overlooked a bit throughout his career, Jordan was always a consistent performer who could be counted on to bring some excitement to whatever music he played on this CD. Jordan is joined by a superior rhythm section (pianist Cedar Walton, bassist Sam Jones, and drummer Billy Higgins) for "Blue Monk," three group originals (including his own complex "Highest Mountain"), and Bill Lee's "John Coltrane," which has a bit of chanting by the players. — *Scott Yanow*

Two Tenor Winner! / Oct. 1984 / Criss Cross ✦✦✦✦

Royal Ballads / Dec. 23, 1986 / Criss Cross ✦✦✦✦

Brilliant interpretations. — *Ron Wynn*

Live at Condon's, New York/Down Through the Years / Oct. 7, 1991 / Milestone ✦✦✦✦

With an extraordinary big band. — *Michael G. Nastos*

Duke Jordan (Irving Sidney Jordan)

b. Apr. 1, 1922, New York, NY

Piano / Bop, Hard Bop

Although he has had a long career, Duke Jordan will always be best-known for being pianist with Charlie Parker's classic 1947 quintet. A little earlier he had worked with the Savoy Sultans, Coleman Hawkins, and the Roy Eldridge big band (1946). After his year with Parker, (his piano introductions to such songs as "Embraceable You" were classic), Jordan worked with the Sonny Stitt-Gene Ammons Quintet (1950-51) and Stan Getz (1949 and 1952-53). He started recording as a leader in 1954, debuting his most famous composition "Jor-du" the following year. Although he worked steadily during the next few decades (writing part of the soundtrack for the French film *Les Liaisons Dangereuses*), Jordan was in obscurity until he began recording on a regular basis for SteepleChase in 1973. Duke Jordan, who was married for a time to the talented jazz singer Sheila Jordan, has lived in Denmark since 1978 and has recorded through the years for Prestige, Savoy, Blue Note, Charlie Parker Records, Muse, Spotlite, and SteepleChase. Still possessing an unchanged bop style, Jordan remains active in the mid-'90s. — *Scott Yanow*

★ **Flight to Jordan** / Aug. 4, 1960 / Blue Note ✦✦✦✦✦

Duke Jordan, who played regularly with the Charlie Parker Quintet in 1947, has long been known as a superior bebop pianist whose style was touched by the genius of Bud Powell's innovations. This quintet album (which also features trumpeter Dizzy Reece and the young tenor Stanley Turrentine) gave Jordan an opportunity to record six of his originals and, although none became as well known as his "Jordu," the music has plenty of strong melodies and variety. This is one of Duke Jordan's better recordings and is quite enjoyable. — *Scott Yanow*

Brooklyn Brothers / Mar. 16, 1973 / Muse ✦✦✦✦

A nice session with fellow reed player Cecil Payne. — *Ron Wynn*

Flight to Denmark / Nov. 25, 1973+Dec. 2, 1973 / SteepleChase ✦✦✦✦

Pianist Duke Jordan has recorded a long series of sessions for the Danish SteepleChase label starting with this 1973 set which has been reissued on CD with four additional selections (three of which are alternate takes). Performing in a trio with bassist Mads Vinding and drummer Ed Thigpen, Jordan plays five of his originals (including "No Problem," "Flight to Denmark," and "Jordu") plus four standards. The pianist's style is easily recognizable (it had not changed much or lost its enthusiasm since 1947 when he achieved fame playing with Charlie Parker), and this CD is a good example of his talents. — *Scott Yanow*

Lover Man / Aug. 1975 / SteepleChase ✦✦✦

Duke's Delight / Nov. 18, 1975 / SteepleChase ✦✦✦✦

Lovely ballads and fine uptempo pieces. — *Ron Wynn*

Tivoli One / Oct. 1984 / SteepleChase ✦✦✦✦

This is a fine all-around trio date for veteran pianist Duke Jordan. Possessor of a rather pure bop style, Jordan (accompanied by bassist Wilbur Little and drummer Dannie Richmond) is in fine form on four of his originals (including a brief rendition of his famous "Jordu," which he uses as a closing theme) and three familiar standards. Bop fans should enjoy this

one, along with virtually all of Jordan's SteepleChase recordings. — *Scott Yanow*

Tivoli Two / Oct. 1984 / SteepleChase ✦✦✦✦

The second of two recordings, this set also finds the classic bop pianist Duke Jordan being joined by bassist Wilbur Little and drummer Dannie Richmond, live from the Tivoli Gardens in Copenhagen. This time around Jordan interprets three originals (a lengthy "No Problem" and "Jordu," which functions as a closing theme), along with three standards. Jordan is heard at the top of his game during these swinging and probing performances. — *Scott Yanow*

Louis Jordan

b. Jul. 8, 1908, Brinkley, AR, d. Feb. 4, 1975, Los Angeles, CA

Saxophone, Vocals / Swing, Jump Blues, Early R&B

Effervescent saxophonist Louis Jordan was one of the chief architects and prime progenitors of the R&B idiom. His pioneering use of jumping shuffle rhythms in a small combo context was copied far and wide during the '40s.

Jordan's sensational hit-laden run with Decca Records contained a raft of seminal performances, featuring inevitably infectious backing by his band, the Tympany Five, and Jordan's own searing alto sax and street corner jive-loaded sense of humor. Jordan was one of the first Black entertainers to sell appreciably in the pop sector; his Decca duet mates included Bing Crosby, Louis Armstrong, and Ella Fitzgerald.

The son of a musician, Jordan spent time as a youth with the Rabbit Foot Minstrels and majored in music later on at Arkansas Baptist College. After moving with his family to Philadelphia in 1932, Jordan hooked up with pianist Clarence Williams. He joined the orchestra of drummer Chick Webb in 1936 and remained there until 1938. Having polished up his singing abilities with Webb's outfit, Jordan was ready to strike out on his own.

The saxist's first 78 for Decca in 1938, "Honey in the Bee Ball," billed his combo as the Elks Rendezvous Band (after the Harlem nightspot that he frequently played at). From 1939 on, though, Jordan fronted the Tympany Five, a sturdy little aggregation often expanding over quintet status that featured some well known musicians over the years: pianists Wild Bill Davis and Bill Doggett, guitarists Carl Hogan and Bill Jennings, bassist Dallas Bartley, and drummer Chris Columbus all passed through the ranks.

From 1942 to 1951, Jordan scored an astonishing 57 R&B chart hits (all on Decca), beginning with the humorous blues "I'm Gonna Leave You on the Outskirts of Town" and finishing with "Weak Minded Blues." In between, he drew up what amounted to an easily followed blueprint for the development of R&B (and for that matter, rock 'n' roll—the accessibly swinging shuffles of Bill Haley & the Comets were directly descended from Jordan; Haley often pointing to his Decca labelmate as profoundly influencing his approach).

"G.I. Jive," "Caldonia," "Buzz Me," "Choo Choo Ch' Boogie," "Ain't That Just like a Woman," "Ain't Nobody Here but Us Chickens," "Boogie Woogie Blue Plate," "Beans and Cornbread," "Saturday Night Fish Fry," and "Blue Light Boogie"—every one of those classics topped the R&B lists, and there were plenty more that did precisely the same thing. Black audiences coast-to-coast were breathlessly jitterbugging to Jordan's jumping jive (and one suspects, more than a few Whites kicked up their heels to those same platters as well).

The saxist was particularly popular during World War II. He recorded prolifically for the Armed Forces Radio Service and the V-Disc program. Jordan's massive popularity also translated onto the silver screen—he filmed a series of wonderful short musicals during the late '40s that were decidedly short on plot but long on visual versions of his hits (*Caldonia, Reet Petite & Gone, Look Out Sister,* and *Beware,* along with countless soundies) that give us an enlightening peek at just what made him such a beloved entertainer. Jordan also cameoed in a big-budget Hollywood wartime musical, *Follow the Boys.*

A brief attempt at fronting a big band in 1951 proved an ill-fated venture, but it didn't dim his ebullience. In 1952, tongue firmly planted in cheek, he offered himself as a candidate for the highest office in the land on the amusing Decca outing "Jordan for President."

Even though his singles were still eminently solid, they weren't selling like they used to by 1954. So after an incredible run of more than a decade and a half, Jordan moved over to the Mesner brothers' Los Angeles-based Aladdin logo at the start of the year. Alas, time had passed the great pioneer by—"Dad Gum Ya Hide Boy," "Messy Bessy," "If I Had Any Sense," and the rest of his Aladdin output sound great in retrospect, but they were not what young R&B fans were searching for at the time. In 1955, he switched to RCA's short-lived "X" imprint, where he tried to remain up-to-date by issuing "Rock 'N' Roll Call."

A blistering Quincy Jones-arranged date for Mercury in 1956 deftly updated Jordan's classics for the rock 'n' roll crowd, with hellfire renditions of "Let the Good Times Roll," "Salt Pork, West Virginia," and "Beware" benefiting from the blasting lead guitar of Mickey Baker and Sam "The Man"

Taylor's muscular tenor sax. There was even time to indulge in a little torrid jazz at Mercury; "The JAMF," from a 1957 LP called *Man, We're Wailin'*, was a sizzling indication of what a fine saxist Jordan was.

Ray Charles had long cited Jordan as a primary influence (he lovingly covered Jordan's "Don't Let the Sun Catch You Crying" and "Early in the Morning"), and paid him back by signing Jordan to the Genius' Tangerine label. Once again, the fickle public largely ignored his worthwhile 1962-64 offerings.

Lounge gigs still offered the saxman a steady income, though, and he adjusted his onstage playlist accordingly. A 1973 album for the French Black & Blue logo found Jordan covering Mac Davis' "I Believe in Music" (can't get much loungier than that!). A heart attack silenced this visionary in 1975, but not before he acted as the bridge between the big-band era and the rise of R&B.

His profile continues to rise posthumously, in large part due to the recent acclaimed Broadway musical *Five Guys Named Moe*, based on Jordan's bubbly, romping repertoire and charismatic persona. —*Bill Dahl*

☆ **Let the Good Times Roll: The Complete Decca Recordings 1938-54** / 1938-1954 / Bear Family ✦✦✦✦✦
The price of this multi-disc import boxed set is indeed a hefty one, but it contains every track the pioneering saxman waxed for Decca—the multitude of hits that inexorably influenced the future of R&B and eventually rock 'n' roll. Bear Family's attention to detail in its presentation is always immaculate, and sound quality follows suit. —*Bill Dahl*

Louis Jordan 1940-1941 / Mar. 13, 1940-Nov. 1940 / Classics ✦✦✦✦

★ **The Best of Louis Jordan** / Nov. 15, 1941-Jan. 1941 / MCA ✦✦✦✦✦
For the rest of us who can't quite finance the Bear Family extravaganza, here's the perfect introduction to the founding father of R&B. Twenty of his all-time classics, including the jumping "Choo Choo Ch'Boogie," "Let the Good Times Roll," "Caldonia," "Blue Light Boogie," and "Five Guys Named Moe," in their seminal Decca configurations. —*Bill Dahl*

1941-43 / Nov. 15, 1941-Nov. 1941 / Classics ✦✦✦✦

Jazz Heritage: Greatest Hits, Vol. 2 (1941-1947) / Nov. 15, 1941-Apr. 23, 1947 / MCA ✦✦✦
Another package of Louis Jordan's R&B hits, this one covering the early and mid-'40s. Jordan was among the biggest stars in the nation during this period, and not only did he have smash songs for himself, others like Woody Herman, Ella Fitzgerald, and even Pearl Bailey and Moms Mabley covered his material. —*Ron Wynn*

Five Guys Named Moe: Original Decca Recordings, Vol. 2 / Jul. 21, 1942-May 8, 1952 / Decca ✦✦✦
Another 18 of Jordan's Decca label classics (although "Five Guys Named Moe" turns up again, in deference to the hit Broadway production). "Is You Is or Is You Ain't (My Baby)," "Jack, You're Dead," "Texas and Pacific," "Boogie Woogie Blue Plate," and "G.I. Jive" are high on the list of gems this time, along with his persuasive 1952 campaign "Jordan for President." —*Bill Dahl*

Just Say Moe! Mo' Best of Louis / Jul. 21, 1942-1973 / Rhino ✦✦✦✦
A nice across-the-board compilation spanning his Decca, Aladdin, RCA, Mercury, and Tangerine label stints. The Decca standouts include "Don't Worry 'Bout That Mule" and the often-covered "Ain't That Just like a Woman," while his Mercury output includes "Big Bess" and "Cat Scratchin'." Could have done without the live "I Believe in Music" at the end, though—that isn't the way we want to remember this wonderful performer. —*Bill Dahl*

1943-45 / Nov. 22, 1943-Jul. 12, 1945 / Classics ✦✦✦✦

One Guy Named Louis / 1954 / Blue Note ✦✦✦

Rock 'n' Roll Call / 1955 / RCA ✦✦✦✦
Only a dozen numbers on this disc, but that's all the saxist made during his 1955-1956 pause at RCA's Vik and "X" subsidiaries. The saxist tried hard to keep up with the times, waxing a stomping title track written by Jack Hammer and Rudy Toombs and a Winfield Scott-penned "Slow, Smooth and Easy" and "Let's Do It Up Baby," but the teenagers just weren't buying. No reason we shouldn't! —*Bill Dahl*

Rock 'n' Roll / Oct. 22, 1956-Aug. 1956 / Verve ✦✦✦

No Moe!—Greatest Hits / Oct. 22, 1956-Aug. 1956 / Verve ✦✦✦

Complete Recordings 1938-1941 / Affinity ✦✦✦✦
Just what it says—two discs' worth of Jordan's earliest Decca work, filled with jivey novelties and lusty sax work by the leader of the Tympany Five. Ends with a couple of his earliest hits, "Knock Me a Kiss" and "I'm Gonna Move to the Outskirts of Town." Forty-nine tracks in all. —*Bill Dahl*

Sheila Jordan

b. Nov. 18, 1928, Detroit, MI
Vocals / Bop, Post-Bop
One of the most consistently creative of all jazz singers, Sheila Jordan has a relatively small voice but has done the maximum with her instrument. She is one of the few vocalists who can improvise logical lyrics (which

often rhyme!), she is a superb scat singer and is also an emotional interpreter of ballads. Despite her talents, Jordan spent much of the '60s and '70s working at a conventional day job! She studied piano when she was 11 and early on sang vocalese in a vocal group. Jordan moved to New York in the '50s, was married to Duke Jordan (1952-62), studied with Lennie Tristano, and worked in New York clubs. George Russell used her on an unusual recording of "You Are My Sunshine," and she became one of the few singers to lead her own Blue Note album (1962). However, it would be a decade before she appeared on records again, working with Carla Bley, Roswell Rudd, and co-leading a group with Steve Kuhn in the late '70s. Jordan recorded a memorable duet album with bassist Arild Andersen for SteepleChase in 1977 and has since teamed up with bassist Harvie Swartz on many occasions. By the '80s Sheila Jordan was finally performing jazz on a full-time basis and gaining the recognition she deserved 20 years earlier. She has recorded as a leader (in addition to the Blue Note session) for East Wind, Grapevine, SteepleChase, Palo Alto, Blackhawk, and Muse. —*Scott Yanow*

★ **Portrait of Sheila Jordan** / Sep. 19, 1962+Oct. 12, 1962 / Blue Note ✦✦✦✦
This innovative date with Barry Galbraith (g), Steve Swallow (b), and Denzil Best (d) is the one to get —*Richard Lieberson*

Sheila / Aug. 27, 1977-Aug. 28, 1977 / SteepleChase ✦✦✦✦
This was a breakthrough recording for Sheila Jordan. She recorded a superb album for Blue Note in 1962 and then was off records (and only working in jazz on a part-time basis) up until the mid-'70s. She cut two albums for tiny labels and then came this, the first of her vocal-bass duet recordings. While in later years bassist Harvie Swartz would be her frequent musical partner, Jordan's SteepleChase set features the talented Arild Andersen on bass. The communication between the two often borders on the miraculous, and it is a pleasure to hear Sheila Jordan's fresh and original interpretations of such songs as "Lush Life," "On Green Dolphin Street," "Don't Explain," and "Better than Anything." —*Scott Yanow*

Songs from Within / Mar. 1989 / MA ✦✦✦✦
Sheila Jordan is one of the few singers to record duets frequently with just a string bass, usually Harvie Swartz. Jordan and Swartz interpret a wide variety of standards on their CD along with two originals. Although the always-inventive singer is clearly the lead voice, Swartz is not restricted to merely an accompanying role; he often shares center stage in close interplay with Jordan, and his lines are almost as unpredictable as Sheila's. Their versions of such veteran songs as "Waltz for Debbie," "St. Thomas," "My Shining Hour," and "In a Sentimental Mood" sound quite original and fresh. As is the custom with M-A, this CD concludes with a selection taken from another release on the label, a melancholy showcase for Marty Krystall's bass clarinet. —*Scott Yanow*

Lost and Found / Sep. 28, 1989-Sep. 29, 1989 / Muse ✦✦✦✦
Superb singer who—sadly—doesn't record very often. —*Ron Wynn*

★ **One for Junior** / Sep. 1991 / Muse ✦✦✦✦✦
This CD is a real gem. Singers Sheila Jordan and Mark Murphy both possess unusual and immediately recognizable voices and are among the top jazz improvisers around. On a typically intelligent and chance-taking program there are many highlights, including a humorous conversation between hipsters on "Where or When," a couple of ballad medleys, and Jordan's witty lyrics on "The Bird." Assisted by pianist Kenny Barron, bassist Harvie Swartz, drummer Ben Riley, and Bill Mays on occasional synthesizer, the two vocalists sound mutually inspired. —*Scott Yanow*

Stanley Jordan

b. Jul. 31, 1959, Chicago, IL
Guitar / Instrumental Pop, Bop
Stanley Jordan's discovery in the early '80s rightfully earned a lot of headlines in the jazz world for he came up with a new way of playing guitar. Although he was not the first to use tapping, Jordan's extensive expertise gave him the ability to play two completely independent lines on the guitar (as if it were a keyboard) or, when he wanted, two guitars at a time. He had originally studied piano, although he switched to guitar when he was 11. After graduating from Princeton in 1981, Jordan played for a time on the streets of New York. Soon he was discovered, had the opportunity to play with Benny Carter and Dizzy Gillespie, and, after recording a solo album for his own Tangent label, signed with Blue Note. Since then his career has been surprisingly aimless. Stanley Jordan can play amazing jazz but he often wastes his talent on lesser material, so one has to be picky in deciding which of his recordings to acquire. —*Scott Yanow*

Touch Sensitive / 1982 / Tangent ✦✦✦✦
He first featured the two-handed touch style, which he has perfected, on this rare independent release. —*Paul Kohler*

Magic Touch / 1985 / Blue Note ✦✦✦✦
This is the debut album by a musician who helped to redefine how a guitar is played. —*Paul Kohler*

Standards, Vol. 1 / 1986 / Blue Note ✦✦✦✦
A stunning collection of jazz standards, it's done to perfection by a superb guitarist. —*Paul Kohler*

Flying Home / 1988 / EMI ✦✦✦
Album from contemporary guitar hero who sometimes justifies his reputation, particularly when he stretches out on standards or jazz anthems and showcases his unique way of playing guitar. Jordan's strumming technique enables him to present unusual chords, phrases, and statements, and when done in a non-gimmicky manner, offers a genuine alternative to the traditional and fusion guitar vocabulary. —*Ron Wynn*

El Huracan / 1989 / Rounder ✦✦✦

● **Stolen Moments** / Nov. 7, 1990-Nov. 9, 1990 / Somethin' Else ✦✦✦✦
Guitarist Stanley Jordan's acclaimed technique, in which he roams over the fret board strumming and gliding rather than picking, has earned him both plaudits and brickbats. His albums have been inconsistent affairs, but he quieted critics with his '91 session. He took standards and anthems that had been done to death and made them sound fresh through invigorating, explosive guitar solos. —*Ron Wynn*

Bolero / Feb. 15, 1994 / Arista ✦✦

Richie Kamuca

b. Jul. 23, 1930, Philadelphia, PA, d. Jul. 22, 1977, Los Angeles, CA
Sax (Tenor) / Cool
An excellent cool-toned tenor who found his own voice in the Lester Young-influenced "Four Brothers" sound, Richie Kamuca tended to be overshadowed by those who came first (such as Stan Getz, Zoot Sims, and Al Cohn), but musicians knew how good he was. Kamuca was a soloist with the orchestras of Stan Kenton (1952-53) and Woody Herman (1954-56) and then worked steadily on the West Coast with such groups as those led by Chet Baker, Maynard Ferguson, the Lighthouse All-Stars (1957-58), Shorty Rogers and Shelly Manne (1959-61). He recorded one album apiece as a leader for Liberty, Mode, and Hi Fi (1956-57); the latter two have been reissued by V.S.O.P. Moving to New York in 1962, Kamuca worked with Gerry Mulligan, Gary McFarland, and Roy Eldridge (1966-71) but was fairly obscure. In 1972 he moved back to Los Angeles to work in the studios but he also played jazz locally with small groups and with Bill Berry's L.A. Big Band. In his later years (1977) before his death from cancer (the day before his 47th birthday), Richie Kamuca recorded three wonderful albums for Concord. —*Scott Yanow*

Richie Kamuca Quartet / Jun. 1957 / VSOP ✦✦✦

West Coast Jazz in Hi Fi / 1959 / Original Jazz Classics ✦✦✦✦
Originally recorded for the Hi Fi label, this CD reissue features tenor saxophonist Richie Kamuca as the main soloist on a variety of standards and basic material arranged by Bill Holman who plays baritone with the octet. Also heard from are trumpeters Conte Candoli and Ed Leddy, trombonist Frank Rosolino, pianist Vince Guaraldi, bassist Monty Budwig and drummer Stan Levey. The music, although based on the West Coast, is not as cool-toned or as laidback as one might expect. High points of the consistently swinging session include "Blue Jazz" (a Kamuca blues), "Star Eyes," "Linger Awhile," and "Indiana." —*Scott Yanow*

★ **Richie** / 1977 / Concord Jazz ✦✦✦✦✦
Richie Kamuca, a hard-swinging but cool-toned tenorman, did not lead any record sessions after 1958 until he recorded three albums for Concord in early 1977, ironically just months before his death at age 47 from cancer. This particular set may very well have been Kamuca's most rewarding. Accompanied by guitarist Mundell Lowe, bassist Monty Budwig, and drummer Nick Ceroli, Kamuca is quite lyrical on the eight superior standards, taking a surprisingly effective vocal on "'Tis Autumn" and coming up with memorable melodic statements on the other songs. —*Scott Yanow*

Charlie / 1977 / Concord Jazz ✦✦✦✦
Richie Kamuca's death from cancer at age 47 just months after this final session was a major loss to jazz. One of the top proponents of the Four Brothers sound on tenor, Kamuca always swung and his tone was quite attractive. This particular set is a tribute to Charlie Parker featuring Kamuca's quintet (which includes trumpeter Blue Mitchell, pianist Jimmy Rowles, bassist Ray Brown, and drummer Donald Bailey). Most unusual is the fact that Kamuca decided to play alto instead of tenor throughout this set and, although this was clearly not his strongest ax, he solos quite well on this date. The music (bop standards and blues) receives favorable and swinging treatment from the talented veterans. —*Scott Yanow*

Roger Kellaway

b. Nov. 1, 1939, Newton, MA
Piano / Bop, Hard Bop
A virtuosic pianist whose phenomenal technique rivals Dick Hyman's, Roger Kellaway's work in commercial settings prior to the '80s led to him being initially overlooked in the jazz world. He played piano and bass at the New England Conservatory (1957-59) and actually left school to play bass with Jimmy McPartland. Switching permanently to piano, Kellaway picked up experience working with Kai Winding, Al Cohn/Zoot Sims, and Clark Terry/Bob Brookmeyer (1963-65). He recorded with many players

including Ben Webster, Maynard Ferguson, Wes Montgomery, and Sonny Rollins and in 1966 moved to Los Angeles where he waxed with Don Ellis' innovative orchestra. Kellaway became Bobby Darin's musical director, worked in the studios (his piano is heard playing the theme of *All in the Family*), wrote film scores, experimented with electric keyboards, played with Tom Scott, and recorded with his popular (but mostly nonjazz) Cello Quartet. Although he gigged locally with Zoot Sims and Harry "Sweets" Edison, it was not until the mid-'80s that Kellaway started playing jazz nearly full-time. His many records since then (for Concord, All Art, Stash, and Chiaroscuro) attest to his impressive talents. —*Scott Yanow*

In Japan / Jun. 5, 1986-Jun. 6, 1986 / All Art Jazz ✦✦✦✦

Alone Together / Jul. 1988 / Dragon ✦✦✦✦

That Was That / Jan. 1991 / Dragon ✦✦✦✦

★ **Live at Maybeck Recital Hall, Vol. 11** / Mar. 10, 1991 / Concord Jazz ✦✦✦✦✦
A recent view of Kellaway's style, it's melodic yet driving, with a strong stride-piano influence. —*Hank Davis*

Concord Duo Series, Vol. 1 (Life's a Take) / May 31, 1992 / Concord Jazz ✦✦✦✦

Wynton Kelly

b. Dec. 2, 1931, Kingston, Jamaica, d. Apr. 12, 1971, Toronto, Canada
Piano / Hard Bop
A superb accompanist loved by Miles Davis and Cannonball Adderley, Wynton Kelly was also a distinctive soloist who decades later would be a strong influence on Benny Green. He grew up in Brooklyn and early on played in R&B bands led by Eddie "Cleanhead" Vinson, Hal Singer, and Eddie "Lockjaw" Davis. Kelly, who recorded 14 titles for Blue Note in a trio (1951), worked with Dinah Washington, Dizzy Gillespie, and Lester Young during 1951-52. After serving in the military he made a strong impression with Washington (1955-57), Charles Mingus (1956-57), and the Dizzy Gillespie big band (1957), but he would be most famous for his stint with Miles Davis (1959-63), recording such albums with Miles as *Kind of Blue*, *At the Blackhawk*, and *Someday My Prince Will Come*. When he left Davis, Kelly took the rest of the rhythm section (bassist Paul Chambers and drummer Jimmy Cobb) with him to form his trio. The group actually sounded at its best backing Wes Montgomery. Before his early death, Kelly recorded as a leader for Blue Note, Riverside, Vee-Jay, Verve, and Milestone. —*Scott Yanow*

Piano Interpretations / Jul. 25, 1951-Aug. 1, 1951 / Blue Note ✦✦✦✦
Recorded at WOR Studios, NYC. Trio. His first solo recording sessions. Even the uptempo pieces have a gentle quality. Very nice mainstream jazz. —*Michael Erlewine*

Piano / Jan. 31, 1958 / Riverside ✦✦✦

Whisper Not / Jan. 31, 1958 / Riverside ✦✦✦

Wynton Kelly / Jan. 31, 1958 / Original Jazz Classics ✦✦✦✦
With the exception of an album for Blue Note in 1951, this was pianist Wynton Kelly's first opportunity to record as a leader. At the time he was still a relative unknown but would soon get a certain amount of fame as Miles Davis' favorite accompanist. With guitarist Kenny Burrell, bassist Paul Chambers and, (on four of the seven selections) drummer Philly Joe Jones, Kelly performs four jazz standards, Oscar Brown, Jr.'s "Strong Man" and two of his originals. Kelly became a major influence on pianists of the '60s and '70s, and one can hear the genesis of many other players in these swinging performances. —*Scott Yanow*

Kelly Blue / Feb. 19, 1959-Mar. 10, 1959 / Original Jazz Classics ✦✦✦✦
Classic Kelly. Bluesy, bright, nice. There is magic in this album. —*Michael Erlewine*

Trio and Sextet / Feb. 19, 1959-Mar. 1959 / Riverside ✦✦✦

Kelly at Midnight / Apr. 27, 1960 / Vee-Jay ✦✦✦

★ **Someday My Prince Will Come** / Sep. 20, 1961-Sep. 21, 1961 / Vee-Jay ✦✦✦✦✦
Pianist Wynton Kelly is heard on this CD reissue (the ten songs from the original LP plus five "new" alternate takes) with either bassist Sam Jones and drummer Jimmy Cobb or bassist Paul Chambers and drummer Philly Joe Jones. His light touch and perfect taste are very much present along with a steady stream of purposeful single-note lines that are full of surprising twists. Trumpeter Lee Morgan and tenor-saxophonist Wayne Shorter drop by for one song (the blues "Wrinkles") but otherwise this recommended set (a definitive Wynton Kelly release), showcases magical trio performances. —*Scott Yanow*

Smokin' at the Half Note / Jun. 1965+Sep. 22, 1965 / Verve ✦✦✦✦
Some recorded Sept 22, 1965, at Englewood Cliffs, NJ. Wynton Kelly Trio with Wes Montgomery (g). Slow to mid-tempos—very listenable. Both Wynton and Wes are in fine form. A rare chance to hear Montgomery in a small-group setting. —*Michael Erlewine*

Last Trio Session / Aug. 4, 1968 / Delmark ✦✦✦

Stan Kenton

b. Dec. 15, 1911, Wichita, KS, **d.** Aug. 25, 1979, Los Angeles, CA
Piano / Progressive Jazz

There have been few jazz musicians as consistently controversial as Stan Kenton. Dismissed by purists of various genres while loved by many others, Kenton ranks up there with Chet Baker and Sun Ra as jazz's top cult figure. He led a succession of highly original bands that often emphasized emotion, power, and advanced harmonies over swing, and this upset listeners who felt that all big bands should aim to sound like Count Basie. Kenton always had a different vision.

Stan Kenton played in the '30s in the dance bands of Vido Musso and Gus Arnheim, but he was born to be a leader. In 1941 he formed his first orchestra, which later was named after his theme song "Artistry in Rhythm." A decent Earl Hines-influenced pianist, Kenton was much more important in the early days as an arranger and inspiration for his loyal sidemen. Although there were no major names in his first band (bassist Howard Rumsey and trumpeter Chico Alvarez come the closest), Kenton spent the summer of 1941 playing regularly before a very appreciative audience at the Rendezvous Ballroom in Balboa Beach, CA. Influenced by Jimmie Lunceford (who, like Kenton, enjoyed high-note trumpeters and thick-toned tenors), the Stan Kenton Orchestra struggled a bit after its initial success. Its Decca recordings were not big sellers, and a stint as Bob Hope's backup radio band was an unhappy experience; Les Brown permanently took Kenton's place.

By late 1943 with a Capitol contract, a popular record in "Eager Beaver" and growing recognition, the Stan Kenton Orchestra was gradually catching on. Its soloists during the war years included Art Pepper, briefly Stan Getz, altoist Boots Mussulli, and singer Anita O'Day. By 1945 the band had evolved quite a bit. Pete Rugolo became the chief arranger (extending Kenton's ideas), Bob Cooper and Vido Musso offered very different tenor styles, and June Christy was Kenton's new singer; her popular hits (including "Tampico" and "Across the Alley from the Alamo") made it possible for Kenton to finance his more ambitious projects. Calling his music "Progressive Jazz," Kenton sought to lead a concert orchestra as opposed to a dance band at a time when most big bands were starting to break up. By 1947 Kai Winding was greatly influencing the sound of Kenton's trombonists, the trumpet section included such screamers as Buddy Childers, Ray Wetzel, and Al Porcino, Jack Costanzo's bongos were bringing Latin rhythms into Kenton's sound and a riotous version of "The Peanut Vendor" contrasted with the somber "Elegy for Alto." Kenton had succeeded in forming a radical and very original band that gained its own audience.

In 1949 Stan Kenton took a year off. In 1950 he put together his most advanced band, the 39-piece Innovations in Modern Music orchestra that included 16 strings, a woodwind section, and two French horns. Its music ranged from the unique and very dense modern classical charts of Bob Graettinger to works that somehow swung despite the weight. Such major players as Maynard Ferguson (whose high-note acrobatics set new standards), Shorty Rogers, Milt Bernhart, John Graas, Art Pepper, Bud Shank, Bob Cooper, Laurindo Almeida, Shelly Manne, and June Christy were part of this remarkable project but, from a commercial standpoint, it was really impossible. Kenton managed two tours during 1950-51 but soon reverted to his usual 19-piece lineup. Then quite unexpectedly, Stan Kenton went through a swinging period. The charts of such arrangers as Shorty Rogers, Gerry Mulligan, Lennie Niehaus, Marty Paich, Johnny Richards, and particularly Bill Holman and Bill Russo began to dominate the repertoire. Such talented players (in addition to the ones already named) as Lee Konitz, Conte Candoli, Sal Salvador, Stan Levey, Frank Rosolino, Richie Kamuca, Zoot Sims, Sam Noto, Bill Perkins, Charlie Mariano, Mel Lewis, Pete Candoli, Lucky Thompson, Carl Fontana, Pepper Adams, and Jack Sheldon made strong contributions. The music was never predictable and could get quite bombastic, but it managed to swing while still keeping the Kenton sound.

Stan Kenton's last successful experiment was his mellophonium band of 1960-63. Despite the difficulties in keeping the four mellophoniums (which formed their own separate section) in tune, this particular Kenton Orchestra had its exciting moments. However, from 1963 on, the flavor of the Kenton big band began to change. Rather than using talented soloists, Kenton emphasized relatively inexpensive youth at the cost of originality. While the arrangements (including those of Hank Levy) continued to be quite challenging, after Gabe Baltzar's "graduation" in 1965, there were few new important Kenton alumni (other than Peter Erskine and Tim Hagans). For many of the young players, touring with Stan Kenton would be the high point of their careers rather than just an important early step. *Kenton Plays Wagner* (1964) was an important project, but by then the bandleader's attention was on jazz education. By conducting a countless number of clinics and making his charts available to college and high-school stage bands, Kenton insured that there would be many bands that sounded like his, and the inverse result was that his own young orchestra sounded like a professional college band! Kenton continued leading and touring with his big band up until his death in 1979. Stan Kenton recorded

for Capitol for 25 years (1943-68) and in the '70s formed his Creative World label to reissue most of his Capitol output and record his current band. In recent times Capitol has begun reissuing Kenton's legacy on CD, and there have been two impressive Mosaic box sets. *— Scott Yanow*

☆ **Complete Capitol Studio Recordings of Stan Kenton 1943-47** / Nov. 19, 1943-Dec. 22, 1947 / Mosaic ✦✦✦✦✦
Documenting Stan Kenton's always controversial but never sleepy music, the seven-CD *Complete Capitol Studio Recordings of Stan Kenton 1943-47* features the orchestra at a time when it was reaching its greatest popularity, evolving from using Kenton's charts into the Pete Rugolo era. In addition to some unreleased tracks, there are also several rare sessions included that were recorded at the time strictly for radio airplay. Most of Kenton's biggest hits ("Artistry in Rhythm," "Eager Beaver," "And Her Tears Flowed Like Wine," "Tampico," "Southern Scandal," "Artistry Jumps," "Intermission Riff," "Across the Alley from the Alamo," and "The Peanut Vendor" are here as are many concert works). A classic reissue. *— Scott Yanow*

★ **Retrospective** / Nov. 19, 1943-Jul. 18, 1968 / Capitol ✦✦✦✦✦
This four-CD set has virtually all of Stan Kenton's most significant recordings from his prime years. Although Kenton completists will prefer to pick up dozens of his individual Creative World releases instead, all other jazz collectors are well advised to get this very well conceived release. Starting with the original version of "Artistry in Rhythm" from 1943 and continuing through all of the different editions of Kenton's orchestras up to 1968's "How Are Things in Glocca Morra" this set includes not only all of the band's most popular recordings but some of its most inventive and esoteric ones, too. Whether it be "Tampico," "Concerto to End All Concertos," "Jolly Rogers," "Art Pepper," "Orange Colored Sky" (with guest Nat King Cole), "All About Ronnie," "Peanut Vendor," and "Maria" or a section of "City of Glass" and a number from the Kenton/Wagner album, the remarkable career of Stan Kenton is covered definitively on this package. It's highly recommended for all jazz collections. *— Scott Yanow*

☆ **Complete Capitol Recordings of the Bill Holman** / Feb. 3, 1950-Sep. 11, 1963 / Mosaic ✦✦✦✦✦
This limited-edition box set is a bit unusual, for rather than reissuing the complete output of a particular artist during a certain era as Mosaic usually does, these four CDs contain all of Stan Kenton's recordings of arrangements by either Bill Holman or Bill Russo. There are three selections from the Innovations band of 1950-51, many recordings from the more swinging 1952-55 period (featuring such soloists as trumpeters Maynard Ferguson and Conte Candoli, trombonist Frank Rosolino, altoists Lee Konitz and Charlie Mariano, tenors Zoot Sims and Bill Perkins, and singer Chris Connor) and Holman's three charts for Kenton's mellophonium band of 1961 in addition to less significant vocal features for Ann Richards and Jean Turner. Kenton completists will already have much of this material (only an early version of "All About Ronnie" was previously unissued) but this attractive box (which is overflowing with classics) will still be treasured by true Kentonites. *— Scott Yanow*

☆ **City of Glass** / Dec. 5, 1951 / Capitol ✦✦✦✦✦
Bob Graettinger was arguably the most radical arranger to ever work in jazz. In fact, it is doubtful that any other big-band leader other than Stan Kenton (who always encouraged adventurous writers) would have used his very complex charts during this era. Graettinger's works, which were influenced by aspects of modern classical music (but were not at all derivative) are all included on this fascinating, if difficult, CD reissue. The four-part "City of Glass," the pieces that comprised "This-Modern World," and a variety of shorter works (including the remarkably dense "Thermopylae") make for some very stimulating listening! This is avant-garde music that still sounds futuristic 45 years later. *— Scott Yanow*

23 Degrees North, 82 / Sep. 2, 1952-Apr. 23, 1953 / Natasha ✦✦✦

● **New Concepts of Artistry in Rhythm** / Sep. 8, 1952-Sep. 16, 1952 / Capitol ✦✦✦✦
Stan Kenton's 1952 orchestra was a very interesting transitional band, still performing some of the complex works of the prior Innovations orchestra but also starting to emphasize swing. This CD contains the rather pompous "Prologue" and Bill Holman's complex "Invention for Guitar and Trumpet" (starring guitarist Sal Salvador and trumpeter Maynard Ferguson) but also Gerry Mulligan's boppish "Young Blood" and Bill Russo's features for trumpeter Conte Candoli ("Portrait of a Count"), trombonist Frank Rosolino ("Frank Speaking"), and altoist Lee Konitz ("My Lady"). *— Scott Yanow*

Cuban Fire / May 22, 1956-May 24, 1956 / Capitol ✦✦✦✦
This CD contains one of the classic Stan Kenton albums, a six-part suite composed and arranged by Johnny Richards. The Kenton orchestra was expanded to 27 pieces for these dates including six percussionists, two French horns, and six trumpets. With such soloists as tenor-great Lucky Thompson (on "Fuego Cubano," trombonist Carl Fontana, altoist Lennie Niehaus, Bill Perkins on tenor, and trumpeters Sam Noto and Vinnie

Tanno), and plenty of raging ensembles, this is one of Stan Kenton's more memorable concept albums of the '50s. — *Scott Yanow*

West Side Story / Mar. 15, 1961-Apr. 11, 1961 / Capitol ✦✦✦✦
When the producers of the film *West Side Story* heard a sampling of what the Stan Kenton Orchestra had done to their score, they were disappointed that they had not thought to ask the band to play on the soundtrack. Johnny Richards' arrangements of ten of the famous play's melodies are alternately dramatic and tender with plenty of the passion displayed by the characters in the story. Soloists include altoist Gabe Baltazar, veteran tenor Sam Donahue, and trumpeter Conte Candoli, but it is the raging ensembles that are most memorable about the classic recording. This CD reissue is highly recommended. — *Scott Yanow*

Freddie Keppard

b. Feb. 27, 1890, New Orleans, LA, **d.** Jul. 15, 1933, Chicago, IL
Cornet / Classic New Orleans Jazz
One of the New Orleans cornet "kings" (succeeding Buddy Bolden and preceding King Oliver), Freddie Keppard was one of the few innovators of the 1910 era who had a chance to record later on, giving listeners a glimpse of his abilities. Keppard was active from around 1906, leading the Olympia Orchestra and freelancing in New Orleans. In 1914 he helped bring jazz to Los Angeles with his Original Creole Band. After settling in Chicago in the early '20s, Keppard worked with Doc Cook's Dreamland Orchestra (with whom he recorded on several occasions), Erskine Tate, Ollie Powers, and Charles Elgar. He could have been the first jazz musician to record (back in 1916), but passed on the opportunity because he was afraid that competitors would steal his ideas. Keppard did record between 1923 and 1927 (his best sides were with his own Jazz Cardinals, particularly "Stock Yard Strut"), and those performances feature him using a staccato phrasing influenced by brass bands and displaying a spirited tone. Unfortunately, Keppard was an alcoholic by the mid-'20s and was soon in a decline just when he should have been entering his prime. He died of tuberculosis in 1933 at the age of 43. All of his recordings are currently available on a single CD put out by the European King Jazz label. — *Scott Yanow*

● **The Complete Freddie Keppard 1923/27** / Jun. 23, 1923-Jan. 1927 / King Jazz ✦✦✦✦

Barney Kessel

b. Oct. 17, 1923, Muskogee, OK
Guitar / Bop, Cool
One of the finest guitarists to emerge after the death of Charlie Christian, Barney Kessel was a reliable bop soloist throughout his career. He played with a big band fronted by Chico Marx (1943), was fortunate enough to appear in the classic jazz short "Jammin' the Blues" (1944), and then worked with the big bands of Charlie Barnet (1944-45) and Artie Shaw (1945); he also recorded with Shaw's Gramercy Five. Kessel became a busy studio musician in Los Angeles but was always in demand for jazz records. He toured with the Oscar Peterson Trio for one year (1952-53) and then, starting in 1953, led an impressive series of records for Contemporary that lasted until 1961 (including several with Ray Brown and Shelly Manne in a trio accurately called "The Poll Winners"). After touring Europe with George Wein's Newport All-Stars (1968), Kessel lived in London for a time (1969-70). In 1973 he began touring and recording with the Great Guitars, a group also including Herb Ellis and Charlie Byrd. A serious stroke in 1992 put Barney Kessel permanently out of action, but many of his records (which include dates for Onyx, Black Lion, Sonet, and Concord in addition to many of the Contemporaries) are currently available along with several video collections put out by Vestapol. — *Scott Yanow*

★ **Barney Kessel, Vol. 3: To Swing or Not to Swing** / Mar. 28, 1955 / Original Jazz Classics ✦✦✦✦✦
High-caliber interpretations. — *Ron Wynn*

Music to Listen to Barney Kessel By / Aug. 6, 1956-Dec. 4, 1956 / Original Jazz Classics ✦✦✦✦
Featured is Kessel's guitar with five woodwinds and a rhythm section. 12 songs were recorded with Buddy Collette (fl), Andre Previn (p), Shelly Manne (d), Jimmy Rowles (p), Red Mitchell (b), Buddy Clark (b), and others. — *AMG*

The Poll Winners with Ray Brown and Shelly Manne / Mar. 18, 1957-Mar. 19, 1957 / Original Jazz Classics ✦✦✦✦
Because guitarist Barney Kessel, bassist Ray Brown, and drummer Shelly Manne all won the *Downbeat, Metronome,* and *Playboy* jazz polls of 1956, it was decided to team the trio together for this and a few other future recordings. Kessel is generally the lead voice of the pianoless group, although Brown and Manne also have plenty of solo space. Together they perform swinging yet quiet versions of a variety of standards (in addition to the guitarist's "Minor Mood") in a relaxed and thoughtful set, reissued on this CD. — *Scott Yanow*

The Poll Winners Ride Again / Aug. 19, 1958 + Aug. 21, 1958 / Original Jazz Classics ✦✦✦✦
Guitarist Barney Kessel, bassist Ray Brown, and drummer Shelly Manne

were dubbed "the Poll Winners" when they swept the *Downbeat, Metronome,* and *Playboy* polls during 1956-57. They recorded several albums together, and this CD reissue features the pianoless trio playing a variety of material, some of it a little odd (including "Volare," "Custard Puff," "When the Red, Red Robin Comes Bob, Bob Bobbin' Along," and "The Merry Go Round Broke Down"). This is a good outing, particularly for bop guitarist Barney Kessel. — *Scott Yanow*

Poll Winners Three! / Nov. 1959 / Original Jazz Classics ✦✦✦✦
'91 reissue of superb 1959 release by a topflight trio with guitarist Barney Kessel, bassist Ray Brown, and drummer Shelly Manne. It was a follow-up to their two previous outstanding records, and the third of four they cut for the Contemporary Records family. — *Ron Wynn*

★ **Limehouse Blues** / Jun. 24, 1969 / Black Lion ✦✦✦✦✦

● **The Poll Winners Straight Ahead** / Jul. 12, 1975 / Original Jazz Classics ✦✦✦✦
15 years after their last joint recordings, the Poll Winners (a trio with guitarist Barney Kessel, bassist Ray Brown, and drummer Shelly Manne) had a reunion for this excellent session, which has been reissued on CD. All three players had grown quite a bit musically since the '50s, and Kessel in particular is heard in excellent form on the three standards and three swinging originals. Overall this is the best all-around recording by the Poll Winners and is easily recommended to bop fans. — *Scott Yanow*

☆ **Straight Ahead** / Jul. 12, 1975 / Contemporary ✦✦✦✦✦
From 1975 with Shelly Manne (d) and Ray Brown (b). — *Michael Erlewine*

Jellybeans / Apr. 1981 / Concord Jazz ✦✦✦

Solo / Apr. 1981 / Concord Jazz ✦✦✦
Superb—some of Kessel's best playing in the '80s. — *Ron Wynn*

Red Hot and Blues / Mar. 15, 1988-Mar. 17, 1988 / Contemporary ✦✦✦✦
One of guitarist Barney Kessel's final recordings before a stroke put him out of action, this is an excellent quintet session with vibraphonist Bobby Hutcherson, pianist Kenny Barron, bassist Rufus Reid, and drummer Ben Riley. Three of Kessel's originals (a pair of blues and a bossa nova) alternate with four standards and Laurindo Almeida's dedication to the guitarist ("Barniana") on this well-paced and consistently swinging set; the uptempo version of "By Myself" is a high-point. — *Scott Yanow*

Steve Khan

b. Apr. 28, 1947, Los Angeles, CA
Guitar / Fusion, Post-Bop
The son of lyricist Sammy Cahn, Steve Khan is best known for his fusion records but has proven on a few occasions that he can also play more straightahead. He originally played piano and drums, not starting on guitar until he was 20. After graduating from UCLA in 1969, Khan moved to New York and worked steadily in jazz, pop, and R&B settings, including such musicians as Maynard Ferguson, Buddy Rich, the Brecker Brothers, Joe Zawinul's Weather Update, and fellow guitarist Larry Coryell. In 1981 he formed the quartet Eyewitness, which worked on an occasional basis throughout the '80s. Steve Khan's most intriguing recordings are a 1980 solo exploration of Thelonious Monk tunes for Novus and a trio outing for Bluemoon named *Let's Call This* (1991). — *Scott Yanow*

The Blue Man / Feb. 1978 / Columbia ✦✦✦

● **Evidence** / Jul. 1980 / Novus ✦✦✦✦
A 1990 reissue of a fusion/jazz-rock set. — *Ron Wynn*

Eyewitness / Nov. 7, 1981-Nov. 8, 1981 / Antilles ✦✦✦✦
Unlike his previous all-star sets, guitarist Steve Khan features his regular group on this album, and the results are quite superior. Whether one calls this music fusion or modern funk, the interplay between Khan, electric bassist Anthony Jackson, drummer Steve Jordan, and percussionist Manolo Badrena is quite impressive; in fact, the four of them share composer credits on three of the five originals. It's one of Steve Khan's best fusion-oriented efforts of the 1980s. — *Scott Yanow*

Local Colour / Apr. 1983-May 1987 / Denon ✦✦✦

Casa Loco / May 21, 1983-May 22, 1983 / Antilles ✦✦✦

Public Access / Jan. 1989 / GRP ✦✦✦

Let's Call This / Jan. 19, 1991-Jan. 20, 1991 / Blue Moon ✦✦✦✦
Best known for his fusion recordings, Steve Khan (ten years after recording the purely acoustic solo date Evidence) stretches out on this pure jazz date. Accompanied by bassist Ron Carter and drummer Al Foster, Khan explores a variety of superior jazz standards (including songs by Thelonious Monk, Wayne Shorter, Larry Young, Freddie Hubbard, and Lee Morgan) along with his own "Buddy System." This is one of Steve Khan's finest recordings to date and is highly recommended to those listeners not familiar with this side of his musical personality. — *Scott Yanow*

Headline / 1992 / Blue Room ✦✦✦✦

Crossings / Dec. 28, 1993-Dec. 30, 1993 / Verve Forecast ✦✦✦✦

John Kirby

b. Dec. 31, 1908, Baltimore, MD, **d.** Jun. 14, 1952, Hollywood, CA
Bass, Tuba / Swing

John Kirby led a most unusual group during the height of the big-band era, a sextet comprising trumpeter Charlie Shavers, clarinetist Buster Bailey, altoist Russell Procope, pianist Billy Kyle, drummer O'Neil Spencer, and his own bass. Although Shavers and Bailey could be quite extroverted, the tightly arranged ensembles tended to be very cool-toned and introverted yet virtuosic. Kirby, originally a tuba player, switched to bass in 1930 when he joined Fletcher Henderson's Orchestra. He was one of the better bassists of the '30s, playing with Henderson (1930-33 and 1935-36) and Chick Webb's big band (1933-35). By 1937 Kirby had his own group at the Onyx Club; Frankie Newton and Pete Brown passed through the band before the personnel was set. With Maxine Sullivan (Kirby's wife at the time) offering occasional vocals, the John Kirby Sextet was quite popular during 1938-42. Shavers' "Undecided" became a hit, and the band's abilities to "swing the classics" caught on. The sextet gradually declined in the '40s. Spencer became ill and was replaced by Specs Powell and later Bill Beason; Kyle was drafted and Procope was replaced by George Johnson. By 1945 (with Shavers' departure to join Tommy Dorsey), the only original members still in the group were Bailey and Kirby himself. The following year the band disbanded and despite some attempts by the bassist to form another similar sextet (including a poorly attended Carnegie Hall reunion in 1950), John Kirby was never able to duplicate his earlier successes. Classics has reissued all of Kirby's prime recordings. —*Scott Yanow*

Boss of the Bass / Dec. 3, 1930-Jan. 15, 1941 / Columbia ✦✦✦✦
John Kirby was never actually the "boss of the bass," even back in the '30s, but he was an important bandleader. The second half of this admirable two-LP set features his unique group on 14 of their more rewarding recordings from 1939-41. The complex yet tight arrangements and concise solos by the virtosi (trumpeter Charlie Shavers, bassist Buster Bailey, altoist Russell Procope, pianist Billy Kyle, drummer O'Neil Spencer, and Kirby on bass) gave the John Kirby Sextet a unique sound of its own. The first of these two LPs contains 14 selections featuring Kirby as a sidemen with such groups as the Chocolate Dandies, Fletcher Henderson, Chick Webb, Putney Dandridge, Teddy Wilson, Charlie Barnet, and Lucky Millinder along with backup work with early versions of his sextet behind singers Midge Williams, Maxine Sullivan, and Mildred Bailey. A well conceived reissue, it contains more than its share of exciting swing performances. —*Scott Yanow*

☆ **John Kirby 1938-1939** / Oct. 28, 1938-Oct. 12, 1939 / Classics ✦✦✦✦✦
☆ **John Kirby 1939-1941** / Oct. 12, 1939-Jan. 15, 1941 / Classics ✦✦✦✦✦
★ **1941-1943** / Jan. 2, 1941-Dec. 1943 / Classics ✦✦✦✦ Procope
The third John Kirby CD from the European Classics label has 21 performances that trace Kirby's unique sextet from the peak of its popularity in 1941 through the war years. In addition to a dozen songs originally released by Victor, this set has nine rarer numbers that appeared on V-Discs. With trumpeter Charlie Shavers, clarinetist Buster Bailey, and altoist Russell Procope, (along with pianist Billy Kyle and drummer O'Neil Spencer), Kirby was able to form an unusual and very distinctive group sound that, although comprising swing virtuosos, looked towards cool jazz of the '50s. By the later tracks of this CD the band was starting to come apart a bit with first Specs Powell and then Bill Beason replacing the late Spencer, George Johnson ably filling in for Procope, and Shavers departing before the final number; the group sound, however, remained intact as among the many highlights of this CD are "Coquette," "Royal Garden Blues," "Night Whispers," "St. Louis Blues," and "9:20 Special." —*Scott Yanow*

Andy Kirk

b. May 28, 1898, Newport, KY, **d.** 1992
Bass, Sax (Bass) / Swing

Andy Kirk was never a major musician (in fact, he never really soloed), arranger, or personality, yet he was a successful big band leader in the '30s and '40s. He started playing bass sax and tuba in Denver with George Morrison's band in 1918. In 1925 he moved to Dallas where he played with Terrence Holder's Dark Clouds of Joy. In 1929 he took over leadership of the band (which was renamed Andy Kirk's Twelve Clouds of Joy) and moved to Kansas City. During 1929-30 they recorded some excellent hot performances with such players as pianist/arranger Mary Lou Williams, violinist Claude Williams, and trumpeter Edgar "Puddinghead" Battle. Surprisingly, Kirk's Orchestra was off records entirely during 1931-35, but in 1936 (the year it relocated to New York) it immediately had a pop hit in "Until the Real Thing Comes Along" featuring the high voice of singer Pha Terrell. In future years such fine soloists as tenor saxophonist Dick Wilson, the early electric guitarist Floyd Smith, Don Byas, Harold "Shorty" Baker, Howard McGhee (1942-43), Jimmy Forrest, and even Fats Navarro and (briefly) Charlie Parker would be among Kirk's sidemen. However, Mary Lou Williams was the most important musician in the band, both as a soloist and an arranger. In 1948 Andy Kirk broke up the band (which had recorded

mostly for Decca) and in later years ran a hotel and served as an official in the Musicians' Union. A lone "reunion" date in 1956 featured the classic charts but almost none of the original sidemen. —*Scott Yanow*

● **Mary's Idea** / Mar. 2, 1936-Jan. 3, 1941 / GRP ✦✦✦✦
This 20-cut disc contains the Kirk band's finest shuffles, rags, stomps, pop covers, and swing pieces, with Dick Wilson's lush tenor floating atop several numbers. Andy Kirk and his Twelve Clouds of Joy made joyful, exuberant music during this period and established Mary Lou Williams' arranging and playing skill. This CD offers an excellent account of the group at its peak. —*Ron Wynn*

Rahsaan Roland Kirk (Ronald T. Kirk)

b. May 15, 1936, Columbus, OH, **d.** Dec. 5, 1977
Clarinet, Flute, Sax (Tenor), Stritch, Manzello / R&B, Avant-Garde, Bop, Swing, Hard Bop, New Orleans Jazz

Sometimes musicians have used flamboyance to mask talent deficiencies. But in other cases, a willingness to have a good time results in talented players skills being downplayed. That was the case with Rahsaan Roland Kirk, who loved clowning, telling outrageous jokes, and enjoying himself in concert. That, coupled with his penchant for playing three horns at once and homemade instruments, convinced some individuals he was more sideshow than legitimately superb soloist. But Kirk's playing three horns was done through skillful use of false fingerings. He modified the keys of his tenor, using the left hand to cover the tenor's range and his right to play the manzello and stritch. It was an incredible combination of musical knowledge and physical dexterity, made even more amazing by the fact the individual doing it had been blind since two. Kirk was a master of circular breathing, another practice that led him to be accused of gimmickry. He could hold and sustain notes for what seemed like hours. Kirk used a siren whistle to punctuate key moments in his solos. He discovered the long forgotten manzello and stritch, a pair of saxophones used in turn-of-the-century Spanish marching bands, in a music store. He made alterations to them with rubber bands and tape, turning them into part of his performing arsenal. Rahsaan Roland Kirk was an amazing musician and personality, who could play lightning-fast bebop, outrageous free solos, heartfelt 12-bar blues, and any and everything in between. He played over 40 instruments, many of his own making. At his concerts it seemed he'd raided a music store, there were so many horns, flutes, and devices on stage. His homemade instruments included the trumpophone (trumpet with soprano sax mouthpiece), slidesophone (miniature trombone resembling Snub Mosley's slide saxophone), black puzzle flute and black mystery pipes. He used flutes like microphones, speaking and sending messages with them. Kirk was one of the funniest people of all time on or back stage, but he didn't find anything humorous about the music business or the treatment jazz musicians received from the general media. He was the leader of the early '70s Jazz and People's Movement, another of those worthy causes that later degenerates into a mutually unproductive series of confrontations. Kirk and Lee Morgan got nationwide press, little of it favorable, in 1970 when they disrupted a taping of "The Merv Griffin Show," protesting the lack of African-American musicians and absence of Black music and compositions from most radio and television shows. The Jazz and People's Movement had a legitimate beef; unfortunately, they were bogged down by publicity-seeking ringers in the ranks, and their tactic of disrupting television tapings cost them points with many of the people they were trying to reach. That was probably the low point of Kirk's great career. He began playing bugle and trumpet as a child, later starting on clarinet and C-melody saxophone. He was a professional at 15, working in R&B bands. He moved from Louisville to Chicago in 1960. Ira Sullivan played on Kirk's second album. Kirk toured Germany in the early '60s, and later played briefly with Charles Mingus. Then he led his own bands exclusively, playing a wide variety of styles and mainly originals while fronting his "Vibration Society." Kirk made his first album for King in 1956, then moved to Argo. He recorded in the '60s and '70s for Argo/Cadet, Prestige, Mercury, Verve, Atlantic, and Warner Bros. Before becoming a leader, Kirk played with Brother Jack McDuff and Jaki Byard. He took the name "Rahsaan" after having a vision during a dream. Such albums as *Volunteered Slavery, Natural Black Inventions*, and *Bright Moments* packed musical and philosophical/political punch. Kirk worked with such guests on his albums as Horace Parlan, Quincy Jones, Al Hibbler, and Leon Thomas. He suffered a stroke in 1975, but continued playing two more years. Kirk founded the Vibration School of Music in 1977 to help saxophonists. It was one of his final acts. Mercury issued a two-record compilation of his early '60s work immediately after his death, then did Kirk justice with a boxed set compilation of his sessions *The Complete Roland Kirk on Mercury*. —*Ron Wynn*

Introducing Roland Kirk / Jun. 7, 1960 / Chess ✦✦✦

☆ **Kirk's Work** / Jul. 11, 1961 / Original Jazz Classics ✦✦✦✦✦
Roland Kirk is in excellent form on this CD reissue of a typically varied (and occasionally amazing) set with organist Jack McDuff, bassist Joe Benjamin, and drummer Art Taylor. Kirk mostly sticks to playing tenor and manzello (with highlights including "Three for Dizzy" and "Makin' Whoopee") but takes "Funk Underneath" as a flute feature and tears into

the ancient "Skater's Waltz" on both stritch and manzello. McDuff plays well but Roland Kirk dominates the set, displaying an encyclopedic knowledge of music and swinging up a storm. —*Scott Yanow*

We Free Kings / Aug. 16, 1961-Aug. 17, 1961 / Mercury ✦✦✦✦
This CD is one of Roland Kirk's finer recordings from his Mercury period. Accompanied by a rhythm section led by pianist Richard Wyands, Kirk on tenor, manzello, stritch (sometimes all three at once), and flute plays some typically miraculous music. Highlights include "Three for the Festival," "Moon Song," "Blues for Alice," and "We Free Kings," but all of the selections contain plenty of Kirk's magic. Twenty years after his death there is still no one around to replace Roland Kirk. This release is recommended to those listeners who do not already have his ten-CD complete Mercury set. —*Scott Yanow*

☆ **Complete Recordings of Roland Kirk** / Aug. 16, 1961-Nov. 17, 1965 / Mercury ✦✦✦✦✦

● **Does Your House Have Lions: The Rahsaan Roland Kirk Anthology** / Nov. 6, 1961-Mar. 1976 / Rhino ✦✦✦✦

Kirk's Work / Mar. 1962 / Prestige ✦✦✦
With Jack McDuff. This is a fine reissue of Kirk in a soul-jazz and mainstream vein. —*Ron Wynn*

Domino / Jan. 1963 / Mercury ✦✦✦✦
Early '60s Kirk vehicle in which his inspired blend of show business, hard bop, and multi-horn/multiphonic solos hadn't yet jelled. It's conventional, straightahead material, well played but not as imaginative or as transcendent as Kirk's music would become in the '70s. —*Ron Wynn*

Rip, Rig & Panic / Now Please Don't . . . / Jan. 13, 1965-Apr. 1967 / EmArcy ✦✦✦✦
Two of Roland Kirk's albums are combined together on this CD. *Rip, Rig & Panic* is one of the remarkable multi-instrumentalist's greatest recordings for it matches him with pianist Jaki Byard (along with bassist Richard Davis and drummer Elvin Jones), who also has the ability to play in virtually every jazz style. With such titles as "No Tonic Pres," "Once in a While", "From Bechet, Byas and Fats," and the electronic "Slippery, Hippery, Flippery," obviously this is an eclectic (and unique) set. While that session has also been included in the ten-CD complete Mercury box, *Now Please Don't You Cry, Beautiful Edith* is a lesser-known recording (originally on Verve) that has Kirk backed up by pianist Lonnie Smith, bassist Ronald Boykins, and drummer Grady Tate. Highlights include "Stompin' Ground," "It's a Grand Night for Swinging," "Alfie," and the title cut. —*Scott Yanow*

The Inflated Tear / Nov. 27, 1967+Nov. 3, 1967 / Atlantic ✦✦✦✦
This is a fine all-around set by the remarkable Rahsaan Roland Kirk which has yet to be fully reissued on CD. The LP, from the Atlantic *Jazzlore* reissue series of the early '80s, features Kirk on tenor, manzello, stritch, clarinet, flute, English horn, flexafone, and whistle performing a wide variety of colorful originals along with Duke Ellington's "Creole Love Call." Highlights include the memorable "The Black and Crazy Blues," "The Inflated Tear," and "A Handful of Fives." It's one of Kirk's better Atlantic sets. —*Scott Yanow*

Left and Right / Jun. 18, 1968 / Atlantic ✦✦✦✦
This LP features two different sides of the unique Rahsaan Roland Kirk. While the first half of the program is dominated by his nine-part suite "Expansions" (a variety of melodies he had written in the 1950s and features Rahsaan's intense playing with a variety of guest artists (including Alice Coltrane on harp, baritonist Pepper Adams, and trumpeter Richard Williams), the second side generally showcases Kirk on one horn at a time performing six ballads while backed by a string section; he plays beautifully and with melodic creativity. —*Scott Yanow*

Volunteered Slavery / Jul. 7, 1969-Jul. 23, 1969 / Rhino ✦✦✦✦
This straight CD reissue of an Atlantic LP has plenty of variety. Rahsaan Kirk (on tenor, flutes, manzello, stritch, and even gong) performs three melodic originals (including the title cut) along with two pop tunes during which he is assisted by "the Roland Kirk Spirit Choir" on background vocals. However, it is his performance at the 1969 Newport Jazz Festival (near-riotous versions of "One Ton" and "Three for the Festival" plus a remarkable John Coltrane three-song medley) that is most memorable. —*Scott Yanow*

Blacknuss / Aug. 1971-Sep. 1971 / Atlantic ✦✦✦

★ **Bright Moments** / Jun. 8, 1973-Jun. 9, 1973 / Rhino ✦✦✦✦✦
This Rhino two-CD set (a straight reissue of an Atlantic two-LP release) is the closest one can come nowadays to hearing what it would be like to see Rahsaan Roland Kirk perform in a club. Kirk, who is joined by a fine four-piece rhythm section for this appearance at San Francisco's legendary Keystone Korner, has colorful (and sometimes very humorous) monologues between the songs and shows off his remarkable virtuosity. Whether it be his emotional renditions of "Prelude to a Kiss" and "If I Loved You," his demonstration of nose flutes on "Fly Town Nose Blues," some authentic New Orleans clarinet playing on "Dem Red Beans and Rice," or a memorable version of his theme "Bright Moments," the music

is exciting and unpredictable. This is the definitive Rahsaan Roland Kirk recording of the 1970s and is essential for any serious jazz collection. —*Scott Yanow*

Simmer, Reduce, Garnish & Serve / 1976-1978 / Warner Archives ✦✦✦✦
This single CD has selections from Rahsaan Roland Kirk's final three albums. His work on his last record *Boogie-Woogie String Along for Real* was quite heroic and miraculous because he had suffered a major stroke that greatly limited his abilities; in fact, Kirk had the use of only one of his hands so his playing was sadly restricted. There is a remarkable amount of variety plus a liberal dose of Kirk's humor on this retrospective, ranging from "Bagpipe Medley" and "Sweet Georgia Brown" (complete with a whistler and Freddie Moore's washboard) to a warm "I'll Be Seeing You" and a tribute to Johnny Griffin, the main influence on Rahsaan's tenor sound. For those listeners who do not already have the three LPs, this is a strong best-of sampler of the saxophonist's final period, although his earlier recordings are recommended first. This CD concludes with an emotional and rather touching collage that pays tribute to Kirk's genius and mourns his premature death. —*Scott Yanow*

I Eye Aye: Live at Montreux 1972 / Rhino ✦✦✦✦
Rahsaan Roland Kirk was at the peak of his powers when he performed at the 1972 Montreux Blues & Jazz Festival. *I Eye Aye: Live at Montreux 1972* features the entirety of his performance, which featured radical but effective interpretations of jazz and pop standards. Though its appeal is basically limited to dedicated Kirk fans, the album has a wealth of wonderful, first-rate music. —*Thom Owens*

Kenny Kirkland

b. Sep. 28, 1955, Newport, NY
Piano, Keyboards / Post-Bop
Closely associated at times with Wynton and Branford Marsalis, Kenny Kirkland has surprisingly only led one CD of his own as of this writing. He started playing piano at age six and later studied at the Manhattan School of Music. Among his early jobs were playing with Michal Urbaniak (on electric keyboards) during 1977, Miroslav Vitous (1979), Terumasa Hino, and Elvin Jones. Influenced by Herbie Hancock, Kirkland was well featured while with Wynton Marsalis' band (1981-85), but his departure in 1985 to play pop music with Sting (along with Branford Marsalis) greatly upset Wynton. After leaving Sting in 1986, Kirkland became a session musician and in the early '90s he joined the *Tonight Show* band (under the direction of Branford Marsalis); his only album as a leader is for GRP (1991). —*Scott Yanow*

● **Kenny Kirkland** / 1991 / GRP ✦✦✦✦
This is a good set with Afro-Latin and hard-bop influences mixed. —*Ron Wynn*

John Klemmer

b. Jul. 3, 1946, Chicago, IL
Sax (Tenor) / Post-Bop, Hard Bop, Crossover
An innovator on the electrified saxophone (using echo effects quite effectively), John Klemmer was also a very strong Coltrane-inspired acoustic tenor saxophonist. He started on tenor when he was 11 in Chicago, toured as a teenager with Ted Weems, and made his first recording as a leader in 1967. Klemmer was a key soloist with Don Ellis' innovative big band (1968-70), started electrifying his horn (using an echoplex), and worked on the West Coast. His easy-listening recordings for ABC in the mid-'70s were quite popular, particularly 1975's *Touch* which found him playing melodies fairly simply. Klemmer alternated the more pop-oriented projects with fiery efforts; his finest jazz album was the two-LP set *Nexus* (mostly reissued on CD), a set of duets and trios with drums and occasional bass. He recorded with Roy Haynes in 1977, cut a few impressive unaccompanied solo saxophone records, and then in 1981 dropped out of music altogether due to physical and mental problems. Other than an erratic MCA album in 1989, little has been heard from John Klemmer since. His many recordings for Cadet, ABC/Impulse, ABC, MCA, and Elektra are mostly out-of-print. —*Scott Yanow*

Waterfalls / Jun. 17, 1972 / Impulse ✦✦✦✦
John Klemmer was (along with Eddie Harris) a pioneer and an innovator at utilizing electrical devices on his saxophone. For this live set, Klemmer used an Echoplex on his tenor and soprano and was joined by keyboardist Mike Nock, electric bassist Wilton Feldman, drummer Eddie Marshall, Victor Feldman on percussion, and (on two of the eight songs) vocalist Diana Lee. Recorded live on June 17, 1972 (with additional recording added five days later), this CD reissue gives one a good example of Klemmer's playing before his mood music records caught on. He certainly achieved some unusual effects at the time, although he never became an influential force. Worth investigating by open-eared listeners. —*Scott Yanow*

★ **Nexus One (for Trane)** / 1979 / Bluebird ✦✦✦✦✦
This CD reissues five of the nine selections from what was arguably tenor

saxophonist John Klemmer's greatest recording session. In addition to forceful versions of "Mr. P.C." and "My One and Only Love" that feature Klemmer joined by bassist Bob Magnusson and drummer Carl Burnett, there are three lengthy explorations (of "Softly as in a Morning Sunrise," "Impressions," and his original "Nexus") that are taken as tenor-drums duets. The music is so powerful that listeners should search for the original double LP, which includes three additional trios and a duet on "Four." Klemmer, who was becoming very popular as a melodic pop saxophonist, must have surprised many of his fans with this very explorative document. —*Scott Yanow*

Earl Klugh

b. Sep. 16, 1954, Detroit, MI
Guitar / New Age, Instrumental Pop, Crossover
An acoustic guitarist with a very pretty tone, Earl Klugh does not consider himself a jazz player and thinks of Chet Atkins as being his most important influence. Klugh played on a Yusef Lateef album when he was 15 and gained recognition in 1971 for his contributions to George Benson's *White Rabbit* record. He played regularly with Benson in 1973, was a member of Return to Forever briefly in 1974 and then in the mid-'70s began recording as a leader. Klugh's popular recordings (for Blue Note, Capitol, Manhattan, and Warner Bros.) tend to use light funk beats, stick closely to the melody, and put the emphasis on his sound; little surprising ever occurs. —*Scott Yanow*

Magic in Your Eyes / 1976 / Liberty ✦✦✦

Earl Klugh / 1976 / EMI ✦✦✦✦
The session that portended his light-touch, fusion-pop approach. —*Ron Wynn*

Finger Paintings / Feb. 1977 / Blue Note ✦✦

● **Solo Guitar** / 1989 / Warner Bros. ✦✦✦✦
Earl Klugh's long-awaited solo album showcased his pretty sound on the acoustic guitar, giving two-to-three-three-minute melodic readings of superior standards. Some of the pieces (notably "I'm Confessin'") found Klugh playing a relaxed "stride" similiar to some of the guitarists of the '30s. —*Scott Yanow*

Move / 1993 / Warner Bros. ✦✦

Lee Konitz

b. Oct. 13, 1927, Chicago, IL
Sax (Alto), Sax (Soprano) / Cool, Post-Bop
One of the most individual of all altoists (and one of the few in the '50s who did not sound like a cousin of Charlie Parker), the cool-toned Lee Konitz has always had a strong musical curiosity that has led him to consistently take chances and stretch himself, usually quite successfully. Early on he studied clarinet, switched to alto, and played with Jerry Wald. Konitz gained some attention for his solos with Claude Thornhill's Orchestra (1947). He began studying with Lennie Tristano, who had a big influence on his conception and approach to improvising. Konitz was with Miles Davis' Birth of the Cool Nonet during their one gig and their early Capitol recordings (1948-50) and recorded with Lennie Tristano's innovative sextet (1949), including the first two free improvisations ever documented. Konitz blended very well with Warne Marsh's tenor (their unisons on "Wow" are miraculous) and would have several reunions with both Tristano and Marsh through the years, but he was also interested in finding his own way; by the early '50s he started breaking away from the Tristano school. Konitz toured Scandinavia (1951) where his cool sound was influential, and he fit in surprisingly well with Stan Kenton's Orchestra (1952-54), being featured on many charts by Bill Holman and Bill Russo. Konitz was primarily a loner from that point on. He almost retired from music in the early '60s but re-emerged a few years later. His recordings have ranged from cool bop to thoughtful free improvisations, and his Milestone set of *Duets* (1967) is a classic. In the late '70s Konitz led a notable Nonet and in 1992 he won the prestigious Jazzpar Prize. He has recorded on soprano and tenor but has mostly stuck to his distinctive alto. Lee Konitz has led consistently stimulating sessions for many labels including Prestige, Dragon, Pacific Jazz, Vogue, Storyville, Atlantic, Verve, Wave, Milestone, MPS, Polydor, Bellaphon, SteepleChase, Sonet, Groove Merchant, Roulette, Progressive, Choice, IAI, Chiaroscuro, Circle, Black Lion, Soul Note, Storyville, Evidence, and Philogy. —*Scott Yanow*

● **Subconscious-Lee** / Jan. 11, 1949-Apr. 7, 1950 / Original Jazz Classics ✦✦✦✦
This very interesting CD has altoist Lee Konitz's first recordings as a leader, taken from a period of time when he was very much under the musical influence of pianist Lennie Tristano. In fact, the program starts off with a quintet date from Jan. 1949 that was actually originally headed by Tristano but features the young altoist. The latter two sessions match Konitz with his fellow Tristano students (including tenor saxophonist Warne Marsh, guitarist Billy Bauer, and Tristano-soundalike Sal Mosca on piano). The original style developed by Tristano, Konitz, and the others (which was different from bop and cool jazz) still sounds fresh today. —*Scott Yanow*

Lee Konitz/Bob Brookmeyer in Paris / Sep. 17, 1953+Jun. 5, 1954 / Vogue ✦✦✦

Jazz at Storyville / Jan. 5, 1954 / Black Lion ✦✦✦✦
This excellent CD gives one a definitive look at altoist Lee Konitz at a period of time when he was breaking away from being a sideman and a student of Lennie Tristano and asserting himself as a leader. With pianist Ronnie Ball, bassist Percy Heath, and drummer Alan Levitt, Konitz explores a variety of his favorite chord changes, some of which were disguised by newer melodies such as "Hi Beck," "Subconscious Lee," and "Sound Lee." Among the other high points of this well recorded set are "Foolin' Myself" and a lengthy exploration of "If I Had You." —*Scott Yanow*

Konitz / Aug. 6, 1954 / Black Lion ✦✦✦✦
The 1954 Lee Konitz Quartet did not last long but they did record some worthwhile performances that still sound fresh over 40 years later. In addition to eight selections (highlighted by "Bop Goes the Leesel," "Mean to Me," "I'll Remember April," and "Limehouse Blues"), there are six previously unissued alternate takes included on this attractive 1989 CD. Altoist Konitz is ably assisted by pianist Ronnie Ball, bassist Peter Ind, and drummer Jeff Morton on cool/bop performances, which give listeners a good sampling of how Konitz sounded in his early prime. —*Scott Yanow*

☆ **Live at the Half Note** / Feb. 24, 1959+Mar. 3, 1959 / Verve ✦✦✦✦✦
The music on this two-CD set has a strange history. Pianist Lennie Tristano had a rare reunion with altoist Lee Konitz and tenor saxophonist Warne Marsh (his two greatest "students") during an extended stay at the Half Note in 1959. Tristano took Tuesday nights off to teach and Bill Evans was his substitute, but the pianist had a couple of those performances recorded for posterity. Years later while listening to his tapes he was so impressed with Marsh's playing that he sent edited versions (comprised entirely of the tenor's solos) to Marsh and somehow they ended up being released in that form by the Revelation label. Finally in 1994 the unedited music was issued by Verve; the consistently exciting playing by Konitz, Marsh, and Evans (with backup by bassist Jimmy Garrison and drummer Paul Motian) makes one wonder what took so long. They perform a dozen extended standards (or "originals" based on the chord changes of familiar tunes) with creativity and inspiration. In fact, of all the Konitz-Marsh recordings, this set ranks near the top. —*Scott Yanow*

★ **The Lee Konitz Duets** / Sep. 25, 1967 / Original Jazz Classics ✦✦✦✦✦
This CD brings back one of altoist Lee Konitz's greatest sessions. In 1967 he recorded a series of very diverse duets, all of which succeed on their own terms. Konitz is matched with valve trombonist Marshall Brown on a delightful version of "Struttin' with Some Barbecue," matches wits with the tenor of Joe Henderson on "You Don't Know What Love Is," plays "Checkerboard" with pianist Dick Katz, "Erb" with guitarist Jim Hall, "Tickle Toe" with the tenor of Richie Kamuca (Konitz switches to tenor on that cut) and an adventurous and fairly free "Duplexity" with violinist Ray Nance, has three different duets on "Alone Together," and, on "Alphanumeric," welcomes practically everyone back for a final blowout. The music ranges from Dixieland to bop and free and is consistently fascinating. —*Scott Yanow*

I Concentrate on You / Jul. 30, 1974 / SteepleChase ✦✦✦✦
Altoist Lee Konitz has always had a desire to play in a wide variety of settings; this duet session with bassist Red Mitchell is a good example. Although Konitz is quite exposed on the 11 Cole Porter songs, he plays in his usual thoughtful and unhurried style, coming up with typically adventurous melodic variations. Mitchell (who switches to piano on "Night and Day") is fine in support, and the CD reissue adds three very different alternate takes to the original program. Well worth picking up. —*Scott Yanow*

Figure and Spirit / Oct. 20, 1976 / Progressive ✦✦✦✦
Altoist Lee Konitz (who doubles on this CD on soprano) teams up with tenor-saxophonist Ted Brown, pianist Albert Dailey, bassist Rufus Reid, and drummer Joe Chambers for this session. The six songs (originals based on standards by Konitz, Brown, and Lennie Tristano) were all performed in one take, and although there are a few minor mistakes, the music is quite exciting and spontaneous. Brown was the best possible substitute for Wayne Marsh (Konitz's original choice for the record) and sounds in prime form. It's worth acquiring by fans of straight-ahead jazz, Lennie Tristano, and Lee Konitz. —*Scott Yanow*

● **Yes, Yes, Nonet** / Apr. 17, 1979 / SteepleChase ✦✦✦✦
It was a tragedy that Lee Konitz's versatile nonet was not able to succeed commercially. Just like its leader, the group was able to stretch from swing standards, bop, and cool jazz to freer improvisations and challenging originals. This SteepleChase release (featuring the nonet when it comprised such fine players as trumpeters Tom Harrell and John Eckert, trombonists Jimmy Knepper and Sam Burtis, baritonist Ronnie Cuber, pianist Harold Danko, bassist Buster Williams, and drummer Billy Hart in addition to Konitz on alto and soprano) features the group at its best on such pieces as "Footprints," "Stardust," "My Buddy," and four songs by Jimmy Knepper. It's an excellent outing from a somewhat neglected group. —*Scott Yanow*

Dovetail / Feb. 25, 1983+Feb. 27, 1983 / Sunnyside ✦✦✦✦

Round and Round / 1988 / Music Masters ✦✦✦

And the Jazzpar All Star Nonet / Mar. 27, 1992-Mar. 29, 1992 / Storyville
✦✦✦✦

On this diverse and highly enjoyable set altoist Lee Konitz is heard in a variety of settings. Five songs (four of them recently composed) feature Konitz interacting with a fine Danish nonet, and on "Subconscious Lee" he is showcased in a quintet with fluegelhornist Allan Botchinsky and pianist Peggy Stern. However, it is his six duets (with Stern, Botchinsky, bassist Jesper Lundgaard, and fellow altoist Jens Sondergaard) that are most notable. Konitz, who can play as freely as any avant-gardist, somehow always sounds relaxed and thoughtful, turning these duets into comfortable dialogues. — *Scott Yanow*

The Jobim Collection / Jan. 6, 1993-Jan. 10, 1993 / Philogy ✦✦✦✦
Altoist Lee Konitz and pianist Peggy Stern (who also plays synthesizer on a few of the tracks) sound like they really enjoyed themselves during this set of 14 Antonio Carlos Jobim songs. The emphasis is very much on melodic improvising (one can hear Jobim's themes throughout these performances), but Konitz as usual sounds very much like himself and Stern is consistently inventive both in reharmonizing some of the songs and in her subtle solos. The results are quite delightful, and this CD is easily recommended to fans of both bossa nova and Lee Konitz. — *Scott Yanow*

Gene Krupa

b. Jan. 15, 1909, Chicago, IL, **d.** Oct. 16, 1973, Yonkers, NY
Drums / Dixieland, Swing

The first drummer to be a superstar, Gene Krupa may not have been the most advanced drummer of the '30s but he was in some ways the most significant. Prior to Krupa, drum solos were a real rarity and the drums were thought of as a merely supportive instrument. Krupa, who with his good lucks and colorful playing became a matinee idol, changed the image of drummers forever.

Gene Krupa made history with his first record. For a session in 1927 with the McKenzie-Condon Chicagoans, he became the first musician to use a full drum set on records. He was part of the Chicago jazz scene of the '20s before moving to New York and worked in the studios during the early years of the Depression. In December 1934 he joined Benny Goodman's new orchestra and for the next three years was an important part of BG's pacesetting big band. Krupa, whose use of the bass drum was never too subtle, starred with Goodman's Trio and Quartet and his lengthy drum feature "Sing, Sing, Sing" in 1937 was historic. After he nearly stole the show at BG's 1938 Carnegie Hall Concert, Krupa and Goodman had a personality conflict and Gene soon departed to form his own orchestra. It took the drummer a while to realize with his band that drum solos were not required on every song! Such fine players as Vido Musso, Milt Raskin, Floyd O'Brien, Sam Donahue, Shorty Sherock and the excellent singer Irene Daye were assets to Krupa's Orchestra and "Drum Boogie" was a popular number but it was not until 1941 when he had Anita O'Day and Roy Eldridge that Krupa's big band really took off. Among his hits from 1941-42 were "Let Me Off Uptown," "After You've Gone," "Rockin' Chair" and "Thanks for the Boogie Ride." Unfortunately Krupa was arrested on a trumped-up drug charge in 1943, resulting in bad publicity, a short jail sentence and the breakup of his orchestra.

In September 1943 he had an emotional reunion with Benny Goodman (who happily welcomed him back to the music world). Krupa also worked briefly with Tommy Dorsey before putting together another big band in mid-1944, one that had a string section. The strings only lasted a short time but Krupa was able to keep his band working into 1951. Tenor saxophonist Charlie Ventura and pianist Teddy Napoleon had a trio hit in "Dark Eyes" (1945), Anita O'Day returned for a time in 1945 (scoring with "Opus No. 1") and, although his own style was unchanged (being a Dixieland drummer at heart), Krupa was one of the first swing big bandleaders to welcome the influence of bebop into his group's arrangements, some of which were written by Gerry Mulligan (most notably "Disc Jockey Jump"). Among the soloists in the second Krupa Orchestra were Don Fagerquist, Red Rodney, Ventura, altoist Charlie Kennedy, tenorman Buddy Wise and in 1949 Roy Eldridge.

After breaking up his band in 1951, Krupa generally worked with trios or quartets (including such sidemen as Ventura, Napoleon, Eddie Shu, Bobby Scott, Dave McKenna, Eddie Wasserman, Ronnie Ball, Dave Frishberg and John Bunch), toured with Jazz at the Philharmonic, ran a drum school with Cozy Cole and had occasional reunions with Benny Goodman. Gradually worsening health in the '60s resulted in him becoming semi-retired but Krupa remained a major name up until his death. Ironically his final recording was led by the same person who headed his first appearance on records, Eddie Condon. Gene Krupa's pre-war big-band records are gradually being released by the Classics label. — *Scott Yanow*

● **Gene Krupa 1935-1938** / Nov. 19, 1935-Jun. 18, 1938 / Classics ✦✦✦✦
The first CD in the European Classics label's "complete" Gene Krupa series starts off with two all-star sessions that preceded the drummer's first dates as a big-band leader. Krupa, Benny Goodman, bassist Israel Crosby (featured on "Blues of Israel"), and several sideman from Goodman's 1935

band jam four songs, and from the following year Krupa is joined by trumpeter Roy Eldridge, tenor saxophonist Chu Berry, pianist Jess Stacy, guitarist Allan Reuss, Crosby, and (on two of the four songs) singer Helen Ward. The two instrumentals ("I Hope Gabriel Likes My Music" and "Swing Is Here") are near-classics that are quite heated. Otherwise, this CD has Krupa's first 15 numbers with his big band, a promising outfit that during 1938 also featured tenor saxophonist Vido Musso, pianist Milt Raskin and the vocals of Irene Daye and Helen Ward. Highlights include "Feeling High and Happy," "Wire Brush Stomp," and the previously unissued "The Madam Swings It." — *Scott Yanow*

Gene Krupa 1938 / Jul. 19, 1938-Dec. 12, 1938 / Classics ✦✦✦✦
The second Gene Krupa CD in Classics complete reissuance of his swing-era recordings has 22 titles from Krupa's Orchestra during the latter half of 1938. The big band did not yet have its own personality, but Irene Day is a fine pop/swing vocalist, Leo Watson is in typically eccentric form singing four happy numbers, the arrangements of Jimmy Mundy and Chappie Willett generally swing hard, Vido Musso and Sam Donahue get off some fine tenor solos, and the leader/drummer really drives the band. Well worth picking up by swing fans. — *Scott Yanow*

Gene Krupa 1939 / Feb. 26, 1939-Jul. 25, 1939 / Classics ✦✦✦✦
The European label's third Gene Krupa set reissues all of the recordings made by the drummer's big band during a five-month period in 1939. Although swinging steadily, Krupa's Orchestra had not broken through yet (it was still two years away from its prime period). With Irene Daye contributing ten pleasing vocals among the 22 selections and such soloists as trumpeter Nate Kazebier, trombonist Floyd O'Brien, tenor saxophonist Sam Donahue, and pianist Milt Raskin (along with the drummer/leader), the group was starting to show some strong potential, particularly on the instrumentals such as "The Madam Swings It" and "Hodge Podge." well played if not overly distinctive swing music. — *Scott Yanow*

Gene Krupa & His Orchestra: 1939-1940 / Jul. 24, 1939-Feb. 12, 1940 / Classics ✦✦✦

Drum Boogie / Jan. 2, 1940-Jan. 17, 1941 / Columbia ✦✦✦✦
Gene Krupa's best-known mark was the one he led during 1941-42, which featured singer Anita O'Day and trumpeter Roy Eldridge. This fine CD has 16 selections from the orchestra that preceded that group, a big band almost on the same level. Although the programming is not in strict chronological order, the swinging music is consistently enjoyable. With Irene Day taking some vocals, and solo space for tenorman Sam Donahue and trumpeters Corky Cornelius and Shorty Sherock, many of the best recordings by this outfit are featured, including the hit "Drum Boogie," "No Name Jive," "Rhumboogie," and "Blue Rhythm Fantasy." Well worth picking up. — *Scott Yanow*

Leave Us Leap / Mar. 30, 1945-1948 / Vintage Jazz Classics ✦✦✦

● **Let Me Off Uptown** / Apr. 5, 1949-Apr. 12, 1949 / Columbia ✦✦✦
Although left out of the history books, drummer Gene Krupa's 1949 big band was very bop-oriented. This Drive Archive CD (which reissues the contents of an Alamac LP), features highlights from three live appearances from an engagement in Hollywood. At the time trumpeter Roy Eldridge was back with the drummer/leader, and he can be heard reviving his routine on "Let Me Off Uptown" with singer Dolores Hawkins and taking a couple of heated solos (including on "After You've Gone"). Also quite prominent are trumpeter Don Fagerquist (a fine bop soloist), trombonist Frank Rosolino (who sings "Pennies from Heaven" and "Lemon Drop") and tenor saxophonist Buddy Wise. The recording quality is a bit erratic, but the music from this forgotten band is often quite exciting. — *Scott Yanow*

Krupa & Rich / Polygram ✦✦✦

Steve Kuhn (Stephen Lewis Kuhn)

b. Mar. 24, 1958, Brooklyn, NY
Piano / Post-Bop

Steve Kuhn has had an interesting career. A talented jazz pianist, he has worked in many types of settings through the years. He began classical piano lessons when he was five, studied with Madame Chaloff, and accompanied her son, baritonist Serge Chaloff, on some gigs when the pianist was 14. He freelanced in Boston as a teenager, graduated from Harvard, and moved to New York where he worked with Kenny Dorham's group (1959-60). Kuhn was the original pianist in John Coltrane's Quartet, playing for two months before McCoy Tyner succeeded him. He was with the bands of Stan Getz (1961-63) and Art Farmer (1964-66), lived in Europe (1967-70), and then returned to the US in 1971. Kuhn doubled on electric piano in the '70s, recorded for ECM, and co-led a group with Sheila Jordan in the latter part of the decade. After a period playing commercial music, he formed an acoustic trio in the mid-'80s, which has been his main vehicle ever since. Steve Kuhn has recorded as a leader for Impulse (1966), Contact, MPS, BYG, Muse, ECM, Black Hawk, New World, Owl, Concord, and Postcards. — *Scott Yanow*

Looking Back / Oct. 1990 / Concord Jazz ✦✦✦✦
Trio. Superior playing and meager compositions. CD version has two bonus cuts. — *Ron Wynn*

Live at Maybeck Recital Hall, Vol. 13 / Nov. 18, 1990 / Concord Jazz ✦✦✦✦

Years Later / Sep. 1992 / Concord Jazz ✦✦✦✦

● **Seasons of Romance** / Apr. 12, 1995-Apr. 13, 1995 / Postcards ✦✦✦✦

Charles Kynard

b. 1933

Organ, Guitar (Bass), Guitar (Electric) / Soul-Jazz, Groove

Organ, electric bass. Kynard is an organist whose jazz-funk leanings rival his predecessors and peers, though not eclipsing them. Solid, though never flashy. He also plays electric bass. Kynard's album *Reelin' with the Feelin'* has been sampled and appears on several acid-jazz releases. —*Michael G. Nastos and Michael Erlewine*

● **Charles Kynard** / 1962-1963 / World Pacific ✦✦✦✦
Kynard's best combo effort. Shows him in a more favorable light as a soul-jazz proprietor. —*Michael G. Nastos*

Where It's At / 1962-1963 / Pacific Jazz ✦✦✦
Kynard with funky guitarist Howard Roberts, Clifford Scott (sax), and Milt Turner (d). This is Kynard's first album and it has not been reissued. —*Michael Erlewine*

Professor Soul / Aug. 6, 1968 / Prestige ✦✦✦✦
Charles Kynard with Cal Green on guitar and Johnny Kirkwood on drums. This 1968 gem, which has not been reissued, has a rendition of "Christo Redentor." —*Michael Erlewine*

The Soul Brotherhood / Mar. 10, 1969 / Prestige ✦✦✦✦
They have got to reissue this one! Here is Kynard with Grant Green on guitar, Blue Mitchell on trumpet, and David "Fathead" Newman on sax. —*Michael Erlewine*

★ **Reelin' with the Feelin'** / Aug. 11, 1969 / Prestige ✦✦✦✦✦
Kynard with Wilton Felder on sax, Joe Pass on guitar, Carol Kaye on bass, and Paul Humphrey on drums. This soul-jazz date has been being sampled and used in recent acid-jazz albums. —*Michael Erlewine*

Afro-Disiac / Apr. 6, 1970 / Prestige ✦✦✦✦
Another Kynard gem that we are waiting for a reissue of. This album features Kynard with Grant Green on guitar and Houston Person on sax. I have not been able to find a copy, but those who know it say that this is the one to hear. I can't wait. —*Michael Erlewine*

Wa-Tu-Wa-Zui / Dec. 14, 1970 / Prestige ✦✦✦
Kynard with Rusty Bryant on sax, Virgil Jones on trumpet, and Melvin Sparks on guitar. —*Michael Erlewine*

Steve Lacy

b. Jul. 23, 1934

Sax (Soprano) / Avant-Garde, Post-Bop, Free Jazz

One of the great soprano saxophonists of all time (ranking up there with Sidney Bechet and John Coltrane), Steve Lacy's career was fascinating to watch develop. He originally doubled on clarinet and soprano (dropping the former by the mid-'50s), inspired by Bechet and playing Dixieland in New York with Rex Stewart, Cecil Scott, Red Allen, and other older musicians during 1952-55. He debuted on record in a modernized Dixieland format with Dick Sutton in 1954. However, Lacy soon jumped over several styles to play free jazz with Cecil Taylor during 1955-57. They recorded together and performed at the 1957 Newport Jazz Festival. Lacy recorded with Gil Evans in 1957 (they would work together on an irregular basis into the '80s), was with Thelonious Monk's quintet in 1960 for four months, and then formed a quartet with Roswell Rudd (1961-64) that exclusively played Monk's music; only one live set (for Emanen in 1963) resulted from that very interesting group.

Steve Lacy, who is considered the first "modern" musician to specialize on soprano (an instrument that was completely neglected during the bop era), began to turn toward avant-garde jazz in 1965. He had a quartet with Enrico Rava that spent eight months in South America. After a year back in New York, he permanently moved to Europe in 1967 with three years in Italy preceding a move to Paris. Lacy's music evolved from free form to improvising off his scalar originals. By 1977 he had a regular group that is still together in the mid-'90s, featuring Steve Potts on alto and soprano, Lacy's wife, violinist/singer Irene Aebi, bassist Kent Carter (later succeeded by Jean-Jacques Avenel), and drummer Oliver Johnson; pianist Bobby Few joined the group in the '80s. Lacy, who has also worked on special projects with Gil Evans, Mal Waldron, and Misha Mengelberg, among others, and in situations ranging from solo soprano concerts, many Monk tributes, big bands, and setting poetry to music, has recorded a countless number of sessions for almost as many labels. His early dates (1957-61) were for Prestige, New Jazz, and Candid, and later on he appeared most notably on sessions for Hat Art, Black Saint/Soul Note and Novus. —*Scott Yanow*

Soprano Saxophone / Nov. 1, 1957 / Original Jazz Classics ✦✦✦✦
A brilliant set. Lacy stakes out his claim as king of soprano sax, years before Coltrane popularizes it. —*Ron Wynn*

Reflections: Steve Lacy Plays Thelonious Monk / Oct. 17, 1958 / Original Jazz Classics ✦✦✦✦
All of soprano saxophonist Steve Lacy's early recordings are quite fascinating for during 1957-64 aspects of his style at times hinted at Dixieland, swing, Monk, and Cecil Taylor, sometimes at the same time! For this CD reissue (a straight reproduction of the original New Jazz LP), Lacy teams up with pianist Mal Waldron, bassist Buell Neidlinger, and drummer Elvin Jones for seven Thelonious Monk compositions. The typical standbys (such as "'Round Midnight," "Straight No Chaser," and "Blue Monk") are avoided in favor of more complex works such as "Four in One," "Bye-Ya," and "Skippy"; the sweet ballad "Ask Me Now" is a high point. Lacy always had an affinity for Monk's music and, even nearly 40 years later, this set is a delight. —*Scott Yanow*

☆ **The Straight Horn of Steve Lacy** / Sep. 1960 / Candid ✦✦✦✦✦
Some of soprano-saxophonist Steve Lacy's most interesting recordings are his earliest ones. After spending periods of time playing with Dixieland groups and then with Cecil Taylor (which was quite a jump), Lacy made several recordings that displayed his love of Thelonious Monk's music plus his varied experiences. On this particular set, Lacy's soprano contrasts well with Charles Davis' baritone (they are backed by bassist John Ore and drummer Roy Haynes) on three of the most difficult Monk tunes ("Introspection," "Played Twice," and "Criss Cross") plus two Cecil Taylor compositions and Charlie Parker's (or is it Miles Davis'?) "Donna Lee." —*Scott Yanow*

Evidence / Nov. 14, 1961 / Original Jazz Classics ✦✦✦✦
This early Steve Lacy album teams the great soprano saxophonist with trumpeter Don Cherry, bassist Carl Brown, and drummer Billy Higgins for four Thelonious Monk songs, an obscurity by Duke Ellington ("The Mystery Song"), and Billy Strayhorn's "Something to Live For." It is quite unusual to hear Cherry during a period when he was regularly performing with Ornette Coleman's Quartet, playing this kind of standard material. Lacy and Cherry approach these standards from a different angle, bringing new life and opening up new possibilities for these songs. Although the playing time of this CD is brief (under 34 minutes), the quality is quite high. —*Scott Yanow*

Trickles / Mar. 11, 1976-Mar. 14, 1976 / Black Saint ✦✦✦✦
One of the early Black Saint albums, this set features a reunion between soprano saxophonist Steve Lacy and trombonist Roswell Rudd; bassist Ken Carter and drummer Beaver Harris complete the quartet. Although Lacy and Rudd had had a group 15 years earlier that exclusively played Thelonious Monk tunes, in this case they perform five of Lacy's diverse originals, stretching themselves on such tunes as "Trickles" and "Robes." The music is less melodic than expected but does have its moments of interest. —*Scott Yanow*

● **Troubles** / May 24, 1979-May 25, 1979 / Black Saint ✦✦✦✦
Lacy and Steve Potts (as) at their best and most frenetic. —*Ron Wynn*

★ **Regeneration** / 1982 / Soul Note ✦✦✦✦✦
The consensus album of the year in 1983, it includes one side of Monk and the other of Herbie Nichols' music. Includes Roswell Rudd (tb), Misha Mengleberg (p), Kent Carter (b), and Hans Bennik (d). —*Michael G. Nastos*

Change of Season / Jul. 2, 1984-Jul. 3, 1984 / Soul Note ✦✦✦✦
This follow-up to *Regeneration* features George Lewis (tb) and Anjen Garter (b). All material by Herbie Nichols. —*Michael G. Nastos*

Only Monk / Jul. 29, 1986-Jul. 31, 1986 / Soul Note ✦✦✦✦
Lacy mines Monk's lode with a vengeance. —*Ron Wynn*

★ **Momentum** / May 20, 1987-May 22, 1987 / Novus ✦✦✦✦✦
On Steve Lacy's first album for an American label in over a decade, his sextet is heard on four extensive originals by the great soprano saxophonist. The music is complex yet often melodic and, although Irene Aebi takes typically eccentric vocals on two of the songs, the main reasons to acquire this album are for the thoughtful yet unpredictable solos of Lacy and altoist Steve Potts. —*Scott Yanow*

The Door / Jul. 4, 1988-Jul. 5, 1988 / Novus ✦✦✦✦
Taut duo and trio cuts. Two bonus tracks on CD. —*Ron Wynn*

Anthem / 1989 / Novus ✦✦✦✦
Some of Lacy's most recent material. The playing equals his past standards. —*Ron Wynn*

★ **Live at Sweet Basil** / Jul. 6, 1991 & Jul. 7, 1991 / Novus ✦✦✦✦✦
Recorded live in a New York club with a sextet. Includes many familiar themes. Soprano saxophonist with regular working band: Steve Potts on alto and soprano sax, Irene Aebi on violin and vocal, Jean Jacques Avenel on bass, Bobby Few on piano, and John Betsch on drums. —*Michael G. Nastos*

Bireli Lagrene

b. Sep. 4, 1966, Saverne, France

Guitar / Swing, Fusion, Post-Bop

When Bireli Lagrene first emerged in 1980 as a 13-year old who sounded exactly like Django Reinhardt, he was considered a marvel. Born (like

Django) to a Gypsy family, he had been playing guitar since he was four. After a few years and several recordings, Lagrene purposely got away from the Reinhardt influence, playing high-powered, rock-oriented fusion and recording with Jaco Pastorius in 1986. He sounded more original but much less interesting during this period. The guitarist has since returned to a quieter form of jazz, playing hard bop versions of standards with hints of his earlier interests in Django and fusion. Bireli Lagrene has recorded thus far for Antilles, Jazzpoint, and Blue Note. —*Scott Yanow*

Bireli Swing '81 / Apr. 1981 / Jazzpoint ✦✦✦✦
Guitarist Bireli Lagrene spent his teenage years sounding very close in style to Django Reinhardt. For this German import, his second recording, the 14-year old (!) romps in Djangoish fashion on such tunes as "Djangology," "Lady Be Good," and "Nuages" but also was starting to show some individuality on his own originals. Most of the selections are performed with one or two rhythm guitarists and a bassist, all Europeans. Lagrene has since grown as a player; if only he had had the opportunity this early to record with violinist Stephane Grappelli before his own style changed! —*Scott Yanow*

Fifteen / Feb. 1982 / Antilles ✦✦✦✦
Recorded shortly before his playing began to change, this Antilles release features guitarist Bireli Lagrene at the age of 15 jamming in the difficult-to-duplicate style of Django Reinhardt. Lagrene, who was one of the best Reinhardt soundalikes ever, is featured in small groups with other Europeans and sounds at his early best on "Sweet Georgia Brown," "Dark Eyes," "Blues for Bireli," and "I Can't Give You Anything but Love." It is a pity that Lagrene (who is so brilliant in this context) does not play this way very often anymore. —*Scott Yanow*

Bireli Lagrene Ensemble Live Featuring Vic Juris / Jun. 1, 1985-Jun. 2, 1985 / Jazzpoint ✦✦✦
Five years after *Routes to Django*, the 18-year-old Lagrene is joined by jazz-fusion guitarist Vic Juris who more than holds his own. Included on this excellent live recording are a few jazz standards and a few Django tunes as well. —*Paul Kohler*

Foreign Affairs / Aug. 10, 1988-Aug. 12, 1988 / Blue Note ✦✦✦
● **Standards** / Jun. 1992 / Blue Note ✦✦✦✦
This is one of guitarist Bireli Lagrene's better jazz albums of the '90s. By this time he had pretty much discarded his original Django Reinhardt influence (even on "Nuages" he sounds nothing like Reinhardt), and he took time off from playing rock to perform a dozen familiar standards with bassist Niels Pedersen and drummer Andre Ceccarelli. Lagrene's technique had been admirable from the start, and on this studio session his own musical personality was allowed to come to the surface. Highlights include "Softly as in a Morning Sunrise," "Autumn Leaves," "Donna Lee," and "Ornithology." —*Scott Yanow*

My Favorite Django / Jan. 1995 / Dreyfus ✦✦✦

Oliver Lake

b. 1942, Marianna, AR
Flute, Sax (Alto), Sax (Soprano) / Reggae, Avant-Garde
An expressive, energetic alto, tenor, and soprano saxophonist and flutist who's led free, hard bop, and reggae bands, Oliver Lake has been a consistently outstanding soloist, composer, and bandleader since the early '70s. His solos, especially on alto, have a pungent, bluesy edge reflecting Lake's bebop and R&B background. He's accomplished on tenor, soprano, and flute, but alto is his best instrument. Lake began playing drums as a child, then turned to alto sax at 18, and later flute. He graduated from Lincoln University in 1968, then taught for a while in public schools and played in R&B bands around the St. Louis area while also serving as a leader in the Black Artists Group (BAG). Lake played in Paris with a quintet of BAG members from 1972 to 1974. He then moved to New York, where he played both free jazz and classical music with combos and as a soloist. He was a founding member with Hamiett Bluiett, David Murray, and Julius Hemphill of the World Saxophone Quartet in 1976, playing in a New Orleans concert. That same year Lake began a trio with Michael Gregory Jackson and Pheeroan Ak Laff. He staged the theatrical presentation *The Life Dance of Is*, for which he also wrote the music and poetry, in 1977. Lake presented a program of compositions for string quartet at Carnegie Hall in 1979. Then he switched gears in the early '80s, forming a reggae/funk/fusion unit Jump Up. They played into the mid-'80s and recorded for Gramavision. Lake recorded in Italy in 1984 and 1985, and performed in New York with a free jazz band that included Kevin Eubanks and Ak Laff. He recorded with Fred Hopkins, Geri Allen, AkLaff, and Rasul Sidik on Gramavision in 1987, and did another session in '88. Lake began recording as a leader in the '70s, and has done sessions for Arista, Sackville, Black Saint, Gramavision, Blue Heron, and Gazell. —*Ron Wynn*

● **Expendable Language** / Sep. 17, 1984+Sep. 20, 1984 / Black Saint ✦✦✦✦
This freebop session (which is often quite free but often has a strong pulse) is one of altoist Oliver Lake's more rewarding sessions. Guitarist Kevin Eubanks sometimes seems a bit out of place (generally he plays in more conservative settings), but pianist Geri Allen, bassist Fred Hopkins, and

drummer Pheeroan AkLaff are quite comfortable thinking on their feet during these spirited performances. —*Scott Yanow*

Boston Duets / 1989 / Music & Arts ✦✦✦✦
The brilliant avant-garde explorer Oliver Lake (here playing alto, soprano, and flute) and the classical pianist Donal Leonellis Fox might seem at first glance to be an odd combination, but this set of duets easily exceeds one's expectations. Fox is fortunately a strong improviser, and he not only sets a strong foundation for Lake's flights but often challenges and inspires the saxophonist. Together they play a variety of moody originals plus Thelonious Monk's "Rhythm-a-ning." This set is a surprise success. —*Scott Yanow*

Again and Again / Apr. 1991 / Gramavision ✦✦✦✦
Altoist Oliver Lake (who also plays a bit of soprano on this session) performs eight of his complex but generally accessible ballads with pianist John Hicks, bassist Reggie Workman, and drummer Pheeroan AkLaff. Although none of these originals are destined to become standards, they inspire Lake to come up with some of his more lyrical solos. —*Scott Yanow*

Virtual Reality: Total Escapism / Oct. 9, 1991 / Gazell ✦✦✦
Edge-ing / Jun. 28, 1993-Jun. 29, 1993 / Soul Note ✦✦✦✦

Lambert, Hendricks & Ross

Group / Bop, Vocalese
Arguably the greatest jazz vocal group of all time, Lambert, Hendricks, and Ross was composed of three masterful bop singers who specialized in vocalese: Dave Lambert (1917-1966), John Hendricks (b. 1921), and Annie Ross (b. 1930). Originally Lambert and Hendricks tried to record re-creations of classic Count Basie performances, but they had difficulty coming up with enough talented singers to fill in for all of the horns. However, once they discovered Ross, it was decided to just use the three of them and overdub the parts; the result was the classic *Sing a Song of Basie*. Lambert, Hendricks, and Ross immediately became a very popular group and during the next few years they recorded several notable albums including a real collaboration with Basie and a collection of Duke Ellington songs. Bad health caused Ross to drop out of the group in 1962, and her replacement, Yolande Bavan (the group was renamed Lambert, Hendricks, and Bavan), was better in ensembles than as a soloist. When Bavan and Lambert both left the band in 1964, the classic group was history. Lambert, Hendricks, and Ross recorded for Impulse, World Pacific, and Columbia, while Lambert, Hendricks, and Bavan made a few albums for RCA. Their influence is still felt in the singing of Manhattan Transfer, the work of the Hendricks Family, and in nearly every jazz vocal group formed during the past 30 years. —*Scott Yanow*

☆ **Sing a Song of Basie** / Aug. 26, 1957-Nov. 26, 1957 / Impulse ✦✦✦✦✦
The premiere jazz vocal group Lambert, Hendricks, and Ross made their recording debut on this classic album, which has been reissued on CD by GRP. After unsuccessfully searching for a dozen singers in 1957 who could sing vocalese in a re-creation of some famous records by the Count Basie Orchestra, Dave Lambert, Jon Hendricks, and Annie Ross decided to overdub their voices several times instead. Utilizing just a rhythm section, the vocalists in note-for-note reproductions of ten Basie records sing the witty and inventive lyrics of Hendricks. Highlights include "It's Sand, Man," "One O'Clock Jump," the uptempo "Little Pony," and "Avenue C." This record was a sensation when it was released, and it is still quite enjoyable and unique. —*Scott Yanow*

The Swingers! / Oct. 1, 1958-Mar. 1959 / Pacific Jazz ✦✦✦
One of the lesser known sets by the classic jazz vocal group Lambert, Hendricks, and Ross, this CD reissue holds its own with their more famous recordings. Assisted by tenor saxophonist Zoot Sims, pianist Russ Freeman, and guitarist Jim Hall, among others, Dave Lambert, Jon Hendricks, and Annie Ross sound their best on such numbers as "Airegin," "Jackie" (a feature for Ross), "Swingin' Til the Girls Come Home," "Four," and "Now's the Time." An instrumental ("Clap Hands! Here Comes Charley") from the same dates but originally issued under drummer Sonny Payne's name has been added to the program. The CD is recommended to fans of this unique and influential vocal trio. —*Scott Yanow*

Everybody's Boppin' / Aug. 6, 1959-Nov. 4, 1959 / Columbia ✦✦✦✦
Lambert, Hendricks, and Ross made their debut on Columbia in 1959, and this CD contains not only all of the music from their first CBS album but five titles from two later records. This set has many memorable classics from the great singers Dave Lambert, Jon Hendricks (the top vocalese lyricist), and Annie Ross. Highlights include the happy "Charleston Alley," a remake of Ross' "Twisted," the heated "Cloudburst," Hendricks' humorous "Gimme That Wine," "Summertime" (a re-creation of Miles Davis' version with Gil Evans), and "Come on Home." Although Lambert, Hendricks, and Ross only lasted a few years, their influence on other vocal groups was enormous. This set is a perfect place for collectors to begin to explore their vocal magic. —*Scott Yanow*

Swingin' Til the Girls Come Home / Sep. 6, 1962-Dec. 21, 1963 / Bluebird ✦✦✦✦
After Yolande Bavan replaced an ill Annie Ross in 1962, the vocal trio of

Lambert, Hendricks, and Bavan recorded three albums before disbanding in early 1964. This CD has some of the high points from each of the three albums: a trio date with guest Pony Poindexter on soprano from Basin Street East, an appearance at the 1963 Newport Jazz Festival (which has spots for trumpeter Clark Terry and tenor saxophonist Coleman Hawkins), and a performance from the Village Gate with cornetist Thad Jones and tenorman Booker Ervin. All of the guests get some solo space, and the vocalists particularly sound strong on "Doodlin'," "Cousin Mary," "Swingin' Till the Girls Come Home," Hendricks' "Gimme That Wine," "Watermelon Man," and "Cloudburst." The Ceylonese singer Bavan definitely gave the group a slightly different sound than it had had with Ross, but she was not as strong a soloist, although Bavan fared well in the ensembles. This CD gives one a definitive look at the group and is well worth picking up. — *Scott Yanow*

★ **The Best of Lambert, Hendricks & Ross** / Columbia ◆◆◆◆◆
Excellent compilation. — *Michael G. Nastos*

Harold Land (Harold de Vance Land)

b. Dec. 18, 1928, Houston, TX
Sax (Tenor) / Hard Bop
Harold Land is an underrated tenor saxophonist whose tone has hardened with time and whose improvising style after the '60s became influenced by (but not a copy of) John Coltrane's. He grew up in San Diego and started playing tenor when he was 16. After working locally and making his recording debut for Savoy (1949), Land had his first high-profile gig in 1954 when he joined the Clifford Brown-Max Roach Quintet. Land performed and recorded with the group until late 1955 when, due to family problems, he had to return home to Los Angeles (where he has been based ever since). He played with Curtis Counce's band (1956-58), recorded a pair of memorable albums for Contemporary (1958-59), led his own groups in the '60s, and co-led groups with Bobby Hutcherson (1967-71) and Blue Mitchell (1975-78). Harold Land has continued freelancing around Los Angeles up to the present time and has recorded as a leader (in addition to Savoy and Contemporary) for such labels as Jazzland, Blue Note, Imperial, Atlantic, Cadet, Mainstream, Concord, Muse, and Postcards. His son Harold Land, Jr., has occasionally played piano with his groups. — *Scott Yanow*

● **Harold in the Land of Jazz** / Jan. 13, 1958-Jan. 14, 1958 / Original Jazz Classics ◆◆◆◆
Steady and entertaining, if predictable. — *Ron Wynn*

The Fox / Aug. 1959 / Original Jazz Classics ◆◆◆◆
Due to his decision to settle in Los Angeles, tenor saxophonist Harold Land has long been underrated. A strong bop stylist who later on would be influenced a great deal by John Coltrane, Land in 1959 had a sound closer to Sonny Rollins. For this excellent straightahead quintet set with trumpeter Dupree Bolton and pianist Elmo Hope, Land performs four of Hope's superior but little-known compositions along with two of his own. This is high-quality hard bop, easily recommended to fans of straightahead jazz. — *Scott Yanow*

West Coast Blues! / May 17, 1960-May 18, 1960 / Original Jazz Classics ◆◆◆◆
Recorded with Wes Montgomery (g), this is another of many excellent Land albums. — *Michael G. Nastos*

Eastward Ho! Harold Land in New York / Jul. 5, 1960-Jul. 8, 1960 / Original Jazz Classics ◆◆◆◆
An exemplary date, with Kenny Dorham (tpt) in top form. — *Ron Wynn*

A Lazy Afternoon / Dec. 28, 1994-Dec. 31, 1994 / Postcards ◆◆◆◆
Harold Land, a long underrated tenor giant based in Los Angeles, is quite melodic yet subtly explorative on his surprising disc. Backed by a string orchestra arranged and conducted by Ray Ellis and a rhythm section led by pianist Bill Henderson, Land explores a dozen standards that are highlighted by "Nature Boy," "Invitation," and "You've Changed." He treats the melodies with respect and taste yet is not shy to stretch the music when called for. Harold Land plays beautifully throughout this memorable release. — *Scott Yanow*

Eddie Lang (Dunn Blind Willie Massaro)

b. Oct. 25, 1902, Philadelphia, PA, **d.** Mar. 26, 1933, New York, NY
Guitar / Classic Jazz
The first jazz guitar virtuoso, Eddie Lang was everywhere in the late '20s; all of his fellow musicians knew that he was the best. A boyhood friend of Joe Venuti, Lang took violin lessons for 11 years but switched to guitar before he turned professional. In 1924 he debuted with the Mound City Blue Blowers and was soon in great demand for recording dates, both in the jazz world and in commercial settings. His sophisticated chord patterns made him a superior accompanist who uplifted everyone else's music, and Lang was also a fine single-note soloist. He often teamed up with violinist Venuti (including some classic duets) and played with Red Nichols' Five Pennies, Frankie Trumbauer and Bix Beiderbecke (most memorably on "Singing the Blues"), the orchestras of Roger Wolfe Kahn, Jean Goldkette, and Paul Whiteman (appearing on one short number with Venuti in

Whiteman's 1930 film *The King of Jazz*), and anyone else who would hire him. A measure of Lang's versatility and talents is that he mostly played the chordal parts on a series of duets with Lonnie Johnson (during which he used the pseudonym Blind Willie Dunn), yet on his two duets with Carl Kress (whose chord voicings were an advancement on Lang's), he played the single-note leads. Eddie Lang, who led some dates of his own during 1927-29, worked regularly with Bing Crosby during the early '30s in addition to recording many sessions with Venuti. Tragically, his premature death was caused by a botched tonsillectomy. — *Scott Yanow*

★ **Stringing the Blues** / Nov. 8, 1926-May 8, 1933 / Columbia ◆◆◆◆◆
This two-LP set (which is long overdue to be reissued on CD) contains a definitive cross-section of the recordings of violinist Joe Venuti and guitarist Eddie Lang. The 32 performances include everything from duets and a few of Lang's meetings with fellow guitarist Lonnie Johnson to examples of Venuti's Blue Four and guest appearances with singer Annette Hanshaw, Clarence Williams, Tommy Dorsey (on trumpet!), and Bing Crosby (on a hot "Some of these Days"). Virtually all of these recordings are superb, with solos also heard from bass saxophonist Adrian Rollini, Don Murray (on clarinet and baritone), cornetist King Oliver, the C-melody sax of Frankie Trumbauer, and Jimmy Dorsey (switching between clarinet, alto, and cornet). Highly recommended for all collections. — *Scott Yanow*

☆ **Jazz Guitar** / Apr. 1, 1927-Jan. 15, 1932 / Yazoo ◆◆◆◆◆
Eddie Lang did not lead many sessions during his short life, and the great majority are on this Yazoo LP. The most in-demand guitarist of 1925-33, Lang's rare opportunities to head his own dates put the focus on his single-note lines and gave him a chance to be in the spotlight rather than making other players sound good. This LP has two unaccompanied solos (including Rachmaninoff's "Prelude"), duets with pianists Frank Signorelli, Arthur Schutt, and Rube Bloom, and three of his famous collaborations with fellow guitarist Lonnie Johnson. However, the most memorable music are Lang's two exciting duets with guitarist Carl Kress: "Pickin' My Way" and an alternate take of "Feeling My Way." This is highly recommended music from the best jazz guitarist prior to the rise of Django Reinhardt. — *Scott Yanow*

Pete LaRoca (Peter Sims)

b. Apr. 7, 1938
Drums / Latin Jazz, Hard Bop
Pete LaRoca's decision to leave music in 1968 and become an attorney (under his original name of Pete Sims) cut short a productive career. He started his career playing timbales in Latin bands, changing his name to Pete LaRoca at the time. He played drums with Sonny Rollins (1957-early 1959) and had associations with Jackie McLean, Slide Hampton, the John Coltrane Quartet (where he was the original drummer in 1960), and Marian McPartland. LaRoca led his own group (1961-62), was the house drummer at the Jazz Workshop in Boston (1963-64), and worked with Art Farmer (1964-65), Freddie Hubbard, Mose Allison, Charles Lloyd (1966), Paul Bley, and Steve Kuhn, among others. He led two impressive albums: the classic Blue Note record *Basra* with Joe Henderson, and *Bliss*, a Douglas session (reissued on Muse) featuring Chick Corea and John Gilmore. LaRoca started playing jazz again in 1979 and has performed occasionally up to the present time. — *Scott Yanow*

● **Basra** / May 19, 1965 / Blue Note ◆◆◆◆
It is strange to realize that drummer Pete LaRoca only led two albums in his career, for this CD reissue of his initial date is a classic. LaRoca's three originals ("Basra," which holds one's interest despite staying on one chord throughout, the blues "Candu," and the complex "Tears Come from Heaven") are stimulating, but it is the other three songs that really bring out the best playing in the quartet (which comprises tenor saxophonist Joe Henderson, pianist Steve Kuhn, and bassist Steve Swallow in addition to LaRoca). "Malaguena" is given a great deal of passion, Swallow's "Eiderdown" (heard in its initial recording) receives definitive treatment, and the ballad "Lazy Afternoon" is both haunting and very memorable; Henderson's tone perfectly fits that piece. — *Scott Yanow*

Yusef Lateef (William Evans)

b. Oct. 9, 1920, Chatanooga, TN
Flute, Oboe, Sax (Tenor) / New Age, Hard Bop, Africa, Zimbabwe, Groove
Yusef Lateef has long had an inquisitive spirit, and he was never just a bop or hard bop soloist. Lateef, who does not care much for the name "jazz," has consistently created music that has stretched (and even broke through) boundaries. A superior tenor saxophonist with a soulful sound and impressive technique, Lateef by the '50s was one of the top flutists around. He also developed into the best jazz soloist to date on oboe, is an occasional bassoonist, and introduced such instruments as the argol (a double clarinet that resembles a bassoon), shanai (a type of oboe), and different types of flutes. Lateef played "world music" before it had a name, and his output was much more creative than much of the pop and folk music that passes under that label in the '90s. Lateef grew up in Detroit and began on tenor when he was 17. He played with Lucky Mill-

inder (1946), Hot Lips Page, Roy Eldridge, and Dizzy Gillespie's big band (1949-50). He was a fixture on the Detroit jazz scene of the '50s where he studied flute at Wayne State University. Lateef began recording as a leader in 1955 for Savoy (and later Riverside and Prestige), although he did not move to New York until 1959. By then he already had a strong reputation for his versatility and for his willingness to utilize "miscellaneous instruments." Lateef played with Charles Mingus in 1960, gigged with Donald Byrd, and was well featured with the Cannonball Adderley Sextet (1962-64). As a leader his string of Impulse recordings (1963-66) were among the finest of his career, although his varied Atlantic sessions (1967-76) usually also had some strong moments. He spent some time in the '80s teaching in Nigeria. His Atlantic records of the late '80s were closer to mood music (or new age) than jazz, but in the '90s (for his own YAL label) Yusef Lateef has recorded a wide variety of music (all originals) including some strong improvised music with the likes of Ricky Ford, Archie Shepp, and Von Freeman. — *Scott Yanow*

Every Village Has a Song / May 6, 1949-Mar. 1976 / Rhino/Atlantic ✦✦✦✦
This good two-disc set covers Lateef's tenure at Atlantic as well as featuring formative material from early sessions for Transition, Prestige/Moodsville, Riverside, Impulse, Blue Note, and Savoy. The discs show Lateef honing a thick, bluesy, expressive tenor tone in the beginning, evolving into a superior straight jazz player, then expanding his repertoire and choice of instruments and contexts. His flute playing became arguably superior to his tenor, while his solos on oboe, shenai, and other previously little-known instruments enabled Lateef to create arresting, fresh, and ultimately significant music. While the sampler approach can't fully document his contributions, it's a solid introduction for those unfamiliar with his output. — *Ron Wynn*

Cry! / Tender / Oct. 11, 1957+Oct. 16, 1959 / Original Jazz Classics ✦✦✦✦
This well rounded program, reissued on CD in the OJC program, features Yusef Lateef (tripling on tenor, flute, and oboe) heading a quintet also that includes trumpeter Lonnie Hillyer, pianist Hugh Lawson, bassist Herman Wright, and drummer Frank Gant. The music alternates between straight ahead pieces and more atmospheric and exotic works. An earlier track ("Ecaps") features Lateef with a different quintet that also includes fluegelhornist Wilbur Harden. — *Scott Yanow*

Other Sounds / Oct. 11, 1957 / Original Jazz Classics ✦✦✦✦
These recordings are among his early African/Middle Eastern fusion efforts, with many exotic instruments. — *Myles Boisen*

The Three Faces of Yusef Lateef / May 9, 1960 / Original Jazz Classics ✦✦✦✦
This is one of Yusef Lateef's most accessible sessions with such famous songs as "Goin' Home," "I'm Just a Lucky So and So," and the ancient standard "Ma He's Makin' Eyes at Me." Lateef (featured on tenor, flute, and oboe) is teamed up with pianist Hugh Lawson, cellist Ron Carter, bassist Herman Wright, and drummer Lex Humphries for a set of stimulating music that also includes a few of Lateef's thought-provoking originals. This CD reissue is recommended as are all of his recordings from the era. — *Scott Yanow*

The Centaur and the Phoenix / Oct. 4, 1960+Oct. 6, 1960 / Original Jazz Classics ✦✦✦✦
For this CD reissue of a Riverside date, the great multi-reedist Yusef Lateef (who switches between tenor, flute, oboe, and the argol) is joined on most selections by five other horns (including a bassoonist) and a rhythm section headed by pianist Joe Zawinul. The music has a lot of diversity, from stomps and ballads to Eastern-influenced explorations; two "bonus cuts" from the same date match Lateef with a four-piece rhythm section that includes pianist Barry Harris and two percussionists. Highlights include "Everyday I Fall in Love," "Summer Song," "Jungle Fantasy," and "The Centaur and the Phoenix." Virtually everything that Yusef Lateef recorded during this era is well worth acquiring. — *Scott Yanow*

★ **Eastern Sounds** / Sep. 5, 1961 / Original Jazz Classics ✦✦✦✦✦
Although originally issued on the Moodsville label (a subsidiary of Prestige), this classic Yusef Lateef date is not all ballads. Accompanied by pianist Barry Harris, bassist Ernie Farrow, and drummer Lex Humphries, Lateef (switching between tenor, oboe, and flute) is quite memorable on such pieces as the "Love Theme from *Spartacus*," "Blues for the Orient," "Don't Blame Me," and "The Plum Blossom." He has long been a true original with an active musical curiosity, and this set gives listeners a strong example of his work. — *Scott Yanow*

● **Into Something** / Dec. 29, 1961 / Original Jazz Classics ✦✦✦✦
This superior set (which has been reissued on CD) features Yusef Lateef on some straight-ahead tunes including "When You're Smiling," "I'll Remember April," and "You've Changed." In addition there are some more adventurous and exotic works, too, making this a well rounded program. Lateef is joined by pianist Barry Harris, bassist Herman Wright, and drummer Elvin Jones for a particularly memorable performance. — *Scott Yanow*

★ **Live at Pep's** / Jun. 29, 1964 / Impulse ✦✦✦✦✦
This mid-'60s concert was one of Lateef's finest, as it perfectly displayed his

multiple influences and interests. There were hard bop originals, covers of jazz classics like Oscar Pettiford's "Oscarlypso" (a CD bonus track), and Leonard Feather's "Twelve Tone Blues," as well as an unorthodox but effective version of Ma Rainey's "See See Rider." On "Sister Mamie," "Number 7," and drummer James Black's "The Magnolia Triangle," Lateef moved away from strict jazz, although he retained his improvisational flair. Lateef played meaty tenor sax solos, entrancing flute and bamboo flute offerings, and also had impressive stints on oboe, shenai, and argol. This was a pivotal date in his career, and those unaware of it will get a treat with this disc. — *Ron Wynn*

The Blue Yusef Lateef / Apr. 23, 1968-Apr. 24, 1968 / Atlantic ✦✦✦

The Diverse Yusef Lateef/Suite 16 / Jan. 15, 1970-Nov. 2, 1970 / Atlantic ✦✦✦✦
For this single CD Rhino combined two complete LPs from Yusef Lateef's period on Atlantic. Although there are some period trappings and the use of a vocal group on a few selections, the music sounds fairly fresh and its diversity (ranging from exotic vamps to the adventurous seven-movement "Symphonic Blues Suite") is a major strength. Earl Klugh's solo guitar rendition of "Michelle" is pleasant if out-of-place and there are some forgettable tracks, but Lateef's willingness to take chances, his highly individual sound on his instruments (tenor, flute, oboe, and a rare outing on soprano), and the impressive amount of variety make this a recommended set. — *Scott Yanow*

Part of the Search / Sep. 1, 1971-Dec. 26, 1973 / Atlantic ✦✦✦✦
Yusef Lateef's Atlantic albums tended to be erratic affairs with plenty of chances taken and the overall results being a mixed success. This set (reissued on CD) is one of his better efforts from the era. Lateef, doubling on tenor and alto this time, is backed not only by his trio but a big band, string quartet, three background vocalists, and a variety of electric keyboardists and guitarists. There are enough good tracks (particularly "Lunceford Prance," "Rockhouse," and "I'm Gettin' Sentimental over You") to make this a release worth checking out. — *Scott Yanow*

Tenors of Yusef Lateef & Ricky Ford / 1994 / YAL ✦✦✦✦
Veteran tenors Yusef Lateef and Ricky Ford team up for this frequently explosive set. Their seven originals all pay tribute to various tenormen (James Moody, Stanley Turrentine, Sonny Rollins, Jimmy Heath, Wayne Shorter, Joe Henderson, and Lateef himself), and the two lead voices, while not copying their inspirations, occasionally insert some of their trademark phrases. Electric bassist Avery Sharpe and drummer Kamal Sabir offer fairly accessible and often-funky backings, but one's main focus is on the intense playing of the two great tenors, who battle it out in fiery fashion. — *Scott Yanow*

Hubert Laws

b. Nov. 10, 1939, Houston, TX
Flute / Classical, Instrumental Pop, Hard Bop, Crossover
A talented flutist whose musical interest was never exclusively straight-ahead jazz, Hubert Laws exceeded Herbie Mann in popularity in the '70s when he recorded for CTI. He was a member of the early Jazz Crusaders while in Texas (1954-60), and he also played classical music during those years. In the '60s Laws made his first recordings as a leader (Atlantic dates from 1964-66) and gigged with Mongo Santamaria, Benny Golson, Jim Hall, James Moody, and Clark Terry, among many others. His CTI recordings from the first half of the '70s made Laws famous and were a high point, particularly compared to his generally wretched Columbia dates from the late '70s. He was less active in the '80s but has come back with a pair of fine Music Masters sessions in the '90s. Laws has the ability to play anything well but not always the desire to perform creative jazz. — *Scott Yanow*

★ **In the Beginning** / Feb. 1974 / CTI ✦✦✦✦✦
This double LP features flutist Hubert Laws at his finest. The music ranges from classical-oriented pieces to straight-ahead jazz with touches of '70s funk included in the mix. The supporting cast includes keyboardist Bob James on most tracks, guitarist Gene Bertoncini, bassist Ron Carter, drummer Steve Gadd, three strings, and Hubert's brother Ronnie on tenor (his solo on John Coltrane's "Moment's Notice" is arguably Ronnie's best ever on record). Whether it be works by Satie or Sonny Rollins, this recording is one of the most rewarding of Hubert Laws' career. — *Scott Yanow*

Storm Then the Calm / 1994 / Music Masters ✦✦✦✦

Jeanne Lee

b. Jan. 29, 1939, New York, NY
Synthesizer, Vocals / Avant-Garde, Free Jazz
Jeanne Lee combines acrobatic vocal maneuvers with a deeply moving sound and quality that allows her to alternate between soaring, upper register flights and piercing, emotive interpretations. She's extremely precise and flexible, and moves from a song or solo's top end to its middle and bottom accompanying an instrument with a stunning ease. Though many critics have cited Lee as creating free jazz's most innovative vocal approach, she's done very little recording, almost none of it as a leader and

even less on American labels. She's best known for her many sessions with Gunther Hampel. Lee studied dance rather than music at Bard College, but while a student there she met Ran Blake. They formed a duo, and she did her first recordings with him, which excited many critics. They toured Europe in 1963. Lee moved to California in 1964, and worked with Ian Underwood and sound poet David Hazelton, whom she later married. She and Hampel established their musical relationship while Lee was in Europe in 1967. Lee recorded with Archie Shepp, Sunny Murray, and Hampel in the late '60s, and with Marion Brown, Anthony Braxton, Enrico Rava, and Andrew Cyrille in the '70s, while also working with Cecil Taylor. She began composing extensively in the '80s, and has concentrated in recent years on performing her original material, which frequently includes poetic and dance components. Most of her recordings have either been done for European labels or small independents. —*Ron Wynn*

★ **Legendary Duets** / Nov. 15, 1961-Dec. 7, 1961 / Bluebird ♦♦♦♦♦
With Ran Blake. It's an appropriate title. A must-buy for creative music listeners. Jeanne Lee does vocals; Ran Blake is on piano. —*Ron Wynn*

Michel Legrand

b. Feb. 24, 1932, Paris, France
Piano / Pop, Hard Bop
Michel Legrand has made his fame and fortune from writing for films, but he has done significant work in jazz on an occasional basis. In 1957 he arranged a set of Dixieland and swing standards for a French orchestra (recorded on Phillips), in 1958 he used three different all-star groups for the classic *Legrand Jazz* (with such sidemen as Miles Davis, John Coltrane, Phil Woods, Herbie Mann, Bill Evans, Ben Webster, Art Farmer, and others), and in 1968 he recorded a strictly jazz set with a trio. Legrand has written for albums led by Stan Getz (1971), Sarah Vaughan (1972), and, on several occasions, Phil Woods. Several of his songs (such as "What Are You Doing the Rest of Your Life," "Watch What Happens," and "The Summer Knows") have been recorded many times by jazz musicians. —*Scott Yanow*

★ **Legrand Jazz** / Jun. 25, 1958-Jun. 30, 1958 / Philips ♦♦♦♦♦
Michel Legrand has spent most of his life as a composer in the studios and for films but this release is a jazz classic. Legrand took 11 famous jazz compositions and arranged them for three different groups. Tenor-great Ben Webster, flutist Herbie Mann, four trombonists, and a rhythm section perform pieces by Duke Ellington, Earl Hines, Django Reinhardt ("Nuages"), and the Count Basie-associated "Blue and Sentimental." A big band with trumpeters Art Farmer and Donald Byrd and altoist Phil Woods plays "Stompin' at the Savoy," "A Night in Tunisia," and Bix Beiderbecke's "In a Mist." The most famous session has Miles Davis, John Coltrane, Phil Woods, Herbie Mann, pianist Bill Evans, harp, vibes, baritone, and a rhythm section performing music by Thelonious Monk, John Lewis, Jelly Roll Morton ("Wild Man Blues"), and Fats Waller's "Jitterbug Waltz." Throughout this superlative album, the arrangements are colorful and unusual, making one wish that Legrand had recorded more jazz albums through the years. —*Scott Yanow*

Michel LeGrand at Shelly Manne's Hole / Jan. 1968 / Verve ♦♦♦♦
A good upbeat mainstream session. Legrand shines as an improviser. —*Ron Wynn*

Jazz Grand / Mar. 1978 / Gryphon ♦♦♦

Le Jazz Grand / Mar. 1978 / DCC ♦♦♦♦
A surprisingly nice session. —*Ron Wynn*

Le Grand Piano / 1981 / Columbia ♦♦♦

Castles in Spain / Columbia ♦♦♦♦
Finely produced, orchestrated, and arranged work by a master of moods and textures. —*Ron Wynn*

Sarah Vaughan/Michel Legrand / Mainstream ♦♦♦
A meeting that worked better than anyone might expect. Vaughan was still her dynamic, charismatic vocal self, while Legrand didn't obscure or dilute her singing, and also effectively supported her in his own way. —*Ron Wynn*

George Lewis

b. 1948
Clarinet / New Orleans Jazz
George Lewis never tried to be a virtuoso soloist. He loved to play melodic ensembles where his distinctive clarinet was free to improvise as simply as he desired. When Lewis was inspired and in tune, he could hold his own with any of his contemporaries in New Orleans, and he always sounded beautiful playing his "Burgundy Street Blues." To everyone's surprise (including himself), he became one of the most popular figures of the New Orleans revival movement of the '50s.

It took Lewis a long time to achieve fame. He taught himself clarinet when he was 18 and worked in the '20s with the Black Eagle Band, Buddy Petit, the Eureka Brass Band, Chris Kelly, Kid Rena, the Olympia Orchestra, and other New Orleans groups. He played with Bunk Johnson in Evan Thomas' group in the early '30s but had a day job throughout most of the

decade. When Bunk was discovered in 1942, Lewis became part of his band, playing with him on and off through 1945 and getting opportunities to lead his own sessions during 1943-45. However, Johnson was difficult to get along with and a homesick Lewis returned to New Orleans by 1946. He played locally with his own group (featuring trombonist Jim Robinson) and in 1950 was portrayed in an article for *Look*. That exposure led to him recording regularly and by 1952 Lewis was in such great demand that he was soon working before crowds in California and touring Europe and Japan. In addition to Robinson, Lewis' band in its prime years often featured trumpeter Kid Howard, pianist Alton Purnell, banjoist Lawrence Marrero, bassist Alcide "Slow Drag" Pavageau, and drummer Joe Watkins. George Lewis, who recorded for many labels (a Mosaic box set of his Blue Note sessions is one of the best reissues), became a symbol of what was right and wrong about the New Orleans revival movement, overpraised by his fans and overcritized by his detractors. At his best he was well worth hearing. —*Scott Yanow*

☆ **Complete Blue Note Recordings** / May 15, 1943-Apr. 11, 1955 / Mosaic ♦♦♦♦♦
A centerpiece for the dedicated New Orleans collector, it begins with Lewis' "Climax" session in 1943 and ranges through a variety of studio and concert performances over a twelve-year period—definitely some of the clarinetist's best work (1943-1944, 1954-1955). —*Bruce Raeburn*

☆ **With Kid Shots** / 1944 / American Music ♦♦♦♦♦
Although this music is historic, it is quite erratic. George Lewis was one of the top New Orleans clarinetists when he was on but during most of these titles he is noticeably out-of-tune. Trumpeter Louis "Kid Shots" Madison is also quite streaky and, although trombonist Jim Robinson is consistent and the pianoless rhythm section (banjoist Lawrence Marrero, bassist Alcide "Slow Drag" Pavageau, and drummer Baby Dodds) is solid, the weak frontline sinks this effort even with the inclusion of the earliest version of "Burgundy Street Blues." The CD concludes with three obscure performances by the same group with Bunk Johnson on trumpet; this version of "Sister Kate" was previously unissued. But there are many more rewarding George Lewis performances to be found elsewhere. —*Scott Yanow*

George Lewis of New Orleans / 1946 / Original Jazz Classics ♦♦♦♦
Some great New Orleans standards appear from the Original Zenith Brass Band and the Eclipse Alley Five, featuring Lewis in good company—Isidore Barbarin (Paul's father), Peter Bocage, Jim Robinson, Baby Dodds, and others. —*Bruce Raeburn*

The Beverly Caverns Sessions / May 26, 1953-May 27, 1953 / Good Time Jazz ♦♦♦♦
Clarinetist George Lewis and his usual band of this period (which consisted of trumpeter Kid Howard, trombonist Jim Robinson, pianist Alton Purnell, Lawrence Marrero on banjo, bassist Slow Drag Pavageau, and drummer Joe Watkins) are in better-than-average form on this well recorded live set. Lewis and his group emphasize ensembles on the dozen New Orleans standards, and the clarinetist/leader is in surprisingly extroverted form, easily the most impressive soloist. Fans of traditional jazz should go out of their way to pick up this CD. These performances were released for the first time in 1994. —*Scott Yanow*

★ **Hot Creole Jazz: 1953** / 1953 / DCC ♦♦♦♦♦
Outstanding CD reissue. —*Ron Wynn*

Jazz at Vespers / Feb. 21, 1954 / Original Jazz Classics ♦♦♦♦

Voyager / 1993 / Avant ♦♦♦

John Lewis

b. May 3, 1920, La Grange, IL
Piano / Bop, Cool, Third Stream
The musical director of the Modern Jazz Quartet for its entire history, John Lewis found the perfect outlet for his interest in bop, blues, and Bach. Possessor of a "cool" piano style that (like Count Basie) makes every note count, Lewis with the MJQ has long helped make jazz look respectable to the classical music community without watering down his performances.

After serving in the military, Lewis was in the Dizzy Gillespie big band (1946-48). He recorded with Charlie Parker during 1947-48 (including "Parker's Mood") and played with Miles Davis' Birth of the Cool Nonet, arranging "Move" and "Rouge." He worked with Illinois Jacquet (1948-49) and Lester Young (1950-51) and appeared on many recordings during the era. In 1951 Lewis recorded with the Milt Jackson Quartet, which by 1952 became the Modern Jazz Quartet. Lewis' musical vision was fulfilled with the MJQ, and he composed many pieces, with "Django" being the best known. In addition to constantly touring with the MJQ during 1952-74, Lewis wrote the film scores to *Odds Against Tomorrow, No Sun in Venice,* and *A Milanese Story,* recorded as a leader (including the 1956 cool classic "Two Degrees East, Three Degrees West," collaborations with Gunther Schuller and records with Svend Asmussen and Albert Mangelsdorff), and worked with Orchestra USA. in the mid-'60s. When the MJQ broke up in 1974, Lewis worked as an educator and occasionally recorded as a leader. With the MJQ's rebirth in 1981, he has resumed his former role as its guiding spirit. Most of John Lewis' own projects were recorded for Atlantic. —*Scott Yanow*

★ **Grand Encounter** / Feb. 10, 1956 / Pacific Jazz ✦✦✦✦✦
A 1988 reissue of a topflight date. Chamber jazz meets third stream with Chico Hamilton (d), Jim Hall (g), Percy Heath (b), and Bill Perkins (sax). —*Ron Wynn*

☆ **Wonderful World of Jazz** / Jul. 29, 1960-Sep. 9, 1960 / Atlantic ✦✦✦✦✦
A 1989 reissue of a fine date. —*Ron Wynn*

Kansas City Breaks / May 25, 1982-May 26, 1982 / DRG ✦✦✦✦
Has the interesting instrumentation of a flute, violin, guitar, and piano trio. All selections are Lewis originals, including the especially famous "Django," "Milano," and "Sacha's Mardi." A sweet session. —*Michael G. Nastos*

★ **The Chess Game, Vols. 1 & 2** / 1987-1988 / Verve ✦✦✦✦✦
Wonderful technique. More third stream than jazz. —*Ron Wynn*

● **Midnight in Paris** / Dec. 1988 / EmArcy ✦✦✦✦
A marvelous session. —*Ron Wynn*

Meade "Lux" Lewis (Meade Anderson Lewis)

b. Sep. 4, 1905, Chicago, IL, d. Jun. 7, 1964, Minneapolis, MN
Piano / Boogie-Woogie
One of the three great boogie-woogie pianists (along with Albert Ammons and Pete Johnson) whose appearance at John Hammond's 1938 *Spirituals to Swing* concert helped start the boogie-woogie craze, Meade Lux Lewis was a powerful if somewhat limited player. He played regularly in Chicago in the late '20s, and his one solo record of the time, "Honky Tonk Train Blues" (1927), was considered a classic. However, other than a few sides backing little-known blues singers, Lewis gained little extra work and slipped into obscurity. John Hammond heard Lewis' record in 1935 and after a search found Lewis washing cars for a living in Chicago. Soon Meade Lux Lewis was back on records and after the 1938 concert he was able to work steadily, sometimes in duets or trios with Ammons and Johnson. He became the first jazz pianist to double on celeste (starting in 1936) and was featured on that instrument in a Blue Note quartet date with Edmond Hall and Charlie Christian; he also played harpsichord on a few records in 1941. After the boogie-woogie craze ended, Lewis continued working in Chicago and California, recording as late as 1962, although by then he was pretty much forgotten. Meade Lux Lewis led sessions through the years that have come out on MCA, Victor, Blue Note, Solo Art, Euphonic, Stinson, Atlantic, Storyville, Verve, Tops, ABC-Paramount, Riverside, and Philips. —*Scott Yanow*

★ **Complete Blue Note Recordings** / Jan. 6, 1939-Aug. 22, 1944 / Mosaic ✦✦✦✦✦
With Meade Lux Lewis. 1939-1944. A wonderful, comprehensive compilation of stamping, romping boogie-woogie piano by the masters. —*Ron Wynn*

1939-1954 / Feb. 1939-Sep. 25, 1954 / Story of Blues ✦✦✦✦
Vintage recordings from a premier boogie-woogie stylist detailing the evolution and fruition of his approach. It features recordings done in the '30s, '40s, and '50s, and sessions for various labels, solos, duets with Albert Ammons, and some combo dates. —*Ron Wynn*

● **The Blues Piano Artistry of Meade Lux Lewis** / Nov. 1, 1961 / Original Jazz Classics ✦✦✦✦
Boogie-woogie pianist Meade Lux Lewis' next-to-last record was his first recording in five years and his final opportunity to stretch out unaccompanied. This solo Riverside set (reissued by OJC on CD) as usual finds Lewis generally sticking to the blues (with "You Were Meant for Me" and "Fate" being exceptions), mostly performing originals. On a few of the songs Lewis switches effectively to celeste. It apparently only took Meade Lux Lewis two hours to record the full set and the results are quite spontaneous yet well organized, a fine all-around portrait of the veteran pianist in his later period. —*Scott Yanow*

Mel Lewis (Melvin Sokoloff)

b. May 10, 1929, Buffalo, NY, d. Feb. 1990
Drums / Bop, Post-Bop
Although he was generally reluctant to solo, Mel Lewis was considered one of the definitive big-band drummers, a musician who was best at driving an orchestra but could also play quite well with smaller units. He started playing professionally when he was 15 and worked with the big bands of Boyd Raeburn (1948), Alvino Rey, Ray Anthony, and Tex Beneke. Lewis gained a great deal of recognition in the jazz world for his work with Stan Kenton (1954-57), making the large ensemble swing hard. In 1957 he settled in Los Angeles, became a studio drummer, and worked with the big bands of Terry Gibbs and Gerald Wilson. Lewis went to New York to play with Gerry Mulligan's Concert Jazz Band in 1960, and he toured Europe with Dizzy Gillespie (1961) and the Soviet Union with Benny Goodman (1962). In 1965 Lewis formed an orchestra in New York with Thad Jones, which grew to be one of the top big bands in jazz. When Jones surprised

everyone by suddenly fleeing to Europe in 1979, Lewis became the orchestra's sole leader, playing regularly each Monday night at the Village Vanguard with the band up until his death. Mel Lewis recorded as a leader in the '50s for San Francisco Jazz Records, Mode (reissued on V.S.O.P.), and Andex and, after Thad Jones left their orchestra, Lewis recorded with his big band for Atlantic, Telarc, and Music Masters. —*Scott Yanow*

Mel Lewis and Friends / Jun. 18, 1976 / A&M ✦✦✦✦
This was a fine straight-ahead blowing bop date, with the only electricity being that produced by the players themselves. This was trumpeter Freddie Hubbard's best recorded effort in nearly five years and he deserved support for his work here . . . The trio also shined on "Wind Flower," a John Lewis-type loper by Sarah Cassey on which the horns sat out; Hank Jones, Ron Carter, and Lewis all had outstanding feature spots . . . This was a faultless date with many high moments of musical substance. —*Bob Rusch, Cadence*

Mellifuous / Mar. 31, 1981 / Landmark ✦✦✦

Mel Lewis & the Jazz Orchestra / Jan. 7, 1982-Jan. 11, 1982 / Red Baron ✦✦✦✦
Recorded live at the Village Vanguard, the Mel Lewis big band (which at the time was in the process of finding its own sound) performs arrangements by Bob Brookmeyer. While letting the band swing and leaving space for such soloists as fluegelhornist Tom Harrell, altoist Dick Oatts, Joe Lovano's tenor, pianist Jim McNeely, and altoist Kenny Garrett, Brookmeyer (who sits in on valve trombone during "Goodbye World") nevertheless constructs difficult charts that are more than a little inspired by modern classical music; this version of "My Funny Valentine" is quite eerie. Somehow the Mel Lewis Orchestra sounds relaxed on this rather complex music, and the overall results are rewarding. —*Scott Yanow*

20 Years at the Village Vanguard / Mar. 20, 1985-Mar. 22, 1985 / Atlantic ✦✦✦✦
A portrait of his orchestra with fresh faces and sounds. —*Ron Wynn*

● **Definitive Thad Jones, Vol. 1** / Feb. 11, 1988-Feb. 15, 1988 / Music Masters ✦✦✦✦
The band playing from the book of longtime co-leader Thad Jones. —*Ron Wynn*

Definitive Thad Jones, Vol. 2 / Feb. 11, 1988-Feb. 15, 1988 / Music Masters ✦✦✦✦
A continuation of the series dedicated to Thad Jones' repertory. —*Ron Wynn*

Soft Lights and Hot Music / Feb. 11, 1988-Feb. 15, 1988 / Music Masters ✦✦✦✦
Here are some excellent big-band tracks, with fine solos by Joe Lovano (ts). —*Ron Wynn*

The Lost Art / Apr. 11, 1989-Apr. 12, 1989 / Music Masters ✦✦✦✦
Sextet. This is the definitive small-group album, with pianist Ken Werner. —*Michael G. Nastos*

To You: A Tribute to Mel Lewis / Sep. 10, 1990-Sep. 12, 1990 / Music Masters ✦✦✦✦
Mel Lewis Jazz Orchestra. Fine recent big-band tracks. —*Ron Wynn*

Ramsey Lewis

Piano, Keyboards / Instrumental Pop, Soul-Jazz, Crossover
Ramsey Lewis has long straddled the boundary between bop-oriented jazz and pop music. Most of his recordings (particularly by the mid-'60s) were very accessible and attracted a large nonjazz audience. In 1956 he formed a trio with bassist Eldee Young and drummer Red Holt. From the start (1958) their records for Argo/Cadet were popular, although in the early days they had a strong jazz content. In 1958 Lewis also recorded with Max Roach and Lem Winchester. On the 1965 albums *The In Crowd* and *Hang On*, Ramsey made the pianist into a major attraction, and from that point on his records became much more predictable and pop-oriented. In 1966 his trio's personnel changed with bassist Cleveland Eaton and drummer Maurice White (later the founder of Earth, Wind and Fire) joining Lewis. In the '70s Lewis often played electric piano, although by later in the decade he was sticking to acoustic and hiring an additional keyboardist. He can still play melodic jazz when he wants to, but Ramsey Lewis has mostly stuck to easy-listening pop music during the past 30 years. —*Scott Yanow*

The Sound of Christmas / 1960-1961 / Chess ✦✦✦

★ **The In Crowd** / May 13, 1965-May 14, 1965 / Chess ✦✦✦✦✦
The In Crowd was the Ramsey Lewis Trio's big hit of the time. The title track typified part of the Lewis style, but helped commercially lock it in to a narrow style. Recorded in May 1965 at the once hip Bohemian Caverns in Washington, D.C., it remains a pleasant, easy listen. —*Bob Rusch, Cadence*

Sun Goddess / 1974 / Columbia ✦✦✦✦
Lewis' most popular album since *The In Crowd.* Very good for what it is. Gold album. —*Ron Wynn*

Routes / 1980 / Columbia ✦✦✦

We Meet Again / 1990 / CBS ◆◆◆◆
Billy Taylor (p) takes the date, but Lewis shows chops he seldom taps these days. —*Ron Wynn*

Sky Islands / 1993 / GRP ◆◆

David Liebman

b. Sep. 4, 1946, New York, NY
Flute, Sax (Soprano), Sax (Tenor) / Avant-Garde, Post-Bop
Dave Liebman has developed through time to become one of the top soprano saxophonists in jazz. A highly individual and explorative (yet versatile) improviser who can stretch from bop to free, Liebman studied early on with Lennie Tristano and Charles Lloyd. He gained important experience playing with Ten Wheel Drive (1970), Elvin Jones (1971-73), and Miles Davis' fusion group (1973-74). Liebman formed Lookout Farm in 1974, the first of several groups (including Quest in the '80s) that teamed his reeds with pianist Richie Beirach. By the late '80s he had largely dropped the tenor to concentrate on soprano and occasionally flute, although he made a rare recording on tenor for Double-Time in 1995. Liebman, who is very active in jazz education and has written several books, has recorded for a countless number of labels through the years as a leader including PM, ECM, Horizon, Timeless, Palo Alto, Impulse, Soul Note, Heads Up, Storyville, Owl, CMP, Red, and Candid. —*Scott Yanow*

Lookout Farm / Oct. 10, 1973-Oct. 11, 1973 / ECM ◆◆◆◆
Liebman at the top-of-the-heap as an unabashed improviser. A high-water mark for this period. Completely original post-Tristano piano of Richard Beirach. —*Michael G. Nastos*

Dedications / Sep. 1979 / CMP ◆◆◆◆
'79 septet performances led by saxophonist David Liebman. These mix standards, originals, blues, and ballads, with strong, intense solos from Liebman, fine arrangements and ensemble interaction, and standout contributions from pianist Richie Beiarch and bassist Eddie Gomez. —*Ron Wynn*

The Loneliness of a Long-Distance Runner / Nov. 1985-Dec. 1985 / CMP ◆◆◆◆

★ **Homage to John Coltrane** / Jan. 27, 1987-Jan. 28, 1987 / Owl ◆◆◆◆◆
1991 reissue. An intense tribute to one of Liebman's prime influences. —*Ron Wynn*

Chant / Jul. 1989 / CMP ◆◆◆◆

★ **The Tree** / Apr. 24, 1990 / Soul Note ◆◆◆◆◆
This rather interesting set of solo soprano-saxophone explorations by David Liebman (one of the greats on that instrument) has an odd concept that works. Liebman plays a six-part suite that has titles of "Roots," "Trunk," "Limbs," "Branches," "Twigs," and "Leaves" and then does a second version, playing the sections in the opposite order. The sections farthest from the "Roots" are the most advanced, although all of these movements are fairly free. It's well worth several listens. —*Scott Yanow*

● **West Side Story Today** / Oct. 13, 1990-Oct. 17, 1990 / Owl ◆◆◆◆
With Goldstein. A 1991 reworking of already overworked material. Both musicians are fine players. —*Ron Wynn*

Setting the Standard / May 1992 / Red ◆◆◆◆

Seasons / Dec. 27, 1992-Jan. 19, 1993 / Soul Note ◆◆◆◆
David Liebman is at his best in pastoral, ethereal situations. This trio session, recorded in 1992 and '93, contains both lengthy tunes and shorter works in which Liebman's intense soprano sax and flute and more robust tenor solos are nicely supported by Billy Hart's sensitive yet assertive drumming and Cecil McBee's bass work, which provides whatever is necessary, from interaction to competition. The three never become detached or predictable and don't allow the music to lose its edge. The songs don't have a propulsive rhythmic quality, but never lack appeal or distinction. —*Ron Wynn*

Miles Away / Mar. 12, 1994-Mar. 13, 1994 / Owl ◆◆◆◆

Kirk Lightsey

b. Feb. 15, 1937, Detroit, MI
Piano / Post-Bop, Hard Bop
A pianist who is not a trendsetter but is consistently excellent, Kirk Lightsey long ago developed his own sound within the hard bop tradition. He started playing piano when he was five, although he also played clarinet while in high school. Lightsey worked in Detroit and California in the early '60s, often accompanying singers. He gained some attention in 1965 when he recorded with Sonny Stitt and was on five Prestige records with Chet Baker. However, Lightsey mostly had low-profile gigs until he toured with Dexter Gordon (1979-83) and became part of the Leaders (starting in the late '80s). Lightsey has recorded with Jimmy Raney, Clifford Jordan, Woody Shaw, David Murray, and Harold Land, among others, and has led his own sessions for Criss Cross and Sunnyside including piano duets with Harold Danko. —*Scott Yanow*

★ **Shorter by Two** / Jul. 19, 1983-Jul. 21, 1983 / Sunnyside ◆◆◆◆◆

Everything Is Changed / Jun. 4, 1986-Jun. 5, 1986 / Sunnyside ◆◆◆◆
This excellent album finds pianist Kirk Lightsey exploring five standards and his bassist Santi Wilson Debriano's "Nandi" with a solid quartet. Drummer Eddie Gladden is an asset, but trumpeter Jerry Gonzales (whose muted statements on four of the six selections recall the lyricism of Miles Davis) often comes close to stealing the show. Lightsey, who sounds particularly strong on the ballads, is the obvious leader, and his tasteful yet swinging piano is a joy to hear. —*Scott Yanow*

Kirk 'n' Marcus / Dec. 1986 / Criss Cross ◆◆◆

● **From Kirk to Nat** / Nov. 1990 / Criss Cross ◆◆◆◆
One of the main reasons why this tribute to the Nat King Cole Trio by Kirk Lightsey is a success is that Lightsey (who is from a much later bop-influenced generation) sounds nothing like Cole. Featured in a trio with guitarist Kevin Eubanks and bassist Rufus Reid, Lightsey performs a set of music reminiscent of Cole but several of the songs (including his original "Kirk's Blues," "Never Let Me Go," and "Close Enough for Love") were never actually recorded by Cole; Lightsey takes surprisingly effective vocals on the latter two songs. —*Scott Yanow*

Abbey Lincoln (Anna Marie Wooldridge)

b. Aug. 6, 1930, Chicago, IL
Vocals / Avant-Garde, Post-Bop, Standards
As with her hero Billie Holiday, Abbey Lincoln always means the lyrics she sings. A dramatic performer whose interpretations are full of truth and insight, Lincoln actually began her career as a fairly lightweight supperclub singer. She went through several name changes (including Anna Marie, Gaby Lee, and Gaby Woolridge) before settling on Abbey Lincoln. She recorded with Benny Carter in 1956 and performed a number in the 1957 Hollywood film *The Girl Can't Help It*. Lincoln's first of three albums for Riverside (1957-59) had Max Roach on drums, and he was a major influence on her; she began to be choosy about the songs she sang and to give words the proper emotional intensity. Lincoln held her own on her early dates with such sidemen as Kenny Dorham, Sonny Rollins, Wynton Kelly, Curtis Fuller, and Benny Golson. She was quite memorable on Roach's *Freedom Now Suite*, showing some very uninhibited emotions. Lincoln's Candid date *Straight Ahead* (1961) had among its players Roach, Booker Little, Eric Dolphy, and Coleman Hawkins, and she made some important appearances on Roach's Impulse album *Percussion Bitter Suite*.

Abbey Lincoln and Max Roach were married in 1962, an association that lasted until 1970. They worked together for a while, but Lincoln (who found it harder to get work in jazz due to the political nature of some of her music) became involved in acting and did not record as a leader during 1962-72. She finally recorded for Inner City in 1973 and gradually became more active in jazz. Her two Billie Holiday tribute albums for Enja (1987) showed listeners that the singer was still in her prime, and she has recorded several excellent sets for Verve in the '90s. Because she puts so much thought into each of her recordings, it is not an understatement to say that every Abbey Lincoln set is well worth owning. —*Scott Yanow*

Affair / 1956 / Liberty ◆◆◆

★ **That's Him** / Oct. 28, 1957 / Original Jazz Classics ◆◆◆◆◆
Striking cuts from the late 50s. Sonny Rollins (ts) is a dynamic guest star. —*Ron Wynn*

☆ **It's Magic** / Aug. 23, 1958 / Original Jazz Classics ◆◆◆◆◆

Abbey Is Blue / Mar. 25, 1959-Mar. 26, 1959 / Original Jazz Classics ◆◆◆◆
Simply amazing interpretations by a premier jazz vocalist coming into her own now in terms of public recognition. She's always deserved it. —*Ron Wynn*

☆ **Straight Ahead** / Feb. 22, 1961 / Candid ◆◆◆◆◆
Reissued several times since it originally came out on a Candid LP, this is one of Abbey Lincoln's greatest recordings. It is a testament to the credibility of her very honest music (and her talents) that Abbey's sidemen on this date include the immortal tenor saxophonist Coleman Hawkins (who takes a memorable solo on "Blue Monk"), Eric Dolphy on flute and alto, trumpeter Booker Little (whose melancholy tone is very important in the ensembles), pianist Mal Waldron, and drummer Max Roach. High points include "When Malindy Sings," "Blue Monk," Billie Holiday's "Left Alone," and "African Lady." —*Scott Yanow*

People in Me / Jun. 23, 1973-Jun. 27, 1973 / Inner City ◆◆◆◆
As good as she gets on this recording. A perennial favorite for many. With David Liebman (soprano/tenor and fl.), Al Foster (d), Mtume (per), and two Japanese musicians. "Living Room," "Africa," "Naturally," and the title track stand out. Proud music. —*Michael G. Nastos*

Golden Lady / 1981 / Inner City ◆◆◆◆
Early '80s material by neglected vocalist Abbey Lincoln. Her intonation, delivery, phrasing, and style are unique, and sometimes so distinctive they seem wrong for a song. But Lincoln makes every number come alive, giving even overly familiar lyrics fresh, vibrant treatments. —*Ron Wynn*

You Gotta Pay the Band / Feb. 25, 1991-Feb. 26, 1991 / Verve ✦✦✦✦
Studio date featuring Stan Getz one last time, and Hank Jones Trio. Maxine Roach on viola for two cuts. Six cuts feature either words and/or music written by Moseka. She has lost absolutely none of her brilliance or passion for singing, interpreting, and creating. —*Michael G. Nastos*

Devil's Got Your Tongue / Feb. 24, 1992-Feb. 25, 1992 / Verve ✦✦✦✦

When There Is Love / Oct. 4, 1992-Oct. 6, 1992 / Verve ✦✦✦✦

A Turtle's Dream / May 19, 1994-Nov. 1994 / Verve ✦✦✦✦

Booker Little

b. Apr. 2, 1938, Memphis, TN, **d.** Oct. 5, 1961
Trumpet / Post-Bop
The first trumpeter emerging after Clifford Brown's death to gain his own sound, Booker Little had a tremendous amount of potential before his premature death. He began on trumpet when he was 12 and played with Johnny Griffin and the MJT + 3 while attending Chicago Conservatory. Little was with Max Roach (1958-59) and then freelanced in New York. He recorded with Roach and Abbey Lincoln, was on John Coltrane's *Africa/Brass* album, and was well documented during a July 1961 gig at the Five Spot with Eric Dolphy. Little had a memorable melancholy sound and his interval jumps looked toward the avant-garde, but he also swung like a hard bopper. Booker Little led four sessions (one album apiece for United Artists, Time, Candid, and Bethlehem) but died of uremia at the age of 23, a particularly tragic loss. —*Scott Yanow*

Booker Little 4 and Max Roach / Oct. 1958 / Blue Note ✦✦✦✦
A tremendous showcase of early-'60s sessions that has exceptional musicians and wonderful compositions. Everyone from Phineas and Calvin Newborn to George Coleman and Max Roach. —*Ron Wynn*

Booker Little / Apr. 13, 1960-Apr. 15, 1960 / Bainbridge ✦✦✦✦
A session with the excellent trumpeter Booker Little playing in a slightly more relaxed fashion than usual. But the casual atmosphere didn't prevent him from contributing some extraordinary solos, nor coaxing similar performances from his group that included pianists Tommy Flanagan or Wynton Kelly, bassist Scott LaFaro, and drummer Roy Haynes. This session has been reissued. —*Ron Wynn*

☆ **Out Front** / Mar. 17, 1961-Apr. 4, 1961 / Candid ✦✦✦✦✦
Booker Little was the first trumpet soloist to emerge in jazz after the death of Clifford Brown to have his own sound. His tragically brief life (he died at age 23 later in 1961) cut short what would have certainly been a major career. Little, on this sextet date with multireedist Eric Dolphy, trombonist Julian Priester, and drummer Max Roach, shows that his playing was really beyond bebop. His seven now-obscure originals (several of which deserve to be revived) are challenging for the soloists, and there are many strong moments during these consistently challenging and satisfying performances. —*Scott Yanow*

★ **Victory and Sorrow** / Aug. 1961-Sep. 1961 / Bethlehem ✦✦✦✦✦
Although he only lived to be 23 and recorded for just a little over three years, Booker Little proved to be one of the top young trumpeters of his era. *Victory and Sorrow* was his fourth and final recording as a leader. Little's melancholy tone is heartbreaking on the date's lone standard "If I Should Lose You," and he contributed all of the other six selections. With fine playing from tenor saxophonist George Coleman, trombonist Julian Priester, pianist Don Friedman, bassist Reggie Workman, and drummer Pete LaRoca, this advanced session has many touching and hard-swinging moments. —*Scott Yanow*

Charles Lloyd

b. Mar. 15, 1938, Memphis, TN
Flute, Sax (Tenor) / Hard Bop, Crossover
During 1966-69 Charles Lloyd led one of the most popular groups in jazz, a unit that played at the rock palace Fillmore West in San Francisco and toured the USSR. Lloyd's music, although generally a bit melodic, was not watered-down and managed to catch on for several years during a time when jazz was at its low point in popularity.

Lloyd played locally in Memphis (including with B.B. King and Bobby Blue Bland) and then in the mid-'50s moved to Los Angeles to attend USC. During his six years in Los Angeles, he gigged around town and played alto with Gerald Wilson's Orchestra. In 1961 he joined the Chico Hamilton Quintet on flute and tenor, making his recording debut and gaining a strong reputation. During 1964-65 he was with the Cannonball Adderley Sextet and then in mid-1965 formed his own group. By 1966 the Charles Lloyd Quartet included Keith Jarrett, Cecil McBee (who was later succeeded by Ron McClure), and Jack DeJohnette and the band was the hit of the 1966 Monterey Jazz Festival. They recorded steadily, toured Europe six times, and were remarkably popular. Lloyd, whose most famous composition is "Forest Flower," played tenor in a soft-toned version of John Coltrane, while his lyrical flute playing is more original. After his group changed personnel in 1969, Lloyd gradually faded out of music, becoming a teacher of transcendental meditation. The few records he made in the

'70s were quite spiritual and bordered on new age. However, pianist Michel Petrucciani looked Lloyd up in the early '80s and persuaded him to return to active playing. For a period Petrucciani was in his quartet. By the late '80s Lloyd had a new group with pianist Bobo Stenson, bassist Palle Danielsson, and drummer Jon Christensen that regularly recorded for ECM. Charles Lloyd, whose style remains virtually unchanged from the '60s, has recorded as a leader for Columbia, Atlantic, Kapp, A&M, Blue Note, and ECM. —*Scott Yanow*

Dream Weaver / Mar. 20, 1966 / Atlantic ✦✦✦✦
Sweeping flute, craggy tenor sax solos, and fine piano by Keith Jarrett. —*Ron Wynn*

● **Forest Flower** / Sep. 8, 1966+Sep. 18, 1966 / Atlantic ✦✦✦✦
Live at Monterey. With Keith Jarrett. Definitive Lloyd. —*Michael G. Nastos*

Charles Lloyd in the Soviet Union / May 14, 1967 / Atlantic ✦✦✦✦
The Charles Lloyd Quartet was (along with Cannonball Adderley's band) the most popular group in jazz during the latter half of the '60s. Lloyd somehow managed this feat without watering down his music or adopting a pop repertoire. A measure of the band's popularity is that Lloyd and his sidemen (pianist Keith Jarrett, bassist Ron McClure, and drummer Jack DeJohnette) were able to have a very successful tour of the Soviet Union during a period when jazz was still being discouraged by the communists. This well received festival appearance has four lengthy performances, including an 18-minute version of "Sweet Georgia Bright," and Lloyd (who has always had a soft-toned Coltrane influenced tenor style and a more distinctive voice on flute) is in top form. —*Scott Yanow*

The Call / Jul. 1993 / ECM ✦✦✦✦

Acoustic Masters I / Jul. 1993 / Atlantic ✦✦✦✦

All My Relations / 1995 / ECM ✦✦✦✦

Joe Lovano

b. 1952
Sax (Tenor) / Post-Bop, Hard Bop
One of the top saxophonists of the '90s, Joe Lovano still seems to be improving! His tenor tone is based in the tradition but is fairly original and his chance-taking improvisations are both stimulating and refreshing. His father, Tony "Big T" Lovano, was a fine tenorman who played in Cleveland. Joe originally started on alto when he was six, switching to tenor five years later. He attended Berklee and then worked with Jack McDuff and Lonnie Smith. After three years touring with Woody Herman's Orchestra (1976-79), Lovano moved to New York, playing regularly with Mel Lewis' Big Band, Paul Motian's various groups (since 1981), Charlie Haden's Liberation Music Orchestra, and (in the early '90s) John Scofield in addition to touring Europe with Elvin Jones (1987). Joe Lovano has recorded as a leader for Soul Note, Jazz Club, Label Bleu (reissued by Evidence), Enja, JSL (a date with his father), and a long string of very impressive outings for Blue Note. His 1995 Blue Note set *Rush Hour* features Joe Lovano and his wife, singer Judi Silvano, in top form collaborating with Gunther Schuller on a challenging set of music. —*Scott Yanow*

Landmarks / Aug. 13, 1990-Aug. 14, 1990 / Blue Note ✦✦✦✦
Although the title of this CD makes it sound as if tenor saxophonist Joe Lovano was performing veteran jazz classics on this date, all but one of the ten songs played by his quintet are actually Lovano originals. With strong assistance provided by guitarist John Abercrombie, pianist Ken Werner, bassist Marc Johnson, and drummer Bill Stewart, Lovano often sounds like a mixture of Dewey Redman and early John Coltrane on his enjoyable set. His music has enough variety to hold one's interest, Abercrombie is in particularly strong form, and Lovano is consistently creative during the modern mainstream music. —*Scott Yanow*

From the Soul / Dec. 28, 1991 / Blue Note ✦✦✦✦
Joe Lovano heads a lineup with pianist Michel Petrucciani, bassist Dave Holland, and late drummer Ed Blackwell. It's hard-edged, explosive playing all around, with Blackwell laying down his patented bombs while Petrucciani and Holland converge behind Lovano's dynamic solos. —*Ron Wynn*

Universal Language / Jun. 26, 1992-Jun. 28, 1992 / Blue Note ✦✦✦✦

Tenor Legacy / Jun. 18, 1993 / Blue Note ✦✦✦✦
Joe Lovano welcomes Joshua Redman to his sextet set (which also features pianist Mulgrew Miller, bassist Christian McBride, bassist Lewis Nash, and percussionist Don Alias) and, rather than jam on standards, Joe Lovano composed five new originals, revived three obscurities, and only chose to perform two familiar pieces. By varying the styles and instrumentation (for example) "Bread and Wine" does not have piano or bass), Lovano has created a set with a great deal of variety and some surprising moments. The two tenors (who have distinctive sounds) work together fine and some chances are taken. This matchup works well. —*Scott Yanow*

● **Live at the Village Vanguard** / May 12, 1994-Jan. 22, 1995 / Blue Note ✦✦✦✦

Frank Lowe

b. Jun. 24, 1943, Memphis, TN
Sax (Tenor) / Avant-Garde, Free Jazz
Another saxophonist forging an alliance of R&B, soul, and free music, Frank Lowe's high-energy style has been heard on '60s and '70s sessions. Though his tone sometimes seems to flatten out, his array of screams, shrieks, octave leaps, and bursts is always attention grabbing, if occasionally chaotic. Lowe began on tenor at 12, then studied briefly at the University of Kansas and with Donald Garrett in San Francisco. He played with Sun Ra in New York during the late '60s, returned to study classical music at San Francisco Conservatory, then played with Alice Coltrane, Rashied Ali, Archie Shepp, Milford Graves, and Don Cherry in New York in the early '70s. He's been a leader since the mid-'70s, recording on Survival, ESP, Cadence Jazz, Musicworks, and Soul Note, among others. Lowe has played with Lester Bowie, Bobo Shaw, Joseph Bowie, Anthony Braxton, and many others. —*Ron Wynn*

The Flam / Oct. 1975 / Black Saint ◆◆◆◆
On this free jazz date the powerful tenor Frank Lowe teams up with trumpeter Leo Smith, trombonist Joseph Bowie, bassist Alex Blake, and drummer Charles Bobo Shaw for five group originals including the collaboration "Third St. Stomp." The very explorative and rather emotional music holds one's interest throughout. These often heated performances are better heard than described. —*Scott Yanow*

Exotic Heartbreak / Nov. 1982 / Soul Note ◆◆◆

Decision in Paradise / Sep. 24, 1984+Sep. 28, 1984 / Soul Note ◆◆◆◆
The all-star lineup (tenor saxophonist Frank Lowe, trumpeter Don Cherry, trombonist Grachan Moncur III, pianist Geri Allen, bassist Charnette Moffett and drummer Charles Moffett), practically guarantees that this music will be worth hearing. Although a touch more conservative than one might expect (more of an open-minded, straight-ahead set than music emphasizing sound explorations), all six group originals are of interest including Lowe's unaccompanied performance on Butch Morris' "I'll Whistle Your Name" and Moncur's whimsical "You Dig!" —*Scott Yanow*

★ **Bodies and Soul** / Nov. 18, 1995-Nov. 19, 1995 / CIMP ◆◆◆◆◆
Frank Lowe led his first record date in 1975, but the explorative tenor saxophonist has never gained more than an underground reputation. A masterful improvisor who has retained a free spirit through the years, Lowe's music is actually much more accessible than one might expect. On *Bodies and Soul*, Lowe's sound varies from the gruff roars of prime Archie Shepp to Sonny Rollins. Assisted by bassist Tim Flood (making his recording debut) and veteran drummer Charles Moffett, Lowe explores four originals plus music by John Coltrane ("Impressions"), Pharoah Sanders, Ornette Coleman, Phillip Watson, Don Cherry, and even a melodic and unaccompanied version of Johnny Green's "Body and Soul." The free bop music is often quite thoughtful but never predictable and is well worth an investigation. —*Scott Yanow*

Jimmie Lunceford

b. Jun. 6, 1902, Fulton, MS, **d.** Jul. 12, 1947, Seaside, OR
Sax (Alto) / Swing
The Jimmie Lunceford Orchestra has always been a bit difficult to evaluate. Contemporary observers rated Lunceford's big band at the top with Duke Ellington and Count Basie but, when judging the music solely on their records (and not taking into account their visual show, appearance, and showmanship), Lunceford's ensemble has to be placed on the second tier. His orchestra lacked any really classic soloists (altoist Willie Smith and trombonist Trummy Young came the closest), and a large portion of the band's repertoire either featured the dated vocals of Dan Grissom or were pleasant novelties. And yet, the well rehearsed ensembles were very impressive, and the arrangements (particularly those of Sy Oliver) were quite original, and the use of glee-club vocalists and short, concise solos were pleasing and often memorable. Plus Lunceford's was the first orchestra to feature high-note trumpeters (starting with Tommy Stevenson in 1934) and had a strong influence on the early Stan Kenton Orchestra.

Although he was trained on several instruments and was featured on flute on "Liza" in the '40s, Lunceford was much more significant as a bandleader than as a musician. While teaching music at Manassa High School in Memphis in 1927, Lunceford organized a student band called the Chickasaw Syncopators, recording two songs that year and a pair in 1930. After leaving Memphis, the band (known by then as the Jimmie Lunceford Orchestra) played in Cleveland and Buffalo and cut two songs in 1933 that were not issued until decades later. 1934 was the breakthrough year. The orchestra made a strong impression playing at New York's Cotton Club, waxed a few notable songs for Victor, and then started recording regularly for Decca. Their tight ensembles and colorful shows made them a major attraction throughout the remainder of the swing era. Among their many hits were "Rhythm Is Our Business," "Four or Five Times," "Swanee River," "Charmaine," "My Blue Heaven," "Organ Grinder's Swing," "Ain't She Sweet," "For Dancers Only," "'Tain't What

You Do, It's the Way That Cha Do It," "Uptown Blues," and "Lunceford Special." The stars of the band included arranger Sy Oliver (on trumpet and vocals), Willie Smith, Trummy Young (who had a hit with "Margie"), and tenor saxophonist Joe Thomas.

In 1939 it was a major blow when Tommy Dorsey lured Sy Oliver away (although trumpeters Gerald Wilson and Snooky Young were important new additions). Unfortunately, Lunceford underpaid most of his sidemen, not thinking to reward them for their loyalty in the lean years. In 1942 Willie Smith was one of several key players who left for better-paying jobs elsewhere, and the orchestra gradually declined. Jimmie Lunceford was still a popular bandleader in 1947 when he suddenly collapsed; rumors have persisted that he was poisoned by a racist restaurant owner who was very reluctant about feeding his band. After Lunceford's death, pianist/arranger Ed Wilcox and Joe Thomas tried to keep the orchestra together, but in 1949 the band permanently broke up. —*Scott Yanow*

★ **Jimmie Lunceford** / Dec. 13, 1927-Sep. 4, 1934 / Masters of Jazz ◆◆◆◆◆
1927-1934. A new release covering early material. —*Ron Wynn*

Jimmie Lunceford (1930-1934) / Jun. 6, 1930-Nov. 7, 1934 / Classics ◆◆◆◆
The first in Classics' "complete" Jimmie Lunceford series has two titles apiece from 1930 (when the band was based in Tennessee) and 1933 along with its first six sessions for Decca in 1934. Lunceford's band had an immediately recognizable sound by 1934 and, despite the presence of such top soloists as altoist Willie Smith, tenor saxophonist Joe Thomas, and high-note trumpeter Tommy Stevenson, it was its arranged ensembles (particularly those of Sy Oliver) that gave the orchestra its musical identity. Among the better selections on this CD are "Flaming Reeds and Screaming Brass," "White Heat," "Swinging' Uptown," "Rose Room," "Miss Otis Regrets," and the band's fresh interpretations of Duke Ellington's "Black and Tan Fantasy" and "Mood Indigo." —*Scott Yanow*

● **Stomp It Off** / Sep. 4, 1934-May 29, 1935 / Decca ◆◆◆◆
While European labels (most notably Classics and Masters of Jazz) reissue every Jimmie Lunceford recording, as usual its domestic counterpart only gives consumers "best of" collections. This CD is actually quite good, consisting of highlights from Lunceford's first year with Decca and serving as a fine introduction to his orchestra's music. Nearly all of the 21 numbers are excellent, and among the more colorful selections are reworkings of three Duke Ellington tunes plus "Miss Otis Regrets," "Dream of You," two versions of the happy "Rhythm Is Our Business," and "Sleepy-Time Gal" (which has a remarkable sax section chorus). —*Scott Yanow*

☆ **Vol. 2** / Sep. 5, 1934-Dec. 18, 1934 / Masters of Jazz ◆◆◆◆◆
Five sessions by the Jimmie Lunceford Orchestra are reissued in full on this French CD including three alternate takes. The big band was in its early prime during the period, and these 19 selections include many memorable arrangements by Sy Oliver and Ed Wilcox including "Miss Otis Regrets," "Stomp It Off," "Since My Best Gal Turned Me Down," and "Rhythm Is Our Business." The short solos by altoist Willie Smith (who doubled on clarinet), tenor saxophonist Joe Thomas, and muted trumpeter Sy Oliver compensate for the occasional indifferent vocals of Henry Wells. —*Scott Yanow*

Jimmie Lunceford (1934-1935) / Nov. 1934-Sep. 1935 / Classics ◆◆◆◆
The second of Classics' reissuance of all the master takes of Jimmie Lunceford's recordings finds the orchestra gaining in popularity and in power. Among the highlights (most of the songs were arranged by Sy Oliver or Ed Wilcox) are "Since My Best Gal Turned Me Down," "Rhythm Is Our Business," "Shake Your Head," "Sleepy-Time Gal," "Four or Five Times," and "Swanee River." The high musicianship and clean ensembles (along with the showmanship) are most impressive, and the concise solos (particularly from altoist Willie Smith, tenor saxophonist Joe Thomas, and trumpeter Sy Oliver) are enjoyable and fit in logically as part of the arrangements. —*Scott Yanow*

Jimmie Lunceford (1935-1937) / Sep. 1935-Jun. 1937 / Classics ◆◆◆◆
Although there have been a few GRP/Decca samplers released domestically, the best way for serious collectors to acquire the recordings of Jimmie Lunceford are by getting the reissue CDs put out by the European labels. On Classics' third Lunceford set, the personnel stays the same (except for one minor change) during the 15-month period that is covered. The well rehearsed unit continued to grow and develop during this time. Among the high points of the CD are "My Blue Heaven," "Organ Grinder's Swing," "Harlem Shout," and "Slumming on Park Avenue." Although one can do without the occasional Dan Grissom vocals, the concise solos, tricky charts, and hip singing of Sy Oliver make this music well worth investigating by fans of the swing era. —*Scott Yanow*

For Dancers Only / Oct. 26, 1936-Nov. 5, 1937 / Decca ◆◆◆◆
For this CD, 20 selections by Jimmie Lunceford's highly rated orchestra are reissued. Dating from 1935-37 and not as complete as the Classics series, the release does give listeners a good overview of Lunceford's music. The arrangements by Sy Oliver (including "Swanee River," "My Blue Heaven," "Organ Grinder's Swing," and "For Dancers Only") are generally the most memorable tracks; this CD also contains a previously unissued take of

"Ragging the Scale." Among the main soloists are altoist Willie Smith, tenor saxophonist Joe Thomas, and trumpeter Oliver. —*Scott Yanow*

Jimmie Lunceford (1937-1939) / Jun. 1937-Jan. 1939 / Classics ✦✦✦✦
For this entry in Classics' complete reissuance of Jimmie Lunceford's recordings, the biggest news for the band was the addition of trombonist Trummy Young who, in addition to being a major soloist, had vocal hits in "Margie" and "'Tain't What You Do (It's The Way That You Do It)." Other highlights of this well rounded CD include "Annie Laurie," "Sweet Sue," and "By the River Saint-Marie." —*Scott Yanow*

Jimmie Lunceford (1939) / Jan. 1939-Sep. 1939 / Classics ✦✦✦✦
For this Classics CD, most of the Jimmie Lunceford Orchestra's earlier Vocalion recordings (owned by Columbia) are reissued. The loss of Sy Oliver in August 1939 (he was lured away by Tommy Dorsey) would soon hurt the band, but they were still using Oliver's arrangements in the last session. "Baby, Won't You Please Come Home," "What Is This Thing Called Swing," a classic rendition of "Ain't She Sweet," "Well, All Right Then," and "Belgium Stomp" are among the more memorable selections on this CD, which also has a few typically inferior Dan Grissom ballad vocals. Swing fans will want all of these CDs even if they do not include Lunceford's alternate takes. —*Scott Yanow*

Jimmie Lunceford (1939-1940) / Dec. 1939-Jun. 1940 / Classics ✦✦✦✦
The Jimmie Lunceford Orchestra was at the height of its power and fame during the period covered by this Classics CD. Arranger-trumpeter Sy Oliver's defection to Tommy Dorsey hurt, but his charts were still in the books and his replacement, Snooky Young, proved to be a superior first trumpeter and soloist. With altoist Willie Smith, Joe Thomas on tenor, and trombonist Trummy Young still around as stars, the band was in top form on such numbers as "Uptown Blues," "Lunceford Special," "Bugs Parade," "What's Your Story, Mornin' Glory," and "Swingin' on C." All of the releases in this series are well worth picking up by swing collectors. —*Scott Yanow*

Jimmie Lunceford (1940-1941) / Jul. 1940-Dec. 1941 / Classics ✦✦✦✦
The European Classics label's Jimmie Lunceford series has thus far stopped with this release, one CD short of completing its task. With the loss of arranger-trumpet-vocalist Sy Oliver, Lunceford's band was still pretty strong although it was no longer developing as quickly as it had previously. During the year and a half covered by this CD, such numbers as "Whatcha Know, Joe," "Siesta at the Fiesta," "Yard Dog Maazurka," and the two-part "Blues in the NIght" were recorded along with lesser material (including some dreary vocal features for Dan Grissom). Although not essential, this CD is recommended to Lunceford completists. —*Scott Yanow*

Margie / Apr. 25, 1946-May 1947 / Savoy ✦✦✦✦
The final recordings of the Jimmie Lunceford Orchestra (prior to its leader's death) are included on this excellent CD. The 13 selections (three sessions from 1946-47) generally avoid the influence of bebop and stick to Lunceford's trademark sound and swing style. Tenor saxophonist and vocalist Joe Thomas was the only one of the major Lunceford soloists to still be with the big band, although trumpeter Bob Mitchell, clarinetist Omer Simeon, and altoist Kurt Bradford (featured on "The 'Jimmies'") also have some solo space. Such up-and-coming players as trumpeter Joe Wilder and trombonist Al Grey make early appearances, and former trombone star Trummy Young returns for four numbers, doing a remake of his hit "Margie." This is a historical and easy-to-enjoy CD overall, put out by Savoy in 1989. —*Scott Yanow*

Jimmy Lyons

b. Dec. 1, 1933, Jersey City, NJ, **d.** May 19, 1986, New York, NY
Sax (Alto), Sax (Soprano) / Free Jazz
Jimmy Lyons worked with Cecil Taylor from 1960 until his death in 1986. Although initially influenced by Charlie Parker, Lyons found a niche for his alto in Taylor's dense and passionate music, becoming an indispensable part of the Cecil Taylor Unit for 26 years. He grew up in Harlem and started playing alto when he was 15, being largely self-taught. A relative unknown when he joined Taylor, Jimmy Lyons was from then on always associated with the innovative pianist, although he did have opportunities to lead sessions for BYG (1969), Hat Art, and Black Saint, often utilizing bassoonist Karen Borca. It is not surprising that for his own dates, Lyons never used a pianist! —*Scott Yanow*

Other Afternoons / Aug. 15, 1969 / Affinity ✦✦✦✦
Because he spent virtually his entire career as Cecil Taylor's altoist, Jimmy Lyons had relatively few chances to record as a leader. This Affinity LP was his first opportunity to head a session, and Lyons picked a particularly superior group of sidemen: trumpeter Lester Bowie, bassist Alan Silva, and drummer Andrew Cyrille. Rather than sounding like the Art Ensemble of Chicago (Bowie's group) or Taylor's Unit, the all-star band comes closer at times to seeming like an updated version of Ornette Coleman's Quartet. The renditions of four originals are quite adventurous and passionate, yet thoughtful and logical. An excellent outing that has not yet reappeared on CD. —*Scott Yanow*

● **Jump Up / What to Do About** / Aug. 30, 1980 / Hat Hut ✦✦✦✦
Burnt Offering / May 15, 1982 / Black Saint ✦✦✦✦

Wee Sneezawee / Sep. 26, 1983-Sep. 27, 1983 / Black Saint ✦✦✦✦
Give It Up / Mar. 1985 / Black Saint ✦✦✦✦

M'Boom

Group / Post-Bop
In 1970 Max Roach first organized M'Boom, a ten-piece unit composed entirely of percussionists. By utilizing such instruments as marimba, xylophone, tympani, vibes, bells, gongs, drum sets, and even a musical saw, Roach leads a very colorful and self-sufficient group. Originally a septet comprising Roach, Warren Smith, Freddie Waits, Omar Clay, Joe Chambers, Roy Brooks, and Ray Mantilla, the group grew to ten pieces in later years. A part-time project, M'Boom has recorded for Baystate (1973), Columbia (1979), Soul Note (1984), and Blue Moon (1992) and appeared at the 1994 Monterey Jazz Festival. —*Scott Yanow*

M'Boom / Jul. 25, 1979-Jul. 27, 1979 / Columbia ✦✦✦✦
Max Roach's percussion sextet. —*Michael G. Nastos*

Collage / 1984 / Soul Note ✦✦✦✦
Max Roach, Warren Smith, and Freddie Waits appear on this one. —*AMG*

● **Live at S.O.B.'s New** / 1992 / Blue Moon ✦✦✦✦
Exciting percussion duels, multiple rhythms, and teeming arrangements and performances by the conglomeration of drummers known as M'Boom. This recent release included founding member Max Roach, plus Roy Brooks, Joe Chambers, Omar Clay, Fred King, Ray Mantilla, Warren Smith, and Freddy Waits performing live at the celebrated New York club S.O.B.'s. —*Ron Wynn*

Harold Mabern

b. Mar. 20, 1936, Memphis, TN
Piano / Hard Bop, Groove
One of several excellent hard-bop pianists from the Memphis area, Harold Mabern has led relatively few dates through the years but has always been respected by his contemporaries. He played in Chicago with MJT + 3 in the late '50s and then moved to New York in 1959. Mabern worked with Jimmy Forrest, Lionel Hampton, the Jazztet (1961-62), Donald Byrd, Miles Davis (1963), J.J. Johnson (1963-65), Sonny Rollins, Freddie Hubbard, Wes Montgomery, Joe Williams (1966-67), and Sarah Vaughan. During 1968-70 Mabern led four albums for Prestige, he was with Lee Morgan in the early '70s, and in 1972 he recorded with Stanley Cowell's Piano Choir. In more recent times Harold Mabern recorded as a a leader for DIW/Columbia and Sackville and toured with the Contemporary Piano Ensemble (1993-95). —*Scott Yanow*

Wailin' / Jun. 30, 1969+Jan. 26, 1970 / Prestige ✦✦✦✦
This CD reissue combines together two sessions (*'Workin'' & Wailin''* and *Greasy Kid Stuff*) led by pianist Harold Mabern during 1969-70. The first date utilizes trumpeter Virgil Jones, tenor saxophonist George Coleman, bassist Buster Williams, and drummer Idris Muhammad on four challenging Mabern originals and Johnny Mandel's "A Time for Love." However, it is the second session that is most memorable for, in addition to Mabern, Williams, and Muhammad, it features trumpeter Lee Morgan and flutist Hubert Laws; the latter mostly plays some surprisingly passionate tenor that makes one wish he had performed on tenor more through the years. Excellent advanced hard-bop music that hints at fusion. —*Scott Yanow*

Greasy Kid Stuff! / Jan. 26, 1970 / Prestige ✦✦✦

Live at Cafe Des Copains / Apr. 25, 1984+Jan. 9, 1985 / Sackville ✦✦✦✦
Outstanding piano solos, sturdy compositions. —*Ron Wynn*

Philadelphia Bound / Apr. 15, 1991+Feb. 29, 1992 / Sackville ✦✦✦✦

★ **The Leading Man** / Nov. 9, 1992-Apr. 12, 1993 / Columbia ✦✦✦✦✦
A brilliant pianist who continues to develop and has found his own voice in the modern mainstream, Harold Mabern chose consistently superior tunes for his Columbia CD, ranging from Wes Montgomery's "Full House" (featuring guitarist Kevin Eubanks in a duet with the leader) and songs by Wayne Shorter, Coltrane, and Bird, to his own "B&B" (a ballad dedicated to Clifford Brown and Booker Little) and the pop tune "Save the Best for Last." Although one can hear aspects of McCoy Tyner's chord voicings in some of Mabern's solos, he has plenty of very individual ideas; check out his near-miraculous playing on "Moment's Notice." With strong support from drummer Jack DeJohnette and either Christian McBride or Ron Carter on bass (in addition to two appearances by trumpeter Bill Mobley), this is one of Harold Mabern's most impressive outings to date and is highly recommended. —*Scott Yanow*

Machito (Frank Raul Grillo)

b. 1912, Havana, Cuba, **d.** Apr. 15, 1984, London, England
Maracas, Vocals / Latin Continuum, United States, Afro-Cuban Jazz
An institution in Latin jazz and international music, Machito (Frank Raul Grillo) was a fixture from the early '40s till the mid-'80s. His bands, thanks to the innovations of brother-in-law and longtime musical director Mario Bauza, blended excellent jazz arrangements with frenetic Cuban rhythms,

creating a sound that was fresh and intriguing. Bauza called it Afro-Cuban music, while others labeled it "Cubop." Machito was the leader, vocalist, and maracas player. The son of a cigar manufacturer, he sang and danced with his father's employees as a child and later sang in the group Jovenes de Rendicion. He worked with several Cuban bands in the late '20s and '30s before coming to America in 1937 as a vocalist with the group La Estrella Habanera. Machito recorded with Alfredito Valdez, El Quarteto Caney, El Conjunto Moderno, and La Orchestra Hatuey while working with other groups in the late '30s. He and Bauza formed a band, but shortly disbanded it. Machito worked with the Orchestra Siboney and recorded with Xavier Cugat before forming the Afro-Cubans in 1940. The next year Bauza joined this band and remained until this had another conflict in 1976, one that couldn't be resolved. The band made its first recordings for Decca. Machito's sister Graciela was bandleader while he was in the army in the mid-'40s. The Afro-Cubans became immensely popular. They appeared with Stan Kenton's big band in the late '40s, and played several concerts with jazz groups. Bauza's idea that they employ top non-Latin jazz stars as special guests led to such players as Charlie Parker, Dizzy Gillespie, Flip Phillips, Howard McGhee, Brew Moore, Buddy Rich, Harry Edison, Cannonball Adderley, Curtis Fuller, Herbie Mann, Johnny Griffin, Eddie Bert, and Aaron Sachs working and recording with the band from the late '40s through the '60s. They maintained their popularity through the mambo era of the '50s and early '60s, and were a staple when salsa surged in popularity during the '70s and '80s. The Afro-Cubans kept busy on both the jazz and salsa circuits, and were featured in Carlos Ortiz's documentary film *Machito: A Jazz Legacy* in 1987. They recorded for Verve, Roulette, Trip, Tico, Secco, Forum, Coral, RCA, Pablo, and Timeless. Machito's 1982 LP *Machito and His Salsa Big Band* won a Grammy. He was still working when he suffered a fatal stroke at Ronnie Scott's club in 1984. —*Ron Wynn and Michael G. Nastos*

Dizzy Gillespie/Charlie Parker / 1948 / Verve ✦✦✦✦
A selection of prime Latin jazz cuts with both Parker and Diz plus Machito. —*Ron Wynn*

Afro Cuban Jazz / Dec. 20, 1948-Jan. 1949 / Verve ✦✦✦

\✦**Mucho Macho Machito & His Afro-Cuban Salseros** / 1948 / Pablo ✦✦✦✦✦
Finally on CD, Pablo's old compilation includes some of Machito's finest Cubop classics, by what was perhaps the finest of all his bands. "Asia Minor," "Babarabatiri," "Tea for Two," "St. Louis Blues," even "Donkey Serenade" are among the featured tracks. This great release has fine notes and great old photos. —*John Storm Roberts*

Cubop City / 1949 / Tumbao ✦✦✦

\✦**Afro-Cuban Jazz Moods** / Jun. 4, 1975-Jun. 5, 1975 / Original Jazz Classics ✦✦✦✦✦
Wonderful reunion with Dizzy Gillespie (tpt). —*Ron Wynn*

Machito & His Salsa Big Band / 1982 / Impulse ✦✦✦✦
A dynamite band with Chocolate Armenteros in the trumpet section and Macho's daughter as lead female vocalist, it also has a fine mix of well known and less-familiar numbers including "El Manicero" and a Machito warhorse, "Quimbombo." —*John Storm Roberts*

1983 Grammy Award Winner / Feb. 6, 1982-Feb. 7, 1982 / MCA ✦✦✦

Mahavishnu Orchestra
....
Group / Fusion
One of the premiere fusion groups, the Mahavishnu Orchestra was considered by most observers during its prime to be a rock band, but its sophisticated improvisations actually put its high-powered music between rock and jazz. Founder and leader John McLaughlin had recently played with Miles Davis and Tony Williams' Lifetime. The original lineup of the group was McLaughlin on electric guitar, violinist Jerry Goodman, keyboardist Jan Hammer, electric bassist Rick Laird, and drummer Billy Cobham. They recorded three intense albums for Columbia during 1971-73, and then the personnel changed completely for the second version of the group. In 1974 the band consisted of violinist Jean Luc Ponty, Gayle Moran on keyboards and vocals, electric bassist Ralphe Armstrong, and drummer Michael Warden; by 1975 Stu Goldberg had replaced Moran and Ponty had left. John McLaughlin's dual interests in Eastern religion and playing acoustic guitar resulted in the band breaking up in 1975. Surprisingly, an attempt to revive the Mahavishnu Orchestra in 1984 (using Cobham, saxophonist Bill Evans, keyboardist Mitchell Forman, electric bassist Jonas Hellborg, and percussionist Danny Gottlieb) was unsuccessful; one Warner Bros. album resulted. However, when one thinks of the Mahavishnu Orchestra, it is of the original lineup, which was very influential throughout the '70s. —*Scott Yanow*

★ **Inner Mounting Flame** / Aug. 14, 1971 / Columbia ✦✦✦✦✦
Classic first album. Definitive fusion. —*Michael G. Nastos*

The Best of Mahavishnu Orchestra / 1971 / Columbia ✦✦

☆ **Birds of Fire** / 1973 / Columbia ✦✦✦✦✦
Classic second album. More definitive fusion. —*Michael G. Nastos*

Between Nothingness & Eternity / Aug. 1973 / Columbia ✦✦✦✦
Fine early '70s jazz-rock session from a pioneering group in this genre. The Mahavishnu Orchestra were among a handful of artists who really did achieve a fusion between rock energy and jazz improvisation. This was their last great album, with blistering solos all around and intelligent, captivating compositions. —*Ron Wynn*

Visions of the Emerald Beyond / Dec. 4, 1974-Dec. 14, 1974 / Columbia ✦✦✦

Apocalypse / 1974 / Columbia ✦✦

Inner Worlds / 1975 / Sony ✦✦✦

Mahavishnu / Apr. 1984-May 1984 / Warner Bros. ✦✦✦

Adam Makowicz (Adam Matyszkowicz)
....
b. Aug. 18, 1940, Cesky Tesin, Czechoslovakia
Piano / Bop, Swing
Adam Makowicz made a strong impression when he first came to the US and at the time he was often compared to Art Tatum. Although his technique is nearly on Tatum's level, Makowicz has long had his own style, mixing together different aspects of jazz ranging from swing to hard bop. He started playing jazz in the late '50s and with Tomasz Stanko formed one of the first European free jazz groups, the Jazz Darings. He led his own groups in Warsaw from 1965 on and in 1970 played electric piano in Michal Urbaniak's band. Makowicz also worked with Urszula Dudziak and recorded several albums in Poland before coming to the US in 1977. Although the initial publicity (when he was championed by John Hammond) has long since died down, Makowicz has if anything continued to improve as a pianist. He has recorded many records as a leader for such labels as Columbia, Stash, Choice, Sheffield Lab, Novus, and Concord. —*Scott Yanow*

★ **Live at Maybeck Recital Hall** / Jul. 19, 1992 / Concord Jazz ✦✦✦✦✦
The Music of Jerome Kern / Sep. 1992 / Concord Jazz ✦✦✦✦
Adam Makowicz interprets 11 well known Jerome Kern compositions on his trio date with bassist George Mraz and drummer Alan Dawson. The pianist's arrangements are full of surprising turns and twists and his unpredictable flights result in some of the familiar songs being given unusual treatments. Stimulating and occasionally exciting music. —*Scott Yanow*

Adam Makowicz/George Mraz / May 22, 1993 / Concord Jazz ✦✦✦✦
The fifth volume in the Concord Duo Series matches pianist Adam Makowicz and bassist George Mraz in a concert at the Maybeck Recital Hall; both musicians are virtuosos originally from Eastern Europe who found fame in the US. On what is very much a duo set, Mraz gets nearly as much solo space as Makowicz. Their repertoire mixes together six fresh renditions of standards with four of the pianist's complex originals, and the harmonically advanced music (which features plenty of close interplay) has enough variety to continually hold one's interest. —*Scott Yanow*

My Favorite Things: The Music of Richard Rodgers / Sep. 7, 1993-Sep. 8, 1993 / Concord Jazz ✦✦✦✦

Junior Mance (Julian Clifford Mance, Jr.)
....
b. Oct. 10, 1928, Chicago, IL
Piano / Bop, Soul-Jazz
Junior Mance is well known for his soulful bluesy style, but he is also expert at playing bop standards. He started playing professionally when he was ten. Mance worked with Gene Ammons in Chicago during 1947-49, played with Lester Young (1950), and was with the Ammons-Sonny Stitt group until he was drafted. He was the house pianist at Chicago's Bee Hive (1953-54), worked as Dinah Washington's accompanist (1954-55), was in the first Cannonball Adderley Quintet (1956-57), and then spent two years touring with Dizzy Gillespie (1958-60). After a few months with the Eddie "Lockjaw" Davis-Johnny Griffin group, Mance formed his own trio and has mostly been a leader ever since. He has led sessions for Verve, Jazzland, Riverside, Capitol, Atlantic, Milestone, Polydor, Inner City, JSP, Nilva, Sackville, and Bee Hive, among other labels. —*Scott Yanow*

Junior Mance Trio at the Village Vanguard / Feb. 22, 1961-Feb. 23, 1961 / Original Jazz Classics ✦✦✦✦
Pianist Junior Mance has long been typecast as a soulful blues player so, as if to confuse listeners, he starts off this live set with an uptempo "Looptown" on which he displays technique worthy of Oscar Peterson. Mance's many fans have no reason to despair though, for in addition to a boppish rendition of "Girl of My Dreams," the pianist does perform a generous amount of blues and soulful pieces. Bassist Larry Gales and drummer Ben Riley help out on this reissue LP, which has yet to come out on CD. It's a strong outing. —*Scott Yanow*

Junior Mance Touch / Oct. 1973 / Polydor ✦✦✦

Deep / 1982 / JSP ✦✦✦

The Tender Touch Of / Apr. 1, 1983 / Nilva ✦✦✦

For Dancers Only / Jul. 3, 1983 / Sackville ✦✦✦✦
Outstanding sets that includes some of Mance's flashiest recent playing. —*Ron Wynn*

● **Mance's Special** / Sep. 14, 1986+Nov. 30, 1988 / Sackville ✦✦✦✦
Fine '86 set with pianist Junior Mance running through romping blues, intricate originals, and moving standards and ballads in a solo set. While he's best at blues-tinged material, Mance shows the versatility necessary to do other material, and doesn't substitute cliches and gimmicks for ideas and substance. —*Ron Wynn*

Here 'Tis / 1992 / Sackville ✦✦✦✦

Softly As In a Morning Sunrise / Jul. 21, 1994 / Enja ✦✦✦✦

Albert Mangelsdorff

b. Sep. 5, 1928, Frankfurt, Germany
Trombone / Avant-Garde, Free Jazz
The master of multiphonics (playing more than one note at a time on a horn), Mangelsdorff has been a giant of the European avant-garde for the past 30 years. He originally studied violin and worked as a jazz guitarist before taking up the trombone in 1948. He played bop in the '50s with Hans Koller and local orchestras. In 1958 Mangelsdorff visited the US to play with Marshall Brown's International Youth Band at the Newport Jazz Festival, but his stays in America have always been fairly brief. By the time he recorded an album with John Lewis in 1962, Mangelsdorff was starting to lean toward the avant-garde. He has since recorded unaccompanied solo albums, been documented at a concert with Jaco Pastorius, led trios, and worked with the Globe Unity Orchestra and the United Jazz & Rock Ensemble. Of his many records, the John Lewis set and his valuable MPS albums will be difficult to find, but Albert Mangelsdorff's work for Enja and Sackville can be acquired. —*Scott Yanow*

★ **Tromboneliness** / Jan. 1976+Mar. 1976 / Sackville ✦✦✦✦✦
A full album of unaccompanied solo trombone might seem a bit tedious, but Albert Mangelsdorff is on a different level than most trombonists. For one thing he is a master of multiphonics (playing chords on a horn) and his use of a wa-wa mute is also quite expert. Although an avant-garde master, Mangelsdorff's version of "Creole Love Call" on this solo album is brilliant, as are his seven diverse originals. In addition, there is plenty of humor on these rambunctious performances. —*Scott Yanow*

Chuck Mangione

b. Nov. 29, 1940, Rochester
Trumpet, Fluegelhorn / Instrumental Pop, Bop
Throughout the '70s, Chuck Mangione was a celebrity. His purposely light-weight music was melodic pop that was upbeat, optimistic, and sometimes uplifting. Mangione's records were big sellers, yet few of his fans from the era knew that his original goal was to be a bebopper. His father had often taken Chuck and his older brother Gap (a keyboardist) out to see jazz concerts, and Dizzy Gillespie was a family friend. While Chuck studied at the Eastman School, the two Mangiones co-led a bop quintet called the Jazz Brothers that recorded several albums for Jazzland, often with Sal Nistico on tenor. Chuck Mangione played with the big bands of Woody Herman and Maynard Ferguson (both in 1965) and Art Blakey's Jazz Messengers (1965-67). In 1968, now sticking mostly to his soft-toned fluegelhorn, Mangione formed a quartet that also featured Gerry Niewood on tenor and soprano. They cut a fine set for Mercury in 1972, but otherwise Mangione's recordings in the '70s generally used large orchestras and vocalists (including Esther Satterfield), putting the emphasis on lightweight melodies such as "Hill Where the Lord Hides," "Land of Make Believe," "Chase the Clouds Away," and the huge 1977 hit (featuring guitarist Grant Geissman) "Feels So Good." After a recorded 1978 Hollywood Bowl concert that summed up his pop years and a 1980 two-LP set that alternated pop and bop (with guest Dizzy Gillespie), Mangione gradually faded out of the music scene. In the '70s Chuck Mangione recorded for Mercury and A&M; in the '80s he had a couple of very forgettable Columbia albums and has not been heard from much in the '90s. —*Scott Yanow*

The Jazz Brothers / Aug. 8, 1960 / Milestone ✦✦✦

Spring Fever / Nov. 1961 / Original Jazz Classics ✦✦✦

● **Chuck Mangione Quartet** / Mar. 1972 / Mercury ✦✦✦✦

Bellavia / 1975 / A&M ✦✦

Chase the Clouds Away / 1975 / A&M ✦✦✦

Feels So Good / 1977 / A&M ✦✦✦

Manhattan Transfer

Group / Easy Listening, Bop, Pop
The Manhattan Transfer has never stuck exclusively to performing jazz (other than their classic 1985 album *Vocalese*), but they rank as the top jazz vocal group since Lambert, Hendricks, and Ross. Tim Hauser put together the first version of the band in 1969 and by 1972 he was joined by Alan Paul, Janis Siegel, and Laurel Masse; in 1979 Cheryl Bentyne took

Masse's place. The four singers are versatile, blend together well, and each has his or her own distinct personalities. Whether it be doo wop, recent pop tunes, or swing standards, the Manhattan Transfer has long been at the top of its field. Since 1975 they have recorded for Atlantic. —*Scott Yanow*

The Manhattan Transfer / 1975 / Atlantic ✦✦✦✦
A nice set, more to the jazz side. Gold album. —*Ron Wynn*

Mecca for Moderns / 1981 / Atlantic ✦✦✦✦
Manhattan Transfer's best from a jazz concept. —*Ron Wynn*

Bodies and Souls / 1983 / Atlantic ✦✦✦

● **Vocalese** / 1985 / Atlantic ✦✦✦✦
Clearly their best. It's their roots. —*Michael G. Nastos*

Brasil / 1987 / Atlantic ✦✦✦

The Anthology: Down in Birdland / 1993 / Rhino ✦✦✦✦

● **The Very Best of the Manhattan Transfer** / 1994 / Rhino ✦✦✦✦

Herbie Mann (Herbert Jay Solomon)

b. Apr. 16, 1930, New York, NY
Flute / Instrumental Pop, Bop, Soul-Jazz, Crossover
Herbie Mann has played a wide variety of music throughout his career. He became quite popular in the '60s but in the '70s became so immersed in pop and various types of world music that he seemed lost to jazz. Fortunately, Mann has never lost his ability to improvise creatively as he has shown in recent times.
Herbie Mann began on clarinet when he was nine but was soon also playing flute and tenor. After serving in the Army, he was with Mat Mathews' Quintet (1953-54) and then started working and recording as a leader. During 1954-58 Mann stuck mostly to playing bop, sometimes collaborating with such players as Phil Woods, Buddy Collette, Sam Most, Bobby Jaspar, and Charlie Rouse. He doubled on cool-toned tenor and was one of the few jazz musicians in the '50s who recorded on bass clarinet; he also recorded in 1957 a full album (for Savoy) of unaccompanied flute.
After spending time playing and writing music for television, in 1959 Mann formed his Afro-Jazz Sextet, a group using several percussionists, vibes (either Johnny Rae, Hagood Hardy, or Dave Pike), and the leader's flute. He toured Africa (1960) and Brazil (1961), had a hit with "Comin' Home Baby," and recorded with Bill Evans. The most popular jazz flutist during the era, Mann explored bossa nova (even recording in Brazil in 1962), incorporated music from many cultures (plus current pop tunes) into his repertoire, and had among his sidemen such top young musicians as Willie Bobo, Chick Corea (1965), Attila Zoller, and Roy Ayers; at the 1972 Newport Festival his sextet included David Newman and Sonny Sharrock. By then Mann had been a producer at Embroyo (a subsidiary of Atlantic) for three years and was frequently stretching his music outside of jazz. As the '70s advanced, Mann became much more involved in rock, pop, reggae, and even disco. After leaving Atlantic at the end of the '70s, Mann had his own label for a while and gradually came back to jazz. He recorded for Chesky, made a record with Dave Valentin, and in the '90s founded the Kokopelli label on which he is free to pursue his wide range of musical interests. Through the years Herbie Mann has recorded as a leader for Bethlehem, Prestige, Epic, Riverside, Savoy, Mode, New Jazz, Chesky, Kokopelli, and, most significantly, Atlantic. —*Scott Yanow*

● **Flute Souffle** / Mar. 21, 1957 / Original Jazz Classics ✦✦✦✦
At the time of this Prestige set (reissued on CD), Herbie Mann was a flutist who occasionally played tenor and Bobby Jaspar a tenor saxophonist who doubled on flute. Two of the four songs find them switching back and forth while the other two are strictly flute features. With pianist Tommy Flanagan, guitarist Joe Puma, bassist Wendell Marshall, and drummer Bobby Donaldson contributing quiet support, the two lead voices constantly interact and trade off during this enjoyable performance. High points are the haunting "Tel Aviv" and a delightful version of "Chasing the Bird." —*Scott Yanow*

The Evolution of Mann: Herbie Mann Anthology / Aug. 3, 1960-Apr. 18, 1992 / Rhino ✦✦
Rhino Records' two-CD retrospective of flutist Herbie Mann's career (subtitled "The Evolution of Mann") is put in a typically attractive box and has fine liner notes but is somewhat flawed. There are no selections included from Mann's bop years (1954-58) and far too many cuts from the '70s when his output was much less significant; in fact, several of the numbers on the second disc are so dated as to be practically unlistenable. This two-fer does have some of the high points of Mann's career (including "Comin' Home Baby," "Memphis Underground," and "Hold on, I'm Comin'"), but it is better to get the original sessions instead. —*Scott Yanow*

● **At the Village Gate** / Nov. 17, 1961 / Atlantic ✦✦✦✦
Remarkably few of flutist Herbie Mann's recordings are available on CD, but fortunately, this one did get reissued. Mann's hit version of "Comin' Home Baby" from this live set became his first big hit. The composer Ben Tucker plays second bass on that cut, and Mann's other sidemen include vibraphonist Hagood Hardy, bassist Ahmed Abdul-Malik, drummer Rudy

Collins, and Chief Bey and Ray Mantilla on percussion. In addition to "Comin' Home Baby," Mann and his men perform memorable versions of "Summertime" and "It Ain't Necessarily So"; the latter is 20 minutes long. Recommended. — *Scott Yanow*

Glory of Love / Jul. 26, 1967-Oct. 6, 1967 / A&M ♦♦

Deep Pocket / Apr. 28, 1992-May 26, 1992 / Kokopelli ♦♦♦

Peace Pieces / Mar. 15, 1995-Apr. 17, 1995 / Kokopelli ♦♦♦♦

Shelly Manne

b. Jun. 11, 1920, New York, NY, d. Sep. 26, 1984, Los Angeles, CA
Drums / Cool, Hard Bop
Shelly Manne made a countless number of records from the '40s into the '80s but is best-known as a good-humored bandleader who never hogged the spotlight. Originally a saxophonist, Manne switched to drums when he was 18 and started working almost immediately. He was with Joe Marsala's band (making his recording debut in 1941), played briefly in the big bands of Will Bradley, Raymond Scott, and Les Brown, and was on drums for Coleman Hawkins' classic "The Man I Love" session of late 1943. Manne worked on and off with Stan Kenton during 1946-52, also touring with Jazz at the Philharmonic (1948-49) and gigging with Woody Herman (1949). After leaving Kenton, Manne moved to Los Angeles where he became the most in-demand of all jazz drummers. He began recording as a leader (his first session was cut in Chicago in 1951) on a regular basis starting in 1953 when he first put together the quintet Shelly Manne and His Men. Among the sidemen who were in his band during their long string of Contemporary recordings (1955-62) were Stu Williamson, Conte Candoli, Joe Gordan, Bob Enevoldsen, Joe Maini, Charlie Mariano, Herb Geller, Bill Holman, Jimmy Giuffre, Richie Kamuca, Victor Feldman, Russ Freeman, Ralph Pena, Leroy Vinnegar, and Monty Budwig. Manne, who had the good fortune to be the leader of a date by the Andre Previn Trio that resulted in a major seller (jazz versions of tunes from *My Fair Lady*), always had an open musical mind and he recorded some fairly free pieces on *The Three and the Two* (trios with Shorty Rogers and Jimmy Giuffre that did not have a piano or bass, along with duets with Russ Freeman) and enjoyed playing on an early session with Ornette Coleman. In addition to his jazz work, Manne appeared on many film soundtracks and even acted in *The Man with the Golden Arm*. He ran the popular club Shelly's Manne-Hole during 1960-74, kept his music open to freer sounds (featuring trumpeter Gary Barone and tenor saxophonist John Gross during 1969-72), played with the Los Angeles Four in the mid-'70s, and was very active up until his death. Throughout his career Shelly Manne recorded as a leader for Savoy, Interlude, Contemporary, Jazz Groove, Impulse, Verve, Capitol, Atlantic, Concord, Mainstream, Flying Dutchman, Discovery, Galaxy, Pausa, Trend, and Jazziz in addition to a few Japanese labels. — *Scott Yanow*

★ **Vol. 1: The West Coast Sound** / Apr. 6, 1953-Sep. 13, 1955 / Original Jazz Classics ♦♦♦♦♦
Drummer Shelly Manne's first sessions for Contemporary contain plenty of definitive examples of West Coast jazz. This CD has four titles apiece from a 1953 septet date with altoist Art Pepper, Bob Cooper on tenor, baritonist Jimmy Giuffre and valve trombonist Bob Enevoldsen, four from a few months later with Bud Shank in Pepper's place and four other songs from 1955 when Manne headed a septet with altoist Joe Maini and Bill Holman on tenor in addition to Giuffre and Enevoldsen. With arrangements by Marty Paich (who plays piano on the first two dates), Giuffre, Shorty Rogers, Bill Russo, Holman and Enevoldsen, the music has plenty of variety yet defines the era, ranging from Bill Russo's "Sweets" (a tribute to trumpeter Harry "Sweets" Edison), Giuffre's "Fugue," the Latin folk tune "La Mucura" and updated charts on older swing tunes. Highly recommended and proof (if any is really needed) that West Coast Jazz was far from bloodless. — *Scott Yanow*

The Three and "The Two" / Sep. 10, 1954 / Original Jazz Classics ♦♦♦♦
These two sets for the Contemporary label (reissued on CD in the OJC label) are two of the more unusual sessions led by drummer Shelly Manne in the '50s. *The Three* features trumpeter Shorty Rogers, Jimmy Giuffre alternating on clarinet, tenor, and baritone, and Manne; no piano or bass! Some of the six performances (particularly the four originals) are quite free, particularly the completely improvised "Abstract No. 1." Although these selections were not influential, they rank second in chronological order (behind Lennie Tristano's performances of 1949) among free jazz records. The remainder of this set (*The Two*) is a duet between pianist Russ Freeman and Manne and is also quite advanced in spots, although in general it is a more swinging session while still being unpredictable. Overall, a very interesting reissue! — *Scott Yanow*

More Swinging Sounds / Jul. 16, 1956-Aug. 16, 1956 / Original Jazz Classics ♦♦♦♦
Drummer Shelly Manne and his 1956 quintet (with trumpeter Stu Williamson, altoist Charlie Mariano, pianist Russ Freeman, and bassist Leroy Vinnegar) perform some challenging material on this CD reissue. The longest piece is Bill Holman's 15 1/2 minute four-part suite "Quartet"

which, despite its potential complexity, actually swings pretty well. In addition, Manne and His Men interpret Johnny Mandel's obscure "Tommyhawk," a Mariano blues number, Charlie Parker's "Moose the Mooche," and Russ Freeman's "The Wind." Shelly Manne deserves great credit for being continually open to new directions and fresh material while staying on his own singular path. — *Scott Yanow*

★ **My Fair Lady** / Aug. 17, 1956 / Original Jazz Classics ♦♦♦♦♦
This trio set by Shelly Manne and His Friends (which consists of the drummer/leader, pianist Andre Previn, and bassist Leroy Vinnegar) was a surprise best-seller and is now considered a classic. Previn (who is really the main voice) leads the group through eight themes from the famous play including "Get Me to the Church on Time," "I've Grown Accustomed to Her Face," "I Could Have Danced All Night," and "On the Street Where You Live." A very appealing set that is easily recommended; an audiophile version has also been released on CD by DCC Jazz. — *Scott Yanow*

● **At the Blackhawk, Vols. 1-5** / Sep. 22, 1959-Sep. 24, 1959 / Contemporary ♦♦♦♦
Recorded live at the Black Hawk, San Francisco. Shelly Manne and His Men. These live sessions are mainstream jazz at its most listenable. With Richie Kamuca on tenor sax, and Victor Feldman on piano. Great listening music! — *Michael Erlewine*

Shelly Manne and His Men at the Blackhawk, Vol. 1 / Sep. 22, 1959+Sep. 24, 1959 / Contemporary ♦♦♦

At The Black Hawk, Vol. 1 / Sep. 23, 1959+Sep. 24, 1959 / Original Jazz Classics ♦♦♦♦
Shelly Manne's Quintet recorded extensively at San Francisco's Black Hawk club for three nights in 1959. Although not the most significant group that the drummer led, this edition (with trumpeter Joe Gordon, tenor saxophonist Richie Kamuca, pianist Victor Feldman, and bassist Monty Budwig) was certainly capable of playing high-quality bebop. Originally their output was released on four LPs; the reissue expanded the music to five CDs. The first volume adds an alternate take of Frank Rosolino's "Blue Daniel" to a set that includes swinging version of "Blue Daniel," "Poinciana," "Our Delight," and "Summertime." The extended performances are easily recommended to straight-ahead jazz fans. — *Scott Yanow*

At The Black Hawk, Vol. 2 / Sep. 23, 1959+Sep. 24, 1959 / Original Jazz Classics ♦♦♦♦
Vol. 2 of the five CDs that document drummer Shelly Manne's Quintet at the Black Hawk club in San Francisco during a three-day period adds a new alternate take of Charlie Mariano's "Step Lightly" to the original program ("Step Lightly," "What's New," "Vamp's Blues"). These lengthy performances ("Vamp's Blues" is over 19 minutes long) give trumpeter Joe Gordon, the cool-toned tenor saxophonist Richie Kamuca, pianist Victor Feldman, bassist Monty Budwig, and the leader/drummer a chance to really stretch out. Fine '50s bebop. — *Scott Yanow*

At The Black Hawk, Vol. 3 / Sep. 23, 1959+Sep. 24, 1959 / Original Jazz Classics ♦♦♦♦
Originally released as four LPs, the Shelly Manne's Quintet's three days at San Francisco's Black Hawk club is now documented on five CDs. The third volume adds a second (and longer) version of "Whisper Not" to the original rendition, Cole Porter's "I Am in Love," and the spontaneous 18-minute "Black Hawk Blues." Considering how much music was documented, it is fortunate that trumpeter Joe Gordon, tenorman Richie Kamuca, pianist Victor Feldman, bassist Monty Budwig, and drummer Shelly Manne were in top form for this enjoyable gig. The music is high-quality, straightforward, and uncomplicated bebop. — *Scott Yanow*

At The Black Hawk, Vol. 4 / Sep. 23, 1959+Sep. 24, 1959 / Original Jazz Classics ♦♦♦♦
Shelly Manne's 1959 Quintet (with trumpeter Joe Gordon, tenor saxophonist Richie Kamuca, pianist Victor Feldman, bassist Montyu Budwig, and the drummer/leader) was not his most important but it was a hard-swinging unit well versed in bebop. Their three days at the Black Hawk (a popular San Francisco jazz club during this era) was almost completely documented, originally on four LPs and now expanded to five CDs. As with the first three sets, the fourth volume adds an alternate take (of "Cabu") to the original program ("Cabu," "Just Squeeze Me," "Nightingale," and a full-length version of their theme "A Gem from Tiffany"). The lengthy solos are consistently excellent, making this entire series recommended to straight ahead fans. — *Scott Yanow*

Shelly Manne and His Men at the Blackhawk, Vol. 5 / Sep. 23, 1959-Sep. 24, 1959 / Contemporary ♦♦♦♦
Unlike the first four volumes of this series, which included three or four selections previously released plus a "new" alternate take, the final CD of the extensive documentation of the Shelly Manne Quintet's stint at the Black Hawk club consists entirely of previously unreleased material. Fortunately, the performances by trumpeter Joe Gordon, tenor saxophonist Richie Kamuca, pianist Russ Freeman, bassist Monty Budwig, and the drummer/leader are at the same high level as on the more familiar material. They perform obscure songs by Horace Silver (has anyone else ever

recorded his "How Deep Are the Roots?") and Victor Feldman in addition to a trio feature on "Wonder Why," the ballad "This Is Always," and a new version of the band's theme song "A Gem from Tiffany." —*Scott Yanow*

● **At the Manne-Hole, Vol. 1** / Mar. 3, 1961-Mar. 5, 1961 / Original Jazz Classics ◆◆◆◆

On the first of two CDs (both of which are straight reissues of the original LPs), Shelly Manne and His Men are heard in prime form performing live at their home base, Shelly's Manne-Hole. Trumpeter Conte Candoli was in particularly strong form throughout the stint, showing self-restraint yet playing with power. Tenor saxophonist Richie Kamuca made for a complementary partner, while pianist Russ Freeman and bassist Chuck Berghofer formed an excellent rhythm section with the leader/drummer. For *Vol. 1* they play "Love for Sale," Duke Ellington's fairly obscure "How Could It Happen to a Dream," "Softly as in a Morning Sunrise," and Dizzy Gillespie's uptempo blues "The Champ." This classic music falls between cool jazz and hard bop. —*Scott Yanow*

At the Manne-Hole, Vol. 2 / Mar. 3, 1961-Mar. 5, 1961 / Original Jazz Classics ◆◆◆◆

The second of two CDs (originally an LP for Contemporary) features Shelly Manne's Quintet in superior form at the legendary Shelly's Manne-Hole club in Hollywood. Trumpeter Conte Candoli (in top form) and the cool-toned tenor Richie Kamuca work together very well while the contributions of the rhythm section (pianist Russ Freeman, bassist Chuck Berghofer, and the drummer/leader) should not be overlooked. Together they perform four standards (highlighted by "On Green Dolphin Street" and "If I Were a Bell") plus their closing theme "A Gem from Tiffany." Both of the volumes are easily recommended. —*Scott Yanow*

2-3-4 / Feb. 5, 1962 / Impulse ◆◆◆◆

Alive in London / Jul. 1970 / Original Jazz Classics ◆◆◆

Perk Up / Apr. 1977 / Concord Jazz ◆◆◆◆

This CD reissue brings back one of the oldest recordings ever issued by the Concord label, a set that was already nine years old when it debuted. Drummer Shelly Manne heads a strong quintet comprising trumpeter Conte Candoli, altoist Frank Strozier (who doubles on flute), pianist Mike Wofford, and bassist Monty Budwig. Although the musicians are all associated with the West Coast hard-bop tradition, there are plenty of moments during this stimulating set when they make it obvious that they had been listening with some interest to some of the avant-garde players, allowing the new innovations to open up their styles a bit. The fresh material (two standards and a pair of originals apiece by Strozier, Wofford, and pianist Jimmy Rowles) inspire the soloists, and the music is not at all predictable. Worth investigating. —*Scott Yanow*

Charlie Mariano

b. Nov. 12, 1923, Boston, MA

Sax (Alto), Sax (Soprano) / Bop, World

Charlie Mariano's career can easily be divided into two. Early on he was a fixture in Boston, playing with Shorty Sherock (1948), Nat Pierce (1949-50), and his own groups. After gigging with a band co-led by Chubby Jackson and Bill Harris, Mariano toured with Stan Kenton's Orchestra (1953-55), which gave him a strong reputation. He moved to Los Angeles in 1956 (working with Shelly Manne and other West Coast jazz stars), returned to Boston to teach in 1958 at Berklee, and the following year had a return stint with Kenton. After marrying Toshiko Akiyoshi, Mariano co-led a group with the pianist on and off up to 1967, living in Japan during part of the time and also working with Charles Mingus (1962-63).

The second career began with the formation of his early fusion group Osmosis in 1967. Known at the time as a strong bop altoist with a sound of his own developed out of the Charlie Parker style, Mariano began to open his music up to the influences of folk music from other cultures, pop, and rock. He taught again at Berklee, traveled to India and the Far East, and in the early '70s settled in Europe. Among the groups Mariano has worked with have been Pork Pie (which also featured Philip Catherine), the United Jazz and Rock Ensemble, and Eberhard Weber's Colours. Charlie Mariano's airy tones on soprano and the nadaswaram (an Indian instrument a little like an oboe) fit right in on some new agey ECM sessions, and he also recorded as a leader through the years for Imperial, Prestige, Bethlehem, World Pacific, Candid (with Toshiko Akiyoshi in 1960), Regina, Atlantic, Catalyst, MPS, CMP, Leo, and Calig. —*Scott Yanow*

★ **Boston All Stars** / Dec. 1951-Jan. 27, 1953 / Original Jazz Classics ◆◆◆◆◆

Altoist Charlie Mariano plays very much in a Charlie Parker style on these early recordings from Boston (eight from 1951 and six from 1953), but his arrangements for the octet (six of the pieces from the former session) are quite original and unpredictable; only trumpeter Joe Gordon among the otherwise obscure personnel ever gained much recognition. The later six selections match Mariano with trumpeter Herb Pomeroy and the brilliant pianist Dick Twardzik in a quintet; Twardzik, with his odd mixture of Bud Powell and Lennie Tristano, consistently steals the show. A historical and generally enjoyable set, it's recommended to bop fans. —*Scott Yanow*

● **Charlie Mariano Plays** / Dec. 21, 1953-Jan. 27, 1955 / Fresh Sound ◆◆◆◆

Back in the '50s, Charlie Mariano was one of the most promising of the bop-orietned altoists. This Fresh Sound CD reissues 16 selections from three sessions originally released by Bethlehem. The personnel is consistent with Mariano joined by pianist Claude Williamson, bassist Max Bennett, drummer Stan Levey, trombonist Frank Rosolino (on eight songs), and the cool-toned trumpeter Stu Williamson (on 11). The repertoire mixes together fairly basic group originals and swinging standards with many fine solos by the horns. An excellent example of Charlie Mariano's playing in the '50s. —*Scott Yanow*

Charlie Mariano Quartet / Jul. 11, 1954 / Fresh Sound ◆◆◆◆

This Fresh Sound CD reissues a Bethlehem album by altoist Charlie Mariano from 1954, the prime of his bebop period. Mariano, whose alto tone mixes together Benny Carter and Charlie Parker, is accompanied by a quiet and supportive rhythm section comprising pianist John Williams, bassist Max Bennett, and drummer Mel Lewis. Switching to tenor on four of the dozen selections, Mariano sounds in excellent form on ten standards, a blues, and his own "Floormat." A swinging cool-bop date. —*Scott Yanow*

Crystal Bells / Dec. 1979 / CMP ◆◆◆

Excellent set, with Don Alias first-rate as a percussionist. —*Ron Wynn*

Standard Time, Vols. 1 & 2 / Apr. 1989 / Fresh Sound ◆◆◆

Both volumes feature Charlie Mariano with the Tete Montoliu Trio. —*Ron Wynn*

Branford Marsalis

b. Aug. 26, 1960, Breaux Bridge, LA

Sax (Alto), Sax (Soprano), Sax (Tenor) / Post-Bop, Hard Bop

The oldest of the four musical Marsalis brothers, Branford Marsalis had already had an impressive career. After studying at Southern University and Berklee, Branford toured Europe with the Art Blakey big band in the summer of 1980 (playing baritone), played three months with Clark Terry, and then spent five months playing alto with Art Blakey's Jazz Messengers (1981). He mostly played tenor and soprano while with Wynton Marsalis' influential group (1982-85), at first sounding most influenced by Wayne Shorter but leaning more toward John Coltrane at the end. The musical telepathy between the two brothers (who helped to revive the sound of the mid-'60s Miles Davis Quintet) was sometimes astounding. Branford toured with Herbie Hancock's V.S.O.P. II. in 1983 and recorded with Miles Davis (1984's *Decoy*). In 1985 when he left Wynton to join Sting's pop rock group, it caused a major (if temporary) rift with his brother that made headlines. Marsalis enjoyed playing with Sting but did not let the association cause him to forget his musical priorities. By 1986 he was leading his own group that eventually consisted of pianist Kenny Kirkland, bassist Bob Hurst, and drummer Jeff "Tain" Watts; sometimes the band was a pianoless trio that really allowed Marsalis to stretch out. After a couple of film appearances (in *School Daze* and *Throw Mama from the Train*), Branford Marsalis became even more of a celebrity when he joined Jay Leno's *Tonight Show* as the musical director in 1992. However, being cast in the role of Leno's sidekick rubbed against Marsalis' temperament, and after two years he had had enough. Branford Marsalis, who attempted to mix together hip-hop and jazz in his erratic *Buckshot LeFonque* project, has recorded steadily for Columbia ever since 1983 (including a classical set) and still seems to be searching for his niche. —*Scott Yanow*

Scenes in the City / Apr. 18, 1983-Nov. 29, 1983 / Columbia ◆◆◆◆

Branford Marsalis' debut as a leader is ambitious yet consistently successful. On "Scenes of the City," his narrative is in the same spirit as some of Charles Mingus' recordings of the '50s. Otherwise, the music is in the modern mainstream vein with Marsalis (on tenor and soprano) hinting strongly at Wayne Shorter and John Coltrane, along with a touch of Sonny Rollins. The backup crew includes such notable young lions as pianists Mulgrew Miller and Kenny Kirkland, bassist Charnett Moffett, and drummers Jeff "Tain" Watts and Marvin "Smitty" Smith in addition to bassist Ron Carter. It's an impressive start to a notable career. —*Scott Yanow*

Royal Garden Blues / Mar. 18, 1986-Jul. 2, 1986 / Columbia ◆◆◆◆

Quartet sessions that feature some outstanding piano by Kenny Kirkland. —*Ron Wynn*

Renaissance / Dec. 31, 1986-Jan. 28, 1987 / Columbia ◆◆◆◆

Marsalis' best ensemble with Kenny Kirkland (p), Bob Hurst, and Tony Williams (d). Four standards, two of Williams' originals, and one of Branford's. A very solid album. —*Michael G. Nastos*

Romances for Saxophone / 1986 / Columbia ◆◆◆

Beautiful, exacting sax solos in a classical vein. —*Ron Wynn*

Random Abstract / Aug. 1987 / Columbia ◆◆◆◆

First-rate quartet performances and excellent solos. —*Ron Wynn*

● **Trio Jeepy** / Jan. 3, 1988-Jan. 4, 1988 / Columbia ◆◆◆◆

His exhaustive, well conceived, and impressive tenor solos, plus the nimble bass work . . . and always consistent drumming . . . provide a variation on the theme. . . . —*Ron Wynn, Rock & Roll Disc*

Crazy People Music / Jan. 10, 1990-Mar. 1, 1990 / Columbia ✦✦✦✦
Quartet. In these sessions, Branford moves farther out. —*Ron Wynn*

The Beautyful Ones Are Not Yet Born / May 16, 1991-May 18, 1991 / Columbia ✦✦✦✦
Trio. An exciting pianoless session, plus a cut with guest star British tenor saxophonist Courtney Pine. Intense, deeply personal, and searing pianoless trio sessions for the '90s. —*Ron Wynn, Rock & Roll Disc*

Bloomington / Sep. 23, 1991 / Columbia ✦✦

I Heard You Twice the First Time / 1992 / Columbia ✦✦✦

Delfeayo Marsalis

Trombone / Bop
Imagine being the younger brother of Wynton and Branford Marsalis! It is little surprise that Delfeayo Marsalis took a while before making his debut on records. The son of Ellis Marsalis and the older brother of drummer Jason, Delfeayo was always interested in engineering, and he started off as a busy record producer, studying both trombone and studio production at Berklee. In addition to his producing, Delfeayo has written some of the most absurd liner notes ever seen, raving about his brothers while trying to pretend that he is an impartial observer! More importantly, Delfeayo Marsalis is a fine J.J. Johnson-inspired trombonist who toured with Ray Charles, Art Blakey's Jazz Messengers, and Abdullah Ibrahim before recording his first album as a leader in 1992. He is long overdue for a follow-up. —*Scott Yanow*

● **Pontius Pilate's Dec** / 1992 / Novus ✦✦✦✦
The debut major label project by longtime producer and trombonist Delfeayo Marsalis. It's a concept work based on an instrumental interpretation about events behind Christ being crucified. Marsalis plays some long and harmonically impressive trombone solos, and is joined by his brothers Wynton, Branford, and the newest prodigy, Jason, plus pianists Kenny Kirkland and Marcus Roberts. —*Ron Wynn*

Ellis Marsalis

b. Nov. 14, 1934
Piano / Post-Bop, Hard Bop
It is a bit ironic that Ellis Marsalis had to wait for sons Wynton and Branford to get famous before he was able to record on a regular basis, but Ellis has finally received his long-overdue recognition. The father of six sons (including Wynton, Branford, Delfeayo, and Jason), Ellis Marsalis' main importance to jazz may very well be as a jazz educator; his former pupils (in addition to his sons) include Terence Blanchard, Donald Harrison, Harry Connick, Jr., Nicholas Payton, and Kent and Marlon Jordan, among others. He started out as a tenor saxophonist, switching to piano while in high school. Marsalis was one of the few New Orleans musicians of the era who did not specialize in Dixieland or R&B. He played with fellow modernists (including Ed Blackwell) in the late '50s with AFO, recorded with Cannonball and Nat Adderley in the '60s, played with Al Hirt (1967-70), and was busy as a teacher. Marsalis freelanced in New Orleans during the '70s and taught at the New Orleans Center for Creative Arts. He recorded with Wynton and Branford on *Father and Sons* in 1982, an album that they shared with Chico and Von Freeman. Since then Marsalis has recorded for ELM, Spindletop (a duet session with Eddie Harris), Rounder, Blue Note, and Columbia. —*Scott Yanow*

Father and Sons / 1982 / CBS ✦✦✦✦
The side with sons Wynton and Branford worth the price. They swing very hard. —*Michael G. Nastos*

Piano in E-Solo Piano / Jul. 24, 1986 / Rounder ✦✦✦✦
Ellis Marsalis got his time in the spotlight with this fine solo piano session. His mix of swing, Afro-Latin, classical, and bebop was spotlighted on superbly crafted versions of Horace Silver's "Nica's Dream" and John Lewis' "Django," as well as Bud Powell's "Hallucinations" and Fats Waller's "Jitterbug Waltz." Marsalis' own originals, "Fourth Autumn" and "Zee Blues," were also expertly written, with charming melodies and smooth, relaxed, yet impressive solos. While he'll probably never get as much publicity as sons Wynton and Branford, Ellis Marsalis certainly deserves high praise for his formidable piano skills. —*Ron Wynn*

Ellis Marsalis Trio / Mar. 18, 1990 / Blue Note ✦✦✦✦
Trio. Spiraling piano at times on these trio sessions. —*Ron Wynn*

● **Heart of Gold** / Feb. 1991-Jun. 1991 / Columbia ✦✦✦✦
Pianist Ellis Marsalis' inspired mix of New Orleans and bebop influences has seldom been presented more effectively than on this session, nicely mixing stunning covers and excellent originals. Marsalis' touch, spinning phrases, surging lines, and clever voicings were impressive on such standards as "Spring Can Really Hang You Up the Most" and "Love For Sale." He also conveyed the sense of longing and loss inherent in "Do You Know What It Means To Miss New Orleans," while his own "El-Ray Blues" was alternately funky and vibrant. —*Ron Wynn*

Whistle Stop / Mar. 20, 1993-Jun. 6, 1993 / Columbia ✦✦✦✦
For this CD, veteran pianist Ellis Marsalis performs songs composed by

some of the top modern New Orleans players of the '60s, including drummer James Black, tenor saxophonist Nat Perrilliat, clarinetist Alvin Batiste, saxophonist Harold Battiste, and himself. With the exception of Alvin Batiste's tunes (based on "Cherokee" and a Dixielandish blues), the originals have strong melodies, slightly tricky chord structures, and sound quite fresh even today. Marsalis utilizes his son Branford on tenor and soprano, bassist Robert Hurst, and drummer Jeff "Tain" Watts; the young Jason Marsalis sits in on drums during two numbers. Ellis Marsalis is in particularly inventive form on this unusually obscure material. —*Scott Yanow*

Loved Ones / Aug. 14, 1995-Sep. 11, 1995 / Columbia ✦✦✦✦

Wynton Marsalis

b. Oct. 18, 1961, New Orleans, LA
Trumpet / Classical, Bop, Swing, Post-Bop, New Orleans Jazz
The most famous jazz musician since 1980, Wynton Marsalis made a major impact on jazz almost from the start. In the early '80s it was major news that a young and very talented Black musician would choose to make a living playing acoustic jazz rather than fusion, funk, or R&B. Marsalis' arrival on the scene started the "Young Lions" movement and resulted in major labels (most of whom had shown no interest in jazz during the previous decade) suddenly signing and promoting young players. There had been a major shortage of new trumpeters since 1970, but Marsalis' sudden prominence inspired an entire new crop of brass players. The music of the mid-'60s Miles Davis Quintet had been somewhat overshadowed when it was new, but Marsalis' Quintet focused on extending the group's legacy. Soon other "Young Lion" units were using Davis' late acoustic work as their starting point.

During the past 15 years Wynton Marsalis has managed to be a controversial figure despite his obvious abilities. His selective knowledge of jazz history (considering post-1965 avant-garde playing to be outside of jazz and '70s fusion to be barren) is unfortunately influenced by the somewhat eccentric beliefs of Stanley Crouch, and his hiring policies as musical director of the Lincoln Center Jazz Orchestra led to exaggerated charges of ageism and racism from local writers. However, more than balancing all of this out is Marsalis' inspiring work with youngsters, many of whom he has introduced to jazz; a few young musicians, such as Roy Hargrove, have been directly helped by Marsalis.

Wynton Marsalis' trumpet playing has been both overcriticized and (at least early on) overpraised. When he first arrived on the scene with the Jazz Messengers, his original inspiration was Freddie Hubbard. However, by the time he began leading his own group, Marsalis often sounded very close to Miles Davis (particularly when holding a long tone) although a version of Miles with virtuosic technique. He was so widely praised by the jazz press at the time (due to their belief that the future of jazz finally seemed safe) that there was an inevitable backlash. Marsalis' sometimes inaccurate statements about jazz of the '70s and the avant-garde in general made some observers angry, and his rather derivative tone at the time made it seem as if there was always going to have to be an asterisk by his name when evaluating his talents. Some listeners formed permanent impressions of Marsalis as a Miles Davis imitator, but they failed to take into account that he was still improving and developing. With the 1990 recording *Tune in Tomorrow*, Marsalis at last sounded like himself. He had found his own voice by exploring earlier styles of jazz (such as Louis Armstrong's playing), mastering the wa-wa mute, and studying Duke Ellington. From that point on, even when playing a Miles Davis standard, Marsalis has had his own sound and has finally taken his place as one of jazz's greats.

The son of pianist Ellis Marsalis, the younger brother of Branford, and the older brother of Delfeayo and Jason (the Marsalis clan as a whole can be accurately called "The First Family of Jazz"), Wynton (who was named after pianist Wynton Kelly) received his first trumpet at age six from Ellis' employer, Al Hirt. He studied both classical and jazz and played in local marching bands, funk groups, and classical orchestras. Marsalis played first trumpet in the New Orleans Civic Orchestra while in high school. He went to Juilliard when he was 18, and in 1980 he made his first recordings with the Art Blakey Big Band and joined the Jazz Messengers.

By 1981 the young trumpeter was the talk of the jazz world. He toured with Herbie Hancock (a double-LP record), continued working with Blakey, signed with Columbia, and recorded his first album as a leader. In 1982 Marsalis not only formed his own quintet (featuring brother Branford and soon Kenny Kirkland, Charnett Moffett, and Jeff "Tain" Watts) but recorded his first classical album; he was immediately ranked as one of the top classical trumpeters of all time. His quintet with Branford lasted until late 1985, although a rift developed between the brothers (fortunately temporary) when Branford finally quit the band to tour with Sting's pop group. By that time Wynton was a superstar, winning a countless number of awards and polls.

Marsalis' next group featured pianist Marcus Roberts, bassist Robert Hurst, and drummer Watts. Over time the group grew to become a four-horn septet with trombonist Wycliffe Gordon, altoist Wes Anderson, Todd Williams on tenor, bassist Reginald Veal, drummer Herlin Riley, and (by the early '90s) pianist Eric Reed. Marsalis has really developed his writing during the past decade (being influenced by Duke Ellington), and the septet proved to be a perfect outlet for his arranging. Although Wynton Marsalis broke up the band by 1995, many of the musicians still appear in his special projects or with the Lincoln Center Jazz Orchestra.

With the passing of so many jazz giants during the past few years, Wynton Marsalis' importance (as a trumpeter, leader, writer, and spokesman for jazz) continues to grow. —*Scott Yanow*

Wynton Marsalis / Aug. 1981 / Columbia ✦✦✦✦
Trumpeter Wynton Marsalis' debut on Columbia, recorded when he was only 19, made it clear from the start that he was going to be a major force in jazz. At the time Marsalis (who was originally a bit influenced by Freddie Hubbard) was starting to closely emulate Miles Davis of the mid-'60s, and his slightly older brother Branford took Wayne Shorter as his role model. The inclusion of Davis' rhythm section from that era (pianist Herbie Hancock, bassist Ron Carter, and drummer Tony Williams) on four of the seven selections reinforced the image. The three other numbers feature such up-and-coming talents as pianist Kenny Kirkland, Charles Fambrough or Clarence Seay on bass, and drummer Jeff "Tain" Watts, helping to launch the rise of the Young Lions. But although not overly original, there is a great deal of outstanding playing on this set, including a definitive version of Tony Williams' "Sister Cheryl" and the long trade off between Wynton and Branford on "Hesitation." —*Scott Yanow*

Think of One / 1983 / Columbia ✦✦✦✦
Wynton Marsalis' second Columbia recording as a leader features his working band of 1983: brother Branford on tenor and soprano, pianist Kenny Kirkland, either Phil Bowler or Ray Drummond on bass, and drummer Jeff "Tain" Watts. They perform the ballad "My Ideal," Duke Ellington's "Melancholia," and Thelonious Monk's "Think of One," along with some group originals. Wynton was deep in his Miles Davis period, while Branford (who was still most influenced by Wayne Shorter) was just beginning to come into his own. Of course Wynton was already a remarkable virtuoso a few years earlier. All of his recordings are worth getting, and this early document has more than its share of brilliant playing. —*Scott Yanow*

Hot House Flowers / May 30, 1984-May 31, 1984 / Columbia ✦✦✦✦
Wynton Marsalis, very much in his Miles Davis period, plays quite melodically throughout this ballad-dominated outing with strings. Branford Marsalis (on tenor and soprano), flutist Kent Jordan, pianist Kenny Kirkland, bassist Ron Carter, and drummer Jeff Watts are strong assets, but it is Wynton's subtle creativity on such songs as "Stardust," "When You Wish Upon a Star," Duke Ellington's "Melancholia," and "I'm Confessin'" that makes this recording special. The arrangements by Robert Freedman generally keep the strings from sounding too sticky, and Wynton's tone is consistently beautiful. —*Scott Yanow*

★ **Black Codes (from the Underground)** / Jan. 11, 1985+Jan. 14, 1985 / Columbia ✦✦✦✦✦
This is probably the best Wynton Marsalis recording from his Miles Davis period. With his brother Branford (who doubles here on tenor and soprano) often closely emulating Wayne Shorter and the rhythm section (pianist Kenny Kirkland, bassist Charnett Moffett, and drummer Jeff Watts) sounding a bit like the famous Herbie Hancock-Ron Carter-Tony Williams trio, Wynton is heard at the head of what was essentially an updated version of the mid-to-late-'60s Miles Davis Quintet (despite Stanley Crouch's pronouncements in his typically absurd liner notes about Marsalis' individuality). The music is brilliantly played and displays what the "Young Lions" movement was really about; young musicians choosing to explore acoustic jazz and to extend the innovations of the pre-fusion, modern mainstream style. Marsalis would develop his own sound a few years later, but even at age 23 he had few close competitors. —*Scott Yanow*

J Mood / Dec. 17, 1985-Dec. 20, 1985 / Columbia ✦✦✦✦
When Branford Marsalis and Kenny Kirkland chose to leave Wynton Marsalis' group to make money with Sting, Wynton had to regroup fast. For this quartet recording with bassist Robert Hurst III and drummer Jeff "Tain" Watts, the trumpeter met up with pianist Marcus Roberts for the first time, performing originals by Wynton, Roberts, Ellis Marsalis, and Donald Brown. Marsalis was still very much under Miles Davis' influence at the time, but at age 24 he had rather remarkable technique. He stretches out in explorative and consistently creative fashion on these seven straight ahead and generally unpredictable selections. —*Scott Yanow*

Standard Time, Vol. 1 / May 29, 1986-Sep. 25, 1986 / Columbia ✦✦✦✦
On the first of three volumes, Wynton Marsalis explores ten standards plus two of his originals with his quartet of the period (which consists of pianist Marcus Roberts, bassist Robert Hurst III, and drummer Jeff "Tain" Watts). Marsalis' tone is quite beautiful on the well balanced set; even the ballads have their unpredictable moments. Among the more memorable performances are his treatments of "Caravan," "April in Paris," "New Orleans," "Memories of You," and two versions of "Cherokee." —*Scott Yanow*

Live at Blues Alley / Dec. 19, 1986-Dec. 20, 1986 / Columbia ✦✦✦✦
This double LP features the great trumpeter Wynton Marsalis and his 1986 quartet, a unit featuring pianist Marcus Roberts, bassist Robert Hurst, and

drummer Jeff "Tain" Watts. Although Marsalis during this period still hinted strongly at Miles Davis, his own musical personality was starting to finally shine through. With the versatile Marcus Roberts (who thus far has been the most significant graduate from Marsalis' groups), Wynton Marsalis was beginning to explore older material, including on this set "Just Friends," and "Do You Know What It Means to Miss New Orleans?" Other highlights include lengthy workouts on "Au Privave" and Kenny Kirkland's "Chambers of Tain." This two-fer is recommended, as are virtually all of Wynton Marsalis' recordings. —*Scott Yanow*

Standard Time, Vol. 2: Intimacy Calling / Sep. 1987-Aug. 1990 / Columbia ✦✦✦✦
Wynton Marsalis' second of three standard albums was actually released after the third volume. On most of the selections the brilliant trumpeter is heard in excellent form with his quartet (comprising pianist Marcus Roberts, bassist Reginald Veal or Robert Hurst, and pianist Riley or Jeff Watts on drums); tenorman Todd Williams helps out on "I'll Remember April," and altoist Wes Anderson is also added to "Crepuscule with Nellie." Marsalis' tone really makes the ballads worth hearing, and his unusual choice (and placement) of notes keeps the music stimulating. This mostly bop-oriented set is rounded off by a happy version of "Bourbon Street Parade." —*Scott Yanow*

Levee Low Moan: Soul Gestures in Southern Blue, Vol. 3 / 1988 / Columbia ✦✦✦
Thick in the South: Soul Gestures in Southern Blue, Vol. 1 / 1988 / Columbia ✦✦✦✦
The three volumes that Wynton Marsalis subtitled "Soul Gestures in Southern Blue" (of which this CD is the first) are overall rather disappointing. This initial CD is the strongest of the three due to the inclusion of tenor saxophonist Joe Henderson and (on two of the five numbers) drummer Elvin Jones, but overall Marsalis (who was in the final section of his Miles Davis period), although playing quite well, seemed to have hit a dead-end. His five compositions lack any memorable melodies and his own virtuosic solos do not have any distinctive qualities; pianist Marcus Roberts occasionally emerges as the top soloist. However, once he had gotten his three-part tribute to the blues out of the way, Marsalis would once again make some giant leaps forward. —*Scott Yanow*

Uptown Ruler: Soul Gestures in Southern Blue, Vol. 2 / 1988 / Columbia ✦✦✦

The Majesty of the Blues / Oct. 27, 1988-Oct. 28, 1988 / Columbia ✦✦✦

Original Soundtrack from "The Tune in Tomorrow" / 1989 / Columbia ✦✦✦✦
This soundtrack recording is very significant in the career of Wynton Marsalis. For the first time the trumpeter displayed a sound of his own; the Miles Davis influence was finally gone. In addition Marsalis not only debuted with his septet (which consisted of trombonist Wycliffe Gordon, altoist Wes Anderson, Todd Williams on tenor, soprano, and clarinet, pianist Marcus Roberts, bassist Reginald Veal, and drummer Herlin Riley) but, in writing this score, Marsalis showed how talented an arranger he was; very much in the Duke Ellington tradition but without resorting to copying. The 16 selections are sometimes a bit fragmented (a few use extra personnel including clarinetist Michael White on six tracks and vocals by Shirley Horn and Johnny Adams), but they hold up very well apart from the movie and have plenty of spirit and humor. —*Scott Yanow*

Crescent City Christmas Card / Jan. 24, 1989-Apr. 4, 1989 / Columbia ✦✦✦✦
Due to some of his statements, Wynton Marsalis gained the reputation of not having much of a sense of humor, but the picture of him on this album (plus the music in general) dispelled that notion. Marsalis and his expanded septet (which welcomed such guests as clarinetist Alvin Batiste, baritonist Joe Temperley and, on one song apiece, singers Jon Hendricks and Kathleen Battle) clearly have a good time on this joyous and unpredictable set of holiday cheer. —*Scott Yanow*

Standard Time, Vol. 3 / 1990 / Columbia ✦✦✦

Blue Interlude / 1991 / Columbia ✦✦✦✦
Wynton Marsalis' septet was the perfect outlet both for his playing and his writing. The impressive young personnel (pianist Marcus Roberts, altoist Wessell Anderson, Todd Williams on tenor, soprano, and clarinet, trombonist Wycliffe Gordon, bassist Reginald Veal, and drummer Herlin Riley) was flexible enough to sound like a New Orleans parade band or the David Murray Octet, and Wynton's writing also made them occasionally appear to be a small group from the Duke Ellington Orchestra. On this CD the music is quite strong as are the solos, and the colorful group is heard at their best on a wide variety of challenging material. —*Scott Yanow*

★ **In This House, on This Morning** / May 28, 1992-May 21, 1993 / Columbia ✦✦✦✦✦
For this double CD (which has typically absurd liner notes from Stanley Crouch) trumpeter Wynton Marsalis musically depicts in three parts a lengthy Sunday church service with program music composed for each of the traditional activities. The set does take quite awhile to get going with

much of the first two parts consisting of introductions and transitions to themes that never seem to arrive. There are some exceptions, particularly Marsalis' violent trumpet distortions on "Call to Prayer," a spirited New Orleans blues, and Todd Williams' tenor solo on another blues. However, it is the third section that is most notable. The 28-minute "In the Sweet Embrace of Life" instrumentally portrays a preacher giving a heated sermon, building up to a very feverish level. Marsalis' model in his writing is clearly Duke Ellington. Trombonist Wycliffe Gordon is an expert with mutes, and Todd Williams is able to hint at both Paul Gonsalves on tenor and Dixieland clarinetists on soprano. Altoist Wes Anderson and pianist Eric Reed are also major assets to the septet. Due to the memorable final section, this lengthy work is one of the high points of his career thus far. *—Scott Yanow*

☆ **Citi Movement** / Jul. 27, 1992-Jul. 28, 1992 / Columbia ♦♦♦♦♦
This double CD contains Wynton Marsalis' score for the modern ballet *Griot New York*. Even more than his trumpet playing, his writing skills had developed quickly during the five years prior to this set. Marsalis' superb septet (which included trombonist Wycliffe Gordon, altoist Wes Anderson, Todd Williams on tenor and soprano, pianist Eric Reed, bassist Reginald Veal, and drummer Herlin Riley) performs the complex and consistently colorful music, which goes through a wide variety of styles (including New Orleans jazz, swing, bop, modal music, and even some sections bordering on the avant-garde). The results are unpredictable, exciting, and quite enjoyable. This is one of Wynton Marsalis' finest recordings to date. *—Scott Yanow*

Joe Cool's Blues / Apr. 12, 1994-Aug. 25, 1994 / Columbia ♦♦♦♦
For this CD Wynton and Ellis Marsalis perform music both old and new that is heard on the *Peanuts* television specials. Wynton's septet (altoist Wessell Anderson, Victor Goines on tenor, trombonist Wycliffe Gordon, pianist Eric Reed, bassist Benjamin Wolfe, and drummer Herlin Riley in addition to the trumpeter-leader) jam on eight of Marsalis' compositions and the perennial "Linus & Lucy," Ellis Marsalis' trio performs four of Vince Guaraldi's themes and, on "Little Birdie," an all-star group (including three of the Marsalises but not Wynton) back Germaine Bazzle's vocal. The music is reasonably enjoyable but not too substantial, worth getting even if it is not one of Wynton's more significant albums. *—Scott Yanow*

Warne Marsh

b. Oct. 26, 1927, Los Angeles, CA, **d.** Dec. 18, 1987, Hollywood, CA
Sax (Tenor) / Cool
Along with Lee Konitz, Warne Marsh was the most successful "pupil" of Lennie Tristano and, unlike Konitz, Marsh spent most of his career exploring chordal improvisation the Tristano way. The cool-toned tenor played with Hoagy Carmichael's Teenagers during 1944-45, and then after the Army he was with Buddy Rich (1948) before working with Lennie Tristano (1949-52). His recordings with Tristano and Konitz still sound remarkable today with unisons that make the two horns sound like one. Marsh had occasional reunions with Konitz and Tristano through the years, spent periods outside of music, and stayed true to his musical goals. He moved to Los Angeles in 1966 and worked with Supersax during 1972-77, also filling in time teaching. Marsh, who collapsed and died on stage at the legendary Donte's club in 1987 while playing "Out of Nowhere," is now considered legendary. He recorded as a leader for Xanadu, Imperial, Kapp, Mode (reissued on V.S.O.P.), Atlantic, Wave, Storyville, Revelation, Interplay, Criss Cross, and Hot Club. *—Scott Yanow*

Music for Prancing / Sep. 1957 / VSOP ♦♦♦♦
A swinging date by the master of cool. *—David Szatmary*

★ **Star Highs** / Aug. 14, 1982 / Criss Cross ♦♦♦♦♦
A recent indication of this tenor's considerable and continued talent, it was recorded with Hank Jones (p). *—David Szatmary*

A Ballad Album / Apr. 7, 1983 / Criss Cross ♦♦♦♦
Nicely played quartet session done in 1983 by Lennie Tristano disciple Warne Marsh. His exacting passages, winding solos, and slow, intricately constructed phrases show how much Marsh was affected by Tristano's "cool" conception. His backing band of pianist Lou Levy, bassist Jesper Lundgaard, and drummer James Martin falls in behind Marsh smartly, with Levy also taking a few nice solos. *—Ron Wynn*

Back Home / Mar. 1986 / Criss Cross ♦♦♦

Pat Martino (Pat Azzara)

b. Aug. 25, 1944, Philadelphia, PA
Guitar / Post-Bop
One of the most original of the jazz-based guitarists to emerge in the '60s, Pat Martino made a remarkable comeback after brain surgery in 1980 to correct an aneurysm, which caused him to lose his memory and completely forget how to play. It took years but he regained his ability, partly by listening to his older records!
    Martino began playing professionally when he was 15. He worked early on with groups led by Willis Jackson, Red Holloway, and a series of organists including Don Patterson, Jimmy Smith, Jack McDuff, Richard "Groove"

Holmes, and Jimmy McGriff. After playing with John Handy (1966), he started leading his own bands and heading sessions for Prestige, Muse, and Warner Bros. that found him welcoming the influences of avant-garde jazz, rock, pop, and world music into his advanced hard-bop style. After the operation, Martino did not resume playing until 1984. Although not as active as earlier, Pat Martino has regained his earlier form, recording again for Muse and Evidence. *—Scott Yanow*

● **East!** / Jan. 8, 1968 / Original Jazz Classics ♦♦♦♦
Despite the title and the cover of this CD reissue (which makes it appear that the performances are greatly influenced by music of the Far East), the style played by guitarist Pat Martino's quartet is very much in the hard-bop tradition. Martino was already developing his own sound and is in excellent form with pianist Eddie Green, drummer Lenny McBrowne, and either Ben Tucker or Tyrone Brown on bass during two group originals, Benny Golson's "Park Avenue Petite," John Coltrane's "Lazy Bird," and the standard "Close Your Eyes." It's a good example of Pat Martino's playing in his early period. *—Scott Yanow*

Baiyina (The Clear Evidence) / Jun. 11, 1968 / Original Jazz Classics ♦♦♦♦
Tight, inventive Martino at his best. *—Ron Wynn*

Desperado / Mar. 1970 / Original Jazz Classics ♦♦♦♦
A fine set enlivened by Eric Kloss' wavery alto. *—Ron Wynn*

The Return / Feb. 1987 / Muse ♦♦♦

Interchange / Mar. 1, 1994 / Muse ♦♦♦♦

● **The Maker** / Sep. 11, 1994 / Evidence ♦♦♦♦

Hugh Masekela (Hugh Ramopolo Masekela)

b. Apr. 4, 1939
Trumpet, Fluegelhorn, Vocals / World Fusion, Instrumental Pop, Soul-Jazz
Hugh Masekela has an extensive jazz background and credentials, but has enjoyed major success as one of the earliest leaders in the world fusion mode. Masekela's vibrant trumpet and fluegelhorn solos have been featured in pop, R&B, disco, Afro-pop, and jazz contexts. He's had American and international hits, worked with bands around the world, and played with African, African-American, European, and various American musicians during a stellar career. His style, especially on fluegelhorn, is a charismatic blend of striking upper register lines, half valve effects, repetitive figures and phrases, with some note bending, slurs, and tonal colors. Though he's often simplified his playing to fit into restrictive pop formulas, Masekela's capable of outstanding ballad and bebop work. He began singing and playing piano as a child, influenced by seeing the film "Young Man with a Horn" at 13. Masekela started playing trumpet at 14. He played in the Huddleston Jazz Band, which was led by anti-apartheid crusader and group head Trevor Huddleston. Huddleston was eventually deported, and Masekela co-founded the Merry Makers of Springs along with Jonas Gwangwa. He later joined Alfred Herbert's Jazz Revue, and played in studio bands backing popular singers. Masekela was in the orchestra for the musical "King Kong," whose cast included Miriam Makeba. He was also in the Jazz Epistles with Abdullah Ibrahim, Makaya Ntshoko, Gwanga, and Kippie Moeketsi. Masekela and Makeba, his wife at that time, left South Africa one year before Ibrahim and Sathima Bea Benjamin in 1961. Such musicians as Dizzy Gillespie, John Dankworth, and Harry Belafonte assisted him. Masekela studied at the Royal Academy of Music, then the Manhattan School of Music. During the early '60s, his career began to explode. He recorded for MGM, Mercury, and Verve, developing his hybrid African/pop/jazz style. Masekela moved to California and started his own record label, Chisa. He cut several albums expanding this formula and began to score pop success. The song "Grazing in the Grass" topped the charts in 1968 and eventually sold four million copies worldwide. That year Masekela sold out arenas nationwide during his tour, among them Carnegie Hall. He recorded in the early '70s with Monk Montgomery and the Crusaders. Masekela moved in a more ethnic direction during the '70s. He traveled to London to play with Nigerian Afrobeat great Fela Kuti and his Africa '70; then came a session with Dudu Pukwana, Eddie Gomez, and Ntshoko, among others, that resulted in his finest jazz/African album, *Home Is Where the Music Is*. Masekela toured Guinea with the Ghanian Afropop band Hedzollah Zoundz, then recorded a series of albums with them both in California and Africa with guest stints from the Crusaders, Patti Austin, and others. Masekela alternated between America and Africa, cutting a successful pop/dance album with Herb Alpert in the late '70s. During the '80s, Masekela returned to South Africa. He visited Zimbabwe and Botswana, and recorded two albums with the Kalahari Band that once more merged jazz-rock, funk, and pop. Masekela was part of Paul Simon's Graceland tour in the mid-'80s, while he continued recording and produced sessions by Makeba. Though the jazz content of his work has varied over the years, Hugh Masekela has far more material on the plus side than the negative. *—Ron Wynn*

Trumpet African / 1962 / Mercury ♦♦♦

24 Karat Hits / 1966 / Verve ♦♦♦

Grrr / 1966 / Mercury ✦✦✦✦
Masekela as a young trumpeter from the mid-'60s. Rare, but clearly his best format and playing. —*Michael G. Nastos*

The Promise of a Future / 1968 / One Way ✦✦✦

★ **Masekela** / 1968 / UNI ✦✦✦✦✦
It all comes together here, with a magic synthesis of trumpet-led African sounds, jazz, and R&B. —*Hank Davis*

★ **Home Is Where the Music Is** / Jan. 1972 / Blue Thumb ✦✦✦✦✦
An outstanding blend of Afro-pop and jazz with strong work by Dudu Pukwana. (as) —*Ron Wynn*

Uptownship / 197_ / Jive/Novus ✦✦✦
Fine recordings in a driving Afro groove. —*Ron Wynn*

Tomorrow / 1987 / Warner Bros. ✦✦✦

Stimela / 1994 / Connoisseur Collection ✦✦✦✦

Lyle Mays

b. 1953
Piano, Keyboards / Post-Bop
Lyle Mays' style is difficult to describe, more atmospheric (with plenty of unique colors) than swinging, and an invaluable part of the sound of the Pat Metheny Group. Mays played and composed for the North Texas State University Lab Band in the mid-'70s. He met Metheny in 1975, toured with Woody Herman's Orchestra (1975-76), and then joined Metheny's band, continuing to play with the guitarist's group up to the present time. Mays (who is also an excellent acoustic pianist) has recorded two albums as a leader for Geffen (1986 and 1988). —*Scott Yanow*

Street Dreams / 1988 / Geffen ✦✦✦

● **Fictionary** / Apr. 23, 1992 / Geffen ✦✦✦✦
Lyle Mays, who became famous for his electric collaborations with Pat Metheny, surprised many with this superior outing in an acoustic trio setting. On the liner jacket Mays thanks Herbie Hancock, Keith Jarrett, and Paul Bley for their inspiration. If one adds in Chick Corea and especially Bill Evans, that should give listeners an idea of what to expect. However, to his credit (and with the assistance of bassist Marc Johnson and drummer Jack Dejohnette) Mays avoids performing overly played standards and sticks mostly to originals (including two free improvisations). There is no coasting on this excellent set. —*Scott Yanow*

Les McCann

b. Sep. 23, 1935, Lexington, KY
Piano, Vocals / Soul-Jazz, Hard Bop, Groove
Les McCann reached the peak of his career at the 1968 Montreux Jazz Festival, recording "Compared to What" and "Cold Duck Time" for Atlantic (*Swiss Movement*) with Eddie Harris and Benny Bailey. Although he has done some worthwhile work since then, much of it has been anti-climatic.

Les McCann first gained some fame in 1956 when he won a talent contest in the Navy as a singer that resulted in a television appearance on *The Ed Sullivan Show*. After being discharged, he formed a trio in Los Angeles. McCann turned down an invitation to join the Cannonball Adderley Quintet so he could work on his own music. He signed a contract with Pacific Jazz and gained some fame with his albums *Les McCann Plays the Truth* and *The Shout*. His soulful funk style on piano was influential and McCann's singing was largely secondary until the mid-'60s. He recorded many albums for Pacific Jazz during 1960-64, mostly with his trio but also featuring Ben Webster, Richard "Groove" Holmes, Blue Mitchell, Stanley Turrentine, Joe Pass, the Jazz Crusaders, and the Gerald Wilson Orchestra. McCann switched to Limelight during 1965-67 and then signed with Atlantic in 1968. After the success of *Swiss Movement*, McCann emphasized his singing at the expense of his playing and he began to utilize electric keyboards. His recordings became less interesting from that point on and, after his Atlantic contract ran out in 1976, McCann appeared on records much less often. However, he stayed popular and a 1994 reunion tour with Eddie Harris was quite successful. —*Scott Yanow*

● **Les McCann Anthology: Relationships** / Feb. 1960-Nov. 1972 / Rhino/Atlantic ✦✦✦✦
One of the many two-CD samplers of Atlantic jazz artists put together by Rhino Records, this retrospective has some of the high points of pianist-vocalist Les McCann's career but is far from perfect. The first CD is purely instrumental, showcasing McCann with several of his trios and in collaborations with organist Richard "Groove" Holmes, the tenors of Ben Webster and Stanley Turrentine, the Jazz Crusaders, and Gerald Wilson's Orchestra. The second half of the two-fer has three selections on which McCann backs singer Lou Rawls (why were these included?) and just two vocals from the pianist. "Compared to What" and "Cold Duck Time" (from his famous meeting with Eddie Harris at the 1968 Montreux Jazz Festival) have been reissued several times, there are no selections from the 1973-95 period, and the music is not programmed in strictly chronological order. Taken as a whole, there is plenty of rewarding music on the collection (including "The Truth," "The Shampoo," "A Little 3/4 for God & Co.", and "With These

Hands"), but McCann's vocalizing and his post-1972 music should not have been neglected. —*Scott Yanow*

Les McCann Sings / Aug. 1961 / Pacific Jazz ✦✦✦✦
A super set with Ben Webster (ts) and Groove Holmes on organ. Soul-jazz and blues at their best. —*Ron Wynn*

● **Les McCann Ltd. in New York** / Dec. 1961 / Pacific Jazz ✦✦✦✦
1989 reissue; with hot tenor from Stanley Turrentine. —*Ron Wynn*

★ **Much Les** / Jul. 22, 1968-Jul. 24, 1968 / Atlantic ✦✦✦✦✦
This straight CD reissue of an Atlantic LP offers one a pretty definitive look at Les McCann in his prime. The pianist/singer develops long, funky vamps (but swings, sings "With These Hands," and, even with a string section added to four of the six numbers and three also having two percussionists, the emphasis is on McCann's trio with bassist Leroy Vinnegar and drummer Donald Dean. This is high-quality and intelligent groove music. —*Scott Yanow*

Layers / Nov. 1972 / Atlantic ✦✦

On the Soul Side / Jan. 1994 / Music Masters ✦✦✦✦

★ **Swiss Movement: Montreux 30th Anniversary Edition** / 1996 / Rhino ✦✦✦✦✦
One of the most popular soul-jazz albums of all time, and one of the best, although Harris (and trumpeter Benny Bailey) had never played or rehearsed with the Les McCann Trio before, and indeed weren't even given the music. Perhaps that sparked the spontaneous funk that comes through clearly on the tape of this show, recorded at the Montreux Festival in 1969. It's actually much more of a showcase for McCann than Harris, although the tenor saxist's contributions are significant. The sole vocal, a version of Gene McDaniels' "Compared to What", remains McCann's signature tune. It's worth picking up Rhino's "Montreux 30th Anniversary Edition," as it adds a nine-minute bonus track ("Kaftan") and historical liner notes. —*Richie Unterberger*

Rob McConnell

b. Feb. 14, 1935, London, Ontario
Trombone / Bop, Swing
Although it has always been a part-time venture (working maybe 30 days a year counting an annual recording), Rob McConnell's Boss Brass has been one of the finest big bands since the mid-'70s. An excellent soloist, McConnell has played valve trombone in Toronto (both in the studios and in jazz settings) for nearly four decades. During 1965-69 he was in Nimmons 'n' Nine Plus Six (led by Phil Nimmons) and in 1968 formed the Boss Brass. Originally the group was composed entirely of brass instruments plus a rhythm section and emphasized pop music. Although it added a saxophone section in 1971, the Boss Brass did not record much jazz until 1976. Comprising many of Toronto's top musicians (including Sam Noto, Guido Basso, Ian McDougall, Moe Koffman, Eugene Amaro, Rick Wilkins, Ed Bickert, Don Thompson, and Terry Clarke, among others), the orchestra mostly plays McConnell's swinging but surprising charts. For a period in the late '80s McConnell moved to Los Angeles and the group broke up, but by 1991 it was back together again. Rob McConnell, who has also cut a few small-group dates for Concord, has recorded with his Boss Brass for Pausa, MPS, Dark Orchid, Innovation, and Concord. —*Scott Yanow*

Boss Brass & Woods / Mar. 11, 1985-Mar. 12, 1985 / MCA ✦✦✦✦
Potent solos by Phil Woods (as), excellent playing by Canada's premier big band. Four standards, one each by saxophonist Rick Wilkins, Quincy Jones, two by leader. 23 pieces working as one. Great solos from Guido Basso, Jan McDougal, and Ed Bickert. —*Michael G. Nastos*

The Jive 5 / Aug. 1990 / Concord Jazz ✦✦✦✦
A fine session in swing/traditional style. —*Ron Wynn*

● **The Brass Is Back** / Jan. 28, 1991-Jan. 29, 1991 / Concord Jazz ✦✦✦✦
More emphasis on post-bop from composers Silver and Kai Winding. Tunes from Don Thompson, R. Wilkins, Roger Kellaway, and McConnell. Two standards. —*Michael G. Nastos*

★ **Our 25th Year** / Mar. 1993 / Concord Jazz ✦✦✦✦✦
Rob McConnell's Boss Brass has produced 25 years of solid music making, most in the swinging bebop tradition. The music on this Concord CD has more than its share of surprises such as a bar of 3/4 put in one chorus of "4 B.C.," phrases "borrowed" from Bob Florence and inserted in "Riffs I Have Known," and an inventive version of "Flying Home." Among the other high points are trumpeter Guido Basso's feature on "Imagination," Eugene Amaro's tenor on "What Am I Here For," and a driving "Broadway." This solid effort is recommended to big-band fans. —*Scott Yanow*

Trio Sketches / May 20, 1993-May 21, 1993 / Concord Jazz ✦✦✦✦
The trio of valve trombonist Rob McConnell, guitarist Ed Bickert, and bassist Neil Swainson creates mellow and melodic bop-based music. While Bickert has one of the quietest guitar sounds around and Swainson is often content to play softly in the background, McConnell's cool tone and accessible style are often in the lead. The results are predictably swinging with plenty of subtle interplay. —*Scott Yanow*

Susannah McCorkle

Vocals / Standards

One of the finest interpreters of lyrics who was active in the jazz world during the '80s and '90s, Susannah McCorkle does not improvise all that much, but she brings the proper emotional intensity to the words she sings; a lyricist's dream! She moved to England in 1971 where she worked with Dick Sudhalter and Keith Ingham, among others, performing at concerts with such visiting Americans as Bobby Hackett, Ben Webster, and Dexter Gordon. McCorkle sang at the Riverboat jazz room in Manhattan during 1975 (gaining a lot of attention) and recorded two albums in England (tributes to Harry Warren and Johnny Mercer) that were released domestically by Inner City. By 1980 she was back in the US, recording a Yip Harburg set and a fourth album for Inner City. After that label folded, McCorkle switched over to Pausa but by the late '80s was recording regularly for Concord. She has expanded her pre-bop repertoire to include Brazilian songs and blues, and in the mid-'90s Susannah McCorkle is at the top of her field. —*Scott Yanow*

★ **No More Blues** / Oct. 1988 / Concord Jazz ✦✦✦✦✦
A good vocalist. Her records are solid, though seldom ambitious. CD version has two bonus cuts. —*Ron Wynn*

Sabia / Feb. 1990 / Concord Jazz ✦✦✦

● **I'll Take Romance** / Sep. 15, 1991-Sep. 17, 1991 / Concord Jazz ✦✦✦✦
Her latest. CD has two bonus cuts. —*Ron Wynn*

From Broadway to Bebop / 1994 / Concord Jazz ✦✦✦✦

Easy to Love / Sep. 6, 1995-Sep. 8, 1995 / Concord Jazz ✦✦✦✦

Jack McDuff (Eugene McDuffy)

b. Sep. 17, 1926, Champaign, IL

Organ / Soul-Jazz, Hard Bop, Groove

A marvelous bandleader and organist as well as capable arranger, "Brother" Jack McDuff has one of the funkiest, most soulful styles of all time on the Hammond B-3. His rock-solid bass lines and blues-drenched solos are balanced by clever, almost pianistic melodies and interesting progressions and phrases. McDuff began as a bassist playing with Denny Zeitlin and Joe Farrell. He studied privately in Cincinnati and worked with Johnny Griffin in Chicago. He taught himself organ and piano in the mid-'50s, and began gaining attention working with Willis Jackson in the late '50s and early '60s, cutting high-caliber soul-jazz dates for Prestige. McDuff made his recording debut as a leader for Prestige in 1960, playing in a studio pickup band with Jimmy Forrest. They made a pair of outstanding albums, *Tough Duff* and *The Honeydripper*. McDuff organized his own band the next year, featuring Harold Vick and drummer Joe Dukes. Things took off when McDuff hired a young guitarist named George Benson. They were among the most popular combos of the mid-'60s, and made several excellent albums. McDuff's later groups at Atlantic and Cadet didn't equal the level of the Benson band, while later dates for Verve and Cadet were uneven, though generally good. McDuff experimented with electronic keyboards and fusion during the '70s, then in the '80s got back in the groove with the Muse *Cap'n Jack*. Other musicians McDuff played with in the '60s and '70s include Joe Henderson, Pat Martino, Jimmy Witherspoon, David "Fathead" Newman, Rahsaan Roland Kirk, Sonny Stitt, and Gene Ammons. There are only a few McDuff sessions available on CD, though they include the fine sessions with Forrest. His work with Benson has also been reissued on CD. —*Ron Wynn and Bob Porter*

Rock Candy / Jan. 25, 1960-Oct. 3, 1963 / Prestige ✦✦✦
A '90 compilation covering sessions that Jack McDuff recorded for Prestige in the early '60s, many of which included guitarist George Benson. It also includes material from McDuff's 1960 debut session on Prestige. Gene Ammons and Jimmy Forrest are also featured on some tracks. —*Ron Wynn*

Tough 'Duff / Jul. 12, 1960 / Original Jazz Classics ✦✦✦✦
McDuff's second lead session for Prestige. Good small-group Hammond organ funk—provided you like vibes, which is not a usual funk instrument. The title cut is excellent. Jimmy Forrest (ts) is in top form here. With Lem Winchester (vib). —*Michael Erlewine*

The Honeydripper / Feb. 3, 1961 / Original Jazz Classics ✦✦✦✦
Pure soul-jazz. This is first-rate jazz-funk, perhaps a little more bluesy than average—which is nice. His third album includes Grant Green on guitar and Jimmy Forrest on tenor sax. Just excellent. —*Michael Erlewine*

Goodnight, It's Time to Go / Jul. 14, 1961 / Prestige ✦✦✦
McDuff on the Hammond B-3 along with Grant Green on guitar and Harold Vick on tenor sax. What more could you ask for? —*Michael Erlewine*

On with It / Dec. 1, 1961 / Prestige ✦✦✦
McDuff on the Hammond B-3 along with Grant Green on guitar and Harold Vick on tenor sax. Classic soul-jazz grooves. —*Michael Erlewine*

● **Brother Jack Meets the Boss** / Jan. 23, 1962 / Original Jazz Classics ✦✦✦✦
straightahead bop with some funky organ. A one-time occurrence. A young McDuff recorded within months of the start of his rise to fame. —*Michael Erlewine*

Mellow Gravy / Jan. 23, 1962 / Prestige ✦✦✦
Smoking Gene Ammons (ts) and the great Hammond B-3 from McDuff. —*Ron Wynn*

Best of Sonny Stitt with Jack Mc Duff / Feb. 16, 1962+Sep. 17, 1963 / Prestige ✦✦✦
Jack McDuff and Sonny Stitt? You bet. I'll buy that anytime. Some nasty stuff. —*Michael Erlewine*

Screamin' / Oct. 23, 1962 / Original Jazz Classics ✦✦✦✦
Organist Jack McDuff teams up with his regular drummer Joe Dukes, altoist Leo Wright, and guitarist Kenny Burrell for a spirited blues-oriented set that has been reissued on CD in the OJC series. "Soulful Drums," featuring Dukes' drum breaks, was a minor hit. Other selections on this generally fine organ date include spirited versions of "He's a Real Gone Guy," "After Hours," and "One O'Clock Jump" even if the title cut does not quite live up to its name! —*Scott Yanow*

Somethin' Slick / Jan. 8, 1963 / Prestige ✦✦✦
McDuff with Kenny Burrell on guitar and Harold Vick on tenor sax. —*Michael Erlewine*

Crash! / Jan. 8, 1963+Feb. 26, 1963 / Prestige ✦✦✦✦
Organist Jack McDuff has long had a powerful style, and the two former LPs that are combined on this single CD offer some strong examples of his accessible playing. In both cases McDuff is joined by guitarist Kenny Burrell (in fact, one of the two sets was originally under Burrell's name), drummer Joe Dukes, and occasionally Ray Barretto on congas. In addition, Harold Vick is on tenor for most selections, and Eric Dixon guests on tenor and flute during three songs. Highlights include a driving "How High the Moon," "Love Walked In," and a pair of original blues: "Smut" and "Our Miss Brooks." McDuff and Burrell work together quite well. This 76-minute CD is easily recommended to fans of the jazz organ. —*Scott Yanow*

★ **Live!** / Jun. 5, 1963 / Prestige ✦✦✦✦✦
Good as organist Jack McDuff's studio recordings are from the early '60s, it is his live sets that are truly exciting. This single CD combines together two former in-concert LPs and find McDuff leading a very strong group that features the young guitarist George Benson, tenorman Red Holloway, drummer Joe Dukes, and on a few numbers the second tenor of Harold Vick. The material (cooking blues, standards, Latin numbers, and originals) has plenty of variety and drive, McDuff really pushes Benson and Holloway, and the music is both accessible and creative. —*Scott Yanow*

Best of Brother Jack McDuff / Jun. 5, 1963-Jul. 1964 / Prestige ✦✦✦
Textbook soul-jazz from a founding father. Organist Brother Jack McDuff didn't invent the bluesy, riff-and backbeat-laden instrumental style called soul-jazz, but he sure helped make it popular. This anthology contains some early '60s McDuff material, including some tracks with guitarist George Benson. You can get all this somewhere else, but as a sampler or introductory package, it's a good collection. —*Ron Wynn*

Dynamic! / Feb. 6, 1964-Feb. 7, 1964 / Prestige ✦✦✦

Live It Up / 1967 / Sugar Hill ✦✦✦
Steaming soul-jazz, funk, blues, and ballads keyed by the whirling, soulful solos, bass pedal work, and direction of organist Jack McDuff. This was one of four fine albums he did for Atlantic in 1966 and 1967. —*Ron Wynn*

Moon Rappin' / Dec. 3, 1969-Dec. 11, 1969 / Blue Note ✦✦✦

★ **The Heating System** / 1971 / Cadet ✦✦✦✦✦
Plenty of funk, sax-wallop, and organ soul. —*Ron Wynn*

The Re-Entry / Mar. 1988 / Muse ✦✦✦✦
A late-'80s return to the sound of earlier recordings, it features Houston Person (ts). Not inspired, it's still a solid performance all around. —*Bob Porter*

Color Me Blue / May 1991+Mar. 1992 / Concord Jazz ✦✦✦✦
Recent cuts showing that organist Jack McDuff can still stomp through bluesy wailers, pound the bass pedals, and lead a hot combo through funky, exuberant numbers. He's heading a group with former band members like guitarist George Benson and drummer Joe Dukes, plus saxophonist Red Holloway, guitarist Ron Eschete, and Phil Upchurch, among others. —*Ron Wynn*

Write On, Capt'n / 1993 / Concord Jazz ✦✦✦

Bobby McFerrin

b. Mar. 11, 1950, New York, NY

Vocals / Bop, Pop, Post-Bop

A truly remarkable singer, Bobby McFerrin's ability to make rhythmic sounds while inhaling makes his vocals into nonstop flights of constant creativity. By alternating falsetto quickly with deep bass notes (and somehow not getting lost!), McFerrin can sound like two or three singers at once. His quick reactions and wide knowledge of musical styles plus a strong wit make his solo performances not only remarkable but hugely entertaining. Despite all of that, Bobby McFerrin's career has not yet lived up to his enormous potential. The son of opera singers, McFerrin was trained as a pianist but by 1977 he had shifted to singing. He worked for a time with Jon Hendricks and then recorded his debut for Elektra Musician in 1982. In 1983 he started doing concerts featuring his unaccompanied solos, and his 1984 release *The Voice* is still his finest recording. In 1988 McFerrin had a fluke hit with "Don't Worry, Be Happy" (which was actually on one of his weaker albums) and he seemed somewhat embarassed by his unexpected commercial success. He maintained a much lower profile, conducting classical orchestras (why?), forming a thus far unrecorded "Voicestra" with other singers, and recording on only an infrequent basis for EMI and Blue Note; a joke-filled encounter with Chick Corea was often closer to performance art than to jazz. Bobby McFerrin is still a major name but not the influential force (and poll-winner) that he should be. —*Scott Yanow*

Bobby McFerrin / 1982 / Elektra ✦✦✦✦
McFerrin's debut, which shocked, rocked, and amazed everyone. —*Ron Wynn*

★ **The Voice** / Mar. 17, 1984-Mar. 26, 1984 / Elektra ✦✦✦✦✦
The Voice was a milestone in jazz history; it was the first time a jazz singer had recorded an entire album solo, without accompaniment or overdubbing, for a major label. Bobby McFerrin's amazing ability to switch back and forth between bass notes and falsetto, along with his talent for jumping octaves made this record quite a virtuoso showcase. For those interested in the potential of the human voice and in an important jazz talent, *The Voice* is recommended without reservations. —*Scott Yanow*

Spontaneous Inventions / 1985 / Blue Note ✦✦✦✦
More superb vocal gymnastics are included, on everyone from the Beatles to Dizzy Gillespie. —*Hank Davis*

Simple Pleasures / 1988 / EMI ✦✦✦✦
The breakthrough album contains the mega hit "Don't Worry, Be Happy" and other gems like "Drive My Car." —*Hank Davis*

Don't Worry, Be Happy / 1988 / EMI ✦✦✦

Medicine Music / 1990 / EMI ✦✦

Play / Jun. 23, 1990 / Blue Note ✦✦✦

Hush / Aug. 1991 / Columbia ✦✦✦

Bang! Zoom / 1995 / Blue Note ✦✦

Howard McGhee

b. 1918, **d.** 1987
Trumpet / Bop, Hard Bop
During 1945-49 Howard McGhee was one of the finest trumpeters in jazz, an exciting performer with a sound of his own who among the young bop players ranked at the top with Dizzy Gillespie and Fats Navarro. The "missing link" between Roy Eldridge and Fats Navarro (Navarro influenced Clifford Brown who influenced most of the post-1955 trumpeters), McGhee originally played clarinet and tenor, not taking up trumpet until he was 17. He worked in territory bands, was with Lionel Hampton in 1941, and then joined Andy Kirk (1941-42), being featured on "McGhee Special." McGhee participated in the fabled bop sessions at Minton's Playhouse and Monroe's Uptown House, modernizing his style away from Roy Eldridge and toward Dizzy Gillespie. He was with Charlie Barnet (1942-43), returned to Kirk (where he sat next to Fats Navarro in the trumpet section), and had brief stints with Georgie Auld and Count Basie before traveling to California with Coleman Hawkins in 1945; their concise recordings of swing-to-bop transitional music (including "Stuffy," "Rifftide," and "Hollywood Stampede") are classic. McGhee stayed in California into 1947, playing with Jazz at the Philharmonic, recording and gigging with Charlie Parker (including the ill-fated "Lover Man" date), and having an influence on young players out on the Coast. His Dial sessions were among the most exciting recordings of his career, and back in New York he recorded for Savoy and had a historic meeting on record with Navarro (1948 on Blue Note).

However, drugs began to adversely affect Howard McGhee's career. He traveled on a USO tour during the Korean War, recording in Guam. McGhee also had sessions for Bethlehem (1955-56) but was inactive during much of the '50s. He recorded some strong dates for Felsted, Bethlehem, Contemporary, and Black Lion during 1960-61, and a quartet outing for United Artists (1962) but (with the exception of a Hep big-band date in 1966) was largely off records again until 1976. He had a final burst of activity during 1976-79 for Sonet, SteepleChase, Jazzcraft, Zim, and Storyville, but by then McGhee was largely forgotten and few knew about his link to Fats Navarro and Clifford Brown. —*Scott Yanow*

South Pacific Jazz / Jan. 17, 1952 / Savoy ✦✦✦

● **Maggie's Back in Town** / Jun. 26, 1961 / Original Jazz Classics ✦✦✦✦
Trumpeter Howard McGhee's date was a rather common outing made interesting because of the quality of the individuals. Maggie (McGhee) was

in good command; his rumpled style of playing always seemed to have direction and purpose and rarely dipped into predictable phrasing. Bassist Leroy Vinnegar and drummer Shelly Manne were as you would expect—solid. The added plus was pianist Phineas Newborn, whose quixotic playing provided a strong second voice, adding unexpected zing. —*Bob Rusch, Cadence*

Young at Heart / Oct. 4, 1979-Oct. 6, 1979 / Storyville ✦✦✦
A welcome appearance by Teddy Edwards (ts). —*Ron Wynn*

Wise in Time / Oct. 1979 / Storyville ✦✦

Chris McGregor

b. Dec. 24, 1936, Umtata, South Africa, **d.** May 26, 1990
Piano / Avant-Garde
A revered and respected bandleader and pianist, South African Chris McGregor's life was changed forever hearing the hymns of the Xhosa people in his father's church of Scotland mission. He'd eventually depart his South African homeland in protest against apartheid, and lead several seminal ensembles of expatriate South Africans. McGregor selected several great players at the 1962 Johannesburg Jazz Festival, among them Mongezi Fesa, Dudu Pukwana, and Johnny Dyani, to be in a new band. The Blue Notes as an integrated band were anathema in '60s South Africa, which was ruled by strict apartheid. They left the country in the early '60s on a European tour and never returned. They remained in Switzerland for a year, then moved to London. McGregor led at various times the Chris McGregor Group and the Brotherhood of Breath. This was an African version of Sun Ra's Arkestra or Cecil Taylor's large orchestra, mixing free and avant-garde arrangements with township jive and other African styles. They developed out of a series of big-band concerts McGregor had been presenting weekly at Ronnie Scott's club. McGregor moved to France in the mid-'70s and did solo dates, but periodically revived the Brotherhood of Breath. Its ranks at one time included Pukwana, Fezi, Dyani, and Louis Moholo. McGregor died in 1990 of lung cancer. —*Ron Wynn*

★ **And the Brotherhood of Breath** / Oct. 1970 / Neon ✦✦✦✦✦
Studio release with excellent compositions, particularly "The Bride." —*Michael G. Nastos*

Live at Willisau / Jan. 27, 1973 / Ogun ✦✦✦✦
The pianist/leader with an 11-piece band of South African expatriates and English free-jazz men. Explosive. —*Michael G. Nastos*

Jimmy McGriff

b. Apr. 3, 1936, Philadelphia, PA
Organ / Soul-Jazz, Hard Bop, Groove
The finest blues soloist among organists, Jimmy McGriff can also play superb soul-jazz, though he's turned in dreary performances on fusion and pop dates in the '70s. McGriff studied bass, drums, tenor sax, and vibes in his teens and attended Combe College of Music in Philadelphia and Juilliard. McGriff later studied electric organ with Jimmy Smith, Milt Buckner, and Groove Holmes. His debut record *I Got A Woman* for Sue was a Top 20 hit in 1962, and he followed it with *All About My Girl* and *Kiko* in 1963 and 1964. McGriff began a long relationship with producer Sonny Lester in 1966, when he joined Solid State Records. The two later teamed at Blue Note, Capitol, Groove Merchant, and LRC. McGriff recorded many fine organ combo sides while also cutting R&B-tinged work during the '60s. He had a huge hit with "The Worm" in '68 and '69, but also made the LP *The Big Band*, a stirring tribute to Count Basie. During the '70s McGriff made more solid small combo jazz dates, including some organ battles with Groove Holmes. But he also did trendy material utilizing multiple electronic keyboards. He didn't distinguish himself on several later LRC sessions. McGriff's earlier Groove Merchant recordings were his best in this period. McGriff, like Hank Crawford, got back to basics when he signed with Milestone in 1980. He's done several dates with Hank Crawford and played with Al Grey. McGriff's early '90s Headfirst sessions mix electronic fusion material with organ jazz. —*Ron Wynn and Bob Porter*

★ **At the Apollo** / 1963 / Collectables ✦✦✦✦✦
The third album from McGriff on the Sue label was recorded live at New York's Apollo Theater in 1963. It features McGriff with Rudolph Johnson on tenor sax, Larry Frazier on guitar, and Willie Jenkins on drums. Contains a great version of "Red Sails in the Sunset" and "A Thing for Jug." —*Michael Erlewine*

☆ **I've Got a Woman** / 1963 / Collectables ✦✦✦✦✦
McGriff's first album is great. The title cut was in the Top 20 in 1962. Also on the same album is "M.G. Blues" and "All About My Girl." This session includes McGriff, Richard Easley on drums and Walter Miller on guitar. High-impact early McGriff is the still the best, and this is the album that started it all, on the Sue label. Three cuts available on the collectable CD *A Toast to Jimmy McGriff's Golden Classics.* —*Michael Erlewine*

Jimmy McGriff at the Organ / 1963 / Sue ✦✦✦
McGriff with Rudolph Johnson on soprano and tenor sax, Larry Frazier on guitar, and Jimmie Smith on drums. This album contains the classic

McGriff cut "Kiko," "That's All," and "Hello Betty". This is drum/sax driven McGriff at his best. —*Michael Erlewine*

Topkapi / 1964-1965 / Sue ✦✦✦
This finds McGriff with pre-recorded tracks with a horn section, guitar, bass, drums, and a string section. The material was arranged and directed by Fred Norman. The album consists of 12 movie and TV themes with McGriff and "orchestra." The orchestra sounds like Musak, but McGriff sounds like McGriff. How the two got together beats me. —*Michael Erlewine*

Blues for Mister Jimmy / 1965 / Collectables ✦✦✦
His last date for the Sue label is a trio, McGriff with Larry Frazier on guitar and Jimmie Smith on drums. Nine bluesy tunes including "Turn Blue," a classic McGriff instrumental. —*Michael Erlewine*

Tribute to Basie / 1966 / Lrc Jazz Classics ✦✦✦
Recorded in 1966 with the Jimmy McGriff Big Band, and it is a very large group. At the center of all these instruments is the one-man band organ sound of McGriff. This is a salute to Count Basie and includes ten songs that he wrote or made a part of his repetoire. Actually, this works quite well. —*Michael Erlewine*

A Bag Full of Soul / 1966 / Solid State ✦✦✦

The Worm / Sep. 1968 / Solid State ✦✦✦

Electric Funk / Sep. 1969 / Blue Note ✦✦
With Stanley Turrentine on tenor sax. —*Michael Erlewine*

Come Together / 1973 / Groove Merchant ✦✦
McGriff and Richard Groove Holmes on the same ticket. —*Michael Erlewine*

Main Squeeze / 1976 / Groove Merchant ✦✦✦
McGriff with the funky guitar of Jimmy Ponder and Connie Lester on alto sax. —*Michael Erlewine*

Countdown / Apr. 27, 1983-Apr. 28, 1983 / Milestone ✦✦✦✦
His first for Milestone. Produced by Bob Porter, McGriff with two saxes, trombone, guitar, and drums for what the liner notes call a "big band sound" combo. Plenty of good funky organ. Some of the numbers are a little too smooth (too many horns) for my taste. —*Michael Erlewine*

Skywalk / Mar. 19, 1984-Mar. 20, 1984 / Milestone ✦✦✦
McGriff sometimes veers away from his soul-jazz strength, but it's still a fine set overall. —*Ron Wynn*

The Starting Five / Oct. 14, 1986-Oct. 15, 1986 / Milestone ✦✦✦✦
Here is McGriff with two terrific blues honkin' sax masters—Rusty Bryant and David "Fathead" Newman. Add Mel Brown and Wayne Boyd on guitar plus Bernard Purdie on drums and you have a recipe for funk. Produced by Bob Porter, this is perhaps the best of McGriff's Milestone output. —*Michael Erlewine*

Blue to the Bone / Jul. 19, 1988-Jul. 20, 1988 / Milestone ✦✦✦✦
McGriff with Bill Easley on sax, Melvin Sparks on guitar, Bernard Purdie on drums, and Al Grey on trombone. The trombone is not that often found in the small-organ combo format and may not appeal to everyone. Smooth, yet funky. —*Michael Erlewine & Ron Wynn.*

You Ought to Think / 1990 / Headfirst ✦✦✦

On the Blue Side / May 1990 / Milestone ✦✦✦✦
An updated version of the vintage McGriff formula: bluesy, soulful organ fare with a balance struck between jazz sensibility and a funk/R&B groove. —*Ron Wynn*

In a Blue Mood / 1991 / K-Tel ✦✦
One of his albums on Headfirst, after leaving Milestone and the great production work of Bob Porter. McGriff on organ and keyboards plus a group with synthesizers, sax, guitar, drums, vocals, and what-not make this more pop-oriented fare than organ funk. Where's Bob Porter when you need him. —*Michael Erlewine*

● **Right Turn On Blues** / Jan. 22, 1994-Jan. 23, 1994 / Telarc ✦✦✦✦
There was virtually no prior planning for this meeting between organist Jimmy McGriff and altoist Hank Crawford but none was needed. The veterans had already recorded four prior albums together, so they simply jammed through blues, ballads, and a few basic originals without any difficulty; Crawford could play this material blindfolded. McGriff sets the grooves expertly with his foot-pedal basswork with assistance from guitarist Rodney Jones and drummer Jesse Hameen. The overall result is a happy and enthusiastic session of foot-tapping music. No real surprises occur but lovers of hard-swinging organ combos have nothing to complain about. —*Scott Yanow*

Blues Groove / Jul. 21, 1995-Jul. 22, 1995 / Telarc ✦✦✦✦
Organist Jimmy McGriff and altoist Hank Crawford always make for a potent team. With guitarist Wayne Boyd and drummer Vance James completing the quartet, McGriff and Crawford explore an appealing mixture of blues, soulful ballads, and riff tunes. Few surprises occur but many of the songs (particularly "Movin' Upside the Blues," "The Sermon," "When I Fall in Love" and "Mercy, Mercy, Mercy") are fairly memorable. The fans of these fine players will not be disappointed. —*Scott Yanow*

Funkiest Little Band in the Land / Lrc Jazz Classics ✦✦✦
This is a collection of McGriff with small bands from 1968 to 1974, before he went to the large orchestra format. Produced by Sonny Lester, many of these appeared on the Groove Merchant label. Includes a lot of funky stuff with titles like "Super Funk," "Fat Cakes," "Groove Fly," and "Dig On it." There are 13 cuts and plenty of vintage McGriff. —*Michael Erlewine*

Georgia on My Mind / Lrc Jazz Classics ✦✦✦
This is a compilation of sixteen selections from six sessions in the late '60s and early '70s, tunes from McGriff albums like *Let's Stay Together* (1966 and 1972 versions), *Fly Dude* (1972), and *Groove Grease* (1971). All small or smallish combos. Mostly standards; some few kickers. —*Michael Erlewine*

Toast to Golden Classics / Collectables ✦✦✦✦
This is a compilation of ten cuts taken from the six early Sue albums, one or two from each. The sound is bad, but it will give you a taste of the Sue material—all the best cuts. These early Sue albums are now all available on collectables and worth hearing, despite the sound. —*Michael Erlewine*

Ken McIntyre

b. Sep. 7, 1931, Boston, MA
Flute, Bassoon, Clarinet (Bass), Oboe, Sax (Tenor) / Avant-Garde, Post-Bop
A versatile player with a thoughtful style who can play quite freely, Ken McIntyre has never been a major name in jazz despite his talents. After serving in the military and graduating from the Boston Conservatory, he arrived in New York in 1960 and made a strong impression. He recorded two albums for New Jazz (including one in which he held his own against Eric Dolphy). McIntyre also led two now-scarce records for United Artists during 1962-63 (including one titled *Way Way Out*) but became involved in education, teaching in the public schools starting in 1961. He continued playing on a part-time basis (recording with Cecil Taylor in 1966). McIntyre led five albums for SteepleChase during 1974-78 including his definitive set Hindsight (which finds him spotlighting each of his five horns in a quartet). He also recorded with Craig Harris in 1983 and put together an Eric Dolphy tribute set for Serene in 1991, but McIntyre has never achieved the recognition he deserved. —*Scott Yanow*

● **Stone Blues** / May 31, 1960 / Original Jazz Classics ✦✦✦✦
This early effort by Ken McIntyre (who doubles here on alto and flute) grows in interest with each listen. On a couple of his six originals (including a song called "Cornballs"), McIntyre slides humorously between notes, but other selections are much more serious. McIntyre's sidemen are now somewhat obscure (trombonist John Mancebo Lewis, pianist Dizzy Sal, bassist Paul Morrison, and drummer Bobby Ward) but they fit well into his conception which at this early stage was essentially advanced bop slightly influenced by the "new thing" music of Ornette Coleman. This interesting set has been reissued on CD. —*Scott Yanow*

★ **Hindsight** / Jan. 13, 1974 / SteepleChase ✦✦✦✦✦
Ken McIntyre had not recorded as a leader in 11 years when he cut this quartet set for SteepleChase, but he was more than ready. The well rounded program (which on the CD reissue includes a second version of "Body and Soul") features McIntyre on separate features for his alto, flute, bassoon, oboe and bass clarinet. Although often compared to Eric Dolphy early in his career, McIntyre actually has a style of his own, open to the innovations of the avant-garde but not shy to embrace melodies. With the assistance of pianist Kenny Drew, bassist Bo Stief, and drummer Alex Riel, McIntyre is in consistently brilliant form with the highlights being "Lush Life" (on bassoon), "Body and Soul" (taken on bass clarinet), "Naima" (for his oboe), and a heated alto workout on "Sunnymoon for Two." —*Scott Yanow*

Dave McKenna

b. May 30, 1930, Woonsocket, RI
Piano / Swing
One of the top swing-based pianists of the past 25 years, Dave McKenna's hard-driving bass lines give momentum to uptempo pieces and his vast knowledge of superior songs from the '30s has resulted in many rewarding albums of traditional but fresh music. Although talented from the start, McKenna did not achieve that much recognition until he was 40 years old. He joined the Musicians' Union when he was 15 and picked up early experience playing with Boots Mussulli (1947), Charlie Ventura (1949), and Woody Herman's Orchestra (1950-51). After two years in the military, McKenna had a second stint with Ventura (1953-54) and then worked with a variety of top swing and Dixieland players including Gene Krupa, Stan Getz, Zoot Sims, Al Cohn, Eddie Condon, Bobby Hackett, and Bob Wilber (in the late '70s) and was a soloist at piano bars in Massachusetts. McKenna had recorded for ABC-Paramount (1956), Epic (1958), Bethlehem (a two-piano date shared with Hall Overton in 1960), and Realm (1963) but in 1973 McKenna's talents finally began to be more fully documented. He led sets for Halcyon, Shiah, Famous Door, Inner City (with vocalist Teddi King), and four for Chiaroscuro. And then in 1979 with *No Bass Hit* (a trio date

with Scott Hamilton and Jake Hanna), McKenna debuted with Concord, finding his home. He has made many sessions for Concord ever since, some as a sideman or with small groups but the best ones are unaccompanied recitals. In the mid-'90s Dave McKenna is at the top of his field. —*Scott Yanow*

Solo Piano / Feb. 24, 1973 / Chiaroscuro ✦✦✦

★ **Dancing in the Dark** / Aug. 1985 / Concord Jazz ✦✦✦✦✦
The great swing pianist Dave McKenna performs 11 selections written by Arthur Schwartz, one of the lesser-known (but very talented) songwriters of the golden age of American popular music. Among the pieces that McKenna joyfully revives are "By Myself," "A Shine on Your Shoes," "I Guess I'll Have to Change My Plan," and "Dancing in the Dark." Happy melodic treatments of classic music. —*Scott Yanow*

My Friend the Piano / Aug. 1986 / Concord Jazz ✦✦✦✦
Pianist Dave McKenna fills *My Friend the Piano* with constant surprises; rhythm, tempo, and key changes that somehow seem logical after the fact. There is a slight emphasis on ballads, but one's attention rarely wanders for the music, although tasteful, is never entirely predictable. —*Scott Yanow*

No More Ouzo for Puzo / Jun. 1988 / Concord Jazz ✦✦✦✦
Recorded by a quartet with guitarist Gray Sargent. The title piece was written by McKenna, the rest all standards treated with tender loving care. —*Michael G. Nastos*

★ **Live at Maybeck Recital Hall, Vol. 2** / Nov. 1989 / Concord Jazz ✦✦✦✦✦
Fine technique, wonderful melodies. —*Ron Wynn*

Shadows 'N Dreams / Mar. 1990 / Concord Jazz ✦✦✦✦
As usual, McKenna's playing ranges from good to great. —*Ron Wynn*

A Handful of Stars / Jun. 15, 1992 / Concord Jazz ✦✦✦✦

Concord Duo Series, Vol. 2 / Dec. 16, 1992 / Concord Jazz ✦✦✦✦

Easy Street / May 6, 1994 & May 18, 1994 / Concord Jazz ✦✦✦✦
The perfect way to hear pianist Dave McKenna is on his solo records; fortunately he has recorded quite a few for Concord. McKenna enjoys performing sets of music with thematic titles. The first seven songs on this date all have something to do with a street (from "Broadway" and "Basin Street Blues" to "Street of Dreams" and "On the Street Where You Live"). After playing his original "Cat's Cradle" and "My Honey's Lovin' Arms," McKenna performs four songs with "Gone" in its title before concluding the program with "Theodore the Thumper." McKenna, one of the top swing pianists of the '80s and '90s, features his driving baselines on some of the faster pieces. This is an enjoyable set that gives listeners a strong example of Dave McKenna's talents. —*Scott Yanow*

John McLaughlin

b. Jan. 4, 1942, Yorkshire, England
Guitar / World, Fusion, Post-Bop
A household name since the early '70s, John McLaughlin was an innovative fusion guitarist when he led the Mahavishnu Orchestra and has continued living up to his reputation as a phenomenal and consistently inquisitive player through the years. He started on guitar when he was 11 years old and was initially inspired by blues and swing players. McLaughlin worked with Alexis Korner, Graham Bond, Ginger Baker, and others in the '60s and played free music with Gunter Hampel for six months. His first album was a classic (1969's *Extrapolation*) and was followed by an obscurity for the Dawns label with John Surman, a quintet set with Larry Young (*Devotion*) and *My Goals Beyond* in 1970, which was half acoustic solos and half jams involving Indian musicians.

In 1969 McLaughlin moved to New York to play with Tony Williams' Lifetime and he appeared on two classic Miles Davis records: *In a Silent Way* and *Bitches Brew*. In 1971 McLaughlin formed the Mahavishnu Orchestra, a very powerful group often thought of as rock but having the sophisticated improvisations of jazz. After three influential albums (*The Inner Mounting Flame, Birds of Fire,* and *Between Nothingness and Eternity*), the group broke up in 1973. McLaughlin, who recorded a powerful spiritual album with Carlos Santana that was influenced by John Coltrane, put together a new Mahavishnu Orchestra in 1974 that, despite the inclusion of Jean Luc Ponty, failed to catch on and broke up by 1975. McLaughlin then surprised the music world by radically shifting directions, switching to acoustic guitar and playing Indian music with his group Shakti. They made a strong impact on the world music scene (which was in its infancy) during their three years. Since then McLaughlin has gone back and forth between electric and acoustic guitars, leading the One Truth Band, playing in trios with Al DiMeola and Paco De Lucia, popping up on some mid-'80s Miles Davis records, forming a short-lived third version of the Mahavishnu Orchestra (with saxophonist Bill Evans), recording an introspective tribute to pianist Bill Evans, and in 1993 touring with a rollicking jazz trio featuring Joey DeFrancesco and drummer Dennis Chambers. Throughout his productive career John McLaughlin has recorded as a leader for Marmalade, Dawns, Douglas, Columbia, Warner Bros., and Verve. —*Scott Yanow*

Extrapolation / Jan. 18, 1969 / Polydor ✦✦✦

Devotion / 1970 / Restless ✦✦✦✦
This often-exciting set, John McLaughlin's third as a leader and predating The Mahavishnu Orchestra by just a year, is actually more in the style of Tony Williams' Lifetime than McLaughlin's later groups. That fact is not surprising when one considers that Lifetime's organist Larry Young is an integral part of this rockish but explorative set. None of the individual songs (which also feature bassist Billy Rich and drummer Buddy Miles) caught on, but McLaughlin's guitar style was already becoming distinctive. —*Scott Yanow*

★ **My Goals Beyond** / 1970 / Rykodisc ✦✦✦✦✦
My Goals Beyond ranked among John McLaughlin's finest acoustic guitar projects; it mixed stunning remakes of jazz classics with piercing originals that blended rock energy, jazz technique, and Asian rhythmic patterns. Billy Cobham and Jerry Goodman were later part of the original Mahavishnu Orchestra, and here they demonstrated the empathy they shared with McLaughlin. Dave Liebman's swirling soprano punctuates McLaughlin's brilliant lines on "Peace One" and "Peace Two," while Airto, Badal Roy, and Mahalakshmi found a comfortable meeting place for their Afro-Latin and Indian colorations and beats. —*Ron Wynn*

Between Nothingness & Eternity / Aug. 1973 / Columbia ✦✦✦

Shakti with John McLaughlin / Jul. 5, 1975 / Columbia ✦✦✦✦
Ragas meet jazz. Extraordinary energy. —*Michael G. Nastos*

Electric Guitarist / 1978 / Columbia ✦✦✦✦
1990 reissue of a date with Carlos Santana (g), Chick Corea (k), and Jack Bruce (b). —*Ron Wynn*

Electric Dreams / Nov. 1978-Dec. 1978 / Columbia ✦✦✦

● **Friday Night in San Francisco** / Nov. 1981 / Columbia ✦✦✦✦

Passion, Grace, and Fire / Oct. 1982-Nov. 1982 / Columbia ✦✦✦✦
Two years after they recorded *Friday Night in San Francisco,* John McLaughlin, Al DiMeola, and Paco De Lucia reunited for another set of acoustic guitar trios. If this can be considered a guitar "battle" (some of the playing is ferocious and these speed demons do not let up too often), then the result is a three-way tie. This guitar summit lives up to its title. —*Scott Yanow*

Time Remembered: John McLaughlin Plays Bill Evans / Mar. 25, 1993-Mar. 28, 1993 / Verve ✦✦

Tokyo Live / Dec. 16, 1993 & Dec. 18, 1993 / Verve ✦✦✦✦
Although it is tempting to think that the Free Spirits (the trio featured on this CD), due to the similarity of the instrumentation (guitarist John McLaughlin, organist Joey DeFrancesco, and drummer Dennis Chambers), would be an updating of Tony Williams' groundbreaking fusion group Lifetime, the reality is somewhat different. McLaughlin may get top billing but this music sounds very much like a Joey DeFrancesco-led Jimmy Smith revival date with most of the selections being blues-based. There are some introspective moments for the guitarist (who plays strictly electric here) but DeFrancesco dominates the ensembles and takes the lion's share of the solo space. The music is enjoyable enough although none of the compositions (all but Miles Davis' "No Blues" are by McLaughlin) are all that memorable. —*Scott Yanow*

After the Rain / Oct. 4, 1994-Oct. 5, 1994 / Verve ✦✦✦✦

Jackie McLean

b. May 17, 1932, New York, NY
Sax (Alto) / Post-Bop, Hard Bop
Jackie McLean has long had his own sound, played slightly sharp and with great intensity; he is recognizable within two notes. McLean was one of the few post-bop oriented players of the early '50s who explored free jazz in the '60s, widening his emotional range and drawing from the new music qualities that fit his musical personality.

The son of guitarist John McLean (who played guitar with Tiny Bradshaw), Jackie started on alto when he was 15. As a teenager he was friends with such neighbors as Bud Powell, Thelonious Monk, and Sonny Rollins. He made his recording debut with Miles Davis in 1951 and the rest of the decade could be considered his apprenticeship. McLean worked with George Wallington, Charles Mingus, and Art Blakey's Jazz Messengers (1956-58). He also participated on a string of jam session-flavored records for Prestige and New Jazz which, due to the abysmal pay and his plodding style, he has since disowned. Actually they are not bad but pale compared to McLean's classic series of 21 Blue Note albums (1959-67). On sessions such as *One Step Beyond* and *Destination Out,* McLean really stretches and challenges himself; this music is quite original and intense yet logical. McLean also appeared as a sideman on some sessions for Blue Note, acted in the stage play *The Connection* (1959-61) and led his own groups on a regular basis. By 1968 however he was moving into the jazz education field and other than some SteepleChase records from 1972-74 (including two meetings with his early idol Dexter Gordon) and an unfortunate commercial outing for RCA (1978-79), McLean was less active as a player during the '70s. However in the '80s Jackie McLean returned to a more active playing schedule (sometimes with his son Rene McLean on tenor), recording for Triloka and most recently Antilles with all of the intensity and passion of his earlier days. — *Scott Yanow*

Lights Out / Jan. 27, 1956 / Prestige ✦✦✦✦
Altoist Jackie McLean's second session as a leader is reissued on this CD. The music that he makes with trumpeter Donald Byrd, pianist Elmo Hope, bassist Doug Watkins, and drummer Art Taylor is essentially hard bop with fairly simple (or in some cases nonexistent) melody statements preceding two romps through the "I Got Rhythm" chord changes, a pair of blues, a thinly disguised "Embraceable You," and a straightforward version of "A Foggy Day." Enjoyable if not really essential music from the up-and-coming altoist. — *Scott Yanow*

4, 5 and 6 / Jul. 1956 / Prestige ✦✦✦✦
This is a well rounded CD reissue that brings back altoist Jackie McLean's third recording as a leader. McLean has several fine ballad features ("Sentimental Journey," "Why Was I Born," "When I Fall in Love," and Mal Waldron's "Abstraction") welcomes trumpeter Donald Byrd to Kenny Drew's "Contour" and jams on a lengthy version of Charlie Parker's "Confirmation" with a sextet that includes Byrd and tenor saxophonist Hank Mobley. With pianist Waldron, bassist Doug Watkins, and drummer Art Taylor offering fine support, this is a strong hard bop set that is tied to the tradition of bebop while looking forward. — *Scott Yanow*

Jackie's Pal / Aug. 31, 1956 / Prestige ✦✦✦

McLean's Scene / Dec. 4, 1956-Feb. 15, 1957 / Prestige ✦✦✦✦

Jackie McLean and Co. / Feb. 8, 1957 / Prestige ✦✦✦

Strange Blues / Feb. 15, 1957-Aug. 30, 1957 / Prestige ✦✦✦✦
The last of the Jackie McLean Prestige sessions, this CD reissue has material from two different sets, but fortunately, the music is on a higher level than one might expect of "leftovers." "Strange Blues" is from a marathon quartet set that McLean had with pianist Mal Waldron, bassist Arthur Phipps, and drummer Art Taylor as is a rendition of "What's New" that is an alternate version to the one included on *Makin' the Changes*. In addition, "Disciples Love Affair" and "Millie's Pad" match McLean with the tuba of Ray Draper (who contributed both songs), trumpeter Webster Young, pianist John Meyers, bassist Bill Salter, and drummer Larry Ritchie, while the incomplete "Not So Strange Blues" is all McLean on an explosive blues with the rhythm section. A generally strong set chiefly recommended to Jackie McLean completists. — *Scott Yanow*

Alto Madness / May 3, 1957 / Prestige ✦✦✦

A Long Drink of the Blues / Aug. 30, 1957 / Prestige ✦✦✦✦
This CD reissue begins with what is titled "Take 1" of "A Long Drink of the Blues." After a false start, the musicians argue for two minutes about the tempo; why was this ever released? "Take 2" is a much more successful 20-minute jam featuring Jackie McLean (doubling on alto and tenor), trombonist Curtis Fuller, trumpeter Webster Young, pianist Gil Coggins, bassist Paul Chambers, and drummer Louis Hayes. The second half of this reissue is from a quartet session that showcases McLean on three standard ballads with pianist Mal Waldron, bassist Arthur Phipps, and drummer Art Taylor. Although not quite as intense as McLean's later Blue Note dates, the ballad renditions show just how mature and original a soloist he was even at this early stage. Despite "Take 1," this CD is worth getting. — *Scott Yanow*

Makin' the Changes / Aug. 30, 1957 / New Jazz ✦✦✦✦
This CD reissue of a Jackie McLean LP features the altoist in two different settings. On three selections—a rollicking "Bean and the Boys," an uptempo "I Never Knew" and "I Hear a Rhapsody"—McLean teams up with pianist Mal Waldron in a quartet with bassist Arthur Phipps and drummer Art Taylor. The other three numbers ("What's New," "Chasin' the Bird," and McLean's original "Jackie's Ghost") have more of a jam session feel and feature McLean in a sextet with trumpeter Webster Young, trombonist Curtis Fuller, pianist Gil Coggins, bassist Paul Chambers, and drummer Louis Hayes. In general, the hard bop music is swinging and fairly advanced, a step above the usual jam sessions of the time. — *Scott Yanow*

Jackie's Bag / Jan. 18, 1959-Sep. 1, 1960 / Blue Note ✦✦✦✦
This interesting LP was a giant step forward for altoist Jackie McLean, although it was released after a couple of his other Blue Note albums. For the first time, McLean shows the influence of Ornette Coleman—not in his sound but in his improvising approach—and his freer style bridged the gap between hard bop and the avant-garde. Three of the songs, highlighted by "Quadrangle" and "Fidel," match McLean in 1959 with trumpeter Donald Byrd, pianist Sonny Clark, bassist Paul Chambers, and drummer Philly Joe Jones while the other numbers, including "Appointment in Ghana," showcase McLean in a sextet with trumpeter Blue Mitchell, Tina Brooks on tenor, pianist Kenny Drew, Chambers, and drummer Art Taylor. Jackie McLean's Blue Note albums were the most significant of his career, and this LP is well worth searching for. — *Scott Yanow*

New Soil / May 2, 1959 / Blue Note ✦✦✦✦
This CD reissue adds "Formidable," which was first released on the 1980 LP *Vertigo*, to the original program. A quintet date with trumpeter Donald Byrd, pianist Walter Davis, Jr., bassist Paul Chambers, and drummer Pete

La Roca, this music is far superior to the jam session-oriented sets that altoist Jackie McLean made for Prestige a few years earlier. Rehearsal time gave the musicians an opportunity to learn the two McLean originals and the four songs contributed by Davis; the latter's "Davis' Cup" is the best-known of the pieces. The music is funky but adventurous, beyond hard bop but still tied to chordal improvisation. Stimulating listening. — *Scott Yanow*

Bluesnik / Jan. 8, 1961 / Blue Note ✦✦✦✦
This is one of the most accessible of altoist Jackie McLean's Blue Note sessions, for the six songs, which have been augmented on the CD reissue by "new" alternate versions of "Goin' Way Blues" and "Torchin'," are all blues. McLean teams up with the fiery young trumpeter Freddie Hubbard, pianist Kenny Drew, bassist Doug Watkins, and drummer Pete La Roca for diverse originals by the leader, Drew, and Hubbard that all have the feeling (if not always the exact structure) of the blues. The variety of tempos, moods, and styles make this a highly recommended set. — *Scott Yanow*

A Fickle Sonance / Oct. 26, 1961 / Blue Note ✦✦✦✦
A remarkable merger of new-thing/avant-garde leanings and hard-bop fluidity and feelings. — *Ron Wynn*

☆ **Let Freedom Ring** / Mar. 19, 1962 / Blue Note ✦✦✦✦✦
This is one of altoist Jackie McLean's most significant recordings. A veteran of the hard bop scene of the '50s, McLean was one of the few musicians from his generation to embrace aspects of the avant-garde without losing his own musical personality. McLean kept his own intense sound and opened up his playing to the point where he could improvise without using chord structures or even a steady tempo. His emotional style is heard at its prime on the four selections included on this CD reissue, a quartet date with pianist Walter Davis, bassist Herbie Lewis, and drummer Billy Higgins. Although the music is not quite as free as Ornette Coleman's, it is nearly as innovative, particularly when one considers the expanded vocabulary that McLean uses (with screams and honks being integrated logically into his solos). Even on Bud Powell's ballad "I'll Keep Loving You," McLean's playing is very advanced and, in its own way, free. This is a gem that still sounds quite modern. — *Scott Yanow*

Tippin' the Scales / Sep. 28, 1962 / Blue Note ✦✦✦✦
This fairly straightahead LP by altoist Jackie McLean was released for the first time in 1984. Due to its boppish nature, as opposed to his more adventurous recordings of the period, it languished in the vaults for over 20 years, but the music is actually quite enjoyable. With assistance from pianist Sonny Clark, bassist Butch Warren, and drummer Art Taylor, McLean is in excellent form on two of his originals, three by Clark (including "Nursery Blues" and "Nicely") and the standard ballad "Cabin in the Sky." A fine hard bop session. — *Scott Yanow*

Vertigo / Feb. 11, 1963 / Blue Note ✦✦✦✦
This 1980 LP released for the first time "Formidable" from a 1959 session and five numbers from a 1963 McLean set. While "Formidable" has a strong quintet (with altoist Jackie McLean, trumpeter Donald Byrd, pianist Walter Davis, bassist Paul Chambers, and drummer Pete La Roca), the 1963 session has the recording debut of drummer Tony Williams along with strong contributions from Byrd, pianist Herbie Hancock (then also near the beginning of his career) and bassist Butch Warren. The latter unit sticks to group originals by Byrd, Hancock, and McLean and the music ranges from catchy funk and hard bop to strong hints of the avant-garde. The later session has yet to appear on CD, making this LP worth searching for by Jackie McLean collectors. — *Scott Yanow*

★ **One Step Beyond** / Apr. 30, 1963 / Blue Note ✦✦✦✦✦
One of the great Jackie McLean records, this album features the innovative altoist performing two of his originals plus a pair by trombonist Grachan Moncur, III. With vibraphonist Bobby Hutcherson (on one of his earliest recordings), bassist Eddie Khan, and drummer Tony Williams (McLean's discovery) completing the quintet, this was a group that could play the most advanced material with creativity and improvise freely when it fit the music. The solos and ensembles on the "difficult" material are quite memorable, and it is to Jackie McLean's credit that he was not satisfied to spend his entire career playing hard bop; his musical curiosity led him to listening closely to the music of Ornette Coleman and to adapting aspects of free jazz that fit his distinctive sound. — *Scott Yanow*

● **Destination Out** / Sep. 20, 1963 / Blue Note ✦✦✦✦
Five very talented and versatile jazzmen (altoist Jackie McLean, trombonist Grachan Moncur III, vibraphonist Bobby Hutcherson, bassist Larry Ridley, and drummer Roy Haynes) explore three of Moncur's originals plus McLean's "Kahlil the Prophet" on this CD reissue of their 1963 Blue Note album. McLean was one of the few players of his generation to be influenced by the free jazz movement yet he never lost his musical personality or his distinctive sound. The improvisations by these musicians are both thoughtful and passionate, making expert use of space, tricky time changes, and emotional intensity. — *Scott Yanow*

It's Time / Aug. 5, 1964 / Blue Note ✦✦✦✦
Altoist Jackie McLean and his sidemen on this excellent quintet set (which also features trumpeter Charles Tolliver, pianist Herbie Hancock, bassist

Cecil McBee, and drummer Roy Haynes) explore aspects of free jazz (particularly on "Cancellation") without letting go completely of the concepts of chordal improvisation. Strange as it seems, McLean's sound and highly expressive vocabulary are more advanced than his actual notes while Tolliver's notes are more unpredictable than his Clifford Brown-inspired tone. Ranging from "Cancellation" to the funky "Das' Dat," this is a stimulating LP that has been reissued as part of Mosaic's four-CD Jackie McLean box set. —*Scott Yanow*

☆ **Complete Blue Note 1964-1966** / Aug. 5, 1964-Apr. 18, 1966 / Mosaic ✦✦✦✦✦

Altoist Jackie McLean has recorded so many fine albums throughout his career, particularly in the '60s for Blue Note, that Mosaic could have reissued his complete output without any loss of quality. This four-CD limited-edition box set contains six complete LPs worth of material plus one "new" alternate take. The music (which also features trumpeters Charles Tolliver and Lee Morgan, pianists Herbie Hancock, Larry Willis, and Harold Mabern, vibraphonist Bobby Hutcherson, bassists Cecil McBee, Bob Cranshaw, Larry Ridley, Herbie Lewis, and Don Moore and drummers Roy Haynes, Billy Higgins, Clifford Jarvis, Jack DeJohnette and Billy Higgins) is explorative (showing the influence of Ornette Coleman) but without totally disgarding McLean's bebop roots. The performances straddle the boundaries between advanced hard bop and free jazz with Jackie McLean consistently emerging as the main star; his solos are consistently exciting and full of unexpected twists and turns. —*Scott Yanow*

Action / Sep. 16, 1964 / Blue Note ✦✦✦✦

This LP, whose music has been reissued as part of a Mosaic Jackie McLean box set, has several selections that are quite fascinating. McLean (along with trumpeter Charles Tolliver, vibraphonist Bobby Hutcherson, bassist Cecil McBee, and drummer Billy Higgins) plays quite free on "Action" (which does not have a specific set of chord changes to follow), a pair of Tolliver ballads ("Plight" is best known), and even the standard "I Hear a Rhapsody" (McLean's feature). Only the bluesy "Hootman" is a bit more conventional, although those solos are also far from predictable. This album is full of exciting music that has long been overshadowed. —*Scott Yanow*

Right Now / Jan. 26, 1965 / Blue Note ✦✦✦✦

With the exception of a beautiful ballad version of Larry Willis' "Poor Eric," the music on this CD (which is also available in Mosaic's four-CD Jackie McLean box set) is hard-charging, intense and fairly free. Altoist McLean was at the peak of his powers during this period and, inspired by the versatile rhythm section (pianist Larry Willis, bassist Bob Cranshaw, and drummer Clifford Jarvis), he plays explorative versions of his own "Eco," Willis' "Christel's Time," and Charles Tolliver's "Right Now"; an alternate version of the latter is added on for the CD reissue. This CD offers listeners a particularly strong example of Jackie McLean's unique inside/outside music of the '60s. —*Scott Yanow*

Consequences / Dec. 3, 1965 / Blue Note ✦✦✦✦

Unreleased until 1979, but fortunately currently available in a Mosaic Jackie McLean CD box set, this superior outing features altoist McLean and trumpeter Lee Morgan as equals in a quintet that also includes pianist Harold Mabern, bassist Herbie Lewis, and drummer Billy Higgins. The music is more straightahead than on the altoist's better-known gems of the period but is never predictable. Morgan really challenges McLean on "Bluesanova" and other highlights include McLean's "Consequence" and the calypso feel of "Tolypso." —*Scott Yanow*

Jacknife / Apr. 12, 1966 / Blue Note ✦✦✦✦

Dr. Jackle / Dec. 18, 1966 / SteepleChase ✦✦✦✦

Tune Up / Dec. 18, 1966 / SteepleChase ✦✦✦✦

From the same "live in Baltimore" session that resulted in *Dr. Jackle*, altoist Jackie McLean and his regular quartet of the period (comprised of pianist Lamont Johnson, bassist Scotty Holt and drummer Billy Higgins) explore lengthy versions of three standards ("Tune Up," "I Remember You," and a passionate "Smile") along with McLean's original "Jack's Tune." As well as the altoist plays, it is the solos of the underrated and underrecorded pianist, LaMont Johnson, that make this explorative hard bop release most notable. —*Scott Yanow*

The Meeting / Jul. 20, 1973-Jul. 21, 1973 / SteepleChase ✦✦✦

The Source / Jul. 20, 1973-Jul. 21, 1973 / SteepleChase ✦✦✦

☆ **Dynasty** / Nov. 5, 1988 / Triloka ✦✦✦✦✦

This is one of the great Jackie McLean albums. After nearly a decade off of records, the veteran altoist teamed up with his son Rene (who triples on tenor, soprano, and flute), pianist Hotep Idris Galeta, bassist Nat Reeves, and drummer Carl Allen for a very passionate and high-powered live set. Whether it be originals by Rene McLean (including "J. Mac's Dynasty") or Galeta, a very intense version of "A House Is Not a Home" or Jackie's "Bird Lives," this is dynamic and consistently exciting music. The go-for-broke solos (which transcend any easy categories) and Jackie's unique sharp tone make this an essential CD, one of the top recordings to be released in 1990. —*Scott Yanow*

Rites of Passage / Jan. 29, 1991-Jan. 30, 1991 / Triloka ✦✦✦✦

Recorded two years after his "comeback" album, *Dynasty*, but using the same personnel, altoist Jackie McLean once again sounds in prime form. His intensity and passion had not declined through the years and his sometimes-abrasive tone had, if anything, become even more distinctive. With this particularly strong group (which has son Rene on tenor, alto, and soprano, pianist Hotep Idris Galeta, bassist Nat Reeves, and drummer Carl Allen), McLean pours his heart out on two of his originals plus pieces by Rene And Galeta. Outstanding no-holds-barred music. —*Scott Yanow*

The Jackie Mac Attack Live / Apr. 1991 / Verve ✦✦✦✦

Veteran altoist Jackie McLean is in top form on this live quartet session with pianist Hotep Idris Galeta, bassist Nat Reeves, and drummer Carl Allen. He performs two originals by Galeta, Rene McLean's "Dance Little Mandissa," "'Round Midnight," and his own "Minor March" and "Five." The amount of passion and intensity that McLean puts into his improvisations is quite impressive, and 40 years after his recording debut, he remains in prime form. This strong, advanced hard bop date gives listeners a good example of his abilities. —*Scott Yanow*

Rhythm of the Earth / Mar. 12, 1992-Mar. 13, 1992 / Antilles ✦✦✦✦

Big Jay McNeely (Cecil McNeely)

b. Apr. 29, 1927, Watts, CA

Saxophone / R&B, West Coast Blues, Blues Jazz, Soul-Jazz, Doo-Wop, Groove

His mighty tenor sax squawking and bleating with wild-eyed abandon, Big Jay McNeely blew up a torrid R&B tornado from every conceivable position—on his knees, on his back, being wheeled down the street on an auto mechanic's "creeper" like a modern-day pied piper. As one of the titans who made tenor sax the solo instrument of choice during rock's primordial era, McNeely could peel the paper right off the walls with his sheets of squealing, honking horn riffs.

Cecil McNeely and his older brother Bob (who blew baritone sax lines with Jay in unison precision on some of Jay's hottest instrumentals) grew up in Los Angeles, where jazz reigned on Watts' bustling nightlife strip. Inspired by Illinois Jacquet and tutored by Jack McVea, McNeely struck up a friendship with Johnny Otis, co-owner of the popular Barrelhouse nitery. Ralph Bass, a friend of Otis, produced McNeely's debut date for Savoy Records in 1948 (Savoy boss Herman Lubinsky tagged the saxist Big Jay, in his eyes a more commercial name than Cecil). McNeely's raucous one-note honking on "The Deacon's Hop" gave him and Savoy an R&B chart-topper in 1949, and his follow-up, "Wild Wig," also hit big for the young saxist with the acrobatic stage presence.

From Savoy, McNeely moved to Exclusive in 1949, Imperial in 1950-51, King's Federal subsidiary in 1952-54 (where he cut some of his wildest waxings, including the mind-boggling "3-D"), and Vee-Jay in 1955. McNeely's live shows were the stuff that legends are made of—he electrified a sweaty throng of thousands packing Chicago's Wrigley Field in 1949 by blowing his sax up through the stands and then from home plate to first base on his back! A fluorescently painted sax that glowed in the dark was another of his showstopping gambits.

In 1958, McNeely cut his last hit in a considerably less frantic mode with singer Little Sonny Warner. The bluesy "There Is Something on Your Mind" was committed to tape in Seattle but came out on DJ Hunter Hancock's Swingin' Imprint the next year. McNeely's original was a huge smash, but it was eclipsed the following year by New Orleans singer Bobby Marchan's dramatic R&B chart-topping version for Fire. Since then, it's been covered countless times, including a fine rendition by Conway Twitty!

Honking saxists had fallen from favor by the dawn of the '60s, so McNeely eventually became a mailman and joined Jehovah's Witnesses (no, that's not the name of a combo). Happily, his horn came back out of the closet during the early '80s. Today, McNeely records for his own little label and tours the country and overseas regularly. This deacon's still hopping! —*Bill Dahl*

Big Jay in 3-D / Aug. 26, 1952-Apr. 8, 1954 / Federal ✦✦✦✦

Honking R&B tenor sax giant McNeely blows his brains out on these early-'50s stompers for King. Truly astonishing is the torrid "3-D," where Big Jay and his baritone sax-blowing brother Bob play some incredibly complex riffs over one of the fastest tempos imaginable. —*Bill Dahl*

The Deacon Rides Again / 1957 / Marconi ✦✦✦

From Harlem to Camden / Aug. 1983-Sep. 1983 / Ace ✦✦✦

Meets the Penguins / Oct. 1983 / Ace ✦✦✦

This reissue of raucous, upbeat R&B cuts also includes the doo-wop harmony ensemble The Penguins. —*Ron Wynn*

● **Nervous** / 1995 / Saxophile ✦✦✦✦

A thorough 19-track examination of McNeely's early heyday, incorporating a live 1951 reprise of his signature "Deacon's Hop," the King label classics "3-D," "Nervous Man Nervous," and "Texas Turkey," a handful of live 1957 efforts that include the crazed "Insect Ball," and McNeely's original hit version of the incendiary blues ballad "There Is Something on Your Mind" (with Little Sonny Warner handling the Ray Charles-influenced lead vocal). —*Bill Dahl*

Swingin' / Collectables ✦✦✦✦
Gymnastic sax maniac's output for Los Angeles DJ Hunter Hancock's Swingin' logo during the late '50s and early '60s. Naturally, his smash "There Is Something on Your Mind" is front and center, alongside the oddly titled "Back . . . Shack . . . Track," "Psycho Serenade," and "Blue Couch Boogie." Little Sonny Warner is the vocalist on some sides. —*Bill Dahl*

Live at Birdland: 1957 / Collectables ✦✦✦✦
An amazing artifact from 1957, when live recordings like this one didn't happen very often. A Seattle engineer with a spanking-new stereo tape recorder captured the contents of this disc while McNeely and his swinging combo were working out at a Seattle nightspot called the Birdland. He gets plenty of room to peel the paper from the gin joint's walls as he wails on "Flying Home," "How High the Moon," and "Let It Roll." —*Bill Dahl*

Jimmy McPartland

b. Mar. 15, 1907, Chicago, IL., **d.** Mar. 13, 1991
Cornet / Dixieland
A solid Dixieland cornetist with his own lyrical sound (influenced by Bix Beiderbecke), Jimmy McPartland played the music he loved for over 60 years. The younger brother of guitarist Dick McPartland (1905-1957), Jimmy was a member of the legendary Austin High School Gang in the '20s. He was Bix Beiderbecke's replacement with the Wolverines during 1925, joined Ben Pollack's band in 1927, and recorded with the McKenzie and Condon Chicagoans during their famous session. McPartland was one of the main soloists (along with Benny Goodman) with Pollack and he stayed with the band into 1929. He then moved to Chicago, working steadily through the '30s. While stationed overseas during World War II (1942-44) he met his future wife, the English pianist Marian Turner. McPartland freelanced at Dixieland sessions during the next four decades, working with Eddie Condon, Art Hodes, and other Chicago jazz veterans and often leading his own band. Although eventually divorced from Marian McPartland, they were still close friends and occasionally played together, remarrying just a few weeks before Jimmy McPartland's death two days short of his 84th birthday. Many of his best early recordings were collected on an MCA two-LP set in the '70s. In addition, he recorded as a leader for Harmony, Prestige, MGM, Grand Award, Jazztone, Epic, Mercury, RCA, Design, Jazzology, Halcyon (Marian's label), and Riff. —*Scott Yanow*

★ **Shades of Bix** / Apr. 24, 1936-Feb. 2, 1956 / Brunswick ✦✦✦✦✦
This double LP is long overdue to be reissued on CD. Trumpeter Jimmy McPartland originally succeeded the legendary Bix Beiderbecke with the Wolverines back in 1925. Decades later, although still influenced a bit by Beiderbecke's sound, McPartland had long developed his own musical personality. The first twelve selections on this set (eight from 1953 and the other four from 1956) feature McPartland paying tribute to Beiderbecke by performing a variety of songs associated with him. Such players as trombonist Lou McGarity, clarinetist Peanuts Hucko, tenorman Bud Freeman, and baritonist Ernie Caceres help out on some of the numbers and pianist Marian McPartland is aboard for the later sides. High point is an emotional version of "In a Mist" that utilizes oboe and bassoon in the arrangement. In addition, this twofer includes McPartland's sessions of 1936 and 1939, superior Dixieland performances that, on four selections, are highlighted by rare solos from altoist Boyce Brown. This highly recommended set is rounded out by eight superior ballads from 1943 and 1946 featuring the mellow cornet of Bobby Hackett. —*Scott Yanow*

McPartlands Live at the Monticello / Nov. 1972 / Halcyon ✦✦✦✦

☆ **At the Festival** / 1979 / Concord Jazz ✦✦✦✦✦
This nice small-group session accents McPartland's fortes: touch, delicacy, and melodic interpretation. —*Ron Wynn*

Marian McPartland

b. Mar. 20, 1920, Windsor, England
Piano / Bop, Swing
Marian McPartland has become famous for hosting her *Piano Jazz* radio program since 1978 but she was a well respected pianist decades before. She played in a four-piano vaudeville act in England and performed on the European continent for the troops during World War II. In Belgium in 1944 she met cornetist Jimmy McPartland and they soon married. Marian moved with her husband to the US in 1946 where she sometimes played with him even though her style was more modern than his Dixieland-oriented groups. McPartland eventually had her own trio at the Embers (1950) and the Hickory House (1952-60) which until 1957 included drummer Joe Morello. She recorded regularly for Savoy and Capitol during the '50s and also made sessions for Argo (1958), Time (1960 and 1963), Sesac, and Dot. Although divorced eventually from Jimmy, they remained close friends, sometimes played together and remarried just weeks before his death. She formed her own Halcyon label and recorded several fine albums between 1969-77. McPartland also made three albums for Tony

Bennett's Improv label during 1976-77 before signing with Concord where she has been since 1978. The Jazz Alliance label has made available on over a couple dozen CDs quite a few episodes of Marian McPartland's *Piano Jazz* show. —*Scott Yanow*

A Sentimental Journey / 1972-1973 / Jazz Alliance ✦✦✦✦
Marian McPartland (famous as a modern pianist and for her *Piano Jazz* radio show) was initially introduced to the jazz major leagues through her husband, the late Jimmy McPartland, who was a talented Dixieland-oriented cornetist. During 1972-73 the McPartlands recorded two of their concerts which were later released on Marian's Halcyon label. This CD reissue contains 12 of the 14 selections and these are among Jimmy McPartland's best later recordings. With frontlines that include either trombonist Vic Dickenson and tenorman Buddy Tate or trombonist Hank Berger and clarinetist Jack Maheu, the cornetist performs Dixieland and swing standards with enthusiasm and power, taking an occasional vocal and clearly having a good time. It's recommended for trad fans. —*Scott Yanow*

Maestro and Friend / Jul. 1973 / Halcyon ✦✦✦✦
Violinist Joe Venuti teams up with pianist Marian McPartland for a set of duets, mostly on standards. The music is quite melodic but has some exciting moments; there are not that many violin-piano duet versions of "That's a Plenty." A tasteful outing by two masterful players. —*Scott Yanow*

Solo Concert at Haverford / Apr. 12, 1974 / Halcyon ✦✦✦

Concert in Argentina / Nov. 1974 / Jazz Alliance ✦✦✦✦
This Buenos Aires concert, originally released as a two-LP set, features four different but complementary pianists in solo performances: Marian McPartland, Teddy Wilson, Ellis Larkins, and Earl Hines. The Jazz Alliance CD reissue unfortunately leaves out a selection or two apiece by each of the keyboardists (it should have come out as a double CD) so the LP version is the more highly recommended format. McPartland shows off her versatility on a Duke Ellington medley, Wilson swings impeccably, Larkins is typically subtle on his ballads, and Hines is the most reckless (and exciting) improviser. —*Scott Yanow*

★ **Piano Jazz: McPartland/Evans** / Nov. 6, 1978 / Jazz Alliance ✦✦✦✦✦

Piano Jazz: McPartland/Stacy / Dec. 1, 1981 / Jazz Alliance ✦✦✦✦
This is one of the most valuable of the *Piano Jazz* episodes for the great swing pianist Jess Stacy, who had been semiretired since the late '50s, making his final commercial recording in 1977. After stumbling a bit on "Dancing Fool," he is quite modest while discussing his own playing but he gets stronger as the hour progresses. Although Stacy has four unaccompanied solos and Marian McPartland is fine on her feature "Heavy Hearted Blues," it is their three joyous duets ("Keepin' out of Mischief Now," "I Would Do Anything for You," and "St. Louis Blues") along with the priceless reminiscing that makes this CD highly recommended to swing collectors. —*Scott Yanow*

Marian McPartland's Piano Jazz with Henry Mancini / Mar. 14, 1985 / Jazz Alliance ✦✦✦✦
Henry Mancini saw his role in music as a film and television composer rather than as a songwriter. During his interesting hour on Marian McPartland's *Piano Jazz* radio show, Mancini discusses his life with good humor and modesty. He takes two brief melody choruses (on "Two for the Road" and "Meggie's Theme"), duets with McPartland on several songs (including "The Pink Panther") and a touching version of "Days of Wine and Roses") and enjoys hearing McPartland interpret "Mr. Lucky" and "Charade." Although only one of his songs ("Days of Wine and Roses") really became a jazz standard, Mancini enjoyed jazz and loved to hear improvising musicians develop his themes. This is an enjoyable set worth a few listens. —*Scott Yanow*

Piano Jazz:McPartland/Eldridge / Aug. 18, 1986 / Jazz Alliance ✦✦✦✦

★ **Piano Jazz: McPartland/Konitz** / Sep. 6, 1991 / Jazz Alliance ✦✦✦✦✦
This CD has one of the most rewarding of Marian McPartland's *Piano Jazz* radio shows. Guest Lee Konitz proves to be a very thoughtful and sometimes witty guest. Konitz talks about what he learned from Tristano and in turn what he tries to get across to students himself. He clearly enjoys discussing the magic of improvisation. In addition the music on this program is uniformly outstanding. For "All the Things You Are" the altoist coaxes McPartland to play freely without a chord structure. He takes "Stella by Starlight" unaccompanied, creates some unpredictable duets with McPartland on familiar yet still fresh standards, plays some abstract piano with the host on "Tactile Talk," and sounds beautiful on soprano during "Little Girl Blue"; upon the latter song's conclusion, Konitz admits that he had never played the song before! This CD ranks up there with the Bill Evans show as the most significant of the *Piano Jazz* programs thus far released on CD. —*Scott Yanow*

Charles McPherson

b. Jul. 24, 1939, Joplin, MO
Sax (Alto) / Bop, Hard Bop
A Charlie Parker disciple who brings his own lyricism to the bebop language, Charles McPherson has been a reliable figure in modern main-

stream jazz for the past 35 years. He played in the Detroit jazz scene of the mid-'50s, moved to New York in 1959, and within a year was working with Charles Mingus. McPherson and his friend Lonnie Hillyer succeeded Eric Dolphy and Ted Curson as regular members of Mingus' band in 1961 and he worked with the bassist off and on up until 1972. Although he and Hillyer had a short-lived quintet in 1966, McPherson was not a fulltime leader until 1972. In 1978 he moved to San Diego which has been his home ever since and sometimes he uses his son Chuck McPherson on drums. Charles McPherson, who helped out on the film *Bird* by playing some of the parts not taken from Charlie Parker records, has led dates through the years for Prestige (1964-69), Mainstream, Xanadu, Discovery, and Arabesque. —*Scott Yanow*

● **Be-Bop Revisited** / Nov. 20, 1964 / Original Jazz Classics ◆◆◆◆
Bebop is the thing on this excellent outing as altoist Charles McPherson and pianist Barry Harris do their interpretations of Charlie Parker and Bud Powell. With trumpeter Carmell Jones, bassist Nelson Boyd, and drummer Al "Tootie" Heath completing the quintet, the band romps through such bop classics as "Hot House," "Nostalgia," "Wail," and "Si Si" along with an original blues and "Embraceable You." A previously unissued "If I Love You" is added to the CD reissue. McPherson and Jones make for a potent frontline on these spirited performances, easily recommended to fans of straightahead jazz. —*Scott Yanow*

First Flight Out / Jan. 25, 1994-Jan. 26, 1994 / Arabesque ◆◆◆◆

Come Play With Me / Mar. 2, 1995 / Arabesque Jazz ◆◆◆◆

Carmen McRae

b. Apr. 8, 1920, New York, NY, **d.** Nov. 10, 1994
Piano, Vocals / Bop, Standards
Carmen McRae always had a nice voice (if not on the impossible level of an Ella Fitzgerald or Sarah Vaughan) but it was her behind-the-beat phrasing and ironic interpretations of lyrics that made her most memorable. She studied piano early on and had her first important job singing with Benny Carter's big band (1944) but it would be another decade before her career really had much momentum. McRae married and divorced Kenny Clarke in the '40s, worked with Count Basie (briefly) and Mercer Ellington (1946-47), and became the intermission singer and pianist at several New York clubs. In 1954 she began to record as a leader and by then she had absorbed the influences of Billie Holiday and bebop into her own style. McRae would record pretty steadily up to 1989 and, although her voice was higher in the '50s and her phrasing was even more laidback in later years, her general style and approach did not change much through the decades. Championed in the '50s by Ralph Gleason, Carmen McRae was fairly popular throughout her career. Among her most interesting recording projects were participating in Dave Brubeck's the Real Ambassadors with Louis Armstrong, cutting an album of live duets with Betty Carter, being accompanied by Dave Brubeck and George Shearing, and closing her career with brilliant tributes to Thelonious Monk and Sarah Vaughan. Carmen McRae, who refused to quit smoking, was forced to retire in 1991 due to emphysema. She recorded for many labels including Bethlehem, Decca (1954-58), Kapp, Columbia, Mainstream, Focus, Atlantic (1967-70), Black Lion, Groove Merchant, Catalyst, Blue Note, Buddah, Concord, and Novus. —*Scott Yanow*

Here to Stay / Jun. 14, 1955-Nov. 12, 1959 / GRP/Decca ◆◆◆◆
One of several CDs that reissue singer Carmen McRae's early Decca recordings, this release draws its material from the 1955 small group album *By Special Request* and a 1959 record with the Ernie Wilkins Orchestra (*Something to Swing About*). McRae excels in both settings. While tenor saxophonist Zoot Sims, trumpeter Richard Williams, and pianist Dick Katz get some solo space on the latter album, the former one showcases McRae either with Dick Katz's quartet, accordion player Mat Mathews' quintet (with flutist Herbie Mann), or (on "Something to Live For") with its composer Billy Strayhorn on piano. During an emotional rendition of "Supper Time," McRae herself plays piano. Throughout the 20 selections, the singer is heard in her early prime, hitting high notes that she would not even think of attempting in her later years. Recommended. —*Scott Yanow*

I'll Be Seeing You / Jun. 14, 1955-Mar. 10, 1959 / Decca ◆◆◆

Carmen Mc Rae Sings Great American Songwriters / Jun. 16, 1955-Mar. 4, 1959 / GRP/Decca ◆◆◆◆
Instead of reissuing all of singer Carmen McRae's early records for Decca in chronological order, the GRP program has hedged its bets a bit by coming up with highlights from each of her sessions although, with the various CDs on a whole, nearly everything has being reissued anyway. The 20 numbers on this CD are taken from ten different sessions and find McRae joined by the Mat Mathews Quintet (featuring flutist Herbie Mann), the Ray Bryant trio, and several large orchestras. The repertoire is taken from the songbooks of some of the classic American composers (including Gershwin, Porter, Kern, Rodgers & Hart, and Arlen) and McRae's interpretations are both respectful and swinging. It is particularly interesting to hear

how high her voice could be in the early days. This CD is easily recommended to her fans. —*Scott Yanow*

You're Lookin' at Me (A Collection of Nat King Cole Songs) / Nov. 1983 / Concord Jazz ◆◆◆◆
Carmen McRae's tribute to Nat King Cole (which predated the late-'80s revival of Cole's music) has its strong and weak points. She wisely adds Cole's former guitarist John Collins to her regular trio and picked some fine material (including "I'm an Errand Girl for Rhythm," "I Can't See for Lookin,'" and "Just You, Just Me"). However McRae's phrasing is much different than Cole's and why did she sing "Sweet Lorraine" without changing any of the words? Despite those reservations, this set has enough strong moments to justify its purchase. —*Scott Yanow*

● **For Lady Day** / Dec. 31, 1983 / Novus ◆◆◆◆
Carmen McRae always considered Billie Holiday to be the most important influence not only on her singing but on her life. Six years before she recorded her monumental tributes to Thelonious Monk and Sarah Vaughan, McRae performed a Billie Holiday set at New York's Blue Note Club that was broadcast over the radio. On the first of two volumes McRae, who talks movingly about Lady Day at the beginning of the set and accompanies herself on piano on "I'm Pulling Through," is heard in prime form, combining the power and range of her earlier years with the emotional depth and behind-the-beat phrasing of her last period. Accompanied by her rhythm section of the time (pianist Marshall Otwell, bassist John Leftwich, and drummer Donald Bailey) and occasionally the tenor of Zoot Sims, McRae really digs into the material, interpreting the songs in her own style but with a knowing nod towards Holiday. This wonderful set is far superior to most of the Billie Holiday tribute albums of recent years and reminds us how much Carmen McRae is missed. —*Scott Yanow*

Carmen McRae-Betty Carter Duets / Jan. 30, 1987-Feb. 1, 1987 / Great American Music Hall ◆◆◆◆
This project is an unusual matchup between two very individual vocalists that generally works. Both Carmen McRae and Betty Carter show a lot of good humor during their duets, cracking occasional jokes and often jamming quite spontaneously. With suitable support from pianist Eric Gunnison, bassist Jim Hughart, and drummer Winard Harper along with a very enthusiastic audience at San Francisco's Great American Music Hall, Carter usually takes vocal honors while McRae comes up with the most humorous lines. Some of the ensembles are ragged but this encounter is overall quite successful. The CD reissue adds three previously unreleased selections that feature McRae without Carter. Now if only someone had teamed together Ella Fitzgerald and Sarah Vaughan for a full album! —*Scott Yanow*

★ **Carmen Sings Monk** / Jan. 30, 1988-Feb. 1, 1988 / Novus ◆◆◆◆◆
This is one of McRae's greatest albums ever. —*Ron Wynn*

Sarah: Dedicated to You / Oct. 12, 1990-Oct. 14, 1990 / Novus ◆◆◆◆
Beautiful and masterly tribute to a dear friend. —*Ron Wynn*

Jay McShann

b. Jan. 12, 1916, Muskogee, OK
Piano / Blues, Swing
The great veteran pianist Jay McShann (also known as Hootie) has had a long career and it is unfair to primarily think of him as merely the leader of an orchestra that featured a young Charlie Parker. He was mostly self-taught as a pianist, worked with Don Byas as early as 1931, and played throughout the Midwest before settling in Kansas City in 1936. McShann formed his own sextet the following year and by 1939 had his own big band. In 1940 at a radio station in Wichita, KS, McShann and an octet out of his orchestra recorded eight songs that were not released commercially until the '70s; those rank among the earliest of all Charlie Parker records (he is brilliant on "Honeysuckle Rose" and "Lady Be Good") and also feature the strong rhythm-section team McShann had with bassist Gene Ramey and drummer Gus Johnson. The full orchestra recorded for Decca on two occasions during 1941-42 but they were typecast as a blues band and did not get to record many of their more challenging charts (although very rare broadcasts have since surfaced and been released on CD by Vintage Jazz Classics). In addition to Bird (who had a few short solos), the main stars were trumpeter Bernard Anderson, the rhythm section, and singer Walter Brown. McShann and his band arrived in New York in February 1942 and made a strong impression but World War II made it difficult for any new orchestras to catch on. There was a final session in December 1943 without Parker but McShann was soon drafted and the band broke up. After being discharged later in 1944, McShann briefly reformed his group but soon moved to Los Angeles where he led combos for the next few years; his main attraction was the young singer Jimmy Witherspoon.

McShann was in obscurity for the next two decades, making few records and mostly playing in Kansas City. In 1969 he was rediscovered and McShann (who had first sung on records in 1966) was soon a popular pianist/vocalist. Sometimes featuring violinist Claude Williams, he has toured constantly, recorded frequently, and appeared at many jazz festivals since then, being active into the mid-'90s. Jay McShann, who has recorded through the years for Onyx (the 1940 radio transcriptions), Decca, Capitol, Aladdin, Mercury, Black Lion, EmArcy, Vee-Jay, Black & Blue, Master Jazz, Sackville, Sonet, Storyville, Atlantic, Swingtime, and Music Masters among others, is a vital pianist and an effective blues vocalist who keeps a classic style alive. —*Scott Yanow*

★ **Blues from Kansas City** / Apr. 30, 1941-Dec. 1, 1943 / GRP/Decca ✦✦✦✦✦
Fine 1992 reissue of vintage Kansas City swing featuring groups led by pianist Jay McShann in the early '40s, some of which included alto saxophonist Charlie Parker. These have been available before in either bare-bones domestic or more comprehensive import packages. This is the first time parent label MCA has taken care to sequence, remaster, and annotate this vital music in the manner it deserves. —*Ron Wynn*

☆ **The Jazz Heritage: Early Bird Charlie Parker (1941-1943)** / Apr. 30, 1941-Dec. 1, 1943 / Spotlite ✦✦✦✦✦
1940-1943 air-checks. With Charley Parker (as), Paul Quinichette, and Gus Johnson. —*Michael Erlewine*

● **The Big Apple Bash** / Aug. 3, 1971-Aug. 10, 1971 / New World ✦✦✦✦
Pianist Jay McShann has spent much of his career being classified as a blues pianist when in fact he is a flexible swing stylist. On this excellent release, McShann appears with two groups of all-stars. His original "Crazy Legs and Friday Strut" and "Georgia on My Mind" find him joined by Herbie Mann (on flute and tenor), baritonist Gerry Mulligan, and a rhythm section that includes guitarist John Scofield. The other selections (two standards, Duke Ellington's "Blue Feeling," and McShann's own "Jumpin' the Blues") are performed by an octet also featuring Mann, altoist Earle Warren, trumpeter Doc Cheatham, trombonist Dicky Wells, and Scofield. The unusual grouping of swing, bop, and modern stylists is successful (the material is pretty basic), and Janis Siegel's guest appearance for a vocal duet with McShann on "Ain't Misbehavin'" works. —*Scott Yanow*

Man from Muskogee / Jun. 24, 1972 / Sackville ✦✦✦✦
One of McShann's finest recordings. With Claude Williams (violin). —*Michael Erlewine*

Airmail Special / Aug. 1985 / Sackville ✦✦✦

● **Paris All-Star Blues: A Tribute** / Jun. 13, 1989 / Music Masters ✦✦✦✦
A 1991 tribute album (recorded in 1989) to Charlie Parker by a great cast of veteran and recent jazz musicians under leadership of pianist Jay McShann, who conducted the band that gave Parker his start. The lineup runs from Benny Carter, Al Grey, and James Moody to Terence Blanchard. —*Ron Wynn*

Hootie & Hicks/Missouri Connec / Sep. 14, 1992-Sep. 15, 1992 / Reservoir ✦✦✦

Pat Metheny

b. Aug. 2, 1954, Lee's Summit, MO
Guitar / Avant-Garde, Post-Bop, Crossover
One of the most original guitarists of the past 20 years (he is instantly recognizable), Pat Metheny is a chance-taking player who has gained great popularity but also taken some wild left turns. His records with the Pat Metheny Group are difficult to describe (folk-jazz? mood music?) but managed to be both accessible and original, stretching the boundaries of jazz and making Metheny famous enough so he could perform whatever type of music he wants without losing his audience.

Metheny (whose older brother is the trumpeter Mike Metheny) started on guitar when he was 13 years old. He developed quickly, taught at both the University of Miami and Berklee while he was a teenager, and made his recording debut with Paul Bley and Jaco Pastorius in 1974. He spent an important period (1974-77) with Gary Burton's group, met keyboardist Lyle Mays, and in 1978 formed his Group which originally featured Mays, bassist Mark Egan, and drummer Dan Gottlieb. Within a short period he was ECM's top artist and one of the most popular of all jazzmen, selling out stadiums. Metheny mostly avoided playing predictable music and his freelance projects were always quite interesting. His 1980 album *80/81* featured Dewey Redman and Mike Brecker in a post bop quintet, he teamed up with Charlie Haden and Billy Higgins on a trio date in 1983, and two years later recorded the very outside *Song X* with Ornette Coleman. Among Metheny's other projects away from the Group were a sideman recording with Sonny Rollins, a 1990 tour with Herbie Hancock in a quartet, a trio album with Dave Holland and Roy Haynes, and a collaboration (and tour) with Joshua Redman. Although his *Zero Tolerance for Silence* in 1994 was largely a waste (40 minutes of feedback), Pat Metheny has retained his popularity and remained a consistently creative performer. He has recorded as a leader for ECM (starting in 1975) and Geffen. —*Scott Yanow*

Bright Size Life / Dec. 1975 / ECM ✦✦✦✦
First album, with Jaco Pastorius (b) and Bob Moses (d). Excellent original material. —*Michael G. Nastos*

Watercolours / Feb. 1977 / ECM ✦✦✦✦
The group's second album; important since it shows Metheny breaking away from the style he'd honed with Gary Burton. —*Ron Wynn*

★ **Pat Metheny Group** / Jan. 1978 / ECM ✦✦✦✦✦
The first recording by Pat Metheny's Group features the innovative guitarist along with keyboardist Lyle Mays, bassist Mark Egan, and drummer Dan Gottlieb. The music is quite distinctive, floating rather than swinging, electric but not rockish, and full of folkish melodies. The best known of these six Metheny-Mays originals are "Phase Dance" and "Jaco." This music grows in interest with each listen. —*Scott Yanow*

New Chautauqua / Apr. 1979 / ECM ✦✦✦

American Garage / Feb. 1980 / ECM ✦✦✦✦
This is the session that marked Metheny's coming of age; better songs, more intense playing, and more variety in arrangements. —*Ron Wynn*

● **1980-1981** / May 26, 1980-May 29, 1980 / ECM ✦✦✦✦
The album that showed jazz purists Metheny's guitar chops extended beyond rock fusion. Extensive crisp performances. The CD issue contains two bonus cuts. —*Ron Wynn*

As Wichita Falls So Falls Wichita / Jun. 1981 / ECM ✦✦✦

Offramp / Apr. 1982 / ECM ✦✦✦✦
This 1982 date is the successor to *Wichita Falls* but lacks that album's charm and flair. —*Ron Wynn*

Travels / May 1983 / ECM ✦✦✦✦
Deftly played and nicely recorded, but for fans only. —*Ron Wynn*

● **Rejoicing** / Nov. 29, 1983-Nov. 30, 1983 / ECM ✦✦✦✦
Pat Metheny takes a vacation from his Group and performs advanced material with bassist Charlie Haden and drummer Billy Higgins. In addition to Horace Silver's "Lonely Woman," Haden's "Blues for Pat," and three Ornette Coleman tunes, the guitarist plays three of his originals including "The Calling," a lengthy exploration of sounds with his guitar synthesizer. Throughout this excellent set, Metheny and his sidemen engage in close communication and create memorable and unpredictable music. —*Scott Yanow*

First Circle / Feb. 15, 1984-Feb. 19, 1984 / ECM ✦✦✦✦
A good quintet date, but doesn't break any new ground. —*Ron Wynn*

Song X / Dec. 1985 / Geffen ✦✦✦✦
With Ornette Coleman. Metheny pays tribute to a surprising influence, teaming with Ornette Coleman in a collaboration that shocked everyone with its musical effectiveness. —*Ron Wynn*

Still Life (Talking) / 1987 / Geffen ✦✦✦✦
A standard Metheny session from 1987; he now has the formula down pat. It is well played and well recorded. —*Ron Wynn*

Letter from Home / Mar. 1989 / Geffen ✦✦✦✦
Continuing in the steps of his previous release, *Still Life Talking*, Metheny's band continues to explore the use of Brazilian rhythms in their music with excellent results. —*Paul Kohler*

● **Question and Answer** / Dec. 21, 1989 / Geffen ✦✦✦✦
A great trio. Metheny stretches out. This is highly recommended. —*Michael G. Nastos*

Secret Story / Jul. 1992 / Geffen ✦✦✦
Assisted by The London Symphony Orchestra on several selections, guitarist/composer Metheny displays a true understanding of life's joys and sorrows by letting his music tell the tale of a deep love relationship between a man and a woman. This record is without a doubt his most sensitive and sincere work to date. Compositionally this record will set new standards. —*Paul Kohler*

Secret Storm / 1993 / Geffen ✦✦✦

I Can See Your House From Here / 1993 / Blue Note ✦✦✦✦
Guitar giants John Scofield and Pat Metheny teamed up for the first time on records for this CD. The collaboration does take awhile to get going and it is not until the fourth cut, the bluish "Everybody's Party," that the sparks begin to fly; fortunately the momentum does not let up much throughout the remainder of the CD. All of the selections (including two blues) are originals by either of the guitarists and, with the accompaniment of bassist Steve Swallow and drummer Bill Stewart, this varied set generally lives up to expectations. —*Scott Yanow*

● **We Live Here** / 1994 / Geffen ✦✦✦✦
The first Pat Metheny Group recording in five years is a bit unusual in two ways. The band uses "contemporary" pop rhythms on many of their selections but in creative ways and without watering down the popular group's musical identity. In addition Metheny for the first time in his recording career sounds a bit like his early influence Wes Montgomery on a few of the songs. With his longtime sidemen (keyboardist Lyle Mays, bassist Steve Rodby, and drummer Paul Wertico) all in top form, Metheny successfully reconciles his quartet's sound with that of the pop music world, using modern technology to expand the possibilities of his own unusual vision of creative improvised music. And as a bonus, some of the melodies are catchy. —*Scott Yanow*

Glenn Miller (Alton Glenn Miller)

b. Mar. 1, 1904, Clarinda, IA, **d.** Dec. 15, 1944, English Channel
Trombone / Easy Listening, Swing

Glenn Miller led the most popular band in the world during 1939-42 and the most beloved of all the swing-era orchestras. His big band played a wide variety of melodic music (including swing, vocal ballads, and novelties) and had tremendous success in every area. Jazz was only part of their music and Miller (like Stan Kenton) was just not interested in swinging like Count Basie. He employed some good horn soloists along the way but was most concerned in displaying strong musicianship, well rehearsed ensembles, danceable tempos and putting together an enjoyable and well rounded show.

Miller grew up in Colorado, attended college for a short time and in 1926 joined Ben Pollack's new band. He was with the group for two years, contributing arrangements and taking some trombone solos but, after Jack Teagarden was discovered and signed up, Miller took the hint and quit. In 1928 he was a freelance arranger in New York and he would work most prominently during the next few years with Red Nichols in pit orchestras, as Smith Ballew's musical director and with the Dorsey Brothers. In 1935 he helped organize Ray Noble's American Orchestra and led his first session but even by 1937, Glenn Miller was still obscure. He was inspired by the success of many new big bands and he put together an orchestra of his own. That venture started out promising with some fine recordings but it soon failed, partly because it did not have a personality of its own. In mid-1938 Miller tried again and although he had a recording contract with Bluebird, the first year was mostly a struggle. However this time around, by having a clarinet double the melody of the saxophones an octave higher, he had his own trademark. An engagement at Glen Island Casino in the summer of 1939 earned the orchestra a regular radio broadcast, their recordings of "Moonlight Serenade" (Miller's theme), "Sunrise Serenade," and particularly "Little Brown Jug," became hits and by the end of the year Glenn Miller was a household name and his band was considered a sensation. During 1939-42 there were many additional hits including "In the Mood," "At Last," "Stairway to the Stars," "Tuxedo Junction," "Pennsylvania 6-5000," "Chattanooga Choo Choo," "A String of Pearls," "Elmer's Tune," "Don't Sit Under the Apple Tree," "American Patrol," "I've Got a Gal in Kalamazoo," "Serenade in Blue," and "Jukebox Saturday Night." There was simply no competition!

From the jazz standpoint, Miller's best soloists were trumpeters Clyde Hurley, Johnny Best, and (by 1942) Bobby Hackett. Tex Beneke, who was more famous for his good-natured vocals, was a decent tenor saxophonist who had a lot of short solos. Less tolerable to jazz listeners were the many ballad vocals of Ray Eberle (who often sounded as if he were straining) and the lightweight but cheerful contributions of singer Marion Hutton.

Only Glenn Miller's decision to enlist in the Army stopped his orchestra's success. He did the near-impossible and organized the finest military jazz band ever heard, his Army Air Force band. By 1944, when it had relocated to London, it featured clarinetist Peanuts Hucko, pianist Mel Powell, drummer/singer Ray McKinley, trumpeter Bobby Nichols, and sometimes a string section and a vocal group. Their version of "St. Louis Blues March" became famous and this group's broadcasts and radio transcriptions are well worth searching for. Glenn Miller flew across the English Channel in December 1944 with plans of setting up engagements on the Continent. His plane was shot down (quite possibly in error by the Allies) and lost.

The Army Air Force band stayed together through 1945. There have been many Glenn Miller ghost orchestras since, but all have been stuck in the role of recreating the past including note-for-note duplications of the recorded solos. The oddest case is Tex Beneke who has spent the past 50 years essentially performing over and over again the same routines that he had done with Miller during a three-year period!

All of Glenn Miller's Bluebird recordings (from 1938-42) have been reissued a countless number of times including in "complete" sets. His band appears quite prominently in two Hollywood movies of the '40s (*Sun Valley Serenade* and *Orchestra Wives*) that are recommended viewing. —*Scott Yanow*

Best of the Big Bands: Evolution of a Band / Apr. 25, 1935-May 23, 1938 / Columbia ✦✦✦

☆ **Complete Glenn Miller, Vols. 1-13** / Sep. 27, 1938-Jul. 16, 1942 / Bluebird ✦✦✦✦✦
This 13-CD set (which is enclosed in an attractive and compact black box) completely reissues the contents of the nine double-LP series of the same name, all 277 studio recordings (including 20 alternate takes which have been placed on the 13th disc) that were made by Glenn Miller's extremely popular orchestra. In addition to all of the hits and the occasional jazz performances, the misses (and the many Ray Eberle vocals) are also on this set so general collectors just wanting a taste of Glenn Miller's music would be better off getting a less expensive greatest-hits set. However, true Glenn

Miller fans should consider this remarkable reissue to be essential; it's all here. —*Scott Yanow*

● **Spirit is Willing** / Sep. 27, 1938-Jul. 16, 1942 / Bluebird ✦✦✦✦
This single CD looks at the jazz side of Glenn Miller, reissuing 22 instrumentals from his prime years. Although Miller did not have a great jazz band, his orchestra was capable of swinging and at one time or another had such fine soloists as trumpeters Clyde Hurley, Billy May, and Johnny Best, tenor saxophonist Al Klink, and clarinetist Ernie Caceres. This is an interesting set even if it offers nothing that is not available elsewhere. —*Scott Yanow*

Pennsylvania 6-5000, Vol. 1: The Sustaining Remotes / Dec. 30, 1938-Oct. 7, 1940 / Vintage Jazz Classics ✦✦✦

★ **The Popular Recordings (1938-1942)** / Apr. 4, 1939-Jul. 15, 1942 / Bluebird ✦✦✦✦✦
Of the many compilations of Glenn Miller hits, this three-disc set strikes the best balance between comprehensiveness and economy. More casual listeners might want to try *Pure Gold*, while true scholars will have to have the *Complete Glenn Miller*, but this 60-track collection contains the best of the most popular bandleader of the last part of the swing era. —*William Ruhlmann*

● **Essential Glenn Miller** / Apr. 4, 1939-Jul. 15, 1942 / Bluebird ✦✦✦✦
Glenn Miller's 1939-42 Victor recordings have been reissued a countless number of times in many different ways through the years. This two-CD set does an excellent job of repackaging all of his hits plus a variety of vocal numbers in chronological order. The 47 selections sum up Miller's legacy quite well, making this a definitive set for listeners who do not desire everything that Glenn Miller recorded. —*Scott Yanow*

★ **Legendary Performer** / May 17, 1939-Sep. 24, 1942 / Bluebird ✦✦✦✦✦
On first glance, this CD may appear to be a greatest-hits package since many of the songs were recorded by Glenn Miller's Orchestra in the studios, but actually the set contains (in chronological order) many of Miller's most historic radio performances. Starting with his theme "Moonlight Serenade" from the band's opening appearance at the Glen Island Casino (when they were unknown), one can experience from song-to-song the quick rush to success, a New Year's Eve version of "In the Mood," and a classic rendition of "Chattanooga Choo Choo" (with Miller being awarded the first Gold record in history), all the way up to the announcement of Miller's entry into the Army, a surprise guest appearance by Harry James, and Glenn Miller's emotional farewell to the audience. This is an essential release for anyone with an interest in Glenn Miller's music and life. —*Scott Yanow*

Little Brown Jug, Vol. 3 / Jun. 20, 1939-Dec. 7, 1939 / Vintage Jazz Classics ✦✦✦

Tuxedo Junction (1939-1940) / Jul. 20, 1939-Apr. 5, 1940 / Vintage Jazz Classics ✦✦✦

★ **Major Glenn Miller & the Army Air Force Band (1943-1944)** / Oct. 29, 1943-Apr. 22, 1944 / Bluebird ✦✦✦✦✦
During the two years of its existence the Glenn Miller Army Air Force Band (the greatest orchestra he ever led) performed and recorded frequently although most of its sessions have been difficult to find ever since. The group was filled with talented jazz soloists (including trumpeters Bobby Nichols and Bernie Privin, clarinetist Peanuts Hucko, and pianist Mel Powell), had fine singers in Ray McKinley, Johnny Desmond and the Crew Chiefs and even an occasional 21-piece string section. This CD has many of the best performances by the huge band including "St. Louis Blues March," "Tail-End Charlie," "Anvil Chorus," "Everybody Loves My Baby," and "It Must Be Jelly" and it is highly recommended to swing fans and jazz historians. —*Scott Yanow*

The Glenn Miller V-Disc Sessions: Vol. 1 / Oct. 29, 1943-May 13, 1944 / Mr. Music ✦✦✦✦
Glenn Miller's Army Air Force Band was the finest group that he ever led. Although it did not make any commercially available recordings, the huge outfit did perform 43 songs for V-Discs that were sent to servicemen overseas. The earliest 22 are included on this first of two rewarding CDs. Mood pieces and novelty vocals alternate with some fine jazz, showing the wide variety of music that this impressive group (which often had a full string section) could generate. Highlights include "St. Louis Blues March," "Tail End Charlie," "G.I. Jive," "Stealin' Apples," and "Here We Go Again." Although the exact personnel is not given, clarinetist Peanuts Hucko, pianist Mel Powell, and trumpeter Bobby Nichols are all heard from. —*Scott Yanow*

The Glenn Miller V-Disc Sessions: Vol. 2 / May 20, 1944-Nov. 17, 1945 / Mister Music ✦✦✦✦

Mulgrew Miller

b. Aug. 13, 1955, Greenwood, MS
Piano / Post-Bop, Hard Bop

An excellent pianist who plays in a style influenced by McCoy Tyner, Mulgrew Miller has been quite consistent throughout his career. He was with Mercer Ellington's big band in the late '70s and had important stints with Betty Carter (1980), Woody Shaw (1981-83), and Art Blakey's Jazz Messengers (1983-86). For a long period he was a member of the Tony Williams Quintet (1986-94). In addition, Mulgrew Miller has led his own sessions for Landmark (starting in 1985) and Novus. —*Scott Yanow*

Hand In Hand / Dec. 16, 1992-Dec. 18, 1992 / Novus ✦✦✦✦
Mulgrew Miller, a talented McCoy Tyner-influenced pianist, leads an all-star septet on much of this date. The main stars, however, are Miller's nine diverse originals which range from modal to Monkish. With tenor saxophonist Joe Henderson appearing on five selections, trumpeter Eddie Henderson on six, and altoist Kenny Garrett heard throughout the full CD, Miller has a perfect frontline to interpret his tricky but logical originals. Vibraphonist Steve Nelson, bassist Christian McBride, and drummer Lewis Nash do not exactly get overshadowed either. —*Scott Yanow*

● **With Our Own Eyes** / Dec. 1993 / Novus ✦✦✦✦
The consistent pianist Mulgrew Miller leads his trio (which includes bassist Richie Good and drummer Tony Reedus) through a set dominated by his originals but also including "Body and Soul" and Michel Legran's "Summer Me, Winter Me." The McCoy Tyner influence will probably always remain a significant part of Miller's style but he is such a powerful player in his own right that one really does not mind. His originals on this set range from the modal 6/4 piece "Somewhere Else" and the thoughtful "Dreamin'" to the melancholy "Carousel." As with all of Mulgrew Miller's releases thus far, this one is well worth picking up. —*Scott Yanow*

Charles Mingus

b. Apr. 22, 1922, Nogales, AZ, **d.** Jan. 5, 1979, Cuernavaca, MX
Bass, Piano / Avant-Garde, Bop, Post-Bop
Charles Mingus' accomplishments and stature merit their own category. He was an awesome bassist, phenomenal composer and irascible, beloved, hated and celebrated personality. His music combined numerous influences; gospel, blues, traditional New Orleans, swing, bebop, Afro-Latin, and symphonic. He turned the bass into a percussive, harmonic, melodic, rhythm and lead instrument. Only Ellington and Monk rivaled his creativity; his use of shifting tempos, alternating meters, and trombones, tuba, and baritone sax in his arrangements was inspired. He insisted on individuality among his players, but would also assign parts and time improvisations in rehearsals. Mingus' knowledge of and ability on the piano led him at one point to hire separate bassists and play piano himself at Jazz Workshop concerts. His legendary temper caused many confrontations on and off the bandstand, and often lead to musicians' being fired in mid-performance, or concerts halted so reprimands could be immediately given. His ire would even extend to audiences he felt were inattentive. Mingus' sisters studied classical violin and piano, but his stepmother only allowed religious music in the house. She took the young Mingus to church meetings, where the moans, groans and hollers, as well as pastor/congregation interaction proved ultimately influential. He studied trombone and cello, then switched to bass partly due to exasperation at poor teachers, but also because classmate Buddy Collette informed him the high school band needed a bassist. Others in this band included Chico Hamilton, Dexter Gordon and Ernie Royal. Mingus later studied with Joe Comfort and Red Callender, plus classical player H. Reinschagen, and took composition lessons with Lloyd Reese. Mingus wrote "What Love" in 1939 and "Half-Mast Inhibitions" in 1940 while working with Reese, and these were recorded in the '60s. He played in Barney Bigard's band in 1942 along with Kid Ory, then joined Louis Armstrong in 1943. While in this band, some transcription sessions for broadcast became his first recordings. Mingus briefly replaced Callender in Lee Young's band. There were stints with Howard McGhee, Illinois Jacquet, Dinah Washington and Ivie Anderson, plus a few engagements heading groups. Mingus worked in 1946 and 1947 with Lionel Hampton, and made jazz and R&B recordings, becoming known as "Baron Von Mingus." But his major jazz attention came in the early '50s. Mingus left a Post Office gig to join Red Norvo's trio with Tal Farlow. He exited the ensemble a year later after an incident in which he was temporarily displaced by a white bassist for a New York television show. This ugliness was caused by a combination of union and racial politics. Mingus worked with Billy Taylor, Lennie Tristano, Duke Ellington, Stan Getz, Art Tatum and Bud Powell in the early and mid-'50s. His stint with Ellington ended on a downbeat; his legendary temper erupted during a dispute with trombonist Juan Tizol, and he joined the short list of musicians openly fired by Duke. Mingus participated in the landmark 1953 Massey Hall concert in Canada with Charlie Parker, Dizzy Gillespie, Bud Powell and Max Roach. He began his own record company, Debut, in partnership with Roach in 1952. It lasted until 1955, issuing recordings by Teo Macero, Kenny Dorham, Paul Bley, John La Porta and Sam Most among others. One Debut release, *Four Trombones*, led to Mingus cutting a Savoy session with J.J. Johnson and Kai Winding. He also worked with Thad Jones, Eddie Bert, Willie Jones, George Barrow and many others. From 1953 to 1955, he was one of several musicians who contributed pieces to a Jazz Composers' Workshop. Mingus founded his own Jazz Workshop in 1955, turning it into a top repertory company. He'd present his pieces to musi-

cians partly by dictating them their lines. The personnel ranged from a low of four to a high of 11, and included over the years Eric Dolphy, Booker Ervin, Jackie McLean, Shafi Hadi, John Handy, Rahsaan Roland Kirk, Jaki Byard, Jimmy Knepper and longtime drummer Dannie Richmond. Mingus' unprecedented compositional skills flourished from the mid-'50s through the '60s. He wrote extended suites, open-ended jams, "free" selections, songs with collectively improvised sections colliding with chaotic dialogues, works for large orchestra, tributes, socio-political anthems and songs with Afro-Latin and African rhythms. The list of brilliant compositions included "My Jelly Roll Soul," "Jelly Roll," "Fables of Faubus," "Orange Was The Color of Her Dress," "Goodbye Pork Pie Hat," "Meditations on Integration" and "Wednesday Night Prayer Meeting." There were others like "Epitaph" that were never completely performed or perfected during his lifetime. This proved an equally productive period for albums. Seminal works issued included *Pithecanthropus Erectus, The Clown, East Coasting, Scenes In The City, Tijuana Moods* and *Wonderland*. There were also remarkable dates for Columbia with Mingus leading a superb 8-10 piece unit and cutting unforgettable versions of "Goodbye Pork Pie Hat" and "Fables Of Faubus." His early '60s groups with Dolphy may have been his finest; they were certainly among his most dynamic performance bands. There were artistic triumphs but sales failures for Candid, ambitious dates for Impulse, including one where he played unaccompanied solo piano throughout, and more successful financially successful works for Atlantic. His acclaimed early and mid-'60s European tours with The Dolphy group were later issued on Atlantic and Prestige recordings. Earlier in his career, Mingus had expressed outrage over the treatment and inequities musicians faced. He'd tried to change things before with his record label. He tried again in 1960, organizing a series of concerts to compete with the Newport Jazz Festival. This effort led to the formation of the short-lived Jazz Artists Guild, an organization that was conceived to assist musicians in promoting and controlling their work. Unfortunately, it collapsed in a wave of rancor and discord, and a financially disastrous 1962 Town Hall concert virtually ended his promotional ventures. Mingus tried to start another record company, but the Charles Mingus label issued few titles and made even less money in its brief existence during 1964 and 1965. He stormed off the Monterey Festival stage in 1965, and eventually withdrew from performing, broke and embittered. A 1968 film "Mingus" directed by Thomas Reichman got lots of attention for showing Mingus being booted out of his New York apartment. Mingus resumed his performing career in 1969. Fantasy purchased the Debut masters and provided him vital funds. Early '70s albums on Columbia and Atlantic, including a live sold-out date at Avery Fisher Hall, rekindled public attention. He received a well deserved Guggenheim fellowship in composition. Mingus' controversial autobiography *Beneath The Underdog*, which had been rejected for publication nearly 10 years earlier, was published and triggered widespread discussion and evaluation (though many raised doubts about various chapters and incidents). Sadly, Mingus' health was fading; he had developed amyotrophic lateral sclerosis, better known as Lou Gehrig's disease. He composed more big band music, including the wonderful *Cumbia and Jazz Fusion* in 1977, and led one last great combo before becoming physically unable to play. This group with tenor saxophonist George Adams, trumpeter Jack Walrath, pianist Don Pullen and drummer Dannie Richmond issued superb albums *Mingus Moves, Changes One* and *Changes Two* in the early '70s. Mingus collaborated on an album with folk and rock vocalist Joni Mitchell, and directed his bands from a wheelchair. His last session came in January of 1978, though he did live long enough to be recognized at the White House by President Carter, a truly poignant moment. Charles Mingus' work lives on via reissues galore. Mosaic has reissued both his Candid output and his amazing 1959 Columbia releases. Prestige has issued the complete Debut masters. Atlantic in 1993 issued the Mingus anthology *Thirteen Pictures*, and reissued *Mingus Moves, Changes One & Two*. His piano album and other Impulses are being reissued by MCA. England's Affinity has reissued some of his great late '50s albums. "Epitaph" was finally performed by an orchestra in 1991, and an album featuring it has also been released. The Mingus Dynasty repertory band has recorded and toured in various editions. Brian Priestly's fine 1982 book, *Mingus*, has provided a scholarly and comprehensive view of his achievements. —*Ron Wynn and Mike Katz*

☆ **The Complete Debut Recordings** / Apr. 1951-1958 / Debut ✦✦✦✦✦

Thirteen Pictures: the Charles Mingus Anthology / 1952-1977 / Rhino ✦✦
Even on a loving two-disc anthology, it's impossible to accurately or fully convey the accomplishments of Charles Mingus, arguably jazz's finest modern bassist/composer. *Thirteen Pictures* tries to outline his career achievements by spotlighting his most famous works and also showcase his abilities. But the sequencing is odd, with songs hopping from decade to decade and the older things coming near the end rather than beginning. Still, there are many essential Mingus pieces here, from the sprawling "Cumbia & Jazz Fusion" to the seminal "Goodbye Pork Pie Hat," "Pithecanthropus Erectus," and "Better Git It In Your Soul." The absence of "Fables of Faubus" is puzzling, and the inclusion of only one track featuring Eric Dolphy is bizarre, but for the Mingus newcomer to whom this set was obvi-

ously directed, it fulfills its basic goal of introducing a genius' work. —*Ron Wynn*

Mingus at the Bohemia / Dec. 23, 1955 / Original Jazz Classics ✦✦✦✦
A live performance at the Club Bohemia in New York, this is the first Mingus recording to feature mostly his own compositions. Some are his future standards. Here are his first attempts at future techniques such as combining two songs into one. His bass playing really stands out. —*Michael Katz*

Plus Max Roach / Dec. 23, 1955 / Fantasy ✦✦✦✦
The Mingus/Roach/Mal Waldron dialogs overcome the ordinary stylings of Eddie Bert and George Barrow. —*Ron Wynn*

Charles Mingus / Dec. 23, 1955 / Prestige ✦✦✦✦
This Prestige two-fer combines two LPs recorded at New York's Cafe Bohemia in December 1955, originally known as *Mingus at the Bohemia* and *Mingus Quintet Plus Max Roach*. This is some of his most spirited live work, with a number of experiments in combining themes (e.g., "Septemberly" is a montage of "September" and "Tenderly") It's an almost totally successful date, with Max Roach adding another dimension to the few tracks he's on. Note that Fantasy's exhaustive Complete Debut Recordings adds no less than 11 more tracks to the original 12. —*Stuart Kremsky*

★ **Pithecanthropus Erectus** / Jan. 30, 1956 / Atlantic ✦✦✦✦✦
This Atlantic set has the first truly classic Charles Mingus performance, the lengthy title cut which attempts to depict musically the rise and fall of man. Altoist Jackie McLean, tenor saxophonist J.R. Monterose, pianist Mal Waldron, and drummer Willie Jones join the bassist/leader for some stirring music with the humorous "A Foggy Day," (complete with sirens and horns honking like automobiles), "Profile of Jackie," and "Love Chant" completing the particularly strong program. —*Scott Yanow*

The Clown / Feb. 13, 1957-Mar. 12, 1957 / Atlantic ✦✦✦✦
All of Charles Mingus' Atlantic sessions are well worth picking up, including this LP. "Haitian Fight Song" is a classic, "Reincarnation of a Lovebird" is close, "Blue Cee" gives the principals (which include trombonist Jimmy Knepper and Shafi Hadi on alto and tenor) a chance to stretch out, and Jean Shepherd verbally improvises a memorable story on "The Clown." —*Scott Yanow*

★ **New Tijuana Moods** / Jul. 18, 1957-Aug. 6, 1957 / Bluebird ✦✦✦✦✦
One of the great Charles Mingus recordings, *Tijuana Moods* found the bassist really inspiring his sidemen (trombonist Jimmy Knepper, altoist Shafi Hadi, trumpeter Clarence Shaw, pianist BIll Triglia, and drummer Danny Richmond) to play above their heads. The music, inspired by a trip to Mexico, is intense yet quite accessible and all five selections are memorable. This two-LP set is actually two sets in one, the original program plus a full LP of alternate takes, all longer than the original masters. The music never loses one's interest and is quite innovative for the period. —*Scott Yanow*

East Coasting / Aug. 16, 1957 / Bethlehem ✦✦✦✦
One of Charles Mingus' lesser-known band sessions, this set of five of his originals (plus the standard "Memories of You") features his usual sidemen of the period (trombonist Jimmy Knepper, trumpeter Clarence Shaw, Shafi Hadi on tenor and alto, and drummer Danny Richmond) along with pianist Bill Evans. The music stretches the boundaries of bop, is never predictable and, even if this is not one of Mingus' more acclaimed dates, it is well worth acquiring for the playing is quite stimulating. —*Scott Yanow*

Jazz Portraits / Jan. 16, 1959 / United Artists ✦✦✦✦
This CD, a straight reissue of *Wonderland*, finds bassist/leader Charles Mingus really pushing altoist John Handy and tenor saxophonist Booker Ervin on four lengthy selections, highlighted by "Nostalgia in Times Square" and "No Private Income Blues." The music is advanced bop that looks towards the upcoming innovations of the avant-garde and is frequently quite exciting. —*Scott Yanow*

☆ **Blues and Roots** / Feb. 4, 1959 / Atlantic ✦✦✦✦✦
One of Charles Mingus' finest studio albums, this date finds the bassist utilizing a nonet (including altoists Jackie McLean and John Handy, Booker Ervin on tenor, baritonist Pepper Adams, and the trombones of Jimmy Knepper and Willie Dennis) on six diverse but consistently stimulating originals. Highlights including "Wednesday Night Prayer Meeting," "Cryin' Blues," "E's Flat Ah's Flat Too," and especially "Moanin'." Although "My Jelly Roll Soul" does not really work, the other numbers find Mingus successfully looking both backwards (with group improvising, stop-time breaks, and church-like harmonies) and forward (with advanced improvisations and a wider use of emotions than was being utilized in bop). —*Scott Yanow*

Complete 1959 CBS Charles Mingus Sessions / May 5, 1959-Nov. 13, 1959 / Mosaic ✦✦✦✦
In 1959 Charles Mingus recorded two tightly edited LPs for Columbia titled *Mingus Ah Um* and *Mingus Dynasty*. Both of those albums are recommended in their original form as is this limited edition four-LP set which restores solos originally cut out and adds numerous alternate takes to these fascinating sessions. Such players as altoist John Handy, tenor saxophonists Booker Ervin and Shafi Hadi, trombonists Jimmy Knepper and

Willie Dennis, trumpeters Richard Williams and Don Ellis, pianists Roland Hanna and Horace Parlan are heard on this deluxe set which is highlighted by the original versions of "Better Git It in Your Soul," "Fables of Faubus," "Boogie Stop Shuffle," "Goodbye Pork Pie Hat," and "Song with Orange." —*Scott Yanow*

☆ **Mingus Ah Um** / May 5, 1959-May 12, 1959 / Columbia ✦✦✦✦✦
This LP from 1959 is one of Charles Mingus' classics, highlighted by the original versions of "Better Git It in Your Soul," "Goodbye Pork Pie Hat," "Boogie Stop Shuffle," and "Fables of Faubus." Well deserving of reissue on CD, such top-notch musicians as altoist John Handy, tenors Booker Ervin and Shafi Hadi, trombonists Jimmy Knepper and Willie Dennis, pianist Roland Hanna, and drummer Danny Richmond gave bassist Mingus one of his strongest units. —*Scott Yanow*

Mingus Dynasty / Nov. 1, 1959-Nov. 13, 1959 / Columbia ✦✦✦✦
This CD is a straight reissue of the original LP and finds bassist Charles Mingus leading two overlapping but different nine and ten piece groups. Much of the music was written for soundtracks of the time but they easily stand out on their own with fine solos from trombonist Jimmy Knepper, Booker Ervin on tenor, altoist John Handy, and pianist Roland Hanna uplifting such songs as "Slop," "Song with Orange," "Far Wells, Mill Valley" and two Duke Ellington-associated numbers. The music can also be heard in unedited form (with many solos added back in) on a Mosaic box set. —*Scott Yanow*

★ **Mingus at Antibes** / Jul. 13, 1960 / Atlantic ✦✦✦✦✦
During 1960 bassist Charles Mingus led one of his finest bands, a pianoless quartet with Eric Dolphy (on alto, flute, and bass clarinet), trumpeter Ted Curson, and drummer Danny Richmond. For this live concert, the band is augmented by the great tenor Booker Ervin for some stirring music. All of the music is memorable: "Wednesday Night Prayer Meeting," "Prayer for Passive Resistance," "What Love," "Folk Forms I," and "Better Git It in Your Soul." The immortal pianist Bud Powell sits in on a fine version of "I'll Remember April" and Dolphy and Ervin in particular generate a great deal of heat during some of their solos. —*Scott Yanow*

Charles Mingus Presents Charles Mingus / Oct. 20, 1960 / Candid ✦✦✦✦
This quartet date is probably among the very finest jazz records ever made. Dolphy and Curson make a great front line and Mingus and Richmond seem to share one mind between them. The absence of a piano keeps everyone on their toes. All first takes recorded in one afternoon, the session is presented as if it were a nightclub set of the period, complete with Mingus' spoken introduction. —*Stuart Kremsky*

☆ **Complete Candid Recordings** / Oct. 20, 1960-Nov. 11, 1960 / Mosaic ✦✦✦✦✦
Bassist/leader Charles Mingus cut some of his most exciting and rewarding recordings for Candid in 1960 and this superb four-LP set (which unfortunately is a limited edition) contains all of the music except for a couple of alternate takes that showed up later on. Five selections feature the brilliant pianoless quartet of Eric Dolphy (on alto, bass clarinet, and flute), trumpeter Ted Curson, Mingus, and drummer Dannie Richmond and these are highlighted by the bass clarinet-bass conversation on "What Love" and the interplay between the four musicians on the very memorable "Folk Forms No. 1." Other musicians are added to six other selections (including the 19-minute jam "MDM") and five other numbers feature trumpeter Roy Eldridge who is teamed with altoist Dolphy on three of the songs; those pieces originally appeared on the Newport Rebels LP. This is a highly recommended set that promises to be hard to find in the future. —*Scott Yanow*

Mysterious Blues / Oct. 20, 1960-Nov. 11, 1960 / Candid ✦✦✦✦
Although a Mosaic box set claims to have all of Charles Mingus' Candid recordings, this CD, in addition to four duplications from the box, contains three alternate takes not included elsewhere: "Body and Soul" (featuring trumpeter Roy Eldridge and altoist Eric Dolphy), the Dannie Richmond drum solo "Melody from the Drums," and a septet runthrough on "Reincarnation of a Love Bird." A fine introduction into the music of Charles Mingus, this set still cannot compare to the Mosaic box which has Mingus' pianoless quartet with Dolphy, Richmond, and trumpeter Ted Curson, but completists will have to acquire both releases. —*Scott Yanow*

☆ **Oh Yeah** / Nov. 6, 1961 / Atlantic ✦✦✦✦✦
One of the great Charles Mingus LPs, this Atlantic release (which finds Mingus sticking exclusively to piano and vocal shouts throughout) not only features tenor saxophonist Booker Ervin, trombonist Jimmy Knepper, bassist Doug Watkins, and drummer Dannie Richmond but the amazing Rahsaan Roland Kirk on tenor, manzello, stritch, flute, and siren. The music is quite emotional and passionate with "Hog Callin' Blues," "Wham Bam Thank You Ma'am," and the explosive "Ecclusiastics" being particularly memorable. —*Scott Yanow*

Money Jungle / Sep. 17, 1962 / Blue Note ✦✦✦✦
George Wein, in his liner notes for this classic session, says that "to hear this album is to believe fully in the validity and lasting qualities of jazz." How right he is. Ellington was between recording contracts at the time, and

producer Alan Douglas, hustling to get some product out on United Artists, brought him together with two modern musicians who practically idolized him. The results, which sound much better on CD than they did on LP, reveal the continuity of jazz, grounded in the blues. Mingus was reportedly quite nervous at the session, and perhaps it's this tension that contributes to his energized conversational style. Roach is an equal partner in the group, with his precise and flowing rhythms. It's one of the great piano trio records. —*Stuart Kremsky*

Complete Town Hall Concert / Oct. 12, 1962 / Blue Note ✦✦✦

The Black Saint and the Sinner Lady / Jan. 20, 1963 / Impulse ✦✦✦✦
One of Charles Mingus' most successful longer suites, the six-part "Black Saint and the Sinner Lady" is full of surprising moments with the 11-piece band exploring a wide variety of moods and colors. Of particular note are Quentin Jackson's wa-wa trombone (which lets Mingus hint strongly at Duke Ellington) and Charlie Mariano's passionate alto. —*Scott Yanow*

☆ **Mingus, Mingus, Mingus, Mingus, Mingus** / Jan. 20, 1963 & Sep. 20, 1963 / Impulse ✦✦✦✦✦
This CD features two separate recording sessions with such top players as trumpeter Richard Williams, trombonists Quentin Jackson and Britt Woodman, Dick Hafer and Booker Ervin on tenors, the many reeds of Eric Dolphy and Jerome Richardson, altoist Charles Mariano, and pianist Jaki Byard. Of the seven selections (all of which are memorable), high points include "Mood Indigo," the fiery "Hora Decubitus," and the definitive version of "Better Get Hit in Yo' Soul." —*Scott Yanow*

Mingus Plays Piano / Jul. 30, 1963 / Mobile Fidelity ✦✦✦✦
Bassist Charles Mingus would never qualify as a virtuoso on the piano but his technique was reasonably impressive and his imagination quite brilliant. This unique solo piano CD (a reissue of a date for Impulse) has a few standards ("Body and Soul," "Memories of You," and "I'm Getting Sentimental over You") along with some freely improvised originals, most of which are quite fascinating to hear, as if one were listening to Mingus think aloud. —*Scott Yanow*

Mingus in Europe / Apr. 26, 1964 / Enja ✦✦✦✦
This CD reissues three selections originally on the LP *Mingus in Europe, Vol. 2* ("Orange Was the Color of Her Dress Then Blue Silk," "Sophisticated Lady" and "AT-FW-YOU") and also includes two performances ("Peggy's Blue Sky Light" and the nearly 23-minute "So Long Eric") that do not seem to have been issued previously. The 1964 Charles Mingus Quintet (trumpeter Johnny Coles had departed a few days earlier due to illness) teamed together the unique multi-instrumentalist Eric Dolphy, tenor saxophonist Clifford Jordan, pianist Jaki Byard, drummer Dannie Richmond, and the bassist/leader in one of the great bands of the '60s. There are many recordings currently available from their European tour and all are worth acquiring including this excellent Enja set (at least by Mingus fans not already owning *Vol. 2*). —*Scott Yanow*

Right Now / Jun. 2, 1964-Jun. 3, 1964 / Original Jazz Classics ✦✦✦✦
Soon after Charles Mingus finished touring Europe with his band (the unit that featured Eric Dolphy), he recorded this CD, performed live at The Jazz Workshop in San Francisco. With tenor saxophonist Clifford Jordan and drummer Dannie Richmond still in the group but Jane Getz replacing pianist Jaki Byard and altoist John Handy filling in for Dolphy on one song, the band performs excellent versions of "Meditations on Integration" and "New Fables," both of which are over 23 minutes long. Although not up to the passionate level of the Mingus-Dolphy Quintet, this underrated unit holds its own. —*Scott Yanow*

Shoes of the Fisherman's Wife . . . . / Sep. 23, 1971-Nov. 1, 1959 / Columbia ✦✦✦
Most of the *Mingus Dynasty*, which features the same lineup as *Mingus Ah Um* and has a similar feel but is less driving. Inexplicable inclusion of "Shoes of the . . . ." from *Let My Children Hear Music*, recorded twelve years later. All great music. —*Michael Katz*

Let My Children Hear Music / 1972 / Columbia ✦✦✦
The CD reissue of the original LP adds one selection ("Taurus in the Arena of Life") to the program of original music. Mingus' unique compositions (mostly recent although one was written back in 1939) receive sympathetic treatment by a partly unidentified large orchestra and are full of interesting textures, sound explorations, and surprises. It makes for a stimulating listen. —*Scott Yanow*

Mingus Moves / 1973 / Atlantic ✦✦✦✦
On this Atlantic LP, Charles Mingus introduced his new group which at the time included trumpeter Ronald Hampton, tenor saxophonist George Adams, pianist Don Pullen, and his longtime drummer Dannie Richmond. Together this excellent quintet performed seven recent compositions including one ("Moves") that features the vocals of Honey Gordon and Doug Hammond. Only three of the pieces are by Mingus but all of the music is greatly influenced by his searching and unpredictable style. This out-of-print LP is worth searching for. —*Scott Yanow*

Mingus at Carnegie Hall / Jan. 19, 1974 / Atlantic ✦✦✦✦
Although Charles Mingus is the leader on this date, it is actually a jam ses-

sion featuring an all-star cast (the amazing Rahsaan Roland Kirk, trumpeter Jon Faddis, John Handy on alto and tenor, altoist Charles McPherson, tenor saxophonist George Adams, baritonist Hamiet Bluiett, pianist Don Pullen, drummer Dannie Richmond, and the bassist-leader) playing rather long versions of "C Jam Blues" and "Perdido." Of the soloists, Handy shows off his high note alto on "Perdido" and Faddis (who was then 20) plays some of his favorite Dizzy Gillespie licks but Rahsaan Roland Kirk (who at one point imitates George Adams) cuts everyone. This CD is a straight reissue of the original LP and is often quite exciting. —*Scott Yanow*

Changes One / Dec. 27, 1974-Dec. 30, 1974 / Atlantic ✦✦✦✦
Charles Mingus' finest recordings of his later period are *Changes One* and *Changes Two*, two Atlantic LPs that have been reissued on CD by Rhino. The first volume features four stimulating Mingus originals ("Remember Rockefeller at Attica," "Sue's Changes," "Devil Blues," and "Duke Ellington's Sound of Love") performed by a particularly talented quintet (tenor saxophonist George Adams who also sings "Devil Blues," trumpeter Jack Walrath, pianist Don Pullen, drummer Dannie Richmond, and the leader/bassist). The band has the adventurous spirit and chance-taking approach of Charles Mingus' best groups, making this an easily recommended example of the great bandleader's music. —*Scott Yanow*

Changes Two / Dec. 27, 1974-Dec. 30, 1974 / Atlantic ✦✦✦✦
Along with *Changes One* (both Atlantic LPs have been reissued on CD by Rhino), this set is one of Charles Mingus' most rewarding of his later period. Mingus' band (trumpeter Jack Walrath, tenor saxophonist George Adams, pianist Don Pullen, and drummer Dannie Richmond) was particularly strong. This set is highlighted by a 17-minute version of "Orange Was the Color of Her Dress, Then Silk Blue," Sy Johnson's "For Harry Carney," and Jackie Paris' vocal on "Duke Ellington's Sound of Love." —*Scott Yanow*

Cumbia and Jazz Fusion / Mar. 31, 1976-May 1, 1977 / Atlantic ✦✦✦✦
As Charles Mingus' career (and life) moved into this final phase, his recordings exclusively featured large (and often potentially unruly) ensembles. This CD, which contains two rather long performances originally recorded as soundtracks for films, is better than most of what followed. "Cumbia & Jazz Fusion" has a large percussion section and quite a few woodwinds along with trumpeter Jack Walrath, tenor saxophonist Ricky Ford and trombonist Jimmy Knepper while "Music for 'Todo Modo'" adds five horns to Mingus' Quintet. The music is episodic but generally holds its own away from the film. —*Scott Yanow*

Bob Mintzer

b. 1953
Clarinet (Bass), Sax (Tenor) / Post-Bop
A versatile soloist influenced by Michael Brecker on tenor, Bob Mintzer gained experience playing with Deodato, Tito Puente (1974), Buddy Rich, Hubert Laws, and the Thad Jones-Mel Lewis Orchestra (1977). In addition to leading his own bands starting in 1978, Mintzer worked with Jaco Pastorius, Mike Mainieri, Louie Bellson, Bob Moses, and the American Saxophone Quartet. He has guested with several Philharmonic Orchestras and led a fine big band in New York since the mid-'80s. Mintzer, a member of the Yellowjackets since 1991 (where his bass clarinet in particular adds a great deal of color to the group), has recorded regularly for DMP for the past decade. —*Scott Yanow*

Art of the Big Band / Sep. 22, 1990-Sep. 23, 1990 / DMP ✦✦✦

I Remember Jaco / Mar. 6, 1991-Mar. 7, 1991 / Novus ✦✦✦✦
Nice tribute to the late bassist by tenor saxophonist and bass clarinetist Bob Mintzer. Instead of his usual big band, Mintzer heads a small combo, which provides space for both himself and other soloists, like pianist Joey Calderazzo. —*Ron Wynn*

● **One Music** / 1991 / DMP ✦✦✦✦
This saxophonist's best small-group work, with fellow Yellow Jackets. The best cuts are the title and "Look Around." Ventures funky and creative into neo-bop modes. —*Michael G. Nastos*

Big Band Trane / Dec. 15, 1995-Dec. 16, 1995 / DMP ✦✦✦✦

Blue Mitchell (Richard Allen Mitchell)

b. Mar. 13, 1930, Miami, FL, **d.** May 21, 1979, Los Angeles, CA
Trumpet / Hard Bop
A wonderful hard bop, blues, and ballad player, Blue Mitchell was the kind of hard working, consistent player who gets overlooked because he's not a star or innovator. Mitchell's lyrical sound and luminous timbre were superbly presented in some fine groups and as a leader in his own combos. He began playing trumpet in high school, acquiring both a good reputation and his nickname. Mitchell toured with the R&B bands of Paul Williams, Earl Bostic, and Chuck Willis in the early '50s. He returned to his Miami hometown off the road in the late '50s, and Cannonball Adderley heard him playing at a club. Adderley took Mitchell with him to New York and they recorded for Riverside in 1958. Mitchell joined Horace Silver's quintet that same year and remained until 1964, participating in some

invigorating dates. When Silver disbanded the ensemble, its members stayed together. The original band was Mitchell, Junior Cook, Gene Taylor, and Roy Brooks. Later Chick Corea and Al Foster replaced Taylor and Brooks, with Mitchell and Cook dividing leadership duties. Later Harold Mabern and Billy Higgins replaced Corea and Foster. Mitchell became a prolific pop and soul session player in the late '60s, recording instrumental pop LPs, touring with Ray Charles and John Mayall. During the mid-'70s, Mitchell did various dates in Los Angeles, while often serving as principal soloist for Tony Bennett and Lena Horne. He played in the big bands of Louis Bellson, Bill Holman, and Bill Berry and worked in several bebop bands, including a quintet with Richie Kamauca. Mitchell was also in a quintet with Harold Land, from 1975 until 1978, while cutting more instrumental pop and disco albums in the late '70s. His career was cut short by his death of cancer at 49. —*Ron Wynn*

★ **Big Six** / Jul. 2, 1958-Jul. 3, 1958 / Original Jazz Classics ✦✦✦✦✦
Trumpeter Blue Mitchell was a virtual unknown when he recorded this Riverside album, his first as a leader. Now reissued on CD in the *OJC* series, Mitchell is heard in excellent form in an all-star sextet with trombonist Curtis Fuller, tenor-great Johnny Griffin, pianist Wynton Kelly, bassist Wilbur Ware, and drummer Philly Joe Jones. In addition to some group originals, obscurities, and the standard "There Will Never Be Another You," the group also plays the earliest recorded version of Benny Golson's "Blues March," predating Art Blakey's famous recording. —*Scott Yanow*

Blues on My Mind / Jul. 1958-Sep. 1959 / Riverside ✦✦✦

Out of the Blue / Jan. 1959 / Original Jazz Classics ✦✦✦✦
This early recording by Blue Mitchell finds the distinctive trumpeter in excellent form in a quintet also featuring tenor saxophonist Benny Golson (who contributed "Blues on My Mind"), either Wynton Kelly or Cedar Walton on piano, Paul Chambers or Sam Jones on bass, and drummer Art Blakey. The consistently swinging repertoire includes a surprisingly effective version of "When the Saints Go Marching In." "Studio B," recorded in the same period but formerly available only in a sampler, has been added to the program. It's an easily enjoyable date of high-quality hard bop. —*Scott Yanow*

Blue Soul / Sep. 1959 / Original Jazz Classics ✦✦✦✦
This CD reissue bring back one of trumpeter Blue Mitchell's better sessions from his early period, his third recording as a leader for Riverside. Six of the selections also feature trombonist Curtis Fuller (in excellent form) and the tenor of Jimmy Heath in a sextet with pianist Wynton Kelly, bassist Sam Jones, and drummer Philly Joe Jones; the arrangements were provided by Heath and Benny Golson. The other three numbers are more informal and showcase Mitchell in a quartet with Kelly and the Jones. Excellent hard bop with the repertoire consisting of "The Way You Look Tonight," "Polka Dots and Moonbeams," "Nica's Dream," and two originals apiece from Golson, Heath, and Mitchell. —*Scott Yanow*

Blue's Moods / Aug. 24, 1960-Aug. 25, 1960 / Original Jazz Classics ✦✦✦✦
Smooth 1960 session that blends romantic pieces, soul-jazz, and mainstream. —*Ron Wynn*

Smooth As the Wind / Dec. 27, 1960-Mar. 30, 1961 / Riverside ✦✦✦✦
Trumpeter Blue Mitchell is in excellent form on this very interesting session which has been reissued on CD. Mitchell is accompanied by a brass section, a rhythm section, and strings. The arrangements (seven by Tadd Dameron and three from Benny Golson) are generally quite stimulating, inspiring the trumpeter to come up with many fresh melodic solos. The repertoire includes two songs that Mitchell played regularly with Horace Silver's Quintet, a pair of superior Tadd Dameron tunes (including the title cut), and six standards. By varying tempos and moods, Dameron and Golson helped create one of the better soloist-with-strings jazz dates. —*Scott Yanow*

A Sure Thing / Mar. 7, 1962-Mar. 28, 1962 / Original Jazz Classics ✦✦✦✦
Trumpeter Blue Mitchell is well featured on this CD reissue with a nonet arranged by Jimmy Heath. The music is straightahead but, thanks to Heath's arrangements, sometimes unpredictable. Best is Mitchell's solo on "I Can't Get Started," "Hootie's Blues," and a quintet workout (with Heath, pianist Wynton Kelly, bassist Sam Jones, and drummer Albert "Tootie" Heath) on "Gone with the Wind." —*Scott Yanow*

Cup Bearers / Aug. 28, 1962 & Aug. 30, 1962 / Original Jazz Classics ✦✦✦✦
Trumpeter Blue Mitchell and four-fifths of the Horace Silver Quintet (with Cedar Walton in Silver's place) perform a variety of superior songs on this CD reissue including Walton's "Turquoise," Tom McIntosh's "Cup Bearers," Thad Jones' "Tiger Lily," and a couple of standards. The music swings hard, mostly avoids sounding like a Horace Silver group, and has particularly strong solos from Mitchell, tenor saxophonist Junior Cook, and Walton; excellent hard bop. —*Scott Yanow*

★ **The Thing to Do** / Jul. 30, 1964 / Blue Note ✦✦✦✦✦
With Chick Corea, Jr. Cook (ts), and Al Foster (d). Recommended for jazz/trumpet lovers. —*Michael G. Nastos*

Down with It / Jul. 14, 1965 / Blue Note ✦✦✦✦
One of Mitchell's least-recognized sessions, this has some fervent trumpet pieces, plus nice piano from a then still-emerging Chick Corea. —*Ron Wynn*

Red Mitchell (Keith Moore Mitchell)

b. Sep. 20, 1927, New York, NY, **d.** 1992
Bass / Cool, Hard Bop
A talented bassist who was always in great demand, Red Mitchell was originally a pianist and he doubled on piano on an occasional basis throughout his career. He switched to bass when he was a member of an Army band in Germany. Mitchell played with Jackie Paris (1947-48), Mundell Lowe, Chubby Jackson's big band, and Charlie Ventura (1949), toured with Woody Herman's Orchestra (1949-51), and was a member of the popular Red Norvo Trio (1952-54). He played with the Gerry Mulligan Quartet (1954) and then settled in Los Angeles where during 1954-68 he played with nearly everyone, from West Coast jazz stars (particularly Hampton Hawes) to recording with Ornette Coleman (1959) and being a member of the studio orchestra of MGM. He also co-led a quintet with Harold Land during 1961-62 that recorded for Atlantic. In 1968 Mitchell moved to Stockholm where he led groups, played with European jazzmen, and accompanied visiting Americans including Dizzy Gillespie and Phil Woods. Mitchell made occasional visits to the US and shortly before he died he moved to Oregon. In addition to the Atlantic date, Red Mitchell led albums for Bethlehem (1955), Contemporary, Pacific Jazz, Mercury, SteepleChase, Caprice, Gryphon, Phontastic, Enja, and Capri in addition to a few smaller European labels. —*Scott Yanow*

Presenting Red Mitchell / Mar. 26, 1957 / Original Jazz Classics ✦✦✦✦
One of the earliest sessions for this bassist, pianist, and singer from New York City; it helped launch his career. —*Ron Wynn*

● **Hear Ye!** / Oct. 14, 1961 / Atlantic ✦✦✦✦
In the early '60s bassist Red Mitchell and tenor saxophonist Harold Land co-led a quintet in Los Angeles. The group did not catch on but they did record one Atlantic set which has been reissued on CD. In addition to the co-leaders, the quintet included trumpeter Carmell Jones, pianist Frank Strazzeri, and drummer Leon Pettis and, although their original program of six songs was comprised entirely of group originals, the music falls easily into the hard bop area with plenty of fine solos and swinging ensembles. The CD reissue adds two previously unreleased tracks including a lone standard, "I'm Old Fashioned." This is a fine effort from a group that deserved greater recognition at the time. —*Scott Yanow*

Talking / Jan. 10, 1989-Jan. 11, 1989 / Capri ✦✦✦✦
This Capri CD has trio playing of the highest order. Bassist Red Mitchell welcomes pianist Kenny Barron and drummer Ben Riley and surprisingly only performs three standards along with Thelonious Monk's "Locomotive"; the remainder of the program is comprised of a Kenny Barron song and five originals from the multi-talented Mitchell. The close communication between these three players is quite impressive and the music always swings. —*Scott Yanow*

Roscoe Mitchell

b. Aug. 3, 1940, Chicago, IL
Sax (Alto), Sax (Tenor), Reeds (Multiple) / Avant-Garde, Free Jazz
One of the top saxophonists to come out of Chicago's AACM movement of the mid-'60s, Roscoe Mitchell is a particularly strong and consistently adventurous improviser long associated with the Art Ensemble of Chicago. After getting out of the military, Mitchell led a hard bop sextet in Chicago (1961) which gradually became much freer. He was a member of Muhal Richard Abrams' Experimental Band and a founding member of the AACM in 1965. Mitchell's monumental *Sound* album (1966) introduced a new way of freely improvising, utilizing silence as well as high energy and "little instruments" as well as conventional horns. Lester Bowie and Malachi Favors were on that date and Mitchell's 1967 follow-up *Old/Quartet*. With the addition of Joseph Jarman and Philip Wilson (who was later succeeded by Don Moye), the Art Ensemble of Chicago was born. The colorful unit was one of the most popular groups in the jazz avant-garde and Mitchell was an integral part of the band. Roscoe Mitchell (who, in addition to his main horns, plays clarinet, flute, piccolo, oboe, baritone and bass saxophones) also was involved in individual projects through the years and has recorded as a leader for Delmark, Nessa, Sackville, Moers Music, 1750 Arch, Black Saint, Cecma, and Silkheart in settings ranging from large ensembles to unaccompanied solo concerts. —*Scott Yanow*

★ **Sound** / Aug. 11, 1966 & Sep. 18, 1966 / Delmark ✦✦✦✦✦
Mitchell's first significant statement as a leader has ambitious pieces, amazing solos, and unorthodox arrangements. —*Ron Wynn*

Live at the Knitting Factory / Nov. 1987 / Black Saint ✦✦✦✦

Duets & Solos / Mar. 1990 / Black Saint ✦✦✦✦

This Dance Is for Steve Mc Call / May 1992 / Black Saint ✦✦✦✦

● **Hey Donald** / May 23, 1994-May 25, 1994 / Delmark ✦✦✦✦
Since Roscoe Mitchell (who on this set made his return to the Delmark label after 28 years) is best known as a free jazz pioneer and a longtime member of the Art Ensemble of Chicago, the straightahead nature of a few of the selections will surprise some of his followers. "Walking in the Moonlight" is a sly and witty strut, "Jeremy" a melodic ballad for the leader's flute and "Hey Donald" could have come from the Sonny Rollins songbook. But Mitchell has not forsaken his innovative style. On "Dragons" his soprano playing (with its circular breathing) sounds very African, there are four free duets with bassist Malachi Favors, and the blowouts on "Song for Rwanda" and "See You at the Fair" are pretty adventurous. In general Mitchell (who is joined by a versatile rhythm section comprised of pianist Jodie Christian, bassist Favors, and drummer Tootie Heath) saves the more boppish pieces for his tenor while on soprano his intense sound creates a drone effect reminiscent a bit of bagpipes. All in all his release for Delmark should keep listeners guessing. *—Scott Yanow*

Hank Mobley

b. Jul. 7, 1930, Eastman, GA, **d.** May 30, 1986, Philadelphia, PA
Sax (Tenor) / Hard Bop
Accurately described by critic Leonard Feather as "the middleweight champion of the tenor" due to his sound (not as light as Lester Young's or as heavy as Sonny Rollins), Hank Mobley tended to be taken for granted during his career but recorded a long string of valuable albums for Blue Note. He first gained attention for his work with Max Roach (on and off during 1951-53) and Dizzy Gillespie (1954). An original member of the Jazz Messengers (1954-56), Mobley joined Horace Silver when the pianist broke away from Art Blakey to form his own group (1956-57). Mobley was back with Blakey for a bit in 1959 and spent an unhappy period with Miles Davis (1961-62) but mostly worked as a leader in the '60s. He was in Europe during much of 1968-70 and recorded with Cedar Walton in 1972 but by the mid-'70s was largely retired due to bad health. Hank Mobley led isolated dates for Savoy, Prestige, and Roulette, but it is for his 25 Blue Note albums (recorded during 1955-70) with the who's who of hard bop (including such sidemen as Horace Silver, Art Blakey, Lee Morgan, Milt Jackson, Art Farmer, Donald Byrd, Bobby Timmons, Sonny Clark, Kenny Dorham, Pepper Adams, Wynton Kelly, Freddie Hubbard, Grant Green, Philly Joe Jones, Herbie Hancock, Andrew Hill, Barry Harris, Curtis Fuller, McCoy Tyner, Billy Higgins, James Spaulding, Jackie McLean, Blue Mitchell, Cedar Walton, Ron Carter, and Woody Shaw) that he will be best-remembered. *—Scott Yanow*

Hank Mobley Quartet / Mar. 27, 1955 / Blue Note ✦✦✦✦
This debut of Mobley on Blue Note includes Horace Silver on piano and Doug Watkins on bass, plus someone named Art Blakey on drums. *—Ron Wynn*

The Jazz Message of Hank Mobley, Vol. 1 / Jan. 30, 1956 / Savoy ✦✦✦

Messages / Jul. 20, 1956 & Jul. 27, 1956 / Prestige ✦✦✦✦

Tenor Conclave / Sep. 7, 1956 / Prestige ✦✦✦
With Al Cohn, John Coltrane, Zoot Sims. A hard-blowing, straightahead jam session that matches four identifiable and individualistic voices. All can be heard elsewhere to greater glory, but it's still interesting. *—Ron Wynn*

Hank Mobley and His All-Stars / Jan. 13, 1957 / Blue Note ✦✦✦✦
This CD is a straight reissue of a Hank Mobley LP that features the "Who's Who" of late-'50s hard bop: the tenor-leader, vibraphonist Milt Jackson, pianist Horace Silver, bassist Doug Watkins, and drummer Art Blakey. The quintet performs five Mobley compositions, (best is the lyrical "Mobley's Musings"), songs that are generally more interesting for their chord changes than for their melodies, which is probably why none of them became standards! One's attention is constantly drawn to the inventive solos and Art Blakey's roaring "accompaniment." An above-average effort from some of the best. *—Scott Yanow*

Hank Mobley Quintet / Mar. 9, 1957 / Blue Note ✦✦✦✦
Tenor saxophonist Hank Mobley teamed up with a couple of his more notable employers (pianist Horace Silver and drummer Art Blakey) plus trumpeter Art Farmer and bassist Doug Watkins for this superior Blue Note album which has been reissued (along with two alternate takes) on CD. Mobley's "Funk in Deep Freeze" is the most memorable selection but on a whole the six compositions (all Mobley originals) display his underrated writing talents. It is a particular joy to hear the inspired playing of Silver and Blakey on this lesser-known but consistently stimulating hard bop set. *—Scott Yanow*

Peckin' Time / Feb. 9, 1958 / Blue Note ✦✦✦✦
Tenor saxophonist Hank Mobley, who throughout his career was overshadowed by more influential tenors such as Sonny Rollins and John Coltrane, was himself a talented and fairly original player and a fine composer; many of his originals deserve to be revived. For this Blue Note session, which in its CD reissue includes three alternate takes, Mobley, trumpeter Lee Morgan, pianist Wynton Kelly, bassist Paul Chambers, and drummer Charlie Persip interpret four of the tenor's songs, including

"High and Flighty" and the 12-minute "Gil-Go Blues," along with the standard "Speak Low." The results are high-quality hard bop, the modern mainstream of the era. *—Scott Yanow*

★ **Soul Station** / Feb. 7, 1960 / Blue Note ✦✦✦✦✦
Other than his 1955 debut for Blue Note, this set (reissued on CD) was tenor saxophonist Hank Mobley's first opportunity to record as leader of a quartet without any other competing horns. With the stimulating support of pianist Wynton Kelly, bassist Paul Chambers, and drummer Art Blakey, Mobley is in peak form on four of his originals (of which "This I Dig of You" is best-known), "Remember," and the ballad "If I Should Lose You." Mobley's improvisations are melodic and thoughtful, yet always swinging and full of inner fire. This CD serves as a perfect introduction to the playing and writing abilities of this underrated talent. *—Scott Yanow*

Roll Call / Nov. 13, 1960 / Blue Note ✦✦✦✦
This set, reissued on CD, differs from tenor saxophonist Hank Mobley's *Soul Station* release of nine months earlier in that although he uses the same impressive rhythm section (pianist Wynton Kelly, bassist Paul Chambers, and drummer Art Blakey), Mobley also welcomes young trumpeter Freddie Hubbard. Hubbard actually steals the show on a few of the numbers, but since five of the pieces are Mobley originals, including such forgotten gems as "Roll Call," "My Groove Your Move," and "A Baptist Beat," the tenorman obviously set up this date partly as a way of featuring the fiery Hubbard. Art Blakey took note of the trumpeter's talents and hired him to replace Lee Morgan with the Jazz Messengers a year later. Overall, this is an excellent hard bop date and, as is true of all of Hank Mobley's Blue Note albums, it is easily recommended to fans of straightahead jazz. *—Scott Yanow*

● **Workout** / Mar. 26, 1961 / Blue Note ✦✦✦✦
This is one of the best-known Hank Mobley recordings, and for good reason. Although none of his four originals ("Workout," "Uh Huh," "Smokin'," "Greasin' Easy") caught on, the fine saxophonist is in top form. He jams on the four tunes, plus "The Best Things in Life Are Free," with an all-star quintet of young modernists—guitarist Grant Green, pianist Wynton Kelly, bassist Paul Chambers, and drummer Philly Joe Jones—and shows that he was a much stronger player than his then-current boss Miles Davis seemed to think. This recommended CD reissue adds a version of "Three Coins in the Fountain" from the same date, originally released on *Another Workout*, to the original LP program. *—Scott Yanow*

No Room for Squares / Mar. 7, 1963 & Oct. 2, 1963 / Blue Note ✦✦✦✦
By 1963, Hank Mobley, whose tenor tone perfectly fit the hard bop modern mainstream music of the late '50s and early '60s, had altered his sound slightly to get a harder tone, influenced to an extent by John Coltrane. This CD reissue differs quite a bit from the original LP program, adding alternate takes of "No Room for Squares" and "Carolyn," along with two previously unissued selections ("Comin' Back" and "Syrup and Biscuits") while dropping two songs from the LP which were cut at a slightly earlier session. Mobley leads a top-notch quintet with trumpeter Lee Morgan, pianist Andrew Hill, bassist John Ore, and drummer Philly Joe Jones through a set of high-quality, if obscure, originals written by either the leader or Morgan. The music is as satisfying and adventurous as one would expect. *—Scott Yanow*

Straight No Filter / Jul. 7, 1963-Feb. 4, 1965 / Blue Note ✦✦✦✦
Straight No Filter consists of the last remaining unissued Hank Mobley-led Blue Note recordings. The first half of this disc is often superb with several brilliant solos from Mobley, McCoy Tyner (piano), and the still underrated Lee Morgan (trumpet). *—Scott Yanow*

The Turnaround / Feb. 4, 1965 / Blue Note ✦✦✦✦
The CD reissue of Hank Mobley's *The Turnaround* is different from the original LP in that two songs from a March 7, 1963 date were dropped, while two previously unissued ones from February 4, 1965 were added. Most intriguing about this quintet set with trumpeter Freddie Hubbard, pianist Barry Harris, bassist Paul Chambers, and drummer Billy Higgins are the six likable but complex Mobley compositions. A very underrated writer, many of Hank Mobley's originals deserve to be revived, including these six ("Pat 'N Chat," "Third Time Around," "Hank's Waltz," "The Turnaround," "Straight Ahead," and "My Sin"). Rather than stick to the standard 32-bar format heard on most pre-1970 songs, Mobley's pieces utilize choruses of 44, 20 and 50 bars while still sounding logical. All of the musicians play up to par on these advanced hard bop tunes. *—Scott Yanow*

Dippin' / Jun. 18, 1965 / Blue Note ✦✦✦✦
All of tenor saxophonist Hank Mobley's Blue Note recordings are recommended for his harmonically advanced, tricky yet logical originals, in addition to consistently fine soloing from some of the top modern mainstream players of the era; these albums helped define the Blue Note sound of the '60s. For this date, a straight CD reissue of the original LP, Mobley, trumpeter Lee Morgan, pianist Harold Mabern, bassist Larry Ridley, and drummer Billy Higgins perform four of the tenorman's originals, the highly appealing "Recado Bossa Nova" and the standard ballad "I See Your Face Before Me." An excellent outing, even if no "hits" resulted. *—Scott Yanow*

A Caddy for Daddy / Dec. 18, 1965 / Blue Note ✦✦✦✦
Hank Mobley was a perfect artist for Blue Note in the '60s. A distinctive but not dominant soloist, Mobley was also a very talented writer whose compositions avoided the predictable, yet could often be quite melodic and soulful; his tricky originals consistently inspired the young all-stars in Blue Note's stable. For this CD, which is a straight reissue of a 1965 session, Mobley is joined by trumpeter Lee Morgan, trombonist Curtis Fuller, pianist McCoy Tyner, bassist Bob Cranshaw, and drummer Billy Higgins (a typically remarkable Blue Note lineup) for the infectious title cut, three other lesser-known but superior originals, plus Wayne Shorter's "Venus Di Mildew." Recommended. — *Scott Yanow*

A Slice of the Top / Mar. 18, 1966 / Blue Note ✦✦✦✦
This is one of tenor saxophonist Hank Mobley's more intriguing sessions, for the talented composer had an opportunity to have four of his originals, plus the standard "There's a Lull in My Life," performed by an octet in the cool-toned style of Miles Davis' "Birth of the Cool" nonet, arranged by Duke Pearson. Although recorded in 1966, this date was not released until 1979 and unfortunately has not yet been reissued on CD. Mobley, who continued to evolve into a more advanced player throughout the '60s, fits right in with such adventurous players as altoist James Spaulding, trumpeter Lee Morgan (with whom Mobley recorded frequently), pianist McCoy Tyner, bassist Reggie Workman, and drummer Billy Higgins. The inclusion of Kiane Zawadi on euphonium and Howard Johnson on tuba adds a lot of color to this memorable outing. — *Scott Yanow*

Hi Voltage / 1967 / Blue Note ✦✦✦✦
This is a typically enjoyable Hank Mobley date from the last great year of music from Blue Note, 1967. The talented tenor, who contributed all six compositions, is teamed with trumpeter Blue Mitchell, altoist Jackie McLean, pianist John Hicks, bassist Bob Cranshaw, and drummer Billy Higgins (all Blue Note veterans except Hicks), and everyone plays up to par. The music sticks to advanced hard bop with hints of funk, bossa nova, and modal tunes. Strange that none of these selections, which include the ballad "No More Goodbys," "Bossa De Luxe," and "Flirty Gerty," caught on. — *Scott Yanow*

Third Season / Feb. 24, 1967 / Blue Note ✦✦✦✦

Far Away Lands / Mar. 26, 1967 / Blue Note ✦✦✦✦
Of all the Blue Note artists of the '60s, tenor saxophonist Hank Mobley may very well be the most underrated. A consistent player whose style evolved throughout the decade, Mobley wrote a series of inventive and challenging compositions that inspired the all-stars he used on his recordings while remaining in the genre of hard bop. For this lesser-known outing, Mobley teams up with trumpeter Donald Byrd, pianist Cedar Walton, bassist Ron Carter, and drummer Billy Higgins for four of his songs (given such colorful titles as "A Dab of This and That," "No Argument," "The Hippity Hop," and "Bossa for Baby"), along with a song apiece from Byrd and Jimmy Heath. An excellent outing, fairly late in the productive career of Hank Mobley. — *Scott Yanow*

Thinking of Home / Jul. 31, 1970 / Blue Note ✦✦✦✦

The Modern Jazz Quartet

Group / Cool, Third Stream
Pianist John Lewis, vibraphonist Milt Jackson, bassist Ray Brown, and drummer Kenny Clarke first came together as the rhythm section of the 1946 Dizzy Gillespie Orchestra and they had occasional features that gave the overworked brass players a well deserved rest. They next came together in 1951, recording as the Milt Jackson Quartet. In 1952 with Percy Heath taking Brown's place, the Modern Jazz Quartet (MJQ) became a permanent group. Other than Connie Kay suceeding Clarke in 1955, the band's personnel was set. In the early days Jackson and Lewis both were equally responsible for the group's musical direction but the pianist eventually took over as musical director. The MJQ has long displayed John Lewis' musical vision, making jazz seem respectable by occasionally interacting with classical ensembles and playing concerts at prestigious venues, but always leaving plenty of space for bluesy and swinging improvising. Their repertoire, in addition to including veteran bop and swing pieces, introduced such originals as Lewis' "Django" and Jackson's "Bags' Groove." The group recorded for Prestige (1952-55), Atlantic (1956-74), Verve (1957), United Artists (1959), and Apple (1967-69) and, in addition to the many quartet outings, they welcomed such guests as Jimmy Giuffre, Sonny Rollins, the Beaux Arts String Quartet, a symphony orchestra conducted by Gunther Schuller, singer Diahann Carroll (on one piece), Laurindo Almeida, a big band, and the Swingle Singers. Although the musicians all had opportunities to pursue individual projects, in 1974 Milt Jackson tired of the constant touring and the limitations set on his improvising and he quit the group, causing the MJQ to have a final tour and break up. In 1981 Jackson relented and the Modern Jazz Quartet (which has recorded further albums for Pablo and Atlantic) became active again although on a more part-time basis. Connie Kay's health began to fade in the early '90s (Mickey Roker often filled in for him) and after his death in 1995, Albert "Tootie" Heath became his replacement. — *Scott Yanow*

MJQ / Dec. 22, 1952 & Jun. 16, 1954 / Original Jazz Classics ✦✦✦✦
Two different groups are heard from on this CD reissue. The original Modern Jazz Quartet (with vibraphonist Milt Jackson, pianist John Lewis, bassist Percy Heath, and drummer Kenny Clarke) performs four numbers at the first recording session of the MJQ. In addition there are four selections from a pickup group led by Jackson that also includes pianist Horace Silver and trumpeter Henry Boozier; the latter date introduced Silver's "Opus De Funk." Overall this somewhat brief CD has swinging music that bop fans will want to get. — *Scott Yanow*

The Modern Jazz Quartet Plays Jazz Classics / Dec. 22, 1952-Jan. 9, 1955 / Prestige ✦✦✦✦
An early work that laid out the essence of The Modern Jazz Quartet, a unit that brought both jazz sensibility and classical precision to anything they played. This time they performed classical material with an improvisational backdrop, something that pianist John Lewis particularly loved. Vibist Milt Jackson also executed his parts smoothly, while bassist Percy Heath and drummer Connie Kay were consistently supportive and steady. — *Ron Wynn*

MJQ: 40 years [Boxed Set] / Dec. 22, 1952-Feb. 3, 1988 / Atlantic ✦✦✦✦
To celebrate The Modern Jazz Quartet's 40th anniversary as a group, Atlantic came out with an attractive four-CD box set that has selections (programmed in chronological order) that cover the group's long career. Most of the selections come from the Atlantic catalog although they have leased a few numbers owned by other labels and, with the exception of four songs from a Japanese concert and one previously unissued performance, all of the music is readily available elsewhere. But this well conceived set serves as a perfect introduction for new listeners and as a fine retrospective of this important group's legacy. All of the best-known compositions are included and they find vibraphonist Milt Jackson, pianist John Lewis, bassist Percy Heath, and drummer Connie Kay (along with a few notable guests) playing at their peak. — *Scott Yanow*

The Modern Jazz Quartet Plays for Lovers / Dec. 22, 1952-Jul. 2, 1955 / Prestige ✦✦✦
Lush, sentimental fare played with delicacy and warmth by the Modern Jazz Quartet. Their detractors ignored these kind of sensitive, yet emphatic sessions when they accused the group of lacking soul. Pianist Lewis and vibist Jackson had some exceptional solos, while bassist Heath and drummer Kay even got some time in the spotlight. — *Ron Wynn*

★ **Django** / Jun. 25, 1953-Jan. 9, 1955 / Original Jazz Classics ✦✦✦✦✦
Although it had recorded one prior session, The Modern Jazz Quartet really came into its own during the three dates that comprise this CD reissue. Highlights include the original versions of John Lewis' "Django," "Milano," "Delauney's Dilemma," and the four-part "La Ronde Suite." In addition to vibraphonist Milt Jackson, pianist John Lewis, and bassist Percy Heath, these performances have the last studio appearances of drummer Kenny Clarke with the group. — *Scott Yanow*

Concorde / Jul. 2, 1955 / Original Jazz Classics ✦✦✦✦
This CD reissue is most significant for having the first recordings of drummer Connie Kay as a regular member of The Modern Jazz Quartet. His subtle style fit in perfectly with vibraphonist Milt Jackson, bassist Percy Heath, and pianist John Lewis. Highlights of this rather brief (around 33 minutes) CD are a four-song "Gershwin Medley," "Softly as in a Morning Sunrise," and "Ralph's New Blues." Excellent and somewhat historic music although the brevity of this set makes one wish that it were combined on CD with Prestige's other MJQ sessions. — *Scott Yanow*

The Modern Jazz Quartet / Apr. 5, 1957 / Mobile Fidelity ✦✦✦✦
The audiophile label Mobile Fidelity in 1994 came out with a rare LP, a reissue of a 1957 Modern Jazz Quartet session originally on Atlantic. The emphasis is very much on the MJQ's bebop roots and vibraphonist Milt Jackson stars on a five-song ballad medley and several standards including "Night in Tunisia" and his own "Bags' Groove." Fine straightahead music; this group could always swing. — *Scott Yanow*

At Music Inn, Vol. 2 / Aug. 3, 1958 & Sep. 3, 1958 / Mobile Fidelity ✦✦✦✦
This Mobile Fidelity CD reissues an Atlantic album by the Modern Jazz Quartet. Vibraphonist Milt Jackson, pianist John Lewis, bassist Percy Heath, and drummer Connie Kay perform a pair of Lewis originals (the rather dry "Midsommer" and "Festival Sketch"), Charlie Parker's "Yardbird Suite," and a three-song ballad medley; the latter features Milt Jackson exclusively. The most unusual aspect to this set is that the great tenor Sonny Rollins joins the quartet for "Bags' Groove" (during which he is quite witty) and "Night in Tunisia." Rollins is quite creative and fits in naturally with the group. This very well recorded reissue from the audiophile Mobile Fidelity label is worth picking up. — *Scott Yanow*

Odds Against Tomorrow / Oct. 9, 1959 / Blue Note ✦✦✦✦
The Modern Jazz Quartet never actually recorded for Blue Note but their United Artists date was reissued on this Blue Note CD. The MJQ (vibraphonist Milt Jackson, pianist John Lewis, bassist Percy Heath, and drummer Connie Kay) perform six of Lewis' compositions which were used in the film *Odds Against Tomorrow*. Best known is "Skating in Central Park"

but all of the selections have their memorable moments and it is good to hear this classic unit playing such fresh material. —*Scott Yanow*

Dedicated to Connie / May 27, 1960 / Atlantic Jazz ✦✦✦✦
After drummer Connie Kay passed away, this previously unreleased concert, recorded in Slovenia in 1960, was issued on a double CD and dedicated to him. The Modern Jazz Quartet (which also includes pianist John Lewis, vibraphonist Milt Jackson, and bassist Percy Heath) is heard in surprisingly inspired form playing their usual repertoire of the time. Highlights include a 23-minute medley of John Lewis compositions, "Bag's Groove," "It Don't Mean A Thing," "Django," "How High The Moon," and "Skating In Central Park." Lewis has stated that the group never played better than during this concert. Although that statement is debatable, the MJQ certainly sounds in prime form throughout the easily recommended release. —*Scott Yanow*

Blues at Carnegie Hall / Apr. 27, 1966 / Mobile Fidelity ✦✦✦✦
On this Mobile Fidelity CD reissue of a live Atlantic set from 1966, the Modern Jazz Quartet performs eight blues-based compositions. In addition to such familiar pieces as the inevitable "Bags' Groove," "Ralph's New Blues" (dedicated to jazz critic Ralph Gleason), and "The Cylinder," there are a few newer pieces (including "Home" which is similar to Lee Morgan's hit "The Sidewinder") included for variety. This predictable but consistently swinging set is particularly recommended to fans of vibraphonist Milt Jackson. —*Scott Yanow*

★ **The Last Concert** / Nov. 25, 1974 / Atlantic ✦✦✦✦✦
The Modern Jazz Quartet broke up after the concert documented on this double CD. It would be nearly seven years before the group got back together again but it certainly went out on top. Mostly revisiting their greatest hits, the MJQ is heard on this two-fer playing inspired versions of such songs as "Softly as in a Morning Sunrise," "Bags' Groove," "Skating in Central Park," "Confirmation," "The Golden Striker," and of course, "Django." This set is a real gem (the music is essential for all serious jazz collections), featuring vibraphonist Milt Jackson, pianist John Lewis, bassist Percy Heath, and drummer Connie Kay at their very best. —*Scott Yanow*

Together Again at Montreux Jazz / Jul. 25, 1982 / Pablo ✦✦✦✦
This CD reissue features the revived Modern Jazz Quartet during their 30th year (counting a seven-year "vacation"), playing some of their usual repertoire (such as "Django," "The Cylinder," and "Bags' Groove" which for some reason was renamed "Bags' New Groove") before a happy audience at the 1982 Montreux Jazz Festival. In reality this release adds little to the MJQ's legacy (since all of the songs but vibraphonist Milt Jackson's "Monterey Mist" had been recorded before, some of them many times) but it does show that the band still had its enthusiasm and the ability to make the veteran material sound fresh and swinging. —*Scott Yanow*

● **Celebration** / Jun. 17, 1992-Jul. 16, 1993 / Atlantic ✦✦✦✦
As part of their 40th anniversary, the Modern Jazz Quartet welcomed ten guest artists to their CD: Bobby McFerrin (brilliant on "Billie's Bounce"), Take Six, Phil Woods, Wynton Marsalis (who gets to show off his technique on "Cherokee"), Illinois Jacquet, Harry "Sweets" Edison, Branford Marsalis, Jimmy Heath, Freddie Hubbard, and Nina Tempo. As usual vibraphonist Milt Jackson and pianist John Lewis also have plenty of solo space and bassist Percy Heath is perfect in support. Since drummer Connie Kay was ailing in 1992 (but back in action the following year), Mickey Roker fills in on seven of the 13 selections. With the exception of "Django" (which features Phil Woods), and "Bags' Groove," the music sticks to bop standards rather than MJQ standbys. It's an enjoyable and varied set. —*Scott Yanow*

Grachan Moncur III

b. 1937
Trombone / Avant-Garde
One of the first trombonists to explore free jazz, Grachan Moncur III is still best-known for his pair of innovative Blue Note albums (1963-64) which also featured Lee Morgan and Jackie McLean on the first session and Wayne Shorter and Herbie Hancock on the later date. The son of bassist Grachan Moncur II who played with the Savoy Sultans from 1937-45, Grachan III started on trombone when he was 11. He toured with Ray Charles (1959-62), was with the Jazztet (1962), and in 1963 played advanced jazz with Jackie McLean. Moncur toured with Sonny Rollins (1964) and played and recorded with Marion Brown, Joe Henderson, and Archie Shepp, matching up with fellow trombonist Roswell Rudd in the latter group. He also was part of the cooperative band 360 Degree Music Experience with Beaver Harris. Grachan Moncur, who has also recorded as a leader for BYG (1969) and JCOA (1974), has continued playing challenging music up to the present day and has been an educator. Some of his more recent associations have been with Frank Lowe (1984-85), Cassandra Wilson (1985), and the Paris Reunion Band. —*Scott Yanow*

Evolution / Nov. 21, 1963 / Blue Note ✦✦✦✦
Easily recommended Blue Note date from the '60s with Lee Morgan (tpt) and Jackie McLean (as). —*Michael G. Nastos*

● **Some Other Stuff** / Jul. 6, 1964 / Blue Note ✦✦✦✦
Grachan Moncur III was one of the top trombonists of the jazz avant-garde in the '60s although he had only a few chances to lead his own record sessions. This 1964 set (which has been reissued on CD) was one of his finest, a quintet outing with bassist Cecil McBee, two of the members of the Miles Davis Quintet (pianist Herbie Hancock and drummer Tony Williams), and tenor saxophonist Wayne Shorter just a brief time before he joined Miles. The group performs four of Moncur's challenging originals including "Nomadic" (which is largely a drum solo) and "The Twins" which is built off of one chord. None of the compositions caught on but the strong and very individual improvising of the young musicians is enough of a reason to acquire the advanced music. —*Scott Yanow*

New Africa / Aug. 11, 1969 / Actuel ✦✦✦✦
The trombonist in a modal setting with Archie Shepp (sax), Roscoe Mitchell (reeds), and Dave Burrell (p) in a Paris studio. —*Michael G. Nastos*

Echoes of Prayer / Apr. 11, 1974 / JCOA ✦✦✦✦
The 1974 *Melody Maker* Jazz Album of the Year. Progressive and thought-provoking. A legendary recording, with the Jazz Composers Orchestra. —*Michael G. Nastos*

Thelonious Monk

b. Oct. 10, 1917, Rocky Mount, NC, **d.** Feb. 17, 1982, Weehawken, NJ
Piano / Bop, Post-Bop
The most important jazz musicians are the ones who are successful in creating their own original world of music with its own rules, logic and surprises. Thelonious Monk, who was criticized by observers who failed to listen to his music on its own terms, suffered through a decade of neglect before he was suddenly acclaimed as a genius; his music had not changed one bit in the interim. In fact, one of the more remarkable aspects of Monk's music was that it was fully formed by 1947, and he saw no need to alter his playing or compositional style in the slightest during the next 25 years.

Thelonious Monk grew up in New York, started playing piano when he was around five and had his first job touring as an accompanist to an evangelist. He was inspired by the Harlem stride pianists (James P. Johnson was a neighbor), and vestiges of that idiom can be heard in his later unaccompanied solos. However, when he was playing in the house band of Minton's Playhouse during 1940-43, Monk was searching for his own individual style. Private recordings from the period find him sometimes resembling Teddy Wilson but starting to use more advanced rhythms and harmonies. He worked with Lucky Millinder a bit in 1942 and was with the Cootie Williams Orchestra briefly in 1944 (Williams recorded Monk's "Epistrophy" in 1942 and in 1944 was the first to record "Round Midnight"), but it was when he became Coleman Hawkins' regular pianist that Monk was initially noticed. He cut a few titles with Hawkins (his recording debut), and, although some of Hawkins' fans complained about the eccentric pianist, the veteran tenor could sense this pianist's greatness.

The 1945-54 period was very difficult for Thelonious Monk. Because he left a lot of space in his rhythmic solos and had an unusual technique, many people thought that he was an inferior pianist. His compositions were so advanced that the lazier bebop players (although not Dizzy Gillespie and Charlie Parker) assumed that he was crazy. And Thelonious Monk's name, appearance (he liked funny hats), and personality (an occasionally uncommunicative introvert) helped to brand him as some kind of nut. Fortunately Alfred Lion of Blue Note believed in him and recorded Monk extensively during 1947-48 and 1951-52. He also recorded for Prestige during 1952-54, had a solo date for Vogue in 1954 during a visit to Paris, and appeared on a Verve date with Bird and Gillespie. But work was very sporadic during this era, and Monk had to struggle to make ends meet.

His fortunes slowly began to improve. In 1955 he signed with Riverside and producer Orrin Keepnews persuaded him to record an album of Duke Ellington tunes and one of standards so his music would appear to be more accessible to the average jazz fan. In 1956 came the classic *Brilliant Corners* album, but it was the following year when the situation permanently changed. Monk was booked into the Five Spot for a long engagement, and he used a quartet that featured tenor saxophonist John Coltrane. Finally the critics and then the jazz public recognized Thelonious Monk's greatness during this important gig. The fact that he was unique was a disadvantage a few years earlier when all modern jazz pianists were expected to sound like Bud Powell (who was ironically a close friend), but by 1957 the jazz public was looking for a new approach. Suddenly Monk was a celebrity, and his status would not change for the remainder of his career. In 1958 his quartet featured the tenor of Johnny Griffin (who was even more compatible than Coltrane), in 1959 he appeared with an orchestra at Town Hall (with arrangements by Hall Overton), in 1962 he signed with Columbia, and two years later was on the cover of *Time*. A second orchestra concert in 1963 was even better than the first, and Monk toured constantly throughout the '60s with his quartet which featured the reliable tenor of Charlie Rouse. He played with the Giants of Jazz during 1971-72 but then in 1973 suddenly retired. Monk was suffering from mental illness, and other than a few special appearances during the mid-'70s, he lived the rest of his life in seclusion. After his death it seemed as if everyone was doing Thelonious Monk tributes. There were so many versions of "'Round Midnight" that it was practically a pop hit! But despite the posthumous acclaim and attempts by pianists ranging from Marcus Roberts to Tommy Flanagan to recreate his style, there was no replacement for the original.

Some of Thelonious Monk's songs became standards early on, most notably "'Round Midnight," "Straight No Chaser," "52nd Street Theme," and "Blue Monk." Many of his other compositions have by now been figured out by other jazz musicians and are occasionally performed including "Ruby My Dear," "Well You Needn't," "Off Minor," "In Walked Bud," "Misterioso," "Epistrophy," "I Mean You," "Four in One," "Criss Cross," "Ask Me Now," "Little Rootie Tootie," "Monk's Dream," "Bemsha Swing," "Think of One," "Friday the 13th," "Hackensack," "Nutty," "Brilliant Corners," "Crepuscule with Nellie," "Evidence," and "Rhythm-a-Ning." Virtually all of Monk's recordings (for Blue Note, Prestige, Vogue, Riverside, Columbia, and Black Lion) have been reissued, and among his sidemen through the years were Idrees Sulieman, Art Blakey, Milt Jackson, Lou Donaldson, Lucky Thompson, Max Roach, Julius Watkins, Sonny Rollins, Clark Terry, Gerry Mulligan, John Coltrane, Wilbur Ware, Shadow Wilson, Johnny Griffin, Donald Byrd, Phil Woods, Thad Jones, and Charlie Rouse. His son Thelonious Monk, Jr. (T.S. Monk) has helped keep the hard bop tradition alive with his quintet and has headed the Thelonious Monk Institute whose yearly competitions succeed in publicizing talented young players. —Scott Yanow

☆ **Complete Blue Note Recordings** / Oct. 15, 1947-Apr. 14, 1957 / Blue Note ✦✦✦✦✦
Shortly after Mosaic's limited-edition four-LP box set of pianist/composer Thelonious Monk's Blue Note recordings ran out of stock, Blue Note reissued Monk's entire output plus his recently discovered 1958 live performance with John Coltrane on this four-CD package. The music is unique, highly influential and timeless. Monk did not record often for Blue Note during 1947-52 (six sessions) but the number of classics is quite impressive: "Ruby My Dear," "Well You Needn't," "Off Minor," "In Walked Bud," "'Round Midnight," "Evidence," "Misterioso," "Epistrophy," "I Mean You," "Four in One," "Criss Cross," "Straight No Chaser," and "Ask Me Now." Add to that his two appearances on a 1957 Sonny Rollins date along with the remarkable Coltrane session and the result is a set that should be in every jazz collection. —Scott Yanow

Thelonious Monk Trio / Oct. 15, 1952 & Dec. 18, 1952 / Original Jazz Classics ✦✦✦✦
1952 & 1954. Wonderful trio recordings. The difference between the Max Roach (d) and Art Blakey (d) cuts is quite instructive. These are some of Monk's more captivating solos from the '50s. —Ron Wynn

Monk / Nov. 13, 1953-May 11, 1954 / Prestige ✦✦✦

Blue Monk, Vol. 1 / May 11, 1954-Sep. 22, 1954 / Prestige ✦✦✦

☆ **Complete Black Lion and Vogue** / Jun. 7, 1954-Nov. 15, 1971 / Mosaic ✦✦✦✦✦
This four-LP limited-edition box set from Mosaic contains the nine piano solos recorded by Thelonious Monk while in Paris on June 7, 1954 (most of which have also been issued by GNP Crescendo) and, more importantly, his complete marathon London session of Nov. 15, 1971. The latter, split between solo and trio performances (with bassist Al McKibbon and drummer Art Blakey), was (other than a record with the Giants of Jazz) Monk's final recording and found the unique pianist in brilliant form, really romping on some of his solos. Although the majority of the songs are his originals, the emphasis on this essential music is on the piano playing. Those critics and listeners who feel that Monk was a limited musician should give these final performances a very close listen. —Scott Yanow

Plays Duke Ellington / Jul. 21, 1955 & Jul. 27, 1955 / Original Jazz Classics ✦✦✦✦
One genius tackles the music of another. Superb trio recordings spiced by Oscar Pettiford (b) and Kenny Clarke (d). —Ron Wynn

Riverside Trios / Jul. 21, 1955-Apr. 3, 1956 / Milestone ✦✦✦✦
When Thelonious Monk first signed with Riverside Records in 1955, producer Orrin Keepnews thought that it would be a good idea for the unrecognized giant to record an album of Duke Ellington compositions and follow it up with a set of standards so as to discount his eccentric and forbidding image. The results were quite satisfying, trio performances with bassist Oscar Pettiford and either Kenny Clarke or Art Blakey on drums that made Monk's playing seem more accessible to the regular jazz audience without watering down his style. This two-LP set contains both albums (the program of Ellington's music is particularly unique) and is very enjoyable. —Scott Yanow

Pure Monk / Jul. 21, 1955-Oct. 22, 1959 / Milestone ✦✦✦✦
By "pure," one means a two-LP set of unaccompanied piano solos from one of the most unique stylists in jazz history. Most of these 21 solos were originally on Thelonious Himself and Thelonious Alone in San Francisco while four others were solo tracks that were part of other albums of the period. Nine of the selections feature Monk playing his own originals but it is the other 12 selections (including such songs as "There's Danger in Your Eyes, Cherie," "Remember," and "Everything Happens to Me") that are particularly memorable; no one else strided like Monk and it is a pleasure to hear him play in this setting. —Scott Yanow

☆ **The Complete Riverside Recordings** / Jul. 21, 1955-Apr. 21, 1961 / Riverside ✦✦✦✦✦
Although this 15-CD box set is not inexpensive, this is the most essential of all of Thelonious Monk's releases. It was during his years with Riverside that Monk achieved the fame he had long deserved. Producer Orrin Keepnews was wise enough to feature the unique pianist/composer in a wide variety of settings and they are all here: separate trio sessions comprised of Duke Ellington songs and standards, meetings on record with Sonny Rollins (including "Brilliant Corners"), John Coltrane, Coleman Hawkins, Gerry Mulligan, and Johnny Griffin, the beginnings of Monk's Quartet with Charlie Rouse, a truncated (and previously unissued) session with Shelly Manne, Monk's famous Town Hall concert of 1959 and a full date of unaccompanied piano solos. Most of this music has also been made available on Milestone two-CD sets and single CDs, but this is the best (and most complete) way to acquire these classics. —Scott Yanow

Straight No Chaser: Thelonius Monk / Sep. 1956-1968 / Columbia ✦✦✦✦
This LP, taken from the soundtrack of the fascinating film Straight No Chaser, contains a great deal of previously unissued material by Thelonious Monk. Three songs were released before, but the other eight numbers (two solos from 1956 and the remainder from 1967-68) are "new," including rehearsal and club performances and two numbers from Monk's otherwise forgotten octet of 1967. It's a real bonus for collectors and a fine complement to the highly recommended film. —Scott Yanow

● **Brilliant Corners** / Dec. 17, 1956-Dec. 23, 1956 / Original Jazz Classics ✦✦✦✦
A recording feat features an excellent version of the title tune. Clark Terry (tpt), Sonny Rollins (ts), and Max Roach (d) guest. —Hank Davis

Thelonious Himself / Apr. 5, 1957-Apr. 16, 1957 / Original Jazz Classics ✦✦✦✦
These are mostly solo; with one cut Coltrane (ts) and Wilbur Ware (b). —Ron Wynn

Thelonious Monk & John Coltrane / Apr. 16, 1957-1957 / Milestone ✦✦✦✦
Much of the music on this two-LP set is quite essential for any serious jazz library (all of it is also included in Monk's giant 15-CD box set The Complete Riverside Recordings). Although Thelonious Monk and John Coltrane played together for several months in 1957, until the discovery of a live tape (which has been issued on Blue Note), the music on this two-fer (which includes several tracks with a larger group that also features Coleman Hawkins, "Monk's Mood" by a trio with bassist Wilbur Ware, and three outstanding tracks with a quartet) was all that existed of their historic collaboration. Coltrane developed rapidly during his period with Monk, and he is heard in brilliant form on "Trinkle, Tinkle" and "Nutty." —Scott Yanow

Art Blakey's Jazz Messengers with Thelonious Monk / May 19, 1957 / Atlantic ✦✦✦✦
Thelonious Monk rarely performed or recorded as a sideman, making this Atlantic LP on which he shares co-billing with drummer Art Blakey a rare event. Monk sounds quite comfortable sitting in with the 1957 version of the Jazz Messengers; in fact, tenor saxophonist Johnny Griffin would soon join his own quartet. The Messengers (which also includes trumpeter Bill Hardman and bassist Spanky DeBrest) perform fine versions of five Monk compositions and Griffin's "Purple Shades." This set deserves to be reissued on CD. —Scott Yanow

☆ **Monk's Music** / Jun. 25, 1957-Jun. 26, 1957 / Riverside ✦✦✦✦✦
This superb septet featured tenor greats Coltrane and Coleman Hawkins. —Hank Davis

☆ **Discovery! at the Five Spot** / 1958 / Blue Note ✦✦✦✦✦
The collaboration between pianist Thelonious Monk and tenor saxophonist John Coltrane was considered (along with the 1943 Earl Hines big band with Charlie Parker and Dizzy Gillespie and the music of the pioneering jazz cornetist Buddy Bolden) to be one of the three lost wonders of jazz history. Although they recorded a trio of quartet numbers in the studios (which are included in various Milestone and Riverside reissues), there was apparently no documentation of their lengthy gig at the Five Spot in 1957, until a tape that Coltrane's wife had recorded was recently discovered. This CD has the happy results, five songs performed by Monk, Coltrane, bassist Ahmed Abdul-Malik, and drummer Roy Haynes at the Five Spot. High points of this somewhat miraculous find include "Trinkle Tinkle," "In Walked Bud," and "I Mean You"; there are also shorter versions of "Epistrophy" and "Crepuscule With Nellie." —Scott Yanow

Thelonious in Action: Recorded at the Five Spot Cafe / Aug. 7, 1958 / Original Jazz Classics ✦✦✦✦

● **At the Five Spot** / Aug. 1958 / Milestone ✦✦✦✦
One of Thelonious Monk's finest bands was the quartet he led in 1958 that featured tenor saxophonist Johnny Griffin. Griffin sounded quite comfortable playing Monk's music and his fiery style really inspired the pianist/composer. This two-LP set (whose contents are also available on Monk's massive CD box *The Complete Riverside Recordings*) has many great moments including "In Walked Bud," "Nutty," and "Let's Cool One" and makes one regret that this band did not stay together for a much longer period. — *Scott Yanow*

★ **The Thelonious Monk Orchestra at Town Hall** / Feb. 28, 1959 / Original Jazz Classics ✦✦✦✦✦
Thelonious Monk Orchestra. A great orchestral showpiece for Monk the composer, one of his best live dates. — *Ron Wynn*

Five by Monk by Five / Jun. 1, 1959-Jun. 2, 1959 / Original Jazz Classics ✦✦✦✦
Quintet. The music proves as intriguing as the title. Excellent trumpet solos from Thad Jones. — *Ron Wynn*

Alone in San Francisco / Oct. 21, 1959 & Oct. 22, 1959 / Original Jazz Classics ✦✦✦✦
Solo piano. Exacting, distinctive renditions of such Monk classics as "Blue Monk," "Pannonica," and "Reflections." — *Ron Wynn*

At the Blackhawk / Apr. 29, 1960 / Original Jazz Classics ✦✦✦

April in Paris / Apr. 18, 1961 / Original Jazz Classics ✦✦✦

Monk's Dream / Oct. 31, 1962-Nov. 6, 1962 / Columbia ✦✦✦✦
Most of Thelonious Monk's recordings for Columbia featured his regular working quartet which at the time of his debut consisted of tenor saxophonist Charlie Rouse, bassist John Ore, and drummer Frankie Dunlop. The music on this LP is fairly typical of his repertoire of the period, five originals (only "Bright Mississippi" had not been recorded before) and three standards, two of which are taken as brief piano solos. However, despite a certain amount of predictability, the playing is consistently excellent and enthusiastic; even if the jazz world was starting to catch up to Monk, his highly original music stood on its own merits. — *Scott Yanow*

Criss-Cross / Nov. 6, 1962-Mar. 29, 1963 / Columbia/Legacy ✦✦✦✦
This CD reissue of the Columbia LP adds a previously unissued version of "Pannonica" to the original program along with updated liner notes. The high-quality repertoire (which includes "Hackensack," "Tea for Two," "Criss-Cross," and "Rhythm-A-Ning") and some consistent solos from the leader/pianist and tenor saxophonist Charlie Rouse make this a CD worth picking up. — *Scott Yanow*

Mysterioso / May 1963-Mar. 2, 1965 / Columbia ✦✦✦✦
This LP contains live performances taken from a variety of sources dating from 1963-65. Pianist/composer Thelonious Monk and tenor saxophonist Charlie Rouse are a constant while bassist Butch Warren and drummer Frank Dunlop are succeeded on a few tracks by bassist Larry Gales and drummer Ben Riley. Not many surprises occur although it is good to hear this band playing "All the Things You Are" and "Honeysuckle Rose" in addition to their usual repertoire. Worth picking up, this music should be reissued on CD eventually. — *Scott Yanow*

Underground / Dec. 14, 1967-Feb. 14, 1968 / Columbia ✦✦✦✦
An excellent latter-period Monk group. "Green Chimneys" is a prime cut. Charlie Rouse is on tenor sax. — *Michael G. Nastos*

Wes Montgomery (John Leslie Montgomery)

b. Mar. 6, 1925, Indianapolis, IN, d. Jun. 15, 1968, Indianapolis, IN
Guitar / Hard Bop, Crossover
Wes Montgomery was one of the great jazz guitarists, a natural extension of Charlie Christian whose appealing use of octaves became influential and his trademark. He achieved great commercial success during his last few years, only to die prematurely.
It had taken Montgomery a long time to become an overnight success. He started to teach himself guitar in 1943 (using his thumb rather than a pick) and toured with Lionel Hampton during 1948-50; he can be heard on a few broadcasts from the period. But then Montgomery returned to Indianapolis where he was in obscurity during much of the '50s, working a day job and playing at clubs most nights. He recorded with his brothers vibraphonist Buddy and electric bassist Monk during 1957-59 and made his first Riverside album (1959) in a trio with organist Melvin Rhyne. In 1960 the release of his album *The Incredible Jazz Guitar of Wes Montgomery* made him famous in the jazz world. Other than a brief time playing with the John Coltrane Sextet (which also included Eric Dolphy) later in the year, Montgomery would be a leader for the rest of his life.
Montgomery's recordings can be easily divided into three periods. His Riverside dates (1959-63) are his most spontaneous jazz outings, small-group sessions with such sidemen as Tommy Flanagan, James Clay, Victor Feldman, Hank Jones, Johnny Griffin, and Mel Rhyne. The one exception was the ironically titled *Fusion*, a ballad date with a string section. All of the Riverside recordings have been reissued in a massive 12-CD box set. With the collapse of Riverside, Montgomery moved over to Verve, where

during 1964-66 he recorded an interesting series of mostly orchestral dates with arranger Don Sebesky and producer Creed Taylor. These records were generally a good balance between jazz and accessibility, for even if the best performances were small-group outings with either the Wynton Kelly Trio or Jimmy Smith. In 1967 Wes signed with Creed Taylor at A&M, and during 1967-68 he recorded three best-selling albums that found him merely stating simple pop melodies while backed by strings and woodwinds. His jazz fans were upset, but Montgomery's albums were played on AM radio during the period. He helped introduce listeners to jazz, and his live performances were as freewheeling as his earlier Riverside dates. Unfortunately, at the height of his success, he died of a heart attack. Montgomery's influence is still felt on many young guitarists. — *Scott Yanow*

Beginnings / Dec. 30, 1957-Oct. 1959 / Blue Note ✦✦✦✦
At the time that guitarist Wes Montgomery recorded "Finger Pickin'" on Dec. 30, 1957, he was an unknown guitarist from Indianapolis who a decade earlier had toured a bit with Lionel Hampton. By the final session on this two-LP set, he was on the verge of stardom. The innovative guitarist (who extended the style of Charlie Christian about as far as it could go) is in consistently superior form on these former rarities. Montgomery is heard with his brothers (vibraphonist/pianist Buddy and electric bassist Monk) in a variety of settings. Such sidemen as a 17-year old Freddie Hubbard (the trumpeter's recording debut), tenor saxophonist Harold Land, and altoist Pony Poindexter are also heard from on this straightahead set which has a generous supply of Montgomery's originals (along with a few jammed standards). There is plenty of classic music here, but this two-fer will be difficult to find. — *Scott Yanow*

Far Wes / Apr. 1958-Oct. 1959 / Pacific Jazz ✦✦✦✦
This historical CD contains some of guitarist Wes Montgomery's first recordings; in fact, only three small-group songs predate these performances. The then-obscure guitarist is heard in two different quintets, both of which include his brothers Buddy (on piano) and Monk (playing electric bass). The earlier set has Harold Land's tenor as a lead voice while altoist Pony Poindexter takes his place on the later date. Montgomery's sound was already quite recognizable and he contributes six originals which alternate with Harold Land's "Hymn for Carl" and four standards. — *Scott Yanow*

☆ **The Complete Riverside Recordings [Box Set]** / Oct. 5, 1959-Nov. 27, 1963 / Riverside ✦✦✦✦✦
Wes Montgomery recorded exclusively for the Riverside label during the four years covered by this massive 12-CD box set, and although his later albums for Verve and particularly the pop/jazz A&M dates sold many more copies, it is for his Riverside dates that his legacy was primarily formed. Virtually unknown at the time of his debut on Riverside, Montgomery soon became a major influence whose style is still copied in the '90s. The guitarist is heard in quite a few different settings on this box including in trios with organist Melvin Rhynbe, a quartet with pianist Tommy Flanagan, as a sideman on different sessions with Nat Adderley, Harold Land, and Cannonball Adderley, performing with his brothers Buddy and Monk, holding his own with pianist George Shearing, vibraphonist Milt Jackson, and tenor great Johnny Griffin and (for an album ironically titled *Fusion*) playing with strings for the first time. All in all there are a tremendous amount of rewarding performances included in this essential set, most of which show why Wes Montgomery is still considered one of the all-time great jazz guitarists. — *Scott Yanow*

Guitar on the Go / Oct. 5, 1959 & Nov. 27, 1963 / Original Jazz Classics ✦✦✦
The final Riverside release of Wes Montgomery material (before the important label went completely bankrupt) was similar to his debut four years earlier; a trio with organist Melvin Rhyne and an obscure drummer (this time George Brown). The CD reissue even includes one leftover track from the earliest session ("Missile Blues") along with newer jams and a pair of "bonus tracks": an alternate take of "The Way You Look Tonight" and a brief "Unidentified Solo Guitar" piece. In general the music swings hard (particularly the two versions of "The Way You Look Tonight") and is a worthy if not essential addition to Wes Montgomery's discography. He would have a few straightahead dates for Verve but this release was really the end of an era. — *Scott Yanow*

Wes Montgomery Trio / Oct. 5, 1959-Oct. 6, 1959 / Original Jazz Classics ✦✦✦✦
Wes Montgomery's first of many sessions for Riverside matched his guitar with organist Melvin Rhyne and drummer Paul Parker for some straightahead swinging. Highlights include "Yesterdays," "'Round Midnight," and Montgomery's originals "Missile Blues" and "Jingles." This CD reissue adds two alternate takes to the original program. — *Scott Yanow*

★ **The Incredible Jazz Guitar of Wes Montgomery** / Jan. 26, 1960 & Jan. 28, 1960 / Original Jazz Classics ✦✦✦✦✦
This is one of Wes Montgomery's greatest recordings, a classic that really alerted the world about the talents of the guitarist. In a quartet with pianist Tommy Flanagan, bassist Percy Heath, and drummer Albert Heath, Wes introduced his originals "West Coast Blues," "Four on Six," and "D-Natural Blues," performed his "Mister Walker," and stretched out on "Airegin," the

ballad "Polka Dots and Moonbeams," "In Your Own Sweet Way," and "Gone with the Wind." All of the unique qualities of Montgomery's style are on display on this essential CD reissue which is also available as part of his 12-CD Riverside boxed set. — *Scott Yanow*

Movin' Along / Oct. 11, 1960 / Original Jazz Classics ++++
Because it was recorded between two of Wes Montgomery's best-known albums (*Incredible Jazz Guitar* and *So Much Guitar*), this particular CD is a bit underrated. The great guitarist is teamed with flutist James Clay (who switches to tenor on Wes' "So Do It"), pianist Victor Feldman, bassist Sam Jones, and drummer Louis Hayes for four standards (highlighted by Clifford Brown's "Sandu" and "Body and Soul"), Sam Jones' "Says You" and two Montgomery originals. The reissue also adds a pair of alternate takes to the fine program. Montgomery made many of his finest jazz recordings originally for Riverside. This is an often-overlooked gem. — *Scott Yanow*

Movin' / Oct. 12, 1960 & Jun. 25, 1962 / Milestone ++++
Wes Montgomery's Riverside recordings (which found him really excelling in straightahead bop-oriented jazz) were reissued on attractive double LPs before CDs took over; all of his music has since been repackaged on single CDs and in a 12-CD boxed set. This particular two-fer combines the music that resulted in *Movin' Along* (an underrated quintet set with pianist Victor Feldman and flutist James Clay), and an often-heated live performance with tenor saxophonist Johnny Griffin and pianist Wynton Kelly that was originally titled *Full House*. Highlights include "Tune Up," "Body and Soul," "Sandu," "I've Grown Accustomed to Her Face," "Blue 'N Boogie," and "S.O.S." — *Scott Yanow*

Wes' Best / 1960-1961 / Fantasy +++
Selections from *The Montgomery Brothers* and *The Montgomery Brothers in Canada.* — *Michael Erlewine*

● **So Much Guitar** / Aug. 4, 1961 / Original Jazz Classics ++++
This CD contains one of Wes Montgomery's finest recordings, a Riverside date that showcases the influential guitarist in a quintet with pianist Hank Jones, bassist Ron Carter, drummer Lex Humphries, and the congas of Ray Barretto. All eight performances are memorable in their own way with "Cottontail," "I'm Just a Lucky So and So," and a brief unaccompanied "While We're Young" being high points. — *Scott Yanow*

● **Full House** / Jun. 25, 1962 / Original Jazz Classics ++++
Tenor saxophonist Johnny Griffin lit a fire under guitarist Wes Montgomery during this live set, and the result is quite a bit of memorable playing, not only by the principals but by pianist Wynton Kelly, bassist Paul Chambers, and drummer Jimmy Cobb. Montgomery is heard in the prime of his straightahead Riverside period. Highlights include such numbers as "Blue 'N' Boogie," "Cariba," and "S.O.S." This CD reissue adds two alternate takes and a version of "Born to Be Blue" to the original program. — *Scott Yanow*

Fusion! Wes Montgomery with Strings / Apr. 18, 1963-Apr. 19, 1963 / Original Jazz Classics ++++
Although most Wes Montgomery fans associate his playing with strings with his later A&M and Verve recordings, the influential guitarist actually fronted a string section for the first time on this Riverside date from 1963, which had the ironic name of *Fusion.* As with his later albums, Montgomery's guitar solos here are brief and melodic, but the jazz content is fairly high even if the emphasis is (with the exception of "Tune-Up") on ballads. This CD has three more performances than the original LP and is worth picking up; the music is quite pretty and pleasing. — *Scott Yanow*

Boss Guitar / Apr. 22, 1963 / Original Jazz Classics +++

Portrait of Wes / Oct. 10, 1963 / Original Jazz Classics ++++
Wes Montgomery's first recordings for Riverside were in a trio with organist Mel Rhyne and ironically his final albums for the struggling (and soon to be bankrupt) label were with Rhyne again. The brilliant guitarist is in fine form on these appealing tunes with the highlights including "Freddie the Freeloader," "Blues Riff," and "Moanin'." As is true with most of Montgomery's CD reissues, there are a couple of "bonus" cuts (alternates of "Blues Riff" and "Moanin'") added to bring the playing time up a bit. All of this music is also available as part of Wes Montgomery's 12-CD Riverside box set. — *Scott Yanow*

Movin' Wes / Nov. 11, 1964 & Nov. 16, 1964 / Verve +++
Wes Montgomery's debut for Verve, although better from a jazz standpoint than his later A&M releases, is certainly in the same vein. The emphasis is on his tone, his distinctive octaves and melody statements. Some of the material (such as "People" and "Matchmaker") are pop tunes of the era, and the brass orchestra (arranged by Johnny Pate) is purely in the background, but there are some worthy performances, chiefly the two-part "Movin' Wes," "Born to Be Blue," and "West Coast Blues." — *Scott Yanow*

Plays the Blues / Nov. 11, 1964-Sep. 28, 1966 / Verve +++
A grab-bag set from past efforts. It's good for its mix of sessions pitting Montgomery with Jimmy Smith (organ), but has somewhat of a slapdash quality. — *Ron Wynn*

Talkin' Verve: Roots Of Acid Jazz / Nov. 18, 1964-Sep. 23, 1966 / Verve ++
The title of this compilation tries to make Montgomery viable for a

younger generation, but it's not exactly "acid jazz." Rather, it's an anthology of some of Montgomery's better pop- and soul-oriented material from the mid-'60s. The 16 tracks show Montgomery in both orchestral and small combo settings, a few cuts taken from his collaborations with Jimmy Smith. Purists have long disdained this phase of Montgomery's career. But those who don't measure work by how straightahead it is will find much to enjoy here, in either the cuts with Oliver Nelson's orchestra, or the less elaborate sessions with the likes of Smith, Grady Tate, Ron Carter, and Ray Barretto. — *Richie Unterberger*

Round Midnight / Mar. 27, 1965 / Charly +++
Six selections of small-group Montgomery taken from the two albums, *Impressions* and *Solitude.* — *Michael Erlewine*

Classic Sound Of . . . / Mar. 27, 1965 / Accord +++
With Harold Mabern (p), Arthur Harper (b), and Jimmy Lovelace (d). Consists of material released on the albums *Impressions* and *Solitude.* — *Michael Erlewine*

Bumpin' / May 1965 / Verve ++++
Wes Montgomery's second Verve album was the best of his orchestral performances. With arrangements by Don Sebesky, Montgomery had opportunities to stretch out on a couple of the selections (most notably on the title cut and "Here's That Rainy Day"), and even though the jazz is not up to the level of his freewheeling Riverside performances, this set is a good compromise between the demands of the jazz and pop worlds. Plus some of the melodies are quite memorable. — *Scott Yanow*

★ **Smokin' at the Half Note** / May 1965-Sep. 22, 1965 / Verve +++++
Live two-fer. Can't get better. A must-buy. — *Michael G. Nastos*

Willow Weep for Me / Aug. 1965 / Verve +++
Recorded at the Half Note Club in NYC in the summer and autumn of 1965. With Wynton Kelly (p), Paul Chambers (b), and Jimmy Cobb (d). Includes brass and woodwinds arrangements by Claus Ogerman on three cuts. — *Michael Erlewine*

The Silver Collection / 1965 / Verve ++

Tequila / Mar. 17, 1966-May 18, 1966 / Verve +++

California Dreaming / Sep. 14, 1966-Sep. 16, 1966 / Verve ++

A Day in the Life / Jun. 6, 1967-Jun. 26, 1967 / A&M +++

Tete Montoliu (Vincente Montoliu)

b. Mar. 28, 1933, Barcelona, Spain
Piano / Hard Bop
An outstanding veteran pianist from Spain, Tete Montoliu was born blind. He learned to read music in Braille when he was seven and developed impressive technique on piano. He recorded with Lionel Hampton in 1956, had his first session as a leader in 1958, and played with the touring Roland Kirk in 1963. Through the years he also worked with such visiting Americans as Kenny Dorham, Dexter Gordon, Ben Webster, Lucky Thompson, and even Anthony Braxton. Tete Montoliu's visits to the US have been very infrequent but his SteepleChase albums (starting in 1971) are generally available; he also cut one date for Contemporary in 1979. — *Scott Yanow*

That's All / Sep. 25, 1971 / SteepleChase ++++
The virtuosic Spanish pianist Tete Montoliu is usually heard from in trio settings, making this rare solo outing particularly special. Montoliu digs into eight familiar standards (including "You Go to My Head," "Round Midnight," "A Child Is Born," and "Giant Steps") and to his credit comes up with fresh new variations. Montoliu's style has Bud Powell's bop approach as its foundation but also incorporates the more modern chord voicings of McCoy Tyner and Bill Evans. This album is a fine example of his talents. — *Scott Yanow*

Lunch in L.A. / Oct. 2, 1979 / Contemporary ++++
Fine two-piano set from the early '80s with flamboyant Spanish pianist Tete Montliu dueting with fellow pianist Chick Corea. Their exchanges, sometimes combative, sometimes complementary, and always engaging and gripping, are brilliant. — *Ron Wynn*

The Music I Like to Play, Vol. 1 / Dec. 1, 1986 / Soul Note ++++
The first in a four-part series that featured pianist Tete Montliu doing his favorite material, much of it standards, but also bop and mainstream pieces, ballads, and an occasional blues. — *Ron Wynn*

The Man from Barcelona / Oct. 1990 / Timeless +++

● **A Spanish Treasure** / Jun. 27, 1991 / Concord Jazz ++++

James Moody

b. Mar. 26, 1925, Savannah, GA
Flute, Sax (Alto), Sax (Tenor) / Bop, Hard Bop
James Moody has been an institution in jazz since the late '40s, whether on tenor, flute, occasional alto, or yodelling his way through his "Moody's Mood for Love." After serving in the Air Force (1943-46), he joined Dizzy Gillespie's bebop orchestra and began a lifelong friendship with the trum-

peter. Moody toured Europe with Gillespie and then stayed overseas for several years, working with Miles Davis, Max Roach, and top European players. His 1949 recording of "I'm in the Mood for Love" in 1952 became a hit under the title of "Moody's Mood for Love" with classic vocalese lyrics written by Eddie Jefferson and a best-selling recording by King Pleasure. After returning to the US, Moody formed a septet that lasted for five years, recorded extensively for Prestige and Argo, took up the flute, and then from 1963-68 was a member of Dizzy Gillespie's quintet. He worked in Las Vegas show bands during much of the '70s before returning to jazz, playing occasionally with Gillespie, mostly working as a leader and recording with Lionel Hampton's Golden Men of Jazz. Moody, who has alternated between tenor (which he prefers) and alto throughout his career, has an original sound on both horns. He is also one of the best flutists in jazz. James Moody has recorded as a leader for Blue Note, Xanadu, Vogue, Prestige, EmArcy, Mercury, Argo, DJM, Milestone, Perception, MPS, Muse, Vanguard, and Novus. —*Scott Yanow*

Moody's Mood for Blues / Jan. 6, 1954-Jan. 28, 1955 / Original Jazz Classics ♦♦♦

Hi-Fi Party / Aug. 23, 1955-Aug. 24, 1955 / Original Jazz Classics ♦♦♦♦
For a period in the mid-'50s tenor saxophonist James Moody (who doubled on alto) was able to keep together a swinging septet that played bop in a fairly accessible way. On this CD reissue of two 1955 sessions, Moody and his group (which includes the trumpeter Dave Burns, trombonist William Shepherd, baritonist Pee Wee Moore, pianist Jimmy Boyd, bassist John Lathan, and drummer Clarence Johnson) perform swinging versions of fairly obscure originals including the lengthy "Jammin' with James" (which has a long tradeoff between Moody and Burns), Benny Golson's "Big Ben," and "There Will Never Be Another You." The high point is Eddie Jefferson's one appearance, singing his alternate lyrics to Charlie Parker's famous solo on "Lady Be Good" which he renamed "Disappointed." —*Scott Yanow*

Wail, Moody, Wail / Dec. 12, 1955 / Original Jazz Classics ♦♦♦♦
James Moody's mid-'50s band was a septet featuring four horns including the leader's tenor and alto. The bop-based group had plenty of spirit (as best shown here on the 14-minute title cut) if not necessarily a strong personality. This CD (a straight reissue of the original LP plus two additional titles from the same session) is accessible, melodic, and swinging; trumpeter Dave Burns is the best soloist among the sidemen. —*Scott Yanow*

• **Last Train from Overbrook** / Sep. 13, 1958-Sep. 16, 1958 / Chess ♦♦♦♦

Something Special / Jul. 1986 / Novus ♦♦♦♦
This is the 1986 release that welcomed him to the Novus/RCA family. —*Ron Wynn*

Moving Forward / Nov. 10, 1987 & Nov. 18, 1987 / Novus ♦♦♦♦
Excellent Kenny Barron piano. —*Ron Wynn*

Sweet and Lovely / Mar. 11, 1989 & Mar. 13, 1989 / Novus ♦♦♦♦
Saxophone veteran James Moody stages an impromptu reunion with his longtime friend and onetime leader Dizzy Gillespie on this 1989 session. Their interaction hasn't been dulled by their time apart; they still anticipate each other and mesh effectively. Moody's own solos are mellow, well constructed, and superbly played. The backing band wisely defers to the giants, although keyboardist Marc Cohen has a few good passages. —*Ron Wynn*

Honey / Oct. 4, 1990-Oct. 15, 1990 / Novus ♦♦♦

Airto Moreira (Airto Guimorva Moreira)

b. Aug. 5, 1941, Itaipolis, Brazil
Percussion, Vocals / Latin Jazz, Crossover
The most high-profile percussionist of the '70s and still among the most famous, Airto Moreira (often simply known by his first name) helped make percussion an essential part of many modern jazz groups; his tambourine solos can border on the amazing! Airto originally studied guitar and piano before becoming a percussionist. He played locally in Brazil, collected and studied over 120 different percussion instruments, and in 1968 moved to the US with his wife, singer Flora Purim. Airto played with Miles Davis during part of 1969-70, appearing on several records (most notably *Live Evil*). He worked with Lee Morgan for a bit in 1971, was an original memeber of Weather Report, and in 1972 was part of Chick Corea's initial version of Return to Forever with Flora Purim; he and Corea also recorded the classic *Captain Marvel* with Stan Getz. By 1973 Airto was famous enough to have his own group, signed to CTI and appeared on Purim's sessions. Since then he has stayed busy, mostly co-leading bands with his wife and recording as a leader for many labels including Buddah, CTI, Arista, Warner Bros, Caroline, Rykodisc, In + Out, and B&W. Not all of his music as a leader would be called jazz but Airto remains a very impressive player. —*Scott Yanow*

• **Free** / Apr. 1972-May 1972 / CTI ♦♦♦♦
This great album includes the first version of "Return to Forever." With Chick Corea (k), Keith Jarrett (p), Stanley Clarke (b), and Joe Farrell (ts). —*Michael G. Nastos*

Three-way Mirror / 1985 / Reference ♦♦♦♦
Few vocal/instrumental teams have ever worked more smoothly than the unit of singer Flora Purim, saxophonist and flutist Joe Farrell, and percussionist Airto Moreira. They initially clicked on the first edition of Return to Forever in the early '70s, and they worked together often until Farrell's death in the mid-'80s. The eight songs featured on *Three-Way Mirror* were Farrell's last sessions, but his saxes and flute retained their drive, range, and authority throughout, punctuated as always by Moreira's array of sounds and Purim's floating, ethereal lead vocals. —*Ron Wynn*

The Other Side of This / Aug. 21, 1992 / Rykodisc ♦♦♦

Frank Morgan

b. Dec. 23, 1933, Minneapolis, MN
Sax (Alto) / Bop, Hard Bop
It is a real rarity for a jazz musician to have his career interrupted for a 30-year period and then be able to make a complete comeback. Frank Morgan showed a great deal of promise in his early days, but it was a long time before he could fulfill his potential. The son of guitarist Stanley Morgan (who played with the Ink Spots), he took up clarinet and alto early on. Morgan moved with his family to Los Angeles in 1947 and won a talent contest, leading to him recording a solo with Freddie Martin. Morgan worked on the bop scene of early-'50s Los Angeles, recording with Teddy Charles (1953) and Kenny Clarke (1954) and leading his own album for GNP in 1955. But then 30 years of darkness intruded. A heroin addict following in the footsteps of his idol Charlie Parker, Morgan was arrested for possession of drugs and was in and out of jails for decades. He performed locally on an occasional basis, but it was not until 1985 when he had an opportunity to lead his second date. Morgan managed to permanently kick drugs and after an initial period during which he sounded very close to Charlie Parker, he developed his own bop-based style. Frank Morgan has recorded a string of excellent sets for Contemporary and Antilles and has become an inspiring figure in the jazz world. —*Scott Yanow*

Frank Morgan / 1955 / GNP ♦♦♦♦
In 1955 when altoist Frank Morgan recorded his debut as a leader, he was being hyped as "the new bird." Unfortunately, he followed in Charlie Parker's footsteps mostly by becoming an irresponsible drug addict. Thirty years passed before he cut his second album and seriously began his successful comeback. The GNP album features Morgan back at the beginning, performing four numbers with Machito's rhythm section and six other songs with a septet that also includes tenor saxophonist Wardell Gray (heard on his final recordings). Trumpeter Conte Candoli is a major asset on both of these boppish dates while Frank Morgan shows why he was rated so high at this point in his career. —*Scott Yanow*

★ **Frank Morgan** / 1955 / GNP ♦♦♦♦♦
A reissue of vintage Morgan that includes work with some of the West Coast's best. The guest list includes Wardell Gray (ts), Carl Perkins (p), and James Clay (ts). Also has Morgan with Machito's rhythm section. —*Ron Wynn*

Easy Living / Jun. 1985 / Original Jazz Classics ♦♦♦♦
Solid hard bop, blues, and ballads from a great veteran. —*Ron Wynn*

Lament / Apr. 1986 / Contemporary ♦♦♦♦
A fine, if unambitious, 1986 quartet date. Bonus cut on CD version. With Cedar Wlaton, Buster WIlliams, and Billy Higgins. —*Ron Wynn*

Double Image / May 21, 1986-May 22, 1986 / Contemporary ♦♦♦♦
With George Cables. An excellent collaboration, pairing a great old veteran and a relatively youthful one on piano in Cables. —*Ron Wynn*

You Must Believe in Spring / Mar. 10, 1992-Mar. 11, 1992 / Antilles ♦♦♦♦
A 1992 release by marvelous alto saxophonist Frank Morgan, whose life story and triumph over heroin addiction and imprisonment was one of the '80s' great success tales. Morgan's biting, yet sensitive and rich alto has rightly been traced to Charlie Parker, but Morgan long ago rid his style of any imitative excesses. He was excellently supported on this program of duets by an amazing lineup of rotating pianists: Kenny Barron, Tommy Flanagan, Barry Harris, Roland Hanna, and Hank Jones. —*Ron Wynn*

Listen To The Dawn / Apr. 19, 1993-Nov. 27, 1993 / Antilles ♦♦♦♦

Lee Morgan

b. Jul. 10, 1938, Philadelphia, PA, **d.** Feb. 19, 1972, New York, NY
Trumpet / Hard Bop
One of the great jazz trumpeters of the '60s, Lee Morgan was the natural successor to Clifford Brown, making an impact on the scene shortly after Brown's death and at first playing in a very similar style. He was a bit of a prodigy, working professionally in Philadelphia when he was 15 and joining Dizzy Gillespie's orchestra when he was barely 18. Morgan led his first Blue Note session later that year, and he would record his first two classic albums for the label during 1957-58: *The Cooker* and *Candy*. Morgan was with Gillespie's band into 1958 when he became a member of Art Blakey's Jazz Messengers (1958-61), touring and recording extensively with the

group and sharing the frontline with Benny Golson, Hank Mobley, and finally Wayne Shorter. Drug problems resulted in his quitting the band in 1961 and maintaining a low profile in Philadelphia until 1963. When Morgan came back, his first recording was his biggest hit, "The Sidewinder." He entered his greatest period, recording one memorable album after another, writing "Ceora" and "Speedball" and spending a second period with Blakey (1964-65). Morgan's playing became more adventurous, and by the end of the decade he was exploring modal music, using some avant-garde elements and opening his playing to the influence of funk. On February 19, 1972 he was fatally shot by a girlfriend, ending his life at the age of 33. Lee Morgan recorded many records throughout his career as a sideman, and he led 25 albums for Blue Note (coincidentally the same number as Hank Mobley) plus sessions for Vee-Jay, Roulette, Jazzland, and Trip. —*Scott Yanow*

Presenting Lee Morgan / Nov. 4, 1956 / Blue Note ✦✦✦

Complete Blue Note Lee Morgan Fifties Sessions / Nov. 4, 1956-Feb. 2, 1958 / Mosaic ✦✦✦✦

Introducing Lee Morgan / Nov. 5, 1956 / Savoy ✦✦✦

A-1 / Nov. 5, 1956-Nov. 7, 1956 / Savoy ✦✦✦

Dizzy Atmosphere / Feb. 1957 / Original Jazz Classics ✦✦✦✦
This is an excellent match between Lee Morgan and Wynton Kelly (p), plus stirring tenor from Bill Mitchell and rollicking trombone from Al Grey. Bonus cuts on CD. —*Ron Wynn*

Lee Morgan Indeed!, Vol. 3 / Mar. 24, 1957 / Blue Note ✦✦✦✦
Although trumpeter Lee Morgan (then only 18 years old) was the nominal leader of this set, tenor saxophonist Benny Golson contributed all five of the compositions and did the arrangements for the sextet (which also includes altoist Gigi Gryce, pianist Wynton Kelly, bassist Paul Chambers, and drummer Charlie Persip). Most notable among the songs is the original version of "I Remember Clifford"; Morgan was the perfect trumpeter to play the tribute to Clifford Brown, who had died in a car crash a year earlier. This CD reissue (a fine hard bop date) adds an alternate take of "Tip-Toeing" to the original program. —*Scott Yanow*

The Cooker / Sep. 29, 1957 / Blue Note ✦✦✦✦
The trumpeter, then just 19, teams up with baritonist Pepper Adams, pianist Bobby Timmons, bassist Paul Chambers, and drummer Philly Joe Jones for a particularly strong set that is highlighted by a lengthy and fiery "Night in Tunisia," "Lover Man" and a rapid rendition of "Just One of Those Things." Morgan plays remarkably well for his age (already ranking just below Dizzy Gillespie and Miles Davis), making this an essential acquisition. —*Scott Yanow*

★ **Candy** / Nov. 18, 1957 / Blue Note ✦✦✦✦✦
Lee Morgan's only quartet album is one of his best. Although only 19 years old at the time, Morgan already had a mature style, a sound influenced by Clifford Brown, and a near-complete mastery of the bop vocabulary. With the strong assistance of pianist Sonny Clark, bassist Doug Watkins, and drummer Art Taylor, Morgan is very expressive and creative on this CD reissue, particularly on such songs as "Candy," "Since I Fell for You," "All the Way," and even "Personality." —*Scott Yanow*

● **The Best of Lee Morgan** / 1957-1965 / Blue Note ✦✦✦✦
Very good compilation and good tune choices. —*Michael G. Nastos*

Here's Lee Morgan / Feb. 2, 1960-Feb. 8, 1960 / Vee-Jay ✦✦✦✦
This CD reissue has its original six songs expanded to 11 with the inclusion of five alternate takes. The music is good solid hard bop that finds Lee Morgan (already a veteran at age 21) coming out of the Clifford Brown tradition to display his own rapidly developing style. Matched with Clifford Jordan on tenor, pianist Wynton Kelly, bassist Paul Chambers, and drummer Art Blakey, Morgan's album could pass for a Jazz Messengers set. —*Scott Yanow*

Leeway / Apr. 28, 1960 / Blue Note ✦✦✦✦
This date was one of trumpeter Lee Morgan's more obscure Blue Note sessions, but fortunately it has been reissued on CD. Matched with altoist Jackie McLean, pianist Bobby Timmons, bassist Paul Chambers, and drummer Art Blakey, Morgan interprets two of Calvin Massey's compositions, McLean's "Midtown Blues" and his own blues "The Lion and the Wolff." The music is essentially hard bop with a strong dose of soul; the very distinctive styles of the principals is the main reason to acquire this easily enjoyable music. —*Scott Yanow*

Minor Strain / May 12, 1960 & Jul. 1960 / Roulette ✦✦✦

Expodient / Oct. 14, 1960 / Vee-Jay ✦✦✦

Take Twelve / Jan. 24, 1962 / Original Jazz Classics ✦✦✦✦
This CD reissue (which adds an alternate take of "Second's Best" to the original LP program) was trumpeter Lee Morgan's only recording during an off-period that lasted from mid-1961 to late 1963. Morgan (who sounds in fine form) leads a quintet with tenor saxophonist Clifford Jordan, pianist Barry Harris, bassist Bob Cranshaw, and drummer Louis Hayes through four of his originals, Jordan's "Little Spain," and the title cut, an Elmo Hope composition. The superior material uplifts the set from being a mere

"blowing" date, but it generally has the spontaneity of a jam session. It's one of Morgan's lesser-known dates. —*Scott Yanow*

★ **The Sidewinder** / Dec. 21, 1963 / Blue Note ✦✦✦✦✦
This album is trumpeter Lee Morgan's best-known recording; the catchy title cut became a hit, launched the boogaloo fad and is still performed decades later. The CD reissue (which adds an alternate take of "Totem Pole" to the original set) finds Morgan at the peak of his powers (where he would remain for the next four or five years) as the leading trumpeter in hard bop. The young (and already immediately recognizable) tenor Joe Henderson, pianist Barry Harris, bassist Bob Cranshaw, and drummer Billy Higgins also make strong contributions to this well rounded program which includes four other memorable Morgan originals: "Totem Pole," "Gary's Notebook," "Boy, What a Night," and "Hocus-Pocus." —*Scott Yanow*

☆ **Search for the New Land** / Feb. 15, 1964 / Blue Note ✦✦✦✦✦
This set (the CD reissue is a duplicate of the original LP) is one of the finest Lee Morgan records. The great trumpeter contributes five challenging compositions ("Search for the New Land," "The Joker," "Mr. Kenyatta," "Melancholee," and "Morgan the Pirate") songs that deserve to be revived. Morgan, tenor saxophonist Wayne Shorter, guitarist Grant Green, pianist Herbie Hancock, bassist Reggie Workman, and drummer Billy Higgins are all in particularly creative form on the fresh material and they stretch the boundaries of hard bop (the modern mainstream jazz of the period). The result is a consistently stimulating set that rewards repeated listenings. —*Scott Yanow*

Tom Cat / Aug. 11, 1964 / Blue Note ✦✦✦✦
It seems strange that the music on this CD was not released initially until 1980. Trumpeter Lee Morgan had had an unexpected hit with "The Sidewinder," so his more challenging recordings were temporarily put aside. As it turns out, this was one of Morgan's better sets from the '60s, and he had gathered together quite an all-star cast: altoist Jackie McLean, trombonist Curtis Fuller, pianist McCoy Tyner, bassist Bob Cranshaw, and drummer Art Blakey. They perform "Rigormortis," McCoy Tyner's "Twilight Mist," and three of the trumpeter's originals including the title cut. The advanced hard bop music still sounds fresh decades later despite its initial neglect. —*Scott Yanow*

Rumproller / Apr. 21, 1965 / Blue Note ✦✦✦
To follow up on his unexpected boogaloo hit "The Sidewinder," Lee Morgan recorded Andrew Hill's somewhat similar "The Rumproller," but this time the commercial magic was not there. However, the trumpeter, tenor saxophonist Joe Henderson, pianist Ronnie Mathews, bassist Victor Sproles, and drummer Billy Higgins all play quite well on the title cut, two of Morgan's songs (the bossa nova "Eclipso" is somewhat memorable), a ballad tribute to Billie Holiday, and Wayne Shorter's "Edda." This LP (not yet reissued on CD) is worth picking up, but it is not essential. —*Scott Yanow*

The Gigolo / Jun. 25, 1965 & Jul. 1, 1965 / Blue Note ✦✦✦✦
Lee Morgan was the leading trumpeter in hard bop during the '60s, and he recorded quite a few classic albums for Blue Note. This is one of them. The CD reissue (which adds an alternate take of the title cut to the original five-song program) features Morgan at his best, whether playing his memorable blues "Speed Ball," an explorative ballad version of "You Go to My Head," a lengthy "The Gigolo," or his other two originals ("Yes I Can, No You Can't" and "Trapped"). There are no weak selections on this set, and the playing by the leader, Wayne Shorter on tenor, pianist Harold Mabern, bassist Bob Cranshaw, and drummer Billy Higgins is beyond any serious criticism. —*Scott Yanow*

★ **Cornbread** / Sep. 8, 1965 / Blue Note ✦✦✦✦✦
This session (reissued on CD by Blue Note) is best known for introducing Lee Morgan's beautiful ballad "Ceora," but actually all five selections (which include Morgan's "Cornbread," "Our Man Higgins," "Most like Lee," and the standard "Ill Wind") are quite memorable. The trumpeter/leader performs with a perfectly complementary group of open-minded and talented hard bop stylists (altoist Jackie McLean, Hank Mobley on tenor, pianist Herbie Hancock, bassist Larry Ridley, and drummer Billy Higgins) and creates a Blue Note classic that is heartily recommended. —*Scott Yanow*

Delightfulee / Apr. 8, 1966 & May 27, 1966 / Blue Note ✦✦✦✦
This classic set by trumpeter Lee Morgan was reissued on LP in 1984 but has not yet appeared on CD. Of the four quintet numbers with tenor saxophonist Joe Henderson, pianist McCoy Tyner, bassist Bob Cranshaw, and drummer Billy Higgins, the instantly likable "Ca-Lee-So" is the most memorable, although the other three Morgan originals ("Zambia," "Nite Flite," and "The Delightful Deggie") also find the trumpeter in excellent form. An unusual aspect to this collection is that there are also two ballads ("Yesterday" and "Sunrise Sunset") that have a nonet playing Oliver Nelson arrangements behind Morgan's lyrical horn; Tyner and tenor saxophonist Wayne Shorter have opportunities to take concise solos. —*Scott Yanow*

The Procrastinator / Jul. 14, 1967 / Blue Note ✦✦✦✦
This out-of-print double LP from 1978 released for the first time a pair of "lost" Lee Morgan albums. The music (from 1967 and 1969) falls into the category of advanced hard bop with the influence of the avant-garde and

modal jazz mixing in with the trumpeter's roots in Art Blakey's brand of hard bop. The earlier date has a particularly impressive lineup of talent (tenor saxophonist Wayne Shorter, vibraphonist Bobby Hutcherson, pianist Herbie Hancock, bassist Ron Carter, and drummer Billy Higgins), while the later album is not exactly a throwaway since it features trombonist Julian Priester, George Coleman on tenor, pianist Harold Mabern, bassist Walter Booker, and drummer Mickey Roker. There are many highlights to this enjoyable (but now difficult-to-locate) two-fer as Morgan and his contemporaries perform 12 group originals plus the lone standard "Stormy Weather." —*Scott Yanow*

Live at the Lighthouse / Jul. 10, 1970-Jul. 12, 1970 / Blue Note ◆◆◆◆
This double LP, which was trumpeter Lee Morgan's next-to-last recording, contains four lengthy side-long explorations of the trumpeter's regular quintet of the period (with Bennie Maupin on tenor, flute, and bass clarinet, pianist Harold Mabern, bassist Jymie Merritt, and drummer Mickey Roker). The music is very modal-oriented and probably disappointed many of Morgan's longtime fans, but he had gotten tired of playing the same hard bop-styled music that he had excelled at during the past decade and was searching for newer sounds. The influence of the avant-garde and early fusion is also felt in spots, but the trumpeter's sound was still very much intact, and he takes some fiery solos that still sound lively decades later. —*Scott Yanow*

Lee Morgan / Sep. 17, 1971-Sep. 18, 1971 / Blue Note ◆◆

Jelly Roll Morton (Ferdinand Joseph Lemott)

b. Oct. 20, 1890, New Orleans, LA, **d.** Jul. 10, 1941, Los Angeles, CA
Piano / Classic New Orleans Jazz
One of the very first giants of jazz, Jelly Roll Morton did himself a lot of harm posthumously by exaggerating his worth, claiming to have invented jazz in 1902. Morton's accomplishments as an early innovator are so vast that he did not really need to stretch the truth.

Morton was jazz's first great composer, writing such songs as "King Porter Stomp," "Grandpa's Spells," "Wolverine Blues," "The Pearls," "Mr. Jelly Roll," "Shreveport Stomp," "Milenburg Joys," "Black Bottom Stomp," "The Chant," "Original Jelly Roll Blues," "Doctor Jazz," "Wild Man Blues," "Winin' Boy Blues," "I Thought I Heard Buddy Bolden Say," "Don't You Leave Me Here," and "Sweet Substitute." He was a talented arranger (1926's "Black Bottom Stomp" is remarkable), getting the most out of the three-minute limitations of the 78 record by emphasizing changing instrumentation, concise solos, and dynamics. He was a greatly underrated pianist who had his own individual style. Although he only took one vocal on records in the '20s ("Doctor Jazz"), Morton in his late-'30s recordings proved to be an effective vocalist. And he was a true character.

Jelly Roll Morton's pre-1923 activities are shrouded in legend. He started playing piano when he was ten years old, worked in the bordellos of Storyville while a teenager (for which some of his relatives disowned him), and by 1904 was traveling throughout the South. He spent time in other professions (as a gambler, pool player, vaudeville comedian, and even a pimp) but always returned to music. The chances are good that in 1915 Morton had few competitors among pianists, and he was an important transition figure between ragtime and early jazz. He played in Los Angeles during 1917-22 and then moved to Chicago, where for the next six years he was at his peak. Morton's 1923-24 recordings of piano solos introduced his style, repertoire, and brilliance. Although his earliest band sides were quite primitve, his 1926-27 recordings for Victor with his Red Hot Peppers are among the most exciting of his career. With such sidemen as cornetist George Mitchell, Kid Ory or Gerald Reeves on trombone, clarinetists Omer Simeon, Barney Bigard, Darnell Howard, or Johnny Dodds, occasionally Stomp Evans on C-melody, Johnny St. Cyr or Bud Scott on banjo, bassist John Lindsay, and either Andrew Hilaire or Baby Dodds on drums, Morton had the perfect ensembles for his ideas. He also recorded some exciting trios with Johnny and Baby Dodds.

With the center of jazz shifting to New York by 1928, Morton relocated through 1930, and although some of the performances are sloppy and erratic, there were also a few more classics. Among the musicians Morton was able to use on his New York records were trumpeters Ward Pinkett, Red Allen, and Bubber Miley, trombonists Geechie Fields, Charles Irvis and J.C. Higginbotham, clarinetists Omer Simeon, Albert Nicholas and Barney Bigard, banjoist Lee Blair, guitarist Bernard Addison, Bill Benford on tuba, bassist Pops Foster and drummers Tommy Benford, Paul Barbarin, and Zutty Singleton.

But with the rise of the Depression, Jelly Roll Morton drifted into obscurity. He had made few friends in New York, his music was considered old-fashioned, and he did not have the temperament to work as a sideman. During 1931-37 his only appearance on records was on a little-known Wingy Manone date. He ended up playing in a Washington D.C. dive for patrons who had little idea of his contributions. Ironically, Morton's "King Porter Stomp" became one of the most popular songs of the

swing era, but few knew that he wrote it. However, in 1938 Alan Lomax recorded him in an extensive and fascinating series of musical interviews for the Library of Congress. Morton's storytelling was colorful and his piano playing in generally fine form as he reminisced about old New Orleans and demonstrated the other piano styles of the era. A decade later the results would finally be released on albums.

Morton arrived in New York in 1939 determined to make a comeback. He did lead a few band sessions with such sidemen as Sidney Bechet, Red Allen, and Albert Nicholas and recorded some wonderful solo sides, but none of those were big sellers. In late 1940 an ailing Morton decided to head out to Los Angeles, but when he died at the age of 50, he seemed like an old man. Ironically his music soon became popular again as the New Orleans jazz revivalist movement caught fire, and if he had lived just a few more years, the chances are good that he would have been restored to his former prominence (as was Kid Ory).

Jelly Roll Morton's early piano solos and classic Victor recordings (along with nearly every record he made) have been reissued on CD. —*Scott Yanow*

★ **Jelly Roll Morton** / Jun. 9, 1923-Feb. 1, 1926 / Milestone ◆◆◆◆◆
The legendary Jelly Roll Morton recorded many of his finest piano solos for Gennett and Paramount during 1923-24, and all 20 (counting a second version of "New Orleans Joys") are on this essential CD; high points include the original versions of "King Porter Stomp," "Grandpa's Spells," "Wolverine Blues," and "The Pearls." In addition there are four early (and surprisingly primitive) band performances (including a version of "Mr. Jelly Lord" from 1926) and two piano-cornet duets with King Oliver. This single CD differs from the earlier two-LP set in that it leaves out a few of Morton's less significant 1924 band sides but includes the Oliver duets and the second "New Orleans Joys." —*Scott Yanow*

The Piano Solos (1923-1924) / Jul. 1923-Jun. 1924 / Fountain ◆◆◆◆
1926-1934 / Sep. 15, 1926-Aug. 15, 1934 / ABC ◆◆◆

☆ **Jelly Roll Morton Centennial: His Complete Victor Recording** / Sep. 15, 1926-Sep. 28, 1939 / Bluebird ◆◆◆◆◆
This five-CD set contains the very best band recordings of Jelly Roll Morton's career. There are 111 performances in this reissue including all of the alternate takes. Bypassed are the pianist's recordings with the vaudevillian clarinetist Wilton Crawley, singers Lizzie Miles and Billie Young, and two songs he performed on a radio broadcast in 1940; otherwise all of his Victor recordings are here. The classics (most from the 1926-28 period) include the remarkable "Black Bottom Stomp," "Grandpa's Spells," "The Pearls," "Wolverine Blues" (a trio with clarinetist Johnny Dodds and drummer Baby Dodds), "Shreveport Stomp," "Low Gravy," "Strokin' Away," and "I Thought I Heard Buddy Bolden Say," but listeners will have their own favorites. In general this is New Orleans jazz at its best with Jelly Roll Morton (as with the best jazz composer/bandleaders) creating his own world of music. —*Scott Yanow*

● **Kansas City Stomp: the Library of Congress Recordings, Vol. 1** / May 23, 1938-Jun. 7, 1938 / Rounder ◆◆◆◆
Pianist/composer Jelly Roll Morton, one of the pioneers of New Orleans jazz, was down and out in 1938 when Alan Lomax found him playing in a Washington D.C. dive. Lomax, realizing that Morton had seen and heard many timeless incidents that would otherwise be forgotten, started interviewing him for the Library of Congress on a wire recorder. Released originally on eight LPs, these discussions found Morton talking about the old days and peppering his talk with piano solos. Rounder has reissued all of the music (and done a fine job of correcting the speed) on four CDs but unfortunately decided to leave out Morton's often-fascinating monologues. This first CD has many strong moments including Morton's demonstration of the piano styles of many forgotten players, his depiction of a New Orleans funeral, his famous demonstration of how "Tiger Rag" evolved from being a quadrille into becoming jazz, and comparisons of "Maple Leaf Rag" as played as ragtime and the way Morton preferred it. —*Scott Yanow*

● **Anamule Dance** / May 23, 1938-Jun. 7, 1938 / Rounder ◆◆◆◆
The second of four CDs that reissue the music (but not the verbal monologues) that pianist/composer Jelly Roll Morton recorded for the Library of Congress is, like the other volumes, filled with memorable performances that are sometimes (due to time limitations) incomplete or heard in excerpts. The most interesting selections on this disc are the lengthy "Winin' Boy Blues," Morton's playful "The Anamule Dance," "Mr. Jelly Lord," and a lengthy (and somewhat filthy) version of "Make Me a Pallet on the Floor." —*Scott Yanow*

● **The Pearls** / May 23, 1938-Jun. 7, 1938 / Rounder ◆◆◆◆
The third of four CDs taken from pianist Jelly Roll Morton's *Library of Congress* recordings is highlighted by the nearly half-hour "Murder Ballad" (a sexual fantasy by Morton about women's prisons), "King Porter Stomp," a two-part "Wolverine Blues," and a seven-minute version of "The Pearls." All four of these releases are recommended to collectors of early jazz although the LP equivalent (which runs to eight volumes) also includes all of his storytelling. —*Scott Yanow*

● **Winin Boy Blues** / Jun. 7, 1938-Dec. 14, 1938 / Rounder ✦✦✦✦
The fourth and final CD in Rounder's *Library of Congress* series has the
later recordings from this extensive program, including two numbers from
six months after the original discussions had concluded. Morton, who is
heard very briefly on guitar on "Li'l Liza Jane," takes fine piano solos on
such numbers as "Freakish," "Pep," "Ain't Misbehavin'," and a medley of
"Spanish tinge" songs including "The Crave." This fascinating series (which
Rounder pitch corrected) is recommended to collectors of early jazz.
—*Scott Yanow*

Bennie Moten

b. Nov. 13, 1894, Kansas City, MO, **d.** Apr. 2, 1935, Kansas City, MO
Piano / Classic Jazz
Bennie Moten is today best-remembered as the leader of a band that
partly became the nucleus of the original Count Basie Orchestra, but
Moten deserves better. He was a fine ragtime-oriented pianist who led
the top territory band of the '20s, an orchestra that really set the standard
for Kansas City jazz. In fact, it was so dominant that Moten was able to
swallow up some of his competitors' groups including Walter Page's Blue
Devils, most of whom eventually became members of Moten's big band.
Moten formed his group (originally a sextet) in 1922, and the following
year they made their first recordings. Among Moten's 1923-25 sides for
Okeh was the original version of his greatest hit "South." During 1926-32
Moten's Orchestra recorded for Victor, and although none of his original
musicians became famous, the later additions included his brother
Buster on occasional jazz accordion, Harlan Leonard, Jack Washington,
Eddie Durham, Jimmy Rushing, Hot Lips Page, and (starting in 1929)
Count Basie. So impressed was Moten by Basie's playing that Count
assumed the piano chair for recordings from that point on (although in
clubs Moten would generally play a feature or two). The most famous
Bennie Moten recording session was also his last, ten songs cut on
December 13, 1932 that find the ensemble strongly resembling Basie's
five years later. In addition to Hot Lips Page, Durham, Washington, and
Basie, the band at that point also starred Ben Webster, Eddie Barefield,
and Walter Page. One of the high points was the debut of "Moten Swing."
Tragically Bennie Moten died in 1935 from a botched tonsillectomy.
Buster Moten briefly took over the band, but many of its top members
(along with some important additions like Lester Young) eventually gravitated towards Count Basie. —*Scott Yanow*

● **South (1926-1929)** / Dec. 13, 1926-Jul. 17, 1929 / Bluebird ✦✦✦✦

★ **Basie Beginnings (1929-1932)** / Oct. 23, 1929-Dec. 13, 1932 / Bluebird
✦✦✦✦✦
Bennie Moten's orchestra, arguably the top territory band at the time
Count Basie joined as second pianist in 1929, had been reasonably well
represented on records since 1923. This date has the cream of Moten's 1929
and 1930 sessions, plus seven of the ten songs cut at their superb Dec. 13,
1932 date. Moten himself never again appeared on records after Basie
joined. —*Scott Yanow*

Paul Motian (Stephen Paul Motian)

b. Mar. 25, 1931, Philadelphia, PA
Drums / Avant-Garde, Post-Bop
Paul Motian is a subtle drummer who is equally important as the leader of
several rather stimulating bands and quite a few colorful recording sessions. Born in Philadelphia, Motian grew up in Providence, RI. After moving to New York in 1955, he played with many top jazz musicians from a
wide variety of styles including Tony Scott, Gil Evans, Art Farmer, Lee
Konitz, George Russell, Stan Getz, Lennie Tristano, Thelonious Monk,
Coleman Hawkins, and Roy Eldridge. As a member of Bill Evans' most
famous trio (the one with Scott LaFaro), Motian helped define the role of
the modern drummer in that type of intimate setting. He remained with
Evans after LaFaro's death (Chuck Israels took over as bassist) until 1963.
Motian then played with Paul Bley's Trio (1963-64) and he later had a long
term musical relationship with Keith Jarrett, starting in 1966 and including
work with Jarrett's quintet in the '70s. Motian also freelanced, and among
the many musicians that he worked with were Mose Allison, Charles
Lloyd, Charlie Haden's Liberation Music Ensemble, and Carla Bley. Motian
began leading his own groups in 1977, and these included a trio with Joe
Lovano and Bill Frisell, and the Electric Bebop Band in the '90s with
Joshua Redman and two guitarists. He has recorded many albums as a
leader (starting in 1972) for ECM, GM, Soul Note, and JMT including collaborations with Lee Konitz. —*Scott Yanow*

● **Tribute** / May 1974 / ECM ✦✦✦✦
Quintet with guitarist Sam Brown, Charlie Haden (b), early work of saxo-
phonist Carlos Ward. Coleman's "War Orphans" and Haden's immortal
"Song for Che" are included. —*Michael G. Nastos*

● **Psalm** / Dec. 1981 / ECM ✦✦✦✦
The eight compositions by drummer Paul Motian on this ECM release
(which is available on CD) are rather dry, and none caught on as future
standards. But the playing by Motian's sidemen (tenors Joe Lovano and

Billy Drewes, bassist Ed Schuller, and especially the remarkable guitarist
Bill Frisell) uplifted the music and gave this group a strong personality of
its own. Although the results are not all that memorable, the music should
please adventurous listeners. —*Scott Yanow*

It Should Have Happened a Long Time Ago / Jul. 1984 / ECM ✦✦✦✦
Tenor/guitar/drums trios are not too common since there are few guitarists around (other than Bill Frisell) who can make up for the absence of
both a keyboard and a bass. With Joe Lovano providing some fine tenor
solos, Frisell adding fire along with a wide variety of unique sounds, and
Paul Motian playing some stimulating drums, this is a surprisingly self-sufficient trio. Motian provided all seven originals on the worthy set which
has been reissued on CD by ECM. —*Scott Yanow*

One Time Out / Sep. 21, 1987-Sep. 22, 1987 / Soul Note ✦✦✦✦
Drummer Paul Motian never makes predictable or conventional albums,
and this mid- and late '80s date proves no different. The trio lineup, with
Motian, tenor saxophonist Joe Lovano, and guitarist and synthesizer player
Bill Frisell, offers some unusual voicings, solos, and harmonies, filling in
the space that would normally be completed by a pianist, bassist, or second
horn. It's not hard bop, fusion, or free, but a mix of all three and more.
—*Ron Wynn*

☆ **Monk in Motian** / Mar. 1988 / JMT ✦✦✦✦✦
A top tribute, with sterling work by Frisell (g) and Dewey Redman (ts).
—*Ron Wynn*

Bill Evans: Tribute to the Great Post-Bop Pianist / May 1990 / JMT
✦✦✦✦
An excellent quartet date featuring sensational guitar by Bill Frisell and
nice tenor sax from Joe Lovano. —*Ron Wynn*

Paul Motian & The Electric Bebop Band / Apr. 1992 / JMT ✦✦✦✦

Gerry Mulligan

b. Apr. 6, 1927, New York, NY
Piano, Sax (Baritone) / Cool
The most famous and probably greatest jazz baritonist of all time, Gerry
Mulligan was a giant. A flexible soloist who was always ready to jam
with anyone from Dixielanders to the most advanced boppers, Mulligan
brought a somewhat revolutionary light sound to his potentially awkward and brutal horn and played with the speed and dexterity of an
altoist.
Mulligan started on the piano before learning clarinet and the various
saxophones. His initial reputation was as an arranger. In 1944 he wrote
charts for Johnny Warrington's radio band and soon was making contributions to the books of Tommy Tucker and George Paxton. He moved to
New York in 1946 and joined Gene Krupa's Orchestra as staff arranger;
his most notable chart was "Disc Jockey Jump." The rare times he played
with Krupa's band was on alto, and the same situation existed when he
was with Claude Thornhill in 1948.
Gerry Mulligan's first notable recorded work on baritone was with
Miles Davis' *Birth of the Cool* nonet (1948-50) but once again his arrangements ("Godchild," "Darn That Dream" and three of his originals "Jeru,"
"Rocker" and "Venus De Milo") were more significant than his short solos.
Mulligan spent much of 1949 writing for Elliot Lawrence's orchestra and
playing anonymously in the saxophone section. It was not until 1951 that
he began to get a bit of attention for his work on baritone. Mulligan
recorded with his own nones for Prestige, displaying an already recognizable sound. After he traveled to Los Angeles, he wrote some arrangements
for Stan Kenton (including "Youngblood," "Swing House" and "Walking
Shoes"), worked at the Lighthouse and then gained a regular Monday
night engagement at the Haig. Around this time Mulligan realized that he
enjoyed the extra freedom of soloing without a pianist. He jammed with
trumpeter Chet Baker and soon their magical rapport was featured in his
pianoless quartet. The group caught on quickly in 1952 and made both
Mulligan and Baker into stars.
A drug bust put Mulligan out of action and ended that Quartet but,
when he was released from jail in 1954, Mulligan began a new musical
partnership with valve trombonist Bob Brookmeyer that was just as successful. Trumpeter Jon Eardley and Zoot Sims on tenor occasionally made
the group a sextet and in 1958 trumpeter Art Farmer was featured in Mulligan's Quartet. Being a very flexible player with respect for other stylists,
Mulligan went out of his way to record with some of the great musicians
he admired. At the 1958 Newport Jazz Fetival he traded off with baritonist
Harry Carney on "Prima Bara Dubla" while backed by the Duke Ellington
Orchestra, and during 1957-60 he recorded separate albums with Thelonious Monk, Paul Desmond, Stan Getz, Ben Webster and Johnny Hodges.
Mulligan played on the classic *Sound of Jazz* television special in 1958 and
appeared in the movies *I Want to Live* and *The Subterraneans*.
During 1960-64 Mulligan led his Concert Jazz Band which gave him
an opporunity to write, play baritone and occasionally double on piano.
The orchestra at times included Brookmeyer, Sims, Clark Terry and Mel
Lewis. Mulligan was a little less active after the big band broke up but he
toured extensively with the Dave Brubeck Quartet (1968-72), had a part-

time big band in the '70s (the Age of Steam), doubled on soprano for a period, led a mid-'70s sextet that included vibraphonist Dave Samuels and in 1986 jammed on a record with Scott Hamilton. In the '90s he toured the world with his excellent "no-name" quartet and led a "Rebirth of the Cool Band" that performed and recorded remakes of the Miles Davis Nonet clasics. Up until the end, Gerry Mulligan was always eager to play.

Among Mulligan's compositions were "Walkin' Shoes," "Line for Lyons," "Bark for Barksdale," "Nights at the Turntable," "Utter Chaos," "Soft Shoe," "Bernie's Tune," "Blueport," "Song for Strayhorn," "Song for an Unifinished Woman" and "I Never Was a Young Man" (which he often sang). He recorded extensively over the years for such labels as Prestige, Pacific Jazz, Capitol, Vogue, EmArcy, Columbia, Verve, Milestone, United Artists, Philips, Limelight, A&M, CTI, Chiaroscuro, Who's Who, DRG, Concord and GRP. —*Scott Yanow*

The Arranger / May 21, 1946-Apr. 20, 1957 / Columbia ✦✦✦✦
This LP includes some of Gerry Mulligan's charts for the orchestras of Gene Krupa ("How High the Moon" and "Disc Jockey Jump") and Elliot Lawrence ("Between the Devil and the Deep Blue Sea" and "Elevation"), in addition to featuring his own 1957 big band ("Thruway," "All the Things You Are," "Mullenium," and "Motel"). The Krupa performances are near-classic, the forgotten Lawrence band is in top form, and Jeru's specially assembled orchestra features solos from baritonist Mulligan, trumpeters Jerry Lloyd and Don Joseph, trombonist Bob Brookmeyer, tenor saxophonist Zoot Sims and altoist Lee Konitz. Excellent music although most of it has since been reissued on CD. —*Scott Yanow*

Mulligan—Baker / Aug. 1951-1965 / Prestige ✦✦✦✦
This double LP is full of valuable recordings. The classic Gerry Mulligan pianoless quartet with trumpeter Chet Baker is heard on eight gems including "Line for Lyons," "Lady Is a Tramp," and their hit version of "My Funny Valentine." In addition, Mulligan performs with his unusual tentette of 1951 (which featured two baritones and maracas) and Jeru and Allen Eager head a sextet on a 171-minute version of his original "Mulligan's Too." This two-fer concludes with four numbers taken from Chet Baker's many quintet sessions of 1965 with tenor saxophonist George Coleman and pianist Kirk Lightsey. Most of this music has since appeared on CD, but this was a well packaged set and does not duplicate Mulligan's remarkable Mosaic box. —*Scott Yanow*

☆ **Pacific Jazz and Capitol Recordings** / Jun. 10, 1952-Jun. 10, 1953 / Mosaic ✦✦✦✦✦
This five-LP box set, as its title states, contains all of the Gerry Mulligan Quartet's recordings for Pacific Jazz and Capitol, everything that that classic group ever recorded other than the material issued by Prestige and a half-record recorded for GNP/Crescendo. Unfortunately, this is a limited-edition set that is now out of print, but it is well worth bidding on in auctions, for not only does it have all of the Mulligan Quartet's other recordings but also 15 previously unissued performances, all of the sides on which altoist Lee Konitz sat in with the quartet and the eight recordings by the 1953 Gerry Mulligan Tentette. These highly influential performances set the standard for West Coast cool jazz, made trumpeter Chet Baker a star, and remain some of the high points of Gerry Mulligan's very productive career. —*Scott Yanow*

Gerry Mulligan In Paris, Vol. 1 / Jun. 1, 1954 & Jun. 3, 1954 / Vogue ✦✦✦✦
Formerly available in piecemeal fashion, this CD (and *Vol. 2*) has all of the music recorded at baritonist Gerry Mulligan's Paris concerts of June 1954. This particular unit (with valve trombonist Bob Brookmeyer, bassist Red Mitchell, and drummer Frank Isola) was one of Jeru's finest for his own wit, swing, and cool-toned creativity were matched by Brookmeyer. High points include "Walkin' Shoes," "Love Me or Leave Me," "My Funny Valentine," and "Five Brothers," but every selection is quite enjoyable. The audience is rightfully enthusiastic. —*Scott Yanow*

California Concerts, Vol. 1 / Nov. 12, 1954 / Pacific Jazz ✦✦✦✦
This CD documents a concert by Gerry Mulligan's Quartet when the baritonist's group featured trumpeter Jon Eardley, bassist Red Mitchell, and drummer Chico Hamilton. Half of these ten selections were either previously unissued or only available as part of obscure samplers. The music, comprised of standards, some blues, and a few Mulligan originals, is quite enjoyable, swinging lightly and with plenty of interplay between the horns. —*Scott Yanow*

California Concerts, Vol. 2 / Dec. 14, 1954 / Pacific Jazz ✦✦✦✦
The second of two CDs in this series mostly consists of previously unissued material taken from a high school concert featuring the Gerry Mulligan Quartet (which at the time featured trumpeter Jon Eardley) plus two guests (valve trombonist Bob Brookmeyer and tenor saxophonist Zoot Sims). This swinging and often witty cool bop music is quite enjoyable and highly recommended. —*Scott Yanow*

Blues in Time / Aug. 1, 1957 / Verve ✦✦✦

Gerry Mulligan Meets Stan Getz / Oct. 22, 1957 / Verve ✦✦✦

Songbook / Dec. 4, 1957-Dec. 5, 1957 / Blue Note ✦✦✦✦

☆ **What is There to Say** / Dec. 17, 1958-Jan. 15, 1959 / Columbia ✦✦✦✦✦
The last of the pianoless quartet albums that Gerry Mulligan recorded in the '50s is one of the best, featuring the complementary trumpet of Art Farmer, bassist Bill Crow, and drummer Dave Bailey along with the baritonist/leader. This CD reissue of the LP is a little skimpy on playing time but makes every moment count. Virtually every selection is memorable. "What Is There to Say," "Just in Time," "Festive Minor," "My Funny Valentine," and "Utter Chaos" are the high points. Highly recommended both to Mulligan collectors and to jazz listeners who are just discovering the great baritonist. —*Scott Yanow*

★ **Gerry Mulligan Meets Ben Webster** / Nov. 3, 1959-Dec. 2, 1959 / Verve ✦✦✦✦✦
Baritone-saxophonist Gerry Mulligan, a modern who loved to jam with the older musicians, always had a flexible style. He had the opportunity (due to his popularity) to record with several of the major active saxophonists of the '50s and '60s. This CD finds him sharing the spotlight with the great veteran tenor Ben Webster. Their original six-song LP program is, on this reissue, augmented by five additional selections that were previously unissued but are played at the same high quality. The nearly 77-minute program (during which Mulligan and Webster are joined by pianist Jimmy Rowles, bassist Leroy Vinnegar, and drummer Mel Lewis) is full of solid swing, some witty improvising, and a few beautiful ballads. —*Scott Yanow*

And the Concert Jazz Band / Nov. 19, 1960 / RTE ✦✦✦✦
At a time when all of the important Verve recordings by Gerry Mulligan's Concert Jazz Band of 1960-63 are long out-of-print, this previously unissued concert performance (a two-CD set made available by the European RTE label) helps to fill the gap. There are many exciting moments among the 14 selections, including hot versions of "You Took Advantage of Me," "Apple Core," "Moten Swing," and "Bweebida Bobbida"; the ballads include "Body and Soul" and "My Funny Valentine." With the leader's baritone, trumpeter Conte Candoli, valve trombonist Bob Brookmeyer, and tenor saxophonist Zoot Sims all getting plenty of solo space and drummer Mel Lewis driving the ensembles, the 14-piece big band is heard at its best. One of the high points is the 21-minute medium-tempo blues "Spring Is Sprung" which finds Mulligan soloing and comping happily on piano. Highly recommended. —*Scott Yanow*

Jazz Fest Masters / Jun. 1969 / Scotti Bros. ✦✦✦✦
This is an easy CD to miss since it was part of the Scotti Bros. *Jazzfest Masters*, a series probably destined for complete obscurity. Recorded at the 1969 New Orleans Jazz Festival, this set is highlighted by three wonderful chance-taking performances by a quartet comprising baritonist Gerry Mulligan, altoist Paul Desmond, bassist Milt Hinton, and drummer Alan Dawson, a brilliant unit that otherwise never recorded. Their version of "Line for Lyons" is classic. Two other songs (including a brief "Take Five") have pianist Jaki Byard making the group a quintet, and there are a pair of features for Mulligan with the University of Illinois Orchestra. The final selection showcases altoist Al Belleto with the Loyola University Jazz Band on "What's New." But the reason to acquire this CD is for the unique Mulligan-Desmond quartet. —*Scott Yanow*

Meets Scott Hamilton / Jan. 1986 / Concord Jazz ✦✦✦

● **Re-Birth of the Cool** / Jan. 29, 1992-Jan. 31, 1992 / GRP ✦✦✦✦
In the summer of 1991 Gerry Mulligan decided to revisit Miles Davis' *Birth of the Cool* recordings. He discussed it with Miles Davis himself who said he might be interested in participating, but sadly Davis died a few months later. With Wallace Roney (the perfect sound-alike) in the trumpeter's place, baritonist Mulligan got the band's original pianist and tuba player (John Lewis and Bill Barber), used his own bassist (Dean Johnson) and drummer (Ron Vincent), and found able subtitutes in altoist Phil Woods (unfortunately Lee Konitz was unavailable to play his old parts), trombonist Dave Bargeron, and John Clark on French horn. This GRP CD brings back the dozen *Birth of the Cool* recordings of 1949-50 with Mel Tormé taking Pancho Hagood's vocal on "Darn That Dream." Although the charts are the same (and it is a particular pleasure to listen to them with the improved recording quality), the solos are all different and in many cases have been lengthened; no need to stick to only three minutes apiece. This fascinating disc is most highly recommended to veteran jazz collectors who know the original *Birth of the Cool* records. —*Scott Yanow*

Dream A Little Dream / 1994 / Telarc ✦✦✦✦
At the time of this recording, baritonist Gerry Mulligan had been a jazz giant for 45 years. His slightly bubbly baritone sound has always been distinctive, and he never had difficulty jamming with anyone. In the '90s Mulligan's regular trio has been comprised of pianist Ted Rosenthal, bassist Dean Johnson, and drummer Ron Vincent. The sidemen work together very well on this quartet date (Bill Mays fills in for Rosenthal on two songs) and form a solid foundation for Mulligan to float over. The baritonist performs a variety of superior standards such as "Home," "They Say It's Wonderful" and "My Shining Hour," revives "My Funny Valentine," and revisits a few of his originals (including "Walking Shoes" and "Song for Strayhorn"). This is a fine example of Gerry Mulligan's playing. —*Scott Yanow*

Dragon Fly / Mar. 12, 1995-Jun. 27, 1995 / Telarc ✦✦✦

Mark Murphy

b. Mar. 14, 1932, Syracuse, NY
Vocals / Post-Bop

A creative singer who has spent his entire career dedicated to jazz, Mark Murphy's wilder flights do not always succeed (sometimes his scatting in live performances can get a bit out of control), but they are never dull or predictable. Murphy began performing when he was 16, recorded his first album (for Capitol) in the late '50s, appeared on some television shows and then spent 1963-72 overseas, performing on radio and television and recording in Europe. Since returning to the US, Murphy has recorded a steady string of stimulating sets for Muse, even incorporating the stories and beat poetry of Jack Kerouac quite effectively on his *Bop for Kerouac* album. Mark Murphy has recorded throughout his career for Capitol, Riverside, Fontana, Saba, Audiophile, and Muse. —*Scott Yanow*

● **Rah** / Sep. 1961-Nov. 1961 / Original Jazz Classics ◆◆◆◆
Reissue. You can hear Murphy's style being cemented. —*Ron Wynn*

That's How I Love the Blues / Oct. 1, 1962-Dec. 28, 1962 / Original Jazz Classics ◆◆◆◆
Good reissue. One of the few Murphy releases I treasure. —*Ron Wynn*

Bridging a Gap / Oct. 1973 / Muse ◆◆◆◆
The celebrated bop, ballads, standards, and scat vocalist sings with customary verve, clarity, and confidence, backed by a combo featuring Mike and Randy Brecker, Ron Carter, and more. —*Ron Wynn*

Mark 2 / May 1975 / Muse ◆◆◆

Mark Murphy Sings / Aug. 1976 / Muse ◆◆◆◆
Strong mid-'70s Murphy session, with particularly solid uptempo numbers, emphatic ballads, and mid-tempo pieces. Murphy is backed by a group that includes alto saxophonist Dave Sanborn playing in a different setting, with more subtlety and passion than on his hit recordings. —*Ron Wynn*

★ **Satisfaction Guaranteed** / Nov. 21, 1979 / Muse ◆◆◆◆◆
Good 1979 session with vocalist Mark Murphy putting his stamp on old standards and new tunes, scatting, vocalizing, and extending them in his fiery, dynamic way. His backing band included veteran trombonist Slide Hampton, plus alto saxophonist Richie Cole, and baritone saxophonist Ronnie Cuber. —*Ron Wynn*

Bop for Kerouac / Mar. 12, 1981 / Muse ◆◆◆◆
This is an unusual recording. Singer Mark Murphy teams up with a fine sextet (featuring altoist Richie Cole and guitarist Bruce Forman), alternating bop standards with readings from Jack Kerouac books. Since Kerouac was a big jazz fan in the '50s and his interest in the music influenced the rhythms of his writing, this "poetry and jazz" set works surprisingly well. It also helps that Mark Murphy is heard at the peak of his powers. —*Scott Yanow*

The Artistry of Mark Murphy / Apr. 2, 1982-Apr. 3, 1982 / Muse ◆◆◆◆
Includes a stunning medley of "Babe's Blue/Little Niles/Dat Dere." Recorded with Tom Harrell (tpt), Gene Bertoncini (g), and Ben Aranov (p) in a larger-group setting. —*Michael G. Nastos*

Beauty and the Beast / Sep. 10, 1985-Nov. 23, 1986 / Muse ◆◆◆◆
This is really good Murphy, arranged by Bill Mays. McCoy Tyner's "Effendi" is a highlight, as is "Doxy" and "I Can't Get Started." —*Michael G. Nastos*

What a Way to Go / Sep. 1990 / Muse ◆◆◆

I'll Close My Eyes / Dec. 16, 1991-Dec. 17, 1991 / Muse ◆◆◆◆

Night Mood / Dec. 31, 1991 / Milestone ◆◆◆

Stolen Moments / Jan. 24, 1992 / Muse ◆◆◆◆

Turk Murphy (Melvin Edward Alton Murphy)

b. Dec. 16, 1915, Palermo, CA, d. May 30, 1987, San Francisco, CA
Trombone / Dixieland

Turk Murphy led one of the most popular bands of the San Francisco Dixieland movement. After playing with various big bands (including Mal Hallett and Will Osborne), Murphy first gained fame for his work with Lu Watters' highly influential Yerba Buena Jazz Band (1940-47). He formed his own group in 1947, and in 1960 the group had a permanent home at Earthquake McGoon's; it also toured occasionally. Although not thought of as a virtuoso trombone soloist and his occasional singing was just passable, Murphy's ensemble work was superior; he put together a stimulating repertoire filled with obscurities and favorites from the '20s (along with some newer originals), and his bands were always very musical. Among his sidemen through the years were trumpeters Don Kinch, Bob Short and Leon Oakley, clarinetist Bob Helm, pianists Wally Rose, Pete Clute, and Ray Skjelbred, and singer Pat Yankee. Turk Murphy and his beloved group made many records for such labels as Good Time Jazz, Fairmont, Columbia (1953-56), Verve, Dawn Club, Roulette, RCA, Motherlode, Atlantic, GHB, MPS, Stomp Off, and Merry Makers. —*Scott Yanow*

Turk Murphy, Vol. 1 / May 31, 1949-Jan. 19, 1950 / Good Time Jazz ◆◆◆

● **Turk Murphy's Jazz Band** / May 8, 1950-Jul. 10, 1951 / Good Time Jazz ◆◆◆◆
More Bay Area revival sounds appear from Murphy, this time with Bill Napier, Don Kinch, Wally Rose, and George Bruns among the sidemen on "St. James Infirmary," "Canal Street Blues," "Down by the Riverside," and more. —*Bruce Raeburn*

San Francisco Jazz, Vol. 2 / May 8, 1950-Jul. 10, 1951 / Good Time Jazz ◆◆◆◆

At The Italian Village / 1952-1953 / Merry Makers ◆◆◆◆

David Murray

b. Feb. 19, 1955, Berkeley, CA
Clarinet (Bass), Sax (Tenor) / Avant-Garde, Post-Bop, Free Jazz

A giant of the avant-garde, David Murray has long had a distinctive tone on tenor and the willingness to play anything from completely free improvisations to bop. Among the most recorded of all jazzmen, Murray's trademark is his sudden leaps into the upper register of his horn.

He started on alto when he was nine and played tenor in a soul group that he led as a teenager. In Southern California Murray often gigged with Bobby Bradford and Arthur Blythe, and then in 1975 he moved to New York. He was an original member of the World Saxophone Quartet in 1976 and worked as a sideman with Sunny Murray, James "Blood" Ulmer, Jack DeJohnette's Special Edition, and Clarinet Summit, playing bass clarinet in the latter. However, Murray is best-known as a leader whose groups have ranged from freewheeling quartets to a spirited big band and an acclaimed octet. He started recording as a leader in 1976 and has since made sessions for Adelphi, India Navigation, Circle, Marge, Red, Horo, Palm, Cadillac, Black Saint, Hat Hut, Cecma, Enja, Portrait, Red Baron, and DIW. In 1991 David Murray was awarded the prestigious Danish Jazzpar prize. —*Scott Yanow*

Flowers for Albert / Jun. 16, 1976 / India Navigation ◆◆◆◆
David Murray, who was age 21 at the time, shows a lot of promise on this early recording. The explorative tenor saxophonist joins with trumpeter Olu Dara, bassist Fred Hopkins, and drummer Phillip Wilson for two adventurous pieces (including the title cut which is dedicated to Albert Ayler). In addition, Murray duets with Hopkins on "Ballad for a Decomposed Beauty" and collaborates with Wilson on their duet "Roscoe." The music is often quite free, but it also takes its time, showing high energy in well chosen spots. Since this period David Murray has lived up to his great potential. —*Scott Yanow*

Sweet Lovely / Dec. 4, 1979-Dec. 5, 1979 / Black Saint ◆◆◆◆
David Murray's string of recordings for Black Saint were among the most rewarding of his career. This one differs from many in that the adventurous tenorman improvises in a sparse trio with bassist Fred Hopkins and drummer Steve McCall. Murray stretches out on four of his originals (which clock in between eight and twelve-and-a-half minutes) and shows plenty of fire but also a healthy dose of lyricism. This is exciting music very much in the avant-garde. —*Scott Yanow*

☆ **Ming** / Jul. 25, 1980 & Jul. 28, 1980 / Black Saint ◆◆◆◆◆
Named after his wife, this is arguably his best octet recording. —*Ron Wynn*

Home / Oct. 31, 1981 & Nov. 1, 1981 / Black Saint ◆◆◆◆
Tenor saxophonist David Murray regrouped the same octet that recorded *Ming* and released *Home*. There was not a weak solo moment on the set, and it was that combination of arrangements and ensemble strength which made this more than just another date. —*Bob Rusch, Cadence*

★ **Murray's Steps** / Jul. 14, 1982-Jul. 19, 1982 / Black Saint ◆◆◆◆◆
The octet is the perfect vehicle for David Murray as an outlet for his writing, a showcase for his compositions, and as an inspiring vehicle for his tenor and bass clarinet solos. For the third octet album (all are highly recommended) Murray meets up with altoist Henry Threadgill, trumpeter Bobby Bradford, cornetist Butch Morris, trombonist Craig Harris, pianist Curtis Clark, bassist Wilber Morris, and drummer Steve McCall; quite a talented group of individuals. Their interpretations of four of Murray's originals ("Murray's Steps," "Sweet Lovely," "Sing Song," and "Flowers for Albert") are emotional, adventurous, and exquisite; sometimes all three at the same time. —*Scott Yanow*

Ming's Samba / Jul. 20, 1988 / Portrait ◆◆◆
Recorded at CBS Studios in New York City, this album is named after David Murray's wife Ming. It includes some nice work, in particular the very lovely cut "Spooning." —*Michael Erlewine*

Jazzpar Prize / Mar. 16, 1991-Mar. 17, 1991 / Enja ◆◆◆◆

Black and Black / Oct. 7, 1991 / Red Baron ◆◆◆◆
A powerhouse 1992 session by the prolific tenor saxophonist and bass clarinetist David Murray. He heads a strong quintet, with trumpeter Marcus Belgrave, pianist Kirk Lightsey, bassist Santi Debriano, and drummer Roy Haynes through some bristling uptempo originals, mixed with a couple of nice mid-tempo and ballad pieces for contrast. —*Ron Wynn*

Sunny Murray (James Marcellus Arthur Murray)

b. Sep. 21, 1937, Idabel, OK
Drums / Avant-Garde, Free Jazz

An important early free drummer, Sunny Murray was one of the first to play without keeping a steady rhythm or pulse (interacting directly with the lead voices), although he was always perfectly capable of playing more conventionally. He started on drums when he was nine and in 1956 moved to New York. Murray picked up early experience gigging with Red Allen, Willie "The Lion" Smith, Jackie McLean, and Ted Curson. He made a giant stylistic leap when he started playing with Cecil Taylor (1959-64) and was the perfect "accompanist" for Albert Ayler (1964-67). Murray also worked with Don Cherry, Ornette Coleman, and John Tchicai during this period. He spent 1968-71 in France, playing and recording with Archie Shepp and freelancing. In the '70s Murray moved to Philadelphia and led bands usually called the Untouchable Factor. For a time in the '80s his quintet included Steve Coleman, Grachan Moncur III, pianist Curtis Clark, and bassist William Parker, and he had a recorded reunion with Taylor in 1980. Sunny Murray has led dates for Jihad (a 1965 session with Albert Ayler as a sideman), ESP, Shandar, Pathe, BYG, Kharma, Philly Jazz, Marge, Moers Music, and Circle, although he has maintained a lower profile during the past decade. —*Scott Yanow*

● **Sunny Murray Quintet** / Jul. 23, 1966 / ESP ✦✦✦✦
Dynamic, slashing, left-field jazz, both free-form and more traditional hard bop. —*Ron Wynn*

Hard Cores / 1968 / Philly Jazz ✦✦✦✦
Perhaps his best group, paced by pianist Don Pullen. —*Ron Wynn*

★ **Never Give a Sucker an Even Break** / Nov. 22, 1969 / Affinity ✦✦✦✦✦
Free rhythm, resuscitations, and spiritual quaverings made up an LP of music which sprang directly from the Albert Ayler/John Coltrane roots. It was a solid effort in structured freedom, rather even-handed and with no great peaks or insights revealed. —*Bob Rusch, Cadence*

Najee

Sax (Soprano), Sax (Tenor) / Instrumental Pop, Crossover

A popular multi-instrumentalist whose style is very similiar to Kenny G., Dave Koz, and George Howard. His releases feature heavily produced, tightly arranged covers of urban contemporary songs, often include appearances by R&B vocalists and have very limited solos and improvisational space. A saxophonist, flutist and occasional keyboardist, Najee makes no claims to being a jazz musician, but his releases are marketed as "contemporary" jazz, and he's aired on lite jazz stations. He's recorded several sessions for EMI and Manhattan; all are available on CD. —*Ron Wynn*

● **Songs From the Key of Life** / Nov. 7, 1995 / EMI ✦✦✦✦

Ray Nance

b. Dec. 10, 1913, Chicago, IL, **d.** Jan. 28, 1976, New York, NY
Violin, Cornet, Vocals / Swing

Ray Nance was a multi-talented individual. He was a fine trumpeter who not only replaced Cootie Williams with Duke Ellington's Orchestra but gave the "plunger" position in Duke's band his own personality. In addition Nance was one of the finest jazz violinists of the '40s, an excellent jazz singer, and even a dancer. He studied piano, took lessons on violin, and was self-taught on trumpet. After leading a small group in Chicago (1932-37), spending periods with the orchestras of Earl Hines (1937-38) and Horace Henderson (1939-40), and a few months as a solo act, Nance joined Duke Ellington's Orchestra. His very first night on the job was fully documented as the band's legendary Fargo concert. A very valuable sideman, Nance played a famous trumpet solo on the original version of "Take the 'A' Train" and proved to be a fine wa-wa player; his violin added color to the suite "Black, Brown and Beige" (in addition to being showcased on numerous songs), and his singing on numbers such as "A Slip of a Lip Will Sink a Ship" and "Tulip or Turnip" was an added feature. Nance was with Ellington with few interruptions until 1963; by then the returning Cootie Williams had taken some of his glory. The remainder of Nance's career was relatively insignificant with occasional small group dates, gigs with Brooks Kerr and Chris Barber (touring England in 1974), and a few surprisingly advanced sideman recordings with Jaki Byard and Chico Hamilton. —*Scott Yanow*

Fats Navarro (Theodore Navarro)

b. Sep. 24, 1923, Key West, FL, **d.** Jul. 7, 1958, New York, NY
Trumpet / Bop

One of the greatest jazz trumpeters of all time, Fats Navarro had a tragically brief career, yet his influence is still being felt. His fat sound combined aspects of Howard McGhee, Roy Eldridge, and Dizzy Gillespie, became the main inspiration for Clifford Brown, and through Brown greatly affected the tones and styles of Lee Morgan, Freddie Hubbard, and Woody Shaw.

Navarro originally played piano and tenor before switching to trumpet. He started gigging with dance bands when he was 17, was with Andy Kirk during 1943-44 and replaced Dizzy Gillespie with the Billy Eckstine big band during 1945-46. During the next three years Navarro was second to only Gillespie among bop trumpeters. Navarro recorded with Kenny Clarke's Bebop Boys, Coleman Hawkins, Eddie "Lockjaw" Davis, Illinois Jacquet, and most significantly Tadd Dameron during 1946-47. He had short stints with the big bands of Lionel Hampton and Benny Goodman, continued working with Dameron, made classic recordings with Bud Powell (in a quintet with a young Sonny Rollins) and the Metronome All-Stars, and a 1950 Birdland appearance with Charlie Parker that was privately recorded. However, Navarro was a heroin addict and that affliction certainly did not help him in what would be a fatal bout with tuberculosis that ended his life at a young age. He was well documented during the 1946-49 period, and most of his sessions are currently available on CD, but Fats Navarro could have done so much more! —*Scott Yanow*

Fat Girl / Sep. 6, 1946-Dec. 5, 1947 / Savoy ✦✦✦✦
Landmark Navarro Savoy sessions with Howard McGhee (tp), Ernie Henry (as), and others. —*Ron Wynn*

☆ **The Fabulous Fats Navarro, Vol. 1** / Jan. 29, 1947-Nov. 29, 1948 / Blue Note ✦✦✦✦✦
Here are brilliant trumpet solos from the sadly neglected trumpet master Navarro. Blue Note may have deleted this completely by now. It has six bonus cuts featuring the equally undervalued Tadd Dameron. —*Ron Wynn*

★ **Prime Source** / Sep. 26, 1947-Aug. 8, 1949 / Blue Note ✦✦✦✦✦
Navarro as featured soloist with the Tad Dameron Sextet and Septet, the Howard McGhee/Navarro Boptet, and Bud Powell's Modernists. Reissue compilation of Navarro's prime early work. —*Michael G. Nastos*

★ **Fats Navarro and Tadd Dameron** / Sep. 26, 1947-Aug. 8, 1949 / Blue Note ✦✦✦✦✦
Many valuable performances from the height of the bop era are included on this double-CD. Subtitled "The Complete Blue Note and Capitol Recordings" and comprised of 23 songs and 13 alternate takes, the reissue features the great trumpeter Fats Navarro in peak form with three groups headed by pianist/arranger Tadd Dameron, in trumpet battles with one of his major influences, Howard McGhee, and on a remarkable all-star quintet with pianist Bud Powell and the young tenor Sonny Rollins. Among the other sidemen are altoist Ernie Henry, tenors Charlie Rouse, Allen Eager, Wardell Gray, and Dexter Gordon, and vibraphonist Milt Jackson. In addition to such gems as "Our Delight," "Lady Bird," "Double Talk," "Bouncing with Bud," "Dance of the Infidels," and "52nd Street Theme," Fats is heard with the 1948 Benny Goodman septet ("Stealin' Apples"), and Dameron leads a group with the 22-year-old Miles Davis. On a whole, this double-CD has more than its share of essential music that belongs in all historical jazz collections. —*Scott Yanow*

The Fabulous Fats Navarro, Vol. 2 / Sep. 1947-Aug. 1949 / Blue Note ✦✦✦✦
The importance of this follow-up volume is equal to that of the first one. —*Ron Wynn*

Oliver Nelson

b. Jun. 4, 1932, St. Louis, MO, **d.** Oct. 27, 1975, Los Angeles, CA
Sax (Alto), Sax (Tenor) / Post-Bop, Hard Bop, Groove

Oliver Nelson was a distinctive soloist on alto, tenor, and even soprano, but his writing eventually overshadowed his playing skills. He became a professional early on in 1947, playing with the Jeter-Pillars Orchestra and with St. Louis big bands headed by George Hudson and Nat Towles. In 1951 he arranged and played second alto for Louis Jordan's big band and followed with a period in the Navy and four years at a university. After moving to New York, Nelson worked briefly with Erskine Hawkins, Wild Bill Davis, and Louie Bellson (the latter on the West Coast). In addition to playing with Quincy Jones' Orchestra (1960-61), between 1959-61 Nelson recorded six small-group albums and a big-band date; those gave him a lot of recognition and respect in the jazz world. *Blues and the Abstract Truth* (from 1961) is considered a classic and helped to popularize a song that Nelson had included on a slightly earlier Eddie "Lockjaw" Davis session, "Stolen Moments." He also fearlessly matched wits effectively with the explosive Eric Dolphy on a pair of quintet sessions. But good as his playing was, Nelson was in greater demand as an arranger, writing for big-band dates of Jimmy Smith, Wes Montgomery, and Billy Taylor among others. By 1967 when he moved to Los Angeles, Nelson was working hard in the studios, writing for television and movies. He occasionally appeared with a big band, wrote a few ambitious works, and recorded jazz on an infrequent basis, but Oliver Nelson was largely lost to jazz a few years before his unexpected death at age 43 from a heart attack. —*Scott Yanow*

Meet Oliver Nelson / Oct. 30, 1959 / Original Jazz Classics ✦✦✦✦
Oliver Nelson's debut as a leader found him at the age of 27 already a dis-

tinctive and skilled tenor saxophonist. For this quintet set (reissued on CD in the OJC series), Nelson teams up with the veteran trumpeter Kenny Dorham, pianist Ray Bryant, bassist Wendell Marshall, and drummer Art Taylor for four of his originals plus the ballads "Passion Flower" and "What's New." Although none of these Nelson tunes caught on, this was an impressive beginning to a short but productive career and gives one a strong example of the multi-talented Nelson's tenor playing. — *Scott Yanow*

● **Takin' Care of Business** / Mar. 22, 1960 / Original Jazz Classics ✦✦✦✦
Oliver Nelson would gain his greatest fame later in his short life as an arranger/composer but this superior session puts the emphasis on his distinctive tenor and alto playing. In a slightly unusual group (with vibraphonist Lem Winchester, organist Johnny "Hammond" Smith, bassist George Tucker, and drummer Roy Haynes), Nelson improvises a variety of well constructed but spontaneous solos; his unaccompanied spots on "All the Way" and his hard-charging playing on the medium-tempo blues "Groove" are two of the many high points. Nelson remains a vastly underrated saxophonist and all six performances on this recommended CD reissue (four of them his originals) are excellent. — *Scott Yanow*

Screamin' the Blues / May 27, 1960 / Original Jazz Classics ✦✦✦✦
Oliver Nelson (on tenor and alto) meets Eric Dolphy (alto, bass clarinet, and flute) on this frequently exciting sextet session with trumpeter Richard Williams, pianist Richard Wyands, bassist George Duvivier, and drummer Roy Haynes. Although Dolphy is too unique and skilled to be overshadowed in a setting such as this, Nelson holds his own. He contributed five of the six compositions (including "Screamin' the Blues," "The Meetin'," and "Altoitis") and effectively matches wits and creative ideas with Dolphy. This CD reissue (also available as part of a huge Eric Dolphy box set) is recommended, as is the follow-up record *Straight Ahead*. — *Scott Yanow*

● **Soul Battle** / Sep. 9, 1960 / Original Jazz Classics ✦✦✦✦
This intriguing session matches together three powerful tenor players: Oliver Nelson, King Curtis (in a rare jazz outing), and Jimmy Forrest. With fine backup work by pianist Gene Casey, bassist George Duvivier, and drummer Roy Haynes, the tenors battle to a draw on a set of blues and basic material (including a fine version of "Perdido"). This CD reissue adds one selection ("Soul Street") from the same date to the original LP program and is easily recommended to fans of big-toned tenors and straightahead swinging. — *Scott Yanow*

★ **Blues and the Abstract Truth** / Feb. 23, 1961 / Impulse ✦✦✦✦✦
This was Oliver Nelson's finest recording and one of the top jazz albums of 1961, a true classic. The lineup is an inspired one: Nelson on tenor and alto, Eric Dolphy doubling on alto and flute, a young trumpeter named Freddie Hubbard, baritonist George Barrow for section parts, pianist Bill Evans, bassist Paul Chambers, and drummer Roy Haynes. The contrasting voices of the soloists really uplift these superior compositions which are highlighted by "Stolen Moments" (a future standard), the fun "Hoe-Down," and "Yearnin." Dolphy cuts everyone, but Nelson and Hubbard are also in top form. — *Scott Yanow*

Straight Ahead / Mar. 1, 1961 / Original Jazz Classics ✦✦✦✦
This CD reissue brings back a very interesting quintet set matching together Oliver Nelson (on alto and tenor) and Eric Dolphy (tripling on alto, flute and bass clarinet). With the assistance of pianist Richard Wyands, bassist George Duvivier and drummer Roy Haynes, the two reedmen battle it out on six compositions (five of Nelson's originals plus Milt Jackson's "Ralph's New Blues"). Although none of Nelson's tunes caught on, this is a pretty memorable date. It certainly took a lot of courage for Oliver Nelson to share the frontline with the colorful Eric Dolphy, but his own strong musical personality holds its own on this straightahead date. — *Scott Yanow*

Main Stem / Aug. 25, 1961 / Original Jazz Classics ✦✦✦✦
Unlike most of Oliver Nelson's recordings, this one has the feel of a jam session. A CD reissue of a Prestige set, Nelson (on tenor and alto) teams up with trumpeter Joe Newman (in exciting form), pianist Hank Jones, bassist George Duvivier, drummer Charlie Persip, and Ray Barretto on congas for two superior standards ("Mainstem" and "Tangerine") plus four of Nelson's more basic originals. The spirited solos of Nelson and Newman are strong reasons to get this happy session. — *Scott Yanow*

Afro-American Sketches / Sep. 29, 1961 & Oct. 10, 1961 / Original Jazz Classics ✦✦✦✦
This CD reissue brings back Oliver Nelson's first big-band date as a leader. Meant as a folk album paying tribute to the history of Blacks in America, there are such songs as "Jungleaire," "Emancipation Blues," "Going Up North," and "Freedom Dance." Among the soloists are flutist Jerry Dodgion, trumpeter Joe Newman, and Nelson himself on tenor and alto. Even this early, Nelson's writing had its own sound; his seven-part suite is well worth hearing. — *Scott Yanow*

Sound Pieces / Sep. 27, 1966-Sep. 28, 1966 / Impulse ✦✦✦✦

● **Black, Brown and Beautiful** / Mar. 17, 1970-1974 / Bluebird ✦✦✦✦
The bulk of this CD has a 1970 session that teams together arranger Oliver Nelson, altoist Johnny Hodges, and (on three of the songs) singer Leon Tho-

mas. The big band also includes pianist Earl Hines and the program is highlighted by "Empty Ballroom Blues," "Welcome to New York," and "Creole Love Call"; all of the songs were composed by either Duke Ellington, Nelson or Thomas. That near-classic session is augmented by three numbers from a couple of later dates that feature Nelson's alto playing. Recommended. — *Scott Yanow*

Phineas Newborn

b. Dec. 14, 1931, Whiteville, TN, **d.** May 26, 1989, Memphis, TN
Piano / Hard Bop
Despite having severe personal and mental problems most of his career, Phineas Newborn, Jr. was one of jazz's most accomplished, technically brilliant pianists. Many compared his incredible speed, harmonic knowledge, dexterity, and rhythmic facility with that of Tatum and Bud Powell. But a combination of being repeatedly off the scene due to illness and spending much of his life in the South rather than on the East or West Coast prevented Newborn from attaining its rightful place in jazz history during his lifetime. He studied piano, theory, alto sax, and various brass instruments while in high school. Both his father and brother were musicians, and Newborn played in various Memphis bands during the '40s until he joined Lionel Hampton in the early '50s. He played with Hampton in 1950 and 1952. Newborn was in the service from 1953-55, then moved to New York in 1956. He had a duo with Charles Mingus in 1958, and toured Europe in 1958 and 1959. Newborn made some highly praised records for Atlantic, RCA, and United Artists in the late '50s, gaining enormous respect from critics and musicians alike. He continued recording on Prestige and Roulette through the late '50s, doing a trio date with Roy Haynes and Paul Chambers for Prestige. He moved to Los Angeles in 1960, and made more outstanding trio sessions for Contemporary in the '60s. But his illness, coupled with a hand injury, led to infrequent appearances at best and long absences from playing, touring or recordings. Newborn was hospitalized in Memphis for a time. He returned to a limited schedule of performances and recordings in the early and mid-'70s. His album *Solo Piano* for Atlantic was a brilliant exposition of gospel and blues-tinged modern playing. Newborn made an acclaimed apearance at a 1975 concert sponsored by the World Jazz Association in Los Angeles. There were other sessions for Pablo and some foreign labels. During the '80s Newborn was a familiar sight at Memphis clubs, and he recorded sonatas by Alexander Scriabin for VSOP in 1987. Newborn died in Memphis in 1989. There are several Newborn '50s and '60s dates that have been reissued within the last couple of years on CD. — *Ron Wynn*

While My Lady Sleeps / Apr. 23, 1957-Apr. 3, 1958 / Bluebird ✦✦✦
This CD reissue is mostly comprised of a 1957 set featuring the virtuosic pianist Phineas Newborn backed by a string orchestra led by Dennis Farnon. Although not as vital as his usual trio dates and Farnon's string arrangements are not too inspiring, the music is pleasing and finds Newborn in his early prime. Particularly noteworthy are his versions of Eddie Miller's "Lazy Mood," "While My Lady Sleeps," and "Bali Hati." Also on this set are three quartet numbers and an unaccompanied rendition of "What's New" from the RCA album *Fabulous Phineas*. — *Scott Yanow*

★ **The World of Piano** / Oct. 16, 1961-Nov. 21, 1961 / Original Jazz Classics ✦✦✦✦✦
An A+ album from an A+ player. — *Michael G. Nastos*

★ **The Great Jazz Piano of Phineas Newborn Jr.** / Nov. 21, 1961-Sep. 12, 1962 / Original Jazz Classics ✦✦✦✦✦
This recording lives up to its title. Phineas Newborn at his prime had phenomenal technique (on the level of an Oscar Peterson), a creative imagination, and plenty of energy. These trio sessions (with Leroy Vinnegar or Sam Jones on bass and either Milt Turner or Louis Hayes on drums) feature Newborn displaying plenty of heat and fresh ideas on compositions by Bud Powell, Bobby Timmons, Benny Golson, Duke Ellington, Thelonious Monk, Sonny Rollins, and Miles Davis and two of his own. This is piano jazz at its highest level. — *Scott Yanow*

Newborn Touch / Apr. 1, 1964 / Original Jazz Classics ✦✦✦✦
Pianist Phineas Newborn, Jr. was a keyboard genius; his remarkable forays with independent movements occuring octaves apart in each hand were a marvel to keyboardists and other instrumentalists alike. This mid-'60s trio date, reissued on CD with three bonus cuts, features Newborn covering compositions by Art Pepper, Ornette Coleman, Benny Carter, and Hampton Hawes, among others. Each becomes a rousing, personalized treatment, with Newborn's consistently unpredictable touch, fleeting solos, and uncanny phrasing. This session only reaffirms how much Newborn's insights and skills are missed. — *Ron Wynn*

Solo / 1975 / L & R Music ✦✦✦

Look Out: Phineas Is Back / Dec. 7, 1976-Dec. 8, 1976 / Original Jazz Classics ✦✦✦✦
Phineas Newborn was one of the great jazz pianists, possessing phenominal technique and mastery of the bebop vocabulary, but various illnesses plagued him throughout the '60s and '70s. On what would be one of his final sessions, Newborn is in surprisingly strong form playing in a trio with

bassist Ray Brown and drummer Jimmie Smith. Highlights include "Abbers Song" (a rapid runthrough on "I've Got Rhythm" chord changes), "A Night in Tunisia," a previously unreleased version of "Just in Time" that appeared for the first time on this CD reissue, and a creative version of Stevie Wonder's "You Are the Sunshine of My Life." —*Scott Yanow*

David "Fathead" Newman (David Newman)

b. Feb. 24, 1933, Dallas, TX
Flute, Sax (Alto), Sax (Tenor) / Soul-Jazz, Hard Bop, Groove

A first-rate soul-jazz, blues, R&B, and funk saxophonist and flutist, David "Fathead" Newman has been a star in seminal bands, issued excellent recordings and been featured on several fine sessions. He can certainly play bebop and has shown surprising chops when so inclined, but that's not his strength. Hearing the gorgeous, huge Newman tenor sax tones filling the space left by a singer laying out, ripping through a 12-bar blues, interacting with an organist or guitarist, or just embellishing a melody, is one of jazz and popular music's great pleasures. His taste has sometimes deserted him, but when working in the right arena Newman's a wonderful player and bandleader. He got his "Fathead" nickname from a music teacher as a child. He began playing with local bands in Dallas, and later toured with Lowell Fulson and T-Bone Walker. Newman became a star while working with Ray Charles. He stayed with Charles a full decade in the '50s and '60s, and was a pivotal part of many landmark R&B dates. The sounds he made with Charles still guide Newman's music. He later worked with King Curtis in the mid-'60s. Newman began recording as a leader for Atlantic in the late '50s. He did several small combo sessions, then later worked with larger bands. Newman played with Blue Mitchell, Roy Ayers, Dr. John, and Ron Carter among others. Things began to go astray in the mid-'70s; there were some experiments with overdubbed strings and horns. But Newman returned to soul-jazz and blues basics on Prestige, Muse, and Atlantic in the '80s. He's recorded for Milestone in the late '80s and '90s, still doing reliable blues and soul-jazz, with an occasional bebop date. He's also recorded for Candid and Timeless, and worked with Cornell Dupree and Ellis Marsalis on a fine session for Amazing Records. Newman has a fair number of titles available on CD. Rhino issued a CD anthology of some earlier Atlantic dates in 1993. —*Ron Wynn*

★ **House of David Newman: David "Fathead" Anthology** / 1952 / Rhino ✦✦✦✦✦

There have not been many saxophonists and flutists more naturally soulful than David "Fathead" Newman. This two-disc set captures Newman at his best. He never really was an album artist; each LP has had its nuggets, and that's what this captures. It has Newman wailing the blues, then stretching out in the Ray Charles band. He covers a Beatles tune, then an Aaron Neville number. He backs Aretha Franklin and pays homage to the great Buster Cooper. This is one anthology that can be recommended without hesitation, because there aren't going to be many complete Newman albums coming down the reissue pike. —*Ron Wynn*

Fathead: Ray Charles Presents David Newman / Nov. 5, 1958 / Atlantic ✦✦✦✦

The talented David Newman, who alternates between tenor and alto, made his debut as a leader at this session. Since he was in Ray Charles' band at the time, Newman was able to use Charles on piano along with Hank Crawford (here called Bennie Crawford) on baritone, trumpeter Marcus Belgrave, bassist Edgar Willis, and drummer Milton Turner. The music is essentially soulful bebop with the highlights including "Hard Times," "Fathead," "Mean To Me," and "Tin Tin Deo." Everyone plays well and this was a fine start to David "Fathead" Newman's career. —*Scott Yanow*

House of David / Mar. 4, 1967-Mar. 7, 1967 / Atlantic ✦✦✦

Bigger & Better (The Many Facets of David Newman) / Mar. 5, 1968-Feb. 11, 1969 / Rhino/Atlantic ✦✦

The packaging on this Rhino CD (which is a reissue of two complete Atlantic LPs) is excellent, but these sets are among tenor saxophonist David "Fathead" Newman's more commercial efforts. The sessions that resulted in *Bigger & Better* feature Newman with a string section and studio musicians for forgettable versions of two Beatles songs, a pair of Sam Cooke R&B pieces, and a couple of lesser items. *The Many Facets of David Newman* is less poppish and more blues-oriented with the lengthy "Children of Abraham" showing some passion, but overall the material is rather weak and has not aged very well. Skip this set in favor of Newman's more recent efforts. —*Scott Yanow*

Back to Basics / May 1977-Nov. 1977 / Milestone ✦✦✦✦

A 1991 CD reissue of a late '70s session by tenor saxophonist and flutist David Newman, which emphasized his patented soul-jazz and blues while matching Newman with different players on various tracks, rather than having a fixed rhythm section. The top guest stars included keyboardists Hilton Ruiz and George Cables and guitarist Lee Ritenour. —*Ron Wynn*

Fire! Live at the Village Vanguard / Dec. 22, 1988-Dec. 23, 1988 / Atlantic ✦✦✦✦

A nice outing that matches Newman with Stanley Turrentine (ts) and Hank Crawford (as). —*Ron Wynn*

● **Return to the Wide Open Spaces** / 1990 / Amazing ✦✦✦✦

Texas tenor saxophonists David Newman and James Clay recorded a first-rate album in 1960, which seamlessly fused blues, soul, swing-tinged jazz, and honking R&B styles. Some 30 years later, Newman and Clay reunited for a sequel, joined by pianist Ellis Marsalis. The resulting release was both timely and delightful, as Newman and Clay showed they hadn't lost any energy or facility. Their gutbucket licks, robust exchanges, and alternately soulful, moving, and swaggering solos on a great collection of tunes by everyone from Billy Strayhorn to Buster Smith were entertaining and distinctive. It was one red-hot night at the Caravan of Dreams, and this CD fully captured the night's flavor. —*Ron Wynn*

● **Mr. Gentle Mr. Cool (Tribute)** / 1994 / Kokopelli ✦✦✦✦

David "Fathead" Newman is in excellent form on this tasteful program of 11 Duke Ellington compositions. Performing in a sextet with trombonist Jim Pugh, pianist David Leonhardt, bassist Peter Washington, Ron Carter on piccolo bass, and drummer Lewis Nash, Newman splits his time between tenor and alto and takes a flute solo on "Azure." The music contains few real surprises (other than the utilization of both bass and piccolo bass) but swings nicely and has fine melodic solos. —*Scott Yanow*

Joe Newman

b. Sep. 7, 1922, New Orleans, LA, **d.** Jul. 4, 1992, New York, NY
Trumpet / Swing

Joe Newman was a superb, exciting trumpeter whose style echoed the best of Harry Edison, Dizzy Gillespie, and Thad Jones, seasoned with his own flavoring. He was among a select corps who not only enjoyed playing, but communicated that joy and exuberance in every solo. He provided high note and upper register antics, but functioned best doing soft, enticing melodies or engaging in mildly combative jam sessions. He was also an accomplished player in the traditional New Orleans style. Newman began his professional career with Lionel Hampton in 1942 and 1943, joining him after touring with the Alabama State Teachers College band. Newman became a member of the Count Basie orchestra in 1943, remaining until 1947. He co-led groups with Illinois Jacquet and J.C. Heard, before returning to the Basie band for a great run from 1952 to 1961. During that time, there were periodic outside recording sessions. Newman did sessions for Savoy, Vanguard and RCA in the '50s, most of them small-combo and tasteful, enjoyable outings. The 1956 album *Salute To Satch* was with a big band. *The Happy Cats* was a sextet date. There was a quintet session with Zoot Sims on Roulette and another Roulette recording with an 11-piece band. Newman toured Europe with the Basie band in 1954. During the early '60s, he continued recording and touring with Basie and making other sides on his own. These included sessions with Tommy Flanagan for Prestige and a quartet set for Stash. There was a 1962 Russian tour with Benny Goodman. Newman became involved with Jazz Interaction, an organization promoting awareness and jazz education in the early '60s, and soon became a tireless advocate. He assumed the organization's presidency in 1967. Newman also wrote compositions for their organization. He began playing with the New York Repertory Orchestra in 1974, and toured Europe and the Soviet Union with them in 1975. During the '70s, '80s and '90s, Newman juggled educating, recording, and doing an infrequent reunion with The Basie orchestra. He made nice sessions with Ruby Braff and Jimmy Rowles in the '70s and Joe Wilder and Hank Jones in the '80s. —*Ron Wynn*

★ **The Complete Joe Newman** / Feb. 8, 1955-1956 / RCA ✦✦✦✦✦

Trumpeter Joe Newman, best-known for his playing with Count Basie's Orchestra, led four albums for RCA during 1955-56. This generous two-CD set reissues all the music from these dates and has plenty of swinging performances. The first disc puts the focus on Newman and tenor saxophonist Al Cohn in a pair of octets with arrangements by Ernie Wilkins, Manny Albam, and Cohn. The second disc starts out with a tribute to Louis Armstrong, a dozen of his songs modernized for a big band; Newman takes a few rare vocals. The final session matches Newman with flutist Frank Wess in a two-guitar septet arranged by Wilkins. While most of the other twofers in this French RCA Jazz Tribune series are reissues of earlier two-LP sets, this one was newly compiled and has 48 splendid examples of Basie-ish swing. Highly recommended. —*Scott Yanow*

I Feel Like a Newman / Apr. 1956 / Black Lion ✦✦✦

Jive at Five / May 4, 1960 / Original Jazz Classics ✦✦✦

A hot quintet date sparked by Newman's interaction with Frank Wess (fl/sax). —*Ron Wynn*

Hangin' Out / May ??, 1984 / Concord Jazz ✦✦✦✦

This relaxed, jovial session is co-led by Joe Wilder (tpt). "Smitty" Smith adds fire on drums. —*Ron Wynn*

James Newton

b. May 1, 1953, Los Angeles, CA
Flute / Avant-Garde

James Newton comes closest of any contemporary flutist to invoking the spirit of Eric Dolphy. His soaring, beautiful tones have that same evocative, bird-like quality, and he's nearly as accomplished with his armada of trills, vocal effects, swirling phrases, flutter tonguing, humming, glissandos, and overblowing. Newton once played alto and tenor saxophones, but gave them up to concentrate on flute. He has a classical timbre, but a jazz musician's heart and that's enabled him to execute solos that are astonishing in their harmonic brilliance and performed with what seems a minimum of effort. Newton played electric bass, alto and tenor sax, bass clarinet, and flute in high school, oddly picking up flute last. He attended a California junior college, majoring in music, and studied under Buddy Collette. Newton played flute and sax in a funk band, and performed with Arthur Blythe, David Murray and others in Stanley Crouch's Black Music Infinity in the early '70s. He became a flutist exclusively in the late '70s and joined the exodus of West Coast musicians to New York. He co-led an ensemble with Anthony Davis, and performed in a trio with a Japanese koto player, a flute quartet with Frank Wess and a woodwind quintet. He began recording as a leader on India Navigation in the late '70s, and continued on Circle, ECM, Gramavision, Bvhaast, Celestial Harmonies, and Blue Note in the '80s. James Newton, who has long since returned to California, is an innovative virtuoso active in many areas from straightahead to free form and world music. In the '90s he remains at the top of his field, leading the way for other flutists. —*Ron Wynn and Scott Yanow*

★ **The African Flower** / Jun. 24, 1985-Jun. 25, 1985 / Blue Note ✦✦✦✦✦
On *The African Flower*, flutist James Newton explored the music of Billy Strayhorn and his mentor Duke Ellington; the results were a fresh reappraisal of timeless music. —*Scott Yanow, Cadence*

● **Romance and Revolution** / Aug. 20, 1986-Aug. 21, 1986 / Blue Note ✦✦✦✦
Flutist James Newton's brilliantly written and performed pieces for octet were featured on this '87 session. Trombonists Steve Turre and Robin Eubanks, vibist Jay Hoggard, and pianist Geri Allen, along with Newton, were among the solo stars. —*Ron Wynn*

Albert Nicholas

b. May 27, 1900, New Orleans, LA, **d.** Sep. 3, 1973, Basle, Switzerland
Clarinet / New Orleans Jazz
A superb clarinetist with an attractive mellow tone, Albert Nicholas had a long and diverse career, but his playing was always consistently rewarding. He studied with Lorenzo Tio, Jr. in New Orleans and played with cornet legends Buddy Petit, King Oliver, and Manuel Perez while in his teens. After three years in the Merchant Marine he joined King Oliver in Chicago for much of 1925-7, recording with Oliver's Dixie Syncopators. He spent a year in the Far East and Egypt, arriving in New York in 1928 to join Luis Russell for five years. Nicholas, who had recorded in several settings in the '20s, sounded perfectly at home with Russell, taking his solos alongside Red Allen, J.C. Higginbottham, and Charlie Holmes. He would later rejoin Russell when the pianist had the backup orchestra for Louis Armstrong a few years later, and Nicholas also worked with Jelly Roll Morton in 1939 (he had recorded with Morton previously in 1929). Things slowed down for a time in the early '40s, but the New Orelans revival got him working again in the mid-'40s with Art Hodes, Bunk Johnson, and Kid Ory; by 1948 the clarinetist was playing regularly with Ralph Sutton's trio at Jimmy Ryan's. In 1953 Nicholas followed Sidney Bechet's example and moved to France where, other than returning to the US for recording sessions in 1959 and 1960, he happily remained for his final 20 years. —*Scott Yanow*

● **Albert Nicholas Quartet** / Jul. 19, 1959 & Jul. 27, 1959 / Delmark ✦✦✦✦
Like Sidney Bechet, clarinetist Albert Nicholas moved permanently to France later in his career. Although he was there 20 years (1953 until his death in 1973), Nicholas never received Bechet's fame, but he seemed to prosper overseas, no longer having to be concerned with the lack of interest of Americans in traditional jazz. This particular album, one of two cut by Nicholas during a rare 1959 visit to the States, teams the melodic clarinetist with the great pianist Art Hodes, bassist Earl Murphy, and drummer Freddy Kohlman. They jam happily through a set of standards and blues and the results are easily enjoyable. —*Scott Yanow*

Herbie Nichols

b. Jan. 3, 1919, New York, NY, **d.** Apr. 12, 1963, New York, NY
Piano / Post-Bop
Few jazz musicians have had as frustrating a career as Herbie Nichols. A very original composer and pianist, Nichols' music was largely unknown not only during his lifetime but still up to the present day. After serving in the Army during 1941-43, he played with many different groups including those led by Herman Autrey, Hal Singer, Illinois Jacquet, and John Kirby (1948-49). Although he recorded his originals in trios for Blue Note and Bethlehem during 1955-57, those records were largely overlooked. Nichols spent most of his career making his living not in bop bands but with Dixieland groups, playing music that was unchallenging but sometimes paid the rent. He was just beginning to gain a following with younger musicians (including Roswell Rudd, Archie Shepp, Steve Swallow, and Bill Watrous) when Nichols was fatally stricken with leukemia. Decades later Mosaic

released all of his Blue Note recordings (including many previously unissued) in a box set. A chapter in A.B. Spellman's *Four Lives in The Bebop Business* in definitive fashion tells the Herbie Nichols story, and there have been recent tribute albums by Misha Mengelberg and Buell Neidlinger (the latter's *Blue Chopsticks* interpreted Nichols' originals with two reeds, violin, viola, and cello!), but with the exception of "Lady Sings the Blues" (which Billie Holiday had recorded), Herbie Nichols' music is still pretty obscure. —*Scott Yanow*

The Art of Herbie Nichols / May 6, 1955-Apr. 19, 1956 / Blue Note ✦✦✦✦
An anthology collecting some pieces by neglected and overlooked pianist Herbie Nichols. Nichols had one of the truly unique styles in all of jazz piano history and didn't really borrow from or imitate anyone. This single disc doesn't match either an earlier Blue Note two-record set, now deleted, or the outstanding Mosaic set, but it's a fine introduction to Nichols' music. —*Ron Wynn*

★ **Complete Blue Note** / May 6, 1955-Apr. 19, 1956 / Mosaic ✦✦✦✦✦
This limited-edition five-LP box set from Mosaic salutes one of the unknown greats of jazz and gives him the treatment he never received while he was alive. Pianist/composer Herbie Nichols had a very original style in the '50s but was unable to find work of any kind with modern jazz players; he instead spent nights playing anonymous piano in Dixieland bands before his premature death in 1963. Nichols only recorded three full albums, two on Blue Note and one for Bethlehem. The former's 22 performances have been expanded to 48 (24 never issued before) by Mosaic, and they give listeners as full a picture of Herbie Nichols as is possible. Heard exclusively in trios (with either Al McKibbon or Teddy Kotick on bass and Art Blakey or Max Roach on drums), Nichols plays his unique music and now finally these rare performances can be heard and savored. —*Scott Yanow*

● **The Bethlehem Session** / Nov. 1957 / Affinity ✦✦✦✦
Herbie Nichols was one of the tragedies of jazz, a very original pianist and composer who could not find regular employment for his thought-provoking music and ended up playing in anonymous Dixieland bands. He only recorded three complete albums as a leader, and his *Bethlehem* date was his last. With perfectly suitable accompaniment from bassist George Duvivier and bassist Danny Richmond, Nichols introduces nine of his originals in addition to performing the standard "Too Close for Comfort." —*Scott Yanow*

Red Nichols (Ernest Loring Nichols)

b. May 8, 1905, Ogden, UT, **d.** Jun. 28, 1965, Las Vegas, NV
Cornet / Dixieland, Classic Jazz
Overrated in Europe in the early '30s when his records (but not those of his Black contemporaries) were widely available and then later underrated and often unfairly called a Bix imitator, Red Nichols was actually one of the finest cornetists to emerge from the '20s. An expert improviser whose emotional depth did not reach as deep as Bix or Louis Armstrong, Nichols was in many ways a hustler, participating in as many recording sessions (often under pseudonyms) as any other horn player of the era, cutting sessions as Red Nichols and his Five Pennies, the Arkansas Travelers, the Red Heads, the Louisiana Rhythm Kings, and the Charleston Chasers among others, usually with similar personnel! Nichols studied cornet with his father, a college music teacher. After moving from Utah to New York in 1923 Nichols, an excellent sightreader who could always be relied upon to add a bit of jazz to a dance band recording, quickly became in great demand. His own sessions at first featured trombonist Miff Mole and Jimmy Dorsey on alto and clarinet, playing advanced music that utilized unusual intervals, whole tone scales and often the tympani of Vic Berton along with hot ensembles. Later on in the decade his sidemen included such young greats as Benny Goodman, Glenn Miller, Jack Teagarden, Pee Wee Russell, Joe Venuti, Eddie Lang, Adrian Rollini, Gene Krupa, and the wonderful mellophone specialist Dudley Fosdick among others; their version of "Ida" was a surprise hit. Although still using the main name of the Five Pennies, Nichols' bands were often quite a bit larger, and by 1929 he was alternating sessions featuring bigger commercial orchestras with small combos. At first Nichols weathered the depression well with work in shows, but by 1932 his long string of recordings came to an end. He headed a so-so swing band up until 1942, left music for a couple of years and for a few months in 1944 was with Glen Gray's Casa Loma orchestra. Later that year he reformed the Five Pennies as a dixieland sextet and, particularly after bass saxophonist Joe Rushton became a permanent member, it was one of the finer traditional jazz bands of the next 20 years. Nichols recorded several memorable hot versions of "Battle Hymn Of the Republic," the best being in 1959. That same year that a highly enjoyable if rather fictional Hollywood movie called *The Five Pennies* (and featuring Nichols' cornet solos and Danny Kaye's acting) made Nichols into a national celebrity at the twilight of his long career. Nichols' earlier sessions are just now being reissued on CD in piecemeal fashion, but none of his later albums are in print yet. —*Scott Yanow*

Innovators

Throughout the history of jazz there have been literally thousands of talented improvisers and hundreds who have developed their own individual voices and approaches. There are six, however, whose accomplishments, originality, innovations and influence tower above the rest; each one of the six greatly altered the vocabulary of jazz and permanently changed the music:

Louis Armstrong (trumpet, vocals)
Duke Ellington (composer, arranger, bandleader, piano)
Charlie Parker (alto sax)
Dizzy Gillespie (trumpet)
Miles Davis (trumpet, bandleader)
John Coltrane (tenor sax, soprano sax)

Here is a list of the second level of jazz greats, artists whose music also greatly enhanced jazz. The categories are meant as a guide and do not necessarily sum up the musicians' entire careers:

New Orleans Jazz

Jelly Roll Morton (piano, composer)
King Oliver (cornet)
Red Allen (trumpet)
Kid Ory (trombone)
Johnny Dodds (clarinet)
Sidney Bechet (soprano, clarinet)

Classic Jazz

Bix Beiderbecke (cornet)
Jack Teagarden (trombone, vocals)
Pee Wee Russell (clarinet)
Bud Freeman (tenor)
James P. Johnson (piano)
Fats Waller (piano, composer, vocals)
Earl Hines (piano)
Joe Venuti (violin)
Bessie Smith (vocals)
Eddie Condon (bandleader)

Swing

Roy Eldridge (trumpet)
Bunny Berigan (trumpet)
Charlie Shavers (trumpet)
Clark Terry (flugelhorn)
Benny Goodman (clarinet, bandleader)
Artie Shaw (clarinet, bandleader)
Coleman Hawkins (tenor)
Lester Young (tenor)
Ben Webster (tenor)
Johnny Hodges (alto)
Benny Carter (alto, arranger)
Harry Carney (baritone)
Art Tatum (piano)

–Continued next column–

Teddy Wilson (piano)
Count Basie (piano, bandleader)
Nat King Cole (piano, vocals)
Django Reinhardt (guitar)
Charlie Christian (guitar)
Lionel Hampton (vibes)
Stephane Grappelli (violin)
Jimmy Blanton (bass)
Gene Krupa (drums)
Buddy Rich (drums)
Louis Bellson (drums)
Billie Holiday (vocals)
Ella Fitzgerald (vocals)

Bop

Howard McGhee (trumpet)
Fats Navarro (trumpet)
J.J. Johnson (trombone)
Buddy DeFranco (clarinet)
Dexter Gordon (tenor)
Bud Powell (piano)
Thelonious Monk (piano, composer)
Oscar Peterson (piano)
Erroll Garner (piano)
Milt Jackson (vibes)
Joe Pass (guitar)
Oscar Pettiford (bass)
Max Roach (drums, bandleader)
Sarah Vaughan (vocals)
Lambert, Hendricks & Ross (vocal group)

Cool Jazz

Gerry Mulligan (baritone)
Lennie Tristano (piano, bandleader)

Hard Bop

Clifford Brown (trumpet)
Lee Morgan (trumpet)
Freddie Hubbard (trumpet)
Cannonball Adderley (alto)
Phil Woods (alto)
Art Pepper (alto)
Sonny Rollins (tenor)
Rahsaan Roland Kirk (tenor, stritch, manzello, flutes)
Wes Montgomery (guitar)
Horace Silver (piano, composer)
Jimmy Smith (organ)
Art Blakey (drums, bandleader)

Avant-Garde

Charles Mingus (bass, bandleader)
Eric Dolphy (alto, bass clarinet, flute)
Ornette Coleman (alto, composer)
Anthony Braxton (alto, composer)
Cecil Taylor (piano)

–Continued next page–

Music Map

Innovators – *continued*

Post Bop
Woody Shaw (trumpet)
Jackie McLean (alto)
Joe Henderson (tenor)
Wayne Shorter (tenor, soprano, composer)
Bill Evans (piano)
McCoy Tyner (piano)
Elvin Jones (drums)
Tony Williams (drums)
Gil Evans (arranger)

Fusion
Chick Corea (piano, keyboards)
Herbie Hancock (piano, keyboards)
Joe Zawinul (keyboards)
Jaco Pastorius (electric bass)

Modern Mainstream/1990's Jazz
Wynton Marsalis (trumpet)
Eddie Daniels (clarinet, tenor)
Keith Jarrett (piano)
Pat Metheny (guitar)
John Scofield (guitar)
Bill Frisell (guitar)

Rhythm of the Day / Oct. 1925-Feb. 1932 / ASV/Living Era ♦♦♦
A 1992 reissue of prime mid-'20s and early '30s Red Nichols cuts. Many are among the songs that such players as Benny Goodman, Artie Shaw, and others listened to closely and learned from during their youth. This is among the better Nichols reissues available. *—Ron Wynn*

● **Red Nichols 1925-28** / Nov. 1925-Sep. 1928 / Fountain ♦♦♦♦

Jazz Classics (1925-1930) / 1925-1930 / Mobile Fidelity ♦♦♦♦

● **Syncopated Chamber Music, Vol. 1** / Feb. 8, 1953-Feb. 9, 1953 / Audiophile ♦♦♦♦

Hot Pennies / Apr. 18, 1957 / Capitol ♦♦♦
For this LP, cornetist Red Nichols expanded his Five Pennies from six pieces to twelve, allowing him to arrange some colorful ensembles while still retaining the flavor of Dixieland. With a backup crew that includes trombonist King Jackson, the great bass saxophonist Joe Rushton, and clarinetist Heinie Beau, Nichols revisits such veteran songs as "Louisiana," "Maple Leaf Rag," "Ida" (a big hit for him in the '20s), and "Farewell Blues." The music is easily enjoyable but will be difficult to find since Capitol has yet to reissue any of their many Red Nichols records on CD. *—Scott Yanow*

Parade of the Pennies / Nov. 1958 / Capitol ♦♦♦♦
For part of this LP, cornetist Red Nichols (with the assistance of clarinetist Heinie Beau's arrangements) revisited his earlier "hits" with successful remakes of such songs as "Buddy's Habits," "Japanese Sandman," "Avalon," and "Washboard Blues." In addition there are three newer songs co-written by Nichols and Beau. Red's Five Pennies are augmented by Jackie Coon's mellophone, a couple of reeds, and the percussion (including tympani) of Ralph Hansell. This is an excellent album well deserving (along with most of Nichols' hard-to-find Capitol LP's) of being reissued on CD. *—Scott Yanow*

Red Nichols and the Five Pennies at Marineland / Jun. 11, 1959 / Capitol ♦♦♦

Blues and Old Time Rags / Jun. 1964 / Capitol ♦♦♦

Jimmie Noone (Jimmy Noone)

b. Apr. 23, 1895, New Orleans, LA, **d.** Apr. 19, 1944, Los Angeles, CA
Clarinet / Classic New Orleans Jazz
Considered one of the three top New Orleans clarinetists of the '20s (with Johnny Dodds and Sidney Bechet), Jimmie Noone had a smoother tone than his contemporaries that appealed to players of the swing era (including Benny Goodman). He played guitar as a child and at age 15 took clarinet lessons from Lorenzo Tio, Jr. and Sidney Bechet (the latter was only 13 years old!). Noone developed quickly and he played with Freddie Keppard (1913-14), Buddy Petit, and the Young Olympia Band (1916) which he led. In 1917 he went to Chicago to join Keppard's Creole Band. After it broke up the following year he became a member of King Oliver's band, staying until he joined Doc Cook's Dreamland Orchestra (1920-26). Although Noone recorded with Cook, it was when he started leading a band at the Apex Club that he hit his stride. By 1928 he had

pianist Earl Hines and altoist Joe Poston in the unusual quintet (Poston stuck to playing melodies behind Noone) and was recording for Vocalion, creating classic music including an early version of "Sweet Lorraine" (his theme song) and "Four or Five Times." Noone worked steadily in Chicago throughout the '30s (although he received less attention from the jazz world), he used Charlie Shavers on some of his late-'30s recordings, and welcomed the young singer Joe Williams to the bandstand; unfortunately they never recorded together. In 1944 Noone was in Kid Ory's band on the West Coast and seemed on the brink of greater fame when he unexpectedly died. Thanks to European reissue series, Jimmie Noone's recordings are readily available on CD. His son Jimmie Noone, Jr. suddenly emerged out of obscurity in the '80s to play clarinet and tenor with the Cheathams. *—Scott Yanow*

★ **Apex Blues** / May 16, 1928-Jul. 1, 1930 / Decca ♦♦♦♦♦
This CD reissues the first dozen selections from clarinetist Jimmie Noone's Apex Club Orchestra (all of the numbers with pianist Earl Hines although not the four alternate takes) plus eight slightly later numbers. Noone had an unusual quintet/sextet in which altoist Joe Poston constantly stated the melody (but never actually had any solos), giving the band an unique sound for the period. Many of Noone's greatest recordings are on this CD (including "I Know That You Know," "Four or Five Times," "Apex Blues," "My Monday Date," "Sweet Lorraine," and "My Daddy Rocks Me with One Steady Roll") although serious collectors will prefer to get the more complete two CDs from the Classics label instead. *—Scott Yanow*

Red Norvo (Kenneth Norville)

b. Mar. 31, 1908, Beardstown, IL
Vibes / Cool, Swing
Red Norvo was an unusual star during the swing era, playing jazz xylophone. After he switched to vibes in 1943 Norvo had a quieter yet no less fluent style than Lionel Hampton. Although no match for Hampton popularity-wise, Norvo and his wife, singer Mildred Bailey, did become known as Mr. and Mrs. Swing!

Red Norvo has had a long and interesting career. He started on marimba when he was 14 and soon switched to xylophone. Active in vaudeville in the late '20s as a tap dancer, Norvo joined Paul Whiteman's Orchestra in the early '30s (meeting and marrying Mildred Bailey). He recorded some extraordinary sides in the early-to-mid-'30s that showed off his virtuosity and imagination; two numbers (the atmospheric "Dance of the Octopus" and "In a Mist") had Benny Goodman playing bass clarinet! Norvo led his own bands during 1936-44 which, with its Eddie Sauter arrangements (particularly in the early days), had a unique ensemble sound that made it possible for one to hear the leader's xylophone. In 1944 Norvo (who by then had switched permanently to vibes) broke up his band and joined Benny Goodman's Sextet. Through recordings and appearances, he showed that his style was quite adaptable and open to bop. Norvo welcomed Charlie Parker and Dizzy Gillespie to a 1945 record date, was part of Woody Herman's riotous first Herd in 1946, and recorded with Stan Hasselgard in 1948. At the beginning of the '50s Norvo put together an unusual trio with guitarist Tal Farlow (later Jimmy Raney) and bassist Charles Mingus (later Red Mitchell). The light yet often speedy unisons and telepathic interplay by the musicians was quite memorable. Norvo led larger groups later in the decade, had reunions with Benny Goodman, and made many fine recordings. The '60s found Red Norvo adopting a lower profile after he had a serious ear operation in 1961. He worked with the Newport All-Stars later in the decade and from the mid-'70s to the mid-'80s was once again quite active, making several excellent recordings. However, his hearing eventually worsened, and a serious stroke put Red Norvo out of action altogether after 55 years of music. — *Scott Yanow*

★ **Dance of the Octopus** / Apr. 18, 1933-Mar. 16, 1936 / Hep ◆◆◆◆◆
The first 26 selections that xylophonist Red Norvo ever led are on this essential (and generous) CD. Among the many illustrious sidemen are future bandleaders Benny Goodman (heard on bass clarinet during memorable versions of "In a Mist" and "Dance of the Octopus"), Jimmy Dorsey, Artie Shaw, Jack Jenney, Charlie Barnet, and Bunny Berigan in addition to Chu Berry, Teddy Wilson, and Gene Krupa. While the first half of the program features all-star groups, the later tracks are prime examples of small-group swing with arranger Eddie Sauter's mellophone, trumpeter Stew Pletcher, and Herbie Haymer's tenor playing key roles. This readily available CD from the Scottish label Hep contains more than its share of classic performances and is essential. — *Scott Yanow*

Red Norvo, Featuring Mildred Bailey / Mar. 22, 1937-Jul. 28, 1938 / Columbia ◆◆◆◆
This CD reissue by Columbia in their Legacy series is a bit of a hodge-podge, covering a two and a half year period in the bandleading career of xylophonist Red Norvo. Unfortunately the music is not programmed in chronological order, but since most of these largely enjoyable 18 titles (including two never previously released) have rarely been reissued, this sampler will have to do until a more "complete" session comes along. Norvo's band during this period not only featured the occasional vocals of his wife, Mildred Bailey, but fine solo work from the tenor of Herbie Haymer, clarinetist Hank D'Amico, and trumpeter Stew Pletcher in addition to the leader. The biggest key in Norvo's orchestra achieving a sound of its own, however, was the distinctive and inventive arrangements of Eddie Sauter. This CD contains great music that deserves to be reissued more coherently. — *Scott Yanow*

Red Norvo and Mildred Bailey / 1938 / Circle ◆◆◆
Vol. 1 / Oct. 28, 1943-May 17, 1944 / Vintage Jazz Classics ◆◆◆◆
This CD from the VJC label features vibraphonist Red Norvo's V-Disc sessions of 1943-44. Most of the music (which includes some breakdowns and alternate takes) finds Norvo leading an octet that includes trumpeter Dale Pearce, trombonist Dick Taylor, clarinetist Aaron Sachs, and the tenor of Flip Phillips; Carol Bruce has three vocals and Helen Ward takes two, but the high points are instrumental versions of "1-2-3-4 Jump," "Seven Come Eleven," and "Flyin' Home." The last three titles (from 1944) feature Norvo leading a quintet with clarinetist Aaron Sachs. Overall, this CD contains plenty of fine examples of late swing, just before the influence of bop began to be felt on the principle's styles. Recommended to fans of the era. — *Scott Yanow*

● **Volume Two: The Norvo-Mingus-Farlow Trio** / Oct. 28, 1943-1950 / Vintage Jazz Classics ◆◆◆◆
With the exception of two titles and an alternate take featuring singer Helen Ward that were left over from Red Norvo's V-Disc sessions of 1943 (which were otherwise reissued in full on *Volume One*), this CD is comprised of 30 concise performances by Red Norvo's brilliant 1949-50 trio which, in addition to the vibraphonist/leader, also includes guitarist Tal Farlow and bassist Charles Mingus. These radio transcriptions (which do not duplicate the group's studio recordings) contain melodic but often speedy versions of standards. The near-telepathic communication among the three brilliant players and the very appealing sound of the group make this an easily-recommended disc for lovers of straightahead jazz and vibes. — *Scott Yanow*

The Red Norvo Trios / Sep. 1953-Oct. 1955 / Prestige ◆◆◆◆
Although the most famous of Red Norvo's vibes/guitar/bass trios featured guitarist Tal Farlow and bassist Charles Mingus, he continued the appealing format for a few years after his sidemen departed. This CD features Norvo with guitarist Jimmy Raney and bassist Red Mitchell on 15 enjoyable performances from 1953-54 and is rounded off by four songs from 1955 when Farlow rejoined Norvo and Mitchell. — *Scott Yanow*

With Jimmy Raney and Red Mitchel / Mar. 1954 / Original Jazz Classics ◆◆◆◆
This CD reissues an album by the 1954 version of the Red Norvo Trio which consists of vibraphonist Red Norvo, guitarist Jimmy Raney, and bassist Red Mitchell. Although not quite reaching the heights of the earlier version with Tal Farlow and Charles Mingus, the close interplay between the musicians on such tonal bop versions of such songs as "Just One of Those Things," "Crazy Rhythm," and "Bernie's Tune" is consistently hard-swinging yet light, adventurous yet accessible. An enjoyable set. — *Scott Yanow*

● **Just a Mood** / Sep. 17, 1954-Jan. 18, 1957 / Bluebird ◆◆◆◆
Vibraphonist Red Norvo was among the most flexible of improvisers from his generation. On this Bluebird CD, Norvo is heard with three very different groups. He interacts with trumpeter Harry "Sweets" Edison, tenor saxophonist Ben Webster, and pianist Jimmy Rowles in a swing-oriented sextet; their performances are highlighted by the memorable "Just a Mood." In addition, Norvo plays four songs that have the word "Blue" in their titles with a quintet that is an outgrowth of his trio of a few years earlier (this group consists of flutist Buddy Collette, guitarist Tal Farlow, Monty Budwig or Red Callender on bass, and drummer Chico Hamilton) and four "Rose" songs with the who's who of West Coast Jazz: trumpeter Shorty Rogers, clarinetist Jimmy Giuffre, pianist Pete Jolly, Farlow, Callender, and drummer Larry Bunker. No matter what the setting, Norvo fits in quite comfortably, and the consistent high-quality of the formerly rare music makes this a highly recommended set to bop collectors. — *Scott Yanow*

Just Friends / Aug. 8, 1983-Aug. 9, 1983 / Stash ◆◆◆◆
For what would be one of vibraphonist Red Norvo's final recordings (his recording debut was in 1931, 52 years earlier!), Norvo teams up quite effectively with guitarist Buck Pizzarelli (an old friend), pianist Russ Kassoff, and bassist Jerry Bruno. The seven standards plus John Pizzarelli's "Blues for Red" make for a well rounded session, balancing ballads such as "My Old Flame" and "I Thought About You" with stomps including "Just Friends" and "Sweet Georgia Brown." Although serious hearing problems and a major stroke would soon end Red Norvo's career, this fine record serves as proof that the great vibraphonist never did decline before his forced retirement. — *Scott Yanow*

Anita O'Day (Anita Belle Colton)

Vocals / Bop, Swing
One of the finest singers to emerge from the swing era, Anita O'Day at her prime was a masterful scat singer and a true improviser whose interpretations of standards uplifted and altered even the most familiar songs. After struggling through dance marathons and discovering that she could sing, O'Day picked up valuable experience performing with Max Miller's group in Chicago. Her big break was hooking up with the Gene Krupa Orchestra. During her two years with the drummer's big band (1941-43), O'Day had hits in "Let Me Off Uptown," "Thanks for the Boogie Ride," and "Bolero at the Savoy." She was with Stan Kenton for a year (1944-45), scoring with "And Her Tears Flowed like Wine." When she decided that Kenton's progressive jazz did not suit her, she recommended June Christy as her successor; Christy, Chris Connor, and Helen Merrill would all spend the early parts of their careers trying to emulate O'Day.

After a period back with Krupa (during which she recorded popular versions of "Opus No. 1" and "Boogie Blues"), O'Day went out on her own. She recorded for Signature in 1947 and London in 1950 but did not appear on a regular basis on records until she began her association with Verve in 1952. The singer's finest recordings were for Verve during 1952-63, both with big bands and small groups. Very open to the innovations of bebop, O'Day was one of the top singers of the decade, captured at the peak of her powers at the 1958 Newport Jazz Festival in the film *Jazz on a Summer's Day* during which she performed memorable renditions of "Sweet Georgia Brown" and a scat-filled "Tea for Two." She also appeared briefly in *The Gene Krupa Story*. However, heroin addiction (which she fully outlined in her 1981 memoirs *High Times Hard Times*) took its toll and after 1963 O'Day's life was quite erratic. In 1970 she made a strong comeback at the Berlin Jazz Festival and by the mid-'70s was recording regularly for her Emily label. Anita O'Day's voice has gradually deteriorated through the years, particularly after the mid-'80s, but her prime recordings from the '50s are quite enjoyable and rank with the best of the era. — *Scott Yanow*

Anita O'Day Swings Cole Porter with Billy May / Jan. 22, 1952-Aug. 17, 1960 / Verve ◆◆◆◆
Most of this CD reissue is taken from sessions in April 1959 on which Anita O'Day interprets Cole Porter songs while accompanied by some rather rambunctious big-band arrangements from Billy May. While her emotional range is wider than Ella Fitzgerald's (who had previously recorded her much better-known *Cole Porter Songbook*), strangely enough O'Day's voice does not sound as strong on the Billy May set as it does on the six "bonus" cuts which are Cole Porter songs she recorded on other occasions (from 1952-60). Still this CD does have its moments with highlights including "I Get a Kick out of You," "All of You," "It's Delovely," "You're the Top," and two versions of "Love for Sale." — *Scott Yanow*

● **Anita** / Dec. 6, 1955-Dec. 8, 1955 / Verve ◆◆◆◆
This CD is a straight reissue of the original LP with singer Anita O'Day heard in prime form. Accompanied by an orchestra conducted and arranged by Buddy Bregman, O'Day is heard near the peak of her powers on such songs as "You're the Top," "Honeysuckle Rose," an emotional rendition of "A Nightingale Sang in Berkeley Square," and "As Long as I Live." One of her better recordings, this CD is recommended. — *Scott Yanow*

Pick Yourself Up with Anita O'Day / Dec. 15, 1956 & Dec. 17, 1956 / Verve ✦✦✦✦

For this well rounded CD reissue that adds nine cuts to the original program, Anita O'Day, in her prime period, is mostly heard accompanied by Buddy Bregman's Orchestra, but there are also a few tracks on which she is joined by a jazz combo featuring trumpeter Harry "Sweets" Edison. Highlights include "Don't Be That Way," "Stompin' at the Savoy," "Pick Yourself Up," "Sweet Georgia Brown," and "I Won't Dance." Virtually all of Anita O'Day's '50s recordings are recommended, for her drug use had not yet affected her voice, and her creativity was generally at its height. — *Scott Yanow*

★ **Anita Sings the Most** / Jan. 31, 1957 / Verve ✦✦✦✦✦

Anita O'Day recorded many rewarding albums in the '50s when her voice was at its strongest, and this collaboration with the Oscar Peterson Quartet (comprising pianist Peterson, guitarist Herb Ellis, bassist Ray Brown, and drummer John Poole) may very well be her best. Not only is the backup swinging, giving a *Jazz at the Philharmonic* feel to some of the songs, but O'Day proves that she could keep up with Peterson. "Them There Eyes" is taken successfully at a ridiculously fast tempo, yet the singer displays a great deal of warmth on such ballads as "We'll Be Together Again" and "Bewitched, Bothered and Bewildered." While Peterson and Ellis have some solos, O'Day is never overshadowed (which is saying a lot!) and is clearly inspired by their presence. The very brief playing time (just 33 minutes) is unfortunate on this straight CD reissue of the original LP, but the high quality definitely makes up for the lack of quantity. A gem. — *Scott Yanow*

Anita O'Day Sings the Winners / Sep. 1958 / Verve ✦✦✦✦

For this CD, which is greatly expanded from the original LP, Anita O'Day sings standards associated with other musicians, including "Four" (Miles Davis), "Early Autumn" (Stan Getz), "Four Brothers" (Woody Herman), "Sing, Sing, Sing" (Benny Goodman and Gene Krupa), and "Peanut Vendor" (Stan Kenton). Some of the material is unusual for a singer to interpret, but O'Day, one of the top jazz vocalists of the decade, improvises when the lyrics are not that strong (or barely exist!). The backup by the Russ Garcia Orchestra is not all that memorable, but the focus is entirely on the vocalist, and O'Day really comes through. — *Scott Yanow*

I Get a Kick Out of You / Apr. 25, 1975 / Evidence ✦✦✦✦

At age 55 Anita O'Day was having a bit of a renaissance, having kicked drugs and become more active in the '70s. This live in Japan set (reissued on CD by Evidence) finds the singer stretching out on nine numbers ("Gone with the Wind" is nearly 11 minutes long) and carefully choosing a tune or two from each of six decades ('20s to the '70s). Of the latter "What Are You Doing the Rest of Your Life" and Leon Russell's "A Song for You" (given a definitive treatment) are effective; other highlights include "Undecided," "I Get a Kick out of You," and "Opus One." This is one of O'Day's best recordings of the '70s. — *Scott Yanow*

King Oliver (Joe Oliver)

b. May 11, 1885, New Orleans, LA, d. Apr. 8, 1938, Savannah, GA
Cornet / Classic New Orleans Jazz

Joe "King" Oliver was one of the great New Orleans legends, an early giant whose legacy is only partly on records. In 1923 he led one of the classic New Orleans jazz bands, the last significant group to emphasize collective improvisation over solos, but ironically his second cornetist (Louis Armstrong) would soon permanently change jazz. And while Armstrong never tired of praising his idol, he actually sounded very little like Oliver; the King's influence was more deeply felt by Muggsy Spanier and Tommy Ladnier.

Although originally a trombonist, by 1905 Oliver was playing cornet regularly with various New Orleans bands. Gradually he rose to the top of the crowded local scene, and in 1917 he was billed "King" by bandleader Kid Ory. A master of mutes, Oliver was able to get a wide variety of sounds out of his horn; Bubber Miley would later on be inspired by Oliver's expertise. In 1919 Oliver left New Orleans to join Bill Johnson's band at the Dreamland Ballroom in Chicago. By 1920 he was a leader himself and, after an unsuccessful year in California, King Oliver started playing regularly with his Creole Jazz Band at the Lincoln Gardens in Chicago. He soon sent for his protégé Louis Armstrong and clarinetist Johnny Dodds, trombonist Honore Dutrey, pianist Lil Harden, and drummer Baby Dodds as a core, Oliver had a remarkable band whose brilliance was only hinted at on records. As it is, the group's 1923 sessions far exceeded any jazz previously recorded; Oliver's three-chorus solo on "Dippermouth Blues" has since been memorized by virtually every Dixieland trumpeter.

Unfortunately, the Creole Jazz Band gradually broke up in 1924. Oliver recorded a pair of duets with pianist Jelly Roll Morton but otherwise was off records that year. He took over Dave Peyton's band in 1925 and renamed it the Dixie Syncopators; Barney Bigard and Albert Nicholas were among the members. New recordings resulted (including "Snag It," which has a famous eight-bar passage by Oliver), but when the cornetist moved to New York in 1927, his music was behind the times and

he made some bad business decisions (including turning down a chance to play regularly at the Cotton Club). Worse yet, his dental problems (caused partly by an early liking of sugar sandwiches) made playing cornet increasingly painful and, on many of his later recordings, Oliver is barely present (although he did a heroic job on 1929's "Too Late"). Pianist Luis Russell took over the Dixie Syncopators in 1929 and, although Oliver's last recordings (from 1931) are superior examples of hot dance music, he was quickly becoming a forgotten name. Unsuccessful tours in the South eventually left Oliver stranded there, working as a janitor in a poolroom before his death at age 52. — *Scott Yanow*

★ **Louis Armstrong/King Oliver** / Apr. 6, 1923-Dec. 22, 1924 / Milestone ✦✦✦✦✦

Classic renditions (1923-24) of "Snake Rag," "Dippermouth Blues," and "Canal Street Blues" come from the hottest band of its day—Oliver's Creole Jazz Band. — *Bruce Raeburn*

Sugar Foot Stomp / Mar. 11, 1926-Jun. 11, 1928 / GRP ✦✦✦✦

This Decca reissue CD put out by GRP is a fine sampler of King Oliver's 1926-28 recordings with his Dixie Syncopators. The hot jazz dance music is highlighted by several classics ("Too Bad," "Snag It," Jackass Blues," "Sobbin' Blues," "Farewell Blues," and two versions of "Snag It"). With such sidemen as trombonist Kid Ory, clarinetists Albert Nicholas and Omer Simeon, and Barney Bigard on tenor and clarinet, Oliver's supporting cast is quite strong. The cornetist was himself starting to fade during this period but does take a few heated solos, and his break on "Snag It" remains quite famous. True King Oliver collectors, though, will want to bypass this one and instead acquire the entries in one of the more comprehensive European complete series. — *Scott Yanow*

King Oliver (1926-1928) / Mar. 11, 1926-Jun. 1928 / Classics ✦✦✦✦

King Oliver (1928-1930) / Jun. 1928-Mar. 1930 / Classics ✦✦✦✦

☆ **King Oliver** / Jan. 16, 1929-Sep. 19, 1930 / RCA ✦✦✦✦✦

This double-CD set (part of the French RCA *Jazz Tribune* series) includes all of King Oliver's Victor recordings of 1929-30 except for a few alternate takes. The 32 selections are better than one might expect considering that Oliver's playing abilities were rapidly fading (due to serious gum problems). The cornetist in fact, takes a few memorable solos, particularly on "Too Late" and "Struggle Buggy." But it is the high musicianship of his sidemen (who include trumpeters Dave Nelson, Red Allen, and Bubber Miley (who is outstanding on "St. James Infirmary"), trombonists J.C. Higginbottham and Jimmy Archey, clarinetist Omer Simeon, altoist Charlie Holmes and, filling in for Oliver, cornetists Louis Metcalf and Punch Miller, that makes this set so enjoyable. — *Scott Yanow*

New York Sessions (1929-1930) / Oct. 8, 1929-Sep. 19, 1930 / Bluebird ✦✦✦✦

Rather than reissue all of the Victor recordings released under King Oliver's name, this CD has the 22 recordings that best show off the cornetist's playing during his final period on records, including several alternate takes. Oliver was plagued with dental problems by 1928 but is in generally good form on these late recordings, taking a dramatic solo on "Too Late" and sounding surprisingly strong on "Struggle Buggy." Otherwise, the music would still be well worth getting for Oliver's sidemen alone since together they form a high-quality dance band. This CD is recommended to all 1920s collectors except King Oliver completists, and even they might be forced to acquire this due to the inclusion of a few very rare alterante takes, including the previously unreleased first take of "Olga." — *Scott Yanow*

King Oliver and His Orchestra (1930-1931) / Apr. 1930-Apr. 1931 / Classics ✦✦✦✦

Sy Oliver (Melvin James Oliver)

b. Dec. 17, 1910, Battle Creek, MI, d. May 28, 1988, New York, NY
Trumpet, Vocals / Swing

Sy Oliver's melodic yet sophisticated arrangements helped define the Jimmy Lunceford sound in the '30s and modernized Tommy Dorsey's band in the '40s. A fine trumpeter (excellent with a mute) and a likable vocalist, Oliver made his recording debut with Zack Whyte's Chocolate Beau Brummels in the late '20s and also worked with Alphonse Trent. Joining Lunceford in 1933, Oliver was responsible for such memorable charts as "My Blue Heaven," "Ain't She Sweet," "Organ Grinder's Swing," and "'Tain't What You Do" among many. It was a major blow to Lunceford when Oliver jumped at the chance to make a lot more money arranging and occasionally singing for Tommy Dorsey. The hiring of Sy Oliver was a major help for Dorsey in getting Buddy Rich to join his band. Oliver's arrangement of "On the Sunny Side of the Street" was his biggest hit for Dorsey. After a brief attempt at leading his own orchestra in 1946, Oliver became a freelance arranger and producer for the remainder of his long career. As late as 1975-80 he was regularly leading a band, but Sy Oliver will always be best-known for his classic Lunceford charts. — *Scott Yanow*

● **Oliver's Twist & Easy Walker** / Jul. 7, 1960 & Oct. 18, 1962 / Mobile Fidelity ✦✦✦✦

During the '50s and '60s, arranger Sy Oliver's groups reflected its leader's loyalty to the swing era and lack of interest in newer jazz styles. This audiophile CD from Mobile Fidelity reissues two rare Oliver albums that were originally recorded as radio transcriptions. The 24 concise performances range from folk melodies such as "Oh, Them Golden Slippers," "I'm a Little Teapot," and "Arkansas Traveler" to swing compositions. Trumpeter Charlie Shavers is the star of the earlier set while the tenor of Budd Johnson takes honors on the second session. Overall the music is a bit lightweight but enjoyable enough. —*Scott Yanow*

Oregon

Group / New Age, New Age, Post-Bop
Oregon emerged in 1970 as a splinter band from The Paul Winter Consort. Its members each had experience in jazz, classical, and a variety of non-western musical styles, and were also multi-instrumentalists. Ralph Towner played standard acoustic and 12-string guitar, piano, a variety of electric keyboards, trumpet and fluegelhorn. Paul McCandless' instrumental arsenal included oboe, English horn, soprano sax, bass clarinet, the musette, and tin flute. Collin Walcott handled most of the percussion duties on tabla and various African and Latin rhythm instruments plus sitar, dulcimer, clarinet, and violin. Glen Moore was the bassist, and also played clarinet, viola, piano, and flute. They suffered some snide comments labelling them the "Modern Jazz Quartet of the '70s" or "a white, European imitation of the Art Ensemble of Chicago." In truth, they were an excellent ensemble playing a hybrid style that wasn't exactly jazz, certainly wasn't rock, but liberally quoted and borrowed from free jazz, Asian, African, European, and pop music sources. They began on Vanguard, later moved to ECM, and also issued albums on Elektra and Portrait/Columbia. Collin Walcott's death in a car accident in 1984 was a major blow, but he was eventually successfully replaced by percussionist Trilok Gurtu. Oregon has worked at times with some guest players (including Zbigniew Seifert, Nancy King, and Elvin Jones). Their Elektra albums have been reissued on Discover CDs while many of their Vanguard and ECM albums have also been reissued on CD. In recent times (due to conflicting schedules) Oregon has been touring as a trio without Gurtu. —*Ron Wynn*

Out of the Woods / Apr. 1978 / Discovery ✦✦✦✦
Many familiar themes. Excellent. —*Michael G. Nastos*

★ **Roots in the Sky** / Dec. 1978 / Discovery ✦✦✦✦✦
A 1992 CD reissue of their 1979 album, among their only releases ever issued by a major label. It was characteristically free-wheeling and eclectic, with long stretches of classical, Asian, African, and jazz coming together, and the group mixing structured ensemble work with surging free solos. —*Ron Wynn*

Oregon / Feb. 1983 / ECM ✦✦✦✦
This is among the more memorable ECM releases, and one of their best from an ensemble-playing standpoint. —*Ron Wynn*

Ecotopia / Mar. 1987 / ECM ✦✦✦
New percussionist Trilok Gurtu makes an impact within the group. —*Ron Wynn*

Always, Never and Forever / 1992 / Intuition ✦✦✦✦

Original Dixieland Jazz Band

Group / Classic Jazz
The first jazz group to ever record, the Original Dixieland Jazz Band in 1917 made history. They were not the first group to ever play jazz (Buddy Bolden had preceded them by 22 years!), nor was this White quintet necessarily the best band of the time, but during 1917-23 (particularly in their earliest years) they did a great deal to popularize jazz. The musicians learned about jazz from their fellow New Orleans players (including King Oliver) but happened to get their big break first. In 1916 drummer Johay Stein, cornetist Nick LaRocca, trombonist Eddie Edwards, pianist Henry Ragas, and clarinetist Alcide "Yellow" Nunez played together in Chicago. With Tony Sbarbaro replacing Stein and Larry Shields taking over for Nunez, the band was booked at Resenweber's restaurant in New York in early 1917. Their exuberant music (which stuck exclusively to ensembles with the only solos being short breaks) caused a major sensation. Columbia recorded the ODJB playing "Darktown Strutters Ball" and "Indiana" but was afraid to put out the records. Victor stepped in and recorded the group playing the novelty "Livery Stable Blues" (which found the horns imitating barnyard animals) and the "Dixie Jazz Band One Step" and quickly released the music; "Livery Stable Blues" was a huge hit that really launched the jazz age. During the next few years the ODJB would introduce such future standards as "Tiger Rag," "At the Jazz Band Ball," "Fidgety Feet," "Sensation," "Clarinet Marmalade," "Margie," "Jazz Me Blues," and "Royal Garden Blues." The group (with J. Russel Robinson taking the place of Ragas who died in the 1919 flu epidemic and trombonist Emile Christian filling in for Edwards) visited London during 1919-20, and they once again caused quite a stir, introducing jazz to Europe. However, upon their return to the US, the ODJB was considered a bit out of fashion after the rise of Paul Whiteman and in 1922 the New Orleans Rhythm Kings (a far superior group). By 1923 when many of the first Black jazz giants finally

were recorded, the ODJB was thought of as a historical band, and due to internal dissension they soon broke up. In 1936 LaRocca, Shields, Edwards, Robinson, and Sbarbaro (the latter the only musician to have a full-time career by then) had a reunion and did a few final recordings together before LaRocca permanently retired. Although the cornetist's arrogant claims that the ODJB had invented jazz are exaggerated and tinged with racism, the Original Dixieland Jazz Band did make a strong contribution to early jazz (most groups that recorded during 1918-21 emulated their style), helped supply the repertoire of many later Dixieland bands and were an influence on Bix Beiderbecke and Red Nichols. —*Scott Yanow*

★ **75th Anniversary** / Feb. 26, 1917-Jun. 7, 1921 / Bluebird ✦✦✦✦✦
The Original Dixieland Jazz Band, the first jazz group to record, stuck exclusively to ensembles with no solos, introduced such standard tunes as "Original Dixieland One Step," "At the Jazz Band," "Fidgety Feet," "Sensation," "Clarinet Marmalade," "Margie," "Jazz Me Blues," "Royal Garden Blues," and "Tiger Rag," all of which are included on this release. It's an essential acquisition for any serious jazz library. —*Scott Yanow*

The Complete Original Dixieland Jazz Band / Feb. 26, 1917-Sep. 25, 1936 / RCA ✦✦✦✦

● **In England** / Sep. 1917-Jan. 21, 1924 / EMI Pathe/Jazztime ✦✦✦✦
The original Dixieland Jazz Band's visit to England during 1919-20 caused a sensation and did much to help popularize and even "legitimize" jazz. More importantly for history, the ODJB cut some of their finest recordings while overseas. These very well recorded documents (some of which are around four rather than three minutes long) feature the ODJB at their best. The performances still do not include any real solos (sticking exclusively to ensembles), but many of the melodies are quite strong. Of their 19 London recordings (all of which are on this CD), high points include "At the Jazz Band Ball," "Tiger Rag," "Tell Me," "I'm Forever Blowing," "Sensation, Bubbles" (one of the first jazz waltzes), "I've Lost My Heart in Dixieland," and "Alice Blue Gown." This CD is rounded out by five real obscurities from English bands cut between 1917-24. Spirited as they are, those groups demonstrate that the ODJB was really the pacesetters for the era. —*Scott Yanow*

The Original Memphis Five

Group / Classic Jazz
Founded in 1917 by trumpeter Phil Napoleon and pianist Frank Signorelli, this excellent New Orleans jazz quintet made a ton of records between 1921-31, including many under different names (such as Ladd's Black Aces and the Carolina Cotton Pickers). Napoleon, trombonist Miff Mole (who in 1922 was succeeded by Charles Panelli), clarinetist Jimmy Lytell, Signorelli, and drummer Jack Roth were regular fixtures in the early days; starting in 1926 the personnel changed fairly frequently with cornetist Red Nichols, drummer Ray Bauduc, Mole, and (during one session apiece in 1928, 1929, and 1931), Tommy and Jimmy Dorsey making appearances. The Original Memphis Five's music was melodic, swinging, and very jazz-oriented. Unfortunately most of their hundreds of recordings have not been reissued on CD yet. —*Scott Yanow*

★ **Collection, Vol. 1: 1922-1923** / Apr. 22, 1922-Dec. 10, 1923 / Collectors Classics/Storyville ✦✦✦✦✦

Kid Ory (Edward Ory)

b. Dec. 25, 1886, La Place, LA, d. Jan. 23, 1973, Honolulu, HI
Trombone / Dixieland
Kid Ory was one of the great New Orleans pioneers, an early trombonist who virtually defined the "tailgate" style (using his horn to play rhythmic bass lines in the front line behind the trumpet and clarinet) and who was fortunate enough to last through the lean years so he could make a major comeback in the mid-'40s. Originally a banjoist, Ory soon switched to trombone and by 1911 was leading a popular band in New Orleans. Among his trumpeters during the next eight years were Mutt Carey, King Oliver, and a young Louis Armstrong; his clarinetists included Johnny Dodds, Sidney Bechet, and Jimmie Noone. In 1919 Ory moved to California and in 1922 (possibly 1921) recorded the first two titles by a Black New Orleans jazz band ("Ory's Creole Trombone" and "Society Blues") under the band title of "Spike's Seven Pods of Pepper Orchestra." In 1925 he moved to Chicago, played regularly with King Oliver and recorded many classic sides with Oliver, Louis Armstrong (in his Hot Five and Seven), and Jelly Roll Morton among others.
The definitive New Orleans trombonist of the '20s, Ory (whose "Muskrat Ramble" became a standard) was mostly out of music after 1930, running a chicken ranch with his brother. However, in 1942 he was persuaded to return, and after a stint with Barney Bigard's group, he formed his own band. Ory's group was featured on Orson Welles' radio show in 1944 and the publicity made it possible for the band to catch on. The New Orleans revival was in full swing and Ory (whose group included trumpeter Mutt Carey and clarinetists Omer Simeon or Darnell Howard) was still in prime form. He appeared in the 1946 film *New Orleans* (and later on in *The Benny Goodman Story*) and worked steadily in Los Angeles. After Mutt

Carey departed in 1948, Ory used Teddy Buckner, Marty Marsala, Alvin Alcorn (the perfect musician for his group), and Red Allen on trumpets, and his Dixieland bands always boasted high musicianship (even with the leader's purposely primitive style) and a consistent level of excitement. They recorded regularly (most notably for Good Time Jazz) up to 1960 by which time Ory (already 73) was cutting back on his activities. He retired altogether in 1966, moving to Hawaii. — *Scott Yanow*

Kid Ory (1944-1945) / Aug. 1944-Nov. 1945 / Good Time Jazz ✦✦✦✦
Trombonist Kid Ory led one of the finest and most consistently exciting New Orleans jazz bands of the 1944-60 period. This CD contains 16 selections from 1944-45 when, after a decade out of music, Ory was making what would be a very successful comeback. These studio sides feature veteran trumpeter Mutt Carey and either Omer Simeon or Darnell Howard on clarinet along with a fine rhythm section and Ory's trombone. Highlights include "Blues for Jimmie Noone," "Panama," "Do What Ory Said," "Maryland, My Maryland," "1919 Rag," and "Ory's Creole Trombone." This is fun and often hard-swinging music. — *Scott Yanow*

★ **Creole Jazz Band at Club Hangover** / May 9, 1953-May 16, 1953 / Storyville ✦✦✦✦✦
Ory with Don Ewell (p), Albert Burbank (cl), Ed "Montudie" Garland (b), and others, is captured in remote broadcast. Specialties include "South Rampart Street Parade," "High Society," and "Milneberg Joys." Ewell and Burbank offer some inspired soloing and ensemble work. — *Bruce Raeburn*

This Kid's the Greatest! / Jul. 17, 1953-Jun. 18, 1956 / Good Time Jazz ✦✦✦✦
This CD features selections from some of Kid Ory's finest New Orleans jazz bands, spanning a three-year period; these studio performances never found their way onto the other Good Time Jazz sets. Such excellent players as the colorful cornetist Teddy Buckner (a superior soloist although not as gifted an ensemble player) and his replacement Alvin Alcorn, clarinetists Pud Brown, Bob McCracken, George Probert, and Phil Gomez, pianists Lloyd Glenn, Don Ewell, and Cedric Haywood, bassists Ed Garland, Morty Corb, and Wellman Braud and drummer Minor Hall all make strong contributions on a variety of Dixieland standards including "Milneberg Joys," "Bill Bailey," and "How Come You Do Me Like You Do." Quite spirited and very musical New Orleans jazz. — *Scott Yanow*

Sounds of New Orleans, Vol. 9 / May 8, 1954-Feb. 26, 1955 / Storyville ✦✦✦✦
Although trombonist Kid Ory had formerly used the veteran Mutt Carey and the nearly virtuosic Teddy Buckner as his trumpeters, Alvin Alcorn (who joined The Creole Jazz Band in 1954) proved to be his perfect partner. Alcorn's lyrical but passionate tone was well featured on solos, but it was his ensemble work (building up a song to several climaxes and expertly utilizing dynamics) that made him ideal for this band. This series of broadcasts from Kid Ory's main gig, the Hangover Club in San Francisco, features superior and rather exciting versions of such songs as "Eh, La Bas," "Maryland, My Maryland," "Mahogany Hall Stomp," and "Original Dixieland One-Step." Fans of New Orleans jazz will love this CD. — *Scott Yanow*

★ **Kid Ory's Creole Jazz Band (1954)** / Aug. 9, 1954-Aug. 10, 1954 / Good Time Jazz ✦✦✦✦✦
Although some Kid Ory fans might disagree, the veteran trombonist led his finest bands (at least the ones that recorded) in the '50s. The one heard on this CD is really quite definitive, featuring the brilliant ensemble player (and distinctive soloist) Alvin Alcorn on trumpet, the talented clarinetist George Probert and an excellent rhythm section (pianist Don Ewell, guitarist Bill Newman, bassist Ed Garland, and drummer Minor Hall). Their versions on this set of "That's a Plenty," "Gettysburg March," "Clarinet Marmalade," and even "When the Saints Go Marching In" are true classics of New Orleans jazz. This joyous and exciting music is essential for all serious jazz collections. — *Scott Yanow*

Creole Jazz Band / Nov. 30, 1954-Dec. 2, 1954 / Good Time Jazz ✦✦✦✦
Trombonist Kid Ory, already age 68 at the time of this recording, was at the peak of his powers in the mid-'50s. This particular version of his Creole Jazz Band was one of the finest, featuring trumpeter Alvin Alcorn and clarinetist George Probert, talented soloists who were also superb group players. Alcorn generated a lot of excitement perfectly placing long notes near the end of each ensemble chorus. This Good Time Jazz CD is almost up to the level of its 1954 and 1956 counterparts, highlighted by torrid versions of "Shake That Thing," "Royal Garden Blues," and "Indiana." — *Scott Yanow*

★ **Legendary Kid** / Nov. 22, 1955-Nov. 25, 1955 / Good Time Jazz ✦✦✦✦✦
One of trombonist Kid Ory's greatest recordings, this consistently exciting CD features trumpeter Alvin Alcorn, clarinetist Phil Gomez, and a strong rhythm section that includes bassist Wellman Braud and Ory's longtime drummer Minor Hall. These versions of "Mahogany Hall Stomp," "There'll Be Some Changes Made," "At the Jazz Band Ball," and "Shine" are all gems, giving listeners some of the very best in New Orleans jazz, and showing that the music need not be played haltingly by over-the-hill musicians; one

can capture its spirit and joy without sacrificing musicianship. Every jazz collection should have this music. — *Scott Yanow*

Favorites! / Jun. 1956-Jul.1956 / Good Time Jazz ✦✦✦✦
This single CD contains 15 of the 17 selections performed by Kid Ory's 1956 Creole Jazz Band that were originally issued on a double LP. Trombonist Ory, trumpeter Alvin Alcorn, and clarinetist Phil Gomez make for a very tight but spontaneous frontline, featuring strong melodic solos and exciting ensembles that paid close attention to dynamics and gradually building up the excitement level. New Orleans jazz at its best. Highlights include "Do What Ory Says," "Jazz Me Blues," "Original Dixieland One-Step," "Panama," "Maryland, My Maryland," "1919 Rag," and "Bugle Call Rag." — *Scott Yanow*

Kid Ory Favorites! / Jun. 1956-Jul. 1956 / Good Time Jazz ✦✦✦✦
Trombonist Kid Ory recorded what were arguably his finest recording sessions for Good Time Jazz. This double LP features Ory, trumpeter Alvin Alcorn and clarinetist Phil Gomez (one of his strongest frontlines) on 17 selections that epitomize the best in New Orleans jazz. Highlights include "Do What Ory Says," "Jazz Me Blues," "Original Dixieland One-Step," "Panama," "Maryland, My Maryland," "1919 Rag," and "Bugle Call Rag." Two selections ("Mood Indigo" and "Toot, Toot, Tootsie") have been left off the single-CD reissue. — *Scott Yanow*

Greg Osby

b. Aug. 3, 1960, St. Louis, MO
Sax (Alto) / Avant-Garde, Free Funk
One of the finest talents to emerge in jazz during the '80s, Greg Osby's own recordings are often frustrating to listen to. His chance-taking approach is admirable but mixing rap with jazz (as he occasionally does) is analogous to slabbing bacteria on one's bread! Osby studied jazz at Howard University (1978-80) and attended Berklee. He worked in New York with Woody Shaw, Jon Faddis, Ron Carter, Dizzy Gillespie, and most notably Jack DeJohnette's Special Edition (1985). A member of the so-called M-Base scene (essentially an extension of the free funk of Ornette Coleman's Prime Time), Osby has recorded as a leader for JMT and Blue Note, but some of his finest playing can be heard on Andrew Hill's records. — *Scott Yanow*

● **Greg Osby and the Sound Theatre** / Jun. 1987-Jun. 1987 / JMT ✦✦✦✦
This is Osby's most accomplished ensemble, especially with Michele Rosewoman on piano. — *Ron Wynn*

Man-Talk for Moderns, Vol. 10 / Oct. 1990-Nov. 1990 / Blue Note ✦✦✦

Harold Ousley (Harold Lomax Ousley)

b. Jan. 33, 1929, Chicago, IL
Flute, Saxophone / Blues Jazz, Swing, Soul-Jazz, Groove
A competent funk and soul-jazz saxophonist and flutist, Harold Ousley's bluesy playing on organ combo dates, rock and roll tunes, and backing vocalists was stronger than much of what he did when leading groups. His albums were often uneven, both in terms of compositional quality and playing. Ousley began his professional career in the '40s, and at one point backed Billie Holiday. During the '50s, he played with King Kolax and Gene Ammons and worked in circus bands. Ousley backed Dinah Washington at the 1958 Newport Jazz Festival, an engagement that led to him winning a recording deal. He traveled to Paris the next year with a song revue, then worked with Clark Terry, Howard McGhee, Machito (Frank Grillo Perez), and Joe Newman in the '60s. Ousley began leading his own groups and recording with organ combos, notably Brother Jack McDuff, in the mid-'60s. He worked with Lionel Hampton and Count Basie in the '70s. Ousley currently has no releases available on CD. — *Ron Wynn*

Tenor Sax / 1961 / Bethlehem ✦✦✦

The Kid / Mar. 28, 1972 / Cobblestone ✦✦✦

Sweet Double Hipness / Mar. 28, 1972 / Muse ✦✦✦

★ **The People's Groove** / 1972 / Muse ✦✦✦✦✦
Saxophonist who worked with Dinah Washington. The all-star cast includes Ray McKinney (b), Bobby Rose (g), and Norman Simmons (p). — *Michael G. Nastos*

Makoto Ozone

b. Mar. 25, 1961, Kobe, Japan
Piano / Post-Bop
A premier jazz musician in Japan, Ozone has made a successful transition to America, where he became equally prominent in this nation's improvisational community. He began on organ at four, then took up piano as a teenager. He went to Berklee in 1980 and studied composing and arranging. He was noticed by Gary Burton and later recorded with him and was part of his band. Ozone's striking ability (especially on mid-tempo pieces) and impressive technique made him a big hit at the Kool Jazz Festival. His 1984 debut recording featured Burton and bassist Eddie Gomez. It was a stunning example of complete knowledge and mastery of the full jazz piano spectrum. Ozone later worked with European pianist Michel Petrucciani and spent extensive time studying classical music. — *Ron Wynn*

Now You Know / 1976 / Columbia ✦✦✦

Makoto Ozone / Jun. 23, 1981-Jun. 24, 1981 / Columbia ✦✦✦

After / Oct. 1986 / Columbia ✦✦✦

● **Starlight** / Nov. 1989-Dec. 1989 / JVC ✦✦✦✦

Hot Lips Page (Oran Thaddeus Page)

b. Jan. 27, 1908, Dallas, TX, d. Nov. 5, 1954, New York, NY
Trumpet, Vocals / Blues, Dixieland, Swing
One of the great swing trumpeters and a talented blues vocalist, "Hot Lips" Page's premature passing left a large hole in the jazz world; virtually all musicians (no matter their style) loved him. Page gained early experience in the '20s performing in Texas, playing in Ma Rainey's backup band. He was with Walter Page's Blue Devils during 1928-31 and then joined Bennie Moten's band in Kansas City in time to take part in a brilliant 1932 recording session. Page freelanced in Kansas City and in 1936 was one of the stars in Count Basie's orchestra but, shortly before Basie was discovered, Joe Glaser signed Hot Lips as a solo artist. Although Page's big band did all right in the late '30s (recording for Victor), if he had come east with Basie he would have become much more famous. Page was one of the top sidemen with Artie Shaw's Orchestra in 1941-42 and then mainly freelanced throughout the remainder of his career, recording with many all-star groups and being a welcome fixture at jam sessions. — *Scott Yanow*

★ **The Chronological Hot Lips Page (1938-1940)** / Mar. 10, 1938-Dec. 3, 1940 / Classics ✦✦✦✦✦

Dr. Jazz Series, Vol. 6 / Dec. 21, 1951-Mar. 7, 1952 / Storyville ✦✦✦✦
There are not that many recordings from the later part of Page's career, which makes this CD (comprised of radio broadcasts) of great interest. Page is heard on a variety of Dixieland and swing standards with quite an assortment of all-stars, including cornetist Wild Bill Davison; trombonists Lou McGarity and Sandy Williams; clarinetists Pee Wee Russell, Bob Wilber, Eddie Barefield, Cecil Scott, and Peanuts Hucko; pianists Red Richards, Dick Cary, Joe Sullivan, and Charlie Queener; and drummer George Wettling (who was actually the leader of these groups). Page is in exuberant form, whether singing tunes such as "When My Sugar Walks down the Street" and a riotous "St. Louis Blues" or leading the ensembles. This is one of his best recordings currently available and is often quite exciting. — *Scott Yanow*

Jeff Palmer

b. 1951, Jackson Heights, NY
Organ / Hard Bop
A fine organist who has carved out his own voice from the dominant Jimmy Smith influence, Jeff Palmer started out on accordion. He switched to organ when he was about 15 years old and is completely self-taught, never having been a pianist. Palmer has played with such guitarists as Grant Green, George Benson, John Scofield, and John Abercrombie and recorded as a leader for Statiras, Soul Note, AudioQuest, and Reservoir. — *Scott Yanow*

Ease On / Sep. 1992 / Audioquest ✦✦✦✦

● **Shades of the Pine** / Sep. 14, 1994 / Reservoir ✦✦✦✦
Jeff Palmer is a talented organist whose style (as with virtually all organists) is influenced by Jimmy Smith. For this CD he performs nine similar blues, all of which are given strong solos by the leader, tenor saxophonist Billy Pierce, and guitarist John Abercrombie; drummer Marvin "Smitty" Smith is consistently swinging in support. Despite the sameness of the repertoire (all but Thelonious Monk's "Ba-lue Bolivar Ba-lues-are" are by Palmer), the cooking music holds one's interest and is quite enjoyable. — *Scott Yanow*

Island Universe / Soul Note ✦✦✦✦

Eddie Palmieri

b. Dec. 15, 1936, New York, NY
Piano / Latin Jazz, Latin Continuum, United States
A sometimes dazzling pianist whose technique incorporates bits and pieces of everyone from McCoy Tyner to Herbie Hancock and recycles them through a dynamic Latin groove, Eddie Palmieri has been a Latin jazz and salsa master since the '50s. His approach can be compared to Thelonious Monk's for its unorthodox patterns, odd rhythms, sometimes disjointed phrases, and percussive effects, played in a manner that seems frazzled but is always successfully resolved. It's a free/bebop/Latin blend, with keyboard solos that are never predictable and always stimulating. Palmieri started as a vocalist, but his elder brother, Charlie, influenced him to become a pianist. He began with the neighborhood band of Orlando Marin, then made his professional debut in 1955 with Johnny Sequi's orchestra. After stints with Vicentico Valdes, Pete Terrace, and Tito Rodriguez, Palmieri formed Conjunto La Perfecta in 1962. The group included Barry Rogers, Johnny Pacheco, Manny Oquendo, and George Castro. He developed with Rogers a two-trombone/flute frontline that was a variation on the charanga (flute and violin) style that Palmieri dubbed "trombanga."

The group initially recorded for Alegre, then switched to Tico. They made several albums in the '60s, including two with Cal Tjader, before disbanding due to money problems in 1968. Palmieri worked with the Tico All-Stars and appeared on the Fania All-Stars debut album. He continued recording, working with such players as Alfredo "Chocolate" Armenteros, Israel "Cachao" Lopez, and Justo Betancourt. He made some R&B/Latin "boogaloo" dates, and in the early '70s attracted some R&B and funk interest working with the band Harlem River Drive. Palmieri held concerts at Sing Sing and at the University of Puerto Rico. He began recording for Coco in the mid-'70s and eventually amassed five Grammy awards in the '70s and '80s. Palmieri's productions were elaborate combinations of contemporary Latin, pop, rock and soul, jazz improvisation, Spanish vocals, and Afro-Latin rhythms. He became so popular that even albums he didn't personally like, such as 1976's *Unfinished Masterpiece* on Coco, won Grammys. Every album he issued between 1978 and 1987 was nominated for a Grammy. But Palmieri didn't fare as well with record labels. His superb late '70s album *Lucumi Macumba Voodoo*, recorded for Columbia, was a sales flop despite a huge publicity campaign. Palmieri was later quoted as saying joining Columbia had been a major mistake. He said the same thing about his affiliation with Fania, even though he won a fifth Grammy for the album *La Verdad/The Truth*. Palmieri suffered yet another label disappointment with 1989's *Sueno* on Capitol that included special guest Dave Sanborn. It flopped both sales-wise and aesthetically, as Capitol sought some Latin instrumental filler to plug into the Kenny G./Najee urban contemporary/Quiet Storm market. Palmieri eventually issued another album on Fania in 1990, *EP*. Despite his failure to attain major label success, Eddie Palmieri's artistic triumphs have cemented his place in the Latin jazz, salsa, and international arena. He has very few albums on CD available anywhere except the specialist and mail order route. — *Ron Wynn and Max Salazar*

Mozambique / 1965 / Tico ✦✦✦✦
Eddie Palmieri first hit in the '60s with his classic two-trombone sound. This is one of his finest albums; unassuming, joyous, punchy, and sharp, it has the outstanding Ismael Quintana on vocals and Manny Oquendo on timbales. — *John Storm Roberts*

El Sonido Nuevo / Oct. 1966 / Verve ✦✦✦

★ **Sun of Latin Music** / 1973 / Coco ✦✦✦✦✦
This album almost perfectly combines Palmieri's experimentalism with the devastating swing that kept him ahead on the street. The "Un Dia Bonito" suite got most attention, but "Una Rosa Española," a one-cut mini-history of salsa, is enchanting. — *John Storm Roberts*

Sueno / Mar. 1990 / Intuition ✦✦✦

Arete / 1995 / RMM ✦✦✦✦

● **Unfinished Masterpiece** / Coco ✦✦✦✦
The late-'70s *Unfinished Masterpiece* caused a huge quarrel because he couldn't or wouldn't get it done to his own satisfaction (Coco finally put it out anyway, thus the title). Unfinished or no, it's classic Palmieri from his late Golden Age, and long unavailable. — *John Storm Roberts*

Sentido / Mpl ✦✦✦✦
The Coco Records-era *Sentido* is regarded by some as his greatest album ever. "Puerto Rico" alone would put it hors concours, even without the version of that piano intro in "Adoracion" and the bi-cultural funk of "Condiciones." — *John Storm Roberts*

Verdad: The Truth / Charly ✦✦✦

Salsa-Jazz-Descarga / Mpl ✦✦✦

Vamonos Pa'l Monte / Tico ✦✦✦

Champagne / Tico ✦✦✦✦

Charlie Parker

b. Apr. 29, 1920, Kansas City, d. Mar. 12, 1955, New York, NY
Sax (Alto) / Bop
One of a handful of musicians who can be said to have permanently changed jazz, Charlie Parker("Bird") was arguably the greatest saxophonist of all time. He could play remarkably fast lines that, if slowed down to half speed, would reveal that every note made sense. Bird, along with his contemporaries Dizzy Gillespie and Bud Powell, is considered a founder of bebop; in reality he was an intuitive player who simply was expressing himself. Rather than basing his improvisations closely on the melody as was done in swing, he was a master of chordal improvising, creating new melodies that were based on the structure of a song. In fact Parker wrote several future standards (such as "Anthropology," "Ornithology," "Scrapple from the Apple," and "Ko Ko," along with such blues as "Now's the Time" and "Parker's Mood") that "borrowed" and modernized the chord structures of older tunes. Parker's remarkable technique, fairly original sound, and ability to come up with harmonically advanced phrases that could be both logical and whimsical were highly influential. By 1950 it was impossible to play "modern jazz" with credibility without closely studying Charlie Parker. Charlie Parker grew up in Kansas City, MO. He first played baritone horn before switching to alto. Parker was so

enamored of the rich Kansas City music scene that he dropped out of school when he was 14, even though his musicianship at that point was questionable (with his ideas coming out faster than his fingers could play them). After a few humiliations at jam sessions, Bird worked hard woodshedding over one summer, building up his technique and mastery of the fundamentals. By 1937, when he first joined Jay McShann's Orchestra, he was already a long way toward becoming a major player.

Parker, who was early on influenced by Lester Young and the sound of Buster Smith, visited New York for the first time in 1939, working as a dishwasher at one point so he could hear Art Tatum play on a nightly basis. He made his recording debut with Jay McShann in 1940, creating remarkable solos with a small group from McShann's Orchestra on "Lady Be Good" and "Honeysuckle Rose." When the McShann big band arrived in New York in 1941, Parker had short solos on a few of their studio blues records, and his broadcasts with the orchestra greatly impressed (and sometimes scared) musicians who had never heard his ideas before. Parker, who had met and jammed with Dizzy Gillespie for the first time in 1940, had a short stint with Noble Sissle's band in 1942, played tenor with Earl Hines' sadly unrecorded bop band of 1943, and spent a few months in 1944 with Billy Eckstine's orchestra, leaving before that group made their first records. Gillespie was also in the Hines and Eckstine big bands, and the duo became a team starting in late 1944.

Although Parker recorded with Tiny Grimes' combo in 1944, it was his collaborations with Dizzy Gillespie in 1945 that startled the jazz world. To hear the two virtuosos play rapid unisons on such new songs as "Groovin' High," "Dizzy Atmosphere," "Shaw 'Nuff," "Salt Peanuts," and "Hot House" and then launch into fiery and unpredictable solos could be an upsetting experience for listeners familiar with Glenn Miller and Benny Goodman. Although the new music was evolutionary rather than revolutionary, the recording strike of 1943-44 resulted in bebop arriving fully formed on records, seemingly out of nowhere.

Unfortunately Parker had been a heroin addict ever since he was a teenager, and some musicians who idolized him foolishly took up drugs in the hope that it would elevate their playing to his level. When Gillespie and Parker (known as "Diz and Bird") traveled to Los Angeles and were met with a mixture of hostility and indifference (except by younger musicians who listened closely), it was decided to return to New York. Impulsively Parker cashed in his ticket, ended up staying in Los Angeles, and, after some recordings and performances (including a classic version of "Lady Be Good" with Jazz at the Philharmonic), the lack of drugs (which he combated by drinking an excess of liquor) resulted in a mental breakdown and six months of confinement at the Camarillo State Hospital. Released in January 1947, Parker soon headed back to New York and engaged in some of the most rewarding playing of his career, leading a quintet that included Miles Davis, Duke Jordan, Tommy Potter, and Max Roach. Parker, who recorded simultaneously for the Savoy and Dial labels, was in peak form during the 1947-51 period, visiting Europe in 1949 and 1950 and realizing a lifelong dream to record with strings, starting in 1949, when he switched to Norman Granz's Verve label.

But Charlie Parker, due to his drug addiction and chance-taking personality, enjoyed playing with fire too much. In 1951 his cabaret license was revoked in New York (making it difficult for him to play in clubs) and he became increasingly unreliable. Although he could still play at his best when he was inspired (such as at the 1953 Massey Hall Concert with Gillespie), Bird was heading downhill. In 1954 he twice attempted suicide before spending time in Bellevue. His health, shaken by a very full if brief life of excesses, gradually declined; when he died in March 1955 at the age of 34, he could have passed for 64!

Charlie Parker, a legendary figure during his lifetime, has, if anything, grown in stature since his death. Virtually all of his studio recordings are available on CD, along with a countless number of radio broadcasts and club appearances. Clint Eastwood put together a well intentioned if simplified movie about aspects of his life (*Bird*). Parker's influence, after the rise of John Coltrane, has become more indirect than direct, but jazz would sound a great deal different if Charlie Parker had not existed. The phrase "Bird Lives" (which was scrawled as graffiti after his death) is still true. —*Scott Yanow*

☆ **The Complete "Birth of Bebop"** / May 1940-Dec. 29, 1945 / Stash ✦✦✦✦✦

This is the type of Charlie Parker CD that is essential for Bird collectors but less important to more casual jazz fans. The contents of this set should amaze Parker fanatics: Bird's initial private recording of May 1940 (unaccompanied versions of "Honeysuckle Rose" and "Body and Soul" cut in a private recording booth); four remarkable studio-quality selections from 1942 (including "Cherokee") in which the altoist is backed only by rhythm guitar and quiet drums; rehearsal and jam session numbers from 1943 with Bird on tenor (including an amazing seven-minute version of "Sweet Georgia Brown" by the trio of Parker, trumpeter Dizzy Gillespie, and bassist Oscar Pettiford); and three lengthy cuts from a late-1945 broadcast by Diz and Bird with a sextet. These important recordings fill a major gap,

giving one many clues as to how Charlie Parker sounded before he emerged fully formed on records in 1945. —*Scott Yanow*

Early Bird (1940-1944) / Aug. 1940-1944 / Stash ✦✦✦✦

★ **Complete Savoy Studio Sessions** / Sep. 15, 1944-Sep. 24, 1948 / Savoy ✦✦✦✦✦

This three-CD box set contains all of the recordings Charlie Parker made for the Savoy label, and it is overflowing with gems and an almost countless number of alternate takes. Bird was one of the most important jazzmen of all time, and nearly every note he recorded (in the studios if not live) is well worth hearing. This box starts off with his sideman date with Tiny Grimes in 1944, contains Parker's famous "Ko Ko" session of 1945 (with a young Miles Davis on trumpet and highlighted by "Now's the Time" and "Billie's Bounce"). It continues through his 1947-48 quintet sessions with a more mature Miles Davis; either Bud Powell, John Lewis, or Duke Jordan on piano; bassists Tommy Potter, Curly Russell, or Nelson Boyd; and drummer Max Roach. Together they recorded such classics as "Donna Lee," "Chasin' the Bird," "Milestones," and "Parker's Mood." Every scrap that the great altoist cut for Savoy is in this box. —*Scott Yanow*

☆ **Bird: Complete on Verve** / Jan. 28, 1946-Dec. 10, 1954 / Verve ✦✦✦✦✦

As a leader, Charlie Parker recorded for Savoy and Dial during 1945-48 and then for Verve exclusively (at least in the studios) during 1949-54. This remarkable ten-CD box set, which adds quite a bit of material to an earlier ten-LP set, contains all of these recordings, plus Bird's earlier appearances with Jazz at the Philharmonic. The JATP jams are highlighted by Parker's perfect solo on "Lady Be Good," a ferocious improvisation on "The Closer," and a solo on "Embraceable You" that tops his more famous studio recording. In addition, this box has all of the "Bird and Strings" sides, his meetings with Machito's Cuban orchestra, the 1950 session with Dizzy Gillespie and Thelonious Monk, small-group dates (including a 1951 meeting with Miles Davis), odd encounters with voices and studio bands, the famous "Jam Blues" with fellow altoists Johnny Hodges and Benny Carter, and his final recordings, a set of Cole Porter tunes. The fact-filled 34-page booklet is indispensable. Highly recommended. —*Scott Yanow*

★ **Complete Dial Sessions** / Feb. 5, 1946-Dec. 17, 1947 / Stash ✦✦✦✦✦

Charlie Parker recorded for Dial during the same period he was cutting his better-known sides for Savoy. This four-CD set contains his 89 Dial recordings, including all of the alternate takes. The innovative altoist is heard with Dizzy Gillespie on "Diggin' Diz"; playing definitive versions of "Moose the Mooche," "Yardbird Suite," and "Ornithology" in a septet; struggling during his tragic "Lover Man" date; on excerpts from a poorly recorded live session, backing singer Earl Coleman and interacting with the Erroll Garner Trio; playing his classic "Relaxin' at Camarillo" (four versions); and finally leading several sessions with his classic quintet (which included trumpeter Miles Davis, pianist Duke Jordan, bassist Tommy Potter, and drummer Max Roach) recording such gems as "Dewey Square," "Embraceable You," and "Scrapple from the Apple." The final session adds the great trombonist J.J. Johnson to the group for more classic music. Essential music, highly recommended for all jazz collections. —*Scott Yanow*

Bebop and Bird, Vols. 1 & 2 / 1946 1952 / Rhino ✦✦✦

Here's a 1988 reissue with an intriguing concept, the first of two volumes that collect various cuts from 1946-1952 including Parker and bop elders Miles Davis, Max Roach, and Errol Garner. Great mastering and good selection. —*Ron Wynn*

Bebop & Bird, Vol. 2 / 1946 1952 / Rhino ✦✦✦✦

This is the second volume of '40s and '50s sessions. —*Ron Wynn*

The Dean Benedetti Recordings of Charlie Parker / Mar. 1, 1947-Jul. 1, 1948 / Mosaic ✦✦

The packaging is impeccable, this seven-CD box set has a definitive 48-page booklet, and the recording quality is as good as possible, so why the poor rating? Dean Benedetti, a fanatical Charlie Parker disciple, recorded Bird extensively during three periods in 1947-48 but his best to turn off his wire recorder whenever anyone but Parker was soloing. He became legendary, as did his long lost acetates, and Mosaic has done what it could to make the excerpts coherent; but the results are still unlistenable. None of the performances on this large set is complete; guests such as Thelonious Monk and Carmen McRae are introduced and play or sing two notes and then are cut off. And, although Parker seems to play well, these performances reveal no secrets and add nothing to his legacy. —*Scott Yanow*

★ **Charlie Parker and Stars of Modern Jazz at Carnegie Hall (Christmas 1949)** / Dec. 25, 1949 / Jass ✦✦✦✦✦

This Carnegie Hall concert can be considered the height of the bebop era. Among the top young modernists heard near their early peaks are pianist Bud Powell, trumpeter Miles Davis, baritonist Serge Chaloff, altoist Sonny Stitt, trombonist Kai Winding, tenor saxophonists Stan Getz and Warne Marsh, pianist Lennie Tristano, altoist Lee Konitz, and Sarah Vaughan. But while their performances are consistently oustanding, Charlie Parker and his quintet (which includes trumpeter Red Rodney, pianist Al Haig, bassist Tommy Potter, and drummer Roy Haynes) steal the show. Bird and Rodney rarely sounded more fiery than on their five songs, and Parker's incredible solo on this version of "Ko Ko" might very well be his best. This CD is highly recommended for all collections. —*Scott Yanow*

Bird and Diz / Jun. 6, 1950 / Verve ✦✦✦✦
This session features quite a group: Charlie Parker on alto, trumpeter Dizzy Gillespie, pianist Thelonious Monk, bassist Curly Russell, and drummer Buddy Rich. They perform five Bird originals along with "My Melancholy Baby," and seven alternate takes are included on this CD. This music is available as part of the Verve ten-CD box, but this particular release is enjoyable by itself. Bird and Monk never recorded together otherwise. —*Scott Yanow*

★ **The Greatest Jazz Concert Ever** / May 1953 / Original Jazz Classics ✦✦✦✦✦
The music on this CD features the famous Massey Hall Concert which teamed (for the last time on records) altoist Charlie Parker and trumpeter Dizzy Gillespie, along with pianist Bud Powell, bassist Charles Mingus, and drummer Max Roach. The full quintet performs six of their standards; listen to Bird burn on "Salt Peanuts" as a reaction to Gillespie's clowning. This is timeless and highly recommended music. —*Scott Yanow*

☆ **Charlie Parker with Strings: The Master Takes** / Verve ✦✦✦✦✦

☆ **South of the Border: The Verve Latin-Jazz Sides** / Verve ✦✦✦✦✦

Leo Parker

b. Apr. 18, 1925, Washington, DC, **d.** Feb. 11, 1962, New York, NY
Sax (Baritone) / Bop, Hard Bop
One of the most soulful, as well as skilled, jazz baritonists, Leo Parker unfortunately didn't make many albums or have a lengthy career. But he displayed a sustained excellence and intensity that made his baritone solos memorable. Parker blended the flamboyance and downhome simplicity of blues and R&B with the sophistication of bebop. He initially recorded on alto sax with Coleman Hawkins in 1944. While playing with Billy Eckstine's orchestra in 1944, '45, and '46, Parker switched to baritone. He worked in a group led by Dizzy Gillespie on 52nd Street in 1946, and played briefly in Gillespie's big band. A 1947 recording with Sir Charles Thompson, "Mad Lad," brought Parker some fame and notoriety. He played with Fats Navarro and Illinois Jacquet from 1947 into the '50s, while making his recording debut as a leader for Savoy in 1947. He was most famous for his late '50s Blue Note albums but also did sessions for Columbia and Chess. Parker died of a heart attack in 1962 at 37. There's actually quite a bit of Parker's output available on CD, considering the brevity of his career. —*Ron Wynn*

Back to Back Baritones / 1948-1950 / Collectables ✦✦✦✦
These recordings feature baritone sax work in an early R&B-honker style with some jazz leanings and a small-combo backing. The album's use of multiple and alternate takes will be of particular interest to musicians and collectors. —*Hank Davis*

● **Rollin' with Leo** / Oct. 12, 1961 & Oct. 20, 1961 / Blue Note ✦✦✦✦
Baritonist Leo Parker was in the early stages of a comeback when he recorded this, his second Blue Note album of 1961. He died four months later, at the age of 36. Performing with an obscure cast (trumpeter Dave Burns is the best known of his sidemen), the full-toned baritonist (who was most influenced by Illinois Jacquet and Charlie Parker) is in excellent form on these basic blues, ballads, and jump tunes. —*Scott Yanow*

Horace Parlan

b. Jan. 19, 1931, Pittsburgh, PA
Piano / Hard Bop
Horace Parlan has overcome physical disability to thrive as a pianist. His right hand was partially crippled by polio in his childhood, but Parlan made frenetic, highly rhythmic right-hand phrases part of his characteristic style, contrasting them with striking left hand chords. He's also infused blues and R&B influences in his style, playing in a stark, sometimes somber fashion. Parlan has always cited Ahmad Jamal and Bud Powell as prime influences. He began playing in R&B bands during the '50s, joining Charles Mingus' group from 1957 to 1959 after a move from Pittsburgh to New York. Mingus aided his career enormously, both through his recordings and his influence. Parlan played with Booker Ervin in 1960 and 1961, then in the Eddie "Lockjaw" Davis-Johnny Griffin quintet in 1962. Parlan played with Rahsaan Roland Kirk from 1963 to 1966 and had a strong series of Blue Note recordings in the '60s. He left America for Copenhagen in 1973 and gained international recognition for some stunning albums on SteepleChase, including a pair of superb duet sessions with Archie Shepp. He also recorded with Dexter Gordon, Red Mitchell, and, in the '80s, Frank Foster and Michael Urbaniak. He did sessions in the '80s on Enja and Timeless. —*Ron Wynn*

Movin' and Groovin' / Feb. 29, 1960 / Blue Note ✦✦✦✦
An album of wonderful trio work with Sam Jones and Al Harewood.

Up and Down / Jun. 18, 1961 / Blue Note ✦✦✦✦
Tremendous solos from Booker Ervin and Grant Green, with dynamic and bluesy Parlan piano. —*Ron Wynn*

Back from the Gig / Feb. 15, 1963 / Blue Note ✦✦✦✦
This was later issued under Booker Ervin's name, but it was truly Parlan's date. Ervin's lusty tenor and Parlan's shimmering piano are impressive. —*Ron Wynn*

Happy Frame of Mind / Feb. 15, 1963 / Blue Note ✦✦✦✦
Expatriate pianist on a reissue of one of his best albums, with Booker Ervin. Search for others. —*Michael G. Nastos*

● **Pannonica** / Feb. 11, 1981 / Enja ✦✦✦✦
Good trio session with pianist Horace Parlan working alongside bassist Reggie Johnson and drummer Alvin Queen. The material, mostly standards with some originals and ballads, isn't overly ambitious, but Parlan's dense, strong, blues-influenced solos and good interaction among the three principals keeps things moving. —*Ron Wynn*

Like Someone in Love / Mar. 1983 / SteepleChase ✦✦✦✦

Glad I Found You / Jul. 30, 1984 / SteepleChase ✦✦✦✦
Straightahead blowing date. Eddie Harris almost outdoes Parlan. —*Ron Wynn*

Joe Pass (Joseph Anthony Passalaqua)

b. Jan. 13, 1929, New Brunswick, NJ, **d.** May 23, 1994
Guitar / Bop
Joe Pass did the near-impossible. He was able to play uptempo versions of bop tunes such as "Cherokee" and "How High the Moon" unaccompanied on the guitar. Unlike Stanley Jordan, Pass used conventional (but superb) technique, and his *Virtuoso* series on Pablo still sounds remarkable two decades later.

Joe Pass had a false start in his career. He played in a few swing bands (including Tony Pastor's) before graduating from high school and was with Charlie Barnet for a time in 1947. But after serving in the military, Pass became a drug addict, serving time in prison and essentially wasting a decade. He emerged in 1962 with a record cut at Synanon, made a bit of a stir with his *For Django* set, recorded several other albums for Pacific Jazz and World Pacific, and performed with Gerald Wilson, Les McCann, George Shearing, and Benny Goodman (1973).

However, in general, Pass maintained a low profile in Los Angeles until he was signed by Norman Granz to his Pablo label. *Virtuoso* made him a star in 1973, and he recorded very prolifically for Pablo, unaccompanied, with small groups, on duo albums with Ella Fitzgerald and such masters as Count Basie, Duke Ellington, Oscar Peterson, Milt Jackson, and Dizzy Gillespie. Pass remained very active until his death from cancer. —*Scott Yanow*

Joy Spring / Feb. 6, 1964 / Blue Note ✦✦✦✦
Joe Pass was near the beginning of his career (after a decade of fighting drug addiction) when he recorded the live quartet session included on this CD reissue. The great guitarist was in his early prime, nine years before he started recording for Pablo. Pass is immediately recognizable on the straightahead bebop date and is supported by a fine rhythm section that includes pianist Mike Wofford, bassist Jim Hughart, and drummer Colin Bailey. The group stretches out on five standards (the renditions are six-and-a-half to ten-and-a-half minutes apiece) but never runs out of inventive ideas. Easily recommended. —*Scott Yanow*

★ **Virtuoso, Vol. 1** / Dec. 1973 / Pablo ✦✦✦✦✦
Superior solo performances of well known standards. —*Ron Wynn*

Two for the Road / 1974 / Pablo ✦✦✦

Portraits of Duke Ellington / Jun. 21, 1974 / Pablo ✦✦✦✦
A tremendous set, with Pass paying homage to Ellington. —*Ron Wynn*

Montreux '75 / 1975 / Original Jazz Classics ✦✦✦✦
Outstanding solo guitar by Joe Pass, done at the 1975 Montreux Festival to an appreciative audience. Pass plays with more energy than on his studio works, doing the usual standards, ballads, and mainstream fare, but demonstrating an exuberance and joyful flair that's more understated on most occasions. —*Ron Wynn*

Virtuoso, Vol. 2 / Sep. 14, 1976 & Oct. 26, 1976 / Pablo ✦✦✦✦
The second of Joe Pass' solo guitar albums for Pablo finds the remarkable Pass exploring more recent standards than one might expect. In addition to a few warhorses, there are also "Feelings" (which he somehow manages to make tolerable), "If," two Chick Corea songs ("Five Hundred Miles High" and "Windows"), and even "Giant Steps." Pass' mastery of the guitar is obvious throughout this enjoyable set. —*Scott Yanow*

Montreux '77: Live! / Jul. 1977 / Original Jazz Classics ✦✦✦✦
A CD reissue of a release that was originally included in the Pablo Live series. The digital remastering accents the shadings, voicings, and melodic counterpoint that are Pass' strong points. He's doing familiar material but adding twists and turns that the receptive, aware audience greatly appreciated. —*Ron Wynn*

Northsea Nights / Jul. 1979 / Pablo ✦✦✦✦
Guitarist Joe Pass and bassist Niels Pedersen, a pair of talented virtuosi, are typically outstanding on this live set of standards. With the exception of

their ad-lib "Blues for the Hague," all of the material would qualify as over-done through the years (such as "'Round Midnight" and "Stella by Star-light"), but the duo makes these veteran pieces sound fresh and new again. —*Scott Yanow*

George, Ira and Joe (Joe Pass Loves Gershwin) / Nov. 23, 1981 / Pablo ✦✦✦✦

There aren't many better matches than the lush, innocent songs of George Gershwin and Joe Pass' equally sentimental, spinning guitar phrases embellishing Gershwin's music. Certainly these songs have been done by countless jazz greats, and Pass doesn't necessarily add anything new. But his takes are wonderfully played, and his choices of material are first-rate. —*Ron Wynn*

Appassionato / Aug. 9, 1990-Aug. 11, 1990 / Pablo ✦✦✦✦

Guitarist Joe Pass reunited with the same musicians he had used on his classic 1963 album *For Django* for this relaxed exploration of a dozen jazz standards: rhythm guitarist John Pisano, bassist Jim Hughart, and drum-mer Colin Bailey. Alternating romps with ballads, Pass is in typically fine form throughout, with "Relaxin' at Camarillo," "Red Door," and "That's Earl, Brother" receiving rare revivals. This CD is one of dozens of worthy Joe Pass Pablo recordings. —*Scott Yanow*

Roy Clark and Joe Pass Play Hank Williams / 1994 / Buster Ann Music ✦✦✦✦

Jaco Pastorius (John Francis Pastorius)

b. Dec. 1, 1951, Norristown, PA, **d.** Sep. 21, 1987, Fort Lauderdale, FL
Bass / Fusion, Post-Bop
The Jaco Pastorius story is a tragedy in a music littered with far too many of them, each frustrating and maddening. Pastorius was simply the great-est electric bassist of the jazz-rock/fusion era, an incredibly fast, imagina-tive, and brillant musician and technician, who not only conceived possi-bilities on the instrument no one else considered, but executed them flawlessy. He considered the electric bass a bass guitar and lead, rather than a rhythm/support instrument; even as an accompanist, his lines and phrases had so much depth and form that they stood out within the arrangement. His solos were adventures, performed with a fluidity and harmonic elan that remain unbelievable no matter how many times they're heard. Pastorius knew how good he was, and his personality, cou-pled with repeated drug and alcohol problems, no doubt hastened his demise. "I'm Jaco f-ing Pastorius," was heard far too often at his concerts or in response to quesions from admiring fans about his facility. But there was no faulting his tone or talents. Pastorius accompanied visiting R&B and pop musicians who came to his native Fort Lauderdale when he was in teens. He emerged as a major electric bassist by the mid-'70s, and his work with Pat Metheny attracted so much notice that he was tabbed to join Weather Report in 1976. That long-term role, plus many other sessions, cemented Pastorius' stature within the jazz and rock/pop world. He played with Blood, Sweat and Tears in 1975, and their drummer, Bobby Colomby, helped arrange the session that led to Pastorius' Epic debut as a leader. Pas-torius recorded with Ira Sullivan, Paul Bley, Joni Mitchell, Metheny, and Bireli Lagrene in the '70s and '80s, in addition to his Weather Report duties. He toured with his own group Word of Mouth from 1980 to 1983, record-ing in 1980 with various jazz musicians and in 1982 with a big band. Pas-torius recorded an album in 1983 and 1984 with Brian Melvin. Then he suffered a series of personal reversals and problems that were as monu-mental as his musical talents. There were repeated rumors of sightings in drug-infested inner city hangouts. Pastorius died as a result of injuries suf-fered during a brawl at the Midnight Club in Fort Lauderdale in 1987. Many live performances from his post-Weather Report days have been released posthumously. Bill Milkowski's definitive biography *Jaco* traces the innovative bassist's rise and fall and is well worth picking up. —*Ron Wynn*

Jaco / Jun. 16, 1974 / Improvising Artists ✦✦✦✦

This live recording is quite historic, for it has the earliest documentation of both electric bassist Jaco Pastorius and guitarist Pat Metheny. Recorded by keyboardist Paul Bley for his Improvising Artists label (without the knowl-edge of his sidemen which also included drummer Bruce Ditmas), this CD reissues the same relatively brief program as was on the LP. Metheny is actually a minor figure on this date (the recording quality keeps him from sounding distinctive), but Pastorius' raging solos and heated accompani-ment inspired Bley to make him the leader. The program consists (with one exception) of songs by either Paul or Carla Bley and generally holds one's interest. —*Scott Yanow*

★ **Jaco Pastorius** / Aug. 1976 / Epic ✦✦✦✦✦

Studio group date and first album from this late/great electric bass guitar genius. A must-buy. —*Michael G. Nastos*

Word of Mouth / Dec. 1981 / Warner Bros. ✦✦✦✦

Bassist Jaco Pastorius' Word of Mouth orchestra was an unfulfilled dream, a worthy concept that did not last long enough to live up to its potential. Its debut album was released without a listing of the personnel, so here it is: Wayne Shorter, Michael Brecker, and Tom Scott on reeds; trumpeter Chuck

Findley; the easily recognizable Toots Thielemans on harmonica; Howard Johnson on tuba; drummers Jack DeJohnette and Peter Erskine; and per-cussionist Don Alias. The music ranges from the Beatles' "Blackbird" and some Bach to Pastorius originals that cover straightahead jazz, Coltranish vamps, and fusion. Next to the bassist/leader, Thielemans emerges as the main voice. It's worth checking out but not essential. —*Scott Yanow*

Invitation / Dec. 1983 / Warner Bros. ✦✦✦✦

More big-band music live in Japan. Look for the CD with more tracks. —*Michael G. Nastos*

Honestly: Solo Live / Mar. 1986 / Big World ✦✦✦✦

Bassist Jaco Pastorius' throbbing, booming electric bass lines made him both a celebrity and a marked man during his lifetime. This Italian date caught Pastorius in peak form; both his speed and facility were unequaled, and he truly approached his instrument like a lead guitar, strumming, zip-ping through passages, and executing incredible runs. —*Ron Wynn*

Live in Italy / Mar. 1986 / Jazzpoint ✦✦✦

John Patitucci

Bass / Fusion, Post-Bop
John Patitucci is one of the top bassists of the '90s (on both acoustic and electric); his speed, very clear tone, and versatility are quite impressive. He started playing bass when he was 11 years old, growing up in Northern California, and in 1978 moved near Los Angeles. He played with Gap Man-gione (1979) while going to college and during 1982-85 worked in Los Angeles with Tom Scott, Robben Ford, Stan Getz, Larry Carlton, Dave Grusin, Ernie Watts, and Freddie Hubbard, in addition to becoming a stu-dio musician. In 1985 he gained a high profile when he joined Chick Corea as a regular member of both the Elektric and Akoustic bands. Patitucci toured and recorded extensively with Corea and has made a series of his own diverse sessions for GRP and Stretch (although he is not as strong a composer as he is a bassist). John Patitucci left the Elektric Band in the early '90s but has continued working with Corea on an occasional basis. —*Scott Yanow*

● **Heart of the Bass** / 1991 / Stretch ✦✦✦✦

Fusion standout John Patitucci flashes the speed and facility that made him the darling of the contemporary jazz set. He's joined by the man whose band has showcased him, pianist Chick Corea, plus percussionist Alex Acuna and other guest stars. The songs are pretty routine, but Patitucci and Corea's performances elevate them. —*Ron Wynn*

Another World / 1993 / GRP ✦✦✦✦

John Patitucci has quickly developed into one of the world's great bassists, both acoustic and electric. He is not on the same level as a composer but is steadily improving, as witness the music on this fine release. There are many bass solos, as one would expect (Patitucci's high-note flights often sound like a guitar), but he does leave space for his sidemen, most notably keyboardist John Beasley (who has two numbers without the bassist), trumpeter Jeff Beal, and one selection apiece for the steel drums of Andy Narell and Mike Brecker's tenor. A few tracks are throwaway funk, but there are enough twists and unusual improvisations to make this a recommended disc even for adventurous listeners. —*Scott Yanow*

Mistura Fina / Jun. 23, 1994-Aug. 20, 1994 / GRP ✦✦✦

Don Patterson (Donald B. Patterson)

b. Jul. 22, 1936, Columbus, OH, **d.** Feb. 10, 1988
Organ / Soul-Jazz, Hard Bop, Groove
Columbus, OH, born Don Patterson began his musical career as a pianist, inspired by Erroll Garner. A solid soul, jazz, blues, and hard bop organist with a pianistic background, Patterson didn't use the pedals or play with as much rhythmic drive as some other stylists, but developed a satisfactory alternative approach. Patterson's organ solos were smartly played, and more melodic than explosive. He switched from piano in 1956 after hear-ing Jimmy Smith. Patterson made his organ debut in 1959 and worked with Sonny Stitt, Eddie "Lockjaw" Davis, Gene Ammons, and Wes Mont-gomery in the early '60s. He recorded with Ammons, Stitt, and Eric Kloss in the early and mid-'60s. Patterson worked often in a duo with Billy James and made several recordings in the '60s and '70s as a leader. He and Al Grey worked together extensively in the '80s. Patterson recorded as a leader for Prestige and Muse. He has one session available on CD. —*Ron Wynn and Michael G. Nastos*

Goin' Down Home / Jan. 22, 1963 / Cadet ✦✦✦✦

Trio with Patterson on the Hammond B-3, Paul Weeden on guitar, and Billy James on drums. Includes the Nat Adderley tune "Worksong." —*Michael Erlewine*

The Exciting New Organ of Don Patterson / May 12, 1964 / Prestige ✦✦✦✦

Great album with Booker Ervin on tenor sax. —*Michael Erlewine*

● **Dem New York Blues** / Jun. 5, 1968 & Jun. 2, 1969 / Prestige ✦✦✦✦

Despite claims to the contrary, organist Don Patterson was very much of the Jimmy Smith school, a hard-driving player with fine improvising skills but lacking a distinctive sound of his own. This CD (which reissues two complete LPs) features Patterson in prime form in a quintet with trumpeter Blue Mitchell, Junior Cook on tenor, and guitarist Pat Martino, and with a separate group that features trumpeter Virgil Jones and both George Coleman and Houston Person on tenors. Although "Oh Happy Day" is a throwaway, Patterson's spirited renditions of the blues and standards make this a fairly definitive example of his talents. —*Scott Yanow*

The Return Of . . . / Oct. 30, 1972 / Muse ++++
Quartet with Eddie Daniels, Ted Dunbar, and Freddie Waits. Any Don Patterson album is worthwhile. —*Michael G. Nastos*

The Genius of the B-3 / Oct. 30, 1972 / Muse ++++
A fine album (fast and slow) with Patterson in excellent form. There is some very nice soul-jazz here. CD clocks out at 43 minutes. —*Michael Erlewine*

These Are Soulful Days / Sep. 17, 1973 / Muse ++++
Quartet with this great Hammond B-3 organist, Jimmy Heath, Pat Martino, and A. Heath. —*Michael G. Nastos*

Movin' Up / Jan. 31, 1976 / Muse ++++
Competent, sometimes animated soul-jazz from organist Don Patterson. Although not as blues-oriented as Jimmy McGriff or Jack McDuff, nor as ambitious as Charles Earland, Patterson plays catchy, clever tunes with good solos and interesting rhythm hooks. —*Ron Wynn*

Big John Patton

b. Jul. 12, 1935, Kansas City, MO
Organ / Soul-Jazz, Hard Bop, Groove
John Patton was born in Kansas City in 1935. A first-rate soul, jazz, and blues organist, Big John Patton's dates are among the most danceable, funky, and exuberant ever done at Blue Note. He wasn't as adventurous as Larry Young, but matched any organist for sheer energy and rousing fervor. Patton played piano in the late '40s and toured with Lloyd Price in the mid- and late '50s. He began playing organ in the '60s, and recorded with Lou Donaldson from 1962 to 1964. Patton also did sessions with Harold Vick, Johnny Griffin, Grant Green, and Clifford Jordan in the '60s, while doing his own dates with a trio. At various times Clifford Jarvis and James "Blood" Ulmer were members of Patton's trio. Bobby Hutcherson, Junior Cook, Blue Mitchell, Vick, and Richard Williams served as special guests on different sessions. Patton recorded with Johnny Lytle in 1977 and 1983. In obscurity during the '70s when the Hammond organ was overshadowed by electric pianos and synthesizers, Patton's career was revived in the '80s, thanks in part to John Zorn's singing his praises and using him on some recordings. Many of Patton's earlier recordings are now available on CD. —*Ron Wynn and Scott Yanow*

Blue John / Jul. 11, 1963-Aug. 2, 1963 / Blue Note ++++
This is a fairly bright bit of soul-jazz, not quite as heavy as your normal soul-jazz session. There is nice guitar by Grant Green. The trumpet of Tommy Turrentine and the stritch (two saxophones braced together) of George Braith are not your usual soul-jazz instruments. The dual-horn sound of the stritch ends up sounding too much like honking car horns for my taste. It is hard to stay in the groove in the middle of the freeway. But any John Patton is worth having. —*Michael Erlewine*

Oh Baby / Mar. 8, 1965 / Blue Note +++
Patton's fourth album for Blue Note. Big John Patton with Grant Green on guitar and Harold Vick on tenor sax. With tunes like "Fat Judy" and "Good Juice," there is no worry about a groove. The addition of a trumpet (Blue Mitchell) means you have a horn section, and this tends to be a little much now and again. Although a little on the light side, thanks to Patton and Green, the groove does go down. —*Michael Erlewine*

★ **Let 'em Roll** / Dec. 11, 1965 / Blue Note +++++
Patton with Grant Green (guitar), Otis Finch (drums), and Bobby Hutcherson (vibes). Green provides superb assistance. While vibes is not a usual instrument for soul-jazz sessions, this album works anyway, and the groove is established. Grant Green and Patton are just a great combination. —*Michael Erlewine*

Boogaloo / Aug. 9, 1968 / Blue Note +++
Big John Patton with a trumpet and sax, drums, and conga. Harold Alexander (sax) plays a little out for a standard soul-jazz session and the combination of the horns amounts to what it should be—a horn section. For me, this never gets down to the business of being soul music. The groove is weak or not there. —*Michael Erlewine*

Understanding / Oct. 25, 1968 / Blue Note ++
Patton with saxman Harold Alexander and drums. Alexander is playing sax that is just a tad too "out" for an organ combo than is standard for soul-jazz, thus turning the sound toward something other than a real groove. If you like progressive sax, you might be able to stay in the groove. —*Michael Erlewine*

Memphis To New York Spirit / 1969 / Blue Note ++
Although it was scheduled for release two times, *Memphis to New York Spirit* didn't appear until 1996, more than 25 years after it was recorded.

The album includes the contents of two separate sessions—one recorded in 1970 with guitarist James "Blood" Ulmer, drummer Leroy Williams, and saxophonist/flautist Marvin Cabell; the other recorded in 1969 with Cabell, Williams, and saxophonist George Coleman—that were very similiar in concept and execution. Patton leads his combo through a selection of originals and covers that range from Wayne Shorter and McCoy Tyner to the Meters. Though the group is rooted in soul-jazz, they stretch the limits of the genre on these sessions, showing a willingness to experiment, while still dipping into the more traditional blues and funk reserves. Consequently, *Memphis to New York Spirit* doesn't have a consistent groove like some other Patton records, but when it does click, the results are remarkable; it's a non-essential but worthy addition to a funky soul-jazz collection. —*Stephen Thomas Erlewine*

Blue Planet Man / Apr. 12, 1993-Apr. 13, 1993 / Evidence +++

Gary Peacock

b. May 12, 1935, Burley, ID
Bass / Post-Bop
A subtle but adventurous bassist, Gary Peacock's flexibility and consistently creative ideas have been an asset to several important groups. He was originally a pianist, playing in an Army band while stationed in Germany in the late '50s. Peacock switched to bass in 1956, staying in Germany after his discharge to play with Hans Koller, Attila Zoller, Tony Scott, and Bud Shank. In 1958 he moved to Los Angeles, where he performed with Barney Kessel, Don Ellis, Terry Gibbs, Shorty Rogers, and (most importantly) Paul Bley. After moving to New York in 1962, Peacock worked with Bill Evans (1962-63), the Paul Bley trio, Jimmy Giuffre, Roland Kirk, and George Russell. In 1964, after a brief stint with Miles Davis, Peacock started an association with Albert Ayler in Europe, also playing with Roswell Rudd and Steve Lacy. Peacock alternated between Ayler and Paul Bley for a time and returned briefly to Miles Davis in the late '60s. After a period in Japan (1969-72), Peacock studied biology (1972-76), worked with Bley, and off and on from the late '70s has played (and recorded) in a trio with Keith Jarrett and Jack DeJohnette. —*Scott Yanow*

Tethered Moon / Nov. 1991 / Evidence ++++

● **Oracle** / May 1993 / ECM ++++
This set of duets by bassist Gary Peacock and guitarist Ralph Towner, as one might expect from an ECM album, makes expert use of space and has its quiet moments. But there is a surprising amount of ferocious interplay between the two musicians. They may play at a consistently low volume, but the set of originals has a few rather passionate grooves and a little more energy than one would have predicted. —*Scott Yanow*

Duke Pearson (Columbus Calvin Pearson, Jr.)

b. Aug. 17, 1932, Atlanta, GA, d. Aug. 4, 1980, Atlanta, GA
Piano / Hard Bop
A good pianist who later became a producer and A&R assistant, Duke Pearson was a fine bebop player during the '50s and early '60s, providing nicely constructed solos on many dates. He was a crafty, rather than dazzling, player, as well as a fine composer and arranger. Jordan studied piano and several brass instruments in his youth, then chose piano because problems with his teeth eliminated the trumpet. He worked in the South as a pianist during the mid- and late '50s, then moved to New York. Pearson worked regularly with Donald Byrd and Pepper Adams, and Byrd recorded Pearson's seminal compositions "Cristo Redentor" and "Jeannine." He was briefly in the Jazztet in 1960, and served as Nancy Wilson's accompanist in 1961. Pearson produced many sessions for Blue Note from 1963 to 1970, and co-formed a big band with Byrd. He soon had sole leadership duties, and the Duke Pearson Big Band dueled the Thad Jones-Mel Lewis Orchestra from the late '60s until 1970. Adams, Lew Tabackin, Randy Brecker, Joe Shepley, and Garnett Brown were regular members, and the band provided a forum for Pearson's compositions. He taught at Clark in 1971, then re-formed the big band in 1972. Pearson toured with Carmen McRae in 1972 and 1973; he battled multiple sclerosis in the late '70s, which severely limited his playing. The former husband of jazz vocalist Sheila Jordan, Pearson also accompanied Dakota Staton and Joe Williams. He recorded for Prestige, Polydor, and Atlantic, in addition to Blue Note. —*Ron Wynn and Michael G. Nastos*

Dedication / Aug. 2, 1961 / Prestige ++++
This is among Pearson's finest 60s sessions. Includes sterling solos by Freddie Hubbard and Pepper Adams. —*Ron Wynn*

● **Wahoo** / Nov. 24, 1964 / Blue Note ++++
From the late pianist/composer/arranger and A&R man, Pearson. Many others by him are as excellent. Find this one and as many others as you can. —*Michael G. Nastos*

Sweet Honey Bee / Dec. 7, 1966 / Blue Note ++++
Pianist/composer Duke Pearson leads an all-star group on this runthrough of seven of his compositions. The musicians (trumpeter Freddie Hubbard, altoist James Spaulding, tenorman Joe Henderson, bassist Ron Carter, drummer Mickey Roker, and the pianist/leader) are actually more

impressive than many of the compositions, although the swinging minor-toned "Big Bertha" deserved to become a standard. The frameworks are quite intelligent, and the improvisations are concise and clearly related to each tune's melody and mood. Although not quite essential, this CD reissue has some rewarding music. — *Scott Yanow*

★ **The Right Touch** / Sep. 13, 1967 / Blue Note ✦✦✦✦✦
Duke Pearson rises to the challenge of writing for an all-star octet (with trumpeter Freddie Hubbard, trombonist Garnett Brown, altoist James Spaulding, Jerry Dodgion on alto and flute, Stanley Turrentine heard on tenor, bassist Gene Taylor, drummer Grady Tate, and the leader/pianist) contributing colorful frameworks and consistently challenging composi-tions. The set is full of diverse melodies (the CD reissue has a previously unissued take of "Los Malos Hombres") played by a variety of distinctive soloists; many of these songs deserve to be revived. This is one of the finest recordings of Duke Pearson's career. — *Scott Yanow*

Introducing Duke Pearson's Big Band / Dec. 1967 / Blue Note ✦✦✦✦
With larger ensemble and great compositions. — *Michael G. Nastos*

☆ **Now Hear This!** / Dec. 2, 1968-Dec. 3, 1968 / Blue Note ✦✦✦✦✦
A worthy blend of civil rights advocacy and hard-bop dialogs with Pepper Adams, Frank Foster, and a surprising Randy Brecker. — *Ron Wynn*

I Don't Care Who Knows It / 1968 / Blue Note ✦✦

Ken Peplowski

b. May 23, 1959, Cleveland, OH
Clarinet, Sax (Tenor) / Dixieland, Swing
One of the top clarinetists of the '90s and a very talented tenor player, Ken Peplowski has helped keep the tradition of small-group swing (and occa-sionally Dixieland) alive. He made his professional debut at ten and played locally in Cleveland. After spending 1978-80 touring with the Tommy Dorsey ghost orchestra (directed by Buddy Morrow), Peplowski settled in New York, freelanced in a variety of settings, and played with Benny Good-man. By 1987 he was a Concord artist and has since recorded frequently for that label, backing Mel Tormé and Rosemary Clooney and leading his own sets, including brilliant duets with guitarist Howard Alden. — *Scott Yanow*

★ **Concord Duo Series, Vol.** / Dec. 1992 / Concord Jazz ✦✦✦✦✦

Steppin' with Peps / Mar. 1993 / Concord Jazz ✦✦✦✦
Ken Peplowski is in top form on this consistently exciting swing-based release. Whether playing clarinet (where his Benny Goodman influence is touched by the coolness of Tony Scott) or romping on tenor (mixing Don Byas with touches of Paul Gonsalves), Peplowski excels throughout this well planned, yet spontaneous, session. The dozen performances have many highlights, including the interplay of Peplowski and guitarist Howard Alden on "The Courtship," a very beautiful version of "Lotus Blos-som" (with Joe Wilder's lyrical trumpet), a hot version of "The Lady's in Love with You," and a reasonably "free" version of Ornette Coleman's "Turn Around." Trumpeters Randy Sandke and Joe Wilder appear on sev-eral numbers, and the rhythm section (with Alden, pianist Ben Aronov, bassist John Goldsby, and drummer Alan Dawson) is excellent; but Ken Peplowski emerges as the main star on this memorable set. — *Scott Yanow*

Live / 1994 / Concord Jazz ✦✦✦✦

It's a Lonesome Old Town / 1995 / Concord Jazz ✦✦✦✦

Art Pepper

b. Sep. 1, 1925, Gardenia, CA, d. Jun. 1, 1982
Sax (Alto) / Bop, Cool, Post-Bop
Despite a remarkably colorful and difficult life, Art Pepper was quite con-sistent in the recording studios; virtually every recording he made is well worth getting. In the '50s he was one of the few altoists (along with Lee Konitz and Paul Desmond) able to develop his own sound despite the dominant influence of Charlie Parker. During his last years Pepper seemed to put all of his life's experiences into his music, and he played with startling emotional intensity.
After a brief stint with Gus Arnheim, Pepper played with mostly Black groups on Central Avenue in Los Angeles. He spent a little time in the Benny Carter and Stan Kenton orchestras before serving in the military (1944-46). Some of Pepper's happiest days were during his years with Stan Kenton (1947-52), although he became a heroin addict in that period. The '50s found the altoist recording frequently both as a leader and a sideman, resulting in at least two classics (*Plays Modern Jazz Classics* and *Meets the Rhythm Section*), but he also spent two periods in jail for drug offenses during 1953-56. Pepper was in top form during his Contemporary record-ings of 1957-60, but the first half of his career ended abruptly with long prison sentences that dominated the '60s. His occasional gigs between jail terms found him adopting a harder tone, influenced by John Coltrane, that disturbed some of his longtime followers. He recorded with Buddy Rich in 1968 before getting seriously ill and rehabilitating at Synanon (1969-71). Art Pepper began his serious comeback in 1975, and the unthinkable hap-pened. Under the guidance and inspiration of his wife, Laurie, Pepper not

only recovered his former form but topped himself with intense solos that were unique; he also enjoyed occasionally playing clarinet. His recordings for Contemporary and Galaxy rank with the greatest work of his career. Pepper's autobiography *Straight Life* (written with his wife) is a brutally honest book that details his sometimes horrifying life. When Art Pepper died at the age of 57, he had attained his goal of becoming the world's great altoist. — *Scott Yanow*

Surf Ride / Feb. 7, 1952-Dec. 24, 1953 / Savoy Jazz ✦✦✦

Art Pepper Quartet, Vol. 1, with the Sonny Clark Trio / May 31, 1953 / Time Is ✦✦✦

☆ **The Complete Pacific Jazz Small Group Recordings of Art Pepper** / Jul. 26, 1956-Aug. 12, 1957 / Mosaic ✦✦✦✦✦
This superior three-LP box set reissues all of altoist Art Pepper's small-group dates for the Pacific Jazz label. Virtually all of the music has since been reissued on CD (part of it as *The Artistry of Pepper* and part of it under trumpeter Chet Baker's name), but the Mosaic box, which has an attractive booklet, is the definitive treatment of this chapter in Pepper's musical story. The great altoist is heard in a sextet with Baker and tenor saxophonist Richie Kamuca, on a version of "Tenderly" with Chet Baker's big band, with Baker and tenor Phil Urso in a different sextet, sharing the spotlight with tenor saxophonist Bill Perkins in a quintet, and heading a nonet playing arrangements by Shorty Rogers. The music is very much in the cool/bop tradition, but Art Pepper is instantly recognizable (he never sounded that much like Charlie Parker), and even at this early stage, he was at the top of his form. All 26 performances are quite enjoyable and swinging, making this hard-to-find set worth the search. — *Scott Yanow*

The Way It Was / Nov. 26, 1956-Nov. 23, 1960 / Original Jazz Classics ✦✦✦✦
Despite his very erratic lifestyle, altoist Art Pepper never made a bad record. This collection is better than most. The first four titles team Pepper with tenor saxophonist Warne Marsh, pianist Ronnie Ball, bassist Ben Tucker, and drummer Gary Frommer for generally intriguing explorations of four standards. One can feel the influence of Lennie Tristano (with Pep-per in Lee Konitz's place), although Pepper had his own sound and a more hard-swinging style. The success of the Pepper-Marsh frontline makes one wish that they had recorded together again. The other three selections are leftovers from a trio of classic Pepper albums, and all are quite worthwhile. Pepper is heard backed by three separate rhythm sections, which include pianists Red Garland, Dolo Coker or Wynton Kelly; either Paul Chambers or Jimmy Bond on bass; and Philly Joe Jones, Frank Butler or Jimmie Cobb on drums. Overall this album sticks to bop standards and finds Art Pepper in top form. — *Scott Yanow*

● **The Artistry of Pepper** / Dec. 11, 1956-Aug. 12, 1957 / Pacific Jazz ✦✦✦✦
This CD starts off with four selections from a date led by tenor saxophonist Bill Perkins that features altoist Art Pepper; the remainder of the quintet is comprised of pianist Jimmy Rowles, bassist Ben Tucker, and Mel Lewis. While they perform boppish versions of two standards and a pair of Pepper originals, the remainder of the CD has a particularly strong set that show-cases Pepper in a nonet arranged by Shorty Rogers. The music in the latter date is all Rogers originals, and there are alternate takes of "Diablo's Dance" and "Popo" to round out the program. The other soloists include trum-peter Don Fagerquist, Bill Holman on tenor, baritonist Bud Shank, valve trombonist Stu Williamson, and pianist Russ Freeman. Highly recom-mended to fans of Art Pepper and West Coast jazz. — *Scott Yanow*

★ **Meets the Rhythm Section** / Jan. 19, 1957 / Original Jazz Classics ✦✦✦✦✦
This is one of Art Pepper's greatest recordings. Although he was reportedly nervous to be playing with Miles Davis' rhythm section (pianist Red Gar-land, bassist Paul Chambers, and drummer Philly Joe Jones), the altoist is quite inspired on the nine high-quality tunes. In addition to some bop stan-dards, this album introduces Pepper's "Straight Life," recasts the Dixieland tune "Jazz Me Blues" in a modern setting, and includes Pepper's "Waltz Me Blues." The combination of musicians works very well, making this one of the top jazz albums of a great jazz year, 1957. — *Scott Yanow*

★ **Art Pepper + Eleven: Modern Jazz Classics** / Mar. 14, 1959-May 11, 1959 / Original Jazz Classics ✦✦✦✦✦
This is a true classic. Altoist Art Pepper is joined by an 11-piece band play-ing Marty Paich arrangements of a dozen jazz standards from the bop and cool jazz era. Trumpeter Jack Sheldon has a few solos, but the focus is very much on the altoist, who is in peak form. The CD reissue adds two addi-tional versions of "Walkin'" and one of "Donna Lee" to the original pro-gram. Throughout, Pepper sounds quite inspired by Paich's charts, which feature the band as an active part of the music rather than just in the back-ground. Highlights of this highly enjoyable set include "Move," "Four Brothers," "Shaw Nuff," "Anthropology," and "Donna Lee," but there is not a single throwaway track to be heard. Essential music for all serious jazz collections. — *Scott Yanow*

Modern Jazz Classics / Mar. 14, 1959-May 12, 1959 / Mobile Fidelity ✦✦✦✦
Another outstanding Art Pepper late '50s album, although in a different

style. Pepper was backed by an 11-piece orchestra and applied his torrid solos to works that were arranged by Marty Paich. This has been issued both as *Modern Jazz Classics* on CD and as *Modern Jazz Classics: Art Pepper Plus Eleven* on vinyl. —*Ron Wynn*

Gettin' Together / Feb. 29, 1960 / Original Jazz Classics ✦✦✦
As a sort of follow-up to Art Pepper's matchup with Miles Davis' trio in the 1957 classic *Art Pepper Meets the Rhythm Section*, Pepper uses Davis' sidemen on this 1960 near-classic. In addition to pianist Wynton Kelly, bassist Paul Chambers, and drummer Jimmy Cobb, trumpeter Conte Candoli makes the group a quintet on four of the eight numbers. The CD reissue adds "The Way You Look Tonight" (formerly available only on another LP) and an alternate take of the title cut to the original repertoire. This time around, rather than emphasizing standards, Pepper performs just three ("Softly, As in a Morning Sunrise," Thelonious Monk's "Rhythm-A-Ning," and "The Way You Look Tonight") and includes three originals of his own: "Diane," "Bijou the Poodle," and "Gettin' Together." The music is all very straightahead and bop-oriented, but as usual, Pepper brings something personal and unique to his playing; he sounds like no one else. —*Scott Yanow*

Smack Up / Oct. 24, 1960-Oct. 25, 1960 / Original Jazz Classics ✦✦✦
The title of this recording (which has been reissued on CD with two takes of the otherwise unknown "Solid Citizens" added) is ironic and inadvertently truthful. Within a short period, Art Pepper would begin spending many years in jail due to his heroin addiction; this was his next-to-last album of this period. Despite the bleak future, the great altoist (who never seemed to make an uninspired record during his unstable life) is in excellent form in a quintet with trumpeter Jack Sheldon, pianist Pete Jolly, bassist Jimmy Bond, and drummer Frank Butler. Highlights of this fine album include Harold Land's title cut, the 5/4 blues "Las Cuevas De Mario," and Ornette Coleman's "Tears Inside." —*Scott Yanow*

Intensity / Nov. 23, 1960-Nov. 25, 1960 / Original Jazz Classics ✦✦✦
This album, reissued on CD with an additional song, "Fine Points," was altoist Art Pepper's final one of his early period and was released when he was already serving a long prison sentence due to his heroin addiction. Assisted by pianist Dolo Coker, bassist Jimmy Bond, and drummer Frank Butler, Pepper was just starting to show the influence of John Coltrane and Ornette Coleman in his style, freeing up his playing and displaying a greater intensity during his improvisations. Ironically, Pepper sticks to swinging standards such as "I Can't Believe That You're in Love with Me," "Gone with the Wind," and "I Wished on the Moon" as points of departure on the interesting and largely enjoyable set. Excluding a 1973 recording with Mike Vax' big band, it would be 15 years before Art Pepper led another record date in the studios. —*Scott Yanow*

Living Legend / Aug. 9, 1975 / Original Jazz Classics ✦✦✦
Art Pepper, one of the major bop altoists to emerge during the '50s, started his comeback with this excellent set. After 15 years of prison time and fighting drug addiction, Pepper was finally ready to return to jazz. Accompanied by three of his old friends (pianist Hampton Hawes, bassist Charlie Haden, and drummer Shelly Manne), Pepper displays a more exploratory and darker style than he had previously. He also shows a greater emotional depth in his improvisations and is open to some of the innovations of the avant-garde in his search for greater self-expression. Although this recording would be topped by the ones to come, the music (five Pepper originals and an intense version of "Here's That Rainy Day") is quite rewarding. —*Scott Yanow*

● **The Trip** / Sep. 15, 1976 & Sep. 16, 1976 / Original Jazz Classics ✦✦✦
Although some listeners prefer altoist Art Pepper's playing of the '50s, when he re-emerged in 1975 there was a much greater emotional intensity to his improvisations, and his solos used a wider vocabulary with nonmusical and emotional sounds being added to his ideas as punctuation. This strong quartet date (with pianist George Cables, bassist David Williams, and drummer Elvin Jones) finds Pepper performing Michel Legrand's "The Summer Knows," lesser-known tunes by Woody Shaw and Joe Gordon, and three originals of his own; the CD reissue also has an alternate take of "The Trip." Powerful music. —*Scott Yanow*

A Night in Tunisia / Jan. 23, 1977 / Storyville ✦✦✦

No Limit / Mar. 26, 1977 / Original Jazz Classics ✦✦✦
Art Pepper's third recording in his comeback years was recorded in a studio but has the emotional intensity and chance-taking improvisations of his live concerts of the period. Joined by his regular group (pianist George Cables, bassist Tony Dumas, and drummer Carl Burnett), Pepper performs lengthy versions of three of his originals (including the modal "My Laurie") and "Ballad of the Sad Young Men." "Mambo de la Pinta" is a little unusual, because Pepper overdubbed himself on tenor to join his alto in the ensembles. Throughout this album (and during his final ten years), Art Pepper played every note as if it might be his last one. The passion displayed on this particular album is reason enough to acquire it. —*Scott Yanow*

Thursday Night at the Village Vanguard / Jul. 28, 1977 / Original Jazz Classics ✦✦✦
Art Pepper's appearances at the Village Vanguard in 1977 were a major

success, making the brilliance of the West Coast-based altoist obvious to the New York critics. His historical stint at the Vanguard was originally made available on four LPs (all reissued as CDs with one additional selection on each disc) and more recently in expanded form as a nine-CD box set. The single CD reissue of the Thursday night portion features the great altoist on lengthy versions of "Valse Triste," a particularly passionate version of "Goodbye," "Blues for Les," "My Friend John," and "Blues for Heard." In addition to Pepper, his trio—pianist George Cables, bassist George Mraz, and drummer Elvin Jones—is also in top form, and the music is consistently stimulating and emotional. —*Scott Yanow*

More for Less / Jul. 28, 1977-Jul. 30, 1977 / Original Jazz Classics ✦✦✦
These CD reissues are taken from Art Pepper's three nights at the Village Vanguard in July 1977, as with the other releases, adds one selection ("Scrapple from the Apple") to the music of the original LP; all of the performances on this and the other sets have since been made available as part of a massive nine-CD box set. The great altoist was clearly excited to be playing at the famous New York club, and his rhythm section—pianist George Cables, bassist George Mraz, and drummer Elvin Jones—consistently stimulated his imagination. This release has more variety than usual, for in addition to his alto playing (including a memorable unaccompanied solo on "Over the Rainbow"), Pepper switches to clarinet for the lengthy "More for Les" and interprets the ballad "These Foolish Things" on tenor. The nine-CD set is essential for Art Pepper fanatics, but those just wanting a taste of the great altoist's talents will be satisfied with this release. —*Scott Yanow*

Friday Night at the Village Vanguard / Jul. 29, 1977 / Original Jazz Classics ✦✦✦
The releases here are taken from altoist Art Pepper's very successful stint at the Village Vanguard in July 1977 has been reissued on CD with one extra track, "A Night in Tunisia." Pepper, who is greatly assisted by a highly sympathetic rhythm section (pianist George Cables, bassist George Mraz, and drummer Elvin Jones), is at his best on "Caravan," which finds him doubling on tenor, and on an intense rendition of "But Beautiful." All of this music is currently available as part of a massive nine-CD box set that really documents the historic engagement. —*Scott Yanow*

Saturday Night at the Village Vanguard / Jul. 30, 1977 / Original Jazz Classics ✦✦✦
The CD reissue of this release, of the sets that document Art Pepper's well received engagement at the Village Vanguard, adds "For Freddie" to the original three-song program. The other selections, which feature pianist George Cables, bassist George Mraz, and drummer Elvin Jones in addition to the altoist/leader, are intense interpretations of "You Go to My Head," Pepper's "The Trip," and a 16-minute version of "Cherokee." The altoist was entering his peak period, and the entire gig has been fully documented on a massive nine-CD box set. —*Scott Yanow*

☆ **Complete Galaxy Recordings** / Dec. 1, 1978-Apr. 14, 1982 / Galaxy ✦✦✦✦✦
Altoist Art Pepper was at the height of his career during his final five years. He was a brilliant improviser in the '50s, but by the late '70s the many dark experiences he had had in life were reflected in a deep emotional intensity in his playing. He played each solo as if it might be his last, and his passion was brutally honest. This giant 16-CD Galaxy set features Pepper at the peak of his powers. Most of the performances are in a quartet setting, although there is a session with strings, five unaccompanied alto solos (he also plays clarinet on a few tracks), and a pair of CDs in which Pepper duets with pianist George Cables. Although more general collectors may want to acquire some of the individual sessions first (most of which are available separately on CD), the more dedicated jazz fans are advised to save their money and acquire this essential package. —*Scott Yanow*

★ **Straight Life** / Sep. 21, 1979 / Original Jazz Classics ✦✦✦✦✦
Altoist Art Pepper recorded many albums for the Galaxy label during 1979-82, all of which have been reissued in a massive 16-CD "complete" box set. This single CD is pretty definitive and serves as a perfect introduction to Pepper's second (and most rewarding) period. Not only is there a superior version of Pepper's famous title cut, but there are very emotional (and explorative) renditions of "September Song" and "Nature Boy." Filling out this quartet set (which also features pianist Tommy Flanagan, bassist Red Mitchell, and drummer Billy Higgins) are "Surf Ride," "Make a List," and "Long Ago and Far Away." Brilliant music. —*Scott Yanow*

Goin' Home / May 11, 1982-May 12, 1982 / Original Jazz Classics ✦✦✦
Art Pepper's final recording sessions were comprised of duets with pianist George Cables. Pepper, who splits his time almost evenly here between alto and clarinet, is in surprisingly strong form considering that he only had a month left to live. He is heard at his best on "Goin' Home," "Don't Let the Sun Catch You Cryin'," "Isn't She Lovely," and "Lover Man," really pouring his emotions into the ballads. Two alternate takes were added to the CD reissue, although for the complete picture, one has to acquire Art Pepper's 16-CD Galaxy box set, which contains plenty of otherwise unissued performances. —*Scott Yanow*

Bill Perkins (William Reese Perkins)

b. Jul. 22, 1924, San Francisco, CA

Sax (Baritone), Sax (Soprano), Sax (Tenor) / Cool, Post-Bop, Hard Bop

Among the "coolest" of the West Coast tenor players of the '50s, Bill Perkins in later years became a bit influenced by John Coltrane and modernized his style in a personal way. A flexible and versatile musician who also plays baritone, alto, soprano, and flute, Perkins is best known for his work on tenor. Born in San Francisco, he grew up in Chile, moved to Santa Barbara, and served in the military in World War II. After studying music and engineering, he played in the big bands of Jerry Wald, Woody Herman (1951-53 and 1954), and Stan Kenton (1953-54 and 1955-58). Perkins started recording as a leader in 1956 (most notably Grand Encounter with John Lewis), including sets with Art Pepper and Richie Kamuca. During the '60s he had a dual career as a studio musician and a recording engineer, and during 1970-92 he was a member of the "Tonight Show" band. In recent years Perkins has played baritone and tenor with the Lighthouse All-Stars and been a member of the Bud Shank Sextet, in addition to heading his own sessions for a variety of labels. — Scott Yanow

The Bill Perkins Octet on Stage / Feb. 6, 1956 / Pacific Jazz ◆◆◆

Tenors Head-On / Jul. 1956-Oct. 29, 1956 / Pacific Jazz ◆◆◆◆

Just Friends / Oct. 29, 1956 / Pacific Jazz ◆◆◆

Quietly There / Nov. 23, 1966-Nov. 30, 1966 / Original Jazz Classics ◆◆◆◆

This set by multi-reedist Bill Perkins (who switches between tenor, baritone, bass clarinet, and flute) has been reissued on CD with one extra selection. On what was one of the earliest tributes to film composer Johnny Mandel, Perkins was careful to perform not only ballads, such as "Emily," "A Time for Love," and "The Shadow of Your Smile," but to add some variety by playing a few of Mandel's more obscure medium-tempo numbers. Still, the results are generally pretty relaxed and tasteful on a quintet set with pianist Victor Feldman (who also plays some cheesy-sounding organ and vibes), guitarist John Pisano, bassist Red Mitchell, and drummer Larry Bunker. — Scott Yanow

● Frame Of Mind / May 20, 1993-May 21, 1993 / Interplay ◆◆◆◆

It is typical of Bill Perkins' adventurous spirit that on this Interplay CD, a session on which he had complete control (including repertoire and sidemen), he would perform ten challenging pieces: four Frank Strazzeri originals, and compositions by Mike Stern, Duke Pearson, Jimmy Heath, Thelonious Monk, Billy Strayhorn, and trumpeter Clay Jenkins. A couple of the pieces are blues, but, due to the tricky frameworks, this was far from a routine jam session. Perkins' tenor (he switches to baritone on "You Know I Care") blends in well with Jenkins, while the rhythm seciton (pianist Strazzeri, either Tom Warrington or Ken Filiano on bass, and drummer Bill Berg) benefits from the inclusion of vibraphonist Bob Leatherbarrow on four of the selections. A wide variety of moods are covered on a rather modern set that serves as an excellent showcase for Perkins. — Scott Yanow

Houston Person

b. Nov. 10, 1934, Florence, SC

Sax (Tenor) / Soul-Jazz, Hard Bop, Groove

In the '90s Houston Person has kept alive the soulful, thick-toned tenor tradition of Gene Ammons, particularly in his work with organists. After learning piano as a youth, Person switched to tenor. While stationed in Germany with the Army, he played in groups that included Eddie Harris, Lanny Morgan, Leo Wright, and Cedar Walton. Person picked up valuable experience as a member of Johnny Hammond's group (1963-66) and has been a bandleader ever since, often working with his wife, singer Etta Jones. A duo recording with Ran Blake (a nice change of pace, but most of Houston Person's playing has been done in blues-oriented organ groups. He has recorded a consistently excellent series of albums for Muse. — Scott Yanow

● Basics / Oct. 12, 1987 / Muse ◆◆◆◆

A good session, with blues and bop leanings. — Ron Wynn

Now's the Time / Jan. 1990 / Muse ◆◆◆◆

● Why Not! / Oct. 5, 1990 / Muse ◆◆◆◆

Organ-tenor-trumpet session. Person's album includes hot contributions by the Harper Brothers, plus Joey DeFrancisco on the Hammond Organ. — Ron Wynn

Lion and His Pride / Sep. 13, 1991 / Muse ◆◆◆◆

Oscar Peterson

b. Aug. 15, 1925, Montreal, Canada

Piano / Bop, Swing

Thanks to Norman Granz, Oscar Peterson ranks among the most extensively recorded jazz pianists in history. He's also been more harshly criticized than many who aren't nearly as gifted a stylist. Peterson's technique comes close to, though it isn't as awesome as, Art Tatum's; his phrasing,

facility, speed, harmonic knowledge, ideas, and style are dazzling. But he's been accused of lacking soul, being unable to play the blues (questionable), and making too many records that sound the same (fair criticism). His early work reflected the influence of Teddy Wilson, Earl Hines, and Nat "King" Cole, but he's long since developed his own recognizable, compelling approach. The elegant lines, flashy, yet intricate phrases, and teeming solos represent the work of a genuine piano master, though he does recycle overly familiar standards and ballads. He works best in a trio setting, where he gets the space to create freely. Peterson began studying classical piano at the age of six, and won a local talent contest in Montreal at 14. He was a regular on a weekly radio program during his late teens, and played with the Johnny Holmes Orchestra throughout the mid-'40s. Granz invited him to appear at a 1949 Carnegie Hall Jazz At The Philharmonic concert, and shortly after became his manager. When Granz founded Verve in the '50s, Peterson became the house pianist. The same was true for subsidiaries Norgran, Clef, and Mercury, and again in the '70s, when Granz formed Pablo. The bulk of Peterson's nearly 100 albums as a leader have been on Granz labels. While on Verve, Peterson recorded with Billie Holiday, Lester Young, Louis Armstrong, Ella Fitzgerald, Coleman Hawkins, Fred Astaire, Benny Carter, Roy Eldridge, Buddy DeFranco, Nelson Riddle, and Milt Jackson. He traveled with the JATP revue through the early '50s and formed a trio patterned after the Cole ensemble: guitar, piano, and bass. From 1953 until 1958 the Oscar Peterson Trio with guitarist Herb Ellis and bassist Ray Brown was a popular attraction. When Ellis left, drummer Ed Thigpen replaced him, and this trio stayed intact from 1959 until 1965. Peterson, Brown, Thigpen, and Phil Nimmons established the Advanced School of Contemporary Music in Toronto in 1960. Peterson kept things going for three years. He recorded for MPS/BASF in the late '60s and early '70s. He rejoined Granz on Pablo in the '70s and decided to concentrate on solo recordings, issuing a number of often astonishing, if thematically similiar, releases. Peterson began branching out by mid-decade, working with orchestras and playing with veterans like Gillespie, Terry, Joe Pass, Eddie "Lockjaw" Davis, Count Basie, and Niels-Henning Orsted Pedersen. Peterson has continued his steady touring and recording in the '80s and '90s. Prestige has reissued many of the Pablos, and several Verve dates are also available. Gene Lee's biography, Oscar Peterson: The Will To Swing, was published in 1988 and is must reading for Peterson fans. — Ron Wynn and Michael Erlewine

● The Complete Young Oscar Peterson / Apr. 30, 1945-Nov. 14, 1949 / RCA ◆◆◆◆

This double CD reissues the complete contents of two valuable LPs, the first 32 studio recordings of the great pianist Oscar Peterson. Recorded in Montreal, Canada, with local musicians during 1945-49 before his fame spread worldwide, these trio performances let one hear how Peterson sounded before he fully discovered bop and formed his own distinctive sound; the pianist already had his remarkable virtuosity, along with a taste for boogie-woogie that he later lost. Sticking mostly to swing standards and rollicking blues, Peterson sounds more touched by the style of Teddy Wilson than he would later on. Fascinating and easily enjoyable music, highly recommended for all serious jazz collections. — Scott Yanow

☆ At Zardis' / Nov. 8, 1955 / Pablo ◆◆◆◆◆

The group that Oscar Peterson led between 1953-58 with guitarist Herb Ellis and bassist Ray Brown was one of the great piano trios of all time. It was never so much a matter of Peterson having two other musicians accompany him as it was that they could meet the pianist as near-equals and consistently inspire him. And unlike most trios, Peterson's had many arranged sections that constantly needed rehearsals and were often quite dazzling. This live double CD from 1955 has previously unreleased (and unknown) performances of 31 songs (28 standards plus three of Peterson's originals) that were released for the first time in 1994. The pianist is often in typically miraculous form, Ellis (whether playing harmonies, offering short solos, or getting his guitar to sound like a conga by tapping it percussively) proves to be a perfect partner, and Brown's subtle but sometimes telepathic contributions should not be overlooked. — Scott Yanow

● Oscar Peterson Plays Count Basie / Dec. 27, 1955 / Verve ◆◆◆◆

On the face of it, pianist Oscar Peterson (whose virtuosity always allowed him to play an infinite amount of notes) and Count Basie (who made inventive use of silence and space by emphasizing single rhythmic sounds) would seem to have had little in common. However, they both swung, and there was a definite overlapping in their repertoire. Peterson's Basie tribute is a near-masterpiece. With guitarist Herb Ellis, bassist Ray Brown, and guest drummer Buddy Rich all playing quite sympathetically, Peterson's arrangements make the nine Basie-associated songs (along with Peterson's original "Blues for Basie") all sound fresh and lightly swinging. Quite a few of these renditions (particularly "Easy Does It," "9:20 Special," "Broadway," and "One O'Clock Jump") are instantly memorable. This CD reissue is highly recommended. — Scott Yanow

☆ At the Stratford Shakesperean Festival / Aug. 8, 1956 / Verve ◆◆◆◆◆

This CD contains what is considered by most listeners to be the finest recording of the Oscar Peterson-Herb Ellis-Ray Brown trio, a group that lasted from 1953-58. Although the soloing was always quite passionate and spontaneous, it was the very complex arrangements that really made this unit sound unique. The live CD adds two selections ("Nuages" and the 13-minute "Daisy's Dream") to the original program and contains particularly memorable renditions of "Falling in Love with Love," "How About You," "Swinging on a Star," "How High the Moon," and "52nd Street Theme." Essential music from a classic band. — *Scott Yanow*

☆ **At The Concertgebouw** / Sep. 29, 1957 & Oct. 9, 1957 / Verve ✦✦✦✦✦
Although the music on this CD was originally said to be recorded in Europe, it actually comes from a Chicago concert; and the five additional selections (last issued on an LP shared with the Modern Jazz Quartet), supposedly performed in Chicago, are from an appearance in Los Angeles. But despite the geographical mixups, the music is consistently brilliant and often wondrous. The Oscar Peterson-Herb Ellis-Ray Brown Trio had been together for more than four years, and these were among their last (and finest) recordings. The very tricky arrangements sandwiched remarkable solos with pianist Peterson sounding especially inspired. Together with their *Stratford Shakespearean* CD of the previous year, this set features the Trio at the peak of their powers. Highlights include "The Lady Is a Tramp," "Budo," "Daahoud," "Indiana," and "Joy Spring." — *Scott Yanow*

Oscar Peterson Plays My Fair Lady / Nov. 20, 1958-Jan. 1960 / Verve ✦✦✦

★ **Oscar Peterson Plays Cole Porter Songbook** / Jul. 14, 1959 Aug. 14, 1959 / Verve ✦✦✦✦✦
Peterson reworks Cole Porter and says something original and distinctive. — *Ron Wynn*

The Trio / Sep. 1961-Oct. 1961 / Verve ✦✦✦✦

Very Tall / Dec. 1961 / Verve ✦✦✦✦
Pianist Oscar Peterson and vibraphonist Milt Jackson met up for the first time on record during this studio session, which has been reissued on CD. Peterson here is often content to let Jackson be the main voice during many of the ensembles, although he also works at pushing the vibist to play at his most swinging. With the assistance of bassist Ray Brown and drummer Ed Thigpen, Peterson and Jackson are sensitive on the two ballads and really romp throughout "Green Dolphin Street," "Work Song," "John Brown's Body," and "Reunion Blues." — *Scott Yanow*

West Side Story / Jan. 24, 1962-Jan. 25, 1962 / Verve ✦✦✦

Bursting out with the All Star Big Band / Jun. 13, 1962-Jun. 14, 1962 / Verve ✦✦✦✦
Pianist Oscar Peterson has a rare outing with a big band on this excellent CD reissue. In addition to his usual bassist Ray Brown and drummer Ed Thigpen, Peterson is joined by a particularly strong big band arranged by Ernie Wilkins; there are short solos for several of the sidemen, including altoist Norris Turney, James Moody on tenor, and altoist Cannonball Adderley. However, the main focus is on Peterson, and he is in excellent form on such songs as "West Coast Blues," "Here's That Rainy Day," "Tricotism," and "Manteca," blending very well with the orchestra. — *Scott Yanow*

Live At The London House / Sep. 27, 1962 / Verve ✦✦✦

Night Train, Vol. 1 / Dec. 15, 1962-Dec. 16, 1962 / Verve ✦✦✦✦
Although the repertoire on this CD reissue by the Oscar Peterson Trio (with bassist Ray Brown and drummer Ed Thigpen) is fairly typical (with such veteran standards as "C Jam Blues," "Bags' Groove," "Easy Does It," and "I Got It Bad"), Peterson and his sidemen sound fairly inspired. The high points are the final two selections: Duke Ellington's "Band Call" and the original version of Peterson's "Hymn to Freedom." This CD gives a definitive look at the '60s Oscar Peterson Trio. — *Scott Yanow*

☆ **Exclusively for My Friends [Box Set]** / 1963-Apr. 1968 / Verve ✦✦✦✦✦
Oscar Peterson has stated that he feels his MPS recordings are his finest. That is quite a statement considering the huge number of records that the pianist has produced through the past 50 years. This four-CD set reissues the music from six of his MPS LPs: *Action, Girl Talk, The Way I Really Play, My Favorite Instrument, Mellow Mood,* and *Travelin' On.* While some of the performances feature the 1963 trio with bassist Ray Brown and drummer Ed Thigpen, most of the music dates from 1967-68 and matches Peterson with bassist Sam Jones and either Louis Hayes or Bobby Durham on drums. A special treat is Oscar Peterson's first unaccompanied solo album, which fills up the final CD. Peterson's many fans know what to expect in this set, while other listeners need to discover him to realize what all of the fuss was about. Quite simply, Oscar Peterson has long been one of the greatest pianists the world has ever known; this reissue offers plenty of proof. — *Scott Yanow*

☆ **Oscar Peterson Trio + One** / Aug. 17, 1964 / Verve ✦✦✦✦✦
This is a true classic. Fluegelhornist Clark Terry, who long has had the happiest sound in jazz, performs ten enthusiastic and generally hard-swinging songs with the Oscar Peterson Trio (which at the time included bassist Ray Brown and drummer Ed Thigpen). Terry is quite exuberant on such pieces as "Brotherhood of Man" and "Mack the Knife," and even the ballads ("They Didn't Believe Me" and "I Want a Little Girl" among them) are full of excitement. This session, though, is best known for having introduced

Clark Terry's humorous "Mumbles" vocals, which can be heard on that piece and "Incoherent Blues." This delightful and essential release has fortunately been reissued on CD. — *Scott Yanow*

Blues Etude / Dec. 3, 1965 & May 4, 1966 / Verve ✦✦✦✦
This CD reissue finds pianist Oscar Peterson at a transitional point in his career. Louis Hayes was the new drummer in his trio, and although veteran Ray Brown is on bass during the earlier of the two sessions, by 1966 he would depart after 15 years and be replaced by Sam Jones. However the basic sound of the Oscar Peterson Trio remained unchanged (his was the dominant voice, anyway) and the personality of the group remained intact. Peterson contributed three originals (including the hard-swinging title cut) to this program and also sounds typically fine on "Let's Fall in Love," "The Shadow of Your Smile," "If I Were a Bell," and a definitive version of "Stella by Starlight." — *Scott Yanow*

☆ **My Favorite Instrument** / Apr. 1968 / Verve ✦✦✦✦✦
Oscar Peterson recorded a remarkable number of albums during his career, but surprisingly this was his first full record of unaccompanied piano solos. Some observers consider his MPS recordings to be his best (quite a few are collected in the four-CD reissue *Exclusively for My Friends,* including this one). The solo LP features Peterson (freed from the constraints of his trio) stretching out on nine familiar standards and really tearing into a few of them, including "Perdido," "Bye Bye Blackbird," and "Lulu's Back in Town," while giving "Little Girl Blue" a beautiful lyrical treatment. A prelude to his outstanding Pablo recordings, *My Favourite Instrument* is one of Peterson's top albums of the '60s. — *Scott Yanow*

Tristeza on Piano / 1970 / Verve ✦✦✦

History of an Artist, Vol. 1 / Dec. 27, 1972 / Pablo ✦✦✦✦
It was only fitting that Oscar Peterson's first of many recordings for Norman Granz' Pablo label would revisit the instrumental combinations he had used in the past. This two-CD set has all of the music originally included on three LPs (a two-album set plus a single record). It showcases the great pianist in duets with bassist Ray Brown; in trios that include guitarists Irving Ashby, Barney Kessel, and Herb Ellis; and with other trios that feature such alumni as bassists Sam Jones, George Mraz, and Niels-Henning Orsted Pedersen; guitarist Joe Pass; and drummers Bobby Durham and Louis Hayes. The only fault with this consistently inventive and hard-swinging program is that the formats (particularly those on the second disc) are not in strictly chronological order. But the music (which also features Peterson taking "Lady of the Lavender Mist" as an unaccompanied solo) is superb. — *Scott Yanow*

History of an Artist, Vol. 2 / Dec. 27, 1972 / Pablo ✦✦✦

The Good Life / May 16, 1973-May 19, 1973 / Original Jazz Classics ✦✦✦✦
Taken from the same live sessions that resulted in *The Trio,* this CD reissue of a Pablo album features three remarkable virtuosos: pianist Oscar Peterson, guitarist Joe Pass, and bassist Neils-Henning Orsted Pedersen. Although not quite reaching the heights of the other set, this CD features some extraordinary solos and interplay from the musicians. Highlights include Peterson's "Wheatland," the blues "For Count" (which is referred to in the liner notes as "Miles"), and "The Good Life." — *Scott Yanow*

Oscar Peterson and Dizzy Gillespie / Nov. 28, 1974-Nov. 29, 1974 / Pablo ✦✦✦✦
This album was the first of five projects in which pianist Oscar Peterson dueted with a trumpeter. Now reissued on CD, the encounter finds Dizzy Gillespie (then 57) in good form for the period, interacting with Peterson on such pieces as "Caravan," "Autumn Leaves," "Blues for Bird," and two of Gillespie's originals that have become standards: "Dizzy Atmosphere" and "Con Alma." It's a worthy acquisition for fans of Peterson and Gillespie. — *Scott Yanow*

Oscar Peterson Plays Porgy and Bess / Jan. 26, 1976 / Verve ✦✦✦✦
Oscar Peterson and his trio (with bassist Ray Brown and drummer Ed Thigpen) explore ten of the stronger themes from George Gershwin's *Porgy and Bess* on this CD reissue. It is true that Peterson's version of "Summertime" will not make one forget the classic rendition by Miles Davis with Gil Evans but, as is true with all of these performances, Peterson makes the melodies sound like his own. "It Ain't Necessarily So" and "I Got Plenty O' Nuttin'" are among the more memorable selections. — *Scott Yanow*

Jam Montreux (1977) / Jul. 14, 1977 / Original Jazz Classics ✦✦✦✦
One of many Pablo albums taken from the 1977 Montreux Jazz Festival, this outing teams pianist Oscar Peterson, bassist Niels Pedersen, and drummer Bobby Durham with tenorman Eddie "Lockjaw" Davis and trumpeters Clark Terry and Dizzy Gillespie. The talented (and very competitive) players really dig into the opening uptempo blues ("Ali and Frazier"), and they continue cooking on "If I Were a Bell," "Bye Bye Blues" (which has been added to the CD reissue), "Things Ain't What They Used to Be," and "Just in Time." As often happens in this type of situation, the musicians inspire each other; this is one of Dizzy Gillespie's better sessions of the '70s. There are no losers in these battles. — *Scott Yanow*

Timekeepers / 1978 / Pablo ✦✦✦✦
The pairing of pianists Count Basie and Oscar Peterson might seem unlikely, given their stylistic differences. Basie's notoriety resulted from his ability to say a lot with a little, while Peterson has been celebrated as a modern technical master whose solos were full of riveting phrases, lines, and statements. Yet the duo are effective partners on this reissued 1978 session and often play against their reputations. Basie has several solos where he demonstrates impressive technique, while Peterson, often accused of overkill, shows he can use restraint and delicacy with as much flair as bombast and flash. —*Ron Wynn*

The Paris Concert / Oct. 5, 1978 / Pablo ✦✦✦✦

The London Concert / Oct. 21, 1978 / Pablo ✦✦✦✦
This two-CD set, which reissues a Pablo two-LP release, features pianist Oscar Peterson in a strong and supportive trio with bassist John Heard and drummer Louis Bellson. Although his sidemen get some solo space, the focus is primarily on the remarkable pianist on a variety of standards, his own "Hogtown Blues," and a six-song Duke Ellington medley. Whether on rapid stomps or sensitive ballads, this trio (which was in reality an all-star pickup group) sounds as if they had worked together regularly for years. —*Scott Yanow*

Skol / Jul. 6, 1979 / Pablo ✦✦✦✦
Pianist Oscar Peterson and violinist Stephane Grappelli meet up on this Scandinavian concert. The "backup" crew (guitarist Joe Pass, bassist Niels Pedersen, and drummer Mickey Roker) is not too bad, either. In addition to a closing blues (highlighted by tradeoffs from Peterson and Grappelli), the quintet performs five veteran standards with creativity and swing. This CD, a straight reissue of a Pablo LP, contains plenty of fine music. —*Scott Yanow*

The Personal Touch / Jan. 28, 1980-Feb. 19, 1980 / Pablo ✦✦✦

Nigerian Marketplace / Jul. 16, 1981 / Pablo ✦✦✦✦
For this set with bassist Niels Pedersen and drummer Terry Clarke, the great pianist Oscar Peterson (appearing at the 1981 Montreux Jazz Festival) performs a medley of "Misty" and "Waltz for Debby"; three standards; his own "Cakewalk"; and the debut of "Nigerian Marketplace," the first section of an extended suite not completed at the time. This is a well rounded set (reissued on CD) that finds the remarkable Oscar Peterson in typically swinging and prime form. —*Scott Yanow*

Two of the Few / Jan. 20, 1983 / Original Jazz Classics ✦✦✦✦
This CD reissue brings back a unique duet recording featuring pianist Oscar Peterson and vibraphonist Milt Jackson. One would expect the instrumentation to feature mostly ballads, but the opposite is true as they romp through quite a few uptempo pieces. Highlights include "Lady Be Good," "Limehouse Blues," "Reunion Blues," and "Just You, Just Me." This is a successful and enjoyable outing. —*Scott Yanow*

If You Could See Me Now / Nov. 9, 1983 / Pablo ✦✦✦✦
Oscar Peterson recorded a countless number of albums for Norman Granz' Pablo label during 1972-83, before Granz decided to call a halt (which was temporary) to his company's operations. This set was the pianist's last before a three-year hiatus, and it finds his quartet of the period (with guitarist Joe Pass, bassist Niels Pedersen, and drummer Martin Drew) in typically swinging form on Miles Davis' "Weird Blues," a pair of Peterson originals, two veteran ballads, and a ridiculously rapid "Limehouse Blues," which is taken as a Peterson-Pass duet. —*Scott Yanow*

Last Call / Mar. 16, 1990-Mar. 17, 1990 / Telarc ✦✦✦✦
The third of four Telarc CDs to be released from an Oscar Peterson reunion engagement at New York's Blue Note Club matches the great pianist with guitarist Herb Ellis, bassist Ray Brown, and drummer Bobby Durham. Although the veterans did not rehearse together beforehand, the repertoire is quite fresh, with five standards being balanced by five Peterson originals, including "Bach's Blues," "Wheatland," and "Blues Etude." The performance is as strong as one would expect, although the inclusion of Durham's drums makes the music less exciting and risky than the late-'50s trio recordings. It's worth picking up, as are the other Oscar Peterson Telarc releases from this now-legendary engagement. —*Scott Yanow*

Michel Petrucciani

b. Dec. 28, 1962, Orange, France
Piano / Post-Bop
Michel Petrucciani has overcome the effects of osteogenensis imperfecta (a bone disease that greatly stunted his growth) to become a powerful pianist. Originally greatly influenced by Bill Evans and to a lesser extent Keith Jarrett, Petrucciani has since developed his own individual voice. He started by playing in the family band with his guitarist father and bassist brother. At the age of 15 he had the opportunity to play with Kenny Clarke and Clark Terry, and at 17 he made his first recording. Petrucciani toured France with Lee Konitz in a duo (1980) and moved to the US in 1982. He coaxed Charles Lloyd out of retirement and toured with his quartet, a mutually beneficial relationship. Petrucciani has since then been a strong attraction in the US, usually playing with a quartet (sometimes featuring Adam Holzman's synthesizer for color) or as a soloist; in 1986 he recorded

at Montreux with Jim Hall and Wayne Shorter. Although Petrucciani's ability to overcome his affliction is admirable, his impressive playing stands by itself. —*Scott Yanow*

● **100 Hearts** / Jun. 1983 / George Wein Collection ✦✦✦✦
If it were not for Michel Petrucciani's good taste, it is likely that his very impressive technique would dominate his solos. As it is, the pianist has been able to use his technique in surprising ways, avoiding the obvious and showing self-restraint while coming up with ingenious ideas in his improvisations. This solo album, his first for an American label, finds Petrucciani exploring pieces by Ornette Coleman, Charlie Haden, and Sonny Rollins in addition to two of his own songs and a lengthy, wandering medley that somehow incorporates "Someday My Prince Will Come," "All the Things You Are," "A Child Is Born," and Bill Evans' "Very Early." A very impressive outing. —*Scott Yanow*

Power of Three / Jul. 14, 1986 / Blue Note ✦✦✦✦
It was logical that Michel Petrucciani (piano) and Jim Hall (guitar) would eventually play together. Both are masters of chordal improvisation and possessors of harmonically rich and introverted styles. At the 1986 Montreux Jazz Festival the pair worked together perfectly, sounding as one on the altered blues "Careful" (where their comping behind each other's solos was exquisite) and on a lengthy and well constructed version of "In a Sentimental Mood." —*Scott Yanow*

Live / Nov. 1991 / Blue Note ✦✦✦

Promenade With Duke / 1993 / Blue Note ✦✦✦

Oscar Pettiford

b. Sep. 30, 1922, Okmulgee, OK, **d.** Sep. 8, 1960, Copenhagen, Denmark
Bass, Cello / Bop
Oscar Pettiford was (along with Charles Mingus) the top bassist of the 1945-60 period and the successor to the late Jimmy Blanton. In addition, he was the first major jazz soloist on the cello. A bop pioneer, it would have been very interesting to hear what Pettiford would have done during the avant-garde '60s, but he died unexpectedly in 1960. After starting on piano, Pettiford switched to bass when he was 14 and played in a family band. He played with Charlie Barnet's band in 1942 as one of two bassists (the other was Chubby Jackson) and then hit the big time in 1943, participating on Coleman Hawkins' famous "The Man I Love" session; he also recorded with Earl Hines and Ben Webster during this period. Pettiford co-led an early bop group with Dizzy Gillespie in 1944 and in 1945 went with Coleman Hawkins to the West Coast, appearing on one song in the film *The Crimson Canary* with Hawkins and Howard McGhee. Pettiford was part of Duke Ellington's Orchestra during much of 1945-48 (fulfilling his role as the next step beyond Jimmy Blanton) and worked with Woody Herman in 1949. Throughout the '50s he mostly worked as a leader (on bass and occasional cello,) although he appeared on many records as both sideman and leader, including with Thelonious Monk in 1955-56. After going to Europe in 1958, he settled in Copenhagen, where he worked with local musicians plus Stan Getz, Bud Powell, and Kenny Clarke. Among Pettiford's better-known compositions are "Tricotism," "Laverne Walk," "Bohemia After Dark," and "Swingin' 'til the Girls Come Home." —*Scott Yanow*

The Oscar Pettiford Memorial Album / Mar. 10, 1949 & Mar. 13, 1954 / Prestige ✦✦✦✦
Stunning bass and cello playing from Oscar Pettiford, showing his technical prowess both with bow and plucked. Phenomenal showcase for Pettiford's work and for bass and cello in general. —*Ron Wynn*

Discoveries / Feb. 21, 1952-Oct. 1957 / Savoy ✦✦✦✦
A stunning early work by the bass and cello great. Has some duets with Charles Mingus, plus other examples of his stirring cello technique. —*Ron Wynn*

★ **The New Oscar Pettiford Trio** / Dec. 29, 1953-Aug. 22, 1959 / Debut ✦✦✦✦✦
A wonderful set. Pettiford is in prime form as a bassist and composer. —*Ron Wynn*

★ **Deep Passion** / Jun. 11, 1956-Sep. 6, 1957 / Impulse ✦✦✦✦✦
Two former LPs by big bands led by bassist Oscar Pettiford (who doubles on cello) are reissued in full on this single CD. The arrangements by Gigi Gryce, Lucky Thompson, and Benny Golson feature a lot of concise solos, an inventive use of the harp (either by Janet Putnam or Betty Glamann), and colorful ensembles. Among the many soloists are trumpeter Art Farmer, trombonists Jimmy Cleveland and Al Grey, the French horn of Julius Watkins, the tenors of Thompson or Golson, and the bassist-leader. This formerly rare music is highly recommended to straightahead jazz fans, for it is full of fresh material and subtle surprises. —*Scott Yanow*

Vienna Blues: The Complete Sessions / Jan. 9, 1959 & Jan. 12, 1959 / Black Lion ✦✦✦✦
Tremendous sessions featuring bass and cello giant Oscar Pettiford heading an unusual group with tenor saxophonist Hans Koller, guitarist Atilla Zoller, and drummer Jimmy Pratt. These were recorded near the end of

Pettiford's career but were first-rate, especially Pettiford's cello solos and Koller's tenor. —*Ron Wynn*

Flip Phillips (Joseph Edward Filipelli)

b. Feb. 26, 1915, Brooklyn, NY
Sax (Tenor) / Bop, Swing
Flip Phillips, who angered some critics early on because he gained riotous applause for his exciting solos during Jazz at the Philharmonic concerts, has for more than 50 years been an excellent tenor saxophonist, equally gifted on stomps, ballads, and standards. He played clarinet regularly in a Brooklyn restaurant during 1934-39, was in Frankie Newton's group (1940-41), and spent time in the bands of Benny Goodman, Wingy Manone, and Red Norvo. However, it was in 1944 that he had his breakthrough. As a featured soloist with Woody Herman's Herd (1944-46), Phillips became a big star. His warm tenor was most influenced by Ben Webster but sounded distinctive even at that early stage. He toured regularly with Jazz at the Philharmonic during 1946-57, scoring a bit of a sensation with his honking solo on "Perdido," and holding his own with heavy competition (including Charlie Parker and Lester Young). He occasionally co-led a group with Bill Harris, and that band was the nucleus of the ensemble that Benny Goodman used in 1959. Phillips then retired to Florida for 15 years, playing on just an occasional basis, taking up the bass clarinet as a double and making only a sporadic record date. But by 1975 he was back in music full-time, making quite a few records, and playing at festivals and jazz parties. Even as he passed his 80th birthday, Flip Phillips had lost none of the enthusiasm or ability that he had a half-century earlier. —*Scott Yanow*

★ **A Melody from the Sky** / Sep. 1944-Nov. 1945 / Doctor Jazz ✦✦✦✦✦
This CD is a straight reissue of a Flying Dutchman LP and has all four of tenor saxophonist Flip Phillips' recording sessions as a leader before 1949. At the time he was a key member of Woody Herman's First Herd, and these performances have short solos from other Herman sidemen (including trombonist Bill Harris and Neal Hefti on trumpet) although Phillips is the main star. His jumping tenor was already quite distinctive, whether on romps or ballads. "Sweet and Lovely" and "Stompin' at the Savoy" are high points of this definitive early Flip Phillips set. —*Scott Yanow*

The Claw: Live at the Floating Jazz Festival / 1986 / Chiaroscuro ✦✦✦✦
Veteran tenor Flip Phillips is heard leading a jam session during what was dubbed the 1986 Floating Jazz Festival, since the music took place on the S.S. Norway somewhere in the Caribbean Sea. Phillips and his fellow tenors Buddy Tate, Al Cohn, and Scott Hamilton (along with pianst John Bunch, guitarist Chris Flory, bassist Major Holley, and drummer Chuck Riggs) clearly had a good time stretching out on the five pieces (which all sport fairly basic chord changes); fluegelhornist Clark Terry joins in on three of the pieces. Unfortunately the liner notes do not tell who solos when, but veteran collectors should be able to tell the tenors apart. The only minus to this CD is a surprisingly boring monologue by Phillips (one of Chiaroscuro's few unsuccessful "Jazzspeaks") at the conclusion of this disc. However, his nine minutes of talking is preceded by 64 minutes of hot jamming, making this CD easily recommended to fans of Jazz at the Philharmonic and straightahead jazz. —*Scott Yanow*

★ **Real Swinger** / May 1988-Jun. 1988 / Concord Jazz ✦✦✦✦✦
With Howard Alden, Butch Miles, and this veteran saxophonist. Still swinging after all these years. Highly recommended. —*Michael G. Nastos*

Live At The 1993 Floating Jazz Festival / Nov. 1, 1993 & Nov. 3, 1993 / Chiaroscuro ✦✦✦✦

Courtney Pine

b. Mar. 18, 1964, London, England
Sax (Soprano), Sax (Tenor) / Post-Bop
For a while it appeared that Courtney Pine might be the next Wynton Marsalis. While Marsalis in the mid-'80s was doing close impressions of mid-'60s Miles Davis, Pine's impressive playing was nearly identical to John Coltrane's of the same era. Since then Pine has received less publicity (at least in the US), and his importance has diminished a bit. He played with reggae and funk bands while in school and has always had a strong interest in several forms of music outside of jazz. He played with John Stevens in the early '80s, formed the Jazz Warriors (an open-minded big band) a few years later, and started leading his own small groups. In 1986 he toured with George Russell's Orchestra and sat in with Art Blakey's Jazz Messengers, but since then, despite some fine records for Antilles, Pine's career has seemed a bit directionless. —*Scott Yanow*

● **Journey to the Urge Within** / Jul. 21, 1986-Jul. 23, 1986 / Antilles ✦✦✦✦
This early Courtney Pine recording (the tenor saxophonist was 22 at the time), features some of the most promising Black English jazz musicians of the time, including Pine (who also plays some bass clarinet and soprano), singer Cleveland Watkiss (who often is reminiscent of Bobby McFerrin), vibraphonist Orphy Robinson, and pianist Julian Joseph. While most of these players have not yet lived up to their potential (Pine remains an

expert Coltrane imitator), this disc has its share of strong music. The emphasis is on Courtney Pine's originals, which cover a wide span of emotions and grooves. —*Scott Yanow*

Destiny's Song and the Image of Pursuance / Jul. 29, 1987-Aug. 1, 1987 / Antilles ✦✦✦✦
English young lion Courtney Pine has heart and soul but sometimes lacks ideas and taste. —*Ron Wynn*

The Vision's Tale / 1990 / Antilles ✦✦

Within the Realms of Our Dream / Jan. 20, 1990-Jan. 21, 1990 / Antilles ✦✦✦✦
Ambitious. —*Ron Wynn*

Closer to Home / 1992 / Antilles ✦✦✦

John "Bucky" Pizzarelli (John Paul Pizzarelli, Sr.)

b. Jan. 9, 1926, Paterson, NJ
Guitar / Swing
A superior guitarist whom swing musicians in particular appreciate, John "Bucky" Pizzarelli has been a fixture in jazz and the studios since the early '50s. Self-taught, Pizzarelli has long been a master of the seven-string guitar. He toured with Vaughn Monroe before and after a stint in the military. In 1952 Pizzarelli joined the staff of NBC, and 12 years later he switched to ABC; in addition he worked with the Three Sounds (1956-57) and had several tours with Benny Goodman. In the '70s he was more active in jazz, co-leading a duo with George Barnes and working with Zoot Sims, Bud Freeman, and Stephane Grappelli. Pizzarelli has since kept up a busy recording schedule and plays often at jazz parties. Bucky has also occasionally recorded with his son, John, since the early '80s. —*Scott Yanow*

Solo Flight / 1981 / Stash ✦✦✦

● **Complete Guitar Duos** / Mar. 19, 1984-Apr. 1984 / Stash ✦✦✦✦
Fine guitar vehicle for Bucky Pizzarelli and John, Jr. They team on both uptempo and slow tunes, with some originals, but mostly interpretations of both jazz and non-jazz items. This is wonderful for guitar devotees; others may have problems with the lack of variety and generally sedate production and sound. —*Ron Wynn*

Jean Luc Ponty (Jean-Luc Ponty)

b. Sep. 29, 1942, Avranches, France
Violin / Fusion, Post-Bop, Crossover
A wide-ranging violinist and one of the finest soloists in the instrument's history, French musician Jean Luc Ponty helped popularize the use of electronics among string players and developed a style that mixed swing, bebop, free, and modal jazz, as well as jazz-rock and pop. He sometimes plays dynamic, intricately constructed, harmonically surprising, solos; other times he offers simple, bluesy statements with a prominent rhythmic focus. Ponty moved from amplifying an acoustic violin to using electric violins exclusively. He also began playing a violectra (an electric instrument tuned an octave below the violin.) Ponty creatively used wa wa pedals, fuzztone, echoplex, and phase shifters, sometimes using an electronic device with a conventional mute. He later began using a five-string electric violin, with the lowest string tuned to C. Ponty alternated between acoustic and electric in his '70s bands and added synthesizer. Ponty's father was a violin teacher and director of the music school in Avranches, while his mother taught piano. Ponty began playing piano and violin at five and clarinet at 11. He left school at 13, opting to become a concert violinist. He studied two years at the Paris Conservatory, winning the Premier Prix at 17. Ponty played three years with the Concerts Lamoureux orchestra, where he was introduced to jazz. He started improvising on clarinet and tenor sax and doing violin duets with Jef Gilson. Ponty was in the army during the early '60s, then turned to jazz exclusively. He appeared at the 1964 Antibes-Juan-les-Pins Jazz Festival leading a quartet. Ponty played and recorded in quartets and trios with Eddy Louiss and Daniel Humair in the '60s, also heading a quartet with Wolfgang Dauner, Niels-Henning Orsted Pedersen, and Humair. Ponty paid his first visit to America in the late '60s, playing at a violin workshop at the Monterey Jazz Festival. His quartet went to England in February 1969. Ponty went to Los Angeles in March, where he played and recorded with Frank Zappa, cutting the album *King Kong*. Later that year he joined George Duke's trio. Ponty returned to France and led a free jazz band, the Jean Luc Ponty Experience, in the early '70s. He returned to America in 1973 and toured with Zappa's Mothers of Invention band. He worked in 1974 and 1975 with the second edition of the Mahavishnu Orchestra. Ponty began heading his own bands in 1975. He started recording for European labels in the mid-'60s, cutting sessions for Palm, Phillips, Saba/Pausa, and Electrola, before making his American recording debut on Pacific Jazz with Duke in 1969. Ponty has subsequently recorded for Blue Note, Pausa, MPS/BASF, Inner City, Atlantic, Columbia, Prestige, and Verve in the '70s and '80s. He's recorded with George Benson, Chick Corea, and Giorgio Gaslini, while doing a violin summit LP with Stuff Smith, Svend Asmussen, and Stephane Grappelli. Ponty has included solo tracks on several albums. Several titles, most of

them Atlantic dates from the '70s, are available on CD. —*Ron Wynn and Michael G. Nastos*

Canteloupe Island / Mar. 1969 / Blue Note ✦✦✦

● **Live at Dontes** / Nov. 19, 1969-Dec. 1969 / Blue Note ✦✦✦✦
In October 1969 violinist Jean Luc Ponty recorded a notable live set with keyboardist George Duke, bassist John Heard, and drummer Dick Berk that gained him a lot of exposure in the US. He had actually played at Donte's in Los Angeles with Duke (on acoustic piano), Heard, and drummer Al Cecchi the previous March. Four of the songs came out on a 1981 LP. This CD reissues that program and then doubles it with four more songs from the same engagement. This is a release that is particularly recommended to listeners who are not involved in Ponty's many fusion projects, for his playing here is relatively straightahead and sounds influenced by the work of the mid-'60s Miles Davis Quintet, and not just because he performs Ron Carter's "Eighty-One." Also of great interest are the solos of Duke, who would eventually become a funk keyboardist and then a pop producer. In this context he sounds like a mixture of McCoy Tyner and Herbie Hancock. —*Scott Yanow*

● **Upon the Wings of Music** / Jan. 1975 / Atlantic ✦✦✦✦
Jean Luc Ponty, who at the time was still with the second version of the Mahavishnu Orchestra, is heard playing his own brand of fusion on this excellent recording, which set the standard for his music of the next decade. With keyboardist Patrice Rushen, Dan Sawyer, or Ray Parker on guitars, bassist Ralphe Armstrong, and drummer Ndugu, the violinist performs eight of his highly arranged but spirited originals. His early Atlantic recordings (of which this is the first) remain underrated for their important contributions to the history of fusion. —*Scott Yanow*

Enigmatic Ocean / Jun. 1977-Jul. 1977 / Atlantic ✦✦✦

Bud Powell (Earl Powell)

b. Sep. 27, 1924, New York, NY, d. Jul. 31, 1966, New York, NY
Piano / Bop
One of the giants of the jazz piano, Bud Powell changed the way that virtually all post-swing pianists play their instruments. He did away with the left hand striding that had been considered essential earlier and used his left hand to state chords on an irregular basis. His right often played speedy single-note lines, essentially transforming Charlie Parker's vocabulary to the piano (although he developed parallel to Parker).

After being encouraged and tutored to an extent by his friend Thelonious Monk at jam sessions in the early '40s, Powell was with Cootie Williams' orchestra during 1943-45. In a racial incident, he was beaten on the head by police; Powell never fully recovered and suffered from bad headaches and mental breakdowns throughout his life. Despite this, he recorded some true gems during 1947-51 for Roost, Blue Note, and Verve, composing such major works as "Dance of the Infidels," "Hallucinations" (also known as "Budo"), "Un Poco Loco," "Bouncing with Bud," and "Tempus Fugit." His erratic behavior resulted in lost opportunities (Charlie Parker supposedly told Miles Davis that he would not hire Powell because "he's even crazier than me!"), but Powell's playing during this period was often miraculous.

A breakdown in 1951 and hospitalization that resulted in electroshock treatments weakened him, but Powell was still capable of playing at his best now and then, most notably at the 1953 Massey Hall Concert. Generally in the '50s his Blue Notes find him in excellent form, while he is much more erratic on his Verve recordings. His warm welcome and lengthy stay in Paris (1959-64) extended his life a bit, but even here Powell spent part of 1962-63 in the hospital. He returned to New York in 1964, disappeared after a few concerts, and did not live through 1966.

In later years Bud Powell's recordings and performances could be so intense as to be scary, but other times he sounded quite sad. However, his influence on jazz (particularly up until the rise of McCoy Tyner and Bill Evans in the '60s) was very strong, and he remains one of the greatest jazz pianists of all time. —*Scott Yanow*

● **Early Years of a Genius (1944-1948)** / Jan. 1944-Dec. 19, 1948 / Mythic Sound ✦✦✦✦
This set is the first of ten CDs of privately recorded Bud Powell works owned by his friend Francis Paudras. All of the releases will be wanted by Powell's greatest fans, but some are better than others. *Vol. 1* is the most historic, for ten selections feature the innovative pianist at age 20 in 1944 as a sideman with trumpeter Cootie Williams' Orchestra, and there are some unique moments. Powell plays a duet with Williams on "West End Blues," joins in with Williams' sextet (which also includes altoist Eddie "Cleanhead" Vinson and tenorman Eddie "Lockjaw" Davis) on "Smack Me," and backs guest Ella Fitzgerald on two numbers, in addition to playing six songs with the full big band. This valuable set concludes with versions of "Perdido" and "Indiana" that Powell performed at the Royal Roost on Dec. 19, 1948, with an all-star group including trumpeter Benny Harris, trombonist J.J. Johnson, altoist Lee Konitz, and clarinetist Buddy DeFranco. Bop collectors will have to get this one. —*Scott Yanow*

Bud Powell Trio Plays / Jan. 10, 1947 & 1953 / Roulette ✦✦✦✦
All of the music on this single CD is included in the Blue Note four-CD "complete" set (the best way to acquire these important performances); however, listeners who do not have the larger reissue will not go wrong by getting this CD. The first eight selections (which find the pianist joined by bassist Curley Russell and drummer Max Roach) are from Bud Powell's first trio date, and he is in prime form on such numbers as "I'll Remember April," "Somebody Loves Me," and "Bud's Bubble." The second session (with bassist George Duvivier and drummer Art Taylor in 1953) does not reach the same heights, but it does contain some fine playing from the founder of bop piano. —*Scott Yanow*

☆ **Complete Blue Note and Roost Recordings** / Jan. 10, 1949-Dec. 29, 1958 / Blue Note ✦✦✦✦✦
Although pianist Bud Powell recorded some great albums elsewhere (most notably his first couple of sessions for Verve), on a whole his Blue Note records were his most significant and definitive. This four-CD set has all of the music from his five Blue Note albums, his two sessions for the Roost label, and all known alternate takes. Powell literally changed the way that the piano is played in jazz, and this magnificent set has more than its share of classics. In addition to the many trio performances, trombonist Curtis Fuller sits in on three numbers, there are a few solo cuts, and one date features Powell at the head of a quintet with trumpeter Fats Navarro and the young tenor Sonny Rollins. Although there are a few faltering moments in the later dates, this essential release (unlike the similar Verve reissue) is quite consistent. —*Scott Yanow*

Complete Bud Powell On Verve / Jan. 1949-Sep. 13, 1956 / Verve ✦✦✦✦
This five-CD deluxe set contains an impressive 150-page booklet and reissues every scrap of music that the innovative pianist Bud Powell recorded for Verve. The first disc has the best music, four truly outstanding sessions from 1949-51. The other performances (trio sides from 1954-56) are much more erratic, particularly the alternate takes, with gems followed by completely lost solos. Bop fans will want this set, but more general collectors are advised to pick up the Blue Notes first. —*Scott Yanow*

★ **The Amazing Bud Powell, Vol. 1** / Aug. 8, 1949-May 1, 1951 / Blue Note ✦✦✦✦✦
The CD reissue of the two LPs titled *The Amazing Bud Powell* puts the important recordings in chronological order (which they weren't in the LP version) and adds some alternate takes; all of the music has also been included in a definitive four-CD box set. Although the latter is the best way to acquire the important performances, this CD gives one a strong sampling of pianist Bud Powell at his best. Powell is heard on a classic session with trumpeter Fats Navarro and tenor saxophonist Sonny Rollins (which is highlighted by exciting versions of "Dance of the Infidels," "52nd Street Theme," and "Bouncing with Bud") and in a trio for "Over the Rainbow" and three versions of his intense "Un Poco Loco." —*Scott Yanow*

The Complete Bud Powell Blue Note Recordings (1949-1958) / Aug. 8, 1949-Dec. 29, 1958 / Mosaic ✦✦✦✦

The Amazing Bud Powell, Vol. 2 / May 1, 1951-Aug. 14, 1953 / Blue Note ✦✦✦✦
These two CD volumes (all of the music has also been reissued on a definitive "complete" Blue Note Bud Powell four-CD set) differ from the original two LPs in that, in addition to the inclusion of some alternate takes, they are programmed in strict chronological order. The influential bebop pioneer (who not only set the standard for bop pianists but largely invented the style) is heard on fine trio performances from 1951 (with bassist Curly Russell and drummer Max Roach) and 1953 (during which he is matched with bassist George Duvivier and drummer Art Taylor). Highlights include "A Night in Tunisia," "Reets and I," "I Want to Be Happy," and "Glass Enclosure." —*Scott Yanow*

Time Was / Oct. 5, 1956 & Feb. 11, 1957 / Bluebird ✦✦✦

The Amazing Bud Powell, Vol. 3 / Aug. 3, 1957 / Blue Note ✦✦✦✦
Bud Powell's playing in the late '50s (just prior to his move to Paris) found the troubled pianist in erratic form, often struggling to make it through songs he had written. However his three Blue Note recordings from the era (which include the slightly later *Time Waits* and *The Scene Changes*) feature Powell in surprisingly inspired form; all of the releases have since been reissued on a comprehensive CD set. *Bud!* (which is subtitled *The Amazing Bud Powell, Vol. 3*) has five trio performances with bassist Paul Chambers and drummer Art Taylor (highlighted by "Bud on Bach" and "Some Soul") and three standards on which the group is joined by trombonist Curtis Fuller. This strong bop set is well worth getting. —*Scott Yanow*

Bud Plays Bird / Oct. 14, 1957-Jan. 30, 1958 / Roulette ✦✦✦✦
Previously unissued until 1996, this trio session by pianist Bud Powell with bassist George Duvivier and drummer Art Taylor is better than his Verve recordings of the period, if not quite up to the level of his earlier classic Blue Note dates. Actually it is a mystery how such excellent music could be unknown and go unreleased for so long. Powell performs 13 Charlie Parker compositions (including two versions of "Big Foot") and Dizzy Gillespie's "Salt Peanuts." Although there are some minor missteps, the

music is enjoyable and generally hard-swinging, with the more memorable performances including "Straw 'Nuff," "Yardbird Suite," "Confirmation," and "Ko Ko." —*Scott Yanow*

● **The Complete Essen Jazz Festival Concert** / Apr. 2, 1960 / Black Lion ✦✦✦✦
Pianist Bud Powell is heard in top form throughout this CD, playing six selections with his all-star trio (which includes bassist Oscar Pettiford and drummer Kenny Clarke) and three songs on which the trio is joined by the great tenor Coleman Hawkins. There is plenty of classic bebop throughout the concert performance, with Powell mostly sticking to standards (along with his original "John's Abbey"); Hawkins is best on "Stuffy." This release is recommended as a fine example of the playing of these classic masters. —*Scott Yanow*

At the Golden Circle, Vol. 1 / Apr. 19, 1962 / SteepleChase ✦✦✦

Mel Powell (Melvin Epstein)

b. Feb. 12, 1923, New York, NY
Piano / Swing
One of the finest swing pianists and a prodigy, Mel Powell was playing piano and writing important arrangements for Benny Goodman by the time he was 18. He had previously played with Bobby Hackett, George Brunis, and Zutty Singleton (1939), was the intermission pianist at Nick's, and worked in the short-lived Muggsy Spanier big band. During his stay with Goodman, Powell and the clarinetist struck up a lifelong friendship; among his arrangements for Goodman were "The Earl," "Mission to Moscow," "Clarinade," and "Jersey Bounce." After a period working for the CBS orchestra under Raymond Scott (1942), Powell was one of the stars of the Glenn Miller Army Air Force Band. Powell, whose style was reminiscent of Teddy Wilson's, recorded with Goodman during 1945-47, led a few record dates (his first one was in 1942), and worked in the studios. However, after studying with Paul Hindemith at Yale (1952), he became a classical composer. Powell did record some superior jazz dates for Vanguard during 1953-55 and sat in with Bobby Hackett in the mid-'60s, but was otherwise occupied completely outside of jazz. After decades of work as a well respected serial composer, Mel Powell returned to jazz for cruises in 1986 and 1987 that were recorded by Chiaroscuro. A muscular disease has since knocked him out of action. —*Scott Yanow*

● **Unavailable Mel Powell** / Dec. 10, 1947-Dec. 31, 1947 / PA/USA ✦✦✦✦
Some of his top compositions from a peak period as a jazz writer and player. —*Ron Wynn*

Return of Mel Powell / Oct. 21, 1987 / Chiaroscuro ✦✦✦✦
This Pulitzer Prize winner returns to his jazz roots. Benny Carter makes this session shine. —*Ron Wynn*

Andre Previn (Andreas Ludwig Priwin)

b. Apr. 6, 1929, Berlin, Germany
Piano / Cool
A conductor and classical pianist of immense standing, Andre Previn has also amassed some impressive jazz credentials. While not among the most spectacular or dazzling stylists and certainly not a great soloist, Previn has nonetheless made many creditable recordings and enjoyed major crossover successes. He started piano lessons as a child in his native Berlin and later was booted out of the Conservatory in a blatant anti-Semitic incident. His family immediately went to Paris and then to Los Angeles. Previn played piano and did the score for a Jose Iturbi film at the age of 16. He split time between classical, film, and jazz material until he was drafted in the early '50s. Previn scored numerous films in the '50s, '60s, and early '70s, among them Oscar winners *Gigi*, *Porgy and Bess*, *Irma La Douce*, and *My Fair Lady*. During the '40s, '50s, and '60s, Previn made more than 20 trio albums ranging from Fats Waller material to jazz versions of Broadway shows. The trio of Previn, Leroy Vinnegar, and Shelly Manne struck commercial gold with *My Fair Lady* in 1956. Previn had a string of albums on the charts in the '60s, among them *Like Love*, *A Touch of Elegance*, *Andre Previn in Hollywood*, and a remake of *My Fair Lady*. He concentrated on conducting and classical music during much of the mid- and late '60s and through the '70s. But Previn returned to jazz in the early '80s, working with Manne and Monty Budwig, cutting an album of rags with Itzhak Perlmann, and working in a quintet with Perlmann, Red Mitchell, Manne, and Jim Hall on *A Different Kind of Blue*, which made the pop charts. The same group group did another album in 1981, and Previn recorded with Ella Fitzgerald and Niels-Henning Orsted Pedersen in 1983. He teamed with Ray Brown and Mundell Lowe for a jazz date and with Thomas Stevens for a repertory set of pre-rock standards in the '90s. Previn has many dates available on CD. —*Ron Wynn and Michael G. Nastos*

★ **Previn At Sunset** / Oct. 13, 1945-May 31, 1946 / Black Lion ✦✦✦✦✦

Double Play! / Apr. 30, 1957 & May 11, 1957 / Original Jazz Classics ✦✦✦✦
Pianists Andre Previn and Russ Freeman team up with drummer Shelly Manne in a trio to play eight of their originals (along with the standard "Take Me out to the Ball Game"), all given titles having to do with baseball.

This was advertised as the first time that two pianists recorded what was then modern jazz together. Previn and Freeman had very complementary styles, making it difficult to know who was playing when, although a complete play-by-play is included. —*Scott Yanow*

Pal Joey / Oct. 28, 1957-Oct. 29, 1957 / Original Jazz Classics ✦✦✦✦
Shelley Manne and Red Mitchell put some snap into Previn's musical menu. —*Ron Wynn*

Gigi / Apr. 7, 1958-Apr. 8, 1958 / Original Jazz Classics ✦✦✦

● **Jazz: King Size** / Nov. 26, 1958 / Original Jazz Classics ✦✦✦✦
The multitalented Andre Previn is heard on this straight CD reissue of a Contemporary LP as the leader of a trio with bassist Red Mitchell and drummer Frankie Capp. Previn always had his own swing/bop piano style, and he is in top form on two of his originals (including the bluish "Much Too Late") and four superior standards. This fine release is an excellent example of Previn's skills as a jazz pianist. —*Scott Yanow*

Andre Previn Plays Jerome Kern / Feb. 26, 1959 & Mar. 10, 1959 / Original Jazz Classics ✦✦✦✦
For this solo piano session (a Contemporary date that has been reissued on CD), the remarkably versatile Andre Previn interprets ten Jerome Kern songs, including several ("Sure Thing," "WhipPoor-Will," "Go Little Boat," and "Put Me to the Test") that are quite obscure. Sometimes he treats the melodies with great respect, while other performances find him stretching the themes and coming up with fresh variations; "They Didn't Believe Me" is a high point. This is a well rounded set with plenty of surprises and consistently tasteful playing, one of Previn's better jazz efforts. —*Scott Yanow*

West Side Story / Aug. 24, 1959-Aug. 25, 1959 / Original Jazz Classics ✦✦✦✦
Yet another turning of *West Side Story* into a jazz setting. Not as good as some other renditions. —*Ron Wynn*

Like Previn! / Feb. 20, 1960-Mar. 1, 1960 / Original Jazz Classics ✦✦✦✦
This trio set for Contemporary (reissued on CD in the OJC series) differs from other Andre Previn sessions in that all eight of the selections were composed by the pianist. With fine assistance from bassist Red Mitchell and drummer Frankie Capp, Previn is in consistently swinging form on his originals, and even if none of the songs caught on, they make for a solid and varied set of bop-oriented music. —*Scott Yanow*

Andre Previn Plays Harold Arlen / May 4, 1960-May 5, 1960 / Original Jazz Classics ✦✦✦

A Touch of Elegance / Nov. 9, 1960-Dec. 18, 1962 / Columbia/Legacy ✦✦✦

● **After Hours** / Mar. 29, 1989 / Telarc ✦✦✦✦
The noted symphonic conductor can also play jazz. —*Ron Wynn*

Uptown / Mar. 9, 1990-Mar. 10, 1990 / Telarc ✦✦✦✦
This recent Previn is nicely done but doesn't have the sparkle of his Prestige sessions. —*Ron Wynn*

Old Friends / Aug. 24, 1991 / Telarc ✦✦✦✦
Superb trio recordings that marked the return of well known classical conductor Andre Previn to intimate jazz recording. He teamed with bassist Ray Brown and guitarist Mundell Lowe, and the three complemented each other expertly, while their solos were tasteful and concise. —*Ron Wynn*

Play Show Boat / 1995 / Deutsche Grammophon ✦✦✦✦
Performing in a style a bit reminiscent of Oscar Peterson, pianist Andre Previn plays eight selections from the play *Show Boat*, six of which are standards, plus the obscure "Life on the Wicked Stage" and "I Might Fall Back on You." Previn contributed three newer pieces, with the uptempo blues "Lickety Split" having his most impressive solo. Although the partly bi-tonal treatment given the usually sweet "Make Believe" takes a bit away from the memorable melody, Previn's interpretations of the other pieces are melodic, respectful, and swinging. Guitarist Mundell Lowe has an occasional solo, and bassist Ray Brown and drummer Grady Tate are typically excellent in support. This fine bop-oriented date shows that Andre Previn (who has spent most of the past three decades in the classical music world) is still the top part-time jazz pianist around! —*Scott Yanow*

Julian Priester

b. Jun. 29, 1935, Chicago, IL
Trombone / Avant-Garde, Hard Bop
Julian Priester is a flexible and adventurous trombonist who has not yet achieved the fame he deserves. He originally studied piano and baritone horn, finally switching to trombone. Before moving to New York in 1958 he worked with Muddy Waters, Bo Diddley, Sun Ra (1954-56), Lionel Hampton, and Dinah Washington (1957). Priester gained recognition for his playing with Max Roach (1958-61) during a period when the drummer often used Booker Little and Eric Dolphy. Priester played in a wide variety of settings throughout the '60s, including six months with Duke Ellington (1969-70). Priester's highest profile gig was with Herbie Hancock's sextet, with whom he toured and recorded during 1970-73. Moving to San Francisco in the mid-'70s, he experimented with electronic music while still

playing trombone, recording with Stanley Cowell and Red Garland. Most of the first half of the '90s was spent with Dave Holland's quintet; later in the decade he worked with George Gruntz and Sun Ra. —*Scott Yanow*

● **Keep Swinging** / Jan. 11, 1960 / Original Jazz Classics ✦✦✦✦
Trombonist Julian Priester sounds very much under the influence of J.J. Johnson during his debut as a leader, a Riverside date reissued on CD in the Original Jazz Classic series. The repertoire is comprised of four Priester originals, one apiece by Jimmy Heath (whose tenor makes the group a quintet on five of the eight songs) and baritonist Charles Davis, and two standards. Priester is heard in his early prime on a warm version of "Once in a While" and plays solid hard bop with pianist Tommy Flanagan, bassist Sam Jones, drummer Elvin Jones, and sometimes Heath on this swinging modern mainstream session. —*Scott Yanow*

Love, Love / Jun. 28, 1974-Sep. 12, 1974 / ECM ✦✦✦

Polarization / Jan. 1977 / ECM ✦✦✦

Tito Puente

b. Apr. 20, 1923, New York, NY
Percussion / Latin Jazz, Latin Continuum
Mario Bauza's death in 1993 leaves Tito Puente as the elder, reigning leader of Latin jazz, salsa, and Afro-Cuban/Afro-Latin music. A magnificent timbales player, great bandleader, flamboyant entertainer, underrated vibes soloist, and competent saxophonist, pianist, and conga and bongos player, Puente has done everything in Latin music. His original intention was to be a dancer, but that was ruined by a torn ankle tendon he suffered in an accident. Puente got early lessons in composition from Charlie Spivak, whom he met aboard the USS Santee in World War II. Puente later got formal training at Juilliard. He worked in the bands of Noro Morales, Machito, and Pupi Campo before forming the Piccadilly Boys in the late '40s; they eventually became the Tito Puente Orchestra. With lead vocalist Vincentico Valdes, Puente's group made its recording debut on Secco. Puente was the first signee on Tico, then a new Latin label, in the late '40s. He made several albums for them in the late '40s and '50s, and helped popularize the "mambo" rage. His hit "Abaniquito" was a crossover smash, and RCA lured Puente from Tico for a string of albums in the '50s that mixed spicy dance beats and red-hot jam sessions. His single "Para los Rumberos" was later covered by Santana, and his late '50s singles and albums were prominent in the rise of the chachacha sound. Puente took vintage Cuban chachacha songs and transferred them from the violin/flute charanga format to a brass and reeds, big-band context. His '50s bands included several major stars like Ray Barretto, Mongo Santamaria, Willie Bobo, and Johnny Pacheco. Puente enjoyed more crossover success in the early '60s for GNP, with albums combining Latin interpretations of Broadway shows, bossa nova, and big- band dates. He returned to Tico and stayed there with the '80s, cutting numerous records in the Latin jazz, Afro-Cuban, and Afro-Latin vein. Puente recorded with Santamaria, Bobo, and Carlos "Patato" Valdez; did a live date in Puerto Rico; played with the Tico All Stars and Fania All Stars; backed such vocalists as Manny Roman, Rolando Le Series, and Celia Cruz; cut "boogaloo" and pop dates; and recorded salsa and big band albums. Santana enjoyed a huge hit with a cover of his single "Oye Como Va," and Puente's bands and albums were the place to hear the greatest Latin musicians and vocalists throughout the '70s. Puente was one of the artists featured in Jeremy Marre's television film *Salsa '79*, and he made several tours of Europe with the Latin Percussion Jazz Ensemble. They became an octet in the early '80s, and the album *Tito Puente and His Latin Ensemble on Broadway* won a Grammy in 1983 and gained credibility and exposure for Concord's Picante line. Puente has continued recording for Concord/Picante, winning another Grammy in 1985 for the album *Mambo Diablo* that included special guest George Shearing on "Lullaby of Birdland." Puente also did guest stints with Cal Tjader and Ray Barretto for '70s albums on Fantasy and Atlantic, and another guest stint with Barretto on an 1981 CTI album. He's also recorded for Timeless, and was featured in the 1992 film *The Mambo Kings*. Some of his classic RCA dates are being reissued on CD by RCA/Bluebird, while his recent Concord and Timeless material is also available on CD. Several of his numerous Tico releases are available on CD from Latin music stores. —*Ron Wynn and Michael G. Nastos*

● **Dance Mania** / 1958 / BMG ✦✦✦✦
Many have long despaired of finding anything from the days of Puente's young prime, and here's one of his two best albums reissued in CD. This was Puente's big band at the height of its powers, one of the great documents of New York Latin music, and the sort of thing that established the man's claim to be one of the creators of big-band mambo. —*John Storm Roberts*

New Cha Cha/Mambo Herd / 1958 / Laserlight ✦✦✦✦

On Broadway / Jul. 1982 / Concord Picante ✦✦✦✦
The great Latin bandleader Tito Puente has long been one of the pioneers in fusing bebop with very danceable Latin music. On this Concord disc, Puente plays vibes and timbales and uses an 11-piece band featuring trumpeter Jimmy Frisaura; Mario Rivera on tenor, soprano, and flute; pia-

nist Jorge Dalto; and an infectious rhythm section. Jazz standards (including "Sophisticated Lady," "Bluesette," and even Freddie Hubbard's "First Light") alternate with Latin numbers. —*Scott Yanow*

☆ **El Rey** / May 1984 / Concord Picante ✦✦✦✦✦
This is '80s Puente, with the Latin-jazz ensemble that has brought him back into the limelight and back to the small-group New York sound that was one of the finest of all crossover styles. This album includes the great reed-player Mario Rivera. *El Rey* has the late Jorge (Dalto) on piano. It contains a mix of jazz and Latin numbers and includes "Oye Como Va," "Ran Kan Kan," "Autumn Leaves" (which Puente first recorded back in the '50s), Coltrane's "Giant Steps," and "Equinox." —*John Storm Roberts, Original Music*

Mambo Diablo / May 1985 / Concord Picante ✦✦✦

Sensacion / 1987 / Concord Picante ✦✦✦

Un Poco Loco / Jan. 1987 / Concord Picante ✦✦✦✦
One of his best for the label. Puente's playing in both large and small contexts. —*Ron Wynn*

Salsa Meets Jazz / Jan. 1988 / Concord Picante ✦✦✦✦
Excellent, maybe his best on the label. Phil Woods joins the party and soars. —*Ron Wynn*

Goza Me Timbal / Jul. 31, 1989-Aug. 1, 1989 / Concord Picante ✦✦✦✦
The songs mix Sonny Rollins and Miles Davis landmarks with topical Puente numbers, extending both bop and Latin horizons. —*Ron Wynn*

Out of This World / Dec. 1990 / Concord Picante ✦✦✦

The Mambo King / 1991 / RMM ✦✦✦✦
Puente's 100th album is a celebration of that fact, with a procession of vocalists, most of whom—like Celia Cruz—were professionally associated with him at one time or another. That doesn't make for a very tight concept, but recordings by musicians of his generation didn't have concepts, they had music. So does this one, including a minor riot with Celia Cruz riding a big, burly mambo arrangement by a band full of just everybody, and a wonderful "El Bribon del Aguacero" with Chocolate Armenteros on trumpet. —*John Storm Roberts*

● **Live at the Village Gate** / Apr. 27, 1992 / Sony Discos ✦✦✦✦

Tito Puente and His Latin Jazz All Stars / 1993 / Concord Picante ✦✦✦✦

In Session / 1993 / Bellaphon ✦✦✦✦
This outing from Tito Puente is a throwback to Latin-jazz of the '50s and '60s. Very much a jazz session, most of the selections feature fine solos from trumpeter Charlie Sepulveda, the muscular tenor of Mario Rivera, flutist Dave Valentin, and pianist Hilton Ruiz. Drummer Ignacio Berroa and three percussionists really push the ensembles, and Puente (on timbales and vibes) has plenty of fine spots. As a bonus, James Moody drops by to do a lively version of his "Moody's Mood for Love" (complete with yodeling). It's an excellent Latin-jazz set. —*Scott Yanow*

● **Royal T** / Jan. 18, 1993 & Jan. 19, 1993 / Concord Picante ✦✦✦✦
Tito Puente has long championed Latin-jazz, a combination of Latin percussion and rhythms with bebop-oriented jazz. This release from the Concord Picante label serves as a perfect introduction to his music. For this date Puente (who performs on timbales and marimba) uses six horns, piano, bass, synthesizer, and three other percussionists to play everything from "Donna Lee" and "Stompin' at the Savoy" to his own exotic originals. Soloists include the many reeds (including piccolo) of Mario Rivera, trumpeter Tony Lujan, trombonist Art Velasco, and of course the percussion section. One of Tito Puente's better recordings of recent times. —*Scott Yanow*

Puente's Heat / Herman / Columbia/Legacy ✦✦✦
A CD reissue of a session that matched Afro-Latin bandleader Tito Puente with swingmaster Woody Herman for a mutually beneficial and enjoyable date. The original release was on RCA and was later reissued on vinyl by Everest. —*Ron Wynn*

Don Pullen

b. Dec. 25, 1941, Roanoke, VA, **d.** Apr. 22, 1995
Organ, Piano / Avant-Garde, Post-Bop
Don Pullen rivals Cecil Taylor in his percussive approach to the piano. He incorporates free, blues, and bebop elements in his solos, featuring tone clusters, funk, and R&B backbeats and rhythms, glissandos, and dense, rigorous, right-hand lines. Pullen's also an accomplished organist; his bass pedal work, accompaniment, and soulful melodies and riffs are remniscent of classic soul-jazz combo dates. Pullen began playing gospel in church and R&B in clubs in his youth. He turned to jazz in his teens. Pullen played in Muhal Richard Abrams' Experimental Band during the mid-'60s in Chicago, and Guiseppi Logan's quartet in New York. He also played on R&B sessions backing Big Maybelle, Ruth Brooks, and Arthur Prysock and on organ with soul-jazz groups. Pullen led a group in the '60s and early '70s that included Roland Prince, Tina Brooks, and Al Dreares. He worked in a duo with Milford Graves in the mid-'60s. Pullen was in Charles Mingus' last great '70s combo, along with George Adams and Dannie Richmond.

After that experience, he went solo. Pullen worked with Sam Rivers, David Murray, Hamiett Bluiett, and various Art Ensemble of Chicago members before co-forming a quartet in the '70s with Adams that included Richmond and Cameron Brown. The Don Pullen/George Adams quartet was a super band whose only failing was recording their finest work for an independent label, thus never enjoying the exposure available only through a conglomerate's publicity machine. Pullen also played with Beaver Harris' 360 Degree Music Experience and in the Mingus Dynasty. Since the quartet disbanded, Pullen has led his own bands and records for Blue Note. His recent *Ode tTo Life* has been highly praised in the mainstream jazz press, hip-hop magazines like *Vibe*, and even international publications such as *Latin Beat*. Pullen has recorded for Atlantic, Horo, Timeless, Black Saint, Sackville, and DIW, among others. He's played with Eddie Gomez, Nina Simone, Bobby Battle, Fred Hopkins, Olu Dara, Donald Harrison, Alex Blake, Gary Peacock, Tony Williams, and Chico Freeman. *—Ron Wynn*

The Magic Triangle / Jul. 24, 1979-Jul. 26, 1979 / Black Saint ✦✦✦✦

The Sixth Sense / Jun. 1985 / Black Saint ✦✦✦✦
Studio date with quintet. Another great Pullen album. *—Michael G. Nastos*

Breakthrough / Apr. 30, 1986 / Blue Note ✦✦✦✦
With George Adams Quartet. Pianist Don Pullen and sax/flute/vocalist George Adams (both ex-Mingus players) with drummer Dan Richmond at their creative zenith. *—Michael G. Nastos*

New Beginnings / Dec. 1988 / Blue Note ✦✦✦✦
A slashing, exciting pianist on his own. *—Ron Wynn*

Random Thoughts / Mar. 23, 1990 / Blue Note ✦✦✦✦
A percussive, attacking pianist. *—Ron Wynn*

● **Kele Mou Bana** / Sep. 25, 1991 & Sep. 26, 1991 / Blue Note ✦✦✦✦
This CD features pianist Don Pullen's "African-Brazilian Connection." Always a very percussive player, Pullen gets to romp with two percussionists on this date while altoist Carlos Ward flies over the top and bassist Nilson Matta keeps the foundation solid. The repertoire is comprised of originals and, even in its freer moments, the rhythms keep the music quite accessible. *—Scott Yanow*

Ode to Life / Jun. 29, 1993 / Blue Note ✦✦✦

Sacred Common Ground / 1994 / Blue Note ✦✦

Flora Purim

b. Mar. 6, 1942, Rio de Janeiro, Brazil
Guitar, Percussion, Vocals / Fusion, Brazilian Jazz
Since her husband Airto Moreira ranks as Brazil's most famous percussionist, it's only fitting that Flora Purim qualifies as that nation's most celebrated jazz vocalist, though she's never had a huge hit like Astrud Gilberto's "The Girl from Ipanema." While Purim's thunder has been stolen in the '80s and '90s by newer, more invigorating, progressive types like Margareth Menezes and Tania Maria, Purim is a revelation in the '70s. With a voice that at one time could range over six octaves; a soothing, alluring sound; and superb timing and delivery, she thrilled audiences with her vocals on the debut *Return to Forever* album and as a leader. The daughter of professional musicians, Purim studied piano and guitar, and performed in Sao Paulo and Rio de Janeiro with Moreira. They moved to Los Angeles in the late '60s, then New York. While Moreira worked with Miles Davis, Purim joined Stan Getz' band. She recorded with Duke Pearson, then with Return to Forever and Moreira. The duo left Return to Forever in the mid-'70s to form their own band, but Purim's career was derailed by an arrest for cocaine possession. She was imprisoned in 1974 and 1975, then resumed her career. Purim's records in the late '70s were more pop- and light jazz-oriented. She started her own band in 1978, as her career and Moreira's seemed headed in opposite stylistic directions. But they reteamed in the mid-'80s, and are still working together. Purim recorded in the '70s for Milestone, then for Concord/Crossover, Sobocode, Venture, and Reference with Mickey Hart in the '80s. She's recorded for Fantasy in the '90s. Most of Purim's sessions are available on CD, both her dates and those with Airto. *—Ron Wynn*

★ **Butterfly Dreams** / Dec. 1973 / Original Jazz Classics ✦✦✦✦✦
A wonderful release that she's seldom equalled since. Joe Henderson (sax), George Duke (piano), and Airto Moreira (percussion). *—Ron Wynn*

Stories to Tell / May 1974-Jul. 1974 / Original Jazz Classics ✦✦✦✦
Nice set; reissued in 1991. *—Ron Wynn*

Encounter / Apr. 1976 / Original Jazz Classics ✦✦✦✦
Purim teamed with fellow Afro-Latin vocalist and instrumentalist Hermeto Pascoal, as well as Airto Moreira, on this album. It had more interesting rhythmic elements due to Pascoal's presence; the vocal contrast was also intriguing. *—Ron Wynn*

Humble People / 1985 / Concord Jazz ✦✦✦✦
An all-star band supports Flora and Airto Moreira through jazz, funk, and Latin pop. Guests include David Sanborn, Joe Farrell, Milton Cardona, and

Jerry Gonzalez. This is one of Purim's better later-period albums. *—Michael G. Nastos*

Ike Quebec

b. Aug. 17, 1918, Newark, NJ, **d.** Jan. 16, 1963, New York, NY
Sax (Tenor) / Swing, Early R&B, Groove
A magnificent "populist" saxophonist whose abilities were undervalued by many critics during his lifetime, Ike Quebec showed that simple, compelling music need not be played in a simplistic manner. He had a pronounced swing bent in his style and tone, particularly the sound of Coleman Hawkins. But Quebec didn't simply parrot Hawkins; he displayed a huge, bluesy tone and swooping, jubilant phrases; he played joyous, uptempo tunes and evocative, slow blues and ballads. There were no false fingerings or anything intricate; it was just direct, heartfelt solos. Quebec was once a pianist and part-time soft shoe artist, but switched to tenor in the '40s, playing with the Barons of Rhythm. He worked with several New York bands, among them groups led by Kenny Clarke, Benny Carter, and Roy Eldridge. He co-wrote the song "Mop Mop" with Clarke, which was later recorded by Coleman Hawkins during one of the earliest bebop sessions. Quebec played from the mid-'40s into the early '50s with Cab Calloway's orchestra and his spinoff unit, the Cab Jivers. Quebec cut one of Blue Note's rare 78 albums in the '40s; he also recorded for Savoy. His song "Blue Harlem" became a huge hit. Quebec also worked with Lucky Millinder and recorded with Calloway. Alfred Lion made Quebec Blue Note's A&R man in the late '40s, after Quebec repeatedly informed him about talented prospective signees. Quebec doubled for a while as a bandleader but concentrated until the late '50s on recording and finding acts for the label. Some of the people he brought Lion included Thelonious Monk and Bud Powell. Quebec wrote "Suburban Eyes" for Monk's label debut. He began playing again in the late '50s, doing Blue Note sessions with Sonny Clark, Jimmy Smith, singer Dodo Green, and Stanley Turrentine, plus his own dates. Just as he was attracting renewed attention and some appreciation from critics who'd previously dismissed him as another honking R&B type, Quebec died of lung cancer in 1963. Mosaic has issued some superb Quebec boxed sets, *The Complete Blue Note Forties Recordings of Ike Quebec and John Hardee* and *The Complete Blue Note 45 Sessions*. *—Ron Wynn*

★ **Complete Blue Note Recordings** / Jul. 18, 1944-Sep. 23, 1946 / Mosaic ✦✦✦✦✦
This is an essential compilation of virtually all the early Quebec jazz dates. *—Ron Wynn*

☆ **Complete Blue Note 45 Sessions** / Jul. 1, 1959-Feb. 13, 1962 / Mosaic ✦✦✦✦✦
A wonderful three-disc collection of Quebec's 1959-1962 songs that packed jazz punch, had R&B appeal, and were originally recorded for and designed as singles for jukeboxes. *—Ron Wynn*

The The Art of Ike Quebec / Nov. 13, 1961-Oct. 5, 1962 / Blue Note ✦✦✦
An anthology featuring some super numbers by dynamic saxophonist Ike Quebec, a masterful blues, ballad, and honking R&B player. It's a good introductory set, although Mosaic has cornered the market on Ike Quebec sessions with its boxed sets featuring his full Blue Note dates. *—Ron Wynn*

Heavy Soul / Nov. 26, 1961 / Blue Note ✦✦✦✦
The thick-toned tenor Ike Quebec is in excellent form on this CD reissue of a 1961 Blue Note date. His ballad statements are warm, and he swings nicely on a variety of medium-tempo material. Unfortunately, organist Freddie Roach has a rather dated sound that weakens this session a bit; bassist Milt Hinton and drummer Al Harewood are typically fine in support. Originals alternate with standards, with "Just One More Chance," "The Man I Love," and "Nature Boy" (the latter an emotional tenor-bass duet) being among the highlights. *—Scott Yanow*

● **Blue and Sentimental** / Dec. 16, 1961 & Dec. 23, 1961 / Blue Note ✦✦✦✦
Hot, lusty, and wonderful. Quebec was a rare jazz musician who never lost his appeal in the R&B community. With Sonny Clark, Grant Green, Paul Chambers, and Philly Joe Jones. *—Ron Wynn*

Congo Lament / Jan. 20, 1962 / Blue Note ✦✦✦
Africa meets Harlem with soul in a rousing Quebec date. *—Ron Wynn*

Easy Living / Jan. 20, 1962 / Blue Note ✦✦✦✦
This CD reissue (which adds three songs to the original LP) is really two sets in one. The first five selections are a blues-oriented jam session that matches the contrasting tenors of Ike Quebec and Stanley Turrentine with trombonist Bennie James, pianist Sonny Clark, bassist Milt Hinton, and drummer Art Blakey. However, it is the last three numbers ("I've Got a Crush on You," "Nancy with the Laughing Face," and "Easy Living") that are most memorable. This set gives a definitive look at late-period Ike Quebec. *—Scott Yanow*

Paul Quinichette

b. May 17, 1916, Denver, CO, **d.** May 25, 1983, New York, NY
Sax (Tenor) / Swing
Paul Quinichette was known throughout his career as the "Vice Prez"

because he sounded so similar to Lester Young. While most of Young's other followers emulated his '30s style, Quinichette sounded like Lester Young of the '50s. After getting experience with Nat Towles, Lloyd Sherock, and Ernie Fields, Quinichette was featured with Jay McShann during 1942-44. He played on the West Coast with Johnny Otis (1945-47), traveled to New York with Louis Jordan, and performed with Lucky Millinder (1948-49), Red Allen, and Hot Lips Page. Quinichette was with Count Basie during 1952-53 (when Basie had reformed his orchestra), worked with Benny Goodman in 1955, recorded with Billie Holiday, and held his own on a session with John Coltrane. Otherwise Quinichette mostly led his own group in the '50s, recording several excellent (if obviously derivative) records. He left music in the late '50s to become an electrical engineer, returning to jazz briefly in the early- to mid-'70s, playing with Sammy Price, Brooks Kerr, and Buddy Tate before being forced to retire because of bad health. —*Scott Yanow*

● **Cattin'** / May 17, 1953-1957 / Mobile Fidelity ◆◆◆◆

Kid from Denver / Jul. 16, 1956 / Biograph ◆◆◆

On the Sunny Side / May 10, 1957 / Original Jazz Classics ◆◆◆◆
A standout late '50s blowing date led by tenor saxophonist Paul Quinichette with trombonist Curtis Fuller, alto saxophonists John Jenkins and Sonny Red, pianist Mal Waldrons, bassist Doug Watkins, and drummer Ed Thigpen. This was simply straightahead blues, ballads, and standards, with Jenkins in particular taking some torrid solos. —*Ron Wynn*

The Chase Is on / Aug. 29, 1957 & Sep. 8, 1957 / Bethlehem ◆◆◆

Jimmy Raney

b. Aug. 20, 1927, Louisville, KY, **d.** May 10, 1995
Guitar / Cool
Jimmy Raney was the definitive cool jazz guitarist, a fluid bop soloist with a quiet sound and a great deal of inner fire. He worked with local groups in Chicago before spending nine months with Woody Herman in 1948. From then on he was in the major leagues, having associations with Al Haig, Buddy DeFranco, Artie Shaw, and Terry Gibbs. His work with Stan Getz (1951-52) was historic, as the pair made for a classic musical partnership. Raney was also very much at home in the Red Norvo Trio (1953-54) before spending six years working primarily in a supper club with pianist Jimmy Lyon (1954-60). After playing with Getz during 1962-63, he returned to Louisville and was outside of music until resurfacing in the early '70s. During the '70s Raney recorded often for Xanadu. He worked frequently with his son, Doug Raney, (who has a very similar sound on guitar) and was less active in the late '80s and '90s until his 1995 death. —*Scott Yanow*

Jimmy Raney / May 28, 1954-Feb. 18, 1955 / Original Jazz Classics ◆◆◆◆
Incredibly talented guitarist on A+ record. Near essential. With Teddy Kotick and Hall Overton. —*Michael G. Nastos*

Jimmy and Doug Raney Quartet / Apr. 19, 1979 / SteepleChase ◆◆◆◆

Duets / Apr. 21, 1979 / SteepleChase ◆◆◆◆
It was recorded with Doug Raney. —*AMG*

● **Raney (1981)** / Feb. 27, 1981 / Criss Cross ◆◆◆◆
This was the first release by Criss Cross, one of the top bop-based labels in Europe. The CD reissue adds six alternate takes to the original seven-song program. The cool-toned guitarist Jimmy Raney is teamed with his son Doug (who has a very similar style on guitar), bassist Jesper Lundgaard, and drummer Eric Ineke. Together they perform one original and six standards in light but forcefully swinging style. The interplay between the two guitarists is a major plus. —*Scott Yanow*

Nardis / Mar. 1983 / SteepleChase ◆◆◆

Wisteria / Dec. 30, 1985 / Criss Cross ◆◆◆◆

But Beautiful / 1990 / Criss Cross ◆◆◆

Freddie Redd

b. May 29, 1928, New York, NY
Piano / Hard Bop
Freddie Redd has blended the rough, furious rhythmic pace of early blues and barrelhouse playing with bebop's voicings and structures. The results are a sound that's both dense and sprawling, energetic, yet never cliched or simplistic. Redd's largely a self-taught player. He began working in New York and Syracuse clubs after his discharge from the Army in 1949. He was in a small group led by Johnny Miller, then recorded in the early '50s with Tiny Grimes and toured the South with Cootie Williams. Redd returned to New York in 1952 and worked for a brief period with Oscar Pettiford and Charles Mingus in 1953. Redd played in the Jive Bombers and recorded with Art Farmer and Gigi Gryce's quintet, plus the Gene Ammons all-stars. He toured Sweden with Ernestine Anderson and Rolf Ericson in 1956, recording with Ericson and Tommy Potter and cutting trio sessions. He moved to San Francisco when he retured to America, working for a short time at the Black Hawk with Mingus and serving as house pianist at Bop City. Redd wrote most of the music for Jack Gelber's play *The Connection* and participated in the New York performances in 1959 and 1960, and in

London and Paris in 1961. Redd also played on the soundtrack for the film version. He lived and performed in Europe during the '60s and early '70s, working and playing in Paris, Denmark, and the Netherlands. Redd returned to America in 1974, settling in Los Angeles. He recorded a trio album in 1977 and recorded new sessions for Triloka in 1988 and Milestone in 1990. —*Ron Wynn*

San Francisco Suite for Jazz Trio / Oct. 2, 1957 / Original Jazz Classics ◆◆◆◆
Trio. A fine reissue of a thorough date. Redd in top form. —*Ron Wynn*

Music from "The Connection" / 1960 / Blue Note ◆◆◆◆
Soundtrack. Concept work that features Redd's playing. —*Ron Wynn*

★ **The Complete Blue Note Freddie Redd** / Feb. 15, 1960-Jan. 17, 1961 / Mosaic ◆◆◆◆◆
Available in a box set as either three LPs or two CDs, this limited-edition release has all of the music recorded at pianist Freddie Redd's three Blue Note sessions. In addition to the selections originally included on the LPs *Music from the Connection* and *Shades of Redd*, there is a completely unissued date that adds to the fairly slim Freddie Redd discography. Altoist Jackie McLean (who is on all three sets) and tenor saxophonist Tina Brooks (a key soloist on two) co-star with the pianist; trumpeter Benny Bailey is also heard from on the later date. The music is comprised mostly of Redd's originals (including seven songs written for the stage play *The Connection*) and fits into the style of the mainstream hard bop of the day, although with a few personal touches. Straightahead fans and Blue Note collectors can consider this set to be essential. —*Scott Yanow*

☆ **Shades of Redd** / Aug. 13, 1960 / Blue Note ◆◆◆◆◆
Quintet with Tina Brooks on tenor sax and Jackie McLean on alto sax plays all Redd originals with flair and bluesy poignancy. —*Michael G. Nastos*

Extemporaneous / Aug. 14, 1978-Sep. 23, 1978 / Interplay ◆◆◆◆
This album from Interplay gave Freddie Redd a rare opportunity to record unaccompanied solos. He interprets eight of his own somewhat obscure compositions with swing, taste, and enough variety to hold one's attention. Redd has long been underrated, and this is one of his better recordings. —*Scott Yanow*

Lonely City / Jan. 18, 1985-Jan. 19, 1985 / Uptown ◆◆◆◆
Freddie Redd, an aggressive, emphatic hard bop pianist, has had an erratic recording career due to personal and drug problems that forced him off the scene. He shows on this session the swinging style, distinctive phrasing, and consistently impressive solo skils that made his Blue Note and Prestige dates so popular during the late '50s. —*Ron Wynn*

● **Live at the Studio Grill** / May 19, 1988 & May 26, 1988 / Triloka ◆◆◆◆
An enchanting session with Al McKibbon and Billy Higgins. —*Ron Wynn*

Everybody Loves a Winner / Oct. 9, 1990 & Oct. 10, 1990 / Milestone ◆◆◆◆
Pianist Freddie Redd has not recorded all that much during his 45-year career, but most of his records have been special events. This particular set has eight of Redd's tightly arranged compositions being performed by a fine sextet that also features tenor saxophonist Teddy Edwards, altoist Curtis Peagler, and trombonist Phil Ranelin. —*Scott Yanow*

Dewey Redman (Walter Dewey Redman)

b. May 17, 1931, Fort Worth, TX
Sax (Tenor) / Post-Bop, Free Jazz
One of the great avant-garde tenors, Dewey Redman has never received anywhere near the acclaim that his son, Joshua Redman, gained in the '90s; but ironically, Dewey is a much more innovative player. He began on clarinet when he was 13years old and played in his high school marching band, a group that also included Ornette Coleman, Charles Moffett, and Prince Lasha. Redman was a public school teacher during 1956-59. After getting his master's degree in education from North Texas State, he moved to San Francisco, where he freelanced as a musician for seven years; Pharoah Sanders was among his sidemen. All of this was a prelude to his impressive association with the Ornette Coleman Quartet (1967-74,) during which Redman's tenor playing was a perfect match for Coleman's alto. Redman could play as free as the leader, but his appealing tone made the music seem a little more accessible. He also worked with Charlie Haden's Liberation Music Orchestra and was an important part of Keith Jarrett's greatest group, his quintet of the mid-'70s. Redman guested on Pat Metheny's notable *80/81* album and teamed up with Don Cherry, Charlie Haden, and Ed Blackwell in the Ornette Coleman reunion band called Old and New Dreams. Despite all of this activity and plenty of recordings (including occasional ones as a leader), Dewey Redman has yet to be fully recognized for his innovative talents. —*Scott Yanow*

Look for the Black Star / Jan. 4, 1966 / Freedom ◆◆◆◆
Although always a bit under-recognized and overshadowed by his contemporaries, tenor saxophonist Dewey Redman has long been one of the giants of the avant-garde and free bop. This early recording finds Redman discovering his own individual voice on five of his frequently emotional originals. Assisted by pianist Jym Young, bassist Donald Raphael Gareet,

and drummer Eddie Moore, this San Francisco date is quite adventurous and holds one's interest throughout. —*Scott Yanow*

Musics / Oct. 17, 1978-Oct. 19, 1978 / Galaxy ✦✦✦✦
This is one of tenor saxophonist Dewey Redman's more accessible sessions. With the assistance of pianist Fred Simmons, bassist Mark Helias, and drummer Eddie Moore, Redman is heard on the lyrical ballad "Alone Again (Naturally)," a bossa nova, jamming over parade rhythms, and performing originals that sometimes are advanced bop. The music is excellent, although not as explorative as most of Redman's other recordings. —*Scott Yanow*

● **The Struggle Continues** / Jan. 1982 / ECM ✦✦✦✦
His best shows great teamwork from bassist Mark Helias, drummer Ed Blackwell, and pianist Charles Eubanks. It's a record to make you say "wow." "Turn Over Baby" is a good boogie, and "Joie de Vivre" is one of Redman's best vehicles for improv. —*Michael G. Nastos*

● **Living on the Edge** / Sep. 13, 1989-Sep. 14, 1989 / Black Saint ✦✦✦✦
A first-rate late '80s date by tenor saxophonist Dewey Redman. He's working alongside excellent pianist Geri Allen, and the compositions are rigorously played. Redman, as the only horn player, gets extensive space and offers his patented twisting, slashing solos. Bassist Cameron Brown and drummer Eddie Moore prove equally adept at adjusting to the Redman/Allen team. —*Ron Wynn*

Choices / Jul. 29, 1992-Jul. 30, 1992 / Enja ✦✦✦

African Venus / Dec. 11, 1992 / Evidence ✦✦✦✦

Don Redman

b. Jul. 29, 1900, Piedmont, WV, **d.** Nov. 30, 1964, New York, NY
Clarinet, Sax (Alto) / Swing, Classic Jazz
Don Redman was the first great arranger in jazz history. His innovations as a writer essentially invented the jazz-oriented big band with arrangements that developed, yet left room for solo improvisations.

After graduating from college with a music degree at the age of 20, Redman played for a year with Billy Paige's Broadway Syncopators and then met up with Fletcher Henderson. Redman became Henderson's chief arranger (although Fletcher was often later mistakenly given credit for the innovative charts), in addition to playing clarinet, alto, and (on at least one occasion) oboe. Redman, whose largely-spoken vocals were charming, recorded the first-ever scat vocal on "My Papa Doesn't Two-Time" in early 1924, predating Louis Armstrong. Although his early arrangements were futuristic, they could be a bit stiff; and it was not until Armstrong joined Henderson's Orchestra that Redman (learning from the brilliant cornetist) began to really swing in his writing. "Sugar Foot Stomp" and "The Stampede" are two of his many classic charts.

It was a shock to Fletcher Henderson when Redman was persuaded in 1927 by Jean Goldkette to direct McKinney's Cotton Pickers. Redman soon turned the previously unknown group into a strong competitor of Henderson's, composing such standards as "Gee Baby, Ain't I Good to You" and "Cherry." He sang more, emphasized his alto over his more primitive-sounding clarinet (guesting on some famous recordings with Louis Armstrong's Savoy Ballroom Five in 1928), and made a strong series of memorable records. In 1931 Redman put together his own big band, which lasted (if not prospered) up until 1941. After that he freelanced as an arranger for the remainder of the swing era, led an all-star orchestra in 1946 that became the first band to visit postwar Europe, and eventually became Pearl Bailey's musical director. Although he recorded a few sessions in the late '50s, Don Redman's main significance is for his influential work of the '20s and '30s. —*Scott Yanow*

● **The Chronological Don Redman, 1931-1933** / Sep. 24, 1931-Feb. 2, 1933 / Classics ✦✦✦✦

The Chronological Don Redman, 1933-1936 / Feb. 2, 1933-May 7, 1936 / Classics ✦✦✦✦

Don Redman (1936-1939) / May 7, 1936-Mar. 23, 1939 / Classics ✦✦✦✦

Joshua Redman

b. Feb. 1, 1969, Berkeley, CA
Sax (Tenor) / Post-Bop, Hard Bop
Every few years it seems as if the jazz media go out of their way to hype one young artist, overpraising him or her to such an extent that it is easy to tear him/her down when the next season arrives. In the early '90s Joshua Redman briefly became a media darling, but in his case he largely deserved the attention. A talented, loop-based tenorman, Redman (who will probably never be an innovator) is a throwback to the styles of Red Holloway and Gene Ammons but has an inquisitive spirit and can play intriguing music when inspired.

The son of the great tenor saxophonist Dewey Redman, Joshua graduated from Harvard and (after debating about whether to become a doctor) seemed headed toward studying law at Yale. However Redman came in first place at the 1991 Thelonious Monk competition, landed a recording contract with Warner Brothers, and was soon on the cover of most jazz

magazines. Pat Metheny was a guest on one of his albums (the Redman-Metheny interplay during their engagements was memorable) and, although Redman has had success touring with his own group, it is a pity that his apprentice period as a sideman was so brief. —*Scott Yanow*

Joshua Redman / May 27, 1992-Sep. 15, 1992 / Warner Bros. ✦✦✦

★ **Wish** / 1993 / Warner Bros. ✦✦✦✦✦
Joshua Redman may be the person to unite warring sects, since he is neither a committed neobop conservative nor a jazz/hip-hopper or "acid" player. He is one of the few young lions that has made great music from day one. Redman's soaring tone, intelligently constructed solos, control, and ability to play riveting uptempo, midtempo, or slow works has justifiably made him a sensation. When the lineup includes Pat Metheny offering marvelous solos on electric and acoustic and Charlie Haden and Billy Higgins being their customary masterful selves on bass and drums, you have the kind of great, uncompromising jazz work you seldom get from a major label in the '90s. —*Ron Wynn*

Moodswing / Mar. 8, 1994-Mar. 10, 1994 / Warner Bros. ✦✦✦✦

Spirit of the Moment: Live at the Village Vanguard / 1995 / Warner Bros. ✦✦✦✦
This double-CD gives one a definitive look at how the much-acclaimed tenor saxophonist Joshua Redman sounded in the mid-'90s. Joined by pianist Peter Martin, bassist Christopher Thomas, and drummer Brian Blade, Redman stretches from Gene Ammons (who is saluted on "Jig-A-Jug") to late period John Coltrane, showing off both his wide range and his lyricism. Redman is heard at his best on the four-minute cadenza that opens "St. Thomas," digging into "My One and Only Love" and playing almost outside on "Lyric." Of the 14 songs, nine are his originals, and although Redman was not at this point an innovator, he was well on his way to forming his own personal style. Recommended. —*Scott Yanow*

Dizzy Reece (Alphonso Son Reece)

b. Jan. 5, 1931, Kingston, Jamaica
Trumpet / Hard Bop
Dizzy Reece is a fine, hard-loop trumpeter who has been overshadowed by the innovators of the style. He started on trumpet when he was 14 and moved to Europe in 1949. It was while he was based in England (1954-59) that he achieved some recognition through a series of recordings with top English musicians, plus a 1958 date with Donald Byrd. He moved to New York in 1959, but after a few notable recordings and a bit of publicity, Reece seemed to fade away, despite remaining active. He was with Dizzy Gillespie's Orchestra in 1968 and the Paris Reunion Band in 1985. —*Scott Yanow*

Blues in Trinity / Aug. 24, 1958 / Blue Note ✦✦✦✦

● **Asia Minor** / Mar. 13, 1962 / Original Jazz Classics ✦✦✦✦
This is one of trumpeter Dizzy Reece's finest recordings, a well planned sextet date (reissued on CD) with baritonist Cecil Payne, Joe Farrell on tenor and flute, pianist Hank Jones, bassist Ron Carter, and drummer Charlie Persip that is on the level of a Blue Note album. Reece (who contributed three diverse originals) performs mostly minor-toned songs that seem to really inspire the musicians. The solos tend to be concise but meaningful, and overall this hard bop but occasionally surprising session is memorable. Strange that Reece would not get another opportunity to lead a record date until 1970. —*Scott Yanow*

Django Reinhardt (Jean Baptiste Reinhardt)

b. Jan. 23, 1910, Liverchies, Belgium, **d.** May 16, 1953, Fontainebleau, France
Guitar / Swing
Django Reinhardt was Europe's first influential jazz figure. His melodic and harmonic ideas, solo style, and general technique have been recycled, absorbed, and spread by generations of jazz and blues guitarists. A 1928 fire cost him two fingers on his fret hand. Reinhardt developed a new fingering system and switched from banjo to guitar. He was a spectacular soloist, able to play with furious intensity or incredible sensitivity, and a remarkable accompanist who could complement and support any musician. His switch to electric guitar in the '40s made him even more influential, as he tackled and mastered issues of amplification and volume. Reinhardt wandered through Belgium and France as a gypsy, playing mostly violin and banjo, plus a little guitar. He was already an adult and professional musician when he discovered jazz. Working with vocalist Jean Sablon, Reinhardt synthesized jazz and traditional gypsy music, developing an approach that borrowed from both but wasn't totally defined by either. He formed the Hot Club of France in 1934 with violinist Stephane Grappelli, two other guitarists, and a bassist. One original guitarist was his brother Joseph. The Hot Club recorded more than 200 songs and was a sensation on both sides of the Atlantic. Such Reinhardt compositions as "Love's Melody," "Stomping At Decca," "Djangology," and "Nocturne" became an established part of the jazz vocabulary. Reinhardt recorded with Coleman Hawkins, Benny Carter, Dicky Wells, Rex Stewart, and Barney Bigard between 1937 and 1939; the quintet recorded in London in

1939. Reinhardt's "Nuages" was a fan favorite during World War II. He began experiments with a big band, while also forming a quintet with clarinetist Hubert Rostaing. The Nazis banned jazz in France and murdered 500,000 Gypsies, but Reinhardt continued playing. The quintet was recreated for a 1946 recording session, and Reinhardt arranged the music for the film *Le Village de La colere* with Andre Hodeir. Later that year Reinhardt journeyed to America to tour with Duke Ellington. But the tour was unsuccessful, in part due to Reinhardt's penchant for disappearing. He began to appreciate and play bop and adapt its lines on guitar. There were occasional reunions with Grappelli before Reinhardt died of a stroke in 1953. A documentary film about his life was made by Paul Paviot in 1958. Django Reinhardt remains a highly influential force and can be thought of not only as a top European jazz artist but as the world's top jazz guitarist (along with Charlie Christian) of 1933-53. —*Ron Wynn and Dan Morgenstern*

★ **Djangologie/USA, Vols. 1-7** / Mar. 15, 1928-Oct. 1, 1940 / Swing ✦✦✦✦✦
This seven-LP box set, made available domestically by DRG, features mostly the remarkable guitarist Django Reinhardt with the Quintet of the Hot Club of France during 1936-39, showing that not only could Europeans play swinging jazz as far back as the '30s, but they could be pacesetters and innovators, too. Violinist Stephane Grappelli also stars throughout this set, which includes appearances with bands led by Benny Carter, Coleman Hawkins, Rex Stewart, harmonica wizard Larry Adler, trumpeter Philippe Brun, trumpeter Bill Coleman, violinist Eddie South, and trombonist Dicky Wells, along with many performances by the Quintet. The first album is in some ways the most interesting, for it features Django as a sideman with a wide variety of French groups, including two very early appearances on banjo. A book in the box has a complete discography of Django Reinhardt's career. Highly recommended; it's superior to the CD reissues of some of this material. —*Scott Yanow*

★ **Djangology** / May 4, 1936-Mar. 10, 1948 / EMI ✦✦✦✦✦
This massive ten-CD set of Django Reinhardt's recordings covers some of the same ground as the earlier 20-LP *Djangology* EMI series, duplicating the music on *Vols. 2-15* along with three tracks from the first LP and ten from *Vol. 16*. However, there are 34 additional selections that were formerly overlooked (on some of those songs Reinhardt plays only a minor role). This essential box contains 243 performances taken from a 12-year period, tracing Reinhardt's career from his performances with the Quintet of the Hot Club of France (which co-starred violinist Stephane Grappelli) through the war years (with the guitarist heard in a wide variety of settings) and the formation of his postwar quintet with clarinetist Hubert Rostaing before concluding with a reunion with Grappelli. Recommended to all serious Django Reinhardt collectors. —*Scott Yanow*

Swing Guitar / Oct. 26, 1945-Mar. 1946 / Jass ✦✦✦✦
In late 1945 the great guitarist Django Reinhardt had an opportunity to broadcast regularly with the ATC (Air Transport Command) Orchestra, a big band filled with talented but now-forgotten American servicemen. Reinhardt is the main soloist throughout, whether with the full orchestra or with small groups out of the band; he also takes "Improvisation No. 6" unaccompanied. In addition, the ATC band is heard on six selections without the guitarist. All in all, this is a surprising and consistently interesting release. —*Scott Yanow*

Brussels and Paris / Mar. 21, 1947-Apr. 8, 1953 / DRG ✦✦✦✦
Even collectors with dozens of Django Reinhardt records may not have the formerly rare performances included on this 1996 reissue CD. The great Reinhardt is heard throughout on electric (rather than acoustic) guitar, and he shows that during his last years he was one of the top bop-based guitarists in the world. Reinhardt is teamed with clarinetist Hubert Rostaing in a 1947 quintet for nine songs, but it is the other 16 selections (his final recordings) that are of greatest interest. During 1951-53 Reinhardt was joined by such top young French modernists as trumpeters Bernard Hullin and Roger Guerin, altoist Hubert Fol, pianists Raymond Fol and Martial Solal, and bassist Pierre Michelot. Django Reinhardt shows that, although he maintained a low profile in the early '50s, he was still the top jazz guitarist in the world. Highly recommended. —*Scott Yanow*

★ **Peche a La Mouche** / Apr. 16, 1947-Mar. 10, 1953 / Verve ✦✦✦✦✦
Legend has it that guitarist Django Reinhardt was at his absolute peak in the '30s during his recordings with violinist Stephane Grappelli and that when he switched from acoustic to electric guitar after World War II, he lost a bit of his musical personality. Wrong on both counts. This double CD documents his Blue Star recordings of 1947 and 1953, and Reinhardt (on electric guitar) takes inventive boppish solos that put him at the top of the list of jazz guitarists who were active during the era. Most of the earlier tracks feature Reinhardt in the Quintet of the Hot Club of France with clarinetist Hubert Rostaing, but it is the eight later selections in which he is backed by a standard rhythm section that are most interesting. These well recorded performances hint at what Django Reinhardt might have accomplished had he lived longer. Highly recommended. -*Scott Yanow*

★ **The Quintette of the Hot Club of France** / 1947 / GNP ✦✦✦✦✦
A new set featuring his mid- and late-40s dates with Hot Club. Wondrous playing by Reinhardt and Grappelli (violin). —*Ron Wynn*

● **Djangology 49** / Jan. 1949-Feb. 1949 / Bluebird ✦✦✦✦
In 1949, guitarist Django Reinhardt and violinist Stephane Grappelli met up in Italy, playing several engagements with Italian rhythm sections and recording an extensive series of songs. This Bluebird CD contains 20 of the best performances, and, even if the rhythm section is fairly irrelevant, Django and Grappelli constantly challenge each other to play at their most creative. These recordings do not duplicate the ones reissued by EMI. —*Scott Yanow*

Emily Remler

b. Sep. 18, 1957, New York, NY, **d.** May 4, 1990, Sydney, Australia
Guitar / Hard Bop
Emily Remler's death at age 32 from a heart attack (certainly not helped by her frequent use of heroin) was a shock to the jazz world and a sad waste. She was just beginning to emerge from the Wes Montgomery influence and develop her own voice. Remler began playing guitar when she was ten, attended Berklee (1976-79), and recorded as a leader for the first time in 1980. She played with the Los Angeles version of the show *Sophisticated Ladies* (1981-82) and in 1985 had a duo with Larry Coryell but otherwise worked mostly as a leader with her own small groups. After recording bop-oriented dates for Concord and a contemporary set for Justice, she toured with David Benoit before her sudden death. —*Scott Yanow*

● **Take Two** / Jun. 1982 / Concord Jazz ✦✦✦✦
Tremendous solos and interpretations by a fine player. —*Ron Wynn*

Catwalk / Aug. 1984 / Concord Jazz ✦✦✦✦
Guitarist Emily Remler's fourth recording makes one regret even more her death at age 32. While her earlier dates were very much in the bop mainstream, this one (in a quartet with trumpeter John D'Earth, bassist Eddie Gomez, and drummer Bob Moses) finds her looking ahead and partly finding her own voice on her seven diverse originals. Although she never became an innovator, Remler certainly had a lot to offer the jazz world, and this fairly adventurous effort was one of the finest recordings of her short career. —*Scott Yanow*

East to West / May 1988 / Concord Jazz ✦✦✦✦
With the Hank Jones Trio. —*Michael G. Nastos*

This Is Me / 1990 / Justice ✦✦✦

Buddy Rich (Bernard Rich)

b. Sep. 30, 1917, New York, NY, **d.** Apr. 2, 1987, Los Angeles, CA
Drums / Bop, Swing
When it came to technique, speed, power, and the ability to put together incredible drum solos, Buddy Rich lived up to the billing of "the world's greatest drummer." Although some other drummers were more innovative, none was in his league, even during the early days. Buddy Rich started playing drums in vaudeville as "Traps, the Drum Wonder" when he was only 18 months old; he was completely self-taught. Rich performed in vaudeville throughout his childhood and developed into a decent singer and a fine tap dancer. But drumming was his purpose in life, and by 1938 he had discovered jazz and was playing with Joe Marsala's combo. Rich was soon propelling Bunny Berigan's Orchestra. He spent most of 1939 with Artie Shaw (at a time when the clarinetist had the most popular band in swing), and then from 1939-45 (except for a stint in the military) he made history with Tommy Dorsey. During this era it became obvious that Buddy Rich was the king of drummers, easily de-throning his friend Gene Krupa. Rich had a boppish band during 1945-47 that did not catch on; toured with Jazz at the Philharmonic; recorded with a countless number of All-Stars in the '50s for Verve (including Charlie Parker, Lester Young, Art Tatum, and Lionel Hampton); and worked with Les Brown, Charlie Ventura, Tommy Dorsey (1954-55), and Harry James (off and on during 1953-66). A heart attack in 1959 slowed him down only briefly and, although he contemplated becoming a fulltime vocalist, Rich never gave up the drums.

In 1966 Buddy Rich beat the odds and put together a successful big band that was his main outlet for his final 20 years. His heart began giving him trouble in 1983, but Rich never gave his music less than 100% and was still pushing himself at the end. A perfectionist who expected the same from his sidemen (some of whom he treated cruelly), Buddy Rich is definitively documented in Mel Tormé's book *Traps, the Drum Wonder*. His incredible playing can be viewed on several readily available videotapes, although surprisingly few of his later big-band albums have been made available yet on CD. —*Scott Yanow*

This One's for Basie / Aug. 24, 1956-Aug. 25, 1956 / Verve ✦✦✦✦
Drummer Buddy Rich put together an interesting 11-piece group for this tribute to Count Basie. The only Basie alumnus present is trumpeter Harry "Sweets" Edison, but the other soloists (trombonists Frank Rosolino and Bob Enevoldsen, Bob Cooper on tenor, and pianist Jimmy Rowles) easily fit into the setting. Marty Paich contributed the arrangements. There are

plenty of drum solos, and the music, if not all that memorable, can easily be enjoyed by straightahead jazz fans. — *Scott Yanow*

Buddy Rich vs Max Roach / Apr. 1959 / Mercury ✦✦✦

Rich Versus Roach / Apr. 1959 / Mercury ✦✦✦✦

The idea probably looked good on paper. Why not combine Buddy Rich's Quintet of 1959 (which consisted of altoist Phil Woods, trombonist Willie Dennis, pianist John Bunch, and bassist Phil Leshin) with Max Roach's band of the time (consisting of trumpeter Tommy Turrentine, tenor saxophonist Stanley Turrentine, trombonist Julian Priester, and bassist Bobby Boswell)? This CD reissues all of the music (including four "new" alternate takes), but the excess of drum solos and the relative brevity of space given to the horns results in a great deal of sameness from track to track. An unexpected bore! — *Scott Yanow*

Swingin' New Big Band / Sep. 29, 1966-Oct. 10, 1966 / Pacific Jazz ✦✦✦✦

Big Swing Face / Feb. 22, 1967-Mar. 14, 1967 / Pacific Jazz ✦✦✦

★ **Mercy, Mercy** / Jul. 10, 1968 / World Pacific ✦✦✦✦✦

Jerome Richardson (Jerome C. Richardson)

b. Nov. 15, 1920, Sealy, TX
Flute, Sax (Soprano) / Cool, Hard Bop

Jerome Richardson was once a notable, versatile jazz saxophonist. He remains quite versatile, but his visibility has been limited for years because of his heavy studio output. Since the early '70s, Richardson's often robust saxophone and tart flute were heard mostly on film and television soundtracks. Richardson began playing alto when he was eight years old and was a professional at 14. He worked with Texas dance bands until 1941, then was briefly in Jimmie Lunceford's band before joining the Navy. He worked in a band led by Marshall Royal in the service. Richardson toured with Lionel Hampton after his discharge in the late '40s, then played with Earl Hines in the early '50s. Richardson moved to New York in 1953, led his own band at Minton's, and worked with Oscar Pettiford in 1956 and 1957. He did sessions with Lucky Millinder, Cootie Williams, Chico Hamilton, Johnny Richards, Gerry Mulligan, and Gerald Wilson, then joined Quincy Jones' orchestra in 1959. He was part of the band for the show "Free and Easy," which toured Europe and performed in Paris. Richardson played in bands backing several singers in the '60s, among them Peggy Lee, Billy Eckstine, Brook Benton, and Julie London. He was a founding member of the Thad Jones-Mel Lewis orchestra in the mid-'60s and was its lead alto saxophonist until 1970. Then Richardson moved to Hollywood, and has since frequently collaborated with Jones, doing albums and touring Japan three times. He toured Europe with Nat Adderley in 1980. Richardson recorded in the '60s as a leader for New Jazz and United Artists, among others. He has no sesssions available as a leader but can be heard on CD reissues by Jones and the Thad Jones-Mel Lewis orchestra. — *Ron Wynn*

● **Midnight Oil** / Oct. 10, 1958 / Original Jazz Classics ✦✦✦✦

Flutist Jerome Richardson (who switches to tenor on one of the five selections on this CD reissue) has long been underrated and has had only four opportunities to lead his own record dates up to the present time, of which *Midnight Oil* was the first. The music (three of Richardson's originals plus Artie Shaw's "Lyric" and the standard "Caravan") is performed in swinging fashion by Richardson, trombonist Jimmy Cleveland (the unusual flute-trombone blend heard on three of the songs is quite pleasing), pianist Hank Jones, guitarist Kenny Burrell, bassist Joe Benjamin, and drummer Charlie Persip. This set offers cool-toned bop that is brief (just over 35 minutes) but easy to enjoy. — *Scott Yanow*

Roamin' with Richardson / Oct. 21, 1959 / Original Jazz Classics ✦✦✦✦

The Rippingtons

Group / Instrumental Pop, Crossover

One of the most popular groups in what is loosely termed "contemporary jazz," the Rippingtons were formed (and have been led ever since) by guitarist/keyboardist Russ Freeman (no relation to the veteran West Coast bop pianist of the same name). Freeman (b. Feb. 11, 1960, in Nashville) studied at Cal Arts and UCLA, and recorded *Nocturnal Playground* as a leader in 1985 for the Brainchild label, a one-man project. In 1987 he was approached to record for the Japanese Alfa label and came up with the Rippingtons name for the all-star group he used on the disc (*Moonlighting*), an ensemble featuring David Benoit, Kenny G., and Brandon Fields. Their album was released domestically by Passport and became a hit. Freeman soon formed a regular touring band (usually including saxophonist Jeff Kashiwa, bassist Kim Stone, drummer Tony Morales, and percussionist Steve Reid) and cut a second disc for Passport; the group has since recorded regularly for GRP. Freeman writes all of the music for the Rippingtons, much of which falls in the pop/R&B genre. — *Scott Yanow*

Kilimanjaro / 1988 / GRP ✦✦✦

Tourist in Paradise / 1989 / GRP ✦✦✦

Welcome to the St. James' Club / 1990 / GRP ✦✦✦

Curves Ahead / 1991 / GRP ✦✦

Curves Ahead features Russ Freeman on keyboards and guitar. These nine songs are played on keyboards, acoustic and electric guitars, drums, sax, congas, shakers, bells, blocks, jingle sticks, and an array of other instruments that have become a trademark for the band. — *MusD*

● **Live in L.A.** / Sep. 1992 / GRP ✦✦✦✦

In September 1992, on two separate nights and in two separate venues, the Rippingtons recorded this album before a live audience. Russ Freman is the driving force on electric, acoustic, and classical guitars as well as guitar synthesizer. He is backed by the core members of the group: Tony Morales, drums; Jeff Kashiwa, saxophone; Mark Portmann, keyboards; Steve Reid, percussion; and Kim Stone, bass. The band is augmented by a solid horn section of alto saxophone, trumpet, and trombone. To add to the excitement and pleasure, special guest artists David Benoit and Carl Anderson joined the proceedings. — *MusD*

Lee Ritenour

b. Nov. 1, 1952, Hollywood, CA
Guitar / Instrumental Pop, Crossover

Lee Ritenour has long been the perfect studio musician, one who can melt into the background without making any impact. While he possesses impressive technique, Ritenour has played mostly instrumental pop, sometimes with a Brazilian flavor. His few jazz efforts have found him essentially imitating Wes Montgomery, but despite that, he has been consistently popular since the mid-'70s. After touring with Sergio Mendes' Brasil '77 in 1973, Ritenour became a very busy studio guitarist in Los Angeles, taking time off for occasional tours with his groups and, in the mid-'90s, with Bob James in Fourplay. He has recorded many albums as a leader, most recently for GRP. — *Scott Yanow*

Captain Fingers / 1977 / Epic ✦✦

Captain's Journey / 1978 / Elektra ✦✦✦

Rio / Aug. 1979-Sep. 1979 / GRP ✦✦✦✦

Ritenour on acoustic. Very nice music. — *Michael Erlewine*

Feel the Night / 1979 / Elektra ✦✦

One of the albums that established the guitarist. — *Michael Erlewine*

Festival / May 1988 / GRP ✦✦✦

Color Rit / Mar. 1989 / GRP ✦✦✦

Stolen Moments / 1990 / GRP ✦✦✦✦

● **Larry and Lee** / Jun. 1994-Jan. 1995 / GRP ✦✦✦✦

Larry Carlton and Lee Ritenour have had parallel careers, but this CD is their first meeting on records. The two guitarists complement each other, and there are hints of Wes Montgomery along with a tribute to Joe Pass ("Remembering J.P."), but the songs (all of them their originals) are little more than rhythmic grooves most of the time, with the usual fadeouts. The consistently lightweight music is reasonably pleasing but never too stimulating. — *Scott Yanow*

Sam Rivers

b. Sep. 25, 1930, El Reno, OK
Flute, Sax (Soprano), Sax (Tenor) / Avant-Garde, Post-Bop

Although often overlooked, Sam Rivers has long been one of the most original voices of the avant-garde, equally skilled on tenor, soprano, and flute. Music ran in his family, for his grandfather published a book of hymns and Black folk songs in 1882; his mother played piano; and his father sang with the Fisk Jubilee Singers. Rivers' musical interests, however, were in a different direction. He started on piano when he was five and then learned violin, alto, soprano, and finally tenor. He played regularly in Boston from 1947, when he went to the Boston Conservatory, and during 1955-57 he was freelancing in Florida. By 1958 Rivers was back in Boston with the Herb Pomeroy big band, and in the early '60s he was leading a band that backed R&B and blues singers (including a tour with T-Bone Walker). Rivers, who by then had become very interested in the music of Cecil Taylor and Ornette Coleman, was still pretty obscure as a Boston legend.

In 1964 Tony Williams (who had played with Rivers when he was a teenager) recommended him for the tenor opening with Miles Davis' Quintet. Although Rivers' playing was too advanced for Davis at the time, he did last through a tour of Japan that was recorded. Rivers made a few records for Blue Note before becoming a member of Cecil Taylor's Unit during 1968-73. With his wife, Bea, he opened Studio Rivbea as a jazz loft in New York in 1971 and became involved in teaching in addition to presenting concerts. Other than a late-'80s association with Dizzy Gillespie (where he good-naturedly played bebop and even took an occasional scat vocal), Rivers has mostly been a leader during the past two decades, whether in duets with Dave Holland or heading a large orchestra. He has recorded mostly for European labels. — *Scott Yanow*

★ **Contours** / May 21, 1965 / Blue Note ✦✦✦✦✦

Excellent, with Herbie Hancock and Freddie Hubbard. — *Michael G. Nastos*

Streams: Live at Montreux / Jul. 6, 1973 / Impulse ✦✦✦✦
Streams features Sam Rivers as the lead voice on the album-long "Streams," a lengthy multisectioned free improvisation recorded at the Montreux Jazz Festival. With support from the brillant bassist Cecil McBee and subtle drumming from the pre-disco Norman Connors, Rivers takes a powerful solo on tenor, sings through his flute, rambles a bit on piano, and concludes with a strong dosage of his soprano. *Streams* remains one of Sam Rivers' strongest recordings. —*Scott Yanow*

Sizzle / 1975 / Impulse ✦✦✦✦
Trio with Barry Altschul and Dave Holland. Funky, with electric touches. Fierce. —*Michael G. Nastos*

Sam Rivers/Dave Holland, Vol. 2 / Feb. 18, 1976 / Improvising Artists ✦✦✦

The Quest / Mar. 12, 1976-Mar. 13, 1976 / Red ✦✦✦✦

Colours / Sep. 13, 1982 / Black Saint ✦✦✦

Max Roach

b. Jan. 10, 1924, New Land, NC
Drums / Avant-Garde, Bop, Post-Bop, Hard Bop
On the basis of his persistence, adaptability, and symbolic importance, Max Roach would merit inclusion in jazz's pantheon of special performers. But he's done more than outlive many of his contemporaries. Along with Kenny Clarke, he changed the direction of drummers in the bop revolution. He shifted the rhythmic focus from the bass drum to the ride cymbal, a move that gave drummers more freedom. He emerged as arguably bebop's greatest drum soloist. Roach doesn't simply drop bombs and blast away. He tells a complete story, varying his pitch, tuning, patterns, and volume. He is a brillant brush player and can push, redirect, or break up the beat. Roach has never stood still musically, though the links between what he played in the '40s and today aren't that far apart. He's worked with pianoless trios, played with symphony orchestras, done duos with free and avant-garde musicians, backed gospel choirs, even played with a rapper long before the jazz/hip-hop thing became a media event. He was outspoken about social injustices in the pre-civil rights era, and recorded powerful, undiluted protest material. His mother sang gospel, and Roach began playing drums in gospel bands at age 10. He had formal studies at the Manhattan School of Music, then started playing with Charlie Parker and Dizzy Gillespie at Minton's Playhouse in 1942. He was house drummer and a frequent participant in after-hours jam sessions. One of the other participants was Kenny Clarke. Roach had brief stints with Benny Carter and Duke Ellington's band, then joined Gillespie's quintet in 1943 and was in Parker-led bands in 1945, 1947-49, and 1951-53. He made his recording debut with Coleman Hawkins in 1943, then recorded with Miles Davis and Parker in the late '40s. Roach traveled to Paris with Parker in 1949 and recorded there with him and others, including Kenny Dorham. He also played with Louis Jordan, Red Allen, and Coleman Hawkins, and participated in the Birth of the Cool sessions in 1948-1950. During the early '50s, Roach toured with the Jazz at the Philharmonic revue; played at Massey Hall in an all-star concert with Parker, Gillespie, Charles Mingus, and Bud Powell; and recorded with Howard Rumsey's Lighthouse All-Stars. During the mid-'50s, he co-led the Max Roach/Clifford Brown orchestra, with Powell's brother Richie on piano, and saxophonists Harold Land and Sonny Rollins. His frenetic, yet precise, drumming laid the foundation for Brown's amazing trumpet solos. This group made some landmark records in its short tenure, among them *Study in Brown* and *At Basin Street*. After Brown and Powell were killed in a car crash in 1956, Roach tried to keep the group going using Dorham and Rollins. He became involved in a record label partnership with Charles Mingus as well, forming Debut Records in the mid-'50s. Later Roach led another influential band, this time with trumpeters Dorham or Booker Little, tenor saxophonist George Coleman, trombonist Julian Priester, and sometimes Ray Draper on tuba. They cut seminal dates for Riverside and EmArcy, among them *On the Chicago Scene*, and *Deeds, Not Words*. The Max Roach +4 became a prototype hard bop unit. Then Roach made another change during the early '60s, composing multi-faceted suites and writing openly political, confrontational material featuring his wife, Abbey Lincoln, criticizing American racial injustices. He dispensed with the piano on occasion and experimented with solo drum compositions as wholly independent pieces. There were more albums for Atlantic and Impulse. The list included *Freedom Now Suite; Percussion Bitter Sweet; It's Time; Speak, Brother, Speak; The Legendary Hassan; Lift Every Voice and Sing;* and *Members, Don't Get Weary.* There was also the brillant *Drums Unlimited*, in 1965. The *Freedom Now Suite* was made into a film by Gianni Amici in 1966, but Roach and Lincoln maintain they suffered severe career reprisals as a result. During the '70s Roach continued recording prolifically for various labels, though most were for import companies like Denon and Soul Note. Roach founded M'Boom Re: Percussion in 1970, a co-operative group of 10 percussionists performing works written for them. The group still records and performs 23 years later. He recorded with Cecil Taylor, Anthony Braxton, Archie Shepp, and Abdullah Ibrahim, while maintaining his own bands. Roach also began a career in education, becoming a professor at the Uni-

versity of Massachusetts at Amherst and later holding a position at the Lennox School of Jazz. He's continued in the '80s and '90s, leading at various times a regular quartet, Double Quartet (an acoustic and string quartet together), and M-Boom, while continuing to lecture, perform, and exemplify the meaning of jazz. —*Ron Wynn*

The Max Roach Quartet, Featuring Hank Mobley / Apr. 10, 1953-Apr. 21, 1953 / Original Jazz Classics ✦✦✦

Max Roach Plus Four / Oct. 12, 1956 / EmArcy ✦✦✦✦
After the deaths of trumpeter Clifford Brown and pianist Richie Powell in a car accident a few months earlier, drummer Max Roach regrouped with trumpeter Kenny Dorham and pianist Ray Bryant filling the unfillable holes; tenor great Sonny Rollins and bassist George Morrow remained from the earlier band. This EmArcy CD finds Roach taking plenty of solo space, including almost all of "Dr. Free-zee" and the climaxes of "Just One of Those Things" and "Woody'n You." The horns have plenty of good spots, and other highlights of this worthy set include George Russell's "Ezz-thetic," and a warm rendition of "Body and Soul." —*Scott Yanow*

Max Roach 4 Plays Charlie Parker / Dec. 23, 1957 / EmArcy ✦✦✦✦
The music on this CD finds drummer Max Roach for the first time performing with a pianoless quartet. With the departure of Sonny Rollins (who is replaced on three songs apiece by either Hank Mobley or George Coleman), Roach's group (which also featured trumpeter Kenny Dorham and either George Morrow or Nelson Boyd on bass) was temporarily without any major innovators (outside of the leader). So it was perfectly fitting that Roach would look backward and perform six of Charlie Parker's compositions. Highlighted by "Yardbird Suite," "Confirmation," and "Ko Ko," this set is generally fine, although the lack of a piano is really felt on some of this material. —*Scott Yanow*

Deeds, Not Words / Sep. 4, 1958 / Original Jazz Classics ✦✦✦✦
This CD reissue of a Max Roach Riverside date is notable for featuring the great young trumpeter Booker Little and for using Ray Draper's tuba as a melody instrument; tenor saxophonist George Coleman and bassist Art Davis complete the excellent quintet. Highlights include "It's You or No One," "You Stepped out of a Dream," and Roach's unaccompanied drum piece "Conversation." This is fine music from a group that was trying to stretch beyond hard bop. —*Scott Yanow*

★ **Freedom Now Suite** / Aug. 31, 1960 & Sep. 6, 1960 / Columbia ✦✦✦✦✦
This is a classic. At a time when the civil rights movement was starting to heat up, drummer Max Roach performed and recorded a seven-part suite dealing with Black history (particularly slavery) and racism. "Driva' Man" has a powerful statement by veteran tenor Coleman Hawkins, and there is valuable solo space elsewhere for trumpeter Booker Little and trombonist Julian Priester, but it is the overall performance of Abbey Lincoln that is most notable. Formerly a nightclub singer, Lincoln really came into her own under Roach's tutelage, and she is a strong force throughout this intense set. On "Tryptict: Prayer/Protest/Peace," Lincoln is heard in duets with the drummer, and her wrenching screams of rage are memorable. This timeless protest record is a gem. —*Scott Yanow*

★ **Percussion Bitter Sweet** / Aug. 1961 / Impulse ✦✦✦✦✦
This CD reissue brings back a classic album, one of the finest of drummer Max Roach's very productive career. The illustrious sidemen (trumpeter Booker Little; trombonist Julian Priester; Eric Dolphy on alto, bass clarinet, and flute; tenorman Clifford Jordan; pianist Mal Waldron; and bassist Art Davis, in addition to some guest percussionists), all have opportunitites to make strong contributions. Dolphy's pleading alto solo on "Mendacity" is particularly memorable. Abbey Lincoln has two emotional and very effective vocals, but it is the overall sound of the ensembles and the political nature of the music that make this set (along with Roach's *Freedom Now Suite*) unique in jazz history. —*Scott Yanow*

It's Time / 1961-1962 / Impulse ✦✦✦✦
This Max Roach date had been out-of-print for about 30 years when it was finally reissued on CD by Impulse in 1996. An unusual set, this outing featured the drummer's all-star sextet (which consisted of trumpeter Richard Williams, tenor saxophonist Clifford Jordan, trombonist Julian Priester, pianist Mal Waldron, and bassist Art Davis) joined by a vocal choir conducted by Coleridge Perkinson and orchestrated by Roach (who contributed all six originals). Unlike most other collaborations, the choir was not overly gospel-oriented and was used as a sort of jazz ensemble. Each of the horns has a feature or two, and singer Abbey Lincoln stars on "Lonesome Lover." But despite the sincerity of this effort, there are times when one wishes the choir would leave altogether and let the quintet really stretch out! —*Scott Yanow*

Speak Brother Speak / Oct. 4, 1962 / Original Jazz Classics ✦✦✦

The Max Roach Trio, Featuring the Legendary Hasaan / Dec. 4, 1964 & Dec. 7, 1964 / Atlantic ✦✦✦✦
Pianist Hasaan Ibn Ali made only one recording in his life, this trio set with drummer Max Roach and bassist Art Davis. A very advanced player whose style fell somewhere between Thelonious Monk and Cecil Taylor (with hints of Herbie Nichols), Ali actually had a rather original sound. His performances of his seven originals on this set (a straight CD reissue of a long

out-of-print LP) are intense, somewhat virtuosic and rhythmic, yet often melodic in a quirky way. This is a classic of its kind, and it is fortunate that it was made; but it is a tragedy that Ali would not record again and that he would soon sink back into obscurity. —*Scott Yanow*

Birth and Rebirth / Sep. 1978 / Black Saint ✦✦✦✦
The first of drummer Max Roach's two duet sets with multi-reedist Anthony Braxton consists of seven fairly free improvisations that they created in the studio. Each of the selections (particularly "Birth," which builds gradually in intensity to a ferocious level, the waltz time of "Magic and Music," the atmospheric "Tropical Forest," and "Softshoe") has its own plot and purpose. Braxton (who performs on alto, soprano, sopranino, and clarinet) and Roach continually inspire each other. Stimulating avant-garde music. —*Scott Yanow*

● **M'Boom** / Jul. 25, 1979-Jul. 27, 1979 / Columbia/Legacy ✦✦✦✦
In 1979 Max Roach founded M'Boom, a group consisting of eight percussionists. Their debut recording (which has been reissued on this Columbia CD) is far from being a monotonous drum battle. In fact, through the use of a wide range of instruments that include chimes, timbales, marimba, vibes, xylophone, tympani, various bells, and steel drums, there are quite a lot of melodies to be heard during these nine performances (which are all group originals other than Thelonious Monk's "Epistrophy"). This is a particularly colorful set that is easily recommended not only to jazz and percussion fans but to followers of World music. —*Scott Yanow*

☆ **One in Two, Two in One** / Aug. 1979 / Hat Hut ✦✦✦✦✦
The second of two duet albums by drummer Max Roach and multi-reedist Anthony Braxton was recorded live and released on this two-LP set; this is the more interesting of the two projects, since it is a nearly 78-minute continual improvisation. Braxton gets to stretch out on alto, soprano, sopranino, contra bass clarinet (which really gets a monstrous sound), clarinet, and flute. With Roach pushing Braxton, the results are quite adventurous, yet full of joy. Followers of avant-garde jazz can consider this set essential. —*Scott Yanow*

Historic Concerts (Mc Millin Theatre, Columbia U., Ny, December 15, 1979) / Dec. 1979 / Soul Note ✦✦✦✦
Drummer Max Roach met up with the intense avant-garde pianist Cecil Taylor for a 1979 concert that resulted in this double CD. After Roach and Taylor play separate five-minute solos (Taylor's is surprisingly melodic and bluesy), they interact during a two-part, 78-minute encounter that finds Roach occasionally taking control. The passionate music is quite atonal but coherent, with Taylor displaying an impressive amount of energy and the two masters (who had not rehearsed or ever played together before) communicating pretty well. This set is weakened a bit by a 17-minute radio interview that includes excerpts from the concert one just heard, although some of the anecdotes are interesting. No revelations really occur in the music, but it certainly holds one's interest! —*Scott Yanow*

Scott Free / May 31, 1984 / Soul Note ✦✦✦✦
This strong set from the Max Roach Quartet (one of the finest regular bands of the '80s) finds the group performing a 40-minute version of trumpeter Cecil Bridgewater's "Scott Free." Because the piece has plenty of solo space (two lengthy improvisations apiece for Bridgewater, tenor saxophonist Odean Pope, bassist Tyrone Brown, and drummer Roach, with a medium-tempo section, a rapid segment, and some free interludes), there is more variety than one might expect. This is excellent music, easily recommended as an example of the underrated but consistently brilliant Max Roach Quartet. —*Scott Yanow*

Bright Moments / Oct. 1, 1986-Oct. 2, 1986 / Soul Note ✦✦✦✦
The combination of drummer Max Roach's regular group (which includes trumpeter Cecil Bridgewater, tenor saxophonist Odean Pope, and electric bassist Tyrone Brown) with the Uptown String Quartet to form his Double Quartet works extremely well. Because the strings get to improvise and are not restricted to the background, the interplay between the two groups is a highlight of this particularly strong outing. In addition to works by Pope and Brown (the latter contributed "Tribute to Duke and Mingus"), the Double Quartet interprets Steve Turre's "Double Delight," Randy Weston's "Hi Fly," and Roland Kirk's happy "Bright Moments." A frequently exquisite yet adventurous album, highly recommended. —*Scott Yanow*

★ **To the Max** / Sep. 15, 1990-Jun. 25, 1991 / Blue Moon ✦✦✦✦✦
Max Roach is heard in a variety of settings on this colorful and varied double CD. The three-part "Ghost Dance" features the innovative drummer with a vocal choir and his percussion group, M'Boom. M'Boom also pops up on two other selections, the Max Roach Quartet (with trumpeter Cecil Bridgewater, Odean Pope on tenor, and electric bassist Tyrone Brown) has four features, Roach takes two unaccompanied drum solos, and the Quartet joins up with the Uptown String Quartet to form Roach's Double Quartet on a 21-minute version of "A Little Booker." The music, which crosses quite a few boundaries, is consistently fascinating and forms a definitive portrait of the ageless drummer's wide musical interests in the early '90s. —*Scott Yanow*

Marcus Roberts

b. Sep. 7, 1963, Jacksonville, FL
Piano / Post-Bop, Hard Bop, Stride
Marcus Roberts has begun to get some of the attacks normally reserved for Wynton Marsalis and others regarded as reactionaries by some members of the jazz press. Roberts' seeming obsession with vintage styles, notably stride, and his willingness to speak openly and voice his disdain of contemporary music has not been well accepted in some circles. A notorious *Downbeat* blindfold test in which Roberts casually ripped some major players for an alleged lack of swing also generated heated replies via letters to the editor. But Roberts must be credited with going his own way; he's one of the few contemporary pianists with few or no ties to McCoy Tyner, Ahmad Jamal, or Bill Evans. He has some Thelonious Monk influence, especially in his phrasing, but Roberts' models, at least in the last few years, have been Jelly Roll Morton and Fats Waller. While his earlier work reflected pronounced gospel and blues ties, mixed with bebop, Roberts has now devoted himself to stride and ragtime, a tactical decision wide open to intense scrutiny and second guessing. He hasn't mastered either form, but continues cutting solo piano albums featuring these styles. Roberts studied piano at Florida State after beginning on the instrument in his youth. He won several competitions in the mid-'80s, then joined Wynton Marsalis' band as his first regular pianist since Kenny Kirkland. Roberts emerged as the Marsalis band's second prime soloist and the hub of its rhythm section. His swing prevented Marsalis' music from getting too stiff or introspective. Roberts' own late '80s and '90s albums for RCA/Novus, particularly the 1990 release *Alone With Three Giants*, detail his commitment to classic music. Whether that makes him a dedicated preservationist or a hopeless nostalgia buff remains open to debate. —*Ron Wynn*

The Truth Is Spoken Here / Jul. 26, 1988-Jul. 27, 1988 / Novus ✦✦✦

Deep in the Shed / Aug. 9, 1989-Dec. 10, 1989 / Novus ✦✦✦✦
His second solo project accents the blues, with nicely arranged compositions and a full band that sometimes swells to include alto and tenor sax, trumpet, and trombone, plus bass and drums. —*Ron Wynn*

Alone with Three Giants / Jun. 3, 1990-Sep. 22, 1990 / Novus ✦✦✦✦
Fifteen tracks of solo piano on works by Monk, Ellington, and Jelly Roll Morton. He fares best on the Monk, and there are five of them. —*Michael G. Nastos*

Prayer for Peace / Jun. 5, 1991-Jun. 7, 1991 / Jive/Novus ✦✦✦

● **As Serenity Approaches** / Jun. 1991-Nov. 1991 / Novus ✦✦✦✦
All of pianist Marcus Roberts' recordings thus far are recommended. This outing has 11 impressive solo performances and eight duets with trumpeters Scotty Barnhart, Nicholas Payton, and Wynton Marsalis (the latter on a fun version of Jelly Roll Morton's "King Porter Stomp"), Todd Williams on clarinet and tenor, and trombonist Ronald Westray, in addition to two meetings with fellow pianist Ellis Marsalis. This music finds Roberts using techniques of the past (especially stride and old-time breaks) in both his new originals and revivals of classic tunes. However, he never resorts to mere copying and feels free to update elements of the music or to throw in eccentric ideas. There is a great deal for listeners to investigate on this fascinating recital. —*Scott Yanow*

If I Could Be with You / 1993 / Novus ✦✦✦✦

Gershwin For Lovers / 1994 / Sony ✦✦✦

Plays Ellington / 1995 / Novus ✦✦✦✦

Red Rodney (Robert Chudnick)

b. Sep. 27, 1927, Philadelphia, PA, **d.** May 27, 1994
Trumpet / Bop, Hard Bop
Red Rodney's comeback in the late '70s was quite inspiring and found the veteran bebop trumpeter playing even better than he had during his legendary period with Charlie Parker. He started his professional career by performing with Jerry Wald's orchestra when he was 15, and he passed through a lot of big bands, including those of Jimmy Dorsey (during which Rodney closely emulated his early idol Harry James), Elliot Lawrence, Georgie Auld, Benny Goodman, and Les Brown. He totally changed his style after hearing Dizzy Gillespie and Charlie Parker, becoming one of the brighter young voices in bebop. Rodney made strong contributions to the bands of Gene Krupa (1946), Claude Thornhill, and Woody Herman's Second Herd (1948-49). Off and on during 1949-51, Rodney was a regular member of the Charlie Parker Quintet, playing brilliantly at Bird's recorded Carnegie Hall Concert of 1949. But drugs cut short that association, and Rodney spent most of the '50s in and out of jail. After he kicked heroin, almost as damaging to his jazz chops was a long period playing for shows in Las Vegas. When he returned to New York in 1972, it took Rodney several years to regain his former form. However, he hooked up with multi-instrumentalist Ira Sullivan in 1980, and the musical partnership benefitted both of the veterans; Sullivan's inquisitive style inspired Rodney to play post-bop music (rather than continually stick to bop), and sometimes their quintet (which also featured Garry Dial) sounded like the Ornette Coleman Quartet! After Sullivan went back to Florida a few years

later, Rodney continued leading his own quintet, which in later years featured the talented young saxophonist Chris Potter. Red Rodney, who was portrayed quite sympathetically in the Clint Eastwood film *Bird* (during which he played his own solos), stands as proof that for the most open-minded veterans there is life beyond bop. —*Scott Yanow*

★ **Early Bebop on Keynote** / Jan. 29, 1947 / Mercury ✦✦✦✦✦
A good 20-track overview of Rodney's mid-40s cuts on Keynote. Both his own band and his stints with others are covered. —*Ron Wynn*

Modern Music from Chicago / Jun. 20, 1955 / Original Jazz Classics ✦✦✦✦
This nice reissue features the famous White trumpeter who once passed for both Black and Native American! —*Ron Wynn*

Bird Lives! / Jul. 9, 1973 / Muse ✦✦✦✦
Quintet with Roy Brooks, Charles McPherson, Barry Harris), and Sam Jones. Three Elmo compositions, Monk's rousing "52nd St. Theme," "Round Midnight," and one standard. —*Michael G. Nastos*

Home Free / Dec. 19, 1977 / Muse ✦✦✦✦
Good, consistently-played mainstream fare by trumpeter Red Rodney. This date was one of many he did for the Muse label that followed the same pattern. They minimized the length and extent of Rodney's solos, had him doing anthems and unexacting originals, and got the best takes of him and his group smoothly executing the hard bop and mainstream formulas. —*Ron Wynn*

Live at the Village Vanguard / May 8, 1980-Jul. 7, 1980 / Muse ✦✦✦✦
With Ira Sullivan and quintet. Three Jack Walrath originals, three standouts. This is one of the most together jazz bands of the '80s. A perfect vehicle for both of them to blow. Sullivan plays saxs, flute, and fluegelhorn. —*Michael G. Nastos*

★ **Spirit Within** / Sep. 21, 1981-Sep. 24, 1981 / Elektra ✦✦✦✦✦
The first of two early '80s albums reuniting frequent collaborators Red Rodney and multi-instrumentalist Ira Sullivan. Sullivan plays second trumpet and a variety of saxophones and provides a challenging and complementary presence to Rodney, who sometimes plays in a restrained, easy fashion, then other times turns up his own playing a notch in response to Sullivan. —*Ron Wynn*

Red Giant / Apr. 1988 / SteepleChase ✦✦✦

One for Bird / Jul. 1988 / SteepleChase ✦✦✦

Red Snapper / Jul. 1988 / SteepleChase ✦✦✦

Red Alert! / Oct. 1990-Nov. 1990 / Continuum ✦✦✦

Then and Now / 1992 / Chesky ✦✦✦✦
Rodney gets back to his bop roots and plays in a quartet with Gary Dial, Jay Anderson, and Jimmy Madison. He does both fresh originals and classics from the '40s and '50s. —*Ron Wynn*

Shorty Rogers (Milton M. Rajonsky)

b. Apr. 14, 1924, Great Barrington, MA, **d.** Nov. 7, 1994
Trumpet / Cool
A fine middle-register trumpeter whose style seemed to practically define "cool jazz," Shorty Rogers was actually more significant for his arranging, both in jazz and in the movie studios. After gaining early experience with Will Bradley and Red Norvo and serving in the military, Rogers rose to fame as a member of Woody Herman's First and Second Herds (1945-46 and 1947-49), and somehow he managed to bring some swing to the Stan Kenton Innovations Orchestra (1950-51), clearly enjoying writing for the stratospheric flights of Maynard Ferguson. After that association ran its course, Rogers settled in Los Angeles, where he led his Giants (which ranged from a quintet to a nonet and a big band) on a series of rewarding West Coast jazz-styled recordings and wrote for the studios, helping greatly to bring jazz into the movies. His scores for *The Wild One* and *The Man with the Golden Arm* are particularly memorable. After 1962 Rogers stuck almost exclusively to writing for television and films, but in 1982 he began a comeback in jazz. Rogers reorganized and headed the Lighthouse All-Stars, and, although his own playing was not quite as strong as previously, he remained a welcome presence both in clubs and recordings. —*Scott Yanow*

☆ **The Complete Atlantic and EMI Jazz Recordings** / Oct. 8, 1951-Mar. 30, 1956 / Mosaic ✦✦✦✦✦
Another exhaustive Mosaic box set, this one devoted to the complete material trumpeter Shorty Rogers cut for EMI and Atlantic in the '50s, including both jazz-influenced material and concept "Martians" albums. Art Pepper is featured on some cuts on alto sax, along with Shelly Manne, Jimmy Giuffre, and Curtis Counce. —*Ron Wynn*

● **Short Stops** / Jan. 12, 1953-Mar. 3, 1954 / Bluebird ✦✦✦✦
A thorough reissue that covers his first three RCA albums. For some strange reason, the CD has only 20 of 32 cuts. —*Ron Wynn*

The Swinging Mr. Rogers / Oct. 21, 1955-Nov. 3, 1955 / Atlantic ✦✦✦✦
Trumpeter Shorty Rogers switched labels in the mid-'50s, moving to Atlantic from RCA. This was his Atlantic debut and was an intimate quartet date

featuring Rogers alongside clarinetist and saxophonist Jimmy Giuffre, bassist Curtis Counce, and drummer Shelly Manne. The single "Martians Go Home" proved so popular that it eventually spawned its own album, *Martians Come Back!*—*Ron Wynn*

Martians, Stay Home / Nov. 3, 1955 / Atlantic ✦✦✦✦
The quintet includes Jimmy Giuffre, Pete Jolly, Curtis Counce, and Shelly Manne. There are six Shorty originals and three standards. These are nice groups, with Rogers' sensitive trumpet leading in a non-threatening, mainstream groove. —*Michael G. Nastos*

Swings / Dec. 9, 1958-Feb. 5, 1959 / Bluebird ✦✦✦✦
New reissue with three bonus cuts. Original RCA album. —*Ron Wynn*

Yesterday, Today and Forever / Jun. 1983 / Concord Jazz ✦✦✦✦
This quintet, with Bud Shank on flute and alto sax, plays three Shorty tunes and four standards. They perform fine readings of Tiny Kahn's "TNT" and Bud Powell's "Budo." —*Michael G. Nastos*

Lighthouse All Stars / 1991 / Candid ✦✦✦✦

America the Beautiful / Aug. 4, 1991-Aug. 5, 1991 / Candid ✦✦✦

Sonny Rollins (Theodore Walter [Newk] Rollins)

b. Sep. 7, 1930, New York, NY
Sax (Tenor) / Bop, Post-Bop, Hard Bop
Sonny Rollins has for more than 40 years been one of the true jazz giants, ranking up there with Coleman Hawkins, Lester Young, and John Coltrane as one of the all-time great tenor saxophonists. He started on piano, took up the alto, and then permanently switched to tenor in 1946. After making his recording debut with Babs Gonzales in 1949, Rollins made a major impact on dates with J.J. Johnson and Bud Powell the same year; the latter session also matched him with Fats Navarro. Rollins' abilities were obvious to the jazz world from the start, and he started recording with Miles Davis in 1951 and with Thelonious Monk two years later. After a period out of music, Rollins joined the Max Roach-Clifford Brown Quintet in late 1955, continuing after Brown's death until 1957. From then on he was always a leader.

Sonny Rollins' series of brilliant recordings for Prestige, Blue Note, Contemporary, and Riverside in the '50s found him in peak form, and he was acclaimed as the top tenor saxophonist of the time, at least until John Coltrane rose to prominence. Therefore Rollins' decision to drop out of music from 1959-61 shocked the jazz world. When he came back in 1961 with a quartet featuring Jim Hall, his style was largely unchanged; but he soon became a much freer player who was well aware of Ornette Coleman's innovations; he even used Coleman's cornetist, Don Cherry, for a time. Although his playing was a bit more eccentric than previously, Rollins was a major force until in 1968 he again decided to retire.

Upon his return in 1971, Sonny Rollins was more open to the influence of R&B rhythms and pop music, and his recordings since then have not always been essential (often using sidemen not up to his level); but Rollins remains a vital soloist. His skill at turning unlikely material into jazz, his unaccompanied flights, and his rhythmic freedom and tonal distortions have kept Sonny Rollins one of the masters of jazz into the mid-'90s. Dozens of superior recordings are currently available. —*Scott Yanow*

☆ **The Complete Prestige Recordings** / May 26, 1949-Dec. 7, 1956 / Prestige ✦✦✦✦✦

Sonny Rollins with the Modern Jazz Quartet / Jan. 17, 1951-Oct. 7, 1953 / Original Jazz Classics ✦✦✦✦
Fire meets cool in this excellent reissue of their early-50s collaboration. —*Ron Wynn*

Moving Out / Aug. 18, 1954-Oct. 25, 1954 / Original Jazz Classics ✦✦✦✦
A nice date. —*Ron Wynn*

Tenor Madness / May 24, 1956 / Original Jazz Classics ✦✦✦✦
This CD (whose contents have since been reissued many times) is highlighted by the one meeting on records between Sonny Rollins and John Coltrane, an exciting battle on "Tenor Madness." Otherwise this is a more conventional but no less worthy Rollins quartet session, with his turning such odd material as "My Reverie" and "The Most Beautiful Girl in the World" into creative jazz. —*Scott Yanow*

Plays for Bird / Oct. 5, 1956 / Original Jazz Classics ✦✦✦✦
Quintet. This is an emphatic tribute to one of his idols, influences, and mentors. —*Ron Wynn*

Sonny Boy / Oct. 5, 1956 / Original Jazz Classics ✦✦✦✦
limpressive stints by Kenny Dorham, Kenny Drew), and Max Roach. —*Ron Wynn*

Tour de Force / Dec. 7, 1956 / Original Jazz Classics ✦✦✦✦
A fine session with Kenny Drew setting the rhythm section pace on piano. —*Ron Wynn*

★ **Way out West** / Mar. 7, 1957 / Original Jazz Classics ✦✦✦✦✦
This timeless recording established Sonny Rollins as jazz's top tenor saxophonist (at least until John Coltrane surpassed him the following year). Joined by bassist Ray Brown and drummer Shelly Manne, Rollins is heard

at one of his peaks on such pieces as "I'm an Old Cowhand," his own "Way Out West," "There Is No Greater Love," and "Come, Gone" (a fast stomp based on "After You've Gone"). The William Claxton photo of Rollins wearing Western gear (and holding his tenor) in the desert is a classic. —*Scott Yanow*

The Sound of Sonny / Jun. 11, 1957-Jun. 19, 1957 / Original Jazz Classics ✦✦✦✦

Wonderful standards and originals, with funky, inventive piano from Sonny Clark. —*Ron Wynn*

☆ **A Night at the Village Vanguard** / Nov. 3, 1957 / Blue Note ✦✦✦✦✦

This CD is often magical. Sonny Rollins, one of jazz's great tenors, is heard at his peak with a pair of pianoless trios (either Wilbur Ware or Donald Bailey on bass and Elvin Jones or Pete La Roca on drums) stretching out on particularly creative versions of "Old Devil Moon," "Softly As in a Morning Sunrise," "Sonnymoon For Two," and "A Night in Tunisia." Not only did Rollins have a very distinctive sound, but his use of time, his sly wit, and his boppish but unpredictable style were completely his own by 1957. —*Scott Yanow*

And Contemporary Leaders / Oct. 20, 1958-Oct. 22, 1958 / Original Jazz Classics ✦✦✦

★ **The Bridge** / Jan. 30, 1962-Feb. 13, 1962 / Bluebird ✦✦✦✦✦

One of the more important Sonny Rollins recordings, this set was his first after a highly publicized three-year retirement. The great tenor, joined by guitarist Jim Hall, bassist Bob Cranshaw, and drummer Ben Riley, is in particularly strong form on this session, even if his style was not much changed from 1959. Advanced bop that hints a bit at the avant-garde. —*Scott Yanow*

Alternatives / May 14, 1962-Apr. 14, 1964 / Bluebird ✦✦✦✦

Sonny Rollins' RCA recordings of 1962-64 found him really stretching out his style, listening to and learning from Ornette Coleman without losing his own musical personality. This CD, in addition to two numbers with bassist Bob Cranshaw and the congos of Candido ("Jungoso" and "Bluesongo") that were originally on the album *What's New*, has four selections from *Now's the Time* along with four very different alternate takes. For example, the original version of "52nd Street Theme" was four minutes long, but the alternate is 14. The personnel also differ, with cornetist Thad Jones and pianist Herbie Hancock making appearances, but the emphasis is on the exciting improvisations of Rollins, one of the great tenor saxophonists of all time. —*Scott Yanow*

On the Outside / Jul. 27, 1962-Feb. 20, 1963 / Bluebird ✦✦✦✦

A very interesting CD of material from Sonny Rollins. It reissues the complete *Our Man in Jazz* (three lengthy performances including a 25-minute version of "Oleo") along with three briefer selections previously on a sampler. These are among Rollins' most avant-garde improvisations, for he seems inspired by trumpeter Don Cherry's presence (although Cherry clearly could not keep up with the great tenor). Rollins really digs into "Oleo" and the 15-minute "Doxy" and plays some remarkable music. —*Scott Yanow*

All the Things You Are / Jul. 15, 1963-Jul. 2, 1964 / Bluebird ✦✦✦✦

Sonny Rollins & Co. 1964 / Jan. 24, 1964-Jul. 9, 1964 / Bluebird ✦✦✦✦

This CD from the Bluebird reissue series fills a lot of gaps in Sonny Rollins' discography. The 13 selections are taken from six different sessions from 1964. The personnel changes from date to date with either Ron Carter or Bob Cranshaw on bass and Roy McCurdy or Mickey Roker on drums, along with pianist Herbie Hancock (on five songs) and guitarist Jim Hall on three others. Some of the music is actually alternate takes, and, in contrast to a rambling 16-minute version of "Now's the Time," a few of the briefer songs (seven are under 31 minutes) shut down prematurely. However, the great tenor's improvisations are consistently fascinating as he reconciles his avant-garde flights to the standards he is performing; "Autumn Nocturne" is a high point. —*Scott Yanow*

Sonny Rollins on Impulse! / Jul. 8, 1965 / Impulse ✦✦✦✦

The first of three studio albums that tenor saxophonist Sonny Rollins recorded for Impulse contains the joyous calypso "Hold 'em Joe" and four unusual versions of standards in which the rhythms he plays are more important than the melodies. Joined by pianist Ray Bryant, bassist Walter Booker, and drummer Mickey Roker, Rollins sounds quite distinctive on this brief but enjoyable set. —*Scott Yanow*

☆ **East Broadway Run Down** / May 9, 1966 / Impulse ✦✦✦✦✦

Sonny Rollins' last recording before taking another long retirement (this time six years) is a real gem, one of his top albums of the '60s. This CD includes the 20-minute title cut (which has some rather free moments but always remains quite coherent), the tenor's memorable original "Blessing in Disguise," and his glorious ballad statement on "We Kiss in a Shadow." Trumpeter Freddie Hubbard helps out on "East Broadway Run Down," but otherwise this excellent set showcases Rollins in a trio with bassist Jimmy Garrison and drummer Elvin Jones. —*Scott Yanow*

● **Next Album** / Jul. 1972 / Original Jazz Classics ✦✦✦✦

Sonny Rollins' first album after ending his six-year retirement is a particu-

larly strong effort. The high point is a ten-minute version of "Skylark" that has a long, unaccompanied section by the great tenor. Other memorable selections include "The Everywhere Calypso" and "Playing in the Yard." Rollins plays soprano on "Poinciana" and is heard using electronics (George Cables' electric piano) for the first time, but this music is not all that different from what he was playing before his retirement. —*Scott Yanow*

Horn Culture / Jun. 1973-Jul. 1973 / Original Jazz Classics ✦✦✦

The Cutting Edge / Jul. 6, 1974 / Original Jazz Classics ✦✦✦✦

Sonny Rollins' 1974 appearance at the Montreux Jazz Festival was warmly received. Joined by his usual band of the period (pianist Stanley Cowell, guitarist Masuo, electric bassist Bob Cranshaw, drummer David Lee, and percussionist Mtume), Rollins manages to turn such unlikely material as "To a Wild Rose" and "A House Is Not a Home" into jazz. The world's only jazz bagpipe player (Rufus Harley) makes his presence felt on "Swing Low, Sweet Chariot." —*Scott Yanow*

Easy Living / Aug. 3, 1977-Aug. 6, 1977 / Milestone ✦✦✦✦

One of Sonny Rollins' better recordings of the '70s, this spirited set finds the veteran tenor adopting a thicker and raunchier R&B-ish tone. Although sticking close to the melody, he really tears into Stevie Wonder's "Isn't She Lovely" and finds interesting new variations to play on "My One and Only Love" (on soprano) and "Easy Living." The fine backup group includes keyboardist George Duke and drummer Tony Williams. —*Scott Yanow*

Falling in Love with Jazz / Jun. 3, 1989-Sep. 9, 1989 / Milestone ✦✦✦

Old Flames / 1993 / Milestone ✦✦✦✦

Sonny Rollins sticks mostly to standard ballads on this excellent CD, which finds him joined by trombonist Clifton Anderson, pianist Tommy Flanagan, bassist Bob Cranshaw, drummer Jack DeJohnette, and, on two selections, a five-piece brass choir arranged by Jimmy Heath. Comfortable and occasionally passionate music by one of the classic tenor saxophonists. —*Scott Yanow*

Wallace Roney

b. May 25, 1960, Philadelphia, PA

Trumpet / Post-Bop, Hard Bop

Listening to Wallace Roney can be a frustrating experience for, despite his obvious technical skills, virtually all of his solos sound like an imitation of Miles Davis circa 1965-70. It is not so much that he is copying phrases; but his sound, phrasing, and approach are nearly identical. Now that he is in his mid-30s, one wonders if he is ever going to develop his own voice.

Roney joined Abdullah Ibrahim's Big Band in 1979 and was with Art Blakey's Jazz Messengers in 1981 (subbing for Wynton Marsalis when he was touring with Herbie Hancock). Since that time he has spent a long period with the Tony Williams Quintet, assisted Miles Davis at the 1991 Montreux Jazz Fesitval (in which Davis revisited for one last time the arrangements of Gil Evans), played as a substitute for Davis in both Gerry Mulligan's Rebirth of the Cool and Herbie Hancock's Tribute to Miles Davis quintet, and recorded steadily as a leader. His own records tend to be modal-based, and they all contain strong (if derivative) trumpet playing. —*Scott Yanow*

Seth Air / Sep. 28, 1991 / Muse ✦✦✦✦

Trumpeter Wallace Roney has yet to escape from the shadow of Miles Davis. However, he is one of the stronger brassmen in jazz of the '90s and plays quite well on this set, which includes three numbers by younger brother Antoine Roney (who is heard on this CD on tenor), two from Roney's pianist Jacky Terasson, and three odd standards: "People," Gershwin's "Gone," and Burt Bacharach's "Wives and Lovers." The music is straightahead but occasionally as unpredictable as the repertoire. —*Scott Yanow*

● **Crunchin'** / Jul. 30, 1993 / Muse ✦✦✦✦

Trumpeter Wallace Roney sounds poignant and fabulous throughout the eight tracks on his latest release. His lines on "What's New" and "You Stepped Out of a Dream" are full and gorgeous, while his soloing on "Woody'n You" and "Time After Time" has warmth, intensity, and edge. Alto saxophonist Antonio Hart chimes in with equal facility and spark, while Geri Allen shows that she is just as outstanding an accompanist on standards and hard bop as in trios or as a leader. —*Ron Wynn*

Munchin' / Jul. 30, 1993 / Muse ✦✦✦

Misterios / 1994 / Warner Bros. ✦✦✦✦

Trumpeter Wallace Roney avoids the standard repertoire altogether on this CD, playing pieces by Pat Metheny, the Beatles, Egberto Gismonti, Jaco Pastorius, and even Dolly Parton, but try as he may, he still sounds like Miles Davis every time he hits a long tone or plays a double-time passage. Backed by a small orchestra that mostly interprets Gil Goldstein arrangements, Roney is the main soloist throughout this interesting ballad-dominated set. —*Scott Yanow*

Wallace Roney Quintet / Feb. 20, 1995-Feb. 22, 1995 / Warner Bros. ✦✦✦✦

Michele Rosewoman

b. 1953, Oakland, CA
Piano / Avant-Garde

An exciting, ambitious pianist particularly effective with Afro-Latin rhythms, Michele Rosewoman has been in the forefront of jazz composers and performers anxious to find new frontiers. But instead of fusion or hip-hop, Rosewoman chose Afro-Cuban music. With parents who owned a record store in Oakland and an older brother who's a musician, Rose-woman began playing piano at six and took lessons at 17 from Edwin Kelly. She studied Cuban percussion with Orlando Rios as well as traditional Shona and Yoruba African music. Rosewoman later worked with members of both the Black Artists Group and the Association for the Advancement of Creative Musicians. She moved to New York in 1978 and played with Oliver Lake at a Carnegie Hall concert. Rosewoman worked with Billy Bang in the early '80s and recorded with Los Kimy, a contemporary Cuban band. She formed the 15-piece New Yor-Uba in the mid-'80s and later premiered the production *New Yor-Uba: A Music Celebration of Cuba in America* at the Public Theatre. Rosewoman began recording as a leader for Soul Note in the mid-'80s and formed the quintet Quintessence in 1986. She toured with Carlos Ward in the early '90s and later did a trio date with Rufus Reid and Ralph Peterson, Jr. —*Ron Wynn and Michael G. Nastos*

● **Contrast High** / Jul. 1988 / Enja ◆◆◆◆
With Quintessence. Pianist with intriguing compositions. —*Michael G. Nastos*

Occasion to Rise / Sep. 13, 1990-Sep. 15, 1990 / Evidence ◆◆◆◆
Pianist Michele Rosewoman shows tremendous rhythmic drive, fine harmonic skills, and outstanding phrasing and playing throughout the ten cuts on this 1990 set. With drummer Ralph Peterson briskly outlining the rhythmic direction and bassist Rufus Reid proving the link between his piercing rhythms and Rosewoman's energetic playing, this is not polite or casual piano fare. It is fiery, sometimes slashing ("The Sweet Eye of Hurricane Sally") and sometimes sentimental ("Prelude to a Kiss" and "We Are"). —*Ron Wynn*

Renee Rosnes

b. 1962, Regina, Saskatchewan, Canada
Piano / Post-Bop, Hard Bop

Renee Rosnes, who plays in an advanced and flexible hard bop style, seems on the brink of great success. A native of Canada, she began piano lessons at age three and violin when she was five. She worked throughout Canada, performing on CBC Jazz Radio Canada shows, gigging with her trio regularly at a hotel, and playing on the S.S. Rotterdam Cruise Liner. Rosnes moved to New York in 1985 and has played and/or recorded with a wide variety of artists, including Joe Henderson, Wayne Shorter, J.J. Johnson, Jon Faddis, James Moody, the group Out of the Blue, Gary Thomas, and Robin Eubanks. She has recorded a couple of her own sessions for Blue Note. —*Scott Yanow*

Renee Rosnes / Apr. 18, 1988-Feb. 4, 1989 / Blue Note ◆◆◆◆
High-caliber duet and quartet sessions. Rosnes proves captivating in any context. Guests include Wayne Shorter and Branford Marsalis. —*Ron Wynn*

For the Moment / Feb. 15, 1990-Feb. 16, 1990 / Blue Note ◆◆◆◆
Four Rosnes originals, four others from Monk, Woody Shaw, Walt Weiskopf, and the Warren/Dubin team. Joe Henderson is featured on seven of the eight cuts. —*Michael G. Nastos*

● **Without Words** / Jan. 8, 1992-Jan. 9, 1992 / Blue Note ◆◆◆◆

Frank Rosolino

b. Aug. 20, 1926, Detroit, MI, d. Nov. 26, 1978, Los Angeles, CA
Trombone / Bop

The horrible way that Frank Rosolino's life ended (killing himself after shooting his two sons) has largely overshadowed his musical accomplishments. One of the top trombonists of the '50s, Rosolino's fluid and often humorous style put him near the top of his field for awhile.

He was a guitarist when he was ten but switched to trombone as a teenager. After serving in the military, Rosolino played with the big bands of Bob Chester, Glen Gray, Gene Krupa (1948-49), Tony Pastor, Herbie Fields, and Georgie Auld. However, all of those experiences were just preludes to his high profile association with Stan Kenton (1952-54), which gave him fame. Rosolino recorded frequently in Los Angeles as a member of the Lighthouse All-Stars (1954-60), a freelancer, and as a studio musician. His song "Blue Daniel" became a jazz standard, and Rosolino was a popular attraction as a brilliant trombonist and a comical singer. He was with Supersax for a period in the '70s. Rosolino's shocking ending was a surprise to even his closest associates. —*Scott Yanow*

● **Frankly Speaking** / May 4, 1955-May 5, 1955 / Affinity ◆◆◆◆
Perhaps his greatest album as a leader. Immaculate trombone solos. —*Ron Wynn*

Frank Rosolino Quartet / Jun. 1957 / VSOP ◆◆◆◆
This matchup works out quite well. Trombonist Frank Rosolino and tenor saxophonist Richie Kamuca make for a potent frontline and are accompanied quite ably by pianist Vince Guaraldi, bassist Monty Budwig, and drummer Stan Levey. This 1957 studio session, originally put out on the long-defunct Mode label, has been reissued on CD by V.S.O.P. and is well worth picking up. Rosolino contributes three originals, Bill Holman arranged some of the ensembles, and the solos are consistently enjoyable and swinging. —*Scott Yanow*

Thinking About You / Apr. 21, 1976-Apr. 23, 1976 / Sackville ◆◆◆

Charlie Rouse

b. Apr. 6, 1924, Washington, DC, d. Nov. 30, 1988, Seattle, WA
Sax (Tenor) / Hard Bop

Possessor of a distinctive tone and a fluid bop-oriented style, Charlie Rouse was in Thelonious Monk's Quartet for more than a decade (1959-70) and, although somewhat taken for granted, was an important ingredient in Monk's music. Rouse was always a modern player, and he worked with Billy Eckstine's orchestra (1944) and the first Dizzy Gillespie big band (1945), making his recording debut with Tadd Dameron in 1947. Rouse popped up in a lot of important groups, including Duke Ellington's Orchestra (1949-50), Count Basie's octet (1980), on sessions with Clifford Brown in 1953, and with Oscar Pettiford's sextet (1955). He co-led the Jazz Modes with Julius Watkins (1956-59) and then joined Monk for a decade of extensive touring and recordings. In the '70s he recorded a few albums as a leader, and in 1979 he became a member of Sphere. Charlie Rouse's unique sound began to finally get some recognition during the '80s. He participated on Carmen McRae's classic *Carmen Sings Monk* album, and his last recording was at a Monk tribute concert. —*Scott Yanow*

The Chase Is on / 1957 / Bethlehem ◆◆◆

Takin' Care of Business / May 11, 1960 / Original Jazz Classics ◆◆◆◆
Two numbers penned by Randy Weston, one apiece by Kenny Drew and Rouse, and two standards. This is a supremely confident group that plays strong music in a somewhat cool mood. —*Michael G. Nastos*

Bossa Nova Bacchanal / Nov. 11, 1962 / Blue Note ◆◆◆

The Upper Manhattan Jazz Society / 1981 / Enja ◆◆◆

● **Epistrophy** / Oct. 10, 1988 / Landmark ◆◆◆◆
An adventurous date with Rouse stepping out and handling the challenge posed by Don Cherry, Buddy Montgomery, and George Cables. —*Ron Wynn*

Jimmy Rowles

b. Aug. 19, 1918, Spokane, WA, d. May 28, 1996
Piano / Bop, Swing

Long known for his expertise in coming up with the perfect chord for the perfect situation, the subtle Jimmy Rowles was in demand for decades as an accompanist, while being underrated as a soloist. After playing in local groups in Seattle, Rowles moved to Los Angeles in 1940 and worked with Slim Gaillard, Lester Young, Benny Goodman, and Woody Herman. After serving in the military he returned to Herman (in time to play with the first Herd), recorded with Benny Goodman, and had stints with Les Brown and Tommy Dorsey. Working as a studio musician, Rowles appeared in a countless number of settings in the '50s and '60s but was best-known for his playing behind Billie Holiday and Peggy Lee. In 1973 he moved to New York, where he recorded more extensively in jazz situations (including duets with Stan Getz); but after touring with Ella Fitzgerald during 1981-83, he returned to California. His song "The Peacocks" has become a standard, and Rowles recorded for many labels, and with his daughter, fluegelhornist Stacy Rowles. —*Scott Yanow*

Weather in a Jazz Vane / 1958 / VSOP ◆◆◆

Let's Get Acquainted with Jazz (For People Who Hate Jazz) / Jun. 20, 1958 / VSOP ◆◆◆

The Special Magic of Jimmy Rowles / Apr. 7, 1974 / Halcyon ◆◆◆◆
This album includes duets with Rusty Gilder on bass. Rowles shows he can also do it alone; with Gilder, sparks occasionally fly. Mostly, this is laidback. They play lots of Duke Ellington. There is a good version of Carl Perkin's "Grooveyard." —*Michael G. Nastos*

Grandpaws / Mar. 1976 / Choice ◆◆◆◆
The trio includes Buster Williams on bass and Billy Hart on drums. They play two by Rowles; the others are standards. They do an exquisite medley of "Lush Life/A Train/I Love You/I Hadn't Anyone 'til You/Margie/Chicago/Desert Fire." Rowles shows his ballad skills best. —*Michael G. Nastos*

● **The Peacocks** / 1977 / Columbia ◆◆◆◆

We Could Make Such Beautiful Music Together / Apr. 1978 / Xanadu ◆◆◆◆
Solo, trio, and quartet performances by pianist Jimmy Rowles from the late '70s. These were originally issued on the Xanadu label, then reissued on

CD in '89 for EPM. Rowles plays with bassists Sam Jones or George Mraz, drummers Leroy Williams or Freddie Waits, and trumpeter Sam Noto. His prickly, sometimes humorous and sometimes poignant piano playing provides the disc's high points. —*Ron Wynn*

Paws That Refresh / Sep. 1980 / Choice ✦✦✦

Plus 2, Plus 3, Plus 4 / Dec. 16, 1988-Dec. 20, 1988 / JVC ✦✦✦✦
This CD reissue's title refers to the fact that pianist Jimmy Rowles appears with a drumless trio (including guitarist Larry Koonse and bassist Eric Von Essen) on four numbers, with a quartet on three songs (drummer Ralph Penland is added) on four other pieces. The music throughout is mellow and quiet with Rowles' chordal style very much the dominant force; he also takes half-spoken vocals on "I Never Loved Anyone" and "I've Grown Accustomed to Her Face." Only "I Wished on the Moon," "Sweet Lorraine," and the closing blues move above a medium-slow pace and the overall results are melodic and relaxing if never all that stimulating. —*Scott Yanow*

Lilac Time / 1994 / Kokopelli ✦✦✦✦

Gonzalo Rubalcaba

b. May 27, 1963, Havana, Cuba
Piano / Post-Bop, Cuba, Latin Continuum, Afro-Cuban Jazz
One of the great Cuban jazz musicians, Gonzalo Rubalcaba has only in recent times been able to travel freely in the US. He studied classical piano from 1971-83, toured France and Africa with the Orquesta Aragon in 1983, and formed the Grupo Proyecto in 1985, touring Europe frequently. In 1986 he met Charlie Haden, who sang his praises and helped arrange his appearances at the Montreal and Montreux festivals. By 1990 Gonzalo Rubalcaba had been discovered by the jazz world, and his records began to be released on Blue Note. An advanced improviser with a dense style, Rubalcaba has unlimited potential. —*Scott Yanow*

● **Discovery: Live at Montreux** / Jul. 15, 1990 / Blue Note ✦✦✦✦
A very good Cuban pianist. His best is yet to come. —*Michael G. Nastos*

☆ **The Blessing** / May 12, 1991-May 15, 1991 / Blue Note ✦✦✦✦
The virtuosic Cuban pianist Gonzalo Rubalcaba's first recording to be issued in the US is still one of his best. With strong accompaniment from bassist Charlie Haden (one of his early champions) and drummer Jack DeJohnette, Rubalcaba is in frequently exciting form throughout these performances. Highlights include an outstanding investigation of "Besame Mucho," "Giant Steps," Ornette Coleman's beautiful "The Blessing," and an unusual treatment about Haden's "Blue in Green." —*Scott Yanow*

Suite 4 Y 20 / May 7, 1992-May 12, 1992 / Blue Note ✦✦✦✦
Recorded in Spain, this excellent set features Ruba;caba's working group (trumpeter Reynaldo Melian, electric bassist Felipe Cabrera, and drummer Julio Barreto) with guest bassist Charlie Haden on four songs. The repertoire includes several pieces by Cuban composers, five of Rubalcaba's originals, "Perfidia," "Love Letters," Haden's "Our Spanish Love Song," and the Beatles' "Here, There and Everywhere." Rubalcaba shows maturity and self-restraint throughout much of this disc, performing a well rounded set of advanced music. —*Scott Yanow*

Rapsodia / Nov. 15, 1992-Nov. 21, 1992 / Blue Note ✦✦✦✦
Rubalcaba has such impressive technique that he has the potential of completely overwhelming any song he plays, but he shows admirable restraint throughout much of this quartet date. Influenced to a degree by Chick Corea and Herbie Hancock, Rubalcaba still shows a fresh personality when he uses an electric keyboard on a few of the selections. His quartet (which includes trumpeter Reynaldo Melian, bassist Felipe Cabrera, and drummer Julio Barreto), provides fine support. This is a well rounded set of complex but fairly accessible music. —*Scott Yanow*

Diz / Dec. 14, 1993-Dec. 15, 1993 / Blue Note ✦✦✦

Roswell Rudd

b. Nov. 17, 1935, Sharon, CT
Trombone / Avant-Garde, Free Jazz
One of the pioneer trombonists in free jazz, Roswell Rudd's extroverted style was heard at its best in the mid-'60s, matching wits with Archie Shepp. He studied French horn from age 11 and during 1954-59 played Dixieland trombone with a variety of groups, including Eli's Chosen Six (with whom he recorded). After recording with Cecil Taylor in 1960 and working (but not recording) with Herbie Nichols, Rudd teamed up with another former Dixielander, Steve Lacy, in a quartet that played exclusively the music of Thelonious Monk. He was with Bill Dixon in 1962 and then was a member of the New York Art Quartet with John Tchicai in 1964. He spent 1965-67 mostly with Archie Shepp, although Rudd also recorded a couple of albums of his own. He played with Robin Kenyetta in 1968 and Charlie Haden's Liberation Music Orchestra in 1969; there were also recordings with Gato Barbieri, Beaver Harris, Lonnie Liston Smith, the Jazz Composers' Orchestra, Enrico Rava, Misha Mengelberg, and more as a leader. Rudd taught at Bard College and the University of Maine and by the

'90s was playing in obscurity in the Catskills, forgotten but apparently still in prime form. —*Scott Yanow*

★ **Regeneration** / Jun. 25, 1982-Jun. 26, 1982 / Soul Note ✦✦✦✦✦
One of many intriguing collaborations pairing Rudd and Steve Lacy. —*Ron Wynn*

Hilton Ruiz

b. May 29, 1952, New York, NY
Piano / Bop, Latin Jazz
One of the finest pianists in Afro-Cuban jazz, Hilton Ruiz is also an expert bop player. A child prodigy who appeared at Carnegie Recital Hall when he was eight, Ruiz gigged with Latin bands as a teenager and gained early experience playing with Joe Newman, Frank Foster, and Freddie Hubbard. He studied with Mary Lou Williams and had an important association with Rahsaan Roland Kirk (1973-77). After touring with George Coleman (1978-79) he recorded with Charles Mingus, Betty Carter, Archie Shepp, Clark Terry, and Chico Freeman among others. Hilton Ruiz has mostly led his own groups since the early '80s, and fortunately he has recorded quite a few rewarding discs. —*Scott Yanow*

● **El Camino [The Road]** / Jun. 1988 / Novus ✦✦✦✦
An ambitious, often dazzling set with pianist Hilton Ruiz. He's heading an outstanding band that includes some great players who seldom record on major label sessions. Trombonist Dick Griffin, saxophonist Sam Rivers, and guitarist Rodney Jones are dynamite, while trumpeter Lew Soloff and Ruiz are dependable and entertaining during their solos and more explosive in their exchanges with Griffin, Rivers, and Jones. —*Ron Wynn*

Manhattan Mambo / Apr. 28, 1992 / Telarc ✦✦✦✦
Pianist Hilton Ruiz is heard with a superior group of musicians adept at playing both bebop and Latin-jazz. With a frontline of trumpeter Charlie Sepulveda, David Sanchez on tenor, and trombonist Papo Vazquez in addition to four percussionists, Ruiz' nonet displays plenty of fire on a set of originals, Perez Prado's "Mambo Numero Cinco," and John Coltrane's "Impressions." —*Scott Yanow*

Live At Birdland / Jun. 24, 1992-Jun. 25, 1992 / Candid ✦✦✦

Heroes / Nov. 8, 1993-Nov. 9, 1993 / Telarc ✦✦✦

Hands on Percussion / 1994-1995 / Tropijazz ✦✦✦✦
Ruiz has had a very successful career in both jazz and Latin music. On this Tropijazz release, he combines the two styles to form a very likable brand of Latin jazz. Ruiz uses Tito Puente (playing vibes or timbales on three songs), flutist Dave Valentin, tenor saxophonist David Sanchez, trumpeter Charlie Sepulveda, trombonist Papo Vasquez, bassist Andy Gonzalez, and percussionists (Giovanni Hidalgo, Ignacio Berroa, and Steve Berrios) for Latinized versions of four jazz standards and five group originals (including three by Ruiz). The music is quite catchy, danceable, and reasonably challenging. Recommended to fans of Latin-jazz. —*Scott Yanow*

Jimmy Rushing

b. Aug. 26, 1903, Oklahoma City, OK, **d.** Jun. 8, 1972, New York, NY
Vocals / Blues, Swing
A huge, striking artist, Jimmy Rushing defined and transcended jazz-based blues shouting. His huge voice was dominating and intricately linked to the beat. He could maintain his intonation regardless of volume and could sing sensitively one moment, then bellow and yell in almost frightening fashion the next, making both styles sound convincing. Rushing's parents were musicians, and he studied music theory in high school. He attended Wilberforce University but dropped out. He moved to the West Coast and did odd jobs, sometimes singing at house parties. Composer and pianist Jelly Roll Morton was among the people he met while making these appearances. Rushing joined Walter Page's Blue Devils in the late '20s. He left them to work in his father's cafe in Oklahoma City, but returned to Page's group in 1928. He made his first records with them in 1929. Rushing toured with Bennie Moten from 1929-1935, recording with Moten in 1931, then joined Count Basie in 1936. Basie has credited Rushing with helping hold things together when times got tough. At an early 1936 session with John Hammond producing, things came together. This marked Lester Young's debut with the band. The songs "Boogie-Woogie" (better known as "I May Be Wrong") and "Evenin'" were instant classics. Rushing's booming voice and the Basie orchestra proved a perfect fit until 1950; they recorded for Columbia and RCA, cutting everything from steamy blues to joyous stomps and novelty tunes like "Did You See Jackie Robinson Hit that Ball." When Basie disbanded the orchestra in 1950, Rushing briefly tried retirement. He ended it a short time later, forming his own band. He'd made some solo recordings in 1945 and continued in the mid-'50s and early '60s, this time for Vanguard. Rushing recreated Basie classics, worked with some of his sidemen, and even accompanied himself on piano. He cut other sessions with Buck Clayton, Dave Brubeck, and Earl Hines and frequently had reunions with Basie and/or his sidemen. Rushing appeared in both film shorts and features, among them *Take Me Back, Baby Air Mail Special, Choo Choo Swing,* and *Funzapoppin'* between 1941 and 1943. He participated in the historic 1957 television show "The Sound Of Jazz,"

and was featured on the sixth episode of a 13-part series "The Subject Is Jazz" in 1958. He was also in the 1973 film *Monterey Jazz*, which profiled the 1970 festival. Rushing also had a singing and acting role in the 1969 film *The Learning Tree*. *—Ron Wynn and Bob Porter*

★ **The Essential Jimmy Rushing** / Dec. 1, 1954-Mar. 5, 1957 / Vanguard ✦✦✦✦✦
Fine anthology collecting material done by the great blues shouter for Vanguard during the mid-'50s. Songs include a remake of "Going To Chicago," plus other combo dates, and he is backed by such Basie comrades as Jo Jones and Buddy Tate. This has been reissued on CD. *—Ron Wynn*

Dave Brubeck and Jimmy Rushing / Jan. 29, 1960-Aug. 4, 1960 / Columbia ✦✦✦✦
Pairing of divergent styles proves effective session. *—Ron Wynn*

Rushing Lullabies / Mar. 1960 / Columbia Special Products ✦✦✦

Jimmy Rushing and the Smith Girls / Jul. 7, 1960-Jul. 13, 1960 / Columbia ✦✦✦

Everyday I Have the Blues / Feb. 9, 1967-Feb. 10, 1967 / Bluesway ✦✦✦✦
A CD reissue of the great blues shouter Jimmy Rushing singing recreated versions of his classics with the Basie band. This originally came out in the mid-'50s, when Rushing had left Basie and was heading his own band. While these versions aren't the definitive ones, they're far from bad. *—Ron Wynn*

George Russell

b. Jun. 23, 1923, Cincinnati, OH
Piano / Avant-Garde, Post-Bop
George Russell's "Lydian concept," which he began working on in the '40s, has evolved into one of jazz's major advances. Russell, whose father was a professor of music at Oberlin, derived a system that graded intervals by how far their pitches were from a central tone. This theory provided musicians with a wider choice of notes by making the tonal center of a piece also its center of gravity. He linked the ancient Lydian mode with modern uses of chromaticism. Russell developed this into the "Lydian chromatic concept of tonal organization," and his work was hailed as a historical breakthrough. He was among the first to combine Afro-Latin influences and jazz elements with "Cubana Be/Cubana Bop." Russell studied composition with Stefan Wolpe. He taught at the Lenox School of Jazz, Lund Unversity in Sweden, and at the New England Conservatory. Russell also published several papers and two volumes on the Lydian chromatic concept. He began playing drums in Cincinnati clubs while attending Wilberforce University High School, where he'd won a scholarship. Russell played briefly in Benny Carter's band but was replaced by Max Roach and turned to composing and arranging. He sold his first big band arrangement to Carter and Dizzy Gillespie in the mid-'40s. Russell later wrote for Earl Hines. He moved to New York and wanted to play drums in Charlie Parker's group, but became ill. Russell worked on his Lydian theories during a lengthy recovery period in the mid-'40s. Later, he wrote several pieces for Dizzy Gillespie, including "Cubana Be/Cubana Bop" and compositions for Buddy DeFranco and Lee Konitz. He also wrote for Charlie Ventura, Artie Shaw, and Claude Thornhill. Besides his teaching stints in the '50s, Russell made his recording debut as a leader on RCA and Decca. He turned to piano and formed a group in the early '60s. Its members included Don Ellis, Eric Dolphy, Chuck Israels, and Steve Swallow. There were sessions for Riverside, Decca, MPS, and Flying Dutchman. He also played at the landmark 1962 Washington, D.C., Jazz Festival. Russell moved to Europe in the mid-'60s and spent six years there teaching at various institutions and recording before returning to America in 1969, when he joined the faculty at the New England Conservatory. During the '70s and '80s he recorded for Soul Note, Blue Note, and ECM. Russell stopped composing in the mid-'70s to finish the second volume of the *Lydian Chromatic Concept*. He recorded albums in the late '70s and '80s with the Swedish Radiojazzgruppen and big bands in New York. Russell's compositions have earned him many honors, among them composer awards from *Metronome* and *Downbeat* magazine, a pair of Guggenheim fellowships, the National Music Award, three grants from the National Education Association, and the Oscar du Disque de Jazz. Among his discoveries were vocalist Shelia Jordan, and he was also an early champion of European saxophonist Jan Garbarek. His *African Game* album in 1985 was one of the first issued on the revived Blue Note label and included Russell's compositions inspired by African drum choirs. He toured England in the late '80s and worked with Courtney Pine and Kenny Wheeler, as well other other British jazz and rock musicians. *—Ron Wynn*

● **Jazz Workshop** / Mar. 31, 1956-Dec. 21, 1956 / Bluebird ✦✦✦✦
A CD reissue of an intriguing release from 1956 by George Russell. This was a superb album, marked by brilliant playing and provocative compositions. Russell spearheads everything and occasionally helps out on piano. The band includes another brilliant player in pianist Bill Evans, plus Hal McKusick on alto sax and flute, Art Farmer on trumpet, guitarist Barry Galbraith, bassists Milt Hinton and Teddy Kotick, and Joe Harris, Osie Johnson or Paul Motian on drums. *—Ron Wynn*

● **New York, New York** / Sep. 12, 1958-Mar. 25, 1959 / MCA ✦✦✦✦
This is a landmark of conceptual arranging, production, and playing magnificence. John Coltrane, Max Roach, Bill Evans, and Jon Hendricks all soar. *—Ron Wynn*

Stratusphunk / Oct. 18, 1960 / Original Jazz Classics ✦✦✦✦
Intriguing, often entrancing, compositions. *—Ron Wynn*

Outer Thoughts / Oct. 18, 1960-Aug. 27, 1962 / Milestone ✦✦✦

★ **Ezz-Thetic** / May 8, 1961 / Original Jazz Classics ✦✦✦✦✦
This is a true classic. Composer/pianist George Russell gathered a very versatile group of talents (trumpeter Don Ellis, trombonist Dave Baker, Eric Dolphy on alto and bass clarinet, bassist Steve Swallow, and drummer Joe Hunt) to explore three of his originals, "'Round Midnight" (which is given an extraordinary treatment by Dolphy), Miles Davis' "Nardis," and David Baker's "Honesty." The music is post-bop, and although using ideas from avant-garde jazz, it does not fall into any simple category. The improvising is at a very high level, and the frameworks (which include free and stop-time sections) really inspire the players. Highly recommended. *—Scott Yanow*

The Stratus Seekers / Jan. 31, 1962 / Original Jazz Classics ✦✦✦✦
Fine example of Russell's inside/outside arranging style. Dave Baker is impressive. *—Ron Wynn*

The Outer View / Aug. 27, 1962 / Original Jazz Classics ✦✦✦✦
Composer George Russell's early-'60s Riverside recordings are among his most accessible. For this set (the CD reissue adds an alternate take of the title cut to the original program), Russell and his very impressive sextet (trumpeter Don Ellis, trombonist Garnett Brown, Paul Plummer on tenor, bassist Steve Swallow, and drummer Pete La Roca) are challenged by the complex material; even Charlie Parker's blues "Au Privave" is transformed into something new. It is particularly interesting to hear Don Ellis this early in his career. The most famous selection, a very haunting version of "You Are My Sunshine," was singer Sheila Jordan's debut on records. *—Scott Yanow*

African Game / Jun. 18, 1983 / Blue Note ✦✦

London Concert, Vol. 1 / Aug. 28, 1989 / Stash ✦✦✦

London Concert, Vol. 2 / Aug. 28, 1989-Aug. 31, 1989 / Stash ✦✦✦✦

Pee Wee Russell (Charles Ellsworth Russell)

b. Mar. 27, 1906, St. Louis, MO, **d.** Feb. 15, 1969, Alexandria, VA
Clarinet / Dixieland
Pee Wee Russell, although never a virtuoso, was one of the giants of jazz. A highly expressive and unpredictable clarinetist, Russell was usually grouped in Dixieland-type groups throughout his career, but his advanced and spontaneous solos (which often sounded as if he were thinking aloud) defied classification. A professional by the time he was 15, Pee Wee Russell played in Texas with Peck Kelley's group (meeting Jack Teagarden); in 1925 he was in St. Louis, jamming with Bix Beiderbecke. Russell moved to New York in 1927 and gained some attention for his playing with Red Nichols' Five Pennies. Russell freelanced, making some notable records with Billy Banks in 1932 that matched him with Red Allen. He played clarinet and tenor with Louis Prima during 1935-37, appearing on many records and enjoying the association. After leaving Prima, he started working with Eddie Condon's freewheeling groups and remained in Condon's orbit on and off for the next 30 years. Pee Wee's recordings with Condon in 1938 made him a star in the trad Chicago jazz world. Russell was featured (but often the butt of jokes) on Condon's Town Hall Concerts. Heavy drinking almost killed him in 1950, but Pee Wee Russell made an unlikely comeback and became more assertive in running his career. He started leading his own groups (which were more swing- than Dixieland-oriented), was a star on the 1957 television special "The Sound of Jazz," and by the early '60s was playing in a pianoless quartet with valve trombonist Marshall Brown, whose repertoire included tunes by John Coltrane and Ornette Coleman. He even sat in with Thelonious Monk at the 1963 Newport Jazz Festival and took up abstract painting. But after the death of his wife in 1967, Pee Wee Russell accelerated his drinking and went quickly downhill, passing away less than two years later. *—Scott Yanow*

★ **Jack Teagarden / Pee Wee Russell** / Aug. 31, 1938-Dec. 15, 1940 / Original Jazz Classics ✦✦✦✦✦
This classic set reissues a couple of important sessions that were made for the H.R.S. label and later acquired by Riverside. The great trombonist Jack Teagarden is heard in 1940 with an octet dominated by Duke Ellington sidemen (including cornetist Rex Stewart, clarinetist Barney Bigard, and tenor saxophonist Ben Webster). Recorded when Teagarden was struggling with his big band, it was a rare treat for him to stretch out with a combo, and the results (which include a superior version of "St. James Infirmary") are memorable. In addition, Pee Wee Russell is heard with an all-star octet of his own that co-stars trumpeter Max Kaminsky, trombonist Dicky Wells, and pianist James P. Johnson in 1938; the final two numbers feature the unique trio of Russell, Johnson, and drummer Zutty Singleton. The musi-

cians seem quite inspired, and both trad and swing fans are advised to get this excellent reissue. — *Scott Yanow*

We're in the Money / 1953-Oct. 2, 1954 / Black Lion ✦✦✦✦
His unique clarinet style is featured on this CD with two overlapping groups, both of which include trombonist Vic Dickenson and pianist George Wein. One band has Russell matching wits with the brilliant trumpet of Wild Bill Davison while the other date showcases the more mellow horn of Doc Cheatham, heard in a rare solo spot in the mid-'50s. This music mostly avoids the old warhorses and features superior swing standards by some of the top Condonites. — *Scott Yanow*

Memorial Album / Mar. 29, 1960 / Prestige ✦✦✦✦
Teaming together trumpeter Buck Clayton with clarinetist Pee Wee Russell in 1960 was a logical move. Both of these individual stylists had been stuck often in Dixieland settings in the '50s, yet they were really highly distinctive swing soloists. Joined by a modern rhythm section led by pianist Tommy Flanagan, Clayton and Russell are in top form on six fine standards, making one wish that they had teamed up in this type of setting more often. — *Scott Yanow*

Jazz Reunion / Feb. 23, 1961-Mar. 8, 1961 / Candid ✦✦✦✦
The reunion that took place in this 1961 session was between Russell and tenor great Coleman Hawkins; they had first recorded one of the songs, ("If I Could Be with You") back in 1929. Both Hawkins and Russell had remained modern soloists, and on this unusual but very satisfying date (which also features trumpeter Emmett Berry and trombonist Bob Brookmeyer), they explore such numers as a pair of Ellington classics ("All Too Soon" and "What Am I Here For?"), two Russell originals, and even the boppish "Tin Tin Deo." — *Scott Yanow*

Pee Wee Russell All Stars / Atlantic ✦✦✦

Terje Rypdal

b. Aug. 23, 1947, Oslo, Norway
Guitar / New Age, Avant-Garde, Fusion, Post-Bop
A flexible Norwegian guitarist and composer, Terje Rypdal blends rock and jazz elements as well as contemporary classical and even New Age ingredients into his solos. He has added an unusual touch, sometimes playing electric guitar with a violin bow, and he uses synthesizers and electronic attachments. Rydal is a self-taught guitarist who studied classical piano. He attended Oslo University and took composition with Finn Mortensen and learned the Lydian chromatic concept from its creator, George Russell. Rypdal worked with Jan Garbarek from the late '60s into the '70s and gained significant attention for his performance at the 1969 New Jazz Meeting in Baden-Baden, Germany. He formed the group Oydessy in the early '70s and visited London and America with them. Rypdal recorded with Palle Mikkelborg at the Festpill in Norway in 1978. He led a trio with Audun Kleive and Bjorn Kjellemyr that toured Eastern Europe and England in the mid-'80s. Rypdal played in a duo with Mikkelborg in 1986. He has recorded often as a leader for ECM in the '70s, '80s, and '90s. Rypdal has several sessions available on CD as a leader. — *Ron Wynn*

Waves / Aug. 1973-Sep. 1977 / ECM ✦✦✦✦
This contains some of Rypdal's jazziest music—"Per Ulv" even verges on bebop, despite its chattering rhythm box—alongside the more characteristic free-fall rhapsodies. — *Michael P. Dawson*

● **Works** / 1974-1981 / ECM ✦✦✦✦
An excellent sampler of Rypdal's music, it includes two cuts from his superb (but currently unavailable) early-'70s albums. — *Michael P. Dawson*

Odyssey / Aug. 1975 / ECM ✦✦✦✦
A magnificent effort that combines crushingly powerful rock/jazz ("Over Bierkerot" is a killer) with long, brooding electric ruminations, it was originally a double album; one track has been left off the CD. — *Michael P. Dawson*

Rypdal, Vitous, DeJohnette / 1979 / ECM ✦✦✦

Chaser / May 1985 / ECM ✦✦✦✦
This 1985 release finds Rypdal working in a hard-hitting power-trio format with his new group, The Chasers. — *Michael P. Dawson*

Blue / Nov. 1986 / ECM ✦✦✦✦
The second album with the rock-oriented Chasers adds keyboards to the mixture. — *Michael P. Dawson*

The Singles Collection / Aug. 1988 / ECM ✦✦✦✦
The title is a joke: this is actually the third album by the Chasers. Inspirational song title: "There is a Hot Lady in My Bedroom and I Need a Drink." — *Michael P. Dawson*

Joe Sample

b. Feb. 1, 1939, Houston, TX
Piano / Soul-Jazz, Hard Bop, Crossover
Pianist Sample formed a group with some Texas comrades in the late '50s

that played an aggressive brand of funky blues, instrumental R&B with jazz touches that they called the "Gulf Coast Sound." When the group moved to Los Angeles in 1960, they changed their name to the Jazz Crusaders. Though Sample also worked with some other musicians in the '60s, among them Tom Scott and the Harold Land/Bobby Hutcherson group, the main unit (Sample on keyboards, Wayne Henderson on trombone, Wilton Felder on tenor sax, and Stix Hooper on drums) were unparalleled at playing R&B-infused soul-jazz. The group dropped the Jazz surname in the '70s, becoming the Crusaders, and gradually began doing less ambitious, markedly lighter material without the strong blues and R&B backing. Sample got more involved in production in the '70s and '80s, and his most recent releases have been heavy on studio touches, weaker on content. — *Ron Wynn*

Fancy Dance / Apr. 20, 1969 / Gazell ✦✦✦✦
A different and rather strong session for keyboardist Joe Sample. Rather than the fusion, blues, and funky instrumentals he's done both with and without his fellow Crusaders, this is a mainstream trio session with Sample, bassist Red Mitchell, and drummer J.C. Moses. While there are two spry blues pieces, there are also some demanding standards and bop in which Sample shows he can execute the chord changes and perform conventional jazz with conviction, even if it's not what he does today. — *Ron Wynn*

Ashes to Ashes / 1990 / Warner Bros. ✦✦✦✦
Some very good funk and instrumental R&B from a first-rate pianist. — *Ron Wynn*

Invitation / 1993 / Warner Bros. ✦✦✦✦

● **Did You Feel That?** / 1994 / Warner Bros. ✦✦✦✦
Fans of the Crusaders of the early '70s will want this set. Joe Sample uses a Fender Rhodes keyboard much of the time, and a two-horn frontline (with trumpeter Oscar Brashear and tenorman Joel Peskin) is reminiscent of his former group; even guitarist Arthur Adams returns. This is intelligent and lightly funky and soulful jazz-oriented dance music that is very easy to enjoy. — *Scott Yanow*

David Sanborn (David William Sanborn)

b. Jul. 30, 1945, Tampa, FL
Sax (Alto) / Soul-Jazz, Crossover
David Sanborn has been the most influential saxophonist on pop, R&B, and crossover music of the past 20 years. Most of his recordings have been in the R&B/dance music vein, although Sanborn is a capable jazz player. His greatest contributions to music have been his passionate sound (with its crying and squealing high notes) and his emotional interpretations of melodies, which generally uplift any record he is on. Unlike his countless number of imitators, Sanborn is immediately recognizable within two notes. While growing up in St. Louis, Sanborn played with many Chicago blues greats (including Albert King) and became a skilled alto-saxophonist despite battling polio in his youth. After important stints with Paul Butterfield (he played with the Butterfield Blues Band at Woodstock), Gil Evans, Stevie Wonder, David Bowie, and the Brecker Brothers, Sanborn began recording as a leader in the mid-'70s and racked up a string of pop successes. Over the years he has worked with many pop players but has made his biggest impact leading his own danceable bands. Occasionally Sanborn throws the music world a curve such as his eccentric but rewarding *Another Hand*, a guest stint with avant-gardist Tim Berne on a 1993 album featuring the compositions of Julius Hemphill, and a set of ballads (*Pearls*) on which he is accompanied by a string orchestra arranged by Johnny Mandel. For a couple of years in the early '90s, Sanborn was the host of the syndicated television series "Night Music," which had a very eclectic lineup of musicians (from Sonny Rollins and Sun Ra to James Taylor and heavy-metal players), most of whom were given the opportunity to play together. It displayed David Sanborn's wide interest and musical curiosity even if many of his own recordings remain quite predictable. — *Scott Yanow*

Taking Off / 1975 / Warner Bros. ✦✦✦

David Sanborn / Feb. 1976 / Warner Bros. ✦✦✦

Love Songs / 1976-1988 / Warner Bros. ✦✦✦

Heart to Heart / Jan. 1978 / Warner Bros. ✦✦✦✦
Still potent compositionally. — *Michael G. Nastos*

Hideaway / 1979 / Warner Bros. ✦✦✦✦

Voyeur / 1980 / Warner Bros. ✦✦✦✦

Change of Heart / 1987 / Warner Bros. ✦✦✦

● **Another Hand** / 1991 / Elektra ✦✦✦✦
A return by Sanborn to his real, true love: unadorned (or only partly adorned) jazz. — *Ron Wynn*

Upfront / 1992 / Elektra ✦✦✦✦
Despite an array of session musicians and some heavily arranged material, alto saxophonist Dave Sanborn cuts long with his most expressive, joyous playing in many years. That's partly due to Marcus Miller's bass work,

which is fluid and backbeat-oriented, while others, like trumpeter Herb Robertson and organist Richard Tee, lay in some perfect riffs in support of Sanborn's earnest solos. — *Ron Wynn*

Hearsay / 1994 / Elektra ✦✦✦

● **Pearls** / Mar. 28, 1995 / Elektra ✦✦✦✦

David Sanborn is joined on this CD by an orchestra arranged by Johnny Mandel for a set dominated by melodic versions of standards. Sanborn does not get all that far away from the themes (which include "Try a Little Tenderness," "Smoke Gets in Your Eyes," "For All We Know," "This Masquerade," and a very emotional "Everything Must Change," in addition to a few newer songs); but his sound is so soulful and full of passion that he does not really need to improvise much to make his point. It's a fine change of pace for the highly influential altoist. — *Scott Yanow*

Poncho Sanchez

b. Oct. 30, 1951, Laredo, TX
Percussion / Latin Jazz

Ever since he led his first record date in 1982, Poncho Sanchez has headed one of the most popular and influential Latin-jazz bands around. The youngest of 11 children, Sanchez taught himself to play guitar, flute, drums, and timbales before settling on the congas. After a period playing with local bands, he joined Cal Tjader's band in 1975 and was an important part of Tjader's pacesetting group until his idol's death in 1982. Shortly after, he formed his own band and has since recorded on a regular basis for Concord Picante. Sanchez's group is very active, playing in clubs, concerts, and festivals on a regular basis. — *Scott Yanow*

★ **Papa Gato** / Oct. 1986 / Concord Picante ✦✦✦✦✦

Percussionist Poncho Sanchez has long led one of the top Latin-jazz groups, succeeding his former boss, the late Cal Tjader. On this easily enjoyable release, Sanchez features plenty of solos from Justo Almario (on alto, tenor, and flute), trumpeter Sal Cracchiolo, and trombonist Art Velasco, and the three percussionists have many opportunities to romp. The jazz content is pretty high, with such songs as "Jumpin' with Symphony Sid," "Senor Blues," and "Manteca" alternating with group originals. A fine introduction to the accessible Latin-jazz of Poncho Sanchez. — *Scott Yanow*

A Night at Kimball's East / Dec. 8, 1990 / Concord Picante ✦✦✦

Para Todos / Oct. 25, 1993-Oct. 26, 1993 / Concord Picante ✦✦✦✦

Everyone plays flawlessly, and Sanchez's conga work provides an array of expertly placed accents, multiple rhythms, and support. The songs are uniformly excellent, and Sanchez's group smoothly handles standards, hard bop, and Afro-Latin numbers. — *Ron Wynn*

Soul Sauce: Memories of Cal Tjader / Mar. 7, 1995-Mar. 8, 1995 / Concord Picante ✦✦✦✦

Pharoah Sanders (Farrell Sanders)

b. Oct. 13, 1940, Little Rock, AR
Sax (Tenor) / Avant-Garde, Hard Bop, Free Jazz

Pharoah Sanders has had a rather unique career. He came to fame when he made the John Coltrane Quartet a Quintet, taking ferocious, emotional, and atonal solos that started where Coltrane's left off. For a period after Coltrane's death, Sanders came close to making the avant-garde popular, as his alternately intense and peaceful solos proved to be a perfect team with singer Leon Thomas ("The Creator Has a Master Plan"). Unfortunately, most of Sanders' output since the late '70s has been quite derivative of Coltrane's hard bop-oriented music circa 1959, years before Sanders joined 'Trane. After graduating from high school, Pharoah Sanders freelanced in San Francisco. He moved to New York in 1962, struggled in obscurity for two years, then made his recording debut on ESP. He came to the attention of John Coltrane and from mid-1965 until 'Trane's death in 1967 was usually a part of Coltrane's controversial group, with his role being largely to create violent sound explorations. Sanders' most rewarding recordings took place during the late '60s/early '70s for Impulse with and without Leon Thomas. However, by the mid-'70s his sessions had become predictable, and Sanders' career never seemed to regain its earlier momentum. His decision in the early '80s to explore standards melodically pleased bebop purists but resulted in many of his followers' being disappointed by the absence of his own musical personality. Since that time, Sanders (now a legend) has continued largely in that direction, although occasionally (such as on drummer Franklin Kiermyer's very intense *Evidence* CD) the real Pharoah Sanders shows up and reminds the jazz world of his significance. — *Scott Yanow*

● **Pharoah's First** / Sep. 10, 1964 / ESP ✦✦✦✦

Pharoah Sanders' debut as a leader has been reissued on this ESP CD. Sanders, who is joined by trumpeter Stan Foster, pianist Jane Getz, bassist William Bennett, and drummer Marvin Pattillo, sounds remarkably like John Coltrane on "Seven by Seven"; he had not found his own musical personality yet. "Bethera" is a bit more distinctive, and overall this historic set should greatly interest fans of both Coltrane and Sanders. — *Scott Yanow*

★ **Karma** / Feb. 14, 1969-Oct. 20, 1969 / Impulse ✦✦✦✦✦

Karma was a real rarity, an avant-garde "hit." One could almost call it "free jazz for the masses." Pharoah Sanders, who in 1966 would have easily won a poll for "least likely to succeed commercially," by 1969 was out on his own, featuring his Jekyll-and-Hyde tenor (alternately peaceful and screaming) over rhythmic vamps. With Leon Thomas singing and yodelling, the 33-minute atmospheric "The Creator Has a Master Plan" caught on and received quite a bit of airplay on jazz stations. — *Scott Yanow*

Journey to the One / 1980 / Evidence ✦✦✦✦

Formerly a Theresa double LP, this single CD contains all ten of Pharoah Sanders' performances from the sessions. As usual, Sanders shifts between spiritual peace and violent outbursts in his tenor solos. The backup group changes from track to track but often includes pianist John Hicks, bassist Ray Drummond, and drummer Idris Muhammad. Sanders really recalls his former boss John Coltrane on "After the Rain" (taken as a duet with pianist Joe Bonner) and a romantic "Easy to Remember"; other high points include "You've Got to Have Freedom" (which has Bobby McFerrin as one of the background singers) and the exotic "Kazuko," on which Sanders is accompanied by kato, harmonium, and wind chimes. — *Scott Yanow*

● **Rejoice** / 1981 / Evidence ✦✦✦✦

Originally a two-LP set on Theresa, this single CD (which contains all of the music) features Pharoah Sanders in excellent form in 1981. Sanders sounds much more mellow than he had a decade earlier, often improvising in a style similar to late-'50s John Coltrane, particularly on "When Lights Are Low," "Moment's Notice," and "Central Park West." The personnel changes on many of the selections and includes such top players as pianists Joe Bonner and John Hicks, bassist Art Davis, drummers Elvin Jones and Billy Higgins, vibraphonist Bobby Hutcherson, trombonist Steve Turre, trumpeter Danny Moore, a harpist, and (on "Origin" and "Central Park West") five vocalists. The music always holds one's interest, making this one of Sanders' better later recordings. — *Scott Yanow*

Heart Is a Melody / Jan. 23, 1982 / Evidence ✦✦✦

Crescent with Love / Oct. 19, 1992-Oct. 20, 1992 / Evidence ✦✦✦✦

This two-CD set features tenor saxophonist Pharoah Sanders accompanied by a supportive rhythm section (pianist William Henderson, bassist Charles Fambrough, and drummer Sherman Ferguson). Although there are some passionate moments, this is actually one of his mellower sessions, and he explores such songs as "Misty," "In a Sentimental Mood," "Too Young to Go Steady," "Body and Soul," "Naima," and "After the Rain" in a ballad style not that different than John Coltrane's of the early '60s. There are some heated moments on some of the other selections (such as "Wise One" and "Crescent"), but Sanders' trademark screeches are at a minimum this time around. — *Scott Yanow*

Arturo Sandoval

b. Nov. 6, 1949, Artemisa, Cuba
Trumpet / Bop, Afro-Cuban Jazz

An energetic, often exciting trumpeter whose flashing phrases, high-note acrobatics, and dynamic, charismatic playing style was first noticed in the group Irakere. Arturo Sandoval hasn't made the great records as a leader that many anticipated, but he displays such potential as a soloist it seems only a matter of time before his definitive recording will be issued. His time, range, timbre, and approach are solid, as are his ballad skills. The only thing lacking has been consistency, particularly on record. Sandoval was one of the founding members in the Orquesta Cubana de Musica Moderna in Havana during the '70s, along with Paquito D'Rivera. Various members of this band later formed Irakere. The group recorded with David Amram in 1977. Sandoval left the group in 1981 and toured internationally with his own band and recorded in Cuba. He met his idol Dizzy Gillespie in the '70s and played with him in Cuba, America, Puerto Rico, and Finland, recording together in Finland for Pablo in the early '80s. Sandoval defected to America during the '80s and has since recorded for Messidor and GRP. He and D'Rivera played together on a recent Messidor release. In the '90s his regular Afro-Cuban group reflects his high-energy virtuosic approach, giving Sandoval an opportunity to display not only his remarkable range (his high notes rival Jon Faddis'!) and warm trumpet sound but his skills on timbales and piano and as a vocalist. — *Ron Wynn and Scott Yanow*

● **To a Finland Station** / Sep. 9, 1982 / Original Jazz Classics ✦✦✦

With Dizzy Gillespie in Helsinki. Excellent interplay. Lots of good feeling on this session. — *Michael G. Nastos*

Breaking the Sound Barrier / 1983 / CCAA ✦✦✦✦

Live date in Chicago from Cuban trumpeter Arturo Sandoval, who plays it straight in jazz and Latin veins. No funk. His best. — *Michael G. Nastos*

Tumbaito / 1986 / Messidor ✦✦✦✦

A tremendous session with dynamic trumpeter Arturo Sandoval mixing things up with an all-star lineup. It was originally available only overseas but has now been issued in America through Messidor. — *Ron Wynn*

★ **Straight Ahead** / Aug. 1988 / Ronnie Scott's Jazz House ♦♦♦♦♦
With his remarkable range and phenomenal technique, Arturo Sandoval is one of the world's great trumpeters; he can do virtually anything he wants on his instrument. Some detractors have claimed that he has too much technique (is such a thing possible?) and that his recordings thus far for GRP are a bit erratic. The latter criticism cannot be applied to this 1988 release. Sandoval is heard with a standard quartet comprising the great pianist Chucho Valdes (the leader of Irakere), bassist Ron Matthewson, and drummer Martin Drew. Recorded in England before Sandoval broke ties with Cuba, Arturo is in near-miraculous form on some blues, a lyrical "My Funny Valentine," and a few basic originals. Just listen to him tear through "Blue Monk," playing in the low register with the speed of an Al Hirt before jumping into the stratosphere like Maynard Ferguson. This CD serves as an excellent introduction for the bop lover to the very talented Arturo Sandoval. —*Scott Yanow*

I Remember Clifford / 1992 / GRP ♦♦♦♦
Arturo Sandoval's high-note explosions, racing lines, expressive tone, and charismatic playing style were ideal for the songs of Clifford Brown, a certified jazz legend. Sandoval's exploits were more than matched by a marvelous group that included pianist Kenny Kirkland, saxophonist Ernie Watts, and bassist Charnett Moffett, plus drummer Kenny Washington. —*Ron Wynn*

Dreams Come True / 1993 / GRP ♦♦♦♦
This is one of trumpeter Arturo Sandoval's more restrained sessions, but he cuts loose effectively in some spots. Accompanied by one of two orchestras arranged and conducted by Michel Legrand on most of the selections, Sandoval displays his warm tone and infuses songs such as "Little Sunflower," "Once Upon a Summertime," and "To Diz with Love" with lots of feeling; his duet with Legrand on Dizzy Gillespie's "Con Alma" is touching. The ten-minute "Dahomey Dance" (which also has solos from tenor saxophonist Ernie Watts and trombonist Bill Watrous) and a hyper "Giant Steps" are among the many highlights of this recommended disc. —*Scott Yanow*

Danzon (Dance On) / Oct. 10, 1993-Nov. 24, 1993 / GRP ♦♦♦♦
Trumpeter Arturo Sandoval comes close on *Danzon* to cutting the Afro-Cuban masterpiece everyone's awaited since his glorious sound first surfaced. From the animated solos on "Africa," "Tres Palabras," and "Conjunto" to the flowing, crisply articulated lines on "Groovin' High," Sandoval plays with imagination, verve, and flair, displaying a more original and distinctive concept than on any of his GRP albums to date. He's joined by many top Latin musicians, plus special guest ringers like Vikki Carr, Bill Cosby, and Gloria Estefan, but there's no pandering or stylistic compromises to integrate them into the proceedings. For those who've longed for Sandoval to cut loose, here's the evidence that justifies his reputation. —*Ron Wynn*

Arturo Sandoval and the Latin Train / 1995 / GRP ♦♦♦♦

Mongo Santamaria

b. Apr. 7, 1922, Jesus Maria, Havana, Cuba
Percussion / Latin Jazz, Cuba, Latin Continuum
Mongo Santamaria is arguably the greatest Cuban percussionist of his generation and, outside of Chano Pozo, the most influential in jazz history. His astonishing ability as a player remains impressive, even when he is featured on albums far below his abilities. No one's been more dominant on congas and bongos as long as Santamaria, who's played in bebop, hard bop, big bands, Latin jazz combos, dance bands, and pop groups. He's recorded for major labels, independents, and tiny Latin companies. There aren't many musicians more intense, or as blazing fast, as Santamaria doing a conga solo. He originally studied violin but switched to drums. Santamaria dropped out of school to become a professional conguero. He was an established star in Havana before Castro's takeover. Santamaria left Cuba for Mexico City with his cousin Armanda Peraza in 1948. They arrived in New York City in 1950 and were billed as the Black Cuban Diamonds. Santamaria made his American debut with Perez Prado; he played with him three years, then spent seven fabulous years with Tito Puente. Their multiple percussion barrages and rhythmic assaults were historic in Latin jazz and jazz circles. Santamaria made several first-rate albums of traditional African and Afro-Cuban music in the early '50s, taking the music directly from Cuban religious practices and ceremonies. He began playing Latin jazz with George Shearing in the early '50s; the group included Willie Bobo on timbales, Peraza on bongos, and Cal Tjader on vibes. Santamaria and Bobo later joined Tjader's group in 1958. Santamaria made several fine albums with him for three years, then played with Dizzy Gillespie and Brother Jack McDuff. He began recording for Fantasy in the late '50s. Santamaria's '60s and early '70s releases blended pop, fusion, rock, jazz, and R&B with Latin arrangements and rhythms. He had a Top Ten hit with his cover of Herbie Hancock's "Watermelon Man" in 1963 and employed such jazz stars as Chick Corea and Hubert Laws in various bands. Santamaria's LPs on the Battle and Riverside labels were extremely popular and eventually led to a contract with Columbia. Santamaria issued several albums on Columbia between 1965 and 1970, sev-

eral of which made the pop LP charts. His cover of the Temptations' "Cloud Nine" single also made the Top 40. Santamaria made "boogaloo" recordings and such crossover releases as *Soul Bag, Stone Soul, La Bamba,* and *Workin' on a Groovy Thing.* He continued cutting fusion material in the early '70s for Atlantic, though his band at this time included Israel "Cachao" Lopez and Peraza. But he soon returned to more traditional Latin music. The LP *Up from the Roots* blended Afro-Cuban and conjunto. He signed with Vaya in the early '70s and shared a Yankee Stadium bill with the Fania All Stars, as well as doing a guest stint with them. Santamaria cut a Latin jazz date live at Montreaux for Pablo in the '80s with Dizzy Gillespie and Toots Thielemans. There were also sessions for Roulette, Tropical Buddah, and a reunion date with the Fania All Stars. Santamaria was featured in the documentary film *Salsa* and teamed with Charlie Palmieri on a sensational late-'80s session for Concord Picante, one of Palmieri's final albums. Santamaria has continued into the '90s, recording a new album of Latin music for Chesky in 1993. Several classic Santamaria sessions have been reissued on CD, and he has current releases available. His recordings on Latin labels can be obtained from specialty stores. —*Ron Wynn*

Yambu / Dec. 1958 / Fantasy ♦♦♦
Afro-Roots / Dec. 1958-May 1959 / Prestige ♦♦♦♦
Mongo Santamaria made a pair of superb Latin-jazz albums for Fantasy in the late '50s. These were subsequently reissued on a two-record set on vinyl in the '70s, then repackaged again for CD. The disc contains the full albums *Yambu* and *Mongo,* each one brilliant. —*Ron Wynn*

Our Man in Havana / May 1959 / Fantasy ♦♦♦
Sabroso / May 1959 / Original Jazz Classics ♦♦♦♦
A 1987 reissue of a wonderful album with Willie Bobo (percussion) and Pete Escovedo. —*Ron Wynn*

At the Black Hawk / 1962 / Fantasy ♦♦♦♦
This CD, which includes the contents of two former Mongo Santamaria LPs, is a fine showcase for his Latin-jazz band of the early '60s. The first set is more jazz-oriented, with plenty of solo space for the Stan Getz-inspired tenor of Jose Silva, while the second date has a stronger role for a violinist and has some group vocals that show where Poncho Sanchez came from. With Santamaria and Wilie Bobo leading the four-member percussion section, such songs as "Tenderly," "All the Things You Are," and "Body and Soul" are successfully Latinized; in addition there are many group originals, including three by pianist Joao Donato. —*Scott Yanow*

★ **Skins** / Jul. 9, 1962-1964 / Milestone ♦♦♦♦♦
This CD (originally *So Mongo* and *Mongo Explodes* on Riverside) includes many compositions by trumpeter Marty Sheller. Guests include Hubert Laws, Chick Corea, and Jimmy Cobb. Every track is vital. —*Michael G. Nastos*

Mongo at the Village Gate / Sep. 2, 1963 / Original Jazz Classics ♦♦♦♦
This is a nonet with Pat Patrick, Bobby Capers, Marty Sheller, and Chihuahua Martinez—a Latin, jazz, and soul combo. MC'd by Symphony Sid, it is startlingly fresh for its era. It still sounds fresh. —*Michael G. Nastos*

Ole Ola / May 1989 / Concord Jazz ♦♦♦♦
Band minus one member. —*Ron Wynn*

Live at Jazz Alley / Mar. 1990 / Concord Jazz ♦♦♦♦
Good group. —*Ron Wynn*

Mambo Mongo / Mar. 30, 1992-Mar. 31, 1992 / Chesky ♦♦♦
Mongo Returns / Jun. 28, 1995-Jun. 29, 1995 / Milestone ♦♦♦♦
Mongo y La Lupe / Fantasy ♦♦♦

Diane Schuur

b. 1953, Seattle, WA
Piano, Vocals / Pop, Standards
Diane Schuur, who has thus far been on the periphery of jazz, has the potential to be an important jazz singer, although her screeching in the upper register and her desire to include an over-abundance of pop material in her repertoire have resulted in her significance being much less than originally expected. Blinded at birth by a hospital accident, Schuur (who would later be nicknamed "Deedles") imitated singers as a child. She had her first gig at a Holiday Inn when she was just ten and originally sang country music. The turning point in her career occurred when she sang "Amazing Grace" at the 1979 Monterey Jazz Festival, greatly impressing Stan Getz. After Getz featured her singing at a televised concert from the White House in 1982, Schuur was signed to GRP and began recording regularly. Although her 1987 collaboration with the Count Basie Orchestra was a high point, Diane Schuur's recordings tend to be a mixed success from the jazz standpoint. —*Scott Yanow*

● **Collection** / 1986-1989 / GRP ♦♦♦♦
A good indicator of the artist's career on the label. —*Ron Wynn*

Diane and the Count Basie Orchestra / 1987 / GRP ♦♦♦♦

Love Songs / 1993 / GRP ✦✦✦✦
The jazz content on this CD from singer Diane Schuur is rather slight, but this is actually one of her finest recordings. Schuur (who has a lovely voice) sings straightforward versions of ten veteran ballads while accompanied by one of two string orchestras. Tom Scott on reeds and trumpeter Jack Sheldon have short spots, but this is very much Schuur's show. She really excels in the restrained setting, making this a superior middle-of-the-road pop recording. —*Scott Yanow*

Bob Scobey

b. Dec. 9, 1916, Tucumcari, NM, **d.** Jun. 12, 1963, Montreal, Canada
Trumpet / Dixieland
Throughout his prime years, Bob Scobey was one of the more popular trumpeters in Dixieland. After many low-profile jobs in dance bands in the '30s, in 1938 Scobey met trumpeter Lu Watters. As a member of Watters' Yerba Buena Jazz Band in San Francisco during 1940-49 (with much of 1942-46 spent in the military), Scobey participated in one of the most influential bands of the Dixieland revival movement. In 1949 he left to form his own Frisco Jazz Band, recording frequently (most notably for Good Time Jazz) and often featuring Clancy Hayes or appearing with Lizzie Miles. In 1959 Scobey opened his Club Bourbon Street in Chicago; he died four years later at the age of 46 from cancer. Many of Bob Scobey's Good Time Jazz dates have been reissued on CD, and they still contain stirring and joyful music. —*Scott Yanow*

● **Bob Scobey's Frisco Band, Vol. 1** / Apr. 29, 1950-Nov. 6, 1951 / Good Time Jazz ✦✦✦✦
This rather brief CD (just 35 minutes), a straight reissue of an LP, gives listeners a good example of the playing of trumpeter Bob Scobey. Taken from his earliest period as a bandleader, these Dixieland performances also feature trombonist Jack Buck; either Darnell Howard, Albert Nicholas, or George Probert on clarinet; pianists Burt Bales or Wally Rose; and banjoist Clancy Hayes, who also takes a few vocals. Excellent, good-time music. —*Scott Yanow*

John Scofield

b. Dec. 26, 1951, Dayton, OH
Guitar / Post-Bop
One of the "big three" of current jazz guitarists (along with Pat Metheny and Bill Frisell), Scofield's influence has been growing in recent years. Possessor of a very distinctive rock-oriented sound that is often a bit distorted, Scofield is a masterful jazz improviser whose music generally falls somewhere between post-bop, fusion, and soul-jazz. He started on guitar while at high school in Connecticut, and from 1970 to 1973 studied at Berklee and played in the Boston area. After recording with Gerry Mulligan and Chet Baker at Carnegie Hall, Scofield was a member of the Billy Cobham-George Duke band for two years. In 1977 he recorded with Charles Mingus and later joined the Gary Burton quartet and Dave Liebman's quintet. His own early sessions as a leader were funk-oriented. From 1982 to 1985 Scofield toured the world and recorded with Miles Davis. Since that time he has led his own groups, played with Bass Desires, and recorded frequently as a leader for Gramavision and Blue Note, using such major players as Charlie Haden, Jack DeJohnette, Joe Lovano, and Eddie Harris. —*Scott Yanow*

Rough House / Nov. 27, 1978 / Enja ✦✦✦

Who's Who? / Novus ✦✦

Shinola / Dec. 12, 1981-Dec. 13, 1981 / Enja ✦✦✦✦
Trio set recorded in 1991. Dense, prickly, and lots of space for guitar work. —*Ron Wynn*

Out Like a Light / Dec. 14, 1981 / Enja ✦✦✦✦
Fine trio date, with guitarist John Scofield stretching out in multiple directions and showing his facility with the swing style, mainstream, and jazz-rock genres. Besides his fluid, inventive solos, Scofield works well with bassist Steve Swallow, who approaches his instrument like a second guitar, and drummer Adam Nussbaum. —*Ron Wynn*

Still Warm / Jun. 1986 / Gramavision ✦✦✦

Blue Matter / Sep. 1986 / Gramavision ✦✦✦✦
A 1989 reissue of a fine, expansive Scofield outing. —*Ron Wynn*

Grace Under Pressure / Dec. 1991 / Blue Note ✦✦✦✦
Guitarist John Scofield leads a top-notch group on this session. It's a piano-less band, with Scofield's nimble guitar lines contrasted by those of second guitarist Bill Frisell. They team with trombonist Jim Pugh, bassist Charlie Haden, and drummer Joey Baron, plus Randy Brecker on fluegelhorn and John Clark on French horn. —*Ron Wynn*

What We Do / May 1992 / Blue Note ✦✦✦✦

★ **Hand Jive** / Oct. 1993 / Blue Note ✦✦✦✦✦
Guitarist John Scofield and tenor saxophonist Eddie Harris make a complementary team on this set of funky jazz, for both have immediately identifiable sounds and adventurous spirits. Along with a fine rhythm section that includes Larry Goldings on piano and organ, Scofield and Harris interact joyfully on ten of the guitarist's originals. —*Scott Yanow*

● **Groove Elation** / 1995 / Blue Note ✦✦✦✦
John Scofield has continued to grow and evolve year by year. This 1995 set is quite blues-oriented, sometimes boppish, and fairly laidback, almost sounding like a Jimmy Smith or Groove Holmes date from the '60s. Larry Goldings (who doubles occasionally on piano) is almost as significant in the ensembles as the leader/guitarist and has become the most important arrival on organ since Joey DeFrancesco and Barbara Dennerlein. Many of the tunes (all Scofield originals) use parade-like rhythms propelled by Idris Muhammad and Dennis Irwin (particularly the eccentric "Peculiar" and "Groove Elation"), and the interplay between the two lead voices is quite appealing. Scofield is unselfish as far as taking solo space (he clearly enjoys the light funky grooves set by Goldings), and the results are quite appealing. —*Scott Yanow*

Slo Sco: Best of Ballads / Gramavision ✦✦✦

Shirley Scott

b. Mar. 14, 1934, Philadelphia, PA
Organ / Soul-Jazz, Hard Bop, Groove
Shirley Scott surprised many people in 1992 when she appeared on Bill Cosby's reprise of the Groucho Marx game and personality show "You Bet Your Life." Not surprised that he'd picked her to be his music director, but that she was playing piano. Her reputation was cemented during the '60s on several superb, soulful organ/soul-jazz dates where she demonstrated an aggressive, highly rhythmic attack blending intricate bebop harmonies with bluesy melodies and a gospel influence, punctuating everything with great use of the bass pedals. But Scott demonstrated an equal flair and facility on piano, many days incorporating snatches of anthemic jazz compositions while noodling in the background. The show was a bore, but it was great to see Scott back in the spotlight. She began playing piano as a child, then trumpet in high school. Scott was working a club date in the mid-'50s in Philadelphia when the owner rented her a Hammond B-3. She learned quickly and was soon leading both popular and artistically superior trios featuring either Eddie "Lockjaw" Davis or then-husband Stanley Turrentine on tenor sax. The Scott/Turrentine union lasted until the early '70s, and their musical collaborations in the '60s were among the finest in the field. Scott continued recording in the '70s, working with Harold Vick and Jimmy Forrest, and then, in the early '80s, with Dexter Gordon. She also made a lot of appearances on TV in New York and Philadelphia. Scott recorded prolifically for Prestige in the '50s and '60s, then for Impulse in the mid-'60s and Atlantic in the late '60s. She moved to Chess/Cadet in the early '70s and also did sessions for Strata-East. In recent years Scott has recorded for Muse and Candid. Her later material wasn't as consistent as her best work for Prestige and Impulse. She has only a few dates available on CD. —*Ron Wynn and Bob Porter*

Great Scott! / May 27, 1958 / Prestige ✦✦✦

Shirley's Sounds / May 27, 1958 / Prestige ✦✦✦
From the 1958 recording with Scott, George Duvivier on bass, and Arthur Edgehill on drums. Includes a version of "Cherokee." —*AMG*

Scottie / Oct. 23, 1958 / Prestige ✦✦✦
This is early Scott, several takes from different session for this Prestige release. —*Michael Erlewine*

Workin' / May 27, 1958-Mar. 24, 1960 / Prestige ✦✦✦
One of several trio and/or combo works that organist Shirley Scott recorded for Prestige in the late '50s and early '60s. Her swirling, driving lines, intense bass-pedal support, and bluesy fervor were ideal for the soul-jazz format, and this is a typical example. —*Ron Wynn*

Shirley Scott Trio / May 27, 1958-Apr. 8, 1960 / Moodsville ✦✦✦
A trio recording with Scott, George Tucker on bass, and Earl Coleman (vcl). Originally released on Moodsville. —*Michael Erlewine*

Now's the Time / May 27, 1958-Mar. 31, 1964 / Prestige ✦✦✦

Scottie Plays the Duke / Apr. 24, 1959 / Prestige ✦✦✦
The Shirley Scott Trio with George Duvivier on bass and Arthur Edgehill on drums. This is a collection of Ellington tunes, including "In a Sentimental Mood." —*Michael Erlewine*

Soul Searching / Dec. 4, 1959 / Prestige ✦✦✦
Shirley Scott with Wendell Marshall on bass and Arthur Edgehill on drums. Includes title tune and "Boss." —*AMG*

Stompin' / Apr. 8, 1960-Mar. 24, 1961 / Prestige ✦✦✦
Here is Scott with Ronnell Bring (piano), Wally Richardson (guitar), Peck Morrison (bass), and Roy Haynes (drums). Includes a rendition of Nat Adderley's "Work Song." —*Michael Erlewine*

Mucho, Mucho / Jun. 23, 1960 / Prestige ✦✦✦
An early date with Gene Casey (piano), Bill Ellington (bass), Manny Ramos (timb), Phil Diaz (bongos), and Juan Amalbert (conga). —*Michael Erlewine*

Soul Sisters / Jun. 23, 1960 / Prestige ✦✦✦
With Lem Winchester on vibes, George Duvivier on bass, and Arthur Edgehill on drums. A dauntless, swinging affair. —*Ron Wynn*

Satin Doll / Mar. 7, 1961 / Prestige ✦✦✦
With George Tucker on bass and Jack Simplkins on drums. A bit more prim, though Scott still burns. —*Ron Wynn*

Hip Soul / Jun. 2, 1961 / Prestige ✦✦✦✦
Here is Stanley Turrentine recording under the name Stan Turner. Slashing, aptly titled. —*Ron Wynn*

Blue Seven / Aug. 22, 1961 / Prestige ✦✦✦
A quintet with Roy Brooks (drums), Oliver Nelson (tenor sax) and Joe Newman (trumpet) plays one Scott original, the title song by Sonny Rollins, and an excellent "Wagon Wheels." —*Michael G. Nastos*

Hip Twist / Nov. 17, 1961 / Prestige ✦✦✦
Scott with Stanley Turrentine (sax), George Tucker (bass), and Otis Finch (drums). Any Turrentine/Scott albums are worth hearing, even with a title like this one. —*Michael Erlewine*

Shirley Scott Plays Horace Silver / Nov. 17, 1961 / Prestige ✦✦✦✦
Just what it says. The queen of the Hammond organ (along with Henry Grimes (bass) and Otis Finch (drums)) plays compositions by the funkmaster himself, Horace Silver. Included are "Señor Blues" and "The Preacher." —*Michael Erlewine*

Happy Talk / Dec. 5, 1962 / Prestige ✦✦✦
Trio with Scott with Earl May (bass) and Roy Brooks (drums). —*AMG*

★ **Sweet Soul** / Dec. 5, 1962 / Prestige ✦✦✦✦✦
Reissued from the "Happy Talk" session, this features Earl May on bass and Roy Brooks on drums. It includes a nice "Jitterbug Waltz." All are standards. —*Michael G. Nastos*

Soul Is Willing / Jan. 10, 1963 / Prestige ✦✦✦✦
This is a good album that shows the husband and wife team of Shirley Scott and Stanley Turrentine in their usual, excellent form—a fine example of organ combo soul-jazz. Now part of the Prestige two-fer called *Soul Shoutin'.* —*Michael Erlewine*

★ **Soul Shoutin'** / Jan. 10, 1963 & Oct. 15, 1963 / Prestige ✦✦✦✦✦
Organist Shirley Scott and her then-husband, tenor great Stanley Turrentine, always made potent music together. This CD, which combines the former Prestige LPs *The Soul Is Willing* and *Soul Shoutin',* finds "Mr. T." at his early peak, playing some intense, yet always soulful, solos on such pieces as Sy Oliver's "Yes Indeed," "Secret Love," and his memorable originals "The Soul Is Willing" and "Deep Down Soul." Scott, who found her own niche within the dominant Jimmy Smith style, swings hard throughout the set, and (with drummer Crassella Oliphant and either Major Holley or Earl May on bass) the lead voices play with such consistent enthusiasm that one would think these were club performances. Highly recommended. —*Scott Yanow*

Drag 'Em Out / May 27, 1963 / Prestige ✦✦✦
Scott with Major Holley (b) and Roy Brooks (d). —*AMG*

For Members Only / Aug. 22, 1963 / Impulse ✦✦✦✦
An excellent date with Earl May on bass and Jimmy Cobb on drums. —*AMG*

☆ **For Members Only/Great Scott** / Aug. 22, 1963-May 20, 1964 / Impulse ✦✦✦✦✦
During the '60s, Shirley Scott's Impulse albums were often split between big-band selections (with orchestras arranged by Oliver Nelson) and trio features. This CD reissue from 1989 includes all of the contents from two of Scott's better Impulse albums, *Great Scott* and *For Members Only.* In general the eight trio numbers are the most rewarding performances on the disc, since the material is fairly superior, while the big band tracks emphasize then-current show and movie tunes. Overall, this generous CD gives one a good overview of Shirley Scott's playing talents. —*Scott Yanow*

Travelin' Light / Feb. 6, 1964-Feb. 7, 1964 / Prestige ✦✦✦
Shirley Scott on the Hammond B-3 with Kenny Burrell on guitar. Released on Prestige. —*Michael Erlewine*

Blue Flames / Mar. 31, 1964 / Original Jazz Classics ✦✦✦✦
Recorded in Englewood Cliffs, NJ, with Turrentine and Stanley. This is exactly the kind of straightahead funky music you would expect from the Scott/Turrentine combination. No disappointments; just great groove. Now available on CD (Prestige OJCCD-328). —*Michael Erlewine*

Everybody Loves a Lover / Aug. 23, 1964 / Impulse ✦✦✦
Scott with Stanley Turrentine on tenor sax, Bob Cranshaw on bass, and Otis Finch on drums. —*AMG*

The Great Live Sessions / Sep. 23, 1964 / ABC/Impulse ✦✦✦✦
Recorded live at the Front Room in Newark, NJ, the album includes ten tracks with a quartet including Stanley Turrentine. On a rare night for music, the band delivered on all counts. You can't go wrong here. —*Michael G. Nastos*

Queen of the Organ / Sep. 23, 1964 / Impulse ✦✦✦✦
A steamy hot mid-'60s soul-jazz session with soulful, bluesy organist Shirley Scott providing some booming, funky solos. This was one of several combo works she cut, usually with saxophonist Stanley Turrentine, who

was her husband at the time. Anything Scott recorded from this period is worth hearing. —*Ron Wynn*

Latin Shadows / Jul. 21, 1965 & Jul. 22, 1965 / Impulse ✦✦✦
Scott with Jimmy Raney on guitar. —*AMG*

Roll 'Em / Apr. 15, 1966-Apr. 19, 1966 / Impulse ✦✦✦
Organist Shirley Scott focuses on swing-era tunes throughout this enjoyable CD reissue. Four songs showcase her organ accompanied by a 17-piece big band arranged by Oliver Nelson, while the remaining six numbers find her jamming with a trio that includes either George Duvivier or Richard Davis on bass and Grady Tate or Ed Shaughnessy on drums. Although nothing all that unexpected occurs, it is fun to hear an organ performing such numbers as "For Dancers Only," "Little Brown Jug" and "Stompin' at the Savoy." —*Scott Yanow*

Shirley Scott and the Soul Saxes / Jul. 9, 1969 / Atlantic ✦✦✦

Blues Everywhere / Nov. 1991 / Candid ✦✦✦✦
Recent trio session with Scott and Arthur Harper (bass) and Mickey Roker (drums). The twist is that she is playing acoustic piano throughout. It's not the usual sound, but she can play that thing. —*Michael Erlewine*

Skylark / 1995 / Candid ✦✦✦✦

Tom Scott

b. May 19, 1948, Los Angeles, CA
Reeds, Sax (Alto), Sax (Tenor) / Instrumental Pop, Crossover
Since he was a teenager Tom Scott has been consistent, a talented multireedist with little or no interest in playing creative jazz. His mother was a pianist, and his father a composer. Scott early on became a studio musician and arranger. Able to play most reeds with little difficulty, Scott performed with the Don Ellis and Oliver Nelson bands, and his L.A. Express became one of the most successful pop-jazz groups of the '70s. Associations with Joni Mitchell, Carole King, and George Harrison were just a few of his successful assignments in the pop world. Although his 1992 GRP release *Born Again* was surprisingly inventive, it was a one-time departure from crossover. —*Scott Yanow*

The Best of Tom Scott / 1980 / Columbia ✦✦✦

Keep This Love Alive / 1991 / GRP ✦✦

● **Born Again** / 1992 / GRP ✦✦✦✦
Longtime session and studio saxophonist Tom Scott surprised many inside and outside the jazz community when he made this non-fusion, mainstream, and straightahead session. It showed he could still play strong, undiluted tenor sax solos, and fit in with a group that included such distinguished players as pianist Kenny Kirkland, trumpeter Randy Brecker, and trombonist George Bohannon. Bassist John Patitucci and drummer Will Kennedy were the fusion stars who rounded out the date. —*Ron Wynn*

Reed My Lips / 1993 / GRP ✦✦

Doc Severinsen

b. Jul. 7, 1927, Arlington, OR
Trumpet / Swing, Pop
Though faithful watchers of "The Tonight Show with Johnny Carson" and most of the '70s-and-beyond generation identify Doc Severinsen as a garish dresser and pseudo-hip bandleader with minimal ability, Severinsen has a substantial bebop heritage. He's also a much better trumpeter than he usually showed during his TV years, gifted with great range and excellent timbre and tone. Judging from recent records, issues of taste are another matter, but Severinsen has shown his skill on past sessions. He was a soloist in Tommy Dorsey's big band in the late '40s and early '50s, and had brief stints with Charlie Barnet and Benny Goodman. Severinsen joined NBC in 1949, and 13 years later was assistant leader of the orchestra, with Skitch Henderson running the band. Henderson left in 1967 for reasons that, as of 1993, had never been fully explained (no one, from Henderson to Severinsen to Johnny Carson will address the situation for the record); and Severinsen took over. He lasted until 1992, when Carson retired and Jay Leno brought in a new band. Though it seems like 43 years at one place and 25 years heading a band would be a great run, there were rumors that everyone, including Severinsen, got pushed rather than voluntarily left their posts. He's led brass workshops for years, conducted the Phoenix Pops, played with other orchestras, and led various groups, among them the unctuous Xebron. Severinsen took "Tonight Show" alumni around the nation on a farewell tour in 1993. He has many sessions available on CD, but you'd be better off getting Barnet and Dorsey reissues from the late '40s. His own albums, particularly recent releases, have miminal jazz content at best. —*Ron Wynn*

Tonight Show Band with Doc Severinsen / Aug. 5, 1986 & Aug. 7, 1986 / Amherst ✦✦✦✦
Tonight Show Band. CD version. —*Ron Wynn*

● **Once More, with Feeling!** / 1991 / Amherst ✦✦✦✦
Very restrained big-band dates. —*Ron Wynn*

The Tonight Show Band, Vol. 2 / Amherst ✦✦✦✦
Companion release. —*Ron Wynn*

Bud Shank (Clifford Everett Shank, Jr.)

b. May 27, 1926, Dayton, OH
Flute, Sax (Alto) / Cool, Hard Bop
Alto saxophonist and flutist Bud Shank was a major player in '50s West Coast circles and has continued as an active contributor into the '90s. His light, steady, yet confident and assured style has been featured on bebop, cool, big-band, and Latin dates, and Shank was among the earliest, most accomplished jazz flutists. He studied clarinet, alto and tenor sax, and flute and attended the University of North Carolina in the mid-40s. Shank studied with Shorty Rogers on the West Coast in 1947. He began to specialize on alto in the late '40s, playing with Charlie Barnet, then added flute while with Stan Kenton in 1950 and 1951. Shank played and recorded with Howard Rumsey's Lighthouse All-Stars, Laurindo Almeida, and Bob Cooper in the '50s, as well as with Kenton, Rogers, Jimmy Giuffre, and Gerald Wilson. Shank also recorded extensively for World Pacific as a leader in the '50s and '60s, most of the time working with a combo. He appeared at several festivals in Europe and South America in the '60s. Shank became mainly a studio musician during the '60s, playing on such film scores and soundtracks as *Slippery When Wet, Barefoot Adventure, War Hunt, Assault on a Queen,* and *The Thomas Crown Affair.* He recorded with Sergio Mendes for Capitol in 1965 and with Chet Baker on World Pacific a year later. Their album *Michelle* reached No. 56 on the pop charts. Shank formed the L.A. Four along with Almeida, Ray Brown, and Chuck Flores in 1974. Flores was later replaced by Shelly Manne, then by Jeff Hamilton. Starting in the mid-'80s, Shank dropped the flute to concentrate exclusively on the alto. His tone has become harder, his style more adventurous, and he has continued to grow in importance. He has recorded extensively (most notably for Concord, Contemporary, and Candid), and, in addition to reunions with Shorty Rogers' Lighthouse All-Stars, has generally led his own stimulating quartet and a pianoless sextet. —*Ron Wynn and Scott Yanow*

Live at the Haig / 1956 / Bainbridge ✦✦✦✦
A 1985 CD reissue of a strong Shank set done in the mid-'50s at the Haig. This was among his earliest stereo sessions and features some superb piano solos by Claude Williamson. Shank was finding a comfortable middle ground between swing, cool, and bop and growing stronger and more individualistic as an alto saxophonist. —*Ron Wynn*

Sunshine Express / Jan. 1976 / Concord Jazz ✦✦✦✦
A 1991 reissue of a Shank quintet series and a title in the Concord label's new collector's line. Alto saxophonist Shank was hitting his stride at this point in the late '70s; he decided to begin doing solo sessions after years of session work and was returning to alto, virtually discarding the flute. This was the first among several dates he cut from '76 to '80; this one included Mike Wofford, Bobby Shew, Larry Bunker, and Fred Atwood. —*Ron Wynn*

Heritage / Dec. 19, 1978 / Concord Jazz ✦✦✦✦
Some torrid, energetic alto sax solos by Bud Shank in the midst of a busy late-'70s stretch that saw him re-establish himself on alto after many years of playing mostly flute. He was working with what was his regular band at the time, with pianist Billy Mays providing both an occasional composition and some strong support as the second soloist. —*Ron Wynn*

This Bud's for You / Nov. 14, 1984 / Muse ✦✦✦✦
Arguably his best quartet date ever and certainly among the top three. Alto saxophonist Bud Shank took a page from Art Pepper's book and decided to work with a set rhythm section. Bassist Ron Carter, pianist Kenny Barron, and drummer Al Foster kicked into gear on the opening song and never faltered. Shank soared, playing more aggressively and showing more conviction in his solos than at any time since the '50s. —*Ron Wynn*

California Concert / May 19, 1985 / Contemporary ✦✦✦✦
Interesting, sometimes engaging live set. —*Ron Wynn*

★ **That Old Feeling** / Feb. 17, 1986 & Feb. 18, 1986 / Contemporary ✦✦✦✦✦
After many years of studio work and a period co-leading the L.A. Four, Bud Shank permanently put away his flute and started concentrating exclusively on alto. This modern bop set with pianist George Cables, bassist John Heard, and drummer Tootie Heath finds Shank at his most passionate and creative, stretching out on jazz standards and eccentric blues. He shows listeners just how much he has grown as an improviser since gaining his initial fame in the '50s. —*Scott Yanow*

Drifting Timelessly / 1990 / Capri ✦✦✦

● **The Doctor Is In** / Sep. 9, 1991-Sep. 10, 1991 / Candid ✦✦✦✦
Good session featuring the steady cool and bop-tinged alto sax solos of Bud Shank in a combo setting. He's backed by pianist Mike Wofford, bassist Bob Magnusson, and drummer Sherman Ferguson. They tackle familiar standards and a few originals, and make satisfying, if unchallenging, music. —*Ron Wynn*

I Told You So / Jun. 26, 1992-Jun. 27, 1992 / Candid ✦✦✦✦

Bud Shank Sextet Plays Harold Arlen / 1995 / Jimco ✦✦✦✦

Sonny Sharrock (Warren Harding Sharrock)

b. Aug. 27, 1940, Ossining, NY, d. May 25, 1994
Guitar / Avant-Garde, Free Jazz
Along with Derek Bailey (whose free-form explorations went in a different direction), Sonny Sharrock was the top avant-garde guitarist. His sonic explorations mixed Jimi Hendrix with Pharoah Sanders and were often quite ferocious. From 1953 to 1960 Sharrock was a singer in a doo-wop group; in 1960 he started playing guitar. He studied composition at Berklee in 1961 (although he was thrown out of the guitar class!). Sharrock worked with Byard Lancaster (1966), was with Pharoah Sanders during 1967-68, participated (uncredited) on Miles Davis' *Jack Johnson* album, and had his most high-profile job as a member of Herbie Mann's popular group, where his adventurous guitar contrasted with Mann's flute and David Newman's soulful tenor. A long period of obscurity occurred after he left Mann, but by the '80s Sharrock was being rediscovered, recording with Material in 1982 and Last Exit (a quartet with saxophonist Peter Brotzmann) later in the decade. *Ask the Ages* teamed Sharrock with Sanders, bassist Charnett Moffett, and Elvin Jones. But just when he seemed on the brink of a potential commercial breakthrough, Sonny Sharrock died unexpectedly at the age of 53. —*Scott Yanow*

Seize the Rainbow / May 1987 / Enemy ✦✦✦✦
Some powerful and at times chaotic playing from a plugged-in and turned-on lineup headed by adventurous guitarist Sonny Sharrock. His splintering, rambunctious licks are matched by bassists Melvin Gibbs and Bill Laswell and drummers Abe Speller and Pheeroan akLaff. —*Ron Wynn*

Faith Moves / 1989 / CMP ✦✦✦

Highlife / Oct. 1990 / Enemy ✦✦✦

★ **Ask the Ages** / 1991 / Axiom ✦✦✦✦✦
Sonny Sharrock was often thought of as the "Pharoah Sanders of the guitar," so it was quite fitting that one of his finest recordings is this matchup with Sanders, bassist Charnett Moffett, and drummer Elvin Jones. This fiery outing was also very good for Sanders, who, after many years of recording more lyrical material in the John Coltrane vein, returned to his prime, early form with ferocious solos that match the intensity of Sharrock's. —*Scott Yanow*

Artie Shaw (Arthur Jacob Arshawsky)

b. May 23, 1910, New York, NY
Clarinet / Swing
One of jazz's finest clarinetists, Artie Shaw never seemed fully satisfied with his musical life, constantly breaking up successful bands and running away from success. While Count Basie and Duke Ellington were satisfied to lead just one orchestra during the swing era and Benny Goodman (due to illness) had two, Shaw led five, all of them distinctive and memorable. After growing up in New Haven, CT, and playing clarinet and alto locally, Shaw spent part of 1925 with Johnny Cavallaro's dance band and then played off and on with Austin Wylie's band in Cleveland during 1927-29 before joining Irving Aaronson's Commanders. After moving to New York, Shaw became a close associate of Willie "The Lion" Smith at jam sessions and by 1931 was a busy studio musician. He retired from music for the first time in 1934 in hopes of writing a book, but when his money started running out, returned to New York. A major turning point occurred when he performed at an all-star big-band concert at the Imperial Theatre in May 1936, surprising the audience by performing with a string quartet and a rhythm section. He used a similar concept in putting together his first orchestra, adding a Dixieland-type frontline and a vocalist while retaining the strings. Despite some fine recordings, that particular band disbanded in early 1937, and Shaw put together a more conventional big band. The surprise success of his 1938 recording of "Begin the Beguine" made the clarinetist into a superstar and his orchestra (which featured the tenor of Georgie Auld, vocals by Helen Forrest and Tony Pastor, and, by 1939, Buddy Rich's drumming) into one of the most popular in the world. Billie Holiday was with the band for a few months, although only one recording ("Any Old Time") resulted. Shaw found the pressure of the band business difficult to deal with, and in November 1939 he suddenly left the bandstand and moved to Mexico for two months. When Shaw returned, his first session, one using a large string section, resulted in another major hit, "Frenesi." It seemed that no matter what he did he could not escape from success! Shaw's third regular orchestra, which had a string section and such star soloists as trumpeter Billy Butterfield and pianist Johnny Guarnieri, was one of his finest, waxing perhaps the greatest version of "Stardust" along with the memorable "Concerto for Clarinet." The Gramercy Five, a small group out of the band (using Guarnieri on harpsichord), also scored with the million-selling "Summit Ridge Drive." Despite all this, Shaw broke up the orchestra in 1941, only to form an even larger one later in the year. The latter group featured Hot Lips Page along with Auld and Guarnieri. After Pearl Harbor, Shaw enlisted and led a Navy band before getting a medical discharge in Feb. 1944. Later in the year his new orchestra featured Roy Eldridge, Dodo Marmarosa, and Barney Kessel and found Shaw's own style becoming quite modern, almost boppish. But with the

end of the swing era, Shaw again broke up his band in early 1946 and was semi-retired for several years, playing classical music as much as jazz. His last attempt at a big band was short-lived, a boppish unit that lasted for a few months in 1949 and included Zoot Sims, Al Cohn, and Don Fagerquist; its modern music was a commercial flop. After a few years of only limited musical activity, Shaw returned one last time, recording extensively with a version of the Gramercy Five that featured Tal Farlow or Joe Puma on guitar, along with Hank Jones. Then in 1955 Artie Shaw permanently gave up the clarinet to pursue his dreams of being a writer. He served as frontman (with Dick Johnson playing the clarinet solos) for a reorganized Artie Shaw orchestra in 1983, but Shaw never played again. Although he received plenty of publicity for his six marriages (his wives included Lana Turner, Ava Gardner, and Evelyn Keyes) and his odd autobiography *The Trouble with Cinderella* (which barely touches on the music business or his wives!), the still outspoken Artie Shaw deserves to be remembered as one of the great clarinetists. His recordings are available in piecemeal fashion on Bluebird. — *Scott Yanow*

Best of the Big Bands / Jun. 11, 1936-Oct. 30, 1936 / Columbia ✦✦✦✦
Artie Shaw's first big band was quite unusual, originally comprising four horns, a string quartet, and a four-piece rhythm section. This unimaginatively titled CD (whose chatty liner notes unfortunately do not include personnel and date information) has the first 16 recordings by this fine orchestra, featuring vocals by the forgettable Wesley Vaughn, Peg LaCentra, and the young Tony Pastor, but, more importantly, successfully matching horns with strings on such enjoyable numbers as "Japanese Sandman," "Sugar Foot Stomp," and "The Skeleton in the Closet." Pity that this potentially great orchestra did not catch on. — *Scott Yanow*

● **Begin the Beguine** / Jul. 24, 1938-Jul. 23, 1941 / Bluebird ✦✦✦✦
Since Artie Shaw's Victor recordings have not been reissued in full on CD, this sampler serves as a fine place to start for swing beginners to start. Featured are many of the more popular recordings of his second and third orchestras, including the title cut, "Frenesi," "Star Dust," and "Summit Ridge Drive," giving one a good idea as to why Artie Shaw was so popular and still remains highly rated as a clarinetist today, decades after his retirement. — *Scott Yanow*

Personal Best / Jul. 24, 1938-Jul. 19, 1945 / Bluebird ✦✦✦

☆ **The Complete Gramercy Five Sessions** / Sep. 3, 1940-Aug. 2, 1945 / Bluebird ✦✦✦✦✦
Many swing big-band leaders featured small groups out of their orchestra as added attractions, particularly Benny Goodman, Tommy Dorsey with his Clambake Seven, and Bob Crosby's Bobcats. In contrast, Artie Shaw recorded relatively few sides with his Gramercy Five. His original unit from 1940 found the great pianist Johnny Guarnieri playing harpsichord exclusively and matched Shaw's clarinet with trumpeter Billy Butterfield. Their eight recordings include "My Blue Heaven," "Smoke Gets in Your Eyes" and a million-seller, "Summit Ridge Drive." The remainder of this CD is from 1945 and features Shaw, trumpeter Roy Eldridge, and the two young modernists: pianist Dodo Marmarosa and guitarist Barney Kessel. Shaw would lead a few other Gramercy Fives in the future, but these are his two most famous. The music is consistently brilliant, with every note counting. — *Scott Yanow*

Blues in the Night / Sep. 2, 1941-Jul. 26, 1945 / Bluebird ✦✦✦✦
While Bluebird in the late '70s released all of Shaw's recordings in chronological order on a series of two-LP sets, its CD reissues have thus far been samplers. *Blues in the Night* has ten selections from the 1941 show orchestra that featured trumpeter/singer Hot Lips Page, in addition to 11 by the 1945 big band that showcased trumpeter Roy Eldridge. Filled with such memorable performances as "Blues in the Night," "St. James Infirmary," "Lady Day," "Little Jazz," and a classic Eddie Sauter arrangement of "Summertime," this excellent CD is recommended to those not already possessing the two-fers. — *Scott Yanow*

The Indispensable Artie Shaw, Vols. 5 & 6 / Nov. 23, 1944-Aug. 1, 1945 / RCA ✦✦✦✦
This two-CD set, a straight reissue of the original French RCA two-LP release, has most of the highlights from clarinetist Artie Shaw's final year with the Victor label. Not a "complete" series but more of a "best of," the two-fer features exciting solos from the clarinetist/leader, trumpeter Roy Eldridge, guitarist Barney Kessel, and pianist Dodo Marmarosa, with the more memorable selections including "Lady Day," "S' Wonderful," "The Grabtown Grapple," "Little Jazz," "Summertime," "Love Walked In," "Dancing on the Ceiling," and "Scuttlebutt." The set is well worth picking up by collectors who do not already have the complete LP series of Artie Shaw recordings reissued in the late '70s. — *Scott Yanow*

● **1949** / 1949 / Music Masters ✦✦✦✦
In 1949 the swing era was already past, and the public's enthusiasm for bebop was quickly receding. No matter. Artie Shaw decided that it was time to put together a modern big band. The venture lasted only three months, but the largely forgotten music that it performed was rewarding. This CD consists of private recordings of the barely documented orchestra, valuable performances that feature the always-modern clarinetist with an

outfit that included trumpeter Don Fagerquist, a great saxophone section with the tenors of Al Cohn and Zoot Sims, and guitarist Jimmy Raney. It is a real pleasure to hear Artie Shaw stretching out in this setting and a real pity that this band could not have lasted. — *Scott Yanow*

★ **The Last Recordings, Vol. 1: Rare and Unreleased** / Feb. 19, 1954 / Music Masters ✦✦✦✦✦
The first of two double-CD sets contains a healthy share of the recordings the clarinetist made with his final Gramercy Five, a unit that included pianist Hank Jones, either Tal Farlow or Joe Puma on guitar, and usually Joe Roland's vibes. Unlike his longtime competitor Benny Goodman, Shaw felt perfectly comfortable with younger modernists. In fact, his own clarinet playing had evolved through the years, and sometimes he hints strongly at Buddy DeFranco without losing his own musical personality during these 20 performances. This is very rewarding music that makes one especially regret that Artie Shaw chose to give up the clarinet after this band ran its course. — *Scott Yanow*

Woody Shaw

b. Dec. 24, 1944, Laurinburg, NC, d. May 10, 1989, New York, NY
Trumpet / Post-Bop, Hard Bop
Woody Shaw was one of the top trumpeters of the '70s and '80s, a major soloist influenced by Freddie Hubbard but more advanced harmonically, who bridged the gap between hard bop and the avant-garde. Unfortunately he never broke through to greater stardom (due partly to personal problems and failing eyesight), and his premature death from injuries incurred from being hit by a train was a major loss. Woody Shaw grew up in Newark, NJ, where his father was a member of the Diamond Jubilee Singers. After starting on bugle, he switched to the trumpet when he was 11 years old. Shaw left town for a tour with Rufus Jones when he was 18, then joined Willie Bobo at a time when Bobo's band included Chick Corea. Shaw played and recorded with Eric Dolphy and, after being invited by Dolphy, traveled to Paris in 1964 just a little too late to join the late saxophonist's band. After a period in Europe playing with Bud Powell and Johnny, he spent periods in the groups of Horace Silver (1965-66), Max Roach (1968-69), and Art Blakey (1973), in addition to making many recordings (some as a sideman for Blue Note) with such players as Jackie McLean, Andrew Hill, and McCoy Tyner. Other than playing with Dexter Gordon in 1976, Shaw was primarily a leader from this point on, recording for Columbia (important sessions reissued in a Mosaic box set), Red, Enja, Elektra, Muse, and Timeless, plus two Blue Note dates co-led with Freddie Hubbard. But overshadowed throughout his career by Hubbard, Miles Davis, Dizzy Gillespie, and later on Wynton Marsalis, Woody Shaw would never find much fame or fortune. — *Scott Yanow*

Song of Songs / Sep. 15, 1972 & Sep. 18, 1972 / Original Jazz Classics ✦✦✦✦
With septet and extended compositions. — *Michael G. Nastos*

● **Little Red's Fantasy** / Jun. 29, 1976 / Muse ✦✦✦✦
Woody Shaw was one of the great trumpeters of the '70s. Although influenced soundwise by Freddie Hubbard, Shaw's more advanced improvisations on his modal originals were quite original and fiery. This set has three of his compositions (including "In Case You Haven't Heard") and a song apiece from pianist Ronnie Mathews and bassist Stafford James; altoist Frank Strozier and drummer Eddie Moore complete the quintet. The varied originals give the musicians strong foundations for their freewheeling and spontaneous solos, making this one of Woody Shaw's better recordings. — *Scott Yanow*

★ **Rosewood** / Dec. 15, 1977-Dec. 19, 1977 / CBS ✦✦✦✦✦
This album, Woody Shaw's first for a major label, has been reissued as part of his Mosaic box set. Shaw, one of the top trumpeters of the late '60s and throughout the next decade, is heard with a sextet (either Joe Henderson or Carter Jefferson on tenor, pianist Onaje Allan Gumbs, bassist Clint Houston, and drummer Victor Lewis) on two numbers and with a "concert ensemble" (which reaches as many as 14 pieces) on the other four selections. Shaw is in top form throughout, particularly on "Rosewood," "Rahsaan's Run," and "Theme for Maxine." This modal music ranks with his best work, making the Mosaic box essential. — *Scott Yanow*

★ **The Complete CBS Studio Recordings of Woody Shaw** / Dec. 15, 1977-Mar. 17, 1981 / Mosaic ✦✦✦✦✦
Between late 1977 and early 1981, trumpeter Woody Shaw recorded four albums for Columbia. This Mosaic three-CD set reissues those LPs, plus one previously unissued selection. Shaw was one of the great hard-bop trumpeters, able to improvise comfortably and with creativity over difficult modal progressions, and, although he had a sound that was similar to Freddie Hubbard's, he was a more advanced soloist. These performances feature him in a variety of settings ranging from a 15-piece group to a quintet. The strong supporting cast includes such fine players as tenors Joe Henderson and Carter Jefferson, altoists Gary Bartz and James Spaulding, trombonists Steve Turre and Curtis Fuller, and pianists Mulgrew Miller, Larry Willis, George Cables, and Onaje Allan Gumbs. Shaw wrote the

majority of the compositions but also jams on a couple of standards. This important reissue finds him at the peak of his powers. —*Scott Yanow*

Stepping Stones / Aug. 5, 1978-Aug. 6, 1978 / Columbia ✦✦✦

Woody III / 1978 / Columbia ✦✦✦
Third consecutive wonderful album for Columbia, which responded by cutting him loose. —*Ron Wynn*

Time Is Right / Jan. 1, 1983 / Red ✦✦✦✦

● **Setting Standards** / Dec. 1, 1983 / Muse ✦✦✦✦
Despite a restrictive menu, some brilliant solos. —*Ron Wynn*

In My Own Sweet Way / Feb. 1987 / In + Out ✦✦✦✦

George Shearing

b. Aug. 13, 1919, London, England
Piano / Bop, Cool, Latin Jazz
Pianist George Shearing, who was influenced by Errol Garner, popularized a unique jazz sound in 1949, with a quintet that featured piano, vibes, guitar, bass, and drums. Shearing used a block-chord approach that combined techniques dating back to Milt Buckner that he probably got through Lennie Tristano. He mixed this with the chordal playing style of the Glenn Miller orchestra, whose records he'd closely examined. His sound and touch have been greatly admired. Shearing's ensemble sound, especially the piano/vibes interplay, attracted widespread attention. He later began performing classical concertos with orchestras during his concerts, including orchestrations featuring his quintet. Such talents as Cal Tjader, Gary Burton, Toots Thielemans, Joe Pass, Israel Crosby, and Vernel Fournier passed through the Shearing group. Shearing began playing piano at three but had only limited musical training at the Linden Lodge School for the Blind in London, which he attended from ages 12 to 16. He absorbed the techniques and influence of Fats Waller, Teddy Wilson, and Art Tatum, as well as boogie woogie and blues pianists through records. He played on British Broadcasting Company broadcasts, including appearances with Ambrose. An accomplished jazz accordionist as well as a fine boogie woogie player, Shearing once played for the King of England. He began recording in 1936, then came to America in 1947 with Leonard Feather's assistance, settling in New York, where he immersed himself in bebop. Shearing replaced Erroll Garner in the Oscar Pettiford trio, then led a quartet with Buddy DeFranco in 1948, before forming his famous quintet in 1949. The original members included Marjorie Hyams on vibes, Chuck Wayne on guitar, John Levy on bass, and Denzil Best on drums. Shearing compositions "Conception" (recorded by Miles Davis as "Deception") and "Consternation" were eventually recorded by one of his idols, Bud Powell. Shearing recorded for Discovery, Savoy, and MGM in the late '40s and early '50s. He wrote "Lullaby of Birdland" in 1952 as a theme for both the club and radio shows being broadcast there. He switched to Capitol and remained with that label into the early '70s, enjoying substantial chart success in the late '50s and early '60s. Shearing made albums with Peggy Lee, Nancy Wilson, Dakota Staton, Nat King Cole, Stephane Grappelli, and the Robert Farnon Orchestra. He started his own label, Sheba Records, for a brief period, then in the '70s signed with Concord. He earned critical plaudits and Grammy awards for dates with Mel Tormé. Shearing also worked with Carmen McRae, Jim Hall, and Marian McPartland in the '70s and '80s. He's currently recording for Telarc. Such pianists as Bill Evans and Herbie Hancock are among the many who've been influenced by Shearing. His material from the late '40s to the '90s is available on CD. —*Ron Wynn*

● **The London Years 1939-1943** / Mar. 2, 1939-Dec. 21, 1943 / Hep ✦✦✦✦
Most of pianist George Shearing's earliest recordings are included on this easily enjoyable swing-oriented CD. During the war years, when he was in his early 20s, Shearing was most influenced by Teddy Wilson, Earl Hines, and Art Tatum, but even at that early stage he was developing his own musical personality. A virtuoso from the start, Shearing is in consistently brilliant form on these standards, originals, and a few interesting boogie-woogie stomps. Of the 25 selections, 22 are piano solos, two are duets with drummer Carlo Krahmer, and one song ("Squeezin' the Blues") is a rare outing for Shearing on accordion; his backup group consists of Krahmer and Leonard Feather on piano. Highly recommended. —*Scott Yanow*

● **The Complete Capitol Live Recordings** / Mar. 8, 1958-Jul. 6, 1963 / Mosaic ✦✦✦✦

● **The Swingin's Mutual** / Jun. 29, 1960-Jan. 7, 1961 / Capitol ✦✦✦✦
The music on this set, a dozen selections featuring the George Shearing Quintet, including six that have vocals by a young Nancy Wilson, has been reissued on CD by Capitol with five additional tracks. This was one of Wilson's most jazz-oriented dates (even if she was never a jazz singer) and is highlighted by her vocals on "The Nearness of You" and "The Things We Did Last Summer," along with instrumental versions of "Oh! Look at Me Now," "Blue Lou," and "Lullaby of Birdland." —*Scott Yanow*

George Shearing and the Montgomery Bros. / Oct. 9, 1961 / Original Jazz Classics ✦✦✦✦
Pianist George Shearing meets up with guitarist Wes, vibraphonist Buddy, and bassist Monk Montgomery on this enjoyable, if slightly lightweight,

outing. The performances are a bit too concise at times, but the CD reissue does add three extra takes to the original 11-song program and has some fine soloing by the principals. Highlights include "Love Walked In," "Love for Sale," and "The Lamp Is Low." —*Scott Yanow*

★ **Nat King Cole Sings/George Shearing Plays** / 1961 / Capitol ✦✦✦✦✦
Wonderful duo. A glorious union. —*Ron Wynn*

● **Blues Alley and Jazz** / Oct. 1979 / Concord Jazz ✦✦✦✦
Pianist George Shearing started a productive ten-year association with the Concord label with this live set, a duo outing matching him with the brilliant bassist Brian Torff. Their performances are virtuosic, intuitive, full of sly wit, and always swinging; it is surprising that Torff did not become more famous. The close interaction between the two masterful musicians on such numbers as Billy Taylor's "One for the Woofer," "The Masquerade Is Over," and a humorous "Lazy River" are impressive, as is Shearing's surprisingly effective vocal on "This Couldn't Be the Real Thing." This CD is recommended. —*Scott Yanow*

On a Clear Day / Aug. 1980 / Concord Jazz ✦✦✦✦
George Shearing's second Concord album, which like the previous *Blues Alley Jazz* is a set of duets with bassist Brian Torff, is the equal of the first. The close communication between the duo and their ability to think fast and immediately react to each other makes it possible for them to uplift such songs as "Love for Sale," "On a Clear Day," "Lullaby of Birdland," and even "Happy Days Are Here Again." Brilliant music. —*Scott Yanow*

Alone Together / Mar. 1981 / Concord Jazz ✦✦✦

First Edition / Sep. 1981 / Concord Jazz ✦✦✦✦
This tasteful set matches pianist George Shearing and guitarist Jim Hall in a program of duets. The fresh material (two originals apiece by Shearing and Hall, the obscure "I See Nothing to Laugh About"), and just three standards challenge the pair, and their quiet and subtle styles match well. The pianist's tributes to Antonio Carlos Jobim and Tommy Flanagan are among the more memorable pieces in this interesting and somewhat unexpected musical collaboration. —*Scott Yanow*

Top Drawer / Mar. 1983 / Concord Jazz ✦✦✦✦
A year after their first meeting on record, pianist George Shearing and singer Mel Tormé (this time with Don Thompson on bass) had an equally successful joint recording. The material is often a bit offbeat (including the obscure swing song "Shine on Your Shoes," "How Do You Say Auf Wiedersehen," and the early bop vocal "What's This"), but there are also inventive remakes of "Stardust" and "Hi Fly," along with two instrumentals: "Oleo" and a Shearing piano solo on "Away in the Manger." Obviously this CD is full of surprises; all of the Tormé-Shearing Concord sessions (which bring out the best in both of the principals) are well worth acquiring. —*Scott Yanow*

Elegant Evening / 1985 / Concord Jazz ✦✦✦

Dexterity / Nov. 1987 / Concord Jazz ✦✦✦✦
For his first tour of Japan in 24 years, pianist George Shearing worked for the first time with bassist Neil Swainson, who soon afterward became a regular member of his duo. This CD features Shearing and Swainson performing a variety of material including Charlie Parker's "Dexterity," "You Must Believe in Spring," a traditional Japanese melody, and a couple of ballads. In addition, singer Ernestine Anderson sits in with the group on "As Long as I Live" and a typically soulful "Please Send Me Someone to Love" before the duo concludes the show (recorded at the second annual Fujitsu-Concord Jazz Festival) with a five-song Duke Ellington medley. A well rounded and consistently enjoyable program. —*Scott Yanow*

I Hear a Rhapsody: Live at the Blue Note / Feb. 27, 1992-Feb. 29, 1992 / Telarc ✦✦✦✦
This excellent trio set by George Shearing with bassist Neil Swainson and drummer Grady Tate finds the veteran pianist still in prime form. The repertoire mostly consists of challenging material and tunes not overplayed by Shearing throughout the years. The musical communication between the players on such tunes as "Bird Feathers," "The End of a Love Affair," "The Duke," "The Masquerade Is Over," and an original apiece by Shearing and Swainson is very impressive, and the pianist's solos are typically distinctive. This CD (Shearing's debut on the Telarc label) is a fine example of George Shearing's still-viable playing as he neared his mid-70s. —*Scott Yanow*

That Shearing Sound / Feb. 14, 1994-Feb. 16, 1994 / Telarc ✦✦✦✦
This was pianist George Shearing's first recording in a piano-vibes-guitar-bass-drums quintet since he broke up his original group in 1978 after 30 years of steady work; Shearing sounds surprisingly inspired throughout. With guitarist Louis Stewart, vibraphonist Steve Nelson, bassist Neil Swainson, and drummer Dennis Mackrel, Shearing explores such vintage Quintet standards as "East of the Sun" and "I'll Never Smile Again," along with two Horace Silver compositions, a pair of his own songs ("Conception" and his biggest hit, "Lullaby of Birdland"), and a variety of other suitable material. The music ranges from easy listening to hard-driving bebop. The sound of the George Shearing Quintet remains as appealing as ever. —*Scott Yanow*

Jack Sheldon

b. Nov. 30, 1931, Jacksonville, FL
Trumpet / Bop

One of the great jokesters in jazz (whose spontaneous monologues are as hilarious as they are tasteless), Jack Sheldon's personality has sometimes overshadowed his excellent trumpet playing and effective vocals. Sheldon started playing professionally at age 13. He moved to Los Angeles in 1947, joined the Air Force, and played in military bands. After his discharge, Sheldon became a popular figure on the West Coast, playing and recording with many top musicians, including Jimmy Giuffre, Herb Geller, Wardell Gray, Stan Kenton, Benny Goodman, Curtis Counce, and Art Pepper. He worked as an actor in the '60s (including starring in the short-lived television series "Run Buddy Run"), was seen nightly on "The Merv Griffin Show," and in the '70s and '80s performed with Benny Goodman, Bill Berry's big band, in the studios, and with his own groups. Into the mid-'90s Jack Sheldon (who often uses a big band arranged by Tom Kubis) remains active in the Los Angeles area, recording regularly for Concord and his Butterfly label. —*Scott Yanow*

● **Stand By for Jack Sheldon** / Mar. 1983 / Concord Jazz ✦✦✦✦
This is one of Jack Sheldon's better recordings. His trumpet solos (accompanied by pianist Ross Tompkins, bassist Ray Brown, and drummer Jake Hanna) are consistently excellent; and his five vocals, although not containing the humor one generally hears in his live performances, are also well done. The ten standards and ballads are given swinging and melodic treatment, making this a fine all-round showcase for Sheldon. —*Scott Yanow*

Blues in the Night / Aug. 3, 1984-Aug. 4, 1984 / Phontastic ✦✦✦✦

Hollywood Heroes / Sep. 1987 / Concord Jazz ✦✦✦✦
A quintet of fairly undistinguished sidemen provides good support for Sheldon. Mostly they play early-period swing-era music bordering on bop. —*Michael G. Nastos*

On My Own / Sep. 12, 1991 / Concord Jazz ✦✦✦✦

Archie Shepp

b. May 24, 1937, Fort Lauderdale, FL
Sax (Soprano and Tenor) / Avant-Garde, Hard Bop, Free Jazz

Archie Shepp has been at various times a feared firebrand and radical, a soulful throwback, and a contemplative veteran. He was viewed in the '60s as perhaps the most articulate and disturbing member of the free generation, a published playwright willing to speak on the record in unsparing, explicit fashion about social injustice and the anger and rage he felt. His tenor sax solos were searing, harsh, and unrelenting, played with a vivid intensity. But in the '70s, Shepp employed a fatback/swing-based R&B approach, and in the '80s he mixed straight bebop, ballads, and blues pieces displaying little of the fury and fire from his earlier days. Shepp studied dramatic literature at Goddard College, earning his degree in 1959. He played alto sax in dance bands and sought theatrical work in New York. But Shepp switched to tenor, playing in several free-jazz bands. He worked with Cecil Taylor, co-led groups with Bill Dixon, and played in the New York Contemporary Five with Don Cherry and John Tchicai. He led his own bands in the mid-'60s with Roswell Rudd, Bobby Hutcherson, Beaver Harris, and Grachan Moncur III. His Impulse albums included poetry readings and quotes from James Baldwin and Malcolm X. Shepp's releases sought to paint an aural picture of African-American life, and included compositions based on incidents like Attica or folk sayings. He also produced plays in New York, among them *The Communist* in 1965 and *Lady Day: A Musical Tragedy* in 1972 with trumpeter/composer Cal Massey. But starting in the late '60s, the rhetoric was toned down and the anger began to disappear from Shepp's albums. He substituted a more celebratory and, at times, reflective attitude. Shepp turned to academia in the late '60s, teaching at SUNY in Buffalo and then the University of Massachusetts. He was named an associate professor there in 1978. Shepp toured and recorded extensively in Europe during the '80s, cutting some fine albums with Horace Parlan, Niels-Henning Orsted Pedersen, and Jasper van't Hof. He has recorded extensively for Impulse, Byg, Arista/Freedom, Phonogram, SteepleChase, Denon, Enja, EPM, and Soul Note. Unfortunately his tone declined from the mid-'80 on (his highly original sound was his most important contribution to jazz), and Archie Shepp is a less significant figure in the '90s than one might hope. —*Ron Wynn and Scott Yanow*

● **Archie Shepp in Europe** / Nov. 15, 1963 / Delmark ✦✦✦✦
The New York Contemporary Five was a co-op that in 1963 featured such up-and-coming talent as tenor saxophonist Archie Shepp (who had previously been with Cecil Taylor), altoist John Tchicai, cornetist Don Cherry (well known due to his association with Ornette Coleman), bassist Don Moore, and drummer J.C. Moses. Their music was a bridge between the innovations of Ornette Coleman's Quartet and the avant-garde explosion of 1965. The performances of originals by Cherry, Coleman, Shepp, and Tchicai, in addition to Thelonious Monk's "Crepuscule with Nellie," are not flawless but are generally quite fascinating, as these young talents did

what they could to break through the "rules" of bebop and create new music and sounds. A historic set. —*Scott Yanow*

★ **Four for Trane** / Aug. 10, 1964 / Impulse ✦✦✦✦
Tenor saxophonist Archie Shepp's debut for Impulse is a classic. This LP (not yet reissued on CD) features the avant-garde innovator playing four of John Coltrane's compositions, including "Cousin Mary" and "Naima," along with his own "Rufus." To his great credit, Shepp never sounded like Coltrane—his raspy tone was much closer to a free version of Ben Webster—and he is heard in top form on this studio date with a sextet also including fluegelhornist Alan Shorter, trombonist Roswell Rudd, altoist John Tchicai, bassist Reggie Workman, and drummer Charles Moffett. Shepp's interpretations of the Coltrane tunes are quite fresh and original. Highly recommended to open-eared listeners. —*Scott Yanow*

Fire Music / Feb. 16, 1965 & Mar. 28, 1965 / Impulse ✦✦✦✦
This particular early Archie Shepp recording (reissued on CD) has its strong moments, although it is a bit erratic. Four selections utilize an advanced sextet. Of these songs, "Hambone" has overly repetitive and rather monotonous riffing by the horns behind the soloists, and Shepp's bizarre exploration of "The Girl from Ipanema" gets tedious, but the episodic "Los Olvidaos" is quite colorful, and the tenorman sounds fine on a spacey rendition of "Prelude to a Kiss." "Malcolm, Malcolm-Semper Malcolm" has Shepp reading a brief poem for the fallen Malcolm X before he jams effectively on tenor in a trio with bassist David Izenzon and drummer J.C. Moses. The CD is rounded out by a "bonus" cut not on the original LP—a live version of "Hambone" that is much more interesting than the earlier rendition. Overall, this set, even with its faults, is recommended. —*Scott Yanow*

● **On This Night** / Mar. 9, 1965 & Aug. 12, 1965 / GRP ✦✦✦✦
Tenor saxophonist Archie Shepp made his mark early in his career and reached heights that he had trouble attaining later on. This Impulse reissue gathers all of Shepp's recordings from two dates, some of which were originally scattered on a variety of LPs. Highlights include the three very different versions of the explosive "The Chased," a reworking of "In a Sentimental Mood," and "The Original Mr. Sonny Boy Williamson." Shepp's quintet also features vibraphonist Bobby Hutcherson, who is heard early in his career. This passionate music is not for the fainthearted. —*Scott Yanow*

New Thing at Newport / Jul. 2, 1965 / Impulse ✦✦✦

● **Goin' Home** / Apr. 25, 1977 / SteepleChase ✦✦✦✦
Archie Shepp's two duet albums with pianist Horace Parlan on Steeple-Chase (the other one is '80s *Trouble in Mind*) both find the innovative avant-garde tenor in relaxed and melodic form, respectfully interpreting music of the '20s and before. *Goin' Home* features Shepp (who doubles on soprano) and Parlan playing tasteful versions of nine ancient Black folk melodies including "Swing Low, Sweet Chariot," "Nobody Knows the Troubles I've Seen," and "Deep River." Those listeners familiar only with Shepp's earlier *Fire Music* will find these compelling performances to be a revelation. —*Scott Yanow*

Little Red Moon / Dec. 11, 1985-Dec. 13, 1985 / Soul Note ✦✦

Wayne Shorter

b. Aug. 25, 1933, Newark, NJ
Sax (Soprano and Tenor) / Fusion, Post-Bop, Hard Bop

It's possible to measure some fans' tenures following jazz and popular music by how they recognize Wayne Shorter. There are many who remember him only as the soprano saxophonist in Miles Davis' jazz-rock bands and as co-leader of Weather Report. Those with longer memories harken back to his days as a young lion on Vee-Jay and with Art Blakey. Shorter has perfected on tenor and soprano sax the same evolving, eclectic approach as longtime friend and musical comrade Herbie Hancock on piano. He's combined hard-bop and modal elements in his solos, playing with an intense and original style that includes a biting, terse attack, and soulfulness. His soprano has one of the most elastic, wondrous tones ever; its beauty and lyricism are unparalleled. Shorter has been better known for soprano than tenor since 1969, and during the Weather Report era he played it about twice as often as he did tenor. He's also an excellent composer who was once Blakey's music director and provided such compositions to Miles Davis as "E.S.P.," "Pinocchio," "Nefertiti," and "Sanctuary." His writing was altered and simplified for Weather Report, consisting mainly of lyrical melodies and heavily syncopated funk backbeats. Shorter began playing clarinet at 16, then switched to tenor sax. He studied music at New York University in the '50s, graduating in 1956. Afer working in a local band, Shorter joined Horace Silver for a short time before being drafted. Upon his discharge, he joined Maynard Ferguson in 1958, meeting Joe Zawinul while in this group. Shorter began working with Art Blakey in 1959, and was in the Messengers until 1963. He made his recording debut as a leader on Vee-Jay and made several recordings for Blue Note in the mid-'60s, working with many top musicians, including his latter-day Miles Davis comrades as well as Freddie Hubbard and James Spaulding. Shorter joined Davis' band in 1964, finally filling the vacuum from John Coltrane's departure. He stayed with the band until 1970, playing in two critical eras:

the looser, freer work of the mid-'60s and the jazz-rock of the late '60s and early '70s, when Shorter began playing soprano. He recorded in the late '60s and '70s with Davis' comrade John McLaughlin, Sonny Sharrock, Miroslav Vitous, and others like Chick Corea and Jack DeJohnette, who had also played jazz-rock with Davis. Shorter experimented with Latin and rock on such Blue Note albums as *Super Nova* and *Odyssey of Iska*. In 1970 Shorter and Zawinul co-founded Weather Report, which they continued until 1985. The band began as a jazz-rock group but gradually enjoyed so much success as a funk/rock/fusion outfit that they grew stagnant churning out albums filled with conservative, trendy material and less open-ended, aggressive playing. Shorter was relatively inactive in the '70s outside of working with Weather Report, recording only a Brazilian album (*Native Dancer*) with Milton Nascimento early in the decade that made the *Billboard* charts. He toured with Hancock and other Davis' alumni on the V.S.O.P. acoustic-jazz tour in the late '70s, also recording for Columbia. Shorter did sessions with Joni Mitchell and Steely Dan. He and Zawinul disbanded Weather Report in 1985. Shorter started a new group in 1986 but overloaded it with electronics and generic compositions and arrangements. The results were poorly received albums such as *Atlantis* and *Phantom Navigator*, although the band's tours were more successful in terms of audience response and reaction. Shorter presented in his group a promising discovery, drummer Terri Lyne Carrington. She parlayed the exposure into a contract with talk-show host Arsenio Hall's first "posse" and her own album deal. Shorter performed in the film *'Round Midnight* in 1986 and played on the *Power of Three* album with Michel Petrucciani and Jim Hall. He co-led a Latin jazz-rock group with Carlos Santana in 1988, touring internationally. His 1988 Columbia album *Joy Ryder* didn't recapture past glories. —*Ron Wynn*

Introducing Wayne Shorter / Nov. 10, 1959 / Vee-Jay ✦✦✦

Wayning Moments Plus / 1962 / Vee-Jay ✦✦✦✦
Wayne Shorter's third and final recording for Vee-Jay is reissued on this CD, which augments the original eight songs with seven alternate takes. Shorter had an original sound by this time, and with a young and fiery Freddie Hubbard joining him in the frontline and a fine rhythm section (pianist Eddie Higgins, bassist Jymie Merritt, and drummer Marshall Thompson), the young tenor is heard in his early prime. There are some fine chance-taking solos on this hard-bop date; "Black Orpheus," "Moon of Manakoora," and "All or Nothing at All" are among the highlights. —*Scott Yanow*

Night Dreamer / Apr. 29, 1964 / Blue Note ✦✦✦✦
A 1988 reissue of prime '60s lineup: Lee Morgan (trumpet), McCoy Tyner (piano), Reggie Workman (bass), and Elvin Jones (drums). —*Ron Wynn*

★ **JuJu** / Aug. 3, 1964 / Blue Note ✦✦✦✦✦
On this CD reissue, which adds "new" takes of "Juju" and "House of Jade" to the original six-song LP program, tenor saxophonist Wayne Shorter has an opportunity to play with two then-current members of the John Coltrane Quartet (pianist McCoy Tyner and drummer Elvin Jones) and an alumnus (bassist Reggie Workman). There are times during these performances that Shorter recalls 'Trane, but his brooding sound, relaxed approach, and his ability to compose quirky originals set him apart even then. Of the repertoire on this quartet date, none was destined to become a standard, although "Yes or No," "Twelve More Bars to Go," and "Juju" were all somewhat memorable. With the rhythm section sounding quite advanced, if not as passionate as they usually played with Coltrane, Shorter has the perfect accompaniment for his melancholy and introverted flights. This CD is a fine example of his early work. —*Scott Yanow*

★ **Speak No Evil** / Dec. 24, 1964 / Blue Note ✦✦✦✦✦
Reissue of one of his best: playing and writing. —*Ron Wynn*

The Soothsayer / Mar. 4, 1965 / Blue Note ✦✦✦✦
A 1990 reissue of a prime 1965 effort. —*Ron Wynn*

Et Cetera / Jun. 14, 1965 / Blue Note ✦✦✦✦
It is strange that this classic Blue Note album was not released for the first time until 1980, for it finds tenor saxophonist Wayne Shorter in prime form. His four originals (along with Gil Evans' "Barracudas") are quite inventive, and the rhythm section (pianist Herbie Hancock, bassist Cecil McBee, and drummer Joe Chambers) is state-of-the art for 1965. These challenging performances find the musicians really listening closely to each other and pushing themselves. Although advanced, the music should not be labeled "avant-garde" or "free jazz" as much as "original." —*Scott Yanow*

The All Seeing Eye / Oct. 15, 1965 / Blue Note ✦✦✦✦

☆ **Adam's Apple** / Feb. 3, 1966 / Blue Note ✦✦✦✦✦
This is a galloping romp, one of Shorter's best '60s dates. Great record. —*Ron Wynn*

Schizophrenia / Mar. 20, 1967 / Blue Note ✦✦✦✦
One of his last and best "pure" jazz dates. —*Ron Wynn*

Super Nova / Aug. 29, 1969 & Sep. 2, 1969 / Blue Note ✦✦✦✦
A 1988 reissue of a careening, eventful date with Chick Corea (keyboards), John McLaughin (guitar), and Jack DeJohnette (drums). —*Ron Wynn*

Moto Grosso Feio / Aug. 26, 1970 / Blue Note ✦✦✦

Odyssey of Iska / Aug. 26, 1970 / Blue Note ✦✦✦
An album that is alternately daring and sentimental. Wonderful soprano solos. —*Ron Wynn*

Native Dancer / Sep. 12, 1974 / Columbia ✦✦✦✦
Wayne Shorter surprised the jazz world with this exotic excursion into Brazilian music in 1975. Milton Nascimento, who accompanies Shorter, wrote five of the nine compositions on this album. Reminiscent of the best of the jazz-samba fusion recordings of Stan Getz, *Native Dancer* is every bit as lush and rich. This is an inspired recording and, in a word, lovely. —*Michael Erlewine*

Atlantis / 1985 / Columbia ✦✦

Phantom Navigator/ Jun. 1987 / Columbia ✦✦

Joy Ryder / 1987 / Columbia ✦✦

High Life / 1994-1995 / Verve ✦✦✦✦

Horace Silver

b. Sep. 2, 1928, Norwalk, CT
Piano / Soul-Jazz, Hard Bop, Groove
As a leading composer and hard-bop pioneer, Horace Silver's piano solos have been a jazz force since the early '50s. He blended vintage R&B, bebop, gospel, blues, and Caribbean elements into jazz in an inspired manner, writing and playing works that were rhythmically and melodically simple, yet gripping and compelling. His work has harmonic sophistication but seldom loses its earthiness and grit. He's been among the rare jazz musicians who've composed the bulk of their material. He's written for combos and vocalists equally well, even on many occasions providing lyrics to accompany his instrumental pieces. Silver was a founding member of the original Jazz Messengers with Art Blakey, and his ensembles have helped introduce and/or nurture quite a few careers, including those of Blue Mitchell, Junior Cook, Donald Byrd, Art Farmer, Joe Henderson, Woody Shaw, Tom Harrell, Michael Brecker, and Randy Brecker. Silver began studying saxophone and piano in high school, listening to blues and boogie woogie. He later mixed that with the Cape Verdean folk music he'd heard as a child. Silver worked in 1950 on a date with Stan Getz, who'd come to make a guest appearance in Hartford. Getz tabbed Silver to work with him, and Silver stayed for a year. Getz cut three of his compositions, "Penny," "Potter's Luck" and "Split Kick." The next year Silver moved to New York, where he worked with Coleman Hawkins, Lester Young, Oscar Pettiford, and Art Blakey. He recorded with Lou Donaldson for Blue Note in 1954, and cut his own trio sessions for the label shortly afterward, working with bassists Gene Ramey, Percy Heath, or Curley Russell and with Blakey on drums. This began an association with Blue Note that lasted nearly 30 years. Silver was co-leader from 1953 to 1955 of a band with Blakey known as the Jazz Messengers. When Silver departed in 1956, Blakey took over the leadership role. Silver's groups became quite popular in the '50s and '60s. Such numbers as "The Preacher," "Doodlin'," "Sister Sadie," and "Song for My Father" became jazz classics, and Silver's albums often crossed over to R&B, soul, and blues audiences. Ray Charles covered "Doodlin'"; and Silver band members Mitchell, Joe Henderson, Kenny Dorham, Clifford Jordan, and Hank Mobley went on to lead their own bands. Silver's forays into hard bop, soul-jazz, and funk made Blue Note both an artistic and commercial juggernaut. "Song for My Father" and "Cape Verdean Blues" both charted in the mid-'60s. Silver began to experiment with concept albums in the '70s, doing a trilogy he called "The United States of Mind." The jazz content of some of this was minimal, but he experimented with strings, African and Indian percussion, and multiple vocalists. Silver left Blue Note at the end of the '70s, forming his own label and issuing recordings he called "Holistic Metaphysical Music." Much of Silver's late '70s and early '80s material was in a quasi-religious bent, but he also established Emerald, a subsidiary of Silveto, and issued vintage dates like *Horace Silver Live: 1964*, which had unreleased versions of "Senor Blues" and "Filthy McNasty." A new Silver album was released in 1993 by Columbia, *It's Got to Be Funky*. Plenty of classic Silver sessions are available on CD. —*Ron Wynn*

Horace Silver Trio, Vol. 1: Spotlight on Drums / Oct. 23, 1952 / Blue Note ✦✦✦✦
Most Silver albums are with a combo (quintet, etc). It is refreshing and clarifying to listen to his trio work. Includes the classic "Opus de Funk." —*Michael Erlewine*

★ **The Best of Horace Silver, Vols. 1 & 2** / 1953-1959 / Blue Note ✦✦✦✦✦
Excellent compilation on CD. Two volumes. —*Michael G. Nastos*

★ **Horace Silver and the Jazz Messengers** / Nov. 13, 1954-Feb. 6, 1955 / Blue Note ✦✦✦✦✦
A true classic, this CD found pianist Horace Silver and drummer Art Blakey co-leading the Jazz Messengers; Silver would leave a year later to form his own group. Also featuring trumpeter Kenny Dorham, Hank Mobley on tenor, and bassist Doug Watkins, this set is most notable for the original versions of Silver's "The Preacher" and "Doodlin'," funky standards

that helped launch hard bop and both the Jazz Messengers and Silver's quintet. Essential music. — *Scott Yanow*

Silver's Blue / Jul. 2, 1956-Jul. 17, 1956 / Portrait ✦✦✦✦
This LP documents the birth of the Horace Silver Quintet, recorded shortly after he left the Jazz Messengers along with some of the other original members. The seven selections (three of which are Silver compositions) feature either Joe Gordan or Donald Byrd on trumpets, tenor saxophonist Hank Mobley, bassist Doug Watkins, and either Kenny Clarke or Art Taylor on drums. Although Silver's piano style was already largely formed, his group did not yet have the distinctive sound it would develop. However this hard-bop music is still quite enjoyable and very historical. — *Scott Yanow*

Six Pieces of Silver / Nov. 10, 1956 / Blue Note ✦✦✦✦
The first classic album by the Horace Silver Quintet, this CD is highlighted by "Senor Blues" (heard in three versions including a later vocal rendition by Bill Henderson) and "Cool Eyes." The early Silver quintet was essentially the Jazz Messengers of the year before (with trumpeter Donald Byrd, tenor saxophonist Hank Mobley, and bassist Doug Watkins, while drummer Louis Hayes was in Blakey's place), but already the band was starting to develop a sound of its own. "Senor Blues" officially put Horace Silver on the map. — *Scott Yanow*

Sterling Silver / Nov. 10, 1956-Jan. 28, 1964 / Blue Note ✦✦✦

The Stylings of Silver / May 8, 1957 / Blue Note ✦✦✦✦
The 1957 Horace Silver Quintet (featuring trumpeter Art Farmer and tenor saxophonist Hank Mobley) is in top form on this date, particularly on "My One and Only Love" and their famous version of "Home Cookin." All of Silver's Blue Note quintet recordings are consistently superb and swinging and, although not essential, this is a very enjoyable set. — *Scott Yanow*

Further Explorations by the Horace Silver Quintet / Jan. 3, 1958 / Blue Note ✦✦✦✦
With trumpeter Art Farmer and tenor saxophonist Clifford Jordan as key members of his quintet, it is not surprising that pianist Horace Silver sounds inspired throughout this set. His increasingly distinctive hard-bop group performed five Silver compositions (none of which became standards despite these versions) and the standard "Ill Wind" for this excellent session. — *Scott Yanow*

☆ **Finger Poppin' with the Horace Silver Quintet** / Feb. 1, 1959 / Blue Note ✦✦✦✦✦
The first recording by the most famous version of the Horace Silver Quintet is also one of the high points of the pianist/composer's career. Among the more memorable tracks of this classic set are "Juicy Lucy" (the epitome of funky jazz), "Cookin' at the Continental," and "Come on Home," but all eight performances are superlative. With trumpeter Blue Mitchell, tenor Junior Cook, bassist Eugene Taylor, and drummer Louis Hayes, Horace Silver had found the perfect forum for his piano and his highly accessible songs. Essential music. — *Scott Yanow*

Blowin' the Blues Away / Aug. 10, 1959 / Blue Note ✦✦✦✦
The second recording by the classic version of the Horace Silver Quintet (with trumpeter Blue Mitchell, tenor saxophonist Junior Cook, bassist Eugene Taylor, and drummer Louis Hayes) introduced Silver's compositions "Sister Sadie" and "Peace" (both of which became jazz standards) in addition to the title track. No jazz library is complete without at least three or four Horace Silver albums. — *Scott Yanow*

Horace-Scope / Jul. 9, 1960 / Blue Note ✦✦✦✦
The most famous version of the Horace Silver Quintet lasted five years (1959-64) and resulted in six albums, of which *HoraceScope* was the third. "Strollin'" is the best known of the new Silver compositions introduced on this set, although this "Nica's Dream" (which was already a few years old) is the only standard. With trumpeter Blue Mitchell, tenor saxophonist Junior Cook, bassist Gene Taylor, and his new drummer Roy Brooks, this was the perfect group for Horace Silver's music. — *Scott Yanow*

Doin' the Thing (At the Village Gate) / May 19, 1961-May 20, 1961 / Blue Note ✦✦✦✦
This live set (recorded at the Village Gate) finds pianist/composer Horace Silver and his most acclaimed quintet (the one with trumpeter Blue Mitchell, tenor saxophonist Junior Cook, bassist Gene Taylor, and drummer Roy Brooks) stretching out on four selections, including his new song "Filthy McNasty." Two shorter performances were added to the CD version of this easily enjoyable and always funky hard-bop session. — *Scott Yanow*

The Tokyo Blues / Jul. 13, 1962-Jul. 14, 1962 / Blue Note ✦✦✦✦
Pianist/composer Horace Silver was inspired by a successful tour of Japan to write these four originals (the best known of which was the title cut) for this fine set, which includes Ronnell Bright's "Cherry Blossom." Although the material is now somewhat obscure, the funky music still communicates very well, and the solos of trumpeter Blue Mitchell, tenor saxophonist Junior Cook, and Silver himself are always worth hearing. — *Scott Yanow*

Silver's Serenade / Apr. 11, 1963-Apr. 12, 1963 / Blue Note ✦✦✦✦
The sixth and final recording session by the most famous of Horace Silver's quintets (the version with trumpeter Blue Mitchell and tenor saxophonist

Junior Cook) did not introduce any new classic tunes ("Silver's Serenade" is the best known), but, as with the previous sets, the results are swinging, funky, and quite creative within the idiom. All of Silver's Blue Note quintet recordings are enjoyable. — *Scott Yanow*

Horace Silver Live: 1964 / Jun. 6, 1964 / Emerald ✦✦✦✦
Released by Horace Silver's own label, this LP contains "new" versions of "Filthy McNasty," "The Tokyo Blues," "Señor Blues," and the lesser-known "Skinney Minnie," as played by his quintet with tenorman Joe Henderson and trumpeter Carmell Jones. These renditions make for an interesting comparison with the earlier versions cut by Silver with Junior Cook and Blue Mitchell, and they are reasonably well recorded. Recommended. — *Scott Yanow*

★ **Song for My Father** / Oct. 26, 1964 / Blue Note ✦✦✦✦✦
Horace Silver's most famous album includes the memorable title cut, four of his other recent compositions (including "Calcutta Cutie" and "Lonely Woman"), and Joe Henderson's "The Kicker." Although trumpeter Blue Mitchell and tenor saxophonist Junior Cook are used on "Calcutta Cutie," the remainder of this classic set features Henderson's tenor and trumpeter Carmell Jones. Funky hard bop at its best, this is essential music for any jazz collection. — *Scott Yanow*

Cape Verdean Blues / Oct. 1, 1965-Oct. 22, 1965 / Blue Note ✦✦✦✦
By late 1965 Horace Silver's Quintet featured trumpeter Woody Shaw and tenor saxophonist Joe Henderson and, on half of this set, the great trombonist J.J. Johnson sits in. "The Cape Verdean Blues," "Pretty Eyes," and Henderson's "Mo' Joe" are among the highlights of this high-quality set of funky hard bop by one of the pacesetting groups. — *Scott Yanow*

The Jody Grind / Nov. 2, 1966-Nov. 23, 1966 / Blue Note ✦✦✦✦
This excellent set finds Horace Silver fronting a particularly advanced edition of his quintet. The band features trumpeter Woody Shaw, tenor saxophonist Tyrone Washington, and, on half of the six tracks (all Silver compositions), the alto and flute of James Spaulding. "The Jody Grind" and "Dimples" are the closest any of these songs came to becoming standards, but Silver fans will find much to enjoy here. — *Scott Yanow*

Serenade to a Soul Sister / Mar. 25, 1968 / Blue Note ✦✦✦✦
One of the final classic albums by the Horace Silver Quintet, this set finds Silver using such sidemen as trumpeter Charles Tolliver, either Stanley Turrentine or Bennie Maupin on tenors, and, on half of the tracks, the young drummer Billy Cobham. The six Silver compositions include "Psychedelic Sally" and "Serenade to a Soul Sister." This music is both timeless and very much of the period. — *Scott Yanow*

You Gotta Take a Little Love / Jan. 10, 1969 / Blue Note ✦✦✦✦
One of the final Horace Silver Quintet Blue Note albums, this somewhat forgotten LP, dedicated to "The Brotherhood of Men," is an instrumental set that introduced six new compositions by the pianist/leader (none of which caught on as standards), along with Bennie Maupin's "Lovely's Daughter." Maupin (on tenor and flute), trumpeter Randy Brecker, bassist John Williams, and drummer Billy Cobham comprise Silver's excellent late-'60s hard-bop group. — *Scott Yanow*

Continuity of Spirit / Mar. 25, 1985 / Silveto ✦✦

Music to Ease Your Disease / Mar. 31, 1988 / Silveto ✦✦✦

It's Got to Be Funky / Feb. 1993 / Columbia ✦✦✦✦
After a 13-year period in which he mostly recorded for his private Silveto label, pianist/composer Horace Silver was rediscovered by Columbia for this session. Rather than featuring a standard quintet as he did throughout his career, the funky pianist is heard with his trio, a six-piece brass ensemble, and guest tenors Red Holloway, Eddie Harris, and Branford Marsalis; Andy Bey contributes four vocals. All of the music (except for a remake of "Song for My Father") was new and served as proof that the master of jazz-funk had not lost his stuff. — *Scott Yanow*

Pencil Packin' Papa / 1994 / Columbia ✦✦✦✦
This CD's main assets are the many new compositions by Horace Silver and his colorful arrangements for the six-piece brass section. Although not enough is heard from the brass players on an individual basis (the greatly underrated trumpeter Oscar Brashear and trombonist George Bohanon get just one solo apiece), this is partly alleviated by the guest tenors. Red Holloway solos on seven songs, while James Moody, Eddie Harris, and Rickey Woodard each pop up twice. In addition, O.C. Smith does a fine job on his four vocals, although Silver's abilities as a lyricist are still open to question. However, his piano solos are typically exciting and inventive, and Silver has obviously lost none of his enthusiasm, even after four decades of music-making. — *Scott Yanow*

Zoot Sims (John Haley Sims)

b. Oct. 29, 1925, Inglewood, CA, d. Mar. 23, 1985, New York, NY
Sax (Tenor) / Bop, Cool

Zoot Sims was a tenor sax stylist associated with the cool era whose sound had an exuberant, swinging energy and bluesy zeal, though it maintained a smooth, relaxed feel. Sims was particularly outstanding in a combo setting, though he could also soar in jam sessions, with a large orchestra, or accompanying vocalists. Though inspired by Lester Young, Sims was far from a slavish imitator. Indeed, near the final portion of his career, Sims reverted to playing in a Ben Webster mode rather than either a Lester Young- or a bop-influenced approach. Sims' family were vaudeville artists, and he began playing drums and clarinet as a child, then moved to tenor sax at 13. Two years later he began touring in dance bands. He played with Bobby Sherwood in the early '40s before joining Benny Goodman in 1943, beginning an association that would remain prominent into the '70s. Sims played at Cafe Society in New York during 1944 with Bill Harris, recording with the group under Joe Bushkin's leadership. Then he went to California, performing with Big Sid Catlett. After Army service, Sims worked again with Goodman in 1946 and 1947, and with Gene Roland. He played in Woody Herman's big band from 1947 to 1949, and it was Roland's compositions for four saxes that led to the creation of the Four Brothers section. Sims played with Stan Getz, Jimmy Giuffre, and Herbie Steward. Upon leaving Herman, he spent a brief period with Buddy Rich, another stint with Goodman in 1950, and an even shorter stay with Chubby Jackson. He then worked with Elliot Lawrence in 1951. Sims debuted as a leader on Prestige in the early '50s, and he played in Stan Kenton's group for a while in 1953. He toured Europe and played in Gerry Mulligan's bands from 1954 to 1956, and later was a soloist in Mulligan's Concert Band. Sims began a long-term musical collaboration with Al Cohn in the '50s; the two had a friendly, yet mildly combative, relationship and made some marvelous twin sax recordings. They toured Scandinavia and Japan in the '70s. Some sessions Sims did in a quintet with Bob Brookmeyer eventually found their way to five different labels. He recorded on United Artists, Riverside, and ABC-Paramount in the '50s. Sims visited England and Europe with Jazz at the Philharmonic in 1967 and 1975 and performed at the Grande Parade du Jazz in Nice with various ensembles. He also toured the Soviet Union with Goodman in the early '60s, and played with John Coltrane, Sonny Rollins, and Coleman Hawkins at a 1966 Titans of the Tenor concert in New York City. Sims began playing soprano sax in the '70s and recorded an excellent Pablo album playing soprano exclusively. He remained busy in the '60s and '70s, recording for Pumpkin, Impulse, Sonet, Argo, RCA, Pacific Jazz, Colpix, Famous Door, Choice, Groove Merchant, Ahead, and Pablo. He continued into the mid-'80s, mostly on Pablo. There's lots of Sims available, many sessions featuring his groups, and others matching him with Cohn, Brookmeyer, Harry Edison, Jimmy Rowles, and Joe Pass. — *Ron Wynn and Dan Morgenstern*

The Zoot Sims Quartet in Paris / Jun. 26, 1950 / Discovery ◆◆◆

Quartets / Sep. 16, 1950 / Original Jazz Classics ◆◆◆◆
This CD reissue features the great tenor saxophonist Zoot Sims (who was then 25) leading his first American recording dates. He is heard with two quartets, the team of pianist John Lewis, bassist Curly Russell, and drummer Don Lamond, and with pianist Harry Biss, bassist Clyde Lombardi, and drummer Art Blakey. All but two numbers clock in around the three-minute mark: an over eight-minute alternate version of "Zoot Swings the Blues" and an 11-minute "East of the Sun." Sims is in fine form throughout these cool-toned but hard-swinging sets. — *Scott Yanow*

Zoot Sims in Paris / 1950-1953 / Vogue ◆◆◆◆

The Rare Dawn Sessions / Jan. 11, 1956-Aug. 10, 1956 / Biograph ◆◆◆

● **Tonite's Music Today** / Jan. 31, 1956 / Black Lion ◆◆◆◆
Valve trombonist Bob Brookmeyer's musical partnerships in the '50s with Stan Getz and especially Gerry Mulligan were celebrated, but he also recorded three fine albums with tenor saxophonist Zoot Sims in 1956 that are quite enjoyable, feature colorful jammed ensembles and hard-swinging yet cool-toned solos that owe as much to the swing tradition as to the innovations of bebop. This Storyville CD finds Zoot and Brookmeyer accompanied by pianist Hank Jones, bassist Wyatt Reuther, and drummer Gus Johnson. Highlights include "I Hear a Rhapsody," "Blue Skies," and Sims' first-ever recorded vocal on a "Blues." This release is easily recommended as is its companion Storyville CD *Morning Fun*. — *Scott Yanow*

● **Morning Fun** / Feb. 1956 / Black Lion ◆◆◆◆
Although it claims on the back of this CD that the music was recorded in August 1956, discographies state February, and that seems more logical, since valve trombonist Bob Brookmeyer and tenor saxophonist Zoot Sims did not team up for a very long period (although three records resulted from their valuable collaboration). With assistance from pianist John Williams, bassist Bill Crow, and drummer Jo Jones, Sims and Brookmeyer are in fine form on such selections as a rollicking "The King," "Lullaby of the Leaves," a brief two-song ballad medley, and Brookmeyer's "Whooeeeee!" Sims takes a rare (and fairly effective) vocal on "I Can't Get Started." Recommended, as is the other Black Lion Zoot Sims CD from the same period, *Tonite's Music Today*. — *Scott Yanow*

Zoot! / Dec. 13, 1956 & Dec. 18, 1956 / Original Jazz Classics ◆◆◆

☆ **Zoot Sims and the Gershwin Brothers** / Jun. 6, 1975 / Original Jazz Classics ◆◆◆◆◆
Along with his album with Count Basie (*Basie and Zoot*) during the same period, this is one of Sims' most exciting recordings. Greatly assisted by pianist Oscar Peterson, guitarist Joe Pass, bassist George Mraz, and drum-

mer Grady Tate, he explores ten songs written by George and Ira Gershwin. Somehow the magic was definitely present and, whether it be stomps such as "The Man I Love," "Lady Be Good," and "I Got Rhythm," or warm ballads (including "I've Got a Crush on You" and "Embraceable You"), Zoot Sims is heard at the peak of his powers. A true gem that has been reissued on CD. — *Scott Yanow*

Hawthorne Nights / Sep. 20, 1976-Sep. 21, 1976 / Original Jazz Classics ◆◆◆◆
Unlike most of his Pablo sessions, this Zoot Sims CD is not a quartet outing but an opportunity for his tenor to be showcased while joined by a nine-piece group that includes six horns (three reeds among them). Bill Holman's inventive arrangements are a large part of why the date is successful, but Sims' playing on the five standards, two Holman pieces, and his own "Dark Cloud" should not be overlooked. Fortunately there is also some solo space saved for the talented sidemen (which include Oscar Brashear and Snooky Young on trumpets, trombonist Frank Rosolino, and the woodwinds and reeds of Jerome Richardson, Richie Kamuca, and Bill Hood). A well rounded set of swinging jazz. — *Scott Yanow*

If I'm Lucky / Oct. 27, 1977-Oct. 28, 1977 / Original Jazz Classics ◆◆◆◆
Tenor saxophonist Zoot Sims recorded quite a few albums with pianist Jimmy Rowles during his Pablo years; all are recommended. Rowles assisted Sims in coming up with obscurities to interpret, and this CD reissue is highlighted by such little-performed songs as "If I'm Lucky," "Shadow Waltz," "Gypsy Sweetheart," and "I Wonder Where Our Love Has Gone." The lead voices are backed ably by bassist George Mraz and drummer Mousey Alexander on this easily enjoyable straightahead date. — *Scott Yanow*

Just Friends / Dec. 18, 1978 & Dec. 20, 1978 / Original Jazz Classics ◆◆◆

Blues for Two / Mar. 6, 1982 & Jun. 23, 1982 / Original Jazz Classics ◆◆◆◆
Although guitarist Joe Pass recorded many unaccompanied solo albums, he made relatively few dates as part of a duo. This CD reissue of a session with tenor saxophonist Joe Pass works quite well because Zoot Sims was a natural swinger who did not need a full rhythm section to push him. His playing on the selections (mainly standards including "Dindi," "Poor Butterfly," "Pennies from Heaven," and "I Hadn't Anyone 'til You") is as heated and lyrical as usual. Pass also warms up quickly to the situation (Sims must have been easy to accompany) and takes many fine solos of his own. The pair collaborated on the opening "Blues for Two" and "Takeoff," which wraps up the highly enjoyable set. — *Scott Yanow*

Jimmy Smith

b. Dec. 8, 1925, Norristown, PA
Organ / Soul-Jazz, Hard Bop, Groove
Jimmy Smith ruled the Hammond organ in the '50s and '60s. He revolutionized thinking about the instrument, showing it could be creatively used in a jazz context and popularized in the process. His Blue Note sessions from 1956 to 1963 were extremely influential and are highly recommended. Smith turned the organ into almost an ensemble itself. He provided walking bass lines with his feet, left-hand chordal accompaniment, solo lines in the right hand, and a booming, funky presence that punctuated every song, particularly the uptempo cuts. Smith turned the fusion of R&B, blues, and gospel influences with bebop references and devices into a jubilant, attractive sound that many others immediately absorbed before following in his footsteps. Smith initially learned piano, both from his parents and on his own. He attended the Hamilton School of Music in 1948 and the Ornstein School of Music in 1949 and 1950 in Philadelphia. Smith began playing the Hammond in 1951 and soon earned a great reputation that followed him to New York, where he debuted at the Cafe Bohemia. A Birdland date and 1957 Newport Jazz Festival appearance launched Smith's career. He toured extensively through the '60s and '70s. His Blue Note recordings included superb collaborations with Kenny Burrell, Lee Morgan, Lou Donaldson, Tina Brooks, Jackie McLean, Ike Quebec, and Stanley Turrentine. He also did several trio recordings, some which were a little bogged down by the excessive length of some selections. Smith scored more hit albums on Verve from 1963 to 1972, many of them featuring big bands and using fine arrangements from Oliver Nelson. These include the excellent *Walk on the Wild Side*. But Verve went to the well once too often seeking crossover dollars, loading down Smith's late-'60s album with hack rock covers. His '70s output was quite spotty, though Smith didn't stop touring, visiting Israel and Europe in 1974 and 1975. He and his wife opened a club in Los Angeles in the mid-'70s. Smith resumed touring in the early '80s, returning to New York in 1982 and 1983. He resigned with Blue Note in 1985 and has done representative dates for them and Milestone in the '90s. — *Ron Wynn and Bob Porter*

A New Star—A New Sound: Jimmy Smith at the Organ, Vol. 1 / Feb. 13, 1956 & Feb. 18, 1956 / Blue Note ◆◆◆◆
The debut of organist Jimmy Smith on records (he was already 30) was a major event, for he introduced a completely new and very influential style on the organ, one that virtually changed the way the instrument is played.

This LP, which has not yet appeared on CD, features the already recognizable organist in a trio with guitarist Thornel Schwartz and Bay Perry on drums. Highlights of this very impressive debut include "The Way You Look Tonight," "Lady Be Good," and Horace Silver's "The Preacher."
—*Scott Yanow*

The Champ / Mar. 11, 1956 / Blue Note ✦✦✦✦
Recorded in New York City. When first issued, many thought there were two players here, or overdubs. Just early Smith cookin'. —*Michael Erlewine*

Greatest Hits, Vol. 1 / Mar. 27, 1956-Feb. 8, 1963 / Blue Note ✦✦✦✦
This double LP, even with its clichéd title, is a real gem. It contains eight of the greatest performances recorded by organist Jimmy Smith during his important period with Blue Note. "The Champ" from his second recording features Smith taking around 50 choruses on a blazing blues, and it set a standard that has still not been surpassed. Also included on this valuable two-fer (some of the material has since been reissued on CD) are "All Day Long," a 20-minute "The Sermon," "Midnight Special," "When Johnny Comes Marching Home," "Can Heat," "Flamingo," and "Prayer Meetin'." In the supporting cast are trumpeter Lee Morgan, altoist Lou Donaldson, Tina Brooks and Stanley Turrentine on tenors, guitarists Kenny Burrell, Thornel Schwartz and Quentin Warren, and drummers Art Blakey and Donald Bailey. This set serves as a perfect introduction to Jimmy Smith's early years and has lots of hard swinging and soulful jams. —*Scott Yanow*

Incredible Jimmy Smith at Club Baby Grand, Vol. 2 / Jun. 12, 1956 / Blue Note ✦✦✦
His original trio was recorded at the Club Baby Grand in Wilmington, DE. —*AMG*

A Date with Jimmy Smith, Vol. 1 / Feb. 11, 1957-Feb. 12, 1957 / Blue Note ✦✦✦
After cutting five albums with his trio, organist Jimmy Smith on Feb. 11, 1957, recorded with trumpeter Donald Byrd, altoist Lou Donaldson, and tenor saxophonist Hank Mobley in a sextet that included guitarist Eddie McFadden and drummer Art Blakey. Among the five songs recorded that day, two (lengthy versions of "Falling in Love with Love" and "Funk's Oats") are included on this LP, along with a shorter trio rendition of "How High the Moon" from two days later with McFadden and drummer Donald Bailey in a trio. All of this music has been reissued by Mosaic on a definitive CD box set. —*Scott Yanow*

A Date with Jimmy Smith, Vol. 2 / Feb. 11, 1957-Feb. 12, 1957 / Blue Note ✦✦✦

The Sounds of Jimmy Smith / Feb. 11, 1957 / Blue Note ✦✦✦
This LP, which has been included as part of a Mosaic Jimmy Smith three-CD box set, features the organist taking a pair of rare unaccompanied solos on "All the Things You Are" and a fairly free "The Fight" and jamming several songs ("Zing Went the Strings of My Heart," "Somebody Loves Me," and "Blue Moon") with his trio. Art Blakey fills in for drummer Donald Bailey on "Zing," while guitarist Eddie McFadden is heard throughout the three selections. Excellent straightahead jazz from the innovative organist. —*Scott Yanow*

☆ **The Complete February 1957 Jimmy Smith Blue Note Sessions** / Feb. 11, 1957-Feb. 13, 1957 / Mosaic ✦✦✦✦✦
It would not be an overstatement to say that organist Jimmy Smith was busy Feb. 11-13, 1957, for he recorded enough material for these three CDs, 21 often-lengthy performances that originally appeared on five LPs, plus three others that had been previously unissued. Smith is heard not only early in his career with his regular trio, but also in a sextet with trumpeter Donald Byrd, altoist Lou Donaldson, tenor saxophonist Hank Mobley, and drummer Art Blakey, in duets with Donaldson, and with a quartet that also stars guitarist Kenny Burrell. These jam sessions feature plenty of exciting solos over fairly common chord changes and, despite the heavy competition, Jimmy Smith (who is still the king of the jazz organ) is the dominant force. Recommended. —*Scott Yanow*

Jimmy Smith at the Organ, Vol. 1: All Day Long / Feb. 12, 1957 / Blue Note ✦✦✦
There is a fair amount of variety on this jam session LP. Organist Jimmy Smith plays "Summertime" in duet with altoist Lou Donaldson and, with guitarist Kenny Burrell and drummer Art Blakey completing the all-star quartet, performs swinging versions of "Yardbird Suite," "There's a Small Hotel," and Burrell's "All Day Long." The music (which has been reissued on CD in a Mosaic box set) will be enjoyed by bop fans even though nothing all that essential occurs. —*Scott Yanow*

Jimmy Smith at the Organ, Vol. 2 / Feb. 13, 1957 / Blue Note ✦✦✦

The Best of Jimmy Smith / Feb. 12, 1957-Jan. 3, 1986 / Blue Note ✦✦✦✦
Small-group setting. Selections from some of Smith's best Blue Note albums, such as *The Sermon, Go for Whatcha Know, Midnight Special, Back at the Chicken Shack, A New Sound,* and *At the Organ.* —*Michael Erlewine*

House Party / Aug. 25, 1957 / Blue Note ✦✦✦✦
Music from two different sessions are included on this enjoyable LP. All of organist Jimmy Smith's jam sessions are worth acquiring, although several (such as this one) have long been out of print. Lengthy versions of "Au Privave" and "Just Friends" and more concise renditions of "Lover Man" and "Blues After All" match Smith with quite a variety of all-stars: trumpeter Lee Morgan, trombonist Curtis Fuller, Lou Donaldson or George Coleman on altos, Tina Brooks on tenor, guitarists Kenny Burrell or Eddie McFadden, and Art Blakey or Donald Bailey on drums. Everyone plays up to par, and the passionate solos (and Smith's heated background riffing) keep the proceedings continually exciting. —*Scott Yanow*

Confirmation / Aug. 25, 1957 & Feb. 25, 1958 / Blue Note ✦✦✦✦
Organist Jimmy Smith led a series of exciting jam sessions for Blue Note during 1957-60, including the three selections heard on this LP. These performances were not released for the first time until 1979, but their quality is as strong as Smith's other output from the era. "Confirmation" matches Smith with altoist Lou Donaldson, tenor saxophonist Tina Brooks, trumpeter Lee Morgan, guitarist Kenny Burrell, and drummer Art Blakey, while a 15-minute rendition of "What Is This Thing Called Love" and a 20-minute "Cherokee" has Morgan, Burrell, Blakey, trombonist Curtis Fuller, and George Coleman on alto. The heated solos are quite enjoyable, and the organist keeps the momentum constantly flowing throughout this happy set. —*Scott Yanow*

★ **Groovin' at Small's Paradise, Vols. 1 & 2** / Nov. 14, 1957 & Nov. 18, 1957 / Blue Note ✦✦✦✦✦
Available in two volumes, this live album was recorded at Small's Paradise in New York City. —*AMG*

☆ **The Sermon** / Feb. 25, 1958 / Blue Note ✦✦✦✦✦
This CD reissue has two of the three selections (the 20-minute "The Sermon" and "Flamingo") from the original LP, adding five additional selections that are related. With such soloists as trumpeter Lee Morgan, trombonist Curtis Fuller, altoist Lou Donaldson, Tina Brooks on tenor, either Eddie McFadden or Kenny Burrell on guitar, and Art Blakey or Donald Bailey on drums, the straightahead music is as good as one would expect (with the lengthy title cut being the obvious high point), and the CD overall offers listeners a strong dose of Jimmy Smith's Blue Note period. —*Scott Yanow*

☆ **Cool Blues** / Apr. 7, 1958 / Blue Note ✦✦✦✦✦
This CD should greatly interest all Jimmy Smith collectors, including those who already have the original LP. In addition to four excellent selections (quintets with altoist Lou Donaldson, Tina Brooks on tenor, guitarist Eddie McFadden, either Art Blakey or Donald Bailey on drums, and the organist/leader), there are three previously unissued numbers from the same gig, featuring the quartet of Donaldson, Smith, McFadden, and Bailey. The repertoire is filled with blues and bop standards and the soloing is at a consistently high and hard-swinging level. Jimmy Smith fans will be pleased. —*Scott Yanow*

Home Cookin' / Jul. 14, 1958-Jun. 16, 1959 / Blue Note ✦✦✦✦
Organist Jimmy Smith and guitarist Kenny Burrell always had a close musical relationship, making their joint recordings quite special. This LP features the pair along with drummer Donald Bailey and (on four of the seven songs) the obscure but talented tenor saxophonist Percy France. The emphasis is on blues and basic material, including versions of "See See Rider," Ray Charles' "I Got a Woman" and several group originals. As usual, the performances are swinging and soulful. —*Scott Yanow*

On the Sunny Side / Jul. 15, 1958 / Blue Note ✦✦✦✦
Organist Jimmy Smith recorded quite a bit of material for Blue Note during 1956-63. This 1981 LP released for the first time eight selections cut during four sessions in the late '50s. In all cases, Smith is joined by guitarist Kenny Burrell and drummer Donald Bailey; Stanley Turrentine makes the group a quartet on "The Sunny Side of the Street" while his fellow tenor Percy France does the same on his original "Apostrophe." All of the songs (other than the latter) are standards, and the tunes generally clock in around a concise five minutes. The results are predictably swinging, and highlights include "On the Sunny Side," "Since I Fell for You," "Bye Bye Blackbird," and "I'm Just a Lucky So and So." Excellent music. —*Scott Yanow*

☆ **Crazy! Baby** / Jan. 4, 1960 / Blue Note ✦✦✦✦✦
Unlike most of the Jimmy Smith recordings from the era, this CD reissue (which adds "If I Should Lose You" and "When Lights Are Low" to the original LP program) features organist Jimmy Smith's regular group (rather than an all-star band). With guitarist Quentin Warren and drummer Donald Bailey completing the trio, Smith is heard in peak form on swinging and soulful versions of such tunes as "When Johnny Comes Marching Home," "Makin' Whoopee," "Sonnymoon for Two," and "Mack the Knife." Despite claims and some strong challenges by others, there has never been a jazz organist on the level of Jimmy Smith. —*Scott Yanow*

Open House / Plain Talk / Mar. 22, 1960 / Blue Note ✦✦✦✦
A two-fer with classic Smith albums *Open House* and *Plain Talk* on one CD. Recorded in Hackensack, NJ. Studio session featuring Blue Mitchell

(trumpet), Ike Quebec (tenor sax), and Jackie McClean (alto sax). This is essentially a jam session without Smith's regular sidemen. More mainstream than most, but very nice tracks—fast and slow. This is an excellent album. —*Michael Erlewine*

★ **Back at the Chicken Shack** / Apr. 25, 1960 / Blue Note ✦✦✦✦✦
This may be the quintessential funky soul-jazz album. Period. I know of no better single recording, and this is the one I would have to take to that desert island when I go. The term "all-star" was coined for this group. Jimmy Smith is as hot as he gets, and so is Stanley Turrentine on tenor sax. Just hot! Kenny Burrell is in top form, too, and Donald Bailey keeps the beat tight. Every jazz fan should hear it, and every groove fan must own it. Also see the Smith album *Midnight Special*, which was recorded at the same session. —*Michael Erlewine*

☆ **Midnight Special** / Apr. 25, 1960 / Blue Note ✦✦✦✦✦
Recorded in Englewood Cliffs, NJ. Small group. This was recorded at the same session as *Back at the Chicken Shack*, and it is as fine—that is: magical! This is a must-have for jazz organ fans. With Stanley Turrentine (tenor sax) and Kenny Burrell (guitar). Every collector of groove music should have a copy. —*Michael Erlewine*

Prayer Meetin' / Jan. 13, 1960 & Feb. 8, 1963 / Blue Note ✦✦✦✦
Organist Jimmy Smith's last Blue Note recording until 1986. On this CD reissue, two earlier selections featuring Smith, tenor saxophonist Stanley Turrentine, guitarist Quentin Warren, bassist Sam Jones (the only time on Blue Note that Smith used a bassist), and drummer Donald Bailey jam on versions of "Lonesome Road" and the original "Smith Walk"; both selections went unreleased until popping up on a 1984 Japanese CD. The bulk of this set is from February 8, 1963, featuring the same personnel without Jones. Highlights include the title cut, a soulful version of "When the Saints Go Marching In," and the Gene Ammons blues "Red Top." Excellent music. —*Scott Yanow*

Jimmy Smith Plays Fats Waller / Jan. 23, 1962 / Blue Note ✦✦✦✦
Although Fats Waller was the first jazz organist, he played mostly piano throughout his career. Organist Jimmy Smith's tribute to Waller is not imitative at all but a good excuse to interpret seven jazz standards that were associated with Fats. With assistance from his regular trio—guitarist Quentin Warren and drummer Donald Bailey—Smith plays such unlikely numbers as "Everybody Loves My Baby," "I've Found a New Baby," and Waller's two biggest hits ("Ain't Misbehavin'" and "Honeysuckle Rose") with soul and swing. An easily enjoyable outing. —*Scott Yanow*

☆ **Bashin' the Unpredictable Jimmy Smith** / Mar. 26, 1962 & Mar. 28, 1962 / Verve ✦✦✦✦✦
Although still a regular Blue Note artist (he would make four more albums for the company within the next year), *Bashin'* was organist Jimmy Smith's debut for Verve, a label that he would record extensively for during 1963-72. On the first half of the program (reissued in full on this CD), Smith was for the first time joined by a big band. Oliver Nelson provided the arrangements, trumpeter Joe Newman and altoist Phil Woods have a solo apiece, and "Walk on the Wild Side" became Smith's biggest hit up to that point. The final three numbers feature Smith's regular trio, with guitarist Quentin Warren and drummer Donald Bailey swinging with soul as usual. The historical set (a bit of a turning point for Jimmy Smith's career) has its strong moments although it is not all that essential. —*Scott Yanow*

I'm Movin On / Jan. 31, 1963 / Blue Note ✦✦✦
This CD reissue of a formerly rare date has a perfectly suitable title, for it is the first of four albums that organist Jimmy Smith made within an eight-day period for Blue Note before permanently leaving the label for Verve. Although notable for matching Smith with guitarist Grant Green in what would be their only joint recording (drummer Donald Bailey completes the trio), the music is fairly typical of a Jimmy Smith session, with the repertoire including blues, a couple of standards, and ballads. The solos are well played, but nothing too surprising occurs (except perhaps for the sappiness of "What Kind of Fool Am I"); the original LP program is expanded by the inclusion of two other selections from the same date. —*Scott Yanow*

Rockin' the Boat / Feb. 2, 1963 / Blue Note ✦✦✦✦
Organist Jimmy Smith's next-to-last LP for Blue Note after a very extensive seven-year period is up to his usual level. With altoist Lou Donaldson joining Smith's regular group (which included guitarist Quentin Warren and drummer Donald Bailey), the quartet swings with soul on such fine numbers as "When My Dream Boat Comes Home," "Can Heat," "Please Send Me Someone to Love," and "Just a Closer Walk with Thee." With the exception of the closing ballad, "Trust in Me," all seven of the selections are closely related to the blues. This is fine music well deserving of being reissued on CD someday. —*Scott Yanow*

Plays the Blues / 1963-1968 / Verve ✦✦✦
Recorded in New Jersey and New York City, this is a selection of Smith's Verve output. Three are big-band numbers with Oliver Nelson. The rest are small-combo efforts—"One for Members" is outstanding. —*Michael Erlewine*

Who's Afraid of Virginia Woolf? / Jan. 20, 1964-Apr. 27, 1964 / Verve ✦✦✦

The Cat / Apr. 27, 1964-Apr. 29, 1964 / Verve ✦✦✦✦
Compared to his earlier Blue Note recordings, organist Jimmy Smith's outings for Verve are not as strong from a jazz standpoint. Certainly his renditions of the "Theme from *Joy House*," "The Cat," and the "Main Title from the Carpetbaggers" are not all that significant. However, this CD has some tasteful arrangements for the big band by Lalo Schifrin and some good playing by the great organist on a variety of other blues-oriented material. Also the combination of organ with a big band is sometimes quite appealing, making this CD worth picking up despite its commercial tracks. —*Scott Yanow*

Monster / Jan. 19, 1965-Jan. 20, 1965 / Verve ✦✦
Due to the material, which includes the two-part "Goldfinger," and the themes from "Bewitched," "The Munsters," and *The Man with the Golden Arm*, this is one of organist Jimmy Smith's lesser recordings. The LP does have some reasonably inventive arrangements for the accompanying big band by Oliver Nelson and some spirited organ playing, but overall it is a rather forgettable and overproduced effort. —*Scott Yanow*

Organ Grinder Swing / Jun. 14, 1965-Jun. 15, 1965 / Verve ✦✦✦
Most of organist Jimmy Smith's recordings for Verve during the mid-to-late '60s were with big bands, making this trio outing with guitarist Kenny Burrell and drummer Grady Tate a special treat. This CD reissue is a throwback to Smith's Blue Note sets (which had concluded two years earlier) and gives the organists the opportunity to stretch out on three blues and three standards. This release shows that, even with all of his commercial success during the period, Jimmy Smith was always a masterful jazz player. —*Scott Yanow*

Got My Mojo Workin' / Dec. 16, 1965-Dec. 17, 1965 / Verve ✦✦✦✦
Recorded in Englewood Cliffs, NJ. Smith in his large-band context, with Oliver Nelson and his orchestra. —*Michael Erlewine*

☆ **The Dynamic Duo** / Sep. 21, 1966 & Sep. 28, 1966 / Verve ✦✦✦✦✦
This CD—a straight reissue of the original LP—is a classic. Organist Jimmy Smith and guitarist Wes Montgomery, both the main pacesetters on their instruments at the time, make for a perfect team on quartet renditions (with drummer Grady Tate and percussionist Ray Barretto) of "James and Wes" and "Baby, It's Cold Outside." However, it is the three numbers with a big band arranged by Oliver Nelson (particularly "Night Train" and a very memorable version of "Down by the Riverside") that really stick in one's mind. Although it is unfortunate that the Smith-Wes collaboration was short-lived (just one other album), it is miraculous that they did find each other and created this brilliant music. —*Scott Yanow*

Further Adventures of Jimmy and Wes / Sep. 21, 1966 & Sep. 28, 1966 / Verve ✦✦✦✦
Organist Jimmy Smith and guitarist Wes Montgomery did all of their recordings together during several sessions in September 1966, but despite the relatively low quantity, the results were consistently memorable. This CD, a follow-up to *The Dynamic Duo*, has one selection ("Milestones") in which the two lead voices are joined by Oliver Nelson's big band and several numbers (including the pop hits "King of the Road" and "Call Me") with a quartet that includes drummer Grady Tate and percussionist Ray Barretto. Although not reaching the heights of the other set, this CD has more than its share of exciting solos from the immortal co-leaders. —*Scott Yanow*

Respect / Jun. 2, 1967 & Jun. 14, 1967 / Verve ✦✦

Stay Loose / Jan. 1968 / Verve ✦✦
A large band album recorded in New York City. Nice organ solos, nondescript tunes. —*Ron Wynn*

The Boss / Nov. 20, 1968 / Verve ✦✦✦
Recorded at Paschal's La Carousel in Atlanta, GA. Lots of fine solos. George Benson (guitar) does his best soul-jazz work since the McDuff days. —*Ron Wynn*

Bluesmith / Sep. 11, 1972 / Verve ✦✦✦✦
It is ironic that one of Jimmy Smith's best Verve releases would be his next-to-last for the label. This surprisingly freewheeling but relaxed jam session also features Teddy Edwards on tenor, guitarist Ray Crawford, bassist Leroy Vinnegar, drummer Donald Dean, and the congas of Victor Pantoja. Together they perform five of Smith's fairly basic originals and Harvey Siders' "Mournin' Wes," a tribute for Wes Montgomery. Fine straightahead music that deserves to be reissued. —*Scott Yanow*

Portuguese Soul / Feb. 8, 1973-Feb. 9, 1973 / Verve ✦✦
Smith recorded this in New York City with a large orchestra under the direction of Thad Jones. —*Michael Erlewine*

Other Side of Jimmy Smith / 1973 / MGM ✦✦✦
Another big-band outing by Smith, Johnny Pate, and orchestra. —*Michael Erlewine*

It's Necessary / Jul. 6, 1977-Jul. 7, 1977 / Mercury ✦✦✦

The Cat Strikes Again / Jul. 1980 / Laserlight ✦✦✦
Recorded in Hollywood with Lalo Schifrin and orchestra. —*Michael Erlewine*

All the Way Live / Aug. 29, 1981 / Milestone ◆◆◆◆
Strange as it seems, organist Jimmy Smith and tenor saxophonist Eddie Harris have to this date only played together once. Their recorded collaboration at San Francisco's Keystone Korner in 1981 has recently been released for the first time by Milestone on *All the Way Live*. Harris (who uses an electrified tenor) and Smith (along with drummer Kenny Dixon) jam a couple of blues, the funky "Eight Counts for Rita" (which has some audience participation), and three familiar standards. The recording quality is not state-of-the-art but is certainly listenable, and the high level of the playing overcomes any technical deficiencies. Essentially a hard-bop stylist, Eddie Harris' brilliance and originality are sometimes hidden under his innovative use of electronics, but he has long had his own sound, while Jimmy Smith is the originator of his very influential style. Highlights of the date include "Autumn Leaves," "A Child Is Born," and "Old Folks." This live set easily surpasses Smith and Harris' studio recordings of the time. A reunion is long overdue. — *Scott Yanow*

Off the Top / Jun. 7, 1982 / Elektra ◆◆◆◆
It had been nine years since organist Jimmy Smith recorded for a major label when Bruce Lundvall approached him to make an album for Elektra Musician. Smith plays some unusual material (including Lionel Richie's "Endless Love" and the "Theme from *M.A.S.H.*") on this LP but swings everything and has a particularly strong supporting cast—guitarist George Benson, Stanley Turrentine on tenor, bassist Ron Carter, and drummer Grady Tate. A fine comeback date. — *Scott Yanow*

Keep on Comin' / Sep. 3, 1983 / Elektra ◆◆◆◆
Organist Jimmy Smith's second of two LPs for the Elektra Musician label is unusual in a couple of respects. He had never played organ with tenor saxophonist Johnny Griffin before, and on one piece, "Piano Solo Medley," Smith has a very rare feature on piano. Otherwise the music, which comprises recent originals by Smith, Griffin, and guitarist Kenny Burrell—who with drummer Mike Baker completes the quartet—is in the soulfully swinging vein that one associates with the great organist. — *Scott Yanow*

Go for Whatcha' Know / Jan. 2, 1986 / Blue Note ◆◆◆◆
Twenty-three years after leaving the label, organist Jimmy Smith returned to the Blue Note label. In addition to signing up two of his old associates who had been with him on many classic Blue Note albums of the past (guitarist Kenny Burrell and tenor saxophonist Stanley Turrentine), Smith uses such fine payers as guest pianist Monty Alexander (on two songs), bassist Buster Williams, and drummer Grady Tate (who takes a warm ballad vocal on "She's Out of My Life"). "Fungii Mama" and "Go for Whatcha Know" are the highlights of this enjoyable LP. — *Scott Yanow*

Prime Time / 1989 / Milestone ◆◆◆◆

Fourmost / Nov. 16, 1990-Nov. 17, 1990 / Milestone ◆◆◆◆
Organist Jimmy Smith has a reunion on this CD with his 30-plus-year associates tenor saxophonist Stanley Turrentine and guitarist Kenny Burrell, along with drummer Grady Tate. Together they play spirited and creative versions of standards and blues. The high points include "Midnight Special," a swinging "Main Stem," Tate's warm vocal on "My Funny Valentine," and a lengthy rendition of "Quiet Nights." This all-star date reaches its potential and is recommended to fans of straightahead jazz. — *Scott Yanow*

Sum Serious Blues / 1993 / Milestone ◆◆◆
Organist Jimmy Smith performs a spirited set of blues-based material (only "You've Changed" is a change of pace) with a dozen of his Los Angeles-based friends, including trumpeter Oscar Brashear, the underrated tenor Herman Riley (who is best among the supporting cast), guitarist Philip Upchurch, and singers Marlena Shaw and Bernard Ighner, who have two vocals apiece. Nothing that surprising occurs, other than Smith's surprisingly effective vocal on "Hurry Change, If You're Comin'," but the swinging music, which was arranged by Johnny Pate, should please Jimmy Smith's fans. — *Scott Yanow*

The Masters / Dec. 24, 1993-Dec. 25, 1993 / Blue Note ◆◆◆
Organist Jimmy Smith, in a trio with guitarist Kenny Burrell and drummer Jimmie Smith (no relation) performs six diverse blues and three familiar standards. Although the music is somewhat predictable, it swings hard and is often rollicking. Burrell sounds inspired, and Smith, who largely originated this idiom, shows that he is still an enthusiastic and masterful player. — *Scott Yanow*

Jazz 'round Midnight / Verve ◆◆◆

Walk on the Wild Side: The Best of the Verve Years / Verve ◆◆◆◆
Smith recorded most of his most popular sides for Verve, and this double CD contains 25 tracks taken from his recordings for the label between 1962 and 1973, in both small-combo and big-band settings. There are a few Jimmy Smith compilations out there, and this isn't necessarily the best; some of the later numbers have disagreeable funk/pop overtones, and anthologies that focus on his early and mid-'60s prime might be better values overall. It does have his most famous performances—"Walk on the Wild Side," "Got My Mojo Workin'," and a couple of his great duets with guitarist Wes Montgomery. It's a decent enough pickup if you just want one or two Smith albums for your library, though not so definitive that it's

worth getting if you already have some Smith compilations that cover the Verve era. — *Richie Unterberger*

Lonnie Liston Smith

b. Dec. 28, 1940, Richmond, VA
Keyboards / Fusion, Post-Bop
Pianist Lonnie Liston Smith underwent a great stylistic change during the '70s. At one point he was working with Pharoah Sanders and Gato Barbieri, providing keyboard interludes for their highly charged, explosive settings. Then he played with Miles Davis, plugging into electric funk. When he formed the Cosmic Echoes with his brother Donald, things were radically different. Smith presented low-key arrangements, with Donald singing pseudo-mystic laments and pontifications, with minimal improvisation and solo space. But these albums put Lonnie Liston Smith on the fusion and crossover map; he enjoyed great sales for a string of releases in this pattern that continued through the '80s and into the '90s. He established himself as one of the more popular acts on the Black upper-middle-class professional circuit, playing college campuses and appearing in several cites with heavy African-American populations and high-profile urban-contemporary radio stations. Lonnie Liston Smith had graduated in music education from Morgan State in 1961, then moved to New York. He played with Betty Carter, Rahsaan Roland Kirk, Art Blakey, Joe Williams, and Sanders. Smith has recorded as a leader for Flying Dutchman, Doctor Jazz, and Signature. Several sessions are available on CD. — *Ron Wynn*

Golden Dreams / 1973 / Bluebird ◆◆◆◆
Recent fusion/jazz date. — *Ron Wynn*

★ **Reflections of a Golden Dream** / Sep. 1976 / RCA ◆◆◆◆◆
This is considered the high point of his career. — *AMG*

Renaissance / 1977 / RCA ◆◆◆

Rejuvenation / Feb. 26, 1985-Feb. 27, 1985 / Doctor Jazz ◆◆◆

Make Someone Happy / 1989 / Doctor Jazz ◆◆◆

Lonnie Smith (Lonnie Smith)

Organ / Blues-Jazz, Soul-Jazz, Groove
Not to be confused with Lonnie Liston Smith, organist Lonnie Smith has been on the soul-jazz and jazz scene since the '60s.
    Smith, who hails from Buffalo, NY, began his career as a trumpet player, forming a vocal group soon after high school. When he ran across the Hammon B-3, he was hooked. With his R&B background, he was soon attracting some real attention. He sat in with Jack McDuff's band in New York and met George Benson there. The two were soon recording for Columbia as the George Benson Quartet, releasing the albums *It's Uptown* (1966) and *Cookbook* (1967). Smith made his first solo album, *Finger Lickin' Good* later in 1967. During a recording session for Lou Donaldson, where Benson and Smith were called in to add some new sounds, he was heard by scout Frank Wolff. He was signed to Blue Note in 1968 and contracted for four albums: *Think, Turning Point, Move Your Hand*, and *Drives*. In 1971 Smith recorded *Live at Club Mozambique*, also released on Blue Note. He's worked often with Lou Donaldson and has done sessions on his own. Smith can play the requisite bluesy licks, work the bass pedal, and offer good stomping numbers. Though he's recorded as a leader for Blue Note, CTI, and other labels, and done sessions with Donaldson, George Benson, Hank Crawford, and many other notables, Smith has just started to have a few sessions available on CD. — *Michael Erlewine and Ron Wynn*

● **Think** / Jul. 23, 1968 / Blue Note ◆◆◆◆
This is an excellent 1986 reissue of a fine soul-jazz date by organist Lonnie Smith with Lee Morgan on trumpet. — *Ron Wynn*

Move Your Hand / Aug. 9, 1969 / Blue Note ◆◆◆◆
Move Your Hand was recorded live at Club Harlem in Atlantic City on August 9, 1969. Organist Lonnie Smith led a small combo—featuring guitarist Larry McGee, tenor saxist Rudy Jones, baritone saxist Ronnie Cuber, and drummer Sylvester Goshay—through a set that alternated originals with two pop covers, the Coasters' "Charlie Brown" and Donovan's "Sunshine Superman." Throughout, the band works a relaxed, bluesy, and, above all, funky rhythm; they abandon improvisation and melody for a steady groove, so much that the hooks of the two pop hits aren't recognizable until a few minutes into the track. No one player stands out, but *Move Your Hand* is thoroughly enjoyable, primarily because the group never lets their momentum sag throughout the session. Though the sound of the record might be somewhat dated, its essential funk remains vital. — *Stephen Thomas Erlewine*

● **Mama Wailer** / Jul. 14, 1971-Jul. 15, 1971 / Kudu ◆◆◆◆

Purple Haze: Tribute to Jimi Hendrix / Nov. 7, 1995 / Music Masters ◆◆

Live at Club Mozambique / Blue Note ◆◆◆◆
This previously unreleased live set features heated and reasonably creative jamming by organist Lonnie Smith, his regular group of the time (tenorman Dave Hubbard, baritonist Ronnie Cuber, drummer Joe Dukes, and percussionist Gary Jones), and guest guitarist George Benson. The pro-

gram (of which six of the eight numbers are Smith originals) is highlighted by a rapid run-through of "Expressions" (based on "Impressions") and a racehorse version of "Seven Steps to Heaven." However Smith's unspeakably bad "vocal" on "Peace of Mind" should be bypassed. This CD is actually worth getting chiefly for Cuber's heated baritone. —*Scott Yanow*

Marvin Smith

b. Jun. 24, 1961, Waukegan, IL
Drums / Post-Bop, Hard Bop
A prolific, constantly-in-demand drummer whose sensitive, yet authoritative playing has been heard on dozens of '80s and '90s sessions, Marvin "Smitty" Smith seems to live in the studio. A onetime Berklee student, he played with Jon Hendricks' band in New York during the early '80s, then worked with John Hicks, Bobby Watson, and Slide Hampton. Smith later recorded with Archie Shepp, then with a quintet co-led by Frank Wess and Frank Foster. He did sessions with Hamiett Bluiett, Kevin Eubanks, and David Murray, as well as playing with Ray Brown, Dave Holland, Ron Carter, Hank Jones, and the Jazztet. Smith made his recording debut as a leader in 1987; also that year he recorded with Sonny Rollins and toured with Sting. Since then Smith's been constantly featured on sessions, often paired with Ray Drummond. He has a couple of Concord dates available on CD and can be heard on numerous releases by other musicians. —*Ron Wynn*

Keeper of the Drums / Mar. 1987 / Concord Jazz ✦✦✦✦
● **Carryin' On** / 1993 / Concord Jazz ✦✦✦✦
Good, nicely played date with a harder edge than usual for Concord material. —*Ron Wynn*

Stuff Smith (Hezekiah Leroy Gordon Smith)

b. Aug. 14, 1909, Portsmouth, OH, **d.** Sep. 25, 1967, Munich, Germany
Violin / Swing
Stuff Smith was one of the big three pre-bop violinists, along with Joe Venuti and Stephane Grappelli. Many of his fans said that he could outswing all of his competitors, and certainly Stuff was a major force on the bandstand. Smith, who cited Louis Armstrong as his main influence, studied music with his father and played with the family band as a child. His first major job and recordings were with Alphonse Trent's territory band in the '20s, but it was not until 1936 that he had his breakthrough. Leading a quintet at the Onyx Club with trumpeter Jonah Jones, Smith's comedy vocals and hard-swinging approach made the group a hit on 52nd Street for several years; his novelty "Tse a Muggin'" became a hit. Smith worked regularly with his trios in the '40s but was in danger of being forgotten in the '50s until Norman Granz recorded him fairly extensively for Verve. Stuff also participated in Nat King Cole's *After Midnight* sessions for Capitol. The violinist moved to Copenhagen in 1965 and was active until his death two years later. —*Scott Yanow*

☆ **Stuff Smith and His Onyx Club Boys** / Feb. 11, 1936-Dec. 1939 / Classics ✦✦✦✦✦
Stuff Smith-Dizzy Gillespie-Oscar Peterson / Jan. 21, 1957-Apr. 17, 1957 / Verve ✦✦✦✦
● **Live at the Montmartre** / Mar. 18, 1965 / Storyville ✦✦✦✦
Swingin' Stuff / Mar. 23, 1965 / Storyville ✦✦✦✦
One of two mid-'60s sessions that violinist Stuff Smith recorded with a mostly foreign band, plus expatriate pianist Kenny Drew. He plays with his characteristic fervor, punctuating his rippling phrases with blues licks, smears, and slurs, plus some dazzling phrases. Bassist Niels-Henning Orsted Pedersen emerges as the dominant rhythm-section member besides Drew, while drummer Alex Riel mainly follows their lead. —*Ron Wynn*

Tab Smith

b. Jan. 11, 1909, Kingston, NC, **d.** Aug. 17, 1971, St. Louis, MO
Sax (Alto) / Swing, Early R&B
One of the finest altoists to emerge during the swing era, Tab Smith became a popular attraction in the R&B world of the '50s because of his record *Because of You*. After playinq in territory bands during the '30s, Smith played and recorded with Lucky Millinder's Orchestra (1936-38) and then freelanced with various swing all-stars in New York. He had opportunities to solo with Count Basie's band (1940-42) before returning to Millinder (1942-44); he took honors on a recording of "On the Sunny Side of the Street" with a stunning cadenza that followed statements by Coleman Hawkins, Don Byas, and Harry Carney. After leaving Millinder, Smith led his own sessions, which became increasingly R&B-oriented (he never became involved with bop). His string of recordings for United in the '50s (which are being reissued by Delmark on CD) made him a fairly major name for a time, even though he had a relatively mellow sound and avoided honking. In the early '60s Tab Smith retired to St. Louis and later became involved in selling real estate. —*Scott Yanow*

● **Jump Time** / Aug. 28, 1951-Feb. 26, 1952 / Delmark ✦✦✦✦
Altoist Tab Smith, who first gained recognition with Count Basie's Orchestra in the mid-'40s, became an unexpected R&B star in the early '50s, thanks in large part to his hit version of "Because of You." Between 1951 and 1957, Smith recorded 90 songs for the United Record Company of which only 48 were issued. Delmark, in their CD reissue series, plans to come out with all of the music in chronological order. This first release has the initial 20 (including the hit), and Tab Smith sounds fine on the sweet ballads, blues, and concise jump tunes; the backup crew includes trumpeter Sonny Cohn, tenor Leon Washington, and either Lavern Dillon or Teddy Brannon on piano. —*Scott Yanow*

Because of You / Aug. 28, 1951-1955 / Delmark ✦✦✦
Ace High / Feb. 26, 1952-Apr. 23, 1953 / Delmark ✦✦✦✦

Willie "The Lion" Smith (William Henry Joseph Bonaparte Bertholoff Smith)

b. Nov. 25, 1897, Goshen, NY, **d.** Apr. 18, 1973, New York, NY
Piano / Stride, Classic Jazz
Willie "The Lion" Smith in the '20s was considered one of the big three of stride piano (along with James P. Johnson and Fats Waller), even though he made almost no recordings until the mid-'30s. His mother was an organist and pianist, and Smith started playing piano when he was six. He earned a living playing piano as a teenager, gained his nickname "The Lion" for his heroism in World War I, and after his discharge became one of the star attractions at Harlem's nightly rent parties. Although he toured with Mamie Smith (and played piano on her pioneering 1920 blues record *Crazy Blues*), Smith mostly freelanced throughout his life. He was an influence on the young Duke Ellington (who would later write "Portrait of the Lion") and most younger New York-based pianists of the '20s and '30s. Although he was a braggart and (with his cigar and trademark derby hat) appeared to be a rough character, Smith was actually more colorful than menacing. He was a very sophisticated pianist with a light touch. His recordings with his Cubs (starting in 1935) and particularly his 1939 piano solos for Commodore (highlighted by "Echoes of Spring") cemented his place in history. Because he remained very active into the early '70s (writing his memoirs *Music on My Mind* in 1965), for quite a few decades Willie "The Lion" Smith was a living link to the glory days of early jazz. —*Scott Yanow*

● **Willie "The Lion" Smith 1925-1937** / Nov. 5, 1925-Sep. 15, 1937 / Classics ✦✦✦✦
Willie "The Lion" Smith 1937-1938 / Sep. 15, 1937-Nov. 30, 1938 / Classics ✦✦✦
Echoes of Spring / 1965 / Milan ✦✦✦✦
A 1992 reissue featuring stomps, stride, and gutbucket blues numbers played by the remarkable Willie "The Lion" Smith. Smith, a friend and associate of everyone from James P. Johnson to Fats Waller, could rip through songs when inspired, but he was also a wonderful ballad player and good interpreter. He displayed all these skills on this set. —*Ron Wynn*

Martial Solal

b. Aug. 23, 1927, Algiers, LA
Piano / Post-Bop
One of the finest European jazz pianists of all time, Martial Solal (a unique stylist) has never received as much recognition in the US as he deserves. Born in Algiers to French parents, Solal has been based in Paris since the late '40s. Although a modernist, he was flexible enough to record an album with Sidney Bechet in 1957 and make other records with Django Reinhardt, Don Byas, and Lucky Thompson. Solal has been heard primarily with his own trios through the years, although he has recorded several notable albums with Lee Konitz. —*Scott Yanow*

☆ **Live** / Sep. 14, 1956-Feb. 7, 1985 / Stefanotis ✦✦✦✦✦
Comprehensive four-disc set of his material from 1959 to 1985 in every context. —*Ron Wynn*
● **Four Keys** / May 1979 / PA/USA ✦✦✦✦
An all-star quartet (pianist Martial Solal, altoist Lee Konitz, guitarist John Scofield, and bassist Niels Pedersen) explores seven diverse Solal originals that range from chamberlike pieces to fairly free group improvising. The results are often exciting if cool in both tone and volume. Thoughtful yet unpredictable music. —*Scott Yanow*

Eddie South

b. Nov. 27, 1904, Louisiana, MO, **d.** Apr. 25, 1962, Chicago, IL
Violin / Swing
Classical training and swing in his soul made Eddie South a jazz giant on violin. South's tremendous technique and riveting, left-hand playing style were supported by strong, aggressive bowing and a commanding approach on either uptempo or slow material. His rich, dreamy tone earned him the nickname the "Dark Angel," and he was hypnotic and moving on ballads. South could also blaze and delight on fast-paced mate-

rial. He was a child prodigy who was coached in jazz by Darnell Howard. South became music director of Jimmy Wade's Syncopators in the mid-'20s, after his studies, which included time at Chicago Musical College. He played in Europe during the late '20s, touring and studying in Paris and Hungary. South also recorded with his group, the Alabamians, for HMV in Paris. He returned to Chicago in the early '30s and co-led a band with Everett Barksdale and Milt Hinton that recorded for Victor. He returned to Paris in the late '30s and made seminal recordings with Django Reinhardt and Stephane Grappelli. South later worked in New York, Chicago, and Los Angeles at the end of the decade. He recorded with a West Coast quintet that included Tommy Benford. South led his own groups through the '40s and '50s, mostly combos, but occasionally a big band. He did several radio and TV programs and spent his final years in Chicago. Besides his sessions for HMV and Victor, South recorded for Okeh, Columbia, and Mercury. Some of his early material was reissued in Europe on Swing. *—Ron Wynn and Michael Erlewine*

Eddie South 1923-1937 / Dec. 1923-Nov. 23, 1937 / Classics ✦✦✦✦

In Paris / Mar. 12, 1929-Nov. 25, 1937 / DRG ✦✦✦✦
Rare cuts from the late '30s featuring violinist Eddie South, whose beautiful, swinging solos were unfortunately seldom recorded. These songs were cut when South was living in Paris and playing with such European jazz greats as Django Reinhardt and Stephane Grappelli. *—Ron Wynn*

● **Eddie South 1937-1941** / Nov. 25, 1937-Mar. 12, 1941 / Classics ✦✦✦✦

Muggsy Spanier (Francis Joseph Spanier)

b. Nov. 9, 1906, Chicago, IL, **d.** Feb. 12, 1967, Sausalito, CA
Cornet / Dixieland
Muggsy Spanier was a predictable but forceful cornetist who rarely strayed far from the melody. Perfectly at home in Dixieland ensembles, Spanier was also an emotional soloist (equally influenced by King Oliver and Louis Armstrong) who was an expert at using the plunger mute. He started on cornet when he was 13, played with Elmer Schoebel's band in 1921, and first recorded in 1924. Spanier was a fixture in Chicago throughout the decade (appearing on several important early records) before joining Ted Lewis in 1929. Although Lewis was essentially a corny showman, Spanier's solos gave his band some validity during the next seven years. After a stint with Ben Pollack's orchestra (1936-38), Spanier became seriously ill and was hospitalized for three months. After he recovered, the cornetist formed his famous eight-piece "Ragtime Band" and recorded 16 Dixieland performances for Bluebird (later dubbed "The Great 16") that virtually defined the music of the Dixieland revival movement. But because his group actually preceded the revival by a couple years, it soon had to break up due to lack of work! Spanier joined Bob Crosby for a time, had his own short-lived big band, freelanced with Dixieland bands in New York, and starting in 1950, gradually relocated to the West Coast. During 1957-59 Spanier worked with Earl Hines' band, and he continued playing until his retirement in 1964, touring Europe in 1960 and always retaining his popularity in the Dixieland world. *—Scott Yanow*

☆ **The Great Sixteen** / Jul. 7, 1939-Dec. 12, 1939 / Bluebird ✦✦✦✦✦
During four sessions in 1939, cornetist Muggsy Spanier performed definitive versions of 16 Dixieland standards that, due to the joy of the music and its huge influence on the future revival movement, would later be dubbed "The Great 16." This CD, which adds eight alternate takes, could have been subtitled "The Great 24." Spanier and his octet (which includes trombonist George Brunies, clarinetist Rod Cless, usually pianist Joe Bushkin, and several different tenors) roar their way through such songs as "Big Butter and Egg Man," "That Da Da Strain," "I Wish I Could Shimmy like My Sister Kate," "Dinah," and "Mandy, Make Up Your Mind." Classic music. *—Scott Yanow*

● **Muggsy Spanier 1939-1942** / Jul. 7, 1939-Jun. 1, 1942 / Classics ✦✦✦✦

Spyro Gyra

Group / Crossover
Founded in 1975 by altoist Jay Beckenstein, Spyro Gyra has consistently been one of the commercially successful pop-jazz groups of the past 20 years. Although originally a studio group, the band became a full-time venture in 1979 and has been touring ever since. Critics love to attack this band's lightweight and rarely changing music (which combines R&B and elements of pop with jazz), but its live performances are often stimulating, unlike many of its records, which emphasize the danceable melodies at the expense of the improvising. *—Scott Yanow*

Catching the Sun / Nov. 1980 / MCA ✦✦✦✦
One among many similar-sounding but highly popular albums by premier fusion ensemble Spyro Gyra. The group's songs usually contained catchy melodies, prominent backbeats, and some room for improvisational expression, although it was limited and required quick bursts rather than expansive statements. They were and still are near the top in the light jazz and fusion field. *—Ron Wynn*

Access All Areas / Nov. 17, 1983 & Nov. 19, 1983 / MCA ✦✦✦✦
An excellent live double album, it includes live versions of songs from early albums. *—Paul Kohler*

Alternating Currents / Oct. 1985 / MCA ✦✦✦✦
Featured is great songwriting and playing, and nice work by keyboardist Tom Schuman. *—Paul Kohler*

Breakout / 1986 / MCA ✦✦✦✦
An album with more mid-tempo jazz-style tunes and nice arrangements, it features Julio Fernandez and synth programming by Eddie Jobson. *—Paul Kohler*

Stories Without Words / Jul. 1987 / MCA ✦✦✦

Three Wishes / 1992 / GRP ✦✦✦

Love and Other Obsessions / 1995 / GRP ✦✦

Jess Stacy (Alexandria Stacy)

b. Aug. 11, 1904, Bird's Point, MO, **d.** Jan. 5, 1994, Los Angeles, CA
Piano / Swing
One of the great swing pianists, Jess Stacy's greatest moment of fame was an unexpected one when, during the latter part of "Sing, Sing, Sing" at Benny Goodman's historic 1938 Carnegie Hall Concert, the clarinetist motioned to Stacy to take a solo (which he never had previously on that song). The pianist constructed a remarkable impressionistic improvisation that stole solo honors and that fortunately was documented (and released for the first time in 1950). A mostly self-taught player who performed on riverboats during the early '20s, Stacy was part of the fertile Chicago jazz scene of the '20s, with his style being influenced by both Earl Hines and Bix Beiderbecke. Still obscure when he joined Goodman's big band in 1935, the pianist soon became well known as one of Goodman's top sidemen, working with him through 1939 and on and off during the next five years. Stacy also spent time with the bands of Bob Crosby, Horace Heidt, and Tommy Dorsey, recorded with Eddie Condon, did some solo recordings of his own (starting in 1935), had a short-lived marriage to singer Lee Wiley, and tried twice to lead big bands of his own. He became fairly obscure after moving to California in 1947 (mostly playing in piano bars), and in 1963 Stacy retired from music altogether, only to return briefly on a few special occasions (and for two Chiaroscuro recordings) over the next 20 years. *—Scott Yanow*

● **Jess Stacy 1935-1939** / Nov. 16, 1935-Nov. 30, 1939 / Classics ✦✦✦✦
Pianist Jess Stacy did not lead that many recording sessions during the swing era, since he spent long periods playing with the big bands of Benny Goodman and Bob Crosby. This excellent CD contains his 21 selections as a leader from a four-year period. Stacy's three numbers from 1935 include a solo Bix Beiderbecke medley and two songs with bassist Israel Crosby and drummer Gene Krupa. In addition this set has Stacy's eight piano solos for Commodore, a duet with Bud Freeman on tenor ("She's Funny That Way"), and eight very rare performances (plus an alternate take) cut for Varsity in 1939 that also feature trumpeter Billy Butterfield, tenor saxophonist Eddie Miller, and either clarinetist Hank d'Amico or Irving Fazola in an octet. This CD contains more than its share of gems. *—Scott Yanow*

Mike Stern

b. Jan. 10, 1953, Boston, MA
Guitar / Fusion, Post-Bop
A rocking, experimental guitarist who rose to fame playing in a pair of Miles Davis' bands, Mike Stern's a competent bebop and hard-bop player and an excellent fusion and jazz-rock musician. He's provided some wondrous riffs, blistering lines, complex voicings, and dynamite phrases during fusion, playing with much more force and vigor than on more conventional jazz. Stern attended Berklee in the early '70s, where he studied with Pat Metheny and Mick Goodrick. Metheny recommended him for a vacancy with Blood, Sweat and Tears, and Stern played with them for two years. He later worked with Billy Cobham, then joined Davis' band in 1981. Stern stayed with him two years, then played with Jaco Pastorius' group, Word of Mouth. Stern made his recording debut as a leader in 1985. He later toured with Davis again, played with Steps Ahead, and worked in bands led by Mike Brecker and Harvie Swartz. Stern recorded as a leader for Atlantic in the '80s and '90s. He has several sessions available as a leader. *—Ron Wynn and Michael G. Nastos*

Upside Downside / Mar. 1986-Apr. 1986 / Atlantic ✦✦✦

Time in Place / Dec. 1987 / Atlantic ✦✦✦✦
With Michael Brecker(sax) and Bob Berg(tenor sax). "Gossip" is a good opening track. *—Michael G. Nastos*

Jigsaw / Feb. 1989 / Atlantic ✦✦✦✦
High-powered jazz-rock with the emphasis on rock. *—Michael G. Nastos*

● **Standards (and Other Songs)** / 1992 / Atlantic ✦✦✦✦
Guitarist Mike Stern, best known for playing rock-oriented fusion and in more commercial settings, surprised many listeners by recording an album dominated by standards. Actually there are three originals included among the 11 pieces, but Stern also digs into such songs as "Like Someone

in Love," "Moment's Notice," Chick Corea's "Windows," and "Straight No Chaser." Among Stern's sidemen on this fairly straightahead but adventurous set are trumpeter Randy Brecker, Bob Berg on tenor, and keyboardist Gil Goldstein. This little-known release is well worth acquiring before it inevitably goes out of print. —*Scott Yanow*

Is What It Is / 1993 / Atlantic ✦✦✦✦
Mike Stern is one of the more creative fusion guitarists, playing with the power of rock but often taking sophisticated improvisations. On this passionate set (which consists of nine of his originals), Stern is joined by the keyboards of Jim Beard, bassist Will Lee, Dennis Chambers or Ben Perowsky on drums, and (on three songs apiece) the tenors of Michael Brecker and Bob Malach. Overall this is one of Mike Stern's better recordings. —*Scott Yanow*

Between the Lines / 1995 / Atlantic ✦✦✦✦

Rex Stewart (William Stewart, Jr.)

b. Feb. 22, 1907, Philadelphia, PA, **d.** Sep. 7, 1967, Los Angeles, CA
Cornet / Dixieland, Swing
Rex Stewart achieved his greatest glory in a subsidiary role, playing cornet 11 years in the Duke Ellington Orchestra. His famous "talking" style and half-valve effects were exploited brillantly by countless Ellington pieces containing perfect passages tailored to showcase Stewart's sound. He played in a forceful, gripping manner that reflected the influence of Louis Armstrong, Bubber Miley, and Bix Beiderbecke, whose solos he once reproduced on record. Stewart played on Potomac riverboats before moving to Philadelphia. He went to New York in 1921. Stewart worked with Elmer Snowden in 1925, then joined Fletcher Henderson a year later. But he felt his talents were not at the necessary level and left Henderson's band, joining his brother Horace's band at Wilberforce College. Stewart returned in 1928. He remained five years and contributed many memorable solos. There was also a brief period in McKinney's Cotton Pickers in 1931, a stint heading his own band, and another short stay with Luis Russell before Stewart joined the Ellington Orchestra in 1934. He was a star throughout his tenure, co-writing the classics "Boy Meets Horn" and "Morning Glory." He also supervised many outside recording sessions using Ellingtonians. After leaving Ellington, Stewart led various combos and performed throughout Europe and Australia on an extensive Jazz at the Philharmonic tour from 1947 to 1951. He lectured at the Paris Conservatory in 1948. Stewart settled in New Jersey to run a farm in the early '50s. He was semi-retired but found new success in the media, working in local radio and TV and leading a band part-time in Boston. Stewart led the Fletcher Henderson reunion band in 1957 and 1958, and recorded with them. He played at Eddie Condon's club in 1958 and 1959, then moved to the West Coast. Stewart again worked as a disc jockey and became a critic. A collection containing many of his best reviews came out posthumously, *Jazz Masters of the Thirties.* There's also a Stewart autobiography. —*Ron Wynn*

Rex Stewart and the Ellingtonians / Jul. 23, 1940-1946 / Original Jazz Classics ✦✦✦✦

★ **With Henri Chase** / Jun. 12, 1966 / Polydor ✦✦✦✦✦
Subtle, supple playing. —*Ron Wynn*

Sonny Stitt (Edward Stitt)

b. Feb. 2, 1924, Boston, MA, **d.** Jul. 22, 1982, Washington, DC
Sax (Alto and Tenor) / Bop, Groove
Charlie Parker has had many admirers, and his influence can be detected in numerous styles, but few have been as avid a disciple as Sonny Stitt. There was almost note-for-note imitation in several early Stitt solos, and the closeness remained until Stitt began de-emphasizing the alto in favor of the tenor, on which he artfully combined the influences of Parker and Lester Young. Stitt gradually developed his own sound and style, though he was never far from Parker on any alto solo. A wonderful blues and ballad player whose approach was one of the influences on John Coltrane, Stitt could rip through an uptempo bebop stanza, then turn around and play a shivering, captivating ballad. He was an alto saxophonist in Tiny Bradshaw's band during the early '40s, then joined Billy Eckstine's seminal big band in 1945, playing alongside fellow emerging bebop stars like Gene Ammons and Dexter Gordon. Stitt later played in Dizzy Gillespie's big band and sextet. He began on tenor and baritone in 1949 and at times was in a two-tenor unit with Ammons. He recorded with Bud Powell and J.J. Johnson for Prestige in 1949, then did albums on Prestige, Argo, and Verve in the '50s and '60s. Stitt led many combos in the '50s, and he rejoined Gillespie for a short period in the late '50s. After a brief stint with Miles Davis in 1960, he reunited with Ammons and for a while was in a three-tenor lineup with James Moody. During the '60s Stitt also recorded for Atlantic, cutting the transcendent *Stitt Plays Bird* that finally addressed the Parker question in epic fashion. He continued heading bands, though he joined the Giants of Jazz in the early '70s. This group included Gillespie, Art Blakey, Kai Winding, Thelonious Monk, and Al McKibbon. Stitt did more sessions in the '70s for Cobblestone, Muse, and others, among them

another definitive date, *Tune Up.* He continued playing and recording in the early '80s, recording for Muse, Sonet, and Who's Who in Jazz. He suffered a heart attack and died in 1982. —*Ron Wynn and Bob Porter*

Sonny Stitt with Bud Powell and J.J. Johnson / Oct. 17, 1949-Jan. 26, 1950 / Original Jazz Classics ✦✦✦✦
This superb CD reissues the complete output of three classic bop sessions, including five "new" alternate takes. Sonny Stitt (who plays tenor throughout) is heard in a quintet with trombonist J.J. Johnson, pianist John Lewis, bassist Nelson Boyd and drummer Max Roach (playing three Johnson compositions and the original version of John Lewis' "Afternoon in Paris") and in a quartet with the great pianist Bud Powell, bassist Curly Russell, and Max Roach. The latter two sessions are highlighted by rapid versions of "All God's Chillun Got Rhythm," "Strike Up the Band" and "Fine and Dandy." Highly recommended music. —*Scott Yanow*

Prestige First Sessions, Vol. 2 / Feb. 17, 1950-Aug. 14, 1951 / Prestige ✦✦✦✦
Sonny Stitt is heard in his early prime throughout this CD, sticking to tenor on all but two of the 24 selections. Few could play bebop with Stitt's sincerity, quick reflexes, and large vocabulary. He swings hard throughout the performances, most of which feature him as the only soloist. Three dull vocals aside (by the forgotten Teddy Williams and Larry Townsend), this gap-filling CD is highly recommended to fans of classic bebop. —*Scott Yanow*

Kaleidoscope / Oct. 8, 1950-Feb. 25, 1952 / Original Jazz Classics ✦✦✦✦
Some of Sonny Stitt's better early sessions are collected on this excellent CD. Stitt (switching between tenor, alto, and on two numbers baritone) is heard with a variety of small groups ranging from quartets to an octet with three trumpeters and is the main star throughout these boppish performances. Highlights include "Cherokee," "Liza," "This Can't Be Love," and "Stitt's It." Recommended. —*Scott Yanow*

At the Hi-Hat / Feb. 11, 1954 / Roulette ✦✦✦✦
For this CD Sonny Stitt is in excellent form. Recorded live at a Boston club, Stitt uses a local rhythm section (pianist Dean Earl, bassist Bernie Griggs, and drummer Marquis Foster) as he jams happily through a variety of standards. Stitt mostly switches between alto and tenor, but on "Tri-Horn Blues" he takes solos not only on both of those saxes but also on his rarely heard baritone. This CD gives a good all-around sampling of early Sonny Stitt. —*Scott Yanow*

● **Sonny Stitt Sits in with the Oscar Peterson Trio** / Oct. 10, 1957 & May 18, 1959 / Verve ✦✦✦✦
This CD combines a complete session that Sonny Stitt (doubling on alto and tenor) did with the 1959 Oscar Peterson Trio (which includes the pianist/leader, bassist Ray Brown, and drummer Ed Thigpen) and three titles from 1957 with Peterson, Brown, guitarist Herb Ellis, and drummer Stan Levey. The music very much has the feel of a jam session and, other than a themeless blues, all of the songs are veteran standards. Highlights of this fine effort include "I Can't Give You Anything but Love," "The Gypsy," "Scrapple from the Apple," "Easy Does It," and "I Remember You." Lots of cooking music. —*Scott Yanow*

Sonny Stitt / 1958 / Chess ✦✦✦

Sonny Stitt at the D.J. Lounge / Jun. 1961 / Chess ✦✦✦

☆ **Boss Tenors** / Aug. 27, 1961 / Verve ✦✦✦✦✦

Stitt Meets Brother Jack / Feb. 16, 1962 / Original Jazz Classics ✦✦✦✦
Sonny Stitt (who sticks on this CD reissue to tenor) meets up with organist Brother Jack McDuff (along with guitarist Eddie Diehl, drummer Art Taylor, and Ray Barretto on congas) for a spirited outing. Two standards ("All of Me" and "Time After Time") are performed with a variety of blues-based originals, and the music always swings in a soulful boppish way. Worth picking up although not essential. —*Scott Yanow*

Nuther Fu'ther / Feb. 19, 1962 / Prestige ✦✦✦
Fine soul-jazz with Jack McDuff (organ). —*Ron Wynn*

Boss Tenors in Orbit / Feb. 1962 / Verve ✦✦✦✦

Autumn in New York / 1962-Oct. 18, 1967 / Black Lion ✦✦✦

☆ **Stitt Plays Bird** / Jan. 29, 1963 / Atlantic ✦✦✦✦✦

Primitivo Soul / Dec. 31, 1963 / Prestige ✦✦✦
Excellent soul, jazz, and blues numbers by alto and tenor saxophonist Sonny Stitt, who plays with almost unrelenting energy and drive throughout this session. This was a typical date, but Stitt's earthy playing moved it beyond cliche and convention. —*Ron Wynn*

● **Soul People** / Aug. 25, 1964 / Prestige ✦✦✦✦
There are dozens of Sonny Stitt records available at any particular time; this CD reissue is one of the better ones. Stitt (mostly sticking to tenor) battles fellow tenor Booker Ervin with assistance from the fine organist Don Patterson and drummer Billy James on five selections and a ballad medley from 1964. Because both Stitt and Ervin always had very individual sounds, their tradeoffs are quite exciting and end up a draw. Among the "bonus" cuts of this CD are a feature for Patterson with a trio in 1966 ("There Will Never Be Another You") and a collaboration between Stitt,

Patterson, James, and guitarist Grant Green on a 1966 version of "Tune Up." Easily enjoyable and generally hard-swinging music. *— Scott Yanow*

☆ **Tune-Up!** / Feb. 8, 1972 / Muse ✦✦✦✦
Sonny Stitt recorded over 100 albums as a leader and several dozen in a quartet setting in his productive career, but this one ranks at the top. The bebop tenor and alto stylist is very inspired by the top-notch rhythm section (pianist Barry Harris, bassist Sam Jones, and drummer Alan Dawson) and has rarely sounded more heated than on "Tune Up," "Idaho," "Just Friends," and "Groovin' High." However it is his nine-minute jam on "I Got Rhythm" (which finds Stitt taking blazing solos on both tenor and alto) that is the high point of this essential set. *— Scott Yanow*

☆ **Constellation** / Jun. 27, 1972 / Muse ✦✦✦✦✦
Along with the previous *Tune Up!* this set (which has been reissued by Muse) is one of Sonny Stitt's greatest recordings. The bop master is stunning on most of the eight selections, particularly "Constellation," "Webb City," and "It's Magic," switching between alto and tenor and sounding quite creative. The rhythm section (pianist Barry Harris, bassist Sam Jones, and drummer Roy Brooks) is outstanding and, whether it be the ballad "Ghost of a Chance," Tadd Dameron's "Casbah," or "Topsy," this set has more than its share of great moments. *— Scott Yanow*

Sonny Stitt/12! / Dec. 12, 1972 / Muse ✦✦✦✦
Sonny Stitt was in prime form in the early '70s when he recorded two classics: *Tune Up!* and *Constellation. Sonny Stitt/12!* from a year later tends to get overlooked, but this LP is also one of the saxophonist's most rewarding recordings. Assisted by pianist Barry Harris, bassist Sam Jones, and drummer Louis Hayes, Stitt (switching between alto and tenor) is in superb form on five standards and two blues; highlights include "I Got It Bad," "Every Tub," and "Our Delight." This LP is worth searching for. *— Scott Yanow*

The Champ / Apr. 18, 1973 / Muse ✦✦✦

Last Stitt Sessions, Vols. 1 & 2 / Jun. 8, 1982-Jun. 9, 1982 / Muse ✦✦✦✦
It is difficult to believe, after listening to this two-CD set, that Sonny Stitt had only six weeks left in his life; he already had cancer but did not know it. Switching between tenor and alto, Stitt on the first disc is heard in top form with pianist Junior Mance, bassist George Duvivier, and drummer Jimmy Cobb, while the second CD (recorded the following day) adds trumpeter Bill Hardman and has Walter Davis in Mance's place. As was typical of Stitt's career, the music throughout is high-quality bebop with the saxophonist stretching out creatively over common chord changes. This double CD (a straight reissue of two single LPs) shows that Sonny Stitt went out on top. *— Scott Yanow*

Billy Strayhorn

b. Nov. 29, 1915, Dayton, OH, **d.** May 31, 1967, New York, NY
Piano / Swing
Billy Strayhorn made collaboration an art form; he combined with Duke Ellington on more than 200 numbers in the orchestra's book and enjoyed a creative empathy with him that has been alternately described as spooky, remarkable, and magic. From the time he submitted a piece to Ellington in 1938 and was contacted three months later, until his death in 1967, Strayhorn fuctioned as co-leader, arranger, pianist, confidant, and muse. Among his gems are "Take the 'A' Train," "Lush Life," "Something to Live For," "Day Dream," "After All," "Passion Flower," "Lotus Blossom," "Johnny Come Lately," "U.M.M.G.," and "Blood Count." Strayhorn found time to write, arrange, and participate in many extra-Ellington sessions with such sidemen as Cootie Williams, Barney Bigard, Johnny Hodges, Louie Bellson, the Coronets and Ellingtonians, Ben Webster, and Clark Terry, plus duos and trios with Ellington and an occasional album of his own. Strayhorn received extensive musical training, and the piece he submitted to Ellington surprised him in its depth and structure. The first Strayhorn number they cut was "Something to Live For," with Jean Eldridge's vocal in 1939. They did more Strayhorn that year, including "I'm Checkin' Out," "Goo'm Bye," and "Grievin'," which were co-written with Ellington; "Lost in Two Flats" by Barney Bigard; and an Ellington tribute to Strayhorn, "Weely (A Portrait of Billy Strayhorn)." He served briefly as pianist in Mercer Ellington's Orchestra before officially becoming Ellington's associate arranger and second pianist. Strayhorn helped with both ambitious pieces and pop material; these included "The Perfume Suite," "A Drum Is a Woman" and "Such Sweet Thunder." He directed the band for Ellington's 1963 production "My People." His final composition, "Blood Count," was sent to the band from the hospital where he died of cancer. The Ellington orchestra cut one of its most poignant albums in tribute, *And His Mother Called Him Bill.* Ellington played "Lotus Blossom" solo at the end of the session, while the musicians packed their gear. Other Strayhorn tributes have been recorded by several musicians, including Art Farmer and Marian McPartland. Joe Henderson won widespread acclaim for his 1992 Strayhorn tribute album, and Strayhorn was a prominent influence on Tadd Dameron. *—Ron Wynn*

Great Times! / Sep. 1950-Nov. 1950 / Original Jazz Classics ✦✦✦

● **Cue for Saxophone** / Apr. 14, 1959 / London ✦✦✦✦
Billy Strayhorn Sextet. Fine Strayhorn arrangements for session of top-flight Ellingtonians. Johnny Hodges (sax) takes honors. Reissue of 1959 date. *—Ron Wynn*

Lush Life / Jan. 14, 1964-Aug. 14, 1965 / Red Baron ✦✦✦✦
A 1992 reissue of a rare session issued under the name of noted arranger/composer Billy Strayhorn, providing the inspiration and material for a combo with Duke Ellington, trumpeters Cootie Williams and Cat Anderson, drummer Sam Woodyard, etc., and featuring his most famous composition. *—Ron Wynn*

Ira Sullivan

b. May 1, 1931, Washington, DC
Flute, Sax (Tenor, Soprano, Alto), Trumpet / Bop, Post-Bop
Ira Sullivan, who is equally skilled on trumpet and a variety of reeds, is one of the great talents in jazz. But due to his desire to be away from the spotlight, his contributions have often been overlooked. His father taught him the trumpet and his mother the saxophone. Sullivan was a key part of the Chicago jazz scene of the '50s, jamming with visiting all-stars and in 1956 spending some time with Art Blakey's Jazz Messengers. He settled in Florida in the early '60s, and, although he has been active locally, he emerges on the national jazz scene only on an irregular basis. His most notable association during the past 20 years was with Red Rodney in a brilliant (and fortunately well recorded) quintet that included pianist Garry Dial. Sullivan has retained an open-minded approach to music and has never been afraid to try new things. Virtually all of his recordings offer some surprises. *— Scott Yanow*

Nicky's Tune / Dec. 24, 1958 / Delmark ✦✦✦✦
The talented Ira Sullivan has recorded relatively few sessions throughout his career, considering his skills. This CD brings back his second full album as a leader, adding the previously unissued "Mock and Roll Blues" (a stomping tune) to the original five-song program. Sullivan, who sticks here exclusively to trumpet, is joined by the obscure tenor Nicky Hill, pianist Jodie Christian, bassist Victor Sproles, and drummer Wilbur Campbell. The music (two standards and four originals) is essentially straightahead bop and generally swings quite hard. *— Scott Yanow*

Bird Lives! / Mar. 12, 1962 / Vee-Jay ✦✦✦✦
Ira Sullivan's quintet played at a Charlie Parker Memorial concert in Chicago on Mar. 12, 1962, and the results (six selections) were originally released on a single LP. The release of this double CD greatly expanded the program. The multi-instrumentalist Ira Sullivan sticks to trumpet and fluegelhorn throughout, the legendary tenor Nicky Hill (who made very few recordings), has a rare chance to stretch out on record (combining touches of Coltrane and Booker Ervin with a full tone of his own), and it is interesting to hear some hints of the then-current free-jazz movement (particularly in the playing of bassist Don Garrett). Overall, a fine bop set. *—Scott Yanow*

● **The Incredible** / Jun. 1980 / Stash ✦✦✦✦
Multi-instrumentalist Ira Sullivan puts on an impressive display of technique as he plays several saxes, plus trumpet and flutes. His facility, solos, and spirit are what make this album interesting. *—Ron Wynn*

Maxine Sullivan (Marietta Williams)

b. May 13, 1911, Homestead, PA, **d.** Apr. 7, 1987, New York, NY
Vocals / Swing, Standards
A great singer, and engaging performer, Maxine Sullivan parlayed a subtle, yet undeniable sense of swing with distinctive phrasing and excellent interpretative qualities to become a fine jazz, standards, and pre-rock pop vocalist. She enjoyed success in the swing era, then repeated that success several eras later. Sullivan sang in clubs in Pittsburgh and on radio broadcasts. Her vocals and Claude Thornhill's arrangment of "Loch Lomond" in 1937 resulted in her first hit. That was followed by a series of folk novelty numbers like "Cockles and Mussels," and "If I Had a Rainbow Bow." But Sullivan at last landed a nationwide radio program with then-husband John Kirby. "Flow Gently Sweet Rhythm" aired Sunday afternoons in 1940 and was the only coast-to-coast radio show featuring Black performers. Sullivan even did some acting, appearing on stage in *Swinging the Dream* and in the films *Goin' Places* and *St. Louis Blues.* She toured with Benny Carter in 1941, then retired in 1942. Sullivan returned in the mid-'40s. After tours of England in 1948 and 1954, and another stage appearance in the 1953 play *Take a Giant Step,* Sullivan retired once more. She became a nurse, but came back again in 1958, this time both singing and playing valve trombone and fluegelhorn. She appeared at several festivals, then did sessions with the World's Greatest Jazz Band, Earl Hines, Ike Isaacs, Bob Wilber, and Dick Hyman. In the '80s Sullivan recorded swing standards for Concord, often working with Scott Hamilton. By the time she passed away a month shy of her 76th birthday, this subtle yet always lightly swinging and classy singer had completed 50 years in jazz. *—Ron Wynn*

The Biggest Little Band in the Land / Oct. 10, 1940-Jan. 20, 1941 / Circle ✦✦✦✦
This CD contains music recorded for the Lang-Worth Transcriptions by the John Kirby Sextet plus singer Maxine Sullivan. Actually Sullivan is only on five of the 18 songs, singing in her typically light and straightforward manner. The other selections feature the unique sextet (trumpeter Charlie Shavers, clarinetist Buster Bailey, altoist Russell Procope, pianist Billy Kyle, bassist John Kirby, and drummer O'Neil Spencer) performing a program heavy on adaptations of classical themes and novel melodies. Shavers in particular comes across well, and the set should please Kirby's fans. —*Scott Yanow*

● **Tribute to Andy Razaf** / Aug. 30, 1956 / DCC ✦✦✦✦
Maxine Sullivan always had a cheerful and subtly swinging style. This formerly rare release (originally on the Period label) finds her interpreting a dozen numbers that have the lyrics of Andy Razaf, including such classics as "Keeping Out of Mischief Now," "Stompin' at the Savoy," "Honeysuckle Rose," "Memories of You," and "Ain't Misbehavin'." Joined by a sextet reminiscent of John Kirby's group of 15 years earlier (and featuring such Kirby alumni as trumpeter Charlie Shavers and clarinetist Buster Bailey), Sullivan is in top form on this delightful session. —*Scott Yanow*

Good Morning, Life! / Nov. 13, 1983-Nov. 14, 1983 / Audiophile ✦✦✦✦
Nice sessions with the Loonis McGlohen quartet. —*Ron Wynn*

It Was Great Fun / 1983 / Audiophile ✦✦✦✦
Solid vocals, nice arrangements. —*Ron Wynn*

Uptown / Jan. 1985 / Concord Jazz ✦✦✦✦
Good workout with the Scott Hamilton (tenor sax) Quintet. —*Ron Wynn*

At Vine St. Live / Mar. 4, 1986-Mar. 5, 1986 / DRG ✦✦✦
Swingin' Sweet / Sep. 1986 / Concord Jazz ✦✦✦✦
Successful meeting with the Scott Hamilton (ts) Quintet. —*Ron Wynn*

Sun Ra (Herman "Sonny" Blount)
....
b. May 22, 1914, Birmingham, AL, **d.** May 30, 1993, Birmingham, AL
Piano, Keyboards / Avant-Garde, Free Jazz
Of all the jazz musicians, Sun Ra was probably the most controversial. He did not make it easy for people to take him seriously, for he surrounded his adventurous music with costumes and mythology that looked backwards toward ancient Egypt and forward into science fiction. In addition, Ra documented his music in very erratic fashion on his Saturn label, generally not listing recording dates and giving inaccurate personnel information so one could not really tell how advanced some of his innovations were. It has taken a lot of time to sort it all out (although Robert Campbell's Sun Ra discography has done a miraculous job). In addition, while there were times when Sun Ra's aggregation performed brilliantly, on other occasions they were badly out of tune and showcased absurd vocals. Near the end of his life, Ra was featuring plate twirlers and fire eaters.
Despite all of the trappings, Sun Ra was a major innovator. Born Sonny Blount in Birmingham, AL (although he used to claim he was from another planet), Ra led his own band for the first time in 1934. He freelanced at a variety of jobs in the Midwest, working as a pianist/arranger with Fletcher Henderson in 1946-47. He appeared on some obscure records as early as 1948 but really got started around 1953. Leading a big band (which he called the Arkestra) in Chicago, Ra started off playing advanced bop but was early on open to the influences of other cultures and experimenting with primitive electric keyboards and playing free long before the avant-garde got established. After moving to New York in 1961, Ra performed some of his most advanced work. In 1970 he relocated his group to Philadelphia, and in later years alternated free improvisations and mystical group chants with eccentric versions of swing tunes, sounding like a spaced-out Fletcher Henderson Orchestra. Many of his most important sidemen were with him on and off for decades (most notably John Gilmore on tenor, altoist Marshall Allen, and baritonist Pat Patrick). Ra, who recorded a pair of fine solo piano albums for JAI, has been well served by Evidence's extensive repackaging of many of his Saturn dates, which have at last been outfitted with correct dates and personnel details. —*Scott Yanow*

Sound Sun Pleasure / 1953 / Evidence ✦✦✦✦
Sun Ra's kaleidoscope of sounds was just taking shape in the '50s and early '60s when the 13 tracks comprising this CD were recorded. His Astro-Infinity Arkestra included several emerging musicians who would later become major stars, like baritone saxophonist Charles Davis, Bob Northern on fluegelhorn, and James Spaulding, who is featured on various reeds. The great jazz violinist Stuff Smith is even along on "Deep Purple," providing a dazzling, bluesy solo right at home in the Ra mix. —*Ron Wynn*

Super-Sonic Jazz / 1956 / Evidence ✦✦✦
Sun Song / Jul. 12, 1956 / Delmark ✦✦✦✦
Other than the title cut (a spacey electronic fantasy that concludes this CD reissue), the music on the early effort from Sun Ra and his Arkestra is

mostly pretty conventional. Although the leader offers some slightly left-of-center piano, Robert Herndon has a couple of colorful tympani solos, and there are some futuristic song titles (such as "Call for All Demons," "Street Named Hell," and "Brainville"), the music could otherwise pass for a typical "territory band" of the mid-'50s. Most notable among the soloists are tenor saxophonist John Gilmore (an influence on John Coltrane), baritonist Pat Patrick, and trombonist Julian Priester. This is a historic set that only hints in spots at Ra's upcoming innovations. —*Scott Yanow*

Sun Ra Visits Planet Earth / Intersteller Low Ways / 1956 / Evidence ✦✦✦✦
We Travel the Spaceways / Bad and Beautiful / 1956 / Evidence ✦✦✦✦
The opening numbers range from the humorous and futuristic bent of "Interplanetary Music" and "We Travel the Spaceways" to the more musically expansive "New Horizons" and "Space Loneliness." Trumpeter Phil Cochran and the superb horn section of Marshall Allen, John Gilmore, and Pat Patrick sometimes remain in the maze and sometimes explode with short but peppery solos. The other songs mix bop and swing tunes with more experimental fare like "Ankh" and "Exotic Two," where Patrick, Gilmore, Ra, and Allen soar while bassist Ronnie Boykins and drummer Tommy Hunter maintain the rhythmic center. —*Ron Wynn*

Angels and Demons at Play/The Nubians of Plutonia / 1956 / Evidence ✦✦✦✦
Sun Ra ambles between vigorous hard bop, ambitious, adventurous free jazz, and African and Afro-Latin material on the 15 selections featured on this set of '50s and early '60s tracks. The first half was recorded in 1956 and 1960 and includes originals from Ronnie Boykins and Julian Priester, plus futuristic organ from Ra on "Music from the World Tomorrow" and hard-blowing solos from John Gilmore and Marshall Allen. The second half consists of rehearsal tapes from 1960 with the Arkestra steadily progressing and moving beyond conventional jazz modes into multiple rhythms, chants, and twisting, roaring arrangements spiced by vividly expressive solos. Plus, like every other disc in the series, it is superbly remastered. —*Ron Wynn*

Sound of Joy / Nov. 1, 1957 / Delmark ✦✦✦✦
This reissue, prior to the release of many of Sun Ra's Saturn albums on Evidence CDs, was often thought of as Ra's second recording, although now several earlier dates have appeared. The music from Sun Ra's Chicago-based band of the '50s (some of the performances also appear on Evidence's *Planet Earth/Low Ways*) is quite interesting, for its ties to the bop and swing traditions are much more obvious than they would be in the near future. Ra's eccentric piano and occasional electric keyboard look forward as do some of the harmonies and Jim Herndon's colorful timpani. Two previously unissued cuts (which have also surfaced on an Evidence set) augment the original LP program. —*Scott Yanow*

Jazz in Silhouette / 1958 / Evidence ✦✦✦
Planet Earth/Interstellar Low / 1958-1960 / Evidence ✦✦✦✦
★ **The Nubians of Plutonia** / 1959 / Impulse ✦✦✦✦✦
Definitive themes from the Arkestra. Dig for this one. —*Michael G. Nastos*

Holiday for Soul Dance / 1960 / Evidence ✦✦✦✦
Sun Ra never concerned himself with the issues of innovation vs. preservation that seem to be the rage in current jazz circles. Instead, his music was both futuristic and classic, embracing the past and anticipating the future. A prime example is this fine eight-track collection of pre-rock standards done in 1968 and 1969. Of course, Ra didn't simply cover these numbers in a reverential manner; instead, he and the Astro-Infinity Arkestra stomp, romp, twist, strut, and cut through a collection ranging from "But Not for Me" to "Early Autumn" and "Body and Soul." —*Ron Wynn*

Fate in a Pleasant Mood / 1960 / Evidence ✦✦✦✦
Sun Ra left Chicago for New York in the early '60s, and half the sessions on this disc were done at the Choreographers' Workshop in New York during 1962 and 1963. The first half were done in Chicago with Marshall Allen and John Gilmore in the solo forefront on alto sax, flute, tenor sax, and clarinet. Ra's teeming piano, Ronnie Boykins' fluid, throbbing bass lines, and Jon Hardy's drums soar at the rhythmic core as the orchestra executed both short bursts and extensive dialogs. Ra turned even further outside on the second set; his space/futuristic concept was solidifying musically and his keyboard work growing more piercing and ethereal. —*Ron Wynn*

Cosmic Tones for Mental Therapy / Art Forms Of . . . / 1961 / Evidence ✦✦✦
★ **Other Planes of There** / 1964 / Evidence ✦✦✦✦✦
Sun Ra's suites and long pieces rank among the most challenging and compelling in jazz history. He would mix and match horn soloists, incorporate extensive polyrhythmic barrages, accents, textures, and sounds and cleverly weave voices, chants, and vocal effects in and out of the mix. The disc's 22-minute title cut was among his finest extended compositions and seems even more astonishing since it was recorded in 1964. The Solar Arkestra keeps surging ahead through bop numbers, light swing, an almost pop piece, and then a return to another long, rewarding final piece. The Evidence Sun Ra collection offers with each release more proof that Ra

belongs in the pantheon of master jazz composers alongside Ellington, Monk, and Mingus. —*Ron Wynn*

The Magic City / 1965 / Evidence ✦✦✦✦
It is safe to say that no city ever got the kind of tribute Sun Ra paid his Birmingham, AL, hometown with this 1965 selection. The 27-minute title cut ambles, clashes, and slides toward completion as Ra's movements, segues, and sections alternate between blistering dialogs and emphatic solos, especially Marshall Allen playing piccolo with the same abandon and spiraling intensity as an alto sax, flute, or oboe. But Ra leads them right back through another intense outing, the nearly 11-minute "The Shadow World." After these two pieces, the band sounds more relaxed on the last two cuts. —*Ron Wynn*

The Heliocentric Worlds of Sun Ra, Vol. 1 / Apr. 20, 1965 / ESP ✦✦✦
The Heliocentric Worlds of Sun Ra, Vol. 2 / Nov. 16, 1965 / ESP ✦✦✦

Monorails and Satellites / 1966 / Evidence ✦✦✦✦
Although he did not record nearly as much solo piano as he should have, the results were memorable whenever Sun Ra did take the keyboard spotlight. That was certainly the case on this 1966 date, with Ra showing the complete range of his styles and influences. There are rumbling boogie progressions and angular bop harmonies, bluesy passages, free sections, and even stride and Afro-Latin references. —*Ron Wynn*

● **Atlantis** / 1967 / Saturn ✦✦✦✦
Sun Ra was soaring far and wide on these late '60s sessions, most notably the 20-minute-plus title cut. This was one of his earliest dates on nothing but electric keyboards, and his manipulation of sounds, noise, whirling phrases, and rhythms was creative and innovative. The other shorter pieces move from somber, almost morose arrangements on *Mu* to the teaming beats of *Bimini* and the otherworldliness of both the Saturn and Impulse versions of *Yucatan*. As usual, Ra's band meshes hard bop, bebop, cool, free, and swing elements, with John Gilmore, Marshall Allen, and Company alternately wailing, colliding with, and complementing the master's dashing clavinet, synthesizer, and organ journeys. An essential and excellent set. —*Ron Wynn*

My Brother the Wind, Vol. 2 / 1969 / Evidence ✦✦✦✦
Sun Ra's synthesizer, organ and electric keyboard playing were the most underrated elements of his arsenal. His piano and electronic keyboard journeys were often viewed as gimmicky, clowning, or musically illiterate ramblings. Sadly, this ignorance was the prevailing view for much of his career. Now, in retrospect, Ra's playing is being celebrated. The remarkable phrases, rhythms, progressions, statements, and solos he offers throughout this 11-cut late-'60s and early-'70s session are a tribute to his understanding of the Moog synthesizer's possibilities and options. —*Ron Wynn*

Space Is the Place / 1972 / Evidence ✦✦

Cosmos / Aug. 1976 / Inner City ✦✦✦

Strange Celestial Road / 1987 / Rounder ✦✦✦

Blue Delight / Dec. 5, 1988 / A&M ✦✦✦✦
A fabulous date by the legendary Sun Ra, one of the few that he made for a major label. The production and mastering gave the group sound a full, gorgeous quality, while the quirky Ra riffs and solos, coupled with the usual explosive and animated work from the Arkestra members, made this a delight. —*Ron Wynn*

Somewhere Else / Dec. 1988-Nov. 1989 / Rounder ✦✦✦✦
Both small-group and larger Arkestra sessions are included on this recent anthology of late-'80s Sun Ra material. The tune "Priest" includes slashing drum support from Billy Higgins and Buster Smith, twin bass interplay from John Ore and Jerib Shahid, Julian Priester's whiplash trombone, and Ra's equally dynamic piano solos. Other numbers include appearances by Don Cherry on pocket trumpet, James Spaulding on alto sax, and flute teaming with fellow alto stylist Marshall Allen and tenor saxophonist John Gilmore, plus the vocal cries, swoops and hollers of June Tyson and Ra's delightful piano and swirling synthesizer. These selections show that Ra hadn't exhausted his creative faculties by the late '80s. —*Ron Wynn*

At the Village Vanguard / Nov. 1991 / Rounder ✦✦✦✦

Tribute to Stuff Smith / Sep. 1992 / Soul Note ✦✦✦✦
Forty years before recording this interesting CD, keyboardist Sun Ra made his debut on records on a duet with violinist Stuff Smith, playing a haunting version of "Deep Purple." For this CD (one of Ra's final sessions) the quartet workout with violinist Billy Bang finds Ra doing a new version of "Deep Purple" and performing tunes associated with Smith. Actually Ra was a bit hemmed in by the concept, and his conception of time was different than Bang's so there is a certain amount of tension in the music. Also, Billy Bang has a much rougher sound (and a freer style) than Stuff Smith, but the end results are well worth hearing. —*Scott Yanow*

Steve Swallow

b. Oct. 4, 1940, Fair Lawn, NJ
Bass / Post-Bop
Steve Swallow has long been many jazz critics' favorite electric bassist, for,

rather than playing his instrument in a rock-oriented manner, Swallow emphasizes the high notes and approaches the electric bass to an extent as if it were a guitar. He originally started on piano and trumpet before settling on the acoustic bass as a teenager. Swallow joined the Paul Bley trio in 1960, and with Bley was part of an avant-garde version of the Jimmy Giuffre 3 during 1960-62. Swallow recorded with George Russell and was a member of Art Farmer's quartet (1962-65), Stan Getz' band (1965-67), and an important edition of Gary Burton's quartet (1967-70). The latter group (starting with the addition of guitarist Larry Coryell) was actually one of the first fusion groups, and it was during that time that Swallow began playing electric bass; within a few years he stopped playing acoustic altogether. Swallow spent a few years in the early '70s living in Northern California and playing mostly locally. Since the late '70s he has been closely associated with Carla Bley's groups, although he occasionally works on other projects (including a reunion of the Jimmy Giuffre 3). Steve Swallow has also proved to be a talented composer, with "Eiderdown," "Falling Grace," "General Mojo's well Laid Plan," and "Hotel Hello" being among his better-known pieces. —*Scott Yanow*

● **Swallow** / Sep. 1991-Nov. 1991 / ECM ✦✦✦✦
All nine cuts were written by this premier electric bass guitarist and performed by a sextet with guests Gary Burton (vibes) and John Scofield (guitar). —*Michael G. Nastos*

Real Book / Dec. 1993 / ECM ✦✦✦✦

Gabor Szabo

b. Mar. 8, 1936, Budapest, Hungary, **d.** Feb. 26, 1982, Budapest, Hungary
Guitar / Post-Bop, Hungary, Crossover
Gabor Szabo was one of the most original guitarists to emerge in the '60s, mixing his Hungarian folk music heritage and his distinctive sound with advanced jazz settings. He started on guitar when he was 14 and was working in Hungary (composing for films and TV) when the Soviet invasion of 1956 inspired him to defect to the US. Szabo attended Berklee College (1957-59) and made a major impact during his years (1961-65) with the Chico Hamilton Quartet/Quintet. Szabo performed with Charles Lloyd and Gary McFarland and was at his peak with his 1966-68 group, a unit that featured the talented Jimmy Stewart on second guitar. In the '70s Szabo became more involved in studio work, commercial recordings, and trying to allow a strong rock influence in his music without losing his musical personality; he headed the fusion group First Circle starting in 1975. But his later years were rather directionless, and Gabor Szabo returned to his homeland when he died just short of his 46th birthday. —*Scott Yanow*

★ **The Sorcerer** / Apr. 14, 1967-Apr. 15, 1967 / Impulse ✦✦✦✦✦
Excellent playing; gypsy influences; 1990 reissue. —*Ron Wynn*

Greatest Hits / MCA ✦✦✦

Jamaaladeen Tacuma

b. Jun. 11, 1956, Hempstead, NY
Bass / Free Funk
Since his emergence with Ornette Coleman's Prime Time in the mid-'70s, Jamaaladeen Tacuma has been one of the top electric bassists in a style of music that could be called "free funk." Growing up in Philadelphia, Tacuma (who before he converted to Islam was known as Rudy McDaniel) played with Charles Earland. Only 19 when he joined Ornette in 1975, his ability to combine funky rhythms with free jazz helped give Prime Time its distinctive (if overcrowded) sound. Tacuma's own solo career has been a bit erratic, alternating great moments with throwaway tracks. He also has played with a wide variety of advanced musicians (including James "Blood" Ulmer, Olu Dara, Julius Hemphill, and David Murray) but has yet to fulfill his great potential. —*Scott Yanow*

● **Show Stopper** / 1982-1983 / Gramavision ✦✦✦✦
The five-piece electric band shows many positive and eclectic forces rooted in jazz but not stuck in the past. Includes "Bird of Paradise" with the Ebony String Quartet. The title track with Olu Dara and Julius Hemphill is a treat of all-out contempo-bop. Other cameos are by Blood Ulmer on guitar and Cornell Rochester on drums. This is a fun album. —*Michael G. Nastos*

Music World / 1986 / Gramavision ✦✦✦

Jukebox / Oct. 1988 / Gramavision ✦✦✦

Boss of the Bass / 1993 / Gramavision ✦✦

Horace Tapscott

b. Apr. 6, 1934, Houston, TX
Piano / Avant-Garde, Post-Bop
Horace Tapscott has long been Los Angeles' top undiscovered legend, a brilliant pianist who has thus far recorded for only the tiniest (and most obscure) labels. A powerful player perfectly able to interpret bop but heard at his best playing his own rhythmic originals with his quartet, Tapscott has had an original style for 30 years, but his music is surprisingly accessible, even at its most passionate. He moved with his family to Los Angeles

in 1945 and was originally a trombonist. Tapscott caught the tail-end of the legendary Central Avenue Scene (his early associates included Eric Dolphy and Don Cherry) and played with Gerald Wilson's Orchestra during 1950-51. While in the Air Force (1953-57), he took up the piano, which was fortunate, because after touring with Lionel Hampton (1959-61), an automobile accident forced him to give him up the trombone. Tapscott returned to Los Angeles in 1961, formed the Pan Afrikan Peoples Arkestra, and has been a major part of the local jazz community ever since. Among his most famous sidemen have been altoist Arthur Blythe and tenor saxophonist Azar Lawrence. Tapscott wrote the arrangements for the late-'60s Sonny Criss album *Sonny's Dream* and shared a Flying Dutchman album (reissued on CD by Novus as *West Coast Hot*) with the John Carter/Bobby Bradford Quartet. Otherwise his recordings have been made for Nimbus, along with a pair of live sessions for Hat Art. Tapscott's longtime quartet with saxophonist Michael Sessions, bassist Roberto Miranda, and drummer Fritz Wise remains undocumented. —*Scott Yanow*

● **The Dark Tree, Vol. 1** / Dec. 14, 1989-Dec. 17, 1989 / Hat Art ✦✦✦✦
Pianist Horace Tapscott has long been Los Angeles' great undiscovered legend. A very original stylist capable of playing bop, free jazz or anything in between, Tapscott does not sound like anyone else. Unfortunately he has made few recordings through the years and thus far none with his regular working band of the past decade, but his two Hat Art CDs partly fill the gap. Tapscott was teamed during a stint at Catalina's in Hollywood with clarinetist John Carter, bassist Cecil McBee, and drummer Andrew Cyrille. The lengthy renditions they give three of the pianist's compositions (along with trombonist Thurman Green's "One for Lately") allows listeners outside of Los Angeles a rare opportunity to hear Tapscott stretching out on records; his playing and that of the all-stars is near peak form. —*Scott Yanow*

● **The Dark Tree, Vol. 2** / Dec. 14, 1989-Dec. 17, 1989 / Hat Art ✦✦✦✦
Pianist Horace Tapscott, a greatly under-recognized but very original pianist, is showcased even more on this set than on the first volume, for clarinetist John Carter is only on two of the five selections (four of which are Tapscott originals). With bassist Cecil McBee and drummer Andrew Cyrille propelling the all-star group, Tapscott's percussive yet generally melodic style is well featured. But why doesn't some label record his regular working group? —*Scott Yanow*

Aiee! The Phantom / Jun. 1995 / Arabesque Jazz ✦✦✦✦

Buddy Tate (George Holmes Tate)

b. Feb. 22, 1913, Sherman, TX
Clarinet, Sax (Tenor) / Swing, Groove
One of the more individual tenors to emerge from the swing era, the distinctive Buddy Tate came to fame as Herschel Evans' replacement with Count Basie's Orchestra. Earlier he had picked up valuable experience playing with Terrence Holder (1930-33), Count Basie's original Kansas City band (1934), Andy Kirk (1934-35), and Nat Towles (1935-39). With Basie again during 1939-48, Tate held his own with such major tenors as Lester Young, Don Byas, Illinois Jacquet, Lucky Thompson, and Paul Gonsalves. After a period freelancing with Hot Lips Page, Lucky Millinder, and Jimmy Rushing (1950-52), Tate led his own crowd-pleasing group for 21 years (1953-74) at Harlem's Celebrity Club. During this period Tate also took time out to record in a variety of settings (including with Buck Clayton and Milt Buckner), and he was one of the stars of John Hammond's Spirituals to Swing concert of 1967. Tate has kept busy since the Celebrity Club association ended, recording frequently, co-leading a band with Paul Quinichette in 1975, playing and recording in Canada with Jay McShann and Jim Galloway, visiting Europe many times, and performing at jazz parties; he was also a favorite sideman of Benny Goodman's in the late '70s. Although age had taken its toll, in the mid-'90s Buddy Tate played and recorded with both Lionel Hampton and the Statesmen of Jazz. —*Scott Yanow*

Tate-a-Tate / Oct. 18, 1960 / Original Jazz Classics ✦✦✦✦
Bubbly modern mainstream is found on *Tate-a-Tate*, a date with Buddy Tate leading a group with (Clark Terry, trumpet; Tommy Flanagan, piano; Larry Gates, bass; Art Taylor, drums) over six tracks. Terry is right on the money and sounding '60s fresh. —*Bob Rusch, Cadence*

Buddy Tate and His Buddies / Jun. 3, 1973 / Chiaroscuro ✦✦✦

★ **Hard Blowin'** / Aug. 25, 1978-Aug. 26, 1978 / Muse ✦✦✦✦✦
Muse has released at least six albums of material recorded at Sandy's Jazz Revival in Massachusetts during a week in 1978. This is veteran tenor Buddy Tate's most rewarding album from the engagement and a fine all-around showcase. Accompanied by pianist Ray Bryant, bassist George Duvivier, and drummer Alan Dawson, Tate stretches out on four familiar standards and shows listeners that he really had one of the more distinctive tenor sounds of the swing era. Recommended. —*Scott Yanow*

Scott's Buddy / 1981 / Concord Jazz ✦✦✦

Quartet / Oct. 1983 / Sackville ✦✦✦

Just Jazz / Apr. 28, 1984 / Reservoir ✦✦

Art Tatum

b. Oct. 13, 1909, Toledo, OH, **d.** Nov. 5, 1956, Los Angeles, CA
Piano / Swing
Art Tatum was among the most extraordinary of all jazz musicians, a pianist with wondrous technique who could not only play ridiculously rapid lines with both hands (his 1933 solo version of "Tiger Rag" sounds as if there were three pianists jamming together!) but was harmonically 30 years ahead of his time; all pianists have to deal to a certain extent with Tatum's innovations in order to be taken seriously. Able to play stride, swing, and boogie-woogie with speed and complexity that could only previously be imagined, Tatum's quick reflexes and boundless imagination kept his improvisations filled with fresh (and sometimes futuristic) ideas that put him way ahead of his contemporaries.

Born nearly blind, Tatum gained some formal piano training at the Toledo School of Music but was largely self-taught. Although influenced a bit by Fats Waller and the semi-classical pianists of the '20s, there is really no explanation for where Tatum gained his inspiration and ideas. He first played professionally in Toledo in the mid-'20s and had a radio show during 1929-30. In 1932 Tatum traveled with singer Adelaide Hall to New York and made his recording debut accompanying Hall (as one of two pianists!). But for those who had never heard him in person, it was his solos of 1933 (including "Tiger Rag") that announced the arrival of a truly major talent. In the '30s Tatum spent periods working in Cleveland, Chicago, New York, Los Angeles, and (in 1938) England. Although he led a popular trio with guitarist Tiny Grimes (later Everett Barkedale) and bassist Slam Stewart in the mid-'40s, Tatum spent most of his life as a solo pianist who could always scare the competition. Some observers criticized him for having too much technique (is such a thing possible?), working out and then keeping the same arrangements for particular songs, and for using too many notes, but those minor reservations pale when compared to Tatum's reworkings of such tunes as "Yesterdays," "Begin the Beguine," and even "Humoresque." Although he was not a composer, Tatum's rearrangements of standards made even warhorses sound like new compositions.

Tatum, who recorded for Decca throughout the '30s and for Capitol in the late '40s, starred at the Esquire Metropolitan Opera House concert of 1944 and appeared briefly in 1947 in his only film, *The Fabulous Dorseys* (leading a jam session on a heated blues). He recorded extensively for Norman Granz in the '50s, both solo and with all-star groups. All of the music has been reissued by Pablo on seven-CD and six-CD box sets. His premature death from uremia has not resulted in any loss of fame, for Art Tatum's recordings still have the ability to scare modern pianists! —*Scott Yanow*

☆ **Piano Starts Here** / Mar. 21, 1933 & 1949 / Columbia/Legacy ✦✦✦✦✦
There are many Art Tatum records currently available, but this is the one to pull out to amaze friends. This CD consists of Tatum's first studio session as a leader (which resulted in "Tea for Two," "St. Louis Blues," "Tiger Rag," and "Sophisticated Lady") and a remarkable solo concert performance from the spring of 1949. While "Tiger Rag" dwarfs everything else, the live set is highlighted by a very adventurous, yet seemingly effortless exploration of "Yesterdays," a ridiculously rapid "I Know That You Know," and the hard-cooking "Tatum Pole Boogie." This is an essential set of miraculous music that cannot be praised highly enough. —*Scott Yanow*

● **Art Tatum (1932-1934)** / Mar. 1933-Oct. 1934 / Classics ✦✦✦✦
This comprehensive CD contains Art Tatum's very first recording (a broadcast version of "Tiger Rag"), four selections in which he accompanies singer Adelaide Hall (along with a second pianist!) and then his first 20 solo sides. To call this virtuosic piano style remarkable would be a major understatement; he has to be heard to be believed. —*Scott Yanow*

Art Tatum (1934-1940) / Oct. 1934-Jul. 1940 / Classics ✦✦✦✦

☆ **Classic Piano Solos (1934-39)** / 1934-1939 / GRP ✦✦✦✦✦
This excellent CD reissues all of Tatum's early Decca piano solos cut at three sessions in 1934 and one in 1937. He was decades ahead of his contemporaries not only in technique but in harmonic ideas. Highlights of this very impressive set include "Emaline," "After You've Gone," "The Shout," two versions of "Liza," and "The Sheik of Araby." —*Scott Yanow*

Standard Transcriptions / Dec. 1935-1943 / Music & Arts ✦✦✦✦
On this double-CD there are 61 solo piano performances by Art Tatum, the majority of which are quite wondrous. Tatum is featured in 1935, 1938, 1939, and 1943 radio transcriptions. The earlier tunes are particularly startling, as Tatum really rips into such numbers as "After You've Gone," "Tiger Rag," "I Would Do Anything for You," and his own "The Shout." His advanced harmonies (some of which have still not been surpassed), remarkable speed, and incredible technique will amaze most listeners. Highly recommended. —*Scott Yanow*

Standards / 1938-1939 / Black Lion ✦✦✦✦
This Black Lion CD features brilliant piano solos originally cut as noncommercial radio transcriptions during 1938-39. Duplicating part of Tatum's Music & Arts double CD, *Standards* features a great deal of magic from the remarkable virtuoso. —*Scott Yanow*

Solos (1940) / Feb. 22, 1940-Jul. 26, 1940 / MCA/Decca ✦✦✦✦
MCA's short-lived Decca CD-reissue program put out this gem, all of
Tatum's piano solos from 1940, including two versions of the previously
unknown "Sweet Emalina, My Gal." Some of the routines on these standards were a bit familiar by now (this "Tiger Rag" pales next to his 1933
version) but are no less exciting and still sound seemingly impossible to
play. — *Scott Yanow*

The V-Discs / Jan. 18, 1944-Jan. 21, 1946 / Black Lion ✦✦✦✦
This Black Lion CD mostly features the phenomenal Tatum playing solo
during 1945-46, really digging into a variety of standards. A rare version of
"Sweet Lorraine" (with bassist Oscar Pettiford and drummer Sid Catlett in
1944), and two numbers with his 1945 trio (featuring guitarist Tiny
Grimes and bassist Slam Stewart) round out this excellent CD. — *Scott
Yanow*

● **The Complete Capitol Recordings, Vol. 1** / Jul. 13, 1949-Dec. 20, 1952 /
Capitol ✦✦✦✦
Tatum recorded 20 piano solos in 1949 and eight selections with his 1952
trio (which included guitarist Everett Barksdale and bassist Slam Stewart)
for Capitol. Ten solos and four trios are included on each of the two CDs in
this "complete" series; he can be heard here at the height of his powers. (He
never did decline, creating miraculous variations of standards that still
amaze today's pianists.) — *Scott Yanow*

● **The Complete Capitol Recordings, Vol. 2** / Sep. 29, 1949-Dec. 20, 1952
/ Capitol ✦✦✦✦
On the second of two CDs, Art Tatum is heard playing solo in 1949 on ten
standards and interacting with his 1952 trio (which included guitarist Everett Barksdale and bassist Slam Stewart) during four numbers. Tatum
always had the ability to amaze fellow pianists (not to mention fans) and
there are plenty of remarkable moments in this fine set. — *Scott Yanow*

The Complete Pablo Solo Masterpieces / Dec. 28, 1953-Jan. 19, 1955 /
Pablo ✦✦✦✦
During four marathon recording sessions in 1953-55, Norman Granz
recorded Art Tatum playing 119 standards, enough music for a dozen LPs.
The results have been recently reissued separately on eight CDs and on
this very full seven-CD box set. Frankly, Tatum did no real advance preparation for this massive project, sticking mostly to concise melodic variations
of standards, some of them virtual set pieces formed over the past two
decades. Since there are few uptempo performances, the music in this
series has a certain sameness after a while but, heard in small doses, it is
quite enjoyable. A special bonus on this box (and not on the individual volumes) are four numbers taken from a 1956 Hollywood Bowl concert.
— *Scott Yanow*

☆ **The Complete Pablo Group Masterpieces** / Jun. 25, 1954-Sep. 11, 1956
/ Pablo ✦✦✦✦✦
Tatum spent most of his career as a solo pianist; in fact it was often said
that he was such an unpredictable virtuoso that it would be difficult for
other musicians to play with him. Producer Norman Granz sought to
prove that the theory was false, so between 1954 and 1956 he extensively
recorded Tatum with a variety of other classic jazzmen, resulting originally
in nine LPs of material that is now available separately as eight CDs and
on this very full six-CD box set. In contrast to the massive solo Tatum sessions that Granz also recorded during this period, the group sides have
plenty of variety and exciting moments, which is not too surprising when
one considers that Tatum was teamed in a trio with altoist Benny Carter
and drummer Louie Bellson; with trumpeter Roy Eldridge, clarinetist
Buddy DeFranco, and tenor saxophonist Hen Webster in separate quartets;
in an explosive trio with vibraphonist Lionel Hampton and drummer
Buddy Rich; with a sextet including Hampton, Rich, and trumpeter Harry
"Sweets" Edison; and on a standard trio session. — *Scott Yanow*

Art Taylor

b. Apr. 6, 1929, New York, NY, **d.** Feb. 6, 1995
Drums / Bop, Hard Bop
One of the great drummers of the '50s, Art Taylor was on a countless number of hard-bop and jam session-styled sessions. His first important gig
was with Howard McGhee in 1948, and this was followed by associations
with Coleman Hawkins (1950-51), Buddy DeFranco (1952), Bud Powell
(1953 and 1955-57), and George Wallington (1954-56). Taylor seemed to
live in Prestige's studios during the second half of the '50s, although he
found time to lead his Wailers, visit Europe with Donald Byrd in 1958, gig
and record with Miles Davis, and play with Thelonious Monk (including
his acclaimed Town Hall concert) in 1959. In 1963 Taylor moved to Europe,
where he spent most of the next 20 years (living mostly in France and Belgium), playing with Europeans and such Americans as Dexter Gordon and
Johnny Griffin. He interviewed scores of his colleagues and collected many
of the insightful discussions in his very readable book *Notes and Tones*
(which was re-released in 1993). After returning to the US, Taylor resumed
his freelancing. In the early '90s he organized a new version of the Wailers
which, during its short existence before his death, temporarily filled the
gap left by the end of the Jazz Messengers. — *Scott Yanow*

● **Taylor's Wailers** / Feb. 25, 1956-Mar. 22, 1957 / Original Jazz Classics
✦✦✦✦
Five of the six selections on this CD reissue feature drummer Art Taylor in
an all-star sextet of mostly young players: trumpeter Donald Byrd, altoist
Jackie McLean, Charlie Rouse on tenor, pianist Ray Bryant, and bassist
Wendell Marshall. Among the high points of the 1957 hard-bop date are
the original version of Bryant's popular "Cubano Chant" and strong renditions of two Thelonious Monk tunes ("Off Minor" and "Well, You Needn't")
cut just prior to the pianist/composer's discovery by the jazz public. Bryant
is the most mature of the soloists, but the three horn players were already
starting to develop their own highly individual sounds. The remaining
track (a version of Jimmy Heath's "C.T.A.") is played by the quartet of Taylor,
tenor saxophonist John Coltrane, pianist Red Garland, and bassist Paul
Chambers and is a leftover (although a good one) from another session.
— *Scott Yanow*

Taylor's Tenors / Jun. 3, 1959 / Original Jazz Classics ✦✦✦✦
Drummer Art Taylor heads a quintet for a fine jam-session-flavored session featuring the tenors of Charlie Rouse (about the time he joined Thelonious Monk's Quartet) and Frank Foster (then with Count Basie), along
with pianist Walter Davis and bassist Sam Jones. The repertoire on this CD
reissue (which was originally recorded for Prestige's New Jazz subsidiary)
includes two Monk tunes that are ideal for jamming ("Rhythm-Aning" and
"Straight No Chaser"), Jackie McLean's "Fidel" (which is given a memorable performance), and originals by Rouse, Davis, and Taylor. All in all this
is a loose and easily enjoyable hard-bop date. — *Scott Yanow*

Mr. A. T. / 1991 / Enja ✦✦✦✦
Drummer Art Taylor, who spent many years in Europe, re-emerged as an
important bandleader with this Enja CD. Taylor's group (called "Taylor's
Wailers") features four Young Lions: the fine tenor Willie Williams, altoist
Abraham Burton (most heavily influenced by his teacher Jackie McLean),
pianist Marc Cary, and bassist Tyler Mitchell, in addition to the drummer/
leader. On a variety of tunes from the '50s and '60s (highlighted by "Hi-Fly,"
"Soul Eyes," and "Gingerbread Boy") the musicians play some high-quality
modern hard bop. Enjoyable music. — *Scott Yanow*

Wailin' at the Vanguard / Aug. 1992 / Verve ✦✦✦✦

Billy Taylor

b. Jul. 21, 1921, Greenville, NC
Piano / Bop, Swing, Hard Bop
Billy Taylor has been such an articulate spokesman for jazz, and his profiles on CBS' "Sunday Morning" television program (where he has been a
regular since 1981) are so successful at introducing jazz to a wider audience that sometimes one can forget how talented a pianist he has been for
the past half-century. While not an innovator, Taylor has been flexible
enough to play swing, bop, and more advanced styles while always retaining his own musical personality. After graduating from Virginia State College in 1942, he moved to New York and played with such major musicians
as Ben Webster, Eddie South, Stuff Smith (with whom he recorded in
1944), and Slam Stewart. In 1951 he was the house pianist at Birdland, and
soon afterward Taylor formed the first of his many trios. He helped found
the Jazzmobile in 1965, and in 1969 became the first Black band director
for a network television series ("The David Frost Show"). In 1975 he earned
a doctorate at the University of Massachusetts, and he both founded and
served as director for the popular radio program "Jazz Alive." — *Scott
Yanow*

Billy Taylor Trio / Nov. 18, 1952-Dec. 29, 1953 / Prestige ✦✦✦✦
Two albums by pianist Billy Taylor are combined on this single CD reissue.
With fine backing from bassist Earl May and drummer Charlie Smith, Taylor is tasteful, swinging, and creative within the boundaries of bop and
swing on this early set, among his first dates as a leader and excellent
examples of his already individual style. — *Scott Yanow*

● **My Fair Lady Loves Jazz** / Jan. 8, 1957-Feb. 5, 1957 / Impulse ✦✦✦✦
Recorded at a time when *My Fair Lady* was a big Broadway hit (but a few
years before it became a film), this CD reissue brings back one of the very
best jazz interpretations of the classic score. The focus throughout is on the
Billy Taylor trio (which included bassist Earl May and drummer Ed Thigpen), but Quincy Jones' arrangements for the seven horns are quite memorable. There is room for short solos from such players as trumpeter Ernie
Royal, trombonist Jimmy Cleveland, altoist Anthony Ortega, and baritonist
Gerry Mulligan, and their presence clearly inspires pianist Taylor to some
of his finest playing. Highly recommended. — *Scott Yanow*

Billy Taylor with Four Flutes / Jul. 20, 1959 / Original Jazz Classics
✦✦✦✦
In the '50s, pianist Billy Taylor was best known for his work with his trios.
For this Riverside set (reissued on CD in the *OJC* series) Taylor tried some-
thing different, writing arrangements for four flutists (including Frank
Wess, Herbie Mann, and Jerome Richardson), his rhythm section, and the
congas of Chino Pozo. The flutists get their opportunities to solo, and the
music (which includes "The Song Is Ended," "St. Thomas," "Oh Lady Be
Good," "How About You," and four of Taylor's originals) is essentially bop,

but the unusual instrumentation gives the set its own personality. Enjoyable music that certainly stands out from the crowd. *—Scott Yanow*

White Nights and Jazz in Leningrad / Jun. 13, 1988-Jun. 14, 1988 / Taylor Made ◆◆◆◆
Trio. Latter-day piano date, fine solos. *—Ron Wynn*

Solo / Aug. 1, 1988-Aug. 2, 1988 / Taylor Made ◆◆◆◆
Noted authority and journalist shows he's a super soloist. *—Ron Wynn*

It's a Matter of Pride / 1993 / GRP ◆◆◆◆
This is a particularly well constructed session by pianist Billy Taylor, who is featured in a combo with bassist Christian McBride, drummer Marvin "Smitty" Smith, the congas of Ray Mantilla, and, on three songs, tenor saxophonist Stanley Turrentine; Grady Tate also contributes two warm ballad vocals. All nine songs were composed by Taylor (including three pieces taken from a more extended work in tribute to Martin Luther King, Jr.), and the results are melodic, boppish, and swinging. *—Scott Yanow*

Cecil Taylor

b. Mar. 15, 1929, New York, NY
Piano / Avant-Garde, Free Jazz
Soon after he first emerged in the mid-'50s, pianist Cecil Taylor was the most advanced improviser in jazz; four decades later, he is still the most radical. Although in his early days he used some standards as vehicles for improvisation, since the early '60s Taylor has stuck exclusively to originals. To simplify describing his style, one could say that Taylor's intense atonal percussive approach involves playing the piano as if it were a set of drums. He generally emphasizes dense clusters of sound played with remarkable technique and endurance, often during marathon performances. Suffice it to say that Cecil Taylor's music is not for everyone!

Taylor started piano lessons at the age of six and attended the New York College of Music and the New England Conservatory. His early influences included Duke Ellington and Dave Brubeck, but from the start he sounded original. Early gigs included work with groups led by Johnny Hodges and Hot Lips Page, but, after forming his quartet in the mid-'50s (which originally included Steve Lacy on soprano, bassist Buell Neidlinger, and drummer Dennis Charles), Taylor was never a sideman again. The group played at the Five Spot Cafe in 1956 for six weeks and performed at the 1957 Newport Jazz Festival (which was recorded by Verve), but, despite occasional records, work was scarce. In 1960 Taylor recorded extensively for Candid under Neidlinger's name (by then the quartet featured Archie Shepp on tenor) and the next year he sometimes substituted in the play *The Connection*. By 1962 Taylor's quartet featured his longtime associate Jimmy Lyons on alto and drummer Sunny Murray. He spent six months in Europe. Albert Ayler worked with Taylor's group for a time, although no recordings resulted, but upon his return to the US Taylor did not work again for almost a year. Even with the rise of free jazz, his music was considered too advanced. In 1964 Taylor was one of the founders of the Jazz Composer's Guild, and in 1968 he was featured on a record by the Jazz Composer's Orchestra. In the mid-'60s Taylor recorded two very advanced sets for Blue Note, but it was generally a lean decade.

Things greatly improved starting in the '70s. Taylor taught for a time at the University of Wisconsin in Madison, Antioch College, and Glassboro State College. He recorded more frequently, and European tours became common. After being awarded a Guggenheim Fellowship in 1973, the pianist's financial difficulties were eased a bit; he even performed at the White House (during Jimmy Carter's administration) in 1979. A piano duet concert with Mary Lou Williams was a fiasco, but a collaboration with drummer Max Roach was quite successful. Taylor started incorporating some of his eccentric poetry into his performances, and, unlike most musicians, he has not mellowed with age! The death of Jimmy Lyons in 1986 was a major blow, but Taylor has remained quite active, never compromising his musical vision. His forbidding music is still decades ahead of its time. *—Scott Yanow*

Jazz Advance / Dec. 10, 1955 / Blue Note ◆◆◆◆
A 1991 reissue of a super set, one of Taylor's best groups with Steve Lacy (sax). *—Ron Wynn*

Looking Ahead / Jun. 9, 1958 / Original Jazz Classics ◆◆◆
☆ **Complete Candid Recordings of Cecil Taylor** / Oct. 12, 1960-Jan. 10, 1961 / Mosaic ◆◆◆◆◆
The sessions on the four discs on this first-rate Mosaic box set were done in 1960 and 1961 for the short-lived Candid label. Taylor's concept had not yet evolved into a finished package; he wasn't always sure where he was going. There are solos that begin in one direction, break in the middle, and conclude in another. Tenor saxophonist Archie Shepp often sounds unsure about what to play and whether to try and interact or establish his own direction. At the same time, there is plenty of exceptional playing from Taylor, Shepp, and the drum/bass combination of Buell Neidlinger and Dennis Charles. You cannot honestly say everything works on these four discs, but there is never a dull moment. It won't please everyone, but listeners ready for a challenge should step right up. *—Ron Wynn*

New York City R&B / Jan. 9, 1961-Jan. 10, 1961 / Candid ◆◆◆◆
☆ **Unit Structures** / May 19, 1966 / Blue Note ◆◆◆◆◆
The place to start checking out Taylor's amazing style. *—Ron Wynn*

Conquistador / Oct. 6, 1966 / Blue Note ◆◆◆◆
Smashing piano, intense compositions. *—Ron Wynn*

★ **Great Concert of Cecil Taylor** / Jul. 29, 1969 / Prestige ◆◆◆◆◆
Box set with Taylor in searing live concert alongside Sam Rivers (sax) and Jimmy Lyons (alto). Three discs of amazing playing. *—Ron Wynn*

Indent / Mar. 1973 / Freedom ◆◆◆◆

Silent Tongues / Jul. 2, 1974 / Freedom ◆◆◆◆
Lambasting, attacking piano solos. *—Ron Wynn*

Air Above Mountains . . . / 1976 / Enja ◆◆◆◆
Bursting, dynamic piano solos. *—Ron Wynn*

Dark Unto Themselves / Jun. 18, 1976 / Enja ◆◆◆◆
The Cecil Taylor Unit on a 1990 reissue of a pulsating 1976 set. *—Ron Wynn*

★ **Unit** / Apr. 3, 1978-Apr. 6, 1978 / New World ◆◆◆◆◆
A sextet, this is as close to a definitive ensemble as Taylor has launched. With Jimmy Lyons (sax), Raphe Malik (trumpet), Ramsey Ameen (violin), Sirone (bass), and R. Shannon Jackson (drums). It runs 60 minutes on vinyl, including a 30-minute "Holiday en Masque." *—Michael G. Nastos*

Historic Concerts / Dec. 15, 1979 / Soul Note ◆◆◆◆
Great duo with Max Roach on drums. *—Ron Wynn*

Jack Teagarden (Weldon Leo Teagarden)

b. Aug. 29, 1905, Vernon, TX, **d.** Jan. 15, 1964, New Orleans, LA
Trombone, Vocals / Dixieland, Swing
One of the classic giants of jazz, Jack Teagarden was not only the top prebop trombonist (playing his instrument with the ease of a trumpeter) but one of the best jazz singers, too. He was such a fine musician that his younger brother Charlie, an excellent trumpeter, was always overshadowed. Jack started on piano at age five (his mother, Helen, was a ragtime pianist), switched to baritone horn, and finally took up trombone when he was ten. Teagarden worked in the Southwest in a variety of territory bands (most notably with the legendary pianist Peck Kelley) and caused a sensation when he came to New York in 1928. His daring solos with Ben Pollack caused Glenn Miller to de-emphasize his own playing with the band, and during the late-'20s/early Depression era "Mr. T." recorded frequently with many groups, including units headed by Roger Wolfe Kahn, Eddie Condon, Red Nichols, and Louis Armstrong. "Knockin' a Jug" and his versions of "Basin Sreet Blues" and "Beale Street Blues" (songs that would remain in his repertoire for the remainder of his career) were definitive. Teagarden, who was greatly admired by Tommy Dorsey, would have been a logical candidate for fame in the swing era, but he made a strategic error. In late 1933, when it looked as if jazz would never catch on commercially, he signed a five-year contract with Paul Whiteman. Although Whiteman's Orchestra did feature Teagarden now and then (and he had a brief period in 1936 playing with a small group from the band, the Three T's, with Charlie Teagarden and Frankie Trumbauer), the contract effectively kept Teagarden from going out on his own and becoming a star. It certainly prevented him from leading what would eventually became the Bob Crosby Orchestra.

In 1939 Jack Teagarden was finally "free," and he soon put together a big band that would last until 1946. However, it was rather late to be organizing a new orchestra (the competition was fierce), and although there were some good musical moments, none of the sidemen became famous, and the arrangements lacked their own musical personality. By the time the orchestra broke up, Teagarden was facing bankruptcy. The trombonist was, however, still a big name (he had fared quite well in the 1940 Bing Crosby film *The Birth of the Blues*), and he had many friends. Crosby helped Teagarden straighten out his financial problems, and from 1947-51 he was a star sideman with Louis Armstrong's All-Stars; their collaborations on "Rocking Chair" are classic. After leaving Armstrong, Teagarden led a steadily working sextet throughout the remainder of his career, playing Dixieland with such talented musicians as brother Charlie; trumpeters Jimmy McPartland, Don Goldie, and Max Kaminsky; and (during a 1957 European tour) pianist Earl Hines. Teagarden toured the Far East during 1958-59, teamed up one last time with Eddie Condon for a television show/recording session in 1961, and had a heartwarming (and fortunately recorded) musical reunion with Charlie, sister-pianist Norma, and his mother at the 1963 Monterey Jazz Festival. He died from a heart attack four months later. *—Scott Yanow*

★ **The Indispensable** / Mar. 14, 1928-Jul. 8, 1957 / RCA ◆◆◆◆◆
Much more complete than the Bluebird CD, this two-CD set has trombonist Jack Teagarden featured with Roger Wolfe Kahn's orchestra (two takes of "She's a Great, Great Girl"), Eddie Condon's Hot Shots, the Mound City Blue Blowers, eight numbers with Ben Pollack, his better recordings with Paul Whiteman's Orchestra, and a complete session under his own leader-

ship in 1947, in addition to three numbers with Bud Freeman in 1957. This set is highly recommended to those who can locate it. — *Scott Yanow*

That's a Serious Thing / Mar. 14, 1928-Jul. 8, 1957 / Bluebird ✦✦✦✦
This readily available Bluebird CD gives one an excellent overview of the talents of trombonist/singer Jack Teagarden. Mr. T. is featured with Eddie Condon on a pair of classic 1929 selections and with Roger Wolfe Kahn's orchestra ("She's a Great Great Girl"), Ben Pollack, the Mound City Blue Blowers, Fats Waller, Benny Goodman, Paul Whiteman, the Three T's, the Metronome All-Stars, Louis Armstrong (the exciting "Jack Armstrong Blues"), and Bud Freeman, in addition to a version of "St. Louis Blues" with Teagarden's group in 1947. Quite a few of these performances are famous and, although this is not a "complete" set, the consistent high quality of these recordings makes this CD highly recommended to all. — *Scott Yanow*

1930-1934 / Oct. 1, 1930-Mar. 2, 1934 / Classics ✦✦✦✦
This Classics CD has the first 23 titles ever issued under the leadership of trombonist Jack Teagarden. Many of these selections were formerly rare, particularly the earlier titles on Domino, Banner, and Crown. Best is the session that co-starred pianist/vocalist Fats Waller, and, while some of the titles are a bit commercial, Teagarden's playing (and that of his better sidemen) uplift the music; "A Hundred Years from Today" is a classic. — *Scott Yanow*

1934-1939 / Sep. 18, 1934-Jul. 19, 1939 / Classics ✦✦✦✦
The second of three Jack Teagarden Classics CDs contains all of his recordings as a leader during this pivotal period. There are three titles from 1934 with a pickup group also including clarinetist Benny Goodman and Frankie Trumbauer on C-melody sax. But the bulk of this CD is taken up by the first 21 studio performances by Jack Teagarden's ill-fated big band in 1939. The trombonist/leader is easily the most interesting soloist, and his vocals are a joy while those of Linda Keene are okay. Teagarden's swing band did not have its own identity, but its recordings are generally enjoyable. — *Scott Yanow*

Jack Teagarden's Big Eight / Pee Wee Russell's Rhythmakers / Aug. 31, 1938-Dec. 15, 1940 / Original Jazz Classics ✦✦✦✦
With Pee Wee Russell (clarinet). Two titans of classic New Orleans style make a great match. — *Ron Wynn*

1939-1940 / Aug. 23, 1939-Feb. 1940 / Classics ✦✦✦✦
The third in Classics' *Complete* Jack Teagarden series traces the trombonist's big-band recordings during his Columbia period. There were no great soloists among Teagarden's sidemen, and some of these tunes (particularly the nine with Kitty Kallen vocals) are throwaways, but Teagarden's own singing on six songs (including "Beale Street Blues" and "If I Could Be with You") and distinctive trombone give listeners strong reasons to acquire this entry in the worthy series. Other highlights include "Peg of My Heart," "Wolverine Blues," "Swingin' on the Teagarden Gate," and "The Blues." — *Scott Yanow*

● **Jack Teagarden and His All Stars** / May 1958 / Jazzology ✦✦✦✦
Taken from the same period (but not duplicating the music) of Jack Teagarden's Pumpkin LP, this Jazzology CD finds the trombonist leading one of his strongest groups, a band that also features many fine solos from cornetist Dick Oakley, clarinetist Jerry Fuller, and pianist Don Ewell. Even on such tunes as "Someday You'll Be Sorry," "High Society," and "When the Saints Go Marching In," this very enjoyable sextet is able to play with enthusiasm and creativity, coming up with something fresh to say on songs the musicians had performed a countless number of times. — *Scott Yanow*

Hundred Years from Today / Sep. 20, 1963-Sep. 21, 1963 / Memphis Archives ✦✦✦✦
Jack Teagarden's final recording (performed less than four months before his death), finds the trombonist/vocalist in particularly happy spirits at the Monterey Jazz Festival. Mr. T. was reunited not only with his brother (trumpeter Charlie) and sister (pianist Norma) but also with his mother, who performs a couple of ragtime piano solos! The strong supporting cast, in addition to the many Teagardens, features clarinetist Pee Wee Russell, baritonist Gerry Mulligan, and pianist Joe Sullivan. The two sets included on this historical CD are filled with blues, standards, and Dixieland, the results of Jack Teagarden's two sets at Monterey. This important and easily enjoyable music is proof that the great trombonist went out on top. — *Scott Yanow*

Jacky Terrasson

b. Nov. 27, 1966, Berlin, Germany
Piano / Post-Bop
One of the most promising pianists of the mid-'90s, Jacky Terrasson grew up in Paris and started studying classical piano when he was five. He switched to jazz as a teenager, attended Berklee in Boston, and a few years later was a regular in Paris jazz clubs and at European festivals. After a stint working with Dee Dee Bridgewater, Terrasson moved to New York in 1990. He worked and recorded with Art Taylor, Cindy Blackman, and Betty

Carter; won the 1993 Thelonious Monk Jazz Competition; and debuted as a leader for Blue Note. — *Scott Yanow*

Jacky Terrasson / 1994 / Blue Note ✦✦✦✦
Jacky Terrasson delights in turning standards inside out. On his CD he gives odd rhythms to "I Love Paris," purposely speeds up and slows down the tempo on "Bye Bye Blackbird," takes "I Fall in Love Too Easily" very slow, does his best to disguise "Bye Bye Blackbird," and shows a grasp of dynamics worthy of Ahmad Jamal. It is fortunate that bassist Ugonna Okegwo and drummer Leon Parker are very alert (or perhaps well rehearsed), because to the uninitiated listener these eccentric and rather quirky performances are often quite unpredictable and occasionally jarring. Well worth checking out. — *Scott Yanow*

● **Reach** / 1995 / Blue Note ✦✦✦✦
The talented young pianist Jacky Terrasson and his trio (with bassist Ugonna Okegwo and drummer Leon Parker) find something new to say on a few standards (including a rare uptempo version of "For Sentimental Reasons") and introduce five of Terrasson's originals. Although he has does not have an original style yet, Terrasson displays a great deal of potential. Highlights include "I Should Care," "Just One of Those Things," and a medley of his "Reach" with "Smoke Gets in Your Eyes." — *Scott Yanow*

Clark Terry

b. Dec. 14, 1920, St. Louis, MO
Fluegelhorn, Vocals / Bop, Swing
Possessor of the happiest sound in jazz, fluegelhornist Clark Terry always plays music that is exuberant, swinging and fun. A brilliant (and very distinctive) soloist, C.T. gained fame for his "Mumbles" vocals (which started as a satire of the less intelligible ancient blues singers) and is also an enthusiastic educator. He gained early experience playing trumpet in the viable St. Louis jazz scene of the early '40s (where he was an inspiration for Miles Davis) and, after performing in a Navy band during World War II, he gained a strong reputation playing with the big band of Charlie Barnet (1947-48), the orchestra and small groups of Count Basie (1948-51), and particularly with Duke Ellington (1951-59). Terry, a versatile swing/bop soloist who started specializing on fluegelhorn in the mid-'50s, had many features with Ellington (including "Perdido") and started leading his own record dates during that era. He visited Europe with Harold Arlen's unsuccessful *The Free & Easy* show of 1959-60 as part of Quincy Jones' Orchestra and then joined the staff of NBC, where he was a regular member of the Tonight Show Orchestra. He recorded regularly in the '60s, including a classic set with the Oscar Peterson Trio and several dates with the quintet he co-led with valve trombonist Bob Brookmeyer. Throughout the '70s, '80s and '90s, C.T. has remained a major force, recording and performing in a wide variety of settings including at the head of his short-lived big band in the mid-'70s, with all-star groups for Pablo, and as a guest artist who can be expected to provide happiness in every note he plays. — *Scott Yanow*

Serenade to a Bus Seat / Apr. 1957 / Original Jazz Classics ✦✦✦✦
Why it took so long for Clark Terry to be recognized for his fine stylized trumpet work is hard to understand, as even by the time of this date he had quite well established himself as a capable individual voice. — *Bob Rusch, Cadence*

Duke with a Difference / Jul. 29, 1957 & Sep. 6, 1957 / Original Jazz Classics ✦✦✦✦
For this CD reissue of a Riverside set, trumpeter Clark Terry and some of the top Ellington sidemen of the period (trombonist Britt Woodman, altoist Johnny Hodges, tenor saxophonist Paul Gonsalves, Tyree Glenn on vibes, bassist Jimmy Woode, and drummer Sam Woodyard) perform eight songs associated with Duke, but with fresh arrangements. There is plenty of solo space for C.T., Gonsalves, and Hodges, and the arrangements by Terry and Mercer Ellington cast a new light on some of the warhorses; highlights include "C-Jam Blues," "Cottontail," "Mood Indigo," and "Come Sunday." — *Scott Yanow*

In Orbit / May 1958 / Original Jazz Classics ✦✦✦✦
One of Thelonious Monk's rare appearances as a sideman is on this quartet set led by fluegelhornist Clark Terry. With bassist Sam Jones and drummer Philly Joe Jones, Terry and pianist Monk perform a set that surprisingly has only one Thelonious Monk song ("Let's Cool One"). Among the high points of this happy, boppish date are C.T.'s "Globetrotter," "One Foot in the Gutter," and "Zip Co-Ed." — *Scott Yanow*

Top and Bottom Brass / Feb. 24, 1959 & Feb. 26, 1959 / Original Jazz Classics ✦✦✦✦
This lesser-known Clark Terry session (reissued on CD in the *OJC* series) has an unusual lineup, with the fluegelhornist joined by Don Butterfield on tuba, pianist Jimmy Jones, bassist Sam Jones, and drummer Art Taylor. Butterfield has nearly as much solo space as C.T. (and is given a prominent role in the ensembles), while Jimmy Jones' chordal solos are somewhat eccentric. Terry is in fine form on a variety of blues, originals, and obscurities, along with interesting versions of "My Heart Belongs to Daddy" and "A Sunday Kind of Love," but the results overall are not all that significant. — *Scott Yanow*

★ **Color Changes** / Nov. 19, 1960 / Candid ✦✦✦✦✦
This is one of fluegelhornist Clark Terry's finest albums. Terry had complete control over the music and, rather than have the usual jam session, he utilized an octet and arrangements by Yusef Lateef, Budd Johnson, and Al Cohn. The lineup of musicians (C.T., trombonist Jimmy Knepper, Julius Watkins on French horn, Yusef Lateef on tenor, flute, oboe, and English horn, Seldon Powell doubling on tenor and flute, pianist Tommy Flanagan, bassist Joe Benjamin, and drummer Ed Shaughnessy) lives up to its potential, and the charts make good use of the sounds of these very individual stylists. The material, which consists of originals by Terry, Duke Jordan, Lateef, and Bob Wilber, is both rare and fresh, and the interpretations always swing. Highly recommended. — *Scott Yanow*

Mellow Moods / Jul. 21, 1961-May 15, 1962 / Prestige ✦✦✦✦

☆ **Oscar Peterson Trio with Clark Terry** / 1964 / Mercury ✦✦✦✦✦
The Oscar Peterson Trio, with bassist Ray Brown and drummer Ed Thigpen, welcomed fluegelhornist Clark Terry to this very memorable studio session. Whether on "Brotherhood of Man," "Mack the Knife," or "They Didn't Believe Me," all of the players are mutually inspired, and the results are not only joyful, but explosively exuberant. However, this album (reissued on CD) will be best remembered for Clark Terry's introduction of his unique vocal style on "Mumbles" and "Incoherent Blues"; those spontaneous performances still sound funny. A gem. — *Scott Yanow*

Ain't Misbehavin' / Mar. 15, 1976-Mar. 16, 1976 / Pablo ✦✦✦✦
This served as a sprightly showcase for tunes either written or associated with Fats Waller. Outstanding in his role as front-line mate was the underappreciated alto saxophonist Chris Woods. Clark Terry's unforced humor was evident throughout this session. — *Bob Rusch, Cadence*

The Globetrotter / 1977 / Vanguard ✦✦✦✦
For this sextet/septet session, fluegelhornist Clark Terry mostly drew his personnel from the big band that he occasionally fronted during the mid-'70s. Of special interest is a chance to hear tenor saxophonist Ernie Wilkins (better known as an arranger) stretching out as a soloist; C.T.'s other sidemen include pianist Ronnie Mathews, bassist Victor Sproeles, and drummer Ed Soph, with guest spots for pianist Walter Bishop and guitarist Roland Prince. The repertoire is particularly strong, with classic ballads such as "Misty" and "Autumn Leaves" alternating with Terry's three colorful originals: "One Foot in the Gutter," "Zip Co-Ed," and "Globetrotter." This excellent LP is long overdue for reissue on CD. — *Scott Yanow*

Memories of Duke / Mar. 11, 1980 / Original Jazz Classics ✦✦✦✦
Fluegelhornist Clark Terry and a strong quartet (pianist Jack Wilson, guitarist Joe Pass, bassist Ray Brown, and drummer Frank Severino) perform nine songs associated with Duke Ellington, including seven of Ellington's compositions, plus a tune apiece from Billy Strayhorn ("Passion Flower") and Mercer Ellington ("Things Ain't What They Used to Be"). Terry knows these songs, which include "Cottontail," "Come Sunday," and "Sophisticated Lady," backward, but he infuses each of his renditions with enthusiasm and melodic creativity. Recommended. — *Scott Yanow*

Jive at Five / Feb. 1986 & Jul. 1988 / Enja ✦✦✦✦

Having Fun / Apr. 11, 1990-Apr. 12, 1990 / Delos ✦✦✦✦
The title of this CD definitely fits not only its music but Clark Terry's career. The colorful fluegelhornist is teamed with Red Holloway doubling on tenor and alto, bassist Major Holley (who sings along with his bass in his solos), pianist Jon Campbell, and drummer Lewis Nash. Since C.T., Holloway, and Holley were all humorists, the music is not only swinging, but quite enthusiastic. With titles like "Mumbles," "Meet the Flintstones," "The Snapper," and "Mule's Soft Claw," the humor isn't unexpected. An excellent and consistently swinging date. — *Scott Yanow*

What a Wonderful World: For Lou / Feb. 1, 1993 / Red Baron ✦✦✦✦

Toots Thielemans (Jean Baptiste Thielemans)

b. Apr. 29, 1922, Brussels, Belgium
Guitar, Harmonica / Bop, Swing, Brazilian Jazz
Although preceded by Larry Adler (who has actually spent much of his career playing popular and classical music), Toots Thielemans virtually introduced the chromatic harmonica as a jazz instrument. In fact, ever since the mid-'50s he has had no close competitors. He simply plays the harmonica with the dexterity of a saxophonist, and has even successfully traded off with the likes of Oscar Peterson.

Thielemans' first instrument was the accordion, which he started when he was three. Although he started playing the harmonica when he was 17, Thielemans' original reputation was made as a guitarist influenced by Django Reinhardt. Very much open to bop, Thielemans played in American GI clubs in Europe, visited the US for the first time in 1947, and shared the bandstand with Charlie Parker at the Paris Jazz Festival of 1949. He toured Europe as a guitarist with the Benny Goodman Sextet in 1950 and the next year moved to the US. During 1953-59 Toots was a member of the George Shearing Quintet (mostly as a guitarist) and has freelanced ever since. He first recorded his big hit "Bluesette" (which featured his expert whistling and guitar) in 1961, and ever since has been greatly in demand (particularly for his harmonica and his whistling) on

pop records (including many dates with Quincy Jones) and as a jazz soloist. Thielemans' two-volume *Brasil Project* was popular in the '90s and found him smoothly interacting on harmonica with top Brazilian musicians. — *Scott Yanow*

Man Bites Harmonica / Dec. 30, 1957 & Jan. 7, 1958 / Original Jazz Classics ✦✦✦✦
Early period. Definitive harmonicist from Belgium. With Pepper Adams, Kenny Drew, Wilbur Ware, and Art Taylor. — *Michael G. Nastos*

★ **Live in the Netherlands** / Jul. 13, 1980 / Pablo ✦✦✦✦✦

Only Trust Your Heart / Apr. 1988-May 1988 / Concord Jazz ✦✦✦

Footprints / Dec. 19, 1989-Dec. 20, 1989 / EmArcy ✦✦✦✦
A 1991 release. Mulgrew Miller (piano) ups the stakes. — *Ron Wynn*

The Brasil Project / 1992 / Private Music ✦✦✦

The Brasil Project, Vol. 2 / 1993 / Private Music ✦✦✦✦
Guitarist, harmonica player, and whistler Toots Thielemans' followup to the critically acclaimed *Brasil Project* doesn't stray far from its predecessor's path. There are 13 nice Afro-Latin selections, with Thielemans backing such top Brazilian vocalists as Milton Nascimento, Gilberto Gil, Ivan Lins, Caetano Veloso, and Dori Caymmi. Guitarists Oscar Castro-Nieves and Lee Ritenour assist Thielemans with delicate shadings and accompaniment. — *Ron Wynn*

Lucky Thompson

b. Jun. 16, 1924, Columbia, SC
Sax (Soprano and Tenor) / Bop, Hard Bop
Lucky Thompson was one of the great tenors to emerge during the '40s and one of the first "modern" soprano saxophonists (taking up the instrument prior to John Coltrane and around the same time as Steve Lacy), but he was always a bit overshadowed by more spectacular players. After some local gigs he moved to New York in the early '40s, playing briefly with Lionel Hampton and Don Redman in 1943 and with Billy Eckstine and Lucky Millinder in 1944. During 1944-45 he gained some attention with Count Basie (where Thompson had succeeded his main influence, Don Byas). Although his large tone looked toward the swing era, Thompson's advanced improvising fit in well with bop players. He settled on the West Coast after leaving Basie, was hired as "insurance" by Dizzy Gillespie in case Charlie Parker did not show up (he recorded with both), and cut many sessions (his solo on "Just One More Chance" was a personal favorite) during his stay in Los Angeles, performing with Boyd Raeburn and the short-lived Stars of Swing. In 1947 Thompson moved to Detroit, but the next year he returned to New York. He led a band regularly at the Savoy during 1951-53, and in 1954 he starred on Miles Davis' famous *Walkin'* session. In 1956 Thompson was a top soloist with Stan Kenton (appearing on *Cuban Fire*), and during the next two years he cut many sessions, both as a leader and as a sideman. He lived in France 1957-62 and 1968-71. Thompson started doubling on soprano and taught at Dartmouth during 1973-74. And then it all stopped. Lucky Thompson completely dropped out of the music business (despite still being in his musical prime) and, other than a few rumors, has not been heard from since. — *Scott Yanow*

● **The Beginning Years** / Oct. 1945-Jun. 7, 1947 / IAJRC ✦✦✦✦

☆ **Tricotism** / Jan. 24, 1956-Dec. 12, 1956 / GRP ✦✦✦✦✦
Thompson created a host of spectacular improvisations on the 16 songs on this wonderful CD reissue. It is comprised of two 1956 sessions; one featured Thompson heading a trio backed by bassist Oscar Pettiford and guitarist Skeeter Best, and the other has him heading either a quartet or quintet that included the great trombonist Jimmy Cleveland. Cleveland's smooth, superbly articulated phrases and statements rank alongside Thompson's gliding lines in their brilliance, and pianist Hank Jones (on three cuts) also sparkles with some marvelous solos. But Lucky Thompson is the star on this date; his elegant, yet robust and exuberant playing demonstrated again what a loss his voluntary departure from the scene constitutes. — *Ron Wynn*

Happy Days / Mar. 8, 1963 & Feb. 16, 1965 / Prestige ✦✦✦✦
This CD has the full contents of two of Lucky Thompson's LPs. The earlier session, since it was originally released on the Prestige subsidiary Moodsville, emphasizes ballads, as Thompson interprets eight Jerome Kern melodies (none of the obvious ones) plus his own moody original "No More." One of the first "modern" jazz musicians to start doubling on soprano (actually predating John Coltrane), Lucky Thompson displays a light but forceful tone on both soprano and tenor; his versions of "Look for the Silver Lining," "Who," and "They Didn't Believe Me" are particularly memorable. The second date was a six-song tribute to a new singer of the period, Barbra Streisand. Other than "People" (this version is harmless enough) and Thompson's "Safari," the other tunes are veteran standards including "Happy Days Are Here Again" and a rare medium-tempo rendition of "As Time Goes By." Overall this CD is full of excellent music by the always underrated Lucky Thompson. — *Scott Yanow*

Claude Thornhill

b. Aug. 10, 1909, Terre Haute, IN, **d.** Jul. 1, 1965, New York, NY
Piano / Cool
Although some of his recordings were on the periphery of jazz and his orchestra was at its most popular in the early '40s, Claude Thornhill's main importance to jazz was the influence that his arrangements and orchestra's sound had on cool jazz of the late '40s. After studying at a music conservatory and playing piano in bands based in the Midwest, Thornhill worked for Paul Whiteman and Benny Goodman in 1934 and for Ray Noble's American band of 1935-36 (for whom he also arranged). He appeared on some Billie Holiday records, and his arrangement of "Loch Lomond" was a big hit for Maxine Sullivan. Although he recorded as a leader in 1937, it was in 1940 that Thornhill put together his own orchestra. The band, featuring long tones played by horns that de-emphasized vibrato, had an unusual sound that sometimes backed the leader's tinkling piano. The instrumentation included two French horns and a tuba; sometimes all six of the reeds played clarinets in unison. Although classified by some as a sweet rather than swing band (since the group played a lot of ballads), with the addition in 1941 of Gil Evans as one of the arrangers, the orchestra's recordings attracted a lot of attention in the jazz world. After a period in the miliary (1942-45), Thornhill put together a new orchestra, retaining the services of Gil Evans (and sometimes using Gerry Mulligan charts as well) and featuring such soloists as altoist Lee Konitz, clarinetist Danny Polo, and trumpeter Red Rodney. Some of Evans' boppish arrangements for the group were classic, and the Miles Davis Nonet of 1948 was based on many of the cool-toned principles of the Thornhill big band. However by then the pianist's glory days were over. He continued leading bands on a part-time basis up until his death, but Claude Thornhill was largely neglected and forgotten during his final 15 years. — *Scott Yanow*

★ **Tapestries** / Jun. 14, 1937-Dec. 17, 1947 / Affinity ♦♦♦♦♦
A comprehensive, two-disc set of his prime cuts, with 17 arranged by Gil Evans. — *Ron Wynn*

Best of Big Bands / Mar. 10, 1941-Dec. 17, 1947 / Columbia ♦♦♦♦
Nice collection of his label cuts. — *Ron Wynn*

1948 Transcription Performance / Apr. 1948-Oct. 1948 / Hep ♦♦♦♦

Henry Threadgill

b. Feb. 15, 1944, Chicago, IL
Flute, Sax (Alto) / Avant-Garde
Although his music can be somewhat forbidding, Henry Threadgill has been one of the most respected members of the avant-garde for the past 20 years. As an altoist and flutist, he has long had an original tone, but it is his work as an innovative composer that is most impressive. He played percussion in marching bands while a child, learned baritone and clarinet in high school, studied at the American Conservatory of Music, and played gospel music for traveling evangelists. In 1962-63 Threadgill was part of Richard Abrams' Experimental Band, and he became a member of the AACM. After a period in the Army, he worked in the house band at a Chicago blues club and recorded with Abrams. In 1971 Threadgill teamed up with Steve McCall and Fred Hopkins in a trio, and in 1975 the group became known as Air. Threadgill recorded and performed extensively with Air (and its successor New Air) and later led several unique ensembles, including X75 (which had four bassists), his Sextet, and Very Very Circus. His signing to Sony in 1994 was a big surprise, for Threadgill's compositions and improvisations are far from accessible; happily his Sony recordings show no sign of being watered-down. — *Scott Yanow*

● **Just the Facts and Pass the Bucket** / 1983 / About Time ♦♦♦♦
Sextet (actually seven pieces). Dynamite open-ended compositions, especially the surly "Black Blues" and the determined "Man Called Trinity Deliverance." Features Olu Dara, Pheeroan Aklaff, John Betsch, and bassist Fred Hopkins. All pungently original material. — *Michael G. Nastos*

Spirit of Nuff . . . Nuff / Nov. 19, 1990-Nov. 21, 1990 / Black Saint ♦♦♦
Too Much Sugar for a Dime / 1993 / Axiom ♦♦♦♦
Imagine writing for an instrumentation of two electric guitars, two tubas, French horn, drums, and Henry Threadgill's alto. Threadgill was up to the challenge, and his four avant-garde originals utilize the odd combination of tones to great advantage. Two additional songs feature Threadgill, just one tuba, drums, a few exotic instruments, and three strings to create some particularly unusual music. It's for the open-eared listener only. — *Scott Yanow*

Carry the Day / 1994 / Columbia ♦♦♦♦

The Three Sounds (Three Sounds)

Ballads, Soul-Jazz, Post-Bop, Groove
A group formed by pianist Gene Harris in the late '50s that evolved from the original Four Sounds, a 1957 quartet. The trio was enormously popular in the late '50s and early and mid-'60s, despite the fact that much of its music was in light cocktail-lounge or soul-jazz mode. Actually Harris was a fine bluesy stylist, and revisionist looks at Three Sounds' material, espe-

cially a 1963 release with Anita O'Day, have resulted in some observers admitting they overlooked or undervalued this group. — *Ron Wynn*

★ **Introducing the Three Sounds** / Sep. 16, 1958 & Sep. 18, 1958 / Blue Note ♦♦♦♦♦
With Gene Harris on both piano and celeste. This is their first album—easy to listen to, but excellent small-group jazz. The CD is 67 minutes. — *Michael Erlewine*

Babe's Blues / Aug. 31, 1961-Mar. 8, 1962 / Blue Note ♦♦♦♦
Underrated group. This is what many people look and hope for in an easy-listening album: a quality jazz recording that can be played in the foreground or background. 43 minutes on CD. — *Michael Erlewine*

Live at the It Club / Mar. 5, 1996 / Blue Note ♦♦♦

Bobby Timmons

b. Dec. 19, 1935, Philadelphia, PA, **d.** Mar. 1, 1974, New York, NY
Piano / Soul-Jazz, Hard Bop, Groove
Bobby Timmons became so famous for the gospel and funky blues cliches in his solos and compositions that his skills as a Bud Powell inspired bebop player have been long forgotten. After emerging from the Philadelphia jazz scene, Timmons worked with Kenny Dorham (1956), Chet Baker, Sonny Stitt, and the Maynard Ferguson Big Band. He was partly responsible for the commercial success of both Art Blakey's Jazz Messengers and Cannonball Adderley's Quintet. For Blakey (whom he was with during 1958-59), Timmons wrote the classic "Moanin'" and, after joining Adderley in 1959, his song "This Here" (followed later by "Dat Dere") became a big hit. It is little wonder that Adderley was distressed when Timmons in 1960 decided to return to the Jazz Messengers. "Dat Dere" particularly caught on when Oscar Brown, Jr. wrote and recorded lyrics that colorfully depicted his curious son. Timmons, who was already recording as a leader for Riverside, soon formed his own trio, but he was never able to gain the commercial success that his former bosses enjoyed. Stereotyped as a funky pianist (although an influence on many players including Les McCann, Ramsey Lewis, and—much later—Benny Green), Timmons' career gradually declined. He continued working until his death at age 38 from cirrhosis of the liver. — *Scott Yanow*

★ **This Here Is Bobby Timmons** / Jan. 13, 1960-Jan. 14, 1960 / Original Jazz Classics ♦♦♦♦♦
Trio with Sam Jones (bass) and Jimmy Cobb (drums). This is the pianist's single best album. — *Michael G. Nastos*

Soul Time / Aug. 12, 1960 & Aug. 17, 1960 / Original Jazz Classics ♦♦♦♦
Pianist Bobby Timmons, best known for his sanctified and funky playing and composing, is heard mostly in a straightahead vein on this CD reissue of a Riverside session. Timmons' four originals ("So Tired" is most memorable) alternate with three standards and are interpreted by a quartet with trumpeter Blue Mitchell, bassist Sam Jones, and drummer Art Blakey. The swinging music is well played, making this a good example of Bobby Timmons' playing in a boppish (as opposed to funky) setting. — *Scott Yanow*

Easy Does It / Mar. 13, 1961 / Original Jazz Classics ♦♦♦♦
Pianist Bobby Timmons, who became famous for his funky originals and soulful playing, sticks mostly to more bop-oriented jazz on this trio set with bassist Sam Jones and drummer Jimmy Cobb. He provides three originals (none of which really caught on) and is in excellent form on the five standards, with highlights including "Old Devil Moon," "I Thought About You," and "Groovin' High." The Riverside CD reissue shows that Timmons was a bit more versatile than his stereotype; in any case, the music is excellent. — *Scott Yanow*

In Person / Oct. 1, 1961 / Original Jazz Classics ♦♦♦♦
Recorded with the Trio. — *AMG*

Born to Be Blue / Sep. 1963 / Original Jazz Classics ♦♦♦♦
Throughout his career, Bobby Timmons was typecast as a soulful and blues-oriented pianist, due to his hits ("Moanin'," "This Here," and "Dis Dat"). But as he shows on this 1963 trio date (with either Sam Jones or Ron Carter on bass and drummer Connie Kay), Timmons was actually a well rounded player when inspired. The repertoire on his CD ranges from bop to spirituals, from three diverse originals to "Born to Be Blue." This is excellent music, but unfortunately Timmons would not grow much musically after this period. His CD is worth picking up. — *Scott Yanow*

Workin' Out / Oct. 21, 1964 & Jan. 20, 1966 / Prestige ♦♦♦♦
This CD reissues the contents of two of pianist Bobby Timmons' most advanced recordings of the '60s. For an example of how the popular pianist continued to evolve after his early funk hits, listen to his often bitonal solo on "Bags' Groove" from 1964. That session features Timmons in a quartet with vibraphonist Johnny Lytle, bassist Keter Betts, and drummer William "Peppy" Hinnant and is filled with subtle surprises. The second recording is even more interesting, for Timmons is teamed with tenor saxophonist Wayne Shorter, bassist Ron Carter, and drummer Jimmy Cobb in 1966. The immediately recognizable Shorter, in particular, plays very well (this version of his "Tom Thumb" is its earliest recording), and the very modern playing of Carter pushes Timmons to really stretch himself. Both of these

generally overlooked sessions (even Shorter's best fans may not know about his collaboration with Timmons) were formerly rare and are quite adventurous, making this a highly recommended acquisition that falls somewhere between hard bop and early avant-garde. — *Scott Yanow*

The Soul Man / Jan. 20, 1966 / Prestige ✦✦✦

Soul Food / Sep. 30, 1966 & Oct. 14, 1966 / Prestige ✦✦✦

Cal Tjader

b. Jul. 16, 1925, St. Louis, MO, **d.** May 5, 1982, Manila
Vibes / Cool, Latin-Jazz, Latin Continuum
The greatest non-Latin bandleader in Latin-jazz history, Cal Tjader's early interest in the music blossomed into a lifelong love affair. While he wasn't the fastest vibes player, his style matured to the point that he could provide efficient, effective solos while his band maintained the groove. Tjader also played piano and bongos. He studied music at San Francisco State University and began as a drummer with Dave Brubeck's trio in the late '40s and early '50s. He worked with Alvino Rey before beginning his own band. Tjader joined George Shearing in 1953; Shearing's band eventually had Tjader playing vibes and percussion with Willie Bobo, Mongo Santamaria, and Armanda Peraza. His bassist Al McKibbon helped stimulate Tjader's love affair with Latin-jazz and Afro-Latin music. When Tjader left Shearing, he started his own groups, which mixed Latin-jazz, Afro-Cuban, and jazz. Bobo and Santamaria joined him later in the '50s, and Tjader led fine bands in the '60s, '70s, and '80s. He recorded for Fantasy from the '50s to the mid-'60s, then switched to Verve. Tjader's Verve sessions included Lalo Schifrin, Bobo, Donald Byrd, and Kenny Burrell; the albums *Several Shades of Jade* and *Soul Sauce* made the pop albums chart. He recorded with Eddie Palmieri on Verve and Tico and with Charlie Palmieri on Fantasy. Tjader continued on Fantasy in the '70s, working with Stan Getz, Charlie Byrd, Hank Jones, and Clare Fischer. He also began recording for Concord in the '70s, cutting both straight jazz sessions with Scott Hamilton and Jones and Latin dates, one of which included Carmen McRae. He won a Grammy for the 1980 release *La Onda Va Bien* and continued on Concord until his death in 1982. Tjader has many sessions available on CD. — *Ron Wynn*

Ritmos Caliente / Mar. 6, 1954 & Nov. 11, 1957 / Fantasy ✦✦✦

Tjader Plays Mambo / Aug. 1954-Sep. 1954 / Original Jazz Classics ✦✦✦✦

Tjader Plays Mambo and *Mambo with Tjader* feature three Fall 1954 sessions with vibist/pianist Tjader playing two dozen Latinized standards. Four of the tracks found Tjader in the company of a small orchestra for added brass accents. The remainder of the tracks were without the horns and with Verlardi added as a third Latin percussionist. — *Bob Rusch, Cadence*

Mambo with Tjader / Sep. 1954 / Fantasy ✦✦✦

Latin Kick / Nov. 1956 / Original Jazz Classics ✦✦✦✦
A 1991 reissue of a prime session. First-rate Latin-jazz. — *Ron Wynn*

★ **Black Orchid** / 1956-1959 / Fantasy ✦✦✦✦✦
This CD reissues the complete contents of two former Fantasy LPs: *Cal Tjader Goes Latin* and *Cal Tjader Quintet*. The highly influential vibraphonist/bandleader is heard leading his young groups (which include such notable sidemen as flutist Paul Horn, pianist Vince Guaraldi, bassist Eugene Wright, and percussionists Willie Bobo and Mongo Santamaria, among others) through sets dominated by Latinized versions of standards. Highlights of this delightful (and somewhat definitive) program of Latin-jazz include "The Lady Is a Tramp," "Undecided," "Flamingo," "Stompin' at the Savoy," and "Lullaby of Birdland." — *Scott Yanow*

Jazz at the Blackhawk / Jan. 20, 1957 / Original Jazz Classics ✦✦✦✦
Vibraphonist Cal Tjader became such an influential force in Latin-jazz that many have forgotten about his abilities to play standard bop. This live set (a CD reissue of the original LP) features Tjader with a conventional but talented quartet (which includes pianist Vince Guaraldi, bassist Eugene Wright, and drummer Al Torre) playing in a style similar to Milt Jackson and the Modern Jazz Quartet; in fact one song they perform is a Guaraldi original titled "Thinking of You, MJQ." There are no Latin rhythms on this set, and oddly enough, the liner notes do not refer at all to Tjader's success in that area. The music is a touch derivative but enjoyable, one of the versatile Cal Tjader's better straightahead sets. Recommended. — *Scott Yanow*

Latin Concert / Sep. 1958 / Original Jazz Classics ✦✦✦✦
This CD reissue gives one a pretty good sampling of vibraphonist Cal Tjader's influential Latin-jazz of the '50s. With pianist Vince Guaraldi, bassist Al McKibbon, Willie Bobo on timbales and drums, and the congas of Mongo Santamaria, Tjader's impressive unit performs four of his catchy originals and two by Santamaria, in addition to Latinized versions of "The Continental" and Ray Bryant's "Cubano Chant." This highly rhythmic music is difficult to dislike. — *Scott Yanow*

★ **Monterey Concerts** / Apr. 20, 1959 / Prestige ✦✦✦✦✦
Outstanding combination of his sessions with Bobo and Santamaria, plus "Concerts by the Sea" LP linked in a two-record package. — *Ron Wynn*

Latino / 1960 / Fantasy ✦✦✦✦
Vibraphonist Cal Tjader is heard leading five different groups throughout this CD, but the identities of the flutists, bassists, and pianists are less important than knowing that Tjader, Willie Bobo (on drums and timbales), and the great conga player Mongo Santamaria are on every selection. The music really cooks with torrid percussion, inspired ensembles, and occasional solos from the sidemen (which sometimes include pianists Lonnie Hewitt or Vince Guaraldi, bassist Al McKibbon, and flutist Paul Horn). Highlights include Latinized versions of "Key Largo" and "September Song," "Night in Tunisia," "The Continental," and a definitive version of Santamaria's "Afro Blue." This is Latin-jazz at its finest. — *Scott Yanow*

Concert on the Campus / 1960 / Original Jazz Classics ✦✦✦✦
Solid 1987 reissue of a great Tjader live date. — *Ron Wynn*

Cal Tjader Plays / Mary Stallings Sings / 1961 / Original Jazz Classics ✦✦✦

Cal Tjader Plays Harold Arlen / 1961 / Original Jazz Classics ✦✦✦

El Sonid Nuevo (The New Soul Sound) / May 24, 1966-May 26, 1966 / Verve ✦✦✦

Descarga / 1971-1972 / Fantasy ✦✦✦

Amazonas / Jun. 1975 / Original Jazz Classics ✦✦✦

The Shining Sea / Mar. 1981 / Concord Picante ✦✦✦✦
Beautiful playing by Hank Jones (piano); more straight jazz than Latin. — *Ron Wynn*

Good Vibes / Concord Jazz ✦✦✦

Charles Tolliver

b. Mar. 6, 1942, Jacksonville, FL
Trumpet / Post-Bop, Hard Bop
In the early '70s Charles Tolliver was one of the brightest young trumpeters in jazz. Although he is still playing well, Tolliver never broke through to the top as one might have predicted. He studied at Howard University and then moved to New York in 1964, playing and recording with Jackie McLean. Tolliver was on quite a few excellent advanced hard-bop records in the mid-'60s, played with Gerald Wilson's Orchestra in Los Angeles (1966-67), and was a member of Max Roach's group at the same time (1967-69) as the compatible Gary Bartz. In 1969 Tolliver formed a quartet called Music Inc. that often featured pianist Stanley Cowell and was on a few occasions expanded to a big band. Tolliver and Cowell founded the Strata-East label in 1971, which released many fine records in the '70s. Although it was an era when there was a serious shortage of talented young trumpeters (prior to the rise of Wynton Marsalis), Tolliver after the mid-'70s maintained a low profile and was thereafter overshadowed by the Young Lions. Charles Tolliver—whose fat tone was influenced by Freddie Hubbard, while his ideas display bits of John Coltrane—has recorded as a leader for Impulse (two songs from a 1965 concert), Black Lion, Enja, and Strata East. — *Scott Yanow*

Paper Man / Jul. 2, 1968 / Black Lion ✦✦✦✦

☆ **The Ringer** / Jun. 2, 1969 / Freedom ✦✦✦✦✦
Includes five Tolliver originals with the Stanley Cowell Trio. All the cuts are important, but "Plight" and "On the Nile" are particularly gripping. Cowell solos marvelously. — *Michael G. Nastos*

Grand Max / Aug. 9, 1972 / Enja ✦✦✦✦
A brilliant showcase for Charles Tolliver. A superb rhythm section. It makes one realize how consistently underrated he has been. — *Bob Rusch, Cadence*

★ **Impact** / Jan. 17, 1975 / Strata East ✦✦✦✦✦
Six spectacular performances from trumpeters. A 23-piece plus eight-piece string section orchestra. Great solos from Tolliver and pianist Stanley Cowell on "Plight" and throughout by James Spaulding (alto sax), George Coleman (tenor sax), Charles McPherson (sax), and Harold Vick (tenor sax). As powerful a record as you're likely to hear. — *Michael G. Nastos*

Mel Tormé

b. Sep. 13, 1925, Chicago, IL
Drums, Vocals / Bop, Swing
At the age of three, he was singing in public; at four, he was on the radio; at nine, he was acting professionall; and at 15, he published his first composition—an instrumental. After playing drums and singing in Chico Marx's band (1942-1943), he formed a vocal ensemble, the Mel-Tones, for which he wrote exceptional arrangements; it performed with Artie Shaw's band. From the late '40s on, Tormé has pursued a career as a solo singer with consistent success, also acting in films and on television and writing songs ("The Christmas Song" and "Born to Be Blue" have become standards). He has published a novel, a reminiscence of Judy Garland, an autobiography, and a biography of his friend and frequent co-worker, Buddy Rich. Tormé is clearly a man of exceptional gifts; his voice has remained an astonishingly consistent and accurate instrument, and his upper range—always a special feature of his style—remains intact in his seventh decade of per-

forming. Although somewhat overlooked as musical tastes changed in the '60s, Tormé emerged in the late '70s as a superb jazz singer, and his Concord recordings (starting in the early '80s) are among the finest of his career. Amazingly enough, his voice has grown stronger with age (holding long unwavering notes on ballads with apparent ease), and as he passed his 70th birthday, Mel Tormé was at the peak of his powers. —*Ron Wynn and Dan Morgenstern*

Spotlight on Great Gentlemen of Song / Jan. 17, 1949-Oct. 4, 1951 / Capitol ✦✦✦✦
This very interesting CD gives listeners a cross-section of Mel Tormé's Capitol recordings. Caught fairly early in his career, Tormé's voice was already quite recognizable and appealing. Ballads alternate with occasional romps, including several arranged by Frank DeVol in 1949 that are surprisingly boppish; Pete Rugolo, Nelson Riddle, and Sonny Burke take care of the other charts. Highlights of the 18 cuts (four of which were previously unreleased) include a wild "Oh, You Beautiful Doll," "Stompin' at the Savoy," "Blue Moon," a spirited "Sonny Boy," and "You're a Heavenly Thing" (which finds Tormé playing piano in a quartet with guitarist Mary Osborne). —*Scott Yanow*

In Hollywood / Dec. 15, 1954 / GRP/Decca ✦✦✦

It's a Blue World / Aug. 28, 1955-Aug. 30, 1955 / Bethlehem ✦✦✦✦
Mel Tormé had spent the first decade of his solo career being treated by record companies as a pop singer when Bethlehem offered to treat him as a jazz artist in 1955. The label requested that his first album be a collection of ballads, probably noting the recent success of Frank Sinatra's *In the Wee Small Hours*. But Tormé picked the songs, ranging from Jerome Kern and P.G. Wodehouse's "'Til The Clouds Roll By" from 1917 to Duke Ellington and Paul Webster's "I've Got It Bad and That Ain't Good" from 1941. The 15-piece orchestra assembled by his accompanist Al Pellegrini backed the singer, and Pellegrini, Sandy Courage, Andre Previn, Marty Paich, and Russ Garcia wrote the arrangements that with delicate precision, caressing the lyrics. Despite the album title, his interpretations had none of the darkness of Sinatra. Rather, Tormé invested the songs with warmth and confidence. Recorded and released around the time he turned 30, *It's a Blue World* marked a turning point in Tormé's recording career. —*William Ruhlmann*

★ **Tormé Touch** / Jan. 1956 / Bethlehem ✦✦✦✦✦
This Bethlehem LP (last reissued in 1978 and originally known as *Lulu's Back in Town*) is a classic. Singer Mel Tormé was matched for the first time with arranger Marty Paich's ten-piece group, which was called the Dek-tette. Among the sidemen are trumpeters Pete Candoli and Don Fagerquist, valve trombonist Bob Enevoldsen, Bud Shank on alto and flute, and either Bob Cooper or Jack Montrose on tenors; in addition, Paich uses both a French horn and a tuba. The arranged ensembles and cool-toned soloists match perfectly with Tormé's warm voice, and there are many high points to this essential date. "Lulu's Back in Town," "When the Sun Comes Out," "Fascinatin' Rhythm," "The Lady Is a Tramp," and "Lullaby of Birdland" are standouts, but all dozen selections are excellent. This is one of Mel Tormé's finest records of the '50s. —*Scott Yanow*

Back in Town / Apr. 23, 1959-Aug. 10, 1959 / Verve ✦✦✦✦

Duke Ellington and Count Basie Songbooks / Dec. 12, 1960 & Feb. 2, 1961 / Verve ✦✦✦✦
Recorded with the Johnny Mandel Orchestra at sessions in Los Angeles, it includes half Duke Ellington and half Count Basie, plus Leroy Carr's "In the Evening (When the Sun Goes Down)." With all these things going for it, how can Tormé do wrong? —*Michael G. Nastos*

London Sessions / 1977 / DCC ✦✦✦

Encore at Marty's, New York / Mar. 27, 1982 / DCC ✦✦✦✦
This CD reissues a full set of music from Mel Tormé with his 1982 trio: pianist Mike Renzi, bassist Jay Leonhart, and drummer Donny Osborne. No editing took place except for the excision of some chatter, yet the music is consistently rewarding. Tormé, who was already 56, was amazingly just entering his musical prime! His well paced set mixes together older songs (highlighted by a Fred Astaire medley), with some newer but worthy pieces (including the debut of Tormé's own "I'm Gonna Miss You"), alternating scat-filled romps with lyrical ballad interpretations. Tormé succeeds at everything he tries, with a humorous rendition of "I Like to Recognize the Tune" and some heated scatting on "Day In, Day Out" among the memorable moments. This CD reissue of an album originally put out on the Flair label is recommended. —*Scott Yanow*

Evening with George Shearing / Apr. 15, 1982 / Concord Jazz ✦✦✦✦
Grammy winner, a wonderful collaborative effort. —*Ron Wynn*

★ **Mel Tormé, Rob McConnell and the Boss Brass** / May 1986 / Concord Jazz ✦✦✦✦✦
This was a very logical matchup that came out as well on record as it looked on paper. Valve trombonist/arranger Rob McConnell has long led one of the top mainstream jazz big bands, while Mel Tormé blossomed into one of the truly great jazz singers in the '80s. McConnell's charts suited Tormé perfectly, and the result is this consistently enjoyable and swinging

album. The singer is quite enthusiastic and in top form on "Just Friends," a touching "September Song," "Don'cha Go 'way Mad," "A House Is Not a Home," "The Song Is You," a whimsical "Cow Cow Boogie," a "Stars" medley, and an exciting six-song Duke Ellington medley. Highly recommended. —*Scott Yanow*

Vintage Year / Aug. 1987 / Concord Jazz ✦✦✦✦

Reunion / Aug. 1988 / Concord Jazz ✦✦✦✦

Sing Sing Sing / Nov. 1992 / Concord Jazz ✦✦✦✦
Although 14 minutes of this CD is a specific "Tribute to Benny Goodman," actually the entire release is at least an indirect homage to the King of Swing. Tormé and his trio (pianist John Colianni, bassist John Leitham, and drummer Donny Osborne) are joined by clarinetist Ken Peplowski and vibraphonist Peter Appleyard (who are very reminiscent of Goodman and Lionel Hampton), and the emphasis is on swing-era standards. Tormé is in typically fine form on such tunes as "It's All Right with Me," "These Foolish Things," "Three Little Words," and the closing "Ev'ry Time We Say Goodbye." The singer even has some additional fun during this live-in-Japan concert by switching to drums for a rousing "Sing, Sing, Sing" that climaxes the Goodman medley. —*Scott Yanow*

Mel Tormé Collection / 1996 / Rhino ✦✦✦✦
This lavish box set spans 93 songs on four compact discs. The set is the only Tormé compilation that is thoroughly cross-licensed, featuring material from 17 different record labels. That certainly means that all of his major songs and hit singles are included, from "Careless Hands" and "The Christmas Song" to "Comin' Home Baby." However, that very extensiveness perversely works against the set—there is too much music here for anyone but devoted Tormé fans to digest. Listeners who want to invest time and money into the box set will find it worthwhile, but casual fans should stick with more manageable, single-disc compilations. —*Thom Owens*

Ralph Towner

b. Mar. 1, 1940, Chehalis, WA
Guitar / Post-Bop
One of the founders of Oregon, Ralph Towner is one of the few modern jazz musicians to specialize on acoustic guitar. His playing often stretches beyond the boundaries of conventional jazz into world music and is quite distinctive. He started playing piano when he was three and trumpet at five, performing in a dance band when he was 13. Towner studied classical guitar in Vienna and played with classical chamber groups in the mid-'60s. After moving to New York in 1969, Towner worked with Jimmy Garrison, Jeremy Steig, and Paul Winter's Winter Consort (1970-71). In the latter group Towner first met up with Collin Walcott, Glen Moore, and Paul McCandless; in 1971 they broke away to form Oregon, a highly versatile group that ranges from jazz and free improvisations to folk music. Towner (who guested with Weather Report in 1971 and played with Gary Burton a bit during 1974-75) has performed and recorded with Oregon extensively since its formation, in addition to recording as a leader and with many other artists on the ECM label. —*Scott Yanow*

Old Friends, New Friends / Jul. 1979 / ECM ✦✦✦✦
Excellent group work with trumpeter Kenny Wheeler. —*Michael G. Nastos*

★ **Solo Concert** / Oct. 1979 / ECM ✦✦✦✦✦
This very well recorded album features Ralph Towner playing 12-string and classical guitar on "Nardis," two pieces by John Abercrombie, and four of his own originals. The interpretations are typically sensitive, thoughtful, and often introspective, but they also show off Towner's impressive technique. —*Scott Yanow*

Five Years Later / Mar. 1981 / ECM ✦✦✦✦

City of Eyes / Jan. 1988-Nov. 1988 / ECM ✦✦✦✦
Solo guitar and group offerings. A treat. —*Michael G. Nastos*

Open Letter / Jul. 1991 / ECM ✦✦✦

Lennie Tristano

b. Mar. 19, 1919, Chicago, IL, **d.** Nov. 18, 1978, New York, NY
Piano / Cool
There aren't many mavericks in any musical form, and even fewer people whose work represents a legitimate alternative. Pianist Lennie Tristano's was a definite departure from established jazz tradition. It emphasized the same instrumental and harmonic mastery as bebop, but included many other unrelated elements. These included complex time signature changes, even rhythmic backgrounds rather than irregular cross-accents, carefully measured dissonance, and quite jarring polytonal effects. Tristano's music even veered into what would later be considered "free" collective improvisation, and he was a pioneer in multi-track dubbing and recording. Tristano insisted that his students, who included everyone from Bud Freeman to Art Pepper, thoroughly investigate the work of jazz greats from Louis Armstrong to Parker, and he put a premium on advanced ear training. Tristano's mother was an amateur pianist and opera singer, and he

first studied music with her. He continued his studies at a school for the blind, spending ten years there learning piano, wind instruments, and music theory. Tristano then entered the American Conservatory in Chicago, graduating in 1943. He played piano and various instruments in jazz contexts and did some private teaching on the side while attending the Conservatory. By the mid-'40s, Tristano was attracting such musicians as Billy Bauer, Lee Konitz, and Bill Russo. He made his first solo and trio recordings during this period. He moved to New York, performing with Charlie Parker and Dizzy Gillespie in concerts and on broadcasts, and doing arrangements for the Metronome All Stars. He was *Metronome*'s "Musician of the Year" in 1947 and occasionally wrote for the magazine. Warne Marsh became his pupil in 1948; then Konitz and Bauer returned, helping form a sextet. This group recorded in 1949. Tristano founded a school in 1951 and hired as teachers such pupils as Konitz, Marsh, and Sal Mosca. He steadily withdrew from public view, sporadically issuing some recordings. Various pupils and teachers left the fold, and Tristano closed the school in 1956, becoming a private teacher on Long Island. He made periodic appearances at the Half Note between 1958 and 1965, had a European tour in 1965, and made his last American public appearance in 1968. There was a French documentary interview about his life, times and work in 1973. After his death in 1978, there was a deluge of reissued and newly released Tristano recordings. A few Tristano sessions from the '40s and '50s are available on CD. —*Ron Wynn and Dan Morgenstern*

★ **Lennie Tristano on Keynote** / 1946-1947 / Mercury ✦✦✦✦✦
Early period progressive pianist. Quite innovative. —*Michael G. Nastos*

Wow / 1950 / Jazz ✦✦✦✦
As is true of the Jazz label's CDs, there are no liner notes on this release and the total time falls into the range of an LP, but this is a rare live performance by pianist Lennie Tristano's finest group. The identities of the bassist and drummer (who are both relegated to quiet timekeeping) are unknown, but the other musicians are quite distinctive. With altoist Lee Konitz, tenor saxophonist Warne Marsh, and guitarist Billy Bauer contributing their voices, Tristano explores a variety of common chord changes, a brief fugue by Bach, and his remarkable title cut. Well worth acquiring. —*Scott Yanow*

Continuity / Oct. 1958 & Jun. 1964 / Jazz ✦✦✦✦
These valuable recordings document the great pianist Lennie Tristano during his later years, when public appearances were rare and recordings only an infrequent event. Tristano is heard playing at the Half Note on two separate occasions. Warne Marsh is on tenor, altoist Lee Konitz is a major asset to the selections from 1964, and the rhythm sections include either Henry Grimes or Sonny Dallas on bass and Paul Motian or Nick Stabulas on drums. The recording quality is decent, if not admirable, but it is the music (six explorations of common chord changes and a 50-second "Everything Happens to Me") that is wonderful. Tristano, Marsh, and Konitz constantly create new melody lines and make highly original music. —*Scott Yanow*

Steve Turre (Steve Turré)

b. Sep. 12, 1948, Omaha, NE
Trombone, Conch / Bop, Latin Jazz, Hard Bop
One of the finest trombonists of the '80s and '90s, Steve Turre also introduced conch shells to jazz. After a brief period on violin, he switched to trombone when he was ten. Turre worked locally from age 13, played with Rahsaan Roland Kirk off and on from 1968, recorded with Santana in 1970, and in 1972 toured with Ray Charles. Turre had many diverse musical experiences in the '70s, including tours with Art Blakey's Jazz Messengers and the Thad Jones-Mel Lewis Orchestra (both in 1973), an opportunity to play trombone and electric bass regularly with Chico Hamilton (1974-76), and recording with Woody Shaw and Rahsaan Roland Kirk. Kirk inspired Turre to play exotic shells, and his ability to get a wide range of clear tones is quite impressive. Since that time Turre toured with McCoy Tyner, Dexter Gordon, Slide Hampton, Poncho Sanchez, Hilton Ruiz, and Tito Puente. In 1987 he joined Dizzy Gillespie's United Nations Orchestra, and he has played regularly with Lester Bowie's Brass Fantasy, the Leaders, and the Timeless All-Stars. Turre performed with his Sanctified Shells (a group featuring four trombonists doubling on shells, trumpeter E.J. Allen, bass, drums, and several percussionists) at the 1995 Monterey Jazz Festival, and has recorded as a leader for Stash, Antilles, and Verve. —*Scott Yanow*

Viewpoint / Feb. 7, 1987-Feb. 8, 1987 / Stash ✦✦✦✦
Steve Turre covers a lot of styles on his debut as a leader; from tributes to Kid Ory and Duke Ellington to bop, a bit of free form, and Latin-jazz. The trombonist proves that he is comfortable in all of those idioms, making this a rather impressive set. His supporting cast consists of pianist Mulgrew Miller, bassist Peter Washington, drummer Idris Muhammed, occasionally cellist Akua Dixon, extra percussion, and (on the Dixielandish piece) clarinetist Haywood Henry, trumpeter Jon Faddis, and the tuba of Bob Stewart. Everything works. —*Scott Yanow*

Fire and Ice / Feb. 5, 1988-Feb. 6, 1988 / Stash ✦✦✦✦
Steve Turre is one of the most versatile and talented trombonists to emerge during the past 15 years. For his second Stash recording, Turre (who also

plays his conch shells on two of the ten songs) utilizes a superb rhythm section (pianist Cedar Walton, bassist Buster Williams, and drummer Billy Higgins) plus a jazz string quartet (Quartette Indigo) on six of the selections. The music ranges from standards (including "When Lights Are Low," Monk's "Well You Needn't," and "Mood Indigo") to some memorable originals and one complex piece played by the strings alone. Stimulating music with more than its share of variety. —*Scott Yanow*

Sanctified Shells / Jan. 31, 1992-May 11, 1992 / Antilles ✦✦✦✦
● **Rhythm Within** / 1995 / Verve ✦✦✦✦
Trombonist Steve Turre obviously put a lot of work into this CD, for each of the nine selections has its own purpose, and the personnel changes on every cut. Turre doubles on the conch shells and on a few numbers uses a "shell choir"; in addition there are often three percussionists, other notable trombonists (including Britt Woodman, Frank Lacy, and Robin Eubanks), and such guest soloists as trumpeter Jon Faddis, tenor saxophonist Pharoah Sanders, and pianist Herbie Hancock. With highlights including "Funky-T," Yusef Lateef's "Morning," "Since I Fell for You" (a Woodman feature), and "All Blues," this is a particularly memorable and well conceived set, one of Turre's best. —*Scott Yanow*

Stanley Turrentine

b. Apr. 5, 1934, Pittsburgh, PA
Sax (Tenor) / Soul-Jazz, Hard Bop, Groove
While highly regarded in soul-jazz circles, Stanley Turrentine is one of the finest tenor saxophonists in any style in modern times. He excels at uptempo compositions, in jam sessions, interpretating standards, playing the blues, and on ballads. His rich, booming, and huge tone, with its strong swing influence, is one of the most striking of any tenor stylist, and during the '70s and '80s he made otherwise horrendous mood music worth enduring.

He toured with the R&B band of Lowell Fulson (1950-1951), whose featured pianist at the time was a young Ray Charles. From 1953-1954 he worked with Earl Bostic (perhaps the greatest R&B sax player of all time), where he replaced John Coltrane. He also worked and cut his first albums with Max Roach (1959-1960). Turrentine started recording as a leader on Blue Note in 1959 and 1960, while also participating in some landmark Jimmy Smith sessions such as *Midnight Special, Back at the Chicken Shack,* and *Prayer Meeting.*

His decade-plus association with Shirley Scott was both professional and personal, as they were married most of the time they were playing together. They frequently recorded, with the featured leader's name often depending on the session's label affiliation. When they divorced and split musically in the early '70s, Turrentine became a crossover star on CTI. Several of his CTI, Fantasy, Elektra, and Blue Note albums in the '70s and '80s made the charts. Though the jazz content became proportionally lower, Turrentine's playing remained consistently superb. He returned to straightahead and soul-jazz in the '80s, cutting more albums for Fantasy and Elektra, then returning to Blue Note. He's currently on the Musicmasters label. Almost anything Turrentine's recorded, even Stevie Wonder cover songs, are worth hearing for his solos. Much of his material is available on CD.

Turrentine is an original, one of a kind. He does not fit neatly into ordinary jazz categories. What makes Turrentine great is his deep love of the roots of jazz—blues and groove music. He never abandoned these roots to join the more cerebral set of jazz soloists. His recording partnership with Jimmy Smith has given us some of the finest funk groove music of all time. —*Bob Porter, Michael Erlewine, and Ron Wynn*

Stan the Man Turrentine / 1959-1960 / Bainbridge ✦✦✦
His earliest album with Turrentine on sax, Sonny Clark or Tommy Flanagan on piano, George Duvivier on bass, and Max Roach on drums. This tends to be uptempo and mainstream. It lacks the distinctive Turrentine sound that later albums show. —*Michael Erlewine*

Look Out / Jun. 18, 1960 / Blue Note ✦✦✦✦
With Horace Parlan (piano), George Tucker (bass), and Al Harewood (drums). Recorded at Englewood Cliffs, NJ. Small group. A 1987 reissue of excellent soul-jazz. —*Ron Wynn*

Blue Hour / Dec. 16, 1960 / Blue Note ✦✦✦✦
With the Three Sounds: Gene Harris (piano), Andrew Simpkinds (bass), and William Dowdy (drums). Recorded in Englewood Cliffs, NJ. A small group setting. This is a beautiful album of relaxed, bluesy sound. —*Michael Erlewine*

Comin' Your Way / Jan. 20, 1961 / Blue Note ✦✦✦✦
With Tommy Turrentine (trumpet), Horace Parlan (piano), George Tucker (bass), and Al Harewood (drums). Recorded at Englewood Cliffs, NJ. Small group. A 1988 reissue of a sumptuous '60s soul-jazz date. Horace Parlan is at his bluesy best. —*Ron Wynn*

● **Up at Minton's** / Feb. 23, 1961 / Blue Note ✦✦✦✦
This is a particularly solid double CD featuring tenor saxophonist Stanley Turrentine, guitarist Grant Green, pianist Horace Parlan, bassist George Tucker, and drummer Al Harewood during a frequently exciting live set.

Although recorded early in the careers of Turrentine and Green, both lead voices are easily recognizable, with Green actually taking solo honors on several of the pieces. Standards and a couple of blues make up the repertoire, giving listeners a definitive look at the soulful Mr. T. near the beginning of his productive musical life. — *Scott Yanow*

Dearly Beloved / Jun. 8, 1961 / Blue Note ✦✦✦✦
A trio recording from Blue Note has Turrentine with Shirley Scott on Hammond organ and Roy Brooks on drums. This is the first recording with Turrentine and Scott, who would work together for ten years and later get married. — *Michael Erlewine*

Z.T.'s Blues / Sep. 13, 1961 / Blue Note ✦✦✦✦
An all-star lineup has Turrentine with Grant Green on guitar and Tommy Flanagan on piano. The rhythm section has Paul Chambers on bass and Art Taylor on drums. Green and Turrentine made few albums together, but the combination is a natural—the two greatest groove masters, bar none. Flanagan seldom appears in this type of setting, and his playing is very tasteful. A studio recording by Rudy Van Gelder at Englewood Cliffs, NJ. If you can find a copy of this, it is a keeper. — *Michael Erlewine*

● **That's Where It's At** / Jan. 2, 1962 / Blue Note ✦✦✦✦
A Blue Note release with Les McCann on piano, Herbie Lewis on bass, and Otis Finch on drums. Small-group format. Excellent (and exciting) soul-jazz session with Turrentine blowing hot. — *Ron Wynn and Michael Erlewine*

Jubilee Shout / Oct. 18, 1962 / Blue Note ✦✦✦✦
Featuring Turrentine with Sonny Clark on piano and Kenny Burrell on guitar. Includes Tommy Turrentine (trumpet), Butch Warren (bass), and Al Harewood (drums). Recorded at Englewood Cliffs, NJ, by Rudy Van Gelder. Here is a classic, funky, soul-jazz groove, three uptempo, three slow. Sonny Clark (piano) soars, and Turrentine is red-hot. — *Ron Wynn and Michael Erlewine*

Never Let Me Go / Jan. 18, 1963 & Feb. 13, 1963 / Blue Note ✦✦✦
An early Blue Note album with the Stanley Turrentine Quintet: Turrentine, Shirley Scott (organ), Major Bolley (bass), Al Harewood (drums), and Ray Barretto (conga). — *Michael Erlewine*

A Chip Off the Old Block / Oct. 21, 1963 / Blue Note ✦✦✦✦
With Turrentine, Blue Mitchell (trumpet), Shirley Scott (organ), Earl May (bass), and Al Harewood (drums). This is a studio recording by Van Gelder. Bluesy, with tunes like "Midnight Blue" and "Blues in Hoss' Flat." — *Michael Erlewine*

Hustlin' / Jan. 24, 1964 / Blue Note ✦✦✦
A classic small group with Turrentine on tenor sax, Shirley Scott on the Hammond organ, and Kenny Burrell on guitar. The rhythm section has Bob Cranshaw on bass and Otis Finch on drums. Includes a version of "Goin' Home." — *Michael Erlewine*

In Memory Of / Jun. 3, 1964 / Blue Note ✦✦✦✦
The group includes Herbie Hancock (piano), Blue Mitchell (trumpet), Curtis Fuller (trombone), Bob Cranshaw (bass), and Otis Finch (drums). This has not yet been reissued by Blue Note. — *Michael Erlewine*

● **Let It Go** / Sep. 21, 1964 & Apr. 15, 1966 / Impulse ✦✦✦✦
This is vital Turrentine, with Shirley Scott on Hammond organ, Ron Carter on bass, and Mack Simpkins on drums. This album includes some additional tracks that were originally released on the Shirley Scott album *Everybody Loves a Lover*. Recorded in Englewood Cliffs, NJ. Husband-and-wife team Turrentine and Scott produce one classic soul-jazz groove album. — *Michael Erlewine*

Joyride / Apr. 14, 1965 / Blue Note ✦✦✦✦
Recorded at Englewood Cliffs, NJ, with a very large group that includes all kinds of horns, plus Herbie Hancock (piano) and Kenny Burrell (guitar). Arranged by Oliver Nelson. Throbbing tenor solos, with big-band backing. — *Ron Wynn*

Rough 'n Tumble / Jul. 1, 1966 / Blue Note ✦✦✦✦
A somewhat larger group (eight pieces) with Grant Green (guitar), Blue Mitchell (trumpet), James Spaulding (alto sax), Pepper Adams (baritone), and McCoy Tyner on piano. Recorded in New York City. One of his most popular, tightest, soul-jazz releases. — *Ron Wynn*

Easy Walker / Jul. 8, 1966 / Blue Note ✦✦✦✦
A small group with Turrentine, McCoy Tyner on piano, Bob Cranshaw on bass, and Mickey Roker on drums. This Blue Note album has yet to be released in the States. — *Michael Erlewine*

The Spoiler / Sep. 22, 1966 / Blue Note ✦✦✦✦
Turrentine with Blue Mitchell (trumpet), Julian Priester (trombone), James Spaulding (alto sax, flute), Bob Cranshaw (bass), Mickey Roker (drums), and Joseph Rivera (percussion). Still not reissued. — *Michael Erlewine*

New Time Shuffle / Feb. 17, 1967 & Jun. 23, 1967 / Blue Note ✦✦✦
A large-group album for Blue Note. — *Michael Erlewine*

Ain't No Way / May 10, 1968 / Blue Note ✦✦✦
Turrentine in small-group format. The cast includes Shirley Scott on the Hammond organ, McCoy Tyner on piano, Jimmy Ponder on guitar, Bob

Cranshaw on bass, and Ray Lucas on drums. Substitute Gene Taylor (bass) and Billy Cobham (drums) for some cuts. — *Michael Erlewine*

Common Touch! / Aug. 30, 1968 / Blue Note ✦✦✦
Turrentine with Shirley Scott on organ, Jimmy Ponder on guitar, Bob Cranshaw on bass, and Leo Morris on drums. Includes a rendition of "Lonely Avenue." Blue Note album, but not yet reissued. — *Michael Erlewine*

Look of Love / Sep. 29, 1968-Oct. 6, 1968 / Blue Note ✦✦✦✦
Larger group setting that was recorded at Englewood Cliffs, NJ. Both romantic and lusty, nice sessions. — *Ron Wynn*

Always Something There / Oct. 14, 1968 & Oct. 28, 1968 / Blue Note ✦✦
Large-group session recorded by Van Gelder. Includes renditions of "Light My Fire" and "Hey Jude." — *Michael Erlewine*

☆ **Sugar** / Nov. 1970 / CTI ✦✦✦✦✦
First album after Turrentine switched to the CTI label and producer Creed Taylor. Recorded at Englewood Cliffs, NJ. Larger group with arrangements. By far the best thing he ever made on CTI. Among the handful of genuine jazz albums that were cut on that label. Includes George Benson (guitar), Ron Carter (bass), Curtis Fuller (trombone). — *Ron Wynn*

The Best of Stanley Turrentine / Nov. 1970-Jun. 7, 1973 / Columbia ✦✦✦✦
Deceptive title. Decent collection of CTI and '70s pop jazz. — *Ron Wynn*

Cherry / May 17, 1972 / Columbia ✦✦✦✦
Produced by Creed Taylor on CTI. Recorded at Englewood Cliffs, NJ. Small group. Lush, wonderful playing by Turrentine and Jackson, despite very uneven material. — *Ron Wynn*

Pieces of Dreams / May 30, 1974-May 31, 1974 / Original Jazz Classics ✦✦
The Best of Mr. T / 1974-1980 / Fantasy ✦✦✦
Selection of tunes from Turrentine's '70s output, including "Everybody Come on Out," "The Man with the Sad Face," "West Side Highway," "Pieces of Dreams," "Nightwings," "Have You Ever Seen the Rain," and "Use the Stairs." — *Michael Erlewine*

Nightwings / Jun. 1977 & Jul. 1977 / Fantasy ✦✦
Large-group session for Fantasy. — *Michael Erlewine*

Straight Ahead / Nov. 24, 1984 / Blue Note ✦✦✦
Recorded at Power Play Studios, Long Island City, NY. Smaller group. Turrentine with George Benson (guitar), Jimmy Smith (organ), Ron Carter (bass), and Jimmy Madison (drums). Two cuts include Jimmy Ponder (guitar) and Les McCann (piano). This is a great combination of musicians, as on earlier cookers, but the time has passed, and it does not come off. Pleasant enough, but lacks high spots. — *Michael Erlewine*

More Than a Mood / 1992 / Music Masters ✦✦✦✦
For this quartet date with pianist Cedar Walton, bassist Ron Carter, and drummer Billy Higgins (trumpeter Freddie Hubbard sits in on two numbers), Turrentine is in top form on a variety of standards plus Tommy Turrentine's "Thomasville" and Rahsaan Roland Kirk's "Spirits Up Above." A fine session. — *Scott Yanow*

If I Could / May 10, 1993-May 12, 1993 / Music Masters ✦✦✦✦
This session from tenor saxophonist Stanley Turrentine often sounds like a CTI recording from the '70s, although Creed Taylor had nothing to do with it. Backed by Don Sebesky's arrangements and assisted by a strong rhythm section and Hubert Laws' flute, Turrentine's solos are stronger than the melodies, and he generally overcomes the unimaginative use of strings on the ballads. Mr. T. is in fine form, and he makes the most of each selection (particularly on the two blues, "June Bug" and "A Luta Continua"), while Laws comes across as much more creative than he does on most of his own recordings. Recommended. — *Scott Yanow*

Ballads / Blue Note ✦✦✦
Time / MusicMasters ✦✦✦
Turrentine with Kenny Drew, Jr. (keyboards), Dave Strykier (guitar), Dwayne Dolphin (bass), and Mark Johnson (drums). Modern, small-group Turrentine. He plays the horn like few others, but this is not in the style of his vintage soul stuff. — *Michael Erlewine*

McCoy Tyner (Alfred McCoy [Saud, Sulaimon] Tyner)

b. Dec. 11, 1938, Philadelphia, PA
Piano / Post-Bop

It is to McCoy Tyner's great credit that his career after John Coltrane has been far from anti-climatic. Along with Bill Evans, Tyner has been the most influential pianist in jazz of the past 35 years, with his chord voicings being adopted and used by virtually every younger pianist. A powerful virtuoso and a true original (compare his playing in the early '60s with that of anyone else from the time!), Tyner (like Thelonious Monk) has not altered his style all that much from his early days, but he has continued to grow and become even stronger.

McCoy Tyner grew up in Philadelphia, where Bud Powell and Richie Powell were neighbors. As a teenager he gigged locally and met John Coltrane. He made his recording debut with the Art Farmer-Benny Golson Jazztet but after six months left the group to join Coltrane in what (with bassist Jimmy Garrison and drummer Elvin Jones) would become the classic quartet. Few other pianists of the period had both the power and the complementary open-minded style to inspire Coltrane, but Tyner was never overshadowed by the innovative saxophonist. During the Coltrane years (1960-65), the pianist also led his own record dates for Impulse.

After leaving Coltrane, Tyner struggled for a period, working as a sideman (with Ike and Tina Turner!) and leading his own small groups; his recordings were consistently stimulating, even during the lean years. After he signed with Milestone in 1972, Tyner finally began to be recognized as one of the greats, and he has never been short of work since. Although there have been occasional departures (such as a 1978 all-star quartet tour with Sonny Rollins and duo recordings with Stephane Grappelli), Tyner has played mostly with his own groups, which have ranged from a quartet with Azar Lawrence and a big band to his current trio. —*Scott Yanow*

Inception / Nights of Ballads and Blues / Jan. 10, 1962 & Apr. 3, 1963 / Impulse ✦✦✦✦

McCoy Tyner: The Early Trios, Vol. 6 / Jan. 10, 1962-Dec. 8, 1964 / ABC/ Impulse ✦✦✦

Nights of Ballads and Blues / Mar. 4, 1963 / Impulse ✦✦✦
Probing, dense, and electric interpretations. —*Ron Wynn*

Today and Tomorrow / Jun. 4, 1963 / Impulse ✦✦✦✦
A 1991 release, reissued from limited Jazz Masters Series of '70s reissues. Superb music throughout. —*Ron Wynn*

● **The Real McCoy** / Apr. 21, 1967 / Blue Note ✦✦✦✦
With Joe Henderson (sax). —*Michael G. Nastos*

Tender Moments / Dec. 1, 1967 / Blue Note ✦✦✦✦
Small big band. Some extraordinary music. —*Michael Erlewine*

Time for Tyner / May 17, 1968 / Blue Note ✦✦✦✦
Tyner and Bobby Hutcherson (vibraphone) have some sparkling exchanges and dialogs. —*Ron Wynn*

● **Extensions** / Feb. 9, 1970 / Blue Note ✦✦✦✦
This CD has an interesting combination of players. It may be the only recording to include both pianist McCoy Tyner and his successor with the John Coltrane Quartet, Alice Coltrane (who adds atmosphere with her harp). This set also matches the young altoist Gary Bartz with Wayne Shorter (doubling on tenor and soprano) who he succeeded in Miles Davis' group and has reunions between Shorter and bassist Ron Carter and by Tyner and drummer Elvin Jones. The all-star sextet stretches out on lengthy renditions of four of Tyner's modal originals, and there is strong solo space for the leader and the two saxophonists. Wayne Shorter in particular is often quite intense. Stimulating music. —*Scott Yanow*

Asante / Sep. 10, 1970 / Blue Note ✦✦✦✦
The final McCoy Tyner Blue Note album found the innovative pianist during a low point in his career. His records were not selling that well, his mentor John Coltrane had passed away three years earlier, and it was not obvious that Tyner would be able to continue struggling successfully to make a living out of music. Fortunately his fortunes would soon rise when he signed with Milestone in 1972 and the critics began to rediscover him. *Asante* is a bit unusual, for the emphasis is on group interplay rather than individual solos. The four originals feature Tyner with altoist Andrew White, guitarist Ted Dunbar, bassist Buster Williams, drummer Billy Hart, Mtume on congas, and two spots for the voice of Songai. Worth investigating. —*Scott Yanow*

☆ **Sahara** / Jan. 1972 / Original Jazz Classics ✦✦✦✦✦
Remarkable date, both in playing and compositional clout. Vital. —*Ron Wynn*

☆ **Echoes of a Friend** / Nov. 11, 1972 / Original Jazz Classics ✦✦✦✦✦
Stunning solo piano. —*Ron Wynn*

Song for My Lady / Nov. 27, 1972 / Original Jazz Classics ✦✦✦✦
A 1988 reissue of a nice set. —*Ron Wynn*

Song of the New World / Apr. 6, 1973-Apr. 9, 1973 / Original Jazz Classics ✦✦✦✦
This set gave pianist McCoy Tyner his first opportunity to write music for a larger group that included brass, flutes, and—on two of the five songs—a string section. The powerful pianist is in fine form and the main soloist throughout (although there are spots for trumpeter Virgil Jones and the flute of Sonny Fortune). Most memorable are the title cut and a reworking of "Afro Blue." —*Scott Yanow*

★ **Enlightenment** / Jul. 7, 1973 / Milestone ✦✦✦✦✦
This is one of the great McCoy Tyner recordings. The powerful, percussive, and highly influential pianist sounds quite inspired throughout his appearance at the 1973 Montreux Jazz Festival. Azar Lawrence (on tenor and soprano) is also quite noteworthy (why didn't he ever become famous?), and there is plenty of interplay with bassist Juney Booth and drummer Alphonse Mouzon. But Tyner is the main star, whether it be on his three-part "Enlightenment Suite," "Presence," "Nebula," or the 25-minute "Walk Spirit, Talk Spirit." —*Scott Yanow*

Sama Layuca / Mar. 26, 1974-Mar. 28, 1974 / Milestone ✦✦✦✦
Pianist McCoy Tyner is heard at the height of his powers throughout this rewarding set. He contributed all five compositions and has a colorful and diverse group of major players at his disposal to interpret them: vibraphonist Bobby Hutcherson, altoist Gary Bartz, Azar Lawrence on tenor and soprano, John Stubblefield doubling on oboe and flute, bassist Buster Williams, drummer Billy Hart, and both Mtume and Guillherme Franco on percussion. The results (which include a brief Tyner-Hutcherson duet on "Above the Rainbow") are quite rewarding and serve as a strong example of McCoy Tyner's music. —*Scott Yanow*

● **Trident** / Feb. 18, 1975-Feb. 19, 1975 / Original Jazz Classics ✦✦✦✦
Pianist McCoy Tyner's first full-length trio album since 1964 was one of his most popular. Accompanied by bassist Ron Carter and Elvin Jones, Tyner (who uses harpsichord and/or celeste for flavoring on three of the six pieces) shows why he was considered the most influential acoustic pianist of the era (before Bill Evans began to surpass him in that category). Whether it be Jobim's "Once I Loved," "Impressions," "Ruby, My Dear," or Tyner's three powerful originals, this set finds Tyner in peak form. —*Scott Yanow*

★ **Supertrio** / Apr. 9, 1977-Apr. 12, 1977 / Milestone ✦✦✦✦✦
This album features the great pianist McCoy Tyner with two separate trios, either bassist Ron Carter and drummer Tony Williams or bassist Eddie Gomez and drummer Jack DeJohnette. The former session, which has a Tyner/Williams duet on "I Mean You" and a collaboration between Tyner and Carter on "Prelude to a Kiss," is the more interesting of the two, with the pianist interacting with Miles Davis' former rhythm section on six high-quality songs. But the Gomez-DeJohnette date (which includes four Tyner compositions plus "Stella by Starlight" and "Lush Life") also has its classic moments. Throughout, the percussive and highly influential pianist sounds inspired by the opportunity to create music with his peers. Recommended. —*Scott Yanow*

4 X 4 / Mar. 3, 1980-May 29, 1980 / Milestone ✦✦✦✦
This set matches the McCoy Tyner Trio (which includes bassist Cecil McBee and drummer Al Foster) with four different guests. Altoist Arthur Blythe and vibraphonist Bobby Hutcherson fare best, but both trumpeter Freddie Hubbard and guitarist John Abercrombie also have their shining moments. In addition to four Tyner compositions, there is one song apiece from McBee, Abercrombie, and Hutcherson in addition to four jazz standards. This collection is a fine all-around showcase for the brilliant pianist, even if no new ground is broken. —*Scott Yanow*

La Leyenda de la Hora / 1981 / Columbia ✦✦✦✦
There are no weak McCoy Tyner albums, and this relative obscurity is better than average. The great pianist is heard with an all-star nonet that includes Hubert Laws on flute, vibraphonist Bobby Hutcherson, altoist Paquito D'Rivera, Chico Freeman on tenor, and trumpeter Marchus Belgrave plus a seven-piece string section. The music (five Tyner originals) is highly rhythmic and generally quite stimulating. A strong effort. —*Scott Yanow*

★ **Live at Sweet Basil** / May 19, 1989-May 20, 1989 / Evidence ✦✦✦✦✦
This double CD (originally recorded for King in 1989) finds the great pianist McCoy Tyner stretching out with bassist Avery Sharpe and drummer Aaron Scott on five standards, a pair of songs apiece by John Coltrane and Thelonious Monk, and two of his own originals. Tyner has continued to grow in density and power through the years and by this time possessed a technique nearly on the level of an Art Tatum; his version of "Yesterdays," although different, somehow recalls Tatum. With other high points including "Monk's Dream," "Don't Blame Me," and "Just in Time," this two-fer gives one a definitive look at McCoy Tyner in the late '80s. —*Scott Yanow*

The Turning Point / Nov. 19, 1991-Nov. 20, 1991 / Verve ✦✦✦✦
This recording may not have been an actual "turning point" in pianist McCoy Tyner's productive career, but its success gave momentum to his big band. Although only a part-time affair, Tyner's orchestra (seven brass, four reeds, and a four-piece rhythm section) is considered one of the major jazz big bands of the '90s, a perfect outlet for the leader's percussive and modal-oriented piano. With arrangements by Tyner, Dennis Mackrel, Slide Hampton, Steve Turre, and Howard Johnson, many of these performances are quite powerful. It is a pity, though, that the liners do not identify the soloists, since there are several that are quite colorful. Recommended. —*Scott Yanow*

☆ **Infinity** / Apr. 12, 1995-Apr. 14, 1995 / Impulse ✦✦✦✦✦
It seems only fitting that the initial new release on the latest revival of the Impulse label features McCoy Tyner and Michael Brecker. When Impulse started out in 1960, John Coltrane and Tyner were the first artists to be signed, and when Impulse was briefly brought back by MCA in the '80s, two of its most important albums were recordings by Brecker. There are not a lot of surprises on this quartet matchup (with bassist Avery Sharpe and drummer Aaron Scott) except perhaps for how well Tyner and Brecker mesh together. The music is somewhat similar to a set by the pianist's regular trio with a solo piece ("Blues Stride"), a generous number of Tyner originals, and colorful versions of Thelonious Monk's "I Mean You" and

"Good Morning Heartache," but Brecker's presence and consistently powerful playing does inspire Tyner and his sidemen. For a strong example as to why today's saxophonists have such a high opinion of Michael Brecker, his roaring statement on the extended "Impressions" will suffice. Highly recommended. — *Scott Yanow*

James Blood Ulmer

b. Feb. 2, 1942, St. Matthews, SC
Guitar, Vocals / Avant-Garde, Crossover, Free Funk
One of the most individual and intense jazz guitarists, James "Blood" Ulmer has been a controversial figure ever since he started playing with Ornette Coleman. As a child he sang with the Southern Sons (a gospel group), but it was as a guitarist that he began performing professionally in 1959 in Pittsburgh. He spent a few years playing funky jazz with organ groups, and during 1967-71 was based in Detroit. In 1971 Ulmer moved to New York, where he worked regularly at Minton's Playhouse and played briefly with Art Blakey, Paul Bley, Larry Young, and Joe Henderson. The turning point of his career came in 1974, when he studied with Ornette Coleman; soon he would be in Ornette's free-funk band, Prime Time. By the time he made his debut as a leader for Artist's House, Ulmer had a style that mixed the power and sound of rock with Coleman's harmolodics and free-form approach. He recorded with Arthur Blythe, was in groups called Phalanx and the Music Revelation Ensemble, and led his own rather abstract bands. Ulmer's recordings have been inconsistent and erratic. They are both primitive and futuristic, while often being quite noisy; an acquired taste! — *Scott Yanow*

★ **Tales of Captain Black** / Dec. 5, 1978 / Artists House ✦✦✦✦✦
The best Ulmer from a total-package perspective. Everything works. — *Ron Wynn*

Are You Glad to Be in America? / Jan. 17, 1980 / Rough Trade ✦✦✦✦
Visionary guitarist with a unique sound. His best. — *Michael G. Nastos*

Freelancing / 1981 / Columbia ✦✦✦✦
A studio session that is mind-expanding. — *Michael G. Nastos*

● **America: Do You Remember . . .** / 1986 / Blue Note ✦✦✦✦
A 1987 release that is uneven but offers lots of excitement. — *Ron Wynn*

Dave Valentin

b. 1954, Bronx, NY
Flute / Latin-Jazz, Crossover
Dave Valentin, who has recorded more than 15 albums for GRP, combines the influence of pop, R&B, and Brazilian music with Latin-jazz to create a slick and accessible form of crossover jazz. At age nine, Valentin enjoyed playing bongos and congas. He gigged at Latin clubs in New York from age 12, but it was not until he was 18 that he seriously started studying flute. Valentin's teacher Hubert Laws suggested that he not double on saxophone, because of his attractive sound on the flute. In 1977 he made his recording debut with Ricardo Marrero's group, and he was also on a Noel Pointer album. Discovered by Dave Grusin and Larry Rosen, Valentin was the first artist signed to GRP, and he has been a popular attraction ever since. — *Scott Yanow*

Mind Time / 1987 / GRP ✦✦✦

Two Amigos / 1990 / GRP ✦✦✦✦
With Herbie Mann. — *Ron Wynn*

Musical Portraits / Jul. 10, 1990 / GRP ✦✦✦

● **Tropic Heat** / 1993 / GRP ✦✦✦✦
Flutist Dave Valentin's 16th album for GRP is one of his best. His regular group (a quartet with pianist Bill O'Connell, bassist Lincoln Goines, and drummer Robbie Ameen) is augmented by two percussionists and an excellent seven-member horn section that consists of the reeds of Dick Oatts, Mario Rivera, and David Sanchez; trombonist Angel "Papo" Vasquez; and three trumpeters, including Charlie Sepulveda. All of the horns get to solo, and the result is a particularly strong Latin-jazz session. Valentin continues to grow as a player and he cuts loose on several of these tracks. — *Scott Yanow*

Rudy VanGelder

Groove
Van Gelder, who is as "with it" today as in the beginning, made this fascinating response to a question about digital recorders in a 1986 radio interview by Ben Sidran of National Public Radio:

Van Gelder: If I'm going to do a session and I can choose what I want to choose, I will choose a digital recorder. There's just no question about it.

Sidran: What about the technical criticism of digital recording that I've read about, the problems of its feeling in some ways unnatural?

Van Gelder: Digital recording has been totally reliable for me. It finally does what a tape machine should do—really, just store what you're putting into it. No analog machine ever made could do that correctly. None. Not even the best, the most expensive, could ever do what a

properly designed two-track digital machine will do. We're talking about clarity of sound, clean sound, wide range, beautiful, no noise problem. To me, it's made working a pleasure. It's like starting all over again and being excited about things, like being able to play back a great sound to the group right after they've played it, and they can hear it right then. Everybody knowns it's good. Before they go home. (Quoted with permission from Mosaic Records staff.)

Note: Rudy Van Gelder has recorded more hard-bop and funk than any other person alive. And no one has recorded Hammond organ jazz like Van Gelder. If it's a Blue Note or Prestige album that has been recorded in Hackensack or Englewood Cliffs, NJ, then chances are it's a Van Gelder recording. — *Michael Erlewine*

Nana Vasconcelos

b. Aug. 2, 1944, Recife, Brazil
Percussion / World Fusion, Brazil, Latin Continuum
An excellent percussionist known for creating amazing melodies and rhythms, Brazilian percussion ace Nana Vasconcelos had the misfortune to make his American debut during the same era as Airto Moreira. Moreira has had a larger profile, but Vasconcelos need not take a back seat to anyone. His playing on the berimbau and cuica can be mesmerizing in its beauty and flair, and Vasconcelos can also dazzle on bongos, maracas, and drums. He played bongos and maracas in his father's band as a 12-year-old. Vasconcelos later was a drummer in Rio de Janeiro, and he mastered several traditional Brazilian rhythm instruments while playing with Milton Nascimento. He came to America with Gato Barbieri in the early '70s. His berimbau playing and percussive support were featured on several Barbieri Flying Dutchman albums. Vasconcelos later lived for two years in Paris, working primarily with handicapped children and doing some dates in Sweden with Don Cherry. He toured and co-led a group with Egberto Gismonti in the mid-'70s, then co-founded the trio Codona with Don Cherry and Collin Walcott in the late '70s. This group combined African, Asian, and South American ethnic styles, playing them in an improvisatory, but not necessarily jazz-based, manner. They disbanded after Walcott's death in 1984, but made some fine ECM albums during their tenure. Vasconcelos also played with Pat Metheny's band in the early '80s and then was in Don Cherry's group Mu in 1984. In the late '80s Vasconcelos recorded with the Bushdancers and made duet sessions with Gismonti for ECM and with Antonello Salis for Soul Note. His albums with Codona and the duets with Gismonti and Salis are available on CD, as are his earlier dates with Gismonti. — *Ron Wynn*

★ **Saudades** / Mar. 1979 / ECM ✦✦✦✦✦
This 1979 recording is probably Afro-experimentalist Vasconcelos' finest. It presents his various facets—berimbau playing, intricate vocals, fine percussion, even gorgeous guitar—simply and almost overwhelmingly. — *John Swenson, Original Music*

Lester / Dec. 1985 / Soul Note ✦✦✦✦

Bush Dance / 1986 / Antilles ✦✦✦✦
Best recorded example of Vasconcelos' rhythmic mastery. — *Ron Wynn*

Rain Dance / Oct. 1988 / Antilles ✦✦✦

Sarah Vaughan

b. Mar. 27, 1924, Newark, NJ, **d.** Apr. 3, 1990, Los Angeles, CA
Vocals / Bop, Standards
Bop's greatest diva, Sarah Vaughan was among jazz and popular music's supreme vocalists. She treated her voice like an instrument, improvising melodic and rhythmic embellishments, using her contralto range to make leaps and jumps, changing a song's mood or direction by enunciation and delivery, and altering her timbre. She turned sappy novelty tunes and light pop into definitive, jazz-based treatments. She had a distinctive swinging quality and intensity in her style, and was also a great scat singer. Vaughan was a dominant performer from the late '40s until the '80s, when illness forced her to cut back her appearances. Vaughan's recorded legacy stands with that of anyone in modern jazz history. She sang in the Mt. Zion Baptist Church choir as a child and became its organist at 12. Vaughan won the famous Amateur Night at the Apollo talent contest in 1942, and by April of the next year she had joined Earl Hines' band as a second pianist and vocalist. When Billy Eckstine left Hines and formed his own band in 1944, Vaughan soon joined and made her recording debut with his orchestra at the end of December. She went solo a year later and remained that way the rest of her career, except for a brief stint with John Kirby in 1945 and 1946. She became a star by performing pop ballads and show tunes, though she made numerous jazz anthems. Eckstine was a frequent duet partner, and the two collaborated on a fine Irving Berlin repertory record in the mid-'50s. Vaughan showed her jazz capabilities early in her solo career, recording a remarkable version of "Lover Man" with Dizzy Gillespie and Charlie Parker in 1945. But from 1949 to 1954, when she was with Columbia, she made hit albums with studio orchestras and cut only one jazz date, with Miles Davis and Budd Johnson. When Vaughan switched to Mercury in 1954, she won the right to make light pop and straight jazz recordings. She

did jazz material for EmArcy, recording with Clifford Brown, Cannonball Adderley, and Count Basie's sidemen, while cutting pop tracks for Mercury. These included the 1958 smash "Broken-hearted Melody." Vaughan maintained similiar relationships with Roulette, Mercury, and Columbia from 1960 to 1967. After a five year break, she returned to recording in 1971, this time with Norman Granz's Pablo label. Granz made many sessions with Vaughan through the '70s, some excellent, others not so good. She made a *Duke Ellington Songbook*, worked with Count Basie and Oscar Peterson, and even did an album of Afro-Latin and Brazilian material. A marvelous two-record live set was recorded in Japan. Her health worsened in the '80s, but she recorded an album of Gershwin songs with the Los Angeles Philharmonic in 1982 and an interesting concept/vocal album *The Planet Is Alive . . . Let It Live!* in 1985 on Gene Lees' Jazzletter label. This was an album of poems by Pope John Paul II, adapted by Lees, with music by Tito Fontana and Sante Palumbo. It featured Vaughan's vocals backed by an orchestra that included such jazz veterans as Art Farmer, Benny Bailey, and Sahib Shihab. When Vaughan died in 1990, there were tributes and worldwide outpourings of grief. Her albums are being steadily reissued, from the formative '40s dates to the '70s sets. Mercury has issued the mammoth *Complete Sarah Vaughan on Mercury* collection, which breaks down her career at the label into eras, with multi-disc packages for each period. The songbooks have been reissued, and Columbia has a two-disc package of material from the late '40s and early '50s. Single-album reissues are also available from the '50s, '60s, and '70s. —*Ron Wynn and Dan Morgenstern*

Time After Time / Dec. 31, 1944-Dec. 29, 1947 / Drive Archive ✦✦✦

I'll Be Seeing You / 1949 / Vintage Jazz Classics ✦✦✦✦
Shortly after Sarah Vaughan's death in 1990, this CD of previously unreleased live and radio performances was put out by Vintage Jazz Classics. The singer is heard in several different settings and excels in all of them. She sings two songs with a studio orchestra in 1949 (including Duke Ellington's "Tonight I Shall Sleep"), jams with her trio around 1961-62 (Woody Herman guests on clarinet for four songs), performs two short selections with Duke Ellington in 1951, and shares the vocal spotlight on "Love You Madly" with Nat King Cole and with Joe Williams on "Teach Me Tonight." Sassy's fans will want this very interesting release. —*Scott Yanow*

Perdido! Live (1953) / Apr. 21, 1951 / Natasha ✦✦✦✦
Most of this CD features Sarah Vaughan on radio broadcasts from Birdland during March and April 1953. She is top form on the varied material (highlighted by "I Get a Kick Out of You," "Tenderly," and "Perdido"), her trio is quite supportive, and Dizzy Gillespie sits in on a few numbers, backing Sassy with respect. The CD concludes with a couple of fairly primitively recorded but impressive songs from a 1951 Apollo Theatre concert. Overall, this release is quite valuable, for it features Vaughan in her early prime; her voice is beautiful throughout. —*Scott Yanow*

☆ **Complete Sarah Vaughan on Mercury, Vol. 1** / Feb. 10, 1954-Jun. 21, 1956 / Mercury ✦✦✦✦✦
Sarah Vaughan's years on Mercury (and its subsidiary EmArcy) feature inspired jazz performances, commercial recordings with string orchestras, and big-band sides that fall in between jazz and middle-of-the-road pop music. All of her recordings for Mercury are on four impressive box sets that add up to 23 CDs. The first set (six CDs) is the best overall of the four because it has a full set with her trio, the famous session with trumpeter Clifford Brown, a date with the Ernie Wilkins Orchestra (featuring altoist Cannonball Adderley), and a variety of orchestral dates. As with all of these sets, many previously unissued performances are included. More selective fans may want to get some of Sassy's individual packages instead (particularly the Clifford Brown date), but completists and true Sarah Vaughan fanatics will consider these four perfectly done sets to be essential. —*Scott Yanow*

The George Gershwin Songbook, Vol. 1 / Apr. 2, 1954-1957 / EmArcy ✦✦✦✦
With the exception of three songs recorded earlier, all of this set (the first of two CDs) dates from 1957 and finds the great Sarah Vaughan accompanied by her regular pianist Jimmy Jones plus a studio orchestra arranged by Hal Mooney. Since these 15 selections are fairly concise (two to five minutes apiece), the emphasis is on the melody and the original lyrics without all that much improvising taking place. Vaughan, who had a wondrous voice, is in excellent form on the superior material, making this CD a fine complement to Ella Fitzgerald's better-known *Gershwin Songbook*. —*Scott Yanow*

★ **Sarah Vaughan** / Dec. 18, 1954 / EmArcy ✦✦✦✦✦
This CD reissue features a classic (but unfortunately one-time only) collaboration between singer Sarah Vaughan and trumpeter Clifford Brown. In addition to Brownie, there is worthy solo space for flutist Herbie Mann and Paul Quinichette on tenor, who both fit in perfectly. Highlights include "Lullaby of Birdland," "He's My Guy," "You're Not the Kind," and "September Song." It is a special joy to hear Sarah Vaughan romping with her contemporaries in such a spontaneous yet coherent setting, swinging up a storm. All of the music on this CD is also included in *Vol. 1* of the box set titled *The Complete Sarah Vaughan on Mercury, Vol. 1* (and in a Clifford

Brown box) but, for those listeners who just want a strong sampling of Vaughan at her best, this is highly recommended. —*Scott Yanow*

● **In the Land of Hi-Fi** / Oct. 25, 1955 / EmArcy ✦✦✦✦
This single CD (whose contents are also included in the box set *The Complete Sarah Vaughan on Mercury, Vol. 1*) has one of the great singer's best jazz dates for EmArcy. Accompanied by an all-star orchestra arranged by Ernie Wilkins and featuring altoist Cannonball Adderley (who was near the beginning of his career), Vaughan is in superior form during these concise (around three minutes apiece) performances, particularly on "Soon," "Cherokee," "I'll Never Smile Again," and "An Occasional Man." A strong session. —*Scott Yanow*

Complete Sarah Vaughan on Mercury, Vol. 2: Sings Great American Songs (1956-1957) / Oct. 29, 1956-Jul. 12, 1957 / Mercury ✦✦✦✦
This five-CD box set, the second of four volumes that reissue all of Sarah Vaughan's recordings for Mercury and EmArcy (plus many previously unissued performances) contains her exploration of Gershwin songs, 13 vocal duets with her close friend Billy Eckstine, and just five jazz numbers with her trio; all of the other selections feature Vaughan backed by large studio orchestras, usually led by Hal Mooney. Most of the material is a bit commercial (certainly the arrangements tend to be), but Sarah Vaughan generally uplifts the songs and overcomes her surroundings. Still, listeners strictly interested in her jazz performances are advised to get some of her single-CD collections instead. —*Scott Yanow*

Complete Sarah Vaughan on Mercury, Vol. 3: Great Show on Stage (1954-1956) / Aug. 6, 1957-1959 / Mercury ✦✦✦✦
The third of four Sarah Vaughan Mercury box sets (this one has six CDs) traces her career during the last two and a half years of the '50s. There are several very interesting sessions (expanded greatly by the inclusion of many previously unissued performances) on this box, including 21 numbers from a gig at Mister Kelly's in Chicago with her trio (led by pianist Jimmy Jones), a meeting with the Count Basie Orchestra that resulted in the album *No Count Sarah*, and a live set with a septet (which includes cornetist Thad Jones and the tenor of Frank Wess) at the London House in Chicago. In addition, there are quite a few commercial sides with large orchestras (including some sessions arranged by Quincy Jones), so overall this box lets one hear the many sides of Sarah Vaughan; a special highlight is her first recorded version of "Misty." The reissue (and the other three volumes) is a must for Sarah Vaughan's greatest fans, although more general listeners may want to acquire one of the less expensive single CDs instead. —*Scott Yanow*

No Count Sarah / Dec. 1958 / EmArcy ✦✦✦✦
Sarah Vaughan recorded in a variety of settings while with Mercury and EmArcy in the '50s, but this particular matchup with the Count Basie Orchestra (pianist Ronnell Bright substitutes for Count, thus the title) is pure jazz. During the classic encounter, Vaughan fits in comfortably with the band, whether singing lyrics (such as "Darn That Dream," "Cheek to Cheek," or "Doodlin'") or scatting sensuously on "No Count Blues." The wit and constant swing (in addition to the spontaneous creativity) make this one of the best of all Vaughan recordings. Highly recommended, either on this CD or as part of the six-CD set *The Complete Sarah Vaughan on Mercury, Vol. 3*. —*Scott Yanow*

The Roulette Years / 1960 / Roulette ✦✦✦

Complete Sarah Vaughan on Mercury, Vol. 4, Pts. 1 and 2: (1963-1967) / Jul. 19, 196-Jan. 1967 / Mercury ✦✦✦✦
The fourth of four box sets reissuing every recording Sarah Vaughan made for the Mercury and EmArcy labels (including many previously unreleased performances) starts off (after four orchestra tracks) with its strongest selections, no less than 32 songs recorded during a live four-day engagement in Copenhagen, during which the singer is accompanied by the Kirk Stuart Trio. Everything else on this six-CD set is somewhat anticlimactic in comparison, for Vaughan is otherwise hindered a bit by string orchestras, a big band and/or a choir. Better to get the live sessions (released as *Sassy Swings the Tivoli* in addition to a Japanese set by the same name that has extra material) instead, although lovers of Vaughan's voice will want to pick up this large reissue anyway. —*Scott Yanow*

Jazz Fest Masters / Jul. 1969 / Scotti Bros. ✦✦✦✦
Sarah Vaughan made no studio recordings between January 1967 and November 1971, which makes her live performance from 1969 (first released on this 1992 CD) of historic interest. More importantly, the singer is in excellent form during these three different settings from the 1969 New Orleans Jazz Festival. She performs nine numbers with a quintet that includes fluegelhornist Clark Terry (who scats along with her on "Sometimes I'm Happy"), the tenor of Zoot Sims, and pianist Jaki Byard, is accompanied by the University of Illinois Big Band on three Benny Carter arrangements, and (during the most unusual track) collaborates with a Dixieland group and a gospel choir on "A Closer Walk with Thee." Overall, the recording quality is decent, and these lively performances add to the recorded legacy of the remarkable singer. —*Scott Yanow*

★ **Complete: Live in Japan** / Sep. 24, 1973 / Mobile Fidelity ✦✦✦✦
This two-CD set contains all of the music that Sarah Vaughan recorded

during her Tokyo concert for Mainstream. The 49-year-old singer is heard at the height of her powers, really digging into the standards and making magic out of such numbers as "Poor," "Round Midnight," "Willow Weep," "My Funny Valentine," "Summertime," and "Bye Bye Blackbird." This two-fer (which finds Vaughan accompanied by pianist Carl Schroeder, bassist John Gianelli, and drummer Jimmy Cobb) gives one a definitive look at the brilliant (and sometimes miraculous) singer. —*Scott Yanow*

How Long Has This Been Going On / Apr. 25, 1978 / Pablo ✦✦✦✦
This CD reissue features the great Sarah Vaughan in a typically spontaneous Norman Granz Pablo production with pianist Oscar Peterson, guitarist Joe Pass, bassist Ray Brown, and drummer Louie Bellson. Vaughan sounds wonderful stretching out on such songs as "Midnight Sun," "More Than You Know," "Teach Me Tonight," and "Body and Soul." All ten of the melodies are standards that she knew backward but still greeted with enthusiasm. A very good example of late-period Sarah Vaughan. —*Scott Yanow*

Duke Ellington Songbook, Vol. 2 / Aug. 15, 1979-Sep. 13, 1979 / Pablo ✦✦✦✦
The second of two Pablo CDs featuring Sarah Vaughan interpreting Duke Ellington-associated material shows that the veteran singer never did decline. With assistance from trumpeter Waymon Reed, flutist Frank Wess, Eddie "Cleanhead" Vinson on alto and a surprise vocal, and several overlapping rhythm sections, Vaughan sounds in top form throughout this date. Highlights include "I Ain't Got Nothing but the Blues," "Chelsea Bridge," "Rocks in My Bed," "I Got It Bad," and "Mood Indigo," but all 11 numbers are well worth hearing. Both of these well conceived sets are recommended. —*Scott Yanow*

Send in the Clowns / Feb. 16, 1981-May 16, 1981 / Pablo ✦✦✦

Crazy and Mixed Up / Mar. 1, 1982 & Mar. 2, 1982 / Pablo ✦✦✦✦
Sarah Vaughan had complete control over the production of this album (which would be her last small-group recording), and, even if the results are not unique, her voice is often in near-miraculous form. With fine backup work from pianist Roland Hanna, guitarist Joe Pass, bassist Andy Simpkins, and drummer Harold Jones, Vaughan sounds in prime form on such songs as "I Didn't Know What Time It Was," "Autumn Leaves," "The Island," and "You Are Too Beautiful." It is hard to believe, listening to her still-powerful voice on this CD reissue, that she had already been a recording artist for 48 years. —*Scott Yanow*

Joe Venuti (Guiseppi Venuti)

b. Sep. 16, 1903, Philadelphia, PA, **d.** Aug. 14, 1978, Seattle, WA
Violin / Dixieland, Swing, Classic Jazz
Although renowned as one of the world's great practical jokers (he once called a couple of dozen bass players with an alleged gig and asked them to show up with their instruments at a busy corner so he could view the resulting chaos!), Joe Venuti's real importance to jazz is as improvised music's first great violinist. He was a boyhood friend of Eddie Lang (jazz's first great guitarist), and the duo teamed up in a countless number of settings during the second half of the '20s, including recording influential duets. Venuti moved to New York in 1925, and immediately he and Lang were greatly in demand for jazz recordings, studio work, and club appearances. Venuti seemed to play with every top White jazz musician during the segregated era, and in 1929 he and Lang joined Paul Whiteman's Orchestra, appearing in the film *The King of Jazz*.

Lang's death in 1933 was a major blow to Venuti, who gradually faded from the spotlight. In 1935, after visiting Europe, the violinist formed a big band; although it survived quite awhile and helped introduce both singer Kay Starr and drummer Barrett Deems, it was a minor-league orchestra that recorded only four songs (which Venuti characteristically titled "Flip," "Flop," "Something," and "Nothing!"). His brief stint in the military during World War II ended the big band, and when he was discharged, Venuti stuck to studio work in Los Angeles. He was regularly featured on Bing Crosby's early-'50s radio show, but in reality the 1936-66 period was the Dark Ages for Venuti, as he drifted into alcoholism and was largely forgotten by the jazz world.

In 1967 Joe Venuti began a major comeback, playing at the peak of his powers at Dick Gibson's Colorado Jazz Party. His long-interrupted recording career resumed with many fine sessions (matching his violin with the likes of Zoot Sims, Earl Hines, Marian McPartland, George Barnes, Dave McKenna, and Bucky Pizzarelli) and, despite his increasingly bad health, Venuti's final decade was a triumph. —*Scott Yanow*

★ **Joe Venuti and Eddie Lang, Vol. 1** / Sep. 1926-Sep. 1928 / JSP ✦✦✦✦✦

★ **Joe Venuti and Eddie Lang, Vol. 2** / Jun. 1928-Sep. 1931 / JSP ✦✦✦✦✦

☆ **Fiddlesticks** / Oct. 22, 1931-Jan. 25, 1939 / Conifer ✦✦✦✦✦
This CD combines five complete sessions, some of violinist Joe Venuti's finest recordings from the '30s. Venuti, guitarist Eddie Lang, trumpeter Charlie Teagarden, trombonist Jack Teagarden, and clarinetist Benny Goodman team for four classics ("Beale Street Blues," "After You've Gone," "Farewell Blues," and "Someday Sweetheart"). Jimmy Dorsey and Adrian Rollini constantly switch instruments on their wild meeting with Venuti and Lang; the violinist is heard on two worthy dates from 1935; and the only four

recordings made by his unsuccessful big band (titled "Flip," "Flop," "Something," and "Nothing") wrap up this essential CD. Venuti would spend 30 years in obscurity (due partly to his alcoholism), but he is heard at the peak of his powers throughout this essential CD. —*Scott Yanow*

Alone at the Palace / Apr. 27, 1977-Apr. 28, 1977 / Chiaroscuro ✦✦✦✦
For one of violinist Joe Venuti's final recording sessions, he engages in a set of duets with the talented swing pianist Dave McKenna. The original LP had a dozen performances, and the reissue CD adds seven more. In addition to the usual standards, there are several Dixieland tunes (including three versions of "At the Jazz Band Ball") and four Venuti originals. McKenna (with his rolling bass lines) was a perfect partner for the violinist, making this set one of the best of Venuti's later years. —*Scott Yanow*

Harold Vick

b. Apr. 3, 1936, Rocky Mount, NC, **d.** Nov. 13, 1987, New York, NY
Sax (Tenor) / Soul-Jazz, Hard Bop, Groove
An excellent, thick-toned tenor, Harold Vick sounded quite at home in hard-bop and soul-jazz settings. His uncle, Prince Robinson (a reed player from the '20s), gave him a clarinet when he was age 13, and three years later Vick switched to tenor. He rose to prominence playing with organ combos in the mid-'60s, recording and performing with Jack McDuff, Jimmy McGriff, and Big John Patton. He started recording as a leader in 1966. Among his associations were Jack DeJohnette's unusual group Compost (1972), Shirley Scott in the mid-'70s, and Abbey Lincoln, with whom he recorded two Billie Holiday tributes for Enja just a short time before his death. —*Scott Yanow*

● **Steppin' Out** / May 21, 1963 / Blue Note ✦✦✦✦
Don't Look Back / Nov. 1974 / Strata East ✦✦✦✦
Commitment / 1975 / Muse ✦✦✦

Leroy Vinnegar

b. Jul. 13, 1928, Indianapolis, IN
Bass / Cool
A great "walking" bassist who's self-taught player, Leroy Vinnegar was a prolific player on the '50s and '60s West Coast recording scene. He's most famous for his dynamic accompaniment and "walking" lines. Vinnegar plucked open strings with the left hand, adding heavier accents. He doesn't take that many solos, but the ones he delivers are outstanding. Vinnegar and pianist Carl Perkins attended school together in Indianapolis and later became colleagues on the West Coast. Vinnegar worked in Chicago during the early '50s, serving as house bassist at the Beehive and playing with Sonny Stitt and Charlie Parker. He moved to Los Angeles in 1954 and eventually recorded with Stan Getz, Shorty Rogers, Herb Geller, Chet Baker, Gerald Wilson, and Serge Chaloff. He, Shelly Manne, and Andre Previn formed a popular trio that did jazz adaptions of Broadway songs and scores. They enjoyed a huge hit album with *My Fair Lady* in 1956. Vinnegar began cutting his own recordings in 1957, and his "walking" trademark was featured on the Contemporary albums *Leroy Walks* and *Leroy Walks Again*. He worked often with Joe Castro and Teddy Edwards, co-leading groups and touring Europe with them. Vinnegar made some seminal recordings with Sonny Rollins, Phineas Newborn, the Jazz Crusaders, and Kenny Dorham. He remained in demand during the '60s, doing several sessions. Perhaps the most successful was another smash album, *Swiss Movement* with Les McCann and Eddie Harris in 1969. Vinnegar was in a quintet co-led by Howard McGhee and Edwards in the '70s and worked in the Panama Hats, a quasi-Dixieland band that backed actor George Segal and often appeared on late-night TV during the '80s. Health problems resulted in Vinnegar's becoming less active in the late '80s, when he moved to Portland, OR. —*Ron Wynn*

Leroy Walks! / Jul. 15, 1957-Sep. 23, 1957 / Original Jazz Classics ✦✦✦✦
This was bassist Leroy Vinnegar's sextet (Vic Feldman, Gerald Wilson, Teddy Edwards, Carl Perkins, Tony Bazley) date from 1957. Not Vinnegar's best. —*Bob Rusch, Cadence*

● **Leroy Walks Again** / Aug. 1, 1962-Mar. 5, 1963 / Original Jazz Classics ✦✦✦✦
This was a bop session that was, for the most part, music of the moment. It's notable for being Freddy Hill's recorded debut (at 28 years old) and for Roy Ayers' solid solos. —*Bob Rusch, Cadence*

Walkin' the Basses / Mar. 1992 / Contemporary ✦✦✦✦
Bassist Leroy Vinnegar was a familiar figure on the West Coast scene of the late '50s and early '60s and drew praises for his entertaining, yet musically sophisticated, "walking" bass lines. Vinnegar has not lost his prowess, and this album features him heading a group with pianist Geoff Lee, drummer Mel Brown, and percussionist Curtis Craft. While it is Vinnegar's date, he doesn't dominate, but sets the table. Vinnegar produced the session and arranged nine of the 11 songs, co-arranging a tenth with Lee. It isn't so much easy listening as nice, sophisticated material from four established pros who enjoy working with each other. —*Ron Wynn*

Integrity / May 14, 1995 / Jazz Focus ✦✦✦

Eddie "Cleanhead" Vinson

b. Dec. 18, 1917, Houston, TX, **d.** Jul. 2, 1988, Los Angeles, CA

Saxophone, Vocals / R&B, Blues, Electric Jump Blues, Jazz, Bop, Jazz, Early R&B, Groove

An advanced stylist on alto saxophone who vacillated throughout his career between jump-blues and jazz, bald-pated Eddie "Cleanhead" Vinson (he lost his hair in a botched bout with a lye-based hair-straightener) also possessed a playfully distinctive vocal delivery that stood him in good stead with blues fans.

Vinson first picked up a horn while attending high school in Houston. During the late '30s, he was a member of an incredible horn section in Milton Larkin's orchestra, sitting next to Arnett Cobb and Illinois Jacquet. After exiting Larkin's employ in 1941, Vinson picked up a few vocal tricks while on tour with bluesman Big Bill Broonzy. Vinson joined the Cootie Williams Orchestra from 1942 to 1945. His vocals on trumpeter Williams' renditions of "Cherry Red" and "Somebody's Got to Go" were in large part responsible for their wartime hit status.

Vinson struck out on his own in 1945, forming his own large band, signing with Mercury, and enjoying a double-sided smash in 1947 with his romping R&B chart-topper "Old Maid Boogie" and the song that would prove his signature number, "Kidney Stew Blues" (both songs featured Vinson's instantly identifiable vocals). A 1949-52 stint at King Records produced only one hit, the amusing sequel "Somebody Done Stole My Cherry Red," along with the classic blues "Person to Person" (later revived by another King artist, Little Willie John).

Vinson's jazz leanings were probably heightened during 1952-53, when his band included a young John Coltrane. Somewhere along about here, Vinson wrote two Miles Davis classics, "Tune Up" and "Four." Vinson steadfastly kept one foot in the blues camp and the other in jazz, waxing jumping R&B for Mercury (in 1954) and Bethlehem (1957), jazz for Riverside in 1961 (with Cannonball Adderly), and blues for Blues Time and ABC-BluesWay. A 1969 set for Black and Blue, cut in France with pianist Jay McShann and tenor saxophonist Hal Singer, beautifully recounted Vinson's blues-shouting heyday. (It's available on Delmark as *Kidney Stew Is Fine.*) A much later set for Muse teamed him with the sympathetic little-big-band approach of Rhode Island-based Roomful of Blues. Vinson toured the States and Europe frequently until his 1988 death of a heart attack. —*Bill Dahl*

Kidney Stew Is Fine / Mar. 28, 1969 / Delmark ✦✦✦✦
Although its programming has been juggled a bit, and the CD has been given liner notes, this Delmark release is a straight reissue of the original LP. Clocking in at around 38 minutes, the relatively brief set is the only recording that exists of Vinson, pianist Jay McShann, and guitarist T-Bone Walker playing together; the sextet is rounded out by the fine tenor Hal Singer, bassist Jackie Sampson, and drummer Paul Gunther. Vinson, whether singing "Please Send Me Somebody to Love," "Just a Dream," and "Juice Head Baby" or taking boppish alto solos, is the main star throughout this album (originally on Black and Blue), a date that helped launch his commercial comeback. —*Scott Yanow*

The Clean Machine / Feb. 22, 1978 / Muse ✦✦✦✦
What makes this album different from many of Eddie Cleanhead Vinson's is that four of the seven selections are taken as instrumentals. Vinson's alto playing has long been underrated, due to his popularity as a blues singer, so this release gives one the opportunity to hear his bop-influenced solos at greater length. With the assistance of a strong rhythm section led by pianist Lloyd Glenn and some contributions from trumpeter Jerry Rusch and Rashid Ali on tenor, Vinson is in excellent form throughout this enjoyable set. —*Scott Yanow*

● **Hold It Right There!** / Aug. 25, 1978-Aug. 26, 1978 / Muse ✦✦✦✦
After years of neglect, Eddie Cleanhead Vinson was finally receiving long overdue recognition at the time of this live session—one of six albums recorded during a week at Sandy's Jazz Revival. Two of these albums featured tenors Arnett Cobb and Buddy Tate in lead roles. While Vinson has fine blues vocals on "Cherry Red" and "Hold It," it is his boppish alto solos on "Cherokee," "Now's the Time," and "Take the 'A' Train" (the latter also having spots for Cobb and Tate) that recommend this set to blues and bop fans alike. —*Scott Yanow*

☆ **And Roomful of Blues** / Jan. 27, 1982 / Muse ✦✦✦✦✦
If there were justice in the world, Eddie Cleanhead Vinson would have been able to tour with this type of group throughout much of his career. Roomful of Blues, a popular five-horn nonet, has rarely sounded more exciting than on this musical meeting with the legendary singer/altoist. Vinson himself is exuberant on some of the selections, particularly "House of Joy," one of five instrumentals among the eight selections. Whether one calls it blues, bebop, or early R&B, this accessible music is very enjoyable and deserves to be more widely heard. Among the supporting players, tenorman Greg Piccolo, trumpeter Bob Enos, and guitarist Ronnie Earl (in one of his earliest recordings) win honors. —*Scott Yanow*

● **Cherry Red Blues** / King/Gusto ✦✦✦✦
Somehow, amidst all the CD reissues from the King Records vaults

unleashed by Charly, Ace, Rhino, and King's current ownership, this versatile alto saxist has fallen through the cracks. Thus, this two-LP collection, boasting all but a handful of his jumping 1949-1952 outings for King, remains your best introduction to the Cleanheaded one's R&B output (along with the 1945-1947 sides he waxed for Mercury, which grace the seven-disc anthology *Blues, Boogie, & Bop: The 1940s Mercury Sessions*). —*Bill Dahl*

Mal Waldron

b. Aug. 16, 1926, New York, NY
Piano / Post-Bop, Hard Bop

Mal Waldron's piano playing has a pinched, angular sound, as he's among the artists not simply influenced by Thelonious Monk's unorthodox style but able to incorporate it in their own work in an individualized way. Waldron isn't quite as idiosyncratic and scattershot as Monk, but he uses the identical sparse approach and unusual voicings and rhythms. He's written compositions for large and small groups, backed vocalists, and done film and ballet scores. Waldron originally played jazz only on alto sax, preferring to play classical on piano, but he switched while at Queens College. Waldron earned his degree in composition and then worked with various New York bands. He made his recording debut in the late '40s with Ike Quebec. Waldron played with Della Reese, then joined Charles Mingus in 1954, playing at the Newport Jazz Festival in 1955 and 1956. He formed his own group with Gigi Gryce and Idrees Sulieman. Waldron was on countless sessions for Prestige in the mid- to late '50s, often supplying many originals, including one ("Soul Eyes") that became a standard. He was Billie Holiday's accompanist from 1957 until her death in 1959; then he worked with Abbey Lincoln and did studio dates. Waldron was part of the remarkable Eric Dolphy quintet with Booker Little that played at the Five Spot in 1961. He also did a studio session with Dolphy. Waldron composed the film scores *The Cool World* in 1963, plus *Three Bedrooms in Manhattan* and *Sweet Love Bitter* in 1965. But he had to relearn the piano after suffering a nervous breakdown in the mid-'60s. Waldron did this partly by listening to his own recordings. He moved to Europe in 1965 to do more film work, settling in Munich in 1967. A trio album Waldron recorded was one of the first issued on the then-new label ECM. He recorded and worked frequently with Steve Lacy and Archie Shepp in the '70s, toured Japan, and began making return visits to America in 1975. Waldron was featured on numerous Enja releases in the '70s with trios, quartets, and solo. He continued recording in the '80s on Enja, Palo Alto, Muse, Projazz, Hat Art, and Soul Note. Waldron has a full slate of past and present sessions available on CD. —*Ron Wynn*

● **Mal, Vols. 1 & 2** / Nov. 9, 1956-May 17, 1957 / Prestige ✦✦✦✦
Two of pianist Mal Waldron's first three albums as a leader are combined on this two-LP set. Waldron is heard in a quintet with trumpeter Idrees Sulieman and altoist Gigi Gryce, leading a sextet with trumpeter Bill Hardman, altoist Jackie McLean and tenor saxophonist John Coltrane and with a different sextet that also stars Sulieman, Coltrane and altoist Sahib Shihab. Many of the Prestige sessions from the era were essentially jam sessions but Waldron's dates were better organized and had more challenging material. Five of the pianist's originals are among the dozen selections on this two-fer which also includes five standards and two obscurities. These hard bop performances are among Coltrane's lesser-known recordings and show that, even in his early days, Mal Waldron had his style. —*Scott Yanow*

Mal 3: Sounds / Jan. 31, 1958 / Original Jazz Classics ✦✦✦

Mal / Four Trio / Sep. 26, 1958 / Original Jazz Classics ✦✦✦✦
It seems strange that this, pianist Mal Waldron's seventh session as a leader, was his first with a group as small as his trio. With the assistance of bassist Addison Farmer and drummer Kenny Dennis, Waldron performs four standards and three of his moody originals. His sometimes-brooding style was already recognizable, and his inventive use of repetition was impressive. This CD reissue of the original LP gives listeners a definitive look at the early style of Mal Waldron. —*Scott Yanow*

Impressions / Mar. 20, 1959 / Original Jazz Classics ✦✦✦✦
Excellent late-'50s work. —*Ron Wynn*

Free at Last / Nov. 24, 1969 / ECM ✦✦✦✦
Outstanding trio date of early ECM release. A 1989 reissue. —*Ron Wynn*

Black Glory / Jun. 29, 1971 / Enja ✦✦✦✦
This CD reissues one of the first Enja recordings, a trio outing for pianist Mal Waldron, bassist Jimmy Woode, and drummer Pierre Favre. Waldron has continued to evolve through the decades while keeping his basic sound. A master at using repetition and brooding chords, Waldron is in excellent form on five of his originals plus Woode's brief "M.C.," playing with a knowledge of the avant-garde but still connected to the hard-bop tradition. —*Scott Yanow*

Live at the Village Vanguard / Sep. 16, 1986 / Soul Note ✦✦✦✦
This is a high-caliber quartet set, with Woody Shaw (trumpet) triumphant. —*Ron Wynn*

Crowd Scene / 1989 / Soul Note ✦✦✦✦
For this quintet session, Mal Waldron contributed two somewhat episodic originals (titled "Crowd Scene" and "Yin and Yang") that are used as the basis for extended improvisations by altoist Sonny Fortune, tenor saxophonist Ricky Ford, bassist Reggie Workman, drummer Eddie Moore, and the pianist/leader. Despite the obvious talents of these very individual players, there are some rambling moments on these lengthy performances, both of which clock in at over 25 minutes. Still, it is often fascinating to hear what the musicians come up with during these go-for-broke improvisations. — *Scott Yanow*

Bennie Wallace (Bennie Lee Wallace, Jr.)

b. Nov. 18, 1940, Chattanooga, TN
Sax (Tenor) / Post-Bop
Bennie Wallace has long had his own unique style, combining the rapsy tone of Ben Webster with the frequent wide-interval jumps of Eric Dolphy. He has an explorative style that sound-wise looks back toward the swing era. Wallace started on clarinet when he was 12 and a few years later switched to tenor. He graduated from the University of Tennessee in 1968 and in 1971 moved to New York, where he debuted with Monty Alexander. Wallace gigged with Sheila Jordan, played with many avant-garde musicians, was in George Gruntz's Concert Jazz Band in 1979, and led his own trio/quartet on-and-off throughout the '70s and '80s. He recorded frequently before 1985 for Enja, but his mid- to late-'80s Blue Note recordings are more memorable; they find him infusing his appealing sound with touches of New Orleans R&B and a healthy dose of humor. In recent times Wallace has been writing music for films, including *White Men Can't Jump.* — *Scott Yanow*

Sweeping through the City / Mar. 1984-Apr. 1984 / Enja ✦✦✦✦
Large-group date with a blues and gospel element. Unwieldy at times, but effective overall. — *Ron Wynn*

★ **Twilight Time** / 1985 / Blue Note ✦✦✦✦✦

☆ **Border Town** / Jun. 1987 / Blue Note ✦✦✦✦✦
Top mix of blues and jazz. Dr. John (p) and John Scofield (g) are first-rate. — *Ron Wynn*

Old Songs / 1993 / AudioQuest ✦✦✦✦
Much of this date features Bennie Wallace's distinctive tenor in a pianoless trio with bassist Bill Huntington and drummer Alvin Queen. Although it could be said that Wallace combines the sound of Ben Webster with the interval jumps of Eric Dolphy (a very potent combination), he has had his own style for over a decade. These eight standards (along with an original blues "At Lulu White's") are taken at a variety of tempos, and Wallace really digs into these fertile chord changes after showing respect for the melodies. — *Scott Yanow*

Fats Waller (Thomas Wright Waller)

b. May 21, 1904, New York, NY, **d.** Dec. 15, 1943, Kansas City, MO
Organ, Vocals / Swing, Stride, Classic Jazz
Thomas "Fats" Waller was a larger than life figure, a multi-talented individual who was not only one of the great stride pianists of all time but an underrated singer, an often-hilarious personality, jazz's first organist, and a brilliant songwriter. He had a lifestyle full of food, liquor, women, and heated music that was great fun while it lasted. Waller's skill as a melodic creator was unmatched, and he collaborated with lyricist partner Andy Razaf on dozens of classics, among them "Ain't Misbehavin," "Honeysuckle Rose," and "Black and Blue." He was the first pianist to swing in the light, graceful fashion that's now associated with modern jazz. Waller influenced such pianists as Count Basie, Art Tatum, and Dave Brubeck. He made hundreds of records, had his own radio programs, and appeared in three films plus a handful of shorts. His father was a Baptist preacher who conducted open-air religious services in Harlem, at which the young Waller played reed organ. He played jazz at school and by 15 was house organist at Lincoln Theatre. After his mother died in 1920, Waller moved in with pianist Russell Brooks' family, dashing his father's hopes that he'd become a religious organist. Brooks introduced Waller to James P. Johnson, who became a tutor and mentor. Waller began making piano rolls in 1922 and made his recording debut as a soloist for the Okeh label, cutting "Muscle Shoals Blues" and "Birmingham Blues." Waller has claimed he studied piano with Leopold Godowsky and composition with Carl Bohm at the Juilliard School during this early period; this has not been fully verified. During the early '20s, Waller recorded with such blues vocalists as Sara Martin, Alberta Hunter, and Maude Mills. He collaborated with Clarence Williams in 1923, an effort that led to his song "Wild Cat Blues" being published and recorded by Williams' Blue Five with Sidney Bechet. This song and the composition "Squeeze Me," issued that same year, helped make Waller's reputation as a songwriter. He made his radio debut in 1923 on a Newark station, then began regular appearances on WHN in New York while still playing organ regularly at both the Lincoln and Lafayette theaters. He began recording with Victor in 1926, cutting the organ solos "St. Louis Blues" and "Lenox Avenue Blues"; he did most of his sessions for that label

the rest of his career. Waller recorded his song "Whiteman Stomp" with Fletcher Henderson's orchestra in 1927; Henderson added other Waller songs like "Crazy 'Bout My Baby" and "Stealin' Apples" to the band's book. While working with groups like Morris' Hot Babes, McKinney's Cotton Pickers, and his own Fats Waller's Buddies (one of the earliest interracial groups to record), Waller turned heads with a string of marvelous solo recordings in 1929; these included "Handful of Keys," "Smashing Thirds," "Numb Fumblin'," and "Valentine Stomp." But he was attaining equal fame for his collaborations with lyricists. He and Razaff did much of the music for the 1928 Black Broadway musical *Keep Shufflin,* and a year later did songs for the shows *Load of Coal* and *Hot Chocolates,* which marked the debut of "Ain't Misbehavin." Waller made his own debut at Carnegie Hall in 1928, serving as piano soloist in Johnson's "Yamekraw," a fantasy for piano and orchestra. In the '30s, Waller did sessions with Ted Lewis, Jack Teagarden, and Billy Banks' Rhythmakers before starting a lengthy recording series with the six-piece group Fats Waller and his Rhythm. Participants included Al Casey, Gene Sedric or Rudy Powell, and either Herman Autrey, Bill Coleman, or John Hamilton. Waller appeared in the films *Hooray for Love!* and *King of Burlesque* in 1935, while on the West Coast with Les Hite's band. Waller soon formed his own big band and recorded with a unit that mixed some members of Rhythm with additional personnel. Waller toured Europe in 1938 and 1939 and cut solo pipe organ tracks for HMV. He recorded "London Suite," an extended series of six related solo piano pieces, during his 1939 London visit. This was his longest single composition. Waller returned to Hollywood in 1943, making the film *Stormy Weather* with Lena Horne and Bill Robinson. He led an all-star unit for the movie that included Benny Carter and Zutty Singleton. Waller also toured extensively that year, and collaborated with lyricist George Marion, Jr., on the score for the theatrical production *Early to Bed* that had its Boston opening May 24, 1943. A lifetime of overeating and alcohol abuse, plus financial pressures from many years of legal controversy over alimony payments, took its toll. Waller became ill during another visit to the West Coast, where he was solo pianist at the Zanzibar room in Hollywood. He died of pneumonia while returning to New York with his manager, Ed Kirkeby. A volume of articles and several books have been written about Waller; many valuable reissues of his work are available. "Ain't Misbehavin'" has become an oft-recorded classic, cut by everyone from Nell Carter to Hank Williams, Jr. — *Ron Wynn, Dan Morgenstern, and Scott Yanow*

☆ **Piano Masterworks, Vol. 1** / Oct. 21, 1922-Sep. 24, 1929 / EPM ✦✦✦✦✦
Although he would become well known in the '30s for his comic vocals and memorable personality, Fats Waller was always first and foremost a pianist. During the '20s he was purely an instrumentalist, one of the greatest and most powerful stride pianists of all time. This CD has all of Waller's early piano solos, including every one of the alternate takes (two versions of many titles and a very rare third take of "I've Got a Feeling I'm Falling"). With the exception of his initial two sides from 1922 and 1927's "Blue Black Bottom," all of these titles are from 1929, including the original version of "Ain't Misbehavin." — *Scott Yanow*

Classic Jazz from Rare Piano Rolls / Mar. 1923-Jan. 1929 / Music Masters ✦✦✦

☆ **Turn on the Heat: The Fats Waller Piano Solos** / Feb. 16, 1927-May 13, 1941 / Bluebird ✦✦✦✦
With the exception of a third take of "I've Got a Feeling I'm Falling" and his two earliest records from 1922, all of Fats Waller's recorded piano solos are on this superior double-CD set. Over half of these recordings are from 1929, but fortunately he also cut three sessions of piano solos after he became much more famous as a comedy personality with his Rhythm sides. Highlights include the virtuosic "Handful of Keys," the earliest version of "Ain't Misbehavin'," "Clothes Line Ballet," "I Ain't Got Nobody," and "Honeysuckle Rose." A special bonus is a pair of piano duets with Bennie Payne ("St. Louis Blues" and "After You've Gone"). Classic music. — *Scott Yanow*

☆ **Fats Waller and His Buddies** / May 20, 1927-Dec. 18, 1929 / Bluebird ✦✦✦✦✦
This CD has most of Fats Waller's best band recordings of the '20s, including eight selections by his "Buddies" (highlighted by "The Minor Drag" and "Harlem Fuss"), six (counting two alternate takes) from the Louisiana Sugar Babes (an odd quartet featuring Waller's organ and James P. Johnson's piano), and seven selections on which Waller sits in with cornetist Thomas Morris' Hot Babies in 1927. Surprisingly, other than his scat vocal on "Red Hot Dan," Fats Waller is heard strictly as a pianist, but his talents were so giant as an instrumentalist that one never minds. With trombonists Charlie Irvis and Jack Teagarden and trumpeters Red Allen and Jabbo Smith among the strong supporting cast, the one word for this superior CD is "hot." — *Scott Yanow*

● **Breakin' the Ice, The Early Years, Part 1** / May 16, 1934-May 6, 1935 / Bluebird ✦✦✦✦
This two-CD set has the first 42 recordings of Fats Waller with his Rhythm. The brilliant stride pianist/vocalist/composer/personality became very popular due to these 1934-35 recordings, which feature either Herman

Autrey or Bill Coleman on trumpet; Gene Sedric, Ben Whitted, Mezz Mezzrow, or Rudy Powell on reeds; guitarist Al Casey; and a rhythm section. All of Waller's Victor recordings have been reissued on CD, and this two-fer (which includes such memorable numbers as "A Porter's Love Song to a Chambermaid," "Serenade for a Wealthy Widow," "How Can You Face Me," "Honeysuckle Rose," "Believe It, Beloved," "I Ain't Got Nobody," "Oh Suzannah Dust Off That Old Pianna," and "You've Been Taking Lessons in Love") is a perfect place to start. — *Scott Yanow*

The Definitive Fats Waller, Vol. 1: His Piano His Rhythm / Mar. 11, 1935-Aug. 7, 1939 / Stash ✦✦✦✦
In addition to his many studio recordings for Victor, the popular pianist/singer/composer Fats Waller recorded two extensive sessions of radio transcriptions that could be used to fill in time between radio shows. These have now been reissued in full on two CDs. The first volume finds Waller performing seven songs in 1935 (two duets with the reeds of Rudy Powell and five solos with some vocals) in addition to 23 performances from 1939 (17 with his Rhythm, an excerpt from an organ solo, and five unaccompanied piano solos). Throughout, Waller, who never really needed an audience, is in exuberant form, playing material that was generally superior to the dog tunes he was often handed at recording sessions. A fun set. — *Scott Yanow*

The Definitive Fats Waller, Vol. 2: Hallelujah / Mar. 11, 1935-Apr. 3, 1939 / Stash ✦✦✦✦
This second volume of rare Fats Waller items includes 24 selections performed at a marathon radio transcription session in 1935 (there were actually 31 pieces played, seven of which are on *Vol. 1*). Waller is heard solo, singing and playing piano without the assistance of his sidemen, and he is in top form on a wide variety of material. This CD concludes with previously unreleased items from three different occasions: a 1936 solo broadcast from Bluefield, WV, two selections privately recorded in London in 1939, and Waller's appearance on "The George Jessel Show" during the same year. A superior release from the great stride pianist, vocalist, composer, and personality. — *Scott Yanow*

● **I'm Gonna Sit Right Down . . . The Early Years, Part 2** / May 8, 1935-Feb. 1, 1936 / Bluebird ✦✦✦✦
The second in a series of five CD packages that reissue all of Fats Waller's Victor recordings with his Rhythm, this two-CD set traces the pianist/composer/vocalist/personality's career during a nine-month period. Among the sidemen are trumpeter Herman Autrey and either Rudy Powell or Gene Sedric on reeds; highlights include the hit version of "I'm Gonna Sit Right Down and Write Myself a Letter," a rambunctious "There'll Be Some Changes Made," "Truckin'," "Got a Bran' New Suit," and four performances from a big-band session. All of the Waller Victor recordings are full of joy and infectious swing. — *Scott Yanow*

● **Fats Waller and His Rhythm: The Middle Years, Part 1 (1936-1938)** / Dec. 24, 1936-Apr. 12, 1938 / Bluebird ✦✦✦✦
This particular three-CD set (which follows "The Last Years") picks up around where *Vol. 4* of the *Complete* LP series ended and includes no less than 70 recordings from Fats Waller's "Middle Years." — *Scott Yanow*

A Good Man Is Hard to Find, The Middle Years: Part 2 / Apr. 12, 1938-Jan. 12, 1940 / Bluebird ✦✦✦✦
Subtitled "The Middle Years, Part 2," this three-CD set contains all of pianist/vocalist Fats Waller's Victor recordings from a nearly two-year period including all of the alternate takes. In fact, the first five selections (the only ones contained here from his short-lived big band) are all alternate takes to the selections that close "The Middle Years, Part 1." Otherwise these performances are by Waller's septet, with either Herman Autrey or John Hamilton on trumpet and Gene Sedric (who doubled on tenor and clarinet); Chauncey Graham filled in for Sedric on one date. Waller's great popularity resulted in the large number of recordings from this era (68 are on this set), and they range from hits ("Two Sleepy People," "Yacht Club Swing," an amazing version of "Hold Tight," "Your Feet's Too Big," and a new rendition of "Squeeze Me") and fresh originals and novelties to trash that Waller did his best (often through satirization) to uplift. Nearly every selection has a liberal dose of his classic piano, and taken as a whole these much-maligned recordings are quite listenable, enjoyable, and historical. — *Scott Yanow*

Jugglin' Jive of Fats Waller and His Orchestra / Jul. 16, 1938-Oct. 18, 1938 / Sandy Hook ✦✦✦✦
This very enjoyable CD contains three radio broadcasts featuring Fats Waller and his Rhythm in 1938. Despite some dated chatter (and not-so-subtle racism) from a radio announcer, the music on these live performances is quite spirited, with Waller singing and playing heated stride piano with his sextet. While trumpeter Herman Autrey and Gene Sedric's reeds are major assets, Fats Waller is virtually the whole show, really driving his sidemen and stimulating both a memorable party atmosphere and creative swinging jazz. — *Scott Yanow*

● **The Last Years (1940-1943)** / Apr. 11, 1940-Jan. 23, 1943 / Bluebird ✦✦✦✦
Since all of the previous Fats Waller Rhythm reissue series start off in 1934

and get discontinued before reaching the '40s, this time around the newest program has started out with Waller's last recordings and is working its way backward. This essential three-CD set contains the pianist/vocalist/composer's last 63 studio recordings. Some of the titles are quite laughable ("Little Curly Hair in a High Chair," "You're a Square from Delaware," "Abercrombie Had a Zombie," and "Come Down to Earth My Angel") but Waller manages to either satirize or save virtually all of the somewhat dubious material. There are some out-and-out classics on this set, too, including "Fats Waller's Original E Flat Blues," "All That Meat and No Potatoes," and "The Jitterbug Waltz"; this wonderful set of spirited music concludes with "Ain't Misbehavin'" from the soundtrack of *Stormy Weather*. — *Scott Yanow*

Last Testament: 1943 / 1943-Sep. 23, 1943 / Alamac ✦✦✦✦
This CD contains most of pianist/vocalist Fats Waller's final recordings, V-Discs cut for servicemen overseas. These solo performances are priceless, for Waller is often hilarious (his reworking of "Two Sleepy People" is classic) yet still playing at his prime; "Hallelujah" has a particularly heated stride solo. Other highlights include "Ain't Misbehavin'," "You're Slightly Less than Wonderful," "This Is So Nice It Must Be Illegal," and "That's What the Birdie Sang to Me." In addition there is a song taken from the movie *Stormy Weather* ("That Ain't Right") which has Waller giving plenty of backtalk to Ada Brown's vocal) and a rare organ solo, "Bouncin' on a V-Disc." Less than three months later Fats Waller was dead; he definitely went out on top! Recommended. — *Scott Yanow*

George Wallington (Giacinto Figlia)

b. Oct. 27, 1924, Palmero, Sicily, Italy, **d.** Feb. 15, 1993, New York, NY
Piano / Bop
George Wallington was one of the first and best bop pianists, ranking up there with Al Haig and just below Bud Powell. He was also the composer of two bop standards: "Lemon Drop" and "Godchild." Born in Sicily, Wallington and his family moved to the US in 1925. He arrived in New York in the early '40s and was a member of the first bop group to play on 52nd Street, Dizzy Gillespie's combo of 1943-44. After spending a year with Joe Marsala's band, Wallington played with the who's who of bop during 1946-52, including Charlie Parker, Serge Chaloff, Allan Eager, Kai Winding, Terry Gibbs, Brew Moore, Al Cohn, Gerry Mulligan, Zoot Sims, and Red Rodney. He toured Europe with Lionel Hampton's ill-fated big band of 1953, and during 1954-60 he led groups in New York that included Donald Byrd and Jackie McLean (the latter succeeded by Phil Woods). In 1960 Wallington gave up on the music business altogether and retired to work in his family's air-conditioning company. Twenty-four years later he re-emerged, recording two albums of original material before time ran out. — *Scott Yanow*

Live: At Cafe Bohemia / Sep. 9, 1955 / Original Jazz Classics ✦✦✦✦
This live set, although led by pianist George Wallington, is most significant for giving listeners early examples of the playing of trumpeter Donald Byrd and altoist Jackie McLean; bassist Paul Chambers and drummer Art Taylor complete the quintet. The music, although mostly group originals (other than "Johnny One Note" and Oscar Pettiford's "Bohemia After Dark"), is essentially a bebop jam; and it is particularly interesting to hear just how much McLean was influenced by Charlie Parker at this point (although his sound was already quickly recognizable). This was a solid if short-lived group, and their brand of hard bop will be enjoyed by straight-ahead jazz fans. The CD reissue adds a second version of "Minor March" to the original program. — *Scott Yanow*

● **Jazz for the Carriage Trade** / Jan. 20, 1956 / Original Jazz Classics ✦✦✦✦
This date with Donald Byrd (trumpet), Phil Woods (alto sax), Teddy Kotick (bass), and Art Taylor (drums) was also reissued as part of a two-fer. The session has a lasting hard-bop edge and closely parallels the Messengers' sound at the time. It is an exemplary sample of New York-style bop. — *Bob Rusch, Cadence*

The New York Scene / Mar. 1, 1957 / Original Jazz Classics ✦✦✦✦
Before he retired from music in 1960, pianist George Wallington led a series of excellent bop-based quintet albums. For this particular CD (a reissue of a date originally put out by New Jazz), Wallington heads a group featuring altoist Phil Woods, trumpeter Donald Byrd, bassist Teddy Kotick, and drummer Nick Stabulas. With the exception of the standard "Indian Summer," the repertoire is pretty obscure (with now-forgotten originals by Byrd, Woods, and Mose Allison in addition to "Graduation Day") but of a consistent high quality. The emphasis is on hard-swinging, and this set should greatly please straightahead jazz fans. — *Scott Yanow*

Pleasure of a Jazz Inspiration / Aug. 19, 1985 / VSOP ✦✦✦✦
Pianist George Wallington, who retired from jazz in 1960, returned in the mid-'80s and recorded three solo albums; he passed away in 1993. This CD, which contains eight originals (which are subtitled *A Jazz Tone Poem*), is not as adventurous as one might think. Actually a lot of the songs are based on fairly common chord changes. Wallington plays quite well (mixing in his dominant Bud Powell influence with touches of Teddy Wilson), making one regret that the important bop-based pianist took so many

years off. At least his final efforts were impressive, and this CD offers some fine examples of his playing after his "comeback." —*Scott Yanow*

Winston Walls

Organ, Vocals / Soul-Jazz, Hard Bop, Groove

Winston Walls was born in Charleston, WV, the son of well known R&B pianist Harry Van Walls (with Joe Turner). At 15 years of age, Walls knew some piano and had been playing in church and school for several years. He learned drums from Frank Thompson and got a job playing drums for Bill "Honky Tonk" Doggett's band. He soon switched to organ and filled in on breaks for Doggett. He acknowledges Jimmy Smith and Jack McDuff as major influences. Walls has toured the country, playing with the Pointer Sisters, Sonny Stitt, Dionne Warwick, Al Green, Charlie Pride, Ike and Tina Turner, and Lou Donaldson. His jazz organ includes elements of R&B, rock, country, and gospel. He once toured with Jimmy Smith, Groove Holmes, and Jack McDuff but had never recorded a solo album. Then in 1993 he recorded a live session with fellow organist (and friend) Brother Jack McDuff, which has been released on Schoolkids' Records.. —*Michael Erlewine and John Bush*

Boss of the B-3 / Oct. 25, 1993-Oct. 26, 1993 / Schoolkids ◆◆◆◆
Long overdue (like about 30 years!) debut album for Walls, who is, as one reviewer put it, "the best organ player you never heard of." You can hear him now in live concert with longtime friend and rival Jack McDuff. You guessed it. McDuff and Walls battle it out as in days of yore, note for note and screeching chord against chord. This is a classic jam battle with a few vocals thrown in for diversion. McDuff is bound to let Walls (after all these years) be heard, so he does not struggle too hard. Good funk fun. Live set means the balance is a little off, but who cares. —*Michael Erlewine*

Cedar Walton

b. Jan. 17, 1934, Dallas, TX
Piano / Hard Bop

A classy, sophisticated but hard-bop, expressive, and skilled pianist, Cedar Walton has proved the ideal accompanist for numerous combos. He's never been a "star" but has provided tasteful, challenging backing and concise, impressive solos. Walton learned piano from his mother and studied music at the University of Denver in the early '50s. He went to New York in 1955 but was drafted by the Army. He played with Leo Wright, Don Ellis, and Eddie Harris while stationed in Germany. Walton recorded with Kenny Dorham after returning to New York. He played in J.J. Johnson's group (1958-60) and took McCoy Tyner's place with the Jazztet (1960-61). Walton played in Art Blakey's Jazz Messengers during a peak period (1961-64). He replaced Bobby Timmons and was in the very strong edition that included Wayne Shorter and Freddie Hubbard. Walton was Abbey Lincoln's accompanist (1965-66) and Prestige's house pianist during 1967-69. Walton played in a group with Hank Mobley in the early '70s, rejoined Blakey in the mid-'70s for a tour of Japan, and started a quartet that in the '70s and '80s included Clifford Jordan, George Coleman or Bob Berg on tenors, and fellow rhythm-section mates Sam Jones and Billy Higgins. The group took the name Eastern Rebellion in 1975. Walton had a brief fling with fusion and jazz-rock in the early '70s, heading a group called Soundscapes that featured electric instrumentation, funk, fusion, and rock rhythms and compositions. He also did some dates for RCA under the label of Mobius. Walton toured Europe, Japan, and the US in the late '70s in a trio with Higgins; since the '80s, Walton has been a member of the Timeless All-Stars. He has also played with J.J. Johnson's quintet and toured with his own trios. Walton, who remains greatly in demand, has recorded for many labels through the years, including Blue Note, Prestige, Muse, Timeless, SteepleChase, CBS, Clean Cuts, and Red. —*Ron Wynn and Scott Yanow*

Cedar! / Jul. 10, 1967 / Original Jazz Classics ◆◆◆◆
Excellent session with Kenny Dorham (trumpet) and Junior Cook (tenor sax). Typically no-frills, emphatic pieces and solos. —*Ron Wynn*

Plays Cedar Walton / Jul. 10, 1967-Jan. 14, 1969 / Prestige ◆◆◆◆
A 1988 reissue of Walton giving his own work a showcase. A host of great players, among them Kenny Dorham (trumpet) and Clifford Jordan (tenor sax). The CD has a bonus cut. —*Ron Wynn*

Spectrum / May 24, 1968 / Prestige ◆◆◆

★ **Breakthrough** / Feb. 22, 1972 / Muse ◆◆◆◆◆
As strong as pianist Cedar Walton plays on his session, the main honors are taken by two of his sidemen. Tenor saxophonist Hank Mobley, whose career was about to go into a complete eclipse, is in brilliant form, showing how much he had grown since his earlier days. Baritonist Charles Davis, who too often through the years has been used as merely a section player, keeps up with Mobley and engages in a particularly memorable tradeoff on the lengthy title cut. Mobley is well showcased on "Summertime," Davis switches successfully to soprano on "Early Morning Stroll," and Walton (with the trio) somehow turns the "Theme from *Love Story*" into jazz. Highly recommended. —*Scott Yanow*

★ **Eastern Rebellion, Vol. 1** / Dec. 10, 1975 / Timeless ◆◆◆◆◆
This CD reissue brings back a classic set featuring four giants of the modern mainstream: pianist/leader Cedar Walton, tenor saxophonist George Coleman, bassist Sam Jones, and drummer Billy Higgins. All five performances are noteworthy, particularly a definitive version of Walton's most famous composition "Bolivia," Coleman's tricky "5/4 Thing," and Jones' boppish "Bittersweet." The veteran musicians all sound quite inspired on this advanced, straightahead set. A gem. —*Scott Yanow*

● **Among Friends** / Jul. 1982 / Evidence ◆◆◆◆
Cedar Walton is one of jazz's great accompanists and session pianists, but he is even more accomplished in trio situations, where he gets the space to fully develop ideas and offer insightful interpretations. This set includes superb reworkings of the Thelonious Monk classics "Ruby My Dear" and "Off Minor," plus his own mid-tempo gem "Midnight Waltz" and the lushly performed "My Foolish Heart" that includes a nice vibes solo from special guest Bobby Hutcherson. Walton works with a thoroughly experienced rhythm section in bassist Buster Williams and drummer Billy Higgins. These are three longtime musical associates demonstrating what polished, distinctive jazz is all about. —*Ron Wynn*

Bluesville Time / Apr. 21, 1985 / Criss Cross ◆◆◆◆

Maybeck Recital Hall Series, Vol. 25 / Aug. 1992 / Concord Jazz ◆◆◆◆

Manhattan Afternoon / Dec. 26, 1992 / Criss Cross ◆◆◆◆

Dinah Washington (Ruth Lee Jones)

b. Aug. 29, 1924, Tuscaloosa, AL, d. Dec. 14, 1963, Detroit, MI
Vocals / Blues, Standards

One of the most versatile and gifted vocalists in American popular music history, Dinah Washington made extraordinary recordings in jazz, blues, R&B, and light-pop contexts, and could have done the same in gospel had she chosen to record in that mode. But the former Ruth Jones didn't believe in mixing the secular and spiritual, and once she'd entered the non-religious music world professionally, she refused to include gospel in her repertoire. Washington's penetrating, high-pitched voice, incredible sense of drama and timing, crystal clear enunciation, and equal facility with sad, bawdy, celebratory, or rousing material enabled her to sing anything and everything with distinction. Growing up in Chicago, Washington played piano and directed her church choir. For a while she did split her time between clubs, and singing and playing piano in Salle Martin's gospel choir as Ruth Jones. There's some dispute about the origin of her name. Some sources say the manager of the Garrick Stage Bar gave her the name Dinah Washington; others say it was Hampton who selected it. It is undisputed that Hampton heard and was impressed by Washington, who'd been discovered by manager Joe Glaser. She worked in Hampton's band from 1943 to 1946. Some of her biggest R&B hits were written by Leonard Feather, the distinguished critic, who was a successful composer in the '40s. Washington dominated the R&B charts in the late '40s and '50s but also did straight jazz sessions for EmArcy and Mercury, with horn accompanists including Clifford Brown, Clark Terry, and Maynard Ferguson, and pianists Wynton Kelly, a young Joe Zawinul, and Andrew Hill. She wanted to record what she liked, regardless of whether it was considered suitable, and in today's market she would be a crossover superstar.

After "What a Difference a Day Makes," nearly all of her recordings were slow ballads with accompaniment from faceless orchestras that would not have been out of place on a country record! Although she did have a few more hits (including some duets with Brook Benton), Washington's post-1958 output has not aged well at all, unlike the music from her first 15 years of recordings. She was only 39 and still in peak musical form when she died from an accidental overdose of diet pills and alcohol in 1963. Dinah Washington remains the biggest influence on most Black female singers (particularly in R&B and soul) who have come to prominence since the mid-'50s. Virtually all of her recordings are in print on CD's, including a massive reissue series of her Mercury and EmArcy sessions. —*Ron Wynn and Dan Morgenstern*

Mellow Mama / Dec. 10, 1945-Dec. 13, 1945 / Delmark ◆◆◆◆
Dinah Washington's first solo recordings (with the exception of a session supervised by Lionel Hampton in 1943) are included on this Delmark repackaging of her Apollo sides. Recorded in Los Angeles during a three-day period, the 12 selections feature the singer with a swinging jazz combo that has tenor saxophonist Lucky Thompson, trumpeter Karl George, vibraphonist Milt Jackson, and bassist Charles Mingus among its eight members. The 21-year-old Washington was already quite distinctive at this early stage and easily handles the blues and jive material with color and humor. Recommended despite the brevity (34 minutes) of the CD. —*Scott Yanow*

★ **The Complete Dinah Washington on Mercury, Vol. 1 (1946-1949)** / Jan. 14, 1946-Sep. 27, 1949 / Mercury ◆◆◆◆◆
All of Dinah Washington's studio recordings from 1946-1961 have been reissued in definitive fashion by Polygram on seven three CD sets. *Vol. 1* finds the youthful singer (who was 21 on the earliest sessions) evolving

from a little known but already talented singer to a best-selling R&B artist. Ranging from jazz and spirited blues to middle-of-the-road ballads, this set (as with the others in the *Complete* series) includes both gems and duds, but fortunately the great majority fall into the former category. The backup groups include orchestras led by Gerald Wilson, Tab Smith, Cootie Williams, Chubby Jackson, and Teddy Stewart, and there are a dozen strong numbers with just a rhythm section. The first five volumes in this series are highly recommended. — *Scott Yanow*

☆ **The Complete Dinah Washington on Mercury, Vol. 2 (1950-1952)** / Feb. 7, 1950-May 6, 1952 / Mercury ✦✦✦✦✦
Dinah Washington was a best-selling artist on the R&B charts during this period, but she was also a very versatile singer who could easily handle swinging jazz, schmaltzy ballads, blues, and novelties with equal skill. The second of these seven three-CD sets in Mercury's *Complete* program mostly finds Washington being accompanied by studio orchestras, although the Ravens join her on two numbers, and drummer Jimmy Cobb heads a couple of jazz groups (including one with both Ben Webster and Wardell Gray on tenors). Not every selection is a classic; but the quality level is quite high, and the packaging is impeccable. Recomended. — *Scott Yanow*

☆ **Complete Dinah Washington on Mercury, Vol. 3 (1952-1954)** / 1952-Aug. 14, 1954 / Mercury ✦✦✦✦✦
Of the seven three-CD sets in Mercury's *Complete* series of Dinah Washington recordings, this is the most jazz-oriented one. The versatile singer participates in a very memorable jam session with an all-star group (featuring Clifford Brown, Maynard Ferguson, and Clark Terry on trumpets!), meets up with Terry and tenor saxophonist Eddie Lockjaw Davis on another spontaneous date (highlighted by uptempo romps on "Bye Bye Blues" and "Blue Skies"), and has several classic collaborations with the warm Lester Youngish tenor of Paul Quinichette. A few commercial sides with studio orchestras are included (since they took place during the same period), but those are in the minority on this essential volume. — *Scott Yanow*

☆ **Complete Dinah Washington on Mercury, Vol. 4 (1954-1956)** / Nov. 2, 1954-Apr. 25, 1956 / Mercury ✦✦✦✦✦
The fourth of seven three-CD sets in Mercury's *Complete* series alternates between strong swinging jazz with the likes of trumpeter Clark Terry, tenor saxophonist Paul Quinichette, pianist Wynton Kelly, and altoist Cannonball Adderley, and middle-of-the-road pop performances with studio orchestras. The third volume is the strongest in this series, but the first five sets all contain more than enough jazz to justify their purchase. *Vol. 4* really attests to Dinah Washington's versatility. — *Scott Yanow*

☆ **Complete Dinah Washington on Mercury, Vol. 5 (1956-1958)** / Jun. 25, 1956-Jul. 6, 1958 / Mercury ✦✦✦✦✦
Mercury has given the great singer Dinah Washington the complete treatment with seven three-CD sets that contain all of her recordings during the 1946-61 period, practically her entire career. *Vol. 5* is the final volume to be highly recommended, since it has her final jazz recordings. On many of these performances she is backed by orchestras led by Quincy Jones, Ernie Wilkins (including a tribute to Fats Waller), or Eddie Chamblee in arrangements that often leave room for short statements from some of the sidemen; one of the albums with Chamblee has a full set of songs associated with Bessie Smith. *Vol. 5* (which contains only a few commercial sides) concludes with her strong performance at the 1958 Newport Jazz Festival. — *Scott Yanow*

The Bessie Smith Songbook / Dec. 30, 1957-Jan. 20, 1958 / EmArcy ✦✦✦

What a Diff'rence a Day Makes! / Feb. 19, 1959-Aug. 1959 / Mercury ✦✦✦✦
Dinah Washington's career reached a turning point with this album. A very talented singer who could interpret jazz, blues, pop, novelties, and religious songs with equal skill, Washington had an unexpected pop hit with her straightforward version of "What a Diff'rence a Day Makes." From then on she would only record with commercial studio orchestras and stick to middle-of-the-road pop music. This 1959 set is not as bad as what would follow, with such songs as "I Remember You," "I Thought About You," "Manhattan," and "A Sunday Kind of Love" all receiving tasteful melodic treatment (although no chances are taken) by Washington and an orchestra conducted and arranged by Belford Hendricks. — *Scott Yanow*

Complete Dinah Washington on Mercury, Vol. 6 (1958-1960) / Feb. 19, 1959-Nov. 12, 1960 / Mercury ✦✦
Up until 1959, Dinah Washington was able to excel in every musical setting that she found herself. A strong jazz-blues vocalist who had many R&B hits, Washington always sounded confident and soulful even when backed by insipid studio orchestras. However after her Feb. 19, 1959 recording of "What a Diff'rence a Day Makes" became a major hit and she gained fame, Dinah Washington stuck to safely commercial pop music. Even when she was singing superior songs during the 1959-63 period, Washington was always backed by large orchestras outfitted with extremely commercial charts better suited to country-pop stars. The sixth in Mercury's series of three-CD sets starts with the Feb. 19 session and cov-

ers 21 months in Dinah Washington's career. Most of the 73 performances are difficult to sit through. — *Scott Yanow*

Unforgettable / Aug. 1959-Jan. 15, 1961 / Mercury ✦✦

Complete Dinah Washington on Mercury, Vol. 7 (1961) / 1961 / Mercury ✦✦
The seventh and final volume in Mercury's *Complete* series of Dinah Washington's recordings has impeccable packaging and largely inferior music, at least from the jazz standpoint. After recording a surprising hit version of "What a Diff'rence a Day Makes" in 1959, the singer stuck exclusively to middle-of-the-road pop music with large string orchestras on her recordings. This three-CD set (which contains Washington's final 67 recordings for Mercury plus a recently discovered alternate take from 1947) is often difficult to sit through, for it totally lacks surprises, suspense, or spontaneity. For completists only, but get the first five volumes. — *Scott Yanow*

Grover Washington, Jr.

b. Dec. 12, 1943, Buffalo, NY
Sax (Alto, Soprano, and Tenor) / Soul-Jazz, Crossover, Groove
Washington is one of the most commercially successful saxophonists in jazz history. A versatile reed specialist, he is equally at home on soprano, alto, or tenor sax, and has recorded on flute and baritone sax. A much more creative improviser than his hit-making saxophone competitors, Washington has had hits with almost everything he has done since his first album (*Inner City Blues*) for Kudu in 1971. His biggest albums, *Mr. Magic* (Kudu) and *Winelight* (Elektra), have spawned hit singles. His recordings for Kudu, Motown, Elektra, and Columbia are mostly commercial in content, but Washington's saxophone work is always first-rate and a good distance in front of his closest fusion rivals. — *Bob Porter*

Inner City Blues / Sep. 1971 / Motown ✦✦✦✦
Definitive early-'70s soul-jazz date. Washington has seldom been more convincing. — *Ron Wynn*

★ **Mister Magic** / 1975 / Motown ✦✦✦✦✦

Two Classic Albums: Mister Magic / Feels So Good / 1975 / Motown ✦✦
Large group. Arranged and conducted by Bob James. Originally released Feb. 7, 1975. This early (quite cohesive) album of Washington helped establish him as one of the main fusion players. Strings too.— *Michael Erlewine*

Live at the Bijou / 1978 / Motown ✦✦✦

☆ **Winelight** / Jun. 1980 / Elektra ✦✦✦✦✦
Grover Washington, Jr., has long been one of the leaders in what could be called rhythm & jazz, essentially R&B-influenced jazz. *Winelight* is one of his finest albums, and not primarily because of the Bill Withers hit "Just the Two of Us." It is the five instrumentals that find Washington (on soprano, alto, and tenor) really stretching out. If he had been only interested in sales, Washington's solos could have been half as long and he would have stuck closely to the melody. Instead he really pushes himself on some of these selections, particularly the title cut. A memorable set of high-quality and danceable soul-jazz. — *Scott Yanow*

Come Morning / Jun. 1981 / Elektra ✦✦

Strawberry Moon / 1987 / Columbia ✦✦✦

Then and Now / 1988 / Columbia ✦✦✦
This is one of Grover Washington, Jr.'s occasional strays away from R&B-oriented jazz to play in a more straightahead setting. Switching between soprano, alto, and tenor, Grover is accompanied by either Tommy Flanagan or Herbie Hancock on piano during five of the eight selections, and he performs such numbers as Ron Carter's "Blues for D.P.," "Stolen Moments," and "Stella by Starlight" with swing and taste. Tenor saxophonist Igor Butman also helps out on three songs. Worth acquiring. — *Scott Yanow*

Next Exit / 1992 / Columbia ✦✦

Sadao Watanabe

b. Feb. 1, 1933, Utsunomiya, Japan
Sax (Alto) / Instrumental Pop, Bop
Sadao Watanabe has long had a split musical personality. He alternates excellent bebop dates with weak pop albums that pale next to the leaders of the idiom (such as Grover Washington, Jr. and David Sanborn). Watanabe learned clarinet and alto in high school. In the '50s he moved to Tokyo, joining Toshiko Akiyoshi's bop-oriented group in 1953. When the pianist moved to the US in 1956, Watanabe took over the band. He attended Berklee during 1962-65 and had the opportunity to work with Gary McFarland, Chico Hamilton, and Gabor Szabo. However Watanabe has remained based in Japan, where he is a major influence on younger players. He has recorded steadily through the years, most notably with Chick Corea in New York (1970) and with the Galaxy All-Stars (1978). Watanabe's bop records are inspired by Charlie Parker, but his Brazilian-flavored pop dates are instantly forgettable. — *Scott Yanow*

California Shower / Mar. 1978 / JVC ✦✦✦

Morning Island / Mar. 1979 / JVC ✦✦

● **Parker's Mood** / Jul. 13, 1985 / Elektra ✦✦✦✦
Close to his best, both on his merit and thanks to aid from James Williams (piano) and Jeff Watts (drums). —*Ron Wynn*

Jazz and Bossa / Nov. 25, 1986-Dec. 1966 / Denon ✦✦✦

Elis / Feb. 1988 / Elektra ✦✦✦

Benny Waters

b. Jan. 23, 1902, Brighton, MD
Clarinet, Sax (Alto and Tenor) / Swing
At the age of 94 in early 1996, Benny Waters was not only the oldest active jazz musician but a powerful altoist who would be considered impressive if he were only 50. Waters' personal history covers virtually the entire history of recorded jazz, although he never really became a major name. He worked with Charlie Miller from 1918-21, studied at the New England Conservatory and became a teacher; one of his students was Harry Carney! Waters played, arranged for and recorded with Charlie Johnson's Paradise Ten (1925-32), an underrated group that also for a time included Benny Carter and Jabbo Smith. Waters, who was primarily a tenor saxophonist and an occasional clarinetist during this period, was influenced to an extent by Coleman Hawkins, and he recorded with both Clarence Williams and King Oliver in the '20s. During the next two decades, Waters played in many groups including those led by Fletcher Henderson (for a few months), Hot Lips Page, Claude Hopkins, and Jimmie Lunceford. He led his own unit during part of the '40s, played with Roy Milton's R&B band, and in 1949 went to France with the Jimmy Archey Dixieland group. Waters settled in Paris, working steadily although he was largely forgotten at home. By the '80s he was visiting the US more frequently and Waters is heard in brilliant form on a 1987 quartet set for Muse on which he plays tenor, alto, and clarinet in addition to taking some effective vocals. A short time later he went blind and stuck exclusively to playing alto (on which he plays in a jump style reminiscent of Tab Smith that shows the occasional influence of John Coltrane!). The seemingly ageless Benny Waters has continued recording and performing with a remarkable amount of energy, touring with the Statesmen of Jazz in 1995 and creating some miraculous music. —*Scott Yanow*

● **From Paradise (Small's) to Shangrila** / Jun. 26, 1987 / Muse ✦✦✦✦
An always interesting player elevates ordinary material. —*Ron Wynn*

Memories of the Twenties / Sep. 22, 1988-Nov. 15, 1988 / Stomp Off ✦✦✦✦
Nice tribute to past eras. —*Ron Wynn*

Swinging Again / May 4, 1993 / Jazzpoint ✦✦✦✦
Few people listening to this CD would guess that Benny Waters (heard exclusively on alto) was 91. Waters (a veteran of the '20s) plays with such power and confidence throughout the standards and blues that he could pass for 51. With an excellent European rhythm section (pianist Thilo Wagner, bassist Jan Jankeje, and drummer Gregor Beck) helping him out, the underrated but distinctive swing stylist is heard in top form, making this European import CD from Germany highly recommended. —*Scott Yanow*

Plays Songs of Love / Jul. 28, 1993 / Jazzpoint ✦✦✦✦
The remarkable Benny Waters (who sticks here exclusively to alto) was 91 at the time of this recording yet still displays a strong tone and creative ideas. Assisted by guitarist Vic Juris and three nearly ancient veterans (pianist Red Richards, bassist Johnny Williams, Jr., and drummer Jackie Williams), Waters performs ten standards that have love as their main topic (including "What Is This Thing Called Love," "When Your Lover Has Gone," "Always," "Taking a Chance on Love," etc.) but fortunately varies the tempos (not every selection is taken at a ballad pace) and comes up with fresh ideas on these songs. Along with his other Jazzpoint release from the same period (*Swinging Again*), this CD is recommended. —*Scott Yanow*

Ethel Waters

b. Oct. 31, 1896, Chester, PA, **d.** Sep. 1, 1977, Chatsworth, CA
Vocals / Blues, Swing, Classic Jazz
Ethel Waters had a long and varied career and was one of the first true jazz singers to record. Defying racism with her talent and bravery, Waters became a stage and movie star in the '30s and '40s without leaving the US. She grew up near Philadelphia and, unlike many of her contemporaries, developed a clear and easily understandable diction. Originally classified as a blues singer (and she could sing the blues almost on the level of a Bessie Smith), Waters' jazz-oriented recordings of 1921-28 swung before that term was even coined. A star early on at theaters and nightclubs, Waters introduced such songs as "Dinah," "Am I Blue" (in a 1929 movie) and "Stormy Weather." She made a smooth transition from jazz singer of the '20s to pop music star of the '30s, and she was a strong influence on many vocalists, including Mildred Bailey, Lee Wiley, and Connee Boswell. Waters spent the latter half of the '30s touring with a group headed by her husband-trumpeter Eddie Mallory and appeared on Broadway (*Mamba's Daughter* in 1939) and in the 1943 film *Cabin in the Sky;* in the latter she introduced "Taking a Chance on Love," "Good for Nothing Joe," and the

title cut. In later years Waters was seen in nonmusical dramatic roles, and after 1960 she confined her performances mostly to religious work for the evangelist Billy Graham. The European Classics label has reissued all of Ethel Waters' prime recordings, and they still sound fresh and lively today. —*Scott Yanow*

Ethel Waters 1921-1923 / Mar. 21, 1921-Mar. 1923 / Classics ✦✦✦✦
Ethel Waters was one of the few singers from the early '20s whose early recordings are still quite listenable. This CD from the Classics label has her first 22 sides (many previously rare including five interesting instrumentals by Waters' band), and, although not on the same level as her performances from a few years later, the music is quite good for the time period. The sidemen are mostly obscure but include pianist Fletcher Henderson and cornetists Gus Aiken and Joe Smith with the highlights being "The New York Glide," "Down Home Blues," "There'll Be Some Changes Made," and "Midnight Blues." —*Scott Yanow*

1923-1925 / Mar. 1923-Jul. 28, 1925 / Classics ✦✦✦✦
The European Classics label's Ethel Waters program completely wipes out all of the other Waters reissues, for it reissues all of her recordings from her prime years in chronological order. Since the singer was very consistent, there are very few duds and many gems in these sets. This particular CD traces Ethel Waters during a two-year period; both the recording quality and her accompaniment greatly improve during this time; cornetist Joe Smith is a standout and pianist Fats Waller is present on "Pleasure Mad" and "Back-Bitin' Mamma." Highlights include "You Can't Do What My Last Man Did," "Sweet Georgia Brown," "Go Back Where You Stayed Last Night," and "Sympathetic Dan." —*Scott Yanow*

★ **1925-1926** / Aug. 25, 1925-Jul. 29, 1926 / Classics ✦✦✦✦✦
This CD in the Classics *Complete* Ethel Waters series contains plenty of gems including "You Can't Do What My Last Man Did," the original version of "Dinah," "Shake That Thing," "I've Found a New Baby" (which has some memorable cornet playing from Joe Smith), "Sugar," and "Heebies Jeebies." On "Maybe Not at All" Ethel Waters does eerie imitations of both Bessie Smith and Clara Smith. She had few competitors as a jazz singer during this era, and the mostly intimate recordings (12 of the 23 tracks find her backed by just a pianist) feature Waters at her best. —*Scott Yanow*

☆ **1926-1929** / Sep. 14, 1926-May 14, 1929 / Classics ✦✦✦✦✦
Few female jazz singers were on Ethel Waters' level during this period, just Bessie Smith and Annette Hanshaw, and all three were quite different from each other. Waters has rarely sounded better than on the four numbers in which she is backed rather forcefully by pianist James P. Johnson (particularly "Guess Who's in Town" and "Do What You Did Last Night") but she is also in fine form on the other small-group sides. "I'm Coming Virginia," "Home," "Take Your Black Bottom Outside," "Someday Sweetheart," and "Am I Blue" (which she introduced) are among the many gems on this highly recommended entry in Classics' complete series. —*Scott Yanow*

1929-1931 / Jun. 6, 1929-Jun. 16, 1931 / Classics ✦✦✦✦
During the period covered in this CD from Classics' *Complete* Ethel Waters series, the singer was quickly developing into a top musical comedy and Broadway star. Although her backup was not as jazz-oriented as previously (despite the presence of such players as clarinetist Benny Goodman, trombonist Toomy Dorsey, Jimmy Dorsey on clarinet and alto, and trumpeter Manny Klein), Waters' renditions of many of these future standards are definitive, particularly "True Blue Lou," "Waiting at the End of the Road," "Porgy," "You're Lucky to Me," and "When Your Lover Has Gone." Superior jazz-oriented singing from one of the very best. —*Scott Yanow*

1931-1934 / Aug. 10, 1931-Sep. 5, 1934 / Classics ✦✦✦✦
Ethel Waters was one of the very few Black performers who was able to keep working in music during the early years of the Depression; in fact her fame grew during the period covered by this excellent CD from Classics' *Complete* series. Among her backup musicians on these consistently excellent sides are violinist Joe Venuti, the Dorsey Brothers, trumpeter Bunny Berigan, trombonist Jack Teagarden, clarinetist Benny Goodman, members of the Chick Webb big band, and the entire Duke Ellington orchestra (the latter on "I Can't Give You Anything but Love" and "Porgy"). High points include the Ellington tracks, "St. Louis Blues" (with The Cecil Mack Choir), the original version of "Stormy Weather," "A Hundred Years from Today," and a remake of "Dinah." Highly recommended as are all of the Ethel Waters Classics discs. —*Scott Yanow*

Bill Watrous (William Russell Watrous II)

b. Jun. 8, 1939, Middletown, CT
Trombone / Bop
One of the finest bop-oriented trombonists of the past 25 years, Bill Watrous has had a low profile since moving to Los Angeles in the '80s, despite remaining quite active. Possessor of a beautiful tone and remarkable technique, Watrous has been overlooked in jazz popularity polls of the past decade. His father was a trombonist and introduced Bill to music. He played in traditional jazz bands as a teenager and studied with Herbie Nichols while in the military. Watrous made his debut with Billy Butter-

field and was one of the trombonists in Kai Winding's groups during 1962-67. He was a busy New York-based studio musician during the '60s, working and recording with Quincy Jones, Maynard Ferguson, Johnny Richards, and Woody Herman, playing in the band for Merv Griffin's TV show (1965-68), and working on the staff of CBS (1967-69). After playing with the jazz-rock group Ten Wheel Drive in 1971, Watrous led his own big band (the Manhattan Wildlife Refuge) during 1973-77, recording two superb albums for Columbia. After moving to Los Angeles, Watrous continued working in the studios, appearing at jazz parties, playing in local clubs and leading an occasional big band. He has recorded as a leader for Columbia, Famous Door, Soundwings, and GNP/Crescendo, although only the latter releases are currently available on CD. — *Scott Yanow*

● **Bone-Ified** / 1992 / GNP ✦✦✦✦

Time for Love / 1993 / GNP Crescendo ✦✦✦

Bobby Watson

b. Aug. 23, 1953, Lawrence, KS
Sax (Alto) / Post-Bop, Hard Bop
Bobby Watson has long been one of the top altoists in jazz, a flexible player able to play swing (he once recorded a tribute to Johnny Hodges), hard bop, and free jazz. He started playing the alto when he was 13 and was soon arranging and composing for his school bands. After graduating from the University of Miami in 1975, Watson moved to New York, hitting the big time by joining (and soon becoming the musical director of) Art Blakey's Jazz Messengers during 1977-81, participating in what were Wynton Marsalis' first recordings. In the '80s Watson co-led groups with Curtis Lundy (with whom he formed the New Note label) and played with the George Coleman Octet, Charlie Persip's big band, Louis Hayes, Sam Rivers, Dameronia, the 29th Street Saxophone Quartet, and the Savoy Sultans. Quite a wide range of jazz styles! Watson began leading his own regular bands in the mid-'80s, and the following decade he headed a regular hardbop quintet known as Horizon. His many recordings (for Enja, Red, New Note, Blue Note, and Columbia) are stimulating and worth investigating. — *Scott Yanow*

Advance / Aug. 8, 1984 / Enja ✦✦✦✦
A 1991 reissue of a release that heralded the arrival of former Jazz Messenger Bobby Watson as a major figure in 1984. —*Ron Wynn*

● **The Year of the Rabbit** / Feb. 7, 1987 / New Note ✦✦✦✦

Post-Motown Bop / Sep. 17, 1990-Sep. 18, 1990 / Blue Note ✦✦✦✦
Despite the title, this is an excellent and traditional set. Watson is sparkling. —*Ron Wynn*

Tailor Made / Dec. 9, 1992-Dec. 11, 1992 / Columbia ✦✦✦✦
This CD was altoist Bobby Watson's first as the leader of a big band. He leads the orchestra through a dozen of his compositions, none of which they had performed together before meeting in the studio. But due to the high caliber of the players, the music came together smoothly. In performances ranging from modern hard bop to Latin, with subtle hints of freer styles of jazz, Watson is the main soloist (although there are a few short spots for trumpeter Terell Stafford), making the album a sort of "concerto for alto and orchestra." Even if the backup musicians have little opportunity to star, the music is consistently enjoyable and is recommended to fans of modern mainstream jazz. — *Scott Yanow*

Midwest Shuffle / 1993 / Columbia ✦✦✦✦

Lu Watters (Lucious Watters)

b. Dec. 19, 1911, Santa Cruz, CA, **d.** Nov. 5, 1989, Santa Rosa, CA
Trumpet, Bandleader / Dixieland
It would be difficult to overestimate the importance of Lu Watters in the Dixieland revival movement. When he organized the two-trumpet Yerba Buena Jazz Band in late 1939, the New Orleans jazz of King Oliver and Jelly Roll Morton was considered not only old hat, but worthy of extinction. More than 55 years later, there are a countless number of trad bands patterned after the two-beat Watters group, which, like its predecessor King Olivers' Creole Jazz Band, is now considered classic. Lu Watters formed his first jazz band in 1925, but he spent most of the '30s playing in San Francisco in his own big band. By 1939 (at the height of the swing era), he had met fellow trumpeter Bob Scobey, trombonist Turk Murphy, and pianist Wally Rose and was planning to bring back the music of the '20s, which had been largely neglected for quite a few years. In December 1939 his new band started playing regularly at the Dawn Club; and by 1941, when they made their first recordings, the Yerba Buena Jazz Band was building up a large following in San Francisco. The records kept the band's legacy alive when some of their members were drafted; Watters spent 1942-45 in the Navy, leading a 20-piece band in Hawaii. In 1946, when the band regrouped at the Dawn Club on Annie Street, it was more successful than ever, and its records from 1946-47 find the group at its height. In June 1947 the band's base of operations moved to Hambone Kelly's in El Cerrito. The eventual departure of Bob Scobey and Turk Murphy (who would soon lead important groups of their own) weakened the Yerba Buena Band slightly,

but the vocals of its banjoist Clancy Hayes were a crowd-pleaser, and the band remained a powerful force. However, when business fell off in 1950, Lu Watters broke up the band at the end of the year (feeling that its time had passed) and retired from music to be a cook and a geologist. Watters said later that he could see the eventual commercialization of Dixieland coming. He continued following the music scene closely but did not pick up his trumpet again until 1963, when a utility company in Northern California announced plans to build a nuclear power plant on an earthquake fault. Watters appeared at a couple of protest rallies with Turk Murphy's band (playing as well as ever) and recorded one last record before permanently retiring. (The power plant was never built!) —*Scott Yanow*

☆ **The Complete Good Time Jazz Recordings** / Dec. 19, 1941-Aug. 16, 1947 / Good Time Jazz ✦✦✦✦✦
Lu Watters' Yerba Buena Jazz Band was one of the most influential Dixieland groups of all time. With Watters and Bob Scobey on trumpets, trombonist Turk Murphy, clarinetist Bob Helm, pianist Wally Rose, banjo, tuba (or bass), and drums, this band had a lot of power and enthusiasm. At a time when swing dominated jazz and bebop was ready to take over, Watters' successful extension of '20s jazz was a major force in fueling the Dixieland revival movement. This four-CD set has all of the group's studio recordings, plus live broadcasts from 1946-47, and six rare performances by the wartime version of the YBJB featuring the talented but ill-fated trumpeter Benny Strickler. This reissue is absolutely essential for all traditional jazz fans and historians. The heated ensembles and joyous solos are great fun to hear. —*Scott Yanow*

● **San Francisco Style, Vol. 1** / 1946 / Good Time Jazz ✦✦✦✦
The repertoire that turned San Francisco "trad crazy"—Morton's "New Orleans Joys," Richard M. Jones' "Jazzin' Babies Blues," and "Ory's Creole Trombone," among others, are done in revival style. —*Bruce Boyd Raeburn*

San Francisco Style, Vol. 2 / 1946 / Good Time Jazz ✦✦✦✦
It's especially notable for originals by Watters such as "Big Bear Stomp," "Emperor Norton's Hunch," and "Annie Street Rock," as well as Turk Murphy's "Trombone Rag." —*Bruce Boyd Raeburn*

At Hambone Kelly's 1949-50 / Dec. 23, 1949-Mar. 3, 1950 / Merry Makers ✦✦✦✦
The later version of Lu Watters' Yerba Buena Jazz Band is featured on this enjoyable Dixieland CD. The music is taken from ten live performances at Hambone Kelly's, and showcases Watters' octet, which includes the leader's trumpet, clarinetist Bob Helm, trombonist Don Noakes, pianist Wally Rose, Clancy Hayes on banjo and vocals, second banjoist Pat Patton, the tuba of Dick Lammi, and drummer Bill Dart. The recording quality is decent, the playing is quite spirited, and, even though this group had only one trumpet (as opposed to two in Watters' more famous earlier band), the hard-driving rhythm and spirited ensembles sound very much in the tradition of the Yerba Buena Jazz Band. Recommended. —*Scott Yanow*

Together Again / Jul. 28, 1963 / Merry Makers ✦✦✦✦

Ernie Watts

b. Oct. 23, 1945, Norfolk, VA
Sax (Tenor) / Instrumental Pop, Post-Bop, Groove
Because he was involved in many commercial recording projects from the mid-'70s through the early '80s and on an occasional basis ever since, some observers wrote Ernie Watts off prematurely as a pop/R&B tenorman. Actually Watts' main hero has always been John Coltrane, and his more recent work reveals him to be an intense and masterful jazz improviser who has developed his own sheets-of-sound approach, along with a distinctive and soulful sound. After attending Berklee, he had an important stint with Buddy Rich's big band (1966-68) before moving to Los Angeles. Watts worked in the big bands of Oliver Nelson and Gerald Wilson, recorded with Jean Luc Ponty in 1969, and became a staff musician for NBC, performing with the "Tonight Show" band on a regular basis. His own records of the '70s and early '80s were generally poppish (1982's *Chariots of Fire* was a big seller), and Watts played frequently with Lee Ritenour and Stanley Clarke, in addition to recording with Cannonball Adderley (one of his idols) in 1972. However Ernie Watts' work became much more interesting from a jazz standpoint starting in the mid-'80s, when he joined Charlie Haden's Quartet West and started recording no-nonsense quartet dates for JVC. —*Scott Yanow*

Ernie Watts Quartet / Dec. 1987 / JVC ✦✦✦✦
After years of being heard primarily in commercial settings, Ernie Watts finally had an opportunity to record exactly what he wanted as a leader on this JVC CD. Watts, in a quartet with pianist Pat Coil, bassist Joel DiBartolo, and drummer Bob Leatherbarrow, features his Coltrane-influenced tenor and a bit of alto and soprano on some group originals and standards (including "My One and Only Love," "Skylark," and "Body and Soul"). One of his finest recordings to date. —*Scott Yanow*

★ **Reaching Up** / Oct. 7, 1993-Oct. 8, 1993 / JVC ✦✦✦✦✦
For this quartet set with pianist Mulgrew Miller, bassist Charles Fambrough, and drummer Jack DeJohnette, Ernie Watts definitely came to

play. Virtually all of his solos are high-powered, and even his ballad statements are filled with clusters of passionate notes. Trumpeter Arturo Sandval has two appearances and makes the music even more hyper. In addition, the rhythm section keeps the proceedings consistently stimulating. The main focus on these standards and originals is generally on Watts' tenor, and even though there isn't all that much variety, this CD is a strong example of his jazz talents. — *Scott Yanow*

Unity / Dec. 13, 1994-Dec. 14, 1994 / JVC ✦✦✦✦
The most unusual aspect of Ernie Watts' latest recording is that the great tenor is joined by a two-bass quartet. Eddie Gomez on acoustic and Steve Swallow on electric blend quite well, are featured in a delightful version of Oscar Pettiford's "Tricotism," and (with pianist Geri Allen and drummer Jack Dejohnette) keep the accompaniment consistently stimulating. Ernie Watts is in top form throughout this fine modern mainstream date, playing with both passion and lyricism on a variety of standards and originals (which, in addition to four songs from the leader, include one apiece from DeJohnette and Swallow). There is just enough variety to keep the proceedings from getting predictable, making this one of Watts' finest sessions. — *Scott Yanow*

Weather Report

Fusion
Weather Report was among the earliest and most influential of all jazz-rock bands. The unit was co-founded by Wayne Shorter and Joe Zawinul in the early '70s. It equaled the original Mahavishnu Orchestra, Tony Williams Lifetime, the original Return To Forever, and Dreams (minus vocals), as a band that stretched the boundaries and created a fresh hybrid, really blending jazz and rock. Shorter and Zawinul had learned from years of playing with Miles Davis how to combine rock energy, funk rhythms, and a jazz sensibility. Their early lineup included bassist Miroslav Vitous and drummer Alphonze Mouzon. Their self-titled debut and *I Sing the Body Electric* remain seminal jazz-rock classics. Even as they began the game of rotating personnel that would continue until they disbanded in 1986, they continued making intriguing releases into the early '80s. Dom Um Romao, Eric Gravitt, and Alphonso Johnson were in the band during the mid-'70s. But its greatest lineup was the late '70s contingent that included Jaco Pastorius and Peter Erskine. These were virtuosos on their instruments and excellent contributors, able to hold their own in any situation, besides being superb accompanists. The last great Weather Report albums were issued by this group, among them *Black Market, Heavy Weather,* and *Mr. Gone.* But things deteoriated when Pastorius and then Erskine left in the early '80s. Their replacements, Victor Bailey and Omar Hakim, were excellent musicians but neither flamboyant soloists nor imaginative thinkers. Shorter and Zawinul began to coast and grew tired of working in the group concept. The final albums were the detached, polished, and extremely professional output of topflight musicians anxious to finish the gig and move on. Percussionists Jose Rossey, then Mino Cineliu, were in and out of the band, and Erskine returned from Steps Ahead for their final dates. Shorter took an extended leave of absence and then he and Zawinul called it quits. — *Ron Wynn and Stephen Aldrich*

Weather Report / Feb. 16, 1971-Mar. 17, 1971 / Columbia ✦✦✦✦
★ **I Sing the Body Electric** / Nov. 1971-Jan. 13, 1972 / Columbia ✦✦✦✦✦
A great record from the days when they were still a serious jazz band. — *Ron Wynn*

Sweetnighter / 1972-1973 / Columbia ✦✦✦✦
Funkier and more rock-directed. — *Michael Erlewine*

Mysterious Traveller / 1973-1974 / Columbia ✦✦✦✦
Weather Report's fourth recording finds Wayne Shorter (on soprano and tenor) taking a lesser role as Joe Zawinul begins to really dominate the group's sound. Most selections include bassist Alphonso Johnson and drummer Ishmael Wilburn, although the personnel shifts from track to track. "Nubian Sundance" adds several vocalists, while "Blackthorn Rose" is a Shorter-Zawinul duet. Overall the music is pretty stimulating and sometimes adventurous; high-quality fusion from 1974. — *Scott Yanow*

Black Market / 1976 / Columbia ✦✦✦✦
A good one with Jaco Pastorius (b). — *Michael G. Nastos*

☆ **Heavy Weather** / 1977 / Columbia ✦✦✦✦✦
One of their best-selling albums. — *Michael Erlewine*

Mr. Gone / 1978 / Columbia ✦✦

Chick Webb (William Henry Webb)

b. Feb. 10, 1909, Baltimore, MD, **d.** Jun. 16, 1939, Baltimore, MD
Drums / Swing
His career was short, and Chick Webb seemed cursed with only bad luck. He was a hunchback and died at 30 from TB of the spine. But during his short lifetime, Webb was a propulsive, dominating figure behind the drums. He was a dynamo whose speed, power, and rhythmic skills were never fully captured on record, according to many who saw him repeatedly triumph in head-to-head battles with swing era royalty. Gene Krupa

reportedly was in awe of Webb and spoke in shell-shocked tones after being blown away at the Savoy in legendary combat that occurred only a few months before Webb died. Webb overcame being unable to read music by memorizing the arrangements. He led the band from a raised platform in the center, cuing sections via his drumming. He ranged over a huge kit with specially constructed pedals and cymbal holders, and was an imaginative stylist who shoved drum technique ahead through dashing fills and crashing cymbals. He came to New York in 1924 and formed a band two years later. Webb cut his first record in 1927. After a period of struggle, by the early '30s Webb had solidified the personnel in his big band and was playing regularly at the Savoy. By 1933 his orchestra was recording regularly. With fine soloists in trumpeters Taft Jordan (who also sang) and Bobby Stark; trombonist Sandy Williams; Elmer Williams (and later Teddy McRae) on tenor; pioneer flutist Wayman Carver; and, most importantly, arranger Edgar Sampson (who wrote "Stompin at the Savoy," "If Dreams Come True," and "Blue Lou" for the orchestra), Webb had one of the better big bands of the '30s. Other members of the ensemble included bassist John Kirby (early on) and future star Louis Jordan on alto. The turning point occurred when Webb added Ella Fitzgerald to his band in 1935. She soon became a major attraction (her 1938 recording of "A-Tisket, A-Tasket" became a huge hit; and from 1937 on, the majority of the orchestra's recordings were vocal features. Webb started becoming seriously ill in 1938, and his death in June 1939 was mourned by millions of swing fans. Ella Fitzgerald headed the orchestra for two years before the big band finally broke up. — *Ron Wynn and Scott Yanow*

Spinnin the Web / Jun. 14, 1929-Feb. 17, 1939 / Decca ✦✦✦✦
★ **Chick Webb (1935-1938)** / Jun. 12, 1935-May 3, 1938 / Classics ✦✦✦✦✦
To a large extent the Chick Webb big band is now remembered chiefly as the launching pad for Ella Fitzgerald, but during its peak years it was one of the top swing bands. This 25-song CD from the European Classics label reissues all of the band's recordings from a three-year period that did not feature Fitzgerald as a solo singer; she does make a brief appearance on "Wake Up and Live." Although there are nine vocals on this set (including three from a young Louis Jordan), the emphasis is on the band's instrumental talents. Such soloists as trumpeters Taft Jordan and Bobby Stark, trombonist Sandy Williams, Elmer Williams and Ted McRae on tenors, and altoist Edgar Sampson are heard from, while the drummer/leader propels the ensembles. A special highlight is the four numbers by Chick Webb's Little Chicks, an unusual quintet featuring the pioneering jazz flutist Wayman Carver and clarinetist Chauncey Haughton. This CD is highly recommended to swing fans. — *Scott Yanow*

Ben Webster

b. Mar. 27, 1909, Kansas City, MO, **d.** Sep. 20, 1973, Amsterdam, Netherlands
Sax (Tenor) / Swing
Ben Webster was considered one of the "big three" of swing tenors along with Coleman Hawkins (his main influence) and Lester Young. He had a tough, raspy, and brutal tone on stomps (with his own distinctive growls); on ballads he would turn into a pussy cat and play with warmth and sentiment. After violin lessons as a child, Wesbter learned how to play rudimentary piano (his neighbor Pete Johnson taught him to play blues). But after Budd Johnson showed him some basics on the saxophone, Webster played sax in the Young Family Band (which at the time included Lester Young). He had stints with Jap Allen and Blanche Calloway (making his recording debut with the latter) before joining Bennie Moten's Orchestra in time to be one of the stars on a classic session in 1932. Webster spent time with quite a few orchestras in the '30s (including Andy Kirk, Fletcher Henderson in 1934, Benny Carter, Willie Bryant, Cab Calloway, and the short-lived Teddy Wilson big band). In 1940 (after short stints in 1935 and 1936), Ben Webster became Duke Ellington's first major tenor soloist. During the next three years he was on many famous recordings, including "Cotton Tail" (which in addition to his memorable solo had a saxophone ensemble arranged by Webster) and "All Too Soon." After leaving Ellington in 1943 (he would return for a time in 1948-49), Webster worked on 52nd Street, recorded frequently as both a leader and a sideman, had short periods with Raymond Scott, John Kirby, and Sid Catlett, and toured with Jazz at the Philharmonic during several seasons in the '50s. Although his sound was considered out-of-style by that decade, Webster's work on ballads became quite popular, and Norman Granz recorded him on many memorable sessions. Webster recorded a classic set with Art Tatum and generally worked steadily, but in 1964 he moved permanently to Copenhagen, where he played when he pleased during his last decade. Although not all that flexible, Webster could swing with the best, and his tone was an influence on such diverse players as Archie Shepp, Lew Tabackin, Scott Hamilton, and Bennie Wallace. — *Scott Yanow*

● **King of the Tenors** / May 21, 1953 & Dec. 8, 1953 / Norgran ✦✦✦✦
Two sessions are combined on this reissue CD, both of which feature the very distinctive tenor of Ben Webster. Webster is heard with two versions of the Oscar Peterson Quartet plus (on six of the 11 numbers) trumpeter Harry "Sweets" Edison and altoist Benny Carter. The original LP had eight

selections; the CD adds two alternate takes, plus the previously unissued "Poutin'." Webster is in fine form, with the highlights including "Tenderly," "That's All," "Pennies from Heaven," and "Cotton Tail." —*Scott Yanow*

Music for Loving / May 28, 1954-Feb. 3, 1955 / Verve ✦✦✦✦
There is a great deal of music on this two-CD set. Tenor saxophonist Ben Webster is featured on two LPs' worth of performances while backed by a string section arranged by Ralph Burns, there are five previously unissued alternate takes, five quartet numbers (four with the Teddy Wilson trio), and a full album showcasing baritonist Harry Carney (in one of only two dates that he had as a leader) with a string section. The emphasis throughout is, naturally, on ballads, but there are some exceptions and enough variety to hold one's interest. Webster and Carney both play beautifully. —*Scott Yanow*

The Soul of Ben Webster / Mar. 5, 1957-Jul. 1958 / Verve ✦✦✦✦

★ **Soulville** / Oct. 15, 1957 / Verve ✦✦✦✦✦
The veteran tenor saxophonist Ben Webster met up with the Oscar Peterson trio on this CD. Other than two fairly basic originals, the great tenor is showcased on durable standards, and the ballads, in particular, are quite memorable. Peterson, bassist Ray Brown, guitarist Herb Ellis, and drummer Stan Levey are superior in support of the masterful saxophonist. —*Scott Yanow*

Meets Gerry Mulligan / Nov. 3, 1959 / Verve ✦✦✦✦
Just a great pairing, despite different concepts. —*Ron Wynn*

☆ **Meet You at the Fair** / Mar. 11, 1964-Nov. 10, 1964 / Impulse ✦✦✦✦✦
Ben Webster's final American recording was one of his greatest. At 55 the tenor saxophonist was still very much in his prime, but he was considered out of style in the US. He would soon move permanently to Europe, where he was better appreciated. This CD has the nine selections originally on the LP of the same name, a quartet set with either Hank Jones or Roger Kellaway on piano, bassist Richard Davis, and drummer Osie Johnson. Webster's tone has rarely sounded more beautiful than on "Someone to Watch over Me" and "Our Love Is Here to Stay." One song from the same session (but originally released on a sampler) and two tunes featuring Webster on an Oliver Nelson date (*More Blues and the Abstract Truth*) wrap up this definitive CD. —*Scott Yanow*

Stormy Weather / Jan. 30, 1965 / Black Lion ✦✦✦✦
Recorded about a month after the veteran tenor Ben Webster moved to Europe, this high quality set with pianist Kenny Drew, bassist Neils Pederson, and drummer Alex Riel features Webster stretching out on the traditional "Londonderry Air," two originals, and seven familiar but fresh standards. Webster, although neglected in the US, was still in peak form in the mid-'60s, as witness this and his other Black Lion CDs covering the period. —*Scott Yanow*

Masters of Jazz, Vol. 5 / 1968-Sep. 25, 1970 / Storyville ✦✦✦✦
This entry in Storyville's *Masters of Jazz* series (which does not duplicate his *Plays Duke Ellington* and *Plays Ballads* albums) alternates ballads and stomps to give listeners a picture of Ben Webster during his last period. Webster is joined by trios led by pianists Kenny Drew and Teddy Wilson, interacts with a drumless piano-bass duo, plays with a Scandinavian quartet, romps with the Danish Radio Big Band on two numbers, and is accompanied on "Going Home" and "Come Sunday" by a string orchestra. These Copenhagen recordings find the great tenor in consistently fine form. —*Scott Yanow*

Dick Wellstood (Richard McQueen Wellstood)

b. Nov. 25, 1927, Greenwich, CT, **d.** Jul. 24, 1987, Palo Alto, CA
Piano / Stride, Classic Jazz
One of the two great stride pianists (along with Ralph Sutton) to emerge during the '40s when members of their generation were generally playing bebop, Wellstood kept an open mind toward later styles (he loved Monk) while sounding at his best playing classic jazz. A little more subtle than Sutton, Wellstood was also a powerful pianist who was a superb interpreter of the music of James P. Johnson and his contemporaries. He came to New York with Bob Wilber's Wildcats in 1946 and quickly caught on in the trad jazz scene. By 1947 he was playing with Sidney Bechet, and in the '50s he worked mostly with veteran players, including trumpeters Roy Eldridge, Rex Stewart, and Charlie Shavers, and the Eddie Condon gang. He was in the intermission band at Condon's starting in 1956 and later was house pianist at the Metropole and Nick's. After a period with Gene Krupa's quartet, he toured with the World's Greatest Jazz Band. Wellstood remained active throughout his all-too-short life, playing solo concerts, performing at jazz parties, and recording quite a few memorable albums. —*Scott Yanow*

★ **Dick Wellstood and His Famous Orchestra Featuring Kenny** / Jul. 1973-Dec. 1973 / Chiaroscuro ✦✦✦✦✦
Dick Wellstood was (along with Ralph Sutton), the top stride pianist of the '70s and '80s. Two of his most exciting recordings are combined on this definitive CD, with eight of the ten tracks originally on the Chiaroscuro LP *Dick Wellstood and His Famous Orchestra Featuring Kenny Davern* and nine of the ten songs from the Chaz Jazz release *The Blue Three* on the program. Kenny Davern sticks to soprano on the earlier set (their "Famous

Orchestra" is actually a duet) and switches to clarinet for the Blue Three sides with Wellstood and drummer Bobby Rosengarden. The music ranges from Dixieland standards to swing tunes (and even "Blue Monk"), but mostly it falls into the genre of hot small-group swing. Highly recommended. —*Scott Yanow*

Frank Wess

b. Jan. 4, 1922, Kansas City, MO
Flute, Sax (Alto and Tenor) / Bop, Swing
A pioneering jazz flutist, Frank Wess has blended a swinging style with bebop influences and nuances. He was an ideal partner to Frank Foster in the Basie band of the mid-'50s and early '60s, playing a softer, smoother, and lighter sound to Foster's harder and more aggressive mode. Wess' flute work, with its full, upbeat lines and expressive tones, upgraded the instrument's role in jazz. Wess began on alto sax and even played some alto solos with Count Basie, but he became better known for his playing on tenor. He worked with Blanche Calloway before World War II, then served in Army bands. After his discharge, Wess had a brief stint in Billy Eckstine's band and worked short periods with Eddie Heywood, Lucky Millinder, and Bull Moose Jackson. Wess began playing flute in 1949, then joined Count Basie in 1953. He remained until 1964. Wess played alto at Basie's request with the band from the late '50s until the mid-'60s. He became active doing commercials and playing in pit and studio bands for plays and television shows. Wess was in the New York Jazz Quartet during the '70s and the repertory group Dameronia in the '80s, as well as the Toshiko Akiyoshi and Woody Herman big bands. He's performed and recorded with old friend Frank Foster in the '80s and '90s. Some recent Wess dates on Concord and Progressive are available on CD, while earlier material has been reissued on Savoy and Fresh Sound. —*Ron Wynn and Michael G. Nastos*

● **Jazz for Playboys** / Dec. 26, 1956 & Jan. 5, 1957 / Savoy ✦✦✦

I Hear Ya' Talkin' / Dec. 8, 1959 / Savoy ✦✦✦✦
This lightly swinging session is very much in the Count Basie style of blues and swing. Frank Wess (switching between flute, tenor, and alto) heads the septet, but it is trumpeter Thad Jones (who wrote three of the five numbers) who often takes solo honors. Trombonist Curtis Fuller, baritonist Charlie Fowlkes, and pianist Hank Jones are also heard from on this enjoyable session that for some obscure reason was not released until 1984. —*Scott Yanow*

Tryin' to Make My Blues Turn Green / Sep. 7, 1993-Sep. 8, 1993 / Concord Jazz ✦✦✦✦
Frank Wess has always been a steady, reliable swinger, able to play swaggering blues and soulful ballads with equal facility and hold his own on more challenging bop pieces. The 12 tracks on his release range from his own swing-tinged originals to the inevitable standards and fine reworkings of jazz pieces by Kenny Burrell and Horace Parlan. Highly professional, nicely played blues-swing material from an often overlooked, dependable improviser. —*Ron Wynn*

Going Wess / Sep. 20, 1993-Sep. 21, 1993 / Town Crier ✦✦✦✦
This CD gave Frank Wess (doubling on tenor and flute) his first opportunity to record with organ, and he is in top form on this trio outing with organist Bobby Forrester and drummer Clarence "Tootsie" Bean. Burners alternate with warm ballads and Wess, (whether on his tough tenor or fluid flute) matches very well with Forrester's light pre-Jimmy Smith organ style. In fact, this session swings so naturally that it could have been recorded in 1958. The ten superior standards are all given very favorable treatment, making this a highly recommended outing. —*Scott Yanow*

Randy Weston

b. Apr. 6, 1926, Brooklyn, NY
Piano / Post-Bop, Hard Bop
Randy Weston has pioneered a compositional and playing style that merges the influence of Thelonious Monk's unconventional concepts with the multiple rhythms and accents of African music. Weston's also used bebop, blues, and funk, mixing all this into an arresting, energetic style with simple melodies and creative uses of dissonance, Caribbean themes, and gospel-blues riffs. Monk's impact on Weston extends to his early years, when Monk informally trained him on piano during visits to his apartment. Weston started professionally in R&B bands, then worked in bebop groups with Kenny Dorham and Cecil Payne. He played with Art Blakey in the late '40s and became Riverside's first bebop signee in 1954. Weston began leading bands with Ahmed Abdul-Malik, Ray Copeland, Payne, Booker Ervin, and Melba Liston in the late '50s. He also gained fame as a composer, with such works as "Hi-Fly," "Little Niles," and "African Cookbook." Weston worked on the West Coast before heading to Nigeria in the early '60s. He returned to Africa on a tour in 1967, settling in Morocco and remaining there until the early '70s. Weston established a nightclub and led a trio. He continued traveling in the early '70s, appearing at the 1974 Montreux Jazz Festival. Weston started recording in the '50s and has been featured on sessions for United Artists, Jubilee, Dawn, Roulette, Bakton (his own label), Riverside, Trip, Arista/Freedom, Polydor, CTI, Atlantic, Owl,

Inner City, Enja, Verve, and Antilles. After a recording drought in the early '80s, there's now an ample number of Weston sessions available on CD. —*Ron Wynn*

Get Happy / 1956 / Original Jazz Classics ✦✦✦✦

● **Jazz a la Bohemia** / Oct. 25, 1956 / Original Jazz Classics ✦✦✦✦
Randy Weston, who was more under Thelonious Monk's influence in 1956 than he would be in the near future, is in top form during this live set. His quartet features the rarely heard but talented baritonist Cecil Payne, bassist Ahmed Abdul-Malik, and drummer Al Dreares. High points of the straightahead set (which has been reissued on CD) include the calypso "Hold 'em Joe" (recorded almost a decade before Sonny Rollins), "It's All Right with Me" (one of two trio tracks), and the lone Weston original on the date, the stimulating "Chessman's Delight." —*Scott Yanow*

Monterey '66 / Sep. 18, 1966 / Verve ✦✦✦✦

Tanjah / May 21, 1973-May 22, 1973 / Verve ✦✦✦✦
Originally on the Polydor label, this lesser-known classic (reissued on CD) teams pianist/composer Randy Weston and arranger Melba Liston (his musical soulmate) on seven of Weston's originals. The fairly large band is filled with distinctive soloists, including trumpeter Jon Faddis (19 at the time), trombonist Al Grey, Billy Harper on tenor, altoist Norris Turney (heard on three versions of "Sweet Meat," two of which were previously unreleased), and several percussionists. The weak points are Weston's use of the Fender Rhodes on a few songs (it waters down his personality) and Candido's chanting during an otherwise exciting version of "Hi-Fly," but those are easily compensated for by the infectious calypso "Jamaican East" and Liston's inventive reworking of "Little Niles." Recommended. —*Scott Yanow*

Portraits of Monk / Jun. 3, 1989 / Verve ✦✦✦✦
Engaging, thoughtful playing. —*Ron Wynn*

Portraits of Duke Ellington / Jun. 4, 1989 / Verve ✦✦✦✦
Topflight set by Weston, paying his homage to Duke in a very distinctive fashion. —*Ron Wynn*

Self Portraits / Jun. 5, 1989 / Verve ✦✦

● **The Spirits of Our Ancestors** / May 20, 1991-May 22, 1991 / Verve ✦✦✦✦
Weston with 11-piece band and guests Pharoah Sanders and Dizzy Gillespie. The stellar arrangements are by Melba Liston. Familiar themes are "The Healers," "Blue Moses," "African Cookbook," and "African Village/Bedford Stuyvesant." Most of the ten tracks are extended on this two-CD set. —*Michael G. Nastos*

Volcano Blues / Feb. 1993 / Antilles ✦✦✦✦

Kenny Wheeler

b. Jan. 14, 1930, Toronto, Canada
Trumpet, Fluegelhorn / Avant-Garde, Post-Bop
Kenny Wheeler has long been one of the most technically proficient of the avant-garde trumpeters. He started on cornet when he was 12, studied at the Toronto Conservatory, and then in 1952 moved to England. He worked in many big bands during the next decade (including with John Dankworth during 1959-65) and became an excellent bop-based soloist. However, by the mid-'60s his musical curiosity led him to freer forms of jazz, and he did important work with John Stevens' Spontaneous Music Ensemble, Tony Oxley's sextet, the Mike Gibbs Orchestra, the Globe Unity Orchestra (starting in 1972), Anthony Braxton's Quartet, and Azimuth. Wheeler has been a regular on ECM since the mid-'70s, and during 1983-87 he was with the Dave Holland quintet. A thoughtful trumpeter with a wide range, Wheeler's playing is always stimulating, yet generally introspective. —*Scott Yanow*

★ **Gnu High** / Jun. 1975 / ECM ✦✦✦✦✦
This is longwinded but worthwhile, with the Keith Jarrett (piano) Trio. —*Michael G. Nastos*

● **Double, Double You** / May 1983 / ECM ✦✦✦✦
Quintet set. Some good playing by Mike Brecker (sax). —*Ron Wynn*

Flutter By, Butterfly / May 1987 / Soul Note ✦✦

Kayak / May 1992 / Ah Um ✦✦✦✦

Paul Whiteman

b. Mar. 28, 1890, Denver, CO, **d.** Dec. 29, 1967, Doylestown, PA
Violin / Pop, Classic Jazz
Because press agents dubbed him "the King of Jazz" in the '20s, Paul Whiteman has always been considered a controversial figure in jazz history. Actually his orchestra was the most popular during the era, and at times (despite its size) it did play very good jazz; perhaps "King of the Jazz Age" would have been a better title.

Originally a classically trained violinist, Paul Whiteman led a large Navy band during World War I and always had a strong interest in the popular music of the day. In 1918 he organized his first dance band in San Francisco; after short periods in Los Angeles and Atlantic City, he

settled in New York in 1920. His initial recordings ("Japanese Sandman" and "Whispering") were such big sellers that Whiteman was soon a household name. His superior dance band used some of the most technically skilled musicians of the era in a versatile show that included everything from pop tunes and waltzes to semi-classical works and jazz. Trumpeter Henry Busse (featured on "Hot Lips" and "When Day Is Done") was Whiteman's main star during the 1921-26 period. Seeking to "make a lady out of jazz," Whiteman's symphonic jazz did not always swing, but at Aeolian Hall in 1924 he introduced "Rhapsody in Blue" (with its composer George Gershwin on piano) in what was called "An Experiment in Modern Music." Red Nichols and Tommy Dorsey passed through the band; but it was in 1927, with the addition of Bix Beiderbecke, Frankie Trumbauer, and Bing Crosby (the latter originally featured as part of a vocal trio called the Rhythm Boys), that Whiteman finally began to have an important jazz band. Joe Venuti and Eddie Lang soon joined up, and many of Whiteman's recordings of 1927-30 (particularly the ones with Bill Challis arrangements) are among his finest.

After Beiderbecke left the band in 1929 and Whiteman filmed the erratic but fascinating movie *The King of Jazz* in 1930, the Depression forced the bandleader to cut back on his personnel (which at one time included two pianos, tuba, bass sax, string bass, banjo, and guitar in its rhythm section!). Although his orchestra in the '30s at times featured Bunny Berigan, Trumbauer, and both Jack and Charlie Teagarden, Whiteman's music was considered old-hat by the time of the swing era, and he retired (except for special appearances) by the early '40s. Many of his recordings (particularly those with Beiderbecke) have been reissued numerous times and are more rewarding than his detractors would lead one to believe. In the '70s Dick Sudhalter for a time organized and led "the New Paul Whiteman Orchestra," which recorded a couple of fine recreation records. —*Scott Yanow*

Paul Whiteman and His Orchestra / Aug. 30, 1921-Sep. 11, 1934 / Pearl Flapper ✦✦✦

The Complete Capitol Recordings / Jun. 5, 1942-Oct. 26, 1951 / Capitol ✦✦✦

★ **Victor Masters** / RCA ✦✦✦✦✦
Some fine sessions. Regardless of anyone's feeling about whether he was overrated due to racial politics, Whiteman's music was very influential on a certain level. —*Ron Wynn*

Gerald Wiggins

b. May 12, 1922, New York, NY
Piano / Bop, Swing
A veteran pianist who's backed many extraordinary performers, Gerald Wiggins has a swinging style and accomplished technique that's enabled him to adjust in swing, bebop, blues, and hard-bop situations, as well as with different vocalists. Wiggins toured with comedian Step 'n' Fetchit in the early '40s, then worked in Les Hite's orchestra and with Louis Armstrong and Benny Carter. He moved to the West Coast in the early '50s, where he backed Lena Horne and accompanied Kay Starr, Eartha Kitt, and Helen Humes. He was a music director and film coach in the studios during the '60s, while leading and recording with various trios. During the '70s, '80s, and '90s Wiggins has done sessions for Muse, Hemisphere, Trend, Palo Alto, Specialty, Challenge, Black and Blue, and Concord. —*Ron Wynn and Michael G. Nastos*

Gerald Wiggins Trio / Dec. 16, 1953 / VSOP ✦✦✦✦
Due to his skills as an accompanist and his work in Hollywood, Gerald Wiggins has always been a bit underrated, but the pianist has long had his own style within the swing-bop tradition. For this trio date (originally out on Tampa and reissued on LP by VSOP, Wig is teamed with bassist Joe Comfort and drummer Bill Douglas for a set of seven standards and two originals. The music swings with both subtlety and soul, and the results are enjoyable. Highlights include "Love for Sale," Duke Ellington's "I Don't Know What Kind of Blues I Got," "Surrey with the Fringe on Top," and "The Man That Got Away." —*Scott Yanow*

Relax and Enjoy It / 1961 / Original Jazz Classics ✦✦✦✦
Pianist Gerald Wiggins led this trio date (1961) with Joe Comfort (bass) and Jackie Mills (drums). While most people have probably heard Wiggins in support, here is a record which spotlights him (he's made numerous recordings under his name but most for very obscure labels). —*Bob Rusch, Cadence*

● **Live at Maybeck Recital Hall, Vol. 8** / Aug. 1990 / Concord Jazz ✦✦✦✦
Outstanding solo set. —*Ron Wynn*

Soulidarity / Aug. 23, 1995-Aug. 24, 1995 / Concord Jazz ✦✦✦✦
This spirited CD gives listeners a very good example of how pianist Gerry Wiggins was sounding in the mid-'90s. It is strange that it had been many years since his last trio album, for this was always the perfect setting for Wiggins. Joined by bassist Andy Simpkins and drummer Paul Humphrey, the pianist swings happily and creatively on such numbers as "The Way You Look Tonight," "Some Other Spring," "Strip City," "What Is There to

Say," "Lover," and even "Alexander's Ragtime Band." An inspired outing. —*Scott Yanow*

Cool Saturdays / Nouveau ✦✦✦

Bob Wilber

b. Mar. 15, 1928, New York, NY
Clarinet, Sax (Alto), Sax (Soprano) / Dixieland, Swing
Throughout his long career Bob Wilber has done a lot to keep classic jazz alive. A bit misplaced (most jazz players of his generation were much more interested in bop and hard bop), Wilber (along with Kenny Davern, Ralph Sutton, and Dick Wellstood) was one of the few in his age group to stick to prebop music. In high school he formed a band that included Wellstood, and as a teenager he sat in at Jimmy Ryan's club in New York. Early on he became Sidney Bechet's protégé and led his own young group, the Wildcats (with whom he made his recording debut). The close association with the dominant Bechet led to a bit of a personality crisis in the '50s as Wilber sought to find his own voice. He studied with Lennie Tristano and formed the Six, a group that tried to modernize early jazz. When that ended, he played Dixieland with Eddie Condon and in 1957 joined Bobby Hackett's band for a year. Wilber freelanced throughout the '60s, in 1968 became a founding member of the World's Greatest Jazz Band, and in 1973 formed Soprano Summit with Kenny Davern, one of the top swing-oriented groups of the decade. A few years later the band broke up, and Wilber teamed up with his wife, singer Pug Horton, in Bechet Legacy (which also featured either Glenn Zottola or Randy Sandke on trumpet). Bob Wilber worked with the New York Jazz Repertory Company, released music on his own Bodeswell label, wrote the authentic soundtrack to the movie *The Cotton Club* (1984), in 1988 led a band at Carnegie Hall to celebrate the 50th anniversary of Benny Goodman's famous concert, and authored his frank memoir, *Music Was Not Enough.* Influenced on soprano, clarinet, and alto by Bechet, Goodman, and Johnny Hodges, respectively, Wilber has long had his own sound on each of his instruments. He has recorded frequently through the years for many labels, most recently Arbors. —*Scott Yanow*

★ **Soprano Summit: In Concert** / 1974 / Concord Jazz ✦✦✦✦✦
For several years in the '70s, Bob Wilber and Kenny Davern teamed up to co-lead Soprano Summit, a group that featured the pair doubling on clarinets and sopranos. Their appearance at the 1976 Concord Jazz Festival found the group at its peak. With Marty Grosz contributing some perfectly suitable chordal acoustic guitar and vocals, and bassist Ray Brown and drummer Jake Hanna keeping the music moving, Wilber and Davern constantly challenge each other on such hot numbers as "Stompy Jones," "Doin' the New Lowdown," and "Swing That Music." This exciting set is highly recommended. —*Scott Yanow*

★ **Bob Wilber and Bechet Legacy** / Jan. 29, 1984 / Challenge ✦✦✦✦✦
After the breakup of Soprano Summit in the early '80s, Bob Wilber formed a group dedicated to reviving the music of his teacher, Sidney Bechet. Wilber (who triples here on soprano, clarinet, and alto) is heard with his intimate quartet (which also includes trumpeter Randy Sandke, guitarist Mike Peters, and bassist John Goldsby) during a live performance on nine selections associated with Bechet. This CD (its contents were released for the first time in 1995) has plenty of passionate and heated swing, with the high points including "Down in HonkyTonk Town," "Promenade Aux Champs-Elysees," "China Boy," and "Lady Be Good." Quite enjoyable. —*Scott Yanow*

The Bob Wilber-Dick Wellstood Duet / Mar. 27, 1984-May 22, 1984 / Progressive ✦✦✦✦
This CD (which reissues the original Progressive LP plus three previously unissued cuts) has a very logical matchup. Of the musicians to come up in the '40s and '50s and choose to play classic jazz (rather than loop), Bob Wilber and Dick Wellstood were two of the most inventive. Wilber (who switches between clarinet and soprano) has long had his own sound, while pianist Wellstood was capable of doing close impressions of James P. Johnson and Fats Waller but had his own message to communicate too. Their duets focus, with a few exceptions, on lesser-known numbers such as "Ain'tcha Got Music," "You, You, You!" and "Wildcat Blues"; two of the highlights are their interpretations of "Chinatown, My Chinatown" (which can be seen as a tribute to Sidney Bechet), and "The Entertainer." Delightful music. —*Scott Yanow*

Summit Reunion / 1990 / Charoscuro ✦✦✦

Horns A-Plenty / Mar. 14, 1994 / Arbors ✦✦✦✦

Lee Wiley

b. Oct. 9, 1915, Fort Gibson, OK, d. Dec. 11, 1975, New York, NY
Vocals / Swing, Standards
Lee Wiley occupies her own place in jazz history. Although a cool-toned and sophisticated singer, her interpretations of superior standards were often quite sensuous. Even if she did not improvise much, she was a favorite of many musicians, particularly Eddie Condon. She came to New York in the early '30s and at age 17 was singing and recording with Leo Reis-

man's orchestra. She spent most of the that decade singing with commercial radio orchestras (including Victor Young and Johnny Green) but eventually also appeared at clubs, backed by small jazz groups, having a close relationship with Bunny Berigan. Starting in 1939 Lee Wiley became the first singer to devote an entire album to the music of one composer; her George Gershwin, Cole Porter, Harold Arlen, and Rodgers and Hart sessions are considered classic and the high points of her career. Wiley married Jess Stacy in 1943, but after five years both the big band and the marriage were history. She appeared at a few of Eddie Condon's Town Hall concerts, but from the late '40s on, Wiley performed and recorded less frequently. After some sessions for Columbia during 1950-51, Storyville in 1954, and Victor during 1956-57, all that remained was a final record for Monmouth-Evergreen in 1971. By then she was forgotten by all but veteran record collectors, but Lee Wiley had made her mark decades earlier. —*Scott Yanow*

★ **Sings the Songs of Ira and George Gershwin . . .** / Nov. 13, 1939-Apr. 1940 / Audiophile ✦✦✦✦✦

Sings the Songs of Rodgers and Hart & Harold Arlen / Feb. 1940-Apr. 1943 / Audiophile ✦✦✦✦

The Carnegie Hall Concert / 1952 & Jul. 5, 1972 / Audiophile ✦✦✦✦

As Time Goes By / Jun. 12, 1956-Jul. 25, 1957 / Bluebird ✦✦✦✦

Baby Face Willette

Organ, Vocals / Blues, Soul-Jazz, Hard Bop, Groove
Baby Face Willette switched from piano to organ after being inspired by Chicago church organists Herman Stevens and Mayfield Woods. Willette recorded two fine albums with soul-jazz giant Grant Green on guitar, *Face to Face* and *Stop and Listen*, both released in 1961. —*Michael Erlewine*

Face to Face / Jan. 30, 1961 / Blue Note ✦✦✦

● **Stop and Listen** / May 22, 1961 / Blue Note ✦✦✦✦

Mo Rock / Mar. 27, 1964 & Apr. 2, 1964 / Argo ✦✦✦

Behind the 8-Ball / Nov. 30, 1964 / Argo ✦✦✦

Buster Williams (Charles Anthony Williams)

b. Apr. 17, 1942, Camden, NJ
Bass / Post-Bop, Hard Bop
Here's one bassist who prefers the background to the spotlight and regards his role as a supportive rather than starring one. Buster Williams has made subtle swing, precise rhythms, a startling tone, and impeccable technique the hallmark of his playing with numerous bands since the early '60s. He learned both bass and drums from his father, opting for bass after being impressed by recordings featuring Oscar Pettiford solos. Williams studied harmony, composition, and theory at Combs College of Music in Philadelphia in the late '50s, then worked with Jimmy Heath. He toured and recorded with the Gene Ammons/Sonny Stitt quintet in 1960 and 1961. Williams played with vocalists Dakota Staton, Betty Carter, Sarah Vaughan, and Nancy Wilson in the mid- and late '60s, recording with Vaughan and Wilson. Williams moved to Los Angeles while with Wilson, playing and recording with the Jazz Crusaders, Prince Lasha, and the Bobby Hutcherson-Harold Land quintet and working with Miles Davis. He moved to New York in 1969 and joined Herbie Hancock, playing with him until 1972. He worked regularly with Mary Lou Williams (1973-75) and Ron Carter's Quartet (1977-1978) and in the early '80s was a member of both Sphere and the Timeless All Stars. Although opportunities to lead his own sessions were rare (thus far for Muse and Buddah), Williams has appeared as a sideman on countless sessions with the who's who of jazz and remains in great demand in the '90s. —*Ron Wynn and Scott Yanow*

Heartbeat / Mar. 28, 1978-Apr. 3, 1978 / Muse ✦✦✦✦
A diverse session of jazz touches by pop guests on the four originals by bassist Williams, one standard, and one by Jimmie Rowles. Includes Rowles, Kenny Barron, Ben Riley, and vocalist Suzanne Klewan, and strings from Pat and Gayle Dixon. —*Michael G. Nastos*

● **Something More** / Mar. 1989 / In & Out ✦✦✦✦

Cootie Williams (Charles Melvin Williams)

b. Jun. 24, 1910, Mobile, AL, d. Sep. 14, 1985, New York, NY
Trumpet / Swing
Cootie Williams, one of the finest trumpeters of the '30s, expanded upon the role originally formed by Bubber Miley with Duke Ellington's Orchestra. Renowned for his work with the plunger mute, Cootie was also a fine soloist when playing open. Starting as a teenager, Cootie Williams played with a variety of local bands in the South, coming to New York with Alonzo Ross' Syncopators. He played for a short time with the orchestras of Chick Webb and Fletcher Henderson (recording with the latter) before joining Duke Ellington as Miley's replacement in February 1929. He was a fixture with Duke's band during the next 11 years, recording many classics with Ellington (including "Echoes of Harlem" and "Concerto for Cootie") and leading some of his own sessions. He recorded with Lionel Hampton,

Teddy Wilson, and Billie Holiday and was a guest at Benny Goodman's Carnegie Hall Concert in 1938. His decision to leave Ellington and join Goodman's Orchestra in 1940 was considered a major event in the jazz world. During his year with BG, Williams was featured with both the big band and Goodman's sextet. The following year he became a bandleader. His orchestra in the '40s featured such up-and-coming players as pianist Bud Powell, tenorman Eddie "Lockjaw" Davis, altoist-singer Eddie "Cleanhead" Vinson, and even Charlie Parker. Although he had a hit (thanks to Willis Jackson's honking tenor) on "Gator," by 1948 Cootie had cut his group back to a sextet. Playing R&B-oriented music, he worked steadily at the Savoy but by the '50s was drifting into obscurity. However, in 1962, after a 22-year absence, Cootie Williams rejoined Duke Ellington, staying as a featured soloist beyond Duke's death in 1974. By then his solos were much simpler and more primitive than earlier (gone was the Louis Armstrong-inspired bravado), but Cootie remained the master with the plunger mute. He was semi-retired during his final decade, taking a final solo in 1978 on a Teresa Brewer record, and posthumously serving as an inspiration for Wynton Marsalis' own plunger playing. — *Scott Yanow*

● **Sextet and Orchestra: 1944 Recordings** / Jan. 6, 1944-Aug. 22, 1944 / Phoenix ◆◆◆◆

Cootie Williams in Hi Fi / Mar. 25, 1958-Apr. 8, 1958 / RCA ◆◆◆◆

James Williams

b. Mar. 8, 1951, Memphis, TN
Piano / Hard Bop
One of the most consistent and reliable pianists in what could be called modern mainstream jazz, James Williams has made many rewarding recordings through the years. He started playing piano when he was 13, primarily gospel and soul music at first (influences that can still be felt in his solos). He studied at Memphis State University and taught at Berklee during 1972-77. While based in Boston, Williams played regularly with such visiting all-stars as Woody Shaw, Art Farmer, Clark Terry, and Joe Henderson. He came to fame during his period with Art Blakey's Jazz Messengers (1977-81) and since then has performed and recorded frequently with a wide variety of players including Sonny Stitt, Bobby Hutcherson, Tom Harrell, his own trios, and the very interesting Contemporary Piano Ensemble. — *Scott Yanow*

● **Alter Ego** / Jul. 19, 1984 & Jul. 20, 1984 / Sunnyside ◆◆◆◆
Pianist James Williams learned a great deal from his stint with Art Blakey's Jazz Messengers, and when he emerged from the group, he was perfectly qualified to be a bandleader. His Sunnyside session features such up-and-coming players as guitarist Kevin Eubanks, the reeds of Billy Pierce and Bill Easley, bassist Ray Drummond, and drummer Tony Reedus on a set of original material. Five of the seven songs were composed by Williams, while the other two (including the memorable "Waltz for Monk") were contributed by Donald Brown. The frequently exciting music (high-quality modern hard bop) still sounds fresh. — *Scott Yanow*

Magical Trio 1 / Jun. 26, 1987 / EmArcy ◆◆◆◆
With Art Blakey and Ray Brown. — *Michael G. Nastos*

Magical Trio 2 / Nov. 23, 1987-Nov. 24, 1987 / EmArcy ◆◆◆

Meet the Magical Trio / Sep. 2, 1988 / EmArcy ◆◆◆◆
Vigorous solos, excellent composition. — *Ron Wynn*

Meets the Saxophone Masters / Sep. 23, 1991 / DIW/Columbia ◆◆◆◆

Talkin' Trash / Mar. 4, 1993 / DIW/Columbia ◆◆◆◆
Although pianist James Williams is the nominal leader of this CD and there is room for many concise solos from Billy Pierce (mostly on tenor), vibraphonist Steve Nelson, and the remarkable bassist Christian McBride, the star throughout is actually fluegelhornist Clark Terry. Terry, 72 at the time but showing no sign of decline, contributed three of the numbers, sings in his famous Mumbles voice on two humorous pieces (including a preacher routine on "The Orator"), and plays quite well throughout. High points of this straightahead session include the boppish "Serenade to a Bus Seat," the uptempo blues "Chuckles," and Terry's spectacular solo on "Moonglow." — *Scott Yanow*

Joe Williams (Joseph Goreed)

b. Dec. 12, 1918, Cordele, GA
Vocals / Blues, Swing, Standards
Joe Williams was possibly the last great big-band singer, following in the tradition of Jimmy Rushing but carving out his own identity. Equally skilled on blues (including double entendre ad-libs), ballads, and standards, Williams has always been a charming and consistently swinging performer. In the late '30s he performed regularly with Jimmie Noone. Williams gigged with Coleman Hawkins and Lionel Hampton in the early '40s and toured with Andy Kirk during 1946-47. After stints with Red Saunders and Hot Lips Page and recordings with King Kolax (including a 1951 version of "Every Day I Have the Blues"), Williams joined Count Basie's Orchestra in 1954. During the next seven years he and Basie had a mutually satisfying relationship, each making the other more famous! His ver-

sion of "Every Day" with Count became his theme song. Many other pieces (such as "Goin' to Chicago" and "Smack Dab in the Middle") became permanent parts of Williams' repertoire. After leaving Basie in 1961, the singer worked with the Harry Edison quintet for a couple of years and has freelanced as a leader ever since, having occasional reunions with the Basie band. His collaborations with Cannonball Adderley and George Shearing were successful, as was an album with the Thad Jones-Mel Lewis Orchestra. Joe Williams has remained one of the most popular and talented singers in jazz. — *Scott Yanow*

★ **Count Basie Swings / Joe Williams Sings** / Jul. 17, 1955-Jul. 26, 1955 / Verve ◆◆◆◆◆
This is the definitive Joe Williams record, cut shortly after he joined Count Basie's orchestra. Included are his classic versions of "Every Day I Have the Blues," "The Comeback," "Alright, Okay, You Win," "In the Evening," and "Teach Me Tonight." Williams' popularity was a major asset to Basie, and getting to sing with that swinging big band on a nightly basis certainly did not harm the singer. This gem belongs in everyone's jazz collection. — *Scott Yanow*

A Swingin' Night at Birdland / Jun. 1962 / Roulette ◆◆◆◆
In 1961, after six years as one of the main attractions of Count Basie's orchestra, Williams (with Basie's blessing) went out on his own. One of his first sessions was this live recording cut at Birdland with a strong quintet that featured trumpeter Harry "Sweets" Edison and Jimmy Forrest on tenor. Williams mostly sings standards and ballads but also tosses in a few of his popular blues (including "Alright, OK, You Win" and "Goin' to Chicago") during a well rounded and thoroughly enjoyable set. — *Scott Yanow*

Me and the Blues / Jan. 2, 1963-Dec. 5, 1963 / RCA ◆◆◆◆
This CD is a straight reissue of the original LP and features singer Joe Williams backed by a studio orchestra headed and arranged by Jimmy Jones. Williams mostly sticks to blues-oriented material, but there is a surprising amount of mood variation on the dozen selections, along with short solos by trumpeters Thad Jones and Clark Terry, altoist Phil Woods, and Seldon Powell on tenor. Ben Webster has a guest spot on "Rocks in My Bed." Williams, heard at the peak of his powers, is at his best on "Me and the Blues," "Rocks in My Bed," "Work Song," and "Kansas City." — *Scott Yanow*

● **The Overwhelmin'** / Feb. 6, 1963-Jun. 18, 1965 / Bluebird ◆◆◆◆
A sampler taken from five former LPs, this fine CD features Joe Williams doing three songs from Duke Ellington's *Jump for Joy*; five numbers at the 1963 Newport Jazz Festival (during which he is joined by trumpeters Clark Terry and Howard McGhee) and tenor greats Coleman Hawkins, Zoot Sims, and Ben Webster); four blues backed by an all-star jazz group; and five ballads in front of an orchestra. Although it would be preferable to have each of the five original albums intact, this superb collection features Joe Williams on a wide variety of material, and he is heard close to his peak throughout. — *Scott Yanow*

Jump for Joy / Mar. 1963 / RCA ◆◆◆◆
After a remarkable six-year tenure, vocalist Joe Williams left Count Basie's orchestra for a solo career in 1961. He recorded the 12 tracks on this disc two years later (this is a '93 CD reissue), assisted by a crack band under the co-leadership of Jimmy Jones and Oliver Nelson. But unlike the Basie years, Williams' mellow, commanding voice clearly dominates at all times. Although none of these numbers is long, each is superbly sung. Williams' diction, storytelling ability, pacing, and delivery are consistently magnificent. Whether singing sweetly or fiercely, doing love songs or blues, uptempo or ballad cuts, Williams' treatments are memorable despite their brevity. — *Ron Wynn*

☆ **And the Thad Jones/Mel Lewis Orchestra** / Sep. 1966 / Blue Note ◆◆◆◆◆
This CD reissues one of Joe Williams' finest recordings. Accompanied by the Thad Jones/Mel Lewis Orchestra, the singer is heard at the peak of his powers. The big band functions primarily as an ensemble (Snooky Young gets off some good blasts on "Nobody Knows the Way I Feel This Morning"), but the inventive Thad Jones arrangements ensure that his illustrious sidemen have plenty to play. Many of the selections (half of which have been in the singer's repertoire ever since) are given definitive treatment on this set (particularly a humorous "Evil Man Blues," "Gee Baby Ain't I Good to You?" and "Smack Dab in the Middle"), and Williams scats at his best on "It Don't Mean a Thing." Get this one. — *Scott Yanow*

Joe Williams Live / Aug. 7, 1973 / Original Jazz Classics ◆◆◆◆
Williams meets the Cannonball Adderley Septet on this rather interesting session. The expanded rhythm section (which includes keyboardist George Duke and both acoustic bassist Walter Booker and the electric bass of Carol Kaye) gives funky accompaniment to Williams, while altoist Cannonball and cornetist Nat have some solo space. Actually the singer easily steals the show on a rather searing version of "Goin' to Chicago Blues," his own "Who She Do," and a few unusual songs, including Duke Ellington's "Heritage." — *Scott Yanow*

In Good Company / Jan. 19, 1989-Jan. 21, 1989 / Verve ◆◆◆◆
A bit of a grab-bag, this CD finds Joe Williams joined by Supersax on two numbers, doing a pair of vocal duets with Marlena Shaw ("Is You Is or Is

You Ain't My Baby" is excellent), teaming up with vocalist/pianist Shirley Horn for two ballads, and being joined by the Norman Simmons Quartet for the remainder. Sticking mostly to standards, Joe Williams shows that at 70 he still had the magic. —*Scott Yanow*

Live at Orchestra . . . / Nov. 20, 1992 / Telarc ✦✦✦✦
Joe Williams is so closely associated with the Count Basie Orchestra that it is difficult to believe that this Telarc CD was his first recording with jazz's great institution in over 30 years. Williams (in generally fine form despite an occasionally raspy voice) performs a well rounded set of blues, ballads, and standards with the Frank Foster-led Basie orchestra, combining some of his older hits with newer songs such as Grady Tate's "A Little at a Time" and "My Baby Upsets Me." Foster's sidemen are heard mostly in an ensemble role, with all of the instrumental solos being rather brief; there is little interaction with the vocalist. That fault aside, this is one of Joe Williams' better recordings of the past decade. —*Scott Yanow*

Feel the Spirit / Sep. 20, 1994-Sep. 23, 1994 / Telarc ✦✦✦

Mary Lou Williams

b. May 8, 1910, Atlanta, GA, **d.** May 28, 1981, Durham, NC
Piano / Bop, Swing, Post-Bop, Stride
A superb pianist, Mary Lou Williams was among jazz's more progressive and forward-looking stylists. Her early playing fused stride and boogie-woogie elements; she adapted to bop, and by the '60s her solos had become more complex, creatively incorporating dissonance without sacrificing blues feeling or emotional intensity. She was a vital composer and arranger, from pivotal works for Andy Kirk's swing band in the '30s to 1946's "Waltz Boogie," in which Williams adapted jazz to non-duple meters, and her sacred works of the '60s and '70s, masses and a cantata. Williams grew up in Pittsburgh, where she was playing by ear as a six-year-old and working carnival and vaudeville shows at 13. She started performing as Mary Lou Burley, joining a group led by John Williams in 1925. The two married shortly afterward. She became Andy Kirk's deputy pianist and arranger in 1929, when he took over Terrence Holden's band, of which Williams was a member. Her arrangements, compositions, and outstanding solos helped make the Kirk band one of the decade's finest. She was also writing arrangements for Benny Goodman, Earl Hines, and Tommy Dorsey. "Froggy Bottom," "Walkin' and Swingin'," and "Little Joe from Chicago" were among songs for Kirk's orchestra, while she penned "Camel Hop" and "Roll 'em" for Goodman. Williams stayed with Kirk until 1942, then formed her own band in New York with trumpeter Shorty Baker, who'd become her second husband. There was a brief stint as a staff arranger for Duke Ellington in the '40s, and she contributed "Trumpet No End" to his orchestra's book in 1946. One year after Williams played "Zodiac Suite" at Town Hall, the New York Philharmonic performed three movements from it at Carnegie Hall, one of the first times a major symphony orchestra recognized a jazz composer's works. Williams contributed scores to Dizzy Gillespie's big band and continued writing influential songs. "In the Land of Oo-Bla-Dee," which she co-wrote and recorded for King with Pancho Hagood's vocals in 1949, was subsequently recorded by Gillespie. "Satchel-Mouth Baby" in 1947 on Asch was turned into "Pretty-Eyed Baby" for Frankie Laine and Jo Stafford in 1951. She played briefly with Goodman in 1948, then moved to Europe from 1952 to 1954. She left the music world in 1954, became a Catholic, and formed a foundation to help musicians with personal problems. Williams returned in 1957, playing with Gillespie at the Newport Festival. She divided her time in the '60s and '70s between leading groups in New York clubs, recording, and composing sacred pieces for jazz orchestras and voices. These included "Black Christ of the Andes" in 1963 and "Mary Lou's Mass" in 1970, which Alvin Ailey later choreographed. There were memorable '70s albums with Buster Williams, Mickey Roker, Buddy Tate, and the controversial, sometimes compelling, but ultimately uneven *Embraced* in 1977, which paired her with Cecil Taylor. Williams also became a busy educator. She recorded *The History Of Jazz* in 1970, an elaborate project featuring her solo piano and commentary. After getting several honorary doctorates, Williams joined Duke University's faculty in 1977, staying with them until her death in 1981. —*Ron Wynn and Dan Morgenstern*

☆ **1927-40** / Jan. 1927-Nov. 18, 1940 / Classics ✦✦✦✦✦
This CD features the great pianist Mary Lou Williams during her earliest period. She is heard in 1927 on six selections with the Synco Jazzers (a small group that included her then-husband John Williams on alto) and then on the first 19 selections ever recorded under her own name. Performed during the long period when she was the regular pianist with Andy Kirk's Twelve Clouds of Joy, Williams is featured on two hot stride solos in 1930, leading trios in 1936 and 1938, playing "Little Joe from Chicago" unaccompanied in 1939, and heading septets in 1940. Among these sidemen are trumpeter Harold "Shorty" Baker and the legendary tenor Dick Wilson. Many of the compositions were written by Williams, including "Night Life," "New Froggy Bottom," "Mary's Special," and "Scratchin' the Gravel." Her version of Jelly Roll Morton's "The Pearls" is a high point. —*Scott Yanow*

First Ladies of Jazz / Jan. 26, 1940-Feb. 1954 / Savoy ✦✦✦✦
Three female pianists are well showcased on this Muse-sponsored CD reissue of Savoy material. The great Mary Lou Williams leads a septet of musicians from Andy Kirk's Orchestra (including the legendary tenor Dick Wilson) on four numbers. The interesting but now somewhat forgotten pianist Jutta Hipp heads a quartet with tenor saxophonist Hans Koller, and Beryl Booker is featured with a quartet that includes Don Byas on tenor. The high quality music ranges from swing to bop, and these rarities are well worth hearing. —*Scott Yanow*

Town Hall (1945): The Zodiac Suite / Dec. 31, 1945 / Smithsonian/ Folkways ✦✦✦✦
Mary Lou Williams' *Zodiac Suite*, a 12-piece work with a different theme for each of the signs of the zodiac (and keeping in mind the personalities of a few jazz musicians born during each period), was composed and first recorded in 1945. With the assistance of bassist Al Lucas and drummer Jack "The Bear" Parker, pianist Williams performs these moody and often introspective (but occasionally playful) sketches in a forward-looking swing style. Five alternate takes have been added to the original program on this CD reissue which, although not quite essential, has its interesting moments. —*Scott Yanow*

Zoning / 1974 / Smithsonian/Folkways ✦✦✦✦

Free Spirits / Jul. 8, 1975 / SteepleChase ✦✦✦

● **Live at the Cookery** / Nov. 1975 / Chiaroscuro ✦✦✦✦
This CD gives a definitive look at the talented pianist Mary Lou Williams in her later years. In these duets with bassist Brian Torff, Williams takes listeners on a trip through the history of jazz, from hymns and blues to stride, swing, and bop (including "All Blues"). The CD reissue adds three fine performances to the original program. Recommended. —*Scott Yanow*

Tony Williams (Anthony Williams)

b. Dec. 12, 1945, Chicago, IL
Drums / Fusion, Post-Bop, Hard Bop
Although he turned 40 in late 1995, Tony Williams has been a major drummer in jazz for 22 years. The open style that he created while with the Miles Davis Quintet in the mid- to late '60s remains quite influential, and he has had a long list of accomplishments during the past couple of decades. Williams' father, a saxophonist, took his son to clubs that gave him an opportunity to sit in; at 11 the youngster already showed potential. He took lessons from Alan Dawson and at 15 was appearing at Boston-area jam sessions. During 1959-60 Williams often played with Sam Rivers, and in December 1962 (when he was barely 17), the drummer moved to New York and played regularly with Jackie McLean. Within a few months he joined Miles Davis, where his ability to imply the beat while playing quite freely influenced and inspired the other musicians; together with Herbie Hancock and Ron Carter he was part of one of the great rhythm sections. Williams, who was 18 when he appeared on Eric Dolphy's classic *Out to Lunch* album, stayed with Davis into 1969, leading his own occasional sessions and becoming a household name in the jazz world. In addition to his interest in avant-garde jazz, Williams was a fan of rock music; and when he left Miles he formed the fusion band Lifetime, a trio with Larry Young and John McLaughlin. After leading other versions of Lifetime (one of them starring Allan Holdsworth), Williams stuck to freelancing for a time, studied composition, and toured with Herbie Hancock's V.S.O.P. band. By the mid-'80s he was heading his own all-star hard-bop group, which featured Wallace Roney as a surrogate Miles Davis and a repertoire dominated by the drummer's originals (including the standard "Sister Cheryl"). With the breakup of the group after nearly a decade, Tony Williams has left his options open. —*Scott Yanow*

● **Life Time** / Aug. 21, 1964-Aug. 24, 1964 / Blue Note ✦✦✦✦
A re-issue of one of his best solo albums of the '60s. —*Ron Wynn*

Spring / Aug. 12, 1965 / Blue Note ✦✦✦✦
Early-period Blue Note recording with Sam Rivers (sax). Powerful music. —*Michael G. Nastos*

☆ **Emergency** / May 26, 1969 & May 28, 1969 / Polydor ✦✦✦✦✦
One of the anthems of jazz-rock in 1969. —*Ron Wynn*

☆ **The Tony Williams Lifetime** / Jan. 17, 1970 / Polydor ✦✦✦✦✦
Groundbreaking early fusion in the late-'60s with Jack Bruce (bass), Larry Young (organ), and John McLaughlin (guitar). —*Michael G. Nastos*

Believe It / 1975 / Columbia ✦✦✦✦
This is a hard-edged fusion quartet with guitarist Allan Holdsworth. —*Michael G. Nastos*

Foreign Intrigue / Jun. 18, 1985-Jun. 19, 1985 / Blue Note ✦✦✦✦
Williams had never led a straightahead recording session before and is a little higher in the mix than drummers usually rate. But despite the fact that he almost drowns out Bobby Hutcherson's vibes at times, Williams' playing is consistently colorful and would hold one's interest even if he were under-recorded. —*Scott Yanow*

★ **Tokyo Live** / Mar. 2, 1992-Mar. 8, 1992 / Blue Note ✦✦✦✦✦
Drummer Tony Williams recorded quite a few CDs with his modern hard-bop quintet during 1986-93, a unit that included trumpeter Wallace Roney, Bill Pierce on tenor and soprano, pianist Mulgrew Miller, and bassist Ira Coleman. This double CD, their only live recording, is definitive. With the exception of the Beatles' "Blackbird," all 12 selections are Williams' compositions, including the classic "Sister Cheryl," heard here in a 14-minute version. Recommended. *—Scott Yanow*

Cassandra Wilson

b. Dec. 1955, Jackson, MS
Vocals / Blues, Avant-Garde, Free Funk
Although her recording career has been somewhat erratic, Cassandra Wilson is one of the top jazz singers of the '90s, a vocalist blessed with a distinctive and flexible voice who is not afraid to take chances. She began playing piano and guitar when she was nine and was working as a vocalist by the mid-'70s, singing a wide variety of material. After a year in New Orleans, Wilson moved to New York in 1982 and began working with Dave Holland and Abbey Lincoln. After meeting Steve Coleman, she became the main vocalist with the M-Base collective. Although there was really no room for a singer in the overcrowded free-funk ensembles, Wilson did as good a job of fitting in as is possible. She worked with New Air and recorded her first album as a leader in 1985. By her third record, a standards date, she was sounding quite a bit like Betty Carter. After a few more albums in which she performed mostly original and rather inferior material, Cassandra Wilson changed directions and performed an acoustic blues-oriented program for Blue Note called *Blue Light 'til Dawn*. By going back in time, she had found herself, and Wilson has continued interpreting in fresh and creative ways vintage country blues and folk music. *—Scott Yanow*

Blue Skies / Feb. 1988 / JMT ✦✦✦✦
Primarily associated with the M-Base school of creative funk, Cassandra Wilson was having a difficult time finding a place for her vocals in the dense ensembles that usually dominate that music. *Blue Skies* was a real change of pace, a set of nine standards in which Wilson is backed by a creative but conventional trio (pianist Mulgrew Miller, bassist Lonnie Plaxico, and drummer Terri Lyne Carrington). Her voice in this setting (and her improvising style) sounds very much like Betty Carter, but Wilson would develop much more individuality during the next few years. *—Scott Yanow*

★ **Blue Light 'til Dawn** / 1993 / Blue Note ✦✦✦✦✦
Cassandra Wilson has steadfastly refused to be pigeonholed or confined to any stylistic formula. Her highly anticipated Blue Note debut may stir renewed controversy, as she is once again all over the place. She begins the set with her intriguing version of "You Don't Know What Love Is." Then she moves from two Robert Johnson covers ("Come On in My Kitchen" and "Hellhound on My Trail") to rock compositions from Van Morrison and Joni Mitchell, then to her own track track and blues cut "Redbone" and a piercing version of "I Can't Stand the Rain" that can hold up to comparisons with Ann Peebles' classic. She doesn't have Johnson's menacing quality (who does?), but does invoke an equally compelling air. Wilson has great timing, pacing, and delivery and certainly has blues sensibility in her sound. *—Ron Wynn*

New Moon Daughter / 1995 / Blue Note ✦✦✦✦
Singer Cassandra Wilson, who has had a rather diverse career that has ranged from the free funk of M-Base to standards a la Betty Carter, has in recent times adopted a folk-oriented style a little reminiscent of Nina Simone. On this CD her repertoire ranges from U2 to Son House, from Hoagy Carmichael to Hank Williams ("I'm So Lonesome I Could Cry"); it is certainly the only album ever that contains both the Monkees' "Last Train to Clarksville" and "Strange Fruit!" This CD is a surprise best-seller, for Wilson's voice actually sounds quite bored and emotionally detached than deserves great credit for stretching herself, but one has to dig deep to find any warmth in her approach. *—Scott Yanow*

Gerald Wilson

b. Sep. 4, 1918, Shelby, MS
Trumpet / Hard Bop
An outstanding bandleader and arranger as well as a good trumpeter and composer, Gerald Wilson has updated and evolved his approach to big bands from the swing era to the present. His bands have been heralded for containing topflight, well drilled musicians presenting immaculately played and superbly written and arranged material. Wilson studied music in high school after his family moved from Memphis to Detroit. He worked with Jimmie Lunceford's band from 1939 to 1942, where he replaced Sy Oliver and learned how to combine precision and flair in his roles as soloist, composer, and arranger. Wilson moved to Los Angeles in the early '40s and played with Benny Carter and Les Hite. He later worked with Clark Terry and Ernie Royal in Willie Smith's Navy band, then organized his own big band. This intriguing group included Melba Liston and Snooky Young

and played an aggressive, forward-looking blend of swing and bebop. Wilson kept it going from 1944 to 1947. He was off the scene for part of the '50s, then returned with a new band in 1952 in San Francisco. Among Wilson's studio duties in the '50s were sessions for Larry Williams on Specialty. He made several albums for World Pacific in the '60s that were highly successful, most notably *Moment of Truth* that featured Mel Lewis, Carmell Jones, Harold Land, and Joe Pass. His band played at the 1963 Monterey Festival, and its roster included Land, Teddy Edwards, and Pass. Wilson also did song arrangements on albums by Buddy Collette, Johnny Hartman, Nancy Wilson, Ella Fitzgerald, Al Hibbler, Julie London, and Bobby Darin, and played trumpet solos on Leroy Vinnegar's LP *Leroy Walks!* on Contemporary. He did a regular radio program, wrote for symphony orchestra, and did film and television scores. A tune Wilson penned in 1970 titled "Viva Tirado" became a huge pop hit when recorded by the band El Chicano. He continued recording in the '80s for Discovery, World Pacific, and Trend, and ran the house band for Redd Foxx's NBC shows. Wilson has been a fixture in Los Angeles since the '40s as a bandleader, arranger, educator, and radio broadcaster. He celebrated his 75th birthday by recording a new set for the MAMA Foundation, reviving some classic arrangements (including "Carlos") and writing some new ones. *—Ron Wynn*

☆ **Moment of Truth** / Sep. 1962 / Pacific Jazz ✦✦✦✦✦
An excellent reissue of a fine '60s date with Harold Land, Teddy Edwards, and Joe Pass. *—Ron Wynn*

Portraits / 1963 / Pacific Jazz ✦✦✦✦
Wonderful large-group recordings made in the '60s for Pacific Jazz. A 1992 reissue. *—Ron Wynn*

The Golden Sword / 1966 / Discovery ✦✦✦✦
First-rate arrangements and solos. *—Ron Wynn*

Calafia / Nov. 29, 1984-Nov. 30, 1984 / Trend ✦✦✦✦
High-caliber orchestra arrangements and solos. *—Ron Wynn*

Love You Madly / 1988 / Discovery ✦✦✦

Jenna / Jun. 27, 1989-Jun. 28, 1989 / Discovery ✦✦✦✦

● **State Street Sweet** / 1994 / MAMA ✦✦✦✦
Bandleader/arranger Gerald Wilson's first recording in several years is a success. He revisits "Carlos" (featuring trumpeter Ron Barrows) and "Lighthouse Blues" and performs some newer originals, including "State Street Sweet," "Lakeshore Drive," and "Jammin' in C." With such soloists as trumpeters Barrows, Bobby Shew, Tony Lujan, and Snooky Young; altoist Randall Willis; tenors Louis Taylor, Plas Johnson (showcased on "Come Back to Sorrento"), and Carl Randall; pianist Brian O'Rourke; and guitarists Anthony Wilson and Eric Otis, this edition of the Gerald Wilson Orchestra is quite strong, but it is the leader's colorful and distinctive arrangements that give the band its personality. Recommended. *—Scott Yanow*

Nancy Wilson

b. Feb. 20, 1937, Chillicothe, OH
Vocals / R&B, Pop, Standards
Nancy Wilson is called a jazz singer, but in reality most of her work has been in the pop/R&B field. Never much of an improviser and overly mannered in her later years, Wilson's most valuable work can be found in early recordings with George Shearing and Cannonball Adderley (the latter is a classic). Very little of her post-1962 work can be considered relevant to jazz. *—Scott Yanow*

● **Swingin's Mutual** / Jun. 29, 1960-Jan. 7, 1961 / Capitol ✦✦✦✦
Singer Nancy Wilson has made only a few recordings of any interest to jazz listeners. This CD reissue brings back her third album, an excellent collaboration with the George Shearing Quintet. Originally Wilson participated on six of the 12 selections, but since five new tracks (with only one vocal) have been added, she is now on seven out of 17. Very much under the influence of Dinah Washington at this point, Nancy Wilson is in generally good form, particularly on "The Nearness of You," "All Night Long," and "The Things We Did Last Summer." As far as the instrumentals by pianist Shearing's Quintet go, "I Remember Clifford," "Evansville," "Blue Lou," and "Lullaby of Birdland" are most memorable, with short solos from vibraphonist Warren Chaisson and guitarist Dick Garcia. *—Scott Yanow*

Nancy Wilson and Cannonball Adderley / Sep. 1, 1962 / Capitol ✦✦✦✦

Lush Life / 1967 / Blue Note ✦✦✦

But Beautiful / 1969 / Capitol ✦✦✦

Ballads, Blues & Big Bands: Best Of / Apr. 1996 / Capitol ✦✦✦✦

Teddy Wilson (Theodore Shaw Wilson)

b. Nov. 24, 1912, Austin, TX, **d.** Jul. 31, 1986, New Britain, CT
Piano / Swing
Teddy Wilson was the definitive swing pianist, a solid and impeccable soloist whose smooth and steady style was more accessible to the general public than Earl Hines' or Art Tatum's. He picked up early experience playing with Speed Webb in 1929 and appearing on some Louis

Armstrong recordings in 1933. Discovered by John Hammond, Wilson joined Benny Carter's band and recorded with the Chocolate Dandies later that year. In 1935 he began leading a series of classic small-group recordings with swing all-stars, which on many occasions featured Billie Holiday. That was also the year that an informal jam session with Benny Goodman and Gene Krupa resulted in the formation of the Benny Goodman Trio. (Lionel Hampton made the group a quartet the following year.) Although he was a special attraction rather than a regular member of the orchestra, Wilson's public appearances with Goodman broke important ground in the long struggle against segregation.

Between his own dates, many recordings with Benny Goodman's small groups, and a series of piano solos, Teddy Wilson recorded a large number of gems during the second half of the '30s. He left Goodman in 1939 to form his own big band, but, despite some fine records, it folded in 1940. Wilson led a sextet at Cafe Society during 1940-44, taught music at Juilliard during the summers of 1945-52, appeared on radio shows, and recorded regularly with a trio, as a soloist, and with pick-up groups, in addition to occasional reunions with Goodman. Wilson's style never changed, and his playing in 1985 was similar to that of 1935. No matter. The enthusiasm and solid sense of swing were present until the end. —*Scott Yanow*

Teddy Wilson (1934-1935) / May 1934-Dec. 1935 / Classics ✦✦✦✦

Teddy Wilson (1935-1936) / Dec. 3, 1935-Aug. 24, 1936 / Classics ✦✦✦✦

Teddy Wilson (1936-1937) / Aug. 24, 1936-Feb. 18, 1937 / Classics ✦✦✦✦

Teddy Wilson (1937) / Mar. 31, 1937-Aug. 29, 1937 / Classics ✦✦✦✦

Teddy Wilson (1937-1938) / Sep. 5, 1937-Apr. 28, 1938 / Classics ✦✦✦✦

Teddy Wilson (1938) / Apr. 28, 1938-Nov. 28, 1938 / Classics ✦✦✦✦

Teddy Wilson (1939) / Jan. 27, 1939-Sep. 12, 1939 / Classics ✦✦✦✦

★ **Central Avenue Blues** / 1948 / Vintage Jazz Classics ✦✦✦✦✦
Teddy Wilson was the definitive swing pianist, an influential stylist still best known for his association with Benny Goodman; however, Wilson had a long career after his years with Goodman. This CD features him mostly with his brilliant sextet of 1944-45, which includes trumpeter Charlie Shavers and vibraphonist Red Norvo. Also here are three Wilson performances from a V-Disc session that features trumpeter Joe Thomas and clarinetist Edmund Hall, and two numbers in which the pianist is backed by a radio orchestra. —*Scott Yanow*

☆ **With Billie in Mind** / May 1972 / Chiaroscuro ✦✦✦✦✦
The concept seemed so logical that it was surprising that no one had thought of it earlier. Producer Hank O'Neal suggested to the veteran swing pianist Teddy Wilson that he record a set of Billie Holiday tunes, since Lady Day had cut many of her greatest sides with Wilson in the '30s. This solo CD, which was originally a 14-song LP, has been expanded with six solos cut at the same sessions. Wilson, who is in peak form, clearly enjoyed playing several tunes that he had not performed in years, and he is heard at the top of his game. Classic swing music. —*Scott Yanow*

Teddy Wilson Trio Revisits the Goodman Years / Jun. 1986 / Storyville ✦✦✦

Kai Winding

b. May 18, 1922, Aarhus, Denmark, **d.** May 6, 1983, Yonkers, NY
Trombone / Bop
One of the finest trombonists to emerge from the bebop era, Kai Winding was always overshadowed to an extent by J.J. Johnson, and together they formed one of the most popular jazz groups of the mid-'50s. Born in Denmark, Winding came to the US with his family when he was 12. He had short stints with the orchestras of Alvino Rey and Sonny Dunham and played in a service band in the Coast Guard for three years. Winding's first burst of fame occured during his year with Stan Kenton's Orchestra (1946-47), during which his phrasing influenced and was adopted by the other trombonists, leading to a permanent change in the Kenton sound. He also participated in some early bop sessions, played with Tadd Dameron (1948-49), and was on one of the Miles Davis's nonet's famous recording sessions. After playing with the big bands of Charlie Ventura and Benny Goodman, he formed a quintet with J.J. Johnson (1954-56); the two trombonists (who sounded nearly identical at the time) had occasional reunions after going their separate ways. Winding led a four-trombone septet off and on through the latter half of the '50s and into the '60s, was music director for the Playboy clubs in New York, and during 1971-72 worked with the Giants of Jazz (an all-star group with Dizzy Gillespie, Sonny Stitt, and Thelonious Monk). Although he recorded frequently both as a leader and as a sideman throughout his career, most of Winding's sessions are not currently available on CD. —*Scott Yanow*

★ **Kai Winding, Jay Jay Johnson and Bennie Green with Strings** / May 13, 1952 & Dec. 3, 1954 / Original Jazz Classics ✦✦✦✦✦
Two unrelated sessions are combined on this CD reissue of an LP. Trombonist Bennie Green is heard on four ballads from 1952, backed by a rhythm section and six strings. However, the more significant selections are eight songs that for the first time matched trombonists J.J. Johnson and

Kai Winding in a quintet. The J.J. and Kai group would be quite popular during the next two years, and, listening to the colorful and melodic versions of such tunes as "How Long Has This Been Going On," "Dinner for One," and "We'll Be Together Again," it is easy to see why. —*Scott Yanow*

Giant Bones / Apr. 17, 1979 / Sonet ✦✦✦✦
Superior two-trombone set with Curtis Fuller (tb). —*Ron Wynn*

Phil Woods

b. Nov. 2, 1931, Springfield, MA
Clarinet, Sax (Alto) / Bop, Hard Bop
One of bebop's most outspoken advocates and an admired alto saxophonist among numerous musicians, Phil Woods has fought the good fight since the '50s, even though he began playing in a time when other styles were challenging bebop's hegemony. Perhaps the fastest alto saxophonist currently active, Woods's technique, from its bright, shimmering tone to his dynamic interpretative abilities and insertion of humorous musical quotations into solos, is textbook bebop. He rivals Frank Morgan as the closest thing going to Charlie Parker in terms of sound and approach, and probably plays better in-tune than virtually any other modern jazz alto stylist. He could be considered a hard bopper, but his reverence for Parker makes it difficult to not associate Woods with this genre. He began playing sax at 12, and later attended Juilliard. While there he played briefly with Charlie Barnet. Woods then worked with George Wallington, Kenny Dorham and Friedrich Gulda, recorded with George Russell and toured the Near East and South America with Dizzy Gillespie during the mid-'50s. He began heading combos in the late '50s, while playing in Buddy Rich's band, touring Europe with Quincy Jones in 1959 and 1960 (he was a founding member of the big band) and the Soviet Union with Benny Goodman in 1962. There were sessions for Prestige in the late '50s and Candid in the early '60s, some with fellow saxophonist Gene Quill; *Phil & Quill* and *Phil Talks With Quill* were the sax equivalent of the J.J. Johnson and Kai Winding collaborations. *Rights Of Swing* in 1960 for Candid showcased his extended compositions. Woods turned to studio work for a while in the '60s, playing on several commercial, television and film dates. He played on the soundtracks for *The Hustler* and *Blow Up*. He recorded with Benny Carter in 1961, appearing on the *Further Definitions* album. During the summers from 1964 to 1967 he taught at the Ramblerny performing arts camp in Pennsylvania. Woods moved to France in 1968, and returned to straight jazz. He formed a combo called The European Rhythm Machine, with pianist George Gruntz, bassist Henri Texler and drummer Daniel Humair. They remained intact until 1972. Woods moved to Los Angeles and formed an electronic quartet that met with criticism and audience displeasure and soon disbanded. He relocated to the East Coast, and in 1973 started an acoustic group with pianist Mike Melillo, bassist Steve Gilmore and drummer Bill Goodwin. This band was critically acclaimed, and Woods won three Grammy awards in the mid-'70s on the strength of such albums as *Images* and *Live From The Showboat*. He also was recognized for his work with pop and soul musicians; he did solos on vocal recordings by Billy Joel and Aretha Franklin among others. He made fine albums for Muse, Testament, Adelphi, and Clean Cuts. Woods made personnel changes in the '80s, as Hal Galper replaced Melillo in 1981 and trumpeter Tom Harrell came on board in 1983. There were more solid dates for Palo Alto, Red Record, Blackhawk, Denon, Omnisound, and Antilles. Galper and Harrell eventually moved on to form their own bands, but Woods has continued recording and performing into the '90s. He's playing more clarinet and occasionally using synthesizer in his recordings. Woods' earlier albums have been steadily reissued, and he keeps making uncompromising music reflecting the influence of mentor Charlie Parker. He's also among the small corps of jazz saxophonists who continue to tour regularly. —*Ron Wynn*

Early Quintets / Aug. 11, 1954 & Mar. 3, 1959 / Original Jazz Classics ✦✦✦✦
A pair of formerly rare quintet sets featuring altoist Phil Woods are combined on this CD reissue from the *OJC* series. One session was actually led by guitarist Jimmy Raney in 1954 (and includes trumpeter John Wilson, bassist Bill Crow, and drummer Joe Morello), while the other group (with trumpeter Howard McGhee, bassist Teddy Kotick, and drummer Roy Haynes) was headed by pianist Dick Hyman in 1959. Both bop-oriented dates have their moments, with the edge going to Hyman's session. —*Scott Yanow*

● **Pairing Off** / Jun. 15, 1956 / Original Jazz Classics ✦✦✦✦
First-rate '80s reissue of an excellent 1956 date with lots of heavy hitters—Kenny Dorham and Donald Byrd (trumpet), Tommy Flanagan (piano), and Woods. —*Ron Wynn*

Altology / Jun. 15, 1956-Mar. 29, 1957 / Original Jazz Classics ✦✦✦✦

The Young Bloods / Nov. 2, 1956 / Original Jazz Classics ✦✦✦✦
Fine reissue taken from days when Woods, Donald Byrd, and Teddy Kotick were rising stars. —*Ron Wynn*

Four Altos / Feb. 9, 1957 / Original Jazz Classics ✦✦✦

Sugan / Jul. 19, 1957 / Original Jazz Classics ✦✦✦✦
This CD from Fantasy's Original Jazz Classics series is essentially a bebop jam session. The quintet (altoist Phil Woods, trumpeter Ray Copeland, pianist Red Garland, bassist Teddy Kotick, and drummer Nick Stabulas) performs three Charlie Parker compositions and three originals by Woods, but the melodies are quickly discarded in favor of heated solos. Woods and the greatly underrated Copeland work together very well, and Garland is a major asset, both as a soloist and as an accompanist to the horns. This little-known date is quite enjoyable. — *Scott Yanow*

★ **Rights of Swing** / Jan. 26, 1960 / Candid ✦✦✦✦✦
This Candid recording is such a major success that it is surprising that altoist Phil Woods has rarely recorded in this context. The all-star octet features not only the altoist/leader but trumpeter Benny Bailey, trombonist Curtis Fuller, baritonist Sahib Shihab, the innovative French horn player Julius Watkins (a major factor in this music), pianist Tommy Flanagan, bassist Buddy Catlett, and drummer Osie Johnson. This set (reissued by Black Lion on CD) consists entirely of Woods's five-part "Rights of Swing" suite, which clocks in around 38 minutes. The colorful arrangements use the distinctive horns in inventive fashion, and the music (which leaves room for many concise solos) holds one's interest throughout. One of Phil Woods' finest recordings, it's a true gem. — *Scott Yanow*

Bouquet / Nov. 1987 / Concord Jazz ✦✦✦✦
Quintet. A nice set from the 1987 Concord Festival in Japan. The CD version has bonus cut. — *Ron Wynn*

● **Bop Stew** / Nov. 1987 / Concord Jazz ✦✦✦✦
Quintet. First in a series of live dates from the 1987 Concord Festival in Japan. Tom Harrell (trumpet) and Woods are emphatic. The CD version has a bonus track. — *Ron Wynn*

Evolution / May 1988 / Concord Jazz ✦✦✦✦
Strong swing and bop cuts from an ensemble that's neither traditional big band or small combo. — *Ron Wynn*

All Bird's Children / Jun. 1990 / Concord Jazz ✦✦✦✦
Quintet. One of Parker's forthright disciples shows where he got his inspiration. The CD version has two bonus cuts. — *Ron Wynn*

Real Life / Sep. 27, 1990-Sep. 28, 1990 / Chesky ✦✦✦✦
A good combo date with a larger group than on most of his recordings. — *Ron Wynn*

An Affair to Remember / 1993 / Evidence ✦✦✦✦

Reggie Workman

b. Jun. 26, 1937, Philadelphia, PA
Bass / Avant-Garde, Hard Bop
Reggie Workman has long been one of the most technically gifted of all bassists, a brilliant player whose versatile style fits into both hard-bop and very avant-garde settings. He played piano, tuba, and euphonium early on, but settled on bass in the mid-'50s. After working regularly with Gigi Gryce (1958), Red Garland, and Roy Haynes, he was a member of the John Coltrane Quartet for much of 1961, participating in several important recordings and even appearing with Coltrane and Eric Dolphy on a half-hour West German television show ("The Coltrane Legacy") that is currently available on video. After Jimmy Garrison took his place with Coltrane, Workman became a member of Art Blakey's Jazz Messengers (1962-64) and was in the groups of Yusef Lateef (1964-65), Herbie Mann, and Thelonious Monk (1967). He recorded frequently in the '60s, including many Blue Note dates and Archie Shepp's classic *Four for Trane*. Since that time Workman has been an educator, played with everyone from Max Roach and Art Farmer to Mal Waldron and David Murray, and in 1989 recorded with Marilyn Crispell and Jeanne Lee. — *Scott Yanow*

Images: The Reggie Workman Ensemble in Concert / Jan. 31, 1989-Jul. 1989 / Music & Arts ✦✦✦✦

● **Cerebral Caverns** / 1995 / Postcards ✦✦✦✦

World Saxophone Quartet

Group / Avant-Garde
The World Saxophone Quartet has long been an innovative saxophone group that originally consisted of altoists Julius Hemphill and Oliver Lake, David Murray on tenor, and baritonist Hamiett Bluiett. Playing without a rhythm section, this band plays adventurous music that somehow always stays coherent; the baselines and rhythms provided by Bluiett help a great deal. In addition to their original music, they have recorded tributes to Duke Ellington and '60s R&B. With Hemphill's departure in 1993 (replaced at times by Arthur Blythe, James Spaulding, and Eric Person), the group has been weakened. — *Scott Yanow*

Steppin' With / Dec. 1978 / Black Saint ✦✦✦✦
The second recording by the World Saxophone Quartet (which follows by a year their Moers Music release *Point of No Return*) gives one a look at this powerful group. Comprised of altoist Julius Hemphill (who contributes four of the six group originals), altoist Oliver Lake, tenorman David Mur-

ray, and baritonist Hamiet Bluiett, the explorative, yet rhythmic, group is heard in their early prime on this stimulating release. — *Scott Yanow*

W.S.Q. / Mar. 1980 / Black Saint ✦✦✦✦

★ **Revue** / Oct. 14, 1980 / Black Saint ✦✦✦✦✦

Prophet / 1980 / Black Saint ✦✦✦✦

★ **Plays Duke Ellington** / Apr. 1986 / Elektra ✦✦✦✦✦
Brilliant adaption of Ellington catalog. — *Ron Wynn*

Dances and Ballads / Apr. 1987 / Elektra ✦✦✦✦
The Quartet extends its reach and scope to include danceable material. — *Ron Wynn*

You Don't Know Me / 1993 / Elektra ✦✦✦✦

Breath Of Life / 1995 / Elektra/Nonesuch ✦✦✦

Yellowjackets

Group / Post-Bop, Crossover
Although sometimes grouped with Spyro Gyra, the Yellowjackets are actually one of the most creative regular groups in the "rhythm and jazz" genre. Founded in 1981 as an R&B-oriented band that starred guitarist Robben Ford, the group took a giant step forward when altoist Marc Russo took Ford's place. With original members Russell Ferrante on keyboards, electric bassist Jimmy Haslip, and drummer William Kennedy, the band found its own R&Bish sound, sometimes playing original compositions that sounded like Joe Zawinul at his most melodic. Russo chose to go out on his own, and his replacement, Bob Mintzer (on tenor and bass clarinet), has added more jazz credibility to the group's music. The Yellowjackets have become quite popular, releasing excellent-selling records for GRP and touring constantly. — *Scott Yanow*

Politics / 1988 / MCA ✦✦✦✦
Politics features the appealing sax of Marc Russo and the compositions of Russel Ferrante. Unpretentious, melodic, and memorable, it has fine studio sound. — *David Nelson McCarthy*

★ **The Spin** / 1989 / MCA ✦✦✦✦✦
Clearly one of their best albums. It swings. — *Michael G. Nastos*

Green House / 1990 / GRP ✦✦✦✦
Included is guest sax by Bob Mintzer and fine orchestration for a real live string ensemble by Vince Mendoza. Very accessible, it has a high level of musicianship all around. — *David Nelson McCarthy*

Live Wires / Nov. 15, 1991-Nov. 16, 1991 / GRP ✦✦✦

Like a River / Apr. 1992 / GRP ✦✦✦✦
Other than the easy-listening pieces that appear near the beginning of the program, this is one of the Yellowjackets' strongest jazz dates. Bob Mintzer's creative reeds (switching between tenor, bass clarinet, soprano, and the EWI) keep the music stimulating; and keyboardist Russell Ferrante has come a long way as both an improviser (where he is most influenced by Herbie Hancock) and as the band's main composer. With bassist Jimmy Haslip and drummer William Kennedy in strong supporting roles, the ensemble plays intelligent funk grooves, some mood music, and occasional sections of straightahead jamming. The inclusion of the Miles Davis-influenced trumpeter Tim Hagans on half of the selections adds variety to a particularly enjoyable set. — *Scott Yanow*

Run for Your Life / 1993 / GRP ✦✦✦✦
This is one of the Yellowjackets' most jazz-oriented sets. Roughly half the music uses funky rhythms, while the remainder is straightahead. "Jacket Town" sounds as if it could have come from a good Eddie Harris record; Bob Mintzer's tenor is heard on a rapid run-through of rhythm changes on "Runferyerlife"; keyboardist Russell Ferrante hints strongly at Chick Corea's acoustic playing on "Muhammed"; and Mintzer's ballad "Sage" is memorable. This fine release is recommended both to the Yellowjackets' longtime fans and those listeners who mistakenly think that this popular group is a mundane fusion band. — *Scott Yanow*

Dreamland / 1995 / Warner Bros. ✦✦✦✦

Collection / GRP ✦✦✦

Larry Young (Larry [Aziz, Khalid Yasin Abdul] Young)

b. Oct. 7, 1940, Newark, NJ, **d.** Mar. 30, 1978, New York, NY
Organ / Fusion, Post-Bop, Hard Bop, Groove
Larry Young, also known as Khalid Yasin, offered as radical an approach on organ in the '60s as Jimmy Smith posed in the '50s. His free, swirling chords, surging lines, and rock-influenced improvisations were an alternative to the groove-centered blues and soul-jazz sound that had become the organ's dominant direction. He brought John Coltrane's late '60s approach to the organ, generating waves of sound and greatly influencing any session he participated in during the '60s and '70s. Young studied piano rather than organ, though he began playing organ in R&B bands in the '50s. He recorded in 1960 with Jimmy Forrest and did his first session for Blue Note as a leader. He worked and recorded with Grant Green in a hard-bop vein in the mid-'60s, though he was beginning his experiments at that point.

Young worked with Joe Henderson, Lee Morgan, Donald Byrd, and Tommy Turrentine, and toured Europe in 1964. His 1965 album *Into Something* alerted everyone that Young was heading a different way. He played with Coltrane, recorded with Woody Shaw and Elvin Jones, then joined Miles Davis' band in 1969. Young worked with John McLaughlin in 1970 and was in Tony Williams' Lifetime with McLaughlin and Jack Bruce in the early '70s. He only made a couple of other records for Perception and Arista, both of them uneven but with some intriguing moments. Neither label had the vaguest idea what Young was trying to do, nor how they could sell it. He died in 1978 at 38. He'd only made a handful of recordings, and his labels never knew what to make of his music. Mosaic issued a superb box set of Young's Blue Note recordings, a six-CD (nine album) collection *The Complete Blue Note Recordings Of Larry Young*. A very early session, *Testifying*, on New Jazz, was reissued by Fantasy in a limited edition in 1992. Blue Note has an anthology package, *The Art of Larry Young*, available as well. —*Ron Wynn*

Testifying / Aug. 2, 1960 / Original Jazz Classics ✦✦✦
Organist Larry Young was 19 when he made this, his debut recording. Although he would become innovative, Young at this early stage was still influenced by Jimmy Smith, even if he had a lighter tone; the fact that he used Smith's former guitarist, Thornel Schwartz, and a drummer whose name was, coincidentally, Jimmie Smith kept the connection strong. R&B-ish tenor Joe Holiday helps out on two songs; and the music (standards, blues, and ballads) always swings. Recommended to fans of the jazz organ. —*Scott Yanow*

Young Blues / Sep. 30, 1960 / Original Jazz Classics ✦✦✦✦
Organist Larry Young's second recording (cut shortly before he turned 20) is the best from his early period, before he shook off the influence of Jimmy Smith. With guitarist Thornel Schwartz in top form, and bassist Wendell Marshall and drummer Jimmie Smith excellent in support, Young swings hard on a few recent jazz originals, some blues, and two standards ("Little White Lies" and "Nica's Dream"). Recommended as a good example of his pre-Blue Note work. —*Scott Yanow*

Groove Street / Feb. 27, 1962 / Original Jazz Classics ✦✦✦

☆ **Complete Blue Note Recordings** / Sep. 11, 1964-Feb. 7, 1969 / Mosaic ✦✦✦✦✦
Larry Young, one of the most significant jazz organists to emerge after the rise of Jimmy Smith, is heard on this limited edition six-CD set at the peak of his creativity. Young was still very much under Smith's influence on the first four sessions (which feature a trio with Green and drummer Elvin Jones, plus guests Sam Rivers or Hank Mobley on tenor and vibraphonist Bobby Hutcherson). However, starting with the monumental *Unity* session (a quartet outing with Joe Henderson on tenor, trumpeter Woody Shaw, and Elvin Jones), Young emerged as a very advanced and original stylist in his own right. The final four dates are generally explorative and feature such notable sidemen as altoists James Spaulding and Byard Lancaster, guitarist George Benson, and trumpeter Lee Morgan. This definitive Larry Young set is highly recommended. —*Scott Yanow*

Into Somethin' / Oct. 12, 1964 / Blue Note ✦✦✦✦
This album is available as part of the Mosaic box set *The Complete Blue Note Recordings of Larry Young*, with Sam Rivers on tenor sax, Grant Green on guitar, and Elvin Jones on drums. First-rate set from a dynamic organist. —*Ron Wynn*

★ **Unity** / Nov. 10, 1965 / Blue Note ✦✦✦✦✦
With Joe Henderson on tenor sax, Woody Shaw on trumpet, and Elvin Jones on drums. Recorded at Englewood Cliffs, NJ. Innovative, far reaching organist. This album is available as part of the Mosaic box set *The Complete Blue Note Recordings of Larry Young*. —*Ron Wynn*

Contrasts / Sep. 18, 1967 / Blue Note ✦✦✦✦
Larger-group format with Tyrone Washington, Herbert Morgan, Hank White, Eddie Wright, Eddie Gladden, Stacey Edwards, and Althea Young. This is more "out" than the earlier material and does not fit into the standard soul-jazz groove style. This album is available as part of the Mosaic box set *The Complete Blue Note Recordings of Larry Young*. —*Michael Erlewine*

Heaven on Earth / Feb. 9, 1968 / Blue Note ✦✦✦

Mother Ship / Feb. 7, 1969 / Blue Note ✦✦✦

Lawrence of Newark / 1973 / Perception ✦✦
Featuring massive percussion group. Interesting. —*Michael G. Nastos*

Lester Young

b. Aug. 27, 1909, Woodville, MS, d. Mar. 15, 1959, New York, NY
Clarinet, Sax (Tenor) / Swing
Lester Young was one of the true jazz giants, a tenor saxophonist who came up with a completely different conception in which to play his horn, floating over bar lines with a light tone rather than adopting Coleman Hawkins' then-dominant forceful approach. A non-conformist,

Young (nicknamed "Pres" by Billie Holiday) had the experience in the '50s of hearing many young tenors try to sound exactly like him!

Although he spent his earliest days near New Orleans, Lester Young lived in Minneapolis by 1920, playing in a legendary family band. He studied violin, trumpet, and drums, starting on alto at age 13. Because he refused to tour in the South, Young left the family band in 1927 and joined Art Bronson's Bostonians, switching to tenor. He was back with the family band in 1929 and then freelanced for a few years, playing with Walter Page's Blue Devils (1930), Eddie Barefield in 1931, back with the Blue Devils during 1932-33, and with Bennie Moten and King Oliver (1933). He was with Count Basie for the first time in 1934 but left to replace Coleman Hawkins with Fletcher Henderson. Unfortunately it was expected that Young would try to emulate Coleman, and his laidback sound angered Henderson's sidemen, resulting in Young's not lasting long. After a tour with Andy Kirk and a few brief jobs, Lester Young was back with Basie in 1936, just in time to star with the band as they headed East. Young made history during his years with Basie, participating on his record dates and starring with Billie Holiday and Teddy Wilson on a series of classic small-group sessions. In addition on his rare recordings on clarinet with Basie and the Kansas City Six, Young displayed a very original cool sound that sounded almost like altoist Paul Desmond in the '50s. After leaving Basie in 1940, Young's career became a bit aimless, not capitalizing on his fame in the jazz world. He co-led a low-profile band with his brother, drummer Lee Young, in Los Angeles until rejoining Basie in December 1943. Young had a happy nine months back with the band, recorded a memorable quartet session with bassist Slam Stewart, and starred in the short film *Jammin' the Blues* before he was drafted. His experiences dealing with racism in the military were horrifying, affecting his state of mind for the remainder of his life.

Although many critics have written that Lester Young never sounded as good after getting out of the military, despite erratic health he actually was at his prime in the mid- to late '40s. He toured (and was well paid by Norman Granz) with Jazz at the Philharmonic on-and-off through the '40s and '50s, made a wonderful series of recordings for Aladdin, and worked steadily as a single. Young also adapted his style well to bebop (which he had helped pave the way for in the '30s). But mentally he was suffering, building a wall between himself and the outside world and inventing his own colorful vocabulary. Although many of his recordings in the '50s were excellent (showing a greater emotional depth than in his earlier days), Young was bothered by the fact that some of his White imitators were making much more money than he was. He drank huge amounts of liquor and nearly stopped eating, with predictable results. In 1956 the *Jazz Giants* album found him in peak form, as did a well documented engagement in Washington, D.C. with a quartet and a last reunion with Count Basie at the 1957 Newport Jazz Festival. But for the 1957 telecast *The Sound of Jazz*, Young mostly played sitting down (although he stole the show with an emotional one-chorus blues solo played to Billie Holiday). After becoming ill in Paris in early 1959, Lester Young came home and essentially drank himself to death. Nearly 40 years after his death, he is still considered (along with Coleman Hawkins and John Coltrane) one of the three most important tenor saxophonists of all time. —*Scott Yanow*

☆ **The Complete Aladdin Sessions** / Jul. 15, 1942-Dec. 29, 1948 / Blue Note ✦✦✦✦✦
Although it has often been written that the cool-toned tenor saxophonist Lester Young's experiences with racism in the military during his 1944-45 so scarred him that musically he never played at the same level as he had previously, the music on this essential two-CD reissue disproves that theory. It is true that his attitude toward life was affected, and Young became somewhat self-destructive; but his post-war solos rank with the greatest work of his career. This two-fer has four selections from 1942 in which Young is heard in a trio with pianist Nat King Cole and bassist Red Callender. It also includes a rare 1945 session headed by singer Helen Humes (including a previously unknown instrumental "Riffin' Without Helen"), that is mostly taken up with Lester Young's very enjoyable 1945-48 small-group dates. Highlights include "D.B. Blues," "Jumpin' with Symphony Sid" (which was a minor hit), "Sunday," and "New Lester Leaps In." Minor errors aside (trumpeter Snooky Young is left out of the personnel listing for the Humes date and Young's final Aladdin session is from 1948 not 1947), this is a well conceived and brilliant set filled with exciting performances by one of the true greats of jazz. —*Scott Yanow*

★ **The Complete Lester Young on Keynote** / Dec. 28, 1943 & Dec. 28, 1944 / Mercury ✦✦✦✦✦
This is an amazing compilation of powerhouse cuts from the '40s. —*Ron Wynn*

Master Takes / Apr. 18, 1944-Jun. 28, 1949 / Savoy ✦✦✦✦
Lester Young recorded for Savoy three times in four different settings. On Apr. 18, 1944, he performed as part of the Count Basie Orchestra (although Basie himself was absent) for three numbers and then cut four more songs with a septet that included trumpeter Billy Butterfield and pianist Johnny Guarnieri. A few weeks later he was featured on four selections in front of the Count Basie rhythm section. Young made his final Savoy appearance in

1949, fronting a young sextet that included pianist Junior Mance and drummer Roy Haynes. All of those performances are included on this CD, minus the many alternate takes, which can be heard (along with this entire program) on *The Complete Savoy Recordings*. —*Scott Yanow*

Pres: The Complete Savoy Recordings / Apr. 18, 1944-Jun. 28, 1949 / Savoy ✦✦✦✦
This set has only 15 selections but includes 21 alternate takes. Most of the sessions date from 1944, when Lester Young was briefly back with Count Basie's Orchestra. He is heard with the Basie band (minus the pianist), in a septet with trumpeter Billy Butterfield and pianist Johnny Guarnieri, and, best of all, on four titles ("Blue Lester," "Ghost of a Chance," "Indiana," and "Jump Lester Jump") with Basie and his rhythm section. The last part of the set finds Young in 1949 fronting a young sextet (which includes trumpeter Jesse Drakes, trombonist Jerry Elliot, and pianist Junior Mance). Throughout, the cool-toned tenor is in excellent form. Pres collectors will have to get this set, although most listeners would be satisfied with *Master Takes*. —*Scott Yanow*

● **Pres Conferences (1946-1958)** / Mar. 20, 1946-1958 / Jass ✦✦✦✦
The great tenor Lester Young is heard in a variety of different settings on this CD, chiefly taken from radio and television broadcasts. The best performances find Pres playing two songs with the Nat King Cole Trio and drummer Buddy Rich in 1946, jamming three standards with trumpeter Buck Clayton and fellow tenor Coleman Hawkins, sitting in with the Count Basie Orchestra in 1952, and performing three numbers with the Bill Potts Trio in 1956. Throughout this very interesting set, Lester Young is in excellent form, making this an excellent introductory CD for listeners not already familiar with Pres' music, and a bonus for collectors, who probably will not already have most of these rare performances. —*Scott Yanow*

★ **With the Oscar Peterson Trio** / Aug. 4, 1952 / Verve ✦✦✦✦✦
Pres and Sweets / 1955 / Verve ✦✦✦✦
Brilliant duo work with Lester Young and Harry "Sweets" Edison. —*Ron Wynn*

☆ **Pres and Teddy** / 1956 / Verve ✦✦✦✦✦
Textbook music from two master improvisers. —*Ron Wynn*

☆ **The Jazz Giants '56** / Jan. 12, 1956 / Verve ✦✦✦✦✦
Even critics who feel (against recorded evidence to the contrary) that little of tenor saxophonist Lester Young's postwar playing is at the level of his earlier performances make an exception for this session. Young was clearly inspired by the other musicians (trumpeter Roy Eldridge, trombonist Vic Dickenson, pianist Teddy Wilson, guitarist Freddie Green, bassist Gene Ramey, and drummer Jo Jones), who made for a very potent band of swing all-stars. The five songs on this LP include some memorable renditions of ballads and a fine version of "You Can Depend on Me," but it is the explosive joy of the fiery "Gigantic Blues" that takes honors. This set, a real gem, is highly recommended. —*Scott Yanow*

● **Lester Young in Washington, D.C., 1956, Vol. 1** / Dec. 7, 1956 / Pablo ✦✦✦✦
In December 1956 the great tenor saxophonist had a gig in Washington D.C. playing at a club with the house rhythm section, the Bill Potts Trio. This engagement would have been long forgotten except that all of the music from one of the nights was recorded and released decades later on four LPs. The recording quality is excellent (studio quality) and, most importantly, Lester Young was in superb form throughout the night. Although there is nothing distinctive about the trio, they are quite competent and evidently pleased Young. The first volume of this highly enjoyable series features fine versions of five standards, a blues, and Pres' "D.B. Blues." —*Scott Yanow*

Joe Zawinul
b. Jul. 7, 1932, Vienna, Austria
Piano, Keyboards / Soul-Jazz, Fusion, Hard Bop
No one has ever been able to get a more human, funky sound out of electric keyboards and synthesizers than Joe Zawinul, Vienna's gift to the improvisational world. Zawinul began playing the accordion at the age of six and started studying classical music a year later at the Vienna Conservatory. He worked with Austrian jazz saxophonist Hans Koller in 1952, then with various Austrian groups in the mid- and late '50s, while also playing in France and Germany with his own trio. Zawinul won a scholarship to Berklee in 1959. Upon coming to America he spent only a week at Berklee before joining Maynard Ferguson and touring with him for eight months. He became Dinah Washington's pianist after a brief stint with Slide Hampton in 1959 and stayed with her until 1961. After a month in Harry Edison's group, he joined Cannonball Adderley and remained with his band until 1970. There Zawinul's skills flourished, and he become a sturdy blues player, good soloist, and excellent accompanist. In 1969 and throughout 1970 he worked in Miles Davis's electric units, gradually moving away from acoustic and concentrating on electric instruments. He co-founded Weather Report in 1971 with Wayne Shorter, and through the '70s and '80s made many influential recordings. Weather Report, especially in its early years, was a true jazz-rock band, able to make appealing, seminal

work that had loose, adventurous foundations and energetic solos. Zawinul's synthesizer solos were never dry or dependent on gimmicks, but showed it was possible to play with individuality and distinction on what many regarded as simply a technological tool. He and Shorter went their separate ways in 1986; since then Zawinul has worked with his own bands. Composer of such tunes as "Mercy, Mercy, Mercy," "Rumplestiltskin," "Birdland," and "In a Silent Way," the masterful keyboardist (a perennial pollwinner) has in recent years led groups called Weather Update and Zawinul Syndicate. —*Ron Wynn*

● **The Rise and Fall of the Third Stream** / 196512 12 / Rhino/Atlantic ✦✦✦✦
This CD collects two Zawinul solo projects from the late '60s, when he was laying the groundwork for concepts that were later highlighted during his Weather Report tenure. *The Rise and Fall of the Third Stream* featured Zawinul on acoustic and electric piano, where his funky gospel- and blues-drenched solos provided welcome relief in a setting where the large orchestra's arrangements were often ponderous and dense. *Money in the Pocket* also boasted a large group, but was a looser, more vibrant release. Neither release was flawless, but *Money in the Pocket* employed its group more creatively and provided tighter, yet less rhythmically and harmonically restrictive, situations than *The Rise and Fall of the Third Stream*. However, both releases are important. —*Ron Wynn*

The Immigrants / 1988 / Columbia ✦✦✦
Black Water / 1989 / Columbia ✦✦✦✦
His recent band has some strong players. This session is uneven by design, with Zawinul and crew going through many styles. —*Ron Wynn*
Lost Tribes / 1992 / Columbia ✦✦✦

John Zorn
b. Sep. 12, 1953, New York, NY
Sax (Alto) / Avant-Garde
The term avant-garde truly fits John Zorn; he falls into no easily definable category or school of playing or composition. His splaying, screaming alto sax solos, use of duck calls, and fondness for film soundtracks and mixing of rock, free, pop, and bop settings confound foes and friends alike. He's been identified with the New York "downtown" crowd, a tag he disdains. Zorn's work began to get wide attention in the mid-'80s, especially the *Cobra '86* album on Hat Art, with its molecular system for 13 players, and Zorn's live act, which has included his blowing a mouthpiece under water. He's also worked with the Golden Palominos and the Kronos Quartet; been featured on tribute albums to Thelonious Monk and Sonny Clark; done solo, trio, duo, and combo recordings; and used studio technology like multitrack dubbing quite creatively. Recent Zorn projects include an album mixing klezmer and free jazz, sessions of pop and rock covers, and thrash/avant-garde material with the Naked City band. —*Ron Wynn*

Pool / Mar. 1, 1980 & Mar. 4, 1980 / Parachute ✦✦✦
Big Gundown / Sep. 1984-Sep. 1985 / Elektra/Nonesuch ✦✦✦✦
Ambitious, rambling, and reflective of Zorn's flirtations with rock and the New York downtown scene. —*Ron Wynn*

● **Voodoo: The Music of Sonny Clark** / Nov. 25, 1985-Nov. 26, 1985 / Black Saint ✦✦✦✦
This is not an album by Sonny Clark, but a tribute to him by John Zorn. Essential Clark repertoire played by progressivists, with John Zorn on alto sax and Wayne Horvits on piano. —*Michael G. Nastos*

Spillane / Aug. 1986-Sep. 1987 / Elektra/Nonesuch ✦✦✦

☆ **Voodoo** / 1987 / Black Saint ✦✦✦✦✦
His best date. Zorn leads a quartet in tribute to Sonny Clark, doing all his tunes. —*Ron Wynn*

★ **News for Lulu** / Aug. 30, 1987 / Hat Hut ✦✦✦✦✦
This is a great power trio with George Lewis and Bill Frisell. —*Ron Wynn*

Spy vs. Spy: The Music of Ornette Coleman / Aug. 18, 1988-Aug. 19, 1988 / Elektra ✦✦✦✦
John Zorn and his quintet play 17 Ornette Coleman tunes ranging chronologically from 1958's "Disguise" to four selections from 1987's *In All Languages*. The performances are concise, with all but four songs being under three minutes and seven under two, but there is absolutely no variety in mood or routine. —*Scott Yanow, Cadence*

Naked City / 1989 / Elektra/Nonesuch ✦✦✦✦
His most intriguing, nicely conceived and executed date, with sparkling solos by Bill Frisell, Wayne Horovitz, and Joey Baron. The CD has three bonus cuts. —*Ron Wynn*

Various Artists
☆ **The 1940s Mercury Sessions** / Sep. 25, 1945-Oct. 27, 1951 / Mercury ✦✦✦✦✦
This seven-CD set is remarkable in several ways. The packaging is quite unique for the box is a plastic reproduction of a '40s radio. Subtitled *Blues*,

Boogie & Bop, the music lives up to the billing, giving listeners the complete Mercury output of several top artists. There are 34 songs from pianist Albert Ammons (two featuring blues singer Sippie Wallace), which find Ammons turning everything (including "Red Sails in the Sunset," "Roses of Picardy," and "Margie") into boogie-woogie; a session with his son, tenor saxophonist Gene Ammons, is a high point. Singer Helen Humes is showcased on 16 stomps and ballads, pianist Jay McShann (often with vocalists Jimmy Witherspoon or Walter Brown) has 24 songs, and Eddie "Cleanhead" Vinson (on alto and vocals) is heard in a variety of settings on 30 selections. In addition there are nine tunes featuring R&B pianist/singer Professor Longhair; four songs apiece from singers Julia Lee, Myra Taylor, and cornetist Rex Stewart; 12 pieces from Buddy Rich's bebop big band; and ten by trumpeter Cootie Williams, including the Willis "Gator" Jackson R&B hit "Gator Tail." As if that were not enough, the seventh disc has previously unreleased alternate takes from Ammons, Humes, McShann, Vinson, Cootie, and two "new" numbers by pianist Mary Lou Williams. The 80-page booklet (with notes from several writers, including Dan Morgenstern) is definitive. Since this is a limited-edition release, it should be acquired as soon as possible; there are literally dozens of musical highlights. —*Scott Yanow*

52nd Street Swing / Sep. 11, 1934-Apr. 3, 1941 / GRP/Decca ✦✦✦✦✦
This fine CD includes performances from many of the most popular small jazz groups that played in New York's 52nd Street during the swing era. There are two hot numbers by the Delta Four (featuring trumpeter Roy Eldridge and clarinetist Joe Marsala), three from the good time ensemble the Spirits of Rhythm, a trio from violinist Stuff Smith's Onyx Club Band (which co-starred trumpeter Jonah Jones), three others from John Kirby's sextet, four numbers by Leonard Feather's All-Star Jam Band (with altoists Benny Carter and Pete Brown, cornetist Bobby Hackett, and clarinetist Joe Marsala), three from trumpeter/vocalist Hot Lips Page, and a pair of selections by pianist Sam Price's Texas Bluesicians, including "Just Jivin' Around," which has a particularly rare solo from the great tenor Lester Young. Veteran collectors will have most of these performances in more complete fashion elsewhere, but this is an excellent sampler for fans of small-group swing. —*Scott Yanow*

After Hours / Jun. 21, 1957 / OJC ✦✦✦
A leaderless sextet jams on four of pianist Mal Waldron's originals; the performances range from eight to 12 minutes apiece. The all-star lineup (trumpeter Thad Jones, Frank Wess on tenor and flute, guitarist Kenny Burrell, Waldron, bassist Paul Chambers, and drummer Art Taylor) is in fine form on the straightahead material, and bop fans will want to pick up this reissue CD. —*Scott Yanow*

Americans In Europe / Jan. 3, 1960 / GRP/Impulse ✦✦✦
In 1963 writer Joachim Berendt organized a concert in Germany that featured many of the top American jazzmen who were then residing in Europe. The results were released on two Impulse LPs. This CD reissue has all six numbers from *Vol. 1 but only two songs of the seven that were originally on Vol. 2*, skipping over cuts by clarinetist Albert Nicholas, blues vocalist/pianist Champion Jack Dupree, and pianist Curtis Jones. However, the most rewarding performances are on this set, including two workouts by tenor saxophonist Don Byas, a feature for trumpeter Idrees Sulieman on "I Can't Get Started," pianist Bud Powell's interpretation of "'Round Midnight," and two numbers apiece by the Kenny Clarke Trio (with organist Lou Bennett and guitarist Jimmy Gourley), and a quintet with clarinetist Bill Smith and altoist Herb Geller. The boppish music is generally quite enjoyable, with Byas' lengthy exploration of "All The Things You Are" being a high point. —*Scott Yanow*

Americans in Europe, Vol. 1 / Jan. 3, 1963 / Impulse ✦✦✦
German critic Joachim Berendt organized an all-star concert in early 1963 that featured a variety of American jazzmen who were living in Europe. The results were issued on two Impulse LPs and all of the music on the first volume (along with two selections from the second set) was reissued on a single CD by GRP/Impulse. Drummer Kenny Clarke leads a trio with organist Lou Bennett and guitarist Jimmy Grouley for two songs, trumpeter Idrees Sulieman is featured on "I Can't Get Started," clarinetist Bill Smith and altoist Herb Geller team up in a quintet for two of Smith's originals, and the immortal pianist Bud Powell plays "'Round Midnight" with a trio. The bop-based music is consistently excellent, making the CD version easily recommended. —*Scott Yanow*

Americans in Europe, Vol. 2 / Jan. 3, 1963 / Impulse ✦✦✦
This is the second of two LPs documenting a 1963 concert in which many of the top American jazzmen who were living in Europe participated. While all of *Vol. 1* has been reissued on CD, only the two numbers from tenor saxophonist Don Byas on this album were included. Byas tears apart "All the Things You Are" with the assistance of trumpeter Idrees Sulieman and pianist Bud Powell and is excellent on "I Remember Clifford." Otherwise clarinetist Albert Nicholas leads a trad sextet for two songs and takes "Rose Room" as a feature, blues pianist/vocalist Champion Jack Dupree is featured on "Wine, Whiskey and Gin Head Women," and Curtis Jones sings the blues on "Lots of Talk for You." —*Scott Yanow*

Anthology of Big Band Swing (1930-1955) / Jan. 14, 1931-Aug. 1955 / Grp ✦✦✦✦✦
This two-CD set is an unusually successful sampler. Although there are a few hits among the 40 selections, many obscurities are also included and not all of the big bands represented are major names, such as Tiny Bradshaw, Noble Sissle, Spud Murphy, Teddy Powell, and Jan Savitt. The emphasis is very much on jazz, and this worthy reissue is overflowing with forgotten classics. Happily the music is programmed in chronological order so one can experience the evolution of big bands, from Duke Ellington, Fletcher Henderson and Luis Russell to postwar recordings from Artie Shaw, Tommy Dorsey, and Benny Goodman. —*Scott Yanow*

Art Deco: Sophisticated Ladies / Apr. 5, 1929-Dec. 17, 1940 / Columbia/Legacy ✦✦✦✦✦
This is a very rewarding two-CD sampler that introduces listeners to a wide variety of singers who were active in the '30s, ranging from jazz vocalists (Annette Hanshaw, Ethel Waters, Connie Boswell, the Boswell Sisters, Lee Wiley, Helen Ward, Ella Logan, Maxine Sullivan, and Mildred Bailey) to cabaret and pop artists of the time (Ruth Etting, Helen Morgan, Greta Keller, Frances Langford, Alice Faye, Nan Wynn, and Ginny Simms). This set has more than its share of rarities (including some previously unissued alternate takes), and there are many rewarding performances. The set is recommended to anyone with an interest in the singing stylists who rose to prominence between Bessie Smith and Billie Holiday. —*Scott Yanow*

At the Jazz Band Ball: Chicago/New York Dixieland / Feb. 8, 1929-Jul. 19, 1939 / Bluebird ✦✦✦✦✦
This 1988 CD contains what was originally called "the Great 16," the four 1939 recording sessions (16 songs in all) by cornetist Muggsy Spanier's hot Ragtime Band. All of that music (plus eight alternate takes) was reissued on CD by Bluebird in 1994, but this CD also contains two selections from Eddie Condon in 1929 and four songs from Bud Freeman's Summa Cum Laude Orchestra in 1939. For those listeners who do not need his alternates, this is a highly recommended set with plenty of exciting and heated Chicago jazz. —*Scott Yanow*

Atlantic Jazz Keyboards / 1994 / Rhino ✦✦✦✦
Rhino's various-artists sampler series focuses on keyboards on this release, with cuts from 13 players. The opening track features Jimmy Yancey's sparkling boogie piano and continues through several styles, from Erroll Garner's flashy solos through Thelonious Monk's amazing bop improvisations, John Lewis's sedate, sophisticated phrases, Lennie Tristano's intricate material, and bluesier fare from Ray Charles, Junior Mance, and Les McCann. Keith Jarrett and Chick Corea take more adventurous directions, while the Mitchell-Ruff duo with drummer Charlie Smith falls somewhere in the center. The set's compositional variety and artist lineup is impressive; while none of these tracks qualify as particularly rare or obscure, they show the wealth of keyboard talent once on the Atlantic roster. —*Ron Wynn*

Barrelhouse Boogie / May 7, 1936-Jun. 17, 1941 / Bluebird ✦✦✦✦✦
The four most important boogie-woogie pianists are all represented on this easily enjoyable CD. Meade Lux Lewis performs a 1936 remake of his classic "Honky Tonk Train Blues" and accompanies himself on "Whistlin' Blues," the subtle Jimmy Yancey plays ten solos from 1939-40, and Pete Johnson and Albert Ammons (with drummer James Hoskins) jam on nine duets from 1940-41. Although there are more complete reissues of the pianists' work available from European labels, this Bluebird set gives listeners a strong sampling of boogie-woogie during its prime years. —*Scott Yanow*

★ **The Best of Blue Note, Vols. 1 & 2** / Nov. 4, 1991 / Blue Note ✦✦✦✦✦
Japanese import. An incredible (just the best!) collection of the very best cuts from the Blue Note label. A perfect introduction to hard-bop and soul-jazz, if you can find it. —*Michael Erlewine*

Best of the Jazz Pianos / 1957-1969 / Denon ✦✦✦
One of five CDs in Denon's series, this release has some interesting if hard-to-trace material. Bill Evans performs two numbers with his classic 1961 trio (which includes bassist Scott LaFaro and drummer Paul Motian), Bud Powell plays two lengthy songs with a quintet that features trumpeter Clark Terry in 1957, Teddy Wilson's trio runs through a pair of standards, Thelonious Monk and a quintet with Charlie Rouse on tenor and trumpeter Thad Jones play a version of "Light Blue" that is supposedly from a European tour in 1958 (doubtful), and Chick Corea is heard on the out-of-place and rather spacey "Sundance," a lengthy improvisation with a group of modernists in 1969. It's a mixed bag. —*Scott Yanow*

The Best of the Jazz Singers / 1954-1974 / Denon ✦✦✦
Only five singers appear on this sampler (part of a five-CD Denon series also including sets devoted to big bands, piano, saxophones, and trumpets), but they are five of the best. Ella Fitgerald and her trio in 1959 perform eight numbers (including "Air Mail Special"), Sarah Vaughan does a song apiece from 1954 and 1960, Carmen McRae is caught during 1972-73, Ruth Brown sings "Fine Brown Frame" with the assistance of the Thad Jones/Mel Lewis Orchestra and Dakota Staton in 1974 sings two numbers. There is nothing too essential on this set, but, if seen at a budget price, it is worth picking up. —*Scott Yanow*

Big Band Renaissance / Apr. 30, 1941-Jan. 1991 / Smithsonian ✦✦✦✦✦
This five-CD set traces the development of the big band in jazz from the end of the swing era up until the '90s. Fifty-eight different orchestras are heard from, generally in one selection apiece although there are some exceptions (most notably Duke Ellington). The music is divided into four categories (road bands, part-time bands, studio bands and avant-garde bands), but many groups really fall into overlapping genres. The set's greatest fault is that the recordings (which range from Ted Heath to Sun Ra) have not been programmed in strict chronological order, which, more than any other method, would have best shown off the music's evolution. However, there are many rarities included on this set, the 88 page booklet is quite informative, and fans of modern jazz big bands will find much to savor. —*Scott Yanow*

The Big Beat / Sep. 4, 1958-Feb. 20, 1964 / Milestone ✦✦✦
This CD reissue brings back the music of the double LP of the same name except for Max Roach's version of "You Stepped Out of a Dream." The sampler features four different drummer-led units in performances that are available on other Fantasy CDs. Art Blakey's 1962-64 Jazz Messengers (with trumpeter Freddie Hubbard, trombonist Curtis Fuller, and tenor saxophonist Wayne Shorter) performs "Caravan," "The High Priest," and a brief "The Theme"; Max Roach's 1958 Quintet (with trumpeter Booker Little and George Coleman on tenor) plays three selections including Roach's drum solo "Conversation"; Elvin Jones meets with his two brothers (cornetist Thad and pianist Hank) on some sextet sides; and Philly Joe Jones heads two all-star groups that include such top musicians as trumpeters Lee Morgan and Blue Mitchell and flutist Herbie Mann. Because the performances are available elsewhere, this CD is not essential, but it serves as a good example of the talents of the four major drummers. —*Scott Yanow*

Billy Eckstine/Big Joe Turner/Johnny Otis / Oct. 5, 1946-Mar. 21, 1951 / Savoy ✦✦✦
This CD is a bit unusual in that it consists of five selections apiece from Billy Eckstine, Big Joe Turner, and Johnny Otis that were left out of Denon's reissue of former two-LP sets on single CDs. Eckstine is heard singing and playing valve trombone with his combo on three standards and "Blues for Sale" in addition to performing "In a Sentimental Mood" while backed by a string orchestra. Turner belts out such tunes as "Careless Love," "Whistle Stop Blues," and "Howlin' Winds" in 1947, while Johnny Otis' numbers from 1950-51 feature vocalists Little Esther (on "Love Will Break Your Heart for You"), Mel Walker, and Marilyn Scott. None of the music on this CD is essential, but there are some good moments, straddling the boundaries between swing, blues, bop, and R&B. —*Scott Yanow*

★ **Birdland All Stars at Carnegie Hall** / Sep. 25, 1954-Dec. 1, 1954 / Roulette ✦✦✦✦✦
There is a great deal of worthy and often historic music on this double CD. Most of the performances are taken from a Sept. 25, 1954, Carnegie Hall concert. Count Basie's Orchestra is in superb form on their seven selections; tenors Frank Foster and Frank Wess in particular blow up a storm. Billie Holiday (backed by the Basie band and pianist Carl Drinkard) is a bit out of it on her six numbers, sometimes getting remarkably far behind the beat. Charlie Parker, in a quartet with pianist John Lewis, bassist Percy Heath, and drummer Kenny Clarke, is also a bit sub-par on his two numbers, but Lester Young, having a rare reunion with the Basie orchestra, is wonderful on an emotional "Pennies from Heaven" and a cookin' "Jumpin' at the Woodside." The second half of the concert features Sarah Vaughan (backed at first by the Basie band and then by her trio) in wondrous form on a jazz-oriented set. She has rarely sounded better. This set concludes with the Basie band live at Birdland on Dec. 16, 1954, welcoming Stan Getz to sit in on five enjoyable numbers. —*Scott Yanow*

● **Birth of the Cool, Vol. 2** / Jan. 23, 1951-Jan. 31, 1953 / Capitol ✦✦✦✦✦
Although its title might lead some to believe that this CD contains more "Birth of the Cool" recordings from Miles Davis, it actually consists of West Coast jazz performances that were influenced by those records. Trumpeter/arranger Shorty Rogers leads an octet that features altoist Art Pepper and Jimmy Giuffre on tenor for six numbers; that date launched what became Shorty Rogers and His Giants. There are also eight performances by Gerry Mulligan's tentet (featuring trumpeter Chet Baker) and two selections from the 1951 Metronome All-Stars, an 11-piece unit that includes altoist Lee Konitz, Stan Getz on tenor, pianist George Shearing, and Miles Davis himself. The music overall is both historically significant and quite enjoyable, making this a highly recommended set. —*Scott Yanow*

Black & White & Reeds All Over / Mar. 4, 1944-Sep. 1, 1944 / Pickwick ✦✦✦✦✦
One of six Pickwick CDs drawn from the Black & White catalog, this release has four complete sessions from 1944 that feature clarinetists in small groups. Rod Cless is heard with trumpeter Sterling Bose, the great pianist James P. Johnson and bassist Pops Foster; the obscure Bingie Madison plays tenor and clarinet with pianist Hank Duncan; the erratic Mezz Mezzrow interacts with pianist Gene Schroeder and drummer George Wettling; and Pee Wee Russell takes solo honors with a group also including pianist Cliff Jackson. All of the releases in this short-lived series are recommended to collectors of '40s small-group jazz. —*Scott Yanow*

Blue Break Beats, Vol. 1-2 / 1993 / Capitol ✦✦✦✦
Blue Note released the two-volume *Blue Break Beats* compilation in the early '90s. The music on *Blue Break Beats* dates from the late '60s and early '70s, when a large portion of Blue Note's soul-jazz artists began experimenting with funk and rock, creating dense electric fusions that concentrated on rhythm, not improvisation. None of this music has ever received much critical praise from jazz purists, but in the late '80s and early '90s, scores of hip-hop and dance DJs discovered these old records and began sampling the original tracks to use in new rap and dance songs. By the early '90s, this jazz/rap/funk fusion had become hip and profitable, which led Blue Note to assemble the *Blue Break Beats* compilations. All of the tracks on the two discs are rare tracks from out-of-print late-'60s and early-'70s albums, featuring multilayered percussion, organs, and guitars. Every song on the two discs—which are sold separately—is hot, with a deep funky groove, and there are no dull spots on the albums. Though it's designed to appeal to fans of contemporary funk and rap, fans of rock-influenced soul-jazz will find *Blue Break Beats* a necessary purchase. —*Stephen Thomas Erlewine*

Blue Guitar / Feb. 5, 1941-Nov. 1989 / Blue Note ✦✦✦
This sampler contains music by 17 guitarists who recorded for Blue Note. Four (including Charlie Christian's acoustic feature on "Jammin' in Four" and the rare "Jimmy's Blues" by Jimmy Shirley) songs are from Blue Note's early days, seven are from its prime bop and hard bop years, and the remaining six (ranging from Earl Klugh to Al DiMeola) are of more recent vintage. The CD gives one a good introduction to these talented players, although this release is not too essential. —*Scott Yanow*

Blue Note Rare Grooves / Jan. 9, 1967-May 19, 1971 / Blue Note ✦✦✦✦✦
Balancing previously unreleased tracks with obscure gems from out-of-print albums, *Blue Note Rare Grooves* is an excellent collection of extremely funky soul-jazz. All of the tracks were recorded between 1967 and 1971, with the majority dating between 1968 and 1969. Though some of the tracks on the disc have been featured on other Blue Note collections, none of the albums they were pulled from are easily available, which makes *Blue Note Rare Grooves* all the more valuable. A good cross-section of artists—featuring John Patton, Richard "Groove" Holmes, Larry Young, Stanley Turrentine, Jack McDuff, Jimmy McGriff, Donald Byrd, Candido, Reuben Wilson, and several others—are included, and every single track has a raw, intoxicating groove. *Blue Note Rare Grooves* may not be for jazz purists, but for listeners looking for a first-rate jazz-funk sampler, it's essential. —*Stephen Thomas Erlewine*

Blue Piano, Vol. 1 / Jan. 6, 1939-Nov. 23, 1953 / Blue Note ✦✦✦
On this sampler there are 14 performances by a variety of pianists from the first 15 years of Blue Note Records. Few of the recordings are particularly rare, but the CD does give one a fine sampling of boogie-woogie (Albert Ammons, Meade Lux Lewis, and Pete Johnson), swing and stride (Earl Hines, James P. Johnson, Nat Cole, Art Tatum, and Art Hodes), and bop (Bud Powell, Lennie Tristano, Thelonious Monk, Wynton Kelly, Al Haig, and Horace Silver). The music is consistently excellent, with none of the groups being larger than a quartet. —*Scott Yanow*

Blue Piano, Vol. 2 / Aug. 1, 1955 / Blue Note ✦✦✦
The second of two CDs containing a sampling of the many great pianists who recorded for Blue Note and its related labels, this program has performances from a dozen masters (Duke Ellington, Herbie Nichols, Cecil Taylor, Sonny Clark, Bill Evans, Herbie Hancock, Chick Corea, Michel Petrucciani, Benny Green, McCoy Tyner, Don Pullen, and Andrew Hill) with three recordings from the '50s, four dating from the '60s, and five from 1987-90, after Blue Note's rebirth. Overall these two sets give one a strong (if not really complete) sampling into the music of some of the great jazz pianists. —*Scott Yanow*

Blue Series: Female Vocals / Jan. 1945-Feb. 1990 / Blue Note ✦✦✦
Eighteen different female vocalists are heard from, on one selection apiece, during this CD reissue; *Vol.1* dealt with the male singers. Some of the material is rarer than others, but there are quite a few worthy tracks from the likes of Anita O'Day, Billie Holiday ("Detour Ahead"), Kay Starr, Abbey Lincoln (during her earliest recording session), Annie Ross, Peggy Lee, Sheila Jordan, Sarah Vaughan, Carmen McRae, and even Rachelle Ferrell. It's a good introduction to these diverse stylists. —*Scott Yanow*

Blue Series: Male Vocals / Jun. 12, 1942-Jan. 1989 / Blue Note ✦✦✦
The first of two CDs from Blue Note has vocals from 19 different male vocalists, including Louis Armstrong and Bing Crosby (collaborating on "Now You Has Jazz"), Nat King Cole, Charles Brown, a previously unreleased item from Mel Tormé, Chet Baker, Mark Murphy, King Pleasure, Jon Hendricks, Joe Williams, Tony Bennett (how did he get here?), and Billy Eckstein. The emphasis is very much on the swing and bop stylist and once one eliminates Lou Rawls' 1989 outing, all of the music is from 1942-62. —*Scott Yanow*

Capitol Jazz Sings the Gershwin Songbook / Jul. 23, 1946-May 1976 / Blue Note ✦✦✦
The music of George Gershwin (and in most cases the lyrics of Ira Gershwin) is interpreted by 16 fine singers on a sampler CD taken from sessions

currently owned by Capitol and its related labels. The music jumps around chronologically and is not programmed with all that much coherence, but the music is consistently enjoyable, with such notable vocalists as Nat King Cole, Carmen McRae, Chet Baker, Sarah Vaughan, Annie Ross, Mel Tormé, Peggy Lee, Johnny Hartman, and Nina Simone ("Summertime") being among the stars. With one exception, all of the music is from the 1946-63 period. — *Scott Yanow*

Celebration of Duke / Sep. 12, 1979-May 13, 1980 / Pablo ✦✦✦✦
Although Sarah Vaughan gets top billing on this set, she takes vocals on just two of the ten songs. Four different groupings of Pablo's All-Star musicians are heard from during a tribute to Duke Ellington, and there are many strong moments. Guitarist Joe Pass, vibraphonist Milt Jackson, bassist Ray Brown, and drummer Mickey Roker make for a potent quartet on three songs; fluegelhornist Clark Terry heads a quintet; Zoot Sims is featured on his lyrical soprano during memorable versions of "Rockin' in Rhythm" and the beautiful "Tonight I Shall Sleep"; and Sassy (backed by just pianist Mike Wofford and guitarist Joe Pass) comes up with fresh interpretations of "I Ain't Got Nothin' but the Blues" and "Everything but You." This is a well rounded and easily enjoyable set with plenty of variety. — *Scott Yanow*

Chartbusters! / Jan. 3, 1995-Jan. 4, 1995 / NYC ✦✦✦
For this unusual CD, eight songs from the prime years of Blue Note (compositions by Horace Silver, Hank Mobley, Bobby Timmons, Sonny Clark, Kenny Dorham, Freddie Hubbard, McCoy Tyner, and the standard "If Ever I Would Leave You") are revisited. What is different from the original versions are not the styles of the solos but the instrumentation. Although tenor saxophonist Craig Handy is on six of the songs (two of which find trombonist Papo Vazquez blending with Handy to create a Jazz Crusaders feel), the dominant forces are organist Lonnie Smith (who with drummer Lenny White is on every selection) and a variety of guitarists. There are no trumpeters, and it is the guitarists (either John Scofield, David Fiuczynski, or Hiram Bullock) who make it obvious that these recordings are not from 1965; they generally take solo honors, particularly Scofield. Organist Smith happily avoids getting into the cliched boogaloo rhythm that he often played on his Blue Note recordings of the late '60s, and the overall music is quite satisfying and swinging in its own way. — *Scott Yanow*

● **Chicago Jazz Summit** / Jun. 22, 1986 / Atlantic ✦✦✦✦✦
Trad jazz fans can consider this set to be essential, for in reality it was the last Eddie Condon record (even though Condon had passed away several years earlier). While Vince Giordano's Nighthawks (a group including the then-unknown clarinetist Ken Peplowski and trumpeter Randy Sandke) act as the "house band," such classic jazz veterans as trumpeters Wild Bill Davison, Yank Lawson, Max Kaminsky, and Jimmy McPartland (the latter two making their final recordings), the tenors of Eddie Miller and Franz Jackson, clarinetists Clarence Hutchenrider, Frank Chace, and Kenny Davern, trombonist George Masso, guitarist Ikey Robinson, pianists Art Hodes, Marian McPartland, and George Wein, bassists Truck Parham and Milt Hinton, and drummer Barrett Deems all have their moments. This historic and spirited set of Dixieland standards could have been titled "We're All Together Again for the Last Time." — *Scott Yanow*

★ **Classic Jazz** / Smithsonian ✦✦✦✦✦
The Smithsonian Collection of Classic Jazz is itself somewhat of a classic, referred to in many books, and used as the main learning source in at least one. If you don't know what you like in jazz and are looking for a well put-together introduction, this set is a good bet. It starts with ragtime's Scott Joplin, and proceeds through Bessie Smith, Louis Armstrong, Art Tatum, Duke Ellington . . . all the way up to and including the free jazz of Ornette Coleman, and even the World Saxophone Quartet. Of course John Coltrane, Thelonious Monk, Miles Davis, and all the other big guns are there—even Horace Silver and Lennie Tristano. This five-CD set (94 tracks) contains classic cuts in most cases. This set is a great place to begin. — *Michael Erlewine*

☆ **Complete Blue Note Recordings of Hall/Johnson/Deparis/Dick** / Feb. 5, 1941-Jun. 24, 1952 / Mosaic ✦✦✦✦
To say that this limited-edition six-LP Mosaic box is overflowing with classics is an understatement. Included are a variety of small-group sessions (with overlapping personnel) from the early days of Blue Note. The Edmond Hall Celeste Quartet has five songs that are the only examples that exist of Charlie Christian playing acoustic guitar; clarinetist Hall, Meade Lux Lewis (on celeste), and bassist Israel Crosby complete the unique group. The king of stride piano, James P. Johnson, is heard on eight solos, and other combos are led by Johnson, Hall (who heads four groups in all), trumpeter Sidney DeParis, and trombonist Vic Dickenson (heard in a 1952 quartet with organist Bill Doggett). Among the other key soloists are vibraphonist Red Norvo, pianist Teddy Wilson, tenor great Ben Webster, baritonist Harry Carney, clarinetist Omer Simeon, and trombonist Benny Morton. But more important than the all-star personnel is the fact that the musicians are consistently inspired and that the performances (ranging from Dixieland to advanced swing) are well planned yet spontaneous. The accompanying 26-page booklet is a major plus, too. Essential music; get this box while you can. — *Scott Yanow*

★ **Complete Commodore Jazz Recordings, Vol. 1** / Apr. 1929-Dec. 21, 1943 / Mosaic ✦✦✦✦
The punchline for this 23-LP limited-edition box set is in its title, *Vol. 1*. On a total of 66 albums, Mosaic has reissued the entire jazz output of Milt Gabler's Commodore label, one of the most important jazz record companies of all time. There is an incredible amount of music included on this first set (the most essential of the three). After five early titles that Commodore acquired from other labels (featuring Cow Cow Davenport, Fletcher Henderson, and Django Reinhardt), one hears the birth of Commodore with the exciting Jan. 17, 1938, outing by Eddie Condon. In addition to a lot more of Condon's freewheeling sessions (much of his best work was for Commodore), there are dates led by Bud Freeman, the Kansas City Five and Six (with Lester Young), Teddy Wilson, Jess Stacy, Chu Berry, Willie "The Lion" Smith, Billie Holiday, Stuff Smith, Jelly Roll Morton, Jack Teagarden, Art Hodes, Joe Marsala, Joe Bushkin, Coleman Hawkins, Lee Wiley, Pee Wee Russell, Bunk Johnson, Mel Powell (with Benny Goodman), Wild Bill Davison, George Brunies, and Edmond Hall. There are many previously unissued performances (not just alternate takes) and literally dozens of classics. Fans of Chicago jazz and small-group swing should bid as much as necessary to acquire this out-of-print box (along with the other two volumes). — *Scott Yanow*

☆ **Complete Commodore Jazz Recordings, Vol. 2** / Feb. 5, 1944-Mar. 16, 1945 / Mosaic ✦✦✦✦
The second of three "volumes" put out by Mosaic that reissues the entire Commodore catalog is, like the first, a 23-LP set; all of the music in this massive box was recorded within 13 months. The limited-edition series is a must (although it will be quite difficult to locate) for collectors of Chicago jazz and small-group swing for it is literally overflowing with classics. The first box is the most essential, but *Vol. 2* is pretty close, with recording sessions led by Sidney and Wilbur DeParis, Albert Ammons, Eddie Heywood, Hot Lips Page, Sid Catlett, Billie Holiday, the Kansas City Six with Lester Young, George Zack, Muggsy Spanier, Miff Mole, Joe Bushkin, Max Kaminsky, Edmond Hall, George Wettling, Bobby Hackett, Pee Wee Russell, Red McKenzie, Jess Stacy, Jack Teagarden, and Wild Bill Davison. In addition to the usual performances (many of which were previously hard to find), there are quite a few previously unissued alternate takes and some selections (including an entire Joe Bushkin Trio date) that were never out before. This set (if it can be found) will be expensive but worth it. — *Scott Yanow*

☆ **Complete Commodore Jazz Recordings, Vol. 3** / Jul. 12, 1938-Jul. 9, 1957 / Mosaic ✦✦✦✦
The third and final Mosaic box set that reissues all of the valuable recordings from Milt Gabler's Commodore label is the smallest of these reissues, a mere 20-LP set. All three of the volumes (which total 66 albums) are wonderful, but since they were originally limited-edition releases (just 2,500 copies apiece) and have gone out-of-print, they will be difficult to locate and expensive to acquire; buy them anyway if you have any interest in small-group swing and Chicago dixieland. *Vol. 3* starts out with some recently discovered alternate takes by Bud Freeman, Chu Berry, Bunk Johnson, and Billie Holiday from 1938-44 before concentrating mostly on the 1945-46 period. There are sessions led by Red Norvo, Bill Coleman, Gene Krupa, Stuff Smith, Teddy Wilson, and the duo of Don Byas and Slam Stewart (all of those are from a legendary 1945 Town Hall concert) plus dates headed by George Zack, Jonah Jones, Wild Bill Davison, Eddie Edwards, George Brunies, and Mel Powell; in addition there are later sets by Bob Wilber, Ralph Sutton, Sidney Bechet, Johnny Wiggs, Willie "The Lion" Smith, Frank Wess, and Peck Kelley. One exhausts superlatives when discussing this remarkable project. — *Scott Yanow*

★ **The Complete Keynote Collection** / Mar. 14, 1941-May 23, 1947 / Polygram ✦✦✦✦
This is an incredible set, a 21-LP box that has all of the jazz recordings ever made for Harry Lim's Keynote label. Much of this music has been reissued in piecemeal fashion on CD by Polygram, but this is the way to get it, complete and in chronological order with all of the alternate takes. Lim had impeccable taste and recorded Chicago jazz, small-group swing, and bop by many of the top musicians of the period; all but the first session (George Hartman Dixieland sides from 1941) are from Dec. 1943 to May 1947. This box has dates by Lester Young, Dinah Washington, Roy Eldridge, Coleman Hawkins, Cozy Cole, the Kansas City Seven, Charlie Shavers with Earl Hines, Benny Morton, Rex Stewart, the Keynoters, Pete Brown, Red Norvo, bassist Billy Taylor, Jonah Jones, George Wettling, Chubby Jackson, Barney Bigard, Bill Harris, Willie Smith, Corky Corcoran, Milt Hinton, J.C. Heard, Irving Fazola, Bud Freeman, Ted Nash, Babe Russin, Manny Klein, Herbie Haymer, Clyde Hurley, Arnold Ross, Juan Tizol, Benny Carter, Marie Bryant, Bernie Leighton, Ann Hathaway, Joe Thomas, George Barnes, Lennie Tristano, Danny Hurd, Dave Lambert and Buddy Stewart, Gene Sedric, Neal Hefti, and Red Rodney, and that is only the leaders. There is so much music (334 performances, including 115 that were not previously released) that in addition to the 21 LPs included is a 45 with an extra Lennie Tristano song. This box will be very difficult to locate, but fans of small-group swing and historic jazz should get it at any price. — *Scott Yanow*

• **The Complete Master Jazz Piano Series** / Mar. 11, 1969-Jan. 9, 1974 / Mosaic ✦✦✦✦✦

During a five-year period the Master Jazz label recorded 11 swing-based pianists in solo settings. Although the label went under later in the decade, the recordings were treasured by collectors. Mosaic, on this four-CD set, brought back all of the music from the original five-volume *Master Jazz Piano* series, adding two unissued selections and a full album released separately of Ram Ramirez's playing. In addition to Ramirez (who is heard on 13 numbers), there are 13 performances by Earl Hines; four apiece from Claude Hopkins, Cliff Jackson, Keith Dunham, Sonny White, Teddy Wilson, Cliff Smalls, and the obscure Gloria Hearn; eight by Jay McShann; and two from Sir Charles Thompson. Most of these pianists (other than Hines and Wilson) rarely recorded during this period in their careers, making this box very important both musically and historically. —*Scott Yanow*

Concord Jazz Festival: Live 1990, First Set / Aug. 18, 1990 / Concord Jazz ✦✦✦

The first of three CDs taken from the 1990 Concord Jazz Festival features three trombonists (Rob McConnell, Al Grey, and Benny Powell), trumpeter Harry "Sweets" Edison, and a fine rhythm section (guitairst Ed Bickert, pianist Gene Harris, bassist Neil Swainson, and drummer Alan Dawson) playing straightahead jazz. Edison, Powell, Harris, Grey, and Bickert have individual features, the full group plays "Cottontail," and the trombonists (without Edison) get to stretch out on "Undecided." Nothing too surprising occurs, but the good-humored music (Grey's "St. James Infirmary" is a high point) is fun and swinging. —*Scott Yanow*

Concord Jazz Festival: Live 1990, Second Set / 1990 / Concord Jazz ✦✦✦

The second of three Concord CDs documenting this 1990 festival matches together four veteran horn soloists (Frank Wess on tenor, and flute, altoist Marshal Royal, Rick Wilkins on tenor and fluegelhornist Pete Minger) with a fine rhythm section (pianist Gerry Wiggins, bassist Lynn Seaton, and drummer Harold Jones) for a variety of jazz standards. Wess, Royal, and Minger each have features (Royal's outing on "Don't Get Around Much Anymore" is a high point), Seaton sings "Just Squeeze Me" in humorous fashion, and the full group jams on "The Blues Walk" and "Broadway." Few surprises occur, but fans of straightahead jazz should enjoy this music. —*Scott Yanow*

Concord Jazz Festival: Live 1990, Third Set / Aug. 18, 1990 / Concord Jazz ✦✦✦✦✦

Although there is no official leader on the CD, this is really an Ernestine Anderson date. Pianist Gene Harris and his quartet (with guitarist Ed Bickert, bassist Lynn Seaton, and drummer Harold Jones) romp through Oscar Pettiford's "Blues in the Closet" and then the singer takes over for the final six numbers; Frank Wess guests on tenor during "I Should Care," and altoist Marshall Royal is heard on "Skylark." Ernestine Anderson is in top form during her well rounded set, with highlights including the lengthy "I Should Care," a swinging "There Is No Greater Love," "On My Own," and a definitive 15-minute version of "Never Make Your Move Too Soon." —*Scott Yanow*

Don't You Feel My Leg / Aug. 25, 1946-May 15, 1950 / Delmark ✦✦✦✦

Subtitled *Apollo's Lady Blues Singers*, this Delmark CD has nine numbers (three previously unissued) by Blue Lu Barker, five from Wea Bea Booze, and four by Baby Dee. Barker was rather limited but ironically was easily the best-known singer of the three. She is assisted on some cuts (all outfitted by Danny Barker lyrics) by trumpeter Shad Collins and either Teddy McRae or Jerry Jerome on tenor and is at her best on the remake of her hit "Don't You Feel My Leg." Wea Bea Booze (joined by a quartet that includes tenorman George Kelly and organist Larry Johnson) and Baby Dee (backed by an unidentified but talented sextet) were actually stronger vocalists despite being long forgotten, and are the main reasons to acquire this fine early R&B/jump music set. —*Scott Yanow*

Early Black Swing: The Birth of Big Band Jazz: 1927-1934 / Apr. 27, 1927-Aug. 4, 1936 / Bluebird ✦✦✦

The music on this CD is quite historic but available in more complete fashion elsewhere. However, listeners wishing to acquire an overview of early swing (mostly prior to the rise of Benny Goodman) could certainly do much worse than these 22 performances. Included are strong examples of the big band music of Fletcher Hederson, Duke Ellington, Bennie Moten, McKinney's Cotton Pickers, Earl Hines, Charlie Johnson's Paradise Ten, the Missourians, Red Allen, Jimmie Lunceford, and Louis Armstrong. —*Scott Yanow*

Esquire 2nd Annual All-American Jazz Concert / Jan. 17, 1945 / Sunbeam ✦✦✦✦✦

This double LP, although not reaching the heights of *Esquire* magazine's famous jazz concert of the previous year, has a large assortment of interesting performances that originated from three different locations on the same day, with celebrities enlisted to present awards to the *Esquire* poll-winners. The radio broadcast begins in New Orleans with selections featuring clarinetist Irving Fazola, guitarist Mary Osborne, pianist James P. Johnson, and Louis Armstrong. Satch appears with Bunk Johnson on "Basin Street Blues" (their only joint recording) and reunites with Sidney

Bechet on "Perdido Street Blues." Switching to New York, the Benny Goodman Sextet is heard on two romps and backing singer Mildred Bailey on "Downhearted Blues." The Los Angeles portion has Duke Ellington's Orchestra as the "house band" with spots for altoist Willie Smith ("Tea for Two"), singer Anita O'Day, pianist Art Tatum, Billie Holiday, and guitarist Al Casey. The show concludes with an attempt to have Duke Ellington's, Louis Armstrong, and Benny Goodman all play "Things Ain't What They Used to Be" together (through a radio hookup) despite being thousands of miles apart. It's a nice, try although it is obvious that they were having trouble hearing each other. But overall this is a set that jazz historians will have little trouble enjoying. —*Scott Yanow*

• **Exciting Battle: JAPT Stockholm '55** / Feb. 2, 1955 / Pablo ✦✦✦✦

This is one of the great JATP recordings. Norman Granz's traveling jam session was at its height whenever trumpeter Roy Eldridge and Dizzy Gillespie teamed up. The octet heard on this CD reissue also includes trombonist Bill Harris, tenor saxophonist Flip Phillips, pianist Oscar Peterson, guitarist Herb Ellis, bassist Ray Brown, and drummer Louie Bellson. They all play well on the jam "Birks" and a four-song ballad medley; "Ow" is a drum feature for Bellson. However, it is the blues "Little David" that is quite classic, for Oscar Peterson sets the groove with a masterful solo and then (after the other horns have their say) Roy Eldridge has one of the finest improvisations of his career. He builds up his solo ever so gradually and dramatically through chorus after chorus, and while the other players riff, Eldridge makes every sound fit, climaxing with some perfectly placed notes in the upper register. It is one of the great moments in recorded jazz history and enough of a reason by itself to acquire this CD. —*Scott Yanow*

Fire / DRZ ✦✦✦✦✦

Various nice cuts from albums by Cannonball Adderley, Yusef Lateef, Gene Ammons, Lee Morgan, Wayne Shorter, Wynton Kelly, Eddie Harris, Paul Chambers, Frank Strozier, and Sonny Stitt—11 in all. Vee-Jay classics. —*Michael Erlewine*

☆ **The First Esquire All-American Jazz Concert** / Jan. 18, 1944 / Radiola ✦✦✦✦✦

This set has one of the great jazz concerts of all time, one that features the who's who of the jazz world of 1944. In 1943 *Esquire* magazine held the first Critics Poll and sponsored a concert featuring many of the winners (those in first or second place); the results are released on this two-fer in its entirety. The high point is a remarkable version of "I Got Rhythm" that has Louis Armstrong and Roy Eldridge on trumpets, trombonist Jack Teagarden, clarinetist Barney Bigard, Coleman Hawkins on tenor, xylophonist Red Norvo, pianist Art Tatum, guitarist Al Casey, bassist Oscar Pettiford, and drummer Sid Catlett. In addition there are individual features and notable appearances by clarinetist Benny Goodman, Lionel Hampton on vibes and drums, pianists Teddy Wilson and Jess Stacy, bassist Sid Weiss, drummer Morey Feld (the latter three on "Rachel's Dream" with Benny Goodman), and vocals from Billie Holiday and Mildred Bailey. The recording quality of the performances (some of which were broadcast over the radio) is generally quite good, and getting to hear Tatum backing Louis Armstrong and Coleman Hawkins' playing on "Basin Street Blues" are two of the many reasons to acquire this unique set. —*Scott Yanow*

Forty Years of Women in Jazz / 1949-1989 / Jass ✦✦✦

While the history of female jazz artists still needs extensive documentation, this 1989 two-disc set goes a long way toward correcting oversights, noting and citing pivotal performers and showing that women have occupied roles in the music besides singers. It begins with pianist Lovie Austin and continues to Hazel Scott, with cuts from vital, underrecorded players such as guitarist Mary Osborne, pianist Beryl Booker, and trombonist Melba Liston. Certainly not every worthy female jazz artist could be included on this one two-disc sampler, but this 44-cut package ranks as a fine start in documenting contributions from women instrumentalists. —*Ron Wynn*

Four French Horns / Apr. 14, 1957 / Savoy ✦✦✦

This is an unusual session. Accordionist Mat Methews came up with the idea of utilizing four French horns as the leading voices on a jazz date, so, with guitarist Joe Puma, bassist Milt Hinton, and drummer Osie Johnson, Mathews welcomed the French horns of Julius Watkins, David Amram, Fred Klein, and Tony Miranda. Watkins has the lion's share of the solo space on this CD release, but all of the horns are heard from both as soloists and in the colorful (and sometimes imaginative) ensembles. This is a moody bop-oriented date that succeeds beyond its novelty value. —*Scott Yanow*

★ **From Spirituals to Swing: Carnegie Hall Concerts, 1938-1939** / 1938-1939 / Vanguard ✦✦✦✦✦

During a pair of Carnegie Hall concerts in late 1938 and late 1939, producer John Hammond had an opportunity to present many of his favorite artists, tracing the evolution of music (as its title said) from spirituals to swing. This double CD is a reissue of the previous double LP and features quite a few historic performances. Featured in good form are the Benny Goodman Sextet (with vibraphonist Lionel Hampton and guitarist Charlie Christian), the Count Basie Orchestra with singer Helen Humes and guest Hot Lips Page (the latter is wonderful on "Blues with Lips"), the Kansas City Six (an all-star group with Lester Young, Buck Clayton, and Charlie

Christian), pianist James P. Johnson, the hot New Orleans Feetwarmers which features the soprano of Sidney Bechet, blues singer Ida Cox, the blues harmonica of Sonny Terry, Big Bill Broonzy, Mitchell's Christian Singers, singer Joe Turner with boogie-woogie pianists Pete Johnson, Meade Lux Lewis, and Albert Ammons and a jam session version of "Lady Be Good" that includes many of these musicians. The recording quality is decent for the period, and the music is generally quite timeless. It's an essential acquisition for all serious jazz collections. —*Scott Yanow*

From the Newport Jazz Festival: Tribute to Charlie Parker / Jul. 1964-Feb. 15, 1967 / Bluebird ✦✦✦✦✦
Although it is not apparent from the outside of this CD, these performances are actually taken from two separate occasions. Trumpeter Howard McGhee, trombonist J.J. Johnson, Sonny Stitt (sticking to tenor), pianist Harold Mabern, bassist Arthur Harper Jr., and drummer Max Roach are heard at the 1964 Newport Jazz Festival jamming on three songs in tribute to Charlie Parker: "Buzzy," "Now's the Time," and "Wee." In addition the MC, Father Norman O'Connor, gets a few of the veterans to say a few words about Bird. The remainder of the CD features altoist Jackie McLean with his quartet at a studio session in 1967 performing searing ballad versions of "Embraceable You" and "Old Folks." A very interesting and well rounded program, worth picking up. —*Scott Yanow*

Fujitsu-Concord 25th Jazz Festival: Silver Anniversary Set / 1993 / Concord ✦✦✦
This two-disc set was recorded at the Fujitsu/Concord Jazz Festival in Concord, CA. The performing roster includes guitarist Howard Alden, a fine if restrained stylist, and his trio, plus soulful, bluesy pianist Gene Harris and award-winning broadcaster/pianist Marian McPartland. Harris' group is augmented by special guest Scott Hamilton, still among the better swing-tinged soloists. McPartland's elegant voicings get some fire and energy from a special guest, tenor saxophonist Chris Potter. The 20 selections comprise the Concord formula—a few originals, but mostly well done reworkings of standards and jazz flagwavers like "The Very Thought of You" and "Sweet Georgia Brown." This is a nice celebration of a company that's earned its place in the hearts of jazz fans for its devotion to unadorned, sophisticated compositions and performances. —*Ron Wynn*

★ **Giants of Funk Tenor Sax** / Prestige ✦✦✦✦
A great two-disc introduction to both honking-blues and funk (soul-jazz) tenor saxophone. Great for beginners, but should be in any collection. Over three hours of blues-funk greats like Arnett Cobb, Eddie "Lockjaw" Davis, Sonny Stitt, Willis Jackson, Houston Person, Stanley Turrentine, Rusty Bryant, and Gene Ammons. A classic collection. —*Michael Erlewine*

Giants of Small Band Swing, Vol. 1 / 1946 / Riverside ✦✦✦
The first of two CDs reissuing material originally on the H.R.S. label has generally strong performances by a variety of small swing-oriented bands from 1946. The personnel overlaps in five groups headed by pianist Billy Kyle, altoist Russell Procope, trombonist Sandy Williams, pianist Jimmy Jones, and trombonist Dicky Wells; the sidemen include such veteran greats as trumpeters Dick Vance, Harold Baker, and Pee Wee Erwin, trombonist Trummy Young, clarinetist Buster Bailey, altoists Lem Davis and Tab Smith, and the tenors of John Hardee and Budd Johnson. Although the music overall is not that essential (the bop recordings of the period are much more significant), there are some memorable performances on this well conceived set. —*Scott Yanow*

Giants of Small Band Swing, Vol. 2 / Nov. 5, 1945-Jun. 3, 1946 / Riverside ✦✦✦
The second of two CDs put out in the *Original Jazz Classics* series that reissues material originally on the H.R.S. label, this volume has fine performances from bands led by three trombonists (Dicky Wells, Sandy Williams, and J.C. Higginbotham) and trumpeter Joe Thomas; among the sidemen are Budd Johnson and Ted Nash on tenors, altoists Tab Smith, Lem Davis, and Johnny Hodges, trumpeters Pee Wee Erwin and Sidney DeParis, and baritonist Harry Carney. Although none of the recordings are classic, and one can argue that the music is slightly behind the times, the solos are quite enjoyable and will be savored by small-group swing fans. —*Scott Yanow*

Giants of the Blues Tenor Sax/Giants of the Funk Tenor Sax / Prestige ✦✦✦
If you can locate it, this three-CD box from Prestige is worth whatever it takes to find it. What it is: 23 fat tracks—12 classic blues sax tracks and 11 more prime funk sax gems. The liner notes and selections are by Atlantic producer Bob Porter, who is *the* authority when it comes to blues in jazz—honkers, bar walkers, original funk, soul-jazz, whatever. This is your guide to some of the best of blues in jazz, not (mind you) jazz tinged with blues, but tunes that will scratch that blues itch plus some real ear-scorchin' rockers. —*Michael Erlewine*

Good Time Jazz Story / Good Time Jazz ✦✦✦✦
The Good Time Jazz label was formed in 1949 to record the Firehouse Five Plus Two, and during its 20 years (particularly during 1949-59) it was one of the top Dixieland labels. It has been revived in the '90s, most of its

releases have been reissued on CD, and there have even been a few new recordings. This four-CD box set is a definitive overview of the label. There is no previously unreleased material included, but virtually every group that recorded for GTJ is represented: Jelly Roll Morton (1938 solos acquired years later), Burt Bales, Paul Lingle, Luckey Roberts, Willie "The Lion" Smith, Wally Rose, the Banjo Kings, Jesse Fuller, Bunk Johnson, George Lewis, Johnny Wiggs, Eddie Pierson, Santo Pecora, Armand Hug, Sharkey Bonano, Paul Barbarin, Bill Matthews, George Girard, the Silver Leaf Jazz Band, Scott Black's Hot Horns, Lu Watters, Benny Strickler, Turk Murphy, Bob Scobey, the Bay City Jazz Band, Don Ewell, Clancy Hayes, Pete Daily, Kid Ory, the Castle Jazz Band, and the Firehouse Five Plus Two. Although completists will prefer to get the full sessions (except for some of the Banjo Kings titles, virtually all of the selections are available elsewhere on CD), the very attractive 60-page booklet and the definitive nature of the box will make it a tempting purchase. —*Scott Yanow*

The Great Saxophones (1951-1970) / May 3, 1951-Aug. 2, 1970 / Chess ✦✦✦
This sampler features 15 different tenor and alto saxophonists on 14 selections taken from the vaults of Chess. Although it would be preferable to acquire these performances as part of the original complete albums, the CD reissue can serve as an introduction of sorts to the many fine players. Featured are Gene Ammons, Zoot Sims, Johnny Griffin, Paul Gonsalves, Johnny Hodges, Yusef Lateef, Sonny Stitt, Roland Kirk, Benny Golson, James Moody, Budd Johnson, Illinois Jacquet, Harold Land, Dexter Gordon, and Von Freeman; the latter two join together on a jam session version of "Billie's Bounce." In general these are excellent bop-oriented performances. —*Scott Yanow*

● **The Greatest Jazz Concert in the World** / Mar. 26, 1967+Jul. 1, 1967 / Pablo ✦✦✦✦✦
In addition to having a somewhat immodest title, this three-CD set was not actually one single concert but two. That reservation aside, the music on the reissue is often quite special. There is a jam session in the Jazz at the Philharmonic vein with fluegelhornist Clark Terry, altoist Benny Carter, the tenors of Zoot Sims and Paul Gonsalves, and the Oscar Peterson Trio, with the all-stars playing a ballad medley and heated run throughs of a few familiar standards. In addition the Oscar Peterson Trio has a few features, an aging Coleman Hawkins does what he can on two numbers, Hawk teams up with altoists Benny Carter and Johnny Hodges on "C Jam Blues," and special guest T-Bone Walker sings and plays a couple of blues with assists from C.T., Gonsalves, Hodges, and Peterson. But that's not all. The Duke Ellington Orchestra is in prime form, performing a great deal of new material plus having guest spots for Sims (along with fellow tenors Gonsalves and Jimmy Hamilton on "Very Tenor"), Oscar Peterson (who gets to lead the band through a unique version of "Take the 'A' Train"), and Carter; Johnny Hodges is also well showcased. Ella Fitzgerald completes the memorable set with her usual classy performance (accompanied by The Jimmy Jones Trio and sometimes the Ellington Orchestra), finishing the show with some hot scatting on "Cotton Tail." Maybe this really was "the Greatest Jazz Concert" after all. —*Scott Yanow*

Greenwich Village Jazz / Sep. 29, 1944-Jan. 5, 1945 / Pickwick ✦✦✦✦
One of six Pickwick CDs drawn from the mid-'40s Black & White catalog, this set has a lot of valuable swing and Dixieland-oriented performances. Clarinetist Barney Bigard leads two dates, one with trumpeter Joe Thomas and tenorman George Auld and the other one with Thomas, a tenor player by the same name, and the great pianist Art Tatum. Pianist Willie "The Lion" Smith heads a spirited Dixieland set with trumpeter Max Kaminsky and clarinetist Rod Cless, while pianist Cliff Jackson's Village Cats is a particularly impressive group with trumpeter Sidney DeParis, trombonist Wilbur DeParis, Gene Sedric on tenor, and the unique Sidney Bechet on soprano. There is plenty of enjoyable music on this easily recommended set. —*Scott Yanow*

● **Greenwich Village Sound** / Nov. 29, 1944-Jan. 12, 1945 / Pickwick ✦✦✦✦✦
Of the six Pickwick CD reissues drawn from the Black & White catalog of the mid-'40s, this one is the most valuable. Clarinetist Joe Marsala leads ten of the 14 performances. The first six songs feature his septet with trumpeter Joe Thomas and the brilliant jazz harpist Adele Girard, who happily has a fair amount of solo space. However, it is the other four selections that really grab one's attention, for the swing-oriented Marsala is matched with stride pianist Cliff Jackson and bebop innovator and trumpeter Dizzy Gillespie. On "My Melancholy Baby" all three of the stylists are heard in uncompromising fashion, first in individual solos and then (much too briefly) battling it out in a unique ensemble. This CD is rounded out by singer Etta Jones (backed by a Barney Bigard combo) interpreting four blues from Dinah Washington's repertoire. This is a highly recommended set. —*Scott Yanow*

GRP Super Live in Concert / Oct. 8, 1987 / GRP ✦✦✦
This double CD is most notable for its second half, which has a strong outing from Chick Corea's Elektric Band, his pacesetting fusion band with guitarist Frank Gambale, altoist Eric Marienthal, bassist John Patitucci, and drummer Dave Weckl. The first CD is of lesser interest since it contains

three routine vocals by Diane Schuur and some dull R&B jams with guitarist Lee Ritenour, keyboardist Dave Grusin, and saxophonist Tom Scott. This set is worth buying for Corea's contributions if seen at a budget price. —*Scott Yanow*

History of Chess Jazz / Jan. 16, 1996 / GRP ♦♦♦
History of Chess Jazz is a double-disc set featuring highlights from the label's overlooked jazz catalog. Among the artists included are Kenny Burrell, Woody Herman, Ramsey Lewis, Etta James, Ahmad Jamal, and Zoot Sims. Jazz wasn't one of Chess' strong points, but there is plenty of fine music here, making it a worthwhile sampler. —*Stephen Thomas Erlewine*

★ **History of Classic Jazz** / May 1921-Dec. 1953 / Riverside ♦♦♦♦♦
This three-CD reissue of an earlier Riverside five-LP set gives listeners a perfect introduction to early jazz. The 60 selections are divided into ten categories: Backgrounds (including African music, a sermon, and marching music), Ragtime (both piano rolls and solo recordings), Blues, New Orleans Style, Boogie Woogie, South Side Chicago, Chicago Style, Harlem, New York Style, and New Orleans Revival. The performances contain many highlights (nearly every selection is a gem), and although emphasizing the '20s, they do not neglect later developments in Dixieland. The informative booklet is also a major asset. It's a highly recommended acquisition even to collectors who may already have the majority of these recordings. —*Scott Yanow*

● **Hot British Dance Bands** / Oct. 7, 1925-Jul. 8, 1937 / Timeless ♦♦♦♦♦
When one thinks of British music of the '30s, it is of polite society dance bands and sappy vocalists. This 22-song CD gives one a very different picture of the scene overseas. Twenty-two different bands (including those led by Fred Elizalde, Jack Hylton, Spike Hughes, Billy Cotton, Ray Noble, and Ambrose) are represented by some of their hottest recordings. The music ranges from Dixieland-oriented tracks to sophisticated swing, and whether it be the Devonshire Restaurant Dance Band's rendition of "Sugar Foot Stomp," the Rhythm Maniacs' "That's a Plenty," or Ambrose's classic "Cotton Pickers' Congregation," this is a historic and very enjoyable reissue, made available by the Dutch Timeless label. Highly recommended to fans of swing who are tired of hearing the same familiar bands all the time. —*Scott Yanow*

Jam Session in Swingville / Apr. 14, 1961+May 19, 1961 / Prestige ♦♦♦
This single CD has all of the music reissued in the mid-'70s on a two-LP set. Although sometimes issued under the names of Coleman Hawkins and Pee Wee Russell, the two great jazzmen actually do not appear together. The music in general (which is performed by two all-star groups with arrangements by either Jimmy Hamilton or Al Sears) is modern swing. Hawkins' band is comprised of trumpeter Joe Newman, trombonist J.C. Higginbotham, clarinetist Hamilton, altoist Hilton Jefferson, and a four-piece rhythm section; pianist Cliff Jackson plays "I Want to Be Happy," and clarinetist Russell's outfit also features trumpeter Joe Thomas, trombonist Vic Dickenson and both Al Sears and Buddy Tate on tenors. Nothing all that memorable or innovative occurs, but the performances are enjoyable. —*Scott Yanow*

James Moody/Frank Foster in Paris / Jul. 13, 1951-Apr. 4, 1954 / Vogue ♦♦♦
On this Vogue CD there are three different sessions, none of which have been available domestically in many years. James Moody plays alto with a French quintet (which includes trumpeter Roger Guerin and pianist Raymond Fol) on six standards and two of his originals; "This Is Always" and "That's My Desire" are particularly memorable. Moody is also heard doubling on tenor and alto while backed by a string section on six French melodies. The emphasis is on ballads, and there is little on that date to grab one's attention. This CD concludes with a 1954 hard-bop set from tenor Frank Foster in which he is backed by a quiet French trio led by pianist Henri Renaud. Overall this is a CD that bop collectors will want because unlike many of the Vogue reissues, this music did not appear on the American Inner City label in the '70s. —*Scott Yanow*

● **Jazz Band Ball** / Dec. 24, 1947-May 5, 1951 / Good Time Jazz ♦♦♦♦♦
Four different New Orleans jazz bands are heard from on three or four selections apiece on this CD, a straight reissue of the original LP; none of the music is available elsewhere. Clarinetist George Lewis and his 1950 group (with Elmer Talbert on trumpet and the reliable trombonist Jim Robinson), Turk Murphy's 1947 band (recorded shortly after he left Lu Watters and featuring trumpeter Bob Scobey), trombonist Kid Ory's 1951 Creole Jazz Band (with trumpeter Teddy Buckner and clarinetist Joe Darensbourg), and the 1947 edition of trumpeter Pete Daily's Rhythm Kings are all in excellent form. This set offers listeners a good sampling of their work, and considering that Lewis, Murphy, and Ory led three of the most popular traditional jazz bands of the '50s (although each sounded quite different from each other), this CD is well worth picking up. —*Scott Yanow*

Jazz Classics in Digital Stereo, Vol. 3: New York / May 29, 1925-Aug. 26, 1935 / ABC ♦♦♦
On the third of four CDs in the Robert Parker series that reissues a cross-section of early jazz recordings from a regional area, the music ranges from the famous (Jelly Roll Morton, Fletcher Henderson, Bessie Smith, and

Duke Ellington) to the lesser known (Charlie Johnson's Paradise Ten, Lloyd Scott, and Freddy Jenkins). Veteran collectors will prefer to skip this sampler and get the complete sessions elsewhere, but listeners just beginning to explore early jazz should find these early recordings (which range from pre-swing to some heated jams) worth investigating. —*Scott Yanow*

Jazz Classics in Digital Stereo, Vol. 4: Hot Town / Feb. 27, 1927-Dec. 4, 1933 / ABC ♦♦♦
This CD sampler in the Robert Parker series mostly features territory bands from cities other than New York, Chicago, and New Orleans. Other than a selection apiece from Jimmie Lunceford ('30s "In Dat Mornin'"), Duke Ellington, Andy Kirk, and Benny Moten, all of the groups are quite obscure (such as those led by Alonzo Ross, Charley Williamson, Troy Floyd, and Slatz Randall), making this release of greater-than-usual interest, although unfortunately complete sessions are not reissued. Excellent music most highly recommended to listeners who want a general sampling of early rarities. —*Scott Yanow*

Jazz Fest Masters / 1969 / Scotti Bros. ♦♦♦
This is one of five CDs taken from the 1969 New Orleans Jazz Festival and released by Scott Bros. in 1992. The set consists of fine Dixieland from groups led by trombonist Jim Robinson, trumpeter Johnny Wiggs, drummer Barry Martyn, and trombonist Papa Bue; sidemen include clarinetist Louis Cottrell, drummer Zutty Singleton, Danny Barker on banjo, and clarinetist Raymond Burke. There are plenty of heated moments from these similar but distinctive groups, and the music is consistently joyful and swinging. —*Scott Yanow*

Jazz Fest Masters / 1969 / Scotti Bros. ♦♦♦
A lot of classic greats are heard on this CD, taken from the 1969 New Orleans Jazz Festival. Roy Eldridge performs four songs while backed by pianist Jaki Byard, bassist Richard Davis, and drummer Alan Dawson; on "Perdido" fellow trumpeters Bobby Hackett and Clark Terry sit in. Dizzy Gillespie plays two obscure numbers with his quintet of the time (with James Moody on tenor and flute), while Buck Clayton heads an octet on "St. Louis Blues" that also includes Buddy (not Bunny as it says in the scanty liner notes) Tate and trombonist Dickie Wells. The performances are quite enjoyable, obscure, and well recorded. This CD is worth getting for Roy Eldridge's playing by itself. —*Scott Yanow*

Jazz Fest Masters: Bourbon Street Swings / 1969 / Jazz Masters ♦♦♦
Taken from a series released by Scotti Bros. that was recorded at the 1969 New Orleans Jazz Festival, this CD has selections from a variety of Dixieland veterans, including trumpeter Sharkey Bonano's band, clarinetist Tony Parenti, the flashy trumpeter Murphy Campo, and pianist Armand Hug, who is heard on a trio version of "Tiger Rag." The music is not all that essential, but New Orleans jazz collectors will enjoy these somewhat historic performances. There are four other releases in this interesting series. —*Scott Yanow*

Jazz Festival / Aug. 12, 1994 / Concord Jazz ♦♦♦
Recorded at the 26th annual Concord Jazz Festival, this two-CD set features music from three different performances. The first disc has a well rounded set with guitarist Charlie Byrd, Hendrik Meurkens on harmonica, clarinetist Ken Peplowski, and a fine rhythm section paying tribute to the music of Antonio Carlos Jobim. A group billed as "Seven Sensational Saxophones" is good but not all that sensational, with four altos being featured on two songs, four tenors on two others, and six of the saxes soloing on "Tryin' to Make My Blues Turn Green"; the horns are altoists Jesse Davis, Gary Foster, tenors Ken Peplowski, Chris Potter, and Frank Wess, Bill Ramsay on alto and baritone, and Rickey Woodard doubling on tenor and alto. The remainder of this two-fer has eight numbers from what was dubbed "the Gene Harris/Rob McConnell/Frank Wess Concord Jazz All-Star Big Band." The three leaders are the main soloists and Jeannie Cheatham takes a couple of spirited guest vocals. Overall, this set should easily please fans of Concord's usual mainstream output. —*Scott Yanow*

Jazz in L.A.: The 1940s / Sep. 1, 1941-1949 / KLON ♦♦♦♦♦
This CD, issued by radio station KLON in anticipation of presenting the Hollywood Jazz Festival (a major event that never occurred due to the Los Angeles riots), will be a tough one to find but is worth the search. Most of its material (all recorded in Los Angeles in the '40s) is extremely rare. Its contents include a medley from the play "Jump for Joy" that features Duke Ellington, Herb Jeffries, Ivie Anderson, and Joe Turner; a jam from a broadcast by the Lee and Lester Young band; live performances by Cee Pee Johnson's Orchestra, Benny Carter's big band, Dizzy Gillespie with Charlie Parker, the Nat King Cole Trio, Howard McGhee's Sextet, and Boyd Raeburn's Orchestra; plus mostly obscure studio sides by Lucky Thompson, the orchestras of Gerald Wilson, Earle Spencer, and Lyle Griffin, Teddy Edwards, Dexter Gordon with Wardell Gray ("The Chase"), and Charles Mingus (in 1949). The program traces the evolution of bop in Los Angeles, and nearly every selection is quite successful. Historic music that deserves much better distribution. —*Scott Yanow*

Jazz Ltd., Vol. 1 / Feb. 1949-1951 / Delmark ♦♦♦♦♦
Starting in 1947 and continuing throughout the '50s, Bill Reinhardt and his wife Ruth ran Jazz Ltd. a Chicago club that served as a haven for Dixieland.

Reinhardt (a fine clarinetist) led the house band, a unit that invariably left a spot open for guest artists. This Delmark CD features the Jazz Ltd. group on 13 selections with such all-stars as soprano great Sidney Bechet, cornetist Muggsy Spanier, trumpeter Doc Evans, trombonist Miff Mole, and pianist Don Ewell; the disc is rounded off by an informative five-minute interview with the Reinhardts from the '60s. The freewheeling music is quite enjoyable; Dixieland fans are advised to pick up this exciting disc. — *Scott Yanow*

Jazz Masters: Verve at 50 / 1994 / Verve ✦✦✦
Verve Records celebrated the 50th anniversary of Norman Granz's first Jazz at the Philharmonic concert with an all-star get-together at Carnegie Hall. Different groups of top players from Verve's legacy (both past and present) had opportunities to perform, and this CD has many of the highlights. Pianist Peter Delano plays "Tangerine" with a trio, Dee Dee Bridgewater sings "Shiny Stockings" with the Carnegie Hall Jazz Band, Hank Jones pays tribute to Art Tatum, Abbey Lincoln sings "I Must Have That Man," Joe Henderson meets up with Antonio Carlos Jobim (who made his final concert appearance) on "Desafinado," "Manteca" features trumpeter Roy Hargrove and trombonist Steve Turre, pianist Yosuke Yamashita pays tribute to Bud Powell, Betty Carter scats on "How High the Moon," Herbie Hancock and John McLaughlin play a restrained acoustic version of Bill Evans' "Turn Out the Stars," Hargrove teams up with altoist Jackie McLean and guitarist Pat Metheny for "The Eternal Triangle," organist Jimmy Smith revisits Oliver Nelson's arrangement of "Down by the Riverside," Art Porter and Jeff Lorber play some crossover, and J.J. Johnson contributes a few trombone solos. Not that many special moments occur (too many of the original Verve stars had long since passed away), but jazz historians and bop fans may want to get this one. — *Scott Yanow*

Jazz Piano / Apr. 1924-Jan. 1972 / Smithsonian ✦✦✦
This four-CD boxed set attempts to trace the history of jazz piano through 68 recordings by 42 pianists. Actually the avant-garde is largely ignored (with no examples of the playing of Cecil Taylor, Paul Bley, or Don Pullen), but otherwise the various acoustic styles are fairly well covered, even with the absence of Ralph Sutton and Dick Wellstood. One can argue with the individual choices, but the music is generally quite excellent. There are one or two selections from each of these players: Jelly Roll Morton, James P. Johnson, Willie "The Lion" Smith, Fats Waller, Earl Hines (who gets four songs), Teddy Wilson, Jimmy Yancey, Meade Lux Lewis, Pete Johnson, Avery Parrish, Count Basie, Billy Kyle, Mary Lou Williams, Art Tatum (five performances), Duke Ellington, Jess Stacy, Nat King Cole, Erroll Garner, Jimmy Jones, Bud Powell, Lennie Tristano, Dodo Marmarosa, Ellis Larkins, Dave McKenna, Al Haig, Oscar Peterson, Jimmy Rowles, Thelonious Monk, Phineas Newborn, Jr., Horace Silver, Martial Solal, Herbie Nichols, Hank Jones, Tommy Flanagan, John Lewis, Randy Weston, Ray Bryant, Bill Evans, McCoy Tyner, Chick Corea, Keith Jarrett, and Herbie Hancock. — *Scott Yanow*

★ **Jazz Scene** / Mar. 1946-Feb. 4, 1955 / Verve ✦✦✦✦✦
In 1949 producer Norman Granz released a remarkable album of 78s that consisted of a dozen selections (many of them specially recorded for the occasion) that perfectly summed up the modern jazz scene of the time. The deluxe set consisted of two Duke Ellington features for baritonist Harry Carney with strings, a pair of complex Neal Hefti arrangements, small-group sides by Lester Young, Charlie Parker, Bud Powell, and altoist Willie Smith, Machito's "Tanga," major works by arrangers Ralph Burns and George Handy and, as the piece de resistance, Coleman Hawkins' pioneering unaccompanied tenor solo "Picasso." Now all of this music has been reissued on a very attractive double-CD set that also contains five alternate takes plus three previously unknown Billy Strayhorn piano solos, further examples of Lester Young and Willie Smith, an obscure Hawkins session with J.J. Johnson from 1949, a few numbers from a forgotten Flip Phillips session, and three selections by Ralph Burns in 1955, two of which feature explosive trumpet work from Roy Eldridge. The new packaging is magnificent, with many Gjon Mili photographs of the jazzmen of the era and extensive liner notes. This was one of the top reissues of 1994 and is essential for all serious historical jazz collections. — *Scott Yanow*

★ **The Jazz Singers** / Prestige ✦✦✦✦✦
Good range of featured artists aimed at novices and new fans. Very fine two-record set with an extensive cross-section from early Armstrong to Flora Purim. This is worth having, regardless of your jazz knowledge. — *Ron Wynn*

Jazz Sketches on Sondheim / Sony ✦✦✦
With so few major composers still alive by the mid-'90s, it was logical that jazz musicians would try to expand their repertoire by exploring the works of non jazz writers. None of Stephen Sondheim's compositions have thus far become jazz standards, but that may change after the release of this CD. Three of the tracks unfortunately feature vocals by the overdramatic Nancy Wilson and the R&Bish Peabo Bryson, but Holly Cole (on two numbers) fares much better. The most interesting moments are provided by the all-star musicians, which include such players as tenors Joshua Redman and Grover Washington, Jr., guitarist Jim Hall, pianist Herbie Hancock, Wayne Shorter on soprano, and trumpeter Terence Blanchard, among oth-

ers. Sondheim himself makes a guest appearance in a piano duet with Hancock on "They Ask Me Why I Believe in You." And best of all, there is no version here of "Send in the Clowns." This varied set has its memorable performances. — *Scott Yanow*

● **Jazz Women: A Feminist Retrospective** / Jun. 1923-Nov. 1957 / Stash ✦✦✦✦✦
This double LP from Stash gives one a fine overview of some of the top female jazz musicians from the '20s through the '50s. Although it is true that there were not that many females fortunate enough to record during that era, there are strong examples here of such excellent players as pianists Lovie Austin, Mary Lou Williams, Lil Armstrong, Una Mae Carlisle, Norma Teagarden, Dorothy Donegan, and Marian McPartland, cornetist Dolly Jones, country blues guitarist/vocalist Memphis Minnie, trumpeters Valaida Snow and Billie Rogers, guitarist Mary Osborne, organist Sarah McLawler, harpist Adele Girard, tenor saxophonist Kathleen Stobart, Ina Ray Hutton's Orchestra, and the International Sweethearts of Rhythm. Quite a few of these recordings remain difficult to find, making this a two-fer well worth picking up. — *Scott Yanow*

Jazz at Lincoln Center Presents: The Fire of the Fundamentals / Aug. 8, 1991-Feb. 14, 1993 / Columbia ✦✦✦
This CD, which actually features the Lincoln Center Jazz Orchestra on only two selections, has highlights from a variety of concerts held at Lincoln Center during 1991-93. A fine octet with clarinetist Michael White, trumpeter Wynton Marsalis, and pianist Marcus Roberts do an effective reinterpretation of Jelly Roll Morton's "Jungle Blues," pianist Kenny Barron strides enthusiastically on a solo version of Thelonious Monk's "Trinkle Tinkle," and Jimmy Heath's soprano playing is showcased on "Ellington's Stray-Horn." Pianist/vocalist Jay McShann recreates "Hootie Blues," pianist Marcus Roberts romps through Monk's "Bolivar Blues," and then "Dahomey Dance" offers particularly strong solos from a septet with Marsalis and tenorman Todd Williams. Betty Carter sings a spacey version of "You're Mine You," Marcus Roberts returns for a solo rendition of Morton's "The Crave," Marsalis' Sextet interprets Miles Davis'moody "Flamenco Sketches," and vocalist Milt Grayson finishes the CD anticlimactically with the ballad "Multi Colored Blue." It's an interesting if not essential set with plenty of variety and many worthwhile performances. — *Scott Yanow*

● **Jazz at Santa Monica Civic '72** / Aug. 2, 1972 / Pablo ✦✦✦✦✦
The Pablo label (and Norman Granz's return as a full-time producer) was launched with this wonderful package, first released as a three-LP set and now available as a three-CD reissue. The 1972 concert was originally supposed to mainly feature the Count Basie Orchestra and Ella Fitzgerald, but Granz surprised everyone by inviting some "guests": trumpeters Roy Eldridge and Harry "Sweets" Edison, the tenors of Stan Getz and Eddie "Lockjaw" Davis, pianist Oscar Peterson, and bassist Ray Brown! Together with Basie trombonist Al Grey, they formed the Jazz at the Philharmonic All-Stars and play wonderfully on three jams (listen to Elridge's break on "In a Mellow Tone") and a ballad medley. In addition there are four selections from Basie's band (featuring the tenor of Jimmy Forrest, trumpeter Pete Minger, and altoist Curtis Peagler), a full set from Fitzgerald, and a Peterson-Brown duet on "You Are My Sunshine." The high point of the concert, however, is the final song, a classic version of "C Jam Blues" which finds Fitzgerald trading off in very humorous fashion with Grey, Getz, Sweets, Lockjaw, and Eldridge; each of the encounters has at least one remarkable moment. This gem is highly recommended. — *Scott Yanow*

★ **Jazz in the Thirties** / Feb. 28, 1933-Dec. 13, 1935 / Disques Swing ✦✦✦✦✦
There is a great deal of remarkable music included on this two-hour two-CD set. Among the 40 selections (all dating from the early years of swing) are sessions led by violinist Joe Venuti, bass saxophonist Adrian Rollini, Benny Goodman (in an all-star group with trombonist Jack Teagarden), Bud Freeman, trumpeter Bunny Berigan, Gene Krupa, and piano solos by Joe Sullivan and Jess Stacy. The recording sessions are all complete and the music is quite rewarding and often very exciting. It's highly recommended, as is the companion set *Ridin' in Rhythm*. — *Scott Yanow*

The John Reid Collection 1940-1944 / Jun. 17, 1940-Jun. 24, 1944 / American Music ✦✦✦
This is a very unusual CD which will be of greatest interest to collectors of New Orleans jazz of the Bunk Johnson variety. A radio broadcast from 1944 features trumpeter Peter Bocage and the clarinets of Big Eye Louis Nelson and Alphone Picou in a septet. In addition there are two piano solos from Burnell Santiago, a "talking record" from 1944 (in which one can hear the voices of Sidney Bechet, Manuel Perez, Nelson, Picou, and Santiago), a couple of unaccompanied Bechet solos, his "Message to Bunk," in which he urges the veteran trumpeter to come up north, and a 1940 performance by clarinetist George Bacquet in a small group; Bechet guests on one selection. This is a very historical (if "low-fi") release that fills a few gaps in the story of the New Orleans jazz revival. — *Scott Yanow*

Krupa & Rich / May 16, 1955-Nov. 1, 1955 / Verve ✦✦✦✦✦
Although drummers Gene Krupa and Buddy Rich are pictured together on this CD's cover, they actually only play together on one selection, a lengthy "Bernie's Tune." The first five performances (with two songs apiece for Rich and Krupa) also feature short solos from trumpeters Dizzy Gillespie and

Roy Eldridge, tenors Flip Phillips and Illinois Jacquet, and pianist Oscar Peterson; Rich is reasonably restrained on his numbers but has his explosive moments. "Bernie's Tune" is far superior to the in-concert Rich/Krupa drum battles that were recorded at other times. The final two performances find Rich leading a different all-star group with consistently excellent solos from trumpeters Thad Jones and Joe Newman and tenors Ben Webster and Frank Wess. This swinging set (which contains formerly rare recordings) is easily recommended to fans of straightahead and bop-oriented jazz. —*Scott Yanow*

The Ladies / Jan. 2, 1946-Oct. 22, 1955 / Savoy ✦✦✦

Four different jazz singers are heard from on this CD reissue released by Muse in 1989. Ernestine Anderson swings two songs (including "Social Call") with the assistance of altoist Gigi Gryce's all-star band. Etta Jones is accompanied by the swing-oriented Pete Johnson All-Stars on "Man Wanted" and two takes of "I May Be Wonderful." The underrated Mary Ann McCall is heard on six numbers, while Annie Ross (who is accompanied by a quartet with vibraphonist Milt Jackson) is in superior form on four songs. Overall the set has formerly rare material that is consistently enjoyable, offering valuable early looks at four talented vocalists. —*Scott Yanow*

The Legendary Big Band Singers / Mar. 3, 1931-Jan. 24, 1951 / GRP/Decca ✦✦✦

Twenty-one different singers from the swing era are mostly heard backed by big bands on this interesting but not essential sampler. Generally the performances give one a good idea as to the vocalist's abilities (such as Cab Calloway's "Minnie the Moocher," Louis Armstrong's "Thanks a Million," Jimmy Rushing's "Sent for You Yesterday" and Sister Rosetta Tharpe's "Trouble in Mind"), and some of the singers (particularly June Richmond, Bon Bon, and Ella Johnson, who is heard on the original version of "Since I Fell for You") deserve the recognition. On the minus side, the decision not to list the personnel of the many orchestras may lead one to wonder who is playing various tenor, trumpet, and piano solos, information that should have been provided. —*Scott Yanow*

Live at the Festival / 1970-1973 / Enja ✦✦✦

This very interesting CD contains four unrelated performances from three editions of Yugoslavia's Ljublijana Jazz Festival. The Bill Evans Trio (with bassist Eddie Gomez and a slightly out-of-place Tony Oxley on drums) plays "Nardis," "Round Midnight" is explored by the duo of Karin Krog (who half-speaks her vocal) and bassist Arild Andersen, tenor saxophonist Archie Shepp and his quintet romp through the uptempo blues "Sonny's Back" in fairly straightahead if ragged fashion, and best of all, the 1970 Bobby Hutcherson-Harold Land quintet explores an original in 7/8; Land in particular is outstanding. This CD offers listeners four examples of the jazz modern mainstream of the early '70s. —*Scott Yanow*

• **Live at the New School 1972** / Apr. 1972 / Chiaroscuro ✦✦✦✦✦

This CD reissue (which adds two previously unreleased and rather loose selections to the original program) is historic because it has the final recordings of both rhythm guitarist Eddie Condon and drummer Gene Krupa (who ironically back in 1927 made their recording debut together). More importantly the spirited music made by this quintet (which also features cornetist Wild Bill Davison, Kenny Davern on soprano, and pianist Dick Wellstood) is quite enjoyable and creative within the boundaries of Dixieland and swing. Wellstood in particular is in excellent form, making up for the absence of a bass, and it is very rewarding to hear Krupa in such a spontaneous setting on what may have been the best recording of his final decade. —*Scott Yanow*

Looking for a Boy / Savoy ✦✦✦✦

Three different female pianists from the '50s are featured on this interesting (if brief) CD reissue. Adelaide Robbins, who had a style somewhere between bebop and Dave Brubeck, is heard in 1956 on the only date that she ever led; her trio on the four selections includes bassist Wendell Marshall and drummer Teddy Sommer. Barbara Carroll is featured at the beginning of her career with a trio in 1950 (highlighted by "Barbara's Carroll"), and Marian McPartland (with bassist Vinnie Burke and drummer Joe Morello) performs four numbers before a club audience. A fine all-round set, one of the better CD reissues in the Savoy series put out by Denon. —*Scott Yanow*

Lost Grooves / Blue Note ✦✦✦✦✦

Nine soul-jazz cuts from the Blue Note vaults from between 1967 and 1970, all previously unreleased, alternate takes, or (in one case) only released on a single, by major figures such as Grant Green, Lou Donaldson, John Patton, Lonnie Smith, and John Patton. This doesn't really rate with the cream of the genre—all of the aforementioned artists have better work in the style available on their own full-length albums, and some of the cuts are fairly unremarkable adaptations of late-'60s soul and pop hits. It's a good deal for the collector though, offering over 70 minutes of material unavailable elsewhere. —*Richie Unterberger*

Masters of the Black & Whites / Jul. 29, 1944-Dec. 1945 / Pickwick ✦✦✦

Pickwick in 1989 came out with six CDs whose material was taken from the Black & White catalog of the mid-'40s. This particular release has trios led by pianists Errol Garner (in an early set), Gene Schroeder (a rare fea-

ture for the Eddie Condon-associated pianist), the forgotten Ray Stokes, and bassist Red Callender, whose combo with guitarist Leonard Enois and pianist William McDaniel has group vocals a la the Nat King Cole Trio. The music overall is not really essential, but swing fans will find it quite enjoyable. —*Scott Yanow*

Masters of the Modern Piano / Apr. 25, 1955-Feb. 1966 / Verve ✦✦✦✦✦

This excellent two-LP set (which draws its material from the vaults of Verve) has a strong cross-section of modern pianists covering a ten-year period. Bud Powell is heard on six numbers with bassist George Duvivier and drummer Art Taylor in 1955, and although Powell was no longer in peak form, in general he plays well. There is also music from Mary Lou Williams (performing "The Zodiac Suite" and "Carioca" with the Dizzy Gillespie Orchestra), Paul Bley (three fairly free trios from 1961 with clarinetist Jimmy Giuffre and bassist Steve Swallow), Wynton Kelly (who plays "Blues on Purpose" in 1965), and two songs from the 1966 Bill Evans Trio. The most interesting selections, however, are the three numbers performed by the Cecil Taylor Quartet (with Steve Lacy on soprano, bassist Buell Neidlinger, and drummer Dennis Charles) at the 1957 Newport Jazz Festival. It is fascinating to hear Taylor take apart Billy Strayhorn's "Johnny Come Lately," a blues, and his own "Tune 2"; this is as accessible as Cecil Taylor ever got. Although some of the music on this two-fer has been reissued on CD, the attractive set is still recommended to those listeners who happen to run across it. —*Scott Yanow*

Mercury 40th Anniversary / Dec. 5, 1945-Mar. 27, 1965 / Mercury ✦✦✦✦✦

To celebrate its 40th birthday and revival, Mercury came up with this attractive and valuable four-LP box set which is comprised of material largely unreleased at the time. The performances (mostly from the '50s) feature such greats as Erroll Garner, Arnett Cobb, Clark Terry, Dinah Washington, Paul Quinichette, Junior Mance, Paul Bley, Helen Merrill, Clifford Brown, John Williams, Herb Geller, Maynard Ferguson, Jimmy Cleveland, Cannonball Adderley, the Quincy Jones Orchestra, Billy Taylor, the Jazztet, Bob James (as an acoustic pianist in 1962), and Dizzy Gillespie. Some but not all of this material has resurfaced on CD and virtually all of the music is quite enjoyable. —*Scott Yanow*

• **New Orleans Collective** / Dec. 28, 1992 / Evidence ✦✦✦✦✦

Trumpeter Nicholas Payton is teamed up with Wessell Anderson (who doubles on sopranino and alto), pianist Peter Martin, bassist Christopher Thomas, and drummer Brian Blade for an unusual set of music that shifts between hard bop and New Orleans jazz. While "Rhonda Mile" (which uses the chord changes to "Indiana") is pure bop, other selections combine the two idioms, and "Four or Five Times" (listed as an Anderson original but actually a standard from the '20s) is strictly Dixieland. A high point is the 16-minute "He Was a Good Man, Oh Yes He Was," which musically depicts a New Orleans funeral. Throughout, Anderson (particularly on the sopranino, which he plays like a clarinet) and Payton work together quite well in the exciting ensembles and show impressive knowlege of earlier forms of jazz while carving out their own individual voices. —*Scott Yanow*

New Orleans Jazz Giants: 1936-1940 / Jan. 15, 1936-Jun. 5, 1940 / JSP ✦✦✦✦✦

There are 26 recordings on this imported CD from the English JSP label. These interesting and often historical performances feature a variety of New Orleans veterans, particularly clarinetists Jimmie Noone and Johnny Dodds. Noone is heard on 14 performances including a session with trumpeter Guy Kelly and trombonist Preston Jackson, a particularly strong outing with trumpeter Charlie Shavers and altoist Pete Brown, and on two songs with a group that includes the erratic cornetist Natty Dominique. Dodds' final session uses the same Dominique group, but his earlier sextet set with Shavers is much more rewarding. In addition there are two songs apiece from trumpeter Red Allen and drummer Zutty Singleton, both recorded the same day in 1940 with the identical personnel. In general the music is quite enjoyable and, Dominique excepted, the veterans and relative youngsters (Shavers was 20) play quite well. —*Scott Yanow*

New Orleans Trumpets / Nov. 1, 1950-May 16, 1954 / Storyville ✦✦✦

On ten LPs (and reissued as ten CDs), the European Storyville label came out with a variety of rare performances recorded in New Orleans during the '50s. None of the 13 selections on this particular volume were included in the other entries in this series. The focus is very much on trumpeters, and there are selections featuring Ernie Cagnolatti, Alvin Alcorn, Papa Celestin ("The Saints"), Percy Humphrey, Lee Collins, Johnny Wiggs (who gets two songs), George Hartman, the forgotten Johnny Bayersdorffer (who is unfortunately not in good shape), Sharkey Bonano and the ill-fated but talented George Girard. These mostly live and freewheeling performances (a few are previously unreleased alternate takes) are generally quite rewarding and easily recommended to lovers of New Orleans jazz. —*Scott Yanow*

The New Wave in Jazz / Mar. 28, 1965 / Impulse ✦✦✦

On March 28, 1965, several of the top "New Thing" artists who were then recording for Impulse performed at a heated concert at the Village Gate that was fully documented. This CD reissue adds two selections to the original LP while dropping an Albert Ayler performance that will be included in an Ayler reissue in the future. There is plenty of fire on the release, including a searing version of "Nature Boy" from the John Coltrane Quartet, a workout from "Hambone" by tenor saxophonist Archie Shepp's Septet, and two numbers apiece from trumpeter Charles Tolliver (with altoist James Spaulding) and trombonist Grachan Moncur, III (with a young Bobby Hutcherson on vibes). Some of the performances are free and ferocious, while other tracks are on the advanced side of bop. Over 30 years later the music still sounds adventurous and full of life. — *Scott Yanow*

New York Jazz in the Roaring Twenties / Apr. 16, 1926-Jan. 27, 1928 / Biograph ◆◆◆◆◆
This CD is subtitled *Tommy Dorsey—Red Nichols—Jimmy Dorsey* but in reality the Dorsey Brothers are only heard as sidemen. Included on the enjoyable set are four selections from Red & Miff's Stompers (co-led by cornetist Nichols and trombonist Miff Mole), seven selections by the California Ramblers, two featuring the obscure Joe Herlihy's Orchestra, and one by Phil Napoleon. The music ranges from hot (if complicated) '20s jazz to some jazz-oriented dance music. An improvement on Biograph's LP of the same name (due to the inclusion of a couple of extra tracks), these performances (originally released by the Edison label) are longer than the usual recordings of the era, often over four (as opposed to three) minutes long. Fans of '20s jazz will want to get this one. — *Scott Yanow*

New York Stories / 1992 / Blue Note ◆◆◆◆◆
This interesting outing by an all-star group (guitarist Danny Gatton, altoist Bobby Watson, trumpeter Roy Hargrove, Joshua Redman on tenor, pianist Franck Amsallem, bassist Charles Fambrough, and drummer Yuron Israel) is most notable for featuring the brilliant Gatton in a jazz setting. Together the septet performs nine originals by group members, and Gatton And Watson emerge as the main solo stars. Despite its somewhat generic name, this advanced hard bop date is quite memorable. — *Scott Yanow*

Newport Jazz All Stars / Jul. 1, 1966+Jul. 3, 1966 / Jazz Band ◆◆◆◆◆
The music on this CD can easily be divided into two parts. Pianist George Wein put together a particularly interesting version of the Newport Jazz All Stars in 1966, featuring cornetist Ruby Braff, tenorman Bud Freeman, baritonist Gerry Mulligan (who also takes a hot solo on alto on "Bernie's Tune"), bassist Jack Lesberg, and drummer Buddy Rich. Each of the horn players and Rich have their own features, but it is the two "free-for-alls" ("Rose Room" and "Bernie's Tune") that are most exciting. In addition pianist Teddy Wilson (with Rich and bassist Gene Taylor) swings on four standards and welcomes trumpeter Clark Terry on three others, two of which feature C.T.'s exuberant vocals ("I Want a Little Girl" and "Mumbles"). This is a happy set of reasonably well recorded music, put out for the first time on this English CD. — *Scott Yanow*

The Newport Jazz Festival All Stars / Jul. 1985 / Concord Jazz ◆◆◆
Nice, loose date with a specially assembled group of mostly veterans plus one or two younger players performing in vintage jam session style. This is modeled after old *Jazz at the Philharmonic* dates, and the atmosphere and musical performances come close to equaling that fervor. — *Ron Wynn*

Newport Rebels / Nov. 1, 1960-Nov. 11, 1960 / Candid ◆◆◆
In 1960 bassist Charles Mingus helped to organize an alternative Newport Jazz Festival in protest of Newport's conservative and increasingly commercial booking policy. The music on this LP (which has been reissued on CD) features some of the musicians who participated in Mingus' worthy if short-lived venture. Trumpeter Roy Eldridge performs three numbers with pianist Tommy Flanagan, Mingus, and drummer Jo Jones; of greatest interest is "Mysterious Blues," for it adds trombonist Jimmy Knepper and the unique altoist Eric Dolphy successfully to the group. The other selections match up drummers Max Roach and Jo Jones with Roach's quintet (featuring trumpeter Booker Little) on "Cliff Walk" and feature singer Abbey Lincoln on "Tain't Nobody's Bizness If I Do." — *Scott Yanow*

● **Obscure and Neglected Chicagoans** / 1925-Dec. 21, 1929 / IAJRC ◆◆◆◆◆
This CD from the International Association of Jazz Record Collectors (IAJRC) is one of their most exciting, particularly for collectors of '20s jazz. Even fanatics of the era will probably not have the great majority of the 25 selections included on this very valuable disc. Released for the first time anywhere are two numbers from a demonstration record by Dud Mecum's Wolverines in 1925 that feature the remains of the group that launched the career of Bix Beiderbecke; it is miraculous that these well recorded performances (starring the tenor of George Johnson) still exist. Also included on this set are six numbers from the Original Wolverines in 1927-28 with cornetist Jimmy McPartland, eleven selections by Ray Miller's hot dance orchestra from 1928-29 (some of which have cornet solos from Muggsy Spanier), and six songs from the totally forgotten but enjoyable band Thelma Terry and Her Boyfriends, a group that also includes a young Gene Krupa. Highly recommended to serious collectors of vintage jazz. — *Scott Yanow*

● **One Night with Blue Note Preserved** / Feb. 22, 1985 / Blue Note ◆◆◆◆◆
This four-LP set, whose material was also made available as single LPs and

single CDs, not only extensively documented a historic concert that paid tribute to the Blue Note label's legacy but was the start of that important record company's comeback. *Vol. 1* features veterans Herbie Hancock on piano, trumpeter Freddie Hubbard, tenor saxophonist Joe Henderson, bassist Ron Carter, drummer Tony Williams, and vibraphonist Bobby Hutcherson on remakes of "Canteloupe Island" and "Recorda Me" and a pair of Hutcherson pieces, but flutist James Newton takes honors with his version of Eric Dolphy's "Hat and Beard." The second set features strong advanced hard-bop music from an all-star quintet (pianist McCoy Tyner, altoist Jackie McLean, trumpeter Woody Shaw, bassist Cecil McBee, and drummer Jack DeJohnette), a trio workout by tenor Bennie Wallace, and a typically intense piano solo from Cecil Taylor. The third album has an Art Blakey reunion band playing "Moanin'," numbers featuring either tenor Stanley Turrentine or altoist Lou Donaldson with organist Jimmy Smith, guitarist Kenny Burrell, and drummer Grady Tate, and two songs in which Grover Washington, Jr. (on soprano) plays with Burrell, Tate, and bassist Reggie Workman. The final set has five numbers by Charles Lloyd (on tenor and flute at the beginning of a successful comeback), pianist Michel Petrucciani, bassist Cecil McBee, and drummer Jack Dejohnette but saves the best for last, two amazing guitar solos from Stanley Jordan. Obviously this music on a whole is highly recommended for all jazz collections. — *Scott Yanow*

Original V-Disc Collection / Jun. 1943-Dec. 30, 1944 / Pickwick ◆◆◆◆◆
This two-CD set contains 40 selections taken from V-Discs, special recordings made specifically for servicemen abroad during World War II. Since a Musicians Union recording strike was taking place during the period, these performances are even more valuable than usual because they document musicians at a time when they were not on commercial records. Nearly all of the music was previously included in Time-Life's four-CD V-Disc set, but those collectors who do not have that reissue will find the selections of great interest. Not all of the performances are jazz (Marian Anderson, Perry Como, Andre Kostelanetz, Josh White, Paul Robeson, and Kay Kyser make appearances) but most are, and the highlights are many: Hot Lips Page's "The Sheik of Araby," Pee Wee Russell's strange vocal on "Pee Wee Speaks," Louis Jordan's "Is You Is or Is You Ain't My Baby," Tony Pastor's alternate lyrics to "Makin' Whoopee," Johnny Long's "In a Shanty in Old Shantytown," a re-creation of the Original Dixieland Jazz Band's version of "Tiger Rag," Woody Herman's early rendition of "Apple Honey," and Art Tatum's reworking of "Liza." — *Scott Yanow*

The Pete Johnson/Earl Hines/Teddy Bunn Blue Note Sessions / Jul. 29, 1939-Mar. 28, 1940 / Mosaic ◆◆◆◆◆
One of Mosaic's pet projects was the complete reissue of all of the Blue Note label's early pre-bop recordings. This single LP has three unrelated but enjoyable small-group sessions originally cut for Blue Note. Pete Johnson is heard on two piano solos and in a trio for four other songs with guitarist Ulysses Livingston and bassist Abe Bolar. Earl Hines takes a couple of typically miraculous piano solos ("The Father's Getaway" and "Reminiscing at Blue Note") and guitarist Teddy Bunn is featured unaccompanied on four cuts plus an alternate take, one of his very rare opportunities to lead a recording session. Although this set is now out of print, swing fans will want to go out of their way to find it if they do not have the music elsewhere. — *Scott Yanow*

A Piano Anthology / Apr. 20, 1926-Mar. 8, 1968 / GRP/Decca ◆◆◆
This CD contains selections from 20 pianists, all but two (Dodo Marmarosa and Bill Evans) who play in pre-bop styles. Taken mostly from the Decca catalog, the collection has many fine performances, highlighted by Jelly Roll Morton's "The Pearls," Fats Waller and James P. Johnson playing together on Johnny Dunn's "What's the Use of Being Alone," Joe Sullivan's "Little Rock Getaway," an alternate take of Art Tatum's "Deep Purple," and rare performances from Frank Melrose, Billy Kyle, Clarence Profit, and Ralph Sutton. Not essential but this reissue has plenty of enjoyable music for fans of swing piano. — *Scott Yanow*

Piano Wizards / Feb. 16, 1927-Jan. 30, 1939 / Memphis Archives ◆◆◆◆
This CD features 16 different pianists from the '20s and '30s on a total of 18 selections. The programming is pretty random and some selections (such as Reginald Forsythe's "St. Louis Blues" and Clarence Williams' "Wild Flower Rag") are rarer than others. The other pianists are Meade Lux Lewis, Albert Ammons, Pete Johnson (the latter three individually and together in a trio), Fats Waller (one number apiece on piano and organ), Jelly Roll Morton, Earl Hines, Duke Ellington, Bix Beiderbecke ("In a Mist"), Jess Stacy, Art Tatum ("Tiger Rag"), Earl Hines, Jabo Williams, Little Brother Montgomery, and Cow Cow Davenport. This collection serves as a good introduction to pre-bop piano styles, although the absence of James P. Johnson and Teddy Wilson keeps it from being definitive. — *Scott Yanow*

Playboy's 40th Anniversary: Four Decades of Jazz 1953-1993 / Jul. 1953-1993 / Verve ◆◆◆
To celebrate the 40th anniversary of *Playboy* magazine, this four-CD box set was compiled and released. The music is drawn from many catalogs (in addition to Verve) and is a sampler of some of the jazz styles from the 40-year period, with the emphasis on greatest hits. From Charlie Parker's "Now's the Time," Errol Garner's "Misty," Dave Brubeck's "Take Five," John

Coltrane's "Giant Steps," Astrud Gilberto's "The Girl from Ipanema," and Lee Morgan's "Sidewinder," to Donald Byrd's "Black Byrd," Grover Washington, Jr.'s "Mister Magic," Kenny G's "Songbird," and Bobby McFerrin's "Don't Worry, Be Happy," many famous numbers are included, although Dixieland, the avant-garde, and creative fusion are completely ignored. The general collector may want to pick up this set as an introduction to some of these jazz artists, but they should be warned that this reissue does not give listeners the entire picture of the jazz world. —*Scott Yanow*

Playing the Black & Whites / Jul. 17, 1942-Dec. 21, 1944 / Pickwick ✦✦✦✦✦

The accent is on pianists throughout this Pickwick CD, one of six released in 1989 that focus on music from the mid-'40s Black & White catalog. Art Hodes' four 1942 piano solos were the earliest Black & White recordings, and they are joined here by a pair of duets by pianist Dick Cary and drummer George Wettling, four Cliff Jackson piano solos, and four numbers from the trio of pianist Nat Jaffe, guitarist Remo Palmieri, and bassist Leo Guarnieri. The music rangs from swing to stride and is consistently enjoyable and formerly rare. All of the Pickwick CDs in this valuable series are recommended to fans of the era. —*Scott Yanow*

● **Prestige 1st Sessions, Vol. 2** / Feb. 17, 1950-Aug. 14, 1951 / Prestige ✦✦✦✦✦

The second volume in the series devoted to the early recordings issued on the Prestige label in 1949 and 1950. More from Don Lanphere, Leo Parker, Tubby Phillips, Al Haig, and Max Roach, among others. —*Ron Wynn*

Prestige 1st Sessions, Vol. 3 / Feb. 7, 1950-Oct. 5, 1951 / Prestige ✦✦✦✦✦

This enjoyable CD combines together four sessions from the first days of the Prestige label. Tenor saxophonist Eddie "Lockjaw" Davis plays with intensity on two songs and backs singer Carl Davis on two others; both of the latter tunes were previously unreleased. Dizzy Gillespie heads a sextet, singing "She's Gone Again" and taking a fine solo on "Nice Work If You Can Get It." Trumpeter Red Rodney is heard on his first session as a leader, seven boppish songs with a quintet. And finally trombonist Bennie Green leads a heated septet that features the tenors of Big Nick Nicholas and Eddie Davis and baritonist Rudy Williams on two spirited numbers. Bop collectors are advised to pick up all three volumes in this series. —*Scott Yanow*

● **RCA Victor Jazz Workshop: The Arrangers** / Mar. 3, 1956-Jul. 8, 1965 / Bluebird ✦✦✦✦✦

A lot of unusual music appears on this Bluebird CD. Altoist Hal McKusick (with arrangements contributed by George Russell and Gil Evans) performs five numbers (including a version of "Blues for Pablo" that was cut a year before Miles Davis' recording) with a variety of musicians, including trumpeter Art Farmer and trombonist Jimmy Cleveland. Arranger John Carisi (heard here on trumpet) interprets seven previously unreleased numbers with an octet, and trombonist Rod Levitt performs five of his arrangements with his own advanced octet. Although these performances would have little influence on future developments in jazz (the free-jazz movement of the '60s overshadowed the trend towards using elements of modern classical music in charts), the music still sounds quite fresh and unpredictable today. —*Scott Yanow*

● **RCA Victor Jazz: The First Half-century—The Twenties Through the Sixties** / Mar. 25, 1918-Aug. 18, 1967 / Bluebird ✦✦✦✦✦

RCA has long had an up-and-down relationship with jazz, and that is reflected in this very interesting five-CD box set drawn completely from their archives. Each disc focuses on a specific decade, and the producers did an excellent job of picking representative recordings. The '20s and '30s are covered particularly well (with 23 selections on each disc); virtually every major name is heard at their prime. The '40s disc also contains many valuable recordings (although RCA had been slow to record bop), but by the '50s and '60s RCA was not in the forefront of discovering up-and-coming artists; there are only hints of the avant-garde, and many of the giants (Miles Davis, John Coltrane and Thelonious Monk to name three) never made it into the label's studios. However, even in the later decades, a variety of great veterans and modernists did make significant recordings for the label, and there is not a loser among the 96 recordings. Overall this reissue gives one a superb overview of RCA jazz activities through the years (from Coleman Hawkins' "Body and Soul" to Sonny Rollins' "The Bridge") and is recommended to all jazz historians along with beginners just starting to explore this classic music. —*Scott Yanow*

Reminiscin' at Blue Note / May 3, 1994 / Blue Note ✦✦✦

This 16-cut CD spotlights three great pianists who recorded for Blue Note in its infancy. Earl Hines was mainly heading big bands at this point, but cut a few tunes for the fledgling label in 1939, including the opening two numbers. Boogie-woogie stylist Pete Johnson takes center stage for five selections, three with guitarist Ulysses Livington and bassist Abe Bolar. On those cuts, Johnson is more restrained and careful than on the solo numbers. James P. Johnson, widely regarded as the father of stride piano, completes the disc with six brilliant pieces that include blistering rags played in much looser fashion than usual for that idiom, stomps, a marvelous version of Bessie Smith's "Backwater Blues," and the entertaining "Improvisations on Pinetop's Boogie Woogie." —*Ron Wynn*

● **Return to the Wide Open Spaces** / 1990 / Amazing ✦✦✦✦✦

Texas tenor saxophonists David Newman and James Clay recorded a first-rate album in 1960, which seamlessly fused blues, soul, swing-tinged jazz, and honking R&B styles. Some 30 years later, Newman and Clay reunited for a sequel, joined by pianist Ellis Marsalis. The resulting release was both timely and delightful, as Newman and Clay showed they hadn't lost any energy or facility. Their gut-bucket licks, robust exchanges, and alternately soulful, moving, and swaggering solos on a great collection of tunes by everyone from Billy Strayhorn to Buster Smith were entertaining and distinctive. It was one red-hot night at the Caravan of Dreams, and this CD fully captured the night's flavor. —*Ron Wynn*

★ **Ridin' in Rhythm** / Feb. 15, 1933-May 26, 1939 / Disques Swing ✦✦✦✦✦

This two-hour two-CD set (a companion to *Jazz in the Thirties*) has more than its share of classic performances. There are big-band sessions by Duke Ellington, Mills Blue Rhythm Band, Benny Carter, Fletcher Henderson and Horace Henderson, piano solos from Buck Washington and Meade Lux Lewis, plus quite a few selections from tenor saxophonist Coleman Hawkins just prior to his decision to move to Europe (in addition to a 1939 date with Jack Hylton's Orchestra). High points include "Sophisticated Lady," "Six Bells Stampede," "Nagasaki," "The Day You Came Along," "Symphony in Riffs," "Honky Tonk Train Blue," and many others. —*Scott Yanow*

● **Saturday Night Swing Club** / Jun. 12, 1937 / Memphis Archives ✦✦✦✦✦

This double CD brings back an entire radio broadcast, the first anniversary show of the legendary *Saturday Night Swing Club*. The many performances are often classic, the recording quality is excellent (except for three songs by Django Reinhardt and Stephane Grappelli that were performed live in France and are very full of static), and even the announcing by Paul Douglas is lively. Such musicians as Duke Ellington, harpist Casper Reardon, vibraphonist Adrian Rollini, trumpeter Bunny Berigan, the Raymond Scott Quintet, the Casa Loma Orchestra, pianist Claude Thornhill, the Benny Goodman Trio and Quartet, the guitar duo of Carl Kress and Dick McDonough, and an impressive house band are all in excellent form. To use a cliche, it is almost like being there. One can truly feel the excitement of the swing era during this highly recommended release. —*Scott Yanow*

Sax Appeal / 1954-1956 / Vee-Jay ✦✦✦✦✦

The corny cover photo (a female model allegedly playing a saxophone, the hodgepodge nature of the program, and the barely adequate liner notes mask the fact that this CD contains a great deal of interesting music. Most of the 24 performances (nine previously unissued) put the emphasis on its tenor soloists, and the music generally falls somewhere between bop and early rhythm & blues. Included are complete sessions by Julian Dash, bassist David Shipp (whose sidemen include altoist Porter Kilbert and pianist Andrew Hill), keyboardist Tommy Dean (one of his songs features altoist Oliver Nelson), the great tenor Wardell Gray (the four numbers from his final session), honker Big Jay McNeely ("Big Jay's Hop"), Al Smith (featuring the tenor of Red Holloway), Arnett Cobb, and Noble "Thin Man" Watts. Collectors in particular will want to pick up this very interesting set. —*Scott Yanow*

● **Stars of Jazz, Vol. 1** / 1972 / Jazzology ✦✦✦✦✦

On the first of two CDs (and originally released on three LPs), pianist Art Hodes leads a particularly strong all-star group through a variety of familiar Dixieland standards. Presented to the audience in an informative and educational way, this music is often quite exciting, not a surprise when one considers the lineup: cornetist Wild Bill Davison (in peak form), trombonist Jim Beebe, clarinetist Barney Bigard, guitarist Eddie Condon, bassist Rail Wilson, and drummer Hillard Brown. This CD would be worth getting if only to hear Davison's highly expressive (and sometimes sarcastic) playing on "Just a Closer Walk with Thee." Traditional jazz fans should consider the two volumes in this series to be essential. —*Scott Yanow*

● **Stars of Jazz, Vol. 2** / 1972 / Jazzology ✦✦✦✦✦

The second of two CDs taken from a single concert (which was originally released as three LPs) features pianist Art Hodes leading a brilliant Chicago-style jazz group (with cornetist Wild Bill Davison in top form, trombonist Jim Beebe, clarinetist Barney Bigard, guitarist Eddie Condon, bassist Rail Wilson, and drummer Hillard Brown) on a variety of mostly familiar Dixieland and swing standards. Hodes presents the music in an entertaining and educational fashion for the audience, and this concert is rounded out by a version of "Kansas City Blues" which was recorded before the concert, at the group's soundcheck. Both of the volumes in this short series are highly recommended, particularly for Davison's emotional and often-humorous solos. —*Scott Yanow*

Stars of the Apollo / Mar. 31, 1927-Jan. 7, 1965 / Columbia/Legacy ✦✦✦

This double CD is a straight reissue of the original double LP. Its 28 selections mostly focus on singers and bands from the swing era that performed at one time or another at the Apollo; all but eight of the numbers are from the 1927-42 period. High points of this hodgepodge collection include Bessie Smith's "Gimme a Pigfoot," the Mills Brothers' "Sweet Sue," Bill "Bojangles" Robinson's "Doin' the New Lowdown," Slim Gaillard's "Sploghm," Sarah Vaughan's "Ain't Misbehavin'," Screamin' Jay Hawkins'

remarkable "I Put a Spell on You," and Aretha Franklin's "Evil Gal Blues."
—*Scott Yanow*

Straight No Chaser / 1994 / Blue Note ✦✦✦✦✦
Blue Note keeps the "concept" packages coming with this two-disc set presenting catalog tracks sampled by the hip-hop/jazz ensemble Us3. The 15 selections include dialogue snippets from Birdland's irrepressible Pee Wee Marquette and the great Art Blakey, with the other material divided between hard bop and soul-jazz, and Herbie Hancock, Horace Silver, and Donald Byrd getting two tracks each. John Patton, Reuben Wilson, Grant Green, Lou Donaldson, Thelonious Monk, Blakey, and Bobby Hutcherson are other featured artists. The songs are first rate, but Blue Note could have also included the recording years of the tracks as an additional service to listeners, particularly those coming from rap with little knowledge of the label's accomplishments or legacy. —*Ron Wynn*

● **Sunset Swing** / Mar. 1, 1945-Nov. 12, 1945 / Black Lion ✦✦✦✦✦
This CD contains 22 generally exciting performances from jazz's transitional years. While the music technically falls into the swing idiom, one can often hear the influence of bop (and even early rhythm & blues) creeping in. Nine different groups are heard from. Trumpeter Howard McGhee and tenor saxophonist Charlie Ventura head a sextet; the 16-year-old pianist Andre Previn makes his recording debut on a trio version of "California Clipper" and joins trumpeter Buddy Childers, altoist Willie Smith, and the tenor of Vido Musso in a sextet; McGhee, Willie Smith and tenor great Lucky Thompson join forces on another date; guitarist Les Paul is heard in a sextet; with trumpeter Harry Edison; pianist Arnold Ross duets with bassist Red Callender; trumpeter Emmett Berry, trombonist Vic Dickenson and altoist Lem Davis swing in a sextet and drummer Ray Bauduc leads an unidentified group. Recommended. —*Scott Yanow*

Swing Is Here / May 13, 1935-Sep. 6, 1939 / Bluebird ✦✦✦
The music on this CD is often quite exciting, but much of it is issued her in incomplete fashion. There are all four titles from Gene Krupa's Swing Band (a superb pickup group with trumpeter Roy Eldridge, clarinetist Benny Goodman, and Chu Berry on tenor in additon to two Helen Ward vocals) but just three numbers from a session led by arranger Gene Gifford with trumpeter Bunny Berigan, six of the ten titles recorded by Mezz Mezzrow's bands during 1936-37 (featuring trumpeter Frankie Newton, Bud Freeman on tenor, and a rare outing outside of the Jimmy Lunceford orchestra by trumpeter Sy Oliver), two jams by Frankie Newton in 1939, and seven songs from Wingy Manone. These important performances deserve better treatment in a more coherent reissue program. —*Scott Yanow*

● **Swing Time! (1925-1955)** / May 14, 1925-Feb. 15, 1955 / Columbia ✦✦✦✦✦
This three-CD box set does an excellent job of covering the big-band era through 66 recordings (by almost as many orchestras) owned by Columbia. The selections (programmed in chronological order), although emphasizing the 1934-45 era, also include 18 earlier and six later recordings. Although the package has some of the familiar hits (such as Glenn Miller's "In the Mood" and Tommy Dorsey's "Marie"), there are also many lesser-known performances, and such forgotten bands as those led by Eddie Stone, Fred Elizalde, and Jack Jenney are represented along with Benny Goodman, Duke Ellington, and Count Basie. Perfect for beginners, this set should also interest collectors who will probably find several "new" gems that they had been unfamiliar with. The accompanying booklet is also excellent. —*Scott Yanow*

Tenor Giants / Feb. 1, 1964+Jul. 14, 1973 / Enja ✦✦✦✦
This CD actually reissues two former live LPs, one featuring Ben Webster and the other a later session from Gene Ammons. Webster is heard at a Providence, RI, gig playing five standards and one original (his medium-tempo blues "Cookin' for T") less than a year before he moved permanently to Europe. Assisted by a top-notch rhythm section (pianist Junior Mance, bassist Bob Cranshaw, and drummer Mickey Roker), the great tenor is in fine form throughout the set, so the familiar repertoire and merely adequate recording quality should not scare anyone away. Gene Ammons' performance with a trio headed by pianist Horace Parlan and including bassist Red Mitchell and drummer Ed Jones) was performed in Sweden just 13 months before Jug's death, but there is no obvious decline in his playing. Ammons (like Art Pepper) was a more intense and freer improviser after serving a long prison sentence than he had been earlier, while remaining quite recognizable. The music is purely straightahead, unlike some of Ammons' studio albums of the era, with three hard-swingers and a two-song ballad medley (Parlan is showcased on "Polka Dots and Moonbeams"). It is particularly nice to hear Gene Ammons verbally introducing the songs, and his performance overall makes for a fine complement to the otherwise unrelated Webster date. —*Scott Yanow*

Tribute to Black Entertainers / Dec. 1, 1919-Jul. 19, 1982 / Columbia ✦✦✦
This two-CD set is rather odd. Programmed loosely (but not exactly) in alphabetical order, the first 41 selections mostly stick to early jazz of the pre-1950 era, with the emphasis on vocalists ranging from the comedian Bert Williams and Louis Armstrong to Cab Calloway and Sarah Vaughan.

The final nine numbers attempt to sum up the past 40 years in Black pop music (jazz is notably absent so was probably judged not "entertaining") and has performances from the likes of Aretha Franklin, Little Richard, and Marvin Gaye. This sampler (which does contain some formerly rare early recordings) is a bit of a hodgepodge, making jazz appear to be a historical music that ceased to exist 45 years ago. —*Scott Yanow*

A Tribute to Duke / 1977 / Concord Jazz ✦✦✦
For this tribute to Duke Ellington, Rosemary Clooney (making her debut on Concord) and Tony Bennett take two vocals apiece, Woody Herman plays "In a Sentimental Mood," and Bing Crosby guests on "Don't Get Around Much Anymore." Actually the three instrumentals are most significant, for the quintet (which includes pianist Nat Pierce, trumpeter Bill Berry, bassist Monty Budwig, and drummer Jake Hanna) helped introduce the young tenor Scott Hamilton. The CD is a straight reissue of the original LP, a historic if not all that essential release. —*Scott Yanow*

Tribute to Duke Ellington / Jul. 2, 1974 / Black Lion ✦✦✦✦
At the 1974 Montreux Jazz Festival (which occurred shortly after Duke Ellington's death), producer Claude Nobs thought it would be a good idea if each solo pianist would play an Ellington song or two. This Black Lion CD (which contains performances also available as part of each player's complete sets) features Randy Weston (playing a quote-filled "Dedication to Edward Kennedy Ellington"), Sir Roland Hanna, Jay McShann, Earl Hines (whose version of "Solitude" is quite emotional), and even Cecil Taylor (who plays a brief but free ballad "After All"). Recommended. —*Scott Yanow*

Tribute to Miles / 1992 / Qwest ✦✦✦
This Miles Davis tribute set brings back four-fifths of his second classic quintet, with Wallace Roney the logical choice to fill in for the late trumpeter. Roney comes across as a sideman and is not as forceful here as one would have hoped. Wayne Shorter, Herbie Hancock, Ron Carter, and Tony Williams had all grown with time, and this reunion has Hancock and Williams taking on more prominent leadership roles than in the earlier days. With the exception of the drummer's "Elegy," all of the music ("So What," "RJ," "Little One," "Pinocchio," "Eighty One," and "All Blues") was regularly performed by the quintet back in the '60s. In general this reunion is a success even if it contains no new revelations. It is particularly nice to hear Wayne Shorter in this setting again. —*Scott Yanow*

Triumphant Sax! / 1975-1993 / GRP ✦✦✦
GRP begins its new Gold Encore anthology series with a good nine-track collection featuring great swing, bop, and hard-bop performances and decent fusion cuts. Any set that begins with a superb Johnny Hodges track and includes wonderful, robust solos from Coleman Hawkins, John Coltrane, and Gerry Mulligan can be forgiven for the routine squawks of Tom Scott and John Klemmer. Michael Brecker's song is humdrum, but his playing has far more strength and energy than the tune merits. Stanley Turrentine shows no one is better at soulful, bluesy tenor, offering an astonishing rendition of "Ciao, Ciao." This should convince newcomers (for whom these sets are clearly designed) to further investigate the music of these greats. —*Ron Wynn*

The Trumpet Summit Meets the Oscar Peterson Big 4 / Mar. 10, 1980 / OJC ✦✦✦✦✦
To call this CD (a reissue of a Pablo date) an all-star session would be an understatement. Joining pianist Oscar Peterson, guitarist Joe Pass, bassist Ray Brown, and drummer Bobby Durham are three classic trumpeters: Dizzy Gillespie, Clark Terry, and Freddie Hubbard. They clearly inspire each other (Gillespie flew in from the East Coast specifically for this date), and the music ("Daahoud", "Just Friends", the new blues "Chicken Wings," and a torrid version of "The Champ") has plenty of exciting moments. Other performances from the same date can be heard on *The Alternate Blues*, an LP overdue to be reissued on CD. —*Scott Yanow*

An Uptown Christmas / Dec. 14, 1984-Jul. 7, 1988 / Uptown ✦✦✦
Uptown was one of the first independent jazz labels to come out with a multiartist Christmas jazz collection. This easily enjoyable CD has performances by the Claudio Roditi-Don Sickler quintet, Frank Wess, Johnny Coles, Kenny Barron, Charlie Rouse, Richard Wyands, Maria Muldaur (who sings the lusty "Santa Baby"), Walter Davis, Jr., Carl Fontana, Al Cohn, Barry Harris, Jack Sheldon, Sahib Shahib, and Tommy Flanagan. The bop-based music has plenty of wit and solid swing along with more variety than one might expect. Recommended. —*Scott Yanow*

● **V-Disc: The Songs That Went to War** / Aug. 27, 1943-Jul. 1948 / Time-Life ✦✦✦✦✦
During World War II a strike by the Musicians Union kept professional players off records for a long period. To fill the gap, a special "V-Disc" program was instituted to provide new music for military personnel serving overseas. This attractive four-CD box set from Time-Life contains 79 performances by a wide variety of artists from the period. Most of the music is jazz, but there are some numbers from pop performers; such notables as Benny Goodman, Woody Herman, Stan Kenton, Lionel Hampton, Glenn Miller, the Nat King Cole Trio, Muggsy Spanier, Hoagy Carmichael, Ella Fitzgerald, Roy Eldridge, Paul Robeson, Hot Lips Page, Stan Kenton, Mar-

ian Anderson, Jack Teagarden, Louis Armstrong, Bunk Johnson, Les Paul, and even Ethel Merman make strong appearances. There is a lot of valuable music on this well conceived reissue. — *Scott Yanow*

Warner Jams, Vol. 1 / 1995 / Warner Bros. ✦✦✦
On this CD some of the top young jazz players from the Warner Brothers roster (trumpeter Wallace Roney, altoist Kenny Garrett, Joshua Redman on tenor, guitarist Peter Bernstein, organist Larry Goldings, pianist Brad Mehldau, bassist Clarence Seay, and drummer Brian Blade) are featured both individually and collectively. There are five showcases (for the three horns and the two keyboards), three songs in which a different duo of horns gets to extensively trade off, and three looser numbers including an opening medium-up blues ("Blue Grass") that sounds like an outtake from a Jimmy Smith jam session. In general Kenny Garrett and Larry Goldings come across best. Garrett is the most advanced soloist on the date (sometimes hinting at the ideas of the M-Base players), while Goldings constantly pushes the horns in the ensembles and drives the rhythm section. Joshua Redman and Wallace Roney (the latter at his best on "Nature Boy") also have their strong moments. Although nothing all that innovative occurs during the hard bop-oriented performances, the straightahead music from these Young Lions is enjoyable and consistently swinging. — *Scott Yanow*

● **West Coast Hot** / Jan. 3, 1969-Apr. 1, 1969 / Jive/Novus ✦✦✦✦✦
The music on this CD reissue is a bit historic and also stands as proof that there was a healthy (artistically if not commercially) avant-garde jazz scene in Los Angeles in the late '60s. John Carter (here switching between clarinet, tenor, and alto) teams up with trumpeter Bobby Bradford in a pianoless quartet for four numbers, while the masterful pianist/composer Horace Tapscott leads a two-bass quintet on four other songs (including the over-17-minute "The Giant Is Awakened") that also feature the then-unknown altoist Arthur Blythe. The performances still sound explorative and have not really dated at all in the quarter-century since. — *Scott Yanow*

West Coast Jive / Aug. 2, 1945-Feb. 27, 1946 / Delmark ✦✦✦
This Delmark CD features music recorded in Los Angeles during 1945-46 that puts the focus on its colorful vocals yet is generally pretty jazz-oriented. Wynonie Harris shouts out three numbers, Duke Henderson is backed by such musicians as tenors Lucky Thompson and Wild Bill Moore in addition to bassist Charles Mingus, the barely documented Cee Pee Johnson Band is heard on six songs, and there are features for the obscure Al "Stomp" Russell Trio and singer Frank Haywood. None of the music is really all that essential, but these often jivey performances are quite accessible and fun. — *Scott Yanow*

The Women (Classic Female Jazz Artists: 1939-1952) / Nov. 24, 1931-Jun. 4, 1955 / Bluebird ✦✦✦
Many of the Bluebird reissues are a bit disappointing due to their sampler nature, programming a lot of unrelated highlights together instead of coming out with the original complete sessions. This set jumps all over the place, with some rare items by Mary Lou Williams, Beryl Booker, Vivien

Garry, the International Sweethearts of Rhythm, and Hazel Scott preceding generally familiar vocals by Edythe Wright, Albert Hunter, Ethel Waters, Mildred Bailey, Helen Ward, Helen Forrest, and Kay Davis. If this CD had stuck to instrumentals by women, this would have been a very valuable set instead of being merely a pleasing curiosity. It is still worth getting until a more coherent reissue comes along. — *Scott Yanow*

World's Greatest Jazz Concert #1 / Feb. 22, 1947 / Jazzology ✦✦✦✦✦
With a title such as this one, it is impossible for the music to quite live up to the billing. However, the performances (released for the first time on this Jazzology CD) are often quite special. On the first of two volumes (the second set was recorded at a different concert two months later), cornetist Wild Bill Davison, clarinetist Albert Nicholas, and trombonist George Brunies (with the assistance of pianist Joe Sullivan, bassist Pops Foster, and drummer Baby Dodds) form a very potent front line on three songs. Brunies and Davison also have individual features, veteran blues singer Bertha "Chippie" Hill takes a vocal, trumpeter Muggsy Spanier leads a group (with Brunies, pianist Art Hodes, and clarinetist Cecil Scott) on two songs, and trumpeter-vocalist Hot Lips Page heads a hard-charging septet with clarinetist Tony Parenti. With all of those classic players, the music (not too surprisingly) is very enjoyable and spirited. Recommended. — *Scott Yanow*

World's Greatest Jazz Concert #2 / Apr. 26, 1947 / Jazzology ✦✦✦✦✦
The second of two CDs in this series was recorded two months after the earlier Jazzology release. Trumpeter Muggsy Spanier, trombonist George Brunies, and the great soprano saxophonist Sidney Bechet are heard on five spirited numbers, trombonist Jack Teagarden teams up in separate performances with Spanier and trumpeter Johnny Windhurst; Windhurst is heard with pianist Dick Wellstood in a quartet; Bechet has a couple of features; The Two Gospel Keys sing a couple of traditional numbers; and finally Spanier, Windhurst, Brunies and clarinetist Bob Wilber team up for the closing "Dippermouth Blues." Dixieland and New Orleans jazz fans are urged to pick up both of these Jazzology sets. — *Scott Yanow*

☆ **Young Lions** / May 25, 1960 / Vee-Jay ✦✦✦✦✦
The '80s and '90s aren't the first time record companies have generated a publicity blitz about youthful jazz musicians. During the '60s, there was another wave of hype about talented prodigies. *The Young Lions* was an album designed to showcase these developing stars, and it included not only Lee Morgan, Wayne Shorter, and Bobby Timmons, but Frank Strozier on alto sax, Bob Cranshaw on bass, and Louis Hayes alternating drum duties with Albert Heath. Each of these musicians developed their own signature sound, even though some (Morgan) didn't enjoy overly long careers, and others (Cranshaw, Hayes) became better known for their contributions to groups than their prowess as leaders. But their potential is fully displayed throughout this eight-track anthology, which includes three bonus cuts. — *Ron Wynn*

MUSIC RESOURCES

Aside from the music itself, there are many fine resources available that make your music journey more comfortable and fun. There is no room here for a comprehensive review of all the music books, magazines, mail-order firms, and record companies out there, but here are some that we feel provide a real service.

Record Companies

Mosaic Records • It seems that every generation has a few record labels where there is real magic happening. Jazz is no exception. If Blue Note was the standard-bearer of the '60s, then, in our time, it has to be Mosaic Records. Mosaic is not your average record label. Instead of recording jazz artists, they are expert at picking up on jazz gems neglected by other major labels and obtaining a license to publish them in very limited editions. Mosaic offers complete, chronologically ordered recordings (many previously unavailable) by acknowledged jazz masters at the peak of their careers. The sets include thoroughly researched booklets, including discographies and many photos, which, with the recordings, constitute definitive research documents for the featured musician. The quality of these Mosaic packages sets a standard for our times. Scholarship aside, what makes Mosaic founders Charlie Lourie and Michael Cuscuna great is their ability to search out pockets of recorded jazz that have been overlooked or forgotten and reissuing them. A class act. Best of all, Mosaic has found some of the very best jazz recordings ever made, and made them available. Here is some incredible music, and Mosaic sets never seem to get far from my stereo system. These albums can be obtained only through the mail. A detailed catalog is available by writing to 35 Melrose Place, Stamford, CT 06902; or call 203/327-7111. —*Michael Erlewine*

Smithsonian Recordings • There are two different companies that share a legitimate tie to the Smithsonian; Smithsonian Recordings is first. You won't see these recordings in stores (you may get a flyer in the mail if you have used your credit card lately). These are, for the most part, boxed sets (CDs and albums) on different music generes—folk, country, jazz, big band, classical, and others. Many of these sets are well conceived and serve as good introductions to a particular kind of music. —*Michael Erlewine*

Smithsonian/Folkways Recordings • Folkways Recordings, started by Moses Asch and Marian Distler in 1947, introduced baby boomers to real folk music. Folkways was *the* folk/world label back in the '60s. With 2,100-plus albums in their catalog, Folkways is the way many of us first heard the likes of the New Lost City Ramblers, The Country Gentlemen, Woody Guthrie, Cisco Houston, Leadbelly, and others, not to mention a wealth of indigenous world music. But for a while it looked like Folkways (a real national treasure) would be gone forever. But since 1987, every original Folkways album is once again available under a new company called Smithsonian/Folkways. New and priceless recordings from the archives have been added to the catalog. The complete Folkways catalog is available by writing to: Smithsonian/Folkways Recordings, Mail Order, 414 Hungerford Dr., Suite 444, Rockville MD 20850. —*Michael Erlewine*

Time-Life Series • The Time-Life Series is available only by mail order. You will find it advertised everywhere—on TV and in many magazines. Time-Life offers sets of recordings on R&B, country, the music of the '70s, hit parade ('40s and '50s hits), classic rock & roll, the rock & roll era, and others. Each set consists of many separate albums, each one containing the big hits for a particular year. In the case of rock, there are often sec-

ond and third albums for a given year featuring additional minor hits. The bad news is that these CDs are expensive. By the time you pay the shipping and handling, each one costs about $20 a shot, which is just too much. For this reason, I wish I could suggest that you ignore the Time-Life Series, that they were poorly done or there was some other reason not to buy them. But the truth is that these CDs are, for the most part, well conceived and well executed. No other hits collection series is even near as comprehensive. Perhaps some of the early albums in the rock series are a little shabby; still, they are worth having. Typically, there are from 20 to 24 hits per disc, with good liner notes (and complete discographies!) written by well-known music writers. I am not alone in this opinion. After talking with some of the other editors of the *All Music Guide*, the word is: this series is expensive but a real value. The R&B series is especially nice. —*Michael Erlewine*

World Music Resources

Original Music
R.D. 1, P.O. Box 190, Lasher Road
Tivoli, New York 12583
See review in mail order section.

Music of the World
P. O. Box 3667
Chapel Hill, NC 27515-3667
(919) 932-9600
(Free Catalog)

Center for Cuban Studies
124 W. 23rd St.
New York, NY 10011
Not a record store, but they do sell records and videos imported from—as opposed to licensed from—Cuba; the selection is unpredictable but worth checking out.

Qbadisk
P. O. Box 1256
Old Chelsea Station
New York, NY 10011
This address is for mail-ordering Qbadisk albums.

Round World Music
491 Aguerro Street
San Francisco, CA 94110
415/255-8411

Jacob's Judaic Book & Gift Center
13896 Cedar Road
University Heights, OH 44118
216/321-7200
Contact Jay Steingroot. This and the following two listings are resources for recordings of Jewish music.

Musique Internationale
3012 West Jarvis
Chicago, IL 60645
312/743-3012
This is a resource for Jewish cantorial music.

Dor (Israeli)
21 Edgewood Tenafly, NJ 07670
800/762-4944
Contact Dubi Gerber.

Mail Order

For those millions of us unlucky enough to reside in places outside the realm of superstores (in other words, most folks), trying to find even the lastest hyped major label jazz item in a mall store, standard retail outlet or neighborhood mom-and-pop one-stop can be disastrous. Assuming the clerk even knows what you're talking about "Duke who?", you've got a better chance of striking oil in the back yard than you do of finding much jazz. Thus, you're inevitably forced to the option of mail order. Granted, there are many disadvantages to this. For one, unless you're a preferred customer, by the time you find out about sales, most of the prime items are gone. Frequently you send the money in for six titles and two weeks later get four, with either a refund check or an inquiry asking if you want to back order. Plus, nothing's preferable to walking into a store, browsing, winnowing down a pile of potential buys and finally walking out with records (discs/tapes) in hand. Anyway, here are a few places that we've personally dealt with over the years without problems. This means they have reasonable shipping rates, will actually send you what you order, the product arrives in playable shape, and they issue catalogs in a timely manner.

By no means are these the only options available: such magazines as *Goldmine*, *Record Collector* and *Discoveries* are full of ads for stores that deal in jazz mail order; there are also many collectors nationwide who regularly hold auctions and set sales. But, if you have never ventured into the wild world of mail order, here are some good places to start. The following is just a selection of some of the longest-lived and most extensive mail-order outfits specializing in rock recordings (and often, those of rock-related genres). Note that this listing just covers a few of the many useful companies of this sort; listeners should also check the advertisements in collector-oriented magazines, especially *Goldmine*, the leader in that field. Most mail-order operations will send their catalog for a small fee, or for free.

Midnight Records • The world's largest mail-order company specializing in independent and reissued rock CDs and LPs. Astonishing depth of selection, with thousands of imports from all over the world in addition to domestic titles. Especially strong in '50s and '60s rock and independent alternative rock, but also good in vintage soul, blues, some '50s pop. They also have a long list of out-of-print rarities. P.O. Box 390, New York, NY 10113-390; (212)675-2768.

Wayside Music • The most extensive selection of avant garde/experimental/progressive rock music by mail. P.O. Box 8427, Silver Spring, MD 20907-8427.

Metro Music • A similar focus as Midnight, on '60s reissues and new independent rock, lots of imports. Not as deep a selection as Midnight, but always offers some stuff no one else has, plus lots of out-of-print LPs and 45s. P.O. Box 10004, Silver Spring, MD 20904-0004; (301) 622-2473.

Eurock • Archie Patterson, a journalist for more than 20 years, started Eurock Ltd. in 1973 to promote and distribute electronic and progressive music from around the world. He's written about some of today's name artists, before they broke into the mainstream and continues today exploring the far corners of the globe for adventurous new music. Eurock, P.O. Box 13718, Portland, OR 97213; (503) 281-0247.

Cadence Mail Order • Among its many other functions, each month *Cadence* magazine also conducts monthly sales of CDs, books, and records. It carries numerous labels, including many European imports and American independents. The address is Cadence, Cadence Building, Redwood, New York 13679.

Coda Sales • Canada's premier jazz publication also sells records, videos, and books. Contact Coda Publications, P.O. Box 1002, Station O, Toronto, Ontario M4A 2N4, Canada.

Roots and Rhythm • Formerly known as Down Home Music, this operation is now Roots and Rhythm. Otherwise, nothing has changed. It remains among the finest and most diverse mail-order services in the world. It has plenty of domestic and foreign label/import jazz, though some of the import prices are a bit to the high side. It also publishes periodic newsletters and has catalogs for many categories. Roots and Rhythm, 10341 San Pablo Avenue, El Cerrito, California 94530.

Double-Time Jazz • Double-Time can compete with any mail-order service for volume in old and new titles. It handles domestic independent and major-label products, as well as reissues, cutouts, and imports, while also carrying albums and videos in addition to CDs. Double-Time, P.O. Box 1244, New Albany, Indiana 47151-1244.

Original Music • Original Music is founded and still operated by John Storm Roberts. If there is anyone who knows more about "world" music and its permutations, combinations, hybrids, and multiple genres, I'd sure like to know who it is. Original Music, R.D. 1, P.O. Box 190, Lasher Road, Tivoli, New York 12583. *—Ron Wynn*

Magazines and Newsletters

Goldmine Magazine • Published since 1974, *Goldmine* is just that — a goldmine of discographical information, extended articles, and great album reviews. Nowhere else will you find in-depth articles on individual artists and groups of this length and breadth. And almost every article is accompanied by a complete discography. *Goldmine* is geared to the record collector. In fact, a good part of each issue is filled with the ads of collectors. Reading through these is an experience in itself. Those of us who don't collect may have little idea of the amount of activity in out-of-print and hard-to-find albums. Thanks to these folks, it is possible to find almost any hard-to-find album. *Goldmine* has some of the best writers in the business, and almost every major freelance writer has written for them at one time or another. It is a tabloid-size magazine of about 170 pages published bi-weekly! There is a lot of information here. If you have never browsed through a copy, you have an experience in store for you. It's an eye-opener. Write to them and mention the *All Music Guide* and you will receive a free sample issue. 700 E. State St., Iola, WI 54990; (715)445-2214 *—Michael Erlewine*

Alternative Press • The writing and production quality aren't up to the level of *Option*, but this monthly offers comprehensive coverage of the alternative rock scene, focusing almost wholly on the bands to be found on college radio stations. Given over almost entirely to features, interviews, and reviews, it's a barometer of sorts as to what's getting played and listened to by the alternative rock crowd. Not as slick or imaginative as some of the competition, but there's a lot of info here. It's stuck to a regular publishing schedule for a long time (a rare feat in the alternative rock world), and it's steadily improved over the years. (P.O. Box 17136, N. Hollywood, CA 91615-9817) *—Richie Unterberger*

Country Music • Country may be the most popular music in the land bar rock, but the quality of journalistic coverage and criticism given to the music is surprisingly poor. *Country Music* is, by a wide margin, the best national publication devoted to the style. In fact, it is the only country magazine worth recommending, and the only one to offer intelligent, knowledgeable criticism. Adhering mostly to the standard feature/ interview/ review format, it covers the entire spectrum of country: the Nashville superstars, of course, get a bigger chunk than anyone else, but there's also a goodly amount of space for more rootsy and acoustic-based performers, independent label releases, vintage reissues, and hillbilly. Includes regular contributions from nationally renowned writers like Rich Kienzle and John Morthland. (329 Riverside Ave., Westport, CT 06880) *—Richie Unterberger*

Dirty Linen • The leading American magazine devoted to "folk, electric folk, traditional and world music," by a long shot. This bi-monthly has plenty of features, oodles of CD, tape, video, concert, and book reviews, roundups of neglected genres and old recordings, listings of new releases, and lots of miscellaneous news. Also offers tour information via several online services. Not as glossy, well-written, or wide-ranging as *Folk Roots*, but almost as informative, complementing that British magazine's coverage well. (P.O. Box 66600, Baltimore, MD 21239-6600) *—Richie Unterberger*

ICE • Steeply priced ($3.95 for 20-page issues), but this newsletter is extremely useful for the hard-bitten record collector, as well as for those involved in the music industry at almost any level. Includes the most comprehensive schedule of upcoming releases, both new and reissues; lots of news about in-the-works projects and reissue packages; items about hard-to-find imports; a column devoted to complaints about inadequate CD remastering, track selection, or packaging, featuring responses from the labels themselves; and listings (with brief comments) of CD bootlegs. Most interesting are the feature stories about major reissues, box sets, or new releases, which often highlight in-depth, inside scoops from the label, compilers, or artists themselves. Mostly rock-oriented, with some coverage of jazz, country, blues, and other genres. (P.O. Box 3043, Santa Monica, CA 90408). *—Richie Unterberger*

Living Blues • Absolutely the best blues publication available, and in fact one of the best specialized music magazines of any kind. Features huge, definitive interviews with major and minor blues performers, a big review section that covers almost every blues release available (lots of imports included), news, obituaries, and miscellaneous other features. It's upgraded its production values recently without sacrificing the depth and integrity of the content. Well-written and accessible to the general reader, not just a scholarly publication for blues fanatics. (Center for the Study of Southern Culture, The University of Mississippi, University, MS 38677-9836) *—Richie Unterberger*

Musician • Perhaps the most intelligent and well-written mainstream U.S. music publication, with the emphasis on long (but not exhausting) features and interviews. Leans a bit toward the classic rock side of the coin, or new performers in the classic rock mold, but there's reasonable coverage of alternative rock, as well as some jazz and other music (hip-hop and Black pop gets a pretty thin slice). Also a fair amount of technology info, including equipment reviews and details of specific musicians' instruments, along with comments about them from the artists themselves. —*Richie Unterberger*

New Musical Express • This weekly tabloid remains the most widely read and circulated British music publication. Resolutely trendy, *NME* is so eager to find and hype The Next Big Thing that there's a certain breathless tone to the coverage, with fickle, mercurial critical evaluations that can run from gushing praise to merciless putdowns within a matter of weeks. Americans may find the prose difficult to follow at times, occasionally approaching impenetrability. They may also be surprised at the intense importance attached to musicians' opinions on all sorts of matters not strictly musical, including politics, sex, personal relationships, and other bands. That said, it's the best source for keeping up with the volatile U.K. music scene, including scads of reviews, and many profiles of upcoming bands (or even stars) months and years before they become known, or release records, on U.S. shores. (P.O. Box 272, Oakfield House, Perrymount Rd, Haywards Heath, West Sussex RH16 3ZA, England) —*Richie Unterberger*

Option • The production values have gotten steadily slicker in the decade since this bi-monthly started, and the coverage of widely known, major label acts has expanded, with a corresponding (but slighter) decrease in the articles about total unknowns. Still, it's the leading international publication devoted to coverage of alternative and indie music of all kinds, and there's still plenty of space for way-underground acts in both the features and reviews sections. Reviews about 200 releases, mostly independent, in every issue, and contains columns devoted to alternative music industry trends and developments, other media, and miscellaneous news. —*Richie Unterberger*

Q • This glossy British monthly is probably the best general interest rock and pop music publication. The review section of each issue covers literally hundreds of new releases, including a lot of British imports and reissues. In-depth features on major performers covering the entire rock and pop spectrum, departments for up-and-coming bands and gossip, book and movie reviews, cool "where are they now?" reports, and eyewitness recollections of major moments in rock history. The writing is much more straightforward and accessible to Yankee readers than the more whimsical and personality-oriented British rock weeklies. Expensive, but worth it, and widely distributed in the U.S. (Tower Publishing Services Ltd., Tower House, Lathkill St., Sovereign Park, Market Harborough LE16 9EF, U.K.) —*Richie Unterberger*

Rolling Stone • Still the most widely circulated music-oriented publication in the United States. At this point, it's pretty widely disdained by the alternative community for moving squarely into the mainstream of the marketplace. As one staff member admitted in a book about the magazine, it has become a tracker of American taste, rather than a pacesetter of American taste. There are still plenty of well-written features about both established and emerging performers, and a small review section with in-depth evaluations of noteworthy new releases. It has given more space to alternative rock of late, though that may be as much of a reflection of that style's radically increased commercial presence as a conscious decision. —*Richie Unterberger*

The Source • "The magazine of hip-hop music, culture & politics" has experienced some well-circulated internal conflicts of late, but remains the most in-depth rap magazine. The writing is erratic, and those who are not immersed in this aspect of African-American culture will find the lingo that peppers much of the writing occasionally difficult to understand impenetrable at times. But it gets the interviews with a lot of performers who are hard to read about elsewhere, not shying away from controversial gangsta rappers, and includes departments for record reviews, radio, film/TV, and gossip. (P.O. Box 586, Mt. Morris, IL 61054) —*Richie Unterberger*

Spin • Launched as the principal competitor to *Rolling Stone* in the mid-'80s, *Spin* is clearly here to stay, after some wobbly crises in it's early days. Covers alternative rock much more aggressively than its rival, ranging from the very popular to the absolutely unknown, and everything in between, though pieces on historical figures and classic rock are seldom presented. Considering its high profile as the second largest music publication in the United States, the writing and focus remain surprisingly erratic. Much more personality-oriented (both in terms of the acts it covers and the writers themselves) than the other big rock magazine in New York, which leads to both liveliness and self-indulgence. Also includes a fair amount of coverage of politics and popular culture. —*Richie Unterberger*

Urb • Devoted mostly to dance music, usually of Black origin, but not always. Covers hip-hop, acid house, acid jazz, club music, some soul, reggae, and rock. Consisting mostly of reviews, features, and interviews, it's distinguished from the somewhat overlapping coverage of *The Source* and *Rap Pages* by a wider scope, more readable format, higher produc-

tion values, and better writing. (1680 N. Vine, Suite 1012, Los Angeles., CA 90028) —*Richie Unterberger*

Vibe • Certainly the slickest and biggest magazine devoted to African-American music, this monthly covers Black pop of all sorts — urban contemporary, soul, hip-hop, dance, and more. Usually fairly mainstream in its coverage, but there are plenty of deviations into emerging and more obscure acts, as well as some White rock releases that have heavy debts to R&B, funk, and hip-hop. Also includes coverage of African-American popular culture. —*Richie Unterberger*

Mojo • Fat, glossy general interest British monthly rock magazine with much more of a historical perspective than most. Coverage is about equally divided between current acts and artists from the past, with a bit (not much) of a bias toward "classic rock" performers. The in-depth interviews, historical surveys, and eyewitness recollections of all sorts of interesting star and cult rock icons of the past are often fascinating, and usually considerably more well-written and less oriented toward collector details than those that appear in *Goldmine*. Also includes record and book reviews, news bits, and other interesting columns. (Tower House, Sovereign Park, Lathkill St., Market Harborough, Leics. LE 16 9EF, U.K.) —*Richie Unterberger*

Latin Beat • No publication covers Afro-Latin music in such a comprehensive manner. From salsa to Latin jazz and all things in between, *Latin Beat* is the best bet. It is even a great inducement to polish up on your high school Spanish, as it is a true bilingual magazine. It comes out 10 times a year. Subscriptions are currently $25 for 10 issues. International orders need an additional $10 for postage. The address: *Latin Beat*, 15900 Crenshaw Blvd., Suite 1-223, Gardena, California 90249.

CCM • *CCM* is the premiere publication in contemporary Christian music, one of the fastest growing genres in the music business today. The magazine covers a wide range of music, including pop, rock, alternative, R&B, hip-hop, and country; all with a decidedly Christian point of view. Send $19.95 for 12 monthly issues to *CCM*, P.O. Box 55996, Boulder, CO 80321-5996.

Rejoice! The Gospel Music Magazine • With very few publications devoted to gospel music, *Rejoice!* is a welcome find. Lots of articles, pictures, and more on your favorite gospel groups, Black and White. It is published bi-monthly by the Center for the Study of Southern Culture, The University of Mississippi, University, MS 38677. Write to the editors of *Rejoice!*, c/o The University of Mississippi, University, MS 38677. —*Michael Erlewine*

The Beat • *The Beat* is a bimonthly publication of reggae, African, Caribbean, and world music, providing information, news, interviews, discographies, reviews, and cultural features to an international market of music fans. It features the work of top writers, artists, and photographers who chronicle this rapidly expanding area of music and the increasing popularity of its associated lifestyle. Today, *The Beat* is the most widely circulated magazine in the country dedicated exclusively to world music. While feature articles still emphasize Jamaican and African artists, recent issues have been devoted to Brazilian pop and music of the Indian subcontinent. But the magazine's real crackle lies with its host of opinionated reviewers, who leave no corner of the world unexplored in their quest for the latest trends or the most obscure sounds. While not as slick as *Spin*, *Rolling Stone*, or *Option*, *The Beat's* newsprint format (black and white) gives it an immediacy these other publications lack, highlighting it as an excellent source of news today on the inevitable influences on mainstream pop in years to come. *The Beat* can be reached at P.O. Box 65856, Los Angeles, CA 90065. —*Bob Tarte*

Cadence • *Cadence* is a monthly founded in 1976 that is edited and published by Bob Rusch. No other magazine in the world reviews as many jazz recordings and their coverage ranges from bop and the avant-garde to Dixieland, blues, reissues, imports and more commercial jazz-related genres. Its subtitle is "The Review of Jazz & Blues Creative Improvised Music" and *Cadence* lives up to the billing. No matter what label a recording comes out on, it receives equal consideration based purely on the quality of the music. In each issue, in addition to hundreds of reviews of CDs, books and videos, *Cadence* generally has two or three oral history interviews (some of them quite lengthy) with jazz and blues artists, both obscure and famous. The middle third of the approximately 112 pages has thousands of recordings for sale through *Cadence* at reasonable prices and fortunately there is no correlation between what is offered and whether a review is favorable or not. In fact *Cadence* is proud of its noncommercial status and even releases put out by Cadence Records have received negative reviews now and then. This magazine is essential for the true jazz record collector who wants to be informed as to what is available and its value from the jazz standpoint. Unfortunately *Cadence* is found on few newsstands so a subscription ($30 per year in the US, $35 outside) is essential. Its address is Cadence, Cadence Building, Redwood, NY 13679. —*Scott Yanow*

Coda • A consistent force in the jazz scene since 1958, *Coda* (which is co-run by John Norris and Bill Smith) has been Canada's top jazz magazine for decades. A bi-monthly, *Coda* has an interesting (if sometimes out-of-date) news section, extensive coverage of the Canadian scene, many CD reviews (which are packaged together as articles) and interviews. Its coverage ranges from veteran bop and swing stars to the avant-garde with little notice taken of fusion or so-called contemporary jazz. Along with *Cadence*, *Coda* is the least commercial of all the jazz magazines and consistently makes for stimulating reading. Subscriptions are available for $24 annually in the U.S., $25.68 in Canada and $30 elsewhere. Its address is Coda Publications, Box 1002, Station 0, Toronto, Ontario M4A 2N4 CANADA. *—Scott Yanow*

Down Beat • Founded in 1934, *Down Beat* remains the most famous jazz magazine in the world. Its prime years were from about the mid-'40s up until the late '60s (some of its older articles and controversies are fascinating to read now) when its only competitor (at least up until 1960) was *Metronome*. However when it opened the door to covering rock in 1967, *Down Beat* alienated some of its audience who did not feel that the Beatles and the Rolling Stones should be covered in a jazz magazine. Even today its motto, "Jazz, Blues & Beyond" keeps it from being taken completely seriously in the jazz community. However *Down Beat*'s articles and interviews are consistently excellent and its CD reviews are generally quite informative if occasionally erratic. There are also transcriptions and articles geared toward student musicians. *Down Beat* does not cover the jazz world with as much depth as *Jazz Times* (and virtually ignores the West Coast) but the two-thirds of each issue that deals with jazz is well worth reading. Subscription rates are $29 for one year, $40.50 for foreign subscribers. Its mailing address is Down Beat, P.O. Box 906, Elmhurst, IL 60126-0906. *—Scott Yanow*

Jazz Now • Founded in 1991 by its editor/publisher Haybert Houston, *Jazz Now* (originally called *California Jazz Now*) is based in the Bay Area and seems to be attempting to fill the gap caused by the demise of *Jazz Forum*. It calls itself "The Jazz World Magazine" and *Jazz Now* has correspondents and regular columns from Germany, the United Kingdom, Poland and New York but it remains primarily a West Coast publication. Published 11 times a year (every month but January), this interesting magazine features news and reviews from a variety of cities, emphasizes noncommercial jazz and generally has a few major interviews along with some CD and book reviews. An unusual innovation is a series of articles focusing on jazz fans who frequent Bay Area clubs. This magazine's progress during the next few years will be worth watching. Subscriptions are $21.65 in California and $20 for the rest of the U.S. Their offices are located at the Jazz Now Building, 3733 California Street, Oakland, CA 94619-1413. *—Scott Yanow*

The Jazz Report • Second to *Coda* among Canadian jazz magazines, the *Jazz Report* is a promising quarterly that was founded in 1988 by publisher Bill King and editor Greg Sutherland. Boasting slick paper and interesting photos, the *Jazz Report* generally has around three interviews per issue along with some CD and book reviews and news. Subscription rates are $18 in the U.S. and overseas and $15 in Canada. Its address is The Jazz Report, 14 London St, Toronto, Ontario M6G 1M9 CANADA. *—Scott Yanow*

Jazz Times • Founded in 1970 by Ira Sabin as *Radio Free Jazz* and published ten times a year (every month but January and August), *Jazz Times* has become what is arguably the number one jazz magazine in the world. Certainly when it comes to its news section and keeping on top of the latest developments, *Jazz Times* has surpassed *Down Beat* and stayed ahead of *Jazziz*, retaining its credibility and becoming an influential force. Most issues have around 100 CD reviews (second to *Cadence*), six or seven major articles, up to ten shorter interviews and a few live reviews. *Jazz Times*'s weaknesses include a general neglect of the West Coast, an occasional tendency to copy *Down Beat* and an inconsistent coverage of fusion and so-called "contemporary" jazz, perhaps in reaction to *Jazziz*. All jazz followers can consider *Jazz Times* and *Cadence* to be the two essential monthly purchases. Yearly subscription rates are $21.95 in the U.S., $35.95 in Canada and $59.95 overseas. Its address is Jazz Times, 7961 Eastern Avenue, Suite 303, Silver Spring, MD 20910-4898. *—Scott Yanow*

Jazziz • The most improved jazz magazine of the past two years, *Jazziz* still confuses many readers. Its coverage of the jazz scene through probing interviews, columns and individual CD reviews is quite impressive but it has a tendency to praise nearly everything. Because its publishers Michael and Lori Fagien (both of whom founded *Jazziz* in 1983) have always enjoyed pop music and crossover, the monthly stretches in coverage from Henry Threadgill to Paul Simon, featuring profiles on world music, and pop and ethnic music pacesetters in addition to jazz artists (most of whom have recent releases out). A very attractive-looking magazine with quite a few unusual and unique articles, *Jazziz* is both innovative and a bit inconsistent, a very useful tool in opening up one's musical horizons. *Jazziz*'s subscriptions are $7.77 per issue (which includes a spe-

cial CD compilation each month) or $3.98 on the newsstand. Its mailing address is 3620 N.W. 43rd Street, Gainesville, FL 32606. *—Scott Yanow*

The Mississippi Rag • Founded in 1973 by editor/publisher Leslie Johnson, the *Mississippi Rag* (which is actually located in Minnesota) has been the top classic jazz monthly ever since. Full of interesting interviews, CD reviews and news dealing with Dixieland, New Orleans jazz and swing, this newspaper is quite informative, even handed and both historical and up-to-date. Fans of early jazz will find lots of valuable information in this important paper. Subscriptions are $18 in the U.S., $20 elsewhere, and its mailing address is The Mississippi Rag, P.O. Box 19068, Minneapolis, MN 55419. *—Scott Yanow*

The West Coast Rag • Since its formation in 1989, the *West Coast Rag* has attracted a growing audience with its lively mixture of classic jazz news, festival listings, nostalgic articles, a growing CD review section and a bit of corn. Founded by Woody Laughnan (who retired in 1995) and now run by Don Jones, the Dixieland-oriented *West Coast Rag* is generally less serious than the *Mississippi Rag* but informative when it comes to listing upcoming festivals and is becoming a bit more national in scope. It accurately describes itself as "An independent, write-it-yourself newspaper concerned with vintage jazz, ragtime and other early American music forms as well as some Americana and period humor." It is published 11 times a year (no January issue), subscriptions are $18 in the U.S. ($20 in Canada and $25 elsewhere) and its mailing address is West Coast Rag, P.O. Box 4127, Fresno, CA. *—Scott Yanow*

Blues Access • The brainchild of radio show host Cary Wolfson (who won a W.C. Handy Award in 1987 and 1991), Blues Access Magazine was inspired by the Whole Earth Catalog's byline "Access to Tools"—thus, access to blues. It was first published in February of 1990 at 16 pages (all newsprint), but today is almost 100 pages with four-color glossy covers. What you find between these covers is a lot of eye and mind candy for the blues lover. It contains everything from full-length feature articles to some twenty columns—filled with info (departments). Lots of pictures too. Issues include many well-written reviews, hundreds of new releases (with descriptions), guitar patterns, societies, resources—the works. There is enough information in one issue to seriously tie up your spare time for days. And the ads are just as interesting—major labels, releases, tours, and festivals. When you are done looking at the ads alone, you have a pretty fair idea of what's happening out there in blues world. If you have never seen a copy, go out and get one. You'll not regret it. You can reach them at (303) 443-7245 or write to Blues Access, 1455 Chestnut Place, Boulder, CO 80304-3153. Internet fans can reach them at their web address of http://www.he.net/~blues *—Michael Erlewine*

Blue Suede News • This doesn't deal with the blues exclusively or primarily, concentrating on roots musics of various sorts (blues, R&B, rockabilly, rock & roll, country) past and present (more past than present). The writing and production standards are also closer to fanzine territory than the blues glossies, although they've come a long way over the years. Blues specialists may find it worth picking up for the occasional blues feature and its huge review section, which always covers lots of contemporary blues albums and reissues. (Box 25, Duvall, WA 98019-0025)—*Richie Unterberger*

Blues & Rhythm • Britain's top blues periodical is less comprehensive than its U.S. counterparts, and more devoted to retrospectives and reissue reviews than the contemporary scene. It's a high-quality operation, though, with lively and informed writing, combining interviews/features with an extensive review section. Doesn't limit itself to blues exclusively, also covering some R&B and a little bit of soul. There are also columns for news, live reports, obits, and in-depth examinations of rare recordings. (Byron Foulger, 1 Cliffe Lane, Thornton, Bradford BD13 3DX, UK)—*Richie Unterberger*

Blues Review • Bimonthly glossy is a bit slicker in the production department than the two other major blues mags (*Living Blues* and *Blues Access*). There's a similar concentration of features and new release/reissue reviews, as well as some special-interest columns for live reviews, product surveys, "Cyberblues" (blues on the Internet), and guitar transcriptions. The coverage is perhaps more inclusive of White acts than its peers, and less devoted to historical pieces. That shouldn't be taken as implied criticism—there's room for all three major U.S. blues magazines, which basically cover much of the same thematic ground without duplicating each other too often. (916 Douglas Dr., #101, Endwell, NY 13760)—*Richie Unterberger*

Living Blues • With the establishment of *Blues Access* and *Blues Revue* as class productions in the 1990s, *Living Blues* is no longer as dominant in its field as it once was. But the bimonthly probably remains the best blues publication available, and in fact one of the best specialized music magazines of any kind. Features huge (if occasionally rambling) interviews with major and minor blues performers, a big review section that covers a high percentage of available blues releases and reissues (lots of imports included), news, obituaries, and miscellaneous other features.

It's upgraded its production values recently without sacrificing the depth and integrity of the content. Well-written and accessible to the general reader, not just a scholarly publication for blues fanatics. (Hill Hall, Room 301, University, MS 38677-9836) —*Richie Unterberger*

Books on Music

The following are a few of the books that you will find on the shelves of record collectors and that were helpful in checking information listed in the *All Music Guide*.

Record Research • Of particular interest to music lovers is the series of books by Joel Whitburn and his company, Record Research. These books are standard items on the shelves of most music collectors and DJs. Originally basing these books on the various chart and sales data (such as #1 hits) coming out of *Billboard* magazine (the industry newsletter of the record business), Whitburn has (in recent years) continued to add more and more valuable information. A few of these books may turn up in your local bookstore, but many are known only to DJs and record collectors. These books include (where possible) the complete Billboard chart statistics: the date an album entered the charts, its peak, and the number of weeks on the charts. Most also have the RIAA Platinum/Gold or million-seller album status. Great reference works. Record Research Inc. can be contacted by writing to P. O. Box 200, Menomonee Falls, WI 53052-0200; or call 414/251-5408. —*Michael Erlewine*

Christgau's Record Guide: Rock Albums of the '70s *by Robert Christgau* (Da Capo Press, 1990) As the longtime rock critic for the *Village Voice*, Christgau is one of the most famous American rock journalists. In a monthly column, he offers paragraph-long reviews of recent significant releases, assigning each of them a grade, from A to E. This is a book-length compilation, almost 500 pages worth, of such reviews from the '70s, refurbished a bit from their original publication. Very few people feel neutral about Christgau; the blunt viciousness of some of his putdowns is bound to make all of his readers angry at some point or another, and the academic obtuseness of some of his evaluations can be infuriating. As a reference book, though, this is pretty valuable, covering just about every release of major significance from the decade, and quite a few of minor significance. You will often disagree with him, but he almost always knows what he's talking about, and most of the pithy reviews convey the essential characteristics of the disc, even if you find his "grade" incorrect. Covers all kinds of rock and soul, and a fair number of reggae, jazz, and other sundry non-rock releases as well. —*Richie Unterberger*

Christgau's Record Guide: The '80s *by Robert Christgau* (Pantheon, 1990) All of the comments for his '70s volume apply here, though it seems as though there's a higher percentage of frustratingly obtuse reviews. Again, covers all kinds of aboveground and underground rock and soul, as well as plenty of world music, reggae, country, and other kinds of non-rock. The most significant gap is the absence of quite a few indie alternative rock records; as Christgau himself notes in his opening essays, the '80s were categorized by fragmentation and increasing diversity, and he drew the line at absorbing and reviewing a lot of records he might have found time for in previous years. Includes extensive introductory remarks about '80s rock. —*Richie Unterberger*

Country on Compact Disc *by the Country Music Foundation, edited by Paul Kingsbury* (1993, Grove Press) There's a major shortage of good critical reference works on country records – country of all kinds, encompassing traditional sounds, bluegrass, and Nashville. This is by far the best, strongly resembling the *Rolling Stone Album Guide* in format, with its one-to-five star rating system and combination career/discography overviews. The writing's very good – a rarity in country journalism – and very catholic in taste, viewing Jimmie Rodgers and Garth Brooks as part of the same spectrum, in the manner that rock critics can view Elvis Presley and Madonna as part of the same phenomenon. Some might find their assessments of the current Nashville crop too generous, but in treating the so-called "Hats" with seriousness, they are according them respectful evaluations that are merited by the fact that much of mainstream America listens to such music more than anything else. The chief flaw is the limited scope of the volume – as the title implies, only albums which have been issued on compact disc are reviewed, which makes the guide extremely strong on records of the late '80s and early '90s, but omits quite a few vintage albums that hadn't come out on CD by 1993. —*Richie Unterberger*

The Penguin Guide To Jazz On CD, LP & Cassette *by Richard Cook & Brian Morton* (1994, Penguin) One of the most impressive musical reference books of any sort, this has 1,400 pages of informed, detailed criticism of several thousands of jazz albums of every stripe. The authors really know their stuff, and rate each record on a scale from one to four stars. Some minor reservations: the listings, as mammoth as they are, include only albums that are in print, excluding quite a few noteworthy,

even classic, works; the writing can be a bit obtuse; and the entries usually plunge right into reviews of specific albums, without supplying thumbnail biographical data or a summary/perspective of the artists' significance and their overall contribution to jazz. It's still an essential reference work, one which no jazz fan should be without. —*Richie Unterberger*

Rolling Stone Album Guide *edited by Anthony DeCurtis & James Henke with Holly George-Warren* (Straight Arrow, 1992). There's a lot to criticize about this 800+ page reference work, if you're so inclined. Many worthwhile performers are not listed, particularly alternative and independent rock artists; the reviewers are sometimes brief to a fault; they are often churlish, even brutally nasty, in their assessment of some acts that do not measure up to current standards of hipness. The fact remains, though, that this is the best overall guide to rock recordings available. The writing is informed and passionate, if occasionally smug; virtually all artists of truly major significance are included; the discographies are pretty thorough, with a handy (if unavoidably inconsistent) rating system ranging from one to five stars. Incidentally, this is the third edition of the book, completely revised from the original 1979 volume, which was edited by Dave Marsh. That red-covered edition, called *The Rolling Stone Record Guide*, is well worth picking up if you find it used; the reviews are entirely different, and the entries cover quite a few artists and out-of-print albums that didn't make it into the current revision. The second edition (identifiable by its blue cover), from the mid-1980s, is dispensable. —*Richie Unterberger*

The Rolling Stone Illustrated History Of Rock & Roll *by Anthony DeCurtis & James Henke with Holly George-Warren* (Straight Arrow, 1992). Still the best general history of rock music, comprising about 100 succinct essays on rock's most important performers and most important genres. Many of the best rock journalists contribute to this volume, including Greil Marcus, Dave Marsh, Peter Guralnick, Robert Palmer, Robert Christgau, Lester Bangs, and Greg Shaw. It is packed with both critical insight and historical detail, with excellent discographies and many wonderful photos. Only two flaws to consider: unavoidably, a lot of interesting performers were omitted (you'd need several volumes of this size to satisfactorily cover every worthwhile rock musician). More seriously, the coverage is heavily weighted towards, and much stronger on, pre-1980 rock; it really seems to run out of steam, in both breadth and quality, when it approaches the modern era. Hold on to the original mid-'70s edition as well, if you still have it; many photos were reproduced in larger formats in that volume, and some essays that appeared in the initial version have been excised or revised for no good reason. —*Richie Unterberger*

The Rough Guide To World Music (1994, Rough Guides) Easily the best reference book currently available for world music, which in the editors' terms covers everything except western classical music and Anglo-American rock, soul, rap, jazz, and country. That leaves 700 pages covering traditional and popular sounds from all continents, from Celtic folk to Indonesian pop to soukous and zouk to reggae and gamelan to flamenco and Indian film music. The chapters are divided into lengthy scene overviews, with sidebars covering musical terms, notable festivals, and portraits of/interviews with important performers like Youssou N'Dour, Baaba Maal, Ruben Blades, Caetano Veloso, and many others. The variety of focus, skilled, passionate writing, and plenty of photos make this a much more enjoyable experience than the typical reference work. It's not a discography or compendium of record reviews, if that's what you're looking for, although there are numerous brief capsule descriptions of the most essential recordings of each region/country/genre. —*Richie Unterberger*

The Trouser Press Record Guide *edited by Ira A. Robbins* (Collier, 1991). A necessary supplement to the more mainstream *Rolling Stone* guides, this 750-page volume focuses almost entirely on post-1975 punk, new wave, and alternative rock (a little rap, reggae, and other odds and ends slip in). Reviewing about 2,500 artists and almost 10,000 records, it covers a great many indies and imports. The writing could be better; the assessments are sometimes lacking in precise descriptive detail, and the evaluations are on the whole too nondescript and generous. Nonetheless, it's easily the best (and one of the few) reference works of its kind. It has gone through four editions, and unless the fifth is on the way soon, the latest one, published in 1991, has started to date substantially. —*Richie Unterberger*

Blues Who's Who • Sheldon, 1987, 775 pages, Da Capo Press. No blues enthusiast should be without this. It contains in-depth career highlights for known blues singers, plus much useful data. —*Michael Erlewine*

Both Sides Now • Interested in oldies on CD? Compilations of your favorite artist? Collections of various artists? Hard to wade through a mass of reissues to find the performances you listened to 20 years ago? Here is a book that lists 3,000 CDs, including track listings for almost

2,000 of these; stereo information on some 1,500; ratings on 1,000; also the SPARS code, playing time, and year the CD was released (when available). Of special interest is the section on artist compilations and collections. This alone makes *Both Sides Now* invaluable and virtually unique in pop-music literature. The CDs are listed both by label and title and indexed by artist. Its author is a stickler for indicating which cuts are mono and which are stereo (just what we buyers need to know). This is a great find! (A *Both Sides Now* newsletter is available on a subscription basis by writing to Both Sides Now Stereo Newsletter, Box 384, Fairfax Station, VA 22039.) *—Michael Erlewine*

Rock Record 4 *by Terry Hounsome,* 1991, Record Research Publications. Indispensible reference work containing not only a huge number of albums but sidemen and instruments for most of these as well. *—Michael Erlewine*

Rock Movers and Shakers *by Dafydd Rees and Luke Crampton,* 1991, 585 pages, Billboard Books, classic rock reference work. Contains details not available elsewhere. *—Michael Erlewine*

Collectible Record Albums 1949-1989 *by Neal Umphred,* Krause Publications. What makes Umphred's books (he has one on 45s and one on jazz albums) useful is that they privide prices for each album listed. A useful book even for non-collectors because it provides a thorough list of albums for each artist. *—Michael Erlewine*

The New Grove Dictionary of Jazz *by Barry Kernfeld,* 1988, 1360 pages, Macmillan Press Limited. If you can afford it (some $300), this

huge two-volume set deserves to be on your bookshelf. It is the best single work on jazz that we have seen. *—Michael Erlewine*

Penguin Encyclopedia of Popular Music *by Donald Clarke,* 1990, 1378 pages, Penguin Books. A fine reference work providing biographical details plus a list of major albums and their release dates. Worth owning. *—Michael Erlewine*

All Music Guide to Rock *edited by Michael Erlewine, Vladimir Bogdanov, Chris Woodstra, Stephen Thomas Erlewine, Richie Unterberger, and William Ruhlmann* (1995, Miller Freeman) If you are looking for more in-depth coverage of rock than is possible in the present book, check out the AMG rock guide. For 15,500 CDs, albums and tapes by 2,500 artists—everything from doo-wop to hip-hop—you get concise reviews, expert ratings and detailed career profiles, plus historical music maps and dozens of essays on rock styles and influences.

All Music Guide to The Blues *edited by Michael Erlewine, Chris Woodstra, Vladimir Bogdanov, and Cub Koda* (1996, Miller Freeman) Our new blues guide provides far more bios and reviews than in the general *All Music Guide*—more than 2,600 top recordings, plus profiles of over 500 key artists.

All Music Guide to Jazz *edited by Michael Erlewine, Chris Woodstra, Vladimir Bogdanov, and Scott Yanow* (Second Edition, 1996, Miller Freeman) This updated edition of our jazz guide reviews the best jazz CDs and albums. Noted jazz critics profile the lives and work of 1,400 key artists, and review and rate each one's best recordings—more than 13,000 in all.

INDEX

A

Evenson, Dean **1058**
Evenson, Dudley 1058
Everett, Betty 64, **134**, 374, 569
Everett, Charles 726
Everlast 456
Everly Brothers, The 1, 7, 17, 36, 37, 125, 129,
    134, 135, 147, 170, 181, 275, 285, 320, 339,
    382, 412, 415, 619, 622, 623, 637, 679, 681,
    721, 767
Everly, Don 134, 135, 695
Everly, Phil 134, 695
Everything But The Girl **136**, 977
Evie (Tornquist) **586**
Ewell, Don 1345, 1396, 1431
Ewen, Alvin 932
Ewing, Tom 728
Exciters, The **136**, 235
Exile **640**, 667, 711
Exkano, Paul 587
Experience Seven 869
Explainer **873**
Exploited, The 7
Ezrin, Bob 153, 154, 211, 312

F

Fabares, Shelley 429
Fabian 9, **136**, 633
Fabulous Pop Tarts **958**
Fabulous Thunderbirds, The 2, 129, **136**, 491,
    498, 503, 536
Faces 7, 44, **136**, 137, 298, 346, 363, 364, 387
Fadden, Jimmie 673, 674
Faddis, Jon 966, 1150, **1219**, 1233, 1262, 1282,
    1322, 1345, 1369, 1401, 1416
Fadela, Chaba **829**, 830
Faeltskog, Agnetha 9
Fagen, Donald **137**, 360, 361, 971
Fagenson, Don 408
Fagerquist, Don 1259, 1291, 1351, 1378
Fahey, John **744**, 745, 747, 756, 757, **1103**
Fair, David 169
Fair, Jad 169
Fairbairn, Bruce 13, 228
Fairchild, Barbara 694
Fairfield Four **586**
Fairport Convention **137**, 138, 247, 378, 383,
    384, 740, 742, 743, 745, 746, 761, 763, 766,
    777, 778, 790, 795, 798, 812, 817, 941
Faith No More **138**, 181
Faith, Adam 9, 336
Faith, Percy **1035**, 1045
Faithfull, Marianne 114, **139**, 223, 955, 980,
    1066, 1071
Fakir, Abdul 149
Fakroun, Ahmed 829
Fal Frett **866**
Falcon, Joseph **821**
Falcons **139**, 146, 288, 561
Fall, The 112, **139**, 140, 155, 223
Fallen Angels 649
Falls, Mildred 592
Faltermeyer, Harold 966
Falzone, Sam 1216
Fambrough, Charles 1165, **1220**, 1373, 1413,
    1433
Fame, Georgie 151, 258
Family 48
Fang, Forrest **1058**
Fania All Stars 1157, 1346, 1374
Fankhauser, Merrell & HMS Bounty **140**, 263
Fanny 948, 949
Fantastic Baggies 344
Fapardokly **140**, 263
Far East Family Band 1068
Farafina 1062
Farah, Ardeshir 1081
Fardon, Don 351
Fargo, Donna **640**
Farian, Frank 55
Farina, Mimi 736, **745**, 787
Farina, Richard 745, 751
Farina, Richard and Mimi **745**

Farlow, Billy C. 94
Farlow, Tal 720, 1205, **1220**, 1320, 1340, 1342,
    1378
Farmer, Addison 1149, 1220, 1221, 1407
Farmer, Art 1149, 1182, **1220**, 1221, 1228,
    1236, 1247, 1248, 1256, 1272, 1281, 1291,
    1294, 1296, 1324, 1333, 1334, 1361, 1371,
    1382, 1390, 1392, 1402, 1405, 1418, 1422,
    1434
Farmer, Mylene **141**
Farndon, Pete 297
Farnon, Robert 1005, 1249, 1279
Farr, Hugh & Karl 686, 690
Farrar, Jay 395
Farrell, Bobby 55
Farrell, Joe 1157, 1195, 1196, 1221, 1279, 1280,
    1282, 1310, 1330, 1360
Farrell, Perry 196, 293
Fashek, Majek **916**
Fast Forward 1089, **1104**
Fastway 260
Fat Boys, The 32, **452**, 453, 460, 464, 472, 604
Fatima Mansions 179
Fatis 919
Fatool, Nick 1226
Faulkner, Eric 32
Faulkner, John **801**, 803, 805
Faure, Duncan 32
Faust 5
Favors, Malachi 1152, 1167, 1323, 1324
Faye, Alice 1012
Fazola, Irving 1226, 1388, 1428
Fear 433
Fearnley, James 291
Feather, Leonard 1014, 1246, 1262, 1271, 1295,
    1324, 1379, 1410, 1425
Feathers, Charlie 592
Fedchock, John 1260
Federici, Danny 357
Feelies **141**
Feidman, Gloria **902**
Feinstein, Michael **1010**
Feld, Morey 1204, 1428
Felder, Don 126
Felder, Wilton 1157, 1198, 1372
Feldman, Alan 800
Feldman, Maxine 939
Feldman, Morton 1089, **1103**
Feldman, Trevor 1221
Feldman, Victor **1221**, 1266, 1282, 1304, 1305,
    1328, 1329, 1353, 1406
Felice, John 317
Feliciano, Cheo 894, 896
Feliciano, Jose **1010**, 1011
Fell, Terry 504
Fender, Freddy 9, 342, **640**, 640
Fenton, David 398
Ferguson, Bob 677
Ferguson, Dave 718
Ferguson, Maureen 1398
Ferguson, Maynard 891, 1162, 1177, 1198,
    1209, 1216, 1217, **1221**, 1222, 1230, 1248,
    1266, 1285, 1286, 1287, 1303, 1367, 1374,
    1380, 1413, 1424
Ferguson, Sherman 1176, 1373, 1377
Ferguson, Steve 271, 591
Fernandez, Julio 1388
Fernando **586**
Ferneyhough, Brian 1139
Ferrante & Teicher **1036**
Ferrante, Art 1036
Ferrante, Russell 1422
Ferrari, Luc **1103**
Ferrell, Rachelle 1426
Ferrer, Jose 968
Ferris, Glen 1216
Ferron **944**, 949, 954
Ferrone, Steve 24
Ferry, Bryan 10, **141**, 302, 324, 971
Fetchit, Stepin 268
Few, Bobby 1292
Feza, Mongezi 843, 1311
Fialho, Francisco **881**

Ficca, Billy 377
Fiedler, Arthur 1033, **1036**, 1041
Fieger, Doug 212
Fielder, Jim 49, 66
Fields, Brandon 1364
Fields, Dorothy 1014
Fields, Ernie 438, 1212, 1217, 1361
Fields, Geechie 1332
Fields, Johnny 586
Fields, Kansas 1194
Fier, Anton 141, 161, 163, 178, 785
Fife, Fay 316
Fifth Dimension **141**, 318, 408
Fig, Anton 22, 211
Figgy Duff **801**, 809
Fight 205
Figure Eight 1235
Filarfolket **883**
File **821**
Filiano, Ken 1353
Finch, Richard 206
Fincher, Dan 495
Findley, Chuck 1349
Fine Young Cannibals 132, **141**, 978
Fineberg, Jeanie 940
Finer, Jem 291
Fingerett, Sally **745**
Fingers, Johnnie 57
Fink, Cathy **944**, 953
Fink, Sue 939, 940, 941, **945**, 954
Finn [ROCK] 104, **142**, 355
Finn, Alec 801
Finn, Mickey 389
Finn, Neil 104, 142, 354, 355
Finn, Tim 16, 104, 142, **142**, 354, 355
Finster, Howard 577
Fiorito, Ed 1041
Fireballs 182, 438, 706
Firefall 147, 155
Firehose **142**, 251
Firm 218
First Edition 685
First Gear 590
First, David **1103**
Fischer, Clare **1222**, 1249, 1399
Fischer, Jens 1082
Fishbone 3
Fishell, Steve 695
Fisher Family **801**
Fisher, Archie 773, **801**
Fisher, Bob 574
Fisher, Cilla 801, 806
Fisher, David Dudu **902**, 902
Fisher, Eddie **1011**
Fisher, Matthew 300, 1069
Fisher, Ray 801
Fisher, Sonny 438
Fitzgerald, Alan 269
Fitzgerald, Ella 843, 1007, 1041, 1159, 1173,
    1185, 1213, 1217, **1222**, 1223, 1224, 1233,
    1247, 1280, 1283, 1317, 1342, 1348, 1357,
    1358, 1405, 1414, 1425, 1431
Fitzgerald, Patrik 269
Fitzgerald, Winston **801**
Fitzroy, Edi 937
Fitzsimmons, Michael 1054
Five Americans 173
Five Blind Boys 971
Five Blind Boys of Alabama, The **586**
Five Blind Boys of Mississippi, The 580, **587**
Five Breezes 477
Five Chinese Brothers **745**
Five Crowns 123, 208
Five Du Tones 302, 412, 439, 440
Five Keys 498
Five Pennies 1339
Five Royales 27, **142**, 485
Five Satins 143, 382, 969
Five Singing Stars 583
Five Stairsteps **143**
Fixx, The **143**
Fjell, Judy **945**
Flack, Roberta 23, **143**, 173, 418

H

When it comes to music, we wrote the book

All Music Guide to Rock
The Best CDs, Albums & Tapes
Rock, Pop, Soul, R&B, and Rap
Edited by Michael Erlewine, Vladimir Bogdanov, and Chris Woodstra, with S.T. Erlewine, R. Unterberger, W. Ruhlmann

This is the ultimate guide to rock recordings. For 15,500 CDs, albums and tapes by 2,500 artists—everything from doo-wop to hip-hop—you get concise reviews, expert ratings and revealing career profiles, plus historical music maps and dozens of essays on rock styles and influences.

Softcover, 970pp, 6-1/8 x 9-1/4, ISBN 0-87930-376-X, $24.95

All Music Guide to Jazz
The Experts' Guide to the Best JazzRecordings
Second Edition • Edited by Michael Erlewine, Vladimir Bogdanov, Chris Woodstra, and Scott Yanow

Completely updated and expanded. An indispensable book for both the serious and casual jazz listener, this guide profiles the lives and work of 1,440 key jazz artists, reviewing and rating over 13,000 of their best recordings. Also includes fascinating essays and music maps that put in context the various jazz styles, innovators, and instruments.

Softcover, 913pp, 6-1/8 x 9-1/4, ISBN 0-87930-407-3, $24.95

All Music Guide to The Blues
The Experts' Guide to the Best Blues Recordings
Edited by Michael Erlewine, Vladimir Bogdanov, Chris Woodstra, and Cub Koda

The essential reference for starting, expanding, or fine-tuning a prime collection of the best in blues recordings. Noted critics profile the lives and work of 560 key artists, and review and rate over 2,600 top recordings.

Softcover, 400pp, 6-1/8 x 9-1/4, ISBN 0-87930-424-3, $17.95

All Music Book of Hit Albums
The Top 10 US & UK Album Charts from 1960 to the Present Day
Compiled by Dave McAleer

From the birth of album charts in 1960, this unique book lists the Top 10 albums in both the US and the UK through the present. Also filled with photos and fascinating trivia. *Softcover, 352pp, 8 x 9-1/2, ISBN 0-87930-393-X, $22.95*

All Music Book of Hit Singles
Top Twenty Charts from 1954 to the Present Day
Compiled by Dave McAleer

This musical time capsule compares U.S. and U.K. Top 20 charts for the past 40 years. The book is studded with photos, trivia and chartfacts featuring the stars and styles of pop music.

Softcover, 432pp, 8 x 9-1/2, ISBN 0-87930-330-1, $22.95

Jaco
The Extraordinary and Tragic Life of Jaco Pastorius, "The World's Greatest Bass Player" • by Bill Milkowski

The fascinating tale of Jaco Pastorius' brilliant musical achievements and tragic life—a fond tribute to the man who revolutionized the electric bass' role in modern music. Bonus CD sampler features 3 songs capturing Jaco in his prime.

Softcover, with CD, 264pp, 6 x 9, ISBN 0-87930-426-X, $14.95

Secrets from the Masters
40 Great Guitar Players
Edited by Don Menn

Featuring the most influential guitarists of the past 25 years: Jimi Hendrix, Les Paul, Eric Clapton, Eddie Van Halen, Chuck Berry, Andrés Segovia, Pete Townshend and many more. Combines personal biography, career history, and playing techniques. *Softcover, 300 pp, 8-1/2 x 11, ISBN 0-87930-260-7, $19.95*

Blues Guitar • The Men Who Made the Music
Second Edition • Edited by Jas Obrecht

Readers get a look inside the lives and music of thirty great bluesmen, through interviews, articles, discographies, and rare photographs. Covers Buddy Guy, Robert Johnson, John Lee Hooker, Albert King, B.B. King, Muddy Waters, and more. *Softcover, 280pp, 8-1/2 x 11, ISBN 0-87930-292-5, $19.95*

Bass Heroes
Styles, Stories & Secrets of 30 Great Bass Players
Edited by Tom Mulhern

Thirty of the world's greatest bass players in rock, jazz, studio/pop, and blues & funk share their musical influences, playing techniques, and opinions. Includes Jack Bruce, Stanley Clarke, James Jamerson, Paul McCartney, and more.

Softcover, 208pp, 8-1/2 x 11, ISBN 0-87930-274-7, $17.95

1000 Great Guitarists
By Hugh Gregory

Profiling the world's outstanding guitarists from A to Z, this inviting "encyclopedia" covers all kinds of guitar music. Superstars and lesser-knowns are listed with full details on their styles, guitars, best recordings, and more.

Softcover, 164pp, 7-1/4 x 9-1/2, ISBN 0-87930-307-7, $19.95

How to Play Guitar
The Basics & Beyond—Chords, Scales, Tunes & Tips
By the Editors of Guitar Player

For anyone learning to play acoustic or electric guitar, this book and CD set is packed with music, licks, and lessons from the pros. The CD guides readers through nine lessons.

Softcover, 80 pp, 8-1/2 x 11, ISBN 0-87930-399-9, $14.95

Hot Guitar
Rock Soloing, Blues Power, Rapid-Fire Rockabilly, Slick Turnarounds, Hot Country, and Cool Licks
By Arlen Roth

Drawing on ten years of the "Hot Guitar" column from *Guitar Player*, this book covers string bending, slides, picking and fingering techniques, soloing, and rock, blues, and country licks.

Softcover, 160pp, 8-1/2 x 11, ISBN 0-87930-276-3, $19.95

Guitar Player Repair Guide
How to Set Up, Maintain, and Repair Electrics and Acoustics • By Dan Erlewine—Second Edition

Whether you're a player, collector, or repairperson, this hands-on guide provides all the essential information on caring for guitars and electric basses. Includes hundreds of photos and drawings detailing techniques for guitar care and repair.

Softcover, 309pp, 8-1/2 x 11, ISBN 0-87930-291-7, $22.95

Available at fine book and music stores, or contact:
Miller Freeman Books • 6600 Silacci Way, Gilroy, CA 95020 • Phone (800) 848-5594 • Fax (408) 848-5784
E-Mail: mfbooks@mfi.com • **World Wide Web:** http://www.mfi.com/mf-books/